Children's Books In Print®

2016

This edition of

CHILDREN'S BOOKS IN PRINT® 2016
was prepared by R.R. Bowker's Database Publishing Group
in collaboration with the Information Technology Department.

Kevin Sayar, Senior Vice President & General Manager
Angela D'Agostino, Vice President Business Development
Mark Van Orman, Senior Director Content Operations

International Standard Book Number/Standard Address Number Agency
Beat Barblan, Director Identifier Services
John Purcell, Manager, ISBN Agency
Richard Smith, Product Manager, Identifier Services
John D'Agostino, Lisseth Montecinos, Cheryl Russo, Publisher Relations
Representatives

Data Services
Lisa Heft, Senior Manager Content Operations
Adrene Allen, Kathleen Cunningham, Managers Content Operations
Ron Butkiewicz, Latonia Hall, Ila Joseph, John Litzenberger,
Rhonda McKendrick, Tom Lucas,
Beverly Palacio, Cheryl Patrick and Mervaine Ricks, Senior Data Analysts QA
Jenny Marie Adams, Supervisor Data Quality
Terry Campesi, Chris Flinn, Suzanne Franks, E-Content Editors II
Mark Ahmad, Lynda Keller, Rosemary Walker, Profilers

Publisher Relations
Patricia Payton, Senior Manager Publisher Relations and Content Development
Ralph Coviello, Jack Tipping Publisher Relations Managers
Erica Ferris, Publisher Liaison
Claire Edwards, Publisher Relations Administrator
Joanne Firca, Assistant Publisher Relations Analyst

Data Services Production
Andy K. Haramasz, Manager Data Distribution & QA

Editorial Systems Group
Mark Heinzelman, Chief Data Architect

Computer Operations Group
Ed Albright, UNIX Administrator
John Nesselt, UNIX Administrator

Bowker®

Children's Books In Print® 2016

An Author, Title, and Illustrator Index to Books for Children and Young Adults

VOLUME 2

- ❖ Authors
- ❖ Illustrators
- ❖ Publishers, Wholesalers &

GREY HOUSE PUBLISHING

R.R. Bowker LLC
630 Central Avenue
New Providence, NJ 07974
Toll-free: 1-888-269-5372
ISBN Agency: 877-310-7333
Fax: 908-795-3518
E-mail: info@bowker.com
URL: http://www.bowker.com

Grey House Publishing, Inc.
4919 Route 22
Amenia, NY 12501
Phone: 518-789-8700
Toll-free: 1-800-562-2139
Fax: 518-789-0545
E-mail: books@greyhouse.com
URL: http://www.greyhouse.com

Kevin Sayar, Senior Vice President & General Manager

Children's Books In Print® 2016 is published by Grey House Publishing, Inc. under exclusive license from R.R. Bowker LLC.

Publishers may update or add to their listings by accessing one of Bowker's online portals: **BowkerLink** for international publishers at http://www.bowkerlink.com and **MyIdentifiers** for USA publishers at http://www.myidentifiers.com.

No payment is either solicited or accepted for the inclusion of entries in this publication.

International Standard Book Numbers

ISBN 13: 978-1-61925-661-3 (set)
ISBN 13: 978-1-61925-662-0 (Vol. 1)
ISBN 13: 978-1-61925-663-7 (Vol. 2)

International Standard Serial Number

0069-3480

Library of Congress Control Number

70-101705

Printed and bound in Canada

CONTENTS

How to Use Children's Books In Print® vii
Publisher Country Codes xi
Country Sequence xiii
Language Codes xv
List of Abbreviations xvii

Volume 1

TITLE INDEX 1

Volume 2

AUTHOR INDEX 2005
ILLUSTRATOR INDEX 2843
PUBLISHER NAME INDEX 3349
WHOLESALER & DISTRIBUTOR NAME INDEX 3521

How To Use
CHILDREN'S BOOKS IN PRINT®

This 47th edition of R.R. Bowker's ***Children's Books In Print®*** is produced from the Books In Print database. Volume 1 contains the Title Index to approximately 265,365 books available from some 16,741 United States publishers. Volume 1 includes books published after 2003. Volume 2 includes the Author and Illustrator indexes, with listings for approximately 55,523 contributors. The Name Publishers index with full contact information for all of the publishers listed in the bibliographic entries is included at the end of the book, followed by a separate index to wholesalers and distributors.

RELATED PRODUCTS

In addition to the printed version, the entire Books In Print database (more than 25 million records, including OP/OSI titles, ebooks, audio books and videos) can be searched by customers on Bowker's Web site, http://www.booksinprint.com. For further information about subscribing to this online service, please contact Bowker at 1-888-269-5372.

The Books In Print database is also available in an array of other formats such as online access through Books In Print site licensing. Database vendors such as OVID Technologies, Inc. make the Books In Print database available to their subscribers. Intota, a new assessment tool for libraries, also utilizes the Books in Print database. It was developed by Serial Solutions which, like Bowker, is a ProQuest affiliate.

COMPILATION

In order to be useful to subscribers, the information contained in ***Children's Books In Print®*** must be complete and accurate. Publishers are asked to review and correct their entries prior to each publication, providing current price, publication date, availability status, and ordering information, as well as recently published and forthcoming titles. Tens of thousands of entries are added or updated for each edition.

DATA ACQUISITION

Bowker aggregates bibliographic information via ONIX, excel and text data feeds from publishers, national libraries, distributors, and wholesalers. Publishers may also add to or update their listings using one of Bowker's online portals: **BowkerLink** for international publishers at http://www.bowkerlink.com and **MyIdentifiers** for USA publishers at http://www.myidentifiers.com.

Larger publishing houses can submit their bibliographic information to the Books In Print database from their own databases. Bowker's system accepts publisher data 24 hours a day, 7 days a week via FTP. The benefits to this method are: no paper intervention, reduced costs, increased timeliness, and less chance of human error that can occur when re-keying information.

To communicate new title information to Books In Print, the quality of the publisher's textual data must be up to—or extremely close to—reference book standards. Publishers interested in setting up a data feed are invited to access the Bowker Title

Submission Guide at http://www.bowker.com or contact us at Data.Submissions@Bowker.com.

Updated information or corrections to the listings in *Books In Print* can now be submitted at any time via email at Data.Submissions@bowker.com. Publishers can also submit updates and new titles to ***Children's Books In Print®*** through one of Bowker's online portals: **BowkerLink** for international publishers at http://www.bowkerlink.com and **MyIdentifiers** for USA publishers at http://www.myidentifiers.com.

To ensure the accuracy, timeliness and comprehensiveness of data in ***Children's Books In Print®***, Bowker has initiated discussions with the major publishers. This outreach entails analyzing the quality of all publisher submissions to the Books In Print database, and working closely with the publisher to improve the content and timeliness of the information. This outreach also lays the groundwork for incorporating new valuable information into ***Children's Books In Print®***. We are now collecting cover art, descriptive jacket and catalog copy, tables of contents, and contributor biographies, as well as awards won, bestseller listings, and review citations.

Bowker will make this important additional information available to customers who receive *Books In Print* in specific electronic formats and through subscriptions to http://www.booksinprint.com.

ALPHABETICAL ARRANGEMENT OF AUTHOR, TITLE, AND ILLUSTRATOR INDEXES

Within each index, entries are filed alphabetically by word with the following exception:

Initial articles of titles in English, French, German, Italian, and Spanish are deleted from both author and title entries.

Numerals, including years, are written out in some cases and are filed alphabetically.

As a general rule, U.S., UN, Dr., Mr., and St. are filed in strict alphabetical order unless the author/publisher specifically requests that the abbreviation be filed as if it were spelled out.

Proper names beginning with "Mc" and "Mac" are filed in strict alphabetical order. For example, entries for contributor's names such as MacAdam, MacAvory, MacCarthy, MacDonald, and MacLean are located prior to the pages with entries for names such as McAdams, McCarthy, McCoy, and McDermott.

Entries beginning with initial letters (whether authors' given names, or titles) are filed first, e.g., Smith, H. C., comes before Smith, Harold A.; B is for Betsy comes before Babar, etc.

Compound names are listed under the first part of the name, and cross references appear under the last part of the name.

SPECIAL NOTE ON HOW TO FIND AN AUTHOR'S OR ILLUSTRATOR'S LISTING

In sorting author and illustrator listings by computer, it is not possible to group the entire listing for an individual together unless a standard spelling and format for each name is used. The information in R.R. Bowker's ***Children's Books In Print®*** is based on data received from the publishers. If a name appears in various forms in this data, the listing in the index may be divided into several groups.

INFORMATION INCLUDED IN AUTHOR, TITLE, AND ILLUSTRATOR ENTRIES

Entries in the Title and Illustrator indexes include the following bibliographic information, when available: author, co-author, editor, co-editor, translator, co-translator, illustrator, co-illustrator, photographer, co-photographer, title, title supplement, sub-title, number of volumes, edition, series information, language if other than English, whether or not illustrated, number of pages, (orig.) if an original paperback, grade range, year of publication, price, International Standard Book Number, publisher's order number, imprint, and publisher name.

Titles new to this edition are indicated by bolding the ISBN. Information on the International Standard Book Numbering System is available from R.R. Bowker.

Author Index entries provide the contributor(s) name(s), title, subtitle, title supplement, and a page number cross reference to the full bibliographic entry in the Title Index (in Volume 1).

The prices cited are those provided by the publishers and generally refer to either the trade edition or the Publisher's Library Bound edition. The abbreviation "lib. bdg." is used whenever the price cited is for a publisher's library bound edition.

ISBN AGENCY

Each title included in **Children's Books In Print®** has been assigned an International Standard Book Number (ISBN) by the publisher. All ISBNs listed in this directory have been validated by using the check digit control, ensuring accuracy. ISBNs allow order transmission and bibliographic information updating using publishing industry supported EDI formats (e.g., ONIX). Publishers not currently participating in the ISBN system may request the assignment of an ISBN Publisher Prefix from the ISBN Agency by calling 877-310-7333, faxing 908-795-3518, or through the ISBN Agency's web site at **http://www.myidentifiers.com**. Please note: The ISBN prefix 0-615 is for decentralized use by the U.S. ISBN Agency and has been assigned to many publishers. It is not unique to one publisher.

SAN AGENCY

Another listing feature in **Children's Books In Print®** is the Standard Address Number (SAN), a unique identification number assigned to each address of an organization in or served by the publishing industry; it facilitates communications and transactions with other members of the industry.

The SAN identifies either a bill to or ship to address for purchasing, billing, shipping, receiving, paying, crediting, and refunding, and can be used for any other communication or transaction between participating companies and organizations in the publishing supply chain.

To obtain an application or further information on the SAN system, please email the SAN Agency at **SAN@bowker.com,** or visit **www.myidentifiers.com**

PUBLISHER NAME INDEX

A key to the abbreviated publisher names (e.g., "Middle Atlantic Pr.") used in the bibliographic entries of ***Children's Books In Print®*** is found after the Illustrator Index in Volume 2. Entries in this index contain each publisher's abbreviated name, followed by its ISBN prefix(es), business affiliation (e.g., "Div. of International Publishing") when available, ordering address(es), SAN (Standard Address Number), telephone, fax, and toll-free numbers. Editorial address(es) (and associated contact numbers) follows. Addresses without a specific label are for editorial offices rather than ordering purposes.

Abbreviations used to identify publishers' imprints are followed by the full name of the imprint. E-mail and Web site addresses are then supplied. A listing of distributors associated with the publisher concludes each entry; each distributor symbol is in bold type, followed by its abbreviated name.

A dagger preceding an entry and the note "CIP" at the end of the entry both indicate that the publisher participates in the Cataloging in Publication Program of the Library of Congress.

Foreign publishers with U.S. distributors are listed, followed by their three-character ISO (International Standards Organization) country code ("GBR," "CAN," etc.), ISBN prefix(es), when available, and a cross-reference to their U.S. distributor, as shown below:

Atrium (GBR) *(0-9535353) Dist by* **Dufour**.

Publishers with like or similar names are referenced by a "Do not confuse with . . ." notation at the end of the entry. In addition, cross-references are provided from imprints and former company names to the new name.

WHOLESALER & DISTRIBUTOR NAME INDEX

Full information on distributors as well as wholesalers is provided in this index. Note that those publishers who also serve as distributors may be listed both here and in the Publisher Name Index.

SAMPLE ENTRY TITLE INDEX

❶ Anti-Boredom Book: ❷ 133 Completely Unboring Things to Do! ❸ Owl & Chikadee Magazines Editors ❹ rev. ed ❺ 2000 ❻ 128 p. ❼ (J) ❽ (gr. k-4). ❾ (Illus.). ❿ pap. ⓫ 12.95 ⓬ (978-1-8956889-9-3(X)); ⓭ 22.95 ⓮ (1-894379-00-4) ⓯ GDPD ⓰ CAN ⓱ (Owl Greey). ⓲ *Dist:* Firefly Bks Limited

Note: Items containing a distributor symbol should be ordered from the distributor, not the publisher.

KEY

❶ Title
❷ Subtitle
❸ Contributor
❹ Edition information
❺ Publication year
❻ Number of pages
❼ Audience
❽ Grade information
❾ Illustrated
❿ Binding type
⓫ Price
⓬ International Standard Book Number
⓭ Additional price
⓮ Corresponding ISBN
⓯ Publisher symbol
⓰ Foriegn publisher ISO code
⓱ Imprint symbol
⓲ U.S. distributor symbol-see note

SAMPLE ENTRY PUBLISHER NAME INDEX

❶ † ❷ **Mosby, Inc.,** ❸ *(0-323; 0-7234; 0-8016; 0-8151; 0-88416; 0-941158; 1-55664; 1-56815),* ❹ Div. of Harcourt, Inc., A Harcourt Health Sciences Co., ❺ Orders Addr.: 6227 Sea Harbor Dr., Orlando, FL 32887 ❻ Toll Free Fax: 800-235-0256 ❼ Toll Free: 800-543-1918 ❽ Edit Addr.: 11830 Westline Industrial Dr., Saint Louis, MO 63146 ❾ (SAN 200-2280) ❿ Toll Free: 800-325-4177
⓫ Web site: http://www.mosby.com/
⓬ Dist(s): ***PennWell Corp.*** ⓭ *CIP.*

KEY

❶ CIP Identifier
❷ Publisher Name
❸ ISBN Prefixes
❹ Division of
❺ Orders Address
❻ Orders Fax
❼ Orders Telephone
❽ Editorial Address
❾ SAN
❿ Toll-Free
⓫ Web site
⓬ Distributors
⓭ Cataloging in Publication

SAMPLE ENTRY WHOLESALER & DISTRIBUTOR NAME INDEX

❶ **New Leaf Distributing Co., Inc.,** ❷ *(0-9627209),* ❸ Div. of Al-Wali Corp.,
❹ 401 Thornton Rd., Lithia Springs, GA 30122-1557 ❺ (SAN 169-1449)
❻ Tel: 770-948-7845; ❼ Fax: 770-944-2313; ❽ Toll Free Fax: 800-326-1066;
❾ Toll Free: 800-326-2665
❿ Email: NewLeaf-dist.com
⓫ Web site: http://www.NewLeaf-dist.com

KEY

❶ Distributor name
❷ ISBN prefix
❸ Division of
❹ Editorial address
❺ SAN
❻ Telephone
❼ Fax
❽ Toll free fax
❾ Toll free
❿ E-mail
⓫ Web site

PUBLISHER COUNTRY CODES

Foreign Publishers are listed with the three letter International Standards Organization (ISO) code for their country of domicile. This is the complete list of ISO codes though not all countries may be represented. The codes are mnemonic in most cases. The country names here may be shortened to a more common usage form.

AFG	AFGHANISTAN
AGO	ANGOLA
ALB	ALBANIA
AND	ANDORRA
ANT	NETHERLANDS ANTILLES
ARE	UNITED ARAB EMIRATES
ARG	ARGENTINA
ARM	ARMENIA
ASM	AMERICAN SAMOA
ATA	ANTARCTICA
ATG	ANTIGUA & BARBUDA
AUS	AUSTRALIA
AUT	AUSTRIA
AZE	AZERBAIJAN
BDI	BURUNDI
BEL	BELGIUM
BEN	BENIN
BFA	BURKINA FASO
BGD	BANGLADESH
BGR	BULGARIA
BHR	BAHRAIN
BHS	BAHAMAS
BIH	BOSNIA & HERZEGOVINA
BLR	BELARUS
BLZ	BELIZE
BMU	BERMUDA
BOL	BOLIVIA
BRA	BRAZIL
BRB	BARBADOS
BRN	BRUNEI DARUSSALAM
BTN	BHUTAN
BWA	BOTSWANA
BWI	BRITISH WEST INDIES
CAF	CENTRAL AFRICAN REP
CAN	CANADA
CH2	CHINA
CHE	SWITZERLAND
CHL	CHILE
CHN	CHINA
CIV	IVORY COAST
CMR	CAMEROON
COD	ZAIRE
COG	CONGO (BRAZZAVILLE)
COL	COLOMBIA
COM	COMOROS
CPV	CAPE VERDE
CRI	COSTA RICA
CS	CZECHOSLOVAKIA
CUB	CUBA
CYM	CAYMAN ISLANDS
CYP	CYPRUS
CZE	CZECH REPUBLIC
DEU	GERMANY
DJI	DJIBOUTI
DMA	DOMINICA
DNK	DENMARK
DOM	DOMINICAN REPUBLIC
DZA	ALGERIA
ECU	ECUADOR
EG	East Germany
EGY	EGYPT
EI	EUROPEAN UNION
EN	England
ESP	SPAIN
EST	ESTONIA
ETH	ETHIOPIA
FIN	FINLAND
FJI	FIJI
FLK	FALKLAND ISLANDS
FRA	FRANCE
FRO	FAEROE ISLANDS
FSM	MICRONESIA
GAB	GABON
GBR	UNITED KINGDOM
GEO	GEORGIA
GHA	GHANA
GIB	GIBRALTAR
GIN	GUINEA
GLP	GUADELOUPE
GMB	GAMBIA
GNB	GUINEA-BISSAU
GNQ	EQUATORIAL GUINEA
GRC	GREECE
GRD	GRENADA
GRL	GREENLAND
GTM	GUATEMALA
GUF	FRENCH GUIANA
GUM	GUAM
GUY	GUYANA
HKG	HONG KONG
HND	HONDURAS
HRV	Croatia
HTI	HAITI
HUN	HUNGARY
IDN	INDONESIA
IND	INDIA
IRL	IRELAND
IRN	IRAN
IRQ	IRAQ
ISL	ICELAND
ISR	ISRAEL
ITA	ITALY
JAM	JAMAICA
JOR	JORDAN
JPN	JAPAN
KAZ	KAZAKSTAN
KEN	KENYA
KGZ	KYRGYZSTAN
KHM	CAMBODIA
KNA	ST. KITTS-NEVIS
KO	Korea
KOR	SOUTH KOREA
KOS	KOSOVA
KWT	KUWAIT
LAO	LAOS
LBN	LEBANON
LBR	LIBERIA
LBY	LIBYA
LCA	ST. LUCIA
LIE	LIECHTENSTEIN
LKA	SRI LANKA
LSO	LESOTHO
LTU	LITHUANIA
LUX	LUXEMBOURG
LVA	LATVIA
MAC	MACAO
MAR	MOROCCO
MCO	MONACO
MDA	MOLDOVA
MDG	MALAGASY REPUBLIC
MDV	MALDIVE ISLANDS
MEX	MEXICO
MHL	MARSHALL ISLANDS
MKD	MACEDONIA
MLI	MALI
MLT	MALTA
MMR	UNION OF MYANMAR
MNE	MONTENEGRO
MNG	MONGOLIA
MOZ	MOZAMBIQUE
MRT	MAURITANIA
MSR	MONTESERRAT
MTQ	MARTINIQUE
MUS	MAURITIUS
MWI	MALAWI
MYS	MALAYSIA
NAM	NAMIBIA
NCL	NEW CALEDONIA
NER	NIGER
NGA	NIGERIA
NIC	NICARAGUA
NLD	THE NETHERLANDS
NOR	NORWAY
NPL	NEPAL
NRU	NAURU
NZL	NEW ZEALAND
OMN	SULTANATE OF OMAN
PAK	PAKISTAN
PAN	PANAMA
PER	PERU
PHL	PHILIPPINES
PNG	PAPUA NEW GUINEA
POL	POLAND
PRI	Puerto Rico
PRK	NORTH KOREA
PRT	PORTUGAL
PRY	PARAGUAY
PYF	FRENCH POLYNESIA
REU	REUNION
ROM	RUMANIA
RUS	RUSSIA
RWA	RWANDA
SAU	SAUDI ARABIA
SC	Scotland
SCG	SERBIA & MONTENEGRO
SDN	SUDAN
SEN	SENEGAL
SGP	SINGAPORE
SLB	SOLOMON ISLANDS
SLE	SIERRA LEONE
SLV	EL SALVADOR
SMR	SAN MARINO
SOM	SOMALIA

PUBLISHER COUNTRY CODES

STP	SAO TOME E PRINCIPE
SU	Soviet Union
SUR	SURINAM
SVK	Slovakia
SVN	SLOVENIA
SWE	SWEDEN
SWZ	SWAZILAND
SYC	SEYCHELLES
SYN	SYNDETICS
SYR	SYRIA
TCA	TURKS NDS
TCD	CHAD
TGO	TOGO
THA	THAILAND
TKM	TURKMENISTAN
TON	TONGA
TTO	TRINIDAD AND TOBAGO
TUN	TUNISIA
TUR	TURKEY
TWN	TAIWAN
TZA	TANZANIA
UGA	UGANDA
UI	UNITED KINGDOM
UKR	UKRAINE
UN	UNITED NATIONS
URY	URUGUAY
USA	UNITED STATES
UZB	UZBEKISTAN
VAT	VATICAN CITY
VCT	ST. VINCENT
VEN	VENEZUELA
VGB	BRITISH VIRGIN ISLANDS
VIR	U.S. VIRGIN ISLANDS
VNM	VIETNAM
VUT	VANUATU
WA	Wales
WSM	WESTERN SAMOA
YEM	REPUBLIC OF YEMEN
YUG	YUGOSLAVIA
ZAF	SOUTH AFRICA
ZMB	ZAMBIA
ZWE	ZIMBABWE

COUNTRY SEQUENCE

AFGHANISTAN	AFG
ALBANIA	ALB
ALGERIA	DZA
AMERICAN SAMOA	ASM
ANDORRA	AND
ANGOLA	AGO
ANGUILLA	AIA
ANTARCTICA	ATA
ANTIGUA & BARBUDA	ATG
ARGENTINA	ARG
ARMENIA	ARM
ARUBA	ABW
AUSTRALIA	AUS
AUSTRIA	AUT
AZERBAIJAN	AZE
BAHAMAS	BHS
BAHRAIN	BHR
BANGLADESH	BGD
BARBADOS	BRB
BELARUS	BLR
BELGIUM	BEL
BELIZE	BLZ
BENIN	BEN
BERMUDA	BMU
BHUTAN	BTN
BOLIVIA	BOL
BOSNIA & HERZEGOVINA	BIH
BOTSWANA	BWA
BOUVET ISLAND	BVT
BRAZIL	BRA
BRITISH INDIAN OCEAN TERRITORY	IOT
BRITISH WEST INDIES	BWI
BRUNEI DARUSSALAM	BRN
BULGARIA	BGR
BURKINA FASO	BFA
BURUNDI	BDI
CAMBODIA	KHM
CAMEROON	CMR
CANADA	CAN
CAPE VERDE	CPV
CAYMAN ISLANDS	CYM
CENTRAL AFRICAN REPUBLIC	CAF
CHAD	TCD
CHILE	CHL
CHINA	CHN
CHRISTMAS ISLAND	CXR
COCOS (KEELING) ISLANDS	CCK
COLOMBIA	COL
COMOROS	COM
CONGO	COG
CONGO, THE DEMOCRATIC REPUBLIC OF THE CONGO	COD
COOK ISLANDS	COK
COSTA RICA	CRI
COTE' D' IVOIRE	CIV
CROATIA	HRV
CUBA	CUB
CYPRUS	CYP
CZECH REPUBLIC	CZE
CZECHOSLOVAKIA	CSK
DENMARK	DNK
DJIBOUTI	DJI
DOMINICA	DMA
DOMINICAN REPUBLIC	DOM
EAST TIMOR	TMP
ECUADOR	ECU
EGYPT (ARAB REPUBLIC OF EGYPT)	EGY
EL SALVADOR	SLV
EQUATORIAL GUINEA	GNQ
ERITREA	ERI
ESTONIA	EST
ETHIOPIA	ETH
EAST GERMANY	DDR
FALKLAND ISLANDS	FLK
FAROE ISLANDS	FRO
FEDERATED STATES OF MICRONESIA	FSM
FIJI	FJI
FINLAND	FIN
FRANCE	FRA
FRENCH GUIANA	GUF
FRENCH POLYNESIA	PYF
FRENCH SOUTHERN TERRITORIES	ATF
GABON	GAB
GAMBIA	GMB
GEORGIA	GEO
GERMANY	DEU
GHANA	GHA
GIBRALTAR	GIB
GREECE	GRC
GREENLAND	GRL
GRENADA	GRD
GUADELOUPE	GLP
GUAM	GUM
GUATEMALA	GTM
GUINEA	GIN
GUINEA-BISSAU	GNB
GUYANA	GUY
HAITI	HTI
HEARD ISLAND & MCDONALD ISLANDS	HMD
HONDURAS	HND
HONG KONG	HKG
HUNGARY	HUN
ICELAND	ISL
INDIA	IND
INDONESIA	IDN
IRAN, ISLAMIC REPUBLIC OF	IRN
IRAQ	IRQ
IRELAND	IRL
ISRAEL	ISR
ITALY	ITA
JAMAICA	JAM
JAPAN	JPN
JORDAN	JOR
KAZAKSTAN	KAZ
KENYA	KEN
KIRIBATI	KIR
KOREA, DEMOCRATIC PEOPLE'S REPUBLIC OF	PRK
KOREA, REPUBLIC OF	KOR
KUWAIT	KWT
KYRGYZSTAN	KGZ
KOSOVA	KOS
LAO PEOPLE'S DEMOCRATIC REPUBLIC	LAO
LATVIA	LVA
LEBANON	LBN
LESOTHO	LSO
LIBERIA	LBR
LIBYAN ARAB JAMAHIRIYA	LBY
LIECHTENSTEIN	LIE
LITHUANIA	LTU
LUXEMBOURG	LUX
MACAU	MAC
MACEDONIA, THE FORMER YUGOSLAV REPUBLIC OF	MKD
MADAGASCAR	MDG
MALAWI	MWI
MALAYSIA	MYS
MALDIVE ISLANDS	MDV
MALI	MLI
MALTA	MLT
MARSHALL ISLANDS	MHL
MARTINIQUE	MTQ
MAURITANIA	MRT
MAURITIUS	MUS
MAYOTTE	MYT
MEXICO	MEX
MOLDOVA, REPUBLIC OF	MDA
MONACO	MCO

COUNTRY SEQUENCE

MONGOLIA	MNG
MONTENEGRO	MNE
MONTSERRAT	MSR
MOROCCO	MAR
MOZAMBIQUE	MOZ
MYANMAR	MMR
NAMIBIA	NAM
NAURU	NRU
NEPAL	NPL
NETHERLANDS	NLD
NETHERLANDS ANTILLES	ANT
NEW CALEDONIA	NCL
NEW ZEALAND	NZL
NICARAGUA	NIC
NIGER	NER
NIGERIA	NGA
NIUE	NIU
NORFOLK ISLAND	NFK
NORTHERN MARIANA ISLANDS	MNP
NORWAY	NOR
OMAN	OMN
OCCUPIED PALESTINIAN TERRITORY	PSE
PAKISTAN	PAK
PALAU	PLW
PANAMA	PAN
PAPUA NEW GUINEA	PNG
PARAGUAY	PRY
PERU	PER
PHILIPPINES	PHL
PITCAIRN	PCN
POLAND	POL
PORTUGAL	PRT
PUERTO RICO	PRI
QATAR	QAT
REUNION	REU
ROMANIA	ROM
RUSSIAN FEDERATION	RUS
RWANDA	RWA
SAINT HELENA	SHN
SAINT KITTS & NEVIS	KNA
SAINT PIERRE & MIQUELON	SPM
SAINT VINCENT & THE GRENADINES	VCT
SAMOA	WSM
SAN MARINO	SMR
SAO TOME E PRINCIPE	STP
SAUDI ARABIA	SAU
SENEGAL	SEN
SERBIA	SRB
SERBIA & MONTENEGRO	SCG
SEYCHELLES	SYC
SIERRA LEONE	SLE
SINGAPORE	SGP
SLOVAKIA	SVK
SLOVENIA	SVN
SOLOMON ISLANDS	SLB
SOMALIA	SOM
SOUTH AFRICA	ZAF
SOUTH GEORGIA & THE SANDWICH ISLANDS	SGS
SPAIN	ESP
SRI LANKA	LKA
ST. LUCIA	LCA
SUDAN	SDN
SURINAME	SUR
SVALBARD & JAN MAYEN	SJM
SWAZILAND	SWZ
SWEDEN	SWE
SWITZERLAND	CHE
SYRIAN ARAB REPUBLIC	SYR
TAIWAN, REPUBLIC OF CHINA	TWN
TAJIKISTAN	TJK
TANZANIA, UNITED REPUBLIC OF	TZA
THAILAND	THA
TOGO	TGO
TOKELAU	TKL
TONGA	TON
TRINIDAD & TOBAGO	TTO
TUNISIA	TUN
TURKEY	TUR
TURKMENISTAN	TKM
TURKS & CAICOS ISLANDS	TCA
TUVALU	TUV
U.S.S.R.	SUN
UGANDA	UGA
UKRAINE	UKR
UNITED ARAB EMIRATES	UAE
UNITED KINGDOM	GBR
UNITED STATES	USA
UNITED STATES MINOR OUTLYING ISLANDS	UMI
URUGUAY	URY
UZBEKISTAN	UZB
VANUATU	VUT
VATICAN CITY STATE (HOLY SEE)	VAT
VENEZUELA	VEN
VIET NAM	VNM
VIRGIN ISLANDS, BRITISH	VGB
VIRGIN ISLANDS, U. S.	VIR
WALLIS & FUTUNA	WLF
WESTERN SAHARA	ESH
West Germany	BRD
YEMEN	YEM
YUGOSLAVIA	YUG
ZAMBIA	ZMB
ZIMBABWE	ZWE
ZAIRE	ZAR

LANGUAGE CODES

ACE	Achioli
AFA	Afro-Asiatic
AFR	Afrikaans
AKK	Akkadian
ALB	Albanian
ALE	Aleut
ALG	Algonquin
AMH	Amharic
ANG	Anglo-Saxon
APA	Apache
ARA	Arabic
ARC	Aramaic
ARM	Armenian
ARN	Araucanian
ARP	Arapaho
ARW	Arawak
ASM	Assamese
AVA	Avar
AVE	Avesta
AYM	Aymara
AZE	Azerbaijani
BAK	Bashkir
BAL	Baluchi
BAM	Bambara
BAQ	Basque
BAT	Baltic
BEJ	Beja
BEL	Belorussian
BEM	Bemba
BEN	Bengali
BER	Berber Group
BIH	Bihari
BLA	Blackfoot
BRE	Breton
BUL	Bulgarian
BUR	Burmese
CAD	Caddo
CAI	Central American
CAM	Cambodian
CAR	Carib
CAT	Catalan
CAU	Caucasian
CEL	Celtic Group
CHB	Chibcha
CHE	Chechen
CHI	Chinese
CHN	Chinook
CHO	Choctaw
CHR	Cherokee
CHU	Church Slavic
CHV	Chuvash
CHY	Cheyenne
COP	Coptic
COR	Cornish
CRE	Cree
CRO	Croatian
CRP	Creoles and Pidgins
CUS	Cushitic
CZE	Czech
DAK	Dakota
DAN	Danish
DEL	Delaware
DIN	Dinka
DOI	Dogri
DRA	Dravidian
DUA	Duala
DUT	Dutch
EFI	Efik
EGY	Egyptian
ELX	Elamite
ENG	English
ENM	English, Middle
ESK	Eskimo
RUM	Romanian
RUN	Rundi
RUS	Russian
SAD	Sandawe
SAG	Sango
SAI	South American
SAM	Samaritan
SAN	Sanskrit
SAO	Sampan
SBC	Serbo-Croatian
SCO	Scots
SEL	Selkup
SEM	Semitic
SER	Serbian
SHN	Shan
SHO	Shona
SID	Sidamo
SIO	Siouan Languages
SIT	Sino-Tibetan
SLA	Slavic
SLO	Slovak
SLV	Slovenian
SMO	Samoan
SND	Sindhi
SNH	Singhalese
SOG	Sogdian
SOM	Somali
SON	Songhai
ESP	Esperanto
EST	Estonian
ETH	Ethiopic
EWE	Ewe
FAN	Fang
FAR	Faroese
FEM	French, Middle
FIJ	Fijian
FIN	Finnish
FIU	Finno-Ugrian
FLE	Flemish
FON	Fon
FRE	French
FRI	Frisian
FRO	French, Old
GAA	Ga
GAE	Gaelic
GAG	Gallegan
GAL	Galla
GEC	Greek, Classical
GEH	German, Middle h
GEM	Germanic
GEO	Georgian
GER	German
GLG	Galician
GOH	German, Old High
GON	Gondi
GOT	Gothic
GRE	Greek
GUA	Guarani
GUJ	Gujarati
HAU	Hausa
HAW	Hawaiian
HEB	Hebrew
HER	Herero
HIL	Hiligaynon
HIN	Hindi
HUN	Hungarian
HUP	Hupa
IBA	Iban
IBO	Igbo
ICE	Icelandic
IKU	Inuktitut
ILO	Ilocano
INC	Indic
IND	Indonesian
INE	Indo-European
INT	Interlingua
IRA	Iranian
IRI	Irish
IRO	Iroquois
ITA	Italian
JAV	Javanese
JPN	Japanese
KAA	Karakalpak
KAC	Kachin
KAM	Kamba
KAN	Kannada
KAR	Karen
KAS	Kashmiri
KAU	Kanuri
KAZ	Kazakh
KHA	Khasi
KHM	Khmer, Central
KIK	Kikuyu
KIN	Kinyarwanda
KIR	Kirghiz
KOK	Konkani
KON	Kongo
KOR	Korean
KPE	Kpelle
KRO	Kru
KRU	Kurukh
SOT	Sotho, Southern
SPA	Spanish
SRD	Sardinian
SRR	Serer
SSA	Sub-Saharan
SUK	Sukuma
SUN	Sundanese
SUS	Susu
SUX	Sumerian
SWA	Swahili
SWE	Swedish
SYR	Syriac
TAG	Tagalog
TAJ	Tajik
TAM	Tamil
TAR	Tatar
TEL	Telugu
TEM	Temne
TER	Tereno
THA	Thai
TIB	Tibetan
TIG	Tigre
TIR	Tigrinya
TOG	Tonga, Nyasa

TON	Tonga, Tonga
TSI	Tsimshian
TSO	Tsonga
TSW	Tswana
KUA	Kwanyama
KUR	Kurdish
LAD	Ladino
LAH	Lahnda
LAM	Lamba
LAO	Laotian
LAP	Lapp
LAT	Latin
LAV	Latvian
LIN	Lingala
LIT	Lithuanian
LOL	Lolo
LUB	Luba
LUG	Luganda
LUI	Luiseno
MAC	Macedonian
MAI	Maithili
MAL	Malayalam
MAN	Mandingo
MAO	Maori
MAP	Malayo-Polynesian
MAR	Marathi
MAS	Masai
MAY	Malay
MEN	Mende
MIC	Micmac
MIS	Miscellaneous
MLA	Malagasy
MLT	Malteses
MNO	Manobo
MOL	Moldavian
MON	Mongol
MOS	Mossi
MUL	Multiple Languages
MUS	Muskogee
MYN	Mayan
NAI	North American
NAV	Navaho
NBL	Ndebele, Southern
NDE	Ndebele, Northern
NEP	Nepali
NEW	Newari
NIC	Niger-Congo
NNO	Norwegian
NOB	Norwegian Bokmal
NOR	Norwegian
NSO	Sotho, Northern
NUB	Nubian
NYA	Nyanja
NYM	Nyamwezi
NYO	Nyoro Group
OES	Ossetic
OJI	Ojibwa
ORI	Oriya
OSA	Osage
OTO	Otomi
PAA	Papuan-Australian
PAH	Pahari
PAL	Pahlavi
PAN	Panjabi
PEO	Persian, Old
PER	Persian, Modern
PLI	Pali
POL	Polish
POR	Portuguese
PRA	Prakrit
PRO	Provencal
PUS	Pushto
QUE	Quechua
RAJ	Rajasthani
ROA	Romance
ROH	Romanish
ROM	Romany
TUK	Turkmen
TUR	Turkish
TUT	Turko-Tataric
TWI	Twi
UGA	Ugaritic
UIG	Uigur
UKR	Ukrainian
UMB	Umbundu
UND	Undetermined
URD	Urdu
UZB	Uzbek
VIE	Vietnamese
VOT	Votic
WAL	Walamo
WAS	Washo
WEL	Welsh
WEN	Wendic
WOL	Wolof
XHO	Xhosa
YAO	Yao
YID	Yiddish
YOR	Yoruba
ZAP	Zapotec
ZEN	Zenaga
ZUL	Zulu
ZUN	Zuni

LIST OF ABBREVIATIONS

Abr.	abridged
act. bk.	activity book
adapt.	adapted
aft.	afterword
alt.	alternate
Amer.	American
anniv.	anniversary
anno.	annotated by
annot.	annotation(s)
ans.	answer(s)
app.	appendix
Apple II	Apple II disk
approx.	approximately
assn.	association
audio	analog audio cassette
auth.	author
bd.	bound
bdg.	binding
bds.	boards
bibl(s).	bibliography(ies)
bk(s).	book(s)
bklet(s).	booklet(s)
boxed	boxed set, slipcase or caseboard
Bro.	Brother
C	college audience level
co.	company
comm.	commission, committee
comment.	commentaries
comp.	complied
cond.	condensed
contrib.	contributed
corp.	corporation
dept.	department
des	designed
diag(s).	diagram(s)
digital audio	digital audio cassette
dir.	director
disk	software disk or diskette
dist.	distributed
Div.	Division
doz.	dozen
ea.	each
ed.	edited, edition, editor
eds.	editions, editors
educ.	education
elem.	elementary
ency.	encyclopedia
ENG	English
enl.	enlarged
epil.	epilogue
exp.	expanded
expr.	experiments
expurg.	expurgated
fac.	facsimile
fasc.	fascicule
fict.	fiction
fig(s).	figure(s)
flmstrp.	filmstrip
footn.	
for.	foreign
frwd.	foreword
gen.	general
gr.	grade(s)
hndbk.	handbook
illus.	Illustrated, illustration(s), Illustrator(s)
in prep.	in preparation
incl.	includes, including
info.	information
inst.	institute
intro.	introduction
ISBN	International Standard Book Number
ISO	International Standards Organization
ITA	Italian
i.t.a.	initial teaching alphabet
J.	juvenile audience level
JPN	Japanese
Jr.	Junior
jt. auth.	joint author
jt. ed.	joint editor
k	kindergarten audience level
lab	laboratory
lang(s).	language(s)
LC	Library of Congress
lea.	leather
lib.	library
lib. bdg.	library binding
lit.	literature, literary
lp	record, album, long playing
l.t.	large type
ltd.	limited
ltd. ed.	limited edition
mac hd	144M, Mac
mac ld	800K, Mac
mass mkt.	mass market paperbound
math.	mathematics
mic. film	microfilm
mic form	microform
mod.	modern
MS(S)	manuscript(s)
natl.	national
net	net price
no(s).	number(s)
o.p.	out of print
orig.	original text, not a reprint (paperback)
o.s.i.	out of stock indefinitely
p.	pages
pap.	paper
per.	perfect binding
photos	photographer, photographs
pop. ed.	Popular edition
prep.	preparation
probs.	problems
prog. bk.	programmed books
ps.	preschool audience level
pseud.	pseudonym
pt(s).	part(s)
pub.	published, publisher publishing
pubn.	publication
ref(s).	reference(s)
rep.	reprint
reprod(s).	reproduction(s)
ret.	retold by
rev.	revised
rpm.	revolution per minute (phono records)
SAN	Standard Address Number
S&L	signed and limited
sec.	section
sel.	selected
ser.	series
Soc.	society
sols.	solutions
s.p.	school price
Sr. (after given name)	Senior
Sr. (before given name	Sister
St.	Saint
stu.	student manual, study guide, etc.
subs.	subsidiary
subsc.	subscription
suppl.	supplement
tech.	technical
text ed.	text edition
tr.	translated, translation translator
trans.	transparencies
unabr.	unabridged
unexpurg.	unexpurgated
univ.	university
var.	variorum
vdisk	videodisk
VHS	video, VHS format
vol(s).	volume(s)
wkbk.	workbook
YA	Young adult audience level
yrbk.	yearbook
3.5 hd	1.44M, 3.5 disk, DOS
3.5 ld	720, 3.5 Disk, DOS
5.25 hd	1.2M, 5.25 Disk, DOS
5.25 ld	360K, 5.25 Disk, DOS

AUTHOR INDEX

A

Numeric

09' Young Writers Conf. Havana Elem. Words Have Wings. (p. 1951)
123 Sesame Street, ed. see Galvin, Laura Gates.
123 Sesame Street, ed. Abby in Wonderland. (p. 2)
—When Zoe Grows Up. (p. 1906)
—Year Starts Here. (p. 1969)
14 Outstanding American Artists Staff, illus. see Nikola-Lisa, W.
1st World Publishing, jt. auth. see CHARLES, A. M. A. N.
1stWorld Library, ed. see James, Henry.
2006-2007 Tongue River Elementary 3rd Graders, text. Sheridan County History ABC Coloring & Activity Book - 2007. (p. 1565)
2nd and 7 Foundation. Hog Mollies & the Amazing Aquatic Adventure (Soft Cover) (p. 787)
2nd and 7 Foundation Staff. Hog Mollies & the Amazing Aquatic Adventure. (p. 787)
2nd and 7th Foundation Staff. Hog Mollies & the Great Golden Gizmo (Case Version) (p. 787)
—Hog Mollies & the Great Golden Gizmo (Paperback Version) (p. 787)
43 Degrees North LLC Staff. Tailgate Trivia National Parks (p. 1695)
4RV Publishing LLC Staff. Case of the Missing Coach. (p. 274)
50 Cent Staff. Playground. Akana, Lizzi, illus. (p. 1372)
826 Valencia Writing Project Student Staff. Time to Eat Cake. (p. 1753)
826 Valencia Writing Project Student Staff, jt. auth. see San Francisco Bay Area Students Staff.

A

A. Alphabet Quest. (p. 50)
A., Aaron. Serenity Rose: Working Through the Negativity. Vol. 1 (p. 1552)
A and J Studios Staff. Dora's Three Little Fairy Tales. (p. 471)
A and J Studios Staff, illus. see Ricci, Christine.
A and J Studios Staff, jt. auth. see Beinstein, Phoebe.
A and J Studios Staff, jt. auth. see Wax, Wendy.
A Boy And His Dog & Bozak, Jon. Demo: The Story of the Junkyard Dog. (p. 425)
A Caribbean Experience Con Amor. There's a Coqui in My Shoe! (p. 1730)
A. Gunderson, Jessica. Pick your Poison Apple. (p. 1354)
A, Julie. Roger & the Bum Bubble. (p. 1484)
A. L. O. E. Triumph over Midian. (p. 1788)
A Lady. Tales from Ariosto: Retold for Children. (p. 1701)
A Mother's Pen. Adventures of Backwards Bear & Baby Curl. (p. 16)
A. Pryor, Scott, jt. auth. see Misseijer, Tamra K.
A to Z. Weathered Pages: The Poetry Pole. Bodeen, Jim et al, eds. (p. 1870)
A., Vartika. Secrets of Destiny. (p. 1545)
A Yusuf, Ali. Three Travellers to India. (p. 1744)
A12, jt. auth. see Young, Judy.
AA Publishing. French. (p. 635)
—Spanish. (p. 1620)
AAA Staff. Here, There & Everywhere: A Guide to Fun & Safe Travel. (p. 770)
—Wheels, Wings & Other Things: A Guide to Fun & Safe Travel. (p. 1901)
Aadland, Dan & Michaelides, Marina. Women & Warriors of the Plains: The Pioneer Photography of Julia E. Tuell. Tuell, Julia E., photos by. (p. 1945)
Aakeson, Kim Fupz & Garde, Ruth. Vitello Becomes a Businessman. Bojesen, Niels Bo, illus. (p. 1846)
—Vitello Carries a Knife. Bojesen, Niels Bo, illus. (p. 1846)
—Vitello Gets a Yucky Girlfriend. Bojesen, Niels Bo, illus. (p. 1846)
—Vitello Scratches a Car. Bojesen, Niels Bo, illus. (p. 1846)
—Vitello Wants a Dad. Bojesen, Niels Bo, illus. (p. 1846)
Aalborg, Gordon. Cat Tracks. (p. 278)
Aalgaard, Wendy. East Indians in America. (p. 498)
—Venezuela in Pictures. (p. 1835)
Aaltio, Maija-Hellikki. Finnish for Foreigners II (p. 589)
A&C Black Staff & Ganeri, Anita. Keystones: Hindu Mandir. Kilby, Jak, illus. (p. 951)
A&C Black Staff & Singh, Kanwaljit Kaur. Keystones: Sikh Gurdwara. (p. 951)
Aardema, John, illus. see Diamond, Charlotte.
Aardema, John, illus. see Gillespie, Jane.
Aardema, John, illus. see Plourde, Lynn.
Aardema, Verna. Koi & the Kola Nuts: A Tale from Liberia. Cepeda, Joe, illus. (p. 966)
—Who's in Rabbit's House? (p. 1920)
—Why Mosquitoes Buzz in People's Ears. (p. 1925)
Aardman Animations Staff, illus. see Candlewick Press, Candlewick.
Aardvark, D. Congraduation Fish. Aardvark, D., illus. (p. 357)
—Merry Kissmoose. Aardvark, D., illus. (p. 1129)
—Punkin's upside down Day. (p. 1417)
Aardvark, E. Gartner Jake. (p. 657)
—Giacco il Giardiniere. (p. 673)
—Jakke, den Traedgaardaren. (p. 906)
Aardvark, E. S. Jakke Puutarhurina. (p. 906)
—Joao o Jardineiro. (p. 919)
Aardvark, Esperanza. Jaap de Tuinman. Zimmer, Dirk, illus. (p. 902)
Aardvark, Nathan, illus. see Murtagh, Ciaran.
Aaron, Chester. Alex, Who Won His War. (p. 36)
—American Ghost. (p. 60)
—Gideon. (p. 674)
—Home to the Sea (p. 793)
—Willa's Poppy. (p. 1933)
Aaron, Jason. Avengers vs. X-Men. Cho, Frank & Romita, John, Jr., illus. (p. 119)
—Other Side. McCaig, Dave & Brosseau, Pat, illus. (p. 1306)
—Scalped - Indian Country Vol. 1 Guera, R. M. & Jock, illus. (p. 1519)
—Wolverine & the X-Men by Jason Aaron - Volume 3. (p. 1944)
Aaron, Rich, illus. see Heydt, Scott.
Aaron, Scott. Jewish U: A Contemporary Guide for the Jewish College Student. (p. 917)
Aaron, Taylor. Pumpkin Goblin Makes Friends. (p. 1416)
Aaron-Barrada, prod. PottieStickers 3-pack Sports Equipment, Seashells & Butterflies: How to Toilet Train in 7 Days with Success with the #1 Portable Toilet Training Reward System for today's family-on-the-go-lifestyle... because consistency Counts! (p. 1388)
Aaron-Barrada, Tammie, creator. PottieStickers 3-Pack Fireflies, Kites & Fish Tank: How to Toilet Train in 7 Days with Success with the #1 Portable Toilet Training Reward System for Today's Family-on-the-Go-Lifestyle... Because Consistency Counts! (p. 1388)
—PottieStickers 3-Pack Tools, Sea Horses & Flowers: How to Toilet Train in 7 Days with Success! #1 Portable Toilet Training Reward System for today's family-on-the-go-lifestyle... because consistency Counts! (p. 1388)
AaronG, Driftin'. Claude Henry, the Iditarod Mouse: The Adventures Begin. (p. 329)
Aarons, Jacob. Stormy Weather. (p. 1656)
Aarons, Maureen & Gittens, Tessa. Autism: A Social Skills Approach for Children & Adolescents. (p. 117)
—Social Skills Programmes: An Integrated Approach from Early Years to Adolescence. (p. 1604)
Aarsen, Carolyne. All in One Place. (p. 44)
Aarvig, Cindy, illus. see Honeycutt, Scarlet.
Aaseng, Maury. Learn to Draw American Landmarks & Historical Heroes: Step-by-Step Instructions for Drawing National Monuments, State Symbols, & More! (p. 983)
Aaseng, Nathan. Business Builders in Broadcasting. (p. 244)
—Business Builders in Sweets & Treats. (p. 244)
—Business Builders in Toys. (p. 244)
—Michael Jordan: Hall of Fame Basketball Superstar. (p. 1134)
—Weird Meat-Eating Plants. (p. 1872)
AB Publishing Staff. Peep Behind the Scenes. (p. 1335)
Abadie, M. J. Teen Dream Power: Unlock the Meaning of Your Dreams. (p. 1713)
Abadzis, Nick. Laika. (p. 972)
—Laika. Abadzis, Nick & Sycamore, Hilary, illus. (p. 972)
Abanu, Vanessa, et al, eds. Conexão Aparentada / Apparent Connection: Quilombo Project magazine, an exploration of arts & culture in the African Diaspora. (p. 356)
Abasta, Mary, illus. see Mendoza, Madeleine.
Abate, Betelhem, photos by see Quarto Generic Staff.
Abato, Andrew. Alphabet Mandalas - Beautiful Letter-Based Mandalas for Colouring in, Learning & Meditation. (p. 49)
—Car Mandalas - Beautiful Mandalas Featuring Cars for Colouring In. (p. 265)
—Celtic Mandalas - Beautiful Mandalas & Patterns for Colouring in, Relaxation & Meditation. (p. 286)
—Christmas Mandalas - Beautiful Christmas Mandalas for Colouring In. (p. 314)
—Decorative Mandalas - Beautiful Mandalas & Patterns for Colouring in, Relaxation & Meditation. (p. 422)
—Fantasy Mandalas - Beautiful Mandalas & Ornamentation for Colouring in, Relaxation & Meditation. (p. 572)
—Farmyard Mandalas - Beautiful Mandalas with a Farmyard Theme for Colouring In. (p. 575)
—Horse Mandalas - Beautiful Horse Mandalas for Colouring in & Meditation. (p. 799)
—Love Mandalas - Beautiful Love Mandalas for Colouring in, Dreaming, Relaxation & Meditation. (p. 1060)
Abawi, Atia. Secret Sky. (p. 1543)
Abay, Ismail, illus. see Ozgur, Lynne Emily.
Abazov, Rafis. Tajikistan. (p. 1696)
Abbaszadeh, Paul. One Love: A True Love Story. (p. 1296)
Abbate, Jason. Welcome to Xooxville. (p. 1874)
Abbeville Press Staff, jt. auth. see Calino.
Abbey. Señor Manzana & Amigos. (p. 1550)
Abbey, Cherie D. & Hillstrom, Kevin, eds. Biography Today: Scientists & Inventors Volume 9. (p. 189)
—Biography Today Sports: Profiles of People of Interest to Young Readers. (p. 189)
Abbey, Cherie D., ed. Annual Cumulation 2008. (p. 87)
—Biography Today: Profiles of People of Interest to Young Readers. (p. 189)
—Biography Today, Annual Cumulation 2003: Profiles of People of Interest to Young Readers. (p. 189)
—Biography Today Annual Cumulation 2004: Profiles of People of Interest to Young Readers. (p. 189)
—Biography Today Authors: Profiles of People of Interest to Young Readers. (p. 189)
Abbey, Cherie, ed. 2009 Biography Today Annual Cumulation. (p. 2003)
—2010 Annual Cumulation. (p. 2003)
—2012 3-Issue Subscription. (p. 2003)
—2012 3-Issue Subscription + 2012 Annual Cumulation. (p. 2003)
—2012 Annual Cumulation. (p. 2003)
—2012 Issue 1. (p. 2003)
—2012 Issue 2. (p. 2003)
—2012 Issue 3. (p. 2003)
Abbey, Jed. Life of George Washington. (p. 1012)
Abbink, Emily. Monterey Bay Area Missions. (p. 1170)
Abboreno, Joseph F., illus. see Fu, Shelley.
Abbot, Belle K. Leah Mordecai. (p. 982)
Abbot, Jacob. History of King Charles the Second of England. (p. 784)
Abbot, Judi, illus. see Murray, Tamsyn.
Abbot, Judi, illus. see Walsh, Joanna.
Abbot, Willis J. Blue Jackets of 1876: A History of the Naval Battles of the American Revolution Together with a Narrative of the War with Tripoli. (p. 203)
Abbott, Bud & Costello, Lou. Who's on First? (p. 1921)
Abbott, Candy, ed. see Betts, McKenzie Leigh.
Abbott, Charles R. Patches & Leif. (p. 1328)
Abbott, Cindy. Reaching Beyond the Clouds: from Undiagnosed to Climbing Mt. Everest. (p. 1442)
Abbott, D. K. Mrs. Potter's Cat. McKenzie, Josie, illus. (p. 1187)
Abbott, David. Conflict in the Middle East. (p. 357)
—Is the Media Too Powerful? (p. 890)
—Pakistan. (p. 1319)
—Twin Towers. (p. 1802)
Abbott, Donna. Cjam, the Unique Camel. (p. 326)
Abbott, Ellen Jensen. Centaur's Daughter (p. 287)
—Keeper (p. 947)
—Watersmeet (p. 1864)
Abbott, G., jt. auth. see Abbott, Geoffrey.
Abbott, Geoffrey & Abbott, G. What a Way to Go: The Guillotine, the Pendulum, the Thousand Cuts, the Spanish Donkey, & 66 Other Ways of Putting Someone to Death. (p. 1878)
Abbott Gidel, Susan, ed. see Abbott, L. A.
Abbott, Halley. Boy Crazy. (p. 217)
—Bridesmaid. (p. 227)
—Forbidden Boy. (p. 616)
—Getting Lost with Boys. (p. 669)
—Girls in Love. (p. 680)
—Last Summer. (p. 978)
—Next Summer. (p. 1249)
—Other Boy. (p. 1306)
—Perfect Boy. (p. 1341)
—Secrets of Boys. (p. 1545)
—Summer Boys. (p. 1674)
—Summer Girls. (p. 1674)
—Waking up to Boys. (p. 1853)
Abbott, Henry. Buzzards. (p. 249)
—Hormigueros (Inside Anthills) (p. 798)
—Inside Anthills. (p. 876)
Abbott, Henry, jt. auth. see Mills, Nathan.
Abbott, J. S. C. History of Henry the Fourth, King of France & Navarre. (p. 784)
Abbott, Jacob. Alexander the Great. (p. 36)
—Aunt Margaret; or, How John True Kept His Resolutions. (p. 115)
—Ellen Linn a Franconia Story. (p. 514)
—Hannibal. (p. 743)
—History of King Charles the Second of en. (p. 784)
—History of King Richard the First of England. (p. 784)
—History of King Richard the Second of England. (p. 784)
—History of William the Conqueror. (p. 785)
—History of Xerxes the Great. (p. 785)
—Jonas on a Farm in Winter (Illustrated E. (p. 925)
—Julius Caesar. (p. 932)
—King Alfred of England. (p. 958)
—King Alfred of England, Makers of Histor. (p. 958)
—Nero. (p. 1241)
—Rollo at Play. (p. 1485)
—Rollo at Work. (p. 1485)
—Rollo at Work & Rollo at Play. (p. 1485)
—Rollo in Holland. (p. 1485)
—Rollo in London. (p. 1485)
—Rollo in Naples. (p. 1485)
—Rollo in Paris. (p. 1485)
—Rollo on the Atlantic. (p. 1485)
—Stories Told to Rollo's Cousin Lucy. (p. 1655)
Abbott, Jane. Janny. (p. 908)
Abbott, Jane, illus. see Robinson, Hilary.
Abbott, Jason, illus. see Edwards, Wysteria.
Abbott, Jason, illus. see Fuerst, Jeffrey B.
Abbott, Jason, illus. see Smith, Carrie.
Abbott, John A. Press-Out & Play Autoshop Fun. (p. 1397)
—Press-Out & Play Construction Crew. (p. 1397)
—Press-Out & Play Dino Park. (p. 1397)
Abbott, Kristin, illus. see Ford, Adam B.
Abbott, Kristin, illus. see Garay, Erin.
Abbott, Kristin, illus. see Hegerhorst, Bethany.
Abbott, L. A. House by the Side of the Road: Stories of 20th Century Farm Life beside Illinois' Lincoln Highway. Abbott Gidel, Susan & Abbott Landow, Jan, eds. (p. 803)
Abbott Landow, Jan, ed. see Abbott, L. A.
Abbott, Laura. Daddy's Shoulders. (p. 399)
—I Love You Infinity. (p. 843)
Abbott, Monica. L T Makes New Friends. (p. 969)
Abbott Orloff, Chrissy. Lady Humming Fly's Lesson on Staying Safe. (p. 970)
Abbott, Raymond. Rosie Finds A Home. (p. 1490)

Abbott, Rosalind. Pet for Me. Seltzer, Jerry, illus. (p. 1345)
Abbott, Roz. Bump in the Road. Seltzer, Jerry Joe, illus. (p. 241)
Abbott, Simon. Animals Everywhere. (p. 82)
—Big Body Book. (p. 178)
—Cafe. (p. 250)
—Dinosaurs. (p. 443)
—Habitación de Mis Sueños. (p. 734)
—Happy Street: Pet Shop. (p. 746)
—I Want to Draw Dinosaurs. (p. 848)
—I Want to Draw Dragons. (p. 848)
—I Want to Draw Fairy Princesses. (p. 848)
—I Want to Draw Monsters. (p. 848)
—Journey Through the Solar System. (p. 928)
—Land of the Dinosaur. (p. 973)
—Learn to Draw: Dragons. (p. 983)
—Learn to Draw: Fairies. (p. 983)
—Learn to Draw: Monsters. (p. 983)
—Little Mouse Visits Grandma: Mouse on Ribbon, Flaps, Acetates. Abbott, Simon, illus. (p. 1032)
—Meet the Ancient Egyptians: More Than Just Mummies. (p. 1122)
—Meet the Incredible Romans: More Than Just Gladiators. (p. 1122)
—My Big Sketchy Doodle Book: Dinosaur Valley. (p. 1197)
—My Big Sketchy Doodle Book: in the Jungle. (p. 1197)
—Planes, Trains & Cars. (p. 1367)
—Pop & Play: Pets. (p. 1384)
—Pop & Play: Things That Go. (p. 1384)
—Pop & Play: under the Sea. (p. 1384)
—Pop & Play: Zoo Animals. (p. 1384)
—Sensational Senses: With Flaps, Tabs & a Pop-Up Surprise! (p. 1551)
—Supermarket. (p. 1684)
—Toy Shop: With a Pop-Out Shop & Play Places! (p. 1774)
—Wonderful World of Simon Abbott - Pirates. (p. 1948)
Abbott, Simon, illus. see Beeson, Samantha & Tango Books Staff.
Abbott, Simon, illus. see Biggs, Brian.
Abbott, Simon, illus. see David, Juliet.
Abbott, Simon, illus. see Goldsmith, Mike.
Abbott, Simon, illus. see Hayes, Susan.
Abbott, Simon, illus. see Tango Books Staff.
Abbott, Tony. Battle Begins. (p. 145)
—Becca & the Prisoner's Cross. (p. 155)
—City in the Clouds. Jessell, Tim, illus. (p. 323)
—Crazy Classroom Caper. (p. 377)
—Firegirl. (p. 592)
—Flight of the Genie. Jessell, Tim, illus. (p. 604)
—Forbidden Stone. (p. 616)
—Fortress of the Treasure Queen. Merrell, David, illus. (p. 623)
—Ghost Road. (p. 671)
—Golden Vendetta. (p. 695)
—Ha-Ha-Haunting of Hyde House. (p. 734)
—Hidden Stairs & the Magic Carpet. Jessell, Tim, illus. (p. 776)
—Ice Dragon. (p. 850)
—Ice Dragon. Caparó, Antonio Javier, illus. (p. 850)
—In the Ice Caves of Krog. Adams, Gil & Jessell, Tim, illus. (p. 866)
—Magic Escapes. Jessell, Tim, illus. (p. 1072)
—Moon Scroll. Jessell, Tim, illus. (p. 1172)
—Mysterious Talent Show Mystery. (p. 1223)
—Postcard. (p. 1387)
—Race to Doobesh. (p. 1431)
—Riddle of Zorfendorf Castle. Merrell, David, illus. (p. 1471)
—Secrets of Droon: City in the Clouds; The Great Ice Battle; The Sleeping Giant of Goll. Vol. 2 (p. 1545)
—Serpent's Curse. (p. 1552)
—Startling Story of the Stolen Statue. (p. 1644)
—Wade & the Scorpion's Claw. (p. 1852)
Abbott, Tony & Jessell, Tim. Genie King. Fitzgerald, Royce, illus. (p. 661)
Abbott, Wes. Dogby Walks Alone Volume 1. (p. 462)
Abboud, Adela, tr. see Benjamin, Ruth.
Abboud, Tony. Al Kindi: The Father of Arab Philosophy. (p. 32)
Abbrederis, Christoph & McLellen, Christoph Elizabeth. Sleeping Beauty. (p. 1589)
Abbruzzi, Danielle. Penelope's Piggies. Sampson, Kathleen, illus. (p. 1336)
Abbs, Brian, et al. Postcards 1. (p. 1387)
Abbs, Peter. Viva la Vida. (p. 1846)
Abby, Mitchell, illus. see Bradford, Wilson D.
ABC-CLIO Inc. Staff, Inc. Encyclopedia of North American Indian Wars, 1607-1890: A Political, Social, & Military History Set (p. 525)
—Events That Formed the Modern World: From the European Renaissance Through the War on Terror Findling, John E. & Thackeray, Frank W., eds. (p. 541)
Abdel Karim Al Sayed, Abdel Maqsud, tr. see Blumenthal, Karen.
Abdel-Fattah, Randa. Does My Head Look Big in This? (p. 460)
—Does My Head Look Big in This? Altuwayya, Zuwaina, tr. (p. 460)
—Friendship Matchmaker. (p. 639)
—Friendship Matchmaker Goes Undercover. (p. 639)
Abdelsalam, Lisa. Song for Me: A Muslim Holiday Story. Nielsen, Janet Marie, illus. (p. 1611)
Abdo. Ancient Civilizations. (p. 68)
ABDO. Daily Life in US History. (p. 400)
—Essential Library of Cultural History. (p. 537)
—Greatest Events in Sports History. (p. 719)
—History of Science. (p. 784)
—How the US Government Works. (p. 813)
—Inside Martial Arts. (p. 876)
—Inside MLB. (p. 876)
—Newsmakers. (p. 1249)
—Ready for Military Action. (p. 1447)
—Sports' Best Ever. (p. 1632)
Abdo, Kenny. All for a Game. Doucet, Bob, illus. (p. 44)
—Comic Relief. Doucet, Bob, illus. (p. 348)
—Duck, Dive, Rock & Roll. Doucet, Bob, illus. (p. 488)
—Give Me Liberty or Give Me Detention! Doucet, Bob, illus. (p. 681)
—Psych-Out! Doucet, Bob, illus. (p. 1413)
—Triple Take. Doucet, Bob, illus. (p. 1787)
Abdo Publishing. My Little Pony. (p. 1212)
ABDO Publishing Company. Action Sports. (p. 10)
—American Moments Set 2. (p. 62)
—Animal Kingdom Set 1 (p. 78)
—Animal Kingdom Set 2 (p. 78)
—Beginning to End Set 1. (p. 159)
—Earth's Treasures. (p. 498)
—Explore the Countries: Set Of 16. (p. 550)
—Girls' SportsZone: Set Of 8. (p. 680)
—Great Explorers: Set Of 6. (p. 715)
—Great Predators: Set Of 8. (p. 718)
—Haven't Got a Clue! Set Of 6. (p. 754)
—History's Greatest Disasters: Set Of 8. (p. 785)
—Holidays Set 1. (p. 788)
—Jokes (p. 924)
—More Super Simple Science. (p. 1175)
—Ultimate Cars Set II (p. 1809)
—Xtreme Fish. (p. 1967)
ABDO Publishing Company Staff. Amazing Reptiles. (p. 55)
—American Moments Set 1. (p. 62)
—Animals: Resource Guide. (p. 81)
—Archie Set of 6 (p. 95)
—Australian Animals. (p. 116)
—Awesome Athletes. (p. 121)
—Betty & Veronica (p. 172)
—Big Buddy Biographies Set 7. (p. 180)
—Cat Craze Set 2. (p. 277)
—Cats Set 2 *2015. (p. 281)
—Chet Gecko Mysteries - 10 Titles. (p. 298)
—Climate Change. (p. 332)
—Comeback Kids. (p. 347)
—Comic Book Creators. (p. 348)
—Conservationists. (p. 359)
—Contemporary Lives Set 2. (p. 360)
—Continents. (p. 360)
—Cool Cupcakes & Muffins. (p. 363)
—Cool Fiber Art. (p. 363)
—Cool Young Chefs. (p. 364)
—Countries of the World (p. 372)
—Countries of the World Set 2. (p. 372)
—Creature Features. (p. 380)
—Creatures of Legend. (p. 380)
—Critter Chronicles. (p. 384)
—Curious George (p. 393)
—Digging up the Past. (p. 439)
—Dinosaurs Set 4. (p. 445)
—Doreen Cronin: Click-Clack & More. (p. 471)
—Dragon Slayer's Academy. (p. 478)
—Easy Reader Classics - 8 Titles. (p. 500)
—Emergency Workers. (p. 518)
—Essential Critiques Set 2. (p. 536)
—Essential Events. (p. 537)
—Essential Events Set 2-Set Of 8. (p. 537)
—Essential Events Set 7. (p. 537)
—Essential Issues (p. 537)
—Essential Issues Set 4. (p. 537)
—Essential Library of the US Military. (p. 537)
—Essential Lives. (p. 537)
—Essential Lives Set 7. (p. 537)
—Essential Viewpoints (p. 537)
—Essential Viewpoints Set 2 (Set Of 8) (p. 537)
—Explore the Countries Set 2. (p. 550)
—Extreme Jobs. (p. 556)
—Extreme Sports Stars. (p. 557)
—Fact & Fiction: Animal Tales: Set of 24. (p. 561)
—Fairy Realm - 10 Titles. (p. 564)
—First Biographies Set 5. (p. 593)
—First Drawings. (p. 594)
—Fish & Game. (p. 598)
—Food Dudes Set 2. (p. 613)
—Good Manners in Relationships. (p. 698)
—Great Achievements in Engineering. (p. 713)
—Great Battles. (p. 714)
—Great Minds of Science. (p. 717)
—Great Moments in Olympic Sports. (p. 717)
—Hank Zipzer: World's Best Underachiever. (p. 742)
—Hardy Boys - 3 Titles. (p. 748)
—Heroes of America. (p. 773)
—Hispanic American History. (p. 781)
—Holidays II. (p. 788)
—Holidays Set 3. (p. 788)
—Innovative Technologies. (p. 875)
—Inside College Basketball Set 2. (p. 876)
—Inside the NBA. (p. 877)
—Inside the Speedway. (p. 877)
—Issues in Sports. (p. 893)
—Jokes & More Jokes! Set Of 8. (p. 924)
—Jughead with Archie - 6 Titles (p. 932)
—Kid Squad Saves the World. (p. 951)
—Let's See A to Z. (p. 1000)
—Little Whistle - 4 Titles. Bowers, Tim, illus. (p. 1037)
—Magic Readers. (p. 1073)
—Major League Baseball's Best Ever. (p. 1078)
—Medical Marvels. (p. 1118)
—Men's Mirror. (p. 1127)
—Mighty Movers. (p. 1140)
—Military Vehicles. (p. 1143)
—Monster Hunters. (p. 1167)
—More Professional Tools. (p. 1174)
—Mr. & Mrs. Green - 4 Titles. (p. 1184)
—Nancy Drew - 4 Titles. (p. 1228)
—Nancy Drew & the Clue Crew - 4 Titles. (p. 1228)
—National Parks Set 1. (p. 1233)
—Native Americans. (p. 1234)
—Natural Disasters. (p. 1235)
—NBA's Best Ever. (p. 1238)
—NFL's Best Ever. (p. 1250)
—NFL's Greatest Teams. (p. 1250)
—Numbers 1-20. (p. 1272)
—Prehistoric Animals Set 2. (p. 1395)
—Pro Wrestling Superstars. (p. 1408)
—Rabbit Ears: A Classic Tale. (p. 1429)
—Rhyme Time. (p. 1468)
—Rocks & Minerals. (p. 1483)
—Science of Life. (p. 1527)
—Shapes Everywhere. (p. 1560)
—Short Tales Chinese Myths. (p. 1569)
—Sight Words. (p. 1574)
—Smartest Animals. (p. 1593)
—South American Animals. (p. 1616)
—Sports' Biggest Moments. (p. 1632)
—Storm Cliff Stables. (p. 1656)
—Story of Exploration. (p. 1658)
—Story of the United States. (p. 1662)
—Story Time for Little Monsters. (p. 1663)
—Super Simple Cultural Art Set 2. (p. 1681)
—Super Simple Exercise. (p. 1681)
—Super Simple Nature Crafts. (p. 1681)
—This or That? (p. 1737)
—Time Soldiers - 6 Titles. (p. 1752)
—Tom Swift, Young Inventor - 4 Titles. (p. 1764)
—Underwater World. (p. 1817)
—Unusual Pets. (p. 1823)
—What We Stand For. (p. 1895)
—World in Conflict-the Middle East. (p. 1956)
—World of Horror: Set Of 12. (p. 1956)
—World War I. (p. 1958)
—World War II. (p. 1959)
—Xtreme Adventure. (p. 1967)
—Xtreme Motorcycles. (p. 1967)
—Xtreme Pets. (p. 1967)
—Xtreme Rodeo. (p. 1967)
—Zoo Animals (p. 1988)
ABDO Publishing Company Staff, jt. auth. see Devillier, Christy.
ABDO Publishing Company Staff, jt. auth. see Gomez, Rebecca.
ABDO Publishing Company Staff, jt. auth. see Magic Wagon Staff.
ABDO Publishing Company Staff, jt. auth. see Molter, Carey.
ABDO Publishing Company Staff, jt. auth. see Rondeau, Amanda.
ABDO Publishing Company Staff, jt. auth. see Scheunemann, Pam.
ABDO Publishing Company Staff & Archer, Claire. Big Cats. (p. 180)
ABDO Publishing Company Staff & Borth, Teddy. On the Farm. (p. 1290)
ABDO Publishing Company Staff & Dash, Meredith. National Holidays. (p. 1233)
ABDO Publishing Company Staff & Doudna, Kelly. Character Concepts. (p. 291)
—Dollars & Cents (p. 463)
—Science Made Simple. (p. 1526)
—Weather (p. 1869)
ABDO Publishing Company Staff & Hansen, Grace. Insects. (p. 875)
—Reptiles. (p. 1461)
—United States President Biographies. (p. 1820)
ABDO Publishing Company Staff & Hanson, Anders. 3-D Shapes. (p. 1991)
ABDO Publishing Company Staff & Howard, Lee. Scooby-Doo Comic Storybook. Alcadia SNC Staff, illus. (p. 1529)
ABDO Publishing Company Staff & Kompelien, Tracy. Math Made Fun. (p. 1106)
—Synonyms. (p. 1693)
ABDO Publishing Company Staff & Lennie, Charles. Construction Machines. (p. 359)
—Dinosaurs. (p. 443)
ABDO Publishing Company Staff & Marcovitz, Hal. Fair Trade. (p. 562)
ABDO Publishing Company Staff & Molter, Carey. Dollars & Cents Set 1. (p. 463)
ABDO Publishing Company Staff & Murray, Julie. Transportation. (p. 1779)
—U. S. Armed Forces. (p. 1806)
ABDO Publishing Company Staff & Rondeau, Amanda. What Should I Eat? (p. 1893)
ABDO Publishing Company Staff & Salzmann, Mary Elizabeth. Animal Homes. (p. 78)
—Antonyms. (p. 90)
—Building Character (p. 239)
—First Sounds: Set Of 47. (p. 597)
—Sports Gear. (p. 1632)
ABDO Publishing Company Staff & Scheunemann, Pam. United We Stand (p. 1820)
ABDO Publishing Company Staff & Wheeler, Jill C. Barack Obama. (p. 137)
ABDO Publishing Company Staff & Wood, Brian. Star Wars: In the Shadow of Yavin. D'Anda, Carlos, illus. (p. 1641)
ABDO Publishing Company Staff, ed. World of Mythology Set 2. (p. 1957)
Abdul Kalam, A. P. J. Children Ask Kalam. Kathuria, Rohit, illus. (p. 302)
Abdulai, David, ed. see Fann, Linsey.
Abdulaya, Lina. Once upon a Time in Oromiy: Sheekko Sheekoo. (p. 1293)
Abdul-Jabbar, Kareem. Streetball Crew Book One Sasquatch in the Paint. (p. 1667)
Abdul-Jabbar, Kareem & Obstfeld, Raymond. Sasquatch in the Paint. (p. 1515)
—Streetball Crew Book Two Stealing the Game. (p. 1667)
—What Color Is My World? The Lost History of African-American Inventors. Boos, Ben & Ford, A. G., illus. (p. 1881)
Abdullah, Aanyah, jt. auth. see Abdullah, Shaila.
Abdullah, Noorah Kathryn. What Do We Say... A Guide to Islamic Manners. (p. 1882)
Abdullah, Patricia Noor. Saving Daddy. Cabri, Alexandra, illus. (p. 1517)
Abdullah, Shaila. Manual for Marco: Living, Learning, & Laughing with an Autistic Sibling. Tejpar, Iman, illus. (p. 1089)
Abdullah, Shaila & Abdullah, Aanyah. My Friend Suhana: A Story of Friendship & Cerebral Palsy. (p. 1209)
Abdullah, Tariq, illus. see Brown, Mia.
Abdul-Rauf, Muhammad. Story of Tawaddud: A Brilliant & Beautiful Girl & a Model of Good Moral Conduct. (p. 1660)
Abe, Hiroshi, illus. see Kimura & North, Lucy.
Abe, Kentaro. Nonsense Kunoichi Fiction (p. 1263)
Abe, Sayori, illus. see Takita, Yoshihiro & Takita, Yoshihiro.
Abe, Sayori, illus. see Takita, Yoshihiro.
Abebe, Elsi. Grandma's Humongous Suitcase: A Tale of Ethiopian History & Culture in A Child Voice... (p. 708)
Abedi, C. J. Fae. (p. 562)
Abedi, Isabel. Farewell, Grandpa Elephant: What Happens When a Loved One Dies? Cordes, Miriam, illus. (p. 573)
Abedi, Isabel & Neuendorf, Abedi -. No Quiero Verte Mas! Neuendorf, Silvio, illus. (p. 1260)
Abeel, Samantha. My Thirteenth Winter: A Memoir. (p. 1220)
Abegg, Rainbow. Mom, Are You There? (p. 1161)
Abegg, Rainbow G. Peaches & Prayers. (p. 1332)
Abel and Haron, jt. auth. see Abel, Simone.
Abel, Cheyanne. It's Better by Far, When You Are Who You Are. (p. 896)
Abel, Jessica & Madden, Matt. Drawing Words & Writing Pictures. (p. 482)
Abel, Mary Bilderback. Los Terribles, Horribles, Horrorosos Achus! / the Terrible, Awful, Horrible Ah-Choos! (p. 1054)
Abel, Melanie. Kitten up a Tree. Lederhos, Anne, illus. (p. 962)
Abel, Simone. Cuddly Critters: Animal Nursery Rhymes (p. 389)
—First Look - Science (p. 596)
—Mother Goose Rhymes (p. 1178)
—Where Is Caterpillar Look & Play. (p. 1908)
Abel, Simone, illus. see Edom, Helen.
Abel, Simone, illus. see Godwin, Sam.
Abel, Simone, illus. see Llewellyn, Claire.
Abel, Simone, illus. see Lodge, Yvette.
Abel, Simone, illus. see Marks, Anthony.
Abel, Simone, jt. auth. see Hartman, Bob.
Abel, Simone & Abel and Haron. Spanking Writers. Volume 2. (p. 1622)
Abela, Deborah. Final Curtain. (p. 586)
—Haunted School. (p. 753)
—Hollywood. O'Connor, George, illus. (p. 789)
—In Search of the Time & Space Machine. Murphy, Jobi, illus. (p. 865)
—Max Remy Superspy: In Search of the Time & Space Machine & Spyforce Revealed (p. 1111)
—Max Remy Superspy: The French Code. (p. 1111)
—Mission: The Nightmare Vortex. O'Connor, George, illus. (p. 1153)
—Mission in Malta. (p. 1153)
—New Kid. (p. 1245)
—Transylvanian Tale. (p. 1779)
Abela, Deborah, jt. auth. see Warren, Johnny.
Abela, Deborah & Warren, Johnny. Jasper Zammit: Soccer Legend (p. 910)
Abela, Donna. Princess & the Pea: Band 15/Emerald. Vol. 9 Stewart, Chantal, illus. (p. 1402)
Abele, Robert. Twilight Saga: The Complete Film Archive. (p. 1801)
Abell, Angel Morgan. Alphabliss of Miss: Poems & Pictures. (p. 50)
Abella, Tomas. E de Escuela. (p. 492)
Abello, Patricia, ed. see Rosa-Mendoza, Gladys.
Abello, Patricia, tr. see Blackaby, Susan.
Abello, Patricia, tr. see Blair, Eric.
Abello, Patricia, tr. see Jones, Christianne C.
Abello, Patricia, tr. see Meachen Rau, Dana.
Abello, Patricia, tr. see Salas, Laura Purdie.
Abello, Patricia, tr. see White, Mark.
Abello, Patricia, tr. see Williams, Jacklyn.
Abello, Susan Davis. Pumpkin & Buster & the Right Thing to Do: About a Bully. (p. 1416)
Abendroth, Teresa, jt. auth. see Baldridge, Kim.
Aber, Linda. Chiller Thrillers: Attack of the Leaping Lizards. Roe, David, illus. (p. 305)
Aber, Linda W. Carrie esta a la Altura. Allen, Joy, illus. (p. 271)
Aber, Linda Williams. Attack of the Leaping Lizards: Library Edition. Roe, David, illus. (p. 113)
—Quien Tiene Manchas; Who's Got Spots? (p. 1427)
Aberback, Brian. Black Sabbath: Pioneers of Heavy Metal. (p. 196)
Abercrombie, Barbara. Show-and-Tell Lion. Cravath, Lynne Avril & Avril, Lynne, illus. (p. 1570)
Abercrombie, Bethaney, illus. see Garces lii, Joseph Louis.
Abercrombie, Josephine. Charlie the Horse. Vincent, Benjamin, illus. (p. 293)
Abercrombie, Sandra K. Puppy Dog Tales: Toby's Story. (p. 1418)
Abercrumbie, Tyla. Red Wine & the Bles'sed Monkey. (p. 1455)
Abere, Jenni. Left Alone. (p. 987)
Aberg, Rebecca. Claves de Mapas. (p. 329)
—Latitud y Longitud. (p. 979)
Aberle, Xylena Apotheloz, illus. see Doerr, Bonnie J.
Aberth, John. Black Death: The Great Mortality of 1348-1350 - A Brief History with Documents. (p. 195)
Abier, Gilles, jt. auth. see Ytak, Cathy.
Abignale, Michelle. School Food Drive: Extend the Counting Sequence. (p. 1522)
Abingdon. Aventuras en Cancion. (p. 119)
—By the Waters: Preschool Kit. (p. 249)
—By the Waters: Older Elementary Kit. (p. 249)
—By the Waters: Younger Elementary Kit. (p. 249)
—Faithsongs: Songs & Activities for Children Grades 2-6. (p. 565)
—In a Dilemma: Living Your Faith Through the Tough Stuff. (p. 863)
—Man with a Mission. (p. 1086)
—PowerXpress Christmas Around the World. (p. 1391)
—PowerXpress David the Boy Disciple. (p. 1391)
—PowerXpress David the King Disciple. (p. 1391)
—PowerXpress Psalms & Songs. (p. 1391)
—PowerXpress Samuel Disciple. (p. 1391)

—Promises for Girls Living Faithfully with God & Neighbor. (p. 1411)
—Promises Leader's Guide Living Faithfully with God & Neighbor. (p. 1411)
—Reel to Real: Making the Most of the Movies with Youth. Vol. 3, No. 1 (p. 1456)
—Reel to Real: Making the Most of the Movies with Youth. Vol. 3, No. 3 (p. 1456)
—Reel to Real: Making the Most of the Movies with Youth. Vol. 4, No. 2 (p. 1456)
—Toddlers & Twos Bible Verse Picture Cards Summer. (p. 1761)
—Under the Baobab Tree. (p. 1813)
—Under the Baobab Tree Older Student. (p. 1813)
—Under the Baobab Tree Preschool Bk. (p. 1813)
Abingdon Press. What Is a United Methodist? (p. 1888)
Abingdon Press, creator. Children's Bible-NRSV. (p. 303)
—Children's Bible-NRSV-Noah Cover. (p. 303)
—More Tween Bible Puzzles: Another Year's Worth of Fun. (p. 1175)
—One Room Sunday School: Resource Kit. (p. 1296)
—Praise God! Jesus Is Born! Easy Dramas, Recitations, & Speeches for Children. (p. 1393)
—What a Story! And Five Other Dramas for Tweens. (p. 1878)
Abingdon Press, ed. What Is a Christian? (p. 1888)
Abingdon Press Staff. Reel to Real: Making the Most of the Movies with Youth. Vol. 5, No. 1 (p. 1456)
—Reel to Real: Making the Most of the Movies with Youth. Vol. 5, No. 2 (p. 1456)
Abio, Carlos, tr. see Ahlberg, Allan.
Abissi, Katherine Alexandra. I Love to Dance! (p. 843)
Abissi, Kristina. Dot. (p. 472)
Abitz, Diana, et al. Know-the-Facts Review Game: 100 Must-Know Facts in a Q & A Game Format to Help Kids Really Remember Standards-Based Social Studies Information. (p. 965)
Ables, Troy. Around This Old House. (p. 101)
Ablett, Barry. Great Expectations. (p. 715)
Ablett, Barry, illus. see Dickens, Charles.
Ablett, Barry, illus. see Dickins, Rosie & Pratt, Leonie.
Ablett, Barry, illus. see Jones, Rob Lloyd.
Ablett, Barry, illus. see Sebag-Montefiore, Mary, ed.
Abley, Mark. Camp Fossil Eyes: Digging for the Origins of Words. Adams, Kathryn, illus. (p. 257)
—Ghost Cat. Reczuch, Karen, illus. (p. 670)
Ablondi, Richard. Ball, the Bat, & the Unforgiving BRAT. (p. 134)
Ablow, Gail. Horse in the House & Other Strange but True Animal Stories. Osborn, Kathy, illus. (p. 799)
Abner, Jessil. Kingsview Kids Adventures: Internet Friend & Adventure in Africa. (p. 961)
Abner, Kirk. Thinking Like Jesus. (p. 1734)
Abnett, Dan. Abraham Lincoln & the Civil War. (p. 6)
—Abraham Lincoln y la Guerra Civil. (p. 7)
—Battle of Gettysburg: Invasion of the North! (p. 146)
—Battle of Gettysburg: Spilled Blood on Sacred Ground. (p. 146)
—Battle of Gettysburg: Spilled Blood on Sacred Ground. Verma, Dheeraj, illus. (p. 146)
—Battle of Midway: The Destruction of the Japanese Fleet. Elson, Richard, illus. (p. 146)
—Battle of the Wilderness: Deadly Inferno. (p. 147)
—Battle of the Wilderness: Deadly Inferno. Verma, Dheeraj, illus. (p. 147)
—Christopher Columbus & the Voyage Of 1492. (p. 317)
—Christopher Columbus & the Voyage of 1492. Q2A Staff, illus. (p. 317)
—Cristóbal Colón y el Viaje de 1942. (p. 383)
—George Washington & the American Revolution. (p. 664)
—George Washington y la Guerra de Independencia. (p. 665)
—Harriet Tubman & the Underground Railroad. (p. 750)
—Harriet Tubman y el Ferrocarril Clandestino. (p. 750)
—Hernan Cortes & the Fall of the Aztec Empire. (p. 771)
—Hernán Cortés y la Caída Del Imperio Azteca. (p. 771)
—Hernán Cortés y la Caída Del Imperio Azteca. Abregón, José María, tr. (p. 772)
—Monitor versus the Merrimac: Ironclads at War. (p. 1164)
—Monitor versus the Merrimac: Ironclads at War. Verma, Dheeraj, illus. (p. 1164)
—Monitor vs. the Merrimack: Ironclads at War! (p. 1164)
—Pier Too Far. Hansen, Jimmy, illus. (p. 1357)
—Sitting Bull & the Battle of the Little Bighorn. (p. 1582)
—This Ghost Is Toast! Williams, Anthony, illus. (p. 1735)
—Toro Sentado y la Batalla de Little Bighorn. (p. 1770)
Abnett, Dan & Lanning, Andy. Dragon Frontier. (p. 477)
—Marvel's Guardians of the Galaxy Prelude. Alves, Wellington et al, illus. (p. 1099)
Abney, Joseph. Anaiya Lives with Daddy, Anaiya Visits Mommy. (p. 66)
Abney, Paula, jt. auth. see Watson, Sherri.
Abodehman, Ahmed. Cinturón. Lovillo, Pilar Ortiz, tr. (p. 321)
Aboff, Marcie. Analyzing Doggie Data (p. 67)
—Do You Really Want to Meet a Polar Bear? Fabbri, Daniele, illus. (p. 458)
—Everyone Feels Sad Sometimes Ward, Damian, illus. (p. 544)
—Everyone Feels Scared Sometimes Ward, Damian, illus. (p. 544)
—Fantastic Fruit Group Swift, Gary, illus. (p. 571)
—Giant Jelly Bean Jar. Billin-Frye, Paige, illus. (p. 673)
—Giant Jelly Bean Jar. Billin-Frye, Paige & Frye, Paige Billin, illus. (p. 673)
—Great Grains Group Poling, Kyle, illus. (p. 716)
—Guatemala ABCs: A Book about the People & Places of Guatemala Trover, Zachary, illus. (p. 728)
—Hot Shots. Manning, Maurie, illus. (p. 802)
—Hurricanes! Sotirovski, Aleksandar, illus. (p. 830)
—If You Were a Polygon Dillard, Sarah, illus. (p. 855)
—If You Were a Polygon Carabelli, Francesca & Dillard, Sarah, illus. (p. 855)
—If You Were a Pound or a Kilogram Carabelli, Francesca, illus. (p. 855)
—If You Were a Prefix Gray, Sara, illus. (p. 855)
—If You Were a Quart or a Liter Carabelli, Francesca, illus. (p. 855)
—If You Were a Set Dillard, Sarah, illus. (p. 855)
—If You Were a Set [LTD Commodities]. Dillard, Sarah, illus. (p. 855)
—If You Were a Suffix Gray, Sara, illus. (p. 855)
—If You Were a Triangle Dillard, Sarah, illus. (p. 855)
—If You Were an Even Number Dillard, Sarah, illus. (p. 855)
—If You Were an Even Number [LTD Commodities]. Dillard, Sarah, illus. (p. 855)
—If You Were an Even Number [Scholastic]. Dillard, Sarah, illus. (p. 855)
—If You Were an Inch or a Centimeter Dillard, Sarah, illus. (p. 855)
—If You Were an Odd Number Dillard, Sarah, illus. (p. 855)
—If You Were an Odd Number [LTD Commodities]. Dillard, Sarah, illus. (p. 855)
—If You Were an Odd Number [Scholastic]. Dillard, Sarah, illus. (p. 855)
—Incredible Vegetable Group Poling, Kyle, illus. (p. 869)
—India ABCs: A Book about the People & Places of India Moore, Frances, illus. (p. 870)
—Pigs, Cows, & Probability (p. 1358)
—Santa's Big Red Helper. Haefele, Steve, illus. (p. 1513)
—Sorting Fur, Feathers, Tails, & Scales (p. 1614)
—Tornadoes! Sotirovski, Aleksandar, illus. (p. 1770)
—Uncle Willy's Tickles: A Child's Right to Say No. Gartner, Kathleen, illus. (p. 1812)
—World's Biggest Machines (p. 1960)
—World's Fastest Machines (p. 1960)
Aboff, Marcie & Gray-Wilburn, Renée. First Graphics: Wild Earth. Sotirovski, Aleksandar, illus. (p. 595)
Aboff, Marcie & Lee, Sally. First Graphics: Myplate & Healthy Eating. Poling, Kyle & Swift, Gary, illus. (p. 595)
Aboff, Marcie & Shaskan, Trisha Speed. Math Fun Carabelli, Francesca & Dillard, Sarah, illus. (p. 1106)
Aboff, Marcie, et al. Giant Jelly Bean Jar. Billin-Frye, Paige, illus. (p. 673)
Aboitiz, Victoria De & Afraz. Mystery of the Breast. (p. 1225)
Abolade, Caroline, told to. I'm Going to Be a Big Brother. (p. 859)
Abolafia, Yossi, illus. see Porte, Barbara Ann.
Abolafia, Yossi, illus. see Prelutsky, Jack.
Abondolo, Daniel. Colloquial Finnish: The Complete Course for Beginners. (p. 341)
Abondolo, Daniel Mario. Colloquial Finnish Mp3. (p. 341)
Abos, Elena, tr. see Sachar, Louis & Sachar, Louis.
Abos, Regine, illus. see Wang, Gabrielle.
Abou El Azm, Mohsen, illus. see Kheneigar, Ahmed Abou.
Aboukhair, Rachel. Grumpy Girl's Guide to Good Manners. (p. 727)
Abouraya, Karen Leggett, jt. auth. see Roth, Susan L.
About Pets Staff. Hamsters. (p. 740)
—Tropical Fish. (p. 1789)
Abraham, Arnetta. Miss Robbie's House. (p. 1152)
Abraham, Chuck. Intricate Eggs: 45 Easter Designs to Color. (p. 881)
—Intricate Jack O'Lanterns: 45 Halloween Designs to Color. (p. 881)
—Intricate under the Sea: 45 Underwater Designs to Color. (p. 881)
—Intricate Valentines: 45 Lovely Designs to Color. (p. 882)
Abraham, Denise Gonzales, jt. auth. see Abraham, Susan Gonzales.
Abraham, Henry & Pfeffer, Irwin. Enjoying Global History. (p. 530)
Abraham, Isaiah. My Great Grandmother's Memorial Service. (p. 1210)
Abraham, Joe, illus. see Giffen, Keith & DeMatteis, J. M.
Abraham, Ken. Armed & Dangerous: Ephesians 6:11 Straight Answers from the Bible. (p. 99)
—Jesus Loves Me Bible Storybook & Devotional Combo. (p. 915)
Abraham, M. K. Piko the Penguinaut. Jan, R. R., illus. (p. 1358)
Abraham, Michelle Shapiro. Be a Mensch Campaign. (p. 148)
—Good Morning, Boker Tov. Alko, Selina, illus. (p. 698)
—Good Night, Lilah Tov. Alko, Selina, illus. (p. 699)
—Great Balancing Act. (p. 713)
—My Cousin Tamar Lives in Israel. Koffsky, Ann D., illus. (p. 1200)
—Repairing My World. (p. 1460)
—Where Is Grandpa Dennis? Fried, Janice, illus. (p. 1908)
Abraham, Michelle Shapiro & Koffsky, Ann D. Shavua Tov! A Good Week. (p. 1563)
Abraham, Philip. Extreme Sports Stars. (p. 557)
—How to Draw the Life & Times of George Washington. (p. 819)
—Language Development Grammer Usage. (p. 975)
—Language Development Writing Process. (p. 975)
Abraham, Rayna M. Just Imagine: Rayna Abraham's Creative Collection for Kids. (p. 938)
Abraham, Susan Gonzales & Abraham, Denise Gonzales. Cecilia's Year. (p. 283)
—Surprising Cecilia. (p. 1686)
Abrahams, Alayne. Dreams & Daydreams. (p. 484)
Abrahams, Marion. Thomas Goes to the Se. (p. 1738)
Abrahams, Peter. Behind the Curtain. (p. 160)
—Down the Rabbit Hole. (p. 474)
—Into the Dark. (p. 881)
—Outlaws of Sherwood Street: Stealing from the Rich. (p. 1313)
—Outlaws of Sherwood Street: Giving to the Poor. (p. 1313)
—Quacky Baseball. Morrison, Frank, illus. (p. 1422)
—Reality Check. (p. 1449)
Abrahams, Peter, see Quinn, Spencer, pseud.
Abrahams, Peter, et al. Up All Night: A Short Story Collection. (p. 1824)
Abrahamson, Alan, jt. auth. see Phelps, Michael.
Abrahamson, Bobbie. Sunflower: A Pony's Story. (p. 1676)
Abrahamson, Jean. Manners Are Magic. (p. 1088)
Abrahamson, Ruth Ann. Adventures of Magic Cookie Bean: A Precocious Calico Shares Christian-Principled Tales; Purrfect for Ages 5 & Up! (p. 20)
—Paris & the Purple Purse: Continuing Adventures of Magic Cookie Bean. (p. 1324)
Abraitis, M., et al. Science for 5-7 Year Olds. (p. 1526)
Abramavitz. Online Privacy & Healthcare. (p. 1298)
Abramovitz, Melissa. 100th Day of School. (p. 1999)
—Abc's of Health & Safety. Morris, Alexander, illus. (p. 4)
—Amazing Feats of Biological Engineering. (p. 54)
—Big Cars (p. 180)
—Bowling. (p. 216)
—Copd. (p. 365)
—Cystic Fibrosis. (p. 397)
—Emergency Vehicles. (p. 518)
—Famous Cars (p. 569)
—How Are Digital Devices Impacting Society? (p. 805)
—How Do Computers Talk to One Another? (p. 806)
—Lou Gehrig's Disease. (p. 1057)
—Lupus. (p. 1066)
—Mental Retardation. (p. 1126)
—Military Airplanes (p. 1142)
—Military Helicopters (p. 1143)
—Military Trucks (p. 1143)
—Military Vehicles. (p. 1143)
—Muscular Dystrophy. (p. 1192)
—Old Cars (p. 1283)
—Osteoporosis. (p. 1306)
—Parkinson's Disease. (p. 1325)
—Silly Cars. (p. 1575)
—Skiing. Lucent Books, ed. (p. 1584)
—Stem Cells. (p. 1647)
—Transplants. (p. 1779)
—Unbelievable Military Aircraft. (p. 1811)
—Volleyball. Greenhaven Press Editors, ed. (p. 1849)
—West Nile Virus. (p. 1876)
—What Is Schizophrenia? (p. 1890)
—World's Smallest Country & Other Geography Records. (p. 1961)
Abramovitz, Melissa, ed. see Mackay, Jennifer.
Abramovitz, Melissa, jt. auth. see Alpert, Barbara.
Abramovitz, Melissa, jt. auth. see Cella, Clara.
Abramovitz, Melissa & Alpert, Barbara. Cars, Cars, Cars. (p. 272)
—Military Machines. (p. 1143)
Abramovitz, Melissa & Cella, Clara. Let's Celebrate. (p. 995)
Abramovitz, Melissa & Clay, Kathryn. Wild about Wheels. (p. 1928)
Abramowski, Christina. Something Special. (p. 1610)
Abramowski, Kerry, jt. auth. see Vercoe, Elizabeth.
Abrams, Amir. Caught Up. (p. 282)
—Diva Rules. (p. 454)
Abrams, Amir, jt. auth. see Simone, Ni-Ni.
Abrams, Dennis. America Ferrera. (p. 59)
—Angelina Jolie. (p. 74)
—Anthony Horowitz. (p. 89)
—Barbara Park. (p. 137)
—Barbara Walters. (p. 137)
—Beastie Boys. (p. 152)
—Coco Chanel. (p. 337)
—Cotton Mather. (p. 369)
—David "Dav" Pilkey. (p. 411)
—Dorado. (p. 471)
—Ehud Olmert. (p. 507)
—Eminem. (p. 519)
—Ernest J. Gaines. (p. 533)
—Ernesto Che Guevara. (p. 534)
—Gary Soto. (p. 657)
—George Washington Carver: Scientist & Educator. (p. 664)
—Georgia O'Keeffe. (p. 665)
—Gregory Hines. (p. 723)
—H. G. Wells. (p. 734)
—Hamid Karzai. (p. 739)
—Hillary Rodham Clinton: Politician. (p. 780)
—Invention of the Moving Assembly Line. (p. 884)
—Jay-Z. (p. 910)
—Johnny Depp. (p. 923)
—Julia Child. (p. 932)
—L. Frank Baum. (p. 969)
—Lemony Snicket: Daniel Handler. (p. 991)
—Maxine Hong Kingston. (p. 1112)
—Mexican War of Independence. (p. 1131)
—Rachael Ray: Food Entrepreneur. (p. 1431)
—S. E. Hinton. (p. 1499)
—Sandra Day O'Connor: U. S. Supreme Court Justice. (p. 1511)
—Taylor Swift. (p. 1708)
—Thabo Mbeki. (p. 1724)
—Treaty of Nanking. (p. 1783)
—Ty Cobb. (p. 1804)
—Viktor Yushchenko. (p. 1842)
Abrams, Dennis & Ludwig, Elisa. Judy Blume. (p. 931)
Abrams, Douglas Carlton, jt. auth. see Tutu, Desmond.
Abrams, Douglas Carlton & Tutu, Desmond. God's Dream. Pham, LeUyen, illus. (p. 691)
Abrams, Elise, jt. auth. see Rendall, Richard.
Abrams, Majella. Reading Pals: Short & Long Vowels Gr. K-1. Taylor, Jennifer, ed. (p. 1446)
Abrams Noterie Staff, jt. auth. see Marabout.
Abrams, Pam. Can I Push the Button. (p. 258)
—Finger Fun. (p. 589)
—Gadgetology: Kitchen Fun with Your Kids, Using 35 Cooking Gadgets for Simple Recipes, Crafts, Games, & Experiments. Punch, Melissa, photos by. (p. 652)
—Now I Eat My ABC's. Wolf, Bruce, illus. (p. 1269)
Abrams, Pam, jt. auth. see Rudy, Maggie.
Abrams, Pam, jt. auth. see Wolf, Laurie Goldrich.
Abrams, Pam, et al. Candy 1 To 20. (p. 261)
Abrams, Patricia. Noah & the Search Dogs. (p. 1261)
Abrams, Penny. Calabash Tales. Mikki, illus. (p. 252)
Abrams, Suzanne, jt. auth. see Lewis, Sue.
Abrams, Taharra. Growing up Porcupine! (p. 727)
Abramsen, Ruth M. Akeelah's Spider. (p. 32)
Abramson, Andra, jt. auth. see Cider Mill Press, Cider Mill.
Abramson, Andra Serlin. Kids Meet the Sharks & Other Giant Sea Creatures. (p. 954)
Abramson, Andra Serlin, jt. auth. see Jordan, Meredith.
Abramson, Andra Serlin & Ross, Paula Kovacs. Kids Meet the Reptiles. (p. 954)
Abramson, Andra Serlin, et al. Inside Stars. (p. 877)
Abramson, Ann. Who Was Anne Frank? Harrison, Nancy, illus. (p. 1918)
Abramson, Beverley. Off We Go! (p. 1279)
Abramson, Cathy, illus. see Arbuthnoy, Nancy.
Abramson, Danny. Andruw Jones. (p. 72)
Abramson, Jill & O'Connor, Jane. Holiday Helper. Melmon, Deborah, illus. (p. 788)
—Puppy Parade. (p. 1418)
—Puppy Parade. Melmon, Deborah, illus. (p. 1418)
Abramson, Laurin. Coco. Abramson, Stephen, photos by. (p. 337)
Abramson, Marcie F. Painless Math Word Problems. (p. 1318)
Abramson, Stephen, photos by see Abramson, Laurin.
Abramson, Susan & Dvorkin, Aaron. Who Hogged the Hallah? A Shabbat Shabang. (p. 1915)
Abrashoff, D. Michael. It's Your Ship: Management Techniques from the Best Damn Ship in the Navy. (p. 899)
Abraxas, Matt, illus. see Carr, Simonetta.
Abrefah, Nana K. My Amazing Short Stories & Questions. (p. 1196)
Abregón, José María, tr. see Abnett, Dan.
Abremski, Kathy, illus. see Burr, Holly.
Abreu, Aline, jt. auth. see Dias, Christina.
Abreu, Carlos, tr. see DiTerlizzi, Tony, et al.
Abreu, Raquel. Little Ruth Reddingford (and the Wolf) An Old Tale retold by Hank Wesselman, PH. D. (p. 1036)
Abreu, Raquel, illus. see Griffith, Travis.
Abril, Paco & Francisco, Abril Berán. Colores que se Aman. Decis, Anne, illus. (p. 344)
Abromovitz, Jaime. Baby Dreamer Ding-A-Ling: Ding-A-Lings. (p. 126)
—Dreamer Ding-A-Ling: Ding-A-Lings: the Banana Phone. (p. 484)
—Zazzy-Q Ding-A-Ling: Ding-A-Lings: the Magic Wand. (p. 1985)
Abron Drache, Sharon. Lubavitchers Are Coming to Second Avenue: A Hanukkah Story. (p. 1062)
Abruzzo, Emily, ed. Dimension. (p. 440)
Abruzzo, Nancy. Pop Flop's Great Balloon Ride. Chilton, Noel, illus. (p. 1384)
Abs, Renata, illus. see Foelker, Rita.
ABS Staff. Bible Now: 101 Amazing Storie. (p. 175)
Abshier, Stan. Teddy's Journal: Cruise to Japan, China, & Singapore. (p. 1713)
Abshire, Lisa D. Sam's Magical Day. (p. 1509)
Abt, Diana, tr. see Mycek-Wodecki, Anna.
Abts, Stacey, illus. see Perry, Janice Kapp.
Abts, Stacey & Kleinman, Bertha A. I Have Two Little Hands. (p. 839)
Abu-Bakr, Sandra. Tales of Lovable Spike: Spike- on the Go! (p. 1702)
Abuelita, Little Grandma. Broccoli with Cheese. (p. 230)
—Clara Jean. (p. 326)
Abuhamda, Nasser. 6 Tales of Adventure. (p. 1992)
—Flower in the Rain. (p. 607)
—Short Stories. (p. 1569)
Abulafia, Yossi, illus. see Nirgad, Lia.
Abuli, Enrique Sanchez, tr. see Eisner, Will.
Abuli, Enrique Sanchez, tr. see Kubert, Joe.
Abuli, Enrique Sanchez, tr. see Mignola, Mike.
Abuli, Enrique Sanchez, tr. see Sfar, Joann & Trondheim, Lewis.
Aburto, Jesus, illus. see Ciencin, Scott & Maese, Fares.
Aburto, Jesus, illus. see Ciencin, Scott, et al.
Aburto, Jesus, illus. see Gunderson, Jessica.
Aburto, Jesus, illus. see Kreie, Chris & Maese, Fares.
Aburto, Jesus, illus. see Kreie, Chris, et al.
Aburto, Jesus, illus. see Maddox, Jake.
Aburto, Jesus, illus. see Peters, Stephanie True & Cano, Fernando M.
Aburto, Jesus, illus. see Renner, C. J., et al.
Aburto, Jesus, illus. see Tullen, Sean & Maese, Fares.
Aburtov, illus. see Ciencin, Scott.
Aburtov, illus. see Maddox, Jake.
Aburtov, illus. see Sonneborn, Scott.
Aburtov, Jesus, illus. see Maddox, Jake.
Aburtov, Jesus Aburto, illus. see Kreie, Chris, et al.
Aburtov, Jesus Aburto, illus. see Maddox, Jake.
Abushanab, Lynn, jt. auth. see Winckelmann, Thom.
Acacia Publishing, creator. My Little Black Book of Numbers/Mi Libro Chiquito Negro de Numeros: Coutning from/Contar de 0 To 20. (p. 1212)
—My Little White Book of Numbers/Mi Libro Chiquito Blanco de Numeros: Counting from/Contar de 20 To 40. (p. 1213)
Academy of American Poets Staff. Poem in Your Pocket for Young Poets. (p. 1375)
Acampora, Michael V. Battle of the Blue Lanterns Schoening, Dan, illus. (p. 146)
—Escape from the Orange Lanterns Schoening, Dan, illus. (p. 535)
—Red Lanterns' Revenge Schoening, Dan, illus. (p. 1454)
Acampora, Michael Vincent. Escape from the Orange Lanterns Schoening, Dan, illus. (p. 535)
—Red Lanterns' Revenge Schoening, Dan, illus. (p. 1454)
Acampora, Paul. I Kill the Mockingbird. (p. 840)
—Rachel Spinelli Punched Me in the Face. (p. 1432)
Acar, Sinan, illus. see Cox, Miss Karin & Cox, Karin.
Acayen, Alex, illus. see Starkey, Ines.
Accardo, Anthony, illus. see Baca, Ana.
Accardo, Anthony, illus. see Bertrand, Diane Gonzales.
Accardo, Anthony, illus. see Griswold del Castillo, Richard.
Accardo, Anthony, illus. see Lainez, René Colato.
Accardo, Jus. Tremble. (p. 1784)
Accardo, Reba, told to. Surgery for Me? (p. 1685)
Access Matrix Staff, jt. auth. see London, Jack.
Acclaim Press. Jasper County, Illinois a Pictorial History. (p. 910)
Accord Publishing Staff. Bugs. (p. 237)
—Colors: A Butterfly-Shaped Book. (p. 345)
—Dinosaurs: A Mini Animotion Book. (p. 444)
—Flip & Click Bingo. (p. 604)
—Flip & Click Christmas Bingo. (p. 604)

—Flip & Click Christmas Hangman. (p. 604)
—Flip & Click Christmas Memory Match. (p. 604)
—Flip & Click Hangman. (p. 604)
—Flip & Click Sports Bingo. (p. 604)
—Flip & Click Sports Hangman. (p. 604)
—Flip & Click Sports Memory Match. (p. 604)
—Go Fun! Big Book of Puzzles. (p. 686)
—Go Fun! Doodle: Summer Fun. (p. 686)
—Go Fun! Dot-to-Dot: Summer Fun. (p. 686)
—Go Fun! Paper Airplanes. (p. 686)
—Go Fun! Unicorns. (p. 686)
—Go Fun! Word Search: Summer Fun. (p. 686)
—Numbers: A Caterpillar-Shaped Book. (p. 1272)
—Oliver's First Christmas. Valiant, Kristi, illus. (p. 1286)
—Ready, Set, Go! (p. 1447)
—Santa's Workshop: A Mini Animotion Book. Idle, Molly, illus. (p. 1513)
—Trucks: A Mini Animotion Book. (p. 1791)
—Twelve Days of Christmas. Fang, Jade, illus. (p. 1800)
—What Do You See? A Lift-The-Flap Book. (p. 1883)
—Where Does Love Come From? Kirkova, Milena, illus. (p. 1907)
—Zoo Babies. (p. 1988)
Accord Publishing Staff, jt. auth. see Brown, Heather.
Accord Publishing Staff, jt. auth. see Chandler, Shannon.
Accord Publishing Staff, jt. auth. see Hannigan, Paula.
Accord Publishing Staff, jt. auth. see Price, Roger.
Accord Publishing Staff, jt. auth. see Riegelman, Rianna.
Accord Publishing Staff, jt. auth. see Stone, Kate.
Accord Publishing Staff, jt. auth. see Young, Rebecca.
Accord Publishing Staff & Andrews McMeel Publishing, LLC Staff. Bugs. (p. 237)
—Numbers: A Silly Slider Book. Cole, Jeff, illus. (p. 1272)
Accord Publishing Staff & Andrews McMeel Publishing Staff. San Francisco. (p. 1510)
Accord Publishing Staff & Hannigan, Paula. Oliver's First Christmas: A Mini AniMotion Book. Valiant, Kristi, illus. (p. 1286)
Accord Publishing Staff & Ohrt, Kate. Hanukkah: A Mini AniMotion Book. (p. 744)
Accord Publishing Staff & Stone, Kate. One Spooky Night: A Halloween Adventure. (p. 1297)
Accord Publishing Staff, et al. Stick to It - Pets: A Magnetic Puzzle Book. (p. 1649)
Accorsi, William. How Big Is the Lion? My First Book of Measuring. (p. 805)
Accrocco, Anthony, illus. see Seltz, Melissa.
Ace Academics & Burchard, Elizabeth R., eds. Algebra 1: A Whole Course in a Box! (p. 38)
Ace Academics, ed. Algebra 1: Exam Prep Software on CD-ROM! Exambusters CD-ROM Study Cards. (p. 38)
—Algebra 2-Trig: A Whole Course in a Box! (p. 38)
—Algebra 2-Trig: Exam Prep Software on CD-ROM! EXambusters CD-ROM Study Cards. (p. 38)
—American History: A Whole Course in a Box!: Study Cards. (p. 61)
—American History: Exam Prep Software on CD-ROM! Exambusters CD-ROM Study Cards. (p. 61)
—American Sign Language: Exam Prep Software on CD-ROM! Exambusters CD-ROM Study Cards. (p. 63)
—Arithmetic: A Whole Course in a Box! (p. 98)
—Arithmetic: Exam Prep Software on CD-ROM! Exambusters CD-ROM Study Cards. (p. 98)
—Biology: A Whole Course in a Box! (p. 189)
—Biology: Exam Prep Software on CD-ROM! Exambusters CD-ROM Study Cards. (p. 189)
—Chemistry: A Whole Course in a Box! (p. 297)
—Chemistry: Exam Prep Software on CD-ROM! Exambusters CD-ROM Study Cards. (p. 297)
—Chinese: Exam Prep Software on CD-ROM! Exambusters CD-ROM Study Cards. (p. 307)
—Coop/hspt: Exam Prep Software on CD-ROM! Exambusters CD-ROM Study Cards. (p. 365)
—Earth Science-Geology: A Whole Course in a Box! (p. 496)
—Earth Science-Geology: Exam Prep Software on CD-ROM! Exambusters CD-ROM Study Cards. (p. 496)
—English Vocabulary: A Whole Course in a Box! (p. 530)
—English Vocabulary: Exam Prep Software on CD-ROM! Exambusters CD-ROM Study Cards. (p. 530)
—Even More Sign Language: A Whole Course in a Box! (p. 541)
—French: Exam Prep Software on CD-ROM! Exambusters CD-ROM Study Cards. (p. 635)
—Geometry: A Whole Course in a Box! (p. 662)
—Geometry: Exam Prep Software on CD-ROM! Exambusters CD-ROM Study Cards. (p. 662)
—German: A Whole Course in a Box! (p. 666)
—German: Exam Prep Software on CD-ROM! Exambusters CD-ROM Study Cards. (p. 666)
—Hebrew: Exam Prep Software on CD-ROM! Exambusters CD-ROM Study Cards. (p. 761)
—Italian: A Whole Course in a Box! (p. 894)
—Italian: Exam Prep Software on CD-ROM! Exambusters CD-ROM Study Cards. (p. 894)
—Japanese: A Whole Course in a Box! (p. 909)
—Japanese: Exam Prep Software on CD-ROM!: Exambusters CD-ROM Study Cards. (p. 909)
—More Sign Language: Exambusters Study Cards: Exambusters Study Cards (p. 1175)
—New SAT: A Whole Course in a Box! (p. 1247)
—New York State Regents: Exam Prep Software on CD-ROM! Exambusters CD-ROM Study Cards. (p. 1248)
—Physics: A Whole Course in a Box! (p. 1353)
—Physics: Exam Prep Software on CD-ROM! Exambusters CD-ROM Study Cards. (p. 1353)
—Russian: Exam Prep Software on CD-ROM! Exambusters CD-ROM Study Cards. (p. 1498)
—Sign Language: A Whole Course in a Box! Pt. 1 (p. 1574)
—Spanish: A Whole Course in a Box! (p. 1620)
—Spanish: Exam Prep Software on CD-ROM! Exambusters CD-ROM Study Cards. (p. 1620)
—Ssat/isee: Exam Prep Software on CD-ROM!: Exambusters CD-ROM Study Cards. (p. 1637)
—World-European History: A Whole Course in a Box! (p. 1955)
—World-European History: Exam Prep Software on CD-ROM! Exambusters CD-ROM Study Cards. (p. 1955)
Ace Academics Staff, ed. Hebrew: A Whole Course in a Box! (p. 761)
Ace, Jane, ed. see Griffin, Randall C.
Ace, Jane, ed. see Renshaw, Amanda.
Ace, Jane, ed. see Williams, Gilda, et al.
Acedera, Kei, illus. see Greven, Alec.
Acedera, Kei, illus. see Oliver, Lauren.
Acen Staff, jt. contrib. by see Gwent (Wales), Staff Development Unit Staff.
Acer, David. Gotcha! 18 Amazing Ways to Freak Out Your Friends. MacEachern, Stephen, illus. (p. 704)
Acerno, Gerry, illus. see Gunderson, Jessica Sarah, et al.
AcesGraphics, illus. see Pie, Corey.
Acevedo, Adriana, tr. see Thompson, Kate.
Acevedo, Ari. Juan Bobo Sends the Pig to Mass. Wrenn, Tom, illus. (p. 930)
Acevedo, Jenny. Ginger's Grand Adventure. (p. 677)
Acevedo, Merlina Hilda. Fionna the Water Fairy. (p. 590)
Acey, Mtaalamu, mem. Eyes Free: The Memoir (p. 558)
Achampong, Nana S. It Pays to Be Kind. (p. 894)
Acharya, Sankarshan. Prosperity: Optimal Governance: Banking, Capital Markets, Global Trade, Exchange Rate. (p. 1412)
Achatz, Eric. Adventures of Ryan Alexander: The Great Space Chase. (p. 22)
Aché, illus. see Pennac, Daniel & Benacquista, Tonino.
Achebe, Chinua. Chike & the River. Rodriguez, Edel, illus. (p. 301)
Achebe, Chinua & Iroaganachi, John. How the Leopard Got His Claws. GrandPré, Mary, illus. (p. 813)
Acher, Gabriela. Amor en Tiempos del Colesterol. (p. 65)
Acheson, A. S. Fighting Words. (p. 586)
Acheson, Alison. Grandpa's Music: A Story about Alzheimer's. Farnsworth, Bill, illus. (p. 710)
—Molly's Cue (p. 1161)
—Mud Girl (p. 1188)
Acheson, Alison & Gutiérrez, Elisa. Cul-De-Sac Kids (p. 390)
Acheson, James & Ross, Sarah C. E. Contemporary British Novel Since 1980. (p. 360)
Achi, Taro. Mamoru the Shadow Protector Volume 1. (p. 1085)
Achieve Now Institute Staff. ESR Anthology (p. 536)
—ESR Student Resource Book. (p. 536)
Achikeobi-Lewis, Omileye. E. Rainbow Goddess. (p. 1435)
Achilles, Carole. Jocelyn's Theatre. Scoggins, Jocelyn, illus. (p. 919)
Achilles, Pat, illus. see Finnan, Kristie.
Achilles, Pat, illus. see Smith, Chrysa.
Achor, Shawn & Blankson, Amy. Ripple's Effect. O'Malley, Judy, ed. (p. 1474)
Aciman, André. Out of Egypt: A Memoir. (p. 1311)
Ackelsberg, Amy. Berry Best Friends Journal. Thomas, Laura, illus. (p. 167)
—Berry Bitty Bakers. MJ Illustrations Staff, illus. (p. 167)
—Day at the Apple Orchard. Thomas, Laura, illus. (p. 412)
—Easter Surprise. Thomas, Laura, illus. (p. 499)
—Happy New Year! (p. 746)
—Puppy Love! Artful Doodlers Limited Staff, illus. (p. 1418)
—Snow Dance. Thomas, Laura, illus. (p. 1598)
—Sweetest Friends. (p. 1690)
—Ultimate Collector's Guide. (p. 1809)
—Valentine's Day Mix-Up. MJ Illustrations Staff, illus. (p. 1830)
Acken, John M., jt. auth. see Acken, Mary P.
Acken, Mary P. & Acken, John M. Learning to Read by Topic: Chess. (p. 986)
Acker, Kerry. Dorothea Lange. (p. 471)
—Everything You Need to Know about the Goth Scene. (p. 546)
—Nina Simone. (p. 1256)
Acker, Rick. Lost Treasure of Fernando Montoya (p. 1057)
Ackerley, Sarah. Patrick the Somnambulist. Ackerley, Sarah, illus. (p. 1329)
Ackerley, Sarah, illus. see Deak, JoAnn.
Ackerman, Arlene. Glimmer de Gloop de Monkey Face: The Elf Named Pee-U & What He Knew. (p. 683)
Ackerman, Bettie Bennett, jt. auth. see Faison, Ashley Starr.
Ackerman, Dena, illus. see Glick, Dvorah.
Ackerman, Helen. Casper's Paper Caper. (p. 276)
Ackerman, Jane. Louis Pasteur & the Founding of Microbiology. (p. 1058)
Ackerman, Jill. Hey, Diddle Diddle! Berg, Michelle, illus. (p. 774)
—My Favorite Pets. (p. 1203)
—Old MacDonald: A Hand-Puppet Board Book. Berg, Michelle, illus. (p. 1284)
—Peek-a-Zoo. Land, Fiona, illus. (p. 1335)
—Please & Thank You! Berg, Michelle, illus. (p. 1373)
—This Little Piggy. Berg, Michelle, illus. (p. 1737)
—Uh-Oh! I'm Sorry. Berg, Michelle, illus. (p. 1808)
—Welcome Summer. Davis, Nancy, illus. (p. 1873)
Ackerman, Jill, jt. auth. see Scholastic, Inc. Staff.
Ackerman, Jill, jt. auth. see Smith, Justine.
Ackerman, Jill & Bryan, Beth. Petting Farm Karp, Ken, photos by. (p. 1348)
Ackerman, Jill & Landers, Ace. I Am a Train. Scholastic, Inc. Staff, ed. (p. 832)
Ackerman, Jill & Smith, Justine. Colors. Land, Fiona, illus. (p. 344)
—Shapes. Land, Fiona, illus. (p. 1560)
Ackerman, Jon. Girls' Volleyball. (p. 681)
Ackerman, Karen. Song & Dance Man. Gammell, Stephen, illus. (p. 1611)
Ackerman, Michele L., illus. see James, Annabelle.
Ackerman, Peter. Lonely Phone Booth. Dalton, Max, illus. (p. 1046)
Ackerman, Peter & Dalton, Max. Lonely Typewriter. (p. 1046)
Ackerman, Tova. Group Soup. Gorbachev, Valeri, illus. (p. 725)
Ackison, Wendy Wassink, illus. see Costanzo, Charlene A. & Costanzo, Charlene.
Ackison, Wendy Wassink, illus. see Crowe, Duane E.
Ackland, Nick. Animals. (p. 81)
—Colors. (p. 344)
—First Words. (p. 597)
—Numbers. (p. 1271)
Ackley, Peggy Jo, illus. see Child, Lydia Maria.
Ackley, Peggy Jo, illus. see Witkowski, Teri.
Ackroyd, Patricia. Where's Polygon? (p. 1910)
Ackroyd, Peter. Ancient Greece. (p. 69)
Aclin, Justin. Akaneiro. Marshall, Dave, ed. (p. 32)
Acocella, Nunzio. Nunu & His Best Friend. (p. 1273)
Acock, Anthony W., jt. auth. see Canas-Jovel, Lourdes E.
Acopiado, Ginger. Dinosaurs Went Marching On. Crenshaw, Derek, illus. (p. 445)
—Over the Rainbow with Joey. Fuglestad, R. A., illus. (p. 1314)
Acorn, Alesa. Diary of the Beloved Book One: The Hidden. (p. 435)
Acorn, John. Bugs of the Rockies. Sheldon, Ian, illus. (p. 237)
—Butterflies of British Columbia. (p. 247)
Acorn, John & Bezener, Andy. Compact Guide to Alberta Birds (p. 351)
Acorn, John Harrison. Bugs of Ontario. Sheldon, Ian, illus. (p. 237)
Acosta, Ivan. Cubiche en la Luna: Tres Obras Teatrales. (p. 389)
Acosta, Jamey & Apodaca, Blanca. Miss Molly's Dolly. (p. 1151)
Acosta, Jamey & Reid, Stephanie. Health & Safety. (p. 757)
Acosta, Jamey & Rice, Dona. Use Your Brain. (p. 1827)
Acosta, Margarita. Girl on the Bench. (p. 678)
—Summer at Grandma's. (p. 1673)
Acosta, Marta. Dark Companion. (p. 407)
Acosta, Naomi. Christmas with Abba. (p. 316)
Acosta, Olivia, tr. see Fisher, Tammy, ed.
Acosta, Patricia, illus. see Dostoevsky, Fyodor.
Acosta, Patricia, illus. see Ibanez, Francisco Montana.
Acosta, Patricia, illus. see Nino, Jairo Anibal.
Acosta, Patricia, illus. see Pombo, Rafael.
Acosta, Patricia, illus. see Ramirez, Gonzalo Canal.
Acosta, Patricia, illus. see Zambrano, Alicia.
Acosta, Patrick. Gabriel of Noah's Ark. (p. 652)
Acosta, Robert. Chibi. Kantz, John, illus. (p. 299)
—Next Generation! (p. 1249)
Acosta, Robert, ed. see Bevard, Robby, et al.
Acosta, Robert & Kilpatrick, Paul. AP You Can Draw Manga Master Course (p. 91)
Acosta, Tatiana, tr. see Barnham, Kay.
Acosta, Tatiana, tr. see Brown, Jonatha A.
Acosta, Tatiana, tr. see Gorman, Jacqueline Laks & Laks Gorman, Jacqueline.
Acosta, Tatiana, tr. see Gorman, Jacqueline Laks.
Acosta, Tatiana, tr. see Mezzanotte, Jim.
Acraman, Helen, illus. see Wright, Danielle.
Acredolo, Linda & Goodwyn, Susan. Baby Signs for Animals. Gentieu, Penny, illus. (p. 128)
—I Can Sign! Animals. (p. 836)
—I Can Sign! Playtime. (p. 836)
—My First Spoken Words: Babies. (p. 1208)
Acreman, Hayley. Found You Rabbit! Acreman, Hayley, illus. (p. 624)
Acreman, Hayley, illus. see Davies, Lewis.
Active Spud Press & Ettinger, Steve. Wallie Exercises. Proctor, Peter, illus. (p. 1855)
Activision Publishing, Inc., Staff, jt. auth. see Grosset and Dunlap Staff.
Activision Publishing Staff, jt. auth. see Creative Shubrook Staff.
Activity Books, jt. auth. see Fulcher, Roz.
Activity Books, jt. auth. see Gaffney, Sean Kevin.
Activity Books, jt. auth. see Levy, Barbara Soloff.
Activity Books, jt. auth. see Wellington, Monica.
Activity Books Staff, jt. auth. see Kurtz, John.
Activity Books Staff, jt. auth. see Shaw-Russell, Susan.
Activity Books Staff, jt. auth. see Tallarico, Tony, Sr.
Acton, Sara, illus. see Kane, Kim.
Act-Two Staff. Bug Safari. (p. 236)
—Space Mission. (p. 1619)
Acuff, Becky. Peanut Pond. (p. 1332)
Acuff, Daniel Stewart. Golf Is the Teacher, Life Is the Lesson. (p. 696)
—Mysteries of Quan. (p. 1222)
Acuña, Daniel, illus. see Brubaker, Ed & Breitweiser, Mitch.
Acuña, Daniel, illus. see Brubaker, Ed.
Acuña, Daniel, illus. see Liu, Marjorie M.
Ada, Alma Flor, illus. see Mora, Pat, et al.
Ada, Alma Flor, et al. Pio Peep! Traditional Spanish Nursery Rhymes. Escrivá, Viví, illus. (p. 1361)
Ada, Alma Flora. Island Treasures: Growing up in Cuba: Includes Where the Flame Trees Bloom, under the Royal Palms, & Five Brand New Stories. Martorell, Antonio, illus. (p. 892)
Ada, Alma Flora, tr. see Floyd, Lucy.
Ada, Alma Flora, tr. see Howard, Reginald.
Adachi, Mitsuri. Cross Game, Vol. 2. Adachi, Mitsuri, illus. (p. 385)
Adachi, Mitsuru. Cross Game, Vol. 4. Adachi, Mitsuru, illus. (p. 385)
Adahan, Miriam. Torah Tigers. (p. 1769)
Adair, Amy. Jay Jay's Special Delivery. (p. 910)
Adair, Dick. Story of Aloha Bear. Britt, Stephanie, illus. (p. 1657)
Adair, Gilbert. Alice Through the Needle's Eye: The Further Adventures of Lewis Carroll's Alice. Thorne, Jenny, illus. (p. 39)
Adair, Pam, tr. see Adair Scott, Paul.
Adair, Rick. Beryllium. (p. 168)
—Boron. (p. 214)
Adair Scott, Paul. Benito Botón e Isabel Hilo. Adair, Pam, tr. (p. 164)
Adair Scott, Paula. Blue Button & Red Thread. (p. 202)
Adair, Tammi. Heart of a Christmas Tree. Rudd, Benton, illus. (p. 759)
Adalbert. Soul, God & Buddha. (p. 1614)
Adam, Adam, et al. Who Is It? Two Yellow Eyes Shining in the Dark... (p. 1916)
Adam, Agnes. Devil Goes Riding. (p. 432)
—Home Sweet Home. (p. 793)
—Miss Primrose's Husband. (p. 1152)
Adam D. Levine. Knights: Reign of Hellfire. (p. 964)
Adam, Jamal, tr. see Moriarty, Kathleen M.
Adam, Mccauley, illus. see Scieszka, Jon.
Adam, Paul. Escape from Shadow Island. (p. 535)
Adam, Sally. Adventures of Rex Adam. (p. 22)
—Cats of Ellis Island. (p. 281)
Adam, Sarah E. Abby in Vermont Coloring & Activity Book. (p. 2)
Adam, Winky. Around the World Coloring Book. (p. 100)
—Color by Number. (p. 342)
—Native American Mazes. (p. 1234)
—Playground Fun Sticker Activity Book. (p. 1372)
Adamac, Matt, jt. auth. see Kelly, Martin.
Adamchuk, Rachelle G. Disappearance: The First Part of Trickery & Honest Deception. (p. 446)
Adame, Marie. Lemonade & Piglet in the Curse of the Rock of Musim. (p. 991)
Adamec, Christine. Opium. (p. 1300)
Adamec, Christine, jt. auth. see Gwinnell, Esther.
Adamec, Christine A., jt. auth. see Petit, William.
Adamec, Christine & Triggle, David J. Amphetamines & Methamphetamine. (p. 65)
—Barbiturates & Other Depressants. (p. 138)
Adamick, Mike. Dad's Book of Awesome Science Experiments: 30 Inventive Experiments to Excite the Whole Family! (p. 399)
Adamowski, Rob. Bernice: Oh my gosh It's a Bear! (p. 167)
Adam-Rita, Susan, jt. auth. see Coach Pedro.
Adams, Alces P. Not Forgotten, Not Gone: La Famille de Mon Pere; A Cajun History. (p. 1267)
Adams, Alison. Androcles & the Lion: Classic Tales Series. Greenhead, Bill, illus. (p. 72)
—Brer Rabbit Hears a Noise: Classic Tales Series. Greenhead, Bill, illus. (p. 226)
—Butterflies & Moths. (p. 247)
—Butterflies & Moths & Las mariposas y las Polillas: 6 English, 6 Spanish Adaptations (p. 247)
—Deserts. (p. 429)
—Gingerbread Man: Classic Tales Edition. Rogers, Jacqueline, illus. (p. 677)
—How the Turtle Cracked Its Shell: Classic Tales Edition. Greenhead, Bill, illus. (p. 813)
—Jack & the Beanstalk: Classic Tales Edition. Magnuson, Diana, illus. (p. 902)
—Las Mariposas y Las Polillas: Set Of 6. (p. 976)
—Las Montañas: Set Of 6. (p. 977)
—Light. (p. 1014)
—Mountains. (p. 1181)
—Mountains & Las Montañas: 6 English, 6 Spanish Adaptations (p. 1181)
—Our Moon. (p. 1309)
—Three Billy Goats Gruff: Classic Tales Edition. Harpster, Steve, illus. (p. 1741)
—Three Little Pigs: Classic Tales Edition. Greenhead, Bill, illus. (p. 1743)
—Two Hungry Hippos Math Game & Dos Hipopótamos con Hambre: 6 English, 6 Spanish Adaptations (p. 1803)
—Why Mosquitoes Buzz in People's Ears: Classic Tales Edition. Greenhead, Bill, illus. (p. 1925)
Adams, Allysa, illus. see Megerdichian, Janet.
Adams, Amy. Muscular System (p. 1192)
Adams, Andrea. If We Were Girlfriends, This Is What I'd Tell You: Straight Talk for Teenage Girls. (p. 854)
Adams, Andy. African Ivory Mystery: A Biff Brewster Mystery Adventure. (p. 27)
—Alaska Ghost Glacier Mystery: A Biff Brewster Mystery Adventure. (p. 34)
—Mystery of the Ambush in Indi: A Biff Brewster Mystery. (p. 1225)
—Mystery of the Mexican Treasure: A Biff Brewster Mystery Adventure. (p. 1225)
Adams, Angela, jt. auth. see Adams, Angela.
Adams, Angela & Adams, Angela. Angela Adams Enclosure Cards. (p. 74)
Adams, Ann. Moppet the Hero. (p. 1173)
Adams, Anne. See It/Say It Bible Storybook. Incrocci, Rick, illus. (p. 1546)
Adams, Anne Marie. Essence of Li: A Spiritual Journey into the Nature of Being. (p. 536)
Adams, Ansel. Ansel Adams: 400 Photographs. Stillman, Andrea G., ed. (p. 88)
—Sierra Nevada: The John Muir Trail. Adams, Ansel, photos by. (p. 1573)
Adams, Arlene, illus. see Bennett, Leonie.
Adams, Art, illus. see Perez, George.
Adams, Arthur, et al. New Mutants Classic (p. 1246)
Adams, B. How to Make Paper Airplanes. Oseid, Kelsey, illus. (p. 820)
—Magic Tricks with String. Oseid, Kelsey, illus. (p. 1074)
Adams, Barbara. World of Tools. (p. 1957)
Adams, Ben. Chico Plays Hide & Seek. Cameron, Craig, illus. (p. 301)
—Pig with the Curliest Tail. Cameron, Craig, illus. (p. 1357)
—Polly the Farm Puppy. Cameron, Craig, illus. (p. 1381)
Adams, Ben, illus. see O'Toole, Janet & Anness Publishing Staff.
Adams, Ben, illus. see O'Toole, Janet.
Adams, Ben, jt. auth. see Baxter, Nicola.
Adams, Beth, illus. see Ludwig, Trudy.
Adams, Bob. Roup. (p. 1491)
Adams, Bradley J. Forensic Anthropology. (p. 617)
Adams, Brenda Thompson. All about Abby: Abby Learns a Lesson about Bullying. (p. 42)
Adams, C. On My Sled: Learning the SL Sound. (p. 1289)
—Planes Go Places: Learning the PL Sound. (p. 1367)
Adams, Carly. Queens of the Ice: They Were Fast, They Were Fierce, They Were Teenage Girls (p. 1425)
Adams, Carol J. God Listens to Your Care: Prayers for All the Animals of the World. (p. 689)
—God Listens to Your Love: Prayers for Living with Animal Friends. (p. 689)
—God Listens When You're Afraid: Prayers for When Animals Scare You. (p. 689)

Adams, Carolyn Lee. Ruthless. (p. 1499)
Adams, Chanelle. Myra. (p. 1222)
Adams, Christine. Learning to Be a Good Friend: A Guidebook for Kids. Alley, R. W., illus. (p. 985)
Adams, Christine A. Worry, Worry Go Away. Alley, R. W., illus. (p. 1961)
Adams, Cindy. Living a Dog's Life: Jazzy, Juicy, & Me. (p. 1040)
Adams, Clarinda. Semi Sweetness in Cookie Dough Land. (p. 1550)
Adams, Clint. Angst Ist Nicht Alles. (p. 75)
—Don't Be Afraid of Heaven. (p. 466)
—Fear Ain't All That (p. 579)
—My Watch Doesn't Tell Time. (p. 1221)
—Seventh Ritual: A race for Survival. (p. 1555)
Adams, Colleen. At the Toy Store. (p. 111)
—Benjamin Franklin: American Inventor. (p. 164)
—Big Day! (p. 180)
—Carlos's Cubby. (p. 270)
—Courage of Helen Keller. (p. 372)
—Everglades: Analyzing Graphs, Tables, & Charts. (p. 542)
—Exploring the Grand Canyon. (p. 553)
—Hawaii: The Aloha State. (p. 755)
—Jake Gyllenhaal. (p. 906)
—Johnny Depp. (p. 923)
—Jugando en la nieve (Playing in the Snow) (p. 931)
—Keira Knightley. (p. 948)
—Kelly Clarkson. (p. 948)
—Magic Squares: Learning the Inverse Relationships Between Addition & Subtraction. (p. 1073)
—Orlando Bloom. (p. 1304)
—Playing in the Snow. (p. 1372)
—Pocahontas: The Life of an Indian Princess. (p. 1375)
—Pocahontas. (p. 1375)
—Primary Source Guide to Italy. (p. 1399)
—Results of the American Revolution: Summarizing Information. (p. 1464)
—School Is Cool! (p. 1523)
—Tangram Puzzles: Describing & Comparing Attributes of Plane Geometric Shapes. (p. 1705)
—True Story of Pocahontas. (p. 1793)
—True Story of the Battle of the Alamo. (p. 1793)
—True Story of the First Thanksgiving. (p. 1793)
—Usher. (p. 1828)
—Weekend in the City: Adding & Subtracting Times to the Nearest Minute. (p. 1871)
Adams, Colleen, jt. auth. see Day, Meredith.
Adams, Colleen, jt. auth. see Schimel, Kate.
Adams, Craig, illus. see Cash, M. A.
Adam's Creations Publishing. Enchanted Fairyland: A Sphinx & Trevi Adventure. Bishop, Christina, illus. (p. 523)
Adams, Cynthia. Mysterious Case of Sir Arthur Conan Doyle. (p. 1223)
Adams, D. A. Brotherhood of Dwarves. (p. 231)
Adams, David. One, Two, Three: A Collection of Songs, Verses, Riddles, & Stories for Children of Grades 1- 3. Mitchell, David, ed. (p. 1297)
Adams, David J. Good Night Vancouver. Veno, Joe & Rosen, Anne, illus. (p. 700)
Adams, David J., jt. auth. see Gamble, Adam.
Adams, Dena C. & Clark, Claire D. This Is Music! Preschool, Vol 1: Itsy Bitsy Music, Book & CD. (p. 1736)
Adams, Denise H. Annabelle's Angels. Adams, Denise H., illus. (p. 85)
—Itchy the Witch. Adams, Denise H., illus. (p. 895)
Adams, Derek. Karen Casey's Adventures in Band: Book One. (p. 943)
Adams, Diane. I Can Do It Myself! Hayashi, Nancy, illus. (p. 835)
—Teacher's Little Helper Hayashi, Nancy, illus. (p. 1709)
—Two Hands to Love You. Davis, Jon & Keiser, Paige, illus. (p. 1803)
—Zoom! Luthardt, Kevin, illus. (p. 1989)
Adams, Ea "Beth". Tiny Wish Granted: A tiny fairy meets a tiny Troll. (p. 1757)
Adams, Elissa, ed. see Children's Theatre Company Staff.
Adams, Elizabeth. Boy Who Cried Wolf. (p. 219)
Adams, Emma, jt. auth. see Pullman, Philip.
Adams, Eunice, jt. auth. see Adams, Rodney.
Adams, Eustace L. Plane Without a Pilot. (p. 1367)
Adams, Fernie. Antelope Was a Beautiful Woman. (p. 89)
Adams, Frank, illus. see Perrault, Charles.
Adams, Gail & Brown, Sheron. Six-Minute Solution: A Reading Fluency Program. (p. 1582)
Adams, Gary. Ladybug Story. (p. 971)
—Little Clock Who Had No Hands. (p. 1026)
Adams, Georgia & Utton, Peter. Cuentame la Biblia. (p. 389)
Adams, Georgie. Noah's Ark. Leplar, Anna C., illus. (p. 1261)
ADAMS, GEORGIE, jt. auth. see Adams, Georgie.
Adams, Georgie & ADAMS, GEORGIE. Historias de Hadas Contadas Por Hadas. Gardner, Sally, tr. (p. 782)
Adams, Georgie & Utton, Peter. Cuéntame y Cántame: Historias y Canciones de la Biblia. (p. 389)
Adams, Gil, illus. see Abbott, Tony.
Adams, H. J. Twice Six Tales All Told. (p. 1801)
Adams, Hazel, illus. see Mataya, Marybeth.
Adams, Hazel, illus. see Vogel, Julia.
Adams, Herschelle. Color Blind. (p. 342)
Adams, Ian. Drumming. (p. 487)
Adams, Ivy. International Kissing Club. (p. 880)
Adams, Ivy, jt. auth. see Deebs, Tracy.
Adams, J. Handler: Second Edition. (p. 740)
Adams, Jackie. Without a Blink. (p. 1942)
Adams, Jacqueline. Obsessive-Compulsive Disorder. (p. 1275)
Adams, James, jt. auth. see Garcia, Cecelia.
Adams, James D. Creepy Campfire Tales: Halloween Campout (p. 381)
—Creepy Campfire Tales: Halloween Campout. Vol. 1 (p. 381)
Adams, Jay C. Squanto: The Squirrel Who Learned to Save. (p. 1636)
Adams, Jean Ekman. Clarence & the Purple Horse Bounce into Town. Adams, Jean Ekman, illus. (p. 326)
—Cowgirl & her Horse. (p. 374)
—When Dogs Dream. (p. 1902)
Adams, Jeanette. Within the Circle (p. 1942)
Adams, Jeanne. Tyler's Safe Day, Everyday Safety for Children. (p. 1805)
Adams, Jeff. Philemon: Real Friendships in an Unreal World. (p. 1350)
Adams, Jennifer. Adventures of Huckleberry Finn: A Camping Primer. Oliver, Alison, illus. (p. 18)
—Alice in Wonderland: A Colors Primer Oliver, Alison, illus. (p. 39)
—Alice in Wonderland Playset: A Babylit(r) Color Primer Board Book & Playset Oliver, Alison, illus. (p. 39)
—Anna Karenina: A BabyLit Fashion Primer Oliver, Alison, illus. (p. 85)
—Christmas Carol: A BabyLit Colors Primer Oliver, Alison, illus. (p. 313)
—Dana's First Fish. (p. 402)
—Don Quixote: A Spanish Language Primer Oliver, Alison, illus. (p. 465)
—Dracula: A BabyLit Counting Primer Oliver, Alison, illus. (p. 476)
—Edgar & the Tattle-Tale Heart. Stucki, Ron, illus. (p. 504)
—Edgar & the Tattle-Tale Heart Board Book (p. 504)
—Edgar Gets Ready for Bed Stucki, Ron, illus. (p. 504)
—Edgar Gets Ready for Bed Board Book (p. 504)
—Frankenstein: An Anatomy Primer. Oliver, Alison, illus. (p. 629)
—Jabberwocky: A Nonsense Primer Oliver, Alison, illus. (p. 902)
—Jane Eyre: A Counting Primer Oliver, Alison, illus. (p. 908)
—Jungle Book: An Animal Primer. Oliver, Alison, illus. (p. 935)
—Moby-Dick: Board Book & Playset Oliver, Alison, illus. (p. 1157)
—Moby-Dick. Oliver, Alison, illus. (p. 1157)
—Pride & Prejudice: A Counting Primer Oliver, Alison, illus. (p. 1399)
—Pride & Prejudice: Counting Primer Book & Playset. Oliver, Alison, illus. (p. 1399)
—Romeo & Juliet: A BabyLit Counting Primer Oliver, Alison, illus. (p. 1486)
—Secret Garden: A Flowers Primer Oliver, Alison, illus. (p. 1541)
—Sense & Sensibility: An Opposites Primer Oliver, Alison, illus. (p. 1551)
—Wonderful Wizard of Oz. Oliver, Alison, illus. (p. 1948)
—Wuthering Heights: A Weather Primer. Oliver, Alison, illus. (p. 1966)
Adams, Jennifer, jt. auth. see Carabine, Sue.
Adams, Jennifer, jt. auth. see Gibbs Smith.
Adams, Jennifer Lynn. For I Am Always with You: Valerie's True Fairy Tale. (p. 615)
Adams, Jesse. Farmer Dillo Counts His Chickens. Speer, Julie & Rogers, David, illus. (p. 574)
—Farmer Dillo Paints His Barn. Speer, Julie & Davis, Christopher Owen, illus. (p. 574)
—Farmer Dillo Shapes Things Up. Speer, Julie & Polhamus, Bruce, illus. (p. 574)
Adams, Jessica. Astrology: What Do the Stars Say about You? (p. 109)
—Psychic Powers: Do You Have a Secret Sixth Sense? (p. 1413)
Adams, Jim, Sr., creator. Math Made Easy As 1+2+3= (p. 1106)
Adams, Jjt. Adventures of Junior & Mousey in the Land of Puttin Pow: Don't Talk to Strangers. Adams, Ronald, illus. (p. 19)
Adams, John Joseph, ed. Under the Moons of Mars: New Adventures on Barsoom. (p. 1813)
—Under the Moons of Mars: New Adventures on Barsoom. Various Artists, illus. (p. 1813)
Adams, Julia. Fruits. (p. 645)
—Grains. (p. 705)
—Proteins. (p. 1412)
—Vegetables. (p. 1834)
Adams, Julie. Kern's Adventures: The Fishing Trip. (p. 949)
Adams, Karen S. Introducing Marion! Your Cancer-Fighting Friend! A Story to Help a Child Learn How to Use Visual Imagery to Fight Cancer. (p. 882)
Adams, Karin. Lights! Curtains! Cows! (p. 1016)
—No TV? No Fair! (p. 1260)
Adams, Katharine. Blackthorn. (p. 197)
Adams, Kathryn, illus. see Abley, Mark.
Adams, Keith. Tales of Henry Tuffin - Henry Goes to School. Hewitt, Geoff, ed. (p. 1702)
—Tales of Henry Tuffin - Henry's Christmas. Geoff Hewitt, ed. (p. 1702)
—Tales of Henry Tuffin - Henry's Sore Foot & a New Arrival. Hewitt, Geoff, ed. (p. 1702)
—Tales of Henry Tuffin - the Day the Light Went Out. Hewitt, Geoff, ed. (p. 1702)
Adams, Kevin. Stegosaurus Named Sam. Adams, Kevin & Price, Michael, illus. (p. 1646)
Adams, Kylie. Beautiful Disaster. (p. 153)
—Bling Addiction: Fast Girls, Hot Boys Series. (p. 199)
Adams, L. Happy Memories: A Continuing Family Saga for Young Adults. (p. 746)
Adams, Lacole Sessions. Maggie & Her Tree. (p. 1071)
Adams, Laurie Gifford. Finding Atticus. (p. 587)
Adams, Lenora. Baby Girl. (p. 126)
Adams, Leon. Dragon Pearls. (p. 477)
—Jewel of Light. (p. 917)
—Land of the Dragons. (p. 973)
—Mystic Lord. (p. 1226)
Adams, Leonard. Two Girls & Two Monsters. (p. 1803)
Adams, Linda. Make & Learn Bible Toys. (p. 1079)
Adams, Linda Paulson. Refining Fire. (p. 1456)
Adams, Lisa. Twelve Days of Christmas in New York City. Adams, Lisa, illus. (p. 1800)
Adams, Lisa K. Dealing with Teasing/Que Hacer con Las Burlas. Velazquez De Leon, Mauricio, tr. from SPA. (p. 418)
Adams, "Little John". Legend of the Mono Gnome: A Story from Gnome Hollow. (p. 989)
Adams, Liz, illus. see Jones, Jen.
Adams, Lucas, illus. see Carlson, Lavelle.
Adams, Lynn. Penguin Sticker Paper Doll. (p. 1337)
Adams, Lynn, illus. see Dussling, Jennifer.
Adams, Lynn, illus. see Friedman, Mel, et al.
Adams, Lynn, illus. see Lawrence, Mary.
Adams, Lynn, illus. see Penner, Lucille Recht.
Adams, Lynn, illus. see Pollack, Pam & Belviso, Meg.
Adams, Lynn, tr. see Dussling, Jennifer.
Adams, Lynne, illus. see Penner, Lucille Recht.
Adams, Lynne, jt. auth. see Williamson, Hilary.
Adams, Marcella Ryan, illus. see Redman-Waldeyer, Christine.
Adams, Mark. Boy Named Bucky Dolan, Amy, illus. (p. 218)
—Bucky's Best Friend Dolan, Amy, illus. (p. 234)
Adams, Mark, ed. see Life Magazine Editors.
Adams, Mark W., illus. see Rubenstein, Lauri.
Adams, Mark Wayne, illus. see Benchimol, Brigitte.
Adams, Mark Wayne, illus. see Hinman, Bobbie.
Adams Marks, Elizabeth, illus. see Hemminger, Marcia.
Adams Marks, Elizabeth, illus. see Koumpouras, Sally.
Adams Marks, Elizabeth, illus. see Meinke, Amanda & Stegmann, Lisa.
Adams, Marlene. Slinkie the courageous Snail. Gonzalez., Jose L., illus. (p. 1590)
Adams, Matt, illus. see Brian, Janeen.
Adams, Matthew R. Kord & Harley. O'Reilly, Sean Patrick, ed. (p. 967)
Adams, Megan Weeks & Gamble, Adam. Good Night Martha's Vineyard. Rosen, Anne, illus. (p. 699)
Adams, M.H. Small Means & Great Ends (Illustrated. (p. 1592)
Adams, Michael. Help Yourself to a Blue Banana: Awakening Your Eyes to Art, Design & Visual Living. (p. 766)
—Little King & the Honeybee. (p. 1030)
Adams, Michael, illus. see Roos, Am & Hamilton, A.
Adams, Michael A. & Nehme, Marina. Business Organisations Law Guidebook. (p. 245)
Adams, Michelle. Cliff Lee. (p. 332)
—Katy Perry. (p. 946)
—Sarah Boone: A Lowcountry Girl Brewster, Jane, illus. (p. 1514)
—Zumba Fitness. (p. 1990)
Adams, Michelle M. I Will Not Be Afraid. Tugeau, Jeremy, illus. (p. 848)
Adams, Michelle M., jt. auth. see Adams, Michelle Medlock.
Adams, Michelle Medlock. Care for a Puppy. (p. 266)
—God Is Always with You. Siewert, Pauline, illus. (p. 689)
—Ha! Ha! Halloween. Johnson, Meredith, illus. (p. 734)
—Hooray for Easter! Devaney, Adam, illus. (p. 796)
—How Much Does God Love You? Keiser, Paige, illus. (p. 811)
—Jessica Simpson. (p. 914)
—Kenny Chesney. (p. 949)
—Life & Times of Cleopatra. (p. 1008)
—Little Colt's Palm Sunday. Parmenter, Wayne, illus. (p. 1026)
—Memories of the Manger. Ettlinger, Doris, illus. (p. 1126)
—My Funny Valentine. Johnson, Meredith, illus. (p. 1209)
—Sparrow's Easter Song. Eldridge, Marion, illus. (p. 1622)
—Story of Jesus Activity Book. Reed, Lisa, illus. (p. 1658)
—Story of Noah Activity Book. Reed, Lisa, illus. (p. 1659)
—Tim Mcgraw. (p. 1750)
—What Is Christmas? (p. 1889)
—What Is Christmas? Wummer, Amy, illus. (p. 1889)
—What Is Easter? Wummer, Amy, illus. (p. 1889)
—What Is Halloween? Wummer, Amy, illus. (p. 1889)
—What Is Thanksgiving? Wummer, Amy, illus. (p. 1890)
—Why I Love you, God. (p. 1925)
—Why I Praise You, God. Chapman, Susan, illus. (p. 1925)
—Why I Thank You, God. Koeller, Carol, illus. (p. 1925)
—Why I Trust You, God. Munger, Nancy, illus. (p. 1925)
Adams, Michelle Medlock, jt. auth. see Holl, Kristi.
Adams, Michelle Medlock & Adams, Michelle M. Sister for Sale! Brooks, Karen Stormer, illus. (p. 1581)
Adams, Misty Pedersen. Grandma Goes Home (p. 708)
Adams, Najla. Adventures of Mama Deer. (p. 20)
Adams, Neal. First X-Men. (p. 598)
Adams, Neal, illus. see Thomas, Roy & Buscema, Sal.
Adams, Neal, et al. 1970s (p. 2002)
Adams, Nick K. Uncivil War: Battle in the Classroom. (p. 1811)
Adams, Pam. Dolphin. (p. 464)
—Farmer in the Dell. (p. 574)
—First Day. (p. 594)
—Kitten. (p. 962)
—Mrs. Honey's Hat. (p. 1187)
—Old Macdonald. (p. 1284)
—Puppy. (p. 1418)
—There Was an Old Lady Who Swallowed a Fly. (p. 1730)
—There Was an Old Lady Who Swallowed the Sea. (p. 1730)
—This Is the House That Jack Built. (p. 1736)
—This Old Man. (p. 1737)
—Tiger. (p. 1748)
Adams, Pam, illus. see Twinn, M.
Adams, Pam, jt. auth. see Kubler, Annie.
Adams, Pam, tr. Old Macdonald Had a Farm. (p. 1284)
—There Was an Old Lady Who Swallowed a Fly. (p. 1730)
Adams, Pamela L. Once upon a Family: A Son's Journey of Love, Loss, & Hope. Henderson, Ken, illus. (p. 1292)
Adams, Patricia E. Break Free, Recover & Be Restored: From Wrong Choices & Their Consequences (p. 224)
—Fiery Darts of the Assassin - Satan: Know the Nature of the Enemy Satan (p. 584)
—Help My Fears' Shadow Is Chasing Me (PTSD) Traumas Aftershock (p. 766)
—Salvation - Unpack It & Use It: Its More Than a Ticket to Heaven (p. 1506)
—Set Free to Praise Him - a Childs Rights Violated: Her Terrors & Traumas (p. 1553)
Adams, Paul Robert. Buntley's Wing Kit. Oliver, Liana, illus. (p. 243)
Adams, Pauline Jacqueline. Valentine's Journey. (p. 1830)
Adams, Pauline M. Exciting Adventures of Amy: The Day We Filled Our Larder. (p. 547)
Adams, Peggy, jt. auth. see Klitzner, Irene.
Adams, Peggy J. Arnie Aardvark & Friends. (p. 100)
Adams, Peter. Why Rain & Fire Are Enemies. (p. 1925)
Adams, Peyton. Firemen Don't Wear Glasses. Carey, Katey, illus. (p. 592)
—Mermaids Don't Wear Glasses. Carey, Katey, illus. (p. 1128)
Adams, Phillip G. Decisions, Decisions, Decisions. (p. 421)
Adams, Presley. Let's Go to Acadia National Park: Solve Problems Involving the Four Operations (p. 997)
Adams, Renee. Can Thunder Hurt Me? Adams, Renee, illus. (p. 258)
Adams, Rich, illus. see Staman, A. Louise.
Adams, Richard. Tyger Voyage. Bayley, Nicola, illus. (p. 1805)
—Watership Down. (p. 1864)
Adams, Robert. Growing up in Charis. (p. 726)
Adams, Rodney & Adams, Eunice. Ooooooooo, You Said A Bad Wooord! How A Group of Young People Outgrew 'Adult' Language. (p. 1298)
Adams, Ronald, illus. see Adams, Jjt.
Adams, Ross. Brandonburg Christmas. (p. 222)
Adams, Rusty, jt. auth. see White-Adams, Beverly.
Adams, S. Great Adventures of Thomas Trumpet. (p. 713)
Adams, S. J. Sparks: The Epic, Completely True Blue, (Almost) Holy Quest of Debbie. (p. 1622)
Adams, Sabrina, jt. auth. see Page, Julie.
Adams, Samuel, jt. auth. see Young, Ben.
Adams, Sandi. Watch What You Wish: Kajsa Conquers Her World. (p. 1861)
Adams, Sarah. Gary & Ray. (p. 657)
Adams, Sarah, tr. see Durand, Delphine.
Adams, Sarah, tr. see Pennac, Daniel.
Adams, Scott. Ben's Bug Collection: Understanding Addition. (p. 165)
—Stick to Drawing Comics, Monkey Brain! Cartoonist Explains Cloning, Blouse Monsters, Voting Machines, Romance, Monkey Gods, How to Avoid Being Mistaken for a Rodent, & More. (p. 1649)
Adams, Sean. Tim Duncan. (p. 1750)
Adams, Sheila Murphy. Beads, Bands, & a Brass Ring. (p. 149)
Adams, Sherred Willc. Five Little Friends. (p. 600)
Adams, Sherred Willco. Five Little Friends. (p. 600)
Adams, Sherred Willcox. Five Little Friends. (p. 600)
Adams, Shireen, illus. see Gilani, Fawzia.
Adams, Shireen, illus. see Mair, J. Samia.
Adams, Simon. 50 Thing You Should Know about the Second World War. (p. 1997)
—Alexander the Great: The Boy Soldier Who Conquered the World. (p. 36)
—Artillery. (p. 104)
—Best Book of Volcanoes. (p. 168)
—Best Book of Weather. (p. 168)
—Cinderella. Askew, Amanda, ed. (p. 320)
—Elizabeth I: The Outcast Who Became England's Queen. (p. 513)
—Hansel & Gretel. Askew, Amanda, ed. (p. 743)
—Iraq War. (p. 887)
—Kingfisher Atlas of the Ancient World. Baxter, Katherine, illus. (p. 960)
—Kingfisher Atlas of World History: A Pictoral Guide to the World's People & Events, 10000BCE-Present. (p. 960)
—Politics. (p. 1380)
—Presidents of the United States. (p. 1397)
—Russia. (p. 1498)
—Sleeping Beauty. Askew, Amanda, ed. (p. 1589)
—Tanks. (p. 1705)
—Titanic. (p. 1757)
—Warplanes. (p. 1858)
—Warships. (p. 1859)
—World History Biographies: Alexander: The Boy Soldier Who Conquered the World. (p. 1955)
—World War I. (p. 1958)
—World War II. (p. 1959)
Adams, Simon, jt. auth. see Dorling Kindersley Publishing Staff.
Adams, Simon, et al. Geography of the World. (p. 662)
Adams, Stacey. Home for Brooks. (p. 792)
Adams, Stephanie Irwin. Ethan's Chocolate Chip Cookie. (p. 539)
Adams, Steve, illus. see Frazee, Randy.
Adams, Steve, illus. see Whelan, Gloria.
Adams, Steve, illus. see Wojtowicz, Jen & Wojzowitz, Jen.
Adams, Steve, illus. see Wojtowicz, Jen.
Adams, Steve, illus. see Yolen, Jane.
Adams, Tanya. Under Raging Skies. (p. 1813)
Adams, Ted, ed. Transformers Animated (p. 1778)
Adams, Thomas J. My Mommy Went to Sea Today. (p. 1214)
Adams, Tina. Chris Mouse & the Promise. (p. 311)
Adams, Tom. Super Science: Matter Matters! Flintman, Thomas, illus. (p. 1680)
Adams, Tonya. Sam the Walrus: A Grumpy Day to Play. Johnson, Amber W., illus. (p. 1507)
Adams, Tracey, jt. auth. see Young, Ed.
Adams, Tracy. Violent Passions: Managing Love in the Old French Verse Romance. (p. 1843)
Adams, Troon Harrison, jt. auth. see Harrison Adams, Troon.
Adams, Trudy. Judging Meghan. (p. 930)
Adams, W. Royce. Computer's Nerd. (p. 355)
—Jay. (p. 910)
—Raid on Rairarubi. (p. 1433)
—Rairarubia: The Rairarubia Tales Bk. 1 (p. 1436)
—Return to Rairarubi. (p. 1465)
—Ring from Rairarubia. (p. 1473)
Adams, Wayne. Laci the Ladybug. Kern, Shelly, illus. (p. 970)
Adams, William J. Goin' to the Zoo / Vamos Al Zoologico. Stiglich, Tom, illus. (p. 692)
—Goin' to the Zoo Coloring Book: Vamos Al Zoologico. Stiglich, Tom, illus. (p. 692)
—Hate that Thunder. Stiglich, Tom, illus. (p. 752)
—Hate That Thunder/Odio Ese Trueno Stiglich, Tom, illus. (p. 752)
—Visiting the Farm / Visitando la Granja. Stiglich, Tom, illus. (p. 1845)
—Visiting the Farm / Visitando la Granja Coloring Book. Stiglich, Tom, illus. (p. 1845)
Adams, William Taylor, see Optic, Oliver, pseud.
Adams-Cantrell;, Renee. Peanut Bunny & the Christmas Lights. Daley-Prado, M. J., illus. (p. 1332)
Adamson, Bonnie, illus. see Bardhan-Quallen, Sudipta.
Adamson, Bonnie, illus. see Brunell, Heather.
Adamson, Bonnie, illus. see Crawford, Laura.

Adamson, Bonnie, illus. see Heling, Kathryn & Hembrook, Deborah.
Adamson, Bonnie, illus. see Heling, Kathryn, et al.
Adamson, Bonnie, illus. see Rashkin, Rachel.
Adamson, Deanna. Other Side of the Lines: Southern Heroes of the US Civil War. (p. 1306)
Adamson, Ged. Meet the Mckaws. (p. 1123)
Adamson, Ged & Rylance, Ulrike. Elsie Clarke & the Vampire Hairdresser. Adamson, Ged, illus. (p. 516)
Adamson, Gil. Help Me, Jacques Cousteau (p. 765)
Adamson, Heather. Ancient Egypt: An Interactive History Adventure (p. 68)
—Animals with Speed. (p. 84)
—Best of Pro Soccer (p. 170)
—Big Animals. (p. 177)
—Bird Nests. (p. 190)
—Birthday Parties. (p. 193)
—Blue in Nature. (p. 203)
—Challenger Explosion Bascle, Brian, illus. (p. 289)
—Charles Darwin & the Theory of Evolution Purcell, Gordon & Milgrom, Al, illus. (p. 292)
—Civil Rights Movement: An Interactive History Adventure (p. 325)
—Civil Rights Movement [Scholastic]: An Interactive History Adventure. (p. 325)
—Clothes in Many Cultures (p. 334)
—Clothes in Many Cultures Saunders-Smith, Gail, ed. (p. 334)
—Day in the Life of a Child Care Worker (p. 413)
—Day in the Life of a Construction Worker (p. 413)
—Day in the Life of a Dentist (p. 413)
—Day in the Life of a Doctor (p. 413)
—Day in the Life of a Firefighter (p. 413)
—Day in the Life of a Police Officer (p. 413)
—Day in the Life of a Veterinarian (p. 413)
—Families in Many Cultures (p. 567)
—Families in Many Cultures Saunders-Smith, Gail, ed. (p. 567)
—Family Vacations. (p. 569)
—Grocery Store. (p. 725)
—Homes in Many Cultures (p. 793)
—Homes in Many Cultures Saunders-Smith, Gail, ed. (p. 793)
—In My Country. (p. 864)
—In My World. (p. 864)
—Let's Play Soccer! (p. 1000)
—Measure It! (p. 1117)
—My Continent. (p. 1200)
—School in Many Cultures Saunders-Smith, Gail, ed. (p. 1523)
—¡Vamos a Jugar al Fútbol! (p. 1831)
Adamson, Heather, jt. auth. see Adamson, Thomas K.
Adamson, Heather, jt. auth. see Adamson, Tom.
Adamson, Heather, jt. auth. see Rustad, Martha.
Adamson, Heather, jt. auth. see Schuh, Mari C.
Adamson, Heather, et al. Wow! (p. 1962)
Adamson, John H. Pictorial History of Shenandoah County: Fifty Years through the Lens of Hugh Morrison, Jr. (p. 1355)
Adamson, Lisbeth. Tokens: Kingdoms Through the Doorways. (p. 1762)
Adamson, Lynda G. Literature Links to World History, K-12: Resources to Enhance & Entice (p. 1023)
Adamson, Lynne, illus. see Caffrey, Jaye Andras.
Adamson, Peter, jt. auth. see Haywood, David.
Adamson, Thomas K. American Revolution. (p. 63)
—Astronauts Saunders-Smith, Gail, ed. (p. 109)
—Baseball: The Math of the Game (p. 140)
—Basketball: The Math of the Game. (p. 143)
—Big Air Skateboarding. (p. 177)
—BMX Freestyle. (p. 204)
—BMX Racing. (p. 204)
—Bowhunting (p. 216)
—Civil War. (p. 325)
—Deer Hunting (p. 423)
—Do You Really Want to Visit Mars? Fabbri, Daniele, illus. (p. 458)
—Do You Really Want to Visit Mercury? Fabbri, Daniele, illus. (p. 458)
—Do You Really Want to Visit the Moon? Fabbri, Daniele, illus. (p. 458)
—Do You Really Want to Visit Venus? Fabbri, Daniele, illus. (p. 458)
—Dragsters (p. 479)
—Duck Hunting (p. 488)
—Earth. (p. 495)
—Earth [Scholastic]: Revised Edition. (p. 496)
—Exploring the Galaxy (p. 553)
—First Moon Landing Purcell, Gordon & Beatty, Terry, illus. (p. 596)
—Freestyle Motocross (p. 635)
—Hot Rods (p. 802)
—Jupiter. (p. 937)
—Jupiter [Scholastic]: Revised Edition. (p. 937)
—Kids' Guide to Sports Design & Engineering (p. 954)
—Learning about South America. (p. 984)
—Lowriders (p. 1061)
—Luna. Saunders-Smith, Gail, ed. (p. 1065)
—Mars. (p. 1096)
—Mars [Scholastic]: Revised Edition. (p. 1096)
—Mercury. (p. 1127)
—Mercury [Scholastic]: Revised Edition. (p. 1127)
—Moon [Scholastic]. (p. 1172)
—Motocross Freestyle. (p. 1179)
—Motocross Racing (p. 1179)
—Motocross Racing. (p. 1179)
—Neptune. (p. 1241)
—Neptune [Scholastic]: Revised Edition. (p. 1241)
—Pluto: A Dwarf Planet (p. 1374)
—Pluto [Scholastic]: A Dwarf Planet. (p. 1374)
—Saturn. (p. 1515)
—Saturno/Saturn. Guzman Ferrer, Martin Luis, tr. from ENG. (p. 1516)
—Secrets of Jupiter. (p. 1545)
—Secrets of Neptune. (p. 1545)
—Secrets of Uranus. (p. 1546)
—Skateboarding Street Style. (p. 1583)
—Sol/the Sun. Saunders-Smith, Gail, ed. (p. 1608)
—South Dakota. (p. 1617)
—Stars [Scholastic]. (p. 1643)
—Stock Cars (p. 1651)
—Sun, Moon, & Stars Pack [Scholastic]. (p. 1676)
—Sun [Scholastic]. (p. 1676)
—Technology of Baseball (p. 1711)
—Uranus. (p. 1825)
—Uranus [Scholastic]: Revised Edition. (p. 1825)
—Venus. (p. 1836)
—Venus [Scholastic]: Revised Edition. (p. 1836)
—World War I. (p. 1958)
—World War II. (p. 1959)
Adamson, Thomas K., jt. auth. see Winrich, Ralph.
Adamson, Thomas K. & Adamson, Heather. 2, 4, Skip Count Some More (p. 1991)
—Give Probability a Chance! (p. 681)
—Half You Heard of Fractions? (p. 737)
—How Do You Measure Length & Distance? (p. 808)
—How Do You Measure Liquids? (p. 808)
—How Do You Measure Time? (p. 808)
—How Do You Measure Weight? (p. 808)
—World's Tallest House of Cards & Other Number Records (p. 1961)
—¿Cómo Mides el Peso? (p. 351)
—¿Cómo Mides el Tiempo? (p. 351)
—¿Cómo Mides los Líquidos? (p. 351)
Adamson, Thomas K. & Capstone Press Editors. Moon Saunders-Smith, Gail, ed. (p. 1171)
Adamson, Thomas K. & Capstone Press Staff. Sun Saunders-Smith, Gail, ed. (p. 1675)
Adamson, Thomas K. & Frederick, Shane. Sports Math. (p. 1633)
Adamson, Thomas K. and Heather. 2, 4, Skip Count Some More. (p. 1991)
—Fun with Numbers. (p. 648)
—Give Probability a Chance! (p. 681)
—Half You Heard of Fractions? (p. 737)
—How Do You Measure Length & Distance? (p. 808)
—How Do You Measure Liquids? (p. 808)
—How Do You Measure Time? (p. 808)
—How Do You Measure Weight? (p. 808)
—Mídelo. (p. 1138)
Adamson, Thomas K. & Heather. Tae Kwon Do. (p. 1695)
Adamson, Thomas K. & Wacholtz, Anthony. Basketball: The Math of the Game (p. 143)
Adamson, Thomas K., et al. High-Tech Sports. (p. 778)
Adamson, Tom & Adamson, Heather. How Do You Measure Time? (p. 808)
—How Do You Measure Weight? (p. 808)
Adan, Jennifer. I Don't See Heaven. (p. 838)
Adanac, Victoria & Smith, Barbara. Bathroom Book of Canadian History (p. 144)
Adappur, Georgekutty. Jack Batson & the Secret in the Manuscript. (p. 902)
Adaptor. Graphic Horror Set 3. (p. 711)
Adare, Sierra. Greece: The Culture. (p. 720)
—Greece - The Culture. (p. 720)
—Greece - The Land. (p. 720)
—Greece - The People. (p. 720)
—Greece - The People. (p. 720)
Adasiewicz, Sue. Your Papers, Please: Crossing Borders. (p. 1981)
Adasikov, Igor, illus. see Lamar, Brad A.
Adatto, Miryam. Creative Haven Dreamscapes Coloring Book. (p. 379)
Adbusters, et al, contrib. by. Reactive Graphics. (p. 1442)
Adcock, Donald C., jt. auth. see Pulver, Beth A.
Adcock, Kerry, illus. see Pearson, Mary Rose.
Adcock, Michael. Cambridge Checkpoints VCE History - Revolutions 2005. (p. 255)
Adcock, Will. Guia Practica Del I Ching. (p. 730)
Addabbo, Carole. Dina the Deaf Dinosaur. Valentine, illus. (p. 440)
Addams, Kelly, jt. auth. see Lewis, JoAnn.
Addario, Yvonne. Treasure Diving with Captain Dom - Special Archival Section: Special Archival Section. (p. 1781)
Addasi, Maha. Time to Pray. Albitar, Nuha, tr. (p. 1753)
—White Nights of Ramadan. Gannon, Ned, illus. (p. 1913)
Addasi, Maha, jt. auth. see Dennis, Yvonne Wakim.
Adderholdt-Elliott, Miriam. Perfeccionista? Descubre lo Malo de Ser Demasiado Bueno. (p. 1341)
Adderley, Peter, illus. see Godfrey, Jan.
Adderly, Brenda D., jt. auth. see Dubrow, Terry J.
Adderson, Caroline. Bruno for Real Flook, Helen, illus. (p. 232)
—I, Bruno Flook, Helen, illus. (p. 834)
—Jasper John Dooley: Star of the Week. Clanton, Ben, illus. (p. 910)
—Middle of Nowhere (p. 1137)
—Middle of Nowhere. (p. 1137)
—Simple Case of Angels (p. 1577)
Adderson, Caroline, jt. auth. see Livingston, Billie.
Addicott, Sara, ed. see O'Neill, Joe.
Addie, Boswell, jt. auth. see Boswell, Addie.
Addington, Judith. A-Z Leader Alphabook. (p. 2)
—Building Blocks for Leaders. (p. 239)
Addino, Victoria. Sadie's Wish: Three Little Elves. Garafalo, Beatrice, illus. (p. 1501)
Addis, Bill. Building: 3,000 Years of Design, Engineering & Construction. (p. 238)
Addison, Angelee. Nanny & the Noomies. (p. 1229)
Addison, D. R. Bulldozers at Work. (p. 240)
—Cement Mixers at Work. (p. 286)
—Cranes at Work. (p. 376)
—Diggers at Work. (p. 439)
—Garbage Trucks at Work. (p. 655)
—Tractors at Work. (p. 1775)
Addison, George R. III. When Mom Came Home. (p. 1903)
Addison, Joseph. Cato (Cato of Utica) Landes, William-Alan, ed. (p. 280)
Addison, Joseph, et al. Cato: A Tragedy, & Selected Essays. Henderson, Christine Dunn, ed. (p. 280)
Addison, Karl. Dinosaurs Coloring Book: Artwork by Karl Addison. Addison, Karl, illus. (p. 444)
Addison, Kenneth, illus. see Schertle, Alice.
Addison, Nicholas & Burgess, Lesley, eds. Issues in Art & Design Teaching. (p. 893)
Adds, John, et al. Exchange & Transport, Energy & Ecosystems. (p. 547)
—Genetics, Evolution & Biodiversity. Furness-Smith, Martin, ed. (p. 661)
—Molecules & Cells. Furness-Smith, Martin, ed. (p. 1160)
—Respiration & Co-Ordination. Furness-Smith, Martin, ed. (p. 1463)
Addy, Sean, illus. see Chin-Lee, Cynthia.
Addy, Sean, illus. see Farmer, Jacqueline.
Addy, Sean, illus. see Hubbell, Patricia.
Addy, Sean, illus. see Winter, Jonah.
Addy, Sean, illus. see Zimmer, Tracie Vaughn.
Addy, Sean, jt. auth. see Winter, Jonah.
Addy, Sharon. In Grandpa's Woods. Akins, Tamlyn, illus. (p. 863)
Adedjouma, Davida. Palm of My Heart: Poetry by African American Children. Christie, Gregory R., illus. (p. 1320)
Adee, Donna & Adee, Ed. Jonathan Finds True Treasure. Rectenbaugh, Marci, illus. (p. 925)
Adee, Ed, jt. auth. see Adee, Donna.
Adeff, Jay, photos by see Dzidrums, Christine & Rendon, Leah.
Adel, Deborah. Tiego's Love. (p. 1747)
Adel, Kaveh N. Boy & the Red Balloon. Rezayazdi, Soheil & Michalopulos, Anastasios, eds. (p. 217)
Adele, Amy, illus. see Gehl, Laura.
Adele, Gloria. My Wild Backyard: Wild Hogs. (p. 1221)
Adele, Oroma. Berry Bear. (p. 167)
Adeleke, Abraham Ajibade. Beauty Contest in the Animal Kingdom. (p. 154)
Adell, Montse, jt. auth. see Queralt, Elisenda.
Adelman, Beth. Cool Cats. (p. 363)
—Killer Whales. (p. 956)
—Pony Guide. (p. 1382)
Adelman, Bob, ed. see Bolden, Tonya.
Adelman, Bob, jt. auth. see Johnson, Charles.
Adelman, Heidi. Beautiful Ballerinas. (p. 153)
—Weird Pets. (p. 1872)
Adelman, Nechama Dina. Bedtime. Blau, Nicole, illus. (p. 156)
Adelman, Penina, et al. JGirl's Guide: The Young Jewish Woman's Handbook for Coming of Age. (p. 917)
Adelman, Tom. Black & Blue: Sandy Koufax, the Robinson Boys, & the World Series That Stunned America. (p. 195)
—Long Ball: The Summer of '75 - Spaceman, Catfish, Charlie Hustle & the Greatest World Series Ever Played. (p. 1047)
Adelson, Leone. Mystery Bear: A Purim Story. Howland, Naomi, tr. (p. 1224)
Adelsperger, Charlotte. Amazing Miracles of Jesus. (p. 55)
Adeney, Anne. Five Teddy Bears. Shimmen, Cathy, illus. (p. 601)
—Two Hungry Birds. O'Kif, illus. (p. 1803)
—Where Are My Glasses? Vagnozzi, Barbara, illus. (p. 1906)
Adeney, Anne & Kavanagh, Peter. George & the Dragon. (p. 663)
Adeniyi, Bab. Servant, the King, & the Princess. (p. 1552)
Adeola, Ogechi. Jo & Skippa: I want to be You! (p. 919)
Aderman, James A. Elijah: Fiery Prophet. (p. 512)
Adewoyin, Beverly. Inside the Mommie Pond. (p. 877)
Adey, et al. Galería de arte y Vida. (p. 653)
Adey, Margaret & Albini, Louis. Glencoe Spanish Tesoro Literario Activities Workbook. (p. 683)
Adey, Margaret, et al. Galería de Arte y Vida: Nivel Avanzado. (p. 653)
—Glencoe Spanish Tesoro Literario: Nivel Avanzado. (p. 683)
Adeyemi, Sam. Parable of Dollars: Proven Strategies for Your Financial Success. (p. 1323)
Adhikary, Anita. N Is for Nepal. Mundy, Jen, illus. (p. 1227)
Adhikary, Anita B. My Daughters Are Smart! D Is for Daughters & S Is for Smart. Russo, Blythe, illus. (p. 1201)
Adhikary, Qiron. Feminist Folktales from India. (p. 581)
Adie, Alasdair. Moca-do-poo Bird. (p. 1157)
Adil, Hajjah Amina & Sperling, Karima. My Little Lore of Light: A Child's Version of Lore of Light. (p. 1212)
Adil, Janeen. Johnny Appleseed. (p. 923)
Adil, Janeen R. Cleopatra (p. 331)
—Dr. Seuss. (p. 475)
—Gods & Goddesses of Ancient Egypt (p. 690)
—Goods & Services (p. 701)
—Mississippi River: The Largest River in the United States. (p. 1154)
—Mississippi River. (p. 1154)
—Northeast Indians: Daily Life in The 1500s (p. 1265)
—Supply & Demand (p. 1684)
—Why Is the Sahara So Dry? A Book about Deserts (p. 1925)
Adil, Janeen R. & Capstone Press Staff. Scotland: A Question & Answer Book (p. 1530)
Adiletta, Dawn. Elizabeth Cady Stanton: Women's Suffrage & the First Vote. (p. 513)
Adilman, Katarzyna, illus. see Campbell, Diana & Mosher, Nancy, eds.
Adina Bates, Shelley. Lady of Spirit: A Steampunk Adventure Novel. (p. 971)
Adinolfi, JoAnn, illus. see Donohue, Moira Rose.
Adinolfi, JoAnn, illus. see Hays, Anna Jane.
Adinolfi, JoAnn, illus. see Hopkins, Lee Bennett.
Adinolfi, JoAnn, illus. see Murphy, Stuart J.
Adinolfi, JoAnn, illus. see Rocklin, Joanne.
Adinolfi, JoAnn, illus. see Spinelli, Eileen.
Adinolfi, JoAnn, illus. see Weiner, Marcella Bakur & Neimark, Jill.
Adinolfi, JoAnn, illus. see Wilson, Zachary.
Adinolfi, JoAnn, jt. auth. see Wilson, Zachary.
Adinolfi, Joanne. Tina's Diner. Adinolfi, Joanne, illus. (p. 1755)
Adjovi, Benoit, photos by see Enwezor, Okwui, et al.
Adkins, Danielle N. Little Lamb's Gift. (p. 1030)
Adkins, Jan. Bertha Takes a Drive. Adkins, Jan, illus. (p. 168)
—Frank Lloyd Wright. (p. 628)
—Line: Tying It up, Tying It Down. (p. 1019)
—Moving Heavy Things. Adkins, Jan, illus. (p. 1183)
—Storm Without Rain. (p. 1656)
—Thomas Edison. (p. 1738)
—What If You Met a Cowboy? Adkins, Jan, illus. (p. 1887)
Adkins, Kurt. Summer of Mucus Mcbain. (p. 1674)
Adkins, Laura. Ordinary Oscar. Hearn, Sam, illus. (p. 1302)
Adkins, Lesley & Adkins, Roy. Handbook to Life in Ancient Greece. (p. 740)
—Handbook to Life in Ancient Rome. (p. 740)
Adkins, Linda. Dog Who Couldn't Wag His Tail: A True Story about a Stray Who Made a Difference. Dilworth, Kristopher & Rhodes, Sean C., eds. (p. 462)
Adkins, Loretta B., illus. see Vogel, Cara Lynn.
Adkins, Patricia. Jeremy & the Crocodile Dentist. (p. 913)
Adkins, Roy, jt. auth. see Adkins, Lesley.
Adkins, Ryan. Dream Catcher. (p. 483)
Adkins, Samantha. Subgirl. (p. 1671)
Adkinson, Gma Mary. Growing up with Princess Lizzy: Little Life Lessons. (p. 727)
Adl, Kamyar, photos by see Adl, Shirin & Quarto Generic Staff.
Adl, Shirin, illus. see Chatterjee, Debjani & D'Arcy, Brian, eds.
Adl, Shirin, illus. see Chatterjee, Debjani & D'Arcy, Brian.
Adl, Shirin, illus. see Chatterjee, Debjani & Quarto Generic Staff.
Adl, Shirin, illus. see Laird, Elizabeth.
Adl, Shirin, illus. see Robert, Na'ima B.
Adl, Shirin & Quarto Generic Staff. Book of Dreams. (p. 211)
—I Is for Iran. Adl, Kamyar, photos by. (p. 839)
Adlard, Charlie, illus. see Petrucha, Stefan, et al.
Adler, Cs. Magic of the Glits: A Tale of Loss, Love, & Lasting Friendship. (p. 1073)
Adler, Dahlia. Behind the Scenes. (p. 160)
Adler, David. Time Zones. Miller, Edward, illus. (p. 1753)
Adler, David A. America's Champion Swimmer: Gertrude Ederle. Widener, Terry, illus. (p. 64)
—Andy & Tamika. Hillenbrand, Will, illus. (p. 72)
—Babe & I. Widener, Terry, illus. (p. 123)
—Barking Treasure Mystery. Natti, Susanna, illus. (p. 139)
—Basketball Mystery Allen, Joy, illus. (p. 143)
—Birthday Mystery. Natti, Susanna, illus. (p. 193)
—Bones & the Apple Pie Mystery. Newman, Barbara, illus. (p. 209)
—Bones & the Big Yellow Mystery Newman, Barbara Johansen, illus. (p. 209)
—Bones & the Big Yellow Mystery. Newman, Barbara Johansen, illus. (p. 209)
—Bones & the Birthday Mystery Newman, Barbara, illus. (p. 209)
—Bones & the Clown Mix-Up Mystery. Newman, Barbara Johansen, illus. (p. 209)
—Bones & the Cupcake Mystery Newman, Barbara, illus. (p. 209)
—Bones & the Dinosaur Mystery Newman, Barbara, illus. (p. 209)
—Bones & the Dinosaur Mystery. Newman, Barbara Johansen, illus. (p. 209)
—Bones & the Dog Gone Mystery Newman, Barbara Johansen, illus. (p. 209)
—Bones & the Dog Gone Mystery. Newman, Barbara Johansen, illus. (p. 209)
—Bones & the Football Mystery. (p. 209)
—Bones & the Math Test. (p. 209)
—Bones & the Math Test Mystery. Newman, Barbara, illus. (p. 209)
—Bones & the Roller Coaster Mystery Newman, Barbara, illus. (p. 209)
—Brothers in Egypt. (p. 231)
—Cam Jansen: The Mystery of the Babe Ruth Baseball. (p. 255)
—Cam Jansen: The Wedding Cake Mystery Allen, Joy, illus. (p. 255)
—Cam Jansen: The Mystery of the Stolen Diamonds. Natti, Susanna, illus. (p. 255)
—Cam Jansen & the Basketball Mystery. Allen, Joy, illus. (p. 255)
—Cam Jansen & the Catnapping Mystery. Natti, Susanna, illus. (p. 255)
—Cam Jansen & the Graduation Day Mystery. (p. 255)
—Cam Jansen & the Joke House Mystery. Allen, Joy, illus. (p. 255)
—Cam Jansen & the Millionaire Mystery. Allen, Joy, illus. (p. 255)
—Cam Jansen & the Spaghetti Max Mystery. Allen, Joy, illus. (p. 255)
—Cam Jansen & the Sports Day Mysteries: A Super Special. (p. 255)
—Cam Jansen & the Sports Day Mysteries: A Super Special. Allen, Joy, illus. (p. 255)
—Cam Jansen & the Sports Day Mysteries. Allen, Joy, illus. (p. 255)
—Cam Jansen & the Summer Camp Mysteries. Allen, Joy, illus. (p. 255)
—Cam Jansen - The First Day of School Mystery Natti, Susanna, illus. (p. 255)
—Cam Jansen - The Tennis Trophy Mystery. Natti, Susanna, illus. (p. 255)
—Catnapping Mystery Natti, Susanna, illus. (p. 280)
—Chocolate Fudge Mystery Natti, Susanna, illus. (p. 309)
—Colonel Theodore Roosevelt. (p. 341)
—Danny's Doodles: the Dog Biscuit Breakfast. (p. 406)
—Danny's Doodles: The Donut Dilemma. (p. 406)
—Danny's Doodles: The Dog Biscuit Breakfast. (p. 406)
—Danny's Doodles: The Jelly Bean Experiment. (p. 406)
—Danny's Doodles: the Squirting Donuts. (p. 406)
—Day I Lost My Hampster: And Other True School Stories. (p. 413)
—Don't Talk to Me about the War. (p. 468)
—Don't Throw It to Mo! Ricks, Sam, illus. (p. 468)
—Dr. Martin Luther King, Jr.: A Historical Perspective. Bootman, Colin, illus. (p. 475)
—Enemies of Slavery. Smith, Donald A., illus. (p. 527)
—Fractions, Decimals, & Percents. Miller, Edward, illus. (p. 627)
—Frederick Douglass: A Noble Life. (p. 633)
—Fun with Roman Numerals. Miller, Edward, illus. (p. 649)
—George Washington: An Illustrated Biography. (p. 664)

A

—Ghostly Mystery Natti, Susanna, illus. (p. 672)
—Green School Mystery Allen, Joy, illus. (p. 722)
—Hanukkah Cookies with Sprinkles. Ebbeler, Jeffrey, illus. (p. 744)
—Harriet Tubman & the Underground Railroad. (p. 750)
—Helen Keller. Wallner, John, illus. (p. 762)
—Helen Keller. Wallner, John C. & Wallner, John, illus. (p. 762)
—Heroes for Civil Rights. Farnsworth, Bill, illus. (p. 772)
—Heroes of the Revolution. Smith, Donald A., illus. (p. 773)
—Honest Abe Lincoln: Easy-to-Read Stories about Abraham Lincoln. Wallner, John C., illus. (p. 794)
—House on the Roof. Hirsh, Marilyn, illus. (p. 803)
—It's a Baby, Andy Russell. Franson, Leanne, illus. (p. 895)
—It's Time to Sleep, It's Time to Dream. Chorao, Kay, illus. (p. 899)
—Kids' Catalog of Hanukkah. (p. 953)
—Little at a Time. Tong, Paul, illus. (p. 1023)
—Many Troubles of Andy Russell. (p. 1089)
—Many Troubles of Andy Russell. Hillenbrand, Will, illus. (p. 1089)
—Millions, Billions, & Trillions: Understanding Big Numbers. Miller, Edward, illus. (p. 1144)
—Millions, Billions, & Trillions. Miller, Edward, illus. (p. 1144)
—Molly Shoe Mystery Natti, Susanna, illus. (p. 1161)
—Money Madness. Miller, Edward, illus. (p. 1164)
—Mystery at the Haunted House Natti, Susanna, illus. (p. 1224)
—Mystery Math: A First Book of Algebra. Miller, Edward, illus. (p. 1224)
—Mystery of Flight 427: Inside a Crash Investigation. Natti, Susanna, illus. (p. 1224)
—Mystery of Flight 54 Natti, Susanna, illus. (p. 1224)
—Mystery of the Carnival Prize Natti, Susanna, illus. (p. 1225)
—Mystery of the Circus Clown Natti, Susanna, illus. (p. 1225)
—Mystery of the Gold Coins Natti, Susanna, illus. (p. 1225)
—Mystery of the Monkey House. Natti, Susanna, illus. (p. 1225)
—Mystery of the Monster Movie Natti, Susanna, illus. (p. 1225)
—Mystery of the Stolen Corn Popper Natti, Susanna, illus. (p. 1226)
—Mystery of the Television Dog Natti, Susanna, illus. (p. 1226)
—Mystery of the U. F. O. Natti, Susanna, illus. (p. 1226)
—Not Wanted by the Police. Franson, Leanne, illus. (p. 1267)
—Perimeter, Area, & Volume: A Monster Book of Dimensions. Miller, Edward, illus. (p. 1343)
—Perimeter, Area, & Volume. Miller, Edward, illus. (p. 1343)
—Picture Book of Amelia Earhart. Fisher, Jeff, illus. (p. 1355)
—Picture Book of Benjamin Franklin Wallner, John & Wallner, Alexandra, illus. (p. 1355)
—Picture Book of Benjamin Franklin. (p. 1355)
—Picture Book of Benjamin Franklin. Wallner, John & Wallner, Alexandra, illus. (p. 1355)
—Picture Book of Cesar Chavez. Adler, Michael S. & Olofsdotter, Marie, illus. (p. 1355)
—Picture Book of Dwight David Eisenhower. (p. 1355)
—Picture Book of Frederick Douglass. Byrd, Samuel, illus. (p. 1355)
—Picture Book of George Washington Carver. Brown, Dan, illus. (p. 1355)
—Picture Book of Harriet Beecher Stowe. Bootman, Colin, illus. (p. 1355)
—Picture Book of Harriet Tubman. Byrd, Samuel, illus. (p. 1355)
—Picture Book of Lewis & Clark. (p. 1355)
—Picture Book of Lewis & Clark. Himler, Ronald, illus. (p. 1355)
—Picture Book of Martin Luther King, Jr. Casilla, Robert, illus. (p. 1355)
—Picture Book of Patrick Henry. Wallner, John et al, illus. (p. 1355)
—Picture Book of Rosa Parks. Casilla, Robert, illus. (p. 1355)
—Picture Book of Sacagawea. Brown, Dan, illus. (p. 1355)
—Place Value. Miller, Edward, illus. (p. 1366)
—President George Washington. Wallner, John C. & Wallner, John, illus. (p. 1397)
—Prices! Prices! Prices! Why They Go up & Down. Miller, Edward, illus. (p. 1398)
—Scary Snake Mystery. Natti, Susanna, illus. (p. 1520)
—School Play Mystery. Natti, Susanna, illus. (p. 1523)
—School Trouble for Andy Russell. Hillenbrand, Will, illus. (p. 1523)
—Secret Service Mystery. Natti, Susanna, illus. (p. 1543)
—Simple Machines: Wheels, Levers, & Pulleys. Raff, Anna, illus. (p. 1578)
—Snowy Day Mystery Natti, Susanna, illus. (p. 1601)
—Speedy Car Mystery Natti, Susanna, illus. (p. 1624)
—Story of Hanukkah. Weber, Jill, illus. (p. 1658)
—Story of Passover. Weber, Jill, illus. (p. 1659)
—Summer Camp Mysteries. Allen, Joy, illus. (p. 1674)
—Things That Float & Things That Don't. Raff, Anna, illus. (p. 1733)
—Time Zones. Miller, Edward, illus. (p. 1753)
—Triangles. Miller, Edward, illus. (p. 1785)
—Triceratops Pops Mystery Natti, Susanna, illus. (p. 1786)
—Valentine Baby Mystery. Natti, Susanna, illus. (p. 1830)
—Working with Fractions. Miller, Edward, illus. (p. 1953)
—You Can, Toucan, Math: Word Problem-Solving Fun. Miller, Edward, illus. (p. 1974)
—Young Cam Jansen & the 100th Day of School Natti, Susanna, illus. (p. 1978)
—Young Cam Jansen & the 100th Day of School Mystery Natti, Susanna, illus. (p. 1978)
—Young Cam Jansen & the Circus Mystery. Natti, Susanna, illus. (p. 1978)
—Young Cam Jansen & the Double Beach Mystery. Natti, Susanna, illus. (p. 1978)
—Young Cam Jansen & the Goldfish Mystery. (p. 1978)
—Young Cam Jansen & the Goldfish Mystery. Natti, Susanna, illus. (p. 1978)
—Young Cam Jansen & the Knock Knock Mystery. (p. 1978)
—Young Cam Jansen & the Lions' Lunch Mystery Natti, Susanna, illus. (p. 1978)
—Young Cam Jansen & the Magic Bird Mystery Natti, Susanna, illus. (p. 1978)
—Young Cam Jansen & the Spotted Cat Mystery Natti, Susanna & Natti, S., illus. (p. 1978)

Adler, David A. & Adler, Michael. Picture Book of Cesar Chavez. (p. 1355)
Adler, David A. & Adler, Michael S. Picture Book of Daniel Boone. Collins, Matt, illus. (p. 1355)
—Picture Book of Dolley & James Madison. Himler, Ronald, illus. (p. 1355)
—Picture Book of Harry Houdini. Collins, Matt, illus. (p. 1355)
—Picture Book of Harry Houdini. Matt, Collins, illus. (p. 1355)
—Picture Book of John & Abigail Adams. Himler, Ronald, illus. (p. 1355)
—Picture Book of John Hancock. Himler, Ronald, illus. (p. 1355)
—Picture Book of Sam Houston. Collins, Matt, illus. (p. 1355)
—Picture Book of Samuel Adams. Himler, Ronald, illus. (p. 1355)
Adler, David A. & Adler, Peter S. Heroes of the Revolution. (p. 773)
Adler, Denise. Thank You for Looking for Me. (p. 1725)
Adler, Dennis. John Bianchi - an American Legend: 50 Years of Gunleather. (p. 921)
Adler, Irene. Cathedral of Fear. McGuinness, Nanette, tr. from ITA. (p. 280)
—Dark Lady Bruno, Iacopo, illus. (p. 407)
—Mystery of the Scarlet Rose. McGuinness, Nanette, tr. from ITA. (p. 1226)
—Sherlock, Lupin, & Me Bruno, Iacopo, illus. (p. 1566)
—Soprano's Last Song Iacopo, Bruno & Bruno, Iacopo, illus. (p. 1614)
Adler, Jack. Chinese Americans. (p. 307)
Adler, Jonathan. Patterns. (p. 1329)
Adler, Karen A. Maybe Donna Wants a Cheeseburger! (p. 1113)
Adler, Kathy. Wild Waters: The Continuing Adventures of Farley & Breezy. Keith, Doug, illus. (p. 1930)
Adler, Kenton. Silver Pipes of Tir Nan Og. (p. 1576)
Adler, Lillian W., jt. auth. see Castberg, C.
Adler, Mary & Rougle, Eija. Building Literacy Through Classroom Discussion: Research-Based Strategies for Developing Critical Readers & Thoughtful Writers in Middle School. (p. 239)
Adler, Mia Sharon. Essential Proteen-Student Journal: A Life Skills Program for Helping Teens Succeed: Student Journal. (p. 537)
Adler, Michael, jt. auth. see Adler, David A.
Adler, Michael S., illus. see Adler, David A.
Adler, Michael S., jt. auth. see Adler, David A.
Adler, Penny, jt. auth. see Zmich, Elizabeth.
Adler, Peter S., jt. auth. see Adler, David A.
Adler, Rebecca. Keep Me Safe at Home & in My Community: A handbook on Safety for Young Children & their Families. (p. 947)
Adler, Tasha, jt. auth. see Segal, Robin.
Adler, Victoria. All of Baby Nose to Toes. Nakata, Hiroe, illus. (p. 45)
—All of Baby, Nose to Toes. Nakata, Hiroe, illus. (p. 45)
Adlerman, Daniel. Rock-a-Bye Baby. Adlerman, Kimberly M., illus. (p. 1481)
Adlerman, Kimberly M., illus. see Adlerman, Daniel.
Adlington, L. J. Cherry Heaven. (p. 298)
—Diary of Pelly D. (p. 435)
—Glittering Eye. (p. 684)
Adly, Muhammad S. Learn & Color (For Children) (p. 982)
—Let's Count in Arabic (p. 995)
Adnet, Bernard, illus. see Harvey, Jayne.
Adnet, Bernard, illus. see Williams, Rozanne Lanczak.
Adoff, Arnold. Black Is Brown Is Tan. McCully, Emily Arnold, illus. (p. 196)
—Roots & Blues: A Celebration. Christie, R. Gregory, illus. (p. 1488)
Adoff, Jaime. Names Will Never Hurt Me. (p. 1228)
Adolph, Anthony. Who Am I? The Family Tree Explorer. (p. 1914)
Adolphe, Bruce. Piano Puzzlers: Thirty Popular Melodies & Folk Tunes in the Styles of Famous Composers. (p. 1354)
Adolphe, Joseph, illus. see Moore, Clement C.
Adonis. Sufism & Surrealism. Cumberbatch, Judith, tr. from ARA. (p. 1672)
Adonis, et al. Victims of a Map: A Bilingual Anthology of Arabic Poetry. Al-Udhari, Abdullah, tr. (p. 1840)
Adornetto, Alexandra. Ghost House. (p. 670)
—Hades. (p. 735)
—Halo. (p. 739)
—Heaven. (p. 761)
—Lampo Circus. (p. 972)
—Shadow Thief. (p. 1558)
Adrian, Emily. Like It Never Happened. (p. 1017)
Adrian, Marti, illus. see Boudin, Jonathan.
Adrian, Mikel. Iza & Her Magic Seashell. Cotton, Sue Lynn, illus. (p. 901)
Adrian, Susan. Tunnel Vision: A Novel. (p. 1797)
Adriana. Things to Be Happy About. (p. 1733)
Adrien, Gilles & Broders, Alain. Planet of the Giant. Elyum Studio, illus. (p. 1368)
Adsit, Kim, jt. auth. see Jordano, Kimberly.
Adson, Patricia R. Princess & Her Garden: A Fable of Awakening & Arrival. (p. 1402)
Aduddell, Angie. Little Lost Shoe. (p. 1031)
Advance Cal-Tech Inc. Staff. Let's Praise & Play: Children's Christian Mini-Piano Book. Kung, Edward, ed. (p. 1000)
Advocate-Art Staff, tr. see Kalz, Jill.
Adyashanti. My Secret Is Silence: Poetry & Sayings of Adyashanti. (p. 1218)
Aebersold, Carol, jt. auth. see Bell, Chanda.
Aebersold, Carol V. & Bell, Chanda. Elf on the Shelf: Spanish Boy Dark Elf. Steinwart, Coe, illus. (p. 512)
—Elf on the Shelf - a Christmas Tradition: Girl Dark. Steinwart, Coe, illus. (p. 512)
Aebersold, Carol V. & Chanda, Bell. Elf on the Shelf: Spanish Girl Dark Elf. Steinwart, Coe, illus. (p. 512)
Aebersold, Carol V., et al. Elf on the Shelf - Girl LT: Light Girl. (p. 512)
Aery, Roxanne. ABC's of Kids (Paperback) (p. 4)
Aeschylus. Aeschylus: Agamemnon. (p. 25)
—Persians. Landes, William-Alan, ed. (p. 1344)
—Prometheus Bound. Browning, Elizabeth Barrett, tr. from GRE. (p. 1411)
—Seven Against Thebes. Landes, William-Alan, ed. (p. 1554)
Aesop. Aesop for Children. Winter, Milo, illus. (p. 25)
—Aesop's Fables. (p. 25)
—Aesop's Fables. Winter, Milo, illus. (p. 25)
—Aesop's Fables. Townsend, George Fyler, tr. (p. 25)
—Aesop's Fables. Jones, V. S. Vernon, tr. from GEC. (p. 25)
—Animal Fables from Aesop. (p. 77)
—Animal Fables from Aesop. Mcclintock, Barbara, illus. (p. 77)
—Ant & the Grasshopper. (p. 88)
—Bat's Big Game. Nobati, Eugenia, illus. (p. 145)
—Belling the Cat. (p. 163)
—Brazier & His Dog. (p. 224)
—Cat & the Birds: And Other Fables by Aesop. Rackham, Arthur, illus. (p. 277)
—Country Mouse & the City Mouse. (p. 372)
—Crow & the Pitcher: A Tale about Problem Solving. Heyer, Carol, illus. (p. 385)
—Dog & the Shadow. (p. 461)
—Donkey & the Load of Salt. (p. 466)
—Fables of Aesop. (p. 559)
—Fabulas de Esopo. (p. 559)
—Fox & the Crane. (p. 626)
—Frog & the Ox. (p. 640)
—Grasshopper & the Ant: A Tale about Planning. Hockerman, Dennis, illus. (p. 711)
—Lion & the Mouse Tuff Book. (p. 1020)
—Lion Classic Aesop's Fables. Hall, Amanda, illus. (p. 1020)
—Lion, the Wolf, & the Fox. (p. 1020)
—Mercury & the Workmen. (p. 1127)
—Miller & the Donkey: A Tale about Thinking for Yourself. Branch, Beverly, illus. (p. 1143)
—Peasant & the Eagle. (p. 1333)
—Rooster & the Fox: A Tale about Being Clever. (p. 1488)
—Sheperd Boy & the Wolf. (p. 1565)
—Swollen Fox. (p. 1692)
—Thief & the Housedog. (p. 1732)
—Two Goats. (p. 1803)
—Two Travelers & a Bear. (p. 1804)
—Wind & the Sun. (p. 1935)
—Wolf in Sheep's Clothing: A Tale about Appearances. (p. 1944)
Aesop, jt. auth. see Award, Anna.
Aesop, jt. auth. see Berendes, Mary.
Aesop, jt. auth. see Crow, Kristyn.
Aesop, jt. auth. see Gehl, Laura.
Aesop, jt. auth. see Guillain, Charlotte.
Aesop, jt. auth. see Hansen, Doug.
Aesop, jt. auth. see Holden, Pam.
Aesop, jt. auth. see Lowry, Amy.
Aesop, jt. auth. see Morpurgo, Michael.
Aesop, jt. auth. see Parker, Emma.
Aesop, jt. auth. see Piumini, Roberto.
Aesop, jt. auth. see Potter, Beatrix.
Aesop, jt. auth. see Sommer, Carl.
Aesop, jt. auth. see Ward, Helen.
Aesop, jt. illus. see Zwerger, Lisbeth.
Aesop Enterprise Inc. Staff. Lion & the Mouse. Watts, Bernadette, illus. (p. 1020)
Aesop Enterprise Inc. Staff, jt. auth. see Blair, Eric.
Aesop Enterprise Inc. Staff, jt. auth. see Testa, Fulvio.
Aesop Enterprise Inc. Staff, jt. auth. see White, Mark.
Aesop Enterprise Inc. Staff & Baruzzi, Agnese. Aesop's Fables. Baruzzi, Agnese, illus. (p. 25)
AEVAC, Inc. Staff, ed. see O'Keefe, Ruth A.
Afanasyev, Alexander. Russian Fairy Tales. Bilibin, Ivan, illus. (p. 1498)
—Russian Folk Tales - Russkie Narodnye Skazki. Bilibin, Ivan, illus. (p. 1498)
—Tale of Tsarevich Ivan, the Firebird, & the Grey Wolf. Bilibin, Ivan, illus. (p. 1700)
Afandalor, Indu. Moooooooom, Do You Love Me? (p. 1173)
Afcan, Paschal, ed. see Joe, Anna Rose.
Afcan, Paschal, tr. see Joe, Anna Rose.
Afetian, "Uncle Ted". Adventures of Midas & the Little Red Airplane. (p. 20)
Affaya, Colett & Affaya, Otman. Arkam, Numero & Numbers Affaya, Colette, illus. (p. 99)
Affaya, Colette, illus. see Affaya, Colett & Affaya, Otman.
Affaya, Otman, jt. auth. see Affaya, Colett.
Affleck, D. S. Wish. (p. 1940)
Affleck, Judith & Letchford, Clive. Aristophanes: Frogs. (p. 98)
Afflerbach, Peter. Seeing Is Believing. (p. 1548)
Afraz, jt. auth. see Aboitiz, Victoria De.
Afrika, Llaila. African Holistic Health. (p. 27)
Afshar, Bethany, ed. see Huff, Charlotte.
Afyouni. Ed.D., Hassan. Lucky Penny: The Lucky Series. (p. 1063)
Afyouni, Hassan. Lucky Shirt: The Lucky Series. (p. 1063)
Afzal, Uz. Dance to the Beat. (p. 402)
—Dance to the Beat. Lumb, Steve, illus. (p. 402)
AG Jatkowska, illus. see Ghigna, Charles.
AG Publishers Editors. Sparkle Card Kit: Everything You Need to Create More than 20 Glittery Greetings! (p. 1622)
Aga Khan Museum (Toronto, Ont.) Staff. Astounding ABC. (p. 109)
Agard, John. Goldilocks on CCTV. Kitamura, Satoshi, illus. (p. 696)
—Hello H2O. Kitamura, Satoshi, illus. (p. 764)
—Young Inferno. Kitamura, Satoshi, illus. (p. 1978)
Agard, John, jt. auth. see Cattell, Bob.
Agard, John & Quarto Generic Staff. Goldilocks on CCTV. Kitamura, Satoshi, illus. (p. 696)
Agard, Nadema, illus. see Sneve, Virginia Driving Hawk.
Agarwal, Chitra, jt. auth. see Agarwal, Nikita.
Agarwal, Nikita & Agarwal, Chitra. Friends & Foes of Harry Potter: Names Decoded. Vincent, Benjamin, illus. (p. 638)
Agassi, Martine. Hands Are Not for Hitting. Heinlen, Marieka, illus. (p. 741)
Agassi, Martine, jt. auth. see Verdick, Elizabeth.
Agassi, Martine & Verdick, Elizabeth. Manos No Son para Pegar. Heinlen, Marieka, illus. (p. 1088)
Agassi, Martine, et al. Manos No Son para Pegar. Heinlen, Marieka, illus. (p. 1088)
Agatha Jane. Ces Mignonnes Autres Créatures: L'Histoire de Ben. Mais Est-Elle Vraie ? (p. 288)
—Those Sweet Other Beings: Ben's Story. (p. 1740)
Agatston, Arthur. South Beach Diet: The Delicious, Doctor-Designed, Foolproof Plan for Fast & Healthy Weight Loss. (p. 1616)
—South Beach Diet Quick & Easy Cookbook: 200 Delicious Recipes Ready in 30 Minutes or Less. (p. 1616)
Agbaje, Salihah. Mouth Almighty a Play. Akhtar, Waheed, illus. (p. 1182)
Age, Heroic, jt. auth. see Beechen, Adam.
Age, Heroic, jt. auth. see Fisch, Sholly.
Agee, James. James Agee - Selected Poems. Hudgins, Andrew, ed. (p. 906)
Agee, Jon. Incredible Painting of Felix Clousseau. (p. 869)
—It's Only Stanley. (p. 898)
—Little Santa. (p. 1036)
—Mi Rinoceronte. (p. 1133)
—Nothing. Agee, Jon, illus. (p. 1268)
—Other Side of Town. Agee, Jon, illus. (p. 1306)
—Palindromania! Agee, Jon, illus. (p. 1320)
—Why Did the Chicken Cross the Road? Agee, Jon et al, illus. (p. 1923)
Agee, Jon, illus. see Lillegard, Dee.
Agee, Jon, illus. see Steig, William.
Ageledis, Ida. First Foil Poetry Seasons Berg, Michelle, illus. (p. 595)
Aggarwal, Eash. Paradox. (p. 1323)
Aggarwal, Madhu, tr. see Kumar, Monica.
Aggs, Patrice. Deux Trois: First French Rhymes. (p. 431)
—Dos Tres: My First Spanish Rhymes. (p. 472)
—Strawberry Squirt. (p. 1666)
—Yi Er San: My First Chinese Nursery Rhymes. (p. 1971)
Aggs, Patrice, illus. see Elliott, Odette.
Aggs, Patrice, illus. see Stewart, Maddie.
Aggs, Patrice, tr. see Stewart, Maddie.
Agha-Khan, Aliyar. Cyrus & Kaleo Go Rock Hunting. (p. 397)
Agin, Élodie, et al. 18 Historias de Princesas y de Hadas. Oyaga, Irene, tr. from FRE. (p. 1995)
Agin, Sue, illus. see Shaw, Mary.
Agins, Donna Brown. Jacqueline Kennedy Onassis: Legendary First Lady. (p. 905)
—Maya Angelou: Diversity Makes for a Rich Tapestry. (p. 1112)
—Maya Angelou: A Biography of an Award-Winning Poet & Civil Rights Activist. (p. 1112)
Agnew, Alicia, illus. see Slanina, Anne M.
Agnew, Kate. Dinosaur Disasters. Jones, Anna, illus. (p. 442)
—Shout, Show & Tell! Monks, Lydia, illus. (p. 1570)
—Shout, Show, & Tell. Monks, Lydia, illus. (p. 1570)
—Space Saver. Castle, Frances, illus. (p. 1619)
—Would You Believe It? Parsons, Gary, illus. (p. 1962)
Agnew, Kate, jt. auth. see Forde, Patricia.
Agnew, Kate, ed. Life & Death: A Collection of Classic Poetry & Prose. (p. 1007)
—Love & Longing: A Collection of Classic Poetry & Prose. (p. 1059)
—War & Peace: A Collection of Classic Poetry & Prose. (p. 1857)
Agnew, Kate, et al. Gweiddi, Dangos a Dweud. (p. 733)
Agnew, Lincoln, illus. see Reeder, Kim Cooley.
Agnew, Lincoln, illus. see Van Camp, Katie.
Agocs, Irisz, jt. auth. see Innes, Shona.
Agora Publications Staff, tr. see Anderson, Al.
Agosin, Marjorie. I Lived on Butterfly Hill. White, Lee, illus. (p. 841)
Agosta, Loredana, jt. auth. see McRae, Anne.
Agostinelli, Enrica, jt. auth. see Munari, Bruno.
Agraso, Alberto & Dojeiji, Mony. I Am Happy. Agraso, Alberto, illus. (p. 833)
—Je Suis Heureuse. Agraso, Alberto, illus. (p. 911)
—Soy Feliz. (p. 1618)
—Soy Feliz. Agraso, Alberto, illus. (p. 1618)
Agredo, Javier, jt. auth. see Agredo, Mary.
Agredo, Mary & Agredo, Javier. Creative Haven Hamsa Designs Coloring Book. (p. 379)
—Creative Haven Nature Fractals Coloring Book. (p. 379)
Agrell, Lewis, illus. see April, Elyse.
Agresti, Aimee. Illuminate: A Gilded Wings Novel, Book One. (p. 857)
—Infatuate: A Gilded Wings Novel, Book Two. (p. 873)
Agria, Mary A. Second Leaves. (p. 1539)
Agroff, Patti, illus. see Paluch, Belly.
Agroff, Patti, illus. see Rosenfeld, Dina.
Agro-Melina, Robert Joseph. Joe & the Mysteries of Dream Hall: The Extra Dwarf & the Purloined Parchment. (p. 920)
Aguado, Bill & Newirth, Richard. Paint Me Like I Am: Teen Poems from WritersCorps. (p. 1318)
Aguayo, Sal. Tiny Detective. (p. 1756)
—Tiny Telepaths: A Continuing Saga (p. 1757)
Aguerre, Elizabeth Suarez. Classroom Literature Circles: A Practical, Easy Guide. Carson-Dellosa Publishing Staff, ed. (p. 329)
—Classroom Literature Circles for Primary Grades. (p. 329)
Aguilar, Judy Lee. Littlest Camel: And the Journey of the Three Kings. Rodriguez, Tom, illus. (p. 1039)
Aguilar, Nadia. Lost Island of Tamarind. (p. 1056)
Aguila, Alicia del, illus. see Written By Tori Velle; Illustrated By Al.
Aguila, Priscilla. As Different As Can Be. (p. 105)
—Unexpected Visitor. (p. 1817)
Aguilar, Arelys, illus. see Ballard, George Anne & Bolton, Georgia Helen.
Aguilar, Carmen, tr. see Morpurgo, Michael.
Aguilar, Carmen, tr. see Potter, Ellen.
Aguilar, David A. 13 Planets: The Latest View of the Solar System. (p. 1995)
—Alien Worlds: Your Guide to Extraterrestrial Life. (p. 41)
—Planets, Stars, & Galaxies: A Visual Encyclopedia of Our Universe. Aguilar, David A., illus. (p. 1368)
—Space Encyclopedia: A Tour of Our Solar System & Beyond. Aguilar, David A., illus. (p. 1619)

—Super Stars: The Biggest, Hottest, Brightest, & Most Explosive Stars in the Milky Way. (p. 1682)
Aguilar, David A., illus. see Hughes, Catherine D.
Aguilar, Gaby. Guspar the Fish: A Story of Perseverance. (p. 732)
Aguilar, Joaquina, tr. see Minarik, Else Holmelund.
Aguilar, Jose. Jovenes piratas/Youngs Pirates. (p. 929)
Aguilar, Jose, illus. see Fuertes, Gloria.
Aguilar, José, jt. auth. see García Lorca, Federico.
Aguilar, Laia, illus. see Cano, Felipe.
Aguilar, Sandra, illus. see Grindley, Sally.
Aguilar, Sandra, illus. see Rider, Cynthia.
Aguilar Sisters Staff, illus. see Weill, Cynthia.
Aguilar-Moreno, Manuel. Handbook to Life in the Aztec World. (p. 740)
Aguiler, Manny, jt. auth. see Smith, Michael.
Aguilera, Dana, et al. Character in Motion! Real Life Stories Series 5th Grade Student Workbook. (p. 291)
Aguileta, Gabriela. Diarios Inconclusos I. (p. 434)
Aguileta, Gabriela, jt. auth. see Chavez, Ricardo.
Aguillo, Don Ellis. Boomer, the Missing Pomeranian. (p. 213)
Aguinaco, Carmen F. Amigos de Jesús 2009: A Bilingual Catechetical Program. un Programa Catequético BilingüE. Advent 2008 - November 2009. Petersen, William, illus. (p. 65)
Aguirre, Alfredo, illus. see Mansour, Vivian.
Aguirre, Ann. Enclave. (p. 524)
—Grimspace. (p. 724)
—Horde. (p. 797)
—Mortal Danger. (p. 1176)
—Outpost. (p. 1313)
—Public Enemies. (p. 1414)
—Queen of Bright & Shiny Things. (p. 1425)
Aguirre, Barbara, tr. see Mitchell, Melanie.
Aguirre, Barbara, tr. see Nelson, Robin.
Aguirre Cox, Ernest, jt. auth. see Aguirre Cox, Maria Victoria.
Aguirre Cox, Maria Victoria & Aguirre Cox, Ernest. Patch. (p. 1328)
Aguirre, Diego, illus. see Joyce, Kelley A.
Aguirre, Jorge. Dragons Beware! (p. 479)
—Dragons Beware! Rosado, Rafael, illus. (p. 479)
—Giants Beware! Rosado, Rafael, illus. (p. 674)
Aguirre, Rigo, tr. see Munsch, Robert.
Aguirre, Sergio. Vecinos Mueren en Las Novelas. (p. 1834)
Aguirre, Sonia Montecino. Lucila Se Llama Gabriela. Vicente, Luise San, illus. (p. 1062)
Aguirre, Zuriñe. Sardines of Love. Aguirre, Zuriñe, illus. (p. 1515)
Aguirre-Sacasa, Roberto. Archie Meets Glee. Parent, Dan, illus. (p. 95)
—Divine Time Muniz, Jim, illus. (p. 454)
—Thor: The Trials of Loki. (p. 1739)
—Wolf at the Door. (p. 1943)
Aguirre-Sacasa, Roberto & Nguyen, Peter. Route 666. (p. 1491)
Agusta, Autum. Rita & Rascal. (p. 1475)
Agustin, Jose. Panza del Tepozteco. Tino, illus. (p. 1321)
Ahamed, S. V., tr. see Tahrike Tarsile Qur'an Editors.
Ahamed, Syed Vickar, tr. from ARA. Quran: English Translation of the Meaning Of. (p. 1429)
Aharoni, Nesta, jt. auth. see Aharoni, Nesta A.
Aharoni, Nesta A. & Aharoni, Nesta. My Goodness - My Kids: Cultivating Decency in a Dangerous World. Kahaney, Phyllis, ed. (p. 1210)
Ahdieh, Renée. Wrath & the Dawn. (p. 1962)
Ahearn, Dan. Time for Kids Readers. (p. 1751)
Ahearn, Dan & Ahearn, Janet. Animal Adventures. (p. 76)
—Olympic Dreams. (p. 1287)
—Storm Chasers. (p. 1655)
Ahearn, Janet, jt. auth. see Ahearn, Dan.
Ahearn, Janet Reed. Bird's-Eye View. (p. 191)
—Lady Liberty. (p. 971)
Ahern, Carolyn L. Tino Turtle Travels to Beijing, China. Burt-Sullivan, Neallia, illus. (p. 1756)
—Tino Turtle Travels to Kenya - the Great Safari. Burt Sullivan, Neallia, illus. (p. 1756)
—Tino Turtle Travels to London, England. Burt Sullivan, Neallia, illus. (p. 1756)
—Tino Turtle Travels to Mexico City, Mexico. Burt Sullivan, Neallia, illus. (p. 1756)
—Tino Turtle Travels to Paris, France. Burt Sullivan, Neallia, illus. (p. 1756)
Ahern, Cecelia. One Hundred Names LP. (p. 1295)
Ahern, Dianne. Break-in at the Basilica: Adventures with Sister Philomena, Special Agent to the Pope. Larson, Katherine, illus. (p. 224)
—Curse of the Coins: Adventures with Sister Philomena, Special Agent to the Pope. (p. 395)
—Lost in Peter's Tomb: Adventures with Sister Philomena, Special Agent to the Pope. Larson, Katherine, illus. (p. 1055)
—Today I Made My First Reconciliation. Larson, Katherine, illus. (p. 1760)
—Today Someone I Love Passed Away. Shurtliff, William, illus. (p. 1761)
Ahern, Frank, illus. see Beckman, Amy.
A.H.Hashmi. Children's Science Encyclopedia. (p. 304)
Ahlberg, Allan. Chicken, Chips & Peas. (p. 300)
—Everybody Was a Baby Once: And Other Poems. Ingman, Bruce, illus. (p. 543)
—Gato Que Desapareció Misteriosamente. Abio, Carlos & Villegas, Mercedes, trs. (p. 658)
—Goldilocks Variations: A Pop-Up Book. Ahlberg, Jessica, illus. (p. 696)
—Hooray for Bread. Ingman, Bruce, illus. (p. 795)
—Master Track's Train. Amstutz, Andre, illus. (p. 1103)
—Miss Dirt the Dustman's Daughter. Ross, Tony, illus. (p. 1151)
—Mrs. Vole the Vet. Clark, Emma Chichester, illus. (p. 1188)
—Pencil. Ingman, Bruce, illus. (p. 1336)
—Previously. Ingman, Bruce, illus. (p. 1398)
—Starting School. (p. 1644)
Ahlberg, Allan, jt. auth. see Ahlberg, Janet.
Ahlberg, Allan, jt. auth. see Ingman, Bruce.
Ahlberg, Allan & Ahlberg, Janet. It Was a Dark & Stormy Night. (p. 894)
—Starting School. (p. 1644)
Ahlberg, Allan & Guene, Faiza. Funnybones. (p. 650)
Ahlberg, Janet, jt. auth. see Ahlberg, Allan.
Ahlberg, Janet & Ahlberg, Allan. Adiós Pequeño! Ahlberg, Janet, illus. (p. 12)
—Adiós Pequeño! Ahlberg, Janet & Ahlberg, Allan, illus. (p. 12)
—Each Peach Pear Plum. (p. 492)
—Starting School. (p. 1644)
Ahlberg, Jessica, illus. see Ahlberg, Allan.
Ahlberg, Jessica, illus. see French, Vivian.
Ahlberg, Jessica, illus. see Tellegen, Toon.
Ahlers, Joan & Tallman, Cheryl. All about Me Diary: The Ultimate Record of Your Child's Day! (p. 43)
Ahlers, Lena C. Sons Known to Fame. (p. 1613)
Ahlers, Oly. Following My Magical Dream (p. 612)
Ahlman, Larry. Mittens at Sea (p. 1156)
—Terror in the Tetons. Larsen, Chuck, ed. (p. 1722)
Ahlstrand, Alan. Ford Escort & Mercury Tracer: 1991 Thru 2002. (p. 617)
Ahlstrom, Leonard. Christmas Shoes for Children. (p. 315)
Ahlstrom, Peter, ed. Romance of the Three Kingdoms Manga: The Oath in the Peach Orchard Kirsch, Alexis, tr. from CHI. (p. 1486)
Ahlstrom, Susan. Project: Owen Ritter. (p. 1410)
Ahluwalia, Libby, jt. auth. see Mayled, Jon.
Ahluwalia, Libby & Cole, Peter. Religious Experience. (p. 1458)
Ahmad, Aadil, illus. see Vigil, Angel.
Ahmad, Iftikhar. World Cultures: A Global Mosaic (p. 1954)
Ahmad, M. I. Aldebaram. (p. 35)
Ahmad, Maryam, illus. see Persaud, Sandhya S.
Ahmad, Shakil, tr. see Saqr, Abdul B.
Ahmad, Tazeen. Abc's of Islam. (p. 4)
—Ali's Special Cure. (p. 41)
Ahmed, Farida. White Unicorn & a Blue Butterfly. (p. 1913)
Ahmed, Naval. Blue Moon on Bandideau. (p. 203)
Ahmed, Rehana. Walking a Tightrope: New Writing from Asian Britain. (p. 1854)
Ahmed, Said Salah. Lion's Share/Qayb Libaax: A Somali Folktale. Dupre, Kelly, illus. (p. 1021)
Ahmed, Said Salah, tr. Travels of Igal Shidad/Safarada Cigaal Shidaad: A Somali Folktale. Amir, Amin Abd al-Fattah Mahmud, illus. (p. 1780)
Ahmed, Shabbir, et al. Jesus: Prophet of Islam. (p. 914)
Ahmed, Suhel. Monsters. Bassani, Srimalle, illus. (p. 1168)
—Princesses. Silver Dolphin Books, Silver Dolphin, ed. (p. 1406)
Ahmed, Syed Z. Chaghatai. (p. 288)
—Manchukou. (p. 1087)
Ahn, H. M. & Lee, T. S. Darwin Story: A Lifetime of Curiosity, a Passion for Discovery. (p. 409)
Ahn, JiYoung, illus. see Kenyon, Sherrilyn.
Aho, Kirsti, ed. see Dharkar, Anuja & Tapley, Scott.
Aho, Kirsti, jt. auth. see Underwood, Dale.
Aho, Kirsti & Underwood, Dale, contrib. by. Town Website Project Using Macromedia Dreamweaver MX 2004: Communicating Information & Ideas on the Web. (p. 1773)
Aho, Sheila Ann. Hooty's Christmas Present. (p. 796)
—Hooty's Forest Adventure. (p. 796)
Ahokangas, Anne Margit. Adventures of Velvet Series: I Am Who I Am. (p. 24)
Ahour, Paravish. All Children of the World Smile in the Same Language: Iran, the Cradle of Civilization. (p. 44)
Ahouse, Jeremy John & Barber, Jacqueline. Fingerprinting. Bevilacqua, Carol & Klofkorn, Lisa, illus. (p. 589)
Ahranjani, Maryam, et al. Youth Justice in America (p. 1982)
Ahrends, Susan, illus. see Turner, Deborah & Mohler, Diana.
Ahrens, Albrecht. Simply Out in the Woods: An Inspirational Children's Story. (p. 1578)
Ahrens, Donald L. Concrete & Concrete Masonry. (p. 355)
Ahrens, Edward P. Already Walks Tomorrow. (p. 50)
Ahrens, Mario. Tapiz Argentino. (p. 1705)
Ahrin, Jacob, illus. see Pearl, David R. & Pearl, Tamara R.
Ahrndt, Paula D. Toof Fairy Tales. (p. 1767)
Ahumada. Juguemos a Leer-Texto. (p. 932)
AIC College of Design Staff, illus. see Ramirez, Jeannette.
Aida, Yu. Gunslinger Girl (p. 732)
Aidinoff, Elsie V. Garden. (p. 656)
Aiello, Ron, jt. auth. see Goldish, Meish.
Aigner-Clark, Julie. Asomate y Ve Las Figuras. Zaidi, Nadeem, illus. (p. 106)
—Asomate Y Ve Los Numeros. Zaidi, Nadeem, illus. (p. 106)
—Aves. (p. 119)
—Baby Einstein Colores: Libro con Ventanas. Zaidi, Nadeem, illus. (p. 126)
—Baby Einstein: Lullabies & Sweet Dreams. (p. 126)
—Baby Einstein: on the Farm. Zaidi, Nadeem, illus. (p. 126)
—Baby Einstein Poemas Preciosos: Pretty Poems & Wonderful Words. Zaidi, Nadeem, illus. (p. 126)
—Bebes. (p. 155)
—Gatos. (p. 658)
—Guarderia de Idiomas (The Guarderia Language) (p. 728)
—Master Pieces. Zaidi, Nadeem, illus. (p. 1103)
—Mundo de Color de Van Gogh. (p. 1191)
—Perros. (p. 1344)
—Ventana Al Color. Zaidi, Nadeem, illus. (p. 1836)
Aihara, Chris. Nikkei Donburi: A Japanese American Cultural Survival Guide. Iwasaki, Glen, illus. (p. 1255)
Aihara, Masaaki, jt. ed. see Sarris, Eno.
Aihara, Masaaki & Sarris, Eno, eds. Grade 1 Addition: Kumon Math Workbooks. (p. 705)
—Grade 1 Subtraction: Kumon Math Workbooks. (p. 705)
—Grade 3 Addition & Subtraction: Kumon Math Workbooks. (p. 705)
—Grade 3 Division: Kumon Math Workbooks. (p. 705)
—Grade 3 Multiplication: Kumon Math Workbooks. (p. 705)
—Grade 4 Decimals & Fractions: Kumon Math Workbooks. (p. 705)
—Grade 4 Division: Kumon Math Workbooks. (p. 705)
—Grade 4 Multiplication: Kumon Math Workbooks. (p. 705)
—Grade 5 Decimals & Fractions: Kumon Math Workbooks. (p. 705)
—Grade 6 Fractions: Kumon Math Workbooks. (p. 705)
Aihara, Miki. Hot Gimmick (p. 801)
—Hot Gimmick Aihara, Miki, illus. (p. 801)
—Tokyo Boys & Girls (p. 1762)
—Tokyo Boys & Girls. Aihara, Miki, illus. (p. 1762)
Aikawa, Yu. Dark Edge. (p. 407)
—Dark Edge. Aikawa, Yu, illus. (p. 407)
Aiken, David, illus. see Aiken, Zora & David.
Aiken, David, illus. see Cummings, Priscilla.
Aiken, David, illus. see Hagman, Harvey Dixon.
Aiken, David, jt. auth. see Aiken, Zora.
Aiken, David & Aiken, Zora. All about Boats: A to Z Aiken, David, illus. (p. 42)
Aiken, George. Reminiscences: Leaves from an Actor's Life. (p. 1460)
Aiken, Joan. Black Hearts in Battersea (p. 196)
—Gato Mog. (p. 658)
—Midwinter Nightingale. (p. 1139)
—Necklace of Raindrops & Other Stories. Hawkes, Kevin, illus. (p. 1239)
—Pequeno Dragon. Wiley, Bee, illus. (p. 1341)
—Serial Garden. (p. 1552)
—Snow Horse & Other Stories. (p. 1599)
Aiken, Joan, jt. auth. see Aiken, Joan.
Aiken, Joan & Aiken, Joan. Arabel's Raven. Blake, Quentin, illus. (p. 94)
—Bridle the Wind. (p. 227)
—Go Saddle the Sea. (p. 687)
—Teeth of the Gale. (p. 1715)
Aiken, Nick. Being Confirmed. Jenkins, Simon, illus. (p. 161)
Aiken, Nick, compiled by. Prayers for Teenagers. (p. 1393)
Aiken, Zora, jt. auth. see Aiken, David.
Aiken, Zora & Aiken, David. A to Z: Pick What You'll Be. Aiken, David, illus. (p. 1)
—Busy Bodies: Play Like the Animals (p. 245)
—Camp ABC: A Place for Outdoor Fun Aiken, David, illus. (p. 257)
—Chesapeake Play Day (p. 298)
Aiken, Zora & David. Double-Talk: Word Sense & Nonsense Aiken, David, illus. (p. 473)
Aikins, Anne Marie. Authority: Deal with It Before It Deals with You Murray, Steven, illus. (p. 117)
—Misconduct: Deal with It Without Bending the Rules Murray, Steven, illus. (p. 1150)
—Racism: Deal with It Before It Gets under Your Skin Murray, Steven, illus. (p. 1432)
Aikins, Dave. Baby's Busy Year: A Book of Seasons. (p. 128)
—Baby's First Christmas. (p. 129)
—Bailando Al Rescate. (p. 132)
—Big Sister Dora! (p. 183)
—Birthday Dance Party: Daisy's Fiesta de Quinceañera. (p. 192)
—Dora Saves the Snow Princess. (p. 470)
—Haunted Houseboat. (p. 753)
—Race to the Tower of Power. (p. 1431)
—Watch Me Draw Dora's Favorite Adventures: Let's Draw! (p. 1861)
—Who's My Baby? (p. 1920)
Aikins, Dave, illus. see Carbone, Courtney.
Aikins, Dave, illus. see Chipponeri, Kelli.
Aikins, Dave, illus. see Driscoll, Laura.
Aikins, Dave, illus. see Golden Books Staff.
Aikins, Dave, illus. see Golden Books.
Aikins, Dave, illus. see Grosset & Dunlap.
Aikins, Dave, illus. see Grosset and Dunlap Staff.
Aikins, Dave, illus. see Inches, Alison.
Aikins, Dave, illus. see Katschke, Judy.
Aikins, Dave, illus. see Marchesani, Laura.
Aikins, Dave, illus. see McMahon, Kara.
Aikins, Dave, illus. see Posner-Sanchez, Andrea.
Aikins, Dave, illus. see Rabe, Tish.
Aikins, Dave, illus. see Random House Dictionary Staff.
Aikins, Dave, illus. see Random House Staff.
Aikins, Dave, illus. see Reisner, Molly.
Aikins, Dave, illus. see Ricci, Christine.
Aikins, Dave, illus. see Rodriguez, Daynali Flores, tr.
Aikins, Dave, illus. see Unknown.
Aikins, Dave, illus. see Ziegler, Argentina Palacios, tr.
Aikins, Dave & Marchesani, Laura. Baby Sees: A First Book of Faces. (p. 128)
Aikins, David. Good, the Bad, & the Krabby! (p. 700)
Aikins, David, illus. see Depken, Kristen L.
Aikins, David, illus. see Golden Books.
Aikins, David, illus. see Inches, Alison.
Aikins, David, illus. see Random House Children's Books Staff.
Aikins, David, illus. see Random House Editors.
Aikins, David, illus. see Random House Staff.
Aikins, David, illus. see Random House.
Aikins, David, illus. see Reisner, Molly.
Aikins, David, illus. see Stevens, Cara.
Aikins, David, illus. see Tillworth, Mary.
Aikman, Louise. North American Dress. (p. 1264)
Aikman, Louise & Harvey, Matthew. Pilates Step-By-Step. (p. 1358)
Aikwawa, Yu. Dark Edge (p. 407)
Aileen Co, illus. see Watson Manhardt, Laurie.
Ailes, Mark Cusco. Snow Dargles: Book Two: the Chronicles of Weekland. (p. 1598)
—Tree of No Boundaries: Book One. (p. 1783)
Aili, Olivia. Portrait Pathway. (p. 1386)
Aillaud, Cindy. Recess at 20 Below. (p. 1451)
Aimard, Gustave. Indian Scout: a Story of the Aster City. (p. 871)
Aimé, Elizabeth Mary. Peaceful Home for Red Rock Hen. (p. 1332)
Aime, Luigi, illus. see Dahl, Michael.
Aime, Luigi, jt. auth. see Dahl, Michael.
Aimone, Logan, jt. auth. see Hall, Homer L.
Aimone, Logan H., jt. auth. see Hall, Homer L.
AIMS Education Foundation. Looking at Lines: Interesting Objects & Linear Functions. (p. 1051)
—Ray's Reflections. (p. 1441)
—Through the Eyes of the Explorers: Minds-on Math & Mapping. (p. 1745)
—Weather Sense: Moisture. (p. 1870)
AIMS Education Foundation, et al. Jaw Breakers & Heart Thumpers. (p. 910)
—Machine Shop. (p. 1068)
Ain, Beth. Starring Jules (As Herself) (p. 1642)
—Starring Jules (As Herself) Higgins, Anne Keenan, illus. (p. 1642)
—Starring Jules (in Drama-Rama) (p. 1642)
—Starring Jules (in Drama-Rama) Higgins, Anne Keenan, illus. (p. 1642)
—Starring Jules (Super-Secret Spy Girl) (p. 1642)
—Starring Jules (Third Grade Debut) (p. 1642)
Aina, Olaiya. Boy, the Dove, & the Hawk. (p. 219)
Aina, Olaiya E. Ijapa, the Lion, & the Boar. (p. 856)
Aine, Mhari. Little Children & the Fairies. (p. 1026)
Aines, Diane, illus. see McClafferty, Lisa.
Ainley, Christian. Enchanted Amulet: The Chronicles of Peraluda (Book One) (p. 523)
Ainslie, Tamsin. I Can Say Please. Ainslie, Tamsin, illus. (p. 836)
—I Can Say Thank You. Ainslie, Tamsin, illus. (p. 836)
Ainslie, Tamsin, illus. see Hathorn, Libby.
Ainslie, Tamsin, illus. see May, Ruthie.
Ainslie, Tamsin, illus. see Norrington, Leonie.
Ainsworth, Kimberly. Hootenanny! A Festive Counting Book. Brown, Jo, illus. (p. 796)
—Little Monkey. Berg, Michelle, illus. (p. 1032)
—Little Panda. Berg, Michelle, illus. (p. 1033)
—Moustache Up! A Playful Game of Opposites. Roode, Daniel, illus. (p. 1182)
Ainsworth, Marlane. Offbeat. Allingham, Andrew, illus. (p. 1279)
AIO Team. 90 Devotions for Kids. (p. 1998)
—Official Guide: A Behind-the-Scenes Look at the World's Favorite Family Audio Drama. (p. 1280)
AIO Team & Buchanan, Kathy. Candid Conversations with Connie: A Girl's Guide to Growing Up. Vol. 1 (p. 261)
Aiosssa, Janet M. Deep in the Woods. Gabel, Deborah Boudreau, illus. (p. 423)
Aira, Luis. Somewhere. (p. 1610)
Aird, Forbes. Race Car Chassis: Design, Structures & Materials for Road, Drag & Circle Track Open- & Closed-Wheel Chassis. (p. 1430)
Aird, Hamish. Pericles: The Rise & Fall of Athenian Democracy. (p. 1343)
Airgood, Ellen. Education of Ivy Blake. (p. 505)
—Prairie Evers. (p. 1392)
Aish, Carolyn Ann. Stepping Stones. (p. 1648)
Aisha. Parsley, Sage, Rosemary & Thyme. (p. 1325)
Aitchison, Jim & Sparks, Marilyn. Tin Pot Puppy. (p. 1755)
Aitchison, Kathleen, jt. auth. see McAdam, Jessica.
Aitchison, Mary Wemyss. Caught in the Crossfire: The Story of Janina Pladek. (p. 282)
Aitchison, Stewart. Traveler's Guide to Monument Valley. (p. 1780)
Aitken, Amber. Perfect Match (p. 1342)
Aitken, Martin, tr. see Teller, Janne.
Aitken, Stephen. Earth's Fever. (p. 498)
—Ecosystems at Risk. (p. 503)
—Fever at the Poles. (p. 583)
—Fever in the Oceans. (p. 583)
—Fever on the Land. (p. 583)
—How to Cure Earth's Fever. (p. 816)
—Ocean Life. (p. 1276)
—People. (p. 1338)
—People in Trouble. (p. 1339)
—Plants & Insects. (p. 1370)
Aiwel, Daniel B. CM Punk: Pro Wrestling Superstar (p. 336)
—John Cena: Pro Wrestling Superstar (p. 921)
Aiyetoro, Nicia. Children of the State. (p. 302)
Aizen, Marina. Mary Had a Little Lamb. (p. 1100)
Aizlewood, R., ed. Kharms: The Old Woman (Starukha) (p. 951)
Aizpuriete, Amanda. Latvia. Hartgers, Katarina, tr. (p. 980)
Ajhar, Brian. Pinocchio. (p. 1360)
Ajhar, Brian, illus. see Beck, Glenn.
Ajhar, Brian, illus. see Greene, Rhonda Gowler.
Ajiri, Ijeoma. Why, Oh Why, Why Must I Be So Shy!?! Izenwata, Chinwendu, illus. (p. 1925)
Ajmera, Maya. Global Baby Bedtimes. (p. 684)
—Global Baby Boys. (p. 684)
Ajmera, Maya & Derstine, Elise Hofer. Music Everywhere! Pon, Cynthia, illus. (p. 1193)
Ajmera, Maya & Hirschfelder, Arlene. Children of Native America Today. (p. 302)
Ajmera, Maya & Ivanko, John D. Be My Neighbor. (p. 148)
—Ser Vecinos. Canetti, Yanitzia, tr. from ENG. (p. 1552)
—To Be a Kid. (p. 1758)
—To Be an Artist. (p. 1758)
Ajmera, Maya, et al. Faith. (p. 565)
—Healthy Kids. (p. 758)
—Our Grandparents: A Global Album. (p. 1309)
—What We Wear: Dressing up Around the World. (p. 1895)
Akaba, Suekichi, illus. see Ishii, Momoko.
Akahori, Kotoyoshi. Saber Marionette J (p. 1499)
Akahori, Satoru. Abenobashi: Magical Shopping Arcade Deguchi, Ryusei, illus. (p. 4)
—Saber Marionette J Fukami, Yuko, tr. from JPN. (p. 1499)
—Saber Marionette J Kotoyoshi, Yumisuke, illus. (p. 1499)
Akainy, Boma. Angel Legn. (p. 73)
Akaishi, Shinobu & Sarris, Eno, eds. Animals - My Book of Mazes, Ages 5-6-7. (p. 82)
—My Book of Mazes: Things That Go! (p. 1199)
Akamastsu, Ken, creator. A. I. Love You (p. 1)
Akamatsu, Ken. A. I. Love You Ury, David, tr. from JPN. (p. 1)
—Ai Love You (p. 30)
—Ai Love You Akamatsu, Ken, illus. (p. 30)
—Love Hina (p. 1059)
—Love Hina Rymer, Nan, tr. (p. 1059)
—Love Hina Rymer, Nan, tr. from JPN. (p. 1059)
—Negima!, Volume 13: Magister Negi Magi. Yoshida, Toshifumi, tr. (p. 1240)
Akana, Lizzi, illus. see 50 Cent Staff.

Akass, Susan. My First Origami Book. (p. 1207)
—My First Sewing Book. (p. 1207)
Akass, Susan, ed. see Hardy, Emma.
Akbarpour, Ahmad. Good Night, Commander Eskandani, Shadi & Mixter, Helen, trs. from PER. (p. 699)
—That Night's Train Saghafi, Majid, tr. from PER. (p. 1726)
Akchurin, Sergo. Blackie & the Magic Stone. (p. 197)
—Canadian Story. (p. 260)
Ake, Anne. Everglades: An Ecosystem Facing Choices & Challenges. (p. 542)
Akech, Martha Arual, jt. auth. see Dau, John Bul.
Aker, Don. Fifth Rule. (p. 584)
—First Stone. (p. 597)
—One on One. (p. 1296)
—Space Between. (p. 1618)
Aker, Frank. October 1973. (p. 1277)
Akerman, Emma, illus. see Dahlin, Adam A.
Akeroyd, John. Plant: An Eyewitness 3-D Book. (p. 1368)
Akers, Darla G. Man, the Moon, & the Star. (p. 1085)
Akers, Ellery. Sarah's Waterfall: A Healing Story about Sexual Abuse. Benicio, Angelique, illus. (p. 1514)
Akers, Martin & Benchmark Education Co., LLC Staff. Fran Grabs It. (p. 627)
—Night Hunt for Food. (p. 1253)
Akers-Bell, Mary, illus. see Greene, Daryl C.
Akerson, Julie Chicos. Life of Riley the Cat. Taylor, Jennifer, illus. (p. 1012)
Akey, Maureen. Adventures of Molly the Monarch Butterfly & Friends Series: Molly. (p. 20)
Akhila Rajan And Ananya Rajan. Crafabets Adventure. (p. 375)
Akhtar, Waheed, illus. see Agbaje, Salihah.
Aki, Katsu. Psychic Academy. (p. 1413)
—Psychic Academy Aki, Katsu, illus. (p. 1413)
—Psychic Academy. Aki, Katsu, illus. (p. 1413)
—Psychic Academy. Frazier, Jan Scott, tr. from JPN. (p. 1413)
—Vision of Escaflowne Bourque, Jeremiah, tr. from JPN. (p. 1844)
—Vision of Escaflowne (p. 1845)
—Vision of Escaflowne Bourque, Jeremiah, tr. from JPN. (p. 1845)
Aki, Katsu, creator. Vision of Escaflowne. (p. 1845)
Aki, Michelle, et al. Uniquely Kentucky (p. 1818)
Aki, Shimizu. Succeccor of Fate. (p. 1671)
Akib, Jamel, illus. see Brill, Marlene Targ.
Akib, Jamel, illus. see Chronicle Books Staff & Markle, Sandra.
Akib, Jamel, illus. see Crane, Stephen.
Akib, Jamel, illus. see Defoe, Daniel.
Akib, Jamel, illus. see Dumas, Alexandre.
Akib, Jamel, illus. see Grahame, Kenneth.
Akib, Jamel, illus. see Hyde, Heidi Smith.
Akib, Jamel, illus. see Iyengar, Malathi Michelle.
Akib, Jamel, illus. see Krishnaswami, Uma.
Akib, Jamel, illus. see Olmstead, Kathleen & Porter, Eleanor H.
Akib, Jamel, illus. see Porter, Eleanor H.
Akib, Jamel, illus. see Rahaman, Vashanti.
Akib, Jamel, illus. see Sasaki, Chris & Wells, H. G.
Akib, Jamel, illus. see Shelley, Mary.
Akib, Jamel, illus. see Spyri, Johanna.
Akib, Jamel, illus. see Stevenson, Robert Louis.
Akib, Jamel, illus. see Stoker, Bram.
Akib, Jamel, illus. see Swift, Jonathan.
Akib, Jamel, illus. see Tait, Chris & Wyss, Johann David.
Akib, Jamel, illus. see Twain, Mark, pseud.
Akib, Jamel, illus. see Verne, Jules.
Akib, Jamel, illus. see Wells, H. G.
Akib, Jamel, illus. see Wiggin, Kate Douglas.
Akib, Jamel, illus. see Woodside, Martin & Grahame, Kenneth.
Akib, Jamel, illus. see Wyss, Johann David.
Akib, Jamel, illus. see Yoo, Paula.
Akihiro. Light of Love, Forever. (p. 1015)
Akimine, Kamijyo. Samurai Deeper Kyo (p. 1509)
—Samurai Deeper Kyo Akimine, Kamijyo, illus. (p. 1509)
—Samurai Deeper Kyo: Volume 15 Akimine, Kamijyo, illus. (p. 1509)
—Samurai Deeper Kyo: Volume 17 Akimine, Kamijyo, illus. (p. 1509)
Akimine, Kamijyo, jt. auth. see Kamijyo, Akimine.
Akimoto, Nami. Miracle Girls (p. 1148)
—Miracle Girls Akimoto, Nami, illus. (p. 1148)
Akin, Daniel. Discovering the Biblical Jesus. (p. 449)
—Discovering the Biblical Jesus Leader. (p. 449)
Akin, Ferruh, jt. auth. see Taykutgul, Selcuk.
Akin, Galan, tr. see Thompson, Margaret.
Akin, Ian, illus. see Stern, Roger.
Akin, Jean Foster. Filigree Slippers. (p. 586)
Akin, Sara Laux. Three Scoops & a Fig Hartung, Susan Kathleen, illus. (p. 1743)
Akin, Sean. Henny Penny. (p. 767)
Akinje, Wale. Adventures of Imhotep. Young, Craig, illus. (p. 19)
Akino, Matsuri. Genju No Seiza Akino, Matsuri, illus. (p. 661)
—Pet Shop of Horrors - Tokyo (p. 1345)
—Pet Shop of Horrors - Tokyo Akino, Matsuri, illus. (p. 1345)
—Pet Shop of Horrors - Tokyo Bourque, Jeremiah, tr. from JPN. (p. 1345)
—Pet Shop of Horrors - Tokyo Iwo, Tomoharu & Masumoto, Bryan, trs. from JPN. (p. 1345)
Akino, Matsuri, creator. Pet Shop of Horrors - Tokyo (p. 1345)
Akins, David. Tyler's Toys & the Bully. (p. 1805)
Akins, Joni. Dean the Bean. (p. 418)
Akins, Karen. Loop. (p. 1052)
—Twist. (p. 1802)
Akins, Tamlyn, illus. see Addy, Sharon.
Akinyemi, Rowena. Under the Moon, Level 1. Oxford University Press Staff & Bassett, Jennifer, eds. (p. 1813)
Akinyemi, Rowena & Marryat. Children of the New Forest, Level 2. Bassett, Jennifer, ed. (p. 302)
Akio, Irene. T Is for Tokyo. Akio, Irene, illus. (p. 1694)
Akiona, Micalynn. My Mom Can Do Anything. (p. 1214)
Akira, Shouko. Times Two. Akira, Shouko, illus. (p. 1754)
Akira, Shouko, jt. auth. see Toriyama, Akira.
Akira, Shouko & Toriyama, Akira. Dr. Slump (p. 475)
Akister, Finola, et al. Sea Poems & Space Poems. (p. 1535)
—Sports Poems & Mouse Poems. (p. 1633)
Akister, Finola, et al, selected by. Sea Poems & Space Poems. (p. 1535)
—Sports Poems & Mouse Poems. (p. 1633)
Akita, Yoshinobu. Orphen (p. 1305)
—Orphen Sawada, Hajime, illus. (p. 1305)
Akita, Yoshinobu & Sawada, Hajime. Orphen (p. 1305)
Akiyama, Tamayo. Mouryo-Kiden: Legend of the Nymphs (p. 1181)
—Mouryou Kiden (p. 1181)
Akiyama, Tamayo, creator. Mouryou Kiden: Legend of the Nymph. Vol. 2 (p. 1181)
Akizuki, Ryo, jt. auth. see Xebec.
Akkari, Hélène. Saving Kanki the Antelope. (p. 1517)
Akley, Jason. Candlestick. (p. 261)
—Sweet Pea & the Bumblebee. (p. 1690)
Akridge, Bill, illus. see Bonner, Anne.
Akselrad, January & Young, Jennifer. Matzah & Miracles: A Passover Musical & Chapter Book. Palagonia, Peter, illus. (p. 1110)
Aksimovich, Natalja, ed. see AZ Books Staff.
Aksinovich, Natalia, ed. see AZ Books Staff.
Aksomitis, Gerard. Solving the Mysteries of the Past. (p. 1608)
Aksomitis, Gerard, jt. auth. see Askomitis, Gerard.
Aksomitis, Linda. Adeline's Dream (p. 12)
—Choosing a Career. (p. 310)
—Downloading Music. (p. 474)
—L Is for Land of Living Skies: A Saskatchewan Alphabet. Bennett, Lorna, illus. (p. 969)
—Sports Champions. (p. 1632)
—Teen Driving. (p. 1713)
Aksomitis, Linda, jt. auth. see Boudreau, Hélène.
Aktar, Nasreen. Samira's Eid. Attard, Enebor, illus. (p. 1507)
Akubue, Chira. Azuka. (p. 122)
Akutagawa. En el Bosque. (p. 522)
Akwudike, Joshua. Mom, Mitchell Refuses to Play with Me. (p. 1161)
Akyroyd, Clarrissa. Native American Horsemanship. Johnson, Troy, ed. (p. 1234)
Al Adely, Laith Muhmood, jt. auth. see Hassig, Susan M.
Al Bahrani, Jawad. Tales of Bul Bul Adventures. (p. 1702)
Al Mansour, Haifaa. Green Bicycle. (p. 721)
Al Mehairi, Maitha. Sally Ride's Adventure: The Dangerous Sea Monster Zelurius. (p. 1505)
Al, Parker, illus. see Miller, Arthur.
Al Shaikh, Latifa. I'm Still Waiting for that Chocolate. (p. 860)
AlaBee. "When Will My Mommy Come?" World & Cross-Cultural Philosophy. (p. 1905)
Aladdin Books. Really Big Awesome Book: Monsters of the Deep, the Universe, Volcanoes, Prehistoric Animals, & Tornadoes. Paiva, Johannah Gilman, ed. (p. 1449)
—Really Big I Didn't Know That Book: Bugs, Sharks, Dinosaurs, Cars, & Trains. Paiva, Johannah Gilman, ed. (p. 1449)
Alagna, Magdalena. Billie Holiday. (p. 187)
—Elvis Presley. (p. 517)
—Everything You Need to Know about Chemotherapy. (p. 545)
—Everything You Need to Know about the Dangers of Binge Drinking. (p. 546)
—Everything You Need to Know about the Dangers of Cosmetic Surgery. (p. 546)
—Great Fire of London of 1666. (p. 716)
—Louisiana Purchase: Expanding America's Boundaries. (p. 1059)
—Mae Jemison: The First African American Woman in Space. (p. 1070)
—Monroe Doctrine: An End to European Colonies in America. (p. 1166)
—War Correspondents: Life under Fire. (p. 1857)
—Wyatt Earp: Sheriff del legano Oeste. (p. 1966)
—Wyatt Earp: Lawman of the American West. (p. 1966)
—Wyatt Earp: Lawman of the American West / Sheriff del oeste Americano. (p. 1966)
—Wyatt Earp: Sheriff del oeste americano (Wyatt Earp: Lawman of the American West) (p. 1966)
Alagna, Magdalena, jt. auth. see Schimel, Kate.
Alaina, Maria. Adding Animals (p. 11)
—Both Sides Are the Same (p. 215)
—Both Sides Are the Same. (p. 215)
—Counting Money (p. 371)
—Estimating (p. 538)
—Fractions (p. 626)
—Graphs (p. 711)
—Measuring Time (p. 1117)
—Patterns in Nature (p. 1329)
—Rainforest. (p. 1436)
—Shapes. (p. 1560)
—Shapes in the City (p. 1560)
—Sumemos Los Animales (p. 1673)
—Wonder Readers Next Steps: Math. (p. 1947)
—Wonder Readers Next Steps: Science. (p. 1947)
—Wonder Readers Next Steps: Social Studies. (p. 1947)
—You Can Count! (p. 1974)
Alaire, Lacey. Oh, the Places We Have Been. (p. 1281)
Alakija, Polly. Catch That Goat! (p. 279)
—Catch That Goat! A Market Day in Nigeria. Alakija, Polly, illus. (p. 279)
—Counting Chickens. (p. 371)
—Has Visto Mi Cabra? (p. 752)
Alakija, Polly, illus. see House, Catherine & Quarto Generic Staff.
Alakija, Sarah. Getting into Oxford & Cambridge. (p. 669)
Al-Allaf, Mashhad, tr. see Al-Ghazali, Abu Hamid.
Alam, Sarah H. Enchanting Fables. (p. 523)
Alamán, Eduardo, jt. auth. see Dunn, Mary R.
Alamán, Eduardo, jt. auth. see Gibbs, Maddie.
Alamán, Eduardo, jt. auth. see Keogh, Josie.
Alamán, Eduardo, tr. see Albright, Rosie.
Alaman, Eduardo, tr. see Dayton, Connor.
Alamán, Eduardo, tr. see Drumlin, Sam.
Alaman, Eduardo, tr. see Hoffman, Mary Ann.
Alamán, Eduardo, tr. see Keogh, Josie.
Alaman, Eduardo, tr. see Poolos, J.
Alaman, Eduardo, tr. see Randolph, Joanne.
Alamn, Eduardo, ed. see Gaspar, Joe.
Alampi, Janet L. Look It Up! Over 600 Definitions for Catholic Kids & Their Parents & Teachers. (p. 1049)
Alan E. And Lisa J. Laird. Cows Can Be Scary. (p. 374)
Alanguilan, Gerry. Elmer. (p. 515)
Alani, Melissa. God's Biggest Treasures. (p. 691)
Alanis, Erik Valdez Y., illus. see Andersen, Hans Christian & Stone Arch Books Staff.
Alanis, Erik Valdez Y., illus. see Stone Arch Books Staff.
Alaniz, Adam, illus. see Kornberg, Arthur.
Alaníz, Eduardo Martínez. Hugo Sanchez. (p. 825)
Alaniz, Joshua. Unfortunate yet Fortunate Squirrel. (p. 1817)
Alaniz, Valeria & García, Sarah Rafael. Barrio Writers: Empowering Teens Through Creative Writing—: A Collection of Works by Teens for Teens, Teachers & Our Communities. (p. 140)
Alano, Benny. Attack of the Vampire Snowmen. Geis, Jessica, illus. (p. 114)
—Hand Puppet Horror. Geis, Jessica, illus. (p. 740)
—Wheel of Fate: Brian Mead's Ghost. (p. 1900)
Alape, Arturo. Caballo y Su Sombra. (p. 250)
—Caiman Sonador. (p. 252)
Al-Araimi, Saif & Al-Rawahi, Thuria. Smart Parents Meet Mr Motivation (V2) (p. 1593)
Alarcao, Renato, illus. see Asai, Carrie & Gray, Mitchel.
Alarcao, Renato, illus. see Asai, Carrie.
Alarcao, Renato, illus. see Javaherbin, Mina.
Alarcao, Renato, illus. see Marcantonio, Patricia Santos, et al.
Alarcao, Renato, illus. see Paterson Jr., John B. & Paterson Sr, John B.
Alarcao, Renato, illus. see Paterson, John B., Jr. & Paterson, John B., Sr.
Alarcao, Renato, illus. see Torres, Jennifer.
Alarcón Ariza, Pedro Antonio de, jt. auth. see de Alarcón, Pedro Antonio.
Alarcon, Claudia, jt. auth. see Blumenthal, Bliss.
Alarcon, Francisco, jt. auth. see Alarcón, Francisco X.
Alarcón, Francisco X. Angels Ride Bikes & Other Fall Poems: Los Angeles Andan Bicicletas y Otros Poemas de Otono. Gonzalez, Maya Christina, illus. (p. 75)
—Animal Poems of the Iguazu. Gonzalez, Maya Christina, illus. (p. 79)
—From the Bellybutton of the Moon & Other Summer Poems (Del Ombligo de la Luna y Otros Poemas de Verano) Gonzalez, Maya Christina, illus. (p. 644)
—Iguanas in the Snow & Other Winter Poems: Iguanas en la Nieve y Otros Poemas. Gonzalez, Maya Christina, illus. (p. 856)
—Laughing Tomatoes & Other Spring Poems (Jitomates Risueños y Otros Poemas de Primavera) Gonzalez, Maya Christina, illus. (p. 980)
—Poems to Dream Together: Poemas para soñar Juntos. Barragán, Paula, illus. (p. 1376)
Alarcón, Francisco X., tr. see Ata, Te.
Alarcón, Francisco X. & Alarcon, Francisco. Iguanas in the Snow & Other Winter Poems. Gonzalez, Maya Christina, illus. (p. 856)
Alarcón, Francisco X., et al. Border Voices (BV10) The San Diego Celebration of Poetry & Music: the 10th Annual Anthology of Poetry. (p. 214)
Alarcon, Jill, jt. auth. see Muhall, Jill K.
Alarcon, Roben. American Indians in the 1800s. (p. 62)
—Constitution & the Bill of Rights. (p. 359)
—John Jay. (p. 922)
—Librarians Then & Now. (p. 1005)
—Sitting Bull. (p. 1582)
—Teachers Then & Now. (p. 1709)
Alarid, Carilyn & Markel, Marilyn. Hits With His Fist Gives a Helping Hand: Mimbres Children Learn about Caring. (p. 786)
—Old Grandfather Teaches a Lesson: Mimbres Children Learn Respect. Alarid, Carilyn & Markel, Marilyn, illus. (p. 1283)
—Talks All Day Has the Courage to Speak: Mimbres Children Learn Citizenship. Alarid, Carilyn & Markel, Marilyn, illus. (p. 1704)
Alarid, Jason & Alarid, Melissa. My Kaya & Me in the Forest. Alarid, Jason, illus. (p. 1211)
Alarid, Melissa, jt. auth. see Alarid, Jason.
Alary, Laura. Mira & the Big Story. Todd, Sue, illus. (p. 1148)
Alaska Boys and Girls Clubs Staff. Is for Alaska. McCann, Michelle, ed. (p. 889)
Alasko, Carl. Emotional Bullshit: The Hidden Plague That Is Threatening to Destroy Your Relationships-And How to Stop It. (p. 520)
Alastra, Stephanie, illus. see Laurent, Karine.
Alaverdy, Melissa, illus. see O'Brien, Eileen.
Alba, Elisabeth, illus. see Earhart, Kristin.
Alba, Elisabeth, illus. see Norwich, Grace.
Albala, Ken. Cooking in Europe, 1250-1650 (p. 362)
Albala, Ken & Cox, Caroline. Opening up North America, 1497-1800, Revised Edition. (p. 1300)
Alban, Andrea, jt. auth. see Gosline, Andrea.
Alban, Rafael Segovia, tr. see Hendry, Diana.
Albanell, Pep. Grito de la Botella. Tobella, Montse, illus. (p. 724)
Albani, Rob. Whole World Laughing at Once. (p. 1920)
Albano, Jennifer, illus. see Schultz, Brenda.
Albarn, Jessica. Boy in the Oak. (p. 218)
Albee, Jo. American Heroes (p. 61)
Albee, Jo & Capstone Press Staff. American Heroes (p. 61)
Albee, Michael J. Elements of Research: The Student's Guide to Avoiding Plagiarism in the Information Age. (p. 511)
Albee, Sarah. Blue's Checkup. Chernichaw, Ian, illus. (p. 204)
—Bugged: How Insects Changed History. Leighton, Robert, illus. (p. 236)
—Bunny Hop. Swanson, Maggie, illus. (p. 242)
—Bunny Hop (Sesame Street) (p. 242)
—Chimpanzees. (p. 306)
—Clever Trevor. Billin-Frye, Paige, illus. (p. 331)
—Dolphins. (p. 464)
—Elephants. (p. 511)
—Elmo Says... Leigh, Tom, illus. (p. 515)
—Elmo's 12 Days of Christmas. Swanson, Maggie, illus. (p. 515)
—Elmo's Lucky Day. Chartier, Normand, illus. (p. 515)
—Elmo's Tricky Tongue Twisters. Swanson, Maggie, illus. (p. 516)
—Fun in the Sun. Williams, Sue, illus. (p. 648)
—Giraffes. (p. 677)
—Halloween ABC. Woolf, Julia, illus. (p. 737)
—Hello, Cat, Hello, Dog. Leigh, Tom, illus. (p. 763)
—Hic! Brannon, Tom, illus. (p. 775)
—Julius Caesar, Cleopatra. (p. 933)
—Kidoozle Kids & the Great Color Chase! (p. 952)
—Kidoozle Kids & the Great Shape Rescue! (p. 952)
—Lions. (p. 1021)
—Max Can Fix That. Schick, Joel, illus. (p. 1111)
—Monsters on the Bus (Sesame Street) Ewers, Joe, illus. (p. 1169)
—Off to Bed. Ebert, Len, illus. (p. 1279)
—One for Me, One for You: A Book about Sharing. Craig, Karen, illus. (p. 1295)
—Poop Happened! A History of the World from the Bottom Up. Leighton, Robert, illus. (p. 1383)
—Time for Bed, Elmo! (Sesame Street) Swanson, Maggie, illus. (p. 1751)
—Trevor el Ingenioso. Billin-Frye, Page, illus. (p. 1785)
—Trevor el Ingenioso; Clever Trevor. (p. 1785)
—Tummies! Moroney, Christopher, illus. (p. 1796)
—Where Is Pig? Velez, Walter, illus. (p. 1909)
—Why'd They Wear That? From Hair Shirts to Hoop Skirts, Platform Shoes to Tattoos, a Fashion History of of the World. (p. 1927)
—World of Dinosaurs. (p. 1956)
Albee, Sarah, jt. auth. see Allen, Constance.
Albee, Sarah & Benchmark Education Co., LLC. Thomas Jefferson: American Architect. (p. 1739)
Albee, Sarah & Delaney, Kate. Cheetahs. (p. 296)
Albee, Sarah & Hood, Susan. Blue's Bad Dream. Chernichaw, Ian, illus. (p. 204)
—Blue's Opposites Game. (p. 204)
—Snappy Heads Andy Alligator. Brown, Jo, illus. (p. 1597)
—Snappy Heads Tommy T Rex. Brown, Jo, illus. (p. 1597)
Albee, Sarah & Sesame Street Staff. I Can Do It! DiFiori, Larry, illus. (p. 835)
Albee, Sarah, et al. Elmo's Little Library (Sesame Street) Swanson, Maggie & Leigh, Tom, illus. (p. 515)
—Read Around Sesame Street (Sesame Street) Mathieu, Joe, illus. (p. 1443)
—To the Center of the Earth! (p. 1759)
Albee, Sarah, retold by. Stone Soup. (p. 1652)
Alber, Christopher. Casey Jones. (p. 275)
Alberg, Nathan, illus. see Berg, Brook.
Alberini, Teresa, illus. see Dawson, Emily C.
Alberini, Teresa, illus. see Pimentel, Annette Bay.
Alberini, Teresa, illus. see Shaffer, Jody Jensen.
Albers, Christine, jt. auth. see Albers, Megan.
Albers, Lisa, ed. see Bonnice, Sherry.
Albers, Lisa, ed. see Brinkerhoff, Shirley.
Albers, Lisa, ed. see Esherick, Joan.
Albers, Lisa, ed. see Lange, Donna.
Albers, Lisa, ed. see Libal, Autumn.
Albers, Lisa, ed. see Libal, Joyce.
Albers, Lisa, ed. see Souder, Patricia.
Albers, Megan & Albers, Christine. Attack of Mr. Crohn's. Albers, Randy, ed. (p. 113)
Albers, Randy, ed. see Albers, Megan & Albers, Christine.
Albert, Beatrice. Adventure's Unlimited: Great Stories for Great Kids. (p. 25)
Albert, Becky. Roxy the Rabbit. (p. 1492)
Albert, Burton. Journey of the Nightly Jaguar. Roth, Robert, illus. (p. 928)
—Where Does the Trail Lead? Pinkney, Brian, illus. (p. 1907)
—Windsongs & Rainbows. (p. 1936)
Albert, Dar, illus. see Cardillo, Linda.
Albert, Edoardo. Call to Prayer: The Story of Bilal. (p. 254)
Albert, Lisa. Mercy Lily. (p. 1127)
Albert, Lisa Rondinelli. Lois Lowry: The Giver of Stories & Memories. (p. 1045)
—So You Want to Be a Film or TV Actor? (p. 1602)
—Stephenie Meyer: Author of the Twilight Saga. (p. 1648)
Albert, Louise. Less Than Perfect. (p. 993)
Albert, Robert, illus. see Irbinskas, Heather.
Albert, Sarah, jt. auth. see Thomson, Elizabeth.
Albert, Susan Wittig. Cat's Claw. (p. 281)
—Mourning Gloria (p. 1181)
Albert, Toni Diana. Saving the Rain Forest with Cammie & Cooper. Bowles, Carol, illus. (p. 1517)
Albertalli, Becky. Simon vs. the Homo Sapiens Agenda. (p. 1577)
Albertazzi, Anne Marie. Salman Rushdie. Bloom, Harold, ed. (p. 1505)
Alberti, Mario, illus. see Gage, Christos.
Alberti, Rafael. Rafael Alberti para Ninos. Gaban, Jesus, illus. (p. 1433)
Alberti, Robert. Mitlanyal: The Gods of Stability (p. 1156)
—Mitlanyal: The Gods of Change (p. 1156)
Alberti, Theresa. Vietnam ABCs: A Book about the People & Places of Vietnam Blanks, Natascha Alex, illus. (p. 1841)
Albertine, illus. see Zullo, Germano.
Alberto, Daisy. Horse & a Hero. RH Disney Staff, illus. (p. 799)
—No Rules for Rex! Smath, Jerry, illus. (p. 1260)
—Pete for President! Sims, Blanche, illus. (p. 1346)
Alberto, Eliseo. Del Otro Lado de los Sueños. Martinez, Enrique & Graullera, Fabiola, illus. (p. 424)
Alberts, Katharine O. Boo on the Loose. (p. 210)
Alberts, Nancy Markham. Just One More? Butler, John, illus. (p. 939)
Alberts, Nancy Markham & Alley, R. W. Joselina Piggy Goes Out. (p. 926)
Alberts, Scott, illus. see Whittaker, Heather.
Albertson, Bernard. Angry Angel. (p. 75)
—So, You Think There Is No Santa (p. 1602)
Albertson, Donald W. Catch A Rising Star: The Adult Game of Youth Sports. (p. 279)
Albertson, Patricia. Trick or Treat: The Tricks on You. (p. 1786)

Albin, Colin. Tom's Tales. (p. 1765)
Albin, Gennifer. Altered. (p. 50)
—Crewel - Chapters 1-5 (p. 382)
—Crewel, Chapters 1-5. (p. 382)
—Unraveled. (p. 1822)
Albini, Louis, jt. auth. see Adey, Margaret.
Albitar, Nuha, tr. see Addasi, Maha.
Albo, Pablo. Glutton. Quarello, Maurizio A. C., illus. (p. 685)
Albon, Lucie. Little Ballerina: A Children's Book Inspired by Edgar Degas. (p. 1023)
Alborghetti, Marci. Miracle of the Myrrh. Blondon, Herve, illus. (p. 1148)
Alborough, Jez. Billy the Goat's Big Breakfast. Alborough, Jez, illus. (p. 187)
—Duck in the Truck. Alborough, Jez, illus. (p. 488)
—Gobble Gobble Moooooo Tractor Book. Alborough, Jez, illus. (p. 688)
—Hug. Alborough, Jez, illus. (p. 824)
—Nat the Cat's Sunny Smile. Alborough, Jez, illus. (p. 1230)
—Six Little Chicks. (p. 1582)
—Super Duck. Alborough, Jez, illus. (p. 1679)
—Watch Out! Big Bro's Coming! (p. 1861)
—Yes. Alborough, Jez, illus. (p. 1970)
Alborozo. Acrobat. (p. 9)
Alborozo, Gabriel. Colour Thief. (p. 346)
—Good Night, Firefly. Alborozo, Gabriel, illus. (p. 699)
Albout, Corrine & Mabire, Grégoire. All Aboard. (p. 41)
Albrecht, Jeff, illus. see Moberg, Julia.
Albrecht, John, Jr. Chocolate Milk Likes Me. Ashby, Chris, illus. (p. 309)
Albrecht, Joshua. Victims of a Tragedy. (p. 1840)
Albrecht, Oliver, et al. Build Your Own Galaxy: The Big Unofficial Lego Builder's Book. (p. 238)
Albrecht, Sally K. & Althouse, Jay. I Sing, You Sing, Too! 30 Echo Songs for Young Singers. (p. 845)
—Rhythm All Around! 10 Songs That Explore Rhythm in Our World. (p. 1468)
Albrecht, Sally K., et al. I Sing, You Sing, Too! 30 Echo Songs for Young Singers. (p. 845)
—Snow Way Out! A Vacation in Winter's Wonderland: A Mini-Musical for Unison & 2-Part Voices. (p. 1599)
Albrecht-Smith, Angie. Willie's Critter Tales: Willie Meets a Possum. (p. 1934)
—Willie's Critter Tales: Willie's Friend Visits. (p. 1934)
Albright, Ann. Samuel Sparrow & the Tree of Light. Albright, Ann, illus. (p. 1509)
Albright, Audrey, illus. see Kaye, Christian Thomas.
Albright, David Edward. Journals of Aiden Hunter: The Marakata Shard. Haight, Joelle, illus. (p. 927)
Albright, Kendra S. & Gavigan, Karen W., eds. AIDS in the Endzone. Petrulis, Sarah, illus. (p. 30)
Albright, Rosie. Bedbug-Sniffing Beagles & Other Scent Hounds: Beagles Cazadores de Chinches y Otros Sabuesos. Alamán, Eduardo, tr. from ENG. (p. 156)
—Bedbug-Sniffing Beagles & Other Scent Hounds. (p. 156)
—Bee Detectives: Abejas Detectives. Alamán, Eduardo, tr. from ENG. (p. 157)
—Bee Detectives. (p. 157)
—Detection Rats: Ratas Detectoras. Alamán, Eduardo, tr. from ENG. (p. 431)
—Detection Rats. (p. 431)
—Military Dolphins: Delfines Del Ejército. Alamán, Eduardo, tr. (p. 1142)
—Military Dolphins. (p. 1142)
—Pig Detectives. (p. 1357)
—Police Dogs: Perros Policías. Alamán, Eduardo, tr. from ENG. (p. 1380)
—Police Dogs. (p. 1380)
Albright, Sawyer. Emeril Lagasse. (p. 518)
Albright, Tawnya, illus. see VonSeggen, Liz.
Albright, Tawnya, et al. Puppetry Clip Art Book & CD. (p. 1417)
Albright, Thomas B. Universal English: Second Language for All. (p. 1820)
Albritton, Leslie. Sally o'Mally's Incredible Day. (p. 1505)
Albuquerque, Blossom. Dashing Duke & His Dodgy Adventures. Flinn, Hannah, illus. (p. 409)
Albuquerque, Jessica. Jessica & the Caramuri. (p. 914)
Albuquerque, Rafael, illus. see Cosby, Andrew & Stokes, Johanna.
Albuquerque, Rafael, illus. see Giffen, Keith, et al.
Albuquerque, Rafael, illus. see Rogers, John, et al.
Alcadia SNC Staff, illus. see ABDO Publishing Company Staff & Howard, Lee.
Alcadia SNC Staff, illus. see Howard, Lee.
Alcamo, I. Edward, ed. see Brock, David.
Alcamo, I. Edward, ed. see Ferreiro, Carmen.
Alcamo, I. Edward, ed. see O'Donnell, Judith A., et al.
Alcamo, I. Edward, ed. see Sfakianos, Jeffrey N.
Alcamo, I. Edward, ed. see Siderovski, Susan.
Alcamo, I. Edward, ed. see Smith, Tara C.
Alcamo, I. Edward, ed. see Walker, David H.
Alcamo, I. Edward, ed. Deadly Diseases & Epidemics. (p. 417)
Alcamol, I. Edward, ed. Deadly Diseases & Epidemics. (p. 417)
Alcantara, Felipe Ugalde, illus. see Villasenor, Victor.
Alcantara, Ignacio, illus. see Vision, David & Vision, Mutiya Sahar.
Alcantara, Ignacio, illus. see Vision, David, et al.
Alcantara, Ignacio, illus. see Vision, David.
Alcantara, Ignacio, illus. see Vision, Mutiya & Vision, David.
Alcantara, Ignacio, illus. see Vision, Mutiya Sahar.
Alcántara, Ricardo. Betania. (p. 171)
Alcantara, Ricardo. Casa de los Miedos. Maier, Ximena, illus. (p. 273)
Alcántara, Ricardo. Cuenta Estrellas. (p. 389)
—Disfraces de Tento. Gusti, illus. (p. 450)
—Hijo Del Viento. (p. 779)
—Huy, Que Miedo! (p. 830)
—Mauro Ojos Brillantes. (p. 1110)
—Quien Ayuda en Casa? (p. 1427)
—Quien Dice No a las Drogas? (p. 1427)
—Quién es Tento? Gusti, illus. (p. 1427)
—Quien Manea el Esqueleto? (p. 1427)
—Quien Quire a los Viejos? (p. 1427)
—Quien USA las Papeleras? (p. 1427)
—Ronda de Cada Dia. (p. 1487)
—Tento Busca su Osito. Gusti, illus. (p. 1720)
—Tento y el Color del Mar. Gusti, illus. (p. 1720)
—Tento y el Diente. Gusti, illus. (p. 1720)
—Tento y el Perro Grandullon. Gusti, illus. (p. 1720)
—Tento y la Tormenta. Gusti, illus. (p. 1720)
—Tento y Su Amigo Gusti, illus. (p. 1720)
—Tento y Su Prima Encarna. (p. 1720)
—Tento y Su Sombra. (p. 1720)
Alcantara, Ricardo. Tomas y el Lapiz Magico. Gusti, illus. (p. 1764)
Alchin, Nicholas. Theory of Knowledge. (p. 1729)
Alciati, Andrea. Book of Emblems: The Emblematum Liber in Latin & English. (p. 211)
Alcock, Deborah. King's Service: A Story of the Thirty Years' War. (p. 961)
Alcoholics Anonymous World Services. Twenty-Four Hours a Day for Teens: Daily Meditations. (p. 1801)
Alcolea, Ana. Cuentos de la Abuela Amelia. Lopiz, Violeta, illus. (p. 390)
Alcorn, Anita C. Caught in the Crossfire: A Boy's View of the Battle of Mill Springs, KY. (p. 282)
Alcorn, John, illus. see McCain, Murray.
Alcorn, Miah, illus. see Chin, Oliver Clyde.
Alcorn, Miah, illus. see Chin, Oliver.
Alcorn, Randy. Lord Foulgrin's Letters. (p. 1052)
—Tell Me about Heaven. DiCianni, Ron, illus. (p. 1716)
—Wait until Then. Ben-Ami, Doron, illus. (p. 1852)
Alcorn, Randy & Washington, Linda. Heaven for Kids. (p. 761)
Alcorn, Stephen. Gift of Days: The Greatest Words to Live By. Alcorn, Stephen, illus. (p. 675)
Alcorn, Stephen, illus. see Dray, Philip.
Alcorn, Stephen, illus. see Hopkins, Lee Bennett, ed.
Alcorn, Stephen, illus. see Hopkins, Lee Bennett.
Alcorn, Stephen, illus. see Hopkinson, Deborah.
Alcorn, Stephen, jt. auth. see Hopkins, Lee Bennett.
Alcorn, Steve. Everything in Its Path: A Novel about the St. Francis Dam Disaster. (p. 545)
Alcott, Jessica. Even When You Lie to Me. (p. 541)
Alcott, Louisa May. Alcott: Little Women, Little Men, Jo's Boys. Showalter, Elaine, ed. (p. 35)
—Comic Tragedies: Written by Jo & Meg & Acted by the Little Women. (p. 348)
—Comic Tragedies. (p. 348)
—Comic Tragedies/ Written by Jo & Meg & Acted by the Little Women. (p. 348)
—Eight Cousins. (p. 507)
—Eight Cousins, or, the Aunt-Hill. (p. 507)
—Flower Fables. (p. 607)
—Garland for Girls. (p. 657)
—Good Wives. (p. 700)
—Hombrecitos. (p. 791)
—Jack & Jill: A Village Story. (p. 902)
—Jack & Jill. (p. 902)
—Jo's Boys. (p. 926)
—Kitty's Class Day. (p. 963)
—Kitty's Class Day & Other Stories. (p. 963)
—Kitty's Class Day, & Other Stories. (p. 963)
—Little Men: Life at Plumfield with Jo's Boys. (p. 1031)
—Little Men. (p. 1031)
—Little Men. Andreasen, Dan, illus. (p. 1031)
—Little Men & Jo's Boys. (p. 1031)
—Little Women: Bring the Classics to Life. (p. 1038)
—Little Women: With a Discussion of Family. Lauter, Richard, illus. (p. 1038)
—Little Women. (p. 1038)
—Little Women. Dunn, Robert, illus. (p. 1038)
—Little Women. Corvino, Lucy, illus. (p. 1038)
—Little Women. McKowen, Scott, illus. (p. 1038)
—Little Women. Eiselein, Gregory & Phillips, Anne K., eds. (p. 1038)
—Louisa Alcott Reader: A Supplementar. (p. 1058)
—Louisa Alcott Reader. (p. 1058)
—Modern Cinderella. (p. 1158)
—Modern Cinderella or the Little Old Shoe. (p. 1158)
—Modern Mephistopheles. (p. 1158)
—Muchachos de Jo. (p. 1188)
—Mujercitas. (p. 1189)
—Old-Fashioned Girl. (p. 1283)
—Old-Fashioned Thanksgiving. Wheeler, Jody, illus. (p. 1283)
—Old-Fashioned Thanksgiving. Bernardin, James, illus. (p. 1283)
—Quatre Filles du Docteur March. (p. 1423)
—Short Stories. (p. 1569)
—Silver Pitchers & Independence. (p. 1576)
—Spinning-Wheel Stories. (p. 1628)
—Under the Lilacs. (p. 1813)
—Works of Louisa May Alcott. (p. 1953)
Alcott, Louisa May, jt. auth. see Francis, Pauline.
Alcott, Louisa May, jt. auth. see Luna, Sagrario.
Alcott, Louisa May & Barbarese, J. T. Little Men. (p. 1031)
Alcott, Louisa May & Meg, Meg. Comic Tragedies/ Written by Jo & Meg & Acted by the Little Women. (p. 348)
Alcott, Louisa May & Messina, Lynn. Little Vampire Women. (p. 1037)
Alcott, Louisa May & Naxos of America Staff. Little Women. Mims, Ashley, illus. (p. 1038)
Alcott, Louisa May & Pratt, Anna Bronson Alcott. Comic Tragedies. (p. 348)
Alcott, Louisa May & Steadman, Barbara. Little Women Coloring Book. (p. 1038)
Alcraft, Rob. Dubai from the Sky. (p. 487)
—France (p. 627)
—Germany (p. 666)
—Mexico (p. 1131)
Alda, Arlene. Book of ZZZs. (p. 212)
—Did You Say Pears? (p. 437)
—Except the Color Grey. (p. 547)
—Hello, Good-Bye. (p. 764)
—Here a Face, There a Face. (p. 769)
—Iris Has a Virus. Desimini, Lisa, illus. (p. 887)
—Lulu's Piano Lesson. Desimini, Lisa, illus. (p. 1065)
Aldana, Jacquelyn. 15-Minute Miracle Revealed. Carroll, Cheri Sunshine, ed. (p. 1995)
—Miracle Manifestation Manual II. (p. 1148)
Aldana, Patricia, ed. Winter Book. Berner, Rotraut Susanne, illus. (p. 1938)
Aldecoa, Josefina. Cuento para Susana. Maier, Ximena, tr. (p. 389)
ALDEN, B. E. A., illus. see Craig, Joni.
Alden, Carol, illus. see Fane, Judy B.
Alden, Peter C. Mammals. Reid, Fiona, illus. (p. 1085)
Alden, Peter C. & Peterson, Roger Tory. Birds. Peterson, Roger Tory, ed. (p. 191)
Alden, Raymond MacDonald. Once There Was a King: A Tournament of Stories. Copelman, Evelyn, illus. (p. 1292)
Alden, Raymond MacDonald & Greenland, Katharine Hayward. Why the Chimes Rang: And Other Stories. (p. 1926)
Alden-Tirrill, Anna. Alabaster Jar. (p. 33)
—Promise Box. (p. 1411)
Alder, Charlie. Daredevil Duck. (p. 406)
Alder, Charlie, illus. see Dale, Jay.
Alder, Charlie, illus. see Hall, Kirsten.
Alder, Charlie, illus. see Manushkin, Fran.
Alder, Charlotte, illus. see Crowne, Alyssa.
Alder, Kelynn. Moments of Wonder: Life with Moritz. (p. 1162)
Alderfer, Jonathan. National Geographic Kids Bird Guide of North America: The Best Birding Book for Kids from National Geographic's Bird Experts. (p. 1232)
Alderfer, Jonathan, ed. see White, Mel.
Alderfer, Jonathan, ed. Arizona & New Mexico. (p. 98)
—Washington & Oregon. (p. 1859)
Alderfer, Lauren. Mindful Monkey, Happy Panda. MacLean, Kerry Lee, illus. (p. 1145)
Alderman, Daniel, et al. Rub a Dub Dub. (p. 1493)
Alderman, Derrick, illus. see Allen, Nancy Kelly.
Alderman, Derrick, illus. see Bridges, Sarah.
Alderman, Derrick, illus. see Dahl, Michael.
Alderman, Peter, jt. auth. see McGrath, Barbara Barbieri.
Alderman, Rusty. Daddy S Little Princess. (p. 398)
Alderman, Tanya. Alexis Learns to Love. (p. 37)
Alderman, Tyrone. Mining & Ranching in Early Colorado: Boom & Bust, & Back Again. (p. 1147)
Alders, Willa. Leafy Finds a Home. Burns, Sandra, illus. (p. 982)
Alderson, Kevin. Grade Power: The Complete Guide to Improving Your Grades Through Self-Hypnosis. (p. 705)
Alderson, Lisa. Snow Family: A Winter's Tale. (p. 1599)
Alderson, Lisa, illus. see Feldman, Thea & Auerbach, Annie.
Alderson, Lisa, illus. see Moore, Clement C.
Alderson, Phil. Busy Kids Dinosaurs Magnetic Playbook. (p. 246)
Alderson, Sarah. Sound. (p. 1614)
—Sound Where Secrets are Buried. (p. 1615)
Alderson, Sue Ann. Eco-Diary of Kiran Singer Ballance, Millie, illus. (p. 502)
—Wherever Bears Be. Johnson, Arden, illus. (p. 1911)
Alderton, David. How to Look after Your Budgie: A Practical Guide to Caring for Your Pet, in Step-By-Step Photographs. (p. 820)
—How to Look after Your Goldfish: A Practical Guide to Caring for Your Pet, in Step-By-Step Photographs. (p. 820)
—How to Look after Your Guinea Pig: A Practical Guide to Caring for Your Pet, in Step-By-Step Photographs. (p. 820)
—How to Look after Your Hamster: A Practical Guide to Caring for Your Pet, in Step-By-Step Photographs. (p. 820)
Alderton, John, illus. see Michael, Melanie.
Alderton, Sylvia. Real Name for Puppy. McCartney, Michael David, illus. (p. 1448)
Aldis, Dorothy & Collins, Heather. Hiding. (p. 777)
Aldis, Dorothy Keeley. We're Going to Town! Gehr, Mary, illus. (p. 1875)
Aldous, Kate, illus. see Burnett, Frances Hodgson.
Aldous, Kate, illus. see Sewell, Anna.
Aldous, Kate & McGairy, James. Little Women. (p. 1038)
Aldovini, Giulia. Hielito, el Pinguino. Brignole, Giancarla, tr. (p. 777)
Aldredge, Terry Beckham, illus. see Laubach, Frank.
Aldrete, Gregory S. Daily Life in the Roman City: Rome, Pompeii, & Ostia (p. 400)
Aldrich, Andrew R. How My Family Came to Be - Daddy, Papa & Me. (p. 811)
Aldrich, Christie. Lukie-Bug & the Mittens: Coping with Bullies Can Be Tricky Business. (p. 1064)
—Suzie Magoo & the Lesson: We Must Always Be Considerate of Those Around Us. (p. 1688)
Aldrich, Jodi. Bee Mumble & Wug. (p. 157)
Aldrich, Lisa J. Cyrus McCormick: And the Mechanical Reaper. (p. 397)
—Nikola Tesla & the Taming of Electricity. (p. 1255)
Aldrich, Sandra D. Danny Dolphin. (p. 405)
—Lenny Lobster Saves the Day. (p. 991)
—Trouble in the Park. (p. 1790)
—Willie's Lesson. (p. 1934)
Aldrich, Thomas Bailey. Story of a Bad Boy. (p. 1657)
—Story of a Cat. (p. 1657)
Aldrich, William & Williamson, Don. Best Garden Plants for Illinois (p. 169)
—Gardening Month by Month in Illinois (p. 656)
—Tree & Shrub Gardening for Illinois (p. 1783)
Aldrich, William, et al. Annuals for Illinois. (p. 87)
—Perennials for Illinois. (p. 1341)
Aldrick, Shirley H. F. Gordon, the Great Gobbley Grasshopper. (p. 702)
—Hazel, the Hoppity Kangaroo. (p. 756)
—Tobias & the Pale, Pale Leprechaun. (p. 1760)
Aldridge, Alan, illus. see Plomer, William.
Aldridge, James. Marvellous Mongolian (p. 1099)
Aldridge, Janet. Meadow Brook Girls Afloat: Or the Stormy Cruise of the Red Rover. (p. 1116)
—Meadow Brook Girls Afloat. (p. 1116)
—Meadow-Brook Girls Afloat. (p. 1116)
—Meadow-Brook Girls Afloat (Illustrat. (p. 1116)
—Meadow-Brook Girls by the Sea, or Th. (p. 1116)
—Meadow-Brook Girls in the Hills: Or the Missing Pilot of the White Mountains. (p. 1116)
—Meadow-Brook Girls under Canvas (Ill. (p. 1116)
Aldridge, Rebecca. Apolo Anton Ohno. (p. 92)
—Ban Ki-Moon: United Nations Secretary-General. (p. 135)
—Hoover Dam. (p. 796)
—Italian Americans. (p. 894)
—Sinking of the Titanic. (p. 1580)
—Stella Mccartney. (p. 1647)
Aldridge, Sheila, illus. see Hall, Matthew Henry.
Aldridge, Susan. AIDS. (p. 30)
—Cloning. (p. 333)
Aldrin, Buzz. Look to the Stars. Minor, Wendell, illus. (p. 1050)
—Reaching for the Moon. Minor, Wendell, illus. (p. 1442)
Aldrin, Buzz & Dyson, Marianne J. Welcome to Mars: Making a Home on the Red Planet. (p. 1873)
Aldritt, Jeremy. Thomas Paine & the Power of Common Sense. (p. 1739)
Ale, Leandra. Spoiled by Grandp. (p. 1630)
Aleekuk, Pam, jt. auth. see Bouchard, David.
Alegre, Mari. Destiny. (p. 430)
Alegria, Ciro. Fabulas y Leyendas Americanas. (p. 559)
—Sacha en el Reino de los Arboles. (p. 1500)
Alegria, Malin. Border Town #1: Crossing the Line. (p. 214)
—Border Town #2: Quince Clash. (p. 214)
Alegria, Malin. Border Town #3: Falling Too Fast. (p. 214)
Alegria, Malin. Border Town #4: No Second Chances. (p. 214)
—Crossing the Line. (p. 385)
—Cruzar el Limite (Crossing the Boundary) (p. 387)
—Estrella's Quinceañera. (p. 538)
—Falling Too Fast. (p. 567)
—Guerra de Quinceaneras (Quince Clash) (p. 728)
—Pueblo Fronterizo: Guerra de Quinceañeras. No. 2 (p. 1414)
—Quince Clash. (p. 1428)
—Sofi Mendoza's Guide to Getting Lost in Mexico. (p. 1605)
Aleixandre, Marilar, jt. auth. see Aleixandre, Marilar.
Aleixandre, Marilar & Aleixandre, Marilar. Branda Sin Futuro. (p. 222)
Alejandro, Alis, tr. see Grejniec, Michael.
Alekos, illus. see Tolstoy, Leo.
Alekseyeva, Alla, illus. see Lond, Laura.
Al-Emadi, Hesham. Savior's Threshold: The Chronicles of Dourren. (p. 1518)
Alemagna, Beatrice. Bug Next Door. David, Annette, tr. from FRE. (p. 236)
—Bugs in a Blanket. (p. 237)
—Bugs in the Garden. (p. 237)
—Lion in Paris. (p. 1020)
Alemagna, Beatrice, illus. see Rodari, Gianni.
Alemagna, Beatrice, illus. see Soussana, Nathalie, et al.
Alemagne, Beatrice. Bugs at Christmas. Gordon, Sam, tr. from FRE. (p. 237)
Aleman, Mateo. Guzman de Alfarache (p. 733)
Alemán, Mateo, jt. auth. see Aleman, Mateo.
Aleman, Mateo & Alemán, Mateo. Guzman de Alfarache (p. 733)
Alemanno, Andrea. Surprise for Lady Lily. (p. 1685)
Alemayehu, Tsehay. Bee-Come! A Collection of Short Stories. (p. 157)
Alembi, Ezekiel. Jaramogi Oginga Odinga: People's Revolutionary. (p. 909)
Alemian, Kimberlee, illus. see Masella, Rosalie Tagg.
Alemián, Manuel, tr. see Gillis, Jennifer Blizin.
Alen, Antonia. My Three Little Dogs. (p. 1220)
Alender, Katie. As Dead as It Gets. (p. 105)
—Bad Girls Don't Die. (p. 131)
—Famous Last Words. (p. 569)
—From Bad to Cursed. (p. 642)
—Marie Antoinette, Serial Killer. (p. 1093)
Alerson, Sue Ann, et al. Time for Flowers Time for Snow (p. 1751)
Aleshina, Nonna, illus. see Holub, Joan.
Aleshire & Peter. Ocean Ridges & Trenches. (p. 1276)
Aleshire, Peter. Deserts. (p. 429)
—Mountains. (p. 1181)
Alessandrello, Anna. Tierra. (p. 1748)
Alessi, Jolene. Zombie Crabs. (p. 1988)
—Zombie Fish. (p. 1988)
—Zombie Grasshoppers. (p. 1988)
—Zombie Snails. (p. 1988)
Alessi, Patty. Rreggie T Rex's Vacation on Maui (p. 1493)
Alessio, Amy. Taking the High Ground. (p. 1698)
Alex, Alicia. Adventures of Lothlorlas the White Hamster: The Beginning. (p. 20)
—Adventures of Lothlorlas the White Hamster: Journey to the Garden. (p. 20)
Alex, Ben. Great Bible Stories: For Children Age 5 & Up. Scandinavia Publishing House Staff, ed. (p. 714)
—Great Bible Stories. (p. 714)
Alex, Ioan. My First Words. (p. 1208)
Alex, Joanne DeFilipp. I Wonder What's Out There: A Vision of the Universe for Primary Classes. (p. 849)
Alex, N. L. Smile All the While. (p. 1594)
Alex, Nan. North Carolina. (p. 1264)
Alex, Nino, jt. auth. see London, Jack.
Alex, Smith. Home. Alex, Smith, illus. (p. 791)
Alexan, Julie. Nolia Fasolia: Read-Along Book: Arabic & English. El-Ahraf, Amer, ed. (p. 1263)
Alexander. Phonic Comics: Princess School - Level 1. (p. 1351)
Alexander, Adam. Flurple Woozle. (p. 608)
Alexander, Alie. Wee Boys. (p. 1871)
Alexander, Alison, et al. Science Interact 7. (p. 1526)
Alexander, Alma. Gift of the Unmage. (p. 675)
—Spellspam. (p. 1625)
Alexander, Annette M. Snow Magic & the Sad Little Christmas Tree. (p. 1599)
Alexander, Archibald. History of Colonization on the West Coast of Africa by the Free People of Color of the United States. (p. 783)
Alexander, Audrey. Angels, Demons, & Religious Rituals. (p. 75)
—Witches & Wicca. (p. 1941)
Alexander, Basia, jt. auth. see Conroy, Jim.

Alexander, Bob. Dangerous Dan Tucker: New Mexico's Deadly Lawman. (p. 404)
Alexander, Brad. Antiniak: A Different Kind of Village. (p. 89)
Alexander, Brenda A. Family Tapestry. (p. 568)
Alexander, Brianna. Heaven Sent. (p. 761)
Alexander, Brooke. Little Mia's Big Heart. (p. 1031)
Alexander, Bryan, jt. auth. see Alexander, Cherry.
Alexander, Carmen. Floating Around in the Middle. Tsosie, Dennison, illus. (p. 605)
—Garden Stories: Rosemarie's Garden, Rosemarie's Roof Garden & Rosemarie Returns to Her Garden. Roswell, Stacey, illus. (p. 656)
—Rosemarie Returns to Her Garden. Roswell, Stacey, illus. (p. 1489)
—Rosemarie's Garden. Roswell, Stacey, illus. (p. 1489)
—Rosemarie's Roof Garden. Roswell, Stacey, illus. (p. 1489)
—Zoo 1000 Miles. Henderson, Cecil, illus. (p. 1988)
Alexander, Carol. Bean Trees. Friedland, Joyce & Kessler, Rikki, eds. (p. 150)
—Bessie Coleman. (p. 168)
—Big Squeal: A True Story about a Homeless Pig's Search for Life, Liberty & the Pursuit of Happiness. (p. 184)
—Big Squeal: A True Story about a Homeless Pig's Search for Life, Liberty & the Pursuit of Happiness. Kalpart Designs, illus. (p. 184)
—Book Thief. Friedland, Joyce & Kessler, Rikki, eds. (p. 212)
—Class Clown. Friedland, Joyce & Kessler, Rikki, eds. (p. 327)
—Florence Nightingale. (p. 606)
—Golden Compass: A Study Guide. Friedland, Joyce & Kessler, Rikki, eds. (p. 694)
—Grains. (p. 705)
—Percy Mcgoo. (p. 1341)
—Planet of Junior Brown. Friedland, Joyce & Kessler, Rikki, eds. (p. 1367)
—When My Name Was Keoko. Friedland, Joyce & Kessler, Rikki, eds. (p. 1904)
Alexander, Carol, jt. auth. see Miller, Reagan.
Alexander, Carol & DiCamillo, Kate. Tiger Rising: Novel-Ties Study Guide. Friedland, Joyce & Kessler, Rikki, eds. (p. 1748)
Alexander, Carol & Vargus, Nanci Reginelli. Florence Nightingale. (p. 606)
Alexander, Carrie, et al. Honk If You Love Real Men: Four Tales of Erotic Romance. (p. 795)
Alexander, Cecil F. All Things Bright & Beautiful. Bryan, Ashley, illus. (p. 46)
Alexander, Cecil Frances. All Things Bright & Beautiful. Vojtech, Anna, illus. (p. 46)
Alexander, Cherry & Alexander, Bryan. Inuit. (p. 883)
Alexander, Chris. Difficult Origami. (p. 438)
—Sort-of-Difficult. (p. 1614)
Alexander, Chris, jt. auth. see Meinking, Mary.
Alexander, Claire. Back to Front & Upside Down. (p. 130)
—Lucy & the Bully Alexander, Claire, illus. (p. 1063)
—Millie Shares. (p. 1144)
—Monkey & the Little One. (p. 1165)
—Small Florence, Piggy Pop Star. Alexander, Claire, illus. (p. 1592)
Alexander, Claudia. Windows to Adventure: Windows to the Morning Star. (p. 1936)
Alexander, David E. Myths of the Lechuza. Smith, Duriel, illus. (p. 1227)
Alexander, Dennis, et al. Alfred's Premier Piano Course: Lesson 3. (p. 38)
—Alfred's Premier Piano Course: Performance 3. Manus, Morton, ed. (p. 38)
—Alfred's Premier Piano Course Assignment Book: Level 1A-6. Manus, Morton, ed. (p. 38)
—Alfred's Premier Piano Course - Theory 3. Manus, Morton, ed. (p. 38)
—Premier Piano Course, Technique Manus, Morton, ed. (p. 1395)
Alexander, Devin. Fast Food Fix: 75+ Amazing Recipe Makeovers of Your Fast Food Restaurant Favorites. (p. 576)
Alexander, Don. Damia's Quest. (p. 409)
Alexander, Dorothy. Ce Ce & Her Shadow. (p. 283)
Alexander, Elizabeth. Praise Song for the Day. Diaz, David, illus. (p. 1393)
Alexander, Elizabeth & Nelson, Marilyn. Miss Crandall's School for Young Ladies & Little Misses of Color. Cooper, Floyd, illus. (p. 1151)
Alexander, Elye J., tr. see Kurimoto, Kaoru.
Alexander, Emmett. Formas / Sort It by Shape. de la Vega, Eida, tr. (p. 620)
—Sort It by Color. (p. 1614)
—Sort It by Shape. (p. 1614)
—Sort It by Size. (p. 1614)
—Tamaños / Sort It by Size. de la Vega, Eida, tr. (p. 1704)
Alexander, Florence. Dare to Be... Martin Luther King Jr. Whitmore, Yvette, illus. (p. 406)
—When God Touched My Life... the Power of His Word. (p. 1902)
Alexander, Florence & Alexander, Stanley. Come with Me & See... African People. (p. 347)
—Come with Me & See... Animals of the World. (p. 347)
—Come with Me & See... Birds of the World. (p. 347)
—Come with Me & See... Children of the World. (p. 347)
—Come with Me & See— African People: Venga Conmigo y Vea— la Gente de Africa. (p. 347)
—Jesus Child Is Born: Dare to Be Great. (p. 915)
—Jesus Christ Is Born. (p. 915)
—Space Exploration. (p. 1619)
Alexander, Florence, et al. Come with Me & See... A Total Eclipse in Africa. Alexander, Florence et al, illus. (p. 347)
Alexander, Geoff. Toothbugs! Carole, Isaacs, illus. (p. 1768)
Alexander, Goldie. Body & Soul. (p. 207)
—Hedgeburners: An A-Z PI Mystery. Gardner, Marjory, illus. (p. 761)
Alexander, Goldie, jt. auth. see Edwards, Hazel.
Alexander, Greg, jt. auth. see Smart, Bradford D.
Alexander, Gregory, illus. see Rowe, John, ed.
Alexander, Greshena. Lessons & Fables: Growing up Is a Part of Life. (p. 993)
Alexander, Hartley Burr. Latin-American Mythology. (p. 979)
—Religious Spirit of the American Indian, as Shown in the Development of His Religious Rites & Customs. (p. 1458)
Alexander, Heather. Allie Gator's Halloween Hayride. Running Press Staff, ed. (p. 47)
—Be a Star! Le Feyer, Diane, illus. (p. 148)
—Case of the Tattooed Cat. (p. 275)
—Easy Desserts from Around the World. (p. 500)
—Easy Main Dishes from Around the World. (p. 500)
—Easy Snacks from Around the World. (p. 500)
—Junior Groovies - Bugs! (p. 936)
—Step into the Spotlight! Le Feyer, Diane, illus. (p. 1648)
Alexander, Heather, jt. auth. see Simmons, Carl.
Alexander, Heather & Hamilton, Meredith. Child's Introduction to Art: The World's Greatest Paintings & Sculptures. Hamilton, Meredith, illus. (p. 305)
Alexander, Ian. Do You See a Dozen? (p. 458)
Alexander, J. H. De la Oscuridad a la Luz. Klemetz, Leticia, tr. from ENG. (p. 416)
Alexander, James W. Good - Better - Best: Classic Treatment of a Christian's Duty to the Poor. (p. 697)
Alexander, Janice Marie. Princess Panny - Not Princess Nobody. Arkanov, Elvira, illus. (p. 1405)
Alexander, Jason. Alice's Adventures in Wonderland. (p. 39)
Alexander, Jen. Aftermath. (p. 28)
Alexander, Jenine. Other Lover. (p. 1306)
Alexander, Jenny. Bullies, Bigmouths & So-Called Friends. (p. 240)
—Rugged Off-Roader. (p. 1494)
—Speedy Sports Car. (p. 1624)
—Taxi about Town. (p. 1707)
Alexander, Jessica, jt. auth. see Shore, Diane Z.
Alexander, Jessica, jt. auth. see Shore, Diane ZuHone.
Alexander, Jessica & Shore, Diane Z. This Is the Dream. Ransome, James E., illus. (p. 1736)
Alexander, Jill S. Sweetheart of Prosper County. (p. 1690)
Alexander, John. Adventures of Thunder & Avalanche: Up & Away. Alexander, John, illus. (p. 24)
—Adventures of Thunder & Avalanche: Laws of Nature. Alexander, John, illus. (p. 24)
Alexander, Johnna A., illus. see Flora, B. David.
Alexander, Katie Norwood, illus. see Bateman, Claire Boudreaux.
Alexander, Kay. Drawing & Painting Activities: Clear: Drawing & Painting Activities: Using Masterworks As Inspiration: Using Masterworks As Inspiration. (p. 481)
Alexander, Kwame. Acoustic Rooster & His Barnyard Band. Bowers, Tim, illus. (p. 9)
—Book Party. (p. 212)
—Crossover. (p. 385)
—Crush: Love Poems. (p. 386)
—He Said, She Said. (p. 756)
Alexander, Kwame, et al. Love & Profanity: A Collection of True, Tortured, Wild, Hilarious, Concise, & Intense Tales of Teenage Life. (p. 1059)
Alexander, Larry, jt. auth. see Gillis, Peter.
Alexander, Lestat. Blue-Eyed Alligator. (p. 202)
Alexander, Linda. As-Easy-As-ABC-123. (p. 105)
—As-Easy-As-ABC-123 Bilingual. (p. 105)
—Collection 1 Bilingual. (p. 339)
Alexander, Linda B. & Kwon, Nahyun, eds. Multicultural Programs for Tweens & Teens. (p. 1190)
Alexander, Lloyd. Arkadians. (p. 99)
—Black Cauldron. (p. 195)
—Black Cauldron. Wyatt, David, illus. (p. 195)
—Book of Three. Wyatt, David, illus. (p. 212)
—Castle of Llyr. (p. 277)
—Castle of Llyr. Wyatt, David, illus. (p. 277)
—Cat Who Wished to Be a Man. (p. 278)
—Dream-of-Jade: The Emperor's Cat. Burkett, D. Brent, illus. (p. 483)
—Foundling: And Other Tales of Prydain. Wyatt, David, illus. (p. 624)
—High King. (p. 778)
—High King. Wyatt, David, illus. (p. 778)
—Iron Ring. (p. 888)
—Remarkable Journey of Prince Jen. (p. 1458)
—Rope Trick. (p. 1488)
—Taran Wanderer. (p. 1706)
—Taran Wanderer. Wyatt, David, illus. (p. 1706)
—Time Cat: The Remarkable Journeys of Jason & Gareth. (p. 1751)
—Xanadu Adventure. (p. 1967)
Alexander, Lloyd, et al. Firebirds: An Anthology of Original Fantasy & Science Fiction. Sharyn, November, ed. (p. 591)
Alexander, Lori. Backhoe Joe. Cameron, Craig, illus. (p. 130)
Alexander, Louise. My Little Pony: School Spirit! (p. 1213)
Alexander, Lyndi. Windmills. (p. 1936)
Alexander, Marilee. Wise Man's Last Wish: A Christmas Tale. Nash, Gisele, illus. (p. 1940)
Alexander, Mark. Incredible Incas. (p. 869)
—Whose Toes Are Those? (p. 1922)
Alexander, Markus. Mesut Ozil Superstar. (p. 1130)
Alexander, Martha. Max & the Dumb Flower Picture. (p. 1110)
—Poems & Prayers for the Very Young. (p. 1376)
—You're Adorable. Alexander, Martha, illus. (p. 1982)
Alexander, Martha, illus. see McGrath, Barbara Barbieri.
Alexander, Martha, et al. Teatro para Niños. Tenorio, Miguel A., ed. (p. 1711)
Alexander, Mary Helen. Please & Thank You. (p. 1373)
Alexander, Michael. Until Wishes Are Fulfilled II: Alec's Story. (p. 1823)
Alexander, Nick. 50 Reasons to Say Goodbye - A Novel. (p. 1997)
Alexander, Nicole "Nikki". Nicole's Rules of Life. (p. 1251)
Alexander, Pat. Lion First Bible. Baxter, Leon, illus. (p. 1020)
Alexander, R. C. Unfamiliar Magic. (p. 1817)
Alexander, R. W. Dr. Wolfgang's Cure. (p. 475)
—Mating Megan. (p. 1109)
—Protecting Pookie. (p. 1412)
—Spark of Life. (p. 1622)
—Spider Fight. (p. 1626)
Alexander, Ric Douglas. Victory over Fat: 6 steps to Permanent Fat Loss & Super Health. (p. 1840)
Alexander, Richard. Broken Treaties: Native American Migrations. (p. 230)
—Colony of Connecticut. (p. 342)
—Counting To 10: Number Names & Count Sequence. (p. 371)
—Inuit: People of the North. (p. 883)
—Que Hacen Los Recolectores de Basura? / What Do Garbage Collectors Do? (p. 1423)
—What Do Garbage Collectors Do? (p. 1882)
Alexander, Robert, jt. auth. see Alexander, Sally Hobart.
Alexander, Rod. BMX Racing: A Step-by-Step Guide. (p. 204)
Alexander, Ron. And God Created Squirrels. (p. 71)
Alexander, Rosemary, jt. auth. see Scholastic, Inc. Staff.
Alexander, S. L. Media & American Courts: A Reference Handbook (p. 1118)
Alexander, Sally Hobart & Alexander, Robert. She Touched the World: Laura Bridgman, Deaf-Blind Pioneer. (p. 1564)
Alexander, Samantha. Flying Start. (p. 610)
—Jodie. (p. 919)
—Mission. (p. 1153)
—Peak Performance (p. 1332)
—Rachel (p. 1431)
—Team Spirit (p. 1710)
—Trapped. (p. 1779)
Alexander, Scott L. My Dog Named Whatever. (p. 1202)
Alexander, Stanley, illus. see Alexander, Florence, et al.
Alexander, Stanley, jt. auth. see Alexander, Florence.
Alexander, Stefany. Sith the Snake. (p. 1582)
Alexander, Stephanie J. Sociology: The Study of Human Social Behavior. (p. 1605)
Alexander, Susanne L. Adventures of the Pixies of Penny Brook Village: Reeza's Revenge. (p. 23)
Alexander, Suzanna M., et al. Prehistoric People of Moccasin Bend, Chattanooga, Tennessee: An Educational Coloring Book. (p. 1395)
Alexander, Sy. Pinksta & the Polka Dotted-Pinstriped-Pants-Wearing Princess. Young, Aviance, illus. (p. 1360)
Alexander, Tom. Foundations for Success. (p. 624)
Alexander, Tonia. Sometimes I Forget to Breathe. (p. 1610)
Alexander, Troas. Cat's Tale. Roberts, Ramona, illus. (p. 281)
Alexander, Troas James. Stray's Great Adventure. Mitchell Jr., Leonard, illus. (p. 1666)
Alexander, Wade F. Sister Elizabeth Kenny: Maverick Heroine of the Polio Treatment Controversy. (p. 1581)
Alexander, William. Ambassador. (p. 56)
—Ghoulish Song. (p. 673)
—Goblin Secrets. (p. 688)
Alexander, Yvonne. Adventure in Autou. (p. 14)
Alexander, Yvonne Rabdau, illus. see MacPherson, Lorry.
Alexander-Heaton, Susanne & Gabriell, Chantal T. ABC Field Guide to Faeries: Inspiring Reminders of Respect for Ourselves, Each Other & the Environment. (p. 3)
Alexandria, Chris. Pick-A-Woowoo: Have You Ever Wondered about Angels? Levitas, Alex, illus. (p. 1354)
—Pick-A-Woowoo - Have You Ever Wondered about Angels? Levitas, Alex, illus. (p. 1354)
Alexandria, Shalayne. Nyville High No. 1: Welcome to Nyville. (p. 1274)
—Nyville High No. 2: Mother May I. (p. 1274)
Alexandria, Vincent. Marvelous Martin: Case of the Freckle-Faced Bully. (p. 1099)
—Marvelous Marvin. (p. 1099)
Alexanyan, Karina. African Odyssey. (p. 28)
Alexie, Oscar. How the Bear Lost This Tail. Sloat, Teri, illus. (p. 812)
Alexie, Sherman. Absolutely True Diary of a Part-Time Indian. (p. 7)
—Absolutely True Diary of a Part-Time Indian. Forney, Ellen, illus. (p. 7)
—Flight. (p. 604)
Alexios, Rene. Pirate & the Mermaid: The Story of Their Song. Pryka, Aaron et al, eds. (p. 1362)
Alexiou, Michelle. Bully for Berl: Playground Escapades. (p. 241)
Alexiou, Xenia, jt. auth. see Baldwin, Kim.
Alexis, André. Ingrid & the Wolf. (p. 874)
Alexopolous, George. Go with Grace Alexopolous, George, illus. (p. 687)
Alexovich, Aaron. Goodbye, Crestfallen Vol. 2. (p. 700)
—Kimmie66. (p. 957)
Al-Fakhri, Patricia, illus. see Johnson, Julia.
Al-Fakhri, Patricia, illus. see Sheffield, Marilyn.
Alfandolo, Koffi, illus. see Gorg, Gwyn.
Alfano, Doreen D. Adventures of Hermie the Hermit Crab: Finding a New Shell. (p. 18)
Alfano, Maria B., jt. auth. see Silvestri, Cris.
Alfano, Vicki D. Pound Puppy to Fire Dog. (p. 1389)
Alfano, Wayne, illus. see Dedomenico, Elizabeth Marie.
Alfano, Wayne, illus. see Marsh, Emily Beata.
Alfano, Wayne, illus. see Wallace, Susan Helen.
Alfaro, Luis, illus. see Salinas, Sonia.
Alfaro, Manuel. Griego el Magnifico y la Gotita Verde Golosa Pegajos. Harrington, David, illus. (p. 724)
—Super Griego the Great & the Secret Mission to the Moon. Harrington, David, illus. (p. 1680)
Alfaro Sifontes, Manuel Guillermo. Alboroto en un Lugar Remoto. (p. 35)
Alfassa, Shelomo. Palm Tree of Deborah. (p. 1320)
Alfau, Georgette. Alfred & Alex & the Toy Eating Monster. (p. 37)
Alfonseca, Manuel. Rubi del Ganges. (p. 1493)
Alfonsi, Alice. Almost Invisible Cases. Harrington, Rich, illus. (p. 48)
—Code Red Cases. Harrington, Rich, illus. (p. 338)
—Freaked Out. (p. 631)
—Lizzie for President. (p. 1043)
—Playing Card Cases. Harrington, Rich, illus. (p. 1372)
Alfonsi, Alice, jt. auth. see Jones, Jasmine.
Alfonsi, Alice, adapted by. Face-off. (p. 560)
—'Rents: Lizzie Mcguire. (p. 1460)
Alfonso, Velia De Guevara. Sandy Comes Home. (p. 1511)
Alfonso, Velia DeGuevara. Kittys' Moving Day. (p. 963)
Alford, Doug. Ogs, Zogs & Useful Cogs. (p. 1280)
Alford, Douglas. Cozy Clozy: From Fibers to Fabrics. Hayes, Betsy, illus. (p. 375)
Alford, Douglas J. Cozy Clozy. (p. 375)
Alford, Douglas J. & Alford, Pakaket. How Do Hedgehogs Hug? Anderson, Jane A., illus. (p. 807)
Alford, Pakaket, jt. auth. see Alford, Douglas J.
Alford, Wade. Princess & the Golden Ring. (p. 1402)
Alford-Craig, Lakiesha. Joe's Dreams of Adventure. (p. 920)
Alfred Publishing Staff. Alfred's Kid's Piano Course Complete: The Easiest Piano Method Ever!, Book & CD. (p. 38)
—Classic FM — Classics for Children. (p. 328)
—Complete Idiot's Guide to Acoustic Guitar Songs. (p. 353)
—Complete Idiot's Guide to Rock Guitar Songs. (p. 353)
Alfred Publishing Staff, jt. auth. see Suzuki, Shinichi.
Alfred Publishing Staff, et al. Alfred's Kid's Ukulele Course 1 Starter Pack: Everything You Need to Play Today!, Book, CD, DVD & Ukulele Boxed Set. (p. 38)
—Classroom Music for Little Mozarts - The Big Music Book: 10 Sequential Lessons for Ages 4-6, Big Book. (p. 329)
—Kid's Guitar Course Movie & TV Songbook 1 & 2: 13 Fun Arrangements That Make Learning Even Easier! (p. 954)
Alfred Sole. Pandi's Adventures in Afric. Patradol Kitcharoen, illus. (p. 1321)
Alfreda. Be Somebody Be Yourself Lesson Plan Reproducibles. Alfreda, illus. (p. 149)
—Story Time Stories Without Rhyme. (p. 1663)
—Taestella A Black Cinderella Folder Leaf Edition. (p. 1695)
Alfreda, Ms. Story Time Stories That Rhyme 100 Stories. (p. 1663)
Alfredson, Murray. Gleaming Clouds. (p. 682)
Alfrey, Eunice, et al. Turtle Who Went to War: And Other Sioux Stories. (p. 1798)
Algar, James, illus. see Tierney, John.
Algeo, Matthew. Abe & Fido: Lincoln's Love of Animals & the Touching Story of His Favorite Canine Companion. (p. 4)
Alger, Horatio. Abraham Lincoln: The Backwoods Boy: Or, How a Young Rail-Splitter Became President. (p. 6)
—Adrift in New York: Or, Tom & Florence Braving the World. (p. 13)
—Andy Grant's Pluck. (p. 73)
—Ben Bruce: Scenes in the Life of a Bowery Newsboy. (p. 163)
—Ben Logan's Triumph: Or, The Boys of Boxwood Academy. (p. 163)
—Bob Burton: Or, The Young Ranchman of the Missouri. (p. 205)
—Bound to Rise: Or: up the Ladder. (p. 216)
—Brave & Bold: The Fortunes of Robert Rushton. (p. 223)
—Brave & Bold. (p. 223)
—Dan, the Newsboy. (p. 402)
—Debt of Honor: The Story of Gerald Lane's Success in the Far West. (p. 421)
—Do & Dare: Or, A Brave Boy's Fight for Fortune. (p. 456)
—Driven from Home: Carl Crawford's Experience. (p. 485)
—Erie Train Boy. (p. 533)
—Errand Boy: Or, How Phil Brent Won Success. (p. 534)
—Errand Boy. (p. 534)
—Facing the World: Or, The Haps & Mishaps of Harry Vane. (p. 561)
—Facing the World. (p. 561)
—Falling in with Fortune: Or, The Experiences of a Young Secretary. (p. 567)
—Fame & Fortune: Or, The Progress of Richard Hunter. (p. 567)
—Fame & Fortune: Or: the Progress of Richard Hunter. (p. 567)
—Finding a Fortune. (p. 587)
—Five Hundred Dollars: Or: Jacob Marlowe's Secret. (p. 600)
—Frank & Fearless: Or, The Fortunes of Jasper Kent. (p. 628)
—Frank & Fearless or the Fortunes of Jasper Kent. (p. 628)
—Frank Fowler, the Cash Boy. (p. 628)
—Frank Hunter's Peril. (p. 628)
—Frank's Campaign: Or, The Farm & the Camp. (p. 631)
—From Canal Boy to President: Or the Boyhood & Manhood of James A. Garfield. (p. 642)
—From Canal Boy to President. (p. 642)
—From Canal Boy to President or the Boyhood & Manhood of James a Garfield. (p. 642)
—From Farm Boy to Senator: Being the History of the Boyhood & Manhood of Daniel Webster. (p. 642)
—Hector's Inheritance: Or: the Boys of Smith Institute. (p. 761)
—Hector's Inheritance: Or, the Boys of Smith Institute. (p. 761)
—Helping Himself. (p. 766)
—Herbert Carter's Legacy: Or: the Inventor's Son. (p. 769)
—Herbert Carter's Legacy. (p. 769)
—In a New World: Or, Among the Gold-Fields of Australia. (p. 863)
—Jack's Ward: Or, The Boy Guardian. (p. 904)
—Jack's Ward. (p. 904)
—Jed, the Poorhouse Boy. (p. 911)
—Joe the Hotel Boy: Or, Winning Out by Pluck. (p. 920)
—Joe the Hotel Boy: Or, Winning Out by Pluck. (p. 920)
—Joe the Hotel Boy. (p. 920)
—Joe's Luck: Or, Always Wide Awake. (p. 920)
—Joe's Luck. (p. 920)
—Lester's Luck. (p. 994)
—Luke Walton: Or, The Chicago Newsboy. (p. 1064)
—Making His Mark. (p. 1081)
—Making His Way: Frank Courtney's Struggle Upward. (p. 1081)
—Making His Way. (p. 1081)
—Mark Stanton. (p. 1095)
—Ned Newton: Or, The Fortunes of a New York Bootblack. (p. 1239)
—Nelson the Newsboy: Or, Afloat in New York. (p. 1241)
—New York Boy. (p. 1248)
—Nothing to Do: A Tilt at Our Best Society. (p. 1268)
—Number 91: Or, The Adventures of a New York Telegraph Boy. (p. 1271)
—Odds Against Him: Or, Carl Crawford's Experience. (p. 1278)
—Only an Irish Boy: Or, Andy Burke's Fortunes & Misfortunes. (p. 1298)
—Out for Business: Or, Robert Frost's Strange Career. (p. 1311)

—Paul Prescott's Charge. (p. 1330)
—Paul the Peddler: Or, The Fortunes of a Young Street Merchant. (p. 1330)
—Paul the Peddler: Or, The Adventures of a Young Street Merchant. (p. 1330)
—Paul the Peddler. (p. 1330)
—Phil the Fiddler. (p. 1350)
—Ragged Dick: Or, Street Life in New York with the Bootblacks. (p. 1433)
—Ragged Dick: Or, Street Life in New York with the Boot-Blacks. (p. 1433)
—Ralph Raymond's Heir: Or, The Mechant's Crime. (p. 1437)
—Randy of the River: Or, The Adventures of a Young Deckhand. (p. 1438)
—Risen from the Ranks: Or, Harry Walton's Success. (p. 1475)
—Risen from the Ranks. (p. 1475)
—Robert Coverdale's Struggle: Or, On the Wave of Success. (p. 1478)
—Rolling Stone: Or, The Adventures of a Wanderer. (p. 1485)
—Rough & Ready: Or, Life among the New York Newsboys. (p. 1491)
—Rufus & Rose: Or, The Fortunes of Rough & Ready. (p. 1494)
—Rupert's Ambition. (p. 1497)
—Sam's Chance: And How He Improved It. (p. 1509)
—Seeking His Fortune, & Other Dialogues. (p. 1548)
—Shifting for Himself: Or, Gilbert Greyson's Fortunes. (p. 1566)
—Slow & Sure: Or, From the Street to the Shop. (p. 1591)
—Store Boy: Or, The Fortunes of Ben Barclay. (p. 1654)
—Store Boy. (p. 1654)
—Strive & Succeed: Or, The Progress of Walter Conrad. (p. 1668)
—Strive & Succeed. (p. 1668)
—Strong & Steady: Or, Paddle Your Own Canoe. (p. 1668)
—Struggling Upward: Or, Luke Larkin's Luck. (p. 1668)
—Struggling Upward; or, Luck Larkin's Luck. (p. 1668)
—Tattered Tom: Or, The Story of a Street Arab. (p. 1707)
—Telegraph Boy. (p. 1716)
—Timothy Crump's Ward. (p. 1755)
—Tin Box & What It Contained. (p. 1755)
—Tom Brace: Who He Was & How He Fared. (p. 1762)
—Tom Temple's Career. (p. 1764)
—Tom Thatcher's Fortune. (p. 1764)
—Tom Tracy: Or, The Trials of a New York Newsboy. (p. 1764)
—Tom Turner's Legacy. (p. 1764)
—Tony the Hero. (p. 1766)
—Tony the Tramp: Or, Right Is Might. (p. 1766)
—Train Boy. (p. 1777)
—Try & Trust: Or, The Story of a Bound Boy. (p. 1794)
—Wait & Win: The Story of Jack Drummond's Pluck. (p. 1852)
—Walter Sherwood's Probation. (p. 1856)
—World Before Him. (p. 1954)
—Young Acrobat. (p. 1978)
—Young Acrobat of the Great North American Circus. (p. 1978)
—Young Bank Messenger. (p. 1978)
—Young Boatman of Pine Point. (p. 1978)
—Young Book Agent: Or, Frank Hardy's Road to Success. (p. 1978)
—Young Captain Jack: Or, The Son of a Soldier. (p. 1978)
—Young Circus Rider: Or, The Mystery of Robert Rudd. (p. 1978)
—Young Miner: Or, Tom Nelson in California. (p. 1979)
—Young Musician. (p. 1979)
—Young Outlaw: Or, Adrift in the Streets. (p. 1979)
—Young Salesman. (p. 1979)
Alger, Horatio & Stratemeyer, Edward. Young Captain Jack: The Son of a Soldier. (p. 1978)
Alger, Horatio, Jr. Frank Hunter's Peril. (p. 628)
—Mark Manning's Mission: The Story of A Shoe Factory Boy. (p. 1095)
—Rufus & Rose or the Fortunes of Rough & Ready. (p. 1494)
—Tom Temple's Career. (p. 1764)
Alger Jr. Horatio Staff. Andy Grants Pluck. (p. 73)
—Do & Dare. (p. 456)
—Frank's Campaign. (p. 631)
—Hector's Inheritance. (p. 761)
—Herbert Carter's Legacy. (p. 769)
—Only an Irish Boy. (p. 1298)
—Struggling Upward. (p. 1668)
Alger, Liz, illus. see Kelly, Bernadette & Ward, Krista.
Al-Ghani, Haitham, illus. see Al-ghani, K. I.
Al-Ghani, Haitham, illus. see Al-Ghani, K.I.
Al-ghani, K. I. Red Beast: Controlling Anger in Children with Asperger's Syndrome. Al-Ghani, Haitham, illus. (p. 1453)
Al-Ghani, K.I. Baby Blue Has the Blues Al-Ghani, Haitham, illus. (p. 125)
—Bertie Bumble Bee: Troubled by the Letter B. Al-Ghani, Haitham, illus. (p. 168)
—Ronnie Raven Recycles Al-Ghani, Haitham, illus. (p. 1487)
Al-Ghazali, Abu Hamid. Beginning of Guidance. Al-Allaf, Mashhad, tr. (p. 159)
Al-Ghussinu, Wa'ad Diab, illus. see Tommalieh, Fakhri & Hujeer, Majeda.
Algie, Jim. Phantom Lover & Other Thrilling Tales of Thailand. (p. 1349)
Algozzine, Bob, jt. auth. see Lambert, Monica.
Algozzine, Bob & Ysseldyke, Jim. Tips for Beginning Teachers. (p. 1757)
Algranati, Melissa J. Talk about It: Family Fun for Girls 8-11. (p. 1703)
Al-Greene, Bob, illus. see at Science, Editors.
Al-Hamdi, Ahmed, tr. see McKee, David.
Ali, Amani Elcheikh. Under the Rubble. (p. 1814)
Ali, Anila & Gottlieb, Karen. Mommy, Am I A? Seiders, Marian, illus. (p. 1162)
Ali, Daud. Ancient India. (p. 69)
—Hands-On History! Ancient India: Discover the Rich Heritage of the Indus Valley & the Mughal Empire, with 15 Step-By-Step Projects & 340 Pictures. (p. 741)
Ali, Dominic. Media Madness: An Insider's Guide to Media. Cho, Michael, illus. (p. 1118)
Ali, Intelaq Mohammed, illus. see Sharafeddine, Fatima.
Ali, Jameela. I Can Make It Through the Rain. (p. 836)
Ali, Khayyam Esab. Wormhole Kids Visit President Kennedy. (p. 1961)
Ali, Maryum. I Shook up the World: The Incredible Life of Muhammad Ali. Johnson, Patrick, illus. (p. 845)
Ali, Raydin. Mystic Museum. (p. 1226)
Ali, S. V. Mir Ahmed, jt. auth. see Yazdi, Ayatullah Agha H. M. M. Pooya.
Ali, Saleena. Behind My Eyes & Truly in Love Stories of Friendship & Love: Book Two. (p. 160)
Ali, Sharifah Enayat. Afghanistan. (p. 26)
Ali, Sharifah Enayat, jt. auth. see Sheehan, S.
Ali, Tariq. Leopard & the Fox: A Pakistani Tragedy. (p. 992)
Aliaga, Roberto. Camión de Papel. Ranucci, Claudia, illus. (p. 256)
—Dorothy: A Different Kind of Friend. (p. 471)
—Night Time Story. (p. 1254)
—Sueño del Osito Rosa. Bansch, Helga, illus. (p. 1672)
Alibert, Eric, illus. see Craipeau, Jean-Lou & Dutrieux, Brigitte.
Alibert, Eric, illus. see Craipeau, Jean-Lou & Dutrieux, Julien.
Alicavusoglu, Leyla, jt. auth. see Hawker, Frances.
Alice, Alex. Valkyrie Alice, Alex, illus. (p. 1831)
Alice B. Emerson. Betty Gordon at Mountain Camp. (p. 172)
—Ruth Fielding of the Red Mill: Or Jasper Parloe's Secret. (p. 1498)
Alice, Dalgliesh. Courage of Sarah Noble. (p. 372)
Alice in Wonderland. Alice in Wonderland Storybook & CD 8x8. (p. 39)
Alice Johannesen, jt. auth. see Sonja Johannesen.
Alice, Kathy. Hanging with Timmy & Spinner. (p. 742)
Alice, Legm. Bizenghast (p. 194)
Alice Turner Curtis. Yankee Girl at Fort Sumter. (p. 1968)
Alighieri, Dante. Divina Comedia. (p. 454)
—Divine Comedy. Bergin, Thomas G., ed. (p. 454)
—Purgatorio Kirkpatrick, Robin, tr. from ITA. (p. 1419)
Alighieri, Dante, see Alighieri, Dante.
Alighieri, Dante & Birk, Sandow. Dante's Inferno Birk, Sandow, tr. from ITA. (p. 406)
Ali-Karamali, Sumbul. Growing up Muslim: Understanding the Beliefs & Practices of Islam. (p. 727)
Alikhan, Salima. Pied Piper of Austin Alikhan, Salima, illus. (p. 1356)
Alikhan, Salima, illus. see Gribnau, Joe.
Alikhan, Salima, illus. see Justice, Joseph.
Alikhan, Salima, illus. see Rockliff, Mara.
Aliki. Ah, Music! Aliki, illus. (p. 30)
—All by Myself! (p. 44)
—All by Myself! Aliki, illus. (p. 44)
—Digging up Dinosaurs. (p. 439)
—My Five Senses. (p. 1208)
—My Five Senses. Aliki, illus. (p. 1208)
—Play's the Thing. Aliki, illus. (p. 1373)
—Push Button. Aliki, illus. (p. 1420)
—Quiet in the Garden. Aliki, illus. (p. 1428)
—¡Musica! (p. 1193)
Aliki, jt. auth. see Brandenberg, Aliki.
Alily, Joseph. Untold- the Never Ending Tales: The Boy & the Wolf - Children's Story. (p. 1823)
Alimo, Brendan Guy. Hunting of Salyut 7. (p. 829)
Alimonti, Frederick. Fix-It Shop: A Story of Music, Magic, a Baseball Bat, & a Toaster. (p. 601)
—Inside Out: A Modern Fable. (p. 877)
Alimonti, Frederick, jt. auth. see Tedesco, Ann.
Alimonti, Frederick & Tedesco, Ann. Tommy & the T-Tops: Helping Children Overcome Prejudice. Hazard, John, illus. (p. 1764)
Alinas, Marv. Bulldozers. (p. 240)
—Cranes. (p. 376)
—Diggers. (p. 438)
—Garbage Trucks. (p. 655)
Alingue, Andebeng-Abeu, tr. see Rousseau, Jean-Jacques.
Alinsky, Shelby. National Geographic Readers: Flutter, Butterfly! (p. 1233)
—National Geographic Readers: Hoot, Owl! (p. 1233)
—National Geographic Readers: Sleep, Bear! (p. 1233)
—National Geographic Readers: Slither, Snake! (p. 1233)
Aliotti, Johnny. Johnny's Simple Dumbbell Workout. (p. 924)
Alipio, Byron P. Jambo Nation Board Game 1st Edition: The game of wild animal Football. (p. 906)
Alirez, Ben, jt. auth. see Langan, Paul.
Alison, Hart. Spy on the Home Front. Jean-P, Tibbles, illus. (p. 1636)
Alison, Jay, illus. see Barefoot Books Staff.
Alixe, Pascal & Klein, Nic. Iron Nail - Captain America (p. 888)
Alizadeh, Kate, illus. see Hughes, John Ceirlog.
Aljure, Luis Carlos. Frédéric Chopin -el Espíritu de la Música. (p. 633)
Al-Kinani, Maarja. All in One. (p. 44)
—Arabic alphabet III. (p. 94)
—Islamic. (p. 891)
Alkire, Don. Mischief's Big Night Out. (p. 1150)
Alkire, J. L. Roar of the Grumkies. (p. 1478)
Alko, Selina. B Is for Brooklyn. Alko, Selina, illus. (p. 123)
—Case for Loving: The Fight for Interracial Marriage. Alko, Selina & Qualls, Sean, illus. (p. 273)
—Daddy Christmas & Hanukkah Mama. (p. 398)
—Every-Day Dress-Up. (p. 542)
—My Fathers World. (p. 1203)
Alko, Selina, illus. see Abraham, Michelle Shapiro.
Alko, Selina, illus. see Brichto, Mira Pollak.
Alko, Selina, illus. see Jacobs, Paul DuBois & Swender, Jennifer.
Alko, Selina, illus. see Pollack-Brichto, Mira.
Alkonada, Jesus Muñoz. Kid Silverhair. Viñals, Noemi, illus. (p. 951)
Alkouatli, Claire. Islam. (p. 891)
Allabach, P. R. Dragon & Captain. Turnbloom, Lucas, illus. (p. 476)
Allaby, Michael. Animals. Garratt, Richard, illus. (p. 81)
—Atmosphere: A Scientific History of Air, Weather, & Climate. Garratt, Richard, illus. (p. 113)
—Deserts. Garratt, Richard, illus. (p. 429)
—Discovering the Earth Garratt, Richard, illus. (p. 449)
—Earth Science: A Scientific History of the Solid Earth. Garratt, Richard, illus. (p. 496)
—Ecology: Plants, Animals, & the Environment. Garratt, Richard, illus. (p. 502)
—Environment. (p. 531)
—Exploration. Garratt, Richard, illus. (p. 550)
—Grasslands. Garratt, Richard, illus. (p. 712)
—Oceans: A Scientific History of Oceans & Marine Life. Garratt, Richard, illus. (p. 1277)
—Plants. Garratt, Richard, illus. (p. 1369)
—Temperate Forests. Garratt, Richard, illus. (p. 1717)
—Tropical Forests. Garratt, Richard, illus. (p. 1789)
—Visual Encyclopedia of Earth. (p. 1846)
—Weather Science: Fog. Garratt, Richard, illus. (p. 1870)
—Weather Science: Floods. Garratt, Richard, illus. (p. 1870)
—Weather Science: Blizzards. Garratt, Richard, illus. (p. 1870)
—Weather Science: Rain & Hail. Garratt, Richard, illus. (p. 1870)
—World's Weather. (p. 1961)
Allaby, Michael, et al. Biomes of the Earth Set. (p. 190)
—Deserts & Semideserts (p. 429)
Allah in Person, Royall. Center Page, Volume 1. (p. 287)
Allahverdi, Artin. My Good Friend Walt Disney. (p. 1210)
Allaire, Caroline, jt. auth. see Fuhr, Ute.
Allaire, Caroline, jt. auth. see Fuhr, UteSautai.
Allaire, Caroline, jt. auth. see Krauczyk, Sabine.
Allaire, Caroline, jt. auth. see Krawczyk, Sabine.
Allaire, Caroline, jt. auth. see Moonlight Publishing Ltd Staff.
Allaire, Caroline & Krawczyk, Sabine. Let's Look at the Hedge. Hugo, Pierre de, illus. (p. 999)
Allaire, M. J. Dragon's Blood: Denicalis Dragon Chronicles - Book One. (p. 479)
—Dragon's Tear: Denicalis Dragon Chronicles - Book Three. (p. 479)
Allamand, Maite. Alamito el Largo. (p. 33)
Allan, David & Brown, Vinson. Illustrated Guide to Common Rocks & Their Minerals. Kelley, D. G. et al, illus. (p. 857)
Allan, Delores. Magical Moments with Roy & Toni: Have You Ever. (p. 1075)
—Magical Moments with Roy & Toni: Come on Lets Go. (p. 1075)
—Magical Moments with Roy & Toni: Fun at the Fair. (p. 1075)
—Magical Moments with Roy & Toni: Do You Ever Wonder. (p. 1075)
—Magical Moments with Roy & Toni: The Magic of Music. (p. 1075)
—Magical Moments with Roy & Toni: Have You Hugged Your Mother Today. (p. 1075)
Allan, Gill, illus. see Rose, Dilys.
Allan, Jasper. Let's Go to the Supermarket. (p. 997)
Allan, Jayne. PC Polly to the Rescue. Mercer, Lynn, illus. (p. 1331)
Allan, Jo. Hungry Hettie (p. 828)
Allan, Joe. 5 Seconds of Summer: The Unauthorized Biography. (p. 1992)
Allan, June, illus. see Robinson, Anthony & Young, Annemarie.
Allan, June, illus. see Robinson, Anthony, et al.
Allan, June, jt. auth. see Robinson, Anthony.
Allan, Nancy P., jt. auth. see Johnson, Randy.
Allan, Nicholas. Android in the Attic. (p. 72)
—Father Christmas Needs a Wee! Allan, Nicholas, illus. (p. 577)
—More & More Rabbits. Allan, Nicholas, illus. (p. 1174)
—Royal Nappy. Allan, Nicholas, illus. (p. 1492)
Allan, Nicholas, illus. see Kelly, Mij.
Allan, Patsy. Boy Who Loved Drums. (p. 219)
—Tessa the Runaway Teapot. (p. 1722)
Allan, Robert Marshall, et al. War Diaries. (p. 1857)
Allan, Shaun. Zits'n'bits. (p. 1987)
Allan, Stewart, jt. auth. see O'Mara Books, Michael.
Allan, Tony. Ancient China. (p. 68)
—Causes of World War I. (p. 282)
—Exploring the Life, Myth, & Art of Ancient Rome. (p. 554)
—Exploring the Life, Myth, & Art of Ancient Vikings. (p. 554)
—Exploring the Life, Myth, & Art of the Vikings. (p. 554)
—Irish Famine: The Birth of Irish America. (p. 887)
—Rainforests. (p. 1436)
—True Ghost Stories. (p. 1792)
—Wild Water: Floods (p. 1930)
Allan, Tony & Dowswell, Paul. True Ghost Stories. (p. 1792)
Allan-Meyer, Kathleen. Play Fair, Little Bear. Garvin, Elaine, illus. (p. 1371)
Allanson, Patricia. Parallella's Problem. Allanson, Patricia, illus. (p. 1324)
Allard Cox, Monica, ed. Public Access to the Rhode Island Coast. (p. 1414)
Allard, Harry. Miss Nelson Is Missing! Marshall, James, illus. (p. 1151)
Allard, Harry & Marshall, James. Miss Nelson Has a Field Day. (p. 1151)
—Sheep Out to Eat. (p. 1564)
Allard, Harry G., Jr. Miss Nelson Has a Field Day Marshall, James, illus. (p. 1151)
—Miss Nelson Is Back Marshall, James, illus. (p. 1151)
Allard, Harry G., Jr. & Marshall, James. Miss Nelson Collection. (p. 1151)
Allard, Melanie, illus. see Glickman, Susan.
Allard, Toni. Anything but Nuts. (p. 91)
Allaway, Al. Laughing Flowers & Blooming Animals. (p. 980)
Allaynalee, jt. auth. see Coyle, Greg.
Allberti, Frances C. Finding Rover. Gremillion, Barry, illus. (p. 588)
Allbritton, Emily. Henry I'm. (p. 768)
Allbritton, Jan. Super Sweetie to the Rescue. (p. 1682)
Allbritton, Stacy. Diary of Marie Landry, Acadian Exile Haynes, Joyce, illus. (p. 435)
Allchin, Rosalind. Frog Princess. (p. 640)
—Frog Princess. Allchin, Rosalind, illus. (p. 640)
Allee, Anita L. Child of the Heart. (p. 301)
—High Country Adventure. (p. 777)
Allegra, Mike. Sarah Gives Thanks: How Thanksgiving Became a National Holiday. Gardner, David, illus. (p. 1514)
Allegretti, Jan & Sommers, Katy. Complete Holistic Dog Book: Home Health Care for Our Canine Companions. (p. 353)
Allegri, Natasha. Adventure Time - Fionna & Cake. (p. 14)
—Fionna & Cake Mathematical. Allegri, Natasha, illus. (p. 590)
Allem, Jolyia. Maiden & the Prince: A Tale of Devotion. (p. 1077)
Alleman, Roy V. Judge, the Gavel & the Gun: Taming of Nebraska's Wild Frontier. (p. 930)
Allen, A. Richard, illus. see Milisic, Roman.
Allen, Alejandro & Rountree, Benjamin. Jirafante Luis: The Giraffephant Luis. (p. 919)
Allen, Amanda & Allen, Cliff. Bad Company Corrupts Good Squirrels. (p. 131)
Allen, Amy Ruth. Queen Latifah: From Jersey Girl to Superstar. (p. 1425)
Allen, Ann Taylor. Feminism & Motherhood in Western Europe, 1890-1970: The Maternal Dilemma. (p. 581)
Allen, Audrey. Jennifer Lawrence. (p. 912)
Allen, Betsy. Mystery of the Ruby Queens: Connie Blair Mystery Series. (p. 1226)
—Silver Secret: A Connie Blair Mystery. (p. 1577)
Allen, Brian. Rickety Rackety Rhymes. (p. 1470)
Allen, Bryony. Otoli. (p. 1307)
Allen, C. William. African Interior Mission. Lee, Xiongpao, illus. (p. 27)
Allen, Carolyn. My Bedtime Prayer. (p. 1196)
Allen, Carter. And the Sky Turned White... (p. 71)
Allen, Cassandra, illus. see Carriger, Candace.
Allen, Cassandra R. Morty the Alien: The Beginnings... (p. 1176)
Allen, Catherine Judge. Corals, Jellyfish, Sponges & Other Simple Animals. Harris, Madeline S. et al, eds. (p. 366)
Allen, Catherine Judge, et al. Fishes. (p. 599)
Allen, Charles F. David Crockett: Scout, Small Boy, Pilgrim, Mountaineer, Soldier, Bear-Hunter, & Congressman, Defender of the Alamo. (p. 411)
Allen, Charlsie. Unexpected Destinies. (p. 1817)
Allen, Chris, illus. see Dunn, Joeming W.
Allen, Chris, illus. see Farrens, Brian & Shakespeare, William.
Allen, Chris, illus. see Goodwin, Vincent.
Allen, Chris, illus. see Shakespeare, William.
Allen, Chris, et al. How to Draw Adventure Friends & Other Cartoon Heroes. (p. 816)
Allen, Christina. Micro-Chip on my Shoulder: A True Story of a Little Poult. (p. 1136)
Allen, Christina G. Hippos in the Night: Autobiographical Adventures in Africa. (p. 781)
Allen, Cindi N. Take a Bite Out of Ryme: Poetry Unit. (p. 1696)
Allen, Cliff, jt. auth. see Allen, Amanda.
Allen, Connie & Harper, Valerie. Essentials of Anatomy & Physiology Laboratory Manual. (p. 537)
Allen, Constance. Elmo! Swanson, Maggie, illus. (p. 515)
—My Name Is Elmo (Sesame Street) Swanson, Maggie, illus. (p. 1215)
—Peekaboo, Elmo! (Sesame Street) Prebenna, David, illus. (p. 1335)
—Shake a Leg! Swanson, Maggie, illus. (p. 1558)
Allen, Constance & Albee, Sarah. Elmo's Little Golden Book Favorites (Sesame Street) Swanson, Maggie & Ewers, Joe, illus. (p. 515)
Allen, Crystal. How Lamar's Bad Prank Won a Bubba-Sized Trophy. (p. 810)
—Laura Line. (p. 980)
Allen, Dana K., illus. see Deskins, Charlotte H.
Allen, Dav. Spy in My Ointment. (p. 1636)
Allen, Dave, jt. auth. see Midland, Greg.
Allen, David. Early Maps of Greenfield, Massachusetts, 1717-1918: With A Narrative History. (p. 493)
—Early Maps of Greenfield, Massachusetts, 1717-1918. (p. 493)
Allen, David L. H. Early Maps of Brattleboro, Vermont, 1745-1912 (p. 493)
Allen, Debbie. Dancing in the Wings. Nelson, Kadir, illus. (p. 403)
—Winker & the Kitten. (p. 1936)
Allen, Douglas, illus. see Mathewson, Robert F.
Allen, Elaine. Mallory the Forgetful Duck Nash, Kelli, illus. (p. 1083)
Allen, Elaine Ann. Olly Explores 7 Wonders of the Chesapeake Bay Nash, Kelli, illus. (p. 1287)
—Olly the Oyster Cleans the Bay Nash, Kelli, illus. (p. 1287)
—Olly's Treasure Nash, Kelli, illus. (p. 1287)
Allen, Elanna. Itsy Mitsy Runs Away. Allen, Elanna, illus. (p. 900)
Allen, Elanna, illus. see Branford, Anna.
Allen, Elanna, illus. see Cohen, Jeff.
Allen, Eleanor. Mouse Monk in a Christmas Adventure. (p. 1182)
Allen, Elise. Barbie: A Fashion Fairytale. (p. 138)
Allen, Elise, jt. auth. see Duff, Hilary.
Allen, Elise & Conners, Daryle. Gabby Duran & the Unsittables. (p. 652)
Allen, Elise & Stanford, Halle. Autumn's Secret Gift. Pooler, Paige, illus. (p. 118)
—Spring's Sparkle Sleepover. Pooler, Paige, illus. (p. 1635)
—Summer's Friendship Games. Pooler, Paige, illus. (p. 1675)
—Winter's Flurry Adventure. Pooler, Paige, illus. (p. 1938)
Allen, Elizabeth, illus. see Meiners, Cheri J.
Allen, Elizabeth, jt. auth. see Meiners, Cheri J.
Allen, Ethan. Narrative of Col. Ethan Allen's Captivity. (p. 1229)
Allen, F. M. Brayhard. (p. 224)
Allen, Francesca. Creepy-Crawlies. (p. 381)
—First Picture Fairytales. (p. 596)
—Under the Sea. (p. 1814)
—Vacation. (p. 1829)
Allen, Francesca, illus. see Litchfield, Jo.
Allen, Francesca, jt. auth. see Brooks, Felicity.
Allen, Francesca, jt. illus. see Litchfield, Jo.
Allen, Francesca & Brooks, Felicity. Busy Truck. Crisp, Dan, illus. (p. 246)
Allen, Gardner W. Our Naval War with France. (p. 1309)
Allen, Graham, jt. ed. see Sellars, Roy.

Allen, Gregory G. Chicken Boy: The Amazing Adventures of a Super Hero with Autism. Culver, Dennis, illus. (p. 300)

Allen, Gwendolyn. Legend of the Four Trees. (p. 989)

Allen, Harry. Ibarajo Road. (p. 849)

Allen, Heather. BOOST Earth Day Is Every Day! Activity Book. (p. 213)

—Earth Day Is Every Day! (p. 495)

Allen, J. J. Hello Kitty's Fun Friend Day! (p. 764)

Allen, J. Kent. Embritt Waters & the Mark of the Rattlesnake. (p. 517)

Allen, James L. Kentucky Cardinal. (p. 949)

Allen, James Lane. Kentucky Warbler. (p. 949)

Allen, Jan. Now I Know the 10 Commandments. Allen, Russ, illus. (p. 1269)

—Now I Know the Story of Samson. (p. 1269)

Allen, Janet. Best Little Wingman. Postier, Jim, illus. (p. 170)

Allen, Jean. Esmerelda Finds a Friend. (p. 536)

—Natural Disasters (p. 1235)

Allen, Jean M. Tangled Web. (p. 1705)

Allen, Jessica, illus. see Teitelbaum, Michael.

Allen, Joan deRis, ed. see Goethes Fairy Tale Staff.

Allen, Joe, illus. see Horner, Susan.

Allen, Joey. Gospel: Big Thoughts for Little Thinkers. (p. 703)

—Mission: Big Thoughts for Little Thinkers. (p. 1153)

—Scripture: Big Thoughts for Little Thinkers. (p. 1533)

—Trinity: Big Thoughts for Little Thinkers. (p. 1786)

Allen, John. Anime & Manga. (p. 84)

—Cause & Effect World War II: World War II. (p. 282)

—High-Tech Weapons. (p. 778)

—Holocaust Survivors. (p. 789)

—How Gene Therapy Is Changing Society. (p. 809)

—Idi Amin. (p. 852)

—Robert Boyle: Father of Chemistry. (p. 1478)

—Robert Boyle. (p. 1478)

—Thinking Critically: Legalizing Marijuana. (p. 1734)

Allen, Jonathan. Banana! Allen, Jonathan, illus. (p. 135)

—I'm Not Reading! (p. 859)

—I'm Not Ready! (p. 859)

—I'm Not Sleepy! (p. 859)

—Is That My Cat? (p. 890)

Allen, Jonathan, illus. see Doyle, Malachy.

Allen, Jonathan, illus. see Thomson, Pat.

Allen, Joshua, illus. see Beverly-Barrier, Essie.

Allen, Joshua, illus. see Hordos, Sandra.

Allen, Joy. Baby Signs. (p. 128)

—Baby Sounds. (p. 128)

—Princess Party. Allen, Joy, illus. (p. 1405)

Allen, Joy, illus. see Aber, Linda W.

Allen, Joy, illus. see Adler, David A.

Allen, Joy, illus. see Buchanan, Sue, et al.

Allen, Joy, illus. see Derico, Laura.

Allen, Joy, illus. see Glatt, Lisa & Greenberg, Suzanne.

Allen, Joy, illus. see Packard, Mary.

Allen, Joy, illus. see Parker, David.

Allen, Joy, illus. see Scelsa, Greg.

Allen, Joy, illus. see Simon, Charnan.

Allen, Joy, illus. see Spirn, Michele Sobel & Spirn, Michele S.

Allen, Joy, illus. see Spirn, Michele Sobel.

Allen, Joy, illus. see Williams, Rozanne Lanczak.

Allen, Judy. Are You a Bee? (p. 96)

—Are You a Bee? Allen, Judy & Humphries, Tudor, illus. (p. 96)

—Are You a Butterfly? Humphries, Tudor, illus. (p. 96)

—Are You a Dragonfly? Humphries, Tudor, illus. (p. 97)

—Are You a Grasshopper? Humphries, Tudor, illus. (p. 97)

—Are You a Ladybug? Humphries, Tudor, illus. (p. 97)

—Are You a Snail? Humphries, Tudor, illus. (p. 97)

—Are You a Spider? (p. 97)

—Are You a Spider? Humphries, Tudor, illus. (p. 97)

—Are You an Ant? Humphries, Tudor, illus. (p. 97)

—Flip the Flaps: Dinosaurs. Humphries, Tudor, illus. (p. 605)

—Flip the Flaps: Whales & Dolphins. Bostock, Mike, illus. (p. 605)

Allen, Judy, jt. auth. see Humphries, Tudor.

Allen, Judy & Mendez, Simon. Flip the Flaps: Animal Homes. (p. 605)

Allen, Julia & Iggulden, Fleur. African Adventure. (p. 26)

Allen, Julie K., tr. see Andersen, Hans Christian.

Allen, Justin. American. (p. 59)

Allen, K. Kurt Busch. (p. 968)

Allen, Katherine E. Festival of Light: Deepavali Legends from Around India. (p. 582)

Allen, Kathleen. Nina. (p. 1256)

—Witch Hunter. (p. 1941)

Allen, Kathryn L., ed. Study Skills: A Student Survival Guide. (p. 1670)

Allen, Kathryn Madeline. Kiss Means I Love You. Futran, Eric, illus. (p. 961)

—Show Me Happy. Futran, Eric, photos by. (p. 1570)

Allen, Kathy. Ancient Egyptian Hieroglyphs. (p. 69)

—Cell Phone Safety. (p. 286)

—Deformed Frogs: A Cause & Effect Investigation (p. 424)

—Drew Brees. (p. 485)

—Elephants under Pressure: A Cause & Effect Investigation (p. 512)

—First American Flag Feeney, Siri Weber, illus. (p. 593)

—First Independence Day Celebration Sperling, Tom, illus. (p. 595)

—Giant Pandas in a Shrinking Forest: A Cause & Effect Investigation (p. 674)

—Girls Race! Amazing Tales of Women in Sports (p. 680)

—Horrible, Miserable Middle Ages: The Disgusting Details about Life During Medieval. (p. 798)

—Horrible, Miserable Middle Ages: The Disgusting Details about Life During Medieval Times. (p. 798)

—Human Head. (p. 826)

—Labradoodle: A Cross Between a Labrador Retriever & a Poodle (p. 970)

—Polar Bears (p. 1379)

—President George Washington Ebert, Len, illus. (p. 1397)

—Science of a Rock Concert: Sound in Action. (p. 1527)

—Sea Turtles' Race to the Sea: A Cause & Effect Investigation (p. 1536)

—Tom Brady. (p. 1762)

—Tony Romo. (p. 1766)

—U. S. Constitution. (p. 1806)

—U. S. Constitution. Saunders-Smith, Gail, ed. (p. 1806)

—Why Do Geese Fly South in the Winter? A Book about Migration. (p. 1923)

—Why Do Geese Fly South in Winter? A Book about Migration. (p. 1923)

—Wind Power. (p. 1935)

Allen, Kathy, illus. see Blake, Edna L. & Boatwright, Edith.

Allen, Kathy, jt. auth. see Krueger, Jenny.

Allen, Kathy & Krueger, Jennifer. When Did Columbus Arrive in the Americas? And Other Questions about Columbus's Voyages. (p. 1901)

Allen, Kathy & Krueger, Jenny. Best of Figure Skating. (p. 170)

—Human Head. (p. 826)

Allen, Kathy, et al. Girls Rock! (p. 680)

—Tech Safety Smarts. (p. 1711)

Allen, Katy C. Dingo & Willy's Donuts. DePaolo, Daniel, illus. (p. 440)

Allen, Kd, illus. see Jordan, Lana.

Allen, Kenny. Aircraft Carriers. (p. 31)

—Bird Builds a House. (p. 190)

—Drilling Rigs. (p. 485)

—Earthmovers. (p. 497)

—Giant Cranes. (p. 673)

—Great Day to Skate. (p. 715)

—Jose Visits the Fire Station. (p. 926)

—Jumbo Jets. (p. 933)

—Kurt Busch. (p. 968)

—My School. (p. 1218)

—Submarines. (p. 1671)

Allen Klein, Laurie, illus. see Kizer Whitt, Kelly.

Allen, LaTasha Diane. Christopher & the Blessing Tree. (p. 316)

Allen, Laurie. Acting Duets for Young Women: Eight- to ten-minute duo scenes for practice & Competition (p. 9)

—Comedy Duos for High School: A Collection of Five Skits (p. 347)

—Comedy Scenes for Student Actors: Short sketches for young Performers (p. 348)

—Middle School Mania: A Collection of Five Skits (p. 1137)

—Middle School Mania: Comedy Duos for Guy / Girl (p. 1137)

—Thirty Short Comedy Plays for Teens: Plays for a Variety of Cast Sizes (p. 1735)

—Thirty-Three Short Comedy Plays for Teens: Plays for Small Casts. (p. 1735)

Allen, Lisa & Sharp, Julis. Time for Bed - The Secret of Shadows: Shadow Theater Inside. Johnson, Vickie, illus. (p. 1751)

Allen, Lisette. Amulet. (p. 66)

—Nicole's Revenge. (p. 1251)

Allen, Lynn Marie. Asperger's? God Bless You! (p. 107)

Allen, M. Misty, Mattie, or Kim. (p. 1155)

Allen, M. E. Gotta Get Some Bish Bash Bosh. (p. 704)

Allen, Margaret. Everyone's a Star. Hults, Alaska, ed. (p. 544)

—Fables & Folklore Reader's Theater: Develop Reading Fluency & Text Comprehension Skills. Hults, Alaska, ed. (p. 559)

—Fairy Tales Reader's Theater: Develop Reading Fluency & Text Comprehension Skills. Hults, Alaska, ed. (p. 564)

—Jingle Jangles: Fun, Interactive Reading Selections for Fluency Practice. Vol. 2256 Walter, LaDawn, ed. (p. 918)

—Reading Pals: Rhyming Words Using Blends & Digraphs Gr. K-1. Taylor, Jennifer, ed. (p. 1446)

Allen, Marie, illus. see Baxter, Nicola.

Allen, Marie, illus. see David, Juliet.

Allen, Marie, illus. see Mckenzie, Precious.

Allen, Marie, illus. see Pennington, Stacey & Pennington, J. C. D.

Allen, Marie, illus. see Robertson, J. Jean.

Allen, Marie, illus. see Suen, Anastasia.

Allen, Marie, illus. see Williamson, Karen.

Allen, Mark, ed. New Tales of Euterpe: The Star of India as a British Emigrant Ship. (p. 1247)

Allen, Mary Beth. Iamadore. (p. 849)

Allen, Michelle. Grandma Nell's Basement. (p. 708)

Allen, Mike. Little on a Road Trip. (p. 1032)

Allen, Miles. Christmas Lore & Legend. (p. 314)

Allen, Molly. Reading Pals: Sight Words Gr. K-1. Taylor, Jennifer, ed. (p. 1446)

Allen, Mongo. Bobo's: The Trip to the Zoo - a Book on Bully Intervention. (p. 206)

Allen, Nancy. Amazing Grace: A Kentucky Girl with Gumption During World War II. (p. 54)

—Hopping on the Number Line. (p. 797)

—Midwest & Great Lakes Regions. (p. 1139)

—My Math Toolbox. (p. 1214)

—Northeast & Metropolitan Regions. (p. 1265)

—Trouble in Troublesome Creek. Crawford, K., illus. (p. 1790)

—Underground Railroad. (p. 1814)

—What's a Fraction? (p. 1896)

Allen, Nancy Kelly. Barreling over Niagara Falls Fields, Lisa, illus. (p. 140)

—Daniel Boone: Trailblazer Waites, Joan C., illus. (p. 405)

—Earth's Rock Cycle. (p. 498)

—Granite & Other Igneous Rocks. (p. 710)

—Happy Birthday: The Story of the World's Most Popular Song Undercuffler, Gary, illus. (p. 744)

—Identifying Rocks. (p. 852)

—Is It Symmetrical? (p. 889)

—Limestone & Other Sedimentary Rocks. (p. 1018)

—Minerals & Rocks. (p. 1146)

—My Life As an Early Settler. (p. 1212)

—My Life As an Immigrant. (p. 1212)

—On the Banks of the Amazon/en Las Orillas del Amazonas. de La Vega, Eida, tr. (p. 1289)

—On the Banks of the Amazon/en las orillas del Amazonas. de la Vega, Eida, tr. (p. 1289)

—Slate & Other Metamorphic Rocks. (p. 1588)

—Trouble in Troublesome Creek: A Troublesome Creek Kids Story. Crawford, K. Michael, illus. (p. 1790)

—Truth about Princesses Kim, Youngsun, illus. (p. 1794)

—What Is an Attribute? (p. 1888)

—What Sea Creature Is This? Brown, Gloria, illus. (p. 1893)

—What's an Election? (p. 1896)

—Whose Food Is This? A Look at What Animals Eat - Leaves, Bugs, & Nuts. Alderman, Derrick & Shea, Denise, illus. (p. 1921)

—Whose Is It? Alderman, Derrick & Shea, Denise, illus. (p. 1921)

—Whose Work Is This? A Look at Things Animals Make - Pearls, Silk, & Honey. Alderman, Derrick & Shea, Denise, illus. (p. 1922)

Allen, Page. Madison's Descent: A Child's Journey. (p. 1070)

—Way to Davis: On the River of Stars. (p. 1864)

Allen, Pamela. Mr. Archimedes' Bath. Allen, Pamela, illus. (p. 1184)

Allen, Pamela, jt. auth. see Carthew, Mark.

Allen, Pat. Field by the Sea. (p. 583)

Allen, Patrick. History of the American Flag. (p. 784)

—Look at Glaciers. (p. 1048)

Allen, Patrick D. Look at Glaciers. (p. 1048)

Allen, Paula Gunn. Pocahontas: Medicine Woman, Spy, Entrepreneur, Diplomat. (p. 1525)

Allen, Pauline. Science & Technology for the Early Years: Purposeful Play Activities. (p. 1525)

Allen, Peter. Ancient Egypt Jigsaw Book. (p. 68)

Allen, Peter, illus. see Daynes, Katie.

Allen, Peter, illus. see Reid, Struan & Stowell, Louie.

Allen, Peter, illus. see Reid, Struan.

Allen, Peter, illus. see Stowell, Louie.

Allen, Peter, jt. auth. see Daynes, Katie.

Allen, Quinc. Outdoor Chums: The First Tour of the. (p. 1312)

—Outdoor Chums. (p. 1312)

—Outdoor Chums after Big Game (Illust. (p. 1312)

—Outdoor Chums on the Gulf. (p. 1312)

Allen, Quincy. Outdoor Chums: The First Tour of the Rod, Gun & Camera Club. (p. 1312)

—Outdoor Chums at Cabin Point: Or the Golden Cup Mystery. (p. 1312)

—Outdoor Chums at Cabin Point or the Golden Cup Mystery. (p. 1312)

Allen, Rachael. 17 First Kisses. (p. 1995)

—Revenge Playbook. (p. 1459)

Allen, Richard, contrib. by. Charlie Parker Played Be Bop. (p. 293)

—Mysterious Thelonious. (p. 1223)

Allen, Richard L. Cool to Be in School. (p. 364)

—Kindergarteners on Their First School Bus. (p. 957)

Allen, Rick, illus. see Schultz, Jan Neubert.

Allen, Rick, illus. see Sidman, Joyce.

Allen, Rinne, jt. auth. see Ignatow, Amy.

Allen, Robert. Mensa Mighty Mindbusters for Kids. (p. 1126)

—Mensa Presents Secret Codes for Kids. (p. 1126)

Allen, Robert, jt. auth. see Carlton Books Staff.

Allen, Robert, et al. Train Your Brain: Super Tricky Teasers - Expert. (p. 1777)

—Train Your Brain: Mind-Twisting Puzzles - Beginner. (p. 1777)

—Train Your Brain: Brain-Bending Challenges - Intermediate. (p. 1777)

Allen, Roger MacBride, jt. auth. see Allen, Thomas B.

Allen, Russ, illus. see Allen, Jan.

Allen, S. Joan, illus. see Graham, Janice C.

Allen, Sandra. Bankruptcy Law. (p. 136)

Allen, Sandra Hutchins, illus. see Pirnot, Karen Hutchins.

Allen, Sharrel. Great Flea Rescue. (p. 716)

Allen, Shira, illus. see Zoldan, Yael.

Allen, Susan. Remarkable Ronald Reagan: Cowboy & Commander in Chief. Harrington, Leslie, illus. (p. 1459)

Allen, Susan, jt. auth. see Allen, Tom.

Allen, Susan & Lindaman, Jane. Read Anything Good Lately? Enright, Vicky, illus. (p. 1443)

—Used Any Numbers Lately? Enright, Vicky, illus. (p. 1827)

—Written Anything Good Lately? Enright, Vicky, illus. (p. 1965)

Allen, Teresa R. Laura, the Bichon Frise: My New Home. (p. 980)

—Tale of the Teeny, Tiny Black Ant: Helping Children Learn Persistence. Seroya, Tea, illus. (p. 1700)

Allen, Thomas B. George Washington, Spymaster: How the Americans Outspied the British & Won the Revolutionary War. Harness, Cheryl, illus. (p. 664)

—Harriet Tubman, Secret Agent: How Daring Slaves & Free Blacks Spied for the Union During the Civil War. (p. 750)

—Harriet Tubman, Secret Agent: How Daring Slaves & Free Blacks Spied for the Union During the Civil War. Bauer, Carla, illus. (p. 750)

—Remember Pearl Harbor: American & Japanese Survivors Tell Their Stories. (p. 1459)

—Remember Pearl Harbor: Japanese & American Survivors Tell Their Stories. (p. 1459)

—Remember Valley Forge: Patriots, Tories, & Redcoats Tell Their Stories. (p. 1459)

Allen, Thomas B., illus. see Roop, Connie & Roop, Peter.

Allen, Thomas B., illus. see Turner, Ann.

Allen, Thomas B. & Allen, Roger MacBride. Mr. Lincoln's High-Tech War: How the North Used the Telegraph, Railroads, Surveillance Balloons, Ironclads, High-Powered Weapons, & More to Win the Civil War. (p. 1185)

Allen, Thomas Gaskell, Jr. & Sachtleben, William Lewis. Across Asia on a Bicycle: The Journey of Two Americans Students from Constantinople to Peking. Perry, Michael W., ed. (p. 9)

Allen, Tim, jt. ed. see Duncan, Andrew.

Allen, Timothy, illus. see McKee, Ruby.

Allen, Tina. Copycat Chick Series: The Dragon & the Woman. (p. 366)

Allen, Tol Lynn. Game Day/Test Day: Who's Keeping Score? (p. 654)

Allen, Tom & Allen, Susan. American Oil Cans Identification & Price Guide. Allen, Tom & Allen, Susan, eds. (p. 62)

Allen, Tony. Irish Famine: The Birth of Irish America (p. 887)

Allen, Traudi. Knife & the Fork Go Dancing. (p. 964)

—Squeaky Door. (p. 1636)

Allen, Troy, jt. auth. see Dowswell, Paul.

Allen, Valerie. Age of Chaucer. (p. 29)

Allen, Vivian Ogea & Redman, Charles. Edna May of Thumbprint Hill. (p. 504)

Allen, Will. Swords for Hire: Two of the Most Unlikely Heroes You'll Ever Meet. Beck, David Michael, illus. (p. 1692)

Allen, William H., creator. TEH Learns to Read: Primary Words. (p. 1715)

—TEH Learns to Read: (13 Volume Set) (p. 1715)

Allenbach, Danielle Reese. Night Plane. (p. 1254)

Allenbaugh, Kay. Chocolate for a Teen's Dreams: Heartwarming Stories about Making Your Wishes Come True. (p. 309)

Allen-Conn, B. J. & Rose, Kim. Powerful Ideas in the Classroom Using Squeak to Enhance Math & Science Learning. (p. 1390)

Allende, Isabel. Bosque de los Pigmeos. (p. 214)

—Cidade das Feras. (p. 319)

—City of the Beasts. (p. 324)

—City of the Beasts. Peden, Margaret Sayers, tr. from SPA. (p. 324)

—Ciudad de las Bestias. (p. 324)

—Forest of the Pygmies. (p. 618)

—Forest of the Pygmies. Peden, Margaret Sayers, tr. from SPA. (p. 618)

—Kingdom of the Golden Dragon. (p. 960)

—Kingdom of the Golden Dragon. Peden, Margaret Sayers, tr. from SPA. (p. 960)

—Reino del Dragón de Oro. (p. 1457)

Allen-Dillon, Rachel. Through Endangered Eyes: A Poetic Journey into the Wild. (p. 1744)

Allen-Powell, Rebecca, et al. Pathfinder Handbook. (p. 1328)

Allen-Wilson, Regina. Bobo & the Pooch. (p. 206)

Aller, Eduardo Murias, et al. Cervantes: Un Escritor en Busca de la Libertad. (p. 288)

Aller, Susan Bivin. Anne Hutchinson. (p. 86)

—Beyond Little Women: A Story about Louisa May Alcott. Wang, Qi Z., illus. (p. 174)

—Florence Nightingale. Butler, Tad, illus. (p. 606)

—George Eastman. (p. 663)

—Madam C. J. Walker. (p. 1069)

—Tecumseh. (p. 1712)

—What Difference Could a Waterway Make? And Other Questions about the Erie Canal. (p. 1882)

Allette, Dawne. Barack Obama: The Making of a President. (p. 137)

—North American Animals. Baker, Alan, illus. (p. 1264)

Allette, Dawne A. Wellington Willowby Weeks. (p. 1874)

Alley, illus. see Heinrichs, Ann.

Alley, Ashleigh, illus. see Gerstler, J. C.

Alley, Marybeth, jt. auth. see Orehovec, Barbara.

Alley, R., illus. see Alley, Zoe.

Alley, R. W. Bratty Brothers & Selfish Sisters: All about Sibling Rivalry. (p. 223)

—Making Christmas Count! A Kid's Guide to Keeping the Season Sacred. (p. 1080)

—Prince's Tooth Is Loose! (p. 1402)

Alley, R. W., illus. see Adams, Christine A.

Alley, R. W., illus. see Adams, Christine.

Alley, R. W., illus. see Alley, Zoe.

Alley, R. W., illus. see Auer, Jim.

Alley, R. W., illus. see Bond, Michael.

Alley, R. W., illus. see Cheshire, Simon.

Alley, R. W., illus. see Clements, Andrew.

Alley, R. W., illus. see Demas, Corinne.

Alley, R. W., illus. see deRubertis, Barbara & DeRubertis, Barbara.

Alley, R. W., illus. see deRubertis, Barbara.

Alley, R. W., illus. see Derubertis, Barbara.

Alley, R. W., illus. see deRubertis, Barbara.

Alley, R. W., illus. see Derubertis, Barbara.

Alley, R. W., illus. see deRubertis, Barbara.

Alley, R. W., illus. see Dotlich, Rebecca Kai.

Alley, R. W., illus. see Falkenhain, John Mark.

Alley, R. W., illus. see Grippo, Daniel.

Alley, R. W., illus. see Hamilton, Kersten.

Alley, R. W., illus. see Harley, Bill.

Alley, R. W., illus. see Jackson, J. S.

Alley, R. W., illus. see Krieb & Kreib.

Alley, R. W., illus. see Lewis, Alaric.

Alley, R. W., illus. see McMullan, Kate.

Alley, R. W., illus. see Mills, Claudia.

Alley, R. W., illus. see Morrow, Carol.

Alley, R. W., illus. see Mundy, Michaelene.

Alley, R. W., illus. see O'Keefe, Susan Heyboer.

Alley, R. W., illus. see O'Neal, Ted.

Alley, R. W., illus. see Parker, Marjorie Blain.

Alley, R. W., illus. see Prelier, James.

Alley, R. W., illus. see Pulver, Robin.

Alley, R. W., illus. see Rothman, Cynthia Anne.

Alley, R. W., illus. see Ryan, Victoria.

Alley, R. W., illus. see Skofield, James.

Alley, R. W., illus. see Stein, Garth.

Alley, R. W., illus. see Trumbore, Cindy.

Alley, R. W., jt. auth. see Alberts, Nancy Markham.

Alley, R. W., jt. illus. see Alley, Zoë B.

Alley, R. W., tr. see Clements, Andrew.

Alley, R. W., tr. see Jackson, J. S.

Alley, Zoe. There's a Wolf at the Door. Alley, R. W. & Alley, R., illus. (p. 1731)

Alley, Zoë B. & Alley, R. W. There's a Princess in the Palace. (p. 1731)

Alleyne, Pat. Night They Came Out to Play (p. 1254)

Allgeier, Steve. Christmas with Norky the Adventure Begins... (p. 316)

—Christmas with Norky, the Adventure Begins.... (p. 316)

Allgoewer, Claudia, tr. see von Mackensen, Manfred, et al.

Allgood, Jean. Come Follow Me: Understanding One's Worth: Color Orange. Bk. 1 Smith, Sandra, illus. (p. 347)

Allgor, Marie. Endangered Animals of Africa. (p. 526)

—Endangered Animals of Antarctica & the Arctic. (p. 526)

—Endangered Animals of Asia. (p. 526)

—Endangered Animals of Australia. (p. 526)

—Endangered Animals of North America. (p. 526)

—Endangered Desert Animals. (p. 526)

—Endangered Forest Animals. (p. 526)

—Endangered Grassland Animals. (p. 526)

—Endangered Ocean Animals. (p. 526)

—Endangered Rain Forest Animals. (p. 527)

—Endangered Tundra Animals. (p. 527)

For book reviews, descriptive annotations, tables of contents, cover images, author biographies & additional information, updated daily, subscribe to **www.booksinprint2.com**

2017

Alliata, Brandon. First Day of Second Grade in the Third Room on the Fourth Floor. (p. 594)
Allibone, Judith, illus. see Morpurgo, Michael.
Allie, Beverly, ed. American Schoolhouse Reader: A Colorized Children's Reading Collection from Post-Victorian America 1890-1925. (p. 63)
—American Schoolhouse Reader: A Colorized Children's Reading Collection from Post-Victorian America 1890-1925. Allie, Beverly, illus. (p. 63)
—American Schoolhouse Reader, Book II: A Colorized Children's Reading Collection from Post-Victorian America 1890-1925. (p. 63)
Allie, Beverly J. American Schoolhouse Reader Collection: A Colorized Children's Reading Collection from Post-Victorian America: 1890 - 1925 (p. 63)
Allie, Scott. Devil's Footprints (p. 432)
Allie, Scott, ed. see Baltazar, Art & Franco.
Allie, Scott, ed. see Gage, Christos.
Allie, Scott, ed. see Jackson, Dan.
Allie, Scott, ed. see Jeanty, Georges, et al.
Allie, Scott, ed. see Mignola, Mike.
Allie, Scott, ed. see Niles, Steve & Santoro, Matt.
Allie, Scott, ed. see Tobin, Paul.
Allie, Scott, ed. see Whedon, Joss, et al.
Allie, Scott, et al. Buffy the Vampire Slayer Allie, Scott & Hahn, Sierra, eds. (p. 236)
Alligator Books Staff & Fabiny, Sarah. Ben Bunny Is Very Hungry. Hughes, Cathy, illus. (p. 163)
—Katie Kitten Finds a Friend. Hughes, Cathy, illus. (p. 945)
—Pip Puppy Looks for Mom. Hughes, Cathy, illus. (p. 1361)
Alliger, Richard, illus. see Jordan, Pat.
Allingham, Andrew, illus. see Ainsworth, Marlane.
Allingham, William. Rhymes for the Young Folk. (p. 1468)
Allio, Mark R. R Is for Rhode Island Red: A Rhode Island Alphabet. Begin, Mary Jane, illus. (p. 1429)
Allirol, Melusine. My Football - Buggy Buddies. (p. 1209)
Allison, Carol. Missionary Adventures: Stories for Boys & Girls. (p. 1153)
Allison, Catherine. Dear Daddy, I Love You. McNicholas, Shelagh, illus. (p. 418)
Allison, Charles T., illus. see Allison, Teresa J.
Allison, Elizabeth, ed. see Dzidrums, Christine & Rendon, Leah.
Allison, Elizabeth, ed. see Dzidrums, Christine.
Allison, Hugh A. Intrigue of Love. (p. 882)
Allison, Jennifer. Bone of the Holy. (p. 209)
—Dead Drop. (p. 416)
—Ghost Sonata. (p. 671)
—Gilda Joyce: Psychic Investigator. (p. 676)
—Gilda Joyce, Psychic Investigator. (p. 676)
—Iggy Loomis, a Hagfish Called Shirley. Moran, Michael, illus. (p. 855)
—Ladies of the Lake. (p. 970)
—Superkid in Training. Moran, Michael, illus. (p. 1683)
Allison, John. Bad Machinery Volume 2: The Case of the Good Boy. (p. 132)
—Case of the Team Spirit. (p. 275)
Allison, Joseph. Petal Peel & the Ghost Dragon. (p. 1346)
Allison, Lauren & Perry, Lisa. Woman Who Is Always Tan & Has a Flat Stomach: And Other Annoying People. (p. 1945)
Allison, Maria T. & Schneider, Ingrid E., eds. Diversity & the Recreation Profession: Organizational Perspectives. (p. 454)
Allison, Pamela S. Emerald's Journal: A summer with Hatchlings. Cepeda, Joseph C., photos by. (p. 518)
Allison, R. Bruce. If Trees Could Talk: Stories about Wisconsin Trees. (p. 854)
Allison, Ralph, illus. see Allison, Ray.
Allison, Ray. Where Did They Go? Allison, Ralph, illus. (p. 1906)
Allison, Rose. Everything You Need to Know about Anemia. (p. 545)
Allison, Samuel B. American Robinson Crusoe. (p. 63)
Allison, Samuel Buel. American Robinson Crusoe. (p. 63)
Allison, T. A. Noah's Harbour. (p. 1262)
Allison, Teresa J. Bobble Stories: The Bobbleup Pup. Allison, Charles T., illus. (p. 206)
—Bobble Stories: The Oddbobble's Visit. Allison, Charles T., illus. (p. 206)
—Bobble Stories: The Humbobble's Lost Hum. Allison, Charles T., illus. (p. 206)
Allien, Katherine. Gloves down Under. Allien, Katherine, illus. (p. 685)
Allman, jt. auth. see Litchfield.
Allman, Barbara. Banking. (p. 136)
—Musical Genius: A Story about Wolfgang Amadeus Mozart. Hamlin, Janet, illus. (p. 1194)
Allman, Cynthia, illus. see Lucht, Susan & Wilson, Mollie.
Allman, Howard, jt. photos by see MMStudios.
Allman, Howard, photos by see Andrews, Georgina & Knighton, Kate.
Allman, Howard, photos by see Brooks, Felicity & Litchfield, Jo.
Allman, Howard, photos by see Doherty, Gillian, ed.
Allman, Howard, photos by see Durber, Matt, illus.
Allman, Howard, photos by see Gibson, Ray.
Allman, Howard, photos by see Gilpin, Rebecca.
Allman, Howard, photos by see Johnson, Sue & Evans, Cheryl.
Allman, Howard, photos by see Litchfield, Jo & Jones, Stephanie, illus.
Allman, Howard, photos by see Litchfield, Jo & Sanchez Gallego, Maria Isabel.
Allman, Howard, photos by see Litchfield, Jo.
Allman, Howard, photos by see Patchett, Fiona, et al.
Allman, Howard, photos by see Patchett, Fiona.
Allman, Howard, photos by see Pratt, Leonie & Atkinson, Catherine.
Allman, Howard, photos by see Watt, Fiona, et al.
Allman, Howard, photos by see Watt, Fiona.
Allman, Joy. Hailey's Magic Stone. (p. 735)
Allman, Kari, illus. see Rankin, Stephanie.
Allman, Paul Limbert. Careers in Video & Digital Video. (p. 268)
Allman, Toney. Animal Life in Groups. (p. 78)
—Asperger's Syndrome. (p. 107)
—Diabetes. (p. 433)
—Distracted Driving. (p. 454)
—Downloading Music. (p. 474)
—Enlightenment. (p. 530)
—Food in Schools. (p. 613)
—Food in the Schools. (p. 613)
—From Insect Wings to Flying Robots. (p. 643)
—From Spider Webs to Man-Made Silk. (p. 643)
—Homicide Detective. (p. 794)
—Importance of Germ Theory. (p. 862)
allman, toney. Infectious Disease Research. (p. 873)
Allman, Toney. Internet Predators. (p. 880)
—J. Robert Oppenheimer: Theoretical Physicist, Atomic Pioneer. (p. 902)
—Jaws of Life. (p. 910)
—Life in a Cave. (p. 1010)
—Mean Behind the Screen: What You Need to Know about Cyberbullying (p. 1116)
—Medical Examiner. (p. 1118)
—Medieval Medicine & Disease. (p. 1119)
—Miracles. (p. 1148)
—Nexi Robot. (p. 1249)
—Obesity. (p. 1275)
—Poisoning. (p. 1377)
—Radiation Sickness. (p. 1432)
—Recycled Tires. (p. 1453)
—School Violence. (p. 1523)
—Stem Cells. (p. 1647)
—Stonehenge. (p. 1653)
—Tuberculosis. (p. 1795)
Allman, Toney, ed. Whooping Cough. (p. 1920)
Allman-Varty, Faye. Kitten Tales of Pumpkin & Parsnip 'Fairy Fields. Knott, Stephen, illus. (p. 962)
Allocca, John A. Guide to A Healthy Life. (p. 730)
Allon, Jeffrey, illus. see Goldin, Barbara Diamond, et al.
Allon, Jeffrey, illus. see Schram, Peninnah.
Allosso, Dan. Outside the Box. (p. 1313)
Allott, Andrew & Mindorff, David. Biology, 2014 (p. 189)
Allouche, José. Corporate Social Responsibility: Concept, Accountability & Reporting. Vol. 1 (p. 368)
Alloway, Kit. Dreamfire. (p. 484)
Allport, Alan. American Military Policy. (p. 62)
—Battle of Britain. (p. 146)
—British Industrial Revolution. (p. 229)
—Congress of Vienna. (p. 357)
—England. (p. 529)
—Gordon Brown. (p. 702)
—Jacques Chirac. (p. 905)
Allport, Alan, jt. auth. see Ferguson, John E.
Allport, Alan, et al. Freedom of Speech. (p. 634)
Allred, Chris Ross. Sir E. Bobbo! (p. 1580)
Allred, Erin. 5-Alarm Cookbook: For Those Who Just Can't Get It Hot Enough. (p. 1992)
Allred, Michael & Allred, Mike. Electric Allegories (p. 508)
Allred, Mike. Atomics: Spaced Out & Grounded in Snap City. (p. 113)
Allred, Mike, illus. see Milligan, Peter.
Allred, Mike, jt. auth. see Allred, Michael.
Allred, Scott, illus. see Olson, Tod.
Allred, Sylvester. DesertAlphabet Encyclopedia. Iverson, Diane, illus. (p. 429)
—ForestAlphabet: Encyclopedia. Iverson, Diane, illus. (p. 618)
—Freshwater Alphabet. Iverson, Diane, illus. (p. 636)
—Rascal, the Tassel-Eared Squirrel. Iverson, Diane, illus. (p. 1439)
Allred, Sylvester & Iverson, Diane. Rascal, the Tassel-Eared Squirrel. (p. 1439)
Allshouse, Sara & Burns, Adam. University of San Francisco College Prowler off the Record. (p. 1821)
Allsop, Marcus. Nos Gusta Ayudar A Cocinar. (p. 1266)
—Nos gustan nuestros dientes / we like our Teeth. (p. 1266)
—We Like Our Teeth. (p. 1867)
—We Like to Help Cook: Nos Gusta Ayudar a Cocinar. Iverson, Diane, illus. (p. 1867)
Allsop, Marcus & Iverson, Diane. Nos Gusta Ayudar a Cocinar: We Like to Help Cook. Iverson, Diane, illus. (p. 1266)
Allsop, Sophie, illus. see Sparklington, Madame & Gurney, Stella.
Allsopp, Sophie. Thank You, God! A Year of Blessings & Prayers for Little Ones. (p. 1725)
Allsopp, Sophie, illus. see Carlson, Melody.
Allsopp, Sophie, illus. see Castle, Kate.
Allsopp, Sophie, illus. see Corderoy, Tracey.
Allsopp, Sophie, illus. see Nellist, Glenys.
Allsopp, Sophie, illus. see Piper, Sophie.
Allsopp, Sophie, illus. see Rock, Lois.
Allsopp, Sophie, illus. see Stoddard, Rosie & Marshall, Phillip.
Allsopp, Sophie, jt. auth. see Frank, Penny.
Allstun, Gina. Related. (p. 1457)
Allsup, Becky. Purple Scarf. (p. 1419)
Allum, Margaret. Best Kind of Kiss. Bentley, Jonathan, illus. (p. 170)
—Daddy Kiss. Bentley, Jonathan, illus. (p. 398)
Allum, Margaret & Watson, Judy. How Many Peas in a Pod? (p. 811)
Allvord, Crash & Luiso, Lisa. Heroes of the Diamond. (p. 773)
Allwright, Deborah, illus. see Blackman, Malorie.
Allwright, Deborah, illus. see Edwards, Pamela Duncan.
Allwright, Deborah, illus. see Green, Alison.
Allwright, Deborah, illus. see Harris, Peter.
Allwright, Deborah, illus. see Lewis, Jill.
Allwright, Deborah, illus. see Roberts, Victoria.
Allwright, Deborah, illus. see Rooney, Rachel.
Allwright, Deborah, illus. see Wallace, Karen.
Allwright, Deborah, illus. see Whybrow, Ian.
Allwright, Deborah, jt. auth. see Lebihan, Kara.
Ally, Daisy. Solar Eclipses. (p. 1606)
Allyn, Daisy. Animal Families. (p. 77)
—Deadly Blue-Ringed Octopuses. (p. 417)
—Earth: The Blue Planet. (p. 495)
—Jupiter: The Largest Planet. (p. 937)
—Killer Whales Are Not Whales! (p. 956)
—Moon: Earth's Satellite. (p. 1171)
—Python. (p. 1421)
—Python / Pitón. (p. 1421)
—Saturn: The Ringed Planet. (p. 1515)
—Seeds & Plants. (p. 1547)
—Triceratops. (p. 1785)
—Tyrannosaurus Rex. (p. 1805)
—What Happens When I Hiccup? (p. 1886)
—Wheels & Axles. (p. 1900)
—Where Does the Bathwater Go? (p. 1907)
—Which Has More? (p. 1911)
Allyn, Daisy, jt. auth. see Mills, Nathan.
Allyn, Daisy & Flynn, Michael. Glowworms Are Not Worms! (p. 685)
Allyn, Pam. Pam Allyn's Best Books for Boys: How to Engage Boys in Reading in Ways That Will Change Their Lives. (p. 1320)
—What to Read When: The Books & Stories to Read with Your Child—And All the Best Times to Read Them. (p. 1894)
Allyn, Pam, jt. auth. see Pastore, Laurie.
Allyn, Virginia, illus. see McLeod, Kris Aro.
Allyson, Jackie. Antonio the Magician Esfandiari. (p. 90)
—Chris Jesus Ferguson. (p. 311)
—Doyle Texas Dolly Brunson. (p. 474)
—Gus the Great Dane Hansen. (p. 732)
—Howard the Professor Lederer. (p. 823)
—Phil Unabomber Laak. (p. 1350)
Allyson, Libby. Scottie Rides the Bus. (p. 1531)
Alma, Ann. Brave Deeds: How One Family Saved Many from the Nazis. (p. 223)
—Skateway to Freedom. (p. 1584)
Alma, Baxter. Snowflakes. (p. 1600)
Almada, Ariel Andres. Walking Through a World of Aromas. (p. 1854)
Almanstotter, Susanne, illus. see Beggs, Melissa.
Almanza, Rafael. Libro de Joveno (p. 1006)
Almanza, Roberto, illus. see Tamez, Juliza.
Almara, Dono Sanchez, illus. see Dickens, Charles.
Almarcegui, Jose Maria, jt. auth. see Lalana, Fernando.
Almarode, John. Dylan Discovers His Brain ! Norcross, David, illus. (p. 491)
Almeida, Artie. Recorder Express (Soprano Recorder Method for Classroom or Individual Use) Soprano Recorder Method for Classroom or Individual Use, Book & CD. (p. 1452)
—Ultimate Game & Activity Pack for Orchestra: Grades 3-6. (p. 1809)
Almeida, Artie, jt. auth. see Heritage.
Almeida, Jose-Gabriel. Lodiville: Adventure Land. (p. 1045)
Almeida, Michelangelo, illus. see Teitelbaum, Michael.
Almekinder, Stephen. Backyardia. (p. 131)
Almena, Fernando & Artigot, Manuel. Companero de Suenos. López, Nivio, tr. (p. 351)
Almena, Fernando & Fernando, Almena. Profesor Desinflado. (p. 1409)
Almendro, Herminio, jt. auth. see Robes, Ruth.
Almeyda, Tonito Avalon, illus. see Arnold, Ginger Fudge.
Almhjell, Tone. Twistrose Key. Schoenherr, Ian, illus. (p. 1803)
Almog, Vered, tr. see Grossman, David.
Almon, Harold. Budgeting & Bill Paying Organizing & Money Management Things to Do & Things to Know Growing Your (FICO) Credit Score (p. 235)
—Business Social Etiquette: Harold Almon's Guide to: Traditions Governing Social Behavior (p. 245)
—Correctly Creatively Setting a Table Service & Seating Assignments Etiquette Lessons for Couples & College & University Students Sharing Drink Atmosphere Food & Honor (p. 368)
—Eight Station Space Organizing: Harold Almon's Guide to: Interior Ambient & Intercultural Views (p. 507)
—Mastering Your Away Trip: Harold Almon's Guide to: Travel Rules of Thumb (TROT) (p. 1103)
—Mens Business Dressing Etiquette Things Someone Meant to Tell You When You Bought Your Best Male Business Dress the Rules on How to Wear It (p. 1126)
—Mens Personal Grooming Etiquette Lessons for College Students Things to Do Things Expected from the Male Half & That Talk (p. 1126)
—Mens Surviving the Parent Company Life's Little Talks Things of Which to Be Mindful When You Thinik You Have Had It (p. 1126)
—Midsection Muscle Management Make Your Current Weight Look Great (p. 1139)
—Personal File Organizing: Harold Almon's Guide to: What Is Done Before Saying I Do (p. 1344)
—Personal Transportation: Harold Almon's Guide to:Factors to Consider When Acquiring a Car (p. 1344)
—Plan for Just in Case & Budgeting & Bill Paying Having Things Done the Way That You Want & Things to Do & Things to Know Growing Your FICO Credit Score Organization & Money Management (p. 1366)
—Resume Writing Etiquette Advantages to List on Your Resume & Other Things to Do What the Job Requires - Get a Better Invitation to Get a Better Offer (p. 1464)
—Rose Haroutunitan (San Luis Obispo CA) Is a Liar & a Thief Court Stop Her Crime Getting a Desired Change: Harold Almon's Guide to What Is Done after a Tort & Before a Gun - Get Help - Get Your Name Back - Get Paid (p. 1489)
—Social & Business Hospitality: Harold Almon'Guide to: Giving Back (p. 1604)
—Using Social & Business Writing Paper What Your Paper Can Say to Others & Do for You Meeting Expectations in Writing Paper Form & Design (p. 1828)
—What the Job Pays: What Is Left after Withholdings (p. 1893)
Almond, David. Boy Who Climbed into the Moon. Dunbar, Polly, illus. (p. 219)
—Boy Who Swam with Piranhas. Jeffers, Oliver, illus. (p. 219)
—Clay. (p. 330)
—En el Lugar de las Alas. (p. 522)
—Fire-Eaters. (p. 590)
—Half a Creature from the Sea: A Life in Stories. Taylor, Eleanor, illus. (p. 736)
—Kit's Wilderness. (p. 962)
—Mouse Bird Snake Wolf. Mckean, Dave, illus. (p. 1182)
—My Dad's a Birdman. Dunbar, Polly, illus. (p. 1201)
—My Name Is Mina. (p. 1215)
—Raven Summer. (p. 1441)
—Savage. McKean, Dave, illus. (p. 1516)
—Skellig. (p. 1584)
—Skelling. (p. 1584)
—Slog's Dad. McKean, Dave, illus. (p. 1591)
—Tightrope Walkers. (p. 1749)
Almond, David, et al. Great War: Stories Inspired by Items from the First World War. Kay, Jim, illus. (p. 719)
Almond, Robert Johnson. Emery's Secret! (p. 518)
Al-Mouhawaka, Kira. Learn to Read Arabic: Drills. (p. 984)
—Learn to Read Arabic: Exercise Book. (p. 984)
—Learn to Read Arabic. (p. 984)
Almquist, Beth, et al. Growing up in Jesus: Weekly Meeting Plans for Voyager Leaders. (p. 726)
Almukahhal, Raja. Physics Laboratory Experiments for the Gifted: Middle & High School. (p. 1353)
Al-Muzher, Engineer Khalid Mohammed. Smart Boy Diary: How smartly can you keep your innovative Ideas? (p. 1592)
Almy, Judy. My Name Is Ick: A Rhyming Story of an Alaska Caribou. (p. 1215)
Al-Naimi, Faisal, jt. auth. see Gillespie, Frances.
Aloian, Molly. Amazon: River in a Rain Forest. (p. 56)
—Andes. (p. 72)
—Appalachians. (p. 92)
—Atoms & Molecules. (p. 113)
—Bugatti. (p. 236)
—Camions de Pompiers. (p. 256)
—Canada Day. (p. 260)
—Christmas. (p. 312)
—Columbus Day. (p. 346)
—Constitution Day. (p. 359)
—Cultural Traditions in Australia. (p. 391)
—Cultural Traditions in Brazil. (p. 391)
—Cultural Traditions in South Africa. (p. 391)
—Cultural Traditions in Thailand. (p. 391)
—Cultural Traditions in the United States. (p. 391)
—Deep-Diving Submarines. (p. 422)
—Different Kinds of Soil. (p. 438)
—Earth Day. (p. 495)
—Eating Green. (p. 501)
—Ellis Island. (p. 514)
—Emancipation. (p. 517)
—Ferrari. (p. 582)
—Fire Trucks: Racing to the Scene. (p. 591)
—Ganges: India's Sacred River. (p. 655)
—Gobi Desert. (p. 688)
—Going Green at School. (p. 692)
—Green Energy. (p. 721)
—Green Gardening & Composting. (p. 721)
—Halloween. (p. 737)
—Hanukkah. (p. 743)
—Hélicoptères. (p. 763)
—Himalayas. (p. 780)
—Hovering Helicopters. (p. 804)
—How Are Insects Helpful? (p. 805)
—How Do We Know It Is Spring? (p. 807)
—How Do We Know It's Fall? (p. 807)
—How Do We Know It's Winter? (p. 807)
—Independence Day. (p. 870)
—Jennifer Lawrence. (p. 912)
—Josh Hutcherson. (p. 926)
—Kalahari Desert. (p. 941)
—Kwanzaa. (p. 968)
—Lady Gaga. (p. 970)
—Life Cycles of Insects. (p. 1010)
—Live It: Honesty. (p. 1040)
—Live It: Respect. (p. 1040)
—Live It: Responsibility. (p. 1040)
—Living Green at Home. (p. 1041)
—Mardi Gras & Carnival. (p. 1092)
—Mixtures & Solutions. (p. 1156)
—Mojave Desert. (p. 1160)
—Motocyclettes. (p. 1179)
—Motorcycles. (p. 1179)
—Nile: River in the Sand. (p. 1255)
—Passover. (p. 1327)
—Plants Are Alive! (p. 1370)
—Ramadan. (p. 1437)
—Remembrance Day. (p. 1460)
—Rocky Mountains. (p. 1484)
—Sahara Desert. (p. 1503)
—Saint Patrick's Day. (p. 1504)
—What Are Bulbs & Roots? (p. 1879)
—What Are Crystals? (p. 1879)
—What Are Igneous Rocks? (p. 1879)
—What Are Metamorphic Rocks? (p. 1879)
—What Are Seeds? (p. 1879)
—What Are Stems? (p. 1879)
—What Does It Mean to Go Green? (p. 1884)
—What Is an Insect? (p. 1888)
—What Is Hearing? (p. 1889)
—What Is Sight? (p. 1890)
—What Is Smell? (p. 1890)
—What Is Taste? (p. 1890)
—What Is Touch? (p. 1891)
—Where Do Insects Live? (p. 1907)
—Why We Need Carbohydrates. (p. 1926)
—Why We Need Fats. (p. 1926)
—Yangtze: China's Majestic River. (p. 1968)
Aloian, Molly, jt. auth. see Corporate Contibutor Staff.
Aloian, Molly, jt. auth. see Crabtree Staff.
Aloian, Molly, jt. auth. see Kalman, Bobbie.
Aloian, Molly, jt. auth. see Miller, Reagan.
Aloian, Molly, jt. auth. see Peppas, Lynn.
Aloian, Molly & Kalman, Bobbie. Antarctic Habitat. (p. 88)
—Arctic Habitat. (p. 96)
—Cadenas Alimentarias del Bosque Tropical. (p. 250)
—Ciclo de Vida de la Flor. (p. 319)
—Ciclo de Vida del Escarabajo. (p. 319)
—Des Animaux de Toutes Sortes. (p. 427)

—Endangered Frogs. (p. 526)
—Endangered Monkeys. (p. 526)
—Explora America del Norte. (p. 549)
—Explore Europe. (p. 550)
—Explore North America. (p. 550)
—Explore South America. (p. 550)
—Fleurs. (p. 603)
—Forêts Humides. (p. 619)
—Hábitat de Bosque Tropical. (p. 734)
—Hábitat de la Antardia. (p. 734)
—Hábitat de la Antárdia. (p. 734)
—Hábitat de la Antártida. (p. 734)
—Hábitat de Pantano. (p. 734)
—Hábitat del Artico. (p. 734)
—Habitat del Artico. (p. 734)
—Habitats Acuaticos. (p. 734)
—Habitats Subterráneos. (p. 735)
—Hábitats Subterraneos. (p. 735)
—Helpful & Harmful Insects. (p. 766)
—Insect Bodies. (p. 875)
—Insect Life Cycles. (p. 875)
—Insectes: Utiles Ou Nuisibles? (p. 875)
—Insects That Work Together. (p. 876)
—L'Amérique du Nord. (p. 972)
—L'Amérique du Sud. (p. 972)
—L'Europe. (p. 1003)
—Life Cycle of a Beetle. (p. 1008)
—Life Cycle of a Flower. (p. 1009)
—Life of the California Coast Nations. (p. 1012)
—Many Kinds of Animals. (p. 1089)
—Muchos Tipos de Animales. (p. 1188)
—Nations of the Northeast Coast. (p. 1234)
—Nations of the Southeast. (p. 1234)
—Race Cars: Start Your Engines! (p. 1430)
—Racecars: Start Your Engines! (p. 1431)
—Rainforest Food Chains. (p. 1436)
—Rainforest Habitat. (p. 1436)
—Singes. (p. 1579)
—Water Habitats. (p. 1862)
—Wetland Habitat. (p. 1877)
Aloian, Molly & Peppas, Lynn. Cultural Traditions in Mexico. (p. 391)
Aloian, Molly & Peppas, Lynne. Cultural Traditions in Mexico. (p. 391)
Aloian, Molly, et al. Coleopteres. (p. 339)
Aloian, Sam. How a Ship Is Built. (p. 804)
Aloise, Frank, illus. see Sootin, Harry.
Alon Curiel, Gil-Ly, illus. see Tepper, Yona.
Alongi, Anthony, jt. auth. see Davidson, MaryJanice.
Alongi, Anthony & Davidson, MaryJanice. Jennifer Scales & the Ancient Furnace. (p. 913)
—Jennifer Scales & the Messenger of Light. (p. 913)
Alonso, jt. auth. see Figuerola.
Alonso & Perello. Pendientes Del Tio de Juan. (p. 1336)
Alonso Benito, L. E. Employment Relations in a Changing Society: Assessing the Post-Fordist Paradigm. Lucio, Miguel Martínez & Alonso, Luis, eds. (p. 521)
Alonso Blanco, Maria Victoria, tr. see Bennett, William J.
Alonso Blanco, Victoria, tr. see Molloy, Michael.
Alonso Blanco, Victoria, tr. see Silverstein, Shel & Margolin, Phillip.
Alonso Blanco, Victoria, tr. see Silverstein, Shel.
Alonso Blanco, Victoria, tr. see Stine, R. L., ed.
Alonso Curiel, Jorge David. Lasl Guerras Han Terminado. (p. 977)
ALONSO CURIEL, Jorge David, jt. auth. see Robles Echeverria, Maria De Jesus.
Alonso, Denis, illus. see Gunderson, Jessica & Loewen, Nancy.
Alonso, Denis, illus. see Gunderson, Jessica.
Alonso, Denis, illus. see Loewen, Nancy.
Alonso Díaz-Toledo, Juan Ramón, illus. see Lowry, Lois.
Alonso Díaz-Toledo, Juan Ramón, illus. see Narváez, Concha López, et al.
Alonso Díaz-Toledo, Juan Ramón, illus. see Olaizola, José Luis.
Alonso, Fernando. Arbol de los Suenos. Urberuaga, Emilio, illus. (p. 94)
—Arbol Que No Tenia Hojas (The Tree Without Leaves) (p. 94)
—Celiana y la Ciudad Sumergida. (p. 286)
—Fantasias de la Lechera. (p. 571)
—Hombrecito Vestido de Gris. Wendell, Ulises, illus. (p. 791)
—Hombrecito Vestido de Gris y Otros Cuentos. (p. 791)
—Milkmaid's Daydreams. (p. 1143)
—Sopaboba. (p. 1613)
—Tree Without Leaves. (p. 1784)
Alonso, Fernando & Fernando, Alonso. Historia de un Hombrecillo de Papel. (p. 782)
—Viejo Reloj. Escriva, Ana Lopez, illus. (p. 1841)
Alonso, Fernando, et al. Spring & the Forgotten City. (p. 1635)
Alonso Gómez, Manuel L., jt. auth. see Alonso, Manuel L.
Alonso, Jesus, illus. see Santillana U. S. A. Publishing Co, Inc. Staff.
Alonso, Juan Ramon, illus. see Cameron, Ann.
Alonso, Juan Ramon, illus. see Farias, Juan & Juan, Farias.
Alonso, Juan Ramon, illus. see Hernández, Miguel & Hernández, Miguel.
Alonso, Juan Ramon, illus. see Lowry, Lois.
Alonso, Juan Ramon, illus. see Olaizola, José Luis.
Alonso, Juan Ramón, tr. see Olaizola, José Luis.
Alonso, Luis, ed. see Alonso Benito, L. E.
Alonso, Manuel L. Algodon. (p. 38)
—Extrano, Muy Extrano. Schubert, Karin, illus. (p. 555)
—Rumbo Sur. (p. 1495)
Alonso, Manuel L., jt. auth. see Alonso, Manuel L.
Alonso, Manuel L. & Alonso Gómez, Manuel L. Aventura Del Zorro. Santoiaya, Antonia, tr. (p. 119)
—Isla de las Montanas Azules. (p. 891)
—Tiempo de Nubes Negras. Gaban, Jesus, illus. (p. 1747)
Alonso, Manuel L. & Alonso, Manuel L. Juego de Adultos. (p. 931)
Alonso, Maria, tr. see Funke, Cornelia.
Alonso, Maria, tr. see Schindler, Nina.
Alonso, Mellissa, jt. auth. see Nations, Susan.
Alonso, Tony. Great Three Days: Understanding & Celebrating the Easter Triduum. (p. 718)
Alonso, Victoria, tr. see Stine, R. L.
Alouette Enterprises. Reflections from the Glass Ceiling. (p. 1456)
—Year of the Butterfly. (p. 1969)
Alpern, Eliyahu, illus. see Ofanansky, Allison.
Alpern, Eliyahu, photos by see Ofanansky, Allison.
Alpers, Jody. T Is for Tortilla: A Southwestern Alphabet Book. Johnson, Celeste, illus. (p. 1694)
Alpert. Attack of the Sugar Bugs. (p. 114)
Alpert, Barbara. Electricity All Around (p. 509)
—Fast Cars. (p. 576)
—Look at Magnets (p. 1048)
—Military Amphibious Vehicles (p. 1142)
—Military Robots (p. 1143)
—Military Ships (p. 1143)
—Small Cars. (p. 1592)
—True Meaning of Christmas, the Greatest Gift of All. Zamboni, David, illus. (p. 1792)
—U. S. Military Fighter Planes (p. 1806)
—U. S. Military Robots (p. 1806)
—U. S. Military Submarines (p. 1806)
—U. S. Military Warships (p. 1806)
Alpert, Barbara, jt. auth. see Abramovitz, Melissa.
Alpert, Barbara, jt. auth. see Schuh, Mari.
Alpert, Barbara & Abramovitz, Melissa. Cars, Cars, Cars. (p. 272)
—Military Machines. (p. 1143)
Alpert, Barbara & Shank, Carol. U. S. Military Technology. (p. 1806)
Alpert, Mark. Six. (p. 1582)
Alpert, Sandra F. Horrible Howard: The Bully & Coward. (p. 798)
Alpert, Sherri. Cassandra Gets Her Smile Back: Teaching Children to Care for Their Teeth. Seroya, Tea, illus. (p. 276)
Alpha Omega Publishing Staff. Bible. (p. 175)
—Mathematics (p. 1107)
Alphabet Soup (Firm) Staff, contrib. by. Let's Look at Tractors. (p. 999)
Alphen, Nick Van. One Day. (p. 1294)
Alphenaar, Pamela L., illus. see Dorner, Nancy L.
Alphin, Arthur B., jt. auth. see Alphin, Elaine Marie.
Alphin, Elaine. Unspeakable Crime: The Prosecution & Persecution of Leo Frank. (p. 1822)
Alphin, Elaine Marie. Counterfeit Son. (p. 370)
—Dinosaur Hunter. Bolognese, Don, illus. (p. 442)
—Germ Hunter: A Story about Louis Pasteur. Verstraete, Elaine, illus. (p. 666)
—Perfect Shot. (p. 1342)
—Picture Perfect. (p. 1355)
—Simon Says. (p. 1577)
Alphin, Elaine Marie & Alphin, Arthur B. I Have Not Yet Begun to Fight: A Story about John Paul Jones. Casale, Paul, tr. (p. 839)
Alphona, Adrian. Runaways - Parental Guidance (p. 1497)
—Runaways - Pride & Joy (p. 1497)
Alphona, Adrian, illus. see Vaughan, Brian K.
Alphona, Adrian, illus. see Vaughn, Brian K.
Alphona, Adrian & Miyazawa, Takeshi. Runaways - Teenage Wasteland (p. 1497)
Alphona, Adrian & Norton, Mike. Runaways - Live Fast (p. 1497)
Alpin, Sue, et al. GCSE Business Studies for Edexcel. (p. 659)
Alpine, Rachele. Canary. (p. 260)
Al-Qawasmi, Jamal, ed. Regional Architecture & Identity in the Age of Globalization (p. 1457)
Al-Rawahi, Thuria, jt. auth. see Al-Araimi, Saif.
Alrawi, Karim. Mouse Who Saved Egypt. Willey, Bee, illus. (p. 1182)
Alsaid, Adi. Let's Get Lost. (p. 997)
—Never Always Sometimes. (p. 1242)
Alsbrooks, Stephanie. Cow Moooves Through the Books of the Bible: Job. Burg, Donna, illus. (p. 373)
—Cow Moooves Through the Books of the Bible: Genesis. Burg, Donna, illus. (p. 373)
—Cow Moooves Through the Books of the Bible - Exodus. Burg, Donna, illus. (p. 373)
—Ten Commandments: The Second Commandment. (p. 1718)
—Ten Commandments. Meier, Paul, illus. (p. 1718)
Alsdurf, Phyllis. It's Milking Time. Sheban, Chris et al, illus. (p. 897)
Alsenas, Linas. Beyond Clueless. (p. 173)
—Princess of 8th Street. (p. 1404)
Alshalabi, Firyal M. & Drexler, Sam. Sky Changed Forever. (p. 1586)
Alsheimer, Jeanette E. & Friedle, Patricia J. Path to Punishment. (p. 1328)
Alsius, Lourdes. Padres Para Aruna. (p. 1317)
Alsonso, Denis, illus. see Loewen, Nancy.
Alsonso, Denis, illus. see Shaskan, Trisha Speed & Loewen, Nancy.
Alsop, Bonnie. Sharing Me: Helping Young Children Deal with Divorce. McKay, Siobhan, illus. (p. 1561)
Alsop - Jinks, A. G. Kylie & the Butterfly. (p. 969)
Alspach, Kate M. Farts Are Fantastic. (p. 575)
Alston, Brad, illus. see Green, Elaine.
Alston, Colin. Invisible Boy. (p. 885)
Alston, E. B. 4 Women. (p. 1992)
—Last Voyage of the Dan-D. Garrett, Toni, illus. (p. 979)
Alston, Sheila Y., photos by see Alston, Stanley E.
Alston, Stanley E. Faith, Love & Life. Sharps, Angelique, ed. (p. 565)
Alt, David, ed. see Chronic, Halka.
Alt, David, ed. see Frye, Keith.
Alt, David, ed. see Van Diver, Bradford B.
Alt, David D. & Hyndman, Donald W. Northwest Exposures: A Geologic Story of the Northwest. (p. 1266)
—Roadside Geology of Idaho. (p. 1477)
—Roadside Geology of Montana. (p. 1477)
—Roadside Geology of Northern & Central California. (p. 1477)
Alt, David D., et al. Roadside Geology of Washington. (p. 1477)
Alt, Madelyn. Hex Marks the Spot (p. 774)
Alt, Matt, tr. see Sasaki, Joh.
Alt, Susan. My Personal Story in ABCs. Van Dijk, Jerianne, illus. (p. 1216)
—Very Special Twin Story. Campbell, Jenny, illus. (p. 1838)
Altabe, Joan B. Art Behind the Scenes: One Hundred Old & Modern Masters in & Out of Their Studios. (p. 101)
Altamirano, Ignacio M., jt. auth. see López, Samuel Salinas.
Altbacker, E. J. Battle of Riptide (p. 146)
—Enemy of Oceans. (p. 527)
—Into the Abyss (p. 881)
—Kingdom of the Deep. (p. 960)
—Last Emprex. (p. 977)
—Shark Wars. (p. 1562)
Altebrando, Tara. Battle of Darcy Lane. (p. 146)
—Best Night of Your (Pathetic) Life. (p. 170)
—My Life in Dioramas. (p. 1212)
Altebrando, Tara, jt. auth. see Zarr, Sara.
Altein, Chani. Aleph Bias Ship on the Aleph Bias Trip. Rosenfeld, D. L. & Leverton, Yossi, eds. (p. 35)
—Gift of Friendship. (p. 675)
—Hashem Is Truly Everywhere. Rosenfeld, D. L. & Leverton, Yossi, eds. (p. 752)
—Olf der Aleph Bais Shif. Brod, Chani, tr. from ENG. (p. 1282)
Alten, Steve. Primal Waters. (p. 1399)
—Sharkman. (p. 1562)
Alter, Anna. Francine's Day. Alter, Anna, illus. (p. 627)
Alter, Anna, illus. see Broyles, Anne.
Alter, Anna, illus. see Jennings, Patrick.
Alter, Austin & Lyon, Abby. Rhode Island School of Design College Prowler off the Record. (p. 1468)
Alter, Judy. Discovering Australia's Land, People, & Wildlife: A MyReportLinks. com Book. (p. 449)
—Discovering North America's Land, People, & Wildlife: A MyReportLinks. com Book. (p. 449)
—Henrietta King: Rancher & Philanthropist. Messersmith, Patrick, illus. (p. 767)
—Illinois: A MyReportLinks.com Book. (p. 857)
—Martín de León: Tejano Empresario. Messersmith, Patrick, illus. (p. 1097)
—Mirabeau B. Lamar: Second President of Texas. Messersmith, Patrick, illus. (p. 1148)
—Miriam Ma Ferguson: First Woman Governor of Texas. Messersmith, Patrick, illus. (p. 1149)
—Missouri: A MyReportLinks.com Book. (p. 1154)
—Montana: A MyReportLinks.com Book. (p. 1170)
—North Carolina: A MyReportLinks. Com Book. (p. 1264)
—Oprah Winfrey. (p. 1301)
—Passenger Ships. (p. 1326)
—Sam Houston Is My Hero. (p. 1506)
—Souvenirs from Space: The Oscar E. Monnig Meteorite Gallery. Normand, Hal, illus. (p. 1618)
—Surgery. (p. 1685)
—Vaccines. (p. 1830)
—Washington, D. C. A MyReportLinks. Com Book. (p. 1860)
—Women's Rights. (p. 1946)
Alter, Judy, jt. auth. see Alter, Judy.
Alter, Judy & Alter, Judy. Laura Ingalls Wilder: Pioneer & Author. (p. 980)
Alter, Judy & Rosenberg, Pam. Jane Addams: Social Reformer & Nobel Prize Winner. (p. 908)
Altés, Marta. My Grandpa. (p. 1210)
Altes, Marta. No! (p. 1257)
Althea, Erin, illus. see Petrella, Angela, et al.
Althouse, A. D & Turnquist, C. H. Modern Refrigeration & Air Conditioning Instructor's Manaul. (p. 1159)
Althouse, A. D., et al. Modern Refrigeration & Air Conditioning: Teaching Package Teacher's Resource Binder. (p. 1159)
—Modern Refrigeration & Air Conditioning: Teaching Package Powerpoint Presentations Site License. (p. 1159)
—Modern Refrigeration & Air Conditioning: Teaching Package PowerPoint Presentations Individual License. (p. 1159)
Althouse, Andrew D., et al. Modern Refrigeration & Air Conditioning. (p. 1158)
—Modern Welding. (p. 1159)
—Modern Welding Instructor's Manual. (p. 1159)
Althouse, Jay, jt. see Albrecht, Sally K.
Althouse, Jay, jt. auth. see Albrecht, Sally K.
Altieri, Maria. Mom, Tell Me a Story. (p. 1161)
Altieri, Marion. Claude, the Clumsy Clydesdale. Romero, Gina, illus. (p. 329)
Altiero, Carl. Alvora & Vulture Mountain. (p. 51)
Altinay, Ayse Gül, tr. see Mater, Nadire.
Altman, Adam. Lifeshaker: The First Tasmear Novel. (p. 1013)
Altman, Alexandra Jessup. Waiting for Benjamin: A Story about Autism. Keeter, Susan, illus. (p. 1852)
Altman, Denise. Clinics in Human Lactation: History & Assessment - It's All in the Details. Vol. 3 (p. 333)
Altman, Joel. Gapper's Grand Tour: A Voyage Through Great American Ball Park. Williams, Tim, illus. (p. 655)
Altman, Linda Jacobs. Adolf Hitler: Evil Mastermind of the Holocaust. (p. 13)
—African Mythology. Bock, William Sauts, illus. (p. 27)
—African Mythology Rocks! Bock, William Sauts, illus. (p. 27)
—American Civil Rights Movement: The African-American Struggle for Equality. (p. 60)
—Bioethics: Who Lives, Who Dies, & Who Decides? (p. 188)
—California. (p. 253)
—California Gold Rush: Stories in American History. (p. 253)
—California Gold Rush. (p. 253)
—Camino de Amelia. (p. 256)
—Celebrate Kwanzaa. (p. 284)
—Crimes & Criminals of the Holocaust. (p. 382)
—Escape-Teens on the Run: Primary Sources from the Holocaust. (p. 535)
—Forgotten Victims of the Holocaust. (p. 620)
—Genocide: The Systematic Killing of a People. (p. 661)
—Hidden Teens, Hidden Lives: Primary Sources from the Holocaust. (p. 776)
—Hitler, Goebbels, Himmler: The Nazi Holocaust Masterminds. (p. 786)
—Hitler, Goebbels, Himmler: The Nazi Holocaust Masterminds. (p. 786)
—Hitler's Rise to Power & the Holocaust. (p. 786)
—Impact of the Holocaust. (p. 862)
—Jewish Victims of the Holocaust. (p. 917)
—Politics of Slavery: Fiery National Debates Fueled by the Slave Economy. (p. 1381)
—Resisters & Rescuers: Standing up Against the Holocaust. (p. 1463)
—Shattered Youth in Nazi Germany: Primary Sources from the Holocaust. (p. 1563)
—Story of Slavery & Abolition in United States History. (p. 1660)
—Trade & Commerce. (p. 1776)
—Warsaw Ghetto Uprising: Striking a Blow Against the Nazis. (p. 1859)
—Warsaw, Lodz, Vilna: The Holocaust Ghettos. (p. 1859)
Altman, Linda Jacobs & Benduhn, Tea. Texas. (p. 1724)
Altman, Linda Jacobs & Fitzgerald, Stephanie. Colorado. (p. 343)
Altman, Linda Jacobs, et al. Arkansas. (p. 99)
Altman, Scott, illus. see Doyle, Bill H.
Altman, Scott, illus. see Doyle, Bill.
Altman, Steven-Elliot & Reaves, Michael. Irregulars. (p. 888)
Altmann, Scott. 3-D Coloring Book—Mermaids. (p. 1991)
—3-D Mazes—Vampires. (p. 1991)
—Fairy Fashion. (p. 563)
—Glow-in-the-Dark Tattoos Hearts. (p. 685)
—Guitar Rock Star Sticker Activity Book. (p. 731)
—Mermaids — Sirens of the Sea. (p. 1128)
—Skulls. (p. 1586)
—Vampire Mazes. (p. 1832)
Altmann, Scott, illus. see Fields, Jan.
Altmann, Scott, illus. see Hood, Ann.
Altmann, Scott, illus. see Lethcoe, Jason.
Altmann, Scott, illus. see O'Hearn, Michael.
Altmann, Scott, jt. auth. see Hood, Ann.
Altmann, Scott, et al. 3-D Coloring Book—Fairies. (p. 1991)
Altobello, Albert & Wadhams, Doyle. 10 Most Important Civil Rights Decisions. (p. 1994)
Altomare, Deborah. God Gives. (p. 688)
Alton, Steve. Firehills. (p. 592)
Altreche, Jeanine. Talula Goes to New York. (p. 1704)
Altscheler, Joseph A. Rock of Chickamauga: A Story of the Western Crisis. (p. 1482)
—Star of Gettysburg: a Story of Southern High Tide. (p. 1640)
Altsheler, Joseph A. Border Watch: A Story of the Great Chief's Last Stand. (p. 214)
—Colonial Frontier Novels: The Young Trailers & The Forest Runners. Vol. 1 (p. 341)
—Colonial Frontier Novels: The Free Rangers & The Riflemen of the Ohio. Vol. 3 (p. 341)
—Colonial Frontier Novels: The Scouts of the Valley & The Border Watch. Vol. 4 (p. 341)
—Colonial Frontier Novels: The Keepers of the Trail & The Eyes of the Woods. Vol. 2 (p. 341)
—Complete 'Great War' Series: The Guns of Europe, the Forest of Swords & the Hosts of the Air. (p. 353)
—Eyes of the Woods: A Story of the Ancient Wilderness. (p. 558)
—Eyes of the Woods: A Story of the Ancient Wilderness. Hutchison, D. C., illus. (p. 558)
—Forest of Swords: A Story of Paris & the Marne. (p. 618)
—Forest Runners: A Story of the Great War Trail in Early Kentucky. (p. 618)
—Free Rangers: A Story of the Early Days along the Mississippi. (p. 634)
—Free Rangers. (p. 634)
—French & Indian War Novels: The Lords of the Wild & The Sun of Quebec (p. 635)
—French & Indian War Novels: The Hunters of the Hills & The Shadow of the North (p. 635)
—French & Indian War Novels: The Rulers of the Lakes & The Masters of the Peaks (p. 635)
—Great Sioux Trail: A Story of Mountain & Plain. (p. 718)
—Great Sioux Trail: A Story of Mountain & Plain. Wrenn, Charles L., illus. (p. 718)
—Guns of Bull Run: A Story of the Civil War's Eve. (p. 732)
—Guns of Bull Run (Webster's French Thesaurus Edition) (p. 732)
—Guns of Bull Run (Webster's Spanish Thesaurus Edition) (p. 732)
—Guns of Europe. (p. 732)
—Guns of Europe. Wrenn, Charles, illus. (p. 732)
—Guns of Shiloh. (p. 732)
—Hosts of the Air: The Story of a Quest in the Great War. (p. 801)
—Hosts of the Air: The Story of a Quest in the Great War. Wrenn, Charles, illus. (p. 801)
—Hunters of the Hills: A Story of the Great French & Indian War. (p. 829)
—Keepers of the Trail: A Story of the Great Woods. (p. 947)
—Last of the Chiefs; a Story of the Great Sioux War. (p. 978)
—Lords of the Wild: A Story of the Old New York Border. (p. 1052)
—Lords of the Wild: A Story of the Old New York Border. (p. 1053)
—Lost Hunters: A Story of Wild Man & Great Beasts. (p. 1055)
—Riflemen of the Ohio: A Story of Early Days along the Beautiful River. (p. 1471)
—Rock of Chickamauga: A Story of the Western Crisis. (p. 1482)
—Rulers of the Lakes: A Story of George & Champlain. (p. 1495)
—Rulers of the Lakes: A Story of George & Champlain. Henry, J., illus. (p. 1495)
—Scouts of Stonewall: The Story of the Great Valley Campaign. (p. 1532)
—Scouts of the Valley: A Story of Wyoming & the Chemung. (p. 1532)
—Scouts of the Valley. (p. 1532)
—Scouts of the Valley (Webster's French Thesaurus Edition) (p. 1532)
—Shades of the Wilderness: A Story of Lee's Great Stand. (p. 1557)

—Shadow of the North: A Story of Old New York & a Lost Campaign. (p. 1557)
—Star of Gettysburg: A Story of Southern High Tide. (p. 1640)
—Star of Gettysburg (Webster's Korean Thesaurus Edition) (p. 1640)
—Sun of Quebec: A Story of a Great Crisis. (p. 1676)
—Sun of Quebec: A Story of a Great Crisis. Wrenn, Charles L., illus. (p. 1676)
—Sword of Antietam: A Story of the Nation's Crisis. (p. 1692)
—Sword of Antietam (Webster's French Thesaurus Edition) (p. 1692)
—Texan Scouts: A Story of the Alamo & Goliad. (p. 1723)
—Texan Scouts. (p. 1723)
—Texan Star: The Story of a Great Fight for Liberty. (p. 1723)
—Texan Triumph: A Romance of the San Jacinto Campaign. (p. 1723)
—Tree of Appomattox: A Story of the Civil War's Close. (p. 1783)
—Tree of Appomattox: A Story of the Civil War's Close. Wrenn, Charles L., illus. (p. 1783)
—Young Trailers: A Story of Early Kentucky. (p. 1979)
—Young Trailers. (p. 1979)
—Young Trailers - A Story of Early Kentucky. (p. 1979)
Altsheler, Joseph A., ed. Masters of the Peaks: A Story of the Great North Woods. (p. 1103)
Altshuler, Bruce & Phaidon Editors. Salon to Biennial: Exhibitions That Made Art History, 1863-1959. Vol. 1 (p. 1505)
Altson, John. A to Z of Forgotten Animals. (p. 2)
Altson, John & Miliotis, Patti Rae. What Happened to Grandpa? A Child Views the Hereafter Through the World's Major Religions. (p. 1885)
Altuna, Horacio. Hot L.A. Volume 1. (p. 801)
Altuney, Aldwyn, photos by see Lynn, Auntie.
Altuwayya, Zuwaina, tr. see Abdel-Fattah, Randa.
Al-Udhari, Abdullah, tr. see Adonis, et al.
Alumbaugh, Michelle. Dream Away. (p. 483)
Alumenda, Stephen. Toko & the Lost Kittens. (p. 1762)
Aluri, Rao. Backcountry Fury: A Sixteen-Year-Old Patriot in the Revolutionary War. (p. 130)
alurista, et al. Calaca Review: Un Bilingual Journal of Pensamiento & Palabra. Vélez, Manuel J., ed. (p. 252)
Alva, Kristian. Balborite Curse: Book Four of the Dragon Stones Saga. (p. 133)
Alvarado, Andrea E., illus. see Madelag.
Alvarado, Andrea E., tr. see Madelag.
Alvarado, Beatriz. Juliana: A girl from the Andes. (p. 932)
Alvarado, Carol, illus. see Benz, Suzanne.
ALVARADO, Claudia. plastic Bottle. (p. 1370)
Alvarado, Dalia, illus. see Romero, Alfonso Suárez.
Alvarado, Eladia, illus. see Gigi.
Alvarado, I. J. Adventures of Saleiah & Emm: Book 1. Zacker, Sandi, illus. (p. 22)
Alvarado, Juan, illus. see Renick, Sam X.
Alvarado, Paulo, illus. see Wagner, Jeff.
Alvarado, Tom, illus. see O'Donnell, Liam.
Alvarado, Tomas, tr. see Drake, Tim.
Alvarez Boccardo, Johanna, jt. auth. see Tello, Antonio.
Alvarez, Carlos. AC-130H/U Gunships. (p. 7)
—AH-1W Super Cobras. (p. 30)
—AH-6 Little Birds. (p. 30)
—Arleigh Burke Destroyers. (p. 99)
—Army Delta Force. (p. 100)
—Army Night Stalkers. (p. 100)
—Army Rangers. (p. 100)
—CH-46 Sea Knights. (p. 288)
—EA-6B Prowlers. (p. 492)
—F/A-18E/F Super Hornets. (p. 559)
—F-35 Lightning IIs. (p. 559)
—M109A6 Paladins. (p. 1067)
—Marine Expeditionary Units. (p. 1094)
—MH-53E Sea Dragons. (p. 1131)
—MH-53J Pave Lows. (p. 1132)
—Salt Flat Racers. (p. 1505)
—Strykers. (p. 1668)
—Ticonderoga Cruisers. (p. 1747)
—UH-60 Black Hawks. (p. 1808)
—V-22 Ospreys. (p. 1829)
Alvarez, Carlos & Von Finn, Denny. Supersonic Jets. (p. 1684)
Alvarez, Cecilia Concepcion, jt. auth. see Argueta, Jorge.
Alvarez, Cecilia Concepcion, jt. auth. see González, Rigoberto.
Alvarez, David, illus. see Leon, Georgina Lazaro.
Alvarez, Diego, illus. see Durán, Rosa Dopazo.
Alvarez, Diego, illus. see Villegas, Aline Guevara.
Alvarez, et al. Maquinas Termicas Motoras. (p. 1091)
Alvarez, Jennifer Lynn. Guardian Herd - Stormbound. McClellan, David, illus. (p. 728)
—Pet Washer. (p. 1346)
—Starfire. (p. 1642)
Alvarez, Jordan. Heavy or Light? Describe & Compare Measurable Attributes. (p. 761)
Alvarez, Jose M., illus. see Santillana U. S. A. Publishing Co, Inc. Staff.
Alvarez, Juan. Chocolate, Chipmunks, & Canoes: An American Indian Words Coloring Book. Alvarez, Juan, illus. (p. 309)
—José Rabbit's Southwest Adventures: An ABC Coloring Book with Spanish Words. Alvarez, Juan, illus. (p. 926)
Alvarez, Juan Ramón. Maximiliano el Nino Que Hablaba con Las Chuparrosas. (p. 1112)
Alvarez, Julia. Antes de Ser Libres. (p. 89)
—Antes de Ser Libres. Valenzuela, Liliana, tr. (p. 89)
—Before We Were Free. (p. 159)
—Como la Tia Lola Aprendio a Ensenar. (p. 351)
—De Como Tia Lola Salvo el Verano. (p. 416)
—De Como Tia Lola Termino Empezando Otra Vez. (p. 416)
—Devolver Al Remitente. (p. 432)
—En Busca de Milagros. (p. 522)
—Finding Miracles. (p. 588)
—How the Garcia Girls Lost Their Accent. (p. 813)
—How Tia Lola Came to Visit Stay. (p. 814)
—How Tia Lola Ended up Starting Over. (p. 814)
—How Tia Lola Ended up Starting Over. (p. 814)
—How Tia Lola Learned to Teach. (p. 814)
—How Tia Lola Saved the Summer. (p. 814)
—mejor regalo del mundo: La leyenda de la vieja Belén. Nuñez, Ruddy, illus. (p. 1124)
—Mejor Regalo del Mundo; The Best Gift of All: La Leyenda de la Vieja Belen; The Legend of La Vieja Belen. Espaillat, Rhina P., tr. (p. 1124)
—Return to Sender. (p. 1465)
Alvarez, Lamberto, illus. see Campos, Tito.
Alvarez, Laura, illus. see Luna, Tom.
Alvarez, Leticia Herrera. Dia de Reyes. Alvarez, Leticia Herrera, illus. (p. 433)
—Pais de las Sombras. Martinez, Enrique & Graullera, Fabiola, illus. (p. 1319)
Alvarez, Lourdes. Reyes Magos. (p. 1467)
Alvarez, Lourdes, tr. see Moore, Clement C.
Alvarez, Lourdes, tr. see Navillus, Nell.
Alvarez, Lourdes M. Colores. (p. 344)
—Mi Primer Libro Alfabeto. Brooks, David, illus. (p. 1133)
—Mi Primer Libro Animales. Brooks, David, illus. (p. 1133)
—Mi Primer Libro Cosas. Brooks, David, illus. (p. 1133)
—Mi Primer Libro Formas. Brooks, David, illus. (p. 1133)
—Mi Primer Libro Numeros. Brooks, David, illus. (p. 1133)
—My First Book Alphabet. Brooks, David, illus. (p. 1205)
—My First Book Colors. Brooks, David, illus. (p. 1205)
—My First Book Numbers. Brooks, David, illus. (p. 1205)
—My First Book Shapes. Brooks, David, illus. (p. 1205)
—My First Book Things. Brooks, David, illus. (p. 1206)
Alvarez, Maria Jesus, illus. see Argueta, Jorge.
Alvarez, Maria Jesus, illus. see Flor Ada, Alma.
Alvarez, Mark, jt. auth. see Cleveland, Will.
Alvarez, Mateo. Diego Rivera: Famous Mexican Painter. (p. 437)
—Frida Kahlo: Famous Mexican Artist. (p. 637)
Alvarez, Michel J. WonderChess - Chess Kit for Kids: Featuring unique, prize-fillable pieces & 3D illustrated lesson Book. Scauzillo, Tony, illus. (p. 1948)
—WonderChess - Chess Kit for Kids - Deluxe Edition in Tin: Featuring, unique prize fillable pieces & 3D illustrated lesson Book Scauzillo, Tony, illus. (p. 1948)
Alvarez, Michel J., creator. WonderCheckers - Checkers Kit for Kids: Featuring Unique Prize-fillable Pieces, Incentive Charts & Motivational Stickers - plus 3D Tic-Tac-Toe. (p. 1947)
Alvarez, Miguel, et al. Why, Mommy!! Pastrovicchio, Lorenzo, illus. (p. 1925)
Alvarez, Mrinali. Pon, Pon: ¡A Jugar con el Bebé! (p. 1382)
Alvarez, Mrinali, illus. see Barceló, Josefina.
Alvarez, Mrinali, illus. see Rivera Lassén, Carmen & Maldonado, Víctor.
Alvarez, Mrinali, illus. see Rivera, Carmen & Maldonado, Victor.
Alvarez, Mrinali, illus. see Rivera, Lassen.
Alvarez, Mrinali & Alvarez, Oneill J. Verde Navidad. (p. 1836)
Alvarez, Oneill J., jt. auth. see Alvarez, Mrinali.
Alvarez O'Neill, Juan. Grano a grano... Refranes Populares. (p. 710)
—¡Vamos a Jugar! (p. 1831)
Alvarez Quintero, Joaquin, jt. auth. see Alvarez Quintero, Serafin.
Alvarez Quintero, Serafin & Alvarez Quintero, Joaquin. Sunny Morning. Landes, William-Alan, ed. (p. 1677)
Alvarez, Rosanela, jt. auth. see Rhijn, Patricia van.
Alvarez-Slater, Luan. Souvenirs. (p. 1618)
Alvariz, Naiara & Naiara, Alvarez. Lo de Sonar. (p. 1044)
Alvergue, Anne, jt. auth. see Kimlan, Lanie.
Alvermann, Donna E., jt. auth. see Strickland, Dorothy S.
Alves, Jeff. Production Assistant's Handbook. (p. 1409)
Alves, Josh, illus. see Green, D. L.
Alves, Wellington. Power Man & Iron Fist: The Comedy of Death. (p. 1389)
—Shadowland: Blood on the Streets. (p. 1558)
Alves, Wellington, illus. see Abnett, Dan & Lanning, Andy.
Alvin, Schwartz, jt. auth. see Schwartz, Alvin.
Alvis, Cheyenne. Don't Open This Book!! (p. 468)
Alvord, David Myron. Albert & His Journey Through the Mountains. (p. 34)
Alvord, Douglas, illus. see Jewett, Sarah Orne.
Alvord, Larry. Down by Ol' Chooster's Pond. (p. 474)
Alward, Diane. Pedals & Promises: An Adventure Devotional for Kids. (p. 1334)
Alward, Jeff, illus. see Boyd, David.
Alward, Jeff, illus. see Lundy, Kathleen Gould.
Alward, Jeff, illus. see Piotrowski, Robert.
Alyce, Kathie. Flip Flop Block Quilts (p. 605)
Alyn, Kimberly. 101 Leadership Reminders. (p. 1999)
Alyson, Jackie. Howard the Professor Lederer. (p. 823)
Al-Zeheri, Ali. Princess & the Gold. (p. 1402)
Amadeo, Diana M. Holy Friends: Thirty Saints & Blesseds of the Americas. Curreli, Augusta & Lombardo, Irina, illus. (p. 791)
Amado, Antonio, illus. see Ibarrola, Begonia.
Amado, Defne, illus. see Dordick, Barry.
Amado, Elisa. Barrilete: Para el Dia de los Muertos Hairs, Joya, photos by. (p. 140)
—Primas Iribarren, Elena & Iribarren, Leopoldo, trs. from ENG. (p. 1400)
—Triciclo Ruano, Alfonso, illus. (p. 1786)
—What Are You Doing? Monroy, Manuel, illus. (p. 1880)
—Why Are You Doing That? Monroy, Manuel, illus. (p. 1922)
Amado, Elisa, jt. auth. see Argueta, Jorge.
Amado, Elisa, tr. see Argueta, Jorge.
Amado, Elisa, tr. see Cardenas, Teresa.
Amado, Elisa, tr. see Cottin, Menena.
Amado, Elisa, tr. see Isol.
Amado, Elisa, tr. see Kurusa, Monika.
Amado, Elisa, tr. see Liniers & Lindgren, Barbro.
Amado, Elisa, tr. see Lujan, Jorge Elias & Luján, Jorge.
Amado, Elisa, tr. see Luján, Jorge.
Amado, Elisa, tr. see Machado, Ana Maria.
Amado, Elisa, tr. see Olmos, Gabriela.
Amado, Elisa, tr. see Ramirez, Antonio.
Amado, Elisa, tr. see Ramírez, Antonio.
Amado, Elisa, tr. see Rueda, Claudia.
Amado, Elisa, tr. see Toledo, Natalia.
Amador, Brian, jt. auth. see Witte, Anna.
Amador Family Staff, jt. auth. see Barefoot Books Staff.
Amador Family Staff & Barefoot Books Staff. Wheels on the Bus. Williamson, Melanie, illus. (p. 1901)
Amador, Xavier. I'm Right, You're Wrong, Now What? Break the Impasse & Get What You Need. (p. 860)
Amagi, Seimaru. Remote Koshiba, Tetsuya, illus. (p. 1460)
Amanda, photos by see Amanda, Grant.
Amanda, Grant. Cook School. Amanda, photos by. (p. 361)
Amanda, Hopkins. Daisy Dog: My Rabbit Buddies. (p. 400)
Amanda Rose. Sara James & the Mermaid Tale. (p. 1514)
Amani, Ahmad. Math City. (p. 1105)
Amani, Alexander. Guardians. (p. 728)
Amann, Remy, photos by see Gomel, Luc.
Amano, Akira. Reborn! Amano, Akira, illus. (p. 1451)
Amano, Jeff. Fade from Grace. (p. 562)
—Kiss & Tell. Brusco, Giulia, illus. (p. 961)
—Ronin Hood of the 47 Samurai. (p. 1487)
Amano, Shiro. Chain of Memories. (p. 288)
—Kingdom Hearts (p. 959)
—Kingdom Hearts Amano, Shiro, illus. (p. 959)
Amano, Shiro, adapted by. Kingdom Hearts II, Volume 1. (p. 959)
Amano, Yoshitaka. Yoshitaka Amano's HERO Party of One Definitive Edition Gaiman, Neil, tr. (p. 1972)
Amant, Kathleen. On Your Potty, Little Rabbit. Van den Abeele-Kinget, Inge, tr. from DUT. (p. 1292)
Amar, Cindy. Tommy's Discovery. (p. 1765)
Amar, Elisheva. One Word Too Many: Stories for Kids about the Life Changing Impact of Words. (p. 1297)
Amar, Raquel, tr. see Bassan, Malca.
Amara, Phil. Treehouse Heroes: The Forgotten Beast. Chau, Alina, illus. (p. 1784)
Amara, Phil, et al. All the Heroes! (p. 45)
Amara, Philip. So, You Want to Be a Comic Book Artist? The Ultimate Guide on How to Break into Comics! (p. 1602)
Amari, Rafat N. Islam in Light of History. (p. 891)
Amarone, Morgan. Madison's Journey. Ruocco, Paul, illus. (p. 1070)
Amarsingh, Bahia. It's Okay to Be Me! D'souza, Maris, illus. (p. 898)
Amaso, Marcellus Chigbo. 100 Tips for a School Child's Daily Safety Guide. (p. 1999)
Amatangelo, Sergio Lino. Forever Four, Finally Five. (p. 619)
Amateau, Gigi. Chancey of the Maury River. (p. 289)
—Claiming Georgia Tate. (p. 326)
—Come August, Come Freedom: The Bellows, the Gallows, & the Black General Gabriel. (p. 347)
—Dante of the Maury River. (p. 406)
—Macadoo of the Maury River. (p. 1067)
—Two for Joy. Marble, Abigail, illus. (p. 1803)
Amatisto, Brandi, illus. see Coleman, William L.
Amato, Anne McCoy. Moving Shelly: A Novel. (p. 1184)
Amato, Carol J. Lost Treasure of the Golden Sun. (p. 1057)
Amato, Gaetano. Upside Right: A Children's Guide to Movement. (p. 1825)
Amato, Mary. Chicken of the Family. Durand, Delphine, illus. (p. 300)
—Drooling & Dangerous: The Riot Brothers Return! Long, Ethan, illus. (p. 485)
—Edgar Allan's Official Crime Investigation Notebook. (p. 504)
—Naked Mole-Rat Letters. (p. 1228)
—Please Write in This Book. Brace, Eric, illus. (p. 1373)
—Snarf Attack, Underfoodle, & the Secret of Life: The Riot Brothers Tell All. Long, Ethan, illus. (p. 1597)
—Stinky & Successful: The Riot Brothers Never Stop! Long, Ethan, illus. (p. 1651)
—Take the Mummy & Run: The Riot Brothers Are on a Roll. Long, Ethan, illus. (p. 1697)
—Word Eater. Ryniak, Christopher, illus. (p. 1950)
Amato, Mary Anne. Where Are My Pictures, Mommy? (p. 1906)
Amato, William. Aircraft Carriers. (p. 31)
—Aviones Supersonicos. (p. 120)
—Bullet Trains. (p. 240)
—Cruceros. (p. 386)
—Cruceros (Cruise Ships) (p. 386)
—Cruise Ships. (p. 386)
—Nuclear Submarines. (p. 1270)
—Portaaviones. (p. 1386)
—Portaaviones (Aircraft Carriers) (p. 1386)
—Space Shuttle. (p. 1619)
—Submarinos Nucleares. (p. 1671)
—Submarinos nucleares (Nuclear Submarines) (p. 1671)
—Supersonic Jets. (p. 1684)
—Transbordadores Espaciales. (p. 1778)
—Transbordadores espaciales (the Space Shuttle) (p. 1778)
—Trenes Bala. (p. 1784)
—Trenes bala (Bullet Trains) (p. 1784)
Amatrula, Michele, illus. see Olds, Barbara Anne.
Amatrula, Michele, jt. auth. see Herman, Gail.
Amaya, Laura, tr. see Page, Lawana.
Ambatchew, Daniel. Mimi Mystery. (p. 1145)
Ambau, Getty. Desta & the Winds of Washaa Umera: The Winds of Washaa Umera (p. 430)
Ambaum, Gene. Poopy Claws. (p. 1383)
Amber, Holly, illus. see Johnson, Rhonda & Paladin, Frank.
Amber, Holly, illus. see Paladin, Frank.
Amberson, Mary. Brave Boy & a Good Soldier: John C. C. Hill & the Texas Expedition to Mier. (p. 223)
Amberson, Mary, jt. auth. see Magruder, Jana.
Amblard, Odile. Privacy, Please! Gaining Independence from Your Parents. Guyot, Céline, illus. (p. 1407)
Ambler, Laura, illus. see Henry, Kristina.
Amboba, Ethan & Lyon, Abby. Occidental College College Prowler off the Record. (p. 1275)
Ambramson, Andra Serlin. Emergency & Rescue Vehicles. (p. 518)
Ambrose. Diseño Simplificado de Edificios Para Cargas de Viento y Sismo. (p. 450)
Ambrose, Adrianne. What I Learned from Being a Cheerleader. (p. 1886)
—Xoxo, Betty & Veronica: In Each Other's Shoes. (p. 1967)
Ambrose, Dave. Chew on This: 31 Biblical Devotions into the Heart of Christ (p. 299)
Ambrose, Marylou. Diabetes: Examining Insulin & Blood Sugar. (p. 433)
—Investigating Diabetes: Real Facts for Real Lives. (p. 884)
Ambrose, Marylou & Deisler, Veronica. Eating Disorders: Examining Anorexia, Bulimia, & Binge Eating. (p. 501)
—Investigate Alcohol. (p. 884)
—Investigate Cocaine & Crack. (p. 884)
—Investigate Methamphetamines. (p. 884)
—Investigating STDs (Sexually Transmitted Diseases) Real Facts for Real Lives. (p. 885)
—Sexually Transmitted Diseases: Examining STDs. (p. 1556)
Ambrosek, Renee. America Debates United States Policy on Immigration. (p. 59)
—Shawn Fanning: The Founder of Napster. (p. 1563)
—Team Roping. (p. 1710)
Ambrosio, Michael. Destiny, Valor & a Lizard Named Louie. Langan, Bob, illus. (p. 431)
—It Takes a Lot of Love. Awes, Jennifer, illus. (p. 894)
Ambrosio, Stefano. Mouse Magic. Pastrovicchio, Lorenzo, illus. (p. 1182)
—Wizards of Mickey - Grand Tournament Pastrovicchio, Lorenzo & Magic Eye Studios, illus. (p. 1943)
Ambroz, Mark, illus. see Frances, Nelle.
Ambrus, Victor, illus. see Thomas, Paul.
Ambrus, Victor G. Busca a Dracula (Search for Dracula) (p. 244)
—Cuenta con Dracula (Count with Dracula) (p. 389)
—Iliad. (p. 856)
—Lee Con Dracula (Read with Dracula) (p. 987)
—Que Hora Es, Dracula? (What Time Is It, Dracula?) (p. 1424)
Ambrus, Victor G., illus. see Miles, Bernard.
Ambush, Peter, illus. see Lyons, Kelly Starling.
Amchin, Robert. Alto Antics - Teacher's Edition: A Beginning Alto Recorder Ensemble Book. Holl, Brent, ed. (p. 50)
Amdahl Elco, Anita & Weikert Stelmach, Katherine. Who Is in That Shell? Patch, Michael, illus. (p. 1916)
Amechazurra, G., illus. see Lowry, Lois.
Amédékanya, Ben-Kofi. Pillars of Pride. (p. 1359)
Ameen, Judith. Harold & the Magic Books. (p. 749)
Ameet Studio, Ameet, illus. see Farshtey, Greg.
Ameet Studio, Ameet, illus. see Landers, Ace.
Ameet Studio, Ameet, illus. see Scholastic, Inc. Staff & Hapka, Cathy.
Ameet Studio (Firm) Staff, illus. see Landers, Ace.
Ameet Studio Staff. LEGO Friends: Andrea's Wish (Activity Book #3) Ameet Studio Staff, illus. (p. 990)
—LEGO Legends of Chima: Wolves & Crocodiles (Activity Book #2) (p. 990)
—LEGO Mixels: Activity Book with Figure. Ameet Studio Staff, illus. (p. 990)
—Piece of Resistance. (p. 1356)
—Ravens & Gorillas Ameet Studio Staff, illus. (p. 1441)
—These Aren't the Droids You're Looking For: A Search & Find Book. Ameet Studio Staff, illus. (p. 1731)
—Tournament of Elements. (p. 1773)
—Where's the Pizza Boy? (p. 1911)
Ameet Studio Staff, illus. see Farshtey, Greg.
Ameet Studio Staff, illus. see Holmes, Anna.
Ameet Studio Staff, illus. see Kotsut, Rafat.
Ameet Studio Staff, illus. see Simon, Jenne.
Ameiss, Bill & Graver, Jane. Love, Sex & God: For Young Women Ages 15 & Up. (p. 1060)
Amelio, Paul. Jack & Zach: The Talk of the Town. (p. 902)
Amen, Henry J., jt. auth. see Park, Kyubyong.
Amend, Allison. Hispanic-American Writers. (p. 781)
Amend, Allison, jt. auth. see McCage, Crystal D.
Amendola, Dominique, illus. see Greene, Joshua M.
Amenii, Nehpril. Memories of the Little Elephant. (p. 1126)
Amenta, Charles A. Russell's World: A Story for Kids about Autism. (p. 1498)
—Russell's World: A Story for Kids about Autism. Pollak, Monika, illus. (p. 1498)
Amer, Fatmah. Islam. (p. 891)
Amer, Joseph. War on Terror. (p. 1858)
Amerel. Summer Holidays: A Story for Childre. (p. 1674)
America, illus. see Greenway, Bethany.
American Academy of Pediatrics Staff, contrib. by. Blast! - Babysitter Lessons & Safety Training. (p. 198)
American Ballet Theatre Staff, et al. Book of Ballet: Learning & Appreciating the Secrets of Dance. Ellison, Nancy, photos by. (p. 210)
American Bible Society Editors. Life of Christ. (p. 1011)
American Bible Society Staff. Amazing Bible Factbook for Kids. (p. 54)
—American Bible Society Favorite Bible Stories & Amazing Facts. (p. 60)
—Four Gospels. (p. 625)
—Read & Learn Bible. Duendes Del Sur Staff, illus. (p. 1442)
American Bible Society Staff, jt. auth. see Scholastic, Inc. Staff.
American Bible Society Staff, ed. My First Read & Learn Bible. (p. 1207)
American Camping Association Staff. Outdoor Living Skills. (p. 1312)
American Cancer Society Staff. Mission: Sunwise (Story Book) Sunwise (Story Book) Environmental Protection Atgency (US), ed. (p. 1153)
American Education Publishing Staff, et al, compiled by. Everyday Success Second Grade. (p. 544)
American Girl, creator. Elizabeth Trading Cards. (p. 513)
—Emily Trading Cards. (p. 519)
—You Can Do It! A Kit to Help You Do Just about Anything. (p. 1974)
American Girl Editorial Staff. Coconut Cookbook: Fun & Fluffy Treats to Eat. (p. 337)
—Coconut Quiz Book: Tear & Share Quizzes for You & a Friend. (p. 337)
American Girl Editorial Staff, ed. see Walton, Rick.
American Girl Editorial Staff, ed. Coconut Photo Journal. Casey, Lukatz, illus. (p. 337)
American Girl Editors. Girls Love Gymnastics. Yoshizumi, Carol, illus. (p. 680)
—Molly's Cooking Studio. Backes, Nick, illus. (p. 1161)

—Samantha's Cooking Studio. Backes, Nick, illus. (p. 1507)
—Scrapbook Studio: Everything You Need to Make a Fresh & Funky Scrapbook—In a Flash! (p. 1532)
American Girl Editors, ed. see Magruder, Trula.
American Girl Editors, jt. ed. see Falligant, Erin.
American Girl Editors, jt. ed. see Magruder, Trula.
American Girl Editors, jt. ed. see Richards, Mary.
American Girl Editors & Anton, Carrie, eds. Poster Pack: 60 Cute, Fun, & Inspiring Posters from American Girl! (p. 1388)
American Girl Editors & Magruder, Trula, eds. Oodles of Ocean Fun: A Collection of Posters, Puzzles, Doodles, Cards, Crafts, Stickers, Frames. (p. 1298)
American Girl Editors & Richards, Mary, eds. Oodles of Sweet Stuff. (p. 1298)
American Girl Publishing Staff, jt. ed. see Chobanian, Elizabeth.
American Heritage, American, jt. auth. see King, David C.
American Heritage Dictionaries Editors, ed. 100 Words Every 4th Grader Should Know. (p. 1999)
American Heritage Dictionaries, Editors of the. American Heritage Children's Dictionary. (p. 61)
—American Heritage First Dictionary. (p. 61)
—American Heritage Picture Dictionary. (p. 61)
—American Heritage Student Dictionary. (p. 61)
American Heritage Dictionaries, Editors of the, ed. Curious George's Dictionary. (p. 394)
American Heritage Dictionary Editors. 100 Words Every Middle Schooler Should Know. (p. 1999)
—American Heritage Children's Science Dictionary. (p. 61)
—American Heritage Essential Student Thesaurus. (p. 61)
—Qué Día Es? Zagarenski, Pamela, illus. (p. 1423)
—What Day Is It? Zagarenski, Pamela, illus. (p. 1881)
—Where Am I Hiding? Zagarenski, Pamela, illus. (p. 1906)
American Heritage Dictionary Editors & Hellweg, Paul. American Heritage Children's Dictionary. (p. 61)
—American Heritage Children's Thesaurus. (p. 61)
—American Heritage Picture Dictionary. (p. 61)
American Heritage Dictionary Editors, ed. American Heritage First Dictionary. (p. 61)
—American Heritage Student Science Dictionary, Second Edition. (p. 61)
—My Very Own Big Spanish Dictionary. Zagarenski, Pamela, illus. (p. 1221)
—Qué Juego? Zagarenski, Pamela, illus. (p. 1424)
—What Can I Do When It Rains? Zagarenski, Pamela, illus. (p. 1880)
—What Can I Do When It Rains? (Qué Puedo Hacer Cuando Llueve?) Zagarenski, Pamela, illus. (p. 1880)
—¿Dónde Me Escondo? Zagarenski, Pamela, illus. (p. 466)
American Heritage Dictionary Editors, et al. American Heritage Student Thesaurus. (p. 61)
American Heritage Dictionary Staff, ed. American Heritage Children's Science Dictionary. (p. 61)
American Heritage Publishing Staff. American Heritage Student Grammar Dictionary. (p. 61)
American LaserTechnic, ed. see Gregory, Daniel.
American Locomotive Company, creator. Articulated Compound Locomotives of the American Locomotives Company. (p. 104)
American Map Corporation Staff, ed. American Map Maze Mania. (p. 62)
—American Map Travel Activities Atlas. (p. 62)
—American Map Us Word Search. (p. 62)
American Map Publishing Staff. Student's Notebook Atlas. (p. 1669)
American Medical Association Staff, jt. auth. see Pfeifer, Kate Gruenwald.
American Museum of Natural History. ABC Universe. (p. 3)
American Museum of Natural History Staff. 1-2-3 Dinosaurs Bite: A Prehistoric Counting Book. (p. 1990)
—ABC Dinosaurs. Hartman, Scott, illus. (p. 3)
—ABC Insects. (p. 3)
—ABC Oceans. (p. 3)
—Spot the Animals: A Lift-the-Flap Book of Colors. (p. 1633)
American Museum of Natural History Staff, jt. auth. see Carson, Mary Kay.
American Museum of Natural History Staff, jt. auth. see Feldman, Thea.
American Museum of Natural History Staff, jt. auth. see Norman, Kim.
American Museum of Natural History Staff, jt. auth. see Pfeffer, Wendy.
American Museum of Natural History Staff, jt. auth. see Stewart, Melissa.
American Museum of Natural History Staff, et al. Inside Dinosaurs. (p. 876)
—Inside Dinosaurs. Brougham, Jason, illus. (p. 876)
American Poets Society Staff, compiled by. Poetry Gems. (p. 1376)
—Wellsprings. (p. 1874)
American Sunday School Union. Allis Family or Scenes of Western Life. (p. 47)
American Tract Society Staff, compiled by. Tract Primer: First Lessons in Sound Doctrine for Young Children. (p. 1775)
American-French Genealogical Society Staff, ed. see Letourneau, Armand.
America's Math Teacher. Mastering Essential Math Skills Book Two: Middle Grades/High School: 20 Minutes a Day to Success. (p. 1103)
Amerikaner, Susan. Dusty Flies High. (p. 490)
—Dusty Flies High. RH Disney Staff, illus. (p. 490)
—Game On! (p. 654)
—Goofy at Bat. (p. 702)
—Let's Look for Colors. (p. 999)
Amerikaner, Susan, jt. auth. see Jordan, Apple.
Amerikaner, Susan & Disney Book Group Staff. Clubhouse Christmas. Loter Inc. Staff, illus. (p. 335)
—Mickey & Friends Goofy at Bat. Disney Storybook Artists Staff, illus. (p. 1136)
Amery & Cartwright. Curly the Pig Kid Kit. (p. 394)
Amery, H. Bible Stories Jigsaw Book. (p. 176)
—Complete Book of Farmyard Tales. (p. 352)
—Cuentos Populares del Mundo. (p. 390)
—Daniel & the Lions. (p. 404)
—First 100 Words in French. (p. 592)
—First Hundred Words. (p. 595)
—First Thousand Words. (p. 597)
—First Thousand Words in German. (p. 597)
—First Thousand Words in Spanish IL. (p. 597)
—Jonah & the Whale. (p. 925)
—Joseph & the Amazing Coat. (p. 926)
—Mini Greek Myths. (p. 1146)
—Mini Stories from Around the World. (p. 1146)
—Moses in the Bulrushes. (p. 1176)
—Navidad en la Granja Libro Con Paginas Puzzle. (p. 1238)
—New Testament. (p. 1247)
—Noah's Ark. (p. 1261)
—Steam Train Jigsaw Book. (p. 1646)
—Stories from Around the World. (p. 1654)
—Telling the Time. (p. 1717)
—Usborne Book of Christmas Carols. (p. 1827)
—Where's Curly? Cartwright, Stephen, illus. (p. 1910)
Amery, H. & Cartwright, S. ABC Jigsaw Book. (p. 3)
—Alphabet Lotto. (p. 49)
—Christmas Jigsaw Book. (p. 314)
—Cinderella. (p. 320)
—Farm Animal Jigsaw Book. (p. 573)
—First Spanish Word Book. (p. 597)
—Little Red Riding Hood. (p. 1035)
—Pairs. (p. 1318)
—Royal Broomstick. (p. 1492)
—Sleeping Beauty. (p. 1589)
—Story of Rumpelstiltskin. (p. 1659)
—Three Little Pigs. (p. 1742)
—Tournament. (p. 1773)
—Where's Rusty? (p. 1910)
Amery, Heather. Bible Stories. Young, Norman, illus. (p. 176)
—Book of Bible Stories with CD (Combined Volume) (p. 211)
—Camping Out. Cartwright, Stephen, illus. (p. 257)
—Christmas Story Jigsaw Book. (p. 315)
—Christmas Treasury. (p. 316)
—Cinderella Kid Kit with Pop Out Coach. Cartwright, Stephen, illus. (p. 320)
—Curly the Pig Board Book. Cartwright, Stephen, illus. (p. 394)
—Dinosaurs. (p. 443)
—Dolly & the Train Sticker Book. Cartwright, Stephen, illus. (p. 464)
—Donkey Cards. Cartwright, Stephen, illus. (p. 466)
—Easter Story. (p. 499)
—Farm. Cartwright, Stephen, illus. (p. 573)
—Farmyard Tales Christmas Flap Bk And. (p. 575)
—Farmyard Tales First Word Book. (p. 575)
—Farmyard Tales Storybook. (p. 575)
—Farmyard Tales Treasury - Internet Referenced. Cartwright, Stephen, illus. (p. 575)
—First 100 Words in French. (p. 592)
—First Hundred Words. Tyler, Jenny, ed. (p. 595)
—First Hundred Words Coloring Book. (p. 595)
—First Hundred Words in Chinese. (p. 595)
—First Hundred Words in French II. (p. 595)
—First Thousand Words: With Internet-Linked Pronunciation Guide. MacKinnon, Mairi, ed. (p. 597)
—First Thousand Words in Arabic. Cartwright, Stephen, illus. (p. 597)
—First Thousand Words in Chinese: With Internet-Linked Pronunciation Guide. MacKinnon, Mairi, ed. (p. 597)
—First Thousand Words in English. Irving, Nicole, ed. (p. 597)
—First Thousand Words in Italian. Cartwright, Stephen, illus. (p. 597)
—First Thousand Words in Japanese. Cartwright, Stephen, illus. (p. 597)
—First Thousand Words in Maori. Cartwright, Stephen, illus. (p. 597)
—Goldilocks & the Three Bears. Tyler, Jenny, ed. (p. 696)
—Greek Myths. (p. 720)
—Greek Myths for Young Children. Edwards, Linda, illus. (p. 721)
—Grumpy Goat. Cartwright, Stephen, illus. (p. 727)
—Hungry Donkey. Tyler, Jenny, ed. (p. 828)
—Illustrated Children's Bible Stories. (p. 857)
—Little Book of First Stories. (p. 1025)
—Little Book of Stories of Jesus. Edwards, Linda, illus. (p. 1025)
—Little Red Riding Hood. Tyler, Jenny, ed. (p. 1035)
—Market Day. Cartwright, Stephen, illus. (p. 1095)
—Mini Children's Bible. (p. 1146)
—New Pony. Cartwright, Stephen, illus. (p. 1246)
—Old Steam Train. Cartwright, Stephen, illus. (p. 1284)
—Old Steam Train Kid Kit. Cartwright, Stephen, illus. (p. 1284)
—Old steam train sticker Book. Cartwright, Stephen, illus. (p. 1284)
—Old Testament: A Collection of Bible Stories. (p. 1284)
—Old Testament, Children's New Testament. (p. 1284)
—Oveja Rizos. Cartwright, Stephen, illus. (p. 1313)
—Princess Stories. (p. 1405)
—Red Tractor Board Book. Cartwright, Stephen, illus. (p. 1455)
—Runaway Tractor. Cartwright, Stephen, illus. (p. 1496)
—Rusty's Train Ride. Cartwright, Stephen, illus. (p. 1498)
—Scarecrow's Secret. Tyler, Jenny, ed. (p. 1519)
—Seaside. Cartwright, Stephen, illus. (p. 1538)
—Snowy Christmas Jigsaw Book. Cartwright, Stephen, illus. (p. 1601)
—Stories from Around the World. (p. 1654)
—Stories from Around the World. Edwards, Linda, illus. (p. 1654)
—Surprise Visitors. Cartwright, Stephen, illus. (p. 1686)
—Telling the Time. Tyler, Jenny & Lacey, Minna, eds. (p. 1717)
—Then & Now. Firmin, Peter, illus. (p. 1729)
—Three Little Pigs. Tyler, Jenny, ed. (p. 1742)
—Traditional Fairy Tales. (p. 1776)
—Usborne Greek Myths Jigsaw Book. Edwards, Linda, illus. (p. 1827)
—What's Biology All About? (p. 1896)
—What's Happening at the Seaside? Cartwright, Stephen, illus. (p. 1897)
—What's Happening on the Farm? Cartwright, Stephen, illus. (p. 1897)
—Where's Woolly? Tyler, Jenny, ed. (p. 1911)
—Wind-up Plane. (p. 1935)
—Woolly Stops the Train. Cartwright, Stephen, illus. (p. 1950)
—Woolly the Sheep. Cartwright, Stephen, illus. (p. 1950)
—Zoo Talkabout Board Book. Cartwright, Stephen, illus. (p. 1989)
Amery, Heather, ed. see Mayes, Susan.
Amery, Heather, jt. auth. see Cartwright, Stephen.
Amery, Heather & Cartwright, Stephen. Céad Focal: The First Hundred Words. (p. 283)
—First French Word Book. (p. 595)
—First Hundred Words in Spanish. (p. 595)
—First Hundred Words Words in Spanish. (p. 595)
—First One Hundred Words Sticker Book. (p. 596)
—First Thousand Words. (p. 597)
—Rusty's Train Ride. (p. 1498)
Amery, Heather & Doherty, Gillian. Wind-Up Tractor Book. (p. 1935)
—Wind-up Train Book. (p. 1935)
Amery, Heather & Harrison, Paul. T. Rex & Other Dangerous Dinosaurs. (p. 1694)
Amery, Heather & Temporin, Elena. Family Bible. (p. 568)
Amery, Heather, ed. Biblia para Ninos. Edwards, Linda, illus. (p. 176)
Amery, Heather, et al. First Hundred Words in Maori. (p. 595)
—Usborne Book of KnowHow. King, Colin, illus. (p. 1827)
Ames, Allison. Susie & Sasha's Tea Party (p. 1688)
Ames, Heidi L. Gisselle's Adventures in Color. del Valle, Clara J., photos by. (p. 681)
Ames, Joseph B. Pete Cow Puncher a Story of the Texas Plains. Perard, Victor, illus. (p. 1346)
Ames, Lee J. Draw 50 Airplanes, Aircraft, & Spacecraft: The Step-by-Step Way to Draw World War II Fighter Planes, Modern Jets, Space Capsules, & Much More... (p. 480)
—Draw 50 Airplanes, Aircraft, & Spacecraft. (p. 480)
—Draw 50 Animals: The Step-by-Step Way to Draw Elephants, Tigers, Dogs, Fish, Birds, & Many More... (p. 480)
—Draw 50 Animals. (p. 480)
—Draw 50 Athletes: The Step-by-Step Way to Draw Wrestlers & Figure Skaters, Baseball & Football Players, & Many More. (p. 480)
—Draw 50 Athletes. (p. 480)
—Draw 50 Baby Animals. (p. 480)
—Draw 50 Beasties: The Step-By-Step Way to Draw 50 Beasties & Yugglies & Turnover Uglies & Things That Go Bump in the Night. (p. 480)
—Draw 50 Beasties. (p. 480)
—Draw 50 Boats, Ships, Trucks, & Trains: The Step-by-Step Way to Draw Submarines, Sailboats, Dump Trucks, Locomotives, & Much More... (p. 480)
—Draw 50 Boats, Ships, Trucks, & Trains. (p. 480)
—Draw 50 Buildings & Other Structures: The Step-by-Step Way to Draw Castles & Cathedrals, Skyscrapers & Bridges, & So Much More... (p. 480)
—Draw 50 Buildings & Other Structures. (p. 480)
—Draw 50 Cars, Trucks, & Motorcycles: The Step-by-Step Way to Draw Dragsters, Vintage Cars, Dune Buggies, Mini Coopers, & Many More... (p. 480)
—Draw 50 Cars, Trucks, & Motorcycles. (p. 480)
—Draw 50 Cats: The Step-by-Step Way to Draw Domestic Breeds, Wild Cats, Cuddly Kittens, & Famous Felines. (p. 480)
—Draw 50 Cats. (p. 480)
—Draw 50 Dinosaurs & Other Prehistoric Animals: The Step-by-Step Way to Draw Tyrannosauruses, Wooly Mammoths, & Many More... (p. 480)
—Draw 50 Dinosaurs & Other Prehistoric Animals. (p. 480)
—Draw 50 Dogs. (p. 480)
—Draw 50 Endangered Animals. (p. 480)
—Draw 50 Famous Cartoons. (p. 480)
—Draw 50 Flowers, Trees, & Other Plants. (p. 480)
—Draw 50 Horses: The Step-by-Step Way to Draw Broncos, Arabians, Thoroughbreds, Dancers, Prancers, & Many More... (p. 480)
—Draw 50 Horses. (p. 480)
—Draw 50 Monsters: The Step-by-Step Way to Draw Creeps, Superheroes, Demons, Dragons, Nerds, Ghouls, Giants, Vampires, Zombies, & Other Scary Creatures. (p. 480)
—Draw 50 Monsters. (p. 480)
—Draw 50 Sharks, Whales, & Other Sea Creatures. (p. 480)
—Draw 50 Vehicles: The Step-by-Step Way to Draw Speedboats, Spaceships, Fire Trucks, & Many More... (p. 480)
—Draw 50 Vehicles. (p. 480)
—Draw the Draw 50 Way. (p. 481)
Ames, Lee J. & Ames, P. Lee. Draw 50 Flowers, Trees, & Other Plants: The Step-by-Step Way to Draw Orchids, Weeping Willows, Prickly Pears, Pineapples, & Many More... (p. 480)
Ames, Lee J. & Budd, Warren. Draw 50 Endangered Animals: The Step-by-Step Way to Draw Humpback Whales, Giant Pandas, Gorillas, & More Friends We May Lose... (p. 480)
—Draw 50 Sharks, Whales, & Other Sea Creatures: The Step-by-Step Way to Draw Great White Sharks, Killer Whales, Barracudas, Seahorses, Seals, & More... (p. 480)
Ames, Lee J. & Burns, Ray. Draw 50 Creepy Crawlies: The Step-by-Step Way to Draw Bugs, Slugs, Spiders, Scorpions, Butterflies, & Many More... (p. 480)
—Draw 50 Creepy Crawlies. (p. 480)
Ames, Lee J. & D'Adamo, Tony. Draw 50 Birds: The Step-By-Step Way to Draw Chickadees, Peacocks, Toucans, Mallards, & Many More of Our Feathered Friends. (p. 480)
—Draw 50 Birds. (p. 480)
Ames, Lee J. & Estrada, Ric. Draw 50 Aliens: The Step-by-Step Way to Draw UFOs, Galaxy Ghouls, Milky Way Marauders, & Other Extraterrestrial Creatures. (p. 480)
—Draw 50 Aliens. (p. 480)
Ames, Lee J. & Mitchell, Andrew. Draw 50 Magical Creatures: The Step-By-Step Way to Draw Unicorns, Elves, Cherubs, Trolls, & Many More. (p. 480)
—Draw 50 Magical Creatures. (p. 480)
Ames, Lee J. & Moylan, Holly Handler. Draw 50 Princesses. (p. 480)
Ames, Lee J. & Zak, Murray. Draw 50 Baby Animals: The Step-by-Step Way to Draw Kittens, Lambs, Chicks, & Other Adorable Offspring. (p. 480)
Ames, Michelle. Firefighters in Our Community. (p. 591)
—Librarians in Our Community. (p. 1005)
—Police Officers in Our Community. (p. 1380)
—Teachers in Our Community. (p. 1709)
—Veterinarians in Our Community. (p. 1839)
Ames, Mildred. Anna to the Infinite Power. (p. 85)
Ames, P. Lee, jt. auth. see Ames, Lee J.
Ames, Philippe, illus. see Hanh, Thich Nhat.
Amestoy, Jennifer. Junkyard Junction: The Story of the Magic Microwave. (p. 936)
Amft, Robert. Peter's ABC Book: Peter Learns about Animals, Birds, Fishes, & Insects. (p. 1347)
Amholt, Laurence. Collins Big Cat - Royal Rap. Morenton, Alice, illus. (p. 340)
Amici, Raffaele Roncalli. History of the American Association of Veterinary Parasitologists (1956-2005) (p. 784)
Amico, Erin. Viol. (p. 1843)
Amico, Sal. Come Back, Zack! (p. 347)
Amidon Lusted, Marcia. Career Building Through Using Multimedia Art & Animation Tools. (p. 266)
—Civic Unrest: Investigate the Struggle for Social Change. Chandhok, Lena, illus. (p. 324)
—Jump-Starting a Career in Physical Therapy & Rehabilitation. (p. 934)
—Roaring Twenties: Discover the Era of Prohibition, Flappers, & Jazz. Keller, Jennifer, illus. (p. 1478)
Amidon Lusted, Marcia, jt. auth. see Leusted, Marcia Amidon.
Amihud, Zohar. Look Mom! I Built My Own Web Site. (p. 1049)
Amin, Ahmed. Mountains of Kohqaf. (p. 1181)
Amin, Heba, illus. see Maydell, Natalie & Riahi, Sep.
Amini, Mehrdokht, illus. see Khan, Hena.
Amini-Holmes, Liz, illus. see Jordan-Fenton, Christy & Pokiak-Fenton, Margaret.
Amini-Holmes, Liz, illus. see Jordan-Fenton, Christy, et al.
Amiot, Karine-Marie, et al. Catholic Bible for Children. Bienfait, Andree, illus. (p. 280)
Amir, Amin Abd al-Fattah Mahmud, illus. see Ahmed, Said Salah, tr.
Amir, Amin Abd al-Fattah Mahmud, illus. see Moriarty, Kathleen M.
Amirault, Ras Steven. Rastafarian Mysticism: An Introduction to the Mysteries of Nyahbinghi. (p. 1440)
Amirkhan, Michele. Princess Elian's Quest. (p. 1403)
Amis, John M., ed. see Rutsky, R. L.
Amitzahandreanias. Weebles & the Cake Walk (p. 1871)
Amler, Jane Frances. Haym Salomon: Patriot Banker of the American Revolution. (p. 755)
Amma, Jill. Indaba Tree Odyssey: An African Tale. (p. 870)
Amman, Jurg. Fairy Tale of the World. Bhend, Kathi, illus. (p. 564)
—Ten Birds. Gebert, Helga, illus. (p. 1718)
Ammann, Michael. Exos. (p. 548)
Ammann, Victor. Shepherd Boy & the Bethlehem Star. (p. 1565)
Ammary, Neyal J. In Mommy's Garden: A Book to Help Explain Cancer to Young Children. Risch, Christopher, illus. (p. 864)
Ammassari, Rita, illus. see MacKenzie, Catherine.
Ammerman, Michelle. Amos's Beautiful Day. (p. 65)
Ammirati, Christelle, illus. see Souza, Cláudia.
Ammirato, Lidia. Why Does the Dog Chase the Cat & the Cat Chase the Mouse? (p. 1924)
Ammon, Richard. Valley Forge. Farnsworth, Bill, illus. (p. 1830)
Ammon, Rob, Jr., et al. Sport Facility Management: Organizing Events & Mitigating Risks. (p. 1631)
Ammons, David F., ed. see Garza, Amy Ammons.
Ammons, Sherilyn, ed. see Garza, Amy Ammons.
Amnesty International Australia Staff, told to. We Are All Born Free: The Universal Declaration of Human Rights in Pictures. (p. 1865)
Amnesty International Staff. Dreams of Freedom: In Words & Pictures. (p. 484)
—We Are All Born Free: The Universal Declaration of Human Rights in Pictures. (p. 1865)
Amnesty International Staff, ed. Free? Stories about Human Rights. (p. 633)
Amnesty International Staff, told to. We Are All Born Free: The Universal Declaration of Human Rights in Pictures. (p. 1865)
Amo, Javier del, see del Amo, Javier.
Amo, Montserrat del, jt. auth. see Del Amo, Montserrat.
Amodei, Michael, jt. auth. see Sawyer, Kieran.
Amodeo, Cristina, illus. see Friedman, Samantha & Matisse, Henri.
Amodeo, Darlene. Samantha & the Soldier: A Letter of Love. (p. 1507)
Amodeo, Jessica & Pecsenye, Jessica. University of Colorado College Prowler off the Record. (p. 1820)
Amollo, Regina. When Mother Leaves Home. (p. 1903)
Amon, Evelyne, et al. Vis-a-Vis: Beginning French. (p. 1844)
Amon, Ras Ran. Gerald, Fish of the Spirit! A Caribbean Tale of Fortune & Greed. Betiku, Olatukunbo, illus. (p. 666)
—Gerald Fish of the Spirit! Activity Book. (p. 666)
Amon, Ras Ran, adapted by. Gerald, Fish of the Spirit! A Caribbean Tale of Fortune & Greed. (p. 666)
Amooti. Grandma Yarumia Fireside Stories: Bible Stories for Children. (p. 708)
Amore, Dani, et al. Samurai Summer Carlsson, Per, tr. (p. 1510)
Amore, Joanne. Joe's Fruit Store (p. 920)
Amore, Sandra. Princess Who Lived on the 174th Floor. (p. 1406)
Amoroso, Cynthia. Airplanes. (p. 32)
—Courage. (p. 372)
—Dump Trucks. (p. 489)
—Fire Trucks. (p. 591)
—Forgiveness. (p. 619)

—Friendliness. (p. 637)
—Generosity. (p. 660)
—Hold Your Horses! (And Other Peculiar Sayings) Cole, Memie & Gallagher-Cole, Memie, illus. (p. 788)
—Honesty. (p. 794)
—Hot Pot: The Sound of Short O. (p. 802)
—I'm All Thumbs! (and Other Odd Things We Say) Gallagher-Cole, Memie, illus. (p. 858)
—It's a Long Shot! (and Other Strange Sayings) Gallagher-Cole, Memie, illus. (p. 895)
—Loyalty. (p. 1061)
—On the Boat: The Sound of Long O. (p. 1289)
—Patience. (p. 1328)
—Patriotism. (p. 1329)
—Responsibility. (p. 1463)
—Ten Pets: The Sound of Short E. (p. 1719)
—Thankfulness. (p. 1725)
—That's the Last Straw! (And Other Weird Things We Say) Gallagher-Cole, Memie, illus. (p. 1727)
—Tolerance. (p. 1762)
—Tow Trucks. (p. 1773)
—William Mckinley. (p. 1933)
Amoroso, Cynthia, jt. auth. see Ballard, Peg.
Amoroso, Cynthia, jt. auth. see Noyed, Bob.
Amoroso, Cynthia & Noyed, Bob. What a Week: The Sound of Long E. (p. 1878)
Amoroso, Cynthia & Noyed, Robert B. Drums. (p. 487)
—Fall. (p. 566)
—Guitars. (p. 731)
—Pianos. (p. 1354)
—Spring. (p. 1634)
—Summer. (p. 1673)
—Trumpets. (p. 1793)
—Winter. (p. 1937)
Amory, Deanna, illus. see Neuhofer, Sheri L.
Amory, Jay. Fledging of Az Gabrielson. (p. 603)
Amos, Angela. 'Twas the Fight Before Christmas. (p. 1799)
Amos, Eduardo & Pearson Education Staff. Amazon Rally. (p. 56)
Amos, H. D. & Lang, A. G. These Were the Greeks. (p. 1732)
Amos, Janine. After You. (p. 28)
—Courteous Kids Spenceley, Annabel, illus. (p. 373)
—Death. (p. 419)
—Divorce. (p. 455)
—Don't Do That! How Not to Act. (p. 467)
—Going to the Hospital. (p. 693)
—Hello! (p. 763)
—I'm Sorry. (p. 860)
—Is Helen Pregnant. (p. 889)
—Moving. (p. 1183)
—No, Thank You. (p. 1260)
—Please. (p. 1373)
—Thank You. (p. 1725)
Amos, Janine & Spenceley, Annabel. Don't Do That! How Not to Act. (p. 467)
—Don't Say That! Let's Talk Nicely. (p. 468)
—Go Away! What Not to Say. (p. 686)
—It Won't Work! Let's Try Again. (p. 894)
—It's Mine! Let's Try to Share. (p. 897)
—Let's Be Kind (p. 994)
—Let's Be Kind. (p. 994)
—Let's Help Out! (p. 998)
—Let's Make Friends. (p. 999)
—Let's Own Up. (p. 999)
—Let's Share. (p. 1000)
—Let's Take Turns. (p. 1001)
—Move Over! Learning to Share Our Space. (p. 1183)
Amos, Michael Paul. Rocktastic Corduroy Peach. (p. 1484)
Amos, Muriel & Olrun, Prudy. Animals of Nunivak Island. Amos, Muriel & Olrun, Prudy, illus. (p. 83)
Amos, Ruth. Race for Chi. (p. 1430)
Amos, Ruth, jt. auth. see Dorling Kindersley Publishing Staff.
Amoss, Berthe. Draw Yourself into a Starlit Journey. (p. 481)
—Draw Yourself into the Ark with Noah & His Family. (p. 481)
—Loup Garou Amoss, Berthe, illus. (p. 1059)
—Mischief & Malice. (p. 1150)
—Secret Lives. (p. 1541)
Amowitz, Lisa. Vision. (p. 1844)
Ampel, Kenneth Robert, illus. see Westra, Elizabeth.
Amper, Susan. Bloom's How to Write about Edgar Allan Poe. (p. 201)
Ampudia, María Jesús, tr. see Nöstlinger, Christine.
Amrein, Paul, illus. see Soundar, Chitra.
Amrine, Matt. Mook the Ranger & the Seed of Fear. (p. 1171)
AMSCO Publications Staff & Hal Leonard Corp. Staff, creators. Super Songbook for Kids. (p. 1682)
Amsden, Charles Avery. America's Earliest Man. (p. 64)
Amsel, Sheri. Human Body Book: All You Need to Know about Your Body Systems - From Head to Toe! (p. 825)
—Kids' Environment Book: Learn How You Can Help the Environment - By Getting Involved at School, at Home, or at Play. (p. 953)
Amstel, Marsha. Horse-Riding Adventure of Sybil Ludington, Revolutionary War Messenger. Hammond, Ted & Carbajal, Richard, illus. (p. 800)
—Horse-Riding Adventure of Sybil Ludington, Revolutionary War Messenger. Hammond, Ted & Carbajal, Richard Pimentel, illus. (p. 800)
Amster, Linda, ed. see New York Times Staff.
Amstutz, Andre, illus. see Ahlberg, Allan.
Amstutz, L. J. Ancient Egypt. (p. 68)
—Investigating Animal Life Cycles. (p. 884)
—Investigating Plant Life Cycles. (p. 885)
Amstutz, Lisa. Cicadas (p. 318)
Amstutz, Lisa J. All Kinds of Bikes: Off-Road to Easy-Riders (p. 44)
—Backyard Birds. (p. 131)
—Bicycle Basics: Let It Roll! (p. 177)
—Bike Safety: A Crash Course (p. 185)
—Cardinals. (p. 266)
—Centipedes (p. 287)
—Cockroaches (p. 337)
—Creepy Crawlers. (p. 381)
—Giraffes Are Awesome! (p. 678)
—Goldfinches. (p. 695)
—House Sparrows. (p. 803)
—Lions Are Awesome! (p. 1021)
—Meerkats Are Awesome! (p. 1120)
—Polar Animal Adaptations (p. 1378)
—Rain Forest Animal Adaptations (p. 1434)
—Robins. (p. 1480)
—Show Me Polar Animals: My First Picture Encyclopedia (p. 1570)
—Simple Bike Maintenance: Time for a Tune-Up! (p. 1577)
—Spokes (p. 1630)
—Thorny Devil Lizards & Other Extreme Reptile Adaptations (p. 1740)
—Titanic. (p. 1757)
—What Eats What in a Forest Food Chain McLaughlin, Zack, illus. (p. 1884)
—What Eats What in a Rain Forest Food Chain Wertheim, Anne, illus. (p. 1884)
—Which Seed Is This? (p. 1911)
—Whose Egg Is This? (p. 1921)
Amstutz, Lisa J., jt. auth. see Murphy, Julie.
Amstutz, Lisa J., et al. Awesome African Animals. (p. 120)
—My First Picture Encyclopedias. (p. 1207)
Amstutz, Lorraine Stutzman, jt. auth. see Zehr, Howard.
Amundsen, Allen. Olive Juice: A Ten-Minute Dramatic Duet. (p. 1285)
—Soul Solution: A Ten-Minute Comedy Duet. (p. 1614)
Amundson, Sandi. Zach & Dougie Dragonfly's Adventure. (p. 1984)
Amundson, Susan. Free to Be Me: The Eskimo Way. Geiken, Brenda, illus. (p. 634)
Amundson, Susan D. Three Little Lambs— Somewhere. Geiken, Brenda Joy, illus. (p. 1742)
Amy Belle Elementary School, illus. see Stoll, Scott.
Amy, Brooks. Princess Polly Stories. (p. 1405)
Amy Brooks. Randy & Her Friends. (p. 1438)
Amy, Holloway, illus. see Trimper, Marty.
Amy Huntington, illus. see Anderson, Jill.
Amya Penny Anysia Turpin. Jesus & Me. (p. 915)
An, Carlos, illus. see Harbo, Christopher L.
An, Jiyoung, illus. see Frazer, Rebecca.
An, Jiyoung, illus. see Man-Kong, Mary.
An, Sang, photos by see Nebens, Amy M.
Ana, Moh. Kookaburra Tales: Shy Not, My Friend. (p. 967)
—Kookaburra Tales # 3: Laugh Not at Others. (p. 967)
Anagost, Karen, illus. see Gandolfi, Claudine.
Anagost, Karen, illus. see Unser, Virginia.
Anaiah, Ruth, text. Through it All: A Journey through Life's Adversities. (p. 1745)
Ananda, Kul & Houlder, Dominic J. Mind Fulness & Money: The Buddhist Path of Abundance. (p. 1145)
Ananda, Linda. Rainbow Childrenr-Magical Moving Stories: Stories with Movement, Dance, Yoga, & Song. (p. 1435)
Ananthanarayanan, Ashraya. Ring of Hope. (p. 1473)
Anasal, Arshes, ed. see Bemelmans, Ludwig.
Anastas, Margaret. Hug for You. Winter, Susan, photos by. (p. 824)
—Mommy's Best Kisses. Winter, Susan, illus. (p. 1162)
Anastasi, Donna. Gerbils: The Complete Guide to Gerbil Care. Bellini, Ellen, photos by. (p. 666)
Anastasia School, Amerigo. Powerful Hands. (p. 1390)
Anastasio, Andrea, jt. auth. see Wolf, Gita.
Anastasio, Antonio. Agujero en el Ala. Garcia de la Viuda, Miriam, tr. (p. 30)
Anastasio, Dina. Everyone Clapped for Jason: Set Of 6. (p. 544)
—Hiding in the Sea & Escondidos en el Mar: 6 English, 6 Spanish Adaptations. (p. 777)
—How Raven Became Black & Owl Got Its Spots & Por qué el cuervo es negro y el búho tiene Manchitas: 6 English, 6 Spanish Adaptations. (p. 812)
—Magic Turtle: Set Of 6. (p. 1074)
—Magic Turtle. (p. 1074)
—Magic Turtle & la tortuga Mágica: 6 English, 6 Spanish Adaptations. (p. 1074)
—Mask Making Around the World: Set Of 6. (p. 1102)
—Mask Making Around the World. (p. 1102)
—Math Fun at the Fair & Matemáticas divertidas en la Feria: 6 English, 6 Spanish Adaptations. (p. 1106)
—My Secret Book. (p. 1218)
—Number Games: Set Of 6. (p. 1271)
—Number Games. (p. 1271)
—Question of Time. (p. 1426)
—Who Was Steve Irwin? (p. 1919)
—Who Was Steve Irwin? Eldridge, Jim, illus. (p. 1919)
Anastasio, Dina & Brown, Dinah. Who Is Malala Yousafzai? Thomson, Andrew, illus. (p. 1916)
Anastasio, Dina & Jenkins, Amanda. Jake Digs a Hole, Luke & the Bug Man: (p. 906)
Anastasio, Dina, retold by. How Raven Became Black & Owl Got Its Spots: Set Of 6. (p. 812)
Anastasiu, Heather. Glitch. (p. 683)
—Override. (p. 1314)
—Shutdown. (p. 1572)
Anastos, Ernie. Ernie & the Big Newz. (p. 534)
Anawalt, Seth. Harry Had A Good Day. (p. 750)
—Treasure of Santa Maria. (p. 1782)
Anaxos Inc. Staff, contrib. by. UXL Encyclopedia of Weather & Natural Disasters. (p. 1829)
Anaya, Hector. Cuenta Cuenta. Moreno, Sergio, illus. (p. 389)
Anaya, Josefina, tr. see Friedman, Laurie.
Anaya Publishers Staff. Aprender a Vivir 1. (p. 93)
—Aprender a Vivir 2: Propuesta Didactica. (p. 93)
—Aprender a Vivir 2. (p. 93)
—Aprender a Vivir 3: Propuesta Didactica. (p. 93)
—Aprender a Vivir 3. (p. 93)
—Aprender a Vivir 4: Propuesta Didactica. (p. 93)
—Aprender a Vivir 4. (p. 93)
—Aprender a Vivir 5: Propuesta Didactica. (p. 93)
—Aprender a Vivir 5. (p. 93)
—Aprender a Vivir 6: Propuesta Didactica. (p. 93)
—Aprender a Vivir 6. (p. 93)
Anaya, Rudolfo. ChupaCabra & the Roswell UFO. (p. 318)
—Curse of the ChupaCabra. (p. 395)
—First Tortilla: A Bilingual Story. Lamadrid, Enrique R., tr. (p. 597)
—How Hollyhocks Came to New Mexico. Garcia, Nasario, tr. (p. 809)
Anaya, Rudolfo, jt. auth. see Anaya, Rudolfo A.
Anaya, Rudolfo A. First Tortilla. (p. 597)
—How Chile Came to New Mexico. Nasario, Garcia, tr. (p. 805)
—Llorona: The Crying Woman. Lamadrid, Enrique R., tr. (p. 1043)
—Santero's Miracle: A Bilingual Story. Lamadrid, Enrique R., tr. (p. 1513)
Anaya, Rudolfo A. & Anaya, Rudolfo. Curse of the ChupaCabra. (p. 395)
—First Tortilla: A Bilingual Story. Lamadrid, Enrique R., tr. from ENG. (p. 597)
—Tortuga: A Novel. (p. 1771)
Anbinder, Adrienne. Clarence Blooms in Winter. Pickman, Marian, illus. (p. 327)
Ancell, Carolyn. World of Saints. (p. 1957)
Anchin, Lisa, illus. see Lewis, Suzanne.
Ancona, George. Can We Help? Kids Volunteering to Help Their Communities. Ancona, George, illus. (p. 258)
—Capoeira: Game! Dance! Martial Art! (p. 263)
—Come & Eat! (p. 347)
—Come & Eat! Ancona, George, photos by. (p. 347)
—Fiesta Fireworks. (p. 584)
—It's Our Garden: From Seeds to Harvest in a School Garden. Ancona, George, illus. (p. 898)
—Let's Eat. (p. 996)
—Mi Casa: My House. (p. 1132)
—Mi Escuela: My School. (p. 1132)
—Mi Familia. (p. 1132)
—Mi Musica. (p. 1133)
—Mis Comidas - My Foods. (p. 1150)
—Mis Fiestas: My Celebrations. (p. 1150)
—Mis Juegos/My Games. (p. 1150)
—Mis Quehaceres - My Chores. (p. 1150)
—Murals: Walls That Sing (p. 1192)
—Olé Flamenco! Ancona, George, photos by. (p. 1285)
—Self Portrait. Ancona, George, photos by. (p. 1549)
Ancona, George, photos by see Becker, Michelle Aki.
Ancona, George, photos by see Bredeson, Carmen.
Ancona, George, photos by see De Capua, Sarah.
Ancona, George, photos by see Mora, Pat.
Anctil, Chad. Midnight Tree. (p. 1139)
And Bean. Pronouns on the Farm. (p. 1411)
and Ellen Brenneman, John W. Lane. Friend Indeed. (p. 637)
& Packer, Knife & McCoshan, Duncan. Captain Fact's Creepy Crawly Adventure. (p. 264)
Andelin, Darline. Easy String Art for All Seasons. (p. 500)
Ander, jt. auth. see Ander.
Ander & Ander. Me & My Bike. (p. 1115)
Anders, Bill. Becoming Noah. (p. 156)
Anders, C. R. Just Me. (p. 939)
—One Great Love We All Wished We Had. (p. 1295)
Anders, Isabel. Easter ABCs. (p. 499)
—Easter ABCs. Rasche, Shelly, illus. (p. 499)
Anders, Lou. Frostborn. (p. 644)
—Nightborn. (p. 1255)
Anders, Shirley. Land of Alphabet: Adventures of Mr. Scribe. (p. 973)
Andersdatter, Karla. Never-Nuff Nasty. (p. 1243)
Andersdatter, Karla Margaret. Marissa the Tooth Fairy. Koff, Deborah, illus. (p. 1094)
Andersen, jt. auth. see Andersen, Hans Christian.
Andersen, Alan Lance. Wizard Academies - Rumpots, Crackpots, & Pooka-Mazed Halfwits. (p. 1942)
Andersen, Amy Elliott, illus. see Elliott, Chris.
Andersen, Bethane, illus. see Sasso, Sandy Eisenberg.
Andersen, Bethanne, illus. see Bryant, Jen.
Andersen, Bethanne, illus. see Hearne, Betsy.
Andersen, Bethanne, illus. see McDonough, Yona Zeldis.
Andersen, C. B. Book of Mormon Sleuth: The Hidden Path. Vol. 3 (p. 211)
—Forgotten Treasure. (p. 620)
—Secret Mission. (p. 1542)
Andersen, D. R. Matter Marvels. (p. 1109)
—Paul Bunyan Builds a Mighty Mountain. (p. 1330)
—Why the Moon Changes in the Night Sky. (p. 1926)
Andersen, Dana Lynne, illus. see Morgan, Jennifer.
Andersen, David W. Tell Us a Story about Flying. (p. 1717)
Andersen, Flemming, illus. see Laban, Terry.
Andersen, Gregg, photos by see Ayers, Amy.
Andersen, Gregg, photos by see Early Macken, JoAnn.
Andersen, Gregg, photos by see Freese, Joan.
Andersen, Gregg, photos by see Gorman, Jacqueline Laks & Laks Gorman, Jacqueline.
Andersen, Gregg, photos by see Gorman, Jacqueline Laks.
Andersen, Gregg, photos by see Knowlton, MaryLee & Dowdy, Penny.
Andersen, Gregg, photos by see Knowlton, MaryLee.
Andersen, Gregg, photos by see Laks Gorman, Jacqueline.
Andersen, Gregg, photos by see Rauen, Amy & Ayers, Amy.
Andersen, Hans Christian. Andersen's Fairy Tales. (p. 72)
—Ariel & the Secret Grotto. (p. 98)
—Constant Tin Soldier. (p. 359)
—Elf of the Rose & Other Tales. (p. 512)
—Emperor & the Nightingale. Van Nutt, Robert, illus. (p. 520)
—Emperor's New Clothes: The Graphic Novel Timmins, Jeffrey Stewart, illus. (p. 521)
—Emperor's New Clothes: An All-Star Illustrated Retelling of the Classic Fairy Tale. (p. 521)
—Emperor's New Clothes. (p. 521)
—Emperor's New Clothes. Van Nutt, Robert, illus. (p. 521)
—Fairy Tales from Many Lands. Rackham, Arthur, illus. (p. 564)
—Fairy Tales of Hans Christian Andersen. (p. 564)
—Fairy Tales of Hans Christian Andersen. Daniel, Noel & Kobler, Florian, eds. (p. 564)
—For Sure! for Sure! White, Mus, tr. from DAN. (p. 616)
—Hans Andersen's Fairy Tales: A Selection. Kingsland, L. W., tr. from DAN. (p. 743)
—Hans Andersen's Fairy Tales. Lewis, Naomi, tr. from DAN. (p. 743)
—Hans Christian Andersen: Illustrated Fairy Tales. (p. 743)
—Hans Christian Andersen: The Complete Stories Hersholt, Jean, tr. from DAN. (p. 743)
—Hans Christian Andersen: The Complete Fairy Tales. Hersholt, Jean P., tr. from DAN. (p. 743)
—Hans Christian Andersen. Tatar, Maria, ed. (p. 743)
—Hans Christian Andersen 1805-75: The Collected Tales. (p. 743)
—Hans Christian Andersen Illustrated Fairytales: The Brave Tin Soldier; Clod Hans; A Gift for Hans; The Ugly Duckling. Vol. V (p. 743)
—Hans Christian Andersen Illustrated Fairytales: The Wild Swans; The Traveling Companion; The Jewish Maiden; The Toad. Vol. VI (p. 743)
—Hans Christian Andersen Illustrated Fairytales: The Snow Queen; The Little Match Girl; The Little Mermaid; She Was Good for Nothing. Vol. 1 (p. 743)
—Hans Christian Andersen Illustrated Fairytales: It's Absolutely True; The Pigkeeper; Little Claus & Big Claus; The Racers; The Buckwheat. Vol. II (p. 743)
—Hans Christian Andersen Illustrated Fairytales: The Snowdrop; There Is a Difference; The Emperor's New Clothes; Thumbelina; What the Old Man Does. Vol. IV (p. 743)
—Hans Christian Andersen Illustrated Fairytales. (p. 743)
—Hans Christian Andersen Tales. (p. 743)
—Hans Christian Andersen's Fairy Tales. Bell, Anthea, tr. from GER. (p. 743)
—Ice-Maiden & Other Tales. Fuller, Fanny, tr. (p. 850)
—IceMaiden & Other Tales. (p. 851)
—Little Match Girl. (p. 1031)
—Little Match Seller. (p. 1031)
—Little Mermaid. (p. 1031)
—Little Mermaid. Capdevila, Francesc, illus. (p. 1031)
—Little Mermaid & Other Fairy Tales. (p. 1031)
—Little Mermaid & Other Fairy Tales. Kliros, Thea, illus. (p. 1031)
—Little Mermaid & Other Tales. (p. 1031)
—Little Mermaid & the Princess & the Pea: Two Tales & Their Histories. Brown, Carron, ed. (p. 1031)
—Little Mermaid Retold. Charlotte, J. M., illus. (p. 1031)
—Little Tin Soldier. (p. 1037)
—Nightingale. Oleynikov, Igor, illus. (p. 1255)
—Patito Feo. (p. 1328)
—Pictures of Sweden. (p. 1356)
—Princess & the Pea: The Graphic Novel Lamoreaux, M. A., illus. (p. 1402)
—Princess & the Pea: The Graphic Novel Lamoreaux, M. A. & Lamoreaux, Michelle, illus. (p. 1402)
—Princess & the Pea. (p. 1402)
—Princess & the Pea. Pixley, Pippa, illus. (p. 1402)
—Princess & the Pea. Kolanovic, Dubravka, illus. (p. 1402)
—Princess & the Pea (La Princesa y el Guisante) Estrada, Pau, illus. (p. 1402)
—Pulgarcilla. (p. 1415)
—Racers: A Tale about Fairness. Goodell, Jon, illus. (p. 1431)
—Red Shoes. (p. 1455)
—Reina de las Nieves. (p. 1457)
—Reina de las Nieves. Bravo-Villasante, Carmen, tr. (p. 1457)
—Ruisenor. (p. 1494)
—Snezhnaya Koroleva - the Snow Queen. Pym, T., illus. (p. 1597)
—Snow Queen. (p. 1599)
—Snow Queen. Lynch, P. J., illus. (p. 1599)
—Snow Queen. Dulac, Edmund, illus. (p. 1599)
—Snow Queen. Bogdanovic, Toma, illus. (p. 1599)
—Snow Queen. Sumberac, Manuel, illus. (p. 1599)
—Snow Queen. Tatamikov, Pavel, illus. (p. 1599)
—Snow Queen. Ibatoulline, Bagram, illus. (p. 1599)
—Snow Queen & Other Tales. (p. 1599)
—Steadfast Tin Soldier. Jorgensen, David, illus. (p. 1645)
—Stories from Hans Andersen. (p. 1654)
—Swineherd. (p. 1691)
—Tales of Hans Christian Andersen. Stewart, Joel, illus. (p. 1702)
—Thumbelina: Hans Christian Andersen Illustrated Fairytales. (p. 1745)
—Thumbelina. (p. 1745)
—Thumbelina. Johnson, David, illus. (p. 1745)
—Thumbelina. Lai, Hsin-Shih, illus. (p. 1745)
—Thumbelina. Pinkney, Brian, illus. (p. 1745)
—Thumbelina. Vivanco, Kelly, illus. (p. 1745)
—Thumbelina. Ibatoulline, Bagram, illus. (p. 1745)
—Traje Nuevo del Emperador. (p. 1777)
—Ugly Duckling: The Graphic Novel Blecha, Aaron, illus. (p. 1808)
—Ugly Duckling: Hans Christian Andersen Illustrated Fairytales. (p. 1808)
—Ugly Duckling. Van Nutt, Robert, illus. (p. 1808)
—Ugly Duckling & Other Fairy Tales. Golden, Harriet, illus. (p. 1808)
—Ugly Duckling & Other Tales. (p. 1808)
—We Both Read-The Emperor's New Clothes. (p. 1866)
—We Both Read-Thumbelina (Picture Book) Bell, Elizabeth, tr. from FRE. (p. 1866)
—What the Moon Saw & Other Tales. (p. 1893)
—Wild Swans: A Tale of Persistence. Lohmann, Renate, illus. (p. 1930)
—Wild Swans. (p. 1930)
—Wild Swans. Lewis, Naomi, tr. from DAN. (p. 1930)
—Wild Swans. Maguire, Thomas Aquinas, illus. (p. 1930)
—Wild Swans & Other Tales. (p. 1930)
Andersen, Hans Christian, jt. auth. see Boada, Francesc.
Andersen, Hans Christian, jt. auth. see Brothers Grimm.
Andersen, Hans Christian, jt. auth. see Filipek, Nina.
Andersen, Hans Christian, jt. auth. see Guillain, Charlotte.
Andersen, Hans Christian, jt. auth. see McFadden, Deanna.
Andersen, Hans Christian, jt. auth. see Namm, Diane.
Andersen, Hans Christian, jt. auth. see Olmstead, Kathleen.

Andersen, Hans Christian, jt. auth. see Poole, Amy Lowry.
Andersen, Hans Christian, jt. auth. see Rylant, Cynthia.
Andersen, Hans Christian, jt. auth. see Sneed, Brad.
Andersen, Hans Christian, jt. auth. see Woodward, Kay.
Andersen, Hans Christian & Andersen. Cuentos de Andersen. Rackham, Arthur, illus. (p. 389)
Andersen, Hans Christian & Capstone Press Editors. Bella y la Bestia: La Novela Grafica. Feldman, Luke, illus. (p. 162)
Andersen, Hans Christian & Capstone Press Staff. Caperucita Roja. Rivas, Victor, illus. (p. 262)
—Cenicienta. Feely, Maria Luisa, tr. (p. 286)
—Hansel y Gretel: La Novela Grafica. Dietrich, Sean, illus. (p. 743)
—Jack y los Frijoles Magicos. Tercio, Ricardo, illus. (p. 903)
—Rumpelstiltskin: La Novela Grafica. Valdez Y Alanis, Erik, illus. (p. 1495)
Andersen, Hans Christian & Christian, Andersen Hans. Cisnes Salvajes. (p. 322)
—Cuentos de Andersen. (p. 389)
Andersen, Hans Christian & Combel Editorial Staff. Patito Feo. Bordoy, Irene, illus. (p. 1328)
Andersen, Hans Christian & Falloon, Jane. Thumbelina. Chichester Clark, Emma, illus. (p. 1745)
Andersen, Hans Christian & Fowler, Gloria. Red Shoes. Yung Yoo, Sun, illus. (p. 1455)
Andersen, Hans Christian & Kurt, Robert. Ugly Duckling. Watts, Bernadette, illus. (p. 1808)
Andersen, Hans Christian & Lewis, Naomi. Steadfast Tin Soldier. Lynch, P. J., illus. (p. 1645)
Andersen, Hans Christian & Sandoval, Gerardo. Thumbelina: The Graphic Novel Horne, Sarah, illus. (p. 1745)
Andersen, Hans Christian & Starbright Foundation Staff. Emperor's New Clothes. Burton, Virginia Lee, illus. (p. 521)
Andersen, Hans Christian & Stevenson, Robert Louis. Swing. Morriss, Deborah & Morstad, Julie, illus. (p. 1691)
Andersen, Hans Christian & Stone Arch Books Staff. Bella y la Bestia: La Novela Grafica Feldman, Luke, illus. (p. 162)
—Caperucita Roja. Rivas, Victor, illus. (p. 262)
—Cenicienta: La Novela Grafica. Timmins, Jeffrey Stewart, illus. (p. 286)
—Hansel y Gretel: La Novela Grafica. Dietrich, Sean, illus. (p. 743)
—Jack y los Frijoles Magicos. Tercio, Ricardo, illus. (p. 903)
—Rumpelstiltskin: La Novela Grafica Alanis, Erik Valdez Y., illus. (p. 1495)
Andersen, Hans Christian & White, Mus. For Sure! for Sure! Czernecki, Stefan, illus. (p. 616)
Andersen, Hans Christian, et al. Best Fairy Tales Boxed Set: Aesop, Hans Christian Andersen, the Brothers Grimm & Celtic Fairy Tales Jacobs, Joseph, ed. (p. 169)
—Stories of Hans Christian Andersen: A New Translation from the Danish. Frank, Diana Crone & Frank, Jeffrey Crone, eds. (p. 1655)
Andersen, Hans Christian, tr. Andersen's Fairy Tales. (p. 71)
—Andersen's Fairy Tales. (p. 72)
Andersen, Jessica. Nightkeepers. (p. 1255)
Andersen, Matthew. Mike & His Marvelous Flying Bike (p. 1141)
Andersen, Neil. WWW: Surfing with Celebrities. (p. 1966)
Andersen, Neil & Capstone Press Staff. At the Controls: Questioning Video & Computer Games (p. 111)
Andersen Press Staff, ed. see Cooper, Susan, et al.
Andersen, Richard. Abraham Rodriguez. (p. 7)
—Arthur Miller. (p. 104)
—Richard III. (p. 1469)
—Toni Morrison. (p. 1765)
—Walter Dean Myers. (p. 1856)
Andersen, Susan. Nephi Breaks His Bow. (p. 1241)
Andersen, Victoria. Toobeez Language Arts Activity Workbook: The Toobeez Language Arts Program Provides Teachers with Collaborative Hands-on Activities for Reading, Writing & Grammar Instruction. Andersen, Victoria, ed. (p. 1767)
Andersen, W. H. Hooray for the Red, White, & Blue: A Content Area Reader-Social Studies. (p. 796)
Andersen-Murphy. If You Believe. (p. 854)
Anderson, ed. see Degenhardt, Scott.
Anderson, A. J. BMX Biking. (p. 204)
Anderson, Aaron, illus. see Pfundstein, Valerie.
Anderson, Abby. Saudi Arabia. (p. 1516)
Anderson, Airlie. Cows in the Kitchen. (p. 374)
—Cows in the Kitchen W/ (p. 374)
—Momo & Snap. (p. 1163)
—Ten Little Ducks. (p. 1719)
—Very Furry Flap Book. (p. 1838)
—Very Patchy Flap Book. (p. 1838)
—Very Spotty Flap Book. (p. 1838)
—Very Stripy Flap Book. (p. 1839)
—What to Doodle? Jr. —Princesses, Fairies, Mermaids & More! (p. 1894)
Anderson, Airlie, illus. see Hayes, Larry E.
Anderson, Airlie, illus. see Hayes, Larry.
Anderson, Al. Adventures with Bingo Borden. Agora Publications Staff, tr. (p. 25)
Anderson, Alan, jt. auth. see Rowe, Ruth.
Anderson, Alasdair, illus. see Hoyle, Geoffrey.
Anderson, Alice. Danny Be Good! (p. 405)
—Penny's Love for Cats. (p. 1338)
Anderson, Amanda. Story of Larry the Hamster. (p. 1658)
Anderson, Amelia, illus. see Teckentrup, Britta.
Anderson, Amy, ed. see Mauerman, Nancy.
Anderson, Andrea Patrice. Heaven's Diary: Our Gift from God. (p. 761)
Anderson, Angela. Civil Wars, 1640-9. (p. 326)
Anderson, Annette Latva. Alone into Darkness: Was It Fate or an Error in Judgment? (p. 48)
Anderson, AnnMarie. When I Grow up - Abraham Lincoln. Kelley, Gerald, illus. (p. 1903)
—When I Grow up - Sally Ride. Kelley, Gerald, illus. (p. 1903)
Anderson, Anya, illus. see Wreggelsworth, Irene.
Anderson, Ashley. My Day with Jesus. (p. 1201)
Anderson, Bendix. Security Dogs. (p. 1546)
Anderson, Bethan, illus. see Bryant, Jen.
Anderson, Bethanne, illus. see Hopkinson, Deborah.
Anderson, Betheny, illus. see Jackson, Penny.
Anderson, Bill, illus. see Biskup, Agnieszka, et al.
Anderson, Bill, illus. see Biskup, Agnieszka.
Anderson, Bill, illus. see Campodonica, Carol A.
Anderson, Bill, illus. see Collins, Terry, et al.
Anderson, Bill, illus. see Harris, Kandi.
Anderson, Bill, illus. see Lemke, Donald B., et al.
Anderson, Bill, illus. see Martin, Michael & Martin, Michael J.
Anderson, Bill, illus. see Martin, Michael J.
Anderson, Bill, jt. auth. see O'Donnell, Liam.
Anderson, Bill & O'Donnell, Liam. World of Food Chains with Max Axiom, Super Scientist Martin, Cynthia, illus. (p. 1956)
Anderson, Billie Ann, illus. see Faircloth, Harry W.
Anderson, Bre. Teaching Joey. (p. 1710)
Anderson, Brent. Power Pack Classic - Volume 3. (p. 1390)
Anderson, Brent, illus. see Claremont, Chris.
Anderson, Brian. Adventures of Commander Zack Proton & the Red Giant. Holgate, Douglas, illus. (p. 17)
—Adventures of Commander Zack Proton & the Warlords of Nibblecheese. Holgate, Douglas, illus. (p. 17)
—Adventures of Commander Zack Proton & the Wrong Planet. Holgate, Douglas, illus. (p. 17)
Anderson, Brian & Anderson, Liam. Monster Chefs. Anderson, Brian, illus. (p. 1166)
Anderson, C. W. Blaze & Thunderbolt. (p. 198)
Anderson, C. W., illus. see Paltenghi, Madalena.
Anderson, Carolyn. No Counting Sheep (p. 1258)
—Water Queen & the Sea of Kings. (p. 1863)
Anderson, Carolyn B. Exchanging God's Glory for the Pleasures of the Flesh. (p. 547)
—Heaven Is a Real Place. (p. 761)
—Running from the Call of God. (p. 1497)
Anderson, Carolyn D. Granny's Farm Friends. (p. 710)
Anderson, Catherine. Daddy Longlegs. (p. 398)
—Morning Light. (p. 1175)
Anderson, Catherine Corley. John F. Kennedy. (p. 921)
Anderson, Cathy, ed. see Charles, R., et al.
Anderson, Cathysue. Through Grandmother's Window. (p. 1745)
Anderson, Charoletta. Mizz Goodie 2 Shoez. (p. 1157)
Anderson, Chizuruoke, jt. auth. see Gresh, Dannah.
Anderson, Christopher C. L. Margaret Bourke-White: Adventurous Photographer. (p. 1092)
Anderson, Claire. Talking to the Stars. (p. 1703)
Anderson, Clay. Beyond the Waterfall. (p. 174)
—Mary Margaret Hammersmith & the Lady of the Roundtable (p. 1100)
Anderson, Connie Kingrey. Haunted Cattle Drive. (p. 753)
—Toadies. (p. 1760)
Anderson, Constance. Smelling Sunshine Anderson, Constance, illus. (p. 1593)
Anderson, D. M. Killer Cows. (p. 956)
Anderson, Dale. Aftermath of the Civil War. (p. 28)
—Al Gore: A Wake-Up Call to Global Warming. (p. 32)
—American Colonies Declare Independence. (p. 60)
—American Revolution: Events & Outcomes. (p. 63)
—Anasazi Culture at Mesa Verde. (p. 67)
—Atom Bomb Project. (p. 113)
—Battle of Yorktown. (p. 147)
—Building the Panama Canal. (p. 239)
—Causes of the American Revolution. (p. 282)
—Causes of the Civil War. (p. 282)
—Chinese Americans. (p. 307)
—Churches & Religion in the Middle Ages. (p. 318)
—Civil War at Sea. (p. 325)
—Civil War in the East (1861-July 1863) (p. 325)
—Civil War in the West (1861-July 1863) (p. 325)
—Cuban Americans. (p. 388)
—Daily Life During the American Revolution. (p. 399)
—FBI & Civil Rights. (p. 578)
—FBI & Organized Crime. (p. 578)
—FBI & White-Collar Crime. (p. 578)
—FBI Files: Successful Investigations. (p. 578)
—First Moon Landing. (p. 596)
—Forming a New American Government. (p. 620)
—Freedom Rides: Campaign for Equality (p. 635)
—Home Fronts in the Civil War. (p. 792)
—How Do We Know the Nature of Human Origins. (p. 808)
—How Do We Know the Nature of Humankind. (p. 808)
—Italian Americans. (p. 894)
—Japanese Americans. (p. 909)
—Key Battles of the American Revolution, 1776-1778. (p. 950)
—Leaders of the American Revolution. (p. 981)
—Lexington & Concord, April 19, 1775. (p. 1004)
—Maria Mitchell. (p. 1093)
—Monks & Monasteries in the Middle Ages. (p. 1166)
—Patriots Win the American Revolution. (p. 1329)
—Polish Americans. (p. 1380)
—Seneca Falls Women's Rights Convention. (p. 1550)
—Soldiers & Sailors in the American Revolution. (p. 1607)
—Soldier's Life in the Civil War. (p. 1607)
—Terrorist Attacks of September, 11, 2001. (p. 1722)
—Tet Offensive: Turning Point of the Vietnam War Anderson, Dale, illus. (p. 1723)
—Union Victory (July 1863-1865) (p. 1818)
—World Almanac Library of the Civil War (p. 1953)
Anderson, Dale, jt. auth. see Crewe, Sabrina.
Anderson, Dale, jt. auth. see Goff, Elizabeth Hudson.
Anderson, Dale, jt. auth. see O'Hern, Kerri.
Anderson, Dale & Compass Point Books Staff. Republican Party: The Story of the Grand Old Party (p. 1462)
Anderson, Dale & Goff, Elizabeth Hudson. First Moon Landing. Floor, Guus & Spay, Anthony, illus. (p. 596)
Anderson, Dale & O'Hern, Kerri. Battle of Gettysburg. McHargue, D., illus. (p. 146)
Anderson, Danny. Santa's Spy. (p. 1513)
Anderson, David. Charlie Sparrow & the Secret of Flight. Anderson, David, illus. (p. 293)
—Emily's Imaginary Airplane. (p. 519)
—Glaciation & Periglacial Environments. (p. 682)
Anderson, David, illus. see Kaner, Etta.
Anderson, David, illus. see McRae, G. c.
Anderson, David A. What You Can See, You Can Be! Jones, Don, illus. (p. 1896)
Anderson, Dawn. Chimpance, Como Yo ! (p. 306)
—Chimpanzee, Like Me! (p. 306)
Anderson, Debby. Every Child Everywhere! Anderson, Debby, illus. (p. 542)
—God Knows My Name. Anderson, Debby, illus. (p. 689)
—Jesus Is Coming Back! Anderson, Debby, illus. (p. 915)
—Kindness Counts! Anderson, Debby, illus. (p. 957)
—Let's Explore God's World. Anderson, Debby, illus. (p. 996)
—Let's Talk about Heaven. (p. 1001)
Anderson, Debby, illus. see Piper, Noël.
Anderson, Debby L. Minnesota for Mini-Sotans. (p. 1147)
Anderson, Debra. Seed Sower, Walter's Special Garden. Lucas, Diane, illus. (p. 1547)
Anderson, Dee. Reading Is Funny! Motivating Kids to Read with Riddles. (p. 1446)
Anderson, Dee, retold by. Otter Gets Tricked! A Cherokee Trickster Story. (p. 1307)
Anderson, Dennis E., photos by. Hidden Treasures of San Francisco Bay. (p. 776)
Anderson, Derek. Blue Burt & Wiggles. Anderson, Derek, illus. (p. 202)
—Gladys Goes Out to Lunch. Anderson, Derek, illus. (p. 682)
—How the Easter Bunny Saved Christmas. Anderson, Derek, illus. (p. 813)
—Romeo & Lou Blast Off. Anderson, Derek, illus. (p. 1486)
—Ten Pigs: An Epic Bath Adventure. Anderson, Derek, illus. (p. 1719)
Anderson, Derek, illus. see Hochman, David & Kennison, Ruth.
Anderson, Derek, illus. see Lord, Cynthia.
Anderson, Derek, illus. see Sierra, Judy.
Anderson, Derek, illus. see Thompson, Lauren.
Anderson, Derek, illus. see Yolen, Jane.
Anderson, Derek, jt. auth. see Thompson, Lauren.
Anderson, Derek, et al. Over the River: A Turkey's Tale. (p. 1314)
Anderson, Dianne & Anderson, Ian. Cambridge Checkpoints VCE English 2005. (p. 255)
Anderson, Dick. African Adventures. (p. 26)
Anderson, Donald. New Practice Readers. (p. 1246)
Anderson, Doug. Hadley & the Bean. (p. 735)
Anderson, Doug, illus. see Frederick, Guy.
Anderson, Dwayne. Partially Human. (p. 1325)
anderson, E. Santa Saves Boswell: How Boswell the Blue-Eyed Beagle Found a Home. (p. 1513)
Anderson, E. Kristin & Kenneally, Miranda. Dear Teen Me: Authors Write Letters to Their Teen Selves. (p. 419)
Anderson, E. Kristin & Kenneally, Miranda, eds. Dear Teen Me: Authors Write Letters to Their Teen Selves. (p. 419)
Anderson, E. V. Many Lives of Lilith Lane (p. 1089)
Anderson, Easter Huggins. Seashells for Lilly. (p. 1538)
Anderson, Ebony. If I Were Just a Little Taller. Barrett, Noah, illus. (p. 853)
Anderson, Eric B. Alena & the Favorite Thing. Kuzma, Jakub, illus. (p. 35)
Anderson, Eric Chase. Chuck Dugan Is AWOL. (p. 318)
Anderson, Erin. Repulsive. (p. 1462)
Anderson, Evelyn Pearl. Knitted with Love. (p. 965)
Anderson, Floyd. Father of the American Navy: John Barry. Orban, Paul, illus. (p. 577)
Anderson, Frank W. Rumrunners: Dodging the Law During Prohibition. (p. 1496)
Anderson, Fred & Cayton, Andrew. Dominion of War: Empire & Liberty in North America, 1500-2000. (p. 465)
Anderson, Gennifer. Celebrations! Baity, Susan, illus. (p. 285)
Anderson, George. Controlling Ourselves. (p. 361)
Anderson, George William, ed. Achieving Success with Faith in God: The Concept of Faith - Based Perseverance. (p. 9)
Anderson, Georgene, jt. auth. see Anderson, Raymond.
Anderson, Georgia Lee. Bullying Is Wrong. Fox, Tom Paul, illus. (p. 241)
Anderson, Geraldine. Bev's Amazing Adventures Book Ii: The Girl from Peru. (p. 173)
Anderson, Gerry. Thunderbirds. (p. 1746)
—Thunderbirds Comic (p. 1746)
Anderson, Ginny. Moon by Day. (p. 1172)
Anderson, Graylin. Seeing the Shapes + Drawing the Shapes = Drawing the Object. (p. 1548)
Anderson, Hans Christian. Little Mermaid. Santore, Charles, illus. (p. 1031)
Anderson, Harold, illus. see Sherman, Harold M.
Anderson, Harry S. & Vail, Martha. Exploring the Pacific, Revised Edition. (p. 554)
Anderson, H.C. Reine des Neiges. (p. 1457)
Anderson, Heidi. Goodnight Tiny Mouse: An Itty Bitty Bedtime Story. (p. 701)
Anderson, Henry Morgan. Timmy the Goat: Spelunking Adventure. Falk, Wendy & Makepeace, Jonathan, eds. (p. 1755)
Anderson, Ho Che, illus. see Pekar, Harvey, et al.
Anderson, Holli. Five: Out of the Dark: Out of the Dark. (p. 599)
Anderson, Holly Lynn. Unexplained Monsters & Cryptids. (p. 1817)
Anderson - Hutchison, Laura M. Toby & Talula Trout. (p. 1760)
Anderson, Ian, jt. auth. see Anderson, Dianne.
Anderson II, Norman E., jt. auth. see Itow, Rebecca Chiyoko.
Anderson II, Norman E. & Itow, Rebecca Chiyoko. Boy, a Dog & Persnickety Log. (p. 217)
Anderson, Irv, illus. see Hillert, Margaret.
Anderson, J. J. Hooyahmi: Stories & poems for children ages 5 To 10. (p. 796)
Anderson, James. Around Home. (p. 100)
—Around Town. (p. 101)
Anderson, James, tr. see Gaarder, Jostein.
Anderson, James O. Poggy, the Stuffed Donkey. (p. 1376)
Anderson, Jameson. Aaron Rodgers. (p. 2)
—Amelia Earhart: Legendary Aviator Whigham, Rod et al, illus. (p. 58)
—Clay Matthews. (p. 330)
—Colin Kaepernick. (p. 339)
—Danica Patrick. (p. 404)
—Dodge Viper (p. 460)
—Dodge Viper/Dodge Viper. (p. 460)
—Gabby Douglas. (p. 652)
—Johnny Manziel. (p. 923)
—Kevin Durant. (p. 950)
—Lebron James. (p. 986)
—Lotus (p. 1057)
—Lotus - Lotus. (p. 1057)
—Miguel Cabrera. (p. 1141)
—Mike Trout. (p. 1141)
—Peyton Manning. (p. 1349)
—Russell Wilson. (p. 1498)
—Z-Boys & Skateboarding Erwin, Steve, illus. (p. 1984)
Anderson, Jan, illus. see Clish, Marian L.
Anderson, Jan, illus. see Day-Bivins, Pat.
Anderson, Jane. Anansi the Spider & the Sky King: A Tale from Africa. (p. 67)
—Harriet Tubman & the Underground Railroad. (p. 750)
—Iktomi Takes to the Sky: A Native American Folktale. (p. 856)
—Inspector Insector. (p. 878)
—My Name Is Deborah Samson. (p. 1215)
Anderson, Jane A., illus. see Alford, Douglas J. & Alford, Pakaket.
Anderson, Janet. Last Treasure. (p. 979)
—Modern Dance. (p. 1158)
—Senate. (p. 1550)
Anderson, Jay, photos by see Campodonica, Carol A.
Anderson, Jean, ed. see Bullock, Harold B.
Anderson, Jean & Lininger, Linda. Queen Mary Mystery (p. 1425)
Anderson, Jeannine. Nightlight. Johnson, Nikki, illus. (p. 1255)
Anderson, Jeff. Zack Delacruz: Me & My Big Mouth. (p. 1984)
Anderson, Jeff, illus. see Beeke, Joel R. & Kleyn, Diana.
Anderson, Jeff, illus. see Foce, Natalia, tr.
Anderson, Jeff, illus. see Mackenzie, Carine & MacKenzie, Carine.
Anderson, Jeff, illus. see MacKenzie, Lachlan.
Anderson, Jeff, illus. see Spurgeon, Charles H.
Anderson, Jeff, jt. auth. see Maddox, Mike.
Anderson, Jenna. How It Happens at the ATV Plant. Wolfe, Bob & Wolfe, Diane, photos by. (p. 810)
—How It Happens at the Building Site. Wolfe, Bob & Wolfe, Diane, photos by. (p. 810)
Anderson, Jennifer. Honey Creek Royalty. (p. 794)
—King of the Lake. (p. 959)
—Spider. (p. 1626)
Anderson, Jennifer Joline. Albert Einstein: Revolutionary Physicist. (p. 34)
—How to Analyze the Music of Michael Jackson. (p. 814)
—John Lennon: Legendary Musician & Beatle. (p. 922)
—Langston Hughes. (p. 974)
—Miley Cyrus: Pop Princess. (p. 1142)
—Wikipedia: The Company & Its Founders. (p. 1928)
—Wilma Rudolph: Track & Field Inspiration. (p. 1934)
—Women's Rights Movement. (p. 1947)
—Writing Fantastic Fiction. (p. 1964)
Anderson, Jeremy. Sealy. (p. 1536)
Anderson, Jesse, illus. see Overstreet, Tommy & Vest, Dale G.
Anderson, Jessica. Case of the Foul Play on a School Day. (p. 274)
—Shaky, Breaky School Sleuth. (p. 1559)
Anderson, Jessica Lee. Border Crossing. (p. 213)
—Calli. (p. 254)
—Trudy. (p. 1791)
Anderson, Jill. Adding with Sebastian Pig & Friends at the Circus. Amy Huntington, illus. (p. 11)
—Adding with Sebastian Pig & Friends at the Circus. Huntington, Amy, illus. (p. 12)
—Counting with Sebastian Pig & Friends on the Farm. Amy Huntington, illus. (p. 372)
—Counting with Sebastian Pig & Friends on the Farm. Huntington, Amy, illus. (p. 372)
—Emperor Penguins. (p. 520)
—Finding Shapes with Sebastian Pig & Friends at the Museum. Amy Huntington, illus. (p. 588)
—Finding Shapes with Sebastian Pig & Friends at the Museum. Huntington, Amy, illus. (p. 588)
—Giraffes. (p. 677)
—Measuring with Sebastian Pig & Friends on a Road Trip. Amy Huntington, illus. (p. 1117)
—Measuring with Sebastian Pig & Friends on a Road Trip. Huntington, Amy, illus. (p. 1117)
—Money Math with Sebastian Pig & Friends at the Farmer's Market. Amy Huntington, illus. (p. 1164)
—Money Math with Sebastian Pig & Friends at the Farmer's Market. Huntington, Amy, illus. (p. 1164)
—Polar Bears. (p. 1379)
—Subtracting with Sebastian Pig & Friends on a Camping Trip. (p. 1671)
—Subtracting with Sebastian Pig & Friends on a Camping Trip. Huntington, Amy, illus. (p. 1671)
—Zebras. (p. 1985)
Anderson, Jill, ed. see Fecher, Sarah & Oliver, Clare.
Anderson, Jill, ed. Let's Get to Work!/Vamos a Trabajar! Evrard, Gaetan, illus. (p. 997)
—Let's Go on Safari!/Vamos de Safari! Utton, Peter, illus. (p. 997)
—Let's Go!/Vamos a Viajar! Evrard, Gaetan, illus. (p. 998)
Anderson, Joan. Single Mother's Book: A Practical Guide to Managing Your Children, Career, Home, Finances, & Everything Else (p. 1579)
Anderson, Joan F. Buster B. Basset Hound, the Label Buster (Book & Music CD) Labeled as ADHD (Attention Deficit Hyperactive Dog) by the Sneaky Label Maker Buster B. Basset Hound Turns into a Hero, the Label Buster. (p. 245)
Anderson, Joanna. Cooking with My Dad: Number Names & Count Sequence. (p. 362)

—Many People of America. (p. 1089)
Anderson, Joanna, jt. auth. see Mills, Nathan.
Anderson, Jodi Lynn. Among the Stars. (p. 65)
—Ever After. (p. 541)
—Loser/Queen. Lee, Brittney, illus. (p. 1054)
—Love & Peaches. (p. 1059)
—May Bird Trilogy: The Ever after; among the Stars; Warrior Princess. (p. 1112)
—My Diary from the Edge of the World. (p. 1202)
—Peaches. (p. 1332)
—Secrets of Peaches. (p. 1545)
—Tiger Lily. (p. 1748)
—Vanishing Season. (p. 1833)
—Warrior Princess. (p. 1859)
Anderson, Jodi Lynn, et al. Americapedia: Taking the Dumb Out of Freedom. (p. 64)
Anderson, John David. Dungeoneers. (p. 490)
—Minion. (p. 1147)
—Sidekicked. (p. 1573)
Anderson, John W. Clutch Bootlegging Love & Tragedy in the 1920's. (p. 336)
—Straight the Highway: The Life Story of Petar & Hannah. (p. 1664)
Anderson, Jon A. My T-Rex. (p. 1219)
Anderson, Josh. Heat on the Street. (p. 760)
—Los Angeles Clippers. (p. 1053)
—Miami Heat. (p. 1133)
Anderson, Joyce. Teen Discussion Guide - Your Parents. (p. 1713)
Anderson, Joyce E. Walking with Grandm. (p. 1854)
Anderson, Judith. Celebrity & Fame. (p. 285)
—Crime. (p. 382)
—Know the Facts about Personal Safety. (p. 965)
—Looking at Settlements. (p. 1051)
—Once There Was a Caterpillar. Gordon, Mike, illus. (p. 1292)
—Once There Was a Raindrop. Gordon, Mike, illus. (p. 1292)
—Once There Was a Seed. Gordon, Mike, illus. (p. 1292)
—Once There Was a Tadpole. Gordon, Mike, illus. (p. 1292)
—War & Conflict. (p. 1857)
—Ways to Do Surveys. (p. 1865)
Anderson, Judith & Flinthart, Dirk. War & Conflict. (p. 1857)
Anderson, Judith & Vaughan, Jenny. Crime. (p. 382)
Anderson, Judy. Virginia. (p. 1844)
Anderson, Julia, ed. see Pakizer, Debi & Sears, Mary A.
Anderson, Julian. View Halloo. (p. 1842)
Anderson, Julie. Erik the Red Sees Green: A Story about Color Blindness. Lopez, David, illus. (p. 533)
Anderson, Julie, illus. see Flora, Sherrill B.
Anderson, Karl A., illus. see Wilson, Jodi L.
Anderson, Kathryn, compiled by. Mom's Summer Survival. (p. 1163)
Anderson, Kathy Archibald. Max the Happy Caterpillar. (p. 1111)
Anderson, Kevin J., jt. auth. see Moesta, Rebecca.
Anderson, Kirsten. Who Was Andy Warhol? (p. 1918)
—Who Was Andy Warhol? Salamunic, Tim et al, illus. (p. 1918)
—Who Was Robert Ripley? (p. 1919)
—Who Was Robert Ripley? Foley, Tim & Harrison, Nancy, illus. (p. 1919)
Anderson, Km. I Want to Be Like... (p. 848)
Anderson, Kris & Pearson Education Staff. Wrong Man. (p. 1965)
Anderson, Lara. Rosalind Franklin (p. 1489)
Anderson, Lars. Compliments of the Domino Lady. Harvey, Rich, ed. (p. 354)
Anderson, Laura Ellen, illus. see Gorman, Karyn.
Anderson, Laura Ellen, illus. see Sutcliffe, William.
Anderson, Laurie Halse. Acting Out (p. 10)
—Catalyst. (p. 278)
—Chains. (p. 288)
—End of the Race (p. 526)
—Fever 1793. (p. 583)
—Fight for Life. (p. 585)
—Forge. (p. 619)
—Frio. (p. 639)
—Hair of Zoe Fleefenbacher Goes to School. Hoyt, Ard, illus. (p. 736)
—Helping Hands. (p. 766)
—Homeless. (p. 793)
—Impossible Knife of Memory. (p. 862)
—Independent Dames: What You Never Knew about the Women & Girls of the American Revolution. Faulkner, Matt, illus. (p. 870)
—Manatee Blues (p. 1086)
—Masks (p. 1102)
—New Beginnings #13 (p. 1243)
—Prom. (p. 1411)
—Say Good-Bye (p. 1518)
—Speak. (p. 1622)
—Storm Rescue. (p. 1656)
—Teacher's Pet. (p. 1709)
—Thank You, Sarah: The Woman Who Saved Thanksgiving. Faulkner, Matt, illus. (p. 1725)
—Ticket to Saudi Arabia. (p. 1747)
—Trapped. (p. 1779)
—Treading Water. (p. 1781)
—Trickster. (p. 1786)
—Twisted. (p. 1802)
—Wintergirls. (p. 1938)
Anderson, Leanne. Great I Am: Meet the Animals in the Stable As They Welcomed the Precious Gift! (p. 716)
Anderson, Lena, illus. see Björk, Christina.
Anderson, Lena & Sandin, Joan. Hedgehog, Pig, & the Sweet Little Friend. Sandin, Joan, tr. from SWE. (p. 762)
Anderson, Leone Castell. Sean's Quest. Welch, Sheila Kelly, illus. (p. 1537)
Anderson, Lesley, illus. see Rottenberg, David Ira & Rottenberg, David Ira.
Anderson, Liam, jt. auth. see Anderson, Brian.
Anderson, Libby. Richest Boy on Earth. (p. 1470)
Anderson, Lil & Szucs, Sandor. Beavers Eh to Bea: Tales from a Wildlife Rehabilitator. (p. 155)
Anderson, Lillian. My Sandwich. Uhlig, Elizabeth, illus. (p. 1218)
Anderson, Linda. Let's Meet the Gickens. (p. 999)
Anderson, Linda A., et al. Big Big God: 13 Amazing Lessons Where Preschoolers Experience God (p. 178)
Anderson, Lindsay. My Spy Adventure. (p. 1219)
Anderson, Lisa & Williams, Zac. No Bake Gingerbread Houses for Kids (p. 1257)
Anderson, Lisa Turner & Barlow, Melissa. Cupcake Cakes Williams, Zac, photos by. (p. 392)
Anderson, Lochlin, illus. see Davis, Trevor.
Anderson, Luleen S. Knack of a Happy Life: Nine Lessons along the Journey. (p. 964)
Anderson, Lynda & Bennett, Melanie. Micro Meanies. (p. 1136)
Anderson, Lynne. Aquarium Adds Up: Set Of 6. (p. 94)
—Aquarium Adds Up. (p. 94)
—Charlie's Championships: Set Of 6. (p. 293)
—Charlie's Championships & Los campeonatos de Charlie: 6 English, 6 Spanish Adaptations. (p. 293)
—Fun with Magnets. (p. 648)
—Make a Marionette. (p. 1078)
—Rocket Ship Shapes: Set Of 6. (p. 1483)
—Rocket Ship Shapes. (p. 1483)
—Taking Photographs. (p. 1698)
Anderson, M. T. Agent Q, or the Smell of Danger! Cyrus, Kurt, illus. (p. 29)
—Astonishing Life of Octavian Nothing, Traitor to the Nation. (p. 108)
—Burger Wuss. (p. 243)
—Chamber in the Sky. (p. 289)
—Clue of the Linoleum Lederhosen. Cyrus, Kurt, illus. (p. 336)
—Empire of Gut & Bone. (p. 521)
—Feed. (p. 580)
—Game of Sunken Places. (p. 654)
—Handel, Who Knew What He Liked. Hawkes, Kevin, illus. (p. 740)
—He Laughed with His Other Mouths. Cyrus, Kurt, illus. (p. 756)
—Jasper Dash & the Flame-Pits of Delaware. Cyrus, Kurt, illus. (p. 910)
—Kingdom on the Waves. (p. 960)
—Me, All Alone, at the End of the World. Hawkes, Kevin, illus. (p. 1115)
—No Such Thing as the Real World. (p. 1260)
—Pox Party (p. 1391)
—Suburb Beyond the Stars. (p. 1671)
—Symphony for the City of the Dead: Dmitri Shostakovich & the Siege of Leningrad. (p. 1693)
—Thirsty. (p. 1734)
—Whales on Stilts! Cyrus, Kurt, illus. (p. 1878)
—Zombie Mommy. Cyrus, Kurt, illus. (p. 1988)
Anderson, Maree. Freaks in the City (p. 631)
Anderson, Margaret J. Bugged-Out Insects. (p. 236)
—Carl Linnaeus: Genius of Classification. (p. 269)
—Charles Darwin: Genius of a Revolutionary Theory. (p. 292)
—Isaac Newton: Greatest Genius of Science. (p. 890)
—Olla-Piska: Tales of David Douglas. (p. 1287)
Anderson, Margaret J., jt. auth. see Cressey, Pamela J.
Anderson, Margaret J. & Stephenson, Karen F. Aristotle: Philosopher & Scientist. (p. 98)
—Aristotle: Genius Philosopher & Scientist. (p. 98)
Anderson, Margaret Jean. Bugged-Out Insects. (p. 236)
—Carl Linnaeus: Father of Classification. (p. 269)
—Charles Darwin: Naturalist. (p. 292)
—Isaac Newton: The Greatest Scientist of All Time. (p. 890)
Anderson, Marilyn D. Arab Americans. (p. 94)
Anderson, Marjorie L. Key: Wise Money Choices for Teens. (p. 950)
Anderson, Marjorie M., illus. see Pearson, Georgene.
Anderson, Mark, ed. see Brown, Gary.
Anderson, Mark, illus. see Entrekin, Allison Weiss.
Anderson, Mark, illus. see Klein, Frederick C.
Anderson, Mark, illus. see Klein, Fredrick C.
Anderson, Mark, illus. see Robins, Sandy.
Anderson, Mark A. Ma Ma, I'm Home (p. 1067)
Anderson, Mary. My Small Backyard: Birds! (p. 1219)
Anderson, Mary, jt. auth. see Latta, Sara L.
Anderson, Matt. Cut the Rope: Strange Delivery. (p. 396)
—Kung Fu Panda 2 Movie Prequel. (p. 968)
—Kung Fu Panda: Kung Fu Crew: Kung Fu Crew. (p. 968)
Anderson, Matt & Hutchins, Eric. White Picket Fences: Double Feature One-shot. (p. 1913)
—White Picket Fences: Red Scare TP: Red Scare TP. (p. 1913)
Anderson, Matt & Johnson, Quinn. Kung Fu Panda: the Slow Fast & Other Stories: The Slow Fast & Other Stories. (p. 968)
Anderson, Matt & Lambert, Chad. Kung Fu Panda: It's Elemental & Other Stories. Vol. 2 (p. 968)
Anderson, Max Elliot. Big Rig Rustlers. (p. 183)
—Legend of the White Wolf. (p. 989)
—Newspaper Caper. (p. 1249)
—North Woods Poachers. (p. 1265)
—Reckless Runaway. (p. 1451)
—Terror at Wolf Lake. (p. 1722)
—When the Lights Go Out. (p. 1904)
Anderson, Max Elliott. Mountain Cabin Mystery. (p. 1180)
—Secret of Abbott's Cave. (p. 1542)
Anderson, Maxine. Amazing Leonardo Da Vinci Inventions: You Can Build Yourself. (p. 54)
—Explore Winter! 25 Great Ways to Learn about Winter. Frederick-Frost, Alexis, illus. (p. 550)
—Great Civil War Projects: You Can Build Yourself. (p. 714)
—Proyectos Impresionantes de la Guerra Civil: Que Puedes Construir Tú Mismo. (p. 1413)
Anderson, Maxine & Berkenkamp, Lauri. Explore Spring! 25 Great Ways to Learn about Spring. Frederick-Frost, Alexis, illus. (p. 550)
Anderson, Mel. Pony Tracks: Renegades & Ranching on the Rez. (p. 1383)
Anderson, Melissa. Big Fib. (p. 181)
Anderson, Melissa & Elrazky, Sumaiyah. Animals A-Z in Arabic - an Arabic / English Easy Reader. (p. 82)
Anderson, Mercedes Padrino. Cities & Towns in the Middle Ages. (p. 322)
Anderson, Mercedes Padrino & Padrino, Mercedes. Cities & Towns in the Middle Ages. (p. 322)
Anderson, Michael. Ancient Greece. (p. 69)
—Ancient Rome. (p. 70)
—Biographies of the American Revolution: Benjamin Franklin to John Paul Jones. (p. 188)
—Biographies of the New World: From Leif Eriksson to Charles Darwin. (p. 188)
—Biographies of the New World Power: Rutherford B. Hayes, Thomas Alva Edison, Margaret Sanger, & More. (p. 188)
—Closer Look at Genes & Genetic Engineering. (p. 334)
—Closer Look at Living Things. (p. 334)
—Closer Look at Plant Reproduction, Growth, & Ecology. (p. 334)
—Early Civilizations of the Americas. (p. 493)
—Earth & Its Moon. (p. 495)
—Elephants Are Coming. (p. 511)
—Football & Its Greatest Players. (p. 615)
—Global Warming. (p. 684)
—Investigating Earth's Oceans. (p. 884)
—Investigating Earth's Weather. (p. 884)
—Investigating Minerals, Rocks, & Fossils. (p. 885)
—Investigating Plate Tectonics, Earthquakes, & Volcanoes. (p. 885)
—Investigating the Global Climate. (p. 885)
—Investigating the History of Earth. (p. 885)
—Nature of Planets, Dwarf Planets, & Space Objects. (p. 1236)
—Politics of Saving the Environment. (p. 1381)
—Sun, Stars, & Galaxies. (p. 1676)
—Woolly Bargains: A Scary Story for Young People. (p. 1950)
Anderson, Michael, contrib. by. Abraham Lincoln. (p. 6)
—Ronald Reagan. (p. 1486)
—Thomas Jefferson. (p. 1738)
Anderson, Michael, ed. Biographies of the American Revolution: Benjamin Franklin, John Adams, John Paul Jones, & More. (p. 188)
—Biographies of the New World: Leif Eriksson, Henry Hudson, Charles Darwin, & More. (p. 188)
—Biographies of the New World Power: Rutherford B. Hayes, Thomas Alva Edison, Margaret Sanger, & More. (p. 188)
—Electricity. (p. 509)
—Light. (p. 1014)
—Pioneers in Astronomy & Space Exploration. (p. 1361)
—Pioneers of the Green Movement: Environmental Solutions. (p. 1361)
Anderson, Michael, Jr. Blaze & the Lost Quarry. (p. 198)
—New Practice Readers: Book A. (p. 1246)
—New Practice Readers: Book B. (p. 1246)
—New Practice Readers: Book C. (p. 1246)
—New Practice Readers: Book D. (p. 1246)
—New Practice Readers. (p. 1246)
Anderson Mitchell, Dolores. Why Am I Here? (p. 1922)
Anderson, Moira. Azul (p. 122)
—Grid Coordinates by Land, Air, & Sea (p. 723)
—Verde (p. 1836)
Anderson, Murphy, illus. see Fox, Gardner, et al.
Anderson, Murphy, et al. Green Lantern Didio, Dan et al, eds. (p. 722)
Anderson, Nathan. Story of Zib. (p. 1663)
Anderson, Neal, illus. see Wells, Anita.
Anderson, Neil & Capstone Press Staff. Music Madness: Questioning Music & Music Videos Anderson, Neil, ed. (p. 1193)
Anderson, Neil J. Active Skills for Reading (p. 10)
Anderson, Neil T. Beta Starter Kit. (p. 171)
Anderson, Neil T. & Warner, Timothy M. Beginner's Guide to Spiritual Warfare. (p. 159)
Anderson, Nicola, illus. see Litton, Jonathan.
Anderson, P. Secret World of Fairies. (p. 1544)
Anderson, P. G. Grandma's Day. Sandford, Barbara, illus. (p. 708)
Anderson, Pamela. My New School: Blonde Boy. Lee, Han & Wu, Stacie, illus. (p. 1216)
—My New School: Blonde Girl. Lee, Han & Wu, Stacie, illus. (p. 1216)
—My New School: Brunette Boy. Lee, Han & Wu, Stacie, illus. (p. 1216)
—My New School: Brunette Girl. Lee, Han & Wu, Stacie, illus. (p. 1216)
—My New School. (p. 1216)
Anderson, Pamela Dell. My New School: Afro Boy. Lee, Hanlim & WU, Stacie, illus. (p. 1216)
—My New School: Afro Girl. Lee, Hanlim & WU, Stacie, illus. (p. 1216)
—My New School: Asian/Latin Boy. Lee, Hanlim & WU, Stacie, illus. (p. 1216)
—My New School: Latin/Asian Girl. Lee, Hanlim & WU, Stacie, illus. (p. 1216)
Anderson, Paris. Sisters Kennington. (p. 1581)
Anderson, Patricia. It's Time for Kindergarten PJ & Parker. (p. 899)
—Tails of a Woodswoman. (p. 1695)
Anderson, Paul C. George Armstrong Custer: The Indian Wars & the Battle of the Little Bighorn. (p. 663)
Anderson, Paul Christopher. George Armstrong Custer: The Indian Wars & the Battle at the Little Bighorn. (p. 663)
—Robert E. Lee: Legendary Commander of the Confederacy. (p. 1479)
Anderson, Paula. Blood Tender. (p. 200)
Anderson, Peggy Perry. I Can Help! (p. 835)
—Joe on the Go. (p. 920)
—Let's Clean Up! (p. 995)
—Time for Bed, the Babysitter Said. (p. 1751)
—To the Tub. (p. 1759)
—To the Tub. Anderson, Peggy Perry, illus. (p. 1759)
Anderson, Peter. Vikings. (p. 1842)
Anderson, Peter, illus. see Redmond, Ian.
Anderson, Phil. Thomas Family Values. (p. 1738)
Anderson, R. J. Pocket Full of Murder. (p. 1375)
—Quicksilver. (p. 1427)
—Spell Hunter. (p. 1625)
—Ultraviolet. (p. 1810)
—Wayfarer. (p. 1865)
Anderson, R. P. Sweet Dreams, Curious George. Obrero, Rudy, illus. (p. 1689)
Anderson, R. P., et al. Happy Easter, Curious George. Young, Mary O'Keefe, illus. (p. 745)
Anderson, Rachael. Mejores Amigos. McNicholas, Shelagh, illus. (p. 1124)
Anderson, Raymond & Anderson, Georgene. Jesse Tree: Stories & Symbols of Advent. (p. 914)
Anderson, Renae. Upon the Heads of the Children. (p. 1825)
Anderson, Reuben. Uniquely Oklahoma (p. 1818)
—Uniquely South Dakota (p. 1818)
Anderson, Rian B. Christmas Prayer. (p. 315)
Anderson, Richard. Home Run for Bunny. Purnell, Gerald, illus. (p. 792)
Anderson, Rick, illus. see Couvillon, Alice & Moore, Elizabeth.
Anderson, Rick, illus. see Shoulders, Michael.
Anderson, Rick, illus. see Townsend, Una Belle.
Anderson, Robert. Italy. (p. 894)
—National Geographic Countries of the World - Italy. (p. 1231)
—Paul Gauguin. (p. 1330)
Anderson, Robert Edward. Story of Extinct Civilizations of the West (p. 1658)
Anderson, Robert Gordon. HalfPast Seven Stories Illustrated Editi. (p. 737)
—Seven O'Clock Stories. (p. 1554)
Anderson, Robert L. Dreamland. (p. 484)
Anderson, Rodney P. Invisible ABC's: Exploring the World of Microbes... (p. 885)
Anderson, Salem. Salem Anderson & Her Private Diary. (p. 1504)
Anderson, Sandra. Rockcliffe. (p. 1482)
Anderson, Sara. Noisy Country Day. (p. 1263)
—Noisy Country Night. (p. 1263)
—Sara's Kitchen. (p. 1514)
Anderson, Scott, illus. see Demuth, Patricia Brennan.
Anderson, Scott, illus. see Frith, Margaret.
Anderson, Scott, illus. see Herman, Gail.
Anderson, Scoular. Bubble Trouble. (p. 233)
—Collins Big Cat - Where on Earth? Band 10/White. Anderson, Scoular, illus. (p. 340)
—Fabulous Creatures - Were They Real? Anderson, Scoular, illus. (p. 560)
—How to Be a Knight in 10 Easy Stages. Anderson, Scoular, illus. (p. 814)
—How to Be a Tudor in 20 Easy Stages. Anderson, Scoular, illus. (p. 815)
—How to Be a Viking in 13 Easy Stages. Anderson, Scoular, illus. (p. 815)
—Pirate Treasure. Anderson, Scoular, illus. (p. 1363)
—Space Pirates: A Map-Reading Adventure. Anderson, Scoular, illus. (p. 1619)
—Super Slosh. (p. 1681)
Anderson, Scoular, illus. see Burnett, Allan.
Anderson, Scoular, illus. see Foster, Jo.
Anderson, Scoular, illus. see North, Laura.
Anderson, Shannon. I Am Not a Pirate. (p. 833)
—Nicken Chuggets. (p. 1251)
—Penelope Perfect: A Tale of Perfectionism Gone Wild. Kath, Katie, illus. (p. 1336)
Anderson, Shauna, illus. see Anderson, Shel.
Anderson, Sheila. America Ferrera: Latina Superstar. (p. 59)
—Are You Ready for Fall? (p. 97)
—Are You Ready for Spring? (p. 97)
—Are You Ready for Summer? (p. 97)
—Are You Ready for Winter? (p. 97)
—Clinic. (p. 333)
—Coasts. (p. 336)
—Fire Station. (p. 590)
—First Step Nonfiction: Animal Adaptations (p. 597)
—Islands. (p. 892)
—Jimmy Carter: A Life of Friendship. (p. 918)
—Landforms: Complete Set. (p. 974)
—Landforms: Classroom Set. (p. 974)
—Library. (p. 1005)
—Lightning Bolt Books: Our Four Seasons (p. 1016)
—Miley Cyrus: Music & TV Superstar. (p. 1142)
—Mountains. (p. 1181)
—Plains. (p. 1366)
—Plateaus. (p. 1370)
—Police Station. (p. 1380)
—Ramadan. Conger, Holli, illus. (p. 1437)
—Roberto Clemente: A Life of Generosity. (p. 1479)
—Roberto Clemente. (p. 1479)
—Valleys. (p. 1831)
—What Can Live in a Desert? (p. 1880)
—What Can Live in A Forest? (p. 1880)
—What Can Live in a Forest? (p. 1880)
—What Can Live in A Grassland? (p. 1880)
—What Can Live in a Grassland? (p. 1880)
—What Can Live in A Lake? (p. 1880)
—What Can Live in a Lake? (p. 1880)
—What Can Live in the Desert? (p. 1880)
—What Can Live in the Mountains? (p. 1880)
—What Can Live in the Ocean? (p. 1880)
Anderson, Shel. Spoofaloof's Adventures: Rainy Day Fun. Anderson, Shauna, illus. (p. 1631)
Anderson, S.N. Desperate for a Family. (p. 430)
Anderson, Sonya, et al, eds. Facing Racism in Education. (p. 561)
Anderson, Sorrel. Clumsies Make a Mess. (p. 336)
—Clumsies Make a Mess of the Big Show. Slater, Nicola, illus. (p. 336)
Anderson, Stephanie, illus. see Aronson, Marc.
Anderson, Stephanie, illus. see Kanevsky, Polly.
Anderson, Stephanie, illus. see Lyon, George Ella.
Anderson, Stephanie, jt. auth. see Lyon, George Ella.
Anderson, Steven. Leap & Twirl. DeAngelo Hout, Sarah, illus. (p. 982)
Anderson, Stuart, ed. Changing Face of America: Immigration Since 1965 (p. 290)
Anderson, Sue, illus. see Yeh, Kat.
Anderson, Susan, illus. see Filakosky, Sandra.
Anderson, Susan, illus. see Gillespie, Tonnika.
Anderson, Susan, illus. see Rutledge, Eddie.
Anderson, Susannah. Susie. (p. 1688)
Anderson, Suzette. Cybertreks: Wildest West. (p. 396)

Anderson, T. L. Fifth Street: The Birthday Wish. (p. 584)
Anderson, T. N. Chiko & the Butterfly. (p. 301)
Anderson, T. Neill. City of the Dead: Galveston Hurricane 1900. (p. 324)
—Horrors of History: Massacre of the Miners. (p. 799)
—Horrors of History: People of the Plague: Philadelphia Flu Epidemic 1918. (p. 799)
—Ocean of Fire: The Burning of Columbia 1865. (p. 1276)
Anderson, Tanya. Dr. Seuss (Theodor Geisel) (p. 475)
—Maid of the Mist. (p. 1076)
—Tillie Pierce: Teen Eyewitness to the Battle of Gettysburg. (p. 1750)
Anderson, Taylor. Storm Surge. (p. 1656)
Anderson, Ted. Pinkie Pie. Bates, Ben, illus. (p. 1360)
Anderson, Ted, et al. My Little Pony: Pony Tales Volume 2: Pony Tales Volume 2. (p. 1213)
Anderson, Tom. Top 40 Fun Facts: Rock & Roll. (p. 1768)
Anderson, Trey. Jesse & Midnight. (p. 914)
Anderson, Vickie S. Pancakes for Supper. (p. 1320)
Anderson, Victoria, ed. see Heck, Tom.
Anderson, Virginia Lynn. Flying Phlox. (p. 610)
—Very Lonely Garden. (p. 1838)
Anderson, W. M. Action Literacy: Elephants. (p. 10)
—Talking about Making Good Choices. (p. 1703)
Anderson, Walter Inglis, jt. auth. see Bass, Hester.
Anderson, Wayne. Brown vs. Board of Education: The Case Against School Segregation. (p. 232)
—Chicago Black Sox Trial: A Primary Source Account. (p. 299)
—ETA: Spain's Basque Terrorists. (p. 539)
—Fighting Racial Discrimination: Treating All Americans Fairly under the Law. (p. 586)
—Tony Stewart: NASCAR Driver. (p. 1766)
Anderson, Wayne, illus. see Berk, Ari.
Anderson, Wayne, illus. see Drake, Ernest.
Anderson, Wayne, illus. see Kerven, Rosalind & Quarto Generic Staff.
Anderson, Wayne, illus. see Passes, David.
Anderson, Wayne, illus. see Pearce, Philippa.
Anderson, Wayne, illus. see Ward, Helen.
Anderson, Wayne, jt. auth. see Sands, Emily.
Anderson, Wayne A. Tony Stewart: NASCAR Driver. (p. 1766)
Anderson, Wayne R. Paula's Perilous Adventure. (p. 1331)
Anderson, Wendy. Expeditions. (p. 548)
Anderson, Wes, jt. auth. see Twentieth Century Fox Home Entertainment Staff.
Anderson, William. Hallie's Bad Day (p. 737)
—Laura Ingalls Wilder: A Biography. (p. 980)
—Les Kelly. Kelly, Leslie A., illus. (p. 993)
—Little House Guidebook. Kelly, Leslie A., illus. (p. 1029)
—Little Woman. (p. 1038)
—M Is for Mount Rushmore: A South Dakota Alphabet. Harness, Cheryl, illus. (p. 1067)
—River Boy: The Story of Mark Twain. Andreasen, Dan, illus. (p. 1475)
—River Boy. (p. 1475)
—V Is for Von Trapp: A Musical Family Alphabet. Graves, Linda, illus. (p. 1829)
Anderson, William T. Almanzo Picture Book Biography. (p. 48)
—Prairie Girl: The Life of Laura Ingalls Wilder. Graef, Renee, illus. (p. 1392)
Anderson, Zachary. Ancient Civilizations of Western Asia & the Mediterranean: From the Hittites to the Phoenicians. (p. 68)
—Ancient Greece: From Tyranny to Democracy. (p. 69)
—Discovering Mission La Purisima Concepción. (p. 449)
—Discovering Mission Nuestra Señora de la Soledad. (p. 449)
—Discovering Mission San Antonio de Padua. (p. 449)
—Fall of Rome & the Rise of Constantinople. (p. 566)
—John Cabot: Searching for a Westward Passage to Asia. (p. 921)
—Origins of Civilization: From Early Humans to the Babylonians. (p. 1304)
—Rise of the Roman Empire. (p. 1475)
—Samuel de Champlain: Exploring the Great Lakes. (p. 1509)
Anderson-Shorter, Susan, illus. see Weldon, Stayton.
Andert, John, illus. see Gamble, Adam.
Andes, Mary Lou. Santa's Prayer. Mattozzi, Patricia, illus. (p. 1513)
Andes, Mary Lou, jt. auth. see Dority, Victoria.
Ando, Natsumi. Arisa 1. (p. 98)
Ando, Yuma. Sherlock Bones. (p. 1565)
—Sherlock Bones Sato, Yuki, illus. (p. 1565)
—Sherlock Bones. (p. 1565)
Ando, Yuma & Sato, Yuki. Sherlock Bones (p. 1565)
Andonian, Mary. Bitsy's Labyrinth. (p. 194)
Andover, Max. Octopuses & Squid. (p. 1278)
Andracki, Andy. Dear Mother Teresa. (p. 419)
Andracki, Zenon. Dear Ashley: A Middle Grade Novel. (p. 418)
Andrada, Javier, illus. see Bailer, Darice, et al.
Andrade Barbosa, Rogerioo. Lendas E Fabulas Dos Bichos De Nossa America. (p. 991)
Andrade, Brigitte. Adventures of Bibi & Friends: Summer Season in Miami Beach (p. 16)
Andrade, J. Jack. Mom, Dad, Tell Me about Money: A Primer. (p. 1161)
Andrade, Marcia. Gust's Maze. (p. 733)
Andrade, Maria J. Why Dear Mrs Sullivan Is Distressed! (p. 1923)
Andrade, Mary J. Day of the Dead in Mexico-Yucatan: Through the Eyes of the Soul. Andrade, Mary J., ed. (p. 414)
—Uarhiri sapirhatiecheri Jukambekua: La velacion de los Angelitos. Murguia, Jose J., illus. (p. 1807)
Andrade, Mary J., photos by. Day of the Dead A Passion for Life: Día de los Muertos Pasión por la Vida. (p. 414)
Andrade Valencia, Esau, illus. see Sáenz, Benjamin Alire.
Andra-Warner, Elle. Hudson's Bay Company Adventures: Tales of Canada's Early Fur Traders. (p. 824)
Andre Alice Norton, jt. auth. see Andre Alice Norton, Alice Norton.
Andre Alice Norton, Alice Norton & Andre Alice Norton. Time Traders. (p. 1753)
André, Julie-Ann, et al. We Feel Good Out Here Macintosh, Tessa, photos by. (p. 1867)
Andre, Richard & Snow, William. Cruise of the Walnut Shell. (p. 386)
Andrea, Kaboos. Windy Hallowed Eve. (p. 1936)
Andrea, Karen. Enchanted Library. (p. 523)
Andrea, Leona. Club de Las Siete Gatas. (p. 335)
Andreacchi, Grace. Little Poems for Children. (p. 1033)
Andreae, Giles. ABC Animal Jamboree. Wojtowycz, David, illus. (p. 3)
—Billy Bonkers. Sharratt, Nick, illus. (p. 187)
—Billy Bonkers & the Wacky World Cup! (p. 187)
—Bustle in the Bushes. Wojtowycz, David, illus. (p. 245)
—Captain Flinn & the Pirate Dinosaurs. Ayto, Russell, illus. (p. 264)
—Cock-a-Doodle-Doo! Barnyard Hullabaloo. Wojtowycz, David, illus. (p. 337)
—Commotion in Ocean. Wojtowycz, David, illus. (p. 349)
—Dinosaurs Galore! Wojtowycz, David, illus. (p. 444)
—Giraffes Can't Dance. Parker-Rees, Guy, illus. (p. 678)
—Giraffes Can't Dance: Number Rumba. Parker-Rees, Guy, illus. (p. 678)
—Heaven Is Having You. Cabban, Vanessa, illus. (p. 761)
—I Love My Daddy. Dodd, Emma, illus. (p. 842)
—I Love My Grandma. Dodd, Emma, illus. (p. 842)
—I Love My Mommy. Dodd, Emma, illus. (p. 842)
—K Is for Kissing a Cool Kangaroo. Parker-Rees, Guy, illus. (p. 941)
—Keep Love in Your Heart, Little One. Vulliamy, Clara, illus. (p. 947)
—Leo, the Lovable Lion. (p. 992)
—Love Is a Handful of Honey. Cabban, Vanessa, illus. (p. 1060)
—Missing Treasure! Ayto, Russell, illus. (p. 1153)
—Morris the Mankiest Monster. McIntyre, Sarah, illus. (p. 1176)
—Pop-Up Dinosaurs Galore! Wojtowycz, David, illus. (p. 1384)
—Purple Ronnie's History of the World. (p. 1419)
—Purple Ronnie's Little Book of Football (p. 1419)
—Purple Ronnie's Little Book of Pants. (p. 1419)
—Purple Ronnie's Little Guide to Doing It (p. 1419)
—Purple Ronnie's Little Guide to Girls. (p. 1419)
—Rumble in Jungle. (p. 1495)
Andreae, Giles, jt. auth. see Purple Ronnie.
Andreae, Giles & Cronin, Janet. Love Poems (p. 1060)
—Purple Ronnie's Little Guide to Life (p. 1419)
Andreae, Giles & Parker-Rees, Guy. Giraffes Can't Dance. (p. 678)
Andreae, Giles & Ronnie, Purple. Purple Ronnie's Little Thoughts about Mums (p. 1419)
Andreae, Giles & World Of Happy Staff. Cow Party: A Story about Love (and Dancing!) Cronin, Janet, illus. (p. 373)
—Dance of Wallowy Bigness. Cronin, Janet, illus. (p. 402)
—Dog Machine. Cronin, Janet, illus. (p. 461)
—Elephant & the Spider. Cronin, Janet, illus. (p. 511)
—Knitting Gorilla. Cronin, Janet, illus. (p. 965)
—Ministry of Niceness. Cronin, Janet, illus. (p. 1147)
—Pink Cricket. Cronin, Janet, illus. (p. 1359)
—Planet of the Bears. Cronin, Janet, illus. (p. 1367)
—Tortoise Football. Cronin, Janet, illus. (p. 1771)
—Two Monkeys. Cronin, Janet, illus. (p. 1804)
Andreasen, Dan. Giant of Seville: A Tall Tale Based on a True Story. (p. 673)
—Saturday with Daddy. Andreasen, Dan, illus. (p. 1515)
—Treasure Bath. Andreasen, Dan, illus. (p. 1781)
—Twelve Days of Christmas. (p. 1800)
Andreasen, Dan, illus. see Alcott, Louisa May.
Andreasen, Dan, illus. see Anderson, William.
Andreasen, Dan, illus. see Barrie, J. M.
Andreasen, Dan, illus. see Bauer, Marion Dane.
Andreasen, Dan, illus. see Capucilli, Alyssa Satin.
Andreasen, Dan, illus. see Carroll, Lewis, pseud.
Andreasen, Dan, illus. see Clements, Andrew.
Andreasen, Dan, illus. see Cochran, Bill.
Andreasen, Dan, illus. see Connick, Harry, Jr.
Andreasen, Dan, illus. see Dickens, Charles.
Andreasen, Dan, illus. see Earhart, Kristin.
Andreasen, Dan, illus. see Goldberg, Judy.
Andreasen, Dan, illus. see Golenbock, Peter.
Andreasen, Dan, illus. see Greene, Rhonda Gowler.
Andreasen, Dan, illus. see Hulme, Joy N.
Andreasen, Dan, illus. see Jackson, Jennifer.
Andreasen, Dan, illus. see Jeffries, Alison.
Andreasen, Dan, illus. see Johnson, Spencer.
Andreasen, Dan, illus. see Kingsbury, Karen.
Andreasen, Dan, illus. see Krensky, Stephen.
Andreasen, Dan, illus. see Kroll, Steven.
Andreasen, Dan, illus. see London, Jack.
Andreasen, Dan, illus. see Martin, Ann M.
Andreasen, Dan, illus. see Marx, Trish.
Andreasen, Dan, illus. see Meadows, Michelle.
Andreasen, Dan, illus. see Montgomery, L. M.
Andreasen, Dan, illus. see Numeroff, Laura Joffe.
Andreasen, Dan, illus. see Rodgers and Hammerstein Organization Staff & Lindsay and Crouse Staff.
Andreasen, Dan, illus. see Rose, Deborah Lee.
Andreasen, Dan, illus. see Sidney, Margaret.
Andreasen, Dan, illus. see Spinelli, Eileen.
Andreasen, Dan, illus. see Tripp, Valerie.
Andreasen, Dan, illus. see Twain, Mark, pseud.
Andreasen, Dan, illus. see Verne, Jules.
Andreasen, Dan, illus. see Wiley, Melissa.
Andreasen, Dan, illus. see Wilson, Karma.
Andreasen, Dan, illus. see Wood, Douglas.
Andreasen, Deborah. Gifted. (p. 675)
Andreasen, Nancy C. Creative Brain: The Science of Genius. (p. 379)
Andreasen, Tim, illus. see Shelton, Carter.
Andregg, Michael. Seven Billion & Counting: The Crisis in Global Population Growth. (p. 1554)
Andrejev, Vladislav, illus. see Forest, Jim.
Andrekson, Judy. Brigadier: Gentle Hero. Parkins, David, illus. (p. 228)
—Fosta: Marathon Master. Parkins, David, illus. (p. 624)
—Gunner: Hurricane Horse. Parkins, David, illus. (p. 732)
—JB Andrew: Mustang Magic. Parkins, David, illus. (p. 911)
—Little Squire: The Jumping Pony. Parkins, David, illus. (p. 1036)
—Miskeen: The Dancing Horse. Parkins, David, illus. (p. 1150)
Andres, Dennis Michael. Insider's Guide to Sedona. Lindahl, Larry, photos by. (p. 878)
Andres, Ken & Johnson, Diane. Math Go Figure Student Book. (p. 1106)
Andres, Kristina. Elephant in the Bathtub. (p. 511)
—Good Little Wolf. (p. 698)
Andressen, Mark, illus. see Monette, Roz.
Andreu Iglesias, Cesar & Hernández, Juan A. Mal Tiempo, Buena Cara: El Humor en el Periodismo Puertorriqueno. (p. 1083)
Andreu, Mabel & Pierola, Mabel. Dona Desastre. (p. 465)
ANDREW A. STOMBERG, ed. see Tegnér, Esaias.
Andrew, Carol B. Animal Alphabet: An Interactive Book to Learn about Letters. (p. 76)
—Colorful Secret: An Interactive Book to Learn about Colors. (p. 344)
—Counting Dinosaurs: An Interactive Book to Learn about Numbers. (p. 371)
—Little Farm Puppy. (p. 1027)
—My Beautiful Ballets. (p. 1196)
—Where's My Mommy? (p. 1910)
Andrew, Charman, jt. auth. see Equipo Staff.
Andrew, Edwards & Fleur, Thornton. Footsteps of the Past: William Booth. (p. 615)
Andrew, Ian, illus. see Berk, Ari & McDermott, Kristen.
Andrew, Ian, illus. see Blake, Spencer.
Andrew, Ian, illus. see Dickinson, Peter.
Andrew, Ian, illus. see Pirotta, Saviour.
Andrew, Ian, illus. see Sands, Emily.
Andrew, Ian, illus. see Twist, Clint.
Andrew, Ian P., illus. see Sands, Emily & Anderson, Wayne.
Andrew, Joe. Three Lady Fish: A Friend in Need. Andrew, Joe, illus. (p. 1742)
Andrew Lang, ed. Orange Fairy Book. H. J. Ford, illus. (p. 1301)
—Pink Fairy Book. H. J. Ford, illus. (p. 1359)
Andrew, Moira, et al. Night Poems & Ghost Poems. (p. 1254)
Andrew, Moira, et al, selected by. Night Poems & Ghost Poems. (p. 1254)
Andrew, Stacy & Davis, Cristine. Morehouse College College Prowler off the Record. (p. 1175)
Andrew-Kollmann, Marcia. Blinky the Magical Elf. Dittus, Jade Moon, illus. (p. 199)
Andrews, jt. auth. see Osborn.
Andrews, A. and A. Adventures of the Walker: The Will of the Chosen. (p. 24)
Andrews, Alexa. At the Beach. (p. 110)
—At the Beach. Keimig, Candice, illus. (p. 110)
—Cat Days. (p. 277)
—Cat Days. John and Wendy, illus. (p. 277)
—In the Forest. Keimig, Candice, illus. (p. 866)
—On a Farm. (p. 1288)
—On a Farm. Keimig, Candice, illus. (p. 1288)
Andrews, Andy. Boy Who Changed the World. (p. 219)
—Henry Hodges Needs a Friend (p. 768)
—Kid Who Changed the World (p. 952)
—Young Traveler's Gift (p. 1979)
Andrews, Barbara. Circulatory System. (p. 321)
—Discover the Circulatory System. (p. 448)
—Discover the Nervous & Digestive Systems. (p. 448)
—Discover the Respiratory System. (p. 448)
—Discover the Southeast Region. (p. 448)
—Discover the Southwest Region. (p. 448)
—Discover the West Region. (p. 448)
—Nervous & Digestive Systems. (p. 1241)
—Respiratory System. (p. 1463)
—Southeast Region. (p. 1617)
—Southwest Region. (p. 1618)
—West Region. (p. 1876)
Andrews, Benny, illus. see Benson, Kathleen & Haskins, Jim.
Andrews, Benny, illus. see Benson, Kathleen.
Andrews, Benny, illus. see Haskins, James.
Andrews, Benny, illus. see Roessel, David & Rampersad, Arnold, eds.
Andrews, Beth. I Miss You! A Military Kid's Book about Deployment. Wright, Hawley, illus. (p. 844)
Andrews, Bruce. Designated Heartbeat. (p. 430)
Andrews, Carol. Giggle Wind. (p. 676)
Andrews, Carolyn. What Are Goods & Services? (p. 1879)
Andrews, Carolyn & Bedesky, Baron. What Is Insurance? (p. 1889)
Andrews, Carolyn & Thompson, Gare. What Is Importing & Exporting? (p. 1889)
Andrews, Catherine, et al. Elson Readers (p. 516)
Andrews, Charlie J. Tales of Animals on Farmer Brown's Farm: Children Stories. (p. 1702)
Andrews, Cheri. Reef Warrior: Embracing Reality. (p. 1456)
—Reef Warrior: Journey to Discovery. (p. 1456)
Andrews, Chris. Aspects of History: The Twentieth Century Lower Pack (p. 107)
—Twentieth Century Higher Pack (p. 1801)
Andrews, Christine. There's Something Lurking. (p. 1731)
Andrews, Cynthia. Molly Goes to Preschool. (p. 1160)
Andrews, D. M. Serpent in the Glass. (p. 1552)
Andrews, David. Wild Work (p. 1930)
Andrews, David, jt. auth. see Leppman, Elizabeth.
Andrews, David, et al. Water Poems & Bug Poems. (p. 1863)
Andrews, David, et al, selected by. Water Poems & Bug Poems. (p. 1863)
Andrews, Emily. Finer Points of Becoming Machine. (p. 589)
Andrews, et al. Uncross My Heart. (p. 1813)
Andrews, Gary, illus. see Dickens, Charles.
Andrews, Gary, illus. see Lamb, Charles & Lamb, Mary.
Andrews, Gary, illus. see Stevenson, Robert Louis.
Andrews, Georgina & Knighton, Kate. 100 Science Experiments. (p. 1999)
—Usborne 100 Science Experiments: Internet-Linked. Chisholm, Jane, ed. (p. 1827)
Andrews, Ilona. Magic Strikes (p. 1073)
Andrews, Jackie. 100 Bible Stories for Children. Biro, Val, illus. (p. 1998)
—David & Goliath. (p. 410)
—Gingerbread Man. Burton, Terry, illus. (p. 677)
—Goldilocks & the Three Bears. Taylor, Lawrie, illus. (p. 696)
—Great Big Enormous Turnip. Taylor, Lawrie, illus. (p. 714)
—Henny Penny. Taylor, Lawrie, illus. (p. 767)
—Joseph & His Wonderful Coat. (p. 926)
—Little Red Hen & the Wheat. Smith, Lesley, illus. (p. 1035)
—Moses in the Bulrushes. de Klerk, Roger, illus. (p. 1176)
—Noah & the First Rainbow. (p. 1261)
—Old Macdonald on His Farm. Bennett, John, illus. (p. 1284)
—On the Farm. (p. 1290)
—Three Billy-Goat Gruff. Bennett, John, illus. (p. 1741)
—Three Little Kittens. Smith, Lesley, illus. (p. 1742)
Andrews, Jackie, retold by. Favourite Tales for Young Readers. (p. 578)
Andrews, Jan. Auction Reczuch, Karen, illus. (p. 114)
—Auction. (p. 114)
—Rude Stories. Blake, Francis, illus. (p. 1494)
—Twelve Days of Summer Jolliffe, Susan Rennick, illus. (p. 1800)
—Very Last First Time Wallace, Ian, illus. (p. 1838)
—When Apples Grew Noses & White Horses Flew: Tales of Ti-Jean Petricic, Dusan, illus. (p. 1901)
Andrews, Jane. Each & All: The Seven Little Sisters Prove Their Sisterhood (Yesterday's Classics) (p. 492)
—Seven Little Sisters Who Live on the Rou. (p. 1554)
—Stories Mother Nature Told Her Child. (p. 1654)
—Stories Mother Nature Told Her Children. (p. 1654)
—Ten Boys Who Lived on the Road from Long Ago to Now (Yesterday's Classics) (p. 1718)
—Young Reader's Series: The stories mother nature told her Children. (p. 1979)
—Young Reader's Series: The seven little sisters who live on the round ball that floats in the Air. (p. 1979)
Andrews, Jane & Hopkins, Louisa Parsons. Seven Little Sisters Who Live on the Round Ball that Floats in the Air. (p. 1554)
Andrews, Jefferri & Andrews, Jonathan. Macos Adventure. (p. 1068)
Andrews, Jennie. Little Mouse Finds a House. (p. 1032)
Andrews, Jennifer M. Good Stuff Is Always on the Inside. (p. 700)
Andrews, Jerome. Initiation. (p. 874)
Andrews, Jesse. Me & Earl & the Dying Girl. (p. 1115)
Andrews, Joan. Best Friend for Thurston. (p. 169)
Andrews, John. Beck's Missing Shoes. (p. 156)
Andrews, Jonathan, jt. auth. see Andrews, Jefferri.
Andrews, Julie. Dumpy's Apple Shop. Walton, Tony, illus. (p. 490)
—Dumpy's Happy Holiday. Walton, Tony, illus. (p. 490)
—Little Bo: The Story of Bonnie Boadicea (p. 1024)
—Little Grey Men: A Story for the Young in Heart. Watkins-Pitchford, Denys, illus. (p. 1028)
—Simeon's Gift. (p. 1577)
Andrews, Julie & Edwards, Julie Andrews. Little Bo in Italy: The Continued Adventures of Bonnie Boadicea. Cole, Henry, illus. (p. 1024)
Andrews, Julie & Hamilton, Emma Walton. Dragon. (p. 476)
—Dumpy & the Firefighters. Walton, Tony, illus. (p. 490)
—Dumpy to the Rescue! Walton, Tony, illus. (p. 490)
—Fairy Merry Christmas. Davenier, Christine, illus. (p. 563)
—Great American Mousical. Walton, Tony, illus. (p. 713)
—Julie Andrews' Collection of Poems, Songs, & Lullabies. McMullan, Jim, illus. (p. 932)
—Julie Andrews' Treasury for All Seasons: Poems & Songs to Celebrate the Year. Priceman, Marjorie, illus. (p. 932)
—Simeon's Gift. Spirin, Gennady, illus. (p. 1577)
—Thanks to You: Wisdom from Mother & Child. (p. 1725)
—Very Fairy Princess: Teacher's Pet. (p. 1837)
—Very Fairy Princess: A Fairy Merry Christmas. (p. 1837)
—Very Fairy Princess: Teacher's Pet. Davenier, Christine, illus. (p. 1837)
—Very Fairy Princess: Here Comes the Flower Girl! Davenier, Christine, illus. (p. 1837)
—Very Fairy Princess. Davenier, Christine, illus. (p. 1837)
—Very Fairy Princess Follows Her Heart. Davenier, Christine, illus. (p. 1838)
—Very Fairy Princess Sparkles in the Snow. Davenier, Christine, illus. (p. 1838)
—Very Fairy Princess Takes the Stage. (p. 1838)
Andrews, Julie & Walton Hamilton, Emma. Very Fairy Princess: a Spooky, Sparkly Halloween. Davenier, Christine, illus. (p. 1837)
—Very Fairy Princess Doodle Book. Davenier, Christine, illus. (p. 1837)
Andrews, Julie, et al. Simeon's Gift. Spirin, Gennady, illus. (p. 1577)
—Very Fairy Princess - Graduation Girl! Davenier, Christine, illus. (p. 1837)
Andrews, Kaare. Astonishing X-Men: Xenogenesis. (p. 109)
—Spider-Man Legend of the Spider-Clan Young, Skott, illus. (p. 1626)
Andrews, Keli. Deadwood. (p. 418)
Andrews, Ken & Johnson, Diane. You Can Be Algebra Ready. (p. 1974)
Andrews, LaMont, Jr. Encyclopedia of Activists & Activism in America, Vol. 2 A-Z (p. 524)
Andrews, LaMont, Jr., illus. see Andrews-McKinney, Joyce.
Andrews, Lawrence. Plague. (p. 1366)
Andrews, Linda. Christmas Village. (p. 316)
Andrews, Linda Wasmer. Emotional Intelligence. (p. 520)
—Intelligence. (p. 879)
—Meditation. (p. 1120)
Andrews, Lindsey. I Walk for Water. Bennett, Jerry, illus. (p. 847)
Andrews, Lisa. Milton the Mouse Starts School. (p. 1144)
Andrews, Luke, illus. see Dontell, Susan L.
Andrews, Lynn V. Spirit Woman: The Teachings of the Shields. Momaday, N. Scott, illus. (p. 1629)
—Teachings Around the Sacred Wheel: Finding the Soul of the Dreamtime. (p. 1710)
Andrews, McKenna. Riding the Storm Out. (p. 1471)

Andrews McMeel Publishing LLC, Andrews McMeel. Go Fun! Big Book of Brain Games. (p. 686)
—Go Fun! Big Book of Crosswords. (p. 686)
—Go Fun! Big Book of Mazes. (p. 686)
—Go Fun! Dinosaur Doodle Book. (p. 686)
Andrews McMeel Publishing LLC Staff. Chicago. (p. 299)
Andrews McMeel Publishing, LLC Staff. Colors. Stone, Kate, illus. (p. 344)
—Hop, Pop, & Play. (p. 796)
—Zoo Babies. (p. 1988)
Andrews McMeel Publishing, LLC Staff, jt. auth. see Accord Publishing Staff.
Andrews McMeel Publishing, LLC Staff, jt. auth. see Cole, Jeff.
Andrews McMeel Publishing, LLC Staff & Cole, Jeff. Eyeball Animation Drawing Book: African Safari Edition. Cole, Jeff, illus. (p. 558)
—Flip & Click Big Book of Games: 100 Games. (p. 604)
Andrews McMeel Publishing, LLC Staff & Wise, Gary. Parents of Flannery McKracken. (p. 1324)
Andrews McMeel Publishing Staff. Dinosaurs. (p. 443)
Andrews McMeel Publishing Staff, jt. auth. see Accord Publishing Staff.
Andrews McMeel Publishing Staff & Broadhurst, Lucy. Ready, Steady, Spaghetti: Cooking for Kids & with Kids. (p. 1447)
Andrews McMeel Publishing Staff & Moore, Clement C. Twas the Night Before Christmas. Goodell, Jon, illus. (p. 1799)
Andrews McMeel Publishing Staff & Vasan, Gandee. Crazy Cats. (p. 377)
—Silly Dogs. (p. 1575)
Andrews McMeel Publishing Staff & Wang, Dorthea Deprisco. Five Minutes until Bed. Vaux, Patricia, illus. (p. 601)
Andrews McMeel Publishing Staff, et al. Happy, Sad, Silly, Mad: My World Makes Me Feel. (p. 746)
Andrews, Melodie, jt. auth. see DeGezelle, Terri.
Andrews, Minnie F., jt. auth. see DeVoss, Joyce A.
Andrews, Natalie. Clara's Witch. (p. 326)
Andrews, Neva. Stormy & Stub. (p. 1656)
Andrews, Pam. Christmas Carol: A Christmas Musical for Children about Giving. (p. 313)
—First Action Heroes: A Musical for Children about the Power of God. (p. 592)
—J-Force to the Rescue: A Kids' Musical Discovering the Ultimate Truth. (p. 901)
—Journey of Praise: An Easy-to-Sing, Easy-to-Stage Musical for Children. (p. 928)
—Joyland: A Children's Christmas Musical Teaching the Blessing of Giving. (p. 930)
—Net: A Kids' Musical about Teaching Evangelism. (p. 1242)
—Shepherd's Story: An Easy-to-Sing Christmas Musical for Children. (p. 1565)
—We Can Praise! An Easy-to-Sing, Easy-to-Stage Mini-Musical for Children. (p. 1866)
Andrews, Pam, jt. auth. see Andrews, Pam.
Andrews, Pam & Andrews, Pam. Cross Country: A Children's Musical That Reminds Us to Race to the Cross. (p. 385)
Andrews, Pam, et al. Easter Tree: An Easy-to-Sing, Easy-to-Stage Children's Easter Musical. (p. 499)
—Power: A Children's Musical about God's Strength in Us. (p. 1389)
Andrews, Phil. Own Goals. (p. 1315)
Andrews, Randall. Last Guardian of Magic. (p. 978)
Andrews, Richard, ed. see Gibson, Rex & Shakespeare, William.
Andrews, Roxanna. Adventures of Super Pig. (p. 23)
Andrews, Sandy. Best Friends - the Depression Years. (p. 169)
Andrews, Tamra. Wonders of the Sky (p. 1949)
Andrews, Ted. Faerie Charms. (p. 562)
Andrews, Troy. Trombone Shorty. Collier, Bryan, illus. (p. 1788)
Andrews, V. C. Garden of Shadows. (p. 656)
—If There Be Thorns/Seeds of Yesterday. (p. 854)
—Petalos al Viento. (p. 1346)
Andrews-Goebel, Nancy. Pot That Juan Built. Diaz, David, illus. (p. 1388)
—Vasija Que Juan Fabrico. Cortes, Eunice, tr. (p. 1833)
Andrews-McKinney, Joyce. Encyclopedia of Activists & Activism in America, Vol. 3 A-Z Andrews, LaMont, Jr., illus. (p. 524)
—Jentle & Jewel Fix Things Andrews-McKinney, Joyce, illus. (p. 913)
—Recognize, Appreciate, Respond: RAR Helping Teens Succeed. (p. 1452)
Andrewson, Natalie, illus. see Lawson, Jessica.
Andreyko, Marc. Street Justice. Palmiotti, Jimmy, illus. (p. 1666)
Andreyko, Marc & Pina, Javier. Manhunter - Trial by Fire. (p. 1087)
Andreyko, Marc & Pins, Javier. Origins. (p. 1304)
Andriani, Renee, illus. see Davis, Kenneth C.
Andriani, Renee, illus. see Murphy, Stuart J.
Andriani, Renee, illus. see Winters, Kay.
Andriani, Renee, jt. auth. see Murphy, Stuart J.
Andriani, Renee W., illus. see Conford, Ellen.
Andriani, Renee W., illus. see Murphy, Stuart J.
Andricain, Sergio. Arco Iris de Poesia: Poemmas de las Americas y Espana. Cuellar, Olga, illus. (p. 95)
Andries, Kathryn. Soul Choices: Six Paths to Find Your Life Purpose. Brill, Darlene, ed. (p. 1614)
Andriotis, Vicky. Prayer in Poetry. (p. 1393)
Andrisani, John. Tiger's New Swing: An Analysis of Tiger Woods's New Swing Technique. (p. 1749)
Andrisano, Micheal. Harold the High Knight & Princess Megan: Harold & Megan. (p. 749)
Andriyevskaya, Yevgeniya, illus. see Lupa, Mary R.
Andronik, Catherine M. Copernicus: Genius of Modern Astronomy. (p. 365)
—Copernicus: Founder of Modern Astronomy. (p. 365)
—Lincoln. (p. 1018)
Andru, Ross, illus. see Conway, Gerry, et al.
Andru, Ross & Kane, Gil. Marvel Masterworks: The Amazing Spider-Man Volume 16. (p. 1099)
Andruetto, María Teresa. País de Juan. Hernández, Gabriel, illus. (p. 1319)
Andrules, Jamie L., illus. see Hamilton, Deborah E.
Andrus, Amy M. Pixie Jane, Too Small. (p. 1365)
Andrusier, Devorah Leah, ed. see Bassan, Malca.
Andryczyk, Mark, tr. see Dergachov, Oleg.
Andryszewski, Tricia. Mass Extinction: Examining the Current Crisis. (p. 1102)
Andujar, Gloria Dearagon, tr. see Paulsen, Gary.
Andurlakis, Anna. Mickey the Mailman Dog. (p. 1136)
Anegon, Tamara, illus. see Nyikos, Stacy.
Anello, Marc, et al. Hip Chick Survival Kit. (p. 780)
Anema, Durlynn. Harriet Chalmers Adams: Adventurer & Explorer. (p. 749)
—Louise Arner Boyd: Arctic Explorer. (p. 1058)
—Ynes Mexia: Botanist & Adventurer. (p. 1971)
Anemone, Robert L. Race Biology & Culture: A Reader. (p. 1430)
Anfousse, Ginette. Mon Ami Pichou. (p. 1163)
—Polo et L'anniversaire. Sarrazin, Marisol, tr. (p. 1381)
Anfousse, Ginette & Sarrazin, Marisol. Polo et le Garde-Manger. (p. 1381)
Anfuso, Dennis, illus. see De Sena, Joseph.
Anfuso, Dennis & Lindsay, Alan. Oz House. (p. 1316)
Ang, Joy, illus. see Heos, Bridget.
Ang, Joy, illus. see Kilabuk, Elisha.
Ang, Joy, illus. see Meng, Cece.
Ang, Joy, illus. see Paquette, Ammi-Joan.
Ang, Joy, illus. see Watson, Stephanie Elaine.
Ang, Karen. Collared Lizard. (p. 339)
—Inside the Ants' Nest. (p. 877)
—Inside the Bee's Hive. (p. 877)
Ang, Selvi, illus. see Ranga, Katherine.
Ang, Tom. How to Photograph Absolutely Everything: Successful Pictures from Your Digital Camera. (p. 821)
Angaramo, Roberta, illus. see Conway, David.
Angaramo, Roberta, illus. see Gormley, Greg.
Angaramo, Roberta, illus. see Harrison, David L.
Angaramo, Roberta, illus. see Perry, Andrea.
Angel. Santa Claus's Journey to Texsuilver. (p. 1511)
Angel, Ann. Amy Tan: Weaver of Asian-American Tales. (p. 66)
—Janis Joplin: Rise up Singing. (p. 908)
—Reader's Guide to Sandra Cisneros's the House on Mango Street. (p. 1444)
—Robert Cormier: Author of the Chocolate War. (p. 1478)
—Such a Pretty Face: Short Stories about Beauty. (p. 1672)
—Things I'll Never Say: Stories about Our Secret Selves. (p. 1733)
Angel, Bruce. I Believe in Santa Claus. (p. 834)
Angel, Carl, illus. see Argueta, Jorge.
Angel, Carl, illus. see Gilles, Almira Astudillo.
Angel, Carl, illus. see Robles, Anthony D.
Angel, Carl, illus. see Robles, Anthony D. & Children's Book Press Staff.
Angel, Embracing. Miranda the Flying Mermaid. (p. 1149)
Angel, Julie Marie. Rhyme Queen. (p. 1468)
Angel, Katharine Ann. Being Forgotten. (p. 161)
Angel, R. P. G. Angel: Investigator's Casebook. (p. 73)
Angela-Lago, illus. see Ventura, Antonio.
Angela's Bookshelf Publishing Staff. Choice Stories for Children. (p. 309)
Angelastro, Yvonne. Four Lost Chicks. (p. 625)
Angelchild, P. Erotic Memoirs Volume 1. (p. 534)
Angelelli, Claudia, et al. Composicion: Proceso y Sintesis. (p. 354)
Angeles, Jiménez Soria, jt. auth. see Soria, Angeles Jimenez.
Angeles, Maria. Tortilla para Emilia. (p. 1770)
Angeletti, Roberta. Cave Painter of Lascaux. (p. 282)
—Golden Goose. (p. 694)
Angeletti, Roberta, illus. see Peters, Polly.
Angeli, Marguerite De, see De Angeli, Marguerite.
Angelillo, Janet. Making Revision Matter: Strategies for Guiding Students to Focus, Organize, & Strengthen Their Writing Independently. (p. 1082)
Angelina, Laura. Little Girl's Wish. (p. 1028)
Angelini, George, illus. see Lucado, Max.
Angelini, Josephine. Dreamless. (p. 484)
—Goddess. (p. 690)
—Starcrossed. (p. 1642)
—Trail of Tears. (p. 1776)
—Trial by Fire. (p. 1785)
Angelini, Josephine & Shields, Gillian. Destiny. (p. 430)
Angelique, A. J. Rose Petals & Ash: Curse of the Red Rose Killer (p. 1489)
Angelique, Aj. Lady Cy. (p. 970)
Angelique, Janice. Ducky Grows Up. (p. 488)
Angelis, Gina De. Hernando Cortes & the Conquest of Mexico. (p. 772)
Angelis, Therese De, see De Angelis, Therese.
Angell, Anne. Promised Land. (p. 1411)
Angell, Ian O. Creative Haven Geometric Allover Patterns Coloring Book. (p. 379)
Angell, Judie. Ronnie & Rosey. (p. 1487)
Angello, Mary L. Legend of the Crystal Skull. (p. 989)
Angelo, Joseph A., Jr. Human Spaceflight. (p. 826)
—Robot Spacecraft. (p. 1480)
—Spacecraft for Astronomy. (p. 1620)
Angelo, Linda. Three Secrets of Happiness. (p. 1743)
Angelo, Tony. Go-bez Nibe: Very Clever Firefly Lubitsky, Maribeth Jenkins, illus. (p. 686)
—Just Inn Time. Freeman, Angela, illus. (p. 938)
Angelou, Maya. Amazing Peace: A Christmas Poem Johnson, Steve et al, illus. (p. 55)
—Cedric of Jamaica. Rockwell, Lizzy, illus. (p. 283)
—My Painted House, My Friendly Chicken, & Me. (p. 1216)
—My Painted House, My Friendly Chicken, & Me. Courtney-Clarke, Margaret, illus. (p. 1216)
Angelou, Maya & Kirkpatrick, Patricia. Maya Angelou. (p. 1112)
Angers, Michelle. Animal Garden. (p. 78)
Angle, Scott, illus. see Fisher, Doris & Gibbs, D. L.
Angle, Scott, illus. see Prokos, Anna & Voege, Debra.
Angleberger, Tom. Art2-D2's Guide to Folding & Doodling: An Origami Yoda Activity Book. (p. 103)
—Crankee Doodle. Bell, Cece, illus. (p. 376)
—Darth Paper Strikes Back: An Origami Yoda Book. (p. 409)
—Darth Paper Strikes Back. (p. 409)
—Emperor Pickletine Rides the Bus. (p. 521)
—Fake Mustache: Or, How Jodie o'Rodeo & Her Wonder Horse (and Some Nerdy Kid) Saved the U. S. Presidential Election from a Mad Genius Criminal Mastermind. (p. 565)
—Fake Mustache. (p. 565)
—Horton Halfpott: Or, the Fiendish Mystery of Smugwick Manor - Or, the Loosening of M'Lady Luggertuck's Corset. (p. 801)
—McToad Mows Tiny Island. Hendrix, John, illus. (p. 1115)
—Origami Yoda Files (p. 1304)
—Poop Fountain! (p. 1383)
—Princess Labelmaker to the Rescue! (p. 1404)
—Rat with the Human Face. (p. 1440)
—Secret of the Fortune Wookiee: An Origami Yoda Book. (p. 1542)
—Secret of the Fortune Wookiee. (p. 1542)
—Secret of the Fortune Wookiee. Bell, Cece, illus. (p. 1542)
—Strange Case of Origami Yoda (p. 1665)
—Strange Case of Origami Yoda. (p. 1665)
—Surprise Attack of Jabba the Puppett. (p. 1685)
Angleberger, Tom, jt. auth. see Hemphill, Michael.
Anglemyer, Jordan. Grandpa's Favorites: A collection of quotes, things to ponder, stories, bits of verse, & Humor. (p. 709)
Anglen, Becca. Nightmare in the Woods. McKeown, Christian, illus. (p. 1255)
Angler, Evan. Spark (p. 1622)
Anglican Church of Canada Staff. Gift of Life: Children's Book for the Eucharist from Life in the Eucharist Program. (p. 675)
—Life in the Eucharist: A Communion Program for Children. (p. 1011)
Anglicas, Louise, illus. see Greve, Meg.
Anglicas, Louise, illus. see Mckenzie, Precious.
Anglicas, Louise, illus. see Mitten, Luana.
Anglicas, Louise, illus. see Robertson, J. Jean.
Anglicas, Louise, illus. see Williamson, Karen.
Anglin, David, tr. see Rodari, Gianni.
Anglin, Dawnice. God's Creation Bible Coloring Book: Bible Coloring Book. (p. 691)
Anglin, Karen L. CliffsQuickReview Math Word Problems. (p. 332)
Anglin, M. R. Lucas: Guardian of Truth. (p. 1062)
Angliss, Sarah & Hewson, Maggie. Matter & Materials. (p. 1109)
—Sound & Light. (p. 1615)
Angliss, Sarah, et al. Hands-On Science: Electricity & Magnets. (p. 741)
—Hands-On Science: Forces & Motion. (p. 741)
—Hands-On Science: Matter & Materials. (p. 741)
—Hands-On Science: Sound & Light. (p. 741)
Anglo, Mick. Young Marvelman Classic - Volume 1. Parlett, George & Bleach, James, illus. (p. 1979)
Anglund, Joan Walsh. Cowboy's Christmas. Anglund, Joan Walsh, illus. (p. 374)
—Little Angels' Book of Christmas. Anglund, Joan Walsh, illus. (p. 1023)
Angom, Matthew, illus. see Pillsbury, Samuel H.
Angst, Frank. Chad Johnson. (p. 288)
Angstrom, Gwen R. Eemlets & Grandma Eema Stories, Book 1: From Rainbow to Sunshine. (p. 505)
—Silent, Snowy Night in Sunriver, Book 2: The Eemlets & Grandma Eema Stories. (p. 1575)
Anguissola, Anna, illus. see Cuffaro, Anna.
Angus, Jennifer. In Search of Goliathus Hercules. (p. 864)
Angus, John. Beautiful Music A Children's Concert. (p. 154)
Angus, Sam. Horse Called Hero. (p. 799)
—Soldier Dog. (p. 1607)
Angwin, Fiona & Foster, Jeff. Last Unicorn: Is It My Responsibility to Protect the Environment? - A Story & Activity Based Approach for 8 to 12 Year Olds. (p. 979)
Anh, Nguyen Nhat. Ticket to Childhood. Naythons, Will, tr. from VIE. (p. 1747)
Anhalt, Ariela. Freefall. (p. 635)
Anhalt, Edward. Raise Your GPA 1 Full Grade. (p. 1436)
Anholt, Catherine, illus. see Anholt, Laurence.
Anholt, Catherine, jt. illus. see Anholt, Laurence.
Anholt, Catherine & Anholt, Laurence. Can You Guess? A Lift-the-Flap Birthday Party Book. (p. 259)
—Catherine & Laurence Anholt's Big Book of Little Children. Anholt, Catherine & Anholt, Laurence, illus. (p. 280)
—Chimp & Zee Play. Anholt, Catherine & Anholt, Laurence, illus. (p. 306)
—First Words & Pictures. (p. 597)
Anholt, Laurence. Anholt's Artists Activity Book. (p. 76)
—Babies, Babies, Babies! Anholt, Catherine, illus. (p. 123)
—Cezanne & the Apple Boy. (p. 288)
—Degas & the Little Dancer. (p. 424)
—Degas y la Pequena Bailarina: Un Cuento Sobre Edgar Degas. (p. 424)
—Eco-Wolf & the Three Pigs Robins, Arthur, illus. (p. 502)
—Jardin Magico de Claude Monet. (p. 909)
—Leonardo & the Flying Boy. (p. 992)
—Magical Garden of Claude Monet. (p. 1074)
—Matisse: the King of Color. (p. 1109)
—Our New Baby & Me: A First Year Record Book for New Brothers & Sisters. Anholt, Catherine, illus. (p. 1309)
—Papa Chagall, Tell Us a Story. (p. 1322)
—Picasso & the Girl with a Ponytail. (p. 1354)
—Stone Girl Bone Girl: The Story of Mary Anning. Moxley, Sheila, illus. (p. 1652)
—Two Nests. Coplestone, Jim, illus. (p. 1804)
—Van Gogh & the Sunflowers. (p. 1833)
Anholt, Laurence, jt. auth. see Anholt, Catherine.
Anholt, Laurence & Anholt, Catherine. Chimp & Zee & the Big Storm. (p. 306)
Anholt, Laurence & Coplestone, Jim. Seven for a Secret. (p. 1554)
Anielski, Angela. My Safe Space: I Don't Know You! (p. 1218)
Animal Hospital Staff. A to Z of Animal Hospital. (p. 2)
Animal Planet Staff. Finding Bigfoot: Everything You Need to Know. (p. 588)
Anin, Ravi & Benchmark Education Co., LLC Staff. In Our Town. (p. 864)
—Pete Mule's Hat. (p. 1346)
Anita D Martinez. Worm Imposters. (p. 1961)
Anita, Ganeri, jt. auth. see Ganeri, Anita.
Anjelais, M. Breaking Butterflies. (p. 225)
Anjou, Colette. Olga's Cats: An ABC Book. Linville, S. Olga, illus. (p. 1285)
—Westie the Dog. Niles, Kim, illus. (p. 1876)
Anke, Robert. Rahoola's Song. (p. 1433)
Ankers, Angela M. Summerbook Readers: Short a & i words (p. 1675)
Anketell, Christine, jt. auth. see Edwards, Hazel.
Ankhnu Feaster, Teraab & Campbell, Rochelle. Magic Seeds. (p. 1073)
Ann. My Name Is Oak... Daytona Oak. (p. 1215)
—We Call Him Puddles. (p. 1866)
Ann, jt. auth. see Buck, Ray.
Ann, Cameron. Most Beautiful Place in the World. (p. 1177)
—Stories Julian Tells. (p. 1654)
Ann Chambers Bsdh Ms. Monty Molar & Friends. (p. 1170)
Ann, Dee. Burden of Silence. (p. 243)
Ann Hollis Rife, illus. see Leland, Debbie.
Ann, Janice. Kenny Breezes the Clouds. (p. 949)
Ann, Melissa. Redfish, Goldfish. (p. 1455)
Ann, Pilling, jt. auth. see Pilling, Ann.
Ann, Sharrie. Granddaughter & King Green Warts. (p. 707)
Ann, Smythe Karen. Fredrick the Butterfly. (p. 633)
Anna. Magic Money Tree. (p. 1072)
Anna, Jennifer. Best Thing: An Almost True Story of Ladybugs & Sisters. (p. 171)
—Grandma's Button Box. (p. 708)
—Maxwell Dreams of Trains. Blue, Buster, illus. (p. 1112)
—Year of the Dragon: The Complete Story Experience Edition. Brandon, Theresa, illus. (p. 1969)
—Year of the Dragon. (p. 1969)
—Yen Shei & the American Bonsai. (p. 1970)
Anna, Sewell, jt. auth. see Sewell, Anna.
Annable, Graham. Further Grickle. (p. 650)
—Stickleback. (p. 1650)
Annaud, Jean-Jacques, et al. Two Brothers: The Tale of Kumal & Sangha. (p. 1803)
AnnDrewArt, illus. see Harris, Donna L.
Anne, Heather. Purple People. (p. 1419)
Anne, Lisa. Heaven's Door. (p. 761)
Anne, Margo. Lily Rose. (p. 1018)
Anne, Paula. Sultry Smith. (p. 1673)
Annear, Tom, et al. Instream Flows: For Riverine Resource Stewardship. (p. 878)
Annelli, Nikki, illus. see Marshall, Judy.
Anne-Marie-Mugwe. Cobjay's Summer Holiday & How to Catch a Squirrel. (p. 336)
Anness Publishing Ltd. Let's Look & See: Vehicles. (p. 998)
—Let's Look & See: Canadian Animals. (p. 998)
Anness Publishing Staff. Nursery Rhymes for Little Ones: Best Ever Rhymes, Action Rhymes, Playtime Rhymes: Mother Goose Collection (p. 1273)
—Step-by-Step Training Manual of Soccer Skills & Techniques. (p. 1647)
Anness Publishing Staff, jt. auth. see O'Toole, Janet.
Anness Publishing Staff, et al. Great Big Book of Things to Make & Do: Cooking, Painting, Crafts, Science, Gardening, Magic, Music & Having a Party - Simple & Fun Step-by-Step Projects for Young Children. (p. 714)
Annette Roeder. Edgar Degas: Coloring Book. (p. 504)
Annie. Giving Children. (p. 681)
Annie Hamilton, Donnell. Three Young Knights & Miss Theodosia's Heartstrings. (p. 1744)
Annie, Johnston. Three Weavers. (p. 1744)
Annie S. Swan. Thankful Rest. (p. 1725)
Annie Starks-Johnson, jt. auth. see Annie Starks-Johnson, Starks-Johnson.
Annie Starks-Johnson, Starks-Johnson & Annie Starks-Johnson. Dottie's Surprise Birthday Party. (p. 472)
Annie's. I Can Bead. Frank, Sharon, ed. (p. 835)
Annie's Staff. I Can Crochet. Ellison, Connie, ed. (p. 835)
Annino, J. G. Florida's Famous Animals: True Stories of Sunset Sam the Dolphin, Snooty the Manatee, Big Guy the Panther, & Others. (p. 607)
Annino, J G. She Sang Promise: The Story of Betty Mae Jumper, Seminole Tribal Leader. Desimini, Lisa, illus. (p. 1564)
Annino, Jan Godown. She Sang Promise: The Story of Betty Mae Jumper, Seminole Tribal Leader. Desimini, Lisa, illus. (p. 1564)
Anniss, Matt. Cold Cases. (p. 338)
—Criminal Profiling. (p. 382)
—Dj-ing. (p. 455)
—Espionage. (p. 536)
—Fighting Cancer. (p. 585)
—History of Modern Music. (p. 784)
—Impact of Technology in Music. (p. 862)
—Impact of Technology in Sports. (p. 862)
—James Watson & Francis Crick. (p. 907)
—Jane Goodall & Mary Leakey. (p. 908)
—Make a Podcast! (p. 1078)
—Music, Fashion, & Style. (p. 1193)
—Music Industry. (p. 1193)
—Performing Live. (p. 1343)
—Planet under Pressure: Too Many People on Earth? (p. 1368)
—Science vs. Disease. (p. 1528)
—Start a Band! (p. 1643)
—Story of Hip-Hop. (p. 1658)
—Story of Pop Music. (p. 1659)
—Story of Punk & Indie. (p. 1659)
—Story of Rock Music. (p. 1659)
—Story of Soul & R & B. (p. 1660)
—Story of Techno & Dance Music. (p. 1660)
—Terrorism. (p. 1722)

—What Is a Database & How Do I Use It? (p. 1888)
—What Is a Website & How Do I Use It? (p. 1888)
Anniss, Matt, jt. auth. see Regan, Lisa.
Anniss, Matthew. Recording & Promoting Your Music (p. 1452)
—Understanding Computer Networks. (p. 1815)
—Understanding Programming & Logic. (p. 1816)
Anniss, Matthew, jt. auth. see Woolf, Alex.
Anniss, Matthew & Mason, Paul. Understanding Computing. (p. 1815)
Annmarie & Emma Chiarenza. Yippee Day. (p. 1971)
Anno, Moyoco. Flowers & Bees. Anno, Moyoco, illus. (p. 608)
—Happy Mania Anno, Moyoco, illus. (p. 746)
Anno, Moyoko. Happy Mania (p. 746)
Anns, Lynn. Tent City Princess. (p. 1720)
Annunziata, Jane, jt. auth. see Nemiroff, Marc A.
Annunziata, Jane & Nemiroff, Marc. Sometimes I'm Scared. Langdo, Bryan, illus. (p. 1610)
Anoli, illus. see Iliand, Valentina.
Anon. Collection of Animal Poems for Children. (p. 339)
—Great Men & Women That Shaped Our World - a Selection of Articles from a Classic Children's Encyclopedi. (p. 717)
Anon & Marshall Cavendish. Step-by-Step Cooking for Kids: Recipes from around the World. (p. 1647)
Anónimo. Juguemos en el Bosque. Bergna, Monica, illus. (p. 932)
Anonimo. Lazarillo de Tormes. (p. 981)
Anónimo. Romancero. (p. 1486)
—Yo Tenia 10 Perritos. Stagno, Laura, illus. (p. 1971)
Anonuevo, Rechelle. Moonlight Serenade. (p. 1173)
Anonymous. Anonymous Diary Collection: Lucy in the Sky; Letting Ana Go; The Book of David. (p. 87)
—Anti-Slavery Alphabet. (p. 89)
—Beauty & the Beast. (p. 154)
—Book of David. (p. 211)
—Book of Old-Time Trades & Tools. (p. 211)
—Child's Book of Poetry a Selection of Poems, Ballads & Hymns. (p. 304)
—Confessions of a Backup Dancer. (p. 356)
—Go Ask Alice. (p. 686)
—Go Ask Alice/Jay's Journal. Sparks, Beatrice, ed. (p. 686)
—Jay's Journal. Sparks, Beatrice, ed. (p. 910)
—Letting Ana Go. (p. 1003)
—Little Cinderella. (p. 1026)
—Lucy in the Sky. (p. 1063)
—Pied Piper of Hamlin. (p. 1356)
—Punky Dunk & the Gold Fish: The Punky Dunk Series. (p. 1417)
—Punky Dunk & the Mouse: The Punky Dunk Series. (p. 1417)
—Punky Dunk & the Spotted Pup: The Punky Dunk Series. (p. 1417)
—Required Poems for Reading & Memorizing: Third & Fourth Grades, Prescribed by State Courses of Study. (p. 1462)
—Rudolph Saves the Day. (p. 1494)
—Rudolph the Red-Nosed Reindeer: Rudolph Saves the Day. (p. 1494)
—STORY of ALADDIN & the MAGICAL LAMP. Craft, Richard et al, eds. (p. 1657)
—STORY of GULNARE of the SEA. Craft, Richard et al, eds. (p. 1658)
—STORY of PRINCE AGIB. Craft, Richard et al, eds. (p. 1659)
—Story of the Fisherman & the Genie. Craft, Richard et al, eds. (p. 1661)
Anonymous & Laughing Elephant Publishing Staff. Kitty's A. B. C. Shape Book. (p. 963)
Anonymus. 'Twas the Night Before Christmas. Tavares, Matt, illus. (p. 1799)
Anorak Press Staff. Anorak: Writing. (p. 87)
—Anorak: The Happy Mag for Kids. Vol. 3 Wright, Jay, illus. (p. 87)
Anorak Press Staff & Olmedillas, Cathy, compiled by. Anorak: The Happy Mag For Kids. (p. 87)
Anrias, Donnan. Targ - the King of Eagles. (p. 1706)
Ansary, Mir Tamim. All Around California: Regions & Resources (p. 43)
—California History (p. 253)
—Columbus Day (p. 346)
—Día de Acción de Gracias. (p. 433)
—Día de la Bandera. (p. 433)
—Día de la Independencia. (p. 433)
—Día de las Elecciones. (p. 433)
—Día de los Caídos. (p. 433)
—Día de los Presidentes. (p. 433)
—Día de los Veteranos. (p. 433)
—Día de Martin Luther King, Jr. (p. 433)
—Día del Trabajo. (p. 433)
—Earth Day (p. 495)
—Flag Day (p. 602)
—Independence Day (p. 870)
—Martin Luther King Jr. Day (p. 1098)
—Memorial Day (p. 1125)
—People of California (p. 1339)
—Presidents' Day (p. 1397)
—Thanksgiving Day (p. 1726)
Ansary, Mir Tamim & Heinemann Library Staff. All Around California: Regions & Resources (p. 43)
—California History (p. 253)
—People of California (p. 1339)
Ansell, Dave, jt. auth. see Smith, Chris.
Ansell, Hilary. Design & Technology. (p. 429)
Ansell, Liz. Unforgettable Snow Lady: And Other Memorable Short Stories, Songs & Rhymes. (p. 1817)
Ansell, Maggi, ed. see Shane, Victor.
Anselmo, Frank D. Ghost Lake Chronicles: Book III- Taylor's Tomb. (p. 671)
Anselmo, Robert Louis. We're All Different & yet Still the Same. (p. 1875)
Ansfield, Elizabeth, ed. see Reiss, Kathryn.
Anshutz, Carrie. Cimarron Chronicles: Saga of the Open Range. (p. 319)
Ansley, Frank, illus. see DePrisco, Dorothea.
Ansley, Frank, illus. see Wheeler, Lisa.
Ansley, Frank & Wheeler, Lisa. Who's Afraid of Granny Wolf? Ansley, Frank, tr. (p. 1920)
Ansong, Anthony. Cunning Kwaku Anansi: Tales by the Fireside. Mahomet, John, illus. (p. 392)
Anstee, Ashlyn. Are We There, Yet? Anstee, Ashlyn, illus. (p. 96)
Anstey, David, illus. see Clynes, Kate.
Anstey, David, illus. see Gregory, Manju.
Anstey, David, jt. auth. see Clynes, Kate.
Ant, Exupery. Giorno con il Piccolo Principe. (p. 677)
—Imparo a Contare con il Picco. (p. 862)
—Journee avec le Petit Prince. (p. 927)
—L apprends a compter avec Le. (p. 969)
—Piccolo Principe el Suio. (p. 1354)
Ant., Mary. Shiniest Treasure: The Journey with Grammy & Grampa! (p. 1566)
—Shiniest Treasure: The Journey with Grammy & Grampa! Part 2. (p. 1566)
Antebi, Marcus, jt. auth. see Emerson, Kim.
Antell, Gerson & Harris, Walter. Economics for Everybody. (p. 502)
Antesberger, Barbara. My Grandma's Hands Are Special (p. 1210)
Anthem Press, compiled by. Modern World School Atlas: USA Edition. (p. 1159)
Anthis, Brian, illus. see Irbinskas, Heather.
Anthoine, Leila, illus. see Cunningham, Edie.
Anthony, Alan, illus. see Watson, George.
Anthony, Camille, et al. Unwanted Child. (p. 1823)
Anthony, Carl Sferrazza. America's Most Influential First Ladies. (p. 64)
Anthony, Carmelo & Brown, Greg. Carmelo Anthony: It's Just the Beginning. (p. 270)
anthony, chance. Princess of Du'val. (p. 1404)
Anthony, David. Bison. (p. 193)
—Who Were the Mound Builders? (p. 1919)
Anthony, David & Clasman, Charles David. Heroes A2Z #13: (Heroes a to Z): Monkey Monster Truck. Blakeslee, Lys, illus. (p. 772)
Anthony, David & David, Charles. Heroes A2Z #1: (Heroes a to Z): Alien Ice Cream. Blakeslee, Lys, illus. (p. 772)
—Heroes A2Z #2: (Heroes a to Z): Bowling over Halloween: Bowling over Halloween. Blakeslee, Lys, illus. (p. 772)
—Knightscares #1: (Knightscares): Cauldron Cooker's Night. No. 1 (p. 964)
—Knightscares #3: (Knightscares): Early Winter's Orb. (p. 964)
—Knightscares #4: (Knightscares) (p. 964)
—Knightscares #5: (Knightscares) (p. 964)
—Knightscares #6: (Knightscares) (p. 964)
Anthony, David H. Freedom: Life after Slavery. (p. 634)
—Langston Hughes: Harlem Renaissance Writer. (p. 974)
Anthony, Erin. I-Ballers: Little Books for Big Minds. (p. 834)
Anthony, Fortuna. Tim Tim the River Crayfish. (p. 1750)
Anthony, Irie. Pants & Shoes & Reading the News. (p. 1321)
Anthony, Jason, jt. auth. see Shipley, Nan.
Anthony, Jessica & Corral, Rodrigo, creators. Chopsticks. (p. 310)
Anthony, Joseph. Dandelion Seed's Big Dream. Arbo, Cris, illus. (p. 403)
—In a Nutshell. (p. 863)
Anthony, Kitty. King's Castles. (p. 960)
Anthony, Mark, illus. see Lucas, Eileen.
Anthony, Mark, et al. Gut Instinct: Diet's Missing Link. (p. 733)
Anthony, Michelle. Big God Story Godbey, Cory, illus. (p. 181)
Anthony, Michelle, jt. auth. see Lindert, Reyna.
Anthony, Michelle & McLaughlin, Dennis R. Gigantic Book of Games for Youth Ministry (p. 676)
Anthony, Mike. Adventures of Henry the Patchwork Whale (p. 18)
Anthony, Nathan & Gardner, Robert. Attack on Pearl Harbor in United States History. (p. 114)
Anthony, Piers. Key to Chroma. (p. 950)
—Key to Havoc. (p. 950)
—Macroscope. (p. 1068)
—Pornucopia. (p. 1386)
Anthony, Rachel. Magic Bee. (p. 1071)
Anthony, Robert. Wake up America. (p. 1853)
Anthony, Roger. Rindin the Puffer. (p. 1473)
Anthony, Ross. Please Don't Step on the Ants. Anthony, Ross, illus. (p. 1373)
Anthony, Stenetta. Love Story. (p. 1060)
Anthony, Susan C. Casting Nines Quick Check For. (p. 276)
Anthony, Wes. Binger & Stumpy the B D Dawg Series - Book. (p. 188)
Anthony-Butt, Lisa. God Speaks Pink: ... to teenage Girls. (p. 690)
Antieau, Kim. Blue Tail. (p. 203)
—Broken Moon. (p. 230)
—Mercy, Unbound. (p. 1127)
Antill, Sara. 10 Ways I Can Earn Money. (p. 1994)
—10 Ways I Can Help My Community. (p. 1994)
—10 Ways I Can Help My Family. (p. 1994)
—10 Ways I Can Live A Healthy Life. (p. 1994)
—10 Ways I Can Save the Earth. (p. 1994)
—Bear's Life. (p. 152)
—Crocodile's Life. (p. 384)
—Curiosity. (p. 392)
—Elephant's Life. (p. 512)
—Giant Anteater. (p. 673)
—Grit. (p. 724)
—Horse's Life. (p. 800)
—Okapi. (p. 1282)
—Platypus. (p. 1370)
—Porcupines. (p. 1386)
—Red Panda. (p. 1454)
—Self-Control. (p. 1549)
—Shark's Life. (p. 1563)
—Social Intelligence. (p. 1604)
—Stonefish. (p. 1653)
—Unusual Animals (p. 1823)
—Whale's Life. (p. 1878)
—Zest. (p. 1986)
Antillano, Laura. Diana en la Tierra Wayuu. Armas, Lourdes, illus. (p. 434)
—Vaca Querida. Ochoa, Ana, illus. (p. 1829)
Antiporda, Enrico. Adventures of Jimbo, the Homeless Cat. Antiporda, Enrico, illus. (p. 19)
Antkowski, Marygrace, illus. see Zipf, Sean.
Antle, Bhagavan. Suryia & Roscoe: The True Story of an Unlikely Friendship. Antle, Bhagavan & Bland, Barry, illus. (p. 1687)
—Suryia Swims! The True Story of How an Orangutan Learned to Swim. Antle, Bhagavan & Bland, Barry, illus. (p. 1687)
—Tiger Cubs & the Chimp: The True Story of How Anjana the Chimp Helped Raise Two Baby Tigers. Antle, Bhagavan, illus. (p. 1748)
Antle, Peg Caryer. Love Never Fails: A Life Lesson Taught to a Child Through His Teddy Bear. (p. 1060)
—Someone Special. (p. 1609)
Antoine, Julia E. Abcs of Caribbean Fruits & Vegetables! (p. 4)
Antoine, Leon. Santa's Destiny: A Legend Reborn (p. 1513)
Antol, Jenna. "Do" The Once Forgotten Little Bunny Who Grew to Become a World Record Holder. (p. 456)
Antologia Staff. Libro de Oro de los Abuelos. (p. 1006)
Anton, jt. auth. see Vilagut.
Anton, Amy Way. Ina the Octopus & Her Shipwreck Adventure. Way, MaryFaye, illus. (p. 868)
Anton, Carrie, ed. see Cryan, Mary Beth.
Anton, Carrie, ed. see Lundsten, Apryl.
Anton, Carrie, jt. ed. see American Girl Editors.
Anton, Carrie, ed. Doll Tees Felt Fashions (Revised) (p. 463)
—Go for It! Start Smart, Have Fun, & Stay Inspired in Any Activity. Laskey, Shannon, illus. (p. 686)
—Paper Doll Fashion Fun: Make paper doll clothes with the supplies Inside! Decaire, Camela, illus. (p. 1322)
Anton de vez, Patricia, tr. see Paver, Michelle & Paver, Michelle.
Anton, Ferdinand. Secret World of the Aztecs. Wynne, Christopher, ed. (p. 1544)
Anton, Howard. Instructor's Solutions Manual to Accompany Contemp Orary Linear Algebra. (p. 878)
Anton, Howard, jt. auth. see Busby, Robert C.
Anton, Howard & Busby, Robert C. Contemporary Linear Algebra. (p. 360)
Anton, Jackie. Backyard Horse Tales Sox: 2nd Edition. (p. 131)
Anton, Madeline Marie, jt. auth. see Anton, Robert Wayne.
Anton, Maggie. Secret Scholar. (p. 1543)
Anton, Mauricio, illus. see Turner, Alan.
Anton, Robert & Marie, Madeline. Flames of Fortune: Dragonia, Tales of the Golden Talon (p. 602)
—Hope for Zargahn: Dragonia, Tales of the Golden Talon. (p. 796)
Anton, Robert Wayne & Anton, Madeline Marie. Portal in the Storm: Dragonia, Tales of the Golden Talon. (p. 1386)
Antonacopoulou, Elena, et al, eds. Learning, Working & Living: Mapping the Terrain of Working Life Learning. (p. 986)
Antonelli, Gina. Who Is Ollie? Antonelli, Gina, illus. (p. 1916)
Antonelli, Paola, jt. auth. see Lovegrove, Ross.
Antonello, Marisa, illus. see Kielburger, Craig.
Antonenkov, Evgeny, illus. see Levin, Vadim.
Antonenkov, Evgeny, illus. see Zunshine, Tatiana.
Antoni, Birgit, jt. auth. see Treiber, Jutta.
Antonia, Miller. Baby's Very First Little Book of Bunnies. (p. 129)
Antoniades, Basil. Having Fun with the Gods & Goddesses of the Ancient Greeks. (p. 755)
Antonian, Armen & Iyer, Lisa H. LA Sensation. (p. 969)
Antonine, Chagmion. Alfred University College Prowler off the Record. (p. 37)
Antonini, Gabriele. Wheels on the Bus. (p. 1901)
Antonini, Gabriele, illus. see Webb, Josh.
Antonini, Gabriele, jt. illus. see Metzger, Steve.
Antonio, illus. see Cerda, Alfredo Gomez.
Antonio, Jose, jt. auth. see Farfan, Flores.
Antoniorrobles. Cuentos de las Cosas Que Hablan. (p. 390)
Antonios, Joseph. Portal:Earth. (p. 1386)
Antonishak, Tom, illus. see Bailer, Darice.
Antonsson, Petur, illus. see Durham, Paul.
Antony, Steve. Betty Goes Bananas. (p. 172)
—Please, Mr. Panda. (p. 1373)
Antor, Max, jt. auth. see Reed, C.
Antosh, Peter, jt. auth. see Dauterman, Mary.
Antram, Dave, illus. see MacDonald, Fiona.
Antram, Dave, illus. see Malam, John.
Antram, David. Extreme Sports. (p. 557)
—Fantasy Castles. (p. 572)
—How to Draw Fairies. (p. 817)
—How to Draw Manga Warriors. (p. 818)
—How to Draw Pets. (p. 818)
—How to Draw Pirates. (p. 818)
—How to Draw Science Fiction. (p. 818)
—How to Draw Vampires, Zombies, & Other Monsters. (p. 819)
—Manga Action Figures. (p. 1087)
—You Wouldn't Want To... (p. 1976)
—You Wouldn't Want To... Ancient Civilization (p. 1976)
Antram, David, illus. see Canavan, Roger.
Antram, David, illus. see Cheshire, Gerard.
Antram, David, illus. see Chesire, Gerald.
Antram, David, illus. see Clarke, Penny.
Antram, David, illus. see Cook, Peter & Salariya, David.
Antram, David, illus. see Cook, Peter.
Antram, David, illus. see Costain, Meredith.
Antram, David, illus. see England, Victoria.
Antram, David, illus. see Ford, Michael & Salariya, David.
Antram, David, illus. see Graham, Ian.
Antram, David, illus. see Hicks, Peter.
Antram, David, illus. see Hynson, Colin.
Antram, David, illus. see Langley, Andrew.
Antram, David, illus. see MacDonald, Fiona & Macdonald, Fiona.
Antram, David, illus. see MacDonald, Fiona.
Antram, David, illus. see Macdonald, Fiona.
Antram, David, illus. see MacDonald, Fiona.
Antram, David, illus. see Macdonald, Fiona.
Antram, David, illus. see Malam, John & Smith, Karen Barker.
Antram, David, illus. see Malam, John.
Antram, David, illus. see Matthews, Rupert.
Antram, David, illus. see Morley, Jacqueline & Salariya, David.
Antram, David, illus. see Morley, Jacqueline.
Antram, David, illus. see Pipe, Jim.
Antram, David, illus. see Ratliff, Thomas.
Antram, David, illus. see Rooney, Anne.
Antram, David, illus. see Stewart, David.
Antram, David, illus. see Woolf, Alex.
Antram, David, jt. auth. see Bergin, Mark.
Antreasyan, Andres, tr. see Masurel, Claire & Kolar, Bob.
Antunes, Ana Claudia. Sea Sons. (p. 1535)
Antwine, Tajiye Lavonne. Changing the World 1 Poem @ a Time. (p. 290)
Anumbor, Justina U. African Girl: African Folklores. (p. 27)
Anwar, Merry, jt. auth. see Cornell, Karl.
Any Kid, ed. see Scholastic, Inc. Staff.
Any Kid Staff, ed. Build a Book: A Book That's All about My Family. (p. 237)
Anyabwile, Dawud, illus. see Sims, Guy A. & Myers, Walter Dean.
Anyanwu, Francis Eze. Awesome Dog: How the Dog Became Man's Best Friend. (p. 121)
Anza, Ana Luisa. Amigos del Otro Lado. Gomez, Eddie Martinez, illus. (p. 65)
—Misterio de la Casa Chueca (y el Bulto Color Mugre) The Mystery of the Crooked House. Escobar, Antonio Rocha, illus. (p. 1155)
Anzai, Nobuyuki. Flame of Recca Anzai, Nobuyuki, illus. (p. 602)
—Flame of Recca. (p. 602)
—Flame of Recca. Anzai, Nobuyuki, illus. (p. 602)
—MÄR (p. 1091)
—MÄR Anzai, Nobuyuki, illus. (p. 1091)
—Märchen Awakens Romance Anzai, Nobuyuki, illus. (p. 1091)
Anzai, Nobuyuki, illus. see Nobuyuki, Anzai, et al.
Anzai, Nobuyuki, jt. auth. see Imai, Yasue.
Anzai, Nobuyuki & Caselman, Lance. Flame of Recca. Anzai, Nobuyuki, illus. (p. 602)
Anzai, Yuko, jt. auth. see Mizuno, Junko.
Anzaldúa, Gloria. Prietita & the Ghost Woman: Prietita y la Llorona. (p. 1399)
—Prietita & the Ghost Woman: Prietita y la Llorona. Gonzalez, Maya Christina, illus. (p. 1399)
Anzalone, Frank, photos by. Images & Art of Santana Row. (p. 860)
Anzalone, Karen. Time in a Bottle. (p. 1752)
Anzalone, Lori, illus. see Haffmann, Janet.
Aoki, Deb, illus. see Sullivan, Kevin.
Aoki, Hisako. Santa's Favorite Story: Santa Tells the Story of the First Christmas. Gantschev, Ivan, illus. (p. 1513)
Aoki, Kotomi. Boku Wa Imoto Ni Koi Wa Suru (p. 208)
—Wa Suru (p. 1851)
Aoki, Shoichi. Fresh Fruits. Sanders, Mark, ed. (p. 636)
—Fresh Fruits Postcards. (p. 636)
Aoki, Takao. Beyblade (p. 173)
—Beyblade: Beyblade Extreme Rotation Shoot Aoki, Takao, illus. (p. 173)
—Beyblade. Aoki, Takao, illus. (p. 173)
Aoki, Yuya, illus. see Takaya, Natsuki.
Aón, Carlos, illus. see Biskup, Agnieszka.
Aón, Carlos, illus. see Harbo, Christopher L.
Aón, Carlos, illus. see Jensen Shaffer, Jody, et al.
Aon, Carlos, illus. see Lynette, Rachel.
Aon, Carlos, illus. see Troupe, Thomas Kingsley.
Aón, Carlos, illus. see Weakland, Mark, et al.
Aón, Carlos, illus. see Weakland, Mark.
Aoyama, Gôshô. Case Closed (p. 273)
—Case Closed Nakatani, Andy, ed. (p. 273)
—Case Closed Aoyama, Gôshô, illus. (p. 273)
—Case Closed. Aoyama, Gôshô, illus. (p. 273)
—Case Closed. Yamazaki, Joe, tr. from JPN. (p. 273)
Aoyama, Gôshô & Nakatani, Andy. Case Closed. Aoyama, Gôshô, illus. (p. 273)
Apa, Ivy Marie, illus. see Brearley, Leeanne.
Apa, Ivy Marie, illus. see Smith, E.
Aparicí Martín, Irene. Dance of Time. (p. 402)
—Mom Goes to War. (p. 1161)
Aparicio, Fernando Soto. Alfajuego. (p. 37)
Aparicio, Raquel, illus. see Lewis, Gill.
A-Park, Gwangjo, illus. see Ruddra, Anshumani.
A-Park, Jung, illus. see Ruddra, Anshumani.
Apel, Lorelei. Dealing with Weapons at School & at Home. (p. 418)
Apel, Melani. Federal Reserve Act: Making the American Banking System Stronger. (p. 580)
Apel, Melanie. Cool Careers Without College for Film & Television Buffs. (p. 362)
—Cool Careers Without College for Film & TV Buffs. (p. 362)
Apel, Melanie Ann. Art & Religion in Ancient Greece. (p. 101)
—Careers in Information Technology. (p. 268)
—Cocaine & Your Nose: The Incredibly Disgusting Story. (p. 337)
—Coping with Leukemia. (p. 365)
—Coping with Stuttering. (p. 365)
—Economy & Industry in Ancient Greece. (p. 503)
—Everything You Need to Know about Diabetes. (p. 545)
—Federal Reserve Act: Making the American Banking System Stronger. (p. 580)
—Home Life in Ancient Greece. (p. 792)
—Land & Resources of Ancient Greece. (p. 973)
—Let's Talk about Being in a Wheelchair. (p. 1001)
—Let's Talk about Feeling Confused. (p. 1001)
—Let's Talk about Feeling Embarrassed. (p. 1001)
—Let's Talk about Feeling Lonely. (p. 1001)
—Let's Talk about Feeling Worried. (p. 1001)
—Let's Talk about Living with Your Single Dad. (p. 1001)
—Let's Talk about Nightmares. (p. 1001)
—Let's Talk about When You Have to Get Stitches. (p. 1001)
—Let's Talk about When You Have to Have Your Appendix Out. (p. 1001)
—Let's Talk about When You Think Nobody Likes You. (p. 1001)
—Politics & Government in Ancient Greece. (p. 1381)
—Technology of Ancient Greece. (p. 1711)

A

—Virginia Apgar: Innovative Female Physician & Inventor of the Apgar Score. (p. 1844)
—Yellowstone Park Fire of 1988. (p. 1970)
Apelian, Virginia. Aliens Celebrating CHRISTMAS. (p. 41)
Apelqvist, Eva. Getting Ready to Drive. (p. 669)
—LGBTQ Families: The Ultimate Teen Guide. (p. 1004)
Apodaca, Blanca. All in a Day's Work: Animator (p. 44)
—Behind the Canvas: An Artist's Life (p. 160)
—Behind the Canvas: An Artist's Life. (p. 160)
Apodaca, Blanca, illus. see Reynolds, Laureen.
Apodaca, Blanca, jt. auth. see Acosta, Jamey.
Apologetics Press, creator. Creation Cards: Exploring God's Creation. (p. 379)
Apologia Educational Ministries, et al. Who Is God? (and Can I Really Know Him?) Worldview Series Book 1. (p. 1915)
Aponte, Jorge. Netx Generation. (p. 1242)
Apostol, Virgil Mayor, jt. auth. see Mayor, Virgil.
Apostoli, Andrea, ed. What Great Music! Classical Selections to Hear & to See. Dufey, Alexandra, illus. (p. 1885)
Apostolina, M. Hazing Meri Sugarman. (p. 756)
Apostolou, Christine Hale, illus. see Thompson, Lauren.
App, Linda Hoogeveen. Emma Pearl, Flower Girl. (p. 520)
Appel, Benjamin & Clark, Henry W. We Were There in the Klondike Gold Rush. Docktor, Irv, illus. (p. 1868)
Appel, Cindy. Best Christmas Gift. Collier, Kevin Scott, illus. (p. 168)
Appel, Dee. Friends in My Garden. Francour, Kathleen, photos by. (p. 638)
—Let's Play Dress Up. Francour, Kathleen, photos by. (p. 1000)
Appel, Julie & Guglielmo, Amy. Find King Henry's Treasure. (p. 587)
—Tickle Tut's Toes. (p. 1747)
Appel, Marty. Pinstripe Pride: The Inside Story of the New York Yankees. (p. 1361)
Appel, Morgan, illus. see Coons, Mary H.
Appelbaum, Barbara G. & Marchant, Peter, told to. Angie's Story. (p. 75)
Appelbaum, Stanley, ed. see Jiménez, Juan Ramón.
Appelbaum, Stanley, jt. auth. see Green, John.
Appelbaum, Stanley, tr. see Balzac, Honoré de.
Appelbaum, Stanley, tr. see Jiménez, Juan Ramón.
Appelbaum, Stanley, ed. Medieval Tales & Stories: 108 Prose Narratives of the Middle Ages. (p. 1119)
Appelbaum, Susannah. Poisons of Caux. Taylor, Jennifer, illus. (p. 1377)
—Shepherd of Weeds Offermann, Andrea, illus. (p. 1565)
Appelhans, Chris, illus. see Offill, Jenny.
Appelhans, Lenore. Level 2: There Has to Be More to the Afterlife Than This. Bk. 1 (p. 1003)
—Memory of After. (p. 1126)
Appelhof, Mary, et al. Worms Eat Our Garbage: Classroom Activities for a Better Environment. Fenton, Mary Frances & Kostecke, Nancy, illus. (p. 1961)
Appello, Lisa K. Zuky's World. (p. 1990)
Appelt, Kathi. Bat Jamboree. Sweet, Melissa, illus. (p. 143)
—Best Kind of Gift. (p. 170)
—Brand-New Baby Blues. Murphy, Kelly, illus. (p. 222)
—Bubba & Beau, Best Friends. Howard, Arthur, illus. (p. 233)
—Counting Crows. Dunlavey, Rob, illus. (p. 371)
—I See the Moon. Jenkins, Debra Reid, illus. (p. 845)
—I See the Moon. Jenkins, Reid Debra, illus. (p. 845)
—Incredible Me! (p. 869)
—Incredible Me! Karas, G. Brian, illus. (p. 869)
—Just People & Paper - Pen - Poem: A Young Writer's Way to Begin. Appelt, Kenneth, photos by. (p. 939)
—Keeper. Hall, August, illus. (p. 947)
—Kissing Tennessee: It's Night for & Love if You Dare. (p. 962)
—Miss Lady Bird's Wildflowers: How a First Lady Changed America. Hein, Joy Fisher, illus. (p. 1151)
—Mogie: The Heart of the House. Rosenthal, Marc, illus. (p. 1160)
—Oh My Baby, Little One. Dyer, Jane, illus. (p. 1280)
—True Blue Scouts of Sugar Man Swamp. (p. 1791)
—True Blue Scouts of Sugar Man Swamp. Bricking, Jennifer, illus. (p. 1791)
—Underneath. (p. 1815)
—Underneath. Small, David, illus. (p. 1815)
—When Otis Courted Mama. Szekeres, Cyndy & McElmurry, Jill, illus. (p. 1904)
Appelt, Kenneth, photos by see Appelt, Kathi.
Apperley, Dawn, illus. see Hall, Kirsten.
Appice, Carmine. Realistic Rock for Kids (My 1st Rock & Roll Drum Method) Drum Beats Made Simple!, Book, 2 CDs & DVD. (p. 1449)
Appignanesi, Richard, jt. auth. see Shakespeare, William.
Apple, Bonnie. Karisma Tales. (p. 943)
Apple, Emma, illus. see Juwayriyah, Umm & Ayed, Juwayriyah.
Apple, Gary, jt. auth. see Kauffman, Dorothy.
Apple, Mali, ed. see Charles, R., et al.
Apple, Margot, illus. see Haas, Jessie.
Apple, Margot, illus. see O'Connor, Jane.
Apple, Margot, illus. see Shaw, Nancy E.
Apple, Margot, illus. see Shaw, Nancy, et al.
Apple, Margot, illus. see Shaw, Nancy.
Apple, Michael W. Rosie the Counting Rabbit. (p. 1490)
Applebaum, Teri L., ed. see Kim, Hy.
Appleby, Alex. Dinosaurs at School. (p. 444)
—Dinosaurs at the Zoo. (p. 444)
—Dinosaur's Five Senses. (p. 444)
—Dinosaurs Help Out. (p. 444)
—Dinosaurs on the Farm. (p. 445)
—Dinosaurs on the Go. (p. 445)
—I Can Be a Ballerina. (p. 835)
—I Can Be a Football Player. (p. 835)
—I Can Be a Singer. (p. 835)
—I Can Be an Artist. (p. 835)
—I Can Be an Astronaut. (p. 835)
—I Can Be the President. (p. 835)
—I See a Bird: Puedo Ver un Pájaro. (p. 845)
—I See a Bird. (p. 845)
—I See a Butterfly: Puedo Ver una Mariposa. (p. 845)
—I See a Butterfly. (p. 845)
—I See a Chipmunk: Puedo Ver una Ardilla Rayada. (p. 845)
—I See a Chipmunk. (p. 845)
—I See a Frog: Puedo Ver una Rana. (p. 845)
—I See a Frog. (p. 845)
—I See a Ladybug: Puedo Ver una Mariquita. (p. 845)
—I See a Ladybug. (p. 845)
—It's Hailing! (p. 897)
—It's Hailing! / Est Granizando! (p. 897)
—It's Rainy! (p. 898)
—It's Rainy! / Est Lloviendo! (p. 898)
—It's Snowing! (p. 898)
—It's Snowing! / Est Nevando! (p. 899)
—It's Stormy! (p. 899)
—It's Stormy!/Es una Tormenta! (p. 899)
—It's Sunny! (p. 899)
—It's Sunny! / Est Soleado! (p. 899)
—It's Windy! (p. 899)
—It's Windy! / Est Ventoso! (p. 899)
—Lo Que Oigo / What I Hear. (p. 1044)
—Lo Que Toco / What I Touch. (p. 1044)
—My Five Senses. (p. 1208)
—Puedo Ser Presidente / I Can Be the President. (p. 1414)
—Puedo Ser un Artista / I Can Be an Artist. (p. 1414)
—Puedo Ser un Astronauta / I Can Be an Astronaut. (p. 1414)
—Puedo Ser un Jugador de Fútbol / I Can Be a Football Player. (p. 1414)
—Puedo Ser una Bailarina / I Can Be a Ballerina. (p. 1414)
—Puedo Ser una Cantante / I Can Be a Singer. (p. 1414)
—What I Hear. (p. 1886)
—What I See. (p. 1887)
—What I Smell. (p. 1887)
—What I Taste. (p. 1887)
—What I Touch. (p. 1887)
Appleby, Alex, jt. auth. see Nagelhout, Ryan.
Appleby, Clifford, ed. Illustrated Bible New Testament. (p. 857)
Appleby, Danny & Pirie, Lauren. Ella & the Balloons in the Sky. Laurence, Laurence, illus. (p. 513)
Appleby, Ellen. Three Billy Goats Gruff. (p. 1741)
—Trois Barbichu (p. 1788)
Appleby, Joyce, ed. see Organization of African Unity Staff.
Appleby, Joyce, et al. American Journey: Early Years. (p. 62)
—American Journey. (p. 62)
—American Republic since 1877. (p. 63)
—American Republic To 1877. (p. 63)
—American Republic to 1877. (p. 63)
—American Vision. (p. 63)
—Republica Estadounidense Hasta 1877. (p. 1462)
—Viaje Estadounidense: Reconstruccion Hasta el Presente. (p. 1839)
—Viaje Estadounidense. (p. 1839)
Appleby, Joyce Oldham, et al. American Journey. (p. 62)
Appleby, R. Scott, jt. auth. see Marty, Martin E.
Applefield, Annie. Beetle & the Berry. Applefield, Annie, illus. (p. 158)
Applegate, Anne. Last Academy. (p. 977)
Applegate, Beverly M. Brave Bart the Shopping Cart: A story of an escape & adventure, of caring & Giving. (p. 223)
Applegate, K. A., pseud. Aftermath. (p. 28)
—Animorphs #7: the Stranger. (p. 84)
—Capture. (p. 265)
—Encounter. (p. 524)
—Invasion. (p. 883)
—Message. (p. 1129)
—Predator. (p. 1394)
—Survival. (p. 1686)
—Visitor. (p. 1845)
Applegate, Katherine. Beach Blondes. (p. 149)
—Buffalo Storm. Ormerod, Jan, illus. (p. 236)
—Capture. (p. 265)
—Crenshaw. (p. 381)
—Don't Swap Your Sweater for a Dog. Biggs, Brian, illus. (p. 468)
—Don't Tap-Dance on Your Teacher. (p. 468)
—Don't Tap-Dance on Your Teacher. Biggs, Brian, illus. (p. 468)
—Home of the Brave. (p. 792)
—Ivan: the Remarkable True Story of the Shopping Mall Gorilla. Karas, G. Brian, illus. (p. 900)
—Never Glue Your Friends to Chairs. Biggs, Brian, illus. (p. 1243)
—Never Race a Runaway Pumpkin. (p. 1243)
—Never Race a Runaway Pumpkin. Biggs, Brian, illus. (p. 1243)
—Never Swim in Applesauce. Biggs, Brian, illus. (p. 1243)
—Never Swipe a Bully's Bear. Biggs, Brian, illus. (p. 1243)
—Never Walk in Shoes That Talk. (p. 1243)
—Never Walk in Shoes That Talk. Biggs, Brian, illus. (p. 1243)
—One & Only Ivan. (p. 1293)
—One & Only Ivan. Castelao, Patricia, illus. (p. 1293)
—Spring Break. (p. 1635)
—Stranger. (p. 1665)
—Sun-Kissed Christmas. (p. 1676)
—Tan Lines: Sand, Surf, & Secrets; Rays, Romance, & Rivalry; Beaches, Boys, & Betrayal. (p. 1704)
Applegate, Katherine, jt. auth. see Grant, Michael.
Applegate, Katherine, see Applegate, K. A., pseud.
Applegate, Katherine & Grant, Michael. Islanders: Nina Won't Tell & Ben's in Love. Vol. 2 (p. 892)
Applehead, Zippy. You Are Who You Be. (p. 1973)
Appleman, Pamela J. Copper Becomes a Farm Dog. (p. 365)
Appleoff, Sandy, illus. see Luebs Shepherd, Rajean.
Applesauce Press Staff. My First American Flag (p. 1204)
Applesauce Press Staff, et al. Gut Busters! Over 600 Jokes That Pack a Punch... . Line! (p. 733)
—Side Splitters: Over 600 Funtastic Jokes & Riddles. (p. 1573)
Appleton, E. R. & Cadman, S. Parkes. Outline of Religion. (p. 1313)
Appleton, Eileen. Leeney & Grandma at the Lake. (p. 987)
Appleton, Nancy. Rescue: Cecelia's Story. (p. 1462)
Appleton, Victor. Adventures of Tom Swift. (p. 24)
—Alien Probe. (p. 41)
—Astral Fortress. (p. 109)
—City in the Stars. (p. 323)
—Into the Abyss. (p. 881)
—Moving Picture Boys at Panama: Stirring Adventures along the Great Canal. (p. 1184)
—Moving Picture Boys at Panama. (p. 1184)
—Moving Picture Boys on the Coast or Showing up the Perils of the Deep. (p. 1184)
—Moving Picture Boys on the War Front or. (p. 1184)
—Rescue Mission. (p. 1462)
—Robot Olympics. (p. 1480)
—Rocket Racers. (p. 1483)
—Space Hotel. (p. 1619)
—Terror on the Moons of Jupiter. (p. 1722)
—Tom Swift among the Diamond Makers. (p. 1763)
—Tom Swift among the Diamond Makers or Th. (p. 1763)
—Tom Swift among the Fire Fighters: Or Battling with Flames from the Air. (p. 1763)
—Tom Swift among the Fire Fighters. (p. 1763)
—Tom Swift & His Aerial Warship: Or the Naval Terror of the Seas. (p. 1763)
—Tom Swift & His Aerial Warship. (p. 1763)
—Tom Swift & His Aerial Warship or the. (p. 1763)
—Tom Swift & His Aerial Warship or the Naval Terror of the Seas. (p. 1763)
—Tom Swift & His Air Glider. (p. 1763)
—Tom Swift & his Air Glider. (p. 1763)
—Tom Swift & His Air Glider or Seeking. (p. 1763)
—Tom Swift & His Air Scout: Or Uncle Sam's Mastery of the Sky. (p. 1763)
—Tom Swift & His Air Scout. (p. 1763)
—Tom Swift & His Air Scout or Uncle Sam. (p. 1763)
—Tom Swift & His Airship. (p. 1763)
—Tom Swift & His Big Tunnel. (p. 1763)
—Tom Swift & His Big Tunnel or the Hidd. (p. 1763)
—Tom Swift & His Electric Locomotive: Or Two Miles a Minute on the Rails. (p. 1763)
—Tom Swift & His Electric Locomotive. (p. 1763)
—Tom Swift & His Electric Locomotive or. (p. 1763)
—Tom Swift & His Electric Rifle. (p. 1763)
—Tom Swift & His Electric Runabout. (p. 1763)
—Tom Swift & His Electronic Electroscope. (p. 1763)
—Tom Swift & His Giant Cannon. (p. 1763)
—Tom Swift & His Giant Cannon or the lo. (p. 1763)
—Tom Swift & His Great Searchlight. (p. 1763)
—Tom Swift & his Great Searchlight. (p. 1763)
—Tom Swift & His Great Searchlight or O. (p. 1763)
—Tom Swift & His Motor Cycle. (p. 1763)
—Tom Swift & His Motor-Boat: Or the Rivals of Lake Carlopa. (p. 1763)
—Tom Swift & his Motor-Boat. (p. 1763)
—Tom Swift & His MotorBoat or the Rival. (p. 1763)
—Tom Swift & His MotorCycle. (p. 1763)
—Tom Swift & his Motor-Cycle. (p. 1763)
—Tom Swift & His MotorCycle or Fun and. (p. 1763)
—Tom Swift & His Motor-Cycle, Tom Swift & His Motor-Boat, Tom Swift & His Airship. (p. 1763)
—Tom Swift & His Photo Telephone. (p. 1763)
—Tom Swift & his Photo Telephone. (p. 1763)
—Tom Swift & His Photo Telephone or the. (p. 1763)
—Tom Swift & His Sky Racer. (p. 1763)
—Tom Swift & his Sky Racer. (p. 1763)
—Tom Swift & His Sky Racer or the Quick. (p. 1763)
—Tom Swift & His Sky Racer or the Quickest Flight on Record. (p. 1763)
—Tom Swift & His Submarine Boat. (p. 1763)
—Tom Swift & His Submarine Boat or Unde. (p. 1763)
—Tom Swift & His Triphibian Atomicar. (p. 1763)
—Tom Swift & His Undersea Search: Or the Treasure on the Floor of the Atlantic. (p. 1763)
—Tom Swift & His Undersea Search. (p. 1763)
—Tom Swift & His Undersea Search or the. (p. 1763)
—Tom Swift & His War Tank. (p. 1763)
—Tom Swift & his War Tank. (p. 1763)
—Tom Swift & His War Tank or Doing His. (p. 1763)
—Tom Swift & His Wireless Message. (p. 1763)
—Tom Swift & his Wireless Message. (p. 1763)
—Tom Swift & His Wireless Message or Th. (p. 1763)
—Tom Swift & His Wizard Camera: Or Thrilling Adventures While Taking Moving Pictu. (p. 1763)
—Tom Swift & his Wizard Camera. (p. 1763)
—Tom Swift & His Wizard Camera or Thril. (p. 1763)
—Tom Swift & the Electronic Hydrolung. (p. 1763)
—Tom Swift & the Visitor from Planet X. (p. 1763)
—Tom Swift Circling the Globe. (p. 1763)
—Tom Swift in Captivity. (p. 1763)
—Tom Swift in Captivity or A Daring Escap. (p. 1763)
—Tom Swift in the Caves of Ice. (p. 1763)
—Tom Swift in the Caves of Ice or the Wre. (p. 1763)
—Tom Swift in the City of Gold. (p. 1763)
—Tom Swift in the City of Gold or Marvelo. (p. 1763)
—Tom Swift in the Land of Wonders. (p. 1763)
—Tom Swift in the Land of Wonders or the. (p. 1763)
—Tom Swift Omnibus #1: Tom Swift & his Motor-Cycle, Tom Swift & His Motor-Boat, Tom Swift & His Airship. (p. 1763)
—Tom Swift Omnibus #2: Tom Swift & His Submarine Boat, Tom Swift & His Electric Runabout, Tom Swift & His Wireless Message. (p. 1763)
—Tom Swift Omnibus #3: Tom Swift among the Diamond Makers, Tom Swift in the Caves of Ice, Tom Swift & His Sky Racer. (p. 1763)
—Tom Swift Omnibus #4: Tom Swift & His Electric Rifle, Tom Swift in the City of Gold, Tom Swift & His Air Glider. (p. 1763)
—Tom Swift Omnibus #5: Tom Swift in Captivity, Tom Swift & His Wizard Camera, Tom Swift & His Great Searchlight. (p. 1764)
—Tom Swift Omnibus #6: Tom Swift & His Giant Cannon, Tom Swift & His Photo Telephone, Tom Swift & His Aerial Warship. (p. 1764)
—Tom Swift Omnibus #7: Tom Swift & His Big Tunnel, Tom Swift in the Land of Wonders, Tom Swift & His War Tank. (p. 1764)
—Tom Swift Omnibus #8: Tom Swift & His Air Scout, Tom Swift & His Undersea Search, Tom Swift among the Fire Fighters, Tom Swift & His Electri. (p. 1764)
—Tom Swift Treasury. (p. 1764)
—War in Outer Space. (p. 1857)
Appleton, Victor & Appleton, Victor, II. Into the Abyss. (p. 881)
—On Top of the World. (p. 1292)
—Under the Radar. (p. 1814)
Appleton, Victor, II, jt. auth. see Appleton, Victor.
Appleton-Smith, Laura. Oh My, It Must Be the Sky! Neel, Preston, illus. (p. 1281)
—Queen Bee Needs to Be Free. Neel, Preston, illus. (p. 1424)
Applin, Barbara, jt. ed. see Simon, Veronica.
Applin, Barbara & Simon, Veronica, eds. Treasure House 1: A Caribbean Anthology. (p. 1781)
Applin, D. G., et al. AQA Modular Science for GCSE. (p. 93)
Appling, Jeffrey R. & Richardson, Jean. Math Survival Guide: Tips for Science Student. (p. 1107)
Apps, Fred, illus. see Christian Focus Publications (CFP) Staff & MacKenzie, Carine.
Apps, Fred, illus. see De Vries, Anne.
Apps, Fred, illus. see Ferguson, Sinclair B.
Apps, Fred, illus. see Foce, Natalia, tr.
Apps, Fred, illus. see Haley, Barbara.
Apps, Fred, illus. see MacKenzie, Carine.
Apps, Fred, illus. see Mackenzie, Carine.
Apps, Fred, illus. see Mackenzie, Carine.
Apps, Fred, illus. see Mackenzie, Carine.
Apps, Fred, illus. see MacKenzie, Carine.
Apps, Fred, illus. see Mackenzie, Carine.
Apps, Fred, illus. see MacKenzie, Catherine.
Apps, Fred, illus. see Michael, Sally.
Apps, Fred, illus. see Reeve, Penny.
Apps, Fred, illus. see Taylor, Jane & MacKenzie, Carine.
Apps, Fred, jt. auth. see MacKenzie, Carine.
Apps, Jerry. Casper Jaggi: Master Swiss Cheese Maker. (p. 276)
—Tents, Tigers & the Ringling Brothers. (p. 1720)
Apps, John, jt. auth. see Metcalfe, Jack.
Apps Ltd, Colossi. Wild Bed Time Stories. (p. 1929)
April, Elyse. Nos Gusta Leer. (p. 1266)
—We Like to Eat Well/Nos Gusta Comer Bien. Agrell, Lewis, illus. (p. 1867)
—We Like to Move - Spanish / English Edition: Exercise Is Fun. (p. 1867)
—We Like to Read: A Picture Book for Pre-Readers & Parents. Thompson, Angie, illus. (p. 1867)
April, Elyse & Ryan, Regina Sara. We Like to Move: Exercise Is Fun. (p. 1867)
April, Elyse, et al. Nos Gusta Movernos: El Ejercicio Es Divertido = We Like to Move: Exercise Is Fun. Iverson, Diane, illus. (p. 1266)
April, Steele. Curious Minds of Mark & Maci: Why Is the Sky Blue? (p. 394)
Apseloff, Stanford S. African Animals Alphabet Book. (p. 27)
Apsley, illus. see Brukner, Lauren.
Apsley, Brenda. Animal Babies. Fotolia, photos by. (p. 76)
—Animal Families. Fotolia, photos by. (p. 77)
—Animal Friends. Fotolia, photos by. (p. 77)
—Animal Fun. Fotolia, photos by. (p. 78)
Apt, Stuart C. Of Wind & Tides. (p. 1279)
Apte, Sunita. Aztec Empire. (p. 122)
—Cesar Chavez: We Can Do It! (p. 288)
—Christopher Reeve: Don't Lose Hope! (p. 317)
—Combat-Wounded Dogs. (p. 346)
—Eating Green. (p. 501)
—Inca: Set Of 6. (p. 868)
—Inca: Text Pairs. (p. 868)
—India. (p. 870)
—March. (p. 1091)
—Mesopotamia: Set Of 6. (p. 1129)
—Mesopotamia: Text Pairs. (p. 1129)
—Mesopotamia. (p. 1129)
—Michael J. Fox: I Can Make a Difference! (p. 1134)
—Polar Regions: Surviving in Antarctica. (p. 1379)
—Police Horses. (p. 1380)
—Pomeranian: Pom Pom Ado. (p. 1382)
—Ride the Whale: A Surfer Tall Tale. Reed, Kyle, illus. (p. 1471)
Apte, Sunita & Hess, Debra. Amistad: Fight for Freedom. (p. 65)
Apte, Sunita, text. Moving Home. (p. 1183)
Apted, Violet. Jasmin & the Nature Fairies. Hollinrake, Chriss, illus. (p. 909)
—Tommy & Jacqui: Laughing with Kookaburras. (p. 1764)
Aptekar, Devan. Darkseid's Revenge. Gordon, Eric A. & Gordon, Steven E., illus. (p. 409)
—How to Train Your Dragon - Befriending a Foe. (p. 822)
Apter, Ronnie, jt. tr. see Herman, Mark.
Aqkay. Jungle Olympics-800 Metres Sprint. (p. 935)
Aquila, J. R. Autumn of the Timber Wolf: The First Book of the Fyrdunian Cycle. (p. 118)
Aquilina, Michael, III. St. Jude: A Friend in Hard Times. Neely, Keith, illus. (p. 1638)
Arabadjis, Heather. Monster Mas. (p. 1167)
árabe, Cuento popular. Ali Baba y Los Cuarenta Ladrones: Ali Baba & the Forty Thieves. (p. 39)
Arac de Nyeko, Monica. Children of the Red Fields. (p. 302)
Aracena, Cynthia, jt. auth. see Prandy, Manuel.
Aracich, Charles. TIME for Kids: Practicing for Today's Tests Language Arts Level 4 (p. 1751)
Aragon Art Studio, illus. see Riddle, Waide Aaron.
Aragón, Carla, et al. Dance of the Eggshells: Baile de los Cascarones. Saville, Kathy Dee, illus. (p. 402)
Aragon, Dolores, illus. see Garcia, Nasario.
Arai, Hiroyuki. Everyone Says Goodnight. (p. 544)
Arai, Kiyoko. Beauty Pop (p. 154)
Arai, Setsuo, illus. see Ching, Tokie.
Arai, Shizuko. Turtle & the Warrior. Maeda, Matsuo, illus. (p. 1798)
Araizumi, Rui, illus. see Kanzaka, Hajime.
Arakawa, Hiromu. Art of Fullmetal Alchemist 2. Arakawa, Hiromu, illus. (p. 102)
—Fullmetal Alchemist. Arakawa, Hiromu, illus. (p. 646)
—Fullmetal Alchemist (p. 647)
—Fullmetal Alchemist. Arakawa, Hiromu, illus. (p. 647)
—Fullmetal Alchemist Box Set (p. 647)
—Hana Yori Dango. Arakawa, Hiromu, illus. (p. 740)

A

Araki, Hirohiko. JoJo's Bizarre Adventure Araki, Hirohiko, illus. (p. 924)
—Jojo's Bizarre Adventure Araki, Hirohiko, illus. (p. 924)
—Jojo's Bizarre Adventure. (p. 924)
—JoJo's Bizarre Adventure. Araki, Hirohiko, illus. (p. 924)
Araki, Mari, illus. see Kashyap, Keshni.
Aramburu, Francisco Gonzalez, tr. see Bierhorst, John.
Arancibia, Janet & Feliz, Guido, eds. Cuaderno de la Rosa Tomo 1 (p. 387)
—Manual de la consejera de Rosas Tomo 1 (p. 1088)
Aranda, Alfredo. My First Music Book: Mi Primer Libro de Musica. (p. 1207)
—My Musical Friends: Mis Amigos Musicales. (p. 1215)
Aranda, Amira, illus. see Malpica, Tono.
Aranda, Julio C., illus. see Plaza, Jose Maria & Plaza, José María.
Aranda, Margaret. Little Missy Two-Shoes: Likes a Ladybug. (p. 1032)
Aranda, Margaret & Ferrante, Marguerite A. Little Missy Two-Shoes Likes to Go to School. (p. 1032)
Aranda, Omar, illus. see Giulieri, Anne.
Aranda, Omar, illus. see Johnson, Jacqueline & Young, Jeanna Stolle.
Aranda, Omar, illus. see Johnson, Young, et al.
Aranda, Omar, illus. see Young, Jeanna & Johnson, Jacqueline Kinney.
Aranda, Omar, illus. see Young, Jeanna & Johnson, Jacqueline.
Aranda, Omar, illus. see Young, Jeanna Stolle & Johnson, Jacqueline.
Aranda, Omar, illus. see Young, Jeanna Stolle & Johnson, Jacqueline Kinney.
Aranda, Tom, illus. see Dreier, David L.
Aranda, Tomás, illus. see Bethea, Nikole Brooks.
Aranega, Merce. DRAGON SIMON Y LOS ESTORNUDOS. CortÉs, Elena Valencia, tr. (p. 478)
—Quiero Escribir un Cuento. (p. 1428)
Aranega, Merce, illus. see Paloma, David.
Aranguren, Dolores, tr. see Carroll, Lewis, pseud.
Aranha, Marc. Queen of Spiders. (p. 1425)
Aranjo, Karl W. Guitar Tab: Blank Manuscript Papaer for Guitar Teachers, Students & Songwriters. (p. 731)
Arant, Bruce, illus. see Cleveland, Lance.
Araque, Ana. My little Seed. (p. 1213)
Araten, Michel. Honey the Hummingbird. (p. 794)
Arato, Rona. Design It! The Ordinary Things You Use Every Day & the Not-So-Ordinary Ways They Came to Be. Newell, Claudia, illus. (p. 429)
—Fossils: Clues to Ancient Life. (p. 624)
—Fukushima Nuclear Disaster. (p. 646)
—Ice Cream Town (p. 850)
—Mrs. Kaputnik's Pool Hall & Matzo Ball Emporium. (p. 1187)
—Protists. (p. 1412)
—Working for Freedom: The Story of Josiah Henson. (p. 1952)
Arato, Rona, jt. auth. see Owlkids Books Inc. Staff.
Arato, Rona & Owlkids Books Inc. Staff. Courage & Compassion: Ten Canadians Who Made a Difference. (p. 372)
Araujo, André. Avengers A. I., 12,000 A. D. (p. 118)
Araujo, Katie, illus. see Irwin, Gayle.
Araujo, Paige Krul, ed. see Richards, Jon.
Aravena, Cristian. Adventures of Marmat. (p. 20)
Arbat, Carles. Barbazul. (p. 137)
Arbaugh, Michelle. Cat & Her Tales. (p. 277)
Arbel, Ilil. Cinnabar Box. (p. 321)
Arbetman, Lee P., et al. Street Law: A Course in Practical Law. (p. 1666)
Arbo, Barbara. Scriptures for Kids. Ross, Melissa, illus. (p. 1533)
Arbo, Cris, illus. see Anthony, Joseph.
Arbo, Cris, illus. see Berkes, Marianne.
Arbo, Cris, illus. see Hodgkins, Fran.
Arbo, Cris, illus. see Mortensen, Lori.
Arbo, Cris, illus. see Steinberg, Laya.
Arbo, Hal, illus. see Morgan, Leon.
Arbogast, Christian Hunt. Heaven's Dentist. (p. 761)
Arbogast, Joan Marie. Buildings in Disguise: Architecture That Looks Like Animals, Food, & Other Things. (p. 239)
Arboleda M.Ed., Teja. What's That Pout All About? Arboleda M.Ed., Teja, illus. (p. 1899)
Arbona, Marion, illus. see Maclear, Kyo.
Arbona, Marion, illus. see Poulin, Andree.
Arbuckle, Katrina & Simpson, Amy. JumpStarters: 100 Games to Spark Discussions. (p. 934)
Arbuckle, Scott, illus. see Woolley, Bryan.
Arbus, Abby. Why Do We Pay Taxes? (p. 1924)
Arbuthnot, Felicity & Van Der Gaag, Nikki. Baghdad. (p. 132)
Arbuthnot, Nancy, tr. see Le, Le Pham.
Arbuthnot, Gill. Chaos Clock (p. 291)
—Chaos Quest (p. 291)
—Keepers' Tattoo. (p. 947)
Arbuthnoy, Nancy. Wild Washington: Animal Sculptures A to Z. Abramson, Cathy, illus. (p. 1930)
Arcana Studio, Arcana, illus. see O'Reilly, Sean.
Arcana Studio Staff, illus. see Everheart, Chris.
Arcana Studio Staff, illus. see O'Reilly, Sean.
Arcayena-Nguyen, Rachelle. Who Me? a Werewolf: Chronicles of Timothy North. (p. 1917)
Arce, Andrea. Under the Influence. (p. 1813)
Arcella, Steven, illus. see Bolin, Frances Schoonmaker, ed.
Arceneaux, Kitty. If Daddy Can, I Can. Isaac, W. Smiley, illus. (p. 852)
Arch Books Staff. Noahs 2 by 2 Adventures Spanis. (p. 1261)
—Spanish David & Goliat. (p. 1621)
—Spanish down Thru the Roof. (p. 1621)
—Spanish Moses Dry Feet. (p. 1621)
Archambault, Ariane, jt. auth. see Corbeil, Jean-Claude.
Archambault, Douglas J. Adventures of Little Buddy & Grizz (p. 19)
Archambault, Jeanne. Larry the Lawnmower. Corey, Victoria, illus. (p. 976)
—Leaping Grasshopper. Smith, Dwight, illus. (p. 982)
Archambault, John. Boom Chicka Rock. Chitwood, Suzanne Tanner & Chitwood, Suzanne, illus. (p. 213)
—By the Baobab Tree. Bender, Robert, illus. (p. 249)
—Cat in the Tree. Cooper, Stephanie, illus. (p. 278)
Archambault, John, jt. auth. see Martin, Bill, Jr.
Archambault, John, jt. auth. see Plummer, David.
Archambault, John & Martin, Bill, Jr. Chicka Chicka ABC. Ehlert, Lois, illus. (p. 299)
—Here Are My Hands. Rand, Ted, illus. (p. 770)
Archambault, John & Plummer, David. Two Birds SAT upon a Stone. Hollander, Sarah, illus. (p. 1803)
Archambault, Marc. Hal the Unwashed Dragon. (p. 736)
—Hal the Unwashed Dragon (perfect Bound) (p. 736)
—Mommy Is Too Tired to Play. (p. 1162)
—Teevert the Little Green Leaf. (p. 1715)
Archambault, Matthew, illus. see Hill, Mary Lea.
Archambault, Matthew, illus. see Ransom, Candice.
Archambault, Matthew, illus. see Stegall, Billy Mark.
Archambeau, Robert. Home & Variations. (p. 792)
Archbold, David M. Amazing Adventures of Chumley, Robin, Snickers & Mac. (p. 52)
Archbold, Tim, illus. see French, Vivian.
Archbold, Tim, illus. see Harmer, David.
Archbold, Tim, illus. see Lisle, Rebecca.
Archbold, Tim, illus. see Morgan, Ruth.
Archbold, Tim, illus. see Rosen, Michael.
Archbold, Tim & Rock, Lois. Good Bad Guy & Other Peculiar Parables. (p. 697)
Archembault, Matthew, illus. see Breault, Christie Merriman.
Archer, Adam, illus. see Elder, Josh.
Archer, Angela, illus. see Womack, Rowena.
Archer, Anita, et al. REWARDS Plus: Application to Social Studies: Reading Excellence: Word Attack & Rate Development Strategies: Student Book. (p. 1467)
Archer, Anita L., et al. REWARDS Plus: Reading Excellence: Reading Strategies Applied to Science Passages. (p. 1467)
Archer, Chris. Aftershock. (p. 29)
Archer, Christine, illus. see Heiman, Diane & Suneby, Elizabeth.
Archer, Claire. Araña Lobo. (p. 94)
—Bird-Eating Spiders. (p. 190)
—Black Widow Spiders. (p. 197)
—Cheetahs. (p. 296)
—Jaguars. (p. 905)
—Jumping Spiders. (p. 934)
—Leones. (p. 992)
—Leopards. (p. 993)
—Lions. (p. 1021)
—Pumas. (p. 1416)
—Tarantula Spiders. (p. 1706)
—Tigers. (p. 1749)
—Trapdoor Spiders. (p. 1779)
—Wolf Spiders. (p. 1944)
Archer, Claire, jt. auth. see ABDO Publishing Company Staff.
Archer, Claire, et al. Arañas Lobo. (p. 94)
—Arañas Saltarinas. (p. 94)
—Arañas Tramperas. (p. 94)
—Arañas Viuda Negra. (p. 94)
—Guepardos. (p. 728)
—Jaguares. (p. 905)
—Leones. (p. 992)
—Leopardos. (p. 993)
—Pumas. (p. 1416)
—Tarántulas. (p. 1706)
—Tarántulas Goliat. (p. 1706)
—Tigres. (p. 1749)
Archer, Colleen Rutherford. Collie Rescue. Umana, Maria Gomez, illus. (p. 340)
—Galloping Goldrush: The Journey Begins. Stafford, Susan, ed. (p. 653)
Archer, Dosh. Big Bad Wolf. Archer, Dosh, illus. (p. 178)
—Humpty's Fall. Archer, Dosh, illus. (p. 827)
—Itsy Bitsy Spider. Archer, Dosh, illus. (p. 900)
—Little Elephant's Blocked Trunk. Archer, Dosh, illus. (p. 1027)
Archer, E. Geek Fantasy Novel. (p. 659)
Archer, James. Travelling Light. (p. 1780)
Archer, Jane. Let Not Your Flight Be in Winter. (p. 994)
Archer, Jeffrey. Purgatory (p. 1419)
Archer, Jennifer. Shadow Girl. (p. 1557)
—Through Her Eyes. (p. 1745)
Archer, Mandy. Ballet. (p. 134)
—Christmas: With 200 Stickers, Puzzles & Games, Fold-Out Pages, & Creative Play. (p. 312)
—Digger to the Rescue. Lightfoot, Martha, illus. (p. 438)
—Diggers & Dumpers. (p. 439)
—Dreadful Dragon Disappearance. (p. 482)
—Fire Truck Is Flashing. Lightfoot, Martha, illus. (p. 591)
—Fluffy Animals. (p. 608)
—Mermaid Kingdom: Over 1000 Reusable Stickers! (p. 1128)
—Pets: Creative Play, Fold-Out Pages, Puzzles & Games, over 200 Stickers! (p. 1348)
—Race Car Is Roaring. Lightfoot, Martha, illus. (p. 1430)
—Robots: Over 1000 Reusable Stickers! (p. 1481)
—Tractor Saves the Day. Lightfoot, Martha, illus. (p. 1775)
—Vacation Creativity Book: Games, Cut-Outs, Art Paper, Stickers, & Stencils. (p. 1829)
Archer, Mary Jane, illus. see Peters, Jean Norman.
Archer, Mary Jane, photos by see Peters, Jean Norman.
Archer, Micha, illus. see Husain, Shahrukh.
Archer, Micha, illus. see Witte, Anna.
Archer, Natalie J. Willy (p. 1934)
Archer, Nick. Rule of Three. (p. 1495)
—Rule of Three. Consolazio, Pamela A., illus. (p. 1495)
Archer, Peggy. From Dawn to Dreams: Poems for Busy Babies. Wakiyama, Hanako, illus. (p. 642)
—Name That Dog! Buscema, Stephanie, illus. (p. 1228)
Archer, Richard. Island Home. (p. 892)
Archer, William, tr. see Ibsen, Henrik.
Archetti, Eduardo P., jt. ed. see Dyck, Noel.
Archeval, Jose, illus. see Brown, Amanda C.
Archibald, A. L., illus. see Gates, Josephine Scribner.
Archibald, Donna, et al. NETS*S Curriculum Series: Social Studies Units for Grades 9-12. McKenzie, Walter, ed. (p. 1242)
Archibald, Laura. Cats of Grand Central. Beckett, Garner, illus. (p. 281)
Archibald Lee Fletcher. Boy Scouts on a Long Hike: Or to the Rescue in the Black Water Swamps. (p. 218)
Archibald, Mary Lynn. Accidental Cowgirl: Six Cows, No Horse & No Clue. (p. 8)
Archibald, Odell, illus. see Skirving, Janet.
Archibold, Tim. Knock Knock! The Best Knock Knock Jokes Ever! (p. 965)
Archie Superstars Staff. Archie 1000 Page Comics Bonanza. (p. 95)
—Archie's Even Funnier Kids' Joke Book. (p. 95)
—Archie's Fun 'n' Games Activity Book. (p. 95)
—Best of Archie Comics. (p. 170)
Archipova, Anastasiya, illus. see Grimm, Jacob & Grimm, Wilhelm.
Archipowa, A., tr. see Grimm, Jacob, et al.
Archuleta, Michael. Metodo Para Aprender a Tocar Guitarra con Mariachi Nivel Elemental. (p. 1130)
Archuleta, Michael, concept. Mariachi Method Book for Vihuela. (p. 1093)
Archuleta, Robert B. Boys' Club: Lost & Found. (p. 220)
Archuleta, Ruben. Eppie Archuleta & the Tale of Juan de la Burra. (p. 532)
Archway Care Sons And Daughters Group, jt. auth. see Archway Care Sons and Daughters Group.
Archway Care Sons and Daughters Group & Archway Care Sons And Daughters Group. How Does Jorge Feel ? (p. 809)
Arciero, Susan, illus. see Gingrich, Callista.
Arciniega Bailey, Yvette. Squiggly Wiggly Lines. (p. 1637)
Arciniega, Triunfo. Amores Eternos. Mantilla, Maria Fernanda, illus. (p. 65)
—Ventana y la Bruja. Vallejo, Esperanza, illus. (p. 1836)
Arciniegas, Triunfo. Caperucita Roja y Otras Historias Perversas. (p. 262)
—Lucy Es Pecosa. Parra, Rocio, illus. (p. 1063)
—Mambro Se Fue a la Guerra. Vallejo, Esperanza, illus. (p. 1084)
—Pirata de la Pata de Palo. Sierra, Juan, illus. (p. 1362)
—Serafin Es un Diablo. Rodriguez, Gonzalo, illus. (p. 1552)
—Vaca de Octavio/la Arana Sube al Monte. Violi, Daniela, illus. (p. 1829)
—Verdadera Historia del Gato con Botas. (p. 1836)
—Yo, Claudia. Sada, Margarita, illus. (p. 1971)
Arco Staff. High Stakes: Writing. (p. 778)
—High-Stakes: Reading. Peterson's Guides Staff, ed. (p. 778)
—Mastering Vocabulary Skills: Entertaining Instruction & Cool Activities for Students Who Want to Get Wise! (p. 1103)
—Science. (p. 1524)
Arcos, Carrie. Out of Reach. (p. 1311)
—There Will Come a Time. (p. 1730)
Arcturus Publishing Staff. Build a Robot. (p. 238)
—Dangerous Book of Dinosaurs. (p. 404)
—Magic Adding & Subtracting. (p. 1071)
—Magical Fairy Activity Book. (p. 1074)
—Paper Planes. (p. 1323)
—Santa's Sleigh. (p. 1513)
Arcturus Publishing Staff, jt. auth. see Harrison, Paul.
Arcudi, John. Thunderbolts: How to Lose. Vol. 1 (p. 1746)
Arcy, Sean & Marshall, Phillip. Freestyle Skateboarding Tricks: Flat Ground, Rails, Transitions. (p. 635)
Arcynski, Charlene. Adventures of Little Sugarbear Boy: The Beginning. (p. 20)
Ard, Catherine. Origami Bugs. (p. 1304)
—Origami Holidays. (p. 1304)
—Origami Monsters. (p. 1304)
—Origami on the Move. (p. 1304)
—Origami Planes. (p. 1304)
—Origami Space. (p. 1304)
Ardagh, Philip. All at Sea. (p. 44)
—High in the Clouds. Dunbar, Geoff, illus. (p. 777)
—Hole in the Road. (p. 788)
—Marie Curie. (p. 1093)
—On the Farm. (p. 1290)
—Up in the Air. (p. 1824)
Ardagh, Philip, jt. auth. see Dunbar, Geoff.
Arden, Adriana. Abandoned Alice. (p. 2)
—Obedient Alice. (p. 1275)
Arden, Carolyn. Goose Moon. Postier, Jim, illus. (p. 702)
—Mountains & Valleys. (p. 1181)
Arden, Lynne. Guess What Happened to Me, Auntie Kate! Marino, Natalie, illus. (p. 729)
Arden, Paul. It's Not How Good You Are, It's How Good You Want to Be: The World's Best Selling Book. (p. 898)
Ardia, Dan & Rice, Elizabeth. Evolution. (p. 546)
Ardila, Carlos, jt. auth. see Rodriguez, Claudia Rodriguez.
Ardis, C. Hill: Oh What A Day Series. (p. 779)
Ardizzone, Edward. Little Tim & the Brave Sea Captain. (p. 1037)
—Sarah & Simon & No Red Paint. Ardizzone, Edward, illus. (p. 1514)
—Tim All Alone. (p. 1750)
—Tim to the Rescue. (p. 1750)
Ardizzone, Edward, illus. see Brand, Christianna.
Ardizzone, Edward, illus. see Estes, Eleanor.
Ardizzone, Edward, illus. see Farjeon, Eleanor.
Ardizzone, Edward, illus. see Langley, Noel.
Ardizzone, Edward, illus. see Quarto Generic Staff.
Ardizzone, Edward, illus. see Trevor, Meriol.
Ardizzone, Edward & Fry, Stephen. Tim's Friend Towser. (p. 1755)
Ardizzone, Edward & Quarto Generic Staff. Tim in Danger. (p. 1750)
Ardizzone, Leonisa. Science—Not Just for Scientists! Easy Explorations for Young Children. (p. 1524)
Ardizzone, Sarah, jt. auth. see Leray, Marjolaine.
Ardizzone, Sarah, tr. see Barroux.
Ardizzone, Sarah, tr. see De Fombelle, Timothée.
Ardizzone, Sarah, tr. see Roy, Sandrine Dumas.
Ardley, Neil. Music. Dorling Kindersley Publishing Staff, ed. (p. 1193)
—Musica. (p. 1193)
Ardley, Neil & Dorling Kindersley Publishing Staff. 101 Great Science Experiments. (p. 1999)
Ardrey, Adam. Finding Merlin: The Truth Behind the Legend of the Great Arthurian Mage. (p. 588)
Ardwin, Juanita. Remember When (p. 1459)
Aree, Bill. Class Vote. (p. 327)
Arefy, Katrin. My First Piano Book 3: Learning the Musical Alphabet Through Stories. (p. 1207)
Arégui, Matthias & Ramstein, Anne-Margot. Before After. Arégui, Matthias & Ramstein, Anne-Margot, illus. (p. 158)
Arellano, Juan Estevan, jt. auth. see Lamadrid, Enrique R.
Arelys, Aguilar, illus. see Ballard, George Anne.
Aremds, Donald L. Norm the Ninja River Mouse. (p. 1264)
Arena, Felice. Sally & Dave: A Slug Story. Arena, Felice, illus. (p. 1505)
Arena, Felice & Kettle, Phil. Basketball Buddies. Gordon, Gus, illus. (p. 143)
—Battle of the Games. Gordon, Gus, illus. (p. 146)
—Bike Daredevils. Cox, David, illus. (p. 185)
—Bull Riding. Cox, David, illus. (p. 240)
—Crawfish Hunt. Vane, Mitch, illus. (p. 376)
—Golf Legends. Gordon, Gus, illus. (p. 696)
—Gone Fishing. Boyer, Susy, illus. (p. 697)
—Halloween Gotcha! Gordon, Gus, illus. (p. 737)
—Hit the Beach. Vane, Mitch, illus. (p. 785)
—Olympics. Cox, David, illus. (p. 1288)
—On the Farm/By Felice Arena & Phil Kettle ; Illustrated by Susy Boyer. Boyer, Susy, illus. (p. 1290)
—Park Soccer. Gordon, Gus, illus. (p. 1324)
—Pirate Ship: By Felice Arena & Phil Kettle: Illustrated by Susy Boyer. Boyer, Susy, illus. (p. 1363)
—Race Car Dreamers. Cox, David, illus. (p. 1430)
—Rock Star. Gordon, Gus, illus. (p. 1482)
—Rotten School Day. Vane, Mitch, illus. (p. 1491)
—Secret Agent Heroes. Vane, Mitch, illus. (p. 1540)
—Tennis Ace. Boyer, Susy, illus. (p. 1720)
—Tree House. Vane, Mitch, illus. (p. 1783)
—Wet World. Vane, Mitch, illus. (p. 1877)
Arena, Felice, et al. Battle of the Games. Gordon, Gus & Vane, Mitch, illus. (p. 146)
Arena, Jacqueline. Basketball Showdown. Foye, Lloyd, illus. (p. 143)
—Horsing Around. Maddock, Monika, illus. (p. 800)
Arena, Jen. Besos for Baby: A Little Book of Kisses. (p. 168)
—Lady Liberty's Holiday. Hunt, Matt, illus. (p. 971)
Arena, Jennifer. One Hundred Snowmen Gilpin, Stephen, illus. (p. 1295)
Arena, Jillayne, illus. see Lainez, René Colato.
Arena Verlag. Kids' Mandalas. (p. 954)
Arena Verlag Staff, jt. auth. see Matthies, Don-Oliver.
Arends, Donald L. Grandpa Grouper, the Fish with Glasses. (p. 709)
Arendt, Hannah. Origins of Totalitarianism: Introduction by Samantha Power. (p. 1304)
Arenella, Betsy Bottino. Isabelle's Dream: A Story & Activity Book for a Child's Grief Journey. Henderson, Dana, illus. (p. 891)
Arengo, Sue. Classic Tales: Thumbelina. Goulding, Celeste, illus. (p. 328)
—Jack & the Beanstalk. (p. 902)
—Jack & the Beanstalk. Ratto, Cinzia, illus. (p. 902)
—Little Red Hen. (p. 1034)
—Mansour & the Donkey. (p. 1088)
Arens, Amanda. Big-Blocks Plan Book Plus. (p. 178)
Arens, Amanda B. & Loman, Karen L. Checklists for Implementing Big Blocks, Grades 4 - 8. (p. 295)
Arens, Amanda B., et al. Teacher's Guide to Big Blocks, Grades 4-8: A Multimethod, Multilevel Framework. (p. 1709)
Arensen, Shel. Carjackers (p. 269)
—First Christmas: Nativity Puzzle Book with 6 Play Pieces. (p. 593)
—Poison Arrow Tree. (p. 1377)
Arenson, Roberta. One, Two, Skip a Few! First Number Rhymes. Arenson, Roberta, illus. (p. 1297)
Arenson, Roberta, illus. see Bird, Fiona.
Arenson, Roberta, illus. see Cohen, Whitney & Life Lab Science Program Staff.
Arenson, Roberta, illus. see Finch, Mary.
Arenson, Roberta & Finch, Mary. Three Billy Goats Gruff. Arenson, Roberta & Asbjørnsen, Peter Christen, illus. (p. 1741)
Arenstam, Peter. Mighty Mastiff of the Mayflower. (p. 1140)
—Nicholas: A Vermont Tale. Holman, Karen Busch, illus. (p. 1250)
—Nicholas: A Maine Tale Bk. 2 Holman, Karen Busch, illus. (p. 1250)
—Nicholas: A New Hampshire Tale. Holman, Karen Busch, illus. (p. 1250)
Arenstam, Peter, et al. MayFlower 1620: A New Look at a Pilgrim Voyage. (p. 1113)
—Mayflower 1620: A New Look at a Pilgrim Village. Brimberg, Sisse & Coulson, Cotton, illus. (p. 1113)
Aresenault, Jane & Cedor, Jean. Guided Meditations for Youth on Personal Themes. Stamschror, Robert P., ed. (p. 730)
Arestis, Philip, et al, eds. Financial Liberalization: Beyond Orthodox Concerns. (p. 587)
Aresty, Reecy. Getting into College & Paying for It: Solutions for High School & College Families Guaranteed to Cut the Cost! (p. 669)
Aretha, David. America's Team: The Dallas Cowboys. (p. 64)
—Amy Winehouse: RandB, Jazz, & Soul Musician. (p. 66)
—Awesome African-American Rock & Soul Musicians. (p. 120)
—Black Power. (p. 196)
—Brown V. Board of Education. (p. 232)
—Cocaine & Crack: A MyReportLinks. com Book. (p. 337)
—Colin Kaepernick. (p. 339)
—Denali National Park & Preserve: Adventure, Explore, Discover. (p. 426)
—Discovering Asia's Land, People, & Wildlife: A MyReportLinks. com Book. (p. 448)
—Dodger Blue: The Los Angeles Dodgers. (p. 460)

—Ecstasy & Other Party Drugs: A MyReportLinks. com Book. (p. 503)
—Eminem: Grammy-Winning Rapper. (p. 519)
—Foul Ball Frame-Up at Wrigley Field: The Baseball Geeks Adventures Book 2. (p. 624)
—Freedom Summer. (p. 635)
—Glacier National Park: Adventure, Explore, Discover. (p. 682)
—Gold Rush to California's Riches. (p. 694)
—Hall Lot of Trouble at Cooperstown: The Baseball Geeks Adventures Book 1. (p. 737)
—Inhalants: A MyReportLinks. com Book. (p. 874)
—Israel in the News: Past, Present, & Future. (p. 893)
—Joe Flacco. (p. 920)
—Lebanon in the News: Past, Present, & Future. (p. 986)
—Magic Johnson: Athlete. (p. 1072)
—Malala Yousafzai & the Girls of Pakistan. (p. 1083)
—Martin Luther King Jr. & the 1963 March on Washington. (p. 1098)
—Methamphetamine & Amphetamines: A MyReportLinks. com Book. (p. 1130)
—Michigan: A MyReportLinks.com Book. (p. 1135)
—Middle Passage. (p. 1137)
—Murder of Emmett Till. (p. 1192)
—No Compromise: The Story of Harvey Milk. (p. 1258)
—On the Rocks: Teens & Alcohol. (p. 1291)
—Political Profiles: Mitt Romney. (p. 1380)
—Power in Pinstripes: The New York Yankees. (p. 1389)
—Rounding Third, Heading Home! (p. 1491)
—Sabotage, Sedition, & Sundry Acts of Rebellion. (p. 1500)
—Salle: French Explorer of the Mississippi. (p. 1505)
—Selma & the Voting Rights Act. (p. 1550)
—Sit-Ins & Freedom Rides. (p. 1581)
—Steel Tough: The Pittsburgh Steelers. (p. 1646)
—Steroids & Other Performance-Enhancing Drugs: A MyReportLinks. com Book. (p. 1649)
—Story of Rosa Parks & the Montgomery Bus Boycott in Photographs. (p. 1659)
—Story of the Birmingham Civil Rights Movement in Photographs. (p. 1660)
—Story of the Civil Rights Freedom Rides in Photographs. (p. 1660)
—Story of the Civil Rights March on Washington for Jobs & Freedom in Photographs. (p. 1660)
—Story of the Little Rock Nine & School Desegregation in Photographs. (p. 1661)
—Story of the Selma Voting Rights Marches in Photographs. (p. 1662)
—Superstars of the Chicago Bulls. (p. 1684)
—Time for Martyrs: The Life of Malcolm X. (p. 1751)
—Top 25 Baseball Skills, Tips, & Tricks. (p. 1768)
—Treasure Hunt Stunt at Fenway Park: The Baseball Geeks Adventures Book 3. (p. 1781)
—Trial of the Scottsboro Boys. (p. 1785)
—With All Deliberate Speed: Court-Ordered Busing & American Schools. (p. 1942)
—Yellowstone National Park: Adventure, Explore, Discover. (p. 1970)
Aretha, David A. Jefferson Davis. (p. 912)
—Tiki Barber. (p. 1749)
Arevalo, Jose Daniel, illus. see Layne, Carmela C.
Arévalo, Josefina. Lo Que Paulito Olvidó. (p. 1044)
Arevalo, Luis Paquime. Juan & the Magic Shoes. (p. 930)
—L. A. 's Riots. (p. 969)
Arevamirp, Esile, jt. auth. see Primavera, Elise.
Arevamirp, Esile & Primavera, Elise. Fred & Anthony Meet the Demented Super-Degerm-O Zombie. Primavera, Elise, illus. (p. 632)
Argent, Kerry. India, the Showstopper. (p. 871)
—Nighty Night! (p. 1255)
Argent, Kerry, illus. see Wild, Margaret.
Argent, Leanne, jt. auth. see Wignell, Edel.
Argenta, Joan. Santa Claus Comes to the Thomas Family. (p. 1511)
—Wicked Princess Torment. (p. 1927)
Argiento, Cindy. Doris in Dreamland. (p. 471)
Argo, Kaitlyn, jt. auth. see Argo, Sandi.
Argo, Sandi & Argo, Kaitlyn. Don't You See It? Jungle Edition Stephens, Sherry & Finnell, Cyndy, illus. (p. 469)
Argoff, Beily, illus. see Paluch, Beily.
Argoff, Patti, illus. see Goldberg, Malky.
Argoff, Patti, illus. see House, Darrell.
Argoff, Patti, illus. see Lieberman, Channah.
Argoff, Patti, illus. see Nutkis, Phyllis.
Argoff, Patti, illus. see Paluch, Beily.
Argoff, Patti, illus. see Stern, Ariella.
Argote-Freyre, Frank. Brief History of the Caribbean. (p. 227)
Arguello, John. Ophelia & the Pet Peeve. (p. 1300)
Arguello, Tito. Dog in Love. (p. 461)
Argueta, Jorge. Alfredito Flies Home Amado, Elisa, tr. from SPA. (p. 37)
—Alfredito Regresa Volando a Su Casa Garay, Luis, illus. (p. 37)
—Arroz Con Leche: Un Poema para Cocinar. Vilela, Fernando, illus. (p. 101)
—Fiesta de Las Tortillas: The Fiesta of the Tortillas. Hayes, Joe & Franco, Sharon, trs. from SPA. (p. 584)
—Fiesta de Las Tortillas. Hayes, Joe & Franco, Sharon, trs. (p. 584)
—Gallinita en la Ciudad: The Little Hen in the City. Castro, Mima, illus. (p. 653)
—Hablando Con Madre Tierra. Perez, Lucia Angela, illus. (p. 735)
—Moony Luna. Gómez, Elizabeth, illus. (p. 1173)
—Pelicula en Mi Almohada. Gomez, Elizabeth & Gómez, Elizabeth, illus. (p. 1336)
—Salsa: Un Poema Para Cocinar / a Cooking Poem Amado, Elisa, tr. (p. 1505)
—Sopa de Frijoles. Yockteng, Rafael, illus. (p. 1613)
—Tamalitos. Amado, Elisa, tr. from SPA. (p. 1704)
—Xochitl & the Flowers. Angel, Carl, illus. (p. 1967)
—Xochitl & the Flowers (Xochitl, la Nina de Las Flores) Angel, Carl, illus. (p. 1967)
—Zipitio Calderon, Gloria, illus. (p. 1987)
Argueta, Jorge & Alvarez, Cecilia Concepcion. Moony Luna: Luna, Lunita Lunera. Gomez, Elizabeth, illus. (p. 1173)
Argueta, Jorge & Amado, Elisa. Guacamole: A Cooking Poem Sada, Margarita, illus. (p. 728)
Argueta, José René & Coleman, Ken. Cultura política de la democracia en Honduras 2008: El impacto de la Gobernabilidad. (p. 390)
Arguilé, Elisa, illus. see Nesquens, Daniel & Martos Sánchez, José Daniel.
Argula, Anne. Homicide My Own. (p. 794)
Argyle, Amber. Winter Queen. (p. 1938)
Argyle, Michelle Davidson. Breakaway. (p. 224)
Argyle, Ray. Boy in the Picture: The Craigellachie Kid & the Driving of the Last Spike. (p. 218)
Arhin, Gerri. Tales of Zeek the Monkey King. (p. 1703)
Arias, Carlos Ballesteros. Magic Forest. (p. 1072)
Arias De Cordoba, Heather & Arias de Cordoba, Kalya. Year Full of Fairies. (p. 1969)
Arias de Cordoba, Kalya, jt. auth. see Arias De Cordoba, Heather.
Arias, Lisa. Dandy Decimals: Add, Subtract, Multiply, & Divide. (p. 403)
—Dazzling Decimals: Decimals & Fractions. (p. 415)
—Dive into Division: Estimation & Partial Quotients. (p. 454)
—Dynamic Denominators: Compare, Add, & Subtract. (p. 491)
—Edgy Equations: One-Variable Equations. (p. 504)
—Fraction Action: Fractions Are Numbers Too. (p. 626)
—Funky Fractions: Multiply & Divide. (p. 649)
—Galactic Geometry: Two-Dimensional Figures. (p. 652)
—Glorious Geometry: Lines, Angles & Shapes, Oh My! (p. 685)
—Groovy Graphing: Quadrant One & Beyond. (p. 725)
—Magical Mathematical Properties: Commutative, Associative, & Distributive. (p. 1074)
—Marvelous Measurement: Conversions. (p. 1099)
—Multiplication Master: Divisibility Rules. (p. 1190)
—Multiplication Meltdown: Factors & Multiples. (p. 1190)
—Positive & Negative Numbers, Oh My! Number Lines. (p. 1387)
—Powerful Place Value: Patterns & Power. (p. 1390)
—Scrumptious Statistics: Show & Recognize Statistics. (p. 1533)
—Time Travel: Intervals & Elapsed Time. (p. 1753)
Aric, Nicholson. I Hope You Dance. (p. 839)
Ariel. Faith. (p. 565)
Arif, Amrana. Allah Gave Me Two Ears to Hear. Clarke, Asiya, illus. (p. 46)
Arif, Tasneem, illus. see Schaefer, Peggy.
Ariga, Hitoshi. Mega Man Gigamix Volume 3 TP (p. 1124)
Ariga, Minatsu & Morita, Kotaro G. Three Little Ones & the Golden Mane. (p. 1742)
Ariganello, Lisa. Henry the Navigator: Prince of Portuguese Exploration. (p. 768)
Arihara, Shino, illus. see Franco, Betsy.
Arihara, Shino, illus. see Lord, Michelle.
Arik, Engin. Crosslinguistic Study of the Language of Space: Sign & Spoken Languages. (p. 385)
Arima, Keitaro. Tsukuyomi - Moon Phase Arima, Keitaro, illus. (p. 1795)
Arima, Keitaro, et al. Tsukuyomi - Moon Phase (p. 1795)
Arin, Dilara, illus. see Menase, Debra.
Arin, Dilara, illus. see Ural, Serpil.
Arinola Awokoya. Adventures of High Jumper. (p. 18)
Arinouchkine, Andrei, jt. auth. see Moncomble, Gerard.
Arinsberg, Norman, illus. see Favorite, Deborah.
Aris, Mary. Bartholomew. (p. 140)
Arisa, Miguel, jt. auth. see Levy, Janice.
Arisa, Miguel, tr. see Levy, Janice.
Arisawa, Mamizu & Matsuzawa, Mari. Inukami! (p. 883)
ARISE Foundation & Benson, Susan. Life Skills Curriculum: ARISE Basic Health 101, Book 1. (p. 1013)
ARISE Foundation Staff. Life Skills Curriculum: ARISE Life Isn't Fair (Instructor's Manual) (p. 1013)
—Life Skills Curriculum: ARISE Sprouts, Book 1. (p. 1013)
ARISE Foundation Staff & Benson, Susan. 31 of Taneka's Urban Life Tales (Instructor's Manual) (p. 1996)
—Life Skills Curriculum: ARISE Rules of the Road (Instructor's Manual) (p. 1013)
Arisman, Marshall. Cat Who Invented Bebop. Arisman, Marshall, illus. (p. 278)
Aristizabal, Luis H. German Arciniegas -un joven de cien Años. (p. 666)
Aristizabal, Nora. Selva Maravillosa/the Wonderful Jungle. Reyes, Maria Margarita, illus. (p. 1550)
Aristophane. Zabime Sisters. Madden, Matt, tr. from FRE. (p. 1984)
Aristophanes. Acharnians. Landes, William-Alan, ed. (p. 8)
—Birds. (p. 191)
—Clouds. Landes, S. H., tr. from GRE. (p. 335)
—Frogs. Landes, William-Alan, ed. (p. 641)
—Knights. Frere, John H., tr. from GRE. (p. 964)
—Lysistrata. Landes, William-Alan, ed. (p. 1067)
—Peace. Landes, William-Alan, ed. (p. 1331)
Arita Vera. All Around the Islands. Moen Cabanting Ruth, illus. (p. 43)
Arita, Vera. Animals Sing Aloha. Louie, Ron, illus. (p. 84)
—Can You Catch a Coqui Frog? Moran, Edna Cabcabin, illus. (p. 258)
Ariye, Shirley. Our Georgia School: A Wildlife Habitat. (p. 1308)
Arjas, Pirkko & Butcher, Sally K. Friend Owl: A Children's Book. (p. 637)
Ark, Dan Vander. Honest to God: A Study of the Psalms. (p. 794)
Arkadina, Mina. Nesmotrya Mina Chto. Arkadina, Mina, ed. (p. 1242)
Arkangel, Brian. Cow Story. Moffat, Ross, illus. (p. 373)
Arkanov, Elvira, illus. see Alexander, Janice Marie.
Arkell, O. E. Adventures of Munchkin-Patch Tabby: How Munchkin Patch-Tabby Got His Name. (p. 21)
Arkham, Thomas. Both Puerto Rican & American. (p. 215)
—Both Puerto Rican & American. Limón, José E., ed. (p. 215)
—Latino American Civil Rights. (p. 979)
—Latino American Civil Rights. Limón, José E., ed. (p. 979)
—Latino Americans & Their Jobs. (p. 979)
—Latino Americans & Their Jobs. Limón, José E., ed. (p. 979)
—Latinos Today. (p. 979)
—Latinos Today. Limón, José E., ed. (p. 979)
—Sirens & Smoke: Firefighters Folklore. (p. 1580)
—Sirens & Smoke: Firefighters Folklore. Jabbour, Alan, ed. (p. 1580)
—You're It! Tag, Red Rover, & Other Folk Games. (p. 1982)
—You're It! Tag, Red Rover, & Other Folk Games. Jabbour, Alan, ed. (p. 1982)
Arkhurst, Joyce Cooper. Further Adventures of Spider: West African Folktales. Pinkney, Jerry, illus. (p. 650)
—Further Adventures of Spider. (p. 650)
Arkin, Alan. Cassie Loves Beethoven. (p. 276)
—Cosmo: A Cautionary Tale. Richards, Jon, illus. (p. 368)
Arledge, Roo, jt. auth. see Crofoot, Betty.
Arlen, Harold, jt. auth. see Harburg, E. Y.
Arlen, Richard. Girls' Boarding School. (p. 679)
Arlene, Sonday. Sonday System - Let's Play Learn: Shapes & Numbers Book. Cindy, Breckman, ed. (p. 1611)
Arline-Hicks, Patience & Hicks, Wendi N. Old Mean Molly Bouthyette, Valerie, illus. (p. 1284)
Arling, Jackie L., illus. see Berning, Terri J.
Arlington, Jane. Night of Nonsense. Reid, Mike, illus. (p. 1253)
Arlington, Jane & Langdon, Sharon. Penguins. (p. 1337)
Arlon, Penelope. Animal Faces. (p. 77)
—Bugs. (p. 237)
—Dinosaurs. (p. 443)
—Dolphins. (p. 464)
—Explorers. (p. 551)
—Granja. (p. 710)
—Insectos: Y Otras Criaturas. (p. 875)
—Mirame Crecer. (p. 1149)
—Penguins: Meet Teh Heroes of a Frozen World. (p. 1337)
—Pingüinos. (p. 1359)
—Planetas. (p. 1368)
—Puppies & Kittens. (p. 1418)
—Rainforest. (p. 1436)
—Really? Ocean. (p. 1449)
—Reptiles. (p. 1461)
—Scholastic Discover More - Ancient Egypt. (p. 1521)
—Scholastic Discover More: Birds. (p. 1521)
Arlon, Penelope, jt. auth. see Arlon, Penny.
Arlon, Penelope, jt. auth. see Scholastic, Inc. Staff.
Arlon, Penelope & Arlon, Penny. Planets. (p. 1368)
Arlon, Penelope & Brown, Laaren. Scholastic Discover More Reader Level 3: Volcanoes. (p. 1521)
—Scholastic Discover More Stickers: Sharks: With 260 Stickers. (p. 1521)
Arlon, Penelope & Buckley, James, Jr. Scholastic Discover More Reader Level 1: Things That Go! (p. 1521)
Arlon, Penelope & Burnie, David. Sharks. (p. 1562)
Arlon, Penelope & Callery, Sean. Scholastic Discover More Reader Level 3: Titanic. (p. 1521)
Arlon, Penelope & Gordon-Harris, Tory. Bugs. (p. 237)
—Dinosaurs. (p. 443)
—Penguins. (p. 1337)
—Planets. (p. 1368)
Arlon, Penelope & Hayes, Susan. Polar Animals. (p. 1378)
Arlon, Penelope & Kosara, Tori. Fantastic Frogs. (p. 571)
Arlon, Penelope & Tuchman, Gail. Scholastic Discover More Reader Level 1: Petting Zoo. (p. 1521)
—Scholastic Discover More Reader Level 2: Shark Attack! (p. 1521)
Arlon, Penelope, et al. Scholastic Discover More Reader Level 1: Planets. (p. 1521)
Arlon, Penny, jt. auth. see Arlon, Penelope.
Arlon, Penny & Arlon, Penelope. Farm. (p. 573)
—See Me Grow. (p. 1546)
Armacost, Betty. Look to the Sky. Arnett, Patty, photos by. (p. 1050)
Armadillo. Let's Look & See: Pets. (p. 998)
—Let's Look & See: Animals. (p. 998)
—Let's Look & See: Kittens. (p. 998)
Armadillo Publishing Staff. Baby's Bible Stories: The Birth of Jesus. Lewis, Jan, illus. (p. 128)
—This Little Pig - Mother Goose Rhymes. Lewis, Jan, illus. (p. 1737)
—Times Table - 1 to 20: Includes Instant Answer Number Matrix Chart. (p. 1754)
—Words - Let's Look & See. (p. 1951)
Armand, Anjale Renee, illus. see Coleman, Alice Scovell.
Armand, Glenda. Ira's Shakespeare Dream Cooper, Floyd, illus. (p. 887)
—Love Twelve Miles Long Bootman, Colin, illus. (p. 1060)
Armand, Louis. Strange Attractors. (p. 1664)
Armand, Villavert. Princess Al: Rumors from the Other Side. Schilling, Christine & Kim, Hyun-Joo, trs. from JPN. (p. 1402)
Armantrout, Denise. Pink & Green Story Time: Book One. (p. 1359)
Armantrout, Linda M., jt. auth. see Minden, Cecilia.
Armas, Lourdes, illus. see Antillano, Laura.
Armas, Teresa. Remembering Grandma / Recordando a Abuela. Ventura, Gabriela Baeza, tr. from ENG. (p. 1459)
Armbrecht, Doug, compiled by. Quiet Time Prepack for Families (Quiet Time Devotionals) (p. 1428)
Armbrust, Janet, illus. see Cecchini, Marie E.
Armbrust, Janet, illus. see Galus, Pamela J.
Armbrust, Janet, illus. see Storey, Melinda.
Armeland, Galia. [Alef] - B [Bet] Yisrael: Aleph Bet Israel. (p. 35)
Armendariz, Anna. Celia's Traditional Mexican Home Cooking: Salsas & Appetizers. (p. 286)
Arment Jd, Laura B. Sixteen Things You Should Know about Work Now: A Guide for Young People. (p. 1583)
Armenteros, Sarah. Emma & the Mashed Potato Monster. (p. 519)
Armentrout, David. Tornadoes. (p. 1770)
—Volcanoes. (p. 1849)
Armentrout, David & Armentrout, Patricia. Animals That Fly & Birds That Don't. (p. 84)
—Annika Sorenstam. (p. 87)
—Bank. (p. 136)
—Biofuels. (p. 188)
—Choppers. (p. 310)
—Crafty Critters. (p. 376)
—Declaration de Independencia. (p. 421)
—Dirt Bikes. (p. 446)
—Doggie Duties. (p. 462)
—Emancipation Proclamation. (p. 517)
—Energia Del Viento. (p. 527)
—Facts on Rats. (p. 561)
—Fire Department. (p. 590)
—Fires. (p. 592)
—George Washington. (p. 664)
—Gettysburg Address. (p. 670)
—Going Green. (p. 692)
—Help! I Have a Hermit Crab. (p. 765)
—Hurricanes. (p. 830)
—Inclined Planes. (p. 869)
—Kitty Care. (p. 963)
—Leaps & Bounds. (p. 982)
—Let's Talk about Pets (p. 1001)
—Levers. (p. 1003)
—Mark Twain. (p. 1095)
—Mayflower Compact. (p. 1113)
—Post Office: Our Community. (p. 1387)
—Pulleys. (p. 1415)
—Raising Rabbits. (p. 1437)
—Screws. (p. 1533)
—Slithering Snakes & How to Care for Them. (p. 1591)
—Speed Demons. (p. 1624)
—Sportbikes. (p. 1631)
—Stunts, Tricks, & Jumps. (p. 1670)
—Tony Hawk. (p. 1766)
—Wedges. (p. 1871)
—Wheels. (p. 1900)
Armentrout, David, et al. Gettysburg Address. (p. 670)
Armentrout, Jennifer L. Don't Look Back. (p. 468)
—Elixir. (p. 513)
—Every Last Breath. (p. 542)
—Lux - Beginnings. (p. 1066)
—Lux - Consequences. (p. 1066)
—Obsidian. (p. 1275)
—Onyx. (p. 1298)
—Opal. (p. 1299)
—Opposition. (p. 1301)
—Origin. (p. 1304)
—Stone Cold Touch. (p. 1652)
—White Hot Kiss. (p. 1913)
Armentrout, Patricia. History of Money. (p. 784)
Armentrout, Patricia, jt. auth. see Armentrout, David.
Armer, Laura Adams. Waterless Mountain. Armer, Sidney, illus. (p. 1863)
Armer, Sidney, illus. see Armer, Laura Adams.
Armijo, Consuelo, jt. auth. see Armijo, Consuelo.
Armijo, Consuelo & Armijo, Consuelo. Aniceto, el Vencecangueles. (p. 76)
Armino, Monica, illus. see Fineman, Kelly Ramsdell.
Armistead, Cal. Being Henry David. (p. 161)
Armistead, John. Return of Gabriel. Gregory, Fran, illus. (p. 1464)
Armistead, John & Gregory, Fran. $66 Summer: A Novel of the Segregated South. (p. 1997)
Armitage, David, jt. auth. see Edwards, Becky.
Armitage, Donald, jt. auth. see Armitage, Ronda.
Armitage, Haley. Into the Realm of Elfrelmey: Kataya's Journey of Destiny. (p. 881)
Armitage, Kimo. Akua Hawaii: Hawaiian Gods & Their Stories. Enos, Solomon, illus. (p. 32)
—Healers. (p. 757)
—Limu: The Blue Turtle & His Hawaiian Garden. Kaneshiro, Scott, illus. (p. 1018)
Armitage, Ronda. Small Knight & George & the Pirates. Robins, Arthur, illus. (p. 1592)
—Wave the Flag & Blow the Whistle: A Railway Adventure. Gordon, Andrew, illus. (p. 1864)
Armitage, Ronda & Armitage, Donald. Lighthouse Keeper's Lunch. (p. 1015)
Armour, Christopher. 40 Daily Devotions. (p. 1996)
Armour, Christopher, jt. auth. see Matens, Margaret H.
Armour, Cy. Earthquakes! (p. 497)
—Tornadoes & Hurricanes! (p. 1770)
—Volcanoes! (p. 1849)
Armour, Michael C. Orca Song. Lee, Katie, illus. (p. 1302)
Armour, Peter. Stop That Pickle! Shachat, Andrew, illus. (p. 1653)
Armour, Steven, illus. see Knoebel, Suzanne B.
Arms. Environmental Science: Enhanced Online Edition. (p. 532)
Armstrong, Alan. Raleigh's Page. Jessell, Tim, illus. (p. 1437)
Armstrong, Alan W. Racing the Moon. Jessell, Tim, illus. (p. 1432)
—Whittington. (p. 1914)
—Whittington. Schindler, S. D., illus. (p. 1914)
Armstrong, Aldona. Every Family Is Special. (p. 542)
Armstrong, Ashley, jt. auth. see Armstrong, Joey.
Armstrong, Ashley Sage-Taylor. Adventures of Starlight & Sunny: Building a Dream, How to Focus & Make Your Dreams Come to Life, with Positive Conscious Morals. Picture Boo. (p. 23)
—Adventures of Starlight & Sunny: The Secret Valley, Book 2, How to Be Happy. to Find Inner Beauty & Peace, with Positive Conscious Morals, P. (p. 23)
—Adventures of Starlight & Sunny: Book Four in the Adventures of Starlight & Sunny Series, ?Princesses Don't Need a Job !? How to Be an Indepen. (p. 23)
—Adventures of Starlight & Sunny: I Am Me ! Who Are You?, How to Find Good Quality Friends & Stand up for One Another, with Positive Morals, Pi. (p. 23)
Armstrong, Bev, illus. see Duby, Marjorie.
Armstrong, Bev, illus. see Klawitter, Pamela Amick.
Armstrong, Bev, illus. see Schwartz, Linda.
Armstrong, Beverly, illus. see Heidrich, Delana.
Armstrong, Beverly, illus. see Klawitter, Pamela Amick.
Armstrong, Beverly, illus. see Schwartz, Linda.
Armstrong, Beverly, illus. see Sylvester, Diane.
Armstrong, Bill. Letters from Ozo (p. 1002)

A

Armstrong, Cara. Moxie: The Dachshund of Fallingwater. (p. 1184)
Armstrong, Carole. Monet: 20 Re-Usable Stickers. (p. 1163)
—My Sticker Art Gallery: Monet. (p. 1219)
Armstrong, Carrie, ed. see Dickins, Rosie.
Armstrong, Carrie, ed. see Miles, Lisa.
Armstrong, Charles. Laugh & Pray Today. (p. 980)
Armstrong, Cindy. Boudreaux & His Buddies. (p. 216)
Armstrong, David. Rising Place. (p. 1475)
Armstrong, E. J., photos by see Cosmic Debris Etc., Inc. Staff & Chronicle Books Staff.
Armstrong, E. J., photos by see Morgan, Diane.
Armstrong, Gregory D. Count with Buddy Coloring Book. (p. 370)
—Day Buddy Flew. (p. 412)
—Don't Laugh at Me. (p. 468)
Armstrong, James. New Mrs. Jones: A One-Act Comedy Play. (p. 1246)
Armstrong, Jeannette C. Dancing with the Cranes. Hall, Ron, illus. (p. 403)
Armstrong, Jennifer. American Story: 100 True Tales from American History. Roth, Roger, illus. (p. 63)
—Fantastic Failure: A True Story. (p. 571)
—Kiln. (p. 956)
—Magnus at the Fire. Smith, Owen, illus. (p. 1076)
—Once upon a Banana. Small, David, illus. (p. 1292)
—Photo by Brady: A Picture of the Civil War. (p. 1352)
—Shattered: Stories of Children & War. (p. 1563)
—Three-Minute Speech: Lincoln's Remarks at Gettysburg. Lorenz, Albert, illus. (p. 1743)
—True Story Behind Lincoln's Gettysburg Address. Lorenz, Albert, illus. (p. 1793)
Armstrong, Jennifer, jt. auth. see Opdyke, Irene Gut.
Armstrong, Jennifer & Butcher, Nancy. Kiln. (p. 956)
Armstrong, Jesse. Big Show. (p. 183)
—Dolph Ziggler. (p. 464)
—Mark Henry. (p. 1095)
—Randy Orton. (p. 1438)
—Triple H. (p. 1787)
Armstrong, Joey & Armstrong, Ashley. God Loves It When... (p. 689)
Armstrong, K. L. & Marr, M. A. Loki's Wolves. (p. 1045)
—Odin's Ravens. (p. 1278)
—Thor's Serpents. (p. 1740)
Armstrong, Kate. David & the Mittens Kitten Stories. (p. 410)
Armstrong, Katharine, illus. see Trelogan, Stephanie.
Armstrong, Kelley. Awakening. (p. 120)
—Awakening. (p. 120)
—Calling. (p. 254)
—Empire of Night. (p. 521)
—Gathering. (p. 658)
—Reckoning. (p. 1451)
—Rising. (p. 1475)
—Sea of Shadows: Age of Legends. (p. 1535)
—Sea of Shadows. (p. 1535)
—Summoning. (p. 1675)
—Summoning. (p. 1675)
Armstrong, Kim. Frosty the Snowbear. (p. 645)
—Petunia in Manhattan. (p. 1349)
Armstrong, Linda. Henry Ford. (p. 768)
—Thinking Kids' Math, Grade 1. Stith, Jennifer & Hoople, Barrie, eds. (p. 1734)
Armstrong, Linda J. African-American Stage, Radio, Film, & TV Entertainers. (p. 27)
—African-American Stage, Radio, Film, & TV Entertainers. Hill, Marc Lamont, ed. (p. 27)
Armstrong, Luanne. Jeannie & the Gentle Giants. (p. 911)
Armstrong, Lynn, jt. ed. see Harris, Nancy.
Armstrong, Mabel. Women Astronomers: Reaching for the Stars. (p. 1945)
Armstrong, Margalynne, jt. auth. see Cates, David.
Armstrong, Matthew S. Jane & Mizmow. Armstrong, Matthew S., illus. (p. 908)
Armstrong, Matthew S., illus. see Davis, Dan T.
Armstrong, Matthew S., illus. see Matte, Johane, et al.
Armstrong, Matthew S., illus. see Prose, Francine.
Armstrong, Michele. Jordyn & Heather in Paris. (p. 925)
—Richard & Ryan's Grand Adventure: Red Turban Rebellion. (p. 1469)
Armstrong, Michelle Hartz, illus. see Beyer, Pamela J. & Bilbrey, Hilary.
Armstrong, Moses K. Orthodox Christian Alphabet Coloring Book. (p. 1305)
Armstrong, Nancy, jt. auth. see Henderson, Elisabeth.
Armstrong, Neal, illus. see Butler, Leah & Peters, Trudy.
Armstrong Nhp, Ashley Sage-Taylor. Adventures of Starlight & Sunny: Book One in, the Adventures of Starlight & Sunny Series, ?the Princess Path?, How to Be True with Good Deeds; (p. 23)
Armstrong, Nicky, illus. see Sunderland, Margot & Hancock, Nicky.
Armstrong, Nicky, illus. see Sunderland, Margot.
Armstrong, Nicky, jt. auth. see Sunderland, Margot.
Armstrong, Nicky, tr. see Sunderland, Margot & Hancock, Nicky.
Armstrong, Nicky, tr. see Sunderland, Margot.
Armstrong, Rachel. Fair Folk in Knob's End. (p. 562)
Armstrong, Reed & Armstrong, Roxlana. Art 4 for Young Catholics. (p. 101)
Armstrong, Robert H., et al. Dragons in the Pond. (p. 479)
Armstrong, Robert W. Big Blue Lake. Broxon, Janet, illus. (p. 178)
Armstrong, Roxlana, jt. auth. see Armstrong, Reed.
Armstrong, Samuel. Gene Autry & the Lost Dogie. (p. 660)
Armstrong, Shelagh, illus. see Smith, David J.
Armstrong, Simon. Cool Art: 50 Fantastic Facts for Kids of All Ages. (p. 362)
Armstrong, Sue. P53: The Gene That Cracked the Cancer Code. (p. 1316)
Armstrong, Susan. Just One?... for Kids! (p. 939)
Armstrong, Thomas. You're Smarter Than You Think: A Kid's Guide to Multiple Intelligences. (p. 1982)
Armstrong, Tiffani. Zach & the Incredible Traveling Hat. (p. 1984)
Armstrong, Tony. My Max Score AP English Literature & Composition: Maximize Your Score in Less Time. (p. 1214)
—Water Troll. (p. 1863)
Armstrong, William H. Sounder. (p. 1615)
Armstrong, Yvette. My Curious Kitty. (p. 1200)
Armstrong, Z. A. Origins of Dexter & Stray, Part: The Man Who Knows Everything. (p. 1304)
Armstrong-Ellis, Carey. I Love You More Than Moldy Ham. (p. 844)
Armstrong-Ellis, Carey, illus. see Newman, Lesléa.
Armstrong-Ellis, Carey, illus. see Rose, Deborah Lee.
Armstrong-Ellis, Carey F. Ten Creepy Monsters. (p. 1718)
Armstrong-Ellis, Carey F., illus. see Rose, Deborah Lee.
Armstrony, Nicky & Sunderland, Margot. Helping Children with Fear - Teenie Weenie in a Too Big World (p. 766)
Armstrony, Nicky, et al. Helping Children Locked in Rage or Hate - How Hattie Hated Kindness. (p. 766)
—Helping Children with Loss & the Day the Sea Went Out & Never Came Back (p. 766)
—Helping Children with Low Self-Esteem & Ruby & the Rubbish Bin. (p. 766)
Arnaktauyok, Germaine, illus. see Bushey, Jeanne.
Arnaktauyok, Germaine, illus. see Christopher, Neil.
Arnaktauyok, Germaine, illus. see Nicol, C. W.
Arnaldo, Monica. Little Book of Big Fears. (p. 1025)
Arnaquq-Baril, Alethea. Blind Boy & the Loon Arnaquq-Baril, Alethea, illus. (p. 199)
Arnau, Eduard. Nuestra Arquitectura Osea. (p. 1270)
Arnau, Marta. cartero de los Suenos. (p. 272)
Arnauld, D. S. Zertelo & the Road of Fire: Book Two. Scott, Sara, ed. (p. 1986)
Arnault, Delphine, illus. see Henry, William.
Arndt, Charles T., illus. see Richardson, Lans.
Arndt, Ingo. Best Foot Forward: Exploring Feet, Flippers, & Claws. (p. 169)
—Best Foot Forward: Exploring Feet, Flippers, & Claws. Arndt, Ingo, photos by. (p. 169)
Arndt, Janna, jt. auth. see Arthur, Kay.
Arndt, Michael. Cat Says Meow & Other Animalopoeia. (p. 278)
Arndt, Rhonda. Mac's Adventure. (p. 1068)
Arne, Robin. Heart of Servanthood. (p. 759)
Arner, Elizabeth. Weather Detectives. (p. 1870)
Arneson, Donald & Drake, Arnold. Dark Shadows: the Complete Series Volume 1: The Complete Series Volume 1 (p. 408)
Arneson, Guy. Kiddy Ditties. (p. 952)
Arnett, Dee. Gifted. (p. 675)
Arnett, John B., Sr. John-John's Greatest Gift. (p. 922)
Arnett, Karen, jt. auth. see Bradford, Jeff.
Arnett, Mindee. Avalon. (p. 118)
—Nightmare Affair. (p. 1255)
—Nightmare Charade. (p. 1255)
—Nightmare Dilemma. (p. 1255)
—Polaris. (p. 1379)
Arnett, Patty, photos by see Armacost, Betty.
Arnett, Robert. Finders Keepers? A True Story. Turakhia, Smita, illus. (p. 587)
Arnéz, Lynda. Father Junipero Serra: Founder of the California Missions. (p. 577)
—My Life As a Pioneer. (p. 1212)
Arni, Samhita & Valmiki. Sita's Ramayana. Chitrakar, Moyna, illus. (p. 1582)
Arno, illus. see Delval, Marie-Hélène.
Arno, Iris Hiskey. Secret of the First One Up. Graef, Renee, illus. (p. 1542)
Arnoff, Rebecca D. Trouble with Tooth Fairies: The Adventures of Sam & Angela. (p. 1790)
Arnold. Fifa Latin America. (p. 584)
Arnold, Adam. Aoi House Omnibus 1 Shiei & Shiei, Shiei, illus. (p. 91)
—Aoi House Omnibus 2 Shiei, illus. (p. 91)
Arnold, Adolf W. Boy Without Toys. (p. 220)
Arnold, Alli, illus. see Burningham, Sarah O'Leary.
Arnold, Alli, illus. see Coombs, Kate.
Arnold, Alli, illus. see Smith, Brooke.
Arnold, Alli, illus. see Weiss, Ellen.
Arnold, Andrew, illus. see Smith, Greg Leitich.
Arnold, Andrew, jt. auth. see Sturm, James.
Arnold, Audrey. Elkin's Tail. (p. 513)
Arnold, Barbara Studebaker. Marmalade. (p. 1096)
Arnold, Beth. Elijah Makes New Friends. Arnold, Beth, illus. (p. 512)
Arnold, Brian. Quick Revision KS3 Science. (p. 1427)
Arnold, Caroline. Birds: Nature's Magnificent Flying Machines. Wynne, Patricia J., illus. (p. 191)
—Caroline Arnold's Animals Arnold, Caroline, illus. (p. 270)
—Caroline Arnold's Black & White Animals. Arnold, Caroline, illus. (p. 270)
—Caroline Arnold's Habitats. Arnold, Caroline, illus. (p. 270)
—Day & Night in the Desert. Arnold, Caroline, illus. (p. 412)
—Day & Night in the Forest. Arnold, Caroline, illus. (p. 412)
—Day & Night in the Rain Forest. Arnold, Caroline, illus. (p. 412)
—Day & Night on the Prairie. Arnold, Caroline, illus. (p. 412)
—Moose's World Arnold, Caroline, illus. (p. 1173)
—Panda's World. Arnold, Caroline, illus. (p. 1321)
—Penguin's World. Arnold, Caroline, illus. (p. 1337)
—Polar Bear's World Arnold, Caroline, illus. (p. 1379)
—Sistema Óseo. Translations.com Staff, tr. (p. 1581)
—Skeletal System. (p. 1584)
—Terrible Hodag & the Animal Catchers. Sandford, John, illus. (p. 1721)
—Too Hot? Too Cold? Keeping Body Temperature Just Right. Patterson, Annie, illus. (p. 1766)
—Walrus' World Arnold, Caroline, illus. (p. 1855)
—Warmer World. Hogan, Jamie, illus. (p. 1858)
—Wiggle & Waggle. Peterson, Mary, illus. (p. 1927)
—Wombat's World Arnold, Caroline, illus. (p. 1945)
—Your Skeletal System. (p. 1981)
—Zebra's World. Arnold, Caroline, illus. (p. 1985)
Arnold, Caroline & Comora, Madeleine. Taj Mahal. Bhushan, Rahul, illus. (p. 1696)
Arnold, Chirley. Double Trouble: A Novel. (p. 473)
Arnold, Clareen. Handwriting - Modern Manuscript. (p. 741)
Arnold, Connie. Count 1, 2, 3 with Me. Nielson, Ginger, illus. (p. 369)
Arnold, Connie & Grady, Kit. Animal Sound -up. (p. 79)
Arnold, Damon. I Am / Mirror Mirror. (p. 831)
Arnold, Darrell. Cowboy Kind. (p. 374)
Arnold, David. Mosquitoland. (p. 1177)
Arnold, Edward Ronny. Rashida. (p. 1439)
Arnold, Elana K. Far from Fair. (p. 572)
—Infandous. (p. 873)
—Question of Miracles. (p. 1426)
—Sacred. (p. 1500)
—Splendor. (p. 1630)
Arnold, Elizabeth. Parsley Parcel. (p. 1325)
Arnold, Ellen L., ed. Salt Companion to Carter Revard. (p. 1505)
Arnold, George. Gatos of the CIA. (p. 658)
Arnold, George "Speedy". What's an Elephant Doing in the Ausable River?!! Arnold, George "Speedy", illus. (p. 1896)
Arnold, Ginger Fudge. Billy's Mountain Adventure Almeyda, Tonito Avalon, illus. (p. 187)
—Two Tipsy Tots Crème, Aurora C., illus. (p. 1804)
Arnold, Ginny. Nomadic Healer (p. 1263)
Arnold, J. Ox Cart Angel. (p. 1315)
Arnold, James R. Aftermath of the French Revolution. (p. 28)
—Saddam Hussein's Iraq. (p. 1501)
Arnold, James R. & Weiner, Roberta. Industrial Revolution (p. 872)
Arnold, James R. & Wiener, Roberta. Robert Mugabe's Zimbabwe. (p. 1479)
Arnold, Janet. Special Number. (p. 1623)
Arnold, Jeanne, illus. see Stevens, Jan Romero.
Arnold, Jerry. Shepherd Boy. (p. 1565)
Arnold, Jude. Lipizzan Reunion: A True Story. (p. 1021)
Arnold, Karen. Leaper Joins the Choir. (p. 982)
Arnold, Katya, illus. see Kimmel, Eric A.
Arnold, Katya, jt. auth. see Arnold, Katya R.
Arnold, Katya R. & Arnold, Katya. Elephants Can Paint Too! Arnold, Katya R. & Arnold, Katya, photos by. (p. 512)
Arnold, Keith A., jt. auth. see Kennedy, Gregory.
Arnold, Laurie B. Hello There, We've Been Waiting for You! (p. 765)
Arnold, Lisa Marie. Creative Short Stories for Smart Kids. (p. 380)
Arnold, Lobel. Frog & Toad Are Friends. (p. 640)
—Frog & Toad Together. (p. 640)
Arnold, Louise. Golden & Grey: The Nightmares That Ghosts Have. (p. 694)
—Golden & Grey: An Unremarkable Boy & a Rather Remarkable Ghost. (p. 694)
—Golden & Grey - A Good Day for Haunting. (p. 694)
Arnold, Michael, illus. see Ross, Brad.
Arnold, Michelle Lee. Mathew Sunburst & the Keepers of the Sky. (p. 1108)
Arnold, N. Xavier. Best Real Estate Investing Method... Ever! (p. 171)
Arnold, Nick. Esa Fascinante Arqueologia. (p. 534)
—How Cars Work: The Interactive Guide to Mechanisms That Make a Car Move. (p. 805)
—Huesos, Sangre y Otros Pedazos del Cuerpo. De Saulles, Tony, illus. (p. 824)
ARNOLD, NICK, jt. auth. see Arnold, Nick.
Arnold, Nick, jt. auth. see Candlewick Press Staff.
Arnold, Nick & ARNOLD, NICK. Esa Repelente Naturaleza. (p. 534)
Arnold, Nick & De Saulles, Tony. Esa Caotica Quimica. De Saulles, Tony, tr. (p. 534)
—Esa Deslumbrante Luz. De Saulles, Tony, tr. (p. 534)
—Esa Electrizante Electricidad. De Saulles, Tony, tr. (p. 534)
—Esas Perversas Plantas. De Saulles, Tony, tr. (p. 534)
—Ese Voluminoso Cerebro. De Saulles, Tony, tr. (p. 535)
—Esos Microscopicos Monstruos. De Saulles, Tony, tr. (p. 536)
Arnold, Nick & Saules, Tony de. Esa Repugnante Digestion. Saules, Tony de, tr. (p. 534)
—Esos Insoportables Sonidos. Saules, Tony de, tr. (p. 536)
Arnold, Nick, et al. Esas Funestas Fuerzas. De Saulles, Tony, tr. (p. 534)
—Sticker Activity Atlas. (p. 1650)
Arnold, Patricia, illus. see Kaderli, Janet.
Arnold, Robyn. Branli Says Bye-Bye to Binky. (p. 222)
Arnold, Sarah. I Told You So! (p. 846)
—Ugh, Eggs! Arnold, Sarah, illus. (p. 1808)
Arnold, Saundra. My Friend Isaac. (p. 1209)
Arnold, Shari. Mystique. (p. 1226)
Arnold, Shauna. Baa. Hines, Irene, illus. (p. 123)
Arnold, Stephen, illus. see Uncle Bob.
Arnold, Tedd. Buzz Boy & Fly Guy. (p. 248)
—Buzz Boy & Fly Guy. Arnold, Tedd, illus. (p. 248)
—Dirty Gert. Arnold, Tedd, illus. (p. 446)
—Even More Parts: Idioms from Head to Toe. Arnold, Tedd, illus. (p. 541)
—Even More Parts. Arnold, Tedd, illus. (p. 541)
—Fix This Mess! Arnold, Tedd, illus. (p. 601)
—Fly Guy & the Frankenfly. (p. 609)
—Fly Guy Meets Fly Girl. (p. 609)
—Fly Guy Meets Fly Girl! Arnold, Tedd, illus. (p. 609)
—Fly Guy Presents: Bats. (p. 609)
—Fly Guy Presents: Space. (p. 609)
—Fly Guy Presents: Sharks. (p. 609)
—Fly Guy Presents: Dinosaurs. (p. 609)
—Fly Guy Presents: Dinosaurs. Arnold, Tedd, illus. (p. 609)
—Fly Guy Presents: Firefighters. Arnold, Tedd, illus. (p. 609)
—Fly Guy vs. the Fly Swatter. (p. 609)
—Fly Guy vs. the Flyswatter! Arnold, Tedd, illus. (p. 609)
—Fly Guy's Amazing Tricks. (p. 609)
—Fly High, Fly Guy! Arnold, Tedd, illus. (p. 609)
—Green Wilma, Frog in Space. Arnold, Tedd, illus. (p. 722)
—Hi! Fly Guy. (p. 775)
—Hi! Fly Guy. Arnold, Tedd, illus. (p. 775)
—Hooray for Fly Guy! (p. 796)
—I Spy Fly Guy! Arnold, Tedd, illus. (p. 846)
—Insects. (p. 875)
—Insects. Arnold, Tedd, illus. (p. 875)
—More Parts. (p. 1174)
—No Jumping on the Bed. (p. 1258)
—Pet for Fly Guy. Arnold, Tedd, illus. (p. 1345)
—Rat Life. (p. 1440)
—Reading Placement Tests: Easy Assessments to Determine Students' Levels of Literacy Development. (p. 1446)
—Reading Placement Tests: Easy Assessments to Determine Students' Levels in Phonics, Vocabulary, & Reading Comprehension. (p. 1446)
—Ride, Fly Guy, Ride! (p. 1471)
—Sharks. Arnold, Tedd, illus. (p. 1562)
—Shoo, Fly Guy! Arnold, Tedd, illus. (p. 1568)
—Space. Arnold, Tedd, illus. (p. 1618)
—Super Fly Guy. Arnold, Tedd, illus. (p. 1680)
—There Was an Old Lady Who Swallowed Fly Guy. Arnold, Tedd, illus. (p. 1730)
—There's a Fly Guy in My Soup. (p. 1730)
—Twin Princes. Arnold, Tedd, illus. (p. 1802)
—Vincent Paints His House. (p. 1842)
Arnold, Tedd, illus. see Agee, Jon.
Arnold, Tedd, illus. see Bagert, Brod.
Arnold, Tedd, et al. Manners Mash-Up: A Goofy Guide to Good Behavior. (p. 1088)
Arnold, Tom. Billy Stargazer's Heavenly Quest. (p. 187)
Arnold, Vickie. Baby Zebra Adventure. (p. 128)
Arnoldi, Katie. Chemical Pink. (p. 297)
Arnone, Marilyn P. & Coatney, Sharon. Mac, Information Detective, in the Case Of— Curious Kids & the Squiggly Question (p. 1067)
—Mac, Information Detective, in ... the Curious Kids & Why Dolphins Visit Curiosity Creek: A Storybook Approach to Introducing Research Skills Picture Book & Educator's Guide Set (p. 1067)
—Mac, Information Detective, in the Curious Kids... - Digging for Answers: A Storybook Approach to Introducing Research Skills Stockley, Gerry, illus. (p. 1067)
Arnone, T. I. Magic Kazoo. (p. 1072)
Arnosky, Deanna, photos by see Arnosky, James.
Arnosky, James. Whole Days Outdoors: An Autobiographical Album. Arnosky, Deanna, photos by. (p. 1920)
Arnosky, Jim. All about Lizards: Y Jim Arnosky. (p. 42)
—All about Manatees. Arnosky, Jim, illus. (p. 42)
—All about Turtles. Arnosky, Jim, illus. (p. 43)
—Babies in the Bayou. Arnosky, Jim, illus. (p. 124)
—Beachcombing: Exploring the Seashore. (p. 149)
—Creep & Flutter: The Secret World of Insects & Spiders. (p. 380)
—Crinkleroot's Guide to Giving Back to Nature. Arnosky, Jim, illus. (p. 383)
—Crinkleroot's Guide to Knowing Animal Habitats. Arnosky, Jim, illus. (p. 383)
—Crocodile Safari. (p. 384)
—Following the Coast. Arnosky, Jim, illus. (p. 612)
—I'm a Turkey! (p. 858)
—Jim Arnosky's Wild World. (p. 917)
—Monster Hunt: Exploring Mysterious Creatures with Jim Arnosky. (p. 1167)
—Pirates of Crocodile Swamp. (p. 1363)
—Rabbits & Raindrops. (p. 1430)
—Raccoon on His Own. Arnosky, Jim, illus. (p. 1430)
—Shimmer & Splash: The Sparkling World of Sea Life. (p. 1566)
—Slither & Crawl: Eye to Eye with Reptiles. (p. 1590)
—Thunder Birds: Nature's Flying Predators. (p. 1746)
—Tooth & Claw: The Wild World of Big Predators. (p. 1768)
—Wild Tracks! A Guide to Nature's Footprints. (p. 1930)
Arnosky, Jim, illus. see Dylan, Bob.
Arnott, Leslie. Underground Worlds. (p. 1815)
Arnov Jr., Boris. Oceans of the World. (p. 1277)
Arnov Jr., Boris & Mindlin, Helen Mather-Smith. Inside Our Earth. Mather-Smith, Charles, illus. (p. 877)
Arnove, Anthony. Iraq: The Logic of Withdrawal. (p. 887)
Arnstein, Bennett Roy. Saturday Afternoon Public Library Origami Club Manual: Not Just Another Origami Book. (p. 1515)
Arntson, Steven. Wrap-Up List. (p. 1962)
Aro, Hiroshi. You & Me (p. 1973)
Aroca, José María, tr. see McCaffrey, Anne.
Aron, Bill, photos by see Hoffman, Lawrence A. & Wolfson, Ron.
Arone, Cathleen. Seababies Come Ashore. (p. 1536)
Aroner, Miriam. Clink Clank Clunk! Catalano, Dominic, illus. (p. 333)
Aronin, Miriam. Ant's Nest: A Huge, Underground City. (p. 90)
—Aye-Aye: An Evil Omen. (p. 121)
—Black-Footed Ferrets: Back from the Brink. (p. 196)
—Earthquake in Haiti. (p. 497)
—How Many People Traveled the Oregon Trail? And Other Questions about the Trail West. (p. 811)
—Mangled by a Hurricane! (p. 1087)
—Merciless Monarchs & Ruthless Royalty. (p. 1127)
—Oklahoma's Devastating May 2013 Tornado. (p. 1283)
—Prairie Dog's Town: A Perfect Hideaway. (p. 1392)
—Saving Animals from Volcanoes. (p. 1517)
—Slammed by a Tsunami! (p. 1587)
—Tuberculosis: The White Plague! (p. 1795)
Aronin, Miriam & Pushies, Fred J. Today's Air Force Heroes. (p. 1761)
Aronnax, Pierre. Oceanology Handbook: A Course for Underwater Explorers. Hawkins, Emily & Twist, Clint, eds. (p. 1277)
Aronofsky, Darren. Fountain. (p. 624)
Aronovsky, Ilona & Gopinath, Sujata. Indus Valley (p. 872)
Arons, Barbara Jean. Pharaoh's Dog. (p. 1349)
Arons, Marsha. Teen Miracles: Extraordinary Life-Changing Stories by America's Teenagers. (p. 1713)
Aronskind, Ofer. Escape from Sunday School. (p. 535)
—That Same Summer. (p. 1726)
Aronson, Billy. Abraham Lincoln. (p. 6)
—Richard M. Nixon. (p. 1469)
—Ulysses S. Grant. (p. 1810)
Aronson, Billy, jt. auth. see Oxley, Jennifer.
Aronson, Billy & Oxley, Jennifer. Chicken Problem. (p. 300)
Aronson, Deb. E. B. White. (p. 491)
Aronson, Deborah. Where's My Tushy? Stevanovic, Ivica, illus. (p. 1910)

Aronson, Emme & Aronson, Phillip. What Are You Hungry For? Feed Your Tummy & Your Heart. Brooks, Erik, illus. (p. 1880)
Aronson, Howard I. Reading Georgian Grammar (p. 1446)
Aronson, Jeff & Aronson, Miriam. Little Mike & Maddie's Black Hill's Adventure. Aronson, Jeff & Zephyr, Jay, illus. (p. 1031)
—Little Mike & Maddie's Christmas Book. Aronson, Jeff & Zephyr, Jay, illus. (p. 1031)
—Little Mike & Maddie's First Motorcycle Ride. Aronson, Jeff & Zephyr, Jay, illus. (p. 1031)
Aronson, Marc. Beyond the Pale: New Essays for a New Era. (p. 174)
—Master of Deceit: J. Edgar Hoover & America in the Age of Lies. (p. 1103)
—Race: A History Beyond Black & White. (p. 1430)
—Real Revolution: The Global Story of American Independence. (p. 1448)
—Trapped: How the World Rescued 33 Miners from 2,000 Feet below the Chilean Desert. (p. 1779)
—Witch-Hunt: Mysteries of the Salem Witch Trials. (p. 1941)
—Witch-Hunt: Mysteries of the Salem Witch Trials. Anderson, Stephanie, illus. (p. 1941)
Aronson, Marc, ed. see Davies, Gill.
Aronson, Marc, jt. auth. see Nelson, Scott Reynolds.
Aronson, Marc, jt. auth. see Parker-Pearson, Mike.
Aronson, Marc, jt. ed. see Campbell, Patty.
Aronson, Marc & Budhos, Marina Tamar. Sugar Changed the World: A Story of Magic, Spice, Slavery, Freedom, & Science. (p. 1672)
Aronson, Marc & Mayor, Adrienne. Griffin & the Dinosaur: How Adrienne Mayor Discovered a Fascinating Link Between Myth & Science. Müller, Chris, illus. (p. 724)
Aronson, Marc & Newquist, H. P. For Boys Only: The Biggest, Baddest Book Ever. Headcase Design, illus. (p. 615)
Aronson, Marc & Smith, Charles R., eds. One Death Nine Stories. (p. 1294)
Aronson, Marc & Smith, Charles R., Jr., eds. Pick-Up Game: A Full Day of Full Court. Smith, Charles R., Jr., illus. (p. 1354)
Aronson, Marc, et al. World Made New: Why the Age of Exploration Happened & How It Changed the World. (p. 1956)
Aronson, Miriam, jt. auth. see Aronson, Jeff.
Aronson, Phillip, jt. auth. see Aronson, Emme.
Aronson, Rosy. Tale of Serendipity: the Adventure Begins! (p. 1700)
Aronson, Sarah. Believe. (p. 161)
—Beyond Lucky. (p. 174)
Aronson, Virginia. Everything You Need to Know about Breast Health & Examinations. (p. 545)
—Everything You Need to Know about Hepatitis. (p. 545)
Aronson, Virginia & Szejko, Allyn. Iguana Invasion! Exotic Pets Gone Wild in Florida. (p. 856)
Arora, Sabina G. Great Migration & the Harlem Renaissance. (p. 717)
Arora, Sabina G., ed. Great Migration & the Harlem Renaissance. (p. 717)
Aros, Angela. Aunt Emma's Secret Recipe (p. 115)
Arpaci, Halis. Eric & Derrick. (p. 533)
Arps, Melissa. Colors. (p. 344)
—Numbers. (p. 1271)
—Opposites. (p. 1300)
—Shapes. (p. 1560)
Arps, Melissa & Lagonegro, Melissa. Friends Forever. RH Disney Staff, illus. (p. 638)
—Polite as a Princess. Harding, Niall & Harchy, Atelier Philippe, illus. (p. 1380)
Arquette, Kerry. Daddy Promises. McCain, Kevin, illus. (p. 398)
Arquillos, Meiko, photos by see Jansdotter, Lotta.
Arrasmith, Patrick, illus. see Carman, Patrick.
Arrasmith, Patrick, illus. see Delaney, Joseph.
Arrasmith, Patrick, illus. see Dunkle, Clare B.
Arrathoon, Leigh A. Men Who Changed the World: The Henry Ford Story. Vol. I Davio, John, ed. (p. 1126)
—Men Who Changed the World: The First Birdmen: Wilbur & Orville Wright. Vol. II Davio, John, ed. (p. 1126)
—Summer of the Bear: An Historical Novel about the Anishinabeg & the Fur Traders in Michigan. (p. 1674)
Arrathoon, Leigh A. & Davio, John. Jody's Travelbooks for Kids: Holland, Michigan. Vol. II Morris, Jeanne L., illus. (p. 920)
—Jody's Travelbooks for Kids: Mackinaw, Michigan. Vol. III Morris, Jeanne L., illus. (p. 920)
—Jody's Travelbooks for Kids: Frankenmuth, Michigan. Vol. I Morris, Jeanne L., illus. (p. 920)
Arrathroon, Leigh A. Magical Adventures in Michigan. (p. 1074)
Arre, N. S. Null: An Intergalactic Affair. (p. 1270)
Arreola Alemón, Roberto, illus. see Galindo-Leal, Carlos.
Arreola, Daniel D. World Geography 2005. (p. 1955)
Arreola, Gil, illus. see Gotsch, Patrice.
Arreola, Manuel, illus. see Arreola, Perla.
Arreola, Perla. Weenz the Cat: What about Me? Arreola, Manuel, illus. (p. 1872)
Arrhenius, Ingela P., illus. see Rundgren, Helen.
Arrieta, Luisa Noguera. Globito Azul. Landinez, Jairo Linares, illus. (p. 685)
Arrieta, Maria Luz. Ultimo Cacique de la Sabana. (p. 1810)
Arrigan, Mary. Grimstone's Ghost. (p. 724)
—Milo & One Dead Angry Druid. Arrigan, Mary, illus. (p. 1144)
—Milo & the Pirate Sisters. (p. 1144)
—Milo & the Raging Chieftains. (p. 1144)
—Pa Jinglebob & the Grabble Gang. (p. 1316)
—Pa Jinglebob - The Fastest Knitter in the West. Paul, Korky, illus. (p. 1316)
—Rabbit Girl. (p. 1429)
Arrigan, Mary & Paul, Korky. PA Jinglebob: The Fastest Knitter in the West. (p. 1316)
Arrigan, Mary & Quarto Generic Staff. Esty's Gold. (p. 539)
Arrington, Aileen. Paper Heart. (p. 1322)
Arrington, Chiquila, illus. see Arrington, Gladys.
Arrington, French L. Exploring the Declaration of Faith. (p. 553)
Arrington, Gladys. Dallas: On Book One: Jo/Jo KIDS. Arrington, Chiquila, illus. (p. 401)
Arrington, Jay, jt. auth. see Harper, Michael J.
Arrington, Linda. Purple Time. (p. 1419)
—Ugly Trees. Arrington, Linda, photos by. (p. 1808)
Arrington, R. Region. Billy Buckins & the Pirates Map (p. 187)
—Tommy Hop the Bunny (p. 1765)
—Voyage of Billy Buckins Harrington, Linda, illus. (p. 1850)
Arriola, Ricardo Ramirez. Vivir en el Circo. Arriola, Ricardo Ramirez, illus. (p. 1846)
Arroba, Doris, ed. see Iturralde, Edna.
Arrott, Nancy, illus. see Avalon-Pai, Phyllis.
Arrowsmith, Colin. Children's World Atlas. (p. 304)
Arrowsmith, Vicker, jt. auth. see Baggott, Stella.
Arrowsmith, Vicky. Sticker Dolly Dressing Costumes & Parties. (p. 1650)
Arroyave, Heidy, tr. see MansBach, Sara.
Arroyo, Andrea. Legend of the Lady Slipper. (p. 989)
Arroyo, David, jt. auth. see Rio, Adam del.
Arroyo, Felipe, photos by see Reddy, Prerana & Strauss, David, eds.
Arroyo, Fian, illus. see Cosgrove, Stephen.
Arroyo, George, jt. auth. see Lynn, Diana.
Arroyo, George, jt. creator see Lynn, Diana.
Arroyo, Kritzia. Angel Princess Star. (p. 74)
Arroyo, Madeline. Calie's Gift. Vavak, S. Dean, illus. (p. 253)
—What Matthias Found. Vavak, S. Dean, illus. (p. 1892)
Arroyo Seppa, Carmen, tr. see Overland, Sarah.
Arroyo, Sheri, et al. How Chefs Use Math. (p. 805)
—How Crime Fighters Use Math. (p. 806)
—How Deep Sea Divers Use Math. (p. 806)
—How Race Car Drivers Use Math. (p. 812)
Arroyo, Yvonne. How the Octopus Got Eight Arms: Two Arms Are Never Enough. (p. 813)
Arruda, Diane. Ancient One, Book II in the Dream River Adventure. (p. 70)
—Undiscovered River: Golden Fish & a True Dream. (p. 1817)
Arruda, Gilda, jt. auth. see Fradkin, Irving.
Arruda, Suzanne M. Stocking for Jesus. Ogden, Betina, illus. (p. 1651)
Arruda, Suzanne Middendorf. Freedom's Martyr: The Story of Jose Rizal, National Hero of the Phillipines. (p. 635)
—Girl He Left Behind: The Life & Times of Libbie Custer. (p. 678)
Arruzza, Rick. No Descanso Para Sparky. Newton, Pilar, illus. (p. 1258)
—No Rest for Sparky. Newton, Pilar, illus. (p. 1260)
—Paseo de Sparky. Newton, Pilar, illus. (p. 1326)
—Sparky's Walk. Newton, Pilar, illus. (p. 1622)
Arscott, Dean, illus. see Baruch, M. P.
ArsEdition. Blossom Magic: Beautiful Floral Patterns to Color. (p. 202)
—Winter Magic: Beautiful Holiday Patterns to Color. (p. 1938)
Arsenal Football Club PLC, jt. auth. see Arsenal Football Club PLC.
Arsenal Football Club PLC & Arsenal Football Club PLC. Official Arsenal Sticker Activity Book. (p. 1280)
, Arsenal Football Club PLC, Arsenal Football Club Plc. Official Arsenal Ultimate Young Gunners' Book: The Ultimate Guide for the Ultimate Fan! (p. 1280)
Arsenal Football Club Staff. Official Arsenal Sticker Colouring Book. (p. 1280)
Arsenault, Elaine. F Is for French: Un Livre d'Alphabet Sur le Quebec - A Quebec Alphabet. Benoit, Renne, illus. (p. 559)
Arsenault, Isabelle, illus. see Akbarpour, Ahmad.
Arsenault, Isabelle, illus. see Britt, Fanny & Ouriou, Susan.
Arsenault, Isabelle, illus. see Dickinson, Emily.
Arsenault, Isabelle, illus. see Maclear, Kyo.
Arsenault, Isabelle, illus. see Trottier, Maxine.
Arsenault, Isabelle, jt. auth. see Maclear, Kyo.
Arsenault, Jane & Cedor, Jean. Guided Meditations for Youth on Sacramental Life. Stamschror, Robert P., ed. (p. 730)
Arsenault, Moira. Bubbles. (p. 233)
Arseneau, Philippe, illus. see Lefrancois, Viateur.
Art Baltazar Comic Book Staff, jt. auth. see Aureliani, Franco.
Art Baltazar Comic Book Staff, jt. auth. see Baltazar, Franco.
Art Baltazar Comic Book Staff & Franco. Tiny Titans - Aw Yeah Titans! (p. 1757)
Art, Henry W. & Robbins, Michael W. WoodsWalk: Peepers, Pikas, & Exploding Puffballs. (p. 1950)
Art Parts, illus. see Lederer, Richard & Gibbs Smith Publisher Staff.
Art, Suzanne Strauss. Story of Islam: From Muhammad to Suleiman the Magnificent. (p. 1658)
Art&Script, illus. see Earley, Catherine.
Arte y Cultura, A.C Staff, illus. see Lascurain, Guadalupe Aleman.
Arte Y Diseno, Tane, illus. see Peredo, Roberto.
Arteaga, Marta. Inside My Imagination. (p. 877)
Artell, Mike. Awesome Alphabets. (p. 120)
—Backyard Bloodsuckers: Questions, Facts & Tongue Twisters about Creepy Crawlers. (p. 131)
—Backyard Bloodsuckers: Questions, Facts & Tongue Twisters about Creepy, Crawly Creatures. (p. 131)
—Drew Brees: Football Superstar (p. 485)
—Funny Cartooning for Kids. (p. 649)
—Hidden Pictures. (p. 776)
—Jacques & de Beanstalk. Harris, Jim, illus. (p. 905)
—Pee-Yew! The Stinkiest, Smelliest Animals, Insects, & Plants on Earth! (p. 1334)
—Petite Rouge. (p. 1348)
—Petite Rouge. Harris, Jim, illus. (p. 1348)
—Peyton Manning: Football Superstar (p. 1349)
—Starry Skies: Questions, Facts, & Riddles about the Universe. (p. 1642)
—Ten-Second Tongue Twisters. Jones, Buck, illus. (p. 1719)
—Three Little Cajun Pigs. Harris, Jim, illus. (p. 1742)
—Weather Whys. (p. 1870)
Artell, Mike, illus. see Moen, Christine Boardman.
Artell, Mike, jt. auth. see Mattern, Joanne.
Artell, Mike, jt. auth. see Rosenbloom, Joseph.
Artell, Mike, et al. Superstar Athletes (p. 1684)
Arterburn, Stephen. Addicted to Love: Understanding Dependencies of the Heart: Romance, Relationships, & Sex. (p. 11)
—Young Believer Gospel of John Sampler. (p. 1978)
Arterburn, Stephen & Florea, Jesse. One Year Every Day Devotions: Devotions to Help You Stand Strong. (p. 1298)
Arterburn, Stephen, et al. Every Young Man's Battle: Strategies for Victory in the Real World of Sexual Temptation. (p. 543)
Artful Doodlers, illus. see Barbo, Maria S. & Bridwell, Norman.
Artful Doodlers, illus. see RH Disney Staff.
Artful Doodlers, illus. see Wax, Wendy.
Artful Doodlers, illus. see Williams, Geoffrey T.
Artful Doodlers Limited Staff. Dora Salva a las Sirenas. (p. 470)
—It's Absolutely True. (p. 896)
Artful Doodlers Limited Staff, illus. see Ackelsberg, Amy.
Artful Doodlers Limited Staff, illus. see Corderoy, Tracey.
Artful Doodlers Limited Staff, illus. see Huelin, Jodi.
Artful Doodlers Limited Staff, illus. see RH Disney Staff.
Artful Doodlers Limited Staff, jt. auth. see Golden Books Staff.
Artful Doodlers Ltd., illus. see Grosset & Dunlap.
Artful Doodlers Ltd., illus. see Grosset and Dunlap Staff.
Artful Doodlers Ltd Staff. Dora Saves Mermaid Kingdom! (p. 470)
Artful Doodlers Ltd Staff, illus. see Huelin, Jodi.
Artful Doodlers Ltd Staff, illus. see Meadows, Daisy.
Arthaud, Sophie, ed. Renyi Picture Dictionary: French/English. (p. 1460)
Arthur, Alex & Dorling Kindersley Publishing Staff. Shell. (p. 1564)
Arthur, Anne. Pigeon with the Sticky Stuck Neck. Liebman, Simean, illus. (p. 1358)
Arthur, Clint. Bleep Blop Bloop Schedeen, Minnie, illus. (p. 199)
Arthur, Felix. Little Book of Alliterations. Capon, Jenny, illus. (p. 1025)
Arthur, Jenny. Little Witch. Arthur, Jenny, illus. (p. 1038)
Arthur, Jenny, illus. see Murphy, Rose.
Arthur, Kay. 2 Peter Pup. (p. 1991)
—Genesis: Pup Leaders Guide (p. 660)
—Genesis Pt. 5: Keeping Your Focus When Your Dreams Are Shattered: A Study on Joseph. (p. 660)
—Jude Pup. (p. 930)
—Lord, I Want to Know You. (p. 1052)
—Lord Teach Me to Pray in 28 Days. (p. 1052)
—Titus Pup. (p. 1758)
Arthur, Kay & Arndt, Janna. Abraham - God's Brave Explorer: Genesis 11-25. (p. 6)
—Becoming God's Champion: 2 Timothy. (p. 156)
—Bible Prophecy for Kids: Revelation 1-7. (p. 176)
—Boy, Have I Got Problems. (p. 218)
—Fast-Forward to the Future: Daniel 7-12. (p. 576)
—God What's Your Name. (p. 690)
—God, What's Your Name? (p. 690)
—How to Study Your Bible for Kids. (p. 821)
—Jesus, to Eternity & Beyond. (p. 916)
—Lord Teach Me to Pray for Kids. (p. 1052)
—You're a Brave Man, Daniel! (p. 1982)
Arthur, Kay & Domeij, Scoti. Wrong Way Jonah. (p. 1965)
—Wrong Way, Jonah! Leite, Eleni, tr. (p. 1965)
Arthur, Kay & Shearer, Cyndy. Jesus in the Spotlight. (p. 915)
Arthur, Kay, et al. How to Study Your Bible for Teens. (p. 821)
—Jesus, Awesome Power, Awesome Love. (p. 915)
—Wrong Way, Jonah! Jonah. (p. 1965)
Arthur, Malcolm, tr. see Perrault, Charles.
Arthur, Martin, jt. auth. see Miller, Reagan.
Arthur, Peggy Ann. Come & Look in Grandma's Garden. (p. 347)
Arthur, Randall. Jordan's Crossing. (p. 925)
Arthur, Sarah. Thinking Theologically about Pop Culture. (p. 1734)
—Walking with Frodo: A Devotional Journey Through the Lord of the Rings. (p. 1854)
Arthur, Sherry. Magical Hallows Eve. (p. 1074)
Arthur, Timothy S. Lady at Home. (p. 970)
Arthur, Tish. Pretty Little Face (p. 1398)
Arthus, Yann B. Tierra explicada a los ninos. (p. 1748)
Arthus-Bertrand, Yann, photos by see Giraudon, David, illus.
Arthus-Bertrand, Yann, photos by see Jankeliowitch, Anne.
Artibani, Francesco, et al. Donald Duck Adventures Clark, John, ed. (p. 466)
Artifact Group Staff, illus. see Golden Books Staff.
Artifact Group Staff, jt. auth. see David, Erica.
Artifact Group Staff, jt. auth. see Pass, Erica.
Artifact Group Staff & Artifact Group, The. Atlantis SquarePantis. (p. 112)
Artifact Group, The. Trash Planet. (p. 1780)
Artifact Group, The, jt. auth. see Artifact Group Staff.
Artifact Group, The, jt. auth. see Lukas, Catherine.
Artifact Group, The & Shepherd, Jodie. Robot Rampage! (p. 1480)
Artigas, Alexandra, illus. see Furfur, Christopher.
Artigas, Alexandra, illus. see Isaacs, Michael.
Artigas de Sierra, Ione M. Bodas del Gallo Perico. (p. 206)
—Chivita del Cebollar. (p. 308)
—Goat in the Onion Patch. (p. 687)
—On the Way to the Wedding. (p. 1292)
Artigot, Manuel, jt. auth. see Almena, Fernando.
Artis, Farrell. Guys, Let's Keep It Real! A Message of Hope for Boys Growing up in Poverty, Racism, & Despair. (p. 733)
Artistic Book and Web Design, illus. see Hood, Karen Jean Matsko.
Artistic Design Service, illus. see Hood, Karen Jean Matsko.
Artistic Design Service Staff, illus. see Hood, James G.
Artistic Design Service Staff, illus. see Hood, Karen Jean Matsko.
Artistic Design Service Staff, illus. see Whispering Pine Press International, ed.
Artistic Design Services, illus. see Hood, Karen Jean Matsko.
Artistic Design Services Staff, illus. see Hood, Kared Jean Matsko.
Artistic Design Services Staff, illus. see Hood, Karen Jean Matsko.
Artistic Studios, Ltd. Staff, creator. Disney Princess Large PlayPad. (p. 452)
Artists of the Kuru Art Project in Botswana, San, illus. see Nelson, Marilyn.
Artists of Troublemaker Studios Staff, illus. see Rodriguez, Robert.
Artists, S. I., illus. see Froeb, Lori C. & Weiss, Ellen.
Artists, Various, illus. see Wadhwa, Vick.
Artley, Bob. Christmas on the Farm Artley, Bob, illus. (p. 315)
Artley, Bob, illus. see Hahn, Cathe.
Artley, Bob, illus. see Townsend, Una Belle.
Artlist Collection Staff. Dog from Arf! Arf! to Zzzzzz. Artlist Collection Staff, illus. (p. 461)
Artman, Townsend, illus. see Wales, Dirk.
Arts, Richa Kinra, illus. see Kats, Jewel.
Arts, Theresa. Dusty Bunny & His Magic Mirror. (p. 490)
Arturo, Corcuera, jt. auth. see Arturo, Corcuera.
Arturo, Corcuera & Arturo, Corcuera. FLAUTA DE KIKIRIKI. (p. 603)
Arturo Miranda Bravo, Jorge. Andres Guardado. (p. 72)
Artus, William. King on the Moon. (p. 959)
Artworks. Blank Journal. (p. 198)
—Faith, Hope & Love. (p. 565)
—Journal. (p. 927)
Artz, D. M. Maggie & the Magic Sparkle Seed. (p. 1071)
Artz, Tracy. Sneaky Leprechaun. (p. 1597)
Artzi, Yocheved. Freedom Chickens: The Story of Lonely Chicken. (p. 634)
Aruego, Jose, illus. see Beaumont, Karen.
Aruego, Jose, illus. see Bruchac, Joseph & Bruchac, James.
Aruego, Jose, illus. see Howard, Reginald.
Aruego, Jose, illus. see Kraus, Robert.
Aruego, Jose, illus. see Shannon, George.
Aruego, Jose, illus. see Sharmat, Mitchell.
Aruego, Jose, illus. see Sierra, Judy.
Aruego, Jose, jt. auth. see Dewey, Ariane.
Aruego, Jose & Dewey, Ariane. Splash! (p. 1629)
Aruffo, Christopher, tr. see Taneda, Naoyuki & Taneda, Ruth.
Aruffo, Christopher, tr. We Hear & Play. (p. 1867)
Arundale, Jackie, jt. auth. see Hart, Greg.
Arvidson, Douglas. Brothers of the Fire Star. Scarborough, Rob, illus. (p. 231)
Arvidson, Douglas N. Eye of the Stallion: The Face in Amber. Bk. 1 (p. 557)
Arvin, Reed. Blood of Angels. (p. 200)
Arvoy, Marsha & Nardi, Dorianne. Area. (p. 97)
—Percentage. (p. 1341)
—Rounding. (p. 1491)
—Using a Calculator. (p. 1828)
Arya, Viki, illus. see Dutta, Arup Kumar.
Aryal, Sia, photos by. 1 2 3s. (p. 1990)
Aryal, Aimee. Cort Spells It Out. De Angel, Miguel, illus. (p. 368)
—Go, Pack, Go! De Angel, Miguel, illus. (p. 687)
—Hello Albert! F. Pflueger, Maura McArdle, illus. (p. 763)
—Hello Aubie! Moore, Danny, illus. (p. 763)
—Hello Baldwin! Goh, Tai Hwa, illus. (p. 763)
—Hello Big Al! Moore, Danny, illus. (p. 763)
—Hello Big Jay! Shrestha, Anuj, illus. (p. 763)
—Hello Big Red! Craig, Megan, illus. (p. 763)
—Hello Blue Devil! Cooper, Blair, illus. (p. 763)
—Hello, Brutus! De Angel, Miguel & Moore, D., illus. (p. 763)
—Hello Bully! Moore, Danny, illus. (p. 763)
—Hello Buzz! Moore, Danny, illus. (p. 763)
—Hello CavMan! Perez, Gerry, illus. (p. 763)
—Hello Cocky! Graybill, Joni, illus. (p. 763)
—Hello, Demon Deacon! Cooper, Blair, illus. (p. 763)
—Hello, Doc! (p. 763)
—Hello Goldy! Sable, Katherine, illus. (p. 764)
—Hello Hairy Dawg. Turnbull, Jesse, illus. (p. 764)
—Hello Herbie Husker! Shrestha, Anuj, illus. (p. 764)
—Hello, Hook 'Em! Craig, Megan, illus. (p. 764)
—Hello Joe Bruin! Perez, Gerry, illus. (p. 764)
—Hello Mr. Wuf! Cooper, Blair, illus. (p. 764)
—Hello Otto! Shrestha, Anuj, illus. (p. 764)
—Hello, Paws! (p. 764)
—Hello, Pistol Pete! Craig, Megan, illus. (p. 764)
—Hello, Ralphie! Perez, Gerry, illus. (p. 765)
—Hello Rameses! Cooper, Blair, illus. (p. 765)
—Hello Smokey! Higgins, Krystal, illus. (p. 765)
—Hello, Testudo! Goh, Tai Hwa, illus. (p. 765)
—Hello Tiger! Graybill, Joni, illus. (p. 765)
—Hello Tommy Trojan! Perez, Gerry, illus. (p. 765)
—Hello Wildcat! Cooper, Blair, illus. (p. 765)
—Here We Go, Steelers! (p. 771)
—How 'Bout Them Cowboys! De Angel, Miguel, illus. (p. 805)
—How 'Bout Them Cowboys! Coloring Book. (p. 805)
—Howdy Reveille! Craig, Megan, illus. (p. 823)
—Let's Go 49ers! (p. 997)
—Let's Go Bears! (p. 997)
—Let's Go Bengals! (p. 997)
—Let's Go, Broncos! (p. 997)
—Let's Go, Chiefs! De Angel, Miguel, illus. (p. 997)
—Let's Go, Colts! (p. 997)
—Let's Go, Giants! De Angel, Miguel, illus. (p. 997)
—Let's Go Hoosiers! Shrestha, Anuj, illus. (p. 997)
—Let's Go Illini! Shrestha, Anuj, illus. (p. 997)
—Let's Go Irish! Shrestha, Anuj, illus. (p. 997)
—Let's Go, Panthers! De Angel, Miguel, illus. (p. 997)
—Let's Go, Seahawks! De Angel, Miguel, illus. (p. 997)
—Let's Go, Vikings! De Angel, Miguel, illus. (p. 998)
—Let's Go, White Sox! De Angel, Miguel & Moore, D., illus. (p. 998)
Aryal, Aimee & Halligan, Chris. Meet Cort the Sport. (p. 1120)

A

Aryal, Aimee Sutter. Hello Hokie Bird! Meadows, Sarah, illus. (p. 764)
Aryal, Kusum. Magic Mermaid Girl. (p. 1072)
Aryal, Naren. Hello, Beaker! Morehead State University. Schartup, Adam, illus. (p. 763)
Aryan, Kiana, illus. see Mohr, Kathryn.
Arzave, Jose. Rabbit the Shepherd. (p. 1429)
Arzoumanian, Alik, illus. see Bass, Hester Thompson & Thompson-Bass, Hester.
Arzoumanian, Alik, illus. see Bass, Hester Thompson.
Arzoumanian, Alik, illus. see MacDonald, Margaret Read.
Asad, Megan Emily. Juggler's Journey. (p. 932)
Asada, Hiroyuki. Tegami Bachi: Letter Bee. Vol. 3 Asada, Hiroyuki, illus. (p. 1715)
—Tegami Bachi. Asada, Hiroyuki, illus. (p. 1715)
Asafo-Agyei Okrah, Kwadwo & Sandy Taylor. African Indigenous Knowledge & Science. (p. 27)
Asai, Carrie. Book of the Flame. Verhoye, Annabelle & Alarcão, Renato, illus. (p. 212)
—Book of the Heart: Heaven's Mission - To Sharpen Her Senses. Alarcao, Renato, illus. (p. 212)
—Book of the Pearl. Verhoye, Annabelle & Alarcao, Renato, illus. (p. 212)
—Book of the Shadow. Alarcao, Renato, illus. (p. 212)
—Book of the Sword. Verhoye, Annabelle, illus. (p. 212)
—Book of the Wind. (p. 212)
Asai, Carrie & Gray, Mitchel. Book of the Wind. Verhoye, Annabelle & Alarcão, Renato, illus. (p. 212)
Asala, Jason, creator. Great Wormwood (p. 719)
Asamiya, Kia. Dark Angel (p. 407)
—Dark Angel: The Path to Destiny Asamiya, Kia, illus. (p. 407)
—Nadesico Asamiya, Kia, illus. (p. 1227)
—Nadesico Cebulski, C. B. & Furuhata, Noriko, trs. from JPN. (p. 1227)
—Silent Mobius. Asamiya, Kia, illus. (p. 1575)
—Steam Detectives. Asamiya, Kia, illus. (p. 1646)
Asamiya, Kia, jt. auth. see Kurihashi, Shinsuke.
Asani, Samantha. Everyone Is Special: A Lesson in Teamwork. (p. 544)
Asano, Atsuko & Imai, Hizuru. Manzai Comics. (p. 1089)
Asare, Meshack. Appel de Sosu (Sosu's Call) Keita, Fatou, tr. (p. 92)
—Sosu's Call. Asare, Meshack, illus. (p. 1614)
Asay, Colleen. What Happened to Grandpa's Hair? (p. 1885)
Asay, Julie. I Wish I Had a Twin Brother. (p. 848)
Asbill, Annette. Mouse's Forever Christmas. Asbill, Annette, illus. (p. 1182)
Asbjornsen, Peter Christen. Three Billy Goats Gruff. Vohra, Sibi, illus. (p. 1741)
—Three Billy Goats Gruff. Sperling, Thomas, illus. (p. 1741)
Asbjornsen, Peter Christen, illus. see Arenson, Roberta & Finch, Mary.
Asbjornsen, Peter Christen, jt. auth. see Crosby, Jeff.
Asbjornsen, Peter Christen, jt. auth. see Roberts, Tom.
Asbjornsen, Peter Christen, jt. auth. see Wright, Rebecca Hu-Van.
Asbury, Terri. Josh's Book of ABC's: Events at the Powwow. (p. 926)
Ascension Press, creator. Theology of the Body for Teens Student Workbook: Discovering God's Plan for Love & Life. (p. 1729)
Asch, Devin, illus. see Asch, Frank.
Asch, Devin, jt. auth. see Asch, Frank.
Asch, Frank. Battle in a Bottle. Kanzler, John, illus. (p. 145)
—Bread & Honey. (p. 224)
—Earth & I. (p. 495)
—Ghost of P. S. 42. Kanzler, John, illus. (p. 671)
—Gravity Buster: Journal 2 of a Cardboard Genius. Asch, Frank, illus. (p. 712)
—Gravity Buster: Journal #2 of a Cardboard Genius. Asch, Frank, illus. (p. 712)
—Happy Birthday, Big Bad Wolf. Asch, Frank, illus. (p. 744)
—Happy Birthday, Moon. Asch, Frank, illus. (p. 745)
—Here Comes the Cat! Vagin, Vladimir, illus. (p. 770)
—Just Like Daddy. (p. 939)
—Milk & Cookies. (p. 1143)
—Milk & Cookies. Asch, Frank, illus. (p. 1143)
—Monsieur Saguette & His Baguette. Asch, Frank, illus. (p. 1166)
—Moonbear's Bargain. (p. 1172)
—Moonbear's Bargain. Asch, Frank, illus. (p. 1172)
—Moonbear's Dream. (p. 1172)
—Moonbear's Pet. (p. 1172)
—Moonbear's Pet. Asch, Frank, illus. (p. 1172)
—Moonbear's Shadow. Asch, Frank, illus. (p. 1172)
—Moonbear's Skyfire. Asch, Frank, illus. (p. 1172)
—Moonbear's Sunrise. Asch, Frank, illus. (p. 1172)
—Mooncake. Asch, Frank, illus. (p. 1172)
—Moondance. (p. 1172)
—Moondance. Asch, Frank, illus. (p. 1172)
—Moongame. Asch, Frank, illus. (p. 1172)
—Mr. Maxwell's Mouse Asch, Devin, illus. (p. 1185)
—Mrs. Marlowe's Mice. Asch, Devin, illus. (p. 1187)
—Pizza. Asch, Frank, illus. (p. 1365)
—Popcorn. (p. 1384)
—Sand Cake. (p. 1510)
—Star Jumper: Journal of a Cardboard Genius. Asch, Frank, illus. (p. 1640)
—Sun Is My Favorite Star. (p. 1676)
—Survival School. Kanzler, John, illus. (p. 1686)
—Time Twister: Journal 3 of a Cardboard Genius. Asch, Frank, illus. (p. 1753)
—Water. (p. 1862)
Asch, Frank, jt. auth. see Asch, Frank.
Asch, Frank & Asch, Devin. Like a Windy Day. (p. 1017)
—Mr. Maxwell's Mouse. Asch, Frank & Asch, Devin, illus. (p. 1185)
Asch, Frank & Asch, Frank. Happy Birthday, Moon. Asch, Frank & Asch, Frank, illus. (p. 745)
—Survival School. Kanzler, John, illus. (p. 1686)
Asch, Sheila. Katy's Time. (p. 946)
Aschermann, Kurt. Bj & the Amazing Doctor Directions. (p. 194)
Ascough, Deirdre Mary. My First Holy Communion. Brown, Lisa, illus. (p. 1206)
Aseervatham, Aloysius & Aseervatham, Leslie. Graduated Numerical Skills: For the Young Scholar. (p. 705)
Aseervatham, Leslie, jt. auth. see Aseervatham, Aloysius.
Asensio, Agusti, illus. see Ende, Michael.
Asfar, Dan. Dear Liza (p. 419)
—Dear Liza. (p. 419)
—Ghost Hunters: Real Stories of Paranormal Investigators. Vol. 1 (p. 670)
—Ghost Hunters of America: Real Stories of Paranormal Investigators. Vol. 1 (p. 670)
—Ghost Stories of Arizona & New Mexico. (p. 671)
—Ghost Stories of Colorado. (p. 671)
—Ghost Stories of Florida. (p. 671)
—Ghost Stories of Louisiana. (p. 671)
—Ghost Stories of Montana. (p. 671)
—Ghost Stories of Virginia. (p. 671)
—Haunted Battlefields (p. 753)
—Haunted Highways (p. 753)
Asfar, Dan, jt. auth. see Chodan, Tim.
Asfar, Dan & Thay, Edrick. Ghost Stories of the Civil War (p. 671)
Asfar, Dan, et al. Ghost Stories of America (p. 671)
Asgedom, Mawi. Code: The 5 Secrets of Teen Success. (p. 338)
—Nothing Is Impossible: The Ultimate Teen Success CDs. Asgedom, Mawi, ed. (p. 1268)
—Win the Inner Battle: The Ultimate Teen Leadership Journal. Berger, Dave, ed. (p. 1935)
Ash. Thrush's Song. (p. 1745)
Ash, illus. see Praveeta.
Ash, Jutta. Rapunzel. (p. 1439)
Ash, Maureen. Death of a Squire (p. 420)
Ash, Russell. Boring, Botty & Spong. (p. 214)
Ash, Russell & Terry, Paul. Top 10 for Boys. (p. 1768)
Ash, Stephanie, jt. auth. see Behan, Abbey Lauren Ash.
Ash Sullivan, Erin, jt. auth. see Sohn, Emily.
Ashabranner, Brent. Gavriel & Jemal: Two Boys of Jerusalem. Conklin, Paul, photos by. (p. 658)
—Great American Memorials Ashabranner, Jennifer, photos by. (p. 713)
Ashabranner, Brent, jt. auth. see Davis, Russell G.
Ashabranner, Jennifer, photos by see Ashabranner, Brent.
Ashar, Linda C. Kerry Bog Pony Sketch & Coloring Book (p. 949)
Ashbe, Jeanne. Adios! (p. 12)
—Cu Cu! (p. 387)
—De Noche se Duerme! Coll-Vinent, Anna, tr. (p. 416)
—Es hora de Recoger: Traduccion Anna Coll-Vinent. (p. 534)
—Eso No Se Hace! (p. 536)
—hora del Bano. (p. 797)
—Oh!, esta Oscuro. (p. 1280)
Ashbee, Edward. Get Set for American Studies. (p. 668)
Ashbrock, Peg, jt. auth. see Moreno, Barry.
Ashburn, Boni. Fort That Jack Built. Helquist, Brett, illus. (p. 623)
—I Had a Favorite Dress. Denos, Julia, illus. (p. 838)
—I Had a Favorite Hat. Ng, Robyn, illus. (p. 838)
—Over at the Castle. Murphy, Kelly, illus. (p. 1313)
Ashburn, Boni & De Giorgi, Sergio. Builder Goose: It's Construction Rhyme Time! (p. 238)
Ashby, Amanda. Demonosity. (p. 426)
—Under a Spell (p. 1813)
—Wishful Thinking. (p. 1940)
—Zombie Queen of Newbury High. (p. 1988)
Ashby, Bonnie Lee, jt. auth. see Turkington, Carol A.
Ashby, Bonnie Lee, jt. auth. see Turkington, Carol.
Ashby, Chris, illus. see Aldrich, John, Jr.
Ashby, Freya Katrina. Summer at the Dunes: A Deirdre Carlisle Mystery. (p. 1673)
Ashby, Gaylene. STORY TIME A Collection of Three Children's Stories. (p. 1663)
Ashby, Lenore. Magic of the Bear. (p. 1073)
Ashby, Mandy Anne. Mindy's Adventure with the Pussycat Witches: Playing in the Rain. (p. 1145)
Ashby, Neal, et al. Goodnight Tiger Stadium. (p. 701)
Ashby, Norman. Magic Fireplace. (p. 1072)
Ashby, Ruth. Amazing Mr. Franklin: Or the Boy Who Read Everything Montgomery, Michael, illus. (p. 55)
—Anne Frank: Young Diarist. (p. 85)
—Caedmon's Song. Slavin, Bill, illus. (p. 250)
—Earth & Its Moon. (p. 495)
—How the Solar System Was Formed. (p. 813)
—John & Abigail Adams. (p. 921)
—My Favorite Dinosaurs. Sibbick, John, illus. (p. 1203)
—Outer Planets. (p. 1312)
—Rocket Man: The Mercury Adventure of John Glenn Hunt, Robert, illus. (p. 1482)
—Rosa Parks: Freedom Rider. (p. 1489)
—Woodrow & Edith Wilson. (p. 1949)
—Young Charles Darwin & the Voyage of the Beagle Duranceau, Suzanne, illus. (p. 1978)
Ashcraft, Carolyn. Hamlet Goes to School. (p. 739)
Ashcraft Jr, D. C., illus. see Hayes, Beverly.
Ashcraft, Shelly & Hunter, Cheryl. Mamaw & the Girls. (p. 1084)
Ashcraft, T. D. Bump the Monster. (p. 241)
Ashcraft, Tami Oldham & McGearhart, Susea. Red Sky in Mourning: A True Story of Love, Loss, & Survival at Sea. (p. 1455)
Ashcroft, Cliff. Dreaming of Still Water. (p. 484)
Ashcroft, Colin Michael, illus. see Sautter, A. J.
Ashcroft, Minnie. Marvelous Map Activities for Young Learners. (p. 1099)
Ashcroft, Minnie & National Geographic Learning Staff. East Asia. (p. 498)
—East Asia - Geography & Environments. (p. 498)
—North America - People & Places. (p. 1264)
Ashdown, Rebecca. Bob & Flo. (p. 205)
—Bob & Flo Play Hide & Seek. (p. 205)
Ashe, E. Happy Horse: A Children's Book of Horses. Ashe, E., illus. (p. 746)
Ashe, Gregory. Imagineer (Fire Eye Edition) A Book of Miracles. Whittaker, Kay, illus. (p. 861)
—Imagineer (Snow Scene Edition) A Book of Miracles. Whittaker, Kay, illus. (p. 861)
Ashe, Jade, jt. auth. see Hinton, S. E.
Ashe, Susan. Cuda of the Celts. (p. 389)
—Cuda of the Celts. Lawrie, Robin, illus. (p. 389)
Asheida. Peach & Pun: The New Family Ferret. (p. 1332)
Asher, Dana. Epidemiologists: Life Tracking Deadly Diseases. (p. 532)
Asher, James, illus. see Burton, K. Melissa.
Asher, James, illus. see Florence, Leigh Anne.
Asher, James, photos by see Burton, K. Melissa.
Asher, Jay. Thirteen Reasons Why. (p. 1735)
Asher, Jay & Mackler, Carolyn. Future of Us. (p. 651)
Asher, Mark J. Old Friends: Great Dogs on the Good Life. Asher, Mark J., photos by. (p. 1283)
Asher, Melissa. Magical, Mystical, Majestic. (p. 1075)
—Toys, Blocks & Cars, Oh My (p. 1774)
Asher, Neal. Brass Man. (p. 222)
Asher, Penny & Booker, Ricki. Mommy & Daddy Are Going on a Trip. Kassab, Selena, illus. (p. 1162)
—My First Day of School. Kassab, Selena, illus. (p. 1206)
—No More Pacifier. Kassab, Selena, illus. (p. 1259)
—We're Having a Baby. Kassab, Selena, illus. (p. 1875)
Asher, Robert, ed. see Paulson, Timothy J.
Asher, Robert, jt. auth. see Ingram, Scott.
Asher, Robert, jt. auth. see Worth, Richard.
Asher, Robert, ed. Explore America's Rich Heritage (p. 550)
Asher, Sandra Fenichel. Blackbirds & Dragons, Mermaids & Mice. (p. 197)
—Somebody Catch My Homework. (p. 1609)
Asher, Sandy. Chicken Storytime. Fearing, Mark, illus. (p. 300)
—Too Many Frogs! Graves, Keith, illus. (p. 1766)
—Why Rabbit's Nose Twitches. (p. 1925)
Asher, Sandy, ed. With All My Heart, with All My Mind: Thirteen Stories about Growing up Jewish. (p. 1942)
Ashes, Dustin. Space-Boot Johnny Recharged. (p. 1618)
Ashford, Deanna. Doctor's Orders. (p. 459)
Ashford Frame, Jeron & Christie, R. Gregory. Yesterday I Had the Blues. (p. 1971)
Ashford, Jeron. Winter Candle. Schuett, Stacey, illus. (p. 1938)
Ashford, Kathy. Around & Back Around Again: A Metaphor (p. 100)
—Little Grace. (p. 1028)
—Spencer's Birthday. (p. 1625)
Ashford, Sylvie, illus. see Ray, Michelle.
Ashforth, Kate. Zap! Fab Things to Draw. Konye, Paul, illus. (p. 1985)
Ashforth, Kate, jt. auth. see Reilly, Carmel.
Ashihara, Hinako. Forbidden Dance (p. 616)
—Forbidden Dance. (p. 616)
—Sos. Ashihara, Hinako, illus. (p. 1614)
Ashkenas, Bruce. Auntie's Ghost. (p. 115)
—Sick Street. (p. 1572)
Ashkenazi, Michael. Handbook of Japanese Mythology (p. 740)
Ashland, Monk & Ashland, Nigel. Sky Village (p. 1587)
Ashland, Nigel, jt. auth. see Ashland, Monk.
Ashley, Bernard. Johnnie's Blitz. (p. 923)
—Present for Paul. Mitchell, David, illus. (p. 1396)
—Solitaire. (p. 1608)
Ashley, Bernard, et al. Angel Boy. (p. 73)
Ashley, Brook, et al. Lonely Doll Makes New Friends. (p. 1046)
Ashley Brown. Geology. (p. 662)
Ashley, Carol, illus. see Swaim, Jessica.
Ashley Comeaux-Foret, illus. see Guillot, Angela K.
Ashley, Elana. Splunkunio Splunkey Detective & Peacemaker: Case One: The Missing Friendship Bracelet. (p. 1630)
—Splunkunio Splunkey Detective & Peacemaker Detective y Pacificador: Case One: The Missing Friendship Bracelet Caso Primero: El Brazalete de la Amistad Desaparecido. Nikolov, Stefan V., tr. (p. 1630)
Ashley, Jane, IV. Blake. Maximilian Press staff, ed. (p. 198)
Ashley, John A. Gathering of the Fairy Horses Series. (p. 658)
Ashley, Kristina. Rescue. (p. 1462)
Ashley, Michele. When Do Trees Look Different? (p. 1902)
—Where Is This Astronaut? (p. 1909)
—Who Has Ears Like These? (p. 1915)
—Who Is This? (p. 1916)
—Why Does the Moon Look Different? (p. 1924)
Ashley, Moana. Wonders of the Worlds. (p. 1949)
Ashley, Sharon. I Wish I Could See. (p. 848)
Ashley, Susan. Ants. (p. 90)
—Bees. (p. 157)
—Butterflies. (p. 247)
—Carro. (p. 271)
—En Autobús. (p. 522)
—Fireflies. (p. 592)
—Going by Bus. (p. 692)
—Going by Car. (p. 692)
—Going by Plane. (p. 692)
—Golden Gate Bridge. (p. 694)
—Grasshoppers. (p. 711)
—I Can Make a Sandwich. (p. 836)
—I Can Read a Map. (p. 836)
—I Can Use a Computer. (p. 836)
—I Can Use a Dictionary. (p. 836)
—I Can Use the Telephone. (p. 837)
—I Can Write a Letter. (p. 837)
—Ladybugs. (p. 971)
—Liberty Bell. (p. 1005)
—Mount Rushmore. (p. 1180)
—Places in American History (p. 1366)
—Por Avión. (p. 1385)
—Por Tren. (p. 1386)
—Washington Monument. (p. 1860)
—Yo-Yo Ma. (p. 1971)
Ashley-Hollinger, Mika. Precious Bones. (p. 1394)
Ashlock, Lisel Jane, illus. see Yolen, Jane.
Ashman, Iain. Egyptian Mummy. (p. 506)
—Wizard's Castle. (p. 1943)
Ashman, Iain, illus. see Beasant, Pam.
Ashman, Linda. Essential Worldwide Monster Guide. Small, David, illus. (p. 537)
—How to Make a Night. Tusa, Tricia, illus. (p. 820)
—Just Another Morning. Muñoz, Claudio, illus. (p. 937)
—Little Baby Buttercup. Byun, You, illus. (p. 1023)
—M Is for Mischief: An A to Z of Naughty Children. Carpenter, Nancy, illus. (p. 1067)
—Mama's Day. Ormerod, Jan, illus. (p. 1084)
—Peace, Baby! Lew-Vriethoff, Joanne, illus. (p. 1331)
—Rain! Robinson, Christian, illus. (p. 1434)
—Sailing off to Sleep. Winter, Susan, illus. (p. 1503)
—Samantha on a Roll. Davenier, Christine, illus. (p. 1507)
—Twelve Days of Christmas in Colorado. (p. 1800)
—When I Was King. McPhail, David, illus. (p. 1903)
Ashman, Linda & Sorra, Kristin. No Dogs Allowed! (p. 1258)
Ashman, Sarah & Parent, Nancy. Holly Bloom's Garden. Mitchell, Lori, illus. (p. 789)
Ashmore, Wayne & Nault, Jennifer. Mark Twain. (p. 1095)
Ashour, Monica. Every Body Is a Gift: God Made Us to Love. Kaminski, Karol, illus. (p. 542)
—Every Body Is Smart: God Helps Me Listen & Choose. Kaminski, Karol, illus. (p. 542)
—Everybody Has a Body: God Made Boys & Girls. Kaminski, Karol, illus. (p. 543)
Ashour, Monica & Harrald-Pilz, Marilee. Everybody Has Something to Give. (p. 543)
—God Has a Plan for Boys & for Girls. (p. 689)
Ashrafizadeh, Maedeh. Life of a Lovebird. (p. 1011)
Ashram, Karen. Seasons & Colors. (p. 1538)
Ashta, Lucia. Perfect Fuzzy-Wuzz. (p. 1341)
Ashton, Anna. Molly & Ben. (p. 1160)
—Our New Puppy. (p. 1309)
Ashton, Brodi. Everbound. (p. 542)
—Everneath. (p. 542)
—Evertrue. (p. 542)
Ashton, Christine. Genie of the Bike Lamp: Level P (p. 661)
Ashton, Kenneth. Gale's Gold Ring: The Legend of Lincoln's Lost Gold. Ashton-Briggs, Shelley, illus. (p. 653)
Ashton, Lisette. Black Widow. (p. 197)
—Hot Pursuit. (p. 802)
Ashton, Lisette, jt. auth. see Nexus Staff.
Ashton, Patricia. Gopher Tortoise: A Life History. (p. 702)
Ashton, Victoria. Confessions of a Teen Nanny. (p. 356)
—Juicy Secrets. (p. 932)
—Rich Girls. (p. 1469)
Ashton-Briggs, Shelley, illus. see Ashton, Kenneth.
Ashworth, Caspian. Copper Smith & the Battle of the Bands. (p. 365)
Ashworth, Deb. Adventures of Laverne & Shirley: In Nebraska. (p. 19)
Ashworth, Leon. Ancient Egypt. (p. 68)
—Gods & Goddesses of Ancient Greece. (p. 690)
—Gods & Goddesses of the Vikings & Northlands. (p. 690)
—Guy Fawkes. (p. 733)
—King Henry VIII. (p. 958)
—Oliver Cromwell. (p. 1285)
Ashworth, Mike, ed. see Ovenden, Mark.
Ashworth, Nichol, illus. see Randolph, Grace, et al.
Ashworth, Sherry. Close-Up. (p. 334)
Ashworth, Susan M. Jo-Jo Helps with the Housework. (p. 919)
Ashworth, William B., Jr. Vulcan's Forge anda Fingal's Cave: Volcanoes, Basalt, & the Discovery of Geological Time. (p. 1851)
Asian Absolute, tr. see Amery, Heather.
Asim, Jabari. Boy of Mine. Pham, LeUyen, illus. (p. 218)
—Fifty Cents & a Dream: Young Booker T. Washington. (p. 585)
—Girl of Mine. Pham, LeUyen, illus. (p. 678)
—Road to Freedom. (p. 1477)
—Whose Knees Are These? Pham, LeUyen, illus. (p. 1921)
—Whose Toes Are Those? Pham, LeUyen, illus. (p. 1922)
Asimov, Isaac. Astronomy Today: Past & Present. (p. 109)
—Solar System: Earth. (p. 1607)
Asimov, Isaac, jt. auth. see Asimov, Janet.
Asimov, Isaac & Asimov, Janet. Norby's Other Secret. (p. 1264)
Asimov, Isaac & Hantula, Richard. Asteroides. Porras, Carlos & D'Andrea, Patricia, trs. from ENG. (p. 108)
—Astronomy in Ancient Times: Past & Present. (p. 109)
—Astronomy Projects. (p. 109)
—Birth of Our Universe. (p. 192)
—Black Holes, Pulsars, & Quasars. (p. 196)
—Comets & Meteors. (p. 348)
—Exploring Outer Space. (p. 553)
—Global Space Programs: Past & Present. (p. 684)
—Is There Life in Outer Space? (p. 890)
—Júpiter. Porras, Carlos & D'Andrea, Patricia, trs. from ENG. (p. 936)
—Legends, Folklore, & Outer Space. (p. 989)
—Life & Death of Stars. (p. 1007)
—Luna. Porras, Carlos & D'Andrea, Patricia, trs. from ENG. (p. 1065)
—Marte: Nuestro Misteriosos Vecino. Porras, Carlos & D'Andrea, Patricia, trs. from ENG. (p. 1097)
—Mercurio. Porras, Carlos & D'Andrea, Patricia, trs. from ENG. (p. 1127)
—Milky Way & Other Galaxies. (p. 1143)
—Neptuno. Porras, Carlos & D'Andrea, Patricia, trs. (p. 1241)
—Our Planetary System. (p. 1309)
—Plutón y Caronte. Porras, Carlos & D'Andrea, Patricia, trs. from ENG. (p. 1374)
—Saturno: El Planeta de los Anillos. Porras, Carlos & D'Andrea, Patricia, trs. from ENG. (p. 1516)
—Science Fiction: Vision of Tomorrow? (p. 1526)
—Sol. Porras, Carlos & D'Andrea, Patricia, trs. from ENG. (p. 1606)
—Space Junk. (p. 1619)
—Stargazer's Guide. (p. 1642)
—Tierra. Porras, Carlos & D'Andrea, Patricia, trs. from ENG. (p. 1748)
—UFOs. (p. 1807)
—Urano: El Planeta Inclinado. Porras, Carlos & D'Andrea, Patricia, trs. from ENG. (p. 1825)
—Venus. Porras, Carlos & D'Andrea, Patricia, trs. from ENG. (p. 1836)
Asimov, Janet, jt. auth. see Asimov, Isaac.

Asimov, Janet & Asimov, Isaac. Norby the Mixed-Up Robot. (p. 1264)
Asirvatham, Sandy. History of Jazz. (p. 784)
Aska, Warabe, illus. see Takamado, Hisako de.
Asker, Niklas, illus. see DuPrau, Jeanne.
Askew, Amanda. Bulldozers. (p. 240)
—Complete Guides Space. (p. 353)
—Cranes. (p. 376)
—Doctor. (p. 459)
—Loaders. (p. 1044)
—Mighty Machines: Diggers. (p. 1140)
—People Who Help Us - Chef. (p. 1340)
—Police Officer. (p. 1380)
—Vet. (p. 1839)
Askew, Amanda, ed. see Adams, Simon.
Askew, Amanda & Crowson, Andrew. Chef. (p. 297)
—Doctor. (p. 459)
—Firefighter. (p. 591)
—Police Officer. (p. 1380)
—Teacher. (p. 1709)
—Vet. (p. 1839)
Askew, Amanda & Marleau, Eve. Visit to the Dentist. Garton, Michael, illus. (p. 1845)
Askew, Claire. Generation V: The Complete Guide to Going, Being, & Staying Vegan as a Teenager. (p. 660)
Askew, Gee. Starstiller. (p. 1643)
Askew, Kim & Helmes, Amy. Anyone but You. (p. 91)
—Exposure. Mitchard, Jacquelyn, ed. (p. 554)
—Tempestuous. (p. 1718)
—Tempestuous. Mitchard, Jacquelyn, ed. (p. 1718)
Askew, Lotonia. God's Creation. (p. 691)
Askew, Shirley. Jean's Magical Moments: Faith of a Child. (p. 911)
Askin, Corrina, illus. see Cashman, Seamus.
Askin, Corrina, jt. auth. see Snell, Gordon.
Askins, Suzan. Riding with Nana. (p. 1471)
Askomitis, Gerard & Aksomitis, Gerard. Solving the Mysteries of the Past. (p. 1608)
Askounis, Christina. Dream of the Stone. (p. 483)
Aslan, Austin. Girl at the Center of the World. (p. 678)
—Islands at the End of the World. (p. 892)
Asleson, Robyn. Albert Moore. (p. 34)
Aslett, Don A. Toilet Cleaner's Attitude. (p. 1762)
Asmus, James. X-Men/Steve Rogers: Escape from the Negative Zone. Bradshaw, Nick & Roberson, Ibraim, illus. (p. 1967)
Asner, Anne-Marie. Klutzy Boy. Asner, Anne-Marie, illus. (p. 964)
—Kvetchy Boy. Asner, Anne-Marie, illus. (p. 968)
—Noshy Boy. Asner, Anne-Marie, illus. (p. 1266)
—Shluffy Girl (p. 1568)
—Shmutzy Girl. Asner, Anne-Marie, illus. (p. 1568)
Asnong, Jocey. Nuptse & Lohtse Go to the Rockies (p. 1273)
Aspen, Laurel. School Reunion. (p. 1523)
Aspen, Lydia, illus. see Holden, Susan.
Aspen-Baxter, Linda. Africa. (p. 26)
—Antarctica. (p. 88)
—Asia. (p. 106)
—Fresh Water. (p. 636)
—Fresh Waters. (p. 636)
—Luna, with Code. (p. 1065)
—Patos. (p. 1328)
—Plants. (p. 1369)
—Rainforests. (p. 1436)
Aspen-Baxter, Linda, jt. auth. see Kissock, Heather.
Aspen-Baxter, Linda & Kissock, Heather. Cabras. (p. 250)
—Cerdos. (p. 287)
—Las Estaciones. (p. 976)
—Las Estrellas. (p. 976)
—Llamas. (p. 1043)
—Los Arcoíris, with Code. (p. 1053)
—Los Planetas, with Code. (p. 1054)
—Ponies. (p. 1382)
—Sol. (p. 1606)
—Vacas. (p. 1829)
Aspen-Baxter, Linda & Lomberg, Michelle. Planets. (p. 1368)
Asper-Smith, Sarah. Have You Ever Seen a Smack of Jellyfish? An Alphabet Book. (p. 754)
—I Would Tuck You In. Watley, Mitchell, illus. (p. 849)
Aspesi, Carol. Tale of the Snail. (p. 1700)
Asphyxia. Mortimer Revealed. (p. 1176)
Aspin, Diana. Ordinary Miracles (p. 1302)
Aspin, Eleanor. Messy Myko & Tidy Tyko (p. 1130)
Aspinall, Marc, illus. see Cave, Holly.
Aspinall, Marc, illus. see Dods, Emma.
Aspinall, Marc, illus. see Dodson, Emma & Woodward, John.
Aspinall, Marc, illus. see Kingfisher Editors & Dods, Emma.
Aspinall, Marc, illus. see Kingfisher Editors, et al.
Aspinall, Marc, illus. see Steele, Philip.
Aspinall, Neal, illus. see McHugh, Erin.
Aspland, G. Choices: Stories for Assembly & P. S. H. E. Lye, Michael, illus. (p. 309)
Aspland, Gordon. Home Stories: Talking about Personal, Social & Health Issues at Home. Lye, Michael, illus. (p. 793)
Aspley, Brenda. I Love Ponies. McNicolas, Shelagh, illus. (p. 842)
Asquith, Ros. Hector & the Cello. (p. 761)
—How to Draw Cartoons. Asquith, Ros, illus. (p. 817)
—Letters from an Alien Schoolboy. (p. 1002)
—Trixie Ace Ghost Buster. (p. 1788)
—Trixie & the Dream Pony of Doom. (p. 1788)
—Trixie Fights for Furry Rights. (p. 1788)
—Trixie Gets the Witch Factor. (p. 1788)
—Vanishing Trick: Poems by Ros Asquith. Asquith, Ros, illus. (p. 1833)
Asquith, Ros, illus. see Cross, Gillian & Quarto Generic Staff.
Asquith, Ros, illus. see Hoffman, Mary Y.
Asquith, Ros, illus. see Hoffman, Mary.
Asquith, Ros, illus. see Moskowitz, Cheryl.
Asquith, Ros, illus. see Quarto Generic Staff.
Asquith, Ros, illus. see Stockdale, Sean & Strick, Alex.
Asquith, Ros, illus. see Strick, Alex & Stockdale, Sean.
Asquith, Ros & Good, Andi. Boo! (p. 209)
Asrani, Megan. Cat on the Windowsill. (p. 278)
Asrar, Mahmud. Shadowland: Power Man. (p. 1558)
Asrar, Mahmud & Bennett, Joe. Indestructible Hulk - Humanity Bomb (p. 870)
Asriningtyas, Visi. What Can We Do with Garbage? Sampah Bisa Diapakan Ya? (p. 1881)
Assaël, Ivan, illus. see Saint Cyr, Vanessa.
Asselin, Kristine Carlson. Ancient Egyptian Myths (p. 69)
—Dangerous Diseases: Scary Illnesses That Frighten the World (p. 404)
—Jennifer Lopez: Actress & Pop Superstar. (p. 913)
—Martin Luther King Jr: Civil Rights Leader. (p. 1098)
—Our Sun (p. 1310)
—Pharaohs & Dynasties of Ancient Egypt. (p. 1349)
—Real Story about Government & Politics in Colonial America (p. 1449)
—Real Story on the Weapons & Battles of Colonial America (p. 1449)
—Smart Research Strategies: Finding the Right Sources. (p. 1593)
—Stars (p. 1643)
—Taurus, Virgo, & Capricorn: All about the Earth Signs. (p. 1707)
—Think for Yourself: Avoiding Plagiarism (p. 1734)
—What You Need to Know about Concussions. (p. 1896)
—Who Really Discovered America? (p. 1917)
—Worst Case of Pasketti-Itis. Luisa, Gioffre-Suzuki, illus. (p. 1961)
Asselin, Kristine Carlson & Hinman, Bonnie. Life in the American Colonies. (p. 1011)
Asselin, Kristine Carlson & Lee, Sally. Scary Science (p. 1520)
Asselin, Kristine Carlson, et al. Research Tool Kit. (p. 1462)
Asselin, Kristine Carlson. TiVo: The Company & Its Founders. (p. 1758)
Assirelli, Francesca. Chicken Licken. (p. 300)
Assirelli, Francesca, illus. see Marshall, Linda Elovitz.
Asso, B., jt. auth. see Rideau, J.
Asso, B. & Bergese, F. Cinebook Recounts: Battle of Britain. (p. 321)
Asso, Bernard & Bergèse, Francis. Battle of Britain. (p. 146)
Asso, Bernard & Rideau, Joel. Biggles Recounts the Falklands War: Volume 1. Chauvin, Daniel & Uderzo, Marcel, illus. (p. 185)
Associated Press Staff. First Pet. (p. 596)
Assorted Staff, jt. auth. see Patten, Brian.
Assunto, Cecelia. God Did Make Little Green Apples. DeMatte, Darcey, illus. (p. 688)
Ast, Bernard. Whiteroser for Tasha. (p. 1914)
Asta, Susan. Evarista's Cart Story: La Historia de la Carretita Segun Evarista. (p. 541)
Astacio, Mrinali Alvarez. Pon, Pon: A Jugar con el Bebé! (p. 1382)
Astacio, Mrinali Alvarez, illus. see Rivera-Lassen, Carmen Leonor.
Aston, Al. Gifts for a King. Hutchinson, Joy, illus. (p. 675)
—Message for Mary. Hutchinson, Joy, illus. (p. 1129)
—Shepherds' Surprise. Hutchinson, Joy, illus. (p. 1565)
Aston, Claire. Wild West Through Time. (p. 1930)
Aston, Dianna. Butterfly Is Patient. Long, Sylvia, illus. (p. 248)
—Egg Is Quiet. (p. 506)
—Seed Is Sleepy. (p. 1547)
Aston, Dianna Hutts. Butterfly Is Patient. (p. 248)
—Butterfly Is Patient. Long, Sylvia, illus. (p. 248)
—Dream Something Big: The Story of the Watts Towers. Roth, Susan L., illus. (p. 483)
—Egg Is Quiet. Long, Sylvia, illus. (p. 506)
—Loony Little: An Environmental Tale. Murphy, Kelly, illus. (p. 1052)
—Moon over Star. Pinkney, Jerry, illus. (p. 1172)
—Nest Is Noisy. Long, Sylvia, illus. (p. 1242)
—Orange in January. Maren, Julie, illus. (p. 1301)
—Rock Is Lively. Long, Sylvia, illus. (p. 1482)
Aston, Dianna Hutts & Hutts Aston, Dianna. Seed Is Sleepy. Long, Sylvia, illus. (p. 1547)
Aston, Neil, contrib. by. Bailed Up. (p. 132)
Aston, Paul, tr. see Anton, Ferdinand.
Aston, Paul, tr. Claude Monet. Kutschbach, Doris, illus. (p. 329)
—Coloring Book: Wassily Kandinsky. Kutschbach, Doris, illus. (p. 344)
Astre, Patrick. Artifact. (p. 104)
Astrella, Mark, illus. see Ryan, Pam Muñoz.
Astro, Ian. Moon School. (p. 1172)
Asuao, Kelcey, illus. see Lesa, Ropeti F.
Asugha, Ruby. Little Sisters, Listen Up! A Message of Hope for Girls Growing up in Poverty Racism, & Despair. (p. 1036)
Asun, Balzola, jt. auth. see Balzola, Asun.
at Science, Editors. League of Scientists: Ghost in the Water. Al-Greene, Bob, illus. (p. 982)
Ata, Te. Baby Rattlesnake. Reisberg, Mira, illus. (p. 127)
—Baby Rattlesnake. Alarcón, Francisco X., tr. (p. 127)
Ata, Te, et al. Baby Rattlesnake. Reisberg, Mira, illus. (p. 127)
Atak. Topsy Turvy World. (p. 1769)
Atamer, Billie. Christmas Party for Santa. (p. 315)
Atamer, Billie. Banjo Billy & the River Rat Kids. (p. 136)
—Little Purple Pumpkin. (p. 1034)
—Magic Sleigh. (p. 1073)
—Pocket Full of Dreams. (p. 1375)
Atanacio, Frank. Aggravating Factors: From the Nick Barnum Sealed Case File a Nick Barnum Novel II. (p. 29)
Atanas, illus. see Johnson, E. Pauline.
Atancibia, Janet, et al, eds. Manual de la consejera de Margaritas Tomo 1 (p. 1088)
Atcheson-Melton, Patty, jt. auth. see Lee, Deborah Baptiste.
Atchison, David. Adventures of Black Bart: the Lone Stranger. (p. 16)
Atchison, David C. Adventures of Black Bart: An Encounter with Regret. (p. 16)
—Adventures of Black Bart: Dry Bones. (p. 16)
Atchison, Doug, jt. auth. see Ellison, James W.
Atchley, Dalton. If I Had a Million Dollars. (p. 853)
—Scared Little Rabbit. (p. 1519)
—Wolf & the Deer. (p. 1943)
Atchley, Kendra, illus. see Johnson, Michael E.
Atha, Anthony, jt. auth. see Frost, Simon.
Atha, Shirley Swigart. Angel with a Wagging Tail. (p. 74)
Athan, Polly, et al. Felicity's Cooking Studio. Mahal, Susan, illus. (p. 581)
Athanassiadis, Kiki, illus. see David, Carole.
Athans, Sandra K. Secrets of the Sky Caves: Danger & Discovery on Nepal's Mustang Cliffs. (p. 1546)
Athans, Sandra K. & Parente, Robin W. Common Core Readiness Guide to Reading. (p. 349)
—Tips & Tricks for Analyzing Text & Citing Evidence. (p. 1757)
—Tips & Tricks for Determining Point of View & Purpose. (p. 1757)
—Tips & Tricks for Evaluating an Argument & Its Claims. (p. 1757)
—Tips & Tricks for Evaluating Multimedia Content. (p. 1757)
Athena Group Inc. Staff, creator. PSI-SIM Science Simulations: The Water Flea Experiment. (p. 1413)
Athens, Sandra & Colarik, Kim. Adventures of Foxy: The Lonely Lost Dog. (p. 18)
Atherton, Isabel. Bad Easter Bunny. Röhr, Stéphanie, illus. (p. 131)
—Ruby Moo's Deep-Sea Adventure! Straker, Bethany, illus. (p. 1493)
—Smelly Ghost. Straker, Bethany, illus. (p. 1593)
Atherton, Isabel & Straker, Bethany. Springy Chicken. Straker, Bethany, illus. (p. 1635)
Atherton, Jim, illus. see London, Adam.
Athey, Victoria. No Peas, Please! Delaney, Molly, illus. (p. 1259)
Atinsky, Steve. Tyler on Prime Time. (p. 1805)
Atinuke. Anna Hibiscus' Song. Tobia, Lauren, illus. (p. 85)
—Good Luck Anna Hibiscus! Tobia, Lauren, illus. (p. 698)
—Have Fun Anna Hibiscus! Tobia, Lauren, illus. (p. 754)
—Hooray for Anna Hibiscus! Tobia, Lauren, illus. (p. 795)
—No. 1 Car Spotter. Cadwell, Warwick Johnson, illus. (p. 1257)
—No 1 Car Spotter & the Firebird. Johnson Cadwell, Warwick, illus. (p. 1257)
—Splash, Anna Hibiscus! Tobia, Lauren, illus. (p. 1629)
Atique, Quazi M. Zahid. Path of Peace: The Complete Code of Life. (p. 1328)
Atkin, Alan, jt. auth. see Kempton, Clive.
Atkin, Jean. Crow House. (p. 386)
Atkin, Pippa. Flexi-RE Evaluation (p. 603)
Atkin, S. Beth. Gunstories: Life-Changing Experiences with Guns. Atkin, S. Beth, illus. (p. 732)
Atkins, A. V. Ishmael: Or, the Origin of the Red Man. (p. 891)
Atkins, Aimee. Billy's Boatshed: MJ Saves the Day. Atkins, Aimee & Franfou Studio, illus. (p. 187)
—Billy's Boatshed - The Project. Atkins, Aimee & Franfou Studio, illus. (p. 187)
Atkins, Alison. Humpty Dumpty & Friends. (p. 827)
—Incy Wincy Spider & Friends. (p. 870)
Atkins, Alison, illus. see Freedman, Claire.
Atkins, Alison, illus. see Henning, Heather.
Atkins, Alison, illus. see Hogg, James.
Atkins, Alison, illus. see Top That Publishing Staff, ed.
Atkins, Ben. Breakaway Kid. Woods, Vanessa, illus. (p. 224)
Atkins, Carla. Kiara & the Butterfly. (p. 951)
Atkins, Catherine. Alt Ed. (p. 50)
—File on Angelyn Stark. (p. 586)
Atkins, Dan. Tony Transitions (p. 1766)
Atkins, Eddie. McCool School: If I ran the School. (p. 1114)
Atkins, Jeannine. Borrowed Names: Poems about Laura Ingalls Wilder, Madam C. J. Walker, Marie Curie, & Their Daughters. (p. 214)
—Girls Who Looked under Rocks: The Lives of Six Pioneering Naturalists. Conner, Paula, illus. (p. 681)
—Preparadas... Listas... Ya! (p. 1395)
Atkins, Jill. Cry, Baby. (p. 387)
—Mom's Robot Leftheri, Eleftheria-Garyfallia, illus. (p. 1163)
—Toad Swims for his Life! Mostyn, David, illus. (p. 1760)
—Tortoise Races Home. Blake, Beccy, illus. (p. 1771)
Atkins, Jill & Dorling Kindersley Publishing Staff. Water Everywhere. (p. 1862)
Atkins, Marcie Flinchum. Ancient China. (p. 68)
Atkins Nutritionals Inc. Staff. Atkins Holiday Recipes: Celebrate the Season with More Than 160 Low-Carb Dishes. (p. 112)
Atkins, Ron. Abby & the Bicycle Caper. (p. 2)
Atkinson, Brett, jt. auth. see Atkinson, Ruth.
Atkinson, C., jt. auth. see Gilpin, R.
Atkinson, Cale. To the Sea. Atkinson, Cale, illus. (p. 1759)
Atkinson, Cale, illus. see Bellisario, Gina.
Atkinson, Cale, illus. see Lakin, Patricia.
Atkinson, Catherine, jt. auth. see Gilpin, Rebecca.
Atkinson, Catherine, jt. auth. see Pratt, Leonie.
Atkinson, Elaine, illus. see McKenzie, Tim A.
Atkinson, Elizabeth. From Alice to Zen & Everyone in Between. (p. 641)
—I, Emma Freke. (p. 838)
—Lisa's Totally Unforgettable Winter. (p. 1022)
Atkinson, Janet I. Colorful Men & Women of the Mother Lode. Atkinson, Janet I., ed. (p. 344)
Atkinson, Joelie & Dinkles. Celeste, Nick & the Magical Tea Party. Oehlers, Adam, illus. (p. 285)
Atkinson, Lawrence. Great Ideas. (p. 716)
Atkinson, Linda. Amazing Chickens at Cliff House. Baker, David, illus. (p. 54)
Atkinson, Mary. Earth Is Flat! (p. 496)
—Pills & Potions: A History of Remedies. (p. 1359)
—What Do You Mean? Communication Isn't Easy. (p. 1883)
Atkinson, Olympia J. Kendahl's Plans. (p. 948)
Atkinson, Peter. Lion Encyclopedia of the Bible. (p. 1020)
Atkinson, Rick. Battle of the Bulge. (p. 146)
—D-Day: The Invasion of Normandy 1944. (p. 397)
Atkinson, Ruth & Atkinson, Brett. Christmas Cutouts. Atkinson, Ruth & Atkinson, Brett, illus. (p. 313)
—Rhyme Templates. Atkinson, Ruth & Atkinson, Brett, illus. (p. 1468)
—Stick Puppet Templates. Atkinson, Ruth & Atkinson, Brett, illus. (p. 1649)
—Story Templates. Atkinson, Ruth & Atkinson, Brett, illus. (p. 1663)
—Traditional Rhyme Templates. Atkinson, Ruth & Atkinson, Brett, illus. (p. 1776)
Atkinson, Stuart. Comets, Asteroids, & Meteors (p. 348)
—Space Tourist: A Traveler's Guide to the Solar System (p. 1620)
Atkinson, Sue. Life Confidence for Kids. (p. 1008)
—New Cambridge Mathematics. (p. 1243)
—Supermaths: Age 4-5. (p. 1684)
—Supermaths 3: Age 3-6. (p. 1684)
—Supermaths 5: Age 4-7. (p. 1684)
Atkinson, Sue & Baxter, Cathy. Modwl 1 - Llyfr Gweithgareddau 5. (p. 1160)
Atkinson, Sue & Canals, Sonia. Modwl 1 - Llyfr Cyswllt Cartref. (p. 1160)
Atkinson, Tim. Discover India. (p. 447)
—Discover the United Kingdom. (p. 448)
Atkinson, Tina Louise. Shape Up. (p. 1560)
Atkinson, William, ed. see Humiston, Sharon & Good, Cynthia.
Atlas. Antarctic Express. (p. 88)
Atlas, Lilly. Journey to the Deep Woods. (p. 929)
Atlas, Ron. Ten Pigs Fiddling. Flint, Stacie, illus. (p. 1719)
Atlee, Nancy. Absolutely Essential Grammar Guide. (p. 7)
Atlus. Persona 4 Arena: Official Design Works: Official Design Works. (p. 1344)
Atmadja, Titin. Liam's Adventure: Liam Meets the King of Java. (p. 1004)
—Liam's Adventure: Liam's Wild Life at Richard's Cabin. (p. 1004)
Atmore, Melanie. From a Butterfly's Eye. (p. 641)
Atnip, Linda. Miranda's Magic Garden. (p. 1149)
—Miranda's Magic Garden. Rothan, Ann, illus. (p. 1149)
Aton, Barbara, illus. see Knight, Betty.
ATP Staff. Carpentry Resource Guide: Resource Guide. (p. 271)
—Concrete Principles Resource Guide. (p. 355)
—HVAC Control Systems Resource Guide. (p. 830)
—Industrial Mechanics Resource Guide. (p. 872)
—Test Masters & Instructor's Guide. (p. 1723)
ATP Staff, A. T. P. PLC Project Organizer: Project Organizer. (p. 1373)
Attaboy. Secret Scheme Book. (p. 1543)
—You Might Be a Monster: And Other Stories I Made Up! (p. 1976)
Attainment Company. Explore Math Classroom Version. (p. 550)
Attanasio, Fabiana. Sweet Side of Fairy Tales. (p. 1690)
Attard, Ebenor. Ali Baba & the Forty Thieves. (p. 39)
Attard, Enebor. Ali Baba & the Forty Thieves. Holland, Richard, illus. (p. 39)
Attard, Enebor, illus. see Aktar, Nasreen.
Attaway, Anelda, ed. see Wheeler, Tonika Yvonne.
Attaway, Kathy. Adventures of Molly Polly Wog. (p. 20)
Attaway-Young, Andrea & Lane Durbin, Deborah. Secret Treasure - A Fairy Tale. (p. 1544)
Atteberry, Kevan. Bunnies!!! Atteberry, Kevan, illus. (p. 242)
Atteberry, Kevan, illus. see Fields, Bryan W.
Atteberry, Kevan, illus. see Gunnufson, Charlotte.
Atteberry, Kevan, illus. see Schaefer, Lola M.
Atteberry, Kevan J., illus. see Bissett, Josie.
Attebury, Nancy Garhan. Out & about at City Hall. Trover, Zachary, illus. (p. 1310)
—Out & about at the Hospital. Trover, Zachary, illus. (p. 1310)
Attema, Martha. Paper Wagon Ross, Graham, illus. (p. 1323)
—Paper Wagon. Ross, Graham, illus. (p. 1323)
—Time to Choose. (p. 1753)
Attenborough, David, jt. auth. see Coast, John.
Attia, Caroline, illus. see Guanci, Anne Marie.
Attia, Stephan. Other Christmas Stories. (p. 1306)
Atticus, C. J. Stranded in Space: The Stellar Life of Jpeg the Robot Dog. Dornschke, Angelika, illus. (p. 1664)
Attinger, Billy. Baby's First Little Book of Prayers. (p. 129)
Atto. Non Non Biyori Vol. 2. (p. 1263)
Attoe, Steve, illus. see Becker, Helaine.
Attrache, Ismael, tr. see Taylor, G. P.
Attwell, James M. Barrie - Mabel Lucie, jt. auth. see Barrie, J. M.
Attwell, Nancy J. Fool's Path. (p. 614)
Attwood, Sarah. Making Sense of Sex: A Forthright Guide to Puberty, Sex & Relationships for People with Asperger's Syndrome. Powell, Jonathan, illus. (p. 1082)
Atwal, Jeet, et al. Children Map the World: Selections from the Barbara Petchenik Children's World Map Competition. Wood, Alberta Auringer, ed. (p. 302)
Atwal, Sam. Paper Cars. (p. 1322)
Atwal, Shalini. Mighty U. S. Mountains. (p. 1140)
Atwarie, Rossi. Adventures of Fox Brown. Bachan, Krystal Ann, illus. (p. 18)
Atwater, Florence, jt. auth. see Atwater, Richard.
Atwater, Jillene. Small & Sassy. DeBroeck, Sarah, illus. (p. 1591)
Atwater, Richard. Mr. Popper's Penguins. (p. 1186)
Atwater, Richard & Atwater, Florence. Mr. Popper's Penguins. (p. 1186)
Atwater-Rhodes, Amelia. Bloodwitch (p. 201)
—Den of Shadows Quartet. (p. 426)
—Falcondance. (p. 565)
—Hawksong. (p. 755)
—Midnight Predator. (p. 1139)
—Persistence of Memory. (p. 1344)
—Poison Tree. (p. 1377)
—Promises to Keep. (p. 1411)
—Shapeshifters: The Kiesha'ra of the Den of Shadows. (p. 1561)
—Snakecharm. (p. 1596)
—Token of Darkness. (p. 1762)
—Wolfcry. (p. 1944)
—Wyvernhail (p. 1966)
Atwell, A. Erika Laura. (p. 533)
Atwell, Debby, illus. see Pinborough, Jan.
Atwood, D. E. If We Shadows. (p. 854)

Atwood, Frederick D. Rocks & Minerals - Pb: A Portrait of the Natural World. (p. 1483)
Atwood, Grace. Meet Nancy Bird Walton. Slaghekke, Harry, illus. (p. 1121)
Atwood, John H., jt. auth. see Baynes, Jenean Atwood.
Atwood, Julie, jt. auth. see Robinson, P. J.
Atwood, Karen. Bible Coloring Book. (p. 175)
—Counting 1-25. (p. 370)
—Halloween Coloring Book. (p. 737)
—Valentine Activity Book. (p. 1830)
Atwood, Kathryn J. Women Heroes of World War II: 26 Stories of Espionage, Sabotage, Resistance, & Rescue. (p. 1945)
Atwood, Kathryn J., jt. auth. see Cornioley, Pearl Witherington.
Atwood, Margaret. Up in the Tree (p. 1824)
Atwood, Megan. Balancing Bears: Comparing Numbers. Holm, Sharon, illus. (p. 133)
—Bridge of Death. (p. 227)
—Busy Beavers: Counting By 5s. Holm, Sharon, illus. (p. 245)
—Cailyn & Chloe Learn about Conjunctions. (p. 252)
—Cailyn & Chloe Learn about Conjunctions. Haus, Estudio, illus. (p. 252)
—Connor & Clara Build a Concrete Poem. Butler, Reginald, illus. (p. 358)
—Cuddly Kittens: Discovering Fractions. Holm, Sharon, illus. (p. 389)
—Cursed Ballet. (p. 395)
—Haunting of Apartment 101. (p. 754)
—How to Face Paint. Oseid, Kelsey, illus. (p. 819)
—Last Desserts. (p. 977)
—Leaping at Shadows. (p. 982)
—Living with Autism. (p. 1042)
—Mayhem on Mohawk Avenue. (p. 1113)
—Monarch Migration: Counting by 10s. Holm, Sharon, illus. (p. 1163)
—Patrick & Paula Learn about Prepositions. Otero, Sole, illus. (p. 1329)
—Piglets Playing: Counting from 11 To 20. Holm, Sharon, illus. (p. 1358)
—Sparrows Singing: Discovering Addition & Subtraction. Holm, Sharon, illus. (p. 1622)
—Stay in the Game. (p. 1645)
—Stolen Luck. (p. 1652)
—Terror of Black Eagle Tavern. (p. 1722)
—Twin Dangers. (p. 1801)
Atwood, Peggy. Levi Jackson the Littlest Gold Prospector & His Donkey Dilbert. (p. 1004)
Atwood, Roger. Stealing History: Tomb Raiders, Smugglers, & the Looting of the Ancient World. (p. 1646)
Atxaga, Bernardo & Costa, Margaret Jull. Adventures of Shola. Valverde, Mikel, illus. (p. 22)
Au, Kathryn. Super Qar for Test-Wise Students: Grade 4 Kit. (p. 1680)
—Super Qar for Test-Wise Students: Grade 5 Kit. (p. 1680)
—Super Qar for Test-Wise Students: Grade 6 Kit. (p. 1680)
—Super Qar for Test-Wise Students: Grade 7 Kit. (p. 1680)
—Super Qar for Test-Wise Students: Grade 8 Kit. (p. 1680)
—Super Qar for Test-Wise Students: Grade 2 5-Pack (p. 1680)
—Super Qar for Test-Wise Students: Grade 3 5-Pack (p. 1680)
—Super Qar for Test-Wise Students: Grade 4 5-Pack (p. 1680)
—Super Qar for Test-Wise Students: Grade 5 5-Pack (p. 1680)
—Super Qar for Test-Wise Students: Grade 6 5-Pack (p. 1680)
—Super Qar for Test-Wise Students: Grade 7 5-Pack (p. 1680)
—Super Qar for Test-Wise Students: Grade 8 5-Pack (p. 1680)
—Super Qar for Test-Wise Students: Grade 1, 5-Pack (p. 1680)
Au, May Parker. Princess Huilua & Kamapuaa. (p. 1404)
Auberson, Blaise, illus. see Auberson, Kim.
Auberson, Kim. Eddy the Electron Goes Solar: A Fun & Educational Story about Photovoltaics. Auberson, Blaise, illus. (p. 504)
Aubert, Elena G., illus. see Editorial, Equipo.
Aubin, Antoine, illus. see Van Hamme, Jean.
Aubin, Henry T. Rise of the Golden Cobra. Taylor, Stephen, illus. (p. 1475)
Auborn, Jodi. Secrets of the North Country: The Hobo's Story. (p. 1545)
Aubrey, Meg Kelleher, illus. see Baglio, Ben M.
Aubuchon, Hope L. Tiger, Ruler of the Universe. (p. 1748)
Auch, Alison. All about Temperature (p. 43)
—Life in the Desert (p. 1011)
—Todo Sobre la Temperatura. (p. 1761)
Auch, Allison. Electrifying Personalities: Set Of 6. (p. 509)
—Electrifying Personalities & Personalidades Electrizantes: 6 English, 6 Spanish Adaptations. (p. 509)
—Women Who Dared: Set Of 6. (p. 1946)
—Women Who Dared & Mujeres que se Atrevieron: 6 English, 6 Spanish Adaptations. (p. 1946)
Auch, Herm, illus. see Auch, Mary Jane.
Auch, Herm, tr. see Auch, Mary Jane.
Auch, M. J. Guitar Boy. (p. 731)
—One Plus One Equals Blue. (p. 1296)
—One-Handed Catch. (p. 1295)
—Wing Nut. (p. 1936)
Auch, Mary Jane. Ashes of Roses. (p. 105)
—Beauty & the Beaks: A Turkey's Cautionary Tale. Auch, Herm, illus. (p. 154)
—Beauty & the Beaks: A Turkey's Cautionary Tale. Auch, Herm & Auch, Mary Jane, illus. (p. 154)
—Buk Buk Buk Festival. Auch, Herm, illus. (p. 240)
—Chickerella. Auch, Herm, tr. (p. 301)
—Chickerella. Auch, Herm, illus. (p. 301)
—Dog on His Own. (p. 461)
—I Was a Third Grade Bodyguard. Auch, Herm, illus. (p. 848)
—I Was a Third Grade Spy. Auch, Herm, illus. (p. 848)
—Journey to Nowhere. (p. 929)
—One-Handed Catch. (p. 1295)
—Plot Chickens. Auch, Mary Jane, illus. (p. 1374)
—Plot Chickens. Auch, Mary Jane & Auch, Herm, illus. (p. 1374)
—Poultrygeist. Jane, Mary & Auch, Herm, illus. (p. 1389)
—Souperchicken. Auch, Herm, illus. (p. 1615)
Auchter, Chris, illus. see Denny, Elizabeth.
Auchter, Christopher, illus. see Wheeler, Jordan.
Auclair, Joan, illus. see Oppenheim, Joanne F. & Oppenheim, Stephanie.
Aucoin, Lee. Mi Comunidad. (p. 1132)
—My Community. (p. 1200)
—Todo Sobre Mí. (p. 1761)
—Todo Sobre Mi. (p. 1761)
—Weather. (p. 1869)
Aucoin, Lee, jt. auth. see Rice, Dona Herweck.
Auden, Scott. Medical Mysteries: Science Researches Conditions from Bizarre to Deadly. (p. 1118)
—New Hampshire 1603-1776. (p. 1245)
Audet, Martine. Que Ferais-Je du Jour? Sylvestre, Daniel, tr. (p. 1423)
Audet, Patrice, jt. auth. see Villeneuve, Marie-Paule.
Audho, Gaitree. Moral Stories for Kids. (p. 1173)
Audia, John P. Creation Story: In Words & Sign Language. Spohn, David, illus. (p. 379)
Audibert, Tara. Matthew Loses His Laugh. (p. 1109)
Audio. Ne Vous Noyez Pas dans une Verre D'Eau. (p. 1238)
Audio & Kidzup Productions Staff. Best Toddler Songbook. (p. 171)
Audouin, Laurent. Keeping It Green! (p. 947)
Audouin, Laurent, illus. see Gamonal, Dulce.
Audouin-Mamikonian, Princess Sophie. Tara Duncan & the Forbidden Book. Rodarmor, William, tr. from FRE. (p. 1706)
—Tara Duncan & the Spellbinders. Rodarmor, Williams, tr. (p. 1706)
Audrey, Colman, illus. see Kotzwinkle, William & Murray, Glenn.
Audrey, Crosby, illus. see Clark, Lucinda.
Audureau, William, jt. auth. see Petronille, Marc.
Auer, Chris. Legend of the Sand Dollar: An Inspirational Story of Hope for Easter Johnson, Rick, illus. (p. 989)
Auer, Jim. Catholic Teen's Guide to Tough Stuff: Straight Talk, Real Issues Art of Choosing Well. (p. 280)
—Handbook for Today's Catholic Teen. (p. 740)
—Know How to Say No to Drugs & Alcohol: A Kid's Guide. (p. 965)
—Standing up to Peer Pressure: A Guide to Being True to You. Alley, R. W., illus. (p. 1639)
Auer, Lois, illus. see Cerone, Diane.
Auerbach, Adam. Edda: A Little Valkyrie's First Day of School. Auerbach, Adam, illus. (p. 503)
Auerbach, Andrea. Dinnertime. (p. 441)
Auerbach, Annie. Attack of the Boggans. (p. 113)
—Cindy Big Hair: A Twisted (and Teased & Braided) Cinderella Story. Maxey, David, illus. (p. 321)
—Despicable Me. (p. 430)
—Eight Chanukah Lights. Iwai, Melissa, illus. (p. 507)
—Epic. (p. 532)
—Grosse Adventures - Trouble at Twilight Cave. (p. 725)
—Hall Monitor (p. 737)
—Horseland - If the Horseshoe Fits. (p. 800)
—Junkyard Dig! Building from A to Z. Shannon, David et al, illus. (p. 936)
—Meet Boulder the Construction-Bot. (p. 1120)
—My Race into Space! A Water Wonder Book. Garofoli, Viviana, illus. (p. 1217)
—Naughty Nautical Neighbors (p. 1237)
—Police on Patrol. Redondo, Jesus & Ivan & Moxo, illus. (p. 1380)
—Pop Goes the Weasel: A Silly Song Book. Gaisey, Christopher, illus. (p. 1384)
—Sinbad: Legend of the Seven Seas Pop-up. McMahon, Brad, illus. (p. 1578)
—Small Fry. Disney Storybook Artists Staff, illus. (p. 1592)
—Spongebob Superstar (p. 1630)
—Squeakquel: Battle of the Bands. (p. 1636)
—Transformers: Rescue Bots: Meet Boulder the Construction-Bot. (p. 1778)
—Traveling in Two's: The Journey to Noah's Ark. Dillard, Sarah, illus. (p. 1780)
—Welcome to Moonhaven. (p. 1873)
—Where's the Chick? Counting Book. Whitehead, Paul, illus. (p. 1910)
Auerbach, Annie, jt. auth. see Disney Book Group Staff.
Auerbach, Annie, jt. auth. see Feldman, Thea.
Auerbach, Annie, jt. auth. see HarperCollins Publishers Ltd. Staff.
Auerbach, Annie, jt. auth. see RH Disney Staff.
Auerbach, Annie, jt. auth. see Rosen, Lucy.
Auerbach, Annie, jt. text see Mayer, Kirsten.
Auerbach, Annie, adapted by. Despicable Me 2: The Junior Novel. (p. 430)
Auerbach, Annie & Berrios, Frank. Off-Road Racers!/Crash Course! RH Disney Staff, illus. (p. 1279)
Auerbach, Annie & Disney Book Group Staff. Air Mater. Disney Storybook Artists Staff, illus. (p. 31)
—P Is for Princess. Disney Storybook Artists Staff, illus. (p. 1316)
Auerbach, Annie & Mike, Norton. Grosse Adventures - The Good, the Bad & the Gassy (p. 725)
Auerbach, Annie & PopCap Games Staff. Plants vs. Zombies: Brains & the Beanstalk. Grosvenor, Charles & Roberts, Jeremy, illus. (p. 1370)
—Three Little Pigs Fight Back. Grosvenor, Charles & Roberts, Jeremy, illus. (p. 1743)
Auerbach, Joshua. Baby Shadows Auerbach, Joshua, illus. (p. 128)
Aufmann, Richard N. Clast Prep Guide: Used with ... Aufmann-Mathematical Excursions. (p. 329)
—Essentials of College Algebra. (p. 537)
—Exploring Intermediate Algebra: A Graphing Approach. (p. 552)
Aufmann, Richard N. & Nation, Richard D. Essentials of College Algebra. (p. 537)
—Essentials of Precalculus. (p. 537)
—Nation's Essentials of Precalculus. (p. 1234)
Aufmann, Richard N., et al. Beginning Algebra with Applications Student Solutions Manual. (p. 159)
—Exploring Intermediate Algebra: A Graphing Approach. (p. 552)
Augarde, Steve. Celandine. (p. 283)
—Garage: A Pop-up Book. Augarde, Steve, illus. (p. 655)
—Winter Wood. (p. 1938)
Augello, Barbara. Dogs. (p. 462)
Augenstein, Marianne R. Quest for Kair (p. 1426)
Auger, Dale. Mwâkwa Talks to the Loon: A Cree Story for Children Auger, Dale, illus. (p. 1195)
Aughe, Roger, illus. see Hildreth, Joann R.
Aughe, Roger, illus. see Hildreth, Ruth Erixon.
Augsburger, A. Don. World Is a Beautiful Place. Ressler-Horst, Lara, illus. (p. 1956)
Augspurger, Eric K. & Fisher, Blake J. 3ds Max & Its Applications, Release 5. (p. 1992)
Augusseau, Stphanie, illus. see Vallat, Christelle.
August, Elaine. Fira Gani: An Earthly Fable. (p. 590)
—It Only Snows in Brooklyn. (p. 894)
—Southern Mischief. (p. 1617)
August, Elaine Schiller. Southern Mischief. (p. 1617)
August House Publishers Staff. August House Book of Scary Stories: Spooky Tales for Telling Out Loud. Parkhurst, Liz, ed. (p. 115)
August, Rachel. Adventures of Libby Nickel: Why Are There Colors? (p. 19)
—Adventures of Libby Nickel: What's your Mommy's First Name? (p. 19)
—Journey of My Untied Shoes. (p. 928)
Augustin, Byron. Andorra. (p. 72)
—Food of Mexico. (p. 613)
—Panama. (p. 1320)
—Paraguay. (p. 1323)
Augustin, Byron & Kubena, Jake. Grand Canyon. (p. 707)
—Yellowstone National Park. (p. 1970)
Augustin, Lucus. Traeh: The Portal. (p. 1776)
Augustin, Yvonne. Rag Doll Tales. (p. 1433)
Augustine, Kristen. Can I Tell You? (p. 258)
Augustine, Peg. Boys Can Be Angels Too & Three Other Christmas Dramas: Easy Dramas, Speeches & Recitations for Children. (p. 220)
—Christmas A to Z. (p. 312)
—Family Time with God: Bible Story Activities for Every Day. (p. 569)
—O Come, All Ye Faithful. Ludlow, Patricia, illus. (p. 1274)
—One Suprising Night/una Noche Sorprendente! Vargas, Emmanuel, tr. (p. 1297)
Augustine, Peg & Flegal, Daphna. Alphabet Rhymes for Bible Times. Easter, Paige, illus. (p. 50)
Augustine, Peg & Vargas, Emmanuel. Take Time for Easter/Descubre la Semana Santa. (p. 1697)
Augustine, Peg, ed. Read to Me: Bible Stories for Preschoolers. (p. 1443)
—Read with Me: Bible Stories for First Readers. (p. 1444)
—Young Reader's Bible Dictionary. (p. 1979)
Augustine, Peggy. It Looks A Lot Like Christmas. (p. 894)
—It Looks A Lot Like Easter. (p. 894)
—Promise of Christmas. (p. 1411)
—Starlit Night. (p. 1642)
Augustine, Saint. Take Time for Christmas Descubre la Navidad. (p. 1697)
Augustyn, Adam. Britannica Guide to Basketball. (p. 229)
Augustyn, Adam, jt. auth. see Day, Meredith.
Augustyn, Brian. Beowulf: Life in the Big City. (p. 166)
—Gotham by Gaslight. Russell, P. Craig & Barreto, Eduardo, illus. (p. 704)
Augustyn, Heather. Chi-Town Coyote. (p. 299)
Auh, Yoonil. Guide to Practicing Repertoire: Level 1 Auh, Yoonil, ed. (p. 730)
—Guide to Practicing Repertoire: Level 2 Auh, Yoonil, ed. (p. 730)
Auh, Yoon-Il. Pre-School Virtuoso (p. 1394)
Auh, Yoonil. Representation Music: A New Approch to Creating Sound & Representing Music. Auh, Yoonil, ed. (p. 1461)
—Representation Music. Auh, Yoonil, ed. (p. 1461)
—Singing Hand: Study of Vibrato. Auh, Yoonil, ed. (p. 1579)
Aukerman, Robert J., illus. see Hoog, Mark E.
Aukerman, Robert J., illus. see Hoog, Mark.
Aulbach, Kathy. ABC's. (p. 3)
—Flower Sprouts: Let's have a Fest! (p. 607)
—Meet the Flowers. (p. 1122)
Auld, Francis, illus. see Mathias, Adeline.
Auld, Mary. Celebrating a Birthday. (p. 284)
—Going on Vacation. (p. 692)
—Meet the Family (p. 1122)
—Mi Hermana. Coffey, Colleen & Carrillo, Consuelo, trs. from ENG. (p. 1132)
—Mi hermano (My Brother) Coffey, Colleen & Carrillo, Consuelo, trs. from ENG. (p. 1132)
—Mi Mamá. Coffey, Colleen & Carrillo, Consuelo, trs. from ENG. (p. 1132)
—Mi Papa. Carrillo, Consuelo & Coffey, Colleen, trs. from ENG. (p. 1133)
—Mis Abuelos. Carrillo, Consuelo & Coffey, Colleen, trs. from ENG. (p. 1149)
—Mis Tíos. Carrillo, Consuelo & Coffey, Colleen, trs. from ENG. (p. 1150)
—My Aunt & Uncle. (p. 1196)
—My Brother. (p. 1199)
—My Dad. (p. 1200)
—My Grandparents. (p. 1210)
—My Mom. (p. 1214)
—My Sister. (p. 1218)
—Sharing a Meal. (p. 1561)
—Welcoming a New Baby. (p. 1874)
Auld, Susan B. Waiting Innocence. (p. 1853)
Aulenback, Stephany. If I Wrote a Book about You. Holmes, Denise, illus. (p. 853)
Ault, Dane, illus. see Hammond, Ashlie.
AULT, Jane M., concept. Heart Connections: Finding Joy through Openness with God. (p. 759)
Ault, Kelly. Let's Sign, Baby! A Fun & Easy Way to Talk with Baby. Landry, Leo, illus. (p. 1000)
Aumann, Jane, jt. auth. see Ladage, Cindy.
Aumann, Jane & Ladage, Cindy. Christmas Tractor. Freitag, Charles, illus. (p. 316)
Auml, Ana, illus. see Lewicki, Krys Val.
Aumuller, Kimberly. Dragon's Hope: Tale of the Guardians. (p. 479)
Aunt Connye. Club House: Stories that Teach. (p. 335)
—Riding Game. (p. 1471)
Aunt Darla. There's a Monster under the Captain's Bed!!! Erik's Monster. Petersen, Darla & Shields, Erik P., illus. (p. 1731)
Aunt Fezzle. Happy-Feliz & Fatso's Heroic School Adventures: Heroes vs. Bullies. (p. 745)
Aunt Judy. Chickens in the Know! Chickens of Different Occupations. Aunt Judy, illus. (p. 300)
—Chickens on the Go! Chickens from different locations around the World. Aunt Judy, illus. (p. 300)
—Chickens on the go! coloring Book. (p. 300)
Aunt Julie. Paddleduck # ABC. (p. 1317)
—Paddleduck! #2: Julie, Living in Texas. (p. 1317)
Auntie Annie. Knute: Dreams of Africa. (p. 966)
—Knute: In the Magical Meadow. (p. 966)
—Knute: Meets Mike in the Magical Meadow. (p. 966)
Auntie Nana. Falling off My Bike. (p. 567)
—Falling off My Bike with Cd. (p. 567)
Aunty Moose, jt. auth. see Aunty Moose, Moose.
Aunty Moose, Moose & Aunty Moose. Gift of a Lifetime. (p. 675)
Aureliani, Franco. Dino-Mike! Aureliani, Franco, illus. (p. 441)
—Dino-Mike & the Jurassic Portal. Aureliani, Franco, illus. (p. 441)
—Dino-Mike & the Museum Mayhem. (p. 441)
—Dino-Mike & the Museum Mayhem. Aureliani, Franco, illus. (p. 441)
—Dino-Mike & the T. Rex Attack. Aureliani, Franco, illus. (p. 441)
—Dino-Mike & the Underwater Dinosaurs. Aureliani, Franco, illus. (p. 441)
Aureliani, Franco, jt. auth. see Baltazar, Art.
Aureliani, Franco, jt. creator see Baltazar, Art.
Aureliani, Franco & Art Baltazar Comic Book Staff. Tiny Titans - Welcome to the Treehouse. (p. 1757)
Aureliani, Franco & Baltazar, Art. Patrick the Wolf Boy. (p. 1329)
Ausbeth-Ajagu, Anuli C. King's Verdict. (p. 961)
Ausburg. Story of the Advent Wreath. (p. 1660)
Auseon, Andrew. Freak Magnet. (p. 631)
—Funny Little Monkey. (p. 650)
—Jo-Jo & the Fiendish Lot. (p. 919)
Auseon, Andrew, jt. auth. see Russell, David O.
Ausona, Roberto De. Robin Hood. (p. 1479)
Austen, Amy. Endangered Animals: Develop Understanding of Fractions & Numbers. (p. 526)
—Life Cycle of a Kangaroo. (p. 1009)
—Look Out for the Dingo! (p. 1049)
—Puffins. (p. 1415)
Austen, Catherine. 26 Tips for Surviving Grade 6 (p. 1996)
—All Good Children (p. 44)
—My Cat Isis. Egger, Virginie, illus. (p. 1200)
—Walking Backward (p. 1854)
Austen, Chuck. Pain of the Gods (p. 1318)
Austen, Chuck, jt. auth. see Jones, Bruce.
Austen, Chuck, jt. auth. see Millar, Mark.
Austen, Chuck & Finn, J. D. In the Name of Gog. (p. 866)
Austen, Chuck & Uy, Steve. Eden's Trail. (p. 504)
Austen, Elizabeth. Baby Animals. (p. 124)
—Living! (p. 1040)
—Seeds. (p. 1547)
—What Do Living Things Need? (p. 1882)
Austen, Jane. Complete Novels of Jane Austen: Emma, Pride & Prejudice, Sense & Sensibility, Northanger Abbey, Mansfield Park, Persuasion, & Lady Susan Oakley, Jacqui, illus. (p. 353)
—Emma. (p. 519)
—Pride & Prejudice. Miralles, Joseph, illus. (p. 1398)
—Pride & Prejudice. (p. 1399)
—Pride & Prejudice. Kronheimer, Ann, illus. (p. 1399)
—Sense & Sensibility. (p. 1551)
—Sense & Sensibility. Kronheimer, Ann, illus. (p. 1551)
Austen, Jane, jt. auth. see Coombs, Kate.
Austen, Jane & Stabler, Jane. Mansfield Park. Kinsley, James, ed. (p. 1088)
Austen, Jane, et al. Sense & Sensibility. Kinsley, James, ed. (p. 1551)
Austen, Mary. Andromeda. (p. 72)
—Ayudantes de la Comunidad / Helping the Community Set. (p. 121)
—I Can Add! Understanding Addition. (p. 834)
—Que Hacen Los Bibliotecarios? / What Do Librarians Do? (p. 1423)
—We Live in a Small Town. (p. 1867)
—What Do Librarians Do? (p. 1882)
Austen, Peter. Everest Canada: The Climb for Hope. (p. 542)
Auster, Michael A. Stone Is Strong! (p. 1652)
—They Led the Way. (p. 1732)
Austic, Greg. Game Design. (p. 654)
Austin, Adam J. 14th Cycle. (p. 1995)
Austin, Antoinette & Austin, John. Little Lobo Who Lost His Howl. Austin, Antoinette & Wooten, Neal, illus. (p. 1030)
Austin, Britta, ed. see Glover, Darryl.
Austin, Cassandra. Born Right Here at Home. (p. 214)
Austin, Cassie Rita. Peppermint. Austin, Cassie Rita, illus. (p. 1340)
Austin, D. & Borgstedt, John. Dinosaurs A 2 Z: The Age of the Dinosaurs. (p. 444)
Austin, Denise. Pilates for Every Body: Strengthen, Lengthen, & Tone— with This Complete 3-Week Body Makeover. (p. 1358)
—Shrink Your Female Fat Zones: Lose Pounds & Inches — Fast! — from Your Belly, Hips, Thighs, & More. (p. 1571)
Austin, Diane Vaughan. Hideout: A Child's Conversations with Jesus. (p. 777)
Austin, Emily Munyungka, jt. auth. see Wingfield, Eileen Wanl.
Austin, Glenda. More Christmas Classics. (p. 1174)
Austin, Heather. Boatyard Ducklings. Austin, Heather, illus. (p. 205)
Austin, Heather, illus. see Perrow, Angeli.
Austin, Howard, jt. auth. see Howard, Elisabeth.
Austin, Jamie Lea-Elizabeth. Reverie. (p. 1466)
Austin, Jeanne J. Unlikely Friends. (p. 1821)

A

Austin, John, jt. auth. see Austin, Antoinette.
Austin, Judi. How Many Cookies? Learning to Subtract 1 from One-Digit Numbers. (p. 811)
—Making My Breakfast: Learning the Sequential Steps of a Process. (p. 1082)
Austin, K. B. Old Mother Turtle & the Three Frogs. (p. 1284)
Austin, Karen D. Jay Jay & the Broken Picture Frame. (p. 910)
Austin, Kate. Everlasting: The Kingdom Key. (p. 542)
Austin, Megan, jt. auth. see Riley, Lehman.
Austin, Michael, illus. see Crunk, Tony.
Austin, Michael, illus. see Deedy, Carmen Agra.
Austin, Michael, illus. see Reiss, Mike & Reiss, Mike.
Austin, Michael Allen. London Bridge Is Falling Down. Austin, Michael Allen, illus. (p. 1046)
Austin, Michael Allen, illus. see Cummins, Julie.
Austin, Michael Allen, illus. see Grandits, John.
Austin, Michael Allen, illus. see Mortensen, Lori.
Austin, Mike. Countdown with Milo & Mouse. (p. 370)
—Fire Engine No. 9. (p. 590)
—Junkyard. Austin, Mike, illus. (p. 936)
—Monsters Love Colors. Austin, Mike, illus. (p. 1169)
—Monsters Love School. Austin, Mike, illus. (p. 1169)
—Where Is Milo's Ball? (p. 1908)
Austin, Mike, illus. see Christopher, Neil.
Austin, Mykel. Pain in the Arms of Joy: Thoughts of a Borderline Personality. (p. 1318)
Austin, Norma J. Baby's Bedtime Poems: Sleepy Time Rhymes. (p. 128)
Austin, Phyllis, et al, eds. On Wilderness: Voices from Maine. (p. 1292)
Austin, Richard. Pocket Piggies Colors! The Teacup Pigs of Pennywell Farm. Austin, Richard, photos by. (p. 1375)
—Pocket Piggies Numbers! Featuring the Teacup Pigs of Pennywell Farm. Austin, Richard, photos by. (p. 1375)
Austin, Rikey. Captain's Treasure: Alice's Bear Shop. (p. 264)
—Chunky & the Bone: Alice's Bear Shop. (p. 318)
—Cobby Goes for a Swim: Alice's Bear Shop. (p. 336)
—Sandy Paints a Picture: Alice's Bear Shop. (p. 1511)
—Tat Gets a Patch: Alice's Bear Shop. (p. 1707)
—Tilly & the Magic Wand: Alice's Bear Shop. (p. 1750)
—Ting Finds a Bell: Alice's Bear Shop. (p. 1755)
—Woodroffe Growls Again: Alice's Bear Shop. (p. 1949)
Austin, Sherlan. Betrayal. (p. 171)
—Kings & a Queen Biblical Timeline with Maps. (p. 960)
Austin, Su. Saltems House Mystery. (p. 1505)
Austin, Tereasa, illus. see McDaniel, Paula.
Austin, Terry, illus. see Dini, Paul.
Austin, Terry, illus. see McCloud, Scott.
Austin, Terry, illus. see Torres, J.
Austin, Terry, jt. auth. see Claremont, Chris.
Austin-Lockhart, Lora. Raindrop Rewards. (p. 1436)
Austin-Smith, Toshiba. I'm Not Your Friend, Mommy. (p. 859)
—Mom, Where's My Father? Substituting Lack with Completeness. (p. 1161)
Australian Museum Archives Staff, jt. auth. see McEvey, Shane F.
Australian Women's Weekly Staff, jt. auth. see Tomnay, Susan.
Austrew, Neva, illus. see Jacobs, Breena.
Auth, Jeannine. Emmy's Question. (p. 520)
Auth, Tony, illus. see Heide, Florence Parry.
Auth, Tony, illus. see Pinkwater, Daniel M.
Auth, Tony, illus. see Rees, Douglas.
Authement, Louise. Diaries of the Fifth Grade Miseries. (p. 434)
Authords, D. K. Being Alone. (p. 161)
Autio, Karen. Saara's Passage (p. 1499)
—Sabotage (p. 1500)
—Second Watch (p. 1540)
Autismfighter. Smunkarellies: Through the Eyes of Children. (p. 1595)
Automobile Association (Great Britain) Staff. AA the Garden Bird Kit. (p. 2)
Autrey, Jacquelyn & Yeager, Alice. U.S. Presidents & Their Animal Friends. Passarella, Jennie, illus. (p. 1826)
Autrey, Nathan W. Purple Penguin Pumpkin Party. (p. 1419)
Autry, Gene. Gene Autry & the Land Grab Mystery. (p. 660)
—Gene Autry Comics V1, No 58, December 1951: The Mysterious Arrows. (p. 660)
—Gene Autry Comics, V1, No 73, March 1953: The Double Game. (p. 660)
Autry, Gene & Haldeman, Dakley. Here Comes Santa Claus. Whatley, Bruce, illus. (p. 770)
Autumn Publishing, jt. auth. see Duck Egg Blue.
Autumn Publishing, Autumn. Party Animals! — Kitten Paper Dolls. (p. 1326)
—Party Animals! — Pony Paper Dolls. (p. 1326)
Autumn Publishing Staff. ABC Learning. (p. 3)
—Adding Up. (p. 11)
—Learn the Alphabet. (p. 983)
—My Skeleton. (p. 1218)
—Numbers 1-100. (p. 1272)
—Solar System. (p. 1607)
—Times Table Wall Chart. (p. 1754)
—World Map. (p. 1956)
—World of Flags. (p. 1956)
Autumn Publishing Staff, illus. see Byeway Wall Charts Staff.
Autumn Publishing Staff, jt. auth. see Duck Egg Blue (Firm) Staff.
Auty, Rob. Hare's Tale 2 - the Golden Hare. Wood, Chaz, illus. (p. 748)
Auty, Robert C. Hare's Tale. (p. 748)
Auvil, Ronnie J. HVAC Control Systems: Answer Key. (p. 830)
—HVAC Control Systems. (p. 830)
Auville, Maggie. Daisy Drew Who Always Knew What to Do. (p. 400)
Auxier, Bryan. Three Days & Four Knights. Daniels, Regina, illus. (p. 1742)
—Where Have All the Fairies Gone? Ramey, Cindy, illus. (p. 1907)
—Where Have All the Unicorns Gone? Daniels, Regina, illus. (p. 1907)
Auxier, Jonathan. Night Gardener. (p. 1253)
—Peter Nimble & His Fantastic Eyes. (p. 1346)
Auzary-Luton, Sylvie, jt. auth. see Pottie, Marjolein.
Auzou Publishing Staff, jt. auth. see Pero, Denis.
Avakian, Arlene Voski, ed. Through the Kitchen Window: Women Explore the Intimate Meanings of Food & Cooking. (p. 1745)
Avakoff, Caroline, ed. see Ellis, Colette.
Avakyan, Tatevik, illus. see Dadey, Debbie.
Avakyan, Tatevik, illus. see Heron, Jackie.
Avakyan, Tatevik, illus. see Higgins, Nadia.
Avakyan, Tatevik, illus. see Kesselring, Susan.
Avakyan, Tatevik, illus. see Loewen, Nancy, et al.
Avakyan, Tatevik, illus. see Loewen, Nancy.
Avalon, Dawn. Bubbels. Een Vochtig Draakje. (p. 233)
—Bubbles. A Wet Dragon. (p. 233)
Avalone, C., jt. auth. see Rouss, Sylvia.
Avalon-Pai, Phyllis. Children's Stories from Around the World. Arrott, Nancy, illus. (p. 304)
Avalos, Cecilia O. Sombrero de Luis Lucero. (p. 1608)
Avalos, Francisco. Amazon Tale. (p. 56)
Avant, Matthew, illus. see Weis, Michael David.
Avanti, Michele. GreeHee the Journey of Five: Tales of Tamoor Book One. (p. 720)
Avasthi, Swati. Chasing Shadows. Phillips, Craig, illus. (p. 294)
—Split. (p. 1630)
Avasti, Smita. Day by Day: The Nineties. (p. 412)
Ave Maria Press, creator. Francis of Assisi: Living Fortitude. (p. 628)
—Therese of Lisieux: Living Justice. (p. 1731)
Avedikian, Linda, jt. auth. see Gigarjian, Ani.
Avedissian, Chant, jt. auth. see Issa, Rose.
Aveline, Erick & Chargueraud, Joyce. Temporary Tattoos. (p. 1718)
Avelino, Kawehi. No Ka Ilio Moo. (p. 1258)
Avelynn, Kate. Flawed. (p. 603)
Aven, Jamie H., illus. see Wallace, Susan F. S. P. & Wright, Melissa.
Aven, Jamie H., illus. see Wallace, Susan Helen & Wright, Melissa.
Avendano, Dolores, illus. see Farina von Buchwald, Martin & Prado Farina, Gabriela.
Avengers Staff, et al. Meet Captain America No. 2. (p. 1120)
Aveni, Anthony. Buried Beneath Us: Discovering the Ancient Cities of the Americas. Roy, Katherine, illus. (p. 243)
Avera, Randy. Truth about Challenger. (p. 1794)
Averbeck, Jim. Except If. Averbeck, Jim, illus. (p. 547)
—Hitch at the Fairmont. Bertozzi, Nick, illus. (p. 786)
—In a Blue Room. Tusa, Tricia, illus. (p. 862)
—Market Bowl. Averbeck, Jim, illus. (p. 1095)
—Oh No, Little Dragon! Averbeck, Jim, illus. (p. 1281)
—One Word from Sophia. Ismail, Yasmeen, illus. (p. 1297)
Averdonz, N. R., jt. auth. see Kreuger, Jim.
Averdonz, N. R., jt. auth. see Simmons, Andrew.
Averett, Edward. Cameron & the Girls. (p. 256)
Averette, Sonya M. Aunt Ruby's Kisses Proulx, Denis, illus. (p. 115)
Averhoff, Claudia Vellozzi, mem. Tomorrow Raising an Angel. (p. 1765)
Averill, Esther. Captains of the City Streets. Averill, Esther, illus. (p. 264)
—Hotel Cat. Averill, Esther, illus. (p. 802)
—Jenny Goes to Sea. Averill, Esther, illus. (p. 913)
—Jenny's Birthday Book. Averill, Esther, illus. (p. 913)
—Jenny's Moonlight Adventure: A Jenny's Cat Club Book. Averill, Esther, illus. (p. 913)
—Jenny's Moonlight Adventure. (p. 913)
—School for Cats. Averill, Esther, illus. (p. 1522)
Averill, Esther H. Jenny & the Cat Club: A Collection of Favorite Stories about Jenny Linsky. Averill, Esther H., illus. (p. 913)
Averill, Leas, ed. see Powers, Alfred.
Averous, Helene. Jaune. Dumont, Madeleine, illus. (p. 910)
—Rouge. Coevoet, Sylvie, illus. (p. 1491)
—Yellow. Dumont, Madeleine, illus. (p. 1969)
Avery, Al. Yankee Flier in the Far East. Laune, Paul, illus. (p. 1968)
Avery & Stella, jt. auth. see Mason & Marisa.
Avery, Ben. Prophet's Oracle Broome, Mat, illus. (p. 1411)
—Tunnel Twist-Up Gaudiamo, Adi Darda, illus. (p. 1797)
Avery, Ben, jt. auth. see Martin, George R. R.
Avery, Ben, jt. auth. see Rogers, Bud.
Avery, Ben, jt. auth. see Rogers, Buddy.
Avery, Ben & Rogers, Bud. Berlin Breakout Gaudiamo, Adi Darda, illus. (p. 167)
Avery, Ben & Zondervan Publishing Staff. Time Trap Wong, Scott, illus. (p. 1753)
Avery, Ben G. Pyramid Peril Gaudiamo, Adi Darda, illus. (p. 1421)
—Turtle Trouble Gaudiamo, Adi Darda, illus. (p. 1798)
Avery, Carrie L. String of Pearls. (p. 1667)
Avery, Emmajane. Wallace Collection Children's Art Book. (p. 1855)
Avery, Fiona. No Honor. (p. 1258)
Avery, Jessie. She Still Has Flowers in Her Hair: A Soul's Journey to Self. (p. 1564)
Avery, John D. & Fellag, Linda Robinson. College Reading (p. 340)
Avery, Kristin. Colcha de Retazos Flor Ada, Alma, tr. (p. 338)
Avery, Lara. Million Miles Away. (p. 1144)
Avery, Matt, illus. see Crockett, Sonja Michelle.
Avery, Michael. Secret Language of Waking Dreams. (p. 1541)
Avery, Mindi. Faith of Our Founding Father. (p. 565)
Avery, Pat McGrath. They Came Home: Korean War POWs Tell Their Stories. (p. 1732)
—Tommy's War: A Parent Goes to War Ray, Eric, illus. (p. 1765)
Avery, Pat McGrath, see McGrath Avery, Pat.
Avery, Sebastian. Landscaper's Tools. (p. 974)
—Porpoises. (p. 1386)
—School Garden: Reason with Shapes & Their Attributes. (p. 1523)
Avery, Sherrie. Miami Metrozoo. (p. 1134)
Avery, Tammy. Molly's Kat Tales (p. 1161)
Avery, Terry. Who Will Save Mr Squeaky? (p. 1919)
Avery, Tom. In Too Deep. (p. 868)
—My Brother's Shadow. (p. 1199)
—Not As We Know It. (p. 1267)
Avett, Harper. Colony of Massachusetts. (p. 342)
—Go Fly a Kite! Reason with Shapes & Their Attributes. (p. 686)
—Watch Out for Alligators! (p. 1861)
Aveyard, Victoria. Red Queen. (p. 1454)
Avi. Barn. (p. 139)
—Beginning, a Muddle, & an End: The Right Way to Write Writing. Tusa, Tricia, illus. (p. 159)
—Catch You Later, Traitor. (p. 279)
—City of Light, City of Dark. (p. 324)
—City of Light, City of Dark. Floca, Brian, illus. (p. 324)
—City of Orphans. Ruth, Greg, illus. (p. 324)
—Crispin: La Cruz de Plomo. (p. 383)
—Crispin: The Cross of Lead. (p. 383)
—Don't You Know There's a War On? (p. 469)
—End of the Beginning: Being the Adventures of a Small Snail (and an Even Smaller Ant) Tusa, Tricia, illus. (p. 526)
—End of Time (p. 526)
—End of Time. (p. 526)
—Ereth's Birthday. Floca, Brian, illus. (p. 533)
—Escape from Home. (p. 535)
—Fighting Ground. (p. 585)
—Good Dog. (p. 697)
—Into the Storm. (p. 881)
—Magia de Medianoche. (p. 1071)
—Mayor of Central Park. Floca, Brian, illus. (p. 1113)
—Midnight Magic. (p. 1139)
—Murder at Midnight. (p. 1192)
—Nothing but the Truth. (p. 1268)
—Old Wolf. Floca, Brian, illus. (p. 1285)
—Perloo the Bold. (p. 1343)
—Poppy. Floca, Brian, illus. (p. 1385)
—Poppy & Ereth. Floca, Brian, illus. (p. 1385)
—Poppy & Rye. Floca, Brian, illus. (p. 1385)
—Poppy's Return. Floca, Brian, illus. (p. 1385)
—Prairie School. Farnsworth, Bill, illus. (p. 1392)
—Ragweed. Howard, E., ed. (p. 1433)
—Romeo & Juliet Together (and Alive!) at Last. (p. 1486)
—Secret School. (p. 1543)
—Seer of Shadows. (p. 1548)
—Silent Movie. Mordan, C. B., illus. (p. 1575)
—Something Upstairs. (p. 1610)
—Sophia's War: A Tale of the Revolution. (p. 1613)
—Strange Happenings: Five Tales of Transformation. (p. 1665)
—Traitors' Gate. Raude, Karina, illus. (p. 1777)
—True Confessions of Charlotte Doyle. (p. 1792)
—What Do Fish Have to Do with Anything? (p. 1882)
—Who Was That Masked Man, Anyway? (p. 1919)
—Wolf Rider. (p. 1944)
Avi, illus. see Canetti, Yanitzia.
Avi, jt. auth. see Vail, Rachel.
Avi, tr. see Canetti, Yanitzia.
Avi & Vail, Rachel. Never Mind! (p. 1243)
Avi, et al. Acting Out: Six One-Act Plays! Six Newbery Stars! (p. 10)
Avia. Sunshine & Ladybug: In Angel Balloons. (p. 1678)
Aviation Staff. Iron Thunder: The Battle Between the Monitor & the Merrimac. (p. 888)
Avignone, June. Peek into the Secret Little Ones of Turtle Back Island. My Wolf Dog, illus. (p. 1335)
Avila, Adrienne, ed. see Pockell, Leslie M.
Avila, Jesus Villicana, illus. see Cerullo, Claudio V.
Avila, Jorge, illus. see Twain, Mark, pseud.
Avila, Juan Casas. DOS Casos de Casas y Algunas Otras Cosas. Jimenez, Leticia Serrano, illus. (p. 472)
Avila, Kat. Hanako Loves Monsters. (p. 740)
Avila, Nelson Moreno. Boy & the Zoo. (p. 217)
Aviles, Donna Nordmark. Fly Little Bird, Fly! (p. 609)
Avilés, Martha, illus. see Costales, Amy.
Avilés, Martha, illus. see Lakritz, Deborah.
Aviles, Martha, illus. see Londner, Renee.
Aviles, Martha, illus. see Mayer, Pamela.
Aviles, Martha, illus. see McCormack, Caren McNelly.
Avilés, Martha, illus. see Meltzer, Amy.
Aviles, Suzanne M. Oglethorpe's Children. (p. 1280)
Avion, Nicole. Happy Quilt. (p. 746)
—tapiz de felicidad feliz (the Happy Quilt) (p. 1706)
Avison, Brigid. I Wonder Why I Sleep: And Other Questions about My Body. (p. 849)
Avista Products. Blackbook Directory & Yearbook 2010-11: Black Business Year in Review Media Write, ed. (p. 197)
Avital, Moshe. Not to Forget, Impossible to Forgive: Poignant Reflections on the Holocaust. (p. 1267)
Avitan, Amos. Your Life in Trade: A Contractor's Guide to Success. (p. 1981)
Avivi, Karen. Shredded. (p. 1571)
Avlon And Matt. Bronsky the Bat. (p. 230)
Avraham, Kate Aver. What Will You Be, Sara Mee? O'Brien, Anne Sibley, illus. (p. 1895)
Avrameli, Maria, tr. see Crouch, Adele.
Avrech, Robert J. Hebrew Kid & the Apache Maiden. (p. 761)
Avrett, Judy, illus. see Taylor, Janelle.
Avril, Adeline & Gravier, Anne. Little Life of Jesus. (p. 1030)
Avril, Francois, illus. see Rozen, Anna.
Avril, Francois, illus. see Surget, Alain & Hirsinger, Julien.
Avril, Lynne. Five Little Monkeys. (p. 600)
Avril, Lynne, illus. see Abercrombie, Barbara.
Avril, Lynne, illus. see Friedman, Laurie.
Avril, Lynne, illus. see Hallowell, George & Holub, Joan.
Avril, Lynne, illus. see Janni, Rebecca.
Avril, Lynne, illus. see Lyon, George Ella.
Avril, Lynne, illus. see Parish, Herman.
Avril, Lynne, illus. see Singer, Marilyn.
Avril, Lynne, illus. see Stewart, Jennifer J.
Avril, Lynne, illus. see Stier, Catherine.
Avril, Lynne, illus. see Zapf, Marlena.
Awa, Simon, et al. Uumajut: Learn about Arctic Wildlife Caron, Romi, illus. (p. 1829)
—Uumajut: Learn More about Arctic Wildlife! Vol. 2 Otak, Leah, tr. (p. 1829)
Awa, Solomon. Igluvigaliurniq Qamusiurnirlu: How to Build an Iglu & a Qamutiik. Breithaupt, Andrew, illus. (p. 856)
Awad, Shelley. Greenhouse Kids: Dan Dellon's Secret. Zonta, Rose, illus. (p. 723)
Awal, Pia. Travel Math. (p. 1780)
Awalt, Barbe. Don't Touch This Book. (p. 469)
AWAN, SHEILA, jt. auth. see Molino.
AWARD & Award, Anna. Bumper Dot to Dot. (p. 241)
—Dot to Dot Count & Colour Fun. (p. 472)
Award, Anna. Animals: Touch & Trace Early Learning Fun! Hewett, Angela et al, illus. (p. 82)
—B C: Touch & Trace Early Learning Fun! Hewett, Angela et al, illus. (p. 122)
—Bridesmaid Ella. (p. 227)
—Cinderella. (p. 320)
—Dally Duck. (p. 401)
—English. Burton, Terry, illus. (p. 529)
—English/French. Burton, Terry, illus. (p. 530)
—Hansel & Gretel. (p. 743)
—Little Red Riding Hood. (p. 1035)
—Moses in the Bulrushes: See the Picture & Say the Word. (p. 1176)
—My First 123. (p. 1203)
—My First ABC. (p. 1204)
—My First Animals. (p. 1204)
—My First Colouring Book. (p. 1206)
—My First Colouring Fun - 123: Copy the Colors to Complete the Picture. (p. 1206)
—My First Colouring Fun - Abc: Copy the Colors to Complete the Pictures. (p. 1206)
—My First Colours. (p. 1206)
—My First Nursery Rhymes. (p. 1207)
—My First Picture Book Farm Animals. (p. 1207)
—My First Shapes. (p. 1207)
—Noah & the Ark. (p. 1261)
—Picture the World of Farm Machines. (p. 1356)
—Picture the World of Working Trucks. (p. 1356)
—Puss in Boots. (p. 1420)
—Story of Goldilocks. (p. 1658)
—Story of Jesus. (p. 1658)
—Story of Puss in Boots: See the Picture & Say the Word. (p. 1659)
—Thumbelina. (p. 1745)
Award, Anna, jt. auth. see Award Publications Staff.
Award, Anna, jt. auth. see Award Staff.
Award, Anna, jt. auth. see AWARD.
Award, Anna, jt. auth. see Calver, Paul.
Award, Anna, jt. auth. see Fry, Jenny.
Award, Anna, jt. auth. see Picthall, Chez.
Award, Anna & Aesop. Lion & the Mouse with the Donkey & the Lapdog. Biro, Val, illus. (p. 1020)
Award, Anna & Award Staff. Mermaid Mia. (p. 1128)
Award, Anna & Biro, Val. Bear & the Travellers & the Ducks & the Tortoise. (p. 150)
Award, Anna, creator. Hansel & Gretel. (p. 743)
Award, Anna, et al. Boy Who Cried Wolf & the Goose That Laid the Golden Eggs. (p. 219)
—Eagle & the Man with the Town Mouse & the Country Mouse. (p. 492)
—Farmer & His Sons & the Donkey in the Lion's Den. (p. 574)
—Fox & the Stork & the Man, His Son & the Donkey. (p. 626)
—Hansel & Gretel. (p. 743)
—Monkey & the Fishermen & the Donkey in the Pond. (p. 1165)
—Sick Lion & Hare & the Tortoise. (p. 1572)
Award Publications Limited, creator. My First Bumper Copy Colouring Book. (p. 1206)
Award Publications Limited Staff, creator. My First Bumper Colouring Fun: ABC & 1 2 3. (p. 1206)
Award Publications Staff. 123. (p. 2000)
—ABC. (p. 2)
—Ballerina Lisa: Glitter Paper Doll. (p. 134)
—Fairy Belle. (p. 563)
—Jack & the Beanstalk. (p. 902)
—Josie & Her Doll: Press-Out Doll. (p. 927)
—Little Stars: My First Words. (p. 1036)
—My First Alphabet: Activities in Key Skills, Parent Tips. (p. 1204)
—My First Book of Prayers. (p. 1205)
—My First Counting. (p. 1206)
—My First Writing. (p. 1208)
—Octopus. (p. 1278)
—Princess Sophia: Glitter Paper Doll. (p. 1405)
—Read along with Me. (p. 1442)
Award Publications Staff, jt. auth. see Smith, Lesley.
Award Publications Staff & Award, Anna. Betty: The Ballerina Press-Out Doll. (p. 172)
—Cathy: Dresses up Press-Out Doll. (p. 280)
—Child's Book of Prayers & Graces. (p. 304)
—Mary & the Fancy-Dress Parties: Press-Out Doll. (p. 1100)
Award Staff. Popstar Chloe: Glitter Paper Doll. (p. 1385)
Award Staff, jt. auth. see Award, Anna.
Award Staff & Award, Anna. Desert Adventure. (p. 428)
—Journey Begins. (p. 928)
—Meerkat Mayhem. (p. 1120)
—Search for the Rainbow Gem. (p. 1537)
—Sticker Fun & Colouring. (p. 1650)
—Yoohoo & Friends. (p. 1972)
Awdry, Rev. W., jt. auth. see Awdry, Wilbert V.
Awdry, W. Animals Everywhere! Courtney, Richard, illus. (p. 82)
—Birthday Express! Stubbs, Tommy, illus. (p. 192)
—Blue Mountain Mystery. Golden Books, illus. (p. 203)
—Brave Little Engines (Thomas & Friends) Durk, Jim, illus. (p. 223)
—Bust My Buffers! (Thomas & Friends) (p. 245)
—Busy, Busy Thomas. Stubbs, Tommy, illus. (p. 246)
—Christmas in Wellsworth. Courtney, Richard, illus. (p. 314)
—Danger at the Dieselworks. Golden Books Staff, illus. (p. 403)
—Dinos & Discoveries / Emily Saves the World. (p. 441)
—Engines & Animals. Yee, Josie, illus. (p. 529)
—Ghost on the Track (Thomas & Friends) (p. 671)
—Henry & the Elephant. Courtney, Richard, illus. (p. 767)
—Hero of the Rails. Golden Books Staff, illus. (p. 772)

—James & the Red Balloon & Other Thomas the Tank Engine Stories. (p. 906)
—King of the Railway. Stubbs, Tommy, illus. (p. 959)
—Legend of the Lost Treasure. (p. 989)
—Lost Crown of Sodor. (p. 1055)
—Lost Ship. Courtney, Richard, illus. (p. 1056)
—Misty Island Rescue. Golden Books Staff, illus. (p. 1155)
—Not So Fast, Bash & Dash! (p. 1267)
—Not So Fast, Bash & Dash! Courtney, Richard, illus. (p. 1267)
—Pirate Treasure. Durk, Jim, illus. (p. 1363)
—Rail Blazers! (Thomas & Friends) Durk, Jim, illus. (p. 1433)
—Ride the Rails with Thomas (Thomas & Friends) Stubbs, Tommy, illus. (p. 1471)
—Rocket Returns. (p. 1483)
—Runaway Engine! Stubbs, Tommy, illus. (p. 1496)
—Santa's Little Engine. (p. 1513)
—Santa's Little Engine (Thomas & Friends) Lapadula, Thomas, illus. (p. 1513)
—Sodor's Legend of the Lost Treasure. (p. 1605)
—Steam Team! Stubbs, Tommy, illus. (p. 1646)
—Story Time Collection. Courtney, Richard & Stubbs, Tommy, illus. (p. 1663)
—Tale of the Brave. (p. 1700)
—Tale of the Brave (Thomas & Friends) Stubbs, Tommy, illus. (p. 1700)
—Thomas & Friends - Go, Thomas Go! (p. 1738)
—Thomas & the Monster (Thomas & Friends) (p. 1738)
—Thomas & the Volcano. (p. 1738)
—Thomas & the Volcano (Thomas & Friends) Courtney, Richard, illus. (p. 1738)
—Thomas' Big Book of Beginner Books. Random House Staff, illus. (p. 1738)
—Thomas Comes to Breakfast. Courtney, Richard, illus. (p. 1738)
—Thomas Goes Fishing. Courtney, Richard, illus. (p. 1738)
—Thomas' Halloween Delivery (Thomas & Friends) Durk, Jim, illus. (p. 1738)
—Thomas, Percy, & the Dragon. Courtney, Richard, illus. (p. 1739)
—Thomas Saves Christmas. Durk, Jim, illus. (p. 1739)
—Thomas the Tank Engine. (p. 1739)
—Thomas the Tank Engine: the Very First Stories (Thomas & Friends) (p. 1739)
—Thomas's Christmas Delivery. Stubbs, Tommy, illus. (p. 1739)
—Treasure on the Tracks. (p. 1782)
—Treasure on the Tracks. Courtney, Richard, illus. (p. 1782)
—Treasure on the Tracks. Random House Staff, illus. (p. 1782)
Awdry, W., jt. auth. see Awdry, Wilbert V.
Awdry, W. & Berrios, Frank. Thomas & Friends Puzzle Book. Random House Staff, illus. (p. 1738)
Awdry, Wilbert V. Big Book of Engines. Golden Books Staff, illus. (p. 179)
—Blue Mountain Mystery. Stubbs, Tommy, illus. (p. 203)
—Blue Train, Green Train. Stubbs, Tommy, illus. (p. 203)
—Close Shave. Courtney, Richard H., illus. (p. 334)
—Cranky's Surprise (Thomas & Friends) Golden Books, illus. (p. 376)
—Day of the Diesels. Stubbs, Tommy, illus. (p. 414)
—Day of the Diesels. Golden Books Staff, illus. (p. 414)
—Easter Engines. (p. 499)
—Easter Engines. Courtney, Richard, illus. (p. 499)
—Fast Train, Slow Train. Stubbs, Tommy, illus. (p. 576)
—Fast Train, Slow Train (Thomas & Friends) (p. 576)
—Flynn Saves the Day. Courtney, Richard, illus. (p. 610)
—Full Steam Ahead! Golden Books, illus. (p. 646)
—Go, Go, Thomas! - Express Coming Through. Random House Staff, illus. (p. 686)
—Go, Go, Thomas!/Express Coming Through. (p. 686)
—Go, Train, Go! Stubbs, Tommy, illus. (p. 687)
—Good Night, Thomas (Thomas & Friends) Random House Staff, illus. (p. 700)
—Gordon's New View. Courtney, Richard, illus. (p. 702)
—Halloween in Anopha. Courtney, Richard, illus. (p. 738)
—Hide-and-Seek Engines. Durk, Jim, illus. (p. 776)
—James & the Red Balloon & Other Thomas the Tank Engine Stories. (p. 906)
—King of the Railway. Golden Books Staff, illus. (p. 959)
—Lost Crown of Sodor. Random House Staff, illus. (p. 1055)
—Making Tracks! (Thomas & Friends) Golden Books Staff, illus. (p. 1082)
—Misty Island Rescue. Golden Books Staff, illus. (p. 1155)
—My Red Railway Book Box. Stubbs, Tommy, illus. (p. 1217)
—Not So Fast, Bash & Dash! Courtney, Richard, illus. (p. 1267)
—Quest for the Golden Crown. Durk, Jim, illus. (p. 1426)
—Risky Rails! (p. 1475)
—Risky Rails! (Thomas & Friends) Random House Staff, illus. (p. 1475)
—Rocket Returns. (p. 1483)
—Rolling on the Rails. Golden Books Staff, illus. (p. 1485)
—Search & Rescue! (Thomas & Friends) Random House Staff, illus. (p. 1537)
—Secret of the Green Engine. (p. 1542)
—Secret of the Green Engine. Awdry, Wilbert V. & Courtney, Richard, illus. (p. 1542)
—Secret of the Mine. Durk, Jim, illus. (p. 1542)
—Slide & Seek! Courtney, Richard, illus. (p. 1590)
—Steam Work! (Thomas & Friends) Golden Books Staff, illus. (p. 1646)
—Tales of Discovery. Golden Books Staff, illus. (p. 1702)
—Thomas' 123 Book. (p. 1737)
—Thomas' 123 Book. Courtney, Richard, illus. (p. 1737)
—Thomas & Friends Sr2. (p. 1738)
—Thomas & the Big, Big Bridge. (p. 1738)
—Thomas & the Shark. (p. 1738)
—Thomas & the Shark. Courtney, Richard, illus. (p. 1738)
—Thomas' Christmas Star. Durk, Jim, illus. (p. 1738)
—Thomas' Favorite Places & Faces. Stubbs, Tommy, illus. (p. 1738)
—Thomas' Giant Puzzle Book (Thomas & Friends) Durk, Jim, illus. (p. 1738)
—Thomas in Charge. (p. 1738)
—Thomas in Charge/Sodor's Steamworks. Random House Staff, illus. (p. 1738)
—Thomas Saves Easter! Stubbs, Tommy, illus. (p. 1739)
—Thomas' Super-Jumbo Coloring Book (Thomas & Friends) Golden Books Staff, illus. (p. 1739)
—Thomas the Tank Engine: The Classic Library Set (p. 1739)
—Thomas' Valentine Party. Durk, Jim, illus. (p. 1739)
—Trains, Cranes & Troublesome Trucks. Stubbs, Tommy, illus. (p. 1777)
—Up, up & Away! Golden Books Staff & Durk, Jim, illus. (p. 1824)
—Valentine's Day in Vicarstown. (p. 1830)
Awdry, Wilbert V., jt. auth. see Corey, Shana.
Awdry, Wilbert V. & Awdry, Rev. W. Thomas' Colorful Ride (Thomas & Friends) Golden Books Staff, illus. (p. 1738)
Awdry, Wilbert V. & Awdry, W. Blue Train, Green Train. Stubbs, Tommy, illus. (p. 203)
—Calling All Engines! Courtney, Richard, illus. (p. 254)
—Cranky Day & Other Thomas the Tank Engine Stories (p. 376)
—Down at the Docks. Courtney, Richard, illus. (p. 474)
—Thomas & the Hide & Seek Animals. Bell, Owain, illus. (p. 1738)
Awdry, Wilbert V. & Hooke, R. Schuyler. Railway Rhymes. Courtney, Richard, illus. (p. 1434)
Awdry, Wilbert V. & Random House Editors. Thomas & Percy & the Dragon. (p. 1738)
Awdry, Wilbert V. & RH Disney Staff. Thomas' Mixed-Up Day - Thomas Puts the Brakes On. RH Disney Staff, illus. (p. 1739)
Awdry, Wilbert V. & Terrill, Elizabeth. Go, Train, Go! Stubbs, Tommy, illus. (p. 687)
Awdry, Wilbert V. & Wrecks, Billy. Thomas Looks up (Thomas & Friends) Random House Staff, illus. (p. 1739)
Awdry, Wilbert Were. Missing Christmas Tree. Stubbs, Tommy, illus. (p. 1152)
Awes, Jennifer, illus. see Ambrosio, Michael.
Awesome Andy. Awesome Art & Coloring Book! (p. 121)
Awiakta, Marilou. Rising Fawn & the Fire Mystery. Bringle, Beverly, illus. (p. 1475)
AWWA Staff, compiled by. Story of Drinking Water (the) (p. 1658)
Axe-Bronk, Susan. Vanishing Gourds: A Sukkot Mystery. Monelli, Marta, illus. (p. 1833)
Axel, Brett. Goblinheart: A Fairy Tale. Biddlespacher, Tara, illus. (p. 688)
Axelrod, Alan. 1001 Events That Made America: A Patriot's Handbook. (p. 2002)
—Encyclopedia of the American Armed Forces (p. 525)
—Encyclopedia of the U. S. Air Force. (p. 525)
—Encyclopedia of the U. S. Marines. (p. 525)
—Encyclopedia of the U. S. Navy. (p. 525)
Axelrod, Alan, jt. auth. see Phillips, Charles.
Axelrod, Alan & Axelrod, Regina. Political History of America's Wars (p. 1380)
Axelrod, Amy. Pigs in the Corner: Fun with Math & Dance. McGinley-Nally, Sharon, illus. (p. 1358)
—Your Friend in Fashion, Abby Shapiro. (p. 1980)
Axelrod, Amy & Axelrod, David. Bullet Catch. (p. 240)
Axelrod, Amy & McGinley-Nally, Sharon. Pigs at Odds: Fun with Math & Games. McGinley-Nally, Sharon, illus. (p. 1358)
Axelrod, David, jt. auth. see Axelrod, Amy.
Axelrod, Kate. Law of Loving Others. (p. 981)
Axelrod, Regina, jt. auth. see Axelrod, Alan.
Axelrod, Toby. Hans & Sophie Scholl: German Resisters of the White Rose. (p. 743)
Axelrod-Contrada, Joan. Animal Debate: A Rip-Roaring Game of Either-Or Questions. (p. 77)
—Facts about Drugs & Society. (p. 561)
—Ghoulish Ghost Stories. (p. 673)
—Halloween & Day of the Dead Traditions Around the World. Chavarri, Elisa, illus. (p. 737)
—Historical Atlas of Colonial America. (p. 782)
—Isabel Allende. (p. 890)
—Kids' Guide to Mummies (p. 953)
—Pesky Critters! Squirrels, Raccoons, & Other Furry Invaders (p. 1345)
—Plessy v. Ferguson: Separate but Unequal. (p. 1374)
—Politics, Government, & Activism. (p. 1381)
—Poverty in America: Cause or Effect? (p. 1389)
—Primary Source History of the Colony of Rhode Island. (p. 1400)
—Reno V. ACLU Internet Censorship. (p. 1460)
—This or That Animal Debate: A Rip-Roaring Game of Either/or Questions. (p. 1737)
—World's Most Famous Ghosts (p. 1960)
Axelsen, Stephen. Vikings Maze Book. (p. 1842)
Axelsen, Stephen, illus. see Ransom, Jeanie Franz.
Axelsson, Carina. Model Undercover: New York. (p. 1157)
—Nigel. (p. 1252)
—Paris. (p. 1324)
Axeman, Lois, illus. see Hillert, Margaret.
Axford, Elizabeth C. Kidtunes Songbook & Activity Guide (p. 955)
Axford, Elizabeth C., ed. see Fant, Donna.
Axford, Elizabeth C., ed. see White, Kimberly.
Axford, Elizabeth C., compiled by. Music Box & Other Delights: Music Classroom Activities. (p. 1193)
Axford, Elizabeth C., ed. My Halloween Fun Book Complete Edition. (p. 1210)
Axiom Press, ed. CultureGrams Kids Edition. (p. 391)
—CultureGrams States Edition. (p. 391)
Axmacher, Denise. Mrs. FireFly. (p. 1187)
Axt, Katie. Can You See the Butterfly? (p. 259)
Axtell, David. We're Going on a Lion Hunt. Axtell, David, illus. (p. 1875)
Axworthy, Ani, illus. see Ganeri, Anita.
Axworthy, Ann, illus. see Ganeri, Anita.
Axworthy, Anni. Dragon Who Couldn't Do Dragony Things. (p. 478)
—Dragon Who Couldn't Do Sporty Things. Axworthy, Anni, illus. (p. 478)
Axworthy, Anni, illus. see Brandreth, Gyles.
Axworthy, Anni, illus. see Langford, Jane.
Axworthy, Anni, illus. see Nash, Margaret.
Axworthy, Anni, jt. auth. see Donaldson, Julia.
Ayache, Avraham, illus. see Mindel, Nissan.
Ayagalria, Julia, et al. Animals of the River. Ayagalria, Julia et al, illus. (p. 83)
Ayala, Anikka & Nash, Kevin. University of Notre Dame College Prowler off the Record. (p. 1821)
Ayala, Joseph, illus. see Hertkorn, Michaela C.
Ayala Poveda, Fernando. Coraje de Vivir. (p. 366)
Ayalomeh, Shedrach, illus. see Uwuigiaren, Omoruyi.
Ayarbe, Heidi. Compromised. (p. 354)
—Compulsion. (p. 354)
—Freeze Frame. (p. 635)
—Wanted. (p. 1856)
Ayasta, Ayasta. Star. (p. 1640)
Ayaz, Huda. Freeze-Land: A New Beginning. (p. 635)
Aycock, Daniel, illus. see Mauro, Paul & Melton, H. Keith.
Aycock, John, jt. auth. see Putnam, Richelle.
Aydelott, Jimmie & Buck, Dianna S. Building Literature Circles. (p. 239)
Ayder, Earl. Longest Shortcut. McGrellis, Cynthia, illus. (p. 1047)
Aydin, Robert, tr. Syriac Bible for Children. (p. 1693)
Aydt, Rachel. Why Me? A Teen Guide to Divorce & Your Feelings. (p. 1925)
Ayduz, Selma, tr. see Öze, Özkan.
Ayed, Juwayriyah, jt. auth. see Juwayriyah, Umm.
Ayer, Eleanor, jt. auth. see Ellsh, Dan.
Ayer, Eleanor H. Everything You Need to Know about Depression. (p. 545)
—Everything You Need to Know about Stress. (p. 546)
—Todo lo que necesitas saber sobre el matrimonio adolescente (Everything You Need to Know about Teen Marriage) (p. 1761)
—Todo lo que necesitas saber sobre la paternidad adolescente (Everything You Need to Know about Teen Fatherhood) (p. 1761)
Ayer, Jane E. Guided Meditations for Junior High: Good Judgment, Gifts, Obedience, Inner Blindness. (p. 730)
Ayer, Joan. Beyond Good Night, Moon - 75 Reviews of Classic Books for Young Children. (p. 174)
Ayer, Paula. Foodprints: The Story of What We Eat. (p. 614)
Ayers, Amy. Adding & Subtracting in Math Club. Andersen, Gregg, photos by. (p. 11)
—Contando en el Zoologico. (p. 360)
—Counting at the Zoo. (p. 370)
—Using Money at the Lemonade Stand. (p. 1828)
Ayers, Amy, jt. auth. see Rauen, Amy.
Ayers, Becky. Secret of Willow Patch. (p. 1543)
—Secret of Willow Patch:the Discovery. (p. 1543)
Ayers, Chris. Daily Zoo: Keeping the Doctor at Bay with a Drawing a Day. Vol. 1 (p. 400)
—MY Daily Zoo. (p. 1201)
Ayers, Linda. Lively Literature Activities for Early Elementary (p. 1040)
—Lively Literature Activities for Pre-K Through Kindergarten (p. 1040)
—My Pet Mosquito. Ayers, Linda, illus. (p. 1217)
—There's Something in My Sandwich. Hunt, Jane, illus. (p. 1731)
—Tiger Does the Write Thing. Hunt, Jane, illus. (p. 1748)
—Tiger Goes Collecting. Hunt, Jane, illus. (p. 1748)
—Time Bridge Travelers Ayers, Ryan, illus. (p. 1751)
—Time Bridge Travelers & the Mysterious Map Ayers, Ryan, illus. (p. 1751)
—Time Bridge Travelers & the Time Travel Station Ayers, Ryan, illus. (p. 1751)
Ayers, Michelle. Michael. (p. 1134)
Ayers, Patricia. Kid's Guide to How Trees Grow. (p. 953)
Ayers, Ryan, illus. see Ayers, Linda.
Ayers, Samuel J. Preston Smith: The Man Who Would Be Governor. (p. 1397)
Ayers, Sanda. Tommy Tractor Goes to the City Young, Sue, illus. (p. 1765)
Ayesenberg, Nina, illus. see Ehlin, Gina.
Ayittey, George B. N. Africa Unchained: The Blueprint for Africa's Future. (p. 26)
Aykroyd, Clarissa. Egypt (p. 506)
—Egypt. (p. 506)
—Government of Mexico. (p. 704)
—Meeting Future Challenges: The Government of Mexico. (p. 1123)
—Pakistan (p. 1319)
—Pakistan. (p. 1319)
—Refugees. (p. 1456)
—Savage Satire: The Story of Jonathan Swift. (p. 1516)
Aylesworth, Jim. Cock-A-Doodle Doo, Creak, Pop-Pop, Moo. Sneed, Brad, illus. (p. 337)
—Cock-a-Doodle-Doo, Creak, Pop-Pop, Moo. Sneed, Brad, illus. (p. 337)
—Gingerbread Man. McClintock, Barbara, illus. (p. 677)
—Goldilocks & the Three Bears. McClintock, Barbara, illus. (p. 696)
—Little Bitty Mousie. Hague, Michael, illus. (p. 1024)
—My Grandfather's Coat. McClintock, Barbara, illus. (p. 1210)
—Naughty Little Monkeys. Cole, Henry, illus. (p. 1237)
—Our Abe Lincoln. McClintock, Barbara, illus. (p. 1307)
Aylett, J. F., jt. auth. see DeMarco, Neil.
Ayliffe, Alex, illus. see Goodings, Christina.
Ayliffe, Alex, illus. see Mayo, Margaret.
Ayliffe, Alex, illus. see Rock, Lois.
Ayliffe, Alex, illus. see Whybrow, Ian.
Ayliffe, Alex, jt. auth. see David, Juliet.
Ayliffe, Alex & Prasadam-Halls, Smriti. My Day - Bedtime. (p. 1201)
—My Day - Playtime. (p. 1201)
Aymaz, Abdullah. No Room for Doubt: Selective Essays for Youth. (p. 1260)
Ayme, Marcel. Cuentos Del Gato Encaramado (p. 390)
Aymez, Carla, illus. see Kraselsky, Rebeca.
Ayotte, Andie C., illus. see Hoppe, Bethany A.
Ayotte-Irwin, Tracy & Jordan, Sara. Bilingual Songs - English-French (p. 186)
Ayoub, Gilda. How Volcanoes Came to Be. (p. 823)
—Little Horatio. (p. 1029)
Ayoub, Hamid, illus. see Hahn, Nancy.
Ayozie, Ben-EL. Ants Everywhere. (p. 90)
—Daddy's Princess. (p. 399)
Ayres, Charlie. Lives of the Great Artists. (p. 1040)
—Story of the World's Greatest Paintings. (p. 1662)
Ayres, Ella, jt. auth. see Nickles, Clay.
Ayres, Honor, illus. see Godfrey, Jan.
Ayres, Honor, illus. see House, Catherine.
Ayres, Honor, illus. see Wright, Sally Ann.
Ayres, Katherine. Family Tree. (p. 569)
—Macaroni Boy. (p. 1067)
—Under Copp's Hill. (p. 1813)
—Up, down, & Around. Westcott, Nadine Bernard, illus. (p. 1824)
—Voices at Whisper Bend. (p. 1848)
Ayres, Michael. A. M. (p. 1)
Ayres, Pam. Piggo & the Fork Lift Truck. (p. 1358)
Ayres, Pamela. Buster & Bella: Best Friends. (p. 245)
Ayres, S. C. Finding the Perfect Fit. Steckler, Megan, illus. (p. 588)
Ayriss, Linda Holt, illus. see Herzog, Brad.
Ayto, Russell, illus. see Andreae, Giles.
Ayto, Russell, illus. see Bently, Peter.
Ayto, Russell, illus. see Burgess, Mark.
Ayto, Russell, illus. see Cowell, Cressida.
Ayto, Russell, illus. see Cutbill, Andy.
Ayto, Russell, illus. see Kelly, Mij.
Ayto, Russell, illus. see Middleton, Julie.
Ayto, Russell, illus. see Mitton, Tony.
Ayto, Russell, illus. see Whybrow, Ian.
Ayto, Russell, jt. auth. see Whybrow, Ian.
Ayton, Shalanna. Adventures of Missy the Moose. (p. 20)
Ayuko, jt. auth. see Tani, Mizue.
Ayuko & Tani, Mizue. Earl & the Fairy. (p. 492)
—Earl & the Fairy. (p. 492)
Ayzenberg, Nina, illus. see Byrd, Bill Scott.
Ayzenberg, Nina, illus. see Ehlin, Gina.
AZ, illus. see Reyes, Carlos José.
AZ Books. Babies. (p. 123)
—Big Knowledge Book. (p. 182)
—Big Zoo Book. (p. 184)
—Bright Colors. (p. 228)
—Forest Animals. (p. 618)
—Forest Life. (p. 618)
—Fruits. (p. 645)
—Hedgehog & His Friends. (p. 761)
—In Hot Africa. (p. 863)
—Our Planet. (p. 1309)
—Prints. (p. 1407)
—Tiger & His Stripes. (p. 1748)
AZ Books, creator. Baby Lion Searches for His Dad. (p. 127)
—Being a Princess. (p. 160)
—Brave & Smart. (p. 223)
—Cinderella. (p. 320)
—Come & Play. (p. 347)
—Construction Machines. (p. 359)
—Cool Races. (p. 364)
—Do Like Me. (p. 457)
—Everyday Machines. (p. 544)
—Farm Animals. (p. 573)
—Fashion Collection. (p. 575)
—Fidget Monkey. (p. 583)
—French Fairy Tales. (p. 635)
—Frog the Hopper. (p. 640)
—Hello, I'm Hippo! (p. 764)
—Hello, I'm Tiger! (p. 764)
—In the Noisy Forest. (p. 867)
—Italian Fairy Tales. (p. 894)
—It's Playtime. (p. 898)
—Kitten Searches for a Friend. (p. 962)
—Lake Animals Moving & Talking. (p. 972)
—Lamb Searches for Her Mom. (p. 972)
—Lion & His Kingdom. (p. 1019)
—Little Magician. (p. 1031)
—Little Physicist. (p. 1033)
—Magic Farm. (p. 1072)
—Magic Forest. (p. 1072)
—Magic Machines. (p. 1072)
—Magic of Velvet. (p. 1073)
—Magic Zoo. (p. 1074)
—Meeting Friends. (p. 1123)
—Musical Farm. (p. 1194)
—My Favorite Pet. (p. 1203)
—My Favorite Toy. (p. 1203)
—Pond Animals. (p. 1382)
—Powerful Machines. (p. 1390)
—Rescue Machines. (p. 1462)
—Sea Adventures. (p. 1534)
—Snow White & the Seven Dwarfs. (p. 1600)
—Space Adventures. (p. 1618)
—Stylish Gifts. (p. 1670)
—Talking Train. (p. 1703)
—Tyler Turtle Travels to Australia. (p. 1805)
—Walk Around a Farm. (p. 1853)
—Walk Around Africa. (p. 1853)
—Water Animals. (p. 1862)
—What Color? (p. 1881)
—What I Say. (p. 1887)
—What Number? (p. 1892)
—What Shape? (p. 1893)
—Who Lives in the Forest? (p. 1916)
—Who Lives in the Ocean? (p. 1916)
AZ Books Staff. About Planet Earth. Petrovskaya, Olga, ed. (p. 6)
—About the Human Body. Petrovskaya, Olga, ed. (p. 6)
—About Wildlife. Petrovskaya, Olga, ed. (p. 6)
—Amazing Space. Ivinskaya, Snezhana, ed. (p. 55)
—Ancient Asia. Kazimirova, Karina & Snezhana, Ivinskaya, eds. (p. 68)
—Ancient Egypt. Ulasevich, Olga, ed. (p. 68)
—Ancient Rome. Naumovets, Elena & Svistunova, Natalia, eds. (p. 70)
—Animal Wonder. (p. 80)
—Animales - Farm Animals: Farm Animals. Gorbachenok, Ekaterina, ed. (p. 80)
—Animals. Slusar, Julia, ed. (p. 81)
—Animals on the Go. (p. 83)
—Asian Fairy Tales. (p. 106)

A

—Atlas for Kids. Kazimirova, Karina, ed. (p. 112)
—Babbling Pond. Tulup, Natalia, ed. (p. 123)
—Bear's Forest. Potapenko, Olga, ed. (p. 152)
—British Fairy Tales. (p. 229)
—Busy Insects Moving & Talking. Dubovik, Ludmila, ed. (p. 246)
—Buzzing Meadow. Tulup, Natalia, ed. (p. 249)
—Cinderella. Zyl, Olga, ed. (p. 320)
—Colores - Colorful Animals: Colorful Animals. Gorbachenok, Ekaterina, ed. (p. 344)
—Colors. Slusar, Julia, ed. (p. 344)
—Colors & Shapes. Petrovskaya, Olga, ed. (p. 345)
—Counting. Petrovskaya, Olga, ed. (p. 370)
—Countries & People. Borovik, Alija et al, eds. (p. 372)
—Discoveries & Inventions. Kazimirova, Karina, ed. (p. 448)
—Discovering the Savanna. Gorojan, Elena, ed. (p. 450)
—Exploring the Ocean. Vasilkova, Elena, ed. (p. 554)
—Farm Animals. Gorojan, Elena, ed. (p. 573)
—Farm Animals Moving & Talking. Harko, Lubov, ed. (p. 573)
—Fashion Ideas. Batan, Natalia, ed. (p. 575)
—Fast Cars. Tulup, Natasha, ed. (p. 576)
—Fast Vehicles Moving & Talking. Harko, Lubov, ed. (p. 576)
—Feathered Singers. Tulup, Natalia, ed. (p. 579)
—Find a Pair. Petrovskaya, Olga, ed. (p. 587)
—Find My Food & Home. Petrovskaya, Olga, ed. (p. 587)
—Flying Planes. Tulup, Natasha, ed. (p. 610)
—Forest Animals. Gorojan, Elena, ed. (p. 618)
—Forest Animals Moving & Talking. Dubovik, Ludmila, ed. (p. 618)
—Frog's Pond. Potapenko, Olga, ed. (p. 641)
—Fruits & Vegetables. Slusar, Julia, ed. (p. 645)
—Great Warriors. Aksinovich, Natalia & Yaroshevich, Angelica, eds. (p. 719)
—Happy Holidays. (p. 746)
—Hello, I'm Bear! Gorbachenok, Ekaterina, ed. (p. 764)
—Hello, I'm Horse! Gorbachenok, Ekaterina, ed. (p. 764)
—History & Discoveries. Shumovich, Nadegda et al, eds. (p. 783)
—Honking Trucks. Tulup, Natasha, ed. (p. 795)
—Horse's Farm. Potapenko, Olga, ed. (p. 800)
—In the Forest. Ulasevich, Olga & Goncharik, Irina, eds. (p. 866)
—In the Jungle. Efimova, Tatiana, ed. (p. 866)
—In the Prairie & Desert. Efimova, Tatiana & Goncharik, Irina, eds. (p. 867)
—In the Savanna. Ulasevich, Olga & Migits, Anna, eds. (p. 867)
—In the Sea & Ocean. Efimova, Tatiana, ed. (p. 867)
—Jungle Animals. Gorojan, Elena, ed. (p. 935)
—Little Thumb. Zyl, Olga, ed. (p. 1037)
—Living Book of Dinosaurs. Latushko, Julia, ed. (p. 1040)
—Living Book of the Forest. Vasilkova, Elena, ed. (p. 1040)
—Living Book of the Jungle. Gasteva, Julia, ed. (p. 1040)
—Living Book of the Ocean. Aksinovich, Natalia, ed. (p. 1040)
—Living Book of the Savanna. Aksimovich, Natalja, ed. (p. 1040)
—Loud Farm. Tulup, Natalia, ed. (p. 1057)
—Meeting Dinosaurs. Vasilkova, Elena, ed. (p. 1123)
—Merry Orchestra. Tulup, Natalia, ed. (p. 1129)
—Movie Star. Puzik, Ulijana, ed. (p. 1183)
—Musical Animals. Tulup, Natalia, ed. (p. 1194)
—Musical Machines. Tulup, Natalia, ed. (p. 1194)
—My Farm. Yaroshevich, Angelica, ed. (p. 1203)
—My Forest. Yaroshevich, Angelica, ed. (p. 1209)
—My Pets. Yaroshevich, Angelica, ed. (p. 1217)
—My Pond. Yaroshevich, Angelica, ed. (p. 1217)
—My Zoo. Yaroshevich, Angelica, ed. (p. 1222)
—Noisy Zoo. Tulup, Natalia, ed. (p. 1263)
—Numeros - Count the Toys: Count the Toys. Gorbachenok, Ekaterina, ed. (p. 1273)
—Ocean Animals. Gorojan, Elena, ed. (p. 1276)
—On the Farm. Ulasevich, Olga, ed. (p. 1290)
—Our Cozy Forest. Zayceva, Irina, ed. (p. 1308)
—Our Faraway Jungle. Zayceva, Irina, ed. (p. 1308)
—Our Friendly Farm. Zayceva, Irina, ed. (p. 1308)
—Polar Animals. Gorojan, Elena, ed. (p. 1378)
—Sailing Ships. Tulup, Natasha, ed. (p. 1503)
—Sam the Auto Mechanic. Boroda, Janna, ed. (p. 1507)
—Sam the Builder. Boroda, Janna, ed. (p. 1507)
—Sam the Constructor. Boroda, Janna, ed. (p. 1507)
—Savanna Animals. Gorojan, Elena, ed. (p. 1516)
—Scouting the Forest. Vasilkova, Elena, ed. (p. 1532)
—Secrets of Pirates. Naumovets, Elena, ed. (p. 1545)
—Shapes. Slusar, Julia, ed. (p. 1560)
—Sleeping Beauty. Zyl, Olga, ed. (p. 1589)
—Sounds of Dinosaurs. Yaroshevich, Angelica, ed. (p. 1615)
—Sounds of the Farm. Sheljagovich, Yana, ed. (p. 1615)
—Sounds of the Forest. Sheljagovich, Yana, ed. (p. 1615)
—Sounds of the Jungle. Migiz, Anna, ed. (p. 1615)
—Sounds of the Savanna & Desert. Migiz, Anna, ed. (p. 1615)
—Sounds of Wild Nature. Naumovets, Elena, ed. (p. 1615)
—Sparrow's Yard. Potapenko, Olga, ed. (p. 1622)
—Squirrel Searches for a Home. (p. 1637)
—Stylish Girls. (p. 1670)
—Terribly Funny Monsters. Shumovich, Nadezhda, ed. (p. 1721)
—Visiting Africa. Zuk, Valentina, ed. (p. 1845)
—Visiting Dinosaurs. Vol, Vera, ed. (p. 1845)
—Visiting the Farm. Zuk, Valentina, ed. (p. 1845)
—Visiting the Forest. Zuk, Valentina, ed. (p. 1845)
—Visiting the Ocean. Lukjanenko, Anna, ed. (p. 1845)
—What Do I Eat? Sisoj, Natalja, ed. (p. 1882)
—Where's My Baby? Sisoj, Natalja, ed. (p. 1910)
—Where's My Toy? Sisoj, Natalja, ed. (p. 1910)
—Who Is the Bear Looking For? Sharipovas, Alesja, ed. (p. 1916)
—Who Is the Hare Looking For? Zajceva, Ira, ed. (p. 1916)
—Who Is the Lion Looking For? Shestakova, Anna, ed. (p. 1916)
—Who Is the Puppy Looking For? Gridina, Anna, ed. (p. 1916)
—Who Is the Tiger Looking For? Gridina, Anna, ed. (p. 1916)
—Who Lives in the Jungle? Gridina, Anna, ed. (p. 1916)
—Who Lives in the Pond? Gridina, Anna, ed. (p. 1916)
—Who Lives in the Savanna? Gridina, Anna, ed. (p. 1916)
—Who Lives on a Farm? Gridina, Anna, ed. (p. 1916)
—Wild Nature. Kokash, Elena et al, eds. (p. 1929)
AZ Books Staff & Evans, Olivia. Haunted Castle. Shumovich, Nadezhda, ed. (p. 753)
Azaceta, Paul, illus. see David, Peter.
Azaceta, Paul, illus. see Golden, Christopher, et al.
Azaceta, Paul, illus. see Waid, Mark & Lee, Stan.
Azadi, Azita. Thank You Sun. (p. 1725)
Azam, Jacques, illus. see Laffon, Martine & De Chabaneix, Hortense.
Azam, Shamim. Sabrina & Her Quest. (p. 1500)
Azaola, Miguel, tr. see Pilkey, Dav.
Azaola, Miguel, tr. see Whybrow, Ian.
Azarian, Mary. Farmers Alphabet. Azarian, Mary, illus. (p. 574)
—Farmer's Alphabet. (p. 574)
—Gardener's Alphabet. (p. 656)
Azarian, Mary, illus. see Brisson, Pat.
Azarian, Mary, illus. see Connor, Leslie.
Azarian, Mary, illus. see Lunge-Larsen, Lise.
Azarian, Mary, illus. see Martin, Jacqueline Briggs.
Azarian, Mary, illus. see Rosen, Michael J.
Azarian, Melissa Eisen. Amistad Mutiny: From the Court Case to the Movie. (p. 65)
Azarov, Max, jt. auth. see Vogel, Rob.
Azerier, Gary. Constellation Station. (p. 359)
Azevedo, Eric. Why Is Blue Bear So Blue? The Adventures of Blue Bear. (p. 1925)
Azhderian, Cecelia, illus. see Richmond, Benjamin.
Azim, Firdous & Zaman, Niaz, eds. Galpa: Short Stories by Bangladeshi Women. (p. 654)
Azima, Cricket. Everybody Eats Lunch. Thomas, Titus V., illus. (p. 543)
Azima, Cricket, jt. auth. see Garfield, Yvette.
Aziz, Khalif. Magikh Series: The Black Phoenix Book 1. (p. 1075)
Aziz, Lamia, illus. see Holden, Pam.
Azizi, Kamran. Leggo of the String... (p. 990)
Azizi, Z., photos by see Dicker, K.
Azizi, Zoha, jt. auth. see Dicker, Katie.
Azman, Hacer. Adventures of Kyle. (p. 19)
—God Loves Us All. (p. 689)
Aznar, Caridad Perez, illus. see Anastasio, Antonio.
Azore, Barbara. Wanda & the Frogs. Graham, Georgia, illus. (p. 1856)
—Wanda & the Wild Hair. Graham, Georgia, illus. (p. 1856)
—Wanda's Freckles. Graham, Georgia, illus. (p. 1856)
Azpuru, Dinorah. Cultura política de la democracia en Guatemala 2008: El impacto de la Gobernabilidad. (p. 390)
Azuma, Kiyohiko. Azumanga Daioh (p. 122)
—Yotsuba! (p. 1972)
—Yotsuba&! Volume 5 (p. 1972)
Azumi, Yukinobu, jt. auth. see Yubuki, Go.
Azurmendi, Mattie. Sock Vacation. (p. 1605)
Azzalin, Stefano, illus. see Colich, Abby.
Azzarelli, Ally. Adele! Singing Sensation. (p. 12)
—Drake! Hip-Hop Celebrity. (p. 479)
—Justin Bieber: Teen Music Superstar. (p. 940)
—Selena Gomez: Latina TV & Music Star. (p. 1549)
—Taylor Lautner: Film Superstar. (p. 1708)
Azzarello, Brian. 100 Bullets: The Hard Way Vol. 8 (p. 1998)
—100 Bullets - First Shot, Last Call Crain, Dale, illus. (p. 1998)
—100 Bullets - Split Second Chance (p. 1998)
—Counterfifth Detective (p. 370)
—Decayed (p. 421)
—For Tomorrow. (p. 616)
—Forgone Tomorrow (p. 619)
—Hang up on the Hang Low (p. 742)
—Kin of Homecoming. (p. 957)
—Lex Luthor: Man of Steel. (p. 1004)
—Samurai (p. 1509)
—Six Feet under the Gun (p. 1582)
—Strychnine Lives (p. 1668)
—Superman: For Tomorrow. (p. 1683)
Azzarello, Brian & Loeb, Jeph. For Tomorrow. Williams, Scott & Sinclair, Alex, illus. (p. 616)
Azzarello, Brian, et al. Absolute Sandman Lee, Jim, illus. (p. 7)
—Thicker Than Blackwater Dell'edera, Werther, illus. (p. 1732)
Azzopardi, Jeannie. Maricio & the Magic Suitcase. (p. 1093)

B

B. Yes I Can for Kids. (p. 1970)
B. A. O'Reilly. You've Got a Friend in Me. (p. 1982)
B alloxk-Dixon, Saige J., jt. auth. see Medina, Sylvia M.
B., Blair. Star Cross'd Destiny: The Fated B., Blair, illus. (p. 1640)
B., David, jt. auth. see Orlan, Pierre Mac.
B., Dick. Henrietta B. Seiberling: The Story of Akron's Pioneer A. A. Christian Fellowship, Its Oxford Group Encounters, & a Non-alcoholic Woman's Role in Helping Found Early A. A. 's Unique Spiritual Program for Curing Alcoholics: Ohio's Lady with a Cause. (p. 767)
—James Club & the Original A. A. Program's Absolute Essentials. (p. 907)
B. Helmer, George. Cow-Giraffe. (p. 373)
B. Lee Schmidt. My Name Is Buttonz. (p. 1215)
B., Lourra. Ouishy Squishy Brain Shop. (p. 1307)
B. Meyer, Deborah. Butterfly Girls. (p. 248)
B., Meyer Deborah. Meet the Brazos Boys. (p. 1122)
B. Robert Clark. Man with Big Hair. (p. 1086)
B. T. B., illus. see Belloc, Hilaire.
Baase, Francesca. Didn't You Hear the Rumor? (p. 437)
Baaumbach, Gerard F., creator. Sadlier We Believe. (p. 1501)
Babajanyan, Sona, illus. see Reiter, David P.
Babajanyan, Sona, illus. see Reiter, David P. & Reiter, David P.
Babarro, Xoan. Tela de Arana Que Todo Lo Apana. (p. 1716)
Babb, Gina. Zain & Zoe's Zoo Adventures: Numbers & Colors. (p. 1984)
Babb, Joanna. Playing with Numbers: A Playbook to Build Numeracy for 3-7 Year Olds, Including Counting, Measuring, Sizes, Shapes, Patterns, Groups & Telling the Time. (p. 1372)
Babbitt, Ellen C. Jataka Tales. (p. 910)
—Jataka Tales I & II. (p. 910)
—Jataka Tales (Yesterday's Classics) (p. 910)
—More Jataka Tales. (p. 1174)
—More Jataka Tales. Young, Ellsworth, illus. (p. 1174)
Babbitt, Ellen C. & Young, Ellsworth. Monkey & the Crocodile: And Other Fables from the Jataka Tales of India. (p. 1165)
Babbitt, Kelli. You Grew in My Heart Instead. (p. 1975)
Babbitt, Natalie. Cerro del Abismo. (p. 287)
—Devil's Storybooks: Twenty Delightfully Wicked Stories. Babbitt, Natalie, illus. (p. 432)
—Elsie Times Eight. Babbitt, Natalie, illus. (p. 516)
—Eyes of the Amaryllis. (p. 558)
—Goody Hall. Babbitt, Natalie, illus. (p. 702)
—Jack Plank Tells Tales. (p. 903)
—Kneeknock Rise. (p. 964)
—Kneeknock Rise. Babbitt, Natalie, illus. (p. 964)
—Misterio Del Manantial. (p. 1155)
—Moon over High Street. (p. 1172)
—Ouch! Marcellino, Fred, illus. (p. 1307)
—Search for Delicious. (p. 1537)
—Search for Delicious. Babbitt, Natalie, illus. (p. 1537)
—Something. (p. 1609)
—Tuck Everlasting. (p. 1795)
Babbs, Gary E. Let Your Light Shine. (p. 994)
Babcock, Allison. Braxton's Potty Chair. (p. 224)
Babcock, Charles A. Bird Day How to Prepare for It. (p. 190)
Babcock, Denise L., et al. World of Communities. (p. 1956)
Babcock, Denise L., et al, texts. Student Activity Book. (p. 1669)
Babcock, Doug. Hark, Hear Harold the Angel Sing. (p. 748)
Babcock, Jeff, illus. see Newman, Gwill York.
Babcock, Lee L. Ghost of Sunday Creek. (p. 671)
Babcock, Nabila. My Child, My Love. (p. 1200)
—To You That Give. (p. 1759)
Babcock, Nona Burroughs. Little Wolf's Adventure: A Medicine Dream & Warrior Ghosts. (p. 1038)
Babeaux, Denise L., jt. auth. see Hall, Terri L.
Babeaux, Dennis, photos by see Hall, Terri L.
Babel, Ann. Little Tree. (p. 1037)
Babel-Worth, Joyce, illus. see Kannenberg, Stacey.
Baber, Maxwell. Map Basics (p. 1089)
Babiak, Alexandra Brittany. Runaway Jacket (p. 1496)
Babich, Elaine. You Never Called Me Princess. (p. 1976)
Babich, Jo Christian. January at the Gate. (p. 908)
Babin, Claire. Gus Is a Fish. Bedrick, Claudia Z., tr. from FRE. (p. 732)
—Gus Is a Tree. Tallec, Olivier, illus. (p. 732)
Babin, Pierre. Debussy. Voake, Charlotte, illus. (p. 421)
Babineaux, Jason James. That's What Big Girls Do! (p. 1727)
Babineaux, Jim. Cody Cottontail Makes a Wise Choice! Babineaux, Jim, illus. (p. 338)
Babinski, Michael, illus. see Draper, Tricia.
Babinsky, Joseph. Magical Dream Forest. (p. 1074)
Babler, Susan E. Look It up-in the Bible, Book 2: Animals, Gardens, & Trees. (p. 1049)
Baboni, Elena, illus. see Lane, Leena.
Babooram, Aasha, illus. see Babooram, Vima.
Babooram, Vima. Poco & His Missing Puppy. Babooram, Aasha, illus. (p. 1375)
Babour Staff & Frazier, April. 3-Minute Devotions for Teen Girls: 180 Encouraging Readings. (p. 1991)
Babra, Neil, illus. see SparkNotes Staff.
Babsky, Irene. Playing with Words. (p. 1373)
Babson, Jane F. Story of Us: The Dolls' History of People of the United States. Babson, Jane F., illus. (p. 1662)
Baby Blessings Staff. Bathtime Bible Stories. (p. 144)
—God Made Me Book W/Plush. (p. 689)
Baby Genius Publishing Staff. 5 Little Monkeys Jumpin' on the Bed: A Sing 'N Count Book. (p. 1992)
—Old MacDonald Had a Farm. (p. 1284)
—Wheels on the Bus. (p. 1901)
Baby Lifeline Staff, jt. auth. see Forbes, E.
Baby Senses Staff, jt. auth. see Beaumont, Susanna.
BabyFirst. BabyFirst How Many? A Counting Book. (p. 128)
Babypants, Caspar. Augie to Zebra: An Alphabet Book! Endle, Kate, illus. (p. 115)
Babypants, Caspar & Ballew, Chris. My Woodland Wish. Endle, Kate, illus. (p. 1221)
Baca, Ana. Benito's Sopaipillas/Las Sopaipillas de Benito. Villarroel, Carolina, tr. (p. 164)
—Chiles for Benito (Chiles para Benito) Colin, Jose Juan, tr. (p. 305)
—Tía's Tamales. Chilton, Noel, illus. (p. 1747)
Baca, Elena, illus. see Murphy, Barbara & Murphy, Barbara Beasley.
Baccala, Gladys, illus. see Harrod-Eagles, Cynthia.
Baccalario, P. D. Suitcase of Stars Pernigotti, Chiara, tr. from ITA. (p. 1673)
Baccalario, Pierdomenico. Century #3: City of Wind. Janeczko, Leah D., tr. from ITA. (p. 287)
—Century #4: Dragon of Seas. Janeczko, Leah D., tr. from ITA. (p. 287)
—City of Wind. Janeczko, Leah D., tr. from ITA. (p. 324)
—Compass of Dreams Pernigotti, Chiara, tr. from ITA. (p. 352)
—Dragon of Seas. Janeczko, Leah D., tr. from ITA. (p. 477)
—Enchanted Emporium. Pernigotti, Chiara, tr. (p. 523)
—Map of the Passages. McGuinness, Nanette, tr. from ITA. (p. 1090)
—Ring of Fire. Janeczko, Leah D., tr. from ITA. (p. 1473)
—Star of Stone. Janeczko, Leah D., tr. (p. 1640)
—Suitcase of Stars Bruno, Iacopo, illus. (p. 1673)
Baccalario, Pierdomenico & McGuinness, Nanette. Thief of Mirrors. Pernigotti, Chiara, tr. from ITA. (p. 1732)
Baccellia, Kim. No More Goddesses. (p. 1259)
Bacchin, Giorgio, illus. see Mayhew, Jon.
Bacchin, Giorgio, jt. auth. see Rees, Celia.
Bacchin, Matteo. Jurassic Mystery: Archaeopteryx. (p. 937)
Bacchin, Matteo, illus. see Shore, Marguerite, tr.
Bacchin, Matteo, illus. see Signore, Marco.
Bacchin, Matteo & Signore, Marco. Journey: Plateosaurus. Shore, Marguerite, tr. from ITA. (p. 927)
—Jurassic Mystery: Archaeopteryx. Shore, Marguerite, tr. from ITA. (p. 937)
Bacchus, Tamika D. Plain Jane Learns to Pray. (p. 1366)
Bach, Alice & Exum, J. Cheryl. Moses' Ark: Stories from the Bible. Dillon, Leo & Dillon, Diane, illus. (p. 1176)
Bach, Annie. Monster Party! (p. 1168)
—Night-Night, Forest Friends. Bach, Annie, illus. (p. 1253)
Bach, Ari. Valhalla. (p. 1830)
Bach, Johann Sebastian. Six Great Secular Cantatas in Full Score. (p. 1582)
Bach, Nancy. Cristoforo Colombo e la Pasta Al Pomodoro - Christopher Columbus & the Pasta with Tomato Sauce: A Bilingual Picture Book (Italian-English Text) Lätti, Leo, illus. (p. 383)
—Galileo Galilei e la Torre Di Pisa - Galileo Galilei & the Pisa Tower: A Bilingual Picture Book about the Italian Astronomer (Italian-English Text) Lätti, Leo, illus. (p. 653)
—Giuseppe Verdi, Compositore d'Opera Italiano - Giuseppe Verdi, Italian Opera Composer: A Bilingual Picture Book (Italian-English Text) Lätti, Leo, illus. (p. 681)
—Maria Montessori & Her Quiet Revolution: A Picture Book about Maria Montessori & Her School Method. Lätti, Leo, illus. (p. 1093)
Bach, Orville E. Tracking the Spirit of Yellowstone: Recollections of 31 Years as a Seasonal Ranger. (p. 1775)
Bach, Richard. Last War: Detective Ferrets & the Case of the Golden Deed. (p. 979)
Bach, Richard & Gardner, Sally. Niña Más Pequeña del Mundo. Tapia, Sonia, tr. (p. 1256)
Bach, Shelby. Of Enemies & Endings. (p. 1279)
—Of Giants & Ice. (p. 1279)
—Of Giants & Ice. Loftis, Cory, illus. (p. 1279)
—Of Sorcery & Snow. (p. 1279)
—Of Witches & Wind. (p. 1279)
Bach, Sherry. Abundant Christmas (p. 7)
Bach, Tamara. Girl from Mars Tanaka, Shelley, tr. from GER. (p. 678)
Bacha, Antoine, jt. auth. see Franco, Liliana.
Bachalo, Chris. Ultimate War (p. 1810)
Bachalo, Chris, illus. see Gischler, Victor.
Bachalo, Chris, jt. illus. see Bradshaw, Nick.
Bachalo, Chris, jt. illus. see Kubert, Adam.
Bachalo, Chris & Irving, Frazier. Uncanny X-Men: Revolution. Vol. 1 (p. 1811)
Bachalo, Chris, et al. Generation X Classic - Volume 2. (p. 660)
—Ultimate X-Men (p. 1810)
—X-Men: With Great Power. (p. 1967)
Bachan, Krystal Ann, illus. see Atwarie, Rossi.
Bachelet, Gilles. My Cat, the Silliest Cat in the World. Bachelet, Gilles, illus. (p. 1200)
Bachelier, Anne, illus. see Carroll, Lewis, pseud.
Bachelor, G. M. No Home Should Be Without. (p. 1258)
Bachem, Paul, illus. see Hart, Alison.
Bächli, Gerhard, et al. Drosophilidae (Diptera) of Fennoscandia & Denmark. (p. 486)
Bachman, Frank P., jt. auth. see McHugh, Michael J.
Bachman, Larry. Where Are You? (p. 1906)
Bachman, Larry B. Where Are You Going? It's about Choice. (p. 1906)
Bachmann, B. L., illus. see Howell, Ruth.
Bachmann, Elaine Rice. While a Tree Grew: The Story of Maryland's Wye Oak. Harrell, Kim, illus. (p. 1911)
Bachmann, Stefan. Peculiar. (p. 1334)
—Whatnot. (p. 1896)
Bachmann, Stefan, et al. Cabinet of Curiosities: 36 Tales Brief & Sinister. Jansson, Alexander, illus. (p. 250)
Bacho, Peter. Leaving Yesler. (p. 986)
Bachoc, Patricia, illus. see Morrison, Kevin.
Bachrach, Anne M. Excuses Don't Count; Results Rule Course: Proven Systems for a Balanced Life. (p. 548)
Bachs, Ramon, illus. see Disney Book Group Staff & Macri, Thomas.
Bachus, Margaret Trimm. Is for Awful! (p. 889)
Bacigalupi, Paolo. Doubt Factory. (p. 473)
—Drowned Cities. (p. 486)
—Ship Breaker. (p. 1567)
—Zombie Baseball Beatdown. (p. 1988)
Back, Francis, illus. see Moore, Christopher.
Back, Samee, illus. see Choi, Robert.
Back-Canevaro, Vanessa. Other Side of Yesterday. (p. 1306)
Backer, Charles. Fireclaw. (p. 591)
Backer, Marni. Food Allergy Friends. (p. 613)
Backer, Miles. Travels with Charlie: Travelin' the Northeast. Nitzberg, Chuck, illus. (p. 1780)
—Travels with Charlie - Down South. Nitzberg, Chuck, illus. (p. 1780)
—Travels with Charlie - Way Out West. Nitzberg, Chuck, illus. (p. 1780)
Backer, Miles, jt. auth. see Bhagat-Clark, Duryan.
Backes, M. Molly. Princesses of Iowa. (p. 1406)
Backes, Nick, illus. see American Girl Editors.
Backes, Nick, illus. see Tripp, Valerie.
Backhouse, Carolyn, illus. see Rivers-Moore, Debbie.
Backland Studio Staff, ed. What Is This? Doubletakes: Picture Puzzles with a Twist! (p. 1891)
Backman, Aidel. Money in the Honey. (p. 1164)
Backman, Aidel, illus. see Weinbach, Shaindel.
Backman, Laura. Lemon the Duck. (p. 991)
Backman, Tisha. Just As I Am. (p. 937)
Backpack Books (Firm) Staff, contrib. by. My Big Animal Book: Includes Touch-And-Feel, Flaps, Pull-Out Tabs, & a Puzzle! (p. 1197)
Backshall, Steve. Steve Backshall's Deadly 60. (p. 1649)
Backues, E. Sharol. Stories of a Dragonfly Spy, a Dog Named Droop & a Little Calf That Wondered Why? (p. 1654)
Backus, Leatha F. Annie & Timmy's Magic Pebbles. (p. 86)

Bacon, Arthur & Bacon, Henry. I Hate Reading: How to Get Through 20 Minutes of Reading a Day Without Really Reading. Hantel, Johanna, illus. (p. 839)
Bacon, C. G. Mean Mandy. (p. 1116)
Bacon, Daskam Josephine. While Caroline Was Growing. (p. 1911)
Bacon, Dolores. Pictures Every Child Should Know (Illust. (p. 1356)
Bacon, Henry, jt. auth. see Bacon, Arthur.
Bacon, Irving R., illus. see Cameron, William J.
Bacon, Josephine Daskam. While Caroline was Growing: Books about Children. (p. 1911)
Bacon, Joy. Oliver Bean, Doctors Aren't Mean! Edward J Russell Elementary School Students, illus. (p. 1285)
Bacon, Lee. Dominion Key. (p. 465)
—Joshua Dread. (p. 927)
—Nameless Hero. (p. 1228)
Bacon, Lizzy. Abortion. (p. 5)
Bacon, Paul. Cats' Letters to Santa. (p. 281)
Bacon, Paul, jt. illus. see O'Sullivan, Tom.
Bacon, Ursula. Shanghai Diary: A Young Girl's Journey from Hitler's Hate to War-Torn China. (p. 1559)
Bacskai, Andrew. Fighting the Legend (p. 586)
Baczynski, Jolanta. Ricky, the Little Elephant. (p. 1470)
Baczynski, Jolanta & Baczynski, Olga. Freddie & Jet. (p. 632)
Baczynski, Olga, jt. auth. see Baczynski, Jolanta.
Bada, Shizzer. Bedtime Stories. (p. 157)
Badalamenti, Andrew. Around the World in One Night. Santa's Secrets Unwrapped! (p. 101)
Badalian, Lucy. George the Dragonslayer & His Friends: On Earth. Badalian, Lucy, illus. (p. 663)
Badaoui, Chad. Lulu & the Purple Pebble. Oehlers, Adam, illus. (p. 1064)
Badasch, Shirley, jt. auth. see Chesebro, Doreen.
Badavino, Jimmy. That's Why They're Called Punkins. Colangione-B, Christie, illus. (p. 1727)
Badcott, Nicholas. Pocket Explorer: African Civilizations. (p. 1375)
Baddeley, Alan, et al. Reading Decision Test: Word Decision 1. (p. 1445)
—Reading Decision Test: Word Decision 2. (p. 1445)
—Reading Decision Test: Letter Decision 1. (p. 1445)
Baddeley, Elizabeth, illus. see Cooper, Ilene.
Baddorf, Robert A. & Perrin, Christopher. Latin for Children, Primer a Activity Book! (p. 979)
Baddorf, Robert & Perrin, Christopher. Latin for Children. Baddorf, Robert, illus. (p. 979)
—Latin for Children, Primer B Activity Book! Baddorf, Robert, illus. (p. 979)
Badeaux, Dewey. Sam & Skully. Ball, Lauren, illus. (p. 1506)
Badegruber, Bernie. 101 Life Skills Games for Children: Learning, Growing, Getting along (Ages 6-12) Jesner, Alois, illus. (p. 1999)
—101 More Life Skills Games for Children: Learning, Growing, Getting Along. (p. 1999)
Badejo, Diedre L. African Union. (p. 28)
Badelt, Klaus. Pirates of the Caribbean - The Curse of the Black Pearl. (p. 1364)
Baden, Jan. Risen Heart: A journal for grieving youth. : the Light Within. (p. 1475)
Baden, Robert. Jesus Returns to Heaven. Hackett, Michael, illus. (p. 916)
—Psalms for Kids. (p. 1413)
Badenhop, Faye D. 'Quacking' the 'Pair O' Ducks' Case. (p. 1422)
Baden-Powell, Robert. Life's Snags & How to Meet Them. (p. 1013)
—Scouting for Boys. (p. 1532)
—Young Knights of the Empire. (p. 1979)
Bader, Amanda. Havana Nights. (p. 754)
Bader, Arlys Elaine. Adventures of Garth & Cloey. (p. 18)
Bader, Bonnie. 100 Monsters in My School. Hendrix, Bryan, illus. (p. 1998)
—Benny the Big Shot Goes to Camp. Warren, Shari, illus. (p. 165)
—Family Reunion. Cole, Mernie Gallagher, illus. (p. 568)
—Fly, Butterfly. (p. 609)
—Go to Bed, Blue. Robertson, Michael, illus. (p. 687)
—Hummingbirds. (p. 826)
—Kit-Kit-Kittens. (p. 962)
—Max's 4 Questions. Hendrix, Bryan & Bryan, Hendrix, illus. (p. 1112)
—Play with Blue. (p. 1371)
—Play with Blue. Robertson, Michael, illus. (p. 1371)
—Pup-Pup-Puppies. (p. 1417)
—Who Was Alexander Graham Bell? (p. 1918)
—Who Was Alexander Graham Bell? Groff, David, illus. (p. 1918)
—Who Was Christopher Columbus? (p. 1918)
—Who Was Christopher Columbus? Harrison, Nancy, illus. (p. 1918)
—Who Was Martin Luther King, Jr. ? Wolf, Elizabeth, illus. (p. 1918)
—Who Was Martin Luther King, Jr. ? Wolf, Elizabeth & Harrison, Nancy, illus. (p. 1918)
—Who Was Robert E. Lee? (p. 1919)
—Who Was Robert E. Lee? Harrison, Nancy & O'Brien, John, illus. (p. 1919)
Bader, Joanne. Abraham, Sarah, & Isaac. (p. 7)
—God Provides Victory Through Gideon. Giliewe, Unada, illus. (p. 690)
—He's Risen! He's Alive! Heroldt, Richard, illus. (p. 774)
—Jesus Heals the Centurion's Servant. (p. 915)
—Jesus resucita a una nina (Jesus Wakes the Little Girl) (p. 916)
—Jesus Wakes the Little Girl. (p. 916)
—Moses & the Long Walk. von der Sterre, Johanna, illus. (p. 1176)
—Widow's Offering. (p. 1927)
Badescu, Ramona. Pomelo Explores Color. Chaud, Benjamin, illus. (p. 1382)
—Pomelo's Big Adventure. Chaud, Benjamin, illus. (p. 1382)
—Pomelo's Opposites. Chaud, Benjamin, illus. (p. 1382)
Badescu, Ramona & Bedrick, Claudia Z. Pomelo Begins to Grow. Chaud, Benjamin, illus. (p. 1382)
Badger, Cynthia. Sara's Secret. (p. 1514)
Badger, Gerry. Photobook: A History. Vol. 1 Parr, Martin, ed. (p. 1353)
Badger, H. Alien Brainwash. (p. 40)
—Brainiacs. (p. 222)
—Dark World. (p. 408)
—Gas Giant. (p. 657)
—Jelly People. (p. 912)
—Kid Kingdom. (p. 951)
—Shrinking Race. (p. 1571)
Badger, Hilary. State of Grace. (p. 1644)
Badger, M. C. Bad News Birthday. Swingler, Simon, illus. (p. 132)
—Baddies vs. Goodies. Swingler, Simon, illus. (p. 132)
—Coolest Pool. (p. 364)
—Excellent Invention. (p. 547)
—Perfect Pet. (p. 1342)
—Very Good Idea. (p. 1838)
—When Robots Go Bad. Swingler, Simon, illus. (p. 1904)
Badger, M. C. & Swingler, Simon. Running Riot. (p. 1497)
Badger, Meredith. Boy Friend? (p. 217)
—Camp Chaos. Oswald, Ash, illus. (p. 257)
—Fairy School Dropout Undercover. (p. 564)
—Genie High School. (p. 661)
—Genie in Charge. Mackintosh, Michelle, illus. (p. 661)
—Go Girl! #12: Back to School. Oswald, Ash, illus. (p. 686)
—How to Boost Your Profile. (p. 815)
—Sophie Bennett Saves the Planet. (p. 1613)
—Things I Don't Know. (p. 1733)
—Undercover. Mackintosh, Michelle, illus. (p. 1814)
Badger, Meredith, jt. auth. see Perry, Chrissie.
Badger, Meredith & McAuley, Rowan. School Spirit (p. 1523)
Badger, Pearstina. Jessica's Journeys: Stories about Life's Lessons. (p. 914)
Badger, Scott. How Big of a Boy are You? (p. 805)
Badger, Ty. Crayons Alive. (p. 377)
Badgett, Sara Ann. Sara's Backyard. (p. 1514)
Badia, Arnhilda. Rourke's Complete History of Our Presidents Encyclopedia 2013 Set. (p. 1491)
Badillo, Steve. Skateboarding: Legendary Tricks. No. 2 (p. 1583)
Badillo, Steve, jt. auth. see Werner, Doug.
Bading, Sarah. Flea on the Farm. (p. 603)
Badiru, Ibrahim Ade. Warty. (p. 1859)
Badoe, Adwoa. Between Sisters (p. 173)
—Nana's Cold Days Junaid, Bushra, illus. (p. 1228)
—Pot of Wisdom. Diakité, Baba Wagué, illus. (p. 1388)
Badoe, Adwoa A. Crabs for Dinner. (p. 375)
Badreddine, Delphine. Tell Me about Colors, Shapes, & Opposites. Guillerey, Aurélie, illus. (p. 1716)
Badt, Karin Luisa. Hair There & Everywhere. (p. 736)
Badu. Learning with the Flowerms: Vol. -1 Hospital Visit. (p. 986)
Bae, Hyun-Joo. New Clothes for New Year's Day. Bae, Hyun-Joo, illus. (p. 1244)
Baehr, Peter R. & Gordenker, Leon. United Nations: Reality & Ideal. (p. 1819)
Baek, Matthew J. Panda & Polar Bear. Baek, Matthew J., illus. (p. 1320)
Baek, Matthew J., illus. see Kushner, Lawrence & Schmidt, Gary.
Baen, Noah, illus. see Lewis, Richard.
Baena, Gloria. Invitacion a la Fiesta del Gran Gorila. Osorno, Laura, illus. (p. 886)
Baer, Brian, illus. see O'Coyne, James.
Baer, Edith. This Is the Way We Go to School. (p. 1736)
—Words are like Faces Teis, Kyra, illus. (p. 1951)
Baer, Jill. Sofia the First: Just One of the Princes. (p. 1605)
Baer, Jill & Disney Book Group Staff. World of Reading: Sofia the First Just One of the Princes: Level 1. Disney Storybook Artists Staff, illus. (p. 1957)
Baer, Julie. I Only Like What I Like. (p. 844)
—Love Me Later. (p. 1060)
Baer, M. Teresa. Indianapolis: A City of Immigrants. (p. 871)
Baer, Marianna. Frost. (p. 644)
Baer, Peter. Wilma Rudolph: Gold-Medal Winner. (p. 1934)
Baer, Peter & Castle, Grace. Olympic Champion: Wilma Rudolph. (p. 1287)
Baer, Sam. 100 Paper Dragons to Fold & Fly. (p. 1998)
—Illustrated Bible Stories. (p. 857)
Baer, Suzie. Peru's MRTA: Tupac Amaru Revolutionary Movement. (p. 1345)
Baer, T. H. Measuring Distance. (p. 1117)
—Measuring Height. (p. 1117)
Baeta, Louisa, tr. from POR. From Another World (p. 641)
Baeta, Luisa, tr. see MacHado, Ana Maria & Machado, Ana Maria.
Baeten, Lieve. Clever Little Witch. Fossey, Wietse, illus. (p. 331)
—Curious Little Witch. (p. 394)
—Curious Little Witch Board Book. (p. 394)
—Happy Birthday, Little Witch! (p. 745)
—Merry Christmas, Little Witch. (p. 1129)
—Up & Away with the Little Witch. (p. 1824)
Baeuerle, Patrick A. & Landa, Norbert. Microexplorers - Physical Science Series (p. 1136)
Báez, Annecy. My Daughter's Eyes & Other Stories. (p. 1201)
Baez, Debra. C a F a S Caring about Fire & Safety. (p. 249)
—Fly, Fly, Little Fly. (p. 609)
—Things That Seem Scary in the Night (p. 1733)
Baez, Josefina. Comrade, Bliss Ain't Playing: Un Cuento de la Republica Dominicana. Cortes, Paulina, illus. (p. 355)
Baez, Marcelo, illus. see Biskup, Agnieszka & Enz, Tammy.
Baez, Marcelo, illus. see Biskup, Agnieszka, et al.
Baez, Marcelo, illus. see Biskup, Agnieszka.
Baez, Marcelo, illus. see Enz, Tammy & Biskup, Agnieszka.
Baez, Marcelo, illus. see Enz, Tammy, et al.
Baez, Marcelo, illus. see Enz, Tammy.
Baeza, Georgina, tr. see Gallegos, Yuliana.
Baeza Ventura, Gabriela, tr. see De Anda, Diane.
Baeza Ventura, Gabriela, tr. see Gonzales Bertrand, Diane.
Baeza Ventura, Gabriela, tr. see Lacamara, Laura.
Baeza Ventura, Gabriela, tr. see Lachtman, Ofelia Dumas.
Baeza Ventura, Gabriela, tr. see Olivas, Daniel.
Baeza Ventura, Gabriela, tr. see Ortiz Cofer, Judith.
Baeza Ventura, Gabriela, tr. see Rivas, Spelile.
Baeza Ventura, Gabriela, tr. see Ruiz-Flores, Lupe.
Baeza Ventura, Gabriela, tr. see Saldaña, René.
Baeza Ventura, Gabriela, tr. see Zepeda, Gwendolyn.
Bagby, Chris, ed. Ode to the Appalachian Trail. (p. 1278)
Bagby, Jeffrey K., illus. see Shawver, Margaret.
Bagby, Lois. Sofie Meets a Wobble. (p. 1605)
Bagby, Susan, jt. auth. see Howe, Maggy G.
Bagdanov, Patricia. Adventures of Charlie & a Dragon Named Trevor. (p. 17)
Bagdasarian, Ross & Karman, Janice. Alvin & the Chipmunks - It's Show Time! With Sound & Music. Running Press Staff, ed. (p. 51)
Bage, Grant & Turner, Jane. Prison Break! And Other Adventures Underground (p. 1407)
Bagert, Brod. Giant Children. Arnold, Tedd, illus. (p. 673)
—Hormone Jungle: Coming of Age in Middle School. (p. 798)
—School Fever. Neubecker, Robert, illus. (p. 1522)
—Shout! Little Poems That Roar. Yoshikawa, Sachiko, illus. (p. 1570)
Bagert, Brod, ed. Edgar Allan Poe. Cobleigh, Carolynn, illus. (p. 504)
—Poetry for Young People: Edgar Allan Poe. Cobleigh, Carolynn, illus. (p. 1376)
Bagge, Peter. Fun with Buddy & Lisa. (p. 648)
—Yeah! Thompson, Kim, ed. (p. 1969)
Baggett, Byrd. Complete Book of Business Success. (p. 352)
Baggett, David, et al, eds. Harry Potter & Philosophy: If Aristotle Ran Hogwarts. (p. 750)
Baggett, Denise. Smithsonian Discover: Space. (p. 1594)
Baggett, Shirley Reed. Adventures of Bandit: A Little Racoon Goes into the Forbidden Forest. (p. 16)
Baggett, Tamara. 52 Weeks of Family Night: Fast & Easy Lessons for Young Families. (p. 1997)
Baggetta, Maria, illus. see Hopkins, Lee Bennett & Boyds Mills Press Staff.
Baggetta, Maria, illus. see Hopkins, Lee Bennett.
Baggetta, Maria, et al. Pastel Step by Step. (p. 1327)
Baggott, Julianna. Burn. (p. 243)
—Fuse. (p. 650)
—Prince of Fenway Park. (p. 1401)
Baggott, Stella. Advent Calendar to Color. (p. 14)
—Around the World Sticker Book. (p. 101)
—Baby's Very First 123 Book. Baggott, Stella, illus. (p. 129)
—Baby's Very First Bath Book. (p. 129)
—Baby's Very First Black & White Library. (p. 129)
—Baby's Very First Colors Book. (p. 129)
—Baby's Very First Little Book of Baby Animals. (p. 129)
—Baby's Very First Noisy Book. Baggott, Stella, illus. (p. 129)
—Baby's Very First Noisy Book Farm. (p. 129)
—Baby's Very First Noisy Nursery Rhymes. (p. 129)
—Baby's Very First Outdoors Book. (p. 129)
—Baby's Very First Stroller Book Animals. (p. 129)
—Baby's Very First Stroller Book Jungle. (p. 129)
—Baby's Very First Touchy-Feely Animals Book. (p. 129)
—Baby's Very First Touchy-Feely Book. (p. 129)
—Baby's Very First Touchy-Feely Christmas Book. Baggott, Stella, illus. (p. 129)
—Baby's Very First Touchy-Feely Lift the Flap Play Book. (p. 129)
—Baby's Very First Toys Book. (p. 129)
—Flip, Flap, Flop. (p. 604)
—Glug, Glug, Glug. Cartwright, Mary, illus. (p. 685)
—Lots of Things to Find & Color in Fairyland. (p. 1057)
Baggott, Stella, illus. see Andrews, Georgina & Knighton, Kate.
Baggott, Stella, illus. see Bowman, Lucy.
Baggott, Stella, illus. see Pratt, Leonie.
Baggott, Stella, illus. see Watt, Fiona, et al.
Baggott, Stella, illus. see Watt, Fiona.
Baggott, Stella & Arrowsmith, Vicker. Popstars & Movie Stars CV. (p. 1385)
Baghcheban, Samineh. Zendigiye Koodakan. (p. 1986)
Baghdasaryan, Rouzanna. Dark. Morchiladze, Manana, illus. (p. 407)
—Moush Wants to Get Lost. Yulia, Lushnikova, illus. (p. 1182)
Baginski, Deanna Fisher. Harvest Time at the Fisher Farms. (p. 752)
Bagley, Conor. Ziggy McFinster's Nantucket Adventure. Bernard Westcott, Nadine, illus. (p. 1986)
Bagley, Jessixa. Boats for Papa. (p. 205)
Bagley, Katie S. Antarctica (p. 88)
—Brush Well: A Look at Dental Care. (p. 232)
—Early American Industrial Revolution, 1793-1850. (p. 493)
—Women Suffrage Movement, 1844-1920. (p. 1946)
Bagley, Mark. Avengers Assemble by Brian Michael Bendis. (p. 118)
—Cats & Kings (p. 281)
—Irresponsible (p. 888)
—Public Scrutiny (p. 1414)
—Ultimate Spider-Man: Carnage. Vol. 11 (p. 1810)
—Ultimate Spider-Man: Superstars. Vol. 12 (p. 1810)
—Ultimate Spider-Man - Legacy (p. 1810)
—Venom (p. 1835)
Bagley, Mark, illus. see Bendis, Brian Michael & Quesada, Joe.
Bagley, Mark, illus. see Busiek, Kurt & David, Peter.
Bagley, Mark, illus. see Defalco, Tom, et al.
Bagley, Mark, illus. see Youngquist, Jeff, ed.
Bagley, Mark & Lim, Ron. Venom: Lethal Protector. (p. 1835)
Bagley, Mark, et al. Tha Amazing Spider-Man. (p. 1724)
Bagley, Pat, illus. see Duffy, Kate & McRedmond, Sarah.
Bagley, Pat, illus. see Kirby, Robert.
Bagley, Tom, illus. see Kyi, Tanya Lloyd.
Bagley, Val. Gospel Truths from the Book of Mormon. (p. 703)
—My Gospel ABCs. (p. 1210)
—My Little Book about Joseph. (p. 1212)
—Who Said Book of Mormon Match Game. (p. 1917)
Bagley, Val Chadwick. I Will Follow God's Plan for Me. (p. 848)
—I Will Trust in Heavenly Father & Jesus. (p. 848)
—Joseph's First Vision. (p. 926)
—My Book about Me. (p. 1198)
Bagley, Val Chadwick, illus. see Mullins, Amy.
Bagley, Val Chadwick & Beckstrand, Tamara, trs. My Little Book about Prayer. Bagley, Val Chadwick, illus. (p. 1212)
Bagley, Val Chadwick & Mullins, Amy. Book of Mormon ABC Book. (p. 211)
—My Favorite Stories from the Bible. (p. 1203)
—My Favorite Stories from the Book of Mormon. (p. 1203)
Baglio, Ben M. Bunny in a Basket. Baum, Ann, illus. (p. 242)
—Cat in the Castle. (p. 278)
—Collie with a Card. Baum, Ann, illus. (p. 340)
—Colt on Christmas Eve. Baum, Ann & Lasher, Mary Ann, illus. (p. 346)
—Come Back, Buddy! (p. 347)
—Corgi in the Cupcakes. Baum, Ann, illus. (p. 367)
—Dalmatian in the Daisies. Baum, Ann & Lasher, Mary Ann, illus. (p. 401)
—Hamster in the Holly. Baum, Ann & Gregory, Jenny, illus. (p. 739)
—Help Find Honey! (p. 765)
—Husky with a Heart. (p. 830)
—Kitty in the Candy Hearts. (p. 963)
—Lost in the Snow. Ettlinger, Doris, illus. (p. 1056)
—Max Is Missing. (p. 1111)
—Midnight Mouse. Ellis, Andy, illus. (p. 1139)
—Puppy in a Puddle Baum, Ann, illus. (p. 1418)
—Puupy in a Present. (p. 1420)
—Runaway Rascal. (p. 1496)
—Searching for Sunshine. Beckett, Andrew & Aubrey, Meg Kelleher, illus. (p. 1537)
—Vanishing Point. Ettlinger, Doris, illus. (p. 1833)
Baglio, Ben M. & Daniels, Lucy. Labrador on the Lawn. Gregory, Jenny, illus. (p. 970)
Baglio, Ben M. & Lasher, Mary Ann. Tabby under the Tree. Baum, Ann, illus. (p. 1694)
Bagnell, Kenneth. Little Immigrants (p. 1029)
Bagnold, Enid. National Velvet. (p. 1234)
Bagnoli, Christine. Miguel's Family Picnic. (p. 1141)
Baguley, Elizabeth. Long Way from Home. Chapman, Jane, illus. (p. 1047)
—Meggie Moon Mabire, Grégoire, illus. (p. 1124)
—Ready, Steady, Ghost! Lindsay, Marion, illus. (p. 1447)
Baguley, Kitt. Venezuela (p. 1835)
Bagwell, Angela. King of Gran Lala's Cats. (p. 958)
Bah, Mariam Kundai. Nature Creatures. (p. 1236)
Baha El Din, Sherif, jt. auth. see Navarro, Dominique.
Bahadur, Gaiutra. Family Ties. (p. 568)
Bahamon, Claire. Peter Fished the Springs of Galilee. Sampson, Anne, ed. (p. 1346)
Bahhur, Hana T. Red Dolphin: Looking for a Friend. (p. 1453)
Bahk, Jane. Juna's Jar. Hoshino, Felicia, illus. (p. 934)
Bahlmann, Clemens. Unterwegs: Lehrwerk Fur Die Mittelstufe: Deutsch Als Fremdsprache (p. 1823)
Bahr, Ann Marie B., ed. Religions of the World. (p. 1458)
Bahr, Mary. If Nathan Were Here. Jerome, Karen A., illus. (p. 853)
Bahrawi, Nazry, jt. auth. see Levy, Patricia.
Bahtuoh, D. G. Nap-Nap, Quack-Quack. (p. 1229)
Bahz, Kahanni. Ants? in My Pants? An Antimated Tale. Fraser, Kevin, illus. (p. 90)
Bai, Durga. Churki-Burki Book of Rhyme. (p. 318)
Bai, Durga, illus. see Rao, Sirish.
Bai, Jenny, illus. see Byrd, Michael.
Baia, Edward. Aikanana. (p. 30)
—Barau Barau. Witnes, Vitus, illus. (p. 137)
—Flying Fox & the Cockatoo. Mape, Michael, illus. (p. 610)
—Isiumanu & Manubada. Ella, Peter Leo, illus. (p. 891)
—Isokau Akuaku: A Traditional Story from Central Province. Mape, Michael & Ella, Peter Leo, illus. (p. 893)
Baicker, Karen. Conquistador: Francisco Pizarro Ravages the Inca Empire. (p. 358)
—Election Activity Book: Dozens of Activities That Help Kids Learn about Voting, Campaigns, Our Government, Presidents, & More. (p. 508)
—Lemurs. (p. 991)
—Napoleon Complex: A Young General Takes France by Storm. (p. 1229)
—Raccoons. (p. 1430)
Baicker, Karen & Chronicle Books Staff. I Can Do It Too! Wilson-Max, Ken, illus. (p. 835)
—You Can Do It Too! Wilson-Max, Ken, illus. (p. 1974)
Baicker, Karen & Scholastic Canada Ltd. Staff. Quick Cloze Passages for Boosting Comprehension Grades 4-6: 40 Leveled Cloze Passages That Give Students Practice in Using Context Clues to Build Vocabulary & Comprehension. (p. 1427)
Baicker, Karen & Scholastic, Inc. Staff. Quick Cloze Passages for Boosting Comprehension: 40 Leveled Cloze Passages That Give Students Practice in Using Context Clues to Build Vocabulary & Comprehension. (p. 1427)
Baicker, Karen, et al. Lemurs. (p. 991)
Baicker-McKee, Carol. Apple Pie for Dinner (p. 92)
Baicker-McKee, Carol, illus. see Stiegemeyer, Julie.
Baidaba. Calila y Diana. (p. 253)
Baier, Ellen & Skindzier, Jon. Franklin & Marshall College College Prowler off the Record. (p. 630)
Baier, Harry. Yo-Yo World Trick Book. (p. 1972)
Baier, Hiltrud. Greta in Schweden. (p. 723)
Baier, Jeanne M. Twins Jeffrey & Jeanne. (p. 1802)
Baifus, Rut, illus. see Grinvald, Zeev & Zryl, Laya.
Baig, Khalid. First Things First: For Inquiring Minds & Yearning Hearts. (p. 597)
Baiker, Karen. Barnyard Friends. (p. 139)
Baikie, Constance N., illus. see Baikie, James.
Baikie, Constance N., jt. auth. see Baikie, James.
Baikie, James. Peeps at Many Lands: Ancient Rome (Yesterday's Classics) (p. 1335)
—Peeps at Many Lands: Ancient Greece (Yesterday's Classics) Fulleylove, John & Baikie, Constance N., illus. (p. 1335)
Baikie, James & Baikie, Constance N. Peeps at Many Lands: Ancient Egypt (Yesterday's Classics) (p. 1335)

B

Bail, Mina Mauerstein. Max & Voltaire Getting to Know You. Choquette, Gabriel, illus. (p. 1110)
Bail, Willow & Fields, April. Is the World Bigger Than a Pond? (p. 890)
Bailen, Leaf, jt. auth. see Bailen, Mark.
Bailen, Mark & Bailen, Leaf. Earf. (p. 492)
Bailer, Darice. African-American Culture. (p. 27)
—Austin & Alex Learn about Adjectives. Girouard, Patrick, illus. (p. 116)
—Australia. (p. 116)
—Dinomite! All about Dinisaurs. (p. 441)
—Donkeys. (p. 466)
—Geese. (p. 659)
—Gran Ferrocarril. Farnsworth, Bill, illus. (p. 706)
—How Do Caterpillars Become Butterflies? (p. 806)
—How Do Tadpoles Become Frogs? (p. 807)
—India. (p. 870)
—Iris & Ian Learn about Interjections. Oseid, Kelsey, illus. (p. 887)
—Last Rail. (p. 978)
—Measuring Length. Petelinsek, Kathleen, illus. (p. 1117)
—Measuring Temperature. Petelinsek, Kathleen, illus. (p. 1117)
—Measuring Time with a Calendar. Petelinsek, Kathleen, illus. (p. 1117)
—Michelangelo. Morrow, J. T., illus. (p. 1135)
—Pablo Picasso. Morrow, J. T., illus. (p. 1316)
—Pony Express. Antonishak, Tom, illus. (p. 1382)
—Prairie Dogs. (p. 1392)
—Railroad!, Level 3: A Story of the Transcontinental Railroad. Farnsworth, Bill, illus. (p. 1434)
—Rembrandt. Morrow, J. T., illus. (p. 1459)
—Ski Slopestyle. (p. 1584)
—Ski Superpipe. (p. 1584)
—Snowboard Cross. (p. 1600)
—Snowboard Superpipe. (p. 1600)
—Snowmobile Snocross. (p. 1601)
—What's Great about Arkansas? (p. 1897)
—What's Great about Kansas? (p. 1897)
—What's Great about Montana? (p. 1897)
—What's Great about Nebraska? (p. 1897)
—What's Great about North Dakota? (p. 1897)
—What's Great about Ohio? (p. 1897)
—What's Great about Vermont? (p. 1897)
—Why Do Bears Hibernate? (p. 1923)
—Why Does It Thunder & Lightning? (p. 1924)
—Will & Wendy Build a Website with Digital Tools. O'Neill, Sean, illus. (p. 1932)
Bailer, Darice, jt. auth. see Shultz, Charles M.
Bailer, Darice & Domínguez, Madelca. Bella Durmiente. Vila Delclòs, Jordi, illus. (p. 162)
—Flautista de Hamelín. Vila Delclòs, Jordi, illus. (p. 603)
—Lobo y Los Siete Cabritos. Montañá, Marta, illus. (p. 1044)
—Ratita Presumida. Curto, Rosa María, illus. (p. 1440)
—Ricitos de Oro y Los Tres Osos. Espluga, María, illus. (p. 1470)
Bailer, Darice, et al. León y el Ratón. Subirana, Joan, illus. (p. 992)
—Pastorcito Mentiroso. Infante, Francesc, illus. (p. 1327)
—Pulgarcita. Andrada, Javier, illus. (p. 1415)
—Ruiseñor. Max, illus. (p. 1494)
—Saltamontes y Las Hormigas. Bassa, illus. (p. 1505)
Bailes, Theanna. Asia & Hopper. (p. 106)
Bailey. Computer Science Tea Man. (p. 355)
Bailey, jt. auth. see Ferreira, Ann Devine.
Bailey, Annette Gentry & McGraw-Hill Education Staff. Discovering Life Skills. (p. 449)
Bailey, Arquilla. Roscoe: I Didn't Do Nuthin. (p. 1489)
Bailey, Arthur Scott. Sleepy Time Tales the Tale of Fatty Coon. (p. 1590)
—Sleepy-Time Tales: The Tale of Brownie B. (p. 1590)
—Sleepy-Time Tales: The Tale of Cuffy Bea. (p. 1590)
—Sleepy-Time Tales: The Tale of Fatty Coo. (p. 1590)
—Sleepy-Time Tales: The Tale of Sandy Chi. (p. 1590)
—Sleepy-Time Tales: The Tale of Tommy Fox. (p. 1590)
—Tale of Benny Badger. (p. 1699)
—Tale of Freddie Firefly. (p. 1699)
—Tale of Grandfather Mole. (p. 1699)
—Tale of Peter Mink. (p. 1700)
—Tale of Sandy Chipmunk. (p. 1700)
—Tale of Tommy Fox. (p. 1700)
—Tuck-Me-in Tales: The Tale of Freddie Fi. (p. 1795)
—Tuck-Me-in Tales: The Tale of Old Mr Cro. (p. 1795)
—Tuck-Me-in Tales: The Tale of Solomon Ow. (p. 1795)
Bailey Association Staff & Gorman, Jacqueline Laks. Modern Feminist Movement. (p. 1158)
Bailey Association Staff & Senker, Cath. Strength in Numbers. (p. 1667)
—Women Claim the Vote. (p. 1945)
Bailey Association Staff, et al. Women of Today. (p. 1946)
Bailey, Beth Burdette. Raining Fish. (p. 1436)
Bailey, Carla R. A. Inner Beauty. (p. 875)
Bailey, Carolyn Sherwin. Boys & Girls of Colonial Days. (p. 220)
—Stories of Great Adventures. Burd, Clara M., illus. (p. 1655)
—Tell Me Another Story: The Book of Story Programs. (p. 1716)
—Wonder Stories the Best Myths for Boys & Girls. (p. 1947)
Bailey, Catherine. Mind Your Monsters. Vidal, Oriol, illus. (p. 1145)
Bailey, Charles. Slick Glickman, Unlikely Hero. (p. 1590)
Bailey, Christine. Girl in the Middle. (p. 678)
Bailey, Court, illus. see Gordon, Leslie M.
Bailey, Dawn Wentz. Joey & the Mighty Oak. (p. 920)
Bailey, Dayna. Perfection. (p. 1342)
Bailey, Debbie. Grandma & Grandpa. Huszar, Susan, photos by. (p. 707)
—Mi Animalito. Huszar, Susan, photos by. (p. 1132)
—Mis Amigos. Huszar, Susan, photos by. (p. 1149)
—My Friends. Huszar, Susan, photos by. (p. 1209)
—My Mom & My Dad. Huszar, Susan, photos by. (p. 1214)
—My Pet. Huszar, Susan, photos by. (p. 1217)
—Sisters & Brothers. Huszar, Susan, photos by. (p. 1581)
Bailey, Debbie R. Domino Effect. (p. 465)
Bailey, Devon. Supercars (p. 1682)
Bailey, Diane. America's Best Dance Crew. (p. 64)
—Ancient Greece. (p. 69)
—Biomedical Engineers! (p. 189)
—Brain Surgeons. (p. 222)
—Coal Power. (p. 336)
—Cyber Ethics. (p. 396)
—Democracy. Colton, Timothy J., ed. (p. 425)
—Dictatorship. Colton, Timothy J., ed. (p. 436)
—Emperor Qin's Terra-Cotta Army. (p. 521)
—Future of Space Exploration. (p. 651)
—General George Thomas: The Rock of Chickamauga. (p. 660)
—Ghosts in America. (p. 672)
—Girls: Being Best Friends. (p. 679)
—Great Moments in World Cup History. (p. 717)
—Harnessing Energy: Coal Power. (p. 749)
—Harnessing Energy: Nuclear Power. (p. 749)
—Harnessing Energy: Solar Power. (p. 749)
—Harnessing Energy: Wind Power. (p. 749)
—History of Dance. (p. 784)
—How Markets Work. (p. 811)
—Hydropower. (p. 831)
—Kansas: Past & Present. (p. 943)
—Kansas Basketball. (p. 943)
—Mary J. Blige. (p. 1100)
—Miley Cyrus. (p. 1142)
—Natural Gas Power. (p. 1235)
—Nuclear Power. (p. 1270)
—Plague. (p. 1366)
—Solar Power. (p. 1606)
—Story of Interscope Records. (p. 1658)
—Suzanne Collins. (p. 1688)
—Tennessee: Past & Present. (p. 1720)
—Texas Football. (p. 1724)
—Top 10 Secrets for Creating & Sticking to a Budget Successfully. (p. 1768)
—Venus & Serena Williams: Tennis Champions. (p. 1836)
—Wind Power. (p. 1935)
—Yamaha: Sport Racing Legend. (p. 1968)
Bailey, Dottie. Great Escape: The Mummy's Walk. (p. 715)
—Great Escape: A Library Adventure. (p. 715)
Bailey, Edward R. Computer Science: A Structure. (p. 355)
Bailey, Ellen. Girls' Summer Book. Ryan, Nellie & Jackson, Lisa, illus. (p. 681)
—Katya's Gold: What Will Her Dreams Cost? (p. 946)
—One Dream, One Direction. (p. 1294)
Bailey, Ellen, jt. auth. see Scholastic, Inc. Staff.
Bailey, Ellen & Mosedale, Julian. London Activity Book: With Palaces, Puzzles & Pictures to Colour. Pinder, Andrew, illus. (p. 1046)
Bailey, Ellen & Williams, Imogen. 5 Seconds of Summer: 100% Unofficial. (p. 1992)
Bailey, Ethel M. T. Lily Pond Village (p. 1018)
Bailey, Frank, illus. see Huberts, Al.
Bailey, Garrick A., ed. Indians in Contemporary Society. (p. 871)
Bailey, Gauvin Alexander. Art of Colonial Latin America. MacKenzie, Julia, ed. (p. 102)
Bailey, Gerry. Adventure Homes. Dreidemy, Joëlle et al, illus. (p. 14)
—Alone in the Arctic. (p. 48)
—Ankylosaurus. Chesterman, Adrian, illus. (p. 84)
—Changing Climate. (p. 290)
—Dry in the Desert. (p. 487)
—Farming for the Future. (p. 574)
—Flight. (p. 604)
—Fragile Planet. (p. 627)
—Out of Energy. (p. 1311)
—Parasaurolophus. McIntosh, Gabe, illus. (p. 1324)
—Powerful Machines. (p. 1390)
—Pressing Down: The Lever. (p. 1397)
—Pteranodon. Carr, Karen, illus. (p. 1413)
—Pulling Up: The Pulley. (p. 1416)
—Rolling Along: Wheels & Axles. (p. 1485)
—Sabre-Tooth Tiger. Reaveley, Trevor, illus. (p. 1500)
—Sea Transportation. (p. 1535)
—Sloping up & Down: The Ramp. (p. 1591)
—Smithsonian Prehistoric Zone (p. 1594)
—Space Challenge. (p. 1618)
—Spinosaurus. Scalf, Chris & McIntosh, Gabe, illus. (p. 1628)
—Splitting Apart: The Wedge. (p. 1630)
—Stegosaurus. Carr, Karen, illus. (p. 1646)
—Storybook Homes. Radford, Karen & Dreidemy, Joëlle, illus. (p. 1663)
—Stranded on an Island. (p. 1664)
—Swept Away by the Storm. (p. 1690)
—Tangled in the Rainforest. (p. 1705)
—Technology. (p. 1711)
—Trapped on the Rock. (p. 1779)
—Triceratops. Carr, Karen, illus. (p. 1785)
—Tylosaurus. Carr, Karen, illus. (p. 1805)
—Tyrannosaurus Rex. Carr, Karen, illus. (p. 1805)
—Velociraptor. Carr, Karen, illus. (p. 1835)
—Winding Around: The Screw. (p. 1936)
—Woolly Mammoth. Carr, Karen, illus. (p. 1950)
—Working Homes. Dreidemy, Joëlle et al, illus. (p. 1952)
Bailey, Gerry, jt. auth. see Ganeri, Anita.
Bailey, Gerry, jt. auth. see Way, Steve.
Bailey, Gerry & Foster, Karen. Armstrong's Moon Rock. Radford, Karen & Noyes, Leighton, illus. (p. 100)
—Cleopatra's Coin. Radford, Karen & Noyes, Leighton, illus. (p. 331)
—Columbus's Chart. Noyes, Leighton & Radford, Karen, illus. (p. 346)
—Columbus's Chart. Radford, Karen & Noyes, Leighton, illus. (p. 346)
—Galileo's Telescope. Noyes, Leighton & Radford, Karen, illus. (p. 653)
—Julius Caesar's Sandals. Noyes, Leighton, illus. (p. 933)
—Leonardo's Palette. Radford, Karen & Noyes, Leighton, illus. (p. 992)
—Marco Polo's Silk Purse. Noyes, Leighton & Radford, Karen, illus. (p. 1092)
—Marco Polo's Silk Purse. Radford, Karen & Noyes, Leighton, illus. (p. 1092)
—Martin Luther King Jr.'s Microphone. Radford, Karen & Noyes, Leighton, illus. (p. 1098)
—Mozart's Wig. (p. 1184)
—Mozart's Wig. Noyes, Leighton & Radford, Karen, illus. (p. 1184)
—Queen Victoria's Diamond. Noyes, Leighton & Radford, Karen, illus. (p. 1425)
—Shakespeare's Quill. Radford, Karen & Noyes, Leighton, illus. (p. 1559)
—Sitting Bull's Tomahawk. Radford, Karen & Noyes, Leighton, illus. (p. 1582)
—Wright Brothers' Glider. Radford, Karen & Noyes, Leighton, illus. (p. 1963)
Bailey, Gerry & Law, Felicia. Circles. Phillips, Mike, illus. (p. 321)
—Cowries, Coins, Credit: The History of Money Phillips, Mike & Brooks, Rosie, illus. (p. 374)
—Energy & Movement. (p. 528)
—Get Rich Quick? Earning Money Phillips, Mike & Brooks, Rosie, illus. (p. 668)
—Money, It's Our Job: Money Careers Phillips, Mike & Brooks, Rosie, illus. (p. 1164)
—Spheres. Phillips, Mike, illus. (p. 1626)
—Stone Age Geometry - Circles. Phillips, Mike, illus. (p. 1652)
—Stone Age Geometry - Cubes. Phillips, Mike, illus. (p. 1652)
—Stone Age Geometry - Triangles. Phillips, Mike, illus. (p. 1652)
—What's It All Worth? The Value of Money Phillips, Mike & Brooks, Rosie, illus. (p. 1898)
—World Money. Beech, Mark, illus. (p. 1956)
—Your Money. Beech, Mark, illus. (p. 1981)
Bailey, Gerry & Reaveley, Trevor. Apatosaurus. (p. 91)
Bailey, Gerry & Way, Steve. Body & Health. (p. 207)
—Communication. (p. 349)
—Water. (p. 1862)
Bailey, Gwen. Perfect Puppy-Newly Revised & Updated: How to Raise a Well-Behaved Dog. (p. 1342)
Bailey, Gwen & Whitehead, Sarah. Why Is My Dog Doing That? (p. 1925)
Bailey, Hannah, illus. see Gallagher, Tara.
Bailey, Heidi Lyn. Beauty Pageant at the Park. (p. 154)
Bailey, Helen. Life at the Shallow End. (p. 1008)
—Swimming Against the Tide. (p. 1691)
—Taking the Plunge. (p. 1698)
—Topaz on Ice. Dare, Bill, illus. (p. 1769)
—Topaz Takes a Chance. Dare, Bill, illus. (p. 1769)
—Topaz - Takes the Stage. Dare, Bill, illus. (p. 1769)
Bailey, J. L. Children's Gate. (p. 303)
Bailey, Jackson. My Love & I. (p. 1213)
Bailey, Jacqui. Charged Up: The Story of Electricity. Lilly, Matthew, illus. (p. 291)
—Cracking Up: A Story about Erosion Lilly, Matthew, illus. (p. 375)
—Debate about Birth Control. (p. 420)
—Drop in the Ocean: The Story of Water. Lilly, Matthew, illus. (p. 485)
—Monster Bones: The Story of a Dinosaur Fossil Lilly, Matthew, illus. (p. 1166)
—Rock Factory: The Story about the Rock Cycle. Lilly, Matthew, illus. (p. 1482)
—Science Works Lilly, Matthew, illus. (p. 1528)
—Sex, Puberty, & All That Stuff: A Guide to Growing Up. McCafferty, Jan, illus. (p. 1556)
—Sun up, Sun Down: The Story of Day & Night. Lilly, Matthew, illus. (p. 1676)
—Taking Action Against Youth Crime. (p. 1698)
—What Happens When You Are Born & Grow? (p. 1886)
—What Happens When You Breathe? (p. 1886)
—What Happens When You Eat? (p. 1886)
—What Happens When You Move? (p. 1886)
—What Happens When Your Heart Beats? (p. 1886)
Bailey, Jennifer P. I Call Mine Mimi. What Do You Call Your Grandmother? (p. 834)
Bailey, Jessica. Van Gogh (p. 1833)
Bailey, Jill. Mosquito (p. 1176)
Bailey, K. C., illus. see Muntean, Michaela.
Bailey, Karen, jt. auth. see Lyon, Jane.
Bailey, Karen, jt. auth. see Lyons, Jane.
Bailey, Katharine. Ferdinand Magellan: Circumnavigating the World. (p. 581)
—Ferdinand Magellan: Circumnavigating the World. (p. 582)
—Muscle Cars. (p. 1192)
—Radisson & des Groseilliers: Fur Traders of the North. (p. 1433)
—Sport Bikes. (p. 1631)
—Sweet Rides. (p. 1690)
—Vasco Da Gama: Quest for the Spice Trade. (p. 1833)
Bailey, Kevin. Anthony Meets the Playground Bully. (p. 89)
Bailey, Kristen. Cosmetic Surgery. (p. 368)
—Sex Education. (p. 1556)
Bailey, Kristin. Average Joe. (p. 119)
—Legacy of the Clockwork Key. (p. 987)
—Rise of the Arcane Fire. (p. 1474)
—Shadow of the War Machine. (p. 1557)
Bailey, LaNiyah. Stand Up! Bully Busters... Coming to Town: Bully Busters Educational Coloring & Activity Book. (p. 1639)
Bailey, LaNiyah & White, LaToya. Not Fat Because I Wanna Be. (p. 1267)
Bailey, Leslie J. Jacub's Journey. DeBroeck, Sarah, illus. (p. 905)
Bailey, Lin. Search for Tommy's Shell. (p. 1537)
—Stanley - the Shark Who Lost His Fin. (p. 1639)
Bailey, Linda. Adventures in Ancient China. Slavin, Bill, illus. (p. 15)
—Adventures in the Ice Age. Slavin, Bill, illus. (p. 15)
—Best Figure Skater in the Whole Wide World. (p. 169)
—Best Figure Skater in the Whole Wide World. Daniel, Alan & Daniel, Lea, illus. (p. 169)
—Farm Team. Slavin, Bill, illus. (p. 574)
—How Can a Brilliant Detective Shine in the Dark? (p. 805)
—If You Happen to Have a Dinosaur. Jack, Colin, illus. (p. 854)
—Joey, the Colt No Man Would Ride. (p. 920)
—Seven Dead Pirates. (p. 1554)
—Stanley at Sea. Slavin, Bill, illus. (p. 1639)
—Stanley's Beauty Contest. Slavin, Bill, illus. (p. 1640)
—Stanley's Little Sister. Slavin, Bill, illus. (p. 1640)
—Stanley's Party. Slavin, Bill, illus. (p. 1640)
—Stanleys Wild Ride. Slavin, Bill, illus. (p. 1640)
—Toads on Toast. Jack, Colin, illus. (p. 1760)
—What's a Serious Detective Like Me Doing in Such a Silly Movie? (p. 1896)
—When Addie Was Scared. (p. 1901)
Bailey, Linda & Masse, Josee. Goodnight, Sweet Pig. Masse, Josee, illus. (p. 701)
Bailey, Lindsey, illus. see Short, Robyn & Williams, Nanon McKewn.
Bailey, Loretta Dovell, illus. see McMahon, V. Karen.
Bailey, Lori Gayle. Dog Who Loved Cucumbers. (p. 462)
Bailey, Lorilyn. Original Dating Questionnaire for Teens: A Great Way to Get to Know Each Other. (p. 1304)
Bailey, Margaret A. Dragonworld & the Room of Strange Hangings. (p. 479)
Bailey, Mark & Oatman, Michael. Tiny Pie. Hemingway, Edward, illus. (p. 1756)
Bailey, Martha. New Mexico: Uno de muchos, de muchos Uno Bailey, Martha, illus. (p. 1246)
Bailey, Martin, illus. see Dale, Jay.
Bailey, Martin, illus. see Giulieri, Anne.
Bailey, Mary. Vhan Zeely & the Time Prevaricators. (p. 1839)
Bailey, Mary R. Vhan Zeely & the Time Prevaricators. (p. 1839)
Bailey, Megan. Fit & Fun. (p. 599)
—Healthy Behaviors. (p. 758)
—Healthy Eating Choices. (p. 758)
Bailey, Melissa. Well, for Goodness Sake Little Jake. (p. 1874)
Bailey, Melissa, illus. see Schuller, Kathleen.
Bailey, Michael. Cartoon Nation Martin, Cynthia, illus. (p. 273)
Bailey, N. C. & Eskeland, N. L. Know Your Gene: A High School Workbook. (p. 965)
Bailey, Pamela J. Sanctuary: Creating a Blessed Place to Live & Love. (p. 1510)
Bailey, Peter. Jack & Rebel, the Police Dog. (p. 902)
Bailey, Peter, illus. see Dyer, Heather.
Bailey, Peter, illus. see Finney, Patricia.
Bailey, Peter, illus. see Pullman, Philip.
Bailey, Peter, illus. see Ward, Nick.
Bailey, Peter, illus. see Wright, Kit.
Bailey, Peter, tr. see Ward, Nick.
Bailey, Preston. Preston Bailey's Fantasy Weddings. (p. 1397)
Bailey Publishing Staff. History of Fashion & Costume Set. (p. 784)
Bailey Publishing Staff & Elgin, Kathy. Elizabethan England. (p. 513)
—Medieval World. (p. 1119)
Bailey Publishing Staff & McEvoy, Anne. 20s & 30s. (p. 1996)
—American West. (p. 64)
Bailey Publishing Staff & Steer, Deirdre Clancy. 1980s & 1990s. (p. 2002)
Bailey Publishing Staff, et al. Colonial America. (p. 341)
Bailey, R. A., jt. auth. see Rittner, Don.
Bailey, Rachel. Superstorm Sandy. (p. 1684)
—Superstorm Sandy Paperback. (p. 1684)
Bailey, Rachel A. Japanese Internment Camps: A History Perspectives Book. (p. 909)
—Triangle Shirtwaist Factory Fire. (p. 1785)
Bailey, Rayna. Immigration & Migration. (p. 861)
Bailey, Rhonda, et al. Matematicas: Applications & Concepts, Course 3. (p. 1104)
—Mathematics: Applications & Concepts. (p. 1107)
Bailey, Rosemary. Benjamin Bunny A Childrens Story. (p. 164)
Bailey, S. D. All While Holding My Ladybug Lunch Pail. (p. 46)
Bailey, Sally, illus. see Leedom, Karen L.
Bailey, Scott. Tales of Billy Woodchuck. (p. 1702)
Bailey, Sheila, illus. see Herman, Debbie.
Bailey, Sheila, illus. see Stortz, Diane M.
Bailey, Sheila, illus. see Stortz, Diane.
Bailey, Sherry. Moments of the Heart. (p. 1162)
Bailey, Sherwin Carolyn. Tell Me Another Story. (p. 1716)
Bailey, Sian, illus. see Muten, Burleigh.
Bailey, Sidney, illus. see Ray, Sandra.
Bailey, Terri L., illus. see Shank, Diane S.
Bailey, Todd, ed. Clue Searcher's Discovery Guide To: A Clue Search Puzzles Book (p. 336)
—Clue Searcher's Discovery Guide To: A Clue Search Puzzles Book: the 50 States (p. 336)
Bailey, Tom. A.G. Gaston: Visionary Businessman. (p. 29)
—Hank Williams Sr: Country Music Legend. (p. 742)
—Jennifer Chandler: Olympic Champion Diver. (p. 912)
—Raphael Semmes: Commander of the Alabama. (p. 1439)
—Red Eagle: Legendary Creek Warrior. (p. 1453)
Bailey, Tressie. Little Box Kittens. (p. 1025)
—Little Box Kittens First Christmas. (p. 1025)
—Little Box Kittens meet Santa Claus. (p. 1025)
—Sebatian's First Day at School. (p. 1539)
—Things Sammy Likes to Do. (p. 1733)
Bailey, Vicki. Catland Adventures. (p. 280)
Bailey, Viola & Wise, Ella. Victorian Times. (p. 1840)
Bailey, Wendy R. Mary the Doll. (p. 1101)
Bailey, William. Shalamar Book I. (p. 1559)
Bailey-Peiffer, Stefanie & Bailey-Yarbrough, Caroline. Modie & the Power of the BellKeys. (p. 1159)
Bailey-Yarbrough, Caroline, jt. auth. see Bailey-Peiffer, Stefanie.
Baille, Helen. Azura Stones. (p. 122)
Baille, James. Steam Genie. (p. 1646)
Baillin, Jill, ed. see McGlotham, L. R. E.
Baillin-Rembar, Jill, ed. see Davies, Donna M.
Baillie, Allan. Archie the Big Good Wolf: Band 15/Emerald. Vol. 9 Ogden, Betina, illus. (p. 95)
—DragonQuest. Harris, Wayne, illus. (p. 478)
Baillie, Jonathan, et al. Animals at the EDGE: Saving the World's Rarest Creatures. (p. 82)
Baillie, Marilyn. Amazing Things Animals Do. Caron, Romi & Owlkids Books Inc. Staff, illus. (p. 56)
—My Pet Puppy. Kurisu, Jane, illus. (p. 1217)

—Whoosh! A Watery World of Wonderful Creatures Mitchell, Susan & Owlkids Books Inc. Staff, illus. (p. 1920)
Baillie, Marilyn, et al. How to Save a Species. (p. 821)
Bailly, Vincent, illus. see Joffo, Joseph.
Baima, Jennifer. Sports Injuries (p. 1632)
Bain, A. Watson, compiled by. Poetry Book for Children. (p. 1376)
Bain, Donald, jt. auth. see Fletcher, Jessica.
Bain, Michelle. Adventures of Thumbs up Johnnie Banker Bill's Guide to Common Cents: Banker Bill's Guide to Common Cents. Lizana, Lorenzo, illus. (p. 24)
—Adventures of Thumbs up Johnnie Body Walk. (p. 24)
—Adventures of Thumbs up Johnnie Jimmy Jam Germ & the Happy Handshake: Jimmy Jam Germ & the Happy Handshake Version 2. Lizana, Lorenzo, illus. (p. 24)
—Adventures of Thumbs up Johnnie Johnnie Finds A Buddy: Johnnie Finds A Buddy Color Version 2. Lizana, Lorenzo, illus. (p. 24)
—Adventures of Thumbs up Johnnie Johnnie's Missing Boot! Johnnie's Missing Boot! Lizana, Lorenzo, illus. (p. 24)
—Adventures of Thumbs up Johnnie Reading Heart to Heart Thumbs up Johnnie, Little Digit & the Special Delivery: Reading Heart to Heart, Coloring & Activity Book. (p. 24)
—Adventures of Thumbs up Johnnie Rules of Thumb for Going Green: Rules of Thumb for Going Green. Lizana, Lorenzo, illus. (p. 24)
—Adventures of Thumbs up Johnnie Thumbs up to Red, White & Blue! Thumbs up to Red, White & Blue! Lizana, Lorenzo, illus. (p. 24)
—Adventures of Thumbs up Johnnie Zipp, Little Digit & the Happy Signs: Zipp, Little Digit & the Happy Signs. Lizana, Lorenzo, illus. (p. 24)
—Las aventuras de Juanito el Pulgarcito Juanito encuentra un Compañerito: Juanito encuentra un Compañerito. Lizana, Lorenzo, illus. (p. 976)
—Las aventuras de Juanito el Pulgarcito Liborio el Microbio y el apretón de Manos: Liborio el Microbio y el apretón de Manos. Lizana, Lorenzo, illus. (p. 976)
—Las aventuras de Juanito el Pulgarcito Zipp, Pequeño Dígito, las señales y las Señas: Zipp, Pequeño Dígito, las señales y las Señas. Lizana, Lorenzo, illus. (p. 976)
Bain, Tracie. Peanuts & Life. (p. 1332)
Bainbridge, Bernadette. Christmas Please & Thank You. (p. 315)
Bainbridge, Bob, illus. see Smith, Clyde.
Bainbridge, Nicki, jt. auth. see Heath, Alan.
Bainbridge, Shane, illus. see Smith, Clyde.
Baine, Celeste. High Tech Hot Shots: Careers in Sports Engineering. (p. 778)
Baines, Andy. I Know a Goldfish That Can't Swim. (p. 840)
Baines, Becky. Bones You Own: A Book about the Human Body. (p. 209)
—Den Is a Bed for a Bear. (p. 426)
—Every Planet Has a Place. (p. 543)
—National Geographic Kids Everything Dogs: All the Canine Facts, Photos, & Fun You Can Get Your Paws On! (p. 1232)
—National Geographic Kids Funny Fill-In: My Backyard Adventure. (p. 1232)
—National Geographic Kids Funny Fill-In: My Safari Adventure. (p. 1232)
—What's in That Egg? A Book about Life Cycles. (p. 1898)
—Your Skin Holds You In. (p. 1981)
—ZigZag - What Did One Elephant Say to the Other? (p. 1986)
—ZigZag: Your Skin Holds You In: A Book about Your Skin. (p. 1986)
Baines, Becky & National Geographic Book Service Staff. Action Journal: Talk Like a Pirate, Analyze Your Dreams, Fingerprint Your Friends, Rule Your Own Country, & Other Wild Things to Do to Be Yourself. (p. 10)
Baines, Emily Ansara. Unofficial Hunger Games Cookbook: From Lamb Stew to Groosling - More Than 150 Recipes Inspired by the Hunger Games Trilogy. (p. 1822)
Baines, Francesca. Mundo de las Plantas. Sanz, Maria Teresa, tr. (p. 1191)
Baines, John. Food for Life. (p. 613)
Baines, John D. Food & Farming. (p. 613)
Baines, Menna, jt. auth. see Orme, David.
Baines, Nigel, illus. see Dave & Matt.
Baines, Nigel, illus. see Ghoulstone, Rotterly.
Baines, Nigel, illus. see Henderson, Stewart.
Baines, Nigel, illus. see MacDonald, Alan.
Baines, Nigel, illus. see Matt & Dave.
Baines, Nigel, illus. see Matt and Dave.
Baines, Nigel, illus. see Matthews, Morgan & Sinden, David.
Baines, Nigel, illus. see Morgan, Matthew, et al.
Baines, Nigel, illus. see Wallace, Karen.
Baines, Rebecca, et al. Arctic Tale: Companion to the Major Motion Picture. (p. 96)
Bains-Fort. It's Keen to Be Green. (p. 897)
Bair, Carolyn. Fireman Dave Goes to School. (p. 592)
Bair, Diane. Western Legends & Leyendas del Oeste: 6 English, 6 Spanish Adaptations. (p. 1876)
Bair, Diane, jt. auth. see Sohn, Emily.
Bair, Diane & Wright, Pamela. Western Legends: Set Of 6. (p. 1876)
Bair, Heather. Flying High with Butterflies: A Pre-K/ K Complete Supplemental Unit. Bruner, Garth, illus. (p. 610)
—I Spy a Butterfly: A Second Grade Complete Supplemental Unit. Bruner, Garth, illus. (p. 846)
—O'H Me O'H My A Butterfly: A First Grade Complete Supplemental Unit. Bruner, Garth, illus. (p. 1280)
Bair, Katie & Bevard, Robby. NHS - Hawaii Bair, Katie, illus. (p. 1250)
Bair, M., illus. see Robinson, James, et al.
Bair, Michael, illus. see Meltzer, Brad.
Bair, Sheila. Bullies of Wall Street: This Is How Greedy Adults Messed up Our Economy. (p. 240)
—Isabel's Car Wash. Stead, Judy, illus. (p. 891)
—Rock, Brock, & the Savings Shock Gott, Barry, illus. (p. 1482)
Baird, Alison. Warding of Willowmere. (p. 1858)
—Witches of Willowmere. (p. 1941)
Baird, Duncan H. & Chronicle Books Staff. Deep Sleep Deck. (p. 423)
Baird, Noah. Southpaw. McMaugh, Kimberly, illus. (p. 1617)
Baird, Patrick. Mr Toad & the Stone of Destiny. (p. 1186)
Baird, Roberta, illus. see Berkes, Marianne.
Baird, Roberta, illus. see Town, Vicky.
Baird Wireman, Ginger. If Wishes Had Wings: A Fall Flight of Fancy. (p. 854)
Baisden, Crystal. Carlie's New Friend. (p. 270)
Baish, Vanessa. Dating. (p. 409)
—Frequently Asked Questions about Dating. (p. 636)
Baish, Vanessa, jt. auth. see Smith, Rita.
Baisley, Maryann Leake, illus. see Beach, Kathleen H. & Weeber, Stephanie B.
Baisley, Stephen, illus. see Matchette, Katharine E.
Baitner, Ray, tr. see Rubinger, Ami.
Baity, Cameron & Zelkowicz, Benny. Foundry's Edg. Foster, John, illus. (p. 624)
Baity, Susan, illus. see Anderson, Gennifer.
Baiz, Mark, jt. auth. see Helmintoller, Matt.
Baizer, Gayle Susan, illus. see Douglas, Donna.
Bajaj, Subash. Three Little Pigs. (p. 1742)
Bajaj, Varsha. How Many Kisses Do You Want Tonight? Bates, Ivan, illus. (p. 811)
—T Is for Taj Mahal: An India Alphabet. Crawford, Robert, illus. (p. 1693)
Bajkiewicz, Thomas A. River Raisin Richie. (p. 1476)
Bajpai, Sneha. Grant Me a Wish: Sometimes... you do get exactly what you wish For. (p. 710)
Bak, Jenny. Color & Poster Book. Middleton, Gayle & Edwards, Ken, illus. (p. 342)
—Ten Gifts from Santa Claus: A Counting Book. Harding, Niall, illus. (p. 1718)
Bak, Robyn. Lucky Little Bison. (p. 1062)
Bakal, Scott, illus. see Hagen, George.
Bakare, Rebecca. Short Stories by Rebecc. (p. 1569)
Baker, Adam. Maury C. Moose & the Forest Noel. (p. 1110)
Baker, Alan. Numeros. (p. 1272)
—Odyssey. (p. 1278)
—Two Tiny Mice: A Mouse-Eye Exploration of Nature. (p. 1804)
—William's Dinosaurs. (p. 1933)
Baker, Alan, illus. see Allette, Dawne.
Baker, Alan, illus. see Martin, Debbie.
Baker, Alison. New England a to Z. Coffey, Kevin, illus. (p. 1244)
Baker, Amanda. Cheesehead Night Before Christmas. (p. 296)
—Zack's Zany Zucchiniland. (p. 1984)
Baker, Amber. Ice Cube Experiment. (p. 850)
Baker, Andrea. Benji's Christmas Letter. (p. 165)
—Benji's Special Christmas Gift. (p. 165)
—Carta a de Santa de Benji / Benji's Christmas Letter. (p. 272)
—Worlds Apart: Leah. (p. 1960)
Baker, Ann. Tree or Three? An Elementary Pronunciation Course. (p. 1783)
Baker, Barbara. Digby & Kate & the Beautiful Day. Winborn, Marsha, illus. (p. 438)
—One Saturday Evening. Duke, Kate, illus. (p. 1296)
Baker, Becky. Lucky Penny. (p. 1063)
Bäker, Bernard. Tall Cotton Gang: Backtracking. (p. 1704)
Baker, Beth. Sylvia Earle. (p. 1692)
Baker, Bill. Alan Moore on His Work & Career. (p. 33)
—Butterfly. RUZICKA, Carol, illus. (p. 247)
—Neil Gaiman on His Work & Career. (p. 1240)
—Talking with Graphic Novelists (p. 1704)
Baker, Bill, jt. auth. see Moore, Alan.
Baker, Bob, et al. Secrets of Halo 2: An Inside Look at the Fantastic Halo Universe! (p. 1545)
Baker, Brant D. Abingdon Children's Sermon Library (p. 5)
Baker, Brynn. Buffalo Soldiers: Heroes of the American West. (p. 236)
—Life in America: Comparing Immigrant Experiences. (p. 1010)
—Military Heroes. (p. 1143)
—Navajo Code Talkers: Secret American Indian Heroes of World War II. (p. 1237)
—Pet Guinea Pigs up Close. (p. 1345)
—Roosevelt's Rough Riders: Fearless Cavalry of the Spanish-American War. (p. 1488)
—Tuskegee Airmen: Freedom Flyers of World War II. (p. 1799)
Baker, Brynn & Kravitz, Danny. U. S. Immigration in The 1900s. (p. 1806)
Baker, Celia M., illus. see Korhel, Erik.
Baker, Chandler. Alive. (p. 41)
Baker, Charles F. & Baker, Charles F., III, eds. Bugs. (p. 237)
Baker, Charles F., ed. Pets: Cats, Dogs, Horses, & Camels, Too! (p. 1348)
—Water Animals. (p. 1862)
—Wild Animals: Lions, Tigers, Bears, & More! (p. 1928)
Baker, Charles F., III, jt. ed. see Baker, Charles F.
Baker, Clara B. & Baker, Edna D. Reading for Children: First Book. Betts, George Herbert, ed. (p. 1446)
Baker, Clara Belle & Kohlsaat, Caroline. Songs for the Little Child. (p. 1612)
Baker, Courtney. Perfect Pet. Snider, Jackie, illus. (p. 1342)
Baker, Craig & Pollitt, Gary. Learn the Word! Understanding Bible Scriptures. (p. 983)
Baker, Cristal. Popsicle Goes to Church. (p. 1385)
Baker, Darrell, illus. see Kreider, Karen.
Baker, David. Allwedd Mathemateg TGAU. (p. 48)
—Exploring Space (p. 553)
—International Space Station. (p. 880)
—Living in Space. (p. 1041)
—Rockets & Launch Vehicles. (p. 1483)
—Roos, A home for Baby. (p. 1488)
—Roos, Baby's new Friend. (p. 1488)
—Satellites. (p. 1515)
—Shuttle. (p. 1572)
Baker, David, illus. see Atkinson, Linda.
Baker, David, illus. see Barry, Debra R.
Baker, David, illus. see Belanger, Kathleen.
Baker, David, illus. see Caligiuri, Susan.
Baker, David, illus. see Camp, V. Ray.
Baker, David, illus. see Carol Hersh.
Baker, David, illus. see Coné, Robert.
Baker, David, illus. see Dalton, Sommer.
Baker, David, illus. see Du Lac, Leo J.
Baker, David, illus. see Dubrule, Jackie.
Baker, David, illus. see Gaulkin, Marianne Quigley.
Baker, David, illus. see Headrick, Julianna.
Baker, David, illus. see Jubilee Jr., Thomas.
Baker, David, illus. see Loccisano, Rina.
Baker, David, illus. see Maranhas, Jayne Ellen.
Baker, David, illus. see Moore, Shawn.
Baker, David, illus. see Moore, Tijon Adamson.
Baker, David, illus. see Narr, Rachel K.
Baker, David, illus. see Norman, Travis D.
Baker, David, illus. see Padua, Grace.
Baker, David, illus. see Phanton, Richard G.
Baker, David, illus. see Sarah Taylor.
Baker, David, illus. see Scott, Gwen.
Baker, David, illus. see Scott, Molly.
Baker, David, illus. see Smith, J. L.
Baker, David, illus. see Spear, Lisa D.
Baker, David, illus. see Swenson, Lynn.
Baker, David, illus. see T.
Baker, David, jt. auth. see Kespert, Deborah.
Baker, David & Kervegant, Ffion. Allwedd Mathemateg 71. (p. 48)
—Allwedd Mathemateg 81. (p. 48)
—Allwedd Mathemateg TGAU. (p. 48)
Baker, David & Kissock, Heather. International Space Station. (p. 880)
—Journey to Mars. (p. 929)
—Living in Space. (p. 1041)
—Living on the Moon. (p. 1041)
—Moon Base: Exploring Space. (p. 1171)
—Probing Space. (p. 1408)
—Rockets & Launch Vehicles. (p. 1483)
—Satellites. (p. 1515)
—Shuttle. (p. 1572)
Baker, David G. & Stewart, Margaret Taylor. Tales of Mike the Tiger: Facts & Fun for Everyone. Lockwood, C. C., photos by. (p. 1702)
Baker, Deborah J., jt. auth. see Benson, Sonia.
Baker, Deirdre. Becca at Sea (p. 155)
Baker, Don, illus. see Klawitter, Pamela Amick.
Baker, E., jt. auth. see Baker, E. D.
Baker, E. D. Bravest Princess. (p. 223)
—Dragon Kiss. (p. 477)
—Dragon Princess. (p. 477)
—Dragon's Breath: Read-Along/Homework Pack (p. 479)
—Fairy Lies. (p. 563)
—Fairy Wings: A Fairy Tale. (p. 564)
—Fairy-Tale Matchmaker. (p. 564)
—Frog Princess (p. 640)
—Prince among Frogs. (p. 1401)
—Princess in Disguise. (p. 1404)
—Question of Magic. (p. 1426)
—Salamander Spell. (p. 1504)
—Unlocking the Spell: A Tale of the Wide-Awake Princess. (p. 1821)
—Wide-Awake Princess. (p. 1927)
Baker, E. D. & Baker, E. No Place for Magic (p. 1259)
—Wings: A Fairy Tale. (p. 1936)
Baker, Ed. Blues Riffs for Piano. (p. 204)
—Story of Kitten Cuckoo. Baker, Ed, illus. (p. 1658)
Baker, Edmund, illus. see Dimarcello, Pete.
Baker, Edmund, illus. see Harpan, Gaile & DiMarcello, Pete.
Baker, Edna D., jt. auth. see Baker, Clara B.
Baker, Ella. Big & Small. (p. 177)
Baker, et al. Nueva Historia de los Estados Unidos. (p. 1270)
Baker, Frank Collins. Cahokia Mounds: Part I. A Report of Progress on the Exploration of the Cahokia Group, by Warren K. Moorehead; Part II. The Geological Aspects of Some of the Cahokia (Illinois) Mounds. (p. 251)
Baker, Frank W., et al. Coming Distractions: Questioning Movies (p. 348)
Baker, Gabi. Angels of Hope. (p. 75)
Baker, Gayle. Cambria: A HarborTown History. (p. 255)
—Denver: A Boomtown History. (p. 427)
—Newport Beach: A HarborTown History. (p. 1249)
—Point Reyes: A HarborTown History. (p. 1377)
—Santa Barbara: A HarborTown History. (p. 1511)
Baker, Georgette. Cantemos Chiquitos (p. 262)
—We're off to the Galapagos: Nos Vamos a Las Islas Galapagos. Baker, Georgette, tr. (p. 1875)
Baker, Ginger. Walking Home Alone. Levy, Pamela R., illus. (p. 1854)
Baker, Grandma Grace. Charlie Crab's Day at the Beach. (p. 293)
Baker, Harriet Li. Book I: Boyduck Goose: His Life & Times. (p. 210)
Baker, Harriet Lila. Book III: Boyduck Goose: His Life & Times. (p. 210)
—Boyduck Goose: His Life & Times (p. 220)
Baker, Helen. Shopping the Cape (p. 1569)
Baker, Ivor, Sr., ed. Philosophy of Life: Stories for Young children (p. 1351)
Baker, Jaime. Bedtime Baby Noble, Roger, illus. (p. 156)
Baker, Janet, illus. see Chesire, Gerald.
Baker, Janet, illus. see Clarke, Penny.
Baker, Janice, ed. see Marsh, Carole.
Baker, Janine. Unraveling: The Patient-to-Patient's Guide Through a Nervous Breakdown. (p. 1822)
Baker, Jason. People Are People. (p. 1339)
Baker, Jayne & Hofstetter, Adam. Insider's Guide to Softball. (p. 878)
Baker, Jeannie. Belonging. Baker, Jeannie, illus. (p. 163)
—Home. Baker, Jeannie, illus. (p. 791)
—Mirror. Baker, Jeannie, illus. (p. 1149)
Baker, Jed. Social Skills Picture Book: For High School & Beyond. (p. 1604)
Baker, Jennifer. Just Like Sisters. (p. 939)
—Lying Game. (p. 1066)
—Most Likely to Deceive. (p. 1177)
—Sworn to Silence. (p. 1692)
Baker, Jennifer, illus. see Mann, Margaret.
Baker, Joan. Beagle Tales. (p. 150)
—Tale of Two Beagles. (p. 1700)
Baker, Joe, illus. see Dongweck, James.
Baker, Jonathan, illus. see Written By Doretta Elaine Wilson; illust.
Baker, Julie. Bread & Roses Strike Of 1912. (p. 224)
Baker, Kage. Hotel under the Sand. Law, Stephanie Pui-Mun, illus. (p. 802)
Baker, Kane. Bobby the Bush Pilot. Swain, Alison Campbell, illus. (p. 206)
Baker, Karle Wilson. Garden of the Plynck (Illustrated Ed. (p. 656)
—Texas Flag Primer. (p. 1724)
Baker, Keith. 1-2-3 Peas. Baker, Keith, illus. (p. 1990)
—Big Fat Hen Big Book. Baker, Keith, illus. (p. 181)
—Camping: A Mr. & Mrs. Green Adventure. (p. 257)
—Cookies: A Mr. & Mrs. Green Adventure. (p. 361)
—Fishing: A Mr. & Mrs. Green Adventure. (p. 599)
—Gallina Grande/Big Fat Hen. Campoy, F. Isabel, tr. (p. 653)
—Gumballs: A Mr. & Mrs. Green Adventure. (p. 731)
—Hickory Dickory Dock. (p. 775)
—Just How Long Can a Long String Be? (p. 938)
—Little Green Peas: A Big Book of Colors. Baker, Keith, illus. (p. 1028)
—LMNO Peas. Baker, Keith, illus. (p. 1044)
—Lucky Days with Mr. & Mrs. Green. Baker, Keith, illus. (p. 1062)
—Meet Mr. & Mrs. Green. (p. 1121)
—Meet Mr. & Mrs. Green. Baker, Keith, illus. (p. 1121)
—More Mr. & Mrs. Green. Baker, Keith, illus. (p. 1174)
—My Octopus Arms. Baker, Keith, illus. (p. 1216)
—No Two Alike. Baker, Keith, illus. (p. 1260)
—On the Go with Mr. & Mrs. Green. Baker, Keith, illus. (p. 1290)
—Peas in a Pod! Baker, Keith, illus. (p. 1333)
—Quack & Count. (p. 1422)
—Sometimes. (p. 1610)
—Sometimes/Algunas Veces. Flor Ada, Alma & Campoy, F. Isabel, trs. from ENG. (p. 1610)
—Talent Show: A Mr. & Mrs. Green Adventure. (p. 1701)
Baker, Keith, illus. see Moran, Alex.
Baker, Kelly A., jt. auth. see Baker, Robin J.
Baker, Ken. Cow Can't Sleep Gray, Steve, illus. (p. 373)
—Fangirl. (p. 571)
—How I Got Skinny, Famous, & Fell Madly in Love. (p. 810)
—Old MacDonald Had a Dragon Santoro, Christopher, illus. (p. 1284)
Baker, Kenneth, ed. Children's English History in Verse. Stower, Adam, illus. (p. 303)
Baker, Kim. Pickle: The (Formerly) Anonymous Prank Club of Fountain Point Middle School. Probert, Tim, illus. (p. 1354)
Baker, Kimberly. Pickle: The (Formerly) Anonymous Prank Club of Fountain Point Middle School. Probert, Tim, illus. (p. 1354)
Baker, Kyle, illus. see Morales, Robert.
Baker, Kyle, jt. auth. see Carroll, Lewis, pseud.
Baker, Larry S. & Landwehr, Karen A. Pebbles in the Pond: Achieving Resilience in Mental Healthl. (p. 1333)
Baker, Lavayne L. Return of the Black Dinosaur. (p. 1464)
Baker, Lawrence W. Cold War Reference Library Cumulative Index. (p. 339)
—Immigration & Migration Reference. (p. 861)
—Reference Library Cumulative Index. (p. 1456)
—Space Exploration - Primary Sources (p. 1619)
Baker, Lawrence W., jt. auth. see Brannen, Daniel E.
Baker, Lawrence W., jt. auth. see Grumet, Bridget Hall.
Baker, Lawrence W., jt. auth. see Howes, Kelly King.
Baker, Lawrence W., jt. auth. see Johnson, Cynthia.
Baker, Lawrence W., jt. auth. see Matuz, Roger.
Baker, Lawrence W., jt. auth. see Outman, James L.
Baker, Lawrence W., jt. auth. see Valentine, Rebecca.
Baker, Leslie. Healing Feelings: A Healing Story for Children Coping with a Grownup's Mental Illness. (p. 757)
Baker, Leslie, illus. see Hippely, Hilary Horder.
Baker, Lisa H., illus. see Gould, Alan.
Baker, Liza. Harold & the Purple Crayon: Under the Sea. (p. 749)
—I Love You Because You're You. McPhail, David, illus. (p. 843)
Baker, Liza, jt. auth. see Johnson, Crockett.
Baker, Liza, et al. I Love You: A Keepsake Storybook Collection. Bryan, Beth, ed. (p. 843)
Baker, Margaret, jt. auth. see Matott, J. P.
Baker, Marina. Marina Baker's Teenage Survival Guide: Everything You Need to Know about Life, Love & Caring for the Planet. (p. 1094)
Baker, Marvin G. Luke's Story: Based on the Gospel of Luke. (p. 1064)
—Mark's Story: An Introduction to the Gospel of Mark. Trittin, Paul S., illus. (p. 1095)
—Matthew's Story: Based on the Gospel of Matthew. (p. 1110)
Baker, Mary. Amy's Apple Butter Granny. (p. 66)
—Christmas Annie. (p. 312)
—English - Spanish Counting Book. Mason, Alfonso & Mason, Ruth, illus. (p. 529)
Baker, Mary E. English - French Counting Book Mason, Alfonso & Mason, Ruth, illus. (p. 529)
Baker, Maryann. My Mom Is a Carpenter: Relate Addition & Subtraction to Length. (p. 1214)
Baker, Matthew. If You Find This. (p. 854)
Baker, Michael. Mind Benders Level 1: Deductive Thinking Skills. (p. 1145)
—Mind Benders Level 2: Deductive Thinking Skills. (p. 1145)
—Thinker Doodles A1: Think, Draw, & Color. (p. 1734)
—Thinker Doodles Beginning: Think, Draw, & Color. (p. 1734)
Baker, Michael O. What Would You Do?: Moral Dilemmas B.k 2 (p. 1895)
—What Would You Do?: Moral Dilemmas Bk. 1 (p. 1895)
Baker, Michelle M. Geese of Belle Isle: Volume I. (p. 659)
Baker, Monica S. Freestyle (p. 635)
Baker, Nancy & Hoffman, Richard L. Exploring Virginia Insects. (p. 554)

B

Baker, Nick, jt. auth. see Dorling Kindersley Publishing Staff.
Baker, Olaf. Dusty Star. (p. 490)
Baker, Patricia. Fashions of a Decade: The 1940s. (p. 576)
—Fashions of a Decade: The 1950s. (p. 576)
Baker, Patrick. Fuzzy the Bear. (p. 651)
Baker, Paul R. & Hall, William H. Nueva Historia de los Estados Unidos. Linder, Bertram L. & Selzer, Edwin, eds. (p. 1270)
Baker, Penny, illus. see Kelman, Louise & Kelman, Suzanne.
Baker, Piers. Ollie & Quentin: An Hilarious Comic Strip about the Unlikely Friendship Between a Seagull & a Lugworm. (p. 1287)
Baker Publishing Group Staff. Boys. (p. 220)
—Girls. (p. 679)
—God's Word. (p. 692)
—God's Word for Boys. (p. 692)
—God's Word for Girls. (p. 692)
Baker Publishing Group Staff, jt. auth. see Kuyper, Vicki J.
Baker Publishing Group Staff, jt. auth. see Larsen, Carolyn.
Baker Publishing Group Staff, jt. auth. see Morrill, Stephanie.
Baker, Rick, jt. auth. see Mills, Nathan.
Baker, Robert. Complete Guides Dinosaurs. (p. 353)
Baker, Robert C. What Happened to Merry Christmas? Hill, Dave, illus. (p. 1885)
Baker, Robin J. & Baker, Kelly A. 3-D Coloring Book—Fish Frenzy! (p. 1991)
—Creative Haven Garden Party Stained Glass Coloring Book. (p. 379)
Baker, Robin J. & McElwain, Kelly A. 3-D Coloring Book—Flower Power! (p. 1991)
—Garden Party! Flower Designs to Color. (p. 656)
Baker, Robin J., et al. Awesome Animal Designs. (p. 120)
—Crazy Paisley. (p. 378)
Baker, Rochelle, illus. see McGrath, Carmelita.
Baker, Rod. Real Healing for Kids: Knowing Jesus as Your Healer. (p. 1448)
—Real Life for Kids: Knowing Jesus As Your Savior. (p. 1448)
—Real Power for Kids: Knowing the Holy Spirit as Your Friend. (p. 1448)
Baker, Roe. What's Wrong with Gretel Goann. (p. 1900)
Baker, Rosalie. In a Word: 750 Words & Their Fascinating Stories & Origins. Lopes, Tom, illus. (p. 863)
Baker, Ryan. How I Would Paint the World? (p. 810)
Baker, Sam. Fashion Victim. (p. 576)
Baker, Samuel White. Cast up by the Sea by Sir Samuel W Baker Complete with Ten Illustrations by Huard. (p. 276)
Baker, Sandy. Colorea Mi Jardin: Un Libro para Colorear Pàjaros, Abejas, Mariposas y Bichos. Thiessen, Carolyn, tr. (p. 343)
Baker, Sara. Ready to Read Goldilocks & the Three Bears. (p. 1448)
—Ready to Read Sleeping Beauty. (p. 1448)
Baker, Sara, illus. see Lynch, Patricia.
Baker, Sara, illus. see Page, Nick & Page, Claire.
Baker, Sara, illus. see Page, Nick.
Baker, Sara, illus. see Zamenhof, Robert.
Baker, Scott. Darby & the Dewberry Fairies: Introduction to the Enchanted Lands Series. (p. 406)
Baker, Sherri, illus. see Noland, Charles.
Baker, Soren. History of Rap & Hip-Hop. (p. 784)
Baker, Stacy. Sammy's Secret. (p. 1508)
Baker, Steve & Golden, Mark. Kings of Christmas. (p. 960)
Baker, Stuart. In Temperate Zones. (p. 865)
—In the Antarctic. (p. 865)
—In the Arctic. (p. 865)
—In the Tropics. (p. 867)
Baker, Sue. Child's Play Weather. (p. 305)
—Scooter: The Little Black Kitty with the White Spot. (p. 1529)
—Scooter's Big Surprise: Book 3. (p. 1529)
—Scooter's New Home. (p. 1530)
Baker, Sue & Stockham, Jessica. Sleep Tight! Stockham, Jess, illus. (p. 1588)
—Wash Day! Stockham, Jess, illus. (p. 1859)
Baker, Susan F. Don't Smoke, Daddy. (p. 468)
Baker, Syd, illus. see Winitz, Harris, et al.
Baker, T. Harri & Browning, Jane. Arkansas History for Young People. (p. 99)
Baker, Tawnya Stout. My Bunny in A Basket. (p. 1199)
Baker, Theo. Hard Hat Zone. (p. 748)
Baker, Theo, jt. auth. see Oliver, Lin.
Baker, Thomas. Fine Lady's Airs. (p. 589)
Baker, Tim. Go: Devotions for Faith on the Move. (p. 686)
Baker, Tim, jt. auth. see Fanning, Mick.
Baker, Tim & Hascall, Glenn. 3-Minute Devotions for Boys: 90 Exciting Readings for Men under Construction. (p. 1991)
Baker, Tommy. Santa Claus, the Fourth Wise Man. (p. 1511)
Baker, Tyrone. Joey & Hoppy. (p. 920)
Baker, Wendy. Experimenta con Insectos (Experiment with Insects) (p. 549)
—Experimenta - Maquinas. (p. 549)
Baker, Wendy & Haslam, Andrew. Electricity. (p. 509)
—Insects. (p. 875)
—Plants. (p. 1369)
Baker, Wendy, et al. Electricity. (p. 509)
—Sound. (p. 1614)
Baker, Willard F. Boy Ranchers among the Indians: Or-Trailing the Yaquis. (p. 218)
—Boy Ranchers among the Indians. (p. 218)
Baker, William F. & O'Malley, Michael. Leading with Kindness: How Good People Consistently Get Superior Results. (p. 982)
Baker, Yaba. Princess Briana. (p. 1403)
Baker-Smith, Grahame. FArTHER. Baker-Smith, Grahame, illus. (p. 575)
Baker-Smith, Grahame, illus. see Calcutt, David.
Bakewell, Lori. Savannah Adventure: Pirate's Treasure. (p. 1516)
Bakhtiar, Laleh. Islamic Ethics: An Interfaith Perspective: Grade 2: the Moral Education Series. (p. 891)

—Islamic Ethics: An Interfaith Perspective: Grade 3: the Moral Education Textbook Series. (p. 891)
Bakker, Jenny, illus. see Swerts, An.
Bakker, Merel. Maks & Mila on a Special Journey. Mini Pois Etc, illus. (p. 1083)
Bakker, R. Scott. Darkness That Comes Before. (p. 408)
—Thousandfold Thought: The Prince of Nothing, Book Three. (p. 1740)
—Warrior Prophet: The Prince of Nothing, Book Two. (p. 1859)
Bakker, Robert T. Big Golden Book of Dinosaurs. Rey, Luis V., illus. (p. 181)
—Dino Babies! Rey, Luis V., illus. (p. 441)
—Dinosaurs! Rey, Luis V., illus. (p. 443)
—Dinosaurs: in Your Face! Rey, Luis V., illus. (p. 445)
—Raptor Pack. Skrepnick, Michael, illus. (p. 1439)
Bakos, Barbara, illus. see Viau, Nancy.
Bakowski, Barbara. What Happens at an Aquarium? (p. 1886)
—What Happens at an Aquarium?/¿Qué Pasa en un Acuario? (p. 1886)
Bakshi, Kelly. First Americans. Bakshi, Kelly, illus. (p. 593)
—Myth-Busting Columbus. (p. 1227)
Balaam, Lisa, jt. auth. see Balaam, Steven.
Balaam, Lisa & Balaam, Steven. Abbey the Cavi in Miami Beach. (p. 2)
Balaam, Steven, jt. auth. see Balaam, Lisa.
Balaam, Steven & Balaam, Lisa. Abbey the Cavi: And Friends. (p. 2)
Balaban, Bob. Boy or Beast. Rash, Andy, illus. (p. 218)
Balaban, Mariah. Scooby-Doo! & the Haunted Diner. (p. 1529)
—Scooby-Doo & the Rotten Robot. Duendes Del Sur Staff, illus. (p. 1529)
—Scooby-Doo & the Scary Snowman. Duendes Del Sur Staff, illus. (p. 1529)
—Scooby-Doo & the Thanksgiving Terror. Duendes Del Sur Staff, illus. (p. 1529)
—Ultimate Handbook. (p. 1809)
—Very Scary Valentine's Day. (p. 1838)
Balaban, Mariah, jt. auth. see Scooby Doo.
Balaban, Mariah, ed. Trucks. Staples, Val, illus. (p. 1791)
Balaban, Mariah T. Scooby-Doo & the Thanksgiving Terror. (p. 1529)
—Very Scary Valentine's Day, Level 2. (p. 1838)
Balachandran, Anitha. Dog Who Loved Red. Balachandran, Anitha, illus. (p. 462)
Balaguer, Nuria, illus. see Glaser, Linda.
Balagura, Saul. Plowing Stones: Poems of the Holocaust. (p. 1374)
Balagura, Saul & Murillo, Alan. Arando Piedras: Poemas del Holocausto. (p. 94)
Balaicius, Robert / Alan. Truth about Ruth: Ruth the Israelite (Bible Commentary) (p. 1794)
Balaji, T., illus. see Scott, Nathan Kumar.
Balance, Millie, illus. see Superle, Michelle.
Balaram, Mahant K. Srimad Bhagavatam Canto 10: The Beautiful Narrations of the Supreme Lord. Vol. 6 (p. 1637)
Balardo, Sharon. I Am Abel. (p. 832)
Balarinji, illus. see Moriarty, Ros.
Balash, Sue Beth. Mimi the Inchworm. (p. 1145)
Balasubramanian, Lalitha. Twins at the Ancient Villa (p. 1802)
Balawajder, Thomas, et al. Ultimate Homework Survival Guide: A Reality Horror Production. Wise, Noreen, ed. (p. 1809)
Balázs, Béla, et al. Cloak of Dreams: Chinese Fairy Tales. (p. 333)
Balazy, Elizabeth M. Prince to the Rescue. (p. 1401)
Balboni, Mary. Birds of Winslow. (p. 192)
Balcazar, Abraham, illus. see Chacek, Karen.
Balcells, Jacqueline. Archipielago de las Puntuadas. (p. 95)
Balcerzak, Kara Garbe. Bizarre Things We've Done to Our Bodies. (p. 194)
Balch, Betty Neff & Poythress, Jean Hill. Tales of the Cinnamon Dragon: Adventures in Farr Elvenhome. Book I Balch, Betty Neff, illus. (p. 1702)
Balch, Glenn. White Ruff: Famous Dog Stories. Priest, Dick, illus. (p. 1913)
Balch, Trudy, tr. see Serrano, Francisco.
Balchin, Jon. Science: 100 Scientists Who Changed the World. (p. 1524)
Balci, jt. auth. see Hasibe, Gul.
Balci, Erkan, jt. auth. see Gul, Hasibe.
Balcom, Katherine. Waterpark. (p. 1864)
Balczon, Mary-Lynne J., jt. auth. see Johnson, Kathryn T.
Bald, Anna, illus. see MacDonald, Hugh.
Baldacci, David. Camel Club. (p. 256)
—Collectors. (p. 340)
—Day of Doom (p. 414)
—Finisher. (p. 589)
Baldanzi, Alessandro, illus. see Facchini, Florenzo.
Baldanzi, Alessandro, illus. see Rossi, Renzo.
Baldanzi, Alessandro, illus. see Silva, Patricia.
Baldassi, Deborah, illus. see Weber, K. E.
Baldeon, David, illus. see Duggan, Gerry.
Baldick, Robert, tr. see Huysmans, Joris-Karl.
Baldick, Robert, tr. see Verne, Jules.
Baldini-Chavez, Cecilia. Silver-Golden Feather Secreted at El Dorado (p. 1576)
Baldner, Jean V. Pebbles in the Wind. Webster, Carroll, illus. (p. 1333)
Baldock, Kirsten. Smoke & Guns. (p. 1594)
Baldoni, John. Lead by Example: 50 Ways Great Leaders Inspire Results (p. 981)
Baldree, Travis. Jumpin' Joey. (p. 934)
Baldridge, Kim & Abendroth, Teresa. Mixing with MerryGold: A Fairy Tale. (p. 1156)
Baldry, Cherith. Emerald Throne. Wyatt, David, illus. (p. 517)
—Lake of Darkness. Wyatt, David, illus. (p. 972)
Balducci, Rita. Nutcracker. Beckett, Sheilah, illus. (p. 1273)
Baldwin, Aaron, ed. see Baldwin, William.
Baldwin, Alisa, illus. see Dagnino, Michelle.
Baldwin, Alisa, illus. see Smedman, Lisa.
Baldwin., C. R. Henry the Spider. (p. 768)
Baldwin, Carol. Acids & Bases (p. 9)
—Chemical Reactions (p. 297)

—Metals (p. 1130)
—Mixtures, Compounds & Solutions (p. 1156)
—Nonmetals (p. 1263)
—States of Matter (p. 1644)
Baldwin, Christopher, illus. see Geltrich, Brigitta, ed.
Baldwin, Christopher, illus. see Peterson, Mike.
Baldwin, Christy. Care for Creation. Draven, Shelly, illus. (p. 266)
—Nine Things Nathan Noticed at Night. Barnes, Sarah, illus. (p. 1256)
—Remembering Wilma. Barnes, Sarah, illus. (p. 1460)
Baldwin, Comingore. Access to Science for Infants & Toddlers. (p. 8)
Baldwin, Douglas. 1920: Canadian Decades. (p. 2002)
—1930: Canadian Decades. (p. 2002)
—War in Afghanistan. (p. 1857)
—War of 1812. (p. 1857)
—World War II. (p. 1959)
Baldwin, Douglas & Baldwin, Patricia. 1920: Canadian Decades. (p. 2002)
Baldwin, Douglas & Baldwin, Patricia L. World War II. (p. 1959)
Baldwin, Douglas & Kissock, Heather. World War I. (p. 1958)
Baldwin, Elizabeth. Horses. (p. 800)
Baldwin, Erin Donoghue, text. Big Fun Guide to Tar Heel Country: 135+ Activities for Families in Chapel Hill, Carrboro, Hillsborough, Pittsboro, & Points in Between! (p. 181)
Baldwin, Faith. Judy: A Story of Divine Corners. Beebe, Robb, illus. (p. 931)
Baldwin, Garrett. Justin Bieber Album. (p. 940)
Baldwin, Guy & Hart, Joyce. Oklahoma. (p. 1283)
—Wyoming. (p. 1966)
Baldwin, J. R. Ashley & Mr. Sunshine. (p. 106)
—Magic Jammies (p. 1072)
Baldwin, James. Fifty Famous People. (p. 585)
—Fifty Famous People (Yesterday's Classics) (p. 585)
—Fifty Famous Stories Retold. (p. 585)
—Fifty Famous Stories Retold (Yesterday's Classics) (p. 585)
—Four Great Americans. (p. 625)
—In My Youth. (p. 864)
—Old Greek Storie. (p. 1283)
—Old Greek Stories. (p. 1284)
—Story of Roland. (p. 1659)
—Story of Siegfried. (p. 1660)
—Thirty More Famous Stories Retold (Yesterday's Classics) (p. 1735)
Baldwin, Kathleen. School for Unusual Girls. (p. 1523)
Baldwin, Kevin. Beetle Dan & the Big Purple Slide: A Beetle Dan Story. (p. 158)
Baldwin, Kim. Breaking the Ice. (p. 225)
Baldwin, Kim & Alexiou, Xenia. Thief of Always. (p. 1732)
Baldwin, Laura. Harry Loves Greens. Marlette, Andy, illus. (p. 750)
—Harry Loves Turnips (Not!) Marlette, Andy, illus. (p. 750)
Baldwin, Lillian. Music for Young Listeners: The Blue Book. (p. 1193)
—Music for Young Listeners: The Crimson Book. (p. 1193)
Baldwin Locomotive Works, creator. Baldwin Locomotive Works Illustrated Catalog. (p. 134)
—Baldwin Logging Locomotives 1913 Catalog. (p. 134)
—History of the Baldwin Locomotive Works 1831-1920. (p. 784)
Baldwin, May. Sarah's School Friend. (p. 1514)
Baldwin, Neil. American Revelation: Ten Ideals That Shaped Our Country from the Puritans to the Cold War. (p. 63)
Baldwin, Patricia, jt. auth. see Baldwin, Douglas.
Baldwin, Patricia, jt. auth. see Fleming, Kate.
Baldwin, Patricia L., jt. auth. see Baldwin, Douglas.
Baldwin, Quinn. Crossover. (p. 385)
Baldwin, Rich & Jones, Sandie. Detective Company. Dawn, Baumer, illus. (p. 431)
Baldwin, Robert F. Fish House Door. Sheckels, Astrid, illus. (p. 598)
Baldwin, Rosalind. Double Rainbow over Blakely. (p. 473)
Baldwin, Sage & Wolfe, Rita M. Puppy's Life. (p. 1418)
Baldwin, Stephen. Spirit Simko, Joe, illus. (p. 1628)
—Spirit Warriors: Number Three. (p. 1629)
Baldwin, Stephen & Rosato, Bruno. Spirit Warriors: Number Two. Simko, Joe & Tidwell, Jeral, illus. (p. 1629)
Baldwin, Stephen & Tabb, Mark. Unusual Suspect: My Calling to the New Hardcore Movement of Faith. (p. 1823)
Baldwin, William. Charleston My Picture Guide to a Holy City. Baldwin, Aaron et al, eds. (p. 292)
Baldyga, Steve. In the Pond. (p. 867)
Bale, K. A., jt. auth. see Duey, K.
Bale, Karen. Preschool Professors Learn about Thunderstorms. (p. 1396)
—Preschool Professors Learn How Seeds Grow. (p. 1396)
—Preschool Professors Meet Madeleine & the Mustangs. (p. 1396)
—Preschool Professors Search for the Easter Bunny. (p. 1396)
Bale, Karen A., jt. auth. see Duey, Kathleen.
Bale, Mary. Oh, No, Pluto! Gace, Mariah, illus. (p. 1281)
Bale, Tim, jt. auth. see Scarrow, Alex.
Balek, Dayna Courtney, illus. see Reynolds Jr., R. A.
Bales, Kevin, et al. Slavery Today. (p. 1588)
Balestier, Courtney. Would You Rather... ? Super Secrets! Over 300 Fiercely Fascinating Questions to Ask Your Friends. Heimberg, Justin & Gomberg, David, eds. (p. 1962)
Balestrieri, James, et al. Meltdown: Aspergers Disorder, Challenging Behavior, & a Families Journey Toward Hope. (p. 1125)
Balestrieri, Mauro, jt. auth. see Boazu, Elena.
Balestrino, Jerry. Pumpkin the Angel Cat: Pumpkins 1st Mission. (p. 1416)
Baley, Arthur. Tale of Brownie Beaver. (p. 1699)
Balfanz, Mary. Princess Emily & the Secret Library. Gorman, Stan, illus. (p. 1403)
Balfe, Roberta Rymer, et al. Young Person's Introduction to the Arts Featuring the Opera La Cenerentola (Cinderella) by Gioachino [sic] Rossini: Music, Drama, Language, Costumes, Games, Puzzles. (p. 1979)

Balfour, Barbara. Great White Sharks. (p. 719)
—Thanksgiving Day. (p. 1726)
Balfour, Melissa. Magic Footprints. Julian, Russell, illus. (p. 1072)
Balfour, Melissa, et al. Yr Olion Traed Hud. (p. 1983)
Balfour, R. C., III. Fishing for the Abundant Life 2 Journey to Faith. (p. 599)
Balian, Lecia, illus. see Balian, Lorna.
Balian, Lorna. Aminal Balian, Lorna & Balian, Lecia, illus. (p. 65)
—Bah! Humbug? (p. 132)
—Fiasco de Bruja (p. 583)
—Fiasco de Bruja Balian, Lorna, illus. (p. 583)
—Garden for a Groundhog. (p. 656)
—Garden for a Groundhog Balian, Lorna, illus. (p. 656)
—Humbug Rabbit. (p. 826)
—Humbug Witch. (p. 826)
—Humbug Witch Balian, Lorna, illus. (p. 826)
—Leprechauns Never Lie Balian, Lorna, illus. (p. 993)
—Mother's Mother's Day (p. 1179)
—Socksnatchers (p. 1605)
—Sometimes It's Turkey, Sometimes It's Feathers (p. 1610)
—Sweet Touch Balian, Lecia, illus. (p. 1690)
—Sweetheart for Valentine Balian, Lorna, illus. (p. 1690)
—Where in the World Is Henry? Balian, Lecia & Balian, Lorna, illus. (p. 1908)
Balika, Susan. Jesus Is My Special Friend. Bolling, Vickey, illus. (p. 915)
Balika, Susan S. Jesus Is My Special Friend. Bolling, Vickey, illus. (p. 915)
Baliko, Janelle. It Doesn't Have to be Pink. Hackmann, Bethany, illus. (p. 894)
Balit, Christina. Escape from Pompeii. (p. 535)
—Lion Book of Wisdom Stories from Around the World. (p. 1020)
—Lion Illustrated Bible for Children. (p. 1020)
Balit, Christina, illus. see Hoffman, Mary.
Balit, Christina, illus. see Joslin, Mary.
Balit, Christina, illus. see Lupton, Hugh & Morden, Daniel.
Balit, Christina, illus. see Mitton, Jacqueline.
Balit, Christina, illus. see Napoli, Donna Jo.
Balit, Christina, illus. see Rock, Lois.
Balit, Christina, jt. auth. see Mitton, Jacqueline.
Balk, Chad. Rundor's Apprentice. (p. 1497)
Balkin, Karen. War on Terrorism. (p. 1858)
Balkin, Karen F. Anorexia. (p. 87)
Balkin, Karen F., ed. Anorexia. (p. 87)
Balkin, Richard, ed. see Selcer, Richard F.
Balkovec, Lisa. Setting It Straight. (p. 1554)
Balkovek, James, illus. see Cather, Willa.
Balkovek, James, illus. see Cohen, Rafael.
Balkovek, James, illus. see McCallum, Ann.
Balkovek, Jim, illus. see Daughtrey, Patricia & Benson, Gary.
Balkwill, Richard. Best Book of Trains. (p. 168)
Ball, Alan, ed. see Hine, Darlene Clark, et al.
Ball, Alexandra, illus. see Robbins, Karen.
Ball, Ann & Will, Julianne. Our Sunday Visitor's Catholic Encyclopedia for Children. (p. 1310)
Ball, Ann & Will, Julianne M. Catholic Bible Stories for Children: 1st Communion Edition. Davidson, Kevin, illus. (p. 280)
—Catholic Bible Stories for Children. Davidson, Kevin, illus. (p. 280)
Ball, Ashley. My Horse Samson. (p. 1211)
Ball, Barbara & Ball, Derek. Task Maths Interactive 1: Sequence Machines. (p. 1706)
—Task Maths Interactive 3: Is it Possible? (p. 1706)
—Task Maths Interactive 4: Number Pyramids. (p. 1706)
Ball, Derek, jt. auth. see Ball, Barbara.
Ball, Donald, et al. International Business: The Challenge of Global Competition. (p. 880)
Ball, Duncan. Case of the Graveyard Ghost & Other Mysteries. David, Mark, illus. (p. 274)
—Emily Eyefinger & the Balloon Bandits. Smith, Craig, illus. (p. 518)
—Emily Eyefinger & the Ghost Ship. Smith, Craig, illus. (p. 518)
—Emily Eyefinger & the Puzzle in the Jungle. Smith, Craig, illus. (p. 518)
—Eyeful of Emily. (p. 558)
—Selby Santa. Stomann, Allan, illus. (p. 1549)
—Selby Scrambled. Stomann, Allan, illus. (p. 1549)
—Selby Screams. Stomann, Allan, illus. (p. 1549)
—Selby Shattered. Stomann, Allan, illus. (p. 1549)
—Selby Snaps. Stomann, Allan, illus. (p. 1549)
—Selby Snowbound. Stomann, Allan, illus. (p. 1549)
—Selby Sorcerer. Stomann, Allan, illus. (p. 1549)
—Selby Spacedog. Stomann, Allan, illus. (p. 1549)
—Selby Speaks. Stomann, Allan, illus. (p. 1549)
—Selby Splits. Stomann, Allan, illus. (p. 1549)
—Selby Supersnoop. Stomann, Allan, illus. (p. 1549)
—Selby Surfs. Stomann, Allan, illus. (p. 1549)
—Selby's Secret. Stomann, Allan, illus. (p. 1549)
—Selby's Selection. Stomann, Allan, illus. (p. 1549)
—Selby's Shemozzle. Stomann, Allan, illus. (p. 1549)
—Selby's Side-Splitting Joke Book. Stomann, Allan, illus. (p. 1549)
—Selby's Stardom. Stomann, Allan, illus. (p. 1549)
Ball, Geoff, illus. see Baxter, Nicola.
Ball, Geoff, illus. see Shone, Rob.
Ball, Geoff, illus. see West, David.
Ball, Geoff, jt. auth. see Baxter, Nicola.
Ball, Georgia. Berry Fun! (p. 167)
—Berry Good Times! (p. 167)
—Croods Prequel GN. (p. 384)
—Snow & Other Stories. (p. 1598)
—Strawberry Shortcake (p. 1666)
—Strawberry Shortcake Digest: The Berry Scary Storm & Other Stories. (p. 1666)
—Strawberry Shortcake Digest: Field Day & Other Stories: Field Day & Other Stories. (p. 1666)
—Strawberry Shortcake: Pineaple Predicament & Other Stories: Pineapple Predicament & Other Stories. (p. 1666)
Ball, Heather. Astonishing Women Artists. (p. 109)
—Magnificent Women in Music (p. 1076)

—Remarkable Women Writers (p. 1459)
—Women Leaders Who Changed the World. (p. 1946)
—Women Writers Who Changed the World. (p. 1946)
Ball, Jacqueline A. Animales Migratorios: Por Aire. (p. 81)
—Blizzard! The 1888 Whiteout. (p. 199)
—Clothing Creations: From T-Shirts to Flip-Flops. (p. 334)
—Conservation & Natural Resources. (p. 358)
—Extreme Animals: Dinosaurs. (p. 556)
—Food Creations: From Hot Dogs to Ice Cream Cones. (p. 613)
—Himeji Castle: Japan's Samurai Past. (p. 780)
—Martin Luther King, Jr: I Have a Dream! (p. 1098)
—Migrating Animals of the Air. (p. 1140)
—Timmy's My Hero, Who's Yours? (p. 1755)
—Tornado! The 1974 Super Outbreak. (p. 1770)
—Traveling Green. (p. 1780)
—Wildfire! The 1871 Peshtigo Firestorm. (p. 1931)
—Windsor Castle: England's Royal Fortress. (p. 1936)
Ball, Jacqueline A., jt. auth. see Ball, Jacqueline A.
Ball, Jacqueline A. & Ball, Jacqueline A. Earthquakes. (p. 497)
—Earth's History. (p. 498)
—Mapping Earth. (p. 1090)
Ball, Jacqueline A. & Behrens, Kristen. Nueva York. Porras, Carlos & D'Andrea, Patricia, trs. from ENG. (p. 1270)
Ball, Jacqueline A., et al. Communication Inventions: From Hieroglyphics to DVDs. (p. 349)
Ball, Jacqueline & Levey, Richard. National Geographic Investigates: Ancient China: Archaeology Unlocks the Secrets of China's Past. (p. 1231)
Ball, Jacqueline & Levey, Richard H. National Geographic Investigates: Ancient China: Archaeology Unlocks the Secrets of China's Past. (p. 1231)
Ball, Jay. Secrets of Creative Pumpkin & Watermelon Carving. (p. 1545)
Ball, Jeff. Son Who Returns. (p. 1611)
Ball, Jennifer L. Byzantine Dress: Representations of Secular Dress in Eighth- to Twelfth-Century Painting. (p. 249)
Ball, Johnny, jt. auth. see Dorling Kindersley Publishing Staff.
Ball, Johnny & Dorling Kindersley Publishing Staff. Go Figure! A Totally Cool Book about Numbers. (p. 686)
Ball, Karen. Pompeii. Cerisier, Emmanuel, illus. (p. 1382)
Ball, Karen, jt. auth. see Dickins, Rosie.
Ball, Lauren, illus. see Badeaux, Dewey.
Ball, Lea. Federalist—Anti-Federalist Debate over States' Rights: A Primary Source Investigation. (p. 580)
—Federalist-Anti-Federalist Debate over States' Rights: A Primary Source Investigation. (p. 580)
Ball, Liz. Bible Stories: Find-the-Picture Puzzles. (p. 176)
—Frog Fun Hidden Treasures: Hidden Picture Puzzles Ball, Liz, illus. (p. 640)
—Miracles & Parables of Jesus: Find-the-Picture Puzzles. (p. 1148)
—Standardbred Star: Learn about Harness Racing with Star & Friends. (p. 1639)
Ball, Liz, illus. see Nathan, Jeff.
Ball, Madeline K. & Seidman, David. Supply & Demand. (p. 1684)
Ball, Marcia. Christmas Fais Do-Do. (p. 313)
Ball, Natalie, illus. see Dale, Jay.
Ball, Nate. Alien in My Pocket: Radio Active. Pamintuan, Macky, illus. (p. 40)
—Alien in My Pocket #5: Ohm vs. Amp. Pamintuan, Macky, illus. (p. 40)
—Alien in My Pocket - Blast Off! Pamintuan, Macky, illus. (p. 40)
—Alien in My Pocket: on Impact! (p. 40)
—Alien in My Pocket - The Science Unfair. Pamintuan, Macky, illus. (p. 40)
—Blast Off! (p. 198)
—On Impact! (p. 1289)
—Radio Active. (p. 1432)
—Science Unfair. (p. 1528)
—Science Unfair. Pamintuan, Macky, illus. (p. 1528)
—Telescope Troubles. Pamintuan, Macky, illus. (p. 1716)
Ball, Pauline E. Chubsey Tucker Tales. (p. 318)
Ball, Robert Stawell. Star-Land: Being Talks with Young People about the Wonders of the Heavens. (p. 1640)
Ball, S. N. Daddies Don't Get Snow Days. Howard, Ellie Nothaus, illus. (p. 398)
Ball, Sara. Flip-O-Storic. Ball, Sara, illus. (p. 605)
Ball, Sara, illus. see Drehsen, Britta.
Ball Sr., Frank J. Bryanna Global Warrior: Attack of the Alaska Aerial Wolf Hunters Pelton, Bonnie L., illus. (p. 233)
—Planet Earth Past, Present, Future: Bryanna Global Warrior Book 3 Pelton, Bonnie L., illus. (p. 1367)
Ball, Susan, et al. Formula One Mathematics Gold. (p. 620)
—Formula One Maths Gold B. (p. 620)
Ball, Tom. Marty Graw Book. (p. 1098)
Ball, Victoria, illus. see Marks, Melanie.
Ballance, Millie, illus. see Alderson, Sue Ann.
Ballantine Books Staff & Cartoon Network Staff. Bakugan Battle Brawlers: The Battle Begins! Montalvo-Lagos, Tomas, illus. (p. 133)
Ballantine, Poe. Decline of the Lawrence Welk Empire. (p. 422)
—God Clobbers Us All. (p. 688)
Ballantyne, R. Coral Island. (p. 366)
Ballantyne, R. M. Battle & the Breeze. (p. 145)
—Blown to Bits; or, the Lonely Man of Rak. (p. 202)
—Coral Island. (p. 366)
—Crew of the Water Wagtail. (p. 382)
—Dog Crusoe. (p. 461)
—Fort Desolation. (p. 623)
—Gascoyne, the Sandal-Wood Trader. (p. 657)
—Gorilla Hunters A Tale of the Wilds of A. (p. 703)
—Hunting the Lions. (p. 829)
—Lighthouse. (p. 1015)
—Norsemen in the West or America Before Columbus. (p. 1264)
—Red Rooney: Or, the Last of the Crew. (p. 1455)
—Saved by the Lifeboat. (p. 1517)
—Silver Lake. (p. 1576)
—Walrus Hunters. (p. 1855)
—World of Ice. (p. 1956)
—Young Trawler. (p. 1979)
Ballantyne, Robert Michael. Battery & the Boiler: Adventures in Laying of Submarine Electric Cables. (p. 145)
—Coxswain's Bride: Also Jack Frost & Sons; & A Double Rescue. (p. 374)
—Crew of the Water Wagtail. (p. 382)
—Fort Desolation: Red Indians & Fur Traders of Rupert's Land. (p. 623)
—Garret & the Garden. (p. 657)
—Jarwin & Cuffy. (p. 909)
—Life in the Red Brigade: London Fire Brigade. (p. 1011)
—Lighthouse. (p. 1015)
—My Doggie & I. (p. 1202)
—Red Rooney: The Last of the Crew. (p. 1455)
—Rover of the Andes: A Tale of Adventure in South America. (p. 1491)
—Silver Lake. (p. 1576)
—Walrus Hunters: A Romance of the Realms of Ice. (p. 1855)
Ballard, Allen. Where Im Bound. (p. 1908)
Ballard & Tighe Publishers Staff. IDEA Picture Dictionary: An IDEA Language Development Resource. (p. 852)
Ballard Beath, Ernest, III & Ruark Gibb, Paula. Golden's Retreat. (p. 695)
Ballard, Ben, illus. see Wallen-Nichols, Missy.
Ballard, Brenda. Boy from Granite Falls. (p. 217)
Ballard, Carol. AIDS & Other Epidemics. (p. 30)
—At the Crime Scene! Collecting Clues & Evidence. (p. 111)
—Cells & Cell Function. (p. 286)
—Crime under the Microscope! In the Forensics Lab. (p. 382)
—Crimebusting! Identifying Criminals & Victims. (p. 382)
—Digestive System (p. 438)
—Digestive System: Injury, Illness & Health. (p. 438)
—Ears (p. 494)
—Earth & the Solar System (p. 495)
—Explaining Food Allergies. (p. 549)
—Exploring Electricity. (p. 552)
—Exploring Forces & Movement. (p. 552)
—Exploring Light. (p. 552)
—Exploring Magnets & Springs. (p. 552)
—Exploring Natural & Man-Made Materials. (p. 552)
—Exploring Sound. (p. 553)
—Eyes (p. 558)
—Fighting Infectious Diseases. (p. 585)
—Food Safety. (p. 614)
—Food Webs. (p. 614)
—Heart & Blood (p. 759)
—How Your Body Moves. (p. 823)
—How Your Brain Works. (p. 823)
—How Your Ears Work. (p. 823)
—Is Our Food Safe? (p. 889)
—Keeping Fit: Body Systems (p. 947)
—Lungs (p. 1065)
—Lungs: Injury, Illness & Health. (p. 1066)
—Muscles (p. 1192)
—Organ Transplants. (p. 1303)
—Plant Variation & Classification. (p. 1369)
—Skeleton & Muscles. (p. 1584)
—Solids, Liquids, & Gases: From Ice Cubes to Bubbles. (p. 1608)
—Understanding Reproduction. (p. 1816)
—Understanding the Senses. (p. 1816)
—Watching Wildlife: Animal Habitats (p. 1861)
—What Happens to Broken Bones? Bones (p. 1886)
—What Is an Asthma Attack? Respiration (p. 1888)
—What Is My Pulse? Blood & Circulation (p. 1890)
—Why Do I Need Glasses? Vision (p. 1923)
—Your Sense of Touch. (p. 1981)
Ballard, Carol & Heinemann Library Staff. Bones (p. 209)
—Digestive System (p. 438)
—Ears (p. 494)
—Earth & the Solar System (p. 495)
—Eyes (p. 558)
—Heart & Blood (p. 759)
—Immune System (p. 862)
—Lungs (p. 1065)
—Mixtures & Solutions (p. 1156)
—Muscles (p. 1192)
Ballard, Donald W. Disneyland Hotel: The Early Years, 1954-1988. (p. 453)
Ballard, Elizabeth Silance. Kate's Fan. Napier, Louise S., illus. (p. 944)
Ballard, George Anne. Flowers along the Way. Ballard, George Anne & Bolton, Georgia Helen, illus. (p. 608)
—Read to Me! James, Melody A. & Arelys, Aguilar, illus. (p. 1443)
—White Fire, the Indian Boy. James, Melody, illus. (p. 1913)
Ballard, George Anne & Bolton, Georgia Helen. Trouble with Cats. Aguilar, Arelys, illus. (p. 1790)
Ballard, John. Shining Thing Hume, Jeff, illus. (p. 1566)
Ballard, John E. & Shiply, Lyn. What Is That Sound! (p. 1890)
Ballard, Kim. Light at Summer's End. (p. 1015)
Ballard, Lee, illus. see P, Michael.
Ballard, Lisa. Moose for Mackenzie. Doucette, Constance, illus. (p. 1173)
Ballard MacKenzie, Laurie. Margarit: One Fair Lady. (p. 1092)
Ballard, Merry, illus. see Crawford, Deborah & Crawford, Ryan.
Ballard, Peg & Amoroso, Cynthia. Fun! The Sound of Short U. (p. 647)
—Little Bit: The Sound of Short I. (p. 1024)
Ballard, Robert. Pieces of Me: Who Do I Want to Be? Voices for & by Adopted Teens. (p. 1356)
Ballard, Robert D. Exploring the Titanic: How the Greatest Ship Ever Lost-Was Found. (p. 554)
Ballard, Shashon. Bruised, Just Not Broken: Our Short Stories. (p. 232)
Ballart, E. Juguemos a Cocinar. (p. 932)
Ballart, Elisabet. Aprendamos a Convivir. Capdevila, Roser, illus. (p. 93)
Ballas, Mark A. Corky. Wedding Waltz: Learn to Waltz at Your Wedding. (p. 1871)
Ballaz, Jesus, jt. auth. see Stevenson, Robert Louis.
Ballen, Karen. Tour of Your Circulatory System Jones, Chris B., illus. (p. 1773)
Ballen, Karen Gunnison. Decoding Our DNA: Craig Venter vs the Human Genome Project. (p. 422)
—Seven Wonders of Medicine. (p. 1555)
Ballengee, Fran. Sara Elizabeth, an Adoption Story. (p. 1514)
Ballentine, Joyce. Nana's Nursery Rhymes 2. (p. 1228)
Ballesta, Alfredo, tr. see Hewitt, Beth Edington.
Ballesta, Juan. Tommy y el Elefante. (p. 1765)
Ballester, Arnal, illus. see Polo, Eduardo.
Ballester Kniska, Lorena Ivonne, ed. see Gonzalez, Aurora Adriana.
Ballesteros, Antonio, tr. see Wilde, Oscar & O'Flahertie Wills Wilde, Oscar Fingal.
Ballesteros, Carles, illus. see Dickens, Rosie.
Ballesteros, Jason. Sideways. (p. 1573)
Ballesteros, Jose Manuel & Manuel, Ballesteros Pastor José. Erase una Vez la Revolucion. (p. 533)
—Foto de Navidad. (p. 624)
—Las Adventuras de Pepe. Martinez, Rocio, illus. (p. 976)
—Ratita Presumida: Adaptacion Teatral. Gonzalez, Tesa, illus. (p. 1440)
Ballesteros, Xose. Tio Lobo. (p. 1757)
Balletta, Janet. Legend of the Colombian Mermaid. Mejia, Estella, illus. (p. 989)
Ballew, Barbara. Ghost of Coalville. (p. 671)
—Sadie, the Goat Lady. (p. 1501)
—Stranger, the Miracle Dog. (p. 1665)
Ballew, Chris, jt. auth. see Babypants, Caspar.
Ballew, Vince & Hvezda, Chris. Make It Happen: Achieving Personal & Professional Goals. (p. 1079)
Ballhaus, Verena, illus. see Mueller, Dagmar H.
Balliett, Blue. Calder Game. Helquist, Brett, illus. (p. 252)
—Chasing Vermeer. Helquist, Brett, illus. (p. 294)
—Danger Box. (p. 403)
—Hold Fast. (p. 787)
—Pieces & Players. (p. 1356)
—Wright 3. Helquist, Brett, illus. (p. 1963)
Ballingall, Peter & Spieler, Marlena. Golf. Harrison, James, ed. (p. 696)
Ballinger, Bryan. Animal Gas. (p. 78)
Ballinger, Bryan, illus. see Big Idea, Inc. Staff & Kenney, Cindy.
Ballinger, Bryan, jt. auth. see Knopf, Susan.
Ballinger, Carolyn, illus. see Zinner, Gennieve.
Ballinger, Wesley, illus. see Minnema, Cheryl.
Ballman, Swanee. Chocolate Kingdom Caper. Brunson, Stephanie, illus. (p. 309)
—Cockadoodlemoo. (p. 337)
—Swords of Angels. (p. 1692)
—Where Do Babies Come From? (p. 1906)
Ballock-Dixon, Saige J., jt. auth. see Medina, Sylvia M.
Ballock-Dixon, Saige J. & Medina, Sylvia M. Chilean Mines. Eagle, Joy, illus. (p. 305)
Balloon Books. Dot to Dot Count to 10. (p. 472)
Balloon Books Staff. Dot to Dot Count to 50. (p. 472)
—I Can Draw. (p. 835)
—Kindergarten Color & Learn. (p. 957)
Balloon Books Staff, ed. see Van Eerbeek, Ton.
Balloon Books Staff, ed. Wild Animals Board Book. (p. 1928)
Balloon Dude Travis. Twisted Adventure in Twisty Town. (p. 1802)
Ballou, Bert. Anthony's Amazing Garden. (p. 89)
—Anthony's Amazing Nativity. (p. 89)
Ballou, Kathy. Tracks Out Back. (p. 1775)
Ballou, Maturin Murray. History of Cuba or, Notes of a Traveler in the Tropics. (p. 783)
Ballou, Miss, ed. see Zielinski, David.
Ballow, Jonah & Gray, Kevan. University of Kansas College Prowler off the Record. (p. 1820)
Balls, Richard. Be Stiff: The Stiff Records Story. (p. 149)
Balmer, Alden J. Mousetrap Racers: The Complete Builder's Manual - Science Secrets You'll Need to Win. (p. 1182)
Balmer, Fred. Festus & His New Job. Newcomb, Kristene, illus. (p. 582)
—Festus & the Hole in the Fence Gang. Newcomb, Kristene, illus. (p. 582)
—Festus & the Missing Bag of Feed. Newcomb, Kristene, illus. (p. 582)
—Festus & the Monster. Newcomb, Kristene, illus. (p. 582)
—Festus & the Stranger. Miller, Callie, ed. (p. 582)
Balmer, Helen, illus. see Pienkowski, Jan.
Balmer, Paul. Big Nursery Rhyme Songbook. (p. 183)
Balmer, Paul & Music Sales Corporation Staff. Lullaby Songbook. (p. 1064)
Balmes, Santi. I Will Fight Monsters for You. Lyona, illus. (p. 848)
Balmet, Jean-Paul, illus. see Fry, Jason.
Balmuth, Deborah L., ed. see Storey Publishing Staff.
Balog, Cyn. Fairy Tale. (p. 564)
—Starstruck. (p. 1643)
Balogh, Andras, illus. see Boutros, Gladys.
Balogh, Jared, illus. see Begum, Dilara.
Balogh, Jared, illus. see Jones, Tina C.
Balogh, Jared, illus. see McNeal, Carl.
Balogh, Jared, illus. see Murray, Rosalie.
Balogh, Jared, illus. see Rhodes, Jennifer.
Balogh, Jared, illus. see Vadney, Jackie.
Balogh, Mary. Under the Mistletoe. (p. 1813)
Balouch, Kristen. Feelings. Balouch, Kristen, illus. (p. 580)
—Little Little Girl with the Big Big Voice. Balouch, Kristen, illus. (p. 1030)
Balouch, Kristen, illus. see Hamilton, Martha & Weiss, Mitch.
Balouch, Kristen, illus. see Karwoski, Gail & Gootman, Marilyn E.
Baloyra, Patricia. Goodnight Miami. Knotz, Sarah, illus. (p. 701)
Balsamello, Melissa. Happy the Hotdog Dog. (p. 747)
—Happy's Adventure at Se: Starring... Happy the Hotdog Dog. (p. 747)
Balsano, Sean, illus. see Raye, Donna.
Balsavar, Deepa & Kaushal, Tara. Seed. (p. 1547)
Balseiro, Maria Luisa, tr. see Mattingley, Christobel.
Balser, Erin & Gardner, Suzanne. Don't Stop Believin' The Unofficial Guide to Glee. (p. 468)
Balsley, Tilda. ABC Hanukkah Hunt. Poole, Helen, illus. (p. 3)
—Eight Is Great. Takahashi, Hideko, illus. (p. 507)
—Let My People Go! Richard, Ilene, illus. (p. 994)
—Lotsa Matzah. Gutierrez, Akemi, illus. (p. 1057)
—Maccabee! The Story of Hanukkah. Harrington, David, illus. (p. 1068)
—Oh No, Jonah! Silver, Jago, illus. (p. 1281)
—Soo's Boo-Boos: She's Got 10! McNicholas, Shelagh, illus. (p. 1613)
Balsley, Tilda & Blalsey, Tilda. Queen Who Saved Her People. Richard, Ilene, illus. (p. 1425)
Balsley, Tilda & Fischer, Ellen. Count's Hanukkah Countdown. Leigh, Tom, illus. (p. 372)
—Grover & Big Bird's Passover Celebration. Leigh, Tom, illus. (p. 725)
—Grover & Big Bird's Passover Journey. Leigh, Tom, illus. (p. 725)
—I'm Sorry, Grover: A Rosh Hashanah Tale. Leigh, Tom, illus. (p. 860)
—I'm Sorry, Grover! A Rosh Hashanah Tale. Leigh, Tom, illus. (p. 860)
—It's a Mitzvah, Grover! Leigh, Tom, illus. (p. 895)
—Shalom Everybodee! Leigh, Tom, illus. (p. 1559)
Balsley, Tilda & Jago. Oh No, Jonah! (p. 1281)
Baltazar, Art. Aw Yeah Comics: Time for.... Adventure! Vol. 2 Baltazar, Franco, illus. (p. 120)
—DC Super-Pets (p. 416)
—Return to the Treehouse. Franco, illus. (p. 1465)
—Starro & the Space Dolphins Baltazar, Art, illus. (p. 1642)
Baltazar, Art, illus. see Bright, J. E.
Baltazar, Art, illus. see Dahl, Michael.
Baltazar, Art, illus. see Korte, Steve.
Baltazar, Art, illus. see Lemke, Donald B.
Baltazar, Art, illus. see Manning, Matthew K.
Baltazar, Art, illus. see Mason, Jane B.
Baltazar, Art, illus. see Sazaklis, John.
Baltazar, Art, illus. see Sonneborn, Scott.
Baltazar, Art, illus. see Stephens, Sarah Hines.
Baltazar, Art, illus. see Stephens, Sarah.
Baltazar, Art, jt. auth. see Aureliani, Franco.
Baltazar, Art & Aureliani, Franco. Adventures Begin! Baltazar, Art, illus. (p. 15)
—And Now... Braniac! (p. 71)
—And Now... Ma Kent! (p. 71)
—Attack of the Toyman! (p. 114)
—Aw Yeah Comics! and. . Action! Baltazar, Art, illus. (p. 120)
—Because You Demanded It... Darkseid! (p. 155)
—Bounty Hunter Brizuela, Dario, illus. (p. 216)
—By Hook or by Web Norton, Mike, illus. (p. 249)
—Counterfeits Brizuela, Dario, illus. (p. 370)
—Enter Bizarro! (p. 531)
—Enter - Nightwing! Baltazar, Art & Aureliani, Franco, illus. (p. 531)
—General Zod Dogs! (p. 660)
—Goldface Attacks! Brizuela, Dario, illus. (p. 695)
—Green Lantern: the Animated Series. Brizuela, Dario, illus. (p. 722)
—Hack & You Shall Find Norton, Mike, illus. (p. 735)
—Haunted Norton, Mike, illus. (p. 753)
—Invisible Destroyer. Brizuela, Dario, illus. (p. 885)
—Meet Tiny Titans East! Baltazar, Art & Aureliani, Franco, illus. (p. 1123)
—Menace of Metallo! Baltazar, Art, illus. (p. 1126)
—Monkey Business Norton, Mike, illus. (p. 1165)
—Monkey Metropolis! Baltazar, Art, illus. (p. 1165)
—Mysterious Alien Menace! (p. 1222)
—Patrick: Wolf Boy. Vol. 4 (p. 1329)
—Penguins in the Batcave! Baltazar, Art & Aureliani, Franco, illus. (p. 1337)
—Report Card Pickup! Baltazar, Art & Aureliani, Franco, illus. (p. 1461)
—Sidekick City Elementary Baltazar, Art & Aureliani, Franco, illus. (p. 1573)
—Superman Family Adventures (p. 1683)
—Super-Pets! Baltazar, Art, illus. (p. 1680)
—Tiny Titans. Baltazar, Art & Aureliani, Franco, illus. (p. 1757)
—Tiny Titans vs. the Fearsome Five Baltazar, Art & Aureliani, Franco, illus. (p. 1757)
—Titans in Space Baltazar, Art & Aureliani, Franco, illus. (p. 1758)
—Welcome to the Treehouse Baltazar, Art & Aureliani, Franco, illus. (p. 1874)
—Who Is the Purple Superman? Baltazar, Art, illus. (p. 1916)
—Young Justice. (p. 1979)
Baltazar, Art & Aureliani, Franco, creators. Patrick the Wolf Boy: Giant Size Collection Vols. 1 & 2 (p. 1329)
—Patrick the Wolf Boy: Giant Size Collection. Vols. 3 & 4 (p. 1329)
Baltazar, Art & Baltazar, Franco. Aw Yeah Titans! (p. 120)
Baltazar, Art & Franco. Green Team: Teen Trillionaires Guara, Ig, illus. (p. 722)
—Itty Bitty Hellboy. Allie, Scott, ed. (p. 900)
Baltazar, Art, et al. Campfire Secrets (p. 257)
—Fears Jones, Christopher, illus. (p. 579)
—Hal Versus Atrocitus Brizuela, Dario, illus. (p. 736)
—Trouble in the Arena! Brizuela, Dario, illus. (p. 1790)
—True Colors Brizuela, Dario, illus. (p. 1792)
Baltazar, Franco, illus. see Baltazar, Art.
Baltazar, Franco, jt. auth. see Baltazar, Art.
Baltazar, Franco & Art Baltazar Comic Book Staff. Tiny Titans - Field Trippin. (p. 1757)
Balthazar, Flore, illus. see Le Gall, Frank & Doo, Robin.
Balthazar, Flore, illus. see Le Gall, Frank.
Balthazar Heitzmann, Kathleen, compiled by. Cane River Genealogy (p. 261)
Baltuck, Naomi. Storytime Stretchers: Tongue Twisters, Choruses, Games, & Charades. (p. 1664)
Baltz, Kimberly. Frieda Tails: Frieda Goes to Town & Frieda, Jack, & the Box. (p. 637)
Baltzer, Rochelle. Dinosaurs & Other Prehistoric Animals. Penfield, James, illus. (p. 444)
—Dogs & Cats. Penfield, James, illus. (p. 462)

B

—Dolphins Eat & Grow: Level 2. Keimig, Candice, illus. (p. 465)
—Dolphins in the Ocean: Level 3. Keimig, Candice, illus. (p. 465)
—Earthquakes. (p. 497)
—Hurricanes. (p. 830)
—Landslides. (p. 974)
—Monsters & Other Mythical Creatures. Penfield, James, illus. (p. 1169)
—Pirates on the High Seas. Penfield, James, illus. (p. 1364)
—Royal Court in Its Kingdom. Penfield, James, illus. (p. 1492)
—Tsunamis. (p. 1795)
—Volcanoes. (p. 1849)
—Wildfires. (p. 1931)
Balukoff, Constance. Mooky's Bad Hair Day . (p. 1171)
Baluschek, Hans, illus. see von Bassewitz, Gerdt.
Balvanz, Gwynessa, illus. see delMazo, Deborah.
Balzac, Honoré de. Pere Goriot. (p. 1341)
—Unknown Masterpiece & Other Stories. Appelbaum, Stanley, tr. from FRE. (p. 1821)
Balzer, Jeremy, illus. see Crawford, Deborah.
Balzer, Jim, ed. see Mason, Christopher.
Balzer, Tracy, text. Discovery Journal. (p. 450)
Balzola, Asun. Munia y el Cocolilo Naranja. (p. 1191)
—Munia y Sra. Piltronera (Munia & Mrs. Piltronera) (p. 1191)
—Santino el Pastelero. (p. 1513)
Balzola, Asun, illus. see Xirinacs, Olga.
Balzola, Asun, illus. see Zubizarreta, Patxi.
Balzola, Asun, tr. see Varios Autores.
Balzola, Asun & Asun, Balzola. Babi es Barbara. (p. 123)
Balzola, Sofia, illus. see Nöstlinger, Christine.
Balzora, Lulrick, jt. auth. see Balzora, Renaud.
Balzora, Renaud & Balzora, Lulrick. Fondation: Doctrines Bibliques en 52 Leçons. (p. 612)
Bama. Lucy Ladybug's Backyard Adventure. (p. 1063)
—What Am I? (p. 1879)
Bama & White, Sherrie. What Am I? (p. 1879)
Bamaton, Paul. Elections: Choosing Our Leaders. (p. 508)
Bambara, Toni Cade. Raymond's Run. Young, Eric, illus. (p. 1441)
Bamber, Lori. Sleep-Easy Investing: The Canadian Guide to Lower-Risk & Income Investing. (p. 1588)
Bambi727, jt. auth. see Bambi727.
Bambi727 & Bambi727. Having Fun with Colors' & Numbers' I wrote this book in hopes our younger children would enjoy & have fun learning their colors' & Numbers' (p. 755)
Bamford, Desmond Nicholas. Beekemose. (p. 157)
Bampton, Bob. Animals in the Wild. (p. 83)
—Animals on the Farm. (p. 83)
Bampton, Bob, illus. see Goldsack, Gaby.
Ban Breathnach, Sarah. Best Part of the Day. Edelson, Wendy, illus. (p. 171)
Banach, Virginia, illus. see Peirce-Bale, Mary.
Banacloche, Julieta & Columbus, Christopher. Tierra a Vista - Viajes Colon (Land Ho! Voyage of Columbus) (p. 1748)
Banana, Red, jt. auth. see Bradman, Tony.
Banas, Sharon L. Character Education (p. 291)
—Dealing with Bullying. (p. 418)
Banas, Sharon L., jt. auth. see Baptiste, Tracey.
Banas, Sharon L., jt. auth. see Clark, Kate Stevenson.
Banas, Sharon L., jt. auth. see Koellhoffer, Tara.
Banas, Sharon L., jt. auth. see McCollum, Sean.
Banas, Sharon L., jt. auth. see Miller, Marie-Therese.
Banas, Sharon L., jt. auth. see Welty, Tara.
Banash, Jennifer. Elite. (p. 513)
—In Too Deep. (p. 868)
—Silent Alarm. (p. 1575)
—Simply Irresistible. (p. 1578)
Bancks, Tristan. Mac Slater Hunts the Cool. (p. 1067)
—Mac Slater vs. the City. (p. 1067)
—My Life & Other Stuff I Made Up. Gordon, Gus, illus. (p. 1211)
—My Life & Other Stuff That Went Wrong. Gordon, Gus, illus. (p. 1211)
—Noob, Amateur Dentist. Gorissen, Dean, illus. (p. 1263)
—Noob & the Librarian Supervillain. Gorissen, Dean, illus. (p. 1263)
—Noob, Crimebuster. Gorissen, Dean, illus. (p. 1263)
—Noob, the Boy Who Could Fly. Gorissen, Dean, illus. (p. 1263)
Bancks, Tristan & Deckert, Tempany. It's Yr Life. (p. 899)
Bancroft, Bronwyn. Australian 1, 2, 3 of Animals. Bancroft, Bronwyn, illus. (p. 116)
—Australian 1,2,3 of Animals. (p. 116)
—Australian ABC of Animals. (p. 116)
—Australian ABC of Animals. Bancroft, Bronwyn, illus. (p. 116)
—E Is for Echidna: My Australian Word Book. Bancroft, Bronwyn, illus. (p. 492)
—Kangaroo & Crocodile: My Big Book of Australian Animals. Bancroft, Bronwyn, illus. (p. 942)
—Patterns of Australia. Bancroft, Bronwyn, illus. (p. 1329)
—Possum & Wattle: My Big Book of Australian Words. (p. 1387)
—Possum & Wattle: My Big Book of Australian Words. Bancroft, Bronwyn, illus. (p. 1387)
—W Is for Wombat: My First Australian Word Book. Bancroft, Bronwyn, illus. (p. 1851)
—Why I Love Australia. Bancroft, Bronwyn, illus. (p. 1925)
Bancroft, Bronwyn, illus. see Morecroft, Judith.
Bancroft, Bronwyn, illus. see Morgan, Sally.
Bancroft, Bronwyn, illus. see Napoli, Donna Jo & Furrow, Elena.
Bancroft, Bronwyn, jt. auth. see Porter, Annaliese.
Bancroft, Greg. Betsy's Day at the Game. Blackmore, Katherine, illus. (p. 172)
Bancroft, Hubert Howe. American Antiquities, Being the Entire Section Devoted to the Subject in the Author's Series on the Native Races. (p. 59)
—Native Races of the Pacific States of North America (p. 1235)
Bancroft, Laura, jt. auth. see Baum, L. Frank.
Bancroft, Myles. Trouble with Adam's Heart. Brouillette, Peter, ed. (p. 1790)
Bancroft, Tom, illus. see Peterson, Eugene H., tr.
Bancroft, Tom, illus. see Sorrells, W. A.
Bancroft, Tom & Hunter, Nick. Animator: The Coolest Jobs on the Planet (p. 84)
Banda, Lo Hartog Van. Fingers. Morris Publishing Company Staff, illus. (p. 589)
Banda, Rey A. Magical City of Northopolis; a Christmas Story. Patlan, Alyssa A., illus. (p. 1074)
Bandala, Luis Rodriguez. Libro, el Escritor y Otros Cuentos. (p. 1006)
Bandelier, Adolph Francis Alphonse. Pioneers in American Anthropology: The Bandelier-Morgan Letters, 1873-1883. (p. 1361)
Bandelin Dacey Studios Staff, illus. see Bullard, Lisa.
Bandelin, Debra, illus. see Bullard, Lisa.
Bandelin, Debra, illus. see Firestone, Mary.
Bandelin, Debra, illus. see Gayle, Sharon Shavers & Gayle, Sharon.
Bandelin, Debra, illus. see Halfmann, Janet.
Bandelin, Debra, illus. see Krensky, Stephen.
Bandelin, Debra, illus. see Lakin, Patricia.
Bandelin, Debra, illus. see Shaskan, Trisha Speed.
Bandelin, Debra, illus. see Thomson, Sarah L.
Bandelin, Debra, illus. see Winstead, Amy.
Bandelin, Debra, tr. see Gayle, Sharon Shavers & Gayle, Sharon.
B&H Editorial Staff. Big Picture Interactive Bible Storybook, Hardcover (Case Of 12) Connecting Christ Throughout God's Story. (p. 183)
B&H Editorial Staff, ed. Big Picture Interactive Bible Stories for Toddlers, from the New Testament: Connecting Christ Throughout God's Story. McPherson, Heath, illus. (p. 183)
—Big Picture Interactive Bible Stories in 5 Minutes: Connecting Christ Throughout God's Story. McPherson, Heath, illus. (p. 183)
—Look & Find Bible: New Testament Stories. Guile, Gill, illus. (p. 1048)
—Look & Find Bible: Old Testament Stories. Guile, Gill, illus. (p. 1048)
—Read to Me Bible for Kids. (p. 1443)
B&H Kids Editorial. Baby Blessings Bible, Padded Boardbook. (p. 125)
B&H Kids Editorial Staff. 50 Bedtime Bible Stories. (p. 1997)
—Devotions off the Map: A 52-Week Devotional Journey. (p. 432)
—Gospel Story. (p. 703)
B&H Kids Editorial Staff, ed. I'm a Christian—Now What? 100 Devotions for Boys. (p. 858)
—I'm a Christian—Now What? 100 Devotions for Girls. (p. 858)
—What It Means to Be a Christian: 100 Devotions for Boys. (p. 1891)
—What It Means to Be a Christian: 100 Devotions for Girls. (p. 1891)
Bandrova, Temenoujka, et al. Children Map the World: Selections from the Barbara Petchenik Children's World Map Competition. Vol. 2 (p. 302)
Bandsuh, Jim. Helmet Hank. (p. 765)
Bandy, Michael S. & Stein, Eric. Granddaddy's Turn. Ransome, James, illus. (p. 707)
—White Water. Stickland, Shadra, illus. (p. 1913)
—White Water. Strickland, Shadra, illus. (p. 1913)
Bandy, Sheena. Magdlynn in Flames. (p. 1071)
Bane, Jeff, illus. see Haldy, Emma E.
Bane, Karen. Raising Tippy. (p. 1437)
Bane, T. Glenn, illus. see Wardell, Joe.
Banegas, Candela & Candela, Pilar. Rayuela: Level 1. Bk. B (p. 1441)
Banegas, Candela, et al. Rayuela: Level 1. Bk. A (p. 1441)
Banek, Yvette, illus. see Hults, Alaska.
Banerjee, Anjali. Looking for Bapu. (p. 1051)
—Seaglass Summer. (p. 1536)
—Silver Spell. Fiegenshuh, Emily, illus. (p. 1577)
Banerjee, Sankha, illus. see Foley, Ryan.
Banerjee, Sankha, illus. see Helfand, Lewis & Teitelbaum, Michael.
Banerjee, Sankha, illus. see Helfand, Lewis.
Banerjee, Timir. Cat & the Kids of Millbrae. Dickman, Michael, illus. (p. 277)
Banerji, Chitrita. Land of Milk & Honey: Travels in the History of Indian Food. (p. 973)
Banes, Graham L. Kingfisher Encyclopedia of Life. (p. 960)
Banes, Graham L., jt. auth. see Kingfisher Editors.
Bang, Derrick, ed. see Schulz, Charles M. & Sasseville, Jim.
Bang, Molly. My Light. Bang, Molly, illus. (p. 1212)
—Ten, Nine, Eight. Bang, Molly, illus. (p. 1719)
—When Sophie Gets Angry - Really, Really Angry. (p. 1904)
—Wiley & the Hairy Man: Adapted from an American Folk Tale. Bang, Molly, illus. (p. 1932)
Bang, Molly, illus. see Harris, Robie H.
Bang, Molly & Chisholm, Penny. Buried Sunlight: How Fossil Fuels Have Changed the Earth. Bang, Molly, illus. (p. 243)
—Living Sunlight: How Plants Bring the Earth to Life. Bang, Molly, illus. (p. 1041)
—Ocean Sunlight: How Tiny Plants Feed the Seas. Bang, Molly, illus. (p. 1276)
Banghart, Tracy E. What the Sea Wants. Blum, Julia C., illus. (p. 1893)
Bangs, Edward. Yankee Doodle. Squier, Robert, illus. (p. 1968)
Bangs, John. Little Book of Christmas. Becher, Arthur, illus. (p. 1025)
Bangs, John Kendrick, et al. Rollo in Emblemland: A Tale Inspired by Lewis Carrol's Wonderland. (p. 1485)
Bangs, Jude Hatcher. Elf King (p. 512)
Bangura, Yusuf & Larbi, George A., eds. Public Sector Reform in Developing Countries: Capacity Challenges to Improve Services. (p. 1414)
Banham, Dale & Luff, Ian. History. (p. 783)
Banham, Dale, et al. Essential Germany, 1918-1945: A Study in Depth. (p. 537)
Bania, Michael. Kumak's Fish: A Tall Tale from the Far North. (p. 968)
—Kumak's Friends & Family: A Coloring & Activity Book. (p. 968)
—Kumak's River: A Tale from the Far North. (p. 968)
—Kumak's River: A Tall Tale from the Far North. (p. 968)
Bania, Michael, illus. see Stihler, Cherie B.
Bania, Michael, illus. see Stihler, Chérie B.
Banicki, Patsy & Staige, Pat. Farmer Carpenter's Barn & the Cow's Saturday Night Dance. Staige, Pat & Stanton, Janet, illus. (p. 574)
Banigan, Chris, illus. see Rowe, W. W.
Banim, Lisa. Case of the Missing She-Geek. (p. 274)
—Hands off My Crush-Boy! (p. 741)
—In the Doghouse. (p. 865)
Banim, Lisa & Minsky, Terri. Case of the Kate Haters. (p. 274)
Banis, Bud. Me & My Shadows -Shadow Puppet Fun ForKids of All Ages: Enhanced with Practical Paper Pastimes. Banis, Bud, illus. (p. 1115)
Banister, Katie Rodriguez & Banister, Steve. Aunt Katie's Visit: A Child's First Book on Disabilities. Whitfield, Eric T., illus. (p. 115)
Banister, Steve, jt. auth. see Banister, Katie Rodriguez.
Baniti, Nailah. Nana's Sweetie-Pie-Chicken. (p. 1228)
—Nia's Dream the Talking Tulips. Bayramoglu, Hatice, illus. (p. 1250)
—Papa's Bella Ros. (p. 1322)
Baniti, Nailah & Bayramoglu, Hatice. Nia's Dream. Bayramoglu, Hatice, illus. (p. 1250)
Bank Street College. Sacajawea: the Jacabee Readers: The Adventures of Dooley, Abby & Baldy. (p. 1500)
Bank Street College of Education. Prado: Family Fold-Out Guide. (p. 1392)
Bankenaar, Dale, illus. see Von Wielligh, G. R.
Bankert, Lisa. Operation: Oddball. Meyers, Nancy, illus. (p. 1300)
Bankert, M. L. Living a Role. (p. 1040)
Bankes, Liz. Irresistible. (p. 888)
Banki, Caspian & Banki, Lynne. What Autism Means to Me. Banki, Caspian & Banki, Damian, illus. (p. 1880)
Banki, Damian, illus. see Banki, Caspian & Banki, Lynne.
Banki, Lynne, jt. auth. see Banki, Caspian.
Bankier, William. Mount St. Helens Volcano. Miller, Zachary N., ed. (p. 1180)
Bankoff, Greg. Cultures of Disaster: Society & Natural Hazard in the Philippines. (p. 391)
Bankoff, Samuel. Famous Coloradans. (p. 569)
Bankole, Adekemi. Rain Beat Dance. (p. 1434)
Bankow, Henriette. Alfie's Angels: Big Book English Only. Garson, Sarah, illus. (p. 37)
Banks, Alex. Jump Boys: Sos. (p. 934)
Banks, Angelica. Finding Serendipity. Lewis, Stevie, illus. (p. 588)
Banks, Ann. Children's Travel Journal. Hartman, Adrienne, illus. (p. 304)
Banks, Anna. Joyride. (p. 930)
—Of Neptune. (p. 1279)
—Of Poseidon (p. 1279)
—Of Poseidon. (p. 1279)
—Of Triton. (p. 1279)
Banks, Anthony, ed. see Mahfouz, Sabrina, et al.
Banks, Calvin J. Beginning Conversations with God: A Prayer & Spiritual Journal for Children. Hayden, Seito & Chandler, Alton, illus. (p. 159)
Banks, Celia. God Loves Me. (p. 689)
—Issy's Gift: A Story about Giving. (p. 893)
—Jacob's Promise: A Story about Faith. Unalp, Janet & Perry, Matt, illus. (p. 904)
Banks, Christopher. Oceans of the World. (p. 1277)
Banks, Delilah & Giacobello, John. Surviving Family Violence. (p. 1687)
Banks, Erin, illus. see Evans, Freddi Williams.
Banks, Erin, illus. see Pritchett, Dylan.
Banks, Erma. Fruit Cocktail. (p. 645)
Banks, J., jt. auth. see Orme, David.
Banks Jackson, Meredith. Puppy & Aidan. (p. 1418)
Banks, Jacqueline Turner. Day for Vincent Chin & Me. (p. 413)
Banks, Jacqueline Turner & Turner Banks, Jacqueline. Egg-Drop Blues. (p. 506)
Banks, Jane Whelen. Liam Knows What to Do When Kids Act Snitty: Coping When Friends Are Tactless. (p. 1004)
—Liam Says "Hi" Learning to Greet a Friend. (p. 1004)
—Liam Wins the Game, Sometimes: A Story about Losing with Grace. (p. 1004)
—Loveable Liam: Affirmations for a Perfectly Imperfect Child. (p. 1061)
Banks, Jane Whelen & Whelen-Banks, Jane. Liam Says "Sorry" Repairing an Encounter Gone Sour. (p. 1004)
Banks, Jewelene. Don't Give That Boy No Gun. (p. 467)
Banks, Kate. And If the Moon Could Talk. Hallensleben, Georg, illus. (p. 71)
—Bear in the Book Hallensleben, Georg, illus. (p. 151)
—Cat Who Walked Across France. Hallensleben, Georg, illus. (p. 278)
—City Cat. Castillo, Lauren, illus. (p. 323)
—Close Your Eyes. Hallensleben, Georg, illus. (p. 334)
—Dillon Dillon. (p. 440)
—Eraserheads. Kulikov, Boris, illus. (p. 533)
—Magician's Apprentice. Sis, Peter, illus. (p. 1075)
—Max's Castle. Kulikov, Boris, illus. (p. 1112)
—Max's Dragon. Kulikov, Boris, illus. (p. 1112)
—Max's Math. Kulikov, Boris, illus. (p. 1112)
—Max's Words. (p. 1112)
—Max's Words. Kulikov, Boris, illus. (p. 1112)
—Night Worker. (p. 1254)
—Night Worker. Hallensleben, Georg, illus. (p. 1254)
—Pajaro, el Mono y la Serpiente en la Selva. Bogacki, Tomek, illus. (p. 1319)
—Please, Papa. Swiatkowska, Gabi, illus. (p. 1373)
—That's Papa's Way. Castillo, Lauren, illus. (p. 1727)
Banks, Kate & Sheldrake, Rupert. Boy's Best Friend. (p. 220)
Banks, Kerry. Baseball's Top 100: The Game's Greatest Records (p. 141)
Banks, Kimberly E. Mask Man. Wroe, Dameon K., ed. (p. 1102)
Banks, L. A., pseud. Wicked. (p. 1927)
Banks, Lois. Learn Your ABC's God's Way. (p. 984)
Banks, Lynne Reid. Adventures of King Midas. (p. 19)
—Angela & Diabola. (p. 74)
—Fairy Rebel. (p. 564)
—Farthest-Away Mountain. (p. 575)
—Harry the Poisonous Centipede: A Story to Make You Squirm. (p. 751)
—Harry the Poisonous Centipede Goes to Sea. Ross, Tony, illus. (p. 751)
—I, Houdini: The Amazing Story of an Escape-Artist Hamster. (p. 839)
—I, Houdini. Riley, Terry, illus. (p. 839)
—Indian in the Cupboard. (p. 871)
—Key to the Indian. (p. 950)
—Key to the Indian. Watling, James, illus. (p. 950)
—Mystery of the Cupboard. (p. 1225)
—Mystery of the Cupboard. Newsom, Tom, illus. (p. 1225)
—Return of the Indian. (p. 1464)
—Secret of the Indian. (p. 1542)
—Tiger, Tiger. (p. 1748)
—Uprooted - a Canadian War Story. (p. 1825)
Banks, Maya. Be with Me. (p. 149)
Banks, Melanee R. Bryana's Biggest Wish: Believe. Give. Imagine. Create. Hope. Love. (p. 233)
Banks, Nancy. Shamoni & Noemi. (p. 1559)
Banks, Pat, illus. see Pack, Linda Hager.
Banks, Piper. Geek Abroad (p. 659)
—Geek High. (p. 659)
—Revenge of the Geek. (p. 1466)
—Summer of the Geek. (p. 1674)
Banks, Radine. Nochi Come Back. (p. 1262)
Banks, Rayelynn, jt. auth. see Metzger, Haley.
Banks, Robin Washington. Big Boy. Morgan, Vincent, illus. (p. 179)
Banks, Rosemary. Moe the Well Dressed Scarecrow. (p. 1160)
Banks, Rosie. Cloud Island. (p. 334)
—Enchanted Palace. (p. 523)
—Glitter Beach. (p. 683)
—Magic Mountain. (p. 1072)
—Mermaid Reef. (p. 1128)
—Secret Kingdom #1: Enchanted Palace. (p. 1541)
—Secret Kingdom #2: Unicorn Valley. (p. 1541)
—Secret Kingdom #3: Cloud Island. (p. 1541)
—Secret Kingdom #4: Mermaid Reef. (p. 1541)
—Secret Kingdom #5: Magic Mountain. (p. 1541)
—Secret Kingdom #6: Glitter Beach. (p. 1541)
—Unicorn Valley. (p. 1818)
Banks, Sandra, illus. see Schult, Sherry.
Banks, Sara Harrell. Everlasting Now (p. 542)
—Remember My Name. (p. 1459)
—Tomo-Chi-Chi: Gentle Warrior. (p. 1765)
Banks, Steven. Art Contest: No Cheating Allowed! Dress, Robert, illus. (p. 101)
—Big Halloween Scare. Martinez, Heather, illus. (p. 181)
—Dear Spongebob ... A Funny Fill-Ins Book. (p. 419)
—Lemonade with a Twist. Miller, Victoria, illus. (p. 991)
—Lost in Time. The Artifact Group, illus. (p. 1056)
—Love Potion. Sasic, Natasha, illus. (p. 1060)
—Pick a Dad, Any Dad! Moore, Harry, illus. (p. 1354)
—Show Me the Bunny! Greenblatt, C. H. & Reiss, William, illus. (p. 1570)
—Show Me the Bunny! (SpongeBob SquarePants) Random House, illus. (p. 1570)
—Song That Never Ends. DePorter, Vince, illus. (p. 1611)
—Special Delivery! DePorter, Vince, illus. (p. 1623)
—Special Delivery. DePorter, Vince, illus. (p. 1623)
—SpongeBob Goes to the Doctor. Saunders, Zina, illus. (p. 1630)
—Spongebob Goes to the Doctor. Saunders, Zina, illus. (p. 1630)
—Stop the Presses! DePorter, Vince, illus. (p. 1653)
—Thanks a Lot, Robo-Turkey! LaPadula, Tom, illus. (p. 1725)
Banks, Steven & Hillenburg, Stephen. Show Me the Bunny! Greenblatt, C. H. & Reiss, William, illus. (p. 1570)
Banks, Steven, et al. For the Love of Bubbles. Osterhold, Jared, illus. (p. 616)
Banks, Sydney. Enlightened Gardener Revisited. (p. 530)
Banks, T. J. Houdini. (p. 802)
Banks, Taylor. Rock Princess. (p. 1482)
Banks, Timothy, illus. see Coles, Michael Joseph, et al.
Banks, Timothy, illus. see Harbo, Christopher L.
Banks, Timothy, illus. see Katz, Jill.
Banks, Timothy, illus. see McCurry, Kristen.
Banks, Timothy, illus. see Sonneborn, Scott.
Banks, Timothy, illus. see Wittrock, Jeni.
Banks, Tyra. Modelland. (p. 1158)
Banks, William. Let This Cup Pass. (p. 994)
Bankston, Carl L., ed. see Salem Press Staff.
Bankston, John. Abby Wambach. (p. 2)
—Alexander Graham Bell & the Story of the Telephone. (p. 36)
—Alexander the Great. (p. 36)
—Alicia Keys. (p. 40)
—Ancient India: Maurya Empire. (p. 69)
—Andre Norton. (p. 72)
—Bow Wow. (p. 216)
—Christina Aguilera. (p. 312)
—Christopher Paolini. (p. 317)
—Daniel Radcliffe. (p. 405)
—Day by Day with Chloe Moretz. (p. 412)
—Diego Rivera. (p. 437)
—Ecstasy = Busted! (p. 503)
—Electric Trains & Trolleys (1880-1920) (p. 508)
—Eminem. (p. 519)
—Evolution of Government & Politics in France. (p. 547)
—F. Scott Fitzgerald. (p. 559)
—Gregor Mendel & the Discovery of the Gene. (p. 723)
—Inhalants = Busted! (p. 874)
—Ja Rule. (p. 902)
—Jack London. (p. 903)
—Jay-Z. (p. 910)
—Joseph Lister & the Story of Antiseptics. (p. 926)
—Karl Benz & the Single Cylinder Engine. (p. 943)
—Katherine Paterson. (p. 944)
—Lance Armstrong. (p. 973)
—Life & Times of Alexander the Great. (p. 1007)

Full bibliographic information is available on the Title Index page number referenced in parentheses at the end of each entry

—Life & Times of Duke Ellington. (p. 1008)
—Life & Times of Scott Joplin. (p. 1008)
—Lois Lowry. (p. 1045)
—Louis Daguerre & the Story of the Daguerreotype. (p. 1058)
—Margaret Mead: Pioneer of Social Anthropology. (p. 1092)
—Missy Elliott: Hip-Hop Superstar. (p. 1154)
—Nellie Bly. (p. 1240)
—Nelly. (p. 1240)
—Randolph J. Caldecott & the Story of the Caldecott Medal. (p. 1438)
—Ray Bradbury. (p. 1441)
—Rudy Giuliani. (p. 1494)
—Shirley Temple. (p. 1567)
—Sigmund Freud: Exploring the Mysteries of the Mind. (p. 1574)
—Stephen Hawking: Breaking the Boundaries of Time & Space. (p. 1648)
—We Visit Ethiopia. (p. 1868)
—We Visit Ghana. (p. 1868)
—We Visit Kenya. (p. 1868)
—We Visit Rwanda. (p. 1868)
—We Visit Singapore. (p. 1868)
—What It's Like to Be Mariano Rivera. (p. 1891)
—What It's Like to Be Selena Gomez. (p. 1891)
Bankston, John, jt. auth. see Todd, Anne M.
Bannatyne, Lesley Pratt. Witches' Night Before Halloween Tans, Adrian, illus. (p. 1941)
Bannatyne-Cugnet, Jo. Day I Became a Canadian: A Citizenship Scrapbook. Zhang, Song Nan, illus. (p. 413)
—Heartland: A Prairie Sampler. Moore, Yvette, illus. (p. 760)
—Prairie Alphabet. Moore, Yvette, illus. (p. 1392)
Banner, Angela. Ant & Bee. (p. 88)
—Ant & Bee & Kind Dog. (p. 88)
—Ant & Bee & the ABC. (p. 88)
—Ant & Bee & the Doctor. (p. 88)
—Ant & Bee & the Rainbow. (p. 88)
—Ant & Bee & the Secret. (p. 88)
—Ant & Bee Count 123. (p. 88)
—Ant & Bee Go Shopping. (p. 88)
—Ant & Bee Time. (p. 88)
—Around the World with Ant & Bee. (p. 101)
—Happy Birthday with Ant & Bee. (p. 745)
—More & More Ant & Bee. (p. 1174)
—More Ant & Bee. (p. 1174)
Banner, Horace. Amazon Adventures. (p. 56)
—Rain Forest Adventures. (p. 1434)
Banner, Melanie Jane. Smoke: A Wolf's Story Kveta, tr. (p. 1594)
Bannerji, Himani. Coloured Pictures. Sasso, illus. (p. 346)
Bannerman, Helen. Boy & the Tigers. Petrone, Valeria, illus. (p. 217)
—Little Black Sambo. (p. 1024)
—Short Works of Helen Bannerman. (p. 1569)
—Story of Little Babaji. (p. 1658)
—Story of Little Black Mingo & the Story of Little Black Sambo. (p. 1658)
—Story of Little Black Mingo (Illustr. (p. 1658)
—Story of Little Black Sambo. (p. 1659)
—Story of the Teasing Monkey. (p. 1662)
Banning, Brianne. Beautiful Bald Princess. (p. 153)
—Brave Bald Knight. (p. 223)
Banning, Greg, illus. see Kingsbury, Karen & Smith, Alex.
Banning, Greg, illus. see Leonetti, Mike.
Banning, Lance. Liberty & Order: The First American Party Struggle. (p. 1005)
Bannister, illus. see Grimaldi, Flora.
Bannister, illus. see Grimaldi.
Bannister, illus. see Nykko.
Bannister, A., illus. see Nykko.
Bannister, Barbara. Christmas Train. Seiler, Jason & Farley, Jason, illus. (p. 316)
—Possum's Three Fine Friends. Baron, Kathy, illus. (p. 1387)
Bannister, Bram. Rupert, the Alien & the Bank Robbery. (p. 1497)
Bannister, Emily, illus. see Rees, Gwyneth.
Bannister, Philip, jt. auth. see Reid, Stef.
Bannon, Anthony & McCurry, Steve. Steve Mccurry. (p. 1649)
Bannon, Laura, illus. see Bowman, James Cloyd, et al.
Bannon, Laura, illus. see Bowman, James Cloyd.
Banqueri, Eduardo. Our Planet. (p. 1309)
Banquieri, Eduardo. Biosphere. (p. 190)
—Life on Earth. (p. 1012)
—Secrets of Earth. (p. 1545)
—Space. (p. 1618)
Banri, Hidaka, jt. auth. see Hidaka, Banri.
Bansch, Helga. Brava, Mimi! (p. 223)
—I Want a Dog! Bansch, Helga, illus. (p. 847)
—Odd Bird Out. (p. 1278)
—Petra. Mejuto, Eva, tr. (p. 1348)
Bansch, Helga, illus. see Aliaga, Roberto.
Bansch, Helga, illus. see Janisch, Heinz.
Bansch, Helga, illus. see Núñez, Marisa.
Bansch, Helga, jt. auth. see Janisch, Heinz.
Bansch, Helga, jt. auth. see Schneider, Antonie.
Banta, Martha, ed. see James, Henry.
Banta, Sandra F. Fancy the Beautiful Little Dragon: Book Number Two Little One's Series. Hecker, Vera, illus. (p. 570)
—Muffy the Dragon. Hecker, Vera, illus. (p. 1189)
Banta, Susan. Leyenda del Coqui. (p. 1004)
Banta, Susan, illus. see Bonnett-Rampersaud, Louise.
Banta, Susan, illus. see Cowan, Charlotte.
Banta, Susan, illus. see Rock, Brian.
Banta, Susan, illus. see Votaw, Carol J.
Banta, Susan, illus. see Votaw, Carol.
Banta, Susan, illus. see Williams, Rozanne Lanczak.
Banting, Celia. I only said I couldn't Cope. (p. 844)
—I Only Said I Didn't Want You Because I Was Terrified. (p. 844)
—I Only Said I Had No Choice. (p. 844)
—I only said I was telling the Truth. (p. 844)
—I Only Said Yes So That They'd Like Me. (p. 844)
Banting, Erinn. Angelina Jolie. (p. 74)
—Caves. (p. 282)
—Civil Rights Movement. (p. 324)
—Condoleeza Rice. (p. 356)
—Condoleezza Rice. (p. 356)
—Cris: Les Autochtones du Canada. Karvonen, Tanjah, tr. from ENG. (p. 383)
—Deserts. (p. 429)
—Empire State Building. (p. 521)
—England: The People. (p. 529)
—England: The Culture. (p. 529)
—England - The Land. (p. 529)
—England - The People. (p. 529)
—Flags & Seals. (p. 602)
—Galapagos Islands: A Unique Ecosystem. (p. 653)
—Galapagos Islands. (p. 653)
—Great Barrier Reef. (p. 713)
—Halle Berry. (p. 737)
—Inventing the Automobile. (p. 883)
—Inventing the Telephone. (p. 883)
—Katie Couric. (p. 945)
—Mary Pope Osbourne. (p. 1101)
—Mountains. (p. 1181)
—Nile River. (p. 1255)
—North America. (p. 1264)
—Rosa Parks. (p. 1488)
—South America. (p. 1616)
—Tundras. (p. 1796)
—Wheels & Axles. (p. 1900)
Banting, Erinn, jt. auth. see De Medeiros, Michael.
Banting, Erinn & Kissock, Heather. Cree. (p. 380)
Bantock, Nick. Windflower. (p. 1935)
Banton, Amy Renee, illus. see Morgan, Robert.
Banville, Vincent. Hennessy. (p. 767)
Banyai, Istvan. Otro Lado. (p. 1307)
Banyai, Istvan, illus. see Park, Linda Sue.
Banyan, Calvin D. Secret Language of Feelings. (p. 1541)
Banyard, Jen. Spider Lies. Gibbs, Tracey, illus. (p. 1626)
Banzet, Dindy. Hoo Hoo's for God & Jesus. (p. 795)
Bao, Julie. Loving Teacher Forever: A True Story of Loving Children, Defying Fate & Achieving Teaching Excellence. (p. 1061)
Bao, Karen. Dove Arising. (p. 473)
Bapiraju Gandham. Wizard of Ants. (p. 1943)
Baptist, Leona. Daniel Boone. (p. 405)
Baptiste, Annette Green, illus. see Lee, Deborah Baptiste & Atcheson-Melton, Patty.
Baptiste, Baron. My Daddy Is a Pretzel: Yoga for Parents & Kids. Fatus, Sophie, illus. (p. 1201)
Baptiste, Tracey. Al Gore. (p. 32)
—Angel's Grace. (p. 75)
—Civil War & Reconstruction Eras. (p. 325)
—Jerry Spinelli. (p. 913)
—Jumbies. (p. 933)
—Madeleine L'Engle. (p. 1070)
—Mathematics: The Study of Numbers, Quantity, & Space (p. 1108)
—Nelson Mandela: Nobel Peace Prize-Winning Warrior for Hope & Harmony. (p. 1241)
—Nelson Mandela: Nobel Peace Prize-Winning Champion for Hope & Harmony. (p. 1241)
—Sharon Creech. (p. 1563)
—Stephenie Meyer. (p. 1648)
Baptiste, Tracey & Banas, Sharon L. Being a Leader & Making Decisions. (p. 160)
—Overcoming Prejudice. (p. 1314)
Baptiste, Tracey, ed. Civil War & Reconstruction Eras. (p. 325)
Baquedano, Lucia Azcona & Lucia, Baquedano Azcona. Divertidos Lios de la Noche. (p. 454)
Bar, Dominique, jt. auth. see Brunor.
Baraba, Joseph Frank. Dusty. (p. 490)
Barabba Entertainment Staff. Drover Drew. (p. 486)
Baraclough, Sue, jt. auth. see Guillain, Charlotte.
Baraclough, Sue, jt. auth. see Oxlade, Chris.
Barad-Cutler, Alexis. Five Hungry Pandas! A Count & Crunch Book. Poling, Kyle, illus. (p. 600)
—Walking with Dinosaurs: Friends Stick Together. (p. 1854)
—Walking with Dinosaurs: Friends Stick Together. (p. 1854)
Barajas Durán, Rafael. Travesuritis Aguda. (p. 1781)
Barajas Mariscal, Libia E. & Mariscal, Libia Barajas. Vida y Fortuna de un Muchacho Inquieto Que Se Convirtio en Cientifico. Bernal, Victor Garcia, illus. (p. 1841)
Barajas, Sal, illus. see alurista, et al.
Barajas, Sal, illus. see Ortiz, Teresa, et al.
Barakat, Ibtisam. Tasting the Sky: A Palestinian Childhood. (p. 1707)
Barakiva, Michael. One Man Guy. (p. 1296)
Baran, Laura, jt. auth. see Mussler-Wright, Richard.
Baran, Laura & Mussler-Wright, Richard. PCS Edventures! Bricklab Kindergarten. (p. 1331)
Baran, Robert J. Bonsai Coloring Book. Steele, Paul, illus. (p. 209)
Barancik, Sue. Guide to Collective Biographies for Children & Young Adults. (p. 730)
Baranda, Maria. Angela en el Cielo de Saturno. Luna, Margarita, illus. (p. 74)
Baranda, María. Marte y Las Princesas Voladores. Odriozola, Elena, illus. (p. 1097)
Baranda, Maria. Risa de los Cocodrilos. Cicero, Julian, illus. (p. 1474)
—Ruge! Magallanes, Alejandro, illus. (p. 1494)
—Sol de los Amigos. Wernicke, Maria, illus. (p. 1606)
—Tulia y la Tecla Magica. Marin, Mary Rodriguez, illus. (p. 1796)
Barandela, Jeremy. United We Stand. (p. 1820)
Baranello, Pat. Adventures of Bible Buddy. (p. 16)
Baranowski, Mark. Day in the Life of the Shifties: Deezer's First Day of Pre-School. Baranowski, Mark, illus. (p. 413)
Baranski, Diane. Summer Fun: Work with Addition & Subtraction Equations. (p. 1674)
Baranski, Marcin, illus. see LeFrak, Karen & Lefrak, Karen.
Baranski, Marcin, illus. see LeFrak, Karen.
Barany, Beth. Henrietta the dragon Slayer. (p. 767)
Baraou, Anne & Sardon, Vincent. Skeleton Family: The Neighbors from Elsewhere. (p. 1584)
Barard, Brooke. Believe in Yourself: Coloring Book. (p. 161)
Baras, Ronit. Be Special, Be Yourself: For Teenagers. (p. 149)
Barasch, Lynne. First Come the Zebra. Barasch, Lynne, illus. (p. 593)
—Hiromi's Hands Barasch, Lynne, illus. (p. 781)
—Knockin' on Wood: Starring Peg Leg Bates. (p. 965)
Barasch, Lynne, illus. see Kerby, Mona.
Barasch, Lynne, illus. see Thayer, Jane.
Barash, Chris. Is It Hanukkah Yet? Psacharopulo, Alessandra, illus. (p. 889)
—Is It Passover Yet? Psacharopulo, Alessandra, illus. (p. 889)
—One Fine Shabbat. Mai-Wyss, Tatjana, illus. (p. 1295)
Barash, Susan Shapiro. Tripping the Prom Queen: The Truth about Women & Rivalry. (p. 1787)
Barasui. Ichigo Mashimaro. (p. 851)
Baratz-Logsted, Lauren. Angel's Choice. (p. 75)
—Annie's Adventures. Weber, Lisa K., illus. (p. 87)
—Crazy Beautiful. (p. 377)
—Durinda's Dangers. Weber, Lisa K., illus. (p. 490)
—Education of Bet. (p. 505)
—Georgia's Greatness. (p. 665)
—Jackie's Jokes. (p. 904)
—Little Women & Me. (p. 1038)
—Me, in Between. (p. 1116)
—Petal's Problems. (p. 1346)
—Rebecca's Rashness (p. 1450)
—Secrets of My Suburban Life. (p. 1545)
—Twin's Daughter. (p. 1802)
—Zinnia's Zaniness. (p. 1987)
Baratz-Logsted, Lauren, et al. Final Battle... for Now Bk. 9. (p. 586)
—Marcia's Madness. Weber, Lisa K., illus. (p. 1092)
Barb Dragony, illus. see Poulter, J. R.
Barba, Corey. Yam. (p. 1968)
Barba, M. J., jt. auth. see Dewin, Howard.
Barba, Núria. Marco Polo Fui el Protagonista Deun Fantastico Viaje a China. (p. 1092)
Barba, Rick. Delta Anomaly. (p. 425)
—Quantum Quandary. (p. 1422)
—Secret of Stoneship Woods. Steccati, Eve, illus. (p. 1542)
Barba, Rick, jt. auth. see Josephs, Rudy.
Barba, Rick & Gratz, Alan. Assassination Game. (p. 107)
Barba, Theresa. How Talia Met Tanner. (p. 812)
Barbara, Cohen. Molly's Pilgrim. (p. 1161)
Barbara, Diane & Donnier, Christine. Mom & Me: A Special Book for You & Your Mom to Fill in Together & Share with Each Other. (p. 1161)
Barbara Stathi. Sacrifice. (p. 1500)
Barbaree, Charlotte. Morgan Mcmouth. (p. 1175)
—Princess & the World's Most Wonderful Blankadoo. (p. 1403)
—Very Merry Gary Derryberry Day. (p. 1838)
Barbaree, Howard E. & Marshall, William L., eds. Juvenile Sex Offender, Second Edition. (p. 941)
Barbarese, J. T., jt. auth. see Alcott, Louisa May.
Barbaresi, Nina. Animal Firefighters Stickers. (p. 77)
—Animal Search-a-Word Puzzles. (p. 79)
—Animal Word Puzzles Coloring Book. (p. 80)
—Bears Stickers. (p. 152)
—Firefighters Coloring Book. (p. 591)
—Glitter Easter Stickers. (p. 684)
—Glitter Rubber Duckies Stickers. (p. 684)
—Glitter Sea Horses Stickers. (p. 684)
—Glitter Tropical Fish Stickers. (p. 684)
—Glitter Valentine Stickers. (p. 684)
—Glow-in-the-Dark Bugs Stickers. (p. 685)
—Glow-in-the-Dark Halloween Stickers. (p. 685)
—Glow-in-the-Dark Tattoos Halloween. (p. 685)
—Horses. (p. 800)
—Little Search-a-Word. (p. 1036)
—Shiny Christmas. (p. 1567)
—Tale of Tom Kitten: A Story about Good Behavior. (p. 1700)
Barbaresi, Nina, jt. auth. see Beylon, Cathy.
Barbaresi, Nina & Beylon, Cathy. Horses & Ponies: Coloring & Sticker Fun. (p. 800)
Barbari, Nader. Eddy the Elephant. (p. 504)
Barbarite, Lynn. Kitty Heaven's in the Sky! (p. 963)
Barbas, Keri, des. Travel Scratch & Sketch. (p. 1780)
Barbas, Kerren. Super Scratch & Sketch: A Cool Art Activity Book for Budding Artists of All Ages. (p. 1681)
Barbas, Kerren, illus. see Gandolfi, Claudine.
Barbas, Kerren, illus. see Peter Pauper Press Staff & Zschock, Heather.
Barbas, Kerren, illus. see Sabin, Ellen.
Barbas, Kerren, illus. see Zschock, Heather.
Barbas, Kerren, des. Scratch & Sketch. (p. 1532)
Barbas Steckler, Kerren, illus. see Nemmers, Tom.
Barbatti, Joyce. Henry the Farsighted Heron. Ferguson, Chaveevah Banks, illus. (p. 768)
Barbauld, Anna. Little Stories for Children; Being Easy. (p. 1037)
Barbe, Walter B. School Year of Poems: 180 Favorites from Highlights. Hockerman, Dennis, illus. (p. 1523)
Barbe-Gall, Françoise. How to Talk to Children about Art. (p. 822)
—How to Understand a Painting: Decoding Symbols in Art. (p. 822)
Barbe-Julien, Colette. Cerditos. (p. 287)
—Conejitos. (p. 356)
—Little Chickens. (p. 1026)
—Little Hippopotamuses. (p. 1029)
—Little Horses. (p. 1029)
—Little Pigs. (p. 1033)
—Little Rabbits. (p. 1034)
Barbé-Julien, Colette, jt. auth. see Barbe-Julien, Colette.
Barbe-Julien, Colette & Barbé-Julien, Colette. Potro. (p. 1388)
Barbelle, illus. see Spivak, Samuel.
Barber, Alison. Little Green Pea. Keiser, Paige, illus. (p. 1028)
Barber, Antonia. Cape of Rushes. (p. 262)
—Dancing Shoes: Lucy's Next Step (p. 403)
—Dancing Shoes Friends & Rivals. (p. 403)
—Tales from Grimm. Chamberlain, Margaret, illus. (p. 1701)
Barber, Antonia & Quarto Generic Staff. Hidden Tales from Eastern Europe. Guild, Shena, ed. (p. 776)
Barber, Barbara E. Allie's Basketball Dream. Ligasan, Darryl, illus. (p. 47)
—Saturday at the New You. Rich, Anna, illus. (p. 1515)
Barber, Barrington. Fundamentals of Oil Painting. (p. 649)
Barber, Benjamin R., jt. ed. see Myers, Sondra.
Barber, Beth. Reading Skills (p. 1446)
Barber, Brian, illus. see Snow, Peggy.
Barber, Carol, illus. see Fripp, Deborah & Fripp, Michael.
Barber, David L., illus. see Martin-Finks, Nancy.
Barber, David L., illus. see Sartori, Rosanne Sheritz.
Barber, Doug. I Know Who Santa Is! (p. 840)
Barber, Elaine R. Billy's First Flight Lesson. (p. 187)
Barber, Genise. Tryouts. (p. 1795)
Barber, H. Chris. Shadow: A Cat for All Seasons. (p. 1557)
Barber, Irene. All about Hurling. (p. 42)
Barber, Jacqueline. Of Cabbages & Chemistry. Bergman Publishing Co. Staff & Fairwell, Kay, eds. (p. 1279)
Barber, Jacqueline, jt. auth. see Ahouse, Jeremy John.
Barber, Jacqueline, et al. Crime Lab Chemistry: Solving Mysteries with Chromatography. Klofkorn, Lisa, illus. (p. 382)
Barber, James. Presidents. (p. 1397)
Barber, James, et al. First Ladies. (p. 595)
Barber, Jill. Baby's Lullaby HildaRose, illus. (p. 129)
—Children in Victorian Times. (p. 302)
—Music Is for Everyone Smith, Sydney, illus. (p. 1193)
Barber, Jill, jt. auth. see Thorold, David.
Barber, Jim. Toronto Maple Leafs: Stories of Canada's Legendary Team. (p. 1770)
Barber, Julia, illus. see Wilcox, Michael.
Barber, Mary Corpening, et al. Bride & Groom: First & Forever Cookbook. Cushner, Susie, photos by. (p. 227)
Barber, N. What They Don't Tell You about Music. (p. 1894)
Barber, N. & Fowke, Robert. What They Don't Tell You about Living Things. (p. 1894)
Barber, Nicola. Afghanistan. (p. 26)
—Air Crash. (p. 31)
—Ancient Roman Jobs. (p. 70)
—Ancient Roman Sports & Pastimes. (p. 70)
—Arab-Israeli Conflict. (p. 94)
—Beijing. (p. 160)
—Brazil. (p. 224)
—Buildings & Structures (p. 239)
—Churchill & the Battle of Britain: Days of Decision (p. 318)
—City Homes. (p. 323)
—Cloning & Genetic Engineering. (p. 333)
—Coping with Population Growth (p. 365)
—Dickens. (p. 436)
—First Day of School. (p. 594)
—Focus on Sweden. (p. 611)
—Going to the Hospital. (p. 693)
—Homes on the Move. (p. 793)
—Homes on the Water. (p. 793)
—Island Homes. (p. 892)
—Los Angeles. Cooper, Adrian, photos by. (p. 1053)
—Lost Cities (p. 1055)
—Mountain Homes. (p. 1180)
—Moving to a New House. (p. 1184)
—New Baby Arrives. (p. 1243)
—Rome. (p. 1486)
—Singapore. (p. 1579)
—Tokyo. (p. 1762)
—Tokyo. Bowden, Rob, photos by. (p. 1762)
—Tomb Explorers (p. 1764)
—Village Homes. (p. 1842)
—Western Front. (p. 1876)
—Who Broke the Wartime Codes? (p. 1914)
—Who Journeyed on the Mayflower? HL Studios Staff, illus. (p. 1916)
—World War I (p. 1958)
Barber, Nicola, jt. auth. see Brownlie Bojang, Ali.
Barber, Nicola, jt. ed. see Newton, Robyn.
Barber, Nicola, et al. Inside Fires & Floods. (p. 876)
—Primary Source Detectives (p. 1399)
Barber, Rachel, et al. Nine Novels by Younger Americans. (p. 1256)
Barber, Ronde, jt. auth. see Barber, Tiki.
Barber, Ronde & Barber, Tiki. Go Long! (p. 686)
Barber, Ross L. Assassin. (p. 107)
Barber, Shirley. Classic Fairies Jigsaw Book: With Four 96-Piece Jigsaws. (p. 328)
—Fairies Alphabet Puzzle Tray: With Five 6-Piece Jigsaw Puzzles. (p. 562)
—Fairy Collection. (p. 563)
—Fairy Stories (p. 564)
—Mermaid Princess Jigsaw Book: With Six 48-Piece Jigsaws. (p. 1128)
—Seventh Unicorn. Barber, Shirley, illus. (p. 1555)
—Spellbound: A Fairytale Jigsaw Book. (p. 1625)
—Spellbound & the Fairy Book: Packed with 3-D Pictures. Barber, Shirley, illus. (p. 1625)
—Tales from Martha B. Rabbit. Barber, Shirley, illus. (p. 1701)
Barber, Stephen. Vanishing Map: A Journey from LA to Tokyo to the Heart of Europe. (p. 1833)
Barber, Tiki. Tiki: My Life in the Game & Beyond. (p. 1749)
Barber, Tiki, jt. auth. see Barber, Ronde.
Barber, Tiki & Barber, Ronde. By My Brother's Side. Root, Barry, illus. (p. 249)
—End Zone. (p. 526)
—Extra Innings. (p. 555)
—Game Day. Root, Barry, illus. (p. 654)
—Game Time: Kickoff!; Go Long!; Wild Card. (p. 654)
—Goal Line. (p. 687)
—Jump Shot. (p. 934)
—Kickoff! (p. 951)
—Red Zone. (p. 1455)
—Teammates. Root, Barry, illus. (p. 1710)
—Wild Card. (p. 1929)
Barber, Tom & Chapman, Lynne. Open Wide! (p. 1299)
Barbera, Anthony. Catching Baby Moses. (p. 279)
Barbera, Katia. Iron Horse (p. 888)
Barbera, Michelle, illus. see Graziano, Claudia.
Barbera, Tony, illus. see Peacock, Ann & Lewis, C. S.
Barbera, Tony, photos by see Peacock, Ann & Lewis, C. S.
Barberán, Maria, tr. see Brookfield, Karen, et al.
Barberet, Denise-Renée. Abraham & Sarah. (p. 6)
—Samson. (p. 1509)

B

Barberi, Carlo, illus. see Beechen, Adam & Wong, Walden.
Barberi, Carlo, illus. see Beechen, Adam.
Barberi, Carlo, illus. see Meredith, Randy.
Barberi, Carlo, illus. see Sumerak, Marc.
Barberi, Carlo, illus. see Torres, J.
Barberi, Carlo, jt. illus. see Medina, Paco.
Barberi, Gladys. Pink Fire Trucks. Safar, Lina, illus. (p. 1359)
Barberi, Marco, et al, trs. Sabelotodo: 1000 Desafíos para Tu Inteligencia. Bertran, Nuria, illus. (p. 1499)
Barberis, France. Would You Like a Parrot? Barberis, Franco, illus. (p. 1962)
Barberis, Franco, illus. see Barberis, France.
Barber-Starkey, Joe. Jason's New Dugout Canoe. Montpellier, Paul, illus. (p. 910)
Barbey, Dorine, et al. Creative Discoveries (p. 379)
Barbie. Barbie & the Secret Door. (p. 138)
—Barbie Dreamhouse Party/ una Fiesta de Ensueno: An English/Spanish Flap Book. (p. 138)
—Barbie Find Your Talent: Book with Microphone. (p. 138)
—Barbie: I Love to Draw! (p. 138)
—Barbie Project - Fashion. (p. 138)
—Barbie the Pearl Princess. (p. 138)
Barbie Staff. Barbie Mariposa & the Fairy Princess. (p. 138)
—Barbie Mariposa & the Fairy Princess Storybook. (p. 138)
Barbier, Mary. U. S. Army. (p. 1806)
Barbieri, Sandra Birriel. Cristal & the Secret of the Enchanted Forest: Cristal y el Secreto Del Bosque Encantado. (p. 383)
Barbini, F. T. Tijaran Tales: White Child. (p. 1749)
Barbo, Maria S. Catnapped Caper. (p. 280)
—Fashionista! Gonzales, Chuck, illus. (p. 576)
—Greatest Battles. (p. 719)
—Hello Kitty, Ice-Skating Princess. (p. 764)
—Pokemon Offical Book 4. (p. 1378)
—Rock Star! Gonzales, Chuck, illus. (p. 1482)
—Treasure Hunt. (p. 1781)
—Velveteen Rabbit & the Boy. (p. 1835)
—Velveteen Rabbit Christmas. Hague, Michael, illus. (p. 1835)
Barbo, Maria S. & Bridwell, Norman. Thanksgiving Parade. Artful Doodlers, illus. (p. 1726)
Barbo, Maria S. & Preller, James. Case of the Four-Leaf Clover. Smith, Jamie, illus. (p. 274)
Barbo, Theresa Mitchell & Webster, W. Russell. Daring Coast Guard Rescue of the Pendleton Crew. Marshall, Julia, illus. (p. 406)
Barbor, Carol, illus. see Fripp, Deborah & Fripp, Michael.
Barborini, Robert, illus. see Hédelin, Pascale.
Barbot, Claudine. Through a Child's Eyes. (p. 1744)
Barbot, Daniel. Auto del Sr. Pulga. Mas, Maribel, illus. (p. 117)
—Rosaura en Bicicleta. Fuenmayor, Morella, illus. (p. 1489)
Barbour, H. S., illus. see Fitzhugh, Percy Keese.
Barbour, H. S., illus. see Roy, Lillian Elizabeth.
Barbour, Karen. Little Nino's Pizzeria Big Book. (p. 1032)
—Mr. Williams. Barbour, Karen, illus. (p. 1187)
—Wonderful Words: Poems about Reading, Writing, Speaking, & Listening. (p. 1948)
Barbour, Karen, illus. see Bunting, Eve.
Barbour, Karen, illus. see Lester, Julius.
Barbour, Karen, illus. see Metaxas, Eric.
Barbour, Karen, illus. see Rampersad, Arnold & Blount, Marcellus, eds.
Barbour Publishing Staff. Choosing Thankfulness. (p. 310)
—My Bible Story Sketchbook: Drawing & Coloring Fun for 8-12 Year Olds! (p. 1197)
Barbour Publishing Staff, jt. auth. see Christian Literature International Staff.
Barbour Publishing Staff, jt. auth. see Hascall, Glenn.
Barbour Publishing Staff & Biggers, Emily. Power Prayers for Girls. (p. 1390)
Barbour Publishing Staff, compiled by. Come Here Often? An Indispensable Guide to Dating. (p. 347)
—Do You Want Fries with That? An Indispensable Guide to: Career. (p. 458)
—Money Doesn't Grow on Trees?! An Indispensable Guide to Money. (p. 1164)
—What's an Alpha-Beta-Soupa? An Indispensable Guide to College. (p. 1896)
Barbour, Ralph Henry. Adventure Club Afloat. (p. 14)
—Behind the Line: A Story of College Life & Football. (p. 160)
—Half-Back. (p. 736)
—Left Tackle Thayer. (p. 987)
—Lilac Girl. (p. 1017)
—New Boy at Hilltop & Other Stories. (p. 1243)
—Right Guard Grant. Crump, Leslie, illus. (p. 1472)
Barbour, Scott. How Can School Violence Be Prevented? (p. 805)
—Is the World Prepared for a Deadly Influenza Pandemic? (p. 890)
—Post-Traumatic Stress Disorder. (p. 1387)
—Should Marijuana Be Legalized? (p. 1569)
Barbour, Scott, ed. Alcohol. (p. 35)
Barbour, Susan, tr. see Tullet, Hervé.
Barbour, William. Censorship. (p. 286)
Barbra K. Mudd, illus. see Vail, Emily Blake.
Barbre, Mark. Cat Named Friend. Smith, Brody, illus. (p. 278)
Barca, Pedro Calderon de la. Life Is a Dream. FitzGerald, Edward, tr. from SPA. (p. 1011)
Barcella, Laura. BFF: A Keepsake Journal of Off-the-Wall Q&As. (p. 174)
—OMG: A Keepsake Journal of Off-the-Wall Q&As. (p. 1288)
Barcellona, Kelley Powell. Hive. (p. 786)
Barcelo, François. My Daddy's Footsteps. Mongeau, Marc, illus. (p. 1201)
—My Mommy's Hands. Mongeau, Marc, illus. (p. 1214)
Barceló, Josefina. Grano a Grano. Álvarez, Mrinalí, illus. (p. 710)
—Pon pon, a jugar con el Bebé. Álvarez, Mrinalí, illus. (p. 1382)
—Vamos a Jugar. Álvarez, Mrinalí, illus. (p. 1831)
Barcelona, Adrian. Little Derek's Dilemm. (p. 1026)
BarCharts Inc., Staff, jt. auth. see Kizlik, S. B.
Barchers, Suzanne. 180 Days of Language for Fifth Grade. (p. 2000)
—180 Days of Language for Fourth Grade. (p. 2000)
—Adventures of Tom Sawyer: An Instructional Guide for Literature (p. 24)
—Big Book of Holidays & Cultural Celebrations. (p. 179)
—Brothers & the Star Fruit Tree: A Tale from Vietnam. Tablason, Jamie, illus. (p. 231)
—Bunyip in the Moon: A Tale from Australia. Clarke, Peter, illus. (p. 243)
—Dragonwings: An Instructional Guide for Literature (p. 479)
—Shipwrecked Sailor: A Tale from Egypt. Hehenberger, Shelly, illus. (p. 1567)
—TIME for Kids: Practicing for Today's Tests Language Arts Level 6 (p. 1751)
—Wounded Lion: A Tale from Spain. (p. 1962)
Barchers, Suzanne I. 2-D Airplane Shapes (p. 1991)
—Big Job. (p. 182)
—Box for Ross. (p. 216)
—Conservation of Energy. (p. 359)
—Dad Wants a Nap. (p. 398)
—Energy. (p. 528)
—Energy in Action. (p. 528)
—Fix It! (p. 601)
—Friction. (p. 637)
—Get to Bed, Ren! (p. 668)
—Graphing the School Cleanup (p. 711)
—Green Peas in Cream. (p. 722)
—Gus in the Tub. (p. 732)
—Harvest Time Subtraction (p. 752)
—How Big Is Kip? (p. 805)
—I've Discovered Sound. (p. 900)
—Kate & Gail. (p. 944)
—Kip Gets Fit. (p. 961)
—Kip Gets Sick. (p. 961)
—Kip Wins! (p. 961)
—Late Kate. (p. 979)
—Luce & Duke. (p. 1062)
—Main Street Block Party. (p. 1077)
—Main Street Game Day. (p. 1077)
—Main Street Parade. (p. 1077)
—Mike Makes up His Mind. (p. 1141)
—On a Walk with Ren. (p. 1288)
—On My Stoop. (p. 1289)
—On the Road with Rose & Bose. (p. 1291)
—One Last Wish: A Tale from India. Todd, Sue, illus. (p. 1295)
—Pack a Bag! (p. 1317)
—Pete Has Fast Feet. (p. 1346)
—Princess & the Giant: A Tale from Scotland. Lafrance, Marie, illus. (p. 1402)
—Read with Gus. (p. 1444)
—Ren in a Mess. (p. 1460)
—Revolution in Space. (p. 1466)
—Rose & Bose. (p. 1489)
—Rose & Dad. (p. 1489)
—Spy It! (p. 1636)
—Tale of the Oki Islands: A Tale from Japan. Yokota, Hiromitsu, illus. (p. 1700)
—To the Dunes with Luce. (p. 1759)
—Top That! (p. 1769)
—Twice as Nice: Long Vowel Storybooks. (p. 1801)
—War Stories for Readers Theatre: World War II (p. 1858)
—War Stories for Readers Theatre. (p. 1858)
—What Can I Read? (p. 1880)
—What Can San Do? (p. 1880)
—What Luck! (p. 1892)
—Wounded Lion: A Tale from Spain. Joven, John, illus. (p. 1962)
—You Can Do It! (p. 1974)
Barchers, Suzanne I. & Pfeffinger, Charla R. Multi-Grade Readers Theatre: Stories about Short Story & Book Authors (p. 1189)
Barchers, Suzanne I. & Ruscoe, Michael. Against All Odds: Readers Theatre for Grades 3-8 (p. 29)
Barchers, Suzanne I. & Teacher Created Materials Staff. Big Day for Kate. (p. 180)
Barchowsky, Damien, illus. see Chopra, Deepak.
Barchus, Nathan, illus. see Wallace, Jim.
Barcilon, Marianne, illus. see Naumann-Villemin, Christine & Naumann.
Barcita, Pamela. Ruby Lee the Bumble Bee Promotional Coloring Book. (p. 1493)
Barcita, Pamela, illus. see Matheson, Dawn.
Barcita, Pamela, illus. see Palazeti, Toulla.
Barcita, Pamela, illus. see Palazzetti, Toulla.
Barcita, Pamela, illus. see Solomon, Sharon K.
Barcita, Pamela, illus. see Solomon, Sharon.
Barcita, Pamela, illus. see Suhay, Lisa.
Barcita, Pamela, illus. see Whipple, Vicky.
Barclay. Chipmunk Joe Takes a Nap. (p. 308)
Barclay, Adrian. Construction Doodles: On-Site Scenes to Complete & Create. (p. 359)
—Outdoor Adventure Doodles: Amazing Scenes to Complete & Create. Running Press Staff, ed. (p. 1312)
Barclay, Aegea, jt. auth. see Barclay, Katerina.
Barclay, Aegea & Barclay, Katrina. Hand of Zeus. (p. 740)
Barclay, Cindy. That Damn Dialysis. (p. 1726)
Barclay, Eric. Counting Dogs. Barclay, Eric, illus. (p. 371)
—Hiding Phil. (p. 777)
—Hiding Phil. Barclay, Eric, illus. (p. 777)
—I Can See Just Fine. (p. 836)
Barclay, Jane. How Cold Was It? (p. 805)
—How Cold Was It? Donato, Janice, illus. (p. 806)
—How Hot Was It? Cole, Kathryn, ed. (p. 809)
—JoJo the Giant. Melo, Esperanca, illus. (p. 924)
Barclay, Judith M. Solving Algebra Word Problems. (p. 1608)
Barclay, Katerina & Barclay, Aegea. Hand of Zeus. Barclay, Katerina, illus. (p. 740)
Barclay, Katrina, jt. auth. see Barclay, Aegea.
Barclay, Marjorie. Flutter: A Very Special Pigeon. (p. 608)
Barclay, William, jt. auth. see Duncan, Denis.
Barcliff, Betty. Gypsy Summer: A Novel. (p. 734)
—Stormy Fall: A Novel. (p. 1656)
Barco, Kathy. READiscover New Mexico: A Tri-Lingual Adventure in Literacy. (p. 1447)
Barcus, Dawn. Go2Guides China Ages 12+ Travel Guides for Kids Who Are Going Places. Dunlop-Kahren, Anne, ed. (p. 687)
—Go2Guides China Ages 5-7: Travel Guides for Kids Who Are Going Places. Dunlop-Kahren, Anne, ed. (p. 687)
—Go2Guides China Ages 8-11: Travel Guides for Kids Who Are Going Places. Dunlop-Kahren, Anne, ed. (p. 687)
Barczak, Marliss, ed. see Stansberry, Don & Cluster Springs Elementary School Staff.
Bard, Mitchell Geoffrey. Israel Matters: Understand the Past, Look to the Future. (p. 893)
Bardack, Amy & Naditch, Beth, eds. Halleli Nafshi: A Weekday Siddur for Children. (p. 737)
Bardakigian, K. D. & Thompson, Robert W. Western Armenian (p. 1876)
Bardaus, Anna W. Bounce, Bounce, Baby! Grove, Christine, illus. (p. 216)
—Dance, Dance, Baby! Grove, Christine, illus. (p. 402)
—Reach, Reach, Baby! Grove, Christine, illus. (p. 1442)
—Read, Read, Baby! Grove, Christine, illus. (p. 1443)
Barden, Christine, et al. Music for Little Mozarts Recital (p. 1193)
Barden, Christine H. & Kowalchyk, Gayle. Music for Little Mozarts — Little Mozarts Go to Hollywood: 10 Favorites from TV, Movies & Radio. (p. 1193)
Barden, Christine H., et al. Alfred's Kid's Piano Course, Bk 1: The Easiest Piano Method Ever!, Book, CD & DVD. (p. 38)
—Alfred's Kid's Piano Course Complete: The Easiest Piano Method Ever!, Book, CD & DVD. (p. 38)
—Little Mozarts Go to Hollywood, Pop Book 1 And 2: 10 Favorites from TV, Movies & Radio. Finn, Christine, illus. (p. 1032)
—Music for Little Mozarts — Little Mozarts Go to Church, Bk 1-2: 10 Favorite Hymns, Spirituals & Sunday School Songs. (p. 1193)
—Music for Little Mozarts Little Mozarts Perform the Nutcracker: 8 Favorites form Tchaikovsky's Nutcracker Suite. (p. 1193)
Barden, Christine H., et al, contrib. by. Alfred's Kid's Piano Course Notespeller, Bk 1 And 2: Music Reading Activities That Make Learning Even Easier! (p. 38)
Barden, Cindy. Using the Standards, Grade 6: Building Grammar & Writing Skills. (p. 1828)
Barden, Cindy & Mark Twain Media Staff. Jumpstarters for the U. S. Constitution: Short Daily Warm-Ups for the Classroom. (p. 934)
—Pre-Algebra, Grades 6+ Short Daily Warm-Ups for the Classroom. (p. 1394)
Barden, Laura. Fail Free Zone. Ebertsch, Ted, illus. (p. 562)
Barden, Stephanie. Cinderella Smith: The More the Merrier. Goode, Diane, illus. (p. 320)
—Cinderella Smith. Goode, Diane, illus. (p. 320)
—More the Merrier. Goode, Diane, illus. (p. 1175)
Bardenhagen-Ludlow, Deborah. Visit to the Neighbors: Mommy, Do You Think Horses Can Talk to Each Other? (p. 1845)
Bardhan-Quallen, Sudipta. AIDS. (p. 30)
—Autism. (p. 117)
—Ballots for Belva: The True Story of a Woman's Race for the Presidency. Martin, Courtney A., illus. (p. 135)
—Chicks Run Wild. Jenkins, Ward, illus. (p. 301)
—Duck, Duck, Moose! Jones, Noah Z., illus. (p. 488)
—Flying Eagle. Ray, Deborah Kogan, illus. (p. 609)
—Hampire! Fine, Howard, illus. (p. 739)
—Hog Prince. Wolff, Jason, illus. (p. 787)
—Nature Science Experiments: What's Hopping in a Dust Bunny? Miller, Edward, illus. (p. 1236)
—Pirate Princess. McElmurry, Jill, illus. (p. 1363)
—Quackenstein Hatches a Family. Jones, Brian T., illus. (p. 1422)
—Rutabaga Boo! Adamson, Bonnie, illus. (p. 1498)
—Snoring Beauty. Manning, Jane, illus. (p. 1598)
—Tyrannosaurus Wrecks! OHora, Zachariah, illus. (p. 1805)
—Worst Twelve Days of Christmas. Wood, Ryan, illus. (p. 1961)
Bardi, Matilde, jt. auth. see Tsakiridis, Dimitra.
Bardin, Matt & Fine, Susan. Zen in the Art of the SAT: How to Think, Focus, & Achieve Your Highest Score. (p. 1986)
Bardley, Kimberly Brubaker. POP! a Book about Bubbles. Miller, Margaret, photos by. (p. 1384)
Bardo, Yuyun, illus. see Hoover, Nadine.
Bardoe, Cheryl. Gregor Mendel: The Friar Who Grew Peas. Smith, Jos. A., illus. (p. 723)
—Mammoths & Mastodons: Titans of the Ice Age. (p. 1085)
—Ugly Duckling Dinosaur: A Prehistoric Tale. Kennedy, Doug & Kennedy, Roy D., illus. (p. 1808)
Bardos, Laszlo C. Amazing Math Projects You Can Build Yourself. Carbaugh, Samuel, illus. (p. 55)
—Amazing Math Projects. Carbaugh, Samuel, illus. (p. 55)
Bardsley, Jacqueline. Dandelion Days. (p. 403)
Bardsley, Maggie, jt. auth. see Rojo, Andrea Szekasy.
Bardsley, Michele. Because Your Vampire Said So (p. 155)
Bardsley-Sirois, Lois. Katherine's Winter Garden. (p. 944)
Bardswich, Elizabeth & Bardswich, Miriam. Out There Travel. (p. 1311)
Bardswich, Miriam, jt. auth. see Bardswich, Elizabeth.
Bardswich, Miriam & Reevely, Lorna. Catastrophe! (p. 278)
Bardugo, Leigh. Ruin & Rising. (p. 1494)
—Shadow & Bone. (p. 1557)
—Siege & Storm. (p. 1573)
—Six of Crows. (p. 1582)
Bardugo, Miriam, illus. see Matov, G.
Bardwell, Harrison. Airplane Girls & the Mystery of Seal Islands. (p. 32)
—Airplane Girls & the Mystery Ship. (p. 32)
—Lurtiss Field Mystery. (p. 1066)
—Roberta's Flying Courage. (p. 1479)
Bardwell, Yvett. My Little Green Book of Numbers. (p. 1212)
—My Little Red Book of Numbers. (p. 1213)
—My Little Yellow Book of Numbers. (p. 1213)
Bare, Bart. Girl. (p. 678)
Baredes, Carla & Lotersztain, Ileana. Preguntas que Ponen los Pelos de Punta: Sobre el Aqua y el Fuego. Basile, Javier, illus. (p. 1395)
—Preguntas que Ponen los Pelos de Punta: Sobre la Tierra y el Sol. Basile, Javier, illus. (p. 1395)
Barefoot Books, jt. auth. see Blackstone, Stella.
Barefoot Books, jt. auth. see Fatus, Sophie.
Barefoot Books, jt. auth. see Finch, Mary.
Barefoot Books, jt. auth. see Krebs, Laurie.
Barefoot Books, jt. auth. see Oppenheim, Joanne F.
Barefoot Books, et al. Dotty Spotty Doodles. (p. 472)
—Pirates Fun Activities. (p. 1363)
Barefoot Books Staff. Clare Beaton's Animal Rhymes. Beaton, Clare, illus. (p. 326)
—Clare Beaton's Garden Rhymes. Beaton, Clare, illus. (p. 326)
—Out of the Blue. Alison, Jay & Jay, Alison, illus. (p. 1311)
Barefoot Books Staff, jt. auth. see Amador Family Staff.
Barefoot Books Staff, jt. auth. see Blackstone, Stella.
Barefoot Books Staff, jt. auth. see Heine, Theresa.
Barefoot Books Staff, jt. auth. see Oppenheim, Joanne F.
Barefoot Books Staff, jt. auth. see Scribens, Sunny.
Barefoot Books Staff, jt. auth. see Williams, Brenda.
Barefoot Books Staff & Amador Family Staff. Wheels on the Bus. Williamson, Melanie, illus. (p. 1901)
Barefoot Books Staff, et al. Zig Zag Zebra. (p. 1986)
Barefoot College Staff, jt. auth. see Harter, Debbie.
Barefoot, Daniel W., ed. Hark the Sound of Tarheel Voices: Firsthand Accounts from 220 Years of UNC History. (p. 748)
Bar-el, Dan. Alphabetter Ross, Graham, illus. (p. 50)
—Audrey (Cow) Mai-Wyss, Tatjana, illus. (p. 115)
—Dream Boats. Wakelin, Kirsti Anne, illus. (p. 483)
—Nine Words Max. Huyck, David, illus. (p. 1256)
—Pussycat, Pussycat, Where Have You Been? Mate, Rae, illus. (p. 1420)
—That One Spooky Night. Huyck, David, illus. (p. 1726)
Bar-el, Dan & Bisaillon, Josee. Fish Named Glub (p. 598)
Bar-el, Dan & Bowers, Tim. Not Your Typical Dragon. (p. 1267)
Barell, John. Surviving Erebus: An Antarctic Adventure Onboard Her Majesty's Ships Erebus & Terror. (p. 1687)
Barella, Laura. Brave Little Tailor. (p. 223)
—Donkey Skin. (p. 466)
—Little Mermaid. (p. 1031)
—Sleeping Beauty. (p. 1589)
—Stonecutter. (p. 1653)
Barenblat, Rachel. Texas. Porras, Carlos & D'Andrea, Patricia, trs. from ENG. (p. 1723)
Barenblat, Rachel, jt. auth. see Siegfried Holtz, Eric.
Barensfeld, Debrae. Fox: Lost & Found. (p. 626)
Barer-Stein, Thelma. You Are What You Eat: People, Culture & Food Traditions. (p. 1973)
Baretz, Susie. You Would Be Surprised. Wulfing, Amy J., illus. (p. 1976)
Barfell, Judith A. Learn & Sign Funtime: Sign with God's Angels. (p. 982)
—Learn & Sign Funtime Beginnings. (p. 983)
—Learn & Sign Funtime-Beginnings-Spanish. (p. 983)
Barfell, Judy. Learn & Sign Funtime: The United States Presidents. (p. 983)
Barfield, Asia. My Inspiration. (p. 1211)
Barfield, Bryce. Jo & Her Blue Block. (p. 919)
—Jo & Her Bright-Green Chair. (p. 919)
Barfield, Maggie. Big Bible Storybook: 188 Bible Stories to Enjoy Together Carpenter, Mark And Anna, illus. (p. 178)
—Little Bible Storybook Carpenter, Mark et al, illus. (p. 1024)
—Welcome the Baby Jesus. (p. 1873)
Barfield, Michelle. Sully Bug. (p. 1673)
—Weezy's Wedding. (p. 1872)
Barg, Soosoonam, illus. see Bowler, Ann Martin.
Bargach, Naim. Wolfen: Beware, even, of little Wolves... (p. 1944)
Barge III, John, illus. see Olive, Gloria D.
Barge III, John S., illus. see Constantine, Cara J.
Barge III, John, illus. see Dtpolk.
Bargellini, Demetrio & Stilton, Geronimo. Coliseum Con. (p. 339)
Bargellini, Demetrio, et al. Secret of the Sphinx. (p. 1543)
Barger, Caroline. Roundup. (p. 1491)
Barger, Jan, illus. see Ross, Kathy.
Barham, Lisa. Project Paris. Rim, Sujean, illus. (p. 1410)
Barham, Paul Richard. Adventures of Damen the Duck. (p. 17)
Barham, Timothy E. Blonds Blending: The Adventures of Suzy Q & You Too. Barham, Timothy E., illus. (p. 200)
Barham, Timothy E., illus. see Cloyd, Suzy.
Bar-hillel, Gili, tr. see Rowling, J. K.
Barhorst, Warren & Burson, Rusty. Game Plan: The Definitive Playbook for Starting or Growing Your Business. (p. 654)
Bari, Ellen. Jumping Jenny. Macia, Raquel Garcia, illus. (p. 934)
—Jumping Jenny. Maciá, Raquel García, illus. (p. 934)
—Our Government: Text Pairs. (p. 1309)
Barichella, Thomas. Star Snatcher's Planet. (p. 1641)
Barickman, Traci. Cooper's Adventures: Facing Our Fears. (p. 365)
Barile, Mary Collins. J. Milton Turner; an American Hero. Guest, Peggy, illus. (p. 901)
Baring-Gould, Sabine. Book of Nursery Songs & Rhymes. (p. 211)
—Crock of Gold: Twelve Fairy Tales, O. (p. 384)
Barish, Jonas A., ed. see Jonson, Ben.
Barkan, Elliott Robert, ed. see Minahan, James.
Barkan, Joanne. Games We Play. (p. 655)
—Looking Good. (p. 1051)
—Rookie Read-About Science: Physical Science (p. 1487)
—Settling the West 1862-1890: Set Of 6. (p. 1554)
—Western Activity Book: Set Of 6. (p. 1876)
—Western Activity Book & Libro de actividades del Oeste: 6 English, 6 Spanish Adaptations. (p. 1876)
—What Is Density? (p. 1889)
—What Is Velocity? (p. 1891)
Barkaw, Henriette. Don't Cry Sly: Big Book English Only. Johnson, Richard, illus. (p. 467)
Barkelew, Pete, compiled by. YaKnow? College Football Trivia (p. 1968)
Barker, Amanda. Bangladesh. (p. 136)
—India. (p. 870)
Barker, Bruce D. Poodle & the Pomeranian: An Original Tails-Tale. (p. 1383)
Barker, C. Penny. Farm. (p. 573)
Barker, Carol. Tibetans: Life in Exile. (p. 1747)

Full bibliographic information is available on the Title Index page number referenced in parentheses at the end of each entry

Barker, Catherine. Spain. (p. 1620)
Barker, Cecily M. Flower Fairies Box Set. (p. 607)
Barker, Charles Ferguson. Under Michigan: The Story of Michigan's Rocks & Fossils. Barker, Charles Ferguson, illus. (p. 1813)
—Under New England: The Story of New England's Rocks & Fossils. Barker, Charles Ferguson, illus. (p. 1813)
—Under Ohio: The Story of Ohio's Rocks & Fossils. Barker, Charles Ferguson, illus. (p. 1813)
Barker, Cicely Mary. Enchanted Garden. (p. 523)
—Fairy Whispers. (p. 564)
—Fairyopolis. (p. 565)
—Flower Fairies Alphabet Coloring Book. (p. 607)
—Flower Fairies Dress up Sticker Bk. (p. 607)
—Flower Fairies Enchanted Parties. (p. 607)
—Flower Fairies Library: A Flower Fairy Alphabet. (p. 607)
—Flower Fairies of the Autumn. (p. 607)
—Flower Fairies Sparkly Sticker Book. (p. 607)
—Flower Fairies Sticker Storybook. (p. 607)
—Flower Fairies Treasury. (p. 607)
—Girls' Book of Flower Fairies. (p. 679)
—How to Find Flower Fairies. (p. 819)
—How to Host a Flower Fairy Tea Party. (p. 820)
—Magical Doors: Discover the Doors to Fairyopolis. (p. 1074)
Barker, Cicely Mary, jt. auth. see Barnham, Kay.
Barker, Cicely Mary, jt. auth. see Warne, Frederick.
Barker, Cicely Mary & Potter, Beatrix. Flower Fairies Paper Dolls. (p. 607)
—Magical Secret Garden. (p. 1075)
—Sunshine & Showers. (p. 1678)
Barker, Cicely Mary & Warne. Flower Fairies. (p. 607)
Barker, Clive. Abarat: Days of Magic, Nights of War Barker, Clive, illus. (p. 2)
—Abarat. (p. 2)
—Abarat. Barker, Clive, illus. (p. 2)
—Absolute Midnight. Barker, Clive, illus. (p. 7)
—Days of Magic, Nights of War. Barker, Clive, illus. (p. 415)
—Thief of Always. (p. 1732)
Barker, Clyde D., jt. auth. see Shipman, James.
Barker, Dan. Mary Had a Little Lamb Songbook. (p. 1100)
Barker, Dan, jt. auth. see Humphrey, Sandra McLeod.
Barker, David. Save the Planet: Compost It. (p. 1516)
—Top 50 Reasons to Care about Great Apes: Animals in Peril. (p. 1768)
Barker, David M. Archaea: Salt-Lovers, Methane-Makers, Thermophiles, & Other Archaeans. (p. 95)
—Archaea. (p. 95)
—Loss of Biodiversity. (p. 1054)
—Science Lab: Soil. (p. 1526)
Barker, Elsa, jt. auth. see Hart, Katherine.
Barker, Gary, illus. see Davis, Jim & Evanier, Mark.
Barker, Gary, illus. see Davis, Jim, et al.
Barker, Geoff. Discover Pakistan. (p. 448)
—How Recycling Works. (p. 812)
—How Renewable Energy Works. (p. 812)
—Hunger. (p. 827)
—Incredible Skyscrapers. (p. 869)
—Mexico. (p. 1131)
—Sports & Leisure Careers. (p. 1632)
—War. (p. 1857)
—Water. (p. 1862)
Barker, Geoff & Hachette Children's Books Staff. Soccer Star: Find Out How Your Favorite Soccer Players Made It! (p. 1603)
Barker, Geoff & Marshall Cavendish Corporation Staff. Sudan. (p. 1672)
Barker, Geoff & Savery, Annabel. Sports & Leisure Careers. (p. 1632)
Barker, Geoff P. Incredible Skyscrapers. (p. 869)
Barker, Geoffrey. How Renewable Energy Works. (p. 812)
Barker, Granville. Madras House. Landes, William-Alan, ed. (p. 1070)
Barker, Henry. Vino del Espacio. Gott, Barry, illus. (p. 1843)
—Vino Del Espacio (It Came from Outer Space) Gott, Barry, illus. (p. 1843)
Barker, Jane Valentine. Building Up. (p. 239)
—Trappers & Traders. Downing, Sybil, ed. (p. 1779)
Barker, Jane Valentine, jt. auth. see Downing, Sybil.
Barker, Jane Valentine & Downing, Sybil. Adventures in the West. (p. 16)
—Colorado Heritage Series (p. 343)
—Mountain Treasures. (p. 1181)
Barker, Juliet. Agincourt: Henry V & the Battle That Made England. (p. 29)
Barker, Laraine Anne. Lord of Obsidian: Quest for Earthlight Trilogy. (p. 1052)
—Obsidian Quest. (p. 1275)
—Third Age of Obsidian: Quest for Earthlight Trilogy. (p. 1734)
Barker, Lesley. Prayer-Walk St. Louis Guidebook & Journal. (p. 1393)
Barker, Leslie. Bailey's Turtle. (p. 133)
Barker, Lori. How Do They Make That? (p. 807)
—Land Animals. (p. 973)
—On the Road: Ratios & Proportions. (p. 1291)
—Our New Car. (p. 1309)
—Sea Creatures. (p. 1534)
—Watch It Grow. (p. 1861)
—What Did I Eat? (p. 1882)
—Where Germs Lurk. (p. 1907)
Barker, Lori, illus. see Nickel, Scott.
Barker, M. A. R. Lords of Tsamra (p. 1053)
Barker, M. P. Difficult Boy. (p. 438)
Barker, Mary Ann. Circus Day Adventure for Emma & Jake. (p. 322)
Barker, Michele. Mending Horses. (p. 1126)
Barker, Peter, ed. see Trebi-Ollennu, Flora.
Barker, Ray & Moorcroft, Christine. Grammar First (p. 706)
—Spelling First (p. 1625)
Barker, Richard H. Citrus Roots Our Legacy: Citriculture to Citrus Culture (p. 323)
Barker, Stephen, illus. see Goodings, Christina.
Barker, Stephen, illus. see Walter Foster Creative Team.
Barker, Stephen, illus. see Walter Foster Custom Creative Team.
Barker, Stephen Elliot. Secret of Spirits Bay. (p. 1542)
Barker, Vicky, illus. see MacKinnon, Mairi.
Barkhouse, Janet, jt. auth. see Barkhouse, Joyce.
Barkhouse, Joyce. Pit Pony (p. 1364)
Barkhouse, Joyce & Barkhouse, Janet. Pit Pony: The Picture Book. Smith, Sydney, illus. (p. 1364)
Barklem, Jill. Adventures in Brambly Hedge. (p. 15)
—Bebes de Amapola. (p. 155)
—Cuento de Invierno. (p. 389)
—Cuento de Mar. (p. 389)
—Cuento de Otono. (p. 389)
—Cuento de Primavera. (p. 389)
—Cuento de Verano. (p. 389)
—Escalera Secreta. (p. 534)
—Montanas Altas. (p. 1170)
Barkley, Brad & Hepler, Heather. Dream Factory. (p. 483)
Barkley, Callie. All about Ellie. (p. 42)
—All about Ellie. Riti, Marsha, illus. (p. 42)
—Amy & the Missing Puppy. (p. 66)
—Amy & the Missing Puppy. Riti, Marsha, illus. (p. 66)
—Amy Meets Her Stepsister. (p. 66)
—Amy Meets Her Stepsister. Riti, Marsha, illus. (p. 66)
—Critter Club: Amy & the Missing Puppy; All about Ellie; Liz Learns a Lesson. Riti, Marsha, illus. (p. 384)
—Ellie & the Good-Luck Pig. Riti, Marsha, illus. (p. 514)
—Ellie's Lovely Idea. (p. 514)
—Ellie's Lovely Idea. Riti, Marsha, illus. (p. 514)
—Liz & the Sand Castle Contest. Riti, Marsha, illus. (p. 1042)
—Liz at Marigold Lake. (p. 1042)
—Liz at Marigold Lake. Riti, Marsha, illus. (p. 1042)
—Liz Learns a Lesson. (p. 1042)
—Liz Learns a Lesson. Riti, Marsha, illus. (p. 1042)
—Marion Strikes a Pose. Riti, Marsha, illus. (p. 1094)
—Marion Takes a Break. (p. 1094)
—Marion Takes a Break. Riti, Marsha, illus. (p. 1094)
—Marion Takes Charge. Riti, Marsha, illus. (p. 1094)
Barkley, Roger C. Johnny Grasshopper. (p. 923)
Barkow, Henriette. Alfie's Angels. (p. 37)
—Alfie's Angels. Garson, Sarah, illus. (p. 37)
—Ali Baba & the Forty Thieves. Brazell, Derek, illus. (p. 39)
—Beowulf: An Anglo-Saxon Epic. Down, Alan, illus. (p. 166)
—Buri & the Marrow. Finlay, Lizzie, illus. (p. 243)
—Buri & the Marrow: Buri Dhe Kungulli. Finlay, Lizzie, illus. (p. 243)
—Buri & the Marrow. Finlay, Lizzie, illus. (p. 243)
—Buskers of Bremen. Reed, Nathan, illus. (p. 245)
—Don't Cry, Sly! Johnson, Richard, illus. (p. 467)
—Don't Cry, Sly! Ne Pleure Pas Sly! Johnson, Richard, illus. (p. 467)
—Giant Turnip: Le Navet Geant. Johnson, Richard, illus. (p. 674)
—Giant Turnip. Johnson, Richard, illus. (p. 674)
—Giant Turnip - Big Book. Johnson, Richard, illus. (p. 674)
—Pandora's Box: English Only. Mayo, Diana, illus. (p. 1321)
—Pandora's Box. Mayo, Diana, illus. (p. 1321)
—Pied Piper. Dry, Roland, illus. (p. 1356)
—That's My Mum: Ajo Eshte Nena Ime. Brazell, Derek, illus. (p. 1727)
—That's My Mum. Brazell, Derek, illus. (p. 1727)
—Three Billy Goats Gruff: English Big Book. Johnson, Richard, illus. (p. 1741)
—Three Billy Goats Gruff. Johnson, Richard, illus. (p. 1741)
—Tom & Sofia Start School. Lamont, Priscilla, illus. (p. 1762)
Barkow, Henriette, illus. see Brazell, Derek.
Barkow, Henriette, jt. auth. see Johnson, Richard.
Barkow, Henriette & Johnson, Richard. Don't Cry, Sly! Mos Qaj Dhelperush! (p. 467)
—Giant Turnip: Rrepa Gjigante. (p. 674)
Barkow, Henriette & Reed, Nathan. Buskers of Bremen: Kengetaret Endacak Te Bremenit. (p. 245)
—Buskers of Bremen: Les Chanteurs de Rues de Bremen. (p. 245)
Barks, Carl. Sheriff of Bullet Valley: Starring Walt Disney's Donald Duck. (p. 1565)
—Uncle Scrooge Clark, John, ed. (p. 1812)
Barks, Carl, illus. see Wheeler, Shannon, et al.
Barks, Carl, jt. auth. see Blum, Geoffrey.
Barks, Carl, jt. auth. see Randolph, Grace.
Barks, Carl, jt. auth. see Rota, Marco.
Barks, Carl & Kinney, Dick. Uncle Scrooge Clark, John, ed. (p. 1812)
Barks, Carl, et al. Uncle Scrooge Clark, John, ed. (p. 1812)
—Uncle Scrooge #387. (p. 1812)
—Uncle Scrooge #389. (p. 1812)
—Walt Disney's Christmas Parade #5. (p. 1855)
—Walt Disney's Comics & Stories #692. Clark, John, ed. (p. 1855)
—Walt Disney's Comics & Stories #702. (p. 1855)
—Walt Disney's Spring Fever Volume 2. Clark, John, ed. (p. 1855)
—Walt Disney's Vacation Parade Volume 5. Clark, John, ed. (p. 1856)
—Walt Disney's Vacation Parade Volume 6. (p. 1856)
Barksdale, Miechel & Dunn, Richard. Mommy, Its Time to Go Pee. (p. 1162)
Barksdale-Hall, Roland. Under African Skies. Murray, Bill, illus. (p. 1813)
Barkus, Mariona. Flower & the Butterfly. Barkus, Mariona, illus. (p. 607)
—Illustrated History No. 13 Barkus, Mariona, illus. (p. 857)
Barland, Dj. Little Ray's Big Rescue. (p. 1034)
Barlas, Robert & Tompsett, Norm. Canada. (p. 260)
Barlas, Robert & Wong, Winnie. Latvia. (p. 980)
Barlas, Robert & Yong, Jui Lin. Bahamas. (p. 132)
—Uganda. (p. 1808)
Barlau, Martin. Lenny Was a Leaf: Learning about Life. (p. 991)
Bar-Lev, Rotem. No More Tears. (p. 1259)
Barlex, David & Wadsworth, Pamela. Rhagor Am Sain a Cherddoriaeth. (p. 1467)
—Sain a Cherddoriaeth. (p. 1503)
Barley-Cohrs, Dayna, illus. see Brewster, James Burd.
Barlics, Brian. Brady Needs a Nightlight. Jones, Gregory Burgess, illus. (p. 221)
Barlone, M. J. Mouse & Rabbits Tale. (p. 1181)
Barlow, Amanda. 1 2 3. (p. 1990)
—Animals. (p. 81)
—Apple Bird ABC. (p. 92)
—Things That Go. (p. 1733)
Barlow, Amanda, illus. see Gibson, Ray.
Barlow, Amanda, illus. see Watt, Fiona.
Barlow, Andrew. Jellytoes Misses the Bus. Barlow, Andrew, illus. (p. 912)
Barlow, Ben. Mimi's Bears. (p. 1145)
Barlow, C. E. Scary Man. Tharp, Lauren R., illus. (p. 1520)
Barlow, Dave. Seekers. (p. 1548)
—Tome of Knowledge; Volcanoes. (p. 1764)
Barlow, Dave, illus. see Bland, Ralph.
Barlow, Helen. Easy Read with Grandma Read: Book 1, Stage 3. (p. 500)
—Easy read with grandma Read: Book 1, Stage 1. (p. 500)
Barlow, J., jt. auth. see Benedetto, K.
Barlow, Jeremy. Star Wars Adventures: Boba Fett & the Ship of Fear. (p. 1641)
Barlow, Melissa. Noodlemania! 50 Playful Pasta Recipes. (p. 1264)
Barlow, Melissa, jt. auth. see Anderson, Lisa Turner.
Barlow, Steve, jt. auth. see Skidmore, Steve.
Barlow, Steve & Skidmore, Steve. Doomsday Virus Buckley, Harriet & Lueth, Nathan, illus. (p. 470)
—Stone Me! Ross, Tony, illus. (p. 1652)
—Touch of Wind! Ross, Tony, illus. (p. 1772)
Barlowe, Dot. America the Beautiful to Paint or Color. (p. 59)
—Birdwatcher's Coloring Book. (p. 192)
—Creative Haven Country Scenes Coloring Book. (p. 379)
—Flower Gardens to Paint or Color. (p. 607)
—Grand Canyon Plants & Animals. (p. 707)
—Let's Explore! - Forest Animals. (p. 996)
—Nautical Scenes to Paint or Color. (p. 1237)
—Rocky Mountains Plants & Animals. (p. 1484)
—Sonoran Desert by Day & Night. (p. 1612)
—Tropical Paradise Scenes to Paint or Color. (p. 1789)
—Walk in the Woods. (p. 1853)
Barlowe, Raleigh Bruce. Campbell's Came. (p. 257)
—Kingmaker. (p. 960)
Barlup, Jessica, illus. see Zaring, Laurie.
Barna, Beverly. Daughter of Dreams, a Fable of Destiny. White, David, illus. (p. 409)
Barna, George & Jackson, Harry, Jr. High-Impact African-American Churches: Leadership Concepts from Some of Today's Most Effective Churches. (p. 777)
Barnabas Fund. Brothers & Sisters: Loving Our Persecuted Family. (p. 231)
—Children of Courage: Raising Tomorrow's Church. (p. 302)
Barnaby, Hannah. Wonder Show. (p. 1947)
Barnacott, Anthony Royce. Permanoids of Chilon. (p. 1343)
Barnard, Alan, illus. see Tanaka, Shelley.
Barnard, Bobbie. Fairies of the Big Forest. (p. 563)
Barnard, Bryn. Genius of Islam: How Muslims Made the Modern World. (p. 661)
—Outbreak: Plagues That Changed History. Barnard, Bryn, illus. (p. 1312)
Barnard, Bryn, illus. see Dubowski, Mark.
Barnard, Bryn, illus. see Nash, Dylan M.
Barnard, Bryn, illus. see Redmond, Shirley Raye.
Barnard, Bryn, illus. see Rotberg, Gene, et al.
Barnard, Bryn, illus. see Rotberg, Gene.
Barnard, Bryn, illus. see Rovetch, L. Bob & Whitman, Emily.
Barnard, Carolyn. Boom Boom's Tale (p. 213)
Barnard, Colleen. Sarah the Seven-Legged Spider. (p. 1514)
Barnard, Edward S. Birds. (p. 191)
—Butterflies. (p. 247)
—Fishes. (p. 599)
—Foxes. (p. 626)
—Frogs. (p. 641)
Barnard, Edward S. & Wilsdon, Christina. Monkeys. (p. 1165)
Barnard, Emma & Cho, Thomas. Really Big Food Project. (p. 1449)
Barnard, Frederick, illus. see Bunyan, John.
Barnard, Irita. Screech Becomes a Hero. (p. 1533)
Barnard, Lucy, illus. see Hodgman, Ann.
Barnard, Lucy, illus. see Lawrence, Trisha.
Barnard, Marietjie & Gous, M. M. Introduction to Accounting for the Senior Phase Learner's Book (Afrikaans Translation) (p. 882)
Barnard, Marietjie & Gous, M.M. Introduction to Accounting for the Senior Phase Learner's Book. (p. 882)
Barnard, Roger & Zemach, Dorothy E. Writing for the Real World, Level 1: An Introduction to General Writing. (p. 1965)
Barnard, Sarah. Map & the Stone. (p. 1089)
Barnas, Aloura, jt. auth. see Frank, Church.
Barnas, Jo-Ann. Great Moments in Olympic Skating. (p. 717)
Barnecut, Suzanne, ed. see Hardman, Ron & Hardman, Jessica.
Barnecutt, Suzanne, ed. see Hardman, Ron & Hardman, Jessica.
Barneda, David, illus. see Reynolds, Aaron.
Barner. Snow. (p. 1598)
Barner, Bob. Animal Baths. (p. 76)
—Animals! Matching Game. (p. 83)
—Bug Safari. (p. 236)
—Bug Safari. Barner, Bob, illus. (p. 236)
—Day of the Dead (El Día de los Muertos) Barner, Bob, illus. (p. 414)
—Día de los Muerto) Barner, Bob, illus. (p. 414)
—Dinosaur Bones. Barner, Bob, illus. (p. 441)
—Dinosaurs! Matching Game. (p. 445)
—I Have a Garden. Barner, Bob, illus. (p. 839)
—Parade Day: Marching Through the Calendar Year. (p. 1323)
—Penguins, Penguins, Everywhere! (p. 1337)
—Sea Bones. (p. 1534)
Barner, Bob, illus. see Lewis, J. Patrick.
Barner, Bob, illus. see McKissack, Patricia C.
Barner, Bob, illus. see Todd, Traci N.
Barner, Bob, illus. see Waters, John F.
Barner, Bob, jt. auth. see Chronicle Books Staff.
Barner, Bob & Chronicle Books Staff. Bears! Bears! Bears! (p. 151)
Barnes, Ben. Don't Eat My Garden. Barnes, Page, illus. (p. 467)
Barnes, Bobbie Jo. Message. (p. 1129)
Barnes, Brenda J. Calvin Compost in Organic City: The Story of an Earthworm. Williams, Nancy E., ed. (p. 255)
—Silas Watts: The Highly Electric Lightning Bug. Williams, Nancy E., ed. (p. 1575)
Barnes, Brynne. Colors of Me. Nelson, Annika M., illus. (p. 345)
Barnes, Charles. Knight Light. (p. 964)
Barnes, Charlotte. Stella Ducktropolis. (p. 1647)
Barnes, Cheryl. Quilting Dot-To-Dot: Patterns for Today's Machine Quilter (p. 1428)
Barnes, Cheryl, jt. auth. see Barnes, Peter W.
Barnes, Cheryl S., illus. see Barnes, Peter W.
Barnes, Cheryl S., jt. auth. see Barnes, Peter W.
Barnes, Cheryl Shaw, illus. see Barnes, Peter W.
Barnes, Cheryl Shaw & Barnes, Peter W. Liberty Lee's Tail of Independence. (p. 1005)
Barnes, Christine E. & Sunset Books Staff. Before & after Bathroom Makeovers. (p. 158)
Barnes, David-Matthew. Fifty Yards & Holding. (p. 585)
—Mesmerized. (p. 1129)
—Swimming to Chicago. (p. 1691)
Barnes, Deb. Inside a Rock Band. (p. 876)
Barnes, Denise Sullivan. Megan's Phone Call. (p. 1124)
Barnes, Derrick. Brand New School, Brave New Ruby. Newton, Vanessa Brantley, illus. (p. 222)
Barnes, Derrick D. Trivia Queen/Supreme. Newton, Vanessa Brantley, illus. (p. 1788)
—We Could Be Brothers. (p. 1867)
Barnes, Derrick D., jt. auth. see Scholastic, Inc. Staff.
Barnes, Garry, illus. see Stone, Connie.
Barnes, Hannah. Rainbow Colored Skin a Father-Son Tattoo Tale. (p. 1435)
Barnes, Helene Teresa. Collection of Children's Poetry. (p. 339)
Barnes, J. Chicks & Chickens: Learning the CH Sound. (p. 301)
Barnes, Jennifer Lynn. Fate. (p. 577)
—Fixer. (p. 601)
—Killer Instinct. (p. 956)
—Perfect Cover. (p. 1341)
—Tattoo. (p. 1707)
Barnes, John. Losers in Space. (p. 1054)
—Tales of the Madman Underground. (p. 1702)
Barnes, John, jt. auth. see John, Antony.
Barnes, John, et al. Culture, Morality, Arts & Humanities. (p. 391)
—Science, Maths & Technology. (p. 1526)
—Society, Politics & the Economy. (p. 1605)
Barnes, John L. C. Clara's Clever Custard. (p. 326)
Barnes, Jon, jt. auth. see Glover, David.
Barnes, Jon, jt. auth. see Parsons, Alexandra.
Barnes, Jon, jt. auth. see Wyse, Liz.
Barnes, Julia. 101 Facts about Deserts. (p. 1999)
—101 Facts about Eagles. (p. 1999)
—101 Facts about Lakes. (p. 1999)
—101 Facts about Lions. (p. 1999)
—101 Facts about Mountains. (p. 1999)
—101 Facts about Oceans. (p. 1999)
—101 Facts about Polar Bears. (p. 1999)
—101 Facts about Rivers. (p. 1999)
—101 Facts about Sharks. (p. 1999)
—101 Facts about Snakes. (p. 1999)
—101 Facts about Tigers. (p. 1999)
—Camels & Llamas at Work. (p. 256)
—Dogs at Work. (p. 462)
—Elephants at Work. (p. 512)
—Horses at Work. (p. 800)
—Pet Cats. (p. 1345)
—Pet Dogs. (p. 1345)
—Pet Goldfish. (p. 1345)
—Pet Guinea Pigs. (p. 1345)
—Pet Parakeets. (p. 1345)
—Pet Rabbits. (p. 1345)
—Secret Lives of Brown Bears. (p. 1541)
—Secret Lives of Dolphins. (p. 1541)
—Secret Lives of Elephants. (p. 1541)
—Secret Lives of Gorillas. (p. 1541)
—Secret Lives of Tigers. (p. 1541)
—Secret Lives of Wolves. (p. 1541)
—Tropical Rain Forests. (p. 1789)
Barnes, Kate & Weston, Steve. Human Body. (p. 825)
Barnes, Kathleen. I Love to See the Temple Reprint. (p. 843)
—Sacrament Time. (p. 1500)
Barnes, Kenneth Edward. Children's Story Collection. (p. 304)
—In Search of A Golden Sparrow. (p. 864)
—Invasion of the Dregs. (p. 883)
—Life on Pigeon Creek. (p. 1012)
Barnes, L. Cats & Kittens: Learning the Hard C & K Sound. (p. 281)
Barnes, Laura T. Ernest & Elston. Cambum, Carol A., illus. (p. 533)
—Ernest's Special Christmas. Cambum, Carol A., illus. (p. 534)
Barnes, Luke. Saints. (p. 1504)
Barnes, M. Craig. Extravagant Mercy. (p. 555)
Barnes, Mary K. Is Today A Stay at Home Day? (p. 890)
Barnes, Morgan. Morgan to the Rescue. (p. 1175)
Barnes, Nico. Basking Sharks. (p. 143)
—Bulldogs. (p. 240)
—German Shepherds. (p. 666)
—Golden Retrievers. (p. 695)
—Great White Sharks. (p. 719)
—Hammerhead Sharks. (p. 739)
—Jack Russell Terriers. (p. 903)
—Labrador Retrievers. (p. 970)
—Mako Sharks. (p. 1083)
—Pugs. (p. 1415)
—Whale Sharks. (p. 1877)
—Zebra Sharks. (p. 1985)
Barnes, Nico, et al. Tiburones Ballena. (p. 1747)
—Tiburones Blancos. (p. 1747)
—Tiburones Cebra. (p. 1747)

B

—Tiburones Mako. (p. 1747)
—Tiburones Martillo. (p. 1747)
—Tiburones Peregrinos. (p. 1747)
Barnes, Page, illus. see Barnes, Ben.
Barnes, Pete. Harley & the Davidsons: Motorcycle Legends. (p. 749)
—Richard Bong: World War II Flying Ace. (p. 1469)
Barnes, Peter W. House Mouse, Senate Mouse. Barnes, Cheryl S., illus. (p. 803)
—Little Miss Patriot. Barnes, Cheryl Shaw, illus. (p. 1032)
—Maestro Mouse: And the Mystery of the Missing Baton. Barnes, Cheryl Shaw, illus. (p. 1070)
—Marshall, the Courthouse Mouse: A Tail of the U. S. Supreme Court. Barnes, Cheryl S., illus. (p. 1096)
—President Adams' Alligator: And Other White House Pets. Barnes, Cheryl Shaw, illus. (p. 1396)
—Woodrow, the White House Mouse. Barnes, Cheryl Shaw, illus. (p. 1949)
Barnes, Peter W., jt. illus. see Barnes, Cheryl Shaw.
Barnes, Peter W. & Barnes, Cheryl. Woodrow for President: A Tail of Voting, Campaigns, & Elections. (p. 1949)
Barnes, Peter W. & Barnes, Cheryl S. Maestro Mouse: And the Mystery of the Missing Baton. (p. 1070)
—President Adams' Alligator: And Other White House Pets. (p. 1396)
Barnes, Roy G. Wildflower Poetry: And poems & stories of Yesterday. (p. 1931)
Barnes, Samantha, ed. see Enright, Dominique, et al.
Barnes, Sarah, illus. see Baldwin, Christy.
Barnes, Shannon. Little Bird Gets His Wings. (p. 1024)
Barnes, Steven John. Hector. (p. 761)
Barnes, Susan. Kelly Karate: Discovers the Ice Princess. (p. 948)
Barnes, Terry, jt. auth. see Webber, Berryl.
Barnes, Tom, photos by see David, Lawrence, ed.
Barnes, Trevor. Biblia ilustrada para Niños. (p. 176)
—World Faiths: Christianity. (p. 1955)
—World Faiths: Hinduism & Other Eastern Religions. (p. 1955)
—World Faiths: Islam. (p. 1955)
—World Faiths: Judaism. (p. 1955)
Barnes, Trisha, ed. see Nix, Pamela.
Barnes, Trisha, illus. see Keyser, William.
Barnes, Vivi. Olivia Twisted. (p. 1287)
—Paper or Plastic. (p. 1322)
Barnes, William, illus. see Hile, Doretta.
Barnes-Murphy, Rowan. Kings & Queens of Britain. (p. 960)
Barnes-Murphy, Rowan, illus. see Blyton, Enid.
Barnes-Murphy, Rowan, illus. see Brennan, Linda Crotta.
Barnes-Murphy, Rowan, illus. see Kemp, Marion, et al.
Barnes-Svarney, Patricia & Svarney, Thomas E. Handy Dinosaur Answer Book. (p. 741)
Barnet, Nancy, illus. see Buchanan, Penelope.
Barnett, Angela. Mystic Grove. (p. 1226)
Barnett, Annette. Myth, Magic, & Mystery: An Introduction to Anthropology for Kids in the 21st Century. (p. 1227)
—One World, Many People: Anthropology Made Fun for Kids. Barnett, Isa, illus. (p. 1297)
Barnett, Brandi. Glamour. (p. 682)
Barnett, Carne S., et al. General Math. (p. 660)
—Pre-Algebra. (p. 1393)
Barnett, Charles, III, illus. see Burgan, Michael & Hoena, Blake A.
Barnett, Charles, III, illus. see Doeden, Matt.
Barnett, Charles, III, illus. see Gianopoulos, Andrea & Capstone Press Editors.
Barnett, Charles, III, illus. see Lassieur, Allison.
Barnett, Charles, III, illus. see Lemke, Donald B.
Barnett, Charles, III, illus. see Miller, Connie Colwell.
Barnett, Charles, III, illus. see Miller, Davis Worth & Brevard, Katherine M.
Barnett, Charles, III, illus. see O'Donnell, Liam & Barnett III, Charles.
Barnett, Charles, III, illus. see O'Donnell, Liam.
Barnett, Charles, III, illus. see O'Hearn, Michael.
Barnett, Charles, III, illus. see Olson, Kay Melchisedech.
Barnett, Charles, III, illus. see Olson, Nathan.
Barnett, Charles, III, illus. see Sautter, Aaron.
Barnett, Charles, III, illus. see Seidman, David & Williams, Keith.
Barnett, Charles, III, illus. see Sohn, Emily.
Barnett, Charles, III, illus. see Wade, Mary Dodson & Capstone Press Staff.
Barnett, Charles, III, illus. see Wade, Mary Dodson.
Barnett, Charles, III, jt. auth. see Gianopoulos, Andrea.
Barnett, Charles, III, jt. auth. see O'Donnell, Liam.
Barnett, Chris. Projectors. (p. 1410)
Barnett III, Charles, illus. see Doeden, Matt.
Barnett III, Charles, jt. auth. see Gianopoulos, Andrea.
Barnett III, Charles, jt. auth. see O'Donnell, Liam.
Barnett III, Charles, jt. auth. see Sohn, Emily.
Barnett, Isa, illus. see Barnett, Annette.
Barnett, Janet, illus. see Bayles, Jennifer L.
Barnett, Linda, illus. see Toombs, Robert.
Barnett, Mac. Billy Twitters & His Blue Whale Problem. Rex, Adam, illus. (p. 187)
—Case of the Case of Mistaken Identity. Rex, Adam, illus. (p. 273)
—Chloe & the Lion. Rex, Adam, illus. (p. 308)
—Danger Goes Berserk. Myers, Matthew, illus. (p. 403)
—Extra Yarn. Klassen, Jon, illus. (p. 555)
—Ghostwriter Secret. Rex, Adam, illus. (p. 673)
—Guess Again! Rex, Adam, illus. (p. 728)
—How This Book Was Made: Based on a True Story. Rex, Adam, illus. (p. 814)
—It Happened on a Train. (p. 894)
—It Happened on a Train. Rex, Adam, illus. (p. 894)
—Leo: A Ghost Story. Robinson, Christian, illus. (p. 991)
—Mustache! Cornell, Kevin, illus. (p. 1194)
—Mysterious Case of Cases: The Case of the Case of Mistaken Identity - The Ghostwriter Secret - It Happened on a Train - Danger Goes Berserk. Rex, Adam & Myers, Matthew, illus. (p. 1222)
—Oh No! Or How My Science Project Destroyed the World. Santat, Dan, illus. (p. 1281)
—Oh No! Not Again! Or How I Built a Time Machine to Save History - Or at Least My History Grade. Santat, Dan, illus. (p. 1281)
—Sam & Dave Dig a Hole. Klassen, Jon, illus. (p. 1506)
—Skunk. McDonnell, Patrick, illus. (p. 1586)
—Telephone. Corace, Jen, illus. (p. 1716)
Barnett, Mac, jt. auth. see Scieszka, Jon.
Barnett, Mac & John, Jory. Terrible Two. Cornell, Kevin, illus. (p. 1721)
Barnett, Mac & Klassen, Barnett -. Sam y Leo Cavan un Hoyo. (p. 1507)
Barnett, Mac, et al. Clock Without a Face. Teplin, Scott & Rex, Adam, illus. (p. 333)
Barnett, Penny. Matilda & Puppy's Beach Adventure. (p. 1109)
Barnett, Raymond A., et al. College Algebra: Graphs & Models with MathZone: Mandatory Package. (p. 340)
Barnett, Russell, illus. see Taylor, Alice.
Barnett, Susanne. Pink & the Mystery of the Stable Room Monster. (p. 1359)
Barnett, Thora, illus. see LeBow, Michael.
Barnett, Tony & Whiteside, Alan. AIDS in the Twenty-First Century: Disease & Globalization. (p. 30)
Barnett, Tracy. Buffalo Soldiers. (p. 236)
—Immigration from South America. (p. 861)
—Oman. (p. 1288)
Barnett, Wm. Billy's Wish. Kiste, Tori Lynn, illus. (p. 187)
Barnette, Brandon. Word Fanatics. (p. 1950)
Barnette, Donald. Is My Skin My Only Sin? Breaking the Color Barrier. (p. 889)
Barnette, Jackie, ed. see Pakizer, Debi & Sears, Mary A.
Barney, Maginel Wright, illus. see Snedeker, Caroline.
Barney, V. J. My Rainy Day. (p. 1217)
Barnham, Kay. Animal Rights. (p. 79)
—Could a Robot Make My Dinner? And Other Questions about Technology. (p. 369)
—Could I Sit on a Cloud? And Other Questions about Science. (p. 369)
—Fall. (p. 566)
—Fried! When Lightning Strikes (p. 637)
—Gory Gladiators, Savage Centurions, & Caesar's Sticky End: A Menacing History of the Unruly Romans! (p. 703)
—Gusto (Taste) Acosta, Tatiana & Gutierrez, Guillermo, trs. (p. 733)
—Hearing. (p. 759)
—Ireland. (p. 887)
—Isaac Newton (p. 890)
—Journeys. (p. 929)
—Mangy Mummies, Menacing Pharaohs, & the Awful Afterlife: A Moth-Eaten History of the Extraordinary Egyptians! (p. 1087)
—Oido. Acosta, Tatiana & Gutierrez, Guillermo, trs. (p. 1282)
—Olfato. Acosta, Tatiana & Gutierrez, Guillermo, trs. (p. 1285)
—Protect Nature. (p. 1412)
—Recycle. (p. 1452)
—Save Energy. (p. 1516)
—Save Water. (p. 1517)
—Sight. (p. 1573)
—Smell. (p. 1593)
—Spring. (p. 1634)
—Summer. (p. 1673)
—Tacto. Acosta, Tatiana & Gutierrez, Guillermo, trs. (p. 1695)
—Taste. (p. 1707)
—Thomas Edison (p. 1738)
—Touch. (p. 1772)
—Vista. Acosta, Tatiana & Gutierrez, Guillermo, trs. (p. 1846)
—Winter. (p. 1937)
Barnham, Kay, jt. auth. see Connolly, Sean.
Barnham, Kay, jt. auth. see Ford, Harry.
Barnham, Kay, jt. auth. see Mason, Paul.
Barnham, Kay & Barker, Cicely Mary. Lavender's Midsummer Mix-Up. (p. 981)
Barnham, Kay & Connolly, Sean. Laugh Out Loud Joke Book. (p. 980)
Barnham, Kay, et al. Science Biographies (p. 1525)
Barnhart, Angie, jt. auth. see Barnhart, Duane.
Barnhart, C. A. What Makes Great Athletes. (p. 1892)
Barnhart, Duane & Barnhart, Angie. Cartooning Basics: Creating the Characters & More. (p. 273)
Barnhart, Judy. Sand Angels in the Snow. (p. 1510)
Barnhart, Nancy, illus. see Grahame, Kenneth.
Barnhart, Norm. Amazing Magic Tricks (p. 55)
—Amazing Magic Tricks, Apprentice Level. (p. 55)
—Amazing Magic Tricks, Beginner Level (p. 55)
—Amazing Magic Tricks [Home Design Alternatives]: Beginner Level. (p. 55)
—Amazing Magic Tricks, Master Level (p. 55)
—Dazzling Card Tricks (p. 415)
—Fantastically Funny Tricks (p. 572)
—Magic Manuals. (p. 1072)
—Marvelous Money Tricks (p. 1099)
—Stunning Stage Tricks (p. 1670)
Barnhart, Norm & Charney, Steve. My First Guide to Magic Tricks. (p. 1206)
Barnhart, Norm, et al. My First Guides. (p. 1206)
Barnhart, Ruth Scheresky. Country Girl: The Story of Lena Dassenka Schild. (p. 372)
Barnhill, Carla. One Year Devotions for Preschoolers 2. Kucharik, Elena, illus. (p. 1298)
Barnhill, Kelly. Iron Hearted Violet. Bruno, Iacopo, illus. (p. 888)
—Mostly True Story of Jack. (p. 1177)
—Witch's Boy. (p. 1941)
Barnhill, Kelly Regan. Animals with No Eyes: Cave Adaptation (p. 84)
—Bizarre, Creepy Hoaxes (p. 194)
—Blood-Sucking, Man-Eating Monsters (p. 200)
—Bloody Book of Blood (p. 201)
—Guess What's Growing: A Photo Riddle Book. (p. 729)
—Mystery Animal Tracks: A Photo Riddle Book. (p. 1223)
—Sewers & the Rats That Love Them: The Disgusting Story Behind Where It All Goes. (p. 1555)
—Sick, Nasty Medical Practices (p. 1572)
—Sweaty Book of Sweat (p. 1689)
—Terrifying, Bone-Chilling Rituals & Sacrifices (p. 1721)
—Wee Book of Pee (p. 1871)
Barnhill, Kelly Regan & Harbo, Christopher L. What's That Shadow? A Photo Riddle Book. (p. 1899)
Barnholdt, Lauren. Aces Up. (p. 8)
—Devon Delaney Should Totally Know Better. (p. 432)
—Fake Me a Match. (p. 565)
—Four Truths & a Lie. (p. 625)
—From This Moment. (p. 644)
—Ghost of a Chance. (p. 671)
—Girl Meets Ghost. (p. 678)
—Hailey Twitch & the Campground Itch. Beaky, Suzanne, illus. (p. 735)
—Hailey Twitch & the Great Teacher Switch. Beaky, Suzanne, illus. (p. 735)
—Hailey Twitch & the Wedding Glitch. Beaky, Suzanne, illus. (p. 735)
—Hailey Twitch Is Not a Snitch. Beaky, Suzanne, illus. (p. 735)
—Harder the Fall. (p. 748)
—Heat of the Moment. (p. 760)
—One Moment in Time. (p. 1296)
—One Night That Changes Everything. (p. 1296)
—Right of Way. (p. 1472)
—Rules for Secret Keeping. (p. 1495)
—Secret Identity of Devon Delaney. (p. 1541)
—Sometimes It Happens. (p. 1610)
—Thing about the Truth. (p. 1732)
—Through to You. (p. 1745)
—Two-Way Street. (p. 1804)
—Watch Me. (p. 1861)
Barnhouse Ms Ncc, Natalie. Shimmy Saves the Day: A Tale about Embracing Your Differences. (p. 1566)
Barnhouse, Rebecca. Book of the Maidservant. (p. 212)
—Peaceweaver. (p. 1332)
—Ring-Giver. (p. 1473)
Barnhurst, Noel, photos by see Spieler, Marlena.
Barnhurst, Noel, photos by see Wong, Richard.
Barnicke Belleghem, Marilyn. Questing Home: Personal Growth Through Travel. (p. 1426)
Barnickle, Angela. Miles Gardner & the Secret of Blissville: A Blissville Mystery Series. (p. 1142)
Barnoski, Karel, illus. see Figueroa, M. A. & Figueroa, P. A.
Barns, Crosby H. Who Programmed the Species? The Theory of Scientific Coincidence. (p. 1917)
Barnum, P. T. Dick Broadhead: A Story of Perilous Adve. (p. 435)
—Jack in the Jungle: A Tale of Land & S. (p. 903)
Barnum, Richard. Mappo the Merry Monkey Illustrated Editi. (p. 1090)
—Squinty the Comical Pig. (p. 1637)
—Squinty the Comical Pig Illustrated Edit. (p. 1637)
Barnum, Tabatha, illus. see Quintanilla, Billie.
Barnum, Vance. Frank & Andy Afloat: The Cave on the Island. (p. 628)
—Frank & Andy Afloat. (p. 628)
—Frank & Andy Afloat or the Cave on the Island. (p. 628)
—Joe Strong the Boy Fire-Eater. (p. 920)
—Joe Strong. the Boy Fire-Eater. (p. 920)
Barnum-Newman, Winifred. To Market, to Market. Newman, Winifred Barnum & Barnum-Newman, Winifred, illus. (p. 1759)
Barnum-Newman, Winifred, illus. see Peterson-Hilleque, Victoria.
Barnwell, Ysaye M. No Mirrors in My Nana's House: Musical CD & Book. Saint James, Synthia, illus. (p. 1259)
Baroff, Raina. Chanukah Puppet Show. (p. 291)
Barois, Lorena Stoopen, tr. see Tudge, Colin.
Barois, Valerian Stoopen, tr. see Garlick, Mark A.
Baroja y Nessi, Pío. Zalacaín el Aventurero. Senabre, Ricardo, ed. (p. 1984)
Baron, Andrew. Adventures of Octopus Rex. (p. 21)
—Pulpo Rex. (p. 1416)
Baron, Celia. Brain Sizzlers: Puzzles for Critical Thinkers. (p. 222)
—Brain Sizzlers. (p. 222)
Baron, Charlie & Gamson, Alyse. Peanut Butter & Jelly. (p. 1332)
Baron, Cheri Ann, illus. see Guiffre, William A.
Baron, Cheri Ann, illus. see Guiffre, William.
Baron Cohen, H. V. Story of Joe & His Magic Snout: An Operetta of Nursery Fairytales for 2 to 10 years Olds. (p. 1658)
Baron, Hyacinthe. Burnt Sienna in Scottsdale: An Art Mystery. (p. 244)
Baron, James. No Pain, No Gain. (p. 1259)
Baron, Jeff. I Represent Sean Rosen. (p. 844)
—Sean Rosen Is Not for Sale. (p. 1537)
Baron, Jessica. Fun with Magnets. (p. 648)
—Let's Make Music. (p. 999)
—Trading Baseball Cards: Learning the Symbols +, -, And = (p. 1776)
—What's in the Garden? Learning to Compare Two Sets of Objects. (p. 1898)
Baron, Kathi. Shattered. (p. 1563)
Baron, Kathy, illus. see Bannister, Barbara.
Baron, L. Day with My Dad: Learning the D Sound. (p. 415)
BarÓN, Lara, illus. see Tsang, Evonne & Jimenez, Adan.
Baron, Lindamichelle. Lion & the Man: A Fable. Huggins, Carl, illus. (p. 1020)
Baron, Lindamichelle, jt. auth. see Sicinski-Skeans, Sharon.
Baron, Lynne Pauls. F. Luis Mora: America's First Hispanic Master. Falk, Peter Hastings, ed. (p. 559)
Baron, Michael. Winter Discovery. (p. 1938)
Baron, Mike. Nexus Omnibus Volume 2. Warner, Chris, ed. (p. 1249)
—Nexus Omnibus Volume 4. Wright, Brendan, ed. (p. 1249)
Baron, Robert C. & Locker, Thomas. Hudson: The Story of a River. Locker, Thomas, illus. (p. 824)
Baron, Robert S. & Kerr, Norbert L. Group Process, Group Decisions, Group Action. (p. 725)
Baron, Ruth. Defriended. (p. 424)
Baroncelli, Silvia, illus. see Heos, Bridget.
Barone, Barbara. Leafy Trees & Bumbly Bees. (p. 982)
Barone, Bill. So Many Scoops! (p. 1602)
Barone, Candy. Dream Star. (p. 484)
Barone, Deborah & Stone, Janet. S. O. S. a simulation solving a scientific mystery by understanding the formation & motion of ocean currents / (p. 1499)
Barone, Luisa T. Abby the Apple. (p. 2)
Barone, Mark, illus. see Young, Mary Beth.
Barone, Michelle. Out of the Ordinary. (p. 1311)
Barosso, Abramo, et al. Uncle Scrooge #378. Clark, John, ed. (p. 1812)
—Uncle Scrooge #386. (p. 1812)
Barozzi, Danilo, illus. see Stilton, Geronimo & Dami, Elisabetta.
Barozzi, Danilo, illus. see Stilton, Geronimo.
Barr, Amelia E. Remember the Alamo. (p. 1459)
Barr, Andrew. Through the Year with Songs of Praise. (p. 1745)
Barr, Bailey, illus. see Skwara, Maike Lena.
Barr, Barbara Jean. My Mom Inside My Pocket Stutz, Chris, illus. (p. 1214)
Barr, Bitsy. Zock's Adventures: Just for Boys ... (p. 1987)
—Zock's Counting Book. (p. 1987)
Barr, Brady & Zoehfeld, Kathleen Weidner. Crocodile Encounters: And More True Stories of Adventures with Animals. (p. 384)
—Crocodile Encounters! And More True Stories of Adventures with Animals. (p. 384)
—National Geographic Kids Chapters: Scrapes with Snakes: And More True Stories of Adventures with Animals. (p. 1232)
—Scrapes with Snakes! True Stories of Adventures with Animals. (p. 1532)
Barr, Brandon, jt. auth. see Lynch, Mike.
Barr, Carolyn Mims. Blue Turtle. (p. 203)
—Waiting Tree. (p. 1853)
Barr, Catherine & Williams, Steve. Story of Life: A First Book about Evolution. Husband, Amy, illus. (p. 1658)
Barr, Gary. Slavery in the United States (p. 1588)
—World War II Home Front (p. 1959)
Barr, Gary E. History & Activities of the Islamic Empire (p. 783)
—History & Activities of the West African Kingdoms (p. 783)
—Mid-Atlantic (p. 1137)
Barr, George. Fascinating Science Experiments for Young People. (p. 575)
—Science Projects for Young People. (p. 1527)
—Sports Science for Young People. (p. 1633)
Barr, Gladys H. Tinker's Armor: The Story of John Bunyan. Hutchinson, William, illus. (p. 1756)
Barr, Gordon. Beginning. (p. 159)
Barr, J. Bennett. Saying Goodbye. (p. 1519)
Barr, Kristen, illus. see Forbes, Harriet H.
Barr, Kristin, illus. see Riggs, Sandy.
Barr, Lester. Robots Land at Manchester Airport. (p. 1481)
Barr, Linda. Advantage Reading Grade 7: High Interest Skill Building for Home & School. Vol. 8135 Hamaguchi, Carla, ed. (p. 14)
—Advantage Reading Grade 8: High Interest Skill Building for Home & School. Vol. 8136 Hamaguchi, Carla, ed. (p. 14)
—Captured (p. 265)
—Long Road to Freedom: Journey of the Hmong (p. 1047)
—Volcano! When a Mountain Explodes (p. 1848)
—Water Patrol: Saving Surfers' Lives in Big Waves. (p. 1863)
—Young Champions: It's All about Attitude. (p. 1978)
Barr, Loel, illus. see Grace, Catherine O'Neill.
Barr, Loel, illus. see Humes, Kristin Joy.
Barr, Lollie. Mag Hags. (p. 1071)
Barr, Mabel. Hamster Huey & the Gooey Kablooie: The Renowned Hero's Most Famous Adventure. (p. 739)
Barr, Margy. Big Adventure of Claire & Carmela Crab. (p. 177)
Barr, Marilyn, illus. see Gross, Arthur.
Barr, Marilynn G. India. (p. 870)
—Miss Pitty Pat & Friends. (p. 1152)
Barr, Marilynn G., illus. see Lingo, Susan L.
Barr, Mary. Trouble with Filly Tucker. (p. 1790)
Barr, Matt & Moran, Chris. Snowboarding. (p. 1600)
Barr, Matthew Bruce. Iron Order. (p. 888)
Barr, Mike W., jt. auth. see Schmidt, Andy.
Barr, Nevada. Hard Truth. (p. 748)
Barr, Robert. Clue of the Silver Spoons. (p. 336)
—Dr. Barr's Tales: Stories of Katharine. (p. 475)
Barr, Steve. 1-2-3 Draw Cartoon Aircraft. (p. 1990)
—1-2-3 Draw Cartoon Monsters. (p. 1990)
—1-2-3 Draw Cartoon People. (p. 1990)
—1-2-3 Draw Cartoon Sea Critters. (p. 1990)
—1-2-3 Draw Cartoon Trucks & Motorcycles. (p. 1990)
—Draw Crazy Creatures. (p. 480)
Barr, Steve, illus. see Schab, Lisa & Gardner, Richard.
Barraclough, John. Jamaica. (p. 906)
—South Africa. (p. 1616)
Barraclough, Lindsey. Long Lankin. (p. 1047)
Barraclough, Sue. Animal Characteristics (p. 77)
—Animal Needs (p. 79)
—Bees (p. 157)
—Circulatory System: Why Does My Heart Beat? (p. 322)
—Digestive System: What Makes Me Burp? (p. 438)
—Earth's Resources (p. 498)
—Earthworms (p. 498)
—Fair Play (p. 562)
—Farm Animals. (p. 573)
—Honestidad (p. 794)
—I Know Someone Who Is Obese (p. 840)
—I Know Someone with Autism (p. 840)
—I Know Someone with Dyslexia (p. 840)
—Jugar Limpio (p. 931)
—Liderazgo (p. 1007)
—Mosquitoes (p. 1176)
—Move & Run. (p. 1183)
—My Body. (p. 1198)
—On the Move. (p. 1291)
—Plants (p. 1369)
—Recycling Materials. (p. 1453)
—Respiratory System: Why Do I Feel Out of Breath? (p. 1463)
—Seasons. (p. 1538)
—Seguridad y el Agua (p. 1548)
—Seguridad y el Hogar (p. 1548)
—Seguridad y las Bicicletas. (p. 1548)
—Seguridad y las Carreteras. (p. 1548)

—Seguridad y Los Incendios (p. 1548)
—Sensory System: Why Am I Ticklish? (p. 1551)
—Sharing (p. 1561)
—Sistema Circulatorio: ¿Por Qué Late Mi Corazón? (p. 1581)
—Sistema Digestivo: ¿Qué Me Hace Eructar? (p. 1581)
—Sistema Respiratorio: ¿Por Qué Me Quedo Sin Aliento? (p. 1581)
—Sistema Sensorial: ¿Por Qué Me Dan Cosquillas? (p. 1581)
—Sistemas Esqueletico y Muscular: ¿Cómo Puedo Pararme de Cabeza? (p. 1581)
—Skeletal & Muscular Systems: How Can I Stand on My Head? (p. 1584)
—Sleep & Rest. (p. 1588)
—Sunlight (p. 1677)
—Tu Seguridad (p. 1795)
—Wash & Clean. (p. 1859)
—Weather & Seasons (p. 1869)
—What Can I Feel? (p. 1880)
—What Can I Hear? (p. 1880)
—What Can I See? (p. 1880)
—What Can I Smell? (p. 1880)
—What Can I Taste? (p. 1880)
Barraclough, Sue & Hachette Children's Books Staff. Be an Eco Hero at Home. (p. 148)
—Be an Eco Hero at School. (p. 148)
—Be an Eco Hero on the Move. (p. 148)
—Be an Eco Hero Outdoors. (p. 148)
Barraclough, Sue & Heinemann Library Staff. Fair Play (p. 562)
—Honesty (p. 794)
—Sharing (p. 1561)
Barraclough, Sue & Lanz, Helen. Eat & Drink. (p. 501)
Barraclough, Sue & Ridley, Sarah. Paper Bag. (p. 1322)
—Plastic Toy. (p. 1370)
Barraclough, Sue, et al. Springtime Tales: A Collection of Animal Stories. (p. 1635)
Barraclough, Susan. Sharks & Other Creatures of the Deep. (p. 1563)
—Snakes & Reptiles: The Scariest Cold-Blooded Creatures on Earth. (p. 1596)
Barradas, Leticia, illus. see Defosse, Rosana Curiel.
Barradas, Michele. Rainbow of Shapes: Learn shapes & Colors. (p. 1435)
Barradel, Isabel. Toyshop Tales. (p. 1774)
Barradell, Isabel. Even More Tales from the Toyshop. (p. 541)
Barragan, Ivy, jt. auth. see Barragan, Sophia.
Barragán, Paula, illus. see Alarcón, Francisco X.
Barragán, Paula, illus. see Shahan, Sherry.
Barragan, Sophia & Barragan, Ivy. Susana Banana the Fantastic Figure Skater. (p. 1688)
Barrager, Brigette, illus. see Clarkson, Stephanie.
Barrager, Brigette, illus. see Evans, Zoe.
Barrager, Brigette, illus. see Grimm, Wilhelm K., et al.
Barrager, Brigette, illus. see Ostow, Micol.
Barrager, Brigette, illus. see Quinton, Sasha.
Barrager, Brigette, illus. see Rosenthal, Amy Krouse.
Barrager, Brigette, illus. see Ziefert, Harriet.
Barrale, Joseph. Adventures of Bobby Bear Baker: Bobby Bear Baker & the Quelt. (p. 16)
Barrance, Reuben, illus. see Dalby, Elizabeth.
Barrance, Reuben & Whatmore, Candice. Birthday. (p. 192)
Barras, Dannette. Esther's Courage. (p. 538)
Barratt, Mark. Joe Rat. (p. 920)
—Wild Man. (p. 1929)
Barraza, Cindy Lou. Mexiroo Dice, ¡Qué Importa! (p. 1131)
—Mexiroo Says, So What!! (p. 1131)
Barredo, Jose Eduardo. Mundo Azul. (p. 1191)
Barreintez, Elsa. I'm Only Eight, by Reynaldo: I Survived Being Eight. (p. 859)
Barreiro, Mike, illus. see Nimoy, Leonard.
Barreneche, Raul A. New Museums. (p. 1246)
Barrera, F. M. Tales of the Blue Wizard: The Children of Jamomere. Barrera, F. M., illus. (p. 1702)
Barrera, J. Mario. Nine Moons. (p. 1256)
—Yak the Alien. (p. 1968)
Barrera, Norma. Diario de Tlauhquechol (1518) (p. 434)
Barrera, Norma Anabel. Artistas de Las Plumas: The Feather Artists. Nepomniatchi, Leonid, illus. (p. 104)
Barret, jt. auth. see Barrett, Judi.
Barret, Marie. Ms. Irene Is so Demanding. Guiza, Victor, illus. (p. 1188)
Barreto, Eduardo, illus. see Augustyn, Brian.
Barreto, Eduardo, illus. see Jones, Bruce.
Barreto, Sonia. Onyx. Switzer, Bobbi, illus. (p. 1298)
Barrett, Angela, illus. see Moore, Clement C.
Barrett, Angela, illus. see Poole, Josephine.
Barrett, Angela, illus. see Schlitz, Laura Amy.
Barrett, Anna Pearl. Neecie & the Sparkling Spring. Weston, Eunice Guy, ed. (p. 1239)
Barrett, Audrey & Vogt, Denis. Adventures of Audrey the Cat. (p. 16)
Barrett, Casey, illus. see Kerns, Kristen.
Barrett, Casey, illus. see Wenning, Jeremy.
Barrett, Cheryl. Andy Goes Crab Fishin' (p. 73)
Barrett, Diana, illus. see Fisher, Meaghan.
Barrett, Ethel. John Welch: The Man Who Couldn't Be Stopped. (p. 923)
Barrett, Granny Rita. Adventures on Granny's Fun-Ee Farm: Book 1. (p. 24)
Barrett, Jennifer. Lethal Delivery, Postage Prepaid. (p. 994)
Barrett, Jennifer & Barrett, Judi. Snake Is Totally Tail. (p. 1596)
Barrett, Jill, jt. auth. see Kiefer, Janet Kennedy.
Barrett, John E. Some Assembly Required: The Not-So-Secret Life of a Transgender Teen. (p. 1609)
Barrett, John E., photos by see Kenney, Sean.
Barrett, John E., photos by see Nelson, Mary Beth & Linn, Laurent, illus.
Barrett, John F. Stories of Jake. (p. 1655)
Barrett, John P. Crows in Our Hands. (p. 386)
Barrett, John S., jt. auth. see Johansen, Hanna.
Barrett, John S., tr. see Johansen, Hanna.
Barrett, Judi. Animales No Deven Actuar Como la Gente. (p. 81)
—Animales No Se Visten. (p. 81)
—Animals Series Barrett, Ron, illus. (p. 84)
—Animals Should Definitely Not Act Like People. Barrett, Ron, illus. (p. 84)
—Animals Should Definitely Not Wear Clothing. Barrett, Ron, illus. (p. 84)
—Cloudy with a Chance of Meatballs. Barrett, Ron, illus. (p. 335)
—Cloudy with a Chance of Meatballs. Barrett, Ronald, illus. (p. 335)
—Cloudy with a Chance of Meatballs 3: Planet of the Pies. Mones, Isidre, illus. (p. 335)
—Complete Cloudy with a Chance of Meatballs: Cloudy with a Chance of Meatballs; Pickles to Pittsburgh. Barrett, Ronald, illus. (p. 352)
—Grandpa's Cloudy with a Chance of Meatballs Cookbook. Barrett, Ronald, illus. (p. 709)
—I Knew Two Who Said Moo: A Counting & Rhyming Book. Moreton, Daniel, illus. (p. 840)
—Never Take a Shark to the Dentist: And Other Things Not to Do. Nickle, John, illus. (p. 1243)
—Pickles to Pittsburgh: Cloudy with a Chance of Meatballs 2. Barrett, Ronald, illus. (p. 1354)
—Pickles to Pittsburgh: The Sequel to Cloudy with a Chance of Meatballs. Barrett, Ron, illus. (p. 1354)
—Santa from Cincinnati. Hawkes, Kevin, illus. (p. 1511)
Barrett, Judi, jt. auth. see Barrett, Jennifer.
Barrett, Judi & Barret. Nublado con Probabilidades de Albondigas. (p. 1269)
Barrett, Judi & Barrett, Ron. Marshmallow Incident. Barrett, Ron, illus. (p. 1096)
Barrett, Judy Ann. Stuff Family. (p. 1670)
Barrett, Karlish, illus. see Jonas, Gennevive.
Barrett, Lauren. My New Mommy: I Got Adopted! (p. 1216)
Barrett, Mary Brigid. All Fall Down. Pham, LeUyen, illus. (p. 44)
—Pat-a-Cake. Pham, LeUyen, illus. (p. 1327)
—Shoebox Sam Morrison, Frank, illus. (p. 1568)
Barrett, Matthew. Jack's Summer Journal 2011: Life at Havertown Elementary: Volume Three. (p. 904)
—Stories by a Ninth Grader. (p. 1654)
Barrett, Michellene. Englisha & David's Adventurous Vacation. (p. 530)
Barrett, Ms S. Moe. Mangoe & Marlie: Mangoe Takes Care of Marlie. (p. 1087)
Barrett, Nana. Terrible Case of the Collywobbles! (p. 1721)
Barrett, Noah, illus. see Anderson, Ebony.
Barrett, Norman S., et al. Great Mystery. (p. 717)
Barrett, Peter, illus. see Barrett, Susan.
Barrett, Peter, illus. see Herriot, James.
Barrett, Peter, illus. see Penner, Lucille Recht.
Barrett, Peter, illus. see Reda, Sheryl A.
Barrett, Phillip. Where's Larry? (p. 1910)
Barrett, Rebecca, illus. see O'Hara, Susan.
Barrett, Richard. Training, Developing, & Motivating People. (p. 1777)
Barrett, Robert. Other Wise Man. (p. 1306)
Barrett, Robert, illus. see Maier, Paul.
Barrett, Robert, illus. see Sandler, Martin W.
Barrett, Robert, illus. see Van Dyke, Henry.
Barrett, Robert, illus. see Weatherford, Carole Boston.
Barrett, Robert, tr. see Schindler, Nina.
Barrett, Robert T., illus. see Maier, Paul L.
Barrett, Ron. Cats Get Famous. Barrett, Ron, illus. (p. 281)
Barrett, Ron, illus. see Barrett, Judi.
Barrett, Ron, illus. see Weitzman, Jacqueline Preiss.
Barrett, Ron, jt. auth. see Barrett, Judi.
Barrett, Ronald, illus. see Barrett, Judi.
Barrett, Selby. Diva Code Diary. (p. 454)
Barrett, Shari & Barrett, Steve. Put That in Writing: Answer Key & Test Bank. Level One (p. 1420)
—Put That in Writing: Mastering the Paragraph. Level One (p. 1420)
Barrett, Steve, jt. auth. see Barrett, Shari.
Barrett, Susan. Day & Night in Forest. Barrett, Peter, illus. (p. 412)
Barrett, Susanna. Isabella Goes to the City. (p. 891)
Barrett, Tracy. 100-Year-Old Secret. (p. 1999)
—Beast of Blackslope. (p. 152)
—Case That Time Forgot. (p. 275)
—Kentucky. (p. 949)
—Missing Heir. (p. 1152)
—Stepsister's Tale. (p. 1648)
—Tennessee. (p. 1720)
—Virginia. (p. 1844)
Barrett, Tracy, jt. auth. see Kleeman, Terry.
Barrett, Tracy & Roberts, Jennifer T. Ancient Greek World. (p. 69)
Barrett, Virginia, illus. see Stott-Thornton, Janet.
Barretta, Gene. Dear Deer: A Book of Homophones. (p. 418)
—Dear Deer: A Book of Homophones. Barretta, Gene, illus. (p. 418)
—Neo Leo: The Ageless Ideas of Leonardo Da Vinci. Barretta, Gene, illus. (p. 1241)
—Now & Ben: The Modern Inventions of Benjamin Franklin. (p. 1269)
—Now & Ben: The Modern Inventions of Benjamin Franklin. Barretta, Gene, illus. (p. 1269)
—On Top of Spaghetti: A Silly Song Book. (p. 1292)
—Timeless Thomas: How Thomas Edison Changed Our Lives. Barretta, Gene, illus. (p. 1754)
—Zoola Palooza: A Book of Homographs. Barretta, Gene, illus. (p. 1989)
Barretta, Gene, illus. see Fretz, Denette.
Barretta, Gene, illus. see Matthies, Janna.
Barretta, Gene, illus. see Pingry, Patricia A.
Barrette, Doris, illus. see Bonnett-Rampersaud, Louise.
Barrette, Doris, illus. see Jackson, Alison.
Barrette, Doris, illus. see Markes, Julie.
Barrette, Doris, illus. see Torme, Mel.
Barrette, Doris, illus. see Tormé, Mel.
Barrette, Doris, jt. auth. see Plourde, Josee.
Barrette, Melanie. Welcome to School: Helping Friends with Autism. James, Colin, ed. (p. 1873)
Barricks, Jerim. I Want to Know??? (p. 848)
Barrie, J. M. Adventures of Peter Pan. (p. 21)
—Complete Adventures of Peter Pan Includes: The Little White Bird, Peter Pan in Kensington Gardens(Illustrated) & Peter. Rackham, Arthur & Bedford, F. D., illus. (p. 352)
—Little White Bird or Adventures in Kensington Gardens. (p. 1037)
—Pantaloon. Landes, William-Alan, ed. (p. 1321)
—Peter & Wendy. (p. 1346)
—Peter Pan. (p. 1346)
—Peter Pan. Cowley, Joy, ed. (p. 1346)
—Peter Pan. Dunn, Ben, illus. (p. 1346)
—Peter Pan. Barrie, J. M., ed. (p. 1346)
—Peter Pan. Press, Jenny, illus. (p. 1346)
—Peter Pan. Bedford, F. D., illus. (p. 1346)
—Peter Pan. Bustelo, Gabriela, tr. (p. 1346)
—Peter Pan. McKowen, Scott, illus. (p. 1346)
—Peter Pan: A Bed Book First Edition Classic. (p. 1347)
—Peter Pan: Complete & Unabridged. Barrie, J. M., illus. (p. 1347)
—Peter Pan: The Story of Peter & Wendy [Photoplay Edition]. (p. 1347)
—Peter Pan: Peter & Wendy & Peter Pan in Kensington Gardens. (p. 1347)
—Peter Pan: The Original Tale of Neverland. Jaramillo, Raquel, illus. (p. 1347)
—Peter Pan: With Three-Dimensional Pop-Up Scenes. Robinson, Nicola, illus. (p. 1347)
—Peter Pan: From the Story by J. M. Barrie. Costa, Patricia Castelao, illus. (p. 1347)
—Peter Pan: An Illustrated Classic for Kids & Young Readers (Excellent for Bedtime & Young Readers) eMusic, Tom, ed. (p. 1347)
—Peter Pan. (p. 1347)
—Peter Pan. Andreasen, Dan, illus. (p. 1347)
—Peter Pan. Bedford, F. D., illus. (p. 1347)
—Peter Pan. Hague, Michael, illus. (p. 1347)
—Peter Pan & Wendy: Centenary Edition. Ingpen, Robert R., illus. (p. 1347)
—Peter Pan & Wendy. (p. 1347)
—Peter Pan & Wendy. Foreman, Michael, illus. (p. 1347)
—Peter Pan, by J. M. Barrie - the Original Classic Edition. (p. 1347)
—Peter Pan in Kensington Gardens. (p. 1347)
—Peter Pan in Kensington Gardens & Peter & Wendy. (p. 1347)
—Peter Pan - the Original Classic Edition. (p. 1347)
—Peter Pan y Wendy. (p. 1347)
—Rosalind. Landes, William-Alan, ed. (p. 1489)
—Story of Peter Pan. Woodward, Alice B., illus. (p. 1659)
—Tommy & Grizel. (p. 1764)
—Will: A Playscript. (p. 1932)
Barrie, J. M., jt. auth. see Hill, Susan.
Barrie, J. M., jt. auth. see Hoena, B. A.
Barrie, J. M., jt. auth. see Hollindale, Peter.
Barrie, J. M., jt. auth. see O'Connor, Daniel.
Barrie, J. M. & Attwell, James M. Barrie - Mabel Lucie. Peter Pan y Wendy. (p. 1347)
Barrie, J. M. & Bedford, F. D. Peter Pan. (p. 1347)
Barrie, J. M. & Lindner, Brooke. Peter Pan. Bedford, Francis Donkin & Rackham, Arthur, illus. (p. 1347)
Barrie, J. M. & RH Disney Staff. Peter Pan. Walt Disney Studios Staff & Dempster, Al, illus. (p. 1347)
Barrie, J. M. & Sterne, Laurence. Life & Opinions of Tristram Shandy, Gentleman. (p. 1007)
Barrie, James Matthew. Peter Pan. Cowley, Joy, ed. (p. 1347)
Barrie, Ruthann. And I Love You, God. (p. 71)
Barrie, Shirley & Sher, Emil, eds. Prepare to Embark: Six Theatrical Voyages for Young Audiences. (p. 1396)
Barriman, Lydia. #8 the Runaway Puppy: A Mystery with Probability. Grutzik, Becky, illus. (p. 1993)
—Runaway Puppy: A Mystery with Probability. Grutzik, Becky, illus. (p. 1496)
—Thr Runaway Puppy: A Mystery with Probability. Grutzik, Becky, illus. (p. 1741)
Barringer, J. M., illus. see Magden, Loretta.
Barringer, Janice & Schlesinger, Sarah. Pointe Book: Shoes, Training, Technique. (p. 1377)
Barringer, Laura, illus. see Rivers, C.
Barrington, Richard. Bands, Tribes & First Peoples & Nations. Wolff, Ariana, ed. (p. 136)
—Bmw: Ultimate Riding Experience. (p. 204)
—Careers in Trucking. (p. 268)
—Ducati: High Performance Italian Racer. (p. 487)
—Junevile Court System: Your Legal Rights. (p. 934)
—Juvenile Court System: Your Legal Rights. (p. 941)
—Sonia Sotomayor. (p. 1612)
—Tom Brady: Super Bowl Champion. (p. 1762)
Barrio, Blanca, illus. see Carballeira, Paula.
Barrionuevo, Al, illus. see Lieberman, A. J.
Barrish, Lily & Pecsenye, Jessice. University of Central Florida College Prowler off the Record. (p. 1820)
Barritt, Carolyn Reed, illus. see Haugaard, Kay.
Barritt, Margaret. Hickory Dickory Dock. East, Jacqueline, illus. (p. 775)
Barron, Ann, illus. see Profilet, Cynthia.
Barron, Ashley, illus. see Flatt, Lizann.
Barron, Ashley, illus. see Thornhill, Jan.
Barron Dc, Philip. Daddy Can't Play Now: A bedtime story of understanding & an introduction to Chiropractic Care. (p. 398)
Barron, Liz. Salcombe Seaside Fairies: Michael the Mussel Fairy. (p. 1504)
—Salcombe Seaside Fairies: Kevin the Crabshell Fairy. (p. 1504)
—Salcombe Seaside Fairies: Louise the Lobster Pot Fairy. (p. 1504)
Barron, Patricia. Meet Judge Patricia Barron. Barron, Robert, photos by. (p. 1121)
Barron, Rachel Stiffler. John Coltrane: Jazz Revolutionary. (p. 921)
—Lise Meitner: Discoverer of Nuclear Fission. (p. 1022)
—Richard Nixon: American Politician. (p. 1469)
Barron, Rex. Showdown at the Food Pyramid. Barron, Rex, illus. (p. 1571)
Barron, Robert, photos by see Barron, Patricia.
Barron, T. A. Ancient One. (p. 70)
—Atlantis in Peril. (p. 112)
—Atlantis Rising. (p. 112)
—Book of Magic Hall, August, illus. (p. 211)
—Child of the Dark Prophecy. (p. 301)
—Doomraga's Revenge. (p. 470)
—Dragon of Avalon (p. 477)
—Eternal Flame: Book 11 (p. 539)
—Ghost Hands. Low, William, illus. (p. 670)
—Great Tree of Avalon: Book 9 (p. 719)
—Heartlight Saga. (p. 760)
—Hero's Trail: A Guide for a Heroic Life. (p. 774)
—Lost Years (p. 1057)
—Lost Years of Merlin. (p. 1057)
—Merlin Effect. (p. 1128)
—Merlin's Dragon. (p. 1128)
—Mirror of Fate (p. 1149)
—Raging Fires (p. 1433)
—Seven Songs (p. 1555)
—Seven Songs of Merlin. (p. 1555)
—Shadows on the Stars: Book 10 (p. 1558)
—Tree Girl. (p. 1783)
—Ultimate Magic (p. 1809)
—Wisdom of Merlin: 7 Magical Words for a Meaningful Life. (p. 1939)
—Wizard's Wings (p. 1943)
Barron's Editorial Staff. Nutcracker. Pagnoni, Roberta & Rigo, Laura, illus. (p. 1273)
Barron's Educational Series & Benton, Lynne. Stranger in the Snow/L'etranger dans la Neige: French/English Edition. Cuthbertson, Ollie, illus. (p. 1665)
Barron's Educational Series Staff & Rigo, L. Off to School. (p. 1279)
Barron's Educational Staff, jt. auth. see Research Masters Staff.
Barroso, Paz, tr. see Bour, Laura & Jeunesse, Gallimard.
Barroso, Paz, tr. see Bour, Laura, et al.
Barroso, Paz, tr. see Chabot, Jean-Philippe, et al.
Barroso, Paz, tr. see Delafosse, Claude & Krawczyk, Sabine.
Barroso, Paz, tr. see Galeron, Henri, et al.
Barroso, Paz, tr. see Houbre, Gilbert & Jeunesse, Gallimard.
Barroso, Paz, tr. see McCaughrean, Geraldine.
Barroso, Paz, tr. see Mettler, René & Jeunesse, Gallimard.
Barroso, Paz, tr. see Moignot, Daniel, et al.
Barroso, Paz, tr. see Pérols, Sylvaine, et al.
Barroux. Draw Patterns with Barroux. (p. 481)
—Draw Patterns with Barroux Drawing Book & Kit: Everything You Need to Start Drawing Shapes, Colors, & Patterns! (p. 481)
—Line of Fire: Diary of an Unknown Soldier. Ardizzone, Sarah, tr. from FRE. (p. 1019)
—Mr Leon's Paris. Ardizzone, Sarah, tr. from FRE. (p. 1185)
Barroux, illus. see Blue Apple Staff.
Barroux, illus. see Leblanc, André.
Barroux, illus. see Owen, Karen.
Barroux, illus. see Ziefert, Harriet.
Barroux, jt. auth. see Owen, Karen.
Barroux, Gilles. Naughty & Nice. (p. 1237)
—Plain & Fancy. (p. 1366)
Barroux, Sophie, illus. see Cadic, Olivier & Gheysens, Francois.
Barroux, Stephane. My Goldfish. (p. 1210)
Barroux, Stephane, illus. see Vidal, Séverine.
Barroux, Stephane-Yves. Mr Leon's Paris. (p. 1185)
Barrow, Alex, illus. see Dawnay, Gabby.
Barrow, Ann, illus. see Brookins, Cara.
Barrow, Ann, illus. see Gill, Shelley.
Barrow, Joy. Sikhism. (p. 1574)
—Sikhism. (p. 1574)
Barrow, Randi. Finding Zasha. (p. 588)
—Saving Zasha. (p. 1518)
Barrow, Shelley. My Life: The Story of a NFL Child. (p. 1211)
Barrowman, Carole E., jt. auth. see Barrowman, John.
Barrowman, John & Barrowman, Carole E. Bone Quill. (p. 209)
—Book of Beasts. (p. 210)
—Hollow Earth. (p. 789)
Barrows, Annie. Bound to Be Bad. (p. 216)
—Ivy & Bean & the Ghost That Had to Go. Blackall, Sophie, illus. (p. 901)
—Ivy & Bean Take the Case. (p. 901)
—Ivy + Bean Blackall, Sophie, illus. (p. 901)
—Ivy + Bean: No News Is Good News. Blackall, Sophie, illus. (p. 901)
—Ivy + Bean. Blackall, Sophie, illus. (p. 901)
—Ivy + Bean & the Ghost That Had to Go. Blackall, Sophie, illus. (p. 901)
—Ivy + Bean Bound to Be Bad. Blackall, Sophie, illus. (p. 901)
—Ivy + Bean Boxed Set: Books 7-9. Blackall, Sophie, illus. (p. 901)
—Ivy + Bean Break the Fossil Record. Blackall, Sophie, illus. (p. 901)
—Ivy + Bean Doomed to Dance. Blackall, Sophie, illus. (p. 901)
—Ivy + Bean Make the Rules Blackall, Sophie, illus. (p. 901)
—Ivy + Bean Make the Rules. (p. 901)
—Ivy + Bean - Make the Rules. Blackall, Sophie, illus. (p. 901)
—Ivy + Bean No News Is Good News. Blackall, Sophie, illus. (p. 901)
—Ivy + Bean Paper Doll Play Set. Blackall, Sophie, illus. (p. 901)
—Ivy + Bean Take Care of the Babysitter. Blackall, Sophie, illus. (p. 901)
—Ivy + Bean Take the Case. Blackall, Sophie, illus. (p. 901)
—Ivy + Bean - What's the Big Idea? Blackall, Sophie, illus. (p. 901)
—Magic Half. (p. 1072)
—Magic in the Mix. (p. 1072)
Barrows, Annie & Blackall, Sophie. Ivy + Bean. (p. 901)
—Ivy + Bean. (p. 901)
—Ivy + Bean & the Ghost That Had to Go (p. 901)
—Ivy + Bean Bound to Be Bad. (p. 901)
—Ivy + Bean Break the Fossil Record (p. 901)
—Ivy + Bean Doomed to Dance. (p. 901)
—Ivy + Bean Take Care of the Babysitter. (p. 901)

B

—Ivy + Bean What's the Big Idea? (p. 901)
Barrows, Annie, et al. Ivy + Bean What's the Big Idea? Blackall, Sophie, illus. (p. 901)
Barrows, Laurie, illus. see Burnett, Karen Gedig.
Barrows, Laurie, illus. see Penberthy, John.
Barrows, Marjorie. Little Duck. Myers, Marie Honre, illus. (p. 1027)
Barrows, Robert. Milestones - the Sixth World. (p. 1142)
Barry, Bridget. Sweet Dreams. (p. 1689)
Barry, Bruce. Roach Approach, Noah's Journey of Faith. (p. 1476)
Barry, Cotter. Adventures of Morgan Morgan the Rhymester. (p. 20)
—By the Numbers. (p. 249)
—Morgan's Family Circle. (p. 1175)
—Rhymester Morgan Morgan In: Elephants Don't Fly. (p. 1468)
Barry, Dave. Worst Class Trip Ever. (p. 1961)
Barry, Dave, jt. auth. see Pearson, Ridley.
Barry, Dave & Pearson, Ridley. Bridge to Never Land. Call, Greg, illus. (p. 227)
—Peter & the Shadow Thieves. Call, Greg, illus. (p. 1346)
—Peter & the Shadow Thieves. Call, Greg & Brown, Roberta, illus. (p. 1346)
—Peter & the Starcatchers. Call, Greg, illus. (p. 1346)
—Peter & the Sword of Mercy. Call, Greg, illus. (p. 1346)
—Peter y los Ladrones. Herrera, Raquel, tr. (p. 1347)
Barry, Debra R. Brady Pickles. (p. 221)
—Debbie's Eyes. Tessier, Beth Marie, photos by. (p. 421)
—Let's Go to the Market. (p. 997)
—Loneliest Leaf. Baker, David, illus. (p. 1046)
Barry, Etheldred B., illus. see Johnston, Annie Fellows.
Barry, Etheldred B., illus. see Johnston, Annie.
Barry, Frances. Big Yellow Sunflower. Barry, Frances, illus. (p. 184)
—Caterpillar to Butterfly. (p. 279)
—Let's Save the Animals. Barry, Frances, illus. (p. 1000)
—Little Eggs, Baby Birds. (p. 1027)
—Salvemos a Los Animales. (p. 1506)
Barry, Holly, et al. Wisdom of Bear. Du Houx, E. M. Cornell, illus. (p. 1939)
Barry, Holly M. Helen Keller's Best Friend Belle. Thermes, Jennifer, illus. (p. 763)
Barry, Jack. Hermit's Handbook. Leue, Mary, ed. (p. 771)
Barry, James, illus. see Hunter, Erin.
Barry, James L., illus. see Hunter, Erin & Jolley, Dan.
Barry, James L., illus. see Hunter, Erin, et al.
Barry, James L., illus. see Hunter, Erin.
Barry, James L., illus. see Jolley, Dan & Hunter, Erin.
Barry, Marian. Baby Moo. (p. 127)
Barry, Maureen. Cumberland Island A to Z, a Scrapbook Journal. Gleason, Anita, illus. (p. 392)
—Freddie the Frog's Adventure. (p. 633)
—Miss Fairfield's Beauty Pageant. (p. 1151)
Barry, Myles. Examining Bridge Collapses. (p. 547)
Barry, Nick. Escape of the Terra-Cotta Soldiers: An Ethan Sparks Adventure. (p. 535)
Barry, Rick. Gunner's Run: A World War II Novel. (p. 732)
—Kiriath's Quest. (p. 961)
Barry, Robert. Mr. Willowby's Christmas Tree. (p. 1187)
Barry, Ron & Fitzgerald, Paula. Me 'n Mom: A Keepsake Scrapbook Journal. Sharp, Chris, illus. (p. 1116)
Barry, Sebastian. Annie Dunne. (p. 86)
—Long Long Way. (p. 1047)
Barry, Sheila Anne, et al. Giant Book of Card Games/Giant Book of Card Tricks: Flip Book. Sterling Publishing Company Staff, ed. (p. 673)
Barry, Steve. Rail Power. (p. 1433)
Barry, Todd J. Pierogies with the Pope: A Tribute to Pope John Paul II, & New Beginnings with Pope Benedict XVI for Young Readers Evenwel, Patricia L., illus. (p. 1357)
—Shoofly Pie with the Pastor: A Journey Through Pennsylvania Dutch Country. Evenwel, Patricia L., illus. (p. 1568)
Barry, Tom. Guerilla Days in Ireland. (p. 728)
Barry, William J. Forever Awakening. (p. 619)
Barsby Ed. D., Carol. Writing Mini-Lessons Grades K-2. (p. 1965)
Barshaw, Ruth McNally. Best Friends Fur-Ever. Barshaw, Ruth McNally, illus. (p. 169)
—Ellie McDoodle: Best Friends Fur-Ever. Barshaw, Ruth McNally, illus. (p. 514)
—Ellie McDoodle: Have Pen, Will Travel. Barshaw, Ruth McNally, illus. (p. 514)
—Ellie McDoodle Diaries: Ellie for President. Barshaw, Ruth McNally, illus. (p. 514)
—Ellie McDoodle Diaries: Most Valuable Player. Barshaw, Ruth McNally, illus. (p. 514)
—Have Pen, Will Travel. Barshaw, Ruth McNally, illus. (p. 754)
—New Kid in School. Barshaw, Ruth McNally, illus. (p. 1245)
—Show Must Go On. Barshaw, Ruth McNally, illus. (p. 1570)
Barske, Dianne. Two Bears There: The Story of Alpun & Oreo. (p. 1803)
Barsocchini, Peter, creator. High School Musical 2 Party Planner. (p. 778)
Barson, Kelly. 45 Pounds. (p. 1997)
—45 Pounds (More or Less) (p. 1997)
Barsony, Piotr. Stories of the Mona Lisa: An Imaginary Museum Tale about the History of Modern Art. (p. 1655)
Barsy, Kalman. Cocodrilo Lloron. Gastaldo, Walter, illus. (p. 337)
—Los Tres Naufragos. Perez-Moliere, Marnie, illus. (p. 1054)
Bart, Kathleen. Global Gourmet: A Multicultural Cookbook. (p. 684)
—Tale of Two Teddies. (p. 1701)
—Town Teddy & Country Bear Go Global. Bart, Kathleen, illus. (p. 1773)
—Town Teddy & Country Bear Tour the USA. Bart, Kathleen, illus. (p. 1773)
—Town Teddy Country Bear. (p. 1773)
Bart, Kathleen, illus. see Dracker, Pune.
Barta, Jeralyn. Rolling with Life. (p. 1485)
Bartalos, Michael. Shadowville. (p. 1558)
Bartch, Lea & Mangrum, Kaylea J. Tucker Goes to Kindergarten: Read & Draw. (p. 1795)
—Tucker Goes to Kindergarten. Mangrum, Kaylea J., illus. (p. 1795)
Bartch, Marian. Math & Stories, Grades K-3. Street Level Studio, illus. (p. 1105)
Bartczak, Peter, illus. see Halter, Loretta.
Bartek, Mary. Funerals & Fly Fishing. (p. 649)
Bartel, Blaine. Little Black Book for Athletes. (p. 1024)
—Little Black Book on Dreaming for Your Future. (p. 1024)
—Little Black Book on How to Get Along with Your Parents. (p. 1024)
—Little Black Book on How to Win a Friend to Christ. (p. 1024)
Bartel, Lynn. Angelina's Angels. (p. 74)
Bartell, Jim. Costa Rica. (p. 368)
—Greece. (p. 720)
—Haiti. (p. 736)
—Kenya. (p. 949)
Bartell, Maggie. Ratsquirrel. (p. 1440)
Bartell, Susan S. Dr. Susan's Girls-Only Weight Loss Guide: The Easy, Fun Way to Look & Feel Good! (p. 475)
Bartelme, Elizabeth. Simon Brute & the Western Adventure. (p. 1577)
Bartels, Korin. Secret in My Shoes. (p. 1541)
Bartels, Lowell. Little Robert: A True Story. Bartels, Mark, illus. (p. 1036)
Bartels, Mark, illus. see Bartels, Lowell.
Barter, James. Ancient Persians. (p. 70)
—Colonial Boston. (p. 341)
—Colonial New York. (p. 341)
—Idi Amin. (p. 852)
—Influential Figures of Ancient Rome. (p. 873)
—Medieval Knight. (p. 1119)
—San Francisco in the 1960s. (p. 1510)
Barter, James E. Colorado. (p. 343)
—Medieval Constantinople. (p. 1119)
Bartfeld, Martha & Hutchinson, Alberta. Infinite Coloring Mandala Designs. (p. 873)
Bartgen M.S. Ccc-Slp-L, Katie Foy. Around the World in a Dream. (p. 101)
Barth, Alexandra, illus. see Mahadeo Rdh, Elizabeth.
Barth, Amy. Annabelle's Secret: A Story about Sexual Abuse. Kinra, Richa, illus. (p. 85)
—Annabelle's Secret. Kinra, Richa, illus. (p. 85)
—Will Was All Boy: A Story about Sexual Abuse. Kinra, Richa, illus. (p. 1932)
Barth, April. Mira nuestros Patrones. (p. 1148)
—¿Cuántos en Total? (p. 388)
Barth, Berndt & Barth, Katrin. Learning Fencing. (p. 985)
—Training Fencing. (p. 1777)
Barth, Daisy. Thank You, Teacher, Because... (p. 1725)
Barth, Kathleen E. Amazing Adventures of Quigley D Pigley & His Friends: How to Become an Astronaut. (p. 52)
—Amazing Adventures of Quigley D Pigley & His Friends. (p. 52)
Barth, Katrin, jt. auth. see Barth, Berndt.
Barth, Katrin & Boesing, Lothar. Learning Basketball. (p. 985)
Barth, Katrin & Dietze, Jurgen. Swimming: Learning. (p. 1691)
—Swimming: Training. (p. 1691)
Barth, Katrin & Heuchert, Richard. Learning Volleyball. (p. 986)
Barth, Katrin & Linkerhand, Antje. Training Volleyball. (p. 1777)
Barth, Katrin & Nordmann, Lutz. Learning Field Hockey. (p. 985)
Barth, Katrin & Sieber, Antonia. Learning Horseback Riding. (p. 985)
—Training Horseback Riding. (p. 1777)
Barth, Katrin & Zempel, Ullrich, trs. from GER. Learning Soccer. (p. 985)
—Training Soccer. (p. 1777)
Barth, Kelly. Rise & Fall of the Taliban. (p. 1474)
Barth, Kelly, ed. Declaration of Independence. (p. 422)
Barth, Kelly L., ed. Declaration of Independence. (p. 422)
barth, lillian. Delma the Duck. (p. 425)
Barth, Lillian. Duchess of Freeman Street. (p. 487)
—Tommy & the Sandman. (p. 1764)
Barth, Linda J. Bridgetender's Boy. Lorenzetti, Doreen, illus. (p. 227)
—Hidden New Jersey. Mitchell, Hazel, illus. (p. 776)
Barth, T. N. L. In the Dragon's Depths. (p. 866)
Bartha, Alysa. Petal's Wish. (p. 1346)
Barthelme, Donald. Slightly Irregular Fire Engine. (p. 1590)
Barthelmes, Andrew, illus. see Michels, Dia L.
Barthelmes, Andrew, illus. see Wallace, Daniel.
Barthes, Roland. Language of Fashion. Stafford, Andy & Carter, Michael, eds. (p. 975)
Bartholomeusz, James. Grey Star. (p. 723)
—White Fox. (p. 1913)
Bartholomew, illus. see Berry, Joy.
Bartholomew, illus. see Berry, Rob & Duey, Kathleen.
Bartholomew, illus. see Leonard, Marcia.
Bartholomew, Al, jt. auth. see Bartholomew, Linda.
Bartholomew, Andrew & Bartholomew, Hailey. Ruby Who? Zinn, Alama, illus. (p. 1493)
Bartholomew, Carl R. Plane Phenomenon: The Pawnshop Mysteries. (p. 1367)
Bartholomew, Hailey, jt. auth. see Bartholomew, Andrew.
Bartholomew, Jane, ed. see Hassler, Jill K.
Bartholomew, Linda & Bartholomew, Al. Adventures in the Tropics. Bartholomew, Linda & Bartholomew, Al, photos by. (p. 16)
—Rain Forest Book for Kids. Bartholomew, Linda & Bartholomew, Al, photos by. (p. 1434)
Bartl, Allison. 101 Pep-Up Games for Children: Refreshing, Recharging, Refocusing. Puth, Klaus, illus. (p. 1999)
—101 Relaxation Games for Children: Finding a Little Peace & Quiet in Between. Puth, Klaus, illus. (p. 2000)
Bartle, Jean Ashworth. Sound Advice: Becoming a Better Children's Choir Conductor. (p. 1615)
Bartlett, Adam. Littlest Giant. (p. 1039)
Bartlett, Alison. Erice the Reindeer. (p. 533)
Bartlett, Alison, illus. see French, Vivian.
Bartlett, Alison, illus. see Ross, Mandy.
Bartlett, Alison, illus. see Thomas, Janet.
Bartlett, Alison, jt. auth. see Puttock, Simon.
Bartlett, Alyssa Joy, illus. see Penley, Janet.
Bartlett, Arthur C. Yankee Doodle: The Story of A Pioneer Boy & His Dog. Cue, Harold, illus. (p. 1968)
Bartlett, Beverly. Cover Girl Confidential. (p. 373)
Bartlett, Brittany D. Cooper the Curious: And the First Snowfall. (p. 365)
Bartlett, Don, jt. auth. see Hole, Stian.
Bartlett, Don, jt. auth. see Hovland, Henrik.
Bartlett, Don, tr. see Hole, Stian.
Bartlett, E. M., contrib. by. Victory in Jesus. (p. 1840)
Bartlett, Helen, jt. auth. see Bartlett, Lorrie.
Bartlett, Irene. New Testament: Bible Poems for Children. (p. 1247)
—Old Testament: Bible Poems for Children. (p. 1284)
Bartlett, J. L., jt. auth. see Helmrath, M. O.
Bartlett, John. Bartlett's Bible Quotations. (p. 140)
—Bartlett's Shakespeare Quotations. (p. 140)
—Bartlett's Words to Live By: Advice & Inspiration for Everyday Life. (p. 140)
Bartlett, Karen T. Kid's Guide to Chicago. Brown, Don, illus. (p. 953)
Bartlett, Lorrie & Bartlett, Helen. Kicker & the Iron Horse: Book Ii. (p. 951)
—Kicker & the Lost Mine: Book Iii. (p. 951)
—Kicker & the Missing Water: Book I. (p. 951)
Bartlett, Mel. Meet President Obama. (p. 1122)
Bartlett, Melissa. What Makes the Sun So Hot? (p. 1892)
Bartlett, Myke. Fire in the Sea. (p. 590)
Bartlett, Philip A. Mystery of the Circle of Fire: A Roy Stover Story. (p. 1225)
Bartlett, Rebecca, illus. see Stern, D. G.
Bartlett, Robert Merrill. Story of Thanksgiving. Compoint, Sally Wern, illus. (p. 1660)
Bartlett, Roberta. How I Met an Alien. (p. 810)
Bartlett, Roger. History of Russia. (p. 784)
Bartlett, Sarah. Women, Sex & Astrology: What Your Star Sign Reveals about Your Sex Life. (p. 1946)
Bartlett, Susan & Wrenn, Luanne. Opening Day. (p. 1300)
Bartlett, T. C. Tuba Lessons. Felix, Monique, illus. (p. 1795)
Bartlett's. Bartlett's Roget's Thesaurus. Little, Brown and Company Staff, ed. (p. 140)
Bartley, Christopher. Indian Philosophy A-Z. (p. 871)
Bartley, Niccole. Land That I Love: Regions of the United States. (p. 974)
—Mid-Atlantic. (p. 1137)
—New England. (p. 1244)
—South. (p. 1616)
—Southwest. (p. 1617)
—West Coast. (p. 1876)
Bartley, Paula. Votes for Women, 1860-1928. (p. 1850)
Barto, Jean S. Critter Chronicles. (p. 384)
Barto, Linda iLham. Where the Ghost Camel Grins: Muslim Fables for Families of All Faiths. (p. 1909)
Bartoletti, Susan Campbell. Black Potatoes: The Story of the Great Irish Famine, 1845-1850. (p. 196)
—Boy Who Dared. (p. 219)
—Down the Rabbit Hole: The Diary of Pringle Rose. (p. 474)
—Flag Maker: A Story of the Star-Spangled Banner. Nivola, Claire A., illus. (p. 602)
—Hitler Youth: Growing up in Hitler's Shadow. (p. 786)
—Kids on Strike! (p. 954)
—Naamah & the Ark at Night. Meade, Holly, illus. (p. 1227)
—Nobody's Diggier Than a Dog. Giacobbe, Beppe, illus. (p. 1262)
—Terrible Typhoid Mary: A True Story of the Deadliest Cook in America. (p. 1721)
—They Called Themselves the K. K. K. The Birth of an American Terrorist Group. (p. 1732)
Bartoletti, Susan Campbell, adapted by. Untold History of the United States, 1898-1945 (p. 1823)
Bartolini, Egle, illus. see Scott, Cavan, et al.
Bartoll, Jean-Claude. Chechen Guerrilla (p. 295)
Bartolome, Teresita Africano. We Lost Our House (p. 1867)
—Where Is Warren D. Worm? (p. 1909)
Bartolomeo, Christina. Snowed In. (p. 1600)
Bartolucci, Marisa, ed. see Young, Lucie.
Barton, Alica, tr. see Shurin, Masha.
Barton, Angie. Hi My Name Is Hanna & I'm Adopted. (p. 775)
Barton, Bethany. I'm Trying to Love Spiders. Barton, Bethany, illus. (p. 860)
Barton, Bethany, illus. see Hasak-Lowy, Todd.
Barton Billman, Hilary. How to Draw the Life & Times of William Henry Harrison. (p. 819)
Barton, Bob. Trouble on the Voyage. (p. 1790)
Barton, Brittney B. Piper & Pickle: Smile. Young, Susan, illus. (p. 1361)
Barton, Bruce, ed. see Beissel, Henry.
Barton, Byron. Boats. Barton, Byron, illus. (p. 205)
—Gallinita Roja. (p. 653)
—My Bike. Barton, Byron, illus. (p. 1197)
—My Bus. Barton, Byron, illus. (p. 1199)
—My Bus Board Book. Barton, Byron, illus. (p. 1199)
—My Car. (p. 1200)
—My Car. Barton, Byron, illus. (p. 1200)
—My House. Barton, Byron, illus. (p. 1211)
Barton, Byron, illus. see Kalan, Robert.
Barton, Carol. Pocket Paper Engineer: How to Make Pop-Ups Step-by-Step. (p. 1375)
Barton, Chris. 88 Instruments. (p. 1998)
—Amazing Age of John Roy Lynch. Tate, Don, illus. (p. 52)
—Attack! Boss! Cheat Code! A Gamer's Alphabet. Spiotto, Joey, illus. (p. 113)
—Can I See Your I. D.? True Stories of False Identities. Hoppe, Paul, illus. (p. 258)
—Day-Glo Brothers: The True Story of Bob & Joe Switzer's Bright Ideas & Brand-New Colors. Persiani, Tony, illus. (p. 413)
—Mighty Truck. Cummings, Troy, illus. (p. 1140)
—Nutcracker Comes to America: How Three Ballet-Loving Brothers Created a Holiday Tradition. Gendron, Cathy, illus. (p. 1274)
—Shark vs. Train. Lichtenheld, Tom, illus. (p. 1562)
Barton, David Charles, creator. Decision for Christ Study of the Bible. (p. 421)
Barton, Deborah, illus. see Norberg, A.
Barton, Elizabeth & Shaw, Natalie. Olivia Leaps! Osterhold, Jared, illus. (p. 1286)
Barton, Elizabeth Dennis, jt. auth. see Shaw, Natalie.
Barton, Harry, illus. see Hubbard, Margaret Ann.
Barton, Jen. If Chocolate Were Purple. Matsuoka, Yoko, illus. (p. 852)
—What's Your Story, Amelia Earhart? (p. 1900)
—What's Your Story, Harriet Tubman? (p. 1900)
Barton, Jenna. C Is for Cure. (p. 250)
Barton, Jill, illus. see Dunbar, Joyce.
Barton, Jill, illus. see Fox, Mem.
Barton, Jill, illus. see Hest, Amy.
Barton, Jill, illus. see King-Smith, Dick.
Barton, Jill, illus. see Root, Phyllis.
Barton, Jill, illus. see Waddell, Martin.
Barton, John. Monkey Boy That Stood Up. (p. 1165)
Barton, Matthew. Winding Road: A Child's Treasury of Poems, Verses, & Prayers. (p. 1936)
Barton, Patrice, illus. see Cheng, Andrea.
Barton, Patrice, illus. see Crum, Shutta.
Barton, Patrice, illus. see Gerber, Carole.
Barton, Patrice, illus. see Hallinan, P. K.
Barton, Patrice, illus. see Hoberman, Mary Ann.
Barton, Patrice, illus. see Ludwig, Trudy.
Barton, Patrice, illus. see McPike, Elizabeth.
Barton, Patrice, illus. see Mora, Pat & Martinez, Libby.
Barton, Patrice, illus. see Shaw, Gina.
Barton, Patrice, illus. see Wortche, Allison.
Barton, Renee. Amagestic: A Caterpillar's Journey. (p. 52)
Barton, Renee L. ABC Story: Featuring: William. (p. 3)
Barton, Roy. Teaching Secondary Science with ICT. (p. 1710)
Barton, Stephen. Violin Improvisation: Fiddle Charts & Finger Patterns. (p. 1843)
Barton, Suzanne, illus. see Metcalf, Paula.
Barton, Tamra Clum. Adventures of Lucky the Leaf. (p. 20)
Barton, Zoe. Always Neverland. (p. 51)
Bartone, Elisa. Peppe the Lamplighter. Lewin, Ted, illus. (p. 1340)
Bartone, John C., Sr. Bioterrorism Potential of Hantaan Virus with Index & Medical Analysis of New Information for Reference & Research: Index & Ana. (p. 190)
Bartos, Judeen. Do Schools Prepare Students for a Global Economy? (p. 457)
—Do U. S. Schools Prepare Students for a Global Economy? (p. 457)
—Food Safety. (p. 614)
—High School Dropouts. (p. 778)
Bartos, Judeen, ed. What Is the Role of Technology in Education? (p. 1890)
Bartoszek, Julie, ed. Chicago Unzipped: A Guidebook to Chicago. (p. 299)
Bartoszko, Alexandra, tr. see Davis, Jim.
Bartoszko, Alexandra, tr. see Watterson, Bill.
Bartow, Philip. T & the Jello Castle-Book 1. (p. 1693)
—T & the Jello Castle-Book 2: Bio Bots. (p. 1693)
Bartowski, Amy. Shapes at the Store: Identify & Describe Shapes. (p. 1560)
Bartowski, Sara. Gavin Volunteers! (p. 658)
Bartram, Bob, illus. see Patten, Lewis B.
Bartram, Simon. Man on the Moon: A Day in the Life of Bob. Bartram, Simon, illus. (p. 1085)
Bartram, Simon, illus. see Lewis, J. Patrick.
Baruch, M. P. Spend the Day with Me. Arscott, Dean, illus. (p. 1625)
Baruffi, Andrea. Henry's Wrong Turn. (p. 769)
Baruffi, Andrea, illus. see Linn, Margot.
Barulich-Liederbach, Terri & Liederbach, Tom. Memory Chair. (p. 1126)
Barutan, Kizaki. Manga Techniques (p. 1087)
—Robot Design Techniques for Beginners. (p. 1480)
Baruzzi, Agnese. Aladdin: A Cut-Paper Book. (p. 33)
—Opposites: A Cut-Paper Book. Baruzzi, Agnese, illus. (p. 1300)
Baruzzi, Agnese, illus. see Ikids Staff.
Baruzzi, Agnese, illus. see Lupton, Hugh.
Baruzzi, Agnese, illus. see Tango Books Staff.
Baruzzi, Agnese, jt. auth. see Aesop Enterprise Inc. Staff.
Baruzzi, Agnese, jt. auth. see Collodi, Carlo.
Baruzzi, Agnese, jt. auth. see Natalini, Sandro.
Baruzzi, Agnese & Natalini, Sandro. True Story of Little Red Riding Hood. Baruzzi, Agnese & Natalini, Sandro, illus. (p. 1793)
Barwell, Matthew W., ed. see Parvensky Barwell, Catherine A.
Barwick. Sail Main5 Weather Alert Nf. (p. 1503)
BARWICK, Adam Mark. Three tales of Twaddle. (p. 1744)
Barwin, Steven. Fadeaway (p. 562)
—Hardball (p. 748)
—Hurricane Heat (p. 829)
—Icebreaker (p. 851)
—Making Select (p. 1082)
—Rock Dogs (p. 1482)
—Sk8er (p. 1583)
—Spiked (p. 1627)
Barwood, Lee. Klassic Koalas: Ancient Aboriginal Tales in New Retellings, BW Edition. (p. 963)
Barwood, Lee, jt. auth. see Barwood, Lee.
Barwood, Lee & Barwood, Lee. Klassic Koalas: Ancient Aboriginal Tales in New Retellings. (p. 963)
Barzak, Christopher. Wonders of the Invisible World. (p. 1949)
Barzyk, Michele Shuptar. Room at the Inn. (p. 1488)
Bas, Mercè Escardó I. Three Little Pigs/Los Tres Cerditos. Joan, Pere, illus. (p. 1743)
Bas, Mercè Escardó I & Boada, Francesc. Ugly Duckling. Capdevila, Francesc, illus. (p. 1808)
Basaar, Holly E. Unwrapping Joy. (p. 1824)
Basal, Patricia. Sammy Discovers Jesus. (p. 1508)
Basaluzzo, Constanza, illus. see Bullard, Lisa.
Basaluzzo, Constanza, illus. see Currie, Robin.
Basaluzzo, Constanza, illus. see Kafka, Rebecca.
Basaluzzo, Constanza, illus. see Lee, Quinlan B.
Basaluzzo, Constanza, illus. see Walter Foster Custom Creative Team.

Basaluzzo, Constanza & Stanford, Elisa. Baby Bible 1,2,3 (p. 125)
Bascle, Brian, illus. see Adamson, Heather.
Bascle, Brian, illus. see Burgan, Michael & Hoena, Blake A.
Bascle, Brian, illus. see Burgan, Michael.
Bascle, Brian, illus. see Collins, Terry.
Bascle, Brian, illus. see Fandel, Jennifer.
Bascle, Brian, illus. see Fein, Eric.
Bascle, Brian, illus. see Lassieur, Allison.
Bascle, Brian, illus. see Martin, Michael & Martin, Michael J.
Bascle, Brian, illus. see Martin, Michael.
Bascle, Brian, illus. see Niz, Xavier & Niz, Xavier W.
Bascle, Brian, illus. see Olson, Nathan & Capstone Press Staff.
Bascle, Brian, illus. see Olson, Nathan.
Bascle, Brian, illus. see Sautter, Aaron.
Bascle, Brian, illus. see Smalley, Roger.
Bascomb, Neal. Nazi Hunters: How a Team of Spies & Survivors Captured the World's Most Notorious Nazi. (p. 1238)
—Nazi Hunters. (p. 1238)
Bascome, Glenn, ed. see Wynn, Mychal.
Bascoul, Eric, jt. auth. see Draper, Sharon M.
Base, Graeme. Enigma: A Magical Mystery. (p. 530)
—Jewel Fish of Karnak. (p. 917)
—Jungle Drums. (p. 935)
—Last King of Angkor Wat. (p. 978)
—Legend of the Golden Snail. (p. 989)
—Little Elephants. (p. 1027)
—Uno's Garden. (p. 1822)
—Water Hole: Coloring Book. (p. 1862)
—Water Hole. Base, Graeme, illus. (p. 1862)
—Water Hole Board Book. (p. 1862)
Base, Graeme, et al. Dinosaurs in Your Backyard: The Coolest, Scariest Creatures Ever Found in the USA! (p. 445)
Basel, Roberta. From Cane to Sugar. (p. 642)
—From Corn to Cereal. (p. 642)
—From Tomato to Ketchup (p. 644)
—What Do Banks Do? (p. 1882)
Basel, Roberta & Compass Point Books Staff. Sequoyah: Inventor of Written Cherokee (p. 1552)
Baseman, Gary, illus. see Harris, John.
Basen, Ryan. Charlotte Bobcats. (p. 293)
—Dwight Howard: Gifted & Giving Basketball Star. (p. 491)
—Georgetown Hoyas. (p. 665)
—Got Your Back: Dealing with Friends & Enemies. (p. 703)
—Jeff Burton: Chasing the Championship. (p. 911)
—Kyle Busch: Gifted & Giving Racing Star. (p. 969)
—Steve Nash: Leader on & off the Court. (p. 1649)
—Texas Rangers. (p. 1724)
—Tony Stewart: Rocket on the Racetrack. (p. 1766)
—Washington Redskins. (p. 1860)
Basford, Johanna. Enchanted Forest. (p. 523)
—Secret Garden: An Inky Treasure Hunt & Coloring Book. (p. 1541)
—Secret Garden: An Inky Treasure Hunt & Colouring Book. (p. 1541)
Bash, Barbara. Shadows of Night: The Hidden World of the Little Brown Bat. Bash, Barbara, illus. (p. 1558)
Bash, Sarah E. My Daddy Is Strong, Handsome, & Tall. (p. 1201)
Basha, Irena Canaj. Birthday Party, It Was Saturday... (p. 193)
Basham, Tom. Accidental Evie. Calvert, Lissa, illus. (p. 8)
—No Vacancy! (p. 1260)
—Sailing Home. Calvert, Lissa, illus. (p. 1503)
Basham, Tom & Calvert, Lissa. Sailing Home. (p. 1503)
Bashe, Kayla. Kitty Cadawell & the Shadowslayers of Fyrn. (p. 963)
Basher, Simon. ABC Kids. (p. 3)
—Algebra & Geometry: Anything but Square! Basher, Simon, illus. (p. 38)
—Basher Basics: Space Exploration. Basher, Simon, illus. (p. 141)
—Basher Science: Climate Change. (p. 141)
—Basher Science: Extreme Biology. Basher, Simon, illus. (p. 141)
Basher, Simon, illus. see Dingle, Adrian, et al.
Basher, Simon, illus. see Field, Jacob & Grant, R. J.
Basher, Simon, jt. auth. see Dingle, Adrian.
Basher, Simon, jt. auth. see Gilpin, Daniel.
Basher, Simon, jt. auth. see Green, Dan.
Basher, Simon & Budzik, Mary. Basher Basics: Creative Writing. Basher, Simon, illus. (p. 141)
—Grammar. Basher, Simon, illus. (p. 706)
—Mythology: Oh My! Gods & Godesses. (p. 1227)
—Punctuation: The Write Stuff! Basher, Simon, illus. (p. 1417)
Basher, Simon & Dingle, Adrian. Periodic Table: Elements with Style! Basher, Simon, illus. (p. 1343)
Basher, Simon & Gilpin, Dan. Planet Earth: What Planet Are You On? Basher, Simon, illus. (p. 1367)
Basher, Simon & Green, Dan. Astronomy: Out of This World! Basher, Simon, illus. (p. 109)
—Basher Science: Microbiology. Basher, Simon, illus. (p. 141)
—Basher Science - Technology: A Byte-Sized World! Basher, Simon, illus. (p. 141)
—Chemistry: Getting a Big Reaction! Basher, Simon, illus. (p. 297)
—Dinosaurs: The Bare Bones! Basher, Simon, illus. (p. 444)
—Human Body: A Book with Guts! Basher, Simon, illus. (p. 825)
—Math: A Book You Can Count On! Basher, Simon, illus. (p. 1105)
—Music. Basher, Simon, illus. (p. 1193)
—Oceans: Making Waves! Basher, Simon, illus. (p. 1277)
—Physics: Why Matter Matters! Basher, Simon, illus. (p. 1353)
—Rocks & Minerals: A Gem of a Book! Basher, Simon, illus. (p. 1483)
—Technology: A Byte-Sized World! Basher, Simon, illus. (p. 1711)
—Weather: Whipping up a Storm! Basher, Simon, illus. (p. 1869)
Basher, Simon, et al. States & Capitals: United We Stand! (p. 1644)
—U. S. Presidents: Oval Office All-Stars! (p. 1807)
—U. S. Presidents: The Oval Office All-Stars! (p. 1807)
Bashline, Trent. How Jake & Daisy Stopped Bullying at Dogwood Elementary. (p. 810)
Basic Skills Agency Staff, jt. auth. see Croft, Andy.
Basic Skills Agency Staff & Blackmore, Sarah. Titanic. (p. 1757)
Basic Skills Agency Staff, et al. Being a Dj. (p. 160)
Basic, Zdenko. Steampunk Charles Dickens' a Christmas Carol. (p. 1646)
Basic, Zdenko, illus. see Gurney, Stella.
Basic, Zdenko, illus. see Worms, Penny.
Basic, Zdenko & Sumberac, Manuel. Steampunk: H. G. Wells. (p. 1646)
Basil, Timothy, illus. see DiCamillo, Kate.
Basile, Javier, illus. see Baredes, Carla & Lotersztain, Ileana.
Basile, Javier, illus. see Cerda, Marcelo.
Basilico, Gabriele, photos by see Bonami, Francesco.
Basinger, Carol. Everything You Need to Know about Deafness. (p. 545)
Basir, A. As Told By: Sofie. (p. 105)
Baskerville. New Baby. (p. 1243)
Baskerville, Elliott. Nig Peas & Thweebies. (p. 1252)
Baskette, Molly Phinney, jt. auth. see Liss-Levinson, Nechama.
Baskey, Kim, illus. see Hanny, Diane.
Baskey, Teresa. History & Geography: U. S. History (p. 783)
Baskin, Jason, illus. see Flowers, Pam.
Baskin, Leonard, illus. see Michelson, Richard.
Baskin, Lyle, illus. see Inman, Robert.
Baskin, Nora Raleigh. All We Know of Love. (p. 46)
—Anything but Typical. (p. 91)
—Basketball (or Something Like It) (p. 143)
—Nine, Ten: A September 11 Story. (p. 1256)
—Ruby on the Outside. (p. 1493)
—Runt. (p. 1497)
—Subway Love. (p. 1671)
—Summer Before Boys. (p. 1674)
—Surfacing. (p. 1685)
—Truth about My Bat Mitzvah. (p. 1794)
Baskwill, Jane. If Peace Is... Carter, Stephanie, illus. (p. 854)
—Langage Integre Et L'Evalua... Whole Language Checklists. (p. 974)
Basmadjian, E. E. B-2 Spirit. (p. 122)
Basman, Michael. Jovenes Jugadores de Ajedrez. (p. 929)
Basman, Michael & Ling, Mary. Chess for Kids. (p. 298)
Basmenji, Kaveh. Tehran Blues: Youth Culture in Iran. (p. 1715)
Basner, Shannon. Mojo's Magical Ride: True Story of Courage, Transformation & Love; an Alaskan Dog Rescue Story. (p. 1160)
Basoff, Kathleen. Merdove Cove. (p. 1127)
Basora, Bettye. Pride's Prize. (p. 1399)
Basore, Polly M. Santa's Stray. Williams, Carlene H., illus. (p. 1513)
—Santa's Stray in A Piano for Christmas. Williams, Carlene H., illus. (p. 1513)
Bass, Alexis. Love & Other Theories. (p. 1059)
—What's Broken Between Us. (p. 1896)
Bass, Barbara. Gus the Bus Driver. (p. 732)
Bass, Barbra. Crocheted Santa. (p. 384)
Bass, Elissa. E-Cigarettes: The Risks of Addictive Nicotine & Toxic Chemicals. (p. 492)
Bass, Elissa, jt. auth. see Hart, Joyce.
Bass, Elissa, jt. auth. see King, David C.
Bass, Guy. Dinkin Dings & the Double from Dimension 9. Williamson, Pete, illus. (p. 440)
—Dinkin Dings & the Frightening Things. Williamson, Pete, illus. (p. 440)
—Ghost of Grotteskew Williamson, Pete, illus. (p. 671)
—Pirate's Eye Williamson, Pete, illus. (p. 1363)
—Spider's Lair. Williamson, Pete, illus. (p. 1627)
—Stitch Head Williamson, Pete, illus. (p. 1651)
Bass, Hester. Secret World of Walter Anderson. Lewis, E. B., illus. (p. 1544)
—Seeds of Freedom: The Peaceful Integration of Huntsville, Alabama. Lewis, E. B., illus. (p. 1547)
Bass, Hester & Anderson, Walter Inglis. Secret World of Walter Anderson. Lewis, E. B., illus. (p. 1544)
Bass, Hester Thompson. So Many Houses. Arzoumanian, Alik, illus. (p. 1602)
Bass, Hester Thompson & Thompson-Bass, Hester. So Many Houses. Arzoumanian, Alik, illus. (p. 1602)
Bass, Jennifer Vogel. Edible Colors. Bass, Jennifer Vogel, photos by. (p. 504)
—Edible Numbers. (p. 504)
Bass, Joy Wine. Flamingephants: Story, Songs, & Illustrations. (p. 602)
Bass, Jules. Herb, the Vegetarian Dragon: Book & Bendo Gift Set. Harter, Debbie, illus. (p. 769)
—Herb, the Vegetarian Dragon. Harter, Debbie, illus. (p. 769)
Bass, Jules, jt. auth. see Blackstone, Stella.
Bass, Jules & Harter, Debbie. Herb the Vegetarian Dragon. (p. 769)
Bass, Karen. Drummer Girl (p. 487)
—Graffiti Knight (p. 705)
—Summer of Fire (p. 1674)
Bass, Keisha Y., creator. Ladybug Ladybug. (p. 971)
Bass, L. G. & Geringer, Laura. Boom Boom Go Away! Ibatoulline, Bagram, illus. (p. 213)
Bass, Patrik Henry. Zero Degree Zombie Zone. Craft, Jerry, illus. (p. 1986)
Bass, Rachel, illus. see Noble, Kate.
Bass, Ron, jt. auth. see Stoltz, Adrienne.
Bass, Ruth. Sarah's Daughter. (p. 1514)
Bass, Saul. Henri's Walk to Paris. (p. 767)
Bass, Scott. Surf! Your Guide to Longboarding, Shortboarding, Tubing, Aerials, Hanging Ten & More. (p. 1685)
Bass, Sheila M. Because You Cared. (p. 155)
Bass, William E. Gift for Sant. Salazar, Vivian Rose, illus. (p. 675)
—Santa Revisits His Secret Little Helper. Salazar, Vivian, illus. (p. 1513)
Bassa, illus. see Bailer, Darice, et al.
Bassan, Malca. Por Tu Propio Bien. Andrusier, Devorah Leah et al, eds. (p. 1386)
Bassani, Srimalie, illus. see Ahmed, Suhel.
Bassarath, Haydn, jt. auth. see Whiteley, Peter.
Basseches, K. B., photos by see Weill, Cynthia.
Bassede, Francine. Dia con los Cerditos. (p. 433)
Bassett, Alisa Cuthbertson. Threads of Time. (p. 1741)
Bassett, Arthur R., et al. Unquiet Grave. Oxford University Press Staff & Bassett, Jennifer, eds. (p. 1822)
Bassett, Jeni, illus. see Kroll, Steven.
Bassett, Jeni, illus. see Ryan, Cheryl, et al.
Bassett, Jeni, jt. auth. see Kroll, Steven.
Bassett, Jennifer. Milo. (p. 1144)
—Watchers. (p. 1861)
Bassett, Jennifer, ed. see Akinyemi, Rowena & Marryat.
Bassett, Jennifer, ed. see Akinyemi, Rowena.
Bassett, Jennifer, ed. see Bassett, Arthur R., et al.
Bassett, Jennifer, ed. see Duckworth, Michael.
Bassett, Jennifer, ed. see Gilbert, Harry.
Bassett, Jennifer, ed. see Grahame, Kenneth & Grahame, Kenneth.
Bassett, Jennifer, ed. see Mowat, Diane.
Bassett, Jennifer, ed. see Nesbit, E.
Bassett, Jennifer, ed. see Shipton, Paul & Henry, O.
Bassett, Jennifer, ed. see Vicary, Tim.
Bassett, Jennifer, jt. auth. see de Bernières, Louis.
Bassett, Jennifer, jt. ed. see Oxford University Press Staff.
Bassett, Jennifer & Stewart, Sue. Recycling. Oxford University Press Staff & Lindop, Christine, eds. (p. 1453)
Bassett, Jennifer, ed. Long White Cloud: Stories from New Zealand. (p. 1047)
Bassett, John. Experiments with Weather & Climate. (p. 549)
Bassett, John M., et al. Laura Secord (p. 980)
Bassett, Kate. Words & Their Meanings. (p. 1951)
Bassett, Madge A. At Bumblebee Farm. Bassett, Madge A., illus. (p. 110)
Bassett, Melvyn, ed. see Wynn, Mychal.
Bassett, Steven. Anatomy & Physiology. (p. 67)
Bassett-Giehtbrock, Dianne. Sissy & Me. (p. 1581)
Bassil, Andrea & van Gogh, Vincent. Vincent Van Gogh. (p. 1842)
—Vincent van Gogh. (p. 1842)
Bassington, Cyril. Your Bones. (p. 1980)
—Your Brain. (p. 1980)
—Your Heart. (p. 1980)
Bassis, Volodymyr & Dhilawala, Sakina. Ukraine. (p. 1808)
Bassler, Grace. It Comes from a Farm! (p. 893)
Bassler, Joni. Chee Choo's Adventures Leonard, Kaycee, illus. (p. 295)
Basso, Bill, illus. see Dadey, Debbie & Dadey, Nathan.
Basso, Bill, illus. see Dadey, Debbie.
Basso, Bill, illus. see McMullan, Kate.
Basso, Michael. Addictions Workbook for Children: For Parents & Teachers Too. Scarfone, Dorothy, ed. (p. 11)
—Autism Spectrum Disorders Workbook: For Kids, Parents & Teachers Too. Scarfone, Dorothy, ed. (p. 117)
—Global Warming & Environmental Workbook: Getting the Attention of Children, Parents & Teachers. (p. 685)
—Health & Wellness Workbook for Children: For Parents & Teachers Too. Scarfone, Dorothy, ed. (p. 757)
—I Miss Grandma Workbook: Teaching Children about Alzheimer's Disease: Photographic Edition. (p. 844)
—Mental & Emotional Health Workbook for Children: For Parents & Teachers Too. Scarfone, Dorothy, ed. (p. 1126)
—Susan, Andy & Milton Learn about the Cycle of Life Workbook: Photographic Edition. Scarfone, Dorothy, ed. (p. 1687)
Basso, Michael J. Underground Guide to Teenage Sexuality. (p. 1814)
Basso, Michael R., Michael R. Susan & Andy's Magical Adventure Workbook. (p. 1687)
Bast, Anya. Chosen Sin. (p. 311)
—Witch Blood. (p. 1941)
Bast, Michael. Death's Academy. (p. 420)
Basta, Mary, illus. see Boule, Mary Null.
Basta, Mary, jt. illus. see Liddell, Daniel.
Basta, Stormie, illus. see Wilson, Angela.
Bastakos, Matina. Emma Emu's Eager Environmental Endeavour: 'E' as in Earth. (p. 519)
Bastedo, Jamie. Free As the Wind Tooke, Susan, illus. (p. 634)
—On Thin Ice (p. 1292)
—Sila's Revenge (p. 1575)
Bastian, Greg. Goldseekers. (p. 696)
Bastian, Kimberlee Ann. Orphan, the Soulcatcher, & the Black Blizzard. (p. 1304)
Bastianich, Lidia Matticchio. Lidia's Christmas Kitchen. Logan, Laura, illus. (p. 1007)
—Lidia's Egg-Citing Farm Adventure. Graef, Renee, illus. (p. 1007)
—Lidia's Family Kitchen: Nonna's Birthday Surprise. Graef, Renee, illus. (p. 1007)
Bastida, Xohana, tr. see Landy, Derek & Landy, Derek.
Bastidas Padilla, Carlos. Intrépido Simon: Aventuras del Libertador. Sierra, Juan Ramon, illus. (p. 882)
Bastien, Valerie, illus. see Vendera, Jaime & McGee, Anne Loader.
Bastin, Marjolein. Christmas with Vera! (p. 316)
Bastone, William, et al. Dog Dialed 911: A Book of Lists from the Smoking Gun. (p. 461)
Bastrya, Judy. Living in Jamaica. (p. 1041)
Basu, Arpon. Hockey's Hottest Players: The on- & off-Ice Stories of the Superstars. (p. 787)
—NHL Enforcers: The Rough & Tough Guys of Hockey. (p. 1250)
Basu, Jayinee. HJBRL - A Nonsense Story by Sukumar Ray. (p. 786)
Basu, Suddhasattwa, illus. see Calasso, Roberto & Parks, Tim.
Basulto, Rita, illus. see MacHado, Ana Maria.
Basurto, Carmen G. Mis Primeras Letras: Lectura y Escritura. (p. 1150)
Basye, Dale E. Blimpo: The Third Circle of Heck. Vol. 3 Dob, Bob, illus. (p. 199)
—Fibble. Dob, Bob, illus. (p. 583)
—Precocia: the Sixth Circle of Heck. Dob, Bob, illus. (p. 1394)
—Rapacia. Dob, Bob, illus. (p. 1439)
—Snivel: the Fifth Circle of Heck. Dob, Bob, illus. (p. 1598)
—Where the Bad Kids Go. Dob, Bob, illus. (p. 1909)
—Wise Acres: the Seventh Circle of Heck. Dob, Bob, illus. (p. 1939)
Basye, Dottie. Angel with Big Feet. (p. 74)
Bataille Lange, Nikki. Extreme Monsters Joke Book. Stuby, Tim, illus. (p. 556)
Bataille, Marion. 10. (p. 1993)
—ABC3D. (p. 3)
—Numero. (p. 1272)
Batan, Natalia, ed. see AZ Books Staff.
Batanda, Jackee Budesta. Blue Marble. (p. 203)
Batcheler, Michelle, jt. auth. see Sikora, Frank.
Batchelor, John. Lighthouses of the World. (p. 1015)
Batchelor, Louise. Whoops! (p. 1920)
Batchelor, Love. Mean Mo & the Christmas Star. (p. 1116)
Batchelor, Mary & Boshoff, Penny. My First Bedtime Bible. (p. 1204)
Batchelor, Melanie. Remember Me. (p. 1459)
Batchelor, R. E. & San José, Miguel Angel. Using Spanish Vocabulary. (p. 1828)
Batchelor, Rhonda. She Loves You. (p. 1564)
Batcher, Jack. Silly Kitty! Joke & Coloring Book. Stockton, Kevin, illus. (p. 1576)
Batchler, Darla. If I Were a Monkey. Parris, Kitty, illus. (p. 853)
Batdorf, Carol. Tinka Coloring Book: A Day in a Little Girl's Life. (p. 1755)
Bate, Helen, illus. see Dunn, James.
Bate, Helen, illus. see Ewart, Francesca, et al.
Bate, Helen, illus. see Ewart, Franzeska G. & Quarto Generic Staff.
Bate, Jonathan, ed. see Clare, John.
Bate, Lucy. Little Rabbit's Loose Tooth. deGroat, Diane, illus. (p. 1034)
Bate, Tharah. White Arrow. (p. 1912)
Bateman. Birds of Prey: An Introduction. (p. 191)
Bateman, Anya. I Just Got a Letter from Allyson Pringle. (p. 840)
—Makeover of James Orville Wickenbee. (p. 1080)
Bateman, Claire Boudreaux. This Little Light of Mine. Alexander, Katie Norwood, illus. (p. 1737)
Bateman, Donna M. Deep in the Swamp. Lies, Brian, illus. (p. 423)
Bateman, Graham, ed. Atoms, Molecules, & States of Matter. (p. 113)
—Chemical Reactions. (p. 297)
—Electricity & Electronics. (p. 509)
—Light & Sound. (p. 1014)
Bateman, Jordan. Dunamis Heroes: Issue #1: the Lost Kingdom. Save, Ken, illus. (p. 490)
Bateman, Julie. Bath, Book, Bed (p. 144)
Bateman, Katherine R. Young Investor: Projects & Activities for Making Your Money Grow. (p. 1979)
Bateman, Marinna. Toogles' Big Move (p. 1767)
Bateman, Robert. Backyard Birds. (p. 131)
—Polar Worlds: Life at the Ends of the Earth. (p. 1379)
Bateman, Teresa. April Foolishness. Westcott, Nadine Bernard, illus. (p. 93)
—April Foolishness Book & DVD Set Westcott, Nadine Bernard, illus. (p. 93)
—Bully Blockers Club. Urbanovic, Jackie, illus. (p. 241)
—Christmas Pups. Kanzler, John, illus. (p. 315)
—Eyes of the Unicorn. Spalenka, Greg, illus. (p. 558)
—Fiona's Luck. Murphy, Kelly, illus. (p. 589)
—Fluffy: Scourge of the Sea. Chesworth, Michael, illus. (p. 608)
—Gus, the Pilgrim Turkey. Sasaki, Ellen Joy, illus. (p. 732)
—Hunting the Daddyosaurus. Huang, Benrei, illus. (p. 829)
—Job Wanted. Sheban, Chris, illus. (p. 919)
—Keeper of Soles. Yayo & Yayo, illus. (p. 947)
—Leprechaun under the Bed. Meisel, Paul, illus. (p. 993)
—Paul Bunyan vs. Hals Halson: The Giant Lumberjack Challenge! Canga, C. B, illus. (p. 1330)
—Plump & Perky Turkey Shelly, Jeff, illus. (p. 1374)
—Traveling Tom & the Leprechaun. Potter, Melisande, illus. (p. 1780)
Bateman, Tracey Victoria. You Had Me at Good-Bye. (p. 1975)
Bateman, Vernon. Mommy I Want 2 Fly. (p. 1162)
Bater, Alison. Another Chance. (p. 87)
Bater, Lucy. Incredible Insects. (p. 869)
Bates, A. W. Technology, e-Learning & Distance Education. (p. 1711)
Bates, Amy. My Puppy's First Year. (p. 1217)
Bates, Amy, illus. see DeGross, Monalisa.
Bates, Amy, illus. see Hest, Amy.
Bates, Amy, illus. see Hopkinson, Deborah.
Bates, Amy, illus. see Meyers, Susan.
Bates, Amy, illus. see Napoli, Donna Jo.
Bates, Amy, illus. see Reich, Susanna.
Bates, Amy, illus. see Stern, Ricki & Worcester, Heidi P.
Bates, Amy, illus. see Turner, Ann.
Bates, Amy, illus. see Twain, Mark, pseud.
Bates, Amy, illus. see Weatherford, Carole Boston.
Bates, Amy June, illus. see Caswell, Deanna.
Bates, Amy June, illus. see Dungy, Tony.
Bates, Amy June, illus. see Hopkinson, Deborah.
Bates, Amy June, illus. see Jewel.
Bates, Amy June, illus. see Krull, Kathleen.
Bates, Amy June, illus. see Kurtz, Jane.
Bates, Amy June, illus. see MacDonald, Maryann.
Bates, Amy June, illus. see MacLachlan, Patricia.
Bates, Amy June, illus. see Meyers, Susan.
Bates, Amy June, illus. see Myers, Laurie.
Bates, Amy June, illus. see Richardson, Justin & Parnell, Peter.
Bates, Amy June, illus. see Sonnichsen, A. L.
Bates, Amy June, illus. see Tolan, Stephanie S.
Bates, Amy June, illus. see Twain, Mark, pseud.
Bates, Amy June, illus. see Wilson, Karma.
Bates, Angie. Hey Baby! (p. 774)
Bates, Ben, illus. see Anderson, Ted.

B

Bates, Ben, illus. see Flynn, Ian.
Bates, Ben, et al. Hedgehog Spaziante, Patrick Spaz, illus. (p. 761)
Bates, Bill, illus. see Written By Pamela McFarland; Illustrated.
Bates, Bob, illus. see Eastman, Gail.
Bates, Brenda J., illus. see Tessin, Kit Elaine.
Bates, Cary, et al. Creepy Archives Volume 17. Simon, Philip, ed. (p. 381)
Bates, Delphine Branon. Help Me Remember the Days of Creation. Bates, Delphine Branon & EsDesignStudio, illus. (p. 765)
Bates, Dianne. Crossing the Line. (p. 385)
—Girl in the Basement. (p. 678)
—Hold-Up Heroes. Wright, Kathryn, illus. (p. 788)
Bates, Emily. Demon's Heart. (p. 426)
Bates, George, illus. see Day, Nancy Raines.
Bates, George, illus. see Perl, Erica S.
Bates, Gordon. Khaki Boys over the Top: Doing & Daring for Uncle Sam. (p. 951)
Bates, Harry, illus. see Hensperger, Beth.
Bates, Ivan, illus. see Bajaj, Varsha.
Bates, Ivan, illus. see Doherty, Berlie.
Bates, Ivan, illus. see Hindley, Judy.
Bates, Ivan, illus. see Jenkins, Martin.
Bates, Ivan, illus. see McBratney, Sam.
Bates, Ivan, illus. see Wheeler, Lisa.
Bates, Janet Costa. Seaside Dream. Davis, Lambert, illus. (p. 1538)
Bates, John, et al. My First Buddhist Alphabet. (p. 1206)
Bates, Katharine, jt. auth. see Bates, Katharine Lee.
Bates, Katharine Lee. America the Beautiful: Together We Stand. Collier, Bryan et al, illus. (p. 59)
—America the Beautiful. Gall, Chris, illus. (p. 59)
Bates, Katharine Lee, ed. see Price, Margaret Evans & Wadsworth, Wallace C.
Bates, Katharine Lee & Bates, Katharine. America the Beautiful. Minor, Wendell & Howell, Troy, illus. (p. 59)
Bates, Katherine. America the Beautiful. (p. 59)
Bates, Katherine Lee. America the Beautiful. Minor, Wendell, illus. (p. 59)
Bates, Kristy A. They Call Me Toaster. (p. 1732)
Bates, Lindsey E., illus. see Roberts, Pauline.
Bates, M. Horse in Danger. (p. 799)
—Perfect Pony. (p. 1342)
—Strangers at the Stables. (p. 1665)
Bates, Marni. Awkward. (p. 121)
—Awkwardly Ever After. (p. 121)
—Invisible. (p. 885)
—Marni: My True Story of Stress, Hair-Pulling, & Other Obsessions. (p. 1096)
—Notable. (p. 1267)
Bates, Martine & Leavitt, Martine. Dragon's Tapestry (p. 479)
Bates, Martine G. Heather Whitestone: Inspirational Miss America. (p. 760)
Bates, Matt. Inside Beehives. (p. 876)
Bates, Matthew. Colmenas (Inside Beehives) (p. 341)
—Ways We Use Water. (p. 1865)
Bates, Megan, ed. see Hino, Matsuri.
Bates, Megan, ed. see Yazawa, Ai.
Bates, Megan, ed. see Yuki, Kaori.
Bates, Melinda. Nick Pricer: An American Heir. (p. 1251)
Bates, Michelle. Dream Pony. (p. 483)
—Horse for the Summer. (p. 799)
—Horse in Danger. (p. 799)
—Midnight Horse. (p. 1138)
—Midnight Horse. (p. 1139)
—Perfect Pony. (p. 1342)
—Ride by Moonlight. (p. 1471)
—Ride by Moonlight. Leigh, Susannah, ed. (p. 1471)
Bates, Michelle, ed. see Civardi, Anne.
Bates, Penny. Murder of Crows. (p. 1192)
Bates, Rhonda. Bible 's Song. (p. 176)
Bates, Robert L. Lopaka's Legends of Hawaii. (p. 1052)
Bates, Ron. How to Lose Friends & Monster Bots (p. 820)
Bates, Shelley. Over Her Head. (p. 1313)
Bates, Sonya. Smuggler's Cave Charko, Kasia, illus. (p. 1595)
—Thunder Creek Ranch Charko, Kasia, illus. (p. 1746)
—Topspin (p. 1769)
—Wildcat Run Charko, Kasia, illus. (p. 1931)
Bates, Sonya Spreen. Marsh Island Charko, Kasia, illus. (p. 1096)
Bates, Susan Welch. Rag Picker's Christmas. (p. 1433)
Bates, Yvonne. Shouldn't I Be Feeling Better by Now? Client Views of Therapy. (p. 1570)
Bateson, Catherine. Airdancer of Glass. (p. 31)
—Being Bee. (p. 161)
—Boyfriend Rules of Good Behavior. (p. 220)
—Magenta Mcphee. (p. 1071)
—Millie & the Night Heron. (p. 1144)
—Mimi & the Blue Slave. (p. 1145)
—Stranded in Boringsville. (p. 1664)
—Wish Pony. (p. 1940)
Bateson Hill, Margaret. Masha & the Firebird. Wilson, Anne, illus. (p. 1102)
Bateson, Maggie. Dinosaur Safari. Forshaw, Louise, illus. (p. 442)
—Fairy Unicorn Riding Stables. Comfort, Louise, illus. (p. 564)
—My Fairy Fashion Show: A Pop-up & Play Book. Comfort, Louise, illus. (p. 1202)
—My Fairy Princess Palace. Comfort, Louise, illus. (p. 1202)
—My Fairy Showtime. Comfort, Louise, illus. (p. 1202)
—My Fairytale Dream Palace. Comfort, Louise, illus. (p. 1202)
—My Pirate Adventure: A Pop-up & Play Book. Eaves, Ed, illus. (p. 1217)
—Palacio de Las Hadas. Sánchez Abuli, Enrique, tr. (p. 1319)
Bateson-Hill, Margaret. Chanda & the Mirror of Moonlight. Littlewood, Karin, illus. (p. 289)
—Goldilocks & the Three Bears. Slater, Kate, illus. (p. 696)
BAtey, Kathey. Exaggeration Aggravation. (p. 547)
—Exaggeration Aggravation. GEBhard, Andy, illus. (p. 547)
Bath, K. P. Flip Side. (p. 605)
Bath, K. P. & McCue, Kerin. Secret of Castle Cant. (p. 1542)
Bath, Louella. Growing Vegetables. (p. 727)
—Mysteries of the Sun. (p. 1222)
Batham, Matthew. Lightsleep. (p. 1016)
Batho-Barth, Angie. Snappy the Squirrel: A Lesson in Friendship. (p. 1597)
Bathroom Readers' Institute Staff. Facts to Annoy Your Teacher. (p. 561)
—Haunted Outhouse: Science, History, Horror, Mystery, and... Eerily Twisted Tales. (p. 753)
—Ogre Drool: 36 Tear-Off Placemats - Puzzles, Mazes, Brainteasers, Weird Facts, Jokes, & More! Merrell, Patrick & Schuna, Sam, illus. (p. 1280)
—Scrambled Brains: 36 Tear-Off Placemats - Puzzles, Mazes, Brainteasers, Weird Facts, Jokes, & More! Merrell, Patrick & Schuna, Sam, illus. (p. 1532)
—Uncle John's Curiously Compelling Bathroom Reader. (p. 1811)
—Uncle John's InfoMania Bathroom Reader for Kids Only! (p. 1811)
—Uncle John's Smell-O-Scopic Bathroom Reader for Kids Only! (p. 1811)
—Uncle John's the Enchanted Toilet Bathroom Reader for Kids Only! (p. 1811)
—Uncle John's Top Secret Bathroom Reader for Kids Only! Collectible Edition. (p. 1811)
—Uncle John's Totally Quacked Bathroom Reader for Kids Only! (p. 1811)
—Uncle John's Unstoppable Bathroom Reader. (p. 1812)
Bathroom Readers' Institute Staff, jt. auth. see Merrell, Patrick.
Bathroom Readers' Institute Staff & BTMS-Portable Press Staff. Uncle John's Creature Feature Bathroom Reader for Kids Only! (p. 1811)
Bathroom Readers' Institute Staff, creator. Uncle John's Bathroom Reader for Kids Only! Collectible Edition. (p. 1811)
—Uncle John's Electrifying Bathroom Reader for Kids Only! (p. 1811)
Batista, Joaquin. Westward Eden. (p. 1876)
Batkhuu, Kh. Doll That Flew Away. Myagmardorj, Enkhtungalag, illus. (p. 463)
Batley, Alan, jt. auth. see Yorke, Peter.
Batlles, Camila, tr. see Kay, Elizabeth.
Batlles, Camila, tr. see Pullman, Philip.
Batlles Vinn, Camila, tr. see Stine, R. L.
Batmanghelidj, F. Water for Health, for Healing, for Life: You're Not Sick, You're Thirsty! (p. 1862)
Batmanglij, Najmieh. Happy Nowruz: Cooking with Children to Celebrate the Persian New Year. (p. 746)
Batonne, Eva, jt. auth. see Marks, Jeffrey Alan.
Bator-Gray, Mary Ann. Jaden & the Weejum: A Cats Angels' Adventure. (p. 905)
Batot, Yvonne & Gose, Senora. Flip Flop French: Ages 3-5: Level 1. (p. 605)
Batres, Ethel. Pin Pon. Ramirez, Elizandro de los Angeles, illus. (p. 1359)
Batson, Alan, illus. see La Rose, Melinda.
Batson, Priscilla. Big Dig Ducks. (p. 181)
Batson, Susann. Duck at the Dog Pound. (p. 488)
—Gilly the Seasick Fish. (p. 676)
—Scaredy: A Cloud Afraid of Thunder. (p. 1519)
—Sparkie: A Star Afraid of the Dark. Batson, Susann, illus. (p. 1622)
Batson, Susann, illus. see Kirkle, Diane Luise.
Batson, Wayne Thomas. Dreamtreaders (p. 484)
—Final Storm (p. 586)
—Isle of Fire (p. 893)
—Isle of Swords (p. 893)
—Search for the Shadow Key (p. 1537)
Batson, Wayne Thomas & Hopper, Christopher. Curse of the Spider King: The Berinfell Prophecies Series - Book One. (p. 395)
Batt, Tanya Robyn. Barefoot Book of Faeries. Newey, Gail, illus. (p. 139)
—Fabrics of Fairytale: Stories Spun from Far & Wide. Griffin, Rachel, illus. (p. 559)
Batt Tanya Robyn. Faeries Gift. Ceccoli Nicoletta, illus. (p. 562)
Batt, Tanya Robyn. Faerie's Gift. Ceccoli, Nicoletta, illus. (p. 562)
—Princess & the White Bear King. Ceccoli, Nicoletta, illus. (p. 1403)
—Princess & White Bear. Ceccoli, Nicoletta, illus. (p. 1403)
Battaglia, Aurelius, illus. see Golden Books Staff.
Battaglia, Stephen. Mr. Mcsymphony's It's All about Classical Music. (p. 1185)
—Mr. Mcsymphony's It's All about Jazz. (p. 1185)
—Mr. Mcsymphony's It's All about Opera. (p. 1185)
—Mr. Mcsymphony's Musicians & their Instruments. (p. 1185)
Battaglioli, Peter. What to Doodle? Crazy Faces. (p. 1894)
Battah, Suzan. Basatai: Outside In. (p. 140)
Battcock, Gregory, ed. see Jeffers, Susan & Ehrlich, Amy.
Battell, Marilynn G. Deadly Deceit. (p. 417)
Batten, Jack. Oscar Peterson: The Man & His Jazz. (p. 1305)
—Silent in an Evil Time: The Brave War of Edith Cavell. (p. 1575)
—War to End All Wars: The Story of World War I. (p. 1858)
Batten, John D., illus. see Jacobs, Joseph, ed.
Batten, John D., illus. see Jacobs, Joseph.
Batten, Mary. Aliens from Earth: When Animals & Plants Invade Other Ecosystems Doyle, Beverly, illus. (p. 41)
—Aliens from Earth: When Animals & Plants Invade Other Ecosystems Doyle, Beverly J., illus. (p. 41)
—Extinct! Creatures of the Past. Doyle, Beverly, illus. (p. 555)
—Hungry Plants. Mirocha, Paul, illus. (p. 828)
—Please Don't Wake the Animals: A Book about Sleep Bond, Higgins, illus. (p. 1373)
—Who Has a Belly Button? Bond, Higgins, illus. (p. 1915)
—Wild Cats. Rowe, Michael Langham, illus. (p. 1929)
Batten, Mary & Sill, Cathryn. About Insects: A Guide for Children Bond, Higgins & Sill, John, illus. (p. 6)
Batten, Scott A. Johnny the Phoenix. (p. 923)
Battersby, Elm. Littlest Survivor. (p. 1039)
Battersby, Katherine. Squish Rabbit. (p. 1637)
Battersea Dogs and Cats Home Staff. Battersea Dogs & Cats Home - Alfie's Story. (p. 145)
—Bruno's Story. (p. 232)
Battersea Dogs and Cats Home Staff & Red Fox Picture Books Staff. Bailey's Story. (p. 133)
Battersea Dogs and Cats Home Staff & Red Fox Staff. Buddy & Holly's Story. (p. 234)
—Coco's Story. (p. 337)
Battersea Dogs and Cats Home Staff & Red Fox Picture Books Staff. Daisy's Story. (p. 401)
Battersea Dogs and Cats Home Staff & Red Fox. Rusty's Story. (p. 1498)
Battersea Dogs Home Staff & Red Fox Staff. Rocky's Story. (p. 1484)
Batterson, Jason. Beast Academy Guide 3B. Owen, Erich, illus. (p. 152)
Batterson, Jason & Rogers, Shannon. Beast Academy Practice 3A. (p. 152)
Batterson, Mark. Circle Maker for Kids: One Prayer Can Change Everything Caparo, Antonio Javier, illus. (p. 321)
Batterson, Mark & Clark, Joel N. Jack Staples & the City of Shadows. (p. 903)
Batterson, Mark, et al. Jack Staples & the Ring of Time. (p. 903)
Batterson, Veronica Randolph. Billy's First Dance. (p. 187)
Batti, Kimberly Rose, illus. see Finger, Mary E.
Batti, Kimberly Rose, illus. see Stegall, Kim.
Battis, Gwen, illus. see Bird, Roy & Harp, Kim.
Battis, Gwen, illus. see McPhail, J. A.
Battista, Emiliano, tr. see Ranciere, Jacques.
Battista, Mary Jane. Danny's Day at the Children's Museum. (p. 406)
Battiste, Alyse. Super Sally's Fantastic Fun Day. (p. 1680)
Battiston, I. My Red Rose: Learning the R Sound. (p. 1217)
Battistoni, I. At the Zoo: Learning the Z Sound. (p. 111)
—I Fight Fires: Learning the Long I Sound. (p. 838)
—What a Whale! Learning the WH Sound. (p. 1878)
Battle, Christina, illus. see Bell, Sophie.
Battle, Cleaton D. Saturday Surprise. Cooper, Emmanuel, illus. (p. 1515)
Battle, Craig. Max Finder Mystery Collected Casebook Pérez, Ramón, illus. (p. 1111)
—Max Finder Mystery Collected Casebook Pérez, Ramón & Owlkids Books Inc. Staff, illus. (p. 1111)
Battle, Craig, jt. auth. see O'Donnell, Liam.
Battle, Timothy. Mr. Bo Finds a New Home & a New Name. (p. 1184)
—Mr. Bo Finds a New Home, Second Edition. (p. 1184)
—Mr. Bo's Big Heart. (p. 1184)
Battle-Lavert, Gwendolyn. Barber's Cutting Edge. Holbert, Raymond, illus. (p. 138)
—Papa's Mark. Bootman, Colin, illus. (p. 1322)
Batton, Doris. Snicker & Snore Griffin, Cheri, illus. (p. 1597)
Batts, Laura. Love Your Pony, Love Your Planet: All about Pony Poo & Other Helpful Things We Can Do! (p. 1061)
Battut, Éric. Little Mouse's Big Secret. (p. 1032)
—Little Pea. Battut, Eric, illus. (p. 1033)
Battut, Eric. Secreto. (p. 1544)
Battuz, Christine, illus. see Jones, Christianne C.
Battuz, Christine, illus. see Nemiroff, Marc A. & Annunziata, Jane.
Battuz, Christine, illus. see Szymona, Marlene L.
Baty, Chris. No Plot? No Problem! A Low-Stress, High-Velocity Guide to Writing a Novel in 30 Days. (p. 1260)
Baty, Danielle Reed, jt. auth. see LeTourneau, Marie.
Baty, Lisa. Does Jesus Wear Jammies? (p. 460)
Batyah, Baraka. Batyah's Realease: One Woman's Journey Out. (p. 147)
Baucham, Voddie, Jr. Ever-Loving Truth. (p. 541)
—Ever-Loving Truth Leader Pack. (p. 541)
Bauchman, 'Della. Many Faces of Sant. (p. 1089)
Bauchner, Elizabeth. Computer Investigation. (p. 355)
—Computer Investigation. Noziglia, Carla Miller & Siegel, Jay A., eds. (p. 355)
—Document Analysis. (p. 459)
—Document Analysis. Noziglia, Carla Miller & Siegel, Jay A., eds. (p. 459)
—Teen Minorities in Rural North America: Growing up Different. (p. 1713)
—Weight Management. McDonnell, Mary Ann & Forman, Sara, eds. (p. 1872)
Baucom, Ian. Through the Skylight. Gerard, Justin, illus. (p. 1745)
Baude, Dawn Michelle. Learning French Book: Fun Exercises to Help You Learn Francais. (p. 985)
Bauder, Julia. Is Iran a Threat to Global Security? (p. 889)
—Media Ethics. (p. 1118)
Bauder, Julia, jt. auth. see Haugen, David M.
Baudet, jt. auth. see Percy, Richard.
Baudet, Stephanie. New Library of Horror: Dracula. (p. 1246)
Baudo, Christopher. Nana & the Scarlett Lady's Spectacular Christmas Day. (p. 1228)
Bauer, A. C. E. Gil Marsh. (p. 676)
—No Castles Here. (p. 1258)
Bauer, A. C. E. & Shakespeare, William. Come Fall. (p. 347)
Bauer, Brandy. Iran: A Question & Answer Book (p. 886)
Bauer, Carla, illus. see Allen, Thomas B.
Bauer, Carole. Tree House Kids. (p. 1783)
Bauer, Cheryl. Our Visit to the Nature Center: Nuestra Visita Al Centro Ecologico. (p. 1310)
Bauer, Christina. Pirate Queen: A Timewalker Journey. (p. 1363)
Bauer, Dana, illus. see Carpenter Czerw, Nancy.
Bauer, Dana, illus. see Layos, Alexandra.
Bauer, Dane. Snow. Wallace, John, illus. (p. 1598)
Bauer, David. Adding Arctic Animals. (p. 11)
—Everything Is Matter! (p. 545)
—My Apple Tree (p. 1196)
—People Change the Land. (p. 1339)
—Sumando Animales del Artico. (p. 1673)
Bauer, David & Reed, Janet. ¡Todos Comen Pan! (p. 1761)
Bauer, Deidre. Silver Mountain. (p. 1576)
Bauer, Dennis. Raphael's Christmas Present. (p. 1439)
Bauer, Helen. Beethoven for Kids: His Life & Music with 21 Activities. (p. 158)
—Verdi for Kids: His Life & Music with 21 Activities. (p. 1836)
Bauer, Jeff. Planets. (p. 1368)
—Renos Asombrosos. (p. 1460)
—What Is an Insect? (p. 1888)
Bauer, Joan. Almost Home. (p. 48)
—Backwater. (p. 130)
—Best Foot Forward. (p. 169)
—Close to Famous. (p. 334)
—Hope Was Here. (p. 797)
—Peeled. (p. 1335)
—Rules of the Road. (p. 1495)
—Squashed. (p. 1636)
—Stand Tall. (p. 1639)
—Sticks. (p. 1650)
—Tell Me. (p. 1716)
—Thwonk. (p. 1746)
Bauer, Joe, illus. see Bauer, Michael Gerard.
Bauer, John, illus. see Lundbergh, Holger, tr.
Bauer, John, illus. see Wilde, Gloria.
Bauer, Jutta. Grandpa's Angel. Bauer, Jutta, illus. (p. 709)
—Madrechillona. (p. 1070)
—Queen of Colors. (p. 1425)
—Selma. Bauer, Jutta, illus. (p. 1550)
Bauer, Jutta, jt. auth. see Stamm, Peter.
Bauer, Larry, illus. see Friedman, Pamela.
Bauer, Larry, illus. see Hanegar, Renee.
Bauer, Larry, jt. auth. see Friedman, Pamela.
Bauer, Linda. Fruits & Flowers & Footprints OH MY!!! (p. 645)
Bauer, Marion Dane. Baby Bear Discovers the World Tekiela, Stan, photos by. (p. 125)
—Blue Ghost. Wang, Suling, illus. (p. 202)
—Celebrating Arizona: 50 States to Celebrate. Canga, C. B., illus. (p. 284)
—Celebrating California. (p. 284)
—Celebrating Florida: 50 States to Celebrate. Canga, C. B., illus. (p. 284)
—Celebrating Florida. (p. 284)
—Celebrating Illinois: 50 States to Celebrate. Canga, C. B., illus. (p. 285)
—Celebrating Massachusetts: 50 States to Celebrate. Canga, C. B., illus. (p. 285)
—Celebrating New York: 50 States to Celebrate. Canga, C. B., illus. (p. 285)
—Celebrating New York. (p. 285)
—Celebrating North Carolina: 50 States to Celebrate. C.B. Canga, C. B., illus. (p. 285)
—Celebrating Texas: 50 States to Celebrate. Canga, C. B., illus. (p. 285)
—Celebrating Texas. (p. 285)
—Celebrating Virginia & Washington, D. C. (p. 285)
—Celebrating Virginia & Washington, D. C. 50 States to Celebrate. Canga, C. B., illus. (p. 285)
—Celebrating Washington State: 50 States to Celebrate. C.B. Canga, C. B., illus. (p. 285)
—Christmas Baby. Cowdrey, Richard, illus. (p. 312)
—Christmas in the Forest. Hearn, Diane Dawson, illus. (p. 314)
—Christmas Lights. Mitchell, Susan, illus. (p. 314)
—Clouds. Wallace, John, illus. (p. 335)
—Crinkle, Crackle, Crack: It's Spring! Shelley, John, illus. (p. 383)
—Cutest Critter Tekiela, Stan, photos by. (p. 396)
—Dinosaur Thunder. Chodos-Irvine, Margaret, illus. (p. 443)
—Double-Digit Club. (p. 472)
—Earthquake! Wallace, John, illus. (p. 497)
—Flood! Wallace, John, illus. (p. 605)
—Golden Ghost. Ferguson, Peter, illus. (p. 694)
—Grand Canyon. Wallace, John, illus. (p. 707)
—Grandmother's Song. Rossi, Pamela, illus. (p. 709)
—Green Ghost. Ferguson, Peter, illus. (p. 721)
—Halloween Forest. Shelley, John, illus. (p. 737)
—Harriet Tubman. Lyon, Tammie, illus. (p. 749)
—How Do I Love You? Church, Caroline Jayne, illus. (p. 807)
—If Frogs Made the Weather. Donohue, Dorothy, illus. (p. 852)
—In Like a Lion, Out Like a Lamb. McCully, Emily Arnold, illus. (p. 864)
—Killing Miss Kitty & Other Sins. (p. 956)
—Little Dog, Lost. Bell, Jennifer A., illus. (p. 1026)
—Longest Night. Lewin, Ted, illus. (p. 1047)
—Love Song for a Baby. Andreasen, Dan, illus. (p. 1060)
—Mama for Owen. Butler, John, illus. (p. 1084)
—Martin Luthur King, Jr. Smith, Jamie, illus. (p. 1098)
—Mighty Mississippi. Wallace, John, illus. (p. 1140)
—Mount Rushmore. Wallace, John, illus. (p. 1180)
—My First Biography: Benjamin Franklin. Lewis, Anthony, illus. (p. 1205)
—My Mother Is Mine. Elwell, Peter, illus. (p. 1214)
—Niagara Falls. Wallace, John, illus. (p. 1250)
—On My Honor. (p. 1289)
—Red Ghost. Ferguson, Peter, illus. (p. 1454)
—Rocky Mountains. Wallace, John, illus. (p. 1484)
—Runt. (p. 1497)
—Shelter from the Wind (p. 1565)
—Snow. Wallace, John, illus. (p. 1598)
—Statue of Liberty. Wallace, John, illus. (p. 1644)
—Thank You for Me! Sweet, Melissa & Stephenson, Kristina, illus. (p. 1725)
—Toes, Ears, & Nose! Katz, Karen, illus. (p. 1761)
—Very Best Daddy of All. Wu, Leslie, illus. (p. 1837)
—Very Little Princess: Rose's Story. Sayles, Elizabeth, illus. (p. 1838)
—Volcano! Wallace, John, illus. (p. 1848)
—Why Do Kittens Purr? Cole, Henry, illus. (p. 1923)
—Wind. Wallace, John, illus. (p. 1935)
—Wonders of America Ready-To-Read Value Pack: The Grand Canyon; Niagara Falls; the Rocky Mountains; Mount Rushmore; the Statue of Liberty; Yellowstone. Wallace, John, illus. (p. 1948)
—Yellowstone. Wallace, John, illus. (p. 1970)
Bauer, Marion Dane, jt. auth. see Katz, Karen.
Bauer, Marion Dane & Rucker, Justin. Celebrating California: 50 States to Celebrate. Canga, C. B., illus. (p. 284)
Bauer, Marion Dane & Wallace, John. Rain. Wallace, John, illus. (p. 1434)
Bauer, Michael. Adventures of Steel Wooly: And my Place on the Farm. (p. 23)
Bauer, Michael G., jt. auth. see Bauer, Michael Gerard.

Bauer, Michael Gerard. Don't Call Me Ishmael! (p. 467)
—Epic Fail. Bauer, Joe, illus. (p. 532)
—Just a Dog. (p. 937)
—Running Man. (p. 1497)
Bauer, Michael Gerard & Bauer, Michael G. Don't Call Me Ishmael. (p. 467)
Bauer Mueller, Pamela. Angry Drum Echoed: Mary Musgrove, Queen of the Creeks. (p. 75)
—Neptune's Honor: A Story of Loyalty & Love. (p. 1241)
Bauer, Patricia. B Is for Battle Cry: A Civil War Alphabet. Geister, David, illus. (p. 122)
Bauer, Robert. C. J. in a Pickle. (p. 250)
Bauer, Roger. Day at the Races: World of Discovery II. Palmer, Kate S., illus. (p. 412)
—Package. Maizel, Karen, illus. (p. 1317)
Bauer, Sepp. Christmas Rose. Wenz-Vietor, Else, illus. (p. 315)
Bauer, Stephanie, illus. see Blackstone, Stella.
Bauer, Stephanie, illus. see Hedlund, Stephanie.
Bauer, Stephanie, illus. see Prochovnic, Dawn Babb.
Bauer, Stephanie, jt. auth. see Blackstone, Stella.
Bauer, Susan Wise. Ancient Times: From the Earliest Nomads to the Last Roman Emperor. Vol. 1 (p. 70)
—Ancient Times: From the Earliest Nomads to the Last Roman Emperor. Vol. 1 West, Jeff, illus. (p. 70)
—Early Modern Times: From Elizabeth the First to the Forty-Niners. Vol. 3 (p. 494)
—Early Modern Times: From Elizabeth the First to the Forty-Niners. Bk. 3 Martirosian, Patty Ann et al, illus. (p. 494)
—Early Modern Times: From Elizabeth the First to the Forty-Niners. Vol. 3 Martirosian, Patty Ann et al, illus. (p. 494)
—Middle Ages: From the Fall of Rome to the Rise of the Renaissance. Vol. 2 (p. 1137)
—Middle Ages. (p. 1137)
—Modern Age: From Victoria's Empire to the End of the USSR. Vol. 4 (p. 1158)
—Modern Age: From Victoria's Empire to the End of the USSR. Vol. 4 Park, Sarah, illus. (p. 1158)
—Story of the World (p. 1662)
Bauer, Susan Wise, jt. auth. see Crandell, Joyce.
Bauer, Susan Wise, jt. auth. see Rountree, Elizabeth.
Bauer, Susan Wise, jt. ed. see Park, Charlie.
Bauer, Tiffany Jamie. Swim Little Swimmy (p. 1690)
Bauer, Walter. Book of Birds, Dreams, & Other Things. (p. 211)
Bauerle, Tanja, illus. see Bertrand, Diane Gonzalez.
Bauerle, Tanja, illus. see Cottrell-Bentley, Lisa M.
Bauerle, Tanja, illus. see Rome, Lori April.
Bauer-Stamper, Judith, jt. auth. see Stamper, Judith Bauer.
Baugh, Ayana Sala. Loopiethotamus, the Chihuahua Who Thinks He Is a Hippopotamus: His Life. (p. 1052)
—Loopiethotamus, the Chihuahua Who Thinks He Is a Hippopotamus: A Loopiethotamus Christmas. (p. 1052)
—Loopiethotamus, the Chihuahua Who Thinks He Is a Hippopotamus Book: His Journey. (p. 1052)
Baugh, Chris. It All Started in Chem Class. . . (p. 893)
Baughan, Brain. Russell Simmons. (p. 1498)
Baughan, Brian. Arab-Israeli Relations, 1950-1979. (p. 94)
—Cesar Chavez. (p. 288)
—Human Rights in Africa. Ojakorotu, Victor & Rotberg, Robert I., eds. (p. 826)
—Liberia. (p. 1005)
—Liberia. Rotberg, Robert I., ed. (p. 1005)
—LL Cool J. (p. 1043)
—Story of Def Jam Records. (p. 1658)
Baughan, Michael Gray. Charles Bukowski. (p. 291)
—Shel Silverstein. (p. 1564)
—Stephen King. (p. 1648)
—Zimbabwe. (p. 1986)
—Zimbabwe. Rotberg, Robert I., ed. (p. 1986)
Baughman, Caitlin. God's Little Family ~the Move to the Mountains. (p. 691)
Baughman, Glenda. Root Rooster Goes to School. (p. 1488)
Baughman, Michelle. Day in the Life of a Cockroach. (p. 413)
Baughman, Trista Herring. Magic Telescope. (p. 1073)
Bauknecht, Julie, illus. see Davidson, Jean.
Bauknecht, Julie, illus. see McCann, David.
Bauknight, Wilfred, illus. see Oelschlager, Vanita.
Bauld, Jane S. Gift of the Gold Coin. Carpenter, Christina D., ed. (p. 675)
Bauld, Jane Scoggins. Hector Saves the Moon Laronde, Gary, illus. (p. 761)
—Hector Visits His Country Cousin Laronde, Gary, illus. (p. 761)
Bauld, Jane Scoggins & Darr, Cynthia G. Firefly's Light. (p. 592)
Bauld, Jane Scoggins & Waldrip, Gayle. Feathered Friends of Texas. (p. 579)
Bauley, Thomas K. Williamsburg A-Z: An Alphabetical Journey (p. 1934)
Baum, Ann, illus. see Baglio, Ben M.
Baum, Ann, illus. see Baglio, Ben M. & Lasher, Mary Ann.
Baum, Diane Ganzer & Olson, Dan. Dakota's Trail. (p. 401)
Baum, Harry Neal, jt. auth. see Miller, Olive Beaupre.
Baum, Kipley, photos by see Sedlacek, Jan Gill.
Baum, L. Frank. 7 Books In: L. Frank Baum's Oz Series, volume 1 of 2. the Wonderful Wizard of Oz, the Marvelous Land of Oz, Ozma of Oz, Dorothy & the Wizard In. (p. 1992)
—7 Books In: L. Frank Baum's Original Oz Series, Volume 1 of 2. the Wonderful Wizard of Oz, the Marvelous Land of Oz, Ozma of Oz, Dorothy & the W. (p. 1992)
—8 Books In: L. Frank Baum's Original Oz Series, volume 2 of 2. Little Wizard Stories of Oz, Tik-Tok of Oz, the Scarecrow of Oz, Rinkitink in Oz, T. (p. 1993)
—Adventures in Oz: The Tin Woodman of Oz, the Magic of Oz, Glinda of Oz. (p. 15)
—Adventures in Oz: The Scarecrow of Oz, Rinkitink in Oz, the Lost Princess of Oz. (p. 15)
—Adventures in Oz: The Wonderful Wizard of Oz, the Marvelous Land of Oz, Ozma of Oz. (p. 15)
—Adventures in Oz: Dorothy & the Wizard in Oz, the Road to Oz, the Emerald City of Oz. (p. 15)
—Adventures in Oz: The Patchwork Girl of Oz, Little Wizard Stories of Oz, Tik-Tok of Oz. (p. 15)
—Adventures of the Magical Monarch of Mo & His People. (p. 23)
—American Fairy Tales. (p. 60)
—Boy Fortune Hunters in Egypt. (p. 217)
—Collected Short Stories of L. Frank Baum. (p. 339)
—Complete Book of Oz: The Wonderful Wizard of Oz, the Marvelous Land of Oz, & Ozma of Oz (p. 352)
—Discontented Gopher: A Prairie Tale. Conahan, Carolyn Digby, illus. (p. 447)
—Dorothy & the Wizard in Oz. (p. 471)
—Dorothy & the Wizard in Oz; the Road to Oz; the Emerald City of Oz (p. 471)
—Dot & Tot of Merryland. (p. 472)
—Emerald City if Oz. (p. 517)
—Emerald City of Oz. (p. 517)
—Enchanted Buffalo. Montileaux, Donald F., illus. (p. 523)
—Enchanted Island of Yew. (p. 523)
—Frank Baum: Oz Books. (p. 628)
—Glinda of Oz. (p. 683)
—Glinda of Oz. John R Neill, illus. (p. 683)
—Kidnapped Santa Claus. (p. 952)
—L Frank Baum's Book of Santa Claus. (p. 969)
—Land of Oz. (p. 973)
—Large Hardback 1: L. Frank Baum's Original Oz Series. Wonderful Wizard of Oz, Marvelous Land of Oz, Ozma of Oz, Dorothy & the Wizard I. (p. 975)
—Life & Adventures of Santa Claus. (p. 1007)
—Life & Adventures of Santa Claus. Clark, Mary, illus. (p. 1007)
—Life & Adventures of Santa Claus. Clark, Mary Cowles, illus. (p. 1007)
—Little Wizard Stories of Oz. (p. 1038)
—Little Wizard Stories of Oz. Neill, John R., illus. (p. 1038)
—Lost Princess of Oz. (p. 1056)
—Magic of Oz. (p. 1073)
—Mago di Oz. (p. 1076)
—Maravillosa Tierra de Oz. (p. 1091)
—Maravilloso Mago de Oz. (p. 1091)
—Marvelous Land of Oz. (p. 1099)
—Mary Louise. (p. 1100)
—Mary Louise & the Liberty Girls. (p. 1100)
—Mary Louise in the Country. (p. 1100)
—Master Key: An Electrical Fairy Tale. (p. 1103)
—Master Key. (p. 1103)
—Michael Foreman's the Wonderful Wizard of Oz. Foreman, Michael, illus. (p. 1134)
—Mirinda Sorchisto de Oz. Broadribb, Donald, tr. (p. 1149)
—Mother Goose in Prose. (p. 1178)
—Navy Alphabet Book. (p. 1238)
—Oz, the Complete Collection, Volume 1: The Wonderful Wizard of Oz; the Marvelous Land of Oz; Ozma of Oz. (p. 1316)
—Oz, the Complete Collection, Volume 2: Dorothy & the Wizard in Oz; the Road to Oz; the Emerald City of Oz. (p. 1316)
—Oz, the Complete Collection, Volume 3: The Patchwork Girl of Oz; Tik-Tok of Oz; the Scarecrow of Oz. (p. 1316)
—Oz, the Complete Collection, Volume 4: Rinkitink in Oz; the Lost Princess of Oz; the Tin Woodman of Oz. (p. 1316)
—Oz, the Complete Hardcover Collection. (p. 1316)
—Ozma of Oz. (p. 1316)
—Patchwork Girl of OZ. (p. 1328)
—Patchwork Girl of Oz. (p. 1328)
—Queen Zixi of Ix: Or the Story of the Magic Cloak. Richardson, Frederick, illus. (p. 1425)
—Rinkitink in Oz. (p. 1473)
—Rinkitink in Oz; the Lost Princess of Oz; the Tin Woodman of Oz (p. 1473)
—Road to Oz. (p. 1477)
—Scarecrow of Oz. (p. 1519)
—Sea Fairies. (p. 1534)
—Sky Island. (p. 1586)
—Tales of Mother Goose. (p. 1702)
—The Patchwork Girl of Oz; Tik-Tok of Oz; the Scarecrow of Oz (p. 1728)
—The Wonderful Wizard of Oz; the Marvelous Land of Oz; Ozma of Oz. (p. 1728)
—Tik-Tok of Oz. (p. 1749)
—Tin Woodman of Oz. (p. 1755)
—Treasury of Oz. (p. 1783)
—Tresury of Oz: The Wonderful Wizard of Oz, the Marvelous Land of Oz, Ozma of Oz, Dorothy & the Wizard in Oz, the Road to Oz, the Emerald City Of. (p. 1785)
—Twinkle & Chubbins. (p. 1802)
—Wizard of Oz: And Other Wonderful Books of Oz - The Emerald City of Oz & Glinda of Oz. Sumpter, Rachell, illus. (p. 1943)
—Wizard of Oz. (p. 1943)
—Wizard of Oz. Denslow, W. W., illus. (p. 1943)
—Wizard of Oz. Zwerger, Lisbeth, illus. (p. 1943)
—Wizard of Oz. Evangelista, Mauro, illus. (p. 1943)
—Wizard of Oz. Michael, Cavallaro et al, illus. (p. 1943)
—Wizard of Oz Book & Charm. (p. 1943)
—Woggle-Bug Book. (p. 1943)
—Wonderful Welcome to Oz: The Marvelous Land of Oz, Ozma of Oz, & the Emerald City of Oz. Maguire, Gregory, ed. (p. 1948)
—Wonderful Wizard of Oz: A Classic Story about Cooperation. (p. 1948)
—Wonderful Wizard of Oz: Daventry Classics Annotated Edition. (p. 1948)
—Wonderful Wizard of Oz: The Marvelous Land of Oz - Ozma of Oz. (p. 1948)
—Wonderful Wizard of Oz. (p. 1948)
—Wonderful Wizard of Oz. Denslow, W. W., illus. (p. 1948)
—Wonderful Wizard of Oz. Wolstenholme, Susan, ed. (p. 1948)
—Wonderful Wizard of Oz. Denslow, W. W. & Menten, Ted, illus. (p. 1948)
—Wonderful Wizard of Oz. Baum, L. Frank & McKowen, Scott, illus. (p. 1948)
Baum, L. Frank, jt. auth. see Shanower, Eric.
Baum, L. Frank, jt. auth. see Thompson, Ruth Plumly.
Baum, L. Frank & Bancroft, Laura. Policeman Bluejay. (p. 1380)
—Twinkle & Chubbins. (p. 1802)
Baum, L. Frank & Denslow, W. W. Wonderful Wizard of Oz. (p. 1948)
Baum, L. Frank & Grahame, Kenneth. All-Action Classics No. 4: the Wonderful Wizard of Oz. Caldwell, Ben, illus. (p. 43)
Baum, L. Frank & Hutchison, David. Land of Oz: the Manga Pocket Manga Volume 2: The Manga Pocket Manga Volume 2 (p. 973)
Baum, L. Frank & Thompson, Ruth Plumly. Oz - The Complete Collection: The Magic of Oz; Glinda of Oz; The Royal Book of Oz. Vol. 5 (p. 1316)
—Royal Book of Oz. (p. 1492)
—The Magic of Oz; Glinda of Oz; the Royal Book of Oz. (p. 1728)
Baum, L. Frank & Van Dyne, Edith. Aunt Jane's Nieces. (p. 115)
Baum, L. Frank & van Dyne, Edith. Mary Louise in the Country. (p. 1100)
—Mary Louise Solves a Mystery. (p. 1100)
Baum, L. Frank & Zwerger, Lisbeth. Wizard of Oz. (p. 1943)
Baum, L. Frank, et al. Children's Treasury. (p. 304)
—Twinkle Tales. Enright, Maginel Wright, illus. (p. 1802)
Baum, L. Frank, told to. Emerald City of Oz. (p. 517)
Baum, Lonna. Monty the Menace: Understanding Differences. Messing, Dave, illus. (p. 1170)
Baum, Robert. Portal Masters: A New Beginning. (p. 1386)
Baum, Roger S. Lion of Oz & the Badge of Courage. Coons, Dean, illus. (p. 1020)
—Oz Odyssey. Seitzinger, Victoria, illus. (p. 1316)
—Toto of Oz & the Surprise Party. Seitzinger, Victoria, illus. (p. 1772)
Bauman, Amy. Everyone Is Special! (p. 544)
—Farm Animal Sounds. (p. 573)
Bauman, Amy & Durman, Laura. History. (p. 783)
—Personalities & Places. (p. 1344)
Bauman, Beth Ann. Jersey Angel. (p. 914)
—Rosie & Skate. (p. 1490)
Bauman, Boomer. One Star at a Time. (p. 1297)
Bauman, Carey. God Controls the Storm. Bauman, Carey, tr. (p. 688)
Bauman, Diane. Agility: Start to Finish. (p. 29)
Bauman, Elizabeth. Private Stories: Monologues for Young Actors Ages 8 to 16 & the Seven Key Questions to Unlock Your Imagination. (p. 1408)
Bauman, Jill. Tale of Squirrel Nutkin. (p. 1700)
Bauman, Lester. Exploring the Epistles of John. (p. 553)
—God's Redeemed Family—the Church: Bible 8 Tests. (p. 691)
Bauman, Marty. Crater Kid Collection. (p. 376)
Bauman, Todd, illus. see Hunter, Julius K.
Bauman Wispe, Lisa. Fritter's Spring: A Pocono Rabbit's Tale. (p. 639)
Baumann, Anne-Sophie, jt. auth. see Texier, Ophélie.
Baumann, Jessica. Bella-Blue Butterfly's Purple Surprise. Kordich, Melinda, illus. (p. 162)
Baumann, Kurt. Joachim. (p. 919)
Baumann, Leigh. Jekyll Island Fun Book. (p. 912)
—St. Simons Island Fun Book. (p. 1638)
Baumann, Margaret. Ajapa the Tortoise: A Book of Nigerian Folk Tales. (p. 32)
Baumann, Marty, illus. see Katschke, Judy.
Baumann, Susan K. Black Civil War Soldiers: The 54th Massachusetts Regiment. (p. 195)
—Harriet Tubman. (p. 749)
—Harriet Tubman: Conductor of the Underground Railroad. (p. 750)
—Middle Passage & the Revolt on the Amistad. (p. 1137)
Baumbach, Gerard F. Sadlier We Believe. (p. 1501)
—Sadlier We Believe, Catechist's Guide. (p. 1501)
—Sadlier We Believe, Parish Edition: God's Law Guides Us. (p. 1501)
—Sadlier We Believe, Parish Edition: We Are God's People. (p. 1501)
—Sadlier We Believe, Parish Edition: Jesus Shares God's Life. (p. 1501)
—Sadlier We Believe, School Edition: God Loves Us. (p. 1501)
Baumbach, Gerard F., creator. Sadlier We Believe. (p. 1501)
—Sadlier We Believe, Catechist's Guide. (p. 1501)
—Sadlier We Believe, Parish Edition: God Loves Us. (p. 1501)
—Sadlier We Believe, Parish Edition: We Are the Church. (p. 1501)
—Sadlier We Believe, Parish Edition: We Meet Jesus in the Sacraments. (p. 1501)
—Sadlier We Believe, School Edition: God's Law Guides Us. (p. 1501)
—Sadlier We Believe, School Edition: Jesus Shares God's Life. (p. 1501)
Baumbach, Rudolph. Summer Legends. (p. 1674)
Baumbusch, Brigitte. Animals in Art. (p. 83)
—Birds in Art. (p. 191)
—Cats in Art. (p. 281)
—Clothing in Art. (p. 334)
—Eyes in Art. (p. 558)
—Faces in Art. (p. 561)
—Festivals in Art. (p. 582)
—Figures in Art. (p. 586)
—Fish in Art. (p. 598)
—Flowers in Art. (p. 608)
—Food in Art. (p. 613)
—Houses in Art. (p. 804)
—Nature in Art. (p. 1236)
—Oceans in Art. (p. 1277)
—Sky in Art. (p. 1586)
—Trees in Art. (p. 1784)
Baumer, Dawn McVay, creator. Dune Daze: Silver Lake. (p. 490)
Baumgard, Sarah. In the Mirror I Saw. (p. 866)
—Little Lady in Red. (p. 1030)
Baumgardner, Jim. Making of a Spy: Sarah's Quest. (p. 1082)
Baumgardner, Julie, illus. see Cope, Steven R.
Baumgardner, Mary Alice, illus. see Carolina Canines for Service & Nowak, Pat.
Baumgart, Brian & Compass Point Books Staff. Teens in Mexico (p. 1715)
Baumgart, Klaus. Laura's Christmas Star. Waite, Judy, tr. from GER. (p. 980)
—Laura's Secret. Waite, Judy, tr. from GER. (p. 980)
Baumgarten, Josephine & Baumgarten, Michael. My Baby Monsters & I went to the Park. (p. 1196)
Baumgarten, Michael, jt. auth. see Baumgarten, Josephine.
Baumgartner, Edward Louis. Wabash Boy. (p. 1851)
Baumgartner, John Robert. Like Losing Your Left Hand. (p. 1017)
—Ron's Ghost: The Secret of the Stone Stairs. (p. 1488)
Baumont, Olivier. Antonio Vivaldi Voake, Charlotte, illus. (p. 90)
Baur, Laura. Riverbank. (p. 1476)
Baurys, Tamra. World Will Never Forget. Bouchal, Renee', illus. (p. 1959)
Bausley, Alicia. Tucker Goes to Heaven. (p. 1795)
Bausman, Mary, illus. see Keith, Brooke.
Bausman, Mary, illus. see Standard Publishing Staff.
Bausum, Ann. Denied, Detained, Deported: Stories from the Dark Side of American Immigration. (p. 426)
—Freedom Riders: John Lewis & Jim Zwerg on the Front Lines of the Civil Rights Movement. (p. 635)
—Marching to the Mountaintop: How Poverty, Labor Fights, & Civil Rights Set the Stage for Martin Luther King Jr.'s Final Hours. (p. 1092)
—Muckrackers: How Ida Tarbell, Upton Sinclair, & Lincoln Steffens Helped Expose Scandal, Inspire Reform, & Invent Investigative Journalism (Large P. (p. 1188)
—Muckrakers: How Ida Tarbell, Upton Sinclair, & Lincoln Steffens Helped Expose Scandal, Inspire Reform, & Invent Investigative Journalism. (p. 1188)
—Our Country's First Ladies. (p. 1308)
—Our Country's Presidents: All You Need to Know about the Presidents, from George Washington to Barack Obama. (p. 1308)
—Our Country's Presidents. (p. 1308)
—Stonewall: Breaking Out in the Fight for Gay Rights. (p. 1653)
—Stubby the War Dog: The True Story of World War I's Bravest Dog. (p. 1668)
—Unraveling Freedom: The Battle for Democracy on the Homefront During World War I. (p. 1822)
—With Courage & Cloth: Winning the Fight for a Woman's Right to Vote. (p. 1942)
Bautista, Cisar Evangelis, illus. see Mariscal, Libia E. Barajas.
Bautista, Gladys, et al. This Poem Called My Body. Garcia Echeverria, Olga, ed. (p. 1737)
Bavati, Robyn. Dancing in the Dark. (p. 403)
—Pirouette. (p. 1364)
Bave, Terry, illus. see Tatchell, Judy.
Baverstock, Alison. 13 British Artists Children Should Know. (p. 1994)
Baviera, Rocco, illus. see Kowalski, Gary A.
Bavosa, Ann. Seasonal Activities for Sensorimotor Development. (p. 1538)
Bawden, Jennifer. Hombre no es la Solucion: Construye una Vida Propia y Luego, una Relacion con Alguien. (p. 791)
Bawden, Juliet & Moxley, Susan. Papier Mache. (p. 1323)
Bawden, Nina. Carrie's War. (p. 271)
Bawtree, Michael. Joe Howe to the Rescue Smith, David Preston, illus. (p. 920)
Baxendale, Trevor & British Broadcasting Corporation Staff. Decide Your Destiny: Claws of the Macra. (p. 421)
Baxley, Ron & Wallace, James. Of Cabbages, Kings & Even (Odd) Queens of Wonderland & Oz: A Gothic Young Adult Crossover Novel. (p. 1279)
Baxter, Alice L. Adam's Atomic Adventures. (p. 11)
Baxter, Anne M. Everybody Needs a Name: The Adventures of Maybe, Book 1. (p. 543)
—Maybe Wins! (p. 1113)
Baxter, Bethany. Armadillos. (p. 99)
—Caimans, Gharials, Alligators, & Crocodiles. (p. 252)
—Conches. (p. 355)
—Indian Rhinoceroses. (p. 871)
—King Crabs. (p. 958)
—Snapping Turtles. (p. 1597)
Baxter, Cathy, jt. auth. see Atkinson, Sue.
Baxter, David. Tournesol Twins. (p. 1773)
Baxter, Fiona, et al. Cambridge Primary Science Stage 4 Learner's Book. (p. 255)
—Cambridge Primary Science Stage 5 Learner's Book. (p. 256)
Baxter, Howard, et al. Succeed in Maths. (p. 1671)
Baxter, Jean Rae. Broken Trail. (p. 230)
—Freedom Bound. (p. 634)
—Way Lies North. (p. 1864)
Baxter, Jennifer. Turned Inside Out. (p. 1798)
Baxter, Judith, ed. Speaking Out: The Female Voice in Public Contexts. (p. 1623)
Baxter, Katherine, illus. see Adams, Simon.
Baxter, Kathleen. Captured History (p. 265)
—Pop Culture Revolutions (p. 1384)
Baxter, Kathleen, jt. contrib. by see McConnell, Robert L.
Baxter, Kathleen A. & Kochel, Marcia Agness. Gotcha for Guys! Nonfiction Books to Get Boys Excited about Reading (p. 704)
Baxter, Kathleen & McConnell, Robert L., contrib. by. Assassination & Its Aftermath: How a Photograph Reassured a Shocked Nation (p. 107)
—Civil War Witness: Mathew Brady's Photos Reveal the Horrors of War (p. 326)
Baxter, Leon, illus. see Alexander, Pat.
Baxter, Mia, illus. see Bush, Jenna.
Baxter, Mia, illus. see Hager, Jenna Bush.
Baxter, Nicola. 3-Minute Animal Stories. Everitt-Stewart, Andy, illus. (p. 1991)
—3-Minute Sleepytime Stories. Stewart, Pauline, illus. (p. 1991)
—Amazing Dragons: Fiendish Tales of Dastardly Deeds. King, Colin, illus. (p. 54)

—Ballet Star: A Little Girl with a Big Dream. Cooper, Gill, illus. (p. 134)
—Bedtime Lullabies: Fall Asleep to Your Free Cd. Finn, Rebecca, illus. (p. 157)
—Bedtime Tales. Press, Jenny, illus. (p. 157)
—Book of Five-Minute Farmyard Tales. Press, Jenny, illus. (p. 211)
—Book of Five-Minute Kitten Tales: A Treasury of over 35 Bedtime Stories. Press, Jenny, illus. (p. 211)
—Book of Five-Minute Teddy Bear Tales: A Treasury of over 35 Bedtime Stories. Press, Jenny, illus. (p. 211)
—Bunny Tales Collection: Twelve Lively Stories of Rascally Rabbits. Shuttleworth, Cathie, illus. (p. 242)
—Celtic Tales & Legends. Shuttleworth, Cathie, illus. (p. 286)
—Children's Classic Poetry Collection: 60 Poems by the World's Greatest Writers. Shuttleworth, Cathie, illus. (p. 303)
—Childrens's Book of Classic Poems & Rhymes. (p. 304)
—Child's Treasury of Classic Stories: Charles Dickens, William Shakespeare, Oscar Wilde. Thorne, Jenny, illus. (p. 305)
—Cinderella: A Sparkling Fairy Tale. Chaffey, Samantha, illus. (p. 320)
—Classic Fairy Tales from Hans Christian Andersen. Shuttleworth, Cathie, illus. (p. 328)
—Classic Fairy Tales from the Brothers Grimm. Shuttleworth, Cathie, illus. (p. 328)
—Classic Folk Tales: 80 Traditional Stories from Around the World. Langton, Roger, illus. (p. 328)
—Classic Nursery Rhymes. Shuttleworth, Cathie, illus. (p. 328)
—Classic Poetry for Children. Shuttleworth, Cathie, illus. (p. 328)
—Dreamland Fairies: Magical Bedtime Stories from Fairyland. Manson, Beverlie, illus. (p. 484)
—Goldilocks & the Three Bears: A Sparkling Fairy Tale. Chaffey, Samantha, illus. (p. 696)
—Great Pirate Adventure: Peek Inside the 3D Windows. Goulding, June, illus. (p. 717)
—Head, Shoulders, Knees & Toes & Other Action Rhymes. Buckingham, Gabriella, illus. (p. 756)
—I Can Learn Times Tables: With Magnetic Numbers to Use Again & Again! Elliott, Rebecca, illus. (p. 836)
—Jewels for a Princess. Chaffey, Samantha, illus. (p. 917)
—Josie the Giraffe & the Starry Night. Fox, Lisa, illus. (p. 927)
—Kaleidoscope Book: My First Book of Learning. Elliott, Rebecca, illus. (p. 941)
—Learn about Our World. Elliott, Rebecca, illus. (p. 982)
—Learn to Count. Elliott, Rebecca, illus. (p. 983)
—Learn to Tell Time: With Magnets to Use Again & Again! Elliott, Rebecca, illus. (p. 984)
—Little Red Riding Hood: A Sparkling Fairy Tale. Chaffey, Samantha, illus. (p. 1035)
—Mermaid & the Star. Rigby, Deborah, illus. (p. 1128)
—My Ballet Theatre: Peek Inside the 3-D Windows. Chaffey, Samantha, illus. (p. 1196)
—My Book of Magical Pony Tales: 12 Beautifully Illustrated Stories. Shuttleworth, Cathie, illus. (p. 1199)
—My Book of Princess Stories. Lyon, Belinda, illus. (p. 1199)
—My First Bedtime Stories. Allen, Marie, illus. (p. 1204)
—My First Fairy Tales: Eight Exciting Picture Stories for Little Ones. Parry, Jo, illus. (p. 1206)
—My First Farmyard Tales: Eight Exciting Picture Stories for Little Ones. Lodge, Ali, illus. (p. 1206)
—My Little Treasury of Bedtime Stories. Press, Jenny, illus. (p. 1213)
—My Little Treasury of Stories & Rhymes. Press, Jenny, illus. (p. 1213)
—My Perfect Doll's House: Peek Inside the 3D Windows. Chaffey, Samantha, illus. (p. 1216)
—My Treasury of Fairies & Elves: A Collection of 20 Magical Stories. Manson, Beverlie, illus. (p. 1220)
—My Wonderful Treasury of Five-Minute Stories. Press, Jenny, illus. (p. 1221)
—Mystery of the Haunted House: Dare You Peek Through the 3-D Windows? Goulding, June, illus. (p. 1225)
—Old MacDonald's: Barnyard Tales. Davis, Caroline, illus. (p. 1284)
—Party at the Fairy Palace: Peek Inside the 3D Windows. Chaffey, Samantha, illus. (p. 1326)
—Perils of Pirates & Other Dastardly Deeds: A Compendium of Swashbuckling Pirate Adventure Stories. King, Colin, illus. (p. 1343)
—Princess Stories. Smith, Helen, illus. (p. 1405)
—Pull the Lever: Who's at Nursery? Lawson, Peter, illus. (p. 1415)
—Puppy Tales Collection: Twelve Silly Stories from Houndsville. Shuttleworth, Cathie, illus. (p. 1418)
—Rhymes for Playtime Fun. Shuttleworth, Cathie, illus. (p. 1468)
—Sing-Along Songs for Children: Join in with Your Free CD. Finn, Rebecca, illus. (p. 1578)
—Snow White: A Sparkling Fairy Tale. Chaffey, Samantha, illus. (p. 1599)
—Sparkly Ballet Story. Pedler, Caroline, illus. (p. 1622)
—Sparkly Pony Story. Pedler, Caroline, illus. (p. 1622)
—Starlight Ballerina. Jones, Deborah, illus. (p. 1642)
—Summer. (p. 1673)
—Tales from the Farmyard: 12 Stories of Grunting Pigs, Quacking Ducks, Clucking Hens, Neighing Horses, Bleating Sheep & Other Animals. Shuttleworth, Cathie, illus. (p. 1701)
—Tales from the Toy Box. Press, Jenny, illus. (p. 1702)
—Teddy Bear's Fun to Learn First 1000 Words. Lacome, Susie, illus. (p. 1712)
—Traditional Fairy Tales from Hans Christian Andersen & the Brothers Grimm. Shuttleworth, Cathie, illus. (p. 1776)
—Trouble in Space: A First Reading Adventure Book. Ball, Geoff, illus. (p. 1790)
—Trouble in Space: First Reading Books for 3-5 Year Olds. Ball, Geoff, illus. (p. 1790)
—Trouble in the Jungle: A First Reading Adventure Book. Ball, Geoff, illus. (p. 1790)
—Trouble on the Ice: First Reading Books for 3-5 Year Olds. Ball, Geoff, illus. (p. 1790)
—Trouble under the Ocean: First Reading Books for 3-5 Year Olds. Ball, Geoff, illus. (p. 1790)
—Trouble with Tippers. Ball, Geoff, illus. (p. 1790)
—Trouble with Tractors. Ball, Geoff, illus. (p. 1790)
—Trouble with Trains. Ball, Geoff, illus. (p. 1790)
—Trouble with Trucks. Ball, Geoff, illus. (p. 1790)
—Ultimate Treasury of Stories & Rhymes: A Collection of 215 Tales & Poems. (p. 1810)
—Visit from the Tooth Fairy: Magical Stories & a Special Message from the Little Friend Who Collects Your Baby Teeth. Manson, Beverlie, illus. (p. 1845)
—We Love Animals on the Farm. Henson, Gaby, illus. (p. 1867)
—Witches, Wizards & Magicians. Morton, Ken, illus. (p. 1941)
Baxter, Nicola, jt. auth. see Maloney, Jim.
Baxter, Nicola, jt. auth. see Wolfe, Jane.
Baxter, Nicola & Adams, Ben. Freddie the Fish, Star of the Show. Cameron, Craig, illus. (p. 632)
Baxter, Nicola & Ball, Geoff. Trouble in the Jungle: First Reading Books for 3-5 Year Olds. (p. 1790)
Baxter, Nicola & Birkinshaw, Marie. Treasury for Little Ones: Hours of Fun for Babies & Toddlers - Stories & Rhymes, Puzzles to Solve, & Things to Make & Do. Endersby, Frank, illus. (p. 1782)
Baxter, Nicola & Francis, Jan. Traditional Fairy Tales: Eight Exciting Picture Stories for Little Ones. Parry, Jo, illus. (p. 1776)
Baxter, Nicola & Jones, Deborah. Rainbow Fairies. (p. 1435)
Baxter, Nicola & Langton, Roger. Children's Stories from the Bible: A Collection of over 20 Tales from the Old & New Testaments, Retold for Younger Readers. Langton, Roger, illus. (p. 304)
Baxter, Nicola & Manson, Beverly. Storybook of Fairy Princesses: Six Tales from an Enchanted Secret World. (p. 1663)
Baxter, Nicola & Morton, Ken. Storybook of Ugly Ogres & Terrible Trolls: Ten Fantastic Tales of Frightful Fun. (p. 1663)
Baxter, Nicola & Shuttleworth, Cathie. Silly Rhymes & Limericks. (p. 1576)
Baxter, Nicola & Siewert, Pauline. Sweet Dreams: Soothing Stories for Peaceful Bedtimes. (p. 1689)
Baxter, Nicola, compiled by. Wonderful World of Fairies: Eight Enchanted Tales from Fairyland. (p. 1948)
Baxter, Nicola, ed. Christmas Lullabies for Children. Finn, Rebecca, illus. (p. 314)
—Classic Stories: Charles Dickens, William Shakespeare & Oscar Wilde: a Treasury for Children. Thorne, Jenny, illus. (p. 328)
—Midsummer Night's Dream & Other Classic Tales of the Plays: Six Illustrated Stories from Shakespeare. Thorne, Jenny, illus. (p. 1139)
Baxter, Nicola, retold by. Terrifying Tales: Nine Stories of Spine-Tingling Suspense. (p. 1722)
Baxter, Pam. Cup of Light: All about the Flaming Chalice. (p. 392)
Baxter, Rob, et al. Iron Kingdoms Character Guide: Full-Metal Fantasy, Volume One. (p. 888)
Baxter, Roberta. Battle of Gettysburg: A History Perspectives Book. (p. 146)
—Battles for Gold & Glory: Civil War Skirmishes in New Mexico Territory. (p. 147)
—Bill of Rights. (p. 186)
—Challenger Explosion. (p. 289)
—Computers. (p. 355)
—Creation of the U. S. Constitution: A History Perspectives Book. (p. 379)
—Dropping of the Atomic Bombs: A History Perspectives Book. (p. 486)
—Fire, Water, & Air: The Story of Antoine Lavoisier. (p. 591)
—First Cars. (p. 593)
—Great Depression: A History Perspectives Book. (p. 715)
—Great Depression. (p. 715)
—Learning about Europe. (p. 984)
—Magna Carta: Cornerstone of the Constitution. (p. 1075)
—Northern Home Front of the Civil War. (p. 1265)
—Particle Model of Matter. (p. 1325)
—Seismology: Our Violent Earth. (p. 1548)
—Skeptical Chemist: The Story of Robert Boyle. (p. 1584)
—Southern Home Front of the Civil War. (p. 1617)
—States of Matter in the Real World. (p. 1644)
Baxter, Stephanie. Adventures of Jack Brown & Friends. (p. 19)
Baxter, Stephen. Phase Space. (p. 1350)
—Proxima. (p. 1413)
Bayard, Janie Domengeaux, illus. see Borland, Jerre Shadrick.
Bayden, Maya. Medical Science. (p. 1118)
Bayden, Maya & Toriello, James. Stomach in 3D. (p. 1652)
Bayer, Linda N. Elie Wiesel: Spokesman for Remembrance. (p. 512)
Bayham, Dalan J. Loch Ness Monster Incident - Junior Explorers Society Episode 2. (p. 1044)
Bayle, B. J. Battle Cry at Batoche. (p. 145)
—Perilous Passage. (p. 1343)
—Red River Rising: A Novel (Large Print 16pt) (p. 1455)
—Red River Rising. (p. 1455)
—Shadow Riders. (p. 1557)
Bayles, Jennifer L. Adventure in Looking & Listening: Exploring Masterworks at the Albright-Knox Art Gallery. Barnett, Janet, illus. (p. 14)
Bayley, Flo, illus. see Hopkinson, Simon.
Bayley, Kimberly & Lawton, Caroline. Bugs A to Z. (p. 237)
Bayley, Nicola, illus. see Adams, Richard.
Bayley, Nicola, illus. see Patten, Brian.
Bayley, Nicola, illus. see Puncel, Maria.
Bayley, Sydney, jt. auth. see Drost, Joost.
Baylies, Peter & Toonkel, Jessica. Stay-at-Home Dad Handbook. (p. 1645)
Baylor, Byrd & Parnall, Peter. Desert Voices. (p. 429)
Baynard, Holland Callaway, jt. auth. see Baynard, Kate Holland.
Baynard, Kate Holland & Baynard, Holland Callaway. Holland Goes to Pompeii: A brief look at the buried city & its famous volcano named Vesuvius. (p. 789)
—Holland Goes to Rome: A brief look at the ancient city, its history & its Culture. (p. 789)
Bayne, Nancy. Great-Grandpa's Chair: A Story about Living & Dying, Shared Between A Great-Grandpa & His 10-year-old Grandson! Graber, Vickie, illus. (p. 716)
Baynes, Jenean Atwood & Atwood, John H. Blue Spots! Yellow Spots! (p. 203)
Baynes, Pauline. I Believe: The Nicene Creed. (p. 834)
—Prince Caspian Baynes, Pauline, illus. (p. 1401)
—Principe Caspian. (p. 1406)
—Questionable Creatures: A Bestiary. Baynes, Pauline, illus. (p. 1426)
Baynes, Pauline, illus. see Green, Roger Lancelyn.
Baynes, Pauline, illus. see Koralek, Jenny.
Baynes, Pauline, illus. see Lewis, C. S.
Baynes, Pauline, illus. see Morgaut, Philippe, tr.
Baynes, Pauline, illus. see Tolkien, J. R. R.
Baynes, Pauline & Lewis, C. S. Prince Caspian. (p. 1401)
Baynton, Martin. Three's a Crowd. Baynton, Martin, illus. (p. 1744)
Baynton, Martin, jt. auth. see Carmine, Mary.
Bayoc, Cbabi, illus. see Forman, Ruth.
Bayramoglu, Hatice, illus. see Baniti, Nailah.
Bayramoglu, Hatice, jt. auth. see Baniti, Nailah.
Bayrock, Fiona. Bubble Homes & Fish Farts. Conahan, Carolyn Digby, illus. (p. 233)
—Ocean Explorer's Handbook. (p. 1276)
—Sound: A Question & Answer Book Collins, Tami & Nei, Molly, illus. (p. 1615)
—States of Matter: A Question & Answer Book McMullen, Anne & Williams, Ted, illus. (p. 1644)
Bays, Gail, illus. see Rothenberger, Charlene.
Bays, Patricia. What Is the Bible? (p. 1890)
Bay-Williams, Jennifer M. & Martinie, Sherri L. Math & Literature, Grades 6-8. (p. 1105)
Bazaldua, Barbara. Boy of Heart Mountain. Ito, Willie, illus. (p. 218)
—Cinderella & the Lost Mice - Belle & the Castle Puppy. Disney Storybook Artists Staff, illus. (p. 320)
Bazaldua, Barbara & Bergen, Lara. Rapunzel & the Golden Rule/Jasmine & the Two Tigers (Disney Princess) Studio IBOIX & Disney Storybook Artists Staff, illus. (p. 1439)
Bazemore, Suzanne. Soccer: How It Works. (p. 1603)
Bazerman. Writing Skills Handbook Fifth Edition & Smarthinking. (p. 1965)
Bazile, Lanetta R. Painted Shapes What Will They Make? (p. 1318)
Bazler, Judith A. Biology Resources in the Electronic Age (p. 189)
Bazzoni, Lainie M. A., illus. see Fox, Alex.
Bb. Matt's 1st Tooth. (p. 1110)
BBC. Time Traveller's Journal. (p. 1753)
Bbc, Bbc. Doctor Who Official Sticker Book. (p. 459)
—How to Be a Time Lord. (p. 815)
—Official Doctionary. (p. 1280)
BBC Books Staff. Doctor Who - 12 Doctors 12 Stories. (p. 459)
BBC Cast Staff. Doctor Who. (p. 459)
BBC Education Staff, jt. auth. see Richards, Justin.
Bbc, Leanne Gl. 100 Scariest Monsters. (p. 1998)
Bdeir, Ayah & Richardson, Matt. Getting Started with LittleBits: Learning & Inventing with Modular Electronics. (p. 669)
Bea, Holly. Lucy Goose Goes to Texas. Boddy, Joe, illus. (p. 1063)
Beach, Annabelle Corrick. Illusions of Spring. (p. 857)
Beach, Bryan, illus. see Hardman, John.
Beach, Bryan, illus. see Weakland, Mark.
Beach, Byron & Keck, Gayle. Stock Matters: An Introduction to Stock & Ownership for Kids. (p. 1651)
Beach, Charles Amory. Air Service Boys in the Big Battle, or, Silencing the Big Guns. (p. 31)
—Air Service Boys over the Atlantic. (p. 31)
—Air Service Boys over the Atlantic, or, the Longest Flight on Record. (p. 31)
Beach, Jeffery. Ten Seconds to Peace: An Every Day Approach to Mindful Living. (p. 1719)
Beach, John & Lubotsky, Dana, readers. Wanderer. (p. 1856)
Beach, John, reader. Moo Cow Kaboom! (p. 1171)
Beach, Kathleen H. & Weeber, Stephanie B. Madison's Mixed-up Flower Girl Magic & Aiden's Amazing Ring Bearer Act Aiden's Amazing Ring Bearer Act. Baisley, Maryann Leake, illus. (p. 1070)
Beach, Kathy Ann. Helping a Garden Grow (p. 766)
Beach, Linda M. Michael's First Word! Gadtan Jean Louis, Rosley, illus. (p. 1135)
Beach, Mark. Simply in Season Children's Cookbook: A World Community Cookbook. (p. 1578)
Beach, Mary FitzGerald, illus. see Harper, Stephan J.
Beach, Rex. Heart of the Sunset. (p. 759)
Beach, Rex E. Heart of the Sunset. (p. 759)
Beach, Stewart. Good Morning-Sun's Up. Sugita, Yataka, illus. (p. 698)
Beach York, Carol, see York, Carol Beach.
Beachamp, Afiyah, illus. see Bush, Vicki-Ann.
Beachy, Elaine. Biff & Becka's Stupendous Vacation. (p. 177)
Beachy, Robert, et al, eds. Women, Business & Finance in Nineteenth-Century Europe: Rethinking Separate Spheres. (p. 1945)
Beacon, Dawn. Peter Piper. Beacon, Dawn, illus. (p. 1347)
Beacon, Dawn, illus. see Guillain, Charlotte & Aesop.
Beacon, Dawn, illus. see Guillain, Charlotte & Andersen, Hans Christian.
Beacon, Dawn, illus. see Guillain, Charlotte & Perrault, Charles.
Beacon, Dawn, illus. see Guillain, Charlotte.
Beacon, Dawn, illus. see Loewen, Nancy.
Beacon Street Girls, creator. Best Friends Journal. (p. 169)
—Flower Power Journal. (p. 607)
—Happy Lucky Thingy Journal. (p. 746)
Beacon Street Girls Staff. Meet the Beacon Street Girls. (p. 1122)
Beadle, David M. Day the Trash Came Out to Play. Faust, Laurie A., illus. (p. 414)
Beadles, Barbara, jt. auth. see Weller, Kathleen.
Beadling, Marilyn. Apple Pie Pickle. (p. 92)
Beagle, Peter S. Tamsin. (p. 1704)
Beagle, Peter S. & Link, Kelly. Superheroes. Horton, Rich, ed. (p. 1683)
Beahm, George. Muggles & Magic: J.K. Rowling & the Harry Potter Phenomenon. Kirk, Tim, illus. (p. 1189)
—Muggles & Magic: An Unofficial Giude to J. K. Rowling & the Harry Potter Phenomenon. Kirk, Tim, illus. (p. 1189)
—Passport to Narnia: A Newcomer's Guide. Kirk, Tim, illus. (p. 1327)
—Passport to Narnia: The Unofficial Giude. Kirk, Tim, illus. (p. 1327)
—Whimsic Alley Book of Spells: Mythical Incantations for Wizards of All Ages. Goldin, Stan, ed. (p. 1911)
Beak, Nick Huckleberry. How to Be a Detective! Crack the Case with 25 Devious Disguises & Devices! (p. 814)
—How to Bend Balloons. (p. 815)
—How to Juggle: 25 Fantastic Juggling Tricks & Techniques to Try! (p. 820)
Beake, Lesley. Home Now. Littlewood, Karin, illus. (p. 792)
—Rough Luck: Diamonds in the Kalahari. (p. 1491)
Beake, Lesley & Williams, Sam. Angel & Elf: Christmas Cookies. (p. 73)
Beakman, Onk. Lightning Rod Faces the Cyclops Queen (p. 1016)
—Mask of Power: Gill Grunt & the Curse of the Fish Master. No. 2 (p. 1102)
—Mask of Power. Santanach, Tino, illus. (p. 1102)
Beakman, Onk, jt. auth. see Grosset & Dunlap.
Beaky, Suzanne. She'll Be Comin' Round the Mountain. (p. 1564)
Beaky, Suzanne, illus. see Barnholdt, Lauren.
Beaky, Suzanne, illus. see Lang, Heather.
Beaky, Suzanne, illus. see Lodding, Linda Ravin.
Beaky, Suzanne, illus. see Owens, Greg.
Beaky, Suzanne, illus. see Schwaeber, Barbie H.
Beaky, Suzanne, illus. see Schwaeber, Barbie H., ed.
Beaky, Suzanne, illus. see Stier, Catherine.
Beal, Abigail. I Love My Beagle. (p. 842)
—I Love My Dachshund. (p. 842)
—I Love My German Shepherd. (p. 842)
—I Love My Golden Retriever. (p. 842)
—I Love My Pug. (p. 842)
—I Love My Yorkshire Terrier. (p. 842)
—Top Dogs (p. 1769)
Beal, Becky. Skateboarding: The Ultimate Guide (p. 1583)
Beal, Denice. Easy Art. (p. 500)
Beal, Duncan, ed. see Croft, Steven.
Beal, Eileen J. Ritalin: Its Use & Abuse. (p. 1475)
Beal, George. Kingfisher First Thesaurus. Chatterton, Martin, illus. (p. 960)
Beal, Jane. Magical poems for Girls. (p. 1075)
Béal, Marjorie, illus. see Cohen, Laurie.
Beal, Scott, ed. Chameleon Toothbrush: New Stories from the Neutral Zone. (p. 289)
Beal, T. J. Wash Day: A Teddy Doonamen Adventure. (p. 1859)
Beal, Tracy Lynn. Puzzle. Cunningham, Charles E., illus. (p. 1420)
Beale, Brian A. My Name Is Colin: ... & this Is Who I Am. (p. 1215)
Beale, C. R. Silly Flop-Flipping Parade. (p. 1576)
Beale, Deborah, jt. auth. see Williams, Tad.
Beale, Edith. Angela's Odyssey. (p. 74)
Beale, Fleur. Boy in the Olive Grove. (p. 218)
—I Am Not Esther. (p. 833)
Beale, G. K. Book of Revelation: A Shorter Commentary. (p. 211)
Beale, Lucy, et al. Complete Idiot's Guide Glycemic Index Cookbook. (p. 353)
Beale, Scott. Millennial Manifesto: A Youth Activist Handbook. (p. 1143)
Bealer-Wynton, Cheryl. Blinky's Island. (p. 199)
Beales, Norma J. Intrepid's Justice: One Woman's Injustice. (p. 881)
Beales, R. A. James Cook: The Pacific Coast & Beyond. (p. 907)
Beall, Kirsten. Jake & the Big Cake Mistake. Desmond, Hillary, illus. (p. 905)
Beall, Linda. Four PAWS & Lucky Little Duke Dog. (p. 625)
—Four Paws & Lucky Little Duke Dog. (p. 625)
Beall, Linda R. We , Four Paws & Me at Yellowstone National Park. (p. 1865)
Beall, Mary Kay. Sleep Tight with Angels Tonight. (p. 1588)
Beall, Pamela Conn & Nipp, Susan Hagen. Best of Wee Sing (p. 171)
—Wee Sing America (p. 1871)
—Wee Sing & Learn ABC (p. 1871)
—Wee Sing & Move. Guida, Liisa Chauncy & Klein, Nancy, illus. (p. 1871)
—Wee Sing & Play (p. 1871)
—Wee Sing Bible Songs (p. 1871)
—Wee Sing Children's Songs & Fingerplays (p. 1871)
—Wee Sing Dinosaurs (p. 1871)
—Wee Sing in the Car (p. 1871)
—Wee Sing Mother Goose Guida, Lisa & Klein, Nancy Spence, illus. (p. 1871)
—Wee Sing Nursery Rhymes & Lullabies (p. 1871)
—Wee Sing Silly Songs (p. 1871)
—Wee Sing Sing-Alongs (p. 1871)
—Who's There on Halloween? Reasoner, Charles, illus. (p. 1921)
Beall, Pamela Conn, et al. Wee Sing Around the World. Chauncey, G., illus. (p. 1871)
—Wee Sing for Baby (p. 1871)
Bealle, John. Old-Time Music & Dance: Community & Folk Revival. (p. 1285)
Beals, Frank Lee. Kit Carson. Merryweather, Jack, illus. (p. 962)
Beals, Kevin, photos by see Barber, Jacqueline, et al.
Beals, Stephen Naayvek, jt. auth. see Gumick, Isabella Grace.
Beam, Cris. I Am J. (p. 833)
Beam, Jon. Jardien's Dream (p. 909)
Beam, Matt, illus. see Schwartz, Joanne.
Beam, Rochelle. Secrets of the Snowman. (p. 1546)

Beamer, Cheryl & Beamer, Frank. Yea, It's Hokie Game Day! De Angel, Miguel, illus. (p. 1969)
Beamer, Frank, jt. auth. see Beamer, Cheryl.
Beamer, Winona Desha & Beamer-Trapp, Kaliko. Pua Polu: The Pretty Blue Hawaiian Flower. Loebel-Fried, Caren Keala, illus. (p. 1414)
Beamer, Winona Desha, et al. Naupaka: By Nona Beamer: Illustrations by Caren Loebel-Fried: Hawaiian Translation by Kaliko Beamer-Trapp: Music by Keola Beamer. Loebel-Fried, Caren, illus. (p. 1237)
Beamer-Trapp, Kaliko, jt. auth. see Beamer, Winona Desha.
Beamish, Diane. Amy's Silent World. (p. 66)
—Brucie Learns a Lesson. (p. 232)
—Gentle Jack. (p. 661)
—Grandma's Magic Button Necklace. (p. 709)
—Treefellows. (p. 1784)
Beamish, Sharon L. Paw Prints. (p. 1331)
Bean. Adverbly: Car-Pet Grammerpals. (p. 25)
—Describe Me: Car-Pet Grammerpals: Adjetives Are All About. (p. 428)
—Pronouns on the Farm: Car-Pet Grammerpals. (p. 1411)
—Umpire's Interjections: Car-Pet Grammerpals. (p. 1810)
Bean, Brett, illus. see Coats, Lucy.
Bean, Izzy, illus. see Donovan, Kim.
Bean, Jennifer. Magic Summer: Adventure by the Lake. (p. 1073)
Bean, Jonathan. At Night. Bean, Jonathan, illus. (p. 110)
—Big Snow. Bean, Jonathan, illus. (p. 184)
—Building Our House. Bean, Jonathan, illus. (p. 239)
Bean, Jonathan, illus. see Jonell, Lynne.
Bean, Jonathan, illus. see Orr, Wendy.
Bean, Jonathan, illus. see Thompson, Lauren.
Bean, Jonathan, illus. see Underwood, Deborah.
Bean, Jonathan, jt. auth. see Hoefler, Kate.
Bean, Margo Cronbaugh. Brutus the Bull. Perry, Aumi Kauffman, illus. (p. 233)
—Buffaloed Badger. Perry, Aumi Kauffman, illus. (p. 236)
Bean, Rachel. United Kingdom. (p. 1818)
Bean, Raymond. Benji Franklin: Kid Zillionaire. Vimislik, Matthew, illus. (p. 165)
—Benji Franklin: Kid Zillionaire Vimislik, Matthew, illus. (p. 165)
—Benji Franklin: Kid Zillionaire Vimislik, Matthew, illus. (p. 165)
—Blown Away (p. 202)
—Building Wealth (and Superpowered Rockets!) Vimislik, Matthew, illus. (p. 239)
—Buying Stocks (and Solid Gold Submarines!) Vimislik, Matthew, illus. (p. 248)
—Investing Well (in Supersonic Spaceships!) Vimislik, Matthew, illus. (p. 885)
—Money Troubles. Vimislik, Matthew, illus. (p. 1164)
—Rippin' It Old School (p. 1474)
—Saving Money (and the World from Killer Dinos!) Vimislik, Matthew, illus. (p. 1517)
—Sweet Farts (p. 1689)
Bean, Shelly. Rooty Toot Rambler: Finds a Home. (p. 1488)
Beander, Lillian. Mylah's Bedtime Stories (p. 1222)
Beane, Abbie, et al. Middlebury College College Prowler off the Record. (p. 1138)
Bear, Andrea, illus. see Santana, Sr. Stella.
Bear, Elizabeth. Ink & Steel (p. 874)
Bear, F. T. Connor Finn: The Secret of Snow. (p. 358)
Bear, Magdalen. Walking Automata: A Collection of Self-Moving Models to Cut Out & Make. (p. 1854)
Bear, Magdalen, jt. auth. see Jenkins, Gerald.
Bearce, Stephanie. All about Electric & Hybrid Cars. (p. 42)
—American Revolution: Spies, Secret Missions, & Hidden Facts from the American Revolution. (p. 63)
—Care for a Kitten. (p. 266)
—Care for a Pet Guinea Pig. (p. 266)
—Civil War: Spies, Secret Missions, & Hidden Facts from the Civil War. (p. 325)
—How to Harness Solar Power for Your Home. (p. 820)
—Kid's Guide to Container Gardening. (p. 953)
—Kid's Guide to Making a Terrarium. (p. 953)
—Top Secret Files: Pirates & Buried Treasure: Secrets, Strange Tales, & Hidden Facts about Pirates. (p. 1769)
—Top Secret Files - The Cold War Spies: Secrets, Special Missions, & Hidden Facts about the CIA, KGB, & MI6. (p. 1769)
—World War I: Spies, Secret Missions, & Hidden Facts from World War I. (p. 1958)
—World War II: Spies, Secret Missions, & Hidden Facts from World War II. (p. 1959)
Beard, Adelia B., jt. auth. see Beard, Lina.
Beard, Adrian. How Texts Work. (p. 812)
—Language Change. (p. 974)
—Language of Literature. (p. 975)
Beard, Alex. Crocodile's Tears. (p. 384)
—Jungle Grapevine. (p. 935)
—Monkey See, Monkey Draw. (p. 1165)
Beard, Chad, ed. see Marsh, Carole.
Beard, Daniel. American Boy's Handy Book: Turn-of-the-Century Classic of Crafts & Activities. (p. 60)
Beard, Daniel C. American Boy's Handy Book. (p. 60)
Beard, Daniel Carter. American Boy's Handy Book: Build a Fort, Sail a Boat, Shoot an Arrow, Throw a Boomerang, Catch Spiders, Fish in the Ice, Camp Without a Tent & 150 Other Activities. (p. 60)
—Shelters, Shacks & Shanties. (p. 1565)
Beard, Darleen B., jt. auth. see Beard, Darleen Bailey.
Beard, Darleen Bailey. Flimflam Man. Christelow, Eileen, illus. (p. 604)
Beard, Darleen Bailey & Beard, Darleen B. Twister. Carpenter, Nancy, illus. (p. 1802)
Beard, Darleen Bailey & Malone, Heather Harms. Annie Glover Is Not a Tree Lover. Malone, Heather Harms, illus. (p. 86)
Beard, Elizabeth. Liza & the Mysteries. (p. 1042)
Beard, George, jt. auth. see Pilkey, Dav.
Beard, Jean J. & Gillespie, Peggy, eds. Nothing to Hide: Mental Illness in the Family. Kaeser, Gigi, photos by. (p. 1268)
Beard, Lauren. Fairytale Hairdresser & Father Christmas. (p. 565)
Beard, Lauren, illus. see Llewellyn, Claire.
Beard, Lauren, illus. see Longstaff, Abie.
Beard, Lauren, jt. auth. see Harvey, Keith.
Beard, Lina & Beard, Adelia B. American Girl's Handy Book: Turn-of-the-Century Classic of Crafts & Activities. (p. 61)
Beard, Linda P. Remember ... Remember Your Name. (p. 1459)
Beard, Robert. Lovenia Little & Her Big Dreams. (p. 1061)
Beard, Robert W. Boy Named Shawn. (p. 218)
—Halcyon. (p. 736)
Beard, Sarah. Porcelain Keys. (p. 1386)
Bearden, Romare. Li'l Dan the Drummer Boy: A Civil War Story. Bearden, Romare, illus. (p. 1017)
Bearden, Thomas E. Oblivion: America at the Brink. (p. 1275)
Beardshaw, Rosalind. I Am a Princess! With Magic Changing Pictures. (p. 832)
—I Am a Spaceman! (p. 832)
—Kiss the Frog. (p. 961)
Beardshaw, Rosalind, illus. see Bedford, David.
Beardshaw, Rosalind, illus. see Black, Birdie.
Beardshaw, Rosalind, illus. see Corderoy, Tracey.
Beardshaw, Rosalind, illus. see Kidd, Pennie.
Beardshaw, Rosalind, illus. see McQuinn, Anna.
Beardshaw, Rosalind, illus. see Pearce, Clemency.
Beardshaw, Rosalind, illus. see Rickards, Lynne.
Beardshaw, Rosalind, illus. see Symes, Sally.
Beardshaw, Rosalind, jt. auth. see Branford, Henrietta.
Beardshaw, Rosalind, jt. auth. see McQuinn, Anna.
Beardslee, Lois. Lies to Live By. (p. 1007)
Beardslee, Nellie L. Glenn's of Newberry Hills. (p. 683)
Beardsley, Kurt. Under Saharan Skies. (p. 1813)
Beardsley, Martyn. Five Naughty Kittens. East, Jacqueline, illus. (p. 601)
—Sir Gadabout. Ross, Tony, illus. (p. 1580)
Beardsley, Sally. 10 Bravest Everyday Heroes. (p. 1993)
Beardwood, Mary. Discovering Islamic Art: A Childrens' Guide with Activity Sheets. (p. 449)
Bearn, Emily. Rose Cottage Tales. (p. 1489)
—Tumtum & Nutmeg: Adventures Beyond Nutmouse Hall. (p. 1796)
—Tumtum & Nutmeg: the Rose Cottage Adventures. Price, Nick, illus. (p. 1796)
Bearport Publishing Staff, contrib. by. They Don't Belong: Tracking Invasive Species. (p. 1732)
Bearss, Patricia, illus. see Paul J McSorley; Illustrated By Patricia.
Bearss, Patricia, jt. auth. see McSorley, Paul J.
Beasant, Pam. How to Draw Buildings. Tatchell, Judy, ed. (p. 817)
Beashel, Paul, et al. AQA Sport Examined. (p. 93)
Beasley, Cassie. Circus Mirandus. (p. 322)
Beasley, Cheryl. Piano Paradise: My Piano Has a Big Secret. (p. 1354)
Beasley, David R. Canoe Trip. Milner, Elizabeth B., illus. (p. 261)
Beasley, Dion, illus. see Bell, Johanna.
Beasley, Gwynneth. Zeke, Ky & the Black Rock. (p. 1985)
—Zeke, Ky & the Jellyfish. (p. 1985)
—Zeke, Ky & the Leeches. (p. 1985)
—Zeke, Ky & the Lightning Rod. (p. 1985)
—Zeke, Ky & the Mountain Stream. (p. 1985)
—Zeke, Ky & the Wooden Wands. (p. 1985)
Beasley, Jonathan & Porter, Rosanna I. Tofu Ling & the Angel: Seeds of Corruptions. Neusca, Guy, Jr. & Porter, Lynda C., illus. (p. 1761)
Beasley, Kama. Delaney's Journal: Dad Loses His Job. (p. 424)
Beasley, Linda L. Meltdowns First Adventure. (p. 1125)
—Meltdown's Next Adventure: The White House. (p. 1125)
Beasley, Nancy Wright. Izzy's Fire: Finding Humanity in the Holocaust. (p. 901)
Beasley, Sterling. Meal Ticket: The Adventures of Captain Miraculous & the Bound-For-Glory Kid Episode Five. (p. 1116)
—Street Kids. (p. 1666)
Beastly Boys Staff, et al. Battle of the Zombies. (p. 147)
Beathard, Patricia. Schools of Yesteryear: History of the One-Room School. (p. 1524)
Beaton. 1 to 20 Gift Wrap (Loose) (p. 1991)
—Mother Goose Gift Wrap (Loose) (p. 1178)
—to Z Gift Wrap (Loose) (p. 1759)
Beaton, Alyson & Bradley, K. J. Grow: An Environmentally Friendly Book. Beaton, Alyson, illus. (p. 725)
Beaton, Clare. Animals Count Dominoes. (p. 82)
—Baby's First Book. (p. 129)
—Baby's First Journal. (p. 129)
—Clare Beaton's Action Rhymes. (p. 326)
—Clare Beaton's Bedtime Rhymes. Beaton, Clare, illus. (p. 326)
—Clare Beaton's Farmyard Rhymes. Beaton, Clare, illus. (p. 326)
—Clare Beaton's Nursery Rhymes. (p. 326)
—Comida/Food. (p. 348)
—Daisy Gets Dressed. (p. 400)
—Easter. (p. 499)
—Easter Activity Book. (p. 499)
—English-Spanish Bilingual First Books (p. 530)
—Halloween: Great Ideas for Making Presents & Decorations Without Breaking the Bank! (p. 737)
—Make & Colour Paper Planes. Beaton, Clare, illus. (p. 1079)
—Make & Colour Wild Animals. (p. 1079)
—Make Your Own Noah's Ark. Beaton, Clare, illus. (p. 1080)
—Make Your Own Theatre Cinderella. (p. 1080)
—Mrs. Moon: Lullabies for Bedtime. (p. 1187)
—My Book of Things to Make & Do. (p. 1199)
—Noah's Ark. (p. 1261)
—Play Castles. Beaton, Clare, illus. (p. 1371)
—Playtime Rhymes for Little People. (p. 1373)
—Snow White. (p. 1599)
—Toys: Los Juguetes. (p. 1774)
Beaton, Clare, illus. see Barefoot Books Staff.
Beaton, Clare, illus. see Blackstone, Stella & Bass, Jules.
Beaton, Clare, illus. see Blackstone, Stella.
Beaton, Clare, illus. see Bruzzone, Catherine.
Beaton, Clare, illus. see Gannij, Joan.
Beaton, Clare, illus. see Gugler, Laurel Dee.
Beaton, Clare, jt. auth. see Blackstone, Stella.
Beaton, Clare, jt. auth. see Gannij, Joan.
Beaton, Clare, jt. illus. see Harter, Debbie.
Beaton, Clare & Blackstone, Stella. Alce, Veinte Ratones. Beaton, Clare, illus. (p. 35)
—Cerdota Grandota. Beaton, Clare, illus. (p. 287)
—How Big Is a Pig? Beaton, Clare, illus. (p. 805)
—How Loud Is a Lion? Beaton, Clare, illus. (p. 810)
Beaton, Clare & Kletter, Dana. Mrs. Moon: Lullabies for Bedtime. (p. 1187)
Beaton, Giff, et al. Birds of Georgia. (p. 191)
Beaton, Jill, ed. see Lewis, Jackie.
Beaton, Jill, ed. see Naifeh, Ted.
Beaton, Kate. Princess & the Pony. (p. 1403)
Beaton, M. C., pseud. Death of a Celebrity. (p. 420)
—Death of a Dreamer. (p. 420)
—Death of a Village. (p. 420)
Beatrice, Chris, illus. see Friedman, J. S.
Beatrice, Chris, jt. illus. see Whatley, Bruce.
Beatrice, Paul. Nifty Plates from the Fifty States: Take a Ride Across Our Great Nation - Learn about the States from Their License Plates! (p. 1252)
Beatrice, Paul, jt. auth. see Rodhe, Paul.
Beatrice, Paul & Rodhe, Paul. Nifty Fifty State Flags. (p. 1252)
Beattie, Amy & Coppin, Sara. Hiking. (p. 779)
Beattie, Julie, jt. auth. see Jay, Gina.
Beattie, Steven M., II. These Are My Sensors. Beattie, Steven M., II, illus. (p. 1731)
Beatty, Charles Clinton. Further Remarks Respecting Indian Affairs. (p. 650)
—Letter to the Rev. John Erskine. (p. 1002)
Beatty, Cherie B. Meet Lewis the Duck. (p. 1121)
Beatty, Connie. Why Owls Say Who. Beatty, Connie & Philippi, Faith, illus. (p. 1925)
Beatty, Hetty Burlingame. Blitz. Tolford, Joshua, illus. (p. 199)
Beatty, Ken. Starship English, Student Book 4. (p. 1643)
Beatty, Ken & Pearson Education Staff. Secret Codes. (p. 1540)
—Theseus & Minotaur. (p. 1732)
Beatty, Nicholas, ed. see Davis, Sharon & Patton, Charlene.
Beatty, Nicholas, jt. auth. see Ross, Barbara.
Beatty, Richard. Boron. (p. 214)
—Lanthanides. (p. 975)
—Manganese. (p. 1087)
—Rivers, Lakes, Streams, & Ponds (p. 1476)
—Wetlands (p. 1877)
Beatty, Richard H. Perfect Cover Letter. (p. 1341)
Beatty, Robert. Serafina & the Black Cloak. (p. 1552)
Beatty, Scott. Criminal Intent Guice, Butch et al, illus. (p. 382)
—Murder in Mind Guice, Butch et al, illus. (p. 1192)
—Scarecrow's Panic Plot. Vecchio, Luciano, illus. (p. 1519)
Beatty, Scott, jt. auth. see Black, Jake.
Beatty, Scott, jt. auth. see Waid, Mark.
Beatty, Scott, et al. In the Mouth of the Whale. Vecchio, Luciano, illus. (p. 866)
Beatty, Susi. Angie the Ant & the Bumblebee Tree. (p. 75)
Beatty, Terry, illus. see Adamson, Thomas K.
Beatty, Terry, illus. see Burgan, Michael & Hoena, Blake A.
Beatty, Terry, illus. see Burgan, Michael.
Beatty, Terry, illus. see Collins, Max Allan & Rowan, Dave.
Beatty, Terry, illus. see Doeden, Matt.
Beatty, Terry, illus. see Jacobson, Ryan.
Beatty, Terry, illus. see Torres, J.
Beaty, Andrea. Artist Ted. Lemaitre, Pascal, illus. (p. 104)
—Attack of the Fluffy Bunnies. (p. 113)
—Attack of the Fluffy Bunnies. Santat, Dan, illus. (p. 113)
—Doctor Ted. Lemaitre, Pascal, illus. (p. 459)
—Dorko the Magnificent. (p. 471)
—Firefighter Ted. Lemaitre, Pascal, illus. (p. 591)
—Fluffy Bunnies 2: The Schnoz of Doom. Santat, Dan, illus. (p. 608)
—Happy Birthday, Madame Chapeau. Roberts, David, illus. (p. 745)
—Hide & Sheep. Mayer, Bill, illus. (p. 777)
—Hush, Baby Ghostling. Lemaitre, Pascal, illus. (p. 830)
—Iggy Peck, Architect. Roberts, David, illus. (p. 855)
—Iggy Peck, Architect. Roberts, David, illus. (p. 856)
—Rosie Revere, Engineer. Roberts, David, illus. (p. 1490)
—Secrets of the Cicada Summer. (p. 1545)
—When Giants Come to Play. Hawkes, Kevin, illus. (p. 1902)
Beaty, Daniel. Knock Knock: My Dad's Dream for Me. (p. 965)
Beaty, Janice C. Jarod & the Mystery of the Joshua Trees: A National Park Adventure Series Book. (p. 909)
Beaty, Janice J. Jarod & the Mystery of the Petroglyphs: A National Park Adventure Series Book. Beaty, Lillian C., illus. (p. 909)
Beaty, Lillian C., illus. see Beaty, Janice J.
Beaty, Mary, et al. George Johnson's War (p. 663)
Beaty, Noel. Legend of Snowy the Shrew. (p. 988)
Beauchamp, David. Agency 32: The Chelten Affair. (p. 29)
Beauchamp, Penny, jt. auth. see Vaughan, Jenny.
Beauchamp, Richard G. Bichon Frise. (p. 177)
Beauchene, Valerie. Voice of the Hummingbird. (p. 1848)
Beauchene, Valerie A. If Wishes Were Wool. (p. 854)
—Middle Child. (p. 1137)
Beaucher, Aleksandra, illus. see Olbrys, Brooks.
Beaude, Pierre Marie. Flora, la Desconocida del Espacio. (p. 606)
Beaudesson, Emmanuel, illus. see Caffery, Don R.
Beaudette, Cathy. Boss of Me. Beaudette, Michelle, illus. (p. 215)
Beaudette, Michelle, illus. see Beaudette, Cathy.
Beaudoin, Beau. Boetry. Beaudoin, Beau, illus. (p. 207)
—Url King. (p. 1826)
Beaudoin, Liliana F. Alton the Unique Alligator: Alton, el Caimán único. (p. 50)
Beaudoin, Sean. Going Nowhere Faster. (p. 692)
—Infects. (p. 873)
—Wise Young Fool. (p. 1940)
—You Killed Wesley Payne. (p. 1975)
Beaudoin, Steven M. Industrial Revolution. (p. 872)
Beaudry, Len. Luther the Looney Bird: In Luther's First Walk. (p. 1066)
Beaufrand, M. J. Rise & Fall of the Gallivanters. (p. 1474)
Beaulieu, Danie. Impact Techniques in the Classroom: 88 Activities to Engage Your Students. (p. 862)
Beaulieu, Jimmé̄y, illus. see Langlois, Annie.
Beaulieu, Jimmy, illus. see Langlois, Annie.
Beaulieu, Jimmy, illus. see Langlois, Suzanne.
Beaumier, Randy P. Snapshot Billy: I Remember. (p. 1597)
Beaumont. Imagerie de Sorcieres. (p. 860)
—Miss Polly Wolly Doodle from T. (p. 1152)
Beaumont, Chris. Amazing Cubeecraft Paper Models: 16 Never-Before-Seen Paper Models. (p. 54)
Beaumont, Holly. Animal Body Coverings. (p. 76)
—Why Do Monkeys & Other Mammals Have Fur? (p. 1923)
—Why Do Owls & Other Birds Have Feathers? (p. 1924)
—Why Do Snails & Other Animals Have Shells? (p. 1924)
Beaumont, Holly & Lewis, Clare. Why Do Snakes & Other Animals Have Scales? (p. 1924)
Beaumont, Jeanne Marie Le Prince De. Beauty & the Beast. Crane, Walter, illus. (p. 154)
Beaumont, Jeanne-Marie Leprince De. Beauty & the Beast: Beauty & the Beast a Tale for the Entertainment of Juvenile Readers. Crane, Walter, illus. (p. 154)
Beaumont, Karen. Crybaby. Yelchin, Eugene, illus. (p. 387)
—Dini Dinosaur. Roode, Daniel, illus. (p. 440)
—Doggone Dogs! Catrow, David, illus. (p. 462)
—Duck, Duck, Goose! A Coyote's on the Loose! Aruego, Jose & Dewey, Ariane, illus. (p. 488)
—Duck, Duck, Goose! (A Coyote's on the Loose!) Aruego, Jose & Dewey, Ariane, illus. (p. 488)
—I Ain't Gonna Paint No More! Catrow, David, illus. (p. 831)
—I Like Myself! Catrow, David, illus. (p. 841)
—Move over, Rover! Dyer, Jane, illus. (p. 1183)
—No Sleep for the Sheep! Urbanovic, Jackie, illus. (p. 1260)
—Shoe-La-La! Pham, LeUyen, illus. (p. 1568)
—Shoe-la-La! Pham, LeUyen, illus. (p. 1568)
—Where's My T-R-U-C-K? Catrow, David, illus. (p. 1910)
—Who Ate All the Cookie Dough? Yelchin, Eugene, illus. (p. 1914)
—Wild about Us! Stevens, Janet, illus. (p. 1928)
Beaumont, Leprince De, see De Beaumont, Leprince.
Beaumont, Marie Leprince de, et al. Beauty & the Beast & Other Fairy Tales. (p. 154)
Beaumont, Peter, illus. see Lowe, Lana.
Beaumont, S. Baby Senses Hearing. (p. 128)
Beaumont, Steve. Drawing Diplodocus & Other Plant-Eating Dinosaurs. (p. 481)
—Drawing Dragons: And Other Cold-Blooded Creatures. (p. 481)
—Drawing Giganotosaurus & Other Giant Dinosaurs. (p. 481)
—Drawing Griffins & Other Winged Wonders. (p. 482)
—Drawing Legendary Monsters (p. 482)
—Drawing Plesiosaurus & Other Ocean Dinosaurs. (p. 482)
—Drawing Pteranodon & Other Flying Reptiles. (p. 482)
—Drawing T. Rex & Other Meat-Eating Dinosaurs. (p. 482)
—Drawing the Kraken & Other Sea Monsters. (p. 482)
—Drawing the Minotaur & Other Demihumans. (p. 482)
—Drawing Triceratops & Other Armored Dinosaurs. (p. 482)
—Drawing Unicorns & Other Mythical Beasts. (p. 482)
—Drawing Werewolves & Other Gothic Ghouls. (p. 482)
—How to Draw Magical Kings & Queens. (p. 818)
—How to Draw Orcs, Elves, & Dwarves. (p. 818)
—How to Draw Warriors. (p. 819)
—How to Draw Witches & Wizards. (p. 819)
—How to Draw Wizards, Warriors, Orcs & Elves. (p. 819)
Beaumont, Susanna. Baby Senses Sight. (p. 128)
—Baby Senses Speech: Look! I'm Talking! (p. 128)
—Baby Senses Taste. (p. 128)
—Baby Senses Touch. (p. 128)
Beaumont, Susanna & Baby Senses Staff. Smell. (p. 1593)
Beaupré, Nathalie. Why Am I Perfect? An Empowering Book Written for Children First. (p. 1922)
Beauregard, Lynda. Great Space Case: A Mystery about Astronomy. Helmer, Der-Shing, illus. (p. 718)
—Hunt for Hidden Treasure: A Mystery about Rocks. Mogorrón, Guillermo, illus. (p. 828)
—In Search of the Fog Zombie: A Mystery about Matter. Helmer, Der-Shing, illus. (p. 864)
—Missing Cuckoo Clock: A Mystery about Gravity. Helmer, Der-Shing, illus. (p. 1152)
—Nighttime Cabin Thief: A Mystery about Light. Helmer, Der-Shing, illus. (p. 1255)
—Summer Camp Science Mysteries. Helmer, Der-Shing, illus. (p. 1674)
—Werewolf Chase: A Mystery about Adaptations. Torres, German, illus. (p. 1875)
—Whispering Lake Ghosts: A Mystery about Sound. Torres, German, illus. (p. 1912)
—Yucky Duck Rescue: A Mystery about Pollution. Torres, German, illus. (p. 1983)
Beausoleil, Dana. Elf in the Oak Tree. (p. 512)
Beausoliel, Loyan & Wells, Leah. Games That Sing: 25 Activities to Keep Children on Their Toes. (p. 655)
Beautement, Tiah, jt. ed. see Fisher, Maire.
Beauvais, Clémentine. Gargoyles Gone AWOL. Home, Sarah, illus. (p. 657)
—Sleuth on Skates. Home, Sarah, illus. (p. 1590)
Beauvais, Den. Alien Parade: Animated Flip Book. Pt. 1 (p. 41)
—Dragonfly Flipz Sampler. (p. 478)
Beauvais, Gailanna. How Are We Blessed? Beauvais, Gailanna, illus. (p. 805)
Beauvisage, Alice. My Blankie. Beauvisage, Alice, illus. (p. 1198)
Beauvois, Nathalie, illus. see Traditional.
Beaver, Simon. Dangerous & Dirty Jobs Low Intermediate Book with Online Access. (p. 404)
—Fantastic Creatures: Monsters, Mermaids, & Wild Men Beginning Book with Online Access. (p. 571)
—Light in the Night: the Moon Beginning Book with Online Access. (p. 1015)
—Paris: City of Light Beginning Book with Online Access. (p. 1324)
—Saved! Heroes in Everyday Life. (p. 1517)

B

—Slice by Slice: The Story of Pizza. (p. 1590)
—Traffic Jams: the Road Ahead Beginning Book with Online Access. (p. 1776)
—Wild Australia! (p. 1928)
—Young & Amazing: Teens at the Top. (p. 1978)
Beaverho, Archie, illus. see Blondin, John.
Beavers, David R. I Am a Manger. (p. 832)
Beavers, Ethen, illus. see Beechen, Adam.
Beavers, Ethen, illus. see Berrios, Frank.
Beavers, Ethen, illus. see Bird, Benjamin.
Beavers, Ethen, illus. see Bright, J. E.
Beavers, Ethen, illus. see Bright, J. E., et al.
Beavers, Ethen, illus. see Buckley, Michael.
Beavers, Ethen, illus. see Eisinger, Justin & Simon, Alonzo, eds.
Beavers, Ethen, illus. see Golden Books.
Beavers, Ethen, illus. see Hoena, Blake.
Beavers, Ethen, illus. see Sazaklis, John.
Beavers, Ethen, illus. see Scaletta, Kurtis.
Beavers, Ethen, illus. see Sutton, Laurie S.
Beavers, Ethen, illus. see Sutton, Laurie.
Beavers, Ethen, illus. see Terrell, Brandon.
Beavers, Ethen, illus. see Wrecks, Billy.
Beavers, Melinda, illus. see Harrigan, Matt.
Beavers, Melinda, illus. see Troupe, Thomas Kingsley.
Beavin, John. Parable of the Stars. (p. 1323)
Beavington, Ruth. Edward Bear. (p. 505)
Beavis, Paul. Hello World! (p. 765)
Beavon, Rod & Jarvis, Alan. Periodicity, Quantitative Equilibrium & Functional Group Chemistry. (p. 1343)
Beazley, Mark, ed. see Marvel Comics Staff.
Beazley, Mark & Marvel Comics Staff, eds. Marvel Universe Roleplaying Game: Guide to the X-Men. (p. 1099)
Beazley, Mark D., ed. see Thomas, Roy.
Bebb, Lynne, jt. auth. see Davies, Carolyn.
Bebirian, Helena, illus. see Mammola-Koravos, Beth A.
Beccaloni, George. Biggest Bugs Life-Size. (p. 185)
Beccard, Helen L., illus. see Windeatt, Mary F.
Beccia, Carlyn. I Feel Better with a Frog in My Throat: History's Strangest Cures. (p. 838)
Beccia, Carlyn, illus. see Krull, Kathleen.
Beccia, Carlyn, illus. see Lachenmeyer, Nathaniel.
Becerra de Jenkins, Lyll. Prision de Honor. (p. 1407)
Bechard, Clem. Mrs. Robinson Finds a Home. (p. 1187)
Bechard, Margaret, jt. auth. see Bechard, Margaret E.
Bechard, Margaret E. & Bechard, Margaret. Hanging on to Max. (p. 742)
Becher, Arthur, illus. see Bangs, John.
Becher, Rudolf. In Search of Yesterday: Mamma, I hate you no More! (p. 865)
Becher, Susan. Silly Friend. (p. 1576)
Bechstein, Ludwig. Rabbit Catcher & Other Fairy Tales. Jarrell, Randall, tr. (p. 1429)
Bechtel, Mark. NASCAR Race Day: Behind the Scenes. (p. 1230)
Bechtold, Chris. Current Adventure: In the Wake of Lewis & Clark. (p. 394)
Bechtold, Lisze. Buster & Phoebe: The Great Bone Game. (p. 245)
—Buster the Very Shy Dog. (p. 245)
—Buster the Very Shy Dog Finds a Kitten. (p. 245)
Bechtold, Phyliss. Seymour Bluffs & the Legend of the Piasa Bird. (p. 1556)
Bechtold, Phyllis. Seymour Bluffs Activities Coloring Book. (p. 1556)
Beck, A. E. Master-E: Travel into Mystical Dragon Dimensions: Collision of Fantasy, Science Fiction & Physics. (p. 1103)
Beck, Adrienne, jt. auth. see Tachibana, Yutaka.
Beck, Alison. Gardening Month by Month in New England (p. 656)
—Gardening Month by Month in Ontario. (p. 656)
—Water Garden Plants for Canada (p. 1862)
Beck, Alison, jt. auth. see Hower, Fred.
Beck, Alison, jt. auth. see Kelbaugh, Duncan.
Beck, Alison, jt. auth. see Knapke, Debra.
Beck, Alison, jt. auth. see Sternberg, Ilene.
Beck, Alison, jt. auth. see Wood, Tim.
Beck, Alison, jt. auth. see Wood, Timothy D.
Beck, Alison & Binetti, Marianne. Gardening Month by Month in British Columbia. (p. 656)
Beck, Alison & Cinque, Maria. Best Garden Plants for New York State. (p. 169)
Beck, Alison & Kelbaugh, Duncan. Gardening Month by Month in the Maritimes (p. 656)
Beck, Alison & Kiefer, Lorraine. Best Garden Plants for New Jersey. (p. 169)
Beck, Alison & Klose, Liz. Best Garden Plants for Ontario (p. 169)
Beck, Alison & Knapke, Debra. Gardening Month by Month in Ohio (p. 656)
Beck, Alison & Mickey, Thomas. Best Garden Plants for New England. (p. 169)
Beck, Alison & Wood, Tim. Gardening Month by Month in Michigan (p. 656)
Beck, Alison, et al. Gardening Month by Month in Washington & Oregon. (p. 656)
Beck, Andrea. Elliot's Emergency. (p. 514)
—Elliot's Fire Truck Beck, Andrea, illus. (p. 514)
—Pierre in the Air! Beck, Andrea, illus. (p. 1357)
—Pierre le Poof! Beck, Andrea, illus. (p. 1357)
—Pierre's Friends Beck, Andrea, illus. (p. 1357)
Beck, Andrea, illus. see Beck, Carolyn.
Beck, Angela. Fish: Keeping & Caring for Your Pet. (p. 598)
—Guinea Pigs: Keeping & Caring for Your Pet. (p. 731)
—Rabbits: Keeping & Caring for Your Pet. (p. 1430)
Beck, Barbara. Bill Every Cloud Has a Silver Lining. (p. 186)
—Future Architect's Handbook (p. 651)
Beck, Bev. Acorn Nuts. Deweese, Susan, illus. (p. 9)
—Benny at the Bop. (p. 165)
—Birthday Present. DeWeese, Susan, illus. (p. 193)
Beck, Blaze, illus. see Beck, Ernie.
Beck, Carolyn. Buttercup's Lovely Day Beck, Andrea, illus. (p. 247)
—Dog Breath Kerrigan, Brooke, illus. (p. 461)
—One Hungry Heron Patkau, Karen, illus. (p. 1295)
—Richard Was a Picker Hodson, Ben, illus. (p. 1470)
—Wellington's Rainy Day Kerrigan, Brooke, illus. (p. 1874)
Beck, Charles, illus. see Steinberg, Alfred.
Beck, Crystall. Adventures of Carter & Vincent. (p. 17)
Beck, David Michael, illus. see Allen, Will.
Beck, David Michael, illus. see Bowyer, Clifford B.
Beck, Dewey. Ledge, a Pie, & Hazel the Fly. (p. 987)
Beck, Ernie. Skinni Mini & Friends in the Valley of Hope. Beck, Blaze, illus. (p. 1585)
Beck, Esther. Cool Spy Supplies: Fun Top Secret Science Projects. (p. 364)
—Ill Help My Chums Learn about Systems! (p. 856)
Beck, Esther & Doudna, Kelly. Im on the Trail to Learn about Scale! (p. 859)
—Please Don't Laugh, I Can Use a Graph! (p. 1373)
—You'll Cause a Stir When You Infer! (p. 1977)
Beck, Gail. Gold: Set Of 6. (p. 693)
—Gold: Text Pairs. (p. 693)
Beck, Glenn. Book of American Heroes. Ajhar, Brian, illus. (p. 210)
Beck, Glenn, et al. Christmas Sweater. Dorman, Brandon, illus. (p. 315)
—Snow Angel. Dorman, Brandon, illus. (p. 1598)
Beck, Greig. Return of the Ancients. (p. 1464)
Beck, Holly. Revenge of the Dorkoids: The Secret Club Begins. (p. 1466)
Beck, Ian. Busy Day. (p. 246)
—Christmas Story. (p. 315)
—Getting Dressed. (p. 669)
—Let's Pretend. (p. 1000)
—Playtime. (p. 1373)
—Secret History of Tom Trueheart. (p. 1541)
—Teddy Robber. (p. 1712)
—Tom Trueheart & the Land of Dark Stories. (p. 1764)
—Ugly Duckling. (p. 1808)
Beck, Ian, illus. see Doherty, Berlie.
Beck, Ian, illus. see McGee, Marni.
Beck, Isabel. Questioning the Author: An Approach for Enhancing Student Engagement with Text. (p. 1426)
Beck, Isabel L., et al. Creating Robust Vocabulary: Frequently Asked Questions & Extended Examples. (p. 379)
—Decodable Books Collections. (p. 422)
—Julian's Glorious Summer. (p. 932)
—Trophies Kindergarten: I Am. (p. 1789)
—Trophies Kindergarten: Soup. (p. 1789)
—Trophies Kindergarten: I Nap. (p. 1789)
—Trophies Kindergarten: We Go. (p. 1789)
—Trophies Kindergarten: Hop In! (p. 1789)
—Trophies Kindergarten: My Bus. (p. 1789)
—Trophies Kindergarten: My Pig. (p. 1789)
—Trophies Kindergarten: Come In. (p. 1789)
—Trophies Kindergarten: Pet Day. (p. 1789)
—Trophies Kindergarten: Sid Hid. (p. 1789)
—Trophies Kindergarten: The Dig. (p. 1789)
—Trophies Kindergarten: The Mat. (p. 1789)
—Trophies Kindergarten: In a Sub. (p. 1789)
—Trophies Kindergarten: The Park. (p. 1789)
—Trophies Kindergarten: But I Can. (p. 1789)
—Trophies Kindergarten: It Is Fun. (p. 1789)
—Trophies Kindergarten: The Party. (p. 1789)
—Trophies Kindergarten: The Salad. (p. 1789)
—Trophies Kindergarten: Hop on Top. (p. 1789)
—Trophies Kindergarten: Up, up, Up. (p. 1789)
—Trophies Kindergarten: We Can Fix. (p. 1789)
—Trophies Kindergarten: Kip the Ant. (p. 1789)
—Trophies Kindergarten: The Big Ram. (p. 1789)
—Trophies Kindergarten: A Hat I Like. (p. 1789)
—Trophies Kindergarten: I Can See It! (p. 1789)
—Trophies Kindergarten: Is It a Fish? (p. 1789)
—Trophies Kindergarten: Is It for Me? (p. 1789)
—Trophies Kindergarten: What Can Hop? (p. 1789)
—Trophies Kindergarten: A Bug Can Tug. (p. 1789)
—Trophies Kindergarten: Tap, Tap, Tap. (p. 1789)
—Trophies Kindergarten: A Big, Big Van. (p. 1789)
—Trophies Kindergarten: Sit on My Chair. (p. 1789)
—Trophies Kindergarten: I Have, You Have. (p. 1789)
—Trophies Kindergarten: Where's My Teddy? (p. 1789)
—Trophies Kindergarten: What Is in the Box? (p. 1789)
—Trophies Kindergarten: First Day at School. (p. 1789)
—Trophies Kindergarten: Little Cat, Big Cat. (p. 1789)
—Wilma Rudolph. (p. 1934)
Beck, Jeanine. Animales, Mis Amigos. (p. 81)
—First Spanish Mi Casa. (p. 597)
Beck, Jerry. Outlaw Animation: Cutting-Edge Cartoons from the Spike & Mike Festivals. (p. 1312)
Beck, Julie. Hangin' Out with Russell. (p. 742)
Beck, Leslie. Healthy Eating for Preteens & Teens: The Ultimate Guide to Diet Nutrition & Food. (p. 758)
Beck, Lynn G. & Sesa. Powercat, the Pacific Tiger. (p. 1390)
Beck, Mary Giraudo. Heroes & Heroines in Tlingit-Haida Legend. DeWitt, Nancy, illus. (p. 772)
Beck, Nina. This Book Isn't Fat, It's Fabulous. (p. 1735)
—This Girl Isn't Shy, She's Spectacular. (p. 1735)
Beck, Pam & Peters, Laura. Best Garden Plants for North Carolina. (p. 169)
Beck, Patricia. Prince Hasmir's High Seas Adventure. (p. 1401)
—Princess Feldings & the Academy of Queens. (p. 1403)
Beck, Paul. Color & Play: Dinosaurs. (p. 342)
—Cuerpo Humano. Fairman, Jennifer, illus. (p. 390)
Beck, Paula. Little Star. (p. 1036)
Beck, Rachel. Bella & the Little Gray Kitten. (p. 162)
Beck, Randy. Teen Quest. (p. 1713)
Beck, Ray, et al. Practicing Basic Skills in Algebra. (p. 1392)
—Practicing Basic Skills in Language Arts. (p. 1392)
—Practicing Basic Skills in Math: Grades 2-3. (p. 1392)
—Practicing Basic Skills in Math: Grades 4-5. (p. 1392)
—Practicing Basic Skills in Math: Grades 6-8. (p. 1392)
—Practicing Basic Skills in Math: Grades K-1. (p. 1392)
—Practicing Basic Skills in Math: Secondary Remedial. (p. 1392)
Beck, Ricky. Puzzled Heart. (p. 1421)
Beck, Robert, illus. see Choat, Beth.
Beck, Roger B. Modern World History: Patterns of Interaction: Pupil's Edition. (p. 1159)
—World History: Patterns of Interaction: Pupil's Edition. (p. 1955)
Beck, Roger B., et al. Ancient World History: Patterns of Interaction. (p. 71)
—Modern World History: Patterns of Interaction. (p. 1159)
—World History: Patterns of Interaction. (p. 1955)
Beck, Scott. Monster Sleepover! (p. 1168)
Beck, Sharon. Fish in Our Class. (p. 598)
Beck, Sunny. In the Children's Meadow. (p. 865)
Beck, Timothy P. Genie & the Lamp: A Story of Creation. McCoy, Jody, illus. (p. 661)
Beck, Tom. David Seymour (Chim) Shneiderman, Ben, photos by. (p. 411)
Beck, W. H. Malcolm at Midnight. Lies, Brian, illus. (p. 1083)
—Malcolm under the Stars. Lies, Brian, illus. (p. 1083)
Beck, William F. Bible Stories in Pictures. Rogers, Ruth W. et al, illus. (p. 176)
—Histori Biblike Me Llustrime: Nga Krijimi Ne Kishen e Hershme. Rogers, Ruth W. et al, illus. (p. 782)
Beckenstein, Cara. True Story of Federico Fish & Ana Alligator. Tanchak, Diane, illus. (p. 1793)
Becker, Aaron. Journey. Becker, Aaron, illus. (p. 927)
—Quest. (p. 1426)
Becker and Mayer! Books Staff. Hello Kitty Super-Sweet Stencils. Sanrio Company, Ltd Staff, illus. (p. 764)
Becker & Mayer, creator. Rock Fashion Design Studio. (p. 1482)
Becker, Ann. Cranes. (p. 376)
—Dinosaurs. (p. 443)
—Fire Engines. (p. 590)
—Monster Trucks. (p. 1168)
—Multiplication. (p. 1190)
—Tractors. (p. 1775)
—Wizards, Witches, & Dragons. (p. 1943)
Becker, Ann, jt. auth. see Dowdy, Penny.
Becker, Ann, jt. auth. see Peppas, Lynn.
Becker, Ann, jt. auth. see Torpie, Kate.
Becker, Ann & Peppas, Lynn. Sorting. (p. 1614)
Becker, Baruch, illus. see Altein, Chani.
Becker, Bill. Jose & Mariano Meet Taotaomon'a (p. 926)
Becker, Bonny. Bedtime for Bear. Denton, Kady MacDonald, illus. (p. 156)
—Birthday for Bear. Denton, Kady MacDonald, illus. (p. 192)
—Library Book for Bear. Denton, Kady MacDonald, illus. (p. 1005)
—Magical Ms. Plum. Portnoy, Amy, illus. (p. 1075)
—Sniffles for Bear. Denton, Kady MacDonald, illus. (p. 1597)
—Visitor for Bear. Denton, Kady MacDonald, illus. (p. 1845)
Becker, Boruch, illus. see Krinsky, Rivkah.
Becker, Boruch, illus. see Rouss, Sylvia.
Becker, Boruch, illus. see Sollish, Ari.
Becker, Brooke. Adventures of Sammy Snowflake Gentry, Kyle, illus. (p. 22)
Becker, Charlotte, illus. see Faulkner, Georgene.
Becker, Christie. You Will Be My Baby Even When. Brayton, Julie, illus. (p. 1976)
Becker, Curt. Sad Sant. Fariss, Michelle, illus. (p. 1501)
Becker, Cynthia S. Chipeta: Ute Peacemaker. (p. 308)
Becker, Frank. You Can TRIUMPH over TERROR: 7 Steps to Plan, Prepare, & Persevere. Becker, Frank, illus. (p. 1974)
Becker, Helaine. AlphaBest: The Zany, Zanier, Zaniest Book about Comparatives & Superlatives. Whamond, Dave, illus. (p. 48)
—Big Green Book of the Big Blue Sea. Dawson, Willow, illus. (p. 181)
—Dirk Daring, Secret Agent (p. 445)
—Insecto-Files: Amazing Insect Science & Bug Facts You'll Never Believe. Dávila, Claudia & Owlkids Books Inc. Staff, illus. (p. 875)
—Juba This, Juba That. Lightburn, Ron, illus. (p. 930)
—Magic up Your Sleeve: Amazing Illusions, Tricks, & Science Facts You'll Never Believe. Dávila, Claudia, illus. (p. 1074)
—Science on the Loose: Amazing Activities & Science Facts You'll Never Believe. Dávila, Claudia & Owlkids Books Inc. Staff, illus. (p. 1527)
—Skateboarding Science. (p. 1583)
—Trouble in the Hills (p. 1790)
—What's the Big Idea? Inventions That Changed Life on Earth Forever. Attoe, Steve & Owlkids Books Inc. Staff, illus. (p. 1899)
Becker, Helaine, jt. auth. see Kain, Bob.
Becker, Helaine, jt. auth. see Kids Can Press Staff.
Becker Holstein, Barbara. Secrets: Diary of a Gutsy Teen. (p. 1544)
—Truth: Diary of a Gutsy Tween. (p. 1794)
—Truth: I'm a Girl, I'm Smart, & I Know Everything! (p. 1794)
Becker, Jacalyn D. I Am No One's Little Girl but God's Own Child (p. 833)
Becker, Jack & Hayhurst, Chris. Brain & Spinal Cord in 3D. (p. 221)
Becker, Jack & Sherman, Josepha. Upper Limbs in 3D. (p. 1825)
Becker, Jaqueline H. Listen, There Are More Than Seven Dwarfs. (p. 1022)
Becker, Jason Earl. Hero Corps: The Rookie. Moutafis, Greg, illus. (p. 772)
Becker, John. Grizzly Bears. (p. 724)
—Wild Cats: Past & Present. Hallett, Mark, illus. (p. 1929)
Becker, John E. California Condor. (p. 253)
—Frenemies for Life: Cheetahs & Anatolian Shepherd Dogs. (p. 636)
—Gray Whales. (p. 713)
—Green Sea Turtles. (p. 722)
—Northern Elephant Seal. (p. 1265)
—Seven Little Rabbits. Cooney, Barbara, illus. (p. 1554)
Becker, Kate M. My Dream Playground. Henry, Jed, illus. (p. 1202)
Becker, Ken, illus. see Posner-Sanchez, Andrea.
Becker, Laura. Wonder of a Summer Day. Steffen, Jennifer, illus. (p. 1947)
Becker, Lisa E., illus. see Winderman, Jay B.
Becker, LuAnne E., illus. see Winderman, Jay B.
Becker, Lynne, creator. Me Too Mommy. (p. 1116)
Becker, May R. Woodland Party. (p. 1949)
—Woodland Party - Color. (p. 1949)
Becker, Michele Joy. What If Marshmallows Fell from the Sky. Joslin, Irene, illus. (p. 1887)
Becker, Michelle Aki. Arizona. (p. 98)
—Arizona. Risco, Eida del, tr. from ENG. (p. 98)
Becker, Pamela, illus. see Bolte, Mari.
Becker, Paula, illus. see Bullard, Lisa.
Becker, Peggy Daniels. Drugs. (p. 487)
—Japanese-American Internment During World War II. (p. 909)
Becker, Rebecca J., illus. see Cox, Joseph J.
Becker, Sandra. Paul Bunyan. (p. 1330)
—Pocahontas. (p. 1375)
Becker, Savan. Starry Night (2nd Edition) (p. 1642)
Becker, Scott. Have A Safe Summer! (p. 754)
Becker, Suzy. Bud & Scooter. (p. 234)
—Bud & Scooter. Becker, Suzy, illus. (p. 234)
—Kate the Great Except When She's Not. Becker, Suzy, illus. (p. 944)
—Kate the Great, Except When She's Not. Becker, Suzy, illus. (p. 944)
—Kids Make It Better: A Write-In, Draw-In Journal. (p. 954)
Becker, Tom. Lifeblood. (p. 1013)
Becker, Tom, et al. Scholastic Almanac 2011: Facts & Stats. (p. 1521)
—World's Cutest Puppies In 3-D. (p. 1960)
Becker, Toni, illus. see Keaster, Diane W.
Becker, Wayne, illus. see Flaxman, Jessica & Hall, Kirsten.
Becker, Wayne, illus. see Jensen, Patricia.
Becker, Wayne, illus. see Namm, Diane.
Becker-Doyle, Eve & Doyle, Evan Brain. Evan Brain's Christmas List & Other Shenanigans: Boy Warrior Fights Evil. Doyle, Evan Brain, illus. (p. 540)
Beckering, Analise. Sight. (p. 1573)
Beckerman, Chad, illus. see Ephron, Delia.
Beckerman, Menucha. Candy Kids. (p. 261)
—Crankytown. (p. 376)
—Crying Clown. (p. 387)
—Friends on the Farm. (p. 638)
—Gitty's Dream Comes True. (p. 681)
—My Middos World: Where Is Michael? (p. 1214)
—My Middos World: Michael Wants Patience (p. 1214)
—My Middos World: Hurray! Michael Is Big. (p. 1214)
—My Middos World: Michael & the Raindrops (p. 1214)
—My Middos World: Michael & the Secret of Making Friends (p. 1214)
—My Middos World: Dina-dee Is a Goody Gaash, Elisheva, illus. (p. 1214)
—My Middos World: Dina-dee Loves Shabbos Gaash, Elisheva, illus. (p. 1214)
—My Middos World: Why Did Dina-dee's Face Shine Gaash, Elisheva, illus. (p. 1214)
—Real Hero. (p. 1448)
—Surprise for Mommy. (p. 1685)
—To Share with Love. (p. 1759)
—Welcome Home. (p. 1873)
—Who Dropped the Chick. (p. 1915)
Beckes, Shirley, illus. see Brandon, Wendy.
Beckes, Shirley, illus. see Crawley, Brian.
Beckes, Shirley, illus. see James, Annabelle.
Beckes, Shirley, illus. see Pugliano-Martin, Carol.
Beckes, Shirley V., illus. see Brandon, Wendy.
Becket. Key the Steampunk Vampire Girl - Book One: And the Dungeon of Despair. (p. 950)
Becket, Jim. Inca Gold: Choose Your Own Adventure #20. (p. 868)
Becket, Nancy, illus. see Sermons, Faye.
Beckett, Andrew, illus. see Baglio, Ben M.
Beckett, Bernard. Lester. (p. 994)
Beckett, David, jt. auth. see Mills, Nathan.
Beckett, G., jt. auth. see Martin, L.
Beckett, Garner, illus. see Archibald, Laura.
Beckett, Harry. Alberta. (p. 35)
—Manitoba. (p. 1087)
—Newfoundland & Labrador. (p. 1249)
—Nova Scotia. (p. 1268)
—Nunavut. (p. 1273)
—Ontario. (p. 1298)
Beckett, Leslie. Miguel Uses a Microscope. (p. 1141)
Beckett, Mike & Platt, Andy. Periodic Table at a Glance. (p. 1343)
Beckett, Samuel & Boxall, Peter. Samuel Beckett: Waiting for Godot-Endgame. Boxall, Peter, ed. (p. 1509)
Beckett, Sheilah, illus. see Balducci, Rita.
Beckett, Sheilah, illus. see Golden Books Staff.
Beckett, Sydney. My Favorite Season. (p. 1203)
Beckett, Wendy, contrib. by. Sister Wendy's American Collection (p. 1581)
Beckett-Bowman, Lucy. Seashore. Donaera, Patrizia & Haggerty, Tim, illus. (p. 1538)
—Sticker Dolly Dressing Bridesmaids. (p. 1650)
—Sticker Dolly Dressing Popstars. (p. 1650)
Beckford, Avril. I Love You 65 Bulldozers. (p. 843)
—Tooth Fairy. (p. 1768)
Beckford, Lois. Interesting Pen Pal. (p. 879)
Beckham, David. Beckham: My World. (p. 156)
—Charlie Barker & the Secret of the Deep Dark Woods. (p. 292)
Beckham, Robert. Who in the World Was the Secretive Printer? The Story of Johannes Gutenberg (Audio CD) (p. 1915)
—Who in the World Was the Secretive Printer? The Story of Johannes Gutenberg. Mickle, Jed, illus. (p. 1915)
Beckhorn, Susan Williams. Moose Eggs: Or, Why Moose Has Flat Antlers. Stevens, Helen, illus. (p. 1173)
—Moose Power! Muskeg Saves the Day. Huntington, Amy, illus. (p. 1173)
—Sarey by Lantern Light. (p. 1515)
Beckingham, Adrian. Diamond Ship. (p. 434)
—GobDrop & Snowshine. (p. 688)
—King of the Things. (p. 959)
Becklake, Sue & Parker, Steve. Astronomy. (p. 109)
Beckler, Bruce. My Daddy Is A Deputy Sheriff. Finney, Simone, illus. (p. 1201)
—My Daddy Is A Fire Fighter: My Daddy Is A Fireman. Peek, Jeannette, illus. (p. 1201)

—My Daddy Is A Police Officer: Wears A Badge Finney, Simone, illus. (p. 1201)
—My Daddy Is a Police Officer: My Daddy Wears a Star. Finney, Simone, illus. (p. 1201)
—My Mommy Is A Deputy Sheriff. Finney, Simone, illus. (p. 1214)
—My Mommy Is A Nurse. Peek, Jeannette, illus. (p. 1214)
—My Mommy Is A Police Officer: My Mommy Wears A Star. Finney, Simone, illus. (p. 1214)
—My Mommy Is A Police Officer: My Mommy Wears A Badge. Finney, Simone, illus. (p. 1214)
—Secret Tunnels of Spring Mountain. (p. 1544)
—Secrets of the Green Mansion. (p. 1545)
—Undercovers in the FBI. (p. 1814)
Beckler, Marion. Carrie: A Story of Early San Diego. (p. 271)
Beckles, Tinyla. Monday with Allie. (p. 1163)
Beckley, N. K. Peggy. (p. 1335)
—Three-Some: Book 2. (p. 1744)
—Writer's Corner: Book 3. (p. 1964)
Becklund, Annette L. Warren Is Wonderful. Gulzeth, Ray, illus. (p. 1858)
Beckman, Amy. Good Night Book. Ahern, Frank, illus. (p. 699)
Beckman, Chris & Beckman, Kelly. It's Not Scary You See... (p. 898)
Beckman, David. Mika & the Queen's Quilt. (p. 1141)
Beckman, Dean A. Making of a Deer Hunter. (p. 1082)
Beckman, Jeff, illus. see Joyce, Kelley A.
Beckman, Kelly, jt. auth. see Beckman, Chris.
Beckman, Rosalind, ed. see UFA National Team.
Beckman, Thea. Crusade in Jeans. (p. 386)
Beckman, Wendy Hart. Dating, Relationships, & Sexuality: What Teens Should Know. (p. 409)
—Harlem Renaissance Artists & Writers. (p. 749)
—National Parks in Crisis: Debating the Issues. (p. 1233)
—Robert Cormier: Banned, Challenged, & Censored. (p. 1478)
Beckmann, Ewaldo, tr. see Stohs, Anita Reight.
Beckom, Sue. Wolf's Boy. (p. 1944)
Beckstead, Lene. Color Me Baptized. (p. 342)
Beckstedt, Cynthia. Hopsy. (p. 797)
Beckstedt, Cynthia M. Great Smoky Mountain Skunk Adventure (p. 718)
Beckstrand, Jared, illus. see Harris, Brooke.
Beckstrand, Jared, illus. see Nelson, Sandi.
Beckstrand, Karl. Crumbs on the Stairs; Migas en las Escaleras: A Mystery (in English & Spanish) (p. 386)
—Crumbs on the Stairs; Migas en las Escaleras: A Mystery (in English & Spanish) Beckstrand, Karl, illus. (p. 386)
—Sounds in the House! A Mystery. Jones, Channing, illus. (p. 1615)
Beckstrand, Tamara, jt. tr. see Bagley, Val Chadwick.
Beckwith, Carrie, et al. Editor in Chief A2: Grammar Disasters & Punctuation Faux Pas. (p. 504)
—Editor in Chief B2: Grammar Disasters & Punctuation Faux Pas. (p. 504)
—Reading Detective A1: Using Higher-Order Thinking to Improve Reading Comprehension. (p. 1445)
—Reading Detective Beginning: Using Higher-Order Thinking to Improve Reading Comprehension. (p. 1445)
Beckwith, Kathy. Critical Mass: I Never Thought It Would Be Like This. . (p. 383)
—Playing War Lyon, Lea, illus. (p. 1372)
Beckwith, Thomas. Indian, or Mound Builder; the Indians, Mode of Living, Manners, Customs, Dress, Ornaments, Etc., Before the White Man Came to the Country, Together with a List of Relics Gathered by the Author (p. 871)
Becky, Morah, jt. auth. see Perlowitz, Rebecca.
Becky, Terri And Melissa. Garden Prayer for Little Farmers: Seeds of Evangelism Series (Book 1) (p. 656)
Becnel, Barbara, ed. Gangs & Drugs: Stanley Tookie Williams Street Peace Series (p. 655)
—Gangs & Friends: Stanley Tookie Williams Street Peace Series (p. 655)
—Gangs & Self-Esteem: Stanley Tookie Williams Street Peace Series (p. 655)
—Gangs & the Abuse of Power: Stanley Tookie Williams Street Peace Series (p. 655)
—Gangs & Violence: Stanley Tookie Williams Street Peace Series (p. 655)
—Gangs & Wanting to Belong: Stanley Tookie Williams Street Peace Series (p. 655)
—Gangs & Weapons: Stanley Tookie Williams Street Peace Series (p. 655)
—Gangs & Your Neighborhood: Stanley Tookie Williams Street Peace Series (p. 655)
Becnel, Kim E. Bloom's How to Write about F. Scott Fitzgerald. (p. 201)
Beco, Alice. Cool Careers Without College for People Who Love Houses. (p. 363)
Bécquer, Gustavo Adolfo, jt. auth. see Bécquer, Gustavo Adolfo.
Bécquer, Gustavo Adolfo & Bécquer, Gustavo Adolfo. Rimas y Leyendas. (p. 1473)
Bécquer, Gustavo Adolpho. Cruz del Diablo (p. 387)
—Rimas y Leyendas. (p. 1473)
—Rimas y Leyendas. Marin Martinez, Juan M., ed. (p. 1473)
Becton, Daniel Walker, illus. see Becton, Sarah Walker, et al.
Becton, Sarah Walker, et al. Wormy Worm. Becton, Daniel Walker, illus. (p. 1961)
Bedard, Kathy, illus. see Miller, Nelson.
Bedard, Michael. Clay Ladies. (p. 330)
—Green Man. (p. 722)
—Painted Devil. (p. 1318)
—William Blake: The Gates of Paradise. (p. 1933)
—Wolf of Gubbio. (p. 1944)
Bedard, Tony. Baptism of Fire Pelletier, Paul et al, illus. (p. 137)
—Breakout. Fernandez, Raul, illus. (p. 225)
—Forget-Me-Not. Donovan, Derec, illus. (p. 619)
—Highway of Horror. Moline, Karl et al, illus. (p. 779)
—Master Class Fiorentino, Fabrizio et al, illus. (p. 1103)
—Most Haunted Moline, Karl et al, illus. (p. 1177)
—Mystic: The Mathemagician Lopresti, Aaron et al, illus. (p. 1226)
—Negation Pelletier, Paul et al, illus. (p. 1240)
—Out All Night Fiorentino, Fabrizio et al, illus. (p. 1310)
—Route 666 Moline, Karl et al, illus. (p. 1491)
—Route 666 Traveler: Highway of Horror. Moline, Karl et al, illus. (p. 1491)
—Shock & Awe Pelletier, Paul et al, illus. (p. 1568)
—Timebreakers. McKenna, Mark, illus. (p. 1753)
Beddor, Frank. Arch Enemy. (p. 95)
—ArchEnemy: The Looking Glass Wars, Book Three (p. 95)
—ArchEnemy. (p. 95)
—Looking Glass Wars (p. 1051)
—Seeing Redd. (p. 1548)
Beddor, Frank & Cavalier, Liz. Hatter M Wrobel, C. J., ed. (p. 752)
—Hatter M: The Looking Glass Wars - Love of Wonder. Wrobel, C. J., ed. (p. 752)
—Hatter M Volume 2: Mad with Wonder: Mad with Wonder. Wrobel, C. J., ed. (p. 752)
—Hatter M Volume 3: the Nature of Wonder: The Nature of Wonder. Wrobel, C. J., ed. (p. 752)
—Nature of Wonder Wrobel, C. J., ed. (p. 1236)
—Zen of Wonder (p. 1986)
Beddows, Eric, illus. see Fleischman, Paul.
Beddows, Eric, illus. see Jam, Teddy.
Beddows, Eric, illus. see Seidler, Tor.
Beddows, Eric, illus. see Wynne-Jones, Tim.
Bedeksy, Baron, jt. auth. see Bedesky, Baron.
Bedeksy, Baron, jt. auth. see Isaacs, Sally.
Bedeksy, Baron & Bedesky, Baron. What Are Taxes? (p. 1879)
Bedell, Barbara, illus. see Kalman, Bobbie & Crossingham, John.
Bedell, Barbara, illus. see Kalman, Bobbie.
Bedell, J. M. Combating Terrorism (p. 346)
—So, You Want to Be a Chef? How to Get Started in the World of Culinary Arts. (p. 1602)
—Teens in Pakistan (p. 1715)
Bedell, Lorraine Frances. Christmas Cat Story (p. 313)
Beder, John, jt. auth. see Crum, Shutta.
Bedesky, Baron. Peary & Henson: The Race to the North Pole. (p. 1333)
Bedesky, Baron, jt. auth. see Andrews, Carolyn.
Bedesky, Baron, jt. auth. see Bedeksy, Baron.
Bedesky, Baron, jt. auth. see Bright-Moore, Susan.
Bedesky, Baron & Bedeksy, Baron. What Are the Levels of Government? (p. 1880)
—What Is a Government? (p. 1888)
Bedford, Annie North. Roy Rogers & the New Cowboy. Helweg, Hans & Crawford, Mel, illus. (p. 1492)
Bedford, Annie North & Golden Books Staff. Scamp. Walt Disney Company Staff & Golden Books Staff, illus. (p. 1519)
Bedford, David. Ahora Me Toca a Mi! Field, Elaine, illus. (p. 30)
—Banned! (p. 136)
—Bath Time. Worthington, Leonie, illus. (p. 144)
—Big Bear Little Bear. Chapman, Jane, illus. (p. 178)
—Big Bears Can! Hansen, Gaby, illus. (p. 178)
—Bouncy Bouncy Bedtime. Julian, Russell, illus. (p. 216)
—Bums. Worthington, Leonie, illus. (p. 241)
—Copy Crocs. Bolam, Emily, tr. (p. 366)
—Daddy Does the Cha Cha Cha! Stevens-Marzo, Bridget, illus. (p. 398)
—Ed's Egg. Sapp, Karen, illus. (p. 504)
—Hound Dog. Williamson, Melanie, illus. (p. 802)
—I've Seen Santa! Warnes, Tim, illus. (p. 901)
—Little Otter's Big Journey Winter, Susan, illus. (p. 1032)
—Mole's Babies. Beardshaw, Rosalind, illus. (p. 1160)
—Mole's in Love. Beardshaw, Rosalind, illus. (p. 1160)
—Mums. Worthington, Leonie, illus. (p. 1191)
—Soccer Camp. Brumpton, Keith, illus. (p. 1603)
—Soccer Machine. Brumpton, Keith, illus. (p. 1603)
—Tails. Worthington, Leonie, illus. (p. 1695)
—Team Bind-up. (p. 1710)
—Tipper, Tipper! Watson, Judy, illus. (p. 1757)
—Top of the League. Brumpton, Keith, illus. (p. 1769)
—Two Tough Crocs. Jellett, Tom, illus. (p. 1804)
—Way I Love You. James, Ann, illus. (p. 1864)
—Who's Yawning? Worthington, Leonie, illus. (p. 1921)
Bedford, David, jt. auth. see Worthington, Leonie.
Bedford, David A. Angela. (p. 74)
—Angela 1: Starting Over. (p. 74)
Bedford, David & James, Ann. Way I Love You. (p. 1864)
—Way I Love You Box Set. (p. 1864)
Bedford, David & Worthington, Leonie. Big. (p. 177)
—Dino-School - Counting. Norrington, Leonie, illus. (p. 441)
—Dino-School - Opposites. (p. 441)
—Mums. (p. 1191)
—Who's Laughing? (p. 1920)
Bedford, F. D., illus. see Barrie, J. M.
Bedford, F. D., jt. auth. see Barrie, J. M.
Bedford, Francis Donkin, illus. see Barrie, J. M. & Lindner, Brooke.
Bedford, Kate. Greeks. (p. 721)
—Vikings. (p. 1842)
Bedford, Kathryn. (True?) Story of Eustace the Monk. (p. 1791)
Bedford, Martyn. Flip. (p. 604)
—Never Ending. (p. 1242)
Bedford, William. Glowworm Who Lost Her Glow. Joyce, Sophie, illus. (p. 685)
—Glow-Worm Who Lost Her Glow. Joyce, Sophie, illus. (p. 685)
Bednar, Chuck. American Idol Profiles Index: Top Finalists from Each Season (82 Contestants) (p. 61)
—Beyoncé. (p. 173)
—David Archuleta. (p. 410)
—David Blaine: Illusionist & Endurance Artist. (p. 410)
—Derek Jeter: All-Star Major League Baseball Player. (p. 427)
—Insights into American Idol. (p. 878)
—Kris Allen. (p. 967)
—Rosa Parks. (p. 1488)
—Tim Duncan. (p. 1750)
—Tony Parker. (p. 1766)
—Tony Romo. (p. 1766)
Bednar, Martin. Sandy's Vision. (p. 1511)
Bednar, Sylvie. Flags of the World. Daneshjoo, Gita, tr. from FRE. (p. 602)
Bednarczyk, Angela, jt. auth. see Vinopol, Corinne.
Bednark, Sara & Ung, Bunheang. Wally's Bedroom Aviary. (p. 1855)
Bednarz, Robert, et al. About My Community. (p. 6)
—Horizons: Us History - Civil War-Present. (p. 797)
Bednarz, Sarah Witham. World Cultures & Geography: Eastern Hemisphere. (p. 1954)
—World Cultures & Geography: Pupil's Edition (c)2005. (p. 1954)
—World Cultures & Geography: Western Hemisphere & Europe. (p. 1954)
Bedore, Bernie. Mythical Mufferaw. (p. 1227)
Bedoyere, Camilla. Creatures of the Night. (p. 380)
—Monsters of the Deep. (p. 1169)
Bédoyère, Guy De la, see De la Bédoyère, Guy.
Bedrick, Claudia Z. People. (p. 1338)
Bedrick, Claudia Z., jt. auth. see Badescu, Ramona.
Bedrick, Claudia Z., tr. see Babin, Claire.
Bedrick, Claudia Z., tr. see Blexbolex.
Bedrick, Claudia Z., tr. see Brun-Cosme, Nadine.
Bedrick, Claudia Z., tr. see Herbauts, Anne.
Bedrick, Claudia Z., tr. see Hong, Chen Jiang.
Bedrick, Claudia Z., tr. see Picouly, Daniel.
Bedrick, Claudia Z., tr. see Pouy, Jean-Bernard.
Bedrick, Jeff, illus. see Emm, David.
Bedry, Christa. Fish. (p. 598)
—Insects. (p. 875)
—Pueblo. (p. 1414)
Bee, Clair. Buzzer Basket: A Chip Hilton Sports Story. (p. 249)
—Clutch Hitter. (p. 336)
—Dugout Jinx: A Chip Hilton Sports Story. (p. 489)
—Dugout Jinx. (p. 489)
—Fourth down Showdown: A Chip Hilton Sports Story. (p. 625)
—Freshman Quarterback: Chip Hilton Sports Story No. 9. (p. 636)
—Hardcourt Upset: A Chip Hilton Sports Story. (p. 748)
—No Hitter: A Chip Hilton Sports Story. (p. 1258)
—Pay-off Pitch: A Chip Hilton Sports Story. (p. 1331)
—Pitcher's Duel: A Chip Hilton Sports Story. (p. 1364)
—Ten Seconds to Play: A Chip Hilton Sports Story. (p. 1719)
—Tournament Crisis: A Chip Hilton Sports Story. (p. 1773)
—Triple Threat Trouble: A Chip Hilton Sports Story. (p. 1787)
Bee, Clair Francis. Pass & a Prayer: A Chip Hilton Sports Story. (p. 1326)
Bee, Ersila. Everywhere Armchair. (p. 546)
Bee, Granny. Laffy the Lamb. Werthiemer, Beverly, ed. (p. 971)
Bee, Harry. Printer Street's War. (p. 1407)
Bee, Kati. Mrs. Flutterbee & the Funny Farm. (p. 1187)
Bee, Nanny. William. (p. 1933)
Bee, Sarah. Yes. Kitamura, Satoshi, illus. (p. 1970)
Bee, Stevie J. Cross Your Heart. (p. 385)
Bee, William. And the Cars Go... Bee, William, illus. (p. 71)
—Digger Dog. Johansson, Cecilia, illus. (p. 438)
—Migloo's Day. Bee, William, illus. (p. 1140)
—Stanley the Farmer Bee, William, illus. (p. 1640)
—Worst in Show. Hindley, Kate, illus. (p. 1961)
BEEBE, Diane. School's Out. (p. 1524)
Beebe, Katherine & Kingsley, Nellie F. First Year Nature Reader. (p. 598)
Beebe, Kathryne. Pilgrim & Preacher: The Audiences & Observant Spirituality of Friar Felix Fabri (1437/8-1502) (p. 1358)
Beebe, Robb, illus. see Baldwin, Faith.
Beebe, Robb, illus. see Stevens, Mark.
Beebe, Susan, illus. see Parker, Vicki Sue.
Beebee, Dorothy, illus. see McCarroll, Tolbert.
Beeby, Betty. Great Granny's Sturdy Stable Picnic Tables. (p. 716)
Beech, Linda. Comprehension Skills: 40 Short Passages for Close Reading - Grade 1. (p. 354)
Beech, Linda, et al. Animals. Scholastic, Inc. Staff, ed. (p. 81)
—City Colors. Scholastic, Inc. Staff, ed. (p. 323)
—Farm Friends. Scholastic, Inc. Staff, ed. (p. 574)
—Find It! Scholastic, Inc. Staff, ed. (p. 587)
—Fly Away. Scholastic, Inc. Staff, ed. (p. 609)
—Go, Go. Scholastic, Inc. Staff, ed. (p. 686)
—Guessing Game. Scholastic, Inc. Staff, ed. (p. 729)
—Helpers. Scholastic, Inc. Staff, ed. (p. 766)
—I Did It! Scholastic, Inc. Staff, ed. (p. 837)
—Little & Big. Scholastic, Inc. Staff, ed. (p. 1023)
—Me Too! Scholastic, Inc. Staff, ed. (p. 1116)
—Party. Scholastic, Inc. Staff, ed. (p. 1325)
—Play Time. Scholastic, Inc. Staff, ed. (p. 1371)
—Ride On! Scholastic, Inc. Staff, ed. (p. 1471)
—Run! Scholastic, Inc. Staff, ed. (p. 1496)
—Sight Word Readers. Scholastic, Inc. Staff, ed. (p. 1574)
—That Hat. Scholastic, Inc. Staff, ed. (p. 1726)
—That Is Funny! Scholastic, Inc. Staff, ed. (p. 1726)
—This Is a Peach. Scholastic, Inc. Staff, ed. (p. 1735)
—Up & Down. Scholastic, Inc. Staff, ed. (p. 1824)
Beech, Linda Ward. 180 Essential Vocabulary Words: Independent Learning Packets That Help Students Learn the Most Important Words They Need to Succeed in School. (p. 2000)
—240 Vocabulary Words - 3rd Grade Kids Need to Know: 24 Ready-to-Reproduce Packets That Make Vocabulary Building Fun & Effective. (p. 2001)
—240 Vocabulary Words 4th Grade Kids Need to Know: 24 Ready-to-Reproduce Packets That Make Vocabulary Building Fun & Effective. (p. 2001)
—240 Vocabulary Words Kids Need to Know: 24 Ready-to-Reproduce Packets That Make Vocabulary Building Fun & Effective. (p. 2001)
—240 Vocabulary Words Kids Need to Know, Grade 3: 24 Ready-to-Reproduce Packets That Make Vocabulary Building Fun & Effective. (p. 2001)
—Compare & Contrast. (p. 351)
—Comprehension Skills: 40 Short Passages for Close Reading, Grade 2. (p. 354)
—Comprehension Skills - 40 Short Passages for Close Reading. (p. 354)
—Comprehension Skills - Short Passages for Close Reading. (p. 354)
—Context Clues. (p. 360)
—Exxon Valdez's Deadly Oil Spill. (p. 557)
—Fact & Opinion. (p. 561)
—Great Grammar Practice: Grade 1. (p. 716)
—Inference. (p. 873)
—Magic School Bus Gets Baked in a Cake: A Book about Kitchen Chemistry. Duchesne, Lucie, tr. from ENG. (p. 1073)
—Magic School Bus in the Haunted Museum: A Book about Sound. Duchesne, Lucie, tr. (p. 1073)
—Main Idea & Details. (p. 1077)
—Predicting. (p. 1395)
Beech, Linda Ward, jt. auth. see Scholastic Coach Magazine Staff.
Beech, Linda Ward, jt. auth. see Scholastic, Inc. Staff.
Beech, Linda Ward, et al. Dinner. Scholastic, Inc. Staff, ed. (p. 440)
—Farm Friends. Scholastic, Inc. Staff, ed. (p. 574)
—My Bear. Scholastic, Inc. Staff, ed. (p. 1196)
—My Dog. Scholastic, Inc. Staff, ed. (p. 1202)
—New Socks. Scholastic, Inc. Staff, ed. (p. 1247)
—Sharing. Scholastic, Inc. Staff, ed. (p. 1561)
Beech, Mark, illus. see Bailey, Gerry & Law, Felicia.
Beech, Mark, illus. see Dakos, Kalli.
Beech, Mark, illus. see Jackson, Robert Bradley.
Beech, Mark, illus. see Mayer, Cassie & Resl, Brigitte.
Beech, Mark, illus. see Pratchett, Terry.
Beech, Mark, illus. see Whitehead, William, et al.
Beech, Mark, illus. see Whitehead, William.
Beech, Sandy. Isle Be Seeing You. Holder, Jimmy, illus. (p. 892)
—Worst Class Trip Ever. Holder, Jimmy, illus. (p. 1961)
Beech, Thomas Michael. Mastering 2D to 3D Conversion. (p. 1103)
Beechen, Adam. Darkseid's Inferno! Beavers, Ethen, illus. (p. 409)
—Divide & Conquer Barberi, Carlo & Wong, Walden, illus. (p. 454)
—Justice League Unlimited. (p. 940)
—Local Hero Barberi, Carlo & Wong, Walden, illus. (p. 1044)
—No More Mr. Smart Guy. LaPadula, Tom, illus. (p. 1259)
—Poker Face Beavers, Ethen, illus. (p. 1378)
—Small Time Barberi, Carlo & Wong, Walden, illus. (p. 1592)
—UFO! (SpongeBob SquarePants) Saunders, Zina, illus. (p. 1807)
Beechen, Adam & Age, Heroic. Mad Mod Is in Vogue! Vedder, Erik, illus. (p. 1069)
Beechen, Adam & Williams, Freddie. Wanted. (p. 1856)
Beechen, Adam & Wong, Walden. In the Dimming Light Barberi, Carlo, illus. (p. 865)
—Monitor Duty Barberi, Carlo, illus. (p. 1164)
—Who Is the Question? Barberi, Carlo, illus. (p. 1916)
Beecher, Elizabeth. Roy Rogers & Cowboy Toby. Crawford, Mel, illus. (p. 1492)
—Roy Rogers & the Sure 'Nough Cowpoke. Steffen, Randy, illus. (p. 1492)
—Roy Rogers' Bullet & Trigger: Wild Horse Roundup. Lenox, August, illus. (p. 1492)
—Roy Rogers on the Double-R Ranch. Nordli, Ernest, illus. (p. 1492)
Beecher, Lyman. Autobiography (p. 117)
Beeching, Henry Charles. Seven Sermons to Schoolboys. (p. 1554)
Beechwood, Beth, adapted by. Check It Out. (p. 295)
—Hannah Montana - Keeping Secrets. (p. 742)
Beecroft, Simon. Ackbar's Underwater Army. (p. 9)
—Chewbacca & the Wookiee Warriors. (p. 299)
—Death Star Battles, Level 3. (p. 420)
—Epic Battles, Level 4. (p. 532)
—Jedi Adventures. (p. 911)
—Pirates ... & Worse! Dorling Kindersley Publishing Staff, ed. (p. 1363)
—Queen's Diary. (p. 1425)
—R2-D2 & Friends. (p. 1429)
—Stand Aside-Bounty Hunters! (p. 1639)
Beecroft, Simon, jt. auth. see Dorling Kindersley Publishing Staff.
Beecroft, Simon & Dorling Kindersley Publishing Staff. Ready, Set, Podrace! Level 1. (p. 1447)
Beecroft, Simon & Fry, Jason. Visual Dictionary. (p. 1846)
Beecroft, Simon & Saunders, Catherine. Join the Rebels. (p. 924)
Beecroft, Simon & Windham, Ryder. Beware the Dark Side. (p. 173)
—I Want to Be a Jedi, Level 3. (p. 847)
Beecroft, Susan. Teddy Goes to Buckingham Palace. (p. 1712)
Beede, John R. Climb On! Dynamic Strategies for Teen Success. (p. 333)
Beede, Mike. Unfunny & Beneath the Puppet Stand. (p. 1817)
Beedle, Tim. Muppet Robin Hood. Villavert, Armand, Jr. & Petersen, David, illus. (p. 1191)
Beedle, Tim, ed. see Randolph, Grace, et al.
Beeghly, Mark. Shocking True Story of Linky & Dinky Plus Uncle Url's Middle-Aged Magic. (p. 1568)
Beehive Illustrations Staff, jt. auth. see Gray-Wilburn, Renée.
Beehler, Doug. Boy Named Jacob. (p. 218)
Beeke, Joel, jt. auth. see Kleyn, Diana.
Beeke, Joel R. & Boorsma, Heidi. God's Alphabet for Life: Devotions for Young Children. (p. 690)
Beeke, Joel R. & Kleyn, Diana. How God Sent a Dog to Save a Family. Anderson, Jeff, illus. (p. 809)
—How God Stopped the Pirates. Anderson, Jeff, illus. (p. 809)
—How God Used a Drought & an Umbrella. Anderson, Jeff, illus. (p. 809)
—How God Used a Snowdrift. Anderson, Jeff, illus. (p. 809)
—How God Used a Thunderstorm. Anderson, Jeff, illus. (p. 809)
Beeke, Tiphanie, illus. see Conte, Paola, et al.
Beeke, Tiphanie, illus. see Fischer, Ellen.
Beeke, Tiphanie, illus. see Rawlinson, Julia & Rawlinson.
Beeke, Tiphanie, illus. see Rawlinson, Julia.

B

Beeke, Tiphanie, illus. see Rudi, Julie A.
Beeke, Tiphanie, illus. see Rylant, Cynthia.
Beeke, Tiphanie, illus. see Whybrow, Ian.
Beeke, Tiphanie, illus. see Zolotow, Charlotte.
Beeke, Tiphanie, tr. see Whybrow, Ian.
Beekman, Kelley Lee. Sir Eli & the Halloween Dragon: The Legend of the Toasted Marshmallow. (p. 1580)
Beel, Rory. Second Informant. (p. 1539)
Beeler, Joe, illus. see Scott, Dan.
Beeler, Selby B. Throw Your Tooth on the Roof. Karas, G. Brian, illus. (p. 1745)
Beeman, Laura. Mojo: The Blind Friesian. (p. 1160)
Beene, Jason, illus. see Bourbeau, Julie.
Beene, Jason, illus. see Farber, E. S.
Beene, Jason, illus. see Farber, Erica.
Beene, Jason, illus. see Graff, Lisa.
Beer, Amy-Jane. Ants. (p. 90)
—Bats. (p. 144)
—Bison. (p. 193)
—Canada Goose. (p. 260)
—Chipmunks. (p. 308)
—Deer. (p. 423)
—Lizards. (p. 1042)
—Pet Rabbits. (p. 1345)
—Puffins. (p. 1415)
—Weasels. (p. 1869)
—Woodchucks. (p. 1949)
Beer, Barbara Vagnozzi. Jack & the Beanstalk. (p. 902)
Beer, Henry, photos by. Girl Defective. (p. 678)
Beer, Josh & Beers, D. G. Sophocles & the Tragedy of Athenian Democracy. (p. 1614)
Beer, Julie. Weird but True Food. (p. 1872)
Beer, Julie, jt. auth. see Honovich, Nancy.
Beer, Julie, jt. auth. see National Geographic Kids Staff.
Beer, Michele, tr. see Reiter, David P. & Reiter, David P.
Beer, Michele, tr. see Vescio, Robert.
Beer, Valorie. Dreamers. (p. 484)
Beernink, Joe. Nowhere Wild. (p. 1269)
Beerntsen, Tammy, photos by see Lawson, Cheri.
Beers. Elements of Literature: Premier Online Edition. (p. 510)
—Elements of Literature: Enhanced Online Edition. (p. 510)
—Elements of Literature. (p. 510)
Beers, jt. auth. see Gafney.
Beers, D. G., jt. auth. see Beer, Josh.
Beers, Gary. Pumpkinroo. (p. 1416)
Beers, Jack. Anchors Grade 1. (p. 67)
—Anchors Grade 1 SP. (p. 67)
—Anchors Grade 2. (p. 67)
—Anchors Grade 2 SP. (p. 67)
—Anchors Grade 3. (p. 67)
—Anchors Grade 3 SP. (p. 67)
—Anchors Grade 4. (p. 67)
—Anchors Grade 5. (p. 67)
—Anchors Grade 5 Student Edition. (p. 67)
—Bridges-Blue. (p. 227)
—Bridges-Gold. (p. 227)
—Bridges-Red. (p. 227)
Beers, Robert Lee, illus. see Freeman, David.
Beers, Robert Lee, illus. see Miller, Judith J.
Beers, Steven. Bumpy the Frog. (p. 241)
Beery, Barbara. Barbara Beery's Pink Princess Party Cookbook. Williams, Zac, photos by. (p. 137)
—Fairies Cookbook (p. 563)
—Mermaid Cookbook Shultz, Kirsten, photos by. (p. 1128)
—Pink Ponies Cookbook (p. 1360)
—Pink Princess Cookbook Snortum, Marty, photos by. (p. 1360)
—Pink Princess Cupcakes (p. 1360)
—Spa Princess Cookbook (p. 1618)
Beesly. Stories from the History of Rome. (p. 1654)
Beeson, J. K. Ali & Friends Adventures. (p. 38)
Beeson, Jan. Mysterious World of the Puffins the Treasure Hunt Book 1. (p. 1223)
Beeson, Jan, illus. see Beeson, Paul & Beeson, Lady Jan.
Beeson, Jan, illus. see Paul & Lady Jan.
Beeson, Lady Jan, jt. auth. see Beeson, Paul.
Beeson, Lea Ann. Leopard Is More Than His Spots. Popovich, Richard E., ed. (p. 992)
Beeson, Paul & Beeson, Lady Jan. Zeela the Zebra of a Different Color. Beeson, Jan, illus. (p. 1985)
Beeson, Sam. White Lies. (p. 1913)
Beeson, Samantha & Tango Books Staff. Baaah! Abbott, Simon, illus. (p. 123)
Beeston, Richard. Looking for Trouble: The Life & Times of a Foreign Correspondent. (p. 1051)
Beeton, Abigail. Pastor's Predicament. (p. 1327)
Beets, Bekah. Renna Can't Remember. (p. 1460)
Beeuwsaert, Matt. I Got Game. Beeuwsaert, Matt, illus. (p. 838)
BEFEC Mulguin and Associates Staff, illus. see Hernandez, Alejandro.
Befus, Tyler. Kid's Guide to Fly Tying. (p. 953)
—Kid's Guide to Flyfishing: It's More Than Catching Fish. (p. 953)
Beg, Sadiql, illus. see Laird, Elizabeth.
Begay, Patrick, illus. see Thomas, Marjorie & Ruffenach, Jessie.
Beggs, Melissa. Pompety-Pooh: Purplest Penguin in Zonkety Zoo. Laible, Steve William, ed. (p. 1382)
Begho, Philip. Adventures in Play-Acting: The TV Producer. (p. 15)
—Aunty Felicia & John Bull Sobo. (p. 116)
—Aunty Felicia & the Bully. (p. 116)
—Aunty Felicia & the Stalkers. (p. 116)
—Aunty Felicia & the Teacher. (p. 116)
—Aunty Felicia Goes for Youth Service. (p. 116)
—Aunty Felicia Goes to Church. (p. 116)
—Aunty Felicia Has an Accident. (p. 116)
—Aunty Felicia Hijacks a Plane. (p. 116)
—Aunty Felicia in the Evil Forest. (p. 116)
—Aunty Felicia Is Stalked Again. (p. 116)
—Aunty Felicia Kidnaps Froggy. (p. 116)
—Aunty Felicia Meets Aunt Daisy. (p. 116)
—Aunty Felicia Plays Soccer. (p. 116)
—Barbie in the Fire. (p. 138)
—Barbie in the Woods. (p. 138)
—Chuma the Terror. (p. 318)
—Crab Story. (p. 375)
—Cucumber Eaters. (p. 389)
—Dream Princess 1. (p. 483)
—Dream Princess 2. (p. 483)
—Dream Princess 3. (p. 483)
—Golden Apples. (p. 694)
—King Omatosan. (p. 959)
—Searching for Barbie. (p. 1537)
—Toju & Tosan Meet Ajayi Crowther. (p. 1762)
—Toju & Tosan Meet Blind Bartimaeus. (p. 1762)
—Toju & Tosan Meet Jezebel. (p. 1762)
—Toju & Tosan Meet Mother Humble. (p. 1762)
—Toju & Tosan Meet the Fastest Sprinter. (p. 1762)
—Toju & Tosan Meet the Rooftop Man. (p. 1762)
—Toju & Tosan Meet the Strange Lion. (p. 1762)
—Toju & Tosan Meet the Water-Walkers. (p. 1762)
Begin, Jean-Guy, illus. see Cotes, Gilles.
Begin, Jean-Guy, illus. see Deslauriers, Anne.
Begin, Jean-Guy, illus. see Lavoie, Rejean.
Begin, Jean-Guy, illus. see Mallet, C. Claire.
Begin, Jean-Guy, illus. see Richard, Martine.
Begin, Mary Jane, illus. see Allio, Mark R.
Begin Smart Books Staff, contrib. by. What Colour Is Your Apple? (p. 1881)
—What Shapes Do You See? (p. 1893)
Beglau, Judy. Mad, Mad, Annabelle Jane. (p. 1069)
Begonia, Ruby, illus. see Binks.
Begum, Dilara. Mama Bird & Her Baby. Balogh, Jared, illus. (p. 1084)
Beha, Eileen. Secrets of Eastcliff-by-the-Sea: The Story of Annaliese Easterling & Throckmorton, Her Simply Remarkable Sock Monkey. Wright, Sarah Jane, illus. (p. 1545)
—Tango: The Tale of an Island Dog. (p. 1705)
Beha, Philippe, illus. see Brière, Paule.
Beha, Philippe, illus. see Goertzen, Glenda.
Beha, Philippe, illus. see Jovanovic, Katarina.
Beha, Philippe, illus. see Poulin, Andree.
Beha, Philippe, illus. see Poulin, Andrée.
Beha, Philippe, illus. see Yolen, Jane & Stemple, Heidi E. Y.
Béha, Philippe, illus. see Yolen, Jane.
Béha, Philippe, jt. auth. see Luppens, Michel.
Beha, Philippe, illus. see Kennedy, X. J.
Behan, Abbey Lauren Ash & Ash, Stephanie. Diary of a Crayon: Red Gets Lost. (p. 434)
—Diary of a Crayon: Green Gets Bullied. (p. 434)
Behan, Rachel A., illus. see Sellers, Amy C., ed.
Behar, Susan & Robinson, Nick. Origami XOXO (p. 1304)
Behar, Yvonne. Out of Spain: Celebrating Sephardi Culture. Vol. 3 Brooks, Andree Aelion, ed. (p. 1311)
Beharrell, Gayle. Adventures of Charlie. (p. 17)
Behe, Mary, jt. auth. see Savitskas, Margaret.
Beheler, Rhonda. They Chose Me: A Story of Grandparent Adoption. (p. 1732)
Behl, Anne-Kathrin, illus. see Wagner, Anke.
Behl, Colin. Noüm. (p. 1268)
Behles, Liza, illus. see Happel, Kathleen.
Behles, Liza, illus. see Lydon, Jeff.
Behling, Silke. Get to Know Horse Breeds: The 100 Best-Known Breeds. (p. 668)
Behling, Steve. Amazing Spider-Man vs. Green Goblin. Disney Book Group Staff, illus. (p. 56)
—Amazing Spider-Man vs. The Green Goblin. (p. 56)
Behme, Thomas, ed. see Pufendorf, Samuel.
Behn, Rosa & Graham, Dora. Adventures of Jenny Duck. (p. 19)
Behnke, Alison. Afghanistan in Pictures. (p. 26)
—Angkor Wat. (p. 75)
—Barbers. (p. 138)
—Botswana in Pictures. (p. 215)
—Can Rats Swim from Sewers into Toilets? And Other Questions about Your Home. (p. 258)
—Chinese in America. (p. 307)
—Conquests of Alexander the Great. (p. 358)
—Conquests of Genghis Khan. (p. 358)
—Cooking the Middle Eastern Way. (p. 362)
—Death of a Dreamer: The Assassination of John Lennon. (p. 420)
—Ecuador in Pictures. (p. 503)
—Kim Jong Il's North Korea. (p. 956)
—Little Black Dress & Zoot Suits: Depression & Wartime Fashions from the 1930s to the 1950s. (p. 1024)
—Mexicans in America. (p. 1131)
—Niger in Pictures. (p. 1252)
—Paraguay in Pictures. (p. 1323)
—Russians in America. (p. 1498)
—Syria in Pictures. (p. 1693)
—Taiwan in Pictures. (p. 1696)
—Timeline History of the Mexican-American War. (p. 1754)
—Timeline History of the Trail of Tears. (p. 1754)
—Timeline History of the Transcontinental Railroad. (p. 1754)
—Up for Sale: Human Trafficking & Modern Slavery. (p. 1824)
—Uruguay in Pictures. (p. 1826)
Behnke, Alison & Duro, Karin L. Cooking the Brazilian Way. (p. 362)
Behnke, Alison & Valens, Victor Manuel. Cooking the Cuban Way. (p. 362)
Behnke, Alison, et al. Cooking the Central American Way. (p. 362)
—Cooking the Mediterranean Way. (p. 362)
Behr, Joyce, illus. see Bolton, Martha.
Behr, Joyce, illus. see Halligan, Terry.
Beh-Rang, Samad. Little Black Fish. Emam, Ruby, tr. (p. 1024)
Behre, Mary. Energized. (p. 528)
Behrendt, Lloyd. Birds of Hope: ... a Primer for the Future. (p. 191)
Behrens, Andy. Fast & the Furriest. (p. 576)
Behrens, Janice. Let's Find Out: Dinosaurs. Courtney, Richard, illus. (p. 996)
—Let's Make Letters: ABC Kids. Michael, Joan, illus. (p. 999)
—Let's Talk Baseball. (p. 1001)
—Let's Talk Swimming. (p. 1001)
—Let's Vote on It! (p. 1001)
—Letters/Numbers Michael, Joan, illus. (p. 1003)
—This Is the Way We Dress. (p. 1736)
—We Are Alike, We Are Different. (p. 1865)
—What Is the Statue of Liberty? (p. 1890)
—What Is the Story of Our Flag? (p. 1890)
Behrens, Janice, jt. auth. see Dancer, Audrey.
Behrens, Kristen, jt. auth. see Ball, Jacqueline A.
Behrens, Rebecca. When Audrey Met Alice. (p. 1901)
Behrman, Carol H. Andrew Jackson. (p. 72)
—James K. Polk. (p. 907)
—Ready-to-Use Writing Proficiency Lessons & Activities. (p. 1448)
—Thomas Jefferson. (p. 1738)
—Writing Proficiency Lessons & Activities. (p. 1965)
Behrman, Carol H., ed. see Rivera, Sheila.
Behruzi, Gulrukh. Mohan the Mynah (p. 1160)
Beier, Anne. Crispus Attucks: Hero of the Boston Massacre. (p. 383)
—Crispus Attucks: Heroe de la Masacre de Boston. (p. 383)
—Crispus Attucks: Heroe de la masacre de Boston. (p. 383)
—Crispus Attucks: Hero of the Boston Massacre / Héroe de la masacre de Boston. (p. 383)
—Crispus Attucks: Héroe de la masacre de Boston (Crispus Attucks: Hero of the Boston Massacre) (p. 383)
—Supreme Court & the Judicial Branch. (p. 1684)
Beier, Ellen, illus. see Christopher, Matt.
Beier, Ellen, illus. see Clements, Andrew.
Beier, Ellen, illus. see Grogan, John & Hill, Susan.
Beier, Ellen, illus. see Helldorfer, M. C.
Beier, Ellen, illus. see Mattern, Joanne & Santrey, Laurence.
Beier, Ellen, illus. see Santrey, Laurence & Mattern, Joanne.
Beier, Ellen, illus. see Silverman, Erica.
Beier, Ellen, illus. see Sneve, Virginia Driving Hawk.
Beifus, Ruth. Shlavim Classics 2-in-1: The Best Reward & the Taste of Truth. Vol. 1 (p. 1567)
—Shlavim Classics 2-in-1: Goodbye to Miri's Mess & Half a Cup of Water. Vol.2 (p. 1567)
Beifus, Ruth, illus. see Rosenberg, Tziporah.
Beighey, Carole La Flamme. Waddodles of Hollow Lake: Ruffed Grouse Courtship Ceremony. (p. 1852)
Beighley, Marci. Strawberry Shortcake's Costume Party. (p. 1666)
Beighley, Marci, illus. see Harimann, Sierra.
Beijing Language Institute Staff. Practical Chinese Reader: Chinese Character Gloss Simplified Character Edition. Bk. 1 (p. 1392)
—Practical Chinese Reader: Chinese Character Gloss Traditional Character Edition. Bk. 1 (p. 1392)
Beiko, S. M. Lake & the Library. (p. 972)
Beil, Karen Magnuson. Jack's House. Wohnoutka, Mike, illus. (p. 904)
—Mooove Over! A Book about Counting by Twos. Meisel, Paul, tr. (p. 1173)
Beil, Michael D. Lantern Sam & the Blue Streak Bandits. (p. 975)
—Mistaken Masterpiece. (p. 1155)
—Red Blazer Girls. (p. 1453)
—Red Blazer Girls: the Mistaken Masterpiece. (p. 1453)
—Red Blazer Girls: the Secret Cellar. (p. 1453)
—Red Blazer Girls: the Vanishing Violin. (p. 1453)
—Secret Cellar. (p. 1540)
—Summer at Forsaken Lake. Kneen, Maggie, illus. (p. 1673)
Beilenson, Evelyn. Warm & Fuzzy Christmas. Giordano, illus. (p. 1858)
—Zoo Is Closed Today! Kennedy, Anne, illus. (p. 1989)
Beilenson, Suzanne. Ancient Egypt Scratch & Sketch. (p. 68)
—Quiz Book: Who R U? (p. 1429)
—Rain Forest Scratch & Sketch: An Art Activity Book for Adventurous Artists & Explorers of All Ages. (p. 1434)
Beilenson, Suzanne, jt. auth. see Bryan, Sarah Jane.
Beiler, Joyce. Kingdom of Laughter. (p. 959)
Beingessner, Laura, illus. see Collins-Philippe, Jane.
Beingessner, Laura, illus. see Lawlor, Laurie.
Beingessner, Laura, illus. see Schwartz, Joanne.
Beinhard, B. J. Sanji's Seed: A Story about Honesty. Hehenberger, Shelly, illus. (p. 1511)
Beinstein, Phoebe. Dora. Mangano, Tom, illus. (p. 470)
—Dora & the Stuck Truck. Roper, Robert, illus. (p. 470)
—Dora Explora los Colores. Hall, Susan & Hall, Susan, illus. (p. 470)
—Dora Goes for a Ride. Fruchter, Jason, illus. (p. 470)
—Los Deseos de Dora. Ziegler, Argentina Palacios, tr. from ENG. (p. 1053)
—Swim, Boots, Swim! Roper, Robert, illus. (p. 1690)
—¡A nadar, Boots! (Swim, Boots, Swim!) Roper, Robert, illus. (p. 1)
—¡Vámonos! / Let's Go! Ziegler, Argentina Palacios, tr. (p. 1831)
—¿Qué Voy a Ser? Saunders, Zina, illus. (p. 1424)
Beinstein, Phoebe & A and J Studios Staff. Di "Aaaa"! Dora Va al Médico. (p. 433)
—Say Ahhh! Dora Goes to the Doctor. (p. 1518)
Beinstein, Phoebe & Silverhardt, Lauryn. Dora's Little Library. (p. 471)
Beinstein, Phoebe, et al. Dora's Stories: A Boxed Set. (p. 471)
Beirne-Keawe, Danielle Ululani. Makaili Sleeps. (p. 1078)
Beisch, Leigh, photos by see Ferreira, Charity.
Beisch, Leigh, photos by see MacNeal, Susan Ella.
Beisch, Leigh, photos by see Shaw, Tucker.
Beiser, Tim. Bradley McGogg: The Very Fine Frog. Berman, Rachel, illus. (p. 221)
—Little Chicken Duck. Slavin, Bill, illus. (p. 1026)
—Miss Mousie's Blind Date. Berman, Rachel, illus. (p. 1151)
Beissel, Henry. Inuk & the Sun (Inuk et le Soleil) Barton, Bruce, ed. (p. 883)
Beissinger, Janet & Pless, Vera. Cryptoclub: Using Mathematics to Make & Break Secret Codes. (p. 387)
Beisswenger, Iffer & Eldred, Margaret. Way We See Things: Middle Schoolers Look at Themselves & Issues They Face Everyday. Krusi, Carolynne, ed. (p. 1864)
—Way We See Things: Middleschoolers Look at Themselves & the Issues They Face Everyday. Krusi, Carolynne, ed. (p. 1864)
Beiter, Anna M. & Beiter, Elizabeth A. Story of the Star-Spangled Banner. (p. 1662)
Beiter, Elizabeth A., jt. auth. see Beiter, Anna M.
Beith, Laura Huliska, illus. see Gerth, Melanie.
Beltia, Sara. Last Good Place of Lily Odilon. (p. 978)
Beitler, Stacey Ann. Willy Goes to School. (p. 1934)
—Willy Goes to the Farm. (p. 1934)
—Willy Helps a Friend. (p. 1934)
Beitz-Grant, Heather, illus. see Shoesmith-Bateman, Amanda.
Beka. Dance Class #6: a Merry Olde Christmas. Crip, illus. (p. 402)
—Dance Class - African Folk Fever. Crip, illus. (p. 402)
—Funny Thing Happened on the Way to Paris... Crip, illus. (p. 650)
—Romeo & Juliets. Crip, illus. (p. 1486)
—So, You Think You Can Hip-Hop? Crip, illus. (p. 1602)
—To Russia, with Love. Crip, illus. (p. 1759)
—We'll Win with Big Class & Huge Style. (p. 1874)
—Why Are We Here Again? Poupard et al, illus. (p. 1922)
Bekele, Aregash, tr. Carry Me (Amharic/English) (p. 271)
Beken, Robert A. Tijuana River Estuary & Border Field State Park: Land of diversity, land of Hope. (p. 1749)
Beker, Jeanne. Big Night Out. Dion, Nathalie, illus. (p. 182)
—Passion for Fashion: Careers in Style. Dion, Nathalie, illus. (p. 1327)
—Strutting It! The Grit Behind the Glamour. (p. 1668)
Bekis, Joanne. Bubble & Butterfly. (p. 233)
Bekkering, Annalise. Bats. (p. 144)
—Frogs. (p. 641)
—Gendarmes: Les Emblèmes Canadiens. McMann, Julie, tr. from ENG. (p. 660)
—Great Lakes. (p. 716)
—Mounties: Canadian Icons. (p. 1181)
—NCAA Basketball. (p. 1238)
—NCAA Basketball Championships. (p. 1238)
—Rabbits. (p. 1429)
—Rabbits. Hudak, Heather C., ed. (p. 1429)
—Seals. (p. 1536)
—Sight. (p. 1573)
—Skunks. (p. 1586)
—Skunks. Hudak, Heather C., ed. (p. 1586)
—Spring. (p. 1634)
—Spring: World of Wonder Seasons. (p. 1635)
Bekoff, Marc. Animals at Play: Rules of the Game. DiMotta, Michael J., illus. (p. 82)
Bekoff, Marc, jt. auth. see Robinson, Jill.
Bekooy Khare, Catherine, jt. auth. see Khare, Pratibha.
Belair, Brenda Brousseau, photos by see Doupe, Pauline Wood.
Beland, Tom. True Story, Swear to God: This One Goes to 11. (p. 1793)
—True Story, Swear to God. (p. 1793)
—True Story, Swear to God: Chances Are: Chances Are. (p. 1793)
Belaney, Archibald Stansfeld. Beavers: Pages from the Writings of Grey Owl. Reynolds, E. E., ed. (p. 155)
—On the Trail: Pages from the Writings of Grey Owl. Reynolds, E. E., ed. (p. 1291)
Belanger, Damon, illus. see Khamis, Johnny.
Belanger, Jeff. Ghosts of War: Restless Spirits of Soldiers, Spies, & Saboteurs. (p. 673)
—Paranormal Encounters: A Look at the Evidence. (p. 1324)
—Real-Life Ghost Encounters. (p. 1448)
—Who's Haunting the White House? The President's Mansion & the Ghosts Who Live There. Powell, Rick, illus. (p. 1920)
—World's Most Haunted Places. (p. 1960)
Belanger, Kathleen. Cooldog's Holiday Adventures. Baker, David, illus. (p. 364)
—Cooldog's New Adventures. (p. 364)
Belanger, Madeleine. Mystical Noise Thoraval, Carly & Buchanan, Jessie, illus. (p. 1226)
Belarde-Lewis, Miranda. Meet Lydia: A Native Girl from Southeast Alaska. Harrington, John, photos by. (p. 1121)
Belasco, Susan. Constructing Literacies. (p. 359)
Belasen, Amy & Osborn, Jacob. Jenny Green's Killer Junior Year. (p. 913)
Belaustegui, Inés, tr. see Mull, Brandon.
Belavilas, Charlotte. Walter, the Carpenter Bee. (p. 1856)
Belback, Elsie. Hidden in Plain Sight: Animal Camouflage. (p. 775)
—Masters of Disguise: Animal Mimicry. (p. 1103)
Belcher, Andy, jt. auth. see Belcher, Angie.
Belcher, Andy & Belcher, Angie. Baby Turtle. (p. 128)
—Rally Challenge: Band 10/White. Belcher, Andy & Belcher, Angie, photos by. (p. 1437)
Belcher, Angie. Storyteller Chapter Books: Fluency - 1 Each of 1 Title: Level T. (p. 1663)
Belcher, Angie, jt. auth. see Belcher, Andy.
Belcher, Angie & Belcher, Andy. Oceans Alive: Band 14. Belcher, Angie, illus. (p. 1277)
—Swimming with Dolphins. (p. 1691)
Belczyk, David. Sometimes Form, Sometimes Vessel. Herning, Kathy, ed. (p. 1610)
Belenky, Alexander. Winning the US Presidency: Rules of the Game & Playing by the Rules. (p. 1937)
Beletic, Kittie Nesius. What Color Is Your Dream? (p. 1881)
Belew, Elizabeth A. There's Always a Place for Mr. Plant. (p. 1731)
Belfield, Annie. Stressed-Out Girl? Girls Dealing with Feelings. (p. 1667)
Belfield, Annie, jt. auth. see Clark, Travis.
Belford, Barbara, jt. auth. see Belford, Bibi.
Belford, Bibi & Belford, Barbara. Canned & Crushed. (p. 261)
Belford, Kevin, jt. auth. see Hubbard, Crystal.
Belge, Kathy, jt. auth. see Bieschke, Marke.
Belgrave, Joanne. Go, Go, Go! ABC: Text & Illustrations. (p. 686)
Belgrove, Teresa. Collection of Children's Poems, Verses & Rhymes for All Ages. (p. 339)

Belgue, Nancy. Casey Little, Yo-Yo Queen (p. 275)
—Colette & the Silver Samovar (p. 339)
—Scream of the Hawk (p. 1532)
—Soames on the Range. (p. 1602)
Beliaev, Edward & Buranbaeva, Oksana. Dagestan. (p. 399)
Believe it or Not! Staff, compiled by. Ripley's Fun Facts & Silly Stories the BIG ONE! (p. 1474)
Belinda, Rochelle. Witnesses to Freedom: Young People Who Fought for Civil Rights. (p. 1942)
Belinkie, Matt, jt. auth. see Stokes, Jordan.
Belinsky, Robin, ed. see Paley, Briyah.
Belisle, Barbara J. Red Hills of Alabama. (p. 1454)
Belisle, John, illus. see Kavanagh, James.
Beliveau, Kathy. Yoga Game. Zaman, Farida, illus. (p. 1972)
—Yoga Game by the Sea. Holmes, Denise, illus. (p. 1972)
Belk, Bradford, jt. auth. see Gangelhoff, Jeanne M.
Belkholm, Erica, illus. see Jacobson, Ryan.
Belknap, Barbara, illus. see Matthews, Kay.
Belknap, Jodi, jt. auth. see Montgomery, Tamara.
Belknap, Jodi P. & Montgomery, Tamara. Kraken Ka The Komodo Dragon. Dodd, Joseph D., illus. (p. 967)
Bell, A. L. Adventures of Captain Zero: I'm the Hero (Special Edition Cover) (p. 17)
—Jr. Comics Coloring (Fun Time) (p. 930)
Bell, Aaron. Jak's Story. (p. 906)
Bell, Albert A., Jr. Secret of the Lonely Grave. (p. 1542)
Bell, Alex. Lex Trent Versus the Gods. (p. 1004)
Bell, Amber Dawn. Cave of Terror. (p. 282)
Bell, Anita & Bell, Belinda. 'Twas Ever. (p. 1799)
Bell, Anthea, jt. auth. see Goscinny, René.
Bell, Anthea, jt. auth. see Sempé, Jean-Jacques.
Bell, Anthea, tr. see Andersen, Hans Christian.
Bell, Anthea, tr. see Bondoux, Anne-Laure.
Bell, Anthea, tr. see Funke, Cornelia.
Bell, Anthea, tr. see Gier, Kerstin.
Bell, Anthea, tr. see Goscinny, Ren&eacute.
Bell, Anthea, tr. see Goscinny, René & Sempé, Jean-Jacques.
Bell, Anthea, tr. see Goscinny, René, et al.
Bell, Anthea, tr. see Goscinny, René.
Bell, Anthea, tr. see Grimm, Jacob & Grimm, Wilhelm.
Bell, Anthea, tr. see Jubert, Herve.
Bell, Anthea, tr. see Jubert, Hervé.
Bell, Anthea, tr. see Kästner, Erich.
Bell, Anthea, tr. see Michaelis, Antonia.
Bell, Anthea, tr. see Mourlevat, Jean-Claude.
Bell, Anthea, tr. see Perrault, Charles.
Bell, Anthea, tr. see Preussler, Otfried.
Bell, Anthea, tr. see Sempé, Jean-Jacques.
Bell, Anthea, tr. see Uderzo, Albert & Goscinny, René.
Bell, Anthea, tr. see Uderzo, Albert, et al.
Bell, Anthea, ed. Bremen Town Musicians. Lai, Hsin-Shih, illus. (p. 226)
Bell, Anthea, tr. from FRE. Nicholas in Trouble. Sempé, Jean-Jacques, illus. (p. 1251)
Bell, Babs. Sputter, Sputter, Sput! Staake, Bob, illus. (p. 1635)
Bell, Barbara. Minimus Secundus Pupil's Book: Moving on in Latin. Forte, Helen, illus. (p. 1147)
—Minimus Secundus Teacher's Resource Book: Moving on in Latin. Forte, Helen, illus. (p. 1147)
Bell, Belinda, jt. auth. see Bell, Anita.
Bell, Bill. Noah: The Incredible Voyager. Bell, Bill, illus. (p. 1261)
Bell, Bill, illus. see Moore, Clement C.
Bell, Bill, illus. see Wilde, Oscar & Hollingsworth, Mary.
Bell, Brad, jt. auth. see Espenson, Jane.
Bell, Braden. Kindling. (p. 957)
—Luminescence. (p. 1065)
—Penumbras. (p. 1338)
Bell, Brian H., jt. auth. see Kennedy, Gregory.
Bell, Bryant. Money Favor: Becoming Financially Empowered Through God's Grace. (p. 1164)
Bell, Cathleen Davitt. Little Blog on the Prairie. (p. 1024)
—Slipping. (p. 1590)
Bell, Cathleen Davitt, jt. auth. see Valentino, Amanda.
Bell, Cece. Deafo. (p. 418)
—Deafo. Lasky, David, illus. (p. 418)
—I Yam a Donkey! (p. 849)
—Itty Bitty. Bell, Cece, illus. (p. 900)
—Rabbit & Robot: The Sleepover. Bell, Cece, illus. (p. 1429)
—Rabbit & Robot. (p. 1429)
—Sock Monkey Boogie-Woogie. Bell, Cece, illus. (p. 1605)
—Sock Monkey Rides Again. Bell, Cece, illus. (p. 1605)
—Sock Monkey Takes a Bath. Bell, Cece, illus. (p. 1605)
Bell, Cece, illus. see Angleberger, Tom.
Bell, Cece, illus. see Mortensen, Denise Dowling.
Bell, Chanda, jt. auth. see Aebersold, Carol V.
Bell, Chanda & Aebersold, Carol. Elf on the Shelf - a Christmas Tradition: Boy Light. Steinwart, Coe, illus. (p. 512)
Bell, Cheryl. Boy Jesus. (p. 218)
Bell, Chris. Deerfield Cats. (p. 423)
—Keycutter's Grandson (p. 950)
—Trapped (p. 1779)
Bell, Christine. Oh No! the Television Won't Work! (p. 1281)
Bell, Clare. Clan Ground. (p. 326)
—Ratha's Challenge. (p. 1440)
—Ratha's Creature. (p. 1440)
Bell, Corydon, illus. see Diggins, Julia E.
Bell, David. Dawn Grays Cosmic Adventure 1. (p. 411)
—Pink Alert! (p. 1359)
—Pyjamas in Space. (p. 1421)
Bell, Debora. Lyssa Lamb. Ronda, Gilger, illus. (p. 1067)
Bell, Diana, illus. see Laguda, Kardy.
Bell, Don, illus. see DeSpain, Pleasant.
Bell, Don, illus. see Young, Richard & Dockrey Young, Judy.
Bell, Don, tr. see DeSpain, Pleasant.
Bell, Donna, jt. auth. see Lee, Carol.
Bell, Eleanor, illus. see Bell, Philip.
Bell, Elisa. Sleepover Movie Scrapbook. (p. 1589)
Bell, Elizabeth, tr. see Andersen, Hans Christian.
Bell, Elvee. Wups. (p. 1966)
Bell, Eric T. Magic of Numbers. (p. 1073)
Bell, Frank. Feng Suey's Special Garden. Seaman, Paul, illus. (p. 581)
—How Slip Slap Slop Got His Name. Seaman, Paul, illus. (p. 812)
—Ma Jong & the Magic Carpet. Seaman, Paul, illus. (p. 1067)
—Panda Patrol to the Rescue. Seaman, Paul, illus. (p. 1320)
Bell, Frank & Bowler, Colin. Panda Patrol Go on Holiday. Seaman, Paul, illus. (p. 1320)
—Panda Power. Seaman, Paul, illus. (p. 1320)
Bell, Fred, illus. see Michels, Dia L.
Bell, G. F. Angel Wings & S'Mores. (p. 74)
Bell, Greg, illus. see Rosen, Barry.
Bell, Hazel. When Silly the Elephant Done His Tricks. (p. 1904)
Bell, Helen Buchanan, tr. see De Monfreid, Henry.
Bell, Hilari. Crown of Earth. Willis, Drew, illus. (p. 386)
—Fall of a Kingdom. (p. 566)
—Forging the Sword. (p. 619)
—Goblin Gate. (p. 688)
—Goblin War. (p. 688)
—Goblin Wood. (p. 688)
—Last Knight. (p. 978)
—Player's Ruse. (p. 1372)
—Prophecy. (p. 1411)
—Rise of a Hero. (p. 1474)
—Rogue's Home. (p. 1485)
—Shield of Stars (p. 1566)
—Sword of Waters. Willis, Drew, illus. (p. 1692)
—Traitor's Son. (p. 1777)
—Trickster's Girl: The Raven Duet Book #1. (p. 1786)
Bell, Hilary. Alphabetical Sydney. Pesenti, Antonia, illus. (p. 50)
Bell, Holly. Abbey Leads the Way. (p. 2)
—Abbey Spells Trouble. (p. 2)
—Emma Saves the Day. (p. 520)
—Ethan Goes Green. Sidwell, Kathy, illus. (p. 539)
—Go, Maddie, Go! (p. 686)
—Kate Plays Detective. (p. 944)
—Matilda's Lost & Found. (p. 1109)
—Olivia Plays Her Part. (p. 1287)
—Olivia's Fantastic Gymnastics. (p. 1287)
Bell, Holly, jt. auth. see Clover, Forever.
Bell, Jaime R. Terra. (p. 1721)
Bell, Jake. Secret Identity Crisis. Giarrusso, Chris, illus. (p. 1541)
Bell, James S., jt. auth. see Bell, James Scott.
Bell, James Scott & Bell, James S. Presumed Guilty (p. 1398)
Bell, James Stuart, et al. Inside the Lion, the Witch & the Wardrobe: Myths, Mysteries, & Magic from the Chronicles of Narnia. (p. 877)
Bell, Janet. Eyes of the Soul. (p. 558)
Bell, Jennifer. My Riding School Pony Logbook. (p. 1217)
—Pony Tale. (p. 1383)
—Smoky Joe's Book of Drawing Ponies: Top Tips, Techniques & Pony Stuff - Straight from the Horse's Mouth! (p. 1595)
Bell, Jennifer, illus. see Carr, Jan.
Bell, Jennifer, illus. see Spinelli, Jerry.
Bell, Jennifer, illus. see Stinson, Kathy.
Bell, Jennifer, illus. see Swinburne, Stephen R.
Bell, Jennifer A., illus. see Bauer, Marion Dane.
Bell, Jennifer A., illus. see Bracken, Beth.
Bell, Jennifer A., illus. see Green, Poppy.
Bell, Jennifer A., illus. see Griffin, Molly Beth.
Bell, Jennifer A., illus. see Hall, Pamela.
Bell, Jennifer A., illus. see Kingsbury, Karen.
Bell, Jennifer A., illus. see Sheinmel, Courtney.
Bell, Jennifer A., illus. see Stanton, Melissa.
Bell, Jennifer A., illus. see Wood, Douglas.
Bell, Jennifer A., jt. auth. see Sheinmel, Courtney.
Bell, Joanne. Juggling Fire (p. 932)
Bell, Johanna. Too Many Cheeky Dogs. Beasley, Dion, illus. (p. 1766)
Bell, John L. & Crow, Jeffrey J. North Carolina: The History of an American State. (p. 1264)
Bell, Jonas Fearon, des. Oh! Christmas Tree: A Fun-To-Find Lift-the-Flap Book. (p. 1280)
Bell, Julia. Massive. (p. 1103)
Bell, Julian. 500 Self-Portraits. (p. 2001)
Bell, Juliet. Kepler's Dream. (p. 949)
Bell, Juliet Clare. Kite Princess. Chapman, Laura-Kate, illus. (p. 962)
Bell, Juliet Clare & Chapman, Laura Kate. Kite Princess. (p. 962)
Bell, Karen. Cookie's Victorian. (p. 361)
Bell, Katja, tr. see Bold, Emily.
Bell, Krista. No Strings. (p. 1260)
Bell, Krista & Smith, Craig. If the Shoe Fits. (p. 854)
Bell, Krista Blakeney. Who Dares? (p. 1914)
—Who Dares? (p. 1915)
Bell, Latarcia. Looking Glass. (p. 1051)
Bell, Leann. Ed & Alma Go Fishing. (p. 503)
—Indianola Santa. (p. 871)
Bell, Liesl, illus. see Rokhsar, Lillian.
Bell, Lindzi. Sherlock Times Three (p. 1566)
Bell, Lisa M. E. I Talked to Mom. (p. 846)
Bell, Liz. Amarie & Her Family. (p. 52)
—Chickee Chickee Chew & Whoo Whoo Whoo. (p. 299)
—Mohawk, Fro or Crew, It Is up to You. (p. 1160)
—Ten Little Babies Bouncing on My Knee. (p. 1719)
—to Z We Write the Words You See. (p. 1759)
Bell, Loman. Old Glory. Bell, Loman, illus. (p. 1283)
—Old Glory Faces the Hurricane. Bell, Loman, illus. (p. 1283)
Bell, Lonnie. History of the New England Patriots. (p. 785)
—History of the New Orleans Saints. (p. 785)
—History of the San Francisco 49ers. (p. 785)
—Story of Coca-Cola. (p. 1657)
—Story of the Ford Motor Company. (p. 1661)
Bell, Lucy. Do Your Ears Hang Low? Doss, Andrea, illus. (p. 458)
Bell, Margie, jt. ed. see Kiser, Penny.
Bell, Marion R. & Geyer, Donna M. Young Cowboys at the Broken Arrow. Stein, Harve, illus. (p. 1978)
Bell, Marvin. Primer about the Flag. Raschka, Chris, illus. (p. 1400)
Bell, Max, et al. Everyday Mathematics: Student Math Journal 2. (p. 544)
—Everyday Mathematics: Mathematics at Home. Bk. 1 (p. 544)
Bell, Megan. Brody the Reading Tutor. (p. 230)
Bell, Megan, jt. auth. see Reader's Digest Editors.
Bell, Melissa. P. S. Lord... (p. 1316)
Bell, Michael & Quie, Sarah. Ancient Egyptian Civilization. D'Ottavi, Francesca, illus. (p. 68)
Bell, Michele Ashman. Dragon's Jaw: A Heart-Pounding Adventure. (p. 479)
—Rescue: A Jungle Adventure. (p. 1462)
—Spyhunt: A Heart-Pounding Adventure: A Novel. (p. 1636)
Bell, Millicent, ed. see James, Henry.
Bell, N. W. Great American Horse Book: A Childrens Guide to Horse's. (p. 713)
Bell, N. Wayne. Childrens' Economics: A Book on Money & Finance. (p. 303)
—Really Big Book of Zoo Animals. (p. 1449)
Bell, Nancy Marie. Step Sideways. (p. 1648)
Bell, Nasherrall, creator. Child Safety at Home, School & Play (p. 301)
Bell, Nick. Mary the Tooth Fairy. Bell, Nick, illus. (p. 1101)
Bell, Ossie S. When Grandma Is Not Grandma: Alzheimer's Steals Family's Treasures. (p. 1902)
Bell, Owain, illus. see Awdry, Wilbert V. & Awdry, W.
Bell, Parker. Tale of the Hundred. (p. 1700)
Bell, Patricia A. Timothy Caterpillar Gets New Shoes. (p. 1755)
Bell, Philip. Elfin Child. (p. 512)
—Jack & Boo's Dinosaur Island. Bell, Eleanor, illus. (p. 902)
Bell, Phillip. Ken the Farmer & His Friend Herbie the Talking Goat. (p. 948)
—Kurt the Dog & His Friend Lisa the Cat. (p. 968)
Bell, Rachael. Australia. (p. 116)
—Italy (p. 894)
—United Kingdom (p. 1819)
Bell, Rebecca. Capitano Ricco. Bell, Rebecca, illus. (p. 263)
—Message from Miami: The Adventures of Sharp-Eye, Book 2. Bell, Rebecca, illus. (p. 1129)
—Princess Sara. Bell, Rebecca, illus. (p. 1405)
—Rebekah Armstronge. (p. 1450)
—Regular Bug: The Adventures of Sharp-Eye, Book 1. Bell, Rebecca, illus. (p. 1457)
Bell, Rob. Love Wins: For Teens. (p. 1060)
Bell, Robin. My Adventure Discovering America. (p. 1195)
—My Adventure Discovering Australia: Advanced My Adventure. (p. 1195)
—My Adventure Discovering Australia. (p. 1195)
—My Adventure with Pirates: Advanced My Adventure. (p. 1195)
Bell, S. Towel Tales: Tub Time. (p. 1773)
Bell, Samantha. Boxfish. (p. 217)
—Copperheads. (p. 366)
—Cuttlefish. (p. 396)
—Hammerhead Sharks. (p. 739)
—How to Survive Being Lost at Sea. (p. 821)
—How to Survive in the Wilderness. (p. 822)
—How to Survive on a Deserted Island. (p. 822)
—I Talk in My Sleep. (p. 846)
—My Fingernails Grow. (p. 1203)
—Perfect Pet (p. 1342)
—Sea Horses. (p. 1534)
—Sea Turtles. (p. 1535)
—Tiger Sharks. (p. 1748)
Bell, Samantha, illus. see Berger, Susan J.
Bell, Samantha, illus. see Chatel, Kim.
Bell, Samantha, illus. see Cox, Tracey M.
Bell, Samantha, illus. see Gladen, Jennifer.
Bell, Samantha, illus. see Stewart, Nancy.
Bell, Samantha, illus. see Tornio, Stacy.
Bell, Samantha S. Cool Military Gear. (p. 364)
—Meet a Baby Elephant. (p. 1120)
—Meet a Baby Giraffe. (p. 1120)
—Meet a Baby Lemur. (p. 1120)
—Meet a Baby Lion. (p. 1120)
—Powerful Military Vehicles. (p. 1390)
Bell, Shelia. Life of Payne: Book II Fairley High Series. (p. 1012)
Bell, Shirley. Boys on the Make. (p. 220)
Bell, Siobhan, illus. see Blackstone, Stella.
Bell, Siobhan, illus. see Roberts, Sheena & Horn, Sandra Ann.
Bell, Siobhan, illus. see Roberts, Sheena.
Bell, Sophie. Lilac Attack! (p. 1017)
—Power to the Purple! Battle, Christina, illus. (p. 1390)
—Ultra Violets. (p. 1810)
Bell, Susan, illus. see Turner, Jennifer.
Bell, Suzanne. Drugs, Poisons, & Chemistry. (p. 487)
—Encyclopedia of Forensic Science. (p. 525)
—Fakes & Forgeries. (p. 565)
Bell, Suzanne, contrib. by. Essentials of Forensic Science (p. 537)
Bell, Taj. Little Night Fairy: Written & illustrated by Taj Bell graphic design & co-illustration by Lisa. (p. 1032)
Bell, Taryn. In the Spotlight. (p. 867)
Bell, Taryn, jt. auth. see Reisfeld, Randi.
Bell, Ted. Nick of Time. (p. 1251)
—Time Pirate. (p. 1752)
Bell, Tom. Where the Lost Things Go. (p. 1909)
Bell, Trudy E. Comets, Meteors, Asteroids, & the Outer Reaches. (p. 348)
—Earth's Journey Through Space. (p. 498)
—Inner Planets. (p. 875)
—Sun: Our Nearest Star. (p. 1675)
Bell, Wade. No Place Fit for a Child. (p. 1259)
Bell, William. Blue Helmet. (p. 203)
—Crabbe (p. 375)
—Death Wind (p. 420)
—Fanatics. (p. 570)
—Five Days of the Ghost (p. 600)
—Only in the Movies. (p. 1298)
—Stones. (p. 1653)
—Tormenta (p. 1770)
Bella Books Staff & Radclyffe. Radical Encounters. (p. 1432)
Bellairs, John. Chessmen of Doom (A Johnny Dixon Mystery: Book Seven) (p. 298)
—Curse of the Blue Figurine (A Johnny Dixon Mystery: Book One) (p. 394)
—Eyes of the Killer Robot (A Johnny Dixon Mystery: Book Five) (p. 558)
—House with a Clock in Its Walls. (p. 804)
—House with a Clock in Its Walls. Gorey, Edward, illus. (p. 804)
—Mansion in the Mist. Gorey, Edward, illus. (p. 1088)
—Mummy, the Will, & the Crypt (A Johnny Dixon Mystery: Book Two) (p. 1191)
—Revenge of the Wizard's Ghost (A Johnny Dixon Mystery: Book Four) (p. 1466)
—Secret of the Underground Room (A Johnny Dixon Mystery: Book Eight) (p. 1543)
—Spell of the Sorcerer's Skull. Gorey, Edward, illus. (p. 1625)
—Spell of the Sorcerer's Skull (A Johnny Dixon Mystery: Book Three) (p. 1625)
Bellamy, David & Dow, Jill. Our Changing World: The River. (p. 1308)
Bellamy, Diane. But I Will Teach You. (p. 246)
Bellamy, Doug. My Blankee. (p. 1198)
Bellamy, Fannie Lillian Miles. Fanning Island. (p. 571)
Bellamy, Jaxon. Galactic Psychic: The Forgotten Race. (p. 652)
Bellamy, Liz. Samuel Johnson. (p. 1509)
Bellamy, Marian Meredith. Goldie & Androcles—A Fable for the 21st Century. Bellamy, Marian Meredith, illus. (p. 695)
Bellamy, Rufus. Backyard Encyclopedia. (p. 131)
—Backyard Heroes. (p. 131)
—Population Growth. (p. 1385)
—Tourism. (p. 1773)
—Waste & Pollution. (p. 1860)
Bellarmine, Robert. Writings on Temporal & Spiritual Authority: On the Laity & on the Temporal Power of the Pope. Tutino, Stefania, ed. (p. 1965)
Bellavia, Rebecca. Planting Sunflowers: Represent & Interpret Data. (p. 1369)
Belle, Annie. KandyKane Kids: Welcome to Kandy Town. (p. 942)
Belle, Deborah A. Day the Sun Called Out Sick!!! Collenberger, Chris, illus. (p. 414)
Belle, Jennifer. Animal Stackers. McPhail, David, illus. (p. 79)
—Little Stalker. (p. 1036)
Belle, Jove. Split the Aces. (p. 1630)
Belle, Magnolia. My Little Pony: Power Ponies to the Rescue! (p. 1213)
—Teen Titans Go!: Chillin' Like a Villain. (p. 1714)
Belle, Monica. Black Lipstick Kisses. (p. 196)
—Office Perks. (p. 1280)
—Pagan Heat. (p. 1317)
—Wild by Nature. (p. 1929)
—Wild in the Country. (p. 1929)
Belle, Sebastian. Exciting! Awesome! Infinite! (Disney Infinity) RH Disney Staff, illus. (p. 547)
Belle, Trixie & Caruso-Scott, Melissa. Beauty & the Beast: Les Petits Fairytales. Lake, Oliver, illus. (p. 154)
—Goldilocks & the Three Bears: Les Petits Fairytales. Lake, Oliver, illus. (p. 696)
—Little Mermaid: Les Petits Fairytales. Lake, Oliver, illus. (p. 1031)
—Little Red Riding Hood: Les Petits Fairytales. Lake, Oliver, illus. (p. 1035)
—Rapunzel. Lake, Oliver, illus. (p. 1439)
—Sleeping Beauty: Les Petits Fairytales. Lake, Oliver, illus. (p. 1589)
Bellefontaine, Kim. ABC of Canada. Gürth, Per-Henrik, illus. (p. 3)
—Canada 123. Gurth, Per-Henrik, illus. (p. 260)
Bellehumeur, Johanne G. Zilch to Zenith. (p. 1986)
Bellemare, Josee, illus. see Lee, Day's.
Bellemare, Paule Trudel, illus. see Zephaniah, Benjamin.
Belleme, John, et al. Japanese Foods That Heal: Using Traditional Japanese Ingredients to Promote Health, Longevity & Well-Being. (p. 909)
Bellen-Berthézène, Cyndie. Cartoon How-To. Workman, Terry & Workman, Lisa, illus. (p. 273)
—Flipping Out! How to Draw Flip Animation. Steck, Jim, illus. (p. 605)
Bellenir, Karen, ed. Accident & Safety Information for Teens: Health Tips about Medical Emergencies, Traumatic Injuries, & Disaster Preparedness. (p. 8)
—Diabetes Information for Teens. (p. 433)
—Eating Disorders Information for Teens. (p. 501)
Beller, Dyan. Creative Bible Crafts: Reproducible Activities. (p. 379)
Beller, Susan Provost. Aftermath of the Mexican Revolution. (p. 28)
—Battling in the Pacific: Soldiering in World War II. (p. 147)
—Billy Yank & Johnny Reb: Soldiering in the Civil War. (p. 187)
—Doughboys over There: Soldiering in World War I. (p. 473)
—History Puzzle: How We Know What We Know about the Past. (p. 785)
—Roman Legions on the March: Soldiering in the Ancient Roman Army. (p. 1486)
—Roots for Kids: A Genealogy Guide for Young People. (p. 1488)
—Siege of the Alamo: Soldiering in the Texas Revolution. (p. 1573)
—Soldiers on the Battlefront (p. 1607)
—Yankee Doodle & the Redcoats: Soldiering in the Revolutionary War. (p. 1968)
—Yankee Doodle & the Redcoats: Soldiering in the Revolutionary War. Day, Larry, illus. (p. 1968)
Belletto, Kimm, jt. auth. see Kubesh, Katie.
Bellevois, Jacqueline. Priestess. (p. 1399)
Bellew, Steve C. Great Walnut War. (p. 719)
Belli, Alfredo, illus. see Dickens, Charles.
Belli, Alfredo, illus. see Morton, Sasha.
Bellin, Joshua David. Survival Colony 9: Forget the Past Fight to Stay Alive. (p. 1686)
Bellinger, Marie, illus. see Harper, Julie-Ann.
Bellingham, Brenda. Captain Lilly & the New Girl MacDonald, Clarke, illus. (p. 264)
—Lilly & the Hullabaloo MacDonald, Clarke, illus. (p. 1017)

B

—Lilly & the Snakes. MacDonald, Clarke, illus. (p. 1017)
—Lilly Babysits Her Brother MacDonald, Clarke, illus. (p. 1017)
—Lilly in the Middle Owen, Elizabeth, illus. (p. 1017)
—Lilly Makes a Friend MacDonald, Clarke, illus. (p. 1017)
—Lilly Makes a Friend. MacDonald, Clarke, illus. (p. 1017)
—Lilly Takes the Lead. MacDonald, Clarke, illus. (p. 1017)
—Lilly Traps the Bullies. MacDonald, Clarke, illus. (p. 1017)
—Lilly's Special Gift MacDonald, Clarke & Kaulbach, Kathy, illus. (p. 1017)
—Lilly's Special Gift. (p. 1017)
—Lilly's Special Gift. MacDonald, Clarke, illus. (p. 1017)
—Maldicion del Cofre de Plata. (p. 1083)
Bellini, Ellen, photos by see Anastasi, Donna.
Bellino, Sarah. Little Miss Detectives: Case Number 1. (p. 1031)
Bellis, Dave, jt. auth. see McDowell, Josh.
Bellis, Jill. Magnificent Six. Farmer, Zoe, illus. (p. 1076)
—Return of the Magnificent Six: A Christmas Adventure. Farmer, Zoe, illus. (p. 1464)
Bellisario, Gina. Be Aware! My Tips for Personal Safety. Kurilla, Renee, illus. (p. 148)
—Choose Good Food! My Eating Tips. Conger, Holli, illus. (p. 310)
—Keep Calm! My Stress-Busting Tips. Kurilla, Renee, illus. (p. 946)
—Let's Meet a Firefighter. Myer, Ed, illus. (p. 999)
—Let's Meet a Librarian. Myer, Ed, illus. (p. 999)
—Let's Meet a Veterinarian. Atkinson, Cale, illus. (p. 999)
—Move Your Body! My Exercise Tips. Kurilla, Renee, illus. (p. 1183)
—Poison Alert! My Tips to Avoid Danger Zones at Home. Conger, Holli, illus. (p. 1377)
—Take a Bath! My Tips for Keeping Clean. Conger, Holli, illus. (p. 1696)
—Twelve Days of Christmas in Illinois. Ebbeler, Jeffrey, illus. (p. 1800)
Bell-Jackson, Sylvia. Bree's Bubble Gum Adventures: The Pajamas from the Bahamas. (p. 226)
Bellm, Dan, jt. auth. see Gallego Garcia, Laura.
Bell-Martin, Janelle. Head & Shoulders. (p. 756)
—Mary Had a Little Lamb. (p. 1100)
—Oh, Mr. Sun. (p. 1280)
Bell-Myers, Darcy. Animal Babies ABC Book of Ballet. (p. 76)
—Animal Babies ABC Book of Princesses. (p. 76)
—Pretty Ponies Paper Dolls. (p. 1398)
Bell-Myers, Darcy, illus. see D'Amico, Christine.
Bell-Myers, Darcy, illus. see Mischel, Jenny Ann.
Bello, Ecrahim, photos by see Nohemi, Esther.
Bello, Rodolfo S. My Baby Doggie. (p. 1196)
Belloc, Hilaire. Cautionary Tales for Children. (p. 282)
—Moral Alphabet: In Words of from One T. (p. 1173)
—More Beasts for Worse Children. B. T. B., illus. (p. 1174)
Belloit, Louquitas. Red Blood, White Lies. (p. 1453)
Bellomy, Gail, illus. see Clawson, Kimberly.
Bellon-Fisher, Linda. Take Note of Tommy-Toe Goat. (p. 1696)
Belloni, Giulia. Anything Is Possible. Trevisan, Marco, illus. (p. 91)
Belloni, Valentina, illus. see Gunderson, Jessica.
Belloni, Valentina, illus. see Meister, Cari.
Bellow, Saul. Mr. Sammler's Planet. (p. 1186)
Bellows, George, jt. auth. see Burleigh, Robert.
Bellows, Greg. Giant. (p. 673)
Bell-Rehwoldt, Sheri. Great World War II Projects: You Can Build Yourself. (p. 719)
—Kids' Guide to Building Cool Stuff (p. 953)
—Kids' Guide to Classic Games. (p. 953)
—Kids' Guide to Duct Tape Projects (p. 953)
—Kids' Guide to Jumping Rope (p. 953)
—Kids' Guide to Pranks, Tricks, & Practical Jokes. (p. 953)
—Maya: Amazing Inventions You Can Build Yourself. Casteel, Tom, illus. (p. 1112)
—Maya: Inventos Increíbles Que Puedes Construir Tu Mismo. Casteel, Tom, illus. (p. 1112)
—Ripley's Believe It or Not! Totally Bizarre. (p. 1474)
—Science Experiments That Surprise & Delight: Fun Projects for Curious Kids (p. 1525)
—Speaking Secret Codes (p. 1623)
—You Think It's Easy Being the Tooth Fairy? Slonim, David, illus. (p. 1976)
Bell-Rehwoldt, Sheri, et al. Kids' Guides. (p. 954)
Bellville, Sharyn. Pirate of Smith Point Beach. (p. 1362)
Bellward, Stacy. Ethiopian Voices: Tsion's Life. Berge, Erlend, illus. (p. 539)
Belmonte, David. Creating Horror Comics. (p. 378)
Belmonte, Kevin. Journey Through the Life of William Wilberforce: The Abolitionist Who Changed the Face of a Nation. (p. 928)
—Travel with William Wilberforce: The Friend of Humanity. (p. 1780)
Belmore, Vickie J. Paul the Pack Rat: Helping Children Learn to Share. Ciaravino, Paul, illus. (p. 1330)
Belmudes, Bonnie. Adventures of Gus & Gunther: How They Met. (p. 18)
Beloat, Betty. Winged Pony. Schwartz, Wendy, illus. (p. 1936)
Belominsky, Alex, illus. see Kurlander, Keith.
Belominsky, M., illus. see Slupskiy, Leon.
Belonie, Shannon. Oliver Andrew Ostrich: My Full Name. (p. 1285)
—Teaching an Ostrich to Fly. (p. 1709)
Belovitch, Jeanne & Bonnevie, Bonnie. New York City Firsts: A Coloring Book for Families about New York History & America's. Belovitch, Jeanne, ed. (p. 1248)
Below, Halina. Chestnut Dreams Below, Halina, illus. (p. 298)
Belpuls, Nathalie, jt. auth. see Belpuls, Peter.
Belpuls, Peter & Belpuls, Nathalie. Dirt: Is That What You're Made Of? (p. 446)
Belpulsi, Nathalie B., jt. auth. see Belpulsi, Peter A.
Belpulsi, Peter A. & Belpulsi, Nathalie B. As the Saying Goes (p. 105)
Belser, Maud Corier. Grace & Marie's Little Farm on the Hill. (p. 704)
Belshaw, Yvonne & Sheldon, Tamia. Toby the Flying Cat. (p. 1760)
Belshe, Judy. Fry Family Goes to Hollywood. (p. 646)
Belt, Christopher R. Adventures of Nate the Gnat. (p. 21)
BELTEI, Nadia. Emily's BOOKS: Coloring & Activity book, age Level: 2-3. (p. 519)
—Emily's BOOKS: Coloring & Activity book, age Level: 2-3 (B&W) (p. 519)
Belthoff, B. A. Porcupine Penny. (p. 1386)
Belton, Blair. Articles of Confederation. (p. 104)
—Be a Zoologist. (p. 148)
Belton, Robyn. Herbert: The True Story of a Brave Sea Dog. Belton, Robyn, illus. (p. 769)
Belton, Robyn, illus. see Sutton, Sally.
Belton, Sandra. Tallest Tree. (p. 1704)
Belton-Fisher, Linda. My Story of Glory. (p. 1219)
Belton-Terrell, Alice F. Kailah & Lyndsey: Sharing Spaces. (p. 941)
Beltran, Andrea. Juliet's Day. (p. 932)
Beltran, Leonardo Arenas, jt. auth. see Gonzalez Montes, Fidencio.
Belval, Brian. Gold. (p. 693)
—Olympic Track & Field. (p. 1288)
—Primary Source History of the Lost Colony of Roanoke. (p. 1400)
—Silver. (p. 1576)
Belval, Brian, ed. Critical Perspectives on Stem Cell Research. (p. 383)
Belverio, Tom. Cindy Learns a Lesson. (p. 321)
Belviso, Meg, jt. auth. see Pollack, Pam.
Belviso, Meg, jt. auth. see Pollack, Pamela D.
Belviso, Meg, jt. auth. see Pollack, Pamela.
Belviso, Meg & Pollack, Pam. What Was the Alamo? Groff, David, illus. (p. 1895)
—Who Is Nelson Mandela? (p. 1916)
Belviso, Meg & Pollack, Pamela. What Was the Alamo? (p. 1895)
Belviso, Meg & Pollack, Pamela D. Who Was Nelson Mandela? Marchesi, Stephen, illus. (p. 1919)
Belyeu, Monti L. Hot Diggity Doggerels: Delightful Ditties about the Dog. (p. 801)
Belzer, Thomas J. Roadside Plants of Southern California. (p. 1477)
Bernal, Luis Dario. Numeros y Palabritas y Otras Locuras Loquitas. (p. 1273)
Bembibre, Cecilia, jt. auth. see Simpson, Joe.
Bembibre, Cecilia, et al. Máscara del Zorro. (p. 1102)
—Niña de Tus Ojos. (p. 1256)
Bemelmans, Ludwig. Madeline: Activity Book with Stickers. (p. 1070)
—Madeline: Edicion en Espanol. Anasal, Arshes, ed. (p. 1070)
—Madeline. (p. 1070)
—Madeline 75th Anniversary Edition. (p. 1070)
—Madeline Christmas Activity Book. (p. 1070)
—Madeline Treasury: The Original Stories by Ludwig Bemelmans. (p. 1070)
—Madeline's Christmas Bemelmans, Ludwig, illus. (p. 1070)
—Madeline's Rescue (p. 1070)
—Madeline's Rescue. (p. 1070)
Bemelmans, Ludwig, illus. see Leaf, Munro.
Bemer Coble, Lynn, ed. see Carpenter, Angie.
Bemis, John Claude. Nine Pound Hammer. (p. 1256)
—Prince Who Fell from the Sky. (p. 1401)
—White City: Book 3 of the Clockwork Dark. (p. 1912)
—Wolf Tree: Book 2 of the Clockwork Dark. (p. 1944)
Bemporad, Alex, photos by see Ollendorff, Valli.
Ben, Mikaelsen. Touching Spirit Bear. (p. 1772)
(Ben Quinn), D. A. Green Glot. (p. 722)
Benacquista, E., jt. auth. see Pennac, D.
Benacquista, Tonino, jt. auth. see Pennac, Daniel.
Ben-Aharon, Ariella. One Day I Was Walking Around. (p. 1294)
Benally, Kendrick, illus. see Powell, Patricia Hruby.
Ben-Ami, Doron, illus. see Alcorn, Randy.
Ben-Ami, Doron, illus. see Byars, Betsy.
Ben-Ami, Doron, illus. see Creel, Ann Howard.
Ben-Ami, Doron, illus. see Cummings, Priscilla.
Ben-Ami, Uzi, jt. auth. see Stern, Judith M.
Benanti, Carol. Real Fossils. Frank, Michael, ed. (p. 1448)
Benard, Federico Vargas, jt. auth. see Vazquez-Lozano, Gustavo.
Benari, Naomi. Early Movement Skills. (p. 494)
Benary-Isbert, Margot. Rowan Farm. (p. 1492)
Benatar, Raquel. Isabel Allende: Memories for a Story: Isabel Allende: Recuerdos para un Cuento. Petersen, Patricia, tr. (p. 890)
—¡Tú También Puedes! La Vida de Barack Obama. Levitas, Alexander, illus. (p. 1795)
Benatar, Raquel & Rubio, Adrian. Go, Milka, Go! The Life of Milka Duno. Benatar, Raquel & Rubio, Adrian, illus. (p. 686)
Benatar, Raquel & Torrecilla, Pablo. Isabel Allende: Recuerdos para un Cuento. Petersen, Patricia, tr. (p. 890)
Benati, R., et al. Meine Freunde und ich. Sammelmappe für Kinder. Mit Audio-CD: Zum Sammeln der Übungsblätter. (p. 1124)
Benator, Eileen. Marching Band for Bears. Benator, Seth, illus. (p. 1091)
Benator, Eileen B. Ballet for Bobcat. Benator, Seth, illus. (p. 134)
Benator, Seth, illus. see Benator, Eileen B.
Benator, Seth, illus. see Benator, Eileen.
Benatova, Sibylla, illus. see David, Ryan.
Benavides, Desiree. Little Henry's Adventures: Henry's Trip to the Supermarket. (p. 1029)
Benavides, Rosa, tr. see Minarik, Else Holmelund.
Benavidez, Barbara. My School Years: Kindergarten Through Graduation. (p. 1218)
Benavidez, Max. Historia de Carlito/ Carlito's Story. (p. 782)
Benavie, Arthur. Social Security under the Gun: What Every Citizen Needs to Know. (p. 1604)
Benbow, Ann & Mably, Colin. Awesome Animal Science Projects. LaBaff, Tom, illus. (p. 120)
—Lively Plant Science Projects. Labaff, Tom & LaBaff, Tom, illus. (p. 1040)
—Master the Scientific Method with Fun Life Science Projects. LaBaff, Tom, illus. (p. 1103)
—Nature's Secret Habitats Science Projects. LaBaff, Tom, illus. (p. 1237)
—Sensational Human Body Science Projects. LaBaff, Tom, illus. (p. 1550)
—Sprouting Seed Science Projects. Labaff, Tom, illus. (p. 1635)
Bencastro, Mario. Promise to Keep. Giersbach-Rascon, Susan, tr. from SPA. (p. 1411)
—Viaje a la Tierra del Abuelo. (p. 1839)
Bence, Deborah L., jt. auth. see Largen, Velda L.
Benchabbat, Edie C., et al. My Little Guardian Storybook. (p. 1212)
Benchimol, Brigitte. Jadyn & the Magic Bubble: I Met Gandhi. Adams, Mark Wayne, illus. (p. 905)
—Jadyn & the Magic Bubble: Discovering India. Benchimol, Brigitte & Zima, Siegfried, illus. (p. 905)
Benchley, Peter. Shark Life: True Stories about Sharks & the Sea. (p. 1562)
Benchmark Education Co. Theodore Roosevelt & the Progressive Era. (p. 1729)
Benchmark Education Co., LLC. Aftermath of World War II. (p. 29)
—Ancient Cultures of Mesoamerica. (p. 68)
—Ancient Cultures of North America. (p. 68)
—At My School Big Book. (p. 110)
—Battles of the American Revolution. (p. 147)
—Battles of World War II. (p. 147)
—Becoming a World Power: 1890-1918. (p. 156)
—Big Trucks Big Book. (p. 184)
—Causes of the American Revolution. (p. 282)
—Causes of World War II. (p. 282)
—Dog Hair EVERYWHERE! Big Book. (p. 461)
—Faces of the American Revolution. (p. 561)
—Families Together Big Book. (p. 567)
—Fun in the Sun Big Book. (p. 648)
—Geography of Africa. (p. 662)
—Geography of Asia & Australia. (p. 662)
—Geography of Europe. (p. 662)
—Geography of North & South America. (p. 662)
—Gold & the Settling of the West. (p. 693)
—Guess Who Lives on My Street Big Book. (p. 729)
—Happy Hippo Holiday Big Book. (p. 746)
—Immigration. (p. 861)
—Industrial Revolution. (p. 872)
—It's Raining, It's Pouring Big Book. (p. 898)
—Look at Me! Big Book. (p. 1048)
—Middle Colonies. (p. 1137)
—Mr. Jitters & the Sleep Machine Big Book. (p. 1185)
—Mrs. MacDonald's Garden Big Book. (p. 1187)
—My Friends Big Book. (p. 1209)
—New England Colonies. (p. 1244)
—OH BRODIE! Big Book. (p. 1280)
—One Frosty Night at the Farm Big Book. (p. 1295)
—Physical & Human Geography. (p. 1353)
—Play, Play, Play All Day Big Book. (p. 1371)
—Roaring Twenties & the Great Depression. (p. 1478)
—Safe at School Big Book. (p. 1502)
—Safety Signs Big Book. (p. 1502)
—Sail with Me Big Book. (p. 1503)
—Show Respect Big Book. (p. 1571)
—Sight Walk Big Book. (p. 1574)
—Southern Colonies. (p. 1617)
—Strawberry Girl Big Book. (p. 1666)
—Trip to Washington, D. C. A Capital Idea Teacher's Guide. (p. 1787)
—Up in the Sky Big Book. (p. 1824)
—We Need a Seed Big Book. (p. 1867)
—Westward Expansion. (p. 1876)
—What Can We Share? Big Book. (p. 1881)
—What Do Bears Eat? Big Book. (p. 1882)
—What Is Papa Cooking? Big Book. (p. 1890)
—What Is That Sound? Big Book. (p. 1890)
—Where Is Moggie? Big Book. (p. 1908)
—Who Do You See? a Rain Forest Rap Big Book. (p. 1915)
—Wind Big Book. (p. 1935)
Benchmark Education Co., LLC, jt. auth. see Albee, Sarah.
Benchmark Education Co., LLC, jt. auth. see Fuerst, Jeffrey B.
Benchmark Education Co., LLC, jt. auth. see Grossman, Max.
Benchmark Education Co., LLC, jt. auth. see Jenkins, Amanda.
Benchmark Education Co., LLC, jt. auth. see Justice, Lee S.
Benchmark Education Co., LLC, jt. auth. see Korba, Joanna.
Benchmark Education Co., LLC, jt. auth. see Martinez, David.
Benchmark Education Co., LLC, jt. auth. see Mika, Christina.
Benchmark Education Co., LLC, jt. auth. see Polydoros, Lori.
Benchmark Education Co., LLC, jt. auth. see Rice, Racheal.
Benchmark Education Co., LLC, jt. auth. see Sanderson, Jeannette.
Benchmark Education Co., LLC, jt. auth. see Sloan, Andy.
Benchmark Education Co., LLC, jt. auth. see Swain, Cynthia.
Benchmark Education Co., LLC, jt. auth. see Walsh, Brendan.
Benchmark Education Co., LLC, jt. auth. see Wood, Greg V.
Benchmark Education Co., LLC, jt. auth. see Worth, Richard.
Benchmark Education Co., LLC Staff, jt. auth. see Akers, Martin.
Benchmark Education Co., LLC Staff, jt. auth. see Anin, Ravi.
Benchmark Education Co., LLC Staff, jt. auth. see Benjamin, Joseph.
Benchmark Education Co., LLC Staff, jt. auth. see Bennett, Liza.
Benchmark Education Co., LLC Staff, jt. auth. see Benton, Celia.
Benchmark Education Co., LLC Staff, jt. auth. see Cochran, Kate.
Benchmark Education Co., LLC Staff, jt. auth. see Davies, Aysha.
Benchmark Education Co., LLC Staff, jt. auth. see Delgado, Ben.
Benchmark Education Co., LLC Staff, jt. auth. see Diego, John.
Benchmark Education Co., LLC Staff, jt. auth. see Flynn, Cam.
Benchmark Education Co., LLC Staff, jt. auth. see Gomez, Sonia.
Benchmark Education Co., LLC Staff, jt. auth. see Green, Lila.
Benchmark Education Co., LLC Staff, jt. auth. see Hassan, Miriam.
Benchmark Education Co., LLC Staff, jt. auth. see Hirsh, Mia.
Benchmark Education Co., LLC Staff, jt. auth. see Hsu, Kim.
Benchmark Education Co., LLC Staff, jt. auth. see Johnson, Tiffany.
Benchmark Education Co., LLC Staff, jt. auth. see Jones, Tambor.
Benchmark Education Co., LLC Staff, jt. auth. see Lane, Tracy.
Benchmark Education Co., LLC Staff, jt. auth. see LaRosa, Paula.
Benchmark Education Co., LLC Staff, jt. auth. see Lee, Kim.
Benchmark Education Co., LLC Staff, jt. auth. see Lee, Wan.
Benchmark Education Co., LLC Staff, jt. auth. see Lewis, Samantha.
Benchmark Education Co., LLC Staff, jt. auth. see Ling, Lei.
Benchmark Education Co., LLC Staff, jt. auth. see Mann, Elsa.
Benchmark Education Co., LLC Staff, jt. auth. see Ochoa, Louisa.
Benchmark Education Co., LLC Staff, jt. auth. see Padilla, Mara.
Benchmark Education Co., LLC Staff, jt. auth. see Robinson, Lisa.
Benchmark Education Co., LLC Staff, jt. auth. see Rogers, Jane.
Benchmark Education Co., LLC Staff, jt. auth. see Rosen, Rachel.
Benchmark Education Co., LLC Staff, jt. auth. see Russo, Gina.
Benchmark Education Co., LLC Staff, jt. auth. see Singer, Beth.
Benchmark Education Co., LLC Staff, jt. auth. see Soto, Luisa.
Benchmark Education Co., LLC Staff, jt. auth. see Stribling, Anne.
Benchmark Education Co., LLC Staff, jt. auth. see Swann, Tammy.
Benchmark Education Co., LLC Staff, jt. auth. see Trevia, Rick.
Benchmark Education Co., LLC Staff, jt. auth. see Uss, John.
Benchmark Education Co., LLC Staff, jt. auth. see Wilkens, Karen.
Benchmark Education Co., LLC Staff & Furgang, Kathy. Light Around Us: Big Book Edition. (p. 1014)
—Light Around Us. (p. 1014)
—Wind & Water Change Earth: Big Book Edition. (p. 1935)
—Wind & Water Change Earth. (p. 1935)
Benchmark Education Co., LLC Staff, et al. Celebrating Earth Day: Big Book Edition. (p. 284)
—Celebrating Earth Day. (p. 284)
—Technology at Home & School: Past & Present. (p. 1711)
—Technology at Home & School: Past & Present: Big Book Edition. (p. 1711)
—Using Technology at Work: Big Book Edition. (p. 1828)
—Using Technology at Work. (p. 1828)
Benchmark Education Co. Staff, jt. auth. see Benjamin, Kathy, Lisa and Kafer.
Benchmark Education Co. Staff, jt. auth. see Benjamin, Lisa.
Benchmark Education Co. Staff, jt. auth. see Brandt, Allison.
Benchmark Education Co. Staff, jt. auth. see da Vinci, Leonardo.
Benchmark Education Co. Staff, jt. auth. see Daniel, Claire.
Benchmark Education Co. Staff, jt. auth. see DeLibero, Nicholas.
Benchmark Education Co. Staff, jt. auth. see Gaestel, Tiffany.
Benchmark Education Co. Staff, jt. auth. see Garcia, Ellen.
Benchmark Education Co. Staff, jt. auth. see Garsteckl, Julia.
Benchmark Education Co. Staff, jt. auth. see Gastel, Tiffany.
Benchmark Education Co. Staff, jt. auth. see Giachetti, Julia.
Benchmark Education Co. Staff, jt. auth. see Grudzina, Joanne, Rebecca and Tangorra.
Benchmark Education Co. Staff, jt. auth. see Hanson, Martina D.
Benchmark Education Co. Staff, jt. auth. see Hanson-Harding, Alexandra.
Benchmark Education Co. Staff, jt. auth. see Hansson, Martina.
Benchmark Education Co. Staff, jt. auth. see Hinman, Bonnie.
Benchmark Education Co. Staff, jt. auth. see Jacobs, Elaina.
Benchmark Education Co. Staff, jt. auth. see Jamieson, Marianne.
Benchmark Education Co. Staff, jt. auth. see Kafer, Kathy.
Benchmark Education Co. Staff, jt. auth. see Kessler, Colleen.

Benchmark Education Co. Staff, jt. auth. see Linde, Barbara M.
Benchmark Education Co. Staff, jt. auth. see Linde, Barbara.
Benchmark Education Co. Staff, jt. auth. see McNeil, Tom.
Benchmark Education Co. Staff, jt. auth. see Melendez, Alicia.
Benchmark Education Co. Staff, jt. auth. see O'Dea, Michael, Rory and Cavanaugh.
Benchmark Education Co. Staff, jt. auth. see O'Dea, Rory.
Benchmark Education Co. Staff, jt. auth. see Peattie, Cindy.
Benchmark Education Co. Staff, jt. auth. see Powless, Justin, Neal and Giles.
Benchmark Education Co. Staff, jt. auth. see Prisco.
Benchmark Education Co. Staff, jt. auth. see Randolph, Jennifer.
Benchmark Education Co. Staff, jt. auth. see Swain, Cynthia.
Benchmark Education Co. Staff, jt. auth. see Wilson, Julius.
Benchmark Education Company. Adaptation (Teacher Guide) (p. 11)
—Aztec World (Teacher Guide) (p. 122)
—Boston Tea Party (Teacher Guide) (p. 215)
—China Long Ago (Teacher Guide) (p. 307)
—Coral Reefs (Teacher Guide) (p. 366)
—Dinosaurs (Teacher Guide) (p. 445)
—Dry As a Desert (Teacher Guide) (p. 487)
—Earthquake! (Teacher Guide) (p. 497)
—Empire of Egypt (Teacher Guide) (p. 521)
—Empires of Mesopotamia (Teacher Guide) (p. 521)
—England Explores the Americas (Teacher Guide) (p. 529)
—Fighting Disease (Teacher Guide) (p. 585)
—Forests (Teacher Guide) (p. 618)
—France Explores the Americas (Teacher Guide) (p. 627)
—George Washington & the American Revolution (Teacher Guide) (p. 664)
—Glaciers (Teacher Guide) (p. 682)
—Great Depression by the Numbers (Teacher Guide) (p. 715)
—Greece Long Ago (Teacher Guide) (p. 720)
—Heredity (Teacher Guide) (p. 771)
—Inca World (Teacher Guide) (p. 868)
—Jamestown Community (Teacher Guide) (p. 907)
—Kingdom of Kush (Teacher Guide) (p. 959)
—Living in a Community (Teacher Guide) (p. 1041)
—Local & State Government (Teacher Guide) (p. 1044)
—Matter Is Everywhere (Teacher Guide) Solids, Liquids, & Gases. (p. 1109)
—Maya World (Teacher Guide) (p. 1113)
—Measuring Matter (Teacher Guide) Solids, Liquids, & Gases. (p. 1117)
—Mesa Verde Communities (Teacher Guide) (p. 1129)
—Midwest Region (Teacher Guide) (p. 1139)
—Newton & His Laws (Teacher Guide) (p. 1249)
—Northeast Region (Teacher Guide) (p. 1265)
—Objects in Motion (Teacher Guide) (p. 1275)
—Ocean Pollution (Teacher Guide) (p. 1276)
—Oil Spills (Teacher Guide) (p. 1282)
—Pacific Northwest Region (Teacher Guide) (p. 1317)
—Plant & Animal Fossils (Teacher Guide) (p. 1368)
—Power of Storms (Teacher Guide) (p. 1389)
—Rome Long Ago (Teacher Guide) (p. 1486)
—Settling the West (Teacher Guide) 1862 To 1890. (p. 1554)
—Seven Wonders of the Ancient World (Teacher Guide) (p. 1555)
—Spain Explores the Americas (Teacher Guide) (p. 1620)
—Symbols of the United States (Teacher Guide) (p. 1693)
—Thirteen Colonies (Teacher Guide) (p. 1735)
—This Is Matter (Teacher Guide) Solids, Liquids, & Gases. (p. 1736)
—Three Laws of Motion (Teacher Guide) (p. 1742)
—Three Twentieth Century Dictators (Teacher Guide) (p. 1744)
—Tropical Rain Forests (Teacher Guide) (p. 1789)
—United States Government (Teacher Guide) (p. 1819)
—Volcanoes (Teacher Guide) Nature's Awesome Power. (p. 1849)
—Water on Earth (Teacher Guide) (p. 1863)
—Weather & Climate (Teacher Guide) (p. 1869)
—Weathering & Erosion (Teacher Guide) (p. 1870)
—Western Legends (Teacher Guide) (p. 1876)
—World War II (Teacher Guide) By the Numbers. (p. 1959)
—Your Skeleton (Teacher Guide) (p. 1981)
Benchmark Education Company, compiled by. Amazing Plants & Plantas Asombrosas. (p. 55)
—Bringing Back the Whooping Crane & ¡Vamos a Rescatar a la Grulla Blanca! (p. 229)
—Classroom Connections - Identifying Cause & Effect Levels S-T (44) Skill Bag. (p. 329)
—Insects Measure up! & ¡Vamos a Medir Insectos! (p. 876)
—Our Family Stories & Las Historias de Nuestras Familias. (p. 1308)
—Spanish & English Theme 5 - Everyday Life: Levels A-E (1-8) (p. 1620)
—Spanish & English Theme Bag 1 - Living Things: Levels A-E (1-8) (p. 1620)
—Spanish & English Theme Bag 2 - Living Things: Levels F-K (10-20) (p. 1620)
—Spanish & English Theme Bag 3 - Family & Friends: Levels A-E (1-8) (p. 1620)
—Spanish & English Theme Bag 4 - Family & Friends: Levels F-K (10-20) (p. 1621)
—Spanish & English Theme Bag 6 - Everyday Life: Levels F-K (10-20) (p. 1621)
—Spanish & English Theme Bags - Set Of 14 (p. 1621)
—Spanish Theme Bag 1 - Living Things: Levels A-E (1-8) (p. 1621)
—Spanish Theme Bag 2 - Living Things: Levels F-K (10-20) (p. 1621)
—Spanish Theme Bag 3 - Family & Friends: Levels A-E (1-8) (p. 1621)
—Spanish Theme Bag 4 - Family & Friends: Levels F-K (10-20) (p. 1621)
—Spanish Theme Bag 5 - Everyday Life: Levels A-E (1-8) (p. 1621)
—Spanish Theme Bag 6 - Everyday Life: Levels F-K (10-20) (p. 1621)
—Spanish Theme Bag 7 the Earth & Its Environments: Levels A-E (1-8) (p. 1621)
—Spanish Theme Bags - Set Of 7 (p. 1621)
Benchmark Education Company, LLC Staff. Cells Teacher's Guide. (p. 286)
—Coming to America: Immigration from 1840 to 1930 Teacher's Guide. (p. 348)
—Disasters of Technology Teacher's Guide. (p. 447)
—Energy Resources Around the World Teacher's Guide. (p. 528)
—Pharaohs, Pyramids & Mummies Teacher's Guide. (p. 1350)
—Reader's Theater for Fluency & Comprehension Handbook. (p. 1444)
—Relationships in Nature Teacher's Guide. (p. 1457)
—Science Measuring Tools Teacher's Guide. (p. 1526)
—Spanish Emergent Supplement. (p. 1621)
—Spanish/English Emergent Supplement. (p. 1622)
—SpiralUp Reading Passages. (p. 1628)
Benchmark Education Company, LLC Staff, compiled by. 19th Century Communities: Theme Set. (p. 1995)
—20th Century History: Theme Set. (p. 1996)
—Adding & Subtracting: Theme Set. (p. 11)
—Addition & Subtraction. (p. 12)
—Algebra. (p. 38)
—AMER Revolution. (p. 58)
—American Beginnings You're Right There! Student Workbooks: Analyze Story Elements Levels S-T (44) (p. 60)
—American Revolution: Theme Set. (p. 63)
—American Revolution. (p. 63)
—Ancient Civilization. (p. 68)
—Ancient Civilizations: Theme Set. (p. 68)
—Ancient Civilizations. (p. 68)
—Animal Adaptation. (p. 76)
—Animal Behavior. (p. 76)
—Arts & Culture: Theme Set. (p. 105)
—Being a Good Citizen: Theme Set. (p. 160)
—Biography Strands Set. (p. 189)
—Biology: Theme Set. (p. 189)
—Bloom & Grow & Simple Systems. (p. 201)
—Bodies in Motion & Body Systems. (p. 206)
—Build up Phonics Readers Add to Pack (p. 238)
—BuildUp Phonics Skill Bag Set. (p. 239)
—Cactus & Canyons & Ecosystems. (p. 250)
—Cactus & Canyons & Regions. (p. 250)
—Career/Biography Emergent Levels A-E (1-8) Texts Set: Early Connections (p. 267)
—Career/Biography Strands Set. (p. 267)
—Celebrations. (p. 285)
—Chemistry: Theme Set. (p. 297)
—Civic Ideals & Practices. (p. 324)
—Civil War: Theme Set. (p. 325)
—Civilizations of the Americas: Theme Set. (p. 326)
—Civilizations of the Americas. (p. 326)
—Classroom Connections - Analyze Character Skill Bag (Levels P-R) (p. 328)
—Classroom Connections - Analyze Story Elements Levels S-T (44) Skill Bag. (p. 328)
—Classroom Connections - Compare & Contrast Skill Bag (Levels J-K) (p. 329)
—Classroom Connections - Draw Conclusions Level T (44) Skill Bag. (p. 329)
—Classroom Connections - Draw Conclusions Level T (44) Student Workbooks (p. 329)
—Classroom Connections - Identify Cause & Effect Skill Bag (Levels L-M) (p. 329)
—Classroom Connections - Identify Fact & Opinion Level S-T (44) Student Workbooks (p. 329)
—Classroom Connections - Identify Fact & Opinon Levels S-T (44) Skill Bag. (p. 329)
—Classroom Connections - Identify Main Idea & Supporting Details Skill Bag (Levels N-O) (p. 329)
—Classroom Connections - Identifying Author's Purpose & Point of View Level T (44) Skill Bag. (p. 329)
—Classroom Connections - Identifying Main Idea & Supporting Details Skill Bag (Levels J-K) (p. 329)
—Classroom Connections - Make Inferences Skill Bag (Levels L-M) (p. 329)
—Classroom Connections - Make Judgments Level T (44) Student Workbooks (p. 329)
—Classroom Connections - Make Predictions Skill Bag (Levels N-O) (p. 329)
—Classroom Connections - Summarize Information Skill Bag (Levels J-K) (p. 329)
—Community Counts & Community Change. (p. 350)
—Community Counts & Local GOVT. (p. 350)
—Comparing Numbers: Theme Set. (p. 352)
—Comprehension Strategy Poster Set Levels A-E (1-8) Emergent. (p. 354)
—Comprehension Strategy Poster Set Levels J-M (18-28) Fluent. (p. 354)
—Comprehension Strategy Posters. (p. 354)
—Comprehension Strategy Posters Set levels F-I (9-16) Early. (p. 354)
—Constitution: Theme Set. (p. 359)
—Counting. (p. 370)
—Data Analysis & Probability. (p. 409)
—Data & Probability. (p. 409)
—Early Explorers: Theme Set. (p. 493)
—Early Explorers. (p. 493)
—Early Math Theme Set. (p. 494)
—Early River Civilizations: Theme Set. (p. 494)
—Early River Civilizations. (p. 494)
—Early Science Theme Set. (p. 494)
—Early/Fluent Math Theme Set. (p. 494)
—Early/Fluent Science Theme Set. (p. 494)
—Earth & Space: Theme Set. (p. 495)
—Earth & Space. (p. 495)
—Earth & Space Science. (p. 495)
—Earth the Inside Story & Earth Systems. (p. 497)
—Earth the Inside Story & Earth's HIST. (p. 497)
—Economics: Theme Set. (p. 502)
—Electricity & Magnetism: Theme Set. (p. 509)
—Electricity & Magnetism. (p. 509)
—Engish Explorers Social Studies Levels 2, 3, 4 (CAN) (p. 529)
—English Explorers Science Set. (p. 529)
—Environment. (p. 531)
—Environment: Theme Set. (p. 532)
—Estimation. (p. 538)
—Eve Bunting's World of Stories & Citizenship. (p. 541)
—Fairness & Equality: Theme Set. (p. 563)
—Families & Friends: Theme Set. (p. 567)
—Family Album & Ancestors. (p. 568)
—Fluency Kit for Independent Practice Levels F-M: Set 1. (p. 608)
—Fluency Kit for Independent Practice Levels N-U: Set 2. (p. 608)
—Fluency Kits for Independent Practice. (p. 608)
—Fluency Kits for Independent Practice - Levels F-U: Sets 1 And 2. (p. 608)
—Forces & Energy: Theme Set. (p. 617)
—Forces & Motion: Theme Set. (p. 617)
—Forces & Motion. (p. 617)
—Freedom's Trail & AMER Revolution. (p. 635)
—Freedom's Trail & U. S. Constitution. (p. 635)
—Geography: Theme Set. (p. 662)
—Geography. (p. 662)
—Geometry. (p. 662)
—Good for You! & Personal Health. (p. 698)
—Government & Citizenship: Theme Set. (p. 704)
—Government & Citizenship. (p. 704)
—GOVT & Citizenship. (p. 704)
—Habitats: Theme Set. (p. 734)
—Habitats. (p. 734)
—Health & Human Body: Theme Set. (p. 757)
—High Frequency Word Component Set. (p. 777)
—HIST & Nature of Science. (p. 781)
—Historical Communities: Theme Set. (p. 783)
—How-to Emergent Levels A-E (1-8) Texts Set: Early Connections (p. 819)
—Human Body: Theme Set. (p. 825)
—Human Body. (p. 825)
—Individual Development & Identity. (p. 872)
—Individuals, Groups & Institutions. (p. 872)
—Individuals, Groups, & Institutions. (p. 872)
—Invention & Technology: Theme Set. (p. 883)
—Jobs. (p. 919)
—Landforms. (p. 974)
—Learning about Earth's Past. (p. 984)
—Life on Earth: Theme Set. (p. 1012)
—Life Science. (p. 1013)
—Light & Sound: Theme Set. (p. 1014)
—Living in Communities: Theme Set. (p. 1041)
—Math Standards Set. (p. 1107)
—Math Strands Set. (p. 1107)
—Math Texts Set. (p. 1107)
—Math Themes. (p. 1107)
—Matter: Theme Set. (p. 1109)
—Matter. (p. 1109)
—Measurement. (p. 1117)
—Measuring: Theme Set. (p. 1117)
—Measuring Time: Theme Set. (p. 1117)
—Money: Theme Set. (p. 1163)
—My First Reader's Theater Lap Books. (p. 1207)
—Native AMER. (p. 1234)
—Native Land & Geography. (p. 1234)
—Native Land & Native AMER HIST. (p. 1234)
—Neighborhoods & Communities: Theme Set. (p. 1240)
—Neighborhoods & Communities. (p. 1240)
—Numbers & Operations: Theme Set. (p. 1272)
—Numbers & Operations. (p. 1272)
—Nutrition & Exercise. (p. 1274)
—One World, Many Cultures: Theme Set. (p. 1297)
—Organisms: Theme Set. (p. 1303)
—Organisms: Past & Present. (p. 1303)
—Organisms Past & Present. (p. 1303)
—Our Changing Earth: Theme Set. (p. 1308)
—Our Environment: Theme Set. (p. 1308)
—Our Environment. (p. 1308)
—Our Solar System: Theme Set. (p. 1310)
—Patterns & Shapes: Theme Set. (p. 1329)
—Patterns & Shapes. (p. 1329)
—People, Places & Environments. (p. 1339)
—People, Places, & Environments. (p. 1339)
—People Who Changed Our World: Theme Set. (p. 1340)
—Phonics Poetry Posters. (p. 1352)
—Phonological Awareness. (p. 1352)
—Physical Science. (p. 1353)
—Plants: Theme Set. (p. 1369)
—Plants & Animal Life: Theme Set. (p. 1369)
—Plants & Animals: Theme Set. (p. 1369)
—Portraits in Greatness Student Workbooks: Identify Author's Purpose & Point of View T (44) (p. 1387)
—Power, Authority, & Governance. (p. 1389)
—Production, Distribution, & Consumption. (p. 1409)
—Reader's Theater Nursery Rhymes & Songs Big Books. (p. 1444)
—Reading First Bookroom COLL. (p. 1445)
—Regions of the U. S. (p. 1457)
—Regions of the U. S. Theme Set. (p. 1457)
—Renaissance: Theme Set. (p. 1460)
—REXExtreme Tutoring Program for Expanding Literacy: Reading Explorers (p. 1467)
—Rocks & Minerals: Theme Set. (p. 1483)
—Rocky Tales & Earth Systems. (p. 1484)
—Safety. (p. 1502)
—Science & Technology. (p. 1525)
—Science As Inquiry. (p. 1525)
—Science as Inquiry. (p. 1525)
—Science Classroom Library. (p. 1525)
—Science in Personal & Social Perspectives. (p. 1526)
—Science in Personal Social Perspectives. (p. 1526)
—Science Standards Set. (p. 1528)
—Science Strands Set. (p. 1528)
—Science, Technology & Society. (p. 1528)
—Science, Technology, & Society. (p. 1528)
—Science Text Set. (p. 1528)
—Science Texts Set. (p. 1528)
—Science Theme: Matter. (p. 1528)
—Science Theme: Weather. (p. 1528)
—Science Theme: Habitats. (p. 1528)
—Science Theme: Life Science. (p. 1528)
—Science Theme: Life on Earth. (p. 1528)
—Science Theme: Forces & Motion. (p. 1528)
—Science Theme: The Environment. (p. 1528)
—Science Theme: Physical Science. (p. 1528)
—Science Theme: Earth & Space Science. (p. 1528)
—Science Theme: What Changes Our Earth. (p. 1528)
—Science Theme: Science in Personal & Social Perspectives. (p. 1528)
—Science Themes: Levels N-P Grade 3. (p. 1528)
—Science Themes: Levels Q-R Grade 4. (p. 1528)
—Science Themes: Levels S-U Grade 5. (p. 1528)
—Science Themes: Levels V-X Grade 6. (p. 1528)
—Science Themes. (p. 1528)
—Scientific Achievements: Theme Set. (p. 1528)
—Senses. (p. 1551)
—Skill Bag #1 Retell Facts/Motion: Levels A-B (1-2) (p. 1584)
—Skill Bag #10 Identify Cause & Effect/Using Data: Levels G-H (12-14) (p. 1584)
—Skill Bag #11 Analyze Story Elements/Arts from Many Cultures: Level I (15-16) (p. 1584)
—Skill Bag #12 Summarize Information/Our Environment: Level I (15-16) (p. 1584)
—Skill Bag #2 Make Connections/Seasons: Levels A-B (1-2) (p. 1584)
—Skill Bag #3 Make Predictions at Home, at School: Level C (3-4) (p. 1584)
—Skill Bag #4 Ask Questions/Counting: Level C (3-4) (p. 1584)
—Skill Bag #5 Compare & Contrast/Families: Levels D-E (5-7) (p. 1584)
—Skill Bag #6 Make Connections/Shapes: Levels D-E (6-8) (p. 1584)
—Skill Bag #7 Identify Sequence of Events/Measuring: Levels F-G (9-12) (p. 1584)
—Skill Bag #8 Make Inferences/Safety: Levels F-G (9-12) (p. 1584)
—Skill Bag #9 Identify Main Idea & Supporting Details/Plants: Levels G-H (12-14) (p. 1584)
—Skill Bags K-3 Set (Set Of 12) (p. 1585)
—Social Studies Theme: Communities. (p. 1604)
—Social Studies Theme: Early Explorers. (p. 1604)
—Social Studies Theme: GOVT & Citizenship. (p. 1604)
—Social Studies Theme: Regions of the U. S. (p. 1604)
—Social Studies Theme: The AMER Revolution. (p. 1604)
—Social Studies Theme: Ancient Civilizations. (p. 1604)
—Social Studies Theme: Early River Civilizations. (p. 1604)
—Social Studies Theme: Time, Continuity & Change. (p. 1604)
—Social Studies Theme: Civilizations of the Americas. (p. 1604)
—Social Studies Theme: People, Places & Environments. (p. 1604)
—Sort & Classify. (p. 1614)
—Spanish Early/Fluent Supplement. (p. 1621)
—Spanish Grade 3 Small Group Set. (p. 1621)
—Spanish Grade 4 Small Group Set. (p. 1621)
—Spanish Grade 5 Small Group Set. (p. 1621)
—Spanish High Frequency Word Vocabulary Kit (p. 1621)
—Spanish Math Standard Sets. (p. 1621)
—Spanish Science Standard Set. (p. 1621)
—Spanish Social Studies Standard Set. (p. 1621)
—Spanish/English Early/Fluent Supplement. (p. 1622)
—Spanish/English Emergent Single Copy Set. (p. 1622)
—SpiralUp Phonics Lesson Resources. (p. 1628)
—SpiralUp Phonics Skill Bag Set. (p. 1628)
—SpiralUp Phonics Support Tools. (p. 1628)
—Start up Phonics Readers Add to Pack: Set Of 26. (p. 1643)
—Start up Phonics Readers Set. (p. 1643)
—Storms: Theme Set. (p. 1656)
—Structures of Life. (p. 1668)
—Telling Time. (p. 1717)
—This State Is Mine & Geography. (p. 1737)
—This State Is Mine & State HIST. (p. 1737)
—Time, Continuity & Change. (p. 1751)
—Time, Continuity, & Change. (p. 1751)
—Tools & Technology. (p. 1767)
—Transportation. (p. 1779)
—Travel Money, U. S. A. & ¿Cuánto costó el Viaje? 6 English, 6 Spanish Adaptations (p. 1780)
—U. S. History. (p. 1806)
—United States History: Theme Set. (p. 1819)
—Universe: Theme Set. (p. 1820)
—Using Maps, Graphs & Charts: Theme Set. (p. 1828)
—Water. (p. 1862)
—Water & Weather: Theme Set. (p. 1862)
—Water & Weather. (p. 1862)
—Watery World & Animal Adaptations. (p. 1864)
—Watery World & Ecosystems. (p. 1864)
—Weather & Seasons. (p. 1870)
—What Changes Our Earth. (p. 1881)
—World Communities: Theme Set. (p. 1954)
—World Cultures: Theme Set. (p. 1954)
—World Geography: Theme Set. (p. 1955)
Bencivengo, Mary Ann. Man in the Moon. (p. 1085)
Bencomo, Martin. Paloma Padilla. (p. 1320)
Benda, Wladyslaw T., illus. see Stratton-Porter, Gene.
Bendall-Brunello, John, illus. see Doyle, Malachy.
Bendall-Brunello, John, illus. see Elliot, Rachel.
Bendall-Brunello, John, illus. see Elliott, Rachel.
Bendall-Brunello, John, illus. see Goodwin, John.
Bendall-Brunello, John, illus. see Grindley, Sally.
Bendall-Brunello, John, illus. see Hodges, Lynn & Buchanan, Sue.
Bendall-Brunello, John, illus. see Hodges, Lynn, et al.
Bendall-Brunello, John, illus. see Murphy, Stuart J.
Bendall-Brunello, John, illus. see Redmond, Diane.
Bendall-Brunello, John, illus. see Schwartz, Betty Ann & Seresin, Lynn.
Bendall-Brunello, John, illus. see Verdick, Elizabeth.
Bendall-Brunello, John, illus. see Wargin, Kathy-jo.
Bendall-Brunello, John, jt. illus. see Wargin, Kathy-jo.
Bendall-Brunello, John, tr. see Grindley, Sally.

B

Bendell, Norm, illus. see Criswell, Patti Kelley.
Bendell, Norm, illus. see Falligant, Erin, et al, eds.
Bender, Abby & Weisgerber, Amy. Purdue University College Prowler off the Record. (p. 1419)
Bender, Albert C. More 'Kids in the Alley' Tales. (p. 1174)
Bender, Alexandra Sabina. Alana's Advice... When There's a Clique, You've Got to Think Quick. (p. 33)
Bender, Carol. Doctor's Little Stowaway. (p. 459)
—Picky Eater, That Peter. (p. 1355)
Bender, Carrie. Forget-Me-Not Lane. (p. 619)
—Hemlock Hill Hideaway: Whispering Brook Series #4. (p. 767)
—Summerville Days: Whispering Brook Series #2. (p. 1675)
—Timber Lane Cove. (p. 1750)
Bender, Carrie, compiled by. Betty Girl & Other Animal Stories. (p. 172)
Bender, Chris. Lion & the Lamb. (p. 1019)
Bender, Esther. Elisabeth & the Windmill. (p. 513)
—Thank God for Rocks. Lard, Mary Anne, illus. (p. 1725)
Bender, Janet. Don't Pop Your Balloon! Get a Grip on Anger. (p. 468)
Bender, Janet & Murray, Amy. Perfect Pals: How to Juggle Your Way from Perfection to Excellence. (p. 1342)
Bender, Janet M. Getting Yourself Together When Your Family Comes Apart: Coping with Family Changes. (p. 670)
—Tyler Tames the Testing Tiger. (p. 1805)
Bender, Lionel. Airplanes & Helicopters. (p. 32)
—Cars & Motorcycles. (p. 272)
—Diggers & Tractors. (p. 439)
—DK Eyewitness Books: Invention: Invention. (p. 456)
—Explaining Blindness. (p. 549)
—Explaining Epilepsy. (p. 549)
—Ships & Boats. (p. 1567)
—Trains & Trams. (p. 1777)
—Trucks & Trailers. (p. 1791)
Bender, Lionel & Dorling Kindersley Publishing Staff. Invention. (p. 883)
Bender, Randy L. Bunko's Journey. LaGrange, Tiffany, illus. (p. 242)
Bender, Robert, illus. see Archambault, John.
Bender, Robert, illus. see Benzwie, Teresa.
Bender, Robert, illus. see Evans, Clay Bonnyman.
Bender, Robert, illus. see Greene, Rhonda Gowler.
Benderly, Beryl Lieff. Jason's Miracle: A Hanukkah Story. (p. 910)
Bendick, Jeanne. Archimedes & the Door of Science: Immortals of Science. (p. 95)
—Herodotus & the Road to History. Bendick, Jeanne, illus. (p. 772)
—Lightning. (p. 1015)
Bendick, Jeanne, illus. see Blough, Glenn O.
Bendick, Jeanne, illus. see Wiker, Benjamin.
Bendinger, Jessica. Seven Rays. (p. 1554)
Bendis, Brian Michael. Blockbuster Finch, David & Thibert, Art, illus. (p. 200)
—Crimson Dynamo. Youngquist, Jeff, ed. (p. 383)
—Daredevil: Out Maleev, Alex, illus. (p. 406)
—Decalogue (p. 421)
—Golden Age. (p. 694)
—Powers: Supergroup. Vol. 4 Oeming, Michael Avon, illus. (p. 1391)
—Takio. Oeming, Michael Avon, illus. (p. 1698)
—Widow. (p. 1927)
Bendis, Brian Michael & Quesada, Joe. Ultimate Six. Bagley, Mark & Hairsine, Trevor, illus. (p. 1810)
Bendis, Brian Michael, et al. What If... ? Why Not? (p. 1887)
Bendis, Brian Michael, text. Ultimate Spider-Man Ultimate Collection (p. 1810)
Bendis, Keith, illus. see Berne, Jennifer.
Bendixen, Alfred, jt. ed. see Serafin, Steven.
Bendoly, Lynne, illus. see Farrell, Steve.
Bendoly, Lynne Anne. Tabetha's Crow. (p. 1694)
Bendon Publishing International Staff. Hello Kitty Sticker W/Poster Book #1705. (p. 764)
—Pooh Workbook Bindup #1040. (p. 1383)
Bendt, Valerie. Creating Books with Children - Book & DVD Set Combo Package. (p. 378)
—Easy-to-Make Bible Story Puppets. DeMicco, Michelle, illus. (p. 500)
—Making the Most of the Preschool Years: 100 Activities to Encourage Independent Play. (p. 1082)
Benduhn, Tea. Ancient Egypt. (p. 68)
—Ancient Greece. (p. 69)
—Ancient Rome. (p. 70)
—Antigua Grecia. (p. 89)
—Antigua Roma. (p. 89)
—Bread & Cereal. (p. 224)
—Bread & Cereal/Pan y Cereales. (p. 224)
—Edad Media. (p. 503)
—Energía del Agua. (p. 527)
—Energía del Viento. (p. 528)
—Energía Nuclear. (p. 528)
—Energía Solar. (p. 528)
—Etanol y Otros Combustibles Nuevos. (p. 539)
—Ethanol & Other New Fuels. (p. 539)
—Fruit: Fruta. (p. 645)
—Fruit. (p. 645)
—Fruit/Fruta. (p. 645)
—Living in Deserts. (p. 1041)
—Living in Mountains. (p. 1041)
—Living in Polar Regions. (p. 1041)
—Living in Tropical Rain Forests. (p. 1041)
—Meat & Beans. (p. 1118)
—Meat & Beans (Carne y Frijoles) (p. 1118)
—Meat & Beans/Carne y Legumbres. (p. 1118)
—Middle Ages. (p. 1137)
—Milk & Cheese. (p. 1143)
—Milk & Cheese/Leche y Queso. (p. 1143)
—Nuclear Power. (p. 1270)
—Oil, Gas, & Coal. (p. 1282)
—Oils. (p. 1282)
—Oils (Aceites) (p. 1282)
—Oils/Aceites. (p. 1282)
—Petróleo, Gas y Carbón. (p. 1348)
—Solar Power. (p. 1606)
—Vegetables. (p. 1834)
—Vegetables (Vegetales) (p. 1834)
—Vegetables/Vegetales. (p. 1834)
—Vida en las Montanas. (p. 1840)
—Vida en las Regiones Polares. (p. 1840)
—Vida en los Desiertos. (p. 1840)
—Water Power. (p. 1863)
—What Is Color? (p. 1889)
—What Is Shape? (p. 1890)
—Wind Power. (p. 1935)
Benduhn, Tea, jt. auth. see Altman, Linda Jacobs.
Benduhn, Tea, jt. auth. see Otfinoski, Steven.
Benduhn, Tea, jt. ed. see Rausch, Monica.
Benedettelli, Daniele. Lego Mindstorms NXT Thinking Robots: Build a Rubik's Cube Solver & a Tic-Tac-Toe Playing Robot. (p. 990)
Benedetti, Debra. Season of Play. Teets, Ashley, illus. (p. 1538)
Benedetti, Hervé & Robin, Nicolas. Planet of the Tortoise Driver. Élyum Studio Staff, illus. (p. 1368)
Benedetti, Hervé, et al. Planet of the Tortoise Driver. Élyum Studio Staff, illus. (p. 1368)
Benedetti, Marie. Fishing with Grandpapa: The Most Important Rules. (p. 599)
Benedetti, Mario. Hombre Que Aprendio a Ladrar y Otros Cuentos. (p. 791)
Benedetti, Martha J. Fantasy Fairytale: 7 short Stories. (p. 572)
Benedetto, Angelo Di, see Di Benedetto, Angelo.
Benedetto, K. & Barlow, J. I See the World. (p. 845)
Benedict, Elizabeth, jt. auth. see Golden Books Staff.
Benedict, Janet, jt. auth. see Benedict, Nicholas.
Benedict, Nicholas & Benedict, Janet. My Mommy Is a Zombie. (p. 1214)
Benedict, Norma. Grammy Hits the Road. (p. 706)
Benedictus, David. Return to the Hundred Acre Wood. Burgess, Mark, illus. (p. 1465)
Benedis-Grab, Daphne. Angel Tree. (p. 74)
—Girl in the Wall. (p. 678)
—Girl in the Wall. Mitchard, Jacquelyn, ed. (p. 678)
Benefield, James. Carnivores. (p. 270)
—Herbivores. (p. 769)
—Omnivores. (p. 1288)
—What Animals Eat. (p. 1879)
Benegas, Candela. Rayuela: Level 1. (p. 1441)
Benenfeld, Rikki. I Go to the Dentist. Rosenfeld, Dina & Leverton, Yossi, eds. (p. 838)
—I Go to the Doctor. Benenfeld, Rikki, illus. (p. 838)
—I Go Visiting. (p. 838)
—Let's Go Shopping. Benenfeld, Rikki, illus. (p. 997)
—Let's Meet Community Helpers. Benenfeld, Rikki, illus. (p. 999)
Benenfeld, Rikki, illus. see Hodakov, Levi.
Benesch, Walter. Adam Cox Meets the CrackleCrunch for Lunch. Jamieson, Sandy, illus. (p. 11)
Benett, Janet M. IJustWantTo SLEEP for KIDS. Kater, Mary, ed. (p. 856)
Benevenia, Rose. Dolly & Babe. Benevenia, Rose, illus. (p. 464)
Beneville, Ed, jt. auth. see Moreira, Joe.
Benfanti, Russell, illus. see James, Brian.
Benfold Haywood, Ian P., illus. see Brindley, John.
Benford, Gregory. Across the Sea of Suns. (p. 9)
—Beyond Infinity. (p. 174)
—In the Ocean of Night. (p. 867)
Benge, Geoff, jt. auth. see Benge, Janet.
Benge, Geoffrey Francis, jt. auth. see Benge, Janet.
Benge, Janet. George Washington Carver: What Do You See? James, Kennon, illus. (p. 664)
—Helen Keller: Facing Her Challenges - Challenging the World James, Kennon, illus. (p. 763)
Benge, Janet & Benge, Geoff. Ben Carson: A Chance at Life. (p. 163)
—Christian Heroes Then & Now - Alan Shepard: Higher & Faster. (p. 311)
—Christian Heroes - Then & Now - Brother Andrew: God's Secret Agent. (p. 311)
—Christian Heroes - Then & Now - C. S. Lewis: Master Storyteller. (p. 311)
—Christian Heroes - Then & Now - C. T. Studd: No Retreat. (p. 311)
—Christian Heroes - Then & Now - Clarence Jones: Mr. Radio. (p. 311)
—Christian Heroes - Then & Now - Count Zinzendorf: First Fruit. (p. 311)
—Christian Heroes - Then & Now - Florence Young: Mission Accomplished. (p. 311)
—Christian Heroes - Then & Now - Ida Scudder: Healing Bodies, Touching Hearts. (p. 311)
—Christian Heroes - Then & Now - John Wesley: The World, His Parish. (p. 311)
—Christian Heroes - Then & Now - Lillian Trasher: The Greatest Wonder in Egypt. (p. 311)
—Christian Heroes - Then & Now - Rachel Saint: A Star in the Jungle. (p. 311)
—Christian Heroes - Then & Now - Rowland Bingham: Into Africa's Interior. (p. 311)
—Christian Heroes - Then & Now - Sundar Singh: Footprints over the Mountains. (p. 311)
—Christian Heroes - Then & Now - Wilfred Grenfell: Fisher of Men. (p. 311)
—Davy Crockett: Ever Westward. (p. 411)
—D.L. Moody: Bringing Souls to Christ. (p. 456)
—Francis Asbury: Circuit Rider. (p. 627)
—Heroes Cristianos de Ayer de Hoy - Peripecia en China: La vida de Hudson Taylor. (p. 772)
—Heroes Cristianos de Ayer y de Hoy - Buenas nuevas en todas las Lenguas: Cameron Townsend. (p. 772)
—Heroes Cristianos de Ayer y de Hoy - la Intrepida Rescatadora: Amy Carmichael. (p. 772)
—Heroes Cristianos de Ayer y de Hoy - Peligro en la Selva: La Vida de Nate Saint. Editorial JUCUM, tr. (p. 772)
—Heroes Cristianos de Ayer y de Hoy - Persecucion en Holanda: La Vida de Corrie Ten Boom. (p. 772)
—Heroes of History - Benjamin Franklin: Live Wire. (p. 773)
—Heroes of History - Christopher Columbus: Across the Ocean Sea. (p. 773)
—Heroes of History - Clara Barton: Courage under Fire. (p. 773)
—Heroes of History - Daniel Boone: Frontiersman. (p. 773)
—Heroes of History - Douglas MacArthur: What Greater Honor. (p. 773)
—Heroes of History - John Smith: A Foothold in the New World. (p. 773)
—Heroes of History - Laura Ingalls Wilder: A Storybook Life. (p. 773)
—Heroes of History - Orville Wright: The Flyer. (p. 773)
—Heroes of History - Theodore Roosevelt: An American Original. (p. 773)
—Heroes of History - Thomas Edison: Inspiration & Hard Work. (p. 773)
—Jacob Deshazer: Forgive Your Enemies. (p. 904)
—Klaus-Dieter John: Hope in the Land of the Incas. (p. 963)
—Louis Zamperini: Redemption. (p. 1058)
—Milton Hershey: More Than Chocolate. (p. 1144)
—Paul Brand: Helping Hands. (p. 1330)
—Ronald Reagan: Destiny at His Side. (p. 1486)
—William Wilberforce: Take up the Fight. (p. 1933)
Benge, Janet & Benge, Geoffrey Francis. Heroes of History - Books 1-5 Gift Set (p. 773)
Benge, Janet and Geoff. Elizabeth Fry. (p. 513)
Benger, Chelsi L., illus. see Zabriskie, Cindy.
Bengtsson, JulieMarie. "What Makes You Special?" (p. 1892)
Bengtz, Ture, illus. see Wheeler, Arville.
Benham, Kelly, jt. auth. see Nielsen, Kelli.
Benham, Tors, illus. see Wolfe, Jane.
Benhamu, Margaret. Pizza Friday. Salanitro, Robert, illus. (p. 1365)
Benhardt, Will. Poseidon's Adventures: My Life as a Raindrop. Mudd, Barbra, illus. (p. 1387)
Benhart, John & Pomeroy, George. South Asia. Gritzner, Charles F., ed. (p. 1616)
Ben-Hur, Roni Amos. Talk Jazz Guitar: A Comprehensive Collection of Be Bop Studies for the Aspiringand Professional Jazz Guitarist. (p. 1703)
Ben-Hur, Roni Amos, text. Talk Jazz: A Comprehensive Collection of Be Bop Studies for All Instrumentalists & Vocalists. (p. 1703)
Beniamino Brady, illus. see George Trad.
Benicio, Angelique, illus. see Akers, Ellery.
Benigni, Maria L. Mi Primer Misalito: My First Missal. (p. 1133)
Benincasa, Sara. Great. (p. 713)
Beninghof, Anne M. Meeting Standards: Instructional Strategies for Struggling Students. (p. 1123)
Benintendi, Stephen F. PowerMark 3-pk Issues 1-3. (p. 1391)
—PowerMark Comics: PM Issue 1 5-Pack. (p. 1391)
—PowerMark Issue 22: Unlikely Heroes. (p. 1391)
—PowerMark Issue 23: Prodigal. (p. 1391)
—PowerMark Issue 24: Apocalypse. (p. 1391)
—PowerMark LightQuest Issue 1: The Hunted. (p. 1391)
—PowerMark Seeker Series Issue 1: Quest for Truth. (p. 1391)
—PowerMark Seeker Series Issue 2: Let there Be... Light. (p. 1391)
—PowerMark Seeker Series Issue 3: Sabotage. (p. 1391)
—PowerMark Seeker Series Issue 4: Redemption. (p. 1391)
—PowerMark Seeker Series Issue 5: Transformation. (p. 1391)
—PowerMark Seeker Series Issue 6: The Pathway. (p. 1391)
—PowerMark Series One Autographed Box Set: Issues 1-12. (p. 1391)
Benintendi, Steve. Betrayal. (p. 171)
—Break Out: Operation: Ascent Part 3 Of 12. (p. 224)
—Cyborg Mayhem. (p. 396)
—Face Off. (p. 560)
—Family Matter. (p. 568)
—Fang Shaw Revealed (p. 571)
—High & Mighty. (p. 777)
—Mission (p. 1153)
—PM Seeker Series # 7 Masquerade: Halloween Edition. (p. 1374)
—PowerMark Comics: PM Issue 2 5-Pack. (p. 1391)
—PowerMark Comics. (p. 1391)
—PowerMark Issue 10 5-Pack. (p. 1391)
—PowerMark Issue 11 5-Pack. (p. 1391)
—PowerMark Issue 12 5-Pack. (p. 1391)
—PowerMark Issue 13 5-Pack. (p. 1391)
—PowerMark Issue 14 5-Pack. (p. 1391)
—PowerMark Issue 15 5-Pack. (p. 1391)
—PowerMark Issue 16 5-Pack. (p. 1391)
—PowerMark Issue 17 5-Pack. (p. 1391)
—PowerMark Issue 4 (5-pk) PM Issue 4 5-Pack. (p. 1391)
—PowerMark Issue 5 (5-pk) PM Issue 5 5-Pack. (p. 1391)
—PowerMark Issue 6 5-PK. (p. 1391)
—PowerMark Issue 8 5-Pack. (p. 1391)
—PowerMark Issue 9 5-Pack. (p. 1391)
—Redemption. (p. 1455)
—Sacrifice: Operation: Ascent Part 4 Of 12. (p. 1501)
—Sinister Plans: Operation: Ascent Part 2 Of 12. (p. 1579)
—Standing Tall: Operation: Ascent Part 1 Of 12. (p. 1639)
—They All Fall Down. (p. 1732)
—Trojan Horse. (p. 1788)
—Underfire. (p. 1814)
—Wake of Leviathan. (p. 1853)
Benioff, Carol, illus. see Lamstein, Sarah Marwil.
Benioff, Carol, illus. see Layne, Steven L.
Benitez, Diana. Butterfly Keeper. (p. 248)
Benitez, Miguel, illus. see Jules, Jacqueline.
Benitez, Miguel, jt. auth. see Jules, Jacqueline.
Benjamin, A. H. Baa! Moo! What Will We Do? Chapman, Jane, tr. (p. 123)
—Hens Don't Crow! Elliot, Rebecca, illus. (p. 769)
—I'm Taller Than You! O'Kif, illus. (p. 860)
—Shamwood. (p. 1559)
—Wanted: Prince Charming. Florin, Fabiano, illus. (p. 1856)
Benjamin, Ali. Thing about Jellyfish. (p. 1732)
Benjamin, Andrew. Pocahontas. (p. 1375)
—World War I: The War to End All Wars. (p. 1958)
Benjamin, Andrew & George, Enzo. World War I: The War to End All Wars. (p. 1958)
Benjamin, Ashley B., et al. Student- Athlete's College Recruitment Guide. (p. 1669)
Benjamin, Christina, illus. see Williams, Rozanne Lanczak.
Benjamin, Cynthia, adapted by. Hare Rescues the Sun: And Other Sky Myths. (p. 748)
Benjamin, Daniel. American Life & Movies from the Ten Commandments to Twilight. (p. 62)
—Extreme Rock Climbing. (p. 556)
—Extreme Snowboarding. (p. 557)
—Marijuana. (p. 1094)
—Steroids. (p. 1649)
Benjamin, Daniel, jt. auth. see Elish, Dan.
Benjamin, Daniel & Simon, Steven. Next Attack: The Failure of the War on Terror & a Strategy for Getting It Right. (p. 1249)
Benjamin, Elizabeth. Learning World of Krystie & Thomas: Investing Starts Early. (p. 986)
Benjamin, Floella. My Two Grandads. Chamberlain, Margaret, illus. (p. 1220)
—My Two Grannies. Chamberlain, Margaret, illus. (p. 1220)
—Sea of Tears. (p. 1535)
Benjamin, Irwin H. Legend of Toad Torrington. (p. 989)
Benjamin, Joseph & Benchmark Education Co., LLC Staff. Ten Red Hens. (p. 1719)
Benjamin, Kathy, Lisa and Kafer & Benchmark Education Co. Staff. Opinions about Science Fiction Technology - from Fiction to Fact. (p. 1300)
Benjamin, Lindsay. Measurement Action! (p. 1117)
Benjamin, Lisa. Baseball Dreams: The Story of Roberto Clemente. (p. 141)
—Jackie Robinson: Changing the Game. (p. 904)
—People of the Wetlands. (p. 1339)
Benjamin, Lisa & Benchmark Education Co. Staff. Rising above - Profiles in Greatness. (p. 1475)
—Story of Casey at the Bat. (p. 1657)
Benjamin, M. A. Jesus the Good Shepherd. (p. 916)
—Psalm 23: The Lord Is My Shepherd. (p. 1413)
Benjamin, Margaret. Johnny Appleseed. (p. 923)
Benjamin, Matthew C. Andy's Discovery. del Conte, Mia, illus. (p. 73)
—Ricky's Adventure. del Conte, Mia, illus. (p. 1470)
Benjamin, Michelle, jt. auth. see Schilling, Vincent.
Benjamin, Michelle & Mooney, Maggie. Nobel's Women of Peace (p. 1262)
Benjamin, Paul. Monsters, Inc: Laugh Factory. Mebberson, Amy, illus. (p. 1169)
Benjamin, Paul & Rosa, Don. Monsters, Inc: Laugh Factory. Mebberson, Amy & Rosa, Don, illus. (p. 1169)
Benjamin, Rachel & Capstone Press Staff. Learn about the Past (p. 982)
Benjamin, Rick A. Hunt for Lost Treasure (p. 828)
Benjamin, Ruth. Lost Treasure of Chelton. (p. 1056)
—My Little Pony: A Secret Gift. Middleton, Gayle, illus. (p. 1213)
—Mysterious Lighthouse of Chelton. (p. 1223)
—Secret Gift/el Regalo Secreto. Abboud, Adela, tr. from ENG. (p. 1541)
—Yesterday's Child. Cohen, Deene, illus. (p. 1971)
Benjamin, Sigalit. Garland of Stars. (p. 657)
Benjamin, Susan J. Speak with Success: A Student's Step-by-Step Guide to Fearless Public Speaking. (p. 1623)
Benjamin, Tina. Let's Dig in the Garden. (p. 995)
—Let's Go Fishing. (p. 997)
—Let's Go to a Pond. (p. 997)
—Let's Have a Picnic. (p. 998)
—Let's Visit the Beach. (p. 1001)
—Let's Walk in the Woods. (p. 1001)
—My Day at School. (p. 1201)
—My Piggy Bank. (p. 1217)
—Where I Live. (p. 1908)
Benjamin, Tina & Bockman, Charlotte. Donde Yo Vivo: Where I Live. (p. 466)
Benjamin-Farren, Joan. Shuli & Me: From Slavery to Freedom A Storybook Omer Calendar. Benjamin-Farren, Joan, illus. (p. 1571)
Benjey, Tom. Doctors, Lawyers, Indian Chiefs: Jim Thorpe & Pop Warner's Carlisle Indian School Football Immortals Tackle Socialites, Bootleggers, Students, Moguls, Prejudice, the Government, Ghouls, Tooth Decay & Rum. (p. 459)
Benke, Karen. Rip the Page! Adventures in Creative Writing. (p. 1473)
Benke, Karen, tr. Leap Write In! Adventures in Creative Writing to Stretch & Surprise Your One-Of-a-Kind Mind. (p. 982)
Benker, Kaily. Great U. S. Rivers. (p. 719)
Ben-Moshe, Jana, illus. see Gurvis, Laura K.
Ben-Moshe, Jana, illus. see Kaye, Terry, et al.
Benn, Carl. War of 1812: The Fight for American Trade Rights. (p. 1857)
Benn, Iris H. Penelope's Big Day: Early Childhood Life Lesson. (p. 1336)
—Penelope's New Friends: Early Childhood Life Lesson. (p. 1336)
Benn, Jente. My Grandma Was There. (p. 1210)
Benn, Lisa. Leroy's Kwanza Lesson. (p. 993)
Bennardo, Charlotte & Zaman, Natalie. Blonde Ops. (p. 200)
—Sirenz. (p. 1581)
—Sirenz Back in Fashion. (p. 1581)
Bennedetti, Eric, jt. auth. see Cassidy, Albert, Jr.
Bennenfeld, Rikki, illus. see Benenfeld, Rikki.
Benner, Leanne. Peanuts in My Life: A Book of Personal Meditations (p. 1332)
Bennese, Kristian, jt. auth. see Bennese, Ray.
Bennese, Ray & Bennese, Kristian. Till the Train Runs Out of Track. (p. 1750)
Bennet, Amy. One Christmas in Lunenburg Kilby, Don, illus. (p. 1294)
Bennet, Archie & Gutiérrez Bello, Marta. Beginner's English/Spanish Dictionary & Guide to Usage. (p. 159)
Bennet, Janice. Flag Fractions! Develop Understanding of Fractions & Numbers. (p. 602)
Bennet, Jill, et al. Cuentos de Terror (p. 390)
Bennet, Tim. Salt for the Supper Table. (p. 1505)
Bennett, Adelaide. Ancient Werewolves & Vampires: The Roots of the Teeth. (p. 71)

—Global Legends & Lore: Vampires & Werewolves Around the World. (p. 684)
Bennett, Amy Culbertson. Little Donkey & the Shadow of the Cross. (p. 1027)
Bennett, Andrea T. & Kessler, James H. Apples, Bubbles, & Crystals: Your Science ABCs. Sarecky, Melody, illus. (p. 93)
—Sunlight, Skyscrapers, & Soda-Pop: The Wherever-You-Look Science Book. Sarecky, Melody, illus. (p. 1677)
Bennett, Andrew. Katherine Mansfield. (p. 944)
Bennett, Andy, illus. see Gerstein, Sherry.
Bennett, Andy, illus. see Weiss, Ellen.
Bennett, Ann Granning, ed. see Goulart, Ron.
Bennett, Anna Elizabeth. Little Witch. Stone, Helen, illus. (p. 1038)
Bennett, Artie. Belches, Burps, & Farts - Oh My! Naujokaitis, Pranas T., illus. (p. 161)
—Butt Book. Lester, Mike, illus. (p. 247)
—Peter Panda Melts Down! Nez, Jon, illus. (p. 1347)
—Poopendous! Moran, Mike, illus. (p. 1383)
Bennett, Beverly, et al. Complete Idiot's Guide to Vegan Cooking. (p. 353)
Bennett, Bonnie. Howard the Worm. (p. 823)
—Meet Cinnamon Bear. (p. 1120)
—My Collection of Short Stories. (p. 1200)
Bennett, Brent, illus. see Justus, Barbara & Starbird, Caroline.
Bennett, Cameron, illus. see Brodsky, Kathy.
Bennett, Carl A., illus. see Reiner, Carl.
Bennett, Carolyn Hart. Seven Sisters: The Voyage. (p. 1554)
Bennett, Carson. Dozen Ways to Play Baseball Without the Ball & Bat. (p. 474)
Bennett, Chris. Robots & Dinosaurs. (p. 1481)
Bennett, Cindy C. Geek Girl. (p. 659)
—Rapunzel Untangled. (p. 1439)
Bennett, Clayton & Mead, Wendy. Montana. (p. 1170)
Bennett, Clinton. Math: Chapter Resource: Indiana Middle School Edition. (p. 1105)
—Math: Chapter Resourses: Florida Middle School Edition. (p. 1105)
—Math: Chapter Resources: Illinois Middle School Edition. (p. 1105)
—Middle School Math Course 1. (p. 1137)
—Middle School Math Course 2. (p. 1137)
Bennett, Cynthia L. Roadside History of Utah. McKenna, Gwen, ed. (p. 1477)
Bennett, David. Big Surprise. (p. 184)
—Lost Teddy. (p. 1056)
Bennett, Davis, illus. see Jurgens, Dan, et al.
Bennett, Dean. Everybody Needs a Hideaway. (p. 543)
Bennett, Deborah. Christmas Star. (p. 315)
Bennett, Debra J. Hip, Hop & Flop's Many Adventures. (p. 780)
Bennett, Diane. Put a Smile on Your Face. (p. 1420)
Bennett, Donna I. Jessica's Bear. Dippold, Jane, illus. (p. 914)
Bennett, Doraine. Appalachian Plateau. (p. 92)
—Atlantic Ocean. (p. 112)
—Blue Ridge Mountains. (p. 203)
—Coast. (p. 336)
—Coastal Plain. (p. 336)
—Coastal Plain (Tidewater) (p. 336)
—Frank Lloyd Wright: Little World Biographies. (p. 628)
—Greece & Our American Heritage. (p. 720)
—Inuit. (p. 883)
—Jackie Robinson. (p. 903)
—Jimmy Carter. (p. 918)
—Kwakiutl. (p. 968)
—Laura Ingalls Wilder: Little World Biographies. (p. 980)
—Lower Coastal Plain. (p. 1061)
—Marsh & Swamp. (p. 1096)
—Mountains. (p. 1181)
—Piedmont. (p. 1356)
—Readers Theatre for Global Explorers (p. 1444)
—Sequoyah. (p. 1552)
—Thomas Jefferson. (p. 1738)
—Tomochichi. (p. 1765)
—Upper Coastal Plain. (p. 1825)
—Valley & Ridge. (p. 1830)
Bennett, Doraine & Scott, Clark C. Benjamin Franklin. (p. 164)
Bennett, Earl. Legend of Bucky the Beaver. (p. 988)
Bennett, Elizabeth, illus. see Schulz, Charles M.
Bennett, Elizabeth, jt. auth. see Harrod-Eagles, Cynthia.
Bennett, Elizabeth, jt. auth. see Schulz, Charles M.
Bennett, Elizabeth & Feldman, Thea, compiled by. Magical Christmas: 86 Bricks. (p. 1074)
Bennett, Eric G. Pull up the Ladder Jack: Seamen Behaving Badly. (p. 1415)
Bennett, Erin Susanne, illus. see Stroud, Bettye.
Bennett, Evelyn & Benson, Jenny, creators. Life Letters: Kid's Stuff. (p. 1011)
Bennett, Felix, illus. see Brenchley, Chaz & Doyle, Arthur.
Bennett, Felix, illus. see Wells, H. G.
Bennett, Frank. Under an African Sun: Memoirs of a Colonial Officer in Northern Rhodesia. (p. 1813)
Bennett, Gretchen. Gina's Great Day. (p. 676)
Bennett, Harry, Jr., illus. see Bumbalough, Jerry.
Bennett, Heath, jt. auth. see Stanley, Andy.
Bennett, Helen. Humanism, What's That? A Book for Curious Kids. (p. 826)
Bennett, Holly. Bonemender. (p. 209)
—Bonemender's Choice (p. 209)
—Bonemender's Oath (p. 209)
—Redwing (p. 1456)
—Shapeshifter (p. 1561)
—Warrior's Daughter (p. 1859)
Bennett, Howard J. Harry Goes to the Hospital: A Story for Children about What It's Like to Be in the Hospital. Weber, M. S., illus. (p. 750)
—It Hurts When I Poop! A Story for Children Who Are Scared to Use the Potty. Weber, M. S., illus. (p. 894)
—Lions Aren't Scared of Shots: A Story for Children about Visiting the Doctor. Weber, M. S., illus. (p. 1021)
—Max Archer, Kid Detective: The Case of the Wet Bed. Gerrell, Spike, illus. (p. 1111)
—Max Archer, Kid Detective: The Case of the Recurring Stomachaches. Gerrell, Spike, illus. (p. 1111)
Bennett, Jack. Tell Me a Story: A Collection of Short Stories. (p. 1716)
Bennett, James, illus. see Brooks, Mel & Reiner, Carl.
Bennett, James, illus. see Krull, Kathleen.
Bennett, James, illus. see McDonough, Yona Zeldis.
Bennett, James, illus. see O'Connor, Jim.
Bennett, James, illus. see Reiner, Carl.
Bennett, James, illus. see Seinfeld, Jerry.
Bennett, James, jt. auth. see Bennett, James W.
Bennett, James W. & Bennett, James. Faith Wish. (p. 565)
Bennett, Jamie, illus. see Birmingham, Maria.
Bennett, Jeffrey. Mago Que Salvo el Mundo. Collier-Morales, Roberta, illus. (p. 1076)
—Max Goes to the Moon: A Science Adventure with Max the Dog. Okamoto, Alan, illus. (p. 1111)
—Max Goes to the Space Station: A Science Adventure with Max the Dog. Carroll, Michael, illus. (p. 1111)
—Wizard Who Saved the World. Collier-Morales, Roberta, illus. (p. 1943)
Bennett, Jeffrey, jt. auth. see Weinman, Logan.
Bennett, Jeffrey, et al. Max Goes to Jupiter: A Science Adventure with Max the Dog. Carroll, Michael, illus. (p. 1111)
Bennett, Jerry, illus. see Andrews, Lindsey.
Bennett, Jill. Grandad's Tree: Poems about Families. Cairns, Julia, illus. (p. 707)
Bennett, Jill & Sharratt, Nick. Noisy Poems. (p. 1263)
Bennett, Joe, illus. see Jurgens, Dan.
Bennett, Joe, illus. see Priest, Christopher.
Bennett, Joe, jt. illus. see Asrar, Mahmud.
Bennett, John, illus. see Andrews, Jackie.
Bennett, Judy, ed. see Stratten, Lou.
Bennett, Kathy. Pony Pointers: How to Safely Care for Your Horse or Pony. Peterson, Carol A., illus. (p. 1382)
Bennett, Katrina. Pandora the Sea Turtle. (p. 1321)
Bennett, Kelly. Dance Y'all, Dance. Murphy, Terri, illus. (p. 402)
—Flag Day. (p. 601)
—Not Norman: A Goldfish Story. Jones, Noah Z., illus. (p. 1267)
—One Day I Went Rambling. Murphy, Terri, illus. (p. 1294)
—Vampire Baby. Meisel, Paul, illus. (p. 1831)
—Your Daddy Was Just Like You. Walker, David, illus. (p. 1980)
—Your Mommy Was Just Like You. Walker, David, illus. (p. 1981)
Bennett, Kelly & Vargus, Nanci Reginelli. Delaware. (p. 424)
Bennett, Kenneth. Gaia Wars. (p. 652)
Bennett, Larry. Attack of the Giant Stink Bugs. Tov, Basia, illus. (p. 113)
Bennett, Leonie. Amazing Dinosaur Facts. (p. 54)
—Dinosaur Babies. (p. 441)
—Dinosaur Fossils. (p. 442)
—Dinosaur Hunting. (p. 442)
—Locket Out. Adams, Arlene, illus. (p. 1045)
—No Problem! Brown, Judy, illus. (p. 1260)
Bennett, Liza & Benchmark Education Co., LLC Staff. I Am Sam. (p. 833)
—I See. (p. 845)
Bennett, Lorna, illus. see Aksomitis, Linda.
Bennett, Lorna, illus. see Chan, Marty.
Bennett, Lorna, illus. see Galat, Joan Marie.
Bennett, Lorna, illus. see Sadler, Judy Ann.
Bennett, Lorna, illus. see Welykochy, Dawn.
Bennett, Lorna & Galat, Joan Marie. Dot-to-Dot in the Sky: Stories in the Stars Bennett, Lorna et al, illus. (p. 472)
Bennett, Lr. Sammy, the Shadow Master. (p. 1508)
Bennett, Marcia. Backpack Cat. (p. 130)
—Backpack Cat. Bennett, Michele & Dunlap, Joan, illus. (p. 130)
Bennett, Marcia Allen. Mystery at Jacob's Well. Eckhardt, Jason C., illus. (p. 1223)
—Mystery at Saddlecreek. (p. 1223)
—Umbrella Town. (p. 1810)
Bennett, Marcia Allen & Eckhardt, Jason C. Mystery at Saddlecreek. (p. 1224)
Bennett, Marian. God Made Kittens. Marlin, Kathryn, illus. (p. 689)
Bennett, Marilyn J. Poinsettia Adventure. (p. 1377)
Bennett, Melanie, jt. auth. see Anderson, Lynda.
Bennett, Michele, illus. see Bennett, Marcia.
Bennett, Michelle & Hart, Joyce. Missouri. (p. 1154)
Bennett, Mike. Percy the Puzzle Piece. (p. 1341)
Bennett, Ned. New Tune a Day Perfomrance Pieces for Flute. (p. 1247)
—New Tune a Day Performace Pieces for Cello. (p. 1247)
—New Tune a Day Performance Pieces for Trombone. (p. 1247)
—New Tune a Day Performance Pieces for Violin. (p. 1247)
Bennett, Nneka, illus. see Lasky, Kathryn.
Bennett, Olivia. Who What Wear! The Allegra Biscotti Collection. (p. 1919)
Bennett, Olivia, jt. auth. see Rifkin, Sherri.
Bennett, Paul. Desert Habitats. (p. 429)
—Freddie, Bill & Irving. Shannon, Kate, illus. (p. 632)
—Ocean Habitats. (p. 1276)
—Seven Harmonies of Music: A Field Guide (p. 1554)
—Tale of a Waggish Dog. (p. 1699)
Bennett, Randle Paul, illus. see Traditional.
Bennett, Richard. Everything I Need to Know I Learned in Boy Scouts. (p. 545)
Bennett, Richard Grant, et al. Secret Santa. (p. 1543)
Bennett, Ron. All Bitter & Twisted. Mould, Paul, ed. (p. 44)
Bennett, Rowena, et al. Monkey Poems & Seed Poems. (p. 1165)
Bennett, Rowena, et al, selected by. Monkey Poems & Seed Poems. (p. 1165)
Bennett, Ruth Elisabeth. Childhood Days: Stories for the Young & Young at Heart (p. 302)
Bennett, Sandra. Gingerbread Aliens. Welsh, Hayley, illus. (p. 677)
Bennett, Saxon. Family Affair. (p. 568)
Bennett, Shirley. Missy - a Tail-Wagging Good Life. (p. 1154)
Bennett, Sophia. Look. (p. 1047)
—Sequins, Secrets, & Silver Linings. (p. 1552)
Bennett, Steven. Adventures of Super Dad: Colossal Encounters (Book #1) (p. 23)
Bennett, Trevor, illus. see Luneau, Terri Robert.
Bennett, Veronica. Angelmonster. (p. 74)
—Cassandra's Sister: Growing up Jane Austen. (p. 276)
Bennett, Virginia. Pigeon Tale. Hardy, E. Stuart, illus. (p. 1357)
Bennett, W. J., Jr. Sydney & Garrett's Great Arkansas Adventury. (p. 1692)
—Vivianna Becomes an Arkansan. (p. 1846)
Bennett, William. Ride to the Black Hills. (p. 1471)
Bennett, William J. libro de la familia y el Hogar para Niños. Alonso Blanco, Maria Victoria, tr. (p. 1006)
Bennett, William J., ed. Book of Virtues for Boys & Girls: A Treasury of Great Moral Stories. Wisnewski, Andrea, illus. (p. 212)
Bennett-Armistead, V. Susan, jt. auth. see Duke, Nell K.
Bennett-Boltinghouse, Jo Ann. Yolandababy: A Pooch Finds Her Purpose! an Adventure in Self-Esteem. Julich, Jenniffer, illus. (p. 1972)
Bennett-Minnerly, Denise. Color Tree. Bennett-Minnerly, Denise, illus. (p. 343)
Bennetts, Nancy. Bed Head. (p. 156)
Bennicke, Rune Brandt. Mystery Hat. Jensen, Jakob Hjort, illus. (p. 1224)
Bennie, Paul. Great Chicago Fire Of 1871. (p. 714)
Bennington, Mark, illus. see Williams, Rose.
Bennion, Anneliese, illus. see Skolmoski, Stephanie.
Bennion, Jay B. From Here to There. (p. 642)
Benny. Socks Heaven. Lau, Benny, illus. (p. 1605)
Benny, Mike, illus. see Crowe, Chris.
Benny, Mike, illus. see Grimes, Nikki.
Benny, Mike, illus. see Raven, Margot Theis.
Benny, Mike, illus. see Whelan, Gloria.
Benoff-Nadel, Phyllis. Magical Garden. (p. 1074)
Benoist, Carol, jt. auth. see Gilmore, Cathy.
Benoist, Cathy & Gilmore, Cathy. Conejito de Pascua: El Cuento de un Dia Extraordinario. Sundy, Jonathan, illus. (p. 356)
Benoit, Brian. Crustacean Vacation Kelley, Marty, illus. (p. 387)
Benoit, Charles. Cold Calls. (p. 338)
—Fall from Grace. (p. 566)
—You. (p. 1972)
Benoît, Debecker, jt. auth. see Debecker, Benoit.
Benoit, Jérôme, illus. see Dorison, Guillaume, et al.
Benoit, Peter. Abraham Lincoln. (p. 6)
—Ancient Greece. (p. 69)
—Ancient Rome. (p. 70)
—Ancient World: Ancient Rome. (p. 71)
—Assassination of JFK. (p. 107)
—Attack on Pearl Harbor. (p. 114)
—Boston Massacre. (p. 215)
—BP Oil Spill. (p. 220)
—British Colonies in North America. (p. 229)
—California Gold Rush. (p. 253)
—Climate Change. (p. 332)
—Confederate States of America. (p. 356)
—Cornerstones of Freedom, Third Series: the Jamestown Colony. (p. 367)
—Cornerstones of Freedom, Third Series: the Trail of Tears. (p. 367)
—D-Day. (p. 397)
—Deserts. (p. 429)
—EXXON Valdez Oil Spill. (p. 557)
—Exxon Valdez Oil Spill. (p. 557)
—Forms of Government. (p. 620)
—Haitian Earthquake of 2010. (p. 736)
—Hindenburg Disaster. (p. 780)
—Hurricane Katrina. (p. 829)
—Immigration. (p. 861)
—Jamestown Colony. (p. 907)
—Krakatau Eruption. (p. 967)
—Louisiana Purchase. (p. 1058)
—Nuclear Age. (p. 1269)
—Nuclear Meltdowns. (p. 1270)
—Oceans. (p. 1277)
—Panama Canal. (p. 1320)
—Salem Witch Trials. (p. 1504)
—September 11, 2001: The 10th Anniversary. (p. 1551)
—September 11 Then & Now. (p. 1551)
—September 11 We Will Never Forget No. 11. (p. 1551)
—Space Race. (p. 1619)
—Supreme Court. (p. 1684)
—Surrender at Appomattox. (p. 1686)
—Temperate Forests. (p. 1717)
—Titanic. (p. 1757)
—Titanic Disaster. (p. 1757)
—Trail of Tears. (p. 1776)
—Tropical Rain Forests. (p. 1789)
—True Book: Disasters (p. 1791)
—True Book: Ecosystems (p. 1791)
—True Book: American Indians (p. 1791)
—Tundra. (p. 1796)
—Vietnam War. (p. 1841)
—Wetlands. (p. 1877)
—Women's Right to Vote. (p. 1946)
Benoit, Peter, jt. auth. see Cunningham, Kevin.
Benoit, Peter, jt. auth. see Dolbear, Emily J.
Benoit, Peter, jt. auth. see Friedman, Mark.
Benoit, Renne, illus. see Arsenault, Elaine.
Benoit, Renné, illus. see de Vries, Maggie.
Benoit, Renne, illus. see Gilmore, Rachna.
Benoit, Renne, illus. see Goldsmith, Howard.
Benoit, Renne, illus. see Jackson, Ellen.
Benoit, Renné, illus. see Manson, Ainslie.
Benoit, Renne, illus. see Seto, Loretta.
Benoit, Renné, illus. see Sleeping Bear Press.
Benoit, Renne, illus. see Stiegemeyer, Julie.
Benoit, Renne, illus. see Upjohn, Rebecca.
Benoit-Renard, Anne. Navani from Delhi. Rigaudie, Mylene, illus. (p. 1237)
Benrali. turtle's dream & Keys. (p. 1799)
Bensch, April, illus. see Wheeler-Cribb, Peggy.
Ben-Shaul, Nitzan. Film: The Key Concepts. (p. 586)
Bensinger, Henry. Ancient Greek Culture. (p. 69)
—Ancient Greek Daily Life. (p. 69)
—Ancient Greek Economy. (p. 69)
—Ancient Greek Geography. (p. 69)
—Ancient Greek Government. (p. 69)
—Ancient Greek Technology. (p. 69)
Bensinger, Lou. Tiny Invaders (p. 1756)
—Tiny Invaders in the Water. (p. 1756)
—Tiny Invaders in Your Backyard. (p. 1756)
—Tiny Invaders in Your Body. (p. 1756)
Bensinger, Marilyn, jt. auth. see O'quinn, Louise.
Benson, Amber. Among the Ghosts. Grace, Sina, illus. (p. 65)
—Ghosts of Albion: Initiation. (p. 672)
Benson, Barbara, illus. see Keilbart, L. S.
Benson, Catherine. It Must Have Been a Sunday. (p. 894)
Benson, Cindy. Chloe & Hairy Go to School. (p. 308)
Benson, Daryl. Alberta: Images. (p. 35)
—Alberta: Images. Benson, Daryl, photos by. (p. 35)
Benson, Don. Harry 'High-Pockets' (p. 750)
Benson, Donald. Tommy Turtle Turns Blue. (p. 1765)
Benson, Donna. Dog Gone Drama, the Cupcakes Club #2. (p. 461)
—Ghost Finds 100ct Diamond in Little Rock. (p. 670)
—Spotlight on the Cupcakes: The Cupcakes Club #3. (p. 1634)
Benson, E. F. Confession of Charles Linkworth. (p. 356)
Benson, Edmund F. & Benson, Susan. Life Skills Curriculum. (p. 1013)
—Life Skills Curriculum: ARISE Basic Health 101, Book 2. (p. 1013)
—Life Skills Curriculum: ARISE Dropout Prevention, Book 1. (p. 1013)
Benson, Elisa & Gohari, Omid. Colgate University College Prowler off the Record. (p. 339)
Benson, Gary, jt. auth. see Daughtrey, Patricia.
Benson, Glenda. Adventures of Pepe & Gracie: Trouble in the Park. (p. 21)
Benson, Irene Elliott. Ethel Hollister's Second Summer As a Campfire Girl. (p. 539)
—How Ethel Hollister Became a Campfire Girl. (p. 809)
Benson, Jeffrey. Adventures of Avortit & Rooney. (p. 16)
Benson, Jenny, jt. creator see Bennett, Evelyn.
Benson, Judith. Noise in Grandma's Attic. (p. 1262)
Benson, Julian. Christmas Dog: Lc's Worst Day Ever! (p. 313)
Benson, Kathleen. Draw What You See: The Life & Art of Benny Andrews. Andrews, Benny, illus. (p. 481)
Benson, Kathleen, jt. auth. see Haskins, James.
Benson, Kathleen, jt. auth. see Haskins, Jim.
Benson, Kathleen & Haskins, Jim. John Lewis in the Lead: A Story of the Civil Rights Movement Andrews, Benny, illus. (p. 922)
Benson, Ken. Leela's Great Life. (p. 987)
Benson, Linda. Finding Chance. Lane, Nancy, illus. (p. 588)
Benson, Linda Sue. Hey Latrell Johnson, Bruce, illus. (p. 774)
—It's Okay, Leon (p. 898)
Benson, Lyn. Who Were the Magi. Joshua, Benson Benson Joshua, illus. (p. 1919)
BENSON, Mary Rubec. Follow the Warrior's Path: Life Story of Ohiyesa Better Known As Dr. Eastman. (p. 612)
Benson, Megan, tr. see Contro, Arturo.
Benson, Megan, tr. see Obregon, Jose M.
Benson, Megan, tr. see Obregon, Jose Maria.
Benson, Megan, tr. see Obregón, José María.
Benson, Megan, tr. see Obregón, José María.
Benson, Michael. Beyond: A Solar System Voyage. (p. 173)
—Bill Clinton. (p. 186)
—Cons & Frauds. (p. 358)
—Drug Crime. (p. 486)
—Lance Armstrong, Cyclist. (p. 973)
—Malcolm X. (p. 1083)
—Organized Crime. (p. 1303)
—U. S. Coast Guard. (p. 1806)
—U. S. Marine Corps. (p. 1806)
—William H. Taft. (p. 1933)
Benson, Nicky. Spirit of Christmas: A Giving Tradition. (p. 1628)
Benson, P. Bryn. Josefina, the Christmas Cow: A Tale of Hope & Faith. Cinelli, Lisa, illus. (p. 926)
Benson, Patrick, illus. see Dowson, Nick.
Benson, Patrick, illus. see Dunbar, Joyce.
Benson, Patrick, illus. see Knapman, Timothy.
Benson, Patrick, illus. see Melville, Herman.
Benson, Patrick, illus. see Morpurgo, Michael.
Benson, Patrick, illus. see Peet, Mal & Graham, Elspeth.
Benson, Patrick, illus. see Waddell, Martin.
Benson, Patrick, illus. see Wise, William.
Benson, Patrick, tr. see Wise, William.
Benson, Patty. Nameless Child. (p. 1228)
—Pretty Little Gipsy. (p. 1398)
Benson, Queen Mary. Lactose Limited. (p. 970)
Benson, Sandra. Tales of the Golden Corpse: Tibetan Folk Tales. Sherup, illus. (p. 1702)
Benson, Sherry. Introducing Jelly Bean. (p. 882)
Benson, Sonia. U. S. Immigration & Migration: Almanac (p. 1806)
—U.S. Immigration & Migration Almanac (p. 1826)
Benson, Sonia & Baker, Deborah J. Almanac, Early Civilizations (p. 48)
—Early Civilizations in the (p. 493)
—Primary Sources, Early Americas (p. 1400)
Benson, Sonia & Stock, Jennifer York. Development of the Industrial U. S. Biographies. (p. 432)
—Development of the Industrial U. S. - Almanac. (p. 432)
—Development of the Industrial U. S. - Primary Sources. (p. 432)
Benson, Sonia, et al. Endangered Species (p. 527)
—UXL Encyclopedia of U.S. History. (p. 1829)
Benson, Susan, jt. auth. see ARISE Foundation Staff.
Benson, Susan, jt. auth. see ARISE Foundation.
Benson, Susan, jt. auth. see Benson, Edmund F.
Benson-Bini, B. From Cancer to Counselor. (p. 642)

Benstock, Hari, et al. Handbook of Literary Feminisms. (p. 740)
Bent, Timothy, ed. see Nothomb, Amélie.
Bentel, Erica & Bentel Family Trust Staff. Can You Crack Them? Elliott, Neil, illus. (p. 258)
Bentel Family Trust Staff, jt. auth. see Bentel, Erica.
Benthre. Do Not Enter. (p. 457)
Bentivegna, Fred. Banking with the Beard. (p. 136)
Bentley, Anita, illus. see Casebolt, Christan.
Bentley, Bernard E. Little Ben's Pledge. (p. 1024)
Bentley, Catherine & Bentley, Dawn. Hoppy Goes to School. Huerta, Catherine, illus. (p. 797)
Bentley, Cheryl. Petronella & the Janjilons. (p. 1348)
—Petronella & the Trogot. (p. 1348)
Bentley, Dawn. Busy Day for Stegosaurus. Carr, Karen, tr. (p. 246)
—Busy Day for Stegosaurus. Carr, Karen, illus. (p. 246)
—Busy Little Beaver. Stover, Beth, illus. (p. 246)
—Buzz-Buzz, Busy Bees: An Animal Sounds Book. Cahoon, Heather, illus. (p. 248)
—Disney Pixar Cars Rhymes on the Go. Schwaeber, Barbie Heit, ed. (p. 452)
—Fuzzy Bear Goes to School. Nagy, Krisztina, illus. (p. 651)
—Fuzzy Bear's Bedtime. Nagy, Krisztina, illus. (p. 651)
—Gingerbread Man. (p. 677)
—Good Night, Sweet Butterflies. Cahoon, Heather, illus. (p. 700)
—Goodnight Bear: A Book & Night Light. Couri, Kathryn A., illus. (p. 701)
—Hoppy Goes to School. Huerta, Catherine, illus. (p. 797)
—Icky Sticky Chameleon. Mack, Jeff, illus. (p. 851)
—It's Tyrannosaurus Rex! (p. 899)
—It's Tyrannosaurus Rex! Carr, Karen, tr. (p. 899)
—It's Tyrannosaurus Rex! Carr, Karen, illus. (p. 899)
—Jack: Lights, Camera, Action! (p. 902)
—Lead the Way, Velociraptor! Carr, Karen, illus. (p. 981)
—Parasaurolophus Escapes. McIntosh, Gabe, illus. (p. 1324)
—Prickly Porcupine. Stover, Beth, illus. (p. 1398)
—Pteranodon Soars. Carr, Karen, illus. (p. 1413)
—Saber-Tooth Trap. (p. 1499)
—Saber-Tooth Trap. Reavely, Trever, illus. (p. 1499)
—Saber-Tooth Trap. Reavely, Trevor, illus. (p. 1499)
—Snack Time, Tyrannosaurus Rex! Carr, Karen, illus. (p. 1595)
—Speedy Little Race Cars. Cahoon, Heather, illus. (p. 1624)
—Surprise, Stegosaurus! Carr, Karen, illus. (p. 1686)
—Three Hungry Spiders & One Fat Fly! Twinem, Neecy, illus. (p. 1742)
—Three Stretchy Frogs. Wallis, Becky, illus. (p. 1744)
—Triceratops Gets Lost. Carr, Karen, illus. (p. 1785)
—Triceratops Gets Lost. Carr, Karen, tr. (p. 1786)
—Triceratops Gets Lost. Carr, Karen, illus. (p. 1786)
—Velociraptor: Small & Speedy. Carr, Karen, tr. (p. 1835)
—Velociraptor: Small & Speedy. Carr, Karen, illus. (p. 1835)
—Velociraptor. Carr, Karen, illus. (p. 1835)
—Velociraptor - Small & Speedy. Carr, Karen, illus. (p. 1835)
—Wake up, Black Bear! Stover, Beth, illus. (p. 1853)
—Watch Out, Triceratops! Carr, Karen, illus. (p. 1861)
—Welcome Back, Puffin! Stover, Beth, illus. (p. 1873)
—Woolly Mammoth in Trouble. (p. 1950)
—Woolly Mammoth in Trouble. Carr, Karen, illus. (p. 1950)
Bentley, Dawn, jt. auth. see Bentley, Catherine.
Bentley, Dawn & Studio Mouse Staff. Dinosaurs & More! Carr, Karent, illus. (p. 444)
—Triceratops. Carr, Karen, illus. (p. 1785)
—Tyrannosaurus Rex. Carr, Karen, illus. (p. 1805)
Bentley, Dawn, et al. Rhyme Time: Rhyme-and-Learn. Schwaeber, Barbie H. & Williams, Tracee, eds. (p. 1468)
Bentley, Douglas W. What Will It Take for a Toad to Kiss a Monkey: The Adventures of Princess Gracie & Prince Wallaby. Bentley, Julia Faye, illus. (p. 1895)
Bentley, Jonathan. Little Big. (p. 1024)
—Ugly Duckling. (p. 1808)
Bentley, Jonathan, illus. see Allum, Margaret.
Bentley, Jonathan, illus. see Holmes, Janet A.
Bentley, Jonathan, illus. see Hughes, Jenny.
Bentley, Jonathan, jt. auth. see Nilsen, Anna.
Bentley, Joyce. Kenya: Our Lives, Our World. (p. 949)
—Rough. (p. 1491)
—Smooth. (p. 1595)
—Soft. (p. 1605)
—St. Lucia. (p. 1638)
—Wet. (p. 1877)
Bentley, Judy, jt. auth. see McConaghy, Lorraine.
Bentley, Julia Faye, illus. see Bentley, Douglas W.
Bentley, Karen. Unsers. (p. 1822)
Bentley, Linda, jt. auth. see Bentley, Linda M.
Bentley, Linda M. & Bentley, Linda. Big Book of Quick & Easy Art Activities: More Than 75 Creative Activities with Curriculum Connections That Keep Kids Creating & Learning All Year Long! (p. 179)
Bentley, Maria. Summer Sounds Level 1 Beginner/Elementary. (p. 1675)
—Summer Sounds Level 1 Beginner/Elementary with CD-ROM/Audio CD. (p. 1675)
Bentley, Nancy. Don't Be a Copycat! Write a Great Report Without Plagiarizing. (p. 466)
Bentley, Nancy Kaye. Mema's back Yard. (p. 1125)
Bentley, Nicolas, illus. see Linklater, Eric.
Bentley, Sue. Chocolate Wishes. (p. 309)
—Chocolate Wishes #1. Swan, Angela, illus. (p. 309)
—Christmas Surprise. Swan, Angela & Farley, Andrew, illus. (p. 315)
—Circus Surprise. (p. 322)
—Circus Surprise #7. Swan, Angela, illus. (p. 322)
—Circus Wish. (p. 322)
—Circus Wish #6 Farley, Andrew & Swan, Angela, illus. (p. 322)
—Classroom Capers. (p. 328)
—Classroom Capers #4. Swan, Angela & Farley, Andrew, illus. (p. 328)
—Classroom Chaos Swan, Angela & Farley, Andrew, illus. (p. 328)
—Classroom Princess. (p. 329)
—Classroom Princess #9. Swan, Angela, illus. (p. 329)
—Cloud Capers Swan, Angela & Farley, Andrew, illus. (p. 334)
—Cloud Capers. (p. 334)
—Dancing Days. (p. 402)
—Dancing Days #5. Swan, Angela & Farley, Andrew, illus. (p. 402)
—Double Trouble Farley, Andrew & Swan, Angela, illus. (p. 473)
—Double Trouble. (p. 473)
—Firelight Friends. (p. 592)
—Firelight Friends #10. Swan, Angela, illus. (p. 592)
—Forest Charm Farley, Andrew & Swan, Angela, illus. (p. 618)
—Forest Charm. (p. 618)
—Friendship Forever. (p. 639)
—Friendship Forever #10. Swan, Angela, illus. (p. 639)
—Glittering Gallop Swan, Angela, illus. (p. 684)
—Glittering Gallop. (p. 684)
—Magic Puppy - A New Beginning. (p. 1073)
—Magic Puppy: Books 1-3. Swan, Angela & Farley, Andrew, illus. (p. 1073)
—Magic Reindeer: a Christmas Wish. Swan, Angela, illus. (p. 1073)
—Moonlight Mischief. (p. 1172)
—Moonlight Mischief #5 Swan, Angela & Farley, Andrew, illus. (p. 1172)
—Muddy Paws Swan, Angela & Farley, Andrew, illus. (p. 1189)
—Muddy Paws. (p. 1189)
—New Beginning Swan, Angela & Farley, Andrew, illus. (p. 1243)
—New Friend Swan, Angela, illus. (p. 1244)
—New Friend. (p. 1244)
—Party Dreams Farley, Andrew & Swan, Angela, illus. (p. 1326)
—Party Dreams. (p. 1326)
—Perfect Secret. (p. 1342)
—Perfect Secret #14. Swan, Angela & Farley, Andrew, illus. (p. 1342)
—Picture Perfect. (p. 1356)
—Picture Perfect #13. Swan, Angela & Farley, Andrew, illus. (p. 1356)
—Pony Camp. (p. 1382)
—Pony Camp #8. Swan, Angela, illus. (p. 1382)
—Puzzle of Paws. (p. 1421)
—Puzzle of Paws #12. Swan, Angela & Farley, Andrew, illus. (p. 1421)
—Riding Rescue. (p. 1471)
—Riding Rescue #6. Swan, Angela, illus. (p. 1471)
—School of Mischief Farley, Andrew & Swan, Angela, illus. (p. 1523)
—Seaside Mystery. (p. 1538)
—Seaside Mystery #9. Swan, Angela, illus. (p. 1538)
—Shimmering Splash. (p. 1566)
—Shimmering Splash #11. Swan, Angela & Farley, Andrew, illus. (p. 1566)
—Show-Jumping Dreams. (p. 1570)
—Show-Jumping Dreams #4. Swan, Angela, illus. (p. 1570)
—Snowy Wishes. (p. 1601)
—Snowy Wishes. Swan, Angela, illus. (p. 1601)
—Sparkling Skates. (p. 1622)
—Sparkling Skates #13. Swan, Angela & Farley, Andrew, illus. (p. 1622)
—Sparkling Steps (p. 1622)
—Sparkling Steps #7 Farley, Andrew & Swan, Angela, illus. (p. 1622)
—Special Wish Swan, Angela, illus. (p. 1623)
—Special Wish. (p. 1623)
—Spellbound at School. (p. 1625)
—Spellbound at School #11. Swan, Angela & Farley, Andrew, illus. (p. 1625)
—Splash of Forever. (p. 1629)
—Splash of Forever #14. Swan, Angela & Farley, Andrew, illus. (p. 1629)
—Splash of Magic. (p. 1629)
—Splash of Magic #3. Swan, Angela, illus. (p. 1629)
—Star Dreams Swan, Angela & Farley, Andrew, illus. (p. 1640)
—Star of the Show Swan, Angela & Farley, Andrew, illus. (p. 1640)
—Star of the Show. (p. 1641)
—Summer Spell. Swan, Angela & Farley, Andrew, illus. (p. 1675)
—Sunshine Shimmers. (p. 1678)
—Sunshine Shimmers #12. Swan, Angela & Farley, Andrew, illus. (p. 1678)
—Twinkle of Hooves. (p. 1802)
—Twinkle of Hooves #3. Swan, Angela, illus. (p. 1802)
—Twirling Tails Farley, Andrew & Swan, Angela, illus. (p. 1802)
—Vacation Dreams. (p. 1829)
—Vacation Dreams #2. Swan, Angela, illus. (p. 1829)
—Winter Wonderland. (p. 1938)
—Winter Wonderland #5. Swan, Angela, illus. (p. 1938)
Bentley, Tadgh. Little Penguin Gets the Hiccups. Bentley, Tadgh, illus. (p. 1033)
Bentley-Davies, Caroline, et al. Writing. Calway, Gareth, ed. (p. 1964)
Bently, Peter. Cat, the Mouse, & the Runaway Train. Cox, Steve, illus. (p. 278)
—Diggory Digger & the Dinosaurs. Parker-Rees, Guy, illus. (p. 439)
—Dustbin Dad. Ayto, Russell, illus. (p. 490)
—Great Balloon Hullaballoo. Matsuoka, Mei, illus. (p. 713)
—Great Dog Bottom Swap. Matsuoka, Mei, illus. (p. 715)
—Great Sheep Shenanigans. Matsuoka, Mei, illus. (p. 718)
—King Jack & the Dragon. Oxenbury, Helen, illus. (p. 958)
—King Jack & the Dragon Board Book. Oxenbury, Helen, illus. (p. 958)
—Lark in the Ark. Chapman, Lynne, illus. (p. 975)
—Look Out, Cub! A Lift-the-Flap Story about Lions. (p. 1049)
—Meet the Parents. Ogilvie, Sara, illus. (p. 1123)
—National Geographic Kids Wild Tales: Ella's Bath: A Lift-The-flap Story about Elephants. (p. 1232)
—National Geographic Kids Wild Tales: Twin Trouble: A Lift-The-flap Story about Bears. (p. 1232)
—National Geographic Little Kids Wild Tales - Charlie & the Banana Monster: A Lift-the-Flap Story about Chimpanzees. (p. 1233)
—Rich Witch, Poor Witch. Field, Jim, illus. (p. 1469)
—Shark in the Dark. Cort, Ben, illus. (p. 1562)
—Tooth Fairy's Christmas. Parsons, Garry, illus. (p. 1768)
—Train Is on Track. Conway, Louise, illus. (p. 1777)
—Yoga Ogre. Rickerty, Simon, illus. (p. 1972)
Bently, Peter, illus. see Wilson, Douglas.
Bently, Peter, jt. auth. see Grant, Richard E.
Bently, Peter, jt. auth. see Roberts, David.
Bently, Peter & McPhillips, Robert. Say Please, Little Bear. (p. 1518)
Bentman, Jonathan & Freeman, Gary. Self-Defense: How to Be a Master at Self-Defense (p. 1549)
Benton, Allie. Inside a Factory (p. 876)
Benton, Allie & Capstone Press Staff. Inside a Factory (p. 876)
Benton, Ann. Ferdinand: The Engine That Went off the Rails. (p. 581)
Benton, Ann & Benton, John. Don't They Make a Lovely Couple? Six Important Questions You Need to Face about Your Marriage. (p. 468)
Benton, Celia. How a Frog Grows (p. 804)
—Our Flag (p. 1308)
—Our Flag. (p. 1308)
Benton, Celia & Benchmark Education Co., LLC Staff. Use It to Pull. (p. 1827)
Benton, Celia & Capstone Press Staff. How a Frog Grows (p. 804)
Benton, Doug. Hummingbird Goose (p. 826)
Benton, James. Case Files of Herman Ootix, B. I. Faith for Life2 Course Five Student Book. Janssen, Patricia E., ed. (p. 273)
—Surprising Stories Teacher Guide: Faith for Life2 Course Five. Janssen, Patricia E., ed. (p. 1686)
Benton, Jim. Am I the Princess or the Frog? Benton, Jim, illus. (p. 51)
—Attack of the 50-Ft. Cupid. Benton, Jim, illus. (p. 113)
—Complete Franny K. Stein, Mad Scientist: Lunch Walks among Us; Attack of the 50-Ft. Cupid - The Invisible Fra - The Fran That Time Forgot - Frantastic Voyage - The Fran with Four Brains - The Frandidate. Benton, Jim, illus. (p. 352)
—Crate of Danger: Lunch Walks among Us - Attack of the 50-Ft. Cupid - The Invisible Fran - The Fran That Time Forgot. Set Benton, Jim, illus. (p. 376)
—Dear Dumb Diary 06: Problem with Here Is It's Where I'm From. (p. 419)
—End (Almost) (p. 526)
—End (Almost) Benton, Jim, illus. (p. 526)
—Five Stinky Socks: A Counting Book. (p. 601)
—Fran That Time Forgot. Benton, Jim, illus. (p. 627)
—Fran with Four Brains. (p. 627)
—Fran with Four Brains. Benton, Jim, illus. (p. 627)
—Frandidate. Benton, Jim, illus. (p. 628)
—Franny K. Stein, Mad Scientist Benton, Jim, illus. (p. 631)
—Frantastic Voyage. Benton, Jim, illus. (p. 631)
—Howard Hubbins Half Hour Hero. (p. 823)
—Invisible Fran. Benton, Jim, illus. (p. 885)
—It's Happy Bunny. Benton, Jim, illus. (p. 897)
—It's Not My Fault I Know Everything. (p. 898)
—It's Not My Fault I Know Everything. Benton, Jim, illus. (p. 898)
—Let's Pretend This Never Happened. Benton, Jim, illus. (p. 1000)
—Life. Get One. (p. 1010)
—Live Each Day to the Dumbest. (p. 1039)
—Live Each Day to the Dumbest. Benton, Jim, illus. (p. 1039)
—Love Bites. (p. 1059)
—Lunch Walks among Us. Benton, Jim, illus. (p. 1065)
—Me (Just Like You, Only Better) Benton, Jim, illus. (p. 1116)
—My Pants Are Haunted! Benton, Jim, illus. (p. 1216)
—Nobody's Perfect. I'm As Close As It Gets. (p. 1262)
—Nobody's Perfect. I'm As Close As It Gets. Benton, Jim, illus. (p. 1262)
—Okay, So Maybe I Do Have Superpowers. Benton, Jim, illus. (p. 1282)
—Piggy Paints. (p. 1358)
—Problem with Here Is That It's Where I'm From. (p. 1408)
—Robot Kitties: An up & down Book. (p. 1480)
—School. Hasn't This Gone on Long Enough? (p. 1523)
—School. Hasn't This Gone on Long Enough? Benton, Jim, illus. (p. 1523)
—Super-Nice Are Super-Annoying. (p. 1680)
—Super-Nice Are Super-Annoying. Benton, Jim, illus. (p. 1680)
—That's What Friends Aren't For. (p. 1727)
—That's What Friends Aren't For. Benton, Jim, illus. (p. 1727)
—What I Don't Know Might Hurt Me. (p. 1886)
—What I Don't Know Might Hurt Me. Benton, Jim, illus. (p. 1886)
—Where's My Fnurgle? (p. 1910)
—Worst Things in Life Are Also Free. Benton, Jim, illus. (p. 1961)
—You Can Bet on That. Benton, Jim, illus. (p. 1974)
Benton, Jim, jt. auth. see Kelly, Jamie.
Benton, Jim & Kelly, Jamie. Can Adults Become Human? (p. 258)
—Never Do Anything, Ever. Benton, Jim, illus. (p. 1242)
—Never Underestimate Your Dumbness. Benton, Jim, illus. (p. 1243)
Benton, John. Gender Questions. (p. 660)
—New Hope Series (p. 1245)
Benton, John, jt. auth. see Benton, Ann.
Benton, Jonathan K. Wicked Kind of Dark. (p. 1927)
Benton, Lynne. Chariot Race/La Carrera de Carrozas. Ursell, Martin, illus. (p. 291)
—Pirate Pete. Chapman, Neil, illus. (p. 1362)
—Sad Princess. Catling, Andy, illus. (p. 1501)
Benton, Lynne, jt. auth. see Barron's Educational Series.
Benton, M. J. Great Book of Dinosaurs. (p. 714)
Benton, Marilyn, illus. see Folmsbee, Judi.
Benton, Michael. Flying Monsters. (p. 610)
—Kingfisher Dinosaur Encyclopedia: One Encylopedia, a World of Prehistoric Knowledge. (p. 960)
—Mighty Giants. (p. 1140)
—Small & Scary. (p. 1591)
Benton, Michael & Cook, Elizabeth. Vida Prehistorica, Dinosaurios Primeros Pobladores. (p. 1841)
Benton, Tim, illus. see Bryant, Ann.
Benton-Banai, Edward. Mishomis Book: The Voice of the Ojibway. (p. 1150)
Bentorah, Chaim. Biblical Truths from Uncle Otto's Farm. (p. 177)
Bentow, Brian. Computer Athlete's Handbook: Your Guide to a Happier, Healthier Techy Lifestyle. Goodwin, Leah, ed. (p. 354)
Bentz, Laurice & Martin, Judy. Land down Under: A Dream Beam Adventure. (p. 973)
Bentz, Lindsay. Really Good Friends. (p. 1449)
Bentz, Lorena Quintana. Cowboy Bill & the Eighth Commandment. (p. 373)
Benway, Robin. Also Known As. (p. 50)
—Audrey, Wait! (p. 115)
—Emmy & Oliver. (p. 520)
—Going Rogue. (p. 693)
Benwell, Sarah. Last Leaves Falling. (p. 978)
Benyo, Richard. South Street Gang vs. the Coalcracker Cyclops. (p. 1617)
Ben-Yosef, Yoni, photos by see Eidelberg, Martin & Cass, Claire.
Benz, Cheryl, jt. auth. see Shuemann, Cynthia.
Benz, Cheryl & Medina, Myra M. College Reading (p. 340)
Benz, Derek & Lewis, J. S. Brimstone Key Bk. 1. (p. 228)
—Brimstone Key. (p. 228)
—Paragon Prison. (p. 1323)
—Relic Hunters: Even Heroes Have to Go to School. (p. 1458)
Benz, Suzanne. Harry's Last Wish: A Story about Forever. Alvarado, Carol, illus. (p. 751)
Benziger, Katherine. Overcoming Depression: The Easy to Read Simple to Use Little Book You Can Use to Turn Your Life Around. (p. 1314)
Benzwie, Teresa. Alphabet Movers. Bender, Robert, illus. (p. 49)
—Numbers on the Move. (p. 1272)
Beop-Ryong, Yeo. Chronicles of Cursed Sword Hui-Jin, Park, illus. (p. 317)
—Chronicles of the Cursed Sword. Hui-Jin, Park, illus. (p. 317)
Beop-Ryong, Yuy. Chronicles of the Cursed Sword Hui-Jin, Park, illus. (p. 317)
Beop-Ryong, Yuy, illus. see Hui-Jin, Park.
Be-Papas. World Exists for Me Saitou, Chiho, illus. (p. 1955)
Be-Papas, illus. see Saito, Chiho.
ber, Gall. Time of the Cats. (p. 1752)
Beraducci, Deborah. Tyler's Halloween Horror Eyre, Jane, illus. (p. 1805)
Beranek, Adam & Beranek, Christian. Dracula vs. King Arthur #1. Moreno, Chris & Fotos, Jay, illus. (p. 476)
Beranek, Adam, et al. Silent Forest Burke, Chris et al, illus. (p. 1575)
Beranek, Christian, jt. auth. see Beranek, Adam.
Beranek, Malinda. Rocky, the Country Squirrel. (p. 1484)
Berard, Robin M. King Tut & the Girl Who Loved Him: The Strange Adventures of Johanna Wilson. (p. 959)
Berardini, Susan, ed. see Clua, Guillem.
Berardy, Lloyd, 1st. Tropical Bear in Hawaii Goes Underwater. (p. 1789)
Berarle, Denis. Little Soul & His Friend. (p. 1036)
Berástegui, Manu, tr. see Santiago Baca, Jimmy.
Bercik, Mark. America's Complete Sports Scholarship Guide: Giving Back Something to the Game. Wilding, Diane, ed. (p. 64)
—America's Complete Sports Scholarship Guide: Giving Something Back to the Game. Wilding, Diane, ed. (p. 64)
Bercowetz, Cynthia. Grandpa Herman's Petting Zoo. (p. 709)
Bercowetz, Cynthia S. Don't Get Ripped Off! (p. 467)
Bercowetz, Cynthia Susan. Tiger, the Singing Cat. (p. 1748)
Bercun, Brenda. I'm Going to Be a Big Brother! Gross, Sue, illus. (p. 859)
—I'm Going to Be a Big Sister! Gross, Sue, illus. (p. 859)
Bercuson, David. How Canada Became Canada (p. 805)
Berdes, George R. Girl Without a Name. (p. 679)
Bereal, JaeMe, illus. see Schroeder, Alan.
Beree, Brian La, see La Beree, Brian.
Bereiter. Open Court Phonemic Awareness & Phonics Kit: Phonics Skills Workbook. (p. 1299)
—Open Court Phonemic Awareness & Phonics Kit: Sounds & Letters Workbook. (p. 1299)
—Open Court Phonics Kit. (p. 1299)
—Phonemic Awareness & Phonics Kit, Grade 1. (p. 1351)
Bereiter, Carl. Open Court Classics: Student Workbook LEVEL 5. (p. 1299)
—Open Court Classics: Teacher's Edition LEVEL 2. (p. 1299)
—Student Anthology: Level 2. (p. 1669)
—Student Anthology: Level 3. (p. 1669)
—Student Anthology: Level 4. (p. 1669)
—Student Anthology: Level 5. (p. 1669)
—Student Anthology: Level 6. (p. 1669)
—Student Workbook: Level 2. (p. 1669)
—Student Workbook: Level 3. (p. 1669)
—Student Workbook: Level 4. (p. 1669)
Beren, Norris L. When Disaster Strikes Home! 101+ Ways to Protect Your Family from Unthinkable Emergencies. (p. 1902)
Berenato, Dave. Medlocks: The Peractio Blackout. (p. 1120)
Berend, Janet Eoff. Vertical. (p. 1837)
Berenda, M. J. Helping with Pocket Change. (p. 766)
Berendes, Mary. Actions/Las Acciones. Petelinsek, Kathleen, illus. (p. 10)
—Animals/Los Animales. Petelinsek, Kathleen, illus. (p. 84)
—Careers/Las Carreras. Petelinsek, Kathleen, illus. (p. 268)
—Clothes/la Ropa. Petelinsek, Kathleen, illus. (p. 334)
—Days & Times (Los Días y Las Horas) Petelinsek, Kathleen, illus. (p. 415)
—Feelings/Las Emociones. Petelinsek, Kathleen, illus. (p. 580)
—Food/la Comida. Petelinsek, Kathleen, illus. (p. 614)
—Good Samaritan. Johnson, Pamela & Squier, Robert, illus. (p. 700)
—Holidays & Celebrations (Los Días de Fiestas y Las Celebraciones) Petelinsek, Kathleen, illus. (p. 788)
—House/la Casa. Petelinsek, Kathleen, illus. (p. 804)
—Independence Day Crafts. Petelinsek, Kathleen, illus. (p. 870)
—Lost Sheep. Squier, Robert, illus. (p. 1056)
—Máquinas. Petelinsek, Kathleen, illus. (p. 1091)

—Neighborhood/el Barrio. Petelinsek, Kathleen, illus. (p. 1240)
—People/Las Personas. Petelinsek, Kathleen, illus. (p. 1340)
—Piranhas. (p. 1362)
—Prodigal Son. Squier, Robert, illus. (p. 1409)
—School/la Escuela. Petelinsek, Kathleen, illus. (p. 1524)
—Sower & the Seeds. Squier, Robert, illus. (p. 1618)
—Sports & Games/Los Deportes y Los Juegos. Petelinsek, Kathleen, illus. (p. 1632)
—St. Patrick's Day Shamrocks. (p. 1638)
—Ten Bridesmaids. Squier, Robert, illus. (p. 1718)
—Unmerciful Servant. Squier, Robert, illus. (p. 1822)
Berendes, Mary & Aesop. Boy Who Cried Wolf. Harrison, Nancy, illus. (p. 219)
—Maid & the Milk Pail. Harrison, Nancy, illus. (p. 1076)
Berendes, Mary & Eick, Jean. Birthday Crafts. Petelinsek, Kathleen, illus. (p. 192)
Berends, Jenny, illus. see Due, Kirsten L.
Berendt, John. My Baby Blue Jays. (p. 1196)
Berenson, Alex. Faithful Spy. (p. 565)
Berenson, Mark. Even Money. (p. 541)
Berenstain, Jan, illus. see Berenstain, Stan, et al.
Berenstain, Jan, jt. auth. see Berenstain, Mike.
Berenstain, Jan, jt. auth. see Berenstain, Stan.
Berenstain, Jan, jt. auth. see Zondervan Publishing Staff.
Berenstain, Jan & Berenstain, Mike. All Aboard! Berenstain, Jan & Berenstain, Mike, illus. (p. 41)
—All Things Bright & Beautiful (p. 46)
—Bear Country Blessings (p. 150)
—Berenstain Bears & a Job Well Done Berenstain, Stan, illus. (p. 166)
—Berenstain Bears & Mama for Mayor! Berenstain, Jan & Berenstain, Mike, illus. (p. 166)
—Berenstain Bears & the Forgiving Tree (p. 166)
—Berenstain Bears & the Gift of Courage Berenstain, Stan, illus. (p. 166)
—Berenstain Bears & the Joy of Giving (p. 166)
—Berenstain Bears & the Little Lost Cub (p. 166)
—Berenstain Bears & the Nutcracker. Berenstain, Jan & Berenstain, Mike, illus. (p. 166)
—Berenstain Bears & the Shaggy Little Pony. Berenstain, Jan & Berenstain, Mike, illus. (p. 166)
—Berenstain Bears & the Tooth Fairy. Berenstain, Jan & Berenstain, Mike, illus. (p. 166)
—Berenstain Bears & the Trouble with Things (p. 166)
—Berenstain Bears at the Aquarium. (p. 166)
—Berenstain Bears at the Aquarium. Berenstain, Jan & Berenstain, Mike, illus. (p. 166)
—Berenstain Bears' Baby Easter Bunny. Berenstain, Jan & Berenstain, Mike, illus. (p. 166)
—Berenstain Bears' Class Trip. Berenstain, Jan & Berenstain, Mike, illus. (p. 166)
—Berenstain Bears Come Clean for School. Berenstain, Jan & Berenstain, Mike, illus. (p. 166)
—Berenstain Bears' Computer Trouble. Berenstain, Jan & Berenstain, Mike, illus. (p. 166)
—Berenstain Bears' Dinosaur Dig. (p. 166)
—Berenstain Bears' Dinosaur Dig. Berenstain, Jan & Berenstain, Mike, illus. (p. 166)
—Berenstain Bears Get Ready for School. Berenstain, Jan & Berenstain, Mike, illus. (p. 166)
—Berenstain Bears Go Green. (p. 166)
—Berenstain Bears Go Out to Eat. (p. 166)
—Berenstain Bears Go Out to Eat. Berenstain, Jan & Berenstain, Mike, illus. (p. 166)
—Berenstain Bears' Old-Fashioned Christmas. Berenstain, Jan & Berenstain, Mike, illus. (p. 167)
—Berenstain Bears' Really Big Pet Show. Berenstain, Jan & Berenstain, Mike, illus. (p. 167)
—Berenstain Bears Say Please & Thank You. Berenstain, Jan & Berenstain, Mike, illus. (p. 167)
—Berenstain Bears' Sleepover. Berenstain, Jan & Berenstain, Mike, illus. (p. 167)
—Berenstain Bears Storybook Bible (p. 167)
—Berenstain Bears - Storybook Bible for Little Ones (p. 166)
—Berenstain Bears Trim the Tree. Berenstain, Jan & Berenstain, Mike, illus. (p. 167)
—Berenstain Bears' Valentine Party. (p. 167)
—Berenstain Bears - We Love Trucks! Berenstain, Jan & Berenstain, Mike, illus. (p. 166)
—Berenstain Bears' Winter Wonderland. Berenstain, Jan & Berenstain, Mike, illus. (p. 167)
—God Bless Our Home. (p. 688)
—God Bless the Animals (p. 688)
—God Made the Colors (p. 690)
—Help the Homeless (p. 766)
—Here's the Church, Here's the Steeple (p. 771)
—Honey Hunt Helpers (p. 794)
—Kitten Rescue (p. 962)
—Let the Bible Be Your Guide. (p. 994)
—Mama's Helpers. (p. 1084)
—Neighbor in Need (p. 1240)
—Safe & Sound! Berenstain, Jan & Berenstain, Mike, illus. (p. 1502)
—Sick Days. Berenstain, Jan & Berenstain, Mike, illus. (p. 1572)
—Trouble with Secrets (p. 1790)
—We Love Our Dad! (p. 1867)
—We Love Our Dad! Berenstain, Jan & Berenstain, Mike, illus. (p. 1867)
—We Love Our Mom! (p. 1867)
—We Love Our Mom! Berenstain, Jan & Berenstain, Mike, illus. (p. 1867)
—We Love Trucks! (p. 1867)
—We Love Trucks! Berenstain, Jan & Berenstain, Mike, illus. (p. 1867)
Berenstain, Jan & Berenstain, Stan. Berenstain Bears: All in the Family. (p. 166)
—Berenstain Bears' Christmas Coloring & Activity Book. (p. 166)
—Berenstain Bears Giant Coloring & Activity Book. (p. 166)
—Berenstain Bears(r)' First Time Do-It! Book. (p. 166)
—Big Book of Berenstain Bears Beginner Books. (p. 178)
Berenstain, Jan, et al. Berenstain Bears. (p. 166)
—Berenstain Bears — a Bear Country Alphabet Coloring Book. (p. 166)
—Berenstain Bears' Count on Numbers Coloring Book. (p. 166)
—Berenstain Bears' Family Reunion. Berenstain, Jan & Berenstain, Mike, illus. (p. 166)
—Berenstain Bears Get Involved (p. 166)
—Berenstain Bears Go on Vacation. Berenstain, Jan & Berenstain, Mike, illus. (p. 166)
—Berenstain Bears Lose a Friend. Berenstain, Jan et al, illus. (p. 167)
—Berenstain Bears' New Kitten. Berenstain, Jan et al, illus. (p. 167)
—Berenstain Bears Play a Good Game (p. 167)
—Berenstain Bears Save Christmas. Berenstain, Mike, illus. (p. 167)
—Big Bedtime Book. Berenstain, Jan & Berenstain, Stan, illus. (p. 178)
—Kindness Counts. (p. 957)
—My Favorite Dog Stories: Learning to Read Box Set. (p. 1203)
Berenstain, Mike. Berenstain Bears & the Biggest Brag (p. 166)
—Berenstain Bears Are SuperBears! Berenstain, Mike, illus. (p. 166)
—Berenstain Bears Blessed Are the Peacemakers (p. 166)
—Berenstain Bears' Country Cookbook: Cub-Friendly Cooking with an Adult (p. 166)
—Berenstain Bears' Easter Parade. Berenstain, Mike, illus. (p. 166)
—Berenstain Bears - Gone Fishin'! Berenstain, Mike, illus. (p. 166)
—Berenstain Bears' Graduation Day. Berenstain, Mike, illus. (p. 166)
—Berenstain Bears' Lemonade Stand. (p. 167)
—Berenstain Bears' Lemonade Stand. Berenstain, Mike, illus. (p. 167)
—Berenstain Bears' Night Before Christmas. Berenstain, Mike, illus. (p. 167)
—Berenstain Bears Phonics Fun. Berenstain, Mike, illus. (p. 167)
—Berenstain Bears' Please & Thank You Book. (p. 167)
—Berenstain Bears' Sleepy Time Book. (p. 167)
—Berenstain Bears: When I Grow Up. Berenstain, Mike, illus. (p. 167)
—Berenstain Bears/Living Lights: The Berenstain Bears' Harvest Festival (p. 167)
—God Made You Special (p. 690)
—Gone Fishin'! (p. 697)
—Hospital Friends. (p. 801)
—Hospital Friends. Berenstain, Mike, illus. (p. 801)
—Valentine Love Bug. Berenstain, Mike, illus. (p. 1830)
Berenstain, Mike, illus. see Berenstain, Jan, et al.
Berenstain, Mike, illus. see Berenstain, Stan & Berenstain, Jan.
Berenstain, Mike, illus. see Berenstain, Stan, et al.
Berenstain, Mike, jt. auth. see Berenstain, Jan.
Berenstain, Mike, jt. auth. see Berenstain, Stan.
Berenstain, Mike & Berenstain, Jan. Berenstain Bears Go to Sunday School (p. 166)
—Berenstain Bears Lose a Friend. Berenstain, Mike & Berenstain, Jan, illus. (p. 167)
—Berenstain Bears Say Their Prayers (p. 167)
Berenstain, Mike & Berenstain, Stan. Berenstain Bears God Bless Our Country (p. 166)
Berenstain, Mike, et al. 5-Minute Berenstain Bears Stories. Berenstain, Mike, illus. (p. 1992)
—Berenstain Bears & the Golden Rule (p. 166)
—Berenstain Bears Give Thanks Berenstain, Stan, illus. (p. 166)
—Faithful Friends Berenstain, Stan, illus. (p. 565)
Berenstain, Stan, illus. see Berenstain, Jan & Berenstain, Mike.
Berenstain, Stan, illus. see Berenstain, Jan, et al.
Berenstain, Stan, illus. see Berenstain, Mike, et al.
Berenstain, Stan, jt. auth. see Berenstain, Jan.
Berenstain, Stan, jt. auth. see Berenstain, Mike.
Berenstain, Stan & Berenstain, Jan. Bears on Wheels. (p. 152)
—Berenstain Bears. (p. 166)
—Berenstain Bears & the Baby Chipmunk. Berenstain, Stan & Berenstain, Jan, illus. (p. 166)
—Berenstain Bears & the Bad Dream. (p. 166)
—Berenstain Bears & the Big Blooper. (p. 166)
—Berenstain Bears & the Blame Game. (p. 166)
—Berenstain Bears & the Mama's Day Surprise. (p. 166)
—Berenstain Bears & the Trouble with Chores. Berenstain, Jan, illus. (p. 166)
—Berenstain Bears & the Wishing Star. Berenstain, Stan & Berenstain, Jan, illus. (p. 166)
—Berenstain Bears & Too Much Car Trip. Berenstain, Stan & Berenstain, Jan, illus. (p. 166)
—Berenstain Bears Bears on Wheels. (p. 166)
—Berenstain Bears' Bedtime Battle. Berenstain, Stan & Berenstain, Jan, illus. (p. 166)
—Berenstain Bears Clean House. (p. 166)
—Berenstain Bears Clean House. Berenstain, Stan & Berenstain, Jan, illus. (p. 166)
—Berenstain Bears down on the Farm. Berenstain, Stan & Berenstain, Jan, illus. (p. 166)
—Berenstain Bears' Family Reunion. (p. 166)
—Berenstain Bears Go on a Ghost Walk. Berenstain, Jan, illus. (p. 166)
—Berenstain Bears Go to School. (p. 166)
—Berenstain Bears Happy Halloween! (p. 166)
—Berenstain Bears' Home Sweet Tree. (p. 166)
—Berenstain Bears Merry Christmas. (p. 167)
—Berenstain Bears' New Pup. Berenstain, Jan, illus. (p. 167)
—Berenstain Bears Out West. Berenstain, Stan & Berenstain, Jan, illus. (p. 167)
—Berenstain Bears' Pet Show. (p. 167)
—Berenstain Bears Play T-Ball. (p. 167)
—Berenstain Bears Play T-Ball. Berenstain, Stan & Berenstain, Jan, illus. (p. 167)
—Berenstain Bears' Report Card Trouble. (p. 167)
—Berenstain Bears Save Christmas. Berenstain, Mike, illus. (p. 167)
—Berenstain Bears' School Days. (p. 167)
—Berenstain Bears' Seashore Treasure. Berenstain, Jan, illus. (p. 167)
—Berenstain Bears' Sleepover (p. 167)
—Berenstain Bears' Stories to Share. (p. 167)
—Berenstain Bears' Storytime Treasury. (p. 167)
—Berenstain Bears' Trouble with Pets. Berenstain, Stan & Berenstain, Jan, illus. (p. 167)
—Berenstain Bears(r) & the Talent Show. (p. 166)
—Osos Berenstain y Demasiada Fiesta. (p. 1306)
—We Like Kites. (p. 1867)
Berenstain, Stan & Berenstain, Mike. Berenstain Bears' Perfect Fishing Spot (p. 167)
Berenstain, Stan, et al. Berenstain Bears & the Bad Influence. Berenstain, Stan et al, illus. (p. 166)
—Berenstain Bears & the Big Spelling Bee Berenstain, Stan et al, illus. (p. 166)
—Berenstain Bears & the Haunted House. (p. 166)
—Berenstain Bears & the Papa's Day Surprise. (p. 166)
—Berenstain Bears & the Trouble with Commercials. Berenstain, Stan et al, illus. (p. 166)
—Berenstain Bears' Big Bedtime Book. Berenstain, Jan & Berenstain, Mike, illus. (p. 166)
—Berenstain Bears' Big Bedtime Book. Berenstain, Stan & Berenstain, Jan, illus. (p. 166)
—Berenstain Bears' Big Book of Science & Nature. (p. 166)
—Berenstain Bears' Christmas Tree (p. 166)
—Berenstain Bears Discover God's Creation (p. 166)
—Berenstain Bears Do Their Best (p. 166)
—Berenstain Bears Go Back to School. Berenstain, Mike, illus. (p. 166)
—Berenstain Bears God Shows the Way Berenstain, Stan & Berenstain, Jan, illus. (p. 166)
—Berenstain Bears Hug & Make Up. Berenstain, Stan & Berenstain, Jan, illus. (p. 167)
—Berenstain Bears Hurry to Help (p. 167)
—Berenstain Bears Learn to Share (p. 167)
—Berenstain Bears Love Their Neighbors Berenstain, Stan, illus. (p. 167)
—Berenstain Bears' Paper Doll Book. (p. 167)
—Berenstain Bears Save Christmas. Berenstain, Stan et al, illus. (p. 167)
—Berenstain Bears' Sleepover Berenstain, Stan et al, illus. (p. 167)
—Berenstain Bears Storybook Treasury. Berenstain, Stan & Berenstain, Jan, illus. (p. 167)
—Do Not Fear, God Is Near (p. 457)
—God Loves You! (p. 689)
—Jobs Around Town (p. 919)
—Nothing Ever Happens at the South Pole. Berenstain, Jan & Berenstain, Mike, illus. (p. 1268)
Berenzy, Alix. Sammy: The Classroom Guinea Pig. Berenzy, Alix, illus. (p. 1507)
Berenzy, Alix, illus. see Guiberson, Brenda Z.
Beres, D. B. Sticky Evidence: Burglar Caught on Tape. (p. 1650)
Beres, D. B. & Franklin, Watts. Dusted & Busted! The Science of Fingerprinting. (p. 490)
Beres, E. Jean. Sugaring Season. (p. 1673)
Beres, Lisa. My Body My House. (p. 1198)
—My body my World. (p. 1198)
Beres, Nancy. Night the Animals Spoke. Schirack, Timm, illus. (p. 1254)
Beres, Samantha. Energy Resources Around the World: Set Of 6. (p. 528)
—Energy Resources Around the World & Recursos energéticos alrededor del Mundo: 6 English, 6 Spanish Adaptations. (p. 528)
Beresford, Elisabeth. Bigfoot Womble. (p. 185)
—Deep Space Womble. (p. 423)
—Ghost of Wimbledon Common. (p. 671)
—Great Cake Mystery. (p. 714)
—Great Womble Explorer. (p. 719)
—Invisible Womble. Price, Nick, illus. (p. 886)
—Snow Womble. Price, Nick, illus. (p. 1600)
—Tomsk to the Rescue. (p. 1765)
—Wandering Wombles. Price, Nick, illus. (p. 1856)
—Wombles: Chaos on the Common. (p. 1945)
—Wombles. Price, Nick, illus. (p. 1945)
—Wombles Buggy Trouble. (p. 1945)
—Wombles Camping & Cloudberries. (p. 1945)
Beresford, Nicholas A., jt. auth. see Smith, Jim.
Beresford, Shane. In the Jungle. (p. 866)
Berg, Aase. Remainland: Selected Poems of Aase Berg. Göransson, Johannes, tr. (p. 1458)
Berg, Adriane. Totally Awesome Money Book for Kids. (p. 1771)
Berg, Albert A., ed. see Bloom, Harold.
Berg & Holland. Tamino Pingüino y el Asunto Del Huevo. (p. 1704)
Berg, Brook. What Happened to Marion's Book? Alberg, Nathan, illus. (p. 1885)
—What Marion Taught Willis. Alberg, Nathan, illus. (p. 1892)
Berg, Carol. Flesh & Spirit. (p. 603)
Berg, Caroline O., illus. see McFarlane, Marilyn.
Berg, Carolyn. Bulletin Boards for Christian. (p. 240)
Berg, David W. & Green, Meg. Savings & Investments. (p. 1518)
Berg, Deva Jean. Tail of Two Sisters. Berg, Deva Jean, illus. (p. 1695)
Berg, Dick. Padunkapoo: The Hawaiian Kangaroo. Berg, Gary, ed. (p. 1317)
Berg, Dorlisa H. Fat Freddy Gets Fit. (p. 577)
Berg, Elizabeth. Egypt. (p. 506)
—Mexico. (p. 1131)
—United States. (p. 1819)
Berg, Elizabeth, jt. auth. see Frank, Nicole.
Berg, Elizabeth & Lau, Ruth. Senegal. (p. 1550)
Berg, Gary, ed. see Berg, Dick.
Berg, Jean Horton. Noisy Clock Shop. Seiden, Art, illus. (p. 1263)
—Pierre, the Young Watchmaker. D'Adamo, Anthony, illus. (p. 1357)
Berg, Kelly, illus. see Sauvageau-Smestad, Sheila.
Berg, Laurna L. Adventures of Lynx & Cheetah: The Unconditional Love of a Beloved Pet Gives Us a Glimpse into the Heart of God. (p. 20)
Berg, Michelle, illus. see Ackerman, Jill.
Berg, Michelle, illus. see Ageledis, Ida.
Berg, Michelle, illus. see Ainsworth, Kimberly.
Berg, Michelle, illus. see Feldman, Thea.
Berg, Michelle, illus. see Karr, Lily.
Berg, Michelle, illus. see Prasadam-Halls, Smriti.
Berg, Michelle, illus. see Prince, April Jones.
Berg, N., jt. auth. see MacKinnon, Mary.
Berg, R. J. Jenny Martin & the Unexpected Gift. (p. 913)
Berg, Rav P. S. Kabbalah Method: The Bridge Between Science & the Soul, Physics & Fulfillment, Quantum & the Creator. Kabbalah Learning Center Staff, ed. (p. 941)
—Power of You: Kabbalistic Wisdom to Create the Movie of Your Life. (p. 1390)
Berg, Ray. Sailing Duck. (p. 1503)
Berg, Rea, jt. auth. see Higgins, Marguerite.
Berg, Rea, jt. auth. see O'Dell, Scott.
Berg, Rebecca L. Great Depression in Literature for Youth: A Geographical Study of Families & Young Lives. (p. 715)
Berg, Ron, illus. see Shire, Poppy.
Berg, Ron, jt. auth. see Deere, John.
Berg, Ron, jt. auth. see John, Deere.
Berg, Ron, jt. auth. see Running Press Staff.
Berg, Vande, et al. Critical Approaches to Television. (p. 383)
Berg, Yehuda. 72 Names of God for Kids: A Treasury of Timeless Wisdom. (p. 1998)
—72 Names of God for Kids. (p. 1998)
Bergamotto, Lori. Skin: The Bare Facts. (p. 1585)
Bergandi, jt. auth. see Solanet.
Bergaust, Erik & Foss, William O. Coast Guard in Action. (p. 336)
Berge, Erlend, illus. see Bellward, Stacy.
Bergen, Brenda, illus. see Singh, Rajinder.
Bergen, Julia, jt. auth. see Patterson, James.
Bergen, Lara. Buzzy Bee Plays Hide & Seek. (p. 249)
—Diego's Birthday Surprise. Mawhinney, Art, illus. (p. 437)
—Don't Throw That Away! A Lift-the-Flap Book about Recycling & Reusing. Snyder, Betsy E., illus. (p. 469)
—Drama Queen. (p. 480)
—Enchanted Library (p. 523)
—Let's Dig It! Shannon, David et al, illus. (p. 995)
—Polar Bears' Home: A Story about Global Warming. Nguyen, Vincent, illus. (p. 1379)
—Sophie the Awesome. Tallardy, Laura, illus. (p. 1613)
—Sophie the Hero. Tallardy, Laura, illus. (p. 1613)
—Stand up & Cheer. (p. 1639)
—Tutu Twins. Pastel, Elyse & Pastel, Elyse, illus. (p. 1799)
Bergen, Lara, jt. auth. see Bazaldua, Barbara.
Bergen, Lara, jt. auth. see Bergen, Lara Rice.
Bergen, Lara, jt. auth. see Disney Book Group Staff.
Bergen, Lara & Disney Book Group Staff. Enchanted Fashions: A Magnetic Book & Playset. Disney Storybook Artists Staff, illus. (p. 523)
—Runaway Hit Disney Storybook Artists Staff, illus. (p. 1496)
Bergen, Lara Rice. Phonics Comics: the Fearless Four - Level 2. Semple, Dave, illus. (p. 1352)
Bergen, Lara Rice & Bergen, Lara. Dora's Sleepover. Miller, Victoria, illus. (p. 471)
Bergens, Teri. Mud Trouble. (p. 1188)
—Problemas de Barro. (p. 1408)
—Xerplek's Schmizzle. (p. 1967)
Berger, Barry W. Passover Haggadah. Hall, Melanie W., illus. (p. 1327)
—Passover Haggadah—Russian. Drazman, Jenya, tr. (p. 1327)
Berger, Bruce. Dazzle of Hummingbirds: The Colorful Life of a Tiny Scrapper. Leon, Vicki, ed. (p. 415)
Berger, Carin. All Mixed Up: A Mix-and-Match Book. (p. 45)
—Finding Spring. Berger, Carin, illus. (p. 588)
—Forever Friends. Berger, Carin, illus. (p. 619)
—Little Yellow Leaf. Berger, Carin, illus. (p. 1038)
—Ok Go. Berger, Carin, illus. (p. 1282)
—Perfect Day. Berger, Carin, illus. (p. 1341)
Berger, Carin, illus. see Peck, Jan & Davis, David.
Berger, Carin, illus. see Prelutsky, Jack.
Berger, Dave, ed. see Asgedom, Mawi.
Berger, Gilda. African Savannah. (p. 28)
—Coral Reef. (p. 366)
—Desert. (p. 428)
—Dinosaurs. (p. 443)
—Matter. (p. 1109)
—Ocean. (p. 1276)
—Planets. (p. 1368)
—Polar Regions. (p. 1379)
—Rain Forest. (p. 1434)
—Restless Earth. (p. 1464)
—Rocks. (p. 1483)
—Sound. (p. 1615)
—Weather. (p. 1869)
Berger, Gilda, jt. auth. see Berger, Melvin.
Berger, Gilda & Berger, Melvin. 101 Animal Secrets. (p. 1999)
—Dangerous Animals. (p. 404)
—Pets. (p. 1348)
—Scholastic Reader Level 2: Ugly Cute Animals. (p. 1522)
Berger, Glenn. Princess Chantik & the Outside World. (p. 1403)
Berger, Joe, illus. see Boyce, Frank Cottrell.
Berger, Joe, illus. see Corderoy, Tracey.
Berger, Joe, illus. see Devlin, Jane V.
Berger, Joe, illus. see Fleming, Ian.
Berger, Joe, illus. see Sauer, Tammi.
Berger, Joe, illus. see Walton, Rick.
Berger, Joe, illus. see Zuckerberg, Randi.
Berger, Lisa, jt. auth. see Millar, Goldie.
Berger, Loretta Oleck. Calm down & Play: Activities to Help Impulsive Children. (p. 254)
Berger, Lou. Dream Dog. Catrow, David, illus. (p. 483)
Berger, Marjorie B., jt. auth. see Knapp, Rene.
Berger, Mary J. Jesus Lives in Us: Activity Book. (p. 915)
Berger, Melvin. Bebés de Animales Polares: Polar Animal Babies. (p. 155)

B

—Germs Make Me Sick! Hafner, Marylin, illus. (p. 667)
—How Do Airplanes Fly? (p. 806)
—Round & Round the Money Goes. (p. 1491)
—Spinning Spiders. Schindler, S. D., illus. (p. 1628)
—Telephones, Televisions, & Toilets. (p. 1716)
—Think Factory: Amazing Inventions. (p. 1734)
—Water, Water Everywhere. (p. 1863)
—What Do Animals Do in Winter? (p. 1882)
—Where Did Your Family Come From? (p. 1906)
—Where Does the Mail Go? (p. 1907)
Berger, Melvin, jt. auth. see Berger, Gilda.
Berger, Melvin & Berger, Gilda. 101 Animal Disguises. (p. 1999)
—101 Animal Records. (p. 1999)
—101 Hidden Animals. (p. 1999)
—Amphibians. (p. 65)
—Animales Polares en Peligro: Polar Animals in Danger. (p. 81)
—Ants. (p. 90)
—Are Mountains Getting Taller? Questions & Answers about the Changing Earth. Carter, Robin, illus. (p. 96)
—Baby Animals. (p. 124)
—Bears. (p. 151)
—Beavers. (p. 155)
—Bees. (p. 157)
—Butterflies. (p. 247)
—Caballitos de Mar: Sea Horses. (p. 250)
—Can You Fly High, Wright Brothers? Dorman, Brandon, illus. (p. 259)
—Caterpillar Grows Up. (p. 279)
—Checkup. (p. 295)
—Chipmunks. (p. 308)
—Cold Weather. (p. 339)
—De Larva a Mariquita: Grub to Ladybug. (p. 416)
—De Renacuajo a Rana: Tadpole to Frog. (p. 416)
—Deer. (p. 423)
—Did It Take Creativity to Find Relativity, Albert Einstein? Dorman, Brandon, illus. (p. 436)
—Dogs Bring Newspapers but Cats Bring Mice: And Other Fascinating Facts about Animal Behavior. (p. 462)
—Dolphins. (p. 464)
—Egg to Robin. (p. 506)
—Flies. (p. 603)
—Foxes. (p. 626)
—Frogs Live on Logs. (p. 641)
—Go to Sleep. (p. 687)
—Grasshoppers. (p. 711)
—Healthy Eating. (p. 758)
—How Do Frogs Swallow with Their Eyes? Questions & Answers about Amphibians. Carr, Karen, illus. (p. 807)
—Hurricanes Have Eyes but Can't See: And Other Amazing Facts about Wild Weather. (p. 830)
—Ice Is Nice. (p. 850)
—Kicking, Running, & Stretching. (p. 951)
—Ladybugs. (p. 971)
—Life on a Coral Reef. (p. 1012)
—Manta Rays. (p. 1088)
—Octopus. (p. 1278)
—Penguins. (p. 1337)
—Penguins Swim but Don't Get Wet: And Other Amazing Facts about Polar Animals. (p. 1337)
—Planets. (p. 1368)
—Polar Animals in Danger. (p. 1378)
—Polar Bears. (p. 1379)
—Raccoons. (p. 1430)
—Real Vikings: Craftsman, Traders, & Fiercesome Raiders. (p. 1449)
—Reptiles. (p. 1461)
—Robin Grows Up. (p. 1479)
—Sea Horses. (p. 1534)
—Seres Vivos: Living Things. (p. 1552)
—Sharks. (p. 1562)
—Shellfish. (p. 1565)
—Sistema Solar: The Solar System. (p. 1581)
—Snake Grows Up. (p. 1596)
—Snowflakes Are Falling. (p. 1600)
—Sunflower Grows Up. (p. 1676)
—Tadpole Grows Up. (p. 1695)
—Think Factory: Solar System. (p. 1734)
—Ugly Cute Animals. (p. 1808)
—Whales. (p. 1877)
—Your Body. (p. 1980)
—Your Bones. (p. 1980)
—Your Brain. (p. 1980)
—Your Heart. (p. 1980)
—Your Muscles. (p. 1981)
—Your Skin. (p. 1981)
Berger, Melvin & Peck, Marshall H., III. Whale Is Not a Fish & Other Animal Mix-Ups. (p. 1877)
Berger, Samantha. Boo-la-La Witch Spa. Roxas, Isabel, illus. (p. 210)
—Crankenstein. Santat, Dan, illus. (p. 376)
—Crankenstein Valentine. Santat, Dan, illus. (p. 376)
—Goldilocks & the Three Bears. Cartwright, Amy, illus. (p. 696)
—Martha Doesn't Say Sorry! Whatley, Bruce, illus. (p. 1097)
—Pirate Potty. Cartwright, Amy, illus. (p. 1363)
—Princess Potty. Cartwright, Amy, illus. (p. 1405)
—Santa's Reindeer Games. Manders, John, illus. (p. 1513)
—Snoozefest. Litten, Kristyna, illus. (p. 1598)
Berger, Samantha & Chanko, Pamela. It's Spring! Sweet, Melissa, illus. (p. 899)
Berger, Sholem, jt. auth. see Rey, H. A.
Berger, Sholem, jt. auth. see Seuss, Dr.
Berger, Susan J. Earthquake! Ruble, Eugene, illus. (p. 497)
—Growing up Dreams. Bell, Samantha, illus. (p. 726)
Berger, Thomas. Stan Bolivan & the Dragon. (p. 1639)
Berger, William E. Living with Asthma. (p. 1042)
—Teen's Guide to Living with Asthma. (p. 1715)
Bergerac. First Book of Christmas Songs for the Beginning Pianist: With Downloadable MP3s. (p. 593)
—First Book of Classical Music for the Beginning Pianist: With Downloadable MP3s. (p. 593)
—My First Book of Chopin: 23 Favorite Pieces in Easy Piano Arrangements. (p. 1205)
Bergeron, Alain, jt. auth. see Quintin, Michel.
Bergeron, Alain M. Abby's Fabulous Season (p. 2)
—Do You Know Dinosaurs? Sampar, illus. (p. 458)
—Do You Know Hyenas? Sampar, illus. (p. 458)
—Do You Know Komodo Dragons? Sampar, illus. (p. 458)
—Do You Know Praying Mantises? Sampar, illus. (p. 458)
Bergeron, Alain M. & Quintin, Michel. Did You Know Chameleons? Sampar, illus. (p. 437)
—Did You Know? Crocodiles! Sampar, illus. (p. 437)
—Did You Know? Spiders! Sampar, illus. (p. 437)
—Did You Know? Toads! Sampar, illus. (p. 437)
—Do You Know Crows? Sampar, illus. (p. 458)
—Do You Know Leeches? Sampar, illus. (p. 458)
—Do You Know Porcupines? Sampar, illus. (p. 458)
—Do You Know Rats? Sampar, illus. (p. 458)
Bergeron, Alain M. & Sampar. Tresor des Tresors. (p. 1785)
Bergeron, Denys. Bottes du Pere Noel. (p. 215)
Bergeron, Joe. Cosmic Cat. (p. 368)
Bergeron, John W., illus. see Hébert-Collins, Sheila.
Bergeron, Pastor Susan "Suzy". Preteens Mothers Best Friend. (p. 1398)
Bergese, F., jt. auth. see Asso, B.
Bergèse, Francis. Ghost Squadron. (p. 671)
Bergese, Francis. Spitfire Parade (p. 1629)
Bergèse, Francis, jt. auth. see Asso, Bernard.
Bergethon, Peter R. Marty's Miraculous Monday Reader. (p. 1098)
—Measuring My World: Student Science Journal. (p. 1117)
—Understanding My World: Student Science Journal. (p. 1816)
Berggren, Jeff. Chicken Cherries. Hansen, Tammy A., ed. (p. 300)
—My Moon Lagoon. Hansen, Tammy A., ed. (p. 1214)
Berggren, Joyce D. Hustle & Bustle of Poor Mrs. Tustle. Muellner, Nancy, illus. (p. 830)
Bergherr, Mary, illus. see Lowery, Linda.
Berghof, Michael. Story of Christmas: Carry-Me Puzzle Book. (p. 1657)
Bergida, Joanna. Wisdom from the Spring: A Collection of Short Storiesbrfrom the Class of 2010brCold Spring Harbor High School. (p. 1939)
Bergin, Jennifer J. Jungle Jim & Jungle Jen in the African Savannahs. (p. 935)
Bergin, Joseph, jt. auth. see Sava, Scott Christian.
Bergin, Mark. Action Fighting Figures. (p. 10)
—Boats. (p. 205)
—Cars. (p. 271)
—Dinosaurs. (p. 443)
—Dinosaurs & Other Prehistoric Creatures. (p. 444)
—Fairies & Mermaids. (p. 562)
—Farm Animals. (p. 573)
—Ghosts & Ghouls. (p. 672)
—How to Draw Cars. (p. 817)
—How to Draw Comic Book Heroes. (p. 817)
—How to Draw Dinosaurs & Other Prehistoric Creatures. (p. 817)
—How to Draw Dragons. (p. 817)
—How to Draw Fantasy Art. (p. 817)
—How to Draw Knights & Castles. (p. 817)
—How to Draw Planes. (p. 818)
—How to Draw Ships. (p. 818)
—It's Fun to Draw Cars, Planes, & Trains. (p. 896)
—It's Fun to Draw Creepy-Crawlies. (p. 896)
—It's Fun to Draw Dinosaurs & Other Prehistoric Creatures. (p. 896)
—It's Fun to Draw Fairies & Mermaids. (p. 896)
—It's Fun to Draw Farm Animals. (p. 897)
—It's Fun to Draw Ghosts & Ghouls. (p. 897)
—It's Fun to Draw Knights & Castles. (p. 897)
—It's Fun to Draw Monsters. (p. 897)
—It's Fun to Draw Pets. (p. 897)
—It's Fun to Draw Pirates. (p. 897)
—It's Fun to Draw Ponies & Horses. (p. 897)
—It's Fun to Draw Princesses & Ballerinas. (p. 897)
—It's Fun to Draw Robots & Aliens. (p. 897)
—It's Fun to Draw Safari Animals. (p. 897)
—It's Fun to Draw Sea Creatures. (p. 897)
—Knights & Castles. (p. 964)
—Magical Creatures & Mythical Beasts. (p. 1074)
—Mammoths & Other Prehistoric Animals. (p. 1085)
—Monsters. (p. 1168)
—Pets. (p. 1348)
—Pirates. (p. 1363)
—Planes. (p. 1367)
—Princesses & Ballerinas. (p. 1406)
—Robots. (p. 1481)
—Robots & Aliens. (p. 1481)
—Rockets. (p. 1483)
—Safari Animals. (p. 1501)
—Sea Creatures. (p. 1534)
—Soldiers. (p. 1607)
—Trains. (p. 1777)
—Trucks. (p. 1791)
Bergin, Mark, illus. see Canavan, Roger.
Bergin, Mark, illus. see Kant, Tanya.
Bergin, Mark, illus. see MacDonald, Fiona.
Bergin, Mark, illus. see Malam, John.
Bergin, Mark, illus. see Matthews, Rupert & Salariya, David.
Bergin, Mark, illus. see Matthews, Rupert.
Bergin, Mark, illus. see Morley, Jacqueline.
Bergin, Mark, illus. see Pipe, Jim.
Bergin, Mark, illus. see Ratliff, Thomas.
Bergin, Mark, illus. see Ratliff, Tom.
Bergin, Mark, illus. see Rooney, Anne.
Bergin, Mark, illus. see Woolf, Alex.
Bergin, Mark, jt. auth. see MacDonald, Fiona.
Bergin, Mark & Antram, David. How to Draw Cartoons. (p. 817)
Bergin, Rory M. & Meyer, Jared. Frequently Asked Questions about Divorce. (p. 636)
Bergin, Thomas G., ed. see Alighieri, Dante.
Bergin, Thomas G., tr. see Alighieri, Dante.
Bergin, Virginia. H2o. (p. 734)
Berglin, Ruth. Dear Big, Mean, Ugly Monster. DiRocco, Carl, illus. (p. 418)
Berglund, Andrea Lloyd. Good Little Horse: Thunder's Morning Stroll. (p. 698)
Berglund, Brad, jt. auth. see Cox, Byron.
Bergman, Carol Ann. Heath Grammar & Composition: Level 5. (p. 760)
Bergman, Dana & Puffin Staff. Merry Christmas, Annie. (p. 1128)
Bergman, Mara. Glitter Kitty. Monks, Lydia, illus. (p. 684)
—Lively Elizabeth! What Happens When You Push Thomas, Cassia, illus. (p. 1040)
—Oliver Who Travelled Far & Wide. Maland, Nick, illus. (p. 1286)
—Oliver Who Would Not Sleep! Maland, Nick, illus. (p. 1286)
—Snip Snap! What's That? Maland, Nick, illus. (p. 1597)
—Yum Yum! What Fun! Maland, Nick, illus. (p. 1983)
Bergman, Mats. Heath Grammar & Composition: Grade 7. (p. 760)
Bergman Publishing Co. Staff, ed. see Barber, Jacqueline.
Bergman Publishing Co. Staff, photos by see Sutter, Debra, et al.
Bergman, Shannon, illus. see Willson, Sarah.
Bergman, Steven. Critic's Carnival: A Ten-Minute Dramatic Monologue. (p. 383)
—History: Ten-Minute Dramatic Duet. (p. 783)
Bergmann, Sarah, illus. see Gordon, Rachel & Gold, Claudia.
Bergmeier-Johnson. Ya Ya's Boom Booms. (p. 1968)
Bergna, Monica. Chico Rey. Broeck, Fabricio Vanden, illus. (p. 301)
Bergna, Monica, illus. see Anónimo.
Bergner, Bobby. Why kitty Is afraid of Poo: A cautionary Tale. Bergner, Bobby, illus. (p. 1925)
Bergquist, Kathie & McDonald, Robert. Field Guide to Gay & Lesbian Chicago. (p. 583)
Bergren, Lisa T. God Found Us You. Bryant, Laura J., illus. (p. 688)
—God Gave Us Angels. Bryant, Laura J., illus. (p. 688)
—God Gave Us Christmas. (p. 688)
—God Gave Us Heaven. (p. 688)
—God Gave Us Love. (p. 688)
—God Gave Us Love. Bryant, Laura J., illus. (p. 688)
—God Gave Us Sleep. Bryant, Laura J., illus. (p. 688)
—God Gave Us So Much: A Limited-Edition Three-Book Treasury. Bryant, Laura J., illus. (p. 688)
—God Gave Us the World. Bryant, Laura J., illus. (p. 688)
—How Big Is God? Bryant, Laura J., illus. (p. 805)
—Season of Fire (p. 1538)
Berg-Seuffert, Barbara. Good Heaven - Eleven! A Tail of Many Cats. (p. 698)
Bergsma, Jody. Wizard. (p. 1942)
Bergstein, Rita M. Your Own Big Bed. Hartung, Susan Kathleen, illus. (p. 1981)
Bergstresser, Kate, jt. tr. see Hind, Devon.
Bergstrom, Amy, et al. Seventh Generation: Native Students Speak about Finding the Good Path. (p. 1555)
Bergstrom, Candace. People of the Prairie. (p. 1339)
Bergstrom, Gunilla. Good Night, Alfie Atkins. Dyssegaard, Elisabeth Kallick, tr. from SWE. (p. 699)
Bergström, Gunilla. Very Tricky, Alfie Atkins. Dyssegaard, Elisabeth Kallick, tr. from SWE. (p. 1839)
Bergström, Gunilla, illus. see Bergstrom, Gunilla.
Bergstrom, Jon T. Denali's Dream. (p. 426)
Bergstrom, Matt. American Landmarks: Miniature Models to Cut & Assemble. (p. 62)
Bergstrom, William. Magic Telescope. (p. 1073)
Bergt, Carolyn. Adventures of Martin Luther. Kirchhoff, Art, illus. (p. 20)
—Child's Garden of Bible Stories Workbooks: New Testament Workbook. (p. 305)
—Child's Garden of Bible Stories Workbooks: Old Testament Workbook. (p. 305)
—What Does This Mean? Mitter, Kathryn, illus. (p. 1884)
Bergt, Carolyn, jt. ed. see Rathmann, Rodney L.
Bergum, Constance R., illus. see Chaconas, Dori.
Bergum, Constance R., illus. see McCormick, Wendy.
Bergum, Constance R., illus. see Stewart, Melissa.
Bergum, Constance Rummel, illus. see Landstrom, Lee Ann & Shragg, Karen.
Bergum, Constance Rummel, illus. see Meyer, Eileen R.
Bergum, Constance Rummel, illus. see Stewart, Melissa.
Bergvall, Caroline. Fig. (p. 585)
Bergvinson, M. E. St. George's Mysterious Cross. (p. 1638)
Bergwerf, Barbara J., illus. see Monroe, Mary Alice.
Bergwerf, Barbara J., illus. see Rathmell, Donna.
Bergwerf, Barbara J., photos by see Rathmell, Donna.
Beringson, Lola. How Can You Lose with a Birthday to Choose? (p. 805)
Berk, Ari. Death Watch. (p. 420)
—Lych Way. (p. 1066)
—Mistle Child. (p. 1155)
—Nightsong. Long, Loren, illus. (p. 1255)
—Secret History of Hobgoblins. (p. 1541)
—Secret History of Mermaids & Creatures of the Deep. Anderson, Wayne, illus. (p. 1541)
Berk, Ari & Dunn, Carolyn. Coyote Speaks: Wonders of the Native American World. (p. 374)
Berk, Ari & McDermott, Kristen. William Shakespeare: His Life & Times. Andrew, Ian et al, illus. (p. 1933)
Berk, Carrie, jt. auth. see Berk, Sheryl.
Berk, Josh. Dark Days of Hamburger Halpin. (p. 407)
—Guy Langman, Crime Scene Procrastinator. (p. 733)
—Say It Ain't So. (p. 1518)
—Strike Three, You're Dead. (p. 1667)
Berk, Sheryl. Dance Divas - On Pointe. (p. 402)
—Dance Divas - Showstopper. (p. 402)
—Dance Divas - Showtime! (p. 402)
—Dance Divas: Step It Up. (p. 402)
—Dance Divas - Step It Up. (p. 402)
—Let's Rock! (p. 1000)
—Showstopper. (p. 1571)
—Showtime! (p. 1571)
—Two to Tango. (p. 1804)
Berk, Sheryl & Berk, Carrie. Baby Cakes. (p. 125)
—Cupcake Club: Truth, Love & Cupcakes. (p. 392)
—Cupcake Club Box Set: Books 1-3. (p. 392)
—Fashion Academy. (p. 575)
—Icing on the Cake. (p. 851)
—Royal Icing: The Cupcake Club. (p. 1492)
—Sugar & Spice: The Cupcake Club. (p. 1672)
—Winner Bakes All: Cupcake Club. (p. 1937)
Berke, Lindsey Jensen. Am I Pretty? (p. 51)
Berkeley, Jon. Between the Light. Dorman, Brandon, illus. (p. 173)
—Hidden Boy. (p. 775)
—Lightning Key No. 3. Dorman, Brandon, illus. (p. 1016)
—Palace of Laughter. Dorman, Brandon, illus. (p. 1319)
—Tiger's Egg. Dorman, Brandon, illus. (p. 1749)
Berkeley, Jon, illus. see Harper, Jessica.
Berkenkamp, Lauri, jt. auth. see Anderson, Maxine.
Berkes, Marianne. Anybody Home? Dickinson, Rebecca, illus. (p. 91)
—árbol Que Trepó el Oso Rietz, Kathleen, illus. (p. 94)
—Daisylocks Morrison, Cathy, illus. (p. 401)
—Going Home: The Mystery of Animal Migration. DiRubbio, Jennifer, illus. (p. 692)
—Hay Alguien en Casa? Dickinson, Rebecca, illus. (p. 755)
—Marsh Morning. Noreika, Robert, illus. (p. 1096)
—Marsh Music. Noreika, Robert, illus. (p. 1096)
—Over in a River: Flowing Out to the Sea. Dubin, Jill, illus. (p. 1313)
—Over in Australia: Amazing Animals down Under. Dubin, Jill, illus. (p. 1313)
—Over in the Arctic: Where the Cold Winds Blow. Dubin, Jill, illus. (p. 1313)
—Over in the Forest: Come & Take a Peek. Dubin, Jill, illus. (p. 1313)
—Over in the Jungle: A Rainforest Rhyme. Canyon, Jeanette, illus. (p. 1313)
—Over in the Ocean: In a Coral Reef. Canyon, Jeanette, illus. (p. 1313)
—Over on a Mountain: Somewhere in the World. Dubin, Jill, illus. (p. 1313)
—Swamp Where Gator Hides. Baird, Roberta, illus. (p. 1688)
—Tortoise & Hare's Amazing Race Morrison, Cathy, illus. (p. 1771)
—Tree That Bear Climbed Rietz, Kathleen, illus. (p. 1783)
—What's in the Garden? Arbo, Cris, illus. (p. 1898)
Berkes, Marianne Collins. Animalogy: Animal Analogies Morrison, Cathy, illus. (p. 81)
—Going Around the Sun: Some Planetary Fun. Mason, Janeen, illus. (p. 692)
—Over in the Jungle: A Rainforest Rhyme. Canyon, Jeanette, illus. (p. 1313)
—Over on the Farm. Morrison, Cathy, illus. (p. 1313)
—Seashells by the Seashore. Noreika, Robert, illus. (p. 1538)
Berkes, Marianne Collins, et al. Plantita Margarita Morrison, Cathy, illus. (p. 1369)
Berkesch, Dennis. Connecting with Gods Love. (p. 358)
Berkey, William A. money question. the legal tender paper monetary system of the United States. an analysis of the specie basis or bank currency system, & of the legal tender paper money System ... (p. 1164)
Berkhof, Louis. Manual of Christian Doctrine, Second Edition. (p. 1089)
Berkin, Carol, jt. auth. see Imbarrato, Susan Clair.
Berkley, Elizabeth. Ask Elizabeth: Real Answers to Everything You Secretly Wanted to Ask about Love, Friends, Your Body... & Life in General. (p. 106)
Berkley, Shea. Fallen Prince. (p. 566)
Berkner, Kathrin, jt. auth. see Yankoglu, Berrin A.
Berkner, Laurie. Laurie Berkner Songbook. (p. 980)
Berkowitz, Barbara. Mouse in the House. (p. 1182)
—Talent Show. (p. 1701)
Berkowitz, Jacob. Jurassic Poop: What Dinosaurs (and Others) Left Behind. Mack, Steve, illus. (p. 937)
—Out of This World: The Amazing Search for an Alien Earth. (p. 1311)
Berkshire, Mary Ann. Black Glove. (p. 196)
—Black Glove Rises. (p. 196)
—Midnight Scream: The Black Glove Book 3. (p. 1139)
Berkson, Suzanne Raphael, illus. see Singer, Isaac Bashevis.
Berlan, Kathryn. Andrew's Amazing Monsters. (p. 72)
Berland, Howard & Polsky, Milton E. Anytime. (p. 91)
—Halloween. (p. 737)
—Holiday. (p. 788)
Berlatsky, Noah. Abortion. (p. 5)
—America's Prisons. (p. 64)
—Animal Rights. Greenhaven Press Staff, ed. (p. 79)
—Anti-Semitism. Greenhaven Press Editors, ed. (p. 89)
—Anti-Semitism. Greenhaven Press Editors & Gale Editors, eds. (p. 89)
—Assassination of Martin Luther King Jr. (p. 107)
—Biodiversity. Greenhaven Press Editors, ed. (p. 188)
—Capital Punishment. (p. 262)
—Catholic Church. (p. 280)
—Celebrity Culture. (p. 285)
—China. (p. 306)
—Cuba. (p. 388)
—Darfur. Greenhaven Press Staff, ed. (p. 406)
—Democratic Party. Greenhaven Press Staff, ed. (p. 425)
—Does the U. S. Two-Party System Still Work? (p. 460)
—Does the World Hate the U. S. ? (p. 460)
—Genetic Engineering. (p. 660)
—Global Financial Crisis. (p. 684)
—H1N1 Flu. (p. 734)
—Hiv/aids. (p. 786)
—Homosexuality. (p. 794)
—Imprisonment. (p. 862)
—Manufacturing Jobs in the U. S. Greenhaven Press Staff, ed. (p. 1089)
—Netiquette & Online Ethics. (p. 1242)
—North & South Korea. Greenhaven Press Editors, ed. (p. 1264)
—Presidential Powers. (p. 1397)
—Republican Party. Greenhaven Press Staff, ed. (p. 1462)
—Social Networking. (p. 1604)
—Sri Lanka. Greenhaven Press Editors & Gale Editors, eds. (p. 1637)
—Stalin's Great Purge. (p. 1638)

—Syria. Greenhaven Press Staff, ed. (p. 1693)
—Taliban. (p. 1703)
—U. S. Intelligence Community. (p. 1806)
—Voting Rights. Greenhaven Press Staff, ed. (p. 1850)
—War on Terror. (p. 1858)
—Water. (p. 1862)
—Water & Ice. (p. 1862)
—Working Women. (p. 1953)
Berlatsky, Noah, ed. see Carroll, Jamuna.
Berlatsky, Noah, ed. Does the World Hate the U. S. ? (p. 460)
—East Pakistan. (p. 498)
—Genetic Engineering. (p. 660)
—Hiv/aids. (p. 786)
—Inflation. (p. 873)
—Interracial America. (p. 880)
—Media Violence. (p. 1118)
—Rap Music. (p. 1439)
—Social Networking. (p. 1604)
—War on Terror. (p. 1858)
Berleth, Richard. Samuel's Choice. Watling, James, illus. (p. 1509)
Berlin, Bill & Berlin, Susan. Kvetch Who Stole Hanukkah Welling, Peter, illus. (p. 968)
Berlin, Eric. Potato Chip Puzzles: The Puzzling World of Winston Breen. (p. 1388)
—Puzzler's Mansion: The Puzzling World of Winston Breen. (p. 1421)
—Puzzling World of Winston Breen. (p. 1421)
Berlin, Irving. Easter Parade. McCue, Lisa, illus. (p. 499)
—White Christmas. Hague, Michael, illus. (p. 1912)
Berlin, Rose Mary, illus. see Capucilli, Alyssa Satin.
Berlin, Rose Mary, illus. see Carpenter Czerw, Nancy.
Berlin, Rose Mary, illus. see Czerw, Nancy Carpenter.
Berlin, Rose Mary, illus. see Ryals, Katherine.
Berlin, Susan, jt. auth. see Berlin, Bill.
Berlinger, Nancy A., illus. see Templeton, Donna L.
Berlitz Editors. Hebrew Phrase Book. (p. 761)
Berlitz Kids Editors, creator. 1000 German Words. (p. 2001)
Berlitz Kids Staff, contrib. by. 1000 Arabic Words. (p. 2001)
Berlitz Publishing. French Flash Cards. (p. 635)
—Spanish Flash Cards. (p. 1621)
Berlitz Publishing Staff. Chinese Flash Cards. (p. 307)
Berlitz Publishing Staff, creator. 1000 Japanese Words. (p. 2001)
Berlitz Publishing Staff, ed. Spanish. (p. 1620)
Berman, Ali. Misdirected: A Novel. (p. 1150)
Berman, Gina Dalpra. Remembering Pets: A Book for Children Who Have Lost a Special Friend. Schneider, Barbara Hoss, illus. (p. 1459)
Berman, Jax, compiled by. Friends: the Family We Choose (Mini Book) (p. 639)
Berman, Laura. Passion Prescription: Ten Weeks to Your Best Sex - Ever! (p. 1327)
Berman, Len. 25 Greatest Baseball Players of All Time. (p. 1996)
—And Nobody Got Hurt! The World's Weirdest, Wackiest True Sports Stories. Gamble, Kent, illus. (p. 71)
—And Nobody Got Hurt 2! The World's Weirdest, Wackiest Most Amazing True Sports Stories. Gamble, Kent, illus. (p. 71)
—Greatest Moments in Sports: Upsets & Underdogs. (p. 720)
Berman, Linda, illus. see Penix, Sherry.
Berman, Melanie & Grishaver, Joel Lurie. My Weekly Sidrah. (p. 1221)
Berman, Neil, jt. auth. see Berman, Valerie.
Berman, Paul, ed. see Sandburg, Carl.
Berman, Rachel, illus. see Beiser, Tim.
Berman, Ron. Biz. (p. 194)
—Fashion. (p. 575)
—Food. (p. 612)
—Future Stars of America. (p. 651)
—Houston Rockets. (p. 804)
—Innovators. (p. 875)
—Kid from Courage. (p. 951)
—Los Angeles Lakers. (p. 1053)
—Sports. (p. 1632)
—Who's Got Next? Future Leaders of America. (p. 1920)
Berman, Ron & McFadden, Stephen. T-Lloyd: In the Trenches. (p. 1694)
Berman, Ruth. American Bison. (p. 60)
—Let's Look at Bats. (p. 998)
—Let's Look at Brown Bears. (p. 998)
—Sharks. (p. 1562)
Berman, Seryl. Around the Shabbos Table. Binus, Ari, illus. (p. 100)
Berman, Steve. Speaking Out: LGBTQ Youth Stand Up. (p. 1623)
Berman, Valerie & Berman, Neil. Bubba Goes to New York: Bubba Travel Series. (p. 233)
Bermann, Flemming. Global Warming for Young Minds: A Global Warming & Sustainability Guide for Children. (p. 685)
Bermejo, Hilbert, illus. see Smith, Mary L.
Bermiss, Aamir Lee, jt. auth. see Scholastic, Inc. Staff.
Bermudez, Raymund, illus. see Sherman, M. Zachary & Lee, Raymund.
Bern, Dave. Best Friends. (p. 169)
Bernabe, Marc. Japones en Vinetas: Curso Basico de Japones a Traves del Manga. March, Guillermo et al, illus. (p. 909)
Bernabe, Tabitha Victoria, illus. see Bernabe, Victor.
Bernabe, Victor. What to Be When I Grow Up. Bernabe, Tabitha Victoria, illus. (p. 1894)
Bernadin, James, illus. see Sobol, Donald J.
Bernadine, Joyce. Teeth Keepers. (p. 1715)
Bernadkin, Mila, jt. auth. see Krueger, Susan L.
Bernado, Jordi, photos by see Varini, Felice.
Bernal, Estela. Can You See Me Now? (p. 259)
Bernal, Mitchell. Skelanimals: Dead Animals Need Love Too Bernal, Mitchell, illus. (p. 1584)
Bernal, Natalia, jt. auth. see Dobbins, Jan.
Bernal, Rafael, illus. see Hoffmann, E. T. A.
Bernal, Richard, illus. see King-Smith, Dick & Fox Busters Ltd. Staff.
Bernal, Sandra Marie. I Want a Pand. (p. 847)
—Wish: Johnny's Story. Merriman, Christi, illus. (p. 1940)
Bernal, Victor Garcia, illus. see Barajas Mariscal, Libia E. & Mariscal, Libia Barajas.
Bernard, C. E. B., illus. see Hamlin, John.
Bernard, Catherine. Celtic Mythology. Bock, William Sauts, illus. (p. 286)
—Celtic Mythology Rocks! Bock, William Sauts, illus. (p. 286)
—E. B. White: Spinner of Webs & Tales. (p. 492)
Bernard, Catherine J. British Empire & Queen Victoria in World History. (p. 229)
Bernard, Cecilia. Inside Divergent: The Initiate's World. (p. 876)
Bernard, Courtney, illus. see Mullarkey, Lisa & Mullarkey, John.
Bernard, Donna, illus. see Sitton, Rebecca.
Bernard, Evslin. Heroes, Gods & Monsters of the Greek Myths. (p. 773)
Bernard, Fred & Roca, François. Jesús Betz. Fortier-Durand, Ghislaine & Dehesa, Juana Inés, trs. (p. 915)
Bernard, Fred, et al. Comedia de Los Ogros. (p. 347)
Bernard, Greg. Alpha Summer. (p. 48)
Bernard, Jan. Daniel Radcliffe. (p. 405)
—Ice Cream Before the Store. McGeehan, Dan, illus. (p. 850)
—Justin Bieber. (p. 940)
—Peanut Butter Before the Store. McGeehan, Dan, illus. (p. 1332)
—Toothpaste Before the Store. McGeehan, Dan, illus. (p. 1768)
Bernard, Janice. Gum. (p. 731)
Bernard, M. My First Mass Book. (p. 1207)
Bernard, Margaret Mitchell. Kate & the Family Tree. Duncan, Shirley, ed. (p. 944)
Bernard, Norah S. CLIVE & BRIE. (p. 333)
Bernard, Romily. Find Me. (p. 587)
—Remember Me. (p. 1459)
Bernard, Shane K. Cajuns & Their Acadian Ancestors: A Young Reader's History. (p. 252)
Bernard, Stephanie. Using Cursive Today (p. 1828)
Bernard, Teko & Wilson, Wayne L. Hoop Kid from Elmdale Park. Diaz, Gabriel, illus. (p. 795)
Bernard Westcott, Nadine, illus. see Bagley, Conor.
Bernard Westcott, Nadine, illus. see Hoberman, Mary Ann.
Bernard Westcott, Nadine, illus. see Miller, Pat.
Bernard Westcott, Nadine, illus. see Reid, Rob.
Bernard, Yves & Fredette, Nathalie. Guide de la Musique du Monde. (p. 730)
Bernardi, Bill. Hockey Sticker Activity Book: Fun, Facts, Puzzles & Ice-Cool Action. (p. 787)
Bernardi, Philip & Havens, Diane. Twice upon a Time. (p. 1801)
Bernardin, James, illus. see Alcott, Louisa May.
Bernardin, James, illus. see Chand, Candy.
Bernardin, James, illus. see Cooney, Doug.
Bernardin, James, illus. see Corey, Shana.
Bernardin, James, illus. see Guy, Ginger Foglesong.
Bernardin, James, illus. see Haddix, Margaret Peterson.
Bernardin, James, illus. see Kimmel, Eric A.
Bernardin, James, illus. see Kinsey-Warnock, Natalie.
Bernardin, James, illus. see Numeroff, Laura Joffe.
Bernardin, James, illus. see Plehal, Christopher J.
Bernardin, James, illus. see Sobol, Donald J.
Bernardin, James, illus. see Star, Nancy.
Bernardin, James, illus. see Walburg, Lori.
Bernardini, Cristian, illus. see Braun, Eric.
Bernardini, Cristian, illus. see Loewen, Nancy & Braun, Eric.
Bernardini, Cristian, illus. see Loewen, Nancy & Gunderson, Jessica.
Bernardini, Cristian, illus. see Loewen, Nancy, et al.
Bernardini, Cristian, illus. see Loewen, Nancy.
Bernard-Nollins, Sonya M. Here I Stand: A Musical History of African Americans in Battle Creek, Michigan. (p. 770)
Bernardo, Anilu. Dia con Mis Tias: A Day with My Aunts. Rodriguez, Christina, illus. (p. 433)
—Fitting In. (p. 599)
—Quedando Bien. Sanmiguel, Rosario, tr. from ENG. (p. 1424)
Bernardy, Catherine J., et al. Let's Investigate (p. 998)
Bernasconi, Pablo. Zoo de Joaquin. (p. 1989)
Bernasconi, Pablo, illus. see McKy, Katie.
Bernasconi, Pablo, jt. auth. see Rodkin, Henry H.
Bernat, Jeff. I'm NOT Complaining, Just Explaining! (p. 859)
Bernatene, Poly. Sorcerer's Apprentice. (p. 1614)
—Which Witch's Wand Works? (p. 1911)
Bernatene, Poly, illus. see Bracegirdle, P. J.
Bernatene, Poly, illus. see Crow, Kristyn.
Bernatene, Poly, illus. see Emmett, Jonathan & Dunn, David H.
Bernatene, Poly, illus. see Emmett, Jonathan.
Bernatene, Poly, illus. see Folgueira, Rodrigo.
Bernatene, Poly, illus. see Hao, K. T.
Bernatene, Poly, illus. see Strathie, Chae.
Bernatene, Poly, illus. see West, Jacqueline.
Bernatene, Poly, jt. auth. see Saracino, Luciano.
Bernath, Stefen. Common Weeds. (p. 349)
—Trees of the Northeast. (p. 1784)
Bernay, Emma. Judaism. (p. 930)
Bernay, Emma, ed. Homosexuality. (p. 794)
—Television. (p. 1716)
Bernd & Richter, Susan. I See You Through My Heart. (p. 845)
Bernd, Penners, illus. see Lohlein, Henning.
Berndl, Klaus & Hattstein, Markus. Contemporary World: From 1945 to the 21st Century. (p. 360)
Berndt, Clarence & Rathmann, Rodney L. Bible History: In the Words of Holy Scripture: With Illustrations, Maps, & Notes. (p. 175)
Berndt, Clarence, ed. Living in Christ. (p. 1041)
Berne, Emma. What Are Graphic Novels? (p. 1879)
Berne, Emma Carlson. Bays. (p. 147)
—Chameleons. (p. 289)
—Coyotes. (p. 374)
—Did Christopher Columbus Really Discover America? And Other Question about the New World. (p. 436)
—Did Christopher Columbus Really Discover America? And Other Questions about the New World. (p. 436)
—Dung Beetles: Stronger Than Ten Men! (p. 490)
—Flesh Flies. (p. 603)
—Frida Kahlo: Groundbreaking Artist. (p. 637)
—Global Warming & Climate Change: Current Issues. (p. 685)
—Hard to Get. (p. 748)
—Hills. (p. 780)
—Hot! Heat Energy. (p. 801)
—Hummingbirds. (p. 826)
—Jewelry Tips & Tricks. Heschke, Elena, illus. (p. 917)
—Lakes. (p. 972)
—Laura Ingalls Wilder. (p. 980)
—Methamphetamine. (p. 1130)
—Nail Care Tips & Tricks. Heschke, Elena, illus. (p. 1227)
—Never Let You Go. (p. 1243)
—Opossums. (p. 1300)
—Paris & Nicky Hilton. (p. 1324)
—Plains. (p. 1366)
—Presidency of Theodore Roosevelt: Leading from the Bully Pulpit (p. 1396)
—Raccoons. (p. 1430)
—Rats: Biting Through Concrete! (p. 1440)
—Ravens. (p. 1441)
—Secrets of Earth. (p. 1545)
—Secrets of Mercury. (p. 1545)
—Secrets of Venus. (p. 1546)
—Today's U. S. Marines (p. 1761)
—Totally Wacky Facts about Exploring Space. (p. 1771)
—Totally Wacky Facts about Space. (p. 1771)
—Under Pressure. (p. 1813)
—What Are Graphic Novels? (p. 1879)
—What's Your Story, Abraham Lincoln? (p. 1900)
—What's Your Story, Cesar Chavez? (p. 1900)
—What's Your Story, Helen Keller? (p. 1900)
—What's Your Story, Jackie Robinson? (p. 1900)
—William Shakespeare: Playwright & Poet. (p. 1933)
—Wood Frogs: Back from the Dead! (p. 1949)
—Yellow Jackets. (p. 1970)
Berne, Emma Carlson, jt. auth. see Destiny, A.
Berne, Emma Carlson, jt. auth. see Maddox, Jake.
Berne, Emma Carlson & Carlson Berne, Emma. Chameleons. (p. 289)
—Dung Beetles. (p. 490)
—Hummingbirds. (p. 826)
Berne, Emma Carlson & Hodge, Marie. Helen Keller: Courage in Darkness. (p. 763)
Berne, Jennifer. Calvin Can't Fly: The Story of a Bookworm Birdie. Bendis, Keith, illus. (p. 255)
—Calvin, Look Out! A Bookworm Birdie Gets Glasses. Bendis, Keith, illus. (p. 255)
—Manfish: A Story of Jacques Cousteau. Puybaret, Éric, illus. (p. 1087)
—Manfish: The Story of Jacques Cousteau. Puybaret, Éric, illus. (p. 1087)
—Nighty-Night, Sleep Tight. Walker, David, illus. (p. 1255)
—On a Beam of Light: A Story of Albert Einstein. Radunsky, Vladimir, illus. (p. 1288)
—Writing-Rich High School Classroom: Engaging Students in the Writing Workshop. (p. 1965)
Berne, Stanley. Empire Sweets: How I Learned to Live & Love in the Greatest Empire on Earth. (p. 521)
—Legal Tender - Or - It's All About Money! (p. 988)
Berneger, Marcia. Buster the Little Garbage Truck. Zimmer, Kevin, illus. (p. 245)
Berner, Beth E. & Riggs, Jenna. Follow That Bee. (p. 612)
Berner, Paulette L., illus. see Berner, R. Thomas.
Berner, R. Thomas. Cottontails & the Jackrabbits. Berner, Paulette L., illus. (p. 369)
Berner, Rotraut Susanne. Definitely Not for Little Ones: Some Very Grimm Fairy-Tale Comics Tanaka, Shelley, tr. from GER. (p. 424)
—Hound & Hare Tanaka, Shelley, tr. from GER. (p. 802)
—In the Town All Year 'Round. Konings, Neeltje & Elliott, Nick, trs. from GER. (p. 867)
Berner, Rotraut Susanne, illus. see Aldana, Patricia, ed.
Berner, Rotraut Susanne, illus. see Richter, Jutta.
Bernet, Marti L. Remember... I Love You! (p. 1459)
Bernet, Roberto, tr. see Isau, Ralf.
Bernhard, Durga. While You Are Sleeping. (p. 1911)
—While You Are Sleeping. Bernhard, Durga, illus. (p. 1911)
Bernhard, Durga, illus. see Lehman-Wilzig, Tami.
Bernhard, Durga Yael. Around the World in One Shabbat: Jewish People Celebrate the Sabbath Together. (p. 101)
—Just Like Me, Climbing a Tree: Exploring Trees Around the World. (p. 939)
Bernhard, Durga Yael, illus. see Jules, Jacqueline.
Bernhard, Durga Yael, illus. see Lehman-Wilzig, Tami.
Bernhard, Durga Yael, illus. see Simpson, Martha Seif.
Bernhardt, Michael J., jt. auth. see Spurlin, Barbara.
Bernhardt, William. Princess Alice & the Dreadful Dragon. McGhee, Kerry, illus. (p. 1402)
Bernheimer, Kate. Girl in the Castle Inside the Museum. Ceccoli, Nicoletta, illus. (p. 678)
—Girl Who Wouldn't Brush Her Hair. Parker, Jake, illus. (p. 679)
—Lonely Book. Sheban, Chris, illus. (p. 1046)
Berni, K. S. Angels of Children: Sarafina Teaches the Importance of Prayer. (p. 75)
Bernice, Janet. Tiny Talks: I Will Follow God's Plan for Me (p. 1756)
Bernieres, Louis De, see de Bernières, Louis.
Bernier-Grand, Carmen. Diego: Bigger Than Life Diaz, David, illus. (p. 437)
Bernier-Grand, Carmen T. Cesar: Si, Se Puede! Yes, We Can! Diaz, David, illus. (p. 288)
—Frida: Viva la Vida! - Long Live Life! Kahlo, Frida, illus. (p. 637)
—Our Lady of Guadalupe Engel, Tonya, illus. (p. 1309)
—Picasso: I the King, Yo el Rey Diaz, David, illus. (p. 1354)
—Sonia Sotomayor: Supreme Court Justice Gonzalez, Thomas, illus. (p. 1612)
—Sonia Sotomayor: Jueza de la Corte Suprema Gonzalez, Thomas, illus. (p. 1612)
Berning, Terri J. Grace Alone Is Enough Arling, Jackie L., illus. (p. 704)
Bernoudy, Jasmine L. Horrible Monster. (p. 798)
Bernreuter, Bob J. Gift. (p. 674)
Berns, J. M., illus. see Chara, Kathleen A., et al.
Berns, Joel M., illus. see Chara, Kathleen A. & Chara, Paul J.
Bernson, Janet. Un-Masking the Soul: A Creative Approach to Working with the Masks in the Mirror (p. 1811)
Bernstein, Charles. Sophist. (p. 1613)
Bernstein, Dan. Tortoise & the Hare Race Again. Glass, Andrew, illus. (p. 1771)
Bernstein, Danielle V. Magic in a Mermaid's Tear. (p. 1072)
Bernstein, Daryl. Better Than a Lemonade Stand! Small Business Ideas for Kids. (p. 172)
—Better Than a Lemonade Stand! Small Business Ideas for Kids. Husberg, Rob, illus. (p. 172)
Bernstein, David. Advertising Outdoors: Watch This Space! (p. 25)
Bernstein, David D. Enchanted Rope. (p. 523)
Bernstein, Gabo León, illus. see Guerra, Elisa Puricelli.
Bernstein, Gabriel León, illus. see Guerra, Elisa Puricelli.
Bernstein, Galia, illus. see Naish, Darren.
Bernstein, Galia, illus. see Schaefer, Carole Lexa.
Bernstein, Galia, illus. see Taylor, Barbara.
Bernstein, Galia, illus. see Walker, Richard.
Bernstein, Jonathan. Bridget Wilder: Spy-In-Training. (p. 227)
Bernstein, Jordan. Bible According to Grandpa. Doehring, Aurora, illus. (p. 175)
Bernstein, Kei. Horsey up & Down: A Book of Opposites. Church, Caroline Jayne, illus. (p. 800)
Bernstein, Laurie & Helm, Joanna. Penny the Penguin Has Pku. (p. 1338)
Bernstein, Leonard. Young People's Concerts. Gottlieb, Jack, ed. (p. 1979)
Bernstein, Nina. Magic by the Book (p. 1072)
Bernstein, Owen. My Turtle & Me. Thompson, Carol, illus. (p. 1220)
Bernstein, Richard. Girl Named Faithful Plum: A True Story of a Dancer from China & How She Achieved Her Dream. (p. 678)
—Girl Named Faithful Plum: The True Story of a Dancer from China & How She Achieved Her Dream. (p. 678)
—Girl Named Faithful Plum. (p. 678)
Bernstein, Robert & Miller, Jack E. Aquaman (p. 93)
Bernstein, Ross. Barry Bonds. (p. 140)
—Shaquille O'Neal. (p. 1561)
—Sports Great Daunte Culpepper. (p. 1632)
Bernstein, Samuel. Mr. Confidential: The Man, His Magazine & the Movieland Massacre That Changed Hollywood Forever. (p. 1184)
Bernstein, Susan H. N. E. Pominonous Epstein & Change. (p. 492)
—E. Pominonous Epstein Minds His Mind. (p. 492)
Bernstein, Vivian. America's Story. (p. 64)
Berocay, Roy. Babu. (p. 124)
—Pateando Lunas. Soulier, Daniel, illus. (p. 1328)
Berquist, Laura M. Harp & Laurel Wreath: Poetry & Dictation for the Classical Curriculum. (p. 749)
Berquist, Nita G. Song of Pounce: Homestead Harmonies. (p. 1611)
Berra, Lawrence Yogi & Ferdenzi, Til. Behind the Plate. (p. 160)
Berra, Yogi. Let's Go, Yankees! Moore, Danny, illus. (p. 998)
Berran, Susan. Bonez. (p. 209)
—Chomp'd. (p. 310)
—Lick'd. (p. 1007)
—Toe Jamm'D (p. 1761)
Berres, et al. Sea Hunt. (p. 1534)
Beresford, Geoffrey C. & Rockett, Andrew M. Finite Mathematics. (p. 589)
Berresford, J. R. Gerald Giraffe's Garage. Parmelee, George, illus. (p. 666)
Berresford, Kay Craig. Maggie & Drew Buy a Birthday Present. (p. 1071)
—Maggie & Drew Make a Mess. (p. 1071)
Berrett, Joshua. Louis Armstrong & Paul Whiteman: Two Kings of Jazz. (p. 1058)
Berrett, Pat, photos by see Hoefer, Jacqueline, ed.
Berri, Victoria L. South Carolina: A MyReportLinks. Com Book. (p. 1616)
Berridge-Burley, Niamh. Shoes That Couldn't Stop Dancing. (p. 1568)
Berrill, Jack. Under the Friday Night Lights! A Gil Thorp Football Collection. (p. 1813)
Berringer, Nick, illus. see Brandreth, Gyles.
Berrios, Frank. Adventure in Arendelle. RH Disney Staff, illus. (p. 14)
—Bad Weather! (DC Super Friends) Beavers, Ethen, illus. (p. 132)
—Big Book of the DC Super Friends. Golden Books, illus. (p. 179)
—Big-Screen Blockbusters! (Disney/Pixar) RH Disney Staff, illus. (p. 183)
—Car Crazy! (Disney/Pixar Cars) RH Disney Staff, illus. (p. 265)
—Cars Animated Short Reader. (p. 272)
—Day in the Sun. (p. 413)
—Deputy Mater Saves the Day! (Disney/Pixar Cars) RH Disney Staff, illus. (p. 427)
—Disney Infinity: the Ultimate Fan Book! (Disney Infinity) RH Disney Staff, illus. (p. 451)
—Drop Zone! (Disney Planes) RH Disney Staff, illus. (p. 486)
—Easter Buggy. (p. 499)
—Easter Buggy (Disney/Pixar Cars) RH Disney Staff, illus. (p. 499)
—Fast Lane. RH Disney Staff, illus. (p. 576)
—Fire Crew! (p. 590)
—Firefighters! (Disney/Pixar Cars) Random House Disney Staff, illus. (p. 591)
—Football with Dad. Biggs, Brian, illus. (p. 615)
—Full Throttle (Disney/Pixar Cars) RH Disney Staff, illus. (p. 646)
—Fur-Ever Friends! (Disney Princess: Palace Pets) RH Disney Staff, illus. (p. 650)
—Heavy Metal Mater & Other Tall Tales. RH Disney Staff, illus. (p. 761)

—Heroes of the Sky/High-Flying Friends (Disney Planes: Fire & Rescue) RH Disney Staff, illus. (p. 773)
—High Gear! (Disney/Pixar Cars) RH Disney Staff, illus. (p. 777)
—High-Speed Adventures. RH Disney Staff, illus. (p. 778)
—Joy's in Charge! RH Disney Staff, illus. (p. 930)
—Just Wing It! (Disney Planes) RH Disney Staff, illus. (p. 940)
—Let Them Eat Cake! (p. 994)
—Let's Cruise! (p. 995)
—Lightning Loves Racing! (p. 1016)
—Lightning Loves Racing! (Disney/Pixar Cars) RH Disney Staff, illus. (p. 1016)
—Mater to the Rescue! (Disney/Pixar Cars) RH Disney Staff, illus. (p. 1104)
—Mater's Amazin' Adventures (Disney/Pixar Cars) RH Disney Staff, illus. (p. 1104)
—Mater's Awesome Easter (Disney/Pixar Cars) RH Disney Staff & Cohee, Ron, illus. (p. 1104)
—Monster Truck Mater (Disney/Pixar Cars) RH Disney Staff, illus. (p. 1168)
—Penny of the Pyramids. (p. 1338)
—Penny of the Pyramids (Mr. Peabody & Sherman) Robinson, Bill, illus. (p. 1338)
—Pirate Puzzles! (SpongeBob SquarePants) Golden Books, illus. (p. 1363)
—Plane Pals. (p. 1367)
—Playful Pets! (Disney Princess: Palace Pets) RH Disney Staff, illus. (p. 1372)
—Power Play! (Disney Infinity) RH Disney Staff, illus. (p. 1390)
—Pretty As a Picture! (Disney Princess) RH Disney Staff, illus. (p. 1398)
—Radiator Springs 500. RH Disney Staff, illus. (p. 1432)
—Ready for Action! (Disney/Pixar Cars) RH Disney Staff, illus. (p. 1447)
—Shakin' in My Tires! RH Disney Staff & Cohee, Ron, illus. (p. 1559)
—Sisters Forever (Disney Frozen) RH Disney Staff, illus. (p. 1581)
—Take to the Sky! RH Disney Staff, illus. (p. 1697)
—Time Travel Mater (Disney/Pixar Cars) RH Disney Staff, illus. (p. 1753)
—To Protect & Serve. Random House Disney Staff, illus. (p. 1759)
—Tow Truck Trouble-Lights Out! RH Disney Staff, illus. (p. 1773)
—Tractor Trouble (Disney/Pixar Cars) RH Disney Staff, illus. (p. 1775)
—Very Mater Christmas (Disney/Pixar Cars) RH Disney Staff, illus. (p. 1838)
—Vote for Mater! (Disney/Pixar Cars) RH Disney Staff, illus. (p. 1850)
—Welcome to Radiator Springs. RH Disney Staff, illus. (p. 1873)
Berrios, Frank, jt. auth. see Auerbach, Annie.
Berrios, Frank, jt. auth. see Awdry, W.
Berrios, Frank, jt. auth. see Golden Books.
Berrios, Frank, jt. auth. see RH Disney Staff.
Berrios, Frank, jt. auth. see Wilson, Mary.
Berrios, Frank & Mangual, Ines. Join the Band! (Fresh Beat Band) Golden Books Staff, illus. (p. 924)
Berrios, Frank & RH Disney Staff. Cars. Disney Storybook Artists Staff, illus. (p. 271)
—Shapes, Colors, Counting & More! (Disney/Pixar Cars) RH Disney Staff, illus. (p. 1560)
—Snow White & the Seven Dwarfs. Disney Storybook Artists Staff, illus. (p. 1600)
—Travel Buddies. Golden Books Staff, illus. (p. 1780)
Berrow, G. M. Applejack & the Honest-To-Goodness Switcheroo. (p. 92)
—My Little Pony: Fluttershy & the Fine Furry Friends Fair. (p. 1213)
—My Little Pony: Discord & the Ponyville Players Dramarama. (p. 1213)
—My Little Pony: Applejack & the Honest-To-Goodness Switcheroo. (p. 1213)
—My Little Pony: Equestria Girls: Through the Mirror. (p. 1213)
—My Little Pony: Pinkie Pie & the Rockin' Ponypalooza Party! (p. 1213)
—My Little Pony: Rarity & the Curious Case of Charity. (p. 1213)
—Pinkie Pie & the Rockin' Ponypalooza Party! (p. 1360)
—Rainbow Dash & the Daring Do Double Dare. (p. 1435)
—Rarity & the Curious Case of Charity. (p. 1439)
—Twilight Sparkle & the Crystal Heart Spell. (p. 1801)
Berry, Andrea. Goalie: The Dynamite Diaries. (p. 687)
Berry, Andrew & Wallace, Alfred Russel. Infinite Tropics: An Alfred Russel Wallace Anthology. Berry, Andrew, ed. (p. 873)
Berry, Bob. Ancient Times: Step-by-Step Instructions for 18 Ancient Characters & Civilizations. (p. 70)
—How to Draw Magical, Monstrous & Mythological Creatures. (p. 818)
—Learn to Draw Pirates, Vikings & Ancient Civilizations: Step-By-step Instructions for Drawing Ancient Characters, Civilizations, Creatures, & More! (p. 983)
Berry, Bob, illus. see Marsocci, Joey & DeBlasio, Allison.
Berry, Bob, illus. see Phan, Sandy.
Berry, Bob, illus. see Torres, Jickie.
Berry, Bob, jt. auth. see Walter Foster Publishing.
Berry, Bob & Destefano, Merrie. How to Draw Magical, Monstrous & Mythological Creatures: Discover the Magic of Drawing More Than 20 Legendary Folklore, Fantasy, & Horror Characters. (p. 818)
Berry, Breanna. Poodles. (p. 1383)
Berry, Carolyn. Buster Tells It All: Stories from Pony Creek Ranch. Cash, Eric, illus. (p. 245)
Berry, Carrie. Diary of Carrie Berry: A Confederate Girl (p. 435)
Berry, Carrie, et al. First-Person Histories (p. 596)
Berry, Connie Lee. Adventure in Africa. (p. 14)
—Criminal in the Caymans. (p. 382)
—Mystery in Mexico. (p. 1224)
—Pirates in Paradise. (p. 1363)
—Treasure in Tahiti. (p. 1781)
Berry, Diane Lambright. Port City Pirates. (p. 1386)
Berry, Eileen M. Buttercup Hill. Harrald-Pilz, Marilee, illus. (p. 247)
—Haiku on Your Shoes. Regan, Dana, illus. (p. 735)
—Looking for Home. Manning, Maurie J., illus. (p. 1051)
Berry, Eileen M., retold by. Sticky Flies, Whirling Squirrels, & Plucky Ducks. (p. 1650)
Berry, Erick. Valiant Captive. (p. 1830)
Berry, Gaynor. Where Are My Pants? A Hide-and-Seek Book W/ Flaps & Slots. Berry, Gaynor, illus. (p. 1906)
Berry, George B. Compassionate Side of a Common Man: Love Poems from the Heart (p. 352)
Berry, Gloria Jean. Open the Door to Great Teacher-Student Rapport: Quick & Easy Classroom Motivators. (p. 1299)
Berry, Holly, illus. see Buzzeo, Toni.
Berry, Holly, illus. see Parker, Marjorie Blain & Matisse, Henri.
Berry, Holly, illus. see Rovetch, L. Bob.
Berry, Holly, illus. see Squires, Janet.
Berry, Holly, illus. see Stanley, Diane.
Berry, Holly, illus. see Weeks, Sarah.
Berry, Jacqueline. Teeny Tiny Topper, the Grasshopper. (p. 1715)
Berry, James. Classic Poems to Read Aloud. Mayhew, James, illus. (p. 328)
—Nest Full of Stars. Bryan, Ashley, illus. (p. 1242)
Berry, Joni. Tent Maker. (p. 1720)
Berry, Joy. Achieve Goals. (p. 8)
—Bad Habits. (p. 131)
—Be a Star. (p. 148)
—Be a Winner. (p. 148)
—Be Assertive. (p. 148)
—Be Beautiful. (p. 148)
—Be Creative. (p. 148)
—Be Happy. (p. 148)
—Be in Control. (p. 148)
—Be Liked. (p. 148)
—Be Organized. (p. 149)
—Be Smart. (p. 149)
—Being Good. (p. 161)
—Being Helpful. (p. 161)
—Being Patient. (p. 161)
—Clean Your Room. (p. 330)
—Criticism & Rejection. (p. 383)
—Fear. (p. 579)
—Feeling Afraid. (p. 580)
—Feeling Angry. (p. 580)
—Fun & Easy Way to Do Your Homework. Bartholomew, illus. (p. 647)
—Fun & Easy Way to Get Good Grades. Bartholomew, illus. (p. 647)
—Get Good Grades. (p. 667)
—Get over It! (p. 668)
—Get over it! Set (p. 668)
—Getting Dressed. (p. 669)
—Good Answers to Tough Questions about Death. (p. 697)
—Good Answers to Tough Questions about Disasters. (p. 697)
—Good Answers to Tough Questions about Divorce. (p. 697)
—Good Answers to Tough Questions about Moving. (p. 697)
—Good Answers to Tough Questions Disasters. Bartholomew, illus. (p. 697)
—Good Answers to Tough Questions Divorce. Bartholomew, illus. (p. 697)
—Good Answers to Tough Questions Moving. Bartholomew, illus. (p. 697)
—Have a Great Future. (p. 754)
—Help Me Be Good about Being a Bad Sport. (p. 765)
—Help Me Be Good about Being Bossy. (p. 765)
—Help Me Be Good about Being Bullied. (p. 765)
—Help Me Be Good about Being Careless. (p. 765)
—Help Me Be Good about Being Forgetful. (p. 765)
—Help Me Be Good about Being Greedy. (p. 765)
—Help Me Be Good about Being Lazy. (p. 765)
—Help Me Be Good about Cheating. (p. 765)
—Help Me Be Good about Gossiping. (p. 765)
—Help Me Be Good about Lying. (p. 765)
—Help Me Be Good about Teasing. (p. 765)
—Help Me Be Good Being a Bad Sport. Bartholomew, illus. (p. 765)
—Help Me Be Good Being Mean. Bartholomew, illus. (p. 765)
—Help Me Be Good Being Selfish. Bartholomew, illus. (p. 765)
—Help Me Be Good Bullying. Bartholomew, illus. (p. 765)
—Help Me Be Good Disobeying. Bartholomew, illus. (p. 765)
—Help Me Be Good Fighting. Bartholomew, illus. (p. 765)
—Help Me Be Good Showing Off. Bartholomew, illus. (p. 765)
—Help Me Be Good Tattling. Bartholomew, illus. (p. 765)
—Help Me Be Good Teasing. Bartholomew, illus. (p. 765)
—Help Me Be Good Whining. Bartholomew, illus. (p. 765)
—I Love Bathtime. Regan, Dana, illus. (p. 841)
—I Love Bedtime. Regan, Dana, illus. (p. 841)
—I Love Being Healthy. Regan, Dana, illus. (p. 841)
—I Love Brothers & Sisters. Regan, Dana, illus. (p. 842)
—I Love Daycare. Regan, Dana, illus. (p. 842)
—I Love Getting Dressed. Regan, Dana, illus. (p. 842)
—I Love Grandmas & Grandpas. Regan, Dana, illus. (p. 842)
—I Love Mealtime. Regan, Dana, illus. (p. 842)
—I Love Mommies & Daddies. Regan, Dana, illus. (p. 842)
—I Love My Friends. Regan, Dana, illus. (p. 842)
—I Love Preschool. Regan, Dana, illus. (p. 842)
—Illness. (p. 857)
—Let's Talk about Being Away from Your Parents. Smith, Maggie, illus. (p. 1001)
—Let's Talk about Being Patient. Smith, Maggie, illus. (p. 1001)
—Let's Talk about Being Shy. Smith, Maggie, illus. (p. 1001)
—Let's Talk about Feeling Afraid. Smith, Maggie, illus. (p. 1001)
—Let's Talk about Feeling Angry. Smith, Maggie, illus. (p. 1001)
—Let's Talk about Feeling Disappointed. Smith, Maggie, illus. (p. 1001)
—Let's Talk about Feeling Jealous. Smith, Maggie, illus. (p. 1001)
—Let's Talk about Feeling Sad. Smith, Maggie, illus. (p. 1001)
—Let's Talk about Getting Hurt. Smith, Maggie, illus. (p. 1001)
—Let's Talk about Needing Attention. Smith, Maggie, illus. (p. 1001)
—Needing Attention. (p. 1239)
—Rude People. (p. 1494)
—Stress. (p. 1667)
—Substance Abuse. (p. 1671)
—Teach Me about Bathtime. (p. 1708)
—Teach Me about Bedtime. (p. 1708)
—Teach Me about Mealtime. (p. 1708)
—Teach Me about Potty Training. (p. 1708)
—Teach Me about Potty Training (Boys) (p. 1708)
—Tough Situations. (p. 1772)
—Trauma. (p. 1780)
—Winning Skills You Can Work It! an Anthology of Six Books. Bartholomew, illus. (p. 1937)
—Work it! Set (p. 1952)
—You Can Go for It! (p. 1974)
—You Can... Work It! Being Smart, Being Creative, Being Assertive, Being in Control, Getting Organized & Attaining Goals! (p. 1974)
Berry, Joy, contrib. by. Go for it! Set. (p. 686)
Berry, Joy Wilt. Book about Being a Bad Sport. (p. 210)
—Book about Being Bossy. (p. 210)
—Book about Being Bullied. (p. 210)
—Book about Being Careless. (p. 210)
—Book about Being Forgetful. (p. 210)
—Book about Being Greedy. (p. 210)
—Book about Being Lazy. (p. 210)
—Book about Being Mean. (p. 210)
—Book about Being Messy. (p. 210)
—Book about Being Rude. (p. 210)
—Book about Being Selfish. (p. 210)
—Book about Being Wasteful. (p. 210)
—Book about Breaking Promise. (p. 210)
—Book about Cheating. (p. 210)
—Book about Complaining. (p. 210)
—Book about Fighting. (p. 210)
—Book about Gossiping. (p. 210)
—Book about Interrupting. (p. 210)
—Book about Lying. (p. 210)
—Book about Overdoing It. (p. 210)
—Book about Showing Off. (p. 210)
—Book about Stealing. (p. 210)
—Book about Tattling. (p. 210)
—Book about Teasing. (p. 210)
—Book about Throwing Tantrums. (p. 210)
—Book about Whining. (p. 210)
—Children's Book about Being Destructive. (p. 303)
—Children's Book about Disobeying. (p. 303)
Berry, Julie. All the Truth That's in Me. (p. 46)
—Amaranth Enchantment. (p. 52)
—Scandalous Sisterhood of Prickwillow Place. (p. 1519)
—Secondhand Charm. (p. 1540)
Berry, Julie Gardner. All the Truth That's in Me. (p. 46)
Berry, Julie Gardner & Gardner, Sally Faye. Curse of the Bizarro Beetle. (p. 394)
—Rat Brain Fiasco. (p. 1440)
Berry, Kenosha, ed. see Crockett, Sonja Michelle.
Berry, Kit. Moondance of Stonewylde. (p. 1172)
—Shadows at Stonewylde. (p. 1558)
—Shaman of Stonewylde. (p. 1559)
—Solstice at Stonewylde. (p. 1608)
Berry, Lynne. Curious Demise of a Contrary Cat. LaMarca, Luke, illus. (p. 392)
—Duck Tents. Nakata, Hiroe, illus. (p. 488)
—Pig & Pug. Correll, Gemma, illus. (p. 1357)
—Squid Kid the Magnificent. (p. 1637)
—What Floats in a Moat? Cordell, Matthew, illus. (p. 1884)
Berry, Max, illus. see Saxby, Claire.
Berry, Minta. Building Sets of Ten. Crabtree Publishing Staff, ed. (p. 239)
—Perimeter. Crabtree Publishing Staff, ed. (p. 1343)
Berry, Minta, jt. auth. see Miller, Reagan.
Berry, Nessa. Protectors of Little Africa. (p. 1412)
Berry, Nina. Notorious Pagan Jones. (p. 1268)
—Othermoon. (p. 1306)
—Othersphere. (p. 1306)
Berry, R. A. Buddy's Blue Day. (p. 235)
—I Can Do It by Myself. (p. 835)
Berry, Rick. Step off the Mat. (p. 1648)
Berry, Rob & Duey, Kathleen. Smart Kids Allowance System: Step-by-Step Money Management Guidebook. Bartholomew, illus. (p. 1592)
Berry, Ron. 123s of How I Love You. Sharp, Chris, illus. (p. 2000)
—Beware the Haunted House. Sharp, Chris, illus. (p. 173)
—Can You Make Peter Rabbit Giggle? Sharp, Chris, illus. (p. 259)
—Can You Make Santa Giggle? (p. 259)
—Can You Roar Like a Lion? Sharp, Chris, illus. (p. 259)
—Charlie the Can-Do Choo-Choo! Sharp, Chris, illus. (p. 293)
—Easter Bunny's Colorful Day! (p. 499)
—It Was a Dark Dark Night. Sharp, Chris, illus. (p. 894)
—Let Your Light Shine. (p. 994)
—Look for the Rainbow! Sharp, Chris, illus. (p. 1049)
—My Boo Boo BK. (p. 1198)
—My First Family Photo Album. Sharp, Chris, illus. (p. 1206)
—My Guardian Angel. Sharp, Chris, illus. (p. 1210)
—Rise & Shine! Sharp, Chris, illus. (p. 1474)
—Silly Safari Bus! Sharp, Chris, illus. (p. 1576)
—We Wish You a Merry Christmas. Sharp, Chris, illus. (p. 1868)
—Where Is Daddy? Smart Kids Publishing Staff, ed. (p. 1908)
—Where Is Mommy? Smart Kids Publishing Staff, ed. (p. 1908)
Berry, Ron, jt. auth. see Mead, David.
Berry, Ron & Mead, David. All Aboard! Charlie the Can-Do Choo Choo. Sharp, Chris, illus. (p. 41)
—Little Drummer Boy. Sharp, Chris, illus. (p. 1027)
Berry, Ron & Sharp, Chris. It's Bedtime. Sharp, Chris & Currant, Gary, illus. (p. 896)
Berry, S. L. E. E. Cummings. (p. 492)
—Langston Hughes. (p. 974)
—Voices in Poetry: E. E. Cummings. (p. 1848)
—Voices in Poetry: Emily Dickinson. (p. 1848)
—Voices in Poetry: Langston Hughes. (p. 1848)
Berry, S. L. & Dickinson, Emily. Emily Dickinson. (p. 518)
Berry, Shilo. E-Mails Home. (p. 492)
Berry, Stéphane, prod. Spies in Disguise (p. 1627)
Berry, VacieAnna, illus. see Laible, Steve William, ed.
Berry, Wendell. Whitefoot: A Story from the Center of the World. Te Selle, Davis, illus. (p. 1914)
Berry, Wendell & Rorer, Abigail. Whitefoot: A Story from the Center of the World. Te Selle, Davis, illus. (p. 1914)
Berryhill, Shane. Dragon Island. (p. 477)
Berryman, Chelsea. Missing Pages. (p. 1152)
Berryman, Jerome W. 20 Core Presentations for Spring (p. 1995)
Bersanetti, Sandra, illus. see Bresanetti, Sandra & Bresanetti, S.
Bersanetti, Sandra, illus. see Brignole, Giancarla, tr.
Bersani, Shennen. Achoo! Why Pollen Counts (p. 9)
Bersani, Shennen, illus. see Cohn, Scotti.
Bersani, Shennen, illus. see Curtis, Jennifer Keats & Frederick, J. Adam.
Bersani, Shennen, illus. see Downer, Ann.
Bersani, Shennen, illus. see Fead, Beverlye Hyman, et al.
Bersani, Shennen, illus. see Haas, Kristin, et al.
Bersani, Shennen, illus. see Haas, Kristin.
Bersani, Shennen, illus. see Halfmann, Janet.
Bersani, Shennen, illus. see Harvey, Jeanne Walker.
Bersani, Shennen, illus. see Love, Donna.
Bersani, Shennen, illus. see Meyers, Barbara & Mays, Lydia.
Bersani, Shennen, illus. see Pallotta, Jerry.
Bersani, Shennen, illus. see Prager, Ellen.
Bersani, Shennen, illus. see Tupper Ling, Nancy.
Bersani, Shennen, illus. see Watson, Lori Ann.
Bersani, Shennen, jt. auth. see Filigenzi, Courtney.
Bersma, Danielle & Visscher, Marjoke. Yoga Games for Children: Fun & Fitness with Postures, Movements & Breath. Evans, Amina Marix, tr. from DUT. (p. 1972)
Berson, Harold, illus. see Chase, Mary.
Bersson, Robert & Shoup, Dolores. Stripes & Stars. Bersson, Robert & Trobaugh, Scott, illus. (p. 1667)
Bert, Ruth J. Everyone Called Her Sister Sarah. Westbeld, Kristine, illus. (p. 544)
Bertagna, Julie. Exodus. (p. 548)
Bertagnolli, Daniel. Now You Seed It, Now You Don't. (p. 1269)
—Whooo Turned Out the Lights? Bertagnolli, Daniel, illus. (p. 1920)
Bertanzetti, Eileen Dunn. Poor Pio. (p. 1383)
Bertch, Barbara A., jt. auth. see Bertch, David P.
Bertch, David P. & Bertch, Barbara A. Dynamic Dinosaur of Faith's History: From Christ to 1000 AD. Vol. I Martin, Terry & Martin, Dyna, eds. (p. 491)
Bertelle, Nicoletta, illus. see Giraldo, Maria Loretta.
Berten, Jinny Powers & Holt, Norah. Littsie of Cincinnati. (p. 1039)
Berthel, Alice H. Power Puzzles: John. (p. 1390)
—Power Puzzles: Luke. (p. 1390)
—Power Puzzles: Mark. (p. 1390)
—Power Puzzles: Matthew. (p. 1390)
Berthiaume, Donna M. Our Cool School Zoo Revue. Jirak, Tracey, illus. (p. 1308)
Berthod, Anne, et al. Slumgirl Dreaming: Rubina's Journey to the Stars. (p. 1591)
Berthold, Joy. Peter on Patrol. (p. 1346)
Bertholf, Bret, illus. see Kurzweil, Allen.
Bertier, Anne, creator. Wednesday. (p. 1871)
Bertino, Mike, illus. see Petrella, Angela, et al.
Bertling, Judy. There's Poo on My Shoe. (p. 1731)
Bertola, Ann Marie, et al, contrib. by. Four in the Afternoon. (p. 625)
Bertolet, J. Where Does Christmas Go? (p. 1907)
Bertoletti, John C., et al. How Baseball Managers Use Math. (p. 805)
—How Fashion Designers Use Math. (p. 809)
Bertolina, Angela. Kids' Acting for Brain Surgeons: Everything You Need to Know to Get Your Kid into Show Business. (p. 952)
Bertolini, Rebecca. Wacky World of Henry Wiloby. (p. 1852)
Bertolo, Constantino, ed. Antologia de Relatos Policiacos. (p. 89)
Bertolucci, Federico, illus. see Bordiglioni, Stephen & Bordiglioni, Stefano.
Berton, Judy. City Dancin' Dancin' at Peppy's. Hernandez, Steven, illus. (p. 323)
Berton, Judy & Guimond, Rick. Do a Dance Picture Book. (p. 456)
Berton, Pierre. Exploring the Frozen North: An Omnibus (p. 553)
—Golden Trail: The Story of the Klondike Rush (p. 695)
—Great Klondike Gold Rush: An Omnibus (p. 716)
Berton, Suzanne. Special Family. (p. 1623)
Bertone, Angela Q. Mary's Christmas. (p. 1101)
Bertoni, Oliver, illus. see Rochelin, Ghyslaine.
Bertouille, Ariane. Otis & Alice Favreau, Marie-Claude, illus. (p. 1307)
Bertozzi, Nick. Diabetes & Me: An Essential Guide for Kids & Parents. (p. 433)
—Lewis & Clark. Bertozzi, Nick, illus. (p. 1004)
—Shackleton: Antarctic Odyssey. Bertozzi, Nick, illus. (p. 1556)
Bertozzi, Nick, illus. see Averbeck, Jim.
Bertram, Charles H. Chipped Beef on Toast (S. O. S.) (p. 308)
—Stone Bear. (p. 1652)
Bertram, Debbie, jt. auth. see Bloom, Susan.
Bertram, Debbie & Bloom, Susan. Best Book to Read. Garland, Michael, illus. (p. 168)
—Best Place to Read. (p. 171)
Bertram, Erica. Spirit Heroes: The Adventure Begins. (p. 1628)
—Spirit Heroes & the Story of Hope. (p. 1628)
—Spirit Heroes & the Titan of Terror. (p. 1628)
Bertram, Esther, jt. auth. see Stonehouse, Bernard.
Bertran, Nuria, illus. see Barberi, Marco, et al, trs.
Bertrand, Cécile, illus. see Laouénan, Christine.
Bertrand, Diane Gonzales. Cecilia & Miguel Are Best Friends. Ventura, Gabriela Baeza, tr. (p. 283)
—Dilema de Trino. Castilla, Julia Mercedes, tr. from ENG. (p. 440)

—Empanadas That Abuela Made/Las Empandas Que Hacia la Abuela. Ventura, Gabriela Baeza, tr. (p. 520)
—F Factor. (p. 559)
—Momento de Trino. Sanmiguel, Rosario, tr. from ENG. (p. 1161)
—My Pal Victor. Sweetland, Robert, illus. (p. 1216)
—Ricardo's Race/la Carrera de Ricardo. Viegas-Barros, Rocio, tr. from ENG. (p. 1469)
—Sip, Slurp, Soup Soup/Caldo Caldo Caldo: CD & Book Set. DeLange, Alex Pardo, illus. (p. 1580)
—Sip, Slurp, Soup, Soup/Caldo, Caldo, Caldo. Castilla, Julia Mercedes, tr. (p. 1580)
—Upside down & Backwards. Hernandez, Karina, tr. (p. 1825)
—We Are Cousins/Somos Primos. Rodriguez, Christina E., illus. (p. 1865)
Bertrand, Diane Gonzales & Ventura, Gabriela Baeza. Bean & Cheese Taco Birthday / Un Cumpleaños con Tacos de Frijoles con Queso. Trujillo, Robert, illus. (p. 150)
—Party for Papá Luis/La Fiesta para Papá Luis. Galindo, Alejandro, illus. (p. 1326)
Bertrand, Diane Gonzales, et al. Adelita & the Veggie Cousins / Adelita y las primas Verduritas. Rodriguez, Tina, illus. (p. 12)
Bertrand, Diane Gonzalez. Park Our Town Built. Bauerle, Tanja, illus. (p. 1324)
—Park Our Town Built/El Parque Que Nuestro Pueblo Construyó. Bauerle, Tanja, illus. (p. 1324)
Bertrand, Frederique, illus. see Leblond, Michaël.
Bertrand, Jessica Dally. Bully Billy. (p. 241)
—Danny & the Dentist. (p. 405)
Bertrand, Lynne. Granite Baby. Hawkes, Kevin, illus. (p. 710)
Berts, Peter, et al. Fish to Fry. Ellipsanime Staff & Dargaud Media Staff, illus. (p. 598)
Berube, John Paul, jt. auth. see Darcy-Bérubé, Françoise.
Berube, Kate, illus. see Manley, Curtis.
Berwick, Gwen & Thorne, Sydney. Voilà! Green, Julie, ed. (p. 1848)
Besant, Annie W. Legends & Tales Lotus Leaves for the Y. (p. 989)
Besel, Jen. Custom Confections (p. 395)
Besel, Jennifer M. Army Rangers (p. 100)
—Baking Bliss! Baked Desserts to Make & Devour (p. 133)
—Christmas Drawing Wonderland! Makuc, Lucy, illus. (p. 313)
—Coldest Places on Earth (p. 339)
—Compass Roses & Directions (p. 352)
—Custom Confections: Delicious Desserts You Can Create & Enjoy (p. 395)
—Delta Force (p. 425)
—Drawing a Christmas Wonderland: A Step-By-Step Sketchpad Makuc, Lucy, illus. (p. 481)
—Drawing a Halloween Spooktacular: A Step-By-Step Sketchpad Makuc, Lucy, illus. (p. 481)
—Green Berets (p. 721)
—Halloween Drawing Spooktacular! Makuc, Lucy, illus. (p. 737)
—Holiday Sketchbook. Makuc, Lucy, illus. (p. 788)
—Hottest Places on Earth. (p. 802)
—Lions & Tigers & Graphs! Oh My! (p. 1021)
—Malia & Sasha Obama (p. 1083)
—Map Scales (p. 1090)
—Maps. (p. 1090)
—Mummies (p. 1190)
—Navy SEALs (p. 1238)
—Robert Pattinson (p. 1479)
—Sugarcoat It! Desserts to Design, Decorate, & Devour (p. 1673)
—Sweet Tooth! No-Bake Desserts to Make & Devour (p. 1690)
—Symbols & Keys (p. 1693)
—Thanksgiving Drawing Feast! Makuc, Lucy, illus. (p. 1726)
—Types of Maps (p. 1805)
—U. S. Navy SEALs: The Missions (p. 1807)
—Valentine's Day Drawing Treat! Makuc, Lucy, illus. (p. 1830)
—Vampires (p. 1832)
—What Is a Map? (p. 1888)
Besel, Jennifer M., jt. auth. see Nobleman, Marc Tyler.
Besel, Jennifer M., et al. American Special Ops. (p. 63)
Beserra, Donna. Twirly Shirley & the Brother Like No Other. (p. 1802)
—Twirly Shirley In Hurricane Shirley. (p. 1802)
Beshears, Linda Gills. Times Table Made Fun & Easy. Theresa Speight, L.L.C. Staff, ed. (p. 1754)
Besheer, Margaret, jt. auth. see Janin, Hunt.
Beshir, Sumaiya, compiled by. Everyday Struggles: The Stories of Muslim Teens. (p. 544)
Beshqoy, Nisreen. Self Taught Arabic Book (p. 1549)
Beshwathy, Steve, illus. see Decary, Marie.
Beshwaty, Steve, illus. see Decary, Marie.
Beshwaty, Steve, illus. see Décary, Marie.
Beshwaty, Steve, illus. see Décary, Marie.
Beshwaty, Steve, illus. see Tremblay, Carole.
Beshwaty, Steve, tr. see Langlois, Annie.
Beskin, Lisa. My Work among the Faithful (p. 1221)
Beskow, Elsa. Aunt Brown's Birthday (p. 115)
—Children of the Forest. (p. 302)
—Land of Long Ago. (p. 973)
—Pelle's New Suit (p. 1336)
—Peter & Lotta's Adventure (p. 1346)
—Peter in Blueberry Land Mini (p. 1346)
—Sun Egg (p. 1676)
Besley, Adrian. How to Fart at School— And Get Away with It! (p. 819)
Besley, Preston, jt. auth. see Croft, Malcolm.
Besom, Mae, illus. see Yamada, Kobi.
Bess, Alex Marie. Scrapper. (p. 1532)
Bess, Clayton, et al. Story for a Black Night. (p. 1657)
Bess Press, creator. From Aloha to Zippy's: A Keiki Alphabet Book. (p. 641)
Bess, Stacey. Planting More Than Pansies: A Fable about Love. Ricks, Melissa, illus. (p. 1369)
Bessen, Luc. Arthur & the Minimoys. Sowchek, Ellen, tr. from FRE. (p. 103)
Besser, Kenneth/R. Arnie Carver & the Plague of Demeverde. (p. 100)
Besserman, Perle. New Kabbalah for Women. (p. 1245)
Bessesen, Brooke. Look Who Lives in the Desert. (p. 1050)
—Look Who Lives in the Ocean: Splashing & Dashing, Nibbling & Quibbling, Blending & Fending. (p. 1050)
—Zachary Z. Packrat & His Amazing Collections. Campbell, Jenney, illus. (p. 1984)
Bessey, Brandan, illus. see Havice, L. K.
Bessey, Lisa. Pretty Little Dot. (p. 1398)
Bessey, Siân Ann. Escape from Germany. (p. 535)
—Uprising in Samoa: A Novel. (p. 1825)
Bessey, Vance, illus. see Heymann, Irene Rommel.
Bessler, edward. Smile for Billy. (p. 1594)
Besson, Luc. Arthur & the Forbidden City. (p. 103)
—Arthur & the Forbidden City. Sowchek, Ellen, tr. (p. 103)
—Arthur & the Minimoys. (p. 103)
Besson, Sam. Coyote: A Trickster Tale (p. 374)
—Coyote: A Trickster Tale. (p. 374)
Best, B. J. Abraham Lincoln, the Emancipation Proclamation, & the 13th Amendment. (p. 7)
—Investing Your Money. (p. 885)
Best, Cari. Ava & the Real Lucille Valentine, Madeline, illus. (p. 118)
—Beatrice Spells Some Lulus & Learns to Write a Letter. Potter, Giselle, illus. (p. 153)
—My Three Best Friends & Me, Zulay. Brantley-Newton, Vanessa, illus. (p. 1220)
—Sally Jean, the Bicycle Queen. Davenier, Christine, illus. (p. 1505)
—Three Cheers for Catherine the Great! Potter, Giselle, illus. (p. 1741)
—When We Go Walking Brooker, Kyrsten, illus. (p. 1905)
Best, Cathy, illus. see DeLoach, Kathleen.
Best, Detra. Sports Edition: The Athlete. (p. 1632)
Best, Gary Dean. Peddling Panaceas: Popular Economists in the New Deal Era. (p. 1334)
Best, Jessica Gabrielle. Wish Giver's Promise. (p. 1940)
Best, Laura. Bitter, Sweet (p. 194)
Best, Michael. Tommy the Turtle. (p. 1765)
Best, Michael S. Tommy the Turtle. (p. 1765)
Best, Rosie. Skulk. (p. 1586)
Best, Roy. Picture Story Book of Peter Pan. (p. 1356)
Best, Susie Montgomery. Glorious Greece & Imperial Rome. (p. 685)
Bester, Marco. Johnny & the Thingamajigs. (p. 923)
Bester, Maryanne. Cool Nguni. Bester, Shayle, illus. (p. 364)
—I Know That! Bester, Shayle, illus. (p. 840)
—Long Trousers. Bester, Shayle, illus. (p. 1047)
—Missing Ball. Bester, Shayle, illus. (p. 1152)
—Three Friends & a Taxi. Bester, Shayle, illus. (p. 1742)
Bester, Maryanne, jt. auth. see Clegg, Maryanne.
Bester, Shayle, illus. see Bester, Maryanne.
Bester, Shayle, illus. see Bloch, Carole.
Bester, Shayle, illus. see Clegg, Maryanne & Bester, Maryanne.
Besterman, Catherine. Extraordinary Education of Johnny Longfoot in His Search for the Magic Hat. Chappell, Warren, illus. (p. 555)
Best-Everette, Shabarbara. Will You Be My Friend? (p. 1932)
Bestful, Scott & Hurteau, Dave. Field & Stream's Guide to Hunting Whitetail. The Editors of Field & Stream, ed. (p. 583)
Beston, Clare. Make Your Own Roman Arena. (p. 1080)
Beston, Henry. Chimney Farm Bedtime Stories. (p. 306)
—Firelight Fairy Book. (p. 592)
—Outermost House: A Year of Life on the Great Beach of Cape Cod. (p. 1312)
Bestor, Sheri Mabry. Substance Abuse: The Ultimate Teen Guide. (p. 1671)
Betances, Abigail. American Holidays. (p. 61)
Betances, Brendan. Granny's Garden. (p. 710)
Betances, Maria. Eva Longoria: Actress & Businesswoman. (p. 540)
—Selena Gomez: Superstar Singer & Actress. (p. 1549)
Betances, Roberto. Lizard Blood. (p. 1042)
Betancourt, Jeanne. Penny & Pepper. Riley, Kellee, illus. (p. 1338)
Betancourt, Raymond, illus. see Hooper, Nancy.
Betanzos, Sue. My New Backyard Garden. (p. 1216)
Beth, Libby. There's a Rainbow in the Mud. (p. 1731)
Beth, Mary, jt. auth. see Chapman, Steven Curtis.
Beth, Robinson. God Made Me: The Safe Touch Coloring Book. Noel, Green, illus. (p. 689)
Beth, Shannon, illus. see Conti, Alexis.
Bethards, David, illus. see Langford, Anne.
Bethea, Nikole. G Is for Grits: A Southern Alphabet Lyne, Alison Davis, illus. (p. 651)
Bethea, Nikole Brooks. Engineering an Awesome Recycling Center with Max Axiom, Super Scientist Pop Art Studios, illus. (p. 529)
—Engineering an Awesome Recycling Center with Max Axiom, Super Scientist Pop Art Studios Staff, illus. (p. 529)
—Oil & Coal. (p. 1282)
—Science of a Bridge Collapse. (p. 1527)
—Science of Basketball with Max Axiom, Super Scientist. (p. 1527)
—Science of Basketball with Max Axiom, Super Scientist. Aranda, Tomás, illus. (p. 1527)
—Science of Football with Max Axiom, Super Scientist. (p. 1527)
—Science of Football with Max Axiom, Super Scientist. Cacau, Caio, illus. (p. 1527)
—Water Cycle. (p. 1862)
Bethea, Nikole Brooks, et al. Science of Sports with Max Axiom. Cacau, Caio, illus. (p. 1527)
Bethea, Terry L. Cabot the Rabbit. (p. 250)
—Why Snails Are Slow. (p. 1926)
Bethel, Ellie. Michael Recycle. (p. 1134)
—Michael Recycle Meets Litterbug Doug. (p. 1134)
—Michael Recycle Saves Christmas. (p. 1134)
Bethel, Ellie & Patterson, Ellie. Michael Recycle Meets Bootleg Peg. (p. 1134)
Bethel, Pamela, photos by see Werker, Kim Piper & Werker, Kim.
Bethers, Linda, retold by. Christmas Oranges. (p. 315)
Bethlehem Steel Corporation, creator. Bethlehem Steel Mine & Industrial Trackwork Catalog. (p. 171)
Bethune, Helen. Barnaby Dell. (p. 139)
—Bright New Day. (p. 228)
—In a Whirl (p. 863)
—Road Trip to Yosemite. (p. 1477)
—Sarah's Journal. (p. 1514)
—Way Back When. (p. 1864)
—Why Do Diamonds Sparkle? All about Earth's Resources. (p. 1923)
—Why Do Glaciers Grind? (p. 1923)
—Why Do Glaciers Move? Level 6 Factbook. (p. 1923)
—Why Do Monkeys Chatter? (p. 1923)
—Why Do Monkeys Chatter? All about Animals. (p. 1924)
—Why Does My Heart Pump? (p. 1924)
Betiku, Olatukunbo, illus. see Amon, Ras Ran.
Betler, Jason. I Have Decided: Beginning Your New life with Jesus. (p. 839)
Bets, Emily. Shirt. (p. 1567)
Bette, Grandma. Excellent Adventures of Max & Madison: Bedtime stories for Youngsters. (p. 547)
Bettenberg, Barbie. Edgar, the Near-Sighted Eagle. Clement, Marilyn, illus. (p. 504)
Bettencourt, Filomena. Priscilla Ballerina. (p. 1407)
Betteo, Patricio, illus. see Clark, Sherryl.
Betteo, Patricio, illus. see Fernández, Bernardo.
Better Homes and Gardens Books Staff. New Junior Cookbook. (p. 1245)
Better Homes and Gardens Books Staff, contrib. by. Big Book of Kids' Crafts: 301 Projects for Kids 4 to 12. (p. 179)
Better-Fitzhugh, Nicole & Fitzhugh, Isaiah C. Take Courage: A Story of Hope & Healing. (p. 1696)
Betteridge, Barbara Dawson. Whittle Your Ears. Mitchell, David S., ed. (p. 1914)
Betteridge, Deirdre, illus. see Stinson, Kathy.
Betteridge, Deirdre, illus. see Toten, Teresa.
Betters, Patricia. Oink a Love Story. (p. 1282)
Betterton, Jerry W. Adventures of Hot Rolls. (p. 18)
Betti, Matthew. Declaration of Independence & the Continental Congress. (p. 422)
Bettinelli, Sara, ed. see Bussagli, Marco.
Bettinger, John & Kina. Koa Becomes a Friend. (p. 966)
Bettino, Teresa Adele. Adventures of Sugarbabe & Thunder. (p. 23)
Bettoli, Delana, illus. see Cotten, Cynthia.
Bettoni, Angela. More Adventures of Edmund & Martha. (p. 1174)
Betts, A. J. Wavelength. (p. 1864)
—Zac & Mia. (p. 1984)
Betts, Bambi. Basic Truths 1-3. (p. 142)
Betts, Betty. Dylan's Adventure. (p. 491)
Betts, Christopher, jt. auth. see Perrault, Charles.
Betts, Edward A. Introduction to Enriched Air Diving: The Textbook for ANDI Limited SafeAir User. (p. 882)
—Openwater Sport Diver: The Textbook for ANDI Openwater Diver. (p. 1300)
Betts, George Herbert, ed. see Baker, Clara B. & Baker, Edna D.
Betts, George Herbert, jt. auth. see Emerson, Charles P.
Betts, Joan D. Bagley B. Butterfield: A Dog Book for People. (p. 132)
Betts, Linda. Place to Grow. (p. 1365)
Betts, Louis, illus. see Wade, Mary H.
Betts, McKenzie Leigh. Blue Bear Finds a Rainbow. Abbott, Candy, ed. (p. 202)
—Pink Bear's Journey: I Love Me, Who Do You Love? Desautels, Stacie, illus. (p. 1359)
Betty Crocker, Betty. Betty Crocker Kids Cook. (p. 172)
Betty Crocker Editors. Betty Crocker Kids Cook! (p. 172)
—Betty Crocker's Cookbook for Boys & Girls. (p. 172)
Betz, Adrienne & Time for Kids Editors. Sharks! (p. 1562)
Betz, Eva K. Priest, Patriot & Leader: The Story of Archbishop Carroll. Dougherty, Charles L., illus. (p. 1399)
Betz, Katy, illus. see Lataif, Nicole.
Betzer, Dan. Dan & Louie: The Greatest Stories Ever Told. Vol. 2 (p. 401)
Beullens, Nathalie, tr. see Khu, Jannell.
Beullens, Nathalie, tr. see Ruffin, Frances E.
Beullens, Nathalie, tr. see Wilson, Natashya.
Beus, Bryan. Westly: A Spider's Tale. Beus, Bryan, illus. (p. 1876)
Beus, Bryan, illus. see Dashner, James.
Beutel, Roger & Spencer, Lauren. Writing a Narrative. (p. 1964)
—Writing about Issues. (p. 1964)
Bevan, C. Scott. Aa-Zz. (p. 2)
Bevan, Clare. Creature in Wide-Mouth Cave (p. 380)
—Great Big Book of Reading Kindergarten Costco. (p. 714)
—Jolly Rascal. (p. 924)
—Said Mouse to Mole. (p. 1503)
—Wobbly Wand (p. 1943)
—Wonderful Gift. (p. 1948)
Bevan, Clare, et al. Party Poems & Out & about Poems. (p. 1326)
Bevan, Clare, et al, selected by. Clothes Poems & Weather Poems. (p. 334)
—Party Poems & Out & about Poems. (p. 1326)
Bevan, Frances. Prayers & Promises. (p. 1393)
Bevan, Lizzie. Never Far When in My Heart. (p. 1242)
Bevan, Sara, jt. auth. see Millward, Andras.
Bevan, Sharon. Sparkles' First Christmas Eve. (p. 1622)
Bevan, Sharon L. Bella Blue Fairy Finds a New Friend. (p. 162)
Bevan, Teleri, jt. auth. see Lemon, Philip.
Bevans, Donna. Don't Do That, Harry! The Puppy Story. (p. 467)
—Sally & Sadie. (p. 1505)
—Scooter & His Friends. (p. 1529)
Bevans Marks And Barrow, illus. see Kaye, Danny.
Bevans, Ph. D. Don't Do That, Harry! The Balloon Story. (p. 467)
Bevard, Robby, jt. auth. see Bair, Katie.
Bevard, Robby, et al. Toning Techniques Acosta, Robert & Dlin, Doug, eds. (p. 1765)
Beveridge, Amy. God Always Cares. Marlin, Kathryn & Julien, Terry, illus. (p. 688)
—God Bless America. Fletcher, Rusty, illus. (p. 688)
—Let's Thank God for Freedom. (p. 1001)
Beveridge, Bruce. Olympic & Titanic: The Truth behind the Conspiracy. (p. 1287)
Beveridge, Cathy. Chaos in Halifax. (p. 291)
—Offside. (p. 1280)
—Shadows of Disaster. (p. 1558)
—Stormstruck. (p. 1656)
Beveridge, Dorothy. Belize Living Alphabet. Beveridge, Jim, photos by. (p. 162)
—Birding in Belize with Colours. Beveridge, Jim, photos by. (p. 191)
—Counting Belize Frogs & Toads. Beveridge, Jim, photos by. (p. 370)
Beveridge, Jim, photos by see Beveridge, Dorothy.
Beveridge, Patricia Tracy Dow. Moonlight of Morgan Hill. (p. 1172)
Beverley, Jo, et al. Dragon Lovers. (p. 477)
Beverley, Naidoo. Journey to Jo'Burg: A South African Story. (p. 928)
Beverley, Virginia, illus. see Savage, Sam.
Beverly, Cleary. Dear Mr. Henshaw. (p. 419)
—Mouse & the Motorcycle. (p. 1182)
Beverly, James. Seamus the Sheltie to the Rescue! (p. 1536)
Beverly, Sonnie. Saved Folk in the House. (p. 1517)
Beverly-Barrier, Essie. Ouse the Mouse. Allen, Joshua, illus. (p. 1310)
Beverly-Patterson, Sylvia Dianne, ed. see S., LaTisha & Lee, Mykle.
Bevilacqua, Carol, illus. see Ahouse, Jeremy John & Barber, Jacqueline.
Bevilacqua, Carol, illus. see Barber, Jacqueline.
Bevilacqua, Carol, illus. see Echols, Jean C.
Bevilacqua, Silvana, illus. see Freedman, Zelda.
Bevin, Shane, illus. see Reiter, David P.
Bevin, Teresa. Tina Springs into Summer/Tina Se Lanza Al Verano. Rodriguez, Perfecto, illus. (p. 1755)
Bevington, David. Twelfth Night Laurel Associates Inc. Staff, ed. (p. 1800)
Bevington, David & Shakespeare, William. Twelfth Night. Gibson, Rex, ed. (p. 1800)
Bevington, Nancy, illus. see Whitfield, Peter.
Bevins, Pegi & Doyle, Arthur. Sherlock Holmes. (p. 1565)
Bevins, Rose. Coming to Terms. (p. 348)
Bevis, Brittany. Two Foals, a Dash of Sprinkles & a Cherry on Top! Talley, Pam, illus. (p. 1803)
Bevis, Mary. Bird on My Hand (hardcover) Making Friends with Chickadees Powell, Consie, illus. (p. 190)
—Bird on My Hand (softcover) Making Friends with Chickadees. Powell, Consie, illus. (p. 190)
—Old Woman Winter. Powell, Consie, illus. (p. 1285)
—Old Woman Winter. Bevis, Mary & Powell, Consie, illus. (p. 1285)
—Wolf Song. Powell, Consie, illus. (p. 1944)
Bevis, Vivian, illus. see New, William.
Bewes, Richard & Thompson, Ian. Top 100 Questions Remix: Spiritual Answers to Real Questions. (p. 1768)
Bewley, Elizabeth. Choose to Recycle. Latimer, Miriam, illus. (p. 310)
—Moon Followed Me Home. Furukawa, Masumi, illus. (p. 1172)
Bewley, Robert, jt. auth. see Dowley, Tim.
Bey, Angelique. Jammin' Jerone! The lamb who played the Saxaphone. Gilbert, Cecilia, illus. (p. 907)
Bey, Charles, illus. see Mac, Cola.
Bey, Kirsten. One Thing or Your Mother. (p. 1297)
Beyer, Mark. Aircraft Carriers: Inside & Out. (p. 31)
—Autos Del Pasado. (p. 117)
—Autos del pasado (Cars of the Past) (p. 118)
—Aviones Del Pasado. (p. 120)
—Aviones del pasado (Planes of the Past) (p. 120)
—Barcos Del Pasado. (p. 138)
—Barcos del pasado (Boats of the Past) (p. 138)
—Bicicletas Del Pasado. (p. 177)
—Bicicletas del pasado (Bicycles of the Past) (p. 177)
—Bicycles of the Past. (p. 177)
—Boats of the Past. (p. 205)
—Cars of the Past. (p. 272)
—Demolition Experts: Life Blowing Things Up. (p. 426)
—Election Of 1800: Congress Helps Settle a Three-Way Vote. (p. 508)
—Election of 1800: Congress Helps Settle a Three-Way Vote. (p. 508)
—Emmanuel Ringelblum: Historian of the Warsaw Ghetto. (p. 520)
—Heinrich Muller: Gestapo Chief. (p. 762)
—Heinrich Müller: Gestapo Chief. (p. 762)
—Homeland Security & Weapons of Mass Destruction: How Prepared Are We? (p. 793)
—Larry Bird. (p. 976)
—Motocicletas Del Pasado. (p. 1179)
—Motocicletas del pasado (Motorcycles of the Past) (p. 1179)
—Motorcycles of the Past. (p. 1180)
—Nuclear Weapons & the Cold War. (p. 1270)
—Planes of the Past. (p. 1367)
—Smokejumpers: Life Fighting Fires. (p. 1594)
—Stevie Wonder. (p. 1649)
—Temperance & Prohibition: The Movement to Pass Anti-Liquor Laws in America. (p. 1717)
—Trains of the Past. (p. 1777)
—Trenes del Pasado. (p. 1784)
—Trenes del pasado (Trains of the Past) (p. 1784)
—War of 1812: The New American Nation Goes to War with England. (p. 1857)
Beyer, Mark T. Aircraft Carriers: Inside & Out. (p. 31)
Beyer, Pamela J. & Bilbrey, Hilary. Little Jake Learns to Stop: A Heartwarming Tale about Determination & Succeeding with Attention Difficulties. Armstrong, Michelle Hartz, illus. (p. 1029)
Beyer, Ramsey. Little Fish: A Memoir. (p. 1027)
Beyer, Ramsey, illus. see Campbell, Jeff.
Beyerl, Paul V. Symbols & Magick of Tarot. (p. 1693)
Beyers, Andrea. Johnny Joins the Army. LeTourneau, Anthony Alex, illus. (p. 923)
Beyers, Kathryn. Babe's Vacation. (p. 123)

B

Beyl, Charles. My Parents Are Divorced Too: A Book for Kids by Kids. (p. 1216)
Beyl, Charles, illus. see Kraus, Jeanne R.
Beyl, Charles, illus. see Nadeau, Kathleen G. & Dixon, Ellen B.
Beyl, Charles, illus. see Weierbach, Jane & Phillips-Hershey, Elizabeth.
Beyle, Thad L., ed. State & Local Government 2004-2005: Politics, Legislatures, Governors, Media, Courts, & Bureaucracies. (p. 1644)
Beylo, Frank. Best of Nothing. (p. 170)
Beylon, Cathy. All Aboard! Trains Activity & Coloring Book. (p. 42)
—Animal Opposites. (p. 79)
—At Day Camp. (p. 110)
—At the Amusement Park. (p. 110)
—At the Aquarium. (p. 110)
—At the Aquarium/en el Acuario: Bilingual Coloring Book. Gongora, Oscar, tr. (p. 110)
—At the Beach. (p. 110)
—At the Circus. (p. 111)
—At the Pet Shop. (p. 111)
—At the Zoo/en el Zoologico: Bilingual Coloring Book. Gongora, Oscar, tr. (p. 111)
—BOOST Mother Goose Coloring Book. (p. 213)
—Camping Fun Sticker Activity Book. (p. 257)
—Christmas Family Fun Coloring Book. (p. 313)
—Color Your Own Bugs Stickers. (p. 343)
—Color Your Own Things That Go Stickers. (p. 343)
—Easy Beauty & the Beast Sticker Picture Puzzle. (p. 500)
—Easy Firehouse Sticker Picture Puzzle. (p. 500)
—Easy Nativity Scene Sticker Picture Puzzle. (p. 500)
—Easy Noah's Ark Sticker Picture Puzzle. (p. 500)
—Favorite Pets. (p. 578)
—Firefighters Tattoos. (p. 591)
—Fun at Nursery School. (p. 647)
—Glitter Ballet Stickers. (p. 683)
—Glitter Tattoos Ballet. (p. 684)
—Going Camping. (p. 692)
—Halloween Stained Glass Coloring Book. (p. 738)
—Happy Halloween Stained Glass Jr. Coloring Book. (p. 745)
—Happy Trains Tattoos. (p. 747)
—Hearts Stained Glass Coloring Book. (p. 760)
—I Love Ballet. (p. 841)
—I Love Ballet/Me Encanta el Ballet: Bilingual Coloring Book. Gongora, Oscar, tr. (p. 841)
—I Love Pets Coloring Book. (p. 842)
—I Love Tropical Fish. (p. 843)
—Kids Cuts. (p. 953)
—Let's Color Together — Horses & Ponies. (p. 995)
—Let's Go Coloring Book. (p. 997)
—Merry-Go-Round Stained Glass Coloring Book. (p. 1129)
—Mother Goose Coloring Book. (p. 1178)
—My Plane Trip. (p. 1217)
—Nature ABC Coloring Book. (p. 1236)
—Noah's Ark Coloring Book. (p. 1261)
—Noah's Ark Stained Glass Coloring Book. (p. 1261)
—Old MacDonald's Farm Coloring Book. (p. 1284)
—Picnic Fun Sticker Activity Book. (p. 1355)
—Rachel to the Rescue Sticker Paper Doll. (p. 1432)
—Safety First Coloring Book. (p. 1502)
—Shiny Dinosaurs. (p. 1567)
—Shiny Toy Trains. (p. 1567)
—Smiley Bugs Tattoos. (p. 1594)
—Teddy Bear Family Stained Glass Coloring Book. (p. 1712)
—Twelve Bugs Bookmarks. (p. 1800)
—Twelve Mother Goose Bookmarks. (p. 1800)
Beylon, Cathy, jt. auth. see Barbaresi, Nina.
Beylon, Cathy & Barbaresi, Nina. I Love Butterflies. (p. 842)
Beynette, Kathy Dezarn. When I Am Not Myself. (p. 1902)
—When Your Porcupine Feels Prickly. (p. 1906)
Beynon, Veronica. My Sister Has Autism & That's Okay. (p. 1218)
Beynon-Davies, Paul, jt. auth. see Charles, Faustin.
Bezanilla, Clara. Pocket Dictionary of Aztec & Mayan Gods & Goddesses. (p. 1375)
Bezdecheck, Bethany. Bailout! Government Intervention in Business. (p. 133)
—Missy Elliott. (p. 1154)
—Relationships: 21st Century Roles. (p. 1457)
Bezdek, Mirasol. Your & You're: Betty the Butterfly. (p. 1979)
Bezek, Lyn. Daisy: The Cripple Creek Donkey. (p. 400)
—Ribbon the Border Collie: From Herder to Healer. (p. 1469)
Bezener, Andy, jt. auth. see Acorn, John.
Bezener, Andy & Kagume, Krista. Compact Guide to Ontario Birds (p. 351)
Bezesky, Tracy, illus. see Jal, David.
Bhabha, Shiraaz, jt. auth. see Krishnaswami, Uma.
Bhachu, Verinder, illus. see Rogers, Kirsteen, et al.
Bhachu, Verindr, illus. see Wilkes, Angela.
Bhadresa, G. N. Tymrose a Fantasy. (p. 1805)
Bhagat-Clark, Duryan & Backer, Miles. Travels with Charlie: Across the Midwest. Nitzberg, Chuck, illus. (p. 1780)
Bhagwat, B. R. Faster Fenay at Fort Pratapgad. Modak, Tejas, tr. (p. 576)
Bhakta, Sanjini. Chocolate Pony. (p. 309)
—My Life as a Dollar Bill. (p. 1212)
Bhandari, D. Growing Wings: Parrot's Day Out. (p. 727)
Bharadwaj, Meenakshi. Lonely Unicorn. (p. 1046)
Bhargava, Neirah, photos by see Jani, Mahendra & Jani, Vandana.
Bhathal, Jenny, jt. auth. see Bhathal, Ragbir.
Bhathal, Ragbir & Bhathal, Jenny. Australian Backyard Astronomy. (p. 116)
Bhatia, Mohini, jt. auth. see Hawker, Frances.
Bhawnani, Henna & Raval, Anuja. Sweet Somethings: For My Cutie "Pie" (p. 1690)
BHB International Staff & Simons, Phillida Brooke. Jock of the Bushveld. (p. 919)
Bhend, Kathi, illus. see Amman, Jurg.
Bhend, Kathi, illus. see Hasler, Eveline.
Bhend, Käthi, illus. see Johansen, Hanna & Barrett, John S.
Bhimji, Saleem, tr. from PER. Islamic Moral System: A Commentary of Surah Al-Hujurat. (p. 892)
Bhinda, Madhu & Marland, Michael. Stories from Asia. (p. 1654)
Bhoola, Prisha. Hashay Says Goodbye & Hello. (p. 752)
Bhote, Tehmina. Medieval Feasts & Banquets: Food, Drink, & Celebration in the Middle Ages. (p. 1119)
Bhote, Themina. Charlemagne: Life & Times of an Early Medieval Emperor. (p. 291)
—Charlemagne: The Life & Times of an Early Medieval Emperor. (p. 291)
Bhugra, Dinesh K. L. & Davies, Dilys. Models of Psychopathology. (p. 1158)
Bhuiyan, Julia, illus. see Sommers, Audrey.
Bhushan, Rahul, illus. see Arnold, Caroline & Comora, Madeleine.
Bhuyan, Sangeetha. Kukola's First School Day. (p. 968)
Biachi, Kelvin K. Tortoise the King. (p. 1771)
Biaggi, Maria Elena, tr. see Plaut, Thomas F.
Biagiotti, Aldo. Escape from Death Valley: A Tale of Two Burros. Biagiotti, Aldo, photos by. (p. 534)
Bial, Morrison D., jt. auth. see Simon, Solomon.
Bial, Raymond. Cree. (p. 380)
—Crow. (p. 385)
—Dripping Blood Cave & Other Ghostly Stories. (p. 485)
—Lifeways (p. 1014)
—Menominee. (p. 1126)
—People & Culture of the Apache. (p. 1339)
—People & Culture of the Cree. (p. 1339)
—People & Culture of the Delaware. (p. 1339)
—People & Culture of the Huron. (p. 1339)
—People & Culture of the Menominee. (p. 1339)
—Shadow Island: A Tale of Lake Superior. (p. 1557)
—Shaker Village. (p. 1559)
—Where Lincoln Walked. (p. 1909)
Bialik, Steve. Minister Jade. (p. 1147)
Bianca & Annie West, illus. see Carmen & Thane Johnson.
Biancakrystal. Clap to Beauty: A toddler self-esteem Book. (p. 326)
Bianchi, Andrew. 10 Rulz. (p. 1994)
Bianchi, Anne. Everything You Need to Know about Family Court. (p. 545)
—Understanding the Law: A Teen Guide to Family Court & Minors' Rights. (p. 1816)
Bianchi, David W. Blue Chip Kids: What Every Child (And Parent) Should Know about Money, Investing, & the Stock Market. (p. 202)
Bianchi, Fausto, illus. see Lucado, Max, et al.
Bianchi, Fausto, illus. see Strasser, Myrna A.
Bianchi, John. Bear Gets a Hat. (p. 150)
—Is the Spaghetti Ready? Edwards, Frank, illus. (p. 890)
—My Ride. Bianchi, John, illus. (p. 1217)
—Over & Under. Bianchi, John, illus. (p. 1313)
—Snowed in at Pokeweed Public School. (p. 1600)
—Sun. Bianchi, John, illus. (p. 1675)
—What Can You Do? Bianchi, John, illus. (p. 1881)
—Where Is Here? (p. 1908)
Bianchi, John, illus. see Edwards, Frank B.
Bianchi, John, illus. see Hileman, Jane & Pitt, Marilyn.
Bianchi, John, illus. see Hileman, Jane.
Bianchi, John, illus. see Pitt, Marilyn & Hileman, Jane.
Bianchi, John, illus. see Pitt, Marilyn & Sanchez, Lucia M.
Bianchi, John, illus. see Pitt, Marilyn, et al.
Bianchi, John, illus. see Pitt, Marilyn.
Bianchi, John, illus. see Rieger, Linda.
Bianchi, John & Edwards, Frank B. Princess Frownsalot (p. 1404)
Bianchi, Leslie, ed. see Takemiya, Masaki.
Bianchi, Mike & Novak, Marisol. Gator Alphabet ABC. Marlette, Andy, illus. (p. 658)
—Swampmeet: A Gator Counting Book. Marlette, Andy, illus. (p. 1688)
Bianchi, Sebastian & Sebastian Bianchi, A. AS Spanish: Tourism & Leisure. (p. 105)
Bianchi, Simone, illus. see Morrison, Grant.
Bianco, David J., jt. auth. see De Angelis, Gina.
Bianco, Francesca, illus. see Campbell, Jeffrey.
Bianco, Guillaume. Ernest & Rebecca Graphic Novels #1: My Best Friend Is a Germ. Dalena, Antonello, illus. (p. 533)
—Grandpa Bug. Dalena, Antonello, illus. (p. 709)
—Land of Waking Stones. Dalena, Antonello, illus. (p. 973)
—Sam the Repulsive. Dalena, Antonello, illus. (p. 1507)
Bianco, Margery Williams. Poor Cecco. Rackham, Arthur, illus. (p. 1383)
—Velveteen Rabbit, or, How Toys Become Real. Nicholson, William, illus. (p. 1835)
—Winterbound. Seredy, Kate, illus. (p. 1938)
Bianco, Margery Williams, jt. auth. see Williams, Margery.
Bianco, Mike, illus. see Blaylock, Josh.
Bianco, Paola. Casa de Bernarda Alba. (p. 273)
Biard, Philippe. Construir. (p. 360)
Biard, Philippe, et al. Dolphins. Peyrols, Sylvaine, illus. (p. 464)
—Fish. Krawczyk, Sabine, illus. (p. 598)
Bib, Betty. Betty Bib's Fairy Handbook: A Field Guide to Fairies & Their Habitats. (p. 172)
Bibeau, Anita, photos by see Muther, Connie.
Bibel, Philip. Tales of the Shtetl. (p. 1703)
Biberstein, Rene. Disasters of Ontario: 75 Stories of Courage & Chaos. (p. 447)
Bibi, Zarina. Bright Night Sky. (p. 228)
Bible Games Company Staff. Bible Characters Card Game. (p. 175)
—Bible Scramble. (p. 176)
Bible, Montré. Heaven Sent. (p. 761)
Bible Visuals International Staff, comment. Conduct of the Church: New Testament. Vol. 24 (p. 356)
—Joseph, a Picture of the Lord Jesus: Old Testament, Pt. 2, Vol. 5 (p. 926)
—Kingdom Forever: Old Testament. Vol. 23 (p. 959)
—Law & Grace: New Testament. Volume 27 (p. 981)
—Prophets to God's People: Old Testament. Vol. 24 (p. 1412)
—Word of God: Old Testament. Vol. 16 (p. 1951)
Bible Visuals International Staff, compiled by. Be the One! the Todd Beamer Story. (p. 149)
—Christ Is God the Son: New Testament. Vol. 34 (p. 311)
—Christ, the Head of the Church: New Testament. Vol. 31 (p. 311)
—Christian Growth: New Testament. Vol. 40 (p. 311)
—Christian Joy: New Testament Volume 30. (p. 311)
—Christian's Belief. (p. 312)
—Christmas Collection. (p. 313)
—Church: New Testament. Vol. 15 (p. 318)
—Condemnation: New Testament. Vol. 19 (p. 355)
—Conversion: New Testament. Volume 17 (p. 361)
—Discovering God's Ways: Old Testament. Vol. 17 (p. 449)
—Disobedience: Old Testament. Vol.20 (p. 453)
—Election: Old Testament. Vol. 06 (p. 508)
—Eternal Salvation: New Testament Volume 35. (p. 539)
—Faith: Old Testament. Volume 02 (p. 565)
—Forgiveness: New Testament Volume 10. (p. 619)
—Future of the Church: New Testament. Vol. 32 (p. 651)
—God Is Sovereign: Old Testament. Vol. 27 (p. 689)
—God (the Trinity): New Testament. Vol. 43 (p. 690)
—Godliness: Old Testament. Vol. 23 (p. 690)
—Godly/Ungodly Living: Old Testament. Vol. 26 (p. 690)
—God's Chosen People: Old Testament Volume 12. (p. 691)
—God's Faithfulness: Old Testament. Vol. 15 (p. 691)
—God's King: Old Testament. Vol. 22 (p. 691)
—Grace of God: Old Testament. Volume 19 (p. 705)
—Hark! the Herald Angels Sing. (p. 748)
—Holy Spirit: New Testament. Vol. 14 (p. 791)
—Human Suffering (Job): Old Testament. Vol. 29 (p. 826)
—In the Beginning: Old Testament. Volume 01 (p. 865)
—Israel: New Testament. Vol. 22 (p. 893)
—Jehovah: Old Testament. Vol. 30 (p. 912)
—Joseph, a Picture of the Lord Jesus: Old Testament. Pt. 1, Vol. 4 (p. 926)
—Justification. (p. 940)
—Law & Faith: New Testament. Volume 26 (p. 981)
—Law & Liberty: New Testament. Volume 28 (p. 981)
—Living by Faith: New Testament Volume 38. (p. 1040)
—Living the Christian Life: New Testament. Volume 23 (p. 1041)
—Lord-He Is God: Old Testament. Vol. 25 (p. 1052)
—Lordship of Christ: New Testament. Volume 07 (p. 1053)
—Nature of Man: Old Testament Volume 03. (p. 1236)
—New Covenant: New Testament. Vol. 37 (p. 1244)
—No Darkness at All: An Adaptation of Patricia St John's Star of Light. (p. 1258)
—Peggy's Christmas Stocking & Socks over Seas. (p. 1335)
—Prayer: New Testament Volume 09. (p. 1393)
—Priesthood of Christ: New Testament. Vol. 36 (p. 1399)
—Prophets of the Messiah: Old Testament. Vol. 32 (p. 1411)
—Providence of God: Old Testament. Vol. 8 (p. 1413)
—Rainbow Garden. (p. 1435)
—Rebellion: Old Testament. Vol. 18 (p. 1451)
—Redemption: Old Testament. Vol. 07 (p. 1455)
—Resurrection: New Testament. Vol. 14 (p. 1464)
—Sanctification: New Testament. Vol. 21 (p. 1510)
—Satan & His Demons: New Testament. Vol. 08 (p. 1515)
—Servants of God: New Testament. Vol. 25 (p. 1552)
—Service: New Testament. Vol. 18 (p. 1552)
—Suffering: New Testament. Vol. 16 (p. 1672)
—Tests of True Faith: New Testament. Vol.39 (p. 1723)
—Until the Letter Came. (p. 1823)
—Wisdom: Old Testament. Vol. 31 (p. 1939)
—Woolly Acres: Psalm 23 Like Never Before! a 4-Act Puppet Drama! (p. 1950)
Bibleco, jt. auth. see Donaher, D F.
Bibleco, jt. auth. see Donaher, D. F.
Bice, Charles. What Lies Beneath. (p. 1891)
Bice, TinaLeAnn. Itty Bitty Fuzzy Worm. (p. 900)
Bichman, David, illus. see Sternfeld, Nathan.
Bick, Ilsa J. Ashes. (p. 105)
—Draw the Dark. (p. 481)
—Drowning Instinct. (p. 486)
—Monsters. (p. 1168)
—Shadows. (p. 1558)
—Sin-Eater's Confession. (p. 1578)
—Sin-Eater's Confession. Elyum Studio, illus. (p. 1578)
Bick, Margaret & Ecker, Catherine. Alive in the Spirit. (p. 41)
—Alive in the Spirit, Family Book. (p. 41)
—Come, Spirit of God. (p. 347)
—Come, Spirit of God, Family Book. (p. 347)
Bickel, Alan M. Fall of Stara Ves. (p. 566)
Bickel, Chris. Nest Seekers. (p. 1242)
Bickel, Cindy, jt. auth. see Nagda, Ann Whitehead.
Bickel, Karla. Animals' Debate. Bickel, Karla, illus. (p. 82)
—Easter Lights. Bickel, Karla, illus. (p. 499)
—Fishnet Valentine. Bickel, Karla, illus. (p. 599)
—Handmade Necklace. Bickel, Karla, illus. (p. 741)
—Heart Petals on the Hearth: A Collection of Children's Stories. (p. 760)
—Heart Petals on the Hearth: A Collection of Children's Stories. Bickel, Karla, illus. (p. 760)
—Heart Petals on the Hearth II: A Collection of Children's Stories. (p. 760)
—Kite Who Was Afraid to Fly. Bickel, Karla, illus. (p. 962)
—Lilac Rose: A Flower's Lifetime. Bickel, Karla, illus. (p. 1017)
—Reading Machine. Bickel, Karla, illus. (p. 1446)
—Surprise Christmas Birthday Party. Bickel, Karla, illus. (p. 1685)
—Teacher's Remarkable Secret. Bickel, Karla, illus. (p. 1709)
Bickerdyke, John. Curiosities of Ale & Beer: An Entertaining History. (p. 392)
Bickerstaff, Linda. Careers in Nutrition. (p. 268)
—Careers in Undercover Narcotics Investigation. (p. 268)
—Frequently Asked Questions about Concussions. (p. 636)
—Kidney Cancer. (p. 952)
—Modern-Day Slavery. (p. 1158)
—Nutrition Sense: Counting Calories, Figuring Out Fats, & Eating Balanced Meals. (p. 1274)
—Oil Power of the Future: New Ways of Turning Petroleum into Energy. (p. 1282)
—Red Badge of Courage & the Civil War. (p. 1453)
—Smart Strategies for Saving & Building Wealth. (p. 1593)
—Stress. (p. 1667)
—Technology & Infertility: Assisted Reproduction & Modern Society. (p. 1711)
—Violence Against Women: Public Health & Human Rights. (p. 1843)
—What Degree Do I Need to Pursue a Career in Nursing? (p. 1881)
—Your Immune System: Protecting Yourself Against Infection & Illness. (p. 1980)
Bickford, Janette. Vern & His Butterfly Migration. (p. 1837)
—Vern's Vacation. (p. 1837)
Bickford, Nicole, jt. auth. see Tennyson, Patrick.
Bickford-Smith, Coralie, illus. see Carroll, Lewis, pseud.
Bickico Enterprises, concept. BabyKids: Easter Book. (p. 128)
—BabyKids: Birthday Book. (p. 128)
—BabyKids: Christmas Book. (p. 128)
—BabyKids: Halloween Book. (p. 128)
Bickico Enterprises Staff, concept. BabyKids: The Color Book. (p. 128)
—BabyKids: The Shapes Book. (p. 128)
—BabyKids: The Counting Book. Bk. 2 (p. 128)
—BabyKids: The Learning Book. Vol. 1 (p. 128)
—BabyKids: El Libro Para Contar. Bk. 1 (p. 128)
—BabyKids: El Libro de los Colores. Bk. 2 (p. 128)
Bicking, Judith, illus. see Margaret I. Pascuzzo.
Bicking, Judith, illus. see Mullican, Judy.
Bicking, Judith, illus. see Pascuzzo, Margaret I.
Bicking, Judith, illus. see Wally, Walter.
Bicking, Judith, illus. see Zadunajsky, Donna M.
Bicking, Judy, illus. see Fogle, Llynda, et al.
Bickle, Laura. Outside. (p. 1313)
Bickle, Mike, jt. auth. see Nysewander, Mark.
Bickley, Mary C. Principles of Financial Services & Products. (p. 1406)
Bickman, Martin. Minding American Education: Reclaiming the Tradition of Active Learning. (p. 1145)
Bicknell, Anita. I Don't Wanna Be Here! (p. 838)
Bicknell, Florence Constable, tr. see Fabre, Jean Henri.
Bicknell, J. Buby Baby 123_Padded. (p. 234)
—Buby Baby Colors_Padded. (p. 234)
—Buby Baby Words_Padded. (p. 234)
—Little Library: Colours. (p. 1030)
Bicknell, Joanna. All Things Bright & Beautiful. (p. 46)
—Build a Story Book. (p. 238)
—Carry-Me Farm Animals. (p. 271)
—Carry-Me Pets. (p. 271)
—Carry-Me Wild Animals. (p. 271)
—Cuddle Buddy: Baby Words. (p. 389)
—Cuddle Buddy: Baby Animals. (p. 389)
—Dress Up: The Christmas Story. (p. 485)
—Emergency. (p. 518)
—Googlies: Pet Pals. (p. 702)
—Googlies: Funny Farm. (p. 702)
—Googlies: Pet Pals. (p. 702)
—My Animal Book. (p. 1196)
—My Digger Book. (p. 1202)
—My First BK of Animals. (p. 1205)
—Touch & Feel Noisy Kitten. (p. 1772)
Bicknell, Joanna & Page, Claire. Magnetics Make Your Own Prayers. (p. 1075)
Bicknell, Joanna & Page, Nick. Finger Friends Tickle Monsters. Saunders, Katie, illus. (p. 589)
—Look at Me! I'm a Ballerina! Snaith, Andy, photos by. (p. 1048)
Bicknell, Joanna & Phillips, Sarah. Time. (p. 1750)
Bicknell, Joanna & Pountney, Beth. Bedtime Buddy: Roarasaurus Loves Buddies. (p. 156)
—Bedtime Buddy: Snugglesaurus Loves Cuddles. (p. 156)
Bicknell, Joanna, ed. Baby Fun Baby Faces. (p. 126)
—Baby Fun Words. (p. 126)
Bickta, Brenda L. Tad's Life in the Lily Pond. (p. 1695)
Bidaisee, Sharlini. Toddler's Basic Knowledge. (p. 1761)
Bidaud, Agnès. Planet of Libris. Elyum Studio, illus. (p. 1367)
Bidder, Alex Von, see McGuirk, Leslie & Von Bidder, Alex.
Bidder, Jane. Inventions We Use at Home. (p. 884)
—Inventions We Use for Information & Entertainment. (p. 884)
—Inventions We Use for Play. (p. 884)
—Inventions We Use to Go Places. (p. 884)
Biddle, Bruce, illus. see Hoenecke, Karen.
Biddle, Bruce, illus. see Hooker, Karen.
Biddle, Charles, Jr. Three Little Pigs. Malak, Annabel, illus. (p. 1742)
Biddle, Megumi, jt. auth. see Biddle, Steve.
Biddle, Steve & Biddle, Megumi. Crane's Gift. (p. 376)
—Make Your Own Greeting Cards. (p. 1079)
—Paper Capers — a First Book of Paper-Folding Fun: Includes 24 Sheets of Origami Paper. (p. 1322)
Biddle, Wendy. Immigrants' Rights After 9/11. (p. 861)
Biddle, Wharton. Story of Timmy Sprite. (p. 1662)
Biddlespacher, Tara, illus. see Axel, Brett.
Biddulph, Rob. Blown Away. Biddulph, Rob, illus. (p. 202)
Bidelman, Jeff. Adventures of Mr. Chicken Butt. Mozi, Jennifer, illus. (p. 20)
Bidias, Kim. Sausage That Didn't Want to Be Eaten: Never Give up on Your Dreams. (p. 1516)
Bidini, Dave. For Those about to Rock: A Road Map to Being in a Band. (p. 616)
—For Those about to Write: How I Learned to Love Books & Why I Had to Write Them. (p. 616)
Bidner, Jenni. Kids' Guide to Digital Photography: How to Shoot, Save, Play with & Print Your Digital Photos. (p. 953)
Bidoli, Katie. Karate Adventures of Kisho, Hana, & Nobu: Karate Is for Everyone! (p. 943)
Bidwell, Dafne. Danger Unlimited: Action, Mystery & Adventure. (p. 404)
Bidzilya, Kristin. Two Girls Dreams Come True. (p. 1803)
Bieber, Hartmut. Busy Bear Around the House. (p. 245)
—Busy Bear Celebrates Christmas. (p. 245)
—Busy Bear Goes to Kindergarten. (p. 245)
—Busy Bear Goes to the Beach. (p. 245)
Bieber, Hartmut, jt. auth. see Schmidt, Hans-Christian.
Bieber, Justin. Justin Bieber: Just Getting Started. (p. 940)
—Justin Bieber: First Step 2 Forever - My Story. (p. 940)
—Justin Bieber - First Step 2 Forever: My Story. (p. 940)
Biebuyck, Valerie. Electra to the Rescue: Saving a Steamship & the Story of Shelburne Museum. (p. 508)

Biederman, Ashley. Eyes Opened. (p. 558)
—Eyes Opened #2. (p. 558)
—Witches Keys. (p. 1941)
Biederman, Judy. Bushy Tail Squirrel's First Day Out. (p. 244)
Biederman, Lynn & Pazer, Lisa. Teenage Waistland. (p. 1714)
Biedinger, Susan A. Reader's Theater Bible Stories. (p. 1444)
Biedrzycki, David. Ace Lacewing: Bug Detective. Biedrzycki, David, illus. (p. 8)
—Ace Lacewing: Bad Bugs Are My Business. Biedrzycki, David, illus. (p. 8)
—Ace Lacewing Bug Detective: The Big Swat. Biedrzycki, David, illus. (p. 8)
—Ace Lacewing, Bug Detective: The Big Swat. Biedrzycki, David, illus. (p. 8)
—Ace Lacewing, Bug Detective: Bad Bugs Are My Business. Biedrzycki, David, illus. (p. 8)
—Breaking News: Bear Alert. Biedrzycki, David, illus. (p. 225)
—Me & My Dragon: Scared of Halloween. Biedrzycki, David, illus. (p. 1115)
—Me & My Dragon. Biedrzycki, David, illus. (p. 1115)
—Santa Retires. Biedrzycki, David, illus. (p. 1513)
—Santa's New Jet. (p. 1513)
—Santa's New Jet. Biedrzycki, David & Bonnet, Rosalinde, illus. (p. 1513)
Biedrzycki, David, illus. see Pallotta, Jerry.
Biedrzycki, David, tr. see Pallotta, Jerry.
Biedrzycki, David & Canetti, Yanitzia. Mi Dragón y Yo. Biedrzycki, David, illus. (p. 1132)
Biegel, Paul. Pais de las Siete Torres. (p. 1319)
Biegert, Melissa Langley. Determining the Cause of Death. (p. 431)
—Finding the Murder Weapon. (p. 588)
—Gathering Blood Evidence. (p. 658)
—Looking for Fingerprints. (p. 1051)
Biehn, Lesley. Humphrey & His Not So Lonely Shell. (p. 827)
Biehn, Mike. Alexander Graham Bell: Famous Inventor. (p. 36)
Biehn, Mike, jt. auth. see Mills, Nathan.
Biel, Timothy Levi. Aranas. Rountree, Monica, tr. (p. 94)
—Osos Polares. Rountree, Monica, tr. (p. 1306)
—Turtles. (p. 1799)
Biel, Valerie. Circle of Nine: Beltany. (p. 321)
Bielby, Paul. Simply the Best: 500 Football Tips for Youngsters. (p. 1578)
Bielling, Ashley Cunningham. Amazing Gracie's Valentine's Day. (p. 54)
Biello, David. Bullet Trains: Inside & Out. (p. 240)
—Portaaviones: Por dentro y por fuera (Aircraft Carriers: Inside & Out) (p. 1386)
—Trenes de Alta Velocidad: Por dentro y por fuera (Bullet Trains: Inside & Out) (p. 1784)
Bielski, Ursula. Creepy Chicago: A Ghosthunter's Tales of the City's Scariest Sites. Noble, Amy, illus. (p. 381)
Biemiller, Carl L. Magic Ball from Mars & Starboy. Voute, Kathleen, illus. (p. 1071)
Bienfait, Andree, illus. see Amiot, Karine-Marie, et al.
Bienik, Stella. Sculpting with Clay: Reason with Shapes & Their Attributes. (p. 1533)
Bier, Andreas. I Wish I Could Fly. Bier, Donna, illus. (p. 848)
Bier, David & Bier, Seth. Bedtime with Rollo: The Nightspryte. (p. 157)
Bier, Donna, illus. see Bier, Andreas.
Bier, Donna, jt. auth. see Bier, Erich.
Bier, Erich & Bier, Donna. Lester the Bear. (p. 994)
Bier, Seth, jt. auth. see Bier, David.
Bierbaum, Tom, et al. Return to Jurassic Park (p. 1465)
Bierce, Ambrose. Devil's Dictionary & Other Works Wilson, Gahan, illus. (p. 432)
—Fantastic Fables. (p. 571)
—Occurrence at Owl Creek Bridge. (p. 1275)
Bierce, Ambrose, et al. Ambrose Bierce Pomplun, Tom, ed. (p. 57)
Bierhorst, John. Nino Espiritu: Una Historia de la Navidad. Aramburu, Francisco Gonzalez, tr. (p. 1257)
Bierman, Carol. Journey to Ellis Island: How My Father Came to America. McGaw, Laurie, illus. (p. 928)
Bierman, Carol, jt. auth. see Brandman, Bronia.
Biers-Ariel, Matt. Seven Species. Goodman, Tama, illus. (p. 1555)
—Solomon & the Trees. Silverberg-Kiss, Esti, illus. (p. 1608)
Bierschwale, Janna. Abby & the Stolen Bone (asi) (p. 2)
—Charlie Horse down by the River. (p. 293)
Biery, Martha. Words Aren't Fair. (p. 1951)
Biesanz, Thomas. EZ Times Table: An easy visual way to learn multiplication & division by playing with patterns & making friends with Numbers. Marsh, Jakob, illus. (p. 559)
Biesanz, Thomas/John. Ez times Table: An easy, visual way to learn multiplication & division by playing with patterns, & making friends with Numbers. (p. 559)
Bieschke, Marke & Belge, Kathy. Queer: The Ultimate LGBT Guide for Teens. Robinson, Christian, illus. (p. 1425)
Biesinger, Joseph. Germany. (p. 666)
Biestman, Margot. Grammie Stories: True Stories about People Living in the Real World. (p. 706)
Biesty, Stephen. Look Inside Cross-Sections: Ships. (p. 1049)
—Look Inside Cross-Sections: Planes. (p. 1049)
Biesty, Stephen, illus. see Dillon, Patrick.
Biesty, Stephen, illus. see Green, Rod.
Biesty, Stephen, illus. see Platt, Richard.
Biesty, Stephen, illus. see Ross, Stewart.
Biesty, Stephen, jt. auth. see Platt, Richard.
Biesty, Stephen & Platt, Richard. Stephen Biesty's Incredible Explosions: Exploded Views of Astonishing Things. (p. 1648)
Biet, Pascal, illus. see Bloom, Becky.
Biever, Rick. Tall Tale of a Barber Named Bill. (p. 1704)
Biffi, Inos. Illustrated Catechism: The Apostles' Creed, the Sacraments, the Ten Commandments, Prayer. Vignazia, Franco, illus. (p. 857)
Biffi, Inos, ed. Life of Mary. Vignazia, Franco, illus. (p. 1012)
Big. Very Best Me. (p. 1837)
Big Bear Books Staff. 1, 2, 3 Baylor: A Little Bear Counting Book. Wiede, Matt, illus. (p. 1990)
Big Blue Bubble Inc., Big Blue & Egmont UK Staff. My Singing Monsters Official Handbook. (p. 1218)
—My Singing Monsters Search & Find. (p. 1218)
Big Blue Bubble Inc. Staff, jt. auth. see Egmont UK, Egmont.
Big Davie. Lady & Her Cat As Told by Bigdavie: A simple easy reading bedtime story that will leave children with delightful images while drifting off to S. (p. 970)
Big Guy Books Staff & Duey, Kathleen. Parche Gould, Robert, photos by. (p. 1324)
Big Idea Design Staff, illus. see Kenney, Cindy.
Big Idea Entertainment, LLC. VeggieTales SuperComics: Vol 1. Jones, Cory, illus. (p. 1834)
Big Idea, Inc. VeggieTales Kids' Worship! Getting to Know God: For Children's Church or Large-Group Programming (p. 1834)
—VeggieTales Kids' Worship! Unit 2 - Wild Bible Adventures: For Children's Church or Large-Group Programming (p. 1834)
Big Idea, Inc. Staff. Pirates Who Don't Do Anything: VBS Superkit. (p. 1364)
Big Idea, Inc. Staff, illus. see Poth, Karen.
Big Idea, Inc. Staff & Kenney, Cindy. God Loves You Very Much! Ballinger, Bryan, illus. (p. 689)
Big Idea, Inc. Staff, et al. Larryboy Meets the Bubblegum Bandit (p. 976)
Big Idea Productions Staff, illus. see Peterson, Doug & Kenney, Cindy.
Big Picture Press, Big Picture. Sticker Style: Shop. Bowers, Jenny, illus. (p. 1650)
Bigalow, Stephen W. Who Is Santa? And How Did He Get to the North Pole? Megenhardt, Bill, illus. (p. 1916)
Bigbee, Rasheda T. Look into My Eyes. (p. 1049)
Bigda, Diane, illus. see Zenkel, Suzanne Siegel.
Bigelow, Barbara C. & Edgar, Kathleen J. UXL Encyclopedia of Drugs & Addictive Substances (p. 1829)
Bigelow, Holly, illus. see Duncan, Leonard C.
Bigelow, Lisa Jenn. Starting from Here (p. 1644)
Biggar, Breanne, illus. see Koffman, Donna Carol.
Biggers, Emily, jt. auth. see Barbour Publishing Staff.
Biggers, Jeff. Chemical Dependency. (p. 297)
Biggers, Liza, illus. see Maxwell, Shannon.
Biggers, Nikki & Mason, Chris. Cal Poly College Prowler off the Record: Inside California Polytechnic State University. (p. 252)
Biggin, Gary, illus. see Butterfield, Moira.
Biggs, Alton, et al. Biology: The Dynamics of Life. (p. 189)
Biggs, Brian. 123 Beep Beep Beep! Biggs, Brian, illus. (p. 2000)
—Blue Bus, Red Balloon: A Book of Colors. Biggs, Brian, illus. (p. 202)
—Everything Goes: Henry in a Jam. (p. 544)
—Everything Goes: On Land. Biggs, Brian, illus. (p. 544)
—Everything Goes: Santa Goes Everywhere! Biggs, Brian, illus. (p. 544)
—Everything Goes: Henry in a Jam. Biggs, Brian & Abbott, Simon, illus. (p. 544)
—Everything Goes - By Sea. Biggs, Brian, illus. (p. 544)
—Everything Goes - What Flies in the Air? Biggs, Brian, illus. (p. 544)
—Good Night, Trucks: A Bedtime Book. Biggs, Brian, illus. (p. 700)
—Henry Goes Skating. Abbott, Simon, illus. (p. 768)
—Henry Goes Skating. Biggs, Brian & Abbott, Simon, illus. (p. 768)
—Henry in a Jam. Biggs, Brian & Abbott, Simon, illus. (p. 768)
—Henry on Wheels. Biggs, Brian & Abbott, Simon, illus. (p. 768)
—In the Air. Biggs, Brian, illus. (p. 865)
—Stop! Go! Biggs, Brian, illus. (p. 1653)
Biggs, Brian, illus. see Applegate, Katherine.
Biggs, Brian, illus. see Berrios, Frank.
Biggs, Brian, illus. see Brunelle, Lynn.
Biggs, Brian, illus. see DiPucchio, Kelly.
Biggs, Brian, illus. see Nix, Garth.
Biggs, Brian, illus. see Rylant, Cynthia.
Biggs, Brian, illus. see Scieszka, Jon.
Biggs, Brian, illus. see Shealy, Dennis.
Biggs, Brian, illus. see Van Draanen, Wendelin.
Biggs, Brian, illus. see Warner, Sally.
Biggs, Fiona, ed. Pocket Irish Legends. (p. 1375)
Biggs, Gene, illus. see Wittels, Harriet & Greisman, Joan.
Biggs, Gina. Red String (p. 1455)
Biggs, Harry, jt. auth. see Heymelaux, Jasmin.
Biggs, K. E. Dawn of Hope. (p. 411)
Biggs, Kathy. Dragonflies of North America: A Color & Learn Book for All Ages, with Activities. Manolis, Tim, illus. (p. 478)
—Dragonflies of North America: A Color & learn Book for All Ages, with Activities. Manolis, Tim, illus. (p. 478)
Biggs, Pauline. Wild Ride. Mayne, Michael, illus. (p. 1930)
Biggs, Stephen. Time Barrel. (p. 1751)
Biggs, Suzanne K. Charlie Christmas. (p. 293)
Biggs-Scribner, Stephanie, comment. Children of the Bible. (p. 302)
—Niñas y niños de la Biblia. (p. 1256)
Bigham, Madge A. Little Folks' Land. Ripperton, Lisa M., ed. (p. 1027)
Bigham, Sean, illus. see Qitsualik-Tinsley, Rachel & Qitsualik-Tinsley, Sean.
Bigler, Ashley Hansen. Once upon a Time: An Adoption Story. Hintz, Amy, illus. (p. 1293)
Bigler, Stephanie, et al. Sir Francis Bacon & the Wolves of Isle Royale: A Little Pig's Big Adventure. (p. 1580)
Bigly, Ashley D., jt. auth. see Bratton, Deboral B.
Bignell, Jonathan. Big Brother: Reality TV in the Twenty-First Century. (p. 179)
Bigonette, John, Jr. Island. (p. 892)
Bigwood, John, illus. see Collins, Tim.
Bihrle, Craig, jt. auth. see Omoth, Tyler.
Bihun, Robb, illus. see Yambar, Chris, ed.
Biklou, Eliyana. Lady Treble & the Seven Notes. (p. 971)
Bilan, Edgar, illus. see Bilan Hochenberg, Nerissa.
Bilan Hochenberg, Nerissa. Mommy Works. Bilan, Edgar, illus. (p. 1162)
Bilan, J. Jack & the Beanstalk. (p. 902)
Bilbrey, Heather. Cookie Man. Green, Megan, illus. (p. 361)
Bilbrey, Hilary, jt. auth. see Beyer, Pamela J.
Bilderback Abel, Mary & Borg, Stan W. Maddy Patti & the Great Curiosity: Helping Children Understand Diabetes. Dey, Lorraine, illus. (p. 1069)
Bildner, Phil. Busted. (p. 245)
—Greatest Game Ever Played. Pullen, Zachary, illus. (p. 719)
—Hallelujah Flight. Holyfield, John, illus. (p. 737)
—Marvelous Cornelius: Hurricane Katrina & the Spirit of New Orleans. Parra, John, illus. (p. 1099)
—Playing the Field. (p. 1372)
—Shoeless Joe & Black Betsy. Payne, C. F., illus. (p. 1568)
—Shot Heard 'Round the World. Payne, C. F., illus. (p. 1569)
—Soccer Fence: A Story of Friendship, Hope, & Apartheid in South Africa. Watson, Jesse Joshua, illus. (p. 1603)
—Turkey Bowl. Payne, C. F., illus. (p. 1797)
—Twenty-One Elephants. Pham, LeUyen, illus. (p. 1801)
—Unforgettable Season: Joe Dimaggio, Ted Williams & the Record-Setting Summer of 1941. Schindler, S. D., illus. (p. 1817)
—Whole New Ballgame. Probert, Tim, illus. (p. 1920)
Bildner, Phil, jt. auth. see Long, Loren.
Bildner, Phil & Long, Loren. Game 3. Long, Loren, illus. (p. 654)
Bileck, Marvin, illus. see Colver, Anne.
Bilen, Tracy. What She Left Behind. (p. 1893)
Biles, Roger. Illinois: A History of the Land & Its People. (p. 857)
Bilgrey, Marc. And Don't Forget to Rescue the Other Princess. (p. 71)
—And Don't Forget to Rescue the Princess. (p. 71)
Bilgrey, Marc, et al. Zombielicious! Noeth, Chris et al, illus. (p. 1988)
Bilibin, Ivan, illus. see Afanasyev, Alexander.
Bilibin, Ivan, illus. see Pushkin, Alexander.
Bilichniansky, Theodore. Adventures of Little Tommy Cabin. (p. 20)
—Adventures of Little Tommy Cabin Part II: Tom Cabin Meets Mittens. (p. 20)
Bilik-Franklin, MidiAna & Griffith, Indigo, photos by. Carseat Tourist. (p. 272)
Bilinsky, Cornelia Mary. God Is with Me: Always & Everywhere. (p. 689)
—Saint Who Fought the Dragon: The Story of St. George. (p. 1504)
Bilkan, Ali Fuat. Tales from Rumi: Mathnawi Selections for Young Readers. (p. 1701)
Bill, Alfred Hoyt & Darlington, Franklin. Highroads of Peril: Being the Adventures of Franklin Darlington. (p. 779)
Bill & Thompson, Dorcas. Iraq (p. 887)
Bill, Graf, illus. see Sparks, Candi, et al.
Bill Henry Edge. Blip & the Seat of Arthur. (p. 199)
Bill, Martin & John, Archambault. Chicka Chicka Boom Boom. (p. 299)
Bill of Rights Institute Staff, contrib. by. Founders & the Constitution: In Their Own Words. (p. 624)
—Founders & the Constitution: In Their Own Words, Volumes One & Two. (p. 624)
Bill of Rights Institute, text. Celebrate the Constitution. (p. 284)
Bill, Poppa. Adventures of Huggyman & Wiggly Worm: The Explorers meet Mr. Moley. (p. 18)
Bill, Stanley, tr. see Tischner, Lukasz.
Bill, Tannis. Pika: Life in the Rocks. Jacobson, Jim, photos by. (p. 1358)
Billam, Rosemary. Elephant Hide & Seek. Lodge, Ali, illus. (p. 511)
—The Mud Monster. Remphry, Martin, illus. (p. 1728)
Bille, Corinna. Transparent Girl & Other Stories. (p. 1779)
Billen-Frye, Paige, illus. see Burgdorf, Larry, et al.
Billen-Frye, Paige, illus. see Burgdorf, Larry.
Biller, Maxim. Poppy's Biggest Wish. (p. 1385)
Billet, Marion. Hello! London. (p. 764)
—Littleland. Billet, Marion, illus. (p. 1038)
—Littleland Around the World. Billet, Marion, illus. (p. 1038)
—London Bus. (p. 1046)
—London Taxi. (p. 1046)
—Make & Do: Ninjas. Quarto Books, Quarto, ed. (p. 1079)
—Make & Do: Pirates. Quarto Books, Quarto, ed. (p. 1079)
—Make & Do: Princesses. Quarto Books, Quarto, ed. (p. 1079)
—Make & Do: Super Cute. Quarto Books, Quarto, ed. (p. 1079)
Billet, Marion, illus. see Nosy Crow.
Billias, George Athan. George Bancroft: Master Historian (p. 663)
Billie, T. J. Dominic Chambers & the Ode to Otis Brown. (p. 465)
Billin-Frye, Page, illus. see Albee, Sarah.
Billin-Frye, Paige. Pease Porridge Hot. Billin-Frye, Paige & Frye, Paige, illus. (p. 1333)
Billin-Frye, Paige, illus. see Aboff, Marcie, et al.
Billin-Frye, Paige, illus. see Aboff, Marcie.
Billin-Frye, Paige, illus. see Albee, Sarah.
Billin-Frye, Paige, illus. see Bruce, Sheila.
Billin-Frye, Paige, illus. see Herman, Gail.
Billin-Frye, Paige, illus. see Janovich, Leah.
Billin-Frye, Paige, illus. see Kesselring, Mari.
Billin-Frye, Paige, illus. see Knudsen, Michelle.
Billin-Frye, Paige, illus. see Kroll, Virginia L.
Billin-Frye, Paige, illus. see Larsen, Kirsten.
Billin-Frye, Paige, illus. see Levine, Abby.
Billin-Frye, Paige, illus. see Moncure, Jane Belk.
Billin-Frye, Paige, illus. see Rottmann, Erik.
Billin-Frye, Paige, illus. see Ziglar, Christy.
Billings. History of Our World 2003. (p. 784)
—How: People, Places, & Ideas. (p. 804)
—Modern World (p. 1159)
Billings, Charlene W. & Tabak, John. Lasers: The Technology & Uses of Crafted Light. (p. 977)
Billings, David. Louie the Buoy. (p. 1058)
Billings, David Joseph. Road Trip with Rabbit & Squash. Billings, David Joseph, illus. (p. 1477)
Billings, Henry & Billings, Melissa. Climbing the World's Highest Mountains. (p. 333)
Billings, Henry, et al. In the Spotlight (p. 867)
—Outer Edge - Cool Science. (p. 1312)
—Outer Edge: Danger Zone. (p. 1312)
Billings, Melissa, jt. auth. see Billings, Henry.
Billings, Tirrea. Monster in the Basement. (p. 1167)
Billingsley, Franny. Big Bad Bunny. Karas, G. Brian, illus. (p. 177)
—Chime. (p. 306)
—Folk Keeper. (p. 611)
Billingsley, Mary. Life of Jesus: Paintings & Meditations on the Rosary. (p. 1012)
Billingsley, ReShonda Tate. Blessings in Disguise. (p. 199)
—Boy Trouble. (p. 219)
—Drama Queens. (p. 480)
—Fair-Weather Friends. (p. 562)
—Friends 'Til the End. (p. 639)
—Getting Even: Good Girlz. (p. 669)
—Nothing but Drama. (p. 1268)
—Rumor Central. (p. 1495)
—Truth or Dare. (p. 1794)
—With Friends Like These. (p. 1942)
—You Don't Know Me Like That. (p. 1975)
Billingsley, Victoria. Happy Hoppy's Orchestra & Other Stories. (p. 746)
Billington, Rachel. Life of Jesus. (p. 1012)
—Life of Saint Francis. (p. 1012)
—Poppy's Angel. (p. 1385)
Billington, Rachel & Quarto Generic Staff. Poppy's Hero. (p. 1385)
Billiot, Christopher. And Heaven Stood Silent. Geist, Hans, illus. (p. 71)
Billiot, Christopher C. And Heaven Stood Silent. (p. 71)
Billiot, Wendy Wilson. Before the Saltwater Came. (p. 158)
Billitteri, Thomas J. & Davis, Catherine. Alternative Medicine. (p. 50)
Billman, Dave, illus. see Thompson, Kim & Carder, Ken.
Billman, Hilary Barton. How to Draw the Life & Times of William Henry Harrison. (p. 819)
Billmayer, Stephanie Joy. Apples to Zebras. (p. 93)
Billout, Guy. Somethings Not Quite Right. (p. 1610)
Billout, Guy, illus. see Hopkins, Lee Bennett.
Billout, Guy, creator. Frog Who Wanted to See the Sea. (p. 640)
Billows, Denis. Cranmead Tales. (p. 376)
—Down in Bluebell Wood. (p. 474)
Bills, Randall N. Detective Mysteries. (p. 431)
Bills, Sherry. Flippy the Frog. (p. 605)
Bills, Taylor. Goldilocks & the Three Bears. (p. 696)
—Jack & the Beanstalk. (p. 902)
—Three Little Pigs. (p. 1742)
—Twas the Night before Christmas. (p. 1799)
—Ugly Duckling. (p. 1808)
Bills, Taylor, illus. see Schwiebert, Pat & DeKlyen, Chuck.
Bills, Taylor, illus. see Schwiebert, Pat.
Billups, Ruth A. No Place for a Horse. (p. 1259)
Billus, Kathleen. Judy Johnson. (p. 931)
Billy, John. Disappearance of the Three Little Pigs: Or Do You Know Where Your Chitlins Are Tonight? (p. 446)
Bilson, Danny, et al. Fastest Man Alive: Lightning in a Bottle. (p. 576)
Bily, Cynthia A. Career & Technical Education. Greenhaven Press Editors, ed. (p. 266)
—Dress Codes in Schools. Gale, ed. (p. 484)
—Endangered Species. (p. 527)
—Gay Marriage. Gale, ed. (p. 659)
—Homosexuality. (p. 794)
—Pollution. (p. 1381)
—Street & Runaway Teens. (p. 1666)
—Welfare. (p. 1874)
Bily, Cynthia A. & Des Chenes, Elizabeth, eds. Endangered Species. (p. 527)
Bily, Cynthia A., ed. Banned Books. (p. 136)
Bily, Ro. My Red Island in the Sky. (p. 1217)
Bilyeu, Dan, illus. see Corriel, Michele.
Bimler, Rich. Sex & the New You: For Young Men 13-15. (p. 1556)
Bimler, Richard. Sex & the New You: For Young Women Ages 13-15. (p. 1556)
Binam, Sharyn. Sidload: Garden. (p. 1573)
Binaohan, Simon. Model President (p. 1157)
Binch, Caroline. Down by the River: Afro-Caribbean Rhymes, Games, & Songs for Children. (p. 474)
—Gregory Cool. (p. 723)
—Princess & the Castle. Binch, Caroline, illus. (p. 1402)
Binch, Caroline, illus. see Cooke, Trish.
Binch, Caroline, illus. see Mitchell, Rita Phillips.
Binchy, Maeve. Nights of Rain & Stars. (p. 1255)
—Quentins. (p. 1425)
Binder, Anita. Bananas & Bears Binder, Lenore, illus. (p. 136)
Binder, Betsy. Wrinkled-at-the Knees Elephant & Other Tuneful Tales. Decenciere, Isabelle, illus. (p. 1963)
Binder, C. F. Black Belt Attitude. (p. 195)
Binder, John. Girl Who Applied Everywhere. (p. 679)
Binder, Lenore, illus. see Binder, Anita.
Binder, Mark. Genies, Giants & a Walrus. (p. 661)
—Kings, Wolves, Princesses & Lions: 28 Illustrated Stories for Young Readers. (p. 961)
Binder, Otto. Shazam! Family Archives (p. 1563)
Binder, Otto, jt. auth. see Siegel, Jerry.
Binder, Otto & Fox, Gardner. Adam Strange. Raboy, Mac, illus. (p. 11)
Binder, Otto, et al. Man of Tomorrow. (p. 1085)
Binder, Pat, illus. see Casad, Mary Brooke.
Bindi, Paulo. Sally Ride: The Sky's the Limit. (p. 1505)
Bindon, John, illus. see Dodson, Peter & Library Association Staff.
Bindon, John, illus. see Dodson, Peter.
Bindon, John, illus. see Lessem, Don.
Bindon, John, illus. see MacLeod, Elizabeth.
Bindon, John, illus. see Walker, Sally M.
Bindrim, Hans-Wolfgang. Wilhelm Hauffs Die Errettung Fatmes: Textanalyse und Interpretation (p. 1932)
Bines, Gary, illus. see Dowswell, Paul.
Bines, Gary, illus. see Fecher, Sarah & Oliver, Clare.
Bine-Stock, Eve Heidi. How to Write a Children's Picture Book: Learning from the Very Hungry Caterpillar, Chicka Chicka Boom Boom, Corduroy, Where the Wild Things

B

Are, the Carrot Seed, Good Night, Gorilla, Sylvester & the Magic Pebble, & Other Favorite Stories. (p. 822)
Bine-Stock, Eve Heidi, ed. see Partin, Charlotte Corry.
Binetti, Marianne, jt. auth. see Beck, Alison.
Binetti, Marianne, jt. auth. see Williamson, Don.
Binfet, Eric. Ninja with Bunny Rabbit Slippers. (p. 1256)
Bing, Christopher, illus. see Denenberg, Barry.
Bing, Christopher H., illus. see Grimm, Jacob & Grimm, Wilhelm.
Bingaman, Jay. Physical Science Student Lab Manual. Matthews, Douglas L., ed. (p. 1353)
Bingaman, Kylie. Good Girl Diva. (p. 698)
Bingaman, Lily. Good Dog Dozer. (p. 697)
Bingamon-Haller, Mary. Great Horned Owl. Burns, Sandra, illus. (p. 716)
—Stillwater River. Burns, Sandra, illus. (p. 1650)
Binger, Christine. Show Me Some Urgency, I'm an Emergency: A trip to the ER. (p. 1570)
Bingham, Caroline & Dorling Kindersley Publishing Staff. First Dinosaur Encyclopedia. (p. 594)
—First Space Encyclopedia. Bingham, Caroline, ed. (p. 597)
Bingham, Chauna. Guide to Middle School Math. (p. 730)
Bingham, Derick. C. S. Lewis - The Storyteller. (p. 250)
—Michael Faraday: Spiritual Dynamo. (p. 1134)
—William Wilberforce: The Freedom Fighter. (p. 1933)
Bingham, Edie. Pride. (p. 1398)
Bingham, Frances. Bedtime Stories for the Inner Child: Reuniting with & Nurturing Your Inner Child. (p. 157)
Bingham, Helen E. Nanny Tess & Emma's Distress. (p. 1229)
Bingham, J., jt. auth. see Wardley, R.
Bingham, J. & Brontë, Emily. Wuthering Heights. (p. 1966)
Bingham, J. Z. Channel Blue: Riders of the Storm. Buhagiar, Jason, illus. (p. 290)
Bingham, Jane. Adventurers. (p. 15)
—Amazon (p. 56)
—Ancient Rome. (p. 70)
—Ancient World. (p. 71)
—Animal Heroes (p. 78)
—Aztec Empire (p. 122)
—Aztec Empire. (p. 122)
—Aztec Empire (Freestyle Express) (p. 122)
—Bermuda Triangle (p. 167)
—Bermuda Triangle. (p. 167)
—Classical Myth: A Treasury of Greek & Roman Legends, Art, & History. (p. 328)
—Courageous Children (p. 372)
—Crop Circles (p. 385)
—Encyclopedia of Ancient World. (p. 524)
—Encyclopedia of World History: Prehistoric, Ancient, Medieval, Last 500 Years. (p. 526)
—Everybody Feels Happy. (p. 543)
—Everybody Feels... Sad. (p. 543)
—Everybody Feels Scared. (p. 543)
—Exploring Australia (p. 551)
—Exploring Europe (p. 552)
—Ghosts & Haunted Houses (p. 672)
—Ghosts & Haunted Houses King, Chris, illus. (p. 672)
—Graffiti (p. 705)
—Great Castle Search. (p. 714)
—Great Prehistoric Search. (p. 718)
—Great Prehistoric Search. Jackson, Ian, illus. (p. 718)
—Gulf Wars with Iraq (p. 731)
—How People Lived in Ancient Egypt. (p. 812)
—How People Lived in Ancient Rome. (p. 812)
—Inca Empire. (p. 868)
—Italy. (p. 894)
—Japan. (p. 908)
—Libro de los Experimentos Científicos. (p. 1006)
—Look Around a Roman Amphitheater. (p. 1048)
—Look Around a Roman Villa. (p. 1048)
—Marie Antoinette (p. 1093)
—Medieval world - internet Linked. Firenze, Inklink, illus. (p. 1119)
—Mexico. (p. 1131)
—Popular Culture: 1920-1939 (p. 1385)
—Post-Impressionism (p. 1387)
—Producing Dairy & Eggs (p. 1409)
—Roald Dahl (p. 1477)
—Ships. King, Colin, illus. (p. 1567)
—Sports Heroes. (p. 1632)
—Stories about Surviving Cancer. (p. 1654)
—Story of Ships. King, Colin, illus. (p. 1660)
—Story of Trains. King, Colin, illus. (p. 1662)
—Stress & Depression. (p. 1667)
—Taking Action Against Bullying. (p. 1698)
—Vampires & Werewolves (p. 1832)
—Vampires & Werewolves King, Chris, illus. (p. 1832)
—Welcome to the Ancient Olympics! Ancient Greek Olympics (p. 1873)
Bingham, Jane, jt. auth. see Parker, Steve.
Bingham, Jane & Hile, Lori. Solving Mysteries with Science. (p. 1608)
Bingham, Jane & Michelangelo Buonarroti. Michelangelo (p. 1135)
Bingham, Jane & Sansom, Fiona. Chinese Myths. Kennedy, Graham, illus. (p. 307)
Bingham, Jane & Turner, Helen. Angry. (p. 75)
—Happy. (p. 744)
—Sad. (p. 1501)
Bingham, Jane, et al. Culture in Action (p. 391)
—Encyclopedia of the Ancient World. (p. 525)
—Encyclopedia of the Roman World. (p. 525)
—Encyclopedia of World History: Prehistoric, Ancient, Medieval, Last 500 Years. (p. 526)
—Usborne Internet-Linked Encyclopedia of World History: Prehistoric, Ancient, Medieval, Last 500 Years. (p. 1827)
Bingham, Jane, retold by. Around the World in Eighty Days. (p. 101)
Bingham, Jennifer. More Than It Seems. Bingham, Salina Gonzales, illus. (p. 1175)
Bingham, Jerry, illus. see Vendera, Jaime & McGee, Anne Loader.
Bingham, John, et al. Running for Mortals: A Commonsense Plan for Changing Your Life Through Running. (p. 1497)
Bingham, Kelly. Circle, Square, Moose. Zelinsky, Paul O., illus. (p. 321)
—Formerly Shark Girl. (p. 620)
—Shark Girl. (p. 1562)
—Z Is for Moose. Zelinsky, Paul O., illus. (p. 1984)
Bingham, Laura. Älvor. (p. 51)
—Wings of Light. (p. 1936)
Bingham, Marjorie. Age of Empires, 1200-1750. (p. 29)
Bingham, Marjorie Wall. Age of Empires, 1200-1750. (p. 29)
Bingham, Mark Jay. Woolie & the Bully. (p. 1950)
Bingham, Pamela E., illus. see Stilwell, Norma Minturn.
Bingham, Salina Gonzales, illus. see Bingham, Jennifer.
Bingley, Thomas. Tales of Shipwrecks & Other Disasters. (p. 1702)
Biniok, Janice. 21st Century Security Dogs. (p. 1996)
—Adopting a Pet. (p. 13)
—Guinea Pigs. (p. 731)
—Mixed Breed Cats. (p. 1156)
—Rabbits. (p. 1429)
—Your First Horse. (p. 1980)
Binion, Wanda E. Mom, How Much Does God Love Me? (p. 1161)
Binkley, Carolyn. Errand: And Stinkbugs & Grasshoppers Green. (p. 534)
Binkow, Howard. Howard B. Wigglebottom Learns about Sportsmanship: Winning Isn't Everything. Cornelison, Susan F., illus. (p. 823)
—Howard B. Wigglebottom Learns to Listen. Cornelison, Susan F., illus. (p. 823)
—Howard B. Wigglebottom Listens to His Heart. Cornelison, Susan F., illus. (p. 823)
—Howard B. Wigglebottom on Yes or No: A Fable about Trust. Long, Taillefer, illus. (p. 823)
Binks. Don't Be a Chicken. Begonia, Ruby, illus. (p. 466)
—Girl with Chipmunk Hands. Begonia, Ruby, illus. (p. 679)
Binning, Eddie. Papaw's Backyard Adventure. (p. 1322)
Binns, B. A. Pull. (p. 1415)
Binns, B. A. & McKenzie, C. Lee. Princess of Las Pulgas. (p. 1404)
Binns, Chris, illus. see Foster, Greg & Quattro, Jacquelyn.
Binns, Paul J. Paul & the Porch Gnome. (p. 1330)
Binns, Tristan Boyer. Ancient Chinese. Taylor, Mike, illus. (p. 68)
—Bright Idea: Conserving Energy (p. 228)
—Clean Planet: Stopping Litter & Pollution (p. 330)
—Edgar Allan Poe: Master of Suspense. (p. 504)
—Exploring Antarctica (p. 551)
—Hermit Crabs (p. 771)
—North America. (p. 1264)
—What Color Is an Orange? Light & Color (p. 1881)
Binns, Tristan Boyer, see Boyer Binns, Tristan.
bint Robert, Na'ima. Welcome to the World, Baby. (p. 1874)
Binus, Ari. Izzy Hagbah. (p. 901)
Binus, Ari, illus. see Berman, Seryl.
Binus, Ari, illus. see Kimmel, Eric A.
Binus, Ari, illus. see Rouss, Sylvia.
Bios Agency, photos by see Le Bloas-Julienne, Renee.
Birch, Ann. Head Lice up Close 6 Pack. (p. 756)
Birch, Beverley. Rift. (p. 1471)
—Shakespeare's Tales. Lambert, Stephen, illus. (p. 1559)
—Transport. (p. 1779)
—Turtle's Party in the Clouds. Jenny, Christine, illus. (p. 1799)
Birch, Beverley, jt. auth. see Shakespeare, William.
Birch, Beverley & Shakespeare, William. Twelfth Night. Williams, Jenny, illus. (p. 1800)
Birch, Kate Jarvik. Perfected. (p. 1342)
Birch, Lawrence. Elephant's Trunk. (p. 512)
Birch, Linda, illus. see Lane, Sheila Mary & Kemp, Marion.
Birch, Manuel James. Dudley the Angel & His Buddy Gabby the Elf. (p. 489)
Birch, Mary. Piggy Wiggy. (p. 1358)
Birch, Penny. Fit to Be Tied. (p. 599)
—Indiscretions of Isabelle. (p. 872)
—Naughty, Naughty. (p. 1237)
—Petting Girls. (p. 1349)
—Plaything. (p. 1373)
—Tickle Torture. (p. 1747)
—Tight White Cotton. (p. 1749)
—When She Was Bad. (p. 1904)
Birch, Penny, jt. auth. see Cruella.
Birch, Reginald, illus. see Burnett, Frances Hodgson.
Birch, Robin. Bird-footed Dinosaurs. (p. 190)
—Bony-skinned Dinosaurs. (p. 209)
—Climate Change. (p. 332)
—Cockroaches up Close (p. 337)
—Dinosaur World Set, 6-Volumes. (p. 443)
—Dwarf Planets. (p. 491)
—Earth. (p. 495)
—Earth's Climate. (p. 498)
—Extreme Weather. (p. 557)
—Hard-headed Dinosaurs. (p. 748)
—How Weather Works. (p. 823)
—Jupiter. (p. 937)
—Living with Weather. (p. 1042)
—Long-necked Dinosaurs. (p. 1047)
—Mars. (p. 1096)
—Meat-eating Dinosaurs. (p. 1118)
—Mercury. (p. 1127)
—Moon. (p. 1171)
—Neptune. (p. 1241)
—New Solar System Set, 12-Volumes. (p. 1247)
—Relatives of Dinosaurs. (p. 1457)
—Saturn. (p. 1515)
—Space Series (p. 1619)
—Stars. (p. 1643)
—Sun. (p. 1675)
—Uranus. (p. 1825)
—Venus. (p. 1836)
—Watching Weather. (p. 1861)
Birch, Sue. Dead Puzzling. (p. 417)
Birch, Vanessa Giancamilli. Seagull by the Shore: The Story of a Herring Gull. (p. 1536)
—Seagull by the Shore: The Story of a Herring Gull. Langford, Alton, illus. (p. 1536)
Birchall, Lorrie L. Purple Glurple. (p. 1419)
—Word Family Game Boards. (p. 1950)
Birchall, Mark. Boni y su Fiesta de Cumpleanos. (p. 209)
—Copy Cat. (p. 366)
Birchall, Mark & McKee, David. Rabbit's Party Surprise. (p. 1430)
Birchard, C. C. Boy Scout Song Book. (p. 218)
Bircher, William. Diary of William Bircher: A Civil War Drummer (p. 435)
Birchfield, D. L. Cherokee. (p. 298)
—Cherokee History & Culture. (p. 298)
—Cheyenne. (p. 299)
—Comanche. (p. 346)
—Navajo. (p. 1237)
Birchfield, D. L., jt. auth. see Crewe, Sabrina.
Birchfield, D. L., jt. auth. see Dwyer, Helen.
Birchfield, Elaine. Wilbur Two the Woodland Road. (p. 1928)
Birck, Jan, illus. see Masannak, Joachim.
Bird, Benjamin. Amazing Adventures of Superman! Levins, Tim, illus. (p. 52)
—Batman Shapes Beavers, Ethen, illus. (p. 144)
—Bubble Trouble! Levins, Tim, illus. (p. 233)
—Cat Is Chasing Me Through This Book! Pérez, Carmen, illus. (p. 278)
—Catwoman Counting Beavers, Ethen & Schigiel, Gregg, illus. (p. 281)
—Don't Give This Book a Bowl of Milk! Pérez, Carmen, illus. (p. 467)
—Magic Monsters! Levins, Tim, illus. (p. 1072)
—Scooby-Doo! Little Mysteries. (p. 1529)
—Scooby-Doo's 1-2-3 Mystery. (p. 1529)
—Scooby-Doo's ABC Mystery. (p. 1529)
—Scooby-Doo's Color Mystery. (p. 1529)
—Scooby-Doo's Shape Mystery. (p. 1529)
—Supergirl's Pet Problem! Levins, Tim, illus. (p. 1683)
—Superman Colors Beavers, Ethen, illus. (p. 1683)
—There's a Mouse Hiding in This Book! Pérez, Carmen, illus. (p. 1731)
—This Book Is Not a Piece of Cheese! Pérez, Carmen, illus. (p. 1735)
—Tom & Jerry (p. 1762)
—Wonder Woman ABCs Beavers, Ethen, illus. (p. 1947)
Bird, Benjamin & Siegel, Jerry. Day of the Bizarros! Levins, Tim, illus. (p. 414)
Bird, Betsy. Giant Dance Party. Dorman, Brandon, illus. (p. 673)
Bird Birdsong, Luci. You're Beautifully Beautiful! (p. 1982)
—You're Wonderfully Wonderful! (p. 1982)
Bird, Fiona. Kids' Kitchen: 40 Fun & Healthy Recipes to Make & Share. Arenson, Roberta, illus. (p. 954)
Bird, Glen, illus. see Pearcey, Alice, ed.
Bird, Glen, illus. see Watt, Fiona.
Bird, Grace. Beetles Ahoy! (p. 158)
Bird, Helen. Balloon Launch. Dimitri, Simona, illus. (p. 135)
—Big Yellow Balloon. Dimitri, Simona, illus. (p. 184)
—Fighting Back. (p. 585)
—Party Time. (p. 1326)
Bird, J. K. Shadow the Dog. (p. 1558)
Bird, Janice W. Freddy in the City: Center City Sites. Bird, Richard E., photos by. (p. 633)
Bird, Janie. Freddy in the City: Memorable Monday. Treffeisen, Brian, photos by. (p. 633)
Bird, Jemima, illus. see Clanchy, Kate.
Bird, Jessica, see Ward, J. R., pseud.
Bird, Jodi Stiriz. Going on a Tree Hunt: A Tree Identification Book for Young Children. (p. 692)
Bird, Julia & Lynch, Annabelle. France. (p. 627)
Bird, Linda. Charlie Bird: The Best Bird Ever. (p. 292)
Bird, Mariko, tr. see Burke, David.
Bird, Matthew, illus. see Bond, Doug.
Bird, Matthew, illus. see Bond, Douglas.
Bird, Matthew, illus. see Gherman, Beverly.
Bird, Nicola. Go! Go! Go! Land, Fiona, illus. (p. 686)
Bird, Nikolai, illus. see Zocchi, Judy.
Bird, Richard E., photos by see Bird, Janice W.
Bird, Roy & Harp, Kim. Hark! I Hear a Meadowlark! Battis, Gwen, illus. (p. 748)
Bird, Sheila May. My Auntie Susan. Postgate, Daniel, illus. (p. 1196)
Bird, Sue & Brown, Greg. Sue Bird: Be Yourself. (p. 1672)
Birdsall, Bridget. Double Exposure. (p. 472)
Birdsall, Jeanne. Flora's Very Windy Day. Phelan, Matt, illus. (p. 606)
—Lucky & Squash. Dyer, Jane, illus. (p. 1062)
—My Favorite Pet by Gus W. for Ms. Smolinski's Class. Bliss, Harry, illus. (p. 1203)
—Penderwicks: A Summer Tale of Four Sisters, Two Rabbits & a Very Interesting Boy. (p. 1336)
—Penderwicks: A Summer Tale of Four Sisters, Two Rabbits, & a Very Interesting Boy. (p. 1336)
—Penderwicks at Point Mouette. (p. 1336)
—Penderwicks in Spring. (p. 1336)
—Penderwicks on Gardam Street. (p. 1336)
Birdseye, Tom. Attack of the Mutant Underwear. (p. 114)
—Storm Mountain. (p. 1656)
—Tough Nut to Crack. (p. 1772)
Birdsong, Michelle. Sneasy the Greasy Babysits Abigail. (p. 1597)
Bireda, Martha. Trabue Woods Book of Values. (p. 1774)
Bireda, Martha R. & Cummings, Jaha F. Ornowali: The Child Returns Home - Reconnecting Our Children with Their True Culture. (p. 1288)
Birenbaum, Barbara. Groundhog Phil's Message: Groundhog Legends & Lore. (p. 725)
—Groundhog Willie's Shadow. (p. 725)
Birk, Robert. Alias Chicano. (p. 39)
Birk, Sandow, illus. see Sanders, Marcus.
Birk, Sandow, jt. auth. see Alighieri, Dante.
Birkas, Carol. Christmas Treena. (p. 316)
Birke, Lisa, tr. see Loughead, Deb.
Birke, Szfra & Mayer, Kathy. Together We Heal. (p. 1762)
Birkelbach, Alan. Smurglets Are Everywhere. Halbower, Susan J., illus. (p. 1595)
Birkemoe, Karen. Strike a Pose: The Planet Girl Guide to Yoga. Collett, Heather, illus. (p. 1667)
Birkenshaw, Lois. Music for Fun, Music for Learning. (p. 1193)
Birkenstock, Michelle M. Harry the Caterpillar. (p. 751)
Birkett, Georgie. Clean It! (p. 330)
—Clean It!/a Limpiar. (p. 330)
—Cook It! (p. 361)
—Cook It!/a Cocinar. (p. 361)
—Fix It! (p. 601)
—Fix It!/a Reparar. (p. 601)
—Grow It! (p. 726)
—Grow It!/a Sembrar. (p. 726)
—Is This My Nose? (p. 890)
—Peekaboo! - Who Are You? Birkett, Georgie, illus. (p. 1335)
—Red, Blue, Peekaboo! Birkett, Georgie, illus. (p. 1453)
Birkett, Georgie, illus. see Edwards, Pamela Duncan.
Birkett, Georgie, illus. see Goodhart, Pippa.
Birkett, Georgie, illus. see Newman, Nanette.
Birkett, Georgie, illus. see Petty, Kate.
Birkett, Georgie, illus. see Simmons, Anthea.
Birkett, Georgie, illus. see Tiger Tales Staff, ed.
Birkett, Georgie, illus. see Toulmin & Piper, Sophie.
Birkett, Georgie, jt. auth. see Goodhart, Pippa.
Birkett, Georgie, jt. auth. see Piper, Sophie.
Birkhead, Jennifer. Peeping Through the Low, Green Grass. (p. 1335)
Birkholz, Gay Lyn. Veheti: Lake Michigan's Treasure. Williamson, Linda K., illus. (p. 1835)
Birkinshaw, Linda, illus. see Richards, Julian.
Birkinshaw, Marie, jt. auth. see Baxter, Nicola.
Birkland, Thomas A., jt. auth. see Schaefer, Todd M.
Birks, Wayne, jt. auth. see Walsh, Ben.
Birky, Joy. Bully Bill. Thompson, Chad, illus. (p. 241)
—Sparkle, the Christmas Star. (p. 1622)
Birky, Rachael, illus. see Shifler, Ann.
Birle, Pete. Boston Celtics. (p. 215)
—Chicago Bulls. (p. 299)
—Cleveland Cavaliers. (p. 331)
—Locals Only. (p. 1044)
—Minnesota Timberwolves. (p. 1147)
—New York Knicks. (p. 1248)
—San Antonio Spurs. (p. 1510)
Birle, Peter. Cleveland Cavaliers. (p. 331)
Birlew, Dan. Resident Evil(r) 4 Official Strategy Guide. (p. 1463)
Birlew, Dan, jt. auth. see BradyGames Staff.
Birmajer, Marcelo. Vida Más: Noticias Extranas IV. (p. 1841)
Birmelin, Immanuel. My Guinea Pig. Lynch, Mary D., tr. from GER. (p. 1210)
Birmingham, Christian. Christmas Treasury. (p. 316)
Birmingham, Christian, illus. see Funke, Cornelia.
Birmingham, Christian, illus. see Haddon, Mark.
Birmingham, Christian, illus. see McCaughrean, Geraldine.
Birmingham, Christian, illus. see Moore, Clement C.
Birmingham, Christian, illus. see Morpurgo, Michael.
Birmingham, Christian & Moore, Clement C. Night Before Christmas. (p. 1252)
Birmingham, John, illus. see Haddon, Mark.
Birmingham, Maria. Tastes Like Music: 17 Quirks of the Brain & Body. Melnychuk, Monika, illus. (p. 1707)
—Weird Zone: Sports. Bennett, Jamie & Owlkids Books Inc. Staff, illus. (p. 1873)
Birnbach, Alece, illus. see Dougherty, Meghan.
Birnbaum, A. Green Eyes. Birnbaum, A., illus. (p. 721)
Birnbaum, A., illus. see Savo, Jimmy.
Birnbaumi, Ricki Korey. Alphabet Jingles. (p. 49)
Birney, Betty G. Adventure According to Humphrey. (p. 14)
—Friendship According to Humphrey. (p. 639)
—Humphrey's Book of Fun Fun Fun. (p. 827)
—Humphrey's Creepy-Crawly Camping Adventure. (p. 827)
—Humphrey's Creepy-Crawly Camping Adventure. Burris, Priscilla, illus. (p. 827)
—Humphrey's Playful Puppy Problem. Burris, Priscilla, illus. (p. 827)
—Humphrey's Really Wheely Racing Day. Burris, Priscilla, illus. (p. 827)
—Humphrey's World of Pets. (p. 827)
—Imagination According to Humphrey. (p. 860)
—Mysteries According to Humphrey. (p. 1222)
—Princess & the Peabodys. (p. 1403)
—School Days According to Humphrey. (p. 1522)
—Secrets According to Humphrey. (p. 1544)
—Seven Wonders of Sassafras Springs. Phelan, Matt, illus. (p. 1555)
—Summer According to Humphrey. (p. 1673)
—Surprises According to Humphrey. (p. 1686)
—Trouble According to Humphrey. (p. 1789)
—Winter According to Humphrey. (p. 1937)
—World According to Humphrey. (p. 1953)
Birney, Roxanne. Johannah's Lazy Eye. (p. 920)
Biro, Sharon. Snaggleloopus. (p. 1595)
Biro, Val. Cinderella: See the Picture & Say the Word. (p. 320)
—For Forever! (p. 615)
—Gumdrop All at Sea. (p. 731)
—Gumdrop & the Bulldozer. (p. 731)
—Gumdrop & the Dinosaur. (p. 731)
—Gumdrop & the Elephant. Biro, Val, illus. (p. 731)
—Gumdrop & the Martians. (p. 731)
—Gumdrop & the Monster. (p. 731)
—Gumdrop & the Secret Switches. (p. 731)
—Gumdrop Finds a Ghost. (p. 731)
—Gumdrop Makes a Start. (p. 731)
—Gumdrops & the Elephant. (p. 731)
—Gumdrop's Magic Journey. (p. 731)
—Gumdrop's Merry Christmas. (p. 731)
—Little Red Riding Hood: See the Picture & Say the Word. (p. 1035)
—Magic Journey. (p. 1072)
—Merry Christmas. (p. 1128)
Biro, Val, illus. see Andrews, Jackie.
Biro, Val, illus. see Award, Anna & Aesop.
Biro, Val, illus. see Blyton, Enid.
Biro, Val, illus. see Claridge, Marit.
Biro, Val, illus. see Fiona Fox Staff, ed.
Biro, Val, illus. see Jennings, Linda.
Biro, Val, jt. auth. see Award, Anna.

Biro, Val, jt. auth. see Blyton, Enid.
Biros, Florence W. Love & Loyalty: The Traits That Made Lincoln Great. (p. 1059)
Birt, Michael. Kody the Conservation Pup: Helps Tori Cross the Road. Trammell, Brandon, illus. (p. 966)
Birt, Pat. Ian Wakes Up. (p. 849)
Birth, Ryan, illus. see Tayler, Amber.
Birtha, Becky. Grandmama's Pride. Bootman, Colin, illus. (p. 708)
—Lucky Beans. Tadgell, Nicole, illus. (p. 1062)
Birtles. Dumb Jokes For Smart Kids. (p. 489)
Birtles, Andrew. Chinese Whispers. (p. 308)
Bisaillon, Josée, illus. see Chang, Hae-Kyung.
Bisaillon, Josee, illus. see Kim, Cecil.
Bisaillon, Josée, illus. see Krensky, Stephen.
Bisaillon, Josée, illus. see Salas, Laura Purdie.
Bisaillon, Josée, illus. see Thornhill, Jan.
Bisaillon, Josée, illus. see Wiviott, Meg.
Bisaillon, Josee, jt. auth. see Bar-el, Dan.
Bisaillon, Josée, jt. auth. see Tibo, Gilles.
Bisbee, Richard J., jt. auth. see Ostendorf, Jenifer Wirth.
Bisbort, Alan. Beatniks: A Guide to an American Subculture. (p. 153)
Bischoff, Marlene A. Charming Chirp. (p. 294)
Biscoe, Cee, illus. see Rumbaugh, Melinda.
Biscontin, Chino. Friend Named Jesus. (p. 637)
Biscontini, Tracey Vasil, ed. see Sparling, Rebecca.
Bise, Jr., jt. auth. see Bise, Jr. J. David.
Bise, Jr. J. David & Bise, Jr. In Search of a Name a Seahorse Story. (p. 864)
Bise, Sharon. Jay's First Day at School. (p. 910)
—Story of Katu. (p. 1658)
Biser, Dee, illus. see Glyman, Caroline A.
Bisgrove, Victoria. Wilgrove Farm. (p. 1932)
Bishara, Cristin. Relativity. (p. 1457)
Bishirjian, Richard J. American Political Tradition & the Nature of Public Philosophy. (p. 62)
Bishop, Amanda. Climate Change. (p. 332)
—Energy Conservation. (p. 528)
—How to Reduce Your Carbon Footprint. (p. 821)
—Soccer Superstars: The Best of the Best. (p. 1603)
—Winning Big: World & Euro Cup Soccer. (p. 1937)
Bishop, Amanda, jt. auth. see Crossingham, John.
Bishop, Amanda, jt. auth. see Kalman, Bobbie.
Bishop, Amanda & Kalman, Bobbie. Life of the Navajo. (p. 1012)
Bishop, Amanda, et al. Nations of the Northwest Coast. (p. 1234)
Bishop, Anne. Anne Bishop's Christmas Dram: The Gift of Three. (p. 85)
—Belladonna. (p. 162)
—Invisible Ring. (p. 886)
Bishop, Barbara L. Children Today Around the U S A. Bishop, Barbara L., illus. (p. 303)
Bishop, Ben, illus. see Fendler, Donn & Plourde, Lynn.
Bishop, Benita. Escape from el Monte. (p. 535)
Bishop, Beverly. My Friend with Autism: Enhanced Edition with FREE CD of Coloring Pages! Bishop, Craig, illus. (p. 1209)
Bishop, Brandy. Christmas Mice. (p. 314)
Bishop, Carol. Chronicles of Rusty. (p. 317)
Bishop, Celeste. Core Math Skills: Measurement & Geometry. (p. 367)
—Crawling Centipedes. (p. 377)
—Creepy Caterpillars. (p. 381)
—Gone Fishing! (p. 697)
—Gone Fishing! Measure Lengths. (p. 697)
—Native American Art of the Northwest Coast. (p. 1234)
—Scrambling Spiders. (p. 1532)
—Slimy Slugs. (p. 1590)
—Tall & Short: Describe & Compare Measurable Attributes. (p. 1704)
—Wandering Woodlice. (p. 1856)
—Why Do Plants Have Flowers? (p. 1924)
—Why Do Plants Have Fruits? (p. 1924)
—Why Do Plants Have Leaves? (p. 1924)
—Why Do Plants Have Roots? (p. 1924)
—Why Do Plants Have Seeds? (p. 1924)
—Wiggly Worms. (p. 1928)
Bishop, Christina, illus. see Adam's Creations Publishing.
Bishop, Christina, illus. see Hayes, Celeste.
Bishop, Claire Huchet. Lafayette: French-American Hero. Brevannes, Maurice, illus. (p. 971)
—Man Who Lost His Head. McCloskey, Robert, illus. (p. 1086)
—Twenty & Ten. (p. 1801)
Bishop, Clive. Trophy Trouble. (p. 1789)
Bishop, Craig, illus. see Bishop, Beverly.
Bishop, Darlene. Transforming Power of Spiritual Desire: A Collection of Devotional Readings. (p. 1778)
Bishop, Debbie. Black Tide: Enter the Game. (p. 197)
—Black Tide: Awakening of the Key. Miller, Mike, illus. (p. 197)
—Fairies of Bladderwhack Pond. Park, Andy, illus. (p. 563)
—MYST of the Lost Shadow Boys. (p. 1222)
Bishop, Desmond. Wizard of Zee. (p. 1943)
Bishop, Elaine, jt. auth. see Frazier, Laverne.
Bishop, Elizabeth. Bishop: Poems, Prose, & Letters. Giroux, Robert & Schwartz, Lloyd, eds. (p. 193)
Bishop, Franklin, jt. illus. see Bishop, Helena Edwards.
Bishop, Gavin, illus. see Cowley, Joy.
Bishop, Gavin, illus. see Mahy, Margaret.
Bishop, Hartley C. Inspired Dating: What Every Woman Needs to Know. (p. 878)
Bishop, Helena Edwards. Lucille Tinderbox. (p. 1062)
—Simon & the Money Tree. (p. 1577)
Bishop, Helena Edwards & Bishop, Franklin. Wayward Haggis. (p. 1865)
Bishop, Ian A. Master's Tree. (p. 1103)
Bishop, Jenna Lucado, jt. auth. see Lucado, Max.
Bishop, Jennie. Garden Wall: A Story of Love Based on I Corinthians 13. Stoddard, Jeff, illus. (p. 656)
—Jesus Must Be Really Special. Wummer, Amy, illus. (p. 916)
—Jonah & the Big Fish Coloring Book. (p. 925)
—Life Lessons from the Squire & the Scroll: Battle Plans for a Pure Heart. (p. 1011)
—Squire & the Scroll: A Tale of the Rewards of a Pure Heart. McDaniels, Preston, illus. (p. 1637)
—Squire & the Scroll Coloring Book. (p. 1637)
—Three Gifts of Christmas. McDaniels, Preston, illus. (p. 1742)
Bishop, Jennie & Henson, Susan. Life Lessons from the Princess & the Kiss: Planting Seeds of Purity in Young Hearts. (p. 1011)
Bishop, John. Goal Setting for Students: Winner of three national parenting book Awards. (p. 687)
Bishop, John E., illus. see Bottiglieri, Tim.
Bishop, Karen C. Christmas Lantern. Donahue, Jim, illus. (p. 314)
Bishop, Kathleen Wong, illus. see Hayashi, Leslie Ann.
Bishop, Mary Harelkin & Coteau Books Staff. Tunnels of Tyranny: A Fourth Moose Jaw Adventure. (p. 1797)
Bishop, Megan, illus. see Blackburn, C. Edward.
Bishop, Meghan, jt. auth. see Bishop, Sherry.
Bishop, Michael. By the River Bank Cloke, Rene, illus. (p. 249)
—In the Wild Wood Cloke, Rene, illus. (p. 868)
—Mr Toad Comes Home Cloke, Rene, illus. (p. 1186)
—Mr Toad in Trouble Cloke, Rene, illus. (p. 1186)
Bishop, Michele. Mummy's Happy Tears. Sharp, Craig, illus. (p. 1191)
Bishop, Nic. Butterflies. Bishop, Nic, photos by. (p. 247)
—Butterflies & Moths. Bishop, Nic, photos by. (p. 247)
—Chameleon! (p. 289)
—Cloud Forest. Bishop, Nic, photos by. (p. 334)
—Frogs. Bishop, Nic, photos by. (p. 641)
—Little Monsters. Bishop, Nic, illus. (p. 1032)
—Lizard, Level 2. Bishop, Nic, illus. (p. 1042)
—Lizards. Bishop, Nic, photos by. (p. 1042)
—Marsupials. Bishop, Nic, photos by. (p. 1097)
—NIC Bishop - Spiders. Bishop, Nic, photos by. (p. 1250)
—Snakes. Bishop, Nic, illus. (p. 1596)
—Spiders. Bishop, Nic, photos by. (p. 1626)
—Spiders. (p. 1627)
Bishop, Nic, illus. see Cowley, Joy.
Bishop, Nic, illus. see Jackson, Ellen.
Bishop, Nic, illus. see Montgomery, Sy.
Bishop, Nic, jt. auth. see Montgomery, Sy.
Bishop, Nic, photos by see Cowley, Joy.
Bishop, Nic, photos by see Jackson, Ellen.
Bishop, Nic, photos by see Montgomery, Sy.
Bishop, Nic & Hughes, Jon. Is There Anybody Out There? Moon, Cliff, ed. (p. 890)
Bishop, Phyllis. Tommy Minor & Tiny Major Danger. (p. 1765)
Bishop, Rhonda. Felix's Fabulous Feathers Roberts, Gaylia, illus. (p. 581)
Bishop, Roma, illus. see Lane, Leena.
Bishop, Rose. Arielle's Pursuit. (p. 98)
Bishop, Sara. Luis the Llam. (p. 1064)
Bishop, Sherry & Bishop, Meghan. Leopold the Leprechaun: A Story of Imagination. (p. 993)
Bishop, Tracey, illus. see Howard, Ian T.
Bishop, Tracy, illus. see Bright, Brad, et al.
Bishop, Tracy, illus. see Roth, Sarra J.
Bishop, Veronica, jt. auth. see Dowley, Tim.
Bishop, W. H. Meltin: The Iceberg. (p. 1125)
Bishop, Wendy & Teague, Deborah Coxwell. Feeling Our Way: A Writing Teacher's Sourcebook. (p. 580)
BishopRoby, Joshua. Animal Kingdom. (p. 78)
—World of Animals. (p. 1956)
Bisiar, Ed. Visitor in the Dark. (p. 1845)
Biskup, Agnieszka. Aliens & Energy Aón, Carlos, illus. (p. 41)
—Amazing Story of Space Travel. Pop Art Properties Staff, illus. (p. 56)
—Amazing Work of Scientists with Max Axiom, Super Scientist Baez, Marcelo, illus. (p. 56)
—Awesome Animals ABC. Brooks, David, illus. (p. 121)
—Batarangs & Grapnels: The Science Behind Batman's Utility Belt (p. 143)
—Batsuits & Capes: The Science Behind Batman's Body Armor (p. 145)
—Captured by Pirates! An Isabel Soto History Adventure Stewart, Roger, illus. (p. 265)
—D-Day: June 6 1944 (p. 397)
—Egypt's Mysterious Pyramids: An Isabel Soto Archaeology Adventure. Stewart, Roger, illus. (p. 507)
—Explorar Ecosistemas con Max Axiom, Supercientífico. Strictly Spanish Translation Services Staff, tr. from ENG. (p. 550)
—Exploring Ecosystems with Max Axiom, Super Scientist Smith, Tod G., illus. (p. 552)
—Exploring Ecosystems with Max Axiom, Super Scientist Smith, Todd Aaron & Smith, Tod G., illus. (p. 552)
—Football: How It Works. (p. 615)
—George Washington: The Rise of America's First President. Mallea, Cristian, illus. (p. 664)
—Graphic Expeditions. Stewart, Roger, illus. (p. 711)
—Gripping Truth about Forces & Motion Lum, Bernice, illus. (p. 724)
—Hockey: How It Works. (p. 786)
—Houdini: The Life of the Great Escape Artist Kinsella, Pat, illus. (p. 802)
—Incredible Work of Engineers with Max Axiom, Super Scientist Baez, Marcelo, illus. (p. 869)
—Obama: The Historic Election of America's 44th President Hayden, Seitu, illus. (p. 1275)
—Powerful World of Energy with Max Axiom, Super Scientist (p. 1391)
—Solid Truth about States of Matter with Max Axiom, Super Scientist Martin, Cynthia & Timmons, Anne, illus. (p. 1607)
—Solid Truth about States of Matter with Max Axiom, Super Scientist Martin, Cynthia & Schulz, Barbara, illus. (p. 1607)
—Solid Truth about States of Matter with Max Axiom, Super Scientist. Martin, Cynthia & Schulz, Barbara, illus. (p. 1607)
—Super Cool Chemical Reaction Activities with Max Axiom. Baez, Marcelo, illus. (p. 1679)
—Super Cool Forces & Motion Activities with Max Axiom. Baez, Marcelo, illus. (p. 1679)
—Thunder Rolling down the Mountain: The Story of Chief Joseph & the Nez Perce Zimmerman, Rusty, illus. (p. 1746)
—Understanding Global Warming with Max Axiom, Super Scientist Martin, Cynthia & Anderson, Bill, illus. (p. 1815)
—Understanding Viruses with Max Axiom, Super Scientist (p. 1816)
—Understanding Viruses with Max Axiom, Super Scientist Derington, Nick, illus. (p. 1816)
—Vampires & Cells Jok, Diego, illus. (p. 1832)
—Vampires & Cells. Jok, illus. (p. 1832)
Biskup, Agnieszka, jt. auth. see Enz, Tammy.
Biskup, Agnieszka, jt. auth. see Yomtov, Nel.
Biskup, Agnieszka & Collins, Terry. American Graphic. Pope, Richie, illus. (p. 61)
Biskup, Agnieszka & Enz, Tammy. Max Axiom Science & Engineering Activities. Baez, Marcelo, illus. (p. 1111)
—Super Cool Science & Engineering Activities. (p. 1679)
Biskup, Agnieszka & Schulz, Barbara. Journey into Adaptation with Max Axiom, Super Scientist Martin, Cynthia, illus. (p. 928)
—Journey into Adaptation with Max Axiom, Super Scientist Martin, Cynthia & Schulz, Barbara, illus. (p. 928)
Biskup, Agnieszka & Sohn, Emily. Ciencia Gráfica. Martin, Cynthia & Dominguez, Richard, illus. (p. 319)
Biskup, Agnieszka, et al. Ciencia Gráfica. Strictly Spanish, LLC., tr. (p. 319)
—Comprender el Calentamiento Global con Max Axiom, Supercientífico. Strictly Spanish Translation Services Staff, tr. from ENG. (p. 354)
—Dynamic World of Chemical Reactions with Max Axiom. (p. 491)
—Exploring Titanic: An Isabel Soto History Adventure (p. 554)
—Graphic Science & Engineering in Action. Baez, Marcelo, illus. (p. 711)
—LOL Physical Science. Lum, Bernice, illus. (p. 1045)
—Surprising World of Bacteria with Max Axiom, Super Scientist (p. 1686)
—Uncovering Mummies: An Isabel Soto Archaeology Adventure (p. 1812)
—Viaje por la Adaptación con Max Axiom, Supercientífico. Strictly Spanish LLC. Staff, tr. (p. 1839)
Biskup, Agnieszka Józefina. George Washington: The Rise of America's First President Mallea, Cristian, illus. (p. 664)
Bissell, Robert. Robert Bissell's Rabbits & Bears. (p. 1478)
Bissell, Sybil A. God & Me: A Journey of Divine Encounters. (p. 688)
—Why Me, Lord? For victims of sexual & physical Abuse Madill, Douglas, illus. (p. 1925)
Bissen, Joe. Minnesota Twins. (p. 1147)
Bissett, Josie. Boogie Monster. Atteberry, Kevan J., illus. (p. 210)
Bissex, Rachel. Dancing With My Mother. Passman, Emily, illus. (p. 403)
Bissing, Ronimund von, see von Bissing, Ronimund.
Bissinger, Wendy & Wendy Bissinger. Sequenced Scale Studies for Cello. (p. 1552)
Bisson, Terry. Nat Turner: Slave Revolt Leader. (p. 1230)
Bissonette, Aimee M. North Woods Girl. McGehee, Claudia, illus. (p. 1265)
Bissonette, Ray. Joe's Story. (p. 920)
Bist, Richard & Skindzier, Jon. Florida State University College Prowler off the Record. (p. 607)
Bist, Vandana, illus. see Raote, Komilla.
Bistline, Lesley. Hairballs in the Morning. (p. 736)
Bistricean, Claudius, illus. see Bistricean, Karen.
Bistricean, Karen. Adventures of Fergus & Lady: The Beginning. Bistricean, Claudius, illus. (p. 18)
—Adventures of Fergus & Lady: Home Sweet Home. Bistricean, Claudius, illus. (p. 18)
Biswas, Pulak, illus. see Gilmore, Rachna.
Biswas, Pulak, illus. see Ravishankar, Anushka.
Bitetto, Marco A. V. Corrections to Article Inaccuracy. (p. 368)
—Errors of Thanks for the Memories. (p. 534)
—Journal of Amateur Computing: Spring/Summer 2003 Issue. Bitetto, Marco A. V., ed. (p. 927)
—Theme Stream: Helicopters. Vol. 10 (p. 1728)
—Theme Stream: Helicopters. Vol. 11 (p. 1728)
—Theme Stream: Helicopters. Vol. 13 (p. 1728)
Bitline S. A. 1010, jt. auth. see Rossouw, Andre J.
Bitner, Amanda Marie. Baby Sister. (p. 128)
Bitner, Pamela. Brother-Sister Team. Poppen, Alex, illus. (p. 231)
Bitner, Pamela, jt. auth. see Sullivan, Therese M.
Bitskoff, Aleksei, illus. see de la Bédoyere, Camilla.
Bitter. Math Calc Explorer 10-Pk. (p. 1105)
Bitterman, Albert. Fortune Cookies. Raschka, Chris, illus. (p. 623)
Bitterman, Kevin. BD's Big Hit (p. 147)
Bitterman, Quinn. Push & Pull: Understanding Force & Motion. (p. 1420)
Bittle Jr., Paul. Me too, Little Puppies, Me Too (p. 1116)
Bittmann, Suzy. Life with Molly Mcgee - Sports Chick: Caught in a Pickle. (p. 1013)
Bittner, M. Winter Angels & Magic Snowflakes. (p. 1938)
Bitto, Ron. Weddings & Funerals. (p. 1871)
Bivens, Arthur Clark. From Sailboats to Submarines. (p. 643)
Biviano, David J. True Moon. (p. 1792)
Bivins, Christopher, illus. see Sensel, Joni.
Bix, Cynthia Overbeck. Fad Mania! A History of American Crazes. (p. 561)
Bix, Daisy. At the Dog Park with Sam & Lucy. Hansen, Amelia, illus. (p. 111)
—Buddy Unchained. Hyatt, Joe, illus. (p. 235)
Bix, Jasper. Let's Go Ice-Skating! (p. 997)
—Let's Go Sledding! (p. 997)
Bix, William T. Sometimes the Best Gets Picked Last. (p. 1610)
Bixby, James F. Mystery of the Christmas Dollhouse. (p. 1225)
Bixby, Sean, illus. see Dongweck, James.
Bixley, Donovan. Little Bo Peep & More ... Favourite Nursery Rhymes. (p. 1024)
Bixley, Donovan, illus. see Falkner, Brian.
Biz, Jen. Letter to My Beagle. (p. 1002)
—Terrible Noise. (p. 1721)
Biz Kid$ & Kotsiovos, Jean. Banking & Financial Systems. (p. 136)
Biz Kids Staff. Banking & Financial Systems. (p. 136)
Bizjak, Donna, illus. see McGovern, Suzanne.
Bizos, Erató-Nadia, et al. Life Skills Matters: Grade 3. (p. 1013)
Bizos, Erató-Nadia, et al. Life Skills Matters Grade 1. (p. 1013)
Bizos, Erató-Nadia, et al. Life Skills Matters Grade 1 Sesotho Translation. (p. 1013)
—Life Skills Matters Grade 1 Xitsonga Translation. (p. 1013)
—Life Skills Matters Grade 3 Workbook Sesotho Translation. (p. 1013)
—Life Skills Matters Grade 3 Workbook Xitsonga Translation. (p. 1013)
Bizzarro, Grace. Christmas on the Internet. Bohart, Lisa, illus. (p. 315)
Bizzozero, Leona Grearson. Unicorn with No Horn. (p. 1818)
Bjarkdottir, Bjork, illus. see Danielsdottir, Sigrun.
Bjarnadottir, Hildur. Triplets. (p. 1787)
Bjarnason, Bjarni Thor, illus. see Snorradottir, Asthildur Bj.
Bjelke, Rolf, photos by see Shapiro, Deborah & Daniel, Lea.
Bjelkier Press. Hero Finds His Path. (p. 772)
Bjerregaard, Malynda. Chatter Batter: Four Stories for Speech. (p. 295)
Björk, Christina. Linnea in Monet's Garden. Sandin, Joan, tr. (p. 1019)
Bjork, Linda. Salmon Cavern. (p. 1505)
Bjorklund, L. F., illus. see Brown, Frances Williams.
Bjorklund, Lynda Hunter & St. James, Rebecca. SHE Teen: Becoming a Safe, Healthy, & Empowered Woman - God's Way. (p. 1564)
Bjorklund, Ruth. Afghanistan. (p. 26)
—Aikido. (p. 30)
—Arthritis. (p. 103)
—Aung San Suu Kyi. (p. 115)
—Blue Whales. (p. 203)
—Cerebral Palsy. (p. 287)
—China. (p. 306)
—Cholera. (p. 309)
—Circulatory System. (p. 321)
—Cree. (p. 380)
—Cystic Fibrosis. (p. 397)
—Eating Disorders. (p. 501)
—Epilepsy. (p. 532)
—Food-Borne Illnesses. (p. 613)
—Gun Control. (p. 731)
—Hopi. (p. 797)
—Hungary. (p. 827)
—Immigration. (p. 861)
—Jamaica. (p. 906)
—Komodo Dragons. (p. 966)
—Liberia. (p. 1005)
—Lizards. (p. 1042)
—Louisiana. (p. 1058)
—Montana. (p. 1170)
—New Mexico. (p. 1246)
—Parrots. (p. 1325)
—Projects about Ancient China. (p. 1410)
—Pros & Cons of Algae Biofuel. (p. 1412)
—Pros & Cons of Natural Gas & Fracking. (p. 1412)
—Puerto Rico. (p. 1414)
—Rabbits. (p. 1429)
—Senses. (p. 1551)
—Sickle Cell Anemia. (p. 1572)
—South Dakota. (p. 1617)
—Tasmanian Devils. (p. 1707)
—Tourette Syndrome. (p. 1773)
—Venus. (p. 1836)
—Wolves. (p. 1944)
Bjorklund, Ruth, jt. auth. see Hantula, Richard.
Bjorklund, Ruth, jt. auth. see Horn, Geoffrey M.
Bjorklund, Ruth, jt. auth. see Todras, Ellen.
Bjorklund, Ruth & Fitzgerald, Stephanie. Massachusetts. (p. 1102)
Bjorklund, Ruth & Hantula, Richard. Puerto Rico. (p. 1414)
Bjorklund, Ruth & Steinitz, Andy. Louisiana. (p. 1058)
Bjorklund, Ruth & Todras, Ellen H. Montana. (p. 1170)
Bjorklund, Ruth & Truett, Trudi Strain. Kansas. (p. 943)
Bjorklund, Ruth, et al. Alaska. (p. 33)
—Nebraska. (p. 1239)
—Oregon. (p. 1302)
Bjorklund, Shawn. G Is for Goat's Groovy Galoshes: Silly ABCs & Other Oddities. (p. 651)
Bjorklung, Lorence, illus. see Selbert, Jerry.
Bjorkman, Lauren. Miss Fortune Cookie. (p. 1151)
—My Invented Life. (p. 1211)
Björkman, Manns, jt. auth. see McGraw, Jay.
Björkman, Steve. Dinosaurs Don't, Dinosaurs Do. (p. 444)
—Dinosaurs Don't, Dinosaurs Do. Björkman, Steve, illus. (p. 444)
—Look Out, Mouse! (p. 1050)
—Look Out, Mouse! Björkman, Steve, illus. (p. 1050)
Björkman, Steve, illus. see Carlson, Melody.
Björkman, Steve, illus. see Cochran, Bill.
Björkman, Steve, illus. see Cox, Judy.
Björkman, Steve, illus. see Foxworthy, Jeff.
Björkman, Steve, illus. see Gibson, Amy.
Björkman, Steve, illus. see Gutch, Michael.
Björkman, Steve, illus. see Heller, Alyson.
Björkman, Steve, illus. see Hom, Susan & Richardson, Phillip.
Björkman, Steve, illus. see Larcombe, Jennifer Rees.
Björkman, Steve, illus. see McGraw, Jay & Björkman, Manns.
Björkman, Steve, illus. see Murphy, Stuart J.
Björkman, Steve, illus. see Post, Peggy & Senning, Cindy Post.
Björkman, Steve, illus. see Senning, Cindy Post & Post, Emily.
Björkman, Steve, illus. see Senning, Cindy Post & Post, Peggy.
Björkman, Steve, illus. see Spurr, Elizabeth.

B

Björkman, Steve, illus. see Stella, Lennon & Stella, Maisy.
Björkman, Steve, illus. see Vande Velde, Vivian.
Björkman, Steve, illus. see Wallace, Carol.
Björkman, Steve, jt. auth. see Gross, Ruth Belov.
bjornlund, lydia. Civil Rights Movement. (p. 324)
Bjornlund, Lydia. History of Video Games. (p. 785)
—How Dangerous Are Performance-Enhancing Drugs? (p. 806)
bjornlund, lydia. Marijuana. (p. 1094)
—Oxycodone. (p. 1315)
Bjornlund, Lydia. Personality Disorders. (p. 1344)
—Rosa Parks & the Montgomery Bus Boycott. (p. 1489)
Bjornlund, Lydia D. Alcohol. (p. 35)
—Angelina Jolie. (p. 74)
—Deforestation. (p. 424)
—Teen Smoking. (p. 1714)
—Trail of Tears: The Relocation of American Indians. (p. 1776)
—Women in Colonial America. (p. 1945)
—Women of the Suffrage Movement. (p. 1946)
Bjornsen, Holly. Red Book Pets Vets & Snakes. Phillips, Linda T., illus. (p. 1453)
Bjornsen, Holly, illus. see White, Elga Haymon.
Bjornson, Barb, illus. see Rosenbaum, Andria Warmflash.
Bjornson, Barb, illus. see Zolkower, Edie Stoltz.
Bjornson, Barbara, illus. see Hills, Jodi.
Bjornson, Nancy. Llamas, Ponies & Pyrite. (p. 1043)
—Mustangs, Fires & Snakes. (p. 1194)
—Sleds, Skins & Snow. (p. 1588)
BJU Press, creator. Worktext for K5: For Christian Schools. (p. 1953)
BJU Staff. Algebra 1 Student Text Grd 9. (p. 38)
—American Republic Activity S 8. (p. 63)
—American Republic Student Grd8. (p. 63)
—Beginnings Write Now Grd K5. (p. 160)
—Bible Truths Stu Materials Gk5. (p. 176)
—Geography Activity Student Gr9. (p. 662)
—Handwriting Worktext Grd 2. (p. 741)
—Reading Student Text Grd 2 If. (p. 1446)
—Reading Student Text Grd 2 Whe. (p. 1446)
—Reading Student Text Grd 3. (p. 1446)
—Reading Student Text Grd 3 B. (p. 1446)
—Reading Worktext Student Grd 2. (p. 1447)
—Science Activity Manual St Gr6. (p. 1524)
—Science Student Notebook Grd 1. (p. 1528)
—Science Student Text Grd 1. (p. 1528)
—Spelling Worktext Grd 2. (p. 1625)
—World Studies Activity St Grd7. (p. 1958)
—Writing Grammar Tests Ak Grd 8. (p. 1965)
—Writing Grammar Tests Grd 8. (p. 1965)
—Writing Grammar Worktext Grd 2. (p. 1965)
Blabey, Aaron. Pearl Barley & Charlie Parsley. (p. 1333)
—Sunday Chutney. Blabey, Aaron, illus. (p. 1676)
Blace, Maria. Lunie Balloonies. Swope, Brenda, illus. (p. 1066)
Blachowicz, Camille & Ogle, Donna. Reading Comprehension: Strategies for Independent Learners. (p. 1445)
Blachowicz, Camille L. Z. Reading Fluency: Reader. (p. 1445)
—Reading Fluency: Reader's Record. (p. 1445)
—Reading Fluency. (p. 1445)
—Reading Fluency, Level C: Reader's Record. (p. 1446)
—Reading Fluency, Level F. (p. 1446)
—Reading Fluency Level G. (p. 1446)
—Reading Fluency Level G: Reader. (p. 1446)
Black, Allyson. Crushed Spaziante, Patrick & Riley, Kellee, illus. (p. 386)
—Fashion Face-off. Johnson, Shane L., illus. (p. 575)
Black, Amber. Day with Miss Sassy. (p. 415)
Black, Andrea, ed. see Black, Chuck.
Black, Angie. Adopting Jake. Lucas, Diane, illus. (p. 13)
Black, Baxter A. Rudolph's Night Off. Patterson, Bill, illus. (p. 1494)
Black, Baxter, frwd. Good Medicine: Humorous Stories & Poems from COWBOY MAGAZINE (p. 698)
Black, Bekka. IDrakula. (p. 852)
Black, Birdie. Just Right for Christmas. Beardshaw, Rosalind, illus. (p. 939)
Black, Brittney, ed. see Black, Chuck.
Black, Bronze, illus. see Duffield, Wendell A.
Black, C. Stewart. Jennifer. (p. 912)
Black, Cary & Schott, Gretchen Victoria. French Quarter Tori & the Red Owl. Travis, Caroline, illus. (p. 636)
Black, Cassandra. Twinkle: A Chapter Book. (p. 1802)
—Twinkle: The Only Firefly Who Couldn't Light Up. Kirk, Tim, illus. (p. 1802)
—When I'm Big & Grown: When I'm Big & Grown: I Want to Be an Entrepreneur When I Grow Up. Tucker, Tracey, illus. (p. 1903)
Black, Chuck. Kingdom's Call. (p. 960)
—Kingdom's Dawn. (p. 960)
—Kingdom's Hope. (p. 960)
—Kingdom's Quest. (p. 960)
—Kingdom's Reign Black, Andrea & Black, Brittney, eds. (p. 960)
—Kingdom's Reign. (p. 960)
—Lady Carliss & the Waters of Moorue. (p. 970)
—Rise of the Fallen: Wars of the Realm, Book 2. (p. 1475)
—Sir Bentley & Holbrook Court. (p. 1580)
—Sir Dalton & the Shadow Heart. (p. 1580)
—Sir Kendrick & the Castle of Bel Lione. (p. 1580)
—Sir Quinlan & the Swords of Valor. (p. 1580)
—Sir Rowan & the Camerian Conquest. (p. 1580)
Black, Clinton L. Why Bad Things Happen to Good Black Women - Where Is God? An Inspiring & Empowering New Book about God's Purpose for Your Misfortunes. (p. 1922)
Black, Cuyler. Goat of Many Colors (p. 687)
Black, Dave. Alfred's Kid's Drum Course 1 Bk & Cd & Drum. (p. 37)
—Kids Drumset Course. (p. 953)
Black, Dave & Houghton, Steve. Alfred's Kid's Drum Course. Shelly, Jeff, illus. (p. 37)
Black, Deirdre. River Run. (p. 1476)
Black, Donnette. Madam C. J. Walker's Road to Success. (p. 1069)
Black, Eldritch. Book of Kindly Deaths. (p. 211)
Black Eye Design, illus. see Lederer, Richard & Gibbs Smith Publisher Staff.
Black Fox, Barbara & Kinnaird, Sara Jane. Princess, the Pickle, & Birdlegs. (p. 1406)
Black, Garry, jt. auth. see Stewart, Michael.
Black, Heidi. Journey to the Ark: Samuel Finds His Way. (p. 929)
Black, Hermann. World War II. (p. 1959)
Black, Holly. Black Heart. (p. 196)
—Coldest Girl in Coldtown. (p. 339)
—Darkest Part of the Forest. (p. 408)
—Doll Bones. (p. 463)
—Doll Bones. Wheeler, Eliza, illus. (p. 463)
—Iron Trial. (p. 888)
—Ironside: A Modern Faery's Tale. (p. 888)
—Kin. Naifeh, Ted, illus. (p. 957)
—Kind. Naifeh, Ted, illus. (p. 957)
—Kith. Naifeh, Ted, illus. (p. 962)
—Modern Faerie Tales: Tithe; Valiant; Ironside. (p. 1158)
—Poison Eaters: And Other Stories. Black, Theo, illus. (p. 1377)
—Red Glove. (p. 1454)
—Tithe: A Modern Faerie Tale. (p. 1758)
—Valiant: A Modern Faerie Tale. (p. 1830)
—White Cat. (p. 1912)
—Zombies vs. Unicorns. (p. 1988)
Black, Holly, jt. auth. see DiTerlizzi, Tony.
Black, Holly & Castellucci, Cecil, eds. Geektastic: Stories from the Nerd Herd. (p. 659)
Black, Holly & Clare, Cassandra. Iron Trial. (p. 888)
Black, Holly & DiTerlizzi, Tony. Arthur Spiderwick's Field Guide to the Fantastical World Around You. DiTerlizzi, Tony, illus. (p. 104)
—Arthur Spiderwick's Field Guide to the Fantastical World Around You. Black, Holly & DiTerlizzi, Tony, illus. (p. 104)
—Field Guide. DiTerlizzi, Tony, illus. (p. 583)
—Giant Problem. DiTerlizzi, Tony, illus. (p. 674)
—Ironwood Tree. DiTerlizzi, Tony, illus. (p. 888)
—Lucinda's Secret. DiTerlizzi, Tony, illus. (p. 1062)
—Seeing Stone DiTerlizzi, Tony, illus. (p. 1548)
—Seeing Stone. DiTerlizzi, Tony, illus. (p. 1548)
—Spiderwick. DiTerlizzi, Tony, illus. (p. 1627)
—Spiderwick Chronicles: The Field Guide - The Seeing Stone - Lucinda's Secret - The Ironwood Tree - The Wrath of Mulgrath. Set DiTerlizzi, Tony, illus. (p. 1627)
—Wrath of Mulgarath. (p. 1962)
—Wrath of Mulgarath. DiTerlizzi, Tony, illus. (p. 1962)
—Wyrm King. DiTerlizzi, Tony, illus. (p. 1966)
Black, Holly & Kushner, Ellen, eds. Welcome to Bordertown. (p. 1873)
Black, Holly & Larbalestier, Justine, eds. Zombies vs. Unicorns. (p. 1988)
Black, Howard, jt. auth. see Parks, Sandra.
Black, Howard & Parks, Sandra. Building Thinking Skills Level 1. (p. 239)
—Dr. Funster's Word Benders B1: Thinking & Vocabulary Fun! (p. 475)
Black, Howard, et al. Learning on Purpose: A Self-Management Approach to Study Skills. (p. 985)
Black, Ilene, illus. see Cowden, Matt.
Black, Jake. Attack of the Man-Bat! Vecchio, Luciano, illus. (p. 113)
—Big Summer Vacation Activity Book. (p. 184)
—Destination: Ooo: Land of Ooo in under 20 Snails a Day. Johnson, Shane L., illus. (p. 430)
—Finn & Jake's Awesome Activities on the Go. (p. 589)
—Official Elmore Junior High School Yearbook. (p. 1280)
—Tales from Regular Show. (p. 1701)
—Totally Top Secret. (p. 1771)
Black, Jake & Beatty, Scott. Batman: Comic Chapter Books (p. 144)
Black, Jake & Brallier, Max. Stuck on Jake. (p. 1669)
Black, Jake & Meredith Books Staff. Race Against Crime. Wallace, Loston, illus. (p. 1430)
—Robo Monster. Stewart, Scott, illus. (p. 1480)
Black, James. Blackbeard's Pirates vs the Evil Mummies. (p. 197)
—Robin Hood vs the Plague Undead. (p. 1480)
Black, Janaya. Breaking Point. (p. 225)
Black, Janet, photos by see McMahon, V. Karen.
Black, Jenna. Glimmerglass. (p. 683)
—Replica. (p. 1461)
—Resistance. (p. 1463)
—Revolution. (p. 1466)
—Shadowspell. (p. 1558)
—Sirensong: A Faeriewalker Novel. (p. 1581)
Black, Jennifer. We Are One Exploration Cards. (p. 1865)
Black, Jeremy, jt. auth. see Doyle, Malachy.
Black, Jess. Dog in Danger! Whitby, Charlotte, illus. (p. 461)
—Fright Night! Whitby, Charlotte, illus. (p. 639)
—Unexpected Arrival. Whitby, Charlotte, illus. (p. 1817)
Black, Jess, jt. auth. see Irwin, Bindi.
Black, Jess & Kunz, Chris. Happy Tails Collection (p. 746)
Black, Jessica L. Why Have Rules? Gillen, Lisa P., illus. (p. 1925)
Black, Jessica L. & Mullican, Judy. Let's Build a Snowman: Cuddle Book. Crowell, Knox, illus. (p. 994)
Black, Jo Ellen. Clyde Mclivingston Takes a Walk. (p. 336)
—Pauline's Secret Pie. (p. 1331)
Black, Joe. Afikomen Mambo. Prater, Linda, illus. (p. 26)
—Afikomen Mambo. Brown, Richard E. & Prater, Linda, illus. (p. 26)
—Boker Tov! Good Morning! Brown, Rick, illus. (p. 208)
Black, Judith. Adult Children of ... Parents. (p. 13)
—Home Front. (p. 792)
Black, Kat. Templar's Apprentice. (p. 1718)
—Templar's Destiny. (p. 1718)
—Templar's Gifts. (p. 1718)
Black, Kieron, illus. see Carville, Declan.
Black Lace Staff, jt. auth. see Strand, Angel.
Black, Laura. Stem Cell Debate: The Ethics & Science Behind the Research. (p. 1647)
Black, Lisa M. My Amazing Hands. (p. 1196)
Black Literary. Chicken Coopers. (p. 300)
Black, Magenta, jt. auth. see Lil Gems.
Black, Melissa, jt. auth. see Black, Natalie.
Black, Michael Ian. Chicken Cheeks. Hawkes, Kevin, illus. (p. 300)
—I'm Bored. Ohi, Debbie Ridpath, illus. (p. 858)
—Naked! Ohi, Debbie Ridpath, illus. (p. 1228)
—Pig Parade Is a Terrible Idea. Hawkes, Kevin, illus. (p. 1357)
—Purple Kangaroo. Brown, Peter, illus. (p. 1419)
—Qué Aburrido! (p. 1423)
Black, Michelle, illus. see Matthews, Camille.
Black, Natalie & Black, Melissa. Double Sided: A Teen Novel. (p. 473)
Black Olive. Outlook - Grim: The Dead Nasties. (p. 1313)
Black, Pam. Candee Bar. (p. 261)
Black, Peter A. Parables from the Pond. (p. 1323)
Black, Peter Jay. Blackout. (p. 197)
—Urban Outlaws. (p. 1825)
Black, Robert. Liberty Girl. (p. 1005)
Black, Robert A. Lunar Pioneers. (p. 1065)
Black, Robyn Hood. Sir Mike. Murphy, David, illus. (p. 1580)
—Wolves. Howard, Colin, illus. (p. 1944)
Black, Ronald, ed. see Swire, Otta.
Black, Rosemary. Sweet Celebrations: A Holiday Dessert Book for Kids. (p. 1689)
Black, Sandi. Vital Skills: How to Build Healthy Family Relationships. (p. 1846)
Black, Sean. Extolziby Gruff & the 39th College. (p. 555)
Black, Shonda. Where Has Grandma Gone? (p. 1907)
Black, Simon. Dog Child. Robledo, Honorio, illus. (p. 461)
Black, Sharnika. Big Cats (p. 180)
Black, Sonia, jt. auth. see Scholastic, Inc. Staff.
Black, Sonia W. Jumping the Broom. Van Wright, Cornelius & Hu, Ying-Hwa, illus. (p. 934)
Black, Tara. Art of Correction. (p. 102)
Black, Ted, et al. Birds of Michigan. (p. 191)
Black, Theo, illus. see Black, Holly.
Black, Theodor, illus. see Palmer, Michele.
Black, Tony, Jr. Free in Mind, Enslaved in Reality. (p. 634)
—Uprising. (p. 1825)
Black, Vickie. Young Chicken Farmers: Tips for Kids Raising Backyard Chickens. (p. 1978)
Black, Wills W. Touch the Moon & Other Adventures of the Fliff Family. (p. 1772)
Black, Yelena. Dance of Shadows. (p. 402)
Blackaby, Henry. Experiencing God Youth Video. (p. 549)
—Your Church Experiencing God Together. (p. 1980)
Blackaby, Susan. Blue Stone Plot Epstein, Len, illus. (p. 203)
—Brownie Groundhog & the February Fox. Segovia, Carmen, illus. (p. 232)
—Brownie Groundhog & the Wintry Surprise. Segovia, Carmen, illus. (p. 232)
—Buds & Blossoms: A Book about Flowers DeLage, Charlene, illus. (p. 235)
—Catching Sunlight: A Book about Leaves Delage, Charlene, illus. (p. 279)
—Classroom Cookout Muehlenhardt, Amy Bailey, illus. (p. 329)
—Cleopatra: Egypt's Last & Greatest Queen. (p. 331)
—De Pesca Ruíz, Carlos, tr. (p. 416)
—Fire Drill with Mr. Dill Muehlenhardt, Amy Bailey, illus. (p. 590)
—Fishing Trip Haugen, Ryan, illus. (p. 599)
—Green & Growing: A Book about Plants. DeLage, Charlene, illus. (p. 721)
—Groceries for Grandpa Lee, Jisun, illus. (p. 725)
—Growing Things DeLage, Charlene, illus. (p. 726)
—Hatching Chicks Muehlenhardt, Amy Bailey, illus. (p. 752)
—Historical Tales Epstein, Len, illus. (p. 783)
—Jenna & the Three R's Holm, Sharon Lane, illus. (p. 912)
—Lugar de Luis Ruíz, Carlos, tr. from ENG. (p. 1064)
—Meg Sale a Pasear Ruíz, Carlos, tr. from ENG. (p. 1124)
—Mejor Futbolista Ruíz, Carlos, tr. from ENG. (p. 1124)
—Moving Day Haugen, Ryan, illus. (p. 1183)
—Nest, Nook & Cranny. Hogan, Jamie, illus. (p. 1242)
—Patito Feo. Ruíz, Carlos, tr. from ENG. (p. 1328)
—Plant Packages: A Book about Seeds Delage, Charlene, illus. (p. 1369)
—Plant Plumbing: A Book about Roots & Stems. DeLage, Charlene, illus. (p. 1369)
—Princesa Del Guisante: Versión Del Cuento de Hans Christian Anderson. Abello, Patricia, tr. from ENG. (p. 1402)
—Read-It! Readers Classroom Tales Muehlenhardt, Amy Bailey, illus. (p. 1443)
—Read-It! Readers Fairy Tales Delage, Charlene, illus. (p. 1443)
—Secret Warning Epstein, Len, illus. (p. 1544)
—Thumbelina: A Retelling of the Hans Christian Andersen Fairy Tale Delage, Charlene, illus. (p. 1745)
—Traje Nuevo Del Emperador. Abello, Patricia, tr. from ENG. (p. 1777)
—Twelve Days of Christmas in Oregon. Conahan, Carolyn Digby, illus. (p. 1800)
—Word of the Day Muehlenhardt, Amy Bailey, illus. (p. 1951)
Blackaby, Susan & Haugen, Ryan. Dan Pone la Mesa Ruíz, Carlos, tr. (p. 402)
Blackaby, Susan & Jones, Christianne C. Cuadro de Mary Ruíz, Carlos, tr. (p. 388)
Blackaby, Tom & Osborne, Rick. Sammy Experiences Jesus. Kung, Isabella, illus. (p. 1508)
Blackall, Sophie. Are You Awake? Blackall, Sophie, illus. (p. 97)
—Baby Tree. Blackall, Sophie, illus. (p. 128)
Blackall, Sophie, illus. see Barrows, Annie, et al.
Blackall, Sophie, illus. see Barrows, Annie.
Blackall, Sophie, illus. see Horvath, Polly.
Blackall, Sophie, illus. see Huxley, Aldous.
Blackall, Sophie, illus. see Jenkins, Emily.
Blackall, Sophie, illus. see Khan, Rukhsana.
Blackall, Sophie, illus. see Lewis, J. Patrick & Yolen, Jane.
Blackall, Sophie, illus. see Marciano, John Bemelmans.
Blackall, Sophie, illus. see Olshan, Matthew.
Blackall, Sophie, illus. see Rosoff, Meg.
Blackall, Sophie, illus. see Shields, Carol Diggory.
Blackall, Sophie, illus. see Shirin Yim, Bridges.
Blackall, Sophie, illus. see Stevens, April.
Blackall, Sophie, illus. see Viorst, Judith.
Blackall, Sophie, illus. see Wheeler, Lisa.
Blackall, Sophie, illus. see Woodson, Jacqueline.
Blackall, Sophie, jt. auth. see Barrows, Annie.
Blackbird. Mr. Hookworm. Blackbird, illus. (p. 1185)
Blackbird Publishing Staff. Mr. HookWorm Coloring Book. (p. 1185)
Blackburn, Abby. My Little Blue Helmet. (p. 1212)
Blackburn, C. Edward. Stories of Christmas: As Told by a Little Lamb. Bishop, Megan, illus. (p. 1654)
Blackburn, Gary. Pickerel Lake (p. 1354)
Blackburn, Joyce. James Edward Oglethorpe. (p. 907)
Blackburn, Ken. Aviation Legend Paper Airplane. (p. 119)
Blackburn, Richard & Carnahan, Rhonda. 'Twas, with a Twist! (p. 1799)
Blackburn, Sheila M. Stewie Scraps & the Easy Rider. (p. 1649)
—Stewie Scraps & the Giant Joggers. (p. 1649)
—Stewie Scraps & the Space Racer. (p. 1649)
—Stewie Scraps & the Super Sleigh. (p. 1649)
Blackburn, Winfrey P. Putney-a little pumpkin with BIG Ideas. (p. 1420)
Blackburne, Livia. Daughter of Dusk. (p. 409)
—Midnight Thief. (p. 1139)
Blackcrane, Gerelchimeg. Black Flame Holmwood, Anna, tr. from CHI. (p. 196)
Blackdog, J. M. Loni Talltree: The world's greatest tree Climber. (p. 1047)
Blacker, Elizabeth A., illus. see Wood, Jane R.
Blacker, Maryanne, ed. Children's Arts & Crafts. (p. 303)
Blacker, Sharnika. Big Cats (p. 180)
Blacker, Terence. Angel Factory. (p. 73)
—Boy2Girl. (p. 220)
—In Control, Ms. Wiz? Ross, Tony, illus. (p. 863)
—In Jail, Ms. Wiz? Ross, Tony, illus. (p. 863)
—In Stitches with Ms. Wiz (p. 865)
—Ms. Wiz Smells a Rat. (p. 1188)
Blacker, Terence & Ross, Tony. En la Carcel. (p. 522)
—Estrella de la Tele. (p. 538)
—Fuera de Control. (p. 646)
—Intrusa en el Hospital. (p. 883)
—Mundo de Problemas. (p. 1191)
Blackett, Dulcibella. Run, Dad, Run! Yelenak, Andy, illus. (p. 1496)
Blackford. Eskdale Herd Boy A Scottish Tale for the Instruction & Amusement of Young Persons. (p. 536)
—Eskdale Herd-boy: The Eskdale Herd-boy. (p. 535)
—Eskdale Herd-boy. (p. 535)
Blackford, Ami. Quest for the Dragon Stone: A Duncan Family Adventure. Blackford, Ami, illus. (p. 1426)
—Quest for the Elfin Elixir: A Duncan Family Adventure Book 2. Blackford, Ami, illus. (p. 1426)
Blackford, Andy. Bill's Bike. (p. 187)
—George & the Dragonfly. Mason, Sue, illus. (p. 663)
—Hungry Little Monkey. (p. 828)
—Jack & the Hungry Bear Van Veldhoven, Marijke, illus. (p. 902)
—Three Little Pigs & the New Neighbor. (p. 1743)
Blackford, Cheryl. Colombia. (p. 341)
—Hungry Coyote. Caple, Laurie, illus. (p. 828)
—Powerful Muscle Cars. (p. 1390)
—This Book Is Top Secret: A Collection of Awesome Military Trivia (p. 1735)
Blackford, Holly. Plight of Persephone in Childrens Literature. (p. 1374)
Blackford, John, illus. see Moore, Helen H.
Blackhurst, Rebecca. Count Grumpula & the Wood Witch. Errington, Rachael, illus. (p. 369)
Blackie. Mels -A-Bob. (p. 1125)
Blackington, Debbie. Mama's Wish/Daughter's Wish. Sommer, Xiaolan, tr. from CHI. (p. 1084)
Blackington, Toni. Put Your Glasses On. Blackington, Toni, illus. (p. 1420)
Blacklaws, Troy. Bafana Bafana: A Story of Soccer, Magic & Mandela. Stooke, Andrew, illus. (p. 132)
Blackledge, Annabel. I Want to Be a Ballerina. (p. 847)
—Let's Go Riding, Level 2. (p. 997)
Blackley Jr., Bobby. Heartfelt Poems of Life. (p. 760)
Blackley, Mary Beth, illus. see Lundy, Charlotte.
Blacklidge, Barbara. Lucky: My Story. (p. 1062)
Blackman, Christy. Mr. Thunder Is Here, but There's No Reason to Fear. (p. 1186)
Blackman, David, et al. Alyawarr Picture Dictionary. (p. 51)
Blackman, Dorothy L. New York Patriots. Gulley, Martha, illus. (p. 1248)
Blackman, Everett A. Wolf Creek Tales. (p. 1943)
Blackman, Haden. Darth Vader & the Lost Command: Vol 1. (p. 409)
—Darth Vader & the Lost Command: Vol 2. Leonardi, Rick, illus. (p. 409)
—Darth Vader & the Lost Command: Vol 3. Leonardi, Rick, illus. (p. 409)
—Darth Vader & the Lost Command: Vol 4. Leonardi, Rick, illus. (p. 409)
—Darth Vader & the Lost Command: Vol 5. Leonardi, Rick, illus. (p. 409)
Blackman, Jizelle. Buddy & Fred: The Adventurous Chronicles. (p. 234)
Blackman, Malorie. Black & White. (p. 195)
—Jessica Strange. (p. 914)
—Knife Edge. (p. 964)
—Naughts & Crosses. (p. 1237)
—Sinclair, Wonder Bear. Allwright, Deborah, illus. (p. 1578)
—Snow Dog. Sweeten, Sami, illus. (p. 1598)
—Space Race. Mier, Colin, illus. (p. 1619)
—Trust Me. (p. 1793)
Blackman, N. S. Dinotek Adventures: Hunters Attack! (p. 445)
—Secret Dinosaur #3: Jurassic Adventure. (p. 1540)
Blackman, S. A. Me & Belinda Gillis. (p. 1115)
—Smickamookum Drinks Belly. Gubitosi, Lillian, illus. (p. 1593)
Blackmon, Clarissa. Join the Club! Foundations for Multiplication. (p. 924)
Blackmon, Kim, illus. see Wilkinson, William L.
Blackmon, Rodney Allan. Kitten Named Buddy: Buddy Stays Clean. (p. 962)
—Kitten Named Buddy: Buddy Goes Outside. (p. 962)
—Kitten Named Buddy: Buddy Makes a Friend. (p. 962)

—Kitten Named Buddy, Buddy's Circus. (p. 962)
Blackmon, Rosalind. Inventions Created by African Americans: An Educational Coloring Book. (p. 884)
Blackmon, Sonya. Hip-Hop Multiplication Workbook. (p. 780)
Blackmore, Charlotte Lozano. Jeanettie Is Called Retard Francis, Amber Rose, illus. (p. 911)
Blackmore, Jeanne C. How Does Sleep Come? Sayles, Elizabeth, illus. (p. 809)
Blackmore, Katherine, illus. see Bancroft, Greg.
Blackmore, Katherine, illus. see Mackall, Dandi.
Blackmore, Katherine, illus. see Newman, Lesléa.
Blackmore, Ruth Benton, jt. auth. see Page, Phil.
Blackmore, Sarah. Livewire Investigates the Black Death. (p. 1040)
Blackmore, Sarah, jt. auth. see Basic Skills Agency Staff.
Blacknall, Sharon. Abc's & 123's of Child Safety. (p. 4)
Blackshaw, Win. David's Dinosaur. (p. 411)
Blackshear, Sue. Tuskaloosa Tales: Stories of Tuscaloosa & Its People. (p. 1799)
Blacksheep, Beverly, illus. see Ruffenach, Jessie, ed.
Blackson, Elizabeth. Our Mortal Days. (p. 1309)
Blackstock, Terri. Southern Storm (p. 1617)
Blackstone, Bellamie. Everyday Magic. (p. 544)
Blackstone, Gay. Around the House Magic. (p. 100)
Blackstone, Margaret, jt. auth. see Guest, Elissa Haden.
Blackstone, Matt. Sorry You're Lost. (p. 1614)
Blackstone, Stella. Alligator Alphabet. Bauer, Stephanie, illus. (p. 47)
—Bear about Town (L'Ours Dans la Ville) Harter, Debbie, illus. (p. 150)
—Bear about Town (Oso en las Ciudad) Harter, Debbie, illus. (p. 150)
—Bear at Home. Harter, Debbie, illus. (p. 150)
—Bear at Home (Oso en Casa) Harter, Debbie, illus. (p. 150)
—Bear at Home/L'ours a la Maison. Harter, Debbie, illus. (p. 150)
—Bear at Work. Harter, Debbie, illus. (p. 150)
—Bear at Work (Oso en el Trabajo) (p. 150)
—Bear in Sunshine. Harter, Debbie, illus. (p. 151)
—Bear Takes a Trip (Oso Se Va de Viaje) Harter, Debbie, illus. (p. 151)
—Bear's Birthday. Harter, Debbie, illus. (p. 151)
—Bear's Birthday (L'Anniversaire de l'Ours) Harter, Debbie, illus. (p. 151)
—Bear's Birthday/El Cumpleanos de Oso. Harter, Debbie, illus. (p. 151)
—Cerdota Grandota. Beaton, Clare, illus. (p. 287)
—Cleo & Caspar. Mockford, Caroline, illus. (p. 331)
—Cleo in the Snow. Mockford, Caroline, illus. (p. 331)
—Cleo on the Move. Mockford, Caroline, illus. (p. 331)
—Cleo the Cat. Mockford, Caroline, illus. (p. 331)
—Cleo's Color Book. Mockford, Caroline, illus. (p. 331)
—Cleo's Counting Book. Mockford, Caroline, illus. (p. 331)
—Come Here, Cleo! Mockford, Caroline, illus. (p. 347)
—Counting Cockatoos. Bauer, Stephanie, illus. (p. 371)
—Dragon on the Doorstep. Harter, Debbie, illus. (p. 477)
—Familia Activa de Oso. Sarfatti, Esther, tr. (p. 567)
—Familia Ocupada de Oso. (p. 567)
—Famille Active de l'Ours. (p. 568)
—Hip Shapes. Bell, Siobhan, illus. (p. 780)
—I Dreamt I Was a Dinosaur. Beaton, Clare, illus. (p. 838)
—I Spy the Sun in the Sky. (p. 846)
—Isla Bajo el Sol. Ceccoli, Nicoletta, illus. (p. 891)
—Jump into January. Carluccio, Maria, illus. (p. 934)
—L'Ours au Travail. (p. 1059)
—Making Minestrone. Brooks, Nan, illus. (p. 1081)
—My Granny Went to Market: A Round-the-World Counting Rhyme. Corr, Christopher, illus. (p. 1210)
—Oso Bajo el Sol. Sarfatti, Esther, tr. (p. 1305)
—Oso en Bicicleta. Sarfatti, Esther, tr. (p. 1305)
—Oso en Casa. Sarfatti, Esther, tr. (p. 1305)
—Oso en la Ciudad. Sarfatti, Esther, tr. (p. 1305)
—Oso en un Cuadrado. Sarfatti, Esther, tr. (p. 1305)
—Secret Seahorse. Beaton, Clare, illus. (p. 1543)
—Ship Shapes. (p. 1567)
—Ship Shapes. Bell, Siobhan, illus. (p. 1567)
—Skip Through the Seasons. Carluccio, Maria, illus. (p. 1586)
—Storytime: First Tales for Sharing. Wilson, Anne, illus. (p. 1664)
—Talk with Me! Mockford, Caroline, illus. (p. 1703)
—Walk with Me! Mockford, Caroline, illus. (p. 1854)
—Walking Through the Jungle. Harter, Debbie, illus. (p. 1854)
—Where's the Cat? Harter, Debbie, illus. (p. 1910)
—Who Are You Baby Kangaroo? Beaton, Clare, illus. (p. 1914)
—Who Are You, Baby Kangaroo? Beaton, Clare, illus. (p. 1914)
—You & Me. Manna, Giovanni, illus. (p. 1973)
—Zoe & Her Zebra. Beaton, Clare, illus. (p. 1987)
Blackstone, Stella, illus. see Harter, Debbie.
Blackstone, Stella, jt. auth. see Beaton, Clare.
Blackstone, Stella, jt. auth. see Krebs, Laurie.
Blackstone, Stella, jt. auth. see Mockford, Caroline.
Blackstone, Stella & Barefoot Books. Baby Talk. (p. 128)
—Bear on a Bike (Oso en Bicicleta) Harter, Debbie, illus. (p. 151)
Blackstone, Stella & Barefoot Books Staff. Bear's School Day. Harter, Debbie, illus. (p. 152)
—Island in the Sun. Ceccoli, Nicoletta, illus. (p. 892)
Blackstone, Stella & Bass, Jules. Hay una Vaca Entre las Coles. Beaton, Clare, illus. (p. 755)
Blackstone, Stella & Bauer, Stephanie. Counting Cockatoos. (p. 371)
—Octopus Opposites. Bauer, Stephanie, illus. (p. 1278)
Blackstone, Stella & Beaton, Clare. How Loud Is a Lion? Beaton, Clare, illus. (p. 810)
—I Dreamt I Was a Dinosaur. Beaton, Clare, illus. (p. 838)
Blackstone, Stella & Broadbent, Jim. Storytime: First Tales for Sharing. Wilson, Anne, illus. (p. 1664)
Blackstone, Stella & Carluccio, Maria. Recorrido Por Las Estaciones. Carluccio, Maria, illus. (p. 1452)
—Skip Through the Seasons. Carluccio, Maria, illus. (p. 1586)
Blackstone, Stella & Champion, Servane. L'Ours au Soleil. Harter, Debbie, illus. (p. 1059)
—L'Ours Dans le Carré. Harter, Debbie, illus. (p. 1059)
Blackstone, Stella & Corr, Christopher. My Granny Went to Market: A Round-the-World Counting Rhyme. (p. 1210)
Blackstone, Stella & Harter, Debbie. Bear at Work: Fun Activities. Harter, Debbie, illus. (p. 150)
—Bear at Work. (p. 150)
—Bear at Work. Harter, Debbie, illus. (p. 150)
—Bear in Sunshine. (p. 151)
—Bear Takes a Trip. (p. 151)
—Can You See the Red Balloon? (p. 259)
—Oso en un Cuadrado. (p. 1305)
—Who Are You? Harter, Debbie, illus. (p. 1914)
Blackstone, Stella & Meza-Riedewald, Leticia. Oso Bajo el Sol. Harter, Debbie, illus. (p. 1305)
—Oso en un Cuadrado. Harter, Debbie, illus. (p. 1305)
Blackstone, Stella & Mockford, Caroline. Cleo's Alphabet Book. (p. 331)
—Cleo's Counting Book. (p. 331)
Blackstone, Stella & Parker, Elizabeth. L'Ours Fait un Voyage. Harter, Debbie, illus. (p. 1059)
Blackstone, Stella, et al. Walking Through the Jungle. (p. 1854)
Blackthorn, Anne. Stallion of Vanishing Island. (p. 1639)
Blackthorn, J. D. & Rinehart, J. D. Crown of Three. (p. 386)
Blackwell, Amy Hackney. Law. (p. 981)
—Law Enforcement & Public Safety. (p. 981)
—Personal Care Services, Fitness & Education. (p. 1344)
Blackwell, Amy Hackney, jt. auth. see Matters, Print.
Blackwell, Amy Hackney, see Hackney Blackwell, Amy.
Blackwell, Archie. Secrets of the Dinosaur World: Jurassic Giants & Other Prehistoric Creatures. (p. 1545)
Blackwell, D. M., jt. auth. see Langan, Paul.
Blackwell, David, illus. see Grasso, Julie A.
Blackwell, David, illus. see Grasso, Julie Anne.
Blackwell, Jodi. Fundamentals: Secret Mission Children's Pack. (p. 649)
—Fundamentals: Secret Mission 001 (Germany) Teaching Pack. (p. 649)
Blackwell, Maxine, jt. auth. see Higgins, Rada/Ruth.
Blackwell, Nancy. Andy the Ant in Precious Cargo. Ettinger, Charles, illus. (p. 73)
Blackwell North America Staff. Matilda. (p. 1109)
Blackwell, Paul. Undercurrent. (p. 1814)
Blackwell, Paul E. Undercurrent. (p. 1814)
Blackwell, Su, jt. auth. see Jones, Wendy.
Blackwell-Burke, Melissa & Kunkel, Kristen. Hide & Seek Sounds. (p. 777)
—Messy Mystery. (p. 1130)
—Pizza Pie Pizzazz. (p. 1365)
—Rhyme Time Party. (p. 1468)
—Summertime Surprise. (p. 1675)
—Sunny Funny Day in May. (p. 1677)
Blackwood, David, illus. see Major, Kevin.
Blackwood, Freya, illus. see Bland, Nick.
Blackwood, Freya, illus. see Doyle, Roddy.
Blackwood, Freya, illus. see Gleeson, Libby.
Blackwood, Freya, illus. see Kobald, Irena.
Blackwood, Freya, illus. see Wild, Margaret.
Blackwood, Freya, jt. auth. see Gleeson, Libby.
Blackwood, Freyda, illus. see Dickens, Rosie.
Blackwood, Gary. Around the World in 100 Days. (p. 100)
—Curiosity. (p. 392)
—Shakespeare's Spy (p. 1559)
—Shakespeare's Spy. (p. 1559)
—Year of the Hangman. (p. 1969)
Blackwood, Gary, jt. auth. see Blackwood, Gary L.
Blackwood, Gary L. Debatable Deaths. (p. 420)
—Enigmatic Events. (p. 530)
—Just-So Woman. Manning, Jane K., illus. (p. 939)
—Legends or Lies. (p. 990)
—Mysterious Messages: A History of Codes & Ciphers. (p. 1223)
—Perplexing People. (p. 1343)
—Second Sight. (p. 1539)
—Shakespeare's Spy. (p. 1559)
—Unsolved History (p. 1822)
Blackwood, Gary L. & Blackwood, Gary. Second Sight. (p. 1539)
—Year of the Hangman. (p. 1969)
Blackwood, Gary L. & Follett, Katherine. Enigmatic Events. (p. 530)
Blackwood, Gary L. & Miller, Susan Martins. Perplexing People. (p. 1343)
Blackwood, Gary L. & Shannon, Terry Miller. Debatable Deaths. (p. 420)
Blackwood, Gary L. & Siburt, Ruth. Legends or Lies? (p. 990)
Blackwood, John. Mathematics Around Us (p. 1108)
Blackwood, Kristin, illus. see Oelschlager, Vanita.
Blackwood, Kristin, illus. see Oeslchlager, Vanita.
Blackwood, Kristin, jt. auth. see Oelschlager, Vanita.
Blackwood, Melissa & Monaghan, Stephen. Letts Monster Practice e Times Tables Age 5-7. Dawson, Liz, illus. (p. 1003)
Blackwood, Melissa, et al. Letts Monster Practice e Maths Age 5-6. (p. 1003)
Blackwood, Paul E., ed. see Hyler, Nelson W.
Blackwood, Sage. Jinx. (p. 919)
—Jinx's Fire. (p. 919)
—Jinx's Magic. (p. 919)
Blade, Adam. Adventurer's Handbook Beast Quest. (p. 15)
—Amictus the Bug Queen. (p. 65)
—Amulet of Avantia: Luna the Moon Wolf. (p. 66)
—Amulet of Avantia: Nixa the Death Bringer. (p. 66)
—Amulet of Avantia: Equinus the Spirit Horse. (p. 66)
—Amulet of Avantia. (p. 66)
—Anoret the First Beast. (p. 87)
—Arachnid the Spider King. (p. 94)
—Arax the Soul Stealer. (p. 94)
—Beast Quest: Ravira Ruler of the Underworld. (p. 152)
—Beast Quest: Early Reader Vedra & Krimon Twin Beasts of Avantia. (p. 152)
—Beast Quest #24: Amulet of Avantia: Stealth the Ghost Panther. (p. 152)
—Beast Quest - Battle of the Beasts - Sepron vs Narga. (p. 152)
—Beast Quest Special Edition #2: Vedra & Krimon the Twin Dragons. (p. 152)
—Brutus the Hound of Horror. (p. 233)
—Call to War. (p. 254)
—Carnivora the Winged Scavenger. (p. 270)
—Cephalox the Cyber Squid. (p. 287)
—Chasing Evil. (p. 294)
—Chronicles of Avantia #3: Call to War. (p. 317)
—Convol the Cold-Blooded Brute. (p. 361)
—Creta the Winged Terror. (p. 381)
—Cypher the Mountain Giant. (p. 397)
—Dagger of Doom. (p. 399)
—Dark Cauldron. (p. 407)
—Dark Realm: Narga the Sea Monster. (p. 408)
—Deep Dive #1: Cephalox the Cyber Squid. (p. 422)
—Deep Dive #2: Silda the Electric Eel. (p. 422)
—Deep Dive #3: Manak the Manta Ray. (p. 422)
—Deep Dive #4: Kraya the Blood Shark. (p. 422)
—Doomskull - The King of Fear (p. 470)
—Elko Lord of the Sea. (p. 513)
—Ellik the Lightning Horror. (p. 514)
—Equinus the Spirit Horse. (p. 533)
—Fang the Bat Fiend. (p. 571)
—Fenro vs Epos. (p. 582)
—Ferrok the Iron Soldier. (p. 582)
—Fire & Fury. (p. 590)
—First Hero. (p. 595)
—Flaymar the Scorched Blaze. (p. 603)
—Grashkor the Beast Guard. (p. 711)
—Hawkite Arrow of the Air. (p. 755)
—Hellion the Fiery Foe. (p. 763)
—Koba - Ghoul of the Shadows. (p. 966)
—Koldo the Arctic Warrior. (p. 966)
—Komodo the Lizard King. (p. 966)
—Koraka the Winged Assassin. (p. 967)
—Krabb Master of the Sea. (p. 967)
—Kragos & Kildor the Two-Headed Demon. (p. 967)
—Krestor the Crushing Terror. (p. 967)
—Linka the Sky Conqueror. (p. 1019)
—Lustor the Acid Dart (p. 1066)
—Madara the Midnight Warrior. (p. 1069)
—Manak the Manta Ray. (p. 1086)
—Minos the Demon Bull. (p. 1148)
—Mortaxe the Skeleton Warrior. (p. 1176)
—Murk the Swamp Man. (p. 1192)
—Muro the Rat Monster. (p. 1192)
—Noctila the Death Owl (p. 1262)
—PINCHO, EL HOMBRE ESCORPION #18. (p. 1359)
—Pirate's Curse. (p. 1363)
—Raksha the Mirror Demon. (p. 1437)
—Serpio the Slithering Shadow. (p. 1552)
—Shamani the Raging Flame (p. 1559)
—Silver: The Wild Terror. (p. 1576)
—Skurik the Forest Demon. (p. 1586)
—Slivka the Cold-Hearted Curse. (p. 1591)
—Spikefin the Water King. (p. 1627)
—Spiros the Ghost Phoenix. (p. 1629)
—Sting the Scorpion Man. Tucker, Ezra, illus. (p. 1651)
—Tagus the Night Horse. Tucker, Ezra, illus. (p. 1695)
—Targro the Arctic Menace. (p. 1706)
—Tarrok the Blood Spike. (p. 1706)
—Tauron the Pounding Fury. (p. 1707)
—Tecton - The Armoured Giant (p. 1712)
—Terra Curse of the Forest. (p. 1721)
—Torgor the Minotaur. (p. 1769)
—Torpix the Twisting Serpent. (p. 1770)
—Trema the Earth Lord. (p. 1784)
—Ursus the Clawed Roar. (p. 1826)
—Vedra & Krimon the Twin Dragons. (p. 1834)
—Vermok the Spiteful Scavenger. (p. 1837)
—Vespick the Wasp Queen. (p. 1839)
—Viktor the Deadly Archer. (p. 1842)
—Vipero the Snake Man. (p. 1844)
—Voltrex the Two-Headed Octopus. (p. 1849)
Blade, Adam, jt. auth. see Scholastic, Inc. Staff.
Bladek, John. Roll up the Streets. (p. 1485)
Blades, Ann, illus. see Laurence, Margaret & James Lorimer and Company Ltd. Staff.
Blades, Ann, illus. see Speare, Jean.
Blades, Ann, illus. see Waterton, Betty.
Blades, Heather. Focus on Canada. (p. 610)
Bladey, Conrad, ed. Beuk of the Sangs of Tommy Armstrong the Pitman's Poet. (p. 173)
Bladholm, Cheri, illus. see Stiegemeyer, Julie.
Bladimir, Trejo, illus. see Sojos, Catalina.
Bladon, Rachel. Improve Your Grammar. (p. 862)
Blagden, Scott. Dear Life, You Suck: A Novel. (p. 419)
—Dear Life, You Suck. (p. 419)
Blaha-Black, Caroline. Anika & the Magic Top. (p. 76)
Blahitka, Vira. Joad the Toad. (p. 919)
Blahnik, Manolo. Blahnik by Boman: Shoes, Photographs, Conversation. Boman, Erik, photos by. (p. 198)
Blaikie, Lynn. Beyond the Northern Lights (p. 174)
Blain, Christophe. Hielos (p. 777)
—Isaac el Pirata: Las Américas. Vol 1 (p. 890)
Blain, Theresa A. Visualize World Geography in 7 Minutes a Day: Let Pictography Take You from Clueless to Knowing the World. Blain, Theresa A., illus. (p. 1846)
Blaine, Jack. Nightworld. (p. 1255)
Blaine, Janice, illus. see Kellerhals-Stewart, Heather.
Blaine, John. Blue Ghost Mystery: A Rick Brant Science Adventure Story. (p. 202)
—Boy Scouts in Russia. (p. 218)
—Boy Scouts on A Submarine. (p. 218)
—Boy Scouts on a Submarine. (p. 218)
—Caves of Fear: A Rick Brant Science Adventure Story. (p. 282)
—Egyptian Cat Mystery: A Rick Brant Science Adventure Story. (p. 506)
—Electronic Mind Reader: A Rick Brant Science Adventure Story. (p. 509)
—Flaming Mountain: A Rick Brant Science Adventure Story. (p. 602)
—Golden Skull: Rick Brant Science Adventure Story. (p. 695)
—Pirates of Shan: A Rick Brant Science Adventure Story. (p. 1364)
—Scarlet Lake Mystery: A Rick Brant Science Adventure Story. (p. 1520)
—Smuggler's Reef: A Rick Brant Science Adventure Story. (p. 1595)
—Wailing Octopus: A Rick Brant Science Adventure Story. (p. 1852)
Blaine, John & Goodwin, Harold Leland. Caves of Fear. (p. 282)
Blaine, Victor. Mis Patines de Ruedas / My Skates (p. 1150)
—My Bike (p. 1197)
—My Ripstik (p. 1217)
—My Scooter (p. 1218)
—My Skateboard (p. 1218)
—My Skates (p. 1218)
—My Sled (p. 1219)
—Watch Me Go! (p. 1861)
Blair, Beth L. Hidden Pictures Book: Hours of Challenging Fun! (p. 776)
Blair, Beth L., illus. see Riccio, Nina M.
Blair, Beth L., jt. auth. see Robinson, Tom.
Blair, Beth L. & Ericsson, Jennifer A. Everything Kids' Mummies, Pharaohs, & Pyramids Puzzle & Activity Book: Discover the Mysterious Secrets of Ancient Egypt. (p. 545)
—Everything Kids' Hanukkah Puzzle & Activity Book: Games, Crafts, Trivia, Songs, & Traditions to Celebrate the Festival of Lights! (p. 545)
—Kids' Animal Puzzles: Slither, Soar, & Swing Through a Jungle of Fun! (p. 952)
—Kids' Christmas Puzzle: Mazes, Activities, & Puzzles for Hours of Holiday Fun. (p. 953)
—Kids Games & Puzzles Book: Secret Codes, Twisty Mazes, Hidden Pictures, & Lots More - For Hours of Fun! (p. 953)
—Kids' Picture Puzzles Book: Hidden Pictures, Matching Games, Pattern Puzzles, & More! (p. 954)
—Kids' Word Search Puzzle: Solve Clever Clues & Hunt for Hidden Words in 100 Mind-Bending Puzzles. (p. 955)
—More Amazing Mazes Book: Wind Your Way Through Hours of Adventurous Fun! (p. 1174)
Blair, Candice. Rosie's Pink House Cato, Andrea, illus. (p. 1490)
Blair, Cathy. About 100 Years of American Musical Theatre in about 100 Minutes: Ten Short Units Covering Broadway Shows from 1900-2000 (CD Enclosed) (p. 5)
—Music Baseball: Name That Style. (p. 1193)
—Rhythm Rally! Level 1, Grades 3-5: Six Fun & Fast-Paced Rhythm Games in One! (p. 1468)
—Rhythms of the World: Discovering the Indigenous Rhythms of Africa, India, Cuba, & Brazil; Grades 5-8. (p. 1468)
Blair, Chris, illus. see Clements, Andrew.
Blair, Culverson, illus. see Brown, Margery W.
Blair, Eric. Annie Oakley Silverman, Dianne, illus. (p. 87)
—Bella Durmiente. Abello, Patricia, tr. from ENG. (p. 162)
—Belling the Cat: A Retelling of Aesop's Fable Silverman, Dianne, illus. (p. 163)
—Blanca Nieves. Abello, Patricia, tr. (p. 198)
—Boy Who Cried Wolf Silverman, Dianne, illus. (p. 219)
—Brave Little Tailor: A Retelling of the Grimm's Fairy Tale Shaw, David, illus. (p. 223)
—Bremen Town Musicians: A Retelling of the Grimm's Fairy Tale Dickson, Bill, illus. (p. 226)
—Country Mouse & the City Mouse: A Retelling of Aesop's Fable Silverman, Dianne, illus. (p. 372)
—Cuervo y la Jarra: Versión de la Fábula de Esopo. Abello, Patricia, tr. (p. 390)
—Daniel Boone Chambers-Goldberg, Micah, illus. (p. 405)
—Donkey in the Lion's Skin: A Retelling of Aesop's Fable Silverman, Dianne, illus. (p. 466)
—Frog Prince: A Retelling of the Grimm's Fairy Tale Ouren, Todd, illus. (p. 640)
—Gato Con Botas: Versión del Cuento de los Hermanos Grimm. Abello, Patricia, tr. from ENG. (p. 658)
—Hansel y Gretel. Abello, Patricia, tr. (p. 743)
—Johnny Appleseed Robledo, Sol, tr. (p. 923)
—Johnny Appleseed Muehlenhardt, Amy Bailey, illus. (p. 923)
—Leyenda de Daniel Boone Robledo, Sol, tr. (p. 1004)
—Lobo y los Siete Cabritos. Abello, Patricia, tr. from ENG. (p. 1044)
—Ninito de Jengibre Abello, Patricia, tr. from ENG. (p. 1256)
—Pastorcito Mentiroso: Versión de la Fábula de Esopo. Abello, Patricia, tr. from ENG. (p. 1327)
—Paul Bunyan Robledo, Sol, tr. from ENG. (p. 1330)
—Pecos Bill Robledo, Sol, tr. from ENG. (p. 1334)
—Pecos Bill Chambers-Goldberg, Micah, illus. (p. 1334)
—Pescador y Su Mujer: Versión del Cuento de los Hermanos Grimm. Abello, Patricia, tr. (p. 1345)
—Principe Encantado. Abello, Patricia, tr. from ENG. (p. 1406)
—Puss in Boots: A Retelling of the Grimm's Fairy Tale Ouren, Todd, illus. (p. 1420)
—Raton de Campo y el Raton de Ciudad: Versión de la Fábula de Esopo. Abello, Patricia, tr. from ENG. (p. 1440)
—Rumpelstiltskin: A Retelling of the Grimm's Fairy Tale Shaw, David, illus. (p. 1495)
—Rumpelstiltskin. Abello, Patricia, tr. from ENG. (p. 1495)
—Shoemaker & His Elves: A Retelling of the Grimm's Fairy Tale Dickson, Bill, illus. (p. 1568)
—Sleeping Beauty: A Retelling of the Grimm's Fairy Tale Ouren, Todd, illus. (p. 1589)
—Tom Thumb: A Retelling of the Grimm's Fairy Tale Ouren, Todd, illus. (p. 1764)
Blair, Eric & Aesop Enterprise Inc. Staff. Belling the Cat: A Retelling of Aesop's Fable Silverman, Dianne, illus. (p. 163)
—Boy Who Cried Wolf: A Retelling of Aesop's Fable Silverman, Dianne, illus. (p. 219)
—Country Mouse & the City Mouse: A Retelling of Aesop's Fable Silverman, Dianne, illus. (p. 372)
—Donkey in the Lion's Skin: A Retelling of Aesop's Fable Silverman, Dianne, illus. (p. 466)
Blair, Eric & Peterson, Ben. Pied Piper (p. 1356)
Blair, Eric, et al. Brave Little Tailor: A Retelling of the Grimm's Fairy Tale Shaw, David, illus. (p. 223)

B

—Bremen Town Musicians: A Retelling of the Grimm's Fairy Tale Dickson, Bill, illus. (p. 226)
—Frog Prince: A Retelling of the Grimm's Fairy Tale Ouren, Todd, illus. (p. 640)
—Puss in Boots: A Retelling of the Grimm's Fairy Tale Ouren, Todd, illus. (p. 1420)
—Sleeping Beauty: A Retelling of the Grimm's Fairy Tale Ouren, Todd, illus. (p. 1589)
—Tom Thumb: A Retelling of the Grimm's Fairy Tale Ouren, Todd, illus. (p. 1764)
Blair, Gregory. Spewing Pulp. (p. 1625)
Blair, Jamie. Leap of Faith. (p. 982)
Blair, Jamie M. Leap of Faith. (p. 982)
Blair, Janet, jt. auth. see Goss, Anthony.
Blair, Jocelyn, illus. see Harkes, Willy.
Blair, Juliet. Arlo & the Vortex Voyage. (p. 99)
Blair, Karen. Baby Animal Farm. Blair, Karen, illus. (p. 124)
Blair, Kathryn S. Diario de Lucia (1939) (p. 434)
Blair, Liza Sparks. Farley Firefly. (p. 573)
Blair, Marcia L. Nana's Birthday Bubbles. (p. 1228)
Blair, Margaret Whitman. Liberty or Death: The Surprising Story of Runaway Slaves Who Sided with the British During the American Revolution. (p. 1005)
—Roaring 20: The First Cross-Country Air Race for Women. (p. 1478)
—Roaring Twenty: The First Cross-Country Air Race for Women. (p. 1478)
—Sand Castle: Blockade Running & the Battle of Fort Fisher. (p. 1510)
Blair, Marion E. Just Beyond a Finger's Reach. (p. 938)
Blair, Mary, illus. see Krauss, Ruth.
Blair, Mary, illus. see Mchugh, Gelolo.
Blair, Mary, illus. see Rylant, Cynthia.
Blair, Monica. Adventures of Mary Ellen: Mary Ellen goes to Day Care. (p. 20)
Blair, Peter, compiled by. Concert Ensembles for Everyone: Works for Instrumental Ensembles with Limited or Non-Traditional Instrumentation, Grades 3-4 (F Horn - Brass 3 And 4) (p. 355)
—Concert Ensembles for Everyone: Works for Instrumental Ensembles with Limited or Non-Traditional Instrumentation, Grades 3-4 (Clarinet A - WW 1 And 2) (p. 355)
—Concert Ensembles for Everyone: Works for Instrumental Ensembles with Limited or Non-Traditional Instrumentation, Grades 3-4 (Trumpet A - Brass 1 And 2) (p. 355)
—Concert Ensembles for Everyone: Works for Instrumental Ensembles with Limited or Non-Traditional Instrumentation, Grades 3-4 (Alto Saxophone - WW 3 And 4) (p. 355)
—Concert Ensembles for Everyone: Works for Instrumental Ensembles with Limited or Non-Traditional Instrumentation, Grades 3-4 (Tenor Saxophone - WW 4 & Brass 4) (p. 355)
—Concert Ensembles for Everyone: Works for Instrumental Ensembles with Limited or Non-Traditional Instrumentation, Grades 3-4 (Trombone/Baritone B. C. /Bassoon - Brass 4 & Bass) (p. 355)
—Concert Ensembles for Everyone: Works for Instrumental Ensembles with Limited or Non-Traditional Instrumentation, Grades 3-4 (Bass - Tuba/Bass, Baritone Saxophone & Bass Clarinet) (p. 355)
Blair, Rachael. Maya's Gossamer: A Gentle Guide on How to Manifest Virtues in Children. (p. 1113)
Blair, Richard P., photos by see Goodwin, Kathleen P.
Blair, Robert W. Power-Glide French Year One Workbook. (p. 1389)
—Power-Glide Spanish Ultimate Year 1 Course. (p. 1389)
—Power-Glide Spanish Ultimate Year One Workbook (p. 1389)
Blair, Thomas L. Sabatini Prophecy. (p. 1499)
Blais, Barb. Little Wally & the Skunk Family. (p. 1037)
Blaisdell, Bette. Backpack Full of Verbs (p. 130)
—Hat Full of Adjectives (p. 752)
—Mouthful of Onomatopoeia (p. 1182)
—Pocket Full of Nouns (p. 1375)
—Words I Know (p. 1951)
Blaisdell, Bob, ed. see Thoreau, Henry.
Blaisdell, Bob, jt. auth. see Green, John.
Blaisdell, Bob & Green, John. Adventures of Hercules Coloring Book. (p. 18)
Blaisdell, Bob, ed. Communist Manifesto & Other Revolutionary Writings: Marx, Marat, Paine, Mao, Gandhi & Others. (p. 349)
Blaisdell, Elinore, illus. see de la Mare, Walter.
Blaisdell, Molly. Can You See the Wind? (p. 259)
—Caves. (p. 282)
—Fossils. (p. 623)
—Hurricane Fury. (p. 829)
—If You Were a Circle Carabelli, Francesca, illus. (p. 854)
—If You Were a Comma Gray, Sara, illus. (p. 854)
—If You Were a Comma [LTD Commodities]. Gray, Sara, illus. (p. 854)
—If You Were a Quadrilateral Carabelli, Francesca, illus. (p. 855)
—If You Were a Quadrilateral Dillard, Sarah & Carabelli, Francesca, illus. (p. 855)
—If You Were Quotation Marks Gray, Sara, illus. (p. 855)
—If You Were Quotation Marks [LTD Commodities]. Gray, Sara, illus. (p. 855)
—If You Were Quotation Marks [Readers World]. Gray, Sara, illus. (p. 855)
—Our Sun. (p. 1310)
—Rembrandt & the Boy Who Drew Dogs: A Story about Rembrandt van Rijn. Lane, Nancy, illus. (p. 1459)
—Truth about Unicorns Yilmaz, Necdet, illus. (p. 1794)
Blaisdell, Molly, jt. auth. see Lyons, Shelly.
Blaisdell, Molly & Lyons, Shelly. If You Were an Apostrophe Gray, Sara, illus. (p. 855)
Blaisdell, Patty. Haunted Shed (p. 753)
Blaisdell, Robert, jt. auth. see Spyri, Johanna.
Blaisdell, Shele. L. A. Teen Project. (p. 969)
Blaise, Kimberly. Reading Response Bookmarks & Graphic Organizers: Reproducible Learning Tools That Prompt Kids to Reflect on Text During & after Reading to Maximize Comprehension. (p. 1446)
Blaivas, C. & Z. Our Beautiful World: The Six Days of Creation. (p. 1307)
Blake. Adventures of Libby the Leaping Learner. (p. 19)
Blake, jt. auth. see Blake, Stephanie.
Blake, Adriana L. Benjamin Bear's Naughtiest Night Ever! (p. 164)
Blake, Angel. Stripped Bare. (p. 1667)
Blake, Anne Catharine, illus. see Ditta-Donahue, Gina.
Blake, Anne Catharine, illus. see Ficocelli, Elizabeth.
Blake, Anne Catharine, illus. see Hawkins-Walsh, Elizabeth & Pierson-Solis, Lennard.
Blake, Anne Catharine, illus. see Lansky, Bruce & Pottle, Robert.
Blake, Anne Catharine, illus. see Stanton, Sue.
Blake, Anne Catharine, tr. see Ficocelli, Elizabeth.
Blake, Ashley Herring. Suffer Love. (p. 1672)
Blake, Beccy, illus. see Atkins, Jill.
Blake, Beccy, illus. see Kelly, Maoliosa.
Blake, Beccy, illus. see Nash, Margaret.
Blake, Beccy, illus. see Shipton, Paul.
Blake, Beccy, illus. see Wallace, Karen.
Blake, Bronwyn. Nick Riley's Ninth Life. (p. 1251)
Blake, Carly. Why Why Why... Are Lions Crazy? (p. 1926)
—Why Why Why... Do Dolphins Squeak? (p. 1926)
—Why Why Why... Do Fish Bite? (p. 1926)
Blake, Carol, illus. see Wilkinson, James H.
Blake, Chris. Egyptian Curse. (p. 506)
—Greek Warriors. (p. 721)
—Pirate Mutiny. (p. 1362)
—Time Hunters - Aztec Attack. (p. 1752)
—Time Hunters - Cowboy Showdown. (p. 1752)
—Time Hunters - Outback Outlaw. (p. 1752)
—Time Hunters - Samurai Assassin. (p. 1752)
—Time Hunters/Mohican Brave 11. (p. 1752)
Blake, Chris & Charismalife. Hover Get's His Wings. (p. 804)
—I'm Just the Right Size. (p. 859)
Blake, Christine & Lopez, Jill. Signs, Signs, Everywhere Signs. (p. 1574)
Blake, Colleen H. Robley. Don't You Wish Your Momma Could Cook Like Mine? Jennings, Randy, illus. (p. 469)
Blake, D M. Achieving Success with Faith in God: The Concept of Faith-Based Perseverance. (p. 9)
Blake, Drew. Engineer's Spell. (p. 529)
Blake, Edna L. & Boatwright, Edith. Grandma & her Amazing Colt, Dripper! Allen, Kathy, illus. (p. 708)
Blake, Emily. Last Goodbye (p. 978)
Blake, Francis, illus. see Andrews, Jan.
Blake, Francis, illus. see Shapiro, Simon & Shapiro, Sheryl.
Blake, Francis, illus. see Swanson, Diane.
Blake, Francis, illus. see Weaver, Janice.
Blake, Jason. Focas Fabulosas. (p. 610)
Blake, Jo, illus. see Box, Su.
Blake, Jo, illus. see Galko, Francine & Heinemann Library Staff.
Blake, Jocelyn. Mama Is on an Airplane. Blake, Jocelyn, illus. (p. 1084)
Blake, Jon. Crazy Party at the House of Fun. Roberts, David, illus. (p. 378)
—Holiday Mania at the House of Fun. Roberts, David, illus. (p. 788)
—House of Fun. Roberts, David, illus. (p. 803)
—Peace & Love Thing. Roberts, David, illus. (p. 1331)
Blake, Joseph D. This Little Village: It Took A Village to Rescue These Little Ducks. (p. 1737)
Blake, Joshua Aaron, illus. see Wood, Debra.
Blake, Kendare. Anna Dressed in Blood. (p. 85)
—Antigoddess. (p. 89)
—Girl of Nightmares. (p. 678)
—Mortal Gods. (p. 1176)
Blake, Kevin. Balto's Story. (p. 135)
—Feral Pigs: Chomp, Chomp! (p. 581)
—Guam's Brown Tree Snakes: Hanging Out. (p. 728)
—Lost in the Antarctic. (p. 1055)
—Rescue Dogs. (p. 1462)
—Roanoke Island: The Town That Vanished. (p. 1478)
—Salton Sea Resort: Death in the Desert. (p. 1506)
Blake, Kevin & Sturdivant, Brad. Bodie: The Town That Belongs to Ghosts. (p. 206)
Blake, Kevin & Yates, Martha. Cliff Dwellings: Empty Windows. (p. 332)
Blake, Lily. Reign: The Prophecy. (p. 1457)
—Reign - Hysteria. (p. 1457)
Blake, Linda. My Pet Rabbit. (p. 1217)
Blake, M. Nation under Siege: Nukes, Mullahs, & the Ultimate Nightmare (p. 1231)
Blake, Max & Chase, Max. Deadly Mission. (p. 417)
—Enemy's Lair. (p. 527)
Blake, Michel. Out to Play. Candlewick Press Staff, illus. (p. 1312)
Blake, Peter. Peter Blake's ABC. Leith, Marcus & Dunkley, Andrew, photos by. (p. 1346)
Blake, Quentin. Cuentame un Cuadro. (p. 389)
—Jack & Nancy. (p. 902)
—Loveykins. Blake, Quentin, illus. (p. 1061)
—Mrs. Armitage, Queen of the Road. Blake, Quentin, illus. (p. 1187)
—Quentin Blake's ABC. (p. 1425)
—Quentin Blake's Nursery Rhyme Book. (p. 1425)
—Quentin Blake's Ten Frogs: A First Book about Numbers. Blake, Quentin, illus. (p. 1425)
—Quentin Blake's Ten Frogs Diez Ranas: A Book about Counting in English & Spanish. Blake, Quentin, illus. (p. 1425)
—Quentin Blake's the Seven Voyages of Sinbad the Sailor. (p. 1425)
—Ten Frogs: A Book about Counting in English & French. Blake, Quentin, illus. (p. 1718)
Blake, Quentin, illus. see Aiken, Joan & Aiken, Joan.
Blake, Quentin, illus. see Dahl, Roald.
Blake, Quentin, illus. see Dickens, Charles.
Blake, Quentin, illus. see Fleischman, Sid.
Blake, Quentin, illus. see Hoban, Russell.
Blake, Quentin, illus. see Luzzati, Emanuele.
Blake, Quentin, illus. see Mahy, Margaret.
Blake, Quentin, illus. see Martin, J. P.
Blake, Quentin, illus. see Morpurgo, Michael.
Blake, Quentin, illus. see Murail, Marie-aude & Murail, Elvire.
Blake, Quentin, illus. see Pennac, Daniel.
Blake, Quentin, illus. see Pitzorno, Bianca & Pitzorno, Bianca.
Blake, Quentin, illus. see Rice, Tim & Webber, Andrew Lloyd.
Blake, Quentin, illus. see Rosen, Michael.
Blake, Quentin, illus. see Steig, William.
Blake, Quentin, illus. see Yeoman, John.
Blake, Robert J. Akiak: A Tale from the Iditarod. Blake, Robert J., illus. (p. 32)
—Akiak. (p. 32)
—Little Devils. Blake, Robert J., illus. (p. 1026)
—Painter & Ugly. Blake, Robert J., illus. (p. 1318)
—Victor & Hugo. (p. 1840)
Blake, Rodger. Good Day: The Adventures of Pompernickel. (p. 697)
Blake Savage. Rip Foster Rides the Gray Planet. (p. 1473)
Blake, Spencer. Spyology. Steer, Dugald A., ed. (p. 1636)
Blake, Stephanie. Poop-Di-Doop! (p. 1383)
Blake, Stephanie & Blake. No Quiero Ir a la Escuela. Blake, Stephanie, illus. (p. 1260)
—Pip Caca. Ros, Rafael, tr. (p. 1361)
Blake, Stephanie J. Marble Queen (p. 1091)
Blake, Susannah. Bread & Pizza. (p. 224)
—Bread & Pizza. Crawford, Andy, photos by. (p. 224)
—Cookies & Cakes. (p. 361)
—Cookies & Cakes. Crawford, Andy, photos by. (p. 361)
—Crafts for Accessorizing That Look. (p. 376)
—Crafts for Pampering Yourself. (p. 376)
—Crafts for Revamping Your Room. (p. 376)
—Crafts for Styling Your Wardrobe. (p. 376)
—Sandwiches & Snacks. (p. 1511)
—Sandwiches & Snacks. Crawford, Andy, photos by. (p. 1511)
—Vegetarian Dishes. (p. 1834)
—Vegetarian Food. Crawford, Andy, photos by. (p. 1834)
Blake, William. Blake: 16 Art Stickers. (p. 198)
—William Blake Stained Glass Colouring Book. (p. 1933)
Blake-Brekke, Carri. Billy Bully Bug: Learns a Lesson in Hawaii. Melton, Jodi, illus. (p. 187)
—Juanita Maria Sophia Bug Diva: Lived down South in the West. Melton, Jo Lynn, illus. (p. 930)
Blake-Garrett, Andrea. Adventures of Izzy & Juju: Twin Detective Investigators (T. D. I.) (p. 19)
—Las Aventuras de Izzy y Juju: Gemelos Detectives Investigadores (G. D. I.) (p. 976)
Blakely, April. Math Brainteasers. (p. 1105)
Blakely, Gloria. Condoleezza Rice. (p. 356)
Blakely-Davis, Vanessa. Got Issues? God's Promises Supersedes Life's Issues. (p. 703)
Blakemore, Megan Frazer. Friendship Riddle. (p. 639)
—Spy Catchers of Maple Hill. (p. 1636)
—Very in Pieces. (p. 1838)
—Water Castle. (p. 1862)
Blakemore, Sally, illus. see Bortz, Trudy & Rappaport, Josh.
Blakemore, Sally, illus. see Piepmeier, Charlotte.
Blakeney, Crystal Denise. Paradise & Cove Counts Feathered Friends. (p. 1323)
—Paradise & Cove Go Camping. (p. 1323)
—Sharing with Paradise & Cove. (p. 1561)
Blakeslee, Ann R. Different Kind of Hero (p. 438)
Blakeslee, Lys, illus. see Anthony, David & Clasman, Charles David.
Blakeslee, Lys, illus. see Anthony, David & David, Charles.
Blakeslee, Lys, illus. see Mackall, Dandi Daley.
Blakeslee, S. E. Once upon a Blue Moon: The Chronicles of the Blue Moon. Blakeslee, S. E., illus. (p. 1292)
Blakeslee, Sandra, jt. auth. see Wallerstein, Judith S.
Blake-Wilson, Pamela. Orange Ray. Pocock, Aaron, illus. (p. 1302)
—Red Ray. Pocock, Aaron, illus. (p. 1454)
Blakley Kinsler, Gwen & Young, Jackie. Crocheting. Melo, Esperanca, illus. (p. 384)
Blakley-Cartwright, Sarah & Johnson, David Leslie. Red Riding Hood. (p. 1454)
Blalock, Rachel. dog & the Flea. (p. 461)
Blalock, Shawna. That Puppy Dog Took My Boots! (p. 1726)
Blalsey, Tilda, jt. auth. see Balsley, Tilda.
Blanc, Esther Silverstein & Eagle, Godeane. Long Johns for a Small Chicken. Dixon, Tennessee, illus. (p. 1047)
Blanc, Katherine. No Dogs, Please! Blanc, Katherine, illus. (p. 1258)
Blanc, Katherine, jt. auth. see Romero, Jordan.
Blanc, Mike, illus. see Oelschlager, Vanita.
Blanc, Mike, jt. auth. see Oelschlager, Vanita.
Blance, Ellen. Monstruo. (p. 1169)
Blance, Ellen & Cook, Ann. Monstruo Compre un Animalito. (p. 1169)
Blance, Ellen & Cook, Tony. Lady Monster Has a Plan. (p. 971)
—Lady Monster Helps Out. (p. 971)
—Monster & Magic Umbrella. (p. 1166)
—Monster & Surprise Cookie. (p. 1166)
—Monster & the Mural. (p. 1166)
—Monster at School. (p. 1166)
—Monster Buys a Pet. (p. 1166)
—Monster Cleans His House. (p. 1167)
—Monster Comes to the City. (p. 1167)
—Monster Gets a Job. (p. 1167)
—Monster Goes Around Town. (p. 1167)
—Monster Goes to Circus. (p. 1167)
—Monster Goes to School. (p. 1167)
—Monster Goes to the Beach. (p. 1167)
—Monster Goes to the Hospital. (p. 1167)
—Monster Goes to the Zoo. (p. 1167)
—Monster Looks for a House. (p. 1167)
—Monster Looks for Friend. (p. 1167)
—Monster Meets Lady Monster. (p. 1167)
—Monster on the Bus. (p. 1168)
—Monstruo Encuentra Trabajo. (p. 1169)
—Monstruo, la Senorita Monstruo y el Paseo en Bicicleta. (p. 1170)
—Monstruo Recorre la Ciudad. (p. 1170)
—Monstruo Va a la Playa. (p. 1170)
—Monstruo Va Al Circo. (p. 1170)
—Monstruo Va Al Hospital. (p. 1170)
—Monstruo y el Muro. (p. 1170)
—Monstruo y la Galleta de Sorpresa. (p. 1170)
—Monstruo y la Liquidacion de Juguetes. (p. 1170)
—Plan de la Senorita Monstruo. (p. 1366)
—Senorita Monstruo Ayuda. (p. 1550)
Blanch, Gregory, jt. auth. see Stathis, Roberta.
Blanch, Gregory & Stathis, Roberta. Renaissance Artists Who Inspired the World. (p. 1460)
Blanch, Ignasi, illus. see Desclot, Miquel.
Blanch, Xavier. Frutas. (p. 646)
—Hortalizas. (p. 801)
Blanchan, Neltje. Birds That Every Child Should Know. (p. 192)
Blanchard, Amy Ella. Sweet Little Maid. (p. 1690)
Blanchard, Anne. Arab Science & Invention in the Golden Age. Brent, R. M., tr. from FRE. (p. 94)
Blanchard, Chad J. Essence & Longing: A Poetic, Conceptual Story of Love. (p. 536)
Blanchard, Cherie & Plant, Cherie A. Word Roots A2: Learning the Building Blocks of Better Spelling & Vocabulary. (p. 1951)
—Word Roots B2: Learning the Building Blocks of Better Spelling & Vocabulary. Bk. 2 (p. 1951)
Blanchard, Daniel. Granddaddy's Secrets: Feeling Good. (p. 707)
Blanchard, Elaine. Help Me Remember: Bible Stories for Children. (p. 765)
Blanchard, Eliza. Child's Book of Animal Poems & Blessings. (p. 304)
Blanchard, Emma. Seeds I See: Work with 11-19 to Gain Foundations for Place Value. (p. 1547)
Blanchard, Jay & Marshall, James. Web-Based Learning in K-12 Classrooms: Opportunities & Challenges. (p. 1870)
—Web-Based Learning in K-12 Classrooms: Opportunites & Challenges. Marshall, James, ed. (p. 1870)
Blanchard, Karen & Root, Christine B. Zero In! Phrasal Verbs in Context. (p. 1986)
Blanchard, Ken. Whale Done, My Wonderful One! (p. 1877)
Blanchard, Ken & Brill, Marietta Abrams. What Your Doctor May Not Tell You Abou Hypothyroidism: A Simple Plan for Extraordinary Results. (p. 1896)
Blanchard, Marianne. Adventures of Red Wing Roussillon, an Irish Setter. (p. 22)
Blanchard, Patricia & Suhr, Joanne. My Bug Box. Sloat, Teri, illus. (p. 1199)
—There Was a Mouse. Gorbachev, Valeri, illus. (p. 1730)
Blanchart, Stephanie, illus. see Quintart, Natalie.
Blanche, David. Day in My Town. (p. 413)
Blanche, Lynn. What Makes It Go? (p. 1892)
Blanchet, Deborah A. Hat. (p. 752)
Blanchet, M. Wylie. Whale Named Henry. Matthews, Miriam & Matthews, Jacqueline M., illus. (p. 1877)
Blanchette, Peg & Thibault, Terri. 12 Easy Knitting Projects. Martin-Jourdenais, Norma Jean, illus. (p. 1994)
—Make Your Own Cool Cards: 40 Awesome Notes & Invitations! (p. 1079)
Blanchin, Matthieu, illus. see Kemoun, Hubert Ben & Grenier, Christian.
Blanck, Cathy. Party for Arty. (p. 1326)
Blanck, Ryan. Engaging the Media: Equipping Young People to Think Critically & Make Biblical Decisions about Entertainment. (p. 529)
Blanco, Alberto. Estrella de Angel. (p. 538)
—Tambien Los Insectos Son Perfectos. Radaviciute, Diana, illus. (p. 1704)
Blanco, César. Hoky the Caring Wolf. (p. 787)
Blanco Freijeiro, Antonio. Arte Griego. (p. 103)
Blanco, Jodee. Bullied Kids Speak Out: We Survived-How You Can Too. (p. 240)
Blanco, Maria, jt. auth. see Palacios, Maria Eugenia Blanco.
Blanco, Martin, illus. see Dahl, Michael.
Blanco, Migy, illus. see Carey, Lorraine.
Blanco, Migy, illus. see Fry, Sonali.
Blanco Moleon, Elena. Talented Demetri. (p. 1701)
Blanco, Ms. Healing Hearts of Nature: Five Therapeutic Fables for Children. (p. 757)
Blanco, Osvaldo, tr. see McCloskey, Robert.
Blanco, Rosa Pilar, tr. see Funke, Cornelia.
Bland, Anita D. Matilda's Apple. (p. 1109)
Bland, Barry, illus. see Antle, Bhagavan.
Bland, Barry, photos by see Antle, Bhagavan.
Bland, Janice. Allie's Class. (p. 47)
Bland, Janice, jt. auth. see Haupt, Wolfgang.
Bland, Joey, ed. see Hall, Dorothy P. & Tillman, CeCe.
Bland, Nick. Runaway Hug. Blackwood, Freya, illus. (p. 1496)
—Very Brave Bear. (p. 1837)
—Very Cranky Bear. Bland, Nick, illus. (p. 1837)
Bland, Nick, illus. see Trewin, Trudie.
Bland, Peter. Formula One Mathematics. (p. 620)
—Formula One Mathematics Gold C Teacher's Resource - Year 9. (p. 620)
—Gold - Teacher's Resource. (p. 693)
Bland, Ralph. Long Long Time. Barlow, Dave, illus. (p. 1047)
Blanda, Dominick. Super Duper Kid Fantastic. (p. 1679)
Blanden, Neale, illus. see Caputo, Antonella, et al.
Blander, Katy, illus. see Robinson, Janice.
Blanding, Allison, illus. see McKechnie, Edward.
Blanding, Dexter, illus. see Longmeyer, C. M.
Blane, Francisco. At the Tag Sale: Lap Book. (p. 111)
—Buildings Around Town: Lap Book. (p. 239)
—Farm Animals: Lap Book. (p. 573)
—I Can Play Music: Lap Book. (p. 836)
—Little Girl with Curl. Kelley, Gerald, illus. (p. 1028)
—Little Jack Horner. Price, Nick, illus. (p. 1029)
—Little Jack Horner Eats Pie. Price, Nick, illus. (p. 1029)
—Looking for the Muffin Man. (p. 1051)
—Muffin Man. Hammond, Andy, illus. (p. 1189)

—My New Clothes: Lap Book. (p. 1216)
—One Raining, Pouring Morning. (p. 1296)
—People at School: Lap Book. (p. 1339)
—Row, Row, Row Your Boat. Kelley, Gerald, illus. (p. 1492)
—Stripes at the Beach: Lap Book. (p. 1667)
—Tim Rows a Boat Gently down the Stream. (p. 1750)
—Up & Down: Lap Book. (p. 1824)
—Vegetables Are Good! Lap Book. (p. 1834)
—What Will You Be? Lap Book. (p. 1895)
Blank, Alison, jt. auth. see Murphy, Jim.
Blank, Carol, jt. auth. see Sanchez, Lorrie Christel.
Blank, Marion. Reading Kingdom, Level 1 (p. 1446)
Blankenbaker, E. Keith. Construction & Building Technology. (p. 359)
—Modern Plumbing: Instructor's Resource. (p. 1158)
—Modern Plumbing: Teaching Package Instructor's Resource Binder. (p. 1158)
—Modern Plumbing. (p. 1158)
—Painting & Decorating: Skills & Techniques for Success. (p. 1318)
Blankenhorn, David. Thrift: A Cyclopedia. (p. 1744)
Blankenship, Julianna. Sally Lumpkin's Party: A story of 6 true Friends. Dionne, Deanna, illus. (p. 1505)
Blankenship, LeeAnn. Mr. Tuggle's Troubles. Dugan, Karen, illus. (p. 1186)
Blankenship, Paula. Los dos leemos-Los Zapatos Perdidos de Lola. Canetti, Yanitzia James, tr. (p. 1053)
—Los dos leemos-Los Zapatos Perdidos de Lola: Nivel K-1. Reinhart, Larry, illus. (p. 1054)
—We Both Read-Lulu's Lost Shoes. Reinhart, Larry, illus. (p. 1866)
—We Both Read-Lulu's Lost Shoes Big Book: Lulu's Lost Shoes Big Book. Reinhart, Larry, illus. (p. 1866)
Blankenship, Robert, illus. see Neer, P. J.
Blankman, Anne. Conspiracy of Blood & Smoke. (p. 359)
—Prisoner of Night & Fog. (p. 1407)
Blanks, Andy, et al. 31 Verses - Identity: Every Teenager Should Know. (p. 1996)
Blanks, Morgan Georgia. Desert Island. (p. 429)
Blanks, Natascha Alex, illus. see Alberti, Theresa.
Blanks, Natascha Alex, illus. see Slade, Suzanne.
Blanksma, Laura. Along the Way with Little Blue. (p. 48)
Blankson, Amy, jt. auth. see Achor, Shawn.
Blanquet, Stephane. Toys in the Basement. (p. 1774)
Blanski, Maribeth, illus. see Pate, Ginger.
Blansten, Gern, jt. auth. see Johanson, Ryan.
Blanton, Edwin. Together We Can. (p. 1762)
Blanton, Ken. Adventures of Glibb Redundant: The Shortcut. (p. 18)
—Adventures of Glibb Redundant: New Friends from the Big City. (p. 18)
Blas, Larry. Adventures of Island Stickman & His Dog Name Pearl. (p. 19)
Blashfield, Jean, jt. auth. see Blashfield, Jean F.
Blashfield, Jean F. Animal Life. (p. 78)
—Argentina. (p. 97)
—Australia. (p. 116)
—England. (p. 529)
—Germany. (p. 666)
—Golda Meir. (p. 694)
—Greenland. (p. 723)
—Hillary Clinton. (p. 779)
—Iowa (Revised Edition) (p. 886)
—Ireland. (p. 887)
—Italy. (p. 894)
—Maryland. (p. 1101)
—Missouri (Revised Edition) (p. 1154)
—Oprah Winfrey. (p. 1301)
—Pakistan (p. 1319)
—Panama - Enchantment of the World. (p. 1320)
—Plant Life. (p. 1369)
—Realm of the Enchanter. (p. 1450)
—We the People - Expansion & Reform (p. 1868)
—Wisconsin. (p. 1939)
—Yemen (p. 1970)
Blashfield, Jean F. & Blashfield, Jean. Haiti. (p. 736)
Blashfield, Jean F. & Ryback, Carol. Animal Life. (p. 78)
Blashfield, Jean F., et al. Countries Around the World. (p. 372)
Blasi, Kathleen McAlpin. Name of Honor. Bowman, Leslie W., illus. (p. 1228)
Blasing, George. and the Raptor Pack: The Journey Begins! Ramirez, Alberto, illus. (p. 71)
—Dinosaur George Prehistoric Safari: Raptor Island. Ramirez, Alberto, illus. (p. 442)
Blasing, George, jt. auth. see Blasing, George.
Blasing, George & Blasing, George. Prehistoric Adventures of Dinosaur George: Jurassic Tigers. Smith, David, illus. (p. 1395)
Blasingame, James B. Gary Paulsen (p. 657)
Blasius, Dan. Hopalong Cassidy Rides Again. (p. 796)
Blask, Tina. I Can Help My Teacher: Use Place Value & Properties of Operation to Add. (p. 835)
—I Can Help My Teacher: Use Place Value & Properties of Operations to Add. (p. 835)
Blaskovic, Eva A. Beyond the Precipice. (p. 174)
Blaskovich, Dominique, illus. see Langley, Karen.
Blasor-Bernhardt, Do. Waltz with Me, Alaska. (p. 1856)
Blassingame, Calvin, illus. see McKinley, Fred B.
Blassingame, Wyatt. Look-It-Up Book of Presidents. Jonaitis, Alice, ed. (p. 1049)
Blassingame, Wyatt & Glendinning, Richard. Mountain Men. (p. 1181)
Blasutta, Mary Lynn, illus. see Falligant, Erin, ed.
Blaszczyk, Regina Lee & Scranton, Philip B. Major Problems in American Business History: Documents & Essays. (p. 1078)
Blatchford, David. Story of Mr Tomkins. (p. 1659)
Blathwayt, Benedict. Dinosaur Disaster. Blathwayt, Benedict, illus. (p. 442)
—Dougal the Digger. Blathwayt, Benedict, illus. (p. 473)
—Great Big Train. (p. 714)
—Little Red Train Jigsaw Book. (p. 1035)
—Well Done, Dougal! Blathwayt, Benedict, illus. (p. 1874)
Blatt, Jane. Books Always Everywhere. (p. 212)
—Books Always Everywhere. Massini, Sarah, illus. (p. 212)
Blatz-Harvey, Elizabeth. Windows of My World. Blatz-Harvey, Elizabeth, illus. (p. 1936)
Blau, Aljoscha, illus. see Janisch, Heinz.
Blau, Nicole, illus. see Adelman, Nechama Dina.
Blauer, Ettagale & Lauré, Jason. Ghana. (p. 670)
—Mali. (p. 1083)
—Mauritania. (p. 1110)
—Morocco. (p. 1175)
Blauer, Ettagale & Laure, Jason. South Africa. (p. 1616)
Blauer, Ettagale & Lauré, Jason. Uganda. (p. 1808)
Blauvelt, Marie. Sacajawea. (p. 1500)
Blaxill, Gina. Forget Me Never (p. 619)
—Saving Silence (p. 1517)
Blaxland, Wendy. American Food. (p. 60)
—Basketballs. (p. 143)
—Bottles & Jars. (p. 215)
—Cans. (p. 261)
—Chinese Food. (p. 307)
—French Food. (p. 635)
—Guitars. (p. 731)
—Helmets. (p. 765)
—Italian Food. (p. 894)
—Knives & Forks. (p. 965)
—Mexican Food. (p. 1131)
—Middle-Eastern Food. (p. 1137)
—Mugs & Plates. (p. 1189)
—Paper. (p. 1322)
—Pencils. (p. 1336)
—Sneakers. (p. 1597)
—Sweaters. (p. 1689)
—T-Shirts. (p. 1694)
Blay, Chuck & Siemers, Robert. Kauai's Geologic History: A Simplified Guide. (p. 946)
Blaylock, Janet. Crissy LeeAnn's Life. (p. 383)
Blaylock, Josh. Misplaced. O'Reilly, Sean Patrick, ed. (p. 1151)
—Penguin Brothers Larter, John & Bianco, Mike, illus. (p. 1336)
—Voltron: A Legend Forged. O'Sullivan, Mike, ed. (p. 1849)
Blaylock, Kathy. Adventures of Buddy Fairy & Friends. (p. 17)
Blaze, Ronan. Echoes from the Hills (p. 502)
Blazej-Yee, Sybil. Leroy Goes to the Olympics: A Graphic Novel. (p. 993)
Blazek, Frank. Phil & His Fabulous Feathers Thomas, Wes, illus. (p. 1350)
Blazek, Sarah. Irish Night Before Christmas Coloring Book Rice, James, illus. (p. 888)
Blazek, Scott R., illus. see Fontenot, Mary Alice.
Blazeman, Christopher. Eagles up Close. (p. 492)
—Horses up Close. (p. 800)
—Snakes up Close. (p. 1597)
Blazon, Nina. Pact of the Wolves. Innes, Sue, illus. (p. 1317)
Blea, Belinda. Passages of Pretty Penny: The Big Race. (p. 1326)
Bleach, James, illus. see Anglo, Mick.
Blecha, Aaron. Goodnight, Grizzle Grump! Blecha, Aaron, illus. (p. 701)
Blecha, Aaron, illus. see Andersen, Hans Christian.
Blecha, Aaron, illus. see Bolger, Kevin.
Blecha, Aaron, illus. see Capstone Press Staff.
Blecha, Aaron, illus. see Donovan, Sandy.
Blecha, Aaron, illus. see Krulik, Nancy.
Blecha, Aaron, illus. see Larsen, C. S.
Blecha, Aaron, illus. see Ocean, Davy.
Blecha, Aaron, illus. see Stone Arch Books Staff.
Blechman, Nicholas. Night Light. (p. 1253)
Blechman, Nicholas, illus. see Rogers, Simon.
Blechman, R. O. Franklin the Fly. (p. 630)
—Juggler of Our Lady: The Classic Christmas Story. (p. 932)
Blechmann, R. O. One & Only 1, 2, 3 Book. Blechmann, R. O., illus. (p. 1293)
Bleck, Linda. Children's Treasury of Lullabies. (p. 304)
—Children's Treasury of Mother Goose. (p. 304)
—Children's Treasury of Poems. (p. 304)
—Pepper Goes to School. Bleck, Linda, illus. (p. 1340)
—What's in My Truck? Bleck, Linda, illus. (p. 1898)
Bleck, Linda, illus. see Pfeffer, Wendy.
Blecker, Lisa. Good in Me from A to Z by Dottie. Blecker, Lisa, illus. (p. 698)
Blecua Perdices, José Manuel, prologue by. Diccionario de Secundaria de la Lengua Espanola Anaya-Vox. (p. 435)
Bledin, David. Bank. (p. 136)
Bledsoe. Environmental Science. (p. 532)
Bledsoe, Amanda. Chores S'mores (p. 310)
—Chores, S'mores! Perry, Jodi, ed. (p. 310)
Bledsoe, C. L. Necro-Files. (p. 1239)
Bledsoe, Glen, jt. auth. see Bledsoe, Karen.
Bledsoe, Glen, jt. auth. see Kiland, Taylor Baldwin.
Bledsoe Jr, Reuben Booo. Bullybuster. (p. 241)
Bledsoe, Karen & Bledsoe, Glen. Fighter Planes: Fearless Fliers. (p. 585)
—Helicopters: High-Flying Heroes. (p. 763)
Bledsoe, Karen E. Chinese New Year Crafts. (p. 307)
—Daredevils of the Air: Thrilling Tales of Pioneer Aviators. (p. 406)
—Fun Chinese New Year Crafts. (p. 647)
—Genetically Engineered Foods. (p. 660)
—Hanukkah Crafts. (p. 744)
Bledsoe, Lucy Jane. How to Survive in Antarctica. (p. 822)
Bledsoe, Michele. Kitty Treats Cookbook. Rupert, Chris et al, illus. (p. 963)
Bledsoe, Michele & Bledsoe, Richard. Secret Kingdom. (p. 1541)
Bledsoe, Richard, jt. auth. see Bledsoe, Michele.
Bledsoe, William B., illus. see Isbell, Rebecca & Buchanan, Marilyn.
Blegen, Daniel. Bob Sakata: American Farmer. (p. 205)
Blegvad, Erik, illus. see Blegvad, Lenore.
Blegvad, Erik, illus. see Bodecker, N. M.
Blegvad, Erik, illus. see Borden, Louise.
Blegvad, Erik, illus. see Hesse, Karen.
Blegvad, Erik, illus. see Stafford, Jean & Van Draanen, Wendelin.
Blegvad, Erik, illus. see Winslow, Marjorie.
Blegvad, Erik, tr. see Blegvad, Lenore.
Blegvad, Lenore. Ana Banana y Yo. Blegvad, Erik, illus. (p. 66)
—Ana Banana y Yo. Puncel, Maria & Blegvad, Erik, trs. (p. 66)
Blehl, Mary F. Spy Is Not a Spy. (p. 1636)
Bleicher, David, illus. see Grishaver, Joel Lurie.
Bleiler, Everett F., ed. see Wells, H. G.
Bleiman, Andrew & Eastland, Chris. 1-2-3 ZooBorns! (p. 1990)
—ABC ZooBorns! (p. 3)
—Hello, Mommy ZooBorns! (p. 764)
—Hello, Mommy Zooborns! (p. 764)
—I Love You, ZooBorns! (p. 844)
—Nighty Night, ZooBorns. (p. 1255)
—Splish, Splash, ZooBorns! (p. 1630)
—Welcome to the World, Zooborns! (p. 1874)
—ZooBorns! Zoo Babies from Around the World. (p. 1989)
Blend from Chicago, D. J. Special. Inner City Youth: The Come Back Show Murders. (p. 875)
Bles, Riemke. Beene & What He Learned about the Atlantic Ocean. (p. 157)
Blesch, Will. Understanding Iraq Today. (p. 1815)
Blessen, Karen, illus. see Gilley, Jeremy.
Blessing, Charlotte. New Old Shoes. Phillips, Gary R., illus. (p. 1246)
Blessing, Marlene, ed. see Ewing, Susan.
Blessing, Victor. Santa Claus Got Sick Because. (p. 1511)
Blevins, Bret, illus. see Jacques, Brian.
Blevins, Bret, illus. see McCloud, Scott.
Blevins, Christine. Midwife of the Blue Ridge. (p. 1139)
Blevins, Don. From Angels to Hellcats: Legendary Texas Women, 1836 to 1880 (p. 641)
Blevins, James. Crones. Whittaker, Stephen, illus. (p. 384)
Blevins, Tim, et al, eds. To Spare No Pains: Zebulon Montgomery Pike & His 1806-1807 Southwest Expedition, A Bicentennial Commemoration. (p. 1759)
Blevins, Wiley. Can You See It? (p. 259)
—Germs (p. 667)
—I'm Not Moving! Cerato, Mattia, illus. (p. 859)
—Is It Hot? Is It Not? (p. 889)
—Magnets (p. 1076)
—Mapping the World (p. 1090)
—Maps (p. 1090)
—Max Finds an Egg. Clanton, Ben, illus. (p. 1111)
—Max Has a Fish. (p. 1111)
—Max Has a Fish. Clanton, Ben, illus. (p. 1111)
—Meat-Eating Plants (p. 1118)
—New Friend. (p. 1244)
—Now & Long Ago (p. 1269)
—Parts of a Plant (p. 1325)
—Phonics from A to Z. (p. 1352)
—Planets (p. 1368)
—Push or Pull? (p. 1420)
—Rice & Beans. Cerato, Mattia, illus. (p. 1469)
—Rocks & Minerals (p. 1483)
—Tools Scientists Use (p. 1767)
—Who Am I? (p. 1914)
—You Can Use a Magnifying Glass. (p. 1974)
Blevins, Wiley, jt. auth. see Boynton, Alice.
Blevins, Wiley, jt. auth. see Douglas, Vincent.
Blevins, Wiley & Capstone Press Editors. Can You See It? (p. 259)
Blevins, Wiley & Capstone Press Staff. Germs (p. 666)
—Is It Hot? Is It Not? (p. 889)
—Magnets (p. 1076)
—Mapping the World (p. 1090)
—Meat-Eating Plants (p. 1118)
—Now & Long Ago (p. 1269)
—Parts of a Plant (p. 1325)
—Rocks & Minerals (p. 1483)
—Tools Scientists Use (p. 1767)
—Who Am I? (p. 1914)
Blevins, Winfred. Roadside History of Yellowstone Park. (p. 1477)
Blevins-Counts, Charlotte. Pot Full of Te. (p. 1388)
—Squirrel, Where Are You? (p. 1637)
Blewett, Ashlee Brown. Horse Escape Artist! And More True Stories of Animals Behaving Badly. (p. 799)
—Mission: Lion Rescue. (p. 1153)
—Mission - Elephant Rescue: All about Elephants & How to Save Them. (p. 1153)
—National Geographic Kids Mission: Elephant Rescue: All about Elephants & How to Save Them. (p. 1232)
—National Geographic Kids Mission: Lion Rescue: All about Lions & How to Save Them. Raven-Ellison, Daniel, ed. (p. 1232)
Blewett, Michael. God's Best Day. (p. 691)
Blewitt, John, jt. auth. see Holden-Rowley, Tim.
Blexbolex. Seasons. Bedrick, Claudia Z., tr. from FRE. (p. 1538)
Blexbolex, creator. Ballad. (p. 134)
Bley-Vroman, Robert, ed. see Miller, Randy & Perron, Jack.
Bligh, Deirdre. Perfect World: I Was Soooo Embarrassed! Martini, Angela, illus. (p. 1342)
Blight, Peter. Lonely Giraffe. Matthewson, Emma, ed. (p. 1046)
—Lonely Giraffe. Terry, Michael, illus. (p. 1046)
Blincoe, Neale. How to Dazzle at Maths Crosswords. (p. 816)
Blishen, Edward, jt. auth. see Garfield, Leon.
Bliss, Barbara. Abigail Elliot & the Dollhouse Family. (p. 5)
Bliss, Bill, jt. auth. see Molinsky, Steven J.
Bliss, Bob. Hardest Lessons: The Lost Babies Series #3. (p. 748)
—Ruby Hind: The Lost Babies Series #1. (p. 1493)
—Too Many Parents: The Lost Babies Series #2. (p. 1767)
Bliss, Bryan. No Parking at the End Times. (p. 1259)
Bliss, Harry. Bailey at the Museum. Bliss, Harry, illus. (p. 133)
—Luke on the Loose. (p. 1064)
—Luke on the Loose. Bliss, Harry, illus. (p. 1064)
Bliss, Harry, illus. see Birdsall, Jeanne.
Bliss, Harry, illus. see Creech, Sharon.
Bliss, Harry, illus. see Cronin, Doreen.
Bliss, Harry, illus. see DiCamillo, Kate.
Bliss, Harry, illus. see Jenkins, Emily.
Bliss, Harry, illus. see McGhee, Alison.
Bliss, Harry, illus. see Menchin, Scott.
Bliss, Harry, illus. see Snyder, Elaine.
Bliss, Harry, illus. see Steig, William & Steig.
Bliss, John. Art That Moves: Animation Around the World. (p. 103)
—Catching & Raising Seafood (p. 279)
—Jewish Migration (p. 917)
—Nineteenth Century Migration to America (p. 1256)
—Pioneers to the West (p. 1361)
—Preening, Painting, & Piercing: Body Art. (p. 1395)
—Processing Your Food (p. 1408)
Bliss, John, jt. auth. see Burgan, Michael.
Bliss, Joy V., jt. auth. see Dybwad, G. L.
Bliss, Pamela. Mystery of Magnets. (p. 1224)
Bliss, Pamela, et al. Introduction to Weather. (p. 882)
Bliss, Robert Woods. Indigenous Art of the Americas, Collection of Robert Woods Bliss. (p. 872)
Bliss, Ryan T. Mooseclumps. Bliss, Ryan T., illus. (p. 1173)
Blissman, Rodger J. Spookster the Halloween Cat. (p. 1631)
Blister Pack Staff. Phase 10 Card Game. (p. 1350)
Blitt, Barry, illus. see Burleigh, Robert.
Blitt, Barry, illus. see Kloske, Geoffrey.
Blitt, Barry, illus. see McNamara, Margaret.
Blitt, Barry, illus. see Offill, Jenny.
Blitt, Barry, illus. see Wilson, Karma.
Blitt, Barry, illus. see Winter, Jonah.
Blitz, Shmuel. Adventures of Aliza & Dovid: Holidays at the Farm. Katz, Tova, illus. (p. 16)
—ArtScroll Children's Book of Berachos: [Sefer Ha-Berakhot Shel]. Katz, Tova, illus. (p. 105)
—Bedtime Stories to Make You Smile. (p. 157)
—Every Story Has a Soul. Katz, Tova, illus. (p. 543)
—[ha-Tehilim Ha-Rishon]: ArtScroll Children's Tehillim. Katz, Tova, illus. (p. 734)
—Megilat Ester: The ArtScroll Children's Megillah. Katz, Tova, illus. (p. 1124)
—[Megilat Rut]: The Artscroll Children's Book of Ruth. Katz, Tova, illus. (p. 1124)
—My First Book of Jewish Holidays. (p. 1205)
—[Sefer Yonah]: The Artscroll Children's Book of Jonah. Katz, Tova, illus. (p. 1548)
—Treasury of Shabbos Bedtime Stories. (p. 1783)
Blitz, Shmuel & Katz, Tova. Artscroll Children's Machzor. [ha-Mahazor Ha-Rishon: Rosh Ha-Shanah Ve-Yom Kipur]. (p. 105)
Blitz, Shmuel & Zakon, Miriam Stark. Search for the Stones. Lumer, Marc, illus. (p. 1537)
Bliven, Bruce, jt. auth. see Bliven, Bruce, Jr.
Bliven, Bruce, Jr. & Bliven, Bruce. Invasion: The Story of D-Day. (p. 883)
Bliven, Jeremy. Captain Stumpy the Pirate Cat. (p. 264)
Blizin Gillis, Jennifer. St. Patrick's Day (p. 1638)
Blob, Anjali, ed. see S., LaTisha & Lee, Mykle.
Blobaum, Cindy. Awesome Snake Science! 40 Activities for Learning about Snakes. (p. 121)
—Explore Gravity! With 25 Great Projects. Stone, Bryan, illus. (p. 550)
—Explore Honey Bees! With 25 Great Projects. Stone, Bryan, illus. (p. 550)
—Explore Night Science! With 25 Great Projects. Stone, Bryan, illus. (p. 550)
—Insectigations: 40 Hands-On Activities to Explore the Insect World. (p. 875)
Blobel, Brigitte. Red Rage. Ward, Rachel, tr. from GER. (p. 1454)
Bloch, Benjamin Jacob. All A's All Ways: A Professor Reveals the Secrets to Success (p. 44)
Bloch, Beth. My Oh My Sweet Potato Pie. Bloch, Beth, illus. (p. 1216)
Bloch, Carole. Hyena & the Seven Little Kids. Morris, Hannah, illus. (p. 831)
—Three Billy Goats Gruff. Bester, Shayle, illus. (p. 1741)
Bloch, Christina. Mommy's Belly Has a Boo Boo. (p. 1162)
Bloch, Joanne. Few Little Lies. (p. 583)
Bloch, Lyudmila & Civitano, Tom. Golden Rules of Etiquette at the Plaza Carroll, Rosemary, illus. (p. 695)
Bloch, Robert. Crowded Earth. (p. 386)
Bloch, Serge. Reach for the Stars: And Other Advice for Life's Journey. (p. 1442)
—You Are What You Eat: And Other Mealtime Hazards. (p. 1973)
Bloch, Serge, illus. see Boudreau, Helene.
Bloch, Serge, illus. see Cali, Davide.
Bloch, Serge, illus. see Lewis, J. Patrick.
Bloch, Serge, illus. see Pouy, Jean-Bernard.
Bloch, Serge, illus. see Rosenthal, Amy Krouse.
Bloch, Serge, illus. see Siegel, Randy.
Block, Betty Mitchell. Magic Pork Chop Bone. (p. 1073)
Block, Cheryl. Rainbow Web. (p. 1436)
—Think Analogies A1: Learning to Connect Words & Relationships. (p. 1734)
—Think Analogies B1: Learning to Connect Words & Relationships. (p. 1734)
—True Blue Friend. Takeshita, Gene, illus. (p. 1791)
Block, Cheryl, et al. Editor in Chief A1: Grammar Disasters & Punctuation Faux Pas. (p. 504)
—Editor in Chief B1: Grammar Disasters & Punctuation Faux Pas. (p. 504)
—Reading Detective Rx: Using Higher-Order Thinking to Improve Reading Comprehension. (p. 1445)
Block, Dakota. Exploring the Solar System. (p. 554)
Block, Dakota, jt. auth. see Mills, Nathan.
Block, Daniel R., jt. auth. see Block, Marta Segal.
Block, Ethel J. Nana's Book. (p. 1228)
—Peter the Worm. (p. 1347)
Block, Francesca Lia. Blood Roses. (p. 200)
—Dangerous Angels. (p. 404)
—Ecstasia. (p. 503)
—Frenzy. (p. 636)
—House of Dolls. McClintock, Barbara, illus. (p. 803)
—How to (Un)Cage a Girl. (p. 822)
—Island of Excess Love. (p. 892)
—Love in the Time of Global Warming. (p. 1060)
—Pink Smog: Becoming Weetzie Bat. (p. 1360)
—Pretty Dead. (p. 1398)
—Primavera. (p. 1400)

B

—Psyche in a Dress. (p. 1413)
—Roses & Bones: Myths, Tales, & Secrets. (p. 1489)
—Teen Spirit. (p. 1714)
—Wasteland. (p. 1860)
—Waters & the Wild. (p. 1864)
—Weetzie Bat. (p. 1872)
Block, Ira, photos by see Lange, Karen.
Block, Joel D. Sex over 50. (p. 1556)
Block, Maggie, jt. auth. see Ellis, Amanda.
Block, Marta Segal. Graphing Global Politics (p. 711)
Block, Marta Segal & Block, Daniel R. Mapping the Land (p. 1090)
—Mapping the United States (p. 1090)
—Mapping the World (p. 1090)
—Mapping Your Community (p. 1090)
—Reading Maps (p. 1446)
Block, Pat and Shelly, jt. auth. see Scarpa, Romano.
Block, Robert S. Collecting Early Machine-Made Marbles: M. F. Christensen & Son Company & Christensen Agate Company (p. 339)
Block, Shelly, jt. auth. see Van Horn, William.
Block, Shelly, et al. Uncle Scrooge Clark, John, ed. (p. 1812)
Block, Thomas, illus. see Pendleton, Paige.
Blocker, Adam P. Joshua & the Spider. Taylor, Josh, illus. (p. 927)
Blocker, Ariel S. Beauty in Me. (p. 154)
Blocksma, Mary. What's on the Beach? A Great Lakes Treasure Hunt. (p. 1899)
—What's on the Beach? A Great Lakes Treasure Hunt. Blocksma, Mary, illus. (p. 1899)
Blodau, Peter, illus. see Snell, Gordon.
Blofield, Robert. How to Make a Movie in 10 Easy Lessons: Learn How to Write, Direct, & Edit Your Own Film Without a Hollywood Budget. (p. 820)
Blohm, Craig E. Catastrophic Events of The 2000s. (p. 278)
—Holocaust Camps & Killing Centers. (p. 789)
—Holocaust Rescue & Liberation. (p. 789)
—Holocaust Resistance. (p. 789)
—O. J. Simpson Case. (p. 1274)
—Possessed. (p. 1387)
—Weapons of Peace: The Nuclear Arms Race. (p. 1869)
Blohm, Judith M. & Lapinksy, Terri. Kids Like Me: Voices of the Immigrant Experience. (p. 954)
Bloker Cantrell, Jeannette, et al. Summer of Joanie & Bobo. (p. 1674)
Bloker, Paula. Just the Right Spot. (p. 940)
Blokland, Suzanne & Hammer, Randy. God's Blue Earth: Teaching Kids to Celebrate the Sacred Gift of Water. (p. 691)
Blom, Jen K. Possum Summer. Rayyan, Omar, illus. (p. 1387)
Blomenkamp Ed.D., Joel. Storm: A Children's Parable for Understanding Life's Hardships. (p. 1655)
Blomfield, Alan. Pendant of Epoch. (p. 1336)
Blomgren, Jennifer. Tale of Alice's Quilt. (p. 1699)
—Where Do I Sleep? A Pacific Northwest Lullaby. Gabriel, Andrea, illus. (p. 1907)
—Where Would I Be in an Evergreen Tree? Gabriel, Andrea, illus. (p. 1910)
—Why Do I Sing? Animal Songs of the Pacific Northwest. Gabriel, Andrea, illus. (p. 1923)
Blomquist, Christopher. BMX in the X Games. (p. 204)
—Desert Tortoises. (p. 429)
—Gopher Tortoises. (p. 702)
—Green Sea Turtles. (p. 722)
—In-Line Skating in the X Games. (p. 864)
—Motocross in the X Games. (p. 1179)
—Primary Source Guide to Chile. (p. 1399)
—Primary Source Guide to Russia. (p. 1399)
—Primary Source Guide to the United Kingdom. (p. 1399)
—Prmiary Source Guide to the United Kingdom. (p. 1408)
—Skateboarding in the X Games. (p. 1583)
—Snapping Turtles. (p. 1597)
—Spiny Soft Shell Turtles. (p. 1628)
—Spiny Softshell Turtles. (p. 1628)
—Street Luge in the X Games. (p. 1666)
—Wakeboarding in the X Games. (p. 1853)
Blomquist, Jean M., jt. auth. see Christen, Carol.
Bloncourt, Nelson. Fanny the Flying French Bulldog. Polyansky, Nikita, illus. (p. 571)
Bloncourt, Nelson & Botero, Fernando. Botero: Paintings & Works on Paper. Polyansky, Nikita, illus. (p. 215)
Blondahl, Samuel, illus. see Callsen, Terri.
Blondel, Jean-Vincent, jt. auth. see Karle, Vincent.
Blondin, George, jt. auth. see Blondin, John.
Blondin, John. Old Man with the Otter Medicine. Sundberg, Mary Rose, tr. (p. 1284)
Blondin, John & Blondin, George. Legend of Caribou Boy. Sundberg, Mary Rose, tr. (p. 988)
Blondon, Herve, illus. see Alborghetti, Marci.
Blonstein, Anne. Blue Pearl. (p. 203)
Blood, Danielle. Multiplication: 22 Super-Motivating, Self-Checking Manipulatives That Help All Kids Practice & Really Learn the Times Table from 1 to 12. (p. 1190)
Blood, Danielle, ed. Around the World Cursive Alphabet Set: 26 Ready-to-Display Letter Cards with Fabulous Photos of Extraordinary Natural Wonders, Ancient Sites, Architecture, & More. (p. 100)
Bloodgood, Dorothy U. Post Card Portrait with Memorabilia of John Burroughs Literary Naturalist. (p. 1387)
Bloodworth, Mark. Blue Bay Mystery. (p. 202)
—Castle Mystery. (p. 277)
Bloodworth, Mark, illus. see Long, Christopher E. & Warner, Gertrude Chandler.
Bloodworth, Mark, illus. see Warner, Gertrude Chandler.
Bloodworth, Mark, jt. illus. see Dubisch, Mike.
Bloom, Amy Beth. Little Sweet Potato. Jones, Noah Z., illus. (p. 1037)
Bloom & Ronzani, Maggie. Mammals: Grades 2 Through 4. (p. 1085)
Bloom, Barbara Lee. Mexican Americans. (p. 1131)
—Nat Love. (p. 1230)
Bloom, Becky. Leo & Lester. Biet, Pascal, illus. (p. 992)
Bloom, C. P. Monkey & the Bee. Raymundo, Peter, illus. (p. 1165)
—Monkey Goes Bananas. Raymundo, Peter, illus. (p. 1165)
Bloom, Carol A. Wishing Closet. (p. 1940)
Bloom, Chrissa. In the Kitchen with Solids, Liquids, & Gases. (p. 866)
Bloom, Clive, illus. see Gliori, Debi.
Bloom, Clive, jt. auth. see Gliori, Debi.
Bloom, Daniel Halevi. Bubbie & Zadie Come to My House: A Story for Hanukkah. Mellichson, Alex, illus. (p. 233)
Bloom, Deb-b. Bird Who Could Fly. (p. 190)
Bloom, Deborah R. Bird Who Could Fly. (p. 190)
Bloom, Denise. More Than a Spoonful. (p. 1175)
Bloom, Denise, et al. More Than a Spoonful. (p. 1175)
Bloom, Harold. Age of Innocence. (p. 29)
—Allan Tate. (p. 46)
—All's Well That Ends Well. (p. 48)
—Ballad of the Sad Cafe. (p. 134)
—Beowulf. (p. 166)
—Bloom's Literary Themes: Dark Humor. (p. 201)
—Bloom's Literary Themes: The Labyrinth. (p. 201)
—Bloom's Literary Themes: The Trickster. (p. 201)
—Bloom's Literary Themes: Human Sexuality. (p. 201)
—Bloom's Literary Themes: Civil Disobedience. (p. 201)
—Bloom's Literary Themes: The American Dream. (p. 201)
—Bloom's Literary Themes: Enslavement & Emancipation. (p. 201)
—Bloom's Literary Themes: Alienation. Hobby, Blake, ed. (p. 201)
—Bloom's Literary Themes: Death & Dying. Hobby, Blake, ed. (p. 201)
—Bloom's Literary Themes: The Grotesque. Hobby, Blake, ed. (p. 201)
—Bloom's Major Short Story Writers. (p. 201)
—Bloom's Modern Critical Views. Henry, W. & Berg, Albert A., eds. (p. 201)
—Charlotte Brontë's Jane Eyre. (p. 293)
—Color Purple - Alice Walker. (p. 343)
—Elie Wiesel's Night. Bloom, Harold, ed. (p. 512)
—Epic. (p. 532)
—Farewell to Arms - Ernest Hemingway. (p. 573)
—Genius: A Mosaic of One Hundred Exemplary Creative Minds. (p. 661)
—Great Expectations. (p. 715)
—Hans Christian Andersen. (p. 743)
—Hispanic-American Writers. (p. 781)
—Jane Austen's Pride & Prejudice. (p. 908)
—London. (p. 1046)
—Man Without Qualities. (p. 1086)
—Midsummer Night's Dream - William Shakespeare. (p. 1139)
—New York. (p. 1247)
—Novelists & Novels: A Collection of Critical Essays. (p. 1268)
—One Flew over the Cuckoo's Nest - Ken Kesey. (p. 1295)
—Paris. (p. 1324)
—Poets & Poems. (p. 1376)
—Road. (p. 1476)
—Robert Hayden. (p. 1479)
—Robert Louis Stevenson. (p. 1479)
—Scarlet Letter. (p. 1520)
—Short Story Writers & Short Stories. (p. 1569)
—Sonnets. Foster, Brett, ed. (p. 1612)
—Thomas Hardy. (p. 1738)
—Twelfth Night. Loos, Pamela, ed. (p. 1800)
—Zora Neale Hurston. (p. 1990)
Bloom, Harold, ed. see Albertazzi, Anne Marie.
Bloom, Harold, ed. see Brontë, Charlotte.
Bloom, Harold, ed. see Carroll, Lewis, pseud.
Bloom, Harold, ed. see Chopin, Kate.
Bloom, Harold, ed. see García Márquez, Gabriel.
Bloom, Harold, ed. see Griffin, Patsy.
Bloom, Harold, ed. see Haley, Alex.
Bloom, Harold, ed. see Homer.
Bloom, Harold, ed. see Hurston, Zora Neale.
Bloom, Harold, ed. see Kafka, Franz.
Bloom, Harold, ed. see Loos, Pamela.
Bloom, Harold, ed. see Marson, Janyce.
Bloom, Harold, ed. see Orwell, George.
Bloom, Harold, ed. see Piorkowski, Sue.
Bloom, Harold, ed. see Remarque, Erich Maria.
Bloom, Harold, ed. see Robbins, Sarah F.
Bloom, Harold, ed. see Shakespeare, William.
Bloom, Harold, ed. see Welsch, Gabe.
Bloom, Harold, ed. see Zuba, Jesse.
Bloom, Harold & Foster, Brett, eds. Hamlet. (p. 739)
Bloom, Harold & Fox, Paul, eds. Oscar Wilde. (p. 1305)
Bloom, Harold & Harley, Alexis, eds. William Blake. (p. 1933)
Bloom, Harold & Hayes, Kevin J., eds. Benjamin Franklin. (p. 164)
Bloom, Harold & Heims, Neil, eds. Henry IV (p. 768)
—King Lear. (p. 958)
—Othello. (p. 1306)
—Tempest. (p. 1717)
Bloom, Harold & Hobby, Blake. Hero's Journey: The Hero's Journey. (p. 773)
Bloom, Harold & Loos, Pamela, eds. As You Like It. (p. 105)
—Taming of the Shrew. (p. 1704)
Bloom, Harold & Marson, Janyce, eds. Midsummer Night's Dream. (p. 1139)
—Romeo & Juliet. (p. 1486)
Bloom, Harold, ed. Adventures of Huckleberry Finn. (p. 18)
—American Fiction Between the Wars. (p. 60)
—Asian-American Writers. (p. 106)
—Beowulf. (p. 166)
—Bible. (p. 175)
—Bloom's BioCritiques. (p. 201)
—Bloom's Biocritiques. (p. 201)
—Bloom's BioCritiques Series (p. 201)
—Bloom's Classic Critical Views (p. 201)
—Bloom's Guides. (p. 201)
—Bloom's Literary Criticism 20th Anniversary Collection. (p. 201)
—Bloom's Literary Places. (p. 201)
—Bloom's Major Literary Characters. (p. 201)
—Bloom's Major Novelists Series (p. 201)
—Bloom's Major Poets. (p. 201)
—Bloom's Major Short Story Writers. (p. 201)
—Bloom's Modern Critical Interpretations. (p. 201)
—Bloom's Modern Critical Views. (p. 201)
—Bloom's Notes. (p. 201)
—Bloom's Period Studies. (p. 201)
—Carlos Fuentes' the Death of Artemio Cruz. (p. 270)
—Catch-22 - Joseph Heller. (p. 279)
—Charles Dickens. (p. 292)
—Chronicles of Narnia. (p. 317)
—Contemporary Poets, New Edition. (p. 360)
—Darkness at Noon. (p. 408)
—David Mamet. (p. 411)
—Dramatists & Drama. (p. 480)
—Dublin. (p. 487)
—Edgar Allan Poe. (p. 504)
—Elizabeth Bennet. (p. 513)
—Emerson's Essays. (p. 518)
—Emile Zola. (p. 518)
—Emily Dickinson. (p. 518)
—Ernest Hemingway. (p. 533)
—Essayists & Prophets. (p. 536)
—F. Scott Fitzgerald. (p. 559)
—Frankenstein. (p. 629)
—Geoffrey Chaucer. (p. 661)
—George Babbitt. (p. 663)
—Guy de Maupassant. (p. 733)
—H. G. Wells. (p. 734)
—Harlem Renaissance. (p. 749)
—Harper Lee's To Kill a Mockingbird. (p. 749)
—Heart of Darkness. (p. 759)
—Herman Melville. (p. 771)
—Herman Melville's Moby-Dick. (p. 771)
—Holden Caulfield. (p. 788)
—House on Mango Street - Sandra Cisneros. (p. 803)
—Iliad. (p. 856)
—Invisible Man. (p. 885)
—Isaac Babel. (p. 890)
—J. D. Salinger. (p. 901)
—J. R. R. Tolkien. (p. 902)
—Jamaica Kincaid. (p. 906)
—James Joyce, New Edition. (p. 907)
—Jane Austen. (p. 908)
—Jane Austen, New Edition. (p. 908)
—Jane Austen's Pride & Prejudice. (p. 908)
—Jay Wright. (p. 910)
—John Knowles's a Separate Peace. (p. 922)
—John Steinbeck. (p. 922)
—John Steinbeck's of Mice & Men. (p. 922)
—John Steinbeck's the Grapes of Wrath. (p. 922)
—Jose Saramago. (p. 926)
—Julio Cortazar. (p. 932)
—Julius Caesar. (p. 932)
—King Arthur. (p. 958)
—Kurt Vonnegut, New Edition. (p. 968)
—Literature of the Holocaust. (p. 1023)
—Long Day's Journey into Night - Eugene O'Neill, New Edition. (p. 1047)
—Love in the Time of Cholera. (p. 1059)
—Macbeth. (p. 1067)
—Marcel Proust. (p. 1091)
—Mark Twain's the Adventures of Huckleberry Finn. (p. 1095)
—Mary Shelley's Frankenstein. (p. 1101)
—Maya Angelou, New Edition. (p. 1112)
—Maya Angelou's I Know Why the Caged Bird Sings. (p. 1112)
—Miguel de Cervantes. (p. 1141)
—Miss Lonelyhearts. (p. 1151)
—Modern American Drama. (p. 1158)
—Modern American Poetry. (p. 1158)
—Modern Critical Views. (p. 1158)
—Nathaniel Hawthorne. (p. 1231)
—Nikolai Gogol. (p. 1255)
—Novelists & Novels. (p. 1268)
—Odyssey. (p. 1279)
—Old Man & the Sea - Ernest Hemingway, New Edition. (p. 1284)
—Passage to India. (p. 1326)
—Ralph Waldo Emerson. (p. 1437)
—Raskolnikov & Svidrigailov. (p. 1439)
—Richard Wright's Black Boy. (p. 1470)
—Robert Louis Stevenson. (p. 1479)
—Rome. (p. 1486)
—Rubaiyat of Omar Khayyam. (p. 1493)
—Rudyard Kipling. (p. 1494)
—Satan. (p. 1515)
—Sir John Falstaff. (p. 1580)
—Sophocles' Oedipus Rex. (p. 1614)
—St. Petersburg. (p. 1638)
—Stories & Poems for Extremely Intelligent Children of All Ages. (p. 1654)
—Streetcar Named Desire. (p. 1667)
—Sylvia Plath's The Bell Jar. (p. 1693)
—T. S. Eliot's the Waste Land. (p. 1694)
—Tale of Two Cities - Charles Dickens. (p. 1700)
—Tennessee Williams's the Glass Menagerie. (p. 1720)
—Toni Morrison's Beloved. (p. 1765)
—Tony Kushner. (p. 1766)
—Walt Whitman. (p. 1856)
—William Golding's Lord of the Flies. (p. 1933)
—Willy Loman. (p. 1934)
—Young Goodman Brown. (p. 1978)
Bloom, Harold, et al. Bloom's Major Dramatists. (p. 201)
—Bloom's Major Novelists. (p. 201)
—Bloom's Major Poets. (p. 201)
Bloom, Harold, intro. Alice Walker. (p. 39)
—American Naturalism. (p. 62)
—Chaim Potok's the Chosen. (p. 288)
—Cry, the Beloved Country. (p. 387)
—E.L. Doctorow's Ragtime. (p. 507)
—Elizabethan Drama. (p. 513)
—Frankenstein. (p. 629)
—Greek Drama. (p. 720)
—Hamlet. (p. 739)
—John Cheever. (p. 921)
—Langston Hughes. (p. 974)
—Leopold Bloom. (p. 993)
—Maggie: A Girl of the Streets. (p. 1071)
—Nick Adams. (p. 1251)
—Tale of Genji. (p. 1699)
—Toni Morrison's the Bluest Eye. (p. 1765)
—William Faulkner. (p. 1933)
Bloom, Harold Ron, ed. see Fitzgerald, F. Scott.
Bloom, Harry, illus. see Danielle, Sara & James, Danielle.
Bloom, J. P. Earth. (p. 494)
—Jupiter. (p. 937)
—Mars. (p. 1096)
—Mercury. (p. 1127)
—Neptune. (p. 1241)
—Planets. (p. 1368)
—Saturn. (p. 1515)
—Uranus. (p. 1825)
—Venus. (p. 1836)
Bloom, Jan. You Track it Weather Lab. Free Jenna Staff, ed. (p. 1976)
Bloom, Janice Stitziel. Grateful Heart under My Bed. Woodcock, Marcy, illus. (p. 712)
—Wonderfully Made under My Bed. Woodcock, Marcy, illus. (p. 1948)
Bloom, Jennifer, jt. auth. see Luterman, Lillian.
Bloom, Jonathan. Must Have Sudoku Holiday Gift 480 Puzzles. (p. 1194)
Bloom, Lloyd, illus. see Walsh, Jill Paton.
Bloom, M. Beth. Don't Ever Change. (p. 467)
—Drain You. (p. 479)
Bloom, Paul. Rules at Lunch. (p. 1495)
—Rules in the Classroom. (p. 1495)
—Rules in the Gym. (p. 1495)
—Rules in the Library. (p. 1495)
—Rules on the Bus. (p. 1495)
—Rules on the Playground. (p. 1495)
—Seal or Sea Lion? (p. 1536)
Bloom, Ronny. Justin Bieber. (p. 940)
Bloom, Stephanie. Drummer Who Lost His Beat. Keylon, Joe, illus. (p. 487)
Bloom, Steve. Polar Animals: In Search of Polar Bears, Penguins, Whales & Seals. (p. 1378)
Bloom, Steve & Wilson, David Henry. Elephants: A Book for Children. (p. 511)
Bloom, Steve, et al. My Favourite Animal Families. (p. 1203)
Bloom, Susan, jt. auth. see Bertram, Debbie.
Bloom, Susan & Bertram, Debbie. Best Book to Read. Garland, Michael, illus. (p. 168)
—Best Place to Read. Garland, Michael, illus. (p. 171)
—City Hall: The Heart of Los Angeles. Leijten, Aileen, illus. (p. 323)
Bloom, Suzanne. Alone Together. Bloom, Suzanne, illus. (p. 48)
—Bus for Us. Bloom, Suzanne, illus. (p. 244)
—Feeding Friendsies. (p. 580)
—Fox Forgets. Bloom, Suzanne, illus. (p. 626)
—Mighty Fine Time Machine. (p. 1140)
—Mighty Fine Time Machine. Bloom, Suzanne, illus. (p. 1140)
—No Place for a Pig. Bloom, Suzanne, illus. (p. 1259)
—Nuestro Autobus. (p. 1270)
—Oh! What a Surprise! (p. 1281)
—Splendid Friend, Indeed. (p. 1630)
—Splendid Friend, Indeed. Bloom, Suzanne, illus. (p. 1630)
—Treasure. (p. 1781)
—We Keep a Pig in the Parlor. (p. 1867)
—What about Bear? (p. 1878)
Bloom, Suzanne, illus. see Brisson, Pat.
Bloom, Suzanne, illus. see Bunting, Eve.
Bloom, Tom, illus. see Zimmerman, Bill.
Bloom, Valerie. Collins Big Cat - Mighty Mountains, Swirling Seas: Lime/Band 11. Cimatoribus, Alessandra, illus. (p. 340)
—Hot Like Fire. Lush, Debbie, illus. (p. 801)
—Let Me Touch the Sky: Selected Poems for Children. (p. 994)
Bloomberg, Georgina, jt. auth. see Hapka, Catherine, pseud.
Bloomberg, Georgina & Hapka, Catherine. Rein It In. (p. 1457)
Bloomberg, Sandi. Ava & the Magic Tutu. (p. 118)
—Michael & the Magic Dinosaur. Collier, Kevin, illus. (p. 1134)
—Veronica & the Magic Fountain. (p. 1837)
Bloomenstein, Susan. Allover Patterns Stained Glass Coloring Book. (p. 47)
—Flower Power Stained Glass Coloring Book. (p. 607)
—Geometric Obsessions Stained Glass Coloring Book. (p. 662)
Bloomer, Nancy Clark. Through the Glass Bottom Boat. (p. 1745)
Bloomer, Rebecca. Willow Farrington Bites Back. (p. 1934)
Bloomfield. Wild Utah Coloring Book. (p. 1930)
Bloomfield, Charlotte. Corridor of Doors. (p. 368)
Bloomfield, Denise. Toby Gets the Brush Off. (p. 1760)
Bloomfield, Glynis. Jake & the Pb's. (p. 906)
—Jake's Secret. (p. 906)
Bloomfield, Kevin. Mr. Biggs at the Circus. (p. 1184)
—Mr. Biggs at the Circus / el Sr. Grande en el Circo. (p. 1184)
—Mr. Biggs in the City. Bloomfield, Kevin, illus. (p. 1184)
—Mr. Biggs in the City/El Sr. Grande en la Ciudad. Bloomfield, Kevin, illus. (p. 1184)
Bloomfield, Susanne George & Reed, Eric Melvin, eds. Adventures in the West: Stories for Young Readers. (p. 16)
Bloomquist, Christopher. BMX in the X Games. (p. 204)
—Skateboarding in the X Games. (p. 1583)
—Street Luge in the X Games. (p. 1666)
Bloomquist, Don/Lee, Jr., ed. see Murphy, Austin.
Bloomquist, Stephen, ed. Sun with Loving Light Dalton, Pamela, illus. (p. 1676)
Bloomsbury Publishing Staff. My Activity Books for Boys. (p. 1195)
—My Activity Books for Girls. (p. 1195)
—My Amazing Adventure Activity & Sticker Book. (p. 1196)
—My Animals Activity & Sticker Book. (p. 1196)
—My Christmas Activity & Sticker Book. (p. 1200)
—My Easter. (p. 1202)
—My Pink Princess Activity & Sticker Book: Bloomsbury Activity Books. (p. 1217)
—My Pirate Activity & Sticker Book: Bloomsbury Activity Books. (p. 1217)

—My Snowman Activity & Sticker Book. (p. 1219)
—My Spooky Halloween Activity & Sticker Book. (p. 1219)
—My Zoo Animals. (p. 1222)
Bloomsbury Publishing Staff, jt. auth. see McAuley, Mary.
Bloor, Edward. London Calling. (p. 1046)
—Plague Year. (p. 1366)
—Story Time. (p. 1663)
—Taken. (p. 1697)
—Tangerine. (p. 1705)
—Tangerine Spanish Edition. de la Vega, Pablo, tr. (p. 1705)
Blos, Joan W. Brothers of the Heart: A Story of the Old Northwest, 1837-1838. (p. 231)
—Letters from the Corrugated Castle: A Novel of Gold Rush California, 1850-1852. (p. 1002)
Bloser, Cheryl. Little Mouse & the Muddy Feet. (p. 1032)
Bloss, Josie. Faking Faith. (p. 565)
Blosser, Connie S. Bear Named Blue. (p. 151)
—Donald Lionz Drought. (p. 426)
—Destiny's Trouble: A True Story. (p. 431)
—Single White Feather. (p. 1579)
Blossom, F. Blossom Kingdom: The Adventures of Emily. (p. 202)
Blossom, J. I Should Have Been a Long Distance Truck. (p. 845)
Blotnick, Elihu. Blue Turtle Moon Queen: The September Book. Robinson, Barbara J., illus. (p. 203)
—Fog Line. Robinson, Barbara J., illus. (p. 611)
—Glimmins: Children of the Western Woods. Blotnick, Elihu, illus. (p. 683)
Blough, Glenn O. After the Sun Goes Down: The Story of Animals at Night. Bendick, Jeanne, illus. (p. 28)
Bloumis, Joy. Adventure in Fairyland. (p. 14)
Blount, Diana. TV Production Student Activity Book. Matthews, Douglas L., ed. (p. 1799)
Blount, Jill Rutland. Tara's Gift. (p. 1706)
Blount, Marcellus, jt. ed. see Rampersad, Arnold.
Blount, Patty. Nothing Left to Burn. (p. 1268)
—Send. (p. 1550)
—Some Boys. (p. 1609)
—TMI. (p. 1758)
Blount, Willie And Ebony. Super Duck Goes Green. (p. 1679)
Blount-Jackson, Evetta. What? No Peanut Butter! (p. 1878)
Blow, Matthew. Behind Evil's Walls. (p. 160)
Blowars, Ryan, illus. see Smale, Denise L.
Blowers, Lisa, illus. see Moulton, Mark Kimball.
Blowers, Norman. Christmas with Carly. (p. 316)
Bloxam, Frances. Beau Beaver Goes to Town. Sollers, Jim, illus. (p. 153)
Bloz, illus. see Plumeri, Arnaud.
Bloze, Eden. Banana Beach. (p. 135)
Blu De Golyer. Adventures of Captain Greenspud. (p. 17)
Blubaugh, Penny. Blood & Flowers. (p. 200)
—Serendipity Market. (p. 1552)
Blue. Corner Stores in the Middle of the Block: That Urban Look. (p. 367)
Blue Apple Staff. Are You Eating Something Green? Sias, Ryan, illus. (p. 97)
—Are You Eating Something Red? Sias, Ryan, illus. (p. 97)
—Chicken Doodle Soup. Zemke, Deborah, illus. (p. 300)
—Count 4, 5, 6. Taback, Simms, illus. (p. 369)
—Extraordinary Pets. Barroux, illus. (p. 555)
Blue Apple Staff, jt. auth. see Dwell Studio Staff.
Blue Apple Staff, jt. auth. see Ernst, Lisa Campbell.
Blue Apple Staff, jt. auth. see Peters, Bernadette.
Blue Apple Staff & Taback, Simms. Mommies & Babies. Taback, Simms, illus. (p. 1162)
—Zoom. Taback, Simms, illus. (p. 1989)
Blue Bananas, jt. auth. see Lewis, Jill.
Blue, Buster, illus. see Anna, Jennifer.
Blue, Buster, illus. see Harrison, Kevin.
Blue, Darcy. Families Rock. (p. 567)
Blue, Duck Egg, et al. 1 2 3: Touch & Trace Early Learning Fun! (p. 1990)
Blue, Elly. Pedal Zombies. (p. 1334)
Blue, Ina. Toady Gets A Bike. (p. 1760)
Blue Lantern Studio Staff, creator. Green Tiger's Illustrated ABC. (p. 722)
Blue, Martha. Little Prankster Girl: At'Eed Adilahi Yazhi. Ruffenach, Jessie, ed. (p. 1033)
Blue, Mary. Sleeping Stranger. (p. 1589)
Blue Ox Technologies Ltd., Blue Ox & York, Christopher. 7 Little Words for Kids: 100 Puzzles. (p. 1992)
Blue, Parker. Try Me. (p. 1794)
Blue, Rose, jt. auth. see Naden, Corinne J.
Blue, Rose & Naden, Corinne J. Dred Scott: Person or Property? (p. 484)
—Exploring the Mississippi River Valley. (p. 554)
Blue, Rose, et al. Harriet Tubman: Riding the Freedom Train. (p. 750)
—Ron's Big Mission. Tate, Don, illus. (p. 1487)
Blue, Sebastien. Liquid Diamond. (p. 1021)
Blue, Sky & Quattro, Jacquelyn. Nature & Me! (p. 1236)
Blue Sky Ink Staff. Congratulations Graduate You Did It! (p. 357)
Blue Talk, Richard, jt. auth. see Fourstar, Jerome.
Bluecheese, Wally, illus. see Heim, Julia & Dami, Elisabetta.
Bluecloud. Space in Time. (p. 1619)
Bluedorn, Hans, jt. auth. see Bluedorn, Nathaniel.
Bluedorn, Harvey. Greek Alphabetarion: A Primer for Teaching How to Read, Write & Pronounce Ancient & Biblical Greek. (p. 720)
—Handy English Encoder Decoder: All the Spelling & Phonics Rules You Could Ever Want to Know. (p. 741)
Bluedorn, Harvey & Bluedorn, Laurie. Ancient History from Primary Sources: A Literary Timeline. (p. 69)
Bluedorn, Johannah. Bless the Lord: The 103rd Psalm. (p. 199)
—Little Bitty Baby Learns Greek. Bluedorn, Johannah, illus. (p. 1024)
—Little Bitty Baby Learns Hebrew. Bluedorn, Johannah, illus. (p. 1024)
—Lord Builds the House: The 127th Psalm. (p. 1052)
—Story of Mr. Pippin. Bluedorn, Johannah, illus. (p. 1659)
Bluedorn, Laurie, jt. auth. see Bluedorn, Harvey.
Bluedorn, Nathaniel. Hand That Rocks the Cradle: Good Books to Read Aloud to Children. (p. 740)
Bluedorn, Nathaniel & Bluedorn, Hans. Thinking Toolbox. (p. 1734)
Bluemel Oldfield, Dawn. Apple. (p. 92)
—Baboon. (p. 124)
—Inside the Cricket's Burrow. (p. 877)
—Patterns at the Seashore. (p. 1329)
—Police Dogs. (p. 1380)
Bluemle, Elizabeth. Dogs on the Bed. Wilsdorf, Anne, illus. (p. 463)
—How Do You Wokka-Wokka? Cecil, Randy, illus. (p. 808)
—My Father the Dog. Cecil, Randy, illus. (p. 1203)
—Tap Tap Boom Boom. Karas, G. Brian, illus. (p. 1705)
Blueraven, Solaris. Mr. Sun & the Halloween Ball. (p. 1186)
Bluestein, Jane & Katz, Eric. High School's Not Forever. (p. 778)
Bluestone, Carol & Irwin, Susan. Washington, D. C. Guidebook for Kids. (p. 1860)
BlueWolf, James Don. Speaking for Fire. Greenlee, Carolyn Wing, illus. (p. 1623)
Bluhm, Joe, illus. see Joyce, William.
Blum, Alex A., et al. Treasure Island. (p. 1781)
Blum, Cinzia Sartini, tr. see Tamaro, Susanna.
Blum, Geoffrey & Barks, Carl. Uncle Scrooge #377. Clark, John, ed. (p. 1812)
Blum, Jeffrey. Raising Amazing Kids Using Ice Cream Sandwiches & a Couch Potato. (p. 1437)
Blum, Joyce. to Z Promises & Prayers for Little Children. (p. 1759)
Blum, Julia C., illus. see Banghart, Tracy E.
Blum, Raymond. Mathamusements. (p. 1107)
Blum, Raymond, et al. Giant Book of Science Fun/Giant Book of Math Fun: Flip Book. Sterling Publishing Company Staff, ed. (p. 673)
Blum, Renon. California Wax Museum. (p. 253)
—Explore Your Dream. (p. 551)
Blum, Vicki. Dragon Prince. Sourwine, David, illus. (p. 477)
—Spitt to the Rescue. (p. 1629)
Blumberg, Christine A., ed. see Sutliff, Jamie.
Blumberg, Margie. Avram's Gift. McGaw, Laurie, illus. (p. 120)
—Sunny Bunnies. Goulding, June, illus. (p. 1677)
Blumberg, Rhoda. Commodore Perry in the Land of the Shogun. (p. 349)
—Shipwrecked! The True Adventures of a Japanese Boy. (p. 1567)
—York's Adventures with Lewis & Clark: An African-American's Part in the Great Expedition. (p. 1972)
Blume, David M. Alcohol Can Be A Gas! Fueling an Ethanol Revolution for the 21st Century. (p. 35)
Blume, Erma Hill. Tattle-Tale Pete. (p. 1707)
Blume, Judy. Are You There God? It's Me, Margaret. (p. 97)
—Bff: Just as Long as We're Together/Here's to You, Rachel Robinson. (p. 174)
—Blubber. (p. 202)
—Cool Zone with the Pain & the Great One. Stevenson, James, illus. (p. 364)
—Deenie. (p. 422)
—Double Fudge. (p. 473)
—Forever... (p. 619)
—Freckle Juice. (p. 632)
—Freckle Juice. Lisker, Sonia, illus. (p. 632)
—Friend or Fiend? With the Pain & the Great One. Stevenson, James, illus. (p. 637)
—Friend or Fiend? with the Pain & the Great One. Stevenson, James, illus. (p. 637)
—Fudge-a-Mania. (p. 646)
—Going, Going, Gone! with the Pain & the Great One. Stevenson, James, illus. (p. 692)
—Here's to You, Rachel Robinson. (p. 771)
—Iggie's House. (p. 855)
—It's Not the End of the World. (p. 898)
—Judy Blume Essentials: Are You There God? It's Me, Margaret; Blubber; Deenie; Iggie's House; It's Not the End of the World; Then Again, Maybe I Won't; Starring Sally J. Freedman As Herself. (p. 931)
—Judy Blume Teen Collection: Are You There God? It's Me, Margaret; Deenie; Forever; Then Again, Maybe I Won't; Tiger Eyes. (p. 931)
—Jugo de Pecas. (p. 932)
—Just As Long As We're Together. (p. 938)
—One in the Middle Is the Green Kangaroo. (p. 1295)
—One in the Middle Is the Green Kangaroo. Ohi, Debbie Ridpath, illus. (p. 1295)
—Otherwise Known As Sheila the Great. (p. 1306)
—Otherwise Known As Sheila the Great. (p. 1306)
—Pain & the Great One. Ohi, Debbie Ridpath, illus. (p. 1318)
—Soupy Saturdays with the Pain & the Great One. Stevenson, James, illus. (p. 1615)
—Starring Sally J. Freedman As Herself. (p. 1642)
—Superfudge. (p. 1683)
—Tales of a Fourth Grade Nothing. (p. 1702)
—Then Again, Maybe I Won't. (p. 1729)
—Tiger Eyes. (p. 1748)
Blume, Lesley M. Wondrous Journals of Dr. Wendell Wellington Wiggins. Foote, David, illus. (p. 1949)
Blume, Lesley M. M. Cornelia & the Audacious Escapades of the Somerset Sisters. (p. 367)
—Julia & the Art of Practical Travel. (p. 932)
—Modern Fairies, Dwarves, Goblins, & Other Nasties: A Practical Guide by Miss Edythe McFate. Foote, David, illus. (p. 1158)
—Rising Star of Rusty Nail. (p. 1475)
—Tennyson. (p. 1720)
—Wondrous Journals of Dr. Wendell Wiggins. Foote, David, illus. (p. 1949)
Blume, Rebecca. Baby Whales. Blume, Rebecca, illus. (p. 128)
—Really, Really, Scary Monster Story! Koji, Jeanette, illus. (p. 1450)
—When the World Was Green! Blume, Rebecca, illus. (p. 1905)
Blume-D'Ausilio, Carole Ed. D. Bronx Bully. (p. 230)
Blumenfeld, Samuel L. Blumenfeld's Alpha-Phonics: A Primer for Beginning Readers. (p. 204)
Blumenstock, Jacqueline & Pool, David. Making New Friends. (p. 1082)
—Making New Friends. Madden, Colleen, illus. (p. 1082)
Blumenthal, Bliss & Alarcon, Claudia. Wiley's Way: El Camino de Wiley. Gonzalez, Ricky & Gonzalez, Crysol, illus. (p. 1932)
Blumenthal, Deborah. Aunt Claire's Yellow Beehive Hair. GrandPré, Mary, illus. (p. 115)
—Blue House Dog Gustavson, Adam, illus. (p. 203)
—Charlie Hits It Big. Brunkus, Denise, illus. (p. 293)
—Different Me. (p. 438)
—Don't Let the Peas Touch! Ering, Timothy Basil, illus. (p. 468)
—Lifeguard. (p. 1013)
—Mafia Girl. (p. 1071)
Blumenthal, Ira, jt. auth. see Wilson, Jerry S.
Blumenthal, Karen. Bootleg: Murder, Moonshine, & the Lawless Years of Prohibition. (p. 213)
—Let Me Play: The Story of Title IX - The Law That Changed the Future of Girls in America. (p. 994)
—Steve Jobs: The Man Who Thought Different. (p. 1649)
—Steve Jobs: The Man Who Thought Different. Abdel Karim Al Sayed, Abdel Maqsud, tr. from ENG. (p. 1649)
—Tommy: The Gun That Changed America. (p. 1764)
Blumenthal, Scott. Explorer's Bible/By Scott E. Blumenthal. (p. 551)
—Great Israel Scavenger Hunt. (p. 716)
—Kid's Mensch Handbook: Step by Step to a Lifetime of Jewish Values. (p. 954)
Blumenthal, Scott & Hodus, Brett. Hoop City. (p. 795)
—Road to the Majors. (p. 1477)
Blumenthal, Walter H. In Old America; Random Chapters on the Early Aborigines. (p. 864)
Blumer, J. Michael. Book of Broken Promises (p. 211)
—Book of Second Chances (p. 211)
Bluming. Hebrew Reading Homework Book: Lamer Shteigin in Ivri. (p. 761)
Blumstein, Amy Beth. Jamie & Tallulah. (p. 907)
Blumstein, Rachel. Everything You Need to Know about Public Speaking. (p. 546)
Blundell, Gerald Lee. Bunkalunken Goes to Washington & Other Stories (p. 242)
Blundell, Gillian & Graham, Noel. Problem Solving Activities with Mottik. (p. 1408)
Blundell, Graham, jt. auth. see Graham, Noel.
Blundell, Jonathan. Cambridge IGCSE Sociology Coursebook. (p. 255)
Blundell, Jonathan, et al. Sociology AS: The Complete Companion AQA. (p. 1605)
Blundell, Judy. Diary of Minnie Bonner: A City Tossed & Broken - San Francisco, California 1906. (p. 435)
—Strings Attached. (p. 1667)
—What I Saw & How I Lied. (p. 1887)
Blundell, Kim, jt. auth. see Tyler, Jenny.
Blundell, Kim, jt. illus. see Cartwright, Stephen.
Blundell, Kim & Tyler, Jenny. Big Book of Mazes. (p. 179)
—Treasure Mazes. (p. 1782)
Blundell, T & TNT Ministries Staff. On the Way for 9 - 11's (p. 1291)
Blundell, T & TNT Resource Material Staff. On the Way for 9 - 11's (p. 1291)
Blundell, Thalia, et al. On the Way for 11-14's (p. 1291)
—On the Way for 9 - 11's (p. 1291)
Blundell, Tony, illus. see Dhami, Narinder.
Blundell, Tony, illus. see Strong, Jeremy.
Blundell, Trevor, et al. Beginning with the Bible: A Child's First Lessons in Knowing God. (p. 159)
—David & Solomon (p. 410)
—Ferrari, 1947-1957 (p. 582)
—Joseph, Job & Moses (p. 926)
—On the Way (p. 1291)
—On the Way for 11 - 14's (p. 1291)
—On the Way for 3 - 9's: \. (p. 1291)
—On the Way for 3 - 9's: Creation, Abraham & Jacob. (p. 1291)
—On the Way for 3 - 9's: The Christmas Story & Miracles of Jesus. Vol. 2 (p. 1291)
—On the Way for 3 - 9's. (p. 1291)
Blunden, Alan. Tommy & the Garden Shed. (p. 1764)
Blunt, Edna M. Margie the Cat. (p. 1092)
Blunt, Fred. Rabbit's Tale. (p. 1430)
Blunt, Fred, illus. see MacKinnon, Mairi.
Blunt, Fred, illus. see Punter, Russell & MacKinnon, Mairi.
Blunt, Fred, illus. see Punter, Russell.
Blunt, Fred, illus. see Ziefert, Harriet.
Blunt, Julia & Gilbert, Dawn. How Donkey Became GREAT. (p. 809)
Blunt, Lucy. Beating the Bullies: How Did Ben Help Himself? (Large Print 16pt) (p. 152)
Blunt, Michele. Walk Through Time. (p. 1854)
Blunt, Patricia. George the Jackdaw. (p. 663)
Bluth, Don, illus. see Mangels, Andy, et al.
Bluthenthal, Diana Cain. I'm a Kid. You're a Baby. (p. 858)
—I'm Not Invited? Bluthenthal, Diana Cain, illus. (p. 859)
Bluthenthal, Diana Cain, illus. see Krensky, Stephen.
Bluthenthal, Diana Cain, illus. see Viorst, Judith.
Bly, Leon, Jenny Turnbull: Kurdistan Mission. Vol. 2 (p. 913)
Bly, Nicole. Liam Goes to Agility School. (p. 1004)
—Liam Likes to Play. (p. 1004)
—Liam Visits the Veterinarian. (p. 1004)
Bly, Scott. Smasher. (p. 1593)
Bly, Stephen A. Lost Wagon Train. (p. 1057)
—Secret of the Old Rifle. (p. 1542)
—Sweet Carolina. (p. 1689)
—Treachery at the River Canyon. (p. 1781)
Blyth, Eileen, illus. see Hawthorne, Grace.
Blyth, Eileen, illus. see Kay, Terry.
Blyth, Eileen C., illus. see Hawthorne, Grace.
Blyth, Joan, et al. Children in History. (p. 302)
—Our Toys. (p. 1310)
Blythe, April. Girlsprouts. (p. 681)
Blythe, Carolita. Revenge of a Not-So-Pretty Girl. (p. 1465)
Blythe, Daniel. Shadow Breakers. (p. 1557)
Blythe, Enid. Adventures of Scamp. (p. 22)
—Three Boys & a Circus. (p. 1741)
Blythe, Gary. Treasury of Princess Stories. (p. 1783)
Blythe, Gary, illus. see Davies, Nicola.
Blythe, Gary, illus. see Sheldon, Dyan.
Blythe, Gary, illus. see Shields, Gillian.
Blythe, Peter, et al. Mathematical Studies: Oxford Ib Diploma Program. (p. 1107)
Blythe, Philip. Nature Hunt! Bewildering Puzzles of the Animal Kingdom. Blythe, Philip, illus. (p. 1236)
Blyton, Enid. Adventure of the Secret Necklace. (p. 14)
—Adventure of the Strange Ruby. (p. 14)
—Adventures of Binkle & Flip. (p. 16)
—Adventures of Mr. Pinkwhistle. (p. 21)
—Adventures of the Six Cousins. Pape, Jane, illus. (p. 23)
—Beauty & the Beast. (p. 154)
—Birthday Kitten. (p. 192)
—Boy Who Wanted a Dog. (p. 219)
—Caravan Family. (p. 265)
—Castle of Adventure. Cobb, Rebecca, illus. (p. 277)
—Children of Green Meadows. (p. 302)
—Children of St. Kidillin. (p. 302)
—Circus of Adventure. (p. 322)
—Circus of Adventure. Cobb, Rebecca, illus. (p. 322)
—Don't Be Silly Mr Twiddle! (p. 467)
—Enid Blyton Adventure Omnibus. (p. 530)
—Enid Blyton Circus Stories. (p. 530)
—Family at Red-Roofs. (p. 568)
—Family Christmas. (p. 568)
—Famous Five. (p. 569)
—Four Cousins. (p. 624)
—Four in a Family. (p. 625)
—Goblin Aeroplane. (p. 688)
—Hedgerow Tales. (p. 762)
—Hello Mr Twiddle. (p. 764)
—Hollow Tree House. (p. 789)
—House at the Corner: Family Adventure. (p. 803)
—Island of Adventure. (p. 892)
—Island of Adventure. Cobb, Rebecca, illus. (p. 892)
—Island of Adventure. Tresilian, Stuart, illus. (p. 892)
—Little Toy Engine & Other Stories. (p. 1037)
—Magic Snow Bird: And Other Stories. Hamilton, Dorothy, illus. (p. 1073)
—Mister Meddle's Muddles. (p. 1155)
—More Hedgerow Tales. (p. 1174)
—Moses in the Bulrushes: See the Picture & Say the Word. (p. 1176)
—Mother Goose: Treasury of Favourite Rhymes. Barnes-Murphy, Rowan, illus. (p. 1177)
—Mountain of Adventure. (p. 1181)
—Mountain of Adventure. Cobb, Rebecca, illus. (p. 1181)
—Mr Meddle Stories. (p. 1185)
—Mr Pink-Whistle Interferes. (p. 1186)
—Mr Pink-Whistle's Party. (p. 1186)
—Mr Twiddle Stories. (p. 1186)
—Naughtiest Girl Again. (p. 1237)
—Naughtiest Girl Is a Monitor. (p. 1237)
—Noah & the Ark: See the Picture & Say the Word. (p. 1261)
—Pretty Star the Pony: And Other Stories. (p. 1398)
—Princess & the Pea. (p. 1402)
—Put-Em-Rights: Family Adventures. (p. 1420)
—Ragamuffin Mystery: A Barney Mystery. (p. 1433)
—Rat-a-Tat Mystery. (p. 1440)
—Rilloby Fair Mystery. (p. 1473)
—Ring O' Bells Mystery. (p. 1473)
—River of Adventure. (p. 1476)
—River of Adventure. Cobb, Rebecca, illus. (p. 1476)
—Rockingdown Mystery. (p. 1483)
—Rubadub Mystery. (p. 1493)
—Sea of Adventure. Cobb, Rebecca, illus. (p. 1535)
—Secret of Cliff Castle: 3 Great Adventure Stories. Downer, Maggie, illus. (p. 1542)
—Secret of Cliff Castle. (p. 1542)
—Secret of the Lost Necklace: 3 Great Adventure Stories. Biro, Val, illus. (p. 1542)
—Ship of Adventure. Cobb, Rebecca, illus. (p. 1567)
—Six Bad Boys. (p. 1582)
—Sleeping Beauty. (p. 1589)
—Stories Jesus Told. (p. 1654)
—Story of Jesus. (p. 1658)
—Strange Umbrella: And Other Stories. Gregory, Sally, illus. (p. 1665)
—Those Dreadful Children: Family Adventure. (p. 1740)
—Tower in Ho-Ho Wood: And Other Stories. (p. 1773)
—Twelve Dancing Princesses. (p. 1800)
—Ugly Old Scarecrow: And Other Stories. (p. 1808)
—Up the Faraway Tree. (p. 1824)
—Valley of Adventure. Cobb, Rebecca, illus. (p. 1831)
—Well, Really, Mr Twiddle! (p. 1874)
Blyton, Enid & Biro, Val. Secret Valley. (p. 1544)
Blyton, Enid & Cinco, Blyton-Los. Cinco en Pelibro. (p. 319)
Blyton, Enid & Wynne, Dudley. Secret Forest. (p. 1540)
—Secret Island. (p. 1541)
—Secret Mountain. (p. 1542)
—Secret of Moon Castle. (p. 1542)
—Secret of Spiggy Holes. (p. 1542)
Blyton, Enid, et al. Fairies' Shoemaker & Other Stories. (p. 563)
—Magical Creatures. (p. 1074)
—My First 123 & Nursery Rhymes. (p. 1203)
—My First Abc. (p. 1204)
—My First Animals. (p. 1204)
—My First Colours & Shapes. (p. 1206)
—Out in Space. (p. 1311)
—Things That Go. (p. 1733)
—Under the Sea. (p. 1814)
BMI Staff, compiled by. Fear Street Collection - Set (p. 579)
Bo, Ben. Skullcrack. (p. 1586)
Bo, Lars, illus. see Wilde, Oscar.
Bo, Zhiyue. History of Modern China. (p. 784)
—History of Modern China. Wang, Jianwei, ed. (p. 784)
Boada, Francesc. Princess & the Pea (la Princesa y el Guisante) A Bilingual Book! Estrada, Pau, illus. (p. 1403)
Boada, Francesc, jt. auth. see Bas, Mercè Escardó I.

Boada, Francesc & Andersen, Hans Christian. Princess & the Pea (La Princesa y el Guisante) Estrada, Pau, illus. (p. 1403)
Boada i Moret, Francesc & Grimm, Jacob i Wilhelm (Germans Grimm). Caperucita Roja. (p. 262)
Boah, Ewuramma Hannah. Jehovah the Lifter of My Head. (p. 912)
Boake, Kathy, illus. see Isabella, Jude.
Boake, Kathy, illus. see Swanson, Diane.
Boake, Terri Meyer. Architecturally Exposed Structural Steel: Specifications, Connections, Details. (p. 95)
Boam, Jon. Colour Me Menagerie. (p. 346)
Board, Jon & Cross, Alan. Cambridge Primary Science Stage 1 Learner's Book. (p. 255)
Board, Kjersti, tr. see Lindenbaum, Pija.
Board, Perry, illus. see Layne, Steven L.
Boardman Moen, Christine. Instant PowerPoint Lessons & Activities: Literary Elements: 16 Model Lessons That Guide Students to Create Easy PowerPoint Presentations That Help Them Analyze Literary Elements in the Books They Read. (p. 878)
Boas, Jacob. We Are Witnesses: Five Diaries of Teenagers Who Died in the Holocaust. (p. 1866)
Boase, Petra. Brilliant Badges to Make Yourself: 25 Amazing Step-By-Step Badge-Making Projects. (p. 228)
—Christmas Crafts for Kids: 50 Step-By-Step Decorations & Gift Ideas for Festive Fun. (p. 313)
—Friendship Bracelets & Beading Fun: 25 Knotty, Dotty, Stripey & Sparkly Designs to Make! (p. 639)
—Terrific T-Shirt Fun: 25 Tremendous T-Shirt Designs & Creations to Try! (p. 1721)
Boase, Petra & Graham, Bettina. Dressing Up! 50 Step-By-Step Amazing Outfits to Make & Faces to Paint. (p. 485)
Boase, Susan, illus. see Orr, Wendy.
Boase, Wendy. Caperucita Roja. Puncel, María, tr. (p. 262)
—Tres Osos. Bull, Carolyn, illus. (p. 1784)
Boat, Patty. Disappointing Homecoming: (A Soldier's Story) (p. 446)
Boatfield, Jonny, illus. see Dalton, Andrew.
Boatman, Marva. Children's Book of Morals. (p. 303)
Boatner, Kay. Funny Fill-In - My Ocean Adventure. (p. 649)
—National Geographic Kids Funny Fill-In: My Medieval Adventure. (p. 1232)
Boatwright, Edith, jt. auth. see Blake, Edna L.
Boatwright-Cook, Jane. Skeleton Leaf Stories: Behind the Shutters. (p. 1584)
Boaz, Ashley. Mystery of the Midnight Blaze. (p. 1225)
Boaz, John. Israeli-Palestinian Conflict. (p. 893)
—Legalizing Drugs. (p. 988)
Boaz, John, ed. U. S. Attack on Afghanistan. (p. 1806)
Boaz, Noel. Evolving Health: The Origins of Illness & How the Modern World Is Making Us Sick. (p. 547)
Boazu, Elena & Balestrieri, Mauro. Lila's Quest. (p. 1017)
Bob, Hippie. Juicy Lucy a Happy Strawberry: A Hippie Bob Tale. (p. 932)
Bob, Schultz. Boyhood & Beyond. (p. 220)
Bob, Steven M. & Howard, Lisa Bob. Bar & Bat Mitzvah Manual: Six Steps to a Meaningful Family Celebration. (p. 137)
Bobak, Cathy, illus. see Janeczko, Paul B.
Bobb, Barry L. Hero of Faith - Johann Sebastian Bach. (p. 772)
Bobbie, Gramma. Bright Stars. (p. 228)
Bobbie, Match. Havdallah Three Stars in the Sky. (p. 754)
Bobbish, John, illus. see Lightfoot, D. J.
Bobeck, Jade. Paxton's Adventures: A Day on Grandpa's Farm. (p. 1331)
Bobek, Joanne R. Day at Pond Snow. (p. 412)
Bober, Natalie S. Countdown to Independence. (p. 370)
—Papa Is a Poet: A Story about Robert Frost. Gibbon, Rebecca, illus. (p. 1322)
—Thomas Jefferson: Draftsman of a Nation. (p. 1739)
Bober, Suzanne, jt. auth. see Merberg, Julie.
Bober, Suzanne & Merberg, Julie. How Is Mona Lisa Feeling? (p. 810)
—Mama, Baby, & Other First Words. (p. 1084)
Bobet, Leah. Above. (p. 6)
—Inheritance of Ashes. (p. 874)
Bobic, Marilyn Kay. My Nana My Special Friend. (p. 1215)
Bobick, Ruth, tr. see Delta, Penelope.
Bobillo, Juan, illus. see Trillo, Carlos.
Bobillo, Juan & Dragotta, Nick. FF (p. 583)
Bobo, W. L. Chickendoodle! Where Are You? (p. 300)
Bobowicz, Pamela. 101 Dalmatians. (p. 1999)
—101 Dalmatians (Disney 101 Dalmatians) RH Disney Staff, illus. (p. 1999)
—Alice in Wonderland (Disney Alice in Wonderland) Disney Storybook Artists Staff, illus. (p. 39)
—Disney Alice in Wonderland. (p. 451)
Bobrick, Benson. Battle of Nashville. (p. 146)
—Fight for Freedom: The American Revolutionary War. (p. 585)
—Passion for Victory: The Story of the Olympics in Ancient & Early Modern Times. (p. 1327)
Bobrick, Julie, ed. see Burke, David.
Bobrick, Julie, ed. Cinderella: Level 1: Learn Mandarin Chinese Through Fairy Tales. Peters, Li Li & Tao, Ming, trs. (p. 320)
Bobrizky, George, illus. see Mara, Thalia.
Bobroff, Ronald P. Roads to Glory: Late Imperial Russia & the Turkish Straits. (p. 1477)
Bobrow, Jerry. California High School Exit Exam - Math. (p. 253)
Bobrow, Laura J. He Listens. (p. 756)
Bobrowsky, Matthew, et al. Using Physics Gadgets & Gizmos, Grades 9-12: Phenomenon-Based Learning. (p. 1828)
Bocanegra, Deborah. Winky Sue's Peppermint Birthday. Buehrle, Jacquelyn, illus. (p. 1936)
Bocanegra, Haley. New Dog Food for Mozart. (p. 1244)
Boccanfuso, Emanuele, illus. see Jeffrey, Gary.
Boccardo, Johanna, illus. see Powell, Jillian.
Bocchino, Serena. What Am I? the Story of an Abstract Painting. Bocchino, Serena, illus. (p. 1879)
Bochenski, Cristina. Emma Has One More. (p. 519)
—Wildlife of the Great Basin. (p. 1931)
Bochinski, Julianne Blair. Complete Handbook of Science Fair Projects. (p. 353)
—Complete Workbook for Science Fair Projects. (p. 353)
—More Award-Winning Science Fair Projects. DiBiase, Judy, illus. (p. 1174)
Bochner, Arthur, et al. New Totally Awesome Business Book for Kids. (p. 1247)
—New Totally Awesome Money Book for Kids. (p. 1247)
Bochynek, Halina. Beagle's Tale. (p. 150)
Bocik, Adam, illus. see Galluzzi, Edward.
Bock, Caroline. Before My Eyes. (p. 158)
—Lie. (p. 1007)
Bock, Danuta. Flying Turtle: A Test of Friendship & Understanding. (p. 610)
Bock, Janna, illus. see Cooper, Sharon Katz.
Bock, Janna, illus. see Langston-George, Rebecca.
Bock, Lee. Oh, Crumps! (p. 1280)
Bock, Suzanne. In the Beginning: Angels with Attitudes (p. 865)
—Meet the Angels (p. 1122)
Bock, Suzanne, illus. see Stimkorb, Patricia.
Bock, William Sauts. Mythology (p. 1227)
Bock, William Sauts, illus. see Altman, Linda Jacobs.
Bock, William Sauts, illus. see Bernard, Catherine.
Bock, William Sauts, illus. see Collier, Irene Dea.
Bock, William Sauts, illus. see Homer, Larona.
Bock, William Sauts, illus. see Houle, Michelle M.
Bock, William Sauts, illus. see Schuman, Michael A.
Bock, William Sauts, illus. see Spies, Karen Bornemann.
Bockemeier, Karen. Patty's Paper Place. (p. 1330)
Bockenhauer, Mark H. & Cunha, Stephen F. National Geographic Our Fifty States. (p. 1233)
Bockman, Charlotte, jt. auth. see Benjamin, Tina.
Bockmann, Melanie. Just Plane Crazy: A Guide True Story Book. (p. 939)
Bockmann, Melanie Scherencel. In the Shadow of the Mob/Melanie Scherencel Bockmann. (p. 867)
Bocknek, Jonathan. Antarctica: The Last Wilderness. (p. 88)
—Plants. (p. 1369)
Bockol, Leslie & Ikids Staff. One Tree. Phillips, Jillian, illus. (p. 1297)
Bocks, Eric Stephen. Wing over Wendover. (p. 1936)
Bocquée, Christian, illus. see Collins, Paul.
Bodach, Marty. Story of My Totem. (p. 1659)
Bodach, Vijaya. Ten Easter Eggs. Logan, Laura, illus. (p. 1718)
Bodach, Vijaya, jt. auth. see Bodach, Vijaya Khisty.
Bodach, Vijaya K. Flowers [Scholastic]. (p. 608)
—Leaves [Scholastic]. (p. 986)
—Roots [Scholastic]. (p. 1488)
—Seeds [Scholastic]. (p. 1548)
Bodach, Vijaya K., jt. auth. see Bodach, Vijaya Khisty.
Bodach, Vijaya Khisty. Electricity. (p. 509)
—Energy. (p. 528)
—Flowers (p. 608)
—Fruits (p. 645)
—Fruits Saunders-Smith, Gail, ed. (p. 645)
—Gráficas Circulares. (p. 705)
—Gráficas de Barras. (p. 705)
—Hacer Gráficas. (p. 735)
—How Does It Grow? (p. 808)
—Leaves (p. 986)
—Leaves Saunders-Smith, Gail, ed. (p. 986)
—Magnets. (p. 1076)
—Making Observations. (p. 1082)
—Measuring. (p. 1117)
—Pictografías. (p. 1355)
—Pictografías/Pictographs. (p. 1355)
—Pictographs (p. 1355)
—Pie Graphs (p. 1356)
—Reflection. (p. 1456)
—Roots (p. 1488)
—Roots Saunders-Smith, Gail, ed. (p. 1488)
—Seeds Saunders-Smith, Gail, ed. (p. 1547)
—Sink or Float? (p. 1579)
—Stems (p. 1647)
—Stems Saunders-Smith, Gail, ed. (p. 1647)
—Tableros de Conteo. (p. 1694)
—Tableros de Conteo/Tally Charts (p. 1694)
—What Is Missing? (p. 1889)
Bodach, Vijaya Khisty & Bodach, Vijaya. Flowers Saunders-Smith, Gail, ed. (p. 608)
Bodach, Vijaya Khisty & Bodach, Vijaya K. Bar Graphs (p. 137)
—Pictographs (p. 1355)
—Pie Graphs (p. 1356)
—Tally Charts (p. 1704)
Bodart, Denis, illus. see Vehlmann, Fabien.
Boddam-Whetham, Jo & Mitchell, Alison. Beginning with God: Book 1: Exploring the Bible with Your Child (p. 159)
Bodden, Michelle. Well My Teacher Said. Williams, Brittney, illus. (p. 1874)
Bodden, Michelle, adapted by. Obara & the Merchants. (p. 1275)
—Obara the Gatekeeper. (p. 1275)
Bodden, Valerie. 9/11 Terror Attacks: Days of Change. (p. 1993)
—9/11 Terror Attacks. (p. 1993)
—Aircraft Carriers. (p. 31)
—Amazing Animals: Polar Bears. (p. 53)
—Amazing Animals: Bison. (p. 53)
—Amazing Animals: Crocodiles. (p. 53)
—Amazing Animals - Crocodiles. (p. 53)
—Amazing Animals: Giraffes. (p. 53)
—Amazing Animals - Giraffes. (p. 53)
—Amazing Animals: Jaguars. (p. 53)
—Amazing Animals: Koalas. (p. 53)
—Amazing Animals - Koalas. (p. 53)
—Amazing Animals: Komodo Dragons. (p. 53)
—Amazing Animals: Lions. (p. 53)
—Amazing Animals - Lions. (p. 53)
—Amazing Animals: Monkeys. (p. 53)
—Amazing Animals: Owls. (p. 53)
—Amazing Animals: Pandas. (p. 53)
—Amazing Animals: Penguins. (p. 53)
—Amazing Animals - Penguins. (p. 53)
—Amazing Animals: Polar Bears. (p. 53)
—Amazing Animals: Rhinoceroses. (p. 53)
—Amazing Animals: Sharks. (p. 53)
—Amazing Animals: Snakes. (p. 53)
—Amazing Animals: Swans. (p. 53)
—Amazing Animals: Tigers. (p. 53)
—Amazing Animals - Tigers. (p. 53)
—Amazon River. (p. 56)
—Ambulances. (p. 57)
—Analyze & Define the Assignment. (p. 67)
—Ancient Civilization: Aztec Empire. (p. 68)
—Ancient Civilization: China. (p. 68)
—Ancient Civilization: Greece. (p. 68)
—Ancient Civilization: Rome. (p. 68)
—Ants. (p. 90)
—Apache. (p. 91)
—Apple. (p. 92)
—Armored Vehicles. (p. 100)
—Assassination of Archduke Ferdinand. (p. 107)
—Assess & Select Your Sources. (p. 107)
—Aztec Empire. (p. 122)
—Aztec Warriors. (p. 122)
—Barbarians. (p. 137)
—Baseball. (p. 140)
—Basketball. (p. 143)
—Battleships. (p. 147)
—Beagles. (p. 150)
—Beetles. (p. 158)
—Being Fit. (p. 161)
—Bicycling. (p. 177)
—Big Time - Calvin Johnson. (p. 184)
—Big Time: Kevin Durant. (p. 184)
—Birds. (p. 191)
—Bison. (p. 193)
—Bombers. (p. 208)
—Bombing of Hiroshima & Nagasaki: Days of Change. (p. 208)
—Bombing of Hiroshima & Nagasaki. (p. 208)
—Brushes with Greatness: History Paintings. (p. 232)
—Brushes with Greatness: Landscapes. (p. 232)
—Bryce Harper: Big Time. (p. 233)
—Built for Battle: Battleships. (p. 239)
—Built for Battle: Fighter Jets. (p. 239)
—Built for Battle: Helicopters. (p. 239)
—Built for Battle: Tanks. (p. 240)
—Bulldogs. (p. 240)
—California. (p. 253)
—Calvin Johnson. (p. 255)
—Caring for Horses. (p. 269)
—Carousels. (p. 271)
—Carrie Underwood: Big Time. (p. 271)
—Castles. (p. 277)
—Cats. (p. 280)
—Centipedes. (p. 287)
—Chameleons. (p. 289)
—Che Guevara: Political Activist & Revolutionary. (p. 295)
—Cherokee. (p. 298)
—City. (p. 323)
—Clouds. (p. 335)
—Club & Prescription Drug Abuse. (p. 335)
—Cockroaches. (p. 337)
—Cold War. (p. 339)
—Columbus Reaches the New World. (p. 346)
—Computers. (p. 355)
—Concrete Poetry. (p. 355)
—Conquistadors. (p. 358)
—Creating a Character: Dialogue & Characterization. (p. 378)
—Creepy Creatures: Ants. (p. 381)
—Creepy Creatures: Beetles. (p. 381)
—Creepy Creatures: Cockroaches. (p. 381)
—Creepy Creatures: Dragonflies. (p. 381)
—Creepy Creatures: Fleas. (p. 381)
—Creepy Creatures: Grasshoppers. (p. 381)
—Creepy Creatures: Mites. (p. 381)
—Creepy Creatures: Moths. (p. 381)
—Creepy Creatures: Slugs. (p. 381)
—Creepy Creatures: Stick Insects. (p. 381)
—Creepy Creatures: Termites. (p. 381)
—Creepy Creatures: Ticks. (p. 381)
—Creepy Creatures - Worms. (p. 381)
—Crickets. (p. 382)
—Critical Plant Life. (p. 383)
—Dairy. (p. 400)
—Declaration of American Independence. (p. 421)
—Deserts. (p. 429)
—Doing Primary Research. (p. 463)
—Eagle. (p. 492)
—Eating Healthy. (p. 501)
—Effective Speeches. (p. 505)
—Egypt. (p. 506)
—Environmental Law. (p. 532)
—Farming Town. (p. 574)
—Ferris Wheels. (p. 582)
—Fetch!: Beagles. (p. 582)
—Fetch!: Bulldogs. (p. 582)
—Fetch!: German Shepherds. (p. 582)
—Fetch!: Poodles. (p. 582)
—Fetch!: Retrievers. (p. 582)
—Fetch!: Terriers. (p. 582)
—Fighter Jets. (p. 585)
—Fire Trucks. (p. 591)
—Fish. (p. 598)
—Fleas. (p. 603)
—Florida. (p. 606)
—Frogs. (p. 641)
—Fruits. (p. 645)
—German Shepherds. (p. 666)
—Giving a Presentation. (p. 681)
—Giving a Presentation. Williams, Nate, illus. (p. 681)
—Glaciers. (p. 682)
—Golf. (p. 696)
—Grains. (p. 705)
—Grand Canyon. (p. 707)
—Grasshoppers. (p. 711)
—Great Barrier Reef. (p. 713)
—Great Warriors: Barbarians. (p. 719)
—Great Warriors: Conquistadors. (p. 719)
—Great Warriors: Mongols. (p. 719)
—Great Warriors: Vikings. (p. 719)
—Greece. (p. 720)
—Grow with Me: Apple. (p. 726)
—Grow with Me: Eagle. (p. 726)
—Grow with Me: Snake. (p. 726)
—Grow with Me: Spider. (p. 726)
—Guinea Pigs. (p. 731)
—Haikus. (p. 735)
—Halloween. (p. 737)
—Hamsters. (p. 740)
—Hanukkah. (p. 743)
—Healthy Plates: Being Fit. (p. 758)
—Healthy Plates: Dairy. (p. 758)
—Healthy Plates: Eating Healthy. (p. 758)
—Healthy Plates: Fruits. (p. 758)
—Healthy Plates: Grains. (p. 758)
—Healthy Plates: Proteins. (p. 758)
—Healthy Plates: Vegetables. (p. 759)
—Helicopters. (p. 763)
—Hiking. (p. 779)
—Hillary Clinton: Historic Leader. (p. 779)
—Holocaust. (p. 789)
—Horsing Around: Caring for Horses. (p. 801)
—Horsing Around: Riding Horses. (p. 801)
—Horsing Around: Showing Horses. (p. 801)
—Horsing Around: Training Horses. (p. 801)
—How to Analyze the Films of George Lucas. (p. 814)
—How to Analyze the Works of Frederick Douglass. (p. 814)
—Hurricanes. (p. 830)
—Identify & Evaluate Advertising. (p. 852)
—Illinois. (p. 857)
—Inclined Planes. (p. 869)
—Internet. (p. 880)
—Jaguars. (p. 905)
—Journalistic Articles. (p. 927)
—Justin Bieber: Musical Phenom. (p. 940)
—Kayaking. (p. 946)
—Kevin Durant. (p. 950)
—Koalas. (p. 966)
—Komodo Dragons. (p. 966)
—Kristen Stewart. (p. 967)
—Levers. (p. 1003)
—Limericks. (p. 1018)
—Man Walks on the Moon: Days of Change. (p. 1086)
—Man Walks on the Moon. (p. 1086)
—Mantises. (p. 1088)
—Mark Twain. (p. 1095)
—Michelle Obama: First Lady & Role Model. (p. 1135)
—Mites. (p. 1156)
—Mongols (Great Warriors) (p. 1164)
—Monkeys. (p. 1165)
—Mosques. (p. 1176)
—Moths. (p. 1179)
—Mount Everest. (p. 1180)
—Mountains. (p. 1181)
—My First Look at - A Town. (p. 1207)
—Navajo. (p. 1237)
—Navigating the Library. (p. 1238)
—New Mexico. (p. 1246)
—New York. (p. 1247)
—Nez Perce. (p. 1249)
—Nonfiction - Writing for Fact & Argument: Truthful Biographies. (p. 1263)
—Northern Lights. (p. 1266)
—Nursery Rhymes. (p. 1273)
—Oceans. (p. 1277)
—One Direction. (p. 1294)
—Oregon. (p. 1302)
—Organized Essays. (p. 1303)
—Our Wonderful Weather: Clouds. (p. 1310)
—Our Wonderful Weather: Hurricanes. (p. 1310)
—Our Wonderful Weather: Snow. (p. 1310)
—Our Wonderful Weather: Thunderstorms. (p. 1310)
—Our Wonderful Weather: Tornadoes. (p. 1310)
—Owls. (p. 1315)
—Painting the Picture: Imagery & Description. (p. 1318)
—Pandas. (p. 1321)
—Parrots. (p. 1325)
—Penguins. (p. 1337)
—Pennsylvania. (p. 1337)
—Photography. (p. 1353)
—Picturing Words in a Poem. (p. 1356)
—Poetry Basics: Concrete Poetry. (p. 1376)
—Poetry Basics: Haiku. (p. 1376)
—Poetry Basics - Limericks. (p. 1376)
—Poetry Basics - Nursery Rhymes. (p. 1376)
—Poking Fun in a Poem. (p. 1378)
—Polar Bears. (p. 1379)
—Poodles. (p. 1383)
—Preparing for an Exam. (p. 1396)
—Print & Subscription Sources. (p. 1406)
—Proteins. (p. 1412)
—Pulleys. (p. 1415)
—Pyramids. (p. 1421)
—Rabbits. (p. 1429)
—Rainforests. (p. 1436)
—Rescue Boats. (p. 1462)
—Research & Synthesize Your Facts. (p. 1462)
—Retrievers. (p. 1464)
—Rhinoceroses. (p. 1467)
—Riding Horses. (p. 1471)
—Rihanna. (p. 1472)
—Robert Griffin III. (p. 1479)
—Roller Coasters. (p. 1485)
—Romance. (p. 1486)
—Rome. (p. 1486)
—Running. (p. 1497)
—Samuel Houston: Army Leader & Historic Politician. (p. 1509)
—Science Fiction. (p. 1526)

—Scorpions. (p. 1530)
—Screws. (p. 1533)
—Scuba Diving. (p. 1533)
—Selena Gomez. (p. 1549)
—Setting the Style: Wording & Tone. (p. 1554)
—Sharks. (p. 1562)
—Showing Horses. (p. 1571)
—Sioux. (p. 1580)
—Skunks. (p. 1586)
—Slugs. (p. 1591)
—Snake. (p. 1596)
—Snakes. (p. 1596)
—Snow. (p. 1598)
—Soccer. (p. 1603)
—Spider. (p. 1626)
—Spiders. (p. 1626)
—Stick Insects. (p. 1649)
—Story of Coca-Cola. (p. 1657)
—Story of Disney. (p. 1658)
—Submarines. (p. 1671)
—Suburb. (p. 1671)
—Suez Canal. (p. 1672)
—Swans. (p. 1689)
—Tanks. (p. 1705)
—Taylor Lautner. (p. 1708)
—Television. (p. 1716)
—Telling The Tale: Narration & Point of View. (p. 1717)
—Temples. (p. 1718)
—Termites. (p. 1721)
—Terriers. (p. 1721)
—Texas. (p. 1723)
—Thanksgiving. (p. 1725)
—Threat of Overpopulation. (p. 1741)
—Through the American West. (p. 1745)
—Thunderstorms. (p. 1746)
—Ticks. (p. 1747)
—To the Heart of Africa. (p. 1759)
—To the Moon. (p. 1759)
—To the Ocean Deep. (p. 1759)
—To the South Pole. (p. 1759)
—To the Top of Mount Everest. (p. 1759)
—Tornadoes. (p. 1770)
—Town. (p. 1773)
—Training Horses. (p. 1777)
—Truthful Biographies. (p. 1794)
—Using the Internet. (p. 1828)
—Valentine's Day. (p. 1830)
—Vegetables. (p. 1834)
—Victoria Falls. (p. 1840)
—Vikings (Great Warriors) (p. 1842)
—Vincent Van Gogh. (p. 1842)
—Volcanoes. (p. 1849)
—Volleyball. (p. 1849)
—Walruses. (p. 1855)
—War on Waste. (p. 1858)
—Water for Life. (p. 1862)
—Water Rides. (p. 1863)
—Wedges. (p. 1871)
—What Are Fiction Genres? (p. 1879)
—What Are Nonfiction Genres? (p. 1879)
—Wheels & Axles. (p. 1900)
—Who Is a Poet? (p. 1915)
—Wildlife in Danger. (p. 1931)
—Worms. (p. 1961)
—Write & Revise Your Project. (p. 1963)
—Write Me a Poem: Finding the Rhyme in a Poem. (p. 1963)
—Writing a Research Paper. (p. 1964)
—Writing a Research Paper. Williams, Nate, illus. (p. 1964)
Bodden, Valerie, jt. auth. see Frisch, Aaron.
Bodden, Valerie & Gehry, Frank O. Frank Gehry. (p. 628)
Boddington, Craig. Buffalo! (p. 235)
Boddy, Gary. Giraffe's Holiday in Sydney. (p. 678)
—This Cow These Cows. (p. 1735)
Boddy, James, illus. see King, Carrie.
Boddy, Joe, illus. see Bea, Holly.
Boddy, Joe, illus. see Daste, Larry, et al.
Bode, Achim, et al. Where We Live. (p. 1910)
Bode, Ann de. I Can't Find You, Mum! (p. 837)
—I Miss You, Grandad. Broere, Rien, illus. (p. 844)
—I Still Love You, Dad. Broere, Rien, illus. (p. 846)
—Leave Me Alone! Broere, Rien, illus. (p. 986)
Bode, Anna de. Can you make me Better? (p. 259)
Bode, Mark, et al. Lizard of Oz. (p. 1042)
Bode, N. E. Anybodies. Ferguson, Peter, illus. (p. 91)
—Slippery Map. Dorman, Brandon, illus. (p. 1590)
—Somebodies. Ferguson, Peter, illus. (p. 1609)
Bodecker, N. M. Mushroom Center Disaster. Blegvad, Erik & Starr, Branka, illus. (p. 1193)
—Quimble Wood. Starr, Branka, illus. (p. 1428)
Bodecker, N. M., illus. see Eager, Edward.
Bodeen, Jim, ed. see A to Z.
Bodeen, S. A. Compound. (p. 354)
—Fallout. (p. 567)
—Gardener. (p. 656)
—Lost. (p. 1054)
—Raft. (p. 1433)
—Shipwreck Island. (p. 1567)
Bodeker, Brian, illus. see Humann, Walter J.
Bodel, Ital, photos by see Herzog, Pearl.
Bodell, Alice L. Matchbook Cover. (p. 1104)
Bodell, Eileen. Last Snapshot. (p. 978)
Bodemann, Y. Michal, jt. ed. see Yurdakul, Gökçe.
Bodenstein, Dan. Steven the Vegan. Ronald, Robrahn, illus. (p. 1649)
—Tale of Eartha the Sea Turtle. (p. 1699)
—Tale of Eartha the Sea Turtle - Special Edition. (p. 1699)
Bodett, Tom. Williwaw! (p. 1934)
Bodett, Tom, illus. see Minor, Wendell.
Bodger, Holly. 5 to 1. (p. 1992)
Bodger, Joan. Tales of Court & Castle. Lang, Mark, illus. (p. 1702)
Bodger, Lorraine, illus. see Javna, John, et al.
Bodi, Sari. Ghost in Allie's Pool. (p. 670)
Bodie, Idella. Heroes & Heroines of the American Revolution. (p. 772)
—Heroines of the American Revolution. (p. 773)
—Light-Horse Harry. (p. 1015)
—Wizard Owl. (p. 1943)
Bodie, Karen. Will You Play Ball with Me? (p. 1932)
Bodily, Michael, illus. see Knudsen, Sherilyn.
Bodin, Alexci. Puke. (p. 1415)
Bodin, Britt. Puppy Named Hope. (p. 1418)
Bodkin, Odds. Belly Button. (p. 163)
—Doing, Doing, Doing. (p. 463)
—Little Proto's T-Rex Adventure: A Musical Dinosaur Story. (p. 1034)
—Perkins Goes Out. (p. 1343)
Bodle, Katharine, jt. auth. see Jennings, Sue.
Bodleian Library Staff, jt. auth. see Collins Publishers Staff.
Bodleian Library Staff & F., Warner. Father Christmas' ABC: A Fascimile. (p. 577)
Bodmer, Karl, illus. see Jackson, John C.
Bodoff, Janet, illus. see Toscano, Leesa.
Bodoh, Tony. Hannah's Animal Farm. (p. 742)
Bodrogi, Michael. Herbert the Tadpole in the Big Change. La Beree, Brian, illus. (p. 769)
Body, Robert J. Bob. I Survived the Bataan Death March. (p. 846)
Body, Wendy. Azio's ABC. (p. 122)
—Blinki's Shopping List. (p. 199)
—Meebie's Magic Box. (p. 1120)
—Minki's Day (p. 1147)
—Mup's Days of the Week (p. 1191)
—Zeebo's Numbers (p. 1985)
—Zia's Colors (p. 1986)
Boecker, Virginia. Witch Hunter. (p. 1941)
Boedoe, Geefwee. Arrowville. Boedoe, Geefwee, illus. (p. 101)
Boehl, Jennifer Lang. That's Mine Sissy. (p. 1727)
Boehm, Ann E., jt. auth. see Brassard, Marla R.
Boehm, Annette, ed. see Hatfield, Ron.
Boehm, Barbara. Bears I'd Like to Meet! A Bear's-Eye View of 101 Notable Figures in History. (p. 152)
Boehm, Gregory A. Big Big Book of Word Search. (p. 178)
Boehm Jerome, Kate. Atlanta, Ga: Cool Stuff Every Kid Should Know. (p. 112)
—Austin & the State of Texas: Cool Stuff Every Kid Should Know. (p. 116)
—Boston & the State of Massachusetts: Cool Stuff Every Kid Should Know. (p. 215)
—Buffalo, Ny: Cool Stuff Every Kid Should Know. (p. 235)
—Charlotte & the State of North Carolina: Cool Stuff Every Kid Should Know. (p. 293)
—Chicago & the State of Illinois: Cool Stuff Every Kid Should Know. (p. 299)
—Columbia & the State of South Carolina: Cool Stuff Every Kid Should Know. (p. 346)
—Columbus & the State of Ohio: Cool Stuff Every Kid Should Know. (p. 346)
—Dallas, Tx: Cool Stuff Every Kid Should Know. (p. 401)
—Houston, Tx: Cool Stuff Every Kid Should Know. (p. 804)
—Jacksonville & the State of Florida: Cool Stuff Every Kid Should Know. (p. 904)
—Orlando, Fl: Cool Stuff Every Kid Should Know. (p. 1304)
—Philadelphia & the State of Pennsylvania: Cool Stuff Every Kid Should Know. (p. 1350)
—Pittsburgh & the State of Pennsylvania: Cool Stuff Every Kid Should Know. (p. 1364)
—Raleigh & the State of North Carolina: Cool Stuff Every Kid Should Know. (p. 1437)
—Richmond & the State of Virginia: Cool Stuff Every Kid Should Know. (p. 1470)
—Rochester & the State of New York: Cool Stuff Every Kid Should Know. (p. 1481)
—San Antonio & the State of Texas: Cool Stuff Every Kid Should Know. (p. 1510)
—Savannah & the State of Georgia: Cool Stuff Every Kid Should Know. (p. 1516)
Boehm, Patricia. Does Noah's Kitten Have Autism Too? Kelly, Robert, illus. (p. 460)
Boehm, Philip, tr. see Laube, Sigrid.
Boehm, Rachel. Ways I Will Love You Gerber, Mary Jane, illus. (p. 1865)
Boehm, Richard G. Building Geography Skills for Life. (p. 239)
Boehm, Richard G. & McGraw-Hill Staff. World Geography. (p. 1955)
Boehm, Richard G., et al. Activity Books: Communities. (p. 10)
—Activity Books: Making a Difference. (p. 10)
—Assessment Programs: Communities. (p. 107)
—Assessment Programs: A Child's Place. (p. 107)
—Assessment Programs: Making a Difference. (p. 107)
—Big Book Libraries. (p. 178)
—Carteles de la Unidad: La Historia de Nuestro Mundo: Relatos de la Historia. (p. 272)
—Daily Geography: Grades K-2. (p. 399)
—Desk Maps: Primary (K-2) Package Of 10. (p. 430)
—Desk Maps: Intermediate (3-7) Package Of 10. (p. 430)
—Game Time! Communities. (p. 654)
—Game Time! United States. (p. 654)
—Game Time! A Child's Place. (p. 654)
—Game Time! Making a Difference. (p. 654)
—Great Beginnings. (p. 714)
—Mundo y Sus Gentes: Hemisferio Occidental, Europa y Rusia. (p. 1191)
—Mundo y Sus Gentes. (p. 1191)
—My World & Me: A Kindergarten Program. (p. 1221)
—Reading Support & Test Preparation: Communities. (p. 1446)
—Reading Support & Test Preparation: A Child's Place. (p. 1446)
—Reading Support & Test Preparation: Making a Difference. (p. 1446)
—Relatos de la Historia: Assessment Program. (p. 1458)
—Relatos de la Historia: Estados y Regiones. (p. 1458)
—Relatos de la Historia: La Historia de Estados Mundo. (p. 1458)
—Relatos de la Historia: La Historia de Estados Unidos. (p. 1458)
—Social Studies Libraries: Making a Difference. (p. 1604)
—Take-Home Review Books. (p. 1696)
—Transparencias: La Historia de Nuestro Mundo: Relatos de la Historia. (p. 1779)
—Vocabulary Picture Cards. (p. 1847)
—World & Its People. (p. 1953)
—World Geography & Cultures. (p. 1955)
—Write-on Charts. (p. 1963)
Boehme, Gerry. Amphetamines. (p. 65)
Boehme, Gerry, jt. auth. see Sanders, Doug.
Boehme, Gerry, et al. New Mexico. (p. 1246)
—Oklahoma. (p. 1282)
Boehnert, Ernest. Magic Christmas Train. (p. 1072)
Boeholt, V. A. Burton the Kind Scarecrow. Christensen, Jennifer Steele, ed. (p. 244)
—Burton's Friendship Garden. Jensen, Nathaniel P., illus. (p. 244)
Boeke, Wanda, tr. see Holtwijk, Ineke & Boyds Mills Press Staff.
Boeke, Wanda, tr. see Moeyaert, Bart.
Boekestein, William. Quest for Comfort: The Story of the Heidelberg Catechism. Hughes, Evan, illus. (p. 1426)
Boekhoff & Kallen, Stuart A. Underground Railroad. (p. 1814)
Boekhoff, P. M. Ben & Jerry. (p. 163)
—Galileo. (p. 653)
—Illinois. (p. 857)
—Missouri. (p. 1154)
—Nifty Thrifty Space Crafts. Ponte, June, illus. (p. 1252)
Boekhoff, P. M., jt. auth. see Brown, Jonatha A.
Boekhoff, P. M. & Brown, Jonatha A. Washington. (p. 1859)
Boekhoff, P. M. & Kallen, Stuart A. Benjamin Franklin. (p. 164)
—Italian Renaissance. (p. 894)
—Navajo. (p. 1237)
—Oregon. (p. 1302)
—Recycling. (p. 1453)
Boelter, Ashaki. Diaries of the Doomed. Boelter, Ashaki, illus. (p. 434)
—Diaries of the Doomed 2: Fate of the Fatal. (p. 434)
—Shut Em' Down # 4: Meltdown of the Maniac Hood Fighter. (p. 1572)
Boelts, Darwin, jt. auth. see Boelts, Maribeth.
Boelts, Maribeth. Before You Were Mine. Walker, David, illus. (p. 159)
—Dogerella. Wu, Donald, illus. (p. 462)
—Happy Like Soccer. Castillo, Lauren, illus. (p. 746)
—PS Brothers. (p. 1413)
—Sleeping Bootsie. Cantor, Patricia, illus. (p. 1589)
—Those Shoes. (p. 1740)
—Those Shoes. Jones, Noah, illus. (p. 1740)
—Those Shoes. Jones, Noah Z., illus. (p. 1740)
Boelts, Maribeth & Boelts, Darwin. Kids to the Rescue! First Aid Techniques for Kids. Megale, Marina, illus. (p. 955)
Boen, Sherry. Fish Who Made a Magical Wish (p. 598)
Boer, Faye, ed. see Chodan, Tim & Asfar, Dan.
Boer, Paula. Brumbies. Evans, Rowena, illus. (p. 232)
Boer, Peter. Bush Pilots: Daredevils of the Wilderness. (p. 244)
—Bush Pilots: Canada's Wilderness Daredevils (p. 244)
—Calgary Flames. (p. 253)
—Canadian Spies & Spies in Canada: Undercover at Home & Abroad. (p. 260)
—Edmonton Oilers. (p. 504)
—Orlando Bloom: Shooting to Stardom (p. 1304)
—Top Canadian Crime Investigations: Hunting Down Serial Killers. (p. 1769)
—Weird Facts about Canadian Hockey: Strange, Wacky & Hilarious Stories. (p. 1872)
Boerema, Deborah Bence. Innkeeper's Dog. (p. 875)
Boerger, Kristin. Hace Viento. (p. 735)
—Let's Read about Wind. (p. 1000)
Boerger, Kristin & Boyett, Suzi. Let's Read about Rain. (p. 1000)
—Llueve. (p. 1043)
Boerke, Arthur Mark, jt. auth. see Plumides, Damon.
Boersma, Heather. Dream Big: 30 Days to Life Beyond All You Could Ask or Imagine. (p. 483)
Boerst, William J. Edgar Rice Burroughs: Creator of Tarzan. (p. 504)
—Galileo Galilei & the Science of Motion. (p. 653)
—Generous Anger: The Story of George Orwell. (p. 660)
—Isaac Asimov: Writer of the Future. (p. 890)
—Johannes Kepler: Discovering the Laws of Celestial Motion. (p. 920)
—Marching in Birmingham. (p. 1092)
—Nicholas Copernicus & the Founding of Modern Astronomy. (p. 1250)
—Time Machine: The Story of H. G. Wells. (p. 1752)
—Tycho Brahe: Mapping the Heavens. (p. 1805)
Boeshaar, Andrea. Wisconsin: Second Time Around. Bk. 3 (p. 1939)
Boesing, Lothar, jt. auth. see Barth, Katrin.
Boettcher, Ashley L. Book of Dreams: The Life Story of a Teenage Girl. (p. 211)
Boeve, Eunice. Echoes of Kansas Past. Peterson-Shea, Julie, illus. (p. 502)
—Summer of the Crow. (p. 1674)
Boey, Stephanie, illus. see Briers, Erica.
Boey, Stephanie, illus. see Harris, Sue.
Boey, Stephanie, illus. see Martin, Ruth.
Boey, Stephanie, illus. see Troupe, Thomas Kingsley.
Bofill, Francesc. Rapunzel: A Bilingual Book. Joma, illus. (p. 1439)
—Rapunzel/Rapunzel. Joma, illus. (p. 1439)
Bofinger, Manfred, illus. see Fuchs, Gerd.
Bofinger, Manfred, tr. see Fuchs, Gerd.
Bogacki, Tomek. Champion of Children: The Story of Janusz Korczak. Bogacki, Tomek, illus. (p. 289)
—Mi Primer Jardin. (p. 1133)
Bogacki, Tomek, illus. see Banks, Kate.
Bogacki, Tomek, illus. see Bruss, Deborah.
Bogacki, Tomek, illus. see Jenkins, Emily.
Bogacki, Tomek, illus. see Tarlow, Ellen.
Bogade, Maria, illus. see Jenkins, Celeste.
Bogade, Maria, illus. see Maier, Inger M.
Bogade, Maria, illus. see Straus, Susan Farber.
Bogaert, Harmen Meyndertsz van den & O'Connor, George. Journey into Mohawk Country. Sycamore, Hilary & O'Connor, George, illus. (p. 928)
Bogaerts, Jorge. Dia Que Hizo Mucho Viento. (p. 433)
Bogan, Lyuba, illus. see Bradford, Amy L.
Bogan, Paulette. Lulu the Big Little Chick. (p. 1065)
—Virgil & Owen. (p. 1844)
Bogan, Paulette, illus. see Reynolds, Aaron.
Bogard, Jennifer M. Strategies to Integrate the Arts in Language Arts (p. 1666)
Bogard, Jerrod. Jack & the Soy Beanstalk. (p. 902)
Bogardus, Karin, jt. auth. see Bogardus, Ray.
Bogardus, Ray & Bogardus, Karin. Hannah the Magic Shelter Dog. Seltzer, Jerry, illus. (p. 742)
Bogarin, Abigail, tr. see Fisher, Tammy, ed.
Bogart, Jill, jt. auth. see Bogart, Jo Ellen.
Bogart, Jo Ellen. Big & Small, Room for All. Newland, Gillian, illus. (p. 177)
—Big Tree Gang Griffiths, Dean, illus. (p. 184)
—Capturing Joy: The Story of Maud Lewis. Lang, Mark, illus. (p. 265)
—Emily Carr: At the Edge of the World. Newhouse, Maxwell, illus. (p. 518)
Bogart, Jo Ellen & Bogart, Jill. Out & about with the Big Tree Gang Griffiths, Dean, illus. (p. 1310)
Bogart, Jo Ellen. Big Tree Gang. Griffiths, Dean, illus. (p. 184)
Bogart, Jon. Animals & Oil Spills. (p. 82)
Bogart, Mike. Henderson Twins in Muckleball! (p. 767)
—Ice Warriors (p. 851)
Bogdan, Diane. Twigs Is a Poet. (p. 1801)
Bogdan, Enache, illus. see Sommer, Carl & Aesop.
Bogdan, Enache, illus. see Sommer, Carl.
Bogdanovic, Toma, illus. see Andersen, Hans Christian.
Bogdanovic, Toma, illus. see Van Nutt, Robert.
Bogel, Rachel Anne. Ride on the Monster's Back. Greenfelder, Jill, illus. (p. 1471)
Boger, Ann. Online Romance. (p. 1298)
Boger-Bass, Vallerie. Mustard Seed: A Christian Promise. Boger-Bass, Vallerie, illus. (p. 1194)
Boggelen-Heutink, Ellen van, illus. see Simons, Alan L.
Boggess, Eileen. Mia the Magnificent: The Mia Fullerton Series. (p. 1133)
—MIA the Meek. (p. 1133)
—Mia the Meek. (p. 1133)
—Mia the Melodramatic. (p. 1133)
Boggs, Danielle. Snow Globe. (p. 1599)
Boggs, Garnett Reed. Totally Katy: Katy Is Always Planning, but Just How Well do Her Plans Work Out? (p. 1771)
Boggs, Patdee. Island of Angels. (p. 892)
Boggs-Johnson, Stefanie. I See You, Little Naomi. (p. 845)
Bogot, Abbey, ed. see Gatchell, Christine.
Bogot, Howard I., et al. Seven Animals Wag Their Tales. Marvin, Fred, illus. (p. 1554)
Bograd, Larry. Uniquely Colorado (p. 1818)
—Uniquely Georgia (p. 1818)
—Uniquely Kansas (p. 1818)
—Uniquely Wyoming (p. 1818)
Bogue, Gary. Raccoon Next Door: And Other Creatures of the Urban Wilderness. Todd, Chuck, illus. (p. 1430)
—There's a Hummingbird in My Backyard. Todd, Chuck, illus. (p. 1731)
—There's an Opossum in My Backyard. Todd, Chuck, illus. (p. 1731)
Bogumill, Mark P. KingMaker: The Swamp Crusade (p. 960)
Bogunya, Angels. Maiz Amargo. (p. 1078)
BOH Staff. Polish EEE-TM. (p. 1380)
Bohan, Thomas L. Crashes & Collapses. (p. 376)
Bohanan, Kacey. All about Me! A fun flip Book! (p. 42)
Bohannan, Pamela. Wades the Duck: The Pammie Sue Collection. (p. 1852)
Bohannon, C. S. Spatula Boy: And the Secret of the Mysterious Old House. (p. 1622)
Bohannon, Debbie. Fred the Furious Frog Forgives & Forgets. (p. 632)
Bohannon, Erin. Crabby & Shoofly. (p. 375)
Bohannon, Lisa Frederiksen. Freedom Cannot Rest: Ella Baker & the Civil Rights Movement. (p. 634)
—Woman's Work: The Story of Betty Friedan. (p. 1945)
—Women's Rights & Nothing Less: The Story of Elizabeth Cady Stanton. (p. 1946)
Bohannon, Lisa Frederkisen. Failure Is Impossible: The Story of Susan B. Anthony. (p. 562)
Bohart, Arthur. Master Student Guide to Academic Success. (p. 1103)
Bohart, Lisa, illus. see Bizzarro, Grace.
Bohart, Lisa, illus. see Chiarello, Robin Taylor.
Bohart, Lisa, illus. see Cooper, Margaret.
Bohart, Lisa, illus. see Cross, Jenny.
Bohart, Lisa, illus. see Desjardins, Margaret M.
Bohart, Lisa, illus. see Harris, Dee.
Bohart, Lisa, illus. see Krueger, T. W.
Bohart, Lisa, illus. see Miranda, Edward.
Bohart, Lisa, illus. see Nelson, Jan.
Bohart, Lisa, illus. see Taylor-Chiarello, Robin.
Bohensky, Anita. Anger Management Workbook for Kids & Teens. (p. 75)
—Self Esteem Workbook for Teens. (p. 1549)
Bohland, Mark. Mystery Disease. (p. 1224)
Bohler, Victoria & Gray, Kevan. Loyola College in Maryland College Prowler off the Record. (p. 1061)
Bohlin, Karen E., ed. see Clifford, Kathleen & Uy, Megan Black.
Bohlken, Robert L. Listening to the Mukies: And Their Character Building Adventures. Veasey, Michele, illus. (p. 1022)
—Listening to the Mukies & Their Character Building Adventures. Veasey, Michele, illus. (p. 1022)
Bohlmann, Katharine. Grandpa, Is There a Heaven? Erickson, David, illus. (p. 709)
Bohlmann, Siegfried, illus. see Hare, Eric B.
Böhm, Florian, et al. KGID - Konstantin Grcic Industrial Deisgn. (p. 951)
Bohm, Janet. What If My House Had Wheels? (p. 1887)

B

Bohman, Jennifer White, illus. see Ford, Ansley Watson & Holt, Denver W.
Bohman, Natasha, illus. see Loever, Charmaine.
Bohmer, Kara Dale. Walking Sarah: First Day Out. (p. 1854)
Bohn, Ken, illus. see Pearce, Claudia & Worley, Karen E.
Bohn, Ken, photos by see Pearce, Claudia & Worley, Karen E.
Bohn, Kendall. Abstract Adventure. (p. 7)
—Abstract Adventure V. (p. 7)
—Fantasy Adventure. (p. 572)
—Original Abstract Adventure. (p. 1304)
Bohn, Kendall, creator. Prehistoric Adventure: A Kaleidoscopia Coloring Book. (p. 1395)
Bohn, Klaus. Healthy Me: I Love Fruit, I Love Veggies. Bohn, Klaus, illus. (p. 758)
Bohnart, Edward R., jt. auth. see Sacks, Raymond J.
Bohner, Charles H. Bold Journey: West with Lewis & Clark. (p. 208)
Bohnet, Christopher, illus. see Fitzsimmons, Kakie.
Bohnet, Christopher, illus. see Pastel, JoAnne & Fitzsimmons, Kakie.
Bohnet, Eric. Christmas Promise. (p. 315)
—From Adam to Easter. Dorenkamp, Michelle, illus. (p. 641)
Bohnet, Eric C. Arch Books: The Centurion at the Cross. Murphy, Terri, illus. (p. 95)
Böhning, W. R., ed. Labour Rights in Crisis: Measuring the Achievement of Human Rights in the World of Work. (p. 970)
Bohorquez, Eduardo, tr. see Kotzwinkle, William & Murray, Glenn.
Bohrer, Erica. 20 Super Spelling Centers: Fun, Ready-to-Go Activities That Help Kids Master the Words on Their Spelling Lists. (p. 1995)
Bohrer, Joe, illus. see Stamp, Jeffrey.
Bohrer, Maddie. Penny's Penny Puzzle. (p. 1338)
Bohrer, Maria. Sofia's Stoop Story: 18th Street, Brooklyn: 18th Street, Brooklyn. Fancher, Lou & Johnson, Steve, illus. (p. 1605)
Bohrer, Melissa Lukeman. Glory, Passion, & Principle: The Story of Eight Remarkable Women at the Core of the American Revolution. (p. 685)
Boie, Kirsten. A los Duendes les Gustan los Pepinillos (Elves Like Pickles) (p. 1)
—King-Kong, el Conejillo de Indias Viajeros. (p. 958)
—King-Kong, Mi Mascota Secreta. (p. 958)
—Princess Plot. (p. 1405)
—Princess Plot. Wilson, David Henry, tr. from GER. (p. 1405)
—Princess Trap. (p. 1406)
—Todo Cambio con Jakob. Raúl, III, illus. (p. 1761)
Boie, Kristen. Little Bitty Story of Austin Q. Peapot Gentile, Christopher, illus. (p. 1024)
Boies, Jennifer. Bonnie Butterfly. (p. 209)
Boiger, Alexandra, illus. see George, Kallie.
Boiger, Alexandra, illus. see Grimm, Jacob & Grimm, Wilhelm K.
Boiger, Alexandra, illus. see Jenkins, Emily.
Boiger, Alexandra, illus. see Lloyd-Jones, Sally.
Boiger, Alexandra, illus. see MacDonald, Betty & Canham, Anne MacDonald.
Boiger, Alexandra, illus. see MacDonald, Betty Bard.
Boiger, Alexandra, illus. see MacDonald, Betty.
Boiger, Alexandra, illus. see MacHale, D. J.
Boiger, Alexandra, illus. see Naylor, Phyllis Reynolds.
Boiger, Alexandra, illus. see Quattlebaum, Mary.
Boiger, Alexandra, illus. see Reichert, Amy.
Boiger, Alexandra, illus. see Singer, Marilyn.
Boileau, Kim. My New Blue Shoes (p. 1216)
Bois, William Pene du. Twenty-One Balloons. (p. 1801)
Bois, William Pene du, see du Bois, William Pène.
Boisrobert, Anouck & Rigaud, Louis. Under the Ocean. (p. 1813)
Boisrond, H. Sean Alexander Series: Loughngoon. Boisrond, H., illus. (p. 1536)
Boissery, Beverley. Sophie's Exile. (p. 1613)
—Sophie's Rebellion. (p. 1613)
—Sophie's Treason. (p. 1613)
Boisteau, Manu, jt. auth. see Martin, Paul.
Boit, Bundy H. Christmas Island. (p. 314)
Bojang, Ali Brownlie. Aid & Development. (p. 30)
Bojesen, Niels Bo, illus. see Aakeson, Kim Fupz & Garde, Ruth.
Bojunga, Lygia. Amigos. (p. 65)
—Cama. (p. 255)
—Casa de la Madrina. (p. 273)
—Cuerda Floja. (p. 390)
—Sofa Estampado. (p. 1605)
Bokhari, Raana. Allah Gave Me Two Hands & Feet. Clarke, Asiya, illus. (p. 46)
Bokma, Cindy, jt. auth. see Brooks, Christalyn.
Bokor, Dina. Alphabet: In the World of Things. (p. 49)
Bokovoy, Melissa K., jt. auth. see Slaughter, Jane.
Bokram, Karen, ed. see Scholastic, Inc. Staff.
Bokram, Karen & Faithgirlz!. Big Book of Quizzes: Fun, Quirky Questions for You & Your Friends (p. 179)
Bokram, Karen & Faithgirlz! and Girls' Life Magazine Editors. Best Party Book Ever! From Invites to Overnights & Everything in Between (p. 171)
Bokram, Karen, ed. Girls' Life Ultimate Guide to Surviving Middle School. Thomas, Bill, illus. (p. 680)
—Head-to-Toe Guide to You. Thomas, Bill, illus. (p. 756)
Bolaffio, Raffaella, illus. see Piumini, Roberto & Aesop.
Bolam, Emily. Around Town. (p. 101)
—Bouncy Garden Bolam, Emily, illus. (p. 216)
—Building Site. (p. 239)
—Bunny. (p. 242)
—Colors. (p. 344)
—Counting. (p. 370)
—Dog. (p. 460)
—Farmyard Friends. Bolam, Emily, illus. (p. 575)
—Father's Day Is Coming! (p. 577)
—Guinea Pig. (p. 731)
—In the Jungle. (p. 866)
—Three Little Pigs. (p. 1742)
—Under the Sea. (p. 1814)
Bolam, Emily, illus. see Bedford, David.
Bolam, Emily, illus. see Coats, Lucy.
Bolam, Emily, illus. see Krensky, Stephen.
Bolam, Emily, illus. see Linn, Margot.
Bolam, Emily, illus. see Prasadam, Smriti.
Bolam, Emily, illus. see Rock, Lois.
Bolam, Emily, illus. see Simon, Francesca.
Bolam, Emily, illus. see St. Pierre, Stephanie.
Bolam, Emily, illus. see Ziefert, Harriet.
Bolam, Emily, tr. see Bedford, David.
Bolan, Michael, illus. see Stephens, Ann Marie.
Bolan, Michael P., illus. see Stephens, Ann Marie.
Bolan, Sandra. Labrador Retriever. (p. 970)
Boland, Gerry. Marco: Master of Disguise. McGuinness, Áine, illus. (p. 1092)
—Marco Moves In. McGuinness, Áine, illus. (p. 1092)
Boland, Hank, jt. auth. see Mueller, Todd.
Boland, Janice. Zippers. Pfeiffer, Judith, illus. (p. 1987)
Boland, John. Amber Road. (p. 57)
Boland, Shalini. Shirtful of Frogs. (p. 1567)
Bolander, Sharon Miller. At the Stroke of Midnight. (p. 111)
—Hiram's Song. (p. 781)
—I Wish That I Could Fly. (p. 849)
Bolchazy, Marie Carducci. Quis Me Amat?/Who Loves Me? (p. 1428)
—Quo Colore Est?/What Color Is It? (p. 1429)
Bold, Emily. Breath of Yesterday Bell, Katja, tr. from GER. (p. 225)
—Curse: Touch of Eternity Heron, Jeanette, tr. from GER. (p. 394)
Bolden, Tanisha N. This Is Why I Rock: A Self-Empowerment Journal for Youth. (p. 1737)
Bolden, Tonya. 12 Days of New York. Ford, Gilbert, illus. (p. 1994)
—Beautiful Moon: A Child's Prayer. Velasquez, Eric, illus. (p. 153)
—Capital Days: Michael Shiner's Journal & the Growth of Our Nation's Capital. (p. 262)
—Cause: Reconstruction America 1863-1877. (p. 282)
—Champ: The Story of Muhammad Ali. Christie, R. Gregory, illus. (p. 289)
—Champ. Christie, R. Gregory, illus. (p. 289)
—Emancipation Proclamation: Lincoln & the Dawn of Liberty. (p. 517)
—FDR's Alphabet Soup: New Deal America, 1932-1939. (p. 578)
—Finding Family. (p. 588)
—George Washington Carver. (p. 664)
—M. L. K. The Journey of a King. Adelman, Bob, ed. (p. 1067)
—Maritcha: A Nineteenth-Century American Girl. (p. 1094)
—Portraits of African-American Heroes. Pitcairn, Ansel, illus. (p. 1387)
—Searching for Sarah Rector: The Richest Black Girl in America. (p. 1537)
—W. E. B. du Bois: A Twentieth-Century Life. (p. 1851)
Bolden-Thompson, Angela. When Company Comes. (p. 1901)
Boldes, Gary. Thoughts of a Sailor. (p. 1740)
Boldi, Florina. Pug in Boots. (p. 1415)
Bolding, Clarissa. Life Is A Song Worth Singing. (p. 1011)
Boldman, Craig, illus. see Entin, Cindy.
Boldt. Politik und Gesellschaft. (p. 1381)
Boldt, Claudia. Melvin: The Luckiest Monkey in the World. (p. 1125)
—Odd Dog. (p. 1278)
—Star Gazers, Skyscrapers & Extraordinary Sausages. Boldt, Claudia, illus. (p. 1640)
—Uugghh! Boldt, Claudia, illus. (p. 1829)
—You're a Rude Pig, Bertie. (p. 1982)
Boldt, Fabienne, illus. see Linke, Uwe.
Boldt, Mike. 123 Versus ABC. Boldt, Mike, illus. (p. 2000)
—Colors Versus Shapes. Boldt, Mike, illus. (p. 345)
—Gophers in Farmer Burrows' Field. (p. 702)
Boldt, Mike, illus. see Petty, Dev.
Boldt, Mike, illus. see Sayres, Brianna Caplan.
Boldt, Peggy A. Misadventures of Choco: Lost. (p. 1150)
—Misadventures of Choco: Hic-Cup. (p. 1150)
—Misadventures of Choco: White Monster. (p. 1150)
—Misadventures of Choco: Four-Legged Friend. (p. 1150)
Boleman-Herring, Elizabeth. First of Everso. (p. 596)
Bolen, Cheryl L. Job E-Search: How to Ignite Your Thermonuclear WMD Without Blowing Yourself Away. (p. 919)
Bolen, Jim, et al. Great Decisions 2007. (p. 715)
Bolen, John. Aurelia's Magic. (p. 116)
Boles, Jim. Ivan the Invacar & the Cave. Cunningham, Bob, illus. (p. 900)
—Ivan the Invacar Helps Big Dog. Cunningham, Bob, illus. (p. 900)
Boles Levy, Anne. Temple of Doubt. (p. 1718)
Boles, Rhonda G. Why Does the Sun Set, Mommy? (p. 1924)
Boles, Terry, illus. see Johns, Linda & Jones, Melanie Davis.
Boles, Terry, illus. see Jones, Melanie Davis.
Boley, Farrell M. Jane & Big Ape/Rails West of Feisty. (p. 908)
Boleyn-Fitzgerald, Miriam, jt. auth. see Faguy, Peter.
Bolger, Janie, et al. Xeriscape for Central Texas, Revised Edition: A Water-Wise Approach to Home Landscaping. Bolger, Janie et al, eds. (p. 1967)
Bolger, Kevin. Gran on a Fan. Hodson, Ben, illus. (p. 707)
—Lazy Bear, Crazy Bear. Hodson, Ben, illus. (p. 981)
—Sir Fartsalot Hunts the Booger. Gilpin, Stephen, illus. (p. 1580)
—Zombiekins. (p. 1988)
—Zombiekins. Blecha, Aaron, illus. (p. 1988)
—Zombiekins 2. Blecha, Aaron, illus. (p. 1988)
Bolger, Z. C. Danny Calloway & the Puzzle House. Robinson, Garrett, ed. (p. 405)
Bolick, Brian, illus. see Saunders, Helen.
Bolin, Corrine, jt. auth. see Bolin, Ken.
Bolin, Frances Schoonmaker, ed. Carl Sandburg. Arcella, Steven, illus. (p. 269)
—Emily Dickinson. Chung, Chi, illus. (p. 518)
—Poetry for Young People: Emily Dickinson. Chung, Chi, illus. (p. 1376)
Bolin, Ken & Bolin, Corrine. Santa SP: Santa Clauses of the South Pole. (p. 1513)
Bolinaga Irasuegui, Iñigo, jt. auth. see Farshtey, Greg.
Bolinao, Mela, jt. auth. see Viau, Nancy.
Boling, Katharine. January 1905. (p. 908)
Boling, Ruth L. Come Worship with Me: A Journey Through the Church Year. Carrier, Tracey Dahle, illus. (p. 347)
Bolinger, Carolyn Lewis. One More. (p. 1296)
Bolitho, Mark. Fold Your Own Origami Air Force. (p. 611)
—Fold Your Own Origami Army. (p. 611)
—Fold Your Own Origami Weapons. (p. 611)
Bolivar, Simon. Champion of Freedom. (p. 289)
Boll, Katherine. Dante the Dancing Goose. (p. 406)
Boll, Rosemarie. Second Trial (p. 1539)
Bolland, Brian. Black & White. (p. 195)
Bolland, Brian, illus. see Morrison, Grant, et al.
Bolland, Brian, illus. see Wagner, John.
Bollard, John. Scholastic Pocket Thesaurus. (p. 1522)
—Scholastic Student Thesaurus. (p. 1522)
Bollard, John, jt. auth. see Bollard, John K.
Bollard, John K. & Bollard, John. Scholastic Children's Thesaurus. Reed, Mike, illus. (p. 1521)
Bollback, Anthony G. Capture of the Twin Dragon. (p. 265)
—Hijacked. (p. 779)
—Mystery of the Counterfeit Money. (p. 1225)
—Rescue at Cripple Creek. (p. 1462)
—Smugglers in Hong Kong. (p. 1595)
—Tiger Shark Strikes Again. (p. 1748)
Bolle, Frank, illus. see Joy, Angelica.
Bollen, Christina. Angel in My Garden Matyuschenko, Tanya, illus. (p. 73)
Bollen, Christine. Flying with the Geese Matyuschenko, Tanya, illus. (p. 610)
—Frogs by the Dozen. Matyschenko, Tanya, illus. (p. 641)
—Three Munch-y Cherries. (p. 1743)
Bollen, Dan. Mother! Secrets of the House. (p. 1178)
Bollen, Roger, illus. see Sadler, Marilyn.
Bollen, Roger, jt. auth. see Sadler, Marilyn.
Bollendorf, Robert F. & Makely, William. Flight of the Loon: One Family's Battle with Recovery. Donlon, Eleanor, ed. (p. 604)
Boller, David, illus. see Wallace, Patrick.
Boller, Gary, illus. see Fecher, Sarah & Oliver, Clare.
Bolles, Joshua. Little Kitty in the City. (p. 1030)
Bollhagen, Nora. Rebecca's Wonderful Day. (p. 1450)
Bolliger, Jeri. Secret of Casa Madera. (p. 1542)
Bolling, Bob. Adventures of Little Archie (p. 19)
Bolling, Vickey, illus. see Balika, Susan S.
Bolling, Vickey, illus. see Balika, Susan.
Bollinger, Carol, illus. see Owens, Robert & Owens, Donna.
Bollinger, Georgia G. Penguins' Perilous Picnic. (p. 1337)
Bollinger, Michele & Tran, Dao X., eds. 101 Changemakers: Rebels & Radicals Who Changed U. S. History. (p. 1999)
Bollinger, Peter. Algernon Graeves Is Scary Enough. Bollinger, Peter, illus. (p. 38)
Bollinger, Peter, illus. see Hirschmann, Kris.
Bollinger, Peter, illus. see Zabludoff, Marc.
Bollinger/Papp. King Kong: Meet Kong & Ann. (p. 958)
Bollow, Ludmilla. Lulu's Christmas Story: A True Story of Faith & Hope During the Great Depression. (p. 1065)
Bolme, Edward Sarah. Baby Bible Board Books Collection: Stories of Jesus No. 1 Gillette, Tim, illus. (p. 125)
—Jesus Feeds the People. Gillette, Tim, illus. (p. 915)
—Jesus Heals a Little Girl. Gillette, Tim, illus. (p. 915)
—Jesus Helps a Blind Man. Gillette, Tim, illus. (p. 915)
—Jesus Stops a Storm. Gillette, Tim, illus. (p. 916)
Bolo the Balloon. Bolo the Balloon. (p. 208)
Bolocan, D. Stephie Learns about Animals: Funny Rhymes for Children about Toys & Animals. (p. 1648)
—Stephie learns about Animals. (p. 1648)
Bologna, Barbara. Bullied over Sandman's Falls. (p. 240)
Bolognese, Don. Warhorse. Bolognese, Don, illus. (p. 1858)
Bolognese, Don, illus. see Alphin, Elaine Marie.
Bolognese, Don, illus. see Brooks, Walter R.
Bolognese, Don, illus. see Shea, George.
Boloz, Sigmund A., jt. auth. see Boloz, Sigmund Adam.
Boloz, Sigmund Adam & Boloz, Sigmund A. Who Speaks for the Children? A Collection of Poems for Children. (p. 1917)
Bolster. Achieving English Proficiency. (p. 9)
—Daily Review Book. (p. 400)
—Exploring Mathematics. (p. 552)
—Math 91 Daily Review. (p. 1105)
—Math 91 Enrichment. (p. 1105)
—Math Ninety-One. (p. 1106)
—Mathematics Grade 3. (p. 1108)
Bolster, Rob, illus. see Garnett, Sammie & Pallotta, Jerry.
Bolster, Rob, illus. see Pallotta, Jerry.
Bolt, Ranjit. Hare & the Tortoise. Potter, Giselle, illus. (p. 748)
Bolt, Sara E., et al. Inclusive Assessment & Accountability: A Guide to Accommodations for Students with Diverse Needs. (p. 869)
Bolt, Susan Collier, illus. see Gopigian, Susan Kadian.
Bolte, Mari. Acrylics Ice, D. C., illus. (p. 9)
—All-American Girl Style: Fun Fashions You Can Sketch Otero, Sole, illus. (p. 43)
—Amazing Outdoor Art You Can Make & Share. (p. 55)
—Amazing Outdoor Art You Can Make & Share. (p. 55)
—Amazing Story of the Combustion Engine. Pop Art Properties Staff, illus. (p. 56)
—Awesome Recipes You Can Make & Share Franco, Paula, illus. (p. 121)
—Colorful Creations You Can Make & Share Franco, Paula, illus. (p. 344)
—Drawing Faces: A Step-By-Step Sketchpad Makuc, Lucy & Dynamo Limited Staff, illus. (p. 481)
—Drawing Faces: A Step-By-Step Sketchbook Makuc, Lucy & Dynamo Limited Staff, illus. (p. 481)
—Drawing Fun Fashions. Rzasa, Jennifer et al, illus. (p. 481)
—Drawing Monsters: A Step-By-Step Sketchpad Makuc, Lucy & Dynamo Limited Staff, illus. (p. 482)
—Drawing Monsters: A Step-By-Step Sketchbook Makuc, Lucy & Dynamo Limited Staff, illus. (p. 482)
—Drawing Pets: A Step-By-Step Sketchpad Makuc, Lucy & Dynamo Limited Staff, illus. (p. 482)
—Drawing Pets: A Step-By-Step Sketchbook Makuc, Lucy & Dynamo Limited Staff, illus. (p. 482)
—Drawing Vehicles: A Step-By-Step Sketchpad Makuc, Lucy & Dynamo Limited Staff, illus. (p. 482)
—Drawing Vehicles: A Step-By-Step Sketchbook Makuc, Lucy & Dynamo Limited Staff, illus. (p. 482)
—Eco Gifts: Upcycled Gifts You Can Make. (p. 502)
—Encountering Ghosts: Eyewitness Accounts Kako, Franco, illus. (p. 524)
—Fab Fashions You Can Make & Share Franco, Paula, illus. (p. 559)
—Flight to Freedom! Nickolas Flux & the Underground Railroad Foster, Brad W. & Simmons, Mark, illus. (p. 604)
—From Me to You: Handmade Gifts for Your VIPs. (p. 643)
—Girly Girl Style: Fun Fashions You Can Sketch Hagel, Brooke, illus. (p. 681)
—Harajuku Style: Fun Fashions You Can Sketch Hagel, Brooke, illus. (p. 747)
—Hollywood Style: Fun Fashions You Can Sketch Dahl, Sarah, illus. (p. 789)
—Homemade Holiday: Gifts for Every Occasion. (p. 793)
—In Good Taste: Great Gifts to Make, Eat, & Share. (p. 863)
—Justin Bieber. (p. 940)
—Make It, Gift It: Handmade Gifts for Every Occasion. (p. 1079)
—Make It, Gift It. (p. 1079)
—My First Sketchbook Makuc, Lucy & Dynamo Limited Staff, illus. (p. 1208)
—Oil Paints Becker, Pamela, illus. (p. 1282)
—Paint It: The Art of Acrylics, Oils, Pastels, & Watercolors Ice, D. C., illus. (p. 1318)
—Paint It. (p. 1318)
—Paper Presents You Can Make & Share. (p. 1323)
—Pastels Becker, Pamela, illus. (p. 1327)
—Rock Star Style: Fun Fashions You Can Sketch Dahl, Sarah, illus. (p. 1482)
—Skater Chic Style: Fun Fashions You Can Sketch Rzasa, Jennifer, illus. (p. 1584)
—Sleepover Girls. Franco, Paula, illus. (p. 1589)
—Sleepover Girls Crafts (p. 1589)
—Sleepover Girls Crafts Franco, Paula, illus. (p. 1589)
—Sleepover Girls Crafts: Amazing Recipes You Can Make & Share Franco, Paula, illus. (p. 1589)
—Sleepover Girls Crafts: Colorful Creations You Can Make & Share Franco, Paula, illus. (p. 1589)
—Sleepover Girls Crafts: Fab Fashions You Can Make & Share Franco, Paula, illus. (p. 1589)
—Spa Projects You Can Make & Share Franco, Paula, illus. (p. 1618)
—Super Science Projects: You Can Make & Share. (p. 1680)
—Super Science Projects You Can Make & Share. (p. 1681)
—Triceratops: Three-Horned Giant Dove, Jason, illus. (p. 1785)
—Unique Accessories: You Can Make & Share. (p. 1818)
—Unique Accessories You Can Make & Share. (p. 1818)
—Watercolors Ice, D. C., illus. (p. 1863)
Bolte, Marissa. Arrested for Witchcraft! Nickolas Flux & the Salem Witch Trials Ginevra, Dante, illus. (p. 101)
—Fashion Drawing Studio: A Guide to Sketching Stylish Fashions Hagel, Brooke et al, illus. (p. 575)
Bolton, Adam, illus. see Thomas, Ian.
Bolton, Anne. Pyramids & Mummies. (p. 1421)
—Rusty Brown's Colorful Day. (p. 1498)
Bolton, Bill. My Magnetic Counting Book: Ten Dancing Dinosaurs. (p. 1213)
Bolton, Bill, illus. see Gunderson, Jessica & Weakland, Mark.
Bolton, Bill, illus. see Lansky, Bruce.
Bolton, Bill, illus. see Miller, Liza.
Bolton, Bill, illus. see Weakland, Mark.
Bolton, Bill, illus. see Williamson, Karen & David, Juliet.
Bolton, Chris A. Smash: Trial by Fire. Bolton, Kyle, illus. (p. 1593)
Bolton, Georgia Helen, illus. see Ballard, George Anne.
Bolton, Georgia Helen, jt. auth. see Ballard, George Anne.
Bolton, John, illus. see Perez, George.
Bolton, John, illus. see Willingham, Bill.
Bolton, Kyle, illus. see Bolton, Chris A.
Bolton, Marth. Who Put Lemons in My Fruit of the Spirit? (p. 1917)
Bolton, Martha. Humorous Monologues. Behr, Joyce, illus. (p. 827)
Bolton, Martha, jt. auth. see Lowry, Mark.
Bolton, Michael. Secret of the Lost Kingdom. Jermann, David, illus. (p. 1542)
—Secreto del Reino Perdido. Jermann, David, illus. (p. 1544)
Bolton, Nicola Joanne. Jasper. (p. 910)
—WeatherGens. (p. 1870)
Bolton, Robin. Roo-Star, the Smartest Chicken in the Coop. (p. 1487)
—Sunny Goes Out to Play. (p. 1677)
Bolton, Violet. Heidi & Huber the Adventures Begin. (p. 762)
Bolton-Eells, Sharon, illus. see Hicks, Rob & Hicks, Kim.
Boltonwood-Castle, Tony. Ben,Jay & Ricardo Karate Adventure: The Night the Thieves Came Calling. (p. 165)
Boltwood, Andrea. Clown Who Came down with a Frown. (p. 335)
Boltwood, Emily. 10 Simple Rules of the House of Gloria. (p. 1993)
Bolund, Inna, illus. see Bulakh, Nadia.
Bolund, Inna, illus. see Finch, Donna.
Bolyard, Dianne. Happily Ever After: The Ultimate True Fairytale. (p. 744)
Boman, Erik, photos by see Blahnik, Manolo.
Bombaci, James J. Million Dollar Dog. (p. 1144)
Bomback, Mark & Craze, Galaxy. Mapmaker. (p. 1090)
Bombay, Cal & Sharpe, Margaret. Slave, Brave & Free (p. 1588)
Bomgaars, Sharon. Best Clubhouse Ever. (p. 168)
Bompart, Juanita A. Anna Pinnelope Poolah. (p. 85)
Bon, Kimberly. Mitchie's Amazing Adventures: Good Bye to Pluto. (p. 1155)
Bonacci, Ross. Rossi & Lucy Go to the Beach. Karla, Nicolee, illus. (p. 1490)

—Show & Tell with Rossi & Lucy: A Daytime Story. (p. 1570)
Bonaddio, T. L. & Tomlinson, Andrew. Stick It! 99 DIY Duct Tape Projects. (p. 1649)
Bonadonna, Davide, illus. see Gordon, David George.
Bonadonna, Davide, jt. auth. see Schatz, Dennis.
Bonami, Francesco. Gabriele Basilico. Basilico, Gabriele, photos by. (p. 652)
Bonanni, Constance, jt. auth. see Hazelton, Tanya.
Bonanno, Joseph T. Monutza the Firefighting Elephant. (p. 1171)
Bonar, Troy A. Safety = Caring. (p. 1502)
Bonasia, Steve. Dominic & the Secret Ingredient. Van Norstrand, Kain, illus. (p. 465)
Bonaste, Sophie. Sacrifices We Make [Library Edition]. (p. 1501)
Bonatakis, Shannon, illus. see Zappa, Ahmet & Muldoon Zappa, Shana.
Bonatakis, Shannon, illus. see Zappa, Ahmet & Zappa, Shane Muldoon.
Bonavita, Madison M., illus. see Martin, Candice J.
Bonawandt, Christian. Dreamers. (p. 484)
Bonazzo, Jennifer. Wings of Peace. (p. 1936)
Bond, A. Russel. Scientific American Boy. (p. 1528)
Bond, A. Russell. Scientific American Boy: Or the Camp at Willow Clump Island. (p. 1528)
Bond, Alan. Tedoul. Swanson, Peter Joseph, illus. (p. 1713)
Bond, Amy, ed. see Goliger, Janet.
Bond, Barbara Higgins, jt. auth. see Masurel, Claire.
Bond, Bob. Illustrated Christmas Story: With 21 Carols, Arranged for Piano & Voice. (p. 857)
Bond, Bob, illus. see Moody, D. L.
Bond, Clint, illus. see Ostrow, Kim.
Bond, Clint & Clark, Andy. Great Snail Race. (p. 718)
Bond, Denis, jt. auth. see Finnis, Anne.
Bond, Denny, illus. see Lowry, Mark & Greene, Buddy.
Bond, Doug. Crown & Covenant Bird, Matthew, illus. (p. 386)
Bond, Douglas. Accidental Voyage: Discovering Hymns of the Early Centuries. (p. 8)
—Guns of Providence. (p. 732)
—Guns of Thunder. (p. 732)
—Hammer of the Huguenots. (p. 739)
—Hand of Vengeance. (p. 740)
—Hostage Lands. (p. 801)
—King's Arrow. Bird, Matthew, illus. (p. 960)
—Mr. Pipes & the British Hymn Makers. (p. 1186)
—Mr. Pipes Comes to America McHugh, Michael J., ed. (p. 1186)
—Rebel's Keep. Bird, Matthew, illus. (p. 1451)
Bond, Felicia. Big Hugs Little Hugs. Bond, Felicia, illus. (p. 181)
—Day It Rained Hearts. Bond, Felicia, illus. (p. 413)
—Halloween Play. Bond, Felicia, illus. (p. 738)
—Poinsettia & the Firefighters. Bond, Felicia, illus. (p. 1377)
—Tumble Bumble. (p. 1796)
Bond, Felicia, illus. see Brown, Margaret Wise.
Bond, Felicia, illus. see Edwards, Pamela Duncan.
Bond, Felicia, illus. see Numeroff, Laura Joffe.
Bond, Felicia, illus. see Numeroff, Laura.
Bond, G. T. 60 Words Toddlers Can Read in Black & White. (p. 1997)
—GT Bond's 24 Words Toddlers Can Read in Color. (p. 728)
—GT Bond's Absolutely Stupendous Book of Colors. (p. 728)
Bond, Gwenda. Fallout. (p. 567)
—Woken Gods. (p. 1943)
Bond, Higgins, illus. see Batten, Mary & Sill, Cathryn.
Bond, Higgins, illus. see Batten, Mary.
Bond, Higgins, illus. see Fraggalosch, Audrey.
Bond, Higgins, illus. see Galvin, Laura Gates.
Bond, Higgins, illus. see Korman, Susan.
Bond, Higgins, illus. see Schneider, Richard H.
Bond, Higgins, illus. see Stewart, Melissa.
Bond, Higgins, illus. see Tan, Sheri.
Bond, Higgins, illus. see Vieira, Linda.
Bond, Jameselle. Poka Dot File. (p. 1377)
Bond, Janice & Fiebelkorn, Claire. Water on Earth. (p. 1863)
Bond, Juliana. Pixie Tales the Wobbly Tooth. (p. 1365)
—Salad Cream. (p. 1504)
Bond, Juliet C. Sam's Sister. Majewski, Dawn, illus. (p. 1509)
Bond, Katherine Grace. Summer of No Regrets. (p. 1674)
Bond, Linda. Retishella & the Dolphins. (p. 1464)
Bond, Michael. Love from Paddington. Fortnum, Peggy & Alley, R. W., illus. (p. 1059)
—More about Paddington. Fortnum, Peggy, illus. (p. 1173)
—Paddington. Alley, R. W., illus. (p. 1317)
—Paddington & the Christmas Surprise. Alley, R. W., illus. (p. 1317)
—Paddington at the Beach. Alley, R. W., illus. (p. 1317)
—Paddington Bear All Day. (p. 1317)
—Paddington Bear All Day. Alley, R. W., illus. (p. 1317)
—Paddington Bear All Day Board Book. Alley, R. W., illus. (p. 1317)
—Paddington Bear Goes to Market. Alley, R. W., illus. (p. 1317)
—Paddington Bear Goes to Market Board Book. Alley, R. W., illus. (p. 1317)
—Paddington Helps Out. Fortnum, Peggy, illus. (p. 1317)
—Paddington Here & Now. Alley, R. W., illus. (p. 1317)
—Paddington in the Garden. Alley, R. W., illus. (p. 1317)
—Paddington Treasury. Alley, R. W., illus. (p. 1317)
Bond, Nancy. String in the Harp. (p. 1667)
Bond, Nancy, illus. see Reeves, Diane Lindsey & Clasen, Lindsey.
Bond, Nancy, illus. see Reeves, Diane Lindsey, et al.
Bond, Nancy, illus. see Reeves, Diane Lindsey.
Bond, Primula. Club Crème. (p. 335)
Bond, Primula, jt. auth. see Hood, Alaine.
Bond, Rebecca. Escape from Baxters' Barn. (p. 534)
—Out of the Woods. (p. 1311)
Bond, Rebecca, illus. see Slade, Suzanne.
Bond, Robert. Iain Sinclair. (p. 849)
Bond, Roland. Harvey Plumstead & the Dinnertime Dog. (p. 752)
Bond, Royce. Princess & the Pirate. (p. 1403)
Bond, Susan. Ride with Me Through ABC. Lemke, Horst, illus. (p. 1471)
Bond, Tammy. I Wish of Things That I Could Be. (p. 849)
Bond, Thomas A. Mill Creek Kids. (p. 1143)
Bond, Victoria & Simon, T. R. Zora & Me. (p. 1990)
Bondanella Filutze, Ann M. On Gramma's Rocker: Animal Tales & Other Short Stories. (p. 1288)
Bonder, Dianna. A, B, Sea: A Deep Sea Symphony (p. 1)
—Accidental Alphabet Bonder, Dianna, illus. (p. 8)
—Accidental Alphabet. (p. 8)
—Dogabet Bonder, Dianna, illus. (p. 462)
Bonder, Dianna, illus. see Grambo, Rebecca L.
Bonder, Dianna, illus. see Harvey, Sarah N. & Buffam, Leslie.
Bonder, Dianna, illus. see Hoppey, Tim.
Bonder, Dianna, illus. see McLellan, Stephanie Simpson.
Bonder, Dianna, illus. see Ruurs, Margriet.
Bonder, Dianna, illus. see Simpson McLellan, Stephanie.
Bonder, Dianna, illus. see StJohn, Amanda.
Bonder, Dianna, illus. see Toews, Marj.
Bondor-Stone, Annabeth & White, Connor. Shivering. Holden, Anthony, illus. (p. 1567)
—Shivers! - The Pirate Who's Afraid of Everything. Holden, Anthony, illus. (p. 1567)
Bondoux, Anne-Laure. Princetta. Bell, Anthea, tr. (p. 1406)
—Time of Miracles. Maudet, Y., tr. from FRE. (p. 1752)
Bondy, Halley. 77 Things You Absolutely Have to Do Before You Finish College. Lloyd, James, illus. (p. 1998)
—Don't Sit on the Baby! The Ultimate Guide to Sane, Skilled, & Safe Babysitting. (p. 468)
Bondy, Natasha, et al. Love Notes: A Random Reference for the Modern Romantic. (p. 1060)
Bone, Emily. 1920's Fashion IR. (p. 2002)
—50 Brain Games. (p. 1997)
—50 Secret Codes. (p. 1997)
—Art Deco Patterns to Color. (p. 101)
—Big Book of Big Bugs. (p. 179)
—Cowboy Things to Make & Do. Harrison, Erica, illus. (p. 374)
—Earthquakes & Tsunamis. (p. 497)
—Helicopters. (p. 763)
—Look Inside Food IR. (p. 1049)
—My Very First Space Book IR (was Book of Space) (p. 1221)
—Owls. Cooper, Jenny & Watson, Richard, illus. (p. 1315)
—See Inside Exploration & Discovery IR. (p. 1546)
—Ships. King, Colin, illus. (p. 1567)
—Solar System (Al Majmoo'a Al Shamsiya) Ibrahim, Nouran, tr. (p. 1607)
—Solar System Internet Referenced. Pastor, Terry & Haggerty, Tim, illus. (p. 1607)
—Sticker Dolly Dressing Around the World. (p. 1650)
—Sticker Dolly Dressing Dream Jobs. (p. 1650)
—Storms & Hurricanes. Weston, Paul, illus. (p. 1656)
—Trains. (p. 1777)
Bone, Emily & King, Colin. See Inside Trains. (p. 1546)
Bone, Emily & Maskell, Hazel. Astronomy & Space Sticker Book IR. (p. 109)
Bone, Emily & Pratt, Leonie. Recycling Things to Make & Do. (p. 1453)
Bone, Emily & Watt, Fiona. Penguins. (p. 1337)
Bone, Ian. Fat Boy Saves World. (p. 577)
Bone, J., illus. see Fisch, Sholly & Age, Heroic.
Bone, J., illus. see Torres, J.
Bone, Jody. Little House That Grew. (p. 1029)
Boné, Thomas H. Teacher Who Would Not Retire Becomes a Movie Star. (p. 1709)
—Teacher Who Would Not Retire Discovers a New Planet. (p. 1709)
—Teacher Who Would Not Retire Goes to Camp. (p. 1709)
Bone, Thomas H. & LeTourneau, Anthony Alex. Mama, Can Armadillos Swim? (p. 1084)
Bonehill, Ralph. Four Boy Hunters. (p. 624)
—Guns & Snowshoes: Or, the Winter Outing of the Young Hunters. (p. 732)
—Guns & Snowshoes. (p. 732)
—Guns & Snowshoes or the Winter Outing of the Young Hunters. (p. 732)
—Out with Gun & Camera. (p. 1312)
—Young Hunters of the Lake. (p. 1978)
Bones. Wolf's Rain. Lida, Toshitsugu, illus. (p. 1944)
Bones & Nobumoto, Keiko. Wolf's Rain Lida, Toshitsugu, illus. (p. 1944)
Bones Brigade Staff & Okamura, Tensai. Darker Than Black (p. 408)
Bonet, Marisabel. Captain. (p. 263)
Bonet, Xavier, illus. see Dahl, Michael.
Bonet, Xavier, illus. see Peterson, Tina L.
Bonetti, Joseph. Magical Castle. (p. 1074)
Bonewitz, Ronald. Rock & Gem. (p. 1481)
Bonforte, Lisa. Farm Animals Coloring Book. (p. 573)
Bonforte, Lisa, illus. see Pollack, Pam & Belviso, Meg.
Bonforte, Lisa, illus. see Smith, Kathie Billingslea.
Bonforte, Lisa, illus. see Zoehfeld, Kathleen Weidner.
Bongaman, jt. auth. see Fredericks, Anthony D.
Bongers, Christine. Dust. (p. 490)
—Henry Hoey Hobson. (p. 768)
Bongiorno, Patti Lynn, text. Tangled Hearts. (p. 1705)
Bongiovanni, Debbie. It's All about Magic or Is It? (p. 896)
—Kindness Pays Off (p. 957)
Bongiovanni-Sharp, Debbie. Mom, but I Don't Want To. (p. 1161)
Bonham, Bob, illus. see Daybell, Chad.
Bonham, Bob, illus. see Setzer, Lee Ann.
Bonham, Frank. Durango Street. (p. 490)
Bonham, T. J. Spi: The Case of the Dark Shadow. (p. 1626)
Bonholtzer, Eric. Remnants & Shadows. (p. 1460)
Bonhomme, Matthieu, illus. see Bonneval, Gwen de & Smith, Owen.
Bonhomme, Matthieu, illus. see De Bonneval, Gwen.
Boni, Simone, illus. see Dixon, Andy.
Bonieskie, Jana. Written in Stone. (p. 1965)
Boniface, William. Adventures of Max the Minnow. Sullivan, Don, illus. (p. 20)
—Extraordinary Adventures of Ordinary Boy: The Great Powers Outage. Bk. 3 Gilpin, Stephen, illus. (p. 555)
—Extraordinary Adventures of Ordinary Boy. Gilpin, Stephen, illus. (p. 555)
—Great Powers Outage. Gilpin, Stephen, illus. (p. 718)
—Hero Revealed. Gilpin, Stephen, illus. (p. 772)
—Lights Out, Night's Out. Kirkova, Milena, illus. (p. 1016)
—There's a Dinosaur in My Soup! Poling, Kyle, illus. (p. 1730)
—Yummy Bunny Easter Treats! Poling, Kyle, illus. (p. 1983)
Bonilla, Barbara Ann. Wacky World of Wendy White! A Whopper of a Tale. (p. 1852)
Bonilla, Daniel. My Magnificent Horse: An Inspirational. (p. 1214)
Bonin, Liane. Idol Talk: Fame Unlimited. (p. 852)
—Pretty on the Outside: Fame Unlimited. (p. 1398)
Bonita, Todd, illus. see Pierce, Terry.
Bonk, John J. Madhattan Mystery. (p. 1070)
—Subway Crush. Trissler, Rebecca Johns, ed. (p. 1671)
Bonk, Michele. Clayton & Evan's Adventures in Farming. (p. 330)
Bonnell, B. T., illus. see Jack, Lizzie.
Bonnell, Kris. Big Hungry Cat. (p. 181)
—Can We Be Friends? (p. 258)
—Clouds Tell the Weather. (p. 335)
—Down in the Sea. (p. 474)
—Flower for a Bee. (p. 607)
—Friend for Jellyfish. (p. 637)
—Frog Fun. (p. 640)
—Garden Is Fun. (p. 656)
—Happy Moon. (p. 746)
—House for Squirrel. (p. 803)
—Lemonade. (p. 991)
—Little Boat. (p. 1025)
—Little Sprout. (p. 1036)
—Look Up! (p. 1050)
—Mmm, Apples. (p. 1157)
—Mother Animals. (p. 1177)
—Mudskipper & the Water. (p. 1189)
—Pets for Us. (p. 1348)
—Picking a Pumpkin. (p. 1354)
—Pizza for Carl. (p. 1365)
—Presents for Mom. (p. 1396)
—Red Apples for Me. (p. 1453)
—Robins in the Spring. (p. 1480)
—Spiders. (p. 1626)
—Spring Is Coming! (p. 1635)
—Too Big to Play. (p. 1766)
—Walk with Dad. (p. 1854)
—We Like the Beach. (p. 1867)
—We Love Pets. (p. 1867)
—What Tigers Do. (p. 1894)
—Where Can Louis Sleep? (p. 1906)
—Where Is a Bear? (p. 1908)
—Where Is the Big Cat? (p. 1909)
—White, White Snow. (p. 1913)
—Who Can Wiggle? (p. 1914)
—Who Has a Hump? (p. 1915)
—Yellow Flowers. (p. 1970)
Bonner, Anne. Intrigue at Pine Haven: Civil War in Florida. Akridge, Bill, illus. (p. 882)
Bonner, Gayle. Life on Peavine Creek: Sam's Story. Johnson, Brandon, illus. (p. 1012)
Bonner, Hannah. When Bugs Were Big, Plants Were Strange, & Tetrapods Stalked the Earth: A Cartoon Prehistory of Life Before Dinosaurs. (p. 1901)
—When Dinos Dawned, Mammals Got Munched, & Pterosaurs Took Flight: A Cartoon PreHistory of Life in the Triassic. (p. 1902)
—When Dinos Dawned, Mammals Got Munched, & Pterosaurs Took Flight: A Cartoon Prehistory of Life in the Triassic. (p. 1902)
—When Fish Got Feet, Sharks Got Teeth, & Bugs Began to Swarm: A Cartoon Prehistory of Life Long Before Dinosaurs. (p. 1902)
—When Fish Got Feet, Sharks Got Teeth, & Bugs Began to Swarm: A Cartoon Prehistory of Life Long Before Dinosaurs. Bonner, Hannah, illus. (p. 1902)
—When Fish Got Feet, When Bugs Were Big, & When Dinos Dawned: A Cartoon Prehistory of Life on Earth. (p. 1902)
Bonner, Janet L. Balloon Wishes. (p. 135)
Bonner, John. Child's History of the United States (p. 305)
Bonner, P. A. I Can Make a Difference: All Around My House. (p. 836)
Bonner, Richard. Boy Inventors Radio Telephone. (p. 218)
Bonner, Sally. Millie's Daydream. (p. 1144)
Bonner, Susan Case. My Whole Self Before You: A Picture Prayer Book Modeled after the Lord's Prayer. (p. 1221)
—My Whole Self Before You: A Child's Prayer & Learning Guide Modeled after the Lord's Prayer. (p. 1221)
Bonner, Valorie J. Gangster Kitty. (p. 655)
Bonnet, Robert L. & Keen, Dan. Home Run! Science Projects with Baseball & Softball. (p. 792)
Bonnet, Rosalind. Animals. (p. 81)
Bonnet, Rosalinde. Alphabet Picture Book. (p. 50)
—Very First Christmas Carols. (p. 1838)
—Very First Words Bedtime. (p. 1838)
—Very First Words Christmas. (p. 1838)
Bonnet, Rosalinde, illus. see Biedrzycki, David.
Bonnet, Rosalinde, illus. see Brooks, Felicity.
Bonnet, Rosalinde, illus. see Eaddy, Susan.
Bonnet, Rosalinde, illus. see Maynor, Megan.
Bonnet, Rosalinde, illus. see McGrath, Barbara Barbieri.
Bonnet, Rosalinde, illus. see Wahl, Jan.
Bonnet, Rosalinde, illus. see Watt, Fiona.
Bonnet, Rosalinde. Very First Nursery Rhymes. Bonnet, Rosaline, illus. (p. 1838)
Bonnett, Rosalind. Santa Flap Book. (p. 1511)
Bonnett, Rosaline. Very First Words on the Farm. (p. 1838)
Bonnett-Rampersaud, Louise. Bubble & Squeak Banta, Susan, illus. (p. 233)
—Dyno-Mite Dog Show McHeffey, Adam, illus. (p. 491)
—How Do You Sleep? Kest, Kristin, illus. (p. 808)
—Never Ask a Bear. Barrette, Doris, illus. (p. 1242)
—Spring Un-Fair (p. 1635)
Bonneval, Gwen de & Smith, Owen. William & the Lost Spirit. Smith, Anne Collins, tr. from FRE. (p. 1933)
Bonnevie, Bonnie, jt. auth. see Belovitch, Jeanne.
Bonney, Joan, illus. see Gauthier, Elizabeth.
Bonnice, Sherry. Adjustment Disorders. McDonnell, Mary Ann & Esherick, Donald, eds. (p. 13)
—Autism. Albers, Lisa et al, eds. (p. 117)
—Children's Folklore. (p. 303)
—Christmas & Santa Claus Folklore. (p. 312)
—Computer Programmer. Riggs, Ernestine G. & Gholar, Cheryl, eds. (p. 355)
—Drug Therapy & Adjustment Disorders. (p. 487)
—Drug Therapy & Premenstrual Disorders. (p. 487)
—Drug Therapy for Adjustment Disorders. (p. 487)
—Financial Advisor. Riggs, Ernestine G. & Gholar, Cheryl, eds. (p. 587)
—Folk Arts & Crafts. (p. 611)
—Folk Dance. (p. 611)
—Folk Fashion. (p. 611)
—Hidden Child: Youth with Autism. (p. 775)
—Hidden Child: Youth with Autism. (p. 775)
—Journalist. Riggs, Ernestine G. & Gholar, Cheryl, eds. (p. 927)
—Premenstrual Disorders. McDonnell, Mary Ann & Esherick, Donald, eds. (p. 1395)
Bonnice, Sherry & Hoard, Carolyn. Cognitive Disorders. McDonnell, Mary Ann & Esherick, Donald, eds. (p. 338)
—Drug Therapy & Cognitive Disorders. (p. 487)
Bonnie, Compton-Hanson. Holly Jean & the Secret of Razorback Ridge (p. 789)
Bonnie, Spino, illus. see Lorraine, Loria.
Bonnin, Jenny, jt. auth. see Mckay, Kim.
Bonnington, P. D. Alexander Smidget & the Green Growth Elixir. (p. 36)
Bonniol, Magali. Ogro De Mariuchi. (p. 1280)
Bono, E., jt. auth. see Bono, Elena.
Bono, Elena & Bono, E. Sombrero de Ramito. Brignole, Giancarla, tr. (p. 1608)
Bono, Ignacio, tr. see Coming, Soon.
Bononno, Robert, tr. see Tajadod, Nahal.
Bonotaux, Gilles. Dirty Rotten Bugs? Arthropods Unite to Tell Their Side of the Story. Bonotaux, Gilles, illus. (p. 446)
Bonsangue, Billy. Nightmare Navigator: When Shadows Lurk. (p. 1255)
Bonstingl, John Jay. Introduction to Social Sciences 91. (p. 882)
—Introduction to the Social Sciences. (p. 882)
Bontempelli, Massimo. Chess Set in the Mirror. Gilson, Estelle, tr. from ITA. (p. 298)
Bontempo, Nancy. Word of Mouth: The Food You Eat. (p. 1951)
Bontinck, Helga. All Around Town. (p. 44)
—Animal Favorites. (p. 77)
—At the Circus. (p. 111)
—At the Seashore. (p. 111)
Bontrager, Stephanie. Social Threat or Social Justice? (p. 1605)
Bonvillain, Nancy. Nez Perce. (p. 1249)
Bonvillain, Nancy & Rosier, Paul C. Zuni. (p. 1990)
Bonwill, Ann. Frazzle Family Finds a Way. Gammel, Stephen, illus. (p. 631)
—I Am Not a Copycat! Rickerty, Simon, illus. (p. 833)
—I Don't Want to Be a Pea! Rickerty, Simon, illus. (p. 838)
—Naughty Toes. Murfin, Teresa, illus. (p. 1237)
Boo, Sue. Baby Finds Love. (p. 126)
Boochever, Annie. Bristol Bay Summer. (p. 229)
Boock, Paula. Dare Truth or Promise. (p. 406)
Boocock, Charles & Yu, Jennifer. 10 Most Memorable Court Cases. (p. 1994)
Boodey, David M. Ruby & Lucy Searching for Silly. Lilagan, Kenneth D., illus. (p. 1493)
Boodey, Erin. Work Your Body Grow Your Brain. Konecny, John, illus. (p. 1952)
Booher, Brock. Charity Chip. (p. 291)
—Healing Stone. (p. 757)
Book Builders, Inc. Staff & Chin, Beverly. How to Ace Any Test. (p. 814)
Book Builders, Inc. Staff, et al. How to Write a Great Research Paper. (p. 822)
Book Company, Popular. Complete English Workout, Volume 1. (p. 352)
—Complete Math Workout, Volume 7. (p. 353)
Book Company Staff. Alphabet Flash Cards. (p. 49)
—Animal Friends. (p. 77)
—Animal World. (p. 80)
—Are You a Dinosaur? (p. 97)
—Are You a Frog? (p. 97)
—Be Bop Bugs. (p. 148)
—Beep Beep. (p. 157)
—Busy Bugs. (p. 246)
—Charmed. Francour, Kathleen, illus. (p. 294)
—Counting. (p. 370)
—Dinosaurs. (p. 443)
—Flitterbyes Photo Frames. Francour, Kathleen, illus. (p. 605)
—Frog Gets Lost. (p. 640)
—Froggy & Friends. (p. 640)
—Hoppity Hop. (p. 797)
—Lift-A-Flap Guess Who. (p. 1014)
—Little Treasures. Francour, Kathleen, illus. (p. 1037)
—Ocean Friends. Lassen, Christian R., illus. (p. 1276)
—Our Precious World Stationery Set. Schimmel, Schim, illus. (p. 1309)
—Treasures of the Sea: Birthday & Address Book. Lassen, Christian R., illus. (p. 1782)
—Who Am I: Pig. (p. 1914)
—Who Am I: Frog. (p. 1914)
—Who Am I: Chick. (p. 1914)
—Who Am I: Rabbit. (p. 1914)
Book Company Staff, jt. auth. see McLean, Wendy.
Book Company Staff, jt. auth. see Simson, Dana.
Book Company Staff, jt. auth. see Volke, Gordon.
Book, Jennie Hale. Baby Dog Beans Comes Home: A Paul & Beans Adventure. (p. 125)
Booker, Carly-Jean, illus. see Hespe, Robert.
Booker, Carolyn. Mr. Green Squash Takes a Journey. (p. 1185)
Booker, Catina M. Granny & Me. (p. 710)
Booker, Ricki, jt. auth. see Asher, Penny.
Booking, Walt. Teddy's Tale. (p. 1713)
Bookins, Daddy. Outside with Lil Boo. Piotti, Dania, illus. (p. 1313)
Bookmiller, Kirsten N. United Nations. (p. 1819)

B

Bookmiller, Kirsten N. & Verloren, Ada. United Nations Children's Fund (UNICEF) (p. 1819)
Books, Appleknobb. Charlie's Monster. Books, Appleknobb, illus. (p. 293)
Books, Atkins. Holy Bible Word Search Puzzles Unscramble the Answers. (p. 791)
Books, D. W. J. & Eisenstark, Reyna. Abolitionism. (p. 5)
Books, D. W. J. & Kearns, Trevor Conan. Terrorism. (p. 1722)
Books, D. W. J. & Kozlowski, Darrell J. Federalism. (p. 580)
Books, D. W. J. & Mauch, Jason. Industrialism. (p. 872)
Books, D. W. J. & Sauers, Richard A. Expansionism. (p. 548)
Books, D. W. J., et al. Isolationism. (p. 893)
—Nationalism. (p. 1234)
Books, Golson. African Americans (p. 27)
—Arab Americans (p. 94)
—Asian Americans (p. 106)
—European Americans (p. 540)
—Hispanic Americans (p. 781)
—Jewish Americans (p. 917)
—Multicultural America (p. 1190)
—Native Americans (p. 1234)
Books, Golson & Purdy, Elizabeth. Celebrating Women in American History (p. 285)
Books, Greenbird, jt. auth. see Talhah, Abu.
BookSource Staff, compiled by. Balloon Blow-Up. (p. 135)
—Crispin: The Cross of Lead. (p. 383)
—Dora's Puppy, Perrito! (p. 471)
—Emerge Additional Books. (p. 518)
—Great Coaster Caper. (p. 714)
—Lights, Camera... Zombies! (p. 1016)
—Obi-Wan Kenobi: Jedi Knight. (p. 1275)
—Petting Zoo. (p. 1349)
—Robot Rumble. (p. 1480)
—Sports Sabotage. (p. 1633)
—Who Saved the Galaxy? (p. 1917)
Bookworks, Downtown. Eye Q Picture Puzzler. (p. 558)
Bookworks, Downtown & Katz, David Bar. My First Batman Book: Touch & Feel. (p. 1204)
—My First Superman Book: Touch & Feel. (p. 1208)
Boom, Rosie. Where Lions Roar at Night. (p. 1909)
Boom Studios Staff, jt. auth. see Lamb, Branden.
Boomgaard, Peter & Stoll, Mark. Southeast Asia: An Environmental History (p. 1617)
Boomgaarden, Larry, jt. auth. see Kallander, Susan.
Boomhower, Ray E. Soldier's Friend: A Life of Ernie Pyle. (p. 1607)
—Sword & the Pen: A Life of Lew Wallace. (p. 1692)
Boon, Brooke. Holy Yoga: Exercise for the Christian Body & Soul. (p. 791)
Boon, Debbie, illus. see Durant, Alan.
Boon, Debbie, illus. see Morgan, Michaela.
Boon, Fiona. My Bible Sticker Backpack. (p. 1197)
—Story of Jesus. Ede, Lara, illus. (p. 1658)
Boon, Fiona & Wickenden, Nadine. My Story David. (p. 1219)
—My Story - Joseph. (p. 1219)
Boon, Fiona, ed. Great Fairy Baking Competition. Ede, Lara, illus. (p. 716)
Boon, Kevin A. F. Scott Fitzgerald. (p. 559)
—George Orwell: Animal Farm & Nineteen Eighty-Four. (p. 663)
—Kurt Vonnegut: Slaughterhouse-Five & Cat's Cradle. (p. 968)
Boon, Kevin Alexander. Ernest Hemingway: The Sun Also Rises & Other Works. (p. 533)
—Kurt Vonnegut. (p. 968)
Boone, Clyde Douglas, told to. Boone Boys: Frontiersmen & Their Great Wild West Show. (p. 213)
Boone, Connie. Lost Zoo. (p. 1057)
Boone, Eugene. Big Book of Pet Names: More Than 10,000 Pet Names - Includes Celebrity Pet Names - the Most Complete Guide to Pet Names & Meanings. (p. 179)
Boone, Mary. 50 Cent. (p. 1997)
—Akon. (p. 32)
—Byzantine Empire. (p. 249)
—Care for a Wild Chincoteague Pony. (p. 266)
—Corbin Bleu. (p. 366)
—David Wright. (p. 411)
—Dizzy Gillespie. (p. 455)
—Jennette McCurdy. (p. 912)
—Ornette Coleman. (p. 1304)
—Pink. (p. 1359)
—Sue Bird. (p. 1672)
—Tim Lincecum. (p. 1750)
—Uniquely Idaho (p. 1818)
—Uniquely Montana (p. 1818)
—Uniquely Oregon (p. 1818)
—Vanessa Anne Hudgens. (p. 1833)
Boone, Mary & Jacobs, Marc. Marc Jacobs. (p. 1091)
Boone, Mary & Sprinkel, Katy. Bieber Fever. (p. 177)
Boone, Melvin, Jr. JD Mc Doil What's up with Oil. (p. 911)
Boone, Patti, illus. see Devol, Laura.
Boone, Robert S., jt. auth. see Larson, Mark H.
Boone, Sheila. Free As a Butterfly. (p. 634)
—Free As a Butterfly. Knox, Susi Grell, illus. (p. 634)
Boone, Stewart. What in the World Is A Palindrome? (p. 1887)
Boonen, Stefan. Totally Lisa. (p. 1771)
—When Pigs Fly! Loufane, illus. (p. 1904)
Boonstra, Juan S. Evangelio en Nuestro Mundo. (p. 541)
Boonyadhistarn, Thiranut. Fingernail Art: Dazzling Fingers & Terrific Toes (p. 589)
—Origami: The Fun & Funky Art of Paper Folding Boonyadhistarn, Thiranut, illus. (p. 1303)
Boonyadhistarn, Thiranut, jt. auth. see Olson, Kay Melchisedech.
Boor, Annarie. Bapsie in the Bushveld. (p. 137)
Boor, Daniele, et al. Bajo la Tierra. (p. 133)
Booraem, Ellen. Small Persons with Wings. (p. 1592)
—Texting the Underworld. (p. 1724)
—Unnameables. (p. 1822)
Booren, Diana. One Friday Afternoon. (p. 1295)
Boorman, Kate A. Winterkill. (p. 1938)
Boorsma, Heidi, jt. auth. see Beeke, Joel R.
Boorstin, Daniel J., et al. History of the United States. (p. 785)
Boos, Andre. Amazing Animal Puzzle Stickers: #2 (p. 53)
—Amazing Animal Puzzle Stickers: #3 (p. 53)
—Amazing Animal Puzzle Stickers: #1. (p. 53)
—Hi! Read, Stick & Learn about Animals. Little Bears are Brown. (p. 775)
—Hi! Read, Stick & Learn about Animals. Little rabbits have Fur. (p. 775)
Boos, Ben. Fantasy: An Artist's Realm. Boos, Ben, illus. (p. 572)
Boos, Ben, illus. see Abdul-Jabbar, Kareem & Obstfeld, Raymond.
Boos, Marcela. Oh No, It's Bedtime! (p. 1281)
Boosel, Brian D. Saint Vincent Coloring Book Gabler, Michael, illus. (p. 1504)
Boot, Chris. Magnum Stories. Magnum Photos Staff, photos by. (p. 1076)
Booth. Health Care Science Technology: Career Foundations: Student Motivation. (p. 758)
Booth & McGraw-Hill Staff. Health Care Science Technology: Career Foundations. (p. 758)
—Health Care Science Technology: Career Foundations, Lab Activity Manual. (p. 758)
Booth, Anita K. Squirrels!!! An Informative & Entertaining Book about Our Favorite Mountain Mammal. Booth, Anita K., illus. (p. 1637)
Booth, Bradley. Adventures in Galilee. (p. 15)
—Escape from Egypt. (p. 535)
—Esther: A Star Is Born. (p. 538)
—Miracles of the Mantle. (p. 1149)
—Noah: The Chosen One. (p. 1261)
—Noah: The End of the World. (p. 1261)
—Plagues in the Palace. (p. 1366)
—Prince of Dreams. (p. 1401)
—Shepherd Warrior. (p. 1565)
Booth, Chrissie. Don't Even Think about It. McMurry, Marena, illus. (p. 467)
Booth, Christina, illus. see French, Jackie.
Booth, Coe. Bronxwood. (p. 230)
—Kinda Like Brothers. (p. 957)
—Tyrell. (p. 1805)
Booth, Crystal. Introducing Tucker. (p. 882)
Booth, David. Doctor Knickerbocker & Other Rhymes. (p. 459)
—Molly Whuppie & the Giant: Band 13/Topaz. Ross, Christine, illus. (p. 1161)
Booth, George, illus. see Fleming, Candace.
Booth, George, illus. see McMullan, Kate.
Booth, George, illus. see Soule, Jean Conder.
Booth, George, illus. see Van Laan, Nancy.
Booth, Graham, illus. see Taylor, Mark.
Booth, Jack. 10 Greatest Accidental Inventions. (p. 1993)
—10 Most Amazing Migrations. (p. 1993)
—10 Most Daring Heists. (p. 1993)
—10 Most Gripping 20th Century War Stories. (p. 1994)
Booth, Karon. Aslan Is on the Move: Romp in Narnia with Study Helps, Art & Play. (p. 106)
Booth, Kathryn A. & Glencoe McGraw-Hill Staff. Health Care Science Technology: Career Foundations. (p. 758)
Booth, Kathryn, et al. Math & Dosage Calculations for Health Care Professionals with Student CD. (p. 1105)
Booth, Martin. War Dog. (p. 1857)
Booth, Philip. Crossing. Ibatoulline, Bagram, illus. (p. 385)
Booth, Richard A. Valley of Gillhista. (p. 1831)
—Where Did You Spend the Night? (p. 1906)
Booth, Sara. Poppy. Horne, Nathan, illus. (p. 1385)
Booth, Scott. How to Draw Superheroes & Super Villains. (p. 818)
Booth, Tanis. Football. (p. 614)
Booth, Vanessa, jt. auth. see Thompson, Sharon.
Booth-Alberstadt, Sheila. Maggie Mcnair Has Sugar Bugs in There. Hall, Norris, illus. (p. 1071)
Boothroyd, Jennifer. All Charged Up: A Look at Electricity. (p. 44)
—Animal Pollinators. (p. 79)
—Animals & the Environment. (p. 82)
—Attract & Repel: A Look at Magnets. (p. 114)
—Attract & Repel. (p. 114)
—Caution in the Kitchen! Germs, Allergies, & Other Health Concerns. (p. 282)
—Combining Shapes. (p. 347)
—Cone. (p. 356)
—Counting. (p. 370)
—Cube. (p. 388)
—Cylinder. (p. 397)
—Ecology: Complete Set. (p. 502)
—Ecology: Classroom Set. (p. 502)
—Endangered & Extinct Birds. (p. 526)
—Endangered & Extinct Fish. (p. 526)
—Endangered & Extinct Invertebrates. (p. 526)
—Endangered & Extinct Mammals. (p. 526)
—Endangered & Extinct Reptiles. (p. 526)
—Energy That Warms Us: A Look at Heat. (p. 528)
—Energy We See: A Look at Light. (p. 529)
—Eye Color: Brown, Blue, Green, & Other Hues. (p. 557)
—Facial Features: Freckles, Earlobes, Noses, & More. (p. 561)
—Feathers. (p. 579)
—From Assembly Lines to Home Offices: How Work Has Changed. (p. 642)
—From Chalkboards to Computers: How Schools Have Changed. (p. 642)
—From Marbles to Video Games: How Toys Have Changed. (p. 643)
—From the Model T to Hybrid Cars: How Transportation Has Changed. (p. 644)
—From Typewriters to Text Messages: How Communication Has Changed. (p. 644)
—From Washboards to Washing Machines: How Homes Have Changed. (p. 644)
—Fur. (p. 650)
—Give it A Push! Give it A Pull! (p. 681)
—Give It a Push! Give It a Pull! A Look at Forces. (p. 681)
—Graphing. (p. 711)
—Grouping. (p. 725)
—Holidays. (p. 788)
—How Big? How Heavy? How Dense? A Look at Matter. (p. 805)
—How Do Hang Gliders Work? (p. 807)
—How Do Helicopters Work? (p. 807)
—How Do Parachutes Work? (p. 807)
—How Does Weather Change? (p. 809)
—How I Care for My Pet. (p. 810)
—How I Do My Homework. (p. 810)
—How I Pack My Lunch. (p. 810)
—In a Cave. (p. 862)
—In a Tree. (p. 863)
—In the Water. (p. 867)
—Insect Pollinators. (p. 875)
—Light Helps Me See. (p. 1015)
—Light Makes Colors. (p. 1015)
—Lightning Bolt Books: Your Amazing Senses (p. 1016)
—Lightning Bolt Books: Exploring Physical Science (p. 1016)
—Lou Gehrig: A Life of Dedication. (p. 1057)
—Loud or Soft? High or Low? A Look at Sound. (p. 1057)
—Many Kinds of Matter: A Look at Solids, Liquids, & Gases. (p. 1089)
—Many Ways to Move: A Look at Motion. (p. 1089)
—Many Ways to Move. (p. 1089)
—Map My Continent. (p. 1090)
—Map My Country. (p. 1090)
—Map My Home. (p. 1090)
—Map My Neighborhood. (p. 1090)
—Map My Room. (p. 1090)
—Map My State. (p. 1090)
—Nelson Mandela: A Life of Persistence. (p. 1240)
—On the Ground. (p. 1290)
—Patterns. (p. 1329)
—People & the Environment. (p. 1339)
—Plants & the Environment. (p. 1370)
—Playing with Light & Shadows. (p. 1372)
—Pyramid. (p. 1421)
—Rectangular Prism. (p. 1452)
—Roald Dahl: A Life of Imagination. (p. 1477)
—Roald Dahl. (p. 1477)
—Scales. (p. 1519)
—Self-Pollination. (p. 1549)
—Sending Messages with Light & Sound. (p. 1550)
—Sensing Light & Sound. (p. 1551)
—Shells. (p. 1565)
—Skin. (p. 1585)
—Skip Counting. (p. 1586)
—Sphere. (p. 1626)
—Susan B. Anthony: A Life of Fairness. (p. 1688)
—Susan B. Anthony: Una Vida de Igualdad. Translations.com Staff, tr. (p. 1688)
—Taste Something New: Giving Different Foods a Try. (p. 1707)
—Transportation. (p. 1779)
—Under the Ground. (p. 1813)
—Vibrations Make Sound. (p. 1840)
—Vision: Nearsightedness, Farsightedness, & More. (p. 1844)
—What Are Elections? (p. 1879)
—What Are Rules & Laws? (p. 1879)
—What Are the Branches of Government? (p. 1880)
—What Does Sunlight Do? (p. 1884)
—What Floats? What Sinks? (p. 1884)
—What Floats? What Sinks? A Look at Density. (p. 1884)
—What Holds Us to Earth? A Look at Gravity. (p. 1886)
—What Holds Us to the Earth? (p. 1886)
—What Is a Democracy? (p. 1888)
—What Is a Forecast? (p. 1888)
—What Is a Gas? (p. 1888)
—What Is a Liquid? (p. 1888)
—What Is a Solid? (p. 1888)
—What Is Citizenship? (p. 1889)
—What Is Climate? (p. 1889)
—What Is Hearing? (p. 1889)
—What Is Severe Weather? (p. 1890)
—What Is Sight? (p. 1890)
—What Is Smell? (p. 1890)
—What Is Taste? (p. 1890)
—What Is Today's Weather? (p. 1891)
—What Is Touch? (p. 1891)
—What's on My Plate? (p. 1899)
—Why Do Moving Objects Slow Down? (p. 1924)
—Why Do Moving Objects Slow Down? A Look at Friction. (p. 1924)
—Why Doesn't Everyone Eat Meat? Vegetarianism & Special Diets. (p. 1924)
Boothroyd, Sa, illus. see Eamer, Claire.
Bootman, Colin. Fish for the Grand Lady. Bootman, Colin, illus. (p. 598)
Bootman, Colin, illus. see Adler, David A.
Bootman, Colin, illus. see Armand, Glenda.
Bootman, Colin, illus. see Battle-Lavert, Gwendolyn.
Bootman, Colin, illus. see Birtha, Becky.
Bootman, Colin, illus. see Malaspina, Ann.
Bootman, Colin, illus. see Nelson, Vaunda Micheaux.
Bootman, Colin, illus. see Rockwell, Anne F.
Bootman, Colin, illus. see Scholastic, Inc. Staff, et al.
Bootman, Colin, illus. see Slade, Suzanne.
Bootman, Colin, illus. see Uhlberg, Myron.
Booton, F. F. Adventures of Elk. (p. 17)
Bootsma, Verner. Talking to the Moon. LaGrange, Tiffany, illus. (p. 1703)
Booty, Don V. Brave Little Starling. (p. 223)
Boraas, Tracey. Creek: Farmers of the Southeast. (p. 380)
—North Carolina. (p. 1264)
—Oklahoma. (p. 1282)
—Puerto Rico. (p. 1414)
Boraks-Nemetz, Lillian. Old Brown Suitcase. (p. 1283)
Boraks-Nemetz, Lillian, jt. compiled by see Watts, Irene N.
Boran, Pat. New & Selected Poems. (p. 1243)
Borando, Silvia. Black Cat, White Cat. (p. 195)
Borando, Silvia, et al. White Book. (p. 1912)
Borchelt, Kelly L. Longest Tunnel. (p. 1047)
Borchini, Ernest. Three Stories about Jonathan, the Computer, & Little Kitty: Three Short Stories about a Boy & His Magic Cat. (p. 1744)
Bordas, Jessica. Dancing Trees. (p. 403)
Borday, Irene, illus. see Parramón, José María.
Bordelois, Augusto, illus. see Hemery, Kathleen Maresh.
Borden, Louise. A+ Custodian. Gustavson, Adam, tr. (p. 1)
—America Is... Schuett, Stacey, illus. (p. 59)
—Baseball Is... Colón, Raúl, illus. (p. 141)
—Big Brothers Don't Take Naps. Dodd, Emma, illus. (p. 180)
—John Hancock Club. Gustavson, Adam, illus. (p. 922)
—Kindergarten Luck. Godbout, Geneviève, illus. (p. 957)
—Last Day of School. Gustavson, Adam, illus. (p. 977)
—Little Ships: The Heroic Rescue at Dunkirk in World War II. Foreman, Michael, illus. (p. 1036)
—Lost-and-Found Tooth. Gustavson, Adam, illus. (p. 1054)
—Off to First Grade. Schindler, S. D. et al, illus. (p. 1279)
—Sea Clocks: The Story of Longitude. Blegvad, Erik, illus. (p. 1534)
Borden, Louise & Borden, Louise W. Across the Blue Pacific: A World War II Story. Parker, Robert Andrew, illus. (p. 9)
—Journey That Saved Curious George: The True Wartime Escape of Margret & H. A. Rey. Drummond, Allan, illus. (p. 928)
Borden, Louise & Daly, Niki. Greatest Skating Race: A World War II Story from the Netherlands. Daly, Niki, illus. (p. 720)
Borden, Louise & Gustavson, Adam. Day Eddie Met the Author. (p. 412)
Borden, Louise & Kroeger, Mary Kay. Fly High! The Story of Bessie Coleman. Flavin, Teresa, illus. (p. 609)
Borden, Louise, et al. Touching the Sky: The Flying Adventures of Wilbur & Orville Wright. Fiore, Peter M., illus. (p. 1772)
Borden, Louise W. His Name Was Raoul Wallenberg. (p. 781)
—Journey That Saved Curious George: The True Wartime Escape of Margret & H. A. Rey. Drummond, Allan, illus. (p. 928)
Borden, Louise W., jt. auth. see Borden, Louise.
Border, Terry. Happy Birthday, Cupcake! Border, Terry, illus. (p. 744)
—Peanut Butter & Cupcake. Border, Terry, illus. (p. 1332)
Borders, Kristy, jt. auth. see Borders, Scott.
Borders, Scott & Borders, Kristy. Globe: Searching for Home. (p. 685)
Bordessa, Kris. Great Colonial America Projects: You Can Build Yourself! (p. 714)
—Great Medieval Projects: You Can Build Yourself. Braley, Shawn, illus. (p. 717)
—Great Medieval Projects. Braley, Shawn, illus. (p. 717)
—Team Challenges: 170+ Group Activities to Build Cooperation, Communication, & Creativity. (p. 1710)
Bordessa, Kris & Martin, W. Eric. Tools of the Ancient Greeks: A Kid's Guide to the History & Science of Life in Ancient Greece. (p. 1767)
Bordiglioni, Stefano, jt. auth. see Bordiglioni, Stephen.
Bordiglioni, Stephen & Bordiglioni, Stefano. Desert Adventure. Bertolucci, Federico, illus. (p. 428)
—Earthquake! Bertolucci, Federico, illus. (p. 497)
—Volcano! Bertolucci, Federico, illus. (p. 1848)
Bordner, Linda. Ten Good Years: Maudie & Win. (p. 1718)
Bordon, David & Winters, Tom. 101 Things You Should Do Before Your Kids Leave Home. (p. 2000)
Bordoni, Chiara, illus. see Watt, Fiona.
Bordons, Paloma, jt. auth. see Bordons, Paloma.
Bordons, Paloma & Bordons, Paloma. Tierra de las Papas. (p. 1748)
Bordowitz, Hank, ed. Led Zeppelin on Led Zeppelin: Interviews & Encounters. (p. 987)
Bordoy, Irene, illus. see Andersen, Hans Christian & Combel Editorial Staff.
Bordoy, Irene, illus. see Sarfatti, Esther, tr.
Bordoy, Irene, illus. see Scholastic, Inc. Staff.
Bordoy, Irene, jt. auth. see Parramón, José María.
Bordoy, Irene, illus. see Sanchez, Isidro.
Bordwell, David & Thompson, Kristin. Film Art: An Introduction & Film Viewers Guide. (p. 586)
Boréal, Carole. I Love Paris, Rome, Berlin, London. (p. 842)
Borene, Mark R. Welcome to the Ground. (p. 1874)
—Welcome to the School. (p. 1874)
Borenstein, Gerri C. Therapy. (p. 1729)
Borer, Christopher. Patrick & Hatrick McDonald, Patrick, illus. (p. 1329)
Boretzki, Anja. Rainy Day Doodles. (p. 1436)
Boretzki, Anja, illus. see Cookson, Paul.
Boretzki, Anja, illus. see Moses, Brian.
Boretzki, Anja, illus. see Prasadam-Halls, Smriti.
Borg, Mary, jt. auth. see Virden, William.
Borg, Richard, jt. auth. see Moon, Alan R.
Borg, Stan W., jt. auth. see Bilderback Abel, Mary.
Borg, Wes. Fakin' Eh! (p. 565)
Borgatti, Katherine, jt. auth. see Painted Daisies Inc. Staff.
Borgeas, Ted. Grandma Is a Giggle (p. 708)
—Grandpa Is a Giggle. (p. 709)
Borgella, Marjorie, illus. see Scholastic, Inc. Staff & Brooks, Regina.
Borgenicht, David. Monkeyfarts! Wacky Jokes Every Kid Should Know. (p. 1165)
Borgenicht, David & Epstein, Robin. Worst-Case Scenario. Gonzales, Chuck, illus. (p. 1961)
Borgenicht, David & Heimberg, Justin. Extreme. (p. 556)
—Worst-Case Scenario Survival Handbook. (p. 1961)
Borgenicht, David & Khan, Hena. Amazon: You Decide How to Survive! Labat, Yancey, illus. (p. 56)
—Mars: You Decide How to Survive! Labat, Yancey, illus. (p. 1096)
Borgenicht, David & Lurie, Alexander. Deadly Seas: You Decide How to Survive! Labat, Yancey, illus. (p. 418)
Borgenicht, David, et al. Survive-O-Pedia. Gonzales, Chuck, illus. (p. 1687)
—The Worst-Case Scenario - Gross. Gonzales, Chuck, illus. (p. 1728)
—Worst-Case Scenario: Everest - You Decide How to Survive! Labat, Yancey, illus. (p. 1961)
—Worst-Case Scenario Survival Handbook. (p. 1961)
Borgens, Matthew Todd, illus. see Rappaport, Doreen.
Borger, Mimi. Story of Mr. Allergyhead. (p. 1659)
Borgert-Spaniol, Megan. Aardvarks. (p. 2)
—American Beavers. (p. 59)
—Anteaters. (p. 89)
—Baboons. (p. 124)
—Baby Foxes. (p. 126)

—Baby Giraffes. (p. 126)
—Baby Hedgehogs. (p. 126)
—Baby Hippos. (p. 126)
—Baby Koalas. (p. 127)
—Baby Squirrels. (p. 128)
—Bighorn Sheep. (p. 185)
—Black Bears. (p. 195)
—Camels. (p. 256)
—Cape Buffalo. (p. 262)
—Capybaras. (p. 265)
—Cheetahs. (p. 296)
—Cranes. (p. 376)
—Dairy Group. (p. 400)
—Flamingos. (p. 602)
—Fruit Group. (p. 645)
—Gazelles. (p. 659)
—Geese. (p. 659)
—Grains Group. (p. 706)
—Grizzly Bears. (p. 724)
—Healthy Eating. (p. 758)
—Jackals. (p. 903)
—Keeping Fit. (p. 947)
—Komodo Dragons. (p. 966)
—Leopards. (p. 993)
—Mongooses. (p. 1164)
—Moose. (p. 1173)
—Nine-Banded Armadillos. (p. 1256)
—Orangutans. (p. 1302)
—Peacocks. (p. 1332)
—Platypuses. (p. 1370)
—Protein Foods Group. (p. 1412)
—Red Foxes. (p. 1454)
—Red Pandas. (p. 1454)
—Red-Tailed Hawks. (p. 1455)
—Salamanders. (p. 1504)
—Sand Tiger Shark. (p. 1510)
—Sloths. (p. 1591)
—Snow Leopards. (p. 1599)
—Spiders. (p. 1626)
—Vegetable Group. (p. 1834)
—Warthogs. (p. 1859)
—Weasels. (p. 1869)
—Whale Shark. (p. 1877)
—Wolverines. (p. 1944)
Borges, Antonion. Cocoa & Company: A Civil War Classic. (p. 337)
Borges, Jorge Luis. Aleph. (p. 35)
—Book of Sand & Shakespeare's Memory. Hurley, Andrew, tr. (p. 211)
—Breve Arte de Ctos Fantastico. (p. 226)
—Breve Antologia de la Poesia Latinoamericana de Vanguardia, 1920-1930. (p. 226)
Borges, Jorge Luis, et al. Cuentos Latinoamericanos: Antologia. (p. 390)
Borgeson, Grace. Douwlina: A Rhino's Story. (p. 473)
Borgia, Mary. Tales of the Texas Mermaid: The Boot. (p. 1703)
—Tales of the Texas Mermaid: The Charro. (p. 1703)
Borgions, Mark, illus. see Brown, Jordan D.
Borgman, Jim, illus. see Scott, Jerry.
Borgman, Jim, jt. auth. see Scott, Jerry.
Borgnon, Liselotte & Olsson, Liselott Mariett. Movement & Experimentation in Young Children's Learning: Deleuze & Guattari in Early Childhood Education. (p. 1183)
Borgo, Deborah Colvin, illus. see Publications International Ltd. Staff, ed.
Borgo, Lacy Finn. Big Mama's Baby. Cote, Nancy, illus. (p. 182)
Borgstedt, John, illus. see Austin, D.
Borgstedt, John, jt. auth. see Zackery, Gary D.
Boricchio, Frances. Adventure of Rodney & Diane. (p. 14)
—Box of Red Dominos. (p. 216)
Borich, Gary D. & Cooper, James M. Field-Based Classroom Observation. (p. 583)
Boring, Mel & Dendy, Leslie. Guinea Pig Scientists: Bold Self-Experimenters in Science & Medicine. Mordan, C. B. & Mordan, C., illus. (p. 731)
—Guinea Pig Scientists. Mordan, C. B., illus. (p. 731)
Borisov, Vadim & Borisova, Alina. Krylataia Mechta. (p. 968)
Borisova, Alina, jt. auth. see Borisov, Vadim.
Borisovna, Gabrielle. Carl Sagan. (p. 269)
Boritzer, Etan. What Is Beautiful? Forrest, Nancy, illus. (p. 1889)
—What Is Death? Forrest, Nancy, illus. (p. 1889)
—What Is Dreaming? Vernon, Jeff, illus. (p. 1889)
—What Is Funny? Day, Jeff, illus. (p. 1889)
—What Is Money? (p. 1889)
—What Is Money? West, Jennifer, illus. (p. 1889)
—What Is Right? Sale, Graham, illus. (p. 1890)
—What Is True? Vernon, Jeff, illus. (p. 1891)
Borja, Richard. Flash! Alphabet Enigma. (p. 602)
Borja, Robert, illus. see McCall, Edith.
Bork, Rhoda. Pioneering: Activities to Live History. (p. 1361)
Borkin, Jeff. Blue's Beach Day. Craig, Karen, illus. (p. 204)
Borkowski, Michael, illus. see Wrecks, Billy.
Borland, Jerre Shadrick. Ferdinand the Frog. Bayard, Janie Domengeaux, illus. (p. 582)
Borland, Kathryn Kilby, jt. auth. see Speicher, Helen Ross.
Borland, Kathryn Kilby & Speicher, Helen Ross. Phillis Wheatley: Young Revolutionary Poet Morrison, Cathy, illus. (p. 1351)
Borland, Polly, photos by see Child, Lauren.
Borlasca, Hector. It's Too Crowded in Here! And Other Jewish Folktales. (p. 899)
Borlasca, Hector, illus. see Fleming, Maria & Scholastic Canada Ltd. Staff.
Borlasca, Hector, illus. see Hapka, Cathy, pseud.
Borlasca, Hector, illus. see Kalz, Jill.
Borlasca, Hector, illus. see Kosara, Tori.
Borlasca, Hector, illus. see Rosa-Mendoza, Gladys.
Borlasca, Hector, illus. see Taylor-Butler, Christine.
Borlasca, Hector, illus. see Williams, Rozanne Lanczak.
Borlasca, Hector, illus. see Zondervan Publishing Staff.
Borlasca, Hector, jt. auth. see D'Andrea, Deborah.
Borlase. Naked Christian. (p. 1228)

Born, Mark Alan. TIDELOG 2003 Graphic Almanac for Southeastern States: Covering the Entire South Carolina Coast, North to Wilmington NC, & South to Brunswick, Ga. Escher, M. C., illus. (p. 1747)
Born, Max, jt. auth. see Einstein, Albert.
Bornemann, Elsa. Cuadernos de un Delfin. (p. 388)
—Cuentos a Salto de Canguro. (p. 389)
—Elefante Ocupa Mucho Espacio. (p. 510)
—Grendelines. Pez, illus. (p. 723)
—Libro de los Chicos Enamorados. (p. 1006)
—Nino Envuelto. Duforu, Sebastian, illus. (p. 1257)
—No Somos Irrompibles. Gaban, Jesus, illus. (p. 1260)
—Socorro! 12 Cuentos para Caerse de Miedo. (p. 1605)
—Socorro Diez y Otros Cuentos. (p. 1605)
—Tinke Tinke. Huadi, illus. (p. 1755)
—Ultimo Mago de Bilembambudin. (p. 1810)
Bornemeier, Pam, ed. see Manton, Charlotte.
Bornholdt, Jenny. Book Is a Book. Wilkins, Sarah, illus. (p. 210)
Borns, Steven, illus. see Brooks, Walter R. & Slayton-Mitchell, Joyce.
Bornstein, Laurie. Angel Cloud. (p. 73)
Bornstein, Micah, jt. auth. see Wolf, Sallie.
Bornstein, Ruth. Little Gorilla Book & CD. (p. 1028)
—Little Gorilla Lap Board Book. (p. 1028)
Bornstein, Ruth Lercher. Gorilita. (p. 703)
—Rabbit's Good News/la Buena Noticia de Conejita. (p. 1430)
Borntrager, Mary Christner. Andy. (p. 72)
—Ellie. (p. 514)
—Polly. (p. 1381)
—Rebecca. (p. 1450)
Boroda, Janna, ed. see AZ Books Staff.
Boroson, Martin & Quarto Generic Staff. Becoming Me: A Story of Creation. Gilvan-Cartwright, Christopher, illus. (p. 156)
Boroughs, Allan. Ironheart. (p. 888)
Borovik, Alija, ed. see AZ Books Staff.
Borovsky, Ivan. Our Trip to the Ocean: Understand Place Value. (p. 1310)
Borowick, Kathleen, illus. see Lawrence, Treat.
Borraga, Charles R. Old Parson's House. (p. 1284)
Borrajero, Judy, illus. see Sprague, Howard Lee.
Borrelli, James, ed. see Chu, C. K.
Borrelli, Kristin K. Sometimes I Make Noises. (p. 1610)
Borrelli, Robert L. & Coleman, Courtney S. Differential Equations: A Modeling Perspective. (p. 438)
Borrelli, Theresa "Terrie". Why Is Jamie Different? (p. 1925)
Borrero, Mari. Daddy Has a New Home, Not a New Heart. (p. 398)
Borrington, Karen. Teaching & Assessing Skills in Business Studies. (p. 1709)
Borris, Albert. Crash into Me. (p. 376)
Borrowman, Mary, jt. auth. see O'Loughlin, Chloe.
Borsage, Charlotte, ed. see Forte, Imogene & Schurr, Sandra.
Borsan, Luis, illus. see Winner, Ramana Moreno.
Borsay, Peter. History of Leisure: The British Experience Since 1500. (p. 784)
Borsin, Kim, illus. see Kline, Joel.
Borsky, Mary. Benny Bensky & the Parrot-Napper. Hendry, Linda, illus. (p. 165)
Borst, Amie & Borst, Bethanie. Little Dead Riding Hood. Caringella, Rachel, illus. (p. 1026)
Borst, Bethanie, jt. auth. see Borst, Amie.
Borstel, Ian von, illus. see Marin, Dale Diane.
Borsten, Joan & Vidov, Oleg, eds. Mikhail Baryshnikov's Stories from My Childhood: Beloved Fairy Tales from the Snow Queen to Ivan & His Magicpony to Cinderella. (p. 1141)
Borth, Teddy. Animal Colors. (p. 77)
—Animals on the Farm. (p. 83)
—Baseball: Great Moments, Records, & Facts. (p. 140)
—Basketball: Great Moments, Records, & Facts. (p. 143)
—Blue Animals. (p. 202)
—Buildings on the Farm. (p. 239)
—Crops on the Farm. (p. 385)
—Farm Life on the Farm. (p. 574)
—Football: Great Moments, Records, & Facts. (p. 615)
—Great Sports. (p. 718)
—Green Animals. (p. 721)
—Gymnastics: Great Moments, Records, & Facts. (p. 734)
—Hockey: Great Moments, Records, & Facts. (p. 786)
—Machines on the Farm. (p. 1068)
—Orange Animals. (p. 1301)
—Red Animals. (p. 1453)
—Soccer: Great Moments, Records, & Facts. (p. 1603)
—Tools on the Farm. (p. 1767)
—White Animals. (p. 1912)
—Yellow Animals. (p. 1970)
Borth, Teddy, jt. auth. see ABDO Publishing Company Staff.
Borth, Teddy, et al. Animales de la Granja. (p. 80)
—Construcciones de la Granja. (p. 359)
—Cultivos de la Granja. (p. 390)
—Herramientas de la Granja. (p. 774)
—Maquinaria de la Granja. (p. 1091)
—Vida en la Granja. (p. 1840)
Borthwick, Paul, et al. Would Jesus Really Do That? (p. 1962)
Bortner, Lynn A. Color My World. (p. 343)
—Stanley's My Name Adventure's My Game. (p. 1640)
Bortnick, Lori. Straw Hat So Big. Santos, Carriel Ann, illus. (p. 1666)
Bortolotti, Dan. Exploring Saturn: From Galileo to Cassini. (p. 553)
—Exploring Saturn. (p. 553)
—Panda Rescue: Changing the Future for Endangered Wildlife. (p. 1320)
—Tiger Rescue: Changing the Future for Endangered Wildlife. (p. 1748)
Borton, Elizabeth. Pollyanna in Hollywood. (p. 1381)
Borton, Eulene, text. Waldenses: The Church in the Wilderness. (p. 1853)
Borton, Paula, ed. see Parker, Steve.
Bortz, Alfred B. Electron. (p. 509)

—Neutrino. (p. 1242)
—Neutron. (p. 1242)
—Photon. (p. 1353)
—Proton. (p. 1412)
—Seven Wonders of Exploration Technology. (p. 1555)
Bortz, Fred. Astrobiology. (p. 109)
—Beyond Jupiter: The Story of Planetary Astronomer Heidi Hammel. (p. 174)
—Big Bang Theory: Edwin Hubble & the Origins of the Universe. (p. 178)
—Charles Darwin & the Theory of Evolution by Natural Selection. (p. 292)
—Double Helix Structure of Dna. (p. 473)
—Electron. (p. 509)
—Envisioning Outer Space: Where Science & Fiction Meet. (p. 532)
—Johannes Kepler & the Three Laws of Planetary Motion. (p. 921)
—Laws of Genetics & Gregor Mendel. (p. 981)
—Laws of Motion & Isaac Newton. (p. 981)
—Neutrino. (p. 1242)
—Neutron. (p. 1242)
—Photon. (p. 1353)
—Proton. (p. 1412)
—Quark. (p. 1422)
—Seven Wonders of Space Technology. (p. 1555)
—Sun-Centered Universe & Nicolaus Copernicus. (p. 1676)
—Understanding Higgs Bosons. (p. 1815)
—Understanding the Large Hadron Collider. (p. 1816)
Bortz, Fred, jt. auth. see Fields, B. H.
Bortz, Fred & Fields, B. H. Understanding Electrons. (p. 1815)
Bortz, Trudy, jt. auth. see Rappaport, Josh.
Bortz, Trudy & Rappaport, Josh. Math Games That Roam the Concept Range. Blakemore, Sally, illus. (p. 1106)
Boruch, Marianne. Poems: New & Selected. (p. 1376)
Borum, Randy & Verhaagen, David Allan. Assessing & Managing Violence Risk in Juveniles. (p. 107)
Borus, Audrey. Kanye West: Grammy-Winning Hip-Hop Artist & Producer. (p. 943)
—Student's Guide to Emily Dickinson. (p. 1669)
—Volunteering: A How-to Guide. (p. 1850)
—Volunteering. (p. 1850)
Borus, Joshua, ed. see Crockett, Kyle A.
Borus, Joshua, ed. see Etingoff, Kim.
Borus, Joshua, ed. see Scott, Celicia.
Borus, Joshua, ed. see Waters, Rosa.
Borza, Joseph. Journey to America. (p. 928)
Borzendowski, Janice. Marie Curie: Mother of Modern Physics. (p. 1093)
Bos, Burny, jt. auth. see de Beer, Hans, pseud.
Bos, Isgar. En Wally va a l'Escola / Wally Goes to School. (p. 523)
—Wally Meets Picasso. (p. 1855)
Bos, Robert C. Gift of Imagination. (p. 675)
Bos, Samone. DK Adventures: Twister! Terrifying Tales of Superstorms. (p. 455)
Bos, Samone & Dorling Kindersley Publishing Staff. Twister! A Terrifying Tale of Superstorms. (p. 1803)
Bosak, Susan V. Dream: A Tale of Wonder, Wisdom & Wishes. Dillon, Leo et al, illus. (p. 483)
—Little Something. McGaw, Laurie, illus. (p. 1036)
—Something to Remember Me By: A Story about Love & Legacies. McGaw, Laurie, illus. (p. 1610)
—Something to Remember Me By. (p. 1610)
Bosak, Virginia, illus. see Buchanan, Johnny & Conway, Beth.
Bosarge, Charlotte, ed. see Forte, Imogene & Schurr, Sandra.
Bosarge, Charlotte, ed. see Forte, Imogene.
Bosarge, Charlotte, ed. see Green, Bea, et al.
Bosarge, Jerusha. Inventing Ott: The Legacy of Arthur C. Guyton. (p. 883)
Boscarelli, Bonnie & Dani. Garden of Weeden: Hector the Hedgehog. (p. 656)
Bosch, David, illus. see Schnee-Bosch, Penny.
Bosch, Hermann. Bedtime Bible Stories for Catholic Children: Loving Jesus through His Word. (p. 156)
Bosch, Meritxell, illus. see Nordling, Lee.
Bosch, Nicole, illus. see Ross, Kathy.
Bosch, Nicole in den, illus. see Medoff, Francine.
Bosch, Nicole in den, illus. see Ross, Kathy.
Bosch, Pseudonymous. Bad Magic. (p. 132)
—If You're Reading This, It's Too Late. (p. 855)
—Name of This Book Is Secret. (p. 1228)
—Name of This Book Is Secret. Ford, Gilbert, illus. (p. 1228)
—Secret Series Complete Collection. (p. 1543)
—This Book Is Not Good for You. (p. 1735)
—This Isn't What It Looks Like. (p. 1737)
—Write This Book: A Do-It-Yourself Mystery. (p. 1964)
—You Have to Stop This. (p. 1975)
Bosch-Abele, Susanne, tr. see Phaidon Press Editors.
Bosco, Antoinette. Charles John Seghers: Pioneer in Alaska. Kalmenoff, Matthew, illus. (p. 292)
—Jesus Garden: An Easter Legend. Mattozzi, Patricia R., illus. (p. 915)
Bosco, Don, jt. auth. see Levy, Patricia.
Bosco, Peter. World War I. (p. 1958)
Bosco, Sally, jt. auth. see Hansen, Lynne.
Boscola, Carolyn, illus. see Camut, LeeAnn.
Bose, Janet Von. Noun Family. (p. 1268)
Bose, Meenekshi, jt. auth. see Gregory, Josh.
Bosgra, Johann, illus. see Gillespie, Jane.
Bosgra, Johann, illus. see Hopkins, Jane.
Boshers, Bo. G Force: Taking Your Relationship with God to a New Level. (p. 651)
Boshers, Martha, illus. see Dixon, Louisa.
Boshier, Rosa. How to Analyze the Works of Martin Luther King Jr. (p. 814)
—How to Analyze the Works of Virginia Woolf. (p. 814)
—Ronald Reagan: 40th US President. (p. 1486)
Boshof, Penny, jt. auth. see Lane, Leena.
Boshoff, Penny. Bible Alive. (p. 175)
—God & Me: 365 Daily Devotions. (p. 688)
Boshoff, Penny, jt. auth. see Batchelor, Mary.

Boshouwers, Suzan. Pirates. Hund, Marjolein, illus. (p. 1363)
Boskey, Elizabeth. America Debates Genetic DNA Testing. (p. 59)
Bosley, Judith A. Sing Christmas. Price, Susan D., illus. (p. 1579)
Bosma, Sam, illus. see Fisher, Sam.
Bosma, Sam, illus. see Smith, Andrew.
Bosnia, Nella, illus. see Turin, Adela.
Boss, Nicco. Message to Badabu. (p. 1129)
Bossano, Patricia. Faery Sight: A Novel. (p. 562)
Bosse, Malcolm. Tusk & Stone. (p. 1799)
Bosse, Nancy Rogers, jt. auth. see Rainbow Bridge Publishing Staff.
Bosse, Tom. Unveiling of the Trinity: A Biblical Account of the Mystery Revealed. (p. 1823)
Bossi, Lisa Burnett, illus. see Gosline, Andrea Alban.
Bossley, Michele Martin. Bear Market. (p. 151)
—Bio-Pirate. (p. 188)
—Cracked. (p. 375)
—Danger Zone. (p. 404)
—Fraud Squad. (p. 631)
—Goon Squad. (p. 702)
—Jumper (p. 934)
—Kicker (p. 951)
—Swiped (p. 1691)
—Tampered (p. 1704)
Bossley, Michele Martin, jt. auth. see Guest, Jacqueline.
Bosson, Jo-Ellen, illus. see Presson, Leslie.
Bosson, Jo-Ellen, jt. auth. see Diaz, Katacha.
Bost, Richard. Taekwon Tales. (p. 1695)
Boster, Jennifer. Case of the Missing Baloney. (p. 274)
Bostian, Laurie, illus. see Webb, Anne Aldridge.
Bostic, Alex, illus. see Collin, Grace.
Bostic, Angie L. Mackenslee's Magic Fountain. (p. 1068)
Bostic, Charles. Da' art of Ravenous Redd. (p. 398)
Bostic, Megan. Never Eighteen. (p. 1242)
Bostick, B. k. Huber Hill & the Brotherhood of Coronado. (p. 824)
—Huber Hill & the Dead Man's Treasure. (p. 824)
—Huber Hill & the Golden Staff of Cibola. (p. 824)
Bostick, Nan. Consumer Spending. (p. 360)
—Managing Money. (p. 1086)
Bostock, Mike, illus. see Allen, Judy.
Bostock, Mike, illus. see Wallace, Karen.
Bostock, Mike, jt. auth. see Wallace, Karen.
Boston, David. Wonder Tales from Around the World. (p. 1947)
Boston, David, illus. see DeSpain, Pleasant.
Boston, L. M. Stones of Green Knowe. Boston, Peter, illus. (p. 1653)
Boston, Peter, illus. see Boston, L. M.
Boston, Ruth. Super Hero for A Day. (p. 1680)
Boston, Vicki, jt. auth. see Stroh, Debbie.
Boston, Vicki & Stroh, Debbie. Christ's Kids Create: Volume 2; Favorite Seasonal Craft Ideas (p. 317)
Boston, Vicki, et al. Wiggles & Squiggles: 60 Bible-Based Classroom Games & Activities. (p. 1928)
Bostrom, Christopher, illus. see Bostrom, Kathleen.
Bostrom, Kathleen. Secret of the Twelve Days of Christmas. Bostrom, Christopher, illus. (p. 1543)
Bostrom, Kathleen Long. Easter Stories & Prayers. Kucharik, Elena, illus. (p. 499)
—Good Morning, God! Lyon, Tammie, illus. (p. 698)
—Good Night, God! Lyon, Tammie, illus. (p. 699)
—Questions from Little Hearts. Kucharik, Elena, illus. (p. 1426)
—Rufus & Ryan Celebrate Easter! Thornburgh, Rebecca, illus. (p. 1494)
—View at the Zoo. Francis, Guy, illus. (p. 1841)
—What about Heaven? Kucharik, Elena, illus. (p. 1878)
—Who Made the World? Kucharik, Elena, illus. (p. 1916)
—Why Is There a Cross? Kucharik, Elena, illus. (p. 1925)
—Winning Authors: Profiles of the Newbery Medalists (p. 1937)
Bostrom, Kathleen Long, jt. auth. see Mackall, Dandi Daley.
Bostrom, Laura, illus. see Propes, Chrysti Carol.
Bostrom, Laura L., illus. see Propes, Chrysti Carol.
Bostrom, Sally, illus. see Kendall, Jack.
Boswall, Nigel. Jerry's Trousers. Melling, David, illus. (p. 914)
Boswell, Addie & Addie, Boswell. Rain Stomper Velasquez, Eric, illus. (p. 1435)
Boswell, John. Healing Your Inner Core: How to Revise Your Life Script & Heal Your Destiny. (p. 757)
Boswell, John, ed. U. S. Armed Forces Survival Guide. (p. 1806)
Boswell, Kelly. Diagrams, Diagrams, Diagrams! (p. 433)
—Displaying Information. (p. 453)
—Graphs, Graphs, Graphs! (p. 711)
—Maps, Maps, Maps! (p. 1090)
—Timelines, Timelines, Timelines! (p. 1754)
Boswell, Lavenia. Victoria's Crossing. (p. 1840)
Boswell, Robert B., tr. see Racine, Jean.
Boswell, Shannon. Savannah's Snorkeling Adventure! Use Place Value Understanding. (p. 1516)
Boswell, William. Wild & Crazy Adventures of a Boy Named Will. (p. 1928)
Bosworth, David, illus. see Campbell, Roy.
Bosworth, Jennifer. Struck. (p. 1668)
Botelho, R. J. Elizabeth & Equines: G. A. R. T. H. V (Genetically Altered Radically Transformed Human) (p. 513)
—G. A. R. T. H. Book IV: A Whale of a Tale. (p. 651)
—G. A. R. T. H. (Genetically Altered Radically Transformed Human) Book III: Downeast Maine: A New Beginning. (p. 651)
Boten, Wallace. From Farm to Store (p. 642)
Boten, Wallace & Capstone Press Staff. From Farm to Store (p. 642)
Botero, Fernando, jt. auth. see Bloncourt, Nelson.
Botha, Ingrid. Chikin & Scrub. (p. 301)
Botha, Si. Goosala Goop. (p. 702)
Botha, Tommy C. I., et al. Natural Sciences Matters Grade 7 Learner's Book. (p. 1236)
—Natural Sciences Matters Grade 7 Learner's Book Afrikaans Translation. (p. 1236)

For book reviews, descriptive annotations, tables of contents, cover images, author biographies & additional information, updated daily, subscribe to www.booksinprint2.com

2085

Botham, Noel. Did Romans Really Wash Themselves in Wee? (p. 436)
—Do Turtles Really Breathe Out of Their Bums? (p. 457)
—How Fast Can You Fart? And Other Weird, Gross & Disgusting Facts. (p. 809)
Bothmer, Gerry, tr. see Lindgren, Astrid.
Botnick, Julie & Linden, Becca. Min Ha'aretz: Making Meaning from Our Food. (p. 1145)
Botsford, Matthew. Johnny Rocket & His Comrades in Faith. (p. 923)
Bott, Paula. Fighting el Fuego. (p. 585)
Botterill, Ron E. Big, Green & Mean, Ogie, the Misunderstood Monster. (p. 181)
Bottiglieri, Tim. Robber Raccoon Bishop, John E., illus. (p. 1478)
Bottner, Barbara. Annoying ABC. Emberley, Michael, illus. (p. 87)
—Feet Go to Sleep. Smith, Maggie, illus. (p. 580)
—Flower Girl Grier, Laura, illus. (p. 607)
—Miss Brooks Loves Books! (And I Don't) Emberley, Michael, illus. (p. 1151)
—Miss Brooks' Story Nook (where Tales Are Told & Ogres Are Welcome) Emberley, Michael, illus. (p. 1151)
—Raymond & Nelda Hayashi, Nancy, illus. (p. 1441)
—Rosa's Room Spiegel, Beth, tr. (p. 1489)
—Rosa's Room Spiegel, Beth, illus. (p. 1489)
—Scaredy Cats. Chess, Victoria, illus. (p. 1519)
Bottner, Barbara & Kruglik, Gerald. Pish & Posh. Bottner, Barbara, illus. (p. 1364)
—Pish & Posh Wish for Fairy Wings. Bottner, Barbara, illus. (p. 1364)
—Wallace's Lists. Landstrom, Olof, tr. (p. 1855)
—Wallace's Lists. Landstrom, Olof, illus. (p. 1855)
Bottoms, Bud. Davey & the GOM Giant Oil Monster. (p. 410)
Bottoms, James. Kid Ethics 2: From A to Z. (p. 951)
Bottoms, James "Bud". Kid Ethics 2: From A to Z. (p. 951)
Bottone, Ann. My National Parks & Monuments Photo Journal. (p. 1215)
Botvin, Gilbert J. Middle School Level 1 - Student Guide. (p. 1137)
Botzakis, Stergios. Entertainment & Gaming (p. 531)
—What's Your Source? Questioning the News. (p. 1900)
Botzakis, Stergios & Capstone Press Editors. Pretty in Print: Questioning Magazines (p. 1398)
Botzman, Harvey. 'Round Lake Erie: A Bicyclist's Tour Guide. (p. 1491)
Bouani, Jennifer. Tyler & His Solve-A-Matic Machine: (1st Edition) (p. 1805)
Boucha, Becky. Kayla Nicole Goes to School: Kayla Nicole Series. (p. 946)
Bouchain, Nava, illus. see Suarez de la Prida, Isabel.
Bouchal, Renee', illus. see Baurys, Tamra.
Bouchard, David. Elders Are Watching. Vickers, Roy Henry, illus. (p. 508)
—For the Love of Reading (p. 616)
—Great Race - The Legend of the Chinese Zodiac. (p. 718)
—I am Raven. Everson, Andy, illus. (p. 833)
—Nokum: Ma Voix et Mon Coeur Sapp, Allen, illus. (p. 1263)
—Rainbow Crow Jean, David, illus. (p. 1435)
—Secret of Your Name Weber, Dennis, illus. (p. 1543)
—That's Hockey Griffiths, Dean, illus. (p. 1726)
—Voices from the Wild: An Animal Sensagoria Parker, Ron, illus. (p. 1848)
Bouchard, David, jt. auth. see Bouchard, David.
Bouchard, David & Aleekuk, Pam. Long Powwow Nights Paul, Leonard, illus. (p. 1047)
Bouchard, David & Bouchard, David. Nokum Is My Teacher Sapp, Allen, illus. (p. 1263)
Bouchard, David & Sapp, Allen. Song Within My Heart (p. 1611)
Bouchard, David & Willier, Shelley. Drum Calls Softly. Poitras, Jim, illus. (p. 487)
Bouchard, Elizabeth. Everything You Need to Know about Sexual Harassment. (p. 546)
Bouchard, Hervé. Harvey Mixter, Helen, tr. from FRE. (p. 752)
Bouchard, James J. Kenpo Student Workbook: Level 3. (p. 949)
Bouchard, Jocelyne, illus. see Love, Ann & Drake, Jane.
Bouchard, John L. Taste of Soda. (p. 1707)
Bouchard, Linda. Sunny the Day Care Cat. (p. 1677)
Bouchard, Margaret. Comprehension Strategies for English Language Learners: 30 Research-Based Reading Strategies That Help Students Read, Understand, & Really Learn Content from Their Textbooks & Other Nonfiction Materials. (p. 354)
Bouchard, Sue, jt. auth. see Burns, Eleanor.
bouche', Ghee. Silly Billy the Horse. (p. 1575)
Boucher, Francoize. I Love Words. (p. 843)
Boucher, Franoize. Book That Will Make You Love Books: Even If You Hate Reading! (p. 212)
—Don't Worry, Be Happy! or Else! (p. 469)
—How Cool Are Your Parents? (or Not) (p. 806)
Boucher, John G., et al. History of Art (p. 783)
Boucher, Julie. Small Fry on the Magnetawan. (p. 1592)
Boucher, Julie, illus. see Desrochers, Diane O.
Boucher, Michel, illus. see Dumont, Virginie, et al.
Boucher, Paul. Stickeee & Gooweee Week of Fun. (p. 1650)
Boucher, Sarah E. Becoming Beauty: A Retelling of Beauty & the Beast. (p. 156)
Bouchet, Paule du, see Du Bouchet, Paule.
Boucquey, Thierry & Diamond, Marie Josephine. Encyclopedia of World Writers, Beginnings to the Twentieth Century. (p. 526)
Boudgourd, Vincent & Owlkids Books Inc. Staff. My Beastly Book of Hilarious Heroes: 150 Ways to Doodle, Scribble, Color & Draw. (p. 1196)
Boudin, Jonathan. Little Red Riding Book. Adrian, Marti, illus. (p. 1035)
Boudreau, Bobby A. Inspirational Stories for Spiritual Youth. (p. 878)
Boudreau, Hélène. Acadian Star (p. 7)
Boudreau, Helene. I Dare You Not to Yawn. Bloch, Serge, illus. (p. 837)
Boudreau, Hélène. Keep Out! Lucas, Diane, illus. (p. 947)
—Life in a Fishing Community. (p. 1010)
—Miraculous Medicines. (p. 1149)
Boudreau, Helene. Real Mermaids Don't Hold Their Breath. (p. 1448)
—Real Mermaids Don't Need High Heels. (p. 1448)
—Real Mermaids Don't Sell Seashells. (p. 1448)
Boudreau, Hélène. Swimming Science. (p. 1691)
Boudreau, Hélène & Aksomitis, Linda. Crimebusting & Detection. (p. 382)
Boudreau, Hélène, et al. Life in a Residential City. (p. 1010)
Boudreaux, Amanda. Birthday Breakfast. (p. 192)
Boudreaux, David. Floating on Faith: The Story of Noah. (p. 605)
Bouganim, Revital, illus. see Ryshpan-Harris, Joanne.
Bougard, Marie-Terese, tr. see Vincent, Jenny & Laird, Elizabeth.
Bougard, Marie-Therese, tr. see Rabley, Stephen.
Boughn, Michael. Into the World of the Dead: Astonishing Adventures in the Underworld. (p. 881)
Boughton, Samantha. Day at the Zoo Adventure Coloring Book. (p. 412)
—Dino Island Adventure Coloring Book. (p. 441)
—Under the Sea Adventure Coloring Book. (p. 1814)
Boujie. Princess from the Heart. (p. 1404)
Boujon, Claude. Bon Appetit Monsieur Renard. (p. 208)
—Paure Verdurette. (p. 1331)
Boukov, Lubima. Magic Swing (p. 1073)
Boulden, James. Buddy Gets Angry: Student Involvement Pack. (p. 235)
—Buddy Gets Angry Video Kit. (p. 235)
—Buddy Learns about Bullying Video Kit. (p. 235)
—Buddy Learns about Tattling: Student Involvement Pack. (p. 235)
—Buddy learns about Teasing: Student Involvement Pack. (p. 235)
—Buddy Learns from His Mistakes: Student Involvement Pack. (p. 235)
Boulden, Lowell E. Why Not Me? (p. 1925)
Bouldin, Anthony Roth & Bouldin, Morshica. Tag along with Momo & Jojo: You're It! Series #2. (p. 1695)
—Tag along with Momo & Jojo: You're IT! Series #1 Jojo's 1st day of School. (p. 1695)
Bouldin, Morshica, jt. auth. see Bouldin, Anthony Roth.
Boule, Mary Null. California Native American Tribes: Mohave Tribe Liddell, Daniel & Basta, Mary, illus. (p. 253)
—Navajo People: SW Region Liddell, Daniel & Basta, Mary, illus. (p. 1237)
Bouler, Olivia. Olivia's Birds: Saving the Gulf. (p. 1287)
Boulet, Susan Seddon. Shaman: The Paintings of Susan Seddon Boulet. (p. 1559)
—Susan Seddon Boulet: The Goddess Paintings. (p. 1688)
Boullosa, Carmen. Solo para Muchachos. Martinez, Enrique, illus. (p. 1608)
Boulter, Carol & Wadsworth, Pamela. Golau. (p. 693)
—Rhagor Am Olau. (p. 1467)
Boulton, Harold, tr. see Hughes, John Ceiriog.
Boulton, M. T. Megan Button & the Brim-Tree. (p. 1124)
Bouma, Paddy. Nelson Mandela: Long Walk to Freedom. (p. 1241)
Bound, Samantha-Ellen. And All That Jazz. (p. 71)
—Hit the Streets. (p. 786)
Bounford, Trevor. Paper Gliders: To Cut Out, Make & Fly. (p. 1322)
—Skeleton. (p. 1584)
Bour, Daniele. Petit ours brun aime Noel. (p. 1348)
—Petit ours brun fait un Cauche. (p. 1348)
—Petit ours brun repond au Teleph. (p. 1348)
Bour, Laura. Am Fluss. (p. 51)
—Rio. (p. 1473)
Bour, Laura & Jeunesse, Gallimard. Oso. Bour, Laura & Barroso, Paz, trs. (p. 1305)
Bour, Laura, et al. Aguila - The Eagle. Bour, Laura & Barroso, Paz, trs. (p. 30)
Bourassa, Barbara. Sports Club. (p. 1632)
Bourbeau, Julie. Wednesdays. Beene, Jason, illus. (p. 1871)
Bourbois, J. M., illus. see Cramer, Kimberley M.
Bourbonniere, Sylvie, illus. see Keens-Douglas, Richardo.
Bourbonnière, Sylvie, illus. see Lacoursiere, Patrick.
Bour-Chollet, Céline, et al. Hora. Bour-Chollet, Céline et al, trs. (p. 797)
Bourcier, Cammy S. Barack Obama. (p. 137)
—Carlos Mencia. (p. 270)
—Malcolm X. (p. 1083)
Bourcier, Noel. André Kertész. (p. 72)
Bourdeau, Marje. Baby's 1st Times, Baby's 1st Rhymes. (p. 128)
Bourdin, Samuel, photos by see Gingeras, Alison M.
Boureau, Silvere, illus. see Hacker, Caryn Sabes.
Bourgeau, Vincent, illus. see Ramadier, Cédric.
Bourgeois, Elodie, tr. see Verrept, Paul.
Bourgeois, Elodie, tr. see Wormell, Chris, et al.
Bourgeois, Paulette. Benjamin et Sa Petite Soeur. (p. 164)
—Benjamin et Son Voisinage. (p. 164)
—Bravo Benjamin! Clark, Brenda, illus. (p. 224)
—Dirt on Dirt. Newbigging, Martha, illus. (p. 446)
—Finders Keepers for Franklin. Clark, Brenda, illus. (p. 587)
—Fire Fighters. LaFave, Kim, illus. (p. 590)
—Franklin & Harriet. Clark, Brenda, illus. (p. 630)
—Franklin & the Baby-Sitter. (p. 630)
—Franklin & the Bubble Gum. (p. 630)
—Franklin & the Computer. Clark, Brenda, illus. (p. 630)
—Franklin & the Thunderstorm. Clark, Brenda, illus. (p. 630)
—Franklin & the Tooth Fairy. Clark, Brenda, illus. (p. 630)
—Franklin Es un Mandon. Varela, Alejandra López, tr. (p. 630)
—Franklin Fibs. Clark, Brenda, illus. (p. 630)
—Franklin Goes to the Hospital. (p. 630)
—Franklin Has a Sleepover. Clark, Brenda, illus. (p. 630)
—Franklin in the Dark: 25th Anniversary Edition. Clark, Brenda, illus. (p. 630)
—Franklin in the Dark. (p. 630)
—Franklin in the Dark. Clark, Brenda, illus. (p. 630)
—Franklin Is Bossy. Clark, Brenda, illus. (p. 630)
—Franklin Is Lost. Clark, Brenda, illus. (p. 630)
—Franklin Is Messy. Clark, Brenda, illus. (p. 630)
—Franklin Rides a Bike. Clark, Brenda, illus. (p. 630)
—Franklin Says I Love You. (p. 630)
—Franklin Says I Love You. Clark, Brenda, illus. (p. 630)
—Franklin Wants a Badge. Clark, Brenda, illus. (p. 630)
—Franklin Wants a Pet. Clark, Brenda, illus. (p. 630)
—Franklin y el Dia de Accion de Gracias. Varela, Alejandra López, tr. (p. 630)
—Franklin's Baby Sister. (p. 631)
—Franklin's Baby Sister. Clark, Brenda, illus. (p. 631)
—Franklin's Bad Day. Clark, Brenda, illus. (p. 631)
—Franklin's Blanket. Clark, Brenda, illus. (p. 631)
—Franklin's Christmas: A Sticker Activity Book. Clark, Brenda, illus. (p. 631)
—Franklin's Christmas Gift. Clark, Brenda, illus. (p. 631)
—Franklin's Class Trip. Clark, Brenda, illus. (p. 631)
—Franklin's Family Treasury. Clark, Brenda, illus. (p. 631)
—Franklin's Halloween. Clark, Brenda, illus. (p. 631)
—Franklin's New Friend. (p. 631)
—Franklin's New Friend. Clark, Brenda, illus. (p. 631)
—Franklin's School Play. Clark, Brenda, illus. (p. 631)
—Franklin's Secret Club. (p. 631)
—Franklin's Secret Club. Clark, Brenda, illus. (p. 631)
—Franklin's Soapbox Derby. (p. 631)
—Fun with Franklin: A Learning to Read Book. Clark, Brenda, illus. (p. 648)
—Garbage Collectors. LaFave, Kim, illus. (p. 655)
—Hurry up, Franklin. Clark, Brenda, illus. (p. 830)
—Manta de Franklin. Varela, Alejandra López, tr. (p. 1088)
—Neighborhood. (p. 1240)
—Nouvel Ami pour Benjamin. (p. 1268)
—Oma's Quilt. (p. 1288)
—Police Workers. LaFave, Kim, illus. (p. 1380)
—Postal Workers. LaFave, Kim, illus. (p. 1387)
—Soleil. Slavin, Bill, illus. (p. 1607)
Bourgeois, Paulette, jt. auth. see Bourgeois, Paulette.
Bourgeois, Paulette, jt. auth. see Jennings, Sharon.
Bourgeois, Paulette & Bourgeois, Paulette. Firefighters. LaFave, Kim, illus. (p. 591)
—Franklin's New Friend. Clark, Brenda, illus. (p. 631)
—Postal Workers. LaFave, Kim, illus. (p. 1387)
Bourgeois, Paulette & Clark, Brenda. Franklin & the Contest. (p. 630)
—Franklin & the Cookies. (p. 630)
—Franklin & the Gecko Games. (p. 630)
—Franklin & the Little Sisters. (p. 630)
—Franklin & the Scooter. (p. 630)
—Franklin Celebrates. (p. 630)
—Franklin in the Stars. (p. 630)
—Franklin Makes a Deal. (p. 630)
—Franklin Snoops. (p. 630)
—Franklin Stays Up. Sinker, Alice, illus. (p. 630)
—Franklin the Detective. (p. 630)
—Franklin's Library Book. (p. 631)
—Franklin's Nickname. Southern, Shelley, tr. (p. 631)
—Franklin's Pumpkin. Southern, Shelley, illus. (p. 631)
—Franklin's Spaceship. (p. 631)
—Franklin's Surprise. (p. 631)
—Franklin's Trading Cards. (p. 631)
—Franklin's Ups & Downs. (p. 631)
Bourgeois, Paulette & Paulette, Bourgeois. Principe y el Mendigo. Jorisch, Stéphane, illus. (p. 1406)
Bourgeois, Paulette & Slavin, Bill. Starting with Space: The Moon. (p. 1644)
Bourgeois, Paulette, et al. Franklin's Big Book of Stories: A Collection of 6 First Readers. (p. 631)
—Franklin's Reading Club. (p. 631)
Bourget, Laëtitia. Aprendizaje Amoroso. (p. 93)
Bourgoing, Pascale de. Apfel. (p. 91)
Bourgoing, Pascale De, see De Bourgoing, Pascale.
Bourgoing, Pascale De, see Jeunesse, Gallimard & De Bourgoing, Pascale.
Bourgoing, Pascale De, see Kniffe, Sophie & De Bourgoing, Pascale.
Bourgoing, Pascale De, see Perols, Sylvaine & De Bourgoing, Pascale.
Bourgoing, Pascale De, et al. Water. (p. 1862)
Bourgonje, Chantal, illus. see Holcroft, Trevor.
Bourguignon, Laurence. Heart in the Pocket. D'Heur, Valérie, illus. (p. 759)
Bourke, Anthony & Rendall, John. Christian the Lion: The True Story of a Lion's Search for a Home. (p. 312)
Bourke, Bob, jt. auth. see Markrich, Mike.
Bourke, Debra. First Day at Bouddi School. Cowley, Ray B., illus. (p. 594)
Bourke, John-Francis, illus. see Hudson, Cheryl Willis.
Bourke, John-Francis, illus. see Willis Hudson, Cheryl.
Bourke, John-Francis, photos by see Hudson, Cheryl Willis.
Bourke, Kenna. Deadly Animals High Beginning Book with Online Access. (p. 417)
—Grammar Lab (p. 706)
—Grammar Lab, Level 1. (p. 706)
—Grammar Lab, Level 2 (p. 706)
—Jeff Corwin: Wild Man. (p. 911)
—Lost: the Mystery of Amelia Earhart High Beginning Book with Online Access. (p. 1056)
—Slime: the Wonderful World of Mucus Low Intermediate Book with Online Access. (p. 1590)
—So Cute! Beginning Book with Online Access. (p. 1602)
Bourke, Nike & Danalis, Stella. What the Sky Knows. (p. 1893)
Bournakis, Maria, illus. see Vardamaskos, Angela.
Bourne, Angela K., jt. ed. see Cini, Michelle.
Bourne, C. L. Sam the Big Blue Bear Bourne, C. L., illus. (p. 1507)
Bourne, Edward Gaylord. Columbus, Ramon Pane, & the Beginnings of American Anthropology. (p. 346)
Bourne, Joanna. Spymaster's Lady. (p. 1636)
Bourne, Malcolm. Tales of Ordinary Madness. (p. 1702)
Bourne, Sylvia. Animal Tales. (p. 80)
Bourne, Tracey. Not Just a Dream! (p. 1267)
Bourque, Jeremiah, tr. see Aki, Katsu.
Bourque, Jeremiah, tr. see Akino, Matsuri.
Bourque, Jeremiah, tr. see Mashima, Hiro.
Bourrouet, Jonathan, illus. see Bumpers, Katrina B.
Bourseiller, Philippe, photos by see Jankéliowitch, Anne.
Boursin, Didier. Easy Origami. (p. 500)
—Folding for Fun: Origami for Ages 4 & Up. (p. 611)
—Paper Folding Fun. (p. 1322)
Boursnell, Clive, photos by see Peters, Rosalind.
Bouse, Biff, illus. see Carroll, John.
Bouse, Susan & Gamble, Adam. Good Night Denver. Veno, Joe, illus. (p. 699)
Boushell, Mike. Freshman Five. (p. 636)
—Gridiron Hero. (p. 723)
Bousquet, Anthea. Counting St. Lucian Style: A delightfully illustrated counting rhyme set in the Caribbean island of St. Lucia. Sandiford, Ted, illus. (p. 371)
—Lucy's St. Lucian Rhyming Alphabet: The ABCs of Caribbean Culture in Upbeat Rhyming Verse. Sandiford, Ted, illus. (p. 1063)
Bousquet, Mark. Adventures of the Five: the Coming of Frost. (p. 23)
Boussarhane, Ericka. Sam & the Boogie Man. (p. 1506)
Bousum, Julie, illus. see Johnson, Gerald J. J.
Boutan, Mila. Renoir & Me. (p. 1460)
—Rousseau: Art Activity Pack. (p. 1491)
Boutavant, Marc. Around the World with Mouk. (p. 101)
Boutavant, Marc, illus. see Butchart, Pamela.
Boutavant, Marc, illus. see Chronicle Books Staff & Leuck, Laura.
Boutavant, Marc, illus. see Davies, Nicola.
Boutavant, Marc, illus. see Desbordes, Astrid.
Boutavant, Marc, illus. see Goldie, Sonia.
Boutavant, Marc, illus. see Guibert, Emmanuel.
Boutavant, Marc, jt. auth. see Guibert, Emmanuel.
Boutenko, Victoria. Green Smoothie Magic. Korobkina, Katya, illus. (p. 722)
Boutet de Monvel, Maurice. Story of Joan of Arc. (p. 1658)
Boutheyette, Valerie, illus. see Teis, Sean P.
Bouthyette, Valerie. Leprechaun Trap. (p. 993)
Bouthyette, Valerie, illus. see Arline-Hicks, Patience & Hicks, Wendi N.
Bouthyette, Valerie, illus. see Costello, Judi.
Bouthyette, Valerie, illus. see Dewees-Gilger, Connie.
Bouthyette, Valerie, illus. see Dowling, Iris Gray.
Bouthyette, Valerie, illus. see Hladik, Terry L.
Bouthyette, Valerie, illus. see Lindemer, C. R.
Boutilier, Joanna. Pigs Aren't Dirty, Bears Aren't Slow: And Other Truths about Misunderstood Animals. Hodson, Ben, illus. (p. 1358)
Boutin, Arnaud. My Beastly Book of Monsters: 150 Ways to Doodle, Scribble, Color & Draw. (p. 1196)
—What's New? What's Missing? What's Different? (p. 1898)
Boutin, Lesa. Amanda Noble, Zookeeper Extraordinaire. Jackson, Bernice, ed. (p. 52)
Bouton, Warren Hussey. Captain's Return: A Spooky Tale from Nantucket. Locke, Barbara Kauffmann, illus. (p. 264)
—Oliver's Ghost: A Spooky Tale from Nantucket. Locke, Barbara K., illus. (p. 1286)
Boutros, Gladys. Bubba & the Sweet Pea: US English Edition. Balogh, Andras, illus. (p. 233)
—Bubba & the Sweet Pea. Balogh, Andras, illus. (p. 233)
Boutros, Jill, et al. Lebanon A to Z: A Middle Eastern Mosaic. Sabbagh, Tatiana, illus. (p. 986)
Boutte, Brock. Gris-Gris & the Cypress Tree: Louisiana. (p. 724)
Bova, Ben. Powersat. (p. 1391)
Bova, Della L. Adventures of Pono: A Puppy Dog's Tale. (p. 21)
Bove, C. M. Sebastian's Secret Excuses to Avoid Cleaning His Room: (Do Not Let Adults Read This Book!!!) (p. 1539)
Bove, Candace Scoble. Calypso: A Day in the Life of a Puppy. (p. 255)
Bové, Lorelay, illus. see LaReau, Kara.
Bove, Neysa, illus. see Merberg, Julie.
Bover, Annie. Mooncorn. (p. 1172)
Bovi, J. K. Wicked Haints: A Savannah Ghost Story (p. 1927)
Bovier, Lionel & Stroun, Fabrice, eds. David Robbins - The Velvet Grind: Selected Essays (1980-2004) (p. 411)
Bovsun, Mara, jt. auth. see Zullo, Allan.
Bow, Erin. Plain Kate. (p. 1366)
—Sorrow's Knot. (p. 1614)
Bow, James. Animal Mysteries Revealed. (p. 79)
—Aston Martin. (p. 108)
—Baseball Science. (p. 141)
—Binge Drinking. (p. 188)
—Cycling Science. (p. 397)
—Dealing with Loss. (p. 418)
—Deep Space Extremes. (p. 423)
—Earth Mysteries Revealed. (p. 496)
—Earth's Climate Change: Carbon Dioxide Overload. (p. 498)
—Earth's Secrets. (p. 498)
—Electrical Engineering & the Science of Circuits. (p. 509)
—Energy from Earth's Core: Geothermal Energy. (p. 528)
—Energy from the Sun: Solar Power. (p. 528)
—Fathom Five: The Unwritten Books. (p. 577)
—Forests Inside Out. (p. 618)
—Gettysburg. (p. 670)
—Grasslands Inside Out. (p. 712)
—Hidden Worlds. (p. 776)
—Impossible Science. (p. 862)
—Lamborghini. Crabtree, ed. (p. 972)
—Mountains Inside Out. (p. 1181)
—Navy Seals. (p. 1238)
—Rescue Missions. (p. 1462)
—Saving Endangered Plants & Animals. (p. 1517)
—Secret Signs. (p. 1543)
—Space Mysteries Revealed. (p. 1619)
—Tundras Inside Out. (p. 1796)
—Unwritten Girl. (p. 1824)
—Wetlands Inside Out. (p. 1877)
—What Is the Executive Branch? (p. 1890)
—What Is the Legislative Branch? (p. 1890)
—Why We Need Minerals. (p. 1926)
—Young City: The Unwritten Books. (p. 1978)
Bow, James, jt. auth. see Crabtree Publishing Company Staff.
Bow, James, jt. auth. see Crabtree Staff.
Bow, James, jt. auth. see Miller, Reagan.
Bow, Patricia. Bone Flute (p. 208)
—Chimpanzee Rescue: Changing the Future for Endangered Wildlife. (p. 306)

—Prism Blade. (p. 1407)
—Ruby Kingdom. (p. 1493)
—Spiral Maze (p. 1628)
—Tennis Science. (p. 1720)
Bowater, Alan. Pig Called Pete. Pascoe, Pete, illus. (p. 1357)
—Pig Called Pete Meets a Cat Called Kitty. Pascoe, Pete, illus. (p. 1357)
—Pig Called Pete Meets a Cow Called Carlotta. Pascoe, Pete, illus. (p. 1357)
—Pig Called Pete Meets a Dog Called Doug. Pascoe, Pete, illus. (p. 1357)
—Pig Called Pete Meets a Sheep Called Sean. Pascoe, Pete, illus. (p. 1357)
Bowater, Charlie, illus. see Thornton, D. S.
Bowater, Charlie, jt. auth. see King, Caro.
Bowcut~, ~Jan. Seasons of Poetry: A Guide for Young Writers Grades 3-6. (p. 1538)
Bowden, Aberdeen O. Day Before Yesterday in America. (p. 412)
Bowden, Cecelia, illus. see Hopper, Missy.
Bowden, Mary Ellen & Rosner, Linda. Joseph Priestley, Radical Thinker. (p. 926)
Bowden, Poona. Juno Wonders. (p. 936)
—Juno¡ 's Dromen. (p. 936)
Bowden, Rob. Africa. (p. 26)
—Africa South of the Sahara (p. 26)
—Asia. (p. 106)
—Building Homes for Tomorrow. (p. 239)
—Cape Town. Maconachie, Roy, photos by. (p. 262)
—Earth's Water Crisis. (p. 498)
—Energy Sources: The Impact of Science & Technology. (p. 528)
—Environments. (p. 532)
—Food & Water. (p. 613)
—Food Industry. (p. 613)
—Istanbul. Parker, Edward, photos by. (p. 893)
—Jerusalem. (p. 914)
—Middle East & North Africa (p. 1137)
—Trade. (p. 1776)
Bowden, Rob, jt. auth. see Brownlie Bojang, Ali.
Bowden, Rob, jt. auth. see Wilson, Rosie.
Bowden, Rob, photos by see Barber, Nicola.
Bowden, Rob, photos by see Mason, Paul.
Bowden, Rob & Foley, Ronan. Focus on Ireland. (p. 610)
Bowden, Rob & Maconachie, Roy. Cairo. (p. 252)
Bowden, Rob & Ransome, Galya. Focus on Russia. (p. 611)
Bowden, Rob & Wilson, Rosie. Ancient Africa (p. 67)
Bowden, Rob, et al. African Culture (p. 27)
—Ancient Africa (p. 67)
—Changing Africa (p. 290)
Bowden, Roger. Tales from Wild Westernville. (p. 1702)
Bowdish, Lynea. How to Be Nice— & Other Lessons I Didn't Learn. Gray, Leslie, illus. (p. 815)
—With Courage: Seven Women Who Changed America. (p. 1942)
Bowditch, Eden Unger. Atomic Weight of Secrets: Or the Arrival of the Mysterious Men in Black. (p. 113)
—Atomic Weight of Secrets or the Arrival of the Mysterious Men in Black. (p. 113)
Bowditch, Kevin E. & Bowditch, Mark A. Oxyfuel Gas Welding Answer Key. (p. 1316)
Bowditch, Kevin E., et al. Oxyfuel Gas Welding. (p. 1316)
Bowditch, Mark A., jt. auth. see Bowditch, Kevin E.
BOWE, Andi. Alphabet book 1: a to z in song & Verse. (p. 49)
—Alphabet book 2: a to z in song & Verse. (p. 49)
Bowe, Brian J. Clash: Punk Rock Band. (p. 327)
—Judas Priest: Metal Gods. (p. 930)
—Ramones: American Punk Rock Band. (p. 1438)
Bowe, Clara Brown. Tubba Toothpaste. (p. 1795)
Bowe, Julie. Birthday Glamour! (p. 192)
—Face the Music. (p. 560)
—Formula for Friends. (p. 620)
—My Best Frenemy. (p. 1196)
—My Extra Best Friend. (p. 1202)
—My Forever Friends. (p. 1209)
—My Last Best Friend. (p. 1211)
—My New Best Friend. (p. 1216)
—Pompom Problems. (p. 1382)
Bowe, Kristine. Seers. (p. 1548)
Bowen, Acton. Escape the Noise: A Thirty-Day Devotional Journey for Students. (p. 535)
Bowen, Ann & Pallister, John. Tackling Geography Coursework. (p. 1694)
Bowen, Anne. I Know an Old Teacher. Gammell, Stephen, illus. (p. 840)
—Que Hacen los Maestros? (Despues de Que Te Vas de la Escuela) Gott, Barry, illus. (p. 1423)
—Scooter in the Outside. Carter, Abby, illus. (p. 1529)
—What Do Teachers Do (after You Leave School)? Gott, Barry, illus. (p. 1882)
Bowen, Anne M. I Loved You Before You Were Born. Shed, Greg, illus. (p. 844)
Bowen, Barbara R. Please! Don't Make Me Kiss Those Pink Socks. (p. 1373)
Bowen, Betsy. Dhegdheer: A Scary Somali Folktale. (p. 433)
Bowen, Betsy, illus. see Hoover, Helen.
Bowen, Betsy, illus. see Root, Phyllis.
Bowen, Carl. Black Anchor Tortosa, Wilson & Fuentes, Benny, illus. (p. 194)
—Quarterback Rush Garcia, Eduardo, illus. (p. 1422)
—Shadow Squadron (p. 1558)
Bowen, Carl & Fuentes, Benny. BMX Breakthrough Sandoval, Gerardo, illus. (p. 204)
—Critical Strike. Tortosa, Wilson, illus. (p. 383)
—Dark Agent Tortosa, Wilson, illus. (p. 407)
—Dragon Teeth. Tortosa, Wilson, illus. (p. 478)
—Eagle Down Tortosa, Wilson, illus. (p. 492)
—Elite Infantry. Tortosa, Wilson, illus. (p. 513)
—Guardian Angel. Tortosa, Wilson, illus. (p. 728)
—Long Shadow. Tortosa, Wilson, illus. (p. 1047)
—Phantom Sun Tortosa, Wilson, illus. (p. 1349)
—Rogue Agent. Tortosa, Wilson, illus. (p. 1485)
—Sand Spider Tortosa, Wilson, illus. (p. 1510)
—Sea Demon Tortosa, Wilson, illus. (p. 1534)
—Sniper Shield Tortosa, Wilson, illus. (p. 1598)
—Steel Hammer. Tortosa, Wilson, illus. (p. 1646)
—White Needle Tortosa, Wilson, illus. (p. 1913)
Bowen, Carl & Poe, Edgar Allen. Murders in the Rue Morgue Dimaya, Emerson & Calero, Dennis, illus. (p. 1192)
Bowen, Cynthia Wiesner. Tamika & Grandpa Jake. (p. 1704)
Bowen, Dean, illus. see Castles, Jennifer.
Bowen, Deangelo. Halloween Surprise. (p. 739)
Bowen, Debbie, ed. see Sargent, Dave.
Bowen, Fred. Dugout Rivals (p. 489)
—Final Cut (p. 586)
—Full Court Fever (p. 646)
—Go for the Goal! (p. 686)
—Golden Glove (p. 694)
—Hardcourt Comeback (p. 748)
—Kid Coach (p. 951)
—No Easy Way: The Story of Ted Williams & the Last .400 Season. Pyle, Charles S. & Pyle, Chuck, illus. (p. 1258)
—Off the Rim (p. 1279)
—On the Line (p. 1290)
—Out of Bounds (p. 1311)
—Perfect Game (p. 1341)
—Playoff Dreams (p. 1373)
—Quarterback Season (p. 1423)
—Real Hoops (p. 1448)
—Soccer Team Upset (p. 1603)
—T. J. 's Secret Pitch (p. 1694)
—Throwing Heat (p. 1745)
—Touchdown Trouble (p. 1772)
—Winners Take All (p. 1937)
Bowen, Gary. Maren's Nest. (p. 1092)
Bowen, J. L. Ryker's Revenge. (p. 1499)
Bowen, James & Jenkins, Garry. My Name Is Bob. (p. 1215)
Bowen, Jessica Tiare. Park Avenue Pound Puppy. (p. 1324)
Bowen, Joe. Real Winners Don't Quit. (p. 1449)
Bowen, John & Patten, Robert, eds. Palgrave Advances in Charles Dickens Studies. (p. 1320)
Bowen, Joshua. Boy Called Jesse. (p. 217)
Bowen, Julie. Sometimes I Can't Talk Well. (p. 1610)
Bowen, Lance. Keiki's First Word Book. (p. 948)
—Keiki's Second Word Book. (p. 948)
Bowen, Lance, illus. see Ching, Carrie.
Bowen, Laura. Julia C. (p. 932)
Bowen, Marvin. Adventures of the Fluffytail Mouse. (p. 23)
Bowen, Michael Dale. Edwarda Opatowska Saved My Life! (p. 505)
Bowen, Rhys, pseud. Evan Blessed (p. 540)
—Evan's Gate. (p. 541)
Bowen, Richard. Captain James Cook: British Explorer. (p. 264)
—Mei Mei - Little Sister: Portraits from a Chinese Orphanage. (p. 1124)
—Socrates: Greek Philosopher. (p. 1605)
—Vincent Van Gogh: Modern Artist. (p. 1843)
Bowen, Richard A., jt. auth. see Moreno, Barry.
Bowen, Robert Sidney. Dave Dawson at Guadalcanal. (p. 410)
—Dave Dawson, Flight Lieutenant. (p. 410)
Bowen, Shane. Out of the Darkness. (p. 1311)
Bowen, Sherry. Little Panda. Wallace, Chad, illus. (p. 1033)
Bowen, Victoria. War's End. (p. 1859)
Bower, Brittany, illus. see Bower, Gary.
Bower, Bugs. Stage Band Jazz Rhythms & Punky Blues: For All Instruments. (p. 1638)
—Stage Bank Jazz Duets: For All Instruments. (p. 1638)
Bower, Gary. Cody's Castle: Encouraging Others. Bower, Jan, illus. (p. 338)
—Garden Where I Grow: And Other Poems for Cultivating a Happy Family. Bower, Jan, illus. (p. 656)
—I'm a Michigan Kid! Bower, Jan, illus. (p. 858)
—I'm a Michigan Kid Coloring & Activity Book. Bower, Jan & Bower, Brittany, illus. (p. 858)
—Jingle in My Pocket. Bower, Jan, illus. (p. 918)
—Mommy Love. Bower, Jan, illus. (p. 1162)
—Person I Marry. Bower, Jan, illus. (p. 1344)
—There's a Party in Heaven! Bower, Jan, illus. (p. 1731)
Bower, Jan, illus. see Bower, Gary.
Bower, Jan, illus. see Layne, Steven L.
Bower, John. Lingering Spirit: A Photographic Tribute to Indiana's Fading, Forlorn, & Forgotten Places. (p. 1019)
Bower, Kevin. Fly Rex Fly. (p. 609)
—Gilbert Grumble. (p. 676)
Bower, Reuben Edward. Unreached Indian; A Treatise on Indian Life & Indian Missions. (p. 1822)
Bower, Tamara. How the Amazon Queen Fought the Prince of Egypt. Bower, Tamara, illus. (p. 812)
—Shipwrecked Sailor: An Egyptian Tale with Hieroglyphs. Bower, Tamara, illus. (p. 1567)
Bower's 2008-2009 4th Grade Class, jt. auth. see Coppock, Phil.
Bowers, A., et al. Mushrooms of the World with Pictures to Color. (p. 1193)
Bowers, Annette. This Reminds Me of Christmas. (p. 1737)
Bowers, Chad, jt. auth. see Sims, Chris.
Bowers, Chuck. Leprechaun Legacy. (p. 993)
Bowers, Elizabeth Shimer, jt. auth. see Ford, Carol A.
Bowers, Elizabeth Shimer & Stark, Clifford D. Living with Sports Injuries. (p. 1042)
Bowers, Jack D. Coming of Age. (p. 348)
Bowers, Jennifer J. Incomplete Patience Only Made Me Stronger. (p. 869)
Bowers, Jenny. Sticker Style: House. Bowers, Jenny, illus. (p. 1650)
Bowers, Jenny, illus. see Big Picture Press, Big Picture.
Bowers, Jenny, illus. see Williams, Rachel.
Bowers, John. Life of Abraham Lincoln. (p. 1011)
Bowers, Linda. Spotlight on Reading Comprehension Making Inferences & Drawing Conclusions. (p. 1634)
Bowers, Linda, et al. No Glamour Language & Reasoning. (p. 1258)
—Social Language Development Test Elementary. (p. 1604)
—Spotlight on Reading Comprehension Characters & Actions. (p. 1634)
—Spotlight on Reading Comprehension Comparing & Contrasting. (p. 1634)
—Spotlight on Reading Comprehension Figurative Language & Exclusion. (p. 1634)
—Spotlight on Reading Comprehension Paraphrasing & Summarizing. (p. 1634)
—Spotlight on Reading Comprehension Sequencing & Problem Solving. (p. 1634)
—Tasks of Problems Solving Elementary. (p. 1707)
—Word Test 2 Elementary Examiner's Manual. (p. 1951)
Bowers, Mary. Faerie Box. (p. 562)
Bowers, Renata. Frieda B. & the Zillabeast. Chesworth, Michael, illus. (p. 637)
Bowers, Shallen. Ladybug & Me: Rainy Days. (p. 971)
Bowers, Tim. New Home. (p. 1245)
Bowers, Tim, illus. see ABDO Publishing Company Staff.
Bowers, Tim, illus. see Alexander, Kwame.
Bowers, Tim, illus. see Clements, Andrew.
Bowers, Tim, illus. see Dickey, R. A.
Bowers, Tim, illus. see Findlay, Lisa.
Bowers, Tim, illus. see Gutman, Dan.
Bowers, Tim, illus. see Heiligman, Deborah.
Bowers, Tim, illus. see Holub, Joan.
Bowers, Tim, illus. see Lewis, J. Patrick, et al.
Bowers, Tim, illus. see Lewis, J. Patrick.
Bowers, Tim, illus. see Lobel, Anita.
Bowers, Tim, illus. see Lodge, Bernard.
Bowers, Tim, illus. see Moran, Alex.
Bowers, Tim, illus. see Palatini, Margie.
Bowers, Tim, illus. see Rylant, Cynthia.
Bowers, Tim, illus. see Scillian, Devin.
Bowers, Tim, illus. see Sierra, Judy.
Bowers, Tim, illus. see Wessels, Marcie.
Bowers, Tim, illus. see Yamaguchi, Kristi.
Bowers, Tim, jt. auth. see Bar-el, Dan.
Bowers, Vivien. Hey Canada! Pavlovic, Milan, illus. (p. 774)
—Wow Canada! Exploring This Land from Coast to Coast to Coast. Eastman, Dianne et al, illus. (p. 1962)
Bowes, Aurette. Someone's Daughter. (p. 1609)
Bowes, Brian, illus. see Brenner, Summer.
Bowes, Deborah. Ballet Book: The Young Performer's Guide to Classical Dance. Pawelak, Lydia, photos by. (p. 134)
Bowes, John P. Black Hawk & the War of 1832: Removal in the North. (p. 196)
—Choctaw. (p. 309)
Bowes, Kyle J. Crossroads of the Other World. (p. 385)
Bowes-Brooks, Yvonne. 100 Ways to Become a Successful Student: Motivational Book for Students. (p. 1999)
Bowie, Barbara Kay. Ready for School: An Activity & Story Book for Parents & Children Entering Kindergarten. (p. 1447)
Bowie, Bob. St Marks Gospel & the Christian Faith. (p. 1638)
Bowie, C. W. Busy Fingers. Willingham, Fred, illus. (p. 246)
—Laboriosos deditos de las Manos. Canetti, Yanitzia, tr. (p. 970)
Bowker, Margie, illus. see Rouse, Walt.
Bowker, Paul. Girls' Lacrosse. (p. 680)
—Kansas City Royals. (p. 943)
—Playing Pro Football. (p. 1372)
—Tampa Bay Rays. (p. 1704)
Bowker, Paul D. New Orleans Pelicans. (p. 1246)
Bowkett, Stephen. Passenger & Other Adventures. (p. 1326)
Bowkett, Steve. Catch Minitales: Short Science Fiction Stories with a Sting! (p. 279)
—Detective Files Burroughs, David, illus. (p. 431)
Bowlby, Linda S. Future Hope. Helms, Dana, illus. (p. 651)
—How Amazon Got Her Name. Helms, Dana, illus. (p. 804)
—Is That So. Helms, Dana, illus. (p. 890)
—Nasaria's Family/la Familia de Nasaria. Helms, Dana, illus. (p. 1230)
—Nentuck's New Family. Helms, Dana, illus. (p. 1241)
—Rock Garden. Helms, Dana, illus. (p. 1482)
Bowler, Ann Martin. All about Korea: Stories, Songs, Crafts & More. Barg, Soosoonam, illus. (p. 42)
—History of the Paso Robles Inn: More Than a Century of Pride. (p. 785)
Bowler, Ann Martin & Bowler, Anna. Gecko's Complaint: A Balinese Folktale. Sukanada, I. Gusti Made, illus. (p. 659)
Bowler, Ann Martin & Tay-Audouard, Lak-Khee. Adventures of the Treasure Fleet: China Discovers the World. (p. 23)
Bowler, Anna, jt. auth. see Bowler, Ann Martin.
Bowler, Colin, illus. see Volke, Gordon.
Bowler, Colin, jt. auth. see Bell, Frank.
Bowler, David, jt. auth. see Harte, Lawrence.
Bowler, Michael J. Children of the Knight. (p. 302)
—Children of the Knight [Library Edition]. (p. 302)
Bowler, Peter J. Interview with Charles Darwin. (p. 881)
Bowler, Tim. Buried Thunder. (p. 243)
—Frozen Fire. (p. 645)
—Playing Dead. (p. 1372)
—Storm Catchers. (p. 1655)
Bowles & Carver. Old English Cuts & Illustrations: For Artists & Craftspeople. (p. 1283)
Bowles, Angelo. Mix-Up: Swift the Cat-Human Book 1. Bowles, Charlene, illus. (p. 1156)
—Swift the Cat-Human: Omnibus. Bowles, Charlene, illus. (p. 1690)
Bowles, B. R. Pauley the Pancake Boy. (p. 1331)
Bowles, Carol, illus. see Albert, Toni Diana.
Bowles, Charlene, illus. see Bowles, Angelo.
Bowles, Doug, illus. see Fredericks, Anthony D.
Bowles, Doug, illus. see Herzog, Brad.
Bowles, Doug, illus. see McCafferty, Catherine.
Bowles, Doug, illus. see Schulz, Walter A.
Bowles, Doug, illus. see Schulz, Walter A. & Schultz, Walter A.
Bowles, Doug, illus. see Scillian, Devin & Scillian, Corey.
Bowles, Doug, jt. auth. see Herzog, Brad.
Bowles, Janice, illus. see Jones, Tammy & Smith, Carrie.
Bowles, Jennifer, illus. see Hawkins, Linda J.
Bowles, Michael J. N., illus. see Michels, Dia L.
Bowles, Michael J. N., photos by see Michels, Dia L.
Bowles, Michael J. N., photos by see Michels, Dia.
Bowles, Paula. Little Lou & the Woolly Mammoth. (p. 1031)
—Scary Mary. (p. 1520)
—What Goes Up. Bowles, Paula, illus. (p. 1885)
Bowlin, Serina. Wandering Sam. Thrasher, Brian, illus. (p. 1856)
Bowlin, William Harrison, jt. auth. see Cooper, Ann Goode.
Bowling, Athena. Malice: The Magicka Barney Chronicles (p. 1083)
Bowling, Joyce E. & Sester, Richard. Path of Stitches (p. 1328)
Bowling, Sarah, jt. auth. see Hickey, Marilyn.
Bowlsby, Tina Marie, illus. see Pereira, William.
Bowman, Andy. Bobby Beaver Learns a Lesson. Travis, Stephanie, illus. (p. 206)
—Indian Slim. Travis, Stephanie, illus. (p. 871)
—Pokey's Garden. Travis, Stephanie, illus. (p. 1378)
—Quilt. Travis, Stephanie, illus. (p. 1428)
Bowman, Anne. Count Them While You Can... Bowman, Anne, illus. (p. 370)
Bowman, Bianca. National Geographic Kids Funny Fill-In: My Pirate Adventure. Tharp, Jason, illus. (p. 1232)
Bowman, Brent, illus. see Fox, Stephen.
Bowman, Challece. Sarah's Camping Trip. (p. 1514)
Bowman, Chris. American Bison. (p. 60)
—Animal Control Officer. (p. 77)
—Attack on Pearl Harbor. (p. 114)
—Bald Eagles. (p. 133)
—Coyotes. (p. 374)
—Firefighter. (p. 591)
—Fossils. (p. 623)
—Gaboon Vipers. (p. 652)
—German Shepherds. (p. 666)
—Golden Retrievers. (p. 695)
—Hindenburg Disaster. (p. 780)
—Iguanas. (p. 856)
—Inland Taipans. (p. 874)
—Judy Blume. (p. 931)
—Labrador Retrievers. (p. 970)
—Minerals. (p. 1146)
—Monster Airplanes. (p. 1166)
—Monster Bulldozers. (p. 1166)
—Oil Field Worker. (p. 1282)
—Parrots. (p. 1325)
—Police Officer. (p. 1380)
—Pronghorn. (p. 1411)
—Raccoons. (p. 1430)
—Rainbow Boas. (p. 1435)
—Rocks. (p. 1483)
—Shel Silverstein. (p. 1564)
—Ski Patroller. (p. 1584)
—Soil. (p. 1606)
—Special Forces Operator. (p. 1623)
—Tree Frogs. (p. 1783)
—Western Diamondback Rattlesnakes. (p. 1876)
—White-Tailed Deer. (p. 1913)
—Wildebeests. (p. 1931)
Bowman, Crystal. Best Thing about My Birthday. (p. 171)
—Elijah & King Ahab Sokolova, Valerie, illus. (p. 512)
—Is God Always with Me? Kucharik, Elena, illus. (p. 889)
—J Is for Jesus: The Sweetest Story Ever Told Gévry, Claudine, illus. (p. 901)
—Jake's Brave Night Maizel, Karen, illus. (p. 906)
—Jesus Feeds the Five Thousand Sokolova, Valerie, illus. (p. 915)
—Jesus Raises Lazarus Sokolova, Valerie, illus. (p. 916)
—Joshua Crosses the Jordan Sokolova, Valerie, illus. (p. 927)
—Little David & His Best Friend. Hartung, Susan Kathleen & Endersly, Frank, illus. (p. 1026)
—Little David Sings for the King Hartung, Susan Kathleen, illus. (p. 1026)
—Little David's Brave Day Hartung, Susan Kathleen & Endersly, Frank, illus. (p. 1026)
—Mommy, May I Hug the Fish? Christensen, Donna, illus. (p. 1162)
—My ABC Bible Lamb, Stacey, illus. (p. 1195)
—My ABC Prayers Lamb, Stacey, illus. (p. 1195)
—My Grandma & Me: Rhyming Devotions for You & Your Grandchild. Kirkland, Katherine, illus. (p. 1210)
—My Happy Pumpkin: God's Love Shining Through Me (p. 1210)
—One Year Devotions for Preschoolers. Kucharik, Elena, illus. (p. 1298)
—Prodigal Son Sokolova, Valerie, illus. (p. 1409)
—Star for Jesus (p. 1640)
—Star for Jesus Gévry, Claudine, illus. (p. 1640)
—Story of the Resurrection Eggs Johnson, Richard G., illus. (p. 1662)
—Thank You, God, for This Day. Fletcher, Rusty, illus. (p. 1725)
Bowman, Crystal & McKinley, Teri. Our Daily Bread for Kids: 365 Meaningful Moments with God. (p. 1308)
Bowman, Crystal & Taylor, Christy Lee. Devotions for Beginning Readers (p. 432)
Bowman, Crystal, et al. My Read & Rhyme Bible Storybook. Engel, Christiane, illus. (p. 1217)
Bowman, Cynthia Ann & Jaeger, Paul T., eds. Guide to High School Success for Students with Disabilities (p. 730)
Bowman, David. Beyond Bethlehem: A Book of Mormon Christmas. (p. 173)
—Great Plan of Happiness. (p. 717)
—Native Americans of the Eastern Woodlands: Set Of 6. (p. 1234)
—Native Americans of the Eastern Woodlands: Text Pairs. (p. 1234)
—Who's Your Greatest Hero? A Book of Mormon Story Applied to Children. (p. 1921)
—Who's Your Hero? Boxed Set of Five Books. (p. 1921)
—Who's Your Hero?: Book of Mormon Stories Applied to Children Vol. 1 (p. 1921)
—Who's Your Hero?: Book of Mormon Stories Applied to Children. Vol. 3 (p. 1921)
—Who's Your Hero?: Book of Mormon Stories Applied to Children. Vol. 4 (p. 1921)
—Who's Your Hero?: Book of Mormon Stories Applied to Children. Vol. 2 Bowman, David, illus. (p. 1921)
Bowman, Debbie. Happy Tree. (p. 747)
Bowman, Donna H. Big Cats. Wald, Christina, illus. (p. 180)

B

—Did Dinosaurs Eat People? And Other Questions Kids Have about Dinosaurs Dumortier, Marjorie, illus. (p. 436)
—What Is the Moon Made Of? And Other Questions Kids Have about Space Lubach, Peter, illus. (p. 1890)
Bowman, Donna Janell. American Indian Life. (p. 62)
—Sioux: The Past & Present of the Dakota, Lakota, & Nakota. (p. 1580)
Bowman, Donna Janell, jt. auth. see Smith-Llera, Danielle.
Bowman, Erin. Forged. (p. 619)
—Frozen. (p. 645)
—Taken. (p. 1697)
—Vengeance Road. (p. 1835)
Bowman, Ethan T., illus. see Hanes, Marina C.
Bowman, Hootie, illus. see Jones, Bryan.
Bowman, James Cloyd. Pecos Bill: The Greatest Cowboy of All Time. Bannon, Laura, illus. (p. 1334)
Bowman, James Cloyd, jt. auth. see Braun, Eric.
Bowman, James Cloyd, et al. Tales from a Finnish Tupa. Kolehmainen, Aili, tr. (p. 1701)
Bowman, John S. Chronology of Wars. (p. 317)
—Exploration in the World of the Ancients, Revised Edition. (p. 550)
Bowman, Laurel, jt. auth. see Glaser, Jason.
Bowman, Leslie, illus. see Ross, Alice & Ross, Kent.
Bowman, Leslie W., illus. see Blasi, Kathleen McAlpin.
Bowman, Linda. Pay Attention: A Self-Monitoring Program for Classroom & Home Behavior Management. (p. 1331)
Bowman, Lucy. Bugs: Level 1. Rivers, Ruth, illus. (p. 237)
—Christmas Sticker Book. (p. 315)
—Drawing, Doodling & Coloring Book Girls. (p. 481)
—Girl's Activity Book. (p. 679)
—Monkeys. Cooper, Jenny & King, Sue, illus. (p. 1166)
—Rainforest (Level 2) - Internet Referenced. (p. 1436)
—Spooky Doodles. (p. 1631)
—Sticker Dolly Dressing Fashion Long Ago. Baggott, Stella, illus. (p. 1650)
—Sticker Dolly Dressing on Vacation (Revised Cover) (p. 1650)
Bowman, Lucy, jt. auth. see MacLaine, James.
Bowman, Lucy & MacLaine, James. Usborne Little Girls' Activity Book. Watt, Fiona, ed. (p. 1827)
Bowman, Mare. Magic Shell. (p. 1073)
Bowman, Patrick. Arrow Through the Axes. (p. 101)
—Torn from Troy. (p. 1770)
Bowman, Patrick & Homer. Cursed by the Sea God. (p. 395)
Bowman, Patty. Amazing Hamweenie Escapes! Bowman, Patty, illus. (p. 54)
Bowman, Peg. Welcomed by Name: Our Child's Baptism. (p. 1874)
Bowman, Rachael Ann. Sammy the Karate Squirrel. (p. 1508)
Bowman, Robert. Three Vests: The New Brilliants. (p. 1744)
Bowman, Sharon, jt. auth. see DiMarco, Carol.
Bowman, Silas. Daudyhouse. Horst, Melisa, illus. (p. 409)
Bowman, Todd A., illus. see Davis, Bertha M.
Bowman, Todd A., illus. see Davis, Bertha.
Bowman, Vicki. Julie Through the Looking Glass. (p. 932)
Bowman-Kruhm, Mary. Day in the Life of a Firefighter. (p. 413)
—Everything You Need to Know about down Syndrome. (p. 545)
—Leakeys: A Biography (p. 982)
Bowman-Kruhm, Mary & Wirths, Claudine G. Coping with Discrimination & Prejudice. (p. 365)
—Day in the Life of a Firefighter. (p. 413)
Bowness, Kim. Brave Engineers. (p. 223)
Bowring, Jane. Billy & Bella. Worthington, Leonie, illus. (p. 187)
Bowring, John, tr. see Von Chamisso, Adelbert.
Bowser, D. M. Enchanting Tales of Lilith. (p. 523)
Bowser, Katya, illus. see Massey, K. J.
Bowser, Ken. Homesick Penguin: Empathy/Caring for Others. Bowser, Ken, illus. (p. 793)
Bowser, Kimberly M. Circus Dogs. (p. 322)
Bowser, Milton. Cartoon Stories from the Teachings of Buddha. (p. 273)
Bowser, Sean T., illus. see Keefer, Nick T.
Bowsher, Melodie. My Lost & Found Life. (p. 1213)
Bowvayne. Spell Behind Bars. Snow, Alan, illus. (p. 1625)
—Turn in the Grave. Snow, Alan, illus. (p. 1797)
Bowyer, Clifford B. Apprentice of Zoldex: The Imperium Saga: the Adventures of Kyria Brigman, June, illus. (p. 93)
—Awakening: The Imperium Saga: the Adventures of Kyria Brigman, June, illus. (p. 120)
—Changing Tides: The Imperium Saga: Fall of the Imperium Trilogy McWeeney, Tom, illus. (p. 290)
—Child of Prophecy: The Imperium Saga: the Adventures of Kyria Brigman, June, illus. (p. 301)
—Continuing the Passion. Flaherty, Tom, photos by. (p. 361)
—Darkness Within: The Imperium Saga: the Adventures of Kyria Brigman, June, illus. (p. 409)
—Ilfanti & the Orb of Prophecy. Beck, David Michael, illus. (p. 856)
—Impending Storm: The Imperium Saga: Fall of the Imperium Trilogy Lubera, Logan, illus. (p. 862)
—Mage's Council: The Imperium Saga: the Adventures of Kyria Brigman, June, illus. (p. 1071)
—Quest for the Shard: The Imperium Saga: the Adventures of Kyria Brigman, June, illus. (p. 1426)
—Rescue of Nezbith: The Imperium Saga: the Adventures of Kyria Brigman, June, illus. (p. 1462)
—Shard of Time: The Imperium Saga: the Adventures of Kyria Brigman, June, illus. (p. 1561)
—Siege of Zoldex: The Imperium Saga: Fall of the Imperium Trilogy McWeeney, Tom, illus. (p. 1573)
—Spread of Darkness: The Imperium Saga: the Adventures of Kyria Brigman, June, illus. (p. 1634)
—Trapped in Time: The Imperium Saga: the Adventures of Kyria Brigman, June, illus. (p. 1779)
Bowyer, Mary. Tony Turtle & Friends. (p. 1766)
Box, Edna. Soul to Soul: A Journey into the Depths of Self. (p. 1614)
Box Girls Staff, creator. Hannukah Box of Questions TM: Cards to Create Great Conversations. (p. 743)
—Shabbat Box of Questions TM. (p. 1556)
—Thanksgiving Box of Questions TM: Cards to Create Great Conversations. (p. 1726)
Box, Marty & McKenna, Allen. Little Red Beetle Goes Shopping. Box, Marty, illus. (p. 1034)
Box, Paul, illus. see Guinn, Dolores Hollyfield.
Box, Su. Baby Jesus. (p. 126)
—Behind the Scenes Christmas. Blake, Jo, illus. (p. 160)
—First Rainbow. Poole, Susie, illus. (p. 596)
—My Very Own Book of Prayers. Cox, Carolyn, illus. (p. 1221)
—Noah's Ark. East, Jacqueline, illus. (p. 1261)
—You Are Very Special: With a Special Surprise for You Inside! Poole, Susie, illus. (p. 1973)
—You Are Very Special. Poole, Susie, illus. (p. 1973)
Box, Su & Brown, Jo. My Rainbow Book of Everyday Prayers. Brown, Jo, illus. (p. 1217)
Boxall, Peter, jt. auth. see Beckett, Samuel.
Boxer, Barbara. Time to Run. (p. 1753)
Boy Scouts of America Staff, creator. Boy Scouts of Americ: The Official Handbook for Boys. (p. 218)
Boyajian, Ann, illus. see Jelenek, Frank X.
Boyajian, Ann, illus. see Scholastic, Inc. Staff & Keenan, Sheila.
Boyce, Catherine & Boyce, Peter. Royal Tea. Sibert, Stephanie Grace, illus. (p. 1492)
—Tea with the Queen. Sibert, Stephanie Grace, illus. (p. 1708)
Boyce, Charles. Critical Companion to William Shakespeare: A Literary Reference to His Life & Work Vol. 2 (p. 383)
Boyce, D. George. Falklands War. (p. 566)
Boyce, Frank Cottrell. Chitty Chitty Bang Bang & the Race Against Time. Berger, Joe, illus. (p. 308)
—Chitty Chitty Bang Bang Flies Again. Berger, Joe, illus. (p. 308)
—Chitty Chitty Bang Bang over the Moon. Berger, Joe, illus. (p. 308)
—Cosmic. (p. 368)
—Cosmic. Lenton, Steven, illus. (p. 368)
—Desirable. (p. 430)
—Framed Lenton, Steven, illus. (p. 627)
—Framed. (p. 627)
—Framed. Lenton, Steven, illus. (p. 627)
—Millions. (p. 1144)
—Unforgotten Coat. (p. 1817)
—Unforgotten Coat. Hunter, Carl & Heney, Clare, illus. (p. 1817)
Boyce, Frank Cottrell, jt. auth. see Boyce, Frank Cottrell.
Boyce, Frank Cottrell & Boyce, Frank Cottrell. Millions Lenton, Steven, illus. (p. 1144)
—Millions. (p. 1144)
Boyce, Natalie Pope, jt. auth. see Osborne, Mary Pope.
Boyce, Natalie Pope & Osborne, Mary Pope. Abraham Lincoln: A Nonfiction Companion to Magic Tree House - Abe Lincoln at Last! No. 47 Murdocca, Sal, illus. (p. 6)
Boyce, P. M. Mom Taught Values with Quotes & Proverbs - a Memoir of Short Stories by P. M. Boyce. (p. 1161)
Boyce, Paul. Hooks Files: Murder, Arson, Robbery, Amnesia. (p. 795)
Boyce, Peter, jt. auth. see Boyce, Catherine.
Boychuk, Bryan. Sword: A Story of Medieval Times. (p. 1692)
Boychuk, Carol. Tiny World: Poems by Carol Boychuk. (p. 1757)
Boyd, Aaron. Smart Money: The Story of Bill Gates. (p. 1593)
Boyd, Aaron, illus. see Kaufmann, Kelli.
Boyd, Aaron, illus. see Paley, Daniel.
Boyd, Aaron, illus. see Scholastic, Inc. Staff & Barnes, Derrick D.
Boyd, Aaron, illus. see Smalls, Irene.
Boyd, Aaron, illus. see Stuve-Bodeen, Stephanie.
Boyd, Amanda. Near & Far at the Beach: Learning Spatial Awareness Concepts. (p. 1238)
—Trip Around Town: Learning to Add 3 One-Digit Numbers. (p. 1787)
Boyd, Annalisa. Special Agents of Christ: A Prayer Book for Young Orthodox Saints. (p. 1623)
Boyd, Anne A. Help Me Decide! (p. 765)
Boyd, Anne, ed. Games 411. (p. 654)
Boyd, Benjamin. Adventures of Kid Humpty Dumpty. (p. 19)
Boyd, Bentley. George Washington Leads the Way. (p. 664)
—Government. (p. 704)
—Moving & Grooving. (p. 1183)
—Reconstruction Junction. (p. 1452)
Boyd, Beverly L. I Am a Blessing in Disguise Rolle, Allison & Rolle, Alexis, eds. (p. 832)
—I Am a Blessing in Disguise Journal for Children. (p. 832)
Boyd, Brian, illus. see Zeckhausen, Dina.
Boyd, Brian A. Secrets of Tallulah: Histories, Mysteries & Colorful Tales from Georgia's Nineteenth Century Mountain Resort. (p. 1545)
Boyd, Candy Dawson. Charlie Pippin. (p. 293)
Boyd, Cathy. Little Snowman's New Hat. (p. 1036)
Boyd, Charles F. What God Has Always Wanted: The Bible's Big Idea from Genesis Through Revelation. Davis, Dennis, illus. (p. 1884)
Boyd, Charles O'Halloran. Mountains of the North. (p. 1181)
Boyd, Christie Brewer. Eminem. Hillstrom, Laurie, ed. (p. 519)
—James Franco. Greenhaven Press Staff, ed. (p. 907)
—Nicki Minaj. Greenhaven Press Staff, ed. (p. 1251)
Boyd, Cindy J., et al. Geometry. (p. 662)
—Glencoe Geometry. (p. 683)
Boyd, D. Rosie & the Treasure of the Three Nuns: A Historical Fiction for Youth. (p. 1490)
Boyd, David. Beware the Vikings. Rooth, Mike, illus. (p. 173)
—Closer to Hamlet. (p. 334)
—Hidden Message. Alward, Jeff, illus. (p. 776)
—Khan of Khans: An Adventure with Genghis Khan. (p. 951)
—Leonardo's Wings: An Adventure with Leonardo da Vinci. (p. 992)
—Little Sure Shot: An Adventure with Annie Oakley. (p. 1037)
—Marco Polo & the Roc. Ng, Drew, illus. (p. 1092)
—Napoleon's Last Stand. Okum, David, illus. (p. 1229)
—Pearl Harbor. Ng, Drew, illus. (p. 1333)
Boyd, Dee, jt. auth. see Scholastic, Inc. Staff.
Boyd, Ervin D., Sr. Help for the Hurting: Getting Beyond This Veil of Tears! (p. 765)
Boyd, G. A. Alchemy Jones & the Source of Magic. (p. 35)
Boyd, Herb. Martin Luther King, Jr. Marcos, Pablo, illus. (p. 1097)
Boyd, Herb, jt. auth. see Wright, Simeon.
Boyd, Ian, et al. Animal Bites: Sharks. (p. 76)
Boyd, John. Annals of Winchester, CT. (p. 85)
Boyd, Johnny. First Tracks. (p. 597)
Boyd, Kassandra, et al. Kids on the Move: Creative Movement for Children of All Ages (p. 954)
Boyd, Kate & Brixton, Iris. Quercus Quest. (p. 1425)
Boyd, Ken. Tinsel Tail Mouse. (p. 1756)
Boyd, Kenneth. Right to Life - & Death? (p. 1472)
Boyd, Lizi. Flashlight. (p. 602)
—I Love Daddy: Super Sturdy Picture Books. Boyd, Lizi, illus. (p. 842)
—I Love Grandma. Boyd, Lizi, illus. (p. 842)
—I Love Grandpa. Boyd, Lizi, illus. (p. 842)
—Inside Outside. Boyd, Lizi, illus. (p. 877)
Boyd, Maria. Will. (p. 1932)
Boyd, Michele. Counting Bunnies. Kenna, Kara, illus. (p. 370)
—Making Shapes with Monkey. Kenna, Kara, illus. (p. 1082)
—Mama's Little Ducklings. Kenna, Kara, illus. (p. 1084)
—My First Words. (p. 1208)
—Rainbow Butterflies. Kenna, Kara, illus. (p. 1435)
Boyd, Nicole. America's Many Regions. (p. 64)
—Clean & Healthy. (p. 330)
—Doctor's Busy Day. (p. 459)
—George Washington: Our First President. (p. 664)
—Let's Brush Our Teeth. (p. 994)
Boyd, Patti, illus. see Kidd, Ron.
Boyd, Roland. Fisherman & His Wife. Wright, Carol, ed. (p. 599)
Boyd, Shelby, illus. see Breshears, Alyce Park.
Boyd, Sheree, illus. see Haugen, Brenda.
Boyd, Sheree, illus. see Rosinsky, Natalie M.
Boyd, Sheree, illus. see Rosinsky, Natalie M. & Picture Window Books Staff.
Boyd, Sheree, illus. see Stille, Darlene R.
Boyd, Sheree, illus. see Stille, Darlene R. & Picture Window Books Staff.
Boyd, Sheree, tr. see Stille, Darlene R.
Boyd, Sonya. I Have What It Takes. (p. 839)
Boyd, William T. Pumpkin Fairy. Roberts, Mary Jo, illus. (p. 1416)
Boydell, Sydney. Cambridge Checkpoints VCE Physics Unit 4 2004. (p. 255)
Boyden, Linda. Boy & Poi Poi Puppy. Boyden, Linda, illus. (p. 217)
—Giveaways: An ABC Book of Loanwords from the Americas. (p. 681)
—Powwow's Coming. (p. 1391)
Boyden, Robin, illus. see Braun, Eric.
Boyds Collection Ltd. Staff. Beary Devilish. (p. 152)
—Beary Sorry You're down (Feel Better Soon!) (p. 152)
—Have Yourself a Beary Little Christmas. (p. 754)
Boyds Mills Press Staff. Drawing Activities. (p. 481)
—Family (p. 568)
—Fun-to-Make Crafts for Halloween. (p. 648)
—Highlights Hidden Pictures 2009. Highlights for Children Editorial Staff, ed. (p. 779)
—Look What You Can Make with Egg Cartons. Ochester, Betsy, ed. (p. 1050)
—Look What You Can Make with Tubes: Creative Crafts from Everyday Objects. Richmond, Margie Hayes, ed. (p. 1050)
—Riddles, Rhymes, & Stories. (p. 1471)
—Sticker Fun. (p. 1650)
—Super Colossal Book of Hidden Pictures (p. 1679)
Boyds Mills Press Staff, jt. auth. see Brown, Elizabeth Ferguson.
Boyds Mills Press Staff, jt. auth. see Clarke, Judith.
Boyds Mills Press Staff, jt. auth. see Dixon, Dougal.
Boyds Mills Press Staff, jt. auth. see Foreman, Wilmoth.
Boyds Mills Press Staff, jt. auth. see Gilbert, Barbara Snow.
Boyds Mills Press Staff, jt. auth. see Highlights for Children Editorial Staff.
Boyds Mills Press Staff, jt. auth. see Holtwijk, Ineke.
Boyds Mills Press Staff, jt. auth. see Hopkins, Lee Bennett.
Boyds Mills Press Staff, jt. auth. see Keyser, Samuel Jay.
Boyds Mills Press Staff, jt. auth. see Petrie, Kathye Fetsko.
Boyds Mills Press Staff, jt. auth. see Russell, Ching Yeung.
Boyds Mills Press Staff, jt. auth. see Vis, Jan.
Boyds Mills Press Staff, jt. auth. see Vis, Leendert Jan.
Boyds Mills Press Staff & Highlights for Children Editorial Staff. Paper Planes That Soar. (p. 1323)
Boye, B. D. Easy As 1, 2, 3. Boye, B. D., illus. (p. 500)
—Look Book. Boye, B. D., illus. (p. 1049)
—Our New Home. Boye, B. D., illus. (p. 1309)
Boyee, Claire & Hains, Harriet. First Cook Book. (p. 593)
Boyer, Allen B. Roberto's Bat. (p. 1479)
Boyer, Allen B. & Hatala, Dan. Roberto's Bat. (p. 1479)
Boyer Binns, Tristan. Chinese Americans. (p. 307)
—German Americans. (p. 666)
—Mexican Americans. (p. 1131)
Boyer, Cecile. Run, Dog! (p. 1496)
Boyer, Cécile. Woof Meow Tweet-Tweet. (p. 1950)
Boyer, Christine M., illus. see Middleton, Leeanne.
Boyer, Colleen McKinnon, jt. auth. see Janowski, Alice.
Boyer, Crispin. National Geographic Kids Everything Ancient Egypt: Dig into a Treasure Trove of Facts, Photos, & Fun. (p. 1232)
—National Geographic Kids Everything Castles: Capture These Facts, Photos, & Fun to Be King of the Castle! (p. 1232)
—National Geographic Kids Ultimate U. S. Road Trip Atlas: Maps, Games, Activities, & More for Hours of Backseat Fun. (p. 1232)
—That's Creepy: Spine-Tingling Facts That Will Test Your Creep-Out Factor. (p. 1726)
—That's Gross! Icky Facts That Will Test Your Gross-Out Factor. (p. 1726)
—That's Sneaky! Spine-Tingling Facts That Will Test Your Creep-Out Factor. (p. 1727)
—That's Sneaky! Stealthy Secrets & Devious Data That Will Test Your Lie Detector. (p. 1727)
—This or That? The Wacky Book of Choices to Reveal the Hidden You. (p. 1737)
Boyer, Gregory. My Little Red Book (p. 1213)
Boyer, Kenneth R. Encyclopedia of Crossword Sticklers. (p. 525)
Boyer, Lyn, illus. see Fetty, Margaret, ed.
Boyer, Lyn, illus. see Grudzina, Rebecca.
Boyer, Lyn, illus. see Harris, Brooke.
Boyer, Lyn, illus. see Nappa, Mike, et al.
Boyer, Marilyn. Character Trails: Learning to Walk in Paths of Righteousness. (p. 291)
—For you they Signed. (p. 616)
Boyer, Marilyn & Turnas, Grace. Profiles of Valor: Character Studies from the War of Independence. (p. 1410)
Boyer, Melody. Great American Pony Ride. Johnson, Dolores Uselman, illus. (p. 713)
Boyer, Paul. Holt American Nation: Modern Era: Online Edition. (p. 789)
—Holt American Nation: Modern Era: Online Edition Plus. (p. 789)
Boyer, Paul S. Holt American Nation: Online Edition Plus. (p. 789)
—Promises to Keep: The United States since World War II. (p. 1411)
Boyer, Paul S., et al. Enduring Vision: A History of the American People. Vol. 2 (p. 527)
—Enduring Vision: A History of the American People to 1877. Vol. 1 (p. 527)
Boyer, Richard G. Oddo Safety Series (p. 1278)
Boyer, Robin, illus. see Burton, Marilee R.
Boyer, Robin, illus. see Giglio, Judy.
Boyer, Robin, illus. see Hall, M. C.
Boyer, Robin, illus. see Hoffman, Joan.
Boyer, Robin, illus. see Irvin, Barbara Bando.
Boyer, Robin, illus. see Jaeger, Elizabeth.
Boyer, Robin, illus. see Robinson, Joanna Jarc.
Boyer, Robin, illus. see School Zone Interactive Staff.
Boyer, Robin, illus. see Veinje, Marie.
Boyer, Susy, illus. see Arena, Felice & Kettle, Phil.
Boyer, Susy, illus. see Giulieri, Anne.
Boyer, Susy, illus. see Walker, Lois.
Boyer-Quick, Sara, jt. auth. see Vittorini, Candace.
Boyer's Staff. American Nation: Modern Era: Online Edition. (p. 62)
Boyes, Alison. What Charlotte Ate: The Story of a Naughty Dog Who Loved to Eat. Boyes, Faye, illus. (p. 1881)
Boyes, Faye, illus. see Boyes, Alison.
Boyes, William. Microeconomics. (p. 1136)
Boyett, Jason. Guy's Guide to Life: How to Become a Man in 224 Pages or Less (p. 733)
Boyett, Suzi. Let's Read about Snow. (p. 1000)
—Nieva. (p. 1251)
Boyett, Suzi, jt. auth. see Boerger, Kristin.
Boyett, Suzi, jt. auth. see Nations, Susan.
Boykin, Antonee. Alex & Tony Learn to Be Gentlemen. (p. 36)
Boykin, Brian, jt. illus. see Lane, Queen.
Boykin, Floyd, Jr. Bare Essence: The Soul of Me. (p. 139)
Boykin, Timothy. Timster's World: So What Makes You So Special? (p. 1755)
Boykins, Corinthia. Too Big for the Tub. (p. 1766)
Boylan, Eleanor. Brementown Musicians: Band 13/Topaz, Vol. 1 Jensz, Penny, illus. (p. 226)
Boylan, Jennifer Finney. Falcon Quinn & the Black Mirror. Dorman, Brandon, illus. (p. 565)
—Falcon Quinn & the Crimson Vapor. (p. 565)
Boylan, Maureen McCourt, jt. auth. see Geiser, Traci Ferguson.
Boyle, Amanda N. Dream. (p. 483)
Boyle, Bill & Hopkins, Dave. My First Atlas. (p. 1204)
Boyle, Bob. Rosie & Rex: A Nose for Fun! Boyle, Bob, illus. (p. 1490)
Boyle, Brendan, jt. auth. see Klutz Editors.
Boyle, Caitlin. Operation Beautiful: One Note at a Time. (p. 1300)
Boyle, Deborah A. Your Geography. (p. 1980)
Boyle, Doe. Coral Reef Hideaway: The Story of a Clown Anemonefish. (p. 366)
Boyle, Joanna. Tip-Tap Dancing Cat. (p. 1757)
Boyle, Karen Cother. Butterhead & the tired Lamb. (p. 248)
—Butterhead's Dream. (p. 248)
Boyle, L. D. Pegram. Trever's Biscuit. (p. 1785)
Boyle, Peter, tr. see Montejo, Eugenio.
Boyle, Sarah B., jt. auth. see Miller, Reagan.
Boyle, T. C. Human Fly & Other Stories. (p. 826)
Boyle, T. Coraghessan, see Boyle, T. C.
Boyles, Jolene, ed. see Surratt, Christopher.
Boyles, Peggy Palo & Prentice Hall Dictionary Editors. Realidades: Level 2 Vol. 2 (p. 1449)
Boyles, Peggy Palo & Prentice Hall Direct Education Staff. Realidades: Level B (p. 1449)
Boyles, Peggy Palo & Prentice Hall Directories Staff. Realidades: Level 1 (p. 1449)
—Realidades: Level A. (p. 1449)
Boyles, Peggy Palo, et al. Realidades, Level 3 (p. 1449)
Boyles, Shawn, illus. see Packard, Albert.
Boyne, John. Boy in the Striped Pajamas. (p. 218)
—Noah Barleywater Runs Away. Jeffers, Oliver, illus. (p. 1261)
—Stay Where You Are & Then Leave. Jeffers, Oliver, illus. (p. 1645)
—Terrible Thing That Happened to Barnaby Brocket. Jeffers, Oliver, illus. (p. 1721)
Boyne, John & Boynejohn. increible caso de Barnaby Brocket. (p. 870)
Boyne, Linda, illus. see White, Cal.
Boynejohn, jt. auth. see Boyne, John.
Boynton. Bath Time! (p. 144)
Boynton, Alice & Blevins, Wiley. Nonfiction Passages with Graphic Organizers for Independent Practice: Selections with Graphic Organizers, Assessments, & Writing Activities That Help Students Understand the Structures & Features of Nonfiction. (p. 1263)
—Teaching Students to Read Nonfiction: 20 Easy Lessons with Color Transparencies, High-Interest Passages, & Practice Pages-Everything You Need to Help Your

Students Learn How to Read All Kinds of Nonfiction. (p. 1710)
Boynton, Bibi. Bats (p. 144)
—Bats (p. 145)
Boynton, Bibi & Capstone Press Staff. Bats (p. 144)
Boynton, Cara. Sam's Secret World. (p. 1509)
Boynton, Colin. Tommy & the Dust Devils. (p. 1764)
Boynton, Jeannette. God Loves Variety. Boynton, Jeannette & Holdeen, Bonnie, illus. (p. 689)
Boynton, Sandra. Amazing Cows: Udder Absurdity for Children. (p. 54)
—Are You a Cow? Boynton, Sandra, illus. (p. 96)
—Azul el Sombrero, Verde el Sombrero. Boynton, Sandra, illus. (p. 122)
—Barnyard Bath! (p. 139)
—Barnyard Dance! (Lap Edition) (p. 139)
—Bath Time! (p. 144)
—Belly Button Book! (p. 163)
—Belly Button Book! (Lap Edition) (p. 163)
—Big Box of Boynton: Barnyard Dance! Pajama Time! Oh My Oh My Oh Dinosaurs! Boynton, Sandra, illus. (p. 179)
—Big Box of Boynton Set 2! Snuggle Puppy! Belly Button Book! Tickle Time! (p. 179)
—Big Box of Little Pookie. (p. 179)
—Blue Moo: 17 Jukebox Hits from Way Back Never. (p. 203)
—Boynton: Moo, Baa, la la La! But Not the Hippopotamus Opposite. Set Boynton, Sandra, illus. (p. 220)
—Buenas Noches a Todos. Boynton, Sandra, illus. (p. 235)
—Bunny Rabbit Show! Boynton, Sandra, illus. (p. 242)
—But Not the Hippopotamus. Boynton, Sandra, illus. (p. 246)
—Christmas Parade. Boynton, Sandra, illus. (p. 315)
—Consider Love. Boynton, Sandra, illus. (p. 359)
—Consider Love (Mini Edition) Its Moods & Many Ways. Boynton, Sandra, illus. (p. 359)
—Dinos to Go/Snoozers Vertical 2-Pack. Boynton, Sandra, illus. (p. 441)
—Dog Train: A Wild Ride on the Rock-and-Roll Side. Boynton, Sandra, illus. (p. 461)
—Fifteen Animals! (p. 584)
—Frog Trouble: And Eleven Other Pretty Serious Songs. (p. 640)
—Fuzzy Fuzzy Fuzzy! A Touch, Skritch, & Tickle Book. Boynton, Sandra, illus. (p. 651)
—Going to Bed Book. Boynton, Sandra, illus. (p. 693)
—Happy Birthday, Little Pookie. (p. 744)
—Happy Hippo, Angry Duck: A Book of Moods. Boynton, Sandra, illus. (p. 746)
—Hey! Wake Up! (p. 774)
—Hippos Go Berserk! Boynton, Sandra, illus. (p. 781)
—Let's Dance, Little Pookie. (p. 995)
—Little Pookie. (p. 1033)
—Moo, Baa, La La La! (p. 1171)
—Moo, Baa, la la La! Boynton, Sandra, illus. (p. 1171)
—Moo Cow Book. Boynton, Sandra, illus. (p. 1171)
—Muu - Beee - ¡Asi Fue! Boynton, Sandra, illus. (p. 1195)
—Night-Night, Little Pookie. (p. 1253)
—Opposites: Special 30th Anniversary Edition! Boynton, Sandra, illus. (p. 1300)
—Opuestos. Ziegler, Argentina Palacios, tr. (p. 1301)
—Pajama Time! (Lap Edition) (p. 1319)
—Perfect Piggies! (p. 1342)
—Perritos: Un Libro para Contar y Ladrar. Boynton, Sandra, illus. (p. 1343)
—Rhinoceros Tap. Boynton, Sandra, illus. (p. 1467)
—Sandra Boynton's Moo, Baa, la la La! Boynton, Sandra, illus. (p. 1511)
—Snuggle Puppy! A Love Song. (p. 1601)
—Spooky Pookie. (p. 1631)
—Tickle Time! (p. 1747)
—What's Wrong, Little Pookie? (p. 1900)
—Your Personal Penguin. (p. 1981)
Boynton, Sandra & King, B. B. One Shoe Blues. (p. 1297)
Boys & Girls Club of Downtown Toronto Staff. C Is for Colorado. (p. 250)
Boys and Girls Club of Greater Fort Worth. T Is for Texas: Written by Kids for Kids. McCann, Michelle, ed. (p. 1694)
Boys and Girls Club of Oklahoma County. O Is for Oklahoma: Written by Kids for Kids. McCann, Michelle, ed. (p. 1274)
Boys & Girls Clubs Rochester, Ny, jt. auth. see NY Boys and Girls Clubs Rochester Staff.
Boys Choir of Harlem Staff. O Holy Night: Christmas with the Boys Choir of Harlem. Ringgold, Faith, illus. (p. 1274)
Boys Town Press Staff. Time to Enrich: Activity Kit. (p. 1753)
Boyter, Constance. Santa 's Secret Trip: The Letter That Changed Everything. (p. 1513)
Boytim, Joan Frey. Daffodils, Violets & Snowflakes: 24 Classical Songs for Young Women, Ages 10 to Mid-Teens. (p. 399)
Boza, Eduardo Robles. Mi Amiga No Qiere Dormir. (p. 1132)
—Mi Amiga No Quiere Comer. (p. 1132)
—Mi Amiga Quiere - Grande (My Friend Wants to Be Big) (p. 1132)
—Mi Amigo - Banarse (My Friend Doesn't Like - Baths) (p. 1132)
—Mi Amigo Se Hace Pipi... (My Friends Wets His Bed) (p. 1132)
—Mi Amigo Tiene Hermanita (My Friend Has a Little Sister) (p. 1132)
Bozak, Jon. Demo: The Story of a Junkyard Dog. Bruns, Scott, illus. (p. 425)
Bozak, Jon, jt. auth. see A Boy And His Dog.
Bozak, Kristin & Cohen, Judith Love. You Can Be a Woman Botanist. Katz, David Arthur, illus. (p. 1973)
Bozanich, Tony L. & Wight, Joe. Nazi Zombies. Isaksen, Patricia, ed. (p. 1238)
Bozarth, Jan. Birdie's Book. Burden, Andrea, illus. (p. 191)
—Fairy Godmother Academy #6: Trinity's Book. (p. 563)
—Kerka's Book. Burden, Andrea, illus. (p. 949)
—Lilu's Book. (p. 1017)
—Sumi's Book. (p. 1673)
—Zally's Book. Burden, Andrea, illus. (p. 1984)
Bozeman, Gary, illus. see Sawyer, J. Scott.
Bozer, Chris, illus. see Parker, Steve.
Bozonelis, Helen Koutras. 200 Years with Abraham Lincoln: One Man's Life & Legacy. (p. 2001)
—Look at the Nineteenth Amendment: Women Win the Right to Vote. (p. 1049)
—Primary Source Accounts of the War of 1812. (p. 1399)
Bozuwa, Titia. In the Shadow of the Cathedral: Growing up in Holland During WW II. (p. 867)
Bozzi, Riccardo. World Belongs to You. Zagnoli, Olimpia, illus. (p. 1954)
Bozzo, Linda. Amazing Animal Feet. (p. 53)
—Amazing Animal Skin. (p. 53)
—Amazing Animal Tails. (p. 53)
—Amazing Animal Teeth. (p. 53)
—Amazing Animal Tongues. (p. 53)
—Amazing Beaks. (p. 54)
—Army Rangers. (p. 100)
—Corny Thanksgiving Jokes to Tickle Your Funny Bone. (p. 367)
—Delta Force. (p. 425)
—Food Jokes to Tickle Your Funny Bone. (p. 613)
—Funny Valentine's Day Jokes to Tickle Your Funny Bone. (p. 650)
—Green Berets. (p. 721)
—Gross Body Jokes to Tickle Your Funny Bone. (p. 725)
—I Like Beagles! (p. 841)
—I Like Collies! (p. 841)
—I Like German Shepherds! (p. 841)
—I Like Labrador Retrievers! (p. 841)
—I Like Mixed-Breed Dogs! (p. 841)
—I Like Poodles! (p. 841)
—Kooky Halloween Jokes to Tickle Your Funny Bone. (p. 967)
—Marine Expeditionary Units. (p. 1094)
—Mi Primer Caballo. (p. 1133)
—Mi Primer Gato. (p. 1133)
—Mi Primer Pajarito. (p. 1133)
—Mi Primer Perro. (p. 1133)
—Mi Primer Pez. (p. 1133)
—Mi Primera Mascota Pequeña. (p. 1133)
—My First Bird. (p. 1205)
—My First Cat. (p. 1206)
—My First Dog. (p. 1206)
—My First Fish. (p. 1206)
—My First Guinea Pig & Other Small Pets. (p. 1206)
—My First Horse. (p. 1206)
—Navy SEALs. (p. 1238)
Bozzo, Linda & Library. At Play in the Past, Present, & Future. (p. 110)
—Community Helpers of the Past, Present, & Future. (p. 350)
—Getting Around in the Past, Present, & Future. (p. 669)
—Houses of the Past, Present, & Future. (p. 804)
—Schools of the Past, Present, & Future. (p. 1524)
—Staying in Touch in the Past, Present, & Future. (p. 1645)
Bozzo, Linda & Library Association Staff. Fire Dog Heroes. (p. 590)
—Guide Dog Heroes. (p. 730)
—Police Dog Heroes. (p. 1380)
—Search & Rescue Dog Heroes. (p. 1537)
—Service Dog Heroes. (p. 1553)
—Therapy Dog Heroes. (p. 1729)
Bozzone, Donna M. Cancer Genetics. (p. 260)
—Causes of Cancer. (p. 282)
Bozzone, Donna M., jt. auth. see Kenny, Paraic.
Bozzuti-Jones, Mark Francisco. Miter Fits Just Fine: A Story about the Rt. Rev. Barbara Clementine Harris, Suffragan Bishop, Diocese of Massachusetts. (p. 1155)
Bozzuti-Jones, Mark Francisco & Haywood, Jennifer Johnson. God Thought of You. (p. 690)
Braasch, Gary, jt. auth. see Cherry, Lynne.
Braasch, Gary, photos by see Cherry, Lynne.
Brabham, Barbara. Donkey Tales — Color with Paco! [English/Spanish Versions]. (p. 466)
Brabourne, Edward Hugessen Knatchbull-Hugessen. River Legends of the Thames & Rhine. Doré, Gustave, illus. (p. 1476)
Bracciano, Alfred F., et al. Modern Refrigeration & Air Conditioning. (p. 1158)
Brace, Eric, illus. see Amato, Mary.
Brace, Maggie D. 'tis Himself: The Tale of Finn Maccool. (p. 1757)
Brace, Nicola, et al. Spss for Psychologists: A Guide to Data Analysis Using SPSS for Windows. (p. 1635)
Bracegirdle, P. J. Dead Family Diaz. Bernatene, Poly, illus. (p. 416)
—Fiendish Deeds. (p. 584)
—Sinister Scenes. (p. 1579)
—Unearthly Asylum. (p. 1817)
Bracey, Ronay. Writing ... Take Small Steps: Improve Students' Writing Skills. (p. 1964)
Bracho, Coral. Jardin del Mar. Suzan, Gerardo, illus. (p. 909)
Brack, Amanda. Big Book of Brick Trucks. (p. 179)
Brack, Amanda, illus. see Moore, Clement C.
Brack, Susan. Horsing Around! (p. 800)
—Mommy & Me Stickers. (p. 1162)
Bracke, Peter M. Crystal Lake Memories: The Complete History of Friday the 13th. (p. 387)
Bracken, Alexandra. Darkest Minds. (p. 408)
—In the Afterlight. (p. 865)
—Never Fade. (p. 1242)
—Never Fade (a Darkest Minds Novel) (p. 1242)
Bracken, Bennett. Chase after the Wind (p. 294)
Bracken, Beth. Henry Helps Clean His Room Busby, Ailie, illus. (p. 768)
—Henry Helps Make Cookies Busby, Ailie, illus. (p. 768)
—Henry Helps Plant a Garden Busby, Ailie, illus. (p. 768)
—Henry Helps Wash the Car Busby, Ailie, illus. (p. 768)
—Henry Helps with Dinner Busby, Ailie, illus. (p. 768)
—Henry Helps with Laundry Busby, Ailie, illus. (p. 768)
—Henry Helps with the Baby Busby, Ailie, illus. (p. 768)
—Henry Helps with the Dog Busby, Ailie, illus. (p. 768)
—Little Bully Bell, Jennifer A., illus. (p. 1025)
—Terrible, Awful, Horrible Manners Watson, Richard, illus. (p. 1721)
—Terrible, Awful, Horrible Manners! Watson, Richard, illus. (p. 1721)
—Too Shy for Show-And-Tell Bell, Jennifer A., illus. (p. 1767)
—Too Shy for Show-and-Tell. Bell, Jennifer A., illus. (p. 1767)
—Wizard of Oz (p. 1943)
Bracken, Beth & Fraser, Kay. At the Edge of the Woods Sawyer, Odessa, illus. (p. 111)
—Believe Sawyer, Odessa, illus. (p. 161)
—Bloodfate Sawyer, Odessa, illus. (p. 201)
—Faerieground Sawyer, Odessa, illus. (p. 562)
—Fate of the Willow Queen. Sawyer, Odessa, illus. (p. 577)
—Hidden Things Sawyer, Odessa, illus. (p. 776)
—Hope Sawyer, Odessa, illus. (p. 796)
—Murder of Crows Sawyer, Odessa, illus. (p. 1192)
—Seventh Kingdom Sawyer, Odessa, illus. (p. 1555)
—Shadows Sawyer, Odessa, illus. (p. 1558)
—Two Mothers. Sawyer, Odessa, illus. (p. 1804)
—Willow Queen's Gate Sawyer, Odessa, illus. (p. 1934)
—Wish Sawyer, Odessa, illus. (p. 1940)
—Wish in the Woods Sawyer, Odessa, illus. (p. 1940)
Bracken, Carolyn, illus. see Capeci, Anne & Cole, Joanna.
Bracken, Carolyn, illus. see Cheshire, Marc.
Bracken, Carolyn, illus. see Cole, Joanna & Capeci, Anne.
Bracken, Carolyn, illus. see Cole, Joanna & Jackson, Tom.
Bracken, Carolyn, illus. see Cole, Joanna & O'Brien, Cynthia.
Bracken, Carolyn, illus. see Cole, Joanna, et al.
Bracken, Carolyn, illus. see Cole, Joanna.
Bracken, Carolyn, illus. see Earhart, Kristin, et al.
Bracken, Carolyn, illus. see Earhart, Kristin.
Bracken, Carolyn, illus. see Egan, Kate & Cole, Joanna.
Bracken, Carolyn, illus. see Fry, Sonali.
Bracken, Carolyn, illus. see O'Connor, Jane.
Bracken, Carolyn, illus. see Rylant, Cynthia.
Bracken, Carolyn, illus. see Schwabacher, Martin, et al.
Bracken, Carolyn, illus. see Smith, Elizabeth.
Bracken, Carolyn, jt. auth. see Rylant, Cynthia.
Bracken- Murphy, Julie. Sammy's Summer Vacation. (p. 1508)
Brackett, Leigh, jt. auth. see Wilson, F. Paul.
Brackett, Leigh & Coppel, Jr., Alfred. Planet Stories - Summer 1949. (p. 1368)
Brackett, Mary Virginia & Gaydosik, Victoria. Facts on File Companion to the British Novel (p. 561)
Brackett, Michael. Adventures of Bunny & Hare. (p. 17)
Brackett, Virginia. Facts on File Companion to British Poetry: 17th & 18th Centuries. (p. 561)
—Home in the Heart: The Story of Sandra Cisneros. (p. 792)
—Restless Genius: The Story of Virginia Woolf. (p. 1464)
—Steve Jobs: Computer Genius of Apple. (p. 1649)
Brackett, Virginia R. F. Scott Fitzgerald: Writer of the Jazz Age. (p. 559)
Brackin, Bob. Further down the Road. (p. 650)
Bradberry, Sarah. Kids Knit! Simple Steps to Nifty Projects. (p. 954)
Bradburn, Ryan. Conditional Following Directions Fun Deck: Fd68. (p. 355)
Bradburn, Ryan, illus. see Webber, Thomas.
Bradburn, Ryan, jt. concept see Webber, Sharon.
Bradbury, Bianca. Flight into Spring. (p. 604)
Bradbury, Jack, illus. see Connell, Del, et al.
Bradbury, Jennifer. Moment Comes. (p. 1161)
—River Runs Deep. (p. 1476)
—Shift. (p. 1566)
—Wrapped. (p. 1962)
Bradbury, Judy. Children's Book Corner: A Read-Aloud Resource with Tips, Techniques, & Plans for Teachers, Librarians & Parents Level Pre-K-K (p. 303)
Bradbury, Ken & Crowe, Robert L. Wait ... Don't Leave Yet. Crowe, Robert L., ed. (p. 1852)
Bradbury, Lynne. Santa Claus Has a Busy Night. (p. 1511)
Bradbury, Ray. Dinosaur Tales. (p. 443)
—Halloween Tree. (p. 739)
—Halloween Tree. Eller, Jon, ed. (p. 739)
—Halloween Tree. Mugnaini, Joseph, illus. (p. 739)
—Switch on the Night. Dillon, Leo & Dillon, Diane, illus. (p. 1691)
Bradby, Marie. Some Friend. (p. 1609)
Braddock, Paige. Jane's World (p. 908)
—Stinky Cecil in Operation Pond Rescue. (p. 1651)
Braddock, Paige, illus. see Schulz, Charles M. & Houghton, Shane.
Braddock, Paige, illus. see Schulz, Charles M. & Scott, Vicki.
Braddock, Pauline. Humbug. (p. 826)
—long way Home. (p. 1047)
Braden, Linda. Mason Jar Crafts for Kids: More Than 25 Cool, Crafty Projects to Make for Your Friends, Your Family, & Yourself! (p. 1102)
Braden, Stephanie. Wishing Well. (p. 1940)
Bradex, Melissa A. Little Gregory. Crane, Eddie, illus. (p. 1028)
Bradfield, Carl. Hawaii Calls Wendell & Myrtle: The Wendells Family Make It to the Big Island. (p. 755)
—Sullivans of Little Horsepen Creek: A Tale of Colonial North Carolina's Regulator Era, Circa: 1760s. (p. 1673)
—Tecumseh's Trail: The Appalachian Trail; Then & Now. (p. 1712)
Bradfield, Jane. Beyond All That Glitters. (p. 173)
Bradfield, Jolly Roger. Benjamin Dilley's Thirsty Camel. Bradfield, Jolly Roger, illus. (p. 164)
—Perfecto Caballero para Dragones. Bradfield, Jolly Roger, illus. (p. 1342)
—Pickle-Chiffon Pie. (p. 1354)
Bradfield, Roger. Hello, Rock. (p. 765)
—!Hola, Piedrita!/Hello, Rock. (p. 787)
—Pickle-Chiffon Pie Olympics. (p. 1354)
Bradfield, Roger, illus. see Hicks, Clifford B.
Bradford, Alice. Bubble-Blowing Bink. (p. 233)
Bradford, Amy L. What God Wants for Christmas: Read along, Sing Along. Bogan, Lyuba, illus. (p. 1884)
Bradford, Amy L. & Larmoyeux, Mary. Resurrection Eggs Activity Book. Wadkins, Fran, illus. (p. 1464)
Bradford, Arthur. Benny's Brigade. Hanawalt, Lisa, illus. (p. 165)
Bradford, Bruce. Angel Named Herald. (p. 73)
Bradford, Chris. Ninja: First Mission. (p. 1256)
—Way of the Dragon. (p. 1864)
—Young Samurai the Way of the Dragon. (p. 1979)
—Young Samurai the Way of the Sword. (p. 1979)
—Young Samurai: the Way of the Sword. (p. 1979)
Bradford, Chris, jt. auth. see Orlean, Susan.
Bradford, Clare. Unsettling Narratives: Postcolonial Readings of Children's Literature. (p. 1822)
Bradford, Danette J. Eric & Winkles Meet the Bunnyworms. Bunker, Thomas, illus. (p. 533)
—Eric & Winkles Meet the Snacker Sneakers. (p. 533)
Bradford, Denise L. Little Jon's Adventures: The Day of the Tumbleweed Travesty. (p. 1029)
Bradford, Gamaliel. Lee the American. (p. 987)
Bradford, Imani. People Can't Save You. (p. 1339)
Bradford, James C. John Paul Jones: And the American Navy. (p. 922)
—John Paul Jones & the American Navy. (p. 922)
Bradford James Nolan. Mouse Who Lived in Fenway Park. Jim Connelly, illus. (p. 1182)
Bradford, Jeff & Arnett, Karen. Masters' Con: A Novel. (p. 1103)
Bradford, Jumanne. Preserving a Young Generation. (p. 1396)
Bradford, June, illus. see MacLeod, Elizabeth.
Bradford, June, illus. see Sadler, Judy Ann & Sadler, Judy.
Bradford, June, illus. see Sadler, Judy Ann, et al.
Bradford, June, illus. see Sadler, Judy Ann.
Bradford, K. B. Grandma's Sunshine. (p. 709)
Bradford, Karleen. Animal Heroes. (p. 78)
—Ghost Wolf Cormack, Allan & Drew-Brook, Deborah, illus. (p. 672)
—Ghost Wolf. Cormack, Allan & Drew-Brook, Deborah, illus. (p. 672)
Bradford, Nell. Little Cheep-Chirp. (p. 1026)
Bradford, Quebe Merritt. In the Absence of My Father: Grief. Grit. Gangs. Guts. Grace. (p. 865)
Bradford, Sarah H. Harriet Tubman- the Moses of Her People: Scenes in the Life of Harriet Tubman. (p. 750)
Bradford, Valerie Ann. Activites Makes Learning Fun. (p. 10)
—Activities Makes Learning Fun: Volume II. (p. 10)
Bradford, Wade. Why Do I Have to Make My Bed? van der Sterre, Johnanna, illus. (p. 1923)
Bradford, William. Jeremy Mcbright Was Afraid of the Night. (p. 913)
—Third Dialogue: Second Lost. Deane, Charles, ed. (p. 1734)
Bradford, Wilson D. Bear & the Price. Abby, Mitchell, illus. (p. 150)
Bradley, A. M. Finnegan's Magic Sunglasses. (p. 589)
Bradley, Adrian. Faraway Kingdom of Oop Loop la Pink. Laurente, Lourdes, illus. (p. 573)
Bradley, Alex. 24 Girls in 7 Days. (p. 1996)
Bradley, B. D. Wonderful Willie: What He & Tommy Did to Spain. (p. 1948)
Bradley, B. J. We the People- the 27 Amendments of the United States Constitution. (p. 1868)
Bradley, Barbara. Hawaiian Kids Cook & Color Book. (p. 755)
Bradley, Carolyn. Gingerbread Heart: Love... a Boy & a Gingerbread Boy with a Gingerbread Heart. (p. 677)
Bradley, Catherine. Freedom of Movement. (p. 634)
Bradley, Danyelle. Learning with Tydi & Froggy: Colors. (p. 986)
Bradley, Debby. Sophie Wonders about Marriage. Guzman, Lula, illus. (p. 1613)
Bradley, Doug. Magnets in My World. (p. 1076)
—Needs & Wants. (p. 1239)
Bradley, F. T. Double Vision: The Alias Men. (p. 473)
—Double Vision. (p. 473)
—Double Vision - Code Name 711. (p. 473)
—Double Vision - The Alias Men. (p. 473)
Bradley, Gerald L., jt. auth. see Hoffmann, Laurence D.
Bradley, Jada. U. S. Territories & Possessions (p. 1807)
Bradley, James. Flyboys: A True Story of Courage. (p. 609)
Bradley, James & Powers, Ron. Flags of Our Fathers: Heroes of Iwo Jima. (p. 602)
—Flags of Our Fathers: A Young People's Edition. (p. 602)
Bradley, James V. Bat. (p. 143)
—Canada Goose. (p. 260)
—Coyote. (p. 374)
—Crows & Ravens. (p. 386)
—How Species Change. (p. 812)
—Mountain Lion. (p. 1181)
—Squirrel. (p. 1637)
Bradley, Jasmine N., jt. auth. see Bradley, Natasha R.
Bradley, Jeff, et al. Hello My Name Is... A Guide to Naming Your Baby. (p. 764)
Bradley, Jeffery & Miller, Britt Ekland. Positive African American Plays for Children Book 2: Building High Self Esteem & Confidence Through Plays. (p. 1387)
Bradley, Jess. I Know Sasquatch. (p. 840)
Bradley, Jessica. Comics Land. (p. 348)
Bradley, Jessica, illus. see Kaplan, Arie.
Bradley, Jessica, illus. see Lemke, Amy J.
Bradley, Jessica, illus. see Lemke, Amy J. & Lemke, Donald B.
Bradley, Jessica, illus. see Nickel, Scott.
Bradley, Jessica, illus. see Sazaklis, John.
Bradley, Jessica, illus. see Sonneborn, Scott.
Bradley, John Ed. Call Me by My Name. (p. 254)
Bradley, John R. Saudi Arabia Exposed: Inside a Kingdom in Crisis. (p. 1516)
Bradley, Judy. Naughty Grandmother. Mitchell, Hazle, illus. (p. 1237)
Bradley, K. J., jt. auth. see Beaton, Alyson.
Bradley, Kathleen. Boy Who Cried Wolf. (p. 219)
Bradley, Kathleen, jt. auth. see Herwick Rice, Dona.
Bradley, Kathleen, jt. auth. see Rice, Dona Herwick.
Bradley, Kathleen E. Making Money Grow. (p. 1081)
Bradley, Kimberly Brubaker. For Freedom: The Story of a French Spy. (p. 615)
—Forces Make Things Move. Meisel, Paul, illus. (p. 617)
—Jefferson's Sons: A Founding Father's Secret Children. (p. 912)
—Lacemaker & the Princess. (p. 970)
—Perfect Pony. Colón, Raúl & McNicholas, Shelagh, illus. (p. 1342)
—War That Saved My Life. (p. 1858)

B

Bradley, Lisa. Abby Wize: Awa. (p. 2)
Bradley, Lois, illus. see Redmond, Shirley Raye.
Bradley, Marion Zimmer. Forest House. (p. 618)
—Planet Savers. (p. 1368)
Bradley, MaryChris, tr. see Louis, Catherine.
Bradley, MaryChris, tr. see Tidholm, Anna-Clara.
Bradley, MaryChris, tr. see Van Straaten, Harmen & Straaten, Harmen Van.
Bradley, Matthew J. Oi! Who Ate My Dinner! & Other Colin the Cat Stories. (p. 1282)
Bradley, Michael. Camaro. (p. 255)
—Cars (p. 272)
—Corvette. (p. 368)
—Derek Jeter. (p. 427)
—Donovan McNabb. (p. 466)
—Escalade. (p. 534)
—Ferrari. (p. 582)
—Ford Truck. (p. 617)
—Generation Next: Superstar Kids of Superstar Athletes. (p. 660)
—GTO. (p. 728)
—Hummer. (p. 826)
—Jaguar. (p. 905)
—Lamborghini. (p. 972)
—Mustang. (p. 1194)
—Prius. (p. 1407)
—Thunderbird. (p. 1746)
—Tony Hawk. (p. 1766)
—Yao Ming. (p. 1968)
Bradley, Michael J. Birth of Mathematics: Anicent Times To 1300. (p. 192)
—Foundations of Mathematics: 1800 To 1900. (p. 624)
—Mathematics Frontiers: 1950 to Present. (p. 1108)
—Modern Mathematics: 1900-1950. (p. 1158)
—Pioneers in Math (p. 1361)
—Yes, Your Parents Are Crazy! A Teen Survival Handbook. Glasbergen, Randy, illus. (p. 1971)
Bradley, Natasha R. & Bradley, Jasmine N. Jessika's Diaries:Life's Not Fair. (p. 914)
Bradley, Nina Leopold, jt. auth. see Hunt, Nancy Nye.
Bradley, Ray. Ultimate Computing Glossary for Advanced Level. (p. 1809)
Bradley, Sandra. Henry Holton Takes the Ice. Palacios, Sara, illus. (p. 768)
Bradley, Sandy, illus. see Niemela, JoAnn Huston.
Bradley, Sharon. Walking Away from Texas. (p. 1854)
Bradley, Simon, ed. Bikes. (p. 185)
Bradley, Steve. Pruner's Bible: A Step-by-Step Guide to Pruning Every Plant in Your Garden. (p. 1413)
Bradley, Tammy L. This Heart of Mine. (p. 1735)
Bradley, Timothy. Bug Builders. (p. 236)
—Hive Mind (p. 786)
—Sci Hi: Ripple Effect. (p. 1524)
—Strange but True: Gross Anatomy. (p. 1664)
—Strange but True: Tiny Creatures. (p. 1664)
—Teddy Bear, Teddy Bear, Say Good Night. Medina, Conni & Stark, Kristy, eds. (p. 1712)
Bradley, Timothy J. Animal Architects. (p. 76)
—Bug Builders. (p. 236)
—Danger in the Desert. (p. 403)
—Demons of the Deep. (p. 426)
—Infestation. Bradley, Timothy J., illus. (p. 873)
—Osito, Osito di Buenas Noches. (p. 1305)
—Osito, Osito, Di Buenas Noches: Teddy Bear, Teddy Bear, Say Good Night. (p. 1305)
—Paleo Bugs: Survival of the Creepiest. Bradley, Timothy J., illus. (p. 1319)
—Strange but True: Gross Anatomy. (p. 1664)
—Strange but True: Bizarre Animals. (p. 1664)
—Strange but True: Bizarre Animals. (p. 1664)
—Strange but True Tiny Creatures. (p. 1665)
—Teddy Bear, Teddy Bear, Say Good Night. (p. 1712)
—Terror in the Tropics. (p. 1722)
—Time Jump (p. 1752)
—Wild Cities. (p. 1929)
—Wild Cities. (p. 1929)
Bradley, Vanessa, illus. see Chase, Diana.
Bradman, Tom. Collins Big Cat Progress - Fiction: White Band 10/Sapphire Band 16. (p. 340)
Bradman, Tom, jt. auth. see Bradman, Tony.
Bradman, Tony. After Happily Ever After Warburton, Sarah, illus. (p. 28)
—Alien. (p. 40)
—Bad Boys. (p. 131)
—Cinderella & the Mean Queen. Warburton, Sarah, illus. (p. 320)
—Dilly & the Birthday Treat. Hellard, Susan & Hellard, Sue, illus. (p. 440)
—Fairy Godmother Takes a Break. Warburton, Sarah, illus. (p. 563)
—Final Cut. (p. 586)
—Flora the Fairy's Magic Spells. Carlow, Emma, illus. (p. 606)
—Frankenstein Teacher. Kavanagh, Peter, illus. (p. 629)
—Frog Prince Hops to It Warburton, Sarah, illus. (p. 640)
—Game Over! (p. 654)
—Ghost Teacher. Kavanagh, Peter, illus. (p. 672)
—Goldilocks & the Just Right Club. Warburton, Sarah, illus. (p. 696)
—It Came from Outer Space. Wright, Carol, illus. (p. 893)
—Jack & the Bean Snacks Warburton, Sarah, illus. (p. 902)
—Michael. Ross, Tony, illus. (p. 1134)
—Mr. Bear Gets Alarmed Warburton, Sarah, illus. (p. 1184)
—Mr. Giant & the Beastly Baron Warburton, Sarah, illus. (p. 1185)
—Mr. Wolf Bounces Back Warburton, Sarah, illus. (p. 1187)
—Mr. Wolf Bounces Back [Scholastic]. Warburton, Sarah, illus. (p. 1187)
—Mummy Family Find Fame. (p. 1191)
—Mummy Family Find Fame. Chatterton, Martin, illus. (p. 1191)
—Perfect Baby. Swain, Holly, illus. (p. 1341)
—Rapunzel Lets Her Hair Down Warburton, Sarah, illus. (p. 1439)
—Red Riding Hood Takes Charge Warburton, Sarah, illus. (p. 1455)
—Sandal. Dupasquier, Philippe, illus. (p. 1510)
—Snow White & the Magic Mirror. Warburton, Sarah, illus. (p. 1599)
—So You Want to Write Fiction. (p. 1602)
—Three Little Pigs Go Camping Warburton, Sarah, illus. (p. 1743)
—Through My Window. Browne, Eileen, illus. (p. 1745)
—Ugly Duckling Returns Warburton, Sarah, illus. (p. 1808)
—Well Done Sam! ELT Edition. (p. 1874)
—Wicked Stepmother Helps Out Warburton, Sarah, illus. (p. 1927)
Bradman, Tony, ed. see Quarto Generic Staff.
Bradman, Tony, jt. auth. see Carlow, Emma.
Bradman, Tony, jt. auth. see Chatterton, Martin.
Bradman, Tony & Banana, Red. Polly & the Pirates. Davies, James, illus. (p. 1381)
Bradman, Tony & Bradman, Tom. My Brother's Keeper. (p. 1199)
Bradman, Tony & Chatterton, Martin. Surprise Party. (p. 1686)
Bradman, Tony & Quarto Generic Staff. In a Minute. Browne, Eileen, illus. (p. 863)
—Wait & See. Browne, Eileen, illus. (p. 1852)
Bradman, Tony, ed. Give Me Shelter. (p. 681)
—Under the Weather: Stories about Climate Change. (p. 1814)
Bradman, Tony, et al. Castle Poems & Dragon Poems. (p. 277)
—Machine Poems & Music Poems. (p. 1068)
—Pirate Poems & Monster Poems. (p. 1363)
Bradman, Tony, et al, selected by. Castle Poems & Dragon Poems. (p. 277)
—Machine Poems & Music Poems. (p. 1068)
—Pirate Poems & Monster Poems. (p. 1363)
Bradmon, Karen. Goldie: A Fishtale of Adventure. (p. 695)
Bradsby, Larry, et al. Algebra 1 Rescue! Student Book: Chapters 1-6. (p. 38)
—Algebra 1 Rescue! Student Book: Chapters 7-12. (p. 38)
Bradshaw, Anne. Dingo. (p. 440)
Bradshaw, Anne, et al, contrib. by. Publishing Secrets: A Comprehensive Guide to Getting Your Book Published in the LDS Market. (p. 1414)
Bradshaw, Brent, jt. auth. see Seigel, Andrea.
Bradshaw, Carrie, illus. see Renert, Gerry.
Bradshaw, Carrie Anne, illus. see Renert, Gerry.
Bradshaw, Cody. Cultures in My Class: Represent & Interpret Data. (p. 391)
Bradshaw, Dustin W. Counting Candles. (p. 371)
Bradshaw, Frances C. F-A-i-t-h: Do You Have It ?? (p. 559)
Bradshaw, Georgine, jt. auth. see Wrighton, Charlene.
Bradshaw, Georgine & Wrighton, Charlene. Basic Kit - Kindergarten. Clark, Irene, illus. (p. 142)
—Kindergarten Zoo-per Kit. Clark, Irene, illus. (p. 957)
—Preschool Zoo-per Kit. Clark, Irene, illus. (p. 1396)
—Set of Color Mini-Books (29 Titles) Clark, Irene, illus. (p. 1554)
Bradshaw, Jennifer. No School Today, My Son. (p. 1260)
Bradshaw, Jim, illus. see Walton, Rick.
Bradshaw, John. Fun Campfire Ghost Stories. (p. 647)
—Fun campfire Stories. (p. 647)
—Fun campfire stories Anthology. (p. 647)
Bradshaw, Nick, illus. see Asmus, James.
Bradshaw, Nick, jt. auth. see Kuhoric, James Anthony.
Bradshaw, Nick & Bachalo, Chris. Wolverine & the X-Men by Jason Aaron - Volume 2. (p. 1944)
Bradshaw, T.S. Goodees. (p. 701)
Brady, Anne Kennedy, jt. auth. see Kennedy, Pamela.
Brady, Annie, illus. see Smith, Michael.
Brady, Bill. Charm for Jo. Brady, Laurie, illus. (p. 294)
Brady, Bill & Brady, Laurie. Charm for Jo. Fargo, Todd, illus. (p. 294)
Brady, Carolyn. Adventures of Pelican Mcfeet: The Big Lumpy Green Monster. Phillips, Deborah, illus. (p. 21)
Brady, Charles. Sword of Clontarf. (p. 1692)
Brady, Games. WWE Slam City. (p. 1966)
Brady, Holly. Adventures of Scooburt Humperdink: Scooburt Steals a Meatball. (p. 22)
Brady, Irene. Campsite Critters ~ Bears: A Camper's Guide. (p. 258)
—Campsite Critters ~ Chipmunks: A Camper's Guide. (p. 258)
—Campsite Critters ~ Mosquitoes, Ticks & Fleas: A Camper's Guide to Bites. (p. 258)
—Campsite Critters ~ Mountain Lion: A Camper's Guide. (p. 258)
—Campsite Critters ~ Wolves: A Camper's Guide. (p. 258)
—Illustrating Nature: Right-brain Art in a Left-Brain World. Brady, Irene, illus. (p. 858)
Brady, James. Mis-Adventures of Don Quixote: The Quest Begins! (p. 1149)
—Scariest Place in the World: A Marine Returns to North Korea. (p. 1520)
Brady, James & Senese, Frederick. Chemistry: Matter & Its Changes: Test Bank. (p. 297)
—Chemistry: Matter & Its Changes: Computerized Test Bank. (p. 297)
—Chemistry: Matter & Its Changes. (p. 297)
Brady, Janeen. Creation. Oswald, Bonnie, illus. (p. 379)
—I Have a Song for You: About People & Nature. Vol. 1 (p. 839)
Brady, Janeen J. Safety Kids: Protect Their Minds. Vol. 3 (p. 1502)
Brady, Jeannette, ed. see Morgan, Beverly.
Brady, Karen. God Is Great: A Collection of 13 Story Book Poems (p. 689)
Brady, Laurel. Bronson Row. (p. 230)
Brady, Laurie, illus. see Brady, Bill.
Brady, Laurie, jt. auth. see Brady, Bill.
Brady, Linzy, ed. As You Like It. (p. 105)
Brady, Lisa, illus. see Tweti, Mira.
Brady, Peter. Bulldozers in Action (p. 240)
—Tractors in Action. (p. 1775)
—Transportation Zone. (p. 1779)
Brady, S. Lamar. Littlest Snowflake. Hegerhorst, Bethany Brady, illus. (p. 1039)
BradyGames. WWE Superstars. (p. 1966)
BradyGames Staff. GameCube/Game Boy Advance Secret Codes 2005 (p. 654)
—Secret Codes 2005. (p. 1540)
BradyGames Staff & Birlew, Dan. Monster Hunter Official Strategy Guide. (p. 1167)
BradyGames Staff & Deats, Adam. Prince of Persia: Warrior Within Official Strategy Guide. (p. 1401)
—PS2 Secret Codes 2004 (p. 1413)
—Secret Codes 2004 (p. 1540)
BradyGames Staff & Ehrlichman, Wes. Onimusha(tm) Blade Warriors. (p. 1298)
BradyGames Staff & Morrell, Chris. Rise to Honor: Official Strategu Guide. (p. 1475)
BradyGames Staff, creator. Secret Codes 2005 (p. 1540)
—Sidmeier's Civilization IV. (p. 1573)
BradyGames Staff, et al. Rock. (p. 1481)
—Sly 2: Band of Thieves Official Strategy Guide. (p. 1591)
—Suikoden IV Official Strategy Guide. (p. 1673)
—WWE Sheamus. (p. 1966)
Braem, Viola Brunette. Woodside: A Novel about the Years from 1930 to 1943. A Fictionalized Autobiography & Funny Events in a One-room School. (p. 1950)
Braestrup, Kate. Here If You Need Me: A True Story. (p. 770)
Braeuner, Shellie. Great Dog Wash. Neubecker, Robert, illus. (p. 715)
Braffet, Holly. If You Were a Dinosaur in Hawaii. (p. 854)
—Kekoa & the Egg Mystery. (p. 948)
Braffet, Holly, illus. see Braffet, Mary.
Braffet, Holly, illus. see Ebie, Mora.
Braffet, Mary. Maile & the Huli Hula Chicken. Braffet, Holly, illus. (p. 1077)
—No Slippers! (p. 1260)
Brafman, Bonnie. Treasure in Marci's House. (p. 1781)
Brafman, Joshua. Death Bunny! (p. 420)
Braga, Humberto, illus. see Schenkman, Richard.
Braganza, Sheraleen. Butterfly Kisses. (p. 248)
Bragaw, Jennie M. Marble Harvest. (p. 1091)
Bragdon, Allen D. & Fellows, Leonard. Juegos de Mente. (p. 931)
Brager, Allison. Off-Colored Rainbows. (p. 1279)
Brager, Bruce L. How You Can Use Waste Energy to Heat & Light Your Home. (p. 823)
—John Kerry: Senator from Massachusetts. (p. 922)
—John Paul Jones: America's Sailor. (p. 922)
—Monitor vs. the Merrimack. (p. 1164)
—There He Stands: The Story of Stonewall Jackson. (p. 1729)
Bragg, Georgia. How They Choked: The Astounding Failures of the Awfully Famous. (p. 813)
—How They Choked: Failures, Flops, & Flaws of the Awfully Famous. (p. 813)
—How They Croaked: The Awful Ends of the Awfully Famous. O'Malley, Kevin, illus. (p. 813)
Bragg, Georgia & O'Malley, Kevin. How They Croaked: The Awful Ends of the Awfully Famous. (p. 813)
Bragg, Jane. Teddy Bears Christmas Miracle. (p. 1712)
Bragg, Ruth E. Changes & Choices: Personal Development & Relationships. (p. 290)
Brahmachari, Sita. Jasmine Skies. (p. 910)
—Mira in the Present Tense. (p. 1148)
Brahney, Jenny. Spotty (p. 1634)
Braidich, S. Little Pigs, Big Pigs: Learning the Short I Sound. (p. 1033)
—Meet Me on the Farm: Learning the Long E Sound. (p. 1121)
Braidich, Shelby. Faith Hill. (p. 565)
—Learning about Clouds. (p. 984)
—What Is a Mountain? (p. 1888)
—Where to Buy It. (p. 1910)
Braidich, V. Dale Earnhardt. (p. 401)
Braidich, Victoria. Animals on the Farm: Learning to Compare Size. (p. 83)
—Copperhead. (p. 366)
—Copperhead / Serpiente Cabeza de Cobre. (p. 366)
—Dale Earnhardt. (p. 401)
—Making History: A Covered Wagon. (p. 1081)
—Monday with Meg. (p. 1163)
—Shapes at Home: Learning to Recognize Basic Geometric Shapes. (p. 1560)
Brailovsky, Anna, tr. see Richter, Jutta.
Brailsford, David. Confessions of Anansi. (p. 356)
Brain, Christine. Edexcel A2 Psychology. (p. 504)
Brain, Helen. No More Secrets. (p. 1259)
Brain Quest Editors. Brain Quest America: 850 Questions 850 Answers Celebrating Our Nation's History People & Culture. (p. 221)
—Brain Quest for the Car: 1100 Questions, 1100 Answers, All about America. (p. 221)
—Brain Quest Presidents. (p. 222)
Brain Quest Editors, jt. auth. see Martinelli, Marjorie.
Brain Quest Editors, jt. auth. see Meyer, Jan.
Brainard, Cecilia M., ed. Growing up Filipino: Stories for Young Adults. (p. 726)
Brainard, Cecilia Manguerra. Cecilia's Diary 1962-1969. (p. 283)
Brainerd, Debbi. Tree That Came Home: An IslandWood Story Inspired by the True Story of a 92-Foot Beam That Returned to Bainbridge Island, Washington. Zecca, Katherine, illus. (p. 1783)
Braithwaite, Doug, illus. see Kruger, Jim.
Braithwaite, Jill. Casa Blanca. Translations.com Staff, tr. from ENG. (p. 273)
—From Tree to Table. (p. 644)
—Police Cars. (p. 1379)
—Statue of Liberty. (p. 1644)
—White House. (p. 1913)
Braithwaite, Lisa. Lucy Goes into the Wild. (p. 1063)
Braithwaite, Pamela. Missing Jessic. (p. 1152)
Braithwaithe, Barrington, illus. see Mohamed, Paloma.
Braithwaithe, Barry, illus. see Mohamed, Paloma.
Brake, Colin & British Broadcasting Corporation Staff. Coldest War. (p. 339)
Brake, Mark. Really, Really Big Questions about Space & Time. Choksi, Nishant, illus. (p. 1450)
Brake, Mark & Jack, Colin. Alien Hunter's Handbook: How to Look for Extra-Terrestrial Life. (p. 40)
Brake, Mark & Lonely Planet Publications Staff. How to Be a Space Explorer: Your Out-of-This-World Adventure (p. 815)
Braley and Thompson, Inc. Staff. Treatment Team Foster Care. (p. 1783)
Braley, Shawn, illus. see Bordessa, Kris.
Braley, Shawn, illus. see Ceceri, Kathy.
Braley, Shawn, illus. see Dickinson, Rachel.
Braley, Shawn, illus. see Reilly, Kathleen M.
Braley, Shawn, jt. auth. see Lopez, Delano.
Brallier, Christine. Night Before Christmas. (p. 1252)
Brallier, Jess M. Tess's Tree. Reynolds, Peter H., illus. (p. 1723)
—Who Was Albert Einstein? Parker, Robert Andrew, illus. (p. 1918)
Brallier, Max. Benson's Big Book of Freak-Outs. (p. 165)
—Best. Journal. Ever. (p. 170)
—BMO's Day Out Reed, Stephen, illus. (p. 204)
—Christmas-Tastic Carol. Warren, Emily, illus. (p. 316)
—Numbers Field Guide. (p. 1272)
—Tales from the Land of Ooo. Reed, Stephen, illus. (p. 1701)
—Unzipped: Uncle Grandpa's Magical Belly Bag Journal. (p. 1824)
—Which Way, Dude? - Jake Goes Bananas Reed, Stephen, illus. (p. 1911)
Brallier, Max, jt. auth. see Black, Jake.
Brallier, Max & Johnson, Shane L. How to Catch a Princess. (p. 815)
Bram, Elizabeth. Rufus the Writer. Groenink, Chuck, illus. (p. 1494)
Bramadat, Dawn, ed. see Brown, Hazel.
Bramall, Dan, illus. see Frost, Adam.
Bramall, Toni. Key Organs: The Fight for Healthy Choices. (p. 950)
Brambles, Lindsay. Becoming Darkness. (p. 156)
Brame, Kimberly. My Abc & Color Bible Book. (p. 1195)
Bramlett, Timothy A. Sharkey Explores the Unknown. (p. 1562)
—Thomas in the Land of the Blips. (p. 1738)
—Visit to Skytropolis. (p. 1845)
Brammer, Deb. Moose. (p. 1173)
—Two Sides to Everything. (p. 1804)
Brammer, Ethriam Cash. My Tata's Guitar / la guitarra de mi Tata. Lechon, Daniel, illus. (p. 1219)
—Rowdy, Rowdy Ranch / Alla en el Rancho Grande. Cruz, D. Nina, illus. (p. 1492)
Brammer, Ethriam Cash, tr. see Caraballo, Samuel.
Brams, Jolie S. How to Do Your Best on Every Test: Test-Taking Skills for Elementary Students. (p. 816)
Bramsch, Joan, ed. see Ruckel, Izidor.
Bramsen, Carin. Hey, Duck! (p. 774)
—Just a Duck? (p. 937)
Bramsen, Carin, illus. see Bramsen, Kirsten.
Bramsen, Kirsten. Yellow Tutu. Bramsen, Carin, illus. (p. 1970)
Bramwell, Martyn. Rocks & Fossils. Bramwell, Martyn, ed. (p. 1483)
Bramwell, Martyn, ed. see Mitchell, Andrew.
Bramwell, Neil D. Ancient China: A MyReportLinks. com Book. (p. 68)
—Ancient Egypt: A MyReportLinks. com Book. (p. 68)
—Ancient Persia: A MyReportLinks. com Book. (p. 70)
—Discover Ancient China. (p. 447)
—Discover Ancient Egypt. (p. 447)
—Discover Ancient Persia. (p. 447)
—James Madison: A MyReportLinks. Com Book. (p. 907)
Bramwell, Wendie & Normand, Bridgid. Rhymitis. Kim, Julie J., tr. (p. 1468)
Bramwell, Wendie, et al. Friendship Alphabet. Ziegler, Michael, illus. (p. 639)
Branam, Sandy, illus. see Chappas, Bess.
Branan, Nellie. Fritzi Finds a New Home. (p. 639)
Branca, James. Adventures of General Azù " Azù Explores the World. (p. 18)
Brancaccio, Terry. Time Out for Gio! (p. 1752)
Brancatelli, Joe, et al. Creepy Archives Volume 18. Simon, Philip, ed. (p. 381)
Brancato, Robin F. Food Choices: The Ultimate Teen Guide. (p. 613)
Branch, Beverly. Nightingale. (p. 1255)
—Thumbelina: A Tale about Being Nice. (p. 1745)
Branch, Beverly, illus. see Aesop.
Branch, Dianne. Logan's Caterpillar. (p. 1045)
—Summer Fun. (p. 1674)
—Sydney Becomes a Big Sister. (p. 1692)
Branch, Elizabeth & Jacque, David, texts. Images in the Mirror: Who Do You See? (p. 860)
Branch, Jennifer. Inspired ABC's. Smith, Jenni, illus. (p. 878)
Branch Jr., Robert F., illus. see Williams, Eula.
Branch, Keith. Forest Elves: Protectors of the Rainforest. (p. 618)
Branch, Ken & Tanguay, Dave. Mr. Who? Mr. Atom! (p. 1187)
Branchaud, R. Gary. Toasty Town! (p. 1760)
Branciforte, Suzanne & Grassi, Anna. Branciforte Parliamo Italiano. (p. 222)
Brand, Axel. Night Medicine. (p. 1253)
Brand, Brandon. Lily Is... Wide Awake. (p. 1018)
Brand, Christianna. Nanny Mcphee: The Collected Tales of Nurse Matilda. Ardizzone, Edward, illus. (p. 1229)
—Nurse Matilda Goes to Hospital. Ardizzone, Edward, illus. (p. 1273)
Brand, Joe. When Grandpa Was a Kid: A Typical Farm Boy Growing up in the 40's & 50's. Whittington, Vi, illus. (p. 1902)
Brand, Mary. Aspen Cat: Adventurer Extraordinaire. Roberts, Tempie, illus. (p. 107)
Brand, Ruth. Joseph. Pennington, Jack & Tank, Daniel, illus. (p. 926)
Brand, Ruth R. Adam & Eve. Vitale, Raoul & Tank, Daniel, illus. (p. 10)
Brand, Ruth Redding. Abraham. White, John, Jr. & Tank, Daniel, illus. (p. 6)
—Jacob (p. 904)
Branda, Barnabus. Myself, I & Me. Villella, Jessica, illus. (p. 1222)

Branda, Barnabus, jt. auth. see Bristol, P. L.
Brandao, Lucia, illus. see MacHado, Ana Maria & Machado, Ana Maria.
Brande, Robin. Evolution, Me & Other Freaks of Nature. (p. 546)
—Fat Cat. (p. 577)
Brandeis, Batsheva. Faiga Finds the Way. Levitas, Alexander, illus. (p. 562)
Brandeis, Gayle. My Life with the Lincolns. (p. 1212)
Brandeis, Madeline. Little Anne of Canad. (p. 1023)
—Little Dutch Tulip Girl. (p. 1027)
—Little Mexican Donkey Boy. (p. 1031)
—Little Philippe of Belgium. (p. 1033)
—Little Spanish Dancer. (p. 1036)
—Little Tom of England. (p. 1037)
—Little Tony of Italy. (p. 1037)
—Mitz & Fritz of Germany. (p. 1156)
—Shaun O'Day of Ireland. (p. 1563)
Brandenberg, Aliki & Aliki. Fiesta Medieval. (p. 584)
Brandenburg, Claire. Monk Who Grew Prayer. (p. 1164)
Brandenburg, Claire, illus. see Hart, Chrissi.
Brandenburg, Claire, illus. see Jackson, Dessi.
Brandenburg, Dale. Computer Kids Coloring Book: Designed to Inspire Children to Think Outside the Box ... but Clor Inside the Lines! (p. 355)
Brandenburg, Jim. Face to Face with Wolves. (p. 560)
Brandenburg, Jim & Brandenburg, Judy. Face to Face with Wolves. (p. 560)
Brandenburg, Judy, jt. auth. see Brandenburg, Jim.
Brandi, Lillian, illus. see Sobol, Donald J.
Brandl, Dave. Gangster Grannies. (p. 655)
Brandman, Bronia & Bierman, Carol. Girl Who Survived: A True Story of the Holocaust. (p. 679)
Brandolini, Anita J. Fizz, Bubble & Flash! Element Explorations & Atom Adventures for Hands-On Science Fun! (p. 601)
Brandon, Anthony G. Moving Day. Yee, Wong Herbert, illus. (p. 1183)
Brandon, Barbara. Homer the H Shaped Tree. (p. 793)
—Survive Your Cancer. (p. 1687)
Brandon, Dan, illus. see Mally, Sarah.
Brandon, Demi. Princess Shakina's Locks. (p. 1405)
Brandon, Lee. At a Glance: Reader. (p. 110)
—Writing Connections: Paragraph & Essays - You, College & Careers. Bk. II (p. 1964)
Brandon, Tanisha Danyette. Bayje's Story: An IVF Tale for Little People (p. 147)
Brandon, Theresa, illus. see Anna, Jennifer.
Brandon, Vicky, illus. see Mcwherter, Barbara.
Brandon, Wendy. Cinderbear: (Imagination in a Box) Winter, Janet, illus. (p. 320)
—Cinderbear: Board Book & Puppet Theater. Winter, Janet, illus. (p. 320)
—Frog Prince: Imagination in a Box. Beckes, Shirley, illus. (p. 640)
—Frog Prince: Board Book & Puppet Theater. Beckes, Shirley V., illus. (p. 640)
Brandreth, Gyles. Madcap Book of Brain Teasers. Axworthy, Anni & Miller, Mike, illus. (p. 1069)
—Madcap Book of Laughs. Hawkins, Colin et al, illus. (p. 1069)
—Super Joke Book. Berringer, Nick, illus. (p. 1680)
Brandsberg, George Thomas. Afoot: A Tale of the Great Dakota Turkey Drive. (p. 26)
Brandstaedter, German H, jt. auth. see Ireland, Mary E.
Brandt, Allison & Benchmark Education Co. Staff. Careers on the Cutting Edge. (p. 268)
Brandt, Beverly. Tiara Club. (p. 1746)
Brandt, Catharine. We Light the Candles: Devotions Related to Family Use of the Advent Wreath. (p. 1867)
Brandt, Chris, tr. see Schitt, Christine.
Brandt, Courney. Fine Line. (p. 589)
Brandt, Courtney. Confessions of a Teenage Band Geek. (p. 356)
Brandt, Daniel A. & Warner, J. C. Metallurgy Fundamentals: Teaching Package Text. (p. 1130)
—Metallurgy Fundamentals: Teaching Package Instructor's Manual. (p. 1130)
Brandt, Diane, et al. AppliCase College Application Organizer: The Complete System for Managing the College Application Process. (p. 93)
Brandt, Heidi. Chicken Pox & Posies. (p. 300)
Brandt, Heike, jt. auth. see Honey, Elizabeth.
Brandt, Keith, jt. auth. see Mattern, Joanne.
Brandt, Keith & Macken, JoAnn Early. Abraham Lincoln: Road to the White House. Lawn, John, illus. (p. 6)
—Daniel Boone: Frontier Explorer. Lawn, John, illus. (p. 405)
—Paul Revere, Son of Liberty. Livingston, Francis, illus. (p. 1330)
Brandt, Keith & Mattern, Joanne. Rosa Parks: Freedom Rider. Griffith, Gershom, illus. (p. 1489)
Brandt, Linda M. Henry's Life As a Tulip Bulb: Developing an Attitude of Gratitude (Book 1) Brandt, Linda M., illus. (p. 769)
Brandt, Lois. Maddi's Fridge. Vogel, Vin, illus. (p. 1069)
Brandt, Michael, illus. see Brandt-Taylor, Diane.
Brandt, Susan, illus. see Harrington, Daniel.
Brandt-Taylor, Diane. Bunny, the Bear, the Bug & the Bee. Brandt, Michael, illus. (p. 242)
Brandvold, Peter. Old Wolves. (p. 1285)
Branen, Kathy. My Life By: D. D. Duck. Robinson, Marcus, illus. (p. 1212)
Braner, Andy. Duplicate This! Showing Your Friends How to Live Like Jesus (p. 490)
Branford, Anna. Violet Mackerel's Brilliant Plot. Allen, Elanna, illus. (p. 1843)
—Violet Mackerel's Natural Habitat. Allen, Elanna, illus. (p. 1843)
—Violet Mackerel's Outside-the-Box: Violet Mackerel's Brilliant Plot; Violet Mackerel's Remarkable Recovery; Violet Mackerel's Natural Habita; Violet Mackerel's Personal Space. Set Allen, Elanna, illus. (p. 1843)
—Violet Mackerel's Personal Space. Allen, Elanna, illus. (p. 1843)
—Violet Mackerel's Possible Friend. Allen, Elanna, illus. (p. 1843)
—Violet Mackerel's Remarkable Recovery. Allen, Elanna, illus. (p. 1843)
Branford, Henrietta. Six Chicks. Elfezzani, Thierry, illus. (p. 1582)
Branford, Henrietta & Beardshaw, Rosalind. Splash! (p. 1629)
Branham, Jan, jt. auth. see Johannes, Avril.
Branigan, Carrie. First Steps in Science: Big Story Book. (p. 597)
—Image Bank. (p. 860)
Branley, jt. auth. see Branley, Franklyn M.
Branley, Franklyn M. Air Is All Around You. O'Brien, John A., illus. (p. 31)
—Earthquakes. Lloyd, Megan, illus. (p. 497)
—Gravity Is a Mystery. (p. 712)
—Gravity Is a Mystery. Miller, Edward, illus. (p. 712)
—Gravity Is a Mystery. Miller, Edward, illus. (p. 713)
—Moon Seems to Change. Emberley, Barbara & Ed, illus. (p. 1172)
—Planets in Our Solar System. O'Malley, Kevin, illus. (p. 1368)
—Sunshine Makes the Seasons. Rex, Michael, illus. (p. 1678)
—Volcanoes. (p. 1849)
—What Makes Day & Night. Dorros, Arthur, illus. (p. 1892)
Branley, Franklyn M. & Branley. Earthquakes. Lloyd, Megan, illus. (p. 497)
—Volcanoes. Lloyd, Megan, illus. (p. 1849)
Branley, Franklyn Mansfield. Gravity Is a Mystery. Miller, Edward, illus. (p. 713)
—Sunshine Makes the Seasons. Rex, Michael, illus. (p. 1678)
Branlyn Community School, Students of the. Claud Learns a Lesson. (p. 329)
Branman, Liz, illus. see Friday, Anita.
Brannan, Dara, ed. ¡Vívelo al extremo! Nivel 1: Lecciones prácticas para aprender de Dios. Tobar, Malena, illus. (p. 1846)
Brannen, Daniel E. & Baker, Lawrence W. Checks & Balances: The Three Branches of the American Government (p. 295)
Brannen, Daniel E., et al. Supreme Court Drama: Cases That Changed America. (p. 1684)
Brannen, Sarah, illus. see Namm, Diane.
Brannen, Sarah S. Madame Martine. (p. 1069)
—Madame Martine. Brannen, Sarah S., illus. (p. 1069)
—Madame Martine Breaks the Rules. Brannen, Sarah S., illus. (p. 1069)
Brannen, Sarah S., illus. see Cline, Eric H. & Rubalcaba, Jill.
Brannen, Sarah S., illus. see Kinney, Jessica.
Brannen, Sarah S., illus. see Levine, Arthur A.
Brannen, Sarah S., illus. see Liu-Perkins, Christine.
Brannen, Sarah S., illus. see Olmstead, Kathleen.
Brannen, Sarah S., illus. see Stewart, Melissa.
Branner, Jenna, jt. auth. see Branner, Toni.
Branner, Toni & Branner, Jenna. Care & Feeding of a Dancer: What You Need to Know on & off the Stage. (p. 266)
Brannin, Kaitlyn & Brannin, Sandy. Return to Arteo. (p. 1465)
Brannin, Sandy, jt. auth. see Brannin, Kaitlyn.
Branning, Debe. Adventures of Chickolet Pigolet: The Bribe of Frankenbeans. Knold, Nijlon, illus. (p. 17)
Brannock, Martha Lee. Freddie, the Frumpy, Grumpy Frog. (p. 633)
—Teddy Bear Too-Too. (p. 1712)
Brannon, Barbara. Discover Adaptation. (p. 447)
—Discover Ancient China. (p. 447)
—Discover Ancient Greece. (p. 447)
—Discover Ancient Rome. (p. 447)
—Discover Coral Reefs. (p. 447)
—Discover Deserts. (p. 447)
—Discover Dinosaurs. (p. 447)
—Discover Disease. (p. 447)
—Discover Earthquakes. (p. 447)
—Discover English Explorers. (p. 447)
—Discover Erosion. (p. 447)
—Discover Forests. (p. 447)
—Discover Fossils. (p. 447)
—Discover French Explorers. (p. 447)
—Discover Gases. (p. 447)
—Discover George Washington. (p. 447)
—Discover Glaciers. (p. 447)
—Discover Heredity. (p. 447)
—Discover Jamestown. (p. 447)
—Discover Liquids. (p. 447)
—Discover Local & State Government. (p. 447)
—Discover Mesa Verde. (p. 447)
—Discover Motion. (p. 447)
—Discover Ocean Pollution. (p. 447)
—Discover Oil Spills. (p. 447)
—Discover Sir Isaac Newton. (p. 448)
—Discover Solids. (p. 448)
—Discover Spanish Explorers. (p. 448)
—Discover Storms. (p. 448)
—Discover Symbols of the United States. (p. 448)
—Discover the Aztec. (p. 448)
—Discover the Boston Tea Party. (p. 448)
—Discover the Empire of Egypt. (p. 448)
—Discover the Empires of Mesopotamia. (p. 448)
—Discover the Inca. (p. 448)
—Discover the Kingdom of Kush. (p. 448)
—Discover the Laws of Motion: Set Of 6. (p. 448)
—Discover the Laws of Motion. (p. 448)
—Discover the Maya. (p. 448)
—Discover the Midwest Region. (p. 448)
—Discover the Northeast Region. (p. 448)
—Discover the Pacific Northwest Region. (p. 448)
—Discover the Thirteen Colonies. (p. 448)
—Discover the United States Government. (p. 448)
—Discover Tropical Rain Forests. (p. 448)
—Discover Water. (p. 448)
—Discover Weather. (p. 448)
—Discover Your Skeleton. (p. 448)
Brannon, Brian, ed. see McChesney, Terry.
Brannon, Dj. Angelic Soldiers: The Way Back. (p. 74)
Brannon, Pat. Filthy Farley O'Charlie Mcbarley. (p. 586)
—Has a Donkey Ever Brought You Breakfast in Bed? Demming, Karen, illus. (p. 752)
—Quirky Kids Zoo. Jimena Pinto-Krowjiline, illus. (p. 1428)
Brannon, Tom. Elmo's Merry Christmas. (p. 515)
—I Love You Valentine Songs. (p. 844)
—Sesame Street All Aboard! (p. 1553)
—What's the Big Idea, Charlie Brown? (p. 1899)
—Where Are You Going, Charlie Brown? (p. 1906)
—Who Cares, Charlie Brown? (p. 1915)
Brannon, Tom, illus. see Albee, Sarah.
Brannon, Tom, illus. see Kleinberg, Naomi.
Brannon, Tom, illus. see Mitter, Matt & Rudko, Che.
Brannon, Tom, illus. see Mitter, Matt.
Brannon, Tom, illus. see Rabe, Tish.
Brannon, Tom, illus. see Random House Editors & Kleinberg, Naomi.
Brannon, Tom, illus. see Reader's Digest Editors, et al.
Brannon, Tom, illus. see Reader's Digest Editors.
Brannon, Tom, illus. see Reader's Digest Staff & Mitter, Matt.
Brannon, Tom, illus. see Reader's Digest Staff.
Brannon, Tom, illus. see Ross, Katharine.
Brannon, Tom, illus. see Sesame Workshop Staff.
Brannon, Tom, illus. see Tabby, Abigail.
Brannon, Tom, illus. see Tieman, Ruth Anne.
Branon, Dave. Heads Up! Sports Devotions for All-Star Kids (p. 757)
Branscomb, Leslie Wolf. Earl Warren. (p. 493)
—Marc Jacobs. (p. 1091)
Branscombe, Allison. All about China: Stories, Songs, Crafts & Games for Kids. Wang, Lin, illus. (p. 42)
Branse, J. L. Day in the Life of a Colonial Glassblower. (p. 413)
Bransom, Paul, illus. see Grahame, Kenneth.
Bransom, Paul, illus. see Kipling, Rudyard.
Branson, Eve. Sarky Puddleboat. Lowe, Wes, illus. (p. 1515)
Branson, Michelle. Texas Doodles (p. 1724)
Branson, Sam. Let's Measure the Weather. (p. 999)
Branson, Terri. Brother Dragon. Taylor, Chet, illus. (p. 231)
—Pete, the Peacock, Goes to Town. (p. 1346)
—Pete, the Peacock, Goes to Town. Taylor, Chet, illus. (p. 1346)
—Tyler on the Moon. Taylor, Chet, illus. (p. 1805)
—Very Dragon Christmas. (p. 1837)
Branson, Terri & Wilks, Jackie. Mirror of the Carousel. (p. 1149)
Brant, Cherie. Legends of Ventura County. (p. 990)
Brant, Dennis, Jr. No Andy No! Sciulli, Erika, illus. (p. 1257)
Brant, John. Duel in the Sun: Alberto Salazar, Dick Beardsley, & America's Greatest Marathon. (p. 489)
Brantley, Meg. Love Family Adventures. (p. 1059)
Brantley-Newton, Vanessa, illus. see Best, Carl.
Brantley-Newton, Vanessa, illus. see Godin, Thelma Lynne.
Brantley-Newton, Vanessa, illus. see Levinson, Cynthia.
Brantley-Newton, Vanessa, illus. see Levy, Debbie.
Brantley-Newton, Vanessa, illus. see Marley, Bob & Marley, Cedella.
Brantley-Newton, Vanessa, illus. see Marley, Cedella & Marley, Bob.
Brantley-Newton, Vanessa, illus. see Marley, Cedella.
Brantley-Newton, Vanessa, illus. see Shapiro, J. H.
Branton, Molly, illus. see Carter, Aubrey Smith.
Brantz, Loryn. Not Just a Dot. (p. 1267)
Brantz, Loryn, illus. see Rebboah, Julie A.
Branum, Anita, jt. auth. see Jeffords, Stephanie.
Branzel, Sylvia. Animal Grossology: The Science of Creatures Gross & Disgusting. Keely, Jack, illus. (p. 78)
—Hands-On Grossology: Really Gross Science Experiments. Keely, Jack, illus. (p. 741)
—History of Vampires & Other Real Blood Drinkers. Keely, Jack, illus. (p. 785)
—Ickstory - Unraveling the History of Mummies Around the World. Keely, Jack, illus. (p. 851)
Brar, Aneel. Super Bowl. (p. 1679)
Braren, Loretta Trezzo, illus. see Press, Judy.
Brasch, Nicholas. Conquering the Sky. (p. 358)
—Hot & Cold (p. 801)
—Inventors Club Meets Again. (p. 884)
—It's All about Physics (p. 896)
—Leonardo Da Vinci: The Greatest Inventor. (p. 992)
—Leonardo Da Vinci. (p. 992)
—Mining (p. 1147)
Brasch, Nicolas. Amazing Built Structures. (p. 54)
—Animal & Plant Survival. (p. 76)
—Baseball Giant. (p. 141)
—Conquering the Sky. (p. 358)
—Ernest Shackleton's Antarctic Expedition. (p. 534)
—Escape from Pacaya. (p. 535)
—Everyday Appliances. (p. 543)
—Foods We Eat. (p. 614)
—Hot Springs & Brown Bears. (p. 802)
—Industrial Revolution: Age of Invention. (p. 872)
—Internet. (p. 880)
—Invention of Money. (p. 883)
—Leonardo Da Vinci: The Greatest Inventor. (p. 992)
—Machines of Speed & Flight. (p. 1068)
—Mystery of the Missing Bike. (p. 1225)
—Natural Disasters. (p. 1235)
—Robots & Artificial Intelligence. (p. 1481)
—Robots of the Future. (p. 1481)
—Sports & Sporting Equipment. (p. 1632)
—Theme Parks, Playgrounds, & Toys. (p. 1728)
—Times, Tides, & Revolutions. (p. 1754)
—Tricks of Sound & Light. (p. 1786)
—Triumphs of Engineering. (p. 1788)
—Why Do Shadows Change? Level 5 Factbook. (p. 1924)
—Why Do Shadows Lengthen? (p. 1924)
—Why Do Shadows Lengthen? All about Light. (p. 1924)
—Why Do Spiders Live in Webs? (p. 1924)
—Why Do Spiders Live in Webs? Level 4 Factbook. (p. 1924)
—Why Do Volcanoes Erupt? (p. 1924)
—Why Do Volcanoes Erupt? All about Earth Science. (p. 1924)
—Why Do Volcanoes Erupt? Level 4 Factbook. (p. 1924)
—Why Does Sound Travel? All about Sound. (p. 1924)
—Why Is It So Loud? (p. 1925)
Brasch, Nicolas & Dawson, Amanda. Chalk Circle. (p. 288)
Brasch, Nicolas & Nickel, Adam. Dad & Dan Go Camping. (p. 398)
—Dad & Dan Go Fishing. (p. 398)
Brasch, Nicolas & Parton, Daron. Riddle of the Camel Race. (p. 1470)
Brasch, Nicolas & Rigby Education Staff. Moving World. (p. 1184)
Brasch, Nicolas & Webb, Melissa. Mystery of the Missing Bike. (p. 1225)
Brasch, Pamela. J Is for Jupiter: A-Z of People, Places & Things in Jupiter, Florida. Kindt, Kathleen G., illus. (p. 901)
Brase, Charles Henry. Understandable Statistics. (p. 1815)
Brase, Charles Henry & Brase, Corrinne Pellillo. Understandable Statistics: Concepts & Methods. (p. 1815)
Brase, Corrinne Pellillo, jt. auth. see Brase, Charles Henry.
Brash, Lorna. Professor Cook's Dynamite Dinners. (p. 1409)
—Professor Cook's Fruity Desserts. (p. 1409)
—Professor Cook's Mind-Blowing Baking. (p. 1409)
—Professor Cook's Smashing Snacks. (p. 1409)
Brashares, Ann. 3 Willows: The Sisterhood Grows. (p. 1991)
—Forever in Blue: The Fourth Summer of the Sisterhood. (p. 619)
—Girls in Pants. (p. 680)
—Here & Now. (p. 769)
—Second Summer of the Sisterhood. (p. 1539)
—Sisterhood of the Traveling Pants: The Sisterhood of the Traveling Pants - The Second Summer of the Sisterhood - Girls in Pants Set (p. 1581)
—Sisterhood of the Traveling Pants. (p. 1581)
Brashear Hopper, Celia. Merry Adventures of Blade & Friends. (p. 1128)
Brashear, Kristina L. Up High in a Tree. (p. 1824)
Brashear-Hopper, Celia. Curious Cricket. (p. 392)
Brasier, Michael. World Through A Child's Eyes: A View of Various Countries & Global Cultures from a Child's Perspective. (p. 1958)
Braslavskii, Felix, illus. see Kovner, Vladimir, tr.
Brass, Alice. Orff Explorations: Classroom Projects in Music, Movement & Poetry. Sakhavarz, Nazy, illus. (p. 1303)
Brassard, France, illus. see Brisson, Pat.
Brassard, France, illus. see Hodge, Deborah.
Brassard, Maria R. & Boehm, Ann E. Preschool Assessment: Principles & Practices. (p. 1396)
Brassel, Sondra, illus. see Coe, Julie L.
Brassey, Richard. George & the Dragon & Other Saintly Stories. (p. 663)
—Greyfriars Bobby. (p. 723)
Brassey, Richard, illus. see McCaughrean, Geraldine.
Brassill, Amber M. My Greatest Mistake (p. 1210)
Braswell, Liz. Fallen. (p. 566)
Braswell, Liz, jt. auth. see Thomson, Celia.
Braswell, Robert William. Jeffrey: Out from the Depths of Innocence. (p. 912)
Bratcher, Shirley Kay. Tudy Goes to the Zoo. (p. 1796)
—Tudy Won't Count - Three. (p. 1796)
Brathwaite, Kamau. Words Need Love Too. (p. 1951)
Bratley, Colleen m. Easter Spirit Eggs. (p. 499)
Bratton, Ashley A., jt. auth. see Bratton, Deboral B.
Bratton, Ashley D., jt. auth. see Bratton, Deboral B.
Bratton, Chris, jt. auth. see Wight, Milan E.
Bratton, Deboral B. & Bigly, Ashley D. Record-a-Sport Golf Organizer. Bratton, Deboral B. & Bigly, Ashley D., eds. (p. 1452)
Bratton, Deboral B. & Bratton, Ashley A. Record-a-Sport Football Sport Organizer. Bratton, Deboral B. & Bratton, Ashley A., eds. (p. 1452)
Bratton, Deboral B. & Bratton, Ashley D. Record-a-Sport Baseball & Softball Organizer. Bratton, Deboral B. & Bratton, Ashley D., eds. (p. 1452)
—Record-a-Sport Basketball Sport Organizer. Bratton, Deboral B. & Bratton, Ashley D., eds. (p. 1452)
—Record-a-Sport Soccer Sport Organizer. Bratton, Deboral B. & Bratton, Ashley D., eds. (p. 1452)
—Record-a-Sport Tennis Organizer. Bratton, Deboral B. & Bratton, Ashley D., eds. (p. 1452)
Bratton, Donna Bowman. From Head to Tail: All about Horse Care (p. 642)
—Saddle Up! Riding & Competitions for Horse Lovers (p. 1501)
Bratton, Donna Bowman, jt. auth. see Kolpin, Molly.
Bratun, Katy. Gingerbread Mouse. Bratun, Katy, illus. (p. 677)
Bratun, Katy, illus. see Cowan, Charlotte.
Bratun, Katy, illus. see Josephs, Mary.
Bratun, Katy, illus. see Lay, Kathryn.
Bratun, Katy, illus. see Morrow, Tara Jaye.
Bratun, Katy, illus. see Schwaeber, Barbie Heit.
Bratvold, Gretchen. Oregon. (p. 1302)
Brauckmann-Towns, Krista, illus. see Lee, Evelyn.
Brauckman-Towns, Krista, illus. see Lee, Evelyn.
Braud, Melissa. World Without Hugs & Kisses. (p. 1959)
Braught, Mark, illus. see Crane, Carol.
Braught, Mark, illus. see Herzog, Brad.
Braught, Mark, illus. see Moore, Cathy.
Braught, Mark, illus. see Scillian, Devin.
Braught, Mark, illus. see Ulmer, Michael.
Braught, Mark, illus. see Ulmer, Mike.
Braulick, Carrie A. Air Force Space Command (p. 31)
—Blue Angels (p. 202)
—Indy Cars (p. 873)
—U. S. Air Force Spy Planes (p. 1806)
—U. S. Air Force Spy Planes [Scholastic]. (p. 1806)
—U. S. Air Force Thunderbirds. (p. 1806)
—U. S. Army Helicopters (p. 1806)
—U. S. Army National Guard (p. 1806)
—U. S. Army Tanks (p. 1806)
Braulick, Carrie A. & Capstone Press Editors. Aviones Espía de la Fuerza Aérea de EE. UU. (p. 120)
Braulick, Carrie A. & Capstone Press Staff. Aviones de Combate de la Fuerza Aérea de EE. UU. (p. 120)
—Blue Angels. (p. 202)
Braulick, J. J. M., jt. auth. see Schultz, Leslie.
Brault, Christopher, illus. see Winkel, Andrew.

B

Braun, Cheskel. Learn to Read (p. 984)
Braun, Chris, illus. see Childress, Jamie.
Braun, Chuck, illus. see Egelberg, Arlene & Clark, Raymond C.
Braun, Eric. Benjamin Banneker (p. 164)
—Bessie Coleman. (p. 168)
—Booker T. Washington: Great American Educator Martin, Cynthia, illus. (p. 212)
—Booker T. Washington: Gran Educador Norteamericano. Martin, Cynthia, illus. (p. 212)
—Canada in Pictures. (p. 260)
—Cesar Chavez: Fighting for Farmworkers Roland, Harry et al, illus. (p. 288)
—Cronus the Titan Tells All: Tricked by the Kids Gilpin, Stephen, illus. (p. 384)
—Fatal Faults: The Story of the Challenger Explosion. (p. 577)
—Football's Greatest (p. 615)
—Football's Greatest Receivers (p. 615)
—Football's Greatest Running Backs (p. 615)
—Gertrude & Reginald the Monsters Talk about Living & Nonliving Bernardini, Cristian, illus. (p. 667)
—Goldilocks & the Three Bears: An Interactive Fairy Tale Adventure. Lopez, Alex, illus. (p. 696)
—Guys' Guide to Making City Life More Awesome (p. 733)
—Guys' Guide to Making Life More Awesome. (p. 733)
—Guys' Guide to Making Sports More Awesome (p. 733)
—Guys' Guide to Making the Outdoors More Awesome (p. 733)
—Guys' Guides (p. 733)
—Hot Rods. (p. 802)
—If I Were a Cowboy Reid, Mick, illus. (p. 853)
—If I Were a Major League Baseball Player. Harmer, Sharon, illus. (p. 853)
—If I Were an Astronaut Harmer, Sharon, illus. (p. 853)
—Jesse Owens. (p. 914)
—Joe-Joe the Wizard Brews up Solids, Liquids, & Gases Boyden, Robin, illus. (p. 920)
—John Green: Star Author, Vlogbrother, & Nerdfighter. (p. 922)
—Lance Dragon Defends His Castle with Simple Machines Briglia, Anthony, illus. (p. 973)
—Let's Rock! Science Adventures with Rudie the Origami Dinosaur Christoph, Jamey, illus. (p. 1000)
—Little Red Riding Hood: An Interactive Fairy Tale Adventure. Epelbaum, Mariano, illus. (p. 1035)
—Lookin' for Light: Science Adventures with Manny the Origami Moth Christoph, Jamey, illus. (p. 1050)
—Loretta Lynch: First African American Woman Attorney General. (p. 1053)
—Mad Margaret Experiments with the Scientific Method Boyden, Robin, illus. (p. 1069)
—Mae Jemison (p. 1070)
—Maurice Sendak (p. 1110)
—Maurice Sendak Saunders-Smith, Gail, ed. (p. 1110)
—Maurice Sendak [Scholastic]. (p. 1110)
—Medea Tells All: A Mad, Magical Love Gilpin, Stephen, illus. (p. 1118)
—Plan a Holiday Party. (p. 1366)
—Plan an Outdoor Party. (p. 1366)
—Plant Parts Smarts: Science Adventures with Charlie the Origami Bee Christoph, Jamey, illus. (p. 1369)
—Simply Sound: Science Adventures with Jasper the Origami Bat Christoph, Jamey, illus. (p. 1578)
—Story of Jamestown Erwin, Steve et al, illus. (p. 1658)
—Super Baseball Infographics. (p. 1679)
—Super Football Infographics. (p. 1680)
—Taking Action to Help the Environment. (p. 1698)
—Tomie Depaola (p. 1764)
—Tomie Depaola [Scholastic]. (p. 1764)
—Tony Hawk. (p. 1766)
—Trust Me, Jack's Beanstalk Stinks! The Story of Jack & the Beanstalk as Told by the Giant. Bernardini, Cristian, illus. (p. 1793)
—Truth about Ogres Tenney, Shawna J. C., illus. (p. 1794)
—Truth about Witches Squier, Robert, illus. (p. 1794)
—Uganda in Pictures. (p. 1808)
—Wilma Rudolph. (p. 1934)
Braun, Eric, ed. see Mather, Anne D. & Weldon, Louise B.
Braun, Eric, jt. auth. see Loewen, Nancy.
Braun, Eric, jt. auth. see Troupe, Thomas Kingsley.
Braun, Eric & Bowman, James Cloyd. Pecos Bill Tames a Colossal Cyclone Weber, Lisa K., illus. (p. 1334)
Braun, Eric & Gunderson, Jessica. Cinderella: An Interactive Fairy Tale Adventure. Lopez, Ayesha, illus. (p. 320)
Braun, Eric & Meister, Cari. American Folk Legends (p. 60)
Braun, Eric & Troupe, Thomas Kingsley. Origami Science Adventures Christoph, Jamey, illus. (p. 1304)
Braun, Lilian Jackson. Cat Who Had 60 Whiskers (p. 278)
Braun, Lisa, illus. see McDermott, Mary.
Braun, Marta. Muybridge & the Riddle of Locomotion. (p. 1195)
Braun, Melinda. Stranded. (p. 1664)
Braun, Philip. Alberto's Dream. (p. 35)
Braun, Sandra. Incredible Women Inventors (p. 869)
—Women Inventors Who Changed the World. (p. 1946)
Braun, Sebastian, illus. see Sperring, Mark.
Braun, Sebastian. I'm a Clown! (p. 858)
—I'm a Monster! (p. 858)
—I'm a Robot! (p. 858)
—I'm an Alien! (p. 858)
—Peekaboo Baby. Braun, Sebastian, illus. (p. 1335)
Braun, Sebastian, illus. see Ziefert, Harriet.
Braun, Sebastien. Back to Bed, Ed! Braun, Sebastien, illus. (p. 130)
—Digger & Tom! Braun, Sebastien, illus. (p. 438)
—I Love My Daddy. Braun, Sebastien, illus. (p. 842)
—I Love You More. Braun, Sebastien, illus. (p. 843)
—Meeow & the Big Box. (p. 1120)
—Meeow & the Blue Table. (p. 1120)
—Meeow & the Little Chairs. (p. 1120)
—Meeow & the Pots & Pans. (p. 1120)
—On Our Way Home. (p. 1289)
—One Sleepy Night. (p. 1297)
—Santa's Noisy House. (p. 1513)
—Shapes & Colors. (p. 1560)
—Toot & Pop! Braun, Sebastien, illus. (p. 1767)
—Who Can Jump? Braun, Sebastien, illus. (p. 1914)
—Who Can Swim? Braun, Sebastien, illus. (p. 1914)
—Whoosh & Chug! Braun, Sebastien, illus. (p. 1920)
—Who's Hiding? (p. 1920)
Braun, Sebastien, illus. see Crow, Nosy.
Braun, Sebastien, illus. see Ford, Bernette G.
Braun, Sebastien, illus. see Ford, Bernette G. & Ford, Bernette.
Braun, Sebastien, illus. see Gates, Susan & Ceredigion, Cymdeithas Lyfrau.
Braun, Sebastien, illus. see Krulik, Nancy.
Braun, Sebastien, illus. see Lobel, Gill.
Braun, Sebastien, illus. see Mongredien, Sue.
Braun, Sebastien, illus. see Nosy Crow.
Braun, Sebastien, illus. see Seltzer, Eric & Hall, Kirsten.
Braun, Sebastien, illus. see Wiley, Melissa.
Braun, Sebastien, illus. see Wood, Julie M.
Brauner, Barbara & Mattson, James Iver. Glitter Trap. Halpin, Abigail, illus. (p. 684)
—Magic Mistake. Halpin, Abigail, illus. (p. 1072)
—Oh My Godmother the Magic Mistake. Halpin, Abigail, illus. (p. 1281)
—Spell Bind. Halpin, Abigail, illus. (p. 1625)
Brauner, Susan. Adventures of Sohi: Mystery of Moon Island. (p. 23)
Brauning, Kate. How We Fall. (p. 823)
Braunius, Marlene, et al. Exploring Language Arts Through Literature Birth - Grade 8. (p. 552)
Braunns, Melissa. Big Bear Cares. (p. 178)
Braunstein, J., jt. auth. see Braunstein, M.
Braunstein, M. & Braunstein, J. Don't Look Smart. (p. 467)
—Don't Look Smart?! (p. 468)
Brave M.A., Kathryn A. & Lavin, Paul J. Fit ting Fairy Tale. (p. 599)
Braver, Vanita. Madison & the New Neighbors Brown, Jonathan, illus. (p. 1070)
—Madison & the Two-Wheeler DiRocco, Carl, illus. (p. 1070)
—Madison's Patriotic Project DiRocco, Carl, illus. (p. 1070)
—Party Princess. Pillo, Cary, illus. (p. 1326)
—Pinky Promise: A Book about Telling the Truth. (p. 1360)
Braverman, Rivkie, jt. auth. see Rosen, Chaya.
Bravi, Soledad. Noisy Book. (p. 1263)
Bravi, Soledad, illus. see Marchon, Benoit.
Bravo, Constanza, illus. see Uribe, Veronica & Esopo.
Bravo, Emile. Goldilocks & the Seven Squat Bears. (p. 696)
—Hunger of the Seven Squat Bears. (p. 828)
Bravo, Fran, illus. see Cano, Carles & Carles, Cano.
Bravo, J. A., tr. see Van Saan, Anita.
Bravo, Juan, illus. see Cano, Carles & Carles, Cano.
Bravo, Leonor. Yo Te Quiero Aiempre. Cornejo, Eduardo, illus. (p. 1971)
Bravo-Villasante, Carmen, tr. see Andersen, Hans Christian.
Brawer, Michael, jt. auth. see Mass, Wendy.
Brawner, Faye. Geraniums: The Complete Encyclopedia (p. 666)
Bray, Adam. Lego Star Wars: Into Battle! (p. 990)
Bray, Adam, jt. auth. see Dorling Kindersley Publishing Staff.
Bray, Barbara, tr. see Giono, Jean & Giono, Aline.
Bray, Carolyn. Classworks - Literacy Year 3. (p. 329)
Bray, Darrell. I Remember Pop's General Store. (p. 844)
Bray, Diane E. B. First Generation: The Story of Annie. (p. 595)
Bray, Libba. Beauty Queens. (p. 154)
—Diviners. (p. 454)
—Going Bovine. (p. 692)
—Great & Terrible Beauty. (p. 713)
—Lair of Dreams. (p. 972)
—Rebel Angels. (p. 1450)
—Sweet Far Thing. (p. 1689)
Bray, Pamela. Day Lonyaie's Life Changed. (p. 413)
—Elephant & Ant. (p. 511)
Bray, Pamela, illus. see Powell, GinaMarie.
Bray, Peter, illus. see Dubosarsky, Ursula.
Bray, Peter, illus. see French, Jackie.
Bray, Phyllis, illus. see Uttley, Alison & Singh, Mahendra.
Bray, Sorcha. Adventures of Powerpup & Wonderboy & the Case of the Wicked Chickens. (p. 21)
Brayley, Genevieve. Noah Saves the Tigers. (p. 1261)
Brayton, Julie, illus. see Becker, Christie.
Brazauski, Vickie. Tweeter the Peachick A True Story (p. 1800)
Brazell, Derek. That's My Mum: Voici Ma Mere. Barkow, Henriette, illus. (p. 1727)
Brazell, Derek, illus. see Barkow, Henriette.
Brazell, Derek, illus. see Mills, David.
Brazell, Derek, illus. see Robert, Na'ima Bint & Petrova-Browning, Nina.
Brazell, Derek, illus. see Robert, Na'ima Bint.
Brazier, Jenny, jt. auth. see Tuxford, Jenny.
Brazier, Vaughan. Zach Zephyr & the Coral Gold. (p. 1984)
Brazier, Yuvonne. Princess Jordan Saves Golden Tree. (p. 1404)
Brazil, Angela. Luckiest Girl in the School. (p. 1062)
—Monitress Merle. (p. 1164)
Brazina, Rhonda & Margolis, Ida R. Carrots for Charlie. (p. 271)
Bre, Norman H. Fehr. Animals in Canad. (p. 83)
Bready, Jane Gilltrap, illus. see Herzog, Brad.
Breakespeare, Andrew, illus. see Gates, Susan.
Brean, Alta. Dear Grandchildren: Growing up on the Frontier. (p. 419)
Brearley, Leeanne. Harlow the Helpful Ghost. Apa, Ivy Marie, illus. (p. 749)
Brearley, Sue. Talk to Me. (p. 1703)
Breast Cancer Fund Staff. Climb Against the Odds: Celebrating Survival on the Mountain. (p. 333)
Breathed, Berkeley. Bloom County: The Complete Collection, 1980-1982 Vol. 1 (p. 201)
—Bloom County: the Complete Library Volume 5: The Complete Library Volume 5 (p. 201)
—Edwurd Fudwupper Fibbed Big. Breathed, Berkeley, illus. (p. 505)
—Flawed Dogs: The Year-End Leftovers at the Piddleton Last Chance Dog Pound. (p. 603)
—Flawed Dogs. Breathed, Berkeley, illus. (p. 603)
—Mars Needs Moms! Breathed, Berkeley, illus. (p. 1096)
—Pete & Pickles. Breathed, Berkeley, illus. (p. 1346)
Breault, Christie Merriman. Logan West, Printer's Devil. Archambault, Matthew, illus. (p. 1045)
Breaux, Joe Ann, illus. see Walker, Gary C.
Breaux, Wayne, Jr., illus. see Siembieda, Kevin.
Brecher, Erwin. Are There Rainbows on the Moon? Over 200 Bizarre, Weird & Wonderful Puzzles with Science. (p. 96)
Brecke, Nicole & Stockland, Patricia M. Airplanes & Ships You Can Draw. Brecke, Nicole, illus. (p. 32)
—Cars, Trucks, & Motorcycles You Can Draw. Brecke, Nicole, illus. (p. 272)
—Cats You Can Draw. Brecke, Nicole, illus. (p. 281)
—Cool Boy Stuff You Can Draw. Brecke, Nicole, illus. (p. 362)
—Cool Girl Stuff You Can Draw. Brecke, Nicole, illus. (p. 363)
—Dinosaurs & Other Prehistoric Creatures You Can Draw. Brecke, Nicole, illus. (p. 444)
—Dogs You Can Draw. Brecke, Nicole, illus. (p. 463)
—Extinct & Endangered Animals You Can Draw. Brecke, Nicole, illus. (p. 555)
—Horses You Can Draw. Brecke, Nicole, illus. (p. 800)
—Insects You Can Draw. Brecke, Nicole, illus. (p. 876)
—Ready, Set, Draw! Brecke, Nicole, illus. (p. 1447)
—Sea Creatures You Can Draw. Brecke, Nicole, illus. (p. 1534)
—Spaceships, Aliens, & Robots You Can Draw. Brecke, Nicole, illus. (p. 1620)
Breckenreid, Julia, illus. see Wing, Natasha.
Breckenridge, Bill. Bernie Bolts Bergen. (p. 167)
Breckenridge, Gerald. Radio Boys Search for the Inca's Treasure. (p. 1433)
Breckenridge, Scott, jt. auth. see Breckenridge, Trula.
Breckenridge, Trula & Breckenridge, Scott. Squiggly the Roach. Breckenridge, Trula & Breckenridge, Scott, illus. (p. 1637)
Breckenridge, Trula & Lynch, Todd. Ricca the Ladybug. Breckenridge, Trula & Lynch, Todd, illus. (p. 1469)
Breckenridge, Trula & Palmore, Iyende. FiFi the Leaf. Breckenridge, Trula & Palmore, Iyende, illus. (p. 584)
Breckman, Cindy, ed. see Fetzer, Erin.
Breckman, Cindy, ed. see Sonday, Arlene.
Brecknell, Annie, illus. see Medina, Sarah.
Breckon, Brett. Dragon Days. (p. 477)
Breckon, Brett, illus. see Morden, Daniel.
Breckwoldt. Story of Craig Winston: An Adopted Bear. (p. 1657)
Brecon, Connah. Frank! (p. 628)
—There's This Thing. Brecon, Connah, illus. (p. 1731)
—Tomorrow. (p. 1765)
Breda, Janette. Adventures of Poppy & Scout. (p. 21)
Bredehoft, Linda. Oh, Where Is My Ducky? (p. 1281)
Bredeson, Carmen. African Elephants up Close. (p. 27)
—Baby Animals of Lakes & Ponds. (p. 124)
—Baby Animals of the Desert. (p. 124)
—Baby Animals of the Frozen Tundra. (p. 124)
—Baby Animals of the Grasslands. (p. 124)
—Baby Animals of the Mountains. (p. 124)
—Baby Animals of the Ocean. (p. 124)
—Baby Animals of the Seashore. (p. 124)
—Baby Animals of the Tropical Rain Forest. (p. 124)
—Baby Animals of the Woodland Forest. (p. 124)
—Boa Constrictors up Close. (p. 205)
—Bomb-Factory Beetles & Other Weird Insects. (p. 208)
—Chocolate Chip Cookie Queen: Ruth Wakefield & Her Yummy Invention. (p. 309)
—Deadly Storm Alert! The Dangerous el Niño & la Niña. (p. 418)
—Don't Let the Barber Pull Your Teeth: Could You Survive Medieval Medicine? Kelley, Gerald, illus. (p. 468)
—Emperor Penguins up Close. (p. 521)
—Fainting Goats & Other Weird Mammals. (p. 562)
—Fiery Volcano: The Eruption of Mount St. Helens. (p. 584)
—Florida. (p. 606)
—Florida. Risco, Eida del, tr. from ENG. (p. 606)
—Flying Geckos & Other Weird Reptiles. (p. 610)
—Fun Facts about Alligators! (p. 647)
—Fun Facts about Frogs! (p. 647)
—Fun Facts about Lizards! (p. 647)
—Fun Facts about Salamanders! (p. 647)
—Fun Facts about Snakes! (p. 647)
—Fun Facts about Turtles! (p. 647)
—Georgia. (p. 665)
—Giant Pandas up Close. (p. 674)
—Giraffes up Close. (p. 678)
—Great White Sharks up Close. (p. 719)
—Hair-Shooting Tarantulas & Other Weird Spiders. (p. 736)
—Kangaroos up Close. (p. 942)
—Leafy Sea Dragons & Other Weird Sea Creatures. (p. 982)
—Lions up Close. (p. 1021)
—Mapas y Globos Terraqueos. (p. 1090)
—Monarch Butterflies up Close. (p. 1163)
—Orangutans up Close. (p. 1302)
—Poison Dart Frogs up Close. (p. 1377)
—Purim. (p. 1419)
—Spindletop Gusher: The Story of the Texas Oil Boom. (p. 1628)
—St. Patrick's Day. (p. 1638)
—Tarantulas up Close. (p. 1706)
—Texas. (p. 1723)
—Weird Birds. (p. 1872)
—Weird but True Animal Homes. (p. 1872)
—Weird but True Food. (p. 1872)
—Weird but True Human Body Facts. (p. 1872)
—Weird but True Rocks. (p. 1872)
—Weird but True Space Facts. (p. 1872)
—Weird but True Weather. (p. 1872)
—What Are Stars? (p. 1879)
—What Do Astronauts Do? (p. 1882)
—What Do You Know about Earth? (p. 1883)
—What Do You Know about the Sun? (p. 1883)
—What Is the Moon? (p. 1890)
—What Is the Solar System? (p. 1890)
Bredeson, Carmen & Cousins, Lindsey. Can You Find These Birds? (p. 259)
—Can You Find These Bugs? (p. 259)
—Can You Find These Butterflies? (p. 259)
—Can You Find These Flowers? (p. 259)
—Can You Find These Rocks? (p. 259)
—Can You Find These Seashells? (p. 259)
—Can You Find These Trees? (p. 259)
Bredeson, Carmen & Dodson Wade, Mary. Texas. (p. 1724)
Bredeson, Carmen & Dyson, Marianne. Astronauts Explore the Galaxy. (p. 109)
—Exploring Earth. (p. 552)
—Exploring the Moon. (p. 554)
—Exploring the Solar System. (p. 554)
—Exploring the Stars. (p. 554)
—Exploring the Sun. (p. 554)
Bredeson, Carmen, et al. Astronauts Explore the Galaxy. (p. 109)
—Exploring Earth. (p. 552)
—Exploring the Moon. (p. 554)
—Exploring the Solar System. (p. 554)
—Exploring the Stars. (p. 554)
—Exploring the Sun. (p. 554)
Bredeson, Michelle. Legends. (p. 989)
Bredhoff, Stacey. Eyewitness: American Originals from the National Archives. (p. 558)
Bredin, Henrietta & McEwen, Priscilla. Prince & the Goosegirl: A Story with Activities Based on the Opera by Humperdinck. (p. 1401)
Bredius, Rein, illus. see Franco, Eloise.
Bredsdorff, Bodil. Crow-Girl: The Children of Crow Cove. Ingwersen, Faith, tr. (p. 386)
—Crow-Girl: The Children of Crow Cove. Ingwersen, Faith, tr. from DAN. (p. 386)
Bree, Loris. Kids' Magic Secrets: Simple Magic Tricks & Why They Work. Bree, Marlin, illus. (p. 954)
Bree, Loris & Bree, Marlin. Kid's Travel Fun Book: Draw. Make Stuff. Play Games. Have Fun for Hours! (p. 955)
—Kid's Trip Diary: Kids! Write about Your Own Adventures & Experiences! (p. 955)
Bree, Marlin, illus. see Bree, Loris.
Bree, Marlin, jt. auth. see Bree, Loris.
Breece, Beverly. Curwood Acorns. DeWeese, Susan, illus. (p. 395)
Breed, Jessica, ed. see Corrie, William E., 3rd & Corrie, Linda D.
Breed, Simon & Butterfield, Moira. Dirty Rotten Pirates. Finlayson, Luke & Mazzara, Mauro, illus. (p. 446)
Breeden, Don, illus. see Swift, Austin Christopher.
Breeden, Neil, jt. auth. see Songhurst, Hazel.
Breeding, Sue. Kaleidoscope of Words. (p. 942)
—Triumph of the Spirit. (p. 1788)
Breems, Beau. Promise. Breems, Beau, illus. (p. 1411)
Breems, Beau A. Gran Historia: The Illustrated Gospel from Creation to Resurrection. Breems, Beau A., illus. (p. 706)
—His Story: The Illustrated Gospel from Creation to Resurrection. Breems, Beau A., illus. (p. 781)
Breems, Beau Alan. His Story: The Illustrated Gospel from Creation to Resurrection. Breems, Beau Alan, illus. (p. 781)
Breen, Krista Michelle. Hardware - the Trouble with Phillip. (p. 748)
—Quicksand: The Mysterious Disappearance of Dakotaroo. (p. 1427)
Breen, M. E. Darkwood. (p. 409)
Breen, Michael, jt. ed. see McEntee, Sean.
Breen, Mirka M. G. Voice of Thunder. (p. 1848)
Breen, Natasha. Sweet Dreamer&Nightmare: And the Power of Positive Thinking. (p. 1689)
Breen, Steve. Stick. (p. 1649)
—Violet the Pilot. (p. 1843)
—Woodpecker Wants Waffles. (p. 1949)
Breen, Steve, illus. see Hale, Bruce.
Breene, Robert G., III. Widow Spider in Its Web. (p. 1927)
Breese, K. Ryer. Future Imperfect. (p. 651)
—Past Continuous. (p. 1327)
Breeze, Johnny & Haws, Dallin. Johnny Bugeyes Christmas. (p. 923)
Brefere, Lisa M., et al. So You Want to Be a Chef? Your Guide to Culinary Careers. (p. 1602)
Brege, K. B. Abominable Snowman A Frozen Nightmare! (p. 5)
—All Isn't Well in Roswell! (p. 44)
—Bigfoot... Big Trouble! (p. 185)
—Champ... A Wave of Terror! Five Ways to Finish. (p. 289)
—Ghost Board Posse London Screaming! (p. 670)
—Grudge of the Gremlins. (p. 727)
Bregman, Ahron. History of Israel. (p. 784)
Bregoli, Jane. Goat Lady. (p. 687)
—Goat Lady. Bregoli, Jane, illus. (p. 687)
Breguet, Amy. Yellowcard. (p. 1970)
Breguet, Amy E. Steve & Bindi Irwin. (p. 1649)
Breguet, Amy E., et al. Diet Pills. (p. 437)
—Junior Drug Awareness: Vicodin, OxyContin, & Other Pain Relievers. (p. 936)
Breheny, Jamie, jt. auth. see Pietras, Jamie.
Brehm, David L. Willy Nilly Volume 1. Claerhout, Paul, illus. (p. 1934)
Brehm, G. Scott. Universal Ride. (p. 1820)
Brehm, Mike. Rising Stars: The 10 Best Young Players in the NHL. (p. 1475)
Brehm, Mike & Russo, Michael. Rising Stars: The 10 Best Young Players in the NHL. (p. 1475)
Breidenthal, Kathryn, illus. see Parr, Ann.
Breiehagen, Per, illus. see Evert, Lori.
Breiehagen, Per, photos by see Evert, Lori.
Breisacher, Cathy. Petunia Pepper's Picture Day. Elden, Christian, illus. (p. 1349)
Breitborde, Mary-Lou & Swiniarski, Louise. Teaching on Principle & Promise: The Foundations of Education. (p. 1710)
Breithaupt, Andrew, illus. see Awa, Solomon.
Breitrose, Prudence & Yue, Stephanie. Mousemobile: When Mice Hit the Road. (p. 1182)
Breitweiser, Mitch, jt. auth. see Brubaker, Ed.

Brekke, Nancy Rose. But Grandma Didn't Mind. (p. 246)
—But That's OK with Grandpa. (p. 246)
Brekke, Robert, ed. see Reed, Rosemary.
Brekke, Robert, photos by see Reed, Rosemary.
Breland, Cathy Easter. Choices! (p. 309)
Brelsfoard, Sam. Life Inside the Arctic Circle. (p. 1011)
Breman, Billy & Watkins, Graham. Searching for Ghosts & Poltergeists. (p. 1537)
BréMaud, R. E. Simon, Friends, & the Dream Stealer: Book One. (p. 1577)
Bremauntz, M. Adventures of Marcela & Little Joey: Little Joey Loves Bugs. (p. 20)
Bremer, Terry. Dandylion: The Most Misunderstood Flower. Pierce, M. Deborah, illus. (p. 403)
Bremmer, Patricia A. Christmas Westie. (p. 316)
—Dolphins' Echo. (p. 465)
Bremner, Shawn, compiled by. Aspire to Something Higher: A Pocket Book of Inspired Thoughts. (p. 107)
Bremner-Lewis, P. L. My Friend, the Unicorn. (p. 1209)
Brenan-Leitner, Rita. Legend of Cricket, the Horse by the Side of the Road. (p. 988)
Brenchley, Chaz & Doyle, Arthur. Lost World. Bennett, Felix, illus. (p. 1057)
Brenda, Baratto, ed. see Clark, Lucinda.
Brenda Jenkins. Trick or Treat Every Night. (p. 1786)
Brenda, Jones. No, I Don't Want to Play Today: An African Tale about Bullying. (p. 1258)
Brenda Seabrooke. Jerry on the Line. (p. 913)
Brenda Slack, jt. auth. see Brenda Slack, Slack.
Brenda Slack, Slack & Brenda Slack. Everybody. (p. 543)
Brenda, Stapleton. Grammar Keys: A Guide for Japanese Students. (p. 706)
Brendler, Carol. Not Very Scary. Pizzoli, Greg, illus. (p. 1267)
—Radio Girl. (p. 1433)
Brendler, Carol & Brendler, Carol H. Winnie Finn, Worm Farmer. Hoyt, Ard, illus. (p. 1937)
Brendler, Carol H., jt. auth. see Brendler, Carol.
Breneman, Terri. Delusional. (p. 425)
Brenes, Carlos A. Private Billy. (p. 1407)
Brenes-Sotela, Guillermo J., tr. see O'Connor, Crystal Ball.
Brenier, Claire, illus. see Moncomble, Gerard & Van den Dries, Sidonie.
Brenn, Lisa, illus. see Grandpa Casey.
Brenna, Beverley. Bug House Family Restaurant Mongeau, Marc, illus. (p. 236)
—Falling for Henry (p. 566)
—Something to Hang on To. (p. 1610)
—Waiting for No One (p. 1852)
—White Bicycle (p. 1912)
Brennah-Nelson, Denise. Maestro Stu Saves the Zoo. (p. 1070)
Brennan, Ann. Hawthorn Bush. (p. 755)
Brennan, Anthony, illus. see Downey, Glen.
Brennan, Ashley Logan. Hockey! Hockey! (p. 786)
Brennan, Cait, illus. see Norfolk, Sherry & Norfolk, Bobby.
Brennan, Carla, illus. see Plaut, Thomas F.
Brennan, Craig, illus. see Samuels, Gregory Robert.
Brennan, Eileen. Bad Astrid. Dunnick, Regan, illus. (p. 131)
Brennan, Finn, jt. auth. see Brennan, Stephen.
Brennan, Francis. Elephants. (p. 511)
Brennan, Frank. Tasty Tales Level 4. (p. 1707)
—Three Tomorrows. (p. 1744)
Brennan, Genevieve. Wellesley College College Prowler off the Record. (p. 1874)
Brennan, George. Creating Beauty: Cosmetic Surgery & the Beauty Industry. (p. 378)
Brennan, Georgeanne. Green Eggs & Ham Cookbook. Seuss, Dr., illus. (p. 721)
Brennan, Gerald T. Man Who Never Died: The Life & Adventures of St. Peter, the First Pope. (p. 1086)
Brennan, Herbie. Doomsday Box: A Shadow Project Adventure. (p. 470)
—Faeman Quest. (p. 562)
—Faerie Lord. (p. 562)
—Faerie Wars. (p. 562)
—Monstruo del Pantano. (p. 1169)
—Purple Emperor. (p. 1419)
—Ruler of the Realm. (p. 1495)
—Secret Prophecy. (p. 1543)
—Shadow Project. (p. 1557)
Brennan, Joseph, jt. auth. see Sohn, Emily.
Brennan, Joseph K. What Is an Oligarchy? Crabtree Publishing Staff, ed. (p. 1889)
Brennan, Joseph K., jt. auth. see Miller, Reagan.
Brennan, Kristine. Burundi. (p. 244)
—Burundi. Rotberg, Robert I., ed. (p. 244)
—City. (p. 323)
—Danica Patrick. (p. 404)
—First World War & the End of the Ottoman Order. (p. 598)
—Indian Americans. (p. 871)
—Native Americans. (p. 1234)
Brennan, Lara, jt. auth. see Brennan, Stephen.
Brennan, Linda. Black Regiment of the American Revolution. Noll, Cheryl Kirk, illus. (p. 196)
Brennan, Linda Crotta. Birth of the United States. (p. 192)
—Boston Tea Party: A History Perspectives Book. (p. 215)
—Franklin Delano Roosevelt's Presidency. (p. 630)
—Geothermal Power. (p. 665)
—Gulf Oil Spill. (p. 731)
—Gulf Oil Spill Paperback. (p. 731)
—Leaves Change Color. (p. 986)
—Managing Money. Barnes-Murphy, Rowan, illus. (p. 1086)
—North Carolina. (p. 1264)
—There Is Day & Night. (p. 1730)
—We Have Earthquakes. (p. 1867)
—We Have Tornadoes. (p. 1867)
—Women of the Ocean State: 25 Rhode Island Women You Should Know. Greenleaf, Lisa, illus. (p. 1946)
Brennan, Lisa, illus. see Casey, Grandpa.
Brennan, Lisa, illus. see Grandpa Casey.
Brennan, Lisa, illus. see McGlotham, L. R. E.
Brennan, Martin. I Saw It in the Garden. Monroe, Michael Glenn, illus. (p. 845)
Brennan, Michael. Imageless World. (p. 860)
Brennan, Neil, illus. see Kurtz, Jane.
Brennan, Patricia. Who Is Bill Gates? (p. 1915)
Brennan, Patricia & Demuth, Patricia Brennan. Who Is Bill Gates? Hammond, Ted & Harrison, Nancy, illus. (p. 1915)
Brennan, Peta, jt. ed. see Jillette, Beatrice.
Brennan, Rosemarie, jt. auth. see Brennan-Nelson, Denise.
Brennan, Sarah. Dirty Story. Harrison, Harry, illus. (p. 446)
—Even Dirtier Story. Harrison, Harry, illus. (p. 541)
—Tale of Chester Choi. Harrison, Harry, illus. (p. 1699)
—Tale of Oswald Ox. Harrison, Harry, illus. (p. 1700)
—Tale of Pin Yin Panda. Harrison, Harry, illus. (p. 1700)
—Tale of Rhonda Rabbit. Harrison, Harry, illus. (p. 1700)
—Tale of Run Run Rat. Harrison, Harry, illus. (p. 1700)
—Tale of Sybil Snake. Harrison, Harry, illus. (p. 1700)
—Tale of Temujin. Harrison, Harry, illus. (p. 1700)
Brennan, Sarah Rees. Demon's Covenant. (p. 426)
—Demon's Lexicon. (p. 426)
—Demon's Surrender. (p. 426)
—Unmade. (p. 1821)
—Unspoken. (p. 1822)
—Unspoken. (p. 1822)
—Untold. Fochesato, Giorgio, illus. (p. 1823)
Brennan, Sarah Rees, jt. auth. see Larbalestier, Justine.
Brennan, Stephen & Brennan, Finn. Adventurous Boy's Handbook: For Ages 9 to 99. Brennan, Stephen & Brennan, Finn, eds. (p. 25)
—Adventurous Boy's Handbook. Brennan, Stephen & Brennan, Finn, eds. (p. 25)
Brennan, Stephen & Brennan, Lara. Adventurous Girl's Handbook. Brennan, Stephen & Brennan, Lara, eds. (p. 25)
—Adventurous Girl's Handbook - For Ages 9 to 99. Brennan, Stephen & Brennan, Lara, eds. (p. 25)
Brennan, Tim. About Teddy: A Story about Tourette's Syndrome. (p. 6)
Brennan, Tim, illus. see Turner, Dona & Dunn, Mark.
Brennan-Nelson, Denise. Buzzy the Bumblebee. Monroe, Michael Glenn, illus. (p. 249)
—He's Been a Monster All Day. Moore, Cyd, illus. (p. 774)
—J Is for Jack-O'-Lantern: A Halloween Alphabet. Wu, Donald, illus. (p. 901)
—Little Colorado. Urban, Helle, illus. (p. 1026)
—Little Halloween. Urban, Helle, illus. (p. 1028)
—Little Michigan. Monroe, Michael Glenn, illus. (p. 1031)
—My Daddy Likes to Say. Donovan, Jane Monroe, illus. (p. 1201)
—My Grandma Likes to Say. Donovan, Jane Monroe, illus. (p. 1210)
—My Momma Likes to Say. Donovan, Jane Monroe, illus. (p. 1214)
—My Teacher Likes to Say. Monroe Donovan, Jane & Donovan, Jane Monroe, illus. (p. 1220)
—Penny: The Forgotten Coin. Monroe, Michael Glenn, illus. (p. 1338)
—Someday Is Not a Day of the Week. O'Malley, Kevin, illus. (p. 1609)
—Willow & the Snow Day Dance. Moore, Cyd, illus. (p. 1934)
Brennan-Nelson, Denise & Brennan, Rosemarie. Willow. Moore, Cyd, illus. (p. 1934)
Brennan-Nelson, Denise & Brennan-Nelson, Dense. Grady the Goose. Monroe, Michael Glenn, illus. (p. 705)
Brennan-Nelson, Dense, jt. auth. see Brennan-Nelson, Denise.
Brenner, Barbara. Boy Who Loved to Draw: Benjamin West. Dunrea, Olivier, illus. (p. 219)
—Good Morning, Garden. Ortakales, Denise, illus. (p. 698)
—One Small Place by the Sea. Leonard, Tom, illus. (p. 1297)
—One Small Place in a Tree. Leonard, Tom, illus. (p. 1297)
Brenner, Barbara, et al. Bunny Tails. Munsinger, Lynn, illus. (p. 242)
Brenner, Emily. On the First Day of Grade School. Whatley, Bruce, illus. (p. 1290)
Brenner, Harriett A. Corky's Humane Tail Tale. Kelly, Julia, illus. (p. 367)
Brenner, Jordyn, jt. auth. see Honowitz, Stacey.
Brenner, Marie, jt. auth. see Thompson, Kay.
Brenner, Martha, jt. auth. see Murphy, Frank.
Brenner, Martha F. Montones de Problemas. Woodruff, Liza, illus. (p. 1170)
—Montones de Problemas; Stacks of Trouble. (p. 1170)
Brenner, Peter. King for One Day. Wyss, Manspeter, illus. (p. 958)
Brenner, Summer. Ivy, Homeless in San Francisco. Bowes, Brian, illus. (p. 901)
Brenner, Tom. And Then Comes Christmas. Christy, Jana, illus. (p. 71)
—And Then Comes Halloween. Meade, Holly, illus. (p. 71)
Brenner, Vida. Magic Music Shop. Sharp, Mary, ed. (p. 1072)
Brenner, William H., jt. ed. see Moyal-Sharrock, Danièle.
Brenning, Juli. Maggi & Milo. Burris, Priscilla, illus. (p. 1071)
Brent, Alexander Michael. Play Date with T-Rex: The Adventures of Jake & Sammy Wiggles. (p. 1371)
Brent, Lance. Dream Secret: Lucid Dreaming. (p. 483)
Brent, Lynette. Chicago (p. 299)
Brent, Lynette & Brent, Lynnette. Acids & Bases. (p. 9)
—Chemical Changes. (p. 297)
Brent, Lynnette. Why Chemistry Matters (p. 1923)
Brent, Lynnette, jt. auth. see Brent, Lynette.
Brent, Lynnette, jt. auth. see Weir, Kirsten.
Brent, Lynnette R. At Home: Long Ago & Today. (p. 110)
—At Play: Long Ago & Today. (p. 110)
—At School: Long Ago & Today. (p. 110)
—At Work: Long Ago & Today. (p. 111)
—I've Discovered Heat! (p. 900)
—I've Discovered Light. (p. 900)
Brent, Mary & Caitlin, Knutsson. Chemo to the Rescue: A Children's Book about Leukemia. (p. 297)
Brent, R. M., tr. see Blanchard, Anne.
Brent-Dyer, Elinor M. Bride Leads the Chalet School. (p. 227)
Brents, Alan. Sheldon the Sheep. (p. 1564)
Brereton, Dan, jt. auth. see Peterson, Brandon.
Brereton, Dan, et al. Buffy the Vampire Slayer Omnibus (p. 236)
Brereton, Erin. Real Girls' Guide to Everything: That Makes It Awesome to Be a Girl! Zalevskaya, Anastacia, illus. (p. 1448)
Brereton, F. S. With Joffre at Verdun: A Story of the Western Front. Webb, Arch, illus. (p. 1942)
Bresanetti, S., jt. auth. see Bresanetti, Sandra.
Bresanetti, Sandra & Bresanetti, S. Regalos de Tia Terciopelina. Brignole, Giancarla, tr. (p. 1457)
Brescia, Leigh. One Wish. (p. 1297)
Breshears, Alyce Park. Friends - a Collection of Stories. (p. 638)
—Run, Girl, Run! Boyd, Shelby, illus. (p. 1496)
Breslin, Jayne. Princess Jelly Tutu Adventures. (p. 1404)
Breslin, Jud. If the Ball's in the Air a Season in Tee-Ball. (p. 854)
Breslin, Theresa. Mutant. (p. 1194)
—Prisoner in Alcatraz. (p. 1407)
—Whispers in the Graveyard. (p. 1912)
Breslin, Theresa, et al. Divided City. (p. 454)
Bresloff, Robert. Wiz Kids of Oz. Ziembo, Daniel, illus. (p. 1942)
Bresnahan, Patrick, illus. see DiBattista, Mary Ann & Finn, Sandra J.
Bresser, Rusty & Holtzman, Caren. Minilessons for Math Practice, Grades 3-5. (p. 1146)
Bressett, Ken, ed. see Yeoman, R. S.
Bret Harte, jt. auth. see Bret Harte, Harte.
Bret Harte, Harte & Bret Harte. Queen of the Pirate Isle. Kate Greenaway, illus. (p. 1425)
Breton, Albert. Economic Theory of Representative Government. (p. 502)
Breton, Katia, illus. see Danesh, H. B.
Brett, Cathy, illus. see Orme, Helen.
Brett, Cathy, illus. see Wallace, Karen.
Brett, Flora. Cat's View of the World. (p. 281)
—Dog's View of the World. (p. 463)
—Get to Know Chameleons. (p. 668)
—Get to Know Geckos. (p. 668)
—Get to Know Gila Monsters. (p. 668)
—Get to Know Komodo Dragons. (p. 668)
—Get to Know Reptiles. (p. 668)
—Horse's View of the World. (p. 800)
—Pet Perspectives. (p. 1345)
—Reptile's View of the World. (p. 1461)
—Your Body Systems. (p. 1980)
—Your Circulatory System Works! (p. 1980)
—Your Digestive System Works! (p. 1980)
—Your Muscular System Works! (p. 1981)
—Your Nervous System Works! (p. 1981)
—Your Respiratory System Works! (p. 1981)
—Your Skeletal System Works! (p. 1981)
Brett, Harold M., illus. see Hale, Lucretia.
Brett, James. Infaeter. Englund, Jonathon, illus. (p. 873)
Brett, Jan. 3 Little Dassies. Brett, Jan, illus. (p. 1991)
—Animals' Santa. Brett, Jan, illus. (p. 83)
—Annie & the Wild Animals. (p. 86)
—Annie & the Wild Animals. Brett, Jan, illus. (p. 86)
—Annie & the Wild Animals Send-A-Story. (p. 86)
—Armadillo Rodeo. Brett, Jan, illus. (p. 99)
—Beauty & the Beast. (p. 154)
—Beauty & the Beast. Brett, Jan, illus. (p. 154)
—Cinders: A Chicken Cinderella. Brett, Jan, illus. (p. 321)
—Daisy Comes Home. Brett, Jan, illus. (p. 400)
—Easter Egg. Brett, Jan, illus. (p. 499)
—First Dog. Brett, Jan, illus. (p. 594)
—Gingerbread Baby. (p. 677)
—Gingerbread Baby. Brett, Jan, illus. (p. 677)
—Gingerbread Friends. Brett, Jan, illus. (p. 677)
—Hedgie Blasts Off! Brett, Jan, illus. (p. 762)
—Home for Christmas. Brett, Jan, illus. (p. 792)
—Honey... Honey... Lion! (p. 794)
—Honey... Honey... Lion! Brett, Jan, illus. (p. 794)
—Honey... Honey... Lion! A Story from Africa. Brett, Jan, illus. (p. 794)
—Mitten: Oversized Board Book. Brett, Jan, illus. (p. 1156)
—Mitten. Brett, Jan, illus. (p. 1156)
—Mossy. Brett, Jan, illus. (p. 1177)
—Night Before Christmas. Brett, Jan, illus. (p. 1252)
—On Noah's Ark. Brett, Jan, illus. (p. 1289)
—Sombrero. (p. 1608)
—Three Snow Bears. Brett, Jan, illus. (p. 1744)
—Town Mouse Country Mouse. (p. 1773)
—Town Mouse Country Mouse. Brett, Jan, illus. (p. 1773)
—Twelve Days of Christmas. Brett, Jan, illus. (p. 1800)
—Umbrella. (p. 1810)
—Umbrella. Brett, Jan, illus. (p. 1810)
Brett, Jan, illus. see Bunting, Eve.
Brett, Jan, illus. see Jane, Pamela.
Brett, Jan, illus. see Simon, Seymour.
Brett, Jeannie. Little Maine. Brett, Jeannie, illus. (p. 1031)
—Wild about Bears. Brett, Jeannie, illus. (p. 1928)
Brett, Jeannie, illus. see Crane, Carol.
Brett, Jeannie, illus. see Fuller, Sandy Ferguson.
Brett, Jeannie, illus. see Noble, Trinka Hakes.
Brett, Jeannie, illus. see Patent, Dorothy Hinshaw.
Brett, Jeannie, illus. see Reynolds, Cynthia Furlong.
Brett, Jeannie, illus. see Stemple, Heidi E. Y.
Brett, Jeannie, illus. see Wilbur, Helen.
Brett, Jessica. Animals on the Go. Cowdrey, Richard, illus. (p. 83)
Brett, Simon. Body on the Beach. (p. 207)
Brett, Tyler & Romano, Tony. False Creek. (p. 567)
Brett-Surman, Michael K., ed. see Brochu, Christopher A., et al.
Brett-Surman, Michael K. & Holtz, Thomas R. Jurassic World Dinosaur Field Guide (Jurassic World) Walters, Robert, illus. (p. 937)
Bretz, Wendy M. Big Move. (p. 182)
Bretzius Matthew. West Virginia University College Prowler off the Record. (p. 1876)
Breuer, Paul, illus. see Jack Stanley.
Breur, Jessica. Division: Grades 4-6. Carlson, Andy et al, illus. (p. 455)
Breutigam-Duden, Martin. Schachturnier: Kniffige Situationen aus Beruehmten Partien. (p. 1521)
Brevannes, Maurice, illus. see Bishop, Claire Huchet.
Brevannes, Maurice, illus. see Peart, Hendry.
Brevard, Katherine M., jt. auth. see Miller, Davis Worth.
Brevard, Katherine McLean, jt. auth. see Miller, Davis Worth.
Brevard, Katherine McLean & Miller, Davis Worth. Story of Oil: How It Changed the World. (p. 1659)
Brevard, Lisa Pertillar. Madame E. Azalia Hackley's the Colored Girl Beautiful (1916) (p. 1069)
Brever, Amy, illus. see Mosby, Pamela.
Brew Ed.D., Ranelle L. Healthy Days. (p. 758)
Brew, Jim. Miz. (p. 1156)
—Pirates. (p. 1363)
Brew, Sean. Teen Assassin. (p. 1713)
Brewe, jt. auth. see Harris, P.
Brewer, Amy J. Mystery of Murder. (p. 1225)
Brewer, Caroline. Kara & Friends Meet Abraham Lincoln. (p. 943)
Brewer, Chris B. Artists: Exploring Art Through the Study of Five Great Lives. (p. 104)
Brewer, Christopher D. Bakersfield & Kern Picture Album. (p. 133)
Brewer, Cristine S. Ilsa, Dad, & Ed. (p. 858)
Brewer, Dan, jt. auth. see Paolilli, Paul.
Brewer, Dean, illus. see Brewer, Sarah.
Brewer, Debbie. Three-Legged Duck. (p. 1742)
Brewer, Dottie A. Jessie's Walk. Naenix, Robin, illus. (p. 914)
—Praying 101 for Kids & Teens. (p. 1393)
—Saul the Pelican. Naenix, Robin, illus. (p. 1516)
Brewer, Duncan. 100 Facts Inventions. (p. 1998)
—1000 Things You Should Know about Mammals. (p. 2001)
—Deserts. (p. 429)
—Inventions. (p. 884)
Brewer, Ebenezer Cobham. Guide to the Scientific Knowledge of Things Familiar by Rev Dr Brewer Carefully Revised, & Adapted for Use in Families & Schools of the U. (p. 730)
Brewer, Elly. Jerry & the Jannans. (p. 913)
Brewer, Heather. Cemetery Boys. (p. 286)
—Chronicles of Vladimir Tod (p. 317)
—Chronicles of Vladimir Tod. (p. 317)
—Eighth Grade Bites. (p. 507)
—Eighth Grade Bites. Laud, Julia, illus. (p. 507)
—Eleventh Grade Burns (p. 512)
—First Kill. (p. 595)
—High School Bites (p. 778)
—Soulbound. (p. 1614)
—Tenth Grade Bleeds. (p. 1720)
—Tenth Grade Bleeds. Preseault, N., ed. (p. 1720)
—The Chronicles of Vladimir Tod. (p. 1728)
—Third Strike. (p. 1734)
—Twelfth Grade Kills. (p. 1800)
Brewer, Janey. Mist & Moonlight. (p. 1155)
Brewer, Jo Ann. Little Girl No One Wanted. (p. 1028)
—Miss Q-Cee & the Sweet Potatoes. (p. 1152)
—Miss Q-Cee Baby Sits. (p. 1152)
Brewer, Kathaleen, illus. see Cruzan, Patricia.
Brewer, Marie. For Smart Girls Only. (p. 616)
Brewer, Mary, jt. auth. see Vincent, Harris T.
Brewer, Melanie. Sweep Away the Bad Day. (p. 1689)
Brewer, Michael. Gotta Have God 2: Ages 10-12. Heiser, Aline, illus. (p. 704)
Brewer, Michelle. Sunrise in My Cup. (p. 1677)
Brewer, Mike, jt. auth. see Harris, Paul.
Brewer, Nancy B. Princess Bertha & the Goose. (p. 1403)
Brewer, Neil. 8 O'Clock Bell. (p. 1993)
Brewer, Paul. Lima Embassy Siege & Latin American Terrorism. (p. 1018)
—September 11 & Radical Islamic Terrorism. (p. 1551)
—You Must Be Joking! Lots of Cool Jokes, Plus 17 1/2 Tips for Remembering, Telling, & Making up Your Own Jokes. (p. 1976)
—You Must Be Joking, Two! Even Cooler Jokes, Plus 11 1/2 Tips for Laughing Yourself into Your Own Stand-Up Comedy Routine. Brewer, Paul, illus. (p. 1976)
Brewer, Paul, illus. see Krull, Kathleen.
Brewer, Paul, illus. see Seuling, Barbara.
Brewer, Paul, jt. auth. see Krull, Kathleen.
Brewer, Sarah. Our New Garden. Brewer, Sarah & Brewer, Dean, illus. (p. 1309)
Brewer, Stephen. Gorillas. (p. 703)
Brewer, Tammy, ed. see McCray, Ed.
Brewer, Terry, illus. see Lepp, Paul & Lepp, Bil.
Brewer, Trish, illus. see Pluto Project Staff & Semkiw, Walter.
Brewin, Barbara. Sidney Snail's Wonderful World of Adventure. (p. 1573)
—Treasure Box of Children's Poetry: A magical world for Children. (p. 1781)
Brewis, Alan. Boris Returns A Hero! (p. 214)
Brewner, J. P. Trifecta: Initiation. (p. 1786)
Brewster, Alicia Wright. Echo. (p. 502)
Brewster, Bobby. Layla the Ridgeless Rhodesian Ridgeback. (p. 981)
Brewster, Chad, et al. Bob's Burgers. (p. 206)
Brewster, David. Wetlands. (p. 1877)
Brewster, Frank. Little Yellow Butterfly Book. (p. 1038)
Brewster, James Burd. Uncle Rocky, Fireman: Fire! Barley-Cohrs, Dayna, illus. (p. 1812)
—Uncle Rocky, Fireman: Something's Missing. Barley-Cohrs, Dayna, illus. (p. 1812)
Brewster, Jane, illus. see Adams, Michelle.
Brewster, Joy. Animales del Mar. Hanner, Albert, illus. (p. 81)
—Animals of the Sea & Animales del Mar: 6 English, 6 Spanish Adaptations (p. 83)
—mundo bajo las Olas. Hanner, Albert, illus. (p. 1191)
—World Beneath the Waves & el mundo bajo las Olas: 6 English, 6 Spanish Adaptations (p. 1954)
Brewster, Patience, illus. see Broach, Elise.
Brewster, Todd, jt. auth. see Jennings, Peter.
Brexel, Bernadette. Badger's Burrow (p. 132)
—Congress. (p. 357)
—Knights of Labor & the Haymarket Riot: The Fight for an Eight-Hour Workday. (p. 964)
—Populist Party: A Voice for the Farmers in an Industrial Society. (p. 1385)
—Populist Party: A Voice for the Farmers in the Industrialized Society. (p. 1385)

B

—Prosecuting Trusts: The Courts Break up Monopolies in America. (p. 1412)
—Yasser Arafat. (p. 1968)
Breyfogle, Norm, illus. see Morgan, Melanie J.
Brez, Lisa. Hickerdoodle Gets Lost. (p. 775)
—Hickerdoodle Gets the Hiccups. (p. 775)
—Hickerdoodle Meets a Chigger. (p. 775)
Brezenoff, Steve. Absolute Value Of -1. (p. 7)
—Absolute Value of -1. (p. 7)
—Alley of Shadows Martin, Cynthia, illus. (p. 47)
—Ballgame with No One at Bat. (p. 135)
—Ballgame with No One at Bat. Calo, Marcos, illus. (p. 135)
—Bites Pinelli, Amerigo, illus. (p. 194)
—Bites. (p. 194)
—Bowling Lane Without Any Strikes. (p. 216)
—Bowling Lane Without Any Strikes. Calo, Marcos, illus. (p. 216)
—Brooklyn, Burning. (p. 231)
—Burglar Who Bit the Big Apple Canga, C. B., illus. (p. 243)
—Burning Secrets Vue, Tou, illus. (p. 244)
—Cave That Shouldn't Collapse Calo, Marcos, illus. (p. 282)
—Cheaters Pinelli, Amerigo, illus. (p. 295)
—Cheaters. (p. 295)
—Crook That Made Kids Cry Calo, Marcos, illus. (p. 384)
—Crook That Made Kids Cry. (p. 384)
—Crook Who Crossed the Golden Gate Bridge Canga, C. B., illus. (p. 384)
—Curses for Sale Percival, Tom, illus. (p. 395)
—Dinosaur That Disappeared Calo, Marcos, illus. (p. 443)
—Dinosaur That Disappeared. (p. 443)
—Everglades Poacher Who Pretended Calo, Marcos, illus. (p. 542)
—Field Trip Mysteries. (p. 584)
—Ghost Who Haunted the Capitol Canga, C. B., illus. (p. 672)
—Grand Canyon Burros That Broke Calo, Marcos, illus. (p. 707)
—Guy in Real Life. (p. 733)
—I Dare You! Hilliker, Phillip, illus. (p. 837)
—Lost Island Pinelli, Amerigo, illus. (p. 1056)
—Lost Island. (p. 1056)
—Mount Rushmore Face That Couldn't See Calo, Marcos, illus. (p. 1180)
—Mummy at Midnight. Prothero, Tiffany, illus. (p. 1191)
—Museum Mysteries. Weber, Lisa K., illus. (p. 1193)
—New in Town Percival, Tom, illus. (p. 1245)
—No Place Like Home Pinelli, Amerigo, illus. (p. 1260)
—No Place Like Home. (p. 1260)
—On the Bus, on the Case Canga, C. B., illus. (p. 1290)
—Overboard Murphy, Scott, illus. (p. 1314)
—Painting That Wasn't There Canga, C. B., illus. (p. 1318)
—Ravens Pass. (p. 1441)
—Ride That Was Really Haunted Calo, Marcos, illus. (p. 1471)
—Seals That Wouldn't Swim Calo, Marcos, illus. (p. 1536)
—Sleeper Percival, Tom, illus. (p. 1588)
—Stowaways Murphy, Scott, illus. (p. 1664)
—Symphony That Was Silent Calo, Marcos, illus. (p. 1693)
—Teacher Who Forgot Too Much Canga, C. B., illus. (p. 1709)
—Thing in the Woods. Pellegrino, Richard, illus. (p. 1732)
—Time Voyage Murphy, Scott, illus. (p. 1753)
—Unsinkable Ship Murphy, Scott, illus. (p. 1822)
—Village That Almost Vanished Canga, C. B., illus. (p. 1842)
—Witch Mayor Percival, Tom, illus. (p. 1941)
—Yellowstone Kidnapping That Wasn't Calo, Marcos, illus. (p. 1970)
—Zombie Who Visited New Orleans Canga, C. B., illus. (p. 1988)
—Zoo with the Empty Cage Canga, C. B., illus. (p. 1989)
Brezenoff, Steve & Calo, Marcos. Field Trip Mysteries (p. 584)
Brezenoff, Steven. Case of the Haunted History Museum. Weber, Lisa K., illus. (p. 274)
—Case of the Missing Museum Archives. Weber, Lisa K., illus. (p. 274)
—Case of the Portrait Vandal. Weber, Lisa K., illus. (p. 275)
—Case of the Stolen Sculpture. Weber, Lisa K., illus. (p. 275)
Brezina. Who Can Open Michelangelo's Seven Seals? (p. 1914)
Brezina, Corona. Alcohol & Drug Offenses: Your Legal Rights (p. 35)
—America's Political Scandals in the Late 1800s: Boss Tweed & Tammany Hall. (p. 64)
—America's Recession: The Effects of the Economic Downturn. (p. 64)
—Arizona: Past & Present. (p. 98)
—Careers as a Medical Examiner. (p. 267)
—Careers in Meteorology. (p. 268)
—Careers in Nanotechnology. (p. 268)
—Careers in the Homicide Unit. (p. 268)
—Celtic Mythology. (p. 286)
—Climate Change. (p. 332)
—Deadly School & Campus Violence. (p. 418)
—Dictatorship: A Primary Source Analysis. (p. 436)
—Disappearing Forests: Deforestation, Desertification, & Drought. (p. 446)
—Discovering Relativity (p. 449)
—Falconry & Game Hawking. (p. 566)
—Fifth Amendment: Double Jeopardy, Self-Incrimination, & Due Process of Law. (p. 584)
—Frequently Asked Questions about Juvenile Detention. (p. 636)
—Frequently Asked Questions about Tanning & Skin Care. (p. 636)
—Getting a Job in Health Care. (p. 668)
—Great Decision-Making Skills. (p. 715)
—Heroin: The Deadly Addiction. (p. 773)
—How Deflation Works. (p. 806)
—How Imports & Exports Work. (p. 810)
—How Stimulus Plans Work. (p. 812)
—How the Group of 20 Works: Cooperation among the World's Major Economic Powers. (p. 813)
—Indiana: Past & Present. (p. 871)
—Industrial Revolution in America: A Primary Source History of America's Transformation into an Industrial Society. (p. 872)
—I've Gotten a DWI/DUI, Now What? (p. 901)
—Jobs in Sustainable Energy. (p. 919)
—Johnny Tremain & the American Revolution. (p. 923)
—Nazi Architects of the Holocaust. (p. 1238)
—New Mexico: Past & Present. (p. 1246)
—Organ Donation: Risks, Rewards, & Research. (p. 1303)
—Sergey Brin, Larry Page, Eric Schmidt, & Google. (p. 1552)
—Top STEM Careers in Math. (p. 1769)
—Treasure Hunters. (p. 1781)
—Understanding the Federal Reserve & Monetary Policy. (p. 1816)
—Understanding the Gross Domestic Product & the Gross National Product. (p. 1816)
—Weapons of Mass Destruction: Proliferation & Control. (p. 1869)
—What Happens to Your Body When You Are Weight Training. (p. 1886)
Brezina, Thomas & Sartin, Laurence. Who Will Find Vincent's Treasury of Colors? (p. 1919)
Brezinova, Ivona. Dorothy & the Glasses. Llapashtica, Mentor, illus. (p. 471)
—To Have a Dog. Delsadze, Zaur, illus. (p. 1759)
Breznak, Irene. Sneezy Louise. Pedersen, Janet, illus. (p. 1597)
Brian, Bethany. How the Rock Cycle Works. (p. 813)
Brian, Dittmar. Mongol Warriors. (p. 1164)
Brian, Harrold, illus. see Thompson, Tolya L.
Brian, Janeen. Adventures of Kingli the Frilled Lizard. (p. 19)
—Cat-Astrophe at the Opera. (p. 277)
—Cat-Astrophe at the Opera. (p. 277)
—I'm a Dirty Dinosaur. James, Ann, illus. (p. 858)
—Maya Monkey. (p. 1112)
—Meet Ned Kelly. Adams, Matt, illus. (p. 1121)
—Mia's Chocolate Challenge. (p. 1134)
Brian, Kate. Endless (a Shadowlands Novel) (p. 527)
—Hereafter (a Shadowlands Novel) (p. 771)
—Private Collection (p. 1407)
—Shadowlands. (p. 1558)
Brian, Kate, pseud. Ambition. (p. 57)
—Beautiful Disaster. (p. 153)
—Book of Spells. (p. 211)
—Confessions. (p. 356)
—Cruel Love. (p. 386)
—Ex-Mas. (p. 547)
—Fake Boyfriend. (p. 565)
—Inner Circle. (p. 875)
—Invitation Only. (p. 886)
—Last Christmas: The Private Prequel. (p. 977)
—Legacy. (p. 987)
—Lucky T. (p. 1063)
—Megan Meade's Guide to the McGowan Boys. (p. 1124)
—Ominous. (p. 1288)
—Paradise Lost. (p. 1323)
—Perfect Mistake. (p. 1342)
—Princess & the Pauper. (p. 1402)
—Private. (p. 1407)
—Privilege. (p. 1408)
—Pure Sin. (p. 1419)
—Revelation. (p. 1465)
—Scandal. (p. 1519)
—Suspicion. (p. 1688)
—Sweet 16. (p. 1689)
—Sweet Deceit. (p. 1689)
—Untouchable. (p. 1823)
—V Club. (p. 1829)
—Vanished. (p. 1833)
—Vengeance. (p. 1835)
—Virginity Club. (p. 1844)
Brian, Sarah Jane. Brainiac's Mindbenders: Fun Activities for Geniuses of All Ages. (p. 222)
—Brainiac's Secret Agent: Fun Activities for Spies of All Ages. (p. 222)
—Forensics Chemistry & Crime: Set Of 6. (p. 617)
—Forensics: Chemistry & Crime: Text Pairs. (p. 617)
Brian Warling Photography (Firm) Staff, jt. contrib. by see Siede Preis Photography (Firm) Staff.
Brian, Williams. Seres Vivos. (p. 1552)
Brian, Williams, jt. auth. see Equipo Staff.
Brian, Williams, jt. auth. see Williams, Brian.
Brianna, et al. Adventures of Sam Spike. (p. 22)
Briant, Ed. Day at the Beach Briant, Ed, illus. (p. 412)
—I Am (Not) the Walrus. (p. 833)
Briant, Ed, illus. see Clough, Lisa.
Briant, Monta Z. & Z, Susan. Songs for Little Hands: Activity Guide & CD. (p. 1612)
Briard, Cheryl. Bear Pond Ferry. (p. 151)
Brice, Ginny. Princess Maddy & Her Blankie. Gary Ripper, illus. (p. 1404)
Briceno, Carole. Turtle's Journey White, Tina Jorgenson, illus. (p. 1799)
Brichto, Mira Pollak. God Around Us: The Valley of Blessings. Vol. 2 Alko, Selina, illus. (p. 688)
Bricker, Chris. Leaping Frogs of Calameris County. (p. 982)
Bricker, Howard Michael, jt. auth. see H M Bricker.
Bricker, Sandra D. Challenger. Miller, Zachary N., ed. (p. 289)
Bricker, Sherry A. Simon & Salina: The Journey Has Begun. (p. 1577)
Brickey, Peter, creator. Coastal Impressions... A photographic journey along the North Carolina Coast. (p. 336)
—From Currituck to Oak Island... A Photo Tour of North Carolina's Lighthouses. (p. 642)
BrickHouse Education. Guess Who: Whose Silhouette Is This? (p. 729)
BrickHouse Education & Colón, Priscilla. Wild ABC's. (p. 1928)
Bricking, Jennifer, illus. see Appelt, Kathi.
Brickman, Robin, illus. see Collard, Sneed B., III.
Brickman, Robin, illus. see Pfeffer, Wendy.
Brickman, Robin, illus. see Sanchez, Anita.
Brickner, Marian, illus. see Levine, Mathea.
Brickweg, Jason. Chris Jericho. (p. 311)
—Christian. (p. 311)
—Santino Marella. (p. 1513)
—Zack Ryder. (p. 1984)
Brickwood, L. M. Children of the Moon. (p. 302)
Bridal, Grania, tr. see Sonik, Madeline.
Bridegam, Martha. Search & Seizure. (p. 1537)
—Unions & Labor Laws. (p. 1818)
Bridge, Chris. Read to Me! (p. 1443)
Bridge, Colin, jt. auth. see Scoffham, Stephen.
Bridge, Emily. O' Happy Day. (p. 1274)
Bridge, George. Jack & the Beanstalk. Flowerpot Press, ed. (p. 902)
Bridgeman, A. M. Place Called Heaven. (p. 1365)
Bridgeman, Kristi, illus. see Hinman, Bobbie.
Bridgeman, Kristi, illus. see Page, P. K.
Bridgemohan, Carolyn, ed. see Esherick, Joan.
Bridgemohan, Carolyn, ed. see Ford, Jean.
Bridgen, Rachel Annie, illus. see Pierres, Marianne De.
Bridger, Maggie. What Time Is It? A Content Area Reader-math. (p. 1894)
Bridges, Andrew. Inside Story of Mars. (p. 877)
Bridges, Charlene. Tell me a Story. (p. 1716)
Bridges, Doreen. Music, Young Children & You: A Parent-Teacher Guide to Music for 0 -5 Year Olds. (p. 1193)
Bridges, Eunice. Day Like Mine. Goodwin, Adrienne Annette, illus. (p. 413)
Bridges, Jeanne Rorex, illus. see Tingle, Tim.
Bridges, Jerry, et al. Chase: Pursuing Holiness in Your Everyday Life. (p. 294)
Bridges, John, illus. see Vrtis, Nikola, ed.
Bridges, LaVon, jt. auth. see Wright, Alice.
Bridges, M. Getting up & Getting On. (p. 670)
Bridges, Madeline. Sing Together, Children. (p. 1579)
Bridges, Moire. Hermanita y el Rey: Una Parabola. Bridges, Moire, illus. (p. 771)
—Sissy & the King: A Parable. Bridges, Moire, illus. (p. 1581)
Bridges, Nancy S., jt. auth. see McKenzie, Marni Shideler.
Bridges, Robin. Katerina Trilogy, Vol. I: the Gathering Storm. (p. 944)
—Katerina Trilogy, Vol. II: the Unfailing Light. (p. 944)
Bridges, Ruby. Ruby Bridges Goes to School: My True Story. (p. 1493)
Bridges, Ruby & Maccarone, Grace. Let's Read About—Ruby Bridges. Van Wright, Cornelius & Hu, Ying-Hwa, illus. (p. 1000)
Bridges, Sarah. I Drive a Backhoe Muehlenhardt, Amy Bailey, illus. (p. 838)
—I Drive a Bulldozer Alderman, Derrick & Shea, Denise, illus. (p. 838)
—I Drive a Fire Engine Muehlenhardt, Amy Bailey, illus. (p. 838)
—I Drive a Freight Train Muehlenhardt, Amy Bailey, illus. (p. 838)
—I Drive a Garbage Truck Alderman, Derrick & Shea, Denise, illus. (p. 838)
—I Drive a Snowplow Alderman, Derrick & Shea, Denise, illus. (p. 838)
—I Drive a Street Sweeper Muehlenhardt, Amy Bailey, illus. (p. 838)
—I Drive an Ambulance Alderman, Derrick & Shea, Denise, illus. (p. 838)
—Muscle Cars (p. 1192)
—Sports Cars (p. 1632)
—Working Wheels Alderman, Derrick & Shea, Denise, illus. (p. 1953)
—Yo Manejo un Camión de la Basura. Alderman, Derrick & Shea, Denise, illus. (p. 1971)
—Yo Manejo un Camión de Volteo. Alderman, Derrick & Shea, Denise, illus. (p. 1971)
—Yo Manejo Una Niveladora. Alderman, Derrick & Shea, Denise, illus. (p. 1971)
Bridges, Shirin Yim. Agrippina: "Atrocious & Ferocious" (p. 30)
—Agrippina: "Atrocious & Ferocious" Malone, Peter, illus. (p. 30)
—Hatshepsut of Egypt. Nguyen, Albert, illus. (p. 752)
—Isabella of Castile. Nguyen, Albert, illus. (p. 891)
—Mary Wrightly, So Politely. Monescillo, Maria, illus. (p. 1101)
—Umbrella Queen. Yoo, Taeeun, illus. (p. 1810)
Bridges, Shirin Yim & Yim Bridges, Shirin. Artemisia of Caria. Nguyen, Albert, illus. (p. 103)
—Horrible Hauntings: An Augmented Reality Collection of Ghosts & Ghouls. Maughan, William, illus. (p. 798)
—Nur Jahan of India. Nguyen, Albert, illus. (p. 1273)
—Qutlugh Terkan Khatun of Kirman. Nguyen, Albert, illus. (p. 1429)
Bridges, Sonya. Snail's Pace. (p. 1596)
Bridges, Taylor. Animals Tall & Short: Describe & Compare Measurable Attributes. (p. 84)
Bridgman, C. A. My Hawaiian Smile. (p. 1210)
—Santa's Hawaiian Vacation. (p. 1513)
Bridgman, L. J., illus. see Smith, Mary P. Wells.
Bridgman, L. T., illus. see Poulsson, Emilie.
Bridgman, Rae. Kingdom of Trolls: A Middlegate Book. (p. 960)
Bridgman, Roger & Dorling Kindersley Publishing Staff. Robot. (p. 1480)
Bridwell, E. Nelson, et al. Shazam! Didio, Dan et al, eds. (p. 1563)
Bridwell, Norman. Clifford & the Halloween Parade. Bridwell, Norman, illus. (p. 332)
—Clifford at the Circus. (p. 332)
—Clifford at the Circus. Bridwell, Norman, illus. (p. 332)
—Clifford Collection. Bridwell, Norman, illus. (p. 332)
—Clifford Goes to Dog School. Bridwell, Norman, illus. (p. 332)
—Clifford Goes to Kindergarten. (p. 332)
—Clifford Goes to Washington. Bridwell, Norman, illus. (p. 332)
—Clifford Loves His Friends. Bridwell, Norman, illus. (p. 332)
—Clifford Makes the Team. Bridwell, Norman, illus. (p. 332)
—Clifford Sees America. (p. 332)
—Clifford Shares. Bridwell, Norman, illus. (p. 332)
—Clifford Takes a Trip. (p. 332)
—Clifford Takes a Trip. Bridwell, Norman, illus. (p. 332)
—Clifford the Big Red Dog. (p. 332)
—Clifford the Big Red Dog. Bridwell, Norman, illus. (p. 332)
—Clifford the Firehouse Dog. Bridwell, Norman, illus. (p. 332)
—Clifford the Small Red Puppy. (p. 332)
—Clifford Va al Doctor. Bridwell, Norman, illus. (p. 332)
—Clifford Visits the Zoo. Bridwell, Norman, illus. (p. 332)
—Clifford y la Hora de Dormir. (p. 332)
—Clifford y la Hora del Baño. (p. 332)
—Clifford y los Sondios de los Animales. (p. 332)
—Clifford's Bedtime Story. Bridwell, Norman, illus. (p. 332)
—Clifford's Birthday Party. (p. 332)
—Clifford's Birthday Party. Bridwell, Norman, illus. (p. 332)
—Clifford's Christmas. Bridwell, Norman, illus. (p. 332)
—Clifford's Christmas Treasury. (p. 332)
—Clifford's Day with Dad. Bridwell, Norman, illus. (p. 332)
—Clifford's Family. Bridwell, Norman, illus. (p. 332)
—Clifford's Field Day. (p. 332)
—Clifford's First Christmas. (p. 332)
—Clifford's First Christmas. Bridwell, Norman, illus. (p. 332)
—Clifford's First Easter. Bridwell, Norman, illus. (p. 332)
—Clifford's First Halloween. Bridwell, Norman, illus. (p. 332)
—Clifford's First Valentine's Day. Bridwell, Norman, illus. (p. 332)
—Clifford's Good Deeds. (p. 332)
—Clifford's Good Deeds. Bridwell, Norman, illus. (p. 332)
—Clifford's Halloween. Bridwell, Norman, illus. (p. 332)
—Clifford's Happy Easter. (p. 332)
—Clifford's Happy Easter. Bridwell, Norman, illus. (p. 332)
—Clifford's Manners. (p. 332)
—Clifford's Pals. (p. 332)
—Clifford's Pals. Bridwell, Norman, illus. (p. 332)
—Clifford's Puppy Days. (p. 332)
—Clifford's School Story Box. Bridwell, Norman, illus. (p. 332)
—Clifford's Sports Day. (p. 332)
—Clifford's Tricks. (p. 332)
—Coleccion. Bridwell, Norman, illus. (p. 339)
—Primera Navidad. (p. 1400)
—Witch Next Door. (p. 1941)
—Witch Next Door. Bridwell, Norman, illus. (p. 1941)
Bridwell, Norman, jt. auth. see Barbo, Maria S.
Bridwell, Norman, jt. auth. see Denega, Danielle.
Bridwell, Norman, jt. auth. see Fisch, Sarah.
Bridwell, Norman, jt. auth. see Herman, Gail.
Bridwell, Norman, jt. auth. see Lee, Quinlan B.
Bridwell, Norman, jt. auth. see Marsoli, Lisa Ann.
Bridwell, Norman, jt. auth. see Pugliano-Martin, Carol.
Bridwell, Norman, jt. auth. see Sander, Sonia.
Bridwell, Norman & Scholastic, Inc. Staff. Big Red Dog. (p. 183)
—Clifford the Big Red Dog. Bridwell, Norman, illus. (p. 332)
—Clifford's Bedtime Story Box. Bridwell, Norman, illus. (p. 332)
—Clifford's Big Dictionary. (p. 332)
Bridy, Dan, illus. see Solomon, Sharon K.
Brie, Erin. Poor Max! (p. 1383)
Briefing Associates Staff. This Is BRIEF! Or Starting Preschool & Homeschool Children Reading Naturally - at Once. Khaiphus, Kosta Demetrius, ed. (p. 1735)
Brieger, Ms. Kirsten, illus. see Kleiman, Deanna.
Brier, Elizabeth, illus. see Morrissey, Tricia.
Brier, Bill. Crystal Heart. (p. 387)
Brier, Howard M. Skycruiser. (p. 1587)
Briere, Charity, illus. see Macaulay, Doug, et al.
Briere, Euphemia. Victor Constantinus, Maximus Augustus: The Life of Saint Constantine, the First Christian Emperor & His Mother, Saint Helena. (p. 1840)
Briere, Marie-Josee, tr. see Crossingham, John & Kalman, Bobbie.
Briere, Marie-Josee, tr. see Dyer, Hadley & Kalman, Bobbie.
Briere, Marie-Josee, tr. see Kalman, Bobbie & Crossingham, John.
Briere, Marie-Josee, tr. see Kalman, Bobbie & Dyer, Hadley.
Briere, Marie-Josee, tr. see Kalman, Bobbie & Larin, Allison.
Briere, Marie-Josee, tr. see Kalman, Bobbie & Macaulay, Kelly.
Briere, Marie-Josee, tr. see Kalman, Bobbie & Sjonger, Rebecca.
Briere, Marie-Josee, tr. see Kalman, Bobbie & Smithyman, Kathryn.
Briere, Marie-Josee, tr. see Kalman, Bobbie.
Briere, Marie-Josee, tr. see Levigne, Heather.
Briere, Marie-Josee, tr. see MacAulay, Kelley & Kalman, Bobbie.
Briere, Marie-Josee, tr. see Sjonger, Rebecca & Kalman, Bobbie.
Briere, Marie-Josee, tr. see Walker, Niki & Dann, Sarah.
Brière, Paule. Undesirables. Beha, Philippe, illus. (p. 1817)
Briere-Haquet, Alice & Chauffrey, Celia. Peter & the Moon (p. 1346)
Brierley, Jane. Life of Jesus Puzzle Book. Lebedev, Aleksandr, illus. (p. 1012)
Briers, A. True Stories about Roman Coins. (p. 1792)
Briers, Audrey. True Stories about Greek Coins. (p. 1792)
Briers, Erica. Little Lamb to the Rescue. Boey, Stephanie, illus. (p. 1030)
—Runaway Chick. Boey, Stephanie, illus. (p. 1496)
Brierton, Maureen. Pride & Peridot: A Tale of Forgiveness. (p. 1398)
Brieske, Joel. Being Different Is Being Normal. (p. 161)
Brigance. Building Reading Skills: Student Response Book. (p. 239)
Brigg, Cathy, illus. see Stewart, Sean & Weisman, Jordan.
Briggett, Marlissa. Compleat Day Tripper-Cape Cod: The Cape's Best Classic & Eclectic Destinations for Kids & Grown-Ups! Pierce, Charlotte, ed. (p. 352)
Briggs, Andy. Council of Evil. (p. 369)
—Dark Hunter. (p. 407)
—Jungle Warrior. (p. 935)
—Rise of the Heroes. (p. 1475)
—Savage Lands. (p. 1516)
—Tarzan: The Greystoke Legacy. (p. 1706)
—Virus Attack. (p. 1844)
Briggs, Betty. Tuff-to-Beat Christmas, A New Edition (p. 1796)
Briggs, Charlotte, illus. see Bush, Leanne.
Briggs, D. Sharon. Mysteries in Knowledge Challenge Your Children: Complete Multiplication Tables. (p. 1222)
Briggs, Eleanor, photos by see Montgomery, Sy.
Briggs, Harry, illus. see Tang, Greg & Greg, Tang.
Briggs, Harry, illus. see Tang, Greg.

Briggs, Jason R. Python for Kids: A Playful Introduction to Programming. (p. 1422)
Briggs, Jay. Giants Child. (p. 674)
Briggs, Karen, illus. see Duroux, Mary.
Briggs, Kelly Paul. Lighthouse Lullaby. (p. 1015)
Briggs, Lucy. Kate Dicamillo. (p. 944)
Briggs, Mark T. Jermaine Peterman & the Encounter in the Forest. (p. 913)
Briggs, Martha Wren. Little Ferry Travels with Virginia: The Little Ferry Goes to Yorktown. Bk. 6 Starbuck-McMillan, Elizabeth, illus. (p. 1027)
Briggs, Mayke Beckmann. Here You Are. Briggs, Mayke Beckmann, illus. (p. 771)
Briggs, Meredith. Polka-Dot Parade. (p. 1381)
Briggs, Molly Anne. Momma's Favorite Rock. (p. 1162)
Briggs, Patricia. Cry Wolf (p. 387)
—Iron Kissed. (p. 888)
Briggs, Paula. Drawing Projects for Children. (p. 482)
Briggs, Raymond. Father Christmas: It's a Blooming Terrible Joke Book. (p. 577)
—Jimmy Murphy & the White Duesenberg. (p. 918)
—Nuvolari & the Alfa Romeo. (p. 1274)
—Puddleman. Briggs, Raymond, illus. (p. 1414)
—Snowman. (p. 1601)
—Snowman & the Snowdog. (p. 1601)
Briggs, Raymond, jt. auth. see Harrison, Joanna.
Briggs, Sandy. Little Steps for New Parents: A Weekly Guide for Developing Your Baby's Intelligence. (p. 1036)
Briggs, Scott, photos by see Kasten, Victoria.
Briggs-Anderson, Naomi. Mattie & Percy: The Story of a Chicken & a Duck. Wooten, Vernon Lee, illus. (p. 1110)
Briggs-Greenberg, Ruthie. Felicity the Dragon. (p. 581)
Briggsw, Anne. Life in the Woolly Lane. (p. 1011)
Brigham, Anthea. Henrietta, World War II Hen. Brigham, Anthea, illus. (p. 767)
Brigham, Marilyn. Swim! Velasquez, Eric, illus. (p. 1690)
Bright, Alasdair, illus. see Giff, Patricia Reilly.
Bright, Amy. Before We Go (p. 159)
—Swimmers (p. 1691)
Bright, Belle. Crash, Bang, Boom, Zing. Bright, Michael, illus. (p. 376)
Bright, Bonnie, illus. see Rothenberg, B. Annye.
Bright, Bonnie, jt. auth. see Elin Hirschman, Jessica.
Bright, Bonnie04, illus. see Rothenberg, B. Annye.
Bright, Brad, et al. Getting to Know Jesus for Little Ones: The Four Keys to Starting a Relationship with God. Bishop, Tracy, illus. (p. 669)
Bright, C. L. Goat Who Wanted to Catch a Fish. (p. 687)
Bright Connections Media. Dragons & Other Legendary Monsters: An Intrepid Wanderer's Guide. (p. 479)
Bright Connections Media, jt. auth. see Grejniec, Michael.
Bright Connections Media, jt. auth. see Sellier, Marie.
Bright, et al. Beginning the Christian Adventure (p. 159)
—Building an Active Faith (p. 238)
—Discover Our Awesome God (p. 448)
Bright, J. E. Batman Versus Man-Bat. (p. 144)
—Batman Versus Man-Bat. Gordon, Steven E. & Gordon, Eric A., illus. (p. 144)
—Batman vs. Catwoman Levins, Tim, illus. (p. 144)
—Best Friends. (p. 169)
—Best Friends - Continental Drift. (p. 169)
—Beware the Shadow Phoenix (Winx Club) Random House Staff, illus. (p. 173)
—Brain Freeze! (p. 221)
—Brain Freeze! Random House Staff, illus. (p. 221)
—Case of the Cheese Thief Neely, Scott, illus. (p. 273)
—Chipwrecked: Brittany Speaks! (p. 308)
—Chipwrecked: Castaway Critters. (p. 308)
—Chipwrecked: Too Cool for Rules. (p. 308)
—Continental Drift: Manny's Big Adventure. (p. 360)
—Cyborg Superman Levins, Tim & DC Comics Staff, illus. (p. 396)
—Cyborg Superman. Levins, Tim, illus. (p. 396)
—DC Super Friends to the Rescue. Doescher, Erik, illus. (p. 415)
—Deepwater Disaster. Schoening, Dan et al, illus. (p. 423)
—Fastest Pet on Earth Baltazar, Art, illus. (p. 576)
—Great Migration. (p. 717)
—Heroes of the High Seas Baltazar, Art, illus. (p. 773)
—Joker on the High Seas McManus, Shawn, illus. (p. 924)
—Lex Luthor & the Kryptonite Caverns Vecchio, Luciano, illus. (p. 1004)
—Manny's Big Adventure. (p. 1088)
—Power of Dragon Flame (Winx Club) Random House Staff, illus. (p. 1389)
—Savage Sands Schoening, Dan, illus. (p. 1516)
—Seed Bank Heist. Beavers, Ethen, illus. (p. 1547)
—Teen Titans Go!: Cyborg Circuit Overload. (p. 1714)
—Walking with Dinosaurs: Patchi's Big Adventure. (p. 1854)
—Walking with Dinosaurs: the Great Migration. (p. 1854)
Bright, J. E., jt. auth. see Digest Readers Staff.
Bright, J. E., jt. auth. see Hult, Gene.
Bright, J. E. & Loughridge, Lee. Deadly Dream Machine. Schigiel, Gregg, illus. (p. 417)
—Joker on the High Seas McManus, Shawn, illus. (p. 924)
Bright, J. E. & Sutton, Laurie S. Wonder Woman vs. Circe Vecchio, Luciano, illus. (p. 1947)
Bright, J. E., et al. Killer Kaleidoscope (p. 956)
—You Choose Stories: Batman. Beavers, Ethen, illus. (p. 1975)
Bright, Jean Hay, see Hay Bright, Jean.
Bright, Joe, illus. see Nichols, Catherine.
Bright, John. Alsager's Secret. (p. 50)
Bright, Laren, jt. auth. see Spanton, Elizabeth.
Bright, Logan Marie Christina. Ruby the Rabbit Goes Exploring. (p. 1493)
Bright, Michael. 3-D Explorer: Sharks. (p. 1991)
—Behavior in Living Things (p. 160)
—Diversity of Species. (p. 454)
—Exploring Nature - Bears & Pandas: An Intriguing Insight into the Lives of Brown Bears, Polar Bears, Black Bears, Pandas & Others, with 190 Exciting Images: Bears & Pandas: Bears & Pandas. (p. 552)
—Extinctions of Living Things (p. 555)
—Future of Life on Earth (p. 651)
—Weather Explained (p. 1870)
Bright, Michael, illus. see Bright, Belle.
Bright, Michael & Fergusson, Ian K. Nature Watch: Sharks. (p. 1237)
Bright, Paul. Bears in the Bed & the Great Big Storm Chapman, Jane, illus. (p. 152)
—Fidgety Fish & Friends. Galloway, Ruth, illus. (p. 583)
—Nobody Laughs at a Lion! Buckingham, Matt, illus. (p. 1262)
Bright, Philip & Ramos, Sarah. Jimmy Rat. (p. 918)
Bright, Phoebe. Lucky Stars #1: Wish upon a Friend. (p. 1063)
—Lucky Stars #2: Wish upon a Pet. (p. 1063)
—Lucky Stars #3: Wish upon a Song. (p. 1063)
—Lucky Stars #5: Wish upon a Superstar. (p. 1063)
—Wish upon a Gift. (p. 1940)
Bright, Phyllis, illus. see Nichele, Neika.
Bright, Rachel. Benjamin & the Super Spectacles. (p. 164)
—Benjamin & the Super Spectacles (the Wonderful World of Walter & Winnie) (p. 164)
—Lion Inside. Field, Jim, illus. (p. 1020)
—Love Monster. (p. 1060)
—Love Monster & the Perfect Present. (p. 1060)
—Side by Side. Gliori, Debi, illus. (p. 1573)
—Walter & the No-Need-To-Worry Suit (the Wonderful World of Walter & Winnie) (p. 1856)
Bright, Todd, illus. see Robinson, Ty, et al.
Brighter Child Publishing Staff, jt. auth. see Hullinger, C. D.
Brighter Child Publishing Staff, creator. Marvel Super Hero Fact Book. (p. 1099)
Brighter Minds, jt. creator see Brighter Minds.
Brighter Minds & Brighter Minds, creators. Birth of Jesus. (p. 192)
Brighter Minds, creator. Animal Sight Words Flashcards. (p. 79)
—Classic Bible Stories: Noah's Ark. (p. 327)
—Fact Book. (p. 561)
—Kung Fu Panda: Create-A-Story. (p. 968)
—Kung Fu Panda Magnetic Storybook. (p. 968)
—My Little Pony Sing & Play: Follow-Th-Lights Paino Songbook. (p. 1213)
Brightfield, Rick. Amazing Mazes: Groovy, Graphic Games. (p. 55)
Brightling, Geoff, illus. see Redmond, Ian.
Brightling, Geoff, photos by see Clarke, Barry & Dorling Kindersley Publishing Staff.
Brightling, Geoff, photos by see Cotterell, Arthur, et al.
Brightman, Michelle. If I Were. (p. 853)
Bright-Moore, Susan & Bedesky, Baron. How Is a Government Elected? (p. 810)
—How Is a Law Passed? (p. 810)
Brighton, Catherine. Brontës: Scenes from the Childhood of Charlotte, Branwell, Emily & Anne. (p. 230)
—Fossil Girl: Mary Anning's Dinosaur Discovery. (p. 623)
—Mozart. (p. 1184)
—My Napoleon. Brighton, Catherine, illus. (p. 1215)
Brighton, Wendy. Bosley Beats the Burglars. (p. 214)
Brightwell, Beverly. Pea Key & Sam. (p. 1331)
—Pea Key & Sam Go to the State Fair. (p. 1331)
Brightwell, Chris R. Nano-Reef Handbook: The Ultimate Guide to Reef Systems under 15 Gallons. (p. 1229)
Brightwell, Emily. Mrs. Jeffries in the Nick of Time. (p. 1187)
Brightwood, Laura. Anansi & the Turtle. (p. 67)
—Banana Fairy Fuss. Pifer, Kimberly, ed. (p. 135)
—Bee Is for Bold. Pifer, Kimberly, ed. (p. 157)
—Bully Goat Grim. (p. 241)
—Buzz off, Bee! Pifer, Kimberly, ed. (p. 248)
—Cheery Garden. Pifer, Kimberly, ed. (p. 296)
—Debate in Sign Language. (p. 421)
—Elephant's Trunk of Confidence. Pifer, Kimberly, ed. (p. 512)
—Ghost House. (p. 670)
—Giraffe's Shocking Surprise. Pifer, Kimberly, ed. (p. 678)
—Growing up in East L. A. (p. 726)
—House That Talked to Itself. (p. 804)
—I Am A Frog. (p. 832)
—Ka-ulu the Strong. (p. 941)
—King Zargon Rules. (p. 959)
—King's New Suit. (p. 960)
—Knot for Singing Parrot. Pifer, Kimberly, ed. (p. 965)
—Left Out. (p. 987)
—Lion & Mousie. (p. 1019)
—Little Freddie & His Whistle. (p. 1028)
—Look What You've Done. (p. 1050)
—Mousanga Bira Mousa. (p. 1181)
—Parrot's Winter Blues. Pifer, Kimberly, ed. (p. 1325)
—Poodle's Broken E. Pifer, Kimberly, ed. (p. 1383)
—Red Hat / Blue Hat. (p. 1454)
—Wise People of Helm. (p. 1940)
—Wolf under the Bed. (p. 1944)
—Woodsman & His Ax. (p. 1950)
Brightwood, Laura & DeRosier, Melissa. LifeStories for Kids K-2: Grades K-2. Brightwood, Laura, illus. (p. 1014)
Brigio, Jack. Digger & Friends. (p. 438)
Brigitte, Smadja, jt. auth. see Miracles, Max.
Brigitte, Smadja, jt. auth. see Smadja, Bridgitte.
Briglia, Anthony, illus. see Braun, Eric.
Brigman, June, illus. see Bowyer, Clifford B.
Brigman, June, illus. see Clay, Kathryn.
Brigman, June, illus. see Sewell, Anna.
Brigman, June, illus. see Simonson, Louise.
Brignall, Richard. Big League Dreams: Baseball Hall of Fame's First African-Canadian, Fergie Jenkins (p. 182)
—Big Train: The Legendary Ironman of Sport, Lionel Conacher (p. 184)
—China Clipper: Pro Football's First Chinese-Canadian Player, Normie Kwong (p. 306)
—Fearless: The Story of George Chuvalo, Canada's Greatest Boxer (p. 579)
—Forever Champions: The Enduring Legacy of the Edmonton Grads (p. 619)
—Forever Champions: The Enduring Legacy of the Edmonton Grads Women's Basketball Team. (p. 619)
—Real Justice: a Police Mr. Big Sting Goes Wrong: The Story of Kyle Unger (p. 1448)
—Summit Series '72: Eight Games That Put Canada on Top of World Hockey (p. 1675)
Brignall, Richard, jt. auth. see Danakas, John.
Brignall, Richard & Sherrard, Brent. China Clipper: Pro Football's First Chinese-Canadian Player, Normie Kwong (p. 306)
Brignaud, Pierre. Baby Caillou: My Farm Friends: A Finger Fun Book. (p. 125)
—Caillou Asks Nicely. (p. 251)
—Caillou - Toddler Essentials: 5 Books about Growing. (p. 251)
—Caillou: Where Is Teddy? (p. 251)
Brignaud, Pierre, illus. see Chouette Publishing Staff.
Brignaud, Pierre, illus. see Decary, Marie.
Brignaud, Pierre, illus. see Egar, Joann.
Brignaud, Pierre, illus. see Johanson, Sarah Margaret.
Brignaud, Pierre, illus. see L'Heureux, Christine & Légaré, Gisèle.
Brignaud, Pierre, illus. see L'Heureux, Christine.
Brignaud, Pierre, illus. see Légaré, Gisèle & L'Heureux, Christine.
Brignaud, Pierre, illus. see Mercier, Johanne.
Brignaud, Pierre, illus. see Nadeau, Nicole.
Brignaud, Pierre, illus. see Paradis, Anne.
Brignaud, Pierre, illus. see Publishing, Chouette.
Brignaud, Pierre, illus. see Rudel-Tessier, Melanie.
Brignaud, Pierre, illus. see Sanschagrin, Joceline.
Brignole, Giancarla, tr. see Aldovini, Giulia.
Brignole, Giancarla, tr. see Bono, Elena & Bono, E.
Brignole, Giancarla, tr. see Bresanetti, Sandra & Bresanetti, S.
Brignole, Giancarla, tr. see Gavioli, Gino & Gavioli, G.
Brignole, Giancarla, tr. see Mostacchi, Massimo.
Brignole, Giancarla, tr. see Ot, Elli & Ot, Eli.
Brignole, Giancarla, tr. see Ot, Elli.
Brignole, Giancarla, tr. see Sartori, Gloria.
Brignole, Giancarla, tr. see Serofilli, Loretta, et al.
Brignole, Giancarla, tr. Gigante y el Mar. Gazzaneo, Lucia, illus. (p. 676)
—Globo de Pablito. Casagrande, Donata Dal Molin, illus. (p. 685)
—Misterio del Condor. Polastri, Rosa Elena, illus. (p. 1155)
—Pueblo de los Silencios. Bersanetti, Sandra, illus. (p. 1414)
—Pulpo Campanero. Meconni, Beppe, illus. (p. 1416)
Briles, Patti, illus. see Williams, Rozanne Lanczak.
Briles, Patty, illus. see Williams, Rozanne Lanczak.
Briley, Jennifer Lenore. Justin's Journey. (p. 940)
Briley, Randy. Mr Underneath. (p. 1187)
Briley, Randy W. Big Pigs & Sock Dances. (p. 183)
Briley, Randy William. Sketchboy. (p. 1584)
Brilis, Michael Nicholas. Joy & Tears in Life: Perspectives of a Greek Immigrant. (p. 929)
Brill, Darlene, ed. see Andries, Kathryn.
Brill, Marietta Abrams, jt. auth. see Blanchard, Ken.
Brill, Marlene Targ. Allen Jay & the Underground Railroad Porter, Janice Lee, illus. (p. 46)
—Allen Jay y el Ferrocarril Subterraneo. Translations.com Staff, tr. from ENG. (p. 46)
—America in the 1900s. (p. 59)
—America in the 1980s. (p. 59)
—America in the 1990s. (p. 59)
—Annie Shapiro & the Clothing Workers' Strike. (p. 87)
—Annie Shapiro & the Clothing Workers' Strike. Akib, Jamel, illus. (p. 87)
—Autism. (p. 117)
—Barack Obama: President for a New Era. (p. 137)
—Bronco Charlie & the Pony Express. Orback, Craig, illus. (p. 230)
—Bronco Charlie y el Pony Express. Translations.com Staff, tr. (p. 230)
—Concrete Mixers. (p. 355)
—Día de los Veteranos. Fitzpatrick, Julia, tr. from ENG. (p. 433)
—Diabetes. (p. 433)
—Down Syndrome. (p. 474)
—Garbage Trucks. (p. 655)
—Illinois. (p. 857)
—Indiana. (p. 871)
—Marshall Major Taylor: World Champion Bicyclist, 1899-1901. (p. 1096)
—Michelle Obama: From Chicago's South Side to the White House. (p. 1135)
—Michigan. (p. 1135)
—Multiple Sclerosis. (p. 1190)
—Nurses. (p. 1273)
—Rough-Riding Adventure of Bronco Charlie, Pony Express Rider. (p. 1491)
—Rough-Riding Adventure of Bronco Charlie, Pony Express Rider. Trover, Zachary, illus. (p. 1491)
—Underground Railroad Adventure of Allen Jay, Antislavery Activist. Hammond, Ted & Carbajal, Richard, illus. (p. 1815)
—Underground Railroad Adventure of Allen Jay, Antislavery Activist. Hammond, Ted & Carbajal, Richard Pimentel, illus. (p. 1815)
—Veterans Day. Wang, Qi Z., illus. (p. 1839)
Brill, Marlene Targ, jt. auth. see Schuman, Michael.
Brill, Marlene Targ & Kaplan, Elizabeth. Minnesota. (p. 1147)
Brill, Marlene Targ & Richards, Marlee. America in the 1910s. (p. 59)
—America in the 1970s. (p. 59)
Brim, Warren & Eglitis, Anna. Creatures of the Rainforest: Two Artists Explore Djabugay Country. Brim, Warren & Eglitis, Anna, illus. (p. 380)
Brimax Publishing, creator. My Little Book of Dinosaurs. (p. 1212)
Brimberg, Sisse, illus. see Arenstam, Peter, et al.
Brimberg, Sisse, photos by see Arenstam, Peter, et al.
Brimberg, Sisse, photos by see Bruchac, Margaret M. & Grace, Catherine O'Neill.
Brimberg, Sisse, photos by see Grace, Catherine O'Neill & Bruchac, Margaret M.
Brimhall, John. My Favorite Classics: Level One. (p. 1203)
Brimmar, A. Help Is on the Way: North America. (p. 765)
Brimmar, A. M. Help Is on the Way:South America. (p. 765)
Brimmer, Debi & Coleson, Julie. How Six Little Ipu Got Their Names. Coleson, Julie, illus. (p. 812)
Brimner, Larry Dane. Baby Bear. (p. 125)
—Birmingham Sunday. (p. 192)
—Bit Is a Bite. Kono, Erin Eitter, illus. (p. 194)
—Black & White: The Confrontation Between Reverend Fred L. Shuttlesworth & Eugene Bull Connor. (p. 195)
—Booker T. Washington: Getting into the Schoolhouse. (p. 212)
—Chief Crazy Horse: Following a Vision. (p. 301)
—Cool Coats. Tripp, Christine, illus. (p. 363)
—Monkey Math. Kulka, Joe, illus. (p. 1165)
—Official M&M's(r) Brand History of the Calendar. Pellaton, Karen E., illus. (p. 1280)
—Pocahontas: Bridging Two Worlds. (p. 1375)
—Strike! The Farm Workers' Fight for Their Rights. (p. 1667)
—Subway: The Story of Tunnels, Tubes, & Tracks. Waldman, Neil, illus. (p. 1671)
—Summer Fun. Tripp, Christine, illus. (p. 1674)
—Trash Trouble. Tripp, Christine, illus. (p. 1780)
—Trick or Treat, Old Armadillo. Catalano, Dominic, illus. (p. 1786)
—We Are One: The Story of Bayard Rustin. (p. 1865)
Brimson, Samuel. Brazil-East Timor (p. 224)
—Ecuador-Honduras (p. 503)
—Hungary-Kiribati (p. 827)
—Korea, North-Nicaragua (p. 967)
—Sierra Leone-United Arab Emirates (p. 1573)
—United Kingdom-Zimbabwe (p. 1819)
Brin, David. Sky Horizon. Hampton, Scott, illus. (p. 1586)
Brin, Susannah. Bad Luck Boy. Miller, Fujiko, illus. (p. 132)
—Climb. Miller, Fujiko, illus. (p. 333)
—Crystal's Chance. Miller, Fujiko, illus. (p. 387)
—Search & Rescue. Miller, Fujiko, illus. (p. 1537)
—Summer Romance. (p. 1675)
—Tough Guy. Miller, Fujiko, illus. (p. 1772)
Brindell, Dennis Fradin. Assassination of Abraham Lincoln. (p. 107)
Brindis, Laura. Cuentos Universales del Barroco a la Vanguardia. (p. 390)
Brindley, John. City of Screams. (p. 324)
—Rule of Claw. Benfold Haywood, Ian P., illus. (p. 1495)
Brine, M. D. Our Little Ones. (p. 1309)
Brinegar, R. L. Ron. Pokey: The Fastest Horse on the Ranch. (p. 1378)
Briner, Elaine. Fairytales of the Wentny Kind. (p. 565)
Briney, Stan. Fantasy Locked in a Criminal Mind. (p. 572)
Bringhurst, Nancy J. A Is for Alligator. Stark, Mindy C., illus. (p. 1)
Bringle, Beverly, illus. see Awiakta, Marilou.
Bringle, Jennifer. Alien Sightings in America. (p. 41)
—Civil Rights Act Of 1964. (p. 324)
—Homelessness in America Today. (p. 793)
—Nebraska: Past & Present. (p. 1239)
—Reproductive Rights: Making the Right Choices. (p. 1461)
—Undertaker: Master of Pain. (p. 1816)
—Vampires in Film & Television. (p. 1832)
—Wing Shooting. (p. 1936)
—Young Women & the HPV Vaccine. (p. 1979)
Bringsvaerd, Tor Age. Ruffen: The Escape to Loch Ness. Hansen, Thore, illus. (p. 1494)
—Ruffen: The Sea Serpent Who Couldn't Swim. Hansen, Thore, illus. (p. 1494)
—When Two Are Angry at Each Other. Vetleseter, Tonje, tr. from NOR. (p. 1905)
—When Two Get Up. Soli, Tina, illus. (p. 1905)
—When Two Say Goodnight. Soli, Tina, illus. (p. 1905)
—When Two Take a Bath. Soli, Tina, illus. (p. 1905)
Brink, Carol Ryrie. Caddie Woodlawn. (p. 250)
Brink Hull, Amanda. Maslyn: A Different Kind of Name for a Delightful Little Girl. (p. 1102)
Brink, LeeAnn. Stuff in the Back of the Desk. Cratty, Aaron, illus. (p. 1670)
Brink-Budgen, Roy van den. Critical Thinking for AS Level. (p. 383)
Brinker, Spencer. Counting to Add with Baron Von Madd. (p. 371)
—Ghost of Skip-Count Castle. (p. 671)
—More or Less & a Vampire's Guess. (p. 1174)
—Odd or Even in a Monstrous Season. (p. 1278)
—Witch's Things: A Counting to 20 Rhyme. (p. 1941)
—Zombie Take Away. (p. 1988)
Brinkerhoff, Phillip. To the Magical Pond. (p. 1759)
Brinkerhoff, Shirley. Anxiety Disorders. McDonnell, Mary Ann & Esherick, Donald, eds. (p. 90)
—Attention—Deficit/Hyperactivity Disorder. (p. 114)
—Childhood & Adolescent Disorders. McDonnell, Mary Ann & Esherick, Donald, eds. (p. 302)
—Contemporary Folklore. (p. 360)
—Drug Therapy & Anxiety Disorders. (p. 487)
—Drug Therapy & Childhood & Adolescent Disorders. (p. 487)
—Drug Therapy & Eating Disorders. (p. 487)
—Drug Therapy & Obsessive-Compulsive Disorders. (p. 487)
—Drug Therapy & Personality Disorders. (p. 487)
—Drug Therapy & Schizophrenia. (p. 487)
—Drug Therapy & Substance-Related Disorders. (p. 487)
—Eating Disorders. McDonnell, Mary Ann & Esherick, Donald, eds. (p. 501)
—Family Folklore. (p. 568)
—Folk Speech. (p. 611)
—Learning Disabilities. Albers, Lisa et al, eds. (p. 985)
—Obsessive-Compulsive Disorder. (p. 1275)
—Obsessive-Compulsive Disorder. McDonnell, Mary Ann & Esherick, Donald, eds. (p. 1275)
—Personality Disorders. McDonnell, Mary Ann & Esherick, Donald, eds. (p. 1344)
—Psychologist. Riggs, Ernestine G. & Gholar, Cheryl, eds. (p. 1413)
—Research Scientist. Riggs, Ernestine G. & Gholar, Cheryl, eds. (p. 1462)
—Schizophrenia. McDonnell, Mary Ann & Esherick, Donald, eds. (p. 1521)
—Social Worker. Gholar, Cheryl & Riggs, Ernestine G., eds. (p. 1605)
—Stuck on Fast Forward: Youth with Attention-Deficit/Hyperactivity Disorder. (p. 1669)
—Stuck on Fast Forward: Youth with Attention Deficit Hyper Activity Disorder. (p. 1669)
—Why Can't I Learn Like Everyone Else? Youth with Learning Disabilities. (p. 1923)

Brinkley, Alan. Unfinished Nation with PowerWeb. (p. 1817)
Brinkley, Inez. Rainbows & Promises. (p. 1436)
Brinkley, Lonnie. I Believe: Lost at the North Pole. (p. 834)
Brinkman, Patricia. Bill of Rights. (p. 186)
—Constitution. (p. 359)
—Discover Earth. (p. 447)
—Discover Minerals. (p. 447)
—Discover Rock Types. (p. 448)
—Discover the Bill of Rights. (p. 448)
—Discover the Constitution. (p. 448)
—Discover the Moon. (p. 448)
—Discover the Rock Cycle. (p. 448)
—Discover the Sun. (p. 448)
—Discover Writing the Constitution. (p. 448)
—Earth. (p. 494)
—Minerals. (p. 1146)
—Moon. (p. 1171)
—Rock Cycle. (p. 1482)
—Rock Types. (p. 1482)
—Sun. (p. 1675)
—Writing the Constitution. (p. 1965)
Brinkman, Paula, illus. see Pierce, Karen F.
Brinks, Jan Herman. Nationalist Myths & Modern Media: Contested Identities in the Age of Globalization. Brinks, Jan Herman et al, eds. (p. 1234)
Brinkworth, Brian. Life in a Coral Reef. (p. 1010)
Brinley, Bertrand R. Big Chunk of Ice: The Last Known Adventure of the Mad Scientists' Club. Geer, Charles, illus. (p. 180)
—Big Kerplop! The Original Adventure of the Mad Scientist's Club. Geer, Charles, illus. (p. 182)
—Mad Scientists' Club. Geer, Charles, illus. (p. 1069)
—Mad Scientists' Club Complete Collection. Geer, Charles, illus. (p. 1069)
Brinsmead, Hesba. Pastures of the Blue Crane. (p. 1327)
Brinson, Connor J., illus. see Brinson, Julie L.
Brinson, Heather. Adventure of the Poisoned Drink. (p. 14)
Brinson, Julie L. Princess Olivia & the Leap Frog Brinson, Connor J., illus. (p. 1405)
Brinster, Dick. Jeff Gordon. (p. 911)
Brinton, Elisa. Courage to Stand: Stories of Young Strength & Triumphs in Adversity. (p. 372)
Brinton, Margaret. 100 Little Language Lessons. (p. 1998)
—100 Little Reading Comprehension Lessons, Grade 1-4: Fun-To-Read Stories with Skill-Building Exercises. Shalansky, Len, illus. (p. 1998)
Brinzel, Daniel, ed. see Coblenz, John.
Brinzel, Daniel, tr. see Coblenz, John.
Briones, Philip. Captain America Corps. (p. 263)
Brischke, D. Wake Up Zoo. (p. 1853)
Brisco, Dianna. Day Marcus Flew. (p. 413)
Brisco, Dianna L. Day Marcus Got a Dog. (p. 413)
Briscoe, Connie, jt. auth. see Cunningham, Michael.
Briscoe, Dean. Hero of Archadeon. (p. 772)
Briscoe, Diana. Bridge Building: Bridge Designs & How They Work. (p. 227)
—Jane Goodall: Finding Hope in the Wilds of Africa. (p. 908)
—Jane Goodall: Finding Hope in the Wilds of Africa Set (p. 908)
Briscoe, Diana C. Bridge Building: Bridge Designs & How They Work Set (p. 227)
Briscoe, Holly. Boy in the Shower. (p. 218)
Brisebois, Ro. Sherlock & Elf: The Mystery of the Thicket Behind the Shed. (p. 1565)
Brisland, Toni. DemiChat & the Lost Mummy. de los reyes Cruz, Cheryl, illus. (p. 425)
Brislane, Niche, illus. see Vaughn, J. D.
Brisley, Joyce Lankester, illus. see Williams, Ursula Moray.
Brissenden, Constance, jt. auth. see Loyle, Larry.
Brissenden, Constance & Larry, Loyle. Goodbye Buffalo Bay (p. 700)
Brisson, Pat. Before We Eat: From Farm to Table. Azarian, Mary, illus. (p. 159)
—Benny's Pennies. (p. 165)
—Hobbledy-Clop. Chambliss, Maxie, illus. (p. 786)
—Melissa Parkington's Beautiful, Beautiful Hair. Bloom, Suzanne, illus. (p. 1125)
—Sometimes We Were Brave. Brassard, France, illus. (p. 1610)
—Star Blanket. Magnus, Erica, illus. (p. 1640)
—Summer My Father Was Ten. Shine, Andrea, illus. (p. 1674)
—Tap-Dance Fever. Cote, Nancy, illus. (p. 1705)
Bristol, Claude M. Magic of Believing for Young People. (p. 1072)
Bristol, Mark, illus. see Neal, Angie & Kjesbo, Rynette.
Bristol, P. L. & Branda, Barnabus. Fiona Faintly: A Goats Tale. Howard, Megz, illus. (p. 589)
Bristow, Catherine. My Strange & Terrible Malady. (p. 1219)
Bristow, David L. Sky Sailors: True Stories of the Balloon Era. (p. 1587)
Bristow, Michael. Backyard Bugs: Understand & Apply Properties of Operations. (p. 131)
Bristow, Sophie. Queen's Beasts. Hiscocks, Dan, ed. (p. 1425)
Brisville, J. C. Invierno en Vid - Grand Oso (Winter - Life of Big Bear) (p. 885)
Brita, Granström, jt. auth. see Manning, Mick.
Britain, Bruce. Jungle Two. (p. 935)
Britain, Lory. My Grandma Died: Child's Story about Death & Loss. Deach, Carol, illus. (p. 1210)
Britain, William. Senor de los Deseos. (p. 1550)
Britan, Denise G. Harry Meets Sam. (p. 750)
Britannica, creator. World Exploration from Ancient Times. (p. 1955)
Britannica Encyclopaedia, Inc. Staff, jt. auth. see Hamel, Raymond.
Britannica, Learning Library. Exploring Space. (p. 553)
—Planet Earth. (p. 1367)
—Religions Around the World. (p. 1458)
—Science & Nature. (p. 1525)
—Technology & Inventions. (p. 1711)
—Wildlife Wonders. (p. 1931)
Britannica Learning Library Staff. Artists Around the World. (p. 104)
—Creatures of the Waters. (p. 380)
—Familiar Animals. (p. 567)
—Remarkable People in History. (p. 1459)
British Broadcasting Corporation Staff. Companion Compendium. (p. 351)
—Doctor Who: Official Annual 2014. (p. 459)
—Doctor Who. (p. 459)
—English Pronunciation: Learning the Sounds of American English. (p. 530)
—Monster Miscellany. (p. 1167)
British Broadcasting Corporation Staff, jt. auth. see Baxendale, Trevor.
British Broadcasting Corporation Staff, jt. auth. see Brake, Colin.
British Broadcasting Corporation Staff, jt. auth. see Santillan, Jorge.
British Broadcasting Corporation Staff, et al. Heart of Stone - Death Riders. (p. 759)
—Monstrous Missions (p. 1169)
—Step Back in Time (p. 1647)
British Museum of Natural History Staff, contrib. by. What Do Animals Eat Colouring Book. (p. 1882)
Britland, Jan. Adventures of Rodger Dodger Dog: First Adventure. Swaim, Mike, illus. (p. 22)
—Adventures of Rodger Dodger Dog: A Christmas Story. Swaim, Mike, illus. (p. 22)
—Adventures of Rodger Dodger Dog: Rodger Saves Bunny. Swaim, Mike, illus. (p. 22)
—Adventures of Rodger Dodger Dog: A Christmas Story. Swaim, Michael, illus. (p. 22)
—Adventures of Rodger Dodger Dog: Rodger Meets Dr. Glee. Swaim, Mike, illus. (p. 22)
—Adventures of Rodger Dodger Dog. Swaim, Michael, illus. (p. 22)
Britner, Melissa, jt. auth. see Britner, Scott.
Britner, Scott & Britner, Melissa. Tyler & Destiny Tales: Lunch at the Zoo. (p. 1805)
Briton, jt. auth. see Britton.
Britsky, Dawn. Children's Yoga Journey. (p. 304)
Britt, Chris. Blabbering Bethann (p. 194)
Britt, Fanny & Ouriou, Susan. Jane, the Fox & Me Morelli, Christelle, tr. from FRE. (p. 908)
Britt, Jeanetta. Pickin' Ground. (p. 1354)
Britt, Joanna, illus. see Doerr, Bonnie J.
Britt, Monica L. Adam to Zacchaeus: the Men of the Bible: An Alphabet Book. (p. 11)
Britt, Paige. Lost Track of Time. White, Lee, illus. (p. 1056)
Britt, Rachel, illus. see Lister, John C.
Britt, Stephanie. My Big Little Bible: Includes My Little Bible, My Little Psalms, & My Little Prayers (p. 1197)
—My Little Prayers (p. 1213)
Britt, Stephanie, illus. see Adair, Dick.
Britt, Stephanie, illus. see Dickinson, Rebecca.
Britt, Stephanie, illus. see Kennedy, Pamela.
Britt, Stephanie, illus. see Pingry, Patricia A.
Britt, Stephanie, illus. see Smith, Tamara.
Britt, Stephanie, jt. auth. see Kennedy, Pamela.
Britt, Stephanie M. My Little Bible. (p. 1212)
Britt, Stephanie M., illus. see Hults, Alaska.
Britt, Stephanie McFetridge. My First Book of Prayers. (p. 1205)
Britt, Stephanie McFetridge, illus. see Lashbrook, Marilyn.
Britt, Stephanie McFetridge, illus. see Pingry, Patricia A.
Britt, Stephanie McFetridge, illus. see Potter, Beatrix.
Brittain, Bill. Wizards & the Monster. (p. 1943)
Brittain, Kyle, jt. ed. see Pocket Press.
Brittain, Kyle, ed. Pocket Guide to Wisconsin Traffic Laws. (p. 1375)
Brittany, jt. auth. see Nana B.
Brittany's Books. I Can Too! African American Girls. (p. 836)
Brittingham, Geoffrey, illus. see Smith, Suzanne C.
Brittingham, Jennifer, illus. see Holbrook, James.
Britto, Romero. Color Play! An Interactive Pop Art Book. Britto, Romero, illus. (p. 343)
—My Alphabet Playbook. Britto, Romero, illus. (p. 1196)
—Where Is Friendship Bear? Britto, Romero, illus. (p. 1908)
Britton & Briton. Ferns Family Favourites. (p. 582)
Britton, April Spring. Alphabet Rhymes. (p. 50)
Britton, Arthur K. Life at a Polar Research Station. (p. 1008)
—Life in the Wild West. (p. 1011)
Britton, Daniel. Financial Fairy Tales: Dreams Can Come True. (p. 587)
Britton, Faith. If You'D Only Believe. (p. 855)
Britton, Felicity. Glee Cast: Inspiring Gleek Mania. (p. 682)
—Nicki Minaj: Conquering Hip-Hop. (p. 1251)
Britton, Lorelle. Mourning Glory: A Devotional for Grieving. (p. 1181)
Britton, Matthew, illus. see Hardman, John.
Britton, Tamara L. Barack Obama. (p. 137)
—Bull Terriers. (p. 240)
—Dwight D. Eisenhower. (p. 491)
—Eye on Economics. (p. 558)
—French Bulldogs. (p. 635)
—George Washington. (p. 664)
—Richard Nixon. (p. 1469)
—Ronald Reagan. (p. 1486)
—Rottweilers. (p. 1491)
—Theodore Roosevelt. (p. 1729)
Britton, Terre, illus. see Kuykendall, Anna.
Britton, Vickie & Jackson, Loretta. Ardis Cole Series: Murder & the Monalet Ruby (Book 4) (p. 96)
Britton, Vicky Lynn. Can You Play Today? (p. 259)
Brix, Liz. Josephine Prairie Dog. (p. 926)
Brixler, Andreas, jt. auth. see Rothstein, Arminio.
Brix-Maffei, Angela & Brix-Maffei, John. Christmas Dinosaur. (p. 313)
Brix-Maffei, John, jt. auth. see Brix-Maffei, Angela.
Brixton, Iris, jt. auth. see Boyd, Kate.
Brizendine, Brad, illus. see Cohen, Larry.
Brizuela, Dario, illus. see Baltazar, Art & Aureliani, Franco.
Brizuela, Dario, illus. see Baltazar, Art, et al.
Brizuela, Dario, illus. see Cohen, Ivan, et al.
Brizuela, Dario, illus. see Fisch, Sholly & Age, Heroic.
Brizuela, Dario, illus. see Fisch, Sholly & Ottolini, Horacio.
Brizuela, Dario, illus. see Fisch, Sholly.
Brizuela, Dario, illus. see Manning, Matthew K., et al.
Brizzi, Elisabeth, tr. see Guibert, Emmanuel & Sfar, Joann.
Brnyczka, Piotr. Petrified World (p. 1348)
Broach, Elise. Barnyard Baby. Doerrfeld, Cori, illus. (p. 139)
—Desert Crossing. (p. 429)
—Gumption! Egielski, Richard, illus. (p. 731)
—Masterpiece. (p. 1103)
—Masterpiece. Murphy, Kelly, illus. (p. 1103)
—Masterpiece. Murphy, Kelly & Brewster, Patience, illus. (p. 1103)
—Miniature World of Marvin & James. Murphy, Kelly, illus. (p. 1146)
—Missing on Superstition Mountain. Caparó, Antonio Javier, illus. (p. 1152)
—Revenge of Superstition Mountain. Ivanov, Aleksey & Ivanov, Olga, illus. (p. 1465)
—Revenge of Superstition Mountain. Ivanov, Olga & Ivanov, Aleksey, illus. (p. 1465)
—Seashore Baby. (p. 1538)
—Shakespeare's Secret. (p. 1559)
—Snowflake Baby. Doerrfeld, Cori, illus. (p. 1600)
—Springtime Baby. Doerrfeld, Cori, illus. (p. 1635)
—Treasure on Superstition Mountain. Caparo, Antonio Javier, illus. (p. 1782)
—Treasure on Superstition Mountain. Caparó, Antonio Javier, illus. (p. 1782)
—Wet Dog! Catrow, David, illus. (p. 1877)
—When Dinosaurs Came with Everything. Small, David, illus. (p. 1902)
Broad, Michael. #1 Ghost Diamond! (p. 1991)
—#2 Zombie Cows! (p. 1991)
—#3 Hypno Hounds! (p. 1991)
—#4 Spooky Ballet! (p. 1992)
—Ghost Diamond! Broad, Michael, illus. (p. 670)
—Hypno Hounds! Broad, Michael, illus. (p. 831)
—Spooky Ballet! Broad, Michael, illus. (p. 1631)
—Zombie Cows! Broad, Michael, illus. (p. 1988)
Broad, Michael, illus. see Wilding, Val.
Broad, Neil. Eastern & Central Arrernte Picture Dictionary. (p. 499)
Broad, Sam, illus. see Else, Barbara.
Broadbent, Jim, jt. auth. see Blackstone, Stella.
Broadbent, Paul. Being A Cartoonist. (p. 160)
—Beneath Our Feet. (p. 164)
—Dance Fever. (p. 402)
—Detective Work. (p. 431)
—Down under Vacation. (p. 474)
—Premier Maths. (p. 1395)
—Rock Stars. (p. 1482)
—Scuba Diving. (p. 1533)
—What Are You Scared Of? (p. 1880)
Broadbent, Paul & Patilla, Peter. Premier Maths Quick Tests. (p. 1395)
Broadbent, Paul, et al. English. (p. 529)
Broadbent, Tom & Kosmo, Lisa. Henrietta. (p. 767)
Broadhurst, Colin, illus. see Broadhurst, Sherree.
Broadhurst, Denton. Elvis Orange. (p. 517)
Broadhurst, Lucy, jt. auth. see Andrews McMeel Publishing Staff.
Broadhurst, Sherree. Bella Finds the Hidden Treasure. (p. 162)
—Bella's Adventures: Bella Rescues Gumleaf the Joey. (p. 162)
—Bella's Adventures: Bella in the City. Broadhurst, Colin, illus. (p. 162)
Broadley, Leo, illus. see Jenkins, Saffy.
Broadman and Holman Publishers Staff. Kindergarten. (p. 957)
—Learning Activities from the Bible Series. (p. 985)
—Preschool. (p. 1396)
Broadman and Holman Publishers Staff & Holman Bible Staff. Illustrated Study Bible for Kids. (p. 858)
Broadman and Holman Publishers Staff, ed. Read to Me Bible for Kids. (p. 1443)
Broadnax, Cassandra. Ten Commandments the Foundation of the Kingdom of God. (p. 1718)
Broadnax, Charles, illus. see Kearney Cooper, Nicole.
Broadribb, Donald. Marcia. (p. 1092)
Broadribb, Donald, tr. see Baum, L. Frank.
Broadribb, Donald, tr. see Carroll, Lewis, pseud.
Broadwater, Andrea. Life of Marian Anderson: Diva & Humanitarian. (p. 1012)
—Mary McLeod Bethune: Educator & Activist. (p. 1101)
Broadway, Hannah, illus. see Hayes, Felix.
Broady, Brianna, jt. auth. see Fielder, Barbara L.
Broberg, Janel. Catie the Cute, Curious & Sometimes Crooked Caterpillar. (p. 280)
Broberg, MaryAnn. Stolen Innocence: The Jan Broberg Story. (p. 1652)
Broberg, Penelope Northrop. Sleuthy Gumshoe: The Remarkable Detective. (p. 1590)
Brobst, Sydney. Edgar Allan Pony & the Racetrack Cat: A Story for Young & Not-So-Young People. (p. 504)
—Floyd's Short Tales of a Country Life. (p. 608)
Brochard, Philippe, illus. see Leblanc, Louise.
Brochard, Philippe, illus. see Lemieux, Jean.
Brochu, Christopher A., et al. Dinosaurs. Brett-Surman, Michael K., ed. (p. 443)
Brochu, Christopher & McHenry, Colin. Dinosaurs. (p. 443)
Brochu, Lisa. Dad Still Smiles. Butterfield, Ned, illus. (p. 398)
Brock, jt. auth. see Brock, Betty.
Brock, Betty & Brock. No Flying in the House. Tripp, Wallace, illus. (p. 1258)
Brock Bryant, Anita. Abcs of Advent. (p. 4)
Brock, C. E., illus. see Keary, Annie & Keary, Eliza.
Brock, C. E., illus. see Nesbit, E.
Brock, Charles Edmund, illus. see Nesbit, E.
Brock, Charles Edmund, illus. see Nesbit, Edith.
Brock, David. Infectious Fungi. Alcamo, I. Edward, ed. (p. 873)
Brock, Geoffrey, tr. see Collodi, Carlo.
Brock, George Ann, illus. see Monhollon, Lake Pylant.
Brock, H. M. Beauty & the Beast. (p. 154)
Brock, J. Judd. Ima Toothlusa Is My Name. (p. 860)
Brock, Justin. Have You Seen My Pencil? Poems & Musings. Wright, Christopher, illus. (p. 754)
Brock, Kenneth J., et al. Compact Guide to Indiana Birds. (p. 351)
Brock, Paula. Nudges. (p. 1270)
Brock, Robert E. Little Dott Finds a Home. (p. 1027)
Brockenbrough, Martha. Devine Intervention. (p. 432)
—Dinosaur Tooth Fairy. Sanchez, Israel, illus. (p. 443)
—Game of Love & Death. (p. 654)
Brocker, Susan. Across the Oregon Trail: Level R (p. 9)
—Restless Spirit. (p. 1464)
—Rivers of the World. (p. 1476)
—Sports Legends: Set Of 6. (p. 1633)
—Sports Legends & Leyendas del Deporte: 6 English, 6 Spanish Adaptations. (p. 1633)
—Vision Without Sight: Human Capabilities. (p. 1845)
—Voices from the Civil War: Set Of 6. (p. 1848)
—Voices from the Civil War & Voces de la Guerra Civil: 6 English, 6 Spanish Adaptations. (p. 1848)
—War Heroes: Level U (p. 1857)
Brocker, Susan & Furgang, Kathy. Pioneers in Medicine: Set Of 6. (p. 1361)
—Pioneers in Medicine & Médicos Pioneros: 6 English, 6 Spanish Adaptations. (p. 1361)
Brocket, Jane. 1 Cookie, 2 Chairs, 3 Pears: Numbers Everywhere. (p. 1991)
—1 Cookie, 2 Chairs, 3 Pears: Numbers Everywhere. Brocket, Jane, photos by. (p. 1991)
—Circles, Stars, & Squares: Looking for Shapes. Brocket, Jane, photos by. (p. 321)
—Cold, Crunchy, Colorful: Using Our Senses. Brocket, Jane, photos by. (p. 338)
—Rainy, Sunny, Blowy, Snowy - What Are Seasons? Brocket, Jane, photos by. (p. 1436)
—Ruby, Violet, Lime: Looking for Color. Brocket, Jane, photos by. (p. 1493)
—Spiky, Slimy, Smooth: What Is Texture? Brocket, Jane, photos by. (p. 1627)
—Stickiest, Fluffiest, Crunchiest: Super Superlatives. Brocket, Jane, photos by. (p. 1650)
Brocket, Jane, photos by. Spotty, Stripy, Swirly: What Are Patterns? (p. 1634)
Brock-Jaurequi, Dawn. Dream Big (p. 483)
—From Little Brother to Big Brother (p. 643)
Brocklehurst, R. Introduction to Powerpoint. (p. 882)
—Roman Army. (p. 1485)
Brocklehurst, Ruth. 1001 Animals Que Buscar. Gower, Teri, illus. (p. 2001)
—1001 Animals to Spot. (p. 2001)
—Animal Sticker Atlas. Turnbull, Stephanie, ed. (p. 79)
—Animales: Atlas con Pegatinas. Lucas, Ana Cristina Llompart, tr. (p. 80)
—Clothes & Fashion Sticker Book IR. Lardot, Christopher, illus. (p. 334)
—Mini Children's Picture Atlas. (p. 1146)
—Princess Things to Make & Do. (p. 1406)
—Roman Britain: Internet-Linked. Chisholm, Jane, ed. (p. 1485)
—Usborne Children's Picture Atlas. Edwards, Linda, illus. (p. 1827)
—Vintage Fashion Coloring Book IR. (p. 1843)
Brocklehurst, Ruth, ed. see Milbourne, Anna & Stowell, Louie.
Brocklehurst, Ruth, jt. auth. see Gilpin, Rebecca.
Brocklehurst, Ruth & Brook, Henry. First World War. Chisholm, Jane, ed. (p. 597)
—Usborne Introduction to the First World War. (p. 1827)
Brocklehurst, Ruth & Doherty, Gillian. Illustrated Grimm's Fairy Tales. (p. 857)
Brocklehurst, Ruth, et al. Famous Artists. (p. 569)
Brockman, Craig. Marty & the Far Woodchuck. (p. 1098)
Brockman, Noah. Journey to Neptune (p. 929)
Brockmann, Melanie, jt. auth. see Brockmann, Suzanne.
Brockmann, Suzanne & Brockmann, Melanie. Night Sky. (p. 1254)
Brockschmidt, Kev, illus. see Wood, Anita.
Brockway, Bettina Chevalier. Muff & the Mushroom Forest. (p. 1189)
Brockway, Harry, illus. see Giono, Jean & Giono, Aline.
Brockway, Margaret. David, the Son of Jesse. (p. 411)
Brockway, Stephanie. Mystic Phyles: Beasts. Masiello, Ralph, illus. (p. 1226)
Brod, Chani, tr. see Altein, Chani.
Broda, Ron, illus. see Ruurs, Margriet.
Brode, Robyn. April/Abril. (p. 93)
—April;abril. (p. 93)
—August/Agosto. (p. 115)
—August;agosto. (p. 115)
—December. (p. 421)
—December/Diciembre. (p. 421)
—December;diciembre. (p. 421)
—February/Febrero. (p. 580)
—February;febrero. (p. 580)
—January/Enero. (p. 908)
—January;enero. (p. 908)
—July/Julio. (p. 933)
—July;julio. (p. 933)
—June/Junio. (p. 934)
—June;junio. (p. 934)
—March/Marzo. (p. 1092)
—March;marzo. (p. 1092)
—May/Mayo. (p. 1113)
—May;mayo. (p. 1113)
—November/Noviembre. (p. 1268)
—November;noviembre. (p. 1268)
—October. (p. 1277)
—October/Octubre. (p. 1277)
—October;octubre. (p. 1277)
—September/Septiembre. (p. 1551)
—September;septiembre. (p. 1551)
Brode, Robyn & Nations, Susan. April. (p. 93)
—August. (p. 115)
—February. (p. 580)
—January. (p. 908)
—July. (p. 933)

—June. (p. 934)
—March. (p. 1091)
—May. (p. 1112)
—November. (p. 1268)
—September. (p. 1551)
Brodek, Lorraine Holnback. Tale of Peeky Peeper. (p. 1700)
Broderick, Al R., illus. see Broderick, Lonia R.
Broderick, Damien. Time Zones. (p. 1753)
Broderick, Joe. Samuel Beckett -la tragicomedia de la Vida. (p. 1509)
Broderick, Kathy. Disney Princess: Belle (Giant First Play -a-Sound) (p. 452)
Broderick, Kevin Joyce. JipiJapa Hat. (p. 919)
Broderick, Lonia. Muffy, Fluffy, & Dexter In. (p. 1189)
Broderick, Lonia R. Muffy, Fluffy, & Dexter In. Broderick, Al R., illus. (p. 1189)
Broderick, Pat, illus. see Edelman, Scott & Conway, Gerry.
Broderick, Paula. Quest: The First Toby & Sox Adventure. (p. 1426)
Broderick, Setsu & Moore, Willamarie. Japanese Traditions: Rice Cakes, Cherry Blossoms & Matsuri - A Year of Seasonal Japanese Festivities. (p. 909)
Broderip, W. J. Zoological Recreations. (p. 1989)
Broders, Alain, jt. auth. see Adrien, Gilles.
Brodeur, Tom. Regina Silsby's Phantom Militia. (p. 1457)
—Regina Silsby's Secret War. (p. 1457)
Brodey, Lisette. Mystical High. (p. 1226)
Brodfuehrer, Marc. Measuring the Weather. (p. 1117)
Brodhead, Kimberly. Gaden's Tower: Book One. (p. 652)
Brodhead, Kimberly Renee. Seedling: The Osarian Tales. (p. 1547)
Brodie, Ian. Cameras in Narnia: How the Lion, the Witch & the Wardrobe Came to Life. (p. 256)
Brodie, N. eale, illus. see Zocchi, Judy.
Brodie, Neal, illus. see Dingles, Molly.
Brodie, Neale, illus. see Dingles, Molly.
Brodie, Neale, illus. see James, Yolanda, et al.
Brodie, Neale, illus. see James, Yolanda.
Brodie, Neale, illus. see Zocchi, Judith Mazzeo.
Brodie, Neale, illus. see Zocchi, Judy.
Brodie, Richard /M. Robbed of Their Childhood: America's Children in Crisis. (p. 1478)
Brodien-Jones, Chris. Glass Puzzle. (p. 682)
Brodien-Jones, Christine. Dreamkeepers. (p. 484)
—Glass Puzzle. (p. 682)
—Owl Keeper. Kneen, Maggie, illus. (p. 1315)
—Scorpions of Zahir. Murphy, Kelly, illus. (p. 1530)
Brodine, Linda. Gramma Please Tell Us a Story. (p. 706)
Brodland, Rita, ed. All Dried Out. Freeman, Troy, illus. (p. 44)
Brodman, Larisa. Pom-Pom Pets. Magruder, Trula, ed. (p. 1381)
Brodnax, Stephan. Dillwyn & the Purple Picnic Pack (p. 440)
Brodner, Steve, illus. see Kunstler, James Howard.
Brodrick, William. Sixth Lamentation. (p. 1583)
Brodsky, Alexandra Fanny. In Pursuit of a Dream: A Time in Australia. (p. 864)
Brodsky, Beverly. Buffalo (p. 235)
—Buffalo. (p. 235)
Brodsky, Beverly, contrib. by. Buffalo: With Selections from Native American Song-Poems. (p. 235)
Brodsky, Irene. Adventures of Silly Kitty, Princess Jasmine & First Puppy. (p. 23)
—Queen Esther's New Coloring Book. Steyert, Bill, illus. (p. 1424)
Brodsky, Kathy. CatFish Tale. Bennett, Cameron, illus. (p. 280)
—Just Sniffing Around. Bennett, Cameron, illus. (p. 939)
—My Bent Tree. Bennett, Cameron, illus. (p. 1196)
Brodsky, Slava. Funny Children's Stories (in Russian - Smeshnye detskie Rasskazy) (p. 649)
Brody, Jessica. 52 Reasons to Hate My Father. (p. 1997)
—Karma Club. (p. 944)
—Unchanged. (p. 1811)
—Unremembered. (p. 1822)
Brody, Joyce, illus. see Mann, Gerre.
Brody, Lazer. Worry Worm. Shapiro, Rebecca, illus. (p. 1961)
Brody, Leslie. Bouncing Worry Ball & Mighty Mitt. (p. 216)
Brodzinsky, Anne Braff. Mulberry Bird: An Adoption Story. (p. 1189)
Broeck, Fabricio Vanden, illus. see Bergna, Monica.
Broeck, Fabricio Vanden, illus. see Gunning, Monica.
Broeck, Fabricio Vanden, illus. see Lainez, René Colato.
Broeck, Fabricio Vanden, illus. see Ortiz, Gilberto Rendon & Rendon, Gilberto.
Broeck, Fabricio Vanden, illus. see Romeu, Emma.
Broeders, Rebecca. How to Survive a Thunderstorm. (p. 821)
Broekstra, Lorette. Baby Bbear Goes to the Farm. (p. 125)
—Baby Bear Goes Camping. (p. 125)
—Baby Bear Goes to the Zoo. (p. 125)
Broekstra, Lorette, illus. see Munro, Maisie.
Broekstra, Lorette, illus. see Rippin, Sally.
Broere, Rien. I Don't Like the Dark! (p. 837)
Broere, Rien, illus. see Bode, Ann de.
Broesch, Valerie, jt. illus. see Zabel, Randy.
Bröger, Achim. Historia de Dragolina (Story of Little Dragon) (p. 782)
—Meyers Grosses Kinderlexikon. (p. 1131)
Brogle, Jennifer. Adventures of Jennifer & Sherry: Summertime. (p. 19)
Broich, Erin. Guardians of Light, Book: The Betrayer. (p. 728)
Broida, Marian. Ancient Israelites & Their Neighbors. (p. 69)
—Hands-On History (p. 741)
—Projects about Ancient Greece. (p. 1410)
—Projects about Colonial Life. (p. 1410)
—Projects about Nineteenth-Century European Immigrants. (p. 1410)
—Projects about the American Revolution. (p. 1410)
—Pueblo. (p. 1414)
Brokamp, Elizabeth. Back to School, Picky Little Witch! Welling, Peter, illus. (p. 130)
—Circle of Three: Enough Friendship to Go Around? Stringfield, Joni, illus. (p. 321)
—Picky Little Witch Riti, Marsha, illus. (p. 1355)
Brokenshire, Kim Girvin. Why Did Hannah Have to Die? (p. 1923)
Brolin, Carol, illus. see Fabris, Judith.
Brolsma, Jody. Fez & the Big, Bad Bully: A Bible Memory Buddy Book about Standing up to Bullies. Harrington, David, illus. (p. 583)
Bromfield, Mario. I'm Special? (p. 860)
Bromfield, Val. If You Can't Sleep... & Other Stories. (p. 854)
Bromley, Anne C. Lunch Thief Casilla, Robert, illus. (p. 1065)
Bromley, Nick. Open Very Carefully: A Book with Bite. O'Byrne, Nicola, illus. (p. 1299)
Bromley, Peter David. Aunty Liz the Lollipop Lady. (p. 116)
Brommer, Gerald. Discovering Art History 4th Edition SE. (p. 448)
Brommer, Gerald F. Illustrated Elements of Art & Principles of Design: Full Color Reproductions, Descriptions of Each Concept, Hands-On Activities. (p. 857)
Bromwell, L. Anne. English Grammar Basics. (p. 530)
Bronfeyn, Lily, illus. see Traynor, Tracy.
Bronn, Charles Heil. Sun, the Moon, & the Gardener's Son. Kami, Y. Z., illus. (p. 1676)
Bronner, Simon J. American Children's Folklore. (p. 60)
—Encyclopedia of American Folklife (p. 524)
Bronner, Simon J., ed. Manly Traditions: The Folk Roots of American Masculinities. (p. 1087)
Bronowski, Karen Kmetz, illus. see Rendina, Donna Rae.
Bronson, Bill. Bill Bronson's Guide to Monsters (p. 186)
Bronson, Cary. I am Not a Flying Elephant Fish! A Children's Science Book on the Butterfly. Gomer, William, illus. (p. 833)
Bronson, Franklin. Why Don't Birds get Lost? Differentiated Studies in Bird Migration: Upper Elementary through Secondary Levels. (p. 1924)
Bronson, Jody, illus. see Carmichael, L. E.
Bronson, Linda, illus. see Chessen, Sherri.
Bronson, Linda, illus. see Greene, Carol.
Bronson, Linda, illus. see Jones, Melanie Davis.
Bronson, Linda, illus. see Wargin, Kathy-jo.
Bronson, Linda, illus. see Zolotow, Charlotte.
Bronson, Mary H., et al. Glencoe la Salud. (p. 683)
—Glencoe Teen Health Course 2. (p. 683)
—Health. (p. 757)
—Salud de los Jóvenes: Curso 2. (p. 1506)
—Teen Health. (p. 1713)
Bronson, Matthew Shane & Bronson, Tammy Carter. Kaleidonotes & the Mixed-up Orchestra. Bronson, Tammy Carter, illus. (p. 941)
Bronson, Tammy Carter. Polliwog. Davi, Annou, tr. (p. 1381)
—Polliwog. Bronson, Tammy Carter, illus. (p. 1381)
Bronson, Tammy Carter, jt. auth. see Bronson, Matthew Shane.
Bronson, Wilfrid. Coyotes. (p. 374)
Bronson, Wilfrid S. Cats. (p. 280)
—Grasshopper Book. (p. 711)
—Pinto's Journey. (p. 1361)
—Starlings. (p. 1642)
—Stooping Hawk & Stranded Whale, Sons of Liberty. (p. 1653)
—Turtles. (p. 1798)
—Wonder World of Ants. (p. 1947)
Bronstein, Arlene. How Did Nonnie Get to Heaven? Torres, Diana, illus. (p. 806)
Bronstein, M. J. Photoplay! Doodle. Design. Draw. (p. 1353)
Bronstein, Raquel, et al. Jueguemos con la Musica: Manual para el Conductor. (p. 931)
Bronstein, S. N. Private Eye Cats: Book One: the Case of the Neighborhood Burglars. (p. 1407)
—Private Eye Cats Book Two: The Case of the Kidnapped Dog. (p. 1407)
Brontë, Charlotte. Charlotte Brontë's Jane Eyre. Bloom, Harold, ed. (p. 293)
—Jane Eyre: The Graphic Novel. (p. 908)
—Jane Eyre: From the Story by Charlotte Bronte. Harvey, Bob, illus. (p. 908)
—Jane Eyre. (p. 908)
—Jane Eyre. Sanders, Joe Sutliff, tr. (p. 908)
—Jane Eyre the Graphic Novel Original Text Hardback: American English. (p. 908)
—Tales of the Islanders. (p. 1702)
Brontë, Charlotte, jt. auth. see Hollyer, Belinda.
Brontë, Emily. Darkness & Glory: Selected Poems. (p. 408)
—Wuthering Heights. (p. 1966)
—Wuthering Heights. Bryant, Clive, ed. (p. 1966)
—Wuthering Heights. Singh, Sara, illus. (p. 1966)
—Wuthering Heights. Lubach, Vanessa, illus. (p. 1966)
—Wuthering Heights. Warner, Darrell, illus. (p. 1966)
—Wuthering Heights by Emily Bront' The Graphic Novel. (p. 1966)
Brontë, Emily, jt. auth. see Bingham, J.
Bronte, Jules. Royal Wedding Adventure. (p. 1492)
Bronte, Jules & Oapos, Jem. Castle Adventure. (p. 276)
Bronzan, William M., Sr. Time to Dream. (p. 1753)
Brook. How to Catch a SNU. (p. 815)
Brook, Harry, retold by. Kidnapped. (p. 952)
Brook, Henry. D-Day. (p. 397)
—Moby Dick. (p. 1157)
—Sea Adventures. (p. 1534)
—Special Forces. Frith, Alex, ed. (p. 1623)
—Spying. Frith, Alex, ed. (p. 1636)
—Tanks. (p. 1705)
—True Sea Stories. (p. 1792)
—True Stories of D-Day. (p. 1792)
—True Stories of Gangsters. McNee, Ian, illus. (p. 1792)
—True Stories of the Blitz. McNee, Ian, illus. (p. 1792)
—Warships IR. (p. 1859)
—Wild West. (p. 1930)
Brook, Henry, jt. auth. see Brocklehurst, Ruth.
Brook, Henry, jt. auth. see de Cervantes, Miguel.
Brook, Henry, retold by. Tom Sawyer. (p. 1763)
Brook, L. Sex in Every City: How to Talk Dirty in Every Language. (p. 1556)
Brook, Meljean. Demon Bound. (p. 426)
—Demon Night. (p. 426)
Brooke, Amy/ J., jt. auth. see Green, George.
Brooke, Anna. Working with Children with Special Educational Needs in the Early Years: A Handbook on Identifying & Responding to SEN in the Early Years & Including All Children in Early Years Settings. (p. 1953)
Brooke, Beatrice D. Art & Culture of the Prehistoric World. (p. 101)
Brooke, Beatrice D. & Magalhaes, Roberto Carvalho de. Art & Culture of the Prehistoric World. (p. 101)
Brooke Casad, Mary, jt. auth. see Casad, Mary Brooke.
Brooke, Gun. September Canvas. (p. 1551)
Brooke, Iris. English Costume of the Early Middle Ages. Landes, William-Alan, ed. (p. 529)
Brooke, Iris, illus. see Matthews, C. M., et al.
Brooke, Iris & Landes, William-Alan. Western European Costume Thirteenth to Seventeenth Century. (p. 1876)
Brooke, Janet, illus. see Landaw, Jonathan.
Brooke, Janet, illus. see Vollbracht, James.
Brooke, L. Leslie. Johnny Crow's Picture Book. (p. 923)
—Ring o' Roses, a Nursery Rhyme Picture Book. Brooke, L. Leslie, illus. (p. 1473)
—Ring o' Roses Treasury: Nursery Rhymes & Stories. (p. 1473)
—Story of the Three Little Pig & Other Shorts Works: The Story of the Three Little Pig & Other Shorts Works. (p. 1662)
—Story of the Three Little Pig & Other Shorts Works. (p. 1662)
Brooke, Lauren. All or Nothing. (p. 45)
—Making Strides. (p. 1082)
—New Class. (p. 1244)
Brooke, Rupert. Lithuania. Landes, William-Alan, ed. (p. 1023)
Brooke, S. Snow Diamond: the Fourth Journey (p. 1598)
Brooke, Samantha. Apple-Picking Day! Durk, Jim, illus. (p. 92)
—Best Friends Forever. (p. 169)
—Coral Reefs: In Danger. Bull, Peter, illus. (p. 366)
—Fire in the Forest! (p. 590)
—Lalaloopsy: Star of the Show. (p. 972)
—Makeover Madness. Thomas, Laura, illus. (p. 1080)
—Princess Parade. (p. 1405)
—Spring Showers. Giles, Mike, illus. (p. 1635)
—Star of the Show. (p. 1641)
—Tonka Picture Clues: at the Construction Site. (p. 1765)
—Unikitty: A Cuckoo Adventure. (p. 1818)
—Unikitty - A Cuckoo Adventure. (p. 1818)
—Welcome to Lalaloopsy Land. (p. 1873)
Brooke, Samantha, jt. auth. see Disney Book Group Staff.
Brooke, Samantha & S. I. International. Go Go Goes to the Doctor. (p. 686)
Brooke, Samantha & Scholastic, Inc. Staff. Fire in the Forest! (p. 590)
—Meet the Lalaloopsy Girls. (p. 1123)
Brooke, Samantha, et al. Super Sweet Treasury. MJ Illustrations et al, illus. (p. 1682)
Brooke, Susan Rich, adapted by. Lion King. (p. 1020)
Brooke, Susan Rich & Seuss, Dr. Cat in the Hat Flips His Lid. Enik, Ted, illus. (p. 278)
Brooker, Jo, illus. see Medina, Sarah.
Brooker, Jo, jt. auth. see Medina, Sarah.
Brooker, Kyrsten, illus. see Best, Carl.
Brooker, Kyrsten, illus. see Brooker, Marion.
Brooker, Kyrsten, illus. see Holt, Kimberly Willis.
Brooker, Kyrsten, illus. see Krull, Kathleen.
Brooker, Kyrsten, illus. see McKissack, Patricia C. & Moss, Onawumi Jean.
Brooker, Kyrsten, illus. see Nargi, Lela.
Brooker, Kyrsten, illus. see Rockliff, Mara.
Brooker, Kyrsten, illus. see Schotter, Roni.
Brooker, Marion. Tadeo's Search for Circles Brooker, Kyrsten, illus. (p. 1695)
Brooker, Marion Fargey. Hold the Oxo! A Teenage Soldier Writes Home. (p. 788)
Brooker, Russell & Schaefer, Todd. Public Opinion in the 21st Century: Let the People Speak? (p. 1414)
Brookes, Archer. Vampireology: The True History of the Fallen. Holt, Nick, ed. (p. 1832)
Brookes, Kat. Through the Eyes of a Geek. (p. 1745)
Brookes, Kate. Top Websites for Homework. (p. 1769)
Brookes, Kate, jt. auth. see Farris, D.
Brookes, Olicia. Predators. (p. 1394)
Brookes, Olivia. Age of Giants. (p. 29)
—Animal. (p. 76)
—Bug. (p. 236)
—Dinosaur. (p. 441)
—Plant-Eaters. (p. 1369)
—Rise of the Reptiles. (p. 1475)
—Shark & Other Sea Creatures. (p. 1562)
—Uncover History. Kent, Peter, illus. (p. 1812)
—Uncover Nature. Inklink Staff, illus. (p. 1812)
—Uncover Technology. Kent, Peter, illus. (p. 1812)
Brookfield, Karen, et al. Escritura. Barberán, Maria, tr. from SPA. (p. 535)
Brookfield, Maureen, illus. see Burg, Ann.
Brookfield, Maureen, illus. see Elissa, Grodin.
Brookfield, Maureen K., illus. see Burg, Ann E.
Brookfield, Maureen K., illus. see Grodin, Elissa D.
Brookins, Cara. Doris Free. Barrow, Ann, illus. (p. 471)
Brookins, Tabitha. Beautiful You Are. (p. 154)
Brooklyn. Adventures of the Earth Saver Girl: Don't be a Litterbug. (p. 23)
Brooklyn, Billie. Motorcycle Racing (p. 1179)
—Sports Car Racing (p. 1632)
Brooklyn, Isabella. If You Were Raised by a Dinosaur. Levesque, Haude, illus. (p. 855)
Brookman, Darin. Where Sagebrush Grows. (p. 1909)
Brookover, Brian D. Neddy & Little Roy Go to Town. (p. 1239)
Brook-Piper, Holly. Animal Friends: A Touch-and-Feel Book. (p. 77)
Brook-Piper, Holly, jt. auth. see Little Bee Books Staff.
Brooks. Come Back, Energy Man. (p. 347)
—Mary Will Not Watch Moon. (p. 1101)
—Mary Will Not Watch the Moon. (p. 1101)
Brooks, jt. auth. see Brooks, Gwendolyn.
Brooks, Aaron & Brown, Greg. Aaron Brooks: Rise Above. (p. 2)
Brooks, Amy. Dorothy Dainty's Gay Times. (p. 471)
—Home Songs for Little Darlings: Children. (p. 793)
—Princess Polly Stories. (p. 1405)
—Princess Polly's Gay Winter. (p. 1405)
—Princess Polly's Playmates. (p. 1405)
—Randy's Summer. (p. 1438)
Brooks, Andree Aelion, ed. see Behar, Yvonne.
Brooks, Bearl. Jumbo Cursive Handwriting Yearbook. (p. 933)
—Jumbo Phonics Yearbook. (p. 933)
—Jumbo Reading Yearbook: Kindergarten. (p. 933)
—My Second Grade Yearbook. (p. 1218)
—My Third Grade Yearbook. (p. 1220)
Brooks, Bearl, et al. Jumbo Word Games Yearbook. (p. 933)
Brooks, Bertha. Big Fishing Trip. (p. 181)
Brooks, Brian. Oopsy Daisy's Bad Day. Brooks, Brian, illus. (p. 1299)
Brooks, Brian, illus. see Reger, Rob.
Brooks, Brody. How Animals Survive. (p. 805)
Brooks, Bruce. Moves Make the Man. (p. 1183)
Brooks, Charlie. Greystone Valley. Grundy, Jessica, illus. (p. 723)
Brooks, Chelsey. Yokeville Yokinton. (p. 1972)
Brooks, Christalyn & Bokma, Cindy. Victorious Girls: Kids in Toon Series. (p. 1840)
Brooks, Clare & Garrington, Sally. Focus on the United States. (p. 611)
Brooks, David. Animals. (p. 81)
—You Can Count at the Lake. Brooks, David, illus. (p. 1974)
—You Can Count at the Ocean. (p. 1974)
—You Can Count in the Desert. Brooks, David, illus. (p. 1974)
—You Can Count in the Jungle. (p. 1974)
Brooks, David, illus. see Alvarez, Lourdes M.
Brooks, David, illus. see Biskup, Agnieszka.
Brooks, David, illus. see Howell, Theresa.
Brooks, David, illus. see Turnbaugh, Kay.
Brooks, David, illus. see Viscardi, Dolly.
Brooks, Dawn Marie. Cat-Ice. (p. 278)
Brooks, Diane L. Readings & Activities for Character Education. (p. 1447)
Brooks, Dominic. Is It My Turn Yet? (p. 889)
Brooks, Donna. Amazing Apple Tree. (p. 53)
—Golden Spindle. (p. 695)
—Magic Amphor. (p. 1071)
—Starry Triangle. (p. 1643)
Brooks, E. S. Historic Boys: Their Endeavors, Their Achievements & Their Times. (p. 782)
—Historic Girls: Stories of Girls Who Have Influenced the History of Their Times. (p. 782)
—Historic Girls. (p. 782)
Brooks, E. S., jt. auth. see Brooks, E. s.
Brooks, E. s. & Brooks, E. S. Historic Boys. (p. 782)
Brooks, Elizabeth. Montefiore's Goddaughter. (p. 1170)
Brooks, Elizabeth, illus. see Evans, Mary & Landes, William-Alan.
Brooks, Erik. Polar Opposites (p. 1379)
Brooks, Erik, illus. see Aronson, Emme & Aronson, Phillip.
Brooks, Erik, illus. see Byars, Betsy, et al.
Brooks, Erik, illus. see Byars, Betsy.
Brooks, Erik, illus. see Conford, Ellen.
Brooks, Erik, illus. see Hulbert, Laura.
Brooks, Erik, illus. see Kimmel, Eric.
Brooks, Erik, illus. see Ode, Eric.
Brooks, Erik, illus. see Stihler, Cherie B.
Brooks, Erik, illus. see Vanasse, Deb.
Brooks, Estell. Magic Farm: A Day of Fun & Adventure. (p. 1072)
Brooks, Evelyn. Medical Pioneers & Pioneros de la Medicina: 6 English, 6 Spanish Adaptations (p. 1118)
—Pioneros de la Medicina. (p. 1361)
—Portraits in Greatness & Retratos de Grandeza: 6 English, 6 Spanish Adaptations (p. 1387)
—Retratos de Grandeza. (p. 1464)
—voz de los Animales: Set Of 6. (p. 1851)
Brooks, Evelyn, told to. Voice for the Animals & la voz de los Animales: 6 English, 6 Spanish Adaptations (p. 1847)
Brooks, F. First Encyclopedia of Our World. (p. 594)
—First Encyclopedia of Science II. (p. 594)
Brooks, F., jt. auth. see Litchfield, J.
Brooks, F., jt. auth. see Litchfield, Jo.
Brooks, F. & Litchfield, J. En Casa. (p. 522)
—Mis Primeras Palabras. (p. 1150)
—Nativity Lift-the-Flap. (p. 1235)
—Picture Dictionary: A First Alphabetical Word Book. (p. 1355)
—Primeros Numeros. (p. 1401)
Brooks, Felicity. Animal Rhymes. (p. 79)
—Big Book of Colors. (p. 179)
—Big Red Tractor. Cartwright, Stephen, illus. (p. 183)
—Brush Your Teeth, Max & Millie. (p. 232)
—Build a Picture Cars Sticker Book. Lovell, Katie, illus. (p. 237)
—Build a Picture Tractors Sticker Book. Lovell, Katie, illus. (p. 237)
—Cars. Newell, Keith, illus. (p. 271)
—Children's Encyclopedia. (p. 303)
—Construction Sites. Newell, Keith, illus. (p. 360)
—Counting Rhymes. Gregorio, Giuliana, illus. (p. 371)
—Daisy Doctor. Litchfield, Jo, illus. (p. 400)
—Daisy the Doctor. Litchfield, Jo, illus. (p. 400)
—Diggers Lift-and-Look. (p. 439)
—Dinosarios. Litchfield, Jo, illus. (p. 441)
—Dress the Teddy Bears for Christmas. (p. 485)
—Dress the Teddy Bears Going Shopping. (p. 485)
—Easy English Words Sticker Book. (p. 500)
—Easy Spanish Words Sticker Book. (p. 500)
—Everyday Words in Spanish. Litchfield, Jo, illus. (p. 544)
—Farms lift & Look. Litchfield, Jo, illus. (p. 575)
—Find the Bird. (p. 587)
—Finger Rhymes. Gregorio, Giuliana, illus. (p. 589)
—First Encyclopedia of Our World. (p. 594)
—First Shapes. Litchfield, Jo, illus. (p. 596)
—First Word Book on the Farm. (p. 597)
—Frank the Farmer. Litchfield, Jo, illus. (p. 629)
—Fred the Firefighter. Litchfield, Jo, illus. (p. 632)
—Getting Dressed. Widdowson, Kay, illus. (p. 669)
—Getting Dressed Magnet Book. Widdowson, Kay, illus. (p. 669)
—Goodnight Baby. (p. 701)
—Granja Minilibros Usborne. Litchfield, Jo, illus. (p. 710)
—Jason & the Argonauts. Humphreys, Graham, illus. (p. 910)
—Jobs People Do. Litchfield, Jo, illus. (p. 919)
—Juega con Gabi. (p. 931)
—Lift-out Colors Book. (p. 1014)
—Lift-the-Flap Counting Book. (p. 1014)

B

—Lift-the-Flap Word Book. (p. 1014)
—Max & Millie Start School. Guicciardini, Desideria, illus. (p. 1110)
—Messy Baby. (p. 1130)
—Musical Nativity. (p. 1194)
—My First French Word Book. (p. 1206)
—My First Spanish Word Book. (p. 1208)
—My First Word Book. Bonnet, Rosalinde, illus. (p. 1208)
—Nativity Jigsaw Bk. (p. 1235)
—Naughty Woolly. Cartwright, Stephen, illus. (p. 1237)
—Noisy Noah's Ark. (p. 1263)
—Noisy Town. (p. 1263)
—Planes. (p. 1367)
—Playtime Baby. (p. 1373)
—Rusty's Friends. Cartwright, Stephen, illus. (p. 1498)
—School Look & Say. Litchfield, Jo, illus. (p. 1523)
—Take Turns, Max & Millie. (p. 1697)
—Tales of King Arthur. (p. 1702)
—Tessa the Teacher. Litchfield, Jo, illus. (p. 1723)
—This Is My Duck. (p. 1736)
—This Is My Tractor. Dimitri, Simona, illus. (p. 1736)
—Time for Bed, Max & Millie. (p. 1751)
—Tractors Chunky Jigsaw Book. (p. 1775)
—Trains Chunky Jigsaw Book. (p. 1777)
—Trains lift & Look. Litchfield, Jo, illus. (p. 1777)
—Trucks Lift-and-Look. (p. 1791)
—Under the Sea Lift & Look. (p. 1814)
—Usborne Internet-Linked Children's Encyclopedia. (p. 1827)
—Usborne Lift & Look Emergency Vehicles. Van Wyk, Hanri, illus. (p. 1827)
—Usborne Lift & Look Tractors. Van Wyk, Hanri, illus. (p. 1827)
—Usborne Shapes Jigsaw Book. (p. 1827)
—Very First Animals Board Book. (p. 1838)
—Very First Colors Board Book. (p. 1838)
—Very First Dictionary in French - Internet Referenced. (p. 1838)
—Very First Dictionary in Spanish - Internet Referenced. (p. 1838)
—Very First Numbers. (p. 1838)
—Vicky the Vet. Litchfield, Jo, illus. (p. 1840)
—Vicky the Vet Kid Kit. Litchfield, Jo, illus. (p. 1840)
Brooks, Felicity, ed. see Dixon, Andy.
Brooks, Felicity, ed. see Doherty, Gillian.
Brooks, Felicity, ed. see Needham, Kate.
Brooks, Felicity, ed. see Watt, Fiona.
Brooks, Felicity, jt. auth. see Allen, Francesca.
Brooks, Felicity, jt. auth. see Durber, Matt.
Brooks, Felicity, jt. auth. see Greenwall, Jessica.
Brooks, Felicity, jt. auth. see Helbrough, Emma.
Brooks, Felicity, jt. auth. see Litchfield, Jo.
Brooks, Felicity, jt. auth. see Young, Caroline.
Brooks, Felicity & Allen, Francesca. Baby's Christmas. Wells, Rachel, illus. (p. 128)
—Baby's Potty. Wells, Rachel, illus. (p. 129)
Brooks, Felicity & Durber, Matt. Airport Magnet Book. (p. 32)
—Busy Bus. Crisp, Dan, illus. (p. 246)
—Trucks & Diggers. Mazali, Gustavo, illus. (p. 1791)
Brooks, Felicity & Fearn, Katrina. First Dot-To-Dot Animals. (p. 594)
—First Dot-To-Dot Things That Go. (p. 594)
Brooks, Felicity & Litchfield, J. Usborne Picture Dictionary: A First Alphabetical Word Book. (p. 1827)
Brooks, Felicity & Litchfield, Jo. First Numbers. (p. 596)
—First Numbers. Allman, Howard, photos by. (p. 596)
—First Picture Animals. Van Wyk, Hanri, illus. (p. 596)
—Missing Cat. (p. 1152)
—Runaway Orange. (p. 1496)
—Tales from Littletown. (p. 1701)
Brooks, Felicity & MacKinnon, Mairi. First Picture Spanish. Litchfield, Jo, illus. (p. 596)
—Picture Dictionary in German. (p. 1355)
Brooks, Felicity & Mackinnon, Mairi. Picture Dictionary in Spanish. (p. 1355)
—Spanish Words & Phrases - Internet Referenced. (p. 1622)
Brooks, Felicity & MacKinnon, Mairi. Usborne Picture Dictionary in Spanish. (p. 1827)
—Ya Hablo Ingles. (p. 1968)
Brooks, Felicity & Millbourne, Anna. Usborne Internet-Linked Children's Encyclopedia. (p. 1827)
Brooks, Felicity & Tyler, Jenny. Usborne 1,2,3 Jigsaw Book. Cartwright, Stephen, illus. (p. 1827)
Brooks, Felicity, des. Build a Picture Trains Sticker Book. (p. 237)
—Build a Picture Trucks Sticker Book. (p. 238)
Brooks, Felicity, ed. Runaway Orange. Litchfield, Jo, illus. (p. 1496)
Brooks, Felicity, et al. Counting Train. Cartwright, Stephen, illus. (p. 371)
Brooks, Felicity, et al, eds. Everyday Words. (p. 544)
Brooks, G. Alan & Grandchildren. Adventures of Zumba & Rumb: Book One - the Separation. (p. 24)
Brooks, George W. Spirit Of 1906. (p. 1628)
—Spirit of 1906. (p. 1628)
Brooks, Grace. Asquinn Twins & Grant. (p. 107)
—Asquinn Twins & Keta. (p. 107)
Brooks, Gwendolyn. Bronzeville Boys & Girls. (p. 230)
—Bronzeville Boys & Girls. Ringgold, Faith, illus. (p. 230)
Brooks, Gwendolyn & Brooks. Bronzeville Boys & Girls. Ringgold, Faith, illus. (p. 230)
Brooks, Heather. Bonnies: Healing Hearts. (p. 209)
—Hercules: A Matter of Trust. (p. 769)
—Sapphire - New Horizons. (p. 1514)
Brooks, John. Balloons, Sea Creatures, & Me. (p. 135)
—Bobby Bright Becomes a Professor & Is Lost at Sea: Bobby Bright Meets His Maker: the Shocking Truth Is Revealed. (p. 206)
—Sundarbans Tiger. (p. 1676)
Brooks, John R. Bobby Bright Spends Christmas in Spain. (p. 206)
—Bobby Bright's Christmas Heroics. (p. 206)
—Bobby Bright's Christmas Heroics. Daly, Dan & Gustafson, Troy, illus. (p. 206)
Brooks, Kaarina, tr. see Mäkinen, Kirsti.
Brooks, Kaarina, tr. from FIN. Peikko, the Foolish Ogre. (p. 1335)
Brooks, Karen. Illumination. (p. 857)
—Tallow. (p. 1704)
—Votive. (p. 1850)
Brooks, Karen Stormer, illus. see Adams, Michelle Medlock & Adams, Michelle M.
Brooks, Karen Stormer, illus. see Gillis, Jennifer Blizin.
Brooks, Karen Stormer, illus. see Sederman, Marty & Epstein, Seymour.
Brooks, Karl. Pros & Cons of an Outdoor John. Dixon, Carol, illus. (p. 1412)
Brooks, Katie, illus. see Miller, R. L.
Brooks, Kaye. Symphony of Creation. (p. 1693)
Brooks, Kevin. Being. (p. 160)
—Black Rabbit Summer. (p. 196)
—Bunker Diary. (p. 242)
—Candy. (p. 261)
—Dawn. (p. 411)
—iBoy. (p. 849)
—Johnny Delgado: Private Detective. (p. 923)
—Martyn Pig. (p. 1098)
Brooks, Kiana Michelle. Rush into Romance - Caught. (p. 1498)
Brooks, Laurie. Franklin's Apprentice. (p. 630)
Brooks, Linda. Wait for Me!!!!!!!! The Misadventures of Smokie & Leroy. (p. 1852)
Brooks, Linda Grace. Asquinn Twins & Where the Trail Forks. (p. 107)
Brooks, Linda Sue. Meet Toado & Friends. Mills, Lori, illus. (p. 1123)
Brooks, Lou. Twimericks: The Book of Tongue-Twisting Limericks. (p. 1801)
Brooks, Marie, et al. Pet Poems & Special Days Poems. (p. 1345)
Brooks, Marie, et al, selected by. Pet Poems & Special Day Poems. (p. 1345)
Brooks, Mark. Thor: The World Eaters. (p. 1739)
Brooks, Mark, illus. see Hickman, Jonathan & Dragotta, Nick.
Brooks, Mark, illus. see Youngquist, Jeff, ed.
Brooks, Martha. Being with Henry (p. 161)
—Bone Dance (p. 208)
—Paradise Cafe & Other Stories. (p. 1323)
—Queen of Hearts. (p. 1425)
—Traveling on into the Light: And Other Stories. (p. 1780)
—True Confessions of a Heartless Girl (p. 1792)
—True Confessions of a Heartless Girl. (p. 1792)
Brooks, Max, jt. auth. see Caceres, Raulo.
Brooks, Mel & Reiner, Carl. 2000 Year Old Man Goes to School. Bennett, James, illus. (p. 2003)
Brooks, Melanie, jt. auth. see Spenser.
Brooks, Melanie & Spenser and Mom Staff. Spenser Goes to el Paso. Jacobsen, Amie, illus. (p. 1625)
Brooks, Minnie. Carl, Colonel of the Carrot Colony. (p. 269)
Brooks, Nan. This Little Piggy. (p. 1737)
Brooks, Nan, illus. see Blackstone, Stella.
Brooks, Nan, illus. see Hillert, Margaret.
Brooks, Nan, illus. see Morton, Debra & Stover, Elizabeth.
Brooks, Nan, illus. see Schwaeber, Barbie.
Brooks, Nan, illus. see Soundprints Staff.
Brooks, Nan, illus. see Tyrell, Melissa.
Brooks, Noel. Sometimes I Hear Bad Words. (p. 1610)
Brooks, Pamela J., et al. Insurance Operations. (p. 879)
Brooks, Philip. Hannibal: Rome's Worst Nightmare. (p. 743)
—Hannibal. (p. 743)
—King George III: America's Enemy. (p. 958)
—Maroon Knights: A Novel. (p. 1096)
—Radio. (p. 1432)
—Story of Ancient Civilizations. (p. 1657)
—Story of Prehistoric Peoples. (p. 1659)
—Tuskegee Airmen. (p. 1799)
Brooks, Phillip. Exploring History: Prehistoric People. (p. 552)
—Exploring History: Ancient Civilizations. (p. 552)
Brooks, Regina, jt. auth. see Scholastic, Inc. Staff.
Brooks, Riley. Carrie Underwood - American Dream. (p. 271)
—Cast of Fame. (p. 276)
—Debby Ryan: Her Sweet Life! (p. 421)
—Mega Movie Stars. (p. 1124)
—One Direction: Superstardom! (p. 1294)
—Rachel Crow: from the Heart. (p. 1432)
—Sterling Knight. (p. 1649)
—Taylor Swift: Fearless Star. (p. 1708)
—Up Close! [25 of Your Fave Stars Inside!]. (p. 1824)
—Willow Smith: Pop's Newest Princess. (p. 1934)
Brooks, Riley, jt. auth. see Scholastic, Inc. Staff.
Brooks, Riley & Hodgin, Molly. One Direction: Quiz Book. (p. 1294)
—One Direction: Straight to the Top! (p. 1294)
Brooks, Robert. Sonreta. Urban, Helle, illus. (p. 1613)
Brooks, Ron, illus. see Wild, Margaret.
Brooks, Ronald, jt. auth. see Fisher, Chris C.
Brooks, Rosetta, jt. auth. see Rian, Jeff.
Brooks, Rosie. What to Doodle? Everyday. (p. 1894)
—What to Doodle? - Jr. Everything! (p. 1894)
Brooks, Rosie, illus. see Bailey, Gerry & Law, Felicia.
Brooks, S. G., illus. see Hopkins, Jackie Mims.
Brooks, S. G., illus. see Slater, David Michael.
Brooks, Sheldon. Life in the Arctic. (p. 1011)
Brooks, Shunda K. What Should I Be? It's All up to Me! The Opportunities Are Endless! (p. 1893)
Brooks, Susie. Amazonian Indians. (p. 56)
—Animals: Enjoy Great Art - Then Create Your Own! (p. 81)
—Brazil. (p. 224)
—Five Silly Monkeys. Tarbett, Debbie, illus. (p. 601)
—Get into Art Animals: Enjoy Great Art—Then Create Your Own! (p. 667)
—Get into Art People: Enjoy Great Art—Then Create Your Own! (p. 667)
—Get into Art Places: Discover Great Art & Create Your Own! (p. 667)
—Get into Art Telling Stories: Enjoy Great Art—Then Create Your Own! (p. 667)
—Greece. (p. 720)
—India. (p. 870)
—Let's Visit France. (p. 1001)
—Let's Visit Greece. (p. 1001)
—Let's Visit Italy. (p. 1001)
—Let's Visit Poland. (p. 1001)
—Let's Visit Spain. (p. 1001)
—People: Discover Great Art & Create Your Own! (p. 1339)
—Plains Indians. (p. 1366)
—Prehistoric People. (p. 1395)
—Reptiles. (p. 1461)
—Space Lift-The-Flap. Lewis, Anthony, illus. (p. 1619)
—St. Lucia. (p. 1638)
Brooks, Susie, jt. auth. see Murrell, Deborah.
Brooks, Tyrice M. Only the Truth Will Tell. (p. 1298)
Brooks, Walt. Walter's Pet Bee. (p. 1856)
Brooks, Walter R. Clockwork Twin: A Freddy the Pig Book on Everything. Wiese, Kurt, illus. (p. 333)
—Freddy & Mr. Camphor. Wiese, Kurt, illus. (p. 633)
—Freddy & Simon the Dictator. Wiese, Kurt, illus. (p. 633)
—Freddy & the Baseball Team from Mars. Wiese, Kurt, illus. (p. 633)
—Freddy & the Dragon. Wiese, Kurt, illus. (p. 633)
—Freddy & the Flying Saucer Plans. Wiese, Kurt, illus. (p. 633)
—Freddy & the Ignormus (p. 633)
—Freddy & the Ignormus. Wiese, Kurt, illus. (p. 633)
—Freddy & the Men from Mars. Wiese, Kurt, illus. (p. 633)
—Freddy & the North Pole. Wiese, Kurt, illus. (p. 633)
—Freddy & the Perilous Adventure. Wiese, Kurt, illus. (p. 633)
—Freddy & the Popinjay. Wiese, Kurt, illus. (p. 633)
—Freddy & the Space Ship. Wiese, Kurt, illus. (p. 633)
—Freddy Goes Camping. Wiese, Kurt, illus. (p. 633)
—Freddy Goes to Florida. Wiese, Kurt, illus. (p. 633)
—Freddy Plays Football. Wiese, Kurt, illus. (p. 633)
—Freddy Rides Again. Wiese, Kurt, illus. (p. 633)
—Freddy the Cowboy. Wiese, Kurt, illus. (p. 633)
—Freddy the Detective. Wiese, Kurt, illus. (p. 633)
—Freddy the Magician. Wiese, Kurt, illus. (p. 633)
—Freddy the Pied Piper. Wiese, Kurt, illus. (p. 633)
—Freddy the Pilot. Wiese, Kurt, illus. (p. 633)
—Freddy's Cousin Weedly. Wiese, Kurt, illus. (p. 633)
—Jimmy Takes Vanishing Lessons. Bolognese, Don, illus. (p. 918)
—Story of Freginald. Wiese, Kurt, illus. (p. 1658)
Brooks, Walter R. & Slayton-Mitchell, Joyce. Knuckleboom Loaders Load Logs: A Trip to the Sawmill. Wiese, Kurt & Borns, Steven, illus. (p. 965)
Brooks, Whitney, ed. see Thompson, Sharon.
Brooks, Yolanda. Do Animals Have Rights? (p. 456)
Brooks, Yvonne. Kids Finance 101: A Guide to Financial Success for Parents & their Children. (p. 953)
Brooks, Yvonne & Grant, Steven. Goat Kids Explore the Woods. (p. 687)
—Meet the Goat Kids. (p. 1122)
Brooksbank, Angela. My Busy Patterns. (p. 1199)
Brooksbank, Anne. Big Thursday. (p. 184)
Brookshire, Breezy, illus. see Smith, Angie.
Brooks-Scrivanich, Olivia. Fiscal Pear & Shimmer in the Call of River Whale. (p. 598)
Broom, Jenny. Animalium. Scott, Katie, illus. (p. 81)
—ArtCards: Accessorize. Haworth, Hennie, illus. (p. 103)
—Artcards: Fashion. Haworth, Hennie, illus. (p. 103)
—Color Create: Animals. Nój, Nahta, illus. (p. 342)
—Lion & the Mouse: Turn-And-Tell Tales. Noj, Nahta, illus. (p. 1020)
—Walk This World. Nieminen, Lotta, illus. (p. 1854)
Brooman, Josh & Mason, James. Era of the Second World War. (p. 533)
Broome, Errol. Judas Donkey. Thompson, Sharon, illus. (p. 930)
—My Grandad Knew Phar Lap. (p. 1210)
—What a Goat! Thompson, Sharon, illus. (p. 1878)
Broome, John. All Star Comics - Archives. (p. 45)
Broome, John, jt. auth. see Fox, Gardner.
Broome, John, jt. auth. see Kanigher, Robert.
Broome, John & Fox, Gardner. Flash Archives (p. 602)
Broome, John, et al. Batman (p. 144)
Broome, Mat, illus. see Avery, Ben.
Broome, Shannon, illus. see Miller, Sue.
Brophy, Ann. Novus 3 & Me: Six Short Stories about Friendship. (p. 1268)
Brophy, Brian. From My Eyes: Life from a Ten Year Old Boy's Perspective. Brophy, Doris, ed. (p. 643)
Brophy, David B. Michelle Obama: Meet the First Lady. (p. 1135)
Brophy, David Bergen. Michelle Obama: Meet the First Lady. (p. 1135)
Brophy, Doris, ed. see Brophy, Brian.
Brophy Down, Susan. Irena Sendler: Bringing Life to Children of the Holocaust. (p. 887)
Brophy, Mary-Beth. Last Stop Before Home. (p. 978)
Broqueville, Paulette-Renee. Unraveling Your Past Relationships. (p. 1822)
Brorsen, Jens. Red Face Bear. (p. 1454)
Brosgol, Vera. Anya's Ghost. Brosgol, Vera, illus. (p. 90)
Brosius, Peter, ed. see Children's Theatre Company Staff.
Broski, Julie. Being Me. Vigla, Vincent, illus. (p. 161)
Broslavick, Chris & Pichler, Tony. Totally Lent: A Teen's Journey to Easter 2006. Cannizzo, Karen A., ed. (p. 1771)
—Totally Lent! A Teen's Journey to Easter 2007. (p. 1771)
—Totally Lent! A Teen's Journey to Lent 2005. Cannizzo, Karen, ed. (p. 1771)
—Totally Lent! A Teen's Journey to Easter 2004. Cannizzo, Karen, ed. (p. 1771)
Bross, Lanie. Chaos. (p. 291)
—Fates. (p. 577)
Bross, Lee. Tangled Webs. (p. 1705)
Brosseau, Pat, illus. see Aaron, Jason.
Brost, April. Luckyduck Luckyduck. (p. 1063)
Brost, Corey. Gospel Connections for Teens: Reflections for Sunday Mass, Cycle A. (p. 703)
—Gospel Connections for Teens: Reflections for Sunday Mass - Cycle B. (p. 703)
Brost, Diane. Courage at Crow Wing River (p. 372)
Broster, Marie. Binky Bunny's Day Out & Poems for Children. (p. 188)
Brother, Ernest. Dick of Copper Gap. (p. 436)
Brothers Grimm. Hansel & Gretel. Cowley, Joy, ed. (p. 743)
—Snow White & Rose Red. Vivanco, Kelly, illus. (p. 1599)
—Twelve Dancing Princesses. Duntze, Dorothee, illus. (p. 1800)
Brothers Grimm, jt. auth. see Brothers Grimm, Becky.
Brothers Grimm, jt. auth. see Grimm, J. & W.
Brothers Grimm & Andersen, Hans Christian. Little Golden Book Fairy Tale Favorites. (p. 1028)
Brothers Grimm, Becky. Rapunzel & Other Tales: Includes the Ugly Duckling & the Boy Pirate. (p. 1439)
Brothers Grimm, Becky, jt. auth. see McCann, John.
Brothers Grimm, Becky & Brothers Grimm. Snow White & Rose Red: A Pop-up Fairytale. Cloyne, Rachel, illus. (p. 1599)
—Tales from the Brothers Grimm. Zwerger, Lisbeth, illus. (p. 1701)
Brothers Grimm, Becky & Isadora, Rachel. Fisherman & His Wife. Isadora, Rachel, illus. (p. 599)
Brothers Grimm, Becky & Sweeney, Monica. Loom Magic Charms! 25 Cool Designs That Will Rock Your Rainbow. (p. 1052)
—Loom Magic Creatures! 25 Awesome Animals & Mythical Beings for a Rainbow of Critters. (p. 1052)
Brothers Grimm, Becky, et al. Complete Grimm's Fairy Tales. (p. 353)
—Fairy Tales from the Brothers Grimm: Deluxe Hardcover Classic. Cruikshank, George, illus. (p. 564)
—Grimms' Fairy Tales. (p. 724)
—Little Red Riding Hood. (p. 1035)
—Snow White. Garcia, Camille Rose, illus. (p. 1599)
Brothers Grimm Staff. Hansel & Gretel. Cowley, Joy, ed. (p. 743)
—Little Red Riding Hood. Cowley, Joy, ed. (p. 1035)
—Snow White & Rose Red: A Grimms' Fairy Tale. Marshall, Denise, illus. (p. 1599)
Brothers Hilts Staff, jt. auth. see Czajak, Paul.
Brothers, Karen. Rhythm & Rhyme Literacy Time, Level K. (p. 1468)
Brothers, Marilee. Moon Rise. (p. 1172)
—Moon Spun. (p. 1172)
—Moonstone. (p. 1173)
—Shadow Moon. (p. 1557)
Brothers, Stephanie, ed. see Holland, Gill.
Brothers Washburn Staff, contrib. by. Mojave Green: Dimensions in Death. (p. 1160)
Brotherton, Marcus. Blur: A Graphic Reality Check for Teens Dealing with Self-Image. (p. 204)
—Heat: A Graphic Reality Check for Teens Dealing with Sexuality. (p. 760)
Brott, Ardyth. Here I Am! Miladovich, Dragana, illus. (p. 770)
Brott, Wayne. Shoes! Delosh, Diana Ting, illus. (p. 1568)
Brough, Hazel, illus. see Searcy, Margaret Zehmer.
Brough, Karen, illus. see Hoffman, Diana / Lynne.
Brougham, Jason, illus. see American Museum of Natural History Staff, et al.
Broughton, Ilona, illus. see Nagy, Jennifer.
Broughton, Pamela & Watson, Jane Werner. Miracles of Jesus. Smath, Jerry, illus. (p. 1149)
Broughton, Pamela, et al. Little Golden Book Bible Favorites. (p. 1028)
Broughton, Theresa. Benny's Very Special Trip. Warren, Joyce, illus. (p. 165)
—Three Amazing Farm Animals. (p. 1741)
Brouillard, Anne. Bathtub Prima Donna. Brouillard, Anne, illus. (p. 144)
Brouillet, Chrystine. Cameleon. (p. 256)
—Corbeau. (p. 366)
—Mon Amie Clémentine. (p. 1163)
Brouillette, Kathy. What Makes me Smile. (p. 1892)
Brouillette, Peter. Adventures of Old Henry: Nobody Cares. Lee, Williams, illus. (p. 21)
Brouillette, Peter, ed. see Bancroft, Myles.
Broussard, Kelly D. Paws of Protection: Alex & Anna Belle's Tails on the Farm. (p. 1331)
Brousse, Michel & Matsumoto, David. Century of Dedication, the History of Judo in America. (p. 287)
Broutin, Alain, et al. Baldomero Va a la Escuela. (p. 134)
Broutin & Stehr. Baldomero Va A la Escuela. (p. 134)
Broutin, Chistian. Trees. (p. 1784)
Broutin, Christian. Barco. (p. 138)
—In the Jungle. Broutin, Christian, illus. (p. 866)
—Town. Broutin, Christian, illus. (p. 1773)
—Tree. Broutin, Christian, illus. (p. 1783)
Broutin, Christian, illus. see Peyrols, Sylvaine, et al.
Broutin, Christian, jt. auth. see Delafosse, Claude.
Broutin, Christian & de Bourgoing, Pascale. Arbol. (p. 94)
Broutin, Christian & Delafosse, Claude. Let's Look at Fairies, Witches, Giants & Dragons. (p. 998)
Brouwer, Aafke, illus. see Goodhart, Pippa.
Brouwer, Sigmund. Absolute Pressure (p. 7)
—All-Star Pride (p. 45)
—Ambush. (p. 57)
—Blazer Drive (p. 199)
—Bug's Eye View: Annie Ant, Don't Cry! (p. 237)
—Camp Craziness. (p. 257)
—Chief Honor (p. 301)
—Cobra Strike (p. 336)
—Counterattack. (p. 370)
—Creature of the Mists. (p. 380)
—Daddy Ant, You Never Listen. (p. 398)
—Death Trap. (p. 420)
—Devil's Pass (p. 432)
—Final Battle. (p. 586)
—Fly Trap. (p. 609)
—Hitmen Triumph (p. 786)
—Hurricane Power (p. 830)
—Justine Mckeen & the Bird Nerd Whamond, Dave, illus. (p. 940)
—Justine Mckeen, Eat Your Beets Whamond, Dave, illus. (p. 940)
—Justine Mckeen, Pooper Scooper Whamond, Dave, illus. (p. 940)
—Justine Mckeen, Queen of Green Whamond, Dave, illus. (p. 940)
—Justine McKeen vs. the Queen of Mean Whamond, Dave, illus. (p. 940)

—Justine McKeen, Walk the Talk Whamond, Dave, illus. (p. 940)
—Madness at Moonshiner's Bay. (p. 1070)
—Maverick Mania (p. 1110)
—Mommy Ant, Eat Your Vegetables. (p. 1162)
—Mystery Pennies. (p. 1226)
—Nowhere to Hide. (p. 1269)
—Oil King Courage (p. 1282)
—Phantom Outlaw at Wolf Creek. (p. 1349)
—Rebel Glory (p. 1450)
—Rock the Boat (p. 1482)
—Scarlet Thunder (p. 1520)
—Sewer Rats (p. 1555)
—Sewer Rats. (p. 1555)
—Snowboarding . . . to the Extreme: Rippin' (p. 1600)
—Thunderbird Spirit (p. 1746)
—Tiger Threat (p. 1748)
—Timberwolf Challenge Griffiths, Dean, illus. (p. 1750)
—Timberwolf Chase Griffiths, Dean, illus. (p. 1750)
—Timberwolf Hunt Griffiths, Dean, illus. (p. 1750)
—Timberwolf Prey Ross, Graham, illus. (p. 1750)
—Timberwolf Revenge Griffiths, Dean, illus. (p. 1750)
—Timberwolf Rivals Ross, Graham, illus. (p. 1750)
—Timberwolf Tracks Ross, Graham, illus. (p. 1750)
—Timberwolf Trap Griffiths, Dean, illus. (p. 1750)
—Tin Soldier (p. 1755)
—Titan Clash (p. 1757)
—Wings of an Angel. (p. 1936)
—Winter Hawk Star (p. 1938)
—Wired (p. 1939)
Brouwer, Sigmund & Gingras, Gaston. Course-Poursuite des Loups Gris Griffiths, Dean, illus. (p. 373)
—Défi des Loups Gris Griffiths, Dean, illus. (p. 424)
—Loups Gris à la Chasse Griffiths, Dean, illus. (p. 1059)
—Revanche des Loups Gris Griffiths, Dean, illus. (p. 1465)
Brovelli, Marcela, tr. see Osborne, Mary Pope.
Browder, N. C. At Sea with the MothBall Fleet & Other Experiences. (p. 110)
Brower. Zoe & the Cocoa-Brown Tutu. Steele, Andrea M., illus. (p. 1987)
Brower, Pauline. Inland Valleys Missions in California. (p. 874)
Brower, Sandra Shane. Princess Zoe & the Mer-Bird. Steele, Andrea M., illus. (p. 1406)
Brower, Saundra Scott. Gifts of Christmas. (p. 675)
Brower, William, illus. see Puscheck, Herbert Charles.
Browin, Frances Williams. Captured Words: The Story of A Great Indian. Bjorklund, L. F., illus. (p. 265)
Brown. Wondrous Worlds of the Wishing Well (p. 1949)
Brown, jt. auth. see Brown, Margaret Wise.
Brown, Abbie Farwell. In the Days of Giants. Smith, E. Boyd, illus. (p. 865)
—Tales of the Red Children. (p. 1702)
Brown, Adam. Adventures of Wormie Wormington Book Three: Wormie & the Snowball. Smart, Andy, illus. (p. 24)
—Adventures of Wormie Wormington Book Two: Wormie & the Kite. Smart, Andy, illus. (p. 24)
Brown, Adam & Smart, Andy. Adventures of Wormie Wormington Book One: Wormie & the Fish. Smart, Andy, illus. (p. 24)
Brown, Adele Q. Elvis Presley. (p. 517)
Brown, Adrienne, illus. see RH Disney Staff & Redbank, Tennant.
Brown, Alan. Bible & Christianity. (p. 175)
—Christianity. (p. 312)
—Christianity. (p. 312)
—Incredible Journey of Walter Rat. (p. 869)
Brown, Alan, illus. see Enos, Joel, ed.
Brown, Alan, illus. see Enos, Joel.
Brown, Alan, illus. see Levine, Cory.
Brown, Alan, jt. auth. see Seaman, Alison.
Brown, Alan & Seaman, Alison. Christian Church. Card, Vanessa, illus. (p. 311)
Brown, Alan James. Love-a-Duck. Chessa, Francesca, illus. (p. 1059)
—Michael & the Monkey King. (p. 1134)
Brown, Alex. Mountain Adventures. (p. 1180)
—Secret Missions. (p. 1542)
Brown, Alison. Eddie & Dog (p. 503)
Brown, Alison, illus. see Mitton, Tony.
Brown, Alison, illus. see Prasadam-Halls, Smriti.
Brown, Allison. Perfection. (p. 1342)
Brown, Amanda, illus. see Henry, Kristina.
Brown, Amanda C. Flying Courage. Archeval, Jose, illus. (p. 609)
Brown, Amy Belding. Mr. Emerson's Wife. (p. 1185)
Brown, Anna, illus. see Lawler, Janet.
Brown, Anne. Dumari Chronicles: Year One: Year One. (p. 489)
Brown, Anne Corbett, jt. auth. see Ringley, Patrick.
Brown, Anne K. Virtual Danger: Staying Safe Online (p. 1844)
Brown, Anne K. & Burns, Jan. Gwen Stefani. (p. 733)
Brown, Antoinette & Skindzier, Jon. St John's University NY College Prowler off the Record: Inside Saint Johns New York. (p. 1638)
Brown, Audrey E. Angels of Freedom. (p. 75)
Brown, Ayanna. I Am Beautiful, for All the Children of the World Elliot, Lee, photos by. (p. 832)
Brown, Barbara. Adventures of Captain Crick, Super Hero. (p. 17)
—Hanukkah in Alaska. Schuett, Stacey, illus. (p. 744)
Brown, Barbara J. Many Different Ways to Worship: Is apart of everyday Life. (p. 1089)
Brown, Bea L. Wally the Cockeyed Cricket. (p. 1855)
Brown Bear Books (Firm) Staff, contrib. by. Ocean Life. (p. 1276)
Brown, Benjamin Thomas. Best Dog. (p. 168)
Brown, Berthalicia, jt. auth. see Brown, Luke.
Brown, Betisa Garagozlu. Sister Sun & Sister Moon. (p. 1581)
Brown, Bill, illus. see Mazer, Anne.
Brown, Bill, jt. auth. see Elser, Smoke.
Brown, Billowby. Wibble Named Wally. (p. 1927)
Brown, Binh. Dunley Children & Other Writings. (p. 490)
Brown, Bobby, illus. see Hogan, Micki.
Brown, Brenda, illus. see King, Bart.
Brown, Brenda, illus. see Piven, Joshua, et al.
Brown, Brett T. & Holloway, Julie M. Haley's Comet. Brown, Brett T., illus. (p. 736)
Brown, Brooklyn. Kifaru Tries Something New. (p. 955)
Brown, Bruce. Jack & the Zombie Box. O'Reilly, Sean Patrick, ed. (p. 902)
—Mwumba. O'Reilly, Sean Patrick, ed. (p. 1195)
Brown, Bruce & Kirkman, Robert. Brit - Awol (p. 229)
Brown, Bruce & Shelton, A. Gordon the Giraffe. (p. 702)
Brown, Calef. Boy Wonders. Brown, Calef, illus. (p. 220)
—Dragon, Robot, Gatorbunny: Pick one. Draw it. Make it Funny. (p. 478)
—Flamingos on the Roof. (p. 602)
—Hallowilloween: Nefarious Silliness from Calef Brown. (p. 739)
—Hallowilloween. (p. 739)
—Hypnotize a Tiger: Poems about Just about Everything. Brown, Calef, illus. (p. 831)
—Pirateria: The Wonderful Plunderful Pirate Emporium. Brown, Calef, illus. (p. 1363)
—Polkabats & Octopus Slacks: 14 Stories. (p. 1381)
—Soup for Breakfast. (p. 1615)
—We Go Together! A Curious Selection of Affectionate Verse. (p. 1867)
Brown, Calef, illus. see Harris, John.
Brown, Calef, illus. see Pinkwater, Daniel M.
Brown, Calef, illus. see Winter, Jonah.
Brown, Cameron, jt. auth. see Spyer, Jonathan.
Brown, Cara D. Isabelle's Wish. (p. 891)
Brown, Carl & Brown, Kay. Little Star. (p. 1036)
Brown, Carol. Sassy Pants. (p. 1515)
Brown, Carol A. Sassy Pants Makes Amends. (p. 1515)
Brown, Carolyn A. God's People Worship Teacher Guide. (p. 691)
—My Worship Book Student Book. (p. 1222)
Brown, Carolyn C. Children Celebrate Easter. (p. 302)
Brown, Carron. On the Train: Shine-A-Light. Johnson, Bee, illus. (p. 1291)
—Secrets of the Apple Tree. Nassner, Alyssa, illus. (p. 1545)
—Secrets of the Rain Forest. Nassner, Alyssa, illus. (p. 1545)
—Secrets of the Seashore. Nassner, Alyssa, illus. (p. 1545)
Brown, Carron, ed. see Andersen, Hans Christian.
Brown, Carron, ed. Beauty & the Beast & Jack & the Beanstalk: Two Tales & Their Histories. (p. 154)
—Cinderella & Aladdin: Two Tales & Their Histories. (p. 320)
—Hansel & Gretel & the Pied Piper of Hamelin: Two Tales & Their Histories. (p. 743)
—Sleeping Beauty & Snow White & the Seven Dwarfs: Two Tales & Their Histories. (p. 1589)
—Three Little Pigs & Little Red Riding Hood: Two Tales & Their Histories. (p. 1743)
Brown, Casey. Age of Aquarius Poetry Book. (p. 29)
Brown, Cathie. Today I am a Pirate. (p. 1760)
Brown, Celease N. & Mubarak, Enoch. Color Orange. (p. 343)
Brown, Charlotte L., jt. auth. see Brown, Charlotte Lewis.
Brown, Charlotte Lewis. After the Dinosaurs: Mammoths & Fossil Mammals. Wilson, Phil, illus. (p. 28)
—Beyond the Dinosaurs: Monsters of the Air & Sea. Wilson, Phil, illus. (p. 174)
—Day the Dinosaurs Died. Wilson, Phil, illus. (p. 414)
Brown, Charlotte Lewis & Brown, Charlotte L. After the Dinosaurs: Mammoths & Fossil Mammals. Wilson, Phil, illus. (p. 28)
—Beyond the Dinosaurs: Monsters of the Air & Sea. Wilson, Phil, illus. (p. 174)
—Day the Dinosaurs Died. Wilson, Phil, illus. (p. 414)
Brown, Cherie. Love Doesn't Hurt: Life Lessons for Young Women. (p. 1059)
Brown, Chris. Chief Hawah's Book of Native American Indians. (p. 301)
—Shiver Me Timbers: A Fun Book of Pirates, Sailors, & Other Sea-Farers. (p. 1567)
Brown, Chris L., illus. see Parker, Ms. Alichia R.
Brown, Cindy. Smashed Penny Collecting for the Young... & Young at Heart. (p. 1593)
Brown, Clarkie. Dasher Christmas. (p. 409)
Brown, Clovis, illus. see Richmond, Beulah.
Brown, Clovis, illus. see Wohlt, Julia.
Brown Conroy, Erin. Writing Skillbuilders: A Fun-Filled Book of Prewriting Skills for Beginning Writers. Bk. 1 (p. 1965)
—Writing Skillbuilders: A Fun-Filled Activity Book for Beautiful Cursive Handwriting. Bk. 3 (p. 1965)
—Writing Skillbuilders: A Fun-Filled Activity Book to Build Strong Handwriting Skills. Bk. 2 (p. 1965)
Brown, Corinne. Let's Keep This Secret. (p. 998)
—Stowaway on the Titanic. (p. 1664)
—Wishful Watoosi: The Horse That Wished He Wasn't. (p. 1940)
Brown, Cornelia. Constance the Little Angel Wants Curls. (p. 359)
Brown, Courtney Allison. BJ Goes to School. (p. 194)
Brown, Craig. Mule Train Mail. Brown, Craig, illus. (p. 1189)
—This Is Craig Brown. (p. 1735)
Brown, Craig McFarland, illus. see Ryan, Pam Muñoz.
Brown, Cynthia Light. Amazing Kitchen Chemistry Projects. Shedd, Blair, illus. (p. 54)
Brown, Cynthia Light & Brown, Nick. Explore Rocks & Minerals! 20 Great Projects, Activities, Experiments. Stone, Bryan, illus. (p. 550)
Brown, Cynthia Light & McGinty, Patrick. Mapping & Navigation: Explore the History & Science of Finding Your Way with 20 Projects. Hetland, Beth, illus. (p. 1090)
Brown, D. L. Nevr ZayDie. (p. 1243)
Brown, Dan, illus. see Adler, David A.
Brown, Dan, illus. see Collins, Lori & Koski, Mary.
Brown, Dan, illus. see Galvin, Laura Gates.
Brown, Dan, illus. see Koski, Mary B.
Brown, Dan, illus. see Larkin, Jim & Rambo, Lee Elliot.
Brown, Daniel. Chipper Learns a Lesson. (p. 308)
—Gerard Manley Hopkins. (p. 666)
Brown, Daniel J., illus. see Pulford, Elizabeth.
Brown, David R. Shakespeare for Everyone to Enjoy. (p. 1559)
Brown, Dawn & Poe, Edgar Allen. Ravenous. (p. 1441)
Brown, Deb Austin. Growing Character-99 Successful Strategies for the Elementary Classroom. (p. 726)
Brown, Debbie. Grandma Box. (p. 708)
Brown, Deborah. Here to Save the Day. (p. 770)
Brown, Deborah Deal. My Typical Sunday. (p. 1220)
Brown, Dee. Saga of the Sioux: An Adaptation from Dee Brown's Bury My Heart at Wounded Knee. (p. 1502)
Brown, Dennis L., illus. see Clary, Margie Willis.
Brown, Derrick. Valentine the Porcupine Dances Funny. Lewis, Jenn, illus. (p. 1830)
Brown, Desirae. Pumpkin's Dream (p. 1416)
Brown, Devin. Not Exactly Normal. (p. 1267)
Brown, Dinah, jt. auth. see Anastasio, Dina.
Brown, Don. Across a Dark & Wild Sea. (p. 9)
—All Stations! Distress! April 15, 1912: the Day the Titanic Sank. Brown, Don, illus. (p. 45)
—All Stations! Distress! April 15, 1912 - The Day the Titanic Sank. Brown, Don, illus. (p. 45)
—America Is under Attack: September 11, 2001: the Day the Towers Fell. (p. 59)
—America Is under Attack: The Day the Towers Fell - September 11, 2001. Vol. 4 (p. 59)
—Dolley Madison Saves George Washington. Brown, Don, illus. (p. 464)
—Drowned City: Hurricane Katrina & New Orleans. (p. 486)
—Gold! Gold from the American River! January 24 1848 - The Day the Gold Rush Began. Brown, Don, illus. (p. 693)
—Gold! Gold from the American River! January 24, 1848: the Day the Gold Rush Began. Brown, Don, illus. (p. 693)
—Great American Dust Bowl. Brown, Don, illus. (p. 713)
—He Has Shot the President! April 14, 1865: the Day John Wilkes Booth Killed President Lincoln. Brown, Don, illus. (p. 756)
—Let It Begin Here! The Day the American Revolution Began April 19, 1775. Brown, Don, illus. (p. 994)
—Mack Made Movies. Brown, Don, illus. (p. 1068)
—Odd Boy Out: Young Albert Einstein. (p. 1278)
—Uncommon Traveler: Mary Kingsley in Africa. (p. 1812)
—Voice from the Wilderness: The Story of Anna Howard Shaw. (p. 1848)
—Wizard from the Start: The Incredible Boyhood & Amazing Inventions of Thomas Edison. Brown, Don, illus. (p. 1942)
Brown, Don, illus. see Bartlett, Karen T.
Brown, Donna. Crippled Like Me. (p. 383)
Brown, Douglas. Young Adult's Survival Guide to Communication: Learn to Start a Conversation with Anyone in 30 Seconds or Less. (p. 1978)
Brown, Dustin, jt. ed. see Scieszka, Jon.
Brown, Dwayne, illus. see Labossiere, Julie.
Brown, E. Jackie, illus. see Kline, Spencer.
Brown, E. Jane. Pinkie. (p. 1360)
Brown, E.A. Gossamer. (p. 703)
Brown, Edna. Fig Leaves & Skin Tunics. (p. 585)
Brown, Elbrite, illus. see Deans, Karen.
Brown, Elbrite, illus. see Jackson, Ellen B.
Brown, Eleanor Russell. Break A Leg They Yelled to the Clown. (p. 224)
Brown, Elizabeth. Aristotle: the Firefly's Message. Schuna, Ramona, illus. (p. 98)
—Collection of Children's Tales. (p. 340)
Brown, Elizabeth Ferguson & Boyds Mills Press Staff. Coal Country Christmas. Stevenson, Harvey, illus. (p. 336)
Brown, Elizabeth R. Wineberry Diner. (p. 1936)
Brown, Elizabeth Rhea. Sweet Maneuvers. (p. 1690)
Brown, Ellen Hodgson. Web of Debt: The Shocking Truth about Our Money System & How We Can Break Free. (p. 1870)
Brown, Erin, illus. see Jameson, Steven.
Brown, Erin O'Leary, illus. see Curry, Don L.
Brown, Fannie T. Where Are the Children? (p. 1906)
Brown, Fern. Daisy & the Girl Scouts: The Story of Juliette Gordon Low. DeJohn, Marie, illus. (p. 400)
Brown, Fiona, illus. see Tatchell, Judy & Varley, Carol.
Brown, Frank. Among the Pandemonious Mismaides: A Fantasy. (p. 65)
Brown, Frederick Martin. America's Yesterday. (p. 64)
Brown, Gary. Sam's Mission Call. Tanner, Stephanie, illus. (p. 1509)
—Tribunal. Anderson, Mark, ed. (p. 1785)
Brown, Gina Bates. Zen & Bodhi's Snowy Day. Hinder, Sarah Jane, illus. (p. 1986)
Brown, Gladys. Adventures of King Flapjack. (p. 19)
Brown, Gladys M. Home Away from Home. (p. 792)
Brown, Gloria, illus. see Allen, Nancy Kelly.
Brown, Gloria Dean, illus. see Elpel, Thomas J.
Brown, Grandma. Does He Have to Be My Cousin Forever? (p. 460)
Brown, Greg. Down at the Sea Hotel: A Greg Brown Song. LeVert, Mireille, illus. (p. 474)
Brown, Greg, jt. auth. see Anthony, Carmelo.
Brown, Greg, jt. auth. see Bird, Sue.
Brown, Greg, jt. auth. see Brooks, Aaron.
Brown, Greg, jt. auth. see Carter, Vince.
Brown, Greg, jt. auth. see Eckstein, David.
Brown, Greg, jt. auth. see Gagne, Eric.
Brown, Greg, jt. auth. see Gonzalez, Tony.
Brown, Greg, jt. auth. see Johnson, Brad.
Brown, Gregory. Johnny Appleseed: An American Tall Tale. (p. 923)
Brown, Gregory R. K. My Best Friend Jason. (p. 1196)
Brown, Gwen. Clifford & His Bear. (p. 332)
Brown, Harriet & Witowski, Teri. Kit's World: A Girl's-Eye View of the Great Depression. Rane, Walter & Hood, Philip, illus. (p. 962)
Brown, Hazel. Prince Henry St. Clair Earl of Orkney. Bramadat, Dawn, ed. (p. 1401)
Brown, Heather. Big Chomp. (p. 180)
—Chomp! Zoo: A Pull-Tab Book. (p. 310)
—Robot Book. (p. 1480)
—Robot Book. Brown, Heather, illus. (p. 1480)
Brown, Heather, illus. see Croyle, Paula.
Brown, Heather, illus. see Hannigan, Paula & Accord Publishing Staff.
Brown, Heather, illus. see Hannigan, Paula.
Brown, Heather, illus. see McGuinness, Elle J.
Brown, Heather, jt. auth. see McGuiness, Elle J.
Brown, Heather & Accord Publishing Staff. Chomp! (p. 309)
Brown, Heather E., jt. auth. see Walker, Andrew D.
Brown, Heather E. & Martin, Ashley. How to Improve at Judo. (p. 820)
Brown, Herman. Cut Too Far. (p. 396)
—Option. (p. 1301)
Brown, Hilary. Two-Liners for Kids. (p. 1803)
Brown, Ilknur. Adventures of Little Robert. (p. 20)
—Faces of Little Robert. (p. 561)
Brown, Ina M., jt. auth. see Brown, Jim D.
Brown, Isobel. Domestic Crime. (p. 465)
—Klimt (p. 963)
Brown, Ivorine. Don't Cry but Smile & Remember. Wilson, Teddy, illus. (p. 467)
Brown, J. A. Busy Bee. Knight, Paula, illus. (p. 245)
—Hurray for Elephant. (p. 829)
—Lion's Mane. Knight, Paula, illus. (p. 1021)
—Scaredy Duck. Knight, Paula, illus. (p. 1519)
Brown, J. Darrell. I Play with Words! (p. 844)
Brown, J. Jan. SOL Activities for Virginia Social Studies: Teaching with Jamestowne's Uncovered Treasures, Student Workbook. (p. 1606)
Brown, Jahla. Nathan Is Nathan. (p. 1231)
Brown, Jake. Dr. Dre in the Studio: From Compton, Death Row, Snoop Dogg, Eminem, 50 Cent, the Game & Mad Money - The Life, Times & Aftermath of the Notorious Record Producer - Dr. Dre. (p. 475)
Brown, James. Farm. Brown, James, illus. (p. 573)
Brown, Jami L. Poot: The Pink Boy. (p. 1384)
Brown, Jamie B. Angelo & the Master. (p. 75)
Brown, Jane. Who Has Four Feet? (p. 1915)
Brown, Jane Clark, illus. see Paterson, Katherine.
Brown, Janet. B Is for Bangkok. Q, Likit, illus. (p. 122)
—Gingerbread Man. (p. 677)
—Gingerbread Man (Floor Book) My First Reading Book. Morton, Ken, illus. (p. 677)
—Goldilocks & the Three Bears (Floor Book) My First Reading Book. Morton, Ken, illus. (p. 696)
—Hansel & Gretel: My First Reading Book. Morton, Ken, illus. (p. 743)
—Jack & the Beanstalk: My First Reading Book. Morton, Ken, illus. (p. 902)
—Pinocchio: My First Reading Book. Morton, Ken, illus. (p. 1360)
—Pinocchio: My First Reading Book. Brown, Janet & Morton, Ken, illus. (p. 1360)
—Puss in Boots. Morton, Ken, illus. (p. 1420)
—Puss in Boots (Floor Book) My First Reading Book. Morton, Ken, illus. (p. 1420)
—Red Riding Hood: My First Reading Book. (p. 1454)
—Red Riding Hood (Floor Book) My First Reading Book. Morton, Ken, illus. (p. 1454)
—Snow White & the Seven Dwarves. Morton, Ken, illus. (p. 1600)
—Snow White & the Seven Dwarves (Floor Book) My First Reading Book. Morton, Ken, illus. (p. 1600)
—Three Billy Goats Gruff (Floor Book) Morton, Ken, illus. (p. 1741)
—Three Little Pigs. Morton, Ken, illus. (p. 1742)
—Three Little Pigs (Floor Book) My First Reading Book. Morton, Ken, illus. (p. 1743)
—Ugly Duckling. Morton, Ken, illus. (p. 1808)
—Ugly Duckling (Floor Book) My First Reading Book. Morton, Ken, illus. (p. 1808)
Brown, Janet Allison. Left Hand, Right Hand: A Hands-on Book about Left & Right. Endersby, Frank, illus. (p. 987)
—My First Book of Jobs. (p. 1205)
—My First Book of Opposites. Endersby, Frank, illus. (p. 1205)
Brown, Janet Allison, jt. auth. see Brown, Janet Allison.
Brown, Janet Allison & Brown, Janet Allison. Seasons (p. 1538)
—Seasons. (p. 1538)
Brown, Janet Hubbard. Hernando de Soto & His Expeditions Across the Americas. Goetzmann, William H., ed. (p. 772)
Brown, Jason, illus. see Curtiss, A. B. & Curtiss, A. B.
Brown, Jason Robert. Tickety Tock. GrandPré, Mary, illus. (p. 1747)
Brown, Jason Robert & Elish, Dan. 13. (p. 1994)
Brown, Jean. My Treasure Book of Nursery Rhymes & Hymns. (p. 1220)
Brown, Jean E. & Stephens, Elaine C., eds. Your Reading: An Annotated Booklist for Middle School & Junior High. (p. 1981)
Brown, Jeff. African Safari Discovery. Pamintuan, Macky, illus. (p. 28)
—Amazing Colorado: A Collection of Puzzlers, Mazes, & Fun! (p. 54)
—Amazing Mexican Secret. Pamintuan, Macky, illus. (p. 55)
—Amazing Washington! A Collection of Puzzlers, Mazes, & Fun! (p. 56)
—Australian Boomerang Bonanza No. 8. Pamintuan, Macky, illus. (p. 116)
—Australian Boomerang Bonanza. Pamintuan, Macky, illus. (p. 116)
—Escape to California. (p. 535)
—Flat Stanley: Show & Tell, Flat Stanley! Pamintuan, Macky, illus. (p. 603)
—Flat Stanley. (p. 603)
—Flat Stanley. Nash, Scott, illus. (p. 603)
—Flat Stanley & the Firehouse. Pamintuan, Macky, illus. (p. 603)
—Flat Stanley & the Haunted House. Pamintuan, Macky, illus. (p. 603)
—Flat Stanley & the Very Big Cookie. Pamintuan, Macky, illus. (p. 603)
—Flat Stanley at Bat. (p. 603)
—Flat Stanley at Bat. Pamintuan, Macky, illus. (p. 603)
—Flat Stanley Collection Pamintuan, Macky, illus. (p. 603)
—Flat Stanley Goes Camping. (p. 603)
—Flat Stanley Goes Camping. Pamintuan, Macky, illus. (p. 603)
—Flat Stanley - His Original Adventure! Nash, Scott & Pamintuan, Macky, illus. (p. 603)
—Flat Stanley - On Ice. Pamintuan, Macky, illus. (p. 603)

B

—Flat Stanley's Worldwide Adventures #10: Showdown at the Alamo. Pamintuan, Macky, illus. (p. 603)
—Flat Stanley's Worldwide Adventures #12: Escape to California. Pamintuan, Macky, illus. (p. 603)
—Framed in France. (p. 627)
—Framed in France. Pamintuan, Macky, illus. (p. 627)
—Intrepid Canadian Expedition Vol. 4. Pamintuan, Macky, illus. (p. 881)
—Intrepid Canadian Expedition. (p. 881)
—Intrepid Canadian Expedition. Pamintuan, Macky, illus. (p. 881)
—Invisible Stanley. (p. 886)
—Invisible Stanley. Nash, Scott & Pamintuan, Macky, illus. (p. 886)
—Mount Rushmore Calamity. Pamintuan, Macky, illus. (p. 1180)
—Show & Tell, Flat Stanley! (p. 1570)
—Showdown at the Alamo. (p. 1571)
—Showdown at the Alamo. Pamintuan, Macky, illus. (p. 1571)
—Stanley & the Magic Lamp. (p. 1639)
—Stanley & the Magic Lamp. Nash, Scott & Pamintuan, Macky, illus. (p. 1639)
—Stanley, Flat Again! Nash, Scott & Pamintuan, Macky, illus. (p. 1640)
—Stanley in Space. Nash, Scott, illus. (p. 1640)
—Stanley in Space. Pamintuan, Macky, illus. (p. 1640)
—Stanley's Christmas Adventure. (p. 1640)
—Stanley's Christmas Adventure. Nash, Scott & Pamintuan, Macky, illus. (p. 1640)
—True Joy of Christmas. (p. 1792)
—U. S. Capital Commotion. Pamintuan, Macky, illus. (p. 1806)
—US Capital Commotion. Pamintuan, Macky, illus. (p. 1826)
Brown, Jeff, jt. auth. see Greenhut, Josh.
Brown, Jeff, jt. auth. see Pennypacker, Sara.
Brown, Jeff Allan. Floom Shroom the Battling Mushroom. (p. 606)
Brown, Jeffrey. Incredible Change-Bots. (p. 869)
—Jedi Academy. Brown, Jeffrey, illus. (p. 911)
—Phantom Bully. (p. 1349)
—Return of the Padawan. Brown, Jeffrey, illus. (p. 1464)
—Sulk Volume 3: Kind of Strength Comes from Madness: Kind of Strength Comes from Madness. (p. 1673)
Brown, Jennifer. Hate List. (p. 752)
—How Lunchbox Jones Saved Me from Robots, Traitors, & Missy the Cruel. (p. 810)
—Life on Mars. (p. 1012)
—Perfect Escape. (p. 1341)
—Shade Me. (p. 1556)
—Thousand Words. (p. 1740)
Brown, Jenny. 100 Active Bible Games for Children. (p. 1998)
Brown, Jeremy. God Makes the Seasons. (p. 690)
Brown, Jeremy K. Amelia Earhart. (p. 58)
—Michael Jackson. (p. 1134)
—Stevie Wonder: Musician. (p. 1649)
—Ursula K. le Guin. (p. 1826)
Brown, Jerry. Merc. (p. 1127)
Brown, Jim. Batting Third: A Tim Allison Baseball Story. (p. 145)
—Batting Third: (A Tim Allison Baseball Story) (p. 145)
—Bridge to Cross. (p. 227)
—Foster Twins in the Mystery at Moore's Lake. (p. 624)
—Rose Garden: Living in Concert with Spirit. (p. 1489)
—Willie Nelson: Red Headed Stranger. (p. 1934)
Brown, Jim D. Foster Twins in the Mystery of the House on Joiner Lane. (p. 624)
Brown, Jim D. & Brown, Ina M. Foster Twins in the Mystery of the House on Joiner Lane. (p. 624)
Brown, Jo. Hoppity Skip Little Chick. (p. 797)
—Where's My Mommy? (p. 1910)
—Where's My Mommy? Brown, Jo, illus. (p. 1910)
Brown, Jo, illus. see Ainsworth, Kimberly.
Brown, Jo, illus. see Albee, Sarah & Hood, Susan.
Brown, Jo, illus. see Mitter, Matt.
Brown, Jo, illus. see Sollinger, Emily.
Brown, Jo, jt. auth. see Box, Su.
Brown, Jo, jt. auth. see Froeb, Lori.
Brown, Jo Ann. Fat Tuesday. (p. 577)
Brown, Joanne. Psychosocial Exploration of Love & Intimacy. (p. 1413)
Brown, Joanne Sheehan. Pirate Freddie Meets Santa Claus. (p. 1362)
Brown, Jocelyn. Mitochondrial Curiosities of Marcels 1 to 19. (p. 1156)
Brown, Joe. Race to the Rescue. Marchesi, Stephen, illus. (p. 1431)
Brown, John, tr. see Moers, Walter.
Brown, John Russell. Hamlet. (p. 739)
—Macbeth. (p. 1067)
Brown, Jonatha A. Amelia Earhart. (p. 58)
—Animal Feet & Legs. (p. 77)
—Animal Heads & Necks. (p. 78)
—Animal Skin & Fur. (p. 79)
—Animal Tails. (p. 80)
—Anne Frank. (p. 85)
—Anne Frank. Acosta, Tatiana & Gutierrez, Guillermo, trs. (p. 85)
—Arizona. (p. 98)
—Basketball. (p. 143)
—Bill Gates. (p. 186)
—Bill Gates. Acosta, Tatiana & Gutierrez, Guillermo, trs. (p. 186)
—Cabezas y los Cuellos de los Animales. (p. 250)
—César Chávez. (p. 288)
—Colas de los Animales. (p. 338)
—Delaware. (p. 424)
—Eleanor Roosevelt. (p. 508)
—Florida. (p. 606)
—Football. (p. 614)
—Henry Ford. (p. 768)
—Hermanos Wright. (p. 771)
—Hermanos Wright. Acosta, Tatiana & Gutierrez, Guillermo, trs. from ENG. (p. 771)
—Hockey. (p. 786)
—Idaho. (p. 851)
—Jackie Robinson. Acosta, Tatiana & Gutierrez, Guillermo, trs. (p. 903)
—John F. Kennedy. (p. 921)
—Las patas y los pies de los animales. (p. 977)
—Maine. (p. 1077)
—Martin Luther King, Jr. (p. 1097)
—Maryland. (p. 1101)
—Montana. (p. 1170)
—Muhammad Ali. (p. 1189)
—Nebraska. (p. 1239)
—Neil Armstrong. (p. 1240)
—Nevada. (p. 1242)
—Oklahoma. (p. 1282)
—Oprah Winfrey. (p. 1301)
—Oprah Winfrey. Acosta, Tatiana & Gutierrez, Guillermo, trs. (p. 1301)
—Piel y el Pelo de los Animales. (p. 1357)
—Puerto Rico & Other Outlying Areas. (p. 1415)
—Rosa Parks. (p. 1488)
—Soccer. (p. 1603)
—South Dakota. (p. 1617)
—Steven Spielberg. (p. 1649)
—Tennis. (p. 1720)
—Texas. (p. 1723)
—Tiger Woods. (p. 1749)
—Tiger Woods. Acosta, Tatiana & Gutierrez, Guillermo, trs. (p. 1749)
—Utah. (p. 1829)
—Venus & Serena Williams. (p. 1836)
—Venus y Serena Williams. (p. 1836)
—Vermont. (p. 1837)
—Walt Disney. (p. 1855)
—West Virginia. (p. 1876)
—Wright Brothers. (p. 1963)
Brown, Jonatha A., jt. auth. see Boekhoff, P. M.
Brown, Jonatha A., jt. auth. see Dubois, Muriel L.
Brown, Jonatha A., jt. auth. see Fairley, Melissa.
Brown, Jonatha A., jt. auth. see Goff, Elizabeth Hudson.
Brown, Jonatha A., jt. auth. see Hudson Goff, Elizabeth.
Brown, Jonatha A., jt. auth. see Meachen Rau, Dana.
Brown, Jonatha A. & Boekhoff, P. M. Washington. (p. 1859)
Brown, Jonatha A. & Dubois, Muriel L. Michigan. (p. 1135)
Brown, Jonatha A. & Goff, Elizabeth Hudson. Ana Frank. McHargue, D. et al, illus. (p. 66)
—Anne Frank. Floor, Guus & Timmons, Jonathan, illus. (p. 85)
Brown, Jonatha A. & Orr, Tamra. Indiana. (p. 871)
Brown, Jonatha A. & Orr, Tamra B. Indiana. (p. 871)
Brown, Jonatha A. & Raatma, Lucia. Jackie Robinson. (p. 903)
—Tiger Woods. (p. 1749)
Brown, Jonatha A. & Ruffin, Frances E. Mississippi. (p. 1154)
Brown, Jonatha A., et al. César Chávez. McHargue, D., illus. (p. 288)
Brown, Jonathan, illus. see Braver, Vanita.
Brown, Jordan. Micro Mania: A Really Close-up Look at Bacteria, Bedbugs & the Zillions of Other Gross Little Creatures That Live in, on & All Around You! (p. 1136)
Brown, Jordan D. Crazy Concoctions: A Mad Scientist's Guide to Messy Mixtures. Owsley, Anthony, illus. (p. 377)
—Innings & Outs of Baseball. Kennedy, Kelly & Downey, Dagney, illus. (p. 875)
—Robo World: The Story of Robot Designer Cynthia Breazeal. (p. 1480)
—Thrills & Chills of Amusement Parks. Borgions, Mark, illus. (p. 1744)
Brown, Joy. Spy Hopping. (p. 1636)
Brown, Joyce. Learning to Use My Bible: A Special Study for Children in Grades 3 & 4. (p. 986)
Brown, Jr. Jimmy's Alphabet Garden. (p. 918)
Brown, Jr., David F., illus. see Brown Sr., David F.
Brown, Judy, illus. see Bennett, Leonie.
Brown, Judy, illus. see Burchett, Janet & Vogler, Sara.
Brown, Judy, illus. see Wallace, Karen.
Brown, Judy, jt. auth. see Chayil, Eishes.
Brown, K. D. Hi, God. (p. 775)
Brown, K. T. Adventures of Peter Tucker: Introduction of the Tiger. (p. 21)
Brown, Kait, illus. see Harvey, Keith.
Brown, Karen, illus. see Moore, Judith.
Brown, Kate. Sleepy ABC. (p. 1589)
Brown, Kate, illus. see Harvey, Keith.
Brown, Kathryn. Adventures at Aaron Loch Farm. (p. 15)
—Freddy the Brave. (p. 633)
Brown, Kathryn, illus. see Dotlich, Rebecca Kai.
Brown, Kathryn, illus. see Hyatt, Patricia Rusch.
Brown, Kathryn, illus. see Lindbergh, Reeve.
Brown, Kathryn, illus. see MacLachlan, Patricia.
Brown, Kathryn, illus. see Moser, Lisa.
Brown, Kathryn, illus. see Rylant, Cynthia.
Brown, Kathryn, illus. see Smith, Linda.
Brown, Kathryn, illus. see Stone, Tanya Lee.
Brown, Kathryn Keil. Alpaca-Bet! Abc's of Alpacas. (p. 48)
Brown, Kathy. Wesley's World. Parsloe, Alismarie, illus. (p. 1876)
Brown, Katie. Katie Brown's Outdoor Entertaining: Taking the Party Outside. Whicheloe, Paul, photos by. (p. 945)
Brown, Kaven L. Two Face. (p. 1803)
Brown, Kay, jt. auth. see Brown, Carl.
Brown, Keisha. Too Serious. (p. 1767)
Brown, Kelli. Yellowstone Park. (p. 1970)
Brown, Kelly, illus. see Collins, Terry.
Brown, Kelly, illus. see Skog, Jason.
Brown, Ken. Scarecrow's Hat Brown, Ken, illus. (p. 1519)
—Why Can't I Fly? (p. 1923)
Brown, Ken, illus. see Day, David.
Brown, Ken, jt. auth. see Brown, Ruth.
Brown, Kevin. In a Field of Sunflowers. (p. 863)
Brown, Kevin, illus. see Bruno, Bonnie.
Brown, Kevin, illus. see Hamilton, Linda.
Brown, Kevin, illus. see Knowlton, Laurie Lazzaro.
Brown, Kevin, illus. see Tidd, Louise Vitellaro.
Brown, Kevin Christian, illus. see Vera, J.
Brown, Kimberly. Autumn Castles. (p. 118)
Brown, Kyle. My Wedding Activity Book. (p. 1221)
Brown, L. McDougal's Feast. (p. 1114)
Brown, Laaren. Scary Snakes. (p. 1520)
—Where in the World? (p. 1908)
Brown, Laaren, jt. auth. see Arlon, Penelope.
Brown, Laaren & Dorling Kindersley Publishing Staff. Children's Illustrated Jewish Bible. Thomas, Eric, illus. (p. 303)
Brown, Laurence J. Housecarl. (p. 804)
Brown, Laurie Krasny. How to Be a Friend. Brown, Marc, illus. (p. 814)
Brown Lcsw, Jennifer. Informacion Disexpectad: La historia de Star se permite a los ninos, padres, y profesionales del salud mental al explorer los emociones e Acciones. (p. 873)
—Star Realizes She Is Not Alone. (p. 1641)
—Star's Unexpected News. (p. 1643)
Brown, Lenoard. Adenture of Paul & Page in Louisiana: (Identical Twins) (p. 12)
—Adventure of Paul & Page in Colorado: (Idennital Twins) (p. 14)
—Adventure of Paul & Page in Hawaii (the Big Island) (Identical Twins) (p. 14)
Brown, Leslie. Not Yet. (p. 1267)
Brown, Lillie Wyatt, illus. see Rome, Jacqueline Thomas.
Brown, Linda, jt. auth. see Brown, S.
Brown, Linda Kayse. Jerboth Weaves a Song. Noble, Penny, illus. (p. 913)
Brown, Linda L., illus. see Brown, S. Glenn.
Brown, Linda L. & Brown, Steven. Cats. (p. 280)
Brown, Linnea, illus. see Briefing Associates Staff.
Brown, Linnet. Keep Your Eyes on the Goal. (p. 947)
—Secrets Can Be Told. (p. 1544)
Brown, Lisa. Baby Do My Banking. (p. 125)
—Baby Fix My Car. (p. 126)
—How to Be. Brown, Lisa, illus. (p. 814)
—Vampire Boy's Good Night. Brown, Lisa, illus. (p. 1832)
Brown, Lisa, illus. see Ascough, Deirdre Mary.
Brown, Lisa, illus. see Daly, Cathleen.
Brown, Lisa, illus. see Ewert, Marcus.
Brown, Lisa, illus. see Gary, Meredith.
Brown, Lisa, illus. see Snicket, Lemony, pseud.
Brown, Lisa, jt. auth. see Griffin, Adele.
Brown, Liz. Bully. (p. 241)
—Civics. (p. 324)
—Dark Ryder. Mclanson, Matt, illus. (p. 408)
—Misty's Revenge. (p. 1155)
—Reference Materials. (p. 1456)
Brown, Lois. Encyclopedia of the Harlem Literary Renaissance: The Essential Guide to the Lives & Works of the Harlem Renaissance Writers. (p. 525)
Brown, Lorna, illus. see Frost, Lulu.
Brown, Louann Mattes & Nemeth, Jason D. How to Create Spectacular Halloween Costumes (p. 816)
Brown, Luke. Essie's Kids & the Rolling Calf - 3: Island Style Story. (p. 537)
Brown, Luke & Brown, Berthalicia. Essie's Kids & the Rolling Calf - 4: Island Style Storybook. (p. 537)
—Just Another Day in Essie's Family. (p. 937)
Brown, Lyle C. Study Guide: Used with ... Brown-Practicing Texas Politics. (p. 1670)
Brown, Mae. Adorable You! Cecil, Randy, illus. (p. 13)
Brown, Marc. Arthur & the 1,001 Dads Brown, Marc, illus. (p. 103)
—Arthur & the Baby. Brown, Marc, illus. (p. 103)
—Arthur & the Bad-Luck Brain (p. 103)
—Arthur & the Bad-Luck Brain. (p. 103)
—Arthur & the Big Snow. Brown, Marc, illus. (p. 103)
—Arthur & the Comet Crisis. (p. 103)
—Arthur & the Cootie-Catcher (p. 103)
—Arthur & the Dog Show. (p. 103)
—Arthur & the Double Dare. (p. 103)
—Arthur & the Lost Diary. (p. 103)
—Arthur & the Mystery of the Stolen Bike. (p. 103)
—Arthur & the Nerves of Steal. (p. 103)
—Arthur & the No-Brainer. (p. 103)
—Arthur & the Poetry Contest. (p. 103)
—Arthur & the Popularity Test. (p. 103)
—Arthur & the School Pet. (p. 103)
—Arthur & the True Francine. (p. 103)
—Arthur & the World Record. (p. 103)
—Arthur Goes to Camp. Brown, Marc, illus. (p. 103)
—Arthur Helps Out. (p. 103)
—Arthur in New York. (p. 103)
—Arthur Jumps into Fall. (p. 103)
—Arthur Locked in the Library! (p. 103)
—Arthur Loses His Marbles. (p. 103)
—Arthur Lost & Found. (p. 103)
—Arthur Lost in the Museum. (p. 103)
—Arthur Plays the Blues. (p. 104)
—Arthur Rocks with Binky. (p. 104)
—Arthur Tells a Story. (p. 104)
—Arthur to the Rescue. (p. 104)
—Arthur Turns Green. (p. 104)
—Arthur Writes a Story. (p. 104)
—Arthur's Birthday Surprise. (p. 104)
—Arthur's Classroom Fib. (p. 104)
—Arthur's Classroom Fib (Step-into-Reading Level 3) (p. 104)
—Arthur's Computer Disaster. (p. 104)
—Arthur's Family Vacation. (p. 104)
—Arthur's Heart Mix-Up. (p. 104)
—Arthur's Homework. (p. 104)
—Arthur's Jelly Beans. (p. 104)
—Arthur's Mystery Babysitter. Brown, Marc, illus. (p. 104)
—Arthur's New Puppy. (p. 104)
—Arthur's off to School. (p. 104)
—Arthur's Perfect Christmas. (p. 104)
—Arthur's Pet Business. Brown, Marc, illus. (p. 104)
—Arthur's Reading Trick. (p. 104)
—Arthur's Teacher Trouble. (p. 104)
—Arthur's Tooth. Brown, Marc, illus. (p. 104)
—Arthur's Tree House. (p. 104)
—Arthur's Underwear. (p. 104)
—Arthur's Valentine. (p. 104)
—Arturo y el Misterioso Sobre. Sarfatti, Esther, tr. from ENG. (p. 105)
—Buster Climbs the Walls. (p. 245)
—Buster Hits the Trail. (p. 245)
—Buster Makes the Grade. (p. 245)
—Buster Plays Along. (p. 245)
—Buster's Dino Dilemma. (p. 245)
—Buster's Sugartime. (p. 245)
—D. W. la Quisquillosa. Sarfatti, Esther, tr. from ENG. (p. 398)
—D W's Library Card. (p. 398)
—D. W. Says Please & Thank You. (p. 398)
—D. W. the Big Boss. (p. 398)
—D. W.'s Library Card. Brown, Marc, illus. (p. 398)
—D. W.'s Perfect Present. Brown, Marc, illus. (p. 398)
—Francine, Believe It or Not. (p. 627)
—Good Night, D. W. Brown, Marc, illus. (p. 699)
—In New York. (p. 864)
—King Arthur. (p. 958)
—Marc Brown Arthur: King Arthur; Francine, Believe it or Not; Arthur & the Cootie-Catcher; (p. 1091)
—Marc Brown's Arthur: Arthur & the Scare-Your-Pants-off Club; Arthur Makes the Team. (p. 1091)
—Marc Brown's Arthur: Arthur & the Crunch Cereal Contest; Arthur Accused!; Locked in the Library. (p. 1091)
—Marc Brown's Arthur: Buster's Dino Dilemma; the Mystery of the Stolen Bike; Arthur & the Lost Diary. (p. 1091)
—Marc Brown's Playtime Rhymes: A Treasury for Families to Learn & Play Together. (p. 1091)
—Monkey: Not Ready for the Baby. (p. 1164)
—Monkey: Not Ready for Kindergarten. (p. 1164)
—Mystery of the Stolen Bike. (p. 1226)
—Visita del Senor Rataquemada. Sarfatti, Esther, tr. from ENG. (p. 1845)
—Who's in Love with Arthur? (p. 1920)
Brown, Marc, illus. see Brown, Laurie Krasny.
Brown, Marc, illus. see Christian, Mary Blount.
Brown, Marc, illus. see Craig, Lindsey.
Brown, Marc, illus. see Pinder, Eric.
Brown, Marc, illus. see Sierra, Judy.
Brown, Marc, illus. see Stine, R. L.
Brown, Marc, illus. see Wolkstein, Diane.
Brown, Marc, jt. auth. see Krensky, Stephen.
Brown, Marc, tr. see Sierra, Judy.
Brown, Marc & Sarfatti, Esther. Arturo y la Navidad. (p. 105)
—D. W. y el Carne de Biblioteca. (p. 398)
Brown, Marci, jt. auth. see Haley, Dennis.
Brown, Marcy & Haley, Dennis. We Both Read Bilingual Edition-The Well-Mannered Monster/el Monstruo Debuenos Modales. Raglin, Tim, illus. (p. 1866)
—We Both Read-Just Five More Minutes! Kulka, Joe, illus. (p. 1866)
—We Both Read-The Well-Mannered Monster. Raglin, Tim, illus. (p. 1866)
—We Both Read-the Well-Mannered Monster. Raglin, Tim, illus. (p. 1866)
Brown, Marcy, et al. Well-Mannered Monster: Monstruo de Buenos Modales. Raglin, Tim, illus. (p. 1874)
Brown, Margaret. On Christmas Day. Harris, Phyllis, illus. (p. 1288)
Brown, Margaret, illus. see Schoeningh, Debby.
Brown, Margaret Wise. Around the World We Go! (p. 101)
—Baby's Gift: Goodnight Moon & the Runaway Bunny Hurd, Clement, illus. (p. 129)
—Boa Noite Lua. (p. 205)
—Bonsoir Lune. (p. 209)
—Buenas Noches Conejito. (p. 235)
—Buenas Noches Luna. Mlawer, Teresa, tr. from ENG. (p. 235)
—Buenas Noches Oso. (p. 235)
—Celebration of the Seasons. (p. 285)
—Child's Good Morning Book. Katz, Karen, illus. (p. 305)
—Christmas in the Barn. Goode, Diane, illus. (p. 314)
—Color Kittens. Provensen, Alice & Provensen, Martin, illus. (p. 342)
—Color Kittens. Provensen, Martin & Provensen, Alice, illus. (p. 342)
—Conejito Andarin. Marcuse, Aida E., tr. (p. 356)
—Dead Bird. (p. 416)
—Dead Bird. Robinson, Christian, illus. (p. 416)
—Dirty Little Boy Salerno, Steven, illus. (p. 446)
—Dream Book. (p. 483)
—Fathers Are Coming Home. Savage, Stephen, illus. (p. 577)
—Fierce Yellow Pumpkin. Egielski, Richard, illus. (p. 584)
—Friendly Book. Williams, Garth, illus. (p. 637)
—Give Yourself to the Rain: Poems for the Very Young. Weidner, Teri, illus. (p. 681)
—Golden Bunny. Weisgard, Leonard, illus. (p. 694)
—Golden Egg Book. Weisgard, Leonard, illus. (p. 694)
—Goodnight Moon. Hurd, Clement, illus. (p. 701)
—Goodnight Moon 1 2 3: A Counting Book. Hurd, Clement, illus. (p. 701)
—Goodnight Moon 123: A Counting Book. Hurd, Clement, illus. (p. 701)
—Goodnight Moon 123 Lap Edition. Hurd, Clement, illus. (p. 701)
—Goodnight Moon 123/Buenas Noches, Luna 123: A Counting Book/un Libro para Contar. Hurd, Clement, illus. (p. 701)
—Goodnight Moon ABC: An Alphabet Book. Hurd, Clement, illus. (p. 701)
—Goodnight Moon ABC Padded Board Book: An Alphabet Book. Hurd, Clement, illus. (p. 701)
—Goodnight Moon Board Book & Bunny. Hurd, Clement, illus. (p. 701)
—Goodnight Moon Classic Library: Contains Goodnight Moon, the Runaway Bunny, & My World. Hurd, Clement, illus. (p. 701)
—Goodnight Moon Cloth Book Box. Hurd, Clement, illus. (p. 701)
—Goodnight Moon/Buenas Noches, Luna. Hurd, Clement, illus. (p. 701)
—Goodnight Songs: Illustrated by Twelve Award-Winning Picture Book Artists. (p. 701)
—Gran Granero Rojo. Bond, Felicia, illus. (p. 706)
—Home for a Bunny. Williams, Garth, illus. (p. 792)
—I Like Fish. (p. 841)
—Little Fir Tree. LaMarche, Jim, illus. (p. 1027)

—Little Fur Family. Williams, Garth, illus. (p. 1028)
—Little Island. Weisgard, Leonard, illus. (p. 1029)
—Little Lost Lamb. (p. 1031)
—Little Scarecrow Boy. Diaz, David, illus. (p. 1036)
—Margaret Wise Brown's the Golden Bunny. Weisgard, Leonard, illus. (p. 1092)
—Mister Dog. Williams, Garth, illus. (p. 1155)
—Mon Petit Monde (French edition of My World) (p. 1163)
—My World: A Companion to Goodnight Moon. Hurd, Clement, illus. (p. 1221)
—My World. Hurd, Clement, illus. (p. 1221)
—Nibble Nibble. Minor, Wendell, illus. (p. 1250)
—Noisy Book Treasury. Weisgard, Leonard, illus. (p. 1263)
—Over the Moon: Goodnight Moon, the Runaway Bunny, & My World. Hurd, Clement, illus. (p. 1314)
—Pussycat's Christmas. Mortimer, Anne, illus. (p. 1420)
—Runaway Bunny. Hurd, Clement, illus. (p. 1496)
—Sleepy ABC. Katz, Karen, illus. (p. 1589)
—Sneakers, the Seaside Cat. Mortimer, Anne, illus. (p. 1597)
—Songs from the Earth. (p. 1612)
—Two Little Trains. Dillon, Leo & Dillon, Diane, illus. (p. 1804)
—Where Have You Been? (p. 1907)
—Where Have You Been? Dillon, Leo & Dillon, Diane, illus. (p. 1907)
Brown, Margaret Wise, jt. auth. see Hurd, Edith Thacher.
Brown, Margaret Wise & Brown. Another Important Book. Raschka, Chris, illus. (p. 87)
—Fierce Yellow Pumpkin. Egielski, Richard, illus. (p. 584)
Brown, Margaret Wise & Brown, Wise M. Buenas Noches, Luna. Mlawer, Teresa, tr. from ENG. (p. 235)
Brown, Margaret Wise & Golden Books Staff. Friendly Tales. (p. 638)
Brown, Margery W. Afro-Bets Book of Shapes. Blair, Culverson & Simpson, Howard, illus. (p. 28)
—Baby Jesus Like My Brother. (p. 126)
—Book of Colors: Meet the Color Family. Blair, Culverson & Simpson, Howard, illus. (p. 211)
Brown, Mari, illus. see Rowlinson, Joanne.
Brown, Mari, illus. see Wuehr, Tina L.
Brown, Marilyn, illus. see Kupchella, Rick.
Brown, Marion, illus. see McDonald, Marion.
Brown, Marion, jt. ed. see Taylor, Julie.
Brown, Marjon Brady. Cowgirl Charity's Quest for Kindness. (p. 374)
Brown, Mark. Tommy Books: Faith Mekis, Pete, illus. (p. 1764)
—Tommy Books: Kings Mekis, Pete, illus. (p. 1764)
—Tommy Books: Love Vol. 2 Mekis, Pete, illus. (p. 1764)
—Tommy Books: Praise Vol. 4 Mekis, Pete, illus. (p. 1764)
—Tommy Books: Too Busy Vol. 3 Mekis, Pete, illus. (p. 1764)
Brown, Martin, illus. see Deary, Terry.
Brown, Marty. Infogirl: A Girl's Guide to the Internet. (p. 873)
—Webmaster. (p. 1870)
Brown, Mary. Ear for Graci. (p. 492)
Brown, Mary Barrett, illus. see Esbensen, Barbara Juster.
Brown, Mary Jo. Bailey Brown: Bailey's New Home. (p. 133)
Brown, Matt, photos by see Bunnett, Rochelle.
Brown, Maureen E. Tanker's Adventures in Monterey. Brown, Michael D., illus. (p. 1705)
Brown, Melony A. Solving Word Problems for Life, Grades 6-8 (p. 1608)
Brown, Merry. Gold Manor Ghost House. (p. 693)
—Second Fall. (p. 1539)
Brown, Mia. Goodnight Joy! Abdullah, Tariq, illus. (p. 701)
Brown, Michael, illus. see Claycomb, Patty.
Brown, Michael D., illus. see Brown, Maureen E.
Brown, Michael R. Susquehanna. (p. 1688)
Brown, Michele. New Tales from Alice's Wonderland: Dinah Plays Hide & Seek. Martyr, Paula, illus. (p. 1247)
—New Tales from Alice's Wonderland: The Queen of Hearts & the Wibbly Wobbly Jelly. Martyr, Paula, illus. (p. 1247)
Brown, Michelle Haney. My First Book of Japanese Words: An ABC Rhyming Book. Padron, Aya, illus. (p. 1205)
Brown, Mick. From Round about Midnight until about Five! (p. 643)
Brown, Mike. Rescue Services. (p. 1462)
—Ted's Simple Truth: His First Adventure. (p. 1713)
Brown, Mike, jt. auth. see Harris, Carol.
Brown, Monica. Butterflies on Carmen Street/Mariposas en la Calle Carmen. Ward, April, illus. (p. 247)
—Chavela's Magic Chicle. Morales, Magaly, illus. (p. 295)
—Lado a Lado: La Historia de Dolores Huerta y Cesar Chavez. Cepeda, Joe, illus. (p. 970)
—Marisol McDonald & the Clash Bash/Marisol Mcdonald y la Fiesta Sin Igual. Palacios, Sara, illus. (p. 1094)
—Marisol Mcdonald Doesn't Match / Marisol Mcdonald no Combina. Palacios, Sara, illus. (p. 1094)
—My Name Is Celia: The Life of Celia Cruz. López, Rafael, illus. (p. 1215)
—My Name Is Gabito: The Life of Gabriel Garcia Marquez. Colón, Raúl, illus. (p. 1215)
—My Name Is Gabito/Me Llamo Gabito: The Life of Gabriel Garcia Marquez/la Vida de Gabriel Garcia Marquez. Colón, Raúl, illus. (p. 1215)
—My Name Is Gabriela/Me Llamo Gabriela: The Life of Gabriela Mistral/la Vida de Gabriela Mistral. Parra, John, illus. (p. 1215)
—Pablo Neruda: Poet of the People. Paschkis, Julie, illus. (p. 1316)
—Pelé, King of Soccer (Pelé, el Rey del Fútbol) Gayesky, Fernando, tr. (p. 1335)
—Tito Puente: Mambo King; Rey del Mambo. López, Rafael, illus. (p. 1758)
—Waiting for the Biblioburro. Parra, John, illus. (p. 1853)
Brown, Monica & Dominguez, Adriana. Maya's Blanket Diaz, David, illus. (p. 1113)
Brown, Monica & Musgrave, Hilary. Be Still & know... God Is Here: Be Still. (p. 149)
Brown, Monica & Ventura, Gabriela Baeza. Clara & the Curandera / Clara y la Curandera. Muraida, Thelma, illus. (p. 326)
Brown, Natalie. Who Was Alexander Graham Bell? (p. 1918)
Brown, Natasha. Prodigy. Rosenbaum, Bev, ed. (p. 1409)
Brown, Nick, illus. see Miro.
Brown, Nick, jt. auth. see Brown, Cynthia Light.
Brown, Palmer. Beyond the Pawpaw Trees. Brown, Palmer, illus. (p. 174)
—Cheerful. (p. 296)
—Hickory. Brown, Palmer, illus. (p. 775)
—Silver Nutmeg. Brown, Palmer, illus. (p. 1576)
—Something for Christmas. Brown, Palmer, illus. (p. 1609)
Brown, Pam. Dear Delilia: New & Selected Poems. (p. 418)
Brown, Pamela. Annie's Attitude on Bullying. (p. 87)
—Barnyard Buddies II. Hutchins, Annie H., illus. (p. 139)
Brown, Pat. Penny for Your Thoughts. (p. 1338)
Brown, Patrica A. & Krelle, Ginger R. Classroom Hydroponic Plant Factory (p. 329)
Brown, Paul. Still Another Time , Times Remembered. (p. 1650)
Brown, Paul Henry. Grandpa Still Remembers: Life Changing Stories for Kids of All Ages from a Missionary Kid in Africa. Deborah, Brown Armes, illus. (p. 709)
Brown, Pauline A. Cat Tales. Burke, Ruth Anne, illus. (p. 278)
Brown, Peggy. Little Golden Book of Jokes & Riddles. Sheldon, David, illus. (p. 1028)
Brown, Peggy & Lovett, Nate. Everything Girls Super Cute Kawaii Fun Book: Tons of Creative, Fun Kawaii Activities—Doodles, Games, Crafts, & More! (p. 544)
Brown, Penny & Washington, Joi. How the Tiger Takes Care of Her Babies. Washington, Joi, illus. (p. 813)
Brown, Peter. Children Make Terrible Pets. (p. 302)
—Chowder. (p. 311)
—Curious Garden. (p. 393)
—Flight of the Dodo. (p. 604)
—Mr. Tiger Goes Wild. Brown, Peter, ed. (p. 1186)
—My Teacher Is a Monster! (No, I Am Not.) (p. 1220)
—You Will Be My Friend! (p. 1976)
Brown, Peter, illus. see Black, Michael Ian.
Brown, Peter, illus. see Kimmel, Haven.
Brown, Peter, illus. see Reynolds, Aaron.
Brown, Petra. Hush, Little Baby. (p. 830)
Brown, Petra, illus. see Gilmore, Grace.
Brown, Petra, illus. see Houran, Lori Haskins.
Brown, Petra, illus. see James, Helen Foster.
Brown, Petra, illus. see Morpurgo, Michael.
Brown, Petra, illus. see Raven, Margot Theis.
Brown, Petra, illus. see Shoshan, Beth.
Brown, Philip. Franky Franklyn's Fantastic Adventure. (p. 631)
—Franky Franklyn's Philadelphia Adventure. (p. 631)
Brown, Phillip A. Haywood & Mel: Haywood Wants to Quit (p. 756)
Brown, Phoenix. I Love to Exercise. Collins, Courtney, illus. (p. 843)
Brown, Rachael. Faerie Wings. (p. 562)
Brown, Rachel K. Daily Life in a Southern Colonial Town: St. Augustine. (p. 399)
—Sacramento: Daily Life in a Western Mining Town. (p. 1500)
—Santa Fe: Daily Life in a Western Trading Center. (p. 1511)
Brown, Rebecca. Wisdom of my Youth. (p. 1939)
Brown Reference Group. History of Invention Set. (p. 784)
Brown Reference Group PLC. Encyclopedia of Art for Young People Kwint, Marius, ed. (p. 524)
Brown Reference Group Staff. Revolutionary War. (p. 1466)
Brown, Rena Cherry. Otter Lee Brave Maidment, Mikaila, illus. (p. 1307)
Brown, Rev. Joe. God's Gift, G G Brown: A True Story. (p. 691)
Brown, Rhonda Sue. Misty the Butterfly (p. 1155)
Brown, Rich. Magic Tails Chapter 2: Window to the Universe. (p. 1073)
Brown, Richard. Snow in the Kitchen. (p. 1599)
—Wait for Us! (p. 1852)
—Welsh Lamb. (p. 1874)
Brown, Richard, illus. see Clark, Diane C. & Harcourt, Inc Staff.
Brown, Richard, illus. see Wissinger, Tamera Will & Long, Earlene R.
Brown, Richard, illus. see Ziefert, Harriet.
Brown, Richard E., illus. see Black, Joe.
Brown, Richard P., et al. Rhodiola Revolution: Transform Your Health with the Herbal Breakthrough of the 21st Century. (p. 1468)
Brown, Rick. Hooray for the 4th of July! (p. 796)
Brown, Rick, illus. see Black, Joe.
Brown, Rick, illus. see Jules, Jacqueline & Hechtkopf, Jacqueline.
Brown, Riley S. Edward & the Enfeebled: Book Two of the Wunderland Novels. (p. 505)
Brown, Riley S., ed. Little Taste of Different. (p. 1037)
Brown, Risa. Blake Shelton. (p. 198)
—Day by Day with Carrie Underwood. (p. 412)
—Pit Bull. (p. 1364)
—South America. (p. 1616)
Brown, Robert. We Are Eternal: What the Spirits Tell Me about Life after Death. (p. 1865)
Brown, Robert, illus. see Kudlinski, Kathleen.
Brown, Robert L. Daddy Grows Colors (p. 398)
Brown, Roberta, illus. see Barry, Dave & Pearson, Ridley.
Brown, Roberta Simpson. Queen of the Cold-Blooded Tales. Hall, Wendell E., illus. (p. 1425)
—Scared in School. (p. 1519)
—Walking Trees & Other Scary Stories. (p. 1854)
Brown, Robin. Advanced Verbal Response. (p. 13)
—Practice Papers: Maths. (p. 1392)
—Practice Papers: English. (p. 1392)
—Practice Papers: Advanced Maths. (p. 1392)
—Practice Papers: Advanced Non-Verbal Reasoning. (p. 1392)
Brown, Robin C. Crafts of Florida's First People. (p. 376)
Brown, Rod, illus. see Shange, Ntozake.
Brown, Roger A. Adventures of Woolee the Blanket & Friends: Book Number 1: the Miracle of Giving Love. (p. 24)
Brown, Roland & Scarborough, Kate. Hot Bikes. (p. 801)
Brown, Ron. Three-Toes the Raccoon Visits the Farm. (p. 1744)
Brown, Ron, illus. see Hauser, Sheri.
Brown, Rosie L. Zach & Rob's Journey: The Lost Eggs. (p. 1984)
Brown, Roslind Varghese & Spilling, Michael. Tunisia. (p. 1797)
Brown, Ruby. My Dad Is a Superhero. Vamos, Lesley, illus. (p. 1201)
—My Mum Is a Superhero. Vamos, Lesley, illus. (p. 1215)
Brown, Russ. Daisy the Donkey's First Fare. (p. 400)
—Poppy's Planet! (p. 1385)
Brown, Ruth. Big Sneeze. (p. 184)
—Christmas Mouse. (p. 314)
—Dark, Dark Tale. (p. 407)
—Diez Semillas. Ponce, Mari Luz, tr. (p. 437)
—Gracie, the Lighthouse Cat. Brown, Ruth, illus. (p. 705)
—Greyfriars Bobby. Brown, Ruth, illus. (p. 723)
—Monkey's Friends. Brown, Ruth, illus. (p. 1166)
—Snail Trail. Brown, Ruth, illus. (p. 1596)
—Tale of Two Mice. Brown, Ruth, illus. (p. 1700)
—Ten Seeds. (p. 1719)
Brown, Ruth, illus. see Fine, Anne.
Brown, Ruth, illus. see Forward, Toby.
Brown, Ruth, illus. see Herriot, James.
Brown, Ruth, jt. auth. see Brown, Ruth.
Brown, Ruth Alberta. Tabitha's Vacation. (p. 1694)
Brown, Ruth & Brown, Ken. Lion in the Long Grass. (p. 1020)
Brown, Ruth & Brown, Ruth. Imagine. Brown, Ruth, illus. (p. 860)
Brown, Ruth E. Goontoff Kingdom Chronicles: The Bogus King. (p. 702)
Brown, Ruth Tepper. Smithsonian Discover: Flight. (p. 1594)
Brown, Ryan A., jt. auth. see Wright, R. Thomas.
Brown, Ryan K., jt. auth. see Brown, Walter C.
Brown, S. Storm Girl: Who Knows What's Real? (p. 1656)
Brown, S. & Brown, Linda. Bugs. Brown, S., illus. (p. 237)
Brown, S. Glenn. Cats. Brown, Linda L. & Brown, S. Glenn, illus. (p. 280)
Brown, Sam. Herbert: I Am - I Can. (p. 769)
—Sometimes I Forget You're a Robot. (p. 1610)
Brown, Sam E. One, Two, Buckle My Shoe: Math Activities for Young Children. Libonn, Julia, illus. (p. 1297)
Brown, Samuel. When in Doubt, Check Him Out: You Have the Power. (p. 1903)
Brown, Sandra. Crush. (p. 386)
Brown, Sandra, jt. auth. see St. Claire, Erin, pseud.
Brown, Sandra, see St. Claire, Erin, pseud.
Brown, Sandra L. How to Spot a Dangerous Man Before You Get Involved: Describes 8 Types of Dangerous Men, Gives Defense Strategies & a Red Alert Checklist for Each, & Includes Stories of Successes & Failures. (p. 821)
Brown, Sharon. Nana, Tell Me a Story. (p. 1228)
Brown, Sheila. Crime & Law in Media Culture. (p. 382)
Brown, Sheila M. Dog Named Ben & His Two Best Friends. (p. 461)
Brown, Sheron, jt. auth. see Adams, Gail.
Brown, Skila. Caminar. (p. 256)
Brown, Sonja. David Lawrence & his Game Day Chocolate Chip Pancakes. (p. 411)
Brown Sr., David F. Tabby Goes to School: The First in the Tabatha Adventures Series Brown Jr., David F., illus. (p. 1694)
Brown, Staci. Beary Bad Trouble. (p. 152)
Brown, Stacia Bradley. Family of His Own. DeKnight, Cathy, illus. (p. 568)
Brown, Stephanie Gwyn, jt. auth. see Evans, Nate.
Brown, Steven, jt. auth. see Brown, Steven T.
Brown, Steven, jt. illus. see Brown, Linda L.
Brown, Steven T. & Brown, Steven. Cinema Anime: Critical Engagements with Japanese Animation. (p. 321)
Brown, Stevi, illus. see Goodall, Barry, Jr.
Brown, Susan. Tiny Body, Huge Love: The Story of Skyler Sue. (p. 1756)
Brown, Susan Taylor. Enrique Esparza & the Battle of the Alamo. (p. 531)
—Enrique Esparza & the Battle of the Alamo. Reeves, Jeni, illus. (p. 531)
—Oliver's Must-Do List. Sullivan, Mary, illus. (p. 1286)
—Robert Smalls Sails to Freedom. Marshall, Felicia, illus. (p. 1479)
Brown, Susie, jt. auth. see Warner, Margaret.
Brown, Suzanne. Night Before Christmas in Ski Country. Schlingman, Dana, illus. (p. 1253)
Brown, Suzy, illus. see Kirk, Bill.
Brown, Sylvia & Struck, Mary Dowd. Post-Pregnancy Handbook: The Only Book That Tells What the First Year after Childbirth Is Really All about - Physically, Emotionally, Sexually. (p. 1387)
Brown, Tahiera Monique. Annihilator of Innocence: That Old Man. (p. 87)
Brown, Tameka Fryer. Around Our Way on Neighbors' Day. Riley-Webb, Charlotte, illus. (p. 100)
—My Cold Plum Lemon Pie Bluesy Mood. Evans, Shane, illus. (p. 1200)
Brown, Tami Lewis. Soar, Elinor! Roca, François, illus. (p. 1603)
Brown, Tara. First Kiss. (p. 595)
—Imaginations. (p. 860)
—White Girl Problems. (p. 1913)
Brown, Tempe. Little Dirt People. Brown, Tempe, illus. (p. 1026)
Brown, Tena L. Tena, Joshua & Friends Brown, Tena L., illus. (p. 1719)
Brown, Teri. Born of Deception. (p. 214)
—Born of Illusion. (p. 214)
—Read My Lips. (p. 1443)
—Velvet Undercover. (p. 1835)
Brown, Terrell. Mary J. Blige. (p. 1100)
—Pharell Williams. (p. 1350)
—Pharrell Williams. (p. 1350)
—Reverend Run (Run-D. M. C.) (p. 1466)
Brown, Tessa. Costume Crafts. (p. 368)
Brown, Tiffanie & Duncan, Kathryn. Benny Builds a House. (p. 165)
Brown, Tiffany M. Gallery Eleven Twenty-Two. Sefcik, Wendy, illus. (p. 653)
Brown, Tim, illus. see Vernick, Audrey Glassman & Gidaro, Ellen Glassman.
Brown, Tim, jt. auth. see DeLuise, Dom.
Brown, Timothy E. W. Grandma's Spirit. (p. 709)
Brown, Tina. My Haunted Summer Holiday. (p. 1210)
Brown, Toni Sorenson. Heroes of the Book of Mormon. (p. 773)
—I Can't Go to Church. Jolley, Mack, illus. (p. 837)
Brown, Toni Sorenson, photos by. Heroes of the Bible. (p. 773)
Brown, Tonny. ADV of Jack & Sidney. (p. 13)
Brown, Tori. Today, Every Day, for Always. (p. 1760)
Brown, Tracy. Cyberbullying: Online Safety. (p. 396)
—Facebook Safety & Privacy. (p. 560)
—Frequently Asked Questions about Same-Sex Marriage & When a Parent Is Gay. (p. 636)
—Jeff Hardy: Bound for Glory. (p. 911)
—John Cena: World Wrestling Champ. (p. 921)
—Staging & Choreography. (p. 1638)
—Stephenie Meyer. (p. 1648)
—White Lines. (p. 1913)
Brown, Trent. 3T Chronicles: Talbert the Chef. (p. 1992)
—3T Chronicles. (p. 1992)
Brown, Tricia. Alaskan Night Before Christmas Stacy, Alan, illus. (p. 34)
—Charlie & the Blanket Toss. Martinsen, Sarah, illus. (p. 292)
—Groucho's Eyebrows: An Alaskan Cat Tale. Lavallee, Barbara, illus. (p. 725)
—Itchy Little Musk Ox. Dubac, Debra, illus. (p. 895)
—Musher's Night Before Christmas Dubac, Debra, illus. (p. 1193)
—Patsy Ann of Alaska: The True Story of a Dog. Fowler, Jim, illus. (p. 1329)
Brown, Tryla. Pink Shirt - Blue Shirt. (p. 1360)
Brown, Tyree. Combing Out the N. A. P. S. (p. 347)
Brown, Urian, ed. see Konomi, Takeshi.
Brown, Valcine. Love after Rain. Hayes, Rebecca, ed. (p. 1059)
Brown, Vandella. Mouse... Have Yourself a Merry Little Christmas Day. (p. 1182)
Brown, Vanessa. Alabama. (p. 33)
—Arizona. (p. 98)
—Arkansas. (p. 99)
—Arkansas. Brusca, Maria Cristina, tr. (p. 99)
—Connecticut. (p. 357)
—Delaware. (p. 424)
—District of Columbia. (p. 454)
—District of Columbia/Distrito de Columbia. (p. 454)
—Georgia. (p. 665)
—Idaho. (p. 851)
—Idaho. Brusca, Maria Cristina, tr. (p. 851)
—Illinois. (p. 857)
—Indiana. (p. 871)
—Iowa. (p. 886)
—Kentucky. (p. 949)
—Kentucky. Brusca, Maria Cristina, tr. (p. 949)
—Louisiana. (p. 1058)
—Louisiana/Luisiana. (p. 1059)
—Maryland. (p. 1101)
—Minnesota. (p. 1147)
—Minnesota. Brusca, Maria Cristina, tr. (p. 1147)
—Mississippi. (p. 1154)
—Mississippi. Brusca, Maria Cristina, tr. (p. 1154)
—Montana. (p. 1170)
—Montana. Brusca, Maria Cristina, tr. from ENG. (p. 1170)
—New Jersey. (p. 1245)
—New Jersey/Nueva Jersey. Brusca, Maria Cristina, tr. from ENG. (p. 1245)
—North Dakota. (p. 1265)
—North Dakota/Dakota del Norte. Brusca, Maria Cristina, tr. from ENG. (p. 1265)
—Oklahoma. (p. 1282)
—Oklahoma. Brusca, Maria Cristina, tr. from ENG. (p. 1282)
—South Dakota/Dakota del Sur. Brusca, Maria Cristina, tr. from ENG. (p. 1617)
—Tennessee. (p. 1720)
—Tennessee. Brusca, Maria Cristina, tr. from ENG. (p. 1720)
—Wyoming. (p. 1966)
Brown, Vinson. Californian Wildlife Region. (p. 253)
Brown, Vinson, jt. auth. see Allan, David.
Brown, Virginia Pounds. Gold Disc of Coosa. (p. 693)
Brown, Virginia Pounds & Owens, Laurella. World of the Southern Indians: Tribes, Leaders, & Customs from Prehistoric Times to the Present. Glick, Nathan H., illus. (p. 1957)
Brown, Virginia Pounds & Owens, Laurella, eds. Southern Indian Myths & Legends. Glick, Nathan, illus. (p. 1617)
Brown, W. C. Adventures of Clever Coyote. Hilty, Bertha, illus. (p. 17)
Brown, W. Gregory, 8th. Through the Ocean Window. (p. 1745)
Brown, Walter C. Basic Mathematics: Text. (p. 142)
—Basic Mathematics. (p. 142)
Brown, Walter C. & Brown, Ryan K. Print Reading for Industry. (p. 1406)
Brown, Walter C. & Dorfmueller, Daniel P. Print Reading for Construction: Residential & Commercial. (p. 1406)
—Print Reading for Construction: Teaching Package Powerpoint Presentations. (p. 1406)
—Print Reading for Construction Instructor's Guide: Residential & Commercial. (p. 1406)
Brown, Walter C. & Kicklighter, Clois E. Drafting for Industry. (p. 476)
Brown, Walter M., jt. auth. see George, Pamela.
Brown, Wanda E. Great Escape (from Loneliness) A Dragon Safe Ending Book. (p. 715)
Brown, William Wells. Black Man, His Antecedents, His Genius, & His Achievements. (p. 196)
Brown, Wise M., jt. auth. see Brown, Margaret Wise.
Brown, Zachary. Darkside War. (p. 409)
Brown-Avery, Cheryl. Annie the Mule Goes to the State Fair. (p. 87)
Brown-Brown, Sharon. Daddy Keeps Losing His Keys! (p. 398)
Browne, A. SunBirds: #3 Great Lengths. (p. 1676)
Browne, Anita, illus. see Rice, Ruth Mason & Villar, Rose.
Browne, Anthony. Gorilla (30th Anniversary Edition) (p. 703)

B

—How Do You Feel? Browne, Anthony, illus. (p. 808)
—Little Bear Book. Browne, Anthony, illus. (p. 1024)
—Little Beauty. (p. 1024)
—Little Beauty. Browne, Anthony, illus. (p. 1024)
—Me & You. Browne, Anthony, illus. (p. 1115)
—Mi Mama. Fuentes Silva, Andrea, tr. (p. 1132)
—My Mom. Browne, Anthony, illus. (p. 1214)
—One Gorilla. Browne, Anthony, illus. (p. 1295)
—One Gorilla: a Counting Book. Browne, Anthony, illus. (p. 1295)
—Things I Like. (p. 1733)
—What If... ? Browne, Anthony, illus. (p. 1887)
Browne, Anton & Skinner, Tony. Popular Music Vocals, Grades 1-8. (p. 1385)
Browne, Barber & Browne, Lee. Charles Dickens. (p. 292)
Browne, Eileen. Handa's Hen. (p. 740)
—Handa's Hen. Browne, Eileen, illus. (p. 740)
—Handa's Surprise: Read & Share. (p. 740)
—Handa's Surprise: Read & Share. Browne, Eileen, illus. (p. 740)
—Handa's Surprise. Browne, Eileen, illus. (p. 740)
—Mary Had a Dinosaur. Rivers, Ruth, illus. (p. 1100)
—Wait for Me! (p. 1852)
Browne, Eileen, illus. see Bradman, Tony & Quarto Generic Staff.
Browne, Eileen, illus. see Bradman, Tony.
Browne, Eileen & Habashi, Azza. Handa's Surprise: Read & Share. (p. 740)
Browne, Frank, photos by see O'Donnell, E. E.
Browne, G. Waldo. With Rogers' Rangers: Woodranger Tales. (p. 1942)
Browne, Gordon, illus. see Corkran, Alice.
Browne, Hetty S. & Sarah Withers. Child s World. (p. 301)
Browne, James, illus. see Licht, Sharon.
Browne, Lee, jt. auth. see Browne, Barber.
Browne, Paula. Cumpleanos de la Mona. Isabel, Isaias, tr. (p. 392)
—Paca, la macaca en la Cocina. Isabel, Isaias, tr. (p. 1317)
—Paca, la macaca va al Mercado. Isabel, Isaias, tr. (p. 1317)
—Que Desbarajuste, Paca. Isabel, Isaias, tr. (p. 1423)
Browne, Philippa-Alys. "Bushbaby blinks" (African Animals ABC) (p. 244)
—"Giraffe dozes" (African Animals ABC) (p. 677)
—"Hippo sleeps" (African Animals ABC) (p. 781)
—"Lion roars" (African Animals ABC) (p. 1020)
Browne, Susan Chalker. Freddy's Day at the Races Rose, Hilda, illus. (p. 633)
—Freddy's Hockey Hero Rose, Hilda, illus. (p. 633)
—Hey Freddy! It's Canada's Birthday! Rose, Hilda, illus. (p. 774)
—Land of a Thousand Whales Keating, Nancy, illus. (p. 973)
Browne, Sylvia. Mystical Life of Jesus: An Uncommon Perspective on the Life of Christ. (p. 1226)
Browne, Vee. Stone Cutter & the Navajo Maiden. Manavi, Lorraine Begay, tr. from ENG. (p. 1652)
Browne, Yolanda. Getting Ready for Christmas. Girouard, Patrick, illus. (p. 669)
Brownell, Celia A. & Kopp, Claire B., eds. Socioemotional Development in the Toddler Years: Transitions & Transformations. (p. 1605)
Brownell, Frank R., 3rd. Gunsmith's Firearms Repair Log (p. 732)
Brownell, Richard. Civil War: The Fall of the Confederacy & the End of Slavery. (p. 325)
—Cold War. (p. 339)
—Oklahoma City Bombing. (p. 1283)
—War in Afghanistan. (p. 1857)
—Wrestling. (p. 1962)
Brownell, Richard, ed. Space Exploration. (p. 1619)
Brownell, Rick. Expressive & Receptive One-Word Picture Vocabulary Tests: EOWPVT-2000 Plates. (p. 555)
—Expressive & Receptive One-Word Picture Vocabulary Tests: ROWPVT-2000 Plates. (p. 555)
Browner, Jesse, tr. see Ricard, Matthieu.
Browning. Mega Joke Book For Kids. (p. 1124)
Browning, Barbara T. Adventures of the Polar Bear Cubs. (p. 23)
Browning, Diane. Signed, Abiah Rose. Browning, Diane, illus. (p. 1574)
Browning, Dixie Burrus, illus. see Walser, Richard & Street, Julia Montgomery.
Browning, Elizabeth Barrett, tr. see Aeschylus.
Browning, Frances G. Dillow. Neon Ned. (p. 1241)
Browning, Jane, jt. auth. see Baker, T. Harri.
Browning, Kurt. Is for Axel: An Ice Skating Alphabet. Rose, Melanie, illus. (p. 889)
Browning, Kurt, jt. auth. see Rodriguez, Sonia.
Browning, Leah. Babysitting Rules: A Guide for When You're in Charge (p. 129)
Browning, Lisa Marie, illus. see Shepherd, Sheri Rose.
Browning, Oscar. True Stories from English History from T. (p. 1792)
Browning, Robert. Pied Piper of Hamelin, Illustrated by Hope Dunlap. Dunlap, Hope, illus. (p. 1356)
Browning, Sommer, jt. auth. see Miller, Ron.
Browning, Suzan, illus. see Quisenberry, Stacey.
Browning, Tom & Moore, Clement C. Night Before Christmas. (p. 1252)
Browning, Wilt, ed. Nothing Finer: North Carolina's Sports History & the People Who Made It. (p. 1268)
Brownjohn, Emma. All Kinds of Feelings: A Lift-The-Flap Book. (p. 44)
—All Kinds of Feelings. (p. 44)
—Help Save Our Planet. Brownjohn, Emma, illus. (p. 766)
—Yes I Can! Be Healthy. Brownjohn, Emma, illus. (p. 1970)
Brownjohn, Emma, illus. see Safran, Sheri.
Brownjohn, John, jt. auth. see Reiche, Dietlof.
Brownjohn, John, tr. see Thal, Lilli.
Brown-Johnson, G. C. O. T. K. City Called Heaven: Revelations. (p. 323)
Brownlee, Browne. Bad Breath. (p. 131)
Brownlee, Christen. Beware of (Prairie) Dog! A Pet Swap Goes Viral. (p. 173)
—Cute, Furry, & Deadly: Diseases You Can Catch from Your Pet! (p. 396)
Brownlee, Joan, et al. Geofinity. (p. 661)
Brownlee, Karen, illus. see McTighe, Carolyn.
Brownlee, Kelly Jackson, illus. see Gambassi, Rod.
Brownlee, Sophia Grace & McClelland, Rosie. Show Time with Sophia Grace & Rosie. McNicholas, Shelagh, illus. (p. 1571)
—Tea Time with Sophia Grace & Rosie. McNicholas, Shelagh, illus. (p. 1708)
Brownlee, Sunny, illus. see Rowles, Louis.
Brownlie Bojang, Ali. Discover Nigeria. (p. 447)
—Egypt in Our World. (p. 506)
—India (p. 870)
—Mexico (p. 1131)
Brownlie Bojang, Ali & Barber, Nicola. Focus on India. (p. 610)
Brownlie Bojang, Ali & Bowden, Rob. Focus on Nigeria. (p. 611)
Brownlie, Ian, illus. see Cunningham, Edie.
Brownlie, Ian D., illus. see St. John, Patricia.
Brownlie, Marion. Spirit of Self. (p. 1628)
—Star Is Happy. (p. 1640)
Brownlow, Brooke. Magic of Old Oak Hill. (p. 1073)
Brownlow, Martin. Game Programmer's Arsenal. (p. 654)
Brownlow, Mike. Dinosaurs of Doom! (p. 445)
—Ten Little Pirates (Red Foil Cover) (p. 1719)
Brownlow, Mike, illus. see Crow, Melinda Melton.
Brown-McCracken, Janet, ed. see DeLong, Ron.
Brown-McCracken, Janet, jt. auth. see DeLong, Ron.
Brownstein, Charles, ed. see Eisner, Will & Miller, Frank.
Brownstein, David. Salt: Your Way to Health. (p. 1505)
Brownstone, David M., jt. auth. see Franck, Irene M.
Brown-Wood, Janay. Imani's Moon. Mitchell, Hazell, illus. (p. 861)
Brownworth, Thom & Hickey, Michael. Rock the Test: The New SAT Solutions Manual to the College Board's Official Study Guide. (p. 1482)
Brownworth, Victoria, ed. From Where They Sit: Black Writers Write Black Youth. (p. 644)
Broxon, Janet, illus. see Armstrong, Robert W.
Broxon, Janet, illus. see Hubbell, Patricia.
Broyes, Hub. FBI. (p. 578)
Broyles, Anne. Arturo & the Navidad Birds Lewis, K. E., illus. (p. 105)
—Priscilla & the Hollyhocks. Alter, Anna, illus. (p. 1407)
—Shy Mama's Halloween. Morin, Leane, illus. (p. 1572)
—Synago Signs at the Crossroads Student. (p. 1693)
Broyles, Beverly Ashley. Grandmother's Alligator/Burukenge Wa Nyanya Activity Guide. (p. 709)
Broyles, Beverly Ashley, illus. see Ferrin, Wendy Wakefield.
Broyles, Bill. Desert Babies A-Z. (p. 428)
Broyles, Duane & Ness, Howard. Vintage Postcards from Old Spokane. (p. 1843)
Broyles, Hub. Life, Love & Adventure after the Civil War. (p. 1011)
—Resolution. (p. 1463)
Broyles, Janell. Barrel Racing. (p. 140)
—Careers in Ballistics Investigation. (p. 267)
—Chemical & Biological Weapons in a Post-9/11 World. (p. 297)
—Chemical Biological Incident Response Force. (p. 297)
—Egyptian Mythology. (p. 507)
—Hate Crimes. (p. 752)
—Timeline of the Jamestown Colony. (p. 1754)
—Triangle Shirtwaist Factory Fire of 1911. (p. 1785)
Broyles, Janell, jt. auth. see Dunkell, Barbara.
Broyles, Matthew. Six-Day War. (p. 1582)
—U. S. Air Marshals. (p. 1806)
Broz, Jon. Bosco - The Dog Who Was Once Afraid of the Dark. Rowland-Hill, Hugo, illus. (p. 214)
Brozman, Dave. Littlest Smoke Detector. Roguez, Jesus, illus. (p. 1039)
Brozovich, Richard & Chase, Linda. Say Goodbye to Being Shy: A Workbook to Help Kids Overcome Shyness. (p. 1518)
Brozyna, Andrew, illus. see Doyle, James.
Brtherson, Bill. Secret Weapon. (p. 1544)
Brubacher, Melody. Adventures of Princess Penelope. (p. 22)
Brubaker, Audrey, ed. see Piepgrass, Arlene.
Brubaker, Ed. Captain America: The Trial of Captain America. Acuña, Daniel, illus. (p. 263)
—Captain America. Guice, Jackson et al, illus. (p. 263)
—Marvels Project: Birth of the Super Heroes. Epting, Steve, illus. (p. 1099)
—Mission to Mars Deodato, Mike, illus. (p. 1153)
—Steve Rogers - Super Soldier. Eaglesham, Dale, illus. (p. 1649)
Brubaker, Ed, jt. auth. see Rucka, Greg.
Brubaker, Ed & Breitweiser, Mitch. Captain America: The Trial of Captain America. Guice, Butch & Acuña, Daniel, illus. (p. 263)
Brubaker, Ed & Tieri, Frank. Prisoner of War. Chaykin, Howard et al, illus. (p. 1407)
Brubaker, Jill, ed. see Hocker, Katherine M.
Brubaker, Robert A., illus. see Brubaker, Sherry K.
Brubaker, Sherry K. Cup of Glitter. Brubaker, Robert A., illus. (p. 392)
Brubaker, William. Dark King. (p. 407)
Bruccoli, Matthew J., et al. Conflicts in American History: A Documentary Encyclopedia (p. 357)
—Student's Encyclopedia of American Literary Characters (p. 1669)
Bruce, Ann Elizabeth. Inspire Your Spirit. (p. 878)
Bruce, Cindy, illus. see Robertson, Elysia Hill.
Bruce Clarke, Margaret. Hunter's Marjory. (p. 828)
Bruce, Dan Wingfoot. Thru-Hiker's Handbook 2004: #1 Guide for Long-Distance Hikes on the Appalachian Trail. (p. 1745)
Bruce, David. Manners I. Care. Delehanty, Joan M., illus. (p. 1088)
Bruce, Debra Fulghum, jt. auth. see McIlwain, Harris H.
Bruce, Gordon. Eliot Noyes: A Pioneer of Design & Architecture in the Age of American Modernism. (p. 513)
Bruce, Jill B. & Wade, Jan. Flags & Emblems of Australia. (p. 602)
Bruce, Judith. Hate Crimes. (p. 752)
Bruce, Julia. Conquest! Can You Build a Roman City? Dennis, Peter, illus. (p. 358)
—Fantasmagoria Hb. (p. 571)
—Hunt! Can You Survive the Stone Age? Dennis, Peter, illus. (p. 828)
—Sail! Can You Command a Sea Voyage? Dennis, Peter, illus. (p. 1503)
—Siege! Can You Capture a Castle? Dennis, Peter, illus. (p. 1573)
Bruce, Karl. Annie Apple & the Teleportation Phantoms from Outer Space. (p. 86)
Bruce, Linda, et al. Space Technology. (p. 1620)
Bruce, Lisa. Amazing Alphabets. Gliori, Debi, illus. (p. 52)
Bruce, Mary Grant. Back to Billabong. (p. 130)
—Mates at Billabong. (p. 1104)
Bruce, Rebekah. If There Were No Grown-Ups. (p. 854)
Bruce, Relly. Fun Times with Meekus & Myron. (p. 648)
—Meet Meekus: From the Meekus & Myron Collection (Book 1) (p. 1121)
—Meet My Family: From the Meekus & Myron Collection (Book 4) (p. 1121)
Bruce, Robin. That Old Bike. (p. 1726)
Bruce, Sheila. Todos Ganan! Billin-Frye, Paige, illus. (p. 1761)
Bruchac, James, jt. auth. see Bruchac, Joseph.
Bruchac, Joseph. Bearwalker. Comport, Sally Wern, illus. (p. 152)
—Boy Who Lived with the Bears: And Other Iroquois Stories. Jacob, Murv, illus. (p. 219)
—Buffalo Song. Farnsworth, Bill, illus. (p. 236)
—Code Talker: A Novel about the Navajo Marines of World War Two. (p. 338)
—Crazy Horse's Vision. (p. 377)
—Crazy Horse's Vision. Nelson, S. D., illus. (p. 377)
—Dark Pond. Comport, Sally Wern, illus. (p. 408)
—Dragon Castle. (p. 476)
—Flying with the Eagle, Racing the Great Bear: Tales from Native North America. (p. 610)
—Heart of a Chief. (p. 759)
—How Chipmunk Got His Stripes. (p. 805)
—Hunter's Promise: An Abenaki Tale. Farnsworth, Bill, illus. (p. 829)
—Jim Thorpe, Original All-American. (p. 918)
—Jim Thorpe's Bright Path Nelson, S. D., tr. (p. 918)
—Killer of Enemies (p. 956)
—Many Nations. Goetzl, Robert F., illus. (p. 1089)
—March Toward the Thunder. (p. 1091)
—My Father Is Taller Than a Tree. Halperin, Wendy Anderson, illus. (p. 1203)
—Night Wings. Comport, Sally Wern, illus. (p. 1254)
—On This Long Journey, the Journal of Jesse Smoke, a Cherokee Boy, the Trail of Tears 1838. (p. 1292)
—Pocahontas. (p. 1375)
—Pushing up the Sky. Flavin, Teresa, illus. (p. 1420)
—Return of Skeleton Man. Comport, Sally Wern, illus. (p. 1464)
—Sacajawea: The Story of Bird Woman & the Lewis & Clark Expedition. (p. 1500)
—Sacajawea. (p. 1500)
—Skeleton Man. Comport, Sally Wern, illus. (p. 1584)
—Squanto's Journey: The Story of the First Thanksgiving. (p. 1636)
—Squanto's Journey: The Story of the First Thanksgiving. Shed, Greg, illus. (p. 1636)
—Sware to God. Comport, Sally Wern, illus. (p. 1689)
—Wabi: A Hero's Tale. (p. 1851)
—Walking Two Worlds. (p. 1854)
—Warriors. (p. 1859)
—Way. (p. 1864)
—Whisper in the Dark. Comport, Sally Wern, illus. (p. 1912)
—Winter People. (p. 1938)
—Wolf Mark (p. 1944)
Bruchac, Joseph, ed. see Smelcer, John E., et al.
Bruchac, Joseph & Bruchac, James. How Chipmunk Got His Stripes. Aruego, Jose & Dewey, Ariane, illus. (p. 805)
—Turtle's Race with Beaver. Aruego, Jose & Dewey, Ariane, illus. (p. 1799)
Bruchac, Joseph & Bruchac, Joseph, III. Our Stories Remember: American Indian History, Culture, & Values Through Storytelling. Vol. 1 (p. 1310)
Bruchac, Joseph & Farnsworth, Bill. Buffalo Song (p. 236)
Bruchac, Joseph & Locker, Thomas. Rachel Carson: Preserving a Sense of Wonder. (p. 1431)
Bruchac, Joseph, III, jt. auth. see Bruchac, Joseph.
Bruchac, Joseph, III & Ross, Gayle. Girl Who Married the Moon: Tales from Native North America. (p. 679)
Bruchac, Margaret M., jt. auth. see Grace, Catherine O'Neill.
Bruchac, Margaret M. & Grace, Catherine O'Neill. 1621: A New Look at Thanksgiving. Coulson, Cotton & Brimberg, Sisse, photos by. (p. 2002)
Bruchac, Marge. Malian's Song. Maughan, William L., illus. (p. 1083)
Bruck, Donna. Once upon a Christmas. (p. 1292)
Brucke, Candice Yarbray. Night-Night Town. (p. 1253)
Brucken, Kelli M. Bristlecone Pines. (p. 229)
—Ghosts. (p. 672)
—Haunted Houses. (p. 753)
Brucker, Glenn, illus. see Downey, Glen.
Bruckner, Tai. Lemon Path Encounter Bruckner, Wes, illus. (p. 991)
Bruckner, Wes, illus. see Bruckner, Tai.
Bruder, Eryka Naomi. Lilyen's Worn-Out Brown Boots. (p. 1018)
Bruder Grimm Staff. King Thrushbeard. Dobrescu, Irina, illus. (p. 959)
Bruder, Mikyla. Button Girl: 25 Pretty Projects from Belts to Barrettes. Nobles, Scott, photos by. (p. 248)
Bruderer, Brooke. Lehi & His Dream. Ridges, Kedrick, illus. (p. 991)
Brudlos, Christopher. Alpha Shade Chapter One. Brudlos, Joseph, illus. (p. 48)
Brudlos, Joseph, illus. see Brudlos, Christopher.
Brudos, Susan E., illus. see Downey, Joni J.
Brudos, Susan E. & Rubino, Alisa A. Wayne's Trail. (p. 1865)
Brudzynski, Jack, jt. auth. see Jordan, Sara.
Brueggeman, Bryan, illus. see Brueggeman, Karen & Paddock, Briana.
Brueggeman, Karen & Paddock, Briana. Fruzzle's Mystery Talent: A Bed Time Fantasy Story for Children Ages 3-10. Brueggeman, Bryan, illus. (p. 646)
Brueggemann, Mindy. Who Is Lilly? Brueggemann, Mindy, photos by. (p. 1916)
Bruel, Five Killer C. Return of White Buffalo: The White Buffalo, One of the Most Sacred Symbols of Native American Mythology. (p. 1465)
Bruel, Nick. Bad Kitty. Bruel, Nick, illus. (p. 132)
—Bad Kitty Christmas. Bruel, Nick, illus. (p. 132)
—Bad Kitty Christmas Storytime Set. (p. 132)
—Bad Kitty Does Not Like Candy. (p. 132)
—Bad Kitty Does Not Like Dogs. (p. 132)
—Bad Kitty Drawn to Trouble. (p. 132)
—Bad Kitty for President. (p. 132)
—Bad Kitty Gets a Bath. Bruel, Nick, illus. (p. 132)
—Bad Kitty Makes Comics. (p. 132)
—Bad Kitty Meets the Baby. (p. 132)
—Bad Kitty Meets the Baby. Bruel, Nick, illus. (p. 132)
—Bad Kitty School Daze. (p. 132)
—Bad Kitty Storytime Set. (p. 132)
—Bad Kitty vs. Uncle Murray. (p. 132)
—Bad Kitty vs. Uncle Murray. Bruel, Nick, illus. (p. 132)
—Bad Kitty's Tasty Treats. (p. 132)
—Does Not Like Dogs (p. 460)
—Drawn to Trouble. (p. 482)
—Happy Birthday, Bad Kitty. Bruel, Nick, illus. (p. 744)
—Little Red Bird. Bruel, Nick, illus. (p. 1034)
—Poor Puppy. (p. 1383)
—Poor Puppy & Bad Kitty. Bruel, Nick, illus. (p. 1383)
—Puppy's Big Day. Bruel, Nick, illus. (p. 1418)
—Who Is Melvin Bubble? Bruel, Nick, illus. (p. 1916)
—Wonderful Year. Bruel, Nick, illus. (p. 1948)
Bruel, Nick, illus. see Bruel, Robert O.
Bruel, Nick, illus. see King-Smith, Dick.
Bruel, Robert O. Bob & Otto. Bruel, Nick, illus. (p. 205)
Bruening, Ari & Gordon, Samantha. Sweet Feet: Samantha Gordon's Winning Season. (p. 1689)
Brug, Sandra Gilbert. Soccer Beat. Moseng, Elisabeth, illus. (p. 1603)
Brugger, Ruth L. Count Candy Corn. (p. 369)
Brughera, Pamela, illus. see Pavanello, Roberto.
Brugman, Alyssa. Alex As Well. (p. 36)
—Beginner's Luck. (p. 159)
—Equen Queen. (p. 533)
—For Sale or Swap. (p. 616)
—Girl Next Door. (p. 678)
—Hot Potato. (p. 802)
Bruha, Ginger. Lilly's Breakfast Time. (p. 1017)
Bruha, Victor, illus. see Therian, Francis Patrick.
Bruhn, Aron. Human Body. Ito, Joel & Kemly, Kathleen, illus. (p. 825)
—Inside Human Body. Ito, Joel & Kemly, Kathleen Hadam, illus. (p. 876)
Bruhn, Joan Z., illus. see Johnson, Liliane & Dufton, Jo S.
Bruin, Jessica. Cube Book. (p. 388)
Bruins, David. Legend of Ninja Cowboy Bear. Leung, Hilary, illus. (p. 988)
—Ninja Cowboy Bear Presents the Way of the Ninja. Leung, Hilary, illus. (p. 1256)
Brukner, Lauren. Kids' Guide to Staying Awesome & in Control: Simple Stuff to Help Children Regulate Their Emotions & Senses. Apsley, illus. (p. 954)
Brukoff, Barry, photos by see McPhail, David.
Brulot, Heleen, illus. see Wolfson, Steve.
Brumage, Katherine. Super Silly Yosemite Sticker & Activity Book: Puzzles, Games, Mazes & More! Hansen, Doug, illus. (p. 1681)
Brumbaugh, Renae. Christmas Stories for Bedtime. (p. 315)
Brumbeau, Jeff. Quiltmaker's Journey. de Marcken, Gail, illus. (p. 1428)
Brumer, Andy, jt. auth. see Clampett, Bobby.
Brumfield, Susan. Over the Garden Wall: Children's Songs & Games from England. (p. 1314)
Brummett, Charlotte K. Doozy, the Lonely Firefly. (p. 470)
Brummit, Ariyana. Soldier's Way Home. (p. 1607)
Brumpton, Keith, illus. see Bedford, David.
Brun, Laura. Frosty the Craft Maker. (p. 645)
Bruna, Dick. Apple. (p. 92)
—Farmer John's Seeds. (p. 574)
—I Can Count. (p. 835)
—Miffy Dances. (p. 1139)
—Miffy Goes Swimming. (p. 1139)
—Miffy Says, I Love You! (p. 1139)
—Miffy the Artist. (p. 1139)
—Miffy va a Nadar/Miffy Goes Swimming. (p. 1139)
—Miffy's Happy New Year. (p. 1139)
—My Vest Is White. (p. 1221)
—On My Scooter. (p. 1289)
—Round, Square, Triangle. (p. 1491)
—School. (p. 1522)
Brun-Cosme, Nadine. Big Wolf & Little Wolf: The Little Leaf That Wouldn't Fall. Tallec, Olivier, illus. (p. 184)
—Big Wolf & Little Wolf. Bedrick, Claudia Z., tr. from FRE. (p. 184)
—Big Wolf & Little Wolf, Such a Beautiful Orange! Tallec, Olivier, illus. (p. 184)
Brun-Cosme, Nadine, et al. Hoy lo Hace Papa! (p. 824)
Brundage, Frances. Cats' Pajamas. Brundage, Frances, illus. (p. 281)
—Cinderella: A Fairy Story. (p. 320)
—Three Bears. (p. 1741)
Brundage, George. Vamos a la misa. (p. 1831)
Brundage, Jerome. Princess & the Bear: Book I: the Battle for Aradam. (p. 1402)
Brundage, Scott, illus. see Fields, Jan.
Brundige, Britt, ed. see Johnson, Sandi.
Brundige, Britt, ed. see McCann, David.
Brundige, Britt, illus. see Johnson, Sandi.

Brundige, Patricia. Traveling with Aunt Patty: Aunt Patty Visits London. Wright, Cindy, ed. (p. 1780)
Brundin, Anders & Dranger, Joanna Rubin. Dudley the Daydreamer. Perry, Frank, tr. from SWE. (p. 489)
Bruneau, Clotilde, et al. Planet of Ashkabaar. (p. 1367)
—Planet of Barnalias. (p. 1367)
—Planet of Coppelius. (p. 1367)
—Planet of Okidians. (p. 1367)
—Planet of the Cublix. (p. 1367)
—Planet of the Snake. Nautilus Studio Staff, illus. (p. 1368)
—Planet of Time. Smith, Owen, tr. from FRE. (p. 1368)
Bruneau, Denise J., jt. auth. see Bruneau M. D., Denise J.
Bruneau M. D., Denise J. & Bruneau, Denise J. My Baby: Illustrations by MikeMotz. com. (p. 1196)
Brunel, Aude. Let's Go to Work. Mancek, Marjan, illus. (p. 998)
Brunell, Heather. Bedtime Monster. Adamson, Bonnie, illus. (p. 157)
—Bedtime Monster/A Dormir, Monstruito! de la Vega, Eida, tr. (p. 157)
Brunelle, Lynn. Camp Out! The Ultimate Kids' Guide. Biggs, Brian & Tanguy, Elara, illus. (p. 257)
—Mama's Little Book of Tricks: Keep the Kids Entertained! Eckel, Jessie & Mount, Arthur, illus. (p. 1084)
—Pop Bottle Science. Meisel, Paul, illus. (p. 1384)
—Pop Bottle Science Floor Display. (p. 1384)
—Reading! - Mind-Bending Brainteasers. (p. 1444)
—World Almanac for Kids - Math! Mind-Bending Brainteasers, Ages 7-9, Grades 2-3. (p. 1953)
Brunelle, Lynn & Gave, Marc. Viruses. (p. 1844)
Brunelli, Carol. Chester A. Arthur. (p. 298)
—James A. Garfield. (p. 906)
Brunelli, Jean, jt. auth. see Lindsay, Jeanne Warren.
Bruner, Elaine C., jt. auth. see Engelmann, Siegfried.
Bruner, Elizabeth. Henry, the Frog. (p. 768)
Bruner, Garth, illus. see Bair, Heather.
Bruner, Garth, illus. see Meyers, Carly J. J.
Bruner, Justine, illus. see Edwards, Cindi.
Bruner, Kristi Rae, jt. auth. see Bruner, Roger.
Bruner, Roger & Bruner, Kristi Rae. Found in Translation: An Unforgettable Mission Trip Where Faith, Obedience, & Forgiveness Intersect. (p. 624)
Bruner, Tammy, illus. see Snyder, Jennifer.
Brunet, Joshua S., illus. see Cooper, Sharon Katz.
Brunette, Steffan. Cough, Achoo, & Roar! (p. 369)
Brunetti, Ivan, illus. see Dahl, Roald.
Brunetti, Sara. Casey's Sugar House. (p. 275)
—Rocky Goes for a Walk. (p. 1484)
—Sammy's Adventure. (p. 1508)
Brunhoff, Jean de, see de Brunhoff, Jean.
Brunhoff, Laurent de, see de Brunhoff, Laurent.
Brunhoff, Laurent de, see Rose, Phyllis & de Brunhoff, Laurent.
Bruni, April A. Bella & Her Little Red Wagon. (p. 162)
—Do Inchworms Go to Heaven? (p. 457)
Bruning, Matt. Baby Animal Picture Puzzles (p. 124)
—Mighty Machines Picture Puzzles (p. 1140)
—Sports Picture Puzzles (p. 1633)
—Zoo Picture Puzzles (p. 1989)
Bruning, Matt, jt. auth. see Marks, Jennifer L.
Bruning, Matt & Cerato, Mattia. You Can Draw Dinosaurs Cerato, Mattia, illus. (p. 1974)
—You Can Draw Flowers Cerato, Mattia, illus. (p. 1974)
Bruning, Matt & Ho, Jannie. You Can Draw Monsters & Other Scary Things Ho, Jannie, illus. (p. 1974)
—You Can Draw Zoo Animals Ho, Jannie, illus. (p. 1974)
Bruning, Matt & Marks, Jennifer L. President Barack Obama (p. 1396)
Bruning, Matt & Sexton, Brenda. You Can Draw Planes, Trains, & Other Vehicles Sexton, Brenda, illus. (p. 1974)
Bruning, Richard, illus. see Wagner, Matt & Seagle, Steven.
Brunk, Jason. Fairies by Chance ... Friends by Grace. (p. 563)
Brunke, Dawn Baumann. Animal Voices, Animal Guides: Discover Your Deeper Self Through Communication with Animals. (p. 80)
—Awakening to Animal Voices: A Teen Guide to Telepathic Communication with All Life. (p. 120)
Brunkus, Denise, illus. see Blumenthal, Deborah.
Brunkus, Denise, illus. see Bush, Laura & Bush, Jenna.
Brunkus, Denise, illus. see Bush, Laura & Hager, Jenna Bush.
Brunkus, Denise, illus. see Calmenson, Stephanie.
Brunkus, Denise, illus. see Keane, Dave.
Brunkus, Denise, illus. see Park, Barbara.
Brunkus, Denise, illus. see Sharmat, Marjorie Weinman & Sharmat, Mitchell.
Brunkus, Denise, illus. see Winters, Kay.
Brunkus, Denise, jt. auth. see Levy, Elizabeth.
Brunkus, Denise, jt. auth. see Park, Barbara.
Brunkus, Denise, tr. see Park, Barbara.
Brunn Emmanuele, Susan. Brooms Are Out! (p. 231)
Brunner, Kym. Wanted - Dead or in Love. (p. 1856)
Brunner, Sharon. Christmas Came for Easter. (p. 313)
Brunner, Terry, illus. see McCoy, M. M.
Brunner-Jass, Renata. Designer Digs: Finding Area & Surface Area. (p. 430)
—Science Olympiad: Proportions & Ratios. (p. 1527)
Brunner-Jass, Renata & Loughran, Donna. Designer Digs: Finding Area & Surface Area. (p. 430)
—Science Olympiad: Proportions & Ratios. (p. 1527)
Bruno, Bonnie. God Thought of Everything Strange & Slimy. Brown, Kevin, illus. (p. 690)
—God Thought of Everything Weird & Wacky. Brown, Kevin, illus. (p. 690)
Bruno, Cristina. Mother Store. (p. 1178)
Bruno, Daphnie. I Love My Baby Berimbau: an Introduction to the Berimbau in Capoeira. Manning, Clarice, illus. (p. 842)
Bruno, Debra. Petey's Tale: A Story of Survival Inspired by Actual Events. (p. 1348)
Bruno, Elsa Knight. Punctuation Celebration. Whitehead, Jenny, illus. (p. 1417)
Bruno, Iacopo, illus. see Adler, Irene.
Bruno, Iacopo, illus. see Baccalario, P. D.
Bruno, Iacopo, illus. see Baccalario, Pierdomenico & McGuinness, Nanette.
Bruno, Iacopo, illus. see Baccalario, Pierdomenico.
Bruno, Iacopo, illus. see Barnhill, Kelly.
Bruno, Iacopo, illus. see Chainani, Soman.
Bruno, Iacopo, illus. see Kuhlman, Evan.
Bruno, Iacopo, illus. see Lawson, Jessica & Twain, Mark.
Bruno, Iacopo, illus. see Lawson, Jessica.
Bruno, Iacopo, illus. see Oliver, Lauren.
Bruno, Iacopo, illus. see Preller, James.
Bruno, Iacopo, illus. see Rockliff, Mara.
Bruno, Iacopo, illus. see Sanders, Ted.
Bruno, Iacopo, illus. see Vaughan, M. M.
Bruno, Iacopo, illus. see Voigt, Cynthia.
Bruno, Iacopo, jt. auth. see Preller, James.
Bruno, Linette Arthurton. Three's No Crowd: Two's Company. (p. 1744)
Bruno, Margaret Farrell, illus. see Finnegan, Evelyn M.
Bruno, Pep. Loro en Mi Granja. Mullerova, Lucie, illus. (p. 1053)
Bruno, Pep, jt. auth. see Bruno, Pepe.
Bruno, Pepe & Bruno, Pep. Silly Nanny Goat. Olmos, Roger, illus. (p. 1576)
Bruno, Richard L. Polio Paradox. (p. 1380)
Bruno, Susan. Secret at the Old Beaver Pond: El Secreto de la Lagunita de un Viejo Castor. McMullen, Brad, illus. (p. 1540)
Bruno, Yvonne. Lisa Finds a New Friend. (p. 1022)
Brunor & Bar, Dominique. Saint Joan of Arc: Quest for Peace. (p. 1503)
Brunor, text. Saint Bernadette: The Miracle of Lourdes. (p. 1503)
Brunot, Katerina, illus. see Scretching, Dorothy/Janis.
Bruns, Greg. Sadie of Dun Rovin' Miss Tank. (p. 1501)
Bruns, Roger. Jesse Jackson: A Biography (p. 914)
Bruns, Scott, illus. see Bozak, Jon.
Brunson, April M. Life in the Single Lane: Accepting God's Gift in This Season of Your Life. (p. 1011)
Brunson, Emma. Survivor Spirit Book: Megan's Ark. (p. 1687)
Brunson, Jodi. Year Without Dad. Cramer, illus. (p. 1969)
Brunson, Marya. Light of Rigel. (p. 1015)
Brunson, Stephanie, illus. see Ballman, Swanee.
Brunson Vlasis, Caroline. Mooney Finds a Bed. (p. 1172)
Brunstetter, Wanda E. Back to School. (p. 130)
—Green Fever. Madden, Colleen, illus. (p. 721)
—Humble Pie. Madden, Colleen, illus. (p. 826)
—Humble Pie. Madden, Colleen M., illus. (p. 826)
—Out of Control. (p. 1311)
Brunsvold, Eric. Gardening with Grandma. Mueller, Miranda, illus. (p. 656)
Brunswick, Glen. Non-Humans Volume 1: Runaway American Dream TP: Runaway American Dream TP. (p. 1263)
Brunswick, Nicola. Living with Dyslexia. (p. 1042)
Brurlah, D. Around the Yamim Tovim. (p. 101)
—Let's Welcome Shabbos. (p. 1001)
Brus, Mischa & Schlitz, Matt. Little Full Stop. Brus, Mischa, illus. (p. 1028)
Brusatte, Steve. Walking with Dinosaurs Encyclopedia. (p. 1854)
Brusca, Maria C., tr. see Zuravicky, Orli.
Brusca, Maria Cristina, tr. see Brown, Vanessa.
Brusca, Maria Cristina, tr. see Ellis, Catherine.
Brusca, Maria Cristina, tr. see Galiano, Dean.
Brusca, Maria Cristina, tr. see Glass, Maya.
Brusca, Maria Cristina, tr. see Hipp, Andrew.
Brusca, Maria Cristina, tr. see Obregon, Jose Maria.
Brusca, Maria Cristina, tr. see Randolph, Joanne.
Brusca, Maria Cristina, tr. see Way, Jennifer.
Bruschetti-Weiss, Janet. Starfish Called Rhonda. Bruschetti-Weiss, Janet, illus. (p. 1642)
Brusco, Giulia, illus. see Amano, Jeff.
Brush, jt. auth. see Nixon.
Brush Creations & Holmes, A. M. X. Robbie Virtual vs. Vlad the Vampire: Book 1. (p. 1478)
Brush, Jim. Armed Services. (p. 99)
—Special Forces. (p. 1623)
—Summer Action Sports. (p. 1673)
—Winter Action Sports. (p. 1937)
Brush, Jim, jt. auth. see Gilpin, Dan.
Brush, Jim, jt. auth. see Hyland, Tony.
Brush, Jim & Hachette Children's Books Staff. Custom Cars. (p. 395)
Brush, Jim & Scarborough, Kate. Extreme Survival. (p. 557)
—Roller Coasters. (p. 1485)
Brush, Joan, illus. see Kondonassis, Yolanda.
Brusha, Joe. Dinosaurs & Prehistoric Predators. Dehart, Andy, ed. (p. 444)
—Tales of Adventure - Pirates. (p. 1702)
—Top 10 Deadliest Sharks. (p. 1768)
Brusha, Joe, ed. see Russ, John Paul.
Brusha, Joe, jt. auth. see Zenescope Entertainment Staff.
Brusha, Joe, et al. Grimm Fairy Tales Boxed Set (p. 724)
—Worlds Most Dangerous Animals. (p. 1960)
Brusic, Sharon A., et al. Technology: Today & Tomorrow. (p. 1711)
Bruss, Deborah. Big Box for Ben Bogacki, Tomek, illus. (p. 179)
Brusselmans, Christiane, et al. Sunday: Leaders Weekly Guidebook, Year C. (p. 1676)
—Sunday: Book of Readings Adapted for Children Year C (p. 1676)
Brust, Beth Wagner. Dolphins. (p. 464)
—Great Tulip Trade. Mattheson, Jenny, illus. (p. 719)
Brust, Steven. Book of Athyra. (p. 210)
—Brokedown Palace. (p. 230)
Brust, Steven & Bull, Emma. Freedom & Necessity. (p. 634)
Brust, Steven & Lindholm, Megan. Gypsy. (p. 734)
Brutocao, W. J. Rocky & the Great Bird Race. Marder, Alan, illus. (p. 1484)
—Sancho at the Music Festival: With Rocky the Otter & Corky the Cormorant. Marder, Alan, illus. (p. 1510)
Bruton, Catherine. I Predict a Riot. (p. 844)
—Pop! (p. 1384)
—We Can Be Heroes: One Explosive Summer... (p. 1866)
Bruton, Georgia. Escape. (p. 534)
Bruton, John, ed. see Docalavich, Heather & Indovino, Shaina C.
Bruton, John, ed. see Etingoff, Kim & Indovino, Shaina C.
Bruton, John, ed. see Sadek, Ademola O. & Indovino, Shaina C.
Bruton, John, ed. see Sanna, Jeanine & Indovino, Shaina C.
Bruton, John, ed. see Simons, Rae & Indovino, Shaina C.
Bruton, John, ed. see Simons, Rae & Indovino, Shaina Carmel.
Bruton, John, ed. see Walker, Ida & Indovino, Shaina C.
Bruton, John, ed. see Walker, Ida & Indovino, Shaina Carmel.
Bruton, Seth. I'm So Cute, You Can't Be Mad. Hicks, Kaylee, illus. (p. 860)
Bruton, W. Dogs' Grand Dinner Party. (p. 463)
Brutton, Elizabeth. Tabbies & Tigers in Provence. (p. 1694)
Bruun, Erik. Florida. Peterson, Rick, illus. (p. 606)
Bruzon, Louise A. Grimstone Galleries. (p. 724)
Bruzonic, Lauren Peacock. Español con Cindi y Sus Amigos. (p. 536)
Bruzzone, Catherine. First French with Superchat: Learn French the Super-Fun Way Through Games, Activities & Songs. Beaton, Clare, illus. (p. 595)
—First Spanish with Supergato: Learn Spanish the Super-Fun Way Through Games, Activities & Songs. Beaton, Clare, illus. (p. 597)
—French for Children. (p. 635)
—French on the Move for Kids: Lively Songs & Games for Busy Kids. (p. 636)
—Italian for Children. (p. 894)
—Lucy the Cat at the Farm: Lucie le Chat a la Ferme. Beaton, Clare, illus. (p. 1063)
—Lucy the Cat in Town: Lucie le Chat en Ville. Beaton, Clare, illus. (p. 1063)
—Spanish Fun. (p. 1621)
—Spanish on the Move for Kids: Lively Songs & Games for Busy Kids. (p. 1621)
—Spanish-English Picture Dictionary. (p. 1621)
Bruzzone, Catherine & Martineau, Susan. Hide & Speak Spanish. Comfort, Louise, illus. (p. 777)
Bruzzone, Catherine & Martinneau, Susan. Hide & Speak English. Comfort, Louise, tr. (p. 777)
—Hide & Speak French. Comfort, Louise, illus. (p. 777)
—Hide & Speak Italian. Comfort, Louise, illus. (p. 777)
Bruzzone, Catherine & Millar, Louise. My French Sticker Atlas. (p. 1209)
—My French Sticker Dictionary: Everyday Words & Popular Themes in Colorful Sticker Scenes. Comfort, Louise, illus. (p. 1209)
—My Spanish Sticker Atlas. (p. 1219)
—My Spanish Sticker Dictionary: Everyday Words & Popular Themes in Colorful Sticker Scenes. Comfort, Louise, illus. (p. 1219)
Bruzzone, Catherine, et al. French-English Picture Dictionary. Comfort, Louise & Dix, Steph, illus. (p. 635)
—French-English Word Puzzle Book: 14 Fun French & English Word Games. Comfort, Louise, illus. (p. 635)
—Spanish-English Word Puzzle Book: 14 Fun Spanish & English Word Games. Comfort, Louise, illus. (p. 1621)
Bryan, Alexandra Faer. Green Kitty. (p. 722)
Bryan, Antonia D. United Arab Emirates. (p. 1818)
Bryan, Ashley. All Night, All Day: A Child's First Book of African-American Spirituals. (p. 45)
—Ashley Bryan: Words to My Life's Song. Bryan, Ashley, illus. (p. 106)
—Ashley Bryan's Puppets: Making Something from Everything. Bryan, Ashley, illus. (p. 106)
—Beautiful Blackbird. Bryan, Ashley, illus. (p. 153)
—Can't Scare Me! Bryan, Ashley, illus. (p. 262)
—Let It Shine: Three Favorite Spirituals. Bryan, Ashley, illus. (p. 994)
—Who Built the Stable? A Nativity Poem. Bryan, Ashley, illus. (p. 1914)
Bryan, Ashley, illus. see Alexander, Cecil F.
Bryan, Ashley, illus. see Berry, James.
Bryan, Ashley, illus. see Giovanni, Nikki.
Bryan, Ashley, illus. see Hughes, Langston.
Bryan, Barbara. Holiday Poems for Children. (p. 788)
—Just for Fun. (p. 938)
—Save the Golden Tree. (p. 1516)
—Starfish, Seashells, Coral & Gems. (p. 1642)
—Where Are My Amethysts? (p. 1906)
Bryan, Beth, ed. see Baker, Liza, et al.
Bryan, Beth, jt. auth. see Ackerman, Jill.
Bryan, Bethany. How the Rock Cycle Works. (p. 813)
Bryan, Bethany, jt. auth. see Kidz Bop Kids Staff.
Bryan, Charity. Monkey & the Sock. (p. 1165)
Bryan, Dale-Marie. Anne Hathaway. (p. 86)
—Colorado River. (p. 343)
—Emma Watson. (p. 520)
—Experiments with Magnets. (p. 549)
—Johnny Depp. (p. 923)
—Living with Celiac Disease. (p. 1042)
—Smartphone Safety & Privacy. (p. 1593)
—South Dakota. (p. 1617)
—Tornadoes. (p. 1770)
—William & Kate. (p. 1933)
Bryan, Deborah. Monster's Daughter. (p. 1169)
Bryan, Diana, illus. see Grimm, Jacob & Grimm, Wilhelm K.
Bryan, Diana, illus. see Metaxas, Eric.
Bryan, Dick & Rafferty, Michael. Capitalism with Derivatives: A Political Economy of Financial Derivatives, Capital & Class. (p. 262)
Bryan, E. A., jt. auth. see Bryan, L. A.
Bryan, Gayle. Professional Athlete. (p. 1409)
—Virtual Apprentice: Professional Athlete. (p. 1844)
Bryan, Hendrix, illus. see Bader, Bonnie.
Bryan, Hintz, illus. see Donahue, Laurie.
Bryan, Jennifer. Alien Anarchy (p. 40)
—Dragón Diferente. Hosler, Danamarie, illus. (p. 477)
Bryan, Jennifer Liu. Different Dragon. Hosler, Danamarie, illus. (p. 438)
—Hilda, A Very Loyal Goat. (p. 779)
Bryan, Jennifer Liu & Kendle, Hazel Cole. Cole Family Christmas. Julich, Jenniffer, illus. (p. 339)
Bryan, Jenny. Milagro del Nacimiento: Una Ventana Transparente. (p. 1142)
Bryan, Jessica, jt. auth. see Stone, Andrew.
Bryan, Kanietzko. Avatar: The Last Airbender. Vol. 6 (p. 118)
Bryan, Kathleen & Tarr, Judith. Serpent & the Rose. (p. 1552)
Bryan, L. A. & Bryan, E. A. Programmable Controllers Theory & Applications: Text. (p. 1410)
—Programmable Controllers Theory & Applications: Selected Applications. (p. 1410)
—Programmable Controllers Theory & Applications: Workbook & Study Guide. (p. 1410)
—Troubleshooting & Understanding: DVD or VHS Training Series. (p. 1790)
Bryan, Laura. You Make My Heart Smile. (p. 1976)
Bryan, Lynn. Where Do Plants Grow? (p. 1907)
Bryan, Marcia. Dandy Lion: The Adventure Begins. (p. 403)
Bryan, Philip, jt. auth. see Pearson, Jane.
Bryan, Sabrina & DeVillers, Julia. Princess of Gossip. (p. 1404)
Bryan, Sarah Jane & Bellenson, Suzanne. Mega Magna Forms Princess. McGregor, Barbara, illus. (p. 1124)
—Mega Magna Forms Safari Adventure. Klug, David, illus. (p. 1124)
Bryan, Sean. Boy & His Bunny. Murphy, Tom, illus. (p. 217)
—Girl & Her Gator. Murphy, Tom, illus. (p. 678)
—Juggling Pug. Murphy, Tom, illus. (p. 932)
Bryan, Sean & Thomas, Evan. Bear & His Boy. Murphy, Tom, illus. (p. 150)
Bryan, Suzanne. Bonkers Finds His Way Home. (p. 209)
Bryan, T. Scott. Geysers: What They Are & How They Work. (p. 670)
Bryan, Tayler, illus. see Kesead, Melissa.
Bryan-Brown, Kim. Leaf That Was Left. Curren, Cindy, illus. (p. 982)
Bryan-Hunt, Jan, illus. see O'Neal, Debbie Trafton.
Bryan-Hunt, Jan, illus. see Simon, Charnan.
Bryan-Hunt, Jan, illus. see Trueit, Trudi Strain.
Bryant, Ann. Ballet Magic. (p. 134)
—Billie & the Parent Plan. (p. 187)
—Christmas Nutcracker. (p. 315)
—Dancing Forever. (p. 403)
—Dancing Forever. Benton, Tim, illus. (p. 403)
—Dancing Friends. (p. 403)
—Dancing Princess. (p. 403)
—Dancing Princess. Benton, Tim, illus. (p. 403)
—Dancing with the Stars. Benton, Tim, illus. (p. 403)
—Dragons vs Dinos. (p. 479)
—Hurry Up! (p. 830)
—Jasmine's Lucky Star. (p. 910)
—Jasmine's Lucky Star. Benton, Tim, illus. (p. 910)
—Lost Broomstick. (p. 1055)
—Play Straight Away! Book One - For Recorder (p. 1371)
—Play Straight Away! Book Two - For Recorder (p. 1371)
—Poppy's Secret Wish. Benton, Tim, illus. (p. 1385)
—Princess at Silver Spires. (p. 1403)
—Reading Corner: Kimberley's Scary Day. Collins, Ross, illus. (p. 1445)
—Rose's Big Decision. (p. 1489)
—Rose's Big Decision. Benton, Tim, illus. (p. 1489)
—School Friends - Drama at Silver Spires. (p. 1523)
—School Friends - Welcome to Silver Spires. (p. 1523)
—She's No Angel. (p. 1566)
—Stinky! Elkerton, Andy, illus. (p. 1651)
—Tag. (p. 1695)
—Too Good to Be True. (p. 1766)
Bryant, Anne, jt. auth. see Bryant, Kevin.
Bryant, Annie. Bad News/Good News. (p. 132)
—Charlotte in Paris. (p. 293)
—Crush Alert. (p. 386)
—Fashion Frenzy. (p. 575)
—Freaked Out. (p. 631)
—Freestyle with Avery. (p. 635)
—Ghost Town. (p. 672)
—Great Scavenger Hunt. (p. 718)
—Green Algae & Bubble Gum Wars. (p. 721)
—Isabel's Texas Two-Step. (p. 891)
—Just Kidding. (p. 939)
—Katani's Jamaican Holiday. (p. 944)
—Lake Rescue. (p. 972)
—Letters from the Heart. (p. 1002)
—Lucky Charm. (p. 1062)
—Maeve on the Red Carpet. (p. 1070)
—Out of Bounds. (p. 1311)
—Promises, Promises. (p. 1411)
—Ready! Set! Hawaii! (p. 1447)
—Sweet Thirteen. (p. 1690)
—Time's Up. (p. 1754)
—Worst Enemies/Best Friends. (p. 1961)
Bryant, Bonnie. Horse Play. (p. 800)
Bryant, Carol W., illus. see Shields, Kathleen J.
Bryant, Cathy. Doctor Said I Have Leukemi. Bunker, Thomas, illus. (p. 459)
Bryant, Claire. Make Your Own Southern Belle Cloth Doll & Her Wardrobe. (p. 1080)
Bryant, Clive, ed. see Brontë, Emily.
Bryant, Clive, ed. see Dickens, Charles.
Bryant, Clive, ed. see Priestley, J. B.
Bryant, Clive, ed. see Shakespeare, William.
Bryant, Clive, ed. see Stoker, Bram.
Bryant, Clive, ed. see Wilde, Oscar.
Bryant, Clive, ed. Sweeney Todd: The Demon Barber of Fleet Street. Shalvey, Declan et al, illus. (p. 1689)
Bryant, Clorinda. Imaginary World: The Stone of Amajara. (p. 860)
Bryant, G. E. Nirvana's Sunshine Babies. (p. 1257)
Bryant, Howard. Legends - The Best Players, Games, & Teams in Baseball. (p. 989)
—Legends: the Best Players, Games, & Teams in Football. (p. 990)
Bryant, James. Rising from the Ashes. (p. 1475)
Bryant, James Culver. Coming Together. (p. 348)

B

Bryant, Janine. Yucky Green Beans. (p. 1983)
Bryant, Jen. Call Me Marianne. Johnson, David, illus. (p. 254)
—Fortune of Carmen Navarro. (p. 623)
—Georgia's Bones. Anderson, Bethan, illus. (p. 665)
—Georgia's Bones. Andersen, Bethanne, illus. (p. 665)
—Kaleidoscope Eyes. (p. 941)
—Music for the End of Time. Peck, Beth, illus. (p. 1193)
—Pieces of Georgia. (p. 1356)
—Right Word: Roget & His Thesaurus. Sweet, Melissa, illus. (p. 1472)
—Ringside 1925: Views from the Scopes Trial. (p. 1473)
Bryant, Jennifer. River of Words: The Story of William Carlos Williams. Sweet, Melissa, illus. (p. 1476)
—Six Dots: A Story of Young Louis Braille. Kulikov, Boris, illus. (p. 1582)
—Splash of Red: The Life & Art of Horace Pippin. Sweet, Melissa, illus. (p. 1629)
—Trial. (p. 1785)
Bryant, Jill. John Henry Holliday. (p. 922)
—Medical Inventions: The Best of Health. (p. 1118)
—Phenomenal Female Entrepreneurs. (p. 1350)
—Technology Mysteries Revealed. (p. 1711)
—Wagon Train. (p. 1852)
—Women in the West. (p. 1946)
Bryant, Jill, jt. auth. see Carey, Nicolette.
Bryant, Jill & Second Story Press Staff. Dazzling Women Designers (p. 415)
Bryant, Jim. Apple for Rose. (p. 92)
Bryant, John E. Taking Speech Disorders to School. Schader, Karen, ed. (p. 1698)
Bryant, Julie, illus. see Grant, Rose.
Bryant, Julie, jt. auth. see Hyman, Corine.
Bryant, Justin, jt. auth. see Hubble, Miles.
Bryant, Kendric L. Math Mechanic: Algebra Edition. (p. 1106)
—Math Mechanic: Money & Time Edition. (p. 1106)
—Math Mechanic: Fractions & Mixed Numbers Edition. (p. 1106)
Bryant, Kerry, illus. see Wales, Sid.
Bryant, Kevin & Bryant, Anne. Keepers in the Forgotten Valley. (p. 947)
Bryant, Kim & Meloan, Becky. Prematurely Yours: The Baby Book Designed Exclusively for the Premature Infant. (p. 1395)
Bryant, Konni Jo. Little Miss Tattletale. (p. 1032)
Bryant, Laura, illus. see Metzger, Steve.
Bryant, Laura, illus. see Sampson, Michael R. & Martin, Bill, Jr.
Bryant, Laura J., illus. see Bergren, Lisa T.
Bryant, Laura J., illus. see Callahan, Sean.
Bryant, Laura J., illus. see Giff, Patricia Reilly.
Bryant, Laura J., illus. see Hodgkins, Fran.
Bryant, Laura J., illus. see Lotz, Anne Graham & Graham Lotz, Anne.
Bryant, Laura J., illus. see Martin, Bill, Jr. & Sampson, Michael.
Bryant, Laura J., illus. see Metzger, Steve.
Bryant, Laura J., illus. see Morales, Melita.
Bryant, Laura J., illus. see Murphy, Patricia J.
Bryant, Laura J., illus. see Nolan, Allia Zobel.
Bryant, Laura J., illus. see Nolan, Lucy.
Bryant, Laura J., illus. see Quattlebaum, Mary.
Bryant, Laura J., illus. see Riehle, Mary Ann McCabe.
Bryant, Laura J., illus. see Sampson, Michael & Martin, Bill, Jr.
Bryant, Laura J., illus. see Sampson, Michael R. & Martin, Bill, Jr.
Bryant, Laura J., illus. see Stiegemeyer, Julie.
Bryant, Laura J., illus. see Thomas, Jean Monrad.
Bryant, Laura J., illus. see Tompert, Ann & Lister, Ralph.
Bryant, Laura J., jt. auth. see Ransom, Candice F.
Bryant, Louella. Two Tracks in the Snow. Fargo, Todd, illus. (p. 1804)
Bryant, Margaret A., et al. Learning about Fall with Children's Literature: Cross-Curricular Units Based on the Works of Eric Carle, Robert Kalan, Ludwig Bemelmans, & More. (p. 984)
—Learning about Spring with Children's Literature. (p. 984)
—Learning about Winter with Children's Literature. (p. 985)
Bryant, Mark. Ghosts in the Cloisters: Clerical Tales of Mystery & Supernatural. (p. 672)
Bryant, Mary. Sped Spud: He May Be a Tater, but He's No Dud (p. 1624)
—Sped Spud: He May Be a Tater, but He's No Dud. (p. 1624)
Bryant, Megan. Merida: The Legend of the Emeralds. (p. 1127)
Bryant, Megan & Disney Book Group Staff. Merida: Legend of the Emeralds. Disney Storybook Art Team, illus. (p. 1127)
Bryant, Megan E. Alphasaurus. Powell, Luciana Navarro, illus. (p. 50)
—Colorasaurus. Powell, Luciana Navarro, illus. (p. 343)
—Countasaurus. Powell, Luciana Navarro, illus. (p. 370)
—Fireflies. Schwartz, Carol, illus. (p. 592)
—Oh My Gods! A Look-It-Up Guide to the Gods of Mythology. (p. 1281)
—Olivia Meets Olivia. Mawhinney, Art & Johnson, Shane L., illus. (p. 1287)
—Princess Valentine. (p. 1406)
—Rapunzel. Huxtable, Tonja & Huxtable, John, illus. (p. 1439)
—Shapeasaurus. Powell, Luciana Navarro, illus. (p. 1560)
—She's All That! A Look-It-Up Guide to the Goddesses of Mythology. (p. 1566)
Bryant, Megan E. & O'Ryan, Ellie. Easy to Be Green: Simple Activities You Can Do to Save the Earth. Lola & Ivanke & Lola, illus. (p. 500)
Bryant, Michael, illus. see Nikola-Lisa, W.
Bryant, Nick & Summers, Rowan. Amazing Spot What! (p. 56)
—Fantastical. (p. 572)
—Spectacular Spot What. (p. 1624)
—Wacky World. (p. 1852)
Bryant, P., ed. see Hancock, Nicky & Sunderland, Margot.
Bryant, Patricia White. Jesus, Is Your Daddy Mean? (p. 915)
Bryant, Phoebe. What Is That in the Air? A play date with Sayde. (p. 1890)
Bryant, Ray. Book of Space. (p. 211)
Bryant, Samantha. Innocent Child. (p. 875)
Bryant, Sara. Epaminondas & His Auntie: Ilustrated by Inez Hogan. (p. 532)
Bryant, Sara Cone. Stories to Tell Children: Fifty-Four Stories with Some Suggestions for Telling. (p. 1655)
Bryant, Sharon & Hood, Dana. Beautiful in God's Eyes: Building Character, Wisdom, & Faith in Young Women. (p. 153)
Bryant, Sheree, et al. Glencoe Reader. (p. 683)
—Glencoe Reader British Literature (p. 683)
—Glencoe Reader, Course 2. (p. 683)
—Glencoe Reader Course 4 (p. 683)
—Glencoe Reader World Literature. (p. 683)
Bryant Sr., Lydia. I Love Lydia (p. 842)
Bryant, Stephen D., et al. Companions in Christ: A Small-Group Experience in Spiritual Formation Leader's Guide Revised. (p. 351)
Bryant, Stephen, et al. Has God Called You to Ministry? (p. 752)
Bryant, Tamera. Life & Times of Hammurabi. (p. 1008)
—This Land Is Your Land. (p. 1737)
—Thomas Alva Edison. (p. 1737)
—We Remember: State Monuments & Historic Sites. (p. 1868)
Bryant, Wanda. This Time & Place We Live (p. 1737)
Bryant-Mole, K., ed. see Tyler, Jenny & Gee, R.
Bryant-Mole, Karen. Dot-to-Dot Animals. (p. 472)
—Dot-to-Dot Dinosaurs. (p. 472)
—Dot-to-Dot in Space. (p. 472)
—Dot-to-Dot Machines. Tyler, Jenny, ed. (p. 472)
—Dot-to-Dot Nature. (p. 472)
—Dot-to-Dot on Seashore. Round, Graham, illus. (p. 472)
—Starting to Measure. (p. 1644)
Bryant-Mole, Karen & Tyler, Jenny. Dot-to-Dot Book: Combined Volume. Round, Graham, illus. (p. 472)
Bryce, Celia. Anthem for Jackson Dawes. (p. 89)
Bryce, Clara. Just My Imagination: Children's Poems. (p. 939)
Bryce, Conor. Wesco P. Mcsnaffle & the Great Brave Quest. (p. 1876)
Bryce, Ellen. Once upon a Holy Night: Value Pak. (p. 1293)
—Once upon a Holy Night: Singer's Edition. (p. 1293)
—Once upon a Holy Night: A Musical Christmas Story Based on Luke 2:1-20 & Matthew 2:1-2. (p. 1293)
Bryce, Ellen Woods. Once upon a Holy Night: A Musical Christmas Story Based on Luke 2:1-20 & Matthew 2:1-2. (p. 1293)
Bryce, Frank & MacCall, Terry. How the Days of the Week Got Their Names (p. 813)
Bryce, George. Among the Mound Builders' Remains. (p. 65)
Brycelea, Clifford, illus. see Browne, Vee.
Brychta, Alex, illus. see Hunt, Roderick.
Brydon, Irene M. Fluffy's Story. (p. 608)
Bryer, Estelle. Eurythmy for the Young Child: A Guide for Teachers & Parents. (p. 540)
Bryer, Tom. Fun Poems for Kids. Bryer, Tom, illus. (p. 648)
Bryers, Paul. Kobal. (p. 966)
Bryfonski, Dedria. Breast Cancer. (p. 225)
—Child Custody. (p. 301)
—Class Conflict in a Tale of Two Cities. Greenhaven Press Editors, ed. (p. 327)
—Class Conflict in Charles Dicken's a Tale of Two Cities. Greenhaven Press Editors, ed. (p. 327)
—Death in Old Man & Sea. Greenhaven Press Editors, ed. (p. 420)
—Depression in J. D. Salinger's The Catcher in the Rye. (p. 427)
—Deregulation. (p. 427)
—Human Trafficking. Greenhaven Press Editors, ed. (p. 826)
—Islamophobia. (p. 892)
—Male & Female Roles in Ernest Hemingway's: The Sun Also Rises. (p. 1083)
—Political Issues in J. K. Rowling's Harry Potter Series. (p. 1380)
—Race Relations in Alan Paton's Cry the Beloved Country. (p. 1431)
—Street Teens. (p. 1667)
—Student Loans. Greenhaven Press Editors, ed. (p. 1669)
—Veterans. (p. 1839)
—War in Joseph Heller's Catch-22. (p. 1857)
Bryfonski, Dedria, jt. auth. see Cruden, Alex.
Bryfonski, Dedria, jt. auth. see Greenhaven Press Editors.
Bryfonski, Dedria, jt. auth. see Hawker, Louise.
Bryfonski, Dedria, ed. Family Violence. (p. 569)
—Islamophobia. (p. 892)
—Male & Female Roles in Ernest Hemingway's The Sun Also Rises. (p. 1083)
Bryne, Kelly, illus. see Gallo, Tina.
Brynie, Faith Hickman. 101 Questions... Holm, Sharon Lane, illus. (p. 1999)
—101 Questions about Muscles: To Stretch Your Mind & Flex Your Brain. (p. 1999)
—101 Questions about Reproduction: Or How 1 + 1 = 3 or 4 or More. Holm, Sharon, illus. (p. 1999)
—101 Questions about Sex & Sexuality: With Answers for the Curious, Cautious, & Confused. Holm, Sharon, illus. (p. 1999)
—101 Questions about Sleep & Dreams: That Kept You Awake Nights... until Now. Holm, Sharon, illus. (p. 1999)
—101 Questions Your Brain Has Asked about Itself but Couldn't Answer... until Now. (p. 1999)
—Do Animals Migrate? (p. 456)
—Do Animals Work Together? (p. 456)
—How Do Animal Babies Live? (p. 806)
—How Do Animals Keep Clean? (p. 806)
—How Do Animals Stay Safe? (p. 806)
—Parent's Crash Course: Elementary School Science Fair Projects. (p. 1324)
—Six-Minute Nature Experiments. Whittingham, Kim, illus. (p. 1582)
—What Helps Plants Grow? The Nitrogen Cycle Case. (p. 1886)
—Which Animals Are the Best Athletes? (p. 1911)
—Why Does It Rain? The Water Cycle Case. (p. 1924)
Bryntirion, Gwasg, jt. auth. see Rhys, Ann Gruffydd.
Bryson. Clyde, the Elf That Santa Fired. (p. 336)
Bryson, Bill. Really Short History of Nearly Everything. (p. 1450)
Bryson, Brenda. Adventures of Roo & Winston. (p. 22)
—Adventures of Roo & Winston - Crop Circles. (p. 22)
Bryson, Ernest. Smudgie New Adventure. (p. 1595)
Bryson, Jamie S. War Canoe. (p. 1857)
Bryson, Karen Mueller. Incredibly Awesome Adventures of Puggie Liddel, the Graphic Novel. Tisdel, L. L, illus. (p. 870)
Bryson, Theresa. Costume Party. (p. 368)
—Farm Alarm. (p. 573)
—Farm Work. (p. 574)
—Hungry Fox: Set Of 6. (p. 828)
—Make a Sundial. (p. 1079)
—On Stage. (p. 1289)
Brzezinski, Kathleen. Seed. (p. 1547)
Brzozowski, Christina, illus. see Grimshaw, Luke.
Brzycki, M. L. & Krueger, S. L. It Came from the Freezer ... or Was it the Drapes? (p. 893)
B'seder, Kol. Songs for Growin. (p. 1612)
BTMS-Portable Press Staff, jt. auth. see Bathroom Readers' Institute Staff.
Buada, Joselito, jt. auth. see Laguatan, Alwen.
Bub, Steven, jt. auth. see Bub, Steven.
Bub, Steven & Bub, Steven. Hero Like My Father. (p. 772)
Buba, Joy, illus. see Foster, Elizabeth Vincent.
Bubar, David N. Home Churches: The Biblical Blueprint for Starting a Christian Home Fellowship. (p. 792)
Bubar, Lorraine, illus. see Friedman, Debbie.
Bubble Guppies, Bubble. Bubble Guppies: Let's Play, Bubble Puppy! A PeekABoo Book. (p. 233)
BubbleGirl, Season. Doggy Diary. (p. 462)
Buble, Brandee. O'Shae the Octopus. Liska, Eliska, illus. (p. 1305)
Bubp, Jennifer, illus. see Russell, Allyson.
Bubsy, Nancy, ed. see Vaval, Fisepe.
Bucay, Jorge. King & the Magician. Gusti, illus. (p. 958)
Buccheri, Chiara, illus. see Bullard, Lisa.
Buccheri, Chiara, illus. see Knudsen, Shannon.
Bucchino, John. Grateful: A Song of Giving Thanks. Hakkarainen, Anna-Liisa, illus. (p. 712)
Bucci, Gino, illus. see Ciccone, Tiziana & Linardi, Franca.
Bucci, Gino, illus. see Ciccone, Tiziana & Linardi, Franca.
Buccieri, Lisa Rojany, jt. auth. see Kor, Eva Mozes.
Bucco, Joe, illus. see Goldman, Steven & Goldman, Dan.
Buchan, John. Magic Walking Stick & Stories from the Arabian Nights. Soper, Vernon, illus. (p. 1074)
—Thirty-Nine Steps. (p. 1735)
Buchanan, jt. auth. see Sullivan Associates Staff.
Buchanan, jt. auth. see Sullivan.
Buchanan & Sullivan. Programmed Reading for Adults: Placement Tests. (p. 1410)
—Programmed Reading for Adults: Sound-Symbol Book. (p. 1410)
—Programmed Reading for Adults. (p. 1410)
Buchanan, Andrea J. Gift. (p. 674)
Buchanan, Andrea J. & Peskowitz, Miriam. Daring Book for Girls: Things to Do. (p. 406)
Buchanan, Andrew. Wise Guide NASCAR. (p. 1940)
Buchanan, Andria, jt. auth. see Eimer, Patricia.
Buchanan, Andy, ed. Wise Guide Fenway Park: The Fan Navigator to Fenway. (p. 1940)
—Wise Guide Notre Dame Stadium: The Fan Navigator to Notre Dame. (p. 1940)
—Wise Guide Yankee Stadium: The Fan Navigator to Yankee Stadium. (p. 1940)
Buchanan, Colin. Remember the Lord. (p. 1459)
—Super Saviour. (p. 1680)
Buchanan, Darlene. Smiley's World. (p. 1594)
Buchanan, Edward. Parent/Teacher Handbook: Teaching Older Children Everything They Need to Know about Their Christian Heritage (p. 1324)
Buchanan, Edward A. Parent/Teacher Handbook: Teaching Younger Children Everything They Need to Know about the Bible Vol. 1 (p. 1324)
—Parent/Teacher Handbook: Teaching Younger Children Everything They Need to Know about Their Christian Heritage Vol. 2 (p. 1324)
—Parent/Teacher Handbooks: Teaching Older Children Everything They Need to Know about the Bible. Vol. 3 (p. 1324)
Buchanan, Fannie R. Magic Music Story Interpretations. (p. 1072)
Buchanan, Heather. Logan's Landscaping: Foundations for Multiplication. (p. 1045)
Buchanan, Jane. Mary Tudor: Courageous Queen or Bloody Mary? (p. 1101)
—Seed Magic Riley-Webb, Charlotte, illus. (p. 1547)
Buchanan, Jessie, illus. see Belanger, Madeleine.
Buchanan, Johnny & Conway, Beth. Rachel & the Magic Beads. Bosak, Virginia, illus. (p. 1431)
Buchanan, Kathy, jt. auth. see AIO Team.
Buchanan, Ken. This House Is Made of Mud (Esta Casa Esta Hecha de Lodo) Tracy, Libba, illus. (p. 1735)
Buchanan, Marilyn, jt. auth. see Isbell, Rebecca.
Buchanan, Matt. Ernie's Place: A Play for Young Audiences. (p. 534)
—Prince Ugly: One Act Youth Play. (p. 1401)
—Sleeping Walter: One Act Youth Play. (p. 1589)
Buchanan, Michael, jt. auth. see Lang, Diane.
Buchanan, Nelda. Hall Closet Light. (p. 737)
Buchanan, P., jt. auth. see Buchanan, Paul.
Buchanan, Patrick J. Where the Right Went Wrong: How Neoconservatives Subverted the Reagan Revolution & Hijacked the Bush Presidency. (p. 1909)
Buchanan, Paul & Buchanan, P. Last Place I Want to Be (p. 978)
Buchanan, Paul & Randall, Rod. Misadventures of Willie Plummet Set. (p. 1150)
Buchanan, Pendella. Layers. (p. 981)
Buchanan, Penelope. In the Spell of an Ibis: The Education of Minemheb the Scribe. Barnet, Nancy, illus. (p. 867)
Buchanan, Peter. Renzo Piano Building Workshop (p. 1460)
Buchanan, Selena. Sunday Chimes (p. 1676)
Buchanan, Shelly. Animal Senses. (p. 79)
—Global Warming. (p. 684)
—Our Ever-Changing Environment (p. 1308)
—Our Government: The Three Branches (p. 1309)
—Plant Reproduction. (p. 1369)
—Powerful Ocean. (p. 1390)
—Shaping Our Environment (p. 1561)
—Stars. (p. 1643)
—U. S. Constitution & You. (p. 1806)
Buchanan, Sue, jt. auth. see Hodges, Lynn.
Buchanan, Sue, et al. Mud Pie Annie Allen, Joy, illus. (p. 1188)
Buchanan, Theodore. Circuits. (p. 321)
Buchanan, Yvonne, illus. see Weatherford, Carole Boston.
Buchdahl, Kenneth A. Dismantling the American Dream: Globalization, Free Trade, Immigration, Unemployment, Poverty, Debt, Foreign Dependency, & More. (p. 451)
Bucheimer, Melissa. Matthew the Little Angel. (p. 1109)
Bucher, Barbara Latini, illus. see Evans, Betty J.
Bucher, Cecile, illus. see Trooboff, Rhoda.
Bucher, Charlotte. Cecil Learns to Smile. (p. 283)
Bucher, Heatherly & Menking, Amanda. Happy Dragon Menking, Amanda & Fisher, Sean, illus. (p. 745)
Buchheim, Su Jen, illus. see Marks, Nancy Freeman.
Buchhelt, Mike. Going to Grand Canyon National Park. (p. 693)
Buchholz, Chris. Beckett 81. (p. 156)
Buchholz, Erwin. Born under a Star Legg, Barbara, illus. (p. 214)
Buchholz, Quint. Coleccionista de Momentos. (p. 339)
—Duerme Bien, Pequeño Oso. (p. 489)
Buchholz, Quint, illus. see Richter, Jutta.
Buchholz, Rachel. How to Survive Anything: Shark Attack, Lightning, Embarrassing Parents, Pop Quizzes, & Other Perilous Situations. (p. 821)
Buchignani, Walter. Tell No One Who You Are: The Hidden Childhood of Régine Miller. (p. 1717)
Buchla, David M., jt. auth. see Floyd, Thomas L.
Buchman, M. L. Bring on the Dusk. (p. 229)
Buchmann, Stephen. Honey Bees: Letters from the Hive. (p. 794)
Buchmann, Stephen, jt. auth. see Cohn, Diana.
Buchmann, Stephen & Cohn, Diana. Bee Tree. (p. 157)
Bucholz, Dinah. Unofficial Harry Potter Cookbook: From Cauldron Cakes to Knickerbocker Glory—More Than 150 Magical Recipes for Muggles & Wizards. (p. 1822)
Buchs, Thomas, illus. see Halfmann, Janet.
Buchs, Thomas, illus. see Rau, Dana Meachen.
Buchs, Thomas, illus. see Rau, Dana.
Buchs, Thomas, illus. see Schwaeber, Barbie Heit.
Buchwald, Ann, jt. auth. see Young, Mariabelle.
Buchwald, Claire. Are You Ready for Me? Hansen, Amelia, illus. (p. 97)
—Max Talks to Me. Ritz, Karen, illus. (p. 1111)
Buchwald, Emilie. Floramel & Esteban. Robinson, Charles, illus. (p. 606)
Buck, Alicia. Out of the Ashes. (p. 1311)
Buck, Angela R. Lily Elf. (p. 1018)
Buck, Bryant. My First Christian Abc Bk. (p. 1206)
Buck, Deanna. My First Articles of Faith BK. (p. 1204)
—My First Church HIST Stories. (p. 1206)
—My First NT Stories Reprint. (p. 1207)
—My First Story of the First Easter. (p. 1208)
Buck, Deanna Draper. My First Book of Temples. Nelson, Casey, illus. (p. 1205)
—My First Scripture Stories. Harston, Jerry, illus. (p. 1207)
—My First Story of the First Christmas. (p. 1208)
—My First Story of the First Christmas. Harston, Jerry, illus. (p. 1208)
Buck, Devin. Haikus & Other Poems: A Collection of Poems by Kids for Kids. (p. 735)
Buck, Dianna S., jt. auth. see Aydelott, Jimmie.
Buck, Jason. Teens for Life: The Official Guide to Starting a High School Pro-Life Club. (p. 1715)
Buck, Lewis, jt. auth. see Kimmel, Elizabeth Cody.
Buck, Melissa, ed. see Preschool, Lollipop.
Buck, Nola, jt. auth. see Godwin, Laura.
Buck, Pearl S. House Divided. (p. 803)
—Sons. (p. 1613)
—Three Daughters of Madame Liang. (p. 1742)
Buck, Ray & Ann. Apache Adventure: The Ryan Family Adventure Series. (p. 91)
Buck, Ruth Matheson. Doctor Rode Side-Saddle: The Remarkable Story of Elizabeth Matheson, Frontier Doctor & Medicine Woman. (p. 459)
Buck Young. Men of Lesbos. (p. 1126)
Buckallew, Rodney. One Full Cycle. (p. 1295)
Buckbee, Johnny. Adventures of Bumble Bee. (p. 17)
Buckell, Tobias, ed. see Le Guin, Ursula K., et al.
Buckell, Tobias S. & Monti, Joe, eds. Diverse Energies. (p. 454)
Bucken, Hajo. Button, Button, Who's Got the Button? (p. 248)
Bucker, Jutta, illus. see Moss, Miriam.
Bucker, Jutta, tr. see Moss, Miriam.
Buckeridge, Anthony. Jennings' Little Hut. (p. 913)
Buckett, George, illus. see Joyce, Irma.
Buckey, Sarah Masters. Clue in the Castle Tower: A Samantha Mystery. Ross, Peg, ed. (p. 335)
—Curse of Ravenscourt: A Samantha Mystery. (p. 394)
—Light in the Cellar: A Molly Mystery. (p. 1015)
—Light in the Cellar: A Molly Mystery. Tibbles, Jean-Paul, illus. (p. 1015)
—Stolen Sapphire: A Samantha Mystery. Tibbles, JeanPaul, illus. (p. 1652)
—Stolen Sapphire. (p. 1652)
Buck-Glenn, Judy. Legend of the Donkey's Cross: An Easter Story. (p. 989)
Buckham, Derek. Santa Stories. (p. 1513)
Buckhingham, Mark & Willingham, Bill. Wolves. McManus, Shawn, illus. (p. 1945)
Bucki, Jo Dee & O'Malley, John. Maya Visits a Hospital: Love Is the Best Medicine Hicks, Mindy, ed. (p. 1113)
Buckingham, Alan. Grow Vegetables: Gardens, Yards, Balconies, Roof Terraces. (p. 726)
Buckingham, Dorothea N. Staring down the Dragon. (p. 1642)

Buckingham, Gabriella. Wheels on the Bus & Other Action Rhymes. (p. 1901)
Buckingham, Gabriella, illus. see Baxter, Nicola.
Buckingham, Mark, illus. see Willingham, Bill.
Buckingham, Matt. Bright Stanley. (p. 228)
Buckingham, Matt, illus. see Bright, Paul.
Buckingham, Matt, illus. see Martin, Peter.
Buckingham, Matt, jt. auth. see Powell, Jillian.
Buckingham, Melinda. Christian Alphabet for Children. (p. 311)
Buckingham, Michele, ed. see Stanley, Andy & Hall, Stuart.
Buckingham, Mike, jt. illus. see Wieringo, Mike.
Buckingham, Royce. Dead Boys. (p. 416)
—Demonkeeper. (p. 426)
Buckingham, Royce Scott. Terminals. (p. 1721)
Buckingham, Suzanne. Meet the Bearded Dragon. (p. 1122)
—Meet the Beaver. (p. 1122)
—Meet the Crocodile. (p. 1122)
—Meet the Iguana. (p. 1122)
—Meet the Peacock. (p. 1123)
—Meet the Ring-Tailed Lemur. (p. 1123)
Buckingham-Smith, Celestia. College Life in Paradise: Hawaiian Style (p. 340)
Buckland, Augustus Robert. Empire Annual for Girls: With Illustrations. (p. 521)
Buckland, Belinda. God's Book of Wisdom: A Family Daily Devotional Built on the Wisdom of Proverbs. (p. 691)
Buckland, Francis Trevelyan. Log-Book of a Fisherman & Zoologist. (p. 1045)
Buckland, M. Barbara. Ellen Jane Vennard: Her Life Story. Chase, Arline, ed. (p. 514)
Bucklaschuk, Angela. Movember with My Doggy. Gillen, Rosemarie, illus. (p. 1183)
—My Doggy the Big Helper. (p. 1202)
Buckle, J. A. Half My Facebook Friends Are Ferrets (p. 736)
Buckler, Carol. Feathered Tales from the Barnyard. (p. 579)
Buckler, Rich, illus. see David, Peter.
Buckler, Rich, illus. see Simonson, Walter, et al.
Buckler, Rich, et al. Marvel Saga: Sub-Mariner & the Human Torch. (p. 1099)
Buckley, A. M. Anarchism. (p. 67)
—Arts. (p. 104)
—Disappearance of Amelia Earhart. (p. 446)
—Homelessness. (p. 793)
—India. (p. 870)
—Italy. (p. 894)
—Japan. (p. 908)
—Mexico. (p. 1131)
—Pixar: The Company & Its Founders. (p. 1365)
—Racism. (p. 1432)
Buckley, Anne. Day Mrs. Roosevelt Came to Town. (p. 413)
Buckley, Annie. Be a Better Babysitter. (p. 148)
—Be a Better Biker. (p. 148)
—Breathing Bridge. (p. 226)
—Ellen Ochoa. (p. 514)
—Kids' Yoga Deck: 50 Poses & Games. Buckley, Annie, illus. (p. 955)
—Making Movies. (p. 1081)
—Movies. (p. 1183)
—Music. (p. 1193)
—Photography. (p. 1353)
—Robert L. Johnson. (p. 1479)
—World's Most Beautiful Birds. (p. 1960)
—Yo-Yo Ma. (p. 1972)
Buckley, Annie & Buckley, James, Jr. Inside Photography. (p. 877)
Buckley, Arabella. Fairy Land of Science. (p. 563)
—Fairy-Land of Science. (p. 563)
—Fairy-Land of Science (Yesterday's Classics) (p. 563)
—Plant Life in Field & Garden. (p. 1369)
—Through Magic Glasses & Other Lectures: A Sequel to the Fairyland of Science. (p. 1745)
Buckley, Arabella B. Birds of the Air. (p. 192)
—By Pond & River. (p. 249)
—Insect Life. (p. 875)
—Trees & Shrubs. (p. 1784)
—Wild Life in Woods & Fields (Yesterday's Classics) (p. 1929)
Buckley, Arabella Burton. Fairy Land of Science. (p. 563)
Buckley, Carol. Tarra & Bella: The Elephant & Dog Who Became Best Friends. Buckley, Carol, photos by. (p. 1706)
—Travels with Tarra (p. 1781)
Buckley, Charlie. How to Wash Your Hands. (p. 822)
—Show Jo How to Make a Sandwich. (p. 1570)
Buckley, Claire. Start to Embroider. (p. 1643)
Buckley, Colleen. Grandma Kathy Has Cancer. Sponaugle, Kim, illus. (p. 708)
Buckley, Elizabeth & Keyes, Joan Ross. Oxford Picture Dictionary Content Area for Kids. (p. 1315)
Buckley, Harriet, illus. see Barlow, Steve & Skidmore, Steve.
Buckley, James. Coaching & Scouting Ferrer, Al, ed. (p. 336)
—Discovery Bugopedia. (p. 450)
—Sports Media Relations Ferrer, Al, ed. (p. 1633)
—STEM in Sports. (p. 1647)
—Things That Go! (p. 1733)
—Who Is Muhammad Ali? (p. 1916)
—Who Was Betsy Ross? (p. 1918)
—Who Was Jesse Owens? (p. 1918)
—Who Was Roberto Clemente? (p. 1919)
—Who Were the Wright Brothers? (p. 1919)
Buckley, James, jt. auth. see Kelley, James E.
Buckley, James, jt. auth. see Kelley, K. C.
Buckley, James, jt. auth. see Piazza, Carmelo.
Buckley, James & Buckley, James, Jr. Tom Brady & the New England Patriots: Super Bowl XLIX. (p. 1762)
Buckley, James, Jr. Baseball: Facts, Stats, Stars, & Stuff. (p. 140)
—Bill Bradley. (p. 186)
—Classic Cars. (p. 327)
—Day with a Doctor. (p. 414)
—Day with a Zoo Veterinarian. (p. 414)
—Home Run Heroes: Big Mac, Sammy & Junior. (p. 792)
—Jimmie Johnson. (p. 918)
—Muhammad Ali. (p. 1189)
—NBA on the Inside. (p. 1238)
—Pele - A Photographic Story of a Life. (p. 1335)
—Scholastic Book of Lists 10cp Counter Display. (p. 1521)
—Scholastic Year in Sports 2013. (p. 1522)
—Who Is Muhammad Ali? Marchesi, Stephen & Harrison, Nancy, illus. (p. 1916)
—Who Was Betsy Ross? O'Brien, John & Harrison, Nancy, illus. (p. 1918)
—Who Was Ernest Shackleton? Hergenrother, Max, illus. (p. 1918)
—Who Was Jesse Owens? Copeland, Gregory, illus. (p. 1918)
—Who Was Milton Hershey? Hammond, Ted, illus. (p. 1919)
—Who Was Roberto Clemente? Hammond, Ted & Harrison, Nancy, illus. (p. 1919)
—Who Were the Wright Brothers? Foley, Tim & Harrison, Nancy, illus. (p. 1919)
Buckley, James, Jr., jt. auth. see Arlon, Penelope.
Buckley, James, Jr., jt. auth. see Buckley, Annie.
Buckley, James, Jr., jt. auth. see Buckley, James.
Buckley, James, Jr., jt. auth. see Tuchman, Gail.
Buckley, James, Jr., et al. Space Heroes, Level 3: Amazing Astronauts. (p. 1619)
Buckley, Jeannette. Discovering Mission San Luis Obispo de Tolosa. (p. 449)
—Discovering Mission San Luis Rey de Francia. (p. 449)
Buckley, Jim. Golf. (p. 696)
—Soccer. (p. 1603)
—Who Was Ernest Shackleton? (p. 1918)
—Who Was Milton Hershey? (p. 1919)
Buckley, Joel, illus. see Butler, Heather.
Buckley, Joel, illus. see Willoughby, R.
Buckley, Kate. Choices: A Novel. (p. 309)
Buckley, MacKenzie. Doggy Day. Perilli, Marilena & Tomita, Kuni, illus. (p. 462)
Buckley, Michael. Attack of the Bullies. (p. 113)
—Cheerleaders of Doom Beavers, Ethen, illus. (p. 296)
—Cheerleaders of Doom. (p. 296)
—Council of Mirrors. (p. 369)
—Council of Mirrors. Ferguson, Peter, illus. (p. 369)
—Everafter War. (p. 542)
—Everafter War. Ferguson, Peter, illus. (p. 542)
—Fairy-Tale Detectives: And the Unusual Suspects. Ferguson, Peter, illus. (p. 564)
—Fairy-Tale Detectives. (p. 564)
—Fairy-Tale Detectives. Ferguson, Peter, illus. (p. 564)
—Inside Story (p. 877)
—Inside Story. (p. 877)
—Inside Story. Ferguson, Peter, illus. (p. 877)
—Kel Gilligan's Daredevil Stunt Show. Santat, Dan, illus. (p. 948)
—M Is for Mama's Boy (p. 1067)
—M Is for Mama's Boy. Beavers, Ethen, illus. (p. 1067)
—Magic & Other Misdemeanors. Ferguson, Peter, illus. (p. 1071)
—National Espionage, Rescue, & Defense Society Beavers, Ethen, illus. (p. 1231)
—NERDS: National Espionage, Rescue, & Defense Society. (p. 1241)
—NERDS: National Espionage, Rescue, & Defense Society. Bk. 1 (p. 1241)
—NERDS 2: M für Muttersöhnchen. (p. 1241)
—NERDS - National Espionage, Rescue, & Defense Society. (p. 1241)
—Once upon a Crime. Ferguson, Peter, illus. (p. 1292)
—Porristas del Infierno. (p. 1386)
—Problem Child: The Sisters Grimm. (p. 1408)
—Problem Child. Ferguson, Peter, illus. (p. 1408)
—Sisters Grimm Boxed Set: The Fairy Tale Detectives; The Unusual Suspects; The Problem Child. (p. 1581)
—Tales from the Hood. Ferguson, Peter, illus. (p. 1701)
—Undertow. (p. 1817)
—Unusual Suspects. (p. 1823)
—Unusual Suspects. Ferguson, Peter, illus. (p. 1823)
—Very Grimm Guide. Ferguson, Peter, illus. (p. 1838)
—Villain Virus. (p. 1842)
Buckley, Michael & Ferguson, Peter. Inside Story. (p. 877)
Buckley, Peter J. Challenge of International Business. (p. 289)
Buckley, Ray. Christmas Moccasins. Buckley, Ray, illus. (p. 314)
Buckley, Richard. Foolish Tortoise: Lap Edition. Carle, Eric, illus. (p. 614)
—Foolish Tortoise. Carle, Eric, illus. (p. 614)
—Greedy Python: Lap Edition. Carle, Eric, illus. (p. 720)
—Greedy Python. (p. 720)
—Greedy Python. Carle, Eric, illus. (p. 720)
Buckley, Susan, jt. auth. see Leacock, Elspeth.
Buckley, Susan & Leacock, Elspeth. Journeys in Time: A New Atlas of American History. Prato, Rodica, illus. (p. 929)
Buckley, Susan Washburn & National Geographic Learning Staff. Industrial Revolution. (p. 872)
Buckley, William F., Jr. National Review Treasury of Classic Children's Literature (p. 1233)
Buckley, William F., Jr., jt. auth. see Stamp, Jorgen.
Buckley, William F., Jr., selected by. National Review Treasury of Classic Children's Literature. (p. 1233)
Buckley-Archer, Linda. Time Quake. (p. 1752)
—Time Thief. (p. 1752)
—Time Travelers. (p. 1753)
Buckmaster, Coleen. Ludmilla Drucilla Gorilla at the Old Wild Horse Ranch. (p. 1064)
Buckmaster, Heath L. Box of Hair: A Fairy Tale (p. 216)
—Box of Hair: A Fairy Tale. (p. 216)
—Dragons of Tamack. (p. 479)
—Venus Diary. (p. 1836)
Buckmaster, Marjorie L. Freshwater Fishes. (p. 636)
—Skin Cancer. (p. 1585)
Buckner, Andrew. Grand Poppa's Favorite Chair: No One Is As Special As You. Welker, Matthew S., illus. (p. 707)
Buckner, Chuck. Death of Arkie Baker. (p. 420)
Buckner, Cory & Wagener, Wolfgang. Quincy Jones/Raphael Soriano - Set Of 2. (p. 1428)
Buckner, Julie, illus. see Fisher, Doris.
Buckner, Julie, illus. see Tunks, Karyn.
Buckner, Julie Dupre, illus. see Fontenot, Mary Alice & Fontenot Landry, Julie.
Buckner, Julie Dupre, illus. see Fontenot, Mary Alice.
Buckton, Chris & Corbett, Pie. Searchlights for Spelling Year 2: For Interactive Whole-Class Teaching. (p. 1538)
Buckwalter, Stephanie. Death Poetry: Death, Be Not Proud. (p. 420)
—Early American Poetry: "Beauty in Words" (p. 493)
—Early American Poetry- Beauty in Words. (p. 493)
—Independent Government Agencies: Working for America. (p. 870)
—Student's Guide to Jack London. (p. 1669)
—Volcanoes: Disaster & Survival. (p. 1849)
Buczacki, Beverley, jt. auth. see Buczacki, Stefan.
Buczacki, Beverly, jt. auth. see Buczacki, Stefan.
Buczacki, Stefan & Buczacki, Beverley. Young Gardener. Sieveking, Anthea, photos by. (p. 1978)
Buczacki, Stefan & Buczacki, Beverly. Young Gardener. Sieveking, Anthea, photos by. (p. 1978)
Buczynski, Sandra. Super Smart Information Strategies: Get Ready for a Winning Science Project. (p. 1681)
Budai, Joan. What's in an Egg? (p. 1897)
Budayr, Valarie. Fox Diaries: The Year the Foxes Came to Our Garden. (p. 626)
Budbill, David. Bones on Black Spruce Mountain. (p. 209)
—Snowshoe Trek to Otter River. (p. 1601)
Budd Josselin. Sun Is Not a Yellow Balloon: Fun with the Sun for Kids. (p. 1676)
Budd, Linda S. Living with the Active Alert Child: Groundbreaking Strategies for Parents. (p. 1042)
Budd, Warren, jt. auth. see Ames, Lee J.
Budde, Nadia. Bristly Hair & I Don't Care! (p. 229)
Budden, Diane Phelps. Shade: A Story about a Very Smart Raven. (p. 1556)
Buddenberg, Laura J., jt. auth. see McGee, Kathleen M.
Buddenberg, Laura J. & Montgomery, Alesia K. Friend Me: 10 Awesome Steps to Fun & Friendship. (p. 637)
Buddhist Text Translation Society Staff, contrib. by. Standards for Students: Instructions in Virtue from the Chinese Heritage = [Di Zi Gui]. (p. 1639)
Budds, Laura. Have You Ever Seen a Bear with a Purple Smile? Zimmerman, Kadie, illus. (p. 754)
Budds, Sam. 1000 First Words in Spanish. Lacome, Susie, illus. (p. 2001)
Budensiek, Joy. Jesus My Very Best Friend: Chinese/English. (p. 916)
—Jesus My Very Best Friend: Russian/English. (p. 916)
—Jesus, My Very Best Friend. (p. 916)
Budge, E. A. Wallis, tr. see Romer, John & Winston, Robert P.
Budge, Robyn E. Whoda Thunkit: Rhyming Tales for the Young & Not So. (p. 1919)
Budgell, Gill. Run-Away Game. (p. 1496)
Budgell, Gill & Ruttle, Kate. Cambridge Handwriting at Home: Forming Cursive Letters. (p. 255)
—Cambridge Handwriting at Home: Forming Manuscript Letters. (p. 255)
—Cambridge Handwriting at Home: Forming Uppercase Letters. (p. 255)
—Cambridge Handwriting at Home: Getting Ready for Handwriting. (p. 255)
—Penpals for Handwriting. (p. 1338)
—Penpals for Handwriting Year 1 Big Book. (p. 1338)
—Penpals for Handwriting Year 1 Practice Book. (p. 1338)
—Penpals for Handwriting Year 2. (p. 1338)
—Penpals for Handwriting Years 5/6. (p. 1338)
Budgen, Tim, illus. see Weaver, A. J.
Budhos, Marina. Ask Me No Questions. (p. 106)
—Remix: Conversations with Immigrant Teenagers. (p. 1460)
—Tell Us We're Home. (p. 1717)
Budhos, Marina Tamar, jt. auth. see Aronson, Marc.
Budiansky, Stephen. Bloody Shirt: Terror after the Civil War. (p. 201)
Budic, Hannah Purdy. Ebenezer Flea & the Right Thing to Do Rosendahl, Melissa M., illus. (p. 501)
Budig, Greg. I Hear the Wind. (p. 839)
—Still: A Winter's Journey. Budig, Greg, illus. (p. 1650)
Budliger, Bob. Birds of New York State (p. 191)
Budnick, Stacy Heller, illus. see Dyer, Wayne W.
Budnick, Stacy Heller, illus. see Dyer, Wayne W. & Tracy, Kristina.
Budnik, Mary Ann. ¡Usted Puede Ser un Santo! (p. 1829)
—¡Usted Puede Ser un Santo! Libro de Ejercicios. (p. 1829)
—¿Buscando la Paz? ¡Intente la Confesión! (p. 244)
Budnik-Wills, Mary Terese. You Can Become A Saint! Facilitator's Guide. (p. 1974)
—¡Usted Puede Ser un Santo la Guía Explicativa. (p. 1829)
Budreau, Craig. Trail Map: Barton Creek Greenbelt—Loop 360 to Zilker Park. (p. 1776)
Budwine, Greg, illus. see Sommer, Carl.
Budwine, Greg, illus. see Uglow, Loyd.
Budzik, Mary, jt. auth. see Basher, Simon.
Bué, Henri, jt. auth. see Carroll, Lewis, pseud.
Bueche, Shelley. Ebola Virus. (p. 501)
Buechner, Frederick. Secrets in the Dark: A Life in Sermons. (p. 1544)
Buechner, Sara Davis, ed. see Dvorak, Antonin.
Buehner, Caralyn. Dex: The Heart of a Hero. Buehner, Mark, illus. (p. 432)
—Goldilocks & the Three Bears. Buehner, Mark, illus. (p. 696)
—In the Garden. Dorman, Brandon, illus. (p. 866)
—Snowmen All Year. Buehner, Mark, illus. (p. 1601)
—Snowmen All Year Board Book. Buehner, Mark, illus. (p. 1601)
—Snowmen at Christmas. Buehner, Mark, illus. (p. 1601)
—Snowmen at Night. Buehner, Mark, illus. (p. 1601)
—Snowmen at Play. Buehner, Mark, illus. (p. 1601)
—Snowmen at Work. Buehner, Mark, illus. (p. 1601)
—Superdog: The Heart of a Hero. Buehner, Mark, illus. (p. 1683)
Buehner, Caralyn & Buehner, Mark. Escape of Marvin the Ape. (p. 535)
—Fanny's Dream. Buehner, Caralyn & Buehner, Mark, illus. (p. 571)
Buehner, Jeremy. Crimson Tides. (p. 383)
Buehner, Mark, illus. see Buehner, Caralyn.
Buehner, Mark, illus. see Cowan, Catherine.
Buehner, Mark, illus. see Melmed, Laura Krauss.
Buehner, Mark, jt. auth. see Buehner, Caralyn.
Buehner, Mark, jt. auth. see Cowan, Catherine.
Buehrle, Jackie, illus. see Knesek, Marian.
Buehrle, Jacquelyn, illus. see Bocanegra, Deborah.
Buehrle, Jacquelyn, illus. see Glass, Alberta.
Buehrle, Jacquelyn, illus. see Hazekamp, Michelle R.
Buehrle, Jacquelyn, illus. see Horstmann, Deborah McFillin.
Buehrle, Jacquelyn, illus. see Signor, Priscilla M.
Buehrle, Jacquelyn, illus. see Tardif, Elizabeth.
Buehrle, Jacquelyn, illus. see Trimoglie, Mario.
Buel, Hubert, illus. see Lampman, Evelyn Sibley.
Buel, Richard. America on the Brink: How the Political Struggle over the War of 1812 Almost Destroyed the Young Republic. (p. 59)
Buell, Carl Dennis, illus. see Muir, John.
Buell, Hal, ed. Uncommon Valor, Common Virtue. (p. 1812)
Buell, Janet & Sisters, Write. Women of the Granite State: 25 New Hampshire Women You Should Know. Greenleaf, Lisa, illus. (p. 1946)
Buell, Jean. God's Heroes: A Child's Book of Saints. Larkin, Jean, ed. (p. 691)
—Pray with Mary: A Child's Book of the Rosary. Larkin, Jean, ed. (p. 1393)
Buell, Tonya. Careers with Successful Dot-Com Companies. (p. 268)
—Cool Careers Without College for Web Surfers. (p. 363)
—Crash of United Flight 93 on September 11 2001. (p. 376)
—Crash of United Flight 93 on September 11 2001. (p. 376)
—Slavery in America: A Primary Source History of the Intolerable Practice of Slavery. (p. 1588)
—Slavery in America. (p. 1588)
Buellis, Linda. Pueblo. (p. 1414)
Buelt, Laura, illus. see Hammerslough, Jane & Smithsonian Institution Staff.
Buelt, Laura, illus. see Hammerslough, Jane.
Buelt, Laura, tr. see Hammerslough, Jane.
Bueno, Carlos. Lauren Ipsum: A Story about Computer Science & Other Improbable Things. (p. 980)
Bueno, Julián David. Henry Cartier - Bresson- el azar y el Instante. (p. 767)
Bueno, Lisa, illus. see Hoffmann, Sara E.
Buesser, Jeanne. He Talks Funny: A Heartwarming Story of Everyday Life. (p. 756)
Buethe, Amanda, jt. auth. see Stites, Ranae.
Buevara, Isaias. Revelation: A Visual Journey. (p. 1465)
Buff, Paul Conrad. River Bk. 1 (p. 1475)
Buffagni, Matteo. Avengers Assemble. (p. 118)
Buffagni, Matteo, illus. see Pak, Greg, et al.
Buffalo, Tom And Tracey. Loganæs Big Night Out. (p. 1045)
Buffalohead, Julie & Erdrich, Liselotte. Sacagawea. Buffalohead, Julie, illus. (p. 1500)
Buffam, Leslie, jt. auth. see Harvey, Sarah N.
Buffie, Margaret. Out of Focus. (p. 1311)
—Who Is Frances Rain? (p. 1915)
—Winter Shadows. (p. 1938)
Buffiere, Mélanie, illus. see Mariolle, Mathieu.
Buffinet, Jacqueline, illus. see Payne, Gaynell.
Buffington, Cecil. High School Super-Star: The Junior Year. (p. 778)
Buffington, Perry W. Cheap Psychological Tricks for Parents: 62 Sure-Fire Secrets & Solutions for Successful Parenting Singh, Jen, illus. (p. 295)
Buffolano, Sandra. Coping with Tourette Syndrome: A Workbook for Kids with Tic Disorders. (p. 365)
Buffomante, Maya. How Pandas Became Black & White. (p. 811)
Buffy, R. P. G. Military Monster Squad: Initiative Sourcebook. (p. 1143)
Buford, Bill & Piaggio Foundation Staff. Vespa: Style in Motion. (p. 1839)
Buford, Stanley G. & Gillen, Rosemarie. Thanks Dad! (p. 1725)
Bug. Patty Cat & the Woong: An I've Got Feelings! Feel Better Book. (p. 1329)
Bug, Amy L. Forces & Motion. (p. 617)
Bug, Judy. Day to Play (p. 414)
Bug, June. Legend of the Wooden Bowl. (p. 989)
Bugbee, M. Howe. Beyond the Road: Mayhaven Award for Children's Fiction. (p. 174)
Bugbird, T. Bff Fashion Boutique Designer. (p. 174)
—My Pretty Pink School Purse. Home, J., illus. (p. 1217)
Bugbird, Tim. Best Friends Forever. (p. 169)
—Charm Books Kittens. (p. 294)
—Charm Books Kittens Poly Bag. (p. 294)
—Charm Books Kittens/Puppies Clip Strip. (p. 294)
—Charm Books Kittens/Puppies Pos Rack. (p. 294)
—Charm Books Puppies Poly Bag. (p. 294)
—Dream Room Designer. (p. 483)
—Farm Friends Peek a Boo! (p. 574)
—Me Myself & I. (p. 1116)
—Molly the Muffin Fairy. (p. 1161)
—Peek a Boo Baby Animals. (p. 1334)
—Peek a Boo Perfect Pets. (p. 1334)
—Peek a Boo Wacky Wild Animals. (p. 1335)
Bugbird, Tim & Scholastic, Inc. Staff. My Pretty Pink Purse. (p. 1217)
Bugg, Ann T. Into the Forest & down the Tower. Kramin, Valerie, illus. (p. 881)
Buggs, Matthews. Beach Party. (p. 149)
Buggs, Michael A. Tabard. Buggs, Michael A., illus. (p. 1694)
Buhagiar, Jason, illus. see Bingham, J. Z.
Buhlig Meister, Victoria. Tell Me a Story, Please, Mi-Mi! (p. 1716)
Bui, Chris Van. Yummy Yummy for My Tummy (p. 1983)
Bui, Nam. Fish over Diamond. (p. 598)
Bui, Tak. Spot the Difference. (p. 1633)
Buice, J. W. Silly Squirrel. (p. 1576)
Buie, Nita. Lollipops Song. (p. 1046)
Bui-Quang, Phuong-Mai. Tea Club. (p. 1708)
Buising, Clare. Moshi Moshi. (p. 1176)
Buitendag, Louis L. Bloomswell Diaries. (p. 202)

B

Buitrago, Fanny. Casa del Abuelo. Gonzalez, Henry, illus. (p. 273)
—Casa del Arco Iris: Una Novela de la Infancia. Gonzalez, Henry, illus. (p. 273)
Bujold, Lois McMaster. Ethan of Athos. Lewis, Suford, ed. (p. 539)
Bujor, Flavia. Profecia de las Piedras. (p. 1409)
—Prophecy of the Stones. Coverdale, Linda, tr. (p. 1411)
Bukhari, Mary, ed. see Markowitz, Darryl.
Bukhatir, A. A. Dragon Boy & the Witches of Galz. (p. 476)
Bukiet, Melvin Jules. Undertown. (p. 1817)
Bukiet, Suzanne. Scripts of the World. (p. 1533)
Buklis, Lawrence S. Mysteries from the Yukon: Three Fisheries Adventures for Students. (p. 1222)
Bulakh, Nadia. Play Day Our Way! Finch, Donna, ed. (p. 1371)
Bulanadi, Danny, illus. see Pearl, Michael.
Bulanadi, Danny, jt. auth. see Pearl, Michael.
Bulbring, Edyth. Cornelia Button & the Globe of Gamagion. (p. 367)
Bulfinch, Thomas. Boy Inventor. (p. 218)
—Bulfinch's Mythology. (p. 240)
Bulger, Melissa. We Can Dream. (p. 1866)
Bulger, Roger J. Pioneer for Health, a Portrait in Leadership: The Honorable Paul Grant Rogers. (p. 1361)
Bulger, Roger J. & Sirota Rosenberg, Shirley. Portrait of Leadership, a Fighter for Health: The Honorable Paul Grant Rogers. (p. 1386)
Bulger, Tawnya. Katrina: Growing Wings. (p. 945)
Bulion, Leslie. At the Sea Floor Café: Odd Ocean Critter Poems Evans, Leslie, illus. (p. 111)
—Hey There, Stink Bug! Evans, Leslie, illus. (p. 774)
—Random Body Parts Lowery, Mike, illus. (p. 1438)
—Trouble with Rules (p. 1790)
—Uncharted Waters (p. 1811)
Bulkowski, James. O'Briah: A Bedtime Story. (p. 1275)
Bull, Angela. Story of Martin Luther King, Level 4. (p. 1659)
Bull, Carolyn, illus. see Boase, Wendy.
Bull, Emma, jt. auth. see Brust, Steven.
Bull, George, tr. see Machiavelli, Niccolò.
Bull, Jane. Libro de la Navidad. Cortes, Eunice, tr. (p. 1006)
Bull, Jane & Dorling Kindersley Publishing Staff. Made by Me. (p. 1070)
Bull, Nicola, ed. see Henning, Heather.
Bull, Pat. Academic Word Power 3. (p. 7)
Bull, Peter. Horses. (p. 800)
—Transport. (p. 1779)
—Under the Sea. (p. 1814)
Bull, Peter, illus. see Brooke, Samantha.
Bull, Peter, illus. see Carson, Mary Kay.
Bull, Peter, illus. see Ganeri, Anita.
Bull, Peter, illus. see Gifford, Clive.
Bull, Peter, illus. see Kingfisher Editors & Murrell, Deborah.
Bull, Peter, illus. see Llewellyn, Claire & Johnson, Jinny.
Bull, Peter, illus. see Llewellyn, Claire.
Bull, Peter, illus. see Murrell, Deborah.
Bull, Peter, illus. see Oxlade, Chris.
Bull, Peter, illus. see Regan, Lisa.
Bull, Peter, illus. see Stewart, Melissa.
Bull, Peter, illus. see Stott, Carole.
Bull, Peter, jt. auth. see Gilpin, Dan.
Bull, Peter, jt. auth. see Johnson, Jinny.
Bull, Peter & Ganeri, Anita. Explorers: Whales & Dolphins. (p. 551)
Bull, Schuyler. Crocodile Crossing. Male, Alan, illus. (p. 384)
—Through Tsavo: A Story of an East African Savanna. (p. 1745)
Bull, Schuyler M. Crocodile Crossing. Male, Alan, illus. (p. 384)
Bull Tellman, Gunvor, illus. see Undset, Sigrid.
Bull, Webster. Kittery Kayaker. Decker, Jacqueline, illus. (p. 963)
Bulla, jt. auth. see Bulla, Clyde Robert.
Bulla, jt. auth. see Robert, Bulla Clyde.
Bulla, Clyde Robert. Secret Valley. (p. 1544)
Bulla, Clyde Robert & Bulla. Shoeshine Girl. Grant, Leigh & Burke, Jim, illus. (p. 1568)
Bulla, Lynda. Churkendoose. (p. 318)
—Freedom Rings: An American Parable. (p. 635)
—Katydid. (p. 946)
Bulla, Randy, illus. see Wells, Sherry A.
Bullard, Alan. Sight-Reading Sourcebook. (p. 1574)
Bullard, Joyce, illus. see Price, J. M.
Bullard, Lisa. Ace Your Oral or Multimedia Presentation. (p. 8)
—Avalanches. (p. 118)
—Big & Small [Scholastic]: An Animal Opposites Book. (p. 177)
—Blizzards. (p. 200)
—Brandon's Birthday Surprise. Saunders, Katie, illus. (p. 222)
—Brody Borrows Money. Byrne, Mike, illus. (p. 230)
—Brown Food Fun [Ars Scribendi (Netherlands)]. (p. 232)
—Busy Animals: Learning about Animals in Autumn Takvorian, Nadine, illus. (p. 245)
—Caleb's Hanukkah. Basaluzzo, Constanza, illus. (p. 252)
—Carter's Christmas. Saunders, Katie, illus. (p. 272)
—Chelsea's Chinese New Year. Saunders, Katie, illus. (p. 297)
—Chevrolet Corvette. (p. 299)
—Choose to Reuse. Thomas, Wes, illus. (p. 310)
—Choose to Reuse. Thomas, Wes & Thomas, John, Jr., illus. (p. 310)
—Cloverleaf Books#8482; - Holidays & Special Day. (p. 335)
—Cloverleaf Books#8482; - Holidays & Special Days: 6Pack Set. Saunders, Katie, illus. (p. 335)
—Cloverleaf Books#8482; - Holidays & Special Days: Single Copy Set. Saunders, Katie, illus. (p. 335)
—Cranes. (p. 376)
—Crocheting for Fun! Suker, Ashlee, illus. (p. 384)
—Daniela's Day of the Dead. Conger, Holli, illus. (p. 405)
—Earth Day Every Day. Xin, Xiao, illus. (p. 495)
—Earth Day Every Day. Xin, Xiao & Zheng, Xin, illus. (p. 495)
—Ella Earns Her Own Money. Moran, Mike, illus. (p. 513)
—Ella Earns Her Own Money. Moran, Michael, illus. (p. 513)
—Emma's Easter. Basaluzzo, Constanza, illus. (p. 520)
—Empire State Building. (p. 521)
—Erie Canal. (p. 533)
—Everglades. (p. 542)
—Fast & Slow: An Animal Opposites Book Saunders-Smith, Gail, ed. (p. 576)
—Fast & Slow [Scholastic]: An Animal Opposites Book. (p. 576)
—Ferrari (p. 582)
—Ferrari/Ferrari. (p. 582)
—Ford Mustang (p. 617)
—Ford Mustang/Ford Mustang. (p. 617)
—Gabriel Gets a Great Deal. Moran, Mike, illus. (p. 652)
—Gateway Arch. (p. 658)
—Go Easy on Energy. Thomas, Wes, illus. (p. 686)
—Go Easy on Energy. Thomas, Wes & Thomas, John, Jr., illus. (p. 686)
—Grace's Thanksgiving. Saunders, Katie, illus. (p. 705)
—Grandes y Pequeños: Un Libro de Animales Opuestos. (p. 707)
—Green Food Fun [Ars Scribendi (Netherlands)]. (p. 721)
—Hailey's Halloween. Conger, Holli, illus. (p. 735)
—Hovercraft. (p. 804)
—I'M a Midnight Snacker! - Meet a Vampire. Buccheri, Chiara, illus. (p. 858)
—I'M Casting a Spell!! Meet a Fairy-Tale Witch. Diaz, Diego, illus. (p. 858)
—I'm Fearsome & Furry! Meet a Werewolf. Moran, Mike, illus. (p. 858)
—I'm from Outer Space! Meet an Alien. Moran, Mike, illus. (p. 859)
—Kevin's Kwanzaa. Basaluzzo, Constanza, illus. (p. 950)
—Kyle Keeps Track of Cash. Byrne, Mike, illus. (p. 969)
—Largos, Cortos y Pequeños: Un Libro de Animales Opuestos. Ferrer, Martin Luis Guzman, tr. (p. 975)
—Leaves Fall Down: Learning about Autumn Leaves Takvorian, Nadine, illus. (p. 986)
—Lily Learns about Wants & Needs. Schneider, Christine M., illus. (p. 1018)
—Look Out for Litter. Xin, Xiao, illus. (p. 1049)
—Look Out for Litter. Xin, Xiao & Zheng, Xin, illus. (p. 1049)
—Loud & Quiet [Scholastic]: An Animal Opposites Book. (p. 1057)
—Lowriders. (p. 1061)
—Marco's Cinco de Mayo. Conger, Holli, illus. (p. 1092)
—Marco's Cinco de Mayo. Conger, Hollil, illus. (p. 1092)
—Mojados y Secos. Ferrer, Martin Luis Guzman, tr. (p. 1160)
—My Clothes, Your Clothes. (p. 1200)
—My Clothes, Your Clothes. Kurilla, Renee, illus. (p. 1200)
—My Family, Your Family. (p. 1203)
—My Food, Your Food. Schneider, Christine, illus. (p. 1208)
—My Home, Your Home. (p. 1211)
—My Home, Your Home. Becker, Paula, illus. (p. 1211)
—My Language, Your Language. (p. 1211)
—My Religion, Your Religion. Conger, Holli, illus. (p. 1217)
—Nina & Nolan Build a Nonsense Poem. Girourard, Patrick, illus. (p. 1256)
—Orange Food Fun [Ars Scribendi (Netherlands)]. (p. 1301)
—Porsche (p. 1386)
—Porsche/Porsche. (p. 1386)
—Power up to Fight Pollution. Thomas, Wes, illus. (p. 1390)
—Power up to Fight Pollution. Thomas, Wes & Thomas, John, Jr., illus. (p. 1390)
—Powerboats. (p. 1390)
—Rally for Recycling. Thomas, Wes, illus. (p. 1437)
—Rashad's Ramadan & Eid Al-Fitr. Conger, Holli, illus. (p. 1439)
—Rashad's Ramadan & Eid Al-Fitr. Conger, Hollil, illus. (p. 1439)
—Red Food Fun (p. 1454)
—Red Food Fun [Ars Scribendi (Netherlands)]. (p. 1454)
—Redwood Forests. (p. 1456)
—Sarah's Passover. Basaluzzo, Constanza, illus. (p. 1514)
—Shanti Saves Her Money. Schneider, Christine M., illus. (p. 1559)
—Stock Cars. (p. 1651)
—Suaves y Asperos. (p. 1670)
—Supercross Motorcycles. (p. 1683)
—Supercross Motorcycles. (p. 1683)
—Trick-or-Treat on Milton Street. Oeltjenbruns, Joni, illus. (p. 1786)
—Tsunamis. (p. 1795)
—Turn Left at the Cow. (p. 1797)
—Watch over Our Water. Xin, Xiao, illus. (p. 1861)
—Wet & Dry: An Animal Opposites Book Saunders-Smith, Gail, ed. (p. 1877)
—What's the Difference Between a Leopard & a Cheetah? Bandelin, Debra et al, illus. (p. 1899)
—What's the Difference Between an Alligator & a Crocodile? Dacey, Bob & Bandelin Dacey Studios Staff, illus. (p. 1899)
—White Food Fun [Ars Scribendi (Netherlands)]. (p. 1913)
—Yellow Food Fun [Ars Scribendi (Netherlands)]. (p. 1970)
—You Can Write a Story! A Story-Writing Recipe for Kids. Melmon, Deborah H., illus. (p. 1974)
Bullard, Lisa, jt. auth. see Lerner Classroom Staff.
Bullas, Will, illus. see Domeniconi, David.
Bulleman, Curtis David. Car Crazy: Tricked Out Activity Book. (p. 265)
—Car Crazy Super Sticker Book. (p. 265)
—Let's Color Together — Cool Cars. (p. 995)
Bulleman, Curtis David & Coloring Books Staff. 3-D Coloring Book—Car Crazy! (p. 1991)
Bullen, Alexandra. Wish. (p. 1940)
—Wishful Thinking. (p. 1940)
Bullen, J. B. Byzantium Rediscovered. (p. 249)
Bullen, Marjorie, illus. see Carsonie, Diane Lynn.
Bullen, Marjorie J., illus. see Carsonie, Diane Lynn.
Bullene, Emma Frances Jay. Psychic History of the Cliff Dwellers, Their Origin & Destruction (p. 1413)
Buller, Ginny. Happy Misunderstanding: How Folly Gets his Name. Chettle, Julie, illus. (p. 746)
Buller, Jon, illus. see Schade, Susan.
Buller, Jon, jt. auth. see Schade, Susan.
Buller, Jon & Schade, Susan. I Love You, Good Night: Lap Edition. Pons, Bernadette, illus. (p. 843)
—I Love You, Good Night. Pons, Bernadette, illus. (p. 843)
Buller, Jon & Warner, Sally. Smart about the First Ladies: Smart about History. Buller, Jon et al, illus. (p. 1592)
Buller, Jon, et al. Smart about the Fifty States. Buller, Jon et al, illus. (p. 1592)
—Smart about the Presidents. Buller, Jon et al, illus. (p. 1592)
Buller, Laura. Bugs Hide & Seek. (p. 237)
—DK Readers L1: Star Wars: What Is a Wookiee? Star Wars: What Is a Wookiee? (p. 456)
—What Is a Wookiee? (p. 1888)
Buller, Laura, jt. auth. see Dorling Kindersley Publishing Staff.
Buller, Laura & Dorling Kindersley Publishing Staff. Faith Like Mine: A Celebration of the World's Religions—Seen Through the Eyes of Children. (p. 565)
Bullis, J. Noah Peepkin - a Small Adventure. (p. 1261)
Bullivant, Cecil. Every Boys Book of Hobbies. (p. 542)
Bullman, Carol & Madsen, James. Christmas House. Madsen, James, illus. (p. 314)
Bulloch, Ivan. Watch It Cook. James, Diane, illus. (p. 1861)
Bulloch, Ivan & James, Diane. Learn with Me 123. Pangbourne, Daniel, illus. (p. 984)
—Learn with Me ABC. Pangbourne, Daniel, photos by. (p. 984)
Bullock, Brad, illus. see Jasper, J. J.
Bullock, Cecile Boyd. Grands Visit the Stars: A Trip to the Planetarium. (p. 710)
Bullock, Harold B. Battle for the Worlds. Anderson, Jean, ed. (p. 145)
Bullock, Jodi. Butterfly. (p. 247)
Bullock Jr., Michael A., illus. see Jones, Debra.
Bullock, Kathleen. Clown-Around Kids. Bullock, Kathleen, illus. (p. 335)
Bullock, Kathleen, illus. see Chatel, Kim.
Bullock, Kathleen, illus. see Farnette, Cherrie, et al.
Bullock, Kathleen, illus. see Forte, Imogene & Frank, Marjorie.
Bullock, Kathleen, illus. see Forte, Imogene, et al.
Bullock, Kathleen, illus. see Frank, Marjorie & Norris, Jill.
Bullock, Kathleen, illus. see Frank, Marjorie.
Bullock, Linda. Looking Through a Microscope. (p. 1051)
—Looking Through a Telescope. (p. 1051)
—You Can Use a Balance. (p. 1974)
Bullock, Miranda. Mama Where Are You? (p. 1084)
Bullock, Rob. Noah Ramsbottom & the Cave Elves. (p. 1261)
Bullock, Robert. Sam Marsh & the Battle of the Cloudships: The Sam Marsh Stories - Part 2. (p. 1506)
Bullock, Robert John. Jacob's War. (p. 904)
Bulson, Deacon Michael E. Teach What You Believe: Timeless Homilies for Deacons - Liturgical Cycle A. (p. 1708)
Bultje, Jan Willem. Czech Republic. (p. 397)
—Lithuania. Hoving, Wilma, tr. (p. 1023)
Bultje, Jan Willem, photos by see Alzpurlete, Amanda.
Bultje, Jan Willem, photos by see Hilsjärv, Piret & Hilepuu, Ene.
Bulwer-Lytton, Edward. Ultimos Dias de Pompeya. (p. 1810)
Bulychev, Kirill. Those Who Survive. Guetov, Dimitar D., ed. (p. 1740)
Bumbalough, Jerry. Purple pup girls are grape Jelly. Bennett, Harry, Jr., illus. (p. 1419)
Bumcrot, Curt. Personal Finance Packet. Zyp, Nicole, ed. (p. 1344)
Bumcrot, Curt & Bumcrot, Jenny. Achieving Peak Performance New Edition. Krischke, Nikki, ed. (p. 9)
Bumcrot, Curt & Dunlap, Shiree. Testing Targets: For Streams of Civilization. Zyp, Nicole, ed. (p. 1723)
—Testing Targets: For Streams of Civilization Zyp, Nikki & Robinson, Heidi, eds. (p. 1723)
—Testing Targets: For Science of the Physical Creation. Zyp, Nicole & Robinson, Heidi, eds. (p. 1723)
Bumcrot, Curt, et al. Achieving Peak Performance Practice Test: Grade 10. (p. 9)
—Achieving Peak Performance Practice Test New Edition. (p. 9)
—Achieving Peak Performance Practice Test New Edition. Finley, Mavion, ed. (p. 9)
Bumcrot, Jenny, jt. auth. see Bumcrot, Curt.
Bumgarner, Jennifer Laughlin. Walking in Mommy's Shoes. (p. 1854)
Bumgarner, Sam. Little Sami's Silly Again (p. 1036)
—Silly Little Sami. (p. 1576)
Bumpers, Katrina. Alphabet Fun, Book 2: Coloring & Activity Book. (p. 49)
Bumpers, Katrina B. Alphabet Fun, Book 1: Coloring & Activity Book. Lopez, Eddie, ed. (p. 49)
Bumpus, Tawanna. Tawanna's Children's Short Story Collections. (p. 1707)
Bumstead, Debbie, illus. see Nelson, James Gary.
Bumstead, Pat & Worsley, Norman H. Canadian Skin & Scales. (p. 260)
Bumstead, Robin, jt. auth. see Drez, Jennifer.
Bunanta, Murti. Tiny Boy & Other Tales from Indonesia Hardiyono, illus. (p. 1756)
Bunce, Elizabeth C. Curse Dark as Gold. (p. 394)
—Liar's Moon. (p. 1005)
—StarCrossed. (p. 1642)
Bunce, Margaret. Adventures with Nature: A Story about Olivia & Her Little Dog, Jake. (p. 25)
Bunch, Bryan H. & Tesar, Jenny E. Diseases (p. 450)
Bunch, Elma Lillian. How Many Doodles Does It Take to Make a Doodle Bug? (p. 811)
—I Love You All the Way to Jesus & Back. (p. 843)
Bunch, Paul, illus. see Mason, Alexis.
Bundile, Mike, et al. Make More Than Your Parents: Your Guide to Financial Freedom. (p. 1079)
Bundrick, Lisa. Learning about Feelings (p. 984)
Bundschuh, Rick. Burned (p. 243)
—Clash (p. 327)
Bundschuh, Rick, jt. auth. see Hamilton, Bethany.
Bundy, E. A. Phillip Marrow, Jr. (p. 1350)
Bundy, John. Kimble's New Armor. (p. 957)
Bung, Lee Ann. I See Heart Colors. (p. 845)
Bunk, Tomas, illus. see Eisenkraft, Arthur & Kirkpatrick, Larry D.
Bunker, Thomas, illus. see Bradford, Danette J.
Bunker, Thomas, illus. see Bryant, Cathy.
Bunker, Thomas, illus. see Goodman, Peggy.
Bunker, Tom, illus. see Myers, Bob.
Bunkers, Traci & Maidment, Stella. Print It! (p. 1406)
Bunkley, Anita Richmond. Steppin' Out with an Attitude: Sister, Sell your Dream! (p. 1648)
Bunkus, Denise, illus. see Swallow, Pamela Curtis & Swallow, Pamela C.
Bunn, Bill. Duck Boy. (p. 488)
Bunn, Cullen. Doom Maidens. (p. 470)
Bunnell, Jacinta. Sometimes the Spoon Runs Away with Another Spoon Coloring Book. Kusinitz, Nat, illus. (p. 1610)
Bunnell, James. Night Orbs. (p. 1254)
Bunnett, Rochelle. Amigos en la Escuela Muñoz, Yenny, tr. from ENG. (p. 65)
Bunnett, Rochelle, photos by see Wess, Robert, illus.
Bunney, Ron. All That Glitters. (p. 45)
—No One Owns Me. (p. 1259)
Bunny, Hull. Hidden Treasure. Fleming, Kye, illus. (p. 776)
Bunte, Joan & Madden, Alison. Fred & Fiona Flea: the Crown Jewels Caper: Globetrotters Extraordinaire. (p. 632)
Bunting, Elaine & D'Amario, Patricia. Counties of Maryland's Lower Eastern Shore Ramsey, Marcy Dunn, illus. (p. 370)
Bunting, Eve. Anna's Table. Morley, Taia, illus. (p. 85)
—Baby Can. Chambliss, Maxie, illus. (p. 125)
—Baby Shower. Love, Judy, illus. (p. 128)
—Ballywhinney Girl. McCully, Emily Arnold, illus. (p. 135)
—Big Bear's Big Boat. Carpenter, Nancy, illus. (p. 178)
—Bones of Fred McFee. Cyrus, Kurt, illus. (p. 209)
—Cart That Carried Martin. (p. 272)
—Cart That Carried Martin. Tate, Don, illus. (p. 272)
—Ducky. Wisniewski, David, illus. (p. 488)
—Emma's Turtle. Winborn, Marsha, illus. (p. 520)
—Finn McCool & the Great Fish. Pullen, Zachary, illus. (p. 589)
—Flower Garden. Hewitt, Kathryn, illus. (p. 607)
—Frog & Friends: Party at the Pond. (p. 639)
—Frog & Friends: Book Four: Frog's Flying Adventure. (p. 639)
—Frog & Friends: Outdoor Surprises. Masse, Josée, illus. (p. 639)
—Frog & Friends. (p. 639)
—Frog & Friends. Masse, Josée, illus. (p. 639)
—Frog & Friends: The Best Summer Ever. (p. 640)
—Frog & Friends: Frog's Lucky Day 7. Masse, Josée, illus. (p. 640)
—Girls A to Z. Bloom, Suzanne, illus. (p. 679)
—Gleam & Glow. Sylvada, Peter, illus. (p. 682)
—Have You Seen My New Blue Socks? Ruzzier, Sergio, illus. (p. 754)
—Hey Diddle Diddle. Fraser, Mary Ann, illus. (p. 774)
—Hurry! Hurry! Mack, Jeff, illus. (p. 830)
—I Don't Want to Go to Camp. Cocca-Leffler, Maryann, illus. (p. 838)
—I Have an Olive Tree. (p. 839)
—In the Haunted House. Meddaugh, Susan, illus. (p. 866)
—Jamaica Tag-Along. Hewitt, Kathryn, illus. (p. 906)
—Lambkins. Keegan, Jonathan, illus. (p. 972)
—Man with the Red Bag. (p. 1086)
—My Dog Jack Is Fat Rex, Michael, illus. (p. 1202)
—My Mom's Wedding. Papp, Lisa, illus. (p. 1214)
—My Red Balloon. Life, Kay, illus. (p. 1217)
—My Robot. Fehlau, Dagmar, illus. (p. 1217)
—My Special Day at Third Street School. Bloom, Suzanne, illus. (p. 1219)
—Night of the Gargoyles. Wiesner, David, illus. (p. 1254)
—No Nap. Meddaugh, Susan, illus. (p. 1259)
—One Candle. Popp, K. Wendy, illus. (p. 1294)
—One Green Apple. Lewin, Ted, illus. (p. 1295)
—Our Library. Smith, Maggie, illus. (p. 1309)
—Picnic in October. Carpenter, Nancy, illus. (p. 1355)
—Pirate Boy. Fortenberry, Julie, illus. (p. 1362)
—Pirate Captain's Daughter. (p. 1362)
—Pop's Bridge. Payne, C. F., illus. (p. 1385)
—Presence: A Ghost Story. (p. 1396)
—Reggie. Burkett, D. Brent, illus. (p. 1457)
—Rudi's Pond. Himler, Ronald, illus. (p. 1494)
—S Is for Shamrock: An Ireland Alphabet. Faulkner, Matt & Bunting, Matt, illus. (p. 1499)
—S. O. S. Titanic. (p. 1499)
—Scary, Scary Halloween Brett, Jan, illus. (p. 1520)
—Snowboarding on Monster Mountain. Ritz, Karen, illus. (p. 1600)
—So Far from the Sea. Soentpiet, Chris K., illus. (p. 1602)
—Sudden Silence. (p. 1672)
—That's What Leprechauns Do. McCully, Emily Arnold, illus. (p. 1727)
—Train to Somewhere. Himler, Ronald, illus. (p. 1777)
—Tweak Tweak. Ruzzier, Sergio, illus. (p. 1799)
—Wash Day. Sneed, Brad, illus. (p. 1859)
—Wedding. Trapani, Iza, illus. (p. 1870)
—Whose Shoe? Ruzzier, Sergio, illus. (p. 1922)
—Will It Be a Baby Brother? Spiegel, Beth, illus. (p. 1932)
—Yard Sale. Castillo, Lauren, illus. (p. 1968)
—You Were Loved Before You Were Born. Barbour, Karen, illus. (p. 1976)
Bunting, Eve & Giblin, James Cross. Ghost Children. (p. 670)
Bunting, Jane. My First ABC. (p. 1204)
—My First Action Word Book: A Picture Dictionary of 1,000 First Words. (p. 1204)
Bunting, John D. College Vocabulary (p. 340)
Bunting, Lisa, et al. Harcourt Health & Fitness. (p. 747)
Bunting, Matt, illus. see Bunting, Eve.
Bunting, Robert L. Into Oblivion: The Lives & Times Leading up to the Final Voyage of the Steamship Marine City from the Ghost Town of Alcona, Michigan on Lake Huron 1880. (p. 881)
Bunting, Sarah Clare. Why Are You So Lazy Owl? (p. 1922)
Bunton, M. Star Girl. (p. 1640)
Bunton, M. Catherine. Butterfly Peddler. (p. 248)
—Fairy Tale Keeper. (p. 564)
—Little Maestro: A Forest Club Activity Book. (p. 1031)
Bunyan, John. Pilgrim's Progress (p. 1359)
—Pilgrim's Progress. (p. 1359)
—Pilgrim's Progress. Pooley, Roger, ed. (p. 1359)

—Pilgrim's Progress 2: Christiana's Story. (p. 1359)
—Pilgrim's Progress from This World to That Which Is to Come;Delivered under the Similitude of a Dream. Barnard, Frederick & Linton, J. D., illus. (p. 1359)
—Sacrificio Aceptable. Greendyk, William, tr. from ENG. (p. 1501)
Bunyan, John, jt. auth. see Watson, Jean.
Bunyan, Noah F. Lightning Man #1. (p. 1016)
Buonanno, Graziella Pacini. Dancing on Grapes. Capaldi, Gina, illus. (p. 403)
Burack, Emilie Christie. Runaway's Gold. (p. 1497)
Burak, Kathryn. Emily's Dress & Other Missing Things. (p. 519)
Buranbaeva, Oksana, jt. auth. see Beliaev, Edward.
Buranelli, Vincent. American Spies & Traitors. (p. 63)
Burarrwanga, Laklak, et al. Welcome to My Country. (p. 1873)
Burbank, Addison, illus. see Manousos, Demetrius.
Burbank, Austin. Grandson's Journey to Santa Claus: The Tinmouth Pond Series Book 1. (p. 710)
—Santa Claus's Destiny: The Tinmouth Pond Series Book 3. (p. 1511)
—There's a Bit of Santa Claus in Everyone: Tinmouth Pond Series Book 2. (p. 1730)
Burbank, Shirley Ann. Where Did I Come From? (p. 1906)
Burbank, Vivian. My Grandma's Playhouse. (p. 1210)
Burbridge, Ella. Egg on Their Faces. (p. 506)
Burbridge, William J., illus. see Murphy, D. Cathy.
Burby, Leslie. Grace Figures Out School. (p. 704)
Burcaw, Shane. Laughing at My Nightmare. (p. 980)
Burch, Benjamin, illus. see Depken, Kristen L.
Burch, Benjamin, illus. see Golden Books.
Burch, Christian. Hit the Road, Manny: A Manny Files Novel. (p. 786)
—Manny Files. (p. 1088)
Burch, D. D. Roney & Ben's Super-Duper Mission to Mars. (p. 1487)
Burch, Deborah. God's Greatest Gift. (p. 691)
—God's Greatest Gift. Burch, Deborah, illus. (p. 691)
Burch, Genny. My Name Is Bobby Claus: A fictional Christmas story for Children. (p. 1215)
Burch, Heather. Halflings (p. 737)
Burch, Joann J. Jefferson Davis: Soldier & President of the Confederacy. (p. 912)
Burch, Lynda S. I SEE Seaside Birds! Burch, Lynda S. & Roberts, MarySue, photos by. (p. 845)
—Meet Me at the Park! Burch, Lynda S., photos by. (p. 1121)
—Wicky Wacky Things that Go! Airplanes 1. Roberts, MarySue, photos by. (p. 1927)
—Wicky Wacky Things that Go! Automobiles 1. Burch, Lynda S. & Roberts, MarySue, photos by. (p. 1927)
—Wicky wacky Things that Go! Boats 1. Burch, Lynda S., photos by. (p. 1927)
—Wicky Wacky Things that Go! Busses. Burch, Lynda S., photos by. (p. 1927)
—Wicky Wacky Things that Go! Emergency Vehicles. Burch, Lynda S., photos by. (p. 1927)
—Wicky Wacky Things that Go! Hot Air Balloons. Roberts, MarySue, photos by. (p. 1927)
—Wicky Wacky Things that Go! Tractors. Burch, Lynda S., photos by. (p. 1927)
—Wicky Wacky Things That Go! Trucks. Burch, Lynda S., photos by. (p. 1927)
—Zoom Zoom Zoom Come Count with Me! Burch, Lynda S., photos by. (p. 1989)
Burch, Lynda S., ed. see Ruble, Eugene.
Burch, Lynda S. & Roberts, MarySue, photos by. I SEE Seaside Birds! (p. 845)
Burch, Minnie Kirby. Adventures of Squir Squirrel: A Story of Love & Trust. (p. 23)
Burch, Monte. Antler, Bone, Horn, & Hide: Projects You Can Make at Home. (p. 89)
—Wildlife & Woodlot Management Handbook: A Comprehensive Handbook for Food Plot & Habitat Development. (p. 1931)
Burch, Regina G. Catch 'Em Being Good! Hamaguchi, Carla & Fisch, Teri, eds. (p. 279)
—Character Education Resource Guide. Fisch, Teri L., ed. (p. 291)
Burch, Regina G. & Donovan Guntly, Jenette. I Can Be Responsible. Burris, Priscilla, illus. (p. 835)
—I Can Share with Others. Jarrett, Michael, photos by. (p. 836)
—I Can Show I Care. Jarrett, Michael, photos by. (p. 836)
—I Can Show Respect. Ember, Kathi, illus. (p. 836)
—I Can Tell the Truth. Motoyama, Keiko, illus. (p. 836)
Burch, Robert. Queenie Peavey. (p. 1425)
Burch, Sharon. Freddie the Frog & the Bass Clef Monster. Harris, Tiffany, illus. (p. 632)
—Freddie the Frog & the Mysterious Wahooooo: 3rd Adventure: Tempo Island. (p. 633)
—Freddie the Frog & the Thump in the Night: 1st Adventure - Treble Clef Island. (p. 633)
—Scat Singing for Kids: A Step-By-Step Journey in Jazz. (p. 1521)
—Sticks! (p. 1650)
Burch, Sharon & Watley, Deborah. Freddie the Frog & the Secret of Crater Island: 4th Adventure: Crater Island. (p. 633)
Burcham, David, illus. see Ross, Patrick.
Burchard, Elizabeth R., jt. ed. see Ace Academics.
Burchard, Patti. Cows Really Do Fly Kites: Patti Burchard. (p. 374)
Burchard, Peter. Frederick Douglass: For the Great Family of Man. (p. 633)
Burchartz, Roxanne, illus. see Gogarty, Brian.
Burchell, Graham. Ice Spells of Krollinad. (p. 850)
Burchell, Graham, tr. see Foucault, Michel & Davidson, Arnold I.
Burchell, Graham, tr. see Foucault, Michel.
Burchers, Sam, Jr., et al. Vocabulary Classic Series: The Call of the Wild. (p. 1847)
Burchett. When I Grow Up: Level A. (p. 1903)
Burchett, Author Walter, BA. Christian children's circle the Word. (p. 311)
—Christian children's crossword puzzles/circle the words/fill in the Blanks. (p. 311)
—Christian children's fill in the Blank. (p. 311)
—Christian children's fill in the blank Revised. (p. 311)
—Christian children's questions & answers abraham & keturah to israel & rachel Volume 2. (p. 311)
—Christian children's questions & answers adam & eve to abraham & sarah Volume 1. (p. 311)
—Christian children's questions & answers birth of christ Volume 5. (p. 311)
—Christian children's questions & answers joseph (coat of many colors) Volume 3. (p. 311)
—Christian children's questions & answers moses Volume 4. (p. 311)
—Christian children's questions & answers resurrection of christ Volume 7. (p. 311)
—Christian crossword puzzles for Children. (p. 311)
Burchett, Claudette. Time for Fun. (p. 1751)
Burchett, Jan & Vogler, Sara. Avalanche Alert Le Feyer, Diane, illus. (p. 118)
—Desert Danger Le Feyer, Diane, illus. (p. 429)
—Desert Danger Le Feyer, Diane & Kennedy, Sam, illus. (p. 429)
—Earthquake Escape Le Feyer, Diane, illus. (p. 497)
—Ocean S. O. S. Le Feyer, Diane, illus. (p. 1276)
—Ocean S. O. S. Le Feyer, Diane & Kennedy, Sam, illus. (p. 1276)
—Poacher Panic Le Feyer, Diane, illus. (p. 1374)
—Polar Meltdown Le Feyer, Diane, illus. (p. 1379)
—Rainforest Rescue Le Feyer, Diane, illus. (p. 1436)
—Safari Survival Le Feyer, Diane, illus. (p. 1502)
—Safari Survival Le Feyer, Diane & Kennedy, Sam, illus. (p. 1502)
Burchett, Janet & Vogler, Sara. Bones & Groans. (p. 209)
—Creep from the Deep. Brown, Judy, illus. (p. 381)
—Shiver & Deliver. Brown, Judy, illus. (p. 1567)
Burchett, Loni. Bear & Katie in A Riverboat Ride (p. 150)
Burchett, Loni R. Bear & Katie in a Day at Nestlenook Farm. (p. 150)
—Bear & Katie in a Day with Friends (p. 150)
—Bear & Katie in the Great Searsport Caper. (p. 150)
Burchett, Mary. When Mommy & Daddy Divorce. (p. 1903)
Burchett, Rick, illus. see Dini, Paul.
Burchett, Rick, illus. see Hoena, Blake A. & Loughridge, Lee.
Burchett, Rick, illus. see Kupperberg, Paul & Loughridge, Lee.
Burchett, Rick, illus. see Lemke, Donald & Loughridge, Lee.
Burchett, Rick, illus. see Lemke, Donald B. & Loughridge, Lee.
Burchett, Rick, illus. see Loughridge, Lee & Hoena, Blake A.
Burchett, Rick, illus. see McCloud, Scott.
Burchett, Rick, illus. see Pasko, Martin & Loughridge, Lee.
Burchett, Rick, illus. see Powell, Martin A., et al.
Burchett, Rick, illus. see Slott, Dan, et al.
Burchett, Rick, illus. see Torres, J.
Burchette, Ruby J. Dog Went to School (p. 462)
Burchfield, Cindy. Gimme, Gimme Moocher Marmots. Burchfield, Cindy, illus. (p. 676)
Burchielli, Riccardo, jt. auth. see Wood, Brian.
Burchill, Julie. Sugar Rush. (p. 1673)
—Sweet (p. 1689)
Burchwell, Erin, illus. see Levine, Susan Sachs.
Burchwell, Erin McCauley, illus. see Levine, Susan Sachs.
Burciaga, David. Say Cheese, God! Wisner, Luke, illus. (p. 1518)
Burckhardt, Ann, jt. auth. see Germaine, Elizabeth.
Burckhardt, Marc, illus. see Cash, John Carter.
Burckhardt, Marc, illus. see Creech, Sharon.
Burckhardt, Marc, illus. see Golio, Gary.
Burckhardt, Marc, illus. see Rosen, Michael J.
Burckhardt, Marc, illus. see Slebert, Diane.
Burd, Clara M., illus. see Bailey, Carolyn Sherwin.
Burd, Nick. Vast Fields of Ordinary. (p. 1833)
Burdan, Andrew. Te Po Roa. (p. 1708)
Burden, Andrea, illus. see Bozarth, Jan.
Burden, B. J. My ABC Scripture Book. (p. 1195)
—Nine Pies. (p. 1256)
Burden, Meg. King Commands. (p. 958)
Burden, P. John, illus. see Weber, Ilse.
Burden, Paul, jt. auth. see Cooper, James M.
Burden, Peter. News of the World? Fake Sheikhs & Royal Trappings. Dillon, Julia & Hiscocks, Dan, eds. (p. 1249)
Burden, Sara. Tom's Wheels. (p. 1765)
Burden, Wendy Lynn. Isaiah. (p. 891)
Burden-Evans, Patricia. Steep Mountain to Climb. (p. 1646)
Burden-Patmon, Denise. Imani's Gift at Kwanzaa. (p. 861)
Burdette, Lucy. Fatal Reservations: A Key West Food Critic Mystery. (p. 577)
Burdette, Roger W. Renaissance of American Coinage 1916-1921 (p. 1460)
Burdick, Jeff. Super Sports Trivia. (p. 1682)
Burdick, Mason. Baseball. (p. 140)
Burdick, Mason, jt. auth. see Roza, Greg.
Burdick, Neal S., jt. auth. see Jamieson, Paul F.
Burdziejko, Lisa. Before She Was Babci (p. 158)
Bureau Of Land Management, et al. Junior Explorer Geology & Fossils Activity Book. (p. 936)
Burfoot, Ella. Bear & Me. (p. 150)
—Betty & the Yeti. (p. 172)
—Don't Kiss the Frog! Princess Stories with Attitude. (p. 467)
—How to Bake a Book. (p. 814)
—Louie & the Monsters. Burfoot, Ella, illus. (p. 1058)
Burfoot, Ella, illus. see Claybourne, Anna.
Burfoot, Ella, illus. see McKee, Brett.
Burford, David. Stones of San Re'al: Book One: the Search for Laura. (p. 1653)
Burford, Dinah. If I Could Talk, I Would Say the Adventures of Miss Pink. (p. 853)
Burford, Lorrimer. Jamaican Storyteller's Tale. (p. 906)
Burford, Michelle, jt. auth. see Douglas, Gabrielle.
Burg, Ann. E Is for Empire: A New York State Alphabet. Brookfield, Maureen, illus. (p. 492)
—Rebekkah's Journey: A World War II Refugee Story. Iskowitz, Joel, illus. (p. 1450)
Burg, Ann E. All the Broken Pieces. (p. 45)
—New York Reader. Darnell, K. L., illus. (p. 1248)
—Pirate Pickle & the White Balloon. Janovitz, Marilyn, illus. (p. 1363)
—Serafina's Promise. (p. 1552)
—Times Square: A New York State Number Book. Brookfield, Maureen K., illus. (p. 1754)
Burg, David F. Great Depression. (p. 715)
Burg, David F. & Woodger, Elin. 1980s. (p. 2002)
Burg, Donna, illus. see Alsbrooks, Stephanie.
Burg, Rebecca. ABCs of Advent: Celebrating the Birth of Jesus As a Family. (p. 4)
Burg, Sarah Emmanuelle. Do You Still Love Me? (p. 458)
Burg, Shana. Laugh with the Moon. (p. 980)
—Thousand Never Evers. (p. 1740)
Burg, Shana, jt. auth. see Coombs, Patricia.
Burgan Cpdt-Ka, Kimberly. Poppy & Puppy Are Friends: A Child's First Introduction to Responsible Dog Ownership. (p. 1385)
Burgan, Michael. African Americans in the Thirteen Colonies. (p. 27)
—America in World War II. (p. 59)
—American Capitalism. (p. 60)
—American Patriot: Benjamin Franklin (p. 62)
—Ancient Aztecs. (p. 68)
—Ancient Incas. (p. 69)
—Arapaho. (p. 94)
—Assassination of Abraham Lincoln. (p. 107)
—Barack Obama. (p. 137)
—Bat Researcher. (p. 143)
—Battle of Bunker Hill: An Interactive History Adventure (p. 146)
—Battle of Gettysburg. Erwin, Steve et al, illus. (p. 146)
—Benedict Arnold: American Hero & Traitor Beatty, Terry, illus. (p. 164)
—Berlin Wall: Barrier to Freedom (p. 167)
—Branches of U. S. Government. (p. 222)
—Breaker Boys: How a Photograph Helped End Child Labor (p. 224)
—Buddhist Faith in America. (p. 234)
—Carpenter. (p. 271)
—Changing Nation (p. 290)
—Chile. (p. 305)
—Christopher Columbus: Opening the Americas to European Exploration. (p. 316)
—Colonial America (p. 341)
—Confucius: Chinese Philosopher & Teacher. (p. 357)
—Connecticut, 1614-1776. (p. 358)
—Creation of the U. S. Constitution. Purcell, Gordon & Beatty, Terry, illus. (p. 379)
—Curse of King Tut's Tomb Schulz, Barbara, illus. (p. 394)
—Developing Flu Vaccines (p. 431)
—Dracula's Dark World. (p. 476)
—Ellis Island: An Interactive History Adventure (p. 515)
—Empire of Ancient Persia. (p. 521)
—Empire of the Mongols, Revised Edition. (p. 521)
—European Industrial Revolution. (p. 540)
—Farming Vegetables & Grains (p. 574)
—Food Engineering: From Concept to Consumer. (p. 613)
—Genetic Engineering: Science, Technology, & Engineering. (p. 660)
—George W. Bush. (p. 663)
—Germany in Our World. (p. 666)
—Great Depression: An Interactive History Adventure (p. 715)
—Great Women of the American Revolution. (p. 719)
—Haymarket Square Tragedy. (p. 755)
—Health Careers in Sports Ferrer, Al, ed. (p. 758)
—Hillary Clinton (p. 779)
—Hillary Rodham Clinton: First Lady & Senator (p. 779)
—Hiroshima: Birth of the Nuclear Age. (p. 781)
—Hot Iron: The Adventures of a Civil War Powder Boy. Rodriquez, Pedro, illus. (p. 801)
—Illinois. (p. 857)
—Inuit. (p. 883)
—Inuit History & Culture. (p. 883)
—Inventions of The 1700s (p. 884)
—Italian Immigrants. (p. 894)
—J. Pierpont Morgan: Industrialist & Financier. (p. 902)
—James Buchanan. (p. 907)
—John F. Kennedy HL Studios Staff, illus. (p. 921)
—Kenya. (p. 949)
—Korean War: An Interactive Modern History Adventure (p. 967)
—Lakota. (p. 972)
—Land & Water. (p. 973)
—Life as a Gladiator: An Interactive History Adventure. (p. 1008)
—Life as a Gladiator. (p. 1008)
—Louisiana Purchase: From Independence to Lewis & Clark. (p. 1059)
—Making Food Choices (p. 1081)
—Making of the Social Network: An Interactive Modern History Adventure (p. 1082)
—Malaysia. (p. 1083)
—Massachusetts, 1620-1776. (p. 1102)
—Miranda V. Arizona: The Rights of the Accused. (p. 1149)
—Muhammad Ali: American Champion Bascle, Brian, illus. (p. 1189)
—Mummy Lairs. (p. 1191)
—My Lai Massacre. (p. 1211)
—Negro Leagues (p. 1240)
—New Mexico: Land of Enchantment. (p. 1246)
—New Mexico (Revised Edition) (p. 1246)
—New York, 1609-1776. (p. 1247)
—North over South: Final Victory in the Civil War (p. 1265)
—Not a Drop to Drink: Water for a Thirsty World. (p. 1266)
—Not a Drop to Drink. (p. 1266)
—Nuevo Mexico. (p. 1270)
—Philippines (p. 1350)
—Popular Culture: 1960-1979 (p. 1385)
—Puerto Rico. (p. 1414)
—Puerto Rico & Other Outlying Areas. (p. 1415)
—Puerto Rico y Otras Areas Perifericas. (p. 1415)
—Pullman Strike Of 1894 (p. 1416)
—Raising the Flag: How a Photograph Gave a Nation Hope in Wartime (p. 1437)
—Reconstruction Amendments Burgan, Michael, illus. (p. 1452)
—Refusing to Crumble: The Danish Resistance in World War II (p. 1457)
—Rhode Island (Revised Edition) (p. 1468)
—Ronald Reagan: A Photographic Story of a Life. (p. 1486)
—Ronald Reagan. (p. 1486)
—Scopes Trial: Faith, Science, & American Education. (p. 1530)
—Shadow Catcher: How Edward S. Curtis Documented American Indian Dignity & Beauty. (p. 1557)
—Shays' Rebellion. (p. 1563)
—Sidney Crosby. (p. 1573)
—Soldier & Founder: Alexander Hamilton (p. 1607)
—South Dakota (Revised Edition) (p. 1617)
—Spies & Traitors: Stories of Masters of Deception (p. 1627)
—Spies of the Civil War: An Interactive History Adventure. (p. 1627)
—Spies of World War I: An Interactive History Adventure. (p. 1627)
—Split History of the American Revolution: A Perspectives Flip Book (p. 1630)
—Split History of World War I. (p. 1630)
—Spying & the Cold War (p. 1636)
—Surviving Earthquakes (p. 1687)
—Tank Man: How a Photograph Defined China's Protest Movement (p. 1705)
—Terrorist Groups (p. 1722)
—Thomas Alva Edison: Great American Inventor (p. 1737)
—Titanic (p. 1757)
—Titanic: Truth & Rumors. Doty, Eldon, illus. (p. 1757)
—Today's U. S. Air Force (p. 1761)
—U. S. Constitution. (p. 1806)
—Underground Railroad. Schwarz, Philip, ed. (p. 1814)
—United Kingdom in Our World. (p. 1819)
—United States of America. (p. 1819)
—Unsolved Mystery of Bigfoot. (p. 1822)
—Untold Story of the Battle of Saratoga: A Turning Point in the Revolutionary War. (p. 1823)
—Untold Story of the Black Regiment: Fighting in the Revolutionary War. (p. 1823)
—U.S. Constitution/By Michael Burgan. (p. 1826)
—Valley Forge. (p. 1830)
—Vietnam War: An Interactive Modern History Adventure (p. 1841)
—Vietnam War. (p. 1841)
—Voting & Elections (p. 1850)
—Voting Rights Act of 1965: An Interactive History Adventure. (p. 1850)
—Weapons, Gear, & Uniforms of the American Revolution (p. 1869)
—Weapons, Gear, & Uniforms of World War II (p. 1869)
—Who Is Richard Branson? Hammond, Ted, illus. (p. 1916)
—Who Was Henry Ford? (p. 1918)
—Who Was Henry Ford? Hammond, Ted, illus. (p. 1918)
—Who Was Henry Ford? Hammond, Ted & Harrison, Nancy, illus. (p. 1918)
—Who Was Theodore Roosevelt? (p. 1919)
—Who Was Theodore Roosevelt? Harrison, Nancy & Hoare, Jerry, illus. (p. 1919)
—Working in College Sports Ferrer, Al, ed. (p. 1953)
—World War II Pilots (p. 1959)
—World War II Pilots: An Interactive History Adventure. (p. 1959)
—World War II Spies (p. 1959)
—World War II Spies: An Interactive History Adventure (p. 1959)
—World War II Spies: An Interactive History Adventure. (p. 1959)
—You Choose: History. (p. 1975)
Burgan, Michael, jt. auth. see Carlson Berne, Emma.
Burgan, Michael, jt. auth. see Fitzgerald, Stephanie.
Burgan, Michael, jt. auth. see Heinrichs, Ann.
Burgan, Michael, jt. auth. see Kravitz, Danny.
Burgan, Michael, jt. auth. see Otfinoski, Steven.
Burgan, Michael, jt. auth. see RJF Publishing Staff.
Burgan, Michael & Bliss, John. Processing Your Food (p. 1408)
Burgan, Michael & Compass Point Books Staff. George Washington Carver: Scientist, Inventor, & Teacher (p. 664)
—Monroe Doctrine (p. 1166)
Burgan, Michael & Doeden, Matt. You Choose: Modern History (p. 1975)
Burgan, Michael & Fitzgerald, Stephanie. Connecticut. (p. 357)
—Reconstruction: Rebuilding America after the Civil War (p. 1452)
Burgan, Michael & Hoena, Blake A. Battle of Bunker Hill: An Interactive History Adventure (p. 146)
—Battle of Gettysburg Erwin, Steve et al, illus. (p. 146)
—Bigfoot (p. 184)
—Boston Massacre. Wiacek, Bob et al, illus. (p. 215)
—Creation of the U. S. Constitution Purcell, Gordon & Beatty, Terry, illus. (p. 379)
—Curse of King Tut's Tomb Lohse, Otha Zackariah Edward & Schulz, Barbara, illus. (p. 394)
—Great San Francisco Earthquake & Fire Miller, Phil & Barnett, Charles, III, illus. (p. 718)
—Japan: A Question & Answer Book (p. 909)
—King Tut's Tomb: Ancient Treasures Uncovered (p. 959)
—Muhammad Ali: American Champion. Bascle, Brian, illus. (p. 1189)
—Nat Turner's Slave Rebellion Wiacek, Bob et al, illus. (p. 1230)
—Political Parties Barnett, Charles et al, illus. (p. 1380)
—Valley of the Kings: Egypt's Greatest Mummies. (p. 1831)
Burgan, Michael & McGeveran, William. California. (p. 253)
Burgan, Michael & Raum, Elizabeth. Revolutionary War Experience (p. 1466)
—You Choose: Spies. (p. 1975)
Burgan, Michael, et al. Equipped for Battle. (p. 533)

B

—Hockey Superstars (p. 787)
—U. S. Armed Forces. (p. 1806)
—Water Power. (p. 1863)
—You Choose: History. (p. 1975)
—You Choose: World War II. (p. 1975)
Burganti, Darien. Fun at the Dojo: Use Place Value Understanding & Properties of Operations to Add. (p. 647)
Burgard, Anna Marlis. Flying Feet: A Story of Irish Dance. Dees, Leighanne, illus. (p. 610)
Burgdorf, Larry. Daniel & the Lions. (p. 404)
—How Enemies Became Friends. (p. 809)
—Jonah, The Runaway Prophet. (p. 925)
—Mystery of the Moving Hand. Koehler, Ed, illus. (p. 1225)
—Paul's Great Basket Caper. (p. 1331)
—prudente y el insensato (The Wise & Foolish Builders) (p. 1413)
—Wise & Foolish Builders: A Parable of Jesus, Matthew 7:24-27 & Luke 6:47-49 for Children. Billen-Frye, Paige, illus. (p. 1939)
Burgdorf, Larry, et al. Best-Loved Parables of Jesus. Billen-Frye, Paige et al, illus. (p. 170)
Burgdorf, Stephen. Anesthetics. (p. 73)
Burgdorff, Jean Taylor. It's Not the Money: How I built a $2 billion real estate business based on the Golden Rule. (p. 898)
Burge, Constance M. Seasons of the Witch Simon and Schuster Children's Staff, ed. (p. 1538)
Burge, Constance M., jt. auth. see Ciencin, Scott.
Burge, Constance M., jt. auth. see Dokey, Cameron.
Burge, Constance M., jt. auth. see Gallagher, Diana G.
Burge, Constance M. & Viguié, Debbie. Pied Piper. (p. 1356)
Burge, Constance M., creator. Warren Witches. (p. 1858)
Burgen, Jim. What's the Big Deal about My Parents? Reeves, Dale, ed. (p. 1899)
Burgen, Michael. Empire of Ancient Rome, Revised Edition. (p. 521)
Burger, Deborah. Creative Kids Photo Guide to Crochet. (p. 379)
Burger, Hamilton C. No Exit: The Apple Grove Gang #1. (p. 1258)
Burger, James P. Mountain Men of the West. (p. 1181)
Burger, Kyle. Adventures of Buddy the Motocross Bike: Buddy Learns about Confidence. (p. 17)
Burgess, B. L. Finding Hartagetu. (p. 588)
Burgess, Barbara. Magic Manuscript: The Nine Companions. (p. 1072)
—Magic Manuscript: Voyage to Eve Ilion. (p. 1072)
Burgess, Gelett. Goops - 1900: And How to Be Them. (p. 702)
—Goops & How to Be Them: A Manual of Manners for Polite Infants. (p. 702)
Burgess, Graham, jt. auth. see Watson, John.
Burgess, H., illus. see Optic, Oliver, pseud.
Burgess, James. Memories of Little Jay. (p. 1126)
Burgess, Jennifer. Dj Daring & the Dangerous Dragon. (p. 455)
Burgess, Karin Whiting. It's Always a Good Day for Crabbing. (p. 896)
Burgess, Kulthum, illus. see Gilani-Williams, Fawzia.
Burgess, Lesley, jt. ed. see Addison, Nicholas.
Burgess, Linda, tr. see Ramadier, Cédric.
Burgess, Linda, text. Mount Vernon's Magnificent Menagerie: And the Very Mysterious Guest. (p. 1180)
Burgess, Lisa Maria. Juma & Little Sungura. Gugu, Abdul M., illus. (p. 933)
—Juma Cooks Chapati. Gugu, Abdul M., illus. (p. 933)
—Juma on Safari. Gugu, Abdul M., illus. (p. 933)
—Juma's Dhow Race. Gugu, Abdul M., illus. (p. 933)
Burgess, Lynne. Shapes: Individual Title Six-Packs. (p. 1560)
Burgess, Mark. Mutiny at Crossbones Bay. Cox, Phil Roxbee, ed. (p. 1194)
—Where Teddy Bears Come From. Ayto, Russell, illus. (p. 1909)
Burgess, Mark, illus. see Benedictus, David.
Burgess, Mark, illus. see Gramatky, Hardie.
Burgess, Mary. Most Wonderful Place. (p. 1177)
Burgess, Maryellen. Life in Kenya. (p. 1010)
Burgess, Matt. Skylar & George Washington: An Innovative Learning Experience. (p. 1587)
Burgess, Matthew. Enormous Smallness: The Story of e. e. Cummings. Di Giacomo, Kris, illus. (p. 531)
Burgess, Megan. Multiple Sclerosis: Theory & Practice for Nurses. (p. 1190)
Burgess, Melvin. Angel for May. (p. 73)
—Bloodsong. (p. 201)
—Cry of the Wolf. (p. 387)
—Fantasma tras la Pared. (p. 571)
—Hit. (p. 785)
—Lady: My Life as a Bitch. (p. 970)
—Nicholas Dane. (p. 1250)
—Sara's Face. (p. 1514)
—Smack. (p. 1591)
Burgess, Melvin, et al. Losing It. Gray, Keith, ed. (p. 1054)
Burgess, Melvyn & Pearson Education Staff. Billy Elliot: 'A Writer of the Hightest Quality with Exceptional Powers of Insight' (p. 187)
Burgess, Patricia. Buddy Scissortail. (p. 235)
Burgess, Pauline. Pony Palace Camp. (p. 1382)
—Pony Surprise. (p. 1383)
Burgess, Ron. Kids Make Magic! The Complete Guide to Becoming an Amazing Magician. (p. 954)
Burgess, Starr. Counselor Dynamite: Twas the Day Before Christmas Break. Guiza, Victor, illus. (p. 369)
—Counselor Dynamite Befuddles the Bullyville Crew. Guiza, Victor, illus. (p. 369)
Burgess, Sushila. Jasmine's Unicorn. (p. 910)
Burgess, Thornton W. Adventures of Bob White. (p. 16)
—Adventures of Bob White. Cady, Harrison, illus. (p. 16)
—Adventures of Bobby Coon. (p. 16)
—Adventures of Buster Bear. (p. 17)
—Adventures of Chatterer the Red Squirrel. (p. 17)
—Adventures of Danny Meadow Mouse. (p. 17)
—Adventures of Grandfather Frog. (p. 18)
—Adventures of Happy Jack. (p. 18)
—Adventures of Jerry Muskrat. (p. 19)
—Adventures of Jimmy Skunk. (p. 19)
—Adventures of Johnny Chuck. (p. 19)
—Adventures of Lightfoot the Deer. (p. 19)
—Adventures of Mr Mocker. (p. 20)
—Adventures of Mr. Mocker. (p. 20)
—Adventures of Mr. Mocker. Cady, Harrison, illus. (p. 20)
—Adventures of Ol' Mistah Buzzard. (p. 21)
—Adventures of Old Man Coyote. (p. 21)
—Adventures of Old Mr. Buzzard. Cady, Harrison, illus. (p. 21)
—Adventures of Old Mr Toad. (p. 21)
—Adventures of Old Mr. Toad. (p. 21)
—Adventures of Paddy the Beaver. (p. 21)
—Adventures of Poor Mrs Quack. (p. 21)
—Adventures of Poor Mrs. Quack. (p. 21)
—Adventures of Prickly Porky. (p. 21)
—Adventures of Reddy Fox. (p. 22)
—Adventures of Reddy Fox & Prickly Porky. (p. 22)
—Adventures of Sammy Jay. (p. 22)
—Adventures of Sammy Jay. Cady, Harrison, illus. (p. 22)
—Adventures of Unc' Billy Possum. (p. 24)
—Adventures of Unc' Billy Possum. Cady, Harrison & Stewart, Pat Ronson, trs. (p. 24)
—Big Book of Animal Stories. (p. 178)
—Billy Mink. (p. 187)
—Billy Mink. Cady, Harrison, illus. (p. 187)
—Blacky the Crow. (p. 198)
—Bowser the Hound. (p. 216)
—Burgess Animal Book for Children. (p. 243)
—Burgess Animal Book for Children. Fuertes, Louis Agassiz, illus. (p. 243)
—Burgess Animal Book for Children (Yesterday's Classics) Fuertes, Louis Agassiz, illus. (p. 243)
—Burgess Bird Book for Children. (p. 243)
—Burgess Bird Book for Children. Fuertes, Louis Agassiz, illus. (p. 243)
—Burgess Bird Book for Children (Yesterday's Classics) Fuertes, Louis Agassiz, illus. (p. 243)
—Burgess Sea Shore Book for Children. (p. 243)
—Burgess Seashore Book for Children. Sutton, George Miksch, illus. (p. 243)
—Buster Bear's Twins. (p. 245)
—Christmas Reindeer. Chase, Rhoda, illus. (p. 315)
—Dear Old Briar Patch. (p. 419)
—Fifty Favorite Burgess Stories. Cady, Harrison, illus. (p. 585)
—Happy Jack. (p. 746)
—Jerry Muskrat at Home. (p. 913)
—Little Joe Otter. (p. 1029)
—Longlegs the Heron. (p. 1047)
—Mother West Wind 'How' Stories. (p. 1178)
—Mother West Wind 'Where' Stories. (p. 1178)
—Mother West Wind 'Why' Stories. (p. 1178)
—Mother West Wind's Animal Friends. Kerr, George, tr. (p. 1178)
—Mother West Wind's Children. (p. 1178)
—Mother West Wind's Children. Kerr, George, illus. (p. 1178)
—Mother West Wind's Neighbors. Kerr, George & Stewart, Pat, illus. (p. 1178)
—Mrs Peter Rabbit. (p. 1187)
—Mrs. Peter Rabbit. (p. 1187)
—National Review Treasury of Classic Bedtime Stories. Cady, Harrison, illus. (p. 1233)
—Old Granny Fox. (p. 1283)
—Old Mother West Wind. (p. 1284)
—Old Mother West Wind. Kerr, George, illus. (p. 1284)
—Old Mother West Wind's Children. (p. 1284)
—Old Mother West Wind's "When" Stories. (p. 1284)
—Old Mother West Wind's "Where" Stories. (p. 1284)
—Short Works of Thornton W. Burgess. (p. 1569)
—Stories of the Green Forest Critters: Volume 2. (p. 1655)
—Stories of the Green Forest Critters: Volume 3. (p. 1655)
—Stories of the Green Forest Critters: Volume 1. Cady, Harrison, illus. (p. 1655)
—Tales from the Storyteller's House. (p. 1702)
—Thornton Burgess Bedtime Stories: Includes Downloadable MP3s. Hauge, Carl & Hauge, Mary, illus. (p. 1740)
—Thornton Burgess Five-Minute Bedtime Tales: From Old Mother West Wind's Library. Cady, Harrison, illus. (p. 1740)
—Tommy & the Wishing Stone. (p. 1764)
—Tommy & the Wishing-Stone. Cady, Harrison, illus. (p. 1764)
—Tommy's Change of Heart. (p. 1765)
—Tommy's Wishes Come True. (p. 1765)
—While the Story-Log Burns. (p. 1911)
—Whitefoot the Wood Mouse. (p. 1914)
—Whitefoot the Wood Mouse. Cady, Harrison, illus. (p. 1914)
—Whitefoot the Woodmouse. (p. 1914)
Burgess, Thornton W. & Cady, Harrison. Adventures of Peter Cottontail & His Green Forest Friends. (p. 21)
Burgess, Thornton W. & Fuertes, Louis Agassiz. Burgess Animal Book for Children. (p. 243)
Burgess, Thornton W. & Stewart, Pat. Meet Peter Cottontail. (p. 1122)
Burgess, V. L. Mapmaker's Sons. (p. 1090)
Burgess, W. Thornton. Old Mother West Wind. (p. 1284)
Burgess, Wes. Bipolar Handbook: Real-Life Questions with Up-to-Date Answers. (p. 190)
Burgess, Zack. Meet the 49ers. (p. 1122)
—Meet the Bears. (p. 1122)
—Meet the Bengals. (p. 1122)
—Meet the Bills. (p. 1122)
—Meet the Broncos. (p. 1122)
—Meet the Browns. (p. 1122)
—Meet the Buccaneers. (p. 1122)
—Meet the Cardinals. (p. 1122)
—Meet the Colts. (p. 1122)
—Meet the Cowboys. (p. 1122)
—Meet the Dolphins. (p. 1122)
—Meet the Eagles. (p. 1122)
—Meet the Giants. (p. 1122)
—Meet the Jaguars. (p. 1122)
—Meet the Jets. (p. 1122)
—Meet the Lions. (p. 1123)
—Meet the Packers. (p. 1123)
—Meet the Patriots. (p. 1123)
—Meet the Raiders. (p. 1123)
—Meet the Ravens. (p. 1123)
—Meet the Redskins. (p. 1123)
—Meet the Saints. (p. 1123)
—Meet the Seahawks. (p. 1123)
—Meet the Steelers. (p. 1123)
—Meet the Texans. (p. 1123)
—Meet the Titans. (p. 1123)
—Meet the Vikings. (p. 1123)
Burgett, Cindy. Policy Debate. (p. 1380)
Burggraaf, Deborah. Crow No More. Lumsden, Matt, illus. (p. 386)
Burghall, Johan. Vale of the Faeries. (p. 1830)
Burghard, Marie. Captain's Best Imbecile: A Young Pirate's Story. (p. 264)
—Captain's Best Imbecile: A Young Pirate's Story: Collector's Edition. (p. 264)
Burghoffer, Michael. My First Bible Storybook. (p. 1204)
—My First Bible Storybook (Bilingual - English & Spanish) (p. 1204)
Burgin, Norma. Children's Dinosaur Encyclopedia. (p. 303)
Burgin, Norma, illus. see Cain, Sheridan.
Burgis, Stephanie. Kat, Incorrigible. (p. 944)
—Renegade Magic. (p. 1460)
—Stolen Magic. (p. 1652)
Burgis, Stephanie & Ward, Barnaby. Kat, Incorrigible. (p. 944)
Burglon, Nora. Sticks Across the Chimney: A Story of Denmark. (p. 1650)
Burgo, Ann & Shelton, Sherry. Parable of the Three Little Pigs. (p. 1323)
Burgos, Carl, et al. Marvel Masterworks: Golden Age Marvel Comics - Volume 5. (p. 1098)
Burgos, Mayda, ed. see Burgos, Rosalina.
Burgos, Mayda, ed. see Burgos, Rosalinda.
Burgos, Mayda, ed. see Soto, Nayda.
Burgos, Mayda, ed. see Sánchez, Celeste.
Burgos, Mayda, jt. auth. see Sánchez, Celeste.
Burgos, Rosalina. Comunidad 2: Los grupos Colaboran. Burgos, Mayda, ed. (p. 355)
—Comunidad 2 Cuaderno: Los grupos Colaboran. Burgos, Mayda, ed. (p. 355)
—Comunidad 2 Guía: Los grupos Colaboran. Burgos, Mayda, ed. (p. 355)
Burgos, Rosalinda. Nuestro País 3 Guía: Su gente, su historia y su Cultura. Burgos, Mayda, ed. (p. 1270)
Burgos-Diaz, Mercedes. Meenah, the Mystical Princess of Zantel. (p. 1120)
Burgwyn, Diana. Despin: The Adventures of a Motherless Puffin, a Lonely Great Auk & a Pack of Ferocious White Rats. (p. 430)
Burian, Boris & Zhizhenko, V. A. Nekogda Ne Zabudem: Rasskazy Belorusskikh Rebiat o Dniakh Velikoi Otechestvennoi Voiny. (p. 1240)
Burian, Peter, jt. auth. see Euripides.
Burick Jr., Michael, illus. see Burick, Rebecca.
Burick, Rebecca. Little Daisy Tutu. Burick, Rebecca & Burick Jr., Michael, illus. (p. 1026)
Burk, Josh. Summer of Saint Nick. (p. 1674)
Burk, Mark Simon. Saddy & Gladdy. (p. 1501)
Burk, Rachelle. Don't Turn the Page! Downing, Julie, illus. (p. 469)
—Tree House in a Storm. Schneider, Rex, illus. (p. 1783)
Burk, Robin. Destination White House: Barney's Incredible Journey. (p. 430)
Burk, Sandy. Let the River Run Silver Again! How One School Helped Return the American Shad to the Potomac River & How You Too Can Help Protect & Restore Our Living Waters. (p. 994)
Burkart, Jeff. Once Upon a Clear Dark Night. (p. 1292)
Burkart, Jeffrey. Hidden Prince. (p. 776)
Burkart, Jeffrey E., retold by. Hidden Prince. (p. 776)
Burkart, Jeffrey, narrated by. Week That Led to Easter/Jesus Washes Peter's Feet. (p. 1871)
Burkart, Tammy Jayne. Lillie (p. 1017)
Burke, Anjalena. Siren: Book 3 of the Dead End Series (p. 1580)
Burke, Anjalena Anita. Ghost: The Dead End Series Book 1 (p. 670)
Burke, Anne. That's Entertainment! (p. 1726)
Burke, Arlene Avery & Hamilton, Phyllis McAllister. Grandma's Fairy Tale Museum. (p. 708)
Burke Battistini, Maryanne. Lacey's Story: A Little Tale That Wags. (p. 970)
Burke, Betty & Finer, Susie. Activités de Printemps. (p. 10)
Burke, Bob. Curds & Whey Mystery. (p. 392)
—Third Pig Detective Agency: The Complete Casebook. (p. 1734)
Burke, Bobbye. Daddy's Little Girl. (p. 399)
Burke, Chris, illus. see Beranek, Adam, et al.
Burke, Christina. Melvin et le Grand Match de Hockey. Minguet, Anne, tr. (p. 1125)
Burke, Daniel, illus. see Tsaliovich, Anatoly.
Burke, David. Beauty & the Beast: Level 3: Learn French Through Fairy Tales. Sandoval, Migs, illus. (p. 154)
—Beauty & the Beast: Level 3: Learn German Through Fairy Tales. Sandoval, Migs, illus. (p. 154)
—Beauty & the Beast: Level 3: Learn Spanish Through Fairy Tales. Sandoval, Migs, illus. (p. 154)
—BEAUTY & the BEAST (English to Hebrew - Level 3) Learn HEBREW Through Fairy Tales. (p. 154)
—Beauty & the Beast (English to Italian - Level 3) Learn ITALIAN Through Fairy Tales. (p. 154)
—BEAUTY & the BEAST (English to Japanese - Level 3) Learn JAPANESE Through Fairy Tales. (p. 154)
—BEAUTY & the BEAST (Japanese to English - Level 3) Learn ENGLISH Through Fairy Tales. (p. 154)
—Bella y la Bestia: Nivel 3: Aprende Ingles con Cuentos de Hadas. Redoles, Marcela, tr. (p. 162)
—Cenicienta: Nivel 1: Aprende Ingles con Cuentos de Hadas. Bobrick, Julie, ed. (p. 286)
—Cinderella: Level 1: Learn Hebrew Through Fairy Tales. Obejas, Ofra, tr. (p. 320)
—Cinderella: Level 1: Learn German Through Fairy Tales. Bobrick, Julie, ed. (p. 320)
—Cinderella: Level 1: Learn Italian Through Fairy Tales. Bobrick, Julie, ed. (p. 320)
—Cinderella: Level 1: Learn Spanish Through Fairy Tales. Bobrick, Julie, ed. (p. 320)
—Cinderella: Level 1: Learn Japanese Through Fairy Tales. Bobrick, Julie, ed. (p. 320)
—CINDERELLA (Japanese to English - Level 1) Learn ENGLISH Through Fairy Tales. (p. 320)
—CINDERELLA (Korean to English - Level 1) Learn ENGLISH Through Fairy Tales. (p. 320)
—Goldilocks & the 3 Bears: Level 2: Learn Hebrew Through Fairy Tales. Sandoval, Migs, illus. (p. 696)
—Goldilocks & the 3 Bears: Level 2: Learn Spanish Through Fairy Tales. Sandoval, Migs, illus. (p. 696)
—Goldilocks & the 3 Bears: Level 2: Learn Japanese Through Fairy Tales. Sandoval, Migs, illus. (p. 696)
—Goldilocks (English to German - Level 2) Learn GERMAN Through Fairy Tales. (p. 696)
—Goldilocks (English to Italian - Level 2) Learn ITALIAN Through Fairy Tales. (p. 696)
—GOLDILOCKS (Japanese to English - Level 2) Learn ENGLISH Through Fairy Tales. (p. 696)
—GOLDILOCKS (Korean to English - Level 2) Learn ENGLISH Through Fairy Tales. (p. 696)
—GOLDILOCKS (Spanish to English - Level 2) Learn ENGLISH Through Fairy Tales. (p. 696)
Burke, David, adapted by. GOLDILOCKS (English to Chinese - Level 2) Learn MANDARIN CHINESE Through Fairy Tales. (p. 696)
Burke, Dorothy, ed. see Kirkland, Jane.
Burke, Ellinor Rozecki. Susana Worrywart & the Magical Teddy Bear Balloon: With CD for Relaxation. Perciopelo, illus. (p. 1688)
—Susana Worrywart & the Magical Teddy Bear Balloon. Perciopelo, illus. (p. 1688)
Burke, Frank. Animal Antics. Burke, Frank, illus. (p. 76)
Burke, Gloreen. Mother Nature Dear. (p. 1178)
Burke, J. C. Faking Sweet. (p. 565)
—Nine Letters Long. (p. 1256)
—Ocean Pearl. (p. 1276)
—Red Cardigan. (p. 1453)
—Starfish Sisters. (p. 1642)
—White Lies. (p. 1913)
Burke, James, illus. see Yolen, Jane.
Burke, Jim, illus. see Bulla, Clyde Robert & Bulla.
Burke, Jim, illus. see Levin, Jonathan, ed.
Burke, Jim, illus. see Thompson, Lauren.
Burke, Jim, illus. see Yolen, Jane.
Burke, Johanna. American Civil War in Texas. (p. 60)
—Anaconda. (p. 66)
—Anaconda / Anaconda. (p. 66)
—Kangaroo Mob. (p. 942)
—Kangaroo Mob / una Manada de Canguros. (p. 942)
Burke, Judy, ed. Look What You Can Make with Paper Bags: Creative Crafts from Everyday Objects. Schneider, Hank, photos by. (p. 1050)
Burke, Juliet. Let's Play! (p. 999)
Burke, Kathleen, jt. auth. see Morris, Kimberly.
Burke, Kathryn Schaar, illus. see Gilbert, Joan.
Burke, Kathy & Pearson Education Staff. Mysteries of the Unexplained. (p. 1222)
Burke, Kealan Patrick. Master of the Moors. (p. 1103)
Burke, Kurt. Johnny Action. (p. 923)
Burke, Linda. Knood the Cat. (p. 965)
Burke, Maria. Ark of Dun Ruah. (p. 99)
Burke, Mary F. Four Square: The Personal Writing Coach, Grades 1-3. Radtke, Becky, illus. (p. 625)
Burke, Mary F., jt. auth. see Gould, Judith S.
Burke, Melissa Blackwell & Sharp, Katie John. Presidents: Profiles in Courage of the Men Who Have Led Our Nation. (p. 1397)
Burke, Melissa J. Johanna Pig & the Diamond Kids. (p. 920)
Burke, Merrilee. Dreamcatcher Garden: A Sacred Journey. (p. 484)
Burke, Michelle Prater. Story of the Wright Brothers. Johnson, Meredith, illus. (p. 1662)
Burke, Morgan. Get It Started. (p. 667)
Burke, Patrick J. Getting Your First Allowance. Severino, Philip, illus. (p. 670)
Burke, Richard G. Flop: The Art of Winning at Low-Limit Hold 'Em. (p. 606)
Burke, Rick. Ben Franklin. (p. 163)
—Molly Pitcher. (p. 1161)
—Paul Revere. (p. 1330)
Burke, Ruth. Gowandale Adventure: And other stories for Boys. (p. 704)
Burke, Ruth Anne, illus. see Brown, Pauline A.
Burke, Ruth Anne, illus. see Nash, Nancy.
Burke, Sandra & Flebotte, Morrigan. Crusading Communicator. Flebotte, Morrigan, ed. (p. 386)
—Hercules Novel Study. Flebotte, Morrigan, ed. (p. 769)
Burke, Shane, illus. see Swanson, David C. N.
Burke, Shane, illus. see Swanson, David.
Burke, Theresa, illus. see Owsley, Anthony, et al.
Burke, Zoe. Charley Harper's What's in the Coral Reef? A Nature Discovery Book. (p. 292)
—Charley Harper's What's in the Rain Forest? A Nature Discovery Book. Harper, Charley, illus. (p. 292)
—Charley Harper's What's in the Woods? A Nature Discovery Book. Harper, Charley, illus. (p. 292)
Burkert, Howard, photos by see Ulch, Virginia.
Burkert, Nancy E., illus. see Dahl, Roald.
Burkes-Larrañaga, Dustin. Johnny Appleseed Plants Trees Across the Land (p. 923)
Burkes-Larrañaga, Dustin, illus. see Fandel, Jennifer & Miller, Connie Colwell.
Burket, Sheila. Detective Morris Norris & the Case of the Missing Socks. (p. 431)
—Silver & Gold: Sissy Stringbean Meets Morris Norris. (p. 1576)
Burket, Sheila, illus. see Hunt, Debbie Colleen.
Burkett, D. Brent, illus. see Alexander, Lloyd.
Burkett, D. Brent, illus. see Bunting, Eve.
Burkett, Jim, photos by see Burkett, Pops.

Burkett, Larry, et al. Burkett & Blue Definitive Guide for Securing Wealth to Last: Money Essentials for the Second Half of Life. (p. 243)
Burkett, Molly. Pioneers of the Air. (p. 1361)
Burkett, Pops. Let's Go Exploring in the Backyard: A Read with Me, Pops Book. (p. 997)
—Let's Go See Who Lives in the Sea: A Read with Me, Pops Book. (p. 997)
—Lions, Tigers, Bears & More: A Read with Me, Pops Book. (p. 1021)
—My New Friends at the Zoo: Read with Me, Pops. Burkett, Jim, photos by. (p. 1216)
Burkhard, Balthasar. Click, Said the Camera. (p. 332)
Burkhardt, Jason, jt. auth. see Kendall, Sara.
Burkhardt, Jason & Kendall, Sara. Backdoor Trio: A Lesson in Faith. (p. 130)
Burkhardt, Mary Sue & JIST Publishing Editors. Developing Career & Living Skills Student Activity Book. (p. 431)
Burkhardt, Mary Sue & Terry, Barb. Developing Career & Living Skills. (p. 431)
—Developing Career & Living Skills Teacher's Wraparound Edition. (p. 431)
Burkhardt, Melissa K. Exceptionally Good Friends: Building Relationships with Autism. (p. 547)
Burkhardt, Rocky. Secrets of Life in Poetry. (p. 1545)
Burkhardt, Ross M. Writing for Real: Strategies for Engaging Adolescent Writers. (p. 1964)
Burkhart, Alma J. If You Could See Her Smile. Burns, Sandra, illus. (p. 854)
—Little Witnesses. (p. 1038)
Burkhart, Jessica. Behind the Bit. (p. 160)
—Bella's Birthday Unicorn. Ying, Victoria, illus. (p. 162)
—Best Enemies. (p. 169)
—Canterwood Crest Stable of Stories: Take the Reins; Chasing Blue; Behind the Bit; Triple Fault. (p. 262)
—Chasing Blue. (p. 294)
—City Secrets. (p. 324)
—Comeback. (p. 347)
—Elite Ambition. (p. 513)
—Famous. (p. 569)
—Hidden Treasure. Ying, Victoria, illus. (p. 776)
—Home for Christmas: Super Special. (p. 792)
—Home for Christmas. (p. 792)
—Home Sweet Drama. (p. 793)
—Initiation. (p. 874)
—Jealousy. (p. 911)
—Little White Lies. (p. 1037)
—Masquerade. (p. 1102)
—Popular. (p. 1385)
—Rival Revenge. (p. 1475)
—Scandals, Rumors, Lies. (p. 1519)
—Take the Reins. (p. 1697)
—Triple Fault. (p. 1787)
—Unfriendly Competition. (p. 1817)
—Where's Glimmer? Ying, Victoria, illus. (p. 1910)
—Wild Hearts. (p. 1929)
Burkhart, Jessica & Haley, Patricia. Chosen: Super Special. (p. 310)
Burkhart, Lorene. Raccoon Tales: Hip, Flip, Skip & Boo go to the Zoo. (p. 1430)
—Raccoon Tales: Hip, Flip, Skip & Boo & Their Friend Stu. (p. 1430)
Burkhead, Frank, Jr. Sports Ministry for Christ. (p. 1633)
Burkhead, Jesse & Miner, Jerry. Public Expenditure. (p. 1414)
Burkholder, Diane, jt. auth. see Sommers, Faith.
Burkholder, Edith, illus. see Martin, Mildred A.
Burkholder, Sheila M. Elsie Waits Patiently. (p. 516)
Burkinshaw, Jane, jt. auth. see Johnson, Michael.
Burklow, Shan Williams. Learn to Draw with Quacker & Friends. (p. 984)
Burks, Brian. Corre con Caballos. Vinos, Maria, tr. (p. 368)
Burks, Catherine. Different Friends Lee, Rudolph, illus. (p. 438)
Burks, David. Brynna: Saga of a Viking Princess. (p. 233)
Burks, David W. Full Circle: The Story of Outlaw-Prince Edwin, High King of England. (p. 646)
Burks Ii, Tony Lamair. Tale of Imani the Bunny. (p. 1699)
Burks, James. Beep & Bah. Burks, James, illus. (p. 157)
—Bird & Squirrel on Ice. (p. 190)
—Bird & Squirrel on the Run! (p. 190)
—Gabby & Gator. (p. 652)
Burks, James, illus. see Holub, Joan.
Burks, James, illus. see Krensky, Stephen.
Burks, James, illus. see Lazar, Tara.
Burks, James, illus. see Trine, Greg.
Burks, Megan. Sally the Circle. (p. 1505)
Burkum, Rachel. Matthew's Bible Stories: Esther Is Brave. Keller, Matt, illus. (p. 1110)
Burleigh, Cyril. Hilltop Boys on the River. (p. 780)
Burleigh, Liz. Matilda the Bassett Hound. (p. 1109)
Burleigh, Robert. Abraham Lincoln Comes Home. Minor, Wendell, illus. (p. 6)
—Abraham Lincoln Comes Home. Minor, Wendell, illus. (p. 7)
—Adventures of Mark Twain by Huckleberry Finn. Blitt, Barry, illus. (p. 20)
—Black Whiteness: Admiral Byrd Alone in the Antarctic. Krudop, Walter Lyon, illus. (p. 197)
—Clang! Clang! Beep! Beep! Listen to the City. Giacobbe, Beppe, illus. (p. 326)
—Edward Hopper Paints His World. Minor, Wendell, illus. (p. 505)
—Good-Bye, Sheepie Catalanotto, Peter, illus. (p. 697)
—Hit the Road, Jack. MacDonald, Ross, illus. (p. 786)
—Home Run: The Story of Babe Ruth. Plimpton, George, ed. (p. 792)
—I Love Going Through This Book. Yaccarino, Dan, illus. (p. 842)
—If You Spent a Day with Thoreau at Walden Pond. Minor, Wendell, illus. (p. 854)
—Into the Woods: John James Audubon Lives His Dream. Minor, Wendell, illus. (p. 881)
—Look Up! Henrietta Leavitt, Pioneering Woman Astronomer. Colón, Raúl, illus. (p. 1050)
—Messenger, Messenger. Root, Barry, illus. (p. 1129)
—Night Flight: Amelia Earhart Crosses the Atlantic. Minor, Wendell, illus. (p. 1253)
—One Giant Leap. Wimmer, Mike, illus. (p. 1295)
—Paul Cezanne: A Painter's Journey. (p. 1330)
—Stealing Home: Jackie Robinson: Against the Odds. Wimmer, Mike, illus. (p. 1646)
—Tiger of the Snows: Tenzing Norgay: the Boy Whose Dream Was Everest. Young, Ed, illus. (p. 1748)
—Toulouse-Lautrec: The Moulin Rouge & the City of Light. (p. 1773)
—Zoom! Zoom! Sounds of Things That Go in the City. Carpenter, Tad, illus. (p. 1989)
Burleigh, Robert & Bellows, George. George Bellows: Painter with a Punch! (p. 663)
Burleson, Joe, illus. see Leonhardt, Alice & Hart, Alison.
Burlew, Rich, creator. Order of the Stick Coloring Book. (p. 1302)
Burling, Alexis. Pharrell Williams: Grammy-Winning Singer, Songwriter & Producer. (p. 1350)
Burlingame, Jeff. 50 Cent: Hip-Hop Mogul. (p. 1997)
—Aerosmith: Hard Rock Superstars. (p. 25)
—Alcohol. (p. 35)
—Avril Lavigne: Celebrity with Heart. (p. 120)
—Crystal Meth. (p. 387)
—Demi! Latina Star Demi Lovato. (p. 425)
—Edgar Allan Poe: Deep into That Darkness Peering. (p. 504)
—Eminem: Hip-Hop Mogul. (p. 519)
—Government Entitlement. (p. 704)
—Hillary Clinton: A Life in Politics. (p. 779)
—How to Freshwater Fish Like a Pro. (p. 819)
—Jay-Z: A Biography of a Hip-Hop Icon. (p. 910)
—Jennifer! Film Star Jennifer Lawrence. (p. 912)
—Jesse James: I Will Never Surrender. (p. 914)
—Jesse Owens: I Always Loved Running. (p. 914)
—John Lennon: "Imagine" (p. 922)
—Kanye West: Hip-Hop Mogul. (p. 943)
—Malcolm X: "I Believe in the Brotherhood of Man, All Men" (p. 1083)
—Prisons: Rehabilitate or Severely Punish? (p. 1407)
—Soccer Star Andrés Iniesta. (p. 1603)
—Soccer Star AndrS Iniesta. (p. 1603)
—Soccer Star Kak. (p. 1603)
—Soccer Star Kaká. (p. 1603)
—Taylor Swift: Music Superstar. (p. 1708)
—Titanic Tragedy. (p. 1758)
Burlingham, Abi. All Grown Up. Everitt-Stewart, Andy, illus. (p. 44)
—Best Friends. Everitt-Stewart, Andy, illus. (p. 169)
Burlington, David Allen. Bass Fishing Guide for Lake LBJ. Burlington, David Allen, ed. (p. 143)
Burlington, Marie. Helpful Hannah. (p. 766)
—Lighthouse Joey. (p. 1015)
Burlinson, J. Imagination Goodnight. Perron, Debra, illus. (p. 860)
Burlinson, James, illus. see Farwell, Nick.
Burloux, Gabriel. Body & Its Pain. Woods, Margaret, tr. from FRE. (p. 207)
Burma, Willingham, illus. see Jordan, Dana Hall.
Burman, Andrew, jt. auth. see Burman, Jan.
Burman, Jan & Burman, Andrew. *Follow That Carrot. (p. 612)
Burmeff, Marian. How the Short Vowel Club Got Started. (p. 813)
Burmeister, AimeeLeigh. Perspective for Kids Volume One Introduction to Perspective. (p. 1344)
Burn, Doris. Andrew Henry's Meadow. (p. 72)
—Andrew Henry's Meadow. Burn, Doris, illus. (p. 72)
Burn, Michael. Childhood at Oriol. (p. 302)
Burn, Scott. Agon. (p. 30)
Burn, Ted, illus. see Crane, Carol.
Burnam, Edna Mae. Step by Step Piano Course - Book 6. (p. 1647)
—Write It Right: With Step by Step. Bk. 5 (p. 1963)
Burne, Cristy. Filth Licker. Siku, illus. (p. 586)
—Takeshita Demons: Monster Matsuri. (p. 1697)
—Takeshita Demons. Siku, illus. (p. 1697)
Burnell, Pamela H. Light Keeper: An Epps Kids Mystery. (p. 1015)
Burnell, Terri. Garden of Eden: Book One of the Living Dreams Series. (p. 656)
Burnell Walsh, Avenda, illus. see Smith, Roy.
Burner, Brett, ed. see Lee, Young Shin & Rogers, Buddy.
Burner, Brett, ed. see Rogers, Bud & Lee, Young Shin.
Burnett, Allan. Bonnie Prince Charlie & All That. Anderson, Scoular, illus. (p. 209)
—Columba & All That. Anderson, Scoular, illus. (p. 346)
—Macbeth & All That. Anderson, Scoular, illus. (p. 1068)
—Mary, Queen of Scots. Anderson, Scoular, illus. (p. 1101)
—Robert the Bruce. Anderson, Scoular, illus. (p. 1479)
—Story of Scotland: Inspired by the Great Tapestry of Scotland. (p. 1660)
—William Wallace & All That. Anderson, Scoular, illus. (p. 1933)
—World War I: Scottish Tales of Adventure. (p. 1958)
Burnett, Anne, illus. see Turton, Karalynn Teresa.
Burnett, Betty. Attack on the U. S. S. Cole in Yemen on October 12, 2000. (p. 114)
—Attack on the USS Cole in Yemen on October 12 2000. (p. 114)
—Cool Careers Without College for Math & Science Wizards. (p. 362)
—Coping with Multiple Sclerosis. (p. 365)
—Delta Force: Counterterrorism Unit of the U. S. Army. (p. 425)
—Ferdinand Magellan: The First Voyage Around the World. (p. 582)
Burnett, Betty & Gevertz, Rob. Coping with Multiple Sclerosis. (p. 365)
Burnett, Calvin & Irons, Calvin. Fun Machines: A Book about Addition & Subtraction. (p. 648)
Burnett, Craig. Jeff Wall. (p. 912)
Burnett, Eric. 21st Century Voices. (p. 1996)
—Gymnastics Jenny Stands on Her Own. (p. 734)
Burnett, Frances Hodgson. Editha's Burglar. Sandham, Henry, illus. (p. 504)
—Emily Fox-Seton. (p. 519)
—Esmeralda, Mère Giraud's Little Daughter, Little Saint Elizabeth & Other Stories: A Collection of Short Stories by Frances Hodgson Burnett. (p. 536)
—Frances Hodgson Burnett Children's Stories Omnibus the Secret Garden, a Little Princess, Little Lord Fauntleroy, Racketty-Packetty House. Cady, Harrison, illus. (p. 627)
—Geheidie Garten. (p. 659)
—Head of the House of Coombe. (p. 756)
—jardín secreto. Lee, Hye Ran , illus. (p. 909)
—Lady of Quality. (p. 971)
—Land of Blue Flower. (p. 973)
—Land of the Blue Flower. (p. 973)
—Little Lord Fauntleroy. (p. 1030)
—Little Lord Fauntleroy. Howell, Troy, illus. (p. 1030)
—Little Lord Fauntleroy. Birch, Reginald, illus. (p. 1030)
—Little Princes. (p. 1033)
—Little Princess. (p. 1033)
—Little Princess. Aldous, Kate, illus. (p. 1033)
—Little Princess. Gill, Margery, illus. (p. 1033)
—Little Princess. McKowen, Scott, illus. (p. 1033)
—Little Princess. Engelbreit, Mary, illus. (p. 1033)
—Little Princess: The Story of Sara Crewe. (p. 1034)
—Little Princess: The Story of Sara Crewe. Warren, Eliza, ed. (p. 1034)
—Little Princess: The Story of Sara Crewe. Rust, Graham, illus. (p. 1034)
—Little Princess: Being the whole story of Sara Crewe now told for T. (p. 1034)
—Little Princess: With a Discussion of Generosity. Gribbon, Sean & Jael, trs. (p. 1034)
—Little Princess. (p. 1034)
—Little Princess. Kliros, Thea, illus. (p. 1034)
—Little Princess Coloring Book. Kliros, Thea, illus. (p. 1034)
—Lost Prince. (p. 1056)
—Pequeño Lord. (p. 1341)
—Petit Princesse. (p. 1348)
—Petite Princess. (p. 1348)
—RackettyPackety House. (p. 1432)
—Racketty-Packetty House. (p. 1432)
—Racketty-Packetty House. Halperin, Wendy Anderson, illus. (p. 1432)
—Robin. (p. 1479)
—Sara Crewe. (p. 1514)
—Sara Crewe or What Happened at Miss Minc. (p. 1514)
—Sara Crewe or What Happened at Miss Minchin's. (p. 1514)
—Sara Crewe, or What Happened at Miss Minchin's. (p. 1514)
—Secret Garden. (p. 1540)
—Secret Garden. McKowen, Scott, illus. (p. 1540)
—Secret Garden. Robinson, Charles, illus. (p. 1540)
—Secret Garden: A Young Reader's Edition of the Classic Story. (p. 1541)
—Secret Garden: With a Discussion of Compassion. Lauter, Richard, illus. (p. 1541)
—Secret Garden. (p. 1541)
—Secret Garden. Hunt, Peter, ed. (p. 1541)
—Secret Garden. Moore, Inga, illus. (p. 1541)
—Secret Garden. Tudor, Tasha, illus. (p. 1541)
—Secret Garden. Corvino, Lucy, illus. (p. 1541)
—Secret Garden. Lawrie, Robin, illus. (p. 1541)
—Secret Garden. Engelbreit, Mary, illus. (p. 1541)
—Secret Garden. Ingpen, Robert R., illus. (p. 1541)
—Secret Garden. Robinson, Charles, illus. (p. 1541)
—Secret Garden Book & Charm. Tudor, Tasha, illus. (p. 1541)
—Secret Garden Coloring Book. Kliros, Thea, illus. (p. 1541)
—Titus kommt nicht alle Tage. (p. 1758)
Burnett, Frances Hodgson, jt. auth. see Francis, Pauline.
Burnett, Frances Hodgson, jt. auth. see Zamorsky, Tania.
Burnett, Frances Hodgson & Collins, Reverie. Lost Prince of Samavia. (p. 1056)
Burnett, Frances Hodgson & Naxos of America Staff. Little Princess. (p. 1034)
—Secret Garden. (p. 1541)
Burnett, Garry. Mrs Ockleton's Rainbow Kite & Other Tales: Anthology. (p. 1187)
Burnett, Garry & Jarvis, Kay. Parents First: Parents & Children Learning Together. (p. 1324)
Burnett, Gretel. A-B-C Smarts: Book 2. (p. 1)
Burnett, Iris & Greager, Clay. So You Think You Can Be President? 200 Questions to Determine If You Are Right (Or Left) Enough to Be the Next Commander-in-Chief. (p. 1602)
Burnett, James. Mathementals Ages 10-11: Exercises in Mental Computation. (p. 1108)
—Mathementals Ages 11-12: Exercises in Mental Computation. (p. 1108)
—Mathementals Ages 6-7: Exercises in Mental Computation. (p. 1108)
—Mathementals Ages 7-8: Exercises in Mental Computation. (p. 1108)
—Mathementals Ages 8-9: Exercises in Mental Computation. (p. 1108)
—Mathementals Ages 9-10: Exercises in Mental Computation. (p. 1108)
—Our Sister's Surprise: A Book about Missing-Addend Subtraction. (p. 1310)
Burnett, James, jt. auth. see Stowasser, Peter.
Burnett, James & I, Calvin. Simple Stew: A Book about Growing Number Patterns. (p. 1578)
Burnett, James & Irons, Calvin. Dozen Dizzy Dinosaurs: A Book about Division (Equal Groups) (p. 474)
—Flower Pot Hen: A Book about Representing Data. (p. 607)
—How Many Legs? A Book about Number Combinations. (p. 811)
—Mirror Mirror: A Book about Doubling Numbers One to Five. (p. 1149)
—Pirates' Gold: A Book about Division (sharing) (p. 1363)
—Scaredy Cats: A Book about Combinations of Ten. (p. 1519)
—Stella's Store: Book about Skip Counting by Five. (p. 1647)
—Sweet Dreams: A Book about Counting Quantities to Ten. (p. 1689)
Burnett, Jenifer. My Jungle Quilt. Burnett, Jenifer, illus. (p. 1211)
Burnett, Karen Gedig. Magical, Marvelous Megan G. Beamer: A Day in the Life of A Dreamer. Barrows, Laurie, illus. (p. 1074)
Burnett, Linda. Father Word's Children's Rhymes. (p. 577)
Burnett, Lindy. I Live Here! (p. 841)
Burnett, Lindy, illus. see Hall, Kirsten.
Burnett, Lindy, illus. see Kudlinski, Kathleen V.
Burnett, Lindy, illus. see Rosa-Mendoza, Gladys.
Burnett, Lindy, illus. see Williams, Rozanne Lanczak.
Burnett, Maria. Celebrating Reading, Writing & Math with Your Child. (p. 285)
—No Parent Left Behind. (p. 1259)
—Pact: Can Be Positive. (p. 1317)
Burnett, Mark & Downey, Roma. Story of God & All of Us Young Readers Edition. (p. 1658)
Burnett, Melissa. Even Pirates Need Their Sleep. (p. 541)
Burnett, Roger J. & Burnett, Wilma J. Short Stories & Tall Tales. (p. 1569)
Burnett, Ruth, jt. auth. see Myers, Hortense.
Burnett, Seb, illus. see Jungman, Ann.
Burnett, Seb, illus. see Robson, Kirsteen.
Burnett, Wilma J., jt. auth. see Burnett, Roger J.
Burnette, Leon P. Peeka-Boo Fables: Land of the Golems. (p. 1335)
Burnette, Margarette. Counting in the Crazy Garden. Henson, Brooke, illus. (p. 371)
Burnette, Sam. Fun on the Farm: The Adventures of Bo'Gator, Brer Possum & Blue. (p. 648)
Burnett-Hartwig, Aimee. Bella's First Hunting Adventure. (p. 162)
Burney, Britt. Bone Tree. (p. 209)
Burney, Claudia Mair. Exorsistah (p. 548)
Burney, Laura, illus. see Miller, Karen.
Burnford, Sheila. Bel Ria: Dog of War. (p. 161)
—Incredible Journey. (p. 869)
Burnham & Laurie. Rivers. (p. 1476)
Burnham, Brad. Carlsbad Caverns: America's Largest Underground Chamber. (p. 270)
—Cave of Lascaux: The Cave of Prehistoric Wall Paintings. (p. 282)
—Caves of the Thousand Buddhas: Treasure House of Chinese Art. (p. 282)
—Kazumura Cave: The World's Longest Lava Tube. (p. 946)
—Mammoth Cave: The World's Longest Cave System. (p. 1085)
—Qumran Caves: Hiding Place for the Dead Sea Scrolls. (p. 1429)
Burnham, Erik. Ghostbusters Volume 2. (p. 672)
Burnham, Janet Hayward. Dragoness Mess. (p. 478)
—Jeremy the Puny. Burnham, Janet Hayward, illus. (p. 913)
Burnham, Molly B. Teddy Mars: Almost a World Record Breaker. Spencer, Trevor, illus. (p. 1712)
Burnham, Niki. Goddess Games. (p. 690)
—Royally Crushed: Royally Jacked; Spin Control; Do-Over. (p. 1492)
—Scary Beautiful. (p. 1520)
—Spin Control. (p. 1627)
—Sticky Fingers. (p. 1650)
Burnham, Niki & Saidens, Amy. Royally Jacked. (p. 1492)
Burniac, Lauren, ed. see Square Fish Staff.
Burniac, Lauren, jt. auth. see Courtauld, Sarah.
Burnie, David. Bird. (p. 190)
—Bug Hunter. (p. 236)
—Disasters. (p. 447)
—Eyewitness Plant. (p. 558)
—Kingfisher Animal Encyclopedia. (p. 960)
—Navigators: Mammals. (p. 1238)
—Shrublands (p. 1571)
Burnie, David, jt. auth. see Arlon, Penelope.
Burnie, David & Juniper, Tony. Endangered Planet. (p. 527)
Burningham, Hilary. Julius Caesar. (p. 932)
Burningham, John. Cama Mágica. (p. 255)
—Cloudland. Burningham, John, illus. (p. 334)
—Estaciones. (p. 538)
—Granpa. Burningham, John, illus. (p. 710)
—It's a Secret! Burningham, John, illus. (p. 896)
—John Burningham. Burningham, John, illus. (p. 921)
—Mr. Gumpy's Outing. (p. 1185)
—Picnic. Burningham, John, illus. (p. 1355)
—There's Going to Be a Baby. Oxenbury, Helen, illus. (p. 1731)
—Tug-of-War. Burningham, John, illus. (p. 1796)
—Way to the Zoo. Burningham, John, illus. (p. 1864)
—Where's Julius? (p. 1910)
Burningham, Sarah O'Leary. Girl to Girl: Honest Talk about Growing up & Your Changing Body. Arnold, Alli, illus. (p. 679)
—How to Raise Your Parents: A Teen Girl's Survival Guide. Pilar, Bella, illus. (p. 821)
Burnley, Beverly. Hands-On Computer Activities for Teaching Math: Grades 3-8. (p. 741)
Burns, Adam, ed. see Lee, Brittany.
Burns, Adam, ed. see Zawel, Marc.
Burns, Adam, jt. auth. see Allshouse, Sara.
Burns, Adam, jt. auth. see Cole, Kristin.
Burns, Adam, jt. auth. see Ewing, Drew.
Burns, Adam, jt. auth. see Fassio, Dan.
Burns, Adam, jt. auth. see Fitzgerald, Brendan.
Burns, Adam, jt. auth. see Fleming, Jessica.
Burns, Adam, jt. auth. see Fosyth, Rebekah.
Burns, Adam, jt. auth. see Gunderman, Shelby.
Burns, Adam, jt. auth. see Lang, Alex.
Burns, Adam, jt. auth. see Langlieb, David.
Burns, Adam, jt. auth. see Lewis, Jeff.
Burns, Adam, jt. auth. see Mass, Aaron.
Burns, Adam, jt. auth. see Miller, Kirystan.
Burns, Adam, jt. auth. see Ramin, Nathan.
Burns, Adam, jt. auth. see Turley, Meredith.
Burns, Adam, jt. auth. see Unkovic, Rachel.
Burns, Adam, jt. auth. see Williams, Jacob.
Burns, Ann. Pink Parasol & the French Confection. (p. 1360)
Burns, Bree. America in The 1970s. (p. 59)
Burns, Brian. My Blankey & Me. (p. 1198)
Burns, Catherine Lloyd. Good, the Bad & the Beagle. (p. 700)
Burns, Charles, illus. see Sinclair, Upton.
Burns, Cheryl Am. A-B-Used Me. (p. 1)
Burns Chong, Susan. Community Gardens. (p. 350)

—Step-By-Step Guide to Innovating at School & Work. (p. 1647)
Burns, Christopher. Island Wilderness: Imagining the Early Years of Martha's Vineyard. (p. 892)
Burns, Dal. Adventures of Phoo. (p. 21)
—Kookaburra & Other Stories. (p. 967)
Burns, David. Fasttrack to America's Past. (p. 576)
Burns, Diane L., et al. Jordan in Pictures. Gable, Brian, illus. (p. 925)
Burns, Donna, illus. see Fujii, Jocelyn.
Burns, Donna, illus. see Rabbett, Martin.
Burns, Eleanor & Bouchard, Sue. Underground Railroad Sampler. (p. 1815)
Burns, Elizabeth & Law, Stephen, eds. Philosophy for AS & A2. (p. 1351)
Burns, Ellen Flanagan. Nobody's Perfect: A Story for Children about Perfectionism. Villnave, Erica Pelton, illus. (p. 1262)
Burns, Emily. Manitou Art Caper. (p. 1087)
—Marked Evidence. (p. 1095)
Burns, Heidi A., contrib. by. U. S. Army True Stories: Tales of Bravery. (p. 1806)
Burns, Helen Marie. Ryleigh's Little Bug Book (p. 1499)
—Ryleigh's Little Bug Book Vareberg, Gladys, illus. (p. 1499)
Burns, Ian. Lissie Pendle. (p. 1022)
—Possum & Python. (p. 1387)
—Twevven & the Horrible Big Bigger Biggest Baby Burp. Eldridge-Murray, Lauren, illus. (p. 1801)
Burns, Jan. Build Your Online Community: Blogging, Message Boards, Newsgroups, & More. (p. 238)
—Crop Circles. (p. 385)
—Fairies. (p. 562)
—Friendship: A How-to Guide. (p. 639)
—Kidnapping. (p. 952)
—Shigeru Miyamoto: Nintendo Game Designer. (p. 1566)
Burns, Jan, jt. auth. see Brown, Anne K.
Burns, Jann. Can Democracy Succeed in the Middle East? Einfeld, Jann, ed. (p. 258)
Burns, Jason M. Megamind: Bad, Blue, Brilliant. (p. 1124)
—Pocket God (p. 1375)
—Sesame Street: I Is for Imagination: I Is for Imagination. (p. 1553)
Burns, Jennifer Bobrow. Career Opportunities in Journalism. (p. 267)
Burns, Jennifer N. Magic in Time: Fairy Tale Stories. (p. 1072)
Burns, Jim. Devotions on the Run: Pulling Out of the Fast Lane to Make Time with God. (p. 432)
—How God Makes Babies. (p. 809)
—Purity Code: God's Plan for Sex & Your Body. (p. 1419)
Burns, Jim & DeVries, Mike. Fresh Ideas: Hot Topics. 11 (p. 636)
Burns, Jim & Devries, Mike. Instant Bible Studies. (p. 878)
Burns, Jo. Pookie & Her Polka-Dotted Socks. (p. 1383)
Burns, Joanne. Abigail Is a Big Girl Now. (p. 5)
—Annibelle Is a Big Girl Now Weaning Two Year-Olds. (p. 86)
—Don't Fear Little Deer. (p. 467)
—Frog's Dog Days. (p. 641)
—How & Why Eagles Fly. (p. 804)
—No Says the Baby When You Say Yes, a book about the terrible Twos. (p. 1260)
—Ollie Oyster's Ouch. (p. 1287)
—Pamela Platypus' Problem. (p. 1320)
—What Is Heaven Like? (p. 1889)
Burns, John. Many Adventures of Pengey Penguin. Coles, James, illus. (p. 1089)
Burns, John, jt. auth. see Hansen, Jim.
Burns, John, et al. Juez Dredd: La ley de Megacity. Vol. 2 (p. 931)
Burns, John M., illus. see Brontë, Emily.
Burns, Judith. Hero: It's up to You. Roldan, Patrict, illus. (p. 772)
Burns, Kate. American Teenager. (p. 63)
—Gay Marriage. (p. 659)
—Gay Rights. (p. 659)
—Rap Music & Culture. (p. 1439)
Burns, Kate & Cothran, Helen, eds. Gay Rights. (p. 659)
Burns, Kate & Sharp, Anne Wallace. Right to Die. (p. 1472)
Burns Knight, Margy. Welcoming Babies O'Brien, Anne Sibley, illus. (p. 1874)
Burns Knight, Margy, et al. Who Belongs Here? An American Story. (p. 1914)
—Who Belongs Here? O'Brien, Anne Sibley, illus. (p. 1914)
Burns, Kylie. Biathlon, Cross Country, Ski Jumping, & Nordic Combined. (p. 175)
—Carrie Underwood. (p. 271)
—Cultural Traditions in Kenya. (p. 391)
—Live It: Perseverance. (p. 1040)
—Roman Numerals & Ordinals. (p. 1486)
—Sidney Crosby. (p. 1573)
—Sparta! (p. 1622)
Burns, Kylie, jt. auth. see Crabtree Publishing Co. Staff.
Burns, Kylie, jt. auth. see Kalman, Bobbie.
Burns, Laura J. Bewitched in Oz Peters, Liam, illus. (p. 173)
Burns, Laura J., jt. auth. see Decter, Ed.
Burns, Laura J., jt. auth. see Metz, Melinda.
Burns, Laura J. & Metz, Melinda. Sacrifice. (p. 1500)
Burns, Loree Griffin. Beetle Busters: A Rogue Insect & the People Who Track It. Harasimowicz, Ellen, illus. (p. 158)
—Citizen Scientists: Be a Part of Scientific Discovery from Your Own Backyard. Harasimowicz, Ellen, photos by. (p. 323)
—Handle with Care: An Unusual Butterfly Journey. Harasimowicz, Ellen, illus. (p. 740)
—Hive Detectives: Chronicle of a Honey Bee Catastrophe. Harasimowicz, Ellen, illus. (p. 786)
—Hive Detectives. (p. 786)
—Tracking Trash: Flotsam, Jetsam, & the Science of Ocean Motion. (p. 1775)
Burns, Maggie. In My Bare Feet. (p. 864)
Burns, Marie. Quest for Gold. (p. 1426)
Burns, Marilyn. Greedy Triangle. Silveria, Gordon, illus. (p. 720)
—Spaghetti & Meatballs for All! A Mathematical Story. Tilley, Debbie, illus. (p. 1620)
Burns, Marilyn, jt. auth. see Wickett, Maryann.
Burns, Marilyn & Sheffield, Stephanie. Math & Literature, Grades 2-3. (p. 1105)
Burns, Mary E. Heartwood. Grinvalsky, Peggy, illus. (p. 760)
Burns, Mary Gore. Magic Room: Mandy & the Lily Pond. (p. 1073)
Burns, Mike, illus. see Gunderson, Jessica.
Burns, Monique. Cool Careers Without College for People Who Love to Make Things Grow. (p. 363)
Burns, Phyllis B. Iron Lady at Sea: From Shipyard to Voyage, A Story of the Great Iron-Hulled Sailing Ship, Star of India. (p. 888)
Burns, Ray, jt. auth. see Ames, Lee J.
Burns, Raymond, illus. see Snow, Dorothea J.
Burns, Richard. For the Living: Selected Writings 1: Longer Poems 1965-2000 (p. 616)
Burns, Robert David, jt. auth. see Whited, Wayne.
Burns, Rosalyn, ed. see Paulin, Chrita.
Burns, Sandra, illus. see Alders, Willa.
Burns, Sandra, illus. see Bingamon-Haller, Mary.
Burns, Sandra, illus. see Burkhart, Alma J.
Burns, Sandra, illus. see Wenning, Jeremy.
Burns, Suzanne. Moon Painters. (p. 1172)
Burns, T. D. BOOST Rocks & Minerals Coloring Book. (p. 213)
Burns, T. R. Bad Apple. (p. 131)
—Watch Your Step. (p. 1861)
—World of Trouble. (p. 1957)
Burns, Taurus, illus. see Radley, Gail.
Burns, Theresa. Queen Emileen. Burns, Theresa, illus. (p. 1424)
Burns, Theresa, illus. see Gantry, Chris.
BURNS, Theresa, illus. see Hoffman, Terri.
Burns, Virginia Law. Bold Women in Michigan History. (p. 208)
Burns, William G., ed. see Larson, Eric.
Burnscott, Leela. Big Bangs: Looking at Fires, Explosions & Crashes. (p. 178)
—Body Talk: Looking at Biological Evidence. (p. 207)
—Fact or Fiction? Looking at Forensic Investigations & Technologies. (p. 561)
—Lasting Impressions: Looking at Marks & Imprints. (p. 979)
—Lost & Found: Looking at Traces of Evidence. (p. 1054)
—Nature Tells: Looking at Bugs, Plants & the Environment. (p. 1236)
Burns-Longship & Price, Robin. Beowulf & the Dragon Raiders. (p. 166)
Burnstine, Susan, photos by see Rabbi's of Boca Raton Theological Seminary Staff.
Buron, Kari D. & Buron, Kari Dunn. When My Worries Get Too Big! A Relaxation Book for Children Who Live with Anxiety. (p. 1904)
Buron, Kari Dunn, jt. auth. see Buron, Kari D.
Burow, Ginger. Night That Was Christmas (p. 1254)
Burphon, S., illus. see Gilligan, Shannon.
Burpo, Sonja, jt. auth. see Burpo, Todd.
Burpo, Todd & Burpo, Sonja. Heaven Is for Real for Kids: A Little Boy's Astounding Story of His Trip to Heaven & Back (p. 761)
Burpo, Todd & Vincent, Lynn. Heaven Is for Real for Kids: A Little Boy's Astounding Story of His Trip to Heaven & Back. (p. 761)
Burque, Hannah Adams, illus. see Mendenhall, Emily & Koon, Adam, eds.
Burr, Avril. Naughty Art. (p. 1237)
Burr, Claudia, et al. When the Viceroy Came. (p. 1905)
Burr, Dan, illus. see Durrant, George D.
Burr, Dan, illus. see Freeman, Emily.
Burr, Dan, illus. see Hailstone, Ruth.
Burr, Dan, illus. see Harrison, David L.
Burr, Dan, illus. see Monson, Marianne.
Burr, Dan, illus. see Monson, Thomas S.
Burr, Dan, illus. see Oaks, Kristen M. & Phillips, JoAnn.
Burr, Dan, illus. see Rowley, Deborah Pace.
Burr, Dan E., illus. see Raczka, Bob.
Burr, Debora. In the Country. (p. 865)
—In the Wild. (p. 868)
Burr, Holly. a-Bee-Sea Book. Abremski, Kathy, illus. (p. 1)
—If I Get to Be in Charge of Spelling. Abremski, Kathy, illus. (p. 853)
Burrell, Bill. Path to Glory. (p. 1328)
Burrell, Carol, tr. see Luciani, Brigitte.
Burrell, Carol Klio. Secret Diary. Neel, Julien, illus. (p. 1540)
—Summertime Blues. Neel, Julien, illus. (p. 1675)
Burrell, Carol Klio, jt. auth. see Neel, Julien.
Burrell, Carol Klio, jt. auth. see Schmitt, Michel-Yves.
Burrell, Carol Klio, tr. see Dubos, Delphine.
Burrell, Carol Klio, tr. see Grimaldi, Flora.
Burrell, Carol Klio, tr. see Grimaldi.
Burrell, Carol M. Scavella. Did Greek Soldiers Really Hide Inside the Trojan Horse? And Other Questions about the Ancient World. (p. 436)
Burres, Kimberly. I Love You & I Like You. (p. 843)
Burri, Hillary Hayden. Bedtime Safari. (p. 157)
Burrier, Sara. Watercolor Fairy Art: How to Bring Your Fairy Realm Art to Life. (p. 1863)
Burrier, Sara, illus. see Havener, Katherine.
Burries-Hall, Tracy. Honey the Firefly: Honey the Firefly & the Cub Scout. (p. 794)
Burrill, Gail F., et al. Advanced Modeling & Matrices. (p. 13)
—Exploring Regression. (p. 553)
—Exploring Symbols. (p. 553)
—Probability Models. (p. 1408)
Burrill, John, ed. see Cole, Bethan, et al.
Burrill, Richard L. My Sweet Lord: The Life-Stories of Muhammad & the Five God-Men of History. (p. 1219)
—Somewhere Behind the Eyes: Language Treasures Aha! (p. 1610)
—Somewhere Behind the Eyes: Surprise Images in Nature Aha! (p. 1610)
—Somewhere Behind the Eyes: Surprise Images in Nature Aha! Vol. 3 (p. 1610)
Burrill, Richard L., ed. Closest to God: Humankind's Search for the Supreme Being. (p. 334)
Burrin, Angela M. Family Journey with Jesus through Lent: Prayers & Activities for Each Day. (p. 568)
—Jesus Speaks to Me on My First Holy Communion. Lo Cascio, Maria Cristina, illus. (p. 916)
Burris, Andrea. Tater & Tot. (p. 1707)
Burris, Andrea & Schad, Anna. Dog Lover's Alphabet Book. Burris, Andrea, illus. (p. 461)
Burris, Andrea M. & Schad, Anna M. Kitty Cat Alphabet Book. Burris, Andrea M., illus. (p. 963)
Burris, Damon A. Find (and Keep) Your Ideal Man: Relationship Strategies for Strong, Confident & Independent Women. (p. 587)
Burris, Judy & Richards, Wayne. Nature's Notes: Bite-sized Learning & Projects for All Ages. (p. 1237)
Burris, Peggy. Meet Pappy. (p. 1122)
Burris, Priscilla, illus. see Birney, Betty G.
Burris, Priscilla, illus. see Brenning, Juli.
Burris, Priscilla, illus. see Burch, Regina G. & Donovan Guntly, Jenette.
Burris, Priscilla, illus. see Busath, Isabelle & Thordsen, Isabella.
Burris, Priscilla, illus. see Coven, Wanda.
Burris, Priscilla, illus. see Pence, Shari A.
Burris, Priscilla, illus. see Rusackas, Francesca.
Burris, Priscilla, illus. see Sorenson, Margo.
Burris, Priscilla, illus. see Van Slyke, Rebecca.
Burris, Priscilla, illus. see Vernick, Audrey.
Burris, Priscilla, illus. see Williams, Rozanne Lanczak.
Burris, Priscilla, tr. see Rusackas, Francesca.
Burris, Shana Renee. Bailey the Bear: Sees Stars Everywhere! (p. 133)
Burroughs, Caleb. Animal Rescue Adventure. (p. 79)
—Cars. (p. 271)
—Dora the Explorer to the Moon. Miller, Victoria, illus. (p. 471)
—Transformers. Mawhinney, Art, illus. (p. 1778)
Burroughs, Chrysti, et al. Super Shot, Amazing Story of David & Goliath. Burroughs, Scott et al, illus. (p. 1681)
Burroughs, David, illus. see Bowkett, Steve.
Burroughs, Denise. Story of the Day You Were Born. (p. 1660)
Burroughs, Derrie, illus. see Tika.
Burroughs, Edgar Rice. Land That Time Forgot: Graphic Novel. Jones, K. L., illus. (p. 974)
—Mars Trilogy: A Princess of Mars - The Gods of Mars - The Warlord of Mars. Fischer, Scott M. et al, illus. (p. 1096)
—Tarzan Twins. Grant, Douglas, illus. (p. 1706)
Burroughs, Edgar Rice, jt. auth. see San Souci, Robert D.
Burroughs, John. Fresh Fields. (p. 636)
—Fresh Fields. Fuert, L. A. & Woodbury et al, Charles H., illus. (p. 636)
—Squirrels & Other Fur-Bearers (Yesterday's Classics) (p. 1637)
Burroughs, Polly. Honey Boat (p. 794)
Burroughs, Scott. Balloon Blow-Up. (p. 135)
—Disappearing Dog. (p. 446)
—Fossil Frenzy. (p. 623)
—Great Coaster Caper. (p. 714)
—Hardy Boys Secret Files Collection: Trouble at the Arcade - The Missing Mitt - Mystery Map - Hopping Mad - A Monster of a Mystery. (p. 748)
—Hopping Mad. (p. 797)
—Lights, Camera ... Zombies! (p. 1016)
—Missing Mitt. (p. 1152)
—Monster of a Mystery. (p. 1168)
—Mystery Map. (p. 1224)
—Robot Rumble. (p. 1480)
—Rockin' Mystery. (p. 1483)
—Sports Sabotage. (p. 1633)
—Trouble at the Arcade. (p. 1789)
Burroughs, Scott, illus. see Burroughs, Chrysti, et al.
Burroughs, Scott, illus. see Dixon, Franklin W.
Burroughs, Scott, illus. see Krensky, Stephen.
Burroughs, Scott, illus. see Redford, Marjorie & Rice, Courtney.
Burroughs, Scott, illus. see Shearer, Amelia.
Burroughs, Scott, illus. see Taylor, Mark A.
Burroughs, Scott, illus. see Williams, Bonnie.
Burroughs, Scott, jt. auth. see Zuchora-Walske, Christine.
Burroughs, William S. Live Performance Hoffman, Kathelin, ed. (p. 1040)
Burroway, Janet & Lord, John Vernon. Giant Jam Sandwich (p. 673)
—Giant Jam Sandwich. Lord, John Vernon, illus. (p. 673)
Burrowes, Adjoa J. Grandma's Purple Flowers. (p. 709)
Burrowes, Adjoa J., jt. auth. see Derby, Sally.
Burrows, Bridget. Developing Language Concepts: Programmes for School-Aged Children. (p. 431)
Burrows, Christopher. Alley Cats. (p. 47)
Burrows, David M. & Laing, Zhivargo. College, Career & Money: A Guide for Teens & Young Adults. (p. 340)
Burrows, Jeffrey Scott, illus. see Lement, Wendy.
Burrows, Jennifer. Arlington National Cemetery. (p. 99)
Burrows, Jennifer S. Canada Goose & You. Day, Margery, illus. (p. 260)
—Most Beautiful. (p. 1177)
Burrows, John. Lewis & Clark: Blazing a Trail West. (p. 1004)
Burrows, Mark. Ultimate Gettin' down with Mama Goose: Your Favorite Rhymes in One Big Musical Collection! (p. 1809)
Burrows, Mark, jt. auth. see Lyne, Alison Davis.
Burrows, Roger. Haunted House. (p. 753)
—Hidden Images - Garden: The Ultimate Coloring Experience. (p. 775)
Burrows, Roger, jt. auth. see Haas, Franklin C.
Burrows, Roger & Gilligan, Jeff. Birds of Oregon. Ross, Gary & Nordhagen, Ted, illus. (p. 191)
Burrows, Roger & Petersen, Wayne. Birds of New England. (p. 191)
Burrows, Roger, et al. Atlantic Canada Birds (p. 112)
Burrows, Terry. ¡Oh, No! Es Hipo! (p. 1281)
Burrus, Denise. Heavenly Balloons. (p. 761)
Burruss, Melissa, illus. see LaRocque, Greg.
Burshek, Edward & Burshek, Tonja. Explorers of the Word: Episode 1: the Creation. Peterson, Melanie, illus. (p. 551)
Burshek, Tonja, jt. auth. see Burshek, Edward.
Burshtein, Karen. Lionel Messi: Soccer's Top Scorer. (p. 1021)
Bursi, Simona, illus. see Goodings, Christina.
Bursi, Simona, illus. see Martin, Peter.
Bursi, Simona, illus. see Milbourne, Anna & Stowell, Louie.
Bursill, Henry, jt. auth. see Jacobs, Frank.
Burslem, Diana & Freeman, Diana. Bee Alarm! Webb, Philip, illus. (p. 157)
Burslem, Tobe. Bermendani. (p. 167)
Burson, Rachel. Aalayah's New Hope. (p. 2)
Burson, Ronda Pfohl. Monk-Monk the Monkey. (p. 1164)
Burson, Rusty, jt. auth. see Barhorst, Warren.
Burstein, Chaya M. Kids' Catalog of Animals & the Earth. Burstein, Chaya M., illus. (p. 953)
Burstein, John. Amazing Circulatory System: How Does My Heart Work? (p. 54)
—Astounding Nervous System: How Does My Brain Work? (p. 109)
—Calculating Area: Space Rocket! (p. 252)
—Can We Get Along? Dealing with Differences. (p. 258)
—Collecting Data: Pick a Pancake. Destiny Images Staff, illus. (p. 339)
—Delicious Dairy. (p. 425)
—Dobiar: Estrellas Del Circo. (p. 459)
—Dollars & Sense: Developing Good Money Habits. (p. 463)
—Dynamic Digestive System: How Does My Stomach Work? (p. 491)
—Exciting Endocrine System: How Do My Glands Work? (p. 547)
—Fabulous Fruits. (p. 560)
—Glorious Grains. (p. 685)
—Hacer Decenas: Grupos de Gollyluvas. (p. 735)
—Have You Heard? Active Listening. (p. 754)
—I Said No! Refusal Skills. (p. 845)
—Keeping Track of Time: Go Fly a Kite! Destiny Images Staff, illus. (p. 948)
—Making Maps: Where's the Party? (p. 1081)
—Making Tens: Groups of Gollywomples. Destiny Images Staff, illus. (p. 1082)
—Manners, Please! Why It Pays to Be Polite. (p. 1088)
—Marvelous Meats & More. (p. 1099)
—Measuring: The Perfect Playhouse. (p. 1117)
—Measuring: The Perfect Playhouse. Destiny Images Staff, illus. (p. 1117)
—Mighty Muscular & Skeletal Systems: How Do My Bones & Muscles Work? (p. 1140)
—Mighty Muscular-Skeletal System: How Do My Bones & Muscles Work? (p. 1140)
—Outstanding Oils & Wonderful Water. (p. 1313)
—Past Tense: Healthy Ways to Manage Stress. (p. 1327)
—Patterns: What's on the Wall? (p. 1329)
—Patterns: What's on the Wall? Destiny Images Staff, illus. (p. 1329)
—Remarkable Respiratory System: How Do My Lungs Work? (p. 1459)
—Speak Up! Communicating Confidently. (p. 1623)
—Speak up! Communicating Confidently. (p. 1623)
—Usar Computadoras: Una máquina con ratón. (p. 1826)
—Using Computers: Machine with a Mouse. (p. 1828)
—Using Computers: Machine with a Mouse. Destiny Images Staff, illus. (p. 1828)
—Vital Vegetables. (p. 1846)
—What Should I Do? Making Good Decisions. (p. 1893)
—Why Are You Picking on Me? Dealing with Bullies. (p. 1922)
—Will You Be My Friend? Buddy Building Strategies. (p. 1932)
—Will You Be My Friend? Buddy-Building Strategies. (p. 1932)
Burstein, John, jt. auth. see Goodbody, Slim.
Burstein, Mark, jt. auth. see Carroll, Lewis, pseud.
Burstein, Raya. Visual Perceptual Skill Building (p. 1846)
—Visual Perceptual Skill Building Book 1 (p. 1846)
Burstein, Stanley M. Reign of Cleopatra (p. 1457)
Burston, Chaim & Naiditch, Dov. Babel. Lumer, Marc, illus. (p. 123)
Bursztyn, Alberto M., ed. Childhood Psychological Disorders: Current Controversies (p. 302)
Bursztyn, Dina. Land of Lost Things: El País de las Cosas Perdidas. Bursztyn, Dina, illus. (p. 973)
Bursztynski, Sue. Crime Time: Australians Behaving Badly. Prout, Louise, illus. (p. 382)
—This Book Is Bugged. Vane, Mitch, illus. (p. 1735)
—Wolfborn. (p. 1944)
Bursztynski, Susan. Sea's Secret. Power, Margaret, illus. (p. 1538)
Burt, A. Spelling. (p. 1625)
Burt, A. M. Write with Confidence: Solutions & Examples for Everyday Writing Needs. (p. 1964)
Burt, Barbara & Schifini, Alfredo. Colonial Life. (p. 341)
Burt, Christine. Ghostly Rescue: A Story of Two Horses. (p. 672)
Burt, Donna, jt. auth. see Crayton, Tina.
Burt, Isabel. Toxics. (p. 1774)
Burt, Janet. Mexico's Pacific North States. (p. 1131)
—Pacific North States of Mexico. (p. 1317)
Burt, Jonathan. Rat. (p. 1440)
Burt, Judith. 10 Most Valuable Elements. (p. 1994)
Burt, Kelly, illus. see Henderson, Kris.
Burt, Marissa. Sliver of Stardust. (p. 1591)
—Story's End. (p. 1663)
Burt, Mary Alice. Beginning the Walk: A Tool for Developing A Preschooler's Faith. Burt, Mary Alice, illus. (p. 159)
Burt, Olive Woolley. John Wanamaker: Boy Merchant. Lees, Harry H., illus. (p. 923)
Burt, Steve. Even Odder: More Stories to Chill the Heart. Hagerman, Jessica, illus. (p. 541)
—Oddest Yet: Even More Stories to Chill the Heart. Hagerman, Jessica, illus. (p. 1278)
—Wicked Odd: Still More Stories to Chill the Heart. Hagerman, Jessica, illus. (p. 1927)
Burt Sullivan, Neallia, illus. see Ahern, Carolyn L.
Burt, Vickie. Alvin the Proud Prankster. Thompson, Jessica, illus. (p. 51)
—Hot Dog or Egg Sandwich? Lindsey, Jessica, illus. (p. 801)
Burt, Vicky. Eager Beavers. Lindsey, Jessica, illus. (p. 492)
Burtenshaw, Jenna. Blackwatch. (p. 198)
—Shadowcry. (p. 1558)
—Winterveil. (p. 1939)
Burtinshaw, Julie. Freedom of Jenny. (p. 634)
—Romantic Ghost Stories Wangler, Chris, ed. (p. 1486)
Burtis, Thomson. Flying Blackbirds. Gretta, J. Clemens, illus. (p. 609)

Burtner, Sharon Patricia. Transforming Moments: The Miracle. (p. 1778)
Burton, Anita. Duckey's Adventures. (p. 488)
Burton, Beth Windsor, jt. auth. see Horne, Glenda Burton.
Burton, Bonnie. Girls Against Girls: Why We Are Mean to Each Other & How We Can Change. (p. 679)
Burton, Bonnie, jt. ed. see Klutz Editors.
burton, brain, jt. auth. see Burton, Bria.
Burton, Bria & burton, brain. Lance & Ringo Tails: The Wild Adventures of a Dog & a Cat As Told by Their Human. (p. 973)
Burton, Carl, jt. auth. see Burton, Linda.
Burton, Chanel, jt. auth. see Burton, Chanel.
Burton, Chanel & Burton, Chanel. Wildancer Takes First: Wildancer Wins First Place. (p. 1931)
Burton, Claudia, illus. see Redfern, Holly.
Burton, Daniel, illus. see Glenn, Avery, et al.
Burton, Elizabeth K. Everdark Gate: The Everdark Wars Book 3. (p. 542)
Burton, Frances. Rainy Day Fun. (p. 1436)
Burton, Gina. Adventures of Bill the Seagull. (p. 16)
Burton, Hallie. Tapestry. (p. 1705)
—Tapestry [Library Edition]. (p. 1705)
Burton, Jacky. Other Stable. (p. 1306)
Burton, James, photos by see Howell, Laura.
Burton, Jane, photos by see Howell, Laura.
Burton, Jane, photos by see Parker, Steve.
Burton, Jane, photos by see Rayner, Matthew & BVetMed MRCVS Staff.
Burton, Jane, photos by see Starke, Katherine & Watt, Fiona.
Burton, Jeffery. Whispering to Lilly. (p. 1912)
Burton, Jennifer. Christopher's Dilemma. (p. 317)
—Princess's Journey. (p. 1406)
Burton, John, et al. Consumer Economics & Personal Finance. (p. 360)
Burton, Julie. Miracle of the Missing Puppies. (p. 1148)
Burton, K. Melissa. Kentucky's Boone: The Pioneer Spirit. Asher, James, illus. (p. 949)
—Now That's Interesting Kentucky's Capitol. Asher, James, photos by. (p. 1269)
Burton, Katherine. One Gray Mouse. Fernandes, Kim, illus. (p. 1295)
—Souris Grise. Fernandes, Kim, illus. (p. 1616)
Burton, Kenneth H. And I Shall Speak of Bridges: Selective Writings, Ponderings, Lyrics, & Poems. (p. 71)
Burton, Kevin, ed. see Heigh, Stephen.
Burton, L. DeVere. Fish & Wildlife: Principles of Zoology & Ecology. (p. 598)
Burton, Lamonica. Good Mothers Come in All Colors. (p. 698)
Burton, Leon H. & Kudo, Takeo. Soundplay: Understanding Music Through Creative Movement. (p. 1615)
Burton, LeVar. Best Friends. (p. 169)
Burton, Linda & Burton, Carl. Pay Attention, Emily Brown! Burton, Linda & Burton, Carl, illus. (p. 1331)
Burton, Lynne. Adventures on Ken's Canal: Volume 1. (p. 24)
—Adventures on Ken's Canal: Volume 2. (p. 24)
—Adventures on Ken's Canal: Volume 3. (p. 24)
—Charlotte's Crocodile. (p. 293)
—Little Ladybird Lost. (p. 1030)
Burton, Margie, et al. Alone & Together. (p. 48)
—Alone & Together & Sola y Acompañada: 6 English, 6 Spanish Adaptations. (p. 48)
—Animal Groups. (p. 78)
—Animals' Eyes & Ears. (p. 82)
—Animals' Eyes & Ears & Los Ojos y Los Oídos de Los Animales: 6 English, 6 Spanish Adaptations. (p. 82)
—Are We Hurting the Earth? (p. 96)
—Are We Hurting the Earth? & ¿Dañamos nuestra Tierra? 6 English, 6 Spanish Adaptations. (p. 96)
—Art Around the World & el arte en el Mundo: 6 English, 6 Spanish Adaptations (p. 101)
—Big & Little. (p. 177)
—Bigger Than? Smaller Than? (p. 185)
—Caring for Our Pets. (p. 269)
—Celebrations Around the World. (p. 285)
—Changing Weather. (p. 290)
—Changing Weather & Cambios en el Clima: 6 English, 6 Spanish Adaptations. (p. 290)
—Children as Young Scientists & Los niños Científicos: 6 English, 6 Spanish Adaptations (p. 302)
—Clean Beaches. (p. 330)
—Clean Beaches & Playas Limpias: 6 English, 6 Spanish Adaptations. (p. 330)
—Cleaning My Room. (p. 330)
—Cleaning My Room & ¡a Limpiar Mi Cuarto! 6 English, 6 Spanish Adaptations (p. 330)
—Clouds & Las Nubes: 6 English, 6 Spanish Adaptations (p. 335)
—Community Jobs & Empleos en la Comunidad: 6 English, 6 Spanish Adaptations (p. 350)
—Counting Insects. (p. 371)
—Counting Insects & Encontré muchos Insectos: 6 English, 6 Spanish Adaptations (p. 371)
—Counting Stars. (p. 371)
—Doing Jobs Together. (p. 463)
—Doing My Job. (p. 463)
—Endangered Animals. (p. 526)
—Endangered Animals & Animales en peligro de Extinción: 6 English, 6 Spanish Adaptations. (p. 526)
—Families. (p. 567)
—Families & la Familia: 6 English, 6 Spanish Adaptations (p. 567)
—Food Around the World. (p. 613)
—Food Around the World & la comida alrededor del Mundo: 6 English, 6 Spanish Adaptations (p. 613)
—Friends. (p. 638)
—Friends & Los Amigos: 6 English, 6 Spanish Adaptations (p. 638)
—Going Places. (p. 692)
—Going Places & la Transportación: 6 English, 6 Spanish Adaptations (p. 693)
—Growing Older. (p. 726)
—Growing Older & Crecemos: 6 English, 6 Spanish Adaptations (p. 726)
—Guess How Many I Have. (p. 728)
—Guessing Jar. (p. 729)
—Heat & el Calor: 6 English, 6 Spanish Adaptations (p. 760)
—Homes Around the World. (p. 793)
—How Do Animals Stay Alive? (p. 806)
—How Many Are Left? & ¿Cuántas cosas nos Quedan? 6 English, 6 Spanish Adaptations (p. 811)
—I Hear! (p. 839)
—Insects All Around. (p. 876)
—Insects All Around & Insectos por todas Partes: 6 English, 6 Spanish Adaptations (p. 876)
—Keeping Score & ¿Quién marca más Puntos? 6 English, 6 Spanish Adaptations (p. 947)
—Keeping Time. (p. 948)
—Life in the City & la vida en la Ciudad: 6 English, 6 Spanish Adaptations (p. 1011)
—Life on a Farm. (p. 1012)
—Living on the Farm. (p. 1041)
—Look at the Animals. (p. 1049)
—Looking Down. (p. 1051)
—Looking for Numbers. (p. 1051)
—Looking for Patterns. (p. 1051)
—Looking for Patterns & en busca de Patrones: 6 English, 6 Spanish Adaptations (p. 1051)
—Looking for Shapes. (p. 1051)
—Looking for Shapes & ¿Ves las Figuras? 6 English, 6 Spanish Adaptations (p. 1051)
—Looking into Space. (p. 1051)
—Looking into Space & Observando el Espacio: 6 English, 6 Spanish Adaptations (p. 1051)
—Measure Up! (p. 1117)
—Measure up! & ¡Vamos a Medir! 6 English, 6 Spanish Adaptations (p. 1117)
—My Five Senses. (p. 1208)
—My Models. (p. 1214)
—New Soccer Nets. (p. 1247)
—Ocean Animals & Los animales Marinos: 6 English, 6 Spanish Adaptations (p. 1276)
—One for You & One for Me. (p. 1295)
—One for You & One for Me & uno para tí y uno para Mí: 6 English, 6 Spanish Adaptations (p. 1295)
—Our Class Survey. (p. 1308)
—Our Money. (p. 1309)
—Our Money & Nuestro Dinero (p. 1309)
—Our Sun. (p. 1310)
—Pair of Babies. (p. 1318)
—Parts Make up a Whole. (p. 1325)
—Parts of a Whole. (p. 1325)
—Peaches all the Time. (p. 1332)
—Plants & Las Plantas: 6 English, 6 Spanish Adaptations. (p. 1370)
—Power of Nature. (p. 1389)
—Power of Nature & la fuerza de la Naturaleza: 6 English, 6 Spanish Adaptations (p. 1389)
—Reading a Graph. (p. 1444)
—Reduce, Reuse, & Recycle. (p. 1456)
—Reduce, Reuse, & Recycle & Reducir, reusar, y Reciclar: 6 English, 6 Spanish Adaptations (p. 1456)
—Riches from Nature. (p. 1470)
—Riches from Nature & Riquezas Naturales: 6 English, 6 Spanish Adaptations (p. 1470)
—Rocks. (p. 1483)
—Rules. (p. 1495)
—Rules & Las Reglas: 6 English, 6 Spanish Adaptations (p. 1495)
—Sorting My Money. (p. 1614)
—Sorting My Money & Clasificar mi Dinero: 6 English, 6 Spanish Adaptations. (p. 1614)
—Sounds. (p. 1615)
—Sounds & Los Sonidos: 6 English, 6 Spanish Adaptations (p. 1615)
—Technology Today. (p. 1712)
—Then & Now. (p. 1729)
—Travel Money, U. S. A. (p. 1780)
—Trees & Los árboles: 6 English, 6 Spanish Adaptations (p. 1784)
—Using Magnets. (p. 1828)
—Water. (p. 1862)
—Water Goes up! Water Comes Down! (p. 1862)
—Water Goes up! Water Comes down & ¡el Agua Sube! ¡el Agua Baja! 6 English, 6 Spanish Adaptations (p. 1862)
—We All Scream for Ice Cream. (p. 1865)
—We Use Numbers. (p. 1868)
—We Use Numbers & Usamos los Números: 6 English, 6 Spanish Adaptations (p. 1868)
—We Use Water. (p. 1868)
—Weather. (p. 1869)
—What Are My Chances? & ¿Qué será Probable? 6 English, 6 Spanish Adaptations (p. 1879)
—What Can You Measure with A Lollipop? (p. 1881)
—What Can You Measure with a Lollipop? & ¿Qué puedes medir con una Paleta? 6 English, 6 Spanish Adaptations. (p. 1881)
—What Comes in Twos? (p. 1881)
—What Comes Next? (p. 1881)
—What Comes Next? & ¿Qué Sigue? 6 English, 6 Spanish Adaptations. (p. 1881)
—What Floats? What Sinks? (p. 1884)
—What Pushes? What Pulls? (p. 1893)
—What Pushes? What Pulls? & ¿Qué empuja? ¿Qué Jala? 6 English, 6 Spanish Adaptations. (p. 1893)
—What Will I Be? (p. 1895)
—Where People Live. (p. 1909)
—Where People Live & ¿Dónde vives Tú? 6 English, 6 Spanish Adaptations (p. 1909)
—Your Body. (p. 1980)
—Your Body & Tu Cuerpo: 6 English, 6 Spanish Adaptations. (p. 1980)
Burton, Marilee R. Kindergarten Scholar. Boyer, Robin, illus. (p. 957)
Burton, Martin Nelson. Dear Mr. Leprechaun: Letters from My First Friendship. Hansen, Clint, illus. (p. 419)
—Fooling the Tooth Fairy. Hansen, Clint, illus. (p. 614)
Burton, Melissa. Divided They Stood. (p. 454)
Burton M.Sc., Kathryn Mac. Diarmid. Haley Honeybee: Finds the Magic Rose. Cox, Glendyne Dewhurst, illus. (p. 736)
Burton, Natasha. 101 Quizzes for BFFs: Crazy Fun Tests to See Who Knows Who Best! (p. 2000)
Burton, Nathaniel, illus. see Sheldon, Tom.
Burton, Neel. Heaven & Hell: Psychology of Emotions. (p. 761)
Burton, Neil. How to Be Brilliant at Recording in Science. (p. 815)
—How to Sparkle at Assessing Science. Ford, Kate, illus. (p. 821)
Burton, P. Birds of North America. (p. 191)
Burton, Rebecca. Leaving Jetty Road. (p. 986)
Burton, Robert. Wally A. Bow 21st Century Abow. (p. 1855)
Burton, Ryan. Female Force: Stephenie Meyer. (p. 581)
Burton, Sarah. Miracle in Bethlehem: A Storyteller's Tale. Chapman, Katriona, illus. (p. 1148)
Burton, Sharon Ann. Grammy Loves Me. (p. 706)
—When I Grow Up. (p. 1902)
Burton, Terry, illus. see Andrews, Jackie.
Burton, Terry, illus. see Award, Anna.
Burton, Terry, illus. see Giles, Sophie, et al.
Burton, Terry, illus. see Tango Books Staff.
Burton, Terry, illus. see Tango Books.
Burton, Terry & Ward, Anna. English. Burton, Terry, illus. (p. 529)
Burton, Thomas. Bluey & Dingo's Outback Adventure. (p. 204)
Burton, Tim. Frankenweenie: A Graphic Novel. (p. 629)
—Melancholy Death of Oyster Boy & the Other Stories: Stick Boy's Festive Season. (p. 1125)
Burton, Tim & Disney Book Group Staff. Frankenweenie: a Graphic Novel. Klubien, Jorgen, illus. (p. 629)
—Nightmare Before Christmas. Burton, Tim, illus. (p. 1255)
Burton, Tom. Long Words Bother Me. (p. 1047)
Burton, Tony. Blinded by Darkness. (p. 199)
Burton, Virginia Lee. Casita. (p. 276)
—Katy & the Big Snow. (p. 945)
—Katy & the Big Snow Lap Board Book. (p. 945)
—Life Story. (p. 1013)
—Little House. (p. 1029)
—Little House. (p. 1029)
—Little House. Burton, Virginia Lee, illus. (p. 1029)
—Mike Mulligan & His Steam Shovel Burton, Virginia Lee, illus. (p. 1141)
—Mike Mulligan & His Steam Shovel. (p. 1141)
—Mike Mulligan Travel Activity Kit. (p. 1141)
Burton, Virginia Lee, illus. see Andersen, Hans Christian & Starbright Foundation Staff.
Burton, Wade T. Tell Me the Old, Old Story... in a New Way. (p. 1716)
Burton, Zisca Isabel. Bloom's How to Write about Toni Morrison. (p. 201)
Burton-Hupp, Lynne. Venus the Very Proper Fly Trap. (p. 1836)
Burt-Westvig, Molly, jt. auth. see Schense, Deb.
Burwen, David M. & Burwen, Susan Jo. Carl Roters & the Rendezvous Murals. (p. 269)
Burwen, Susan Jo, jt. auth. see Burwen, David M.
Burwick, Josh. Dad, I Wish I Was Your Age. Monroe, Dan, illus. (p. 398)
Burwitz, Patrick. Mia's Dogcow. (p. 1134)
Burzynski, Roberta. Why Would Anyone Cut a Tree Down? Forest Service (U.S.), Northeastern Area State and Private Forestry, ed. (p. 1927)
Bus, Sabrina. Hail Mary. Deneux, Xavier, illus. (p. 735)
—Our Father. Deneux, Xavier, illus. (p. 1308)
Busaluzzo, Constanza, illus. see Currie, Robin.
Busaluzzo, Constanza, illus. see David C. Cook Publishing Company Staff & Currie, Robin.
Busath, Isabelle & Thordsen, Isabella. Little Book of Rules. Burris, Priscilla, illus. (p. 1025)
Busby, Ailie. Por Qué Soy Tan Pequeño? (p. 1386)
Busby, Ailie, illus. see Bracken, Beth.
Busby, Ailie, illus. see Child's Play Staff.
Busby, Ailie, illus. see Eves, Sue.
Busby, Ailie, illus. see Grant, Carrie and David.
Busby, Ailie, illus. see Metzger, Steve.
Busby, Ailie, illus. see Puttock, Simon.
Busby, Ailie, illus. see Reid, Camilla.
Busby, Ailie, illus. see Sutcliffe, William.
Busby, Barbara Sheen. Car Racing. Greenhaven Press Editors, ed. (p. 265)
—Cerebral Palsy. Kling, Andrew A., ed. (p. 287)
—Walt Disney. Greenhaven Press Editors, ed. (p. 1855)
Busby, Barbara Sheen, jt. auth. see Greenhaven Press Editors.
Busby, Cylin. Blink Once. (p. 199)
Busby, Cylin & Busby, John. Year We Disappeared: A Father-Daughter Memoir. (p. 1969)
Busby, Cylin, ed. First Kiss (Then Tell) (p. 595)
—First Kiss (Then Tell) A Collection of True Lip-Locked Moments. (p. 595)
Busby, Deehna R. Father's Precious Creations Series: Things That Crawl. (p. 577)
Busby, John, jt. auth. see Busby, Cylin.
Busby, Mark. Southwest (p. 1617)
Busby, Peter. First to Fly: How Wilbur & Orville Wright Invented the Airplane. Craig, David, illus. (p. 597)
Busby, Robert C., jt. auth. see Anton, Howard.
Busby, Robert C. & Anton, Howard. Contemporary Linear Algebra, Student Solutions Manual. (p. 360)
Buscema, John. Fantastic Four: Extended Family. Pacheco, Carlos, illus. (p. 571)
Buscema, John, illus. see Conway, Gerry & Lee, Stan.
Buscema, John, illus. see Conway, Gerry & Wein, Len.
Buscema, John, illus. see Wolfman, Marv, et al.
Buscema, John, illus. see Wolfman, Marv.
Buscema, John, jt. auth. see Claremont, Chris.
Buscema, John, jt. illus. see Muth, Jon J.
Buscema, John & Byrne, John. Avengers: The Legacy of Thanos. (p. 118)
Buscema, John & Hall, Bob. Avengers: Assault on Olympus. (p. 118)
Buscema, John, et al. Marvel Masterworks - The Avengers (p. 1099)
Buscema, Sal. Marvel Masterworks - Captain America (p. 1099)
—Marvel Universe Guardians of the Galaxy: Cosmic Team-Up. (p. 1099)
Buscema, Sal, illus. see David, Peter, et al.
Buscema, Sal, illus. see David, Peter.
Buscema, Sal, illus. see Simonson, Walter.
Buscema, Sal, jt. auth. see Thomas, Roy.
Buscema, Sal, et al. Essential Captain America - Volume 7. (p. 536)
—Marvel Masterworks: The Avengers. Vol. 14 (p. 1099)
—Marvel Masterworks: The Defenders - Volume 2. (p. 1099)
Buscema, Stephanie, illus. see Archer, Peggy.
Buscema, Stephanie, illus. see Crimi, Carolyn.
Buscemi, Karen. Split in Two: Keeping It Together When Your Parents Live Apart. (p. 1630)
Buscemi, Santi V. & Smith, Charlotte. 75 Readings: An Anthology. (p. 1998)
Busch, Darcy J. Lily & the Hidden Secrets (p. 1018)
Busch, Janice. Elephant That Fell. (p. 511)
Busch, Jean. Aiden & the Frog Prince (p. 30)
—Cheyenne & the Indian Spirit. (p. 299)
—Colleen & the Willow Fairy. (p. 340)
Busch, Jeffrey, jt. auth. see Irving, Washington.
Busch, Jeffrey, jt. auth. see Kipling, Rudyard.
Busch, Leah, jt. auth. see Gross, Sandra.
Busch, Melinda Kay. Born on Christmas Morn. Hall, Melanie, illus. (p. 214)
—Fiery Furnace. Koehler, Ed, illus. (p. 584)
—God Calls Abraham... God Calls You! Dorenkamp, Michelle, illus. (p. 688)
—Jesus & the Woman at the Well. Clark, Bill, illus. (p. 915)
—Savior of the Nations-Mini BK. Hall, Melanie, illus. (p. 1518)
Busch, Miriam. Lion, Lion. Day, Larry, illus. (p. 1020)
Buscher, Nancy Tancey. Kaleidoscope of Children's Poems. (p. 942)
Buser, Jeanette. I'm A Flea from A to Z. (p. 858)
Bush, Don. Little Brook Series (p. 1025)
—Magic Smith the Chameleon. (p. 1073)
Bush, Emilie P. Steamduck Learns to Fly! Petty, William Kevin, illus. (p. 1646)
Bush, Jenna. Ana's Story: A Journey of Hope. (p. 67)
—Ana's Story: A Journey of Hope. Baxter, Mia, illus. (p. 67)
—Historia de Ana: Un Camino Lleno de Esperanza. Baxter, Mia, illus. (p. 782)
Bush, Jenna, jt. auth. see Bush, Laura.
Bush, John. Mr. Crookodile. Paul, Korky, illus. (p. 1184)
Bush, John & Geraghty, Paul. Bungle in the Jungle. (p. 242)
Bush, Laura & Bush, Jenna. Read All about It! Brunkus, Denise, illus. (p. 1442)
Bush, Laura & Hager, Jenna Bush. Read All about It! Brunkus, Denise, illus. (p. 1442)
Bush, Leanne. Sarah's Happy Harvest Time Briggs, Charlotte, illus. (p. 1514)
—Very Special Christmas with Grandm. (p. 1838)
Bush, Martha Faircloth. Helping Hurting Children: a Journey of Healing: Children's Workbook. (p. 766)
Bush, Maureen. Crow Boy (p. 385)
—Cursed! (p. 395)
—Feather Brain (p. 579)
—Nexus Ring (p. 1249)
Bush, Penelope. Alice in Time. (p. 39)
Bush, Randall. Caterbury Tails. Watson, Ben, illus. (p. 279)
Bush, Randall B. Gabriel's Magic Ornament. Schunemann, Ryan, illus. (p. 652)
Bush, Robert Quacken. Return of Pete Pack Rat. Bush, Robert Quacken, ed. (p. 1464)
Bush, Rosetta Bowman. Chicken Every Sunday. (p. 300)
—Coal Dust Twins. (p. 336)
—My Name Is Violet. (p. 1215)
Bush, Selene. Golden Cape. (p. 694)
Bush, Susan Hussey. Alone on Stage: An American American Actress in 1930s France & America. (p. 48)
Bush, Suzanne & Takes, Deb. Time Will Tell. (p. 1753)
Bush, Timothy. Teddy Bear, Teddy Bear: A Traditional Rhyme. (p. 1712)
Bush, Timothy, illus. see Goodman, Susan E.
Bush, Timothy, illus. see Roy, Ron.
Bush, Timothy, illus. see Roy, Ronald.
Bush, Timothy, tr. see Roy, Ron.
Bush, Todd. Rick Frost & the Alaskan Adventure. (p. 1470)
—Rick Frost & the Sword of Calibum. (p. 1470)
Bush, Ty. Marcus Jones & the Mastery of the Scripture Balls. (p. 1092)
Bush, Valerie Chow, ed. Jump. (p. 933)
Bush, Valerie Chow, et al. Jump Write In! Creative Writing Exercises for Diverse Communities, Grades 6-12 Tannenbaum, Judith, ed. (p. 934)
Bush, Vicki-Ann. Queen of IT. Beachamp, Afiyah, illus. (p. 1425)
Bushar, Carol. Robby the Lion Doesn't Eat Meat. (p. 1478)
Bushell, Abby. Pc Rob Has a Very Important Job: Talking about Strangers. (p. 1331)
Bushell, Nick, jt. auth. see Martineau, Susan.
Bushell, Nick & Martineau, Susan. Cool Circuits & Wicked Wires. Ursell, Martin, illus. (p. 363)
Bushell, Sharon. Bernie Jones & the Blazing Bandits. (p. 167)
—Trouble with Bernie. (p. 1790)
Bushell, Tony. Skills: Activity Masters. (p. 1585)
Bushey, Jeanne. Orphans in the Sky Krykorka, Vladyana, illus. (p. 1305)
—Sled Dog for Moshi Amaktauyok, Germaine, illus. (p. 1588)
Bushman, Janet. Shiny Red Apple. (p. 1567)
Bushnell, Candace. Carrie Diaries. (p. 271)
—Lipstick Jungle. (p. 1021)
—Sex & the City. (p. 1556)
—Summer & the City. (p. 1673)
—Trading Up. (p. 1776)
Bushnell, David Ives. Cahokia & Surrounding Mound Groups. (p. 251)
Bushnell, Jack. Farm Crossing: The Amazing Adventures of Addie & Zachary. Caple, Laurie, illus. (p. 573)
—Night of the White Deer. Co, Miguel, illus. (p. 1254)

Bushnell, Larry. God's Diminishing Power: If We Don't Do It God's Way His Power Is Unavailable. (p. 691)
Bushnell, Steven G. Big Adventures of Little Church Mouse: The Parables of Jesus. (p. 177)
Bushor, Mark. Mission Mania: Crazy to Serve. (p. 1153)
Bushore-Fallis, Martha. Book of Lyrics: Freedom Found, the Musical Drama. (p. 211)
Bush-Retherford, Dody & Clark, Paul. Lil Witches Wheel of the Year Coloring Book. (p. 1017)
Bushweller, Ellie. Tree with A Hundred Hands. (p. 1784)
Busic, Valerie. Jason's First Day. OI Foundation, ed. (p. 910)
Busiek, Kurt. Avengers Assemble (p. 118)
—Camelot Falls (p. 256)
—Liberty Project. (p. 1005)
—Marvels: The Platinum Edition Slipcase. (p. 1099)
—Marvels. Youngquist, Jeff, ed. (p. 1099)
—Superman - Secret Identity. (p. 1683)
—Wizard's Tale. (p. 1943)
Busiek, Kurt, jt. auth. see Johns, Geoff.
Busiek, Kurt, jt. auth. see Slott, Dan.
Busiek, Kurt & David, Peter. Thunderbolts Classic - Volume 1. Bagley, Mark et al, illus. (p. 1746)
Busiek, Kurt, et al. Above & Beyond. (p. 6)
—Albion. Guice, Jackson, illus. (p. 35)
—Avengers Assemble (p. 118)
—Superman - Back in Action. Woods, Pete, photos by. (p. 1683)
Buske, Jody. Wilderness Awakening. (p. 1931)
Busquets, Carlos. Animales Cuentan 365 Historias. (p. 80)
Busquets, Jordi & Susaeta, Equipo. Leo y Veo, las Brujas. (p. 992)
—Leo y Veo, las Hadas. (p. 992)
—Leo y Veo, los Gigantes. (p. 992)
—Leo y Veo, los Gnomos. (p. 992)
Buss, Robin, ed. see Dumas, Alexandre.
Buss, Robin, tr. see Dumas, Alexandre.
Bussagli, Marco. Understanding Architecture Bettinelli, Sara & Galleschi, M. Lucrezia, eds. (p. 1815)
Busse, Gregory D. Morphine. Triggle, David J., ed. (p. 1176)
Busse, Kathy. Generations of Country Kids: Twelve Timeless Stories of Purpose. (p. 660)
Bussell, Darcey. Christmas in Enchantia. (p. 314)
—Delphie & the Glass Slippers. (p. 425)
—Delphie & the Masked Ball. (p. 425)
—Summer in Enchantia. (p. 1674)
Bussell, Darcey & Dorling Kindersley Publishing Staff. Ballet Book. (p. 134)
Bussell, Linda. Exploring Solid Figures on the Web. (p. 553)
—Measuring at the Pond. (p. 1117)
—Multiplicar para Planear una Fiesta. (p. 1190)
—Multiply to Make Party Plans. (p. 1190)
—Pizza Parts: Fractions! (p. 1365)
—Pizza Por Partes: Fracciones! (p. 1365)
—Pizza por Partes: ¡FRACCIONES! (p. 1365)
—Probabilidad con Juegos y Diversión. (p. 1408)
—Probability with Fun & Games. (p. 1408)
—Trabajemos con Números en Las Noticias. (p. 1774)
—Using Division at Sports Camp. (p. 1828)
—Using Division Facts in the Garden. (p. 1828)
—Vamos a Explorar Cuerpos Sólidos en la Red. (p. 1831)
—Vamos a Medir en el Estanque. (p. 1831)
—Vamos a Usar Datos de División en el Jardín. (p. 1831)
—Vamos a Usar la División en el Campamento de Deportes. (p. 1831)
—Working with Numbers in the News. (p. 1953)
Bussereth, Bianca. Sky Rod. (p. 1587)
Bussey, Jennifer. 1820-1840 (Events That Changed the World) (p. 2002)
—Saddam Hussein. (p. 1501)
Bussiere, Desireé. Bowling by the Numbers. (p. 216)
—Golf by the Numbers. (p. 696)
—Gymnastics by the Numbers. (p. 734)
Bussiere, Desirée. Let's Measure More. (p. 999)
Bussiere, Desirée. Skateboarding by the Numbers. (p. 1583)
—Swimming by the Numbers. (p. 1691)
—Tennis by the Numbers. (p. 1720)
Bussiere, Desirée. What in the World Is a Baker's Dozen? & Other Interesting Measurements. (p. 1887)
—What in the World Is a Centimeter? & Other Metric Measurements. (p. 1887)
—What in the World Is a Leap Year? & Other Time Measurements. (p. 1887)
—What in the World Is a Mile? & Other Distance Measurements. (p. 1887)
—What in the World Is a Ton? & Other Weight & Volume Measurements. (p. 1888)
—What in the World Is an Acre? & Other Land & Sea Measurements. (p. 1888)
Bussing-Burks, Marie. Influential Economists. (p. 873)
Bussing-Burks, Marie, jt. auth. see Nichols, Clive.
Bustamante, Frank & Gray, Dan, eds. Testimony of Jacob Hollow. Bustamante, Frank et al, illus. (p. 1723)
Bustamente, Martin, jt. auth. see Nelson, Jo.
Bustani, Juma. Adventure in Nairobi. (p. 14)
Bustard, Ned, ed. see Sanderson, Krystyna.
Bustard, Ned, jt. auth. see Nichols, Stephen J.
Busteed, Kerri J. Will's Bow Hunting Adventure. Byers, Leon, illus. (p. 1934)
—Will's First Hunt. Byers, Leon, illus. (p. 1934)
Bustelo, Ana, tr. see Lowry, Lois.
Bustelo, Gabriela, tr. see Barrie, J. M.
Bustelo, Gabriela, tr. see Cleary, Beverly.
Buster Books. Fun to Finish Animals. (p. 648)
Buster Books Staff. Big Book of Amazing Activities. (p. 178)
—I Love Niall. (p. 842)
Buster Books Staff, jt. auth. see Fearns, Georgie.
Buster Books Staff, jt. auth. see Maloney, Jim.
Buster Books Staff, jt. auth. see Playmobil.
Buster Books Staff, jt. auth. see Schrey, Sophie.
Bustle, Cheryl. Ralphie Goes on a Boat Ride! (p. 1437)
Bustos, Eduardo & Rodríguez, Lucho. Going Ape! (p. 692)
Busuttil, Conor, illus. see O'Sullivan, Helen.
Butch, Hartman. Fairly Oddparents: Gone Too Far. Vol. 6 (p. 563)
Butchart, Francis & Smith, Ron. Elf the Eagle. Campbell, Ruth, illus. (p. 512)
Butchart, Pamela. Never Tickle a Tiger. Boutavant, Marc, illus. (p. 1243)
Butcher, A D. Grandma Can You Tell Me. Dugan, Alan, illus. (p. 708)
Butcher, A. J. Chaos Rising. (p. 291)
—Serpent Scenario. (p. 1552)
—Spy High Mission One. (p. 1636)
Butcher, A. J. & Butcher, Andrew J. Conexión Caos: Spy High, Episodio 2. Vol. 2 Morales, Andrea & Yver, Camila, trs. (p. 356)
Butcher, Alice & Farquhar, Ginny. Sewing for Kids: Easy Projects to Sew at Home. (p. 1556)
Butcher, Andrew. Slave Harvest. (p. 1588)
—The Time of the Reapers (p. 1728)
—Tomorrow Seed. (p. 1765)
Butcher, Andrew & Butcher, Andrew J. Factoria Frankestein. Morales, Andrea, tr. (p. 561)
Butcher, Andrew J., jt. auth. see Butcher, A. J.
Butcher, Andrew J., jt. auth. see Butcher, Andrew.
Butcher, Ben, illus. see Nicholas, Christopher.
Butcher, Derek. Max the ed up Dog: Max & Matts Adventures. (p. 1111)
Butcher, Kristen, jt. auth. see Butcher, Kristin.
Butcher, Kristin. Alibi (p. 39)
—Caching In (p. 250)
—Chat Room (p. 295)
—Chat Room. (p. 295)
—Cheat (p. 295)
—Hemingway Tradition. (p. 766)
—Last Superhero. (p. 979)
—Pharaohs & Foot Soldiers: One Hundred Ancient Egyptian Jobs You Might Have Desired or Dreaded. Newbigging, Martha, illus. (p. 1349)
—Plan de Zee (p. 1366)
—Return to Bone Tree Hill. (p. 1465)
—Trouble with Liberty (p. 1790)
—Truths I Learned from Sam. (p. 1794)
—Zach & Zoe: Bully & the Beagle (p. 1984)
—Zach & Zoe & the Bank Robber (p. 1984)
—Zee's Way (p. 1985)
—Zee's Way. (p. 1985)
Butcher, Kristin & Butcher, Kristen. Tomorrow Tunnel. (p. 1765)
Butcher, Kristin & Labatt, Mary. Sam Finds a Monster. Sarrazin, Marisol, illus. (p. 1506)
Butcher, Nancy. Beauty. (p. 154)
—It Can't Be Done, Nellie Bly! A Reporter's Race Around the World Singh, Jen, illus. (p. 893)
Butcher, Nancy, jt. auth. see Armstrong, Jennifer.
Butcher, Nancy, et al. Island Girls. (p. 892)
—It's Snow Problem (p. 898)
—Two for the Road. (p. 1803)
Butcher, Nicholas. Hand above the Gate. (p. 740)
Butcher, Sally K., jt. illus. see Arjas, Pirkko.
Butcher, Sam. Precious Moments: Storybook Bible & Girl Prayer Pal Set. (p. 1394)
—Precious Moments: Small Hands Bible with Pink Bible Cover. (p. 1394)
—Precious Moments: Small Hands Bible with Lavender Bible Cover. (p. 1394)
—Precious Moments: Angel Kisses & Snuggle Time Prayers with Dolly. (p. 1394)
—Precious Moments: Angel Kisses & Snuggle Time Prayers with Teddy Bear. (p. 1394)
Butcher, Sam, illus. see MacArthur, John.
Butcher, Shannon K. No Regrets. (p. 1260)
Butcher, Tami. My Bonus Mom! Taking the Step Out of Stepmom. Nouf, Feras, illus. (p. 1198)
Butcher, Timothy. ABACA Flows over Niagara Falls: An Illustrated History. (p. 2)
Butefish, Jennifer, photos by see Williamson, Kate T.
Butenas, Jennifer. Moment in Time. Cheng, Charlotte, illus. (p. 1161)
Butineau, W. Turning Thirteen. (p. 1798)
Butkus, Michael. Drawing: Learn the Basics of Drawing. (p. 481)
Butler, Alberta J. Little White Butterflies. (p. 1037)
Butler, Amy. In Stitches: More Than 25 Simple & Stylish Sewing Projects. Redinger, Jacob, illus. (p. 865)
Butler, Andrea. Senor Sol y el Senor Mar Flor Ada, Alma, tr. (p. 1550)
Butler, Anne. Weep for the Living (p. 1872)
Butler, Berwyn. Dinky the Doorknob: The Adventures of Sir Dinkum Wilhelm, the Third Earl of Surridge. (p. 440)
Butler, Berwyn & McClean, Shorty. Dinky the Doorknob. (p. 440)
Butler, Berwyn G. Amazing Moonshine Mcpool. (p. 55)
Butler, Bryan C., illus. see Harvey, Paul, Jr.
Butler, Bryna. Whispering Evil (Midnight Guardian Series, Book 2) (p. 1912)
Butler, Charles. Fetch of Mardy Watt: Can You Believe Your Eyes? (p. 582)
Butler, Charles, jt. auth. see Butler, Charles, Jr.
Butler, Charles, Jr. & Butler, Charles. Death of a Ghost: Birth of a Nightmare. Wyatt, David, illus. (p. 420)
Butler, Chris. My Body. (p. 1198)
Butler, Chris, illus. see Rosa-Mendoza, Gladys.
Butler, Craig. Possum's Christmas. (p. 1387)
Butler, Daphne. What Happens When Food Cooks? (p. 1886)
Butler, Darnell. ABC's of People in the Bible. Uto-Uko, Iniobong, illus. (p. 4)
Butler, Darren J. Helen Keller: Leader Without Sight or Sound. (p. 763)
—Masterpiece: An Abbie Girl Spy Mystery. Casteel, Kay, illus. (p. 1103)
—Secret of Crybaby Hollow. (p. 1542)
Butler, David. Bible Ites: An Illustrated Guide to the People in the Holy Bible. Jeppesen, Ryan, illus. (p. 175)
Butler, Debra Rae. BenjiB. (p. 165)
Butler, Don. North Fork: A Tale of the Southwestern Frontier. (p. 1265)
Butler, Dori. Detective Cluck & the Missing Hens. (p. 431)
—How the Rhino Got Wrinkly Skin: An Adaptation of a Rudyard Kipling Story. (p. 813)
—Late Again! (p. 979)
—Sheep in Wolf's Clothing. (p. 1564)
—Time Capsule. (p. 1751)
—Tortoise & the Hare: An Aesop's Fable. (p. 1771)
Butler, Dori H. Campus Attack, Sabotage! (p. 258)
Butler, Dori Hillestad. Alexandra Hopewell, Labor Coach. (p. 37)
—Buddy Files: The Case of the School Ghost. Tugeau, Jeremy, illus. (p. 234)
—Buddy Files: The Case of the Fire Alarm. Bk. 4 Tugeau, Jeremy, illus. (p. 234)
—Buddy Files: The Case of the Missing Family. Bk. 3 Tugeau, Jeremy, illus. (p. 234)
—Case of the Library Monster. Tugeau, Jeremy, illus. (p. 274)
—Case of the Lost Boy. Tugeau, Jeremy, illus. (p. 274)
—Case of the Missing Family Tugeau, Jeremy, illus. (p. 274)
—Case of the Mixed-Up Mutts Tugeau, Jeremy, illus. (p. 274)
—Case of the Mixed-Up Mutts Bk. 2 Tugeau, Jeremy, illus. (p. 274)
—Case of the School Ghost Tugeau, Jeremy, illus. (p. 275)
—Case of the School Ghost. (p. 275)
—Do You Know the Monkey Man? (p. 458)
—F Is for Firefighting Waites, Joan C., illus. (p. 559)
—Five O'Clock Ghost Damant, Aurore, illus. (p. 601)
—Ghost Backstage Damant, Aurore, illus. (p. 670)
—Ghost in the Attic Damant, Aurore, illus. (p. 670)
—Haunted Library. (p. 753)
—Haunted Library #1. Damant, Aurore, illus. (p. 753)
—Just in Time. Trissler, Rebecca Johns, ed. (p. 938)
—My Grandpa Had a Stroke. Wong, Nicole, illus. (p. 1210)
—P Is for Police Waites, Joan, illus. (p. 1316)
—Porch Swing. Flounders, Anne, ed. (p. 1386)
—Secret Room. (p. 1543)
—Secret Room #5. Damant, Aurore, illus. (p. 1543)
—Sliding into Home (p. 1590)
—Sliding into Home Casale, Paul, illus. (p. 1590)
—Trading Places with Tank Talbott. (p. 1776)
—Truth about Truman School (p. 1794)
—Yes, I Know Monkey Man (p. 1970)
Butler, Ellis Parker. Pigs Is Pigs & Other Favorites. (p. 1358)
Butler, Erin. Be Patient, Petunia. (p. 149)
—Blood Hex. (p. 200)
Butler, Ethel And Steven, creator. Callie the Kangie Traveling America. (p. 254)
Butler, Geoff, illus. see Walsh, Alice.
Butler, Georgia Anne. Of the Wing: The Legend Awakes. (p. 1279)
Butler, Gloria. Lighthouse Lindy. (p. 1015)
Butler, Gregory J., illus. see Toporoff, Debi.
Butler, Heather. Adam & the Tattooed Angel. Buckley, Joel, illus. (p. 11)
—Ellie & the Clown Crisis. Buckley, Joel, illus. (p. 514)
Butler, Heather, ed. Reading for Fluency Resource Guide: Learning to Read Text Accurately & Quickly. (p. 1446)
Butler, Jalen. Helping Man: The Beginning. (p. 766)
Butler, James L. Cow-Pie Chronicles. Millsap, Lonnie, illus. (p. 373)
Butler, Jeremy. Hello, Zippy! (p. 765)
Butler, Jerry, illus. see Pferdehirt, Julia.
Butler, John. Bedtime in the Jungle. Butler, John, illus. (p. 157)
—Can You Cuddle Like a Koala? Butler, John, illus. (p. 258)
—Can You Growl Like a Bear? Butler, John, illus. (p. 259)
—Hush, Little Ones. Butler, John, illus. (p. 830)
—If You See a Kitten Butler, John, illus. (p. 854)
—If Your Dreams Take off & Fly. (p. 855)
—Ten in the Den. Butler, John, illus. (p. 1718)
—Ten in the Meadow. Butler, John, illus. (p. 1718)
—Whose Baby Am I? (p. 1921)
Butler, John, illus. see Alberts, Nancy Markham.
Butler, John, illus. see Bauer, Marion Dane.
Butler, John, illus. see Galbraith, Kathryn O.
Butler, John, illus. see Goldsmith, Mike.
Butler, John, illus. see Hawkins, Emily.
Butler, John, illus. see Henrichs, Wendy.
Butler, John, illus. see Milbourne, Anna.
Butler, John, illus. see Parker, Steve.
Butler, John, illus. see Smith, Alastair.
Butler, John, illus. see Thompson, Lauren.
Butler, John, illus. see Wang, Margaret.
Butler, John, illus. see Wilson, Hannah.
Butler, Jon, et al. Grammar Links Basic: An Introductory Course for Reference & Practice. (p. 706)
Butler, Julie Dupre, illus. see Fontenot, Mary Alice & Fontenot Landry, Julie.
Butler, Kristi T. Big Surprise. Paparone, Pamela, illus. (p. 184)
—Rip's Secret Spot. (p. 1474)
—Rip's Secret Spot. Cepeda, Joe, illus. (p. 1474)
Butler, Kynora. Knowing Is Believing in Reading: Facing Your Fears. (p. 965)
Butler, Lanzi W. Gates of Guilford: Selected poems & Photographs. (p. 658)
Butler, Latrica, ed. see Welch, Michael, Sr.
Butler, Laura. Cellies. (p. 286)
Butler, Leah & Peters, Trudy. Owen's Choice: The Night of the Halloween Vandals. Armstrong, Neal, illus. (p. 1314)
Butler, Linda. Grammar Links Basic: An Introductory Course for Reference & Practice. (p. 706)
Butler, Linda & Podnecky, Janet. Audio Cd: Used with ... Butler-Grammar Links 1: A Theme-Based Course for Reference & Practice. (p. 114)
—Grammar Links: A Theme-Based Course for Reference & Practice. (p. 706)
—Grammar Links 1 (p. 706)
Butler, Linda, et al. Grammar Links 1: A Theme-Based Course for Reference & Practice. (p. 706)
Butler, Lindsay L., illus. see Cudeyro, Erica M.
Butler, Lisa, illus. see Hele, Bonita Jewel.
Butler, Lisa, illus. see Sia, Cress.
Butler, M. Christina. First Snow. Endersby, Frank, illus. (p. 596)
—One Special Christmas. Macnaughton, Tina, illus. (p. 1297)
—Who's Been Eating My Porridge? Howarth, Daniel, illus. (p. 1920)
Butler, Mackay M., jt. auth. see Hooley, Rachelle B.
Butler, Mark. Jonathan's Raspberry Beard. (p. 925)
Butler, Mark J. Unlocking the Groove: Rhythm, Meter, & Musical Design in Electronic Dance Music. (p. 1821)
Butler, Mary. Sojourner Truth: From Slave to Activist for Freedom. (p. 1606)
Butler, Mary Ann. Protect Me Love My World! (p. 1412)
Butler, Mary G. Sojourner Truth: From Slave to Activist for Freedom. (p. 1606)
Butler, Matthew. Billy Goes Hunting: A boy's journey to discover the values & traditions of Hunting. (p. 187)
Butler, Nancy J. Fred the Fireless Dragon. (p. 632)
Butler, Nicola, illus. see Dickins, Rosie.
Butler, Octavia E. Fledgling. (p. 603)
—Seed to Harvest. (p. 1547)
Butler, Ralph M., illus. see Greenfield, Nancy Reuben.
Butler, Reginald, illus. see Atwood, Megan.
Butler, Reginald, illus. see Marsico, Katie.
Butler, Reginald, illus. see Owings, Lisa.
Butler, Reginald, illus. see Sirota, Lyn.
Butler, Robbie. Holocaust: For Use with Holocaust Biographies & Teen Witnesses to the Holocaust: A Teacher's Guide. (p. 789)
Butler, Roberta. Making Shapes. Moon, Jo, illus. (p. 1082)
Butler, Rosemary. My Merry Menagerie: Lighthearted Verses & Drawings. Butler, Rosemary, illus. (p. 1214)
Butler, Sara. Jake & Zach's Special Day. (p. 906)
Butler, Sharon, illus. see Taylor, C. Brian.
Butler, Shirley. First-Class Adventure of Flat Freddie. (p. 593)
Butler, Susan. Hermit Thrush Sings. (p. 771)
Butler, T. Lee. Ghost on Tanner's Mountain. (p. 671)
Butler, Tad, illus. see Aller, Susan Bivin.
Butler, Tad, illus. see Humphrey, Art & Humphrey, Pat.
Butler, Tad, illus. see McPherson, Stephanie Sammartino.
Butler, Tad, illus. see Waxman, Laura Hamilton.
Butler, Tammi. I Am a Ward of the Court. (p. 832)
Butler, Terrold B. Sharing. (p. 1561)
Butler, Tom. My Childhood Stories. (p. 1200)
Butler, William S. Scraper Jones: Treasure Hunter. (p. 1532)
Butler-Moore, Nylea L., jt. auth. see Staton, Rebecca McKown.
Butler-Moore, Nylea L., jt. contrib. by see Cox, Joe.
Butschler, Margaret, photos by see Harley, Avis.
Butt, Kyle. God Made Plants. (p. 690)
—God Made the World. (p. 690)
Butt, Sheila K. Does God Love Michael's Two Daddies. Perkins, Ken, illus. (p. 460)
Butterbaugh, Kelly Ann. Hey, History Isn't Boring Anymore! A Creative Approach to Teaching the Civil War. (p. 774)
Butterfield, Cathy, illus. see Miller, Mark.
Butterfield, M. & Edom, H. Science with Air. (p. 1528)
Butterfield, MaryAnn Milton. You Are Too a Bully! (p. 1973)
Butterfield, Moira. Bible Stories Creativity Book. (p. 176)
—Bulldozers & Other Construction Machines. Lyon, Chris & Biggin, Gary, illus. (p. 240)
—Dolphin Finds a Star. (p. 464)
—Farm Animals. (p. 573)
—Funny Face. (p. 649)
—Genetics. (p. 660)
—Giraffe. (p. 677)
—Golden Eagle. (p. 694)
—Halloween Creativity Book. (p. 737)
—Knight. (p. 964)
—Lady of the Manor. (p. 971)
—Muddypaws. Mendez, Simon, illus. (p. 1189)
—My New Preschool: An Interactive Playbook. Corke, Estelle, illus. (p. 1216)
—Olympics - History. (p. 1288)
—Panda. (p. 1320)
—Protecting Rain Forests. (p. 1412)
—Protecting Temperate Forests. (p. 1412)
—Rabbit. (p. 1429)
—Space. Biggin, Gary & Lipscombe, Nick, illus. (p. 1618)
—Spring. James, Helen, illus. (p. 1634)
—Underwater Creativity Book: Games, Cut-Outs, Art Paper, Stickers, & Stencils! (p. 1817)
—Wannabes Fashion Queen: For Girls Who Know What They Want to Be. (p. 1856)
—Who Eats Who at the Seashore? (p. 1915)
—Who Eats Who in Grasslands? (p. 1915)
—Wild Animals. (p. 1928)
—Wildlife Adventure Creativity Book. (p. 1931)
Butterfield, Moira, jt. auth. see Breed, Simon.
Butterfield, Moira, jt. auth. see Weber, Belinda.
Butterfield, Moira & Golding, Elizabeth. Moonlight Book: Halloween Hide-And-Seek. Gray, Dean, illus. (p. 1172)
Butterfield, Moira & Hachette Children's Books Staff. Olympics Events. (p. 1288)
—Olympics Records. (p. 1288)
—Olympics Scandals. (p. 1288)
Butterfield, Moira & Potter, William. Halloween Pocket Activity Fun & Games: Games, Puzzles, Fold-Out Scenes, Patterned Paper, Stickers! (p. 738)
Butterfield, Moira, et al. Record Breakers & Other Speed Machines. (p. 1452)
Butterfield, Ned, illus. see Brochu, Lisa.
Butterfield, Ned, illus. see Carlson, Melody.
Butterfield, Ned, illus. see Doyle, Arthur.
Butterfield, Ned, illus. see Hugo, Victor.
Butterfield, Ned, illus. see Twain, Mark, pseud.
Butterfield, Ned, illus. see Wyss, Johann David.
Butterfield, Ned, tr. see Doyle, Arthur.
Butterfield, Ned, tr. see Hugo, Victor.
Butterman, Stephen. Rootbeer Beard. (p. 1488)
Butters, Dorothy Gilman, pseud. Bells of Freedom. Wilde, Carol, illus. (p. 163)
Butterworth & Heath, illus. see Leslie, Emma.
Butterworth and Heath, illus. see Leslie, Emma.
Butterworth, Annette. Jake in Trouble. (p. 906)
Butterworth, Annette, jt. auth. see Butterworth, Nick.
Butterworth, Chris. How Did That Get in My Lunchbox? The Story of Food. Gaggiotti, Lucia, illus. (p. 806)
—See What a Seal Can Do. Nelms, Kate, illus. (p. 1547)
—Where Did My Clothes Come From? Gaggiotti, Lucia, illus. (p. 1906)

Butterworth, Christine. How Did That Get in My Lunchbox? The Story of Food. Gaggiotti, Lucia, illus. (p. 806)
—Sea Horse: The Shyest Fish in the Sea. Lawrence, John, illus. (p. 1534)
—See What a Seal Can Do. Nelms, Kate, illus. (p. 1547)
Butterworth, Ian, jt. auth. see Cooper, Helen.
Butterworth Moira. Fall. James, Helen, illus. (p. 566)
—Summer. James, Helen, illus. (p. 1673)
—Winter. James, Helen, illus. (p. 1937)
Butterworth, MyLinda. Monster Run. Day, Linda S., ed. (p. 1168)
Butterworth, MyLinda & Day, Linda S. Frogazoom! Day, Linda S., illus. (p. 640)
Butterworth, Nick. After the Storm. Butterworth, Nick, illus. (p. 28)
—Albert the Bear to the Rescue. (p. 34)
—House on the Rock. Inkpen, Mick, illus. (p. 803)
—Jingle Bells. (p. 918)
—One Snowy Night. Butterworth, Nick, illus. (p. 1297)
—Percy's Bumpy Ride. Butterworth, Nick, illus. (p. 1341)
—Q Pootle 5. Butterworth, Nick, illus. (p. 1422)
—Rescue Party. Butterworth, Nick, illus. (p. 1462)
—Secret Path. Butterworth, Nick, illus. (p. 1543)
—Thud! Butterworth, Nick, illus. (p. 1745)
—Tiger. (p. 1748)
—Tiger. Butterworth, Nick, illus. (p. 1748)
—Tiger in the Snow! (p. 1748)
—Treasure Hunt. Butterworth, Nick, illus. (p. 1781)
—Whisperer. (p. 1912)
—Whisperer. Butterworth, Nick, illus. (p. 1912)
Butterworth, Nick, jt. auth. see Inkpen, Mick.
Butterworth, Nick & Butterworth, Annette. Jake Again. (p. 905)
Butterworth, Nick & Inkpen, Mick. Animal Tales from the Bible: Four Favorite Stories about Jesus (p. 80)
—Favorite Parables from the Bible: Stories Jesus Told (p. 578)
—Wonderful Earth. (p. 1948)
Butterworth, Oliver. Enormous Egg. (p. 531)
Buttler, Elizabeth, illus. see Wong, Janet S.
Buttner, Thom, illus. see Gosselin, Kim.
Button, Joshua. Joshua & the Two Crabs. Button, Joshua, illus. (p. 927)
Button, Kevin. Giving Gnome. Guritz, Linda F., illus. (p. 681)
Button, Lana. Willow Finds a Way. Howells, Tania, illus. (p. 1934)
—Willow's Whispers Howells, Tania, illus. (p. 1934)
Button, Mark. Finding Ti Ming & Tem Po: Legend of the Golf Gods. (p. 588)
Button, Timothy D. Matthew Mcsilly. (p. 1109)
Buttram, Larry. Honor Thy Sister. (p. 795)
Butts, Ed. Bodyguards! From Gladiators to the Secret Service. Plumbe, Scott, illus. (p. 207)
—She Dared: True Stories of Heroines, Scoundrels, & Renegades. Collins, Heather, illus. (p. 1564)
—Shipwrecks, Monsters, & Mysteries of the Great Lakes. (p. 1567)
—Singing Sight Words (p. 1579)
—SOS - Stories of Survival: True Tales of Disaster, Tragedy, & Courage. (p. 1614)
—X Doesn't Mark the Spot: Tales of Pirate Gold, Buried Treasure, & Lost Riches. (p. 1967)
Butts, Edward. Brotherhoods, Death Squads, & the FBI: The Dramatic History of Policing. Williams, Gareth Glyn, illus. (p. 231)
Butz, Christopher. Follow That Letter: From the Post Office to Our Mailbox. (p. 612)
—I Go to Work as a Letter Carrier. (p. 838)
—Red Wolves. (p. 1455)
Butz, Steve. Bone Race: A Quest for Dinosaur Fossils. (p. 209)
—Year Round Project-Based Activities for STEM Grd 2-3. (p. 1969)
Butzer, Anna. Maria Mitchell (p. 1093)
Butzer, Anna & Colich, Abby. Great Women in History (p. 719)
Butzer, C. M. Gettysburg. Butzer, C. M., illus. (p. 670)
Butzer, C. M., illus. see Thompson, Ben.
Buus, Dan and Bonnie. Adventures in the Wild with Mike & Blackie. (p. 16)
Buxton, Jamie. Temple Boys. (p. 1718)
Buxton, Jane H. Undersea Animals: A Dramatic Dimensional Visit to Strange Underwater Realms. Pinkney, Jerry, illus. (p. 1815)
Buxton, Karen & Wallenfels, Linda. Triathlete's Guide to off-Season Training. (p. 1785)
Buxton, Sarah, jt. auth. see Widmer, Kirsten.
Buxton, Ted. Soccer Skills: For Young Players. (p. 1603)
Buxton, W. J. Winkiedough Twinkletoe: Upon the Window Ledge. (p. 1936)
Buyea, Rob. Because of Mr. Terupt. (p. 155)
—Mr. Terupt Falls Again. (p. 1186)
Buyea, Robert W. Saving Mr. Terupt. (p. 1517)
Buyer, Robert & Coute, Ursula T. Family Work & Fun Through the Years: Four Stories about Children & Families Having Fun Working Together. (p. 569)
Buyer, Robert L. & Coute, Ursula T. Following the North Star. (p. 612)
Buyske, Gail. How the Russian Snow Maiden Helped Santa Claus. Voronina, Natasha, illus. (p. 813)
Büyüksahin, Mehmet, et al. Khadija Bint Khuwaylid. (p. 951)
Buzan, Frederick. Rattle. (p. 1440)
Buzan, Tony. Mind Maps for Kids: The Shortcut to Success at School. (p. 1145)
Buzbee, Lewis. Bridge of Time. (p. 227)
—Steinbeck's Ghost. (p. 1646)
Buzel, Alita. Adventures of Jedediah the Muie: Book One. (p. 19)
Buzo, Laura. Love & Other Perishable Items. (p. 1059)
Buzzeo, Toni. Adventure Annie Goes to Kindergarten. Wummer, Amy, illus. (p. 14)
—But I Read It on the Internet! Yoshikawa, Sachiko, illus. (p. 246)
—Fire up with Reading! Yoshikawa, Sachiko, illus. (p. 591)
—Great Dewey Hunt. Yoshikawa, Sachiko, illus. (p. 715)

—Inside the Books: Readers & Libraries Around the World. Daly, Jude, illus. (p. 877)
—Just Like My Papa. Wohnoutka, Mike, illus. (p. 939)
—Library Doors. Westcott, Nadine Bernard, illus. (p. 1006)
—Little Loon & Papa. Spengler, Margaret, tr. (p. 1030)
—My Bibi Always Remembers. Wohnoutka, Mike, illus. (p. 1197)
—No T. Rex in the Library. Yoshikawa, Sachiko, illus. (p. 1260)
—One Cool Friend. Small, David, illus. (p. 1294)
—Our Librarian Won't Tell Us Anything! Yoshikawa, Sachiko, illus. (p. 1309)
—Passion for Elephants: The Real Life Adventure of Field Scientist Cynthia Moss. Berry, Holly, illus. (p. 1327)
—Penelope Popper, Book Doctor. Christy, Jana, illus. (p. 1336)
—R Is for Research. Wong, Nicole, illus. (p. 1429)
—Stay Close to Mama. Wohnoutka, Mike, illus. (p. 1645)
—Toni Buzzeo & You. (p. 1765)
—Whose Tools? Datz, Jim, illus. (p. 1922)
—Whose Truck? Datz, Jim, illus. (p. 1922)
Buzzy. One Sunny Day. Martin, John, ed. (p. 1297)
BVetMed MRCVS Staff, jt. auth. see Rayner, Matthew.
Bwesigye, Brian. Fables Out of Nyanj. (p. 559)
By Kaleena Ma. Glasses for Me? Oh No! Dawn Phillips, illus. (p. 682)
Byars, jt. auth. see Byars, Betsy.
Byars, Betsy. Animal, the Vegetable, & John D. Jones. (p. 80)
—Bingo Brown, Amante Gitano. (p. 188)
—Bingo Brown y el Lenguaje del Amor. (p. 188)
—Black Tower. (p. 197)
—Blossom Promise. (p. 202)
—Blossom Promise. Haley, Amanda, illus. (p. 202)
—Blossoms & the Green Phantom. (p. 202)
—Blossoms & the Green Phantom. Haley, Amanda, illus. (p. 202)
—Blossoms Meet the Vulture Lady. (p. 202)
—Boo's Surprise. Brooks, Erik, illus. (p. 213)
—Burbujas, el Pez de una Tonelada. (p. 243)
—Casa de las Alas. (p. 273)
—Cybil War. (p. 396)
—Dark Stairs. (p. 408)
—Dead Letter. (p. 417)
—Death's Door. (p. 420)
—Disappearing Acts. (p. 446)
—Golly Sisters Go West. Truesdell, Sue, illus. (p. 697)
—Keeper of the Doves. (p. 947)
—King of Murder. (p. 959)
—Moon & I. (p. 1171)
—Not-Just-Anybody Family. (p. 1267)
—Pinballs. (p. 1359)
—Preguntas de Bingo Brown. Gatagan, T., illus. (p. 1395)
—Summer of the Swans. (p. 1674)
—Tarot Says Beware. (p. 1706)
—Tarot Says Beware. (p. 1706)
—Tornado. Ben-Ami, Doron, illus. (p. 1770)
—Trouble River. (p. 1790)
—Wanted... Mud Blossom. (p. 1856)
—Wanted... Mud Blossom. Haley, Amanda, illus. (p. 1856)
Byars, Betsy & Byars. Pinballs. (p. 1359)
Byars, Betsy, et al. Cat Diaries: Secret Writings of the MEOW Society. Brooks, Erik, illus. (p. 277)
—Dog Diaries: Secret Writings of the WOOF Society. Brooks, Erik, illus. (p. 461)
Byars, Bob M., illus. see Woody, John.
Byass, Gershom G. Kaieteur & Poems of Nature, Love & Life. (p. 941)
Byassee, Meghan L. Fallen Heart. (p. 566)
Bybee, Linda & Lawless, Laura. Untwin. (p. 1823)
Byckowski, Mark. Animals Know Their Abc's a to Z So Can You! (p. 83)
Bye, Eric A., tr. see Schliewen, Ulrich.
Bye, K. A. I Like Birthdays! Interactive Book about Me. Ridgell, Earl W., Jr., illus. (p. 841)
Byer, Janice, illus. see Perry, Sondra.
Byer, Stacey, illus. see Picayo, Mario.
Byerly, Kenny Sternin & Eisinger, Justin. Teenage Mutant Ninja Turtles Animated: Never Say Xever/The Gauntlet (p. 1714)
Byerly, Robbie. At the Lake. (p. 111)
Byerly, Robbie, jt. auth. see Warren, Heather.
Byerly, Robbie, jt. auth. see Washington, Joi.
Byerly, Robbie & Kiley, Kieran. Look at the Signs. (p. 1049)
Byerly, Robbie & Warren, Heather. Brown Bear or Black Bear. (p. 231)
Byers, Ann. African-American History from Emancipation to Today: Rising above the Ashes of Slavery. (p. 27)
—American Star Wars Program. (p. 63)
—America's Star Wars Program. (p. 64)
—Anti-Semitism & the Final Solution: The Holocaust Overview. (p. 89)
—Auschwitz, Bergen-Belsen, Treblinka: The Holocaust Camps. (p. 116)
—Blackouts: A Practical Survival Guide. (p. 197)
—Career As a Construction Manager. (p. 266)
—Career As a Dental Hygienist. (p. 266)
—Communication Satellites. (p. 349)
—Communications Satellites. (p. 349)
—Courageous Teen Resisters: Primary Sources from the Holocaust. (p. 373)
—Crash of the Concorde: When Disaster Strikes! (p. 376)
—Crash of the Concorde. (p. 376)
—First Apartment Smarts. (p. 593)
—First Credit Cards & Credit Smarts. (p. 594)
—Frequently Asked Questions about Gangs & Urban Violence. (p. 636)
—Frequently Asked Questions about Puberty. (p. 636)
—Fruits & Vegetables: From the Garden to Your Table. (p. 645)
—Germany: A Primary Source Cultural Guide. (p. 666)
—Great Resume, Application, & Interview Skills. (p. 718)
—History of U.S. Immigration: Coming to America. (p. 785)
—Immigration: Interpreting the Constitution. (p. 861)
—Internship & Volunteer Opportunities for People Who Love Animals. (p. 880)
—Jobs As Green Builders & Planners. (p. 919)
—Kristallnacht & Living in Nazi Germany. (p. 967)
—Lebanon's Hezbollah. (p. 986)

—Menstruation. (p. 1126)
—Ohio State Football. (p. 1282)
—Oskar Schindler: Saving Jews from the Holocaust. (p. 1305)
—Remembering the Holocaust: Anti-Semitism & the "Final Solution." (p. 1460)
—Rescuing the Danish Jews: A Heroic Story from the Holocaust. (p. 1462)
—Saving Children from the Holocaust: The Kindertransport. (p. 1517)
—Sexual Assault & Abuse. (p. 1556)
—Trail of Tears: A Primary Source History of the Forced Relocation of the Cherokee Nation. (p. 1776)
—Trapped-Youth in the Nazi Ghettos: Primary Sources from the Holocaust. (p. 1779)
—West Virginia: Past & Present. (p. 1876)
—Working with Veterans & Military Families Through Service Learning (p. 1953)
—Wyoming: Past & Present. (p. 1966)
—Youth Destroyed-The Nazi Camps: Primary Sources from the Holocaust. (p. 1982)
Byers, Ann, jt. auth. see Klar, Jeremy.
Byers, Betty Bradford. Whitlow Sanction (p. 1914)
Byers, Bradley, illus. see Long, Samantha Gail.
Byers, Brian. Noah's Babies Opposites & Offerings. (p. 1261)
Byers, Brian, illus. see Mead, David.
Byers, Chester. Cowboy Roping & Rope Tricks. (p. 374)
Byers, Edward. Connie & Her Bubble Gum Adventure. (p. 358)
Byers, Helen. Peru. (p. 1344)
Byers, Helen & National Geographic Learning Staff. Japan. (p. 908)
Byers, James. One Nutty Family. Collier, Kevin, illus. (p. 1296)
Byers, Leon, illus. see Busteed, Kerri J.
Byers, Letha. Tesa, the Adopted Cow-bird. (p. 1722)
Byers, Lynne. Critters Following Jesus: Book Two: Donkey. (p. 384)
Byers, Marcella. Mitsy & Marty Mouse Visit Grandpa. Grant, Cheryl, illus. (p. 1156)
Byers, Michael, illus. see Colich, Abby.
Byers, Michael, illus. see Collins, Terry.
Byers, Michael, illus. see Gunderson, Jessica & Collins, Terry.
Byers, Michael, illus. see Hicks, Kelli L.
Byers, Michael, illus. see Kolpin, Molly, et al.
Byers, Michael, illus. see Kolpin, Molly.
Byers, Michael, illus. see Krohn, Katherine.
Byers, Shaunette. Story: The Legend of Fearless Fred. Lollino, Jessica, ed. (p. 1656)
Byeway Books, creator. Colors. (p. 344)
—Rhymes. (p. 1468)
Byeway Wall Charts Staff. Counting to 20. Autumn Publishing Staff, illus. (p. 371)
Bygrave, Linda. Bear. (p. 150)
—Butterfly. (p. 247)
—Crocodile. (p. 384)
—Duck. (p. 488)
—Frog. (p. 639)
—Hippo. (p. 781)
—Rabbit. (p. 1429)
—Tiger. (p. 1748)
Byj, Charlot. Six Little Steppers Paper Dolls. Taliadoros, Jenny, ed. (p. 1582)
Bykowski, Christy. Gluten-Free Me Beckman Goes to School. Thompson, Chad, illus. (p. 685)
Byler, Linda. Big Decisions: A Novel Based on True Experiences from an Amish Writer! (p. 181)
—Little Amish Matchmaker: A Christmas Romance. (p. 1023)
—Running Around (And Such) (p. 1497)
—When Strawberries Bloom: A Novel Based on the True Experiences from an Amish Writer! (p. 1904)
Byles, Monica. Polos. (p. 1381)
Bylsma, Dan & Bylsma, Jay M. Slam Dunks Not Allowed! (p. 1587)
Bylsma, Jay M., jt. auth. see Bylsma, Dan.
Byman, Jeremy. Andrew Grove: And the Intel Corporation. (p. 72)
—Carl Sagan: In Contact with the Cosmos. (p. 269)
—J. P. Morgan: Banker to a Growing Nation. (p. 901)
—Madam Secretary: The Story of Madeleine Albright. (p. 1069)
—Tim Duncan. (p. 1750)
Byng, Georgia. Molly Moon & the Monster Music. (p. 1160)
—Molly Moon & the Morphing Mystery. (p. 1160)
—Molly Moon Detiene el Mundo. (p. 1160)
—Molly Moon, Micky Minus, & the Mind Machine. (p. 1160)
—Molly Moon Stops the World. (p. 1160)
—Molly Moon Viaja a Traes del Tiempo. Crispin, Maria Dolores, tr. (p. 1161)
—Molly Moon y el Increible Libro. (p. 1161)
—Molly Moon's Hypnotic Time Travel Adventure. (p. 1161)
—Molly Moon's Hypnotic Book of Hypnotism. (p. 1161)
Bynum, Betty. I'm a Pretty Little Black Girl! (p. 858)
Bynum, Georgette. Tickle Me Ticklish. (p. 1747)
Bynum, Janie. Twelve Days of Christmas in Texas. Bynum, Janie, illus. (p. 1800)
Bynum, Janie, illus. see Dussling, Jennifer.
Bynum, Janie, illus. see Ginkel, Anne.
Bynum, Jeff. Blinky. (p. 199)
Bynum, Juanita. Heart for Jesus. (p. 759)
Bynum, Juanita, ed. Parable about the King. (p. 1323)
Bynum, Saran, illus. see Neal, Allyson.
Bynum, Steven. Davina's Magical Radio: A KDDF Radio Mystery - Book One. (p. 411)
Bynum-Nwulu, Jane, illus. see Hawkhurst, Joan C.
Byous, Shawn. Because I Stubbed My Toe (p. 155)
Byous, Shawn, illus. see Handloser, Rick.
Byrd, B. N. My Favorite Toy. (p. 1203)
Byrd, Betty. They Call Me Pharaoh. (p. 1732)
Byrd, Bill Scott. Story of Rap & Tap. Ayzenberg, Nina, illus. (p. 1700)
Byrd, Carl Grigsby. Where Did Pop Pop Go? (p. 1906)
Byrd, Debbie. Ayla by the Sea. (p. 121)
Byrd, Jeff. Tale of Two Tails, el Perro con Dos Colas: A children's story in English & Spanish. (p. 1701)
Byrd, Josiah. Makayla's Birthday Money! Work with Money. (p. 1078)

Byrd, Lee Merrill. Lover Boy / Juanito el Carinoso: A Bilingual Counting Book. Delgado, Francisco, illus. (p. 1061)
—Treasure on Gold Street/El Tesoro de la Calle D'Oro: A Neighborhood Story in Spanish & English. Castro L., Antonio, illus. (p. 1795)
—Ttesoro en la Calle Oro: A Neighborhood Story in English & Spanish. Franco, Sharon, tr. (p. 1795)
Byrd, Michael. Adventures of Banter & Jafar: Spoiled Rotten Bai, Jenny, illus. (p. 16)
Byrd, Robert. Brave Chicken Little. Byrd, Robert, illus. (p. 223)
—Electric Ben: The Amazing Life & Times of Benjamin Franklin. (p. 508)
—Leonardo, Hermoso Sonador. Merido, Miguel A., tr. (p. 992)
—Leonardo, the Beautiful Dreamer. Byrd, Robert, illus. (p. 992)
Byrd, Robert, illus. see Edinger, Monica.
Byrd, Robert, illus. see Kroll, Steven.
Byrd, Robert, illus. see Krull, Kathleen.
Byrd, Robert, illus. see Schlitz, Laura Amy.
Byrd, S., illus. see Soto, G., et al.
Byrd, Samuel, illus. see Adler, David A.
Byrd, Sandra. Asking for Trouble. (p. 106)
—Island Girl. (p. 892)
—One Year Be-Tween You & God: Devotions for Girls. (p. 1297)
Byrd, Tracy. Fruits & Vegetables & How They Grow: A to Z. (p. 645)
Byrd, Vince H., et al. Donny Doo-Doos. (p. 466)
Byrd, William. Westover Manuscripts: History of the Dividing Line Between Virginia & North Carolina, a Journey to the Land of Eden, a Progress to the Mines. (p. 1876)
—Writings of Col. William Byrd. (p. 1965)
Byrd-Bredbenner, Carol. Adventures in Food & Nutrition. (p. 15)
—Adventures in Food & Nutrition! Teacher's Annotated Edition. (p. 15)
Byrd-Hill, Ida. Me & My Big Career Hill, Karen, ed. (p. 1115)
Byrne, Andrew. Trilogy of Terror. Mockford, Patricia, ed. (p. 1786)
Byrne, Barbara. Magic Bell On. (p. 1071)
—Megan's Moon. (p. 1124)
Byrne, Beth, illus. see Harrison, Anne-Marie.
Byrne, Bob. Robots Don't Cry. (p. 1481)
Byrne, Bob, illus. see Snell, Gordon & Askin, Corrina.
Byrne, Eileen. Electricity for the Future. (p. 509)
Byrne, Emma, illus. see O'Neill, Karl.
Byrne, Eugene. Darwin: A Graphic Biography. Gurr, Simon, illus. (p. 409)
Byrne, Gayle. Sometimes It's Grandmas & Grandpas: Not Mommies & Daddies. Haverfield, Mary, illus. (p. 1610)
—Sometimes Just One Is Just Right. Haverfield, Mary, illus. (p. 1610)
Byrne, Graham, illus. see Saxby, Claire.
Byrne, Jean Livingstone. Legends of Newgrange. (p. 990)
Byrne, John. Avengers West Coast: Vision Quest. (p. 119)
—Jurassic Park: the Devils in the Desert TP: The Devils in the Desert. TP. (p. 937)
—Spider-Man: Marvel Team-Up. (p. 1626)
Byrne, John, illus. see Claremont, Chris & Wolfman, Marv.
Byrne, John, illus. see Claremont, Chris, et al.
Byrne, John, illus. see Friedrich, Mike.
Byrne, John, illus. see Mantlo, Bill.
Byrne, John, illus. see Stern, Roger & Layton, Bob.
Byrne, John, illus. see Stern, Roger, et al.
Byrne, John, jt. auth. see Mignola, Mike.
Byrne, John, jt. illus. see Buscema, John.
Byrne, John, jt. auth. see Cockrun, Dave.
Byrne, John A. Visionaries Jeff, Youngquist, ed. (p. 1845)
Byrne, John A., jt. auth. see Welch, Jack.
Byrne, John & Cockrum, Dave. Essential X-Men (p. 537)
Byrne, John & Wolfman, Marv. Man of Steel (p. 1085)
Byrne, John, et al. Amazing Spider-Man. (p. 55)
—Man of Steel (p. 1085)
Byrne, John Patrick. Donald & Benoit. Byrne, John Patrick, illus. (p. 465)
Byrne, John, text. Fantastic Four Annual (p. 571)
Byrne, Judy. New Queen. (p. 1247)
Byrne, Lex. Ever Met the Hooferjackal? (p. 541)
Byrne, Marlene. Follow the Leader. Graber, Jesse, illus. (p. 612)
—Kick the Can. Graber, Jesse, illus. (p. 951)
Byrne, Marlene F. Ghost in the Graveyard. Graber, Jesse, illus. (p. 670)
—Treasure Hunt. Graber, Jesse, illus. (p. 1781)
Byrne, Marlene F. & Graber, Jesse. Just a Baseball Game. (p. 937)
Byrne, Mary. Only Children Hear Me: Jake Is a Friend You Can Talk To. (p. 1298)
Byrne, Mary Gregg, illus. see Schmidt, Heidi.
Byrne, Mike. Britain, 1895-1918. (p. 229)
—Twinkle, Twinkle, Little Star ; and, Spaceship, Spaceship, Zooming. (p. 1802)
—Twinkle, Twinkle, Little Star ; and, Spaceship, Spaceship, Zooming High. (p. 1802)
Byrne, Mike, illus. see Bullard, Lisa.
Byrne, Mike, illus. see Coult, Lucy Alice.
Byrne, Mike, illus. see David, Juliet.
Byrne, Mike, illus. see Gale, Emily.
Byrne, Mike, illus. see Graham, Oakley.
Byrne, Mike, illus. see Hapka, Cathy, pseud.
Byrne, Mike, illus. see Hooks, Gwendolyn.
Byrne, Mike, illus. see Jablow, Renee.
Byrne, Mike, illus. see Kushner, Elisabeth.
Byrne, Mike, illus. see Lakritz, Deborah.
Byrne, Mike, illus. see Mckenzie, Precilous.
Byrne, Mike, et al. Great Britain & Irish Question, 1798-1922. (p. 714)
Byrne, Paul J. Cuban Missile Crisis: To the Brink of War. (p. 388)
Byrne, Paul J. & Compass Point Books Staff. Chinese Revolution: The Triumph of Communism (p. 307)
Byrne, Richard. Penguins Can't Fly: Two Friends Become TRUE Friends! (p. 1337)
—Really, Really, Really Big Dinosaur. (p. 1450)
—This Book Just Ate My Dog! Byrne, Richard, illus. (p. 1735)

For book reviews, descriptive annotations, tables of contents, cover images, author biographies & additional information, updated daily, subscribe to www.booksinprint2.com

2113

—We're in the Wrong Book! Byrne, Richard, illus. (p. 1875)
Byrne, Richard, illus. see Weston, Carrie.
Byrnes, Gary. Witch Grannies - the Case of the Lonely Banshee. (p. 1941)
Byrnes, James P. & Wasik, Barbara A. Language & Literacy Development: What Educators Need to Know. (p. 974)
Byrne-Walker, Mary Ann, illus. see Laplante, Carole.
Byron, Kevin, photos by see Russo, Monica.
Byrum, Isabel C. How John Became a Man Life Story of a Motherless Boy. (p. 810)
BYTE ME! ebook inc nonprofit, Georgia C., illus. see Pedroza, Georgina, tr.
Byte Me! P. CLOUDWOMAN in Black & White: And in some shades of Gray. Pedroza, Georgina & Garcia, Eloisa, trs. (p. 335)
Bytheway, John. Are Your Standards Fences or Guardrails? (p. 97)
—How to Be an Extraordinary Missionary. (p. 815)
—Sacrament. Pinnock, Nathan, illus. (p. 1500)
Byun, You. Dream Friends. Byun, You, illus. (p. 483)
Byun, You, illus. see Ashman, Linda.
Bywaters, Mayer. Tempest. (p. 1717)
Bzymek, Izabela, illus. see McKernan, Wendy.
Bzymek, Izabela, illus. see Stranaghan, Crystal.
Bzymek, Izabela, jt. auth. see Madill, Emily Elizabeth.
Bzymek, Izabela, jt. auth. see Stranaghan, Crystal J.

C

C., Brandi & Flanagan, Logan. City Mom Country Dad. (p. 323)
C. Collodi. Adventures of Pinocchio. (p. 21)
C D Stampley Enterprises, creator. Billy & Baxter Learn to Build (p. 187)
—Billy & Baxter on City Streets (p. 187)
C, Danny. English Alphabet in Colors. (p. 529)
C. Larene Hall. Martha's Freedom Train. (p. 1097)
C, Linda. Kiss. (p. 961)
C. Q. Press Staff. Historic Documents of 2004. (p. 782)
—Landmark Events in U. S. History (p. 974)
C. Ridley, Joi & Gray, Kevan. Howard University College Prowler off the Record. (p. 823)
CA HS Speech Association & Curriculum Committee. Speaking Across the Curriculum: Practical Ideas for Incorporating Listening & Speaking into the Classroom. (p. 1623)
Cabal, Graciela Beatriz. Azul. (p. 122)
—Toby. (p. 1760)
Cabala, Edith, jt. auth. see Klenovsky, Daniel.
Caballero, D., tr. see Cuno, Sabine.
Caballero, D., tr. see Droop, Constanza.
Caballero, D., tr. Bomberos. Metzger, Wolfgang, illus. (p. 208)
—Esa Eres Tu y Este Soy Yo. Rubel, Doris, illus. (p. 534)
—Granja. Ebert, Anne, illus. (p. 710)
—Que? Como? Por Que?: Autos y Camiones. Weller, Ursula, illus. (p. 1423)
Caballero, Eduardo. Arte de Vivir Sin Sonar. (p. 103)
—Historia en Cuentos 3: Todo Por un Florero/el Cometa Llanero/el Zapatero Soldado. Torres, Nora Estela & Jaime, Daniel, illus. (p. 782)
Caballero, Erica. Mount Mole. (p. 1180)
Caballero, Manuel Morillo, see Morillo Caballero, Manuel, notes.
Caballero, Sergio, ed. see Claret, Albert.
Caban, Carlos, illus. see Stuart, Kelly.
Caban, Carlos, tr. see Stuart, Kelly.
Caban, Connie. Don't Be Afraid of the Storm. Page, illus. (p. 466)
Caban, Jose Alberto. Travesia del Desierto. (p. 1781)
—Venir del Mar. Mateo, Rosario & Sada, Margarita, illus. (p. 1835)
Cabanillas, Laura Sabin. Abc's of Character. Sebastian, illus. (p. 4)
Cabanting, Ruth, illus. see Gillespie, Jane.
Cabat, Erni. Erni Cabat's Magical ABC: Animals Around the Farm. (p. 534)
Cabatingan, Erin. A Is for Musk Ox. Myers, Matthew, illus. (p. 1)
—Musk Ox Counts. Myers, Matthew, illus. (p. 1194)
—World According to Musk Ox. Myers, Matthew, illus. (p. 1953)
Cabban, Vanessa, illus. see Andreae, Giles.
Cabban, Vanessa, illus. see Catchpool, Michael.
Cabban, Vanessa, illus. see Durant, Alan.
Cabban, Vanessa, illus. see Emmett, Jonathan.
Cabban, Vanessa, illus. see Freedman, Claire.
Cabban, Vanessa, illus. see Schaefer, Carole Lexa.
Cabban, Vanessa, illus. see White, Kathryn.
Cabban, Vanessa, jt. auth. see Freedman, Claire.
Cabe, Neil. How to Take Tests: Secrets Your Teacher Never Wanted You to Know. (p. 822)
Cabell, James. Jurgen. (p. 937)
Cabell, James Branch. Jewel Merchants. (p. 917)
Cabell, Robert W. Mermaid Adventures of Princess Miranda: Volume One. Cabell, Robert W., illus. (p. 1128)
Cabello de Carbonera, Mercedes. Blanca Sol. Voysest, Oswaldo, ed. (p. 198)
Cabello-Argandona, Roberto. Cinco de Mayo: An Illustrated History. (p. 319)
Cabiya, Pedro, creator. Anima Sola: Hambre. (p. 76)
Cabla, Rhonda. Charlie's World. (p. 293)
Cable, Annette, illus. see Cerny, Michele.
Cable, Annette, illus. see Morgan, Cythia.
Cable, Annette, illus. see Stokes, Betty Southard.
Cable, Annette, illus. see Wolpe, Nina.
Cable, George W. Dr. Sevier. (p. 475)
Cable, Ken. Track of the Hunter. (p. 1775)
Cable, Ted T., et al. Compact Guide to Kansas Birds. (p. 351)
Cabot, David, illus. see Richards, Douglas E.
Cabot, Meg. Abandon. (p. 2)
—Abandon Book 3: Awaken. (p. 2)
—Airhead. (p. 31)
—All-American Girl. (p. 43)
—Avalon High. (p. 118)
—Awaken. (p. 120)
—Being Nikki. (p. 161)
—Best Friends & Drama Queens. (p. 169)
—Blast from the Past. (p. 198)
—Forever Princess (p. 619)
—From the Notebooks of a Middle School Princess. (p. 644)
—Glitter Girls & the Great Fake Out. (p. 684)
—Haunted. (p. 753)
—Homecoming. Coronado, Jinky, illus. (p. 793)
—How to Be Popular: When You're a Social Reject Like Me, Steph L. (p. 815)
—Hunter's Moon. Coronado, Jinky, illus. (p. 828)
—In Waiting. (p. 868)
—Jinx. (p. 919)
—Journal d'une Princesse. (p. 927)
—Love You to Death. (p. 1061)
—Mediator: Shadowland & Ninth Key. Vols. 1&2 (p. 1118)
—Merlin Prophecy. (p. 1128)
—Merlin Prophecy. Coronado, Jinky, illus. (p. 1128)
—Missing You. (p. 1153)
—Moving Day. (p. 1183)
—New Girl. (p. 1244)
—Nicola y el Noble Impostor. Tapia, Sonia, tr. (p. 1251)
—Pants on Fire. (p. 1321)
—Party Princess. (p. 1326)
—Princess Diaries. (p. 1403)
—Princess Diaries Box Set: The Princess Diaries; Princess in the Spotlight; Princess in Love. (p. 1403)
—Princess Diaries - Forever Princess. (p. 1403)
—Princess in Love (p. 1404)
—Princess in Love. (p. 1404)
—Princess in Pink. (p. 1404)
—Princess in the Spotlight (p. 1404)
—Princess in the Spotlight Vol. 2. (p. 1404)
—Princess in the Spotlight. (p. 1404)
—Princess in Training (p. 1404)
—Princess in Training. (p. 1404)
—Princess in Waiting. (p. 1404)
—Princess Lessons. McLaren, Chesley, illus. (p. 1404)
—Princess Mia. (p. 1404)
—Princess on the Brink. (p. 1405)
—Princess Present. (p. 1405)
—Project Princess. (p. 1410)
—Ready or Not. (p. 1447)
—Runaway. (p. 1496)
—Safe House - Sanctuary. (p. 1502)
—Stage Fright. (p. 1638)
—Teen Idol. (p. 1713)
—Twilight. (p. 1801)
—Underworld. (p. 1817)
—Valentine Princess. (p. 1830)
—Victoria & the Rogue. (p. 1840)
—When Lightning Strikes; Code Name Cassandra. (p. 1903)
Cabot, Meg, jt. auth. see Carroll, Jenny, pseud.
Cabot, Meg, see Carroll, Jenny, pseud.
Cabot, Meg, et al. Prom Nights from Hell. (p. 1411)
Cabot, Paloma & Larousse Editors, eds. Larousse Children's Spanish Dictionary. (p. 975)
Cabra, Raul, ed. see Young, Lucie.
Cabral, Jeane. All Aboard the Yellow School Bus: Follow the Bus Through the Pages on a Counting Adventure! Top That Publishing Staff, ed. (p. 42)
—Bad Dog Ben. (p. 131)
—Count My Blessing 1 to 10. Kolanovic, Dubravka, illus. (p. 369)
—Good Night Little Moo. Howarth, Daniel, illus. (p. 699)
—Just One Flower. (p. 939)
—Kitty in the Grass. (p. 963)
—Tree Hugs. (p. 1783)
Cabral, Len. Cinturita de Anansi Flor Ada, Alma, tr. (p. 321)
Cabral, Noel. Rachel's Four-Legged Friend. (p. 1432)
Cabrales Arteaga, José Manuel, ed. see Unamuno, Miguel de & Unamuno, Miguel de.
Cabre, Jordi & Escandell, Victor (ALEHOP). Julio Verne. (p. 932)
Cabré, María Angeles, tr. see Rouse, Jeff.
Cabrera, Cozbi A., illus. see Grimes, Nikki.
Cabrera, Dax. Arise: The Stories of the Seven. (p. 98)
Cabrera, Eva, illus. see Defoe, Daniel.
Cabrera, Eva, illus. see Gonzalez, Jorge & Shakespeare, William.
Cabrera, Giovanni, illus. see Portorrico, Silvia.
Cabrera, Jane. 12 Days of Christmas. (p. 1994)
—Baa, Baa, Black Sheep. (p. 123)
—Cat's Colors. (p. 281)
—Fetch. Cabrera, Jane, illus. (p. 582)
—Here We Go Round the Mulberry Bush. Cabrera, Jane, illus. (p. 771)
—If You're Happy & You Know It! Cabrera, Jane, illus. (p. 855)
—Kitty's Cuddles. (p. 963)
—Mommy, Carry Me Please! Cabrera, Jane, illus. (p. 1162)
—Old MacDonald Had a Farm. (p. 1284)
—Old Mother Hubbard. (p. 1284)
—One, Two, Buckle My Shoe. (p. 1297)
—Row, Row, Row Your Boat. (p. 1492)
—Row, Row, Row Your Boat. Cabrera, Jane, illus. (p. 1492)
—Ten in the Bed. Cabrera, Jane, illus. (p. 1718)
—Twinkle, Twinkle, Little Star. (p. 1802)
Cabrera, Marcela, illus. see Manson, Sheri.
Cabrera, Mirna Y. & Esquenazi, Martha E., eds. La Rueda, Rueda: Traditional Latin American Folk Songs for Children. Jones, Juan Luis, illus. (p. 969)
Cabreros, Beryl. Melting Pot of Children's Poetry (p. 1125)
Cabri, Alexandra, illus. see Abdullah, Patricia Noor.
Cabrillo, Cinthya, illus. see Suddard, Lisa.
Cabrini, Joe. Chicco's Nicedream Van - Daniel's Winning Goal. Cabrini, Joe, illus. (p. 299)
Cabrol, Marta. Thumbelina. (p. 1745)
Cacau, Caio, illus. see Bethea, Nikole Brooks, et al.
Cacau, Caio, illus. see Bethea, Nikole Brooks.
Cacau, Caio, illus. see Dreier, David L. & Hoena, Blake.
Cacau, Caio, illus. see Hoena, Blake.
Caccamo, Pepe. A Cazar Palabras. Fernandez, Maria Xose, illus. (p. 1)
Caccia, Christiane, illus. see Wullschleger Daldini, Elena.
Cacciatore, Mark G., jt. auth. see Fare, Dennis.
Cacciatore, Stacy. Candy Around the World. (p. 261)
Caceres, Marangelie, illus. see Casanueva, Idilian.
Caceres, Raulo & Brooks, Max. Max Brooks' the Extinction Parade Volume 1. (p. 1111)
Cach, Lisa. Wake unto Me. (p. 1853)
Cache, Dee. ABC's of Boating Terms (p. 4)
Cachola, Jean Iwata, et al. O Kamehameha III: Kauikeaouli. (p. 1274)
Cadalbert, Julie. God's Beautiful Heaven. (p. 691)
—Have No Fear, Little Flock: A Lamb's Story of the First Christmas. (p. 754)
Cadavid, Jorge. Lewis Carroll -Los Juegos del Lenguaje. (p. 1004)
Caddy, David. Reef. (p. 1456)
—Whammy! (p. 1878)
Cadeau, Michelle. My Unique Family: With JayJay & Totte. Lileng, Kimberly, ed. (p. 1220)
Cadell, Ava. NeuroLoveology: The Power to Mindful Love & Sex. (p. 1242)
Cadet, Guichard, ed. see Owens, Michael T.
Cadet, John. Kangaroo's Adventure. (p. 942)
Cadic, Oliver, et al. Queen Margot - The Bloody Wedding. (p. 1425)
Cadic, Olivier & Gheysens, Francois. Queen Margot - The Age of Innocence. Derenne, Juliette & Barroux, Sophie, illus. (p. 1425)
Cadieux Davignon, Danielle. Promesse. (p. 1411)
Cadman, Mistie. Sophie's Summer Sombrero Adventure. (p. 1613)
Cadman, S. Parkes, jt. auth. see Appleton, E. R.
Cadney, Mary, ed. see Cisneros, Kevin.
Cado, Herman. Early Explorers & Fur Traders in Colorado. (p. 493)
Cadose, Linda A. Hidden Chamber in the Great Sphinx. (p. 775)
Caduto, Michael J. Catch the Wind, Harness the Sun: 22 Super-Charged Projects for Kids. (p. 279)
—Child of God: Stories of Jesus & Stewardship Activities for Children. Tyrol, Adelaide, illus. (p. 301)
—In the Beginning: The Story of Genesis & Earth Activities for Children. (p. 865)
—Riparia's River Pastuchiv, Olga, illus. (p. 1473)
Cadwallader, Doris Jensen. Little Pine's Christmas Story. (p. 1033)
Cadwell, Warwick Johnson, illus. see Atinuke.
Cady, Harrison, illus. see Burgess, Thornton W.
Cady, Harrison, illus. see Burnett, Frances Hodgson.
Cady, Harrison, jt. auth. see Burgess, Thornton W.
Cady, Harrison, tr. see Burgess, Thornton W.
Cady, Jennifer. Jose Limon. (p. 926)
—José Limón. (p. 926)
Caes, Charles J. Discovering the Speed of Light. (p. 450)
—How Do We Know the Speed of Light? (p. 808)
Caes, Charles J., jt. auth. see North, Charles.
Caesor, Ebraska, ed. see Moore, Mary.
Caetano, Joao, illus. see Saramago, José.
Caetano, Joao, jt. auth. see Nuez, Marisa.
Caez, Joshua. To Find an Ivory-billed Woodpecker. (p. 1758)
Cafaro, Phyllis. Captain Mcfinn & Friends Meet Coral Rose. (p. 264)
—Legend of Captain McFinn & Friends. (p. 988)
Cafege, Adam. Of Petals & Hope: Sunny Sunflower Triumphs over Bullying. Calindas, Marconi, illus. (p. 1279)
Caffee, Julie, illus. see Marlow, Herb.
Caffee, Tammie Jenks. Summer of Snail. (p. 1674)
Cafferata, Patty. Goldfield Hotel: Gem of the Desert. (p. 695)
Cafferata, Sue, illus. see Fowler, Allan.
Caffery, Don R. Our Holy Father, the Pope: The Papacy from Saint Peter to the Present. Beaudesson, Emmanuel, illus. (p. 1309)
Caffery, Erasmus. Fonging for the Soul. (p. 612)
Caffey, Don. Yikes-Lice! Girouard, Patrick, illus. (p. 1971)
Caffrey, Jaye Andras. First Star I See. Adamson, Lynne, illus. (p. 597)
Caffrey, Scott. Story of the Boston Celtics. (p. 1660)
—Story of the Buffalo Bills. (p. 1660)
—Story of the Chicago Bulls. (p. 1660)
—Story of the Dallas Cowboys. (p. 1660)
—Story of the Detroit Pistons. (p. 1660)
—Story of the Kansas City Chiefs. (p. 1661)
—Story of the Miami Dolphins. (p. 1661)
—Story of the Oakland Raiders. (p. 1661)
Cafiero, Crystal. Gone Fishing, Just Daddy & Me. (p. 697)
Cafiero, Tara, illus. see Laiz, Jana.
Cafmeyer, Judy. Ready, Set, Show What You Know(r) on the Ohio Acheivement Test for Gr. 3: Student Edition. (p. 1447)
—Ready, Set, Show What You Know(r) on the Ohio Achievement Tests for Gr. 3: Parent/Teacher Edition. (p. 1447)
Cafu, illus. see Parker, Jeff.
Cage, Elizabeth. Covert Affairs: License to Thrill; Live & Let Spy; Nobody Does It Better. (p. 373)
—Covert Affairs 2: Spy Girls Are Forever; Dial V for Vengeance; If Looks Could Kill. (p. 373)
—Dial V for Vengeance. (p. 433)
—If Looks Could Kill. (p. 853)
—License to Thrill. (p. 1007)
—Live & Let Spy. (p. 1039)
—Nobody Does It Better. (p. 1262)
—Spy Girls Are Forever. (p. 1636)
Cage, Josef, illus. see Sherman, M. Zachary & Iligan, Marlon.
Caglar, Atife. Sayabiliyorum. (p. 1519)
Caglaroglu, Nurefsan. My Sweet Grandparents. (p. 1219)
—Night of Wonders (p. 1254)
Cagle, Eddie, illus. see Eterno-Harris, Jacqueline.
Cagle, Erica. My Little Book of Stories. (p. 1212)
Cagle, Terry R., illus. see Gordon, Emily.
Cagle, Terry R., illus. see Sonnenberg, Matthew Martin.
Cagliano, Stefano. Cuerpo Humano. (p. 390)
Cagno, Stefano. Lou, Buc & All the Others. (p. 1057)
Cagol, Andrea, illus. see Capozzi, Suzy.
Cagol, Andrea, illus. see Disney Princess Staff & Disney Book Group Staff.
Cagol, Andrea, illus. see Jordan, Apple.
Cagol, Andrea, illus. see Saxon, Victoria.
Cahill, Bear. We're Brothers & Sisters. Collier, Kevin Scott, illus. (p. 1875)
Cahill, Bernadette. Arkansas Women & the Right to Vote: The Little Rock Campaigns: 1868-1920. (p. 99)
Cahill, Bryon. Freedom from Fear. (p. 634)
—Freedom from Want. (p. 634)
—Freedom of Speech & Expression. (p. 634)
—Freedom to Worship. (p. 635)
Cahill, Byron. Legend of Skywoman. (p. 988)
—Space Pox. (p. 1619)
Cahill, Katina. I Love You This Much. (p. 844)
Cahill, Stacie. My Parents Love Me Too! (p. 1216)
Cahn, Yehudah. Ancient Tale of Rags & Riches. Hinckley, Greg, illus. (p. 70)
Cahoon, Heather, illus. see Bentley, Dawn.
Cahoon, Heather, illus. see Tang, Greg.
Cahoon, Rebecca. Magic Garden. (p. 1072)
Caicco, Joseph. Adventures of the Rainbow Guardians: When the Color Came Down. (p. 23)
Caicedo, Andres. Angelitos Empantanados. (p. 74)
Caicedo, Maria Victoria. En la Casa con la Abuelita. (p. 522)
Cail, Carol. Dibby Witch's Bing Bang Birthday. (p. 435)
—It's a Zoo Around Here. (p. 896)
Caillou, Marie, illus. see Hubert.
Caimite. Voodoo Fantasy: A Romantic Adventure. (p. 1850)
Cain. Tommy Tan & the Bowl of Time. (p. 1765)
Cain, Barbara S. Autism, the Invisible Cord: A Sibling's Diary. (p. 117)
Cain, Betty. Devotions about Kids Stuff. (p. 432)
Cain, Betty Ward. My Trip to the Funny Farm. (p. 1220)
—You Can Count on Me. (p. 1974)
Cain, Bill. Battle of the Bulge. (p. 146)
Cain, Bill, jt. auth. see Hama, Larry.
Cain, Bill & Hama, Larry. Tank of Tomorrow. (p. 1705)
Cain, Candice. Tortoise & the Hare. (p. 1771)
Cain, David, jt. auth. see Martin, Laura C.
Cain, Dece. Seven Angels High. (p. 1554)
Cain, Doreyl Ammons, illus. see Garza, Amy Ammons.
Cain, Doreyl Ammons, illus. see Nolen, Gale.
Cain, Doreyl Ammons, illus. see Pafford, Nancy McIntosh.
Cain, Janan. Roonie B. Moonie: Lost & Alone. (p. 1488)
—Way I Feel. Cain, Janan, illus. (p. 1864)
Cain, Janan, illus. see Metzger, Steve.
Cain, Janan, jt. auth. see Parenting Press Staff.
Cain, Karen L. Squirrel's Curl. (p. 1637)
Cain, Kate & Oakhill, Jane, eds. Children's Comprehension Problems in Oral & Written Language: A Cognitive Perspective. (p. 303)
Cain, Marie Mowery. After the Dinosaurs. (p. 28)
—Air Power. (p. 31)
—All Eyes on You. (p. 44)
—America the Beautiful. (p. 59)
—American Symbols. (p. 63)
—Animals Say. (p. 83)
—Baby Animals. (p. 124)
—Best Friends. (p. 169)
—Beyond the Backyard. (p. 174)
—Big Bad Cats. (p. 178)
—Celebrate Cinco de Mayo. (p. 283)
—Celebrate Kwanzaa. (p. 284)
—Cool Places. (p. 364)
—Dress for the Weather. (p. 484)
—Feathers or Fur. (p. 579)
—Flying Colors. (p. 609)
—For Your Health. (p. 616)
—From Eggs to Geese. (p. 642)
—George Takes a Road Trip, China. (p. 663)
—George Takes a Road Trip, Mexico. (p. 663)
—Insects up Close. (p. 876)
—It's a Matter of Weather. (p. 895)
—Let's Move. (p. 999)
—Look at That Face. (p. 1048)
—Message for You. (p. 1129)
—Monumental America. (p. 1170)
—More & Less. (p. 1174)
—One by One. (p. 1294)
—Slow Slugs & Snails. (p. 1591)
—Something to Snack On. (p. 1610)
—Splash of Colors. (p. 1629)
—Storm Watch. (p. 1656)
—Then & Now. (p. 1729)
—Tiny Acorns, Majestic Oaks. (p. 1756)
—Tools Rule. (p. 1767)
—Tremendous Trees. (p. 1784)
—Trip to the Moon. (p. 1787)
—Under the Waves. (p. 1814)
—Very, Very Big. (p. 1839)
—Water Colors. (p. 1862)
—Weird Bugs. (p. 1872)
—What's Out There. (p. 1899)
—Who Was Amelia Earhart? (p. 1918)
—Who Was Jim Thorpe? (p. 1918)
—Wide Open Space. (p. 1927)
Cain, Mary, illus. see Lobdell, Chanel Mickayla.
Cain, Mary Wimmer. Liver (p. 1040)
Cain, Michael. Mathability: Math in the Real World. (p. 1107)
Cain, Patrick G. BMX Street. (p. 204)
—BMX Vert. (p. 204)
—Komodo Dragon. (p. 966)
—Komodo Dragon Paperback. (p. 966)
—Moto X Best Trick. (p. 1179)
—Moto X Freestyle. (p. 1179)
—Skateboarding Street. (p. 1583)
—Skateboarding Vert. (p. 1583)
Cain, Sheridan. Crunching Munching Caterpillar. Tickle, Jack, illus. (p. 386)
—Crunching Munching Caterpillar Pop-up. Tickle, Jack, illus. (p. 386)
—Donde Dormiras Pequena Liebre? Percy, Sally, illus. (p. 466)

—Pequena Tortuga y la Cancion del Mar. Burgin, Norma, illus. (p. 1341)
—Teeny Weeny Tadpole. Tickle, Jack, illus. (p. 1715)
Cain, Vernice. Little Green Tree. (p. 1028)
Caine, Paul. Jake's Journey. (p. 906)
Caine, Rachel, pseud. Bite Club (p. 194)
—Bitter Blood: The Morganville Vampires. (p. 194)
—Black Dawn. (p. 195)
—Carpe Corpus. (p. 271)
—Daylighters. (p. 415)
—Fade Out. (p. 562)
—Fall of Night. (p. 566)
—Feast of Fools. (p. 579)
—Ghost Town (p. 672)
—Ghost Town. (p. 672)
—Kiss of Death (p. 961)
—Kiss of Death. (p. 961)
—Last Breath (p. 977)
—Lord of Misrule. (p. 1052)
—Midnight Alley. (p. 1138)
—Morganville Vampires. (p. 1175)
—Windfall (p. 1935)
Caine, Rachel, pseud, et al. Immortal: Love Stories with Bite. Cast, P. C., ed. (p. 861)
Caines-Floyd, Eydi. Story of Wanton Desire. (p. 1663)
Caird, Frankie Telfer. Secret of Ellis Meadow. (p. 1542)
Cairn, Barbara. Gatsby's Grand Adventure: Book 2 Renoir's the Apple Seller. Ruble, Eugene, illus. (p. 658)
Cairns, Barbara. Gatsby's Grand Adventures: Book 1 Winslow Homer's Snap the Whip. Ruble, Eugene, illus. (p. 658)
Cairns, Conrad. African Knights: The Armies of Sokotu, Bornu & Bagirmi in the Nineteenth Century. (p. 27)
Cairns, Julia, illus. see Bennett, Jill.
Cairns, Julia, illus. see Chamberlain, Mary, et al.
Cairns, Julia, illus. see Chamberlin, Mary, et al.
Cairns, Julia, illus. see Chamberlin, Richard & Chamberlin, Mary.
Cairns, Julia, illus. see Chamberlin, Richard, et al.
Cairns, Julia, illus. see Krebs, Laurie & Barefoot Books.
Cairns, Julia, illus. see Krebs, Laurie.
Cairns, Julia, jt. auth. see Krebs, Laurie.
Cairns, Julia, jt. auth. see Singer, Marilyn.
Cairo, Anna. Spider in My Shower. (p. 1626)
Cairo, Carlos Villanes. Fuga. (p. 646)
Cairo, Carlos Villanes & Villanes Cairo, Carlos. Ballenas Cautivas. (p. 134)
Caisse, Sebastian. Grimoire: The Journey Begins. (p. 724)
Caitlin, Knutsson, jt. auth. see Brent, Mary.
Cakal, Kimberly. Today I Hugged a Porcupine. (p. 1760)
Cakes, Patty. God: When Will You Answer My Prayers. (p. 688)
Cala, C. J. Mother Dandy's Nonmalmani. (p. 1177)
Calabazza, Della & Monckeberg, Paulina. Ludovico & Ooops 2006. (p. 1064)
Calabrese, Diane Marie. My Dad's off to War. Swope, Brenda, illus. (p. 1201)
Calabrese, Dianne. Inspirational Guide (p. 878)
Calabrese, Linda Lee. It Is What It Is: In a Kid's Mind. (p. 894)
Calabrese, Paul. Bad Bug Book: (and other Annoying Pests) (p. 131)
—Good Bug Book ... (and Other Cool Creatures) (p. 697)
Calabresi, Linda. Human Body. (p. 825)
Calaf, Monica. How You Were Born. Fuentes, Mikel, illus. (p. 823)
—You, Me & the Breast. Fuentes, Mikel, illus. (p. 1976)
Calafiore, Jim, illus. see Carlson, J. P.
Calafiore, Jim, illus. see Winick, Judd.
Calahasen, Stella. Dream Catcher. (p. 483)
Calais-Germain, Blandine & Lamotte, Andree. Anatomy of Movement: Exercises. (p. 67)
Calamandrei, Camilla. Fever. (p. 583)
Calame, Don. Beat the Band. (p. 152)
—Call the Shots. (p. 254)
—Swim the Fly. (p. 1691)
Calander, Sydney, illus. see Danker, Mervyn.
Calarco, Donald Charles. In a Dandelion's World: A Small Book with a Big Story! (p. 863)
Calarnou, Yves, illus. see Le Duc, Michel, et al.
Calasso, Roberto & Parks, Tim. Ka, the Story of Garuda: Based on the English Translation by Tim Parks of the Italian Original by Roberto Calasso. Basu, Suddhasattwa, illus. (p. 941)
Calaway, Bernie L. & Ledford, Jan Roadarmel. Operation Revelation: A Teen's Script to Earth's Final Curtain. (p. 1300)
Calbom, Cherie. Juice Lady's Guide to Juicing for Health: Unleashing the Healing Power of Whole Fruits & Vegetables. (p. 932)
Calcines, Eduardo. Rooftop Clubhouse: A Character Building Book of Virtues. (p. 1487)
Calcines, Eduardo F. Leaving Glorytown: One Boy's Struggle under Castro. (p. 986)
Calcium Staff, contrib. by. Epics of Greek Mythology (p. 532)
—Gods & Goddesses of Greek Mythology (p. 690)
—Heroes & Mortals of Greek Mythology (p. 772)
—Monsters & Creatures of Greek Mythology (p. 1169)
Calcutt, David. Robin Hood. Baker-Smith, Grahame, illus. (p. 1479)
Caldarone, Marybeth Sidoti, jt. auth. see Liu, Carol.
Caldas, Iara. Fisherman Collection: The Fishery. (p. 599)
Caldecott, Randolph. Come Lasses & Lads. (p. 347)
—Farmer's Boy. (p. 574)
—Frog He Would A-Wooing Go. (p. 640)
—Hey Diddle Diddle & Baby Bunting. (p. 774)
—House That Jack Built. (p. 803)
—Queen of Hearts, & Sing a Song for Sixpence. (p. 1425)
—Ride a Cock-Horse to Banbury Cross, & a Farmer Went Trotting upon His Grey Mare. (p. 1471)
—Three Jovial Huntsmen. (p. 1742)
Caldecott, Randolph, illus. see Ewing, Juliana Horatia.
Caldecott, Randolph, illus. see Marcus, Leonard S.
Calder, C. J. Busy Truck Rooney, Ronnie & Peterson, Shauna, illus. (p. 246)
—Fast Truck. Rooney, Ronnie & Peterson, Shauna, illus. (p. 576)
—Muddy Truck Rooney, Ronnie & Peterson, Shauna, illus. (p. 1189)
—Snow Truck Rooney, Ronnie & Peterson, Shauna, illus. (p. 1599)
Calder, Catherine. Teddy Tale. (p. 1712)
Calder, Joan. Airplanes in the Garden: Monarch Butterflies Take Flight. (p. 32)
Calder, Kate. L'Équitation. (p. 993)
Calder, Kate & Rouse, Bonna. Patinage Artistique. (p. 1328)
Calderas, Gloria, illus. see Hall, Kirsten.
Calderisi, Robert. Trouble with Africa: Why Foreign Aid Isn't Working. (p. 1790)
Calderon, Catalina, tr. see Kipling, Rudyard.
Calderón de la Barca, Pedro. Magico Prodigioso. (p. 1075)
—Vida Es Sueno. Rodriguez Cuadros, Evangelina, ed. (p. 1841)
—Vida Es Sueno; el Alcalde de Zalamea. (p. 1841)
Calderón de la Barca, Pedro, jt. auth. see Calderón de la Barca, Pedro.
Calderón de la Barca, Pedro & Calderón de la Barca, Pedro. Alcalde de Zalamea. (p. 35)
—Vida Es Sueno. (p. 1841)
Calderon, Eduardo Caballero. Bolivar: Una Historia que Parece un Cuento. (p. 208)
—Cristo de Espaldas. (p. 383)
—Historia en Cuentos 4: El Almirante Nino/el Caballito de Bolivar/el Sargento de Doce Anos. Torres, Nora Estela & Jaime, Daniel, illus. (p. 782)
—Siervo Sin Tierra. (p. 1573)
Calderón, Emilio. Mapa del Creador. (p. 1090)
Calderon, George. Tahiti. (p. 1695)
Calderon, Gloria, illus. see Argueta, Jorge.
Calderon, Gloria, illus. see Iribarren, Elena, ed.
Calderon, Lee, illus. see Ward, Jennifer.
Calderon, Marcela, illus. see Monkman, Olga.
Calderon, Marcela, illus. see White, Amy.
Calderon, W. Frank. Animal Painting & Anatomy. (p. 79)
Calderwood, Wendy. Kirby Kids: Into the Lungs. (p. 961)
Caldey, Vincent, jt. auth. see D'Lacey, Chris.
Caldicott, Chris. World Food Alphabet. (p. 1955)
Caldwell, Ben. Royale Treatment (p. 1492)
Caldwell, Ben, illus. see Baum, L. Frank & Grahame, Kenneth.
Caldwell, Beth Evans. Ruth Tells the Truth. (p. 1498)
Caldwell, Bruce. Sidecar Scooter. Hawyard, Charlie O., illus. (p. 1573)
Caldwell, Charlotte. Kirby's Journal: Backyard Butterfly Magic. (p. 961)
Caldwell, Christiana Marie Melvin, jt. auth. see Reynolds, Loralyn.
Caldwell, D. W. Roadside Geology of Maine. Ort, Kathleen, ed. (p. 1477)
Caldwell, Daisy L. Sarah the Oh So Silly, but Shy Stegosaurus (p. 1514)
Caldwell, Denise. Our Ellen Friends. (p. 1307)
Caldwell, J. Lynn. Tooth Fairy's Guide to Lost Teeth: A Fortune for Every Day a Tooth Is Lost. Jepson, Beth, illus. (p. 1768)
Caldwell, JoAnne Schudt. Comprehension Assessment: A Classroom Guide. (p. 354)
Caldwell, Mardie M. Adoptingonline. com: Safe & Proven Methods That Have Brought Thousands of Families Together. (p. 13)
Caldwell, S. a. Secrets of the Dragon World: Curiosities, Legends & Lore. (p. 1545)
Caldwell, Sandi. Wailing Waylon. (p. 1852)
Caldwell, Talent, illus. see Morrison, Robbie.
Caldwell, Theo. Finn the Half-Great. (p. 589)
Caldwell, Tiffany & MacKenzie, W. R. Adventures of ForkMan: A Children's Book of Etiquette. (p. 18)
Caldwell, V. M. Runt: Story of a Boy. (p. 1497)
Caleca, James Renny. Hope, the Wonder Chicken. (p. 797)
Calenda, Kristen. Nubian: A True Story about a Very Special Kitty. (p. 1269)
Calero, Dennis. You're Not the Captain of Me! (p. 1982)
Calero, Dennis, illus. see Bowen, Carl & Poe, Edgar Allen.
Calero, Dennis, illus. see Harper, Benjamin & Poe, Edgar Allen.
Calero, Dennis, illus. see Manning, Matthew K. & Poe, Edgar Allen.
Calero, Dennis, illus. see Poe, Edgar Allen & Harper, Benjamin.
Calero, Dennis, illus. see Poe, Edgar Allen.
Calero, Dennis, illus. see Shelley, Mary & Shelley, Mary.
Calero, Dennis, illus. see Tulien, Sean & Poe, Edgar Allen.
Calero, Dennis, illus. see Wells, H. G.
Caleshu, Anthony. Siege of the Body & a Brief Respite. (p. 1573)
Caletti, Deb. Fortunes of Indigo Skye. (p. 623)
—Honey, Baby, Sweetheart. (p. 794)
—Last Forever. (p. 977)
—Love Is All You Need: Wild Roses - The Nature of Jade. (p. 1060)
—Nature of Jade. (p. 1236)
—Queen of Everything. Greenberg, Anne, ed. (p. 1425)
—Secret Life of Prince Charming. (p. 1541)
—Six Rules of Maybe. (p. 1582)
—Stay. (p. 1645)
—Story of Us. (p. 1662)
—Wild Roses. (p. 1930)
Caley, Isabel W., illus. see Gilman, Dorothy Foster.
Calfee, Pat. Issy Books Set 1 Gee, Isybilla, illus. (p. 893)
—Issy Books Set 2 Gee, Isybilla, illus. (p. 893)
—Issy Books Set 3 Gee, Isybilla, illus. (p. 893)
Calford, Farley. Complete Disaster, Rhonda's Birthday Party. (p. 352)
Calhoun, Bonnie S. Thunder: A Novel. (p. 1746)
Calhoun, Crissy. Love You to Death: The Unofficial Companion to the Vampire Diaries. (p. 1061)
Calhoun, David B. Grace Abounding: The Life, Books & Influence of John Bunyan. (p. 704)
Calhoun, Dia. After the River the Sun. Slater, Kate, illus. (p. 28)
—Avielle of Rhia (p. 120)
—Eva of the Farm. Slater, Kate, illus. (p. 540)
—Firegold. (p. 592)
Calhoun, Dorothy Sweet. Six Bees for Children: A Collection of Educational Wisdoms for Children. (p. 1582)
Calhoun, Florence. Choosing a Career in Teaching. (p. 310)
—No Easy Answers: A Teen Guide to Why Divorce Happens. (p. 1258)
Calhoun, Jackie. Wrong Turns. (p. 1965)
Calhoun, Marmaduke Randolph. Story of an Aviator. Twist, Clint, ed. (p. 1657)
Calhoun, Megan. Oscar the Pig: Mommy Goes to Work. (p. 1305)
Calhoun, Sharon Cooper & English, Billie Joan. Oklahoma Adventure. (p. 1283)
Calhoun, Terry. Muggwapps. (p. 1189)
Calhoun, Yael. Earth Science Fair Projects: Using Rocks, Minerals, Magnets, Mud, & More. (p. 496)
—Earth Science Fair Projects, Revised & Expanded Using the Scientific Method. LaBaff, Stephanie & LaBaff, Tom, illus. (p. 496)
—Plant & Animal Science Fair Projects: Using Beetles, Weeds, Seeds, & More. (p. 1368)
—Plant & Animal Science Fair Projects. (p. 1368)
—Water in the News. (p. 1863)
Call, Charlene C. Nature of Study Skills: Hardworking Helen K Honeybee Study Skills 3. Norcross, Harry, illus. (p. 1236)
Cali, Davide. Bear with the Sword. Foli, Gianluca, illus. (p. 151)
—Enemy. Bloch, Serge, illus. (p. 527)
Cali, Davide. I Didn't Do My Homework Because... Chaud, Benjamin, illus. (p. 837)
Cali, Davide. I Love Chocolate. Daviddi, Evelyn, illus. (p. 842)
—I Love Kissing You. Bloch, Serge, illus. (p. 842)
—Mama Robot. Danesi, Marcel, tr. from ITA. (p. 1084)
—Piano, Piano. Rivers, Randi, tr. from FRE. (p. 1354)
—Santa's Suit. Heliot, Éric, illus. (p. 1513)
Cali, Davide, jt. auth. see Chaud, Benjamin.
Cali, Davide & Chaud, Benjamin. Funny Thing Happened on the Way to School... (p. 650)
Cali, Davide & Planina, Vincent. 10 Little Insects. (p. 1993)
Calico World Entertainment Staff, illus. see Knights, Harry B.
Califf, David J. Battle of Actium. (p. 146)
California Publishing-XLNC!. Spirit: That Stranger Inside Us. (p. 1628)
Caligiuri, Susan. Haylie's Haunted Hamper. Baker, David, illus. (p. 755)
Calin, Marisa. Between You & Me. (p. 173)
Calindas, Marconi, illus. see Cafege, Adam.
Calino & Abbeville Press Staff. 123 Caterpillar. Calino, illus. (p. 2000)
—ABC Snake. Calino, illus. (p. 3)
Calishain, Tara, et al. Google Pocket Guide. (p. 702)
Calitri, Susan, illus. see Hawksley, Gerald.
Calitri, Susan, illus. see Masurel, Claire & Bond, Barbara Higgins.
Calitri, Susan, illus. see Masurel, Claire.
Calitri, Susan Chapman, illus. see Cifuentes, Carolina, ed.
Calitri, Susan Chapman, illus. see Cifuentes, Carolina.
Calixto, Melissa. This Father's Love. (p. 1735)
Calkhoven, Laurie. Boys of Wartime: Daniel at the Siege of Boston 1776. (p. 220)
—Daniel at the Siege of Boston 1776. (p. 404)
—Flash, Boom, Blast! Amazing Inventions from the War Front. (p. 602)
—Fork in the Trail. Studios, Arcana, illus. (p. 620)
—George Washington: An American Life. (p. 664)
—I Grew up to Be President. Zomchek, Rebecca, illus. (p. 838)
—Michael at the Invasion of France 1943 (p. 1134)
—Will at the Battle of Gettysburg. (p. 1932)
—Winning Goal. Studios, Arcana, illus. (p. 1937)
Calkhoven, Laurie & Herndon, Ryan. Fearless Feats: Incredible Records of Human Achievement. (p. 579)
Calkhoven, Laurie & Laskey, Shannon. Miles of Smiles: Travel Games & Quizzes to Go. Hunt, Sara, ed. (p. 1142)
Calkin, Abigail B., jt. auth. see Calkin, Author.
Calkin, Author & Calkin, Abigail B. Carolyne Letters: A Story of Birth, Abortion & Adoption. (p. 271)
Calkins, Chris. Auto Tour of Civil War Petersburg: 1861-1865 (p. 117)
Calkins, David. Daddy in Ladyland - A Night at the Ballet. (p. 398)
Calkins, Lucy, et al. Writing Reviews. (p. 1965)
Call, Angela, illus. see Tayler, Sandra.
Call, Brian, illus. see Rowley, Deborah Pace.
Call, Brian D., tr. Sarah's Cloud. (p. 1514)
Call, Greg, illus. see Barry, Dave & Pearson, Ridley.
Call, Greg, illus. see Columbus, Chris & Vizzini, Ned.
Call, Greg, illus. see Elish, Dan.
Call, Greg, illus. see Farley, Terri.
Call, Greg, illus. see Hatfield, Ruth.
Call, Greg, illus. see Holt, Christopher.
Call, Greg, illus. see Levine, Gail Carson.
Call, Greg, illus. see Malone, Marianne.
Call, Greg, illus. see Pearson, Ridley & Barry, Dave.
Call, Greg, illus. see Snyder, Laurel.
Call, Greg, jt. auth. see McCaffrey, Anne.
Call, Ken, illus. see Edwards, Roberta.
Callaghan, Cindy. Just Add Magic. (p. 937)
—Lost in London. (p. 1055)
—Lost in Paris. (p. 1055)
—Lucky Me. (p. 1063)
Callaghan, Melissa. TIME for Kids: Practicing for Today's Tests Language Arts Level 2 (p. 1751)
Callaghan, Paul & Manhire, Bill, eds. Are Angels OK? The Parallel Universes of New Zealand Writers & Scientists. (p. 96)
Callahan, Ann Marie. Sun Tea Fish. Sponheimer, Katheryne, illus. (p. 1676)
Callahan, Charlie. Samantha Loses Her Sweet Tooth. Callahan, Charlie, illus. (p. 1507)
Callahan, Kerry P. Mordechai Anielewicz: Hero of the Warsaw Ghetto Uprising. (p. 1173)
Callahan, Kerry P., jt. auth. see Wolfe, James.
Callahan, Lauren & Callahan, Michael T. Hello, Knightro! Williams, Tim, illus. (p. 764)
Callahan, Mary Ann. Little Heroes: The Story of Charlie & Minette. (p. 1029)
Callahan, Michael P. Daddy Daddy, It's Time for Bed! (p. 398)
Callahan, Michael T., jt. auth. see Callahan, Lauren.
Callahan, Patricia. Flying Colors. RH Disney Staff, illus. (p. 609)
Callahan, Sean. Bear Hug. (p. 150)
—Bear Hug. Bryant, Laura J., illus. (p. 150)
—Leprechaun Who Lost His Rainbow Cote, Nancy, illus. (p. 993)
—Shannon & the World's Tallest Leprechaun. Kemly, Kathleen, illus. (p. 1559)
—Wild Day with Dad. Howarth, Daniel, illus. (p. 1929)
Callahan, Susan. Always Right. (p. 51)
—Fighter. (p. 585)
—New Way. (p. 1247)
Callahan, Thera S. All Wrapped Up. (p. 46)
—All Wrapped Up. Gordon, Mike, illus. (p. 46)
—Regalo Bien Envuelto: All Wrapped Up. Gordon, Mike, illus. (p. 1457)
Callahan, Tim. Dark Days in Morgan County: Kentucky Summers Series. (p. 407)
Callan, Jamie Cat. Writer's Toolbox: Creative Games & Exercises for Inspiring the Write Side of Your Brain. (p. 1964)
Callan, Jim. America in the 1900s And 1910s. (p. 59)
—America in The 1930s. (p. 59)
—America in The 1960s. (p. 59)
Callan, Mary Ann. Spunky Chunks. (p. 1635)
Callanan, Michael I. & Wusinich, Bill. Electrical Systems Based on the 2005 NEC: Text. (p. 509)
—Electrical Systems Based on the 2005 NEC: Answer Key. (p. 509)
—Electrical Systems Based on the 2005 NEC: Resource Guide. (p. 509)
Callaway, Julie. My Haiti, My Homeland. (p. 1210)
Calle, Juan, illus. see Colich, Abby.
Calle, Juan, illus. see McCurry, Kristen.
Calle, Juan & Valentino, Serena. Good Dream, Bad Dream: The World's Legendary Heroes Save the Night! (p. 697)
Calleja, Seve. Planeta del Tesoro. (p. 1368)
Calleja, Seve, et al. Mariposa Transparents. (p. 1094)
Callella, Kim. Build-a-Skill Instant Books Short & Long Vowels. Shiotsu, Vicky & Faulkner, Stacey, eds. (p. 238)
Callella, Kim & Williams, Rozanne Lanczak. Build-a-Skill Instant Books Synonyms & Antonyms. Faulkner, Stacey, ed. (p. 238)
Callella, Trisha. Daily Writing Warm-Ups: Grades 3-4. (p. 400)
—Daily Writing Warm-Ups: Grades 5-6. (p. 400)
—Developing Reading Fluency Grade 1: Using Modeled Reading, Phrasing, & Repeated Oral Reading. Fisch, Teri L., ed. (p. 431)
—Developing Reading Fluency, Grade 2: Using Modeled Reading, Phrasing, & Repeated Oral Reading. Fisch, Teri L., ed. (p. 431)
—Developing Reading Fluency, Grade 3: Using Modeled Reading, Phrasing, & Repeated Oral Reading Fisch, Teri L., ed. (p. 431)
—Developing Reading Fluency, Grade 4: Using Modeled Reading, Phrasing, & Repeated Oral Reading. Fisch, Teri L., ed. (p. 432)
—Greek & Latin Roots: Teaching Vocabulary to Improve Reading Comprehension. Rous, Sheri, ed. (p. 720)
—I Have, Who Has? Language Arts Grades 1-2. Taylor, Jennifer, ed. (p. 839)
—I Have, Who Has? Language Arts, Grades 3-4: 38 Interactive Card Games Hamaguchi, Carla, ed. (p. 839)
—I Have, Who Has? Language Arts, Grades 5-6: 38 Interactive Card Games. Hamaguchi, Carla, ed. (p. 839)
—I Have, Who Has? Math, Grades 3-4: 38 Interactive Card Games. Hamaguchi, Carla, ed. (p. 839)
—More Greek & Latin Roots: Teaching Vocabulary to Improve Reading Comprehension. Faulkner, Stacey, ed. (p. 1174)
—Prefixes & Suffixes: Teaching Vocabulary to Improve Reading Comprehension. Williams, Carolea & Rous, Sheri, eds. (p. 1395)
—Reading Fluency: Using Modeled Reading, Phrasing, & Repeated Oral Reading. Hults, Alaska, ed. (p. 1445)
Callen, Liz, illus. see Crawley, Dave.
Callen, Liz, illus. see Scraper, Katherine.
Callen, Sharon. Anna Goes to Zambia. (p. 85)
—Boris & Bea. (p. 214)
—Boris Keeps Fit. (p. 214)
—Boris the Bassett. (p. 214)
—Curious Café. (p. 392)
—Duck Pond Fun. (p. 488)
—Glass Slippers. (p. 682)
—Grandpa & Me. (p. 709)
—Happy Faces Leave Home. (p. 745)
—How to Be a Kitten. (p. 814)
—Life at the Top (p. 1008)
—Lovely One. (p. 1061)
—Maddy's Mad Hair Day (p. 1070)
—Max. (p. 1110)
—Ms. Wilde & Oscar. (p. 1188)
—My Life as a Bee. (p. 1211)
—Safari Camp. (p. 1502)
—Seb's Train. (p. 1539)
—Soo Yun's Book. (p. 1613)
—Splash Down! (p. 1629)
—What Can You See? (p. 1881)
Callender, Simone. Rosa's Paw-Paw Tree: An inspiring tale about a daughter's deep love for her Mother. Downer, Romeo, illus. (p. 1489)
Callery, Sean. Dark History of America's Old West. (p. 407)
—Dark History of Ancient Greece. (p. 407)
—Dark History of Ancient Rome. (p. 407)
—Dark History of the Aztec Empire. (p. 407)
—Defying Gravity: Surviving Extreme Sports (p. 424)
—Frozen World: Polar Meltdown (p. 645)
—I Wonder Why There's a Hole in the Sky. (p. 849)
—Life Cycles: Desert. (p. 1010)
—Life Cycles: Forest. (p. 1010)

C

—Life Cycles: Grassland. (p. 1010)
—Life Cycles: Polar Lands. (p. 1010)
—Life Cycles - River. (p. 1010)
—Lights Out! Living in 24-Hour Darkness (p. 1016)
—Mountain. (p. 1180)
—Ocean. (p. 1276)
—Rocks & Minerals. (p. 1483)
—Titanic. (p. 1757)
—Treasure Hunt. (p. 1781)
—Victor Wouk: The Father of the Hybrid Car. (p. 1840)
—World War II. (p. 1959)
Callery, Sean, jt. auth. see Arlon, Penelope.
Callery, Sean, jt. auth. see Otero, Hanna.
Calles, Rosa M., illus. see De Aragon, Ray J.
Callfas, Diana, jt. auth. see Warburton, Lianne.
Callicutt, Kenny, illus. see Joyce, William.
Callier, Marie-Isabelle. No, No, No! Masson, Annick, illus. (p. 1259)
Callies, Debi. Frog Mill. (p. 640)
Callies, Pat, jt. auth. see Morgante, Roxanne.
Call-Morin, Katherine. Heart of a Horse. (p. 759)
Callo, Valeria, illus. see Peyron, Gabriela.
Callough, Melanee & Parks, Amy, creators. Do & Does Fun Deck: Fd56. (p. 456)
Calloway, Cassidy. Confessions of a First Daughter. (p. 356)
—Secrets of a First Daughter. (p. 1545)
Calloway, Jill Trotta. There's an Elephant in My Room: A child's unforgettable journey through cancer proved hope was stronger than Fear. (p. 1731)
Calloway, Nathaniel. Missing Tape Recorder: An Original Child's Tale. (p. 1153)
Callsen, Terri. Outdoor Adventures of Charlie & Kaylee: Hunting Fear (book 1) Lignor, Amy, ed. (p. 1312)
Calma, Jocelyn. Little Malia's Big Poi Idea. Robinson, Don, illus. (p. 1031)
Calman, Ross. Treaty of Waitangi. (p. 1783)
Calmenson, Stephanie. 10 Items or Less. Christy, Jana, illus. (p. 1993)
—Birthday at the Panda Palace. Cushman, Doug, illus. (p. 192)
—Frog Principal. Brunkus, Denise, illus. (p. 640)
—Jazzmatazz! Degen, Bruce, illus. (p. 911)
—Late for School! Yoshikawa, Sachiko, illus. (p. 979)
—May I Pet Your Dog? The How-to Guide for Kids Meeting Dogs (and Dogs Meeting Kids) Ormerod, Jan, illus. (p. 1112)
—Ollie's Class Trip: A Yes-And-No Book. Carter, Abby, illus. (p. 1287)
—Ollie's School Day: A Yes-And-No Book. Carter, Abby, illus. (p. 1287)
—Oopsy, Teacher! Yoshikawa, Sachiko, illus. (p. 1299)
—There Are No Moose on This Island Thermes, Jennifer, illus. (p. 1729)
Calmenson, Stephanie, jt. auth. see Cole, Joanna.
Calmenson, Stephanie, jt. auth. see RH Disney Staff.
Calmenson, Stephanie, jt. ed. see Cole, Joanna.
Calmenson, Stephanie & Cole, Joanna. Hot Diggity Dogs. Ross, Heather, illus. (p. 801)
—No Dogs Allowed. Ross, Heather, illus. (p. 1258)
—Teacher's Pets. Ross, Heather, illus. (p. 1709)
Calmes, Nikki. Adorable Bears & the New Arrival. (p. 13)
Calo, Marcos, illus. see Brezenoff, Steve.
Calo, Marcos, illus. see Lay, Kathryn.
Calo, Marcos, illus. see McFadden, Deanna.
Calo, Marcos, illus. see Namm, Diane.
Calo, Marcos, illus. see Olmstead, Kathleen & Andersen, Hans Christian.
Calo, Marcos, illus. see Paris, Harper.
Calo, Marcos, illus. see Wells, Marcia.
Calo, Marcos, jt. auth. see Brezenoff, Steve.
Calonita, Jen. Belles. (p. 163)
—Family Affairs. (p. 568)
—Flunked. (p. 608)
—Grass Is Always Greener. (p. 711)
—On Location. (p. 1289)
—Reality Check. (p. 1449)
—Secrets of My Hollywood Life. (p. 1545)
—Sleepaway Girls. (p. 1588)
—Summer State of Mind. (p. 1675)
—There's No Place Like Home. (p. 1731)
—Winter White. (p. 1938)
Calopisis, Dennis. Hungry Little Crocodile. (p. 828)
—Lonely Little Donkey. (p. 1046)
Calovich, Annie & Peters, Laura. Best Garden Plants for Kansas. (p. 169)
Calu, John & Hart, Dave. Treasure of Tucker's Island. (p. 1782)
Calucag, Angela. Little Freddy S Journey. (p. 1028)
Calumus, Bic-. Tale of Peter Rabbit, the Original Latin Version, C 777 B C Faithfully Translated by Bic-Calamus. (p. 1700)
Calvani, Mayra. Bad Mad Sad Day for Mama Bear. Snider, K. C., illus. (p. 132)
—Chocalin! Pylypchuck, Anna, illus. (p. 309)
—Humberto, the Bookworm Hamster. Grady, Kit, illus. (p. 826)
—Water Cycle: Water Play Series Book 1. Morris, Alexander, illus. (p. 1862)
Calvani, Mayra & Pylypchuk, Anna. Crash! (p. 376)
Calver, Paul. Drawing. (p. 481)
—Painting. (p. 1318)
Calver, Paul, illus. see Giles, Angela & Picthall, Chez.
Calver, Paul & Award, Anna. My Favourite Rescuers Sticker Book. (p. 1203)
Calver, Paul & Gunzi, Christiane. Aircraft: Play & Learn with Stickers. (p. 31)
—Farm: Play & Learn with Stickers. (p. 573)
—Farm Babies: Play & Learn with Stickers. (p. 573)
—Pets: Play & Learn with Stickers. (p. 1348)
—Trucks. Warren Photographic Staff, photos by. (p. 1791)
—Zoo: Play & Learn with Stickers. (p. 1988)
Calver, Paul, ed. Flags & Facts. (p. 602)
Calvert, Deanna. Las Sombras. Lester, Mike, illus. (p. 977)
—Shadows. Lester, Mike, illus. (p. 1558)
—Sombras: Shadows. Lester, Mike, illus. (p. 1608)
Calvert, Ellen Haseneck. Nine Goldfish in David's Pond. Fleming, Diana Trucks, illus. (p. 1256)
Calvert, J. Oliver. Honey Childrens Series Honey Meets the Prince Book One. (p. 794)
Calvert, John. Arabian Peninsula in the Age of Oil. (p. 94)
—Divisions in Islam. (p. 455)
Calvert, Lissa, illus. see Basham, Tom.
Calvert, Lissa, illus. see Horne, Constance.
Calvert, Lissa, illus. see Pavlick, Leon E. & PAVLICK, A. N. N. M.
Calvert, Lissa, jt. auth. see Basham, Tom.
Calvert, Pam. Multiplying Menace: The Revenge of Rumpelstiltskin. Geehan, Wayne, illus. (p. 1190)
—Multiplying Menace Divides! Geehan, Wayne, illus. (p. 1190)
Calvert, Patricia. Bigger. Minor, Wendell, illus. (p. 185)
—Kit Carson: He Led the Way. (p. 962)
—Vasco Da Gama: So Strong a Spirit. (p. 1833)
Calvert, Trudy, illus. see Rice, David L. & RICE, DAVID L.
Calvert, Trudy, tr. see Rice, David L. & RICE, DAVID L.
Calvert, Trudy L., jt. auth. see Rice, David L.
Calvert-Weyant, Linda, illus. see Riggin, Lisa.
Calvetti, Leonello, illus. see Dalla Vecchia, Fabio Marco.
Calway, Gareth, ed. see Bentley-Davies, Caroline, et al.
Calza, Gian Carlo. Japan Style. Kempton, Alexa, ed. (p. 909)
Calza, Gian Carlo, et al. Hokusai. (p. 787)
Cam, Philip. Philosophy Park: A Beginner's Guide to Great Philosophers & Their Ideas. (p. 1351)
Cam, Philip, ed. Thinking Stories 3. (p. 1734)
Camacho, Austin S. Payback Assignment. (p. 1331)
Camacho, Celi C. Bedtime for Meaghan. (p. 157)
Camacho, Norma I. Mikey/Jackster. (p. 1141)
Camacho, Ricardo, illus. see Payno, Manuel.
Camagajevac, Seb. Creating Fantasy Comics. (p. 378)
Camagni, Jacopo, illus. see Tobin, Paul.
Cámara, Noemi, jt. auth. see Rigby, Robert.
Cámara, Noemi, et al. Fantasmas de Goya. (p. 571)
Camara-Macauley, Marcella. Candy Girl. (p. 261)
Camardella, Michele L. America in The 1980s. (p. 59)
Camarena, Cathy & Ruff, Gloria B. Carmen y Carlos. (p. 270)
—Cindi y Cesar. (p. 321)
—Cindi y César. (p. 321)
—Crisma y Cristian. (p. 383)
—Crisma y Cristián. (p. 383)
—Ema y Eduardo. (p. 517)
—Fey y Felix. (p. 583)
—Fey y Félix. (p. 583)
—Florinda y Flavio. (p. 607)
—Gilda y Gilberto. (p. 676)
—Isabel E Ivan. (p. 890)
—Isabel e Iván. (p. 890)
—Kelli y Avellino. (p. 948)
—Oliva y Oscar. Flores-Hanson, Lourdes & Rosso-White, Gloria, eds. (p. 1285)
—Olivia y Oscar. (p. 1287)
—Tonis y Tono. (p. 1765)
—Toñis y Toño. (p. 1765)
—Valeria y Victor. (p. 1830)
—Valeria y Víctor. (p. 1830)
Camargo, F. T. Shanti & the Magic Mandala. (p. 1559)
Cambell, Rod & Wen, Dref. Anifeiliaid y Fferm. (p. 76)
Cambridge ESOL. Cambridge Young Learners English Tests 7 Flyers Answer Booklet: Examination Papers from University of Cambridge ESOL Examinations. (p. 256)
—Cambridge Young Learners English Tests 7 Starters Answer Booklet: Examination Papers from University of Cambridge ESOL Examinations. (p. 256)
Cambridge School Classics Project Staff. Cambridge Latin Course Unit 5. (p. 255)
Cambridge Studios. Interactive World Issues (p. 879)
Cambridge University Press, creator. SMP Interact to Book 9s. (p. 1595)
Cambridge University Press Staff. Business. (p. 244)
—Fractions. (p. 626)
—Joey's Quiet War & Other Stories. (p. 920)
Camburn, Carol A., illus. see Barnes, Laura T.
Camcam, Princesse, illus. see Sabatier-Morel, Francoise & Pellegrini, Isabelle.
Camcam, Princesse, illus. see Yamada, Miho.
Camcam, Princesse, creator. Fox's Garden. (p. 626)
Camden, Jean, illus. see Kids Can Press Staff & Forbes, Scott.
Camden, Marian Louise. Earth Child's Book of the Year. Wright, Diane Beem, illus. (p. 495)
—Earth Child's Book of Verse. Wright, Diane Beem, illus. (p. 495)
Camelleri, Michael, jt. auth. see Norrington, Leonie.
Camelo, Wilson. U. S. Air Force & Military Careers. (p. 1806)
Camelo, Wilson, jt. auth. see Rice, Earle.
Camerena, Rebecca. My Dog Is a Hero. (p. 1202)
Camerena, Rebecca & Ganeri, Anita. My Dog Is a Hero. (p. 1202)
Cameron, Amanda-Jane. Body Armour. (p. 207)
Cameron, Andrea. 10 Most Revolutionary Songs. (p. 1994)
Cameron, Andrea, jt. auth. see Hall, Marcella Runell.
Cameron, Ann. Colibri. (p. 339)
—Gloria Rising. (p. 685)
—Julian, Dream Doctor. Strugnell, Ann, illus. (p. 932)
—Julian, Secret Agent. (p. 932)
—Julian's Glorious Summer. (p. 932)
—Lugar Mas Bonito del Mundo. Alonso, Juan Ramon, illus. (p. 1064)
—Secret Life of Amanda K. Woods. (p. 1541)
—Spunky Tells All. Castillo, Lauren, illus. (p. 1635)
Cameron, Anne. Dreamspeaker. (p. 484)
—Gumboot Geese. Huber, June, illus. (p. 731)
—Lightning Catcher: The Storm Tower Thief. Jamieson, Victoria, illus. (p. 1016)
—Lightning Catcher. Jamieson, Victoria, illus. (p. 1016)
—Lightning Catcher - The Secrets of the Storm Vortex. Jamieson, Victoria, illus. (p. 1016)
Cameron, Antonia & Fosnot, Catherine Twomey. Games for Early Number Sense. (p. 655)
Cameron, Caleb. Kabe Academy. (p. 941)
Cameron, Chad, illus. see Raczka, Bob.
Cameron, Chad, illus. see Rusch, Elizabeth.
Cameron, Charles. Why Lizzie Johnson Matters to Texas. (p. 1925)
—Why Richard King Matters to Texas. (p. 1925)
Cameron, Craig, illus. see Adams, Ben.
Cameron, Craig, illus. see Alexander, Lori.
Cameron, Craig, illus. see Baxter, Nicola & Adams, Ben.
Cameron, Craig, illus. see Hewitt, Sally.
Cameron, Craig, illus. see Klein, Adria F.
Cameron, Craig, illus. see Yasuda, Anita.
Cameron, Don, jt. auth. see Siegel, Jerry.
Cameron, Don & Finger, Bill. World's Finest Comics. (p. 1960)
Cameron, Don, et al. Dark Knight (p. 407)
Cameron, E. Jane, jt. auth. see Wilcox, Jean K.
Cameron, Ed, illus. see Schultze, Gwendolyn.
Cameron, Eileen. G Is for Garden State: A New Jersey Alphabet. Ettlinger, Doris, illus. (p. 651)
Cameron, Eleanor. Stowaway to the Mushroom Planet. (p. 1664)
Cameron, Emma, jt. auth. see Seib, Anke.
Cameron, Erica. Sing Sweet Nightingale. (p. 1579)
Cameron, Eugenia, illus. see St. Julian, Ska.
Cameron, Gerald. Jesus & His Imaginary Dog, Lucky. (p. 915)
Cameron, Harriet. Adventures of Herman Quacker: Herman Goes to School. (p. 18)
—Nomad's Joyous Christmas. (p. 1263)
Cameron, Ian. I Have Not yet Begun to Fight: The Story of John Paul Jones Hero of the American Navy. (p. 839)
—Stirling Bridge. (p. 1651)
Cameron, Jill. Miffy, the Crooked-Eyed Cat. (p. 1139)
Cameron, Julia. Complete Artist's Way: Creativity as a Spiritual Practice. (p. 352)
Cameron, Katheryn Lynn. Christmas That Waited. (p. 316)
Cameron, Kathleen. Chicken Without a Coop. (p. 300)
Cameron, Ken. genética de las Plantas. Hanner, Albert & Hortens, Mike, illus. (p. 660)
—Plant Atlas & Plantas alrededor del Mundo: 6 English, 6 Spanish Adaptations (p. 1368)
—Plant Genetics & la genética de las Planta: 6 English, 6 Spanish Adaptations (p. 1369)
—Plantas alrededor del Mundo. (p. 1369)
Cameron, Kristy. Adventures of Herb the Wild Turkey - Herb Goes Camping. Shickle, Ian, illus. (p. 18)
—Behind the Door of Timothy Moore. Schickle, Ian, illus. (p. 160)
—Other Side of the Window. Ian, Shickle, illus. (p. 1306)
Cameron, Lisa. S Squad: the Camp Mystery. (p. 1499)
Cameron, Marie, illus. see Chodzin, Sherab.
Cameron, Marie, illus. see Hoffman, Mary.
Cameron, Merilee Ann. Violet-Covered Teacup. (p. 1843)
Cameron, Milissa. Faster, Daddy! (p. 576)
Cameron, Peter. Someday This Pain Will Be Useful to You. (p. 1609)
Cameron, Robert A., jt. auth. see McMillan, Gregory K.
Cameron, Sam. Missing Juliet: a Fisher Key Adventure. (p. 1152)
—Mystery of the Tempest: A Fisher Key Adventure. (p. 1226)
Cameron, Scott. William H. Rehnquist: Chief Justice of the U.S. Supreme Court. (p. 1933)
Cameron, Shanda. Feathered & Furry Friends. (p. 579)
Cameron, Sharon. Dark Unwinding. (p. 408)
—Rook. (p. 1487)
—Spark Unseen. (p. 1622)
Cameron, Stephanie. Ella Mae the Courageous Cheerleader. (p. 514)
Cameron, Thomas "Tom". Freddy's Adventure on the Safari River. (p. 633)
—Freddy's Mick Mock Ridge Adventure. (p. 633)
Cameron, W. Bruce. Ellie's Story. (p. 514)
Cameron, Wade. Melvin the Mischievious Mongoose First Day of School. (p. 1125)
Cameron, William J. You & the Ten Commandments. Bacon, Irving R., illus. (p. 1973)
Cameron-Gallo, Vivian. We're Three: A Story About Families & The Only Child. Simcic, Christina, illus. (p. 1875)
Camey, Lacy & Robey, Samantha. Last Name Banks. (p. 978)
Camille, Diana. Treasury of Goops: Timeless Manners for Every Generation. (p. 1783)
Camille, Diana, illus. see Ross, Barbara & Beatty, Nicholas.
Camilleri, Andrea & Sartarelli, Stephen. August Heat. Sartarelli, Stephen, tr. from ITA. (p. 115)
Camilleri, Michael, illus. see Metzenthen, David.
Caminada, Janet Barnett. Yoga, the Kid & the Cricket: A fun & easy illustrated guide to beginner's yoga. A complete yoga workout that follows along with the story. Written. (p. 1972)
Camisa, Kathryn. Hairy Tarantulas. (p. 736)
Camling, Candace, illus. see Davis, David.
Camm, Martin. Meyers Buch der Baeren. (p. 1131)
—Meyers Buch der Wale und Delfine. (p. 1131)
Camm, Martin, illus. see Cheshire, Gerard.
Camm, Sue. Baby Animals. (p. 124)
Cammarata, Jan. Karli's Kritters. (p. 944)
Cammarata, Robert P., jt. auth. see Whitfield, Laurie A.
Cammell, Sandra, illus. see Eggleton, Jill.
Cammell, Sandra, illus. see Holden, Pam.
Cammilleri, Johnathon. White Cat of Big Pine Hills. (p. 1912)
Cammuso, Frank. Big Birthday Bash. (p. 178)
—Cookie Catastrophe. (p. 361)
—Dinosaur Dilemma. (p. 442)
—Dodgeball Chronicles. (p. 460)
—Dragon Players. (p. 477)
—Misadventures of Salem Hyde: Dinosaur Dilemma. (p. 1150)
—Misadventures of Salem Hyde: Spelling Trouble. (p. 1150)
—Misadventures of Salem Hyde - Cookie Catastrophe (p. 1150)
—Spelling Trouble. (p. 1625)
Cammuso, Frank, illus. see Lynch, Jay.
Cammuso, Frank, jt. auth. see Lynch, Jay.
Cammuso, Frank & Lynch, Jay. Otto's Backwards Day. (p. 1307)
Cammy Fox Riley. Truckee's Adventures: Book One. (p. 1791)
Camossa, Silvia. Elecciones Que Brillan. Mesquita, Camila, illus. (p. 508)
Camp, Andrew. Scales. (p. 1519)
Camp, Carole Ann. American Women Inventors. (p. 64)
Camp, John R., see Sandford, John, pseud.
Camp, Lindsay. Keeping up with Cheetah. Newton, Jill, illus. (p. 948)
—Por Que? Ross, Tony, illus. (p. 1385)
—Why? Ross, Tony, illus. (p. 1922)
Camp, Mark J. Roadside Geology of Ohio. (p. 1477)
Camp, Randolph. Wet Matches. (p. 1877)
Camp, Richard Van, see Van Camp, Richard.
Camp, V. Ray. Little Mouse on the Prairie. Baker, David, illus. (p. 1032)
Campagne, Carmen, jt. auth. see Kaldor, Connie.
Campagne, Michelle. Little Blue Doggy. (p. 1024)
Campagne, Michelle & Gallant, Dany. Fabuleuse Melodie De. (p. 559)
Campana, Augustine. Last Fairy. (p. 977)
Campanella, Marco, et al. My Day with Billy Brownmouse. (p. 1201)
Campanelli, Mario, illus. see Jeffrey, Dennis.
Campaniello, Don. 1000 First Words in Italian. Lacome, Susie, illus. (p. 2001)
Campbell, jt. auth. see Glenn, Wendy J.
Campbell, Aileen. Wee Scot Travels. (p. 1871)
Campbell, Alex, illus. see Holland, Gini & O'Hern, Kerri.
Campbell, Alex, illus. see O'Hern, Kerri & Holland, Gini.
Campbell, Alex, illus. see Raatma, Lucia & O'Hern, Kerri.
Campbell, Amy. Fish in My Drain: Ava's Adventures. (p. 598)
Campbell, Andrew. Cosmetic Surgery. (p. 368)
—Ethiopia. (p. 539)
—Organ Transplants. (p. 1303)
—Protecting Wetlands. (p. 1412)
—Who Eats Who in the Desert? (p. 1915)
Campbell, Angella. Angel & Turkish. (p. 73)
—Engel und Turkish. (p. 529)
Campbell, Anna. Silly Rules: Jokes for Kids. Isbell, Toby, illus. (p. 1576)
Campbell, Ann-Jeanette. Espacio Asombro. (p. 536)
Campbell, Ballard C. Disasters, Accidents, & Crises in American History: A Reference Guide to the Nation's Most Catastrophic Events. (p. 447)
Campbell, Barbara. Lets Build Something: A Story Book/Coloring Book/Workbook. (p. 994)
Campbell, Blendon, illus. see Tarbell, Ida M.
Campbell, Brandon L. Embracing Ultimate Reality: A Soul Path (p. 517)
Campbell, Brent, illus. see Schwartz, Marcia.
Campbell, Brian, et al. Vampire: Nomads. (p. 1831)
Campbell, Bruce, photos by see Hawker, Frances & Alicavusoglu, Leyla.
Campbell, Bruce, photos by see Hawker, Frances & Bhatia, Mohini.
Campbell, Bruce, photos by see Hawker, Frances & Paz, Noemi.
Campbell, Bruce, photos by see Hawker, Frances & Resi, Putu.
Campbell, Bruce, photos by see Hawker, Frances & Sunantha Phusomsai.
Campbell, Bruce, photos by see Hawker, Frances & Taub, Daniel.
Campbell, Candy. My Mom Is A Nurse (p. 1214)
Campbell, Carol P. & Orr, Tamra. Frequently Asked Questions about Teen Pregnancy. (p. 636)
Campbell, Charles K. Magic Coin. (p. 1072)
Campbell, Cheryl. Darling Saves Christmas: The Continuing Adventures of Darling the Curly Tailed Reindoe. McGinnis, Steve, illus. (p. 409)
—Darling the Curly Tailed Reindoe. McGinnis, Steve, illus. (p. 409)
Campbell, Ciara. Slavery in America. (p. 1588)
Campbell, Ciara, ed. Slavery in America. (p. 1588)
Campbell, Corbin. Little Blue Man. (p. 1024)
Campbell, Crystal Wood. Grandpa's Pocket. (p. 710)
—Little Paw & the Moon. (p. 1033)
Campbell, D. Andrew. Catharsis. (p. 280)
Campbell, D. B., illus. see Coulton, Mia.
Campbell, Diana & Mosher, Nancy, eds. Everyday Signs for the Newborn Baby. Adilman, Katarzyna, illus. (p. 544)
Campbell, Donna P., illus. see Pierce, AnneMarie.
Campbell, Dorthina A. Step Forward Strategies for Struggling Readers: Student Resource Guide. (p. 1647)
Campbell, Ellen Langas. Raising the Roof (p. 1437)
—Smart Alex (p. 1592)
—Will Stephanie Get the Story? (p. 1932)
Campbell, Eric. Lugar de los Leones. (p. 1064)
Campbell, Erica. Lola Ladybug Says Her Prayers. (p. 1045)
Campbell, Eva, illus. see Walters, Eric.
Campbell, Faith Amelia. Iridescence. (p. 887)
Campbell, Forest G. & Ramen, Fred. Insider's Guide to Basketball. (p. 878)
Campbell, Fran. Trip to the Dentist. (p. 1787)
Campbell, Geoffrey A. Vulnerable America: An Overview of National Security. (p. 1851)
—Weapons of War. (p. 1869)
Campbell, George L., jt. auth. see Moseley, Christopher.
Campbell, Guy. Boys' Summer Book. Moran, Paul, illus. (p. 220)
Campbell, Guy, jt. auth. see Scholastic, Inc. Staff.
Campbell, H. David. Adventurous Jill: And Her Friend Jack. (p. 25)
—Merribell: A Comforting Story. (p. 1128)
—Stanley: The Littlest Elf. (p. 1639)
Campbell, Hannah. Skylanders Universe: Take Flight & Fight! (p. 1587)
Campbell, Hannah S., jt. auth. see Grosset & Dunlap.
Campbell, Hazel. Juice Box & Scandal. (p. 932)
Campbell, Hazel D. Ramgoat Dashalong: Magical Tales from Jamaica. (p. 1438)
Campbell, Herman. Child's Prayer from the Heart. (p. 305)
Campbell, Howard. Dog Named Pavlov: Un Perro Llamado Pavlov. McCloskey, Kevin, illus. (p. 461)
Campbell, Hugh R. Goal Scoring Step-by-Step. (p. 687)
Campbell, Isaiah. Struggles of Johnny Cannon. (p. 1668)
Campbell, J. A. Sabaska's Tale. (p. 1499)
Campbell, J. & McGuire. Confessions of Saint Augustine. (p. 356)

Campbell, Jack. Courageous (p. 372)
Campbell, Jacquie, illus. see Lemay, Didi.
Campbell, James. Boyface & the Quantum Chromatic Disruption Machine. (p. 220)
—Boyface & the Tartan Badger. (p. 220)
Campbell, James & Mould, Chris. Boyface & the Uncertain Ponies. (p. 220)
Campbell, Jane & Hartley, Susan. Bringing Back the Whooping Crane. (p. 229)
Campbell, Janis, jt. auth. see Collison, Cathy.
Campbell, Janis, jt. auth. see Lewis, Anne Margaret.
Campbell, Jan-Ives. League of Super Groovy Crimefighters Trade Paperback. Massey, Mitch & Kelleher, Michael, illus. (p. 982)
Campbell, Jeff. Daisy to the Rescue: True Stories of Daring Dogs, Paramedic Parrots, & Other Animal Heroes. Beyer, Ramsey, illus. (p. 401)
Campbell, Jeffrey. St. Francis & the Christmas Miracle of Greccio. Bianco, Francesca, illus. (p. 1638)
Campbell, Jenney, illus. see Bessesen, Brooke.
Campbell, Jennifer. Elise the Elephant. Cox, Nancy, illus. (p. 513)
Campbell, Jenny, illus. see Alt, Susan.
Campbell, Jenny, illus. see Callella, Kim & Williams, Rozanne Lanczak.
Campbell, Jenny, illus. see Callella, Kim.
Campbell, Jenny, illus. see Cernak, Kim & Williams, Rozanne Lanczak.
Campbell, Jenny, illus. see Cernak, Kim.
Campbell, Jenny, illus. see Cernek, Kim & Shiotsu, Vicky.
Campbell, Jenny, illus. see Cernek, Kim & Williams, Rozanne Lanczak.
Campbell, Jenny, illus. see Cernek, Kim, et al.
Campbell, Jenny, illus. see Cernek, Kim.
Campbell, Jenny, illus. see Jordano, Kimberly & Corcoran, Tebra.
Campbell, Jenny, illus. see Lewis, Dawn & Jacks, Cyndie.
Campbell, Jenny, illus. see Lewis, Sue & Abrams, Suzanne.
Campbell, Jenny, illus. see Lewis, Sue & Stern, Amy.
Campbell, Jenny, illus. see Lubben, Amy & Williams, Rozanne Lanczak.
Campbell, Jenny, illus. see Philipson, Sandra J.
Campbell, Jenny, illus. see Philipson, Sandra.
Campbell, Jenny, illus. see Shiotsu, Vicky.
Campbell, Jenny, illus. see Williams, Rozanne Lanczak.
Campbell, Jim, illus. see Priestley, J. B.
Campbell, Joanna, jt. auth. see Newhall, Mary.
Campbell, Joanna, pseud. Faith in a Long Shot. (p. 565)
—Star of Shadowbrook Farm. (p. 1640)
Campbell, Joe Bill, jt. auth. see Campbell, June M.
Campbell, Jon & Wesley, Jack. Scholastic Discover More Reader Level 2: Military Vehicles. (p. 1521)
Campbell, Jonathan A. & Lamar, William W. Venomous Reptiles of the Western Hemisphere (p. 1836)
Campbell, Josette & Hayhurst, Chris. Euclid: The Father of Geometry. (p. 540)
Campbell, Joy. Jack & Luke & the Paper Airplanes. (p. 902)
Campbell, Judy. Gizmo the Little Crow: Written & Illustrated By. (p. 681)
Campbell, Julie. Gatehouse Mystery. Stevens, Mary, illus. (p. 658)
—Red Trailer Mystery. Stevens, Mary, illus. (p. 1455)
—Secret of the Mansion: Trixie Belden. (p. 1542)
—Secret of the Mansion. Stevens, Mary, illus. (p. 1542)
Campbell, June M. & Campbell, Joe Bill. Thank You, God, for Who I Am. (p. 1725)
Campbell, K. G. Lester's Dreadful Sweaters. Campbell, K. G., illus. (p. 994)
Campbell, K. G., illus. see DiCamillo, Kate.
Campbell, K. G., illus. see Keane, David.
Campbell, K. G., jt. auth. see Dyckman, Ame.
Campbell, Karen, illus. see Vineyard Church of Columbus.
Campbell, Kathy. Down under Advent Calendar of Chrissy Stories: Great Activities for the 2013 Silly Season. (p. 474)
—Let's Draw a Bear with Squares. (p. 995)
—Let's Draw a Bear with Squares / Vamos a dibujar un oso usando Cuadrados. (p. 995)
—Let's Draw a Fish with Triangles. (p. 995)
—Let's Draw a Fish with Triangles / Vamos a dibujar un pez usando Triángulos. (p. 996)
—Let's Draw a Frog with Ovals. (p. 996)
—Let's Draw a Frog with Ovals / Vamos a dibujar una rana Usando óvalos. (p. 996)
Campbell, Kathy Kuhtz. Let's Draw a Bear with Squares: Vamos a Dibujar un Oso Usando Cuadrados. (p. 995)
—Let's Draw a Bear with Squares. Muschinske, Emily, illus. (p. 995)
—Let's Draw a Fish with Triangles: Vamos a Dibujar un Pez Usando Triangulos. Muschinske, Emily, tr. (p. 996)
—Let's Draw a Fish with Triangles. (p. 996)
—Let's Draw a Frog with Ovals: Vamos a Dibujar una Rana Usando Ovalos. Muschinske, Emily, tr. (p. 996)
—Let's Draw a Frog with Ovals. (p. 996)
Campbell, Ken, illus. see Cliffe, Kara.
Campbell, Kenneth. Great Leaps Oral Calculations Addition Mixed Facts. (p. 717)
Campbell, Kimberly. Lois Duncan: Author of I Know What You Did Last Summer. (p. 1045)
—Richard Peck: A Spellbinding Storyteller. (p. 1469)
Campbell, Kumari. United Kingdom in Pictures. (p. 1819)
Campbell, L. A. Cartboy & the Time Capsule. (p. 272)
—Cartboy Goes to Camp. (p. 272)
Campbell, Laura. Tommy Tumbleweed. (p. 1765)
Campbell, Laurence. Girls in White Dresses. (p. 680)
Campbell, Lisa, illus. see Romagnoli, L. M.
Campbell, Lori. Adventures of Tinkerbelle & Peanut. (p. 24)
Campbell, Lori M., jt. auth. see Lear, Edward.
Campbell, Lorne, photos by see Stern, Sam & Stern, Susan.
Campbell, Margaret & Gohari, Omid. Duke University College Prowler off the Record. (p. 489)
Campbell, Margaret Christine & Goldstein, Natalie. Discovering Atoms. (p. 448)
Campbell, Mari. Maggiemoosetracks: Wolf Pack. Jennings, Randy, illus. (p. 1071)
—Maggiemoosetracks: Making Friends. Katsumoto, Sayaka, tr. (p. 1071)
—Maggiemoosetracks: Making Friends. Jennings, Randy, illus. (p. 1071)
Campbell, Mari & Jennings, Randy. Maggiemoosetracks: Christmas Star. (p. 1071)
Campbell, Marie L. Pocketful of Passage. (p. 1375)
Campbell, Marilyn & Columbus, Curt. Crime & Punishment. (p. 382)
Campbell, Marjorie Wilkins. Savage River: Seventy-One Days with Simon Fraser Delainey, James, illus. (p. 1516)
Campbell, Mary Exa Atkins, jt. auth. see Gregory, Kristiana.
Campbell, Matt. God Made Snot. (p. 690)
—Unlocked. (p. 1821)
Campbell, Maureen & Yoerg, Sharon. Bridges to Safety: A Practical Guide for Adults to Help Teens Teach Conflict Resolution & Character Skills to Children. (p. 227)
Campbell, Mel. Caminando con Mapas/Walk on Maps. Mallick, David, tr. from ENG. (p. 256)
Campbell, Mercer. You Look Puny. (p. 1976)
Campbell, Meredith, jt. auth. see Dwyer, Megan.
Campbell, Michelle M. Granpa's Workshop: How Granpa Shows His Love. (p. 710)
Campbell, Morgan. Shots, Lies, & That Party. (p. 1569)
Campbell, Nicola. Shi-Shi-Etko LaFave, Kim, illus. (p. 1566)
Campbell, Nicola I. Shin-Chi's Canoe. Lafave, Kim, illus. (p. 1566)
Campbell, Patsy. Pray Work Win! (p. 1393)
Campbell, Patty & Aronson, Marc, eds. War Is... Soldiers, Survivors, & Storytellers Talk about War. (p. 1857)
Campbell, Polly, jt. auth. see Rice, Simon.
Campbell, Polly, et al. Focus on Spain. (p. 611)
Campbell, R. My Home. (p. 1211)
Campbell, R. W. Merrick Tumbledorf: The Last Talcomite Dragon. (p. 1128)
Campbell, R. Wayne, et al. Compact Guide to British Columbia Birds (p. 351)
Campbell, Ray, illus. see Charlton, Ella Mae.
Campbell, Richard P., photos by see Campbell, Sarah C.
Campbell, Rochelle, jt. auth. see Ankhnu Feaster, Teraab.
Campbell, Rod. Baby's Fluffy Friends. (p. 129)
—Buster's Bedtime. (p. 245)
—Buster's Park. (p. 245)
—Colour Bugs. (p. 346)
—Dear Zoo: From the Zoo. Campbell, Rod, illus. (p. 419)
—Dear Zoo. (p. 419)
—Dear Zoo. Campbell, Rod, illus. (p. 419)
—Jyngl: Sefyll-I-Fyny. (p. 941)
—Simple Ryhming ABC. (p. 1578)
—Who's That? (p. 1921)
—Wild Animals. (p. 1928)
Campbell, Ross. Shadoweyes Volume One. (p. 1558)
—Water Baby. (p. 1862)
Campbell, Ross, illus. see Lynch, Brian.
Campbell, Roy. Song of the Jackalope. Bosworth, David, illus. (p. 1611)
Campbell, Rusty & Porter, Malcolm. Atlas of Africa. (p. 112)
—Atlas of Asia. (p. 112)
Campbell, Ruth, illus. see Butchart, Francis & Smith, Ron.
Campbell, Ruth, illus. see Page, P. K.
Campbell, Ruth, illus. see Payne, Laurie.
Campbell, Ruth, jt. auth. see Ellis, Mark.
Campbell, S. E. Tasting Silver. (p. 1707)
Campbell, S Q. Animals. (p. 81)
—Shapes. (p. 1560)
Campbell, Sally R. Confident Consumer. (p. 356)
Campbell, Sam. Sweet Sue's Adventures. Fox, Charles Philip, photos by. (p. 1690)
Campbell, Sandra. Bears in the City: Andrew & Owen Save the Day. (p. 152)
—Brooklyn's ABC Game - A Camp Fire Game: An ABC Game for Kids. (p. 231)
—Country Vacation! (p. 372)
—Where's Grandma Going? (p. 1910)
Campbell, Sarah C. Growing Patterns: Fibonacci Numbers in Nature. Campbell, Richard P., photos by. (p. 726)
—Mysterious Patterns: Finding Fractals in Nature. Campbell, Sarah C. & Campbell, Richard P., photos by. (p. 1223)
—Wolfsnail: A Backyard Predator. Campbell, Sarah C. & Campbell, Richard P., photos by. (p. 1944)
Campbell, Scott, illus. see DiPucchio, Kelly.
Campbell, Scott, illus. see Dylan, Bob.
Campbell, Scott, illus. see Eversole, Robyn.
Campbell, Shirlene. Ook Ook the Monkey. (p. 1298)
Campbell, Stephanie. Little City Girl Meets the Suburbs. (p. 1026)
Campbell, Susan. Little Jimmy: The Itty Bitty Fifty Foot Tall Giraffe. (p. 1029)
Campbell, Suzy. Hidden Graveyard. (p. 775)
—My Daddy Is a Soldier (p. 1201)
—Pennies for Christmas (p. 1337)
Campbell, Todd M. Puppy Dog's New Friend. (p. 1418)
Campbell, Tom, photos by see Williams, Geoffrey T.
Campbell, Tonie. Highest Stand. (p. 779)
Campbell, Trenton, ed. Gods & Goddesses of Ancient China. (p. 690)
Campbell, Wallis. Angel Island. (p. 73)
Campbell, Wanda Gail. Little Buckets Full of Big Love. (p. 1025)
Campbell, Yma Orne. Manners & Morals in Minutes for Children. (p. 1088)
Campbell-Fells. Blue Ribbon Girls. (p. 203)
Campbell-Quillen, Virginia, illus. see McIntosh, Anne.
Campbell-Rush, Peggy. Ready to Write! 100 Tips & Strategies for Developing Fine-Motor Skills to Help Young Students Build a Strong Foundation for Handwriting. (p. 1448)
Camper, Anne K., jt. auth. see Crewe, Sabrina.
Camper, Cathy. Low Riders in Space. Raúl, III, illus. (p. 1061)
Campher, Jerome C. Path of Purpose: Walking in God's Plan for Your Life. (p. 1328)
Campi, Alex de. Valentine Volume 1: Ice of Death TP: Ice of Death TP. (p. 1830)
Campidelli, Maurizio, illus. see Smith, Brian & Levine, Cory.
Campillo, Carlo Collodi. Ilustrado por Susana. Aventuras de Pinocho. (p. 119)
Campion, Nardi Reeder. Patrick Henry: Firebrand of the Revolution. Mays, Victor, illus. (p. 1329)
Campion, Pascal, illus. see Catherine, Maria.
Campion, Pascal, illus. see Driscoll, Laura.
Campion, Pascal, illus. see Krensky, Stephen.
Campis, Adrian, Jr., illus. see Cook, Beatrice.
Campisi, Stephanie, jt. auth. see Nass, Marcia.
Campling, Jo, ed. see Thompson, Neil.
Campo, Juan. Encyclopedia of Islam. (p. 525)
Campodonica, Carol. Crazy Animal Stories. (p. 377)
Campodonica, Carol A. How Congress Works. Miller, Bondell, ed. (p. 806)
—How to Build a California Mission: Santa Cruz Weber, Francis J. et al, eds. (p. 815)
—How to Build a California Mission: Santa Barbara Wardup, Shirley et al, eds. (p. 815)
Campolo, Tony. You Can Make a Difference (p. 1974)
Campos Eichelberger, Misty. Who Is Santa? & Where Did He Come From? (p. 1916)
Campos F, Angel, illus. see Estrada, Gabriela Aguileta.
Campos, Jacqueline. Adventures of Lil' Wolf, Twinkie, to. (p. 19)
Campos, Leo. Creating Manga Comics (p. 378)
Campos, Maria de Fatima. Victoria's Day. (p. 1840)
Campos, Maria de Fatima, photos by. Cássio's Day: From Dawn to Dusk in a Brazilian Village. (p. 276)
Campos, Paula. Turtle's Shell. Ortega, Macarena, illus. (p. 1799)
Campos, Paz, tr. see Homer & Martín, Jean.
Campos, Tito. Muffler Man en l Hombre Mofle. Alvarez, Lamberto, illus. (p. 1189)
Campoverde Rocha, Jennifer. Aku & the Magnificent Color Scheme. (p. 32)
Campoy, F. Isabel. Mi Dia de la A a la Z. Lavandeira, Sandra, illus. (p. 1132)
—My Day from A to Z. (p. 1201)
Campoy, F. Isabel, jt. auth. see Flor Ada, Alma.
Campoy, F. Isabel, jt. auth. see Willems, Mo.
Campoy, F. Isabel, jt. contrib. by see Flor Ada, Alma.
Campoy, F. Isabel, tr. see Baker, Keith.
Campoy, F. Isabel, tr. see Daniel, Claire & Ernst, Lisa Campbell.
Campoy, F. Isabel, tr. see Douglas, Erin.
Campoy, F. Isabel, tr. see Floyd, Lucy.
Campoy, F. Isabel, tr. see Fox, Mem.
Campoy, F. Isabel, tr. see Howard, Reginald.
Campoy, F. Isabel, tr. see Krull, Kathleen.
Campoy, F. Isabel, tr. see McPhail, David.
Campoy, F. Isabel, tr. see Moran, Alex.
Campoy, F. Isabel, tr. see Most, Bernard.
Campoy, F. Isabel, tr. see Murphy, Mary.
Campoy, F. Isabel, tr. see Parks, Carmen.
Campoy, F. Isabel, tr. see Stevens, Janet & Crummel, Susan Stevens.
Campoy, F. Isabel, tr. see Walsh, Ellen Stoll.
Campoy, F. Isabel & Howell, Theresa. Maybe Something Beautiful. López, Rafael, illus. (p. 1113)
Camprubi, Krystal, illus. see Kloczko, Edouard.
Campy, F. Isabel, tr. see Prap, Lila.
Camuncoli, Giuseppe, illus. see Grayson, Devin, et al.
Camuncoli, Giuseppe, illus. see Hickman, Jonathan.
Camuncoli, Giuseppe, illus. see Slott, Dan & Waid, Mark.
Camus, William. Azules Contra Grises. (p. 122)
—Fabricante de Lluvia. (p. 559)
Camut, LeeAnn. Peacock Parade. Boscola, Carolyn, illus. (p. 1332)
—Toe Jam. Boscola, Carolyn, illus. (p. 1761)
Canaday, Cindi, jt. auth. see Canaday, Matt.
Canaday, Matt & Canaday, Cindi. Book of Mormon Circle a Word Griffin, Grace, ed. (p. 211)
Canadian Books Staff. Canadian Scented Book. (p. 260)
Canadian Museum of Nature Staff, jt. auth. see Conlan, Kathy.
Canady, Mary Monica. Why Is My Name Sam? Papeo, Maria Eugenia & Saumell, Marina, illus. (p. 1925)
Canady, Robert J., jt. auth. see Raines, Shirley C.
Canale, Allison. Ella & the Worry Doll. Lefebure, Ingrid, illus. (p. 513)
Canale, Suzie Hearl. Candy Roses of Cape Care. Coffey, Kevin, illus. (p. 261)
Canales, Veronica, tr. see Saki.
Canales, Viola. Tequila Worm. (p. 1721)
Canals, Mercè, illus. see Farre, Lluis & Farré, Lluís.
Canals, Sonia, illus. see Massey, Kay.
Canals, Sonia, jt. auth. see Atkinson, Sue.
Canas, Alicia, illus. see Garcia Lorca, Federico X & Garcia Lorca, Federico.
Cañas, Alicia, illus. see Sierra I. Fabra, Jordi & Sierra i Fabra, Jordi.
Cañas, Alicia, tr. see Sierra I. Fabra, Jordi & Sierra I Fabra, Jordi.
Canas, José & José, Cañas Torregrosa. Ojos de Botella de Anis. (p. 1282)
—Princesa Que No Sabia Estornudar. Martinez, Rocio, illus. (p. 1402)
Canas-Jovel, Lourdes E. & Acock, Anthony W. Lil' Vegan Monsters' Cookbook. Schiller, Caitlin, ed. (p. 1037)
Canavan, Andrea. Federal Aviation Administration: Your Government: How it Works. (p. 580)
Canavan, Charles Patrick. Rocky's Road to Sunshine. (p. 1484)
Canavan, Jean, illus. see Clinton, Ann M.
Canavan, Roger. Indonesia. (p. 872)
—You Wouldn't Want to Live Without Bacteria! Bergin, Mark, illus. (p. 1977)
—You Wouldn't Want to Live Without Clean Water! Antram, David, illus. (p. 1977)
—You Wouldn't Want to Live Without Extreme Weather! (p. 1977)
—You Wouldn't Want to Live Without the Writing! Bergin, Mark, illus. (p. 1977)
Canavan, Thomas. Computation Skills: 50 Math Super Puzzles. (p. 354)
—Do Plants Really Eat Insects? Questions & Answers about the Science of Plants. (p. 457)
—Does It Really Rain Frogs? Questions & Answers about Planet Earth. (p. 460)
—Fighting Illness & Injury: The Immune System. (p. 585)
—Fit & Healthy: Heart, Lungs, & Hormones. (p. 599)
—Fueling the Body: Digestion & Nutrition. (p. 646)
—Growth & Development: Cells & DNA. (p. 727)
—How Your Body Works: The Ultimate Illustrated Guide. (p. 823)
—Making Connections: 50 Math Super Puzzles. (p. 1081)
—Mental Math: 50 Math Super Puzzles. (p. 1126)
—Problem Solving: 50 Math Super Puzzles. (p. 1408)
—Ready for Action: Bones & Muscles. (p. 1447)
—Sensing the World: The Nervous System. (p. 1551)
—Shapes & Symmetry: 50 Math Super Puzzles. (p. 1560)
—Symbols & Algebra: 50 Math Super Puzzles. (p. 1693)
—What Makes You Hiccup? Questions & Answers about the Human Body. (p. 1892)
—Why Are Black Holes Black? Questions & Answers about Space. (p. 1922)
—Why Do Ice Cubes Float? Questions & Answers about the Science of Everyday Materials. (p. 1923)
—Why Do Zebras Have Stripes? Questions & Answers about Animals. (p. 1924)
Canby, Courtlandt, jt. auth. see Lemberg, David S.
Cancio, Damian, illus. see Gonzalez-Villariny, Natali.
Canda, Chelsea. I Think My Dad's a Superhero. (p. 846)
Candace, Bonnie & Ellen, illus. see Clarke, Lisa Anne.
Candace, Bonnie & Ellen, illus. see Huebner, Dawn.
Candau, Brittany. Amazing Spider-Man 2: Fully Charged. (p. 56)
—Amazing Spider-Man 2 Junior Novel. (p. 56)
—Amazing Spider-Man 2 Junior Novel. Disney Book Group Staff, illus. (p. 56)
—Cinderella. Godbey, Cory, illus. (p. 320)
—Spider-Man vs. Electro. (p. 1626)
Candela, Pilar, jt. auth. see Banegas, Candela.
Candelaria, Michael. Sharks! (p. 1562)
Candelario, Margo. Looking to the Clouds for Daddy. Craft, Jerry, illus. (p. 1051)
Candell, Arianna. Mind Your Manners: In School. Curto, Rosa M., illus. (p. 1145)
Cander, Chris. Word Burglar. Tramonte, Katherine H., illus. (p. 1950)
Candle Books, creator. Carry along Bible Activities. (p. 271)
—More 365 Activities for Kids (p. 1173)
Candler, John. Brief Notices of Hayti with Its Condition, Resources & Prospects. (p. 228)
Candlewick. My Little Bear Library. (p. 1212)
Candlewick Press. Berlin: a 3D Keepsake Cityscape. McMenemy, Sarah, illus. (p. 167)
—Doggie Duties. (p. 462)
—Fizzy's Lunch Lab: Super Supper Throwdown. (p. 601)
—Peppa Pig & the Busy Day at School. (p. 1340)
—Peppa Pig & the Great Vacation. (p. 1340)
—Peppa Pig & the Muddy Puddles. (p. 1340)
—Peppa Pig & the Vegetable Garden. (p. 1340)
—Show's Over. (p. 1571)
Candlewick Press, Candlewick. Australia - A 3D Expanding Country Guide. Trounce, Charlotte, illus. (p. 116)
—FETCH! with Ruff Ruffman: Show's Over. WGBH, illus. (p. 583)
—France. Krauss, Trisha, illus. (p. 627)
—Japan: Panorama Pops. Smith, Anne, illus. (p. 909)
—Louvre: A 3D Expanding Museum. McMenemy, Sarah, illus. (p. 1059)
—Nelly Nitpick, Kid Food Critic. Lunch Lab LLC, Lunch Lab, illus. (p. 1240)
—Peppa Pig & the Busy Day at School. Candlewick Press, Candlewick & Ladybird Books Staff, illus. (p. 1340)
—Peppa Pig & the Day at Snowy Mountain. (p. 1340)
—Peppa Pig & the Great Vacation. (p. 1340)
—Peppa Pig & the Treasure Hunt. (p. 1340)
—Peppa Pig & the Vegetable Garden. (p. 1340)
—Ruff Ruffman's 44 Favorite Science Activities. WGBH, illus. (p. 1494)
—Shaun the Sheep Movie - Shear Madness. Aardman Animations Staff, illus. (p. 1563)
—Shaun the Sheep Movie - the Great Escape. Aardman Animations Staff, illus. (p. 1563)
—Shaun the Sheep Movie - Timmy in the City. Aardman Animations Staff, illus. (p. 1563)
—Story of Flight: Panorama Pops. Holcroft, John, illus. (p. 1658)
—Venice: a 3D Keepsake Cityscape. McMenemy, Sarah, illus. (p. 1835)
Candlewick Press Staff. Creepy-Crawlies: a 3D Pocket Guide. KJA Artists Staff, illus. (p. 381)
—Dinosaurs: a 3D Pocket Guide. KJA Artists Staff, illus. (p. 444)
—FETCH! with Ruff Ruffman: Doggie Duties. WGBH Educational Foundation Staff, illus. (p. 583)
—Fizzy's Lunch Lab: Super Supper Throwdown. Lunch Lab Staff, illus. (p. 601)
—Peppa Pig & the Busy Day at School. Candlewick Press Staff, illus. (p. 1340)
—Peppa Pig & the Great Vacation. (p. 1340)
—Peppa Pig & the Lost Christmas List. (p. 1340)
—Peppa Pig & the Lost Christmas List. Ladybird Books Staff, illus. (p. 1340)
—Peppa Pig & the Lost Christmas List. Candlewick Press Staff, illus. (p. 1340)
—Peppa Pig & the Muddy Puddles. (p. 1340)
—Peppa Pig & the Perfect Day. (p. 1340)
—Peppa Pig & the Vegetable Garden. (p. 1340)
—Rio de Janeiro: a 3D Keepsake Cityscape. Krauss, Trisha, illus. (p. 1473)
Candlewick Press Staff, illus. see Blake, Michel.
Candlewick Press Staff, illus. see McDonald, Megan & Michalak, Jamie.

C

Candlewick Press Staff, illus. see McDonald, Megan.
Candlewick Press Staff, illus. see Michalak, Jamie.
Candlewick Press Staff, jt. auth. see DiCamillo, Kate.
Candlewick Press Staff, jt. auth. see Holcroft, John.
Candlewick Press Staff, jt. auth. see Ladybird Books Staff.
Candlewick Press Staff, jt. auth. see Young, Sarah.
Candlewick Press Staff & Arnold, Nick. Flying Machines. Kearney, Brendan, illus. (p. 610)
Candlewick Press Staff, creator. Brand New Readers Purple (p. 222)
Cando, Kinder. Creatures under the Sea Take Home. (p. 380)
Candoli, Georgia. Dear Baldy. (p. 418)
Candon, Jennifer, illus. see Maier, Inger M.
Candy Cane Press, creator. Baby Panda Book & Toy Gift Set (p. 127)
—Safe at Home! Indoor Safety. (p. 1502)
—Safe at Play: Outdoor Safety. (p. 1502)
Candy, T. M. & Fisher, W. A. Dear Mister Mayor. (p. 419)
Candy, Wolf. Tree, the House & the Hurricane. (p. 1784)
Candybird Staff. My Book of Secrets. (p. 1199)
Cane, David A. Nitro Circus. (p. 1257)
Cane, Ella. Communities in My World (p. 349)
—Continents in My World (p. 361)
—Countries in My World (p. 372)
—Homes in My World (p. 793)
—My World. (p. 1221)
—Neighborhoods in My World (p. 1240)
—Our Government (p. 1309)
—States in My World (p. 1644)
—U. S. House of Representatives (p. 1806)
—U. S. Presidency. (p. 1807)
—U. S. Senate (p. 1807)
—U. S. Supreme Court (p. 1807)
Cane, Rachel. Soy. (p. 1618)
Cane, Sutter. Governing Texas: Local, State, & National Governments. (p. 704)
Cane, William. Art of Kissing. (p. 102)
Canetti, et al. Poquito Mas. (p. 1385)
Canetti, Yanitzia. 1-2-3 Do, Re, Mi Ants. (p. 1990)
—1-2-3, Do, Re, Mi Elephants. (p. 1990)
—1-2-3 Do, Re, Mi Sheep. (p. 1990)
—1-2-3 Do, Re, Mi Spiders. (p. 1990)
—ABC's of Plants. (p. 4)
—ABCs of School. (p. 4)
—Abecedario de Plantas. (p. 4)
—Abecedario de Profesiones y Oficios. (p. 4)
—Abecedario Escolar. (p. 4)
—ABeCedario Musical. (p. 4)
—Abecedario Nutritivo. (p. 4)
—ABeCedario Salvaje. (p. 4)
—Acrobacias: Ellos lo hace bien, ¡nosotros También! (p. 9)
—Acurrucarse: Ellos lo hacen bien nosotros Tambien. (p. 10)
—Adaptación, Qué Sensación Alas. (p. 11)
—Adaptación, ¡qué Sensación! (p. 11)
—adaptación, ¡qué Sensación! Lenguas. (p. 11)
—Adivina, Adivinador: ¿Quién está Escondido? (p. 12)
—Agacharse: Ellos lo hacen bien nosotros Tambien. (p. 29)
—Agarrarse: Ellos lo hacen bien nosotros Tambien. (p. 29)
—Almost the Same. (p. 48)
—Amazing Adaptations! (p. 52)
—Amazing Adaptations! Tongues. (p. 52)
—Canciones para Dormir a Las Munecas: Dulce Compania. (p. 261)
—Canciones para dormir a los Peluches. (p. 261)
—Canta y Cuenta Las Arañas. (p. 262)
—Canta y Cuenta Las Hormigas. (p. 262)
—Canta y Cuenta Las Ovejas. (p. 262)
—Casi Iguales. (p. 276)
—Casos y cosas que dan Risa. (p. 276)
—Colores escolares/School Colors: A World of Color. (p. 344)
—Colorful Shapes/Figuras de Colores: A World of Color. (p. 344)
—Colorful Sights Paisajes de Colores: A World of Color. (p. 344)
—Colors on Colors/Colores Sobre Colores: A World of Color. (p. 345)
—Could It Be? (p. 369)
—De quien es esta Sombra? Adivina Adivinador. (p. 416)
—Doña Flautina Resuelvelotodo. Avi, tr. (p. 465)
—En Tiempos Dificiles. Willy, Romont, illus. (p. 523)
—Friends to the End: Together Is Better. (p. 639)
—Guess Who? Who Crosses Here? (p. 729)
—Guess Who? Who's Hiding? (p. 729)
—Guess Who? Who's Looking at Me? (p. 729)
—Guess Who? Who's Shadow Is This? (p. 729)
—Guess Who? Whose Skin Is This? (p. 729)
—Guess Who? Whose Tracks Are These? (p. 729)
—I'm Proud to Be Me! (p. 859)
—Imagina un mundo Mejor. (p. 860)
—Imagine a Better World. (p. 860)
—Lullaby for My Doll. (p. 1064)
—Lullaby for My Teddy Bear. (p. 1064)
—mundo es una Semilla: Un mundo Mejor. (p. 1191)
—Musical ABCs. (p. 1194)
—Musical Colors/Colores Musicales: A World of Color. (p. 1194)
—No somos tan Diferentes: La alegria de estar Juntos. (p. 1260)
—Not So Different. (p. 1267)
—Our Great Big World. (p. 1309)
—Party Colors/Colores Festivos: A World of Color. (p. 1326)
—Que le Dijo? Bate, bate, Disparates. (p. 1424)
—Quien cruza por Aqui? Adivina, Adivinador. (p. 1427)
—Quien deja esta Huella? Adivina, Adivinador. (p. 1427)
—Quien me mira Asi? ¿quien Me Mira Así? (p. 1427)
—Rhyming Tongue Twisters Animals. (p. 1468)
—Rhyming Tongue Twisters Science: Science. (p. 1468)
—Rhyming Tongue-Twisters Art. (p. 1468)
—Rhyming Tongue-Twisters Math. (p. 1468)
—Say What? (p. 1518)
—Siempre contigo mi Amigo: La alegria de estar Juntos. (p. 1573)
—Soy Original, ¡genial! (p. 1618)
—Sporty Colors/Colores Deportivos: A World of Color. (p. 1633)
—Tasty Colors/Colores de Sabores: A World of Color. (p. 1707)
—Trabalenguas Artisticos. (p. 1774)
—Trabalenguas Cientificos. (p. 1774)
—Trabalenguas Zoológicos. (p. 1774)
—What They Can Do, We Can Too! Crouch. (p. 1894)
—What They Can Do, We Can Too! Curl Up. (p. 1894)
—What They Can Do, We Can Too! Grab. (p. 1894)
—What They Do... We Can, Too! Gymnastics: Gymnastics. (p. 1894)
—When Times Are Tough. Keating, Alison, tr. (p. 1905)
—Yo También Puedo Ser Presidente. (p. 1971)
—Yummy ABC's. (p. 1983)
—¿Quién se oculta tras la Luz? (p. 1427)
—¿Quién tiene esta Piel? (p. 1427)
Canetti, Yanitzia, jt. auth. see Biedrzycki, David.
Canetti, Yanitzia, jt. auth. see Ross, Dev.
Canetti, Yanitzia, tr. see Ajmera, Maya & Ivanko, John D.
Canetti, Yanitzia, tr. see Bowie, C. W.
Canetti, Yanitzia, tr. see Harter, Debbie.
Canetti, Yanitzia, tr. see Macdonald, Alastair.
Canetti, Yanitzia, tr. see McGrath, Barbara Barbieri & Shaw, Brian.
Canetti, Yanitzia, tr. see McKay, Sindy.
Canetti, Yanitzia, tr. see McQuinn, Anna & Beardshaw, Rosalind.
Canetti, Yanitzia, tr. see Munsch, Robert.
Canetti, Yanitzia, tr. see Parenting Press Staff & Cain, Janan.
Canetti, Yanitzia, tr. see Rey, H. A.
Canetti, Yanitzia, tr. see Rey, H. A. & Rey, Margret.
Canetti, Yanitzia, tr. see Ryan, Pam Muñoz.
Canetti, Yanitzia, tr. see Seuss, Dr.
Canetti, Yanitzia & Keating, Alison. I Can Be President, Too! (p. 835)
Canetti, Yanitzia & Yanitzia, Canetti. Blanca Nieve y los Siete Gigantones. Decis, Anne, illus. (p. 198)
—Patito Bello. Costa, Maria, illus. (p. 1328)
Canetti, Yanitzia James, tr. see Blankenship, Paula.
Canetti, Yanitzia James, tr. see Krebs, Laurie & Blackstone, Stella.
Canetti, Yanitzia James, tr. see McKay, Sindy.
Canetti, Yanitzia James, tr. see Ross, Dev.
Canetti, Yanitzia James, tr. see Seuss, Dr.
Canetti, Yanitzia James, et al. Ay, Luna, Luna, Lunita... Peinador, Angeles, illus. (p. 121)
Canetti, Yanitzia, tr. see Lesynski, Loris.
Canfield, Andrea. Sassy the Seahag. Hallinan, Susan, illus. (p. 1515)
Canfield, J. Douglas & Von Sneidern, Maja-Lisa. Broadview Anthology of Restoration & Early Eighteenth-Century Drama. Canfield, J. Douglas, ed. (p. 230)
Canfield, Jack & Hansen, Mark Victor. Chicken Soup for the Teenage Soul Collection. (p. 300)
Canfield, Jack, et al. Chicken Soup for the Child's Soul: Character-Building Stories to Read with Kids Ages 5-8. (p. 300)
Canfield, Michael. Freaky Animal Stories. (p. 631)
Canfield, Muriel. Broken & Battered: A Way Out for the Abused Woman. (p. 230)
Canfield, Nancy Lee. Rose for My Mother: A Memoir. Grey, Andrew, illus. (p. 1489)
Canga, C B, illus. see Bateman, Teresa.
Canga, C B, illus. see Bauer, Marion Dane & Rucker, Justin.
Canga, C. B., illus. see Bauer, Marion Dane.
Canga, C. B., illus. see Brezenoff, Steve.
Canga, C. B, illus. see Gallagher, Diana G.
Canga, C. B., illus. see Kurtz, Jane.
Canga, C. B., illus. see Troupe, Thomas Kingsley.
Cangilla-McAdam, Claudia. Maria's Mysterious Mission. Crum, Anna-Maria, illus. (p. 1093)
Canham, Anne MacDonald, jt. auth. see MacDonald, Betty.
Caniac, Nina. Baby Pets Play! Caniac, Nina, illus. (p. 127)
Caniff, Milton. Milton Caniff's Male Call. (p. 1144)
Caniff, Milton & Caniff, Milton Arthur. Complete Terry & the Pirates, 1934-1936 (p. 353)
Caniff, Milton Arthur, jt. auth. see Caniff, Milton.
Caniglia, illus. see Piccirilli, Tom.
Canine, Craig, ed. see Coxe, Molly.
Canini, Mikko. Genetic Engineering. (p. 660)
—Iran. (p. 886)
Canini, Mikko, jt. ed. see Cothran, Helen.
Canino, Kate. How Trade Deficits Work. (p. 823)
—Maintaining a Healthy Weight. (p. 1077)
—Turkey Hunting. (p. 1797)
Canizares, Susan & Chessen, Betsey. Storms: Tormentas. (p. 1656)
—Wind: El Viento. (p. 1935)
Canizzaro, Angelina Joyce. Daddy's Magic Lunchbox. (p. 399)
Cann, Helen, illus. see Evetts-Secker, Josephine.
Cann, Helen, illus. see Gilchrist, Cherry.
Cann, Helen, illus. see Hopkins, Lee Bennett.
Cann, Helen, illus. see Howell, Gill.
Cann, Helen, illus. see Krebs, Laurie.
Cann, Helen, illus. see Milligan, Bryce.
Cann, Helen, illus. see Riel, Jorn, et al.
Cann, Helen, illus. see Riel, Jörn & Chodzin, Sherab.
Cann, Helen, illus. see Riel, Jörn & Mason, John.
Cann, Helen, illus. see Singh, Rina.
Cann, Helen, illus. see Stemple, Heidi E. Y. & Yolen, Jane.
Cann, Helen, illus. see Watts, Murray.
Cann, Helen, illus. see Yue, Gui & Farrow, Clare.
Cann, Helen, illus. see Yue, Guo & Farrow, Clare.
Cann, Helen, jt. auth. see Gilchrist, Cherry.
Cann, Kate. Consumed. (p. 360)
—Crow Girl. (p. 385)
—Mediterranean Holiday: Or, How I Moved to a Tiny Island & Found the Love of My Life. (p. 1120)
—Possessed. (p. 1387)
—Text Game. (p. 1724)
—Viviendo Juntos. (p. 1846)
Cannarella, Deborah. Kansas (Revised Edition) (p. 943)
Cannavale, Matthew C. Florida, 1513-1821. (p. 606)
—North Carolina, 1524-1776. (p. 1265)
Cannavicci, Luigi A., illus. see Ciccone, Tiziana & Linardi, Franca.
Cannavicci, Luigi A., illus. see Ciccone, Tiziana.
Cannell, Jon, illus. see Holmes, Mary Tavener & Harris, John.
Cannell, Jon, illus. see Holmes, Mary Tavener.
Cannell, Jon, illus. see Jacobson, Ryan.
Cannell, Jon, illus. see Kennedy, Nancy B.
Cannella, Marco, illus. see Montgomery, R. A.
Cannella, Marco & Marron, Jose Luis. Tattoo of Death. (p. 1707)
Cannella, Nicole Derosa. Ribbit Exhibit: One frog's tale of a leap of Faith. (p. 1469)
Canning, Charlie. 89th Temple. (p. 1998)
Canning, Erin, ed. see Canning, Seán.
Canning, Laura A. Molly's Sweet Shop. King, Steve, illus. (p. 1161)
Canning, Seán. Cat That Loves to Eat. Canning, Erin, ed. (p. 278)
Cannizzaro, Debbie. We Live in Mandeville: 0. (p. 1867)
Cannizzo, Karen, ed. see Broslavick, Chris & Pichler, Tony.
Cannizzo, Karen, ed. see Puls, Ruth.
Cannizzo, Karen, ed. see Scully, Michael & Donovan, Patrick J.
Cannizzo, Karen, ed. see Ward, Hadley & Castano, Marie.
Cannizzo, Karen, jt. ed. see Schippe, Cullen.
Cannizzo, Karen A., ed. see Broslavick, Chris & Pichler, Tony.
Cannizzo, Karen A., ed. see Dotterweich, Kass P.
Cannizzo, Karen A., ed. see Olla, Debbie.
Cannizzo, Karen A., ed. see Puls, Ruth.
Cannizzo, Karen A., ed. see Scully, Michael & Donovan, Patrick.
Cannizzo, Karen A., ed. Confirmation: Gifted with the Spirit. (p. 357)
Cannizzo, Karen & Schippe, Cullen, eds. Church Welcomes Me: Grade 2 (p. 318)
—Jesus Loves Me: Grade 1 (p. 916)
—Learning the Way: Grade 3 (p. 985)
Cannizzo, Karen & Schippe, Cullen W., eds. Discovering the Story of God's People: Grade 6 (p. 450)
—Learning to Celebrate: Grade 5 (p. 985)
Cannizzo, Karen, ed. Confirmation: Confirming My Commitment to Christ. (p. 356)
—Confirmation: Confirming My Commitment to Christ/Candidate Edition. (p. 357)
—Mass Prayers: For Young Catholics. (p. 1102)
Cannon, illus. see Potter, Noel Gyro.
Cannon, jt. auth. see Cannon, Janell.
Cannon, A. E. Charlotte's Rose. (p. 294)
—Loser's Guide to Life & Love. (p. 1054)
—Sophie's Fish. White, Lee, illus. (p. 1613)
Cannon, Anita. My Aunt Bonnie: A Child's Story of Love & Loss. (p. 1196)
Cannon, Annie, illus. see Crenson, Victoria.
Cannon, Deborah. Pirate Vortex: Elizabeth Latimer, Pirate Hunter. (p. 1363)
Cannon, Devyn. Noble Mcfee & the Jellybean Epidemic. (p. 1262)
Cannon Hackett, Teresa. Creative Writing: Using Fairy Tales to Enrich Writing Skills. (p. 380)
Cannon, Janell. Crickwing. (p. 382)
—Dog for Sale. (p. 461)
—Pinduli. Cannon, Janell, illus. (p. 1359)
—Stellaluna. (p. 1647)
—Verdi. (p. 1836)
Cannon, Janell & Cannon. Verdi. (p. 1836)
Cannon, Joanne Mary. Girlfriends Party Time Sticker Paper Dolls. (p. 679)
Cannon, Jonathan. Greetings from Scurf Bay: Wish We Weren't Here! (p. 723)
Cannon, Joseph, illus. see Murthy, Amishi & Chou, Vivian.
Cannon, Joseph, illus. see Potter, Noel Gyro.
Cannon, Joseph P., told to. Nutrition Essentials: A Guide for the Fitness Professional. (p. 1274)
Cannon, Julie. Uncharted Passage. (p. 1811)
Cannon, K. L. Mr. Mortimer: The Grapevine That Wouldn't Die. (p. 1185)
Cannon, Kevin, illus. see Ottaviani, Jim.
Cannon, Lyn. Unraveling. (p. 1822)
Cannon, Martin, illus. see Weiner, Brian.
Cannon, Nick, jt. auth. see Scholastic, Inc. Staff.
Cannon, Nick & Carey, Mariah. Roc & Roe's Twelve Days of Christmas. Ford, A. G., illus. (p. 1481)
Cannon, Shannon. Letter Qq: Past & Present Set (p. 1002)
—Letter Uu: Jobs Set (p. 1002)
—Seasons (p. 1538)
Cannon, Shannon & Capstone Press Staff. Letter Qq: Past & Present (p. 1002)
—Letter Uu: Jobs (p. 1002)
Cannon, Sherrill S. Gimme-Jimmy. (p. 676)
—Manner-Man. (p. 1088)
—Peter & the Whimper-Whineys. (p. 1346)
—Santa's Birthday Gift. (p. 1513)
Cannon, William J., ed. see Haugen, Peter.
Cannon, William, Jr. Marine Science. (p. 1094)
Cannon, Zander. Star Trek: the Next Generation: Ghosts: The Next Generation: Ghosts. (p. 1641)
Cannon, Zander, illus. see Ottaviani, Jim.
Cannone, Gregory, illus. see Mittmann, Gerald & Mittmann, Laura.
Cano, Brenda. Caterpillar Named - Gussy. (p. 279)
Cano, Carles. Cuentos para Todo el Año. (p. 390)
Cano, Carles & Cano Peiró, Carles. Arbol de las Hojas Din A-4. (p. 94)
—¡¡¡Papááá—!!! Cano, Carles & Giménez, Paco, trs. (p. 1322)
Cano, Carles & Carles, Cano. Dragon a Dieta. Bravo, Juan & Bravo, Fran, illus. (p. 476)
Cano, Felipe. Bonjour Camille. Aguilar, Laia, illus. (p. 209)
Cano, Fernando, illus. see Hoena, B. A. & Barrie, J. M.
Cano, Fernando, illus. see Hoena, Blake A.
Cano, Fernando, illus. see Hoena, Blake.
Cano, Fernando, illus. see Manning, Matthew K.
Cano, Fernando, illus. see Steele, Michael A.
Cano, Fernando, illus. see Steele, Michael Anthony.
Cano, Fernando, illus. see Terrell, Brandon.
Cano, Fernando, illus. see Tullen, Sean.
Cano, Fernando, jt. auth. see Ciencin, Scott.
Cano, Fernando M., illus. see Ciencin, Scott, et al.
Cano, Fernando M., jt. auth. see Peters, Stephanie True.
Cano Peiró, Carles, jt. auth. see Cano, Carles.
Cantalapiedra, Jose, illus. see Lopez, Minia.
Cantell, Brenda, illus. see Thompson, Lisa.
Canter, David. Mapping Murder: Walking in Killers' Footsteps. (p. 1090)
Canter, Idalia, illus. see Ebel, Julia Taylor, Jr.
Canter, Idalia, illus. see Ebel, Julia Taylor.
Canterbury, David W. Rodeo. (p. 1484)
Canterna, Marcy. Great Saint Patrick's Day Flood Teacher's Study Guide. (p. 718)
—Teacher's Study Guide for the Steps of Pittsburgh: Portrait of a City (p. 1709)
Cantillo, Oscar. Blue Around Me. (p. 202)
—Discovering Mission San Fernando Rey de España. (p. 449)
—Discovering Mission San Francisco de Asís. (p. 449)
—Discovering Mission San Francisco de Solano. (p. 449)
—Green Around Me. (p. 721)
—Purple Around Me. (p. 1419)
Cantin, Emily Wheeler. Tom Turkey the Truthful Storyteller. (p. 1764)
Cantini, Barbara, illus. see Krisp, Caleb.
Canton, William. Childs Book of Saints. (p. 304)
—Child's Book of Saints. Robinson, T. H., illus. (p. 304)
—Child's Book of Warriors. Cole, Herbert, illus. (p. 304)
—Invisible Playmate A Story of the Unseen. (p. 886)
Cantone, Ana Laura. Historia Enredada. (p. 782)
Cantone, Anna Laura, illus. see Piumini, Roberto.
Cantone, Anna-Laura, illus. see Cali, Davide.
Cantone, AnnaLaura, illus. see Madison, Alan.
Cantor, Carrie & Cantor, Carrie Nichols. Mexican War: How the United States Gained Its Western Lands. (p. 1131)
Cantor, Carrie Nichols. Francisco Vásquez de Coronado: The Search for Cities of Gold. (p. 628)
Cantor, Carrie Nichols, jt. auth. see Cantor, Carrie.
Cantor, Don & Cantor, Michael. Perfect Pet: Finding a pet that Is dear to your Heart. Martin, McDonald, illus. (p. 1342)
Cantor, Jillian. Life of Glass. (p. 1012)
—Searching for Sky. (p. 1537)
—September Sisters. (p. 1551)
Cantor, Joanne. Teddy's TV Troubles. Lowes, Tom, illus. (p. 1713)
Cantor, Michael, jt. auth. see Cantor, Don.
Cantor, Patricia, illus. see Boelts, Maribeth.
Cantor, Patricia, illus. see Long, Kathy.
Cantrell, Beth. Leggtowne Chronicles. (p. 990)
Cantrell, Caley. You're Bringing Me a Baby?! (p. 1982)
Cantrell, Julie. God Is with Me Through the Day (p. 689)
Cantrell, Kat. Princess & the Player. (p. 1403)
Cantrell, Katie, illus. see Dunston, Marc.
Cantrell, Pete. Happy Angel: A Fractured Fairy Tale. Farris, Kim, illus. (p. 744)
Cantu, Sarah. Dogs that Follow their Detective Dreams. Adventure No. 1: Find a New Home. (p. 463)
Cantucci, Alessandro, illus. see Wildwood, Gretchen.
Cantwell, Lois. Women Winners: Then & Now. (p. 1946)
Cantwell, Lois & Smith, Pohla. Women Winners: Then & Now. (p. 1946)
Cantwell, Michael. Rising of the Fifth Sun. (p. 1475)
Cantwell, Rebecca & Compass Point Books Staff. Teens in Kenya (p. 1715)
Cantwell, Tom. Seminole & the Slave. (p. 1550)
Canty, Charlotte, illus. see Waddell, Martin.
Canuto, Louise, tr. see Heymelaux, Jasmin.
Canwell, Diane, jt. auth. see Sutherland, Jon.
Canwell, Diane, jt. auth. see Sutherland, Jonathan.
Canwell, Diane & Sutherland, John. Submarines. (p. 1671)
Canwell, Diane & Sutherland, Johnathan. Cruise Ships. (p. 386)
Canwell, Diane & Sutherland, Jonathan. Leisure & Tourism. (p. 991)
Canwell, Nancy. He's Got Your Back: A Daily Devotional for Juniors. (p. 774)
Canwell, Peter & Evry, Philip. Christmas Dove & the Woodcutter. (p. 313)
Canyon, Christopher. John Denver's Take Me Home, Country Roads. (p. 921)
Canyon, Christopher, illus. see Denver, John.
Canyon, Christopher, illus. see Lewis, J. Patrick.
Canyon, Christopher, tr. see Denver, John.
Canyon, Jeanette, illus. see Berkes, Marianne Collins.
Canyon, Jeanette, illus. see Berkes, Marianne.
Canzer, Brahm. E-Business: Strategic Thinking & Practice. (p. 492)
Cap Compass Staff. Life after School, Explained. (p. 1007)
Capa, Robert, photos by see Whelan, Richard.
Capaccio, George. ADD & ADHD. (p. 11)
—Cancer Treatments. (p. 261)
—Countryside. (p. 372)
—Digestive Disorders. (p. 438)
—Iron: Set Of 6. (p. 888)
—Iron: Text Pairs. (p. 888)
—Jupiter. (p. 937)
—Mars. (p. 1096)
—Religion. (p. 1458)
—Religion in Colonial America. (p. 1458)
—Schools. (p. 1524)
—Sun. (p. 1675)
—Tsunamis: Set Of 6. (p. 1795)
—Tsunamis: Text Pairs. (p. 1795)
Capaldi, Gina. Boy Named Beckoning: The True Story of Dr. Carlos Montezuma, Native American Hero. Capaldi, Gina, illus. (p. 218)
Capaldi, Gina, illus. see Buonanno, Graziella Pacini.
Capaldi, Gina, illus. see Lilly, Melinda.
Capaldi, Gina, illus. see Mangrum, Allison.
Capaldi, Gina, illus. see Simmons, Andra.
Capaldi, Gina, jt. auth. see Rife, Douglas M.

Capaldi, Gina & Pearce, Q. L. Red Bird Sings: The Story of Zitkala-Sa, Native American Author, Musician, & Activist. Capaldi, Gina, illus. (p. 1453)

Capaldi, Mario. Odysseus & the Wooden Horse: A Greek Legend. (p. 1278)

Caparo, Antonio, illus. see Wildavsky, Rachel.

Caparó, Antonio Javier, illus. see Abbott, Tony.

Caparo, Antonio Javier, illus. see Batterson, Mark.

Caparo, Antonio Javier, illus. see Broach, Elise.

Caparo, Antonio Javier, illus. see Fairlie, Emily.

Caparó, Antonio Javier, illus. see Findlay, Lisa & Swift, Jonathan.

Caparo, Antonio Javier, illus. see May, Robert L.

Caparo, Antonio Javier, illus. see Prager, Ellen.

Caparo, Antonio Javier, illus. see Prineas, Sarah.

Caparo, Antonio Javier, jt. auth. see Pogue, David.

Capasso, Diana, tr. see Chesne, Sabrina.

Capatti, Bérénice. Klimt & His Cat. Monaco, Octavia, illus. (p. 963)

Capcom. Dragon's Dogma: Official Design Works: Official Design Works. (p. 479)

CAPCOM. Miles Edgworth Files Vol. 2 (p. 1142)

Capcom Japan Staff. Ace Attorney. Nibley, Alethea, tr. from JPN. (p. 8)

Capcom Japan Staff, jt. auth. see Goikeda, Shin-Ya.

Capdevila, Francesc, illus. see Andersen, Hans Christian.

Capdevila, Francesc, illus. see Bas, Mercè Escardó I & Boada, Francesc.

Capdevila, Francesc, illus. see Chronicle Books Staff.

Capdevila, Juan, et al. Teo en la Escuela (Teo at School) (p. 1720)

Capdevila, Roser, illus. see Ballart, Elisabet.

Capdevila, Roser, illus. see Joly, Fanny.

Capdevila, Roser, jt. auth. see Vendrell, Maria Martinez.

Capdevila, Roser & Vendrell, Maria Martinez. Agua Inquieta. (p. 30)

—Cambios y Distancias. (p. 255)

—Como Duele... (p. 350)

—Conflictos de Ana. (p. 357)

—Hola y Adios. (p. 787)

—Reir y Llorar. (p. 1457)

—Uno Mas. (p. 1822)

Capecl, Anne. Danger! Dynamite! Casale, Paul, illus. (p. 403)

—Daredevils Casale, Paul, illus. (p. 406)

—Food Chain Frenzy. Speirs, John, illus. (p. 613)

—Ghost Train Casale, Paul, illus. (p. 672)

—Little Lab or Horrors. (p. 1030)

—Magic School Bus Chapter Book Food Chain Frenzy. No.17: (p. 1073)

—Missing! Casale, Paul, illus. (p. 1152)

Capeci, Anne, jt. auth. see Cole, Joanna.

Capeci, Anne & Cole, Joanna. Magic School Bus Has a Heart. Bracken, Carolyn, illus. (p. 1073)

—Magic School Bus Rides the Wind, Level 2. Bracken, Carolyn, illus. (p. 1073)

Capehart, Staci. Furry Tails: The Adventures of Mr. Mackie. (p. 650)

Capek, Michael. Battle over Slavery: Causes & Effects of the U.S. Civil War. (p. 147)

—Civil Rights Movement. (p. 325)

—Emperor Qin's Terra Cotta Army. (p. 521)

—Jamaica. (p. 906)

—Secrets of the Terracotta Army: Tomb of an Ancient Chinese Emperor (p. 1546)

—Stonehenge. (p. 1653)

—Understanding Iran Today. (p. 1815)

—Understanding Syria Today. (p. 1816)

—Unsolved Archaeological Mysteries. (p. 1822)

Capelle, Joanna, illus. see Evans, Alwyn & Davis, Anne.

Capello, Dominic, jt. auth. see Schwartz, Pepper.

Caper, William. Alexander the Great: Set Of 6. (p. 36)

—Alexander the Great: Text Pairs. (p. 36)

—American Bison: A Scary Prediction. (p. 60)

—Ancient Greece: Set Of 6. (p. 69)

—Ancient Greece: Text Pairs. (p. 69)

—Ancient Greece: An Interactive History Adventure (p. 69)

—Aztec: Set Of 6. (p. 122)

—Aztec: Text Pairs. (p. 122)

—Challenger Space Shuttle Explosion. (p. 289)

—Florida Panthers: Struggle for Survival. (p. 607)

—Gladiators: A Guide to the Deadly Warriors (p. 682)

—India & China: Set Of 6. (p. 871)

—India & China: Text Pairs. (p. 871)

—Nightmare on the Titanic. (p. 1255)

—Platypus: A Century-Long Mystery. (p. 1370)

—Typhoid Fever: Dirty Food, Dirty Water! (p. 1805)

—U. S. Army Rangers: The Missions (p. 1806)

Capetta, Amy Rose. Entangled. (p. 531)

—Unmade. (p. 1821)

Capici, Gaetano. How Did That Get to My House? Mail. (p. 806)

—What Do They Do? Dentists. (p. 1882)

—What Do They Do? Police Officers. (p. 1882)

—What Does It Do? Bulldozer. (p. 1884)

—What Does It Do? Cement Mixer. (p. 1884)

Capildeo, Vahni. No Traveller Returns. (p. 1260)

Capitelli, Yvonne. Daria Rose & the Day She Chose. Forrester Baldy, Sherri, illus. (p. 406)

Caplan, Frank A. Donkey Who Lost His Tail. (p. 466)

Caplan, Jeremy. Franklin D Roosevelt A Leader in Troubled Times. (p. 630)

Caplan, Jeremy B., told to. Volcanoes! (p. 1849)

Caple, Kathy. Duck & Company. Caple, Kathy, illus. (p. 488)

—Duck & Company Christmas. Caple, Kathy, illus. (p. 488)

—Night at the Zoo. Caple, Kathy, illus. (p. 1252)

—Termite Tales. Caple, Kathy, illus. (p. 1721)

—Termite Trouble: Brand New Readers. Caple, Kathy, illus. (p. 1721)

Caple, Laurie, illus. see Blackford, Cheryl.

Caple, Laurie, illus. see Bushnell, Jack.

Caple, Laurie, illus. see Wargin, Kathy-jo.

Caple, Laurie A., illus. see Meyer, Eileen R.

Caplin, Daniel. Grandfather Turtle. (p. 707)

Capoblanco, Sal, et al. Managing Conflict Dynamics: A Practical Approach. (p. 1086)

Capobianco, Sue Murphy. Buttons the Bunny of Button Cove Lane. (p. 248)

Capon, Brian. Plant Survival: Adapting to a Hostile World. Capon, Brian, illus. (p. 1369)

Capon, Jenny, illus. see Arthur, Felix.

Capone, Deb. Dumplings Are Delicious. Jaskiel, Stan, illus. (p. 490)

—Tooth Fairy Tales. (p. 1768)

—Tooth Fairy Tales Learning & Activity Guide. (p. 1768)

Caponigro, Laureen, illus. see Phillips, Dixie.

Capote, Lori. Monster Knows Math. Wass, Chip, illus. (p. 1167)

—Monster Knows Math [6 X 6]. Wass, Chip, illus. (p. 1167)

—Monster Knows More Than, Less Than Wass, Chip, illus. (p. 1167)

—Monster Knows Numbers Wass, Chip, illus. (p. 1167)

—Monster Knows Patterns Wass, Chip, illus. (p. 1167)

—Monster Knows Shapes Wass, Chip, illus. (p. 1167)

Capotosto, Anthony. No Shoes Required. (p. 1260)

Capozzi, Suzy. Frosty the Snowman Big Golden Book (Frosty the Snowman) Laguna, Fabio & Cagol, Andrea, illus. (p. 645)

Capozzi, Suzy & Finnegan, Delphine. Lady & the Tramp. RH Disney Staff, illus. (p. 970)

Capozziello, Vincent. Planning My Career. (p. 1368)

Capozzola, Christine. Angel from Heaven. Nguyen, Cindy, illus. (p. 73)

Capp, Al. Frazetta Years 1960-1961 (p. 631)

Cappa, Marta. Best Grandpa in the World: Stories from Slumber Village - Story 1. (p. 170)

Cappacio, George. Cancer Treatments. (p. 261)

Cappelli, Frank. Violin. (p. 1843)

Cappellino, Marilyn. Mangia! Macaroni. (p. 1087)

Capper, Ann. Big Thighs, Tight Jeans (Should Jan Go O. (p. 184)

Cappetta, Cynthia. Chairs, Chairs, Chairs! Stromoski, Rick, illus. (p. 288)

Cappo, Nan Willard. Cheating Lessons. (p. 295)

Cappoccia, Héloïse. Planet of the Overhearers. (p. 1368)

Cappoen, Jennifer Tipton, illus. see Dixon, Dallas L.

Cappoen, Jennifer Tipton, illus. see Ghani, Samna.

Cappoen, Jennifer Tipton, illus. see Lawrence, Donna.

Cappoli, Sara, illus. see Jeffrey, Gary.

Cappon, Manuela, illus. see Grant, Neil.

Cappon, Manuela, illus. see Leoni, Cristiana.

Cappon, Manuela, tr. see Grant, Neil.

Capps, Edward. Foundations in Brass: A new age cymbal Tutorial. (p. 624)

Capps, Edward Allen, creator. Cymbal Technique 101: Foundations in Brass. (p. 397)

Capps, Leigh, illus. see Samuel, Lynette M.

Capps, Todd. Ahora Soy Cristiano. (p. 30)

—G-Force Leader Guide. (p. 651)

Caprara, Collette, illus. see Hall, Noelle Chason & Joanne Beeker Clurman.

Caprin, K. F. Adventures of the Little Savages. (p. 23)

Caprio, Pattie, illus. see Lin, Joyce, tr.

Capriola, Arlene & Swensen, Rigmor. US History: Reconstruction to the Present. 8 (p. 1826)

—US History: Colonial Period to the Civil War. 7 (p. 1826)

Capriola, Arlene & Swenson, Rigmor. Ancient Civilizations. (p. 68)

—Six Topics in US History (p. 1583)

Capriolo, Paola. Maria Callas. Scandella, Alessandra, illus. (p. 1093)

Caprio-Scalera, Jill. Gramma's Jammas. Caprio-Scalera, Jill & Edrington, Greg Q., illus. (p. 706)

Capron, André, tr. see Carroll, Lewis, pseud.

Capsey, Steve. Let's Draw Cars. (p. 996)

Capstone Press. Alphabet Fun. (p. 49)

—Animals on the Edge. (p. 83)

—Climate. (p. 332)

—Cool Sports Facts. (p. 364)

—Data Mania. (p. 409)

—Dinosaur Wars (p. 443)

—Dirt Bike World (p. 446)

—Disasters. (p. 447)

—Disgusting History. (p. 450)

—Easy Magic Tricks (p. 500)

—First Graphics: Seasons (p. 595)

—First Graphics: My Community (p. 595)

—Full Throttle (p. 646)

—Green Crafts. (p. 721)

—Hay Numeros en Todas Partes (p. 755)

—Jelly Bear Christmas Surprise (p. 912)

—Joke Books. (p. 924)

—Making & Breaking Codes (p. 1080)

—Nasty (But Useful!) Science. (p. 1230)

—Natural Wonders. (p. 1236)

—Paper Airplanes. (p. 1322)

—Passport to World Sports. (p. 1327)

—People & Culture. (p. 1339)

—Play Like the Pros (p. 1371)

—Poet's Toolbox: Set of 4 (p. 1376)

—Real World Math (p. 1449)

—Scary Stories (p. 1520)

—Shark Zone. (p. 1562)

—Spot It. (p. 1633)

—Star Biographies (p. 1640)

—Strange but True. (p. 1664)

—Truth & Rumors Fall 2010 (p. 1794)

—Ultimate Pro Team Guides (p. 1809)

—Unusual Histories. (p. 1823)

—Vampires. (p. 1832)

—Voices of War. (p. 1848)

—Wild Outdoors. (p. 1930)

—Wildcats. (p. 1931)

—Working Dogs. (p. 1952)

—You Choose: Warriors. (p. 1975)

—You Choose Books. (p. 1975)

—Zoo Animal Mysteries. (p. 1988)

Capstone Press Editors. Story of Orion: A Roman Constellation Myth Guerlais, Gérald, illus. (p. 1659)

Capstone Press Editors, jt. auth. see Adamson, Thomas K.

Capstone Press Editors, jt. auth. see Andersen, Hans Christian.

Capstone Press Editors, jt. auth. see Blevins, Wiley.

Capstone Press Editors, jt. auth. see Botzakis, Stergios.

Capstone Press Editors, jt. auth. see Braulick, Carrie A.

Capstone Press Editors, jt. auth. see Doeden, Matt.

Capstone Press Editors, jt. auth. see Endres, Hollie J.

Capstone Press Editors, jt. auth. see Gianopoulos, Andrea.

Capstone Press Editors, jt. auth. see Giglio, Judy.

Capstone Press Editors, jt. auth. see Hollander, Cass.

Capstone Press Editors, jt. auth. see Jones, Jen.

Capstone Press Editors, jt. auth. see Leber, Nancy.

Capstone Press Editors, jt. auth. see Lindeen, Carol K.

Capstone Press Editors, jt. auth. see Lindeen, Mary.

Capstone Press Editors, jt. auth. see Mader, Jan.

Capstone Press Editors, jt. auth. see Michaels, Eric.

Capstone Press Editors, jt. auth. see Miller, Connie Colwell.

Capstone Press Editors, jt. auth. see O'Shei, Tim.

Capstone Press Editors, jt. auth. see Olson, Nathan.

Capstone Press Editors, jt. auth. see Perkins, Wendy.

Capstone Press Editors, jt. auth. see Rake, Jody Sullivan.

Capstone Press Editors, jt. auth. see Rose, Emma.

Capstone Press Editors, jt. auth. see Sandvold, Lynnette B.

Capstone Press Editors, jt. auth. see Schuette, Sarah L.

Capstone Press Editors, jt. auth. see Schwartz, Heather E.

Capstone Press Editors, jt. auth. see Spengler, Kremena T.

Capstone Press Editors, jt. auth. see Wan, Guofang.

Capstone Press Editors & Rake, Jody Sullivan. Jack Russell Terriers Saunders-Smith, Gail, ed. (p. 903)

Capstone Press Geography Department Staff. Illinois. (p. 857)

Capstone Press Staff. Flood Vila, Alvaro F., illus. (p. 605)

—Follow the Drinking Gourd: An Underground Railroad Story Squier, Robert, illus. (p. 612)

—John Henry - Hammerin' Hero. Evergreen, Nelson, illus. (p. 922)

—Johnny Appleseed Millet, Jason, illus. (p. 923)

—Legend of Johnny Appleseed. Lamoreaux, Michelle, illus. (p. 988)

—Pecos Bill, Colossal Cowboy. Weber, Lisa K., illus. (p. 1334)

—Rapunzel. Timmins, Jeffrey Stewart, illus. (p. 1439)

—Shivers, Wishes, & Wolves: Stone Arch Fairy Tales, Volume One Dietrich, Sean et al., illus. (p. 1567)

—Sleeping Beauty. Dietrich, Sean, illus. (p. 1589)

—Snow White. Valdez Y Alanis, Erik, illus. (p. 1599)

—Story of Cassiopeia: A Roman Constellation Myth Squier, Robert, illus. (p. 1657)

—Story of Ursa Major & Ursa Minor: A Roman Constellation Myth Guerlais, Gérald, illus. (p. 1662)

—Tall Tale of Paul Bunyan. Blecha, Aaron, illus. (p. 1704)

—Three Little Pigs. Blecha, Aaron, illus. (p. 1742)

Capstone Press Staff, jt. auth. see Adamson, Thomas K.

Capstone Press Staff, jt. auth. see Adil, Janeen R.

Capstone Press Staff, jt. auth. see Albee, Jo.

Capstone Press Staff, jt. auth. see Andersen, Hans Christian.

Capstone Press Staff, jt. auth. see Andersen, Nell.

Capstone Press Staff, jt. auth. see Anderson, Nell.

Capstone Press Staff, jt. auth. see Benjamin, Rachel.

Capstone Press Staff, jt. auth. see Benton, Allie.

Capstone Press Staff, jt. auth. see Benton, Celia.

Capstone Press Staff, jt. auth. see Blevins, Wiley.

Capstone Press Staff, jt. auth. see Boten, Wallace.

Capstone Press Staff, jt. auth. see Boynton, Bibl.

Capstone Press Staff, jt. auth. see Braulick, Carrie A.

Capstone Press Staff, jt. auth. see Cannon, Shannon.

Capstone Press Staff, jt. auth. see Chapman, Cindy.

Capstone Press Staff, jt. auth. see Cherrington, Janelle.

Capstone Press Staff, jt. auth. see Coleman, Lori.

Capstone Press Staff, jt. auth. see DeGezelle, Terri.

Capstone Press Staff, jt. auth. see Doeden, Matt.

Capstone Press Staff, jt. auth. see Donovan, Barbara A.

Capstone Press Staff, jt. auth. see Endres, Hollie J.

Capstone Press Staff, jt. auth. see Englar, Mary.

Capstone Press Staff, jt. auth. see Giglio, Judy.

Capstone Press Staff, jt. auth. see Johnson, Tami.

Capstone Press Staff, jt. auth. see Jones, Jen.

Capstone Press Staff, jt. auth. see Josephs, Ben.

Capstone Press Staff, jt. auth. see Kras, Sara Louise.

Capstone Press Staff, jt. auth. see Leber, Nancy.

Capstone Press Staff, jt. auth. see Levin, Amy.

Capstone Press Staff, jt. auth. see Lindeen, Carol K.

Capstone Press Staff, jt. auth. see Lindeen, Mary.

Capstone Press Staff, jt. auth. see Mader, Jan.

Capstone Press Staff, jt. auth. see Mann, Rachel.

Capstone Press Staff, jt. auth. see Martin, Michael.

Capstone Press Staff, jt. auth. see Miller, Connie Colwell.

Capstone Press Staff, jt. auth. see O'Shei, Tim.

Capstone Press Staff, jt. auth. see Olson, Nathan.

Capstone Press Staff, jt. auth. see Perkins, Wendy.

Capstone Press Staff, jt. auth. see Ray, Liz.

Capstone Press Staff, jt. auth. see Riehecky, Janet.

Capstone Press Staff, jt. auth. see Robbins, Trina.

Capstone Press Staff, jt. auth. see Rose, Emma.

Capstone Press Staff, jt. auth. see Rusch, Elizabeth.

Capstone Press Staff, jt. auth. see Sautter, Aaron.

Capstone Press Staff, jt. auth. see Schuette, Sarah L.

Capstone Press Staff, jt. auth. see Schwartz, Heather E.

Capstone Press Staff, jt. auth. see Shores, Lori.

Capstone Press Staff, jt. auth. see Shulman, Lisa.

Capstone Press Staff, jt. auth. see Somervill, Barbara A.

Capstone Press Staff, jt. auth. see Sullivan, Jody.

Capstone Press Staff, jt. auth. see Tagliaferro, Linda.

Capstone Press Staff, jt. auth. see Thales, Sharon.

Capstone Press Staff, jt. auth. see Tu, Alice.

Capstone Press Staff, jt. auth. see VanVoorst, Jennifer.

Capstone Press Staff, jt. auth. see Wade, Mary Dodson.

Capstone Press Staff, jt. auth. see Wan, Guofang.

Capstone Press Staff, jt. auth. see Watson, Yolanda.

Capstone Press Staff & Gwynne, Alexander. Robot Rumble (p. 1480)

Capstone Press Staff & Rustad, Martha E. H. Little Scientist (p. 1036)

Capstone Press Staff & Time for Kids Magazine Staff. Little Kids Book of Why (p. 1029)

Capstone Press Staff, et al. Easy to Draw Monsters Cerato, Mattia & Ho, Jannie, illus. (p. 500)

—Famous Firsts (p. 569)

—Little Paleontologist (p. 1033)

—Ultimate Kids' Guide to Fun: Experiments, Projects, Games & Fascinating Facts Every Kid Should Know (p. 1809)

Capstone Publishing, creator. Exploring Materials: Glass Set. (p. 552)

Capt, E. Raymond. Isle of Iona. (p. 893)

Captain, Cliff. Fables by the Sea (p. 559)

Captain, Tamira. When Do You Grow? Thorne, Sean, illus. (p. 1902)

Captured Light Distribution, jt. creator see Chasse, Betsy.

Capua, Sarah De. Life Skills Biographics. (p. 1013)

Capuccio, Elena. Vincent Cleans His Room with the Creature. (p. 1842)

—Vincent Meets the Creature. (p. 1842)

Capucilli, Alyssa Satin. Biscuit. Schories, Pat, illus. (p. 193)

—Biscuit & the Baby. Schories, Pat, illus. (p. 193)

—Biscuit & the Little Pup. Schories, Pat, illus. (p. 193)

—Biscuit & the Lost Teddy Bear. Schories, Pat, illus. (p. 193)

—Biscuit Feeds the Pets. Schories, Pat, illus. (p. 193)

—Biscuit Gives a Gift. Schories, Pat, illus. (p. 193)

—Biscuit Goes Camping. Schories, Pat, illus. (p. 193)

—Biscuit Goes to School. Schories, Pat, illus. (p. 193)

—Biscuit in the Garden. (p. 193)

—Biscuit in the Garden. Schories, Pat, illus. (p. 193)

—Biscuit Is Thankful. Schories, Pat, illus. (p. 193)

—Biscuit Loves Father's Day. Schories, Pat & Young, Mary O'Keefe, illus. (p. 193)

—Biscuit Loves Mother's Day. Schories, Pat & Young, Mary O'Keefe, illus. (p. 193)

—Biscuit Loves School. Schories, Pat, illus. (p. 193)

—Biscuit Loves the Library. (p. 193)

—Biscuit Loves the Library. Schories, Pat, illus. (p. 193)

—Biscuit Meets the Class Pet. (p. 193)

—Biscuit Meets the Class Pet. Schories, Pat, illus. (p. 193)

—Biscuit Phonics Fun. Schories, Pat, illus. (p. 193)

—Biscuit Plays Ball. (p. 193)

—Biscuit Plays Ball. Schories, Pat, illus. (p. 193)

—Biscuit Storybook Collection. Schories, Pat, illus. (p. 193)

—Biscuit Takes a Walk. Schories, Pat, illus. (p. 193)

—Biscuit Visits the Big City. (p. 193)

—Biscuit Visits the Big City. Schories, Pat, illus. (p. 193)

—Biscuit Visits the Doctor. Berlin, Rose Mary & Schories, Pat, illus. (p. 193)

—Biscuit Visits the Pumpkin Patch. Schories, Pat, illus. (p. 193)

—Biscuit Wins a Prize. Schories, Pat, illus. (p. 193)

—Biscuit's 100th Day of School. Young, Mary O'Keefe & Schories, Pat, illus. (p. 193)

—Biscuit's 123. Schories, Pat & Berlin, Rose Mary, illus. (p. 193)

—Biscuit's ABC Adventure. Wenzel, David T. & Schories, Pat, illus. (p. 193)

—Biscuit's ABCs. Schories, Pat, illus. (p. 193)

—Biscuit's Big Field Trip. Schories, Pat, illus. (p. 193)

—Biscuit's Big Friend. Schories, Pat, illus. (p. 193)

—Biscuit's Birthday. Schories, Pat, illus. (p. 193)

—Biscuit's Christmas Eve. Schories, Pat, illus. (p. 193)

—Biscuit's Christmas Storybook Collection. Schories, Pat, illus. (p. 193)

—Biscuit's Day at the Farm. (p. 193)

—Biscuit's Day at the Farm. Schories, Pat, illus. (p. 193)

—Biscuit's Earth Day Celebration. Wenzel, David T. & Schories, Pat, illus. (p. 193)

—Biscuit's First Beach Day. Schories, Pat, illus. (p. 193)

—Biscuit's First Sleepover. Schories, Pat & Berlin, Rose Mary, illus. (p. 193)

—Biscuit's First Trip. (p. 193)

—Biscuit's First Trip. Berlin, Rose Mary & Schories, Pat, illus. (p. 193)

—Biscuit's Hanukkah. Schories, Pat & Young, Mary O'Keefe, illus. (p. 193)

—Biscuit's Pet & Play Christmas. Schories, Pat & Young, Mary O'Keefe, illus. (p. 193)

—Biscuit's Pet & Play Easter. Berlin, Rose Mary & Schories, Pat, illus. (p. 193)

—Biscuit's Pet & Play Halloween. Andreasen, Dan & Schories, Pat, illus. (p. 193)

—Biscuit's Show & Share Day. Schories, Pat & Young, Mary O'Keefe, illus. (p. 193)

—Biscuit's Snowy Day. Schories, Pat & Young, Mary O'Keefe, illus. (p. 193)

—Bizcocho Encuentra un Amigo. Pastemac, Susana, tr. (p. 194)

—Hannah Is a Big Sister. Stott, Dorothy, illus. (p. 742)

—Henry Is a Big Brother. Stott, Dorothy, illus. (p. 768)

—Katy Duck. Cole, Henry, illus. (p. 945)

—Katy Duck & the Tip-Top Tap Shoes. Cole, Henry, illus. (p. 945)

—Katy Duck & the Tip-Top Tap Shoes. (p. 946)

—Katy Duck, Big Sister. Cole, Henry, illus. (p. 946)

—Katy Duck Board Book 4-Pack: Katy Duck; Katy Duck, Big Sister; Katy Duck, Center Stage; Katy Duck, Dance Star. Cole, Henry, illus. (p. 946)

—Katy Duck, Center Stage. Cole, Henry, illus. (p. 946)

—Katy Duck, Dance Star. Cole, Henry, illus. (p. 946)

—Katy Duck, Dance Star/Katy Duck, Center Stage. Cole, Henry, illus. (p. 946)

—Katy Duck, Flower Girl. Cole, Henry, illus. (p. 946)

—Katy Duck Goes to Work. (p. 946)

—Katy Duck Goes to Work. Cole, Henry, illus. (p. 946)

—Katy Duck Makes a Friend. Cole, Henry, illus. (p. 946)

—Katy Duck Meets the Babysitter. Cole, Henry, illus. (p. 946)

—Katy Duck Ready-To-Read Value Pack: Starring Katy Duck; Katy Duck Makes a Friend; Katy Duck Meets the Babysitter; Katy Duck & the Tip-Tap Shoes; Katy Duck, Flower Girl; Katy Duck Goes to Work. Cole, Henry, illus. (p. 946)

—Katy Duck's Happy Halloween. Cole, Henry, illus. (p. 946)

—Meet Biscuit! Schories, Pat, illus. (p. 1120)

C

For book reviews, descriptive annotations, tables of contents, cover images, author biographies & additional information, updated daily, subscribe to www.booksinprint2.com

2119

—Mind Your Manners, Biscuit! Schories, Pat & Young, Mary O'Keefe, illus. (p. 1145)
—Monkey Play. (p. 1165)
—Mrs. McTats & Her Houseful of Cats. Rankin, Joan E. & Rankin, Joan, illus. (p. 1187)
—My Dad & Me. Mitchell, Susan, illus. (p. 1200)
—My First Ballet Class: A Book with Foldout Pages. Jensen, Leyah, illus. (p. 1204)
—My First Gymnastics Class: A Book with Foldout Pages. Hanifin, Laura, photos by. (p. 1206)
—My First Karate Class: A Book with Foldout Pages. Jensen, Leyah, photos by. (p. 1207)
—My First Soccer Game: A Book with Foldout Pages. Jensen, Leyah, photos by. (p. 1208)
—My Mom & Me. Mitchell, Susan, illus. (p. 1214)
—Not This Bear: A First Day of School Story. Hussey, Lorna, illus. (p. 1267)
—Panda Kisses. Widdowson, Kay, illus. (p. 1320)
—Pedro's Burro. Estrada, Pau, illus. (p. 1334)
—Reading Is Fun with Biscuit: Biscuit; Biscuit Wants to Play; Biscuit Finds a Friend. Schories, Pat, illus. (p. 1446)
—Scat, Cat! Meisel, Paul, illus. (p. 1521)
—Starring Katy Duck. Cole, Henry, illus. (p. 1642)
—Tulip & Rex Write a Story. Massini, Sarah, illus. (p. 1796)
—Tulip Loves Rex. Massini, Sarah, illus. (p. 1796)
—Where Is Love, Biscuit? A Pet & Play Book. Berlin, Rose Mary & Schories, Pat, illus. (p. 1908)
Capucilli, Alyssa Satin, jt. auth. see Estrada, Pau.
Capucilli, Alyssa Satin, jt. auth. see Schories, Pat.
Capucilli, Alyssa Satin & Cole, Henry. Katy Duck Is a Caterpillar. (p. 946)
—Katy Duck Makes a Friend. (p. 946)
Capullo, Greg & Robertson, Darick. X-Force: Assault on Graymalkin. (p. 1967)
Capus, Stephen, tr. see Marshak, Samuil.
Caputo, Antonella, illus. see Henry, O., et al.
Caputo, Antonella, et al. Edgar Allan Poe's Tales of Mystery. Pomplun, Tom, ed. (p. 504)
Caputo, Christine A. Birds. (p. 191)
—Fish. (p. 598)
—Insects & Spiders. (p. 876)
—Mammals. (p. 1085)
—Oil Spills. (p. 1282)
—Reptiles & Amphibians. (p. 1461)
Caputo, Frank. Adventures of Jimmy Farrell & the Magic Red Ring. (p. 19)
Caputo, James, illus. see Florence, Debbi Michiko.
Caputo, Jim, illus. see Castaldo, Nancy F.
Caputo, Jim, illus. see Chmielewski, Gary.
Caputo, Jim, illus. see Florence, Debbi Michiko.
Caputo, Jim, illus. see Littlefield, Cindy A.
Caputo, Kenneth. Adventures of Jay & Tay: Our First Karate Class. (p. 19)
Caraballo, Samuel. Estas Manos: Manitas de Mi Familia. Costello, Shawn, illus. (p. 538)
—Mis abuelos y yo / My Grandparents & I. Brammer, Ethriam Cash, tr. (p. 1149)
—Mis Papitos: Heroes de la Cosecha. Gomez, Obed, illus. (p. 1150)
—My Big Sister / Mi Hermana Mayor. Muraida, Thelma, illus. (p. 1197)
Caraballo, Samuel & Torrecilla, Pablo. Estrellita in the Big City/Estrellita en la Ciudad Grande. Caraballo, Samuel & Torrecilla, Pablo, illus. (p. 538)
Carabelli, Francesca, illus. see Aboff, Marcie & Shaskan, Trisha Speed.
Carabelli, Francesca, illus. see Aboff, Marcie.
Carabelli, Francesca, illus. see Blaisdell, Molly.
Carabelli, Francesca, illus. see Shaskan, Trisha Speed.
Carabelli, Francesca, illus. see Stampler, Ann Redisch.
Carabelli, Francesca, illus. see Wax, Wendy A. & Wax, Naomi.
Carabine, Sue & Adams, Jennifer. Christmas in Idaho. Kawasaki, Shauna Mooney, illus. (p. 314)
Carabine, Sue & Smith, Johanna. Night Before Christmas in Michigan. Kawasaki, Shauna Mooney, illus. (p. 1253)
Caraboolad, Arla. Tommy Tortoise Gets the Sugar Blues. Mancell, Doris, illus. (p. 1765)
Caracappa, Michael. Storybook: From Age Three to Young Teenager. (p. 1663)
Caraccilo, Dominic. E-Tailing: Careers Selling over the Web. (p. 492)
Caraccilo, Dominic J. Military Intelligence Technology of the Future. (p. 1143)
Caracino, Leah, illus. see Wilson, Barbara.
Caramagna, Joe. Behind the Mask: Young Readers Novel. (p. 160)
—Iron Man & the Armor Wars. (p. 888)
—Iron Man & the Armor Wars Part 1: Down & Out in Beverly Hills Hosted. (p. 888)
—Iron Man & the Armor Wars Part 2: The Big Red Machine. (p. 888)
—Iron Man & the Armor Wars Part 3: How I Learned to Love the Bomb. (p. 888)
—Iron Man & the Armor Wars Part 4: The Golden Avenger Strikes Back. (p. 888)
—Marvel Universe Avengers Assemble Volume 1. (p. 1099)
Caramagna, Joe, jt. auth. see Eliopoulos, Chris.
Caramagna, Joe, text. Amazing Spider-Man. (p. 55)
—Amazing Spider-Man - Vulture: Young Readers Novel. (p. 56)
—Hulk & the Agents of S. M. A. S. H. (p. 825)
Caran, Rick. Jilli Dog - the Little Dog That Made Mr. Kranby Smile. Caran, Rick, illus. (p. 917)
Carangelo, Audrey. How Unusual! (p. 823)
—On the Street: Poems about Paintings. (p. 1291)
Carangelo, Audrey & Hess, Debra. Radiation, Rats, & Mutant Monsters! (p. 1432)
—Teenage Plant Food. (p. 1714)
Caratsev, Serghei I., et al. Teaching & Learning Strategies for the Thinking Classroom: A Career Development Curriculum for Secondary School Students. Shapiro, Susan G., ed. (p. 1710)
Caravan, Jill. Pandas: A Portrait of the Animal World. (p. 1321)
Caravan Studios Staff, jt. auth. see Valois, Rob.
Caravantes, Peggy. American in Texas: The Story of Sam Houston. (p. 61)
—Battle of the Alamo: A History Perspectives Book. (p. 146)
—Best of Times: The Story of Charles Dickens. (p. 171)
—Cleopatra: Powerful Leader or Ruthless Pharaoh? (p. 331)
—Daughters of Two Nations. Flores, Carolyn Dee, illus. (p. 410)
—French & Indian War. (p. 635)
—Great & Sublime Fool: The Story of Mark Twain. (p. 713)
—Hurricane Katrina. (p. 829)
—Hurricane Katrina Paperback. (p. 830)
—Many Faces of Josephine Baker: Dancer, Singer, Activist, Spy. (p. 1089)
—Marcus Garvey: Black Nationalist. (p. 1092)
—O. Henry: William Sidney Porter: Texas Cowboy Writer. (p. 1274)
—Orphan Trains: A History Perspectives Book. (p. 1304)
—Petticoat Spies: Six Women Spies of the US Civil War. (p. 1348)
—Waging Peace: The Story of Jane Addams. (p. 1852)
—Writing Is My Business: The Story of O. Henry. (p. 1965)
Caravela, Elena, illus. see Italia, John.
Caravela, Elena, illus. see Kraus, Joanna H.
Caraway, James, illus. see Friedman, Estelle.
Carayannis, Elias G. & Sipp, Caroline M. E-Development Towards the Knowledge Economy: Leveraging Technology, Innovation & Entrepreneursip for 'Smart' Development. (p. 492)
Carbajal, Diego, illus. see Dorn, Susy.
Carbajal, Richard, illus. see Amstel, Marsha.
Carbajal, Richard, illus. see Brill, Marlene Targ.
Carbajal, Richard, illus. see Figley, Marthy Rhodes & Figley, Marty Rhodes.
Carbajal, Richard, illus. see Figley, Marty Rhodes.
Carbajal, Richard, illus. see Littlefield, Holly.
Carbajal, Richard, illus. see Neusner, Dena.
Carbajal, Richard, illus. see Patrick, Jean L. S.
Carbajal, Richard, illus. see Ransom, Candice.
Carbajal, Richard Pimentel, illus. see Amstel, Marsha.
Carbajal, Richard Pimentel, illus. see Brill, Marlene Targ.
Carbajal, Richard Pimentel, illus. see Figley, Marty Rhodes.
Carbajal, Richard Pimentel, illus. see Ransom, Candice.
Carballeira, Paula. Paco. Barrio, Blanca, illus. (p. 1317)
Carbaugh, Sam, illus. see Ceceri, Kathy.
Carbaugh, Sam, illus. see Formichelli, Linda & Martin, W. Eric.
Carbaugh, Samuel, illus. see Bardos, Laszlo C.
Carbaugh, Samuel, illus. see Formichelli, Linda, et al.
Carbaugh, Samuel, illus. see Gardner, Jane P.
Carbaugh, Samuel, illus. see Mooney, Carla.
Carbaugh, Samuel, illus. see Reilly, Kathleen M.
Carberry, Edward. Glassblowing: An Introduction to Artistic & Scientific Flameworking. (p. 682)
Carberry, Marie. This Is My House! (p. 1736)
Carbon, Sally & Langer, Justin. I Want to Be a Cricketer. Gollan, Stewart, illus. (p. 847)
Carbone, Courtney. Amazing Animals (the World of Eric Carle) (p. 53)
—Best in Show! (Disney Princess: Palace Pets) RH Disney Staff, illus. (p. 170)
—Disney Princess Joke Book (Disney Princess) RH Disney Staff et al, illus. (p. 452)
—Flower Power! (DC Super Friends) Schoening, Dan, illus. (p. 607)
—Food Fight! (p. 613)
—Food Fight! Random House Editors & Aikins, Dave, illus. (p. 613)
—Forever a Princess (Disney Princess) RH Disney Staff, illus. (p. 619)
—Half-Shell Heroes! (Teenage Mutant Ninja Turtles) Golden Books Staff & Sciarrone, Claudio, illus. (p. 737)
—Happy Easter, Princess! RH Disney Staff, illus. (p. 745)
—Heart of a Hero (DC Super Friends) Golden Books, illus. (p. 759)
—Holiday Hearts (Disney Princess) RH Disney Staff, illus. (p. 788)
—How to Be a Princess (Disney Princess) RH Disney Staff, illus. (p. 814)
—Ice Box. RH Disney Staff, illus. (p. 850)
—In the Game! (Disney Infinity) RH Disney Staff, illus. (p. 866)
—Julius Jr. Story Collection. Golden Books, illus. (p. 933)
—Monster Mania! RH Disney Staff, illus. (p. 1167)
—Monster of Sodor. (p. 1168)
—Monster of Sodor (Thomas & Friends) Courtney, Richard, illus. (p. 1168)
—Palace Pets: Snuggle Buddies. (p. 1319)
—Pet Friends Forever! (p. 1345)
—Power-Packed! (DC Super Friends) Golden Books, illus. (p. 1390)
—Rescue Buddies! (Disney Planes: Fire & Rescue) RH Disney Staff, illus. (p. 1462)
—Royal Runway! (Disney Princess) RH Disney Staff, illus. (p. 1492)
—School Daze/Monster Party! (Disney/Pixar Monsters, Inc. ; Disney/Pixar Monsters University) RH Disney Staff, illus. (p. 1522)
—Snow Day! (p. 1598)
—Snow Day! (Frosty the Snowman) Random House, illus. (p. 1598)
—Snuggle Buddies. RH Disney Staff, illus. (p. 1601)
—Somebunny Special (SpongeBob SquarePants) Golden Books Staff, illus. (p. 1609)
—SpongeBob Movie Tie-In Deluxe Step into Reading (SpongeBob SquarePants) Random House Editors & Aikins, Dave, illus. (p. 1630)
—Star Wars: the Phantom Menace (Star Wars) Martinez, Heather, illus. (p. 1642)
Carbone, Courtney, jt. auth. see Golden Books Staff.
Carbone, Courtney, jt. auth. see Random House Staff.
Carbone, Courtney, jt. auth. see RH Disney Staff.
Carbone, Courtney & Hands, Cynthia. Thrills & Chills! RH Disney Staff, illus. (p. 1744)
—Troll Magic. RH Disney Staff, illus. (p. 1788)
Carbone, Elisa. Blood on the River: James Town 1607. (p. 200)
—Heroes of the Surf. Carpenter, Nancy, illus. (p. 773)
—Pack. (p. 1317)
—Stealing Freedom. (p. 1646)
Carbone, Elisa & Lewis, Earl B. Night Running. (p. 1254)
Carbone, Peter W. Ben the Raindrop: Strength in Leadership. (p. 163)
Carbonel, Paula & Carbonell, Paula. Butterfly Trip. (p. 248)
Carbonell, Mels. Extreme Personality Makeover: How to Develop a Winning Christ-Like Personality to Improve Your Effectiveness. (p. 556)
—So, You're Unique! What's Your Point? (p. 1602)
Carbonell, Oliver. Peter Learns to Ride His Bicycle. (p. 1346)
Carbonell, Paula, jt. auth. see Carbonel, Paula.
Carbonell-Matela, Anna. Whitaker Farm. (p. 1912)
Card, Melanie. Ward Against Darkness. (p. 1858)
Card, Michael. Tell Me Why: Eternal Answers to Children's Timeless Questions. (p. 1717)
Card, Orson Scott. Ender's Game: Response Journal. (p. 527)
—First Meetings: In the Ender Universe. (p. 596)
—Pathfinder. (p. 1328)
—Pathfinder & Ruins: Pathfinder; Ruins. (p. 1328)
—Ruins. (p. 1494)
—Shadow of the Giant. (p. 1557)
—Stonefather. Kidd, Tom, illus. (p. 1653)
Card, Orson Scott, jt. auth. see Chiang, D.
Card, Orson Scott, et al. Great Snape Debate: Is Snape Innocent or Guilty? (p. 718)
Card, Vanessa, illus. see Brown, Alan & Seaman, Alison.
Card, Vanessa, illus. see Ganeri, Anita.
Cardaci, Diane. Realistic Textures: Discover Your Inner Artist as You Explore the Basic Theories & Techniques of Pencil Drawing. (p. 1449)
Cardarelli, Alyn. Captain Virtue & the Champions of Justice. (p. 264)
Cardarelli, Mario. Bunny, an Orphan's Story. (p. 242)
—Kid Jack Adventures: Prevent Bullying. (p. 951)
Cardemil, Carmen, illus. see del Rio, Ana Maria.
Cardemil, Carmen, illus. see Delgado, Luis Cabrera.
Cardemil, Carmen, illus. see Morábito, Fabio.
Cardemil, Carmen, illus. see Schkolnik, Saul.
Carden, Kathleen A. & Godley-Sugrue, Mary. Week-by-Week Lessons: Standards-Based Lessons That Guide Students Through the Writing Process, Teach Conventions, Explore Genres, & Help Second Graders Write Effective Sentences, Paragraphs, & Essays. (p. 1871)
Cardenas, Ernesto A. Amazing Animals. (p. 53)
—Animal World. (p. 80)
—Baby, Mom, & Dad. (p. 127)
—Bee Is an Insect. (p. 157)
—Bodies of Water. (p. 206)
—Butterflies. (p. 247)
—Five Senses. (p. 601)
—Four Seasons of the Year. (p. 625)
—Frogs & Toads. (p. 641)
—Habitats. (p. 734)
—Healthy Habits. (p. 758)
—I Will Grow Strong & Healthy! (p. 848)
—Insects. (p. 875)
—Learn about Plants. (p. 982)
—Legs. (p. 991)
—Liquid or Solid? (p. 1021)
—Measurement. (p. 1117)
—Mixtures & Solutions. (p. 1156)
—Natural Resources. (p. 1235)
—Oceans. (p. 1277)
—Rocks. (p. 1483)
—Science Lab. (p. 1526)
—Soils. (p. 1606)
—Sounds. (p. 1615)
—Spring, Summer, Fall, & Winter. (p. 1635)
—Textures. (p. 1724)
—Two by Two. (p. 1803)
—Vegetables for Me! (p. 1834)
—Water Cycle. (p. 1862)
—Weather. (p. 1869)
—What Do You Use to Measure? (p. 1883)
—What Does A Scientist Use? (p. 1884)
—What Is Matter? (p. 1889)
—What Is the Weather Like Today? (p. 1890)
—Wheels & Motors. (p. 1901)
—Where Does Fruit Come From? (p. 1907)
—Wholes & Parts. (p. 1920)
—Wind. (p. 1935)
—With My Senses. (p. 1942)
—Wood or Paper? (p. 1949)
Cardenas, Ernesto & Saavedra, Patricia. estado del Tiempo. (p. 538)
—laboratorio de Ciencias. (p. 969)
—Medición. (p. 1119)
—Qué es la Materia? (p. 1423)
—Recursos Naturales. (p. 1452)
—Rocas. (p. 1481)
Cardenas, Patricia Karla, illus. see Hernandez, Georgina.
Cardenas, Patricia Karla Marquez, illus. see Hernandez, Georgina.
Cardenas, Teresa. Oloyou. Amado, Elisa, tr. from SPA. (p. 1287)
Carder, Ken, jt. auth. see Thompson, Kim.
Carder, Ken & LaRoy, Sue. Kindergarten: Ages 5-6. Johnson, Mike et al, illus. (p. 957)
Cardero, Patrick & JFA Productions Staff. Hello It's Me: An Ineterview with God. (p. 764)
Cardi, Annie. Chance You Won't Return. (p. 289)
Cardie, John P. How to Beat Granddad at Checkers. Murr, Bob, illus. (p. 815)
Cardillo, Joseph. Be Like Water: Practical Wisdom from the Martial Arts. (p. 148)
Cardillo, Linda. Smallest Christmas Tree. Cardillo, Linda & Albert, Dar, illus. (p. 1592)
Cardillo, Margaret. Just Being Audrey. Denos, Julia, illus. (p. 938)
Cardin, Beth W. Little Red Leaf. (p. 1035)
Cardin, Jodi. Bernice's Bad Hair Days. Chin, Todd, illus. (p. 167)
Cardinal, Daniel, et al. Epistemology: The Theory of Knowledge. (p. 532)
Cardinal, John, illus. see Pinder, Eric.
Cardinale, Christopher, illus. see Lyon, George Ella.
Cardno, Anthony R. Firflake: A Christmas Story. Cornue, Don, illus. (p. 592)
Cardon, Jenny Wilding. Little Box of Baby Quilts. (p. 1025)
Cardon, Laurent, illus. see Machado, Ana Maria.
Cardon, Laurent, illus. see Taylor, Sean.
Cardona, Jose. Mulan (Disney Princess) Golden Books, illus. (p. 1189)
Cardona, Jose, illus. see Hapka, Catherine, pseud.
Cardona, Jose, illus. see Poindexter, Katherine & RH Disney Staff.
Cardona, Nancy. Beethoven. Swope, Brenda, illus. (p. 158)
Cardoni, Paolo, illus. see Lebscky, Ibi.
Cardonick, Isabell, jt. auth. see Feldgus, Eileen G.
Cardoso, Kelly. Thomas & the Toad King. DeBroeck, Sarah, illus. (p. 1738)
Cardoso, Onelio Jorge. Caballito Blanco. (p. 250)
Cardoza, Kristina. Pinky Bunny's First Day of Kindergarten. (p. 1360)
Carducci, Barbara Simpson. Storee Wryter Gets a Dog. (p. 1654)
Carducci, Bernardo J. & Fields, Teesue H. Shyness Workbook for Teens. (p. 1572)
Carduff, Christopher, ed. see Maxwell, William.
Cardwell, Helen. Amber Janusson: Protector of the Magic Lands. (p. 57)
—Amber Janusson & the Battle for the Magic Lands. (p. 57)
Cardwell, Michelle. Seeing the World Through Different Eyes. (p. 1548)
Cardwell, Mike, jt. auth. see Flanagan, Cara.
Cardwell, Mike & Flanagan, Cara. Psychology A2: The Complete Companion. (p. 1413)
—Psychology AS: The Complete Companion. (p. 1413)
—Psychology AS: The Exam Companion AQA 'A' Specification. (p. 1413)
—Psychology AS. (p. 1413)
Cardy, Jason, illus. see Shakespeare, William.
Cardy, Jason, illus. see Shelley, Mary & Shelley, Mary.
Carella, C. J., et al. Buffy the Vampire Slayer Roleplaying Game: Slayer's Handbook. Ferguson, C. Brent, illus. (p. 236)
Carella, C.J. Buffy the Vampire Slayer: Core Rulebook. (p. 236)
Carelli, Anne O'Brien. Amina's New Friends. (p. 65)
Carestio, Michael A. Black Jack Jetty: A Boy's Journey Through Grief. (p. 196)
Carew, Kieran. 1 Block Down. Yan, Stan, illus. (p. 1990)
Carew-Miller, Anna. Buddha: Father of Buddhism. (p. 234)
—Buddha. (p. 234)
—Chief Seattle: Great Chief. (p. 301)
—Confucius: Great Chinese Philosopher. (p. 357)
—Famous People of Mexican History. (p. 569)
—Famous People of Mexico. (p. 569)
—Hans Christian Andersen: Denmark's Famous Author. (p. 743)
—Jordan. (p. 925)
—Jordan. (p. 925)
—Ludwig Van Beethoven: Great Composer. (p. 1064)
—Mark Twain: Great American Fiction Writer. (p. 1095)
—Mark Twain. Di Gennaro, Andrea, illus. (p. 1095)
—Native American Confederacies. Johnson, Troy, ed. (p. 1234)
—Native American Cooking. Johnson, Troy, ed. (p. 1234)
—Palestinians. (p. 1320)
—Tunisia. (p. 1797)
—Vital & Creative: The Art & Architecture of Mexico. (p. 1846)
—William Shakespeare: Great English Playwright & Poet. (p. 1933)
Carew-Miller, Anna, jt. auth. see Miller, Anna Carew.
Carey, Anna. Blackbird. (p. 197)
—Boat Guy: Adventure to Shilo Island. (p. 205)
—Deadfall: The Sequel to Blackbird. (p. 417)
—Eve. (p. 541)
—Once. (p. 1292)
—Rebecca Is Always Right. (p. 1450)
—Rise: An Eve Novel. (p. 1474)
—Rise. (p. 1474)
Carey, Barbara. Carey Formula: Your Ideas Are Worth Millions. (p. 268)
Carey, Becky. 47 Strings: Tessa's Special Code. Stidwell O'Boyle, Carrie, ed. (p. 1997)
—Wilma Goes to the Hospital. (p. 1934)
Carey, Benedict. Island of the Unknowns. (p. 892)
—Poison Most Vial: A Mystery. (p. 1377)
—Unknowns: A Mystery. (p. 1821)
Carey, Bill. Fairy Tales for the 21st Century. (p. 564)
Carey, Bob, illus. see Jackson, Emma.
Carey, Cassandra L. Adventures of Uncle Joe: Uncle Joe & His Bear. (p. 24)
Carey, Catherine Elaine. Colorful & Playful Animal Friends (p. 344)
Carey, Charles W. American Revolution. (p. 63)
—Eugene V. Debs: Outspoken Labor Leader & Socialist. (p. 540)
—Kennedy Assassination. (p. 948)
Carey, Charles W., Jr. Emancipation Proclamation. (p. 517)
Carey, Charles W. Jr, ed. American Revolution. (p. 63)
Carey, Edward. Foulsham: The Iremonger Trilogy: Book 2. (p. 624)
—Heap House: The Iremonger Trilogy: Book One. (p. 759)
Carey, Ernestine Gilbreth, jt. auth. see Gilbreth, Frank B., Jr.
Carey, Gary. On Woolf's Mrs. Dalloway. (p. 1292)
Carey, Jacqueline. Godslayer. (p. 692)
Carey, Janet Lee. Beast of Noor. (p. 152)
—Double Life of Zoe Flynn. (p. 473)
—Dragon's Keep. (p. 479)
—Dragonswood. (p. 479)
—In the Time of Dragon Moon. (p. 867)

—Wenny Has Wings. (p. 1875)
Carey, Jennifer, ed. see Norton, O. Richard.
Carey, Joanna, jt. auth. see Wilson, Jacqueline.
Carey, John. Cook Spies. (p. 361)
Carey, John/E, III. Finding Joy Together: Commonsense Tools for a Better Marriage in Thirty Days or Less. (p. 588)
Carey, Joseph, illus. see Carey, Kathleen.
Carey, Katey, illus. see Adams, Peyton.
Carey, Kathleen. Jack Kat Had a Day Carey, Joseph, illus. (p. 903)
Carey, Keelin, et al. Smart Princess: And Other Deaf Tales Halligan, Kelly C. et al, illus. (p. 1593)
Carey, Lorraine. Cinderella's Stepsister & the Big Bad Wolf. Blanco, Migy, illus. (p. 320)
Carey, Louise, jt. auth. see Carey, Mike.
Carey, Mariah, jt. auth. see Cannon, Nick.
Carey, Michael. Little Kathy Likes Karate. Connors, Jackie, ed. (p. 1029)
Carey, Mike. Collision. Mann, Clay, illus. (p. 341)
—Dalliance with the Damned. (p. 401)
—Devil in the Gateway. Hampton, Scott et al, illus. (p. 432)
—Furies. (p. 650)
—God Save the Queen. (p. 690)
—John Constantine, Hellblazer: Red Sepulchre. Palmiotti, Jimmy, illus. (p. 921)
—Lucifer Kelly, Ryan, illus. (p. 1062)
—My Faith in Frankie. (p. 1202)
—Reasons to Be Cheerful. Ruggiero, Lorenzo, illus. (p. 1450)
—X-Men Legacy: Collison. Mann, Clay, illus. (p. 1967)
Carey, Mike & Carey, Louise. Confessions of a Blabbermouth. (p. 356)
Carey, Mike & Fabry, Glenn. Neil Gaiman's Neverwhere. Quitely, Frank, illus. (p. 1240)
Carey, Mike & Fern, Jim. Cut Here Pennington, Mark & Villarrubia, Jose, illus. (p. 396)
Carey, Mike & Kelly, Ryan. Children & Monsters. (p. 302)
Carey, Mike & Maco, Leonardo. All His Engines. (p. 44)
Carey, Mike, text. Second Coming. (p. 1539)
Carey Molter. Ate As in Skate. (p. 111)
Carey, Nicolette & Bryant, Jill. Women Athletes Who Changed the World. (p. 1945)
Carey, Rosa Nouchette. Esther: A Book for Girls. (p. 538)
—Uncle Max. (p. 1812)
Carey-Costa, Denise. Lucky. Sjostrom, Nicole & Iseminger, Jonathan, illus. (p. 1062)
—Tale of Three Tails. Sjostrom, Nicole & Iseminger, Jonathon, illus. (p. 1700)
Cargile, Phillip & Miss Cheryl. Wagon Man: The Untold Story of the Go-Burn Kids. (p. 1852)
Cargill, Chad. Cargill Consulting's ACT Prep. (p. 268)
Cargill, Chad, et al. Cargill Consulting's ACT Prep. (p. 268)
Carhart, Paul M. One of the Girls. (p. 1296)
Caribe Betania Staff, et al. Biblia Juvenil (p. 176)
Caride, Ramon, et al. futuro Robado/ The Rob Future. (p. 651)
Cariello, Sergio, illus. see Dixon, Chuck.
Cariello, Sergio, illus. see Martin, Gary & Rogers, Bud.
Cariello, Sergio, illus. see Martin, Gary & Zondervan Bibles Staff.
Cariello, Sergio, illus. see Martin, Gary & Zondervan Publishing Staff.
Cariello, Sergio, illus. see Martin, Gary, et al.
Cariello, Sergio, illus. see Mauss, Doug, ed.
Cariello, Sergio, illus. see Rogers, Bud & Martin, Gary.
Cariello, Sergio, illus. see Sapp, Brent.
Cariello, Sergio, illus. see Seeling, Caleb.
Cariello, Sergio, et al. Captain America: Hail Hydra. (p. 263)
Carig, Michael. Counting Silly Faces: Numbers Eleven to Twenty. Craig, Michael, illus. (p. 371)
Carigiet, Alois. Bell for Ursli: A Story from the Engadine in Switzerland. (p. 162)
Carillo, Christina. Life Can Be A Smile. (p. 1008)
Carillo, Christina Martin. Come Smile with Me. (p. 347)
—Mr Plaid. (p. 1186)
Carillo, Fred, illus. see Crane, Stephen.
Carillo, Fred, illus. see London, Jack.
Caring, Angela. Becoming Bryn. (p. 156)
Caringella, Rachel, illus. see Borst, Amie & Borst, Bethanie.
Carisse, Carissa, illus. see Singleton, Glynn.
Carithers, Rochelle. Purple with Pink Polka Dot Ponies. Weber, Caressa, illus. (p. 1419)
Carkhuff Jr., Sam. Ranch Race. Crow, Katie, illus. (p. 1438)
Carl And Betty Coggins. Mr Bowbow. (p. 1184)
Carl, Dave. Super Cyclist. Mack, Kathryn, illus. (p. 1679)
Carl, Grandpa. Of Human Bonding by Ducklings: A Duckling's Story of Love. (p. 1279)
Carl, Jean R., jt. auth. see Kelly, Elaine A.
Carl, JoAnna, pseud. Chocolate Bridal Bash (p. 309)
—Chocolate Frog Frame-Up. (p. 309)
—Chocolate Jewel Case. (p. 309)
—Chocolate Mouse Trap. (p. 309)
—Chocolate Puppy Puzzle (p. 309)
—Crime de Cocoa: Three Chocoholic Mysteries. (p. 382)
Carle, Eric. 10 Little Rubber Ducks. Carle, Eric, illus. (p. 1993)
—10 Little Rubber Ducks Board Book. Carle, Eric, illus. (p. 1993)
—Arana Muy Ocupada. Carle, Eric, illus. (p. 94)
—Artist Who Painted a Blue Horse. Carle, Eric, illus. (p. 104)
—Canguro Tiene Mama? Mlawer, Teresa, tr. (p. 261)
—Chenille Qui Fait des Trous. (p. 297)
—Coccinelle Mal Lune. (p. 337)
—Color My World (the World of Eric Carle) Carle, Eric, illus. (p. 343)
—Colors (Colores) (p. 345)
—Count with the Very Hungry Caterpillar. Carle, Eric, illus. (p. 370)
—De la Cabeza a los Pies. Carle, Eric, illus. (p. 416)
—Die kleine Raupe Nimmersatt: Ein Bilderbuch. (p. 437)
—Does a Kangaroo Have a Mother, Too? Carle, Eric, illus. (p. 460)
—Dragons Dragons: And Other Creatuers That Never Were. (p. 479)
—Eric Carle Classics: The Tiny Seed - Pancakes, Pancakes! - Walter the Baker. Carle, Eric, illus. (p. 533)
—Eric Carle Gift Set: The Tiny Seed; Pancakes, Pancakes!; a House for Hermit Crab; Rooster's off to See the World. Carle, Eric, illus. (p. 533)
—Eric Carle Mini Library: A Storybook Gift Set. Carle, Eric, illus. (p. 533)
—Eric Carle Ready-To-Read Collection: Have You Seen My Cat?; the Greedy Python; Pancakes, Pancakes!; Rooster Is off to See the World; a House for Hermit Crab; Walter the Baker. Carle, Eric, illus. (p. 533)
—Eric Carle's ABC. (p. 533)
—Eric Carle's All Around Us. Carle, Eric, illus. (p. 533)
—Eric Carle's Opposites. (p. 533)
—Friends. Carle, Eric, illus. (p. 638)
—From Head to Toe. Carle, Eric, illus. (p. 642)
—From Head to Toe Soft Book. (p. 642)
—Have You Seen My Cat? (p. 754)
—Have You Seen My Cat? Carle, Eric, illus. (p. 754)
—House for Hermit Crab. Carle, Eric, illus. (p. 803)
—How Things Grow. (p. 814)
—Mister Seahorse. Carle, Eric, illus. (p. 1155)
—My Own Very Busy Spider Coloring Book. Carle, Eric, illus. (p. 1216)
—My Own Very Hungry Caterpillar. Carle, Eric, illus. (p. 1216)
—My Own Very Lonely Firefly Coloring Book. Carle, Eric, illus. (p. 1216)
—My Own Very Quiet Cricket Coloring Book. Carle, Eric, illus. (p. 1216)
—My Very First Book of Animal Homes. Carle, Eric, illus. (p. 1221)
—My Very First Book of Animal Sounds. Carle, Eric, illus. (p. 1221)
—My Very First Book of Colors. Carle, Eric, illus. (p. 1221)
—My Very First Book of Food. Carle, Eric, illus. (p. 1221)
—My Very First Book of Numbers. Carle, Eric, illus. (p. 1221)
—My Very First Book of Numbers (Mi Primer Libro de Numeros) Carle, Eric, illus. (p. 1221)
—My Very First Book of Shapes / Mi Primer Libro de Figuras: Bilingual Edition. Carle, Eric, illus. (p. 1221)
—My Very First Book of Words. Carle, Eric, illus. (p. 1221)
—My Very First Library Carle, Eric, illus. (p. 1221)
—Ours Blanc Dis Moi. (p. 1310)
—Pancakes, Pancakes! (p. 1320)
—Pancakes, Pancakes! Carle, Eric, illus. (p. 1320)
—Piccolo Ragno Tesse e Tace. (p. 1354)
—Rabbit & the Turtle. (p. 1429)
—Rooster Is off to See the World. (p. 1488)
—Rooster Is off to See the World. Carle, Eric, illus. (p. 1488)
—Shapes to See, Shapes to Draw! (the World of Eric Carle) Carle, Eric, illus. (p. 1561)
—Shine with the Very Lonely Firefly. Carle, Eric, illus. (p. 1566)
—"Slowly, Slowly, Slowly," Said the Sloth. (p. 1591)
—"Slowly, Slowly, Slowly," Said the Sloth. Carle, Eric, illus. (p. 1591)
—Tiny Seed. Carle, Eric, illus. (p. 1756)
—Very Busy Doodle Book (the World of Eric Carle) Carle, Eric, illus. (p. 1837)
—Very Busy Spider. (p. 1837)
—Very Busy Spider. Carle, Eric, illus. (p. 1837)
—Very Busy Spider's Favorite Words. Carle, Eric, illus. (p. 1837)
—Very Colorful Day (the World of Eric Carle) Carle, Eric, illus. (p. 1837)
—Very Hungry Caterpillar. Carle, Eric, illus. (p. 1838)
—Very Hungry Caterpillar. (p. 1838)
—Very Hungry Caterpillar. Carle, Eric, illus. (p. 1838)
—Very Hungry Caterpillar (La Oruga Muy Hambrienta) Carle, Eric, illus. (p. 1838)
—Very Hungry Caterpillar's Favorite Words. Carle, Eric, illus. (p. 1838)
—Very Hungry Caterpillar's Finger Puppet Book. (p. 1838)
—Very Lonely Firefly. (p. 1838)
—Very Quiet Cricket. Carle, Eric, illus. (p. 1838)
—Walter the Baker. Carle, Eric, illus. (p. 1856)
—What's Your Favorite Animal? Carle, Eric, illus. (p. 1900)
—World of Eric Carle Big Coloring Book (the World of Eric Carle) Carle, Eric, illus. (p. 1956)
Carle, Eric, illus. see Buckley, Richard.
Carle, Eric, illus. see Eric Carle Museum of Picture Book Art Staff.
Carle, Eric, illus. see Martin, Bill, Jr.
Carle, Eric, illus. see Martin, Bill, Jr. & Priddy, Roger.
Carle, Eric, illus. see Singer, Isaac Bashevis.
Carle, Eric, illus. see Sundgaard, Arnold.
Carle, Eric, jt. auth. see Chronicle Books Staff.
Carle, Eric, jt. auth. see Simon, Seymour.
Carle, Eric & Chronicle Books Staff. 1, 2, 3 to the Zoo Train Flash Cards. (p. 1990)
—Animal. (p. 76)
—Animal Lacing Cards. (p. 78)
—String-Alongs. (p. 1667)
—Very Hungry Caterpillar Lacing Cards. (p. 1838)
—World of Eric Carle the Very Hungry Caterpillar Flash Cards. (p. 1956)
Carle, Eric & Iwamura, Kazuo. Where Are You Going? To See My Friend! Carle, Eric, illus. (p. 1906)
Carle, Gilda. Teen Talk with Dr. Gilda: A Girl's Guide to Dating. (p. 1714)
Carle, Meghan, et al. Teens Cook: How to Cook What You Want to Eat. (p. 1715)
Carles, Cano, jt. auth. see Cano, Carles.
Carleson, J. C. Tyrant's Daughter. (p. 1805)
Carleton, Kate. What Happens to Your Body When You Cycle. (p. 1886)
Carleton, Will. Rhymes of Our Planet, by Will Carleton. (p. 1468)
Carletta-Vietes, Lisa, illus. see Kurstedt, Rosanne.
Carletti, Emanuela, illus. see Goodings, Christina.
Carlile, Candy. Crafts with Rhymes - Growing up God's Way. (p. 376)
—Crafts with Rhymes - Learning from God's Word. (p. 376)
—Crafts with Rhymes - Living in God's World. (p. 376)
Carlile, Vowery D. Monsters, Magic & Make-Believe. (p. 1169)
Carlile-Grattopp, Kari & Grattopp, Matthew. When I Turned Five. (p. 1903)
Carlin, Claire, ed. Imagining Contagion in Early Modern Europe. (p. 861)
Carlin, Daniel. Washington University in St Louis College Prowler off the Record. (p. 1860)
Carlin, George. 3 X Carlin: An Orgy of George. (p. 1992)
Carlin, Laura. World of Your Own. (p. 1958)
Carlin, Laura, illus. see Davies, Nicola.
Carlin, Lydia. Insect Homes. (p. 875)
—Moon. (p. 1171)
Carlin, Pat. Cow Visits Chicago. (p. 373)
Carlin, Patricia, jt. auth. see Pat Carlin, Carlin.
Carlin, Peter Ames. Catch a Wave: The Rise, Fall & Redemption of the Beach Boys' Brian Wilson. (p. 279)
Carlin, Richard. Folk. (p. 611)
Carlin, Richard, ed. American Popular Music (p. 62)
Carling, Amelia Lau. Alfombras de Aserrín. (p. 37)
—Tienda de Mamá y Papá. (p. 1748)
Carling, Amelia Lau, illus. see Mora, Pat & Martinez, Libby.
Carling, Amelia Lau, jt. auth. see Mora, Pat.
Carlinsky, Dan. Do You Know Your Boyfriend? (p. 458)
Carlisi, Alison & Foxx, Teralene S. Forest & the Fire. (p. 618)
Carlisle, A. J. Codex Lacrimae: The Mariner's Daughter & Doomed Knight. (p. 338)
Carlisle, Brady. Tony Dungy. (p. 1766)
Carlisle, Kelly. My Mommy Is A Rocker. (p. 1214)
Carlisle, Rodney P. Afghanistan War. (p. 26)
—Age of Reform, 1890-1920 (p. 29)
—Civil War & Reconstruction, 1860 - 1876 (p. 325)
—Colonial Revolutionary Era: Beginnings To 1783 (p. 341)
—Contemporary America, 1970 to Present (p. 360)
—Early National Period & Expansion, 1783 - 1859 (p. 494)
—Exploring Space, Revised Edition. (p. 553)
—Gilded Age, 1870-1900 (p. 676)
—Great Depression & World War II, 1929-1949 (p. 715)
—Iraq War. (p. 887)
—Postwar America, 1950-1969 (p. 1388)
—Roaring Twenties, 1920 - 1929 (p. 1478)
Carlisle, Rodney P., jt. auth. see Golson Books, Ltd. Staff.
Carlisle, Rodney P. & Golson, J. Geoffrey, eds. Turning Points-Actual & Alternate Histories: Colonial America from Settlement to the Revolution (p. 1798)
Carlisle, Samantha. Day Sam Lost Lucky. (p. 414)
Carlo, Sonja. Christmasmaker: Santa's first Flight. Carlo, Sonja, illus. (p. 316)
Carlon, Mick. Riding on Duke's Train. (p. 1471)
—Travels with Louis. (p. 1780)
Carlone, Sydney. Life in a Marsh. (p. 1010)
Carlos, Martin Ramos Juan, jt. auth. see Martin Ramos, Juan Carlos.
Carlos, Puerto, jt. auth. see Puerto, Carlos.
Carlos, Tio. My Fish Trish. (p. 1208)
Carlow, Emma, illus. see Bradman, Tony.
Carlow, Emma & Bradman, Tony. Flora the Fairy. Carlow, Emma, illus. (p. 606)
Carls, Beth & Looper, Amy, eds. I Wish I Knew What to Do: On What to Say to Get Bullies to Leave You Alone. (p. 849)
Carlsen, Derek. Faith & Courage Commentary on Acts. (p. 565)
Carlsen, GiGi. Yu & the Ewe. (p. 1983)
Carlsen, Wendy Vergoz, jt. ed. see Replogle, Steve.
Carlson, illus. see Carlson, Nancy.
Carlson, Al, illus. see Carlson, Dale.
Carlson, Amanda. Sultenfuss Moose's Lost Slipper. (p. 1673)
Carlson, Amie. My Princesses Learn to Share. Heyworth, Heather, illus. (p. 1217)
Carlson, Andrea, et al. Community Works: Smart Youth Make Safer Communities (p. 350)
Carlson, Andy, illus. see Breur, Jessica.
Carlson, Andy, illus. see Kehl, Esther.
Carlson, Andy, illus. see Morris, Deborah & Morris, Larry.
Carlson, Barbara, ed. see Satifka, Erica L., et al.
Carlson Berne, Emma. Answer! Analyze Your Data. (p. 88)
—Bays. (p. 147)
—Beaches. (p. 149)
—Bright! Light Energy. (p. 228)
—Chameleons: Masters of Disguise! (p. 289)
—Dung Beetles: Stronger Than Ten Men! (p. 490)
—Guess! Research & Form a Hypothesis. (p. 728)
—Hazmat: Disposing Toxic Materials. (p. 756)
—Hills. (p. 780)
—Hummingbirds: Faster Than a Jet! (p. 826)
—Lakes. (p. 972)
—Look! Make Observations & Ask Questions. (p. 1048)
—Loud! Sound Energy. (p. 1057)
—Plains. (p. 1366)
—Predict! Plan an Experiment. (p. 1395)
—Scavengers: Eating Nature's Trash. (p. 1521)
—Search & Rescue: Imminent Danger. (p. 1537)
—Share! Present Your Findings. (p. 1561)
—Shocking! Electricity. (p. 1568)
—Speeding! Mechanical Energy. (p. 1624)
—Test! Collect & Document Data. (p. 1723)
—Transforming! Chemical Energy. (p. 1778)
—Valleys. (p. 1831)
—Whale Sharks: Bulletproof! (p. 1877)
Carlson Berne, Emma, jt. auth. see Berne, Emma Carlson.
Carlson Berne, Emma & Burgan, Michael. Captured World History (p. 265)
Carlson Berne, Emma, et al. Greatest U. S. Presidents (p. 720)
—Planets. (p. 1368)
Carlson, Bert H. Perilous African Adventures of Sir Bert & Sir Gilbert. (p. 1343)
Carlson, Brian & Carlson, Jenny. So Long, Old Hat. (p. 1602)
Carlson, Bryce. Wall- E: Out There. Luthi, Morgan, illus. (p. 1854)
Carlson, Cami. Hey! You're Great! (p. 775)
Carlson, Caroline. Buccaneers' Code. (p. 234)
—Magic Marks the Spot. Phillips, Dave, illus. (p. 1072)
—Terror of the Southlands. Phillips, Dave, illus. (p. 1722)
—Very Nearly Honorable League of Pirates - The Terror of the Southlands. Phillips, Dave, illus. (p. 1838)
Carlson, Cheryl. Charles M. Schulz Saunders-Smith, Gail, ed. (p. 292)
—Dr. Seuss (p. 475)
—Dr. Seuss Saunders-Smith, Gail, ed. (p. 475)
—Dr. Seuss [Scholastic]. (p. 475)
—Favorite Author Bios Pack [Scholastic]. (p. 578)
Carlson, Christine, illus. see Tonderum, Angela.
Carlson, Claudia. Avi the Ambulance Goes to School. (p. 119)
—Avi the Ambulance to the Rescue! (p. 119)
Carlson, Dale. Human Apes. Carlson, Al & Nicklaus, Carol, illus. (p. 825)
—Teen Brain Book: Who & What Are You? Teasdale, Nancy, ed. (p. 1713)
—Understand Your Self: Teen Manual for the Understanding of Oneself. (p. 1815)
—Who Said What? Philosophy Quotes for Teens. Nicklaus, Carol, illus. (p. 1917)
—¿Adonde Vamos? Dentro y Fuera de tu mente. Guix, Joan Carles, tr. from ENG. (p. 13)
Carlson, Dale Bick. Mountain of Truth. Nicklaus, Carol, illus. (p. 1181)
—Talk: Teen Art of Communication. Khalmar, Kishore, ed. (p. 1703)
Carlson, Dale Bick & Carlson, Hannah. Are You Human, or What? Nicklaus, Carol, illus. (p. 97)
Carlson, Dale Bick & Khalmar, Kishore. Cosmic Calendar: The Big Bang to Your Consciousness. (p. 368)
Carlson, Dale, et al. Out of Order: Young Adult Manual of Mental Illness & Recovery. (p. 1311)
Carlson, David Gray, ed. Hegel's Theory of the Subject. (p. 762)
Carlson, Drew. Attack of the Turtle. Johnson, David A., illus. (p. 114)
Carlson, Eric S., illus. see Crum, Sally.
Carlson, George. Fun Time Library Boxed Set. (p. 648)
Carlson, George Leonard, illus. see Martin, John.
Carlson, Geri L. Andrew Goes to the Chiropractor. Kiel, Casey K., illus. (p. 72)
Carlson, Glenn E. Angie the Aviator. Robinson, Helen, ed. (p. 75)
Carlson, Hannah. Addiction: The Brain Disease. (p. 11)
Carlson, Hannah, jt. auth. see Carlson, Dale Bick.
Carlson, J. Kelley. Freeing Golden Eagle. (p. 635)
Carlson, J. P. Rex Riders. Calafiore, Jim, illus. (p. 1467)
Carlson, Jenny, jt. auth. see Carlson, Brian.
Carlson, Josh, illus. see Wiens, Patti.
Carlson, Jr. Autism Coloring Book. Carlson, Kevin, illus. (p. 117)
Carlson, Julie. Uncle Tom's Cabin & the Abolitionist Movement. (p. 1812)
Carlson, Kevin, illus. see Carlson, Jr.
Carlson, Kevin, illus. see Carlson, Richard.
Carlson, Kim, illus. see Schroeder, Frauna.
Carlson, Kirsten, illus. see Cerullo, Mary M. & Simmons, Beth E.
Carlson, Kirsten, illus. see Hirschi, Ron.
Carlson, Kirsten, illus. see Ufer, David A.
Carlson, Laurie, jt. auth. see Carlson, Laurie M.
Carlson, Laurie M. Harry Houdini for Kids: His Life & Adventures with 21 Magic Tricks & Illusions. (p. 750)
Carlson, Laurie M. & Carlson, Laurie. Thomas Edison for Kids: His Life & Ideas, 21 Activities. (p. 1738)
Carlson, Lavelle. Can a Toucan Hoot Too? A Phonemic Awareness Tale Adams, Lucas, illus. (p. 258)
—Eek! I Hear a Squeak & the Scurrying of Little Feet. Loehr, Jenny, illus. (p. 505)
—Fable of Mable with a Ladle at the Table: A Phonemic Awareness Tale. (p. 559)
—Frog Who Could Not Croak: Phonemic Awareness Tale #4. (p. 640)
—Rocks in My Socks & Rainbows Too Adams, Lucas, illus. (p. 1484)
Carlson, Lisa, illus. see Krensky, Stephen.
Carlson, Lisa, illus. see Kropf, Latifa Berry.
Carlson, Lori M., jt. auth. see Carlson, Lori Marie.
Carlson, Lori M., ed. Voices in First Person: Reflections on Latino Identity. Morais, Flavio, illus. (p. 1848)
Carlson, Lori Marie. Cool Salsa: Bilingual Poems on Growing up Latino in the United States. (p. 364)
—Red Hot Salsa: Bilingual Poems on Being Young & Latino in the United States. (p. 1454)
Carlson, Lori Marie & Carlson, Lori M. Moccasin Thunder: American Indian Stories for Today. (p. 1157)
Carlson, Lori Marie, ed. Cool Salsa: Bilingual Poems on Growing up Latino in the United States. (p. 364)
Carlson, Martin D. Rfaud Tastes Wisdom. Oketch, Alphonce Omondi, illus. (p. 1467)
Carlson, Maureen. Clay Characters for Kids. (p. 330)
—Crazy Clay Creatures. (p. 377)
—Freaky Funny Clay. (p. 632)
Carlson, Melody. Bad Connection. (p. 131)
—Benjamin's Box: The Story of the Resurrection Eggs Stockman, Jack, illus. (p. 165)
—Beyond Reach. (p. 174)
—Bitsy's Harvest Party. Reagan, Susan Joy, illus. (p. 194)
—Blade Silver: Color Me Scarred. (p. 198)
—Bright Purple: Color Me Confused. (p. 228)
—Burnt Orange: Color Me Wasted. (p. 244)
—Catwalk (p. 281)
—Charlene's Grumpy Day: A Scoozie Tale about Patience. Fincher, Kathryn Andrews, illus. (p. 291)
—Ciao (p. 318)
—Dark Blue: Color Me Lonely. (p. 407)
—Dating Games #1: First Date. (p. 409)
—Dating Games #2: Blind Date. (p. 409)
—Dating Games #3: Double Date. (p. 409)
—Dating Games #4: Prom Date. (p. 409)
—Day the Circus Came to Town. Butterfield, Ned, illus. (p. 414)
—Deep Green: Color Me Jealous. (p. 423)
—Double Take. (p. 473)
—Face the Music. (p. 560)
—Faded Denim: Color Me Trapped. (p. 562)
—Farmer Brown's Field Trip. Bjorkman, Steve, illus. (p. 574)
—Fool's Gold: Color Me Consumed. (p. 614)
—Forgive Others. Reagan, Susan Joy, illus. (p. 619)

C

—Forgotten: Seventeen & Homeless. (p. 619)
—Glamour (p. 682)
—Goodnight, Angels Allsopp, Sophie, illus. (p. 701)
—Grover Tells a Whopper: A Scoozie Tale about Honesty. Fincher, Kathryn Andrews, illus. (p. 725)
—Harsh Pink: Color Me Burned. (p. 751)
—Hi, I'm Blackbeary: The Fruit of the Spirit Is Peace. Mahan, Ben, illus. (p. 775)
—Homecoming Queen (p. 793)
—I Do! (p. 837)
—Ireland. (p. 887)
—It's a Green Thing. (p. 895)
—Just Another Girl. (p. 937)
—Just Ask. (p. 938)
—Last Dance (p. 977)
—Lost in Las Vegas (p. 1055)
—Meant to Be. (p. 1117)
—Mixed Bags (p. 1156)
—Moon White: Color Me Enchanted. (p. 1172)
—My Name Is Chloe. (p. 1215)
—New York Debut (p. 1248)
—Noah & the Incredible Flood Francisco, Wendy, illus. (p. 1261)
—Notes from a Spinning Planet: Papua New Guinea. (p. 1267)
—Notes from a Spinning Planet - Mexico. (p. 1268)
—Not-So-Simple Life. (p. 1267)
—O Come Let Us Adore Him. (p. 1274)
—Other Brother. Björkman, Steve, illus. (p. 1306)
—Oveja Perdida. (p. 1313)
—Payback. (p. 1331)
—Pitch Black: Color Me Lost. (p. 1364)
—Playing with Fire. (p. 1372)
—Premiere (p. 1395)
—Rendezvous (p. 1460)
—Road Trip. (p. 1476)
—Sold Out. (p. 1607)
—Spotlight (p. 1633)
—Spring Breakdown (p. 1635)
—Stealing Bradford. (p. 1646)
—Torch Red: Color Me Torn. (p. 1769)
—'Twas the Night: The Nativity Story. Reagan, Susan Joy, illus. (p. 1799)
—Viva Vermont! (p. 1846)
—What Matters Most. (p. 1892)
—When the Creepy Things Come Out! Reagan, Susan Joy, illus. (p. 1904)

Carlson, Melody & Rue, Nancy N. Dear Nancy: Answers to Letters from Girls Like You. (p. 419)
Carlson, Nancy. Amie & the Skateboard Gang. Carlson, Nancy, illus. (p. 100)
—Amie Goes to Camp. Carlson, Nancy, illus. (p. 100)
—First Grade, Here I Come! (p. 595)
—Get up & Go! (p. 668)
—Harriet & George's Christmas Treat. (p. 749)
—Harriet & the Roller Coaster. (p. 749)
—Harriet & the Roller Coaster. Carlson, Nancy, illus. (p. 749)
—Harriet & Walt. (p. 749)
—Harriet & Walt. Carlson, Nancy, illus. (p. 749)
—Harriet Series (p. 749)
—Harriet's Halloween Candy. (p. 750)
—Harriet's Halloween Candy. Carlson, Nancy, illus. (p. 750)
—Harriet's Recital. (p. 750)
—Henry & the Bully. (p. 767)
—Henry & the Valentine Surprise. (p. 767)
—Henry's 100 Days of Kindergarten. (p. 769)
—Henry's 100 Days of Kindergarten. Carlson, Nancy, illus. (p. 769)
—Henry's Amazing Imagination. (p. 769)
—Henry's Show & Tell. Carlson, Nancy, illus. (p. 769)
—I Don't Like to Read! Carlson, Nancy & Carlson, Nancy, illus. (p. 838)
—I Like Me! (p. 841)
—It's Going to Be Perfect! Carlson, Nancy, illus. (p. 897)
—Life Is Fun. Carlson, Nancy, illus. (p. 1011)
—Look Out, Kindergarten, Here I Come! Mlawer, Teresa, tr. (p. 1050)
—Louanne Pig in the Mysterious Valentine. (p. 1057)
—Louanne Pig in the Perfect Family. (p. 1057)
—Louanne Pig in Witch Lady. Carlson, Nancy, illus. (p. 1057)
—Louanne Pig Series (p. 1057)
—Loudmouth George & the Big Race. (p. 1057)
—Loudmouth George & the Cornet. (p. 1057)
—Loudmouth George & the Fishing Trip. (p. 1057)
—Loudmouth George & the New Neighbors. (p. 1058)
—Loudmouth George & the Sixth-Grade Bully. (p. 1058)
—Loudmouth George Earns His Allowance. Carlson, Nancy, illus. (p. 1058)
—My Best Friend Moved Away. Carlson, Nancy, illus. (p. 1196)
—My Family Is Forever. Carlson, Nancy, illus. (p. 1203)
—No Es Mi Culpa. Translations.com Staff, tr. from ENG. (p. 1258)
—Poor Carl. Carlson, Nancy, illus. (p. 1383)
—Sit Still! Carlson, Nancy, illus. (p. 1582)
—Smile a Lot! Carlson, Nancy, illus. (p. 1594)
—Snowden. Carlson, Nancy, illus. (p. 1600)
—Sometimes You Barf. Carlson, Nancy, illus. (p. 1610)
—Take Time to Relax! Carlson, Nancy, illus. (p. 1697)
—Think Happy! Carlson, Nancy, illus. (p. 1734)
—This Morning Sam Went to Mars: A Book about Paying Attention. (p. 1737)
—What If It Never Stops Raining? Carlson, Nancy, illus. (p. 1887)
—¡Piensa en Grande! (p. 1357)
—¡Sonríe! Translations.com Staff, tr. from ENG. (p. 1612)
Carlson, Nancy, illus. see Kessel, Joyce K.
Carlson, Nancy, illus. see Lindaman, Jane.
Carlson, Nancy & Isaak, Armond. Armond Goes to a Party: A Book about Asperger's & Friendship. (p. 99)
Carlson, Nancy & McCool, Barry. T Is for Twin Cities: A Minneapolis/St. Paul Alphabet. Geister, David, illus. (p. 1694)
Carlson, Nancy Gayle, illus. see Gregory, Lorraine NAR NEEDED.
Carlson, Nolan. Lame Eagle & Wind Chaser. (p. 972)
Carlson, Patrick, illus. see Wells, Jason & Wells, Jeff.

Carlson, Richard. Ne Vous Noyez Pas dans un Verre d'Eau. (p. 1238)
—Schizophrenia Coloring Book. Carlson, Steven, tr. (p. 1521)
Carlson, Ron. Speed of Light. (p. 1624)
Carlson, Sally Kephart. Your Mission to Neptune. (p. 1981)
Carlson, Steven, tr. see Carlson, Richard.
Carlson-Berne, Emma. Beaches. (p. 149)
—Snoop Dogg. (p. 1598)
—Valleys. (p. 1831)
Carlson-Voiles, Polly. Someone Walks By: The Wonders of Winter Wildlife. (p. 1609)
—Someone Walks By. (p. 1609)
—Summer of the Wolves. (p. 1674)
Carlson, Per, tr. see Amore, Dani, et al.
Carlstrom, Kimberly. Scrambled Letters: Written by Kimberly Carlstrom. Illustrated by Peyton Button. (p. 1532)
Carlstrom, Nancy White. Climb the Family Tree, Jesse Bear! Degen, Bruce, illus. (p. 333)
—Does God Know How to Tie Shoes? McElrath-Eslick, Lori, illus. (p. 460)
—Glory. Jenkins, Debra Reid, illus. (p. 685)
—Guess Who's Coming, Jesse Bear. Degen, Bruce, illus. (p. 729)
—It's Your First Day of School, Annie Claire. Moore, Margie, illus. (p. 899)
—Jesse Bear, What Will You Wear? (p. 914)
—Jesse Bear, What Will You Wear? Degen, Bruce, illus. (p. 914)
—Mama, Will It Snow Tonight? Tong, Paul, illus. (p. 1084)
—Raven & River. Van Zyle, Jon, illus. (p. 1441)
—This Is the Day! Cowdrey, Richard, illus. (p. 1736)
—What a Scare, Jesse Bear. Degen, Bruce, illus. (p. 1878)
—What Does the Sky Say? Ladwig, Tim, illus. (p. 1884)
—Where Is Christmas, Jesse Bear? Degen, Bruce, illus. (p. 1908)
Carlstrom, Nancy White & Saport, Linda. Before You Were Born. Saport, Linda, illus. (p. 159)
Carlton & Regan, Lisa. Epic Sticker Scene Book. (p. 532)
Carlton Books, ed. Eye Twisters: Boggle, Baffle & Blow Your Mind! (p. 558)
—ISolar System. (p. 893)
—Kate & Pippa Dress-Up Sticker Book: Create Stylish Outfits & Design Your Own Accessories! (p. 944)
—Vacation Doodles: Doodle Your Way to Vacation Heaven! (p. 1829)
Carlton Books Staff, ed. see Sipi, Claire.
Carlton Books Staff, ed. see Souter, Gerry & Souter, Janet.
Carlton Books Staff & Alien, Robert. Mensa Mighty Mystery Puzzles for Kids. (p. 1126)
Carlton Books Staff, ed. Fairyland Magic. (p. 564)
Carlton Books UK. Science Museum. (p. 1526)
—Science Museum Kids Handbook. (p. 1526)
Carlton, Heather. Bobby's Lesson on Blessings. (p. 206)
Carlton, Kat. Two Lies & a Spy. (p. 1803)
Carlton Publishing Group & Regan, Lisa. Rio 2 Sticker Scene Book: Complete the Movie Scenes with over 200 Stickers! (p. 1473)
Carlton Publishing Group Staff & Regan, Lisa. Rio 2 Sticker Activity Book: Exciting Puzzles, Fun Games, & over 200 Stickers! (p. 1473)
Carlucci, Jennifer. Stevie Meanie Stinkerpots. (p. 1649)
Carluccio, Maria. Sounds Around Town. (p. 1615)
—Sounds Around Town. Carluccio, Maria, illus. (p. 1615)
Carluccio, Maria, illus. see Blackstone, Stella.
Carluccio, Maria, jt. auth. see Blackstone, Stella.
Carman, Debby. Cha Cha, the Dancing Dog. Carman, Debby, illus. (p. 288)
—Chewdalootie, Doing My Duty. Carman, Debby, illus. (p. 299)
—I'm Gronk & I'm Green. Carman, Debby, illus. (p. 859)
—I'm Maximum Cat, That's a Fact! (p. 859)
—Kittywimpuss Got Game. Carman, Debby, illus. (p. 963)
—Nutcracker Cats of the Kremlin. Carman, Debby, illus. (p. 1274)
—Purrionia's Lullaby. Carman, Debby, illus. (p. 1419)
Carman, Patrick. 3 Below. (p. 1991)
—3:15 Season One Things That Go Bump in the Night. (p. 1992)
—Beyond the Valley of Thorns. (p. 174)
—Black Circle. (p. 195)
—Dark Eden. Arrasmith, Patrick, illus. (p. 407)
—Dark Hills Divide. (p. 407)
—Dark Planet. (p. 408)
—Eve of Destruction. Arrasmith, Patrick, illus. (p. 541)
—Floors. (p. 606)
—Floors. (p. 606)
—Floors #2: 3 Below. (p. 606)
—Floors #3: the Field of Wacky Inventions. (p. 606)
—House of Power. (p. 803)
—Pulse. (p. 1416)
—Quake. (p. 1422)
—Rivers of Fire. (p. 1476)
—Shantorian (p. 1560)
—Stargazer. (p. 1642)
—Tenth City. (p. 1720)
—Thirteen Days to Midnight. (p. 1735)
—Trackers (p. 1775)
—Tremor. (p. 1784)
—Trouble with Fuzzwonker Fizz. Sheesley, Brian, illus. (p. 1790)
—Walnut Cup. James, Steve, illus. (p. 1855)
Carman, Patrick & Scholastic, Inc. Staff. Black Circle. (p. 195)
—Dark Hills Divide. (p. 407)
Carman, Patrick & Studios, P. c. Crossbores. (p. 385)
Carmean, John. Moving Day: Adventures in Hogtown. (p. 1183)
Carmen & Thane Johnson. Dogs Don't Wear Underwear. Bianca & Annie West, illus. (p. 462)
Carmen, Indigo. Princess the Pygmy Goat. Nardi, Tisa, illus. (p. 1406)
—Tee Hee. Diana, illus. (p. 1713)
Carmen Luisa. Adventures of Cotin Mirel: Three Short Stories. (p. 17)
Carmen, Martín Anguita, jt. auth. see Martín Anguita, Carmen.

Carmi, Giora. Circle of Friends (p. 321)
—Circle of Friends Carmi, Giora, illus. (p. 321)
—Rooster Prince. (p. 1488)
Carmi, Giora, illus. see Goldin, Barbara Diamond.
Carmi, Giora, illus. see Kimmel, Eric A.
Carmi, Giora, illus. see Schwartz, Howard.
Carmi, Rebecca. Amazing Magnetism. Speirs, John, illus. (p. 55)
Carmichael, Bruce. Little Path by Shadow Mountain. (p. 1033)
Carmichael, Chris & Rutberg, Jim. Ultimate Ride: Get Fit, Get Fast, & Start Winning with the World's Top Cycling Coach. (p. 1810)
Carmichael, Claire. Gotta B. (p. 704)
—Leaving Simplicity. (p. 986)
Carmichael, Clay. Brother, Brother. (p. 231)
—Wild Things (p. 1930)
—Wild Things. (p. 1930)
Carmichael, David Alan. Faith - the Final Frontier. (p. 565)
Carmichael, Heather. Ellie Finds a New Home. McFarland, Shea, illus. (p. 514)
Carmichael, Katrina. Back Together Again. (p. 130)
Carmichael, L. E. Amazing Feats of Civil Engineering. (p. 54)
—Forensic Science: In Pursuit of Justice. (p. 617)
—Fox Talk. Bronson, Jody, illus. (p. 626)
—Gene Therapy. (p. 660)
—How Do Video Games Work? (p. 807)
—Humpback Whale Migration. (p. 827)
—Hybrid & Electric Vehicles. (p. 831)
—Locust Migration. (p. 1045)
—Scientific Method in Real World. (p. 1528)
—Scientific Method in the Real World. (p. 1528)
—What Are Programs & Apps? (p. 1879)
—Wildebeest Migration. (p. 1931)
—Zebra Migration. (p. 1985)
Carmichael, Leslie. Amulet of Amon-Ra. (p. 66)
—Lyranel's Song. (p. 1066)
Carmichael, Peyton, illus. see Colvin, Adele Bibb.
Carmichael, Peyton, illus. see Colvin, Adele.
Carmichael, Tricia & MacDonald, Allison, eds. Deal with It Series Bullying & Conflict Resource Guide Charette, Geraldine et al, illus. (p. 418)
Carmindy. Bloom: A Girl's Guide to Growing up Gorgeous. (p. 201)
Carmine, Mary & Baynton, Martin. Daniel et Ses Dinosaures. (p. 405)
Carmitchel, Andrew. Wizard on Oak Street. (p. 1943)
Carmody, Isobelle. Ashling. (p. 106)
—Dreamtrails: The Obernewtyn Chronicles. (p. 484)
—Farseekers. (p. 575)
—Fox Called Sorrow. (p. 626)
—Keeping Place. (p. 947)
—Mystery of Wolves. (p. 1226)
—Obernewtyn. (p. 1275)
—Red Queen. (p. 1454)
—Riddle of Green. (p. 1470)
—Stone Key. (p. 1652)
Carmody, Isobelle & McNab, Nan, eds. Wilful Eye. (p. 1932)
Carmody, Michael A. Life with Jesus: Bible Study Workbook. (p. 1013)
Carmona, Adela. Boy Who Could See. Chapman, Robert E., illus. (p. 219)
Carmona, Blanca L. Gone to Heaven: A children's memoir Book. (p. 697)
Carmony, Crystal. Ima Gene's Imagination. (p. 860)
Carmouche, Angelica Drisana. Mommy in Mind. (p. 1162)
Carnagie, Julie. Persian Gulf Wars Cumulative Index: From Operation Desert Storm to Operation Iraqi Freedom. (p. 1344)
Carnagie, Julie, ed. see Hillstrom, Laurie Collier.
Carnagie, Julie L., jt. auth. see Howes, Kelly King.
Carnagie, Julie L., jt. ed. see Gale Editors.
Carnahan, Rhonda, jt. auth. see Blackburn, Richard.
Carnavas, Peter. Blue Whale Blues. Carnavas, Peter, illus. (p. 203)
—Boy on the Page. Carnavas, Peter, illus. (p. 218)
—Children Who Loved Books. Carnavas, Peter, illus. (p. 303)
—Last Tree in the City (Akhr Shajara Fil Madina) Ibrahim, Nouran, tr. (p. 979)
Carnegy, Vicky. Fashions of a Decade: The 1980s. (p. 576)
Carnehl, Jeff, illus. see Trunkhill, Brenda.
Carnelos, Melissa. 10 Most Amazing Animal Heroes. (p. 1993)
Carnes, Conrad D. Green Patch: D-Day & Beyond. (p. 722)
Carnes, Daphane. Grace. (p. 704)
Carnesecca, Michele. How Does the Holy Ghost Make Me Feel? Xanthos, Carol, illus. (p. 809)
Carnesi, Mònica. Little Dog Lost: The True Story of a Brave Dog Named Baltic. Carnesi, Mònica, illus. (p. 1027)
—Sleepover with Beatrice & Bear. Carnesi, Mònica, illus. (p. 1589)
Carnevale, Michael. Hotel Coolidge. (p. 802)
Carney, Audrey McDonald. It's Me Mommy, I've Been Sent from Heaven Above. (p. 897)
Carney, Charles. Day Just for Daddies. (p. 413)
Carney, Charles, jt. auth. see Pebbles.
Carney, Deborah, illus. see Taeckens, Geri.
Carney, Elizabeth. Angry Birds Playground: A Global Geographic Adventure! (p. 75)
—Angry Birds Playground - Atlas: A Global Geographic Adventure! (p. 75)
—Bats. (p. 144)
—Big Cats: Pictures to Purr about & Info to Make You Roar! (p. 180)
—Cats vs. Dogs. (p. 281)
—Dog Finds Lost Dolphins: And More True Stories of Amazing Animal Heroes. (p. 461)
—Dolphins: Dolphin Facts, Photos, & Fun That Will Make You Flip. (p. 464)
—Frogs! (p. 641)
—Great Migrations: Whales, Wildebeests, Butterflies, Elephants, & Other Amazing Animals on the Move. (p. 717)
—Mummies. (p. 1190)

—National Geographic Little Kids First Big Book of the World. (p. 1232)
—National Geographic Readers: Mars. (p. 1233)
Carney, Elizabeth, jt. auth. see Johns, Chris.
Carney, Elizabeth, jt. auth. see Marsh, Laura.
Carney, Elizabeth, jt. auth. see Nichois, Michael.
Carney, Elizabeth, jt. auth. see Rosing, Norbert.
Carney, Elizabeth & Rosing, Norbert. Face to Face with Polar Bears. (p. 560)
Carney, Elizabeth & Zapruder, Alexandra. National Geographic Readers: Anne Frank. (p. 1233)
Carney, John, ed. see McNab, Chris.
Carney, John, ed. see Wilson, Patrick.
Carney, John & Carney, Veta. Teddy's Journey. (p. 1713)
Carney, Karin. Prince Braden's Animal Kingdom. (p. 1401)
—Princess Bailey & Her Animal Friends. (p. 1403)
Carney, Larry. Jeff Gordon. PC Treasures Staff, ed. (p. 911)
—Joe Gibbs Racing 2008. (p. 920)
—NASCAR. (p. 1230)
—NASCAR Hendrick Motorsports 2008. (p. 1230)
—NASCAR Penske Racing. (p. 1230)
—NASCAR Petty Racing 2008. (p. 1230)
—Tony Stewart. PC Treasures Staff, ed. (p. 1766)
Carney, Larry, adapted by. Gingerbread Man's Christmas. (p. 677)
—Jack & the Beanstalk. (p. 902)
—Little Mermaid's Christmas. (p. 1031)
—Rapunzel. (p. 1439)
—Silly Book/CD - Silly Zoo. (p. 1575)
—Silly Farm. (p. 1575)
—Silly Friends. (p. 1576)
—Silly Neighborhood. (p. 1576)
—Sleeping Beauty. (p. 1589)
—Snow White. (p. 1599)
—Three Bears Christmas. (p. 1741)
—Three Billy Goats Gruff. (p. 1741)
—Three Little Pig's Christmas. (p. 1743)
Carney, Mary Lou. Treasure Rock. (p. 1782)
Carney, Mary Lou, jt. auth. see Macomber, Debbie.
Carney, Mary Lou & Peale, Norman Vincent. Power of Positive Thinking for Teens. (p. 1389)
Carney, Patrick, illus. see Kreger, Claire.
Carney, Patrick, photos by see Kreger, Claire.
Carney, Riley. Final Alliance: Book Five of the Reign of the Elements. (p. 586)
—Fire Stone: Book One of the Reign of the Elements. (p. 591)
Carney, Veta, jt. auth. see Carney, John.
Carney-Nunes, Charisse. I Dream for You a World: A Covenant for Our Children. Williams, Ann Marie, illus. (p. 838)
Carney-Nunes Charisse. Nappy. Williams, Ann Marie, illus. (p. 1229)
Carney-Nunes, Charisse & Williams, Ann Marie. I Am Barack Obama. (p. 832)
Carnicelli, C. Something's in the Forest. (p. 1610)
Carnrike, Jason Jg. Much Too Much. (p. 1188)
Caro, Joe. Santa's Christmas Train. Shih, Lin, illus. (p. 1513)
—Santa's Christmas Train Coloring Book. Shih, Lin, illus. (p. 1513)
Caro, Stephen, jt. auth. see Pérez-Foncea, Juan Antonio.
Carol, Darlene. Puppy Called Runt: The Adventure Begins. (p. 1418)
Carol Henson Keesee. Angry Thunderstorm. Rachel Henson, illus. (p. 75)
Carol Hersh. Handy Sandy. Baker, David, illus. (p. 742)
Carol, Light. Chickensing Story Book Board. Carol, Light, illus. (p. 301)
Carol Muller-Funk. Proxmire & the Exodus of Prairieville. (p. 1413)
Carol, Racklin-Siegel, illus. see Goldstein, Jessica & Inker, Inna, eds.
Carol White-Hill. Mommy & Her Makeup. (p. 1162)
Carola, Leslie Conron & Grossman, Andrea. Mrs. Grossman's Sticker Magic. (p. 1187)
Carolan. B Is for Beach: An Alphabet Book. (p. 122)
—Goodnight Hawaiian Moon. (p. 701)
—This Is My Piko. Carolan, Joanna, illus. (p. 1736)
Carolan, Christine, illus. see Jackson, Ellen B.
Carolan, Christine, illus. see Mannone, Christine.
Carolan, Christine, illus. see Wasserman, Mira.
Carolan, Debra. Puppets No Strings Attached. (p. 1417)
Carolan, Dr. Where Are My Slippers? A Book of Colors. Carolan, Joanna F., illus. (p. 1906)
Carolan, Jill. Sadie's Bargain. (p. 1501)
Carolan, Joanna, illus. see Carolan.
Carolan, Joanna & Carolan, Terry. President from Hawaii. Zunon, Elizabeth, illus. (p. 1397)
Carolan, Joanna F. Old Makana Had a Taro Farm. Carolan, Joanna F., illus. (p. 1284)
Carolan, Joanna F., illus. see Carolan, Dr.
Carolan, Terry, jt. auth. see Carolan, Joanna.
Carolane, Sue. AA Is for Alpacas. (p. 2)
Carole, Bonnie. Black & White in Winter. (p. 195)
—Blue & Yellow in Summer. (p. 202)
—Orange & Brown in Fall. (p. 1301)
Carole, Isaacs, illus. see Alexander, Geoff.
Carole, Jane & Stella, Heather. Get Ready for Kindergarten. (p. 668)
—Get Ready for Pre-K Revised & Updated. (p. 668)
Carole Marsh. Ah,Sol Japanese for Kids. (p. 30)
—Alabama Indians. (p. 33)
—Alaska Indians. (p. 34)
—Arizona Indians. (p. 98)
—Arkansas Indians. (p. 99)
—Atlanta Coloring. (p. 112)
—Big Book of Native American Activities. (p. 179)
—California Indians. (p. 253)
—Celebrating Native American Heritage. (p. 285)
—Chicago Coloring & Activity Book. (p. 299)
—Colorado Indians. (p. 343)
—Connecticut Indians. (p. 358)
—Dallas Coloring & Activity Book. (p. 401)
—Delaware Indians. (p. 424)
—False Paw! French for Kids. (p. 567)
—Florida Indians. (p. 607)

—From Russia with Love! Russian for Kids. (p. 643)
—Georgia Indians. (p. 665)
—Hawaii Indians. (p. 755)
—Ho Lee Chow! Chinese for Kids. (p. 786)
—How Our Nation Was Born: the American Revolution. (p. 811)
—Idaho Indians. (p. 852)
—Illinois Indians. (p. 857)
—Indiana Indians. (p. 871)
—Iowa Indians. (p. 886)
—It Really Is Greek to Me! Greek for Kids. (p. 894)
—Kansas Indians. (p. 943)
—Kentucky Indians. (p. 949)
—Los Angeles Coloring & Activity Book. (p. 1053)
—Louisiana Indians. (p. 1058)
—Maine Indians. (p. 1077)
—Maryland Indians. (p. 1101)
—Massachusetts Indians. (p. 1102)
—Michigan Indians. (p. 1135)
—Minnesota Indians. (p. 1147)
—Mississippi Indians. (p. 1154)
—Missouri Indians. (p. 1154)
—Montana Indians. (p. 1170)
—Nebraska Indians. (p. 1239)
—Nevada Indians. (p. 1242)
—New England Coloring. (p. 1244)
—New Hampshire Indians. (p. 1245)
—New Jersey Indians. (p. 1245)
—New Mexico Indians. (p. 1246)
—New York City Coloring & Activity Book. (p. 1248)
—New York Indians. (p. 1248)
—North Carolina Indians. (p. 1265)
—North Dakota Indians. (p. 1265)
—Of All the Gaul! Latin for Kids. (p. 1279)
—Ohio Indians. (p. 1281)
—Oklahoma Indians. (p. 1283)
—Oregon Indians. (p. 1303)
—Patriotic Biographies. (p. 1329)
—Patriotic Projects. (p. 1329)
—Pennsylvania Indians. (p. 1338)
—Presidential Elections. (p. 1397)
—Rhode Island Indians. (p. 1468)
—San Francisco Coloring & Activity Book. (p. 1510)
—Say What When You Sneeze? German for Kids. (p. 1519)
—South Carolina Indians. (p. 1616)
—South Dakota Indians. (p. 1617)
—Tennessee Indians. (p. 1720)
—Texas Indians. (p. 1724)
—Uh,Oh,Amigo! Spanish for Kids. (p. 1808)
—Vermont Indians. (p. 1837)
—Virginia Indians. (p. 1844)
—Washington Dc Coloring & Activity Book. (p. 1860)
—Washington Indians. (p. 1860)
—West Virginia Indians. (p. 1876)
—When Brother Fought Brother: the American Civil War. (p. 1901)
—Wisconsin Indians. (p. 1939)
—Wyoming Indians. (p. 1966)
Carolina Canines for Service & Nowak, Pat. Job for Arabella. Baumgardner, Mary Alice, illus. (p. 919)
Carolina Esquivel Rael. Anthony P the Talker. (p. 89)
Carolina, Philip. My Sister Hates Me ... Only Sometimes. (p. 1218)
Carolinas' Nature Photographers Association Staff & Friends of Congaree Swamp Staff, contrib. by. Images of Congaree National Park. (p. 860)
Caroline, Alyssa. What Etter Is Missing? (p. 1884)
Caroll, Joseph, jt. auth. see Fischer, Stephen David.
Caroll, Robin. Samantha Sanderson at the Movies (p. 1507)
—Samantha Sanderson off the Record (p. 1507)
—Samantha Sanderson on the Scene (p. 1507)
Carolyn, Berg. Jesus Walks Away. Paris, Pat, illus. (p. 916)
Carolyn, Larsen. Grandmas 8 Special Stories for Little Boys. (p. 708)
Carolyn, Reeder. Shades of Gray. (p. 1557)
Caron, Edward, jt. auth. see Caron, Sharon.
Caron, Eleonore. Gizmo & Ellen Mysteries: The Case of the Missing Boy. (p. 681)
Caron, Lucille & Jacques, Philip M. Addition & Subtraction Smarts! (p. 12)
Caron, Lucille & St. Jacques, Philip M. Addition & Subtraction Smarts! (p. 12)
—Fraction & Decimal Smarts! (p. 626)
—Geometry Smarts! (p. 663)
—Math Success (p. 1107)
—Multiplication & Division Smarts! (p. 1190)
—Percent & Ratio Smarts! (p. 1341)
—Pre-Algebra & Algebra Smarts! (p. 1394)
Caron, Lucille, et al. Fraction & Decimal Smarts! (p. 626)
—Geometry Smarts! (p. 663)
—Multiplication & Division Smarts! (p. 1190)
—Percent & Ratio Smarts! (p. 1341)
—Pre-Algebra & Algebra Smarts! (p. 1394)
Caron, Mona. Many Worlds: Native Life along the Anza Trail. (p. 1089)
Caron, Mona, illus. see Shah, Idries.
Caron, Monique. Smiling Scarecrow the Winter Months. Caron, Monique, illus. (p. 1594)
Caron, Romi, illus. see Awa, Simon, et al.
Caron, Romi, illus. see Baillie, Marilyn.
Caron, Romi, illus. see Ducharme, Huguette.
Caron, Romi, illus. see McGuinness, Elle J.
Caron, Romi, jt. auth. see McGuinness, Elle J.
Caron, Sharon & Caron, Edward. Where Do My Kids Go? (p. 1907)
Caron, Susie. Twee' Eckstein, Joe, illus. (p. 1799)
Carosella, Melissa. Dolley Madison: First Lady of the United States. (p. 464)
—Fight for Freedom: Ending Slavery in America. (p. 585)
—Founding Mothers: Women Who Shaped America. (p. 624)
—Frederick Douglass: Leader of the Abolitionist Movement. (p. 633)
—Hillary Rodham Clinton: First Lady, Senator, & Secretary of State. (p. 780)
—Still Marching Strong: Women in Modern America. (p. 1650)
Carothers, Nina. Gold Old Gets a Little Help from His Friends. Nilsen, Richard J., ed. (p. 693)
—Pink Ink's Purpose. Nilsen, Richard J., ed. (p. 1360)
—Red Ed & the True Meaning of Christmas. Nilsen, Richard J., ed. (p. 1453)
—Wonderful World of Color Olors. Nilsen, Richard J., ed. (p. 1948)
Carothers, Sue & Henke, Elizabeth. Human Body: Fun Activities, Experiments, Investigations, & Observations! (p. 825)
—Human Body, Grades 4 - 6: Fun Activities, Experiments, Investigations, & Observations! Hall, Milton, illus. (p. 825)
Carousel Writers' Group Staff, contrib. by. Every Pony Has a Tale. (p. 543)
Carpan, Carolyn. Rocked by Romance: A Guide to Teen Romance Fiction (p. 1482)
Carpenter, Angie. Digewi Deer: The Tale of a Blind Deer. Berner Coble, Lynn, ed. (p. 438)
Carpenter, Ann. Slumber Girls & the Mystical Dollhouse. (p. 1591)
Carpenter, Anne. Animals Tell: Bible Stories As Told by the Animals That Were There. (p. 84)
Carpenter, Anthony, illus. see Osborne, Rick, et al.
Carpenter, Anthony, illus. see Strauss, Ed.
Carpenter, Carole H., jt. auth. see Handy, Femida.
Carpenter, Chad. Morry Moose's Time-Traveling Outhouse Adventure. (p. 1176)
—Tundra Alaska Coloring Book. (p. 1796)
Carpenter, Christina D., ed. see Bauld, Jane S.
Carpenter, Christopher. Lilly's Heart: The Veterinary Clinic Cases Series. (p. 1017)
Carpenter, Cindy. Little Inchworm. (p. 1029)
Carpenter Czerw, Nancy. Friends on the Farm. Berlin, Rose Mary & Bauer, Dana, illus. (p. 638)
—Story of Pilot Star: The First Few Weeks. Bk. 1 (p. 1659)
—Two Miniature Horses. Bauer, Dana, illus. (p. 1804)
Carpenter, Dan, jt. auth. see Kennelly, Sean.
Carpenter, Debra, illus. see Lastoka, Mariann.
Carpenter, Donna. Triple Treat. (p. 1787)
Carpenter, Elizabeth. DinoMazes: The Colossal Fossil Book - 31 Poster-Size Prehistoric Fossil Nazes. (p. 441)
—Mummy Mazes: A Monumental Book. (p. 1191)
—MummyMaze: The Tomb Treasures Maze Book. (p. 1191)
Carpenter, Frances. Tales of a Chinese Grandmother. (p. 1702)
Carpenter, Gloria. Prissy the Persnickety Cat. (p. 1407)
Carpenter, Holly & Chouinard, Karen. Healing Together: An Alphabet Book. (p. 757)
Carpenter, Jake. Snowmobile Best Trick. (p. 1601)
Carpenter, Joyce M. Unexpected Friend. (p. 1817)
Carpenter, Kenneth, ed. Carnivorous Dinosaurs. (p. 270)
Carpenter, Kristie. Adventures of the Angles. (p. 23)
Carpenter, L. J. Out of the Tank. (p. 1311)
Carpenter, Lynette Stutzman. My Brother, the Senator. (p. 1199)
Carpenter, Mark, illus. see Barfield, Maggie.
Carpenter, Mark And Anna, illus. see Barfield, Maggie.
Carpenter, Michael, jt. auth. see Fulton, Roger.
Carpenter, Michelle D. More No Fear here Six Scary Stories to Thrill You & the Kids + Extras. (p. 1174)
—No Fear Here Five Scary Stories to Thrill You & the Kids. (p. 1258)
Carpenter, Mike, illus. see Olsen, Grant Orrin.
Carpenter, Nan. Louisa May Alcott & Thoreau's Flute, Two Letters: The Huntington Library Quarterly V24, No. 1, November 1960. (p. 1058)
Carpenter, Nancy. Queen Victoria's Bathing Machine. (p. 1425)
Carpenter, Nancy, illus. see Ashman, Linda.
Carpenter, Nancy, illus. see Beard, Darleen Bailey & Beard, Darleen B.
Carpenter, Nancy, illus. see Bunting, Eve.
Carpenter, Nancy, illus. see Carbone, Elisa.
Carpenter, Nancy, illus. see Cullen, Lynn.
Carpenter, Nancy, illus. see Facklam, Margery.
Carpenter, Nancy, illus. see Fleming, Candace.
Carpenter, Nancy, illus. see George, Kristine O'Connell.
Carpenter, Nancy, illus. see Hopkinson, Deborah.
Carpenter, Nancy, illus. see Moore, Eva.
Carpenter, Nancy, illus. see Nye, Naomi Shihab.
Carpenter, Nancy, illus. see Offill, Jenny.
Carpenter, Nancy, illus. see White, Linda Arms.
Carpenter, Nancy, illus. see Winters, Kay.
Carpenter, Nancy, jt. auth. see Hopkinson, Deborah.
Carpenter, Nancy, jt. auth. see Winters, Kay.
Carpenter, Ray. Adventures of Benny Bell. (p. 16)
Carpenter, Scott. Little Pepper Muffin. (p. 1033)
Carpenter, Stephen. If Kids Ruled the School: More Kids' Favorite Funny School Poems. (p. 853)
—I've Been Burping in the Classroom. (p. 900)
—Mary Had a Little Jam, & Other Silly Rhymes. (p. 1100)
—What I Did on My Summer Vacation: Kids' Favorite Funny Summer Vacation Poems. (p. 1886)
Carpenter, Stephen, illus. see Lansky, Bruce.
Carpenter, Stephen, illus. see Lansky, Bruce & Meadowbrook Press Staff.
Carpenter, Stephen, illus. see Lansky, Bruce & Wiechmann, Angela, eds.
Carpenter, Stephen, illus. see Lansky, Bruce, ed.
Carpenter, Stephen, illus. see Lansky, Bruce.
Carpenter, Stephen, illus. see Meadowbrook Press Staff.
Carpenter, Stephen, jt. auth. see Lansky, Bruce.
Carpenter, Susan, jt. auth. see Glenn, Suki.
Carpenter, Suzanne. Barti & Bel Whizz Around Wales. (p. 140)
Carpenter, Suzanne, illus. see Morden, Daniel.
Carpenter, Suzanne, illus. see Morgan, Ruth.
Carpenter, Suzanne, illus. see Stephens, Chris S.
Carpenter, Tad. Barnyard Friends. (p. 140)
—I Say, You Say Animal Sounds! (p. 845)
—I Say, You Say Colors! (p. 845)
—I Say, You Say Feelings! (p. 845)
—I Say, You Say Opposites! (p. 845)
—On the Go. (p. 1290)
Carpenter, Tad, illus. see Burleigh, Robert.
Carpenter, Tad, illus. see Galante, Cecilia.
Carpenter, Tad, illus. see Leppanen, Debbie.
Carpenter, Tad, illus. see McCanna, Tim.
Carpenter, Tad, illus. see Natural Resources Defense Council Staff, et al.
Carpenter, Tad, illus. see Pantone.
Carpenter, Tad, illus. see Tuell, Todd.
Carpenter, Thomas. 'Ps' & 'Qs' And 'Ws' (p. 1413)
Carpenter, Tom. Big Game Hunting: Bear, Deer, Elk, Sheep, & More. (p. 181)
—Freshwater Fishing: Bass, Trout, Walleye, Catfish, & More. (p. 637)
—Saltwater Fishing: Snapper, Mackerel, Bluefish, Tuna, & More. (p. 1506)
—Small Game Hunting: Rabbit, Raccoon, Squirrel, Opossum, & More. (p. 1592)
—Upland Bird Hunting: Wild Turkey, Pheasant, Grouse, Quail, & More. (p. 1825)
—Waterfowl Hunting: Duck, Goose, & More. (p. 1863)
Carpenter, Tracy. Country Fair Camp. (p. 372)
—Summer Camp. (p. 1674)
—Winter Camp. (p. 1938)
Carpenter-Pezoldt, Wendy. Grandma's Unique Birthday Songs. (p. 709)
Carpentiere, Elizabeth. Kidnapped (p. 952)
Carper, Mary Ann. My Name Is Tiny: A Children's Devotional about Fitting In. (p. 1215)
Carper, Virginia. Animal Teachings: Mammals. (p. 80)
—Animal Teachings Volume Two: Birds (p. 80)
Carpio, Melvin M. Web of Darkness. (p. 1870)
Carr, A. E. K., illus. see Imholtz, August & Tannenbaum, Alison.
Carr, Aaron. American Flag. (p. 60)
—Animal Patterns. (p. 79)
—Arabian Oryx. (p. 94)
—Armadillos. (p. 99)
—Bird. (p. 190)
—Bison. (p. 193)
—Blues. (p. 204)
—BMX. (p. 204)
—Bmx. (p. 204)
—BMX with Code. (p. 204)
—Bobcats. (p. 206)
—Break Dance. (p. 224)
—Bumblebees. (p. 241)
—Capitol Building. (p. 263)
—Cat. (p. 277)
—Chameleon. (p. 289)
—Chimpanzee. (p. 306)
—Cockroaches. (p. 337)
—Conejo. (p. 356)
—Cougars. (p. 369)
—Country. (p. 372)
—Cruise Ships. (p. 386)
—Diseños de Animales. (p. 450)
—Diseños de Las Plantas. (p. 450)
—Dog. (p. 460)
—Dogs. (p. 462)
—Earthworms. (p. 498)
—Esqui. (p. 536)
—Explorando Los Colores. (p. 550)
—Exploring Colors. (p. 551)
—Ferret. (p. 582)
—Fire Station. (p. 590)
—Fire Trucks. (p. 591)
—Fish. (p. 598)
—Formas. (p. 620)
—Foxes. (p. 626)
—Frog. (p. 639)
—Garbage Trucks. (p. 655)
—Gato. (p. 658)
—Giraffe. (p. 677)
—Golden Gate Bridge. (p. 694)
—Goose. (p. 702)
—Gophers. (p. 702)
—Grandes y Pequeño. (p. 707)
—Great Seal. (p. 718)
—Guinea Pig. (p. 731)
—Gusto. (p. 733)
—Hamster. (p. 739)
—Helicopters. (p. 763)
—Hermit Crab. (p. 771)
—Hippo. (p. 781)
—Horses. (p. 800)
—Hospital. (p. 801)
—Humpback Whale. (p. 827)
—Hyena. (p. 831)
—Iguana. (p. 856)
—Jefferson Memorial. (p. 912)
—Ladybugs. (p. 971)
—Lemur. (p. 991)
—Library. (p. 1005)
—Lincoln Memorial. (p. 1018)
—Magents with Code. (p. 1071)
—Magnets, with Code. (p. 1076)
—Moose. (p. 1173)
—Mosquitoes. (p. 1176)
—Moths. (p. 1179)
—Moto X. (p. 1179)
—Moto X with Code. (p. 1179)
—Motocross. (p. 1179)
—Narwhal. (p. 1230)
—Natural o Hecho Por el Hombre. (p. 1235)
—Natural or Man-Made, with Code. (p. 1235)
—Nature Patterns. (p. 1236)
—Números. (p. 1273)
—Oído. (p. 1282)
—Olfato. (p. 1285)
—Opposites, with Code. (p. 1301)
—Owls. (p. 1315)
—Pájaro. (p. 1319)
—Perro. (p. 1343)
—Pez. (p. 1349)
—Plants. (p. 1369)
—Pledge of Allegiance. (p. 1373)
—Police Station. (p. 1380)
—Pop. (p. 1384)
—Potbellied Pig. (p. 1388)
—Rabbit. (p. 1429)
—Rap. (p. 1438)
—Rat. (p. 1440)
—Rhino. (p. 1467)
—Rock. (p. 1481)
—Salamander. (p. 1504)
—San Francisco 49ers. (p. 1510)
—School. (p. 1522)
—Sea Turtles. (p. 1535)
—Semi Trucks. (p. 1550)
—Shapes. (p. 1560)
—Skateboard. (p. 1583)
—Skateboarding. (p. 1583)
—Skiing. (p. 1584)
—Snow Leopard. (p. 1599)
—Snowboard. (p. 1600)
—Snowboarding. (p. 1600)
—Solids. (p. 1607)
—Soy el Elefante. (p. 1618)
—Spring. (p. 1634)
—Stick Insects. (p. 1649)
—Summer. (p. 1673)
—Surf. (p. 1685)
—Surfing. (p. 1685)
—Tacto. (p. 1695)
—Tiranosaurio Rex. (p. 1757)
—Trains. (p. 1777)
—Turkey. (p. 1797)
—Vista. (p. 1846)
—Washington Monument. (p. 1860)
—Winter. (p. 1937)
—Wolverine. (p. 1944)
—Woodpeckers. (p. 1949)
Carr, Annaleise. Annaleise Carr: How I Conquered Lake Ontario to Help Kids Battling Cancer (p. 85)
Carr, Annie Roe. Nan Sherwood at Pine Camp or the Old Lum. (p. 1228)
—Nan Sherwood at Rose Ranch. (p. 1228)
—Nan Sherwood at Rose Ranch or the Old Me. (p. 1228)
—Nan Sherwood's Winter Holidays. (p. 1228)
—Nan Sherwoods Winter Holidays or Rescuin. (p. 1228)
Carr, Barbara, et al. Revise for Cambridge Primary Checkpoint Maths. (p. 1466)
Carr, Bernie. Jake & Miller's Big Adventure: A Prepper's Book for Kids. Wells, Aja, illus. (p. 905)
Carr, Bret, jt. auth. see Wake, Iam.
Carr, C. Hanna's Way. (p. 743)
Carr, Crystal. Ram, Ham, Strawberry Jam: Identifying Nouns. (p. 1437)
Carr, Dan. God I Need to Talk Bad Temper. (p. 689)
—God I Need to Talk Cheating. (p. 689)
—God I Need to Talk Hurting Oth. (p. 689)
—God I Need to Talk Paying Atte. (p. 689)
—God, I Need to Talk to You about Lying. Clark, Bartholomew & Clark, Bill, illus. (p. 689)
—God, I Need to Talk to You about Sharing. Clark, Bartholomew & Clark, Bill, illus. (p. 689)
—God, I Need to Talk to You about Stealing. Clark, Bartholomew & Clark, Bill, illus. (p. 689)
—God, I Need to Talk to You about Vandalism. Clark, Bartholomew & Clark, Bill, illus. (p. 689)
Carr, David. Trebb the Troll. (p. 1783)
Carr, Debra. Curry Comb Caper. Carr, Stephen, illus. (p. 394)
—Feed Trough Thriller. Carr, Stephen, illus. (p. 580)
—Misty Is Missing. Carr, Stephen, illus. (p. 1155)
Carr, Debra, jt. auth. see Carr, Jon.
Carr, Denis. 10 Most Significant Medical Breakthroughs. (p. 1994)
Carr, Diane. Chattahoochee River. (p. 295)
—River Dragon Activity Book: Just Add Kids. (p. 1475)
Carr, Dorothy. Snow Goes Home. (p. 1599)
Carr, Elias & Karre, Andrew. Combination. (p. 346)
—Fight the Wind. (p. 585)
Carr, Elsie, tr. see Farley, Walter.
Carr, Fran. Wilbur Runs Away. (p. 1928)
Carr, Greg, illus. see Carr, Heather.
Carr, Heather. Jiggleworm. Carr, Greg, illus. (p. 917)
Carr, Holly. What Is Pink? (p. 1890)
Carr, Holly, illus. see Rossetti, Christina.
Carr, Howie. Brothers Bulger: How They Terrorized & Corrupted Boston for a Quarter Century. (p. 231)
Carr, Jacqueline. Tiny Tot Prayers: Baby's First Prayers. (p. 1757)
Carr, Jan. 'Cause I Love You. Howarth, Daniel, illus. (p. 282)
—Greedy Apostrophe: A Cautionary Tale. Long, Ethan, illus. (p. 720)
—Splish, Splash, Spring. Donohue, Dorothy, illus. (p. 1630)
—Sweet Hearts. Donohue, Dorothy, illus. (p. 1689)
—Toe Shoe Mouse. Bell, Jennifer, illus. (p. 1761)
Carr, Jason. Taking off the Wheels. (p. 1698)
—When You Hear the Floor Creak. (p. 1905)
Carr, Jennifer. Be Who You Are. (p. 149)
Carr, Joaquin. American Revolution: Set Of 6. (p. 63)
—American Revolution: Text Pairs. (p. 63)
—Habitats of South America: Set Of 6. (p. 735)
—Habitats of South America: Text Pairs. (p. 735)
Carr, Jon & Carr, Debra. Harry the Hippo. (p. 751)
—Jeremy the Giraffe. (p. 913)
Carr, Josie. IGod: Prayers & Promises to Connect to You with Him. (p. 856)
Carr, Julie B. Countdown to a Miracle: 2nd Edition: the Making of Me. (p. 370)
Carr, Karen. Christmas Wishing Quilt. (p. 316)
Carr, Karen, illus. see Bailey, Gerry.
Carr, Karen, illus. see Bentley, Dawn & Studio Mouse Staff.
Carr, Karen, illus. see Bentley, Dawn.
Carr, Karen, illus. see Berger, Melvin & Berger, Gilda.
Carr, Karen, illus. see Chin, Karen & Holmes, Thom.
Carr, Karen, illus. see Galvin, Laura Gates & Studiomouse Staff.
Carr, Karen, illus. see Wagner, Karen.
Carr, Karen, tr. see Bentley, Dawn.

C

Carr, Karen & Diffily, Deborah. Jurassic Shark. Carr, Karen, illus. (p. 937)
Carr, Karent, illus. see Bentley, Dawn & Studio Mouse Staff.
Carr, Kathy. Granny, Where Did My Mommy Go? (p. 710)
Carr, Lawrence. Under the Peach Tree. (p. 1814)
Carr, Lynn. Marty Likes to Party! (p. 1098)
Carr, Margaret. Colorado Settlers & Native Americans. (p. 343)
Carr, Mary. Great Chocolate Caper: Mystery That Teaches Logic Skills. (p. 714)
Carr, Mary Ann. Great Chocolate Caper: A Mystery That Teaches Logic Skills. (p. 714)
—More One-Hour Mysteries. (p. 1174)
Carr, Mary Jane. Children of the Covered Wagon. (p. 302)
Carr, Melissa S. Who Are the Muslims? (p. 1914)
Carr, Pat. Border Ransom. (p. 214)
Carr, Patrick W. Legend's Granddaughter: Not Quite Super, Book 1. Dabbs, Douglas, illus. (p. 990)
Carr, Paul C. Adventures of Three Cousins. (p. 24)
Carr, Richard. Honey. (p. 794)
Carr, Roger Vaughan. Climb. (p. 332)
Carr, Roger Vaughan & Knapsey, Kath. How to Discover the World. (p. 816)
Carr, Sharleen. Watch for Fallen Rock. (p. 1860)
Carr, Sheryl. Little Drop & the Healing Place. Harris, La Verne Abe, illus. (p. 1027)
Carr, Simonetta. Athanasius. Abraxas, Matt, illus. (p. 112)
—Augustine of Hippo. Lowe, Wes, illus. (p. 115)
—John Calvin. Taglietti, Emanuele, illus. (p. 921)
—John Knox. Abraxas, Matt, illus. (p. 922)
—John Owen. Abraxas, Matt, illus. (p. 922)
Carr, Stephen. Water Views. Smith, Eric, illus. (p. 1863)
Carr, Stephen, illus. see Carr, Debra.
Carr, Suzanna & Crutchfield, Tylicia. Nosey Rosey. Illustrated by: Charles Duke, illus. (p. 1266)
Carr, Tabatha, illus. see Mervyn, Catherine Antolino.
Carradice, Phil. Child's Dylan Thomas. (p. 304)
Carradice, Phil & Thomas, Frances. Hannah Goes to War. (p. 742)
Carragain, Eamonn O. Ritual & the Rood: Liturgical Images & the Old English Poems of the Dream of the Rood Tradition. (p. 1475)
Carrano, Matthew T., jt. auth. see Clencin, Scott.
Carrano, Matthew T., jt. auth. see Kranking, Kathy.
Carranza, Maite, et al. Clan de la Loba. (p. 326)
—Desierto de Hielo. (p. 429)
—maldicio´n de Odi. (p. 1083)
Carrarini, Jean Charles, jt. auth. see Carrarini, Rose.
Carrarini, Rose & Carrarini, Jean Charles. Breakfast, Lunch, Tea. Glanville, Toby, photos by. (p. 225)
Carrasco, Jose Manuel. viaje de las semillas. (p. 1839)
Carrasco, Xavier. Rumpelstiltskin. Infante, Francesc, illus. (p. 1495)
Carrasquilla, Tomas. Cuentos. (p. 389)
Carraway, Rose. Chickens on the Farm. (p. 300)
—Chickens on the Farm / Pollos de Granja. (p. 300)
—Cows on the Farm: Vacas de Granja? (p. 374)
—Cows on the Farm. (p. 374)
—Fun Frogs: Ranas Saltarinas. (p. 647)
—Fun Frogs. (p. 647)
—Goats on the Farm. (p. 688)
—Goats on the Farm / Cabras de Granja. (p. 688)
—Great Guinea Pigs. (p. 716)
—Happy Hermit Crabs: Cangrejos Ermitaños Felices. (p. 746)
—Happy Hermit Crabs. (p. 746)
—Horses on the Farm. (p. 800)
—Horses on the Farm / Caballos de Granja. (p. 800)
—Marvelous Mice: Ratones Maravillosos. (p. 1099)
—Marvelous Mice. (p. 1099)
—Pigs on the Farm: Cerdos de Granja. (p. 1358)
—Pigs on the Farm. (p. 1358)
—Sheep on the Farm: Ovejas de Granja. (p. 1564)
—Sheep on the Farm. (p. 1564)
—Slithering Snakes: Serpientes Resbaladizas. (p. 1591)
—Slithering Snakes. (p. 1591)
—Terrific Turtles: Tortugas Asombrosas. (p. 1721)
—Terrific Turtles. (p. 1721)
Carr-Dudley, Janet. Mama's Last Chance. (p. 1084)
Carre, John Le, see Le Carré, John.
Carre, Lilli. Tippy & the Night Parade. (p. 1757)
Carreiro, Carolyn. Make Your Own Puppets & Puppet Theaters. Jourdenais-Martin, Norma Jean, illus. (p. 1080)
Carrel, Douglas, illus. see Drake, Ernest.
Carrel, Douglas, illus. see Steer, Dugald A.
Carrell, Douglas, illus. see Grey, Allan.
Carrell, Elizabeth. Cat Named Romeo. (p. 278)
Carrer, Chiara. Otto Carrotto. (p. 1307)
Carreras De Sosa, Lydia. Sé Que Estás Allí. (p. 1534)
Carreres, Albert, illus. see Porter, Alan J.
Carreres, Albert, illus. see Smith, Brian & Moore, B. Clay.
Carrero, Jorge & Cody, William. Buffalo Bill. (p. 235)
Carrescia, Reid, illus. see Saccheri, Josephine.
Carretero, M—nica, jt. auth. see Carretero, Mónica.
Carretero, Mónica. Fairy Handbook. (p. 563)
—Manual de Piratas. (p. 1088)
—Pirate Handbook. (p. 1362)
—Witches Handbook. (p. 1941)
Carretero, Monica, illus. see Miranda, Conchita & Miranda Ros, Conchita.
Carretero, Mónica & Carretero, M—nica. Circo de Pulgas. (p. 321)
—Familia Bola. Carretero, Mónica, illus. (p. 567)
Carretero, Monica, et al. Flea Circus. Carretero, Monica, illus. (p. 603)
—Haunted Houses Handbook. Carretero, Monica, illus. (p. 753)
—Roly-Polies. Carretero, Monica, illus. (p. 1485)
Carrick, Carol. Mothers Are Like That. Carrick, Paul, illus. (p. 1178)
—Patrick's Dinosaurs Carrick, Donald, illus. (p. 1329)
—Polar Bears Are Hungry. (p. 1379)
Carrick, Donald, illus. see Carrick, Carol.
Carrick, Paul. Watch Out for Wolfgang. Carrick, Paul, illus. (p. 1861)
Carrick, Paul, illus. see Carrick, Carol.
Carrick, Paul, illus. see Suen, Anastasia.
Carrie C Yakola. Lucy's Shooting Star. (p. 1063)
Carrier, Isabelle. Paseo de Nina. (p. 1326)
Carrier, Jason, illus. see Franklin, Kirk.
Carrier, Jason, illus. see Scali, Jacob, et al.
Carrier, Misty. Who Stole the Hot Sauce? Columbeanu, Alexandra, illus. (p. 1917)
Carrier, Stephen, jt. auth. see Carrier, Therese.
Carrier, Therese & Carrier, Stephen. Josiah's School Fun Day. Hatfield, Tommy, illus. (p. 927)
Carrier, Tracey Dahle, illus. see Boling, Ruth L.
Carrière, Francine. Comme un Conte d'Enfant et le Clochard de New Perry. (p. 348)
Carriere, Jean-Claude. Little Black Book. (p. 1024)
Carrière, Nicole, jt. auth. see Wallace, Stone.
Carrigan, James. That We Are Gentle Creatures. (p. 1726)
Carriger, Candace. Inside My Garden. Allen, Cassandra, illus. (p. 877)
Carriger, Gail. Curtsies & Conspiracies. (p. 395)
—Etiquette & Espionage. (p. 539)
—Waistcoats & Weaponry. (p. 1852)
Carrigg, Susan, illus. see Keltz, Karen.
Carrilho, Andre, illus. see McKissack, Patricia C.
Carrilho, Andre, illus. see Winter, Jonah.
Carrillo, Azalea, photos by see Kassandra, ed.
Carrillo, Charles M., illus. see Church, Peggy Pond.
Carrillo, Consuelo, tr. see Auld, Mary.
Carrillo, Consuelo, tr. see Holland, Gini.
Carrillo, Consuelo, tr. see Macken, JoAnn Early.
Carrillo, J. Raul, illus. see Messick, Maxine.
Carrillo, P. S. Desert Passage. (p. 429)
Carrillo, Summer. Why Being Unique Makes Me Wonderful: Children Can Learn to Understand Why They Are Unique. (p. 1922)
Carrington, Edith. History of the Robins & Keepers Trave. (p. 785)
Carrington, Leonora. Leche Del Sueno. (p. 987)
Carrington, Marsha Gray, illus. see Chaconas, Dori.
Carrington, Marsha Gray, illus. see McDonald, Megan.
Carrington, Matt, illus. see Gors, Steven E.
Carrington, Rachel, et al. Secrets Volume 22 Dark Whispers - the Secrets Collection: The Best in Women's Erotic Romance: Dark Whispers. (p. 1546)
Carrington, Samala. Sally Sunshine Mandy Moon. (p. 1505)
Carrión, Julio & Zárate, Patricia. Cultura política de la democracia en Perú 2008: El impacto de la Gobernabilidad. (p. 390)
Carris, Joan. Magic at the Bed & Biscuit. Jones, Noah Z., illus. (p. 1071)
—Welcome to the Bed & Biscuit. Jones, Noah Z., illus. (p. 1873)
—Wild Times at the Bed & Biscuit. Jones, Noah Z., illus. (p. 1930)
Carris, Joan D. Ghost of a Chance. (p. 671)
Carris, Joan Davenport. Magic at the Bed & Biscuit. Meserve, Jessica & Jones, Noah Z., illus. (p. 1071)
Carroll. Lbd Gka Nf Fun for All Seasons. (p. 981)
Carroll, jt. auth. see Carroll, Lewis, pseud.
Carroll, B. H. Comentario Carroll-Doce: Apocalipsis: Carroll's Commentary-12: Apocalypse. (p. 348)
Carroll, Barbara. Valentine: A Purr-fect Kitty. (p. 1830)
Carroll, Barbara G. 3 Little Pugs & Other Dog Tails. (p. 1991)
—Harry the Mouse Who Lived in My Car. (p. 751)
Carroll, Caroline, jt. auth. see Carroll, Michael.
Carroll, Cheri Sunshine, ed. see Aldana, Jacquelyn.
Carroll, Claudia. Missy Mouse & the Rocket Ship. (p. 1154)
—Old Dumpling & the Rainy Day. (p. 1283)
—Shmadiggle & the Imagination Asteroid. (p. 1568)
Carroll, Colleen. Babies. (p. 123)
—Dogs. (p. 462)
—Elements: Animals - People - Families - Play - Feelings - Weather Set 1 (p. 510)
—Horses. (p. 800)
—How Artists See (p. 805)
—How Artists See: Heroes, Artists, Cities, Elements Set (p. 805)
—How Artists See: Animals - People - Feelings - Weather Set 1 (p. 805)
—How Artists See: Work; Heroes; Cities; Elements; America; Artists Set 2 (p. 805)
—How Artists See Heroes: Myth, History, War, Everyday. (p. 805)
—How Artists See Work/Play/Families/America Set 2 (p. 805)
—Trains. (p. 1777)
Carroll, D. Year of the Turtle. (p. 1969)
Carroll, D. L. Sir Licksalot & the Island Fools. (p. 1580)
Carroll, D. S. Victory over Victory: An Essay Studying our Personal & Cultural Compulsion in Pursuit of Victory, Its Costs, & Its Alternatives of Arrogance or Mo. (p. 1840)
Carroll, Danielle. Great Divide (p. 715)
—Is It Odd or Even? (p. 889)
—Place Value. (p. 1366)
—Tiling with Shapes. (p. 1750)
—What Is a Hundred? (p. 1888)
Carroll, Harlisha. Miracle Mouse & Jesus - Book: (Short Stories 1) (p. 1148)
—Miracle Mouse & Jesus Book #3: Short Stories 2. (p. 1148)
Carroll, Jacquie Lund. Queen's Jewels. Gillen, Rosemarie, illus. (p. 1425)
Carroll, James Christopher. Boy & the Moon. Carroll, James Christopher, illus. (p. 217)
Carroll, Jamuna. America's Youth. (p. 64)
—Do Animals Have Rights? (p. 456)
—India. (p. 870)
—Pharmaceutical Industry. (p. 1350)
—School Reform. Berlatsky, Noah, ed. (p. 1523)
Carroll, Jamuna & Cothran, Helen, eds. Do Children Have Rights? (p. 456)
Carroll, Jason. I Know I Wanna Go to Heaven. (p. 840)
Carroll, Jean E. Shadows of Las Vegas. (p. 1558)
Carroll, Jenny, pseud. Safe House. (p. 1502)
Carroll, Jenny, pseud & Cabot, Meg. Code Name Cassandra. (p. 338)
—Darkest Hour - The Mediator. (p. 408)
—Reunion. (p. 1465)
—Sanctuary. (p. 1510)
—Shadowland (p. 1558)
—Shadowland. (p. 1558)
Carroll, Jillian. Hot Spot. (p. 802)
—Where to Stay. (p. 1910)
—Zoom Around a Moon. (p. 1989)
Carroll, Joan, ed. see Stripling, Joe.
Carroll, Jody. Mitsy Morgan: Six Monkeys Past Midnight. (p. 1156)
Carroll, John. Adventures of Robbie the Raindrop. (p. 22)
—Adventures of Robbie the Raindrop. Mann, Derek & Bouse, Biff, illus. (p. 22)
Carroll, Jonathan. Meet Julius Carmichael: First Day Blues. Koltun, Amy, illus. (p. 1121)
Carroll, Joyce Armstrong. Dr. JAC's Guide to Writing With Depth. (p. 475)
Carroll, Joyce Armstrong, et al. Writing & Grammar: Communication in Action (p. 1964)
—Writing & Grammar: Communication in Action, Bronze Level (p. 1964)
—Writing & Grammar: Communication in Action, Platinum Level (p. 1964)
Carroll, Jr., illus. see Mansur, Motesem.
Carroll, Kathleen. Guide to Great Field Trips. (p. 730)
Carroll, Kathy. Rabbit & the Amazing Hopping Contest. (p. 1429)
Carroll, Katie, illus. see Carroll, Michael Shane.
Carroll, Katie L. Elixir Bound. (p. 513)
Carroll, Lewis. Alice Ihre Obmteier Im Wunderlaund. (p. 39)
Carroll, Lewis, jt. auth. see Rae, John.
Carroll, Lewis, jt. auth. see Richards, Anna Matlack.
Carroll, Lewis, jt. auth. see Sewell, Byron W.
Carroll, Lewis, pseud. Alice's Anters in Ferlielann. McClure, Derrick, tr. from ENG. (p. 30)
—Ailis's Anterins I the Laun o Ferlies. McCallum, Andrew, tr. from ENG. (p. 30)
—Alice au Pays des Merveilles. (p. 39)
—Alice in Wonderland Pérez, Daniel et al, illus. (p. 39)
—Alice in Wonderland. (p. 39)
—Alice in Wonderland. Steadman, Ralph, illus. (p. 39)
—Alice in Wonderland & Through the Looking-Glass. Andreasen, Dan, illus. (p. 39)
—Alice in Wonderland Giant Poster & Coloring Book. Tenniel, John, illus. (p. 39)
—Alice in Wonderland Made Simple for Kids. Sloan, Peter, illus. (p. 39)
—Alice Through the Looking-Glass. Oxenbury, Helen, illus. (p. 39)
—Alice's Abenteuer im Wunderland. Zimmermann, Antonie, tr. (p. 39)
—Alice's Adventirs in Wonderlaand. Johnson, Laureen, tr. from ENG. (p. 39)
—Alice's Adventures in Wonderland. (p. 39)
—Alice's Adventures in Wonderland. Tenniel, John, illus. (p. 39)
—Alice's Adventures in Wonderland. Robinson, Gordon, illus. (p. 39)
—Alice's Adventures in Wonderland Tenniel, John, illus. (p. 40)
—Alice's Adventures in Wonderland: And Other Stories. Tenniel, John, illus. (p. 40)
—Alice's Adventures in Wonderland: With a Discussion of Imagination. Schneider, Rex, tr. (p. 40)
—Alice's Adventures in Wonderland. (p. 40)
—Alice's Adventures in Wonderland. Bloom, Harold, ed. (p. 40)
—Alice's Adventures in Wonderland. Lomie, June, illus. (p. 40)
—Alice's Adventures in Wonderland. Wiley, Nancy, illus. (p. 40)
—Alice's Adventures in Wonderland. Tenniel, John, illus. (p. 40)
—Alice's Adventures in Wonderland. McKowen, Scott, illus. (p. 40)
—Alice's Adventures in Wonderland. Lipchenko, Oleg, illus. (p. 40)
—Alice's Adventures in Wonderland. Oxenbury, Helen, illus. (p. 40)
—Alice's Adventures in Wonderland. Rountree, Harry, illus. (p. 40)
—Alice's Adventures in Wonderland. Ghiuselev, Iassen, illus. (p. 40)
—Alice's Adventures in Wonderland. Ingpen, Robert R., illus. (p. 40)
—Alice's Adventures in Wonderland. Evangelista, Mauro, illus. (p. 40)
—Alice's Adventures in Wonderland. Garcia, Camille Rose, illus. (p. 40)
—Alice's Adventures in Wonderland & Through the Looking Glass. (p. 40)
—Alice's Adventures in Wonderland & Through the Looking-Glass. Haughton, Hugh, ed. (p. 40)
—Alice's Adventures in Wonderland & Through the Looking Glass. Tenniel, John, illus. (p. 40)
—Alice's Adventures in Wonderland, & Through the Looking Glass Bachelier, Anne, illus. (p. 40)
—Alice's Adventures in Wonderland & Through the Looking Glass. Tenniel, John & Bickford-Smith, Coralie, illus. (p. 40)
—Alice's Adventures in Wonderland, & Through the Looking Glass. Haughton, Hugh & Roberge, Thomas, eds. (p. 40)
—Alice's Adventures under Ground: Being the Book Afterwards Developed into Alice's Adventures in Wonderland. (p. 40)
—Alice's Carrànts in Wunnerlan. Morrison-Smyth, Anne, tr. from ENG. (p. 40)
—Alicia en el País de las Maravillas. (p. 40)
—Alicia en el Pais de las Maravillas. Aranguren, Dolores, tr. (p. 40)
—Alicia en el Pais de Las Maravillas, Fantasmagoria, y un Cuento Enredado. (p. 40)
—Anya V Stranye Chudes. Nabokov, Vladimir, tr. from RUS. (p. 90)
—Aventuras de Alicia. (p. 119)
—Aventuras de Alisia en la Pais de Mervelias. Davies, Simon, tr. from ENG. (p. 119)
—Aventuroj de Alicio en Mirlando: Alice's Adventures in Wonderland in Esperanto. (p. 119)
—Aventuros d'Alis in Marvoland. Midgley, Ralph, tr. from ENG. (p. 119)
—Best of Lewis Carroll. (p. 170)
—Eachdraidh Ealasaid Ann an Tir Nan Iongantas. Watson, Moray, tr. from ENG. (p. 492)
—Hunting of the Snark: An Agony in Eight Fits. Lipchenko, Oleg, illus. (p. 829)
—Hunting of the Snark. Peake, Mervyn, illus. (p. 829)
—Jabberwocky. Jorisch, Stéphane, illus. (p. 902)
—Lès-Aventûres D'Alice Ô Pèyis Dès Mèrvèy. Capron, André, tr. from ENG. (p. 993)
—Ma Loko o Ke Aniani Ku a Me Ka Mea I Loaa IaAleka Ma Laila. (p. 1067)
—Michael Foreman's Alice's Adventures in Wonderland. Foreman, Michael, illus. (p. 1134)
—Na Hana Kupanaha a Aleka Ma Ka Aina Kamaha'o. NeSmith, R. Keao, tr. from ENG. (p. 1227)
—Nonsense Verse. Hussey, Lorna, illus. (p. 1263)
—Nursery Alice. (p. 1273)
—Nursery Alice. Tenniel, John, illus. (p. 1273)
—Nursery Alice. Tenniel, John & Thomson, E. Gertrude, illus. (p. 1273)
—Nursery Alice. Tenniel, Sir John & Thomson, E. Gertrude, illus. (p. 1273)
—'O Tafaoga a 'Alise I Le Nu'o O Mea Ofoofogia. Simanu-Klutz, Luafata, tr. from ENG. (p. 1274)
—Sense & Nonsense Stories from Lewis Carroll: Alice, Sylvie & Bruno, & More. Tenniel, John, illus. (p. 1551)
—Story of Sylvie & Bruno. (p. 1660)
—Sylvie & Bruno. (p. 1693)
—Sylvie & Bruno Concluded. (p. 1693)
—Sylvie & Bruno Concluded. Furniss, Harry, illus. (p. 1693)
—Through the Looking Glass. (p. 1745)
—Through the Looking Glass. Tenniel, John, illus. (p. 1745)
—Through the Looking-Glass. (p. 1745)
—Through the Looking-Glass, & What Alice Found There, Original Version: Alice Through the Looking Glass. Tenniel, John, illus. (p. 1745)
—Trans la Spegulo Kaj Kion Alico Trovis Tie. Broadribb, Donald, tr. from ENG. (p. 1778)
Carroll, Lewis, pseud & Baker, Kyle. Through the Looking-Glass. (p. 1745)
Carroll, Lewis, pseud & Bué, Henri. Adventures D'Alice Au Pays des Merveilles. (p. 15)
Carroll, Lewis, pseud & Burstein, Mark. Sonja in a Kingdom of Wonder. (p. 1612)
Carroll, Lewis, pseud & Carroll. Alicia en el País de las Maravillas. (p. 40)
Carroll, Lewis, pseud & Everson, Michael. Alice's Adventures in Wonderland: Retold in Words of One Syllable. (p. 40)
—Dee Erläwnisse Von Alive Em Wundalaund. (p. 422)
Carroll, Lewis, pseud & Faraday, L. Winifred. Sylvie & Bruno. (p. 1693)
Carroll, Lewis, pseud & Fleemin, Sandy. Ailice's Adventures in Wunnerland. (p. 30)
Carroll, Lewis, pseud & Frith, Barbara. Alice's Adventures in Wonderland & Through the Looking-Glass. Tenniel, John, illus. (p. 40)
Carroll, Lewis, pseud & Furniss, Harry. Sylvie & Bruno. (p. 1693)
—Sylvie & Bruno Concluded. (p. 1693)
Carroll, Lewis, pseud & Kearney, Elfric Leofwine. Aventuroj de Alicio en Mirlando: Alice's Adventures in Wonderland in Esperanto. (p. 119)
Carroll, Lewis, pseud & Kontis, Alethea. Wonderland Alphabet: Alice's Adventures Through the ABCs & What She Found There. Lee, Janet K., illus. (p. 1948)
Carroll, Lewis, pseud & Nonnen, Emily. Alices äfventyr I Sagolandet. (p. 40)
Carroll, Lewis, pseud & Roberts, Selyf. Anturiaethau Alys Yng Ngwlad Hud. (p. 90)
Carroll, Lewis, pseud & Sabuda, Robert. Alice's Adventures in Wonderland. (p. 40)
Carroll, Lewis, pseud & Stowell, Brian. Contoyryssyn Ealish Ayns Cheer Ny Yindyssyn. (p. 361)
Carroll, Lewis, pseud & Sweeney, Kevin. Exeunt Alice. (p. 548)
Carroll, Lewis, pseud & Williams, Nicholas. Alys in POW an Anethow: Alice's Adventures in Wonderland in Cornish. (p. 51)
Carroll, Lewis, pseud & _órarinn Eldjárn. Ævintýri Lísu Undralandi. (p. 1843)
Carroll, Lewis, pseud, et al. Sylvie & Bruno. (p. 1693)
Carroll, Michael. Ascension. (p. 105)
—Awakening (p. 120)
—Hunter. (p. 828)
—Stronger: A Super Human Clash. (p. 1668)
—Super Human. (p. 1680)
Carroll, Michael, illus. see Bennett, Jeffrey, et al.
Carroll, Michael, illus. see Bennett, Jeffrey.
Carroll, Michael, illus. see DeCristofano, Carolyn Cinami.
Carroll, Michael & Carroll, Caroline. I Love God's Green Earth: Devotions for Kids Who Want to Take Care of God's Creation. (p. 842)
Carroll, Michael Shane. Brewster's New School. Carroll, Katie, illus. (p. 226)
—Bye-Bye Brewster. Carroll, Katie, illus. (p. 249)
Carroll, Mona. Jacob's Storm (p. 904)
Carroll, Myrna & Manley, Claudia B. Track & Field: Girls Rocking It. (p. 1775)
Carroll, Nick, ed. 30 Years of Flame: California's Legendary Surf Photographer. (p. 1996)
Carroll, Noel. Broken Odyssey. (p. 230)
Carroll, Pam, illus. see Domeniconi, David.
Carroll, Pam, illus. see Furlong, Reynolds Cynthia.
Carroll, Pam, illus. see Scillian, Devin.
Carroll, Quincy. Play Guitar (p. 1371)
Carroll, Raymond, illus. see Pinestein Press.
Carroll, Rosemary, illus. see Bloch, Lyudmila & Civitano, Tom.
Carroll, Sheila, ed. see Treadwell, Harriette Taylor & Free, Margaret.
Carroll, Thomas. Colony. (p. 342)
Carroll, Yvonne. Great Irish Legends for Children Lawrie, Robin, illus. (p. 716)
—Irish Legends for Children Su, Lucy, illus. (p. 888)

Carroll, Yvonne & Waters, Fiona, as told by. Child's Treasury of Irish Stories & Poems. (p. 305)
Carrow, Ian. Jackson's Surprise Party: Shapes & Their Attributes. (p. 904)
—Jackson's Surprise Party. (p. 904)
Carruth, J. A., text. Mary Queen of Scots. (p. 1101)
Carruth, Jane. More Bible Stories for Children. Cloke, Rene, illus. (p. 1174)
Carruthers, Deborah. Olivia's Birthday. Zvonarova, Jenny Desneige, illus. (p. 1287)
Carruthers, Sandy, illus. see Croall, Marie P.
Carruthers, Sandy, illus. see Fontes, Justine & Fontes, Ron.
Carruthers, Sandy, illus. see Storrie, Paul D.
Carryl, Charles E. Admiral's Caravan: A Tale Inspired by Lewis Carroll's Wonderland. (p. 13)
—Davy & the Goblin: Or, What Followed Reading 'Alice's Adventures in Wonderland' (p. 411)
Cars & Disney Book Group Staff. Cars. (p. 271)
Carsey, Alice. Pinocchio. (p. 1360)
—Pinocchio, the Tale of a Puppet. (p. 1361)
Carsey, Alice, illus. see Collodi, C.
Carsey, Alice, illus. see Collodi, Carlo.
Carsey, Alice & Collodi, Carlo. Pinocchio. (p. 1360)
Carson, Brendan. Fantastic Adventures of Pete & Lizzy: Pete & Lizzy Greet the World. (p. 571)
Carson, Brian & Ramen, Catherine. Understanding Your Right to Freedom from Searches. (p. 1816)
Carson, Ciaran, tr. see Penguin Press Staff.
Carson, Diana Pastora. All the Muchos in the World: A Special Story about Love. Pruitt, Ginny, illus. (p. 46)
Carson, Donna Wren. Mystery of Grimly Manor. (p. 1224)
Carson, J. Visiting the Vet: Learning the V Sound. (p. 1845)
—You Can Do It! Learning the Y Sound. (p. 1974)
Carson, Jack. Academy Attack. (p. 7)
—Battle Champions - Terminal Takedown. (p. 145)
—Canyon Clash. (p. 262)
—Swampland Slam. (p. 1688)
Carson, James. Saddle Boys in the Grand Canyon: Or the Hermit of the Cave. (p. 1501)
—Saddle Boys of the Rockies. (p. 1501)
—Saddle Boys of the Rockies or Lost on Th. (p. 1501)
Carson, Jana. We Both Read Bilingual Edition-About Space/Acerca Del Espacio. (p. 1866)
—We Both Read-The Boy Who Carried the Flag. Westerman, Johanna, illus. (p. 1866)
—We Both Read-The New Tribe. Treatner, Meryl, illus. (p. 1866)
Carson, Janet. Camping with Colleen. (p. 257)
—In the Forest: Learning Directional Concepts. (p. 866)
—What Is a Mammal? (p. 1888)
Carson, Jeanelle. Lexi Lou Meets Jadie Bear. (p. 1004)
Carson, Jill. Nuclear Power. (p. 1270)
Carson, John & Carson, Marlene. Ramblin' Rose: The Chinese Fortune Cookie. (p. 1437)
Carson, John E. Last Resort. (p. 978)
Carson, John E., jt. auth. see Carson, Marlene R.
Carson, John E. & Carson, Marlene R. Ramblin' Rose: The Porcelain Mines in Russia. (p. 1437)
—Wire Forest of Peru. (p. 1939)
Carson, Karen. Horseplay: 50 Puzzles & Games for Horse Lovers. (p. 800)
Carson, Marlene, jt. auth. see Carson, John.
Carson, Marlene R., jt. auth. see Carson, John E.
Carson, Marlene R. & Carson, John E. Ramblin' Rose: The Secret in the Arctic Ice. (p. 1437)
Carson, Mary E. 8th Landing: The Yankton Sioux Meet Lewis & Clark. (p. 1993)
Carson, Mary K., jt. auth. see Carson, Mary Kay.
Carson, Mary Kay. Bat Scientists. Uhlman, Tom, photos by. (p. 143)
—Beyond the Solar System: Exploring Galaxies, Black Holes, Alien Planets, & More; a History with 21 Activities. (p. 174)
—Did It All Start with a Snowball Fight? And Other Questions about... the American Revolution. Elliott, Mark & Hunt, Robert, illus. (p. 436)
—Emi & the Rhino Scientist. Uhlman, Tom, photos by. (p. 518)
—Exploring the Solar System: A History with 22 Activities. (p. 554)
—Far-Out Guide to Asteroids & Comets. (p. 572)
—Far-Out Guide to Earth. (p. 572)
—Far-Out Guide to Jupiter. (p. 572)
—Far-Out Guide to Mars. (p. 572)
—Far-Out Guide to Mercury. (p. 572)
—Far-Out Guide to Neptune. (p. 572)
—Far-Out Guide to Saturn. (p. 572)
—Far-Out Guide to the Icy Dwarf Planets. (p. 572)
—Far-Out Guide to the Moon. (p. 572)
—Far-Out Guide to the Sun. (p. 572)
—Far-Out Guide to Uranus. (p. 572)
—Far-Out Guide to Venus. (p. 572)
—How Many Planets Circle the Sun? And Other Questions about Our Solar System. Miller, Ron, illus. (p. 811)
—How Strong Is an Ant? And Other Questions about Bugs & Insects. Schwartz, Carol, illus. (p. 812)
—Inside Biosphere 2: Earth Science under Glass. Uhlman, Tom, photos by. (p. 876)
—Inside Hurricanes. (p. 876)
—Inside Tornadoes. (p. 878)
—Inside Weather. (p. 878)
—Underground Railroad for Kids: From Slavery to Freedom with 21 Activities. (p. 1815)
—Universe: From the Big Bang to Deep Space. (p. 1820)
—Weather Projects for Young Scientists: Experiments & Science Fair Ideas. (p. 1870)
—What Makes a Tornado Twist? And Other Questions about Weather. Mackay, Louis, illus. (p. 1892)
—What Sank the World's Biggest Ship? And Other Questions About... The Titanic. Elliott, Mark, illus. (p. 1893)
—What Sank the World's Biggest Ship? And Other Questions About . . . The Titanic. Elliott, Mark, illus. (p. 1893)
—What Was Your Dream, Dr. King? And Other Questions About... Martin Luther King, Jr. Madsen, Jim, illus. (p. 1895)
—Which Way to Freedom? And Other Questions about the Underground Railroad. (p. 1911)
—Who Invented Home Video Games? Ralph Baer. (p. 1915)
—Who Invented Home Video Games?—Ralph Baer. (p. 1915)
—Who Invented Television? Philo Farnsworth. (p. 1915)
—Who Invented Television?— Philo Farnsworth. (p. 1915)
—Who Was Susan B. Anthony Vote? And Other Questions about Women's Suffrage. (p. 1919)
—Who Was the Hair-Care Millionaire? Madam C. J. Walker. (p. 1919)
—Why Couldn't Susan B. Anthony Vote? And Other Questions about Women's Suffrage. (p. 1923)
—Why Does the Earth Spin? And Other Questions about Our Planet. Bull, Peter, illus. (p. 1924)
—Wright Brothers for Kid: How They Invented the Airplane, 21 Activities Exploring the Science & History of Flight. D'Argo, Laura, illus. (p. 1963)
Carson, Mary Kay, jt. auth. see Cole, Joanna.
Carson, Mary Kay & American Museum of Natural History Staff. Deadly & Dangerous: (Level 2) (p. 417)
Carson, Mary Kay & Carson, Mary K. Extreme Planets Q & A. (p. 556)
Carson, Mary Kay & Library Association Staff. Far-Out Guide to Asteroids & Comets. (p. 572)
—Far-Out Guide to Jupiter. (p. 572)
—Far-Out Guide to Mars. (p. 572)
—Far-Out Guide to Mercury. (p. 572)
—Far-Out Guide to the Moon. (p. 572)
Carson, Nancy & Shannon, Jacqueline. Raising a Star: The Parent's Guide to Helping Kids Break into Theater, Film, Television, or Music. (p. 1437)
Carson, Pat & Peters, Victoria Smith. If the Shoe Fits. (p. 854)
Carson, Penny & Hess, Amy. Simon Goes Camping. (p. 1577)
—Simon's Day of Rain. (p. 1577)
Carson, Rae. Bitter Kingdom. (p. 194)
—Crown of Embers. (p. 386)
—Girl of Fire & Thorns. (p. 678)
—Girl of Fire & Thorns Stories. (p. 678)
—Walk on Earth a Stranger. (p. 1853)
Carson, Shawn, illus. see Tompkins, Bill.
Carson, Shawn, illus. see Tompkins, Robyn Lee.
Carson, Shawn K., illus. see Tompkins, Robyn Lee.
Carson, Shonette. Ian's Bad Choices Turned His Life Around. Dupon-Martinez, Christopher, illus. (p. 849)
—My Dear Child, I Have Gone to Heaven Let's Talk: A Child's Recovery Plan Hearn, Marilyn, illus. (p. 1201)
Carson Sr., Johnny. Little Dog. (p. 1026)
Carson Sr., Johnny Lee. Cookies & Dreams. (p. 361)
Carson-Dellosa Publishing Staff. 101 Easy Reading Games, Grade 5. (p. 1999)
—Add & Subtract, Grade 1. (p. 11)
—Addition 0 to 12. (p. 12)
—Alfabeto. (p. 37)
—Aliens. (p. 41)
—All about Me, Grades Pk - 1. (p. 43)
—Alphabet. (p. 49)
—Alphabet Animals, Grades PK - K. (p. 49)
—Alphabet, Grades PK - K: Dot-to-Dot. (p. 49)
—Alphabet, Grades PK - K: Sounds & Pictures. (p. 49)
—Barns & Farm Animals. (p. 139)
—Beginning Math, Grade 1. (p. 159)
—Beginning Reading, Grade 1. (p. 159)
—Beginning Reading, Grades K. (p. 159)
—Beginning Vocabulary, Grade K. (p. 159)
—Character Education, Grade 5. (p. 291)
—Colors & Shapes. (p. 345)
—Colors, Grades PK - K. (p. 345)
—Complete Library Skills. (p. 353)
—Complete Library Skills, Grades K - 2. (p. 353)
—Crazy Eights. (p. 377)
—Cursive Practice, Grade 2-3. (p. 395)
—Dictionary, Grades 6-12. (p. 436)
—Division 0 to 12. (p. 455)
—Dot-to-Dot Bible Pictures: Make Personal Connections to God's Word! (p. 472)
—Everyday Words in Spanish: Photographic. (p. 544)
—Everything for Early Learning. (p. 544)
—Fill-in-the-Blank Bible Fun: Includes a Riddle for Every Lesson! (p. 586)
—First Grade Skills. (p. 595)
—First Words. (p. 597)
—Fractions. (p. 626)
—Get Ready for Kindergarten. (p. 668)
—Go Fish. (p. 686)
—Hidden Pictures, Grades PK - 1. (p. 776)
—I Can Trace. (p. 836)
—I Lost a Tooth! (p. 841)
—Kindergarten Skills. (p. 957)
—Let's Learn to Cut. (p. 998)
—Letters & Sounds, Grades K - 1. (p. 1002)
—Letters, Grades PK - K: Uppercase & Lowercase. (p. 1002)
—Mailboxes & Letters. (p. 1077)
—Math Fact Book, Grades 4-8. (p. 1106)
—Mazes,Grades PK - 1. (p. 1113)
—Multiplication 0 to 12. (p. 1190)
—Multiplication, Grade 3. (p. 1190)
—Number Play, Grade K. (p. 1271)
—Numbers 0-20, Grades PK - K. (p. 1272)
—Numbers 0-30, Grades K - 1. (p. 1272)
—Numbers 0-30, Grades Pk - K: Dot-to-Dot. (p. 1272)
—Numbers 1 to 100 (Numeros del 1 al 100) (p. 1272)
—Numbers 1 to 26, Grades PK - 1. (p. 1272)
—Numbers 1 to 26 (Numeros del 1 al 26) (p. 1272)
—Phonics. (p. 1351)
—Phonics for First Grade. (p. 1352)
—Phonics for Kindergarten, Grade K. (p. 1352)
—Printing Practice for Beginners. (p. 1407)
—Printing Practice, Grade 2. (p. 1407)
—Puzzles & Games: Word Play. (p. 1421)
—Puzzles & Games for Math, Grade 1. (p. 1421)
—Puzzles & Games, Grade 1. (p. 1421)
—Read, Grade 5. (p. 1443)
—Reading Comprehension, Grade 1. (p. 1445)
—Reading Comprehension, Grades 5-6. Warren, Rebecca, ed. (p. 1445)
—Reading Comprehension, Grades 7-8. (p. 1445)
—Same & Different, Grades Pk - K. (p. 1507)
—Science Fact Book. (p. 1526)
—Scissors Skills, Grades PK - 1. (p. 1529)
—Sequencing. (p. 1552)
—Shapes, Grades PK - K. (p. 1560)
—Social Studies, Grades K - 2. (p. 1604)
—Spelling & Writing for Beginners, Grade 1. (p. 1625)
—Starter Spanish, Grades Preschool - 1. (p. 1643)
—Student Planner, Grades 4-8. (p. 1669)
—Subtraction 0 to 12. (p. 1671)
—Time & Money. (p. 1751)
—Word Play, Grades K - 1: Rhyming. (p. 1951)
Carson-Dellosa Publishing Staff, ed. see Aguerre, Elizabeth Suarez.
Carson-Dellosa Publishing Staff, jt. auth. see Ewald, Thomas.
Carson-Dellosa Publishing Staff, jt. auth. see School Specialty Publishing Staff.
Carson-Dellosa Publishing Staff, jt. auth. see Sutton, Toby.
Carson-Dellosa Publishing Staff & Holmes, Ellen White. Complete Plan Book. (p. 353)
Carson-Dellosa Publishing Staff & Spectrum Staff. Georgia Test Prep, Grade 4. (p. 665)
—Science Test Practice, Grade 3. Thompson, Karen, ed. (p. 1528)
Carson-Dellosa Publishing Staff, compiled by. ABCs of the Bible, Grades PK - K: Coloring Fun from A to Z. (p. 4)
—Alphabet Flash Cards. (p. 49)
—Alphabet, Grades PK - K. (p. 49)
—Animals, Grades 1 - 3. (p. 82)
—Basic Picture Words Flash Cards. (p. 142)
—Basic Sight Words. (p. 142)
—Beginning Vocabulary, Grade 1. (p. 159)
—Daily Character Education Activities, Grades 2 - 3: 180 Lessons for Each Day of the School Year. (p. 399)
—Dot-to-Dot Bible Pictures, Grades 1-3: Make Personal Connections to God's Word! (p. 472)
—Early Skills, Grade 1. (p. 494)
—Early Skills, Grade PK. (p. 494)
—Handwriting, Grades K - 1. (p. 741)
—Name That Bible Character! (p. 1228)
—Numbers 0-10, Grades PK - K. (p. 1272)
—Numbers & Counting, Grades PK - 1. (p. 1272)
—Preschool Skills. (p. 1396)
—Puzzles & Games for Beginners, Grade K. (p. 1421)
—Puzzles & Games for Math, Grade 2. (p. 1421)
—Puzzles & Games, Grade 2: Word Play. (p. 1421)
—Puzzles & Games, Grade 2. (p. 1421)
—Ready Reproducibles, Grades K - 1: Year-Round Instructional & Decorative Resources. (p. 1447)
Carson-Dellosa Publishing Staff, ed. Actividades de Tercer Grado. (p. 10)
Carsonie, Diane Lynn. Little Red Chicken Bullen, Marjorie J., illus. (p. 1034)
—Silly Frog. Bullen, Marjorie, illus. (p. 1576)
Carstairs, Sue. Saving Turtles: A Kids' Guide to Helping Endangered Creatures. (p. 1518)
Carswell, Sarah. Grandma Stories: The Quilt. (p. 708)
Cart, Jen, illus. see Smith, Constance.
Cart, Michael. Necessary Noise: Stories about Our Families as They Really Are. Noruzi, Charlotte, illus. (p. 1239)
Cart, Michael, ed. see Masters, William H.
Cart, Michael, et al. How Beautiful the Ordinary: Twelve Stories of Identity. (p. 805)
—Taking Aim: Power & Pain, Teens & Guns. (p. 1698)
Carta, Karla K. Chocolate in My Pocket. (p. 309)
—Fairy Jane. (p. 563)
Cartaya, Pablo & Howard, Martin. Tina Cocolina: Queen of the Cupcakes. Richards, Kirsten, illus. (p. 1755)
Carte, Donald. Clean Passing. (p. 330)
Cartee, Mary. Go Forth My Angels. (p. 686)
—Patchwork Princess. (p. 1328)
Carter, Abby, illus. see Bowen, Anne.
Carter, Abby, illus. see Calmenson, Stephanie.
Carter, Abby, illus. see Chapman, Susan Margaret.
Carter, Abby, illus. see Dodds, Dayle Ann.
Carter, Abby, illus. see Hermes, Patricia.
Carter, Abby, illus. see Jacobson, Jennifer Richard.
Carter, Abby, illus. see Kenah, Katharine.
Carter, Abby, illus. see Provencher, Rose-Marie.
Carter, Abby, illus. see Sanders-Wells, Linda.
Carter, Abby, illus. see Sitomer, Alan Lawrence.
Carter, Abby, illus. see Williams, Suzanne.
Carter, Aimée. Goddess Inheritance. (p. 690)
—Goddess Interrupted. (p. 690)
—Goddess Legacy. (p. 690)
—Goddess Test. (p. 690)
—Pawn. (p. 1331)
Carter, Alden. Love, Football, & Other Contact Sports. (p. 1059)
Carter, Alden R. Love, Football, & Other Contact Sports. (p. 1059)
—Up Country. (p. 1824)
—Walkaway. (p. 1854)
—Wart, Son of Toad (p. 1859)
Carter, Alex, jt. auth. see Healey, Tim.
Carter, Ally. All Fall Down. (p. 44)
—Cross My Heart & Hope to Spy. (p. 385)
—Don't Judge a Girl by Her Cover. (p. 467)
—Gallagher Girls (p. 653)
—Heist Society. (p. 762)
—I'd Tell You I Love You, but Then I'd Have to Kill You. (p. 851)
—Only the Good Spy Young. (p. 1298)
—Out of Sight, Out of Time. (p. 1311)
—Perfect Scoundrels. (p. 1342)
—Uncommon Criminals. (p. 1812)
—United We Spy. (p. 1820)
Carter, Amy. Not So Wicked, Wicked Witch! (p. 1267)
Carter, Amy, illus. see Carter, Jimmy.
Carter, Andi, illus. see Tourville, Amanda Doering.
Carter, André & Nicholls, Shawn. You Call That a Sport? Strange Sports from Around the Globe. (p. 1973)
Carter, Andrew. Adjectives. Schrey, Sophie, ed. (p. 13)
—Adverbs. (p. 25)
—Adverbs. Edwards, Nicola, ed. (p. 25)
—Nouns & Pronouns. Schrey, Sophie, ed. (p. 1268)
—Prepositions. (p. 1396)
—Prepositions. Schrey, Sophie, ed. (p. 1396)
—Punctuation & Sentences. (p. 1417)
—Punctuation & Sentences. Jones, Bryony, ed. (p. 1417)
—Verbs. Edwards, Nicola, ed. (p. 1836)
Carter, Angela C. Momma, Why Do We Have to Take a Bath? (p. 1162)
Carter, Anne, illus. see Dant, Jennifer.
Carter, Anne Laurel. Night Boy Pelletier, Ninon, illus. (p. 1253)
—Out of the Deeps Debon, Nicolas, illus. (p. 1311)
—Under a Prairie Sky Daniel, Alan & Daniel, Lea, illus. (p. 1813)
Carter, Anne Laurel, et al. Shepherd's Granddaughter (p. 1565)
Carter, Aubrey Smith. Enchanted Lizard: La Lagartijta Mágica. Nelson, Esther Whitt, ed. (p. 523)
Carter, Barbara, illus. see Power, Molly.
Carter, Brei. Della Goes to Dreamland. (p. 424)
Carter, Brian. King of the Pond. (p. 959)
Carter, Brittany. Angel Sin: Book Two. (p. 74)
—Human Sin: Book One. (p. 826)
Carter, Brynn. Puppet Explained. (p. 1417)
Carter, Caela. Me, Him, Them, & It. (p. 1116)
—My Best Friend, Maybe. (p. 1196)
Carter, Candace. Sid's Surprise. Kim, Joung Un, illus. (p. 1573)
Carter, Carol S., creator. Appreciation of Diversity. (p. 93)
Carter, Cassandra. 16 Isn't Always Sweet. (p. 1995)
Carter, Catherine. Anna's Choice. Pittman, Gail, illus. (p. 85)
Carter, Cathy. You Are My Very Best Friend: The Adventures of Mike & Gabe (in English & Spanish) (p. 1973)
Carter, Cheri. Misfitz: A Book of Poems. (p. 1150)
Carter, Cynthia & Weaver, C. Kay. Violence & the Media. (p. 1843)
Carter, Dana, illus. see Davis, Harold.
Carter, Darlene. Little Spit-N-Gasser Finds New Friends. (p. 1036)
Carter, David. David Carter's 100: Lift the Flaps & Learn to Count! (p. 410)
—Nutters of Pendle Forest - Part 1 the Enchanted Valley. (p. 1274)
Carter, David A. 12 Bugs of Christmas: A Pop-Up Christmas Counting Book. Carter, David A., illus. (p. 1994)
—600 Black Spots: A Pop-Up Book for Children of All Ages. Carter, David A., illus. (p. 2001)
—Alpha Bugs: A Pop-Up Alphabet. Carter, David A., illus. (p. 48)
—B Is for Box — the Happy Little Yellow Box: A Pop-Up Book. Carter, David A., illus. (p. 123)
—Beach Bugs. Carter, David A., illus. (p. 149)
—Big Bug Book. Carter, David A., illus. (p. 180)
—Birthday Bugs. Carter, David A., illus. (p. 192)
—Bitsy Bee Goes to School. Carter, David A., illus. (p. 194)
—Blue 2: A Pop-Up Book for Children of All Ages. Carter, David A., illus. (p. 202)
—Blue 2: A Pop-Up Book for Children of All Ages. Vol. 2 Carter, David A., illus. (p. 202)
—Box of Bugs: 4 Pop-Up Concept Books. Carter, David A., illus. (p. 216)
—Bugs That Go! A Bustling Pop-Up Book. Carter, David A., illus. (p. 237)
—Builder Bugs: A Busy Pop-Up Book. Carter, David A., illus. (p. 238)
—Colors: A Bugs Pop-Up Concept Book. Carter, David A., illus. (p. 345)
—Counting: A Bugs Pop-Up Concept Book. Carter, David A., illus. (p. 370)
—Feely Bugs. Carter, David A., illus. (p. 580)
—Glittery Crittery Pop-up Counting Book. (p. 684)
—Halloween Bugs Carter, David A., illus. (p. 737)
—Happy Little Yellow Box: A Pop-Up Book of Opposites. Carter, David A., illus. (p. 746)
—Happy Shiny Blue Circle: A Touch-And-Feel Book of Shapes. (p. 746)
—Hide & Seek. (p. 776)
—How Many Bugs in a Box? Carter, David A., illus. (p. 811)
—Jingle Bugs: A Merry Pop-Up Book with Lights & Music! Carter, David A., illus. (p. 918)
—Love Bugs. Carter, David A., illus. (p. 1059)
—Merry Christmas, Bugs! Carter, David A., illus. (p. 1128)
—One Red Dot: A Pop-Up Book for Children of All Ages. Carter, David A., illus. (p. 1296)
—Opposites: A Bugs Pop-Up Concept Book. Carter, David A., illus. (p. 1300)
—Princess Bugs: A Touch-And-Feel Fairy Tale. Carter, David A., illus. (p. 1403)
—School Bugs. Carter, David A., illus. (p. 1522)
—Snow Bugs: A Wintery Pop-Up Book. Carter, David A., illus. (p. 1598)
—Snowy Day in Bugland! Carter, David A., illus. (p. 1601)
—Spot the Dot. Carter, David A., illus. (p. 1633)
—Springtime in Bugland! Carter, David A., illus. (p. 1635)
—Up & Down: A Bugs Pop-Up Concept Book. Carter, David A., illus. (p. 1824)
—Welcome to Bugland! A Fun Foldout World from David A. Carter. Carter, David A., illus. (p. 1873)
—White Noise: A Pop-Up Book for Children of All Ages. Carter, David A., illus. (p. 1913)
—Yellow Square: A Pop-Up Book for Children of All Ages. Carter, David A., illus. (p. 1970)
Carter, David A., illus. see Weeks, Sarah.
Carter, David A. & Carter, Noelle. Little Mouse & Daddy. Carter, David A. & Carter, Noelle, illus. (p. 1032)
—Little Mouse & Mommy. Carter, David A. & Carter, Noelle, illus. (p. 1032)
—Little Mouse Plays Peek-a-Boo. Carter, David A. & Carter, Noelle, illus. (p. 1032)
—Little Mouse's Christmas. Carter, David A. & Carter, Noelle, illus. (p. 1032)
—Lots of Bots! A Counting Pop-Up Book. (p. 1057)

Carter, David A. & Diaz, James. You Call That Art?! Learn about Modern Sculpture & Make Your Own. (p. 1973)
Carter, David A., creator. Glitter Critters: Dave Carter's Pop-up Book! (p. 683)
Carter, Denine, ed. Gotta Have Graphs. (p. 704)
Carter, Denzel T. Hannah & the Hurricane. (p. 742)
—Tadpole Grows Up. (p. 1695)
Carter, Derek, jt. auth. see DeLuise, Dom.
Carter, Destiny, et al. Freak Files: An Erotic Anthology. (p. 631)
Carter, Dorothy. Wilhe'mina Miles: After the Stork Night. Stevenson, Harvey, illus. (p. 1932)
Carter, E. J. Lewis & Clark Journals. (p. 1004)
—Mayflower Compact. (p. 1113)
Carter, Elizabeth. Everything You Need to Know about Human Papillomavirus. (p. 545)
Carter, Erin. Welcome Back Sun. (p. 1873)
Carter, Fred, illus. see Soles, Henry, ed.
Carter, Grant Matthew. Disaster Caster. Morling, Donovan, illus. (p. 446)
Carter, Greg, illus. see Smalley, Roger.
Carter, Herbert. Boy Scouts' First Camp Fire: Or Scouting with the Silver Fox Patrol. (p. 218)
—Boy Scouts' First Camp Fire. (p. 218)
—Boy Scouts on Sturgeon Island. (p. 218)
—Boy Scouts on Sturgeon Island or Marooned among the Game-Fish Poachers. (p. 218)
—Boy Scouts on the Trail or Scouting. (p. 219)
—The, Boy Scouts on Sturgeon Island. (p. 1728)
Carter, J. A. Green Stone. (p. 722)
Carter, James. Around the World. Moon, Cliff, ed. (p. 100)
—Homes Sweet Homes. (p. 793)
—I'm a Little Alien. (p. 858)
—Journey to the Centre of My Brain (p. 929)
Carter, James & Denton, Graham. Grrr! Dinos, Dragons & Other Beastie Poems. (p. 727)
Carter, Jani R. Long Ago in the African Jungle. (p. 1046)
Carter, Jason Andrew. Stations of the Nativity. (p. 1644)
Carter, Jay. Bully Caterpillar: An Adventurous Journey of the Inner Child. (p. 241)
Carter, Jill, illus. see Maxwell, Andre L. & Maxwell, Amanda L.
Carter, Jimmy. Little Baby Snoogle- Fleejer. Carter, Amy, illus. (p. 1023)
Carter, Joey. Great Airboat Ride! A Cantor Kids! Book. (p. 713)
—Lost in a Submarine! A Cantor Kids! Book. (p. 1055)
Carter, Julie. Mr. Fingers. (p. 1185)
Carter, K. D. Vacation into Nonsense. (p. 1830)
Carter, Kara. Abby's Quilt. (p. 2)
Carter, Kathleen. Bubba the Bullfrog & the Pond at the End of the Street. (p. 233)
Carter, Keisha. Maloni's Shoes. (p. 1084)
Carter, Kelly, illus. see Garcia, Alaycia.
Carter, Kelly, illus. see Wiggins, D. L.
Carter, Kris, illus. see Gill, Heidi.
Carter, Kris, jt. auth. see Gill, Heidi.
Carter, Kristie Freeman. Learning How to Dance. (p. 985)
Carter, Kristin. What Matters Most: A Children's Book of Families. (p. 1892)
Carter, Lara. Crusher Field Opening Day. (p. 387)
Carter, Larry. Red Wallet. (p. 1455)
—Tommie's Bad Dream. (p. 1764)
Carter, Liane. Chronicles of Joy. (p. 317)
Carter, M. Scott. Stealing Kevin's Heart: A Novel (p. 1646)
Carter, Matt, jt. auth. see Titchenell, F. J. R.
Carter, Maureen. Tale of Jemima Puddle-Duck: A Story about Trust. (p. 1699)
Carter, Michael, ed. see Barthes, Roland.
Carter, Mike. Access to the Universe. (p. 8)
Carter, Nikki. Doing My Own Thing. (p. 463)
—Get over It. (p. 668)
—It's All Good: A So for Real Novel. (p. 896)
—Not a Good Look. (p. 1266)
—Step to This. (p. 1648)
Carter, Nikki & Elliott, Kevin. Break-Up Diaries (p. 224)
Carter, Noelle, jt. auth. see Carter, David A.
Carter, Noni. Good Fortune. (p. 698)
Carter, Olivia. Through My Eyes, Book One: Jake. (p. 1745)
Carter, Paula Becker, illus. see Lingo, Susan L.
Carter, Philip, jt. auth. see Russell, Ken.
Carter, Pip. Double Dare. (p. 472)
—Little People. (p. 1033)
Carter, R. J. Alices Journey Beyond Moon Wright, Lucy, illus. (p. 40)
Carter, R J. Alice's Journey Beyond the Moon Wright, Lucy, illus. (p. 40)
Carter, Rachel. Find Me Where the Water Ends. (p. 587)
—So Close to You. (p. 1602)
—This Strange & Familiar Place. (p. 1737)
Carter, Rebecca. Moonlit Daydreams. (p. 1173)
Carter, Richard. Community Shakespeare Company Edition of the TWO GENTLEMEN of VERONA. (p. 350)
Carter, Robert. Windjammers: The Final Story. Carter, Robert, illus. (p. 1936)
carter, robert bob. Magic Eye. (p. 1072)
Carter, Robin, illus. see Berger, Melvin & Berger, Gilda.
Carter, Robin, illus. see Costello, Dee & Keith, Helen.
Carter, Russell Gordon. Teenage Animal Stories. Osborne, Richard, illus. (p. 1714)
Carter, Sandy Lewis, illus. see Reed, Tom.
Carter, Scott. Drawing a Dark Way: Rymadoon. (p. 481)
Carter, Scott William. Last Great Getaway of the Water Balloon Boys. (p. 978)
—Wooden Bones. (p. 1949)
Carter, Sharon, illus. see Murray, Patricia Lei.
Carter, Shawn. Sheldon's First School Bus Ride. (p. 1564)
Carter, Stephanie. Great Zoo Breakout That Never Happened. (p. 719)
Carter, Stephanie, illus. see Baskwill, Jane.
Carter, Susan. Home for Copper: A Story of Adoption. (p. 792)
Carter, Tammy. My Friend, Dinner. (p. 1209)
Carter, Terry G., et al. Preaching God's Word: A Hands-On Approach to Preparing, Developing, & Delivering the Sermon (p. 1394)
Carter, Tod, illus. see Nolan, Allia Zobel.
Carter, Todd. Monarch Universe Package Set: Children's Picture Book. (p. 1163)
Carter, Vince & Brown, Greg. Vince Carter: Choose Your Course. (p. 1842)
Carter, Vincent O. Such Sweet Thunder. (p. 1672)
Carter, Wade. Adventures of Ernie & Ike: Lessons in Life Series. (p. 18)
Carter-Johnson, Helen. Golden Memories of Childhood. (p. 695)
Carteron, Nancy Lee, jt. auth. see Fremes, Ruth.
Carter-Reed, Lorye. Grandpa Isn't Coming Anymore: A Child's Look at Death. (p. 709)
—I Saw God in My Room. (p. 845)
Carter-Stephenson, C. J. Crystal Ship. (p. 387)
Carthage, Lynn. Haunted. (p. 753)
Carthew, Mark. Flabbergaster. (p. 601)
—Footprints on the Moon: Poems about Space (p. 615)
—Hairy Toe. Lindsey, Cath, illus. (p. 736)
—Speak Up! (p. 1622)
—Vroom! Vroom! Poems about Things with Wheels. (p. 1851)
Carthew, Mark & Allen, Pamela. Brown Bread & Honey. Allen, Pamela, illus. (p. 231)
Carthew, Mark & Rosen, Michael. Kaleidoscope. Denton, Terry, illus. (p. 941)
—There Was an Old Lady Who Swallowed a Fly. James, Ann, illus. (p. 1730)
Carthew, Natasha. Winter Damage. (p. 1938)
Cartier, Eric, illus. see Trondheim, Lewis.
Cartier, Wesley. Marco's Run. Ruffins, Reynold, illus. (p. 1092)
Cartlidge, Cherese. Alternative Energy. (p. 50)
—Anne Hathaway. Greenhaven Press Staff, ed. (p. 86)
—Beyonce. (p. 173)
—Celia Cruz. (p. 286)
—Drew Barrymore. (p. 485)
—Home Windmills. (p. 793)
—Jane Lynch. Greenhaven Press Editors, ed. (p. 908)
—Jennifer Lopez. Greenhaven Press Staff, ed. (p. 913)
—Leonardo Dicaprio. Gale, ed. (p. 992)
—Neil Patrick Harris. Greenhaven Press Editors, ed. (p. 1240)
—Reparations for Slavery. (p. 1460)
—Ryan Gosling. Greenhaven Press Editors, ed. (p. 1499)
—Water from Air: Water Harvesting Machines. (p. 1862)
Cartlidge, Michelle. Mouse Christmas House: A Press-Out Model Book. (p. 1182)
Cartmell, C. J. Magic Mailbox. (p. 1072)
Cartmill, Carly. Split Pea Soup Caper. (p. 1630)
Cartobaleno, illus. see Depken, Kristen L.
Cartobaleno, illus. see Tillworth, Mary.
Cartobaleno, jt. auth. see Random House Staff.
Cartobaleno Staff, illus. see Golden Books Staff.
Cartobaleno Staff, jt. auth. see Golden Books Staff.
Cartogna, Eileen. Fun at the Fair: Learning Subtraction Facts To 10. (p. 647)
—Jobs Around Town: Learning to Sort & Classify. (p. 919)
Carton, Gerard. We Four Kings. (p. 1867)
Carton, Rick, illus. see Ogden, Charles.
Cartonia, Lucia. What Shape Is It? (p. 1893)
Cartoon Network Books. Learn to Draw Adventure Time. (p. 983)
Cartoon Network Staff, jt. auth. see Ballantine Books Staff.
Cartoon Network Staff, jt. auth. see McDonnell, Chris.
Cartoon Saloon, illus. see Donbavand, Tommy.
Cartoon Saloon Staff, illus. see Donbavand, Tommy.
Carttar, Debra. Picturing Lucy. (p. 1356)
Cartw, Paul. Where Are the Seeds/Ww/E. (p. 1906)
Cartwheel Editors, jt. auth. see Landers, Ace.
Cartwright, jt. auth. see Amery.
Cartwright, Amy. Dreidel, Dreidel, Dreidel. (p. 484)
—Jack & the Beanstalk. (p. 902)
Cartwright, Amy, illus. see Berger, Samantha.
Cartwright, Christina, illus. see McPherson, Heather L. A.
Cartwright, Deanna Vincent. Disciple's Diary Student Book. (p. 447)
—Jesus & His Followers. (p. 915)
Cartwright, Mary. Splish, Splash, Splosh Bath Bk. Wells, Rachel, illus. (p. 1630)
Cartwright, Mary, illus. see Baggott, Stella.
Cartwright, Mary, told to. Little Book of Little Puppies. (p. 1025)
Cartwright, Nancy & Jones, Joanna. Henry's Adventure at the Franklin Hotel. Feterl, Bill, illus. (p. 769)
Cartwright, Pauline. About Earth (Paperback) Copyright 2016. (p. 5)
Cartwright, Ran. Adventures of Billy Space Boy (p. 16)
Cartwright, Reg, illus. see Flor Ada, Alma.
Cartwright, S. Fairy Jigsaw Puzzle. (p. 563)
Cartwright, S., jt. auth. see Amery, H.
Cartwright, S., jt. auth. see Cox, Phil Roxbee.
Cartwright, S., jt. auth. see Gulliver, A.
Cartwright, S., jt. auth. see Tyler, Jenny.
Cartwright, Shannon. Alaska 1 2 3: Colors & Numbers. (p. 34)
Cartwright, Shannon, illus. see Chamberlin-Calamar, Pat.
Cartwright, Shannon, illus. see Gill, Shelley.
Cartwright, Shannon, jt. auth. see Gill, Shelley.
Cartwright, Stan & Dixon, Edna. Strong Fox: How Fox Came to Help a Village Grow Stronger. (p. 1668)
Cartwright, Stephen. Abc Floor. Cartwright, Stephen, illus. (p. 3)
—Animal Babies. (p. 76)
—Animal Noises. (p. 79)
—Children's Songbook - Internet Referenced. (p. 304)
—Christmas Stencil Book. (p. 315)
—Cinderella. (p. 320)
—Fairytale Jigsaw Book. (p. 565)
—Fairytale Snap. (p. 565)
—Find the Duck. (p. 587)
—Find the Kitten. (p. 587)
—Find the Puppy. (p. 587)
—Hercules. (p. 769)
—Jason & the Golden Fleece. (p. 910)
—Little Book of Train Stories. (p. 1043)
—Ludo. (p. 1064)
—Noisy Animals Board Bk. Cartwright, Stephen, illus. (p. 1262)
—Sleeping Beauty. (p. 1589)
—Three Little Pigs. (p. 1742)
—Ulysses. (p. 1810)
—Usborne Phonics Flashcards: Dog. Cartwright, Stephen, illus. (p. 1827)
Cartwright, Stephen, illus. see Amery, H.
Cartwright, Stephen, illus. see Amery, Heather.
Cartwright, Stephen, illus. see Brooks, Felicity & Tyler, Jenny.
Cartwright, Stephen, illus. see Brooks, Felicity, et al.
Cartwright, Stephen, illus. see Brooks, Felicity.
Cartwright, Stephen, illus. see Civardi, Anna.
Cartwright, Stephen, illus. see Civardi, Anne.
Cartwright, Stephen, illus. see Cox, Phil Roxbee, ed.
Cartwright, Stephen, illus. see Cox, Phil Roxbee.
Cartwright, Stephen, illus. see Hawthorn, Philip & Tyler, Jenny.
Cartwright, Stephen, illus. see Hawthorn, Phillip.
Cartwright, Stephen, illus. see Hawthorne, Philip & Tyler, Jenny.
Cartwright, Stephen, illus. see Marks, Anthony.
Cartwright, Stephen, illus. see Milbourne, Anna.
Cartwright, Stephen, illus. see Rawson, Christopher.
Cartwright, Stephen, illus. see Roxbee-Cox, Phil.
Cartwright, Stephen, illus. see Sheikh-Miller, Jonathan.
Cartwright, Stephen, illus. see Sims, Lesley.
Cartwright, Stephen, illus. see Tyler, Jenny & Hawthorn, Phillip.
Cartwright, Stephen, illus. see Tyler, Jenny.
Cartwright, Stephen, illus. see Watt, Fiona.
Cartwright, Stephen, jt. auth. see Amery, Heather.
Cartwright, Stephen, jt. auth. see Cox, Phil Roxbee.
Cartwright, Stephen, jt. auth. see Watt, Fiona.
Cartwright, Stephen, jt. auth. see Wilkes, Angela.
Cartwright, Stephen & Amery, Heather. Céad Focal Sticker Book: The First Hundred Words. (p. 283)
—First Thousand Words in Russian. (p. 597)
Cartwright, Stephen & Blundell, Kim. Snakes & Ladders. (p. 1596)
Cartwright, Steven. Farmyard Tales Sticker Coloring Book. (p. 575)
Cartwright, Teryl, et al. Humongous Book of Bible Skits for Children's Ministry. (p. 827)
Cartwtright, S., jt. auth. see Tyler, Jenny.
Carty, Amy. Little Girl Who Lied: The Importance of Honesty. Williams, Nancy E., ed. (p. 1028)
Carty, Hilda. Catventure. (p. 281)
Caruncho, Isabel, illus. see Prats, Joan de Déu.
Carus, Andre W. Flint Holds Fire (p. 604)
Carus, Marianne. Higglety Pigglety Pop! Or There Must Be More to Life. (p. 777)
—Sing, Clap, & Dance with Ladybug. (p. 1579)
—Sing Together with Ladybug. (p. 1579)
Carus, Marianne, ed. Celebrate Cricket: 30 Years of Stories & Art. (p. 283)
Carus, Titus Lucretius. Lucretius. (p. 1063)
Caruso, Barbara, reader. Elvis the Rooster Almost Goes to Heaven (p. 517)
Caruso, Carla. Secreto de la Abuela Maria. (p. 1544)
Caruso, D. A. Burning House. (p. 244)
—Cool by the Pool. (p. 362)
—Free Wheelin' Picture Book (English) (p. 634)
—Poison Patrol: Picture Book (English) (p. 1377)
Caruso, Frank, illus. see Vachss, Andrew.
Caruso, Maria Victoria, illus. see Gonzalez, Aurora Adriana.
Caruso, Paul. Lonely Nail. (p. 1046)
Caruso, Rosalie. How I taught my mom... the Law of Attraction. (p. 810)
Caruso-Scott, Melissa, jt. auth. see Belle, Trixie.
Caruth, Jeannette, illus. see Pages, Christina.
Caruthers, William A. Cavaliers of Virginia. (p. 282)
Carvajal, Cheryl, ed. see Cowie, Mabel.
Carvajal, Mario. Polilla del Baul. Saraniti, Carlos, illus. (p. 1380)
Carvajal, Victor. Chipana. (p. 308)
—Como un Salto de Campana. (p. 351)
—Cuentatrapos. (p. 389)
Carvalho, Adelia. There Once Was a Dog. Vaz de Carvalho, Joao, illus. (p. 1730)
Carvalho, Bernardo, illus. see Minhós Martins, Isabel.
Carvalho de Magalhaes, Roberto. Claude Monet. (p. 329)
—Michelangelo. (p. 1135)
Carvalho, et al. Nuestros Derechos. Nazareth, Carla, illus. (p. 1270)
Carvalho, Marcela. Three Sisters, Three Weddings, & One Dress. (p. 1744)
Carvell, Marlene. Sweetgrass Basket. (p. 1690)
Carvell, Tim. Planet Tad. Holgate, Doug, illus. (p. 1368)
—Return to Planet Tad. (p. 1465)
Carver, jt. auth. see Bowles.
Carver, David. Leafy Leafs Where Is Lester? Carver, Erin, illus. (p. 982)
—Lester Returns Home with His New Friend La'doo Carver, Erin, illus. (p. 994)
Carver, Erin, illus. see Carver, David.
Carver Middle School. Voices from the Middle: Stepping into the Real World. (p. 1848)
Carver, Peter, ed. Blue Jean Collection. (p. 203)
—Horrors (p. 799)
Carville, Declan. Day to Remember at the Giant's Causeway. Ellis, Brendan, illus. (p. 414)
—Fairy Glen. (p. 563)
—Incredible Sister Brigid. Black, Kieron, illus. (p. 869)
Carvin, Rose-Mae. Dorning the Popsicle Boy: A Story of the Philippines. Hertzler, Frances H.., illus. (p. 465)
—Ly Huy's Escape: A Story of Vietnam. Neal, Sharon & Mayer, Kristin, eds. (p. 1066)
Cary, illus. see Fox, Mary Virginia.
Cary, illus. see Graves, Charles P.
Cary, illus. see Russell, Solveig Paulson.
Cary, Bob. Born to Pull: The Glory of Sled Dogs. de Marcken, Gail, illus. (p. 214)
Cary, Debbi, illus. see Helm, Julie G.
Cary, Debbi G., photos by see Helm, Julie G.
Cary, Kate. Bloodline. (p. 201)
—Reckoning. (p. 1452)
Cary, Lorene. Free! Great Escapes from Slavery on the Underground Railroad. (p. 633)
Cary, Michael & Kelly, Timothy. This American Courthouse: 100 Years of Service to the People of Westmoreland County Pennsylvania. (p. 1735)
Cary. Rosa Nouchette. Esther: A Book for Girls. (p. 538)
Carzon, Walter, illus. see Huelin, Jodi.
Casad, Mary Brooke. Bluebonnet at the Alamo Vincent, Benjamin, illus. (p. 204)
—Bluebonnet at the Ocean Star Museum Vincent, Benjamin, illus. (p. 204)
—Bluebonnet at the State Fair of Texas Binder, Pat, illus. (p. 204)
Casad, Mary Brooke & Brooke Casad, Mary. Bluebonnet at the East Texas Oil Museum Vincent, Benjamin, illus. (p. 204)
Casad, Patricia E. Bubbykins: (Life on the Farm) (p. 233)
Casado, Alicia, jt. auth. see Casado, Dami.
Casado, Alicia & Casado, Dami. Los Ruidos de la Granja. (p. 1054)
—Luna. (p. 1065)
Casado, Dami. Como Comes Tu? (p. 350)
—Como Te Lavas? (p. 351)
—Como Te Vistes? (p. 351)
—Los Ruidos de Las Mascotas. (p. 1054)
—Mar. (p. 1091)
Casado, Dami, jt. auth. see Casado, Alicia.
Casado, Dami & Casado, Alicia. Bebes de la Selva. (p. 155)
—Bosque. (p. 214)
—Gusto. (p. 733)
—Invierno. (p. 885)
—Las Montanas. (p. 977)
—Lluvia. (p. 1043)
—Los Dientes. (p. 1053)
—Los Ruidos Del Bosque. (p. 1054)
—Nieve. (p. 1252)
—Oido. (p. 1282)
—Olfato. (p. 1285)
—Otono. (p. 1307)
—Palabra. (p. 1319)
—Primavera. (p. 1400)
—Rios y Lagos. (p. 1473)
—Ruidos de la Selva. (p. 1494)
—Sol. (p. 1606)
—Sueño. (p. 1672)
—Tacto. (p. 1695)
—Verano. (p. 1836)
—Vista. (p. 1846)
Casado, Dami Y. Alicia. Bebe Ha Crecido. (p. 155)
—Bebe Ha Llegado. (p. 155)
—Bebe Ya Va Al Cole. (p. 155)
Casagranda, Brigitte. Salt Dough Fun. (p. 1505)
Casagrande, Donata Dal Molin, illus. see Brignole, Giancarla, tr.
Casagrande, Donata Dal Molin, illus. see Perego, Jeanne.
Casagrande, Jerry. Birthday Train. (p. 193)
Casalderrey, Fina & Casalderrey Fraga, Xosefa. Alas de Mosca Para Ángel. Uhía, Manuel & Farias, Juan, trs. (p. 33)
Casalderrey Fraga, Xosefa, jt. auth. see Casalderrey, Fina.
Casale, Karen. Never Let a Ghost Borrow Your Library Book: Book Care Guidelines from the Library Secret Service. Rebora, Cecilia, illus. (p. 1243)
Casale, Paul, illus. see Alphin, Elaine Marie & Alphin, Arthur B.
Casale, Paul, illus. see Butler, Dori Hillestad.
Casale, Paul, illus. see Capeci, Anne.
Casale, Paul, illus. see Diaz, Katacha & Bosson, Jo-Ellen.
Casale, Paul, illus. see Diaz, Katacha.
Casale, Paul, illus. see Keene, Carolyn.
Casale, Paul, illus. see Morris, Rene.
Casale, Paul, tr. see Alphin, Elaine Marie & Alphin, Arthur B.
Casale, Roberto. Little Binky Bear. (p. 1024)
Casaluci, Stacy Manning. Miracles Love a Believer. (p. 1149)
Casanova, Jose Maria, illus. see Llimos Plomer, Anna & Llimós, Anna.
Casanova, Karen. Danica Patrick. (p. 404)
Casanova, Mary. Chrissa Stands Strong England, Tamara, ed. (p. 311)
—Curse of a Winter Moon. (p. 394)
—Danger at Snow Hill. Rayyan, Omar, illus. (p. 403)
—Day Dirk Yeller Came to Town. Hoyt, Ard, illus. (p. 412)
—Dog-Napped! Rayyan, Omar, illus. (p. 461)
—Extreme Stunt Dogs. Rayyan, Omar, illus. (p. 557)
—Frozen. (p. 645)
—Jess. (p. 914)
—Klipfish Code. (p. 963)
—Moose Tracks. (p. 1173)
—One-Dog Canoe. Hoyt, Ard, illus. (p. 1294)
—One-Dog Sleigh. Hoyt, Ard, illus. (p. 1294)
—Riot. (p. 1473)
—Some Cat! Hoyt, Ard, illus. (p. 1609)
—Some Dog! Hoyt, Ard, illus. (p. 1609)
—Stealing Thunder. (p. 1646)
—To Catch a Burglar. Rayyan, Omar, illus. (p. 1758)
—Trouble in Pembrook. Rayyan, Omar, illus. (p. 1790)
—Turtle-Hatching Mystery. Rayyan, Omar, illus. (p. 1798)
—Utterly Otterly Day. Hoyt, Ard, illus. (p. 1829)
—Utterly Otterly Night. Hoyt, Ard, illus. (p. 1829)
—When Eagles Fall. (p. 1902)
—Wolf Shadows. (p. 1944)
Casanueva, Idilian. I Like to Flap My Hands. (p. 841)
—You May Touch Here! Puedes Tocar Aqui! Caceres, Marangelie, illus. (p. 1976)
Casapulla, Louise. Ashlee Simpson. (p. 106)
Casares, Adolfo Bioy. Invesion de Morel. (p. 884)
Casares, Oscar. Brownsville: Stories. (p. 232)
Casarjian, Bethany & Casarjian, Robin. Power Source: Taking Charge of Your Life. (p. 1390)
Casarjian, Robin, jt. auth. see Casarjian, Bethany.
Casas, Dianne de Las. Beware, Beware of the Big Bad Bear! Gentry, Marita, illus. (p. 173)

Casas, Fritz, illus. see Sherman, M. Zachary.
Casas, Lola & Chiva, Francesc. NAM-NAM. (p. 1228)
Casas, Marisol Perez, tr. see Ehrler, Brenda.
Casaus, Lisa May, illus. see Martinez, Demetria & Montoya-Read, Rosalee.
Casciano, Christie & Moziak, Rose Mary Casciano. Haunted Hockey in Lake Placid. (p. 753)
—Puck Hog. (p. 1414)
Casciato, Daniel. Expansion & Reform: Early 1800s-1861. (p. 548)
—Expansion & Reform: (Early 1800s-1861) (p. 548)
Cascino, Jennifer, illus. see Nathan, Nadine Rubin.
Cascio, Maria Cristina Lo, illus. see Davidson, Susanna & Daynes, Katie.
Cascio, Maria Cristina Lo, illus. see Watt, Fiona.
Cascioli, Lucia. Shifters. (p. 1566)
Casco, Maria Cristina Lo, illus. see Mitchell, Patricia.
Cascone, Annette, jt. auth. see Cascone, Gina.
Cascone, Annette & Cascone, Gina. Beast of Baskerville. (p. 152)
—Grandpa's Monster Movies. (p. 710)
—Grave Secrets. (p. 712)
—Invasion of the Appleheads. (p. 883)
—Little Magic Shop of Horrors. (p. 1031)
—Witching Game. (p. 1941)
Cascone, Gina, jt. auth. see Cascone, Annette.
Cascone, Gina & Cascone, Annette. Little Magic Shop of Horrors. (p. 1031)
Casden, Ron, jt. auth. see Mutchnick, Brenda.
Case, Carrie L., jt. auth. see Ecklund, Faith.
Case, Jessica. TIME for Kids: Practicing for Today's Tests Language Arts Level 5 (p. 1751)
Case, Jonathan, illus. see Jenson, Jeff, et al.
Case, Layne. Charlie. (p. 292)
Case, Linda. Brigits Day of Fun. (p. 228)
Case, Maggie. Squirrel's Tale. (p. 1637)
Case, Nikki & Delrio, Martin. Searching for the Loch Ness Monster. (p. 1537)
Case, Richard, illus. see Ennis, Garth.
Casebolt, Christan. Zoey & Bel Bentley, Anita, illus. (p. 1987)
Casebolt, Jerry & Casebolt, Pemela. Butterflies & Buckaroos. (p. 247)
Casebolt, Pemela, jt. auth. see Casebolt, Jerry.
Caseley, Judith. Beauty Day. (p. 154)
—In Style with Grandma Antoinette. (p. 865)
Casella, Jody. Thin Space. (p. 1732)
Caselli, Stefano. Avengers World: A. I. M. Empire. Vol. 1 (p. 119)
Caselli, Stefano, illus. see Spencer, Nick & Hickman, Jonathan.
Caselli, Stefano, jt. auth. see Slott, Dan.
Casello-Atassi, Rosemarie. Camel's Tales: The Journey to Bethlehem. (p. 256)
Caselman, Lance, jt. auth. see Anzai, Nobuyuki.
Caselman, Lance, jt. auth. see Kubo, Tite.
Caselman, Lance, jt. auth. see Oda, Eiichiro.
Caselman, Lance, jt. auth. see Watase, Yuu.
Caselman, Lillian, tr. see Takei, Hiroyuki, et al.
Casero, Joseph M. Patxi of the Pyrenees. (p. 1330)
Casey, Barbara. Cadence of Gypsies. (p. 250)
—Slightest in the House. (p. 1590)
—Two Dogs & a Tail. (p. 1803)
Casey, Bert. Acoustic Guitar Book 2 Deluxe Edition: Book/DVD/CD (p. 9)
Casey, Betty Sidon. Christmas Tail. (p. 316)
Casey, C. A. Dragon Drool. (p. 477)
—Top of the Key. (p. 1769)
Casey, Carin Jayne. Granny Babysits: The Mischievous Five. (p. 710)
Casey, Carolyn. Apache. (p. 91)
—Mary Cassatt: The Life of an Artist. (p. 1100)
Casey, Dawn. Barefoot Book of Earth Tales. Wilson, Ann, illus. (p. 139)
—Barefoot Book of Earth Tales. Wilson, Anne, illus. (p. 139)
—Children of Lir: A Celtic Legend. Mayo, Diana, illus. (p. 302)
—Great Race: The Story of the Chinese Zodiac. Wilson, Anne, illus. (p. 718)
—Isis & Osiris. Mayo, Diana & Mistry, Nilesh, illus. (p. 891)
—Little Bear: A Folktale from Greenland. Corner, Chris, illus. (p. 1023)
—Lullaby for Little One. Fuge, Charles, illus. (p. 1064)
Casey, Dawn, et al. Barefoot Book of Ballet Stories. Wilson, Anne & Guay, Rebecca, illus. (p. 139)
Casey, Grandpa. Meet the Müsh-Mice. (p. 1123)
—Trilogy: Three adventures of the Müsh-Mice. Brennan, Lisa, illus. (p. 1786)
Casey, James, illus. see Eldridge, Les.
Casey, Jane. Bet Your Life. (p. 171)
—Hide & Seek. (p. 776)
—How to Fall. (p. 819)
Casey, Joe. Godland Celestial Edition Book 2 HC. (p. 690)
—Godland Finale. (p. 690)
—Haunt (p. 753)
—Rock Bottom. (p. 1482)
Casey, Joe, jt. auth. see Kirkman, Robert.
Casey, Joe & Gerard, Caleb. Full Moon Fever. (p. 646)
Casey, Joe & Reed, Brian. Amazing Spider-Man: The One & Only. Weeks, Lee et al, illus. (p. 55)
Casey, Joe & Saunders, Catherine. Darth Maul: Sith Apprentice. (p. 409)
Casey, Lukatz, illus. see American Girl Editorial Staff, ed.
Casey, Mark. African Princess: Deasha's Wild Adventure. (p. 28)
Casey, Quinn, illus. see Casey, Sean.
Casey, Robert, photos by see Kinmont, Ritchie.
Casey, Sean. My Dad Cancelled Christmas! Casey, Quinn, illus. (p. 1200)
Casey, Susan. Devil's Teeth: A True Story of Obsession & Survival among America's Great White Sharks. (p. 432)
—Kids Inventing! A Handbook for Young Inventors. (p. 954)
—Wave: In Pursuit of the Rogues, Freaks, & Giants of the Ocean. (p. 1864)
—Women Heroes of the American Revolution: 20 Stories of Espionage, Sabotage, Defiance, & Rescue. (p. 1945)
Cash, Emory, illus. see Neely, Kirk H.
Cash, Eric, illus. see Berry, Carolyn.
Cash, Eric, illus. see Kristen, Judith.
Cash, John Carter. Cat in the Rhinestone Suit. Nash, Scott, illus. (p. 278)
—Daddy Loves His Little Girl. Burckhardt, Marc, illus. (p. 398)
—Momma Loves Her Little Son. Burckhardt, Marc, illus. (p. 1162)
Cash, Lea Michelle. Strawberry Pot. (p. 1666)
Cash, M. A. Edward of Canterbury & the King of Red. Adams, Craig, illus. (p. 505)
Cash, Marie Romero. Santos: A Coloring Book of New Mexican Saints. (p. 1513)
Cash, Megan Montague. Bow-Wow's Nightmare Neighbors. Newgarden, Mark, illus. (p. 216)
Cash, Megan Montague, jt. auth. see Newgarden, Mark.
Cash, Paul, illus. see House, B. J.
Cash, T., jt. auth. see Morrow.
Casher, Debby Lightman. Color Doodles. (p. 342)
Cashford, Brenda. Bobbins Story: The Little Cat That Touched So Many Lives. (p. 206)
Cashin, Herschel V., et al. Under fire with the Tenth U. S. Cavalry. (p. 1813)
Cashin, John. Firearms Safety. (p. 591)
—Keeping up with the Kardashians. (p. 948)
Cashman, Erin. Exceptionals. (p. 547)
Cashman, Mary & Whipple, Cynthia. Merrilee Mannerly & Her Magnificent Manners. Johnson, Meredith, illus. (p. 1128)
Cashman, Seamus. Something Beginning with P: New Poems from Irish Poets. Askin, Corrina & Clarke, Alan, illus. (p. 1609)
Cashmore-Hingley, Michael, illus. see Gabolinscy, Jack.
Cashore, Kristin. Bitterblue. (p. 194)
—Bitterblue. Schoenherr, Ian, illus. (p. 194)
—Fire. (p. 590)
—Fire. November, S., ed. (p. 590)
—Graceling. (p. 705)
Cash-Walsh, Tina, illus. see D'Amico, Joan & Drummond, Karen Eich.
Casil, Amy Sterling. B-1 Lancer. (p. 122)
—Buzz Aldrin: The Pilot of the First Moon Landing. (p. 248)
—Choosing a Career in Aircraft Maintenance. (p. 310)
—Choosing a Career in Aircraft Mechanic. (p. 310)
—Coping with Terrorism. (p. 365)
—Creation of Canyons. (p. 379)
—Department of Labor. (p. 427)
—Hantavirus. (p. 743)
—Lois Duncan. (p. 1045)
—Mississippi: Past & Present. (p. 1154)
—Tony Hawk: Skateboard Mogul. (p. 1766)
—Why Banks Fail. (p. 1922)
Casilio, L. J. Fairy Tales. (p. 564)
Casilla, Robert, illus. see Adler, David A.
Casilla, Robert, illus. see Bromley, Anne C.
Casilla, Robert, illus. see Howard, Elizabeth Fitzgerald.
Casilla, Robert, illus. see Markun, Patricia M.
Casilla, Robert, illus. see Medina, Jane & Median, Jane.
Casilla, Robert, illus. see Mora, Pat & Ventura, Gabriela Baeza.
Casilla, Robert, illus. see Pinkney, Gloria Jean.
Casilla, Robert, illus. see Prince, April Jones.
Casilla, Robert, illus. see Ruiz-Flores, Lupe & Rosales-Yeomans, Natalia.
Casilla, Robert, illus. see Warren, Sarah E.
Casino, Boc. Sara's Simple Hope. (p. 1514)
Casis, Carmen A., tr. see Jepson-Gilbert, Anita.
Caso, Adolph. KaSO English to Italian Dictionary: With a Proposed One-to-One Relationship of Italian Graphemes (Letters) & Phonemes (Sounds) (p. 944)
Caso, Frank. Censorship. (p. 286)
Caso, Frank, jt. auth. see Fattah, Hala.
Caso, George R. Mission. Caso, George R., illus. (p. 1153)
Cason, Anjanette. Praise Puppy's Adventure in Praise. (p. 1393)
Cason, Stephanie. Night-Night Dance. (p. 1253)
Caspe, Jennifer Yap. Boy with One Hand. (p. 219)
Casper, Denise J. U. S. District Court Speaks. (p. 1806)
Casper, Gina R. Corky Beagle. (p. 367)
Casper, Julie Kerr. Agriculture: The Food We Grow & Animals We Raise. (p. 30)
—Animals: Creatures That Roam the Planet. (p. 81)
—Changing Ecosystems. (p. 290)
—Energy: Powering the Past, Present, & Future. (p. 528)
—Forests: More Than Just Trees. (p. 618)
—Fossil Fuels & Pollution: The Future of Air Quality. (p. 623)
—Global Warming (p. 684)
—Greenhouse Gases: Worldwide Impacts. (p. 723)
—Lands: Taming the Wilds. (p. 974)
—Natural Resources Set, 8-Volumes. (p. 1235)
—Water & Atmosphere: The Lifeblood of Natural Systems. (p. 1862)
Caspersen, Barbara, jt. auth. see Williams, Marilyn.
Casplan. Magician in the Attic. (p. 1075)
Cass, Bill, illus. see Owens, Jim.
Cass, Claire, jt. auth. see Eidelberg, Martin.
Cass, Isabella. Don't Stop Believing (p. 468)
—Nobody's Angels. (p. 1262)
Cass, Keysha. Helping Hand. (p. 766)
Cass, Kiera. Elite. (p. 513)
—Élite. (p. 513)
—Happily Ever After. (p. 744)
—Heir. (p. 762)
—Heir Intl. (p. 762)
—One. (p. 1293)
—Selection. (p. 1549)
—Selection Series Box Set. (p. 1549)
—Selection Stories: The Prince; The Guard. (p. 1549)
Cass, Liz. Ouisa & the Big People. (p. 1307)
Cassaday, John. Astonishing X-Men - Gifted (p. 109)
—Dangerous (p. 404)
—Unstoppable (p. 1823)
Cassady, Carolyn. Off the Road: My Years with Cassady, Kerouac, & Ginsberg. (p. 1279)
Cassady, David. Xenosaga Episode II: Strategy Guide. (p. 1967)
Cassady, John, jt. auth. see Nury, Fabien.
Cassady, Marsh. Creating Stories for Storytelling. (p. 379)
—Playwriting Step by Step. (p. 1373)
—Storytelling Step by Step. (p. 1664)
Cassady, Marsh, jt. auth. see Sturkie, Joan.
Cassan, Adolfo. Inside the Human Body. (p. 877)
Cassano, Carol E. Journey to the Bottom of the Ocean: Heavenly Adventures Volume 2. (p. 929)
Cassanos, Lynda Cohen. Indonesia. (p. 872)
—Morocco. (p. 1175)
Cassatt, Mary, illus. see Harris, Lois V.
Casse-Dasilva, Christel. Little Prayers for the Children. (p. 1033)
Cassedy, Patrice, tr. Finance. (p. 587)
Cassel, Katrina. Christian Girl's Guide to Being Your Best. (p. 311)
—Christian Girl's Guide to the Bible. (p. 311)
—Promises for God's Princesses. (p. 1411)
Cassel, Katrina L. Middle School Survival Manual. (p. 1138)
Cassel, Lili, illus. see Weilerstein, Sadie Rose.
Cassell, Dana K. & Rose, Noel R. Encyclopedia of Autoimmune Diseases. (p. 525)
Cassell, Jody. Where's Leon? Storybook & Reader's Guide CD-ROM Kristof Pincheira, Kyra, illus. (p. 1910)
Cassell, John. Marching Book / Marchar. (p. 1092)
Cassella, Lynn. When Parents Divorce. (p. 1904)
Cassells, E. Steve. Tracing the Past: Archaeology along the Rocky Mountain Expansion Loop Pipeline (p. 1775)
Casselman, Grace. Hole in the Hedge. (p. 788)
—Walk in the Park. (p. 1853)
Cassels, Jean. Twelve Days of Christmas in Louisiana. Cravath, Lynne Avril, illus. (p. 1800)
Cassels, Jean, illus. see Cuyler, Margery.
Cassels, Jean, illus. see Larson, Kirby & Nethery, Mary.
Cassels, Jean, illus. see Mock, Chara.
Cassels, Jean, illus. see Nicholas, Melissa.
Cassels, Jean, illus. see Rappoport, Bernice.
Cassels, Rosemary Van Liew. Rainbow Fish (p. 1435)
Cassetta, Andrea, illus. see Frost, Lesley.
Cassetta, Andrea, illus. see Miranda, Edward.
Cassettari, James. Monster Trucks Coloring Book. (p. 1168)
Cassettari, Noeline, jt. auth. see Phillips, Gina.
Cassettari, Noeline, jt. auth. see Turner, Jill.
Cassidy, Al, illus. see Dean, Lani.
Cassidy, Albert, Jr. & Bennedetti, Eric. Amazing Adventures of Dr. Snappy & Sam: Dr. Snappy vs. Subluxor. Romanchick, Jennifer, ed. (p. 52)
Cassidy, Amber, illus. see Goodhart, Pippa.
Cassidy, Anne. Blood Money. (p. 200)
—Butterfly Grave. (p. 248)
—Careless. (p. 268)
—Dead House. (p. 416)
—Dead Time. (p. 417)
—Innocent. (p. 875)
—Killing Rachel. (p. 956)
—Looking for JJ. (p. 1051)
—Toby's Trousers. Lewis, Jan, illus. (p. 1760)
—Wizard Balloon Remphry, Martin, illus. (p. 1942)
—Wizard Woof Remphry, Martin, illus. (p. 1943)
Cassidy, Anne & Durant, Alan. Doing the Double. (p. 463)
Cassidy, Cathy. Dizzy. (p. 455)
—Indigo Blue. (p. 872)
Cassidy, Colette. DIVCO, the Little Milk Truck. (p. 454)
Cassidy, Georgina M. True Make Believe Story: TTMBS Collection. (p. 1792)
Cassidy, Henry. Backyard Ecosystems. (p. 131)
Cassidy, John. World According to Klutz. Klutz Editors, ed. (p. 1953)
Cassidy, John, ed. see Klutz Editors & Boyle, Brendan.
Cassidy, John, jt. auth. see Doherty, Paul.
Cassidy, Maura A. Go Ask Anyone! (p. 686)
—Go Ask Your Father! (p. 686)
—Go Ask Your Girlfriends! (p. 686)
—Go Ask Your Grandparent! (p. 686)
—Go Ask Your Mother! (p. 686)
—Go Ask Your Teenager! (p. 686)
Cassidy, Mike. Skinny on Bullying: Legend of Gretchen. (p. 1585)
Cassidy, Nancy White, illus. see Cheney, Cora.
Cassidy, Sara. Seeing Orange Meissner, Amy, illus. (p. 1548)
—Skylark (p. 1587)
—Slick (p. 1590)
—Windfall (p. 1935)
Cassidy, Sean. Good to Be Small (p. 700)
—Gummytoes (p. 731)
Cassidy, Sean, illus. see Devine, Monica.
Cassidy, Sean, illus. see Ruurs, Margriet.
Cassidy, Tam. White Lady Ghost. (p. 1913)
Cassie, Brian. Tornadoes. (p. 1770)
Cassilly, Barbara. Numbers from the Bible. (p. 1272)
Cassino, Mark, photos by see Nelson, Jon.
Cassin-Scott, Jack. Costumes & Settings for Historical Plays: The Classical Period: Ancient Through Early Middle Ages. (p. 368)
—Elizabethan & Restoration Period 1558-1715. (p. 513)
—Medieval Period (Early Gothic, Late Gothic, Renaissance) (p. 1119)
Cassis, Youssef, jt. ed. see Minoglou, Ioanna.
Cassity, Brittney. Fiddlebug. (p. 583)
Cassius, Sonya. My Beautiful World. (p. 1196)
Casson, Sophia, illus. see Lemieux, Jean.
Casson, Sophie, illus. see Lemieux, Jean.
Casson, Sophie, jt. auth. see Lemieux, Jean.
Cassone, Chris, creator. Great Central Park Treasure Hunt: Interactive Orienteering Map of NYC's Famous Park. (p. 714)
Cassriel, Betsy R. Robot Builders! (p. 1480)
Cassutto, George. Civics Student Activity Book: Student Activities Book. (p. 324)
Cast, Kristin, jt. auth. see Cast, P. C.
Cast, Kristin, et al. Kisses from Hell. (p. 962)
Cast, P. C. Elphame's Choice. (p. 516)
Cast, P. C., ed. see Caine, Rachel, pseud, et al.
Cast, P. C. & Cast, Kristin. Awakened. (p. 120)
—Betrayed. (p. 172)
—Burned. (p. 243)
—Chosen. (p. 310)
—Destined. (p. 430)
—Hidden. (p. 775)
—House of Night: the Beginning: Marked & Betrayed. (p. 803)
—Hunted. (p. 828)
—Kalona's Fall. (p. 942)
—Marcada: Una Casa de la Noche Novela. (p. 1091)
—Marked. (p. 1095)
—Neferet's Curse. (p. 1240)
—Redeemed. (p. 1455)
—Tempted. (p. 1718)
—Untamed. (p. 1823)
Cast, P. C. & Doner, Kim. Fledgling Handbook 101. (p. 603)
Cast, P. C., ed. Eternal: More Love Stories with Bite. (p. 539)
—Nyx in the House of Night: Mythology, Folklore & Religion in the PC & Kristin Cast Vampyre Series. (p. 1274)
Castaldi, Elicia. Food Parade: Healthy Eating with the Nutritious Food Groups. Castaldi, Elicia, illus. (p. 613)
Castaldi, Elicia, illus. see Holm, Jennifer L.
Castaldo, Annalisa, ed. see Shakespeare, William.
Castaldo, Nancy. Race Around the World (Totally True Adventures) Lowe, Wesley, illus. (p. 1430)
Castaldo, Nancy F. Keeping Our Earth Green. Caputo, Jim, illus. (p. 947)
—Leap into Space: Exploring the Universe & Your Place in It. McRae, Patrick, illus. (p. 982)
—Pizza for the Queen. Potter, Melisande, illus. (p. 1365)
—Rainforests: An Activity Guide for Ages 6-9. (p. 1436)
—Sniffer Dogs: How Dogs (and Their Noses) Save the World. (p. 1597)
—Sunny Days & Starry Nights: Nature Activities for Ages 2-6. (p. 1677)
Castaldo, Nancy F., jt. auth. see de Seve, Karen.
Castan, Mike. Fighting for Dontae. (p. 585)
—Price of Loyalty. (p. 1398)
Castaneda, Ana Zelaya. Animal Alphabet. (p. 76)
Castaneda, Huguette. Mariella y Los Obsequios Del Mar. (p. 1093)
—Mariella's Gifts from the Se. (p. 1094)
Castañeda, Omar S. Abuela's Weave. Sanchez, Enrique O., illus. (p. 7)
—Tapiz de Abuela. (p. 1705)
Castaneda, Patricia, jt. auth. see Sosa, Carlos.
Castaneda, Ricardo Chavez. Beso Mas Largo del Mundo(The Longest Kiss in the World) Rodriguez, Mary, illus. (p. 168)
Castañer, Mercedes, tr. see Nelson, Robin.
Castañer, Mercedes P., tr. see Nelson, Robin.
Castanga, Felicity. Incredible Here & Now. (p. 869)
Castano, Clara, jt. auth. see Yazbeck, Peter.
Castano, Marie, jt. auth. see Ward, Hadley.
Castberg, C. & Adler, Lillian W. New Reading Hebrew: A Guided Instruction Course. (p. 1247)
Casteel, Kay, illus. see Butler, Darren J.
Casteel, Kay, illus. see Smith, Annie Laura.
Casteel, Kay, illus. see Taylor, Mary Ann.
Casteel, Seth. Underwater Doggies 1,2,3. (p. 1817)
—Underwater Doggies Colors. (p. 1817)
Casteel, Tom, illus. see Bell-Rehwoldt, Sheri.
Casteel, Tom, illus. see Dodge Cummings, Judy.
Casteel, Tom, illus. see Mooney, Carla.
Casteel, Tom, illus. see Reilly, Kathleen M.
Castelao, Patricia, illus. see Applegate, Katherine.
Castelao, Patricia, illus. see Hapka, Catherine, pseud.
Castelao, Patricia, illus. see Orr, Wendy.
Castellan, Andrea. Mickey Mouse & the Orbiting Nightmare. (p. 1136)
Castellan, Andrea "Casty". Mickey Mouse & the World to Come. Castellan, Andrea "Casty" & Mazzon, Michelle, illus. (p. 1136)
Castellaneta, Paulie. Under the Covers. (p. 1813)
Castellani, Andrea, jt. auth. see Earnhardt, Donna W.
Castellano Boyum, Marie. More Simply Super Storytimes: Programming Ideas for Ages 3-6. (p. 1175)
Castellano, Giuseppe, illus. see Zuravicky, Orli.
Castellano, Marie. Simply Super Storytimes: Programming Ideas. (p. 1578)
Castellano, Peter. Chupacabras. (p. 318)
—Longboard Skateboarding. (p. 1047)
—MMA. (p. 1157)
—Mma. (p. 1157)
—Motocross. (p. 1179)
Castellanos, Diana, illus. see Inkiow, Ditler.
Castellanos, Stacey. Magic in My Head. (p. 1072)
Castellarin, Loretta & Roberts, Ken. Spike (p. 1627)
Castelli, Jeanette. Gatos en la Luna/the Cats on the Moon. Santana, Andrea, illus. (p. 658)
Castellini, Claudio, illus. see Youngquist, Jeff, ed.
Castells, Margarita. Libro de Las Mil y una Noches: Relatos de Hoy y Siempre. Sariola, Eulalia, illus. (p. 1006)
Castellucci, Cecil. Beige. (p. 160)
—Boy Proof (p. 218)
—Boy Proof. (p. 218)
—Grandma's Gloves. Denos, Julia, illus. (p. 708)
—Janes in Love. (p. 908)
—Odd Duck. (p. 1278)
—Plain Janes. (p. 1366)
—Queen of Cool. (p. 1425)
—Rose Sees Red. (p. 1489)
—Tin Star. (p. 1755)
—Year of the Beasts. Powell, Nate, illus. (p. 1969)
Castellucci, Cecil, jt. ed. see Black, Holly.
Casten, Diane. Christmas Doll. (p. 313)
Castenetto, Christiana. Dante's Journey. Ceva, Aline Cantono di, illus. (p. 406)
Caster, Shannon. Brain. (p. 221)
—Eyes. (p. 558)
—Heart. (p. 759)
—Kidneys. (p. 952)
—Lungs. (p. 1065)
—Skin. (p. 1585)
Casterline, L. C. Sounds of Music. Yerkes, Lane, illus. (p. 1615)

C

Casterline, L. C. & Packard, Mary. Beyond the Grave: Ripley's Believe It or Not! (p. 174)
Castile, Muriel, tr. see Montardre, Hélène.
Castile, Muriel, tr. see Royer, Anne.
Castilla, Julia Mercedes. Aventuras de un Nino de la Calle. (p. 119)
—Strange Parents. (p. 1665)
Castilla, Julia Mercedes, tr. see Bertrand, Diane Gonzales.
Castillo, Cesar, illus. see LaRocque, Greg.
Castillo, Elizabeth. Jaden Christian. (p. 905)
Castillo, Gary D. Quesadilla Moon. (p. 1426)
Castillo, Guillermo Graco, illus. see Gomez, Mercedes.
Castillo, Guillermo Graco, illus. see Malpica, Antonio.
Castillo, Ina. Red the Super Wiener. (p. 1455)
Castillo, Jesus, illus. see Riveros, Gabriela.
Castillo, Lauren. Melvin & the Boy. Castillo, Lauren, illus. (p. 1125)
—Nana in the City. (p. 1228)
—Troublemaker. (p. 1790)
Castillo, Lauren, illus. see Banks, Kate.
Castillo, Lauren, illus. see Boelts, Maribeth.
Castillo, Lauren, illus. see Bunting, Eve.
Castillo, Lauren, illus. see Cameron, Ann.
Castillo, Lauren, illus. see Fern, Tracey E.
Castillo, Lauren, illus. see Hest, Amy.
Castillo, Lauren, illus. see King James Bible Staff.
Castillo, Lauren, illus. see Stanek, Linda.
Castillo, Marcos, illus. see Kessler, Cristina.
Castillo, Rachel. Sarah the Octopus. (p. 1514)
Castillo, Rodolfo Iguaran. Freddy Rincon. (p. 633)
Castillon, Carly, illus. see McKendry, Sam.
Castillon, Carly, illus. see Rovetch, L. Bob.
Castle, Amber. Amelia the Silver Sister. Hall, Mary, illus. (p. 58)
—Evie the Swan Sister. Hall, Mary, illus. (p. 546)
—Grace the Sea Sister. Hall, Mary, illus. (p. 705)
—Isabella - The Butterfly Sister. Hall, Mary, illus. (p. 891)
—Sophia the Flame Sister. Hall, Mary, illus. (p. 1613)
—Spell Sisters: Chloe the Storm Sister. Hall, Mary, illus. (p. 1625)
—Spell Sisters: Olivia the Otter Sister. Hall, Mary, illus. (p. 1625)
Castle, Caroline. Big Fuzzy. Howarth, Daniel, illus. (p. 181)
—For Every Child: The UN Convention on the Rights of the Child in Words & Pictures. (p. 615)
Castle, Elizabeth. Because I Love You More Than All the Stars in Heaven. (p. 155)
Castle, Frances, illus. see Agnew, Kate.
Castle, Frances, illus. see Wickings, Ruth.
Castle, George. Chicago Bears. (p. 299)
—Chicago Cubs. (p. 299)
—Chicago White Sox. (p. 299)
—Sammy Sosa: Slammin' Sammy. Rains, Rob, ed. (p. 1508)
Castle, Grace, jt. auth. see Baer, Peter.
Castle, Ian. British Infantryman in South Africa 1877-81. Hook, Christa, illus. (p. 229)
Castle, Jan And Kare. Gracey's Desire. LaFerriere, Suzanne, illus. (p. 705)
Castle, Jennifer. Beginning of After. (p. 159)
Castle, Kate. Ballerina's Handbook. Allsopp, Sophie, illus. (p. 134)
Castle, Lila. Star Shack. (p. 1641)
Castle, Lynn, illus. see Haberstroh, Marilyn & Panik, Sharon.
Castle, Patricia. Gravity. (p. 712)
—In the Garden. (p. 866)
Castle, Regina F. Henry Hopper. (p. 768)
Castleberry, Stephen B., Sr. & Castleberry, Susie. History Mystery. (p. 783)
Castleberry, Stephen B., Sr. & Castleberry, Susie L. Weighty Matters. (p. 1872)
Castleberry, Stephen B., Sr. & Castleberry, Susie. Where There's Smoke. (p. 1910)
Castleberry, Susie, jt. auth. see Castleberry, Stephen B., Sr.
Castleberry, Susie L., jt. auth. see Castleberry, Stephen B., Sr.
Castleforte, Brian. Papertoy Monsters: 50 Cool Papertoys You Can Make Yourself! (p. 1323)
Castlemon, Harry. Boy Trapper. (p. 219)
—Go-Ahead; or, the Fisher-Boy's Motto, by Harry Castlemon [Pseud]. (p. 686)
—No Moss; or, the Career of a Rolling Stone, by Harry Castlemon [Pseud]. (p. 1259)
—Sportsman's Club among the Trappers. (p. 1633)
—Sportsmans Club in the Saddle. (p. 1633)
Castles, Heather, illus. see James, Shilah & James, Michael.
Castles, Heather, illus. see Nejime, Shoichi.
Castles, Jennifer. Song for Lorkie. Bowen, Dean, illus. (p. 1611)
Castleton, Chaffee. Runty's Adventure: A Story of Love. Queen, Dana, illus. (p. 1497)
Castner, K. D. Daughters of Ruin. (p. 410)
Casto, Christina, illus. see Scholl, Jenny.
Castonguay, Leo. Piper Peter. (p. 1361)
Castor, Daniel & Castor, Harriet. Jam Sponge & Sneakers. (p. 906)
—Wondaglop Plot. (p. 1947)
Castor, H. Ballet for Beginners. (p. 134)
—Dinosaurs Next Door. (p. 445)
—Starting Chess. (p. 1644)
Castor, H. M. VIII. (p. 1842)
Castor, Harriet. Ballet Magic Fisher, Chris, illus. (p. 134)
—Dance Off. (p. 402)
—Hit the Beach! (p. 785)
—How to Be a Ballerina. Clifton-Brown, Holly, illus. (p. 814)
—Incredible Present. Young, Norman, illus. (p. 869)
—Trucks. Lyon, Chris, illus. (p. 1791)
—Trucks. Lyon, Chris et al, illus. (p. 1791)
Castor, Harriet, jt. auth. see Castor, Daniel.
Castor, Harriet, jt. auth. see Young, Caroline.
Castrataro, Kristen. Grandpa's Farm Has Lots of Saws. (p. 709)
Castrillón, Melissa, illus. see Rundell, Katherine.
Castro, Adam-Troy. Gustav Gloom & the Cryptic Carousel #4. Margiotta, Kristen, illus. (p. 732)
—Gustav Gloom & the Four Terrors Margiotta, Kristen, illus. (p. 733)
—Gustav Gloom & the Four Terrors #3. Margiotta, Kristen, illus. (p. 733)
—Gustav Gloom & the Inn of Shadows #5. Margiotta, Kristen, illus. (p. 733)
—Gustav Gloom & the Nightmare Vault Margiotta, Kristen, illus. (p. 733)
—Gustav Gloom & the Nightmare Vault #2. Margiotta, Kristen, illus. (p. 733)
—Gustav Gloom & the People Taker Margiotta, Kristen, illus. (p. 733)
—Gustav Gloom & the People Taker #1. Margiotta, Kristen, illus. (p. 733)
Castro, Adam-Troy, jt. auth. see Westerfeld, Scott.
Castro, Anita. Two Hands to Hold. Wroth, Dean, illus. (p. 1803)
Castro, Christopher, illus. see Castro, Shirley.
Castro, Edmund Lee. Crystal & Her Flying Adventure. (p. 387)
—Crystal & the Not-So-Scary Night. (p. 387)
Castro, Eugenio Diaz. Manuela. (p. 1089)
Castro, Giovanni & Chabot, Jacob. Hello Kitty: It's about Time. (p. 764)
Castro, Ivan A. 100 Hispanics You Should Know (p. 1998)
Castro L., Antonio, illus. see Byrd, Lee Merrill.
Castro L., Antonio, illus. see Hayes, Joe.
Castro L., Antonio, illus. see Rivera-Ashford, Roni Capin.
Castro, Luis F., illus. see Tinsley, P. S.
Castro, Maria Elena, illus. see Guerrero, Ernesto, tr.
Castro, Marisol Pales. Diccionario de Sinonimos y Antonimos. (p. 435)
Castro, Mima, illus. see Argueta, Jorge.
Castro, Mima, illus. see Flor Ada, Alma.
Castro, Mima, illus. see White, Amy.
Castro, Nachie. Doomed! Disney Book Group Staff, illus. (p. 470)
—Man in the Ant Hill. Marvel Illustrators, illus. (p. 1085)
—Venom! Disney Book Club Staff & Disney Book Group Staff, illus. (p. 1835)
Castro, Patricia, illus. see Twain, Mark, pseud.
Castro, Shirley. Pelican Family Counting Book. Castro, Christopher, illus. (p. 1335)
—Pelican Family Series — Stelly & the Sticky, Gooey Taffy. Castro, Christopher, illus. (p. 1335)
—Pelican Family Series—Telly's Story. Castro, Christopher, illus. (p. 1335)
Castro-Bran, Rose. Adventures of Port Herman Lighthouse. (p. 21)
Castronova, Jeri. Paint the Sky & Dance: Women & the New Myths Workbook. (p. 1318)
Castronovo, Katy, illus. see Duehl, Kristine.
Castroviejo, Concha & Fedorchek, Robert M., trs. from SPA. Garden with Seven Gates. (p. 656)
Castrovilla, Selene. By the Sword. Farnsworth, Bill, illus. (p. 249)
—Girl Next Door. (p. 678)
—Revolutionary Friends: General George Washington & the Marquis de Lafayette. Kozjan, Drazen, illus. (p. 1466)
—Saved by the Music. (p. 1517)
Castulo Aten, Vicky Talaro, illus. see Talaro, Theresa.
Caswell, Brian. Cruisin' (p. 386)
—Double Exposure. (p. 472)
Caswell, David G. Laughter Prevents Wrinkles. (p. 980)
Caswell, Deanna. Beach House. Bates, Amy June, illus. (p. 149)
Caswell, Kelly. Hickory Dickory Dock. (p. 775)
Caszatt-Allen, Wendy, illus. see PaleoJoe.
Caszatt-Allen, Wendy, jt. auth. see PaleoJoe.
Catagan, Tino, illus. see Andersen, Hans Christian.
Catala, Ellen. Animals in Danger (p. 83)
—How Do You Move? (p. 808)
—On the Ranch. (p. 1291)
—Snakes & Lizards. (p. 1596)
—Up, up, & Away. (p. 1824)
—What Does a Firefighter Do? (p. 1883)
—What Has Changed? (p. 1886)
Catala, Ellen, jt. auth. see Endres, Hollie J.
Catala, Ellen & Ring, Susan. Lo Que Necesitamos y lo Que Queremos. (p. 1044)
Catala, Ellen & Trumbauer, Lisa. Restar. (p. 1464)
—¿Por Qué Medimos? (p. 1385)
Català, Josep Maria, tr. see Rey, H. A. & Rey, Margret.
catalán, Cuento popular. Historia de un Conejito. Ruiz, Margarita, illus. (p. 782)
catalán, Cuento popular, jt. auth. see Combel Editorial Staff.
Catalani, Dorothy Kon & Catalani, Jim. Wethechildren, Future Leaders - Patriotic 123. Stephens, Joan Wilson, illus. (p. 1877)
Catalani, Jim, jt. auth. see Catalani, Dorothy Kon.
Catalano, Angela. Community Needs: Meeting Needs & Wants in the Community. (p. 350)
—Community Plans: Choices about Money Making in Communities. (p. 350)
—Community Plans: Making Choices about Money in Communities. (p. 350)
—Community Resources: The Land & the People in Communities. (p. 350)
—Community Space: How Land & Weather Shape Communities. (p. 350)
Catalano, Dominic. Frog Went A-Courting: A Musical Play in Six Acts. (p. 640)
—Mr. Basset Plays. Catalano, Dominic, illus. (p. 1184)
Catalano, Dominic, illus. see Aroner, Miriam.
Catalano, Dominic, illus. see Brimner, Larry Dane.
Catalano, Dominic, illus. see Coleman, Wim & Perrin, Pat.
Catalano, Dominic, illus. see Goodman, Joan.
Catalano, Dominic, illus. see Grimm, Jacob & Grimm, Wilhelm K.
Catalano, Dominic, illus. see Mackall, Dandi Daley.
Catalano, Dominic, illus. see Williams, Rozanne Lanczak.
Catalano, Nikki. Mitsu: The Dark Witch & the Dream Wilderness. (p. 1156)
Catalano, Tom. Rhymes for Teens: Poems Older Students Can Enjoy. Romango, Jim, illus. (p. 1468)
Catalanotto, Peter. Daisy 1, 2, 3. Catalanotto, Peter, illus. (p. 400)
—Dylan's Day Out. Catalanotto, Peter, illus. (p. 491)
—Emily's Art. Catalanotto, Peter, illus. (p. 519)
—Ivan the Terrier. Catalanotto, Peter, illus. (p. 900)
—Kitten Red, Yellow, Blue. Catalanotto, Peter, illus. (p. 962)
—Matthew A. B. C. Catalanotto, Peter, illus. (p. 1109)
—Monkey & Robot. (p. 1165)
—Monkey & Robot. Catalanotto, Peter, illus. (p. 1165)
—More of Monkey & Robot. Catalanotto, Peter, illus. (p. 1174)
—Newbies. Catalanotto, Peter, illus. (p. 1249)
—Question Boy Meets Little Miss Know-It-All. Catalanotto, Peter, illus. (p. 1426)
Catalanotto, Peter, illus. see Burleigh, Robert.
Catalanotto, Peter, illus. see Lyon, George Ella.
Catalanotto, Peter, illus. see Osborne, Mary Pope.
Catalanotto, Peter, illus. see Ryder, Joanne & Ryder.
Catalanotto, Peter, jt. auth. see Lyon, George Ella.
Catalanotto, Peter & Schembri, Pamela. Veterans Day Visitor. Catalanotto, Peter, illus. (p. 1839)
Cataldo, Melanie, illus. see Yolen, Jane.
Catanese, Donna, illus. see Hamsa, Bobbie.
Catanese, P. W. Brave Apprentice. (p. 223)
—Dragon Games. Ho, David, illus. (p. 477)
—End of Time. Ho, David, illus. (p. 526)
—Eye of the Warlock: A Further Tales Adventure. (p. 558)
—Happenstance Found. (p. 744)
—Mirror's Tale: A Further Tales Adventure. (p. 1149)
—Riddle of the Gnome: A Further Tale Adventure. (p. 1470)
—Riddle of the Gnome. (p. 1470)
—Thief & the Beanstalk: A Further Tales Adventure. (p. 1732)
Catanzarite, Lisa. What the World Is Like to Bea Moore: The Treasure. Miller, Heidi, illus. (p. 1894)
Catchpole, Barbara. Dead Ed in My Head. (p. 416)
Catchpole, Diana, illus. see Mortimer, Sheila.
Catchpole, Diana, illus. see Taylor, Dereen.
Catchpool, Michael. Cloud Spinner. Jay, Alison, illus. (p. 334)
—Grandpa's Boat. Williams, Sophy, illus. (p. 709)
—Where There's a Bear, There's Trouble. Cabban, Vanessa, illus. (p. 1909)
Cate, Annette LeBlanc. Look Up! Bird-Watching in Your Own Backyard. Cate, Annette LeBlanc, illus. (p. 1050)
—Magic Rabbit. (p. 1073)
—Magic Rabbit. Cate, Annette LeBlanc, illus. (p. 1073)
Cate, Marijke Ten. Where Is My Sock? Cate, Marijke Ten, illus. (p. 1909)
Cate, Shari. Dreams of King Neb. (p. 484)
Catel, Patrick. Battles of the Revolutionary War (p. 147)
—China (p. 306)
—Graphing Money (p. 711)
—Home Front of the Revolutionary War (p. 792)
—Japan (p. 908)
—Key People of the Revolutionary War (p. 950)
—Money & Trade (p. 1164)
—Nelson Mandela. (p. 1240)
—Raising Livestock (p. 1437)
—Skiing (p. 1584)
—Soldiers of the Revolutionary War (p. 1607)
—Surviving Stunts & Other Amazing Feats. (p. 1687)
—What Did the Ancient Chinese Do for Me? (p. 1882)
—What Did the Ancient Egyptians Do for Me? (p. 1882)
—What Did the Ancient Greeks Do for Me? (p. 1882)
—Why We Fought: The Revolutionary War Set (p. 1926)
Catel, Patrick & Collins, Frank. Cuba (p. 388)
Cater, Angela. Adventures of Sailor Sam. Cater, Angela, illus. (p. 22)
—Perfect Nest for Mrs Mallard. Cater, Angela, illus. (p. 1342)
Caterer, Claire. Wand & the Sea. (p. 1856)
Caterer, Claire M. Key & the Flame. (p. 950)
Caterisano, Sarah, illus. see Clark, Ruth E.
Caterpillar. My Big Book of Trucks & Diggers. (p. 1197)
Caterpillar Inc. Staff, et al. Big, Bigger, & Biggest Trucks & Diggers. (p. 178)
Cates, Darrin. Look Inside Caves. (p. 1049)
Cates, David. Karl Marx: Philosopher & Revolutionary. (p. 943)
—Scottsboro Boys. (p. 1532)
Cates, David & Armstrong, Margalynne. Plessy v. Ferguson: Segregation & the Separate but Equal Policy. (p. 1374)
Cathcart Jr., George R. Ernie Goes to Kindergarten. (p. 534)
Cathcart, Sharyn, illus. see Smith, Claude Clayton.
Cathcart, Yvonne, illus. see Hutchins, Hazel J. & Hutchins, Hazel.
Cathcart, Yvonne, illus. see Hutchins, Hazel.
Cathcart, Yvonne, illus. see McCarney, Rosemary.
Cather, Willa. My Antonia. (p. 1196)
—Willa Cather. Balkovek, James, illus. (p. 1933)
Catherall, Arthur. Strange Intruder. (p. 1665)
Catherine, Headlam, jt. auth. see Headlam, Catharine.
Catherine, Maria. Me & Grandma. Campion, Pascal, illus. (p. 1115)
—Me & Grandpa. Campion, Pascal, illus. (p. 1115)
—Time Together (p. 1753)
—Time Together: Me & Dad Campion, Pascal, illus. (p. 1753)
Catherine, Mary. Classic Myths. (p. 328)
Catherine, Rose. Fido the Duck: A Short Tale. (p. 583)
Catherine Roth, Alice. Katie & Sally Learn a Lesson: Book One. (p. 944)
Catholic Answers, creator. Truth Is Out There: Brendan & Erc in Exile, Volume 1. (p. 1794)
Catholic Book Publishing Staff, creator. Saints Teach Us. (p. 1504)
—Thank You Prayers. (p. 1725)
Catholic Church, Archdiocese of Birmingham (England) Staff, jt. contrib. by see Maryvale Institute of Religious Education Staff.
Cathy Smentkowski. If the Shoe Fits. (p. 854)
Cathy, Wilcox, illus. see Gervay, Susanne.
Catipon, Atreyu. Wizard's Magic Hat. (p. 1943)
Catlin, George, photos by see Jackson, John C.
Catling, Andy, illus. see Benton, Lynne.
Catling, Andy, illus. see Taylor, Martin.
Catling, Andy, jt. auth. see Robinson, Hilary.
Catling, Patrick S., jt. auth. see Skene, Catling Patrick.
Catling, Patrick Skene. Chocolate Touch. (p. 309)
Catling, S. Mapstart 2. (p. 1091)
Catling, Simon & HarperCollins UK Staff. Collins First Atlas. (p. 340)
Catlow, Nikalas. Do You Doodle? (p. 457)
—Mind Your Own Business: A File of Super Secret Stuff. (p. 1145)
—Oodles of Doodles. (p. 1298)
—Spies vs. Giant Slugs in the Jungle. Wesson, Tim, illus. (p. 1627)
—Trolls vs. Cowboys in the Arctic. Wesson, Tim, illus. (p. 1788)
Catlow, Nikalas, illus. see Enright, Dominique, et al.
Catlow, Nikalas, illus. see Running Press Staff.
Catlow, Nikalas, jt. auth. see Wesson, Tim.
Catlow, Nikalas & Sinden, David. Don't Eat This Book. (p. 467)
Catlow, Nikalas & Wesson, Tim. Aliens vs. Mad Scientists under the Ocean. Catlow, Nikalas & Wesson, Tim, illus. (p. 41)
—Robots vs. Gorillas in the Desert. Catlow, Nikalas & Wesson, Tim, illus. (p. 1481)
—Romans vs. Dinosaurs on Mars. Catlow, Nikalas & Wesson, Tim, illus. (p. 1486)
Catlow, Nikalas, et al. Funny Fingers. (p. 649)
—Funny Fingers Are Having a Party! (p. 649)
Catlow, Niki, illus. see Enright, Dominique, et al.
Catmull, Katherine. Summer & Bird. (p. 1673)
Cato, Andrea, illus. see Blair, Candice.
Cato, Nancy, illus. see Goldberg, Whoopi & Underwood, Deborah.
Cato, Vivienne. Torah & Judaism. (p. 1769)
Caton, Peter. Josh: Hero. (p. 926)
Caton, Tim, illus. see Feierabend, John M.
Catone, Gina. Homework Time with Charlie. (p. 794)
Cator, David. Map Symbols. (p. 1090)
Catran, Ken. Artists Are Crazy & Other Stories. (p. 104)
—Bloody Liggie. (p. 201)
—Dawn Hawk. (p. 411)
—Protus Rising. (p. 1412)
—Tomorrow the Dark. (p. 1765)
—Voyage with Jason. (p. 1850)
Catran, Wendy. Katie Raven's Fire. (p. 945)
Catron, John. Hodder Reading Project 5-6 Reader: Stories of Many Cultures. (p. 787)
Catron, Julie Gaches. Homerun Hitters: No Pride Allowed. (p. 793)
—Homerun Hitters: Book Two: Please Forgive Me. (p. 793)
Catrow, David. Best in Show. (p. 170)
—Dinosaur Hunt. (p. 442)
—Fly Flew In. (p. 609)
—Fly Flew In. Catrow, David, illus. (p. 609)
—Fun in the Sun. (p. 648)
—Funny Lunch. (p. 650)
—Funny Lunch. Catrow, David, illus. (p. 650)
—Monster Mash. (p. 1167)
—Scholastic Reader Level 1: Max Spaniel: Best in Show. Catrow, David, illus. (p. 1522)
—We the Kids: The Preamble of the Constitution of the United States. Catrow, David, illus. (p. 1868)
—We the Kids: The Preamble to the Constitution of the United States. Catrow, David, illus. (p. 1868)
Catrow, David, illus. see Beaumont, Karen.
Catrow, David, illus. see Berger, Lou.
Catrow, David, illus. see Broach, Elise.
Catrow, David, illus. see Crow, Kristyn.
Catrow, David, illus. see Crum, Shutta.
Catrow, David, illus. see Fleming, Candace.
Catrow, David, illus. see Katz, Alan.
Catrow, David, illus. see Lovell, Patty.
Catrow, David, illus. see Mandel, Peter.
Catrow, David, illus. see Nolen, Jerdine & Keliher, Brian.
Catrow, David, illus. see Nolen, Jerdine.
Catrow, David, illus. see Orloff, Karen Kaufman.
Catrow, David, illus. see Reiss, Mike & Reiss, Mike.
Catrow, David, illus. see Reiss, Mike.
Catrow, David, illus. see San Souci, Robert D.
Catrow, David, illus. see Smith, Stuart.
Catrow, David, illus. see Zweibel, Alan.
Cat's Pyjamas. Haunted House: A Touch & Feel Spooky Tour. (p. 753)
Catt, Thessaly. Animal Journeys (p. 78)
—Migrating with the Arctic Tern. (p. 1140)
—Migrating with the Caribou. (p. 1140)
—Migrating with the Humpback Whale. (p. 1140)
—Migrating with the Monarch Butterfly. (p. 1140)
—Migrating with the Salmon. (p. 1140)
—Migrating with the Wildebeest. (p. 1140)
—My Grandparents: MIS Abuelos. (p. 1210)
—My Grandparents. (p. 1210)
—My Mom. (p. 1214)
—My Mom(Mi Mamá) (p. 1214)
—My Uncles & Aunts: MIS Tíos y Tías. (p. 1220)
—My Uncles & Aunts. (p. 1220)
Cattanach, Ann. Malpas the Dragon. Renouf, Michael, illus. (p. 1084)
Cattell, Bob, jt. auth. see Ross, David.
Cattell, Bob & Agard, John. Butter-Finger. Smy, Pam, illus. (p. 247)
—Shine on, Butter-Finger. Smy, Pam, illus. (p. 1566)
Cattie, Ray. Ard Righ: The Sword on the Stone. (p. 96)
Cattish, Anna, illus. see Cobb, Amy.
Cattouse, Tanya. Book 1- a Special Day. (p. 210)
Catusanu, Mircea, illus. see Golden Books Staff, et al.
Catusanu, Mircea, illus. see Hazen, Barbara Shook.
Catusanu, Mircea, illus. see Hissom, Jennie.
Catusanu, Mircea, illus. see Pearson, Peter.
Cauble, Christopher, photos by see Johanek, Durrae.
Caudill, Rebecca. Did You Carry the Flag Today, Charley. Grossman, Nancy, illus. (p. 437)
—Happy Little Family. Merwin, Decie, illus. (p. 746)
—Schoolhouse in the Woods. Merwin, Decie, illus. (p. 1523)
—Schoolroom in the Parlor. Merwin, Decie, illus. (p. 1524)
—Up & down the River. Merwin, Decie, illus. (p. 1824)

Caudle, Brad & Caudle, Melissa. Oceans. (p. 1277)
Caudle, Melissa. Day at the Zoo: Stephen's Big Day. (p. 412)
Caudle, Melissa, jt. auth. see Caudle, Brad.
Caudle, P. L. Tale of Strawberry Snow Simmonds, Frank H., illus. (p. 1700)
Caudle, Ruth. Yvette, Annette & Renette. (p. 1983)
Caudron, Chris & Childs, Caro. Face Painting. (p. 560)
—Usborne Book of Face Painting. Knighton, Kate, ed. (p. 1827)
Caughey, Ellen. Eric Liddell: Gold Medal Missionary. (p. 533)
Caughey, Melissa. Kid's Guide to Keeping Chickens: Best Breeds, Creating a Home, Care & Handling, Outdoor Fun, Crafts & Treats. (p. 953)
Caughill, Jeff. Good Old Hockey Game. (p. 700)
Cauley, Lorinda Bryan, illus. see Roberts, Bethany.
Cauley, Phil. Adventures of Io, the Little Angel: Sticks & Stones. (p. 20)
Caulfield, Annie. Katie Milk Solves Reality-TV Crimes. (p. 945)
—Solves Crimes: And So On... (p. 1608)
Caulk, M. Clara's Golden Find. (p. 326)
Caulson, Kathleen. Power Reading: Games/Mixed P1. (p. 1390)
—Power Reading: Games. Caulson, Kathleen, illus. (p. 1390)
Caun, Chris. Usborne Book of Face Painting. (p. 1827)
Cause, Santa's. Santa's Cause: Celebrating Santa's Favorite Gift. (p. 1513)
Causey, Emma. Reuniting of Lillie. (p. 1465)
Causton, Linda. Lester's Rainy Lake Pony. (p. 994)
Caut, Vincent, illus. see Schmitt, Michel-Yves & Burrell, Carol Klio.
Caut, Vincent, illus. see Schmitt, Michel-Yves.
Cauthen, Joyce, prod. Bullfrog Jumped: Children's Folksongs from the Byron Arnold Collection. (p. 240)
Cauthen, Shawna Renee. God... Why? (p. 690)
Cauthen, Tommy, illus. see DeBray, Sherry.
Cauvin, Raoul. Bluecoats - Greenhorn Lambil, Willy, illus. (p. 204)
—Bluecoats the, Vol. 6: Bronco Benny. Lambil, Willy, illus. (p. 204)
—Cedric 1 - High-Risk Class. Laudec, Calvinaoul, illus. (p. 283)
—Cedric Vol. 4: Hot & Cold. Laudec, illus. (p. 283)
—Dad's Got Class. (p. 399)
—Navy Blues. Lambil, Willy, illus. (p. 1238)
—Robertsonville Prison Lambil, Willy, illus. (p. 1479)
—Rumberley. Lambil, Willy, illus. (p. 1495)
—What Got into Him? Laudec, illus. (p. 1885)
Cavaciuti, Susan. Someone Hurt Me. Cavaciuti, Susan, illus. (p. 1609)
Cavagnaro, Larry, illus. see Cavagnaro, Teresa Dunham.
Cavagnaro, Teresa Dunham. Sweet Sallie's Squirrel Scarf Factory. Cavagnaro, Larry, illus. (p. 1690)
Cavaiola, Alan & Colford, Joseph E. Practical Guide to Crisis Intervention. (p. 1392)
Cavalie. Mystere des Caves Saint Emilion. (p. 1222)
Cavalier, Liz, jt. auth. see Beddor, Frank.
Cavaliere, Katrina. Mom! There's a Monster under My Bed! (p. 1161)
Cavaliere, Lisa. Lainey Lemonade's Cupcake Parade. (p. 972)
Cavaliere, Wanda. Don't Be Afraid of the Dark: Nicky Moonbeam Saves Christmas. (p. 466)
Cavallaro, Mike, illus. see Peterson, Scott.
Cavallaro, Mike, illus. see Sonneborn, Scott.
Cavallaro, Mike, illus. see Weissburg, Paul.
Cavallaro, Mike, illus. see Yolen, Jane.
Cavalli, Frank. Before the Beginning Began. Riley, Kellee, illus. (p. 158)
Cavallini, Linda, illus. see Lobo, Julia.
Cavallini, Valentina, illus. see Robert, Na'ima B.
Cavallini, Valentina, illus. see Robert, Na'ima B. & Quarto Generic Staff.
Cavallo, Anna. Cuba. (p. 388)
—Peru. (p. 1345)
—Tanzania. (p. 1705)
Cavalluzzo, Jean Smith, jt. auth. see Hickman, Pamela.
Cavanagh, Cathy May. Handi-Bear Cares. (p. 740)
Cavanagh, Helen & Norfleet, Celeste O. Getting Played. (p. 669)
Cavanagh, Peter J. Fungie: The Dingle Dolphin. (p. 649)
Cavanah, Frances. Abe Lincoln Gets His Chance. (p. 4)
Cavanaugh, Catherine, jt. auth. see Feinstein, Barbara.
Cavanaugh, Joseph. Who Am I, Really? How Our Wounds Can Lead to Healing. (p. 1914)
Cavanaugh, Karen. My First Prayer Book. Luberoff, William, illus. (p. 1207)
Cavanaugh, Madison. One-Minute Cure: The Secret to Healing Virtually All Diseases. (p. 1296)
Cavanaugh, Nancy J. Always, Abigail. (p. 51)
—This Journal Belongs to Ratchet. (p. 1737)
Cavanaugh, Natalie. Somebody Loves You. (p. 1609)
Cavanaugh, Stacy, illus. see Dalton, Matthew.
Cavanaugh, Wendy. Pumpkin in the Sky: Let's bake a pie together, you & I, with Auntie Wendy. Cavanaugh, Wendy & LeVesque, Sherry, photos by. (p. 1416)
Cavanna, Betty. Touch of Magic. Gretzer, John, illus. (p. 1772)
Cave, Edward. Fifty-Two Secrets for Praying with Scripture: A scriptural look at Praying. (p. 585)
Cave, Holly. Really, Really Big Questions about Science. Aspinall, Marc, illus. (p. 1450)
Cave, Kathryn. W Is for World: A Round-the-World ABC. (p. 1851)
—W Is for World Big Book: A Round-the-World ABC. Oxfam Staff, illus. (p. 1851)
—You've Got Dragons Maland, Nick, illus. (p. 1982)
Cave, Kathryn & Quarto Generic Staff. Troll Wood. Hess, Paul, illus. (p. 1788)
Cave, Kathryn & Riddell, Chris. Counting Sheep: A Bedtime Adventure! Riddell, Chris, illus. (p. 371)
—Horatio Happened. (p. 797)
Cave, Patrick. Selected. (p. 1549)
—Sharp North. (p. 1563)
Cave', Shell. Mind Magik for Kidz. (p. 1145)
Cave, Yvonne, photos by see Paddison, Valda.
Cavender, Barbara. B Is for Ben. (p. 122)
Cavender, Bernie, illus. see Lukas, Catherine.
Cavendish, Grace. Grace Mysteries: Assassin & Betrayal. (p. 705)
Cavendish, Marshall, jt. auth. see Downing, David.
Cavendish, Marshall, jt. auth. see Mason, Paul.
Cavendish Publishing Staff. AS Level Lawcards. (p. 105)
—Law Map in Constitutional & Administrative Law. (p. 981)
—Law Map in Contract Law. (p. 981)
—Law Map in English Legal System. (p. 981)
—Law Map in European Union Law. (p. 981)
—Law Map in Land Law. (p. 981)
—Law Map in Tort Law. (p. 981)
Caveney, Philip. Night on Terror Island. (p. 1254)
—Space Blasters. (p. 1618)
—Spy Another Day. (p. 1635)
Caviezel, Giovanni. Astronaut. Mesturini, C., illus. (p. 109)
—Astronaut. Mesturini, Cristina, illus. (p. 109)
—Ballerina. Mesturini, C., illus. (p. 134)
—Builder. Mesturini, C., illus. (p. 238)
—Christmas Star. Pagnoni, Roberta, illus. (p. 315)
—Cowboy. Mesturini, C., illus. (p. 373)
—Day at the Firehouse. Rigo, Laura, illus. (p. 412)
—Fairy. Mesturini, Cristina, illus. (p. 563)
—Farmer. Mesturini, C., illus. (p. 574)
—Fireman's Safety Hints. Mesturini, C., illus. (p. 592)
—Halloween. Caviezel, Giovanni & Mesturini, C., illus. (p. 737)
—Haunted House. Donati, Giuliana, illus. (p. 753)
—Little Bee. (p. 1024)
—Little Crab. (p. 1026)
—Little Elf. Mesturini, Cristina, illus. (p. 1027)
—Little Gingerbread Man. Donati, Giuliana, illus. (p. 1028)
—Little Snail. (p. 1036)
—Little Snowman. Mesturini, C., illus. (p. 1036)
—My Own Human Body. Mesturini, Cristina, illus. (p. 1216)
—Nurse. Mesturini, C., illus. (p. 1273)
—Pirates! Mesturini, C., illus. (p. 1363)
—Police Officer. Mesturini, Cristina, illus. (p. 1380)
—Policeman's Safety Hints. (p. 1380)
—Princess. Mesturini, C., illus. (p. 1402)
—Princess. Mesturini, Cristina, illus. (p. 1402)
—Race Car Driver. Mesturini, Cristina, illus. (p. 1430)
—Santa. Mesturini, Cristina, illus. (p. 1511)
—Santa's Toyshop. Rigo, Laura, illus. (p. 1513)
—Spring. Pagnoni, Roberta, illus. (p. 1634)
—Summer. Pagnoni, Roberta, illus. (p. 1673)
Caviezel, Giovanni, jt. illus. see Rigo, L.
Caviezel, Giovanni & Mesturini, Cristina. Fireman. (p. 592)
Cavill, Ian. Elle in the Village. (p. 514)
Cavill, Steve. Coursework Techniques for GCSE Maths. (p. 373)
Cavins, Emily. Great Adventure Kids Coloring Book: Bible Story Coloring Book. McCook, Eileen, illus. (p. 713)
Cavins, Emily & Christmyer, Sarah. Great Adventure Kids Chart. (p. 713)
Cavnar, Gracie. Eat It! Food Adventures with Marco Polo: Volume One: Leaving Home Matsick, Anni, illus. (p. 501)
Cavolina, Michael. Barreled Over. (p. 140)
Cavusgil, Sharon, jt. auth. see Tunceren, Li-Lee.
Cawood, Ian. Britain in the Twentieth Century. (p. 229)
Cawthorne, Nigel. Military Commanders: The 100 Greatest Throughout History. (p. 1142)
—Notorious Tyrants. (p. 1268)
—Victory: 100 Great Military Commanders. (p. 1840)
Cayce, Jw & Guy, K. T. Miss Milli's Adventure: Garden Adventure Series. Moore, Elyse, illus. (p. 1151)
Caycedo Garner, Lucia. Student Lab Audio CDs: Used with ... Caycedo Garner-!Claro Que Si!: An Integrated Skills Approach. (p. 1669)
Cayen, Alise. Patty Pom-Poms. (p. 1330)
Cayetano, Eldred Roy, tr. see Resman, Michael.
Caygill, Ronald. Scrope Hall. (p. 1533)
Cayless, Sophie, illus. see Corlett, Mary Lee.
Cayless, Sophie, illus. see Sasscer, Abby.
Cayton, Andrew, jt. auth. see Anderson, Fred.
Cayton, Andrew & Prentice Hall Staff. America: Pathways to the Present. (p. 58)
—America: Pathways to the Present, Modern American History. (p. 58)
Cayton, Andrew R. L. America: Pathways to the Present, Modern American History. (p. 58)
Caza, Sheila. Time to Go: The Growing Erb Series. Koski, Rozanne, illus. (p. 1753)
Cazenave, Florencia. Tengo Fiebre. (p. 1720)
Cazet, Denys. Elvis the Rooster & the Magic Words (p. 517)
—Elvis the Rooster & the Magic Words. Cazet, Denys, illus. (p. 517)
—Grandpa Spanielson's Chicken Pox Stories: The Octopus. No. 1 Cazet, Denys, illus. (p. 709)
—Minnie & Moo: The Case of the Missing Jelly Donut (p. 1147)
—Minnie & Moo: Hooves of Fire. Cazet, Denys, illus. (p. 1147)
—Minnie & Moo: The Night Before Christmas. Cazet, Denys, illus. (p. 1147)
—Minnie & Moo: The Night of the Living Bed. Cazet, Denys, illus. (p. 1147)
—Minnie & Moo: The Attack of the Easter Bunnies. Cazet, Denys, illus. (p. 1147)
—Minnie & Moo: The Case of the Missing Jelly Donut. Cazet, Denys, illus. (p. 1147)
—Minnie & Moo Adventure Series. Cazet, Denys, illus. (p. 1147)
—Minnie & Moo & the Haunted Sweater. Cazet, Denys, illus. (p. 1147)
—Minnie & Moo & the Potato from Planet X (p. 1147)
—Minnie & Moo & the Seven Wonders of the World. Cazet, Denys, illus. (p. 1147)
—Minnie & Moo & the Thanksgiving Tree. (p. 1147)
—Minnie & Moo Holiday Series. Cazet, Denys, illus. (p. 1147)
—Minnie & Moo Meet Frankenswine. (p. 1147)
—Minnie & Moo Meet Frankenswine. Cazet, Denys, illus. (p. 1147)
—Minnie & Moo - The Night of the Living Bed. Cazet, Denys, illus. (p. 1147)
—Night of the Living Bed. Cazet, Denys, illus. (p. 1254)
—Octopus Cazet, Denys, illus. (p. 1278)
—Octopus. Cazet, Denys, illus. (p. 1278)
—Perfect Pumpkin Pie. Cazet, Denys, illus. (p. 1342)
—Shrunken Head. (p. 1571)
—Snout for Chocolate. (p. 1598)
—Snout for Chocolate. Cazet, Denys, illus. (p. 1598)
—Wanted Dead or Alive. (p. 1856)
—Wanted Dead or Alive. Cazet, Denys, illus. (p. 1856)
—Will You Read to Me? Cazet, Denys, illus. (p. 1932)
Cazet, Denys, reader. Minnie & Moo: Will You Be My Valentine? (p. 1147)
—Minnie & Moo & the Potato from Planet X. (p. 1147)
C.B. Canga, C. B., illus. see Bauer, Marion Dane.
Ccar, ed. Mishkan T'filah for Youth (p. 1150)
Ceanadach, Siusaidh. Let's Talk about Elements & the Pagan Wheel. (p. 1001)
—Let's Talk about Pagan Festivals. (p. 1001)
Cearley, Clint, illus. see Pearl, Michael.
Ceasar, Fady, illus. see Alexan, Julie.
Ceasar, Jennifer. Everything You Need to Know about Acne. (p. 545)
Ceaser, Jennifer. Everything You Need to Know about Acne. (p. 545)
Ceballos, Jacalyn Martin. Little Bee the Size of a Pe. O'Connor, Marcy & O'Connor, Bailey, illus. (p. 1024)
Ceballos, Victor M. Mundo Increible. (p. 1191)
Ceban, Bonnie J. Floods & Mudslides: Disaster & Survival. (p. 605)
—Hurricanes, Typhoons, & Cyclones: Disaster & Survival. (p. 830)
—Tornadoes: Disaster & Survival. (p. 1770)
Cebollero, Julie. Lion That Roared. (p. 1020)
Cebulski, C. B., tr. see Asamiya, Kia.
Cebulski, Megan Elizabeth. Brave Little Butterfly. (p. 223)
Cecca, John. Snow Daze: The Storm, Adventure, Children, Educational, Exciting, Family Oriented. Tick, David, ed. (p. 1598)
—Snow Daze (E3) The Storm. Tick, David, ed. (p. 1598)
—Summer Daze: The Brush Fire. Tick, David, ed. (p. 1674)
Ceccarelli, David & Kimmel, Janine L. L' Irresistibile Richiamo Dell'Acciuga. (p. 969)
Cecchetti, Diane. Cheerleading Skills: How to Cheer Like a Champ. (p. 296)
Cecchi, Lorenzo, illus. see McRae, Anne & Agosta, Loredana.
Cecchini, Marie E. Under the Sea: A Cross-Curricular Unit for Grades 1-3. Mitchell, Judy & Lindeen, Mary, eds. (p. 1814)
Ceccoli, Nicoletta. Little Red Riding Hood. (p. 1035)
Ceccoli Nicoletta, illus. see Batt Tanya Robyn.
Ceccoli, Nicoletta, illus. see Batt, Tanya Robyn.
Ceccoli, Nicoletta, illus. see Batt, Tanya Robyn.
Ceccoli, Nicoletta, illus. see Bernheimer, Kate.
Ceccoli, Nicoletta, illus. see Blackstone, Stella & Barefoot Books Staff.
Ceccoli, Nicoletta, illus. see Blackstone, Stella.
Ceccoli, Nicoletta, illus. see Doyle, Malacy.
Ceccoli, Nicoletta, illus. see Duffy, Carol Ann & Stevenson, Juliet.
Ceccoli, Nicoletta, illus. see Duffy, Carol Ann.
Ceccoli, Nicoletta, illus. see Helgerson, Joseph.
Ceccoli, Nicoletta, illus. see Lachenmeyer, Nathaniel.
Ceccoli, Nicoletta, illus. see Ogburn, Jacqueline K.
Ceccoli, Nicoletta, illus. see Thomson, Sarah L.
Ceccolini, Danielle, illus. see Corn, Tori.
Cecelia And Andrew Davis. Budgie Tale: Rascal Meets Emmit. (p. 235)
Ceceri, Kathy. Robotics: Discover the Science & Technology of the Future with 20 Projects. Carbaugh, Sam, illus. (p. 1480)
—Silk Road: Explore the World's Most Famous Trade Route with 20 Projects. Ceceri, Kathy, illus. (p. 1575)
—World Myths & Legends: 25 Projects You Can Build Yourself. Braley, Shawn, illus. (p. 1956)
Cecil, Carrie Gerlach & cecil, charli. Charli & Wilbur a Dancing Dog's Dream. (p. 292)
cecil, charli, jt. auth. see Cecil, Carrie Gerlach.
Cecil, Jennifer, illus. see Rosen, Michael J. & Kaboom! Staff.
Cecil, Kimberly. Adventures of Hebear (p. 18)
Cecil, Laura. Cunning Cat Tales. Chichester Clark, Emma, illus. (p. 392)
Cecil, Lauren. Fresh-n-Fruity Spring. MJ Illustrations Staff, illus. (p. 636)
—Harmony Takes the Stage. (p. 749)
—Lalaloopsy: Christmas Magic. Hill, Prescott, illus. (p. 972)
—Lalaloopsy: Cinder Slippers & the Grand Ball. Hill, Prescott, illus. (p. 972)
—Lalaloopsy: Halloween Surprise. Fruchter, Jason, illus. (p. 972)
—Lalaloopsy: Here Come the Little Sisters! Hill, Prescott, illus. (p. 972)
—Lalaloopsy: Lala-Oopsies: Meet the Lala-Oopsies. (p. 972)
—Lalaloopsy: Let's Grow a Garden! (p. 972)
—Meet the Lalaloopsies. (p. 1122)
—My First Sleepover. Workman, Terry, illus. (p. 1208)
Cecil, Lauren & Scholastic, Inc. Staff. Party Time! Hill, Prescott, illus. (p. 1326)
Cecil, Randy. Duck. Cecil, Randy, illus. (p. 488)
—Gator. Cecil, Randy, illus. (p. 658)
—Horsefly & Honeybee. Cecil, Randy, illus. (p. 800)
Cecil, Randy, illus. see Bluemle, Elizabeth.
Cecil, Randy, illus. see Brown, Mae.
Cecil, Randy, illus. see Elliott, David.
Cecil, Randy, illus. see Howe, James.
Cecil, Randy, illus. see Joosse, Barbara.
Cecil, Randy, illus. see Lowell, Susan.
Cecil, Randy, illus. see Root, Phyllis.
Cecil, Randy, illus. see Sayre, April Pulley & Sayre, Jeff.
Cecil, Randy, illus. see Sayre, Jeff & Sayre, April Pulley.
Cedar, Emily, illus. see Fitzmaurice, John.
Cederborg, Else. Naughty Peteyboy, Sonya & the Magic Word. (p. 1237)
Cedor, Jean, jt. auth. see Arsenault, Jane.
Cedor, Jean, jt. auth. see Arsenault, Jane.
Ceely, Jonatha, et al. Writing a Research Paper. 6th Edition. (p. 1964)
Cefalo, Andrea. Fairytale Keeper: Avenging the Queen. (p. 565)
Cefalo, Maria Raffaella. If Dreams Could Talk. (p. 852)
Cefery, Holly. Coping with Cancer. (p. 365)
—Yasser Arafat. (p. 1968)
Cefrey, Holly. AIDS. (p. 30)
—Antidepressants. (p. 89)
—Biggest NASCAR Races. (p. 185)
—Bounty Hunter. (p. 216)
—Career Building Through Machinima: Using Video Games to Make Movies. (p. 266)
—Career Building Through Music, Video, & Software Mashups. (p. 266)
—Competitive Skateboarding. (p. 352)
—Coniferous Forest. (p. 357)
—Coniferous Forests. (p. 357)
—Coping with Media Violence. (p. 365)
—Deciduous Forest. (p. 421)
—Deserts. (p. 429)
—Exploring Australia: Using Charts, Graphs, & Tables. (p. 551)
—Frequently Asked Questions about Drinking & Driving. (p. 636)
—Frequently Asked Questions about Online Gaming Addiction. (p. 636)
—From Slave to Cowboy: The Nat Love Story. (p. 643)
—Grasslands. (p. 712)
—Hallucinogens & Your Neurons: The Incredibly Disgusting Story. (p. 739)
—Interstate Commerce Act: The Government Takes Control of Trade Between States. (p. 881)
—Interstate Commerce ACT: The Government Takes Control of Trade Between the States. (p. 881)
—Inventions of Alexander Graham Bell: The Telephone. (p. 884)
—Inventions of Amanda Jones: The Vacuum Method of Canning & Food Preservation. (p. 884)
—Inventions of Eli Whitney: The Cotton Gin. (p. 884)
—Inventions of Granville Woods: The Railroad Telegraph System & the Third Rail. (p. 884)
—Inventions of Granville Woods: The Railroad Telegraph System & the "Third Rail" (p. 884)
—Inventions of Martha Coston: Signal Flares That Save Sailors' Lives. (p. 884)
—Inventions of Martha Coston: Signal Flares That Saved Sailors' Lives. (p. 884)
—Inventions of Thomas Alva Edison: Father of the Lightbulb & the Motion Picture Camera. (p. 884)
—Inventions of Thomas Alva Edison: Father of the Light Bulb & the Motion Picture Camera. (p. 884)
—Justin Timberlake. (p. 940)
—Let's Take a Hike! Converting Fractions to Decimals. (p. 1001)
—Oceans. (p. 1277)
—One Life to Lose for My Country: The Arrest & Execution of Nathan Hale. (p. 1295)
—Pinckney Treaty: America Wins the Right to Travel the Mississippi River. (p. 1359)
—Race Car Drivers: Life on the Fast Track. (p. 1430)
—Researching People, Places, & Events. (p. 1463)
—Sherman Antitrust Act: Getting Big Business under Control. (p. 1566)
—Super Jumbo Jets: Inside & Out. (p. 1680)
—Super Jumbo Jets: Por dentro y por fuera (Super Jumbo Jets: Inside & Out) (p. 1680)
—Syphilis & Other Sexually Transmitted Diseases. (p. 1693)
—Taylor Swift. (p. 1708)
—Tundra. (p. 1796)
—United States Constitution & Early State Constitutions: Law & Order in the New Nation & States. (p. 1819)
—Yellow Fever. (p. 1970)
Cefrey, Holly, jt. auth. see Schimel, Kate.
Cefrey, Holly & McPartland, Randall. HIV & AIDS. (p. 786)
Ceh, Kenneth. Nicholas & the Fruit Surprise. (p. 1250)
Cela, Jaume. Pied Piper: El Flautista de Hamelin. Losantos, Cristina, illus. (p. 1356)
Celano, June. Dripsy the Cloud. (p. 485)
Celbridge, Yolanda. Lacing Lisbeth. (p. 970)
—Licked Clean. (p. 1007)
—Punished in Pink. (p. 1417)
—School for Stingers. (p. 1523)
—Submission of Stella. (p. 1671)
—Training of an English Gentleman. (p. 1777)
Celcer, Irene. Gift. Gatto, Horacio, illus. (p. 674)
—Gift of Adoption. Gatto, Horacio, illus. (p. 675)
—Gift of Egg Donation. Gatto, Horacio, illus. (p. 675)
—Gift of Embryo Donation. Gatto, Horacio, illus. (p. 675)
—Gift of Sperm Donation. Gatto, Horacio, illus. (p. 675)
—Gift of Surrogacy. Gatto, Horacio, illus. (p. 675)
—Tirania de Las Dietas. (p. 1757)
Celebrated A Staff. Story Parade: A Collection of Modern Stories for Boys & Girls. (p. 1663)
Celee. Adventures of Remmy Raindrop: Book I. (p. 22)
—My Life with God. (p. 1212)
Celentano, Suzanne C. & Marshall, Kevin. Theatre Management: A Successful Guide to Producing Plays on Commercial & Non-Profit Stages. (p. 1728)
Celenza, Anna Harwell. Bach's Goldberg Variations. Kitchel, JoAnn E., illus. (p. 130)
—Beethoven's Heroic Symphony. Kitchel, JoAnn E., illus. (p. 158)
—Duke Ellington's Nutcracker Suite. Tate, Don, illus. (p. 489)
—Gershwin's Rhapsody in Blue. Kitchell, Joann E., illus. (p. 667)
—Saint-Saëns's Danse Macabre. Kitchel, JoAnn E., illus. (p. 1504)
Celeskey, Matt, illus. see Weaver, Anne H.
Celeste, Ruby. Millie, the Miracle Baby. (p. 1144)
Celestin, Marie. Unaccepted Child. (p. 1811)
Celestino, Cleofas Ramirez, illus. see Farfan, Flores & Antonio, Jose.
Celia, Shannon Casey. Nature's Music: Musical Colors Series (p. 1237)
Celichowska, Renata. Seven Statements of Survival: Conversations with Dance Professionals. (p. 1555)

C

Celik, Vladislav. You Too Can Play Piano & Organ Without Teacher (p. 1976)
Cella, Clara. Earth Day. (p. 495)
—Groundhog Day. (p. 725)
—Martin Luther King Jr. Day. (p. 1098)
—Memorial Day. (p. 1125)
—Presidents' Day. (p. 1397)
Cella, Clara, jt. auth. see Abramovitz, Melissa.
Cella, Clara & Abramovitz, Melissa. Let's Celebrate. (p. 995)
Cella, Kristen, illus. see Mayhall, Robin.
Cellucci, Lucy Lemay. True Colours. (p. 1792)
Cels, Marc. Arts & Literature in the Middle Ages. (p. 105)
—Life on a Medieval Manor. (p. 1012)
Cemmick, Paul, illus. see Hawkins, Elizabeth.
Cendrars, Blaise. Petits Contes Negres pour les Enfants. (p. 1348)
Censullo, Chris. Boy with the Big Blue Hair. (p. 220)
Centelo, Tara Jaye. Mommy Loves Her Baby. (p. 1162)
Center for Learning Network Staff. Catch-22: Curriculum Unit. (p. 279)
—Ceremony: Curriculum Unit. (p. 287)
—Charming Billy/at Weddings & Wakes: Curriculum Unit. (p. 294)
—Cinema & Catechesis: Using Feature Films in the Religion Classroom Vol. 1 (p. 321)
—Cinema & Catechesis: Using Feature Films in the Religion Classroom Vol. 2 (p. 321)
—Endangered Species: Social Issues Series. (p. 527)
—Faith: Minicourse. (p. 565)
—House on Mango Street: Curriculum Unit. (p. 803)
—I Know Why the Caged Bird Sings: Curriculum Unit. (p. 840)
—Paradise Lost: Curriculum Unit. (p. 1323)
—Ponder Heart/One Writer's Beginnings: Curriculum Unit. (p. 1382)
—Sexuality: Connecting Mind, Body, & Spirit — Minicourse. (p. 1556)
—Slaughterhouse-Five: Curriculum Unit. (p. 1588)
—U. S. History & Geography 2: Curriculum Unit Bk. 2 (p. 1806)
—Violence in America. (p. 1843)
Center for Learning Staff. Age of Imperialism: 1895-1930 — Elementary U. S. History Series (p. 29)
—Among the Hidden/among the Impostors: Novel Curriculum Unit. (p. 65)
—As I Lay Dying: Novel Curriculum Unit. (p. 105)
—Doing My Part: Curriculum Unit. (p. 463)
—Doing My Part Student Edition: Curriculum Unit. (p. 463)
—Faith & Belief. (p. 565)
—Habibi/Seven Daughters & Seven Sons: Novel Curriculum Unit. (p. 734)
—Hunger: Social Studies Curriculum Unit. (p. 827)
—Justice & Peace. (p. 940)
—One Hundred Years of Solitude: Novel Currriculum Unit. (p. 1295)
—Piano Lesson: Drama Curriculum Unit — Grades 9-12. (p. 1354)
—Prayer & Worship. (p. 1393)
—Secret Life of Bees: Novel Curriculum Unit — Grades 9-12. (p. 1541)
—Tangerine/Bleachers: Novel Curriculum Unit — Grades 9-12. (p. 1705)
—Using Literature to Teach U. S. History: Elementary U. S. History Series (p. 1828)
—White Mountains/the True Confessions of Charlotte Doyle: Novel Curiculum Unit. (p. 1913)
—World War I: Social Studies Curriculum Unit. (p. 1958)
—World War II: 1935-1945 — Elementary U. S. History Series (p. 1959)
Centineo Durrett, Marjorie. Stick People Stories. (p. 1649)
Cento, Nucci. Maverick & Miss Murphy at Rascal's Rescue Ranch. (p. 1110)
Centore, Michael. India (p. 870)
—Italy (p. 895)
—Japan (p. 909)
—Mexico (p. 1131)
—Renewable Energy (p. 1460)
—Russia (p. 1498)
Centre for Addiction and Mental Health Staff. Can I Catch It Like a Cold? Coping with a Parent's Depression. Weissmann, Joe, illus. (p. 258)
Ceol, Cheryl. Can You Picture This? You Draw It / You Say It / You Find It / You Write It. (p. 259)
Cepeda, Joe. Swing. (p. 1691)
Cepeda, Joe, illus. see Aardema, Verna.
Cepeda, Joe, illus. see Brown, Monica.
Cepeda, Joe, illus. see Butler, Kristi T.
Cepeda, Joe, illus. see Deans, Karen.
Cepeda, Joe, illus. see Galbraith, Kathryn O.
Cepeda, Joe, illus. see Giglio, Judy.
Cepeda, Joe, illus. see Lainez, René Colato.
Cepeda, Joe, illus. see McKissack, Robert L.
Cepeda, Joe, illus. see Montes, Marisa.
Cepeda, Joe, illus. see Morrison, Toni & Morrison, Slade.
Cepeda, Joe, illus. see Pattison, Darcy.
Cepeda, Joe, illus. see Reiche, Dietlof & Brownjohn, John.
Cepeda, Joe, illus. see Ryan, Pam Muñoz.
Cepeda, Joe, illus. see Thomson, Sarah L.
Cepeda, Joseph C., photos by see Allison, Pamela S.
Cephas, Shelley A. Animal Tales: Poetry for Children & the Child at Heart. (p. 80)
Cera, Bobbee. Wags, Woofs & Other Tails. (p. 1852)
Cerami, Matteo, et al. Planet of the Grand Buffoon. Smith, Anne & Smith, Owen, trs. from FRE. (p. 1368)
Cerasi, Chris. Star Wars Adventures: Chewbacca & the Slavers of the Shadowlands. (p. 1641)
Cerasi, Christopher. Star Wars: Fandex Deluxe Edition. (p. 1641)
Cerasini, Marc. Godzilla Saves America: A Monster Showdown In 3-D! Morgan, Tom & Mounts, Paul, illus. (p. 692)
Cerasini, Marc, et al. Keep It Hidden! The Best Places to Stash Your Stuff. (p. 947)
—Spy to Spy: Sharing Your Secrets Safely. (p. 1636)
Cerasoli, Anna. Los Diez Magnificos. (p. 1053)
Cerato, Mattia. Drew the Screw. (p. 485)
—Mom's New Friend. Cerato, Mattia, illus. (p. 1163)
—Sheep in the Closet. Cerato, Mattia, illus. (p. 1564)
—You Can Draw Construction Vehicles Cerato, Mattia, illus. (p. 1974)
—You Can Draw Dragons, Unicorns, & Other Magical Creatures Cerato, Mattia, illus. (p. 1974)
Cerato, Mattia, illus. see Blevins, Wiley.
Cerato, Mattia, illus. see Capstone Press Staff, et al.
Cerato, Mattia, illus. see Kalz, Jill.
Cerato, Mattia, illus. see Plourde, Lynn.
Cerato, Mattia, illus. see Walter Foster Custom Creative Team.
Cerato, Mattia, illus. see Walter Foster Jr. Creative Team.
Cerato, Mattia, jt. auth. see Bruning, Matt.
Cerato, Mattia & Ho, Jannie. Easy-To-Draw Monsters: A Step-By-Step Drawing Book. Cerato, Mattia & Ho, Jannie, illus. (p. 500)
Cerato, Mattia & Sexton, Brenda. Easy-to-Draw Mythical Creatures. Cerato, Mattia & Sexton, Brenda, illus. (p. 500)
—Easy-to-Draw Vehicles: A Step-By-Step Drawing Book. Cerato, Mattia & Sexton, Brenda, illus. (p. 500)
—Easy-to-Draw Vehicles. Cerato, Mattia & Sexton, Brenda, illus. (p. 500)
Cerda, Alfredo Gomez. Manolo Multon y el Mago Guason. Antonio & Covi, illus. (p. 1088)
Cerdá, Alfredo Gómez. Mari Pepa y el Club de los Pirados. Navía, Miguel, illus. (p. 1093)
Cerda, Edward, illus. see Merrick, Sylvia Bach.
Cerda, Gomez, et al. Cuando Miguel No Fue Miguel. (p. 388)
Cerda, Marcelo. Cine No Fue Siempre Asi. Basile, Javier, illus. (p. 321)
Cereales Laforet, Agustin, et al. Argonautas. (p. 98)
—Atalanta, la de los Pies Ligeros. (p. 111)
—Colera de Aquiles. (p. 339)
—Dedalo e Icaro: Historia para un Laberinto. (p. 422)
—Helena y la Guerra de Troya. (p. 763)
—Laurel de Apolo. (p. 980)
—Prometeo. (p. 1411)
—Regreso de Ulises. (p. 1457)
—Teseo y el Minotauro. (p. 1722)
—Trabajos de Hercules. (p. 1774)
Cerebellum Academic Team. Lesson Booster 8 Series Set. (p. 993)
—Lesson Booster Middle School Series. (p. 993)
Cerebellum Corporation, prod. Willow Pond Storybook. (p. 1934)
Ceredigion, Cymdeithas Lyfrau, jt. auth. see Davies, Elgan Philip.
Ceredigion, Cymdeithas Lyfrau, jt. auth. see Gates, Susan.
Cereghino, Sandy. Oscar: The Short Legged Reindeer. (p. 1305)
Cereno, Benito. Invincible Presents: Atom Eve Collected Edition: Atom Eve Collected Edition. (p. 885)
Cerf, Christopher & Peterson, Paige. Blackie: the Horse Who Stood Still: The Horse Who Stood Still. (p. 197)
Cerimele, Ron. Hee, Haw, & a Donkey Named Sam. (p. 762)
—Winup. (p. 1939)
Cerino, Ann. Carmella the Cat. (p. 270)
Cerio, Johnathan. Cathedral. (p. 280)
Cerisier, Emmanuel, illus. see Ball, Karen.
Cerisier, Emmanuel, illus. see Blanchard, Anne.
Cerisier, Emmanuel, illus. see Gifford, Clare.
Cerisier, Emmanuel, illus. see Lacey, Minna & Davidson, Susanna.
Cermele, Joe. Field & Stream's Guide to Catching Bass. The Editors of Field & Stream, ed. (p. 583)
Cernak, Kim. Build-a-Skill Instant Books Consonant Blends & Digraphs. Shiotsu, Vicky & Faulkner, Stacey, eds. (p. 238)
—Build-a-Skill Instant Books R-Controled Vowels & Vowel Digraphs. Shiotsu, Vicky & Faulkner, Stacey, eds. (p. 238)
Cernak, Kim & Williams, Rozanne Lanczak. Build-a-Skill Instant Books Math Facts To 20. Faulkner, Stacey, ed. (p. 238)
Cernak, Linda. Edgar Degas. Morrow, J. T., illus. (p. 504)
—Leonardo Da Vinci. Morrow, J. T., illus. (p. 992)
—Mary Cassatt. Morrow, J. T., illus. (p. 1100)
—Totalitarianism. (p. 1771)
—Vincent Van Gogh. Morrow, J. T., illus. (p. 1842)
Cernek, Kim. Build-a-Skill Instant Books Time & Money. Faulkner, Stacey, ed. (p. 238)
—Consonant Puzzles & Activities Cernek, Kim, ed. (p. 359)
—Life Cycles. Rous, Sheri, ed. (p. 1009)
—Preschool Songs & Fingerplays: Building Language Experience Through Rhythm & Movement. (p. 1396)
Cernek, Kim, ed. see Geiser, Traci Ferguson & Boylan, Maureen McCourt.
Cernek, Kim, ed. see Jordano, Kimberly & Adsit, Kim.
Cernek, Kim, ed. see Lewis, Sue & Stern, Amy.
Cernek, Kim & Shiotsu, Vicky. Mapping. Rous, Sheri, ed. (p. 1090)
Cernek, Kim & Williams, Rozanne Lanczak. Build-a-Skill Instant Books Color, Shape & Number Words. Shiotsu, Vicky & Faulkner, Stacey, eds. (p. 238)
Cernek, Kim, et al. Nutrition. Rous, Sheri, ed. (p. 1274)
—Solar System. Rous, Sheri & Hamaguchi, Carla, eds. (p. 1607)
—Teacher's Ideas 3 Set (p. 1709)
Cerney, Samantha May, illus. see Oldenburg, Richard.
Cerniga, Kira, illus. see D'Amico, Carol.
Cerny, Michele. No More Rules! A Boy's Discovery of What Life is Like Without Rules. Cable, Annette, illus. (p. 1259)
Cerone, Diane. Lucy & the Red-Tailed Hawk. Auer, Lois, illus. (p. 1063)
Cerone, Sal, illus. see DeRosier, Cher.
Cerpok, M. L. Mobile Monk: A Zen Tale. Wagner, Gavin, illus. (p. 1157)
Cerretti, Cristiana. Enormous Turnip. (p. 531)
Cerrillo, et al. Adivina Quien Soy. (p. 13)
Cerrito, Angela. End of the Line. (p. 526)
—Safest Lie. (p. 1502)
Cerrito, Dana. On the Day Love Was Born. Gallegos, Lauren, illus. (p. 1290)
Cerulean, Susan I., et al, eds. Between Two Rivers: Stories from the Red Hills to the Gulf. Meyer, Nancy, illus. (p. 173)
Cerulli, Claudia. Ottavia e I Gatti Di Roma - Octavia & the Cats of Rome: A Bilingual Picture Book in Italian & English. Lätti, Leo, illus. (p. 1307)
Cerullo, Claudio V. Isabella Goes to Kindergarden (p. 891)
—Isabella's Rainy Day with Her Friends. (p. 891)
—Stop Bullying Me. (p. 1653)
—Thankful Day. Avila, Jesus Villicana, illus. (p. 1725)
Cerullo, Jillian. Danger of the River. (p. 404)
Cerullo, Mary M. City Fish, Country Fish Rotman, Jeffrey L., illus. (p. 323)
—Giant Squid: Searching for a Sea Monster. (p. 674)
—Giant Squid: Searching for a Sea Monster Roper, Clyde F. E., photos by. (p. 674)
—Journey to Shark Island: A Shark Photographer's Close Encounters Rotman, Jeffrey L., illus. (p. 929)
—Life under Ice Curtsinger, Bill, photos by. (p. 1013)
—Life under Ice. Curtsinger, Bill, illus. (p. 1013)
—Sea Soup: Zooplankton Curtsinger, Bill, photos by. (p. 1535)
—Searching for Great White Sharks: A Shark Diver's Quest for Mr. Big Rotman, Jeffrey L., photos by. (p. 1537)
—Seeking Giant Sharks: A Shark Diver's Quest for Whale Sharks, Basking Sharks, & Manta Rays Rotman, Jeffrey L., illus. (p. 1548)
—Shark Expedition Rotman, Jeffrey L., photos by. (p. 1562)
—Shark Expedition: A Shark Photographer's Close Encounters. Rotman, Jeffrey L., photos by. (p. 1562)
—Sharks of the Deep: A Shark Photographer's Search for Sharks at the Bottom of the Sea Rotman, Jeffrey L., illus. (p. 1563)
Cerullo, Mary M. & Nardo, Don. Smithsonian. (p. 1594)
Cerullo, Mary M. & Simmons, Beth E. Sea Secrets. Carlson, Kirsten, illus. (p. 1535)
Cervantes, Angela. Gaby, Lost & Found. (p. 652)
Cervantes, Gerard. Hilda Bee's Special Home. (p. 779)
Cervantes, Jennifer. Tortilla Sun. (p. 1770)
Cervantes, Jennifer & Chronicle Books Staff. Tortilla Sun. (p. 1770)
Cervantes, Valeria, illus. see Rivas, Spelile & Plascencia, Amira.
Cervantes, Valeria, illus. see Rivas, Spelile.
Cervasio, Mark. Life's a Ball with Billy the Baseball. (p. 1013)
Cervi, Isaac. Pockets. (p. 1375)
Cervone, Barbara, ed. In Our Village: Boto, Ethiopia Through the Eyes of Its Youth. (p. 864)
Cervone, Shannon. Black Suitcase. Vene, Alessandro, illus. (p. 197)
CES Industries, Inc. Staff. Ed-Lab Nine Hundred & Eighty Experiment Manual: Microcomputer Technology (p. 503)
Cesa, Irene, ed. Chemical Bonding (p. 297)
—Chemical Reactions. (p. 297)
—Chemistry of Food (p. 297)
—Chemistry of Gases (p. 297)
—Gas Laws (p. 657)
—Solubility & Solutions. (p. 1608)
Cesak, Jerry. My Personal Panther. Naughton, Terry, illus. (p. 1216)
Cesena, Denise. Caring - Companion Book. Perez, Maureen T., illus. (p. 269)
—Orderliness. Cesena, Denise & Perez, Maureen T., illus. (p. 1302)
—Orderliness - Companion Book. Cesena, Denise & Perez, Maureen T., illus. (p. 1302)
—Respect. Cesena, Denise & Perez, Maureen T., illus. (p. 1463)
Cesena, Denise, illus. see Perez, Maureen T.
Cesena, Denise, illus. see Smith, Anya.
Cesena, Denise & Perez, Maureen T. Caring. Perez, Maureen T., illus. (p. 269)
Cesler, Margaret E. Bread Book. (p. 224)
Cesmat, Brandon. When Pigs Fall in Love & Other Stories. (p. 1904)
Cesmat, Sheryl. Adopted Kitty from the City. (p. 13)
—Poppy. (p. 1385)
Cestaro, Gregg, photos by see Loving, Vikki.
Cestnik, Jay, jt. auth. see Cestnik, Lisa.
Cestnik, Lisa & Cestnik, Jay. 100 Sight Word Mini-Books: Instant Fill-In Mini-Books That Teach 100 Essential Sight Words. (p. 1999)
Ceva, Aline Cantono di, illus. see Castenetto, Christiana.
Ceville, Laura. My Dog, Jack. (p. 1202)
Cha, Louis. Legendary Couple Wong, Tony, illus. (p. 989)
Chaapel, Barbary. Estuary. (p. 538)
Chaban, Liz. Jules of the World: The California Caper. (p. 932)
Chabert, Clement. Lobo tiene Hambre. (p. 1044)
Chabert, Jack. Eerie Elementary #1: the School Is Alive! (a Branches Book) Ricks, Sam, illus. (p. 505)
—Eerie Elementary #2: the Locker Ate Lucy! (a Branches Book) Ricks, Sam, illus. (p. 505)
—Locker Ate Lucy! (p. 1045)
—Locker Ate Lucy! Ricks, Sam, illus. (p. 1045)
—School Is Alive! (p. 1523)
—School Is Alive! Ricks, Sam, illus. (p. 1523)
Chabon, Daniel, ed. see Craig, Johnny, et al.
Chabon, Daniel, ed. see Freeman, Chris W. & Hunt, Korey.
Chabon, Daniel, ed. see Tobin, Paul.
Chabon, Michael. Astonishing Secret of Awesome Man. Parker, Jake, illus. (p. 109)
—Summerland. (p. 1675)
Chabon, Michael, et al. Amazing Adventures of the Escapist (p. 52)
Chabot, Jacob. Hello Kitty: Work of Art. (p. 764)
—Hello Kitty: Fashion Music Wonderland. (p. 764)
—Hello Kitty: It's about Time. McGinty, Ian et al, illus. (p. 764)
—Hello Kitty: Work of Art. McGinty, Ian et al, illus. (p. 764)
Chabot, Jacob, illus. see Golden Books.
Chabot, Jacob, jt. auth. see Castro, Giovanni.
Chabot, Jacob, jt. auth. see Monlongo, Jorge.
Chabot, Jacob & Mcginty, Ian. Hello Kitty: Delicious! (p. 764)
Chabot, Jacob & Monlongo, Jorge. Hello Kitty: Here We Go! (p. 764)
—Here We Go! (p. 770)
Chabot, Jean-Philippe, jt. auth. see Grant, Donald.
Chabot, Jean-Philippe, et al. Pablo Picasso. Chabot, Jean-Philippe & Barroso, Paz, trs. (p. 1316)
Chabot, Jean-Phillipe. Paul Gauguin. (p. 1330)
Chabot, Jean-Philippe, illus. see Sorbier, Frederic.
Chabot, Shersta. Stars, Stockings, & Shepherds. Egbert, Corey, illus. (p. 1643)
Chabrian, Deborah L., illus. see Mackall, Dandi Daley & Kingsbury, Karen.
Chabvepi-Tudosa, Patricia, tr. see Tudosa-Fundureanu, Lucia.
Chace, Reeve, jt. auth. see Gross, Frederick C.
Chace, Tara, jt. auth. see Harstad, Johan.
Chace, Tara, tr. see Hagerup, Klaus.
Chace, Tara, tr. see Nesbo, Jo.
Chace, Tara, tr. see Nilsson, Per.
Chace, Tara F., tr. see Nesbo, Jo.
Chacek, Karen. Mascota Inesperada. Monroy, Manuel, illus. (p. 1102)
—Nina Complot. Balcazar, Abraham, illus. (p. 1256)
Chachas, George & Wojtak, James. Adventures of Dynamic Doolittle: The Problem with Paulie Python. De Soto, Ben, illus. (p. 17)
—Doolittle's Very, Very Bad Day. De Soto, Ben, illus. (p. 470)
—Story of Doolittle: An Exceptional Young Gorilla. De Soto, Ben, illus. (p. 1658)
Chachi, Abdelkader, jt. auth. see D'Oyen, Fatima M.
Chacko, Miss Hannah. Lie. (p. 1007)
Chaco Culture National Historical Park (N.M.) Staff & Western National Parks Association Staff, contrib. by. Clay, Copper & Turquoise: The Museum Collection of Chaco Culture National Historical Park. (p. 330)
Chacoff, Juan Domingo. Carlos Valderrama. (p. 270)
Chacon, Cesar, tr. see Luetkemeyer, Jenny.
Chacón, Dulce. Voz Dormida. (p. 1851)
Chacon, Pam, illus. see Oppenlander, Meredith.
Chacon, Rick, illus. see Oppenlander, Meredith.
Chaconas, Dori. Babysitters. McCue, Lisa, illus. (p. 129)
—Best Friends No. 1. McCue, Lisa, illus. (p. 169)
—Collectors McCue, Lisa, illus. (p. 340)
—Coriander the Contrary Hen. Carrington, Marsha Gray, illus. (p. 367)
—Cork & Fuzz. McCue, Lisa, illus. (p. 367)
—Cork & Fuzz - The Collectors. McCue, Lisa, illus. (p. 367)
—Dancing with Katya Bergum, Constance R., illus. (p. 403)
—Finders Keepers McCue, Lisa, illus. (p. 587)
—Good Sports. McCue, Lisa, illus. (p. 700)
—Goodnight, Dewberry Bear. (p. 701)
—Hurry down to Derry Fair. Tyler, Gillian, illus. (p. 830)
—Looking for Easter Moore, Margie, illus. (p. 1051)
—Looking for Easter. Moore, Margie, illus. (p. 1051)
—Pennies in a Jar Lewin, Ted, illus. (p. 1337)
—Short & Tall No. 2 McCue, Lisa, illus. (p. 1569)
—Spring Cleaning. McCue, Lisa, illus. (p. 1635)
—Swimming Lesson McCue, Lisa, illus. (p. 1691)
—Swimming Lesson. McCue, Lisa, illus. (p. 1691)
—That Blessed Christmas Night. Perez-Stable, Deborah, illus. (p. 1726)
—Virginnie's Hat. Meade, Holly, illus. (p. 1844)
—Wait a Minute. (p. 1852)
—Wait a Minute. McCue, Lisa, illus. (p. 1852)
Chad, H. Scott. Bad Pups: How It All Began. (p. 132)
Chad, Jon. Leo Geo & His Miraculous Journey Through the Center of the Earth. Chad, Jon, illus. (p. 992)
—Leo Geo & the Cosmic Crisis. Chad, Jon, illus. (p. 992)
Chad, Roberta. When Staying Home Is Not an Option: A Working Mom's Guide to Creative Time with the Young Ones. (p. 1904)
Chadda, Sarwat. City of Death. (p. 323)
—Savage Fortress. (p. 1516)
Chadderdon, Andrea & Nash, Kevin. University of Oklahoma College Prowler off the Record. (p. 1821)
Chadeesingh, D. K. Bettina Bee & the Expedition to Seek Big Treasure. (p. 172)
Chadha, Radhika. Basava & the Dots of Fire. Phatak, Bhakti, illus. (p. 140)
Chadha, Radhika & Kuriyan, Priya. I'm So Sleepy. (p. 860)
Chadow, Alysa. US States. (p. 1826)
Chadwick, Anita. Rosebuds Puppies. (p. 1489)
Chadwick, Cheryl. Adventures of Skinny Little Timmy. (p. 23)
Chadwick, Cindy, illus. see Chastain, Sandra.
Chadwick, Douglas H., jt. auth. see Shapira, Amy.
Chadwick, J. R. Thomas & the Dragon's Pearl. (p. 1738)
Chadwick, Jennie. Peach Tree Kids: Circus Fleas. (p. 1332)
—Peach Tree Kids: Jaws of Dragon. (p. 1332)
Chadwick, Kat, illus. see Rochester, Karen.
Chadwick, Katie. Meet Miss Molly. (p. 1121)
Chadwick, Paul. Concrete Volume 1: Depths: Depths. (p. 355)
—Fragile Creature. (p. 627)
—Heights. (p. 762)
Chadwick, Robert. Vengeful Impulse. (p. 1835)
Chafe, Justin. Bunny Rabbit on the Moon. (p. 242)
Chafe, Wallace, tr. see Weller, Sadie Bedoka.
Chafer, E. I., ed. Illustrated Book of Children's Verse. (p. 857)
Chaffee, Allen. Adventures of Fleet Foot & Her Fawns. (p. 18)
Chaffee, Joel. Atomic & Molecular Structure. (p. 113)
—How to Build a Prize-Winning Robot. (p. 815)
Chaffee, John. Thinking Critically: A Concise Guide. (p. 1734)
Chaffey, Samantha, illus. see Baxter, Nicola.
Chaffey, Tim & Westbrook, Joe. Truth Chronicles: The Ark. (p. 1794)
Chaffin, Daniel, illus. see Lewis, Anna.
Chaffin, Dawn Marie. My Love. (p. 1213)
Chafin, Carolyn. What Did the Animals Think? (p. 1882)
Chafin, T. A. & Luttrull, Polly. Unauthorized Nitpicker's Guide to the SW Saga. (p. 1811)
Chagall, Marc, illus. see Lewis, J. Patrick.
Chaghatzbanian, Sonia, illus. see Gill, J. Duddy.
Chaidez, Cristina. Good Girls with Bad Boys. (p. 698)
Chaikin, Andrew. Man on the Moon: The Voyages of the Apollo Astronauts. (p. 1085)
—Man on the Moon: One Giant Leap: Lunar Explorers: the Odyssey Continues (p. 1085)
—When Dinosaurs Walked. Wynne, Patricia, illus. (p. 1902)
Chaikin, Miriam. Hardlucky: The Story of a Boy Who Learns How to Think Before He Acts. Lisowski, Gabriel, illus. (p. 748)
—Menorahs, Mezuzas, & Other Jewish Symbols. Weihs, Erika, illus. (p. 1126)

Chaikin, Stacey & Feltes Taylor, Kimberly. Fran & Gran. (p. 627)
Chainani, Soman. Last Ever After. (p. 977)
—School for Good & Evil. Bruno, Iacopo, illus. (p. 1522)
—School for Good & Evil Series Complete Box Set. (p. 1522)
—World Without Princes. (p. 1959)
—World Without Princes. Bruno, Iacopo, illus. (p. 1959)
—World Without Princes. (p. 1960)
Chaira, Francesca di, illus. see Taplin, Sam.
Chaisson, Kristen. Dreamland. (p. 484)
Chaisson, Samuel Jam. Larry & Joe's Detective Agency. (p. 976)
Chaisty, Chris, illus. see Caudron, Chris & Childs, Caro.
Chait, Baruch. Lost Treasure of Tikkun Hamiddos Island. Pollack, Gadi, illus. (p. 1057)
—Terrifying Trap of the Bad Middos Pirates Pollack, Gadi, illus. (p. 1722)
Chaitkin, Carol. Barron's English Power Pack (p. 140)
—English. Kostman, Samuel & Chaitkin, Carol, eds. (p. 529)
—Let's Review: English. (p. 1000)
Chakour, Charles M. Mary Magdalene's Story Unit. (p. 1100)
Chakraborty, Tirtha. Dengue Fever & Other Hemorrhagic Viruses. (p. 426)
Chakravorty, Amita. Rupadil's Lighthouse. (p. 1497)
Chalabi, Tamara. Shi'ls of Jabal 'Amil & the New Lebanon: Community & Nation-State, 1918-1943. (p. 1566)
Chaland, Yves. Chaland Anthology: Freddy Lombard. Vol. 2 (p. 288)
Chalberg, John C., ed. Opposing Viewpoints in American History, Volume 1: From Colonial Times to Reconstruction. (p. 1300)
—Opposing Viewpoints in American History, Volume 2: From Reconstruction to the Present. (p. 1300)
Chalek, Sarah, illus. see LaCroix, Debbie Bernstein.
Chalekian, Bobbie. Legend of the Lamb & the Lion. (p. 989)
Chaley, Dimitry. Marty the Martian Learns ABC. (p. 1098)
Chalfant, Patrick. When the Levee Breaks. (p. 1904)
Chalifour, Francis. After. (p. 28)
—Fils du Pendu. (p. 586)
Chalifoux, Lisa M. Bravery Is like Love. Perras, Marielle, illus. (p. 223)
—Spotty & Eddie Visit Percé. (p. 1634)
Chaline, Eric. Martial Arts for Athletic Conditioning: Winning Ways. James, Adam, ed. (p. 1097)
—Martial Arts for Athletic Conditioning. (p. 1097)
—Martial Arts for Women: Winning Ways. James, Adam, ed. (p. 1097)
—Ninjutsu: Winning Ways. James, Adam, ed. (p. 1257)
—Ninjutsu. (p. 1257)
Chalk, Frank. South Africa: Never Again! Greenhaven Press Editors & Gale Editors, eds. (p. 1616)
Chalk, Gary, illus. see Hunter, Erin.
Chalk, Gary, illus. see Jacques, Brian.
Chalk, Gary, illus. see Jones, Allan Frewin.
Chalk, Gary, illus. see Jones, Allan.
Chalk, Gary, illus. see Morrison, Matthew.
Chalk, Gary, jt. auth. see Sutherland, Jon.
Chalk, Miriam, ed. see Keats, John.
Chall, Marsha Wilson. One Pup's Up. Cole, Henry, illus. (p. 1296)
—Pick a Pup. Henry, Jed, illus. (p. 1354)
—Prairie Train. Thompson, John, illus. (p. 1392)
—Secret Keeps. (p. 1541)
Challen, Paul. Checkered Flag (p. 295)
—Culture & Crafts of Canada. (p. 391)
—Culture & Crafts of Egypt. (p. 391)
—Flip It Gymnastics. (p. 605)
—Get to Know Screws. (p. 668)
—Get to Know Wheels & Axles. (p. 668)
—Hail! Ancient Chinese. (p. 735)
—Hurricane & Typhoon Alert! (p. 829)
—Metric System. (p. 1130)
—Smash It Tennis. (p. 1593)
—Spin It Figure Skating. (p. 1627)
—Swing It Golf. (p. 1691)
—Volcano Alert! (p. 1848)
—What Does a Defensive Back Do? (p. 1883)
—What Does a Running Back Do? (p. 1883)
—What Is Supply & Demand? (p. 1890)
Challen, Paul, jt. auth. see Challen, Paul C.
Challen, Paul, jt. auth. see Crabtree Publishing Co. Staff.
Challen, Paul, jt. auth. see Peppas, Lynn.
Challen, Paul & Cipriano, Jeri. How Do Mortgages, Loans, & Credit Work? (p. 807)
Challen, Paul & Peppas, Lynn. Math Words & Symbols. (p. 1107)
Challen, Paul C. Bicycle Racing (p. 177)
—Environmental Disaster Alert! (p. 532)
—Formula 1 Racing (p. 620)
—Kart Racing (p. 944)
—Mighty Tanks. (p. 1140)
—Migration in the 21st Century: How Will Globalization & Climate Change Affect Migration & Settlement? (p. 1141)
—NASCAR Racing (p. 1230)
—Surviving 9/11. (p. 1687)
—Surviving D-Day. (p. 1687)
—Surviving the Boston Marathon Bombing. (p. 1687)
—What Does a Linebacker Do? (p. 1883)
—What Does a Quarterback Do? (p. 1883)
Challen, Paul C. & Challen, Paul. Drought & Heat Wave Alert! (p. 486)
—Environmental Disaster Alert! (p. 532)
—Life in Ancient China. (p. 1010)
—Life in Ancient Egypt. (p. 1010)
Challenger, Robert James. Eagle's Reflection: And Other Northwest Coast Stories (p. 492)
—Grizzly's Home: And Other Northwest Coast Children's Stories (p. 724)
—Nature's Circle: And Other Northwest Coast Children's Stories (p. 1237)
—Raven's Call: And More Northwest Coast Stories (p. 1441)
Challenner, Nena C., jt. auth. see Reese, Pam Britton.
Challiyil, Pradheep. Journey to the Source: Decoding Matrix Trilogy. (p. 929)
Challoner, Audrey, illus. see Roberts, Johanna Lonsdorf.
Challoner, Jack. DK Eyewitness Books: Energy: Energy. (p. 456)
—DK Eyewitness Books: Hurricane & Tornado: Hurricane & Tornado. (p. 456)
—Energy. (p. 528)
—Find Out about Rocks & Minerals: With 23 Projects & More Than 350 Pictures. (p. 587)
—Sound: An Investigation. (p. 1615)
—Start-Up Science (p. 1643)
—What's the Big Idea? Alien Life. (p. 1899)
Chally, Jeanne. Helen Keller: A Triumph of Spirit. (p. 763)
Chalmers, Jason. Camp Sacrowee. (p. 257)
—Fall Nightmares. (p. 566)
—Fall Nightmares 101: A Parody. (p. 566)
Chalmers, Josh, jt. auth. see Moulton, Mark Kimball.
Chalmers, Kirsty, illus. see Darling, Pollyanna.
Chalmers, Mary, illus. see Lindquist, Jennie D.
Chalofsky, Margie, et al. Changing Places: A Kid's View of Shelter Living. (p. 290)
Chaloner, David. Collected Poems. (p. 339)
Chaltas, Thalia. Because I Am Furniture. (p. 155)
Chaman, Lal. Hindu America, Revealing the Story of the Romance of the Surya Vanshi Hindus & Depicting the Imprints of Hindu Culture on the Two Americas. (p. 780)
Chamber, Catherine. Elephants' Ears. Mockford, Caroline, illus. (p. 512)
Chamberlain, Adrian. Rock Star (p. 1482)
Chamberlain, Alexander Francis. Contributions of the American Indian to Civilization. (p. 361)
Chamberlain, Calum, illus. see Gridley, J.
Chamberlain, Catherine. Basic Concept Workbook. (p. 141)
Chamberlain, Jane H., creator. Patriot Dreams: A Nonvoter's Digest of Facts & Feelings about Where We are Now & What to do Next: A User's Manual for Democracy. (p. 1329)
Chamberlain, Karen, et al. Feather for the Queen. (p. 579)
Chamberlain, Lyn. Quonby & the Tree Den. Weltner, Dave, illus. (p. 1429)
Chamberlain, Margaret, illus. see Barber, Antonia.
Chamberlain, Margaret, illus. see Benjamin, Floella.
Chamberlain, Margaret, illus. see Greaves, Margaret.
Chamberlain, Margaret, illus. see Mahy, Margaret.
Chamberlain, Margaret, illus. see Mooney, Bel.
Chamberlain, Margaret, illus. see Ohanesian, Diane.
Chamberlain, Margaret, illus. see Pomranz, Craig.
Chamberlain, Margaret, illus. see Rickards, Lynne.
Chamberlain, Margaret, illus. see Sheridan, Sara.
Chamberlain, Margaret, illus. see Tierney, Fiona.
Chamberlain, Margaret, illus. see Willis, Jeanne.
Chamberlain, Mary, et al. Las Crepes de Mama Panya: Un Relato de Kenia. Cairns, Julia, illus. (p. 976)
Chamberlain, Nick. Adventures of Papillon. (p. 21)
Chamberlain, Penny. Chasing the Mooon (p. 294)
Chamberlain-Pecorino, Sarah, illus. see Fox, Julie.
Chamberlin, Ann. Dumpling. (p. 490)
Chamberlin, Emily Hall, illus. see Knevels, Gertrude.
Chamberlin, Kate. Charles & David. Wroth, Dean, illus. (p. 291)
Chamberlin, Kathleen H. Marcy Mary: The Memoirs of a Dachshund American Princess. (p. 1092)
Chamberlin, Kylie. Island in the Attic. (p. 892)
Chamberlin, Maggie, illus. see May, Marcie & Zerhusen, Margaret.
Chamberlin, Mary, jt. auth. see Chamberlin, Richard.
Chamberlin, Mary, et al. Mama Panya's Pancakes. Cairns, Julia, illus. (p. 1084)
Chamberlin, Richard & Chamberlin, Mary. Mama Panya's Pancakes: A Market Day in Kenya. Cairns, Julia, illus. (p. 1084)
Chamberlin, Richard, et al. Mama Panya's Pancakes. Cairns, Julia, illus. (p. 1084)
Chamberlin, Thomas Chrowder. Geologic Relations of the Human Relics of Lansing, Kansas, with an Editorial on the Antiquity of Man in America & a Review on Kakabikansing. (p. 662)
Chamberlin-Calamar, Pat. Alaska's 12 Days of Summer. Cartwright, Shannon, illus. (p. 34)
Chambers, Aidan. Breaktime. (p. 225)
—Dying to Know You. (p. 491)
—Kissing Game: Short Stories. (p. 962)
—Now I Know. (p. 1269)
—Postcards from No Man's Land. (p. 1388)
—Toll Bridge. (p. 1762)
Chambers, Ailin. Animals. (p. 81)
—Creepy Crawlies. (p. 381)
—Fairies & Princesses. (p. 562)
—Manga. (p. 1087)
—Robots & Monsters. (p. 1481)
—Superheroes. (p. 1683)
Chambers, Bev R. Bouncer & Friends. (p. 216)
Chambers, Brent, illus. see Eggleton, Jill.
Chambers, Catherine. African Culture (p. 27)
—Alexander Graham Bell (p. 36)
—Are Humans Damaging the Atmosphere? (p. 96)
—Bigfoot. (p. 184)
—Blizzard (p. 199)
—Can We Protect People from Natural Disasters? (p. 258)
—Count Dracula. (p. 369)
—Day at an Indian Market (p. 412)
—Dilma Rousseff (p. 440)
—Earth Debates. (p. 495)
—Earth's Growing Population (p. 498)
—Egyptian Treasures. (p. 507)
—Energy in Crisis. (p. 528)
—Go Green! Lead the Way. (p. 686)
—How Effective Is Recycling? (p. 809)
—How Harmful Are Fossil Fuels? (p. 809)
—Living Forever: The Pharmaceutical Industry. (p. 1041)
—Loch Ness Monster. (p. 1044)
—Neil Armstrong (p. 1240)
—Rain & Life in a Nigerian Village (p. 1434)
—See for Yourself: Body Science. (p. 1546)
—Stopping Pollution (p. 1654)
—Threatened Wetlands. (p. 1741)
—Tooth Fairy. (p. 1768)
—Tornado (p. 1770)
—Why Why Why... Did Knights Wear Heavy Armor? (p. 1926)
Chambers, Catherine, jt. auth. see Dorling Kindersley Publishing Staff.
Chambers, Catherine, jt. auth. see Maxwell, Scott.
Chambers, Catherine, jt. auth. see Shuckburgh, Emily.
Chambers, Catherine & Dorling Kindersley Publishing Staff. School Days Around the World, Level 3. (p. 1522)
Chambers, Catherine & Lapthorn, Nicholas. Lakes (p. 972)
Chambers, Catherine E. Ape Adventures, Level 3. (p. 91)
—DK Adventures: Clash of the Gladiators: Clash of the Gladiators. (p. 455)
—DK Adventures: the Mummy's Curse: The Mummy's Curse. (p. 455)
Chambers, Catherine E., jt. auth. see Dorling Kindersley Publishing Staff.
Chambers, Catherine E. & Dorling Kindersley Publishing Staff. Clash of the Gladiators. (p. 327)
—Mummy's Curse. (p. 1191)
Chambers, Catherine, et al. All about Myths. (p. 43)
—Coolest Jobs on the Planet (p. 364)
, Chambers, Chambers. School Science Dictionary. (p. 1523)
Chambers, Cindy. Beamer Learns the Signs of a Stroke & How to Help. (p. 150)
—Beamer Visits the Children's Rehabilitation Center: The Beamer Book Series. (p. 150)
Chambers, Cindy & Demme, Tina. Beamer Visits the Emergency Room. Huber, Jim, illus. (p. 150)
Chambers, Cindy & Miller, Gabriella. Beamer Learns about Cancer: The Beamer Book Series. (p. 150)
Chambers, Darci. My Name Is Dawson: The Fun Begins. (p. 1215)
Chambers, Don. Entitlement Trap: Families & Money. (p. 531)
—Money Basics for Young Adults: College Edition. (p. 1164)
Chambers, Dori. Princesses' Pink Pillows. (p. 1406)
Chambers Harrap Publishers Staff, jt. auth. see Grandison, Alice.
Chambers, James, ed. see Nimoy, Leonard.
Chambers, Jennifer. Watershed Adventures of a Water Bottle. (p. 1864)
Chambers, Jerry. Cat Who Became a Teacher. (p. 278)
Chambers, Jo. All about Cars. (p. 42)
—Art Gallery. (p. 102)
—Caring for Wild Animals. (p. 269)
—Discovering India. (p. 449)
—Extreme Earth. (p. 556)
—High Tech. (p. 778)
—Making Movies. (p. 1081)
—That's Extreme. (p. 1726)
—Tropical Rainforest. (p. 1789)
Chambers, Joan, et al. Work of Art. (p. 1952)
Chambers, Karen. Cats in Flats. (p. 281)
Chambers, Linda Kandelin. Littlest Bull. (p. 1038)
Chambers, Mal, jt. auth. see Millett, Peter.
Chambers, Mal, jt. auth. see Mitchell, Julie.
Chambers, Mark. Brian the Smelly Bear. (p. 226)
—Five Little Monkeys ; and, Five Little Penguins. (p. 600)
—Five Little Monkeys ; Five Little Penguins. (p. 600)
Chambers, Mark, illus. see Emmett, Jonathan & Dunn, David H.
Chambers, Mark, illus. see Frost, Adam.
Chambers, Mark, illus. see Harper, Charise Mericle.
Chambers, Mark, illus. see Steinberg, D. J.
Chambers, Mark, illus. see Taplin, Sam.
Chambers, Mark, jt. auth. see Colbert, David.
Chambers, Mark A., illus. see Powell, Jillian.
Chambers, Mark L., illus. see Inches, Alison.
Chambers, Mary, illus. see Snider, Cindy Gay.
Chambers, Mary & Meinking, Mary. Who Counts the Penguins? Working in Antarctica. (p. 1915)
—Who Rolls Through Fire? Working on a Movie Set. (p. 1917)
—Who Swings the Wrecking Ball? Working on a Construction Site. (p. 1917)
—Who Walks the Tight Rope? Working at a Circus. (p. 1918)
Chambers, Melinda. Day the Snapdragons Snapped Back. Spiker, Sue Ann, illus. (p. 414)
—We Are Whoooo We Are. Spiker, Sue Ann, illus. (p. 1866)
Chambers, Oswald. Jesus Wants All of Me: Based on the Classic Devotional My Utmost for His Highest. Smouse, Phil A., illus. (p. 916)
Chambers, Pamela G. My Mommy's Getting Married. Stewart, Muriel, illus. (p. 1214)
Chambers, Robert B. Hobee's Quest: In the Deep. (p. 786)
Chambers, Robert W. Purple Emperor. (p. 1419)
Chambers, Sally, illus. see Shulman, Mark.
Chambers, Sally, et al. Waldo'n Ennill y Dydd. (p. 1853)
Chambers, Sam T., et al. Head Case Lacrosse Goalie: Sports Fiction with a Winning Edge. Collins, Don, illus. (p. 756)
Chambers, Tina, photos by see Platt, Richard & Dorling Kindersley Publishing Staff.
Chambers, Veronica. Celia Cruz, Queen of Salsa. Maren, Julie, illus. (p. 286)
—Double Dutch: A Celebration of Jump Rope, Rhyme, & Sisterhood. (p. 472)
—Plus. (p. 1374)
Chambers, Veronica & Clampet, Jason. Papi's Bodega. Miyares, Daniel, illus. (p. 1323)
Chambers, Vickie. In the Silence of the Hills. Taylor, LaVonne, ed. (p. 867)
Chambers, Whittaker, tr. see Salten, Felix.
Chambers, Whittaker, tr. from GER. Bambi. Disney Storybook Artists Staff, illus. (p. 135)
—City Jungle. (p. 323)
Chambers, Z., illus. see Santini, Philip.
Chambers-Goldberg, Micah, illus. see Blair, Eric.
Chambers-Goldberg, Micah, illus. see Ganz-Schmitt, Sue.
Chambers-Goldberg, Micah, illus. see Jones, Christianne C.
Chambers-Goldberg, Micah, illus. see Schroeder, Abraham.
Chambliss Bertman, Jennifer. Book Scavenger. (p. 212)
Chambliss, Marilyn, illus. see Hecker, Cindy.
Chambliss, Matthew, photos by see Houle, Donna Lee.
Chambliss, Maxie, illus. see Brisson, Pat.
Chambliss, Maxie, illus. see Bunting, Eve.
Chambliss, Maxie, illus. see Cole, Joanna.
Chambliss, Maxie, illus. see Fahiner, Paul.
Chambliss, Maxie, illus. see Fleming, Maria.
Chambliss, Maxie, illus. see Namm, Diane.
Chambliss, Maxie, illus. see Snyder, Carol.
Chamisso, Adelbert Von, see Von Chamisso, Adelbert.
Chamorro, Marco, jt. auth. see Iturralde, Edna.
Champagne, Elena. Where Do Raindrops Go? Sama, Billy, illus. (p. 1907)
Champagne, Heather, illus. see Marshall, Denise.
Champagne, Keith, illus. see Kramer, Don & Johns, Geoff.
Champagne, Keith, jt. auth. see Johns, Geoff.
Champagne, Liz, illus. see Pollack, Jeff & Steinberg, Lane.
Champagne, Marklyn, jt. auth. see Walker-Hirsch, Leslie.
Champagne, Melanie. My Aunt Came Back. (p. 1196)
Champier, Jacqueline. Little Piggy Goes South. (p. 1033)
Champion, Chayil. Affiliated. (p. 26)
Champion, Daryl, illus. see Champion, Dionne N., et al.
Champion, Dionne N., et al. Spirit of the Baobab Tree. Champion, Dionne N. & Champion, Daryl, illus. (p. 1628)
Champion, Gina. Anna & Her Mommy. Mitchell, Nanci, illus. (p. 85)
Champion, Neil. Camping & Hiking. (p. 257)
—Finding Food & Water. (p. 588)
—Finding Your Way. (p. 588)
—Fire & Cooking. (p. 590)
—In an Emergency. (p. 863)
—Making Shelter. (p. 1082)
—Orienteering. (p. 1303)
—Rock Climbing. (p. 1482)
—Tools & Crafts. (p. 1767)
—Tropical Rain Forests. (p. 1789)
—Wild Biking: Off-Road Mountain Biking. (p. 1929)
—Wild Rock: Climbing & Mountaineering. (p. 1930)
—Wild Snow: Skiing & Snowboarding. (p. 1930)
—Wild Trail: Hiking & Camping. (p. 1930)
—Wild Underground: Caves & Caving. (p. 1930)
—Wild Water: Canoeing & Kayaking. (p. 1930)
Champion, Neil, jt. auth. see Reid, Struan.
Champion, Neil & Ganeri, Anita. Finding Food & Water. (p. 588)
—Fire & Cooking. (p. 590)
—In an Emergency. (p. 863)
—Making Shelter. (p. 1082)
—Tools & Crafts. (p. 1767)
Champion, Servane, jt. auth. see Blackstone, Stella.
Champion, Vanessa, illus. see Chance, C.
Champlain, Michael. Painful Expressions (p. 1318)
Champlin, DeeAnn. Eddie E & the Eggs. Champlin, DeeAnn, illus. (p. 503)
Champlin, Susan, jt. auth. see Mack, Stan.
Champlin, Tim. Lummox. (p. 1065)
Champman, Joan. Val's Vacation. (p. 1831)
Chan, Arlene. Awakening the Dragon: The Dragon Boat Festival. Zhang, Song Nan, illus. (p. 120)
—Moon Festival: A Chinese Mid-Autumn Celebration. (p. 1172)
Chan, Carol, ed. see Farhat, Michael.
Chan, Crystal. Bird. (p. 190)
Chan, David. Meeting the Computer - One Byte at a Time (Chinese Edition) (p. 1124)
Chan, Gillian. Ocean Apart: The Gold Mountain Diary of Chin Mei-Ling. (p. 1276)
Chan, Harvey, illus. see Storm, Jeff.
Chan, Harvey, illus. see Yee, Paul.
Chan, Harvey, jt. auth. see Lottridge, Celia Barker.
Chan, Hingman. Celebrating Chinese New Year: An Activity Book, Second Edition. Yoon, Selina & Chen, Michael Yoon, eds. (p. 284)
Chan, Irene, illus. see Spiro, Ruth.
Chan, Janette Shipston. Tinny Tiger. (p. 1757)
Chan, Jason, illus. see Haydon, Elizabeth.
Chan, Jimmy, illus. see Thompson, Lisa.
Chan, Mari. Super Fun Kids. (p. 1680)
Chan, Marsha. College Oral Communication. (p. 340)
—College Oral Communication. (p. 340)
Chan, Marty. Barnabas Bigfoot: a Hairy Tangle. (p. 139)
—Barnabas Bigfoot: Bone Eater. (p. 139)
—Devil's Island (p. 432)
—Mystery of the Frozen Brains MacIntyre, R. P., ed. (p. 1225)
—Mystery of the Graffiti Ghoul. (p. 1225)
—Mystery of the Mad Science Teacher. (p. 1225)
—True Story. Bennett, Lorna, illus. (p. 1793)
Chan, Paul D. Why Is Mommy Sad? A Child's Guide to Parental Depression. Faust, Laurie A., illus. (p. 1925)
Chan, Peter, et al. Alien Race: Visual Development of an Original Intergalactic Adventure. Robertson, Scott, ed. (p. 41)
Chan, Queenie. Dreaming (p. 484)
—Dreaming Collection. (p. 484)
Chan, San Wei. Spear & Shield. (p. 1623)
Chan, Suwin, illus. see Gamble, Adam & Jasper, Mark.
Chan, Suwin, illus. see Gamble, Adam.
Chanani, Gloria. Fearful Frannie & Her Fateful Trip to Maui. (p. 579)
—Fearful Frannie's African Safari. (p. 579)
—It's Story Time Grandm. (p. 899)
Chance, C. Trepets Book Three Rabbit Race Day. Champion, Vanessa, illus. (p. 1784)
Chance, Karen. Embrace the Night (p. 517)
Chance, Kitty. Farmer Fran's Funny Friends. (p. 574)
Chance, Megan. Shadows (p. 1558)
Chance, Robyn. C Is for Chin. Chance, Robyn, illus. (p. 249)
—Ewela's Unbaalievable Journey. (p. 547)
Chancellor, Deborah. Ambulance Rescue. (p. 57)
—Animal Sticker Atlas. Lewis, Anthony, illus. (p. 79)
—Camping Trip. Fairclough, Chris, illus. (p. 257)
—Changing Environment. (p. 290)
—Changing Environment, Level 5. (p. 290)
—Christmas Story. Downing, Julie, illus. (p. 315)
—Clothes & Toys. (p. 334)
—Discover Science - Maps & Mapping. (p. 448)
—Fire Rescue. (p. 590)
—Food Waste. (p. 614)
—Good Manners. (p. 698)
—Healthy Eating. (p. 758)

—Lizards. (p. 1042)
—Piranhas. (p. 1362)
—Police Rescue. (p. 1380)
—Rats. (p. 1440)
—Sea Rescue. (p. 1535)
Chancellor, Deborah, jt. auth. see Goldsmith, Mike.
Chancellor, Deborah, jt. auth. see Taylor, Barbara.
Chancellor, Deborah & Goldsmith, Mike. Weather. (p. 1869)
Chancellor, Debroah. Weather. (p. 1869)
Chancey, Loren. Blue Sneaker Breakdown. (p. 203)
Chand, Candy. Twelve Prayers of Christmas. Bernardin, James, illus. (p. 1800)
Chand, Dianne. Hats! (p. 752)
Chand, Emlyn. Courtney Saves Christmas. Giffin, Noelle, illus. (p. 373)
—Davey the Detective: A Bird Brain Book. Shaw, Sarah, illus. (p. 410)
—Farsighted. (p. 575)
—Honey the Hero: A Bird Brain Book. Shaw, Sarah, illus. (p. 794)
—Izzy the Inventor: A Bird Brain Book. Giffin, Noelle, illus. (p. 901)
—Larry the Lonely: A Bird Brain Book. Giffin, Noelle, illus. (p. 976)
—Open Heart. (p. 1299)
—Poppy the Proud: A Bird Brain Book. Shaw, Sarah, illus. (p. 1385)
—Ricky the Runt: A Bird Brain Book. Giffin, Noelle, illus. (p. 1470)
—Vicky Finds a Valentine: Bird Brain Books. Giffin, Noelle, illus. (p. 1840)
Chand, Vimi. World of Peanut Butter Jelly Boy: Peanut Butter Jelly Boy's Stay in the Hospital. (p. 1957)
Chanda, Bell, jt. auth. see Aebersold, Carol V.
Chanda, J-P. Four's a Crowd. Let's Draw Studio Staff, illus. (p. 625)
—Happy Birthday, SpongeBob! Martinez, Heather, illus. (p. 745)
—Turtle Rescue! Redondo, Jesus, illus. (p. 1798)
Chanda, Justin, ed. see Creech, Sharon, et al.
Chandab, Taghred. Perfect Flower Girl. Talib, Binny, illus. (p. 1341)
Chanders, C. R. Through a Daddy's Eyes. (p. 1744)
Chandhok, Lena, illus. see Amidon Lusted, Marcia.
Chandler, Alton. Salute to African American Architects: Learning Activities. Chapman, Loring F., ed. (p. 1506)
—Salute to African American in Medicine: Learning. Chapman, L., ed. (p. 1506)
—Salute to Black Inventor, Dr. Georde Washington Carver: The Peanut Wizard. Chapman, L., ed. (p. 1506)
Chandler, Alton, illus. see Banks, Calvin J.
Chandler, Alton, jt. auth. see Howell, Ann C.
Chandler, Amanda, jt. auth. see Chandler, Andrew.
Chandler, Andrew & Chandler, Amanda. Gertrude & Abigail: The Adventures Thereof. (p. 667)
Chandler, Andrew Robert. Horatio the Half-Hooved Horse. (p. 797)
Chandler, Ann. Kootenay Silver. (p. 967)
—Salute to Black Inventors: Coloring Learning Activities. Vol. 1 Chapman, Loring F., ed. (p. 1506)
—Siena Summer (p. 1573)
Chandler, Ben. Beast Child. (p. 152)
—Quillblade (p. 1428)
Chandler, Bill & Chandler, Marie. Reindeer That Couldn't Fly. Kling, Leslie, illus. (p. 1457)
Chandler, David. Animal Fact Files Birds (p. 77)
Chandler, David & Flegg, Jim. Birds. (p. 191)
Chandler, Elizabeth. Back Door of Midnight. (p. 130)
—Dark Secrets: Legacy of Lies - Don't Tell. (p. 408)
—Deep End of Fear. (p. 423)
—Everafter. (p. 541)
—Evercrossed. (p. 542)
—Everlasting. (p. 542)
—Kissed by an Angel: Evercrossed; Everlasting; Everafter. (p. 961)
—Kissed by an Angel: Kissed by an Angel; the Power of Love; Soulmates. (p. 961)
—Love at First Click. (p. 1059)
—Monsters Are We. (p. 1169)
—No Time to Die - The Deep End of Fear No. 2. (p. 1260)
—Summer in the City. (p. 1674)
Chandler, F. First Encyclopedia of History. (p. 594)
Chandler, Fiona. Ancient world - Internet Linked. McCaffrey, Susie, illus. (p. 71)
—Encyclopedia of World History. (p. 526)
—First Encyclopedia of the Human Body: Internet-Linked. Hancock, David & Woodcock, John, illus. (p. 594)
—First Encyclopedia of the Human Body II. (p. 594)
—First Encyclopedia of the Human Body - Internet Linked. Hancock, David, illus. (p. 594)
—Prehistoric World. (p. 1395)
—Usborne Internet-Linked First Encyclopedia of History. (p. 1827)
—Usborne Little Encyclopedia of the Human Body: Internet-Linked. Hancock, David & Woodcock, John, illus. (p. 1827)
Chandler, Fiona & McCaffrey, Susie. Usborne Internet-Linked Ancient World. (p. 1827)
Chandler, Fiona, et al. Usborne First Encyclopedia of History. Hancock, David, illus. (p. 1827)
—Usborne Internet-Linked Prehistoric World. Firenze, Inklink, illus. (p. 1827)
Chandler, Gary & Graham, Kevin. Making a Better World (p. 1080)
Chandler Goldstein. Georgette: A Little Frog Discovers the Value in Revealing Her True Self! (p. 665)
Chandler, Jean. Adventures of Molly: No Dogs Allowed. (p. 20)
—Adventures of Molly: Molly Visits the Farm. (p. 20)
Chandler, Jeff. Fire Dog Champ. (p. 590)
—New Kitten: A Story about a Foster Puppy (p. 1246)
Chandler, Jeff, illus. see Fisher, Doris & Gibbs, D. L.
Chandler, Jeff, photos by see Fisher, Doris & Gibbs, D. L.
Chandler, Jeffery. Christmas Santa Overslept. (p. 315)
Chandler, Joan. Cat Tales. (p. 278)
Chandler, Kimberley L., et al. Earth Beneath Our Feet: An Earth Science Unit for High-Ability Learners in Grades 3-4. (p. 495)
Chandler, Kristen. Girls Don't Fly. (p. 680)
Chandler, Marie, jt. auth. see Chandler, Bill.
Chandler, Mary Darlene. Tippee's Big Adventure. (p. 1757)
Chandler, Matt. Bachelor's Grove Cemetery & Other Haunted Places of the Midwest (p. 130)
—Bear Hunting for Kids (p. 150)
—Dangerous Times: History's Most Troubled Eras. (p. 404)
—Deer Hunting for Kids (p. 423)
—Ghosts of the Alamo & Other Hauntings of the South (p. 672)
—Outrageous Pro Wrestling Rivalries. (p. 1313)
—Side-By-Side Baseball Stars: Comparing Pro Baseball's Greatest Players (p. 1573)
—Who's Who of Pro Baseball: A Guide to the Game's Greatest Players. (p. 1921)
—World's Most Haunted Places (p. 1960)
Chandler, Matt & Garbe, Suzanne. Haunted America (p. 753)
Chandler, Matt, et al. Into the Great Outdoors. (p. 881)
Chandler, Matt, retold by. Trojan War: A Graphic Retelling. (p. 1788)
Chandler, Matthew Allan. Deer Hunting for Kids (p. 423)
Chandler, Michael. Littlest Cowboy's Christmas Jacobsen, Terry, illus. (p. 1039)
Chandler, Mitzi. I See Something Grand. (p. 845)
Chandler, Murray. Chess Puzzles for Kids. (p. 298)
—Chess Tactics for Kids. (p. 298)
Chandler, Murray & Milligan, Helen. Chess for Children. McCluskey, Cindy, illus. (p. 298)
Chandler, Paul. Mouse of Commons - Mouse of Lords. (p. 1182)
Chandler, Pauline. Mr. Rabbit the Farmer. Smith, Eric, illus. (p. 1186)
—Warrior Girl: A Novel of Joan of Arc. (p. 1858)
Chandler, Samuel. Illustrated Stories for Christmas. Spatz, Caroline, ed. (p. 858)
Chandler, Sean Morgan. Ebony Marshal. (p. 502)
Chandler, Shannon, illus. see Hannigan, Paula & Croyle, Paula.
Chandler, Shannon, illus. see Hannigan, Paula.
Chandler, Shannon, illus. see Riegelman, Rianna & Accord Publishing Staff.
Chandler, Shannon & Accord Publishing Staff. Colors. (p. 344)
Chandler, Simon Cookson & Cookson, Dave. Thinking Skills. (p. 1734)
Chandler, Susan. Welcome to Cuckooville. Durand, Delphine, illus. (p. 1873)
—What I Do with Vegetable Glue. Odriozola, Elena, illus. (p. 1886)
Chandler, Terrence, illus. see Friedman-Brunt, Elyse.
Chandler, Terry Ann. Miss Beula Helps Libby. (p. 1151)
Chandler, Tom. Sad Jazz. (p. 1501)
Chandler, Tony. Journey. (p. 927)
Chandpai - Dhamrai Bangladeshi Students Staff. Shuba & the Cyclone. Kelly, Victoria, ed. (p. 1571)
Chandra, Deborah & Comora, Madeleine. George Washington's Teeth. Cole, Brock, illus. (p. 665)
Chandra, Rohini S. Dragon in the Candle Jar. (p. 477)
Chandraratna, Bandula. Mirage. (p. 1149)
Chandu, illus. see Nagpal, Saraswati.
Chanek, Sherilin & National Geographic Learning Staff. Africa - Geography & Environments. (p. 26)
—Europe & Russia: Geography & Environments. (p. 540)
—Europe & Russia - People & Places. (p. 540)
Chaney, Scott. Christian Warriors: Games, Gear, Gospel - Especially for Christian Youth. (p. 312)
Chang, Bernard, illus. see Cornell, Paul & Venditti, Robert.
Chang, Chong, illus. see Chang, Grace.
Chang, Edward. Easy Chinese - Mandarin Level I: Basic Text & Workbook. (p. 500)
Chang, Grace. Jin Jin & Rain Wizard. Chang, Chong, illus. (p. 918)
—Jin Jin the Dragon. Chang, Chong, illus. (p. 918)
Chang, Hae-Kyung. Oh No, School! Bisaillon, Josée, illus. (p. 1281)
Chang, Heidi. Skin on Your Body (p. 1585)
Chang, Ifay, as told by. Outopians. (p. 1313)
Chang, Lulu, jt. auth. see Chu, Carol.
Chang, MacKerras And Hsiu-Ching, et al. Hanyu for Intermediate Students (p. 744)
Chang, MacKerras, et al. Hanyu for Beginning Students. (p. 744)
—Hanyu for Intermediate Students. (p. 744)
Chang, Margaret. Celia's Robot. (p. 286)
Chang, Maria, jt. auth. see Chang, Maria L.
Chang, Maria L. & Chang, Maria. Classroom Management in Photographs: Full-Color Photographs with Teacher Descriptions & Insights about What Really Works. (p. 329)
Chang, Maria L. & Zile, Susan Van. Science: Graphic Organizers & Mini-Lessons. (p. 1524)
Chang, Michelle, illus. see Cheng, Andrea.
Chang, Nan, tr. Kids Stuff Chinese: Easy Chinese phrases for you & your Kids. (p. 955)
Chang, Perry, jt. auth. see Hart, Joyce.
Chang, Peter & Mackerras, Alyce. Hanyu for Beginning Students. (p. 744)
—Hanyu for Beginning Students Character Writing Book. (p. 744)
—Hanyu for Intermediate Students (p. 744)
—Hanyu for Intermediate Students: Character Writing Book (p. 744)
—Hanyu for Intermediate Students: Teacher's Book Stage 1. (p. 744)
Chang, Raymond, et al. Understanding Chemistry. (p. 1815)
Chang, Roy, illus. see Goldsberry, U'i.
Chang, Roy, illus. see Steele, Margaret.
Chang, Shu-Cheng, et al, eds. Geometric Evolution Equations. (p. 662)
Chang, Tara Larsen, illus. see Miller, Sibley & Lenhard, Elizabeth.
Chang, Tara Larsen, illus. see Miller, Sibley.
Chang, Tristen & Pecsenye, Jessica. UC Davis College Prowler off the Record: Inside University of California Davis. (p. 1807)
Chang, Warren, illus. see Sobol, Donald J.
Chankhamma, Sharl. Sisters' Luck. (p. 1581)
Chanko, Pamela. 101 Content-Building Fingerplays, Action Rhymes, & Songs: Easy & Engaging Activities That Build Important Background Knowledge & Enrich Young Learners' Vocabularies. (p. 1999)
—25 Fun Phonics Plays for Beginning Readers: Engaging, Reproducible Plays That Target & Teach Key Phonics Skills - And Get Kids Eager to Read! (p. 1996)
—Easy Reader Biographies: Betsy Ross: The Story of Our Flag. (p. 500)
—Easy Reader Biographies: Rosa Parks: Bus Ride to Freedom. (p. 500)
—Follow-The-Directions Flip Chart: No-Cook Recipes: 12 Healthy, Month-By-Month Recipes with Fun Activities That Teach Young Learners How to Listen & Follow Directions. (p. 612)
—Leveled Poems for Small-Group Reading Lessons: 40 Just-Right Poems for Guided Reading Levels e-N with Mini-Lessons That Teach Key Phonics Skills, Build Fluency, & Meet the Common Core. (p. 1003)
—Shoe Box Learning Centers: Time & Measurement: 30 Instant Centers with Reproducible Templates & Activities That Help Kids Practice Important Math Skills-Independently! (p. 1568)
—Shoe Box Learning Centers: Word Families: 30 Instant Centers with Reproducible Templates & Activities That Help Kids Practice Important Literacy Skills-Independently! (p. 1568)
—Teaching with Favorite Ezra Jack Keats Books: Engaging, Skill-Building Activities That Help Kids Learn about Families, Friendship, Neighborhood & Community, & More in These Beloved Classics. (p. 1710)
—Teaching with Favorite Lois Ehlert Books: Engaging, Skill-Building Activities That Introduce Basic Concepts, Develop Vocabulary, & Explore Favorite Science Topics. (p. 1710)
—Teaching with Favorite Mem Fox Books: Engaging, Skill-Building Activities That Help Kids Learn about Feelings, Families, Friendship & More. (p. 1710)
—Word Families: 30 Instant Centers with Reproducible Templates & Activities That Help Kids Practice Important Literacy Skills-Independently! (p. 1950)
Chanko, Pamela, jt. auth. see Berger, Samantha.
Channa, Abdul Malik, illus. see Rafi, Natasha.
Channing, Blanche Mary. Zodiac Stories. (p. 1987)
Channing, Margot. Dinosaurs & Other Prehistoric Creatures. (p. 444)
Chanover, Hyman & Zusman, Evelyn. Book of Prayer for Junior Congregations: Sabbath & Festivals. (p. 211)
Chantler, Chris, jt. auth. see Read, Howard.
Chantler, Scott. Captive Prince. Chantler, Scott, illus. (p. 264)
—Northwest Passage (p. 1266)
—Sign of the Black Rock. Chantler, Scott, illus. (p. 1574)
—Tower of Treasure. Chantler, Scott, illus. (p. 1773)
Chao, Eileen. Go Away, Sam! (p. 686)
Chao, Linus, illus. see Matsuura, Richard & Matsuura, Ruth.
Chao, Yu-Han. We Grow Old: Fifty-Three Chinese Love Poems. (p. 1867)
Chapel, Jamie Moore & Eberhardt, Nancy Chapel. ¿Qué Es Diferente ... ¿Qué Es lo Mismo? (p. 1423)
Chapelle, Suzanne Ellery Greene & Phillips, Glenn O. African American Leaders of Maryland: A Portrait Gallery. (p. 27)
Chapin, Jimmy, illus. see Rehberg, Emily.
Chapin, Patricia. Storm. (p. 1655)
Chapin, Patrick, illus. see White, James C.
Chapin, Patrick O., illus. see Giunta, Brian.
Chapin, Tom & Forster, John. Backwards Birthday Party. Groenink, Chuck, illus. (p. 130)
Chaplain, Dawn. One Red Apple. (p. 1296)
Chaple, Glenn F. Outer Planets Jones, Lauren V. & Slater, Timothy F., eds. (p. 1312)
Chapleski, Greg. Golfinitions - the Golf Dictionary. (p. 696)
Chapleski, Gregory. Getting Started in Golf. (p. 669)
Chapleski, Gregory, creator. Moving Ahead in Golf. (p. 1183)
Chaplin, Deborah. Do I Have To? (p. 457)
Chapline, Jo, jt. auth. see Mundy, Charlene.
Chapman. Seasons & Woodman. (p. 1538)
Chapman, Allan W. Mr Wugidgem & the Dark Journey. (p. 1187)
—Mr. Wugidgem & the Phoenix Journey. (p. 1187)
Chapman, Allen. Bart Sterlings Road to Success. (p. 140)
—Bart Stirlings Road to Success or the Yo. (p. 140)
—Bart Stirling's Road to Success; or, the Young Express Agent. (p. 140)
—Frank Roscoes Secret or the Darewell Chu. (p. 629)
—Frank Roscoe's Secret; or, the Darewell Chums in the Woods. (p. 629)
—Radio Boys First Wireless. (p. 1432)
—Radio Boys' First Wireless: The Radio Boys' First Wireless. (p. 1432)
—Radio Boys First Wireless or Winning the. (p. 1432)
—Radio Boys' First Wireless; or, Winning the Ferberton Prize. (p. 1432)
—Tom Fairfield's Pluck & Luck. (p. 1763)
—Tom Fairfields Pluck & Luck or Working. (p. 1763)
—Tom Fairfield's Pluck & Luck; or, Working to Clear His Name. (p. 1763)
Chapman, Amberlee. Smee the One Inch Tall Man & Me. (p. 1593)
Chapman, Andrew. Heroic Feats. (p. 773)
Chapman, Bob. Visitors. (p. 1845)
Chapman, Brenda. Hiding in Hawk's Creek. (p. 777)
—Running Scared. (p. 1497)
—Second Chances. (p. 1539)
—Trail of Secrets. (p. 1776)
—Where Trouble Leads. (p. 1910)
Chapman, Brian & Jarvis, Alan. Organic Chemistry, Energetics, Kinetics & Equilibrium. (p. 1303)
—Transition Metals, Quantitative Kinetics & Applied Organic Chemistry. (p. 1778)
Chapman, Brian, et al. Structure, Bonding & Main Group Chemistry. (p. 1668)
Chapman, Bunny. Shanu the Watcher. (p. 1560)
Chapman, Carlene. Jackson Goes to the Beach. (p. 904)
Chapman, Caroline. Battles & Weapons: Exploring History Through Art. (p. 147)
Chapman, Cat, illus. see MacIver, Juliette.
Chapman, Cat, illus. see Maclver, Juliette.
Chapman, Catherine. Magical Scarecrows' Garden. (p. 1075)
Chapman, Charlotte. Adventures of Little Payton. (p. 20)
Chapman, Cheryl. Pass the Fritters, Critters. Roth, Susan L., illus. (p. 1326)
Chapman, Chris, illus. see Smith, Lucy.
Chapman, Chris & Hvolboll, Eric P., contrib. by. Portraits of Gaviota. (p. 1387)
Chapman, Cindy. Baby Animals (p. 124)
—On a Farm (p. 1288)
—Play It Safe! (p. 1371)
—What Is in the Sky? (p. 1889)
—Where Is Your Home? (p. 1909)
Chapman, Cindy, jt. auth. see Scholastic, Inc. Staff.
Chapman, Cindy & Capstone Press Staff. Baby Animals (p. 124)
—On a Farm (p. 1288)
—Play It Safe! (p. 1371)
—What Is in the Sky? (p. 1889)
—Where Is Your Home? (p. 1909)
Chapman, Clay McLeod. Camp Cannibal. (p. 257)
—Tribe - Homeroom Headhunters. (p. 1785)
Chapman, D. Artist Cards: Level 1. (p. 104)
—Artist Cards: Level 2. (p. 104)
—Artist Cards: Level 3. (p. 104)
—Artist Cards: Level 4. (p. 104)
—Artist Cards: Level 5. (p. 104)
—Artist Cards: Level 6. (p. 104)
—Assessment Masters: Level 1. (p. 107)
—Assessment Masters: Level 2. (p. 107)
—Assessment Masters: Level 3. (p. 107)
—Assessment Masters: Level 4. (p. 107)
—Assessment Masters: Level 5. (p. 107)
—Studio Masters: Level 1. (p. 1670)
—Studio Masters: Level 2. (p. 1670)
—Studio Masters: Level 3. (p. 1670)
—Studio Masters: Level 4. (p. 1670)
—Studio Masters: Level 5. (p. 1670)
—Studio Masters: Level 6. (p. 1670)
—Vocabulary Cards. (p. 1847)
Chapman, David E. Daddy & I Explore... the Caves! (p. 398)
Chapman, Debbie, illus. see Harris, Angela L.
Chapman, Elsie. Divided (Dualed Sequel) (p. 454)
—Dualed. (p. 487)
Chapman, Fern Schumer. Is It Night or Day? (p. 889)
Chapman, Frederica. She Greened the Land: A Fairy Tale for the Earth. (p. 1564)
Chapman, Frederick T., illus. see Coatsworth, Elizabeth.
Chapman, Frederick T., illus. see Downey, Fairfax.
Chapman, Frederick T., illus. see Jewett, Eleanore M.
Chapman, Frederick T., illus. see Meigs, Elizabeth Bleecker.
Chapman, Frederick T., illus. see Undset, Sigrid, ed.
Chapman, Garry. Coal. (p. 336)
—Coffee. (p. 338)
Chapman, Garry & Hodges, Gary. Iron Ore. (p. 888)
—Oil. (p. 1282)
—Sugar. (p. 1672)
—Wheat. (p. 1900)
Chapman, Gary. Love Languages of God. (p. 1060)
—Tiw: A Student's Guide to the Five Love Languages. (p. 1758)
Chapman, Gaye. Little Blue. Chapman, Gaye, illus. (p. 1024)
Chapman, Gaye, illus. see Russell, Paula.
Chapman, Giles. Racing Driver: How to Drive Racing Cars Step by Step. (p. 1432)
Chapman, Gillian. Bible Make & Do (p. 175)
Chapman, Gillian, illus. see Henning, Heather.
Chapman, Gillian, illus. see Lane, Leena.
Chapman, Gillian, jt. auth. see Lane, Leena.
Chapman, Gillian & Robson, Pam. Making Art with Fabric. (p. 1080)
—Making Art with Packaging. (p. 1080)
—Making Art with Paper. (p. 1080)
—Making Art with Rocks & Shells. (p. 1080)
—Making Art with Sand & Earth. (p. 1080)
—Making Art with Wood. (p. 1080)
Chapman, Helen. Happy New Year. (p. 746)
—Landmarks of the World. (p. 974)
Chapman, J. Ant: Learning the Short A Sound. (p. 88)
—Pet Pals: Learning the P Sound. (p. 1345)
Chapman, Jane. Hands off My Honey! Warnes, Tim, illus. (p. 741)
—Is It Christmas Yet? Chapman, Jane, illus. (p. 889)
—No More Cuddles! Chapman, Jane, illus. (p. 1259)
Chapman, Jane, illus. see Baguley, Elizabeth.
Chapman, Jane, illus. see Bedford, David.
Chapman, Jane, illus. see Benjamin, A. H.
Chapman, Jane, illus. see Bright, Paul.
Chapman, Jane, illus. see Corderoy, Tracey.
Chapman, Jane, illus. see Davies, Nicola.
Chapman, Jane, illus. see Dowson, Nick.
Chapman, Jane, illus. see Freedman, Claire.
Chapman, Jane, illus. see French, Vivian.
Chapman, Jane, illus. see Hendry, Diana.
Chapman, Jane, illus. see Jenkins, Martin.
Chapman, Jane, illus. see Jennings, Linda.
Chapman, Jane, illus. see Kavanagh, Peter.
Chapman, Jane, illus. see Lloyd-Jones, Sally.
Chapman, Jane, illus. see Root, Phyllis.
Chapman, Jane, illus. see Sassi, Laura.
Chapman, Jane, illus. see Sykes, Julie.
Chapman, Jane, illus. see Warnes, Tim.
Chapman, Jane, illus. see Wilson, Karma.
Chapman, Jane, jt. auth. see Wilson, Karma.
Chapman, Jane, tr. see Benjamin, A. H.

Chapman, Jane, tr. see Kavanagh, Peter.
Chapman, Jared. Pirate, Viking & Scientist. (p. 1363)
—Steve, Raised by Wolves. (p. 1649)
—Vegetables in Underwear. (p. 1834)
Chapman, Jared & Smeldt, H. W. Farts in the Wild: A Spotter's Guide. (p. 575)
Chapman, Jason. Ted, Bo & Diz: The First Adventure (p. 1712)
—Who's That Singing? A Pull-the-Tab Book. Chapman, Jason, illus. (p. 1921)
—Who's That Snoring? A Pull-the-Tab Bedtime Book. Chapman, Jason, illus. (p. 1921)
Chapman, Jesse, illus. see Tobin, Richard K.
Chapman, Jim, illus. see Chapman, Steven Curtis & Beth, Mary.
Chapman, Joan. Cloud Called Cleo. (p. 334)
—Count the Ways to Get Around: Learning to Count To 5. (p. 370)
—Heavy & Light: Learning to Compare Weights of Objects. (p. 761)
—Living Things. (p. 1041)
—Lonely Crayon. (p. 1046)
—Maps, Maps, Maps. (p. 1090)
—Visiting the Police Station. (p. 1845)
Chapman, K., et al. Icelandic Conversations (p. 851)
Chapman, Karean. Adventures of Northern the Moose & a Dragon Named Zeus. Ciesinka, Izabela, illus. (p. 21)
—Look at Me, a Muscian I Want to Be. Ciesinska, Izabela, illus. (p. 1048)
—Look at Me, a Veterinarian I Want to Be. Ciesinska, Izabela, illus. (p. 1048)
Chapman, Karen B. Marino Mission: One Girl, One Mission, One Thousand Words - 1,000 Need-to-Know New 'SAT Vocabulary Words. (p. 1094)
Chapman, Katriona, illus. see Burton, Sarah.
Chapman, Katriona, illus. see Dale, Jay.
Chapman, Keith. Itsy Bitsy Spider. Tickle, Jack, illus. (p. 900)
Chapman, Kelly. Princess with a Purpose. Lyon, Tammie, illus. (p. 1406)
—Warrior Prince for God. Ebbeler, Jeff, illus. (p. 1858)
—Warrior Prince for God Activity Book. Ebbeler, Jeff, illus. (p. 1858)
—Warrior Prince for God Curriculum Leader's Guide. Ebbeler, Jeff, illus. (p. 1859)
Chapman, L., ed. see Chandler, Alton.
Chapman, L., ed. see Howell, Ann C. & Chandler, Alton.
Chapman, Lara. Flawless. (p. 603)
—XYZs of Being Wicked. (p. 1967)
Chapman, Laura H. Big Book; Level One Bk. 1 (p. 178)
Chapman, Laura Kate, jt. auth. see Bell, Juliet Clare.
Chapman, Laura-Kate, illus. see Bell, Juliet Clare.
Chapman, Lee, illus. see Chapman, Nancy Kapp & Chapman, Nancy.
Chapman, Lee, illus. see Stevens, Carla & Stevens, Chapman.
Chapman, Linda. Flying High. Hull, Biz & Farley, Andrew, illus. (p. 610)
—Starlight Surprise. (p. 1642)
—Starlight Surprise. Hull, Biz, illus. (p. 1642)
—Twilight Magic. Kronheimer, Ann, illus. (p. 1801)
Chapman, Linda & Cole, Steve. Last Phoenix. (p. 978)
Chapman, Loring F., ed. see Chandler, Alton.
Chapman, Loring F., ed. see Chandler, Ann.
Chapman, Lynne. Baby Can Bounce! Chapman, Lynne, illus. (p. 125)
—Baby Goes Baaaaa! Chapman, Lynne, illus. (p. 126)
Chapman, Lynne, illus. see Bently, Peter.
Chapman, Lynne, illus. see Hall, Pam.
Chapman, Lynne, illus. see Jarman, Julia.
Chapman, Lynne, illus. see Love, Pamela.
Chapman, Lynne, illus. see Oram, Hiawyn.
Chapman, Lynne, illus. see Rawlinson, Julia.
Chapman, Lynne, illus. see Rix, Jamie.
Chapman, Lynne, jt. auth. see Barber, Tom.
Chapman, Marian. Purple Pony. (p. 1419)
Chapman, Mary Beth & Chapman, Steven Curtis. Shaoey & Dot: Back in a Bug's Blink. (p. 1560)
—Shaoey & Dot: A Trip to Dr. Betterbee. (p. 1560)
—Shaoey & Dot: Thunder & Lightning Bugs. (p. 1560)
—You Were Always in My Heart: A Shaoey & Dot Adoption Story (p. 1976)
Chapman, Megan Joy. Lion Heart & Alessio Book 2: Mission, Peace, Patience, Kindness. (p. 1020)
Chapman, Michelle, illus. see Crosby, June.
Chapman, Mike. Sport of Lincoln (p. 1631)
Chapman, Nancy, jt. auth. see Chapman, Nancy Kapp.
Chapman, Nancy Kapp & Chapman, Nancy. Tripper's Travels: An International Scrapbook Chapman, Lee, illus. (p. 1787)
Chapman, Neil, illus. see Benton, Lynne.
Chapman, Neil, illus. see North, Laura.
Chapman, Neil, illus. see Stevenson, Robert Louis.
Chapman, Neil, jt. auth. see Wallace, Karen.
Chapman, Neil A., illus. see Graves, Sue.
Chapman, Nichole. You Were Made for Greatness. (p. 1976)
Chapman, Noel & Cheek, Judith. Creative Fashion Drawing. (p. 379)
Chapman, Patricia. Beth. (p. 171)
—Bible in the Hunger Games: A "Bibleizing" Study Guide. Kyle, Margaret, illus. (p. 175)
Chapman, Randy. Greatest Dunk of All. (p. 719)
Chapman, Richard. New Complete Guitarist. (p. 1244)
Chapman, Robert, illus. see Luenn, Nancy.
Chapman, Robert E., illus. see Carmona, Adela.
Chapman, Robyn, jt. auth. see Jakobsen, Lars.
Chapman, S. I. mon. In the Desert. (p. 865)
Chapman, Sherill, et al, adapted by. More Numbers. (p. 1174)
—Vocabulary Puzzles. (p. 1847)
Chapman, Simon. At the North Pole. (p. 111)
—In the Himalayas. Chapman, Simon, illus. (p. 866)
—In the Jungle. Chapman, Simon, illus. (p. 866)
—On Safari. Chapman, Simon, illus. (p. 1289)
—Under the Sea. Chapman, Simon, illus. (p. 1814)
Chapman, Steven, jt. auth. see Saunders, Nigel J.
Chapman, Steven, jt. auth. see Saunders, Nigel.
Chapman, Steven Curtis. Cinderella: The Love of a Daddy & His Princess (p. 320)
Chapman, Steven Curtis, jt. auth. see Chapman, Mary Beth.
Chapman, Steven Curtis & Beth, Mary. Christmas Miracle Chapman, Jim, illus. (p. 314)
Chapman, Susan. Old Ways Mantha, John, illus. (p. 1285)
Chapman, Susan, illus. see Adams, Michelle Medlock.
Chapman, Susan, illus. see Hood, Sue.
Chapman, Susan Margaret. Too Much Noise in the Library. Carter, Abby, illus. (p. 1767)
Chapman, Tammy. Lady Belle. (p. 970)
Chapman, Todd & Judge, Lita. D Is for Dinosaur: A Prehistoric Alphabet. Judge, Lita, illus. (p. 397)
Chapman, Victoria L., ed. see Facts on File, Inc. Staff, et al.
Chapmann, Helen. Art of Maths. (p. 102)
—Shapes & Scapes. (p. 1560)
Chapmanworks Staff, illus. see Parent, Nancy.
Chapmon, Rachelle. Mari. (p. 1093)
Chapoton, Debra. Bullies & Bears (p. 240)
—Mystery's Grave (p. 1226)
—Secret in the Hidden Cave. (p. 1541)
Chapouton, Anne Marie, jt. auth. see Claverie, Jean.
Chappas, Bess. Kiki & the Red Shoes. Branam, Sandy, illus. (p. 955)
Chappell, Aimee. Good Bye Grandpa. (p. 697)
Chappell, Billie-Jean & Williams, Frederick C. Happiness Colouring Book. Williams, Frederick C., illus. (p. 744)
Chappell, Crissa-Jean. More Than Good Enough. (p. 1175)
Chappell, Jackie. Our School Is Like A Family. (p. 1310)
—Our School Is Like a Family. (p. 1310)
—Taking Kindness with Me. (p. 1698)
—When I Ride the Bus. (p. 1903)
Chappell, Mike & Nuttall, Chris. Business & the European Union. (p. 244)
Chappell, Rachel. Solving Science Questions: A Book about the Scientific Process. (p. 1608)
Chappell, Warren, illus. see Besterman, Catherine.
Chappell, Warren, illus. see McCleery, William.
Chappell, Warren, illus. see Richter, Conrad.
Chappelow, Sarah. Caterpillars (p. 279)
Chapus, Julie. Blame Game. (p. 198)
—Your Feelings. (p. 1980)
Char, Harry. Case of the Broken Pipe. (p. 273)
—Case of the Missing Bicycle. (p. 274)
—Man Who Could Not Read. (p. 1086)
Chara, Kathleen A. & Chara, Paul J. Sensory Smarts: A Book for Kids with ADHD or Autism Spectrum Disorders Struggling with Sensory Integration Problems. Berns, Joel M., illus. (p. 1551)
Chara, Kathleen A., et al. Allergy Busters: A Story for Children with Autism or Related Spectrum Disorders Struggling with Allergies. Berns, J. M., illus. (p. 46)
Chara, Paul J., jt. auth. see Chara, Kathleen A.
Charaipotra, Sona & Clayton, Dhonielle. Tiny Pretty Things. (p. 1756)
Charbonneau, Joelle. Graduation Day. (p. 705)
—Independent Study. (p. 870)
—Testing. (p. 1723)
Charbonnel, Olivier, illus. see Hooper, Ruth.
Charbonnel-Bojman, Severine. My Picture Book of Animals. (p. 1217)
—What's in My House? (p. 1897)
Charbonnet, Gabrielle, jt. auth. see Patterson, James.
Chardi, Hannah. Oriental Fairy Tales. (p. 1303)
Charest, Emily MacLachlan, jt. auth. see MacLachlan, Patricia.
Charest, Emily MacLachlan & MacLachlan, Patricia. Before You Came. Diaz, David, illus. (p. 159)
Charest, Jocelyne. Loi du Tallon. Fil & Julie, illus. (p. 1045)
Charette, Beverly. Story of Christmas for Children. (p. 1657)
Charette, Geraldine, illus. see Carmichael, Tricia & MacDonald, Allison, eds.
Charette, Geraldine, illus. see MacEachern, Robyn.
Chargualaf, Cathy. Animal Storybook No. 1: Building Self-Esteem Through Animal Stories. (p. 80)
Chargueraud, Joyce, jt. auth. see Aveline, Erick.
Charing, Douglas, jt. auth. see Dorling Kindersley Publishing Staff.
Chariot, F. Home Allowance & Chore Kit. (p. 791)
Chariot Family Staff. Very Special Birthday. (p. 1838)
Chariot Publishing Staff. Christmas Is Coming. (p. 314)
Charismalife, jt. auth. see Blake, Chris.
Charisse, April. Say Hello to Me: A Story about a Little Girl on the Autism Spectrum. (p. 1518)
Chariton, Dan & Weiss, Stacy. Silver Surfer (p. 1577)
Charko, Kasia, illus. see Bates, Sonya Spreen.
Charko, Kasia, illus. see Bates, Sonya.
Charko, Kasia, illus. see Harvey, Sarah N. & Buffam, Leslie.
Charko, Kasia, illus. see Helmer, Marilyn.
Charko, Kasia, illus. see Manuel, Lynn.
Charko, Kasia, illus. see McDowell, Pamela.
Charko, Kasia, illus. see Olsen, Sylvia & Martin, Ron.
Charko, Kasia, jt. auth. see Olsen, Sylvia.
CHARLES, A. M. A. N. & 1st World Publishing. Dad & Me Go to School. (p. 398)
Charles, Akins, illus. see Heiney, Sue P.
Charles, Aman, jt. ed. see Charles, Anya.
Charles, Antoinette. My Favorite Island Games. (p. 1203)
Charles, Anya & Charles, Aman, eds. Voice of Washington Elementary 2004: An Anthology of Poems. (p. 1848)
Charles, Bob. Trip to the Market: Set Of 6. (p. 1787)
—Trip to the Market & una visita al Mercado: 6 English, 6 Spanish Adaptations. (p. 1787)
Charles, Boyd. What God Has Always Wanted. (p. 1884)
Charles, Donald. Adventures in a Bubble. (p. 15)
Charles, Donald, illus. see Hillert, Margaret.
Charles, Emery. Through My Angel's Eyes: The Story of a Kal-a-Tar. (p. 1745)
Charles, Emmanuel. Punch-Out Dragons: Mix & Match! Sturdy & Easy to Make! (p. 1416)
Charles, et al. Problem-Solving Experiences in Mathematics. (p. 1408)
Charles, Faith. Learn to Fulfill the Needs of Yourself: It's an Inside Job. (p. 984)
Charles, Faustin. Selfish Crocodile. Terry, Michael, illus. (p. 1549)
—Selfish Crocodile Book of Colours. Terry, Michael, illus. (p. 1549)
—Selfish Crocodile Book of Sounds. Terry, Michael, illus. (p. 1549)
—Selfish Crocodile Book of Words. Terry, Michael, illus. (p. 1549)
—Selfish Crocodile Counting Book. Terry, Michael, illus. (p. 1549)
Charles, Faustin & Beynon-Davies, Paul. Selfish Crocodile Book of Numbers. Terry, Michael, illus. (p. 1549)
—Selfish Crocodile Jigsaw Book. Terry, Michael, illus. (p. 1549)
Charles, Faustin & Terry, Michael. Selfish Crocodile Book of Nursery Rhymes. Terry, Michael, illus. (p. 1549)
Charles, Jennifer. What If I Were a Snake? (p. 1887)
Charles, Joan, illus. see Noyce, Pendred.
Charles, John, jt. auth. see Mosley, Shelley.
Charles, K. M. Day of Rest & Gladness. (p. 414)
Charles, Kathy. John Belushi Is Dead. (p. 921)
Charles, Kaye Ellen. Macarthur & Martha. (p. 1067)
Charles Kingsley Staff. Madam How & Lady Why. (p. 1069)
Charles L. Wilson. Search Is On: The Wild Adventures of Lester & Dora. (p. 1537)
Charles, Loren I. Dividing Treasures (p. 454)
Charles, Mae. Pecos Meets Bad Bart. (p. 1334)
Charles, Nancy Linehan. Romeo & Juliet or the Old You-Know-I-Really-Love-You-but-My-Father-Really-Hates-You Blues. (p. 1486)
Charles, Nancy Linehan, adapted by. Midsummer Night's Dream or the Night They Missed the Forest for the Trees. (p. 1139)
Charles, Norma. Boxcar Kid. (p. 217)
—Chasing a Star. (p. 294)
—Girl in the Backseat. (p. 678)
Charles, Norma M. Fuzzy Wuzzy. (p. 651)
—Sophie's Friend in Need. (p. 1613)
Charles, Norma M., jt. auth. see Heneghan, James.
Charles, Novalyn. Wagabuibui, the Four Eyed Eagle. Manasau, Amos, illus. (p. 1852)
Charles, Patrick. Ocean Food Chains. (p. 1276)
Charles, R., et al. Problem-Solving Experience in Mathematics. (p. 1408)
—Problem-Solving Experiences in Mathematics: Grade 2. Anderson, Cathy & Apple, Mali, eds. (p. 1408)
—Problem-Solving Experiences in Mathematics. (p. 1408)
—Problem-Solving Experiences in Mathematics, Grade 2 Anderson, Cathy & Apple, Mali, eds. (p. 1408)
Charles, Randall, et al. Problem-Solving Experiences in Mathematics, Grade 1. (p. 1408)
Charles, Randall I. & Prentice Hall Directories Staff. Pre-Algebra (p. 1393)
Charles, Randall I. & Prentice Hall Staff. Prentice Hall Mathematics (p. 1395)
Charles, Randall I., et al. Problem Solving Experiences: Making Sense of Mathematics. (p. 1408)
—Problem-Solving Experiences in Mathematics: Prob Solv Exper. (p. 1408)
Charles, Rie. Hole in My Heart. (p. 788)
—No More Dragons. (p. 1259)
Charles Robinson, illus. see Oscar Wilde.
Charles, Rodney, ed. see Norsic, Donald.
Charles, Rodney, jt. auth. see Myers, Nancy.
Charles Santore. Velveteen Rabbit (Kohl's Edition) Charles Santore, illus. (p. 1835)
Charles Santore & Williams, Margery. Velveteen Rabbit: Or How Toys Become Real. Set (p. 1835)
Charles, Simpson, illus. see Sonnebeyatta, Kemba.
Charles, Valerie. Dancing Light. (p. 403)
Charles, Veronika. Fairy Tales in the Classroom: Teaching Students to Create Stories with Meaning Through Traditional Tales (p. 564)
Charles, Veronika Martenova. Birdman. Galouchko, Annouchka Gravel & Daigle, Stephan, illus. (p. 191)
—Don't Eat That! Parkins, David, illus. (p. 467)
—Don't Enter the House! Parkins, David, illus. (p. 467)
—Don't Forget! Parkins, David, illus. (p. 467)
—Don't Go in There! Parkins, David, illus. (p. 467)
—Don't Go into the Forest! Parkins, David, illus. (p. 467)
—Don't Go near the Water! Parkins, David, illus. (p. 467)
—Don't Open the Door! Parkins, David, illus. (p. 468)
—Don't Talk to Strangers! Parkins, David, illus. (p. 468)
—Don't Touch That! Parkins, David, illus. (p. 469)
—Don't Walk Alone at Night! Parkins, David, illus. (p. 469)
—It's Not about the Apple! Parkins, David, illus. (p. 898)
—It's Not about the Crumbs! Parkins, David, illus. (p. 898)
—It's Not about the Diamonds! Parkins, David, illus. (p. 898)
—It's Not about the Hunter! Parkins, David, illus. (p. 898)
—It's Not about the Pumpkin! Parkins, David, illus. (p. 898)
—It's Not about the Rose! Parkins, David, illus. (p. 898)
Charles, Veronika Martenova & Parkins, David. It's Not about the Ball! (p. 898)
—It's Not about the Beanstalk! (p. 898)
—It's Not about the Straw! (p. 898)
—It's Not about the Tiny Girl! (p. 898)
Charlesbridge, ed. Sir Cumference Classroom Activities. (p. 1580)
Charlesbridge Publishing Staff, jt. auth. see Lane, Kimberly.
Charlesbridge Publishing Staff, jt. auth. see Osofsky, Randy.
Charlesbridge Publishing Staff, jt. auth. see Richardson, R. Sarah.
Charleston, Janice. Our Country's Holidays. (p. 1308)
Charleston, Janice, jt. auth. see Mills, Nathan.
Charlesworth, Eric. Easy Reader Biographies: Cesar Chavez: A Leader for Change. (p. 500)
—Solve & Match Math Practice Pages: 50+ Motivating, Self-Checking Activities That Help Kids Review & Master Essential Math Skills. (p. 1608)
Charlesworth, Kate & Gribbin, John. Cartoon History of Time. (p. 273)
Charlesworth, Liza. Animal Phonics Readers: A Big Collection of Exciting Informational Books That Target & Teach Key Phonics Skills. (p. 79)
—Guided Science Readers Super Set: Animals: A BIG Collection of High-Interest Leveled Books for Guided Reading Groups. (p. 730)
—Human Body: Exciting Nonfiction Books That Build Kids' Vocabularies. Set (p. 825)
—Introduction to Nonfiction Write-On - Wipe-Off Flip Chart: An Interactive Learning Tool That Teaches Young Learners How to Navigate Nonfiction Text Features for Reading Success. (p. 882)
—My 100th Day (p. 1195)
—Nonfiction Alphabet Readers: A Big Collection of Just-Right Informational Books for Teaching the Letters a to Z. (p. 1263)
—Parts-of-Speech Tales: Lessons, Practice Pages & Reproducible Versions of Each Storybook. (p. 1325)
—Punctuation Tales: A Motivating Collection of Super-Funny Storybooks That Help Kids Master the Mechanics of Writing. (p. 1417)
—Seven Magic Hats. Lewis, Stephen, illus. (p. 1554)
—Three Bouncing Balls. Jones, Doug, illus. (p. 1741)
—Two Bunny Slippers. Jones, Doug, illus. (p. 1803)
—Zero Spots. Jones, Doug, illus. (p. 1986)
Charlesworth, Liza, jt. auth. see Fleming, Maria.
Charlesworth, Liza, jt. auth. see Schecter, Deborah.
Charlesworth, Liza & Schecter, Deborah. Big Collection of Mini-Books for Guided Reading: 75 Reproducible Mini-Books for Levels A, B & C That Give Kids a Great Start in Reading. (p. 180)
Charlesworth, Liza & Scholastic Canada Ltd. Staff. Eight Legs Are Great! Snider, Jackie, illus. (p. 507)
Charlesworth, Liza & Scholastic, Inc. Staff. 100 Wacky Wishes. Kennedy, Kelly, illus. (p. 1999)
—Happy Hippos. Mahoney, Daniel J., illus. (p. 746)
—Monkey's Missing Bananas. Sexton, Brenda, illus. (p. 1166)
—Ten Fingers Can! Kennedy, Anne, illus. (p. 1718)
Charlesworth, Liza, ed. Life Cycles: Exciting Nonfiction Books That Build Kids' Vocabularies. (p. 1009)
—Wild Weather: Weather!, Tornadoes!, Blizzards!, Hurricanes!, Floods!, Lightning! (p. 1930)
Charley, Grace. Trouble with Benny Bubble. (p. 1790)
Charleyboy, Lisa, jt. auth. see Leatherdale, Mary Beth.
Charlier, Jean-Michel, jt. auth. see Giraud, Jean.
Charlip, Remy. Arm in Arm: A Collection of Connections, Endless Tales, Reiterations, & Other Echolalia. (p. 99)
—Little Old Big Beard & Big Young Little Beard: A Short & Tall Tale Charlip, Remy & Rettenmund, Tamara, illus. (p. 1032)
—Perfect Day. (p. 1341)
Charlo, Victor A. Good Enough. Dunsmore, Roger, ed. (p. 698)
Charlotte, jt. auth. see Dickinson, Mary.
Charlotte, Evans, jt. auth. see Evans, Charlotte.
Charlotte Hansen, illus. see Hansen, Diane.
Charlotte, J. M., illus. see Andersen, Hans Christian.
Charlton, Andrew F. Ocean Is My Sky. (p. 1276)
Charlton, Dennis. TWIGS & the Bully. Fine, Steve, illus. (p. 1801)
Charlton, Ella Mae. Landi of Terrebonne Bayou. Campbell, Ray, illus. (p. 974)
Charlton, James, jt. auth. see Cook, Sally.
Charlton-Trujillo, e. E. Fat Angie. (p. 576)
Charly, Harry T. Learning Colors Is Fun. (p. 985)
Charman, Andrew. I Wonder Why Dinosaurs Died Out: And Other Questions about Animals in Danger. (p. 849)
—I Wonder Why Leaves Change Color: And Other Questions about Plants. (p. 849)
—I Wonder Why the Dinosaurs Died Out: And Other Questions about Extinct & Endangered Animals. (p. 849)
Charnee, David. P T Mudd in the Land of Lies: A Novel for Children of All Ages. (p. 1316)
Charner, Kathleen, ed. see Claycomb, Patty.
Charner, Kathleen, ed. see Dowell, Ruth I.
Charner, Kathleen, ed. see Gilbert, LaBritta.
Charner, Kathleen, ed. see Miller, Karen.
Charney, Steve. Abracadabra: Magia para Niños: 50 Divertido Trucos Mágicos. Sims, Blanche, illus. (p. 6)
—Amazing Tricks with Everyday Stuff (p. 56)
—Awesome Coin Tricks (p. 121)
—Cool Card Tricks (p. 362)
—Hocus-Jokus: 50 Funny Magic Tricks Complete with Jokes. (p. 787)
—Kids' Guide to Magic Tricks (p. 953)
Charney, Steve, jt. auth. see Barnhart, Norm.
Charney, Steve & Goldbeck, David. ABC's of Fruits & Vegetables & Beyond: Delicious Alphabet Poems Plus Food, Facts & Fun for Everyone. Larson, Maria Burgaleta, illus. (p. 4)
Charnick, Tim, illus. see Christian, Focus & Tnt Ministries Staff.
Charnstrom, Angela. My Teeny Tiny Brother: A Sibling's Experience & Perspective of Life in the Neonatal Intensive Care Unit. (p. 1220)
Charon Aldredge. Kiddie Rhythms the Show. (p. 952)
Charrier, Lisa. Oh My, Oh No! Domergue, Agnes, illus. (p. 1281)
Charriere, Henri. Papillon (p. 1323)
Charron, Ashley. Hello Green Mountains: It's a Soggy Spring. (p. 764)
—Hello Green Mountains: It's a Winter Wonderland. (p. 764)
Charry, Elias & Segal, Abraham. Eternal People. (p. 539)
Charters, Janet. General. Foreman, Michael, illus. (p. 660)
Charters, Robby. Story of Saint Catrick. (p. 1659)
Chartier, Brent, jt. auth. see Jones, Patrick.
Chartier, Doris E. Ben's Desert Journey. (p. 165)
Chartier, Normand, illus. see Albee, Sarah.
Chartier, Normand, illus. see Icenoggle, Jodi.
Chartier, Normand, illus. see Pochocki, Ethel.
Charton, Barbara. Facts on File Dictionary of Marine Science. (p. 561)
Chartrand, Kenneth. Martian's Dream of Christmas. (p. 1097)
Chartrand, Lili. Fabulous World of Mr. Fred Grimard, Gabrielle, illus. (p. 560)

C

—Smelly Story of Hazel the Weasel. Eid, Jean-Paul, illus. (p. 1593)
—Taming Horrible Harry. Ouriou, Susan, tr. from FRE. (p. 1704)
Charvet, Lilian. Princess Dilly & the Kingdom of Pily: Book 1. (p. 1403)
Chasan, Emily & Gray, Kevan. Tufts University College Prowler off the Record. (p. 1796)
Chase, Andra, illus. see Talley, Linda.
Chase, Andra, jt. auth. see Rebein, Alyssa Chase.
Chase, Anita, et al. Tundra Adventures. Chase, Anita et al, illus. (p. 1796)
Chase, Arline, ed. see Buckland, M. Barbara.
Chase, Dakota. Changing Jamie. (p. 290)
Chase, Diana. Angel in a Gum Tree. (p. 73)
—Daisy Street. Bradley, Vanessa, illus. (p. 400)
—Light House Kids. (p. 1015)
—No More Borders for Josef. (p. 1259)
Chase, et al. Angel in a Gum Tree. (p. 73)
Chase, Frank, Jr. False Roads to Manhoon. (p. 567)
Chase, Gloria. God Is Love, Can't You See? (p. 689)
—Going to Hell from the Church? (p. 693)
—No One: A Great & Terrible God. (p. 1259)
—Open Heaven: Receiving the Revelation of the 23rd Psalm. (p. 1299)
—Pray & Obey. (p. 1393)
—Wake up Sleeping Giant. (p. 1853)
—What in This World Do I Have to Live For? (p. 1888)
Chase, Jeffrey Scott. Andy the Alien. (p. 73)
—Andy the Alien Visits the Outer Planets. (p. 73)
Chase, John, ed. see Crawford, Margaret & Kaliski, John.
Chase, Kit. Lulu's Party. Chase, Kit, illus. (p. 1065)
—Oliver's Tree. Chase, Kit, illus. (p. 1286)
Chase, L. P. Elliot Stone & the Mystery of the Summer Vacation Sea Monster. DiRocco, Carl, illus. (p. 514)
—Elliott Stone & the Mystery of the Backyard Treasure. (p. 514)
—Today Is Tuesday. (p. 1760)
Chase, Linda, illus. see Griner, Jack.
Chase, Linda, jt. auth. see Brozovich, Richard.
Chase, Luke. First Verse: A Collection of Poetry. (p. 597)
Chase, Mary. Loretta Mason Potts. (p. 1053)
—Loretta Mason Potts. Berson, Harold, illus. (p. 1053)
Chase, Max. Crash Landing. (p. 376)
—Lethal Combat. (p. 994)
—Space Wars! (p. 1620)
—STAR FIGHTERS 1: Alien Attack. (p. 1640)
—STAR FIGHTERS 2: Deadly Mission. (p. 1640)
Chase, Max, jt. auth. see Blake, Max.
Chase, Michelle B., illus. see Shea, Christine.
Chase, Odette. This Child's War: A World War II Memoir. (p. 1735)
Chase, Paula. So Not the Drama. (p. 1602)
Chase, Paula Hyman. Flipping the Script. (p. 605)
Chase, Randal S. Making Precious Things Plain: A Book of Mormon Study Guide (p. 1082)
Chase, Rhoda, illus. see Burgess, Thornton W.
Chase, Richard. Grandfather Tales: American-English Folk Tales. (p. 707)
—Jack Tales: Folk Tales from the Southern Appalachians. (p. 903)
Chase, Scott J. What Should I Do When I Grow Up? (p. 1893)
Chase, Sherry. Matthew Loves to Play Nintendo Game Cube. (p. 1109)
Chase, Tanor R., illus. see Shea, Christine.
Chasemore, Richard, jt. auth. see Harvey, Ian.
Chasse, Betsy & Captured Light Distribution, creators. Little Book of Bleeps. (p. 1025)
Chast, Roz. Around the Clock. Chast, Roz, illus. (p. 100)
—Marco Goes to School. Chast, Roz, illus. (p. 1092)
—Too Busy Marco. Chast, Roz, illus. (p. 1766)
Chast, Roz, illus. see Duffy, Chris, ed.
Chast, Roz, jt. auth. see Martin, Steve.
Chastain, Denise. Hanni & David. (p. 743)
Chastain, Donna, ed. see DeLong, Ron.
Chastain, Grant, ed. see O'Reilly, Sean Patrick.
Chastain, Madye Lee, illus. see Courlander, Harold & Herzog, George.
Chastain, Sandra. Kaseybelle: The Tiniest Fairy in the Kingdom Chadwick, Cindy, illus. (p. 944)
Chastain, Zachary. Cocaine: The Rush to Destruction. (p. 337)
—Cocaine: The Rush to Destruction. Henningfield, Jack E., ed. (p. 337)
—Cornmeal & Cider: Food & Drink in the 1800s. (p. 367)
—From the Parlor to the Altar: Romance & Marriage in The 1800s. (p. 644)
—Home Sweet Home: Around the House in the 1800s. (p. 793)
—Passing the Time: Entertainment in The 1800s. (p. 1326)
—Rooting for the Home Team: Sports in The 1800s. (p. 1488)
—Scandals & Glory: Politics in The 1800s. (p. 1519)
—Scandals & Glory: Politics in the 1800s. (p. 1519)
—Sick All the Time: Kids with Chronic Illness. (p. 1572)
—Statistical Timeline & Overview of Gay Life. (p. 1644)
—Sweat of Their Brow: Occupations in the 1800s. (p. 1689)
—Tobacco: Through the Smokescreen. (p. 1760)
—Tobacco: Through the Smoke Screen. Henningfield, Jack E., ed. (p. 1760)
Chastain, Zachary & Flath, Camden. Sick All the Time: Kids with Chronic Illness. (p. 1572)
Chastain, Zachary & Livingston, Phyllis. Youth with Asperger's Syndrome: A Different Drummer. (p. 1982)
Chatel, Kim. Burgher & the Woebegone. Bell, Samantha, illus. (p. 243)
—Clip-Clop, Tippity-Tap French Vocabulary on the Farm. Bullock, Kathleen, illus. (p. 333)
—Horse Camp. (p. 799)
—Talent for Quiet. Chatel, Kim, photos by. (p. 1701)
Chatelain, Eva, illus. see Meyerhoff, Jenny.
Chatelain, Jeremy. May the Stars Drip Down. McClure, Nikki, illus. (p. 1112)
Chater, Mack, illus. see Collins, Terry.
Chater, Mack, illus. see Yomtov, Nel.
Chaterjee. With Our Own Minds: Women Organizing & Developing on Indian Plantation. (p. 1942)
Chatfield, Carl & Johnson, Timothy. Microsoft(r) Office Project 2007. (p. 1136)
Chatham, Dennis J., illus. see Hatch Jr., B. J. Butch.
Chatlien, Michael. Donovan McNabb. (p. 466)
Chatlien, Ruth Hull. Modern American Indian Chiefs. (p. 1158)
Chatlien, Ruth Hull & Cohon, Rhody. Modern American Indian Chiefs. (p. 1158)
Chatlos, Timothy J. Because Daddy's Coming Home Today. Knight, Michael T., illus. (p. 155)
Chatman, Dudley D. I Brush My Teeth & I Smile (p. 834)
Chatman, Michael. Michael the Great. (p. 1135)
Chatten, Vicky. Bonding. (p. 208)
Chatterjee, Debjani & D'Arcy, Brian. Let's Celebrate! Festival Poems from Around the World. Adl, Shirin, illus. (p. 995)
Chatterjee, Debjani & D'Arcy, Brian, eds. Let's Celebrate! Festival Poems from Around the World. Adl, Shirin, illus. (p. 995)
Chatterjee, Debjani & Quarto Generic Staff. Let's Play! Poems about Sports & Games from Around the World. D'Arcy, Brian, ed. (p. 999)
Chatterjee, Sudipto. Colonial Staged: Theatre in Colonial Calcutta. (p. 341)
Chatterjee, Susnata, illus. see Talwar, Ankoor & Talwar, Abhinav.
Chatterji, Somnath, illus. see Denise, Carolyn.
Chatterley, Cedric N., photos by see Lau, Barbara & Nesbitt, Kris.
Chatterley, Cedric N., photos by. Grace: For All the Children. (p. 704)
Chatterton, Chris, illus. see Marshall, Linda Elovitz.
Chatterton, Martin. Brain Finds a Leg (p. 221)
—Brain Finds a Leg. (p. 221)
—Brain Full of Holes (p. 221)
—Brain Full of Holes. (p. 221)
—Can Dogs Fly? Fido's Book of Pop-up Transportation Surprises. (p. 258)
—Chew Bee or Not Chew Bee. Rogers, Gregory, illus. (p. 299)
—Where Is Santa's Suit? (p. 1909)
Chatterton, Martin, illus. see Beal, George.
Chatterton, Martin, illus. see Bradman, Tony.
Chatterton, Martin, illus. see Clarke, Jane.
Chatterton, Martin, illus. see Gibbs, Susie.
Chatterton, Martin, illus. see Griffiths, Mark.
Chatterton, Martin, illus. see Kingfisher Editors.
Chatterton, Martin, illus. see Mandrake, Tiffany.
Chatterton, Martin, jt. auth. see Bradman, Tony.
Chatterton, Martin & Bradman, Tony. Surprise Party. Chatterton, Martin, illus. (p. 1686)
Chattin, A. K. Dust Bunnies (p. 490)
Chatton, Julie. Trains: Safe & Sound. (p. 1777)
Chatzikonstantinou, Danny, illus. see Harbo, Christopher L.
Chatzikonstantinou, Danny, illus. see Harbo, Christopher.
Chatzikonstantinou, Danny, illus. see Tarpley, Todd.
Chatzky, Jean. Not Your Parents' Money Book: Making, Saving, & Spending Your Own Money. Jenkins, Ward & Haya, Erwin, illus. (p. 1267)
Chau, Alina, illus. see Amara, Phil.
Chau, Alina, illus. see Chin, Oliver.
Chau, Alina, illus. see Ling, Nancy Tupper.
Chau, Ming, photos by see Cheung, Shu Pui, et al.
Chaucer, Geoffrey. Canterbury Tales. (p. 262)
—Canterbury Tales - Literary Touchstone Edition. (p. 262)
—Pardoner's Tale. (p. 1324)
Chaud, Benjamin. Bear's Sea Escape. (p. 152)
—Bear's Song. (p. 152)
—Bear's Surprise. (p. 152)
—Farewell Floppy. (p. 573)
Chaud, Benjamin, illus. see Badescu, Ramona & Bedrick, Claudia Z.
Chaud, Benjamin, illus. see Badescu, Ramona.
Chaud, Benjamin, illus. see Cali, Davide.
Chaud, Benjamin, jt. auth. see Cali, Davide.
Chaud, Benjamin & Cali, Davide. I Didn't Do My Homework Because Doodle Book of Excuses. (p. 837)
Chaudet, Annette. Nose Book. (p. 1266)
Chaudhary, Aman, illus. see Hyde, Margaret E.
Chaudhary, Aman, illus. see Hyde, Margaret.
Chaudhary, Shahida. Sammy's Midnight Hunger. Mikle, Toby, illus. (p. 1508)
Chaudhry, Saida. Call to Prophethood. (p. 254)
Chauffrey, Celia, illus. see Don, Lari, et al.
Chauffrey, Celia, jt. auth. see Briere-Haquet, Alice.
Chauncey, G., illus. see Beall, Pamela Conn, et al.
Chausse, Sylvie. Gatos de Maria Tatin. Crozat, Francois, illus. (p. 658)
Chauvin, Belinda N. Megan... A Child of God I Am. Sun Star, Elan & Snyder, Diana, illus. (p. 1124)
Chauvin, D., illus. see Rideau, J. & Asso, B.
Chauvin, Daniel, illus. see Asso, Bernard & Rideau, Joel.
Chava, illus. see Klempner, Rebecca.
Chavarri, Elisa, illus. see Axelrod-Contrada, Joan.
Chavarri, Elisa, illus. see Codell, Esmé Raji.
Chavarri, Elisa, illus. see Cosson, J.
Chavarri, Elisa, illus. see Ingalls, Ann.
Chavarri, Elisa, illus. see Kesselring, Susan.
Chavarri, Elisa, illus. see Lewis, Anne Margaret.
Chavarri, Elisa, illus. see Malaspina, Ann.
Chaveevah, Banks Ferguson, illus. see Hickey, Joshalyn M.
Chavers, Jim. Sharks, Sex & Sun: '60's Lifeguard Stories. (p. 1563)
Chaves, Guido. Capuli. (p. 265)
Chaves, Guido, illus. see Gonzalez, Ana Carlota.
Chaves, Guido, illus. see Iturralde, Edna.
Chavez, Denise & Feyder, Linda, eds. Shattering the Myth: Plays by Hispanic Women. (p. 1563)
Chavez, Emilio. Thurgood Marshall: Supreme Court Justice. (p. 1746)
Chavez, Joe. Benny the Bunny & Jesus. (p. 165)
Chavez, Orlando. Dog for Tommy. (p. 461)
Chavez, R. J. Bob. Bye Bye Butterfly: A True-Life Children's Butterfly Adventure. (p. 249)
Chavez, Ricardo & Aguileta, Gabriela. Nina Que Tenia el Mar Adentro. Lopez, Claudia Navarro, illus. (p. 1256)
Chaviano, Daina. Pais de Dragones. (p. 1318)
Chawarska, Katarzyna, et al, eds. Autism Spectrum Disorders in Infants & Toddlers: Diagnosis, Assessment, & Treatment. (p. 117)
Chawla, Neena, illus. see Doudna, Kelly.
Chawla, Neena, illus. see Hanson, Anders.
Chawla, Neena, illus. see Kompelien, Tracy.
Chawla, Neena, illus. see Salzmann, Mary Elizabeth.
Chawla, Neena, illus. see Scheunemann, Pam.
Chayamach, Suguro. Vergil. (p. 1836)
Chayamachi, Suguro. Devil May Cry Chayamachi, Suguro, illus. (p. 432)
Chayce, Jorden. How High Is Up? (p. 809)
Chayil, Eishes & Brown, Judy. Hush. (p. 830)
Chayka, Doug, illus. see Crowe, Carole.
Chayka, Doug, illus. see Greene, Jacqueline Dembar.
Chayka, Doug, illus. see Jordan, Shirley.
Chayka, Doug, illus. see Malaspina, Ann.
Chayka, Doug, illus. see Williams, Karen Lynn & Mohammad, Khadra.
Chayka, Douglas, illus. see Greene, Jacqueline Dembar.
Chaykin, Howard, illus. see Brubaker, Ed & Tieri, Frank.
Chazen, Lois. Loving Ruby. (p. 1061)
Chbosky, Stephen. Perks of Being a Wallflower. (p. 1343)
Chbosky, Stephen & Perez-Sauquillo, Vanesa. Las Ventajas de Ser Invisible. (p. 977)
Che, Akwanwi Mfonyam. Baby King: Born in a Stable. (p. 126)
Che, Dana. Choice That Changed Her Life: ne Choice Can Change Everything! (p. 309)
Che, Jonnie. Drum & Bell with the Three Chinese Brothers. (p. 487)
Cheadle, Don & Prendergast, John. Not on Our Watch: The Mission to End Genocide in Darfur & Beyond. (p. 1267)
Cheaney, J. B. My Friend the Enemy. (p. 1209)
—Somebody on This Bus Is Going to Be Famous. (p. 1609)
Cheaney, J. B. & Cheaney, Janie. Middle of Somewhere. (p. 1137)
Cheaney, Janie, jt. auth. see Cheaney, J. B.
Cheaney, Janie B. Wordsmith Craftsman Grd 10 + (p. 1952)
—Wordsmith Grd 7-9. (p. 1952)
Cheatham, Mark. Aliens! (p. 41)
—Life of a Colonial Soldier. (p. 1011)
—Mummies. (p. 1190)
—Werewolves! (p. 1875)
—Witches! (p. 1941)
Checchetto, Marco, jt. illus. see De La Torre, Roberto.
Check, Laura. Almost-Instant Scrapbooks. Day, Betsy, tr. (p. 48)
—Create Your Own Candles: 30 Easy-To-Make Designs. (p. 378)
Checkmark Books, creator. Communication Skills. (p. 349)
—Organization Skills. (p. 1303)
—Professional Ethics & Etiquette. (p. 1409)
—Research & Information Management. (p. 1462)
Chedekel, Evelyn. Fake Doughnut. Le, Loanne, illus. (p. 565)
Chedru, Delphine. Spot It! Find the Hidden Creatures. (p. 1633)
—Spot It Again! Find More Hidden Creatures. (p. 1633)
Chee, illus. see Golden, Christopher, et al.
Chee, illus. see Nelson, Michael Alan.
Chee, Cheng-Khee, illus. see Esbensen, Barbara Juster.
Chee, Cheng-Khee, illus. see Johnston, Tony.
Cheehy, Debra/Ilene. I Like Dogs. Hilliard, Carol, illus. (p. 841)
Cheek, Diane. Wiggly Workers. (p. 1928)
Cheek, Judith, jt. auth. see Chapman, Noel.
Cheek, Roland. Gunnar's Mine. (p. 732)
—Lincoln County Crucible. (p. 1018)
Cheek, Stephen. Catfish Cowboy & Mr. Turtle. (p. 280)
Cheel, Richard. Global Warming Alert! (p. 685)
Cheeseboro, Tyrese. Why Did Ronald Break the Rules? Rules at Home & Rules at School! (p. 1923)
Cheetham, Craig. American Cars Before 1950. (p. 60)
—American Cars of The 1950s. (p. 60)
Cheetham, Natasha. Princess of the Sky. (p. 1405)
Cheetham, Stephen. Off to the Park! (p. 1279)
Cheever, Karen J. Tuck-In: (a Child's Event) (p. 1795)
Chef Jeff. Do Cows Eat Cake? (p. 456)
Cheha, Jacob. Today's Okay. Pagano, Mark, illus. (p. 1761)
Chehoski, Robert, jt. auth. see Jaworski, Sabrina K.
Chehoski, Robert, ed. Critical Perspectives on Climate Disruption. (p. 383)
Chekel, Martin, creator. English Linguistics Teacher's Training ELD Program Kit byTalking Page (p. 530)
Chekhov, Anton. Anniversary. Landes, William-Alan, ed. (p. 87)
—Bear: An Extravaganza in One Act. Landes, William-Alan, ed. (p. 150)
—Cherry Orchard: A Comedy in Four Acts. (p. 298)
—Sea Gull. (p. 1534)
—Sea-Gull. Landes, William-Alan, ed. (p. 1534)
—Three Sisters: Tri Sewiry. (p. 1744)
—Uncle Vanya. (p. 1812)
Chekki, F. A. Netherworld Dreams: Little Dante's Journey to the Underworld. (p. 1242)
Chelkowski, Lisa. Sisters' Christmas Tale. (p. 1581)
Chell, Jenny, jt. auth. see Hildebrandt, Laurel.
Chellew, Robert E. Journeyman Electrician's Exam Workbook Based on the 2005 NEC: Text. (p. 929)
—Journeyman Electrician's Exam Workbook Based on the 2005 NEC: Answer Key. (p. 929)
Chellis, Marie. Hayburner (p. 755)
Chelsea House Publishing Staff. Journey into Civilization Set. (p. 928)
Chelsey, Emily, illus. see Donlon, Bridget.
Chemerka, William. Davy Crockett from a to Z (p. 411)
Chemerka, William R. Alamo from A to Z (p. 33)
—Juan Seguin. Collins, Don, illus. (p. 930)
Chemerka, William R. & Collins, Don. Gregorio Esparza: Alamo Defender. Collins, Don, illus. (p. 723)
Chemistry, jt. auth. see Lipscomb, William N.
Chen, Bill. Musical. Sun, Jun, illus. (p. 1194)
Chen, Chih Yuan, illus. see Chou, Yih-Fen.
Chen, Chih-Yuan. Artie & Julie. Chen, Zhiyuan & Chen, Chih-Yuan, illus. (p. 104)
—Best Christmas Ever. (p. 168)
—En Camino a Comprar Huevos. Chen, Chih-Yuan, illus. (p. 522)
—Featherless Chicken. Chen, Chih-Yuan, illus. (p. 579)
—Guji Guji. Chen, Chih-Yuan, illus. (p. 731)
Chen, D. M. & Sun, Michelle. Tie a Wish with Bracelets: Easy & Fun Chinese Knotting. (p. 1747)
Chen, Da. China's Son: Growing up in the Cultural Revolution. (p. 307)
—Sword. (p. 1692)
Chen, E. C. Bad Alphabet. (p. 131)
Chen, Edward, et al. PC Mod Projects: Cool It! Light It! Morph It! (p. 1331)
Chen, Grace, illus. see Rue, Nancy N.
Chen, Jiang Hong, illus. see Morgenstern, Susie Hoch & Morgenstern, Susie.
Chen, John. Helping at the Book Sale: Represent & Solve Subtraction Problems. (p. 766)
Chen, Ju-Hong. Jade Stone: A Chinese Folktale (p. 905)
Chen, Ju-Hong, illus. see Zimmerman, Andrea.
Chen, Julia. On the Way Home. Stewart, Fion, illus. (p. 1291)
Chen, Justina. Blind Spot for Boys. (p. 199)
—Girl Overboard. (p. 678)
—Nothing but the Truth (And a Few White Lies) (p. 1268)
—Return to Me. (p. 1465)
Chen, Justina, jt. auth. see Headley, Justina Chen.
Chen, Kuo Kan, illus. see Frith, Alex.
Chen, Kuo Kang, illus. see Clarke, Catriona.
Chen, Kuo Kang, illus. see Cook, Janet.
Chen, Kuo Kang, illus. see Needham, Kate.
Chen, Kuo Kang, illus. see Oxlade, Chris & Stockley, Corinne.
Chen, Kuo Kang, illus. see Stockley, Corinne, et al.
Chen, Kuo Kang, illus. see Stockley, Corinne.
Chen, Kuo Kang, illus. see Turnbull, Stephanie.
Chen, Kuo Kang, illus. see Unwin, Mike & Woodward, Kate.
Chen, Kuo Kang, tr. see Stockley, Corinne, et al.
Chen, Michael. Expressions of a Son. (p. 555)
Chen, Michael Yoon, ed. see Chan, Hingman.
Chen, Nina. Santa's New Idea. (p. 1513)
Chen, Pauline W. Peiling & the Chicken-Fried Christmas. (p. 1335)
Chen, Sam. Real Meal Table Fable. Peschel, Georgia, illus. (p. 1448)
Chen, Sean, et al. Shadowland: Street Heroes. (p. 1558)
Chen, Shan-Shan & Goodman, Heidi. Mei-Mei's Lucky Birthday Noodles: A Loving Story of Adoption, Chinese Culture & a Special Birthday Treat. (p. 1124)
Chen, W., ed. see Yadav, S. S.
Chen, Wah, jt. auth. see Shum, Chi Wan.
Chen, Wei Dong. Etched in Blood. Long Liang, Xiao, illus. (p. 539)
—Expulsion of Sun Wu Kong. Peng, Chao, illus. (p. 555)
—Family Plot. Long Liang, Xiao, illus. (p. 568)
—Fight to the Death. Peng, Chao, illus. (p. 585)
—Heroes & Chaos Liang, Xiao Long, illus. (p. 772)
—Heroes & Chaos. Long Liang, Xiao, illus. (p. 772)
—Lost Children. Peng, Chao, illus. (p. 1055)
—Monkey King: Three Trials. Peng, Chao, illus. (p. 1165)
—Monkey King: The Sacred Tree. Peng, Chao, illus. (p. 1165)
—Monkey King: The Bane of Heaven. Peng, Chao, illus. (p. 1165)
—Monkey King: Journey to the West. Peng, Chao, illus. (p. 1165)
—Monkey King: Enemies & a New Friend. Peng, Chao, illus. (p. 1165)
—Monkey King: Birth of the Stone Monkey. Peng, Chao, illus. (p. 1165)
—Realm of the Infant King. Peng, Chao, illus. (p. 1450)
—Revenge & Betrayal. Long Liang, Xiao, illus. (p. 1465)
—Stolen Kingdom. Peng, Chao, illus. (p. 1652)
—To Pledge Allegiance. Long Liang, Xiao, illus. (p. 1759)
—Treasures of the Mountain Kings. Peng, Chao, illus. (p. 1782)
Chen, Wei Dong & Liang, Xiao Long. Blood & Honor (p. 200)
—Brotherhood Restored Liang, Xiao Long, illus. (p. 231)
—Etched in Blood (p. 539)
—Family Plot (p. 568)
—Revenge & Betrayal (p. 1465)
—Three Kingdoms Liang, Xiao Long, illus. (p. 1742)
—To Pledge Allegiance (p. 1759)
Chen, Yong. Gift. (p. 674)
Chen, Yong, illus. see Coste, Marion.
Chen, Zhiyuan, illus. see Chen, Chih-Yuan.
Chen, Zhiyuan, illus. see Chou, Yih-Fen.
Chenault, Jean Elkins. What Star? (p. 1893)
Chenette, Roseanne V. Shellaby Willowbee. (p. 1564)
Cheney, Cora. Doll of Lilac Valley. Cassidy, Nancy White, illus. (p. 463)
Cheney, Glenn. Shot Down (p. 1569)
—Trapped (p. 1779)
Cheney, Lynne. A Is for Abigail: An Almanac of Amazing American Women. Glasser, Robin Preiss, illus. (p. 1)
—Our 50 States: A Family Adventure Across America. Glasser, Robin Preiss, illus. (p. 1307)
—Time for Freedom: What Happened When in America. (p. 1751)
—We the People: The Story of Our Constitution. Harlin, Greg, illus. (p. 1868)
—When Washington Crossed the Delaware: A Wintertime Story for Young Patriots. Fiore, Peter M., illus. (p. 1905)
Cheney, Lynne & Fiore, Peter. When Washington Crossed the Delaware: A Wintertime Story for Young Patriots. (p. 1905)
Cheney, Roland. Racing Angelettes. (p. 1432)
Cheng, Ainsley. Being Just Me, Myself, & I! (p. 161)
Cheng & Tsui, ed. see Miocevich, Grant.
Cheng, Andrea. Bear Makers. (p. 151)
—Brushing Mom's Hair. Wong, Nicole, illus. (p. 233)
—Eclipse. (p. 502)
—Etched in Clay: The Life of Dave, Enslaved Potter & Poet. Cheng, Andrea, illus. (p. 539)
—Goldfish & Chrysanthemums. Chang, Michelle, illus. (p. 695)
—Grandfather Counts. (p. 707)

—Honeysuckle House. (p. 795)
—Lace Dowry. (p. 970)
—Only One Year Wong, Nicole, illus. (p. 1298)
—Shanghai Messenger Young, Ed, illus. (p. 1559)
—When the Bees Fly Home McFadden, Joline, illus. (p. 1904)
—Where Do You Stay? (p. 1907)
—Year of the Baby. Barton, Patrice, illus. (p. 1969)
—Year of the Book. Halpin, Abigail, illus. (p. 1969)
—Year of the Fortune Cookie. Barton, Patrice, illus. (p. 1969)
—Year of the Three Sisters. Barton, Patrice, illus. (p. 1969)
Cheng, Charlotte, illus. see Butenas, Jennifer.
Cheng, Christopher. Python. Jackson, Mark, illus. (p. 1421)
—Sounds Spooky. Davis, Sarah, illus. (p. 1615)
Cheng, Christopher, et al. Australia's Greatest Inventions & Innovations. (p. 116)
Cheng, Haw. Sixth Grade Was a Nightmare, & Seventh Is Worse: A 12-Year Old Speaks Out. Thurman, Joann M., ed. (p. 1583)
Cheng, Hong, jt. auth. see Wan, Guofang.
Cheng, Puay Koon, illus. see Humphreys, Neil.
Cheng'en, Wu. Journey to the West. Chiang, Shirley, illus. (p. 929)
Cheng-Liang, Zhu, illus. see Li-Qiong, Yu.
Chenn, Eric. Willie the Wheel. Chenn, Eric, illus. (p. 1934)
Chenous, Brad. Stories from Farmer Ready's. (p. 1654)
Cheong, Colin. China. (p. 306)
Cheongbi, Studio. Bill Gates Story: The Computer Genius Who Changed the World. (p. 186)
Cheong-Lum, Roseline Ng & NgCheong-Lum, Roseline. Maldives. (p. 1083)
Chepokas, Rebecca & Stanchfield, Ronald M. Good-bye, Mitch: Sorrow, Grief, Inspiration (p. 697)
Cheramie, Jessica Dragon. Secrets of the Truth: Meridienne Drake Series: Book 1. (p. 1546)
Cheray, Toni. My Friend Zac. (p. 1209)
Cherfas, Jeremy. Genoma Humano. Yanez, Cecilia, tr. (p. 661)
Cheri, Rae & McKinney, John. Hiking. (p. 779)
Cherian, Raichel, jt. auth. see Cherian, Raichel.
Cherian, Raichel & Cherian, Raichel. Knock Knock... ... Is My Father Here? The Pursuit of a Baby Sheep. Joy, Elvis, illus. (p. 965)
Cherician, David, tr. see Wilde, Oscar.
Cherie, Rachel. Turning of the Tides: Daughters of the High Seas (Book 2) (p. 1798)
Cherif, Jennifer, illus. see Jesse, Mary.
Chering, Don. Acorn That Doubted. (p. 9)
Cherna. Patch's Country Quilt. Cherna, illus. (p. 1328)
Chernesky, Felicia, ed. see Pfundstein, Valerie.
Chernesky, Felicia Sanzari. Cheers for a Dozen Ears: A Summer Crop of Counting. Swan, Susan, illus. (p. 296)
—Pick a Circle, Gather Squares: A Fall Harvest of Shapes. Swan, Susan, illus. (p. 1354)
—Sugar White Snow & Evergreens: A Winter Wonderland of Color. Swan, Susan, illus. (p. 1673)
—Sun above & Blooms Below: A Springtime of Opposites. Swan, Susan, illus. (p. 1675)
Chernett, Dan, illus. see Wooding, Chris.
Chernichaw, Ian, illus. see Albee, Sarah & Hood, Susan.
Chernichaw, Ian, illus. see Albee, Sarah.
Chernichaw, Ian, illus. see Spelvin, Justin.
Chernoff, Maxine. Evolution of the Bridge: Selected Prose Poems. (p. 547)
Chernyak, Inna, illus. see Milhander, Laura Aron.
Cherobin. Zoomy Boomy & the Moon: Zoomy & the Moon Learn the Strength of Love. (p. 1989)
—Zoomy Boomy, the Moon, & the Earth: All in its Season, & Seasons Change. (p. 1989)
Cherobin, jt. auth. see Cherobin.
Cherobin & Cherobin. Zoomy Boomy Lights the Night: Zoomy Conquers Shyness. (p. 1989)
Cherrington, Janelle. Native American Baskets. (p. 1234)
—Native American Baskets. (p. 1234)
—Where Animals Live (p. 1906)
—Who Needs Teeth? (p. 1917)
Cherrington, Janelle & Capstone Press Staff. Native American Baskets (p. 1234)
—Where Animals Live (p. 1906)
Cherrington, Joan. Color Theory for the Young Artist. (p. 343)
Cherrington, Sharnett Felicia. Bitter Sweet. (p. 194)
Cherry, Alison. For Real. (p. 616)
—Red. (p. 1453)
Cherry, Bob. Little Rains. (p. 1034)
Cherry, Gale, illus. see Sues, Grandma.
Cherry, Jason. Sassafras in the Window (p. 1515)
Cherry Lake Publishing Staff. Information Explorer (p. 874)
Cherry Lake Publishing Staff, compiled by. Citizens & their Governments. (p. 323)
—Cool Science Centers. (p. 364)
—Heathy for Life. (p. 760)
—Power Up! (p. 1390)
—Road to Recovery. (p. 1477)
Cherry, Lynne. How Groundhog's Garden Grew. Cherry, Lynne, illus. (p. 809)
—How We Know What We Know about Our Changing Climate: Scientists & Kids Explore Global Warming. Braasch, Gary, photos by. (p. 823)
—River Ran Wild. (p. 1476)
Cherry, Lynne, illus. see Ryder, Joanne.
Cherry, Lynne & Braasch, Gary. How We Know What We Know about Our Changing Climate: Scientists & Kids Explore Global Warming. Braasch, Gary, illus. (p. 823)
Cherry, Michael D. Addventures of Plusmen: Plusmen Meets the Permutation. (p. 12)
Cherry, Winky. My First Doll Book: Hand Sewing. (p. 1206)
—My First Embroidery Book: A Name Sampler. (p. 1206)
—My First Machine Sewing Book: Straight Stitching. (p. 1207)
—My First Quilt Book: Machine Sewing. (p. 1207)
—My First Sewing Book: Hand Sewing. (p. 1207)
Cherryh, C. J. Collected Short Fiction of C. J. Cherryh. (p. 339)
—Downbelow Station. (p. 474)
Cherrywell, Steph. Pepper Penwell & the Land Creature of Monster Lake. (p. 1340)
Cherubini. Pinocchio in Africa. (p. 1361)
Cherubini, E. Pinocchio in Africa. (p. 1361)
Cheryl A. Page; Illustrations By Kimberl. Grammie, What's That? (p. 706)
Cheryl H. Hahn, illus. see Greene, Brenda.
Chesebro, Doreen & Badasch, Shirley. Student Activity Guide for Health Science Fundamentals. (p. 1669)
Cheshire, Gerald. Living World. (p. 1042)
Cheshire, Gerard. Day & Night in Swamp. Camm, Martin, illus. (p. 412)
—Electricity & Magnetism. (p. 509)
—Forces & Motion. (p. 617)
—Jellyfish - Scary Creatures. (p. 912)
—Light & Color. (p. 1014)
—Lizards. (p. 1042)
—Lizards - Scary Creatures. (p. 1043)
—Scary Creatures of the River. Francis, John et al, illus. (p. 1520)
—Scary Creatures of the Soil. Antram, David et al, illus. (p. 1520)
—Solar System & Beyond. (p. 1607)
—Sound & Vibration. (p. 1615)
Cheshire, Gerard & Tango Books Staff. Life in a Watermill. Hutchinson, Tim, illus. (p. 1010)
Cheshire, Giff. Night Riders: A Western Duo. (p. 1254)
Cheshire, Marc. Eloise Dresses Up: 50 Reusable Stickers! Hahner, Chris, illus. (p. 516)
—Merry Christmas, Eloise! Bracken, Carolyn, illus. (p. 1128)
Cheshire, Simon. Boy with Wings. Coburn, Dylan, illus. (p. 220)
—Frankenstein Inheritance. (p. 629)
—Treasure of Dead Man's Lane & Other Case Files: Saxby Smart, Private Detective: Book 2. Alley, R. W., illus. (p. 1782)
Chesire, Gerald. Living Things. Baker, Janet, illus. (p. 1042)
—Living World. Baker, Janet et al, illus. (p. 1042)
—People & Places. Antram, David, illus. (p. 1339)
—People & Places. Antram, David et al, illus. (p. 1339)
Chesne, Sabrina. Lillie's Treasures/Los tesoros de Lili. Capasso, Diana, tr. (p. 1017)
Chesney, Marion, see Beaton, M. C., pseud.
Chess, Victoria, illus. see Bottner, Barbara.
Chess, Victoria, illus. see Hogg, Gary.
Chess, Victoria, illus. see Sierra, Judy.
Chess, Victoria, illus. see Van Laan, Nancy.
Chess, Victoria, illus. see Wise, William.
Chessa, Francesca. Button Muddle. Chessa, Francesca, illus. (p. 248)
—Holly's Red Boots. Chessa, Francesca, illus. (p. 789)
Chessa, Francesca, illus. see Brown, Alan James.
Chessa, Francesca, illus. see Piumini, Roberto.
Chessa, Francesca, illus. see Shields, Gillian.
Chessa, Francesca, illus. see Shipton, Jonathan.
Chessen, Betsey, jt. auth. see Canizares, Susan.
Chessen, Sherri. Gorp's Dream: A Tale of Diversity, Tolerance, & Love in Pumpernickel Park. Masel, Christy, illus. (p. 703)
—Gorp's Secret: An Empowering Tale in Pumpernickel Park. Bronson, Linda, illus. (p. 703)
Chesshir, Judi. My Finny Fin Fin. (p. 1203)
Chester, H. C., jt. auth. see Oliver, Lauren.
Chester, Laura. Hiding Glory. Lippincott, Gary A., illus. (p. 777)
—Marvel the Marvelous. Lippincott, Gary A., illus. (p. 1099)
Chester, Laura & DeMari, Donna. Heartbeat for Horses. (p. 760)
Chester, Malcolm. Elysia: The World in Children's Dreams. (p. 517)
Chester, Michael & Kramer, Saunders B. Discoverer: The Story of A Satellite. (p. 448)
Chesterfield, Jayson. Inuit. (p. 883)
Chesterfield, Sadie. Let's Make a Snowman! (p. 999)
Chesterfield, Sadie & Universal Studios Staff. Minions: The Junior Novel. (p. 1147)
Chesterman, Adrian, illus. see Bailey, Gerry.
Chesterman, Adrian, illus. see Galvin, Laura Gates.
Chesterman, Adrian, illus. see Halfman, Janet.
Chesterman, Adrian, illus. see Halfmann, Janet.
Chesterman, Al, illus. see Winner, Cherie.
Chesterman, Barnaby. Judo: Winning Ways. James, Adam, ed. (p. 931)
—Taekwondo: Winning Ways. James, Adam, ed. (p. 1695)
Chesterman, Barnaby & Willingham, Bob. Judo. (p. 931)
Chesterton, G. K. G. K. Chesterton's Early Poetry: Greybeards at Play, the Wild Knight & Other Poems, the Ballad of the White Horse. (p. 651)
—Magic: A Fantastic Comedy in Three Acts. (p. 1071)
Chesterton, Peter, illus. see Shakespeare, William & Birch, Beverley.
Chestnut, Debi. Murder in Crystal: A Savannah Williams Mystery. (p. 1192)
Chesworth, Michael, illus. see Bateman, Teresa.
Chesworth, Michael, illus. see Bowers, Renata.
Chesworth, Michael, illus. see Crist, James J. & Crist, J. J.
Chesworth, Michael, illus. see Gershenson, Harold P.
Chesworth, Michael, illus. see Lewis, Maggie.
Chesworth, Michael, illus. see Stern, Judith M. & Ben-Ami, Uzi.
Chesworth, Michael D., illus. see Edwards, Nancy.
Chesworth, Michael D., illus. see Wurm, Kristine.
Chetdav, Rain S. Acidrain. (p. 9)
Chetkowski, Emily. Amasa Walker's Spendid Garment. Peterson, Dawn, illus. (p. 52)
—Mabel Takes the Ferry Peterson, Dawn, illus. (p. 1067)
Chetkowski, Emily DiPalma, jt. auth. see DiPalma, Emilio.
Chettle, Julie, illus. see Buller, Ginny.
Chetwin, Grace. Foundling of Snawbyr Crygg: Part 2 of the Lords of Aelyth-kintalyn. (p. 624)
—Jason's Wonderful Week of Fabulous Night Rides. (p. 910)
—Wycan: Part 3 of the Lords of Aelyth-Kintalyn. (p. 1966)
Cheung, Aries, illus. see Libster, Bernard.
Cheung, Charly, illus. see Shakespeare, William.
Cheung, Hyechong. K Is for Korea. Das, Prodeepta, photos by. (p. 941)
Cheung, Irvin, photos by see McQuinn, Anna.
Cheung, Jim, illus. see Marz, Ron.
Cheung, Jim, et al. Young Avengers. (p. 1978)
Cheung, Lisa. 10 Most Destructive Ecosystem Invaders. (p. 1993)
Cheung, Shu Pui, et al. Walking on Solid Ground. Wei, Deborah & Kodish, Debora, eds. (p. 1854)
Cheung, Theresa. Dreams: What Are Your Dreams Trying to Tell You? (p. 484)
—Face & Hand Reading: Discover Their Secret Meanings! (p. 560)
—Numerology: What Do Numbers Reveal about You? (p. 1272)
Cheung, Theresa & Silvers, Terry. Psychic Power for Teens. (p. 1413)
Cheva, Cherry. DupliKate. (p. 490)
—She's So Money. (p. 1566)
Chevannes, Sabrina. Batsford Book of Chess for Children. (p. 145)
Chevat, Richie. Magnetic Learning: Dinosaurs. (p. 1075)
—Marble Book. Cooper, Martha, photos by. (p. 1091)
—Ripley's Birds of Prey. (p. 1474)
Cheverton, Mark. Algae Voices of Azule - Book 3: Finding the Lost. (p. 38)
—Battle for the Nether: An Unofficial Minecrafter's Adventure. (p. 145)
—Confronting the Dragon. (p. 357)
—Invasion of the Overworld: An Unofficial Minecrafter's Adventure. (p. 883)
—Invasion of the Overworld. (p. 883)
—Jungle Temple Oracle. (p. 935)
—Last Stand on the Ocean Shore: Book Three in the Mystery of Herobrine Series: a Gameknight999 Adventure: an Unofficial Minecrafter's Saga. (p. 978)
—Trouble in Zombie-Town. (p. 1790)
Cheviot, Patrice. Twice Blessed: the Special Life of Twins. Rothan, Ann, illus. (p. 1801)
Chevrier, Janet, tr. see Kieffer, Jean-Francois.
Chew, Elizabeth V. Day at Monticello. Elliott, Mark, illus. (p. 412)
Chew, Ruth. Magic in the Park. (p. 1072)
—Matter-Of-Fact Magic Book: the Witch at the Window. (p. 1109)
—Matter-Of-Fact Magic Book: the Would-Be Witch. (p. 1109)
—No Such Thing as a Witch. (p. 1260)
—Trouble with Magic. (p. 1790)
—Wednesday Witch. (p. 1871)
—What the Witch Left. (p. 1894)
—Witch's Broom. (p. 1941)
Chewning, Randy, illus. see Clay, Kathryn.
Chewning, Randy, illus. see Lynette, Rachel.
Chewning, Randy, illus. see Schmauss, Judy Kentor.
Chewning, Randy, illus. see Showers, Paul.
Cheyney, Arnold. History Challenge Level 1: 190 Brainteasers about the United States. (p. 783)
—History Challenge Level 2: 190 Brainteasers about the World. (p. 783)
—Legends of Arts. (p. 990)
—Write Away! 140 Writing Prompts for Grades 4-6. (p. 1963)
Cheyney, Arnold, jt. auth. see Cheyney, Jeanne.
Cheyney, Arnold & Sourcebooks, Inc Staff. Geography Challenge: 180 Fun & Creative Problems for Kids. (p. 662)
Cheyney, Arnold B. Athletes of Purpose. (p. 112)
Cheyney, Jeanne & Cheyney, Arnold. Big Book of Bulletin Boards for Every Month. (p. 179)
Chiacchiera, Moreno. Creating Funny Comics. (p. 378)
Chiacchiera, Moreno, illus. see Kalz, Jill.
Chiacchiera, Moreno, illus. see Taylor, Saranne.
Chiaki, Taro & Sasakishonen. Puri Puri (p. 1419)
Chiang, Andy, illus. see Marsoli, Lisa Ann.
Chiang, D. & Card, Orson Scott. Robota. (p. 1480)
Chiang, Gregory. Language of the Dragon: A Classical Chinese Reader (p. 975)
Chiang, Mona. Isaac Newton & His Laws of Motion: Set Of 6. (p. 890)
—Isaac Newton & His Laws of Motion: Text Pairs. (p. 890)
—Oil Spill: Disaster in the Gulf. (p. 1282)
Chiang, Shirley, illus. see Cheng'en, Wu.
Chiang, Shirley, illus. see Courtauld, Sarah & Davies, Kate.
Chiang, Shirley, illus. see Guanzhong, Luo.
Chiang, Shirley, illus. see MacKey, Cindy.
Chiang, Shirley, illus. see Naian, Shi.
Chiang, Shirley, illus. see Xueqin, Cao.
Chiappini, Lydia. Llama's Tale: Freesia's Little Llama Farm. (p. 1043)
Chiappone, Tanya M. Abc's of the B-I-B-L-E. (p. 4)
Chiara, Francesca De, illus. see Taplin, Sam.
Chiara, Francesca De, illus. see Watt, Fiona.
Chiaramonti, Gregory. Probie: the Space Probe, Mission One: the Ocean of Europa. (p. 1408)
Chiarello, Robin Taylor. Blue Lobster's Holiday! Bohart, Lisa, illus. (p. 203)
—Clam Diggers Ball. Bohart, Lisa, illus. (p. 326)
Chiarini, Chynna. Hippy Potto's Travel Adventure. (p. 781)
Chiasson, Herménégilde. Oiseau Tatoué. Lafrance, David, illus. (p. 1282)
Chiba, Tomohiro. Mobile Suit Gundam Seed Astray R Toda, Yasunari, illus. (p. 1157)
Chiba, Tomohiro & Games, Incbandai. Mobile Suit Gundam Lost War Chronicles Natsumoto, Masato, illus. (p. 1157)
Chibbaro, Julie. Deadly. Sovak, Jean-Marc Superville, illus. (p. 417)
Chibi, Andrew A. English Reformation: The Effect on a Nation. (p. 530)
Chic, Suzy & Touvay, Monique. Watching. (p. 1861)
Chicatelli, Joy. Bailey's Heartstrings. Rottinger, Amy, illus. (p. 133)
Chicault, Cecile, et al. Tales from the Brothers Grimm. (p. 1701)
Chicchelly, Dana. Preparing for FCAT Reading/ Grade 6. (p. 1396)
Chichester Clark, Emma. Amazing Mr. Zooty! (p. 55)
—Amazing Mr. Zooty! Chichester Clark, Emma, illus. (p. 55)
—Beside the Sea. Chichester Clark, Emma, illus. (p. 168)
—Come to School Too, Blue Kangaroo! Chichester Clark, Emma, illus. (p. 347)
—Friends for Life. Chichester Clark, Emma, illus. (p. 638)
—Go to Town. Chichester Clark, Emma, illus. (p. 687)
—Goldilocks & the Three Bears. (p. 696)
—Hansel & Gretel. (p. 743)
—Little Miss Muffet Counts to Ten. Chichester Clark, Emma, illus. (p. 1032)
—McElderry Book of Grimms' Fairy Tales. (p. 1114)
—Mimi's Book of Counting. Chichester Clark, Emma, illus. (p. 1145)
—Mimi's Book of Opposites. Chichester Clark, Emma, illus. (p. 1145)
—No Mas Besos! (p. 1259)
—Piper. Chichester Clark, Emma, illus. (p. 1361)
—Plum & Rabbit & Me Chichester Clark, Emma, illus. (p. 1374)
—We Are Not Fond of Rat! Chichester Clark, Emma, illus. (p. 1865)
Chichester Clark, Emma, illus. see Andersen, Hans Christian & Falloon, Jane.
Chichester Clark, Emma, illus. see Cecil, Laura.
Chichester Clark, Emma, illus. see Crossley-Holland, Kevin.
Chichester Clark, Emma, illus. see Morpurgo, Michael & Aesop.
Chichester Clark, Emma, illus. see Morpurgo, Michael.
Chichester Clark, Emma, illus. see Newman, Nanette.
Chichester Clark, Emma, illus. see Shakespeare, William.
Chichester Clark, Emma, illus. see Whybrow, Ian.
Chick, Bryan. Riddles & Danger. (p. 1471)
—Secret Zoo: Traps & Specters. (p. 1544)
—Secret Zoo. (p. 1544)
—Secret Zoo: Raids & Rescues. (p. 1544)
—Secrets & Shadows. (p. 1544)
—Traps & Specters. (p. 1779)
Chick, Douglas. What All Network Administrators Know. (p. 1879)
Chick, Jack T. First Bite. (p. 593)
—Who Is He? (p. 1915)
Chick, Sandra. Push Me, Pull Me. (p. 1420)
chickaDEE Magazine Staff. Hilarious Adventures of Mish & Mash: The Story of How Two Monsters - And You - Make the Perfect Joke Book! Geoffroi, Remie & Owlkids Books Inc. Staff, illus. (p. 779)
Chickadee Magazine Staff, et al. You Asked? Over 300 Great Questions & Astounding Answers. (p. 1973)
Chidebelu-Eze / Dove Publishing, Chibueze Obi. Lion That Finally Roared: Inspirational Story of Purpose & Destiny. Newborne, David / F., illus. (p. 1020)
Chidebelu-Eze/Dove Publishing, Chibueze / Obi. Tales of Tortoise: Inspirational Stories of Wisdom. Newborne, David / F., illus. (p. 1703)
Chidester, Jeffrey L., jt. auth. see Knott, Stephen F.
Chidgey, Catherine, jt. auth. see Könnecke, Ole.
Chidgey, Catherine, tr. see Könnecke, Ole.
Chidgey, Scarlett, ed. see Roland-James, Patricia & James, Robert L.
Chidley, Howard J. FiftyTwo Story Talks to Boys & Girls D. (p. 585)
Chidvilasananda. Good Night, Sweet Dreams, I Love You! (p. 700)
Chien, Catia, illus. see Rabinowitz, Alan.
Chien, Catia, illus. see Snyder, Laurel.
Chien, Catia, illus. see Young, Jessica.
Chiesa, Lynn. Guess What? (p. 729)
Chiew, Suzanne. What a Wonderful World! McNaughton, Tina, illus. (p. 1878)
Chifamba-Barnes, Sarudzayi Elizabeth. Village Story-Teller: Zimbabwean Folktales. (p. 1842)
Chiger, Arielle. 20 Fun Facts about Beetles. (p. 1995)
Chiger, Arielle & Elkin, Matthew. 20 Fun Facts about Gas Giants. (p. 1995)
Chiger, Arielle & Houk Maley, Adrienne. 20 Fun Facts about Asteroids & Comets. (p. 1995)
Chigeza, Philemon. Measurement Ideas & Possibilities. (p. 1117)
Chihak, Sheena. Kung Fu Panda 3-D Puzzle Book. Salesse, Alain, illus. (p. 968)
—Kung Fu Panda: Paws of Power Activity Kit. (p. 968)
Chihak, Sheena, jt. ed. see Karpinske, Stephanie.
Chihak, Sheena & Loki. Kung Fu Panda. Mada Design Inc, illus. (p. 968)
Chihaya, Masataka, tr. see Ugaki, Matome.
Chikoyak, Andrew J., illus. see Joe, Anna Rose.
Chikuhwa, Jacob. From the Cradle to the Bonfire. (p. 644)
Chikvaidze, Yuriy, illus. see Troyan, Slava & Katya.
Chikwanine, Michel, jt. auth. see Humphreys, Jessica Dee.
Chilcoat, George, jt. auth. see Tunnell, Michael.
Chilcote, Paul Wesley. Changed from Glory into Glory: Wesleyan Prayer for Transformation. (p. 290)
Chilcott-Monk, Julien. Basic Dictionary of Bible People. (p. 141)
Child, David. Santa Visits: Not What You Expect. (p. 1513)
Child, Hamilton. Gazetteer & Business Directory of Sullivan County For 1872-73: Republished on CD-ROM by Between the Lakes Group (p. 659)
Child, Jeremy. Bunny. Davies, Caroline, illus. (p. 242)
—Kitty. Davies, Caroline, illus. (p. 963)
—Mouse. Davies, Caroline, illus. (p. 1181)
—Puppy. Davies, Caroline, illus. (p. 1418)
—Santa. Leach, Emma, illus. (p. 1511)
Child, L. Maria. Over the River & Through the Wood: The New England Boy's Song about Thanksgiving Day. Tavares, Matt, illus. (p. 1314)
Child, Lauren. Beware of the Storybook Wolves. (p. 173)
—But Excuse Me That Is My Book. Child, Lauren, illus. (p. 246)
—But I Am an Alligator. (p. 246)
—But I've Used All My Pocket Change. (p. 246)
—Charlie & Lola: My Best, Best Friend. (p. 292)
—Charlie Is Broken! (p. 293)
—Clarice Bean: The Utterly Complete Collection. Child, Lauren, illus. (p. 327)
—Clarice Bean, Don't Look Now. Child, Lauren, illus. (p. 327)
—Clarice Bean Spells Trouble. Child, Lauren, illus. (p. 327)
—Clarice Bean, That's Me. (p. 327)
—Clarice Bean, That's Me. Child, Lauren, illus. (p. 327)
—Cuidado con los Cuentos de Lobos. (p. 390)

C

—De Verdad Que Podemos Cuidar de Tu Perro. Mendo, Miguel Angel, tr. (p. 416)
—Help! I Really Mean It! (p. 765)
—I Absolutely Must Do Coloring Now or Painting or Drawing. Child, Lauren, illus. (p. 831)
—I Am Collecting a Collection Sticker Stories. (p. 832)
—I Am Going to Save a Panda! (p. 833)
—I Am Not Sleepy & I Will Not Go to Bed. (p. 833)
—I Am Not Sleepy & I Will Not Go to Bed. Child, Lauren, illus. (p. 833)
—I Am Really, Really Concentrating. (p. 833)
—I Am Too Absolutely Small for School. (p. 834)
—I Am Too Absolutely Small for School. Child, Lauren, illus. (p. 834)
—I Can Do Anything That's Everything All on My Own. (p. 835)
—I Can't Stop Hiccuping! (p. 837)
—I Completely Know about Guinea Pigs. (p. 837)
—I Completely Must Do Drawing Now & Painting & Coloring. (p. 837)
—I Really Absolutely Must Have Glasses. (p. 844)
—I Want a Pet. (p. 847)
—I Want to Be Much More Bigger Like You. (p. 848)
—I Will Never Not Ever Eat a Tomato. (p. 848)
—I Will Never Not Ever Eat a Tomato. Child, Lauren, illus. (p. 848)
—I've Won, No I've Won, No I've Won. (p. 901)
—Maude: The Not-So-Noticeable Shrimpton. Krauss, Trisha, illus. (p. 1110)
—My Haircut Sticker Book. (p. 1210)
—My Halloween Sticker Stories. (p. 1210)
—My Wobbly Tooth Must Not Ever Never Fall Out. Child, Lauren, illus. (p. 1221)
—Princesa y el Guisante. Rubio, Esther, tr. (p. 1402)
—Quién Teme al Libro Feroz? (p. 1427)
—Ruby Redfort Catch Your Death (Book #3) Child, Lauren, illus. (p. 1493)
—Ruby Redfort Look into My Eyes. Child, Lauren, illus. (p. 1493)
—Ruby Redfort Take Your Last Breath. Child, Lauren, illus. (p. 1493)
—Sizzles Is Completely Not Here. (p. 1583)
—Slightly Invisible. (p. 1590)
—Soy Demasiado Pequeña para Ir Al Colegio: Protagonizado Por Juan y Totola. (p. 1618)
—Spells Trouble. Child, Lauren, illus. (p. 1625)
—Utterly Me, Clarice Bean. Child, Lauren, illus. (p. 1829)
—What Planet Are You from, Clarice Bean? (p. 1892)
—You Can Be My Friend. (p. 1974)
Child, Lauren, illus. see Lindgren, Astrid.
Child, Lauren, illus. see Oldfield, Jenny.
Child, Lauren, jt. auth. see Grosset and Dunlap Staff.
Child, Lauren & Ingham, Dave. Boo! Made You Jump! (p. 210)
Child, Lauren & Rubio, Esther. Nunca Jamás Comeré Tomates. (p. 1273)
Child, Lauren & Starkey, Anna. I Will Be Especially Very Careful. (p. 848)
Child, Lauren, et al. Carys Blodyn, Dyma Fi. (p. 273)
—F'n Hollol, Carys Blodyn. (p. 586)
—Fydda i Byth Bythoedd yn Bwyta Tomato. (p. 651)
Child, Lee, pseud. Running Blind (p. 1497)
—Without Fail (p. 1942)
Child, Lydia Maria. Bitty Bear's Sleigh Ride. Ackley, Peggy Jo, illus. (p. 194)
—Duty of Disobedience to the Fugitive Slave Act. (p. 491)
—Magician's Show Box & Other Stories. (p. 1075)
—Magician's Show Box, & Other Stories by the Author of Rainbows for Children. (p. 1075)
—Over the River & Through the Wood. Manson, Christopher, illus. (p. 1314)
—Over the River & Through the Woods. Edelson, Wendy, illus. (p. 1314)
Child, Maria. Girls Own Book 1834. (p. 680)
Child, Neil. Creek. (p. 380)
Childers, Amy. You're My Boy! (p. 1982)
Childers, Basil, photos by see Kimmel, Eric A.
Children of Appalachia. Teddy Bear Helps on the Farm. Children of Appalachia, illus. (p. 1712)
Children-Oln, illus. see Terbay, Susan Handle.
Children's Art-Friends of Kateri, illus. see McCauley, Marlene.
Children's Bible Hour Staff. Tesoros Para Niños, Tomo 2: 365 Historias Devocionales Para Ninos y jovenes (p. 1722)
Children's Book Press Staff, jt. auth. see Perez, Amada Irma.
Children's Book Press Staff, jt. auth. see Robles, Anthony D.
Childrens Books Staff, illus. see Ciminera, Siobhan & Testa, Maggie.
Childrens Books Staff, jt. auth. see McElroy, Jean.
Childrens Books Staff & Williams, Avery. Alchemy of Forever: An Incarnation Novel. (p. 35)
Children's Press, contrib. by. Ants Go Marching. (p. 90)
—Family Photo & Other Family Stories. (p. 568)
—Frog in the Pond & Other Animal Stories. (p. 640)
—Piglets Belong to Pigs. (p. 1358)
—Red, Blue, & Yellow Too! (p. 1453)
—Show-and-Tell Sam & Other School Stories. (p. 1570)
—Sing a Song of Seasons. (p. 1578)
—Three Little Kittens Get Dressed. (p. 1742)
Children's Press (New York, N.Y.) Staff & Scholastic, Inc. Staff, contrib. by. Brush, Brush, Brush! (p. 232)
Children's Press (New York, N.Y.) Staff, contrib. by. Can You Find Colors? (p. 258)
Childrens Press Staff. Ants Go Marching. (p. 90)
—Everywhere a Moo, Moo. (p. 546)
Childrens Press Staff, ed. see Falk, Laine.
Childrens Press Staff & Scholastic, Inc. Staff, contrib. by. 5 Busy Ducklings. (p. 1992)
—Can You Find Colors? (p. 258)
—Do You See Shapes? (p. 458)
—Hide-and-Peek. (p. 776)
Childrens Press Staff, contrib. by. Bug Box: Firefly Friend -The Great Bug Hunt - How Many Ants? (p. 236)
Childrens Press Staff, ed. Messy Bessey. (p. 1130)
—Rookie Reader. (p. 1487)
—Rookie Reader - Level A (p. 1487)
Children's Theatre Company Staff. Fierce & True: Plays for Teen Audiences. Brosius, Peter & Adams, Elissa, eds. (p. 584)
—Igniting Wonder: Plays for Preschoolers. Brosius, Peter & Adams, Elissa, eds. (p. 856)
Childres, Roger & Rhoney, Anita. Hopping Higgy: The Happy Hollow Series. (p. 797)
Childress, Boyd. 100 Most Popular Team Sports Heroes for Young Adults: Biographical Sketches & Professional Paths. (p. 1998)
Childress, Diana. Equal Rights Is Our Minimum Demand: The Women's Rights Movement in Iran 2005. (p. 533)
—Johannes Gutenberg & the Printing Press. (p. 920)
—Marco Polo's Journey to China. (p. 1092)
—Omar Al-Bashir's Sudan. (p. 1288)
—War of 1812. (p. 1857)
Childress, Gavin & Dooley, Audrey. Reading Your Bible: A Starter's Guide. Wild, Gill, illus. (p. 1447)
Childress, H. Lee. Cane. (p. 261)
Childress, Jamie. Galactic Treasure Hunt: Lost City of Atlantis. Braun, Chris, illus. (p. 652)
—Galactic Treasure Hunt: Lost City of the Moon. Braun, Chris, illus. (p. 652)
—Lost Universe. Braun, Chris, illus. (p. 1057)
Childress, Jenna Lynn. Dragon Soul: Book One of the Triune Jewels. (p. 478)
Childress, Mark. One Mississippi. (p. 1296)
Childress, Mildred Tickfer. Esmerelda the Silly Goose. Zipperer, Susan Johnson, illus. (p. 536)
Childress, Nancy, ed. see Childress, Robert.
Childress, Robert. Who Ever Heard of a Horse in the House? Childress, Nancy, ed. (p. 1915)
Childress, Story. Blue Moon Cheese. (p. 203)
—Momma, What's Love? (p. 1162)
—Old Codger (p. 1283)
Childs, Barbara. Sammy & the Cow Bird. (p. 1507)
Childs, Caro, jt. auth. see Caudron, Chris.
Childs, Karin Alfelt. Balm of Gilead. (p. 135)
Childs, Maria. Firefighters Don't! (p. 591)
—Noah's Treasure. (p. 1262)
Childs, Mark. Jaloopa: Home of the Poobah Baloo. (p. 906)
Childs, Mattie S. Lesson Helpers. (p. 993)
Childs, Neal. Shaggy Bear & the Three Bees. (p. 1558)
Childs, Pat Nelson. Orphan's Quest: Book One of the Chronicles of Firma. (p. 1305)
Childs, Peter. Fiction of Ian Mcewan. Tredell, Nicholas, ed. (p. 583)
Child's Play, creator. Getting Ready. (p. 669)
—Going Out. (p. 692)
—Penguin. (p. 1336)
Child's Play, ed. 5 Little Men in a Flying Saucer. (p. 1992)
Child's Play Staff. Spring. Busby, Ailie, illus. (p. 1634)
—Summer. Busby, Ailie, illus. (p. 1673)
—Winter. Busby, Ailie, illus. (p. 1937)
Childs, Rob. Keeper's Ball. Sheppard, Kate, illus. (p. 947)
—Wicked Catch! Reid, Michael, illus. (p. 1927)
Childs, Sam, illus. see Friedman, Joe.
Childs, Sam, illus. see Marshall, Jill.
Childs, Tera, jt. auth. see Childs, Tera Lynn.
Childs, Tera Lynn. Fins Are Forever. (p. 589)
—Forgive My Fins. (p. 619)
—Goddess Boot Camp. (p. 690)
—Just for Fins. (p. 938)
—Sweet Legacy. (p. 1690)
—Sweet Shadows. (p. 1690)
—Sweet Venom. (p. 1690)
Childs, Tera Lynn & Childs, Tera. Oh. My. Gods. (p. 1281)
Childs, Tera Lynn & Deebs, Tracy. Powerless. (p. 1391)
Childs, William R. Economic Literacy: A Complete Guide. Driver, Stephanie Schwartz, ed. (p. 502)
Child's World Staff & Kelley, K. C. Weird Water Sports. (p. 1873)
Child's World Staff & Watson, S. B. Weird Sports of the World. (p. 1872)
Child's World Staff, The & Kelley, K. C. Weird Races. (p. 1872)
—Weird Sports Moments. (p. 1872)
Child's World Staff, The & Watson, S. B. Weird Animal Sports. (p. 1872)
—Weird Throwing & Kicking Sports. (p. 1872)
Chilek, Deborah. Trip to the Zoo. (p. 1787)
Chilek, Laurie. Counting at the Zoo: Learning to Add 1 to One-Digit Numbers. (p. 370)
—Scary Slide. (p. 1520)
—¡Qué miedo! ¡un tobogán! (the Scary Slide) (p. 1424)
Chiles, Paul. Granny's Cove. (p. 710)
Chillemi, Stacey. My Daddy Has Epilepsy. (p. 1201)
—My Mommy Has Epilepsy. (p. 1214)
Chillous, Regina Hall. Bible Puzzle Book. (p. 176)
Chilman-Blair, Kim & DeLoache, Shawn. Medikidz Explain Acquired Brain Injury: What's up with Tamara? (p. 1119)
Chilman-Blair, Kim. Medikidz Explain Swine Flu. (p. 1120)
—Que le Pasa a la Abuelita de Sam? Los Medikidz Explican el Cancer de Pulmon. deLoache, Shawn, illus. (p. 1424)
—Que le Pasa a Nuestro Papa? Los Medikidz Explican el Cancer Colorrectal. deLoache, Shawn, illus. (p. 1424)
—Que le Sucede a Lyndon? Los Medikidz Explican el Osteosarcoma. Taddeo, John, illus. (p. 1424)
—Superheroes on a Medical Mission (p. 1683)
—What's up with Jerome's Grandad? Medikidz Explain Prostate Cancer. deLoache, Shawn, illus. (p. 1900)
—What's up with Jo? Medikidz Explain Brain Tumors. Taddeo, John, illus. (p. 1900)
—What's up with Lyndon? Medikidz Explain Osteosarcoma. Taddeo, John, illus. (p. 1900)
—What's up with Our Dad? Medikidz Explain Colorectal Cancer. deLoache, Shawn, illus. (p. 1900)
—What's up with Richard? Medikidz Explain Leukemia. Taddeo, John, illus. (p. 1900)
—What's up with Sam's Grandma? Medikidz Explain Lung Cancer. deLoache, Shawn, illus. (p. 1900)
—¿Qué le Pasa a la Mamá de Bridget? Los Medikidz Explican el Cáncer de Seno. Taddeo, John, illus. (p. 1424)
—¿Qué le Pasa a Richard? Los Medikidz Explican la Leucemia. Taddeo, John, illus. (p. 1424)
—¿Qué le Pasa Al Abuelito de Jerome? Los Medikidz Explican el Cáncer de Prostata. deLoache, Shawn, illus. (p. 1424)
—¿Qué le Pasa Jo? Los Medikidz Explican los Tumores Cerebrales. Taddeo, John, illus. (p. 1424)
Chilman-Blair, Kim & Deloache, Shawn. Medikidz Explain Autism: What's up with Ben? (p. 1119)
Chilman-Blair, Kim & DeLoache, Shawn. Medikidz Explain Burns: What's up with Harry? (p. 1119)
—Medikidz Explain Childhood Glaucoma: What's up with Scott? (p. 1119)
—Medikidz Explain Clinical Trials: What's up with Sara? (p. 1119)
Chilman-Blair, Kim & Deloache, Shawn. Medikidz Explain Depression: What's up with James? (p. 1119)
—Medikidz Explain Depression. (p. 1119)
—Medikidz Explain Growth Hormone Deficiency: What's up with Greg? (p. 1119)
Chilman-Blair, Kim & DeLoache, Shawn. Medikidz Explain Having an Operation. (p. 1119)
—Medikidz Explain Hereditary Angioedema: What's up with Luke? (p. 1119)
—Medikidz Explain Malaria: What's up with Ken? (p. 1119)
Chilman-Blair, Kim & Deloache, Shawn. Medikidz Explain Organ Transplants: What's up with William? (p. 1120)
Chilman-Blair, Kim & DeLoache, Shawn. Medikidz Explain Parkinson's Disease: What's up with Alys' Grandad? (p. 1120)
—Medikidz Explain Rheumatoid Arthritis: What's up with Eloise's Mum? (p. 1120)
—MediKidz Explain Severe Asthma: What's up with Tim? (p. 1120)
Chilman-Blair, Kim & Deloache, Shawn. Medikidz Explain Sleep Apnea. (p. 1120)
Chilman-Blair, Kim & DeLoache, Shawn. Medikidz Explain Slipped Hip: What's up with Jacob? (p. 1120)
—MediKidz Explain Type 1 Diabetes: What's up with Ashleigh? (p. 1120)
—Medikidz Explain Ulcerative Colitis: What's up with Sarah? (p. 1120)
Chilman-Blair, Kim & deLoache, Shawn. What's up with Tiffany's Dad? Medikidz Explain Melanoma. (p. 1900)
Chilman-Blair, Kim & DeLoache, Shawn. ¿Qué le Pasa Al Papá de Tiffany? Los Medikidz Explican el Melanoma. (p. 1424)
Chilman-Blair, Kim & Hersov, Kate. Medikidz Explain Haemophilia: What's up with Louis? Deloache, Shawn, illus. (p. 1119)
—Medikidz Explain Inflammatory Bowel Disease: What's up with Adam? Deloache, Shawn, illus. (p. 1119)
Chilman-Blair, Kim & Kipiniak, Chris. Medikidz Explain Hepatitis A: What's up with George? (p. 1119)
—Medikidz Explain Kidney Transplants: What's up with Jonah? (p. 1119)
—Medikidz Explain Seasonal Flu: What's up with Tom? (p. 1120)
Chilman-Blair, Kim & Lee, Tony. MediKidz Explain HIV: What's up with Jason? (p. 1119)
Chilman-Blair, Kim & Rimmer, Ian. Medikidz Explain Eczema: What's up with Kenzie? (p. 1119)
—Medikidz Explain Multiple Sclerosis: What's up with Ryan's Mum? (p. 1120)
Chilman-Blair, Kim & Taddeo, John. Medikidz Explain ADHD. (p. 1119)
—Medikidz Explain Autism. (p. 1119)
—Medikidz Explain Brain Tumours: What's up with Rachel? (p. 1119)
—Medikidz Explain HIV. (p. 1119)
—Medikidz Explain Swine Flu: What's up with Jasmine? (p. 1120)
—"What's up with Bill?" Medikidz Explain Epilepsy. (p. 1900)
—"What's up with David?" Medikidz Explain Food Allergies. (p. 1900)
—"What's up with Ella?" Medikidz Explain Diabetes. (p. 1900)
—"What's up with Max?" Medikidz Explain Asthma. (p. 1900)
—What's up with Pam? Medikidz Explain Childhood Obesity. (p. 1900)
Chilman-Blair, Kim, et al. Medikidz Explain Dystonia Management. (p. 1119)
—Medikidz Explain Epilepsy: What's up with Wendy? (p. 1119)
—Medikidz Explain Food Allergy: What's up with Paulina? (p. 1119)
—Medikidz Explain Leukaemia: What's up with Richard? (p. 1119)
—Medikidz Explain Living with ADHD. Copter, Steve, illus. (p. 1119)
—Medikidz Explain Scoliosis: What's up with John? (p. 1120)
—"What's up with Sean?" Medikidz Explain Scoliosis. (p. 1900)
Chilson, Martin. Carmen Cooks Healthy! Represent & Solve Problems Involving Division. (p. 270)
—In Search of Great White Sharks. (p. 864)
Chilton, Claire. Shattered. (p. 1563)
Chilton, Noel, illus. see Abbruzzo, Nancy.
Chilton, Noel, illus. see Baca, Ana.
Chilton, Noel, illus. see Steinsiek, Sabra Brown.
Chilton, Noel, tr. see Church, Peggy Pond.
Chilton, Noel Dora, illus. see Steinsiek, Sabra Brown.
Chilton, Pamela & Light, The. Odyssey of the Soul, Light the Act of Creation. (p. 1279)
Chilvers, Nigel, illus. see Peebles, Alice.
Chima, Ahiru & Misu, Max. Ellenâ___- Ellen meets Frog King - (p. 514)
Chima, Cinda Williams. Crimson Crown. (p. 382)
—Demon King. (p. 426)
—Dragon Heir. (p. 477)
—Enchanter Heir. (p. 523)
—Exiled Queen. (p. 548)
—Gray Wolf Throne. (p. 713)
—Seven Realms Box Set. (p. 1554)
—Sorcerer Heir. (p. 1614)
—Warrior Heir. (p. 1858)
—Wizard Heir. (p. 1942)
Chimal, Carlos. Mas Alla de los Dinosaurios. (p. 1101)
Chimal, Monica Genis. Entre Amigos. Flores, Heyliana, illus. (p. 531)
Chime, P. K. Moonrise. (p. 1173)
Chime, Taffeta. Last. (p. 977)
Chimeno del Campo, Ana Belén. Preste Juan: Mito y Leyenda en la Literatura Infantil y Juvenil Contemporánea. (p. 1397)
Chimenti, Maureen. Day My Pet Went to Heaven. (p. 413)
Chimento, Carmen C. Seven Paths to Glory: Simplified Theology for a Troubled World. (p. 1554)
Chimombo, S. Bird Boy's Song. (p. 190)
Chin, Amanda. Pet's Playground: Playing Safe in a Dog-and-Cat World. Feldman, Luke, illus. (p. 1348)
Chin, Amanda, jt. auth. see Feldman, Luke.
Chin, Beverly. Grammar for Writing 2007: Level Orange, Consumable. (p. 706)
Chin, Beverly, jt. auth. see Book Builders, Inc. Staff.
Chin, Carl, illus. see Vermond, Kira.
Chin, Foo Swee. Zeet. Chin, Foo Swee, illus. (p. 1985)
Chin, Jason. Coral Reefs. Chin, Jason, illus. (p. 366)
—Gravedad. (p. 712)
—Gravity. Chin, Jason, illus. (p. 712)
—Island: A Story of the Galápagos. Chin, Jason, illus. (p. 892)
—Redwoods. Chin, Jason, illus. (p. 1456)
Chin, Jason, illus. see Jango-Cohen, Judith.
Chin, Jason, illus. see Paul, Miranda.
Chin, Jason, illus. see Schechter, Lynn R.
Chin, Jason, illus. see Thomson, Sarah L.
Chin, Jason, illus. see Winchester, Simon.
Chin, Jonathan L., jt. auth. see Hamel-Mcevoy, Kristen.
Chin, Karen & Holmes, Thom. Dino Dung: The Scoop on Fossil Feces. Carr, Karen, illus. (p. 441)
Chin, Lili, illus. see Fleck, Denise.
Chin, Marcos, illus. see Kasdan, Mallory.
Chin, Oliver. 9 of 1: A Window to the World. (p. 1993)
—Baltazar & the Flying Pirates. Roth, Justin, illus. (p. 135)
—Julie Black Belt: the Belt of Fire. Chua, Charlene, illus. (p. 932)
—Timmy & Tammy's Train of Thought. McPherson, Heath, illus. (p. 1754)
—Welcome to Monster Isle. Miracola, Jeff, illus. (p. 1873)
—Year of the Dog: Tales from the Chinese Zodiac. Alcorn, Miah, illus. (p. 1969)
—Year of the Dragon: Tales from the Chinese Zodiac. (p. 1969)
—Year of the Horse: Tales from the Chinese Zodiac. Wood, Jennifer, illus. (p. 1969)
—Year of the Ox: Tales from the Chinese Zodiac. Alcorn, Miah, illus. (p. 1969)
—Year of the Pig: Tales from the Chinese Zodiac. Alcorn, Miah, illus. (p. 1969)
—Year of the Sheep. Chau, Alina, illus. (p. 1969)
—Year of the Tiger: Tales from the Chinese Zodiac. Roth, Justin, illus. (p. 1969)
Chin, Oliver Clyde. Adventures of Wonderbaby: From A to Z. Chiodo, Joe, illus. (p. 24)
—Harriet's Hairballs. Crawford, Gregory, tr. (p. 750)
—Julie Black Belt: The Kung Fu Chronicles. Chua, Charlene, illus. (p. 932)
—Year of the Rabbit: Tales from the Chinese Zodiac. Roth, Justin, illus. (p. 1969)
—Year of the Rat: Tales from the Chinese Zodiac. Alcorn, Miah, illus. (p. 1969)
Chin, Oliver, ed. Year of the Snake: Tales from the Chinese Zodiac. Wood, Jennifer, illus. (p. 1969)
Chin, Tiffani. School Sense: How to Help Your Child Succeed in Elementary School. (p. 1523)
Chin, Todd, illus. see Cardin, Jodi.
Chinapen, Joel. Sugar Is Bitter, Sugar Is Sweet. (p. 1673)
Chinchinian, Harry. Princess & the Beggar II: Continuing Adventures. Chinchinian, Harry, illus. (p. 1402)
Chinery, Michael. Animal Kingdom: Life in the Wild. (p. 78)
—Animales Salvajes. (p. 81)
Chinery, Michael & Michael, Chinery. Bosques. (p. 215)
—Costas. (p. 368)
—Desiertos. (p. 429)
—Enciclopedia de los Animales Salvajes (p. 523)
—Lagos y los Rios. (p. 971)
—Oceanos. (p. 1277)
—Polos. (p. 1381)
—Sabanas y las Praderas. (p. 1499)
—Selvas. (p. 1550)
Chinery, Michael, ed. Children's Encyclopedia of Animals: Life in the Wild. (p. 303)
Ching, Barbara, frwd. Country. (p. 372)
Ching, Brent & Santos, Jordan. Little Lima Bean. (p. 1030)
Ching, Brian, illus. see Williams, Rob.
Ching, Carrie. Tons of Things to Do for Hawaii's Kids: Activities, Adventures & Excursions for Keiki Eager to Explore Oahu. Bowen, Lance, illus. (p. 1765)
Ching, Jacqueline. Abigail Adams: A Revolutionary Woman. (p. 5)
—Adventure Racing. (p. 14)
—Cyberterrorism. (p. 396)
—Genocide & the Bosnian War. (p. 661)
—Jobs in Green Travel & Tourism. (p. 919)
—Mission San Fernando Rey de Espana. (p. 1153)
—Mission San Rafael Arcangel. (p. 1153)
—Mission Santa Ines. (p. 1153)
—Utah: Past & Present. (p. 1829)
—Women's Rights. (p. 1946)
Ching, Jacqueline, jt. auth. see Mableton, Barry.
Ching, Jacqueline & Connelly, Jack. Discovering Mission San Rafael Arcángel. (p. 449)
Ching, Jacqueline & Dorling Kindersley Publishing Staff. Thomas Jefferson. (p. 1738)
Ching, Jerry Yu & Onghai, Mike. Greatest King. Ching, Jerry Yu, illus. (p. 720)
Ching, Juliet. Assassination of Robert F. Kennedy. (p. 107)
Ching, Lorilei. He Ping: An Orphan's Destiny. (p. 756)
Ching, Patrick. Tale of Rabbit Island. (p. 1700)
Ching, Tokie. Boy's Day in Hawaii. Arai, Setsuo, illus. (p. 220)
—Girl's Day in Hawaii with Yuki Chan. (p. 680)

Chin-Lee, Cynthia. Akira to Zoltan: Twenty-Six Men Who Changed the World. Addy, Sean & Halsey, Megan, illus. (p. 32)
—Akira to Zoltan: Twenty-Six Men Who Changed the World. Halsey, Megan & Addy, Sean, illus. (p. 32)
—Amelia to Zora: Twenty-Six Women Who Changed the World. Halsey, Megan & Addy, Sean, illus. (p. 58)
Chinn, Jacqueline. How Can I Be Special? Mondragon, Manny, illus. (p. 805)
Chinn, Karen. Sam y el Dinero de la Suerte. Van Wright, Cornelius, illus. (p. 1507)
—Sam y el Dinero de la Suerte. Van Wright, Cornelius & Hu, Ying-Hwa, illus. (p. 1507)
Chinnery, Karen. Secret Agent Squirrel. (p. 1540)
Chinnien, Kim. Tim Tim: The White Gorilla. (p. 1750)
Chinodya, Shimmer. Tale of Tamari. (p. 1700)
Chinsamy-Turan, Anusuya. Famous Dinosaurs of Africa. Rey, Luis, illus. (p. 569)
Chinsang, Wayne, jt. auth. see Shady, Justin.
Chinsang, Wayne, jt. auth. see Waid, Mark.
Chiodi, Maira, illus. see Miller, Connie Colwell.
Chiodo, Charles, illus. see Chiodo, Stephen & Strain, Jim.
Chiodo, Joe, illus. see Chin, Oliver Clyde.
Chiodo, Stephen & Strain, Jim. Chiodo Bros. ' Alien Xmas. Chiodo, Charles, illus. (p. 308)
Chipka, Sandy, illus. see Flaggert, Candy.
Chipley, John. Secret Place: A Boy's Journey into the Woods. (p. 1543)
Chipman, Laura. Dragonspeaker. (p. 479)
Chipman-Sullivan, Lois. What Does Love Mean, God? (p. 1884)
Chippendale, Lisa A. Yo-Yo Ma: A Cello Superstar Brings Music to the World. (p. 1972)
Chipponeri, Kelli. Big Win. Aikins, Dave, illus. (p. 184)
—SpongeBob Rocks! Martinez, Heather, illus. (p. 1630)
Chirco, Antonella, illus. see McCardell, Kenneth/W.
Chiri, et al. Glencoe Keyboarding with Computer Applications: MS Office 2000 Professional Edition Student Manaul. (p. 683)
Chironna, Ronald, illus. see Loeper, John J.
Chirp Magazine Editors. Joking Around with Chirp: More Than 130 Feather-Ruffling Jokes, Riddles, & Tongue Twisters! Kain, Bob & Owlkids Books Inc. Staff, illus. (p. 924)
Chisholm, Donna. Smelly Little Oil Company. (p. 1593)
Chisholm, Donneisha Dee. Baby Patch. (p. 127)
Chisholm, J., jt. auth. see Reid, S.
Chisholm, Jane. First Christmas. (p. 593)
—Timelines of World History. (p. 1754)
Chisholm, Jane, ed. see Andrews, Georgina & Knighton, Kate.
Chisholm, Jane, ed. see Brocklehurst, Ruth & Brook, Henry.
Chisholm, Jane, ed. see Brocklehurst, Ruth.
Chisholm, Jane, ed. see Claybourne, Anna.
Chisholm, Jane, ed. see Dickins, Rosie.
Chisholm, Jane, ed. see Dowswell, Paul, et al.
Chisholm, Jane, ed. see Harvey, Gill.
Chisholm, Jane, ed. see Jones, Rob Lloyd.
Chisholm, Jane, ed. see Lacey, Minna.
Chisholm, Jane & Reid, Straun. Who Built the Pyramids? Stitt, Sue, illus. (p. 1914)
Chisholm, Penny, jt. auth. see Bang, Molly.
Chisiya. Afrikan Lullaby: Folk Tales from Zimbabwe. (p. 28)
Chisman, James Ph. D. Bullette & Jessic. (p. 240)
Chisolm, Melinda. Remembering to Breathe. Cross, Jo Ellen, illus. (p. 1460)
Chissick, Michael. Ladybird's Remarkable Relaxation: How Children (And Frogs, Dogs, Flamingos & Dragons) Can Use Yoga Relaxation to Help Deal with Stress, Grief, Bullying & Lack of Confidence. Peacock, Sarah, illus. (p. 971)
Chisum, William Boyd. Story of God's Grace. (p. 1658)
Chitara, Jagdish, jt. auth. see Scott, Nathan Kumar.
Chitombo, Patience, illus. see Zinjiba-Nyakutya, Peshie.
Chitouras, Barbara, illus. see Lindskoog, Kathryn, ed.
Chitrakar, Manu, illus. see Flowers, Arthur.
Chitrakar, Moyna, illus. see Arni, Samhita & Valmiki.
Chitrakar, Swarna, illus. see Rao, Sirish.
Chittenden, Charlotte E. What Two Children Did. (p. 1894)
Chittenden, George. Boy Who Led Them. (p. 219)
Chitty, Joan E. Charlie Macaffee: Search for the Genie's Body. (p. 293)
Chitwood, Suzanne, illus. see Archambault, John.
Chitwood, Suzanne Tanner, illus. see Archambault, John.
Chiu, Bessie, illus. see Martha, Morales.
Chiu, Bobby, illus. see Epstein, Adam Jay & Jacobson, Andrew.
Chiu, David. Choosing a Career in the Post Office. (p. 310)
—Government Regulation of the Railroads: Fighting Unfair Trade Practicesin America. (p. 704)
—Government Regulation of the Railroads: Fighting Unfair Trade Practices in America. (p. 704)
Chiu, David, jt. auth. see Regis, Natalie.
Chiu, David & Regis, Natalie. Insider's Guide to Wrestling (p. 878)
Chiu, Harry. Enve Lopt Unfolded. (p. 531)
Chiu, Stephen & Lui, Tai-lok. Hong Kong: Becoming a Chinese Global City. (p. 795)
Chiva, Francesc, jt. auth. see Casas, Lola.
Chizuru, Mio. Pirate & the Princess Volume 1: the Timelight Stone: The Timelight Stone. (p. 1362)
—Pirate & the Princess Volume 2: the Red Crystal: The Red Crystal. (p. 1362)
Chizuwa, Masayuki. My Book of Money Counting Coins: Ages 5, 6, 7. (p. 1199)
—My Book of Money Counting Dollars & Cents: Ages 6, 7, 8. (p. 1199)
Chmakova, Svetlana. Nightschool - The Weirn Books (p. 1255)
Chmakova, Svetlana, creator. Dramacon (p. 480)
Chmiel, David & Hensle, Terry W., eds. Golf After 50: Playing Without Pain. (p. 696)
Chmielewski, Gary. Animal Zone: Jokes, Riddles, Tongue Twisters & Daffynitions. Caputo, Jim, illus. (p. 80)
—Animal Zone. Caputo, Jim, illus. (p. 80)
—Classroom Zone: Jokes, Riddles, Tongue Twisters & Daffynitions. Caputo, Jim, illus. (p. 329)
—Classroom Zone. Caputo, Jim, illus. (p. 329)
—Computer Zone: Jokes, Riddles, Tongue Twisters & Daffynitions. Caputo, Jim, illus. (p. 355)
—Computer Zone. Caputo, Jim, illus. (p. 355)
—Fright Zone: Jokes, Riddles, Tongue Twisters & Daffynitions. Caputo, Jim, illus. (p. 639)
—Fright Zone. Caputo, Jim, illus. (p. 639)
—Ghost Zone: Jokes, Riddles, Tongue Twisters & Daffynitions. Caputo, Jim, illus. (p. 672)
—Ghost Zone. Caputo, Jim, illus. (p. 672)
—History Zone: Jokes, Riddles, Tongue Twisters & Daffynitions. Caputo, Jim, illus. (p. 785)
—History Zone. Caputo, Jim, illus. (p. 785)
—How Did That Get to My House? Internet. (p. 806)
—How Did That Get to My House? Television. (p. 806)
—Let's Eat in the Funny Zone: Jokes, Riddles, Tongue Twisters & Daffynitions. Caputo, Jim, illus. (p. 996)
—Let's Eat in the Funny Zone. Caputo, Jim, illus. (p. 996)
—Let's Go in the Funny Zone: Jokes, Riddles, Tongue Twisters & Daffynitions. Caputo, Jim, illus. (p. 997)
—Let's Go in the Funny Zone. Caputo, Jim, illus. (p. 997)
—Medical Zone: Jokes, Riddles, Tongue Twisters & Daffynitions. Caputo, Jim, illus. (p. 1119)
—Medical Zone. Caputo, Jim, illus. (p. 1119)
—Science Zone: Jokes, Riddles, Tongue Twisters & Daffynitions. Caputo, Jim, illus. (p. 1528)
—Science Zone. Caputo, Jim, illus. (p. 1528)
—Sports Zone. Caputo, Jim, illus. (p. 1633)
Cho, Alan. World Series. (p. 1958)
Cho, Charles. Age of Ultron: The Reusable Sticker Book. (p. 29)
—Ant-Man: The Amazing Adventures of Ant-Man. (p. 88)
—Marvel's Ant-Man: the Reusable Sticker Book. (p. 1099)
Cho, Charles & Marvel. Guardians of the Galaxy: The Reusable Sticker Book. (p. 728)
Cho, Frank, illus. see Aaron, Jason.
Cho, Frank, illus. see Millar, Mark & Santoro, Frank.
Cho, Michael, illus. see Ali, Dominic.
Cho, Michael, illus. see O'Donnell, Liam.
Cho, Michael, illus. see Szpirglas, Jeff.
Cho, Michelle. Korean Dream. (p. 967)
Cho, Seung-Yup, illus. see Lee, Ki-Hoon.
Cho, Shinta. Gas We Pass: The Story of Farts. Stinchecum, Amanda M., tr. (p. 657)
Cho, Thomas, jt. auth. see Barnard, Emma.
Choat, Beth. Soccerland Beck, Robert, illus. (p. 1604)
Chobanian, Elizabeth, ed. see Criswell, Patti Kelley.
Chobanian, Elizabeth & American Girl Publishing Staff, eds. Coconut's Guide to Life: Life Lessons from a Girl's Best Friend. Lukatz, Casey, illus. (p. 337)
Chobanian, Elizabeth, ed. Coconut's Guide to Life: Life Lessons from a Girl's Best Friend. Lukatz, Casey, illus. (p. 337)
Chocheli, Niko, illus. see Hart, Chrissi.
Choclate-Brown, Honey. Mama never told Me. (p. 1084)
Chocolate Cupcake Staff. Chocolate Cupcake: Celebrating Our Sweetness. Lacy, Lauren, illus. (p. 309)
Chocolate, Debbi. Pigs Can Fly! The Adventures of Harriet Pig & Friends. Tryon, Leslie, illus. (p. 1358)
Chodagiri, Shanthi, illus. see Heap, Bridgette.
Chodan, Tim. Gabriel Dumont (p. 652)
Chodan, Tim & Asfar, Dan. Louis Riel Boer, Faye, ed. (p. 1058)
Chodos-Irvine, Margaret. Ella Sarah Gets Dressed. (p. 514)
Chodos-Irvine, Margaret, illus. see Bauer, Marion Dane.
Chodos-Irvine, Margaret, illus. see Wong, Janet S.
Chodzin, Sherab. Barefoot Book of Buddhist Tales. Cameron, Marie, illus. (p. 139)
Chodzin, Sherab, jt. auth. see Riel, Jörn.
Choffel, Theodora L. Coat for Ebony. (p. 336)
Choi, Allan, illus. see Dumas, Alexandre.
Choi, Allan, illus. see Landolf, Diane Wright.
Choi, Allan Jai-Ho, illus. see Paigerac, Patricia.
Choi, Anne Soon. Korean Americans. (p. 967)
Choi, Ellen, jt. auth. see Yi, Myong-Jin.
Choi, Eun-gyu. All Kinds of Nests: Birds. Cowley, Joy, ed. (p. 45)
Choi, Eun-Mi. Where Are You, Sun Bear? Malaysia. Cowley, Joy, ed. (p. 1906)
Choi, Haran. Why Me? (p. 1925)
Choi, Il-Ho, illus. see Kim, Sarah, tr.
Choi, Il-Ho, illus. see Shin, Eui-Cheol.
Choi, Jeongim. Who's Coming Tonight? Gang, MinJeong, illus. (p. 1920)
Choi, Jin, tr. see Christian, Cheryl.
Choi, Mike. Astonishing Thor. (p. 109)
Choi, Mike, illus. see Hickman, Jonathan.
Choi, Min-ho, illus. see Brothers Grimm Staff.
Choi, Na-mi. Song of the Mekong River: Vietnam. Cowley, Joy, ed. (p. 1611)
Choi, Robert. Korean Folks Songs: Stars in the Sky & Dreams in Our Hearts. Back, Samee, illus. (p. 967)
Choi, SeoYun. Let's Be Friends. Furukawa, Masumi, illus. (p. 994)
Choi, Sook Nyul. Echoes of the White Giraffe. (p. 502)
—Gathering of Pearls. (p. 658)
Choi, Sooyun. Janie & the Breakfast Fairy. (p. 908)
Choi, Stef, illus. see Look, Lenore.
Choi Sung Hwan, Aragon Noel, illus. see Miller, Jennifer.
Choi Sung Hwan, Aragon Noel, illus. see Ruditis, Paul.
Choi, Yangsook. Name Jar. (p. 1228)
—Name Jar. Choi, Yangsook, illus. (p. 1228)
Choi, Yangsook, illus. see Gill, Janet.
Choi, Yangsook, illus. see Lee, Milly.
Choi, Yangsook, illus. see Thong, Roseanne.
Choi, Yang-sook, illus. see Yun, Yeo-rim.
Choi, Young-Jin. Jesus Feeds Everybody! (p. 915)
—Mary's Big Surprise. (p. 1101)
—Where Are You, Little Lamb? (p. 1906)
Choi, Young-Jin & Kim, Jung-cho. Walk on the Waves. (p. 1854)
Choice Technologies, jt. auth. see Tenney, Bob.
Choices Program - Brown University. Russian Revolution (p. 1498)
Choiniere, Joseph & Golding, Claire Mowbray. What's That Bird? Getting to Know the Birds Around You, Coast to Coast. Robins, James, illus. (p. 1899)
Chojnowski, Bryan. Muffin Time: Origins. (p. 1189)
Choksi, Nishant, illus. see Brake, Mark.
Choksi, Sean. Theft of Time. (p. 1728)
Cholakova, Maila, jt. auth. see Pacheva, Svetla.
Choldenko, Gennifer. Al Capone Does My Homework. (p. 32)
—Al Capone Does My Shirts. (p. 32)
—Al Capone Shines My Shoes. (p. 32)
—Chasing Secrets. (p. 294)
—Giant Crush. Sweet, Melissa, illus. (p. 673)
—If a Tree Falls at Lunch Period. (p. 852)
—No Passengers Beyond This Point. (p. 1259)
—Notes from a Liar & Her Dog. (p. 1267)
—Putting the Monkeys to Bed. Davis, Jack E., illus. (p. 1420)
Choldenko, Gennifer, et al. No Passengers Beyond This Point. (p. 1259)
Cholette, Daniel, jt. auth. see Janelle, Nicole.
Cholij, Mark & Nagaraj, Geetha. English Basics: A Companion to Grammar & Writing. (p. 529)
Chollat, Emilie, illus. see Gallo, Tina.
Chollat, Emilie, illus. see Hazen, Barbara Shook.
Choltus, Rebekah L. Joe's Room. Choltus, Rebekah L., illus. (p. 920)
Chomiak, Joseph, illus. see Tremlin, Nathan, et al.
Chomphootung, Rassamee, illus. see Kundiger, Donovan & Kundiger, Marion.
Chomsky, Noam, jt. auth. see Griffiths, Philip Jones.
Chon, Kye Young. Audition: Volume 1 (p. 115)
Chong, Elaine S. & Hovanec, Erin. Phobias. (p. 1351)
Chong, Luther, photos by see Whitman, Nancy C.
Choo, Brian, illus. see Long, John.
Choo, Missy. What Color Is Monday. (p. 1881)
Chooseco, creator. Choose Your Own Adventure 4 Book Boxed Set #1: The Abominable Snowman/Journey under the Sea/Space & Beyond/the Lost Jewels of Nabooti. (p. 310)
—Choose Your Own Adventure 4 Book Boxed Set #2: Mystery of the Maya/House of Danger/Race Forever/Escape. (p. 310)
Chopin, Kate. Awakening: An Icelandic Classic. Davis, Stephen, illus. (p. 120)
—Kate Chopin's the Awakening. Bloom, Harold, ed. (p. 944)
—Story of an Hour. (p. 1657)
Chopra, Deepak. Fire in the Heart: A Spiritual Guide for Teens. (p. 590)
—Teens Ask Deepak: All the Right Questions. Barchowsky, Damien, illus. (p. 1715)
—You with the Stars in Your Eyes: A Little Girl's Glimpse at Cosmic Consciousness. Zaboski, Dave, illus. (p. 1976)
Choquette, Gabriel, illus. see Bail, Mina Mauerstein.
Choquette, Michel, tr. see Kotzwinkle, William & Murray, Glenn.
Chorao, Kay. Baby's Lap Book. Chorao, Kay, illus. (p. 129)
—Bad Boy, Good Boy. (p. 131)
—D Is for Drums: A Colonial Williamsburg A. B. C. (p. 397)
—D Is for Drums: A Colonial Williamsburg ABC. Chorao, Kay, illus. (p. 397)
—Ed & Kip. Chorao, Kay, illus. (p. 503)
—Rhymes Round the World. Chorao, Kay, illus. (p. 1468)
Chorao, Kay, illus. see Adler, David A.
Chorao, Kay, illus. see Harper, Jo.
Chorao, Kay, illus. see Rose, Deborah Lee.
Chorao, Kay, illus. see Sartell, Debra.
Chorba, April. Dot Jewelry: Make Pretty Paper Bracelets & Necklaces. (p. 472)
—Mini Pom-Pom Pets: Make Your Own Fuzzy Friends. (p. 1146)
—Pom-Pom Puppies: Make Your Own Adorable Dogs. (p. 1382)
—Thumb Doodles: The Epic Saga at Your Fingertips. Klutz Editors, ed. (p. 1745)
—Tissue Paper Crafts. (p. 1757)
Chorba, April, jt. auth. see Scholastic, Inc. Staff.
Chorba, April & Editors of Klutz. Prankster Magic: With Real Fake Gum. (p. 1393)
Chorba, April & Johnson, Anne Akers. Fashion Forms. (p. 575)
Chorba, April & Kane, Barbara. Potholders & Other Loopy Projects. (p. 1388)
Chorba, April & Murphy, Pat. Book of Impossible Objects: 25 Eye-Popping Projects to Make, See & Do. (p. 211)
Chorba, April & Phillips, Karen. It's All about Us (.... Especially Me!) A Journal of Totally Personal Questions for You & Your Friends. (p. 896)
Chorlian, Meg & Hale, Sarah Elder, eds. Ulysses S. Grant: Confident Leader & Hero. (p. 1810)
Chornock, Ruth. Devin's New Bed. (p. 432)
Chorpash, Marci, jt. auth. see Webb, Margot.
Chorpenning, Charlotte B. Indian Captive. (p. 871)
Chorvathova, Michaela, tr. see Krcmár, Karol.
Chotjewitz, David. Daniel Half Human. Orgel, Doris, tr. from GER. (p. 405)
Chotjewitz, David & Orgel, Doris. Daniel, Half Human: And the Good Nazi. (p. 405)
Chottin, Ariane. Little Donkeys. (p. 1027)
—Little Leopards. (p. 1030)
Chou, Joey. Crazy by the Letters. Chou, Joey, illus. (p. 377)
Chou, Joey, illus. see Disney Book Group Staff, et al.
Chou, Joey, illus. see DiTerlizzi, Angela.
Chou, Joey, illus. see Fliess, Sue.
Chou, Joey, illus. see Jones, Karl.
Chou, Joey, illus. see Livingston, A. A.
Chou, Joey, illus. see Sagerman, Evan.
Chou, Joey, illus. see Williams, Dawn.
Chou, Vivian, jt. auth. see Murthy, Amishi.
Chou, Yih-Fen. Mimi Goes Potty. Chen, Zhiyuan, illus. (p. 1145)
—Mimi Loves to Mimic. Chen, Chih-Yuan, illus. (p. 1145)
—Mimi Says No. Chen, Chih Yuan, illus. (p. 1145)
—Mimi Tidies Up. Chen, Zhiyuan, illus. (p. 1145)
—Potty Story. Chen, Zhiyuan, illus. (p. 1388)
Choudhry, Fahima. Snow Surprise. (p. 1599)
Choudhury, Dorbesh, tr. see Hambleton, Laura.
Chouette Publishing Staff. Baby Caillou: Good Morning! Brignaud, Pierre, illus. (p. 125)
—Baby Caillou: Good Night! Brignaud, Pierre, illus. (p. 125)
—Caillou: When I Grow Up ... Sévigny, Eric, illus. (p. 251)
—Caillou: Storybook Treasury. Sévigny, Eric, illus. (p. 251)
—Caillou: Jobs People Do. Brignaud, Pierre, illus. (p. 251)
—Caillou - Learning for Fun: Ages 3-4. Brignaud, Pierre & Sévigny, Eric, illus. (p. 251)
—Caillou - Learning for Fun!, Ages 4-5. Brignaud, Pierre & Sévigny, Eric, illus. (p. 251)
—Caillou - Let's Go to the Park. Brignaud, Pierre, illus. (p. 251)
—Caillou - My Clothes. Brignaud, Pierre, illus. (p. 251)
—Caillou - My First Dictionary. Brignaud, Pierre, illus. (p. 251)
—Caillou - My First Dictionary / Mi Primer Diccionario: In My House / En Mi Casa. Velazquez De Leon, Mauricio, tr. (p. 251)
—Caillou - The Little Artist. Sevigny, Eric, illus. (p. 251)
Chouinard, Karen, jt. auth. see Carpenter, Holly.
Chovanetz, Tabatha Moran. Halley Ann Lindsey Heath. Kickingbird, Samantha, illus. (p. 735)
—Peggy's Pigtails. (p. 1335)
Chow, Candice, illus. see Thielbar, Melinda.
Chow, Cheryl, jt. auth. see Chow, James H.
Chow, James H. & Chow, Cheryl. Encyclopedia of Hepatitis & Other Liver Diseases. (p. 525)
Chow, Michelle Nel. To Be a Nut or Not! (p. 1758)
Chowdary, Daddala Vineesha. Locket of Moonstone. (p. 1045)
Chowdhury, Uttom & Robertson, Mary. Why Do You Do That? A Book about Tourette Syndrome for Children & Young People. Whallett, Liz, illus. (p. 1924)
Chown, Xanna Eve, jt. auth. see Helou, Sandra.
Chown, Xanna Eve, jt. auth. see Miles, Lisa.
Chowning, Judy. Jacki & Jo's Grand Canyon Adventure. (p. 903)
Choy, Howard, jt. auth. see Taylor, Rodney L.
Choyce, Lesley. Big Burn. (p. 180)
—Book of Michael (p. 211)
—Breaking Point (p. 225)
—Carrie Loses Her Nerve Thurman, Mark, illus. (p. 271)
—Crash (p. 376)
—Deconstructing Dylan. (p. 422)
—Dumb Luck (p. 489)
—End of the World As We Know It (p. 526)
—Hell's Hotel (p. 765)
—Last Chance (p. 977)
—Living Outside the Lines (p. 1041)
—Pandemónium (p. 1321)
—Random (p. 1438)
—Rat (p. 1440)
—Reacción (p. 1442)
—Reaction (p. 1442)
—Reckless (p. 1451)
—Refuge Cove. (p. 1456)
—Running the Risk (p. 1497)
—Skate Freak (p. 1583)
—Skunks for Breakfast Jones, Brenda, illus. (p. 1586)
—Smoke & Mirrors. (p. 1594)
—Sudden Impact (p. 1672)
—Sudden Impact. (p. 1672)
—Thunderbowl (p. 1746)
—Wave Warrior (p. 1864)
Chris, Crowe. Mississippi Trial 1955. (p. 1154)
Chris, Healey, illus. see Steinberg, Howard.
Chris, Jerry. Beau, the Story of a Horse. (p. 153)
Chris, Wright. Pilgrim's Progress Puzzle Book. (p. 1359)
Chris, Wright, illus. see Patterson, Eric.
Chrisagis, Brian. Who & What Am I? Good News Gang. Chrisagis, Shawn, illus. (p. 1914)
Chrisagis, Brian, jt. auth. see Chrisagis, Shawn.
Chrisagis, Shawn, illus. see Chrisagis, Brian.
Chrisagis, Shawn & Chrisagis, Brian. Prejudice in Mandi's Garden: Seeds of Kindness. (p. 1395)
Chriscoe, Sharon. Scary Weather, Scaredy Cat (p. 1521)
Chrisemer, Michael, jt. auth. see Lynn, Michaela.
Chrismer, Melanie. Chachalaca Chiquita Harrington, David, illus. (p. 288)
—Comets. (p. 348)
—Mars. (p. 1096)
—Math Tools. (p. 1107)
—Moon. (p. 1171)
—Multiply This! (p. 1190)
—Neptune. (p. 1241)
—Odd & Even Socks. (p. 1278)
—Phoebe Clappsaddle for Sheriff Roeder, Virginia M., illus. (p. 1351)
—Phoebe Clappsaddle Has a Tumbleweed Christmas Roeder, Virginia M., illus. (p. 1351)
—Sun. (p. 1675)
—Venus. (p. 1836)
Chrisotpher, Matt. Top Wing. (p. 1769)
Chrisp, Peter. Dinosaur Detectives, Level 4. (p. 442)
—Explore Titanic: Breathtaking New Pictures, Recreated with Digital Technology Vongrapachanh, Somchith, illus. (p. 550)
—Navigators: Pirates. (p. 1238)
—Victorian Age. (p. 1840)
—World War II: Fighting for Freedom. (p. 1959)
Chrisp, Peter, jt. auth. see Dorling Kindersley Publishing Staff.
Chriss, Granddad. Adventures of Barazaburg. (p. 16)
Christe, Moreno, illus. see Young, Scott Alexander.
Christelow, Eileen. Cinco Monitos Colección de Oro. (p. 319)
—Cinco Monitos Hacen un Pastel de Cumpleanos. (p. 319)
—Cinco Monitos Sin Nada Que Hacer. (p. 319)
—Desperate Dog Writes Again. (p. 430)
—Five Little Monkeys Bake a Birthday Cake. (p. 600)
—Five Little Monkeys Bake a Birthday Cake. Christelow, Eileen, illus. (p. 600)
—Five Little Monkeys Go Shopping. (p. 600)
—Five Little Monkeys Jump in the Bath. (p. 600)
—Five Little Monkeys Jump into Learning Boxed Set. (p. 600)
—Five Little Monkeys Jumping on the Bed. (p. 600)

C

—Five Little Monkeys Jumping on the Bed. Ortiz, Victoria, tr. (p. 600)
—Five Little Monkeys Jumping on the Bed Big Book. (p. 600)
—Five Little Monkeys Jumping on the Bed Lap Board Book. (p. 600)
—Five Little Monkeys Reading in Bed. (p. 600)
—Five Little Monkeys Set for Costco 2005. (p. 600)
—Five Little Monkeys Sitting in a Tree. (p. 600)
—Five Little Monkeys Sitting in a Tree Book & CD (p. 600)
—Five Little Monkeys Wash the Car. (p. 600)
—Letters from a Desperate Dog. (p. 1002)
—Vote! (p. 1850)
—Vote! Christelow, Eileen, illus. (p. 1850)
—What Do Authors & Illustrators Do? (p. 1882)
Christelow, Eileen, illus. see Beard, Darleen Bailey.
Christen, Carol & Blomquist, Jean M. What Color Is Your Parachute? for Teens. (p. 1881)
Christen, Dennis H. Lundon Bridge wa seagae wa Yolsae. Lee, Kathryn, tr. (p. 1065)
—Lundon's Bridge & the Three Keys. (p. 1065)
Christen, Thiel. Night & Day. (p. 1252)
Christenbury, Leila, et al, eds. Handbook of Adolescent Literacy Research. (p. 740)
Christensen, Andrew, illus. see Latham, Donna.
Christensen, Bob. Gaylord Goose. Marsh, Bobbi, illus. (p. 659)
Christensen, Bonnie. Daring Nellie Bly: America's Star Reporter. (p. 407)
—Django: World's Greatest Jazz Guitarist. Christensen, Bonnie, illus. (p. 455)
—Elvis: The Story of the Rock & Roll King. Christensen, Bonnie, illus. (p. 517)
—Fabulous! A Portrait of Andy Warhol. Christensen, Bonnie, illus. (p. 559)
—I, Galileo. (p. 838)
—Plant a Little Seed. Christensen, Bonnie, illus. (p. 1368)
—Single Pebble: A Story of the Silk Road. Christensen, Bonnie, illus. (p. 1579)
—Woody Guthrie: Poet of the People. Christensen, Bonnie, illus. (p. 1950)
Christensen, Bonnie, illus. see Crist-Evans, Craig.
Christensen, Bonnie, illus. see Krensky, Stephen.
Christensen, Bonnie, illus. see Myers, Walter Dean.
Christensen, Bonnie, illus. see Osborne, Mary Pope.
Christensen, Catherine. Emily's Perfect Christmas Tree. (p. 519)
Christensen, D. J., illus. see McCormic, Maxine Griffith.
Christensen, David, illus. see Williams, Rozanne Lanczak.
Christensen, Donald, illus. see Haan, Wanda.
Christensen, Donna, illus. see Bowman, Crystal.
Christensen, Evelyn B. Kentucky Puzzles: Bluegrass Brainteasers for Ages 6 To 106. (p. 949)
Christensen, Gerda. Troll Peter Discovers the Bog-Woman's Secret & Other Stories. (p. 1788)
—Troll Peter Finds A Treasure at the End of the Rainbow & Other Stories: Troll Peter's Adventures, Book 2. (p. 1788)
—Troll Peter Visits His Uncle, the Bridge Troll & Other Stories. (p. 1788)
Christensen, Gerda & Evans, Carol. Troll Peter & His Family Prepare for Winter & Other Stories: Troll Peter's Adventures Book 4. (p. 1788)
Christensen, Jennifer Steele, ed. see Boeholt, V. A.
Christensen, Jo-Anne. Haunted Halloween Stories: A Collection of Ghost Stories. Vol. 1 (p. 753)
—Victorian Ghost Stories. (p. 1840)
Christensen, Laurel. LYFSGUD: If God Sent You a Text Message. (p. 1066)
Christensen, Margaret Kate. Hollyhock Fairies. (p. 789)
Christensen, Sharlene. Why Oh Why Did I Tell a Lie? (p. 1925)
Christensen, Wendy. Empire of Ancient Egypt, Revised Edition. (p. 521)
Christensen-Hall, Nancy. Good Night, Little Kitten. Hockerman, Dennis, illus. (p. 699)
Christensen-Jowers, Rae. Day I Spent Without Tv. (p. 413)
Christenson, Deanna. Best Friends! (p. 169)
Christenson, Debra. Hairy Harry (p. 736)
Christenson, Emme Jo, jt. auth. see Christenson, Lisa.
Christenson, Erik, illus. see Shaskan, Trisha Speed.
Christenson, Jonathan. Maximilian's Mistake. Gerecke, Bretta, illus. (p. 1112)
Christenson, Lisa. Harley Hippo & the Crane Game. Christenson, Lisa, illus. (p. 749)
Christenson, Lisa & Christenson, Emme Jo. Seasons on the Sofa. Christenson, Lisa & Christenson, Emme Jo, illus. (p. 1539)
—Who Ate the Moon? Christenson, Lisa & Christenson, Emme Jo, illus. (p. 1914)
Christenson, Maren. Just Like Joan. (p. 939)
Christenson, Maren, illus. see Dutson, Shelly.
Christenson, Missy. If I Were You... (p. 853)
Christi, C. C. Gorge the Fart. (p. 702)
Christian, Andersen Hans, jt. auth. see Andersen, Hans Christian.
Christian, Anna. Newcomer. (p. 1249)
Christian Art Gifts, creator. Miracles of Jesus Puzzle Bible. (p. 1149)
—My Little Puzzle Bible. (p. 1213)
—My Secret Diary. (p. 1218)
Christian, Betsy & Christian, George. For the Love of Texas: Tell Me about the Colonists! Gruszka, Chris A., illus. (p. 616)
—For the Love of Texas: Tell Me about the Revolution! Gruszka, Chris A., illus. (p. 616)
Christian, Cheryl. How Many? (English/Haitian Creole) Dwight, Laura, photos by. (p. 810)
—How Many? (English/Russian) Dwight, Laura, photos by. (p. 810)
—How Many? (Korean) Choi, Jin, tr. (p. 810)
—How Many? (Portuguese/English) Dwight, Laura, photos by. (p. 810)
—How Many? (Simplified Mandarin) Dwight, Laura, photos by. (p. 810)
—How Many? (Spanish/English) Fiol, Maria A., tr. from ENG. (p. 810)
—How Many? (Traditional Cantonese) Dwight, Laura, photos by. (p. 810)
—How Many? (Vietnamese) Dwight, Laura, photos by. (p. 810)
—What Happens Next? (Haitian Creole/English) Dwight, Laura, photos by. (p. 1886)
—What Happens Next? (Korean) Choi, Jin, tr. (p. 1886)
—What Happens Next? (Russian/English) Dwight, Laura, photos by. (p. 1886)
—What Happens Next? (Simplified Mandarin) Dwight, Laura, photos by. (p. 1886)
—What Happens Next (Spanish/English) Bilingual Edition Dwight, Laura, photos by. (p. 1886)
—What Happens Next? (Traditional Cantonese) Dwight, Laura, photos by. (p. 1886)
—What Happens Next? (Vietnamese) Dwight, Laura, photos by. (p. 1886)
—What's in My Garden? A Book of Colors. Ericsson, Annie Beth, illus. (p. 1897)
—What's in My Toybox: A Book of Shapes Ericsson, Annie Beth, illus. (p. 1898)
—Where Does It Go? (Haitian Creole/English) Dwight, Laura, photos by. (p. 1907)
—Where Does It Go? (Korean) Choi, Jin, tr. from ENG. (p. 1907)
—Where Does It Go? (Russian/English) Dwight, Laura, photos by. (p. 1907)
—Where Does It Go? (Simplified Mandarin) Dwight, Laura, photos by. (p. 1907)
—Where Does It Go? (Spanish/English) Fiol, Maria A., tr. (p. 1907)
—Where Does It Go? (Traditional Cantonese) Dwight, Laura, photos by. (p. 1907)
—Where Does It Go? (Vietnamese) Dwight, Laura, photos by. (p. 1907)
—Where's the Baby? (Haitian Creole/English) Dwight, Laura, photos by. (p. 1910)
—Where's the Baby? (Korean) Choi, Jin, tr. (p. 1910)
—Where's the Baby? (Russian/English) Dwight, Laura, photos by. (p. 1910)
—Where's the Baby? (Simplified Mandarin) Dwight, Laura, photos by. (p. 1910)
—Where's the Baby? (Spanish/English) Bilingual Edition Fiol, Maria A., tr. from ENG. (p. 1910)
—Where's the Baby? (Traditional Cantonese) Dwight, Laura, photos by. (p. 1910)
—Where's the Baby? (Vietnamese) Dwight, Laura, photos by. (p. 1910)
—Where's the Kitten? (Haitian Creole/English) Dwight, Laura, photos by. (p. 1911)
—Where's the Kitten? (Korean) Choi, Jin, tr. (p. 1911)
—Where's the Kitten? (Russian/English) Dwight, Laura, photos by. (p. 1911)
—Where's the Kitten? (Simplified Mandarin) Dwight, Laura, photos by. (p. 1911)
—Where's the Kitten? (Spanish/English) Bilingual Edition Fiol, Maria A., tr. (p. 1911)
—Where's the Kitten? (Traditional Cantonese) Dwight, Laura, photos by. (p. 1911)
—Where's the Kitten? (Vietnamese) Dwight, Laura, photos by. (p. 1911)
—Where's the Puppy? (Haitian Creole/English) Dwight, Laura, photos by. (p. 1911)
—Where's the Puppy? (Korean) Choi, Jin, tr. (p. 1911)
—Where's the Puppy? (Russian/English) Dwight, Laura, photos by. (p. 1911)
—Where's the Puppy? (Simplified Mandarin) Dwight, Laura, photos by. (p. 1911)
—Where's the Puppy (Spanish/English) Bilingual Edition Fiol, Maria A., tr. (p. 1911)
—Where's the Puppy? (Traditional Cantonese) Dwight, Laura, photos by. (p. 1911)
—Where's the Puppy? (Vietnamese) Dwight, Laura, photos by. (p. 1911)
—Witches Williams, Wish, illus. (p. 1941)
Christian, Cheryl, jt. auth. see Ericsson, Annie Beth.
Christian, Claudia D. Vicious Bliss Fallen. (p. 1840)
Christian, David. This Fleeting World: An Overview of Human History. Weidemann, Linda, illus. (p. 1735)
Christian, Diana. Lucky Seven. (p. 1063)
Christian, Focus & Tnt Ministries Staff. God's Zoo. Charnick, Tim, illus. (p. 692)
Christian Focus Publications (CFP) Staff, ed. see Tnt.
Christian Focus Publications (CFP) Staff & Dinnen, Marie. Entering by Faith: A Study in Hebrews. (p. 531)
Christian Focus Publications (CFP) Staff & MacKenzie, Carine. Jesus Is Alive: The Amazing Story. (p. 915)
—Joseph: God's Dreamer. Apps, Fred, illus. (p. 926)
Christian Focus Publications (CFP) Staff & Russell, Dorothy. Men of Courage: A Study of Elijah & Elisha. (p. 1126)
Christian Focus Publications (CFP) Staff & Scrimshire, Hazel. Little Rich Man. (p. 1035)
—Safe at Sea. (p. 1502)
—Special Baby - The Birth of Jesus. (p. 1623)
Christian Focus Publications (CFP) Staff & Tnt. Christmas Story, Preparation for Service & the Promised Messiah. (p. 315)
Christian, George, jt. auth. see Christian, Betsy.
Christian, Heather, illus. see Widmer, Becky.
Christian, Judy, et al. Scribble, Dribble, & Glue: Bible Art Projects for Kids. (p. 1533)
Christian Literature International Staff & Barbour Publishing Staff. Barbour Children's Bible. (p. 138)
Christian, Lmh. Stories from the Red Glass. (p. 1654)
Christian, Mary Blount. Special Ops: Tactical Training (p. 1623)
—Swamp Monsters. Brown, Marc, illus. (p. 1688)
—Working with Immigrants & Migrant Populations Through Service Learning (p. 1953)
Christian Mauricio Constante. What a Catch! (p. 1878)
Christian, Norma. Christmas Mouse. (p. 314)
Christian, Peggy. Chocolate, a Glacier Grizzly. Cottone-Kolthoff, Carol, illus. (p. 309)
—If You Find a Rock. Lember, Barbara Hirsch, photos by. (p. 854)
Christian, Reinar Carl, Sr. Nate: The New Bus on the Block! (p. 1230)
Christian, Sandra J. Colorado. (p. 343)
—Florida. (p. 606)
—Iowa. (p. 886)
—Nebraska. (p. 1239)
—South Carolina. (p. 1616)
Christiana, David, illus. see Levine, Gail Carson.
Christiana, David, illus. see Schwartz, Alvin.
Christiane, illus. see Young, Marlabelle & Buchwald, Ann.
Christiansen, Candace. Mitten Tree. Greenstein, Elaine, illus. (p. 1156)
Christiansen, Candace, jt. auth. see Locker, Thomas.
Christiansen, Diane. Scenes for Teens, by Teens: A collection by Diane Christiansen. (p. 1521)
Christiansen, Diane Mayer, jt. auth. see Christiansen, Jackie.
Christiansen, Jackie & Christiansen, Diane Mayer. Jackie's Journal. (p. 904)
Christiansen, Jennifer. Get to Know Inclined Planes. (p. 668)
—Get to Know Wedges. (p. 668)
Christiansen, Jennifer J. Saucy's Taste of Paris. (p. 1516)
Christiansen, Lee, illus. see Goodman, Susan E. & Goodman, Susan.
Christiansen, Lee, illus. see Vaughan, Richard Lee.
Christiansen, Per. Constrictor Snakes. (p. 359)
—Pests & Parasites. (p. 1345)
—Poisonous Spiders. (p. 1377)
—Prehistoric Beasts. (p. 1395)
—Terrifying & Ugly Sea Creatures. (p. 1721)
Christiansen, Sue. Zoey. (p. 1987)
Christianson, Cornell. Holiday Skits & Contests: With Songs, Quizzes, Jokes & Prayers. (p. 788)
Christianson, Leslie Rose. Adventures of Peter & Paul. (p. 21)
—Malinda Matters: Malinda's Birthday Surprise. (p. 1083)
—Malinda Matters: Malinda's Halloween Adventure. (p. 1083)
—Malinda Matters: And Priscilla the Praying Mantis. (p. 1083)
Christie, Agatha. Asesinato en el Orient Expreso. (p. 105)
—Cita con la Muerte. (p. 322)
Christie, Caroline. Silver Heels: A Story of Blackfeet Indians at Glacier National Park. Wilde, George, illus. (p. 1576)
Christie, Donna. Bobby & the Well. (p. 206)
Christie, Douglas, Jr. Dougie Goes to School. (p. 473)
—Dougie Learns to Ride. (p. 473)
Christie, Ed. Sweet Smell of Rotten Eggs: Volume Two, the Dude Ranch Rangers. (p. 1690)
Christie, Gerschutz. Samuel the Camel & the Lone Star. (p. 1509)
Christie, Gregory, illus. see Seskin, Steve & Shamblin, Allen.
Christie, Gregory R., illus. see Adedjouma, Davida.
Christie, Gregory R., illus. see Miller, William.
Christie, Jackie. Wacky WaterSlide Wipeout. (p. 1852)
Christie, Jacky. Roger's Big Adventure. (p. 1484)
Christie, Jacqueline. Alphabet Animals. (p. 49)
Christie, Lee. Basic Heredity: Set Of 6. (p. 142)
—Basic Heredity: Text Pairs. (p. 142)
Christie, Olivia. French Manners. (p. 636)
Christie, Pamela. King's Lizard: A Tale of Murder & Deception in Old Santa Fe 1782. (p. 960)
Christie, Peter. Animal Snoops: The Wondrous World of Wildlife Spies. (p. 79)
—Curse of Akkad: Climate Upheavals That Rocked Human History. (p. 394)
—Naturally Wild Musicians: The Wondrous World of Animal Song. (p. 1236)
—Well-Schooled Fish & Feathered Bandits: The Wondrous Ways Animals Learn from Animals. (p. 1874)
Christie, Peter & Kinnaird, Ross. 50 Climate Questions: A Blizzard of Blistering Facts. (p. 1997)
Christie, R., illus. see Medina, Tony.
Christie, R., illus. see Seskin, Steve & Shamblin, Allen.
Christie, R. Gregory. It Jes' Happened: When Bill Traylor Started to Draw Tate, Don, illus. (p. 894)
—Mousetropolis. (p. 1182)
Christie, R. Gregory, illus. see Adoff, Arnold.
Christie, R. Gregory, illus. see Bolden, Tonya.
Christie, R. Gregory, illus. see Grimes, Nikki.
Christie, R. Gregory, illus. see Lewis, J. Patrick.
Christie, R. Gregory, illus. see Medina, Tony.
Christie, R. Gregory, illus. see Nelson, Vaunda Micheaux.
Christie, R. Gregory, illus. see Richards, Beah E.
Christie, R. Gregory, illus. see Weatherford, Carole Boston.
Christie, R. Gregory, illus. see Wheeler, Lisa.
Christie, R. Gregory, illus. see Williams, Mary.
Christie, R. Gregory, jt. auth. see Ashford Frame, Jeron.
Christie, Stuart. Worlding Forster: The Passage from Pastoral. (p. 1960)
Christin, Pierre & Mezieres, Jean-Claude. Valerian Volume 1: The New Future Trilogy: on the Frontiers/the Living Weapons/the Circles of Power. Smith, Timothy Ryan, tr. from FRE. (p. 1830)
Christine, Grove, illus. see Snead, Kathi.
Christine Holzhausen, tr. see Stastny, Peter & Lehmann, Peter, eds.
Christine, Nöstlinger, jt. auth. see Nöstlinger, Christine.
Christine, Peymani. Bratz: Super-Bratz. Tan, Anthony, illus. (p. 223)
Christman, Therese, illus. see Ramsay, Betsy.
Christmas, Art E. Who Needs Me? The Christian Answer for Grief. (p. 1917)
Christmas, Dozay, illus. see Trottier, Maxine.
Christmas, Jeryl. Alphabug Bully Busters. (p. 50)
—Alphabugs. (p. 50)
Christmyer, Sarah, jt. auth. see Cavins, Emily.
Christodoulou, Jean, illus. see Foster, Jesse, et al.
Christoph, James, illus. see Donovan, Sandy.
Christoph, Jamey, illus. see Braun, Eric & Troupe, Thomas Kingsley.
Christoph, Jamey, illus. see Braun, Eric.
Christoph, Jamey, illus. see Flash Kids Editors.
Christoph, Jamey, illus. see Troupe, Thomas Kingsley & Braun, Eric.
Christoph, Jamey, illus. see Troupe, Thomas Kingsley.
Christoph, Jamey, illus. see Weatherford, Carole Boston.
Christopher, Dale. Behind the Desk with... Matt Christopher: The #1 Sportswriter for Kids. (p. 160)
Christopher, Danielle. Harley. (p. 749)
Christopher, Danny, illus. see Pelletier, Mia.
Christopher, Garrett. Good Masters! Sweet Ladies! A Study Guide. Friedland, Joyce & Kessler, Rikki, eds. (p. 698)
—Look at These Animals: A Content Area Reader-science. (p. 1049)
—Your Amazing Senses: A Content Area Reader-health. (p. 1979)
Christopher, Garrett & McDonald, Megan. Judy Moody Saves the World! Friedland, Joyce & Kessler, Rikki, eds. (p. 931)
Christopher, Jennifer, illus. see Christopher, Jennifer R.
Christopher, Jennifer R. What If a Fork Was a Spoon. Christopher, Marie & Christopher, Jennifer, illus. (p. 1887)
Christopher, John. Beyond the Burning Lands. (p. 174)
—City of Gold & Lead. (p. 324)
—Pool of Fire. (p. 1383)
—Tripods Collection: The White Mountains - The City of Gold & Lead - The Pool of Fire - When the Tripods Came. (p. 1787)
—When the Tripods Came. (p. 1905)
—White Mountains. (p. 1913)
—Wild Jack. (p. 1929)
Christopher, Kathleen. Janie's First Day of School. (p. 908)
Christopher, Lawrence. Tickle Fingers: Where Is Pinky? Christopher, Lawrence, illus. (p. 1747)
Christopher, Lucy. Flyaway. (p. 609)
—Killing Woods. (p. 956)
—Stolen. (p. 1651)
—Stolen. (p. 1652)
Christopher, Marie, illus. see Christopher, Jennifer R.
Christopher, Matt. Albert Pujols: On the Field With... (p. 34)
—All Keyed Up. Vasconcellos, Daniel, illus. (p. 44)
—All-Star Fever. Dewdney, Anna, illus. (p. 45)
—At the Plate with... Ichiro. (p. 111)
—Babe Ruth: Legends in Sports. (p. 123)
—Babe Ruth. (p. 123)
—Baseball Flyhawk. (p. 141)
—Baseball Turnaround. (p. 141)
—Baseball World Series. (p. 141)
—Basket Counts. (p. 142)
—Body Check. (p. 207)
—Captain Contest. (p. 264)
—Catch That Pass! (p. 279)
—Catching Waves. (p. 279)
—Center Court Sting. (p. 287)
—Centerfield Ballhawk. Beier, Ellen, illus. (p. 287)
—Comeback Challenge. (p. 347)
—Comeback of the Home Run Kid. (p. 347)
—Dale Earnhardt Sr: Matt Christopher Legends in Sports. (p. 401)
—Day of the Dragon (p. 414)
—Dirt Bike Racer. (p. 446)
—Dirt Bike Runaway. (p. 446)
—District Doubleheader. (p. 454)
—Dive Right In. (p. 454)
—Dog That Called the Pitch. (p. 461)
—Dog That Called the Signals. (p. 461)
—Dog That Pitched a No-Hitter. (p. 461)
—Dog That Stole Football Plays. Vasconcellos, Daniel et al, illus. (p. 461)
—Dog That Stole Home. (p. 461)
—Dog That Stole the Football Plays. (p. 461)
—Double Play at Short. (p. 473)
—El Campo de Juego Con... Derek Jeter. (p. 507)
—Extreme Team: Skateboard Moves. Leonard, David, illus. (p. 557)
—Face-Off. (p. 560)
—Fairway Phenom. (p. 563)
—Football Double Threat. (p. 615)
—Great Americans in Sports: Babe Ruth. (p. 713)
—Great Americans in Sports: Mia Hamm. (p. 713)
—Great Moments in American Auto Racing. (p. 717)
—Great Moments in Basketball History. (p. 717)
—Great Moments in the Summer Olympics. (p. 717)
—Great Quarterback Switch. (p. 718)
—Greatest Sports Team Rivalries. (p. 720)
—Halfback Attack. Meyer, Karen, illus. (p. 737)
—Heads Up! Vasconcellos, Daniel, illus. (p. 757)
—Heads Up. Vasconcellos, Daniel, illus. (p. 757)
—Hit-Away Kid. Ulrich, George, illus. (p. 785)
—Hockey Machine. (p. 786)
—Home Run Kid Races On. (p. 792)
—Hook Shot Hero: A Nothin' but Net Sequel. (p. 795)
—Hot Shot. (p. 802)
—Ice Magic. (p. 850)
—Inline Skater. (p. 874)
—Into the Danger Zone. Koelsch, Michael, illus. (p. 881)
—Johnny Long Legs. (p. 923)
—Karate Kick. (p. 943)
—Kick It! Vasconcellos, Daniel, illus. (p. 951)
—Kid Who Only Hit Homers. (p. 952)
—Lacrosse Face-Off. (p. 970)
—Lacrosse Firestorm. (p. 970)
—Little Lefty. (p. 1030)
—Long Arm Quarterback. (p. 1047)
—Long-Arm Quarterback. (p. 1047)
—Lucky Baseball Bat: 50th Anniversary Commemorative Edition. Henneberger, Robert, illus. (p. 1062)
—Lucky Baseball Bat. Henneberger, Robert, illus. (p. 1062)
—Making the Save. Vasconcellos, Daniel, illus. (p. 1082)
—Man Out at First. Beier, Ellen, illus. (p. 1085)
—Master of Disaster. Vasconcellos, Daniel, illus. (p. 1103)
—Michael Jordan: Legends in Sports. (p. 1134)
—Miracle at the Plate. (p. 1148)
—Muchacho Que Bateaba Solo Jonrones. (p. 1188)
—New York Yankees: The Most Successful Team in Major League History. (p. 1248)
—Olympics: Unforgettable Moments of the Games. (p. 1288)
—On the Bike with... Lance Armstrong. (p. 1289)
—On the Court with... Dwight Howard. (p. 1290)

—On the Court with... Lebron James. (p. 1290)
—On the Court With... Shaquille O'Neil. (p. 1290)
—On the Court with... Yao Ming. (p. 1290)
—On the Field With... Peyton & Eli Manning. (p. 1290)
—On the Mound with... Curt Schilling. (p. 1291)
—On Thin Ice. Koelsch, Michael, illus. (p. 1292)
—One Smooth Move. Koelsch, Michael, illus. (p. 1297)
—Out at Second. (p. 1310)
—Perfect Game. (p. 1341)
—Play Ball! (p. 1371)
—Power Pitcher. (p. 1390)
—QB Blitz. (p. 1422)
—Return of the Home Run Kid. (p. 1464)
—Rock On. Koelsch, Michael, illus. (p. 1482)
—Roller Hockey Radicals. (p. 1485)
—Roller Hockey Rumble. Koelsch, Michael, tr. (p. 1485)
—Shadow over Second. Dewdney, Anna, illus. (p. 1557)
—Shoot for the Hoop. (p. 1568)
—Skateboard Tough. (p. 1583)
—Slam Dunk. (p. 1587)
—Slide, Danny, Slide. (p. 1590)
—Snowboard Champ. (p. 1600)
—Snowboard Maverick. (p. 1600)
—Snowboard Showdown. (p. 1600)
—Soccer Halfback. (p. 1603)
—Soccer Scoop. (p. 1603)
—Spy on Third Base. Ulrich, George, illus. (p. 1636)
—State Showdown. (p. 1644)
—State Show-Down. (p. 1644)
—Stealing Home. (p. 1646)
—Stranger in Right Field. Dodson, Bert, illus. (p. 1665)
—Submarine Pitch. (p. 1671)
—Super Bowl: Legendary Sports Events. (p. 1679)
—Switch Play! Vasconcellos, Daniel, illus. (p. 1691)
—Team That Couldn't Lose. (p. 1710)
—Tough to Tackle. (p. 1773)
—Wild Ride. Koelsch, Michael, illus. (p. 1930)
—World Series: Legendary Sports Events. (p. 1958)
—You Lucky Dog. Vasconcellos, Daniel, illus. (p. 1976)
—Zero's Slider. Delaney, Molly, illus. (p. 1986)
Christopher, Matt, jt. auth. see Mantell, Paul.
Christopher, Matt, jt. auth. see Peters, Stephanie.
Christopher, Matt, jt. auth. see Stout, Glenn.
Christopher, Matt & Peters, Stephanie. Great Moments in the Summer Olympics. (p. 717)
Christopher, Matt & Peters, Stephanie True. World Cup. (p. 1954)
Christopher, Matt & Stout, Glenn. On the Mound With... Curt Schilling. (p. 1291)
Christopher, Maynard, jt. auth. see Maynard, Christopher.
Christopher, Neil. Arctic Giants Widermann, Eva, illus. (p. 96)
—Country of Wolves Pérez, Ramón, illus. (p. 372)
—Hidden: A Compendium of Arctic Giants, Dwarves, Gnomes, Trolls, Faeries & Other Strange Beings from Inuit Oral History Austin, Mike, illus. (p. 775)
—Way Back Then Arnaktauyok, Germaine, illus. (p. 1864)
Christopher, Neil, jt. auth. see Flaherty, Louise.
Christopher, Nicholas. True Adventures of Nicolo Zen. (p. 1791)
Christopher, Nick. Dream of Manifest Destiny: Immigrants & the Westward Expansion. (p. 483)
—Janey Adds: Understanding Addition. (p. 908)
—Lice. (p. 1007)
—Que Hacen Los Carteros? / What Do Mail Carriers Do? (p. 1423)
—Que Hacen Los Policias? / What Do Police Officers Do? (p. 1423)
—What Do Mail Carriers Do? (p. 1882)
—What Do Police Officers Do? (p. 1882)
—What Makes a Civilization? (p. 1892)
Christopher, Nick, jt. auth. see Mills, Nathan.
Christopher, Paul. Michelangelo's Notebook. (p. 1135)
—Rembrandt's Ghost. (p. 1459)
Christopher, Peter, photos by see Tanaka, Shelley.
Christopher, Romero, jt. auth. see Joseph, Costa.
Christopher, Wright, illus. see Patterson, Eric.
Christophersen, Christine, illus. see Christophersen, Jane Garlil.
Christophersen, Christine & Christophersen, Jane. My Home in Kakadu. (p. 1211)
Christophersen, Jane, jt. auth. see Christophersen, Christine.
Christophersen, Jane Garlil. Kakadu Calling: Stories for Kids. Christophersen, Christine, illus. (p. 941)
Christopherson, Keven. Adventures of the Sky Kids: Lost Treasure of Kolob Canyon. (p. 23)
Christopherson, Sara Cohen. Living with Epilepsy. (p. 1042)
—Top 50 Reasons to Care about Marine Turtles: Animals in Peril. (p. 1769)
—Top 50 Reasons to Care about Whales & Dolphins: Animals in Peril. (p. 1769)
Christov-Bakarglev, Carolyn. Arte Povera. (p. 103)
Christy, Betty. Easy-to-Cut Silhouette Designs. (p. 500)
Christy, Jana, illus. see Brenner, Tom.
Christy, Jana, illus. see Buzzeo, Toni.
Christy, Jana, illus. see Calmenson, Stephanie.
Christy, Jana, illus. see Clark, Julie Aigner.
Christy, Jana, illus. see Fliess, Sue.
Christy, Jana, illus. see Golden Books.
Christy, Jana, illus. see Karst, Patrice.
Christy, Jana, illus. see MacDonald, Maryann.
Christy, Jana, illus. see Posner-Sanchez, Andrea.
Christy, Jana, illus. see RH Disney Staff & Depken, Kristen L.
Christy, Jana, illus. see RH Disney Staff.
Christy, Jana, illus. see Rosenberg, Madelyn.
Christy, Jana, illus. see Seven, John.
Christy, Jana, illus. see Sweeney, Linda Booth.
Christy, Jana, illus. see Taylor, Chloe.
Christy, Jana, illus. see Thomson, Sarah L.
Christy, Jana, illus. see Thorpe, Kiki & RH Disney Staff.
Christy, Jana, illus. see Thorpe, Kiki.
Christy, Jana, jt. auth. see Jonath, Leslie.
Christy, Jana, jt. auth. see Seven, John.
Christy, Lee Louis. I Go to Work as a Doctor. (p. 838)

—I Go to Work as a Firefighter. (p. 838)
—I Go to Work as a Police Officer. (p. 838)
Christy Mahler Mills. No Regrets. (p. 1260)
Christy, Stephen, ed. see Henson, Jim & Juhl, Jerry.
Christy, Stephen, ed. see Kay, Stan.
Christy, Stephen, ed. see Powers, Mark.
Chronic, Halka. Roadside Geology of Arizona. (p. 1477)
—Roadside Geology of New Mexico. Alt, David & Hyndman, Donald W., eds. (p. 1477)
—Roadside Geology of Utah. (p. 1477)
Chronic, Halka & Williams, Felicie. Roadside Geology of Colorado. (p. 1477)
Chronicle Books Editors. Lately Lily ABC Travel Flash Cards. Player, Micah, illus. (p. 979)
Chronicle Books Editors, jt. auth. see ImageBooks Staff.
Chronicle Books Staff. 101 Things to Do While You Wait. (p. 2000)
—75 Word Puzzles. (p. 1998)
—Aladdin & the Magic Lamp (Aladino y la Lampara Maravillosa) Montserrat, Pep, illus. (p. 33)
—Around the World Matching Game. Player, Micah, illus. (p. 101)
—Fantastical Fairies Matching Game. Medeiros, Giovana, illus. (p. 572)
—Fortune-Telling Birthday Book. (p. 623)
—Just a Minute Teacher's Guide. (p. 937)
—Look at Me! My Photo Book of W. (p. 1048)
—Made in China. (p. 1070)
—My Favorite Things Flash Cards. Siminovich, Lorena, illus. (p. 1203)
—New York, Baby! Jenkins, Ward, illus. (p. 1247)
—Nick Jr. Nursery Rhyme Time: A Touch-and-See Activity Book. (p. 1251)
—Nickelodeon Nighttime Book. (p. 1251)
—Papa Do You Love Me Teacher's. (p. 1322)
—Port-A-Plant. (p. 1386)
—Romeow & Drooliet. (p. 1486)
—Ruby's Wish Teacher's Guide. (p. 1494)
—San Francisco, Baby! Jenkins, Ward, illus. (p. 1510)
—Space Matching Game. (p. 1619)
—Sprout Your Own Leafy Wonders. (p. 1635)
—Stanley Goes Fishing Hc (French) (p. 1640)
—Star Wars Lightsaber Thumb Wrestling. (p. 1641)
—Thumbelina. Capdevila, Francesc, illus. (p. 1745)
—Up to No Good: The Rascally Things Boys Do, as Told by Perfectly Decent Grown Men. Harmon, Kitty, ed. (p. 1824)
—Vunce upon a Time. Seibold, J. Otto & Vivian, Siobhan, illus. (p. 1851)
—Wahine. (p. 1852)
Chronicle Books Staff, jt. auth. see Baicker, Karen.
Chronicle Books Staff, jt. auth. see Baird, Duncan H.
Chronicle Books Staff, jt. auth. see Barner, Bob.
Chronicle Books Staff, jt. auth. see Carle, Eric.
Chronicle Books Staff, jt. auth. see Cervantes, Jennifer.
Chronicle Books Staff, jt. auth. see Cosmic Debris Etc., Inc. Staff.
Chronicle Books Staff, jt. auth. see Gaumont Cinémathèque Muse Staff.
Chronicle Books Staff, jt. auth. see Gherman, Beverly.
Chronicle Books Staff, jt. auth. see Gillingham, Sara.
Chronicle Books Staff, jt. auth. see Gomi, Taro.
Chronicle Books Staff, jt. auth. see Gordon, Lynn.
Chronicle Books Staff, jt. auth. see Image Books Staff.
Chronicle Books Staff, jt. auth. see ImageBooks Staff.
Chronicle Books Staff, jt. auth. see Lenz Mulligan Rights and Co. Staff.
Chronicle Books Staff, jt. auth. see MacColl, Michaela.
Chronicle Books Staff, jt. auth. see Marshall, Rita.
Chronicle Books Staff, jt. auth. see Museum of Modern Art (New York, N.Y.) Staff.
Chronicle Books Staff, jt. auth. see Parr, Todd.
Chronicle Books Staff, jt. auth. see Paul Frank Industries Staff.
Chronicle Books Staff, jt. auth. see Turner Classic Movies Staff.
Chronicle Books Staff, jt. auth. see Williams, Katie.
Chronicle Books Staff & Barner, Bob. Dinosaurs Roar, Butterflies Soar! (p. 445)
Chronicle Books Staff & Carle, Eric. Animal Place Mats: The World of Eric Carle Animal Place Mats. (p. 79)
Chronicle Books Staff & Estellon, Pascale. Giant Play & Learn Book. (p. 674)
Chronicle Books Staff & Frank, Paul. Julius! (p. 932)
—Wild West Bananza. (p. 1930)
Chronicle Books Staff & Image Books Staff. Little Cat: Finger Puppet Book. Put, Klaartje van der, illus. (p. 1025)
Chronicle Books Staff & ImageBooks Staff. Little Bee. van der Put, Klaartje, illus. (p. 1024)
—Little Moose: Finger Puppet Book. Put, Klaartje van der, illus. (p. 1032)
Chronicle Books Staff & Javins, Marie. World Atlas & Tour. (p. 1954)
Chronicle Books Staff & Leuck, Laura. For Just One Day. Boutavant, Marc, illus. (p. 615)
Chronicle Books Staff & Markle, Sandra. Animals Christopher Columbus Saw: An Adventure in the New World. Akib, Jamel, illus. (p. 82)
Chronicle Books Staff & Museum of Modern Art (New York, N.Y.) Staff. String-Along Books. (p. 1667)
Chronicle Books Staff & Powers, Amelia. Giant Pop-Out Bugs. (p. 674)
Chronicle Books Staff & Smith, Molly. Trucks, Trains & More! (p. 1791)
Chronicle Books Staff & Thong, Roseanne. Wish: Wishing Traditions Around the World. Kleven, Elisa, illus. (p. 1940)
Chronicle Books Staff, contrib. by. John Singer Sargent Portraits. (p. 922)
Chronicle Books Staff, et al. Eye-Popping 3-D Pets: Phantogram Animals You Can Practically Pet! (p. 558)
—Little Reindeer. (p. 1035)
Chronicle Guidance Publishers, creator. Chronicle Four-Year College Databook: A Directory of Accredited Four-Year Colleges with Their Major Programs of Study. (p. 317)

—Chronicle Two-Year College Databook: A Directory of Accredited Two-Year Colleges with Their Major Programs of Study. (p. 317)
—Chronicle Vocational School Manual: A Directory of Accredited, Approved, Certified, Licensed or Registered Vocational & Technical Schools with Programs of Study. (p. 317)
Chronicle Staff. Creative Collection of American Short Stories. Nascimbene, Yan, illus. (p. 379)
Chronister, Amanda, illus. see Wallace, Nancy K.
Chronopoulos, Maria, illus. see Desautels, Denise.
Chrustowski, Rick. Bee Dance. Chrustowski, Rick, illus. (p. 157)
Chrustowski, Rick, illus. see Joosse, Barbara M.
Chrystall, Claire, illus. see Harris, Sue.
Chrystall, Claire, illus. see Hunt, Janie.
Chrystyn, Julie. Hachiko: The Story of a Loyal Akita & the Royal Dogs of Japan. (p. 735)
Chu, April, illus. see Jiang, Emily.
Chu, April, illus. see Van, Muon.
Chu, April, illus. see Wallmark, Laurie.
Chu, C. K. Eternal Spring Chi Kung. Borrelli, James, ed. (p. 539)
Chu, Carol. Shoes, Shoes, Shoes: A Delightful Book of Imaginary Footwear for Coloring, Inspiring, & Dreaming. Chwast, Seymour, illus. (p. 1568)
Chu, Carol & Chang, Lulu. Fashion Coloring Book. (p. 575)
Chu, Kate, illus. see Partin, Charlotte Corry.
Chua, Charlene, illus. see Chin, Oliver Clyde.
Chua, Charlene, illus. see Chin, Oliver.
Chua, Maria, jt. auth. see Krause, John.
Chuang, Emily. Francis' Tail. (p. 628)
Chubb, Andrew, jt. auth. see Parley, Peter, pseud.
Chubbs-Rogers, Shannon. Listen... Can You Hear It? (p. 1022)
Chuck D, jt. auth. see Collins, Tracy Brown.
Chuck, Stump & Jim, Strawn. Sad Mad Glad Book: The Anatomy of Your Attitude. (p. 1501)
Chucklebeary, Rosie. Crisis Company. (p. 383)
—Inside a Wish. (p. 876)
Chudacoff, Howard, et al. Major Problems in American Urban & Suburban History: Documents & Essays. (p. 1078)
Chudler, Eric H. Inside Your Brain. (p. 878)
Chui, David. Choosing a Career in the Post Office. (p. 310)
Chui, Patricia. Florida. Porras, Carlos & D'Andrea, Patricia, trs. from ENG. (p. 606)
Chukovsky, Kornei. Doctor Ouch. Seabaugh, Jan, tr. from RUS. (p. 459)
Chuks-Samuel, Mary. Captain Rainbow & the Agents: Value My Vote. (p. 264)
Chukwumerije, Dikeogu. Malaik: A Poetry Collection for Children & Those Who Love Them. Okonji, Azuka, illus. (p. 1083)
Chul, Ahn. Volcano High. (p. 1848)
Chullabrahm, T. M., illus. see Penner, Evelyn.
Chum, Hermit. Vagrant. (p. 1830)
Chumley, Joel. Treasure Tree. (p. 1782)
Chun, C. S., illus. see Oh, Cirro.
Chun, Peggy, jt. auth. see Mecum, Shelly.
Chung, Arree. Ninja! Chung, Arree, illus. (p. 1256)
Chung, Arree, illus. see Spector, Todd.
Chung, Chi, illus. see Bolin, Frances Schoonmaker, ed.
Chung, Chi, illus. see Lowell Gallion, Sue.
Chung, Chi, illus. see Nolan, Allia Zobel.
Chung, Chi, illus. see Viola, Karen.
Chung, Haley, illus. see Jung, Tori.
Chung, Helena. Jennifer, the Special One. (p. 913)
Chung, Helena R. Inside My Special Box. (p. 877)
Chung, Liz. Inside Rabbit Burrows. (p. 877)
—Life in China. (p. 1010)
—Madrigueras de Conejos (Inside Rabbit Burrows) (p. 1070)
Chung, Ruth, illus. see Eissler, Trevor.
Chupack, Edward, ed. Lease Negotiation Handbook—2006 Supplement (p. 986)
Chupeco, Rin. Girl from the Well. (p. 678)
—Suffering. (p. 1672)
Chur, R. G. Crescent Bay. (p. 381)
—Penny the Pink Cloud. (p. 1338)
Churbuck, Esther V., illus. see Gates, Josephine Scribner.
Church, Alfred J. Aeneid for Boys & Girls. (p. 25)
—Stories from Livy. (p. 1654)
—Stories of the East from Herodotus. (p. 1655)
—Story of the Odyssey. (p. 1661)
—Three Greek Children. (p. 1742)
Church, Alfred John. Stories of the Iliad & the Aeneid. (p. 1655)
—Story of the Iliad. (p. 1661)
—Story of the Odyssey. (p. 1661)
Church, Alfred John, adapted by. Story of the Last Days of Jerusalem: From Josephus. (p. 1661)
Church, Anna. Hug-A-Bug Travels to Greece. Taylor, Nicole, illus. (p. 824)
—Hug-A-Bug Travels to Peru. Church, Anna & Taylor, Nicole, illus. (p. 824)
Church, Bryan. Dreamcatcher Bowl. (p. 484)
Church, Caroline Jayne. Creation. (p. 379)
—Giggle! Church, Caroline Jayne, illus. (p. 676)
—Goodnight, I Love You. Church, Caroline Jayne, illus. (p. 701)
—Here Comes Christmas! Church, Caroline Jayne, illus. (p. 770)
—Here Comes Easter! Church, Caroline Jayne, illus. (p. 770)
—Here Comes Halloween! Church, Caroline Jayne, illus. (p. 770)
—I Am a Big Brother! Church, Caroline Jayne, illus. (p. 831)
—I Am a Big Sister! Church, Caroline Jayne, illus. (p. 832)
—I Love You! Church, Caroline Jayne, illus. (p. 843)
—Let's Get Dressed! Church, Caroline Jayne, illus. (p. 997)
—Little Apple Goat. Church, Caroline Jayne, illus. (p. 1023)
—Ping Pong Pig. Church, Caroline Jayne, illus. (p. 1359)
—Potty Time! Church, Caroline Jayne, illus. (p. 1388)
—Rain, Rain, Go Away. (p. 1435)
—Ruff! And the Wonderfully Amazing Busy Day. Church, Caroline Jayne, illus. (p. 1494)

—Sweet Child of Mine: A Caroline Jayne Church Treasury. Church, Caroline Jayne, illus. (p. 1689)
—Ten Tiny Toes. Church, Caroline Jayne, illus. (p. 1719)
—Twinkle, Twinkle, Little Star. Church, Caroline Jayne, illus. (p. 1802)
Church, Caroline Jayne, illus. see Bauer, Marion Dane.
Church, Caroline Jayne, illus. see Bernstein, Kei.
Church, Caroline Jayne, illus. see Davis, Jimmie.
Church, Caroline Jayne, illus. see Holub, Joan.
Church, Caroline Jayne, illus. see Morgan, Michaela & Hinnant, Skip.
Church, Caroline Jayne, illus. see Page, Josephine.
Church, Caroline Jayne, illus. see Randall, Ronne.
Church, Caroline Jayne, illus. see Rossetti-Shustak, Bernadette.
Church, Caroline Jayne, illus. see Waring, Richard & Jayne, Waring -.
Church, Caroline Jayne, jt. auth. see Zadrozny, Alicia.
Church, Elizabeth Comfort, illus. see Church, Peggy Pond.
Church, J. R. Guardians of the Grail: And the Men Who Plan to Rule the World. Griffin, Ralph G. & Stearman, G. G., eds. (p. 728)
Church, Lorraine. Pencilvani. (p. 1336)
Church, Oliver. Living Dead - the Reaper's Reward. (p. 1040)
Church, Peggy Pond. Burro of Angelitos. (p. 244)
—Pancake Stories: Cuentos Del Panqueque. Chilton, Noel, tr. (p. 1320)
—Shoes for the Santo Niño: Zapitillos para el Santo Niño: A Bilingual Tale. Carrillo, Charles M., illus. (p. 1568)
—Shoes for the Santo Niño: Carrillo, Charles M., illus. (p. 1568)
Churches, Richard. Effective Classroom Communication Pocketbook. (p. 505)
Churchill, E. Richard. Tricks & Pranks. (p. 1786)
Churchill, Ginger. Carmen's Sticky Scab. Gott, Barry, illus. (p. 270)
—Wild Rose's Weaving. Wong, Nicole, illus. (p. 1930)
Churchill, Jessica, photos by see Shaboo, Joseph R.
Churchill, Jill. Little Ducks. Yaccarino, Dan, illus. (p. 600)
Churchill, Sue. Australian Bats. (p. 116)
Churchill, Vicki & Fuge, Charles. Sometimes I Like to Curl up in a Ball. (p. 1610)
Churchill, Vicki & McAllister, Angela. Adventures of Little Wombat. Fuge, Charles, illus. (p. 20)
Churchill, Vicky & Fuge, Charles. Butterfly Kiss. (p. 248)
Churilla, Bryan & Shepherd, Jeremy. Engineer - Konstrukt. Churilla, Bryan, illus. (p. 529)
Chuslo-Shur, Lauren, ed. Golden Friendship. (p. 694)
Chuta, Edith N. Straight Talk to Troubled Kids: Finding Wisdom Underneath Our Pains. (p. 1664)
Chuzzlewit, Abraham R., illus. see Vitterito, Joseph A., 2nd.
Chwast, Seymour. Bobo's Smile. Chwast, Seymour, illus. (p. 206)
—Get Dressed! (p. 667)
—She Sells Sea Shells: World Class Tongue Twisters. (p. 1564)
—Tall City, Wide Country. Chwast, Seymour, illus. (p. 1704)
Chwast, Seymour, illus. see Chu, Carol.
Chwast, Seymour, illus. see Linn, Margot.
Chwast, Seymour, illus. see Martin, Judith.
Chwast, Seymour, illus. see Spinelli, Jerry.
Chwast, Seymour & Lofting, Hugh. Dr. Dolittle. Chwast, Seymour, illus. (p. 475)
Chwast, Seymour & Moskof, Martin. Still Another Alphabet Book. (p. 1650)
—Still Another Number Book. (p. 1650)
Chylak, Jolie Catherine, illus. see Steele, Kathleen Marie.
Chyle, Bonnie. Our Pet Show. (p. 1309)
Ciaffaglione, Sebastian, illus. see Newsome, Richard.
Ciaffaglione, Sebastian, illus. see Warner, Margaret & Brown, Susie.
Ciancio, Billie, compiled by. Best Bible Crafts II. (p. 168)
Cianciulli, M. M. Show Me Some More. (p. 1557)
Ciaramitaro, Joseph A., et al. Student Workbook for Use with Welding. (p. 1669)
Ciaravino, Paul, illus. see Belmore, Vickie J.
Ciardi, John. Someone Could Win a Polar Bear. Gorey, Edward, illus. (p. 1609)
—Wish-Tree. Glanzman, Louis S., illus. (p. 1940)
Ciarleglio, Lauren. New Hampshire: Past & Present. (p. 1245)
Ciarrochi, Joseph V., et al. Get Out of Your Mind & into Your Life for Teens: A Guide to Living an Extraordinary Life. (p. 667)
Cibos, Lindsay, jt. auth. see Hodges, Jared.
Cibos, Lindsay & Hodges, Jared. Peach Fuzz, Volume 3. (p. 1332)
Ciccarelli, Gary, illus. see Friden, Chris.
Ciccarelli, Gary, illus. see Sylvester, Diane.
Ciccolini, Marguerite. Pasta Family. Ciccolini, Michael, illus. (p. 1327)
Ciccolini, Michael. Pasta Family 2: First Day of School! Ciccolini, Michael, illus. (p. 1327)
—Pasta Family 5: Macaroni in Space!!! Ciccolini, Michael, illus. (p. 1327)
Ciccolini, Michael, illus. see Ciccolini, Marguerite.
Ciccone, Madonna L., see Madonna, pseud.
Ciccone, Madonna L. & Madonna. Perfect Pair Fulvimari, Jeffrey, illus. (p. 1342)
Ciccone, Tizania & Linardi, Franca. Pancake Princess. Bucci, Gino, illus. (p. 1320)
Ciccone, Tiziana. Taylor, Please Stop Talking! Cannavicci, Luigi A., illus. (p. 1708)
—Tooth Fairy Trouble. (p. 1768)
Ciccone, Tiziana & Linardi, Franca. Lucinda, Queen of Everything. Cannavicci, Luigi A., illus. (p. 1062)
—No More Peanut Butter, Daniel! Bucci, Gino, illus. (p. 1259)
Cicero, Julian, illus. see Baranda, Maria.
Cicero, Julian, illus. see Jinks, Catherine.
Cicero, Julian, illus. see Luna, Arcadio.
Cicero, Julian, illus. see Masera, Mariana.
Cicero, Noah. Burning Babies. (p. 244)
Cichos, Tomek, illus. see Wildfong, Tonya.
Cicola, Amanda, et al. Health & Safety 1: Gym Class; Shopping for Lunch; Good for You; My Happy Heart; Just

For book reviews, descriptive annotations, tables of contents, cover images, author biographies & additional information, updated daily, subscribe to www.booksinprint2.com

2139

Like Me; Staying Safe; Always Brush Your Teeth; A Visit to the Doctor Simon, Sue A. et al, illus. (p. 757)
Ciddor, Anna. Wolfspell. (p. 1944)
Cider Mill Press, Cider Mill & Abramson, Andra. Snoopy's Happy Day: A Finger Puppet Book. Whitlock, Matt, illus. (p. 1598)
Cider Mill Press Staff. Mashmallow Launcher: Make Your Own... Awesome... - Everything You Need to Build Your Owns Blaster! (p. 1102)
Cider Mill Press Staff, ed. see Ewing, Susan.
Cider Mill Press Staff & Copeland, Cynthia L. Secrets of Middle School: Everything You Need to Succeed. (p. 1545)
Cider Mill Press Staff, ed. What's Missing: Look & Look & Look-Can You Find What's Missing? (p. 1898)
Cielo, Ana. Long Journey Home. (p. 1047)
Ciencin, Scott. Attack of the Cling-Ons Crowther, Jeff, illus. (p. 113)
—Cry of the Banshee! Francavilla, Francesco, illus. (p. 387)
—Dino Defenses. (p. 441)
—Escape from Blackbeard's Curse! Francavilla, Francesco, illus. (p. 534)
—Eye for Eye Tocchini, Greg et al, illus. (p. 557)
—Point-Blank Paintball Aburtov, illus. (p. 1377)
Ciencin, Scott, illus. see Salvatore, R. A.
Ciencin, Scott & Burge, Constance M. Luck Be a Lady. (p. 1062)
Ciencin, Scott & Cano, Fernando. Power at the Plate Esparza, Andres et al, illus. (p. 1389)
Ciencin, Scott & Carrano, Matthew T. Growing up Dino. (p. 726)
Ciencin, Scott & Fuentes, Benny. End Zone Thunder Sandoval, Gerardo, illus. (p. 526)
—Full Court Flash Sandoval, Gerardo, illus. (p. 646)
Ciencin, Scott & Maese, Fares. Avalanche Freestyle Aburto, Jesus & Esparza, Andres, illus. (p. 118)
—BMX Blitz Aburto, Jesus & Esparza, Andres, illus. (p. 204)
—BMX Blitz Esparza, Andres & Aburto, Jesus, illus. (p. 204)
Ciencin, Scott, et al. Hoop Rat Aburto, Jesus & Cano, Fernando M., illus. (p. 795)
—Point-Blank Paintball Aburto, Jesus, illus. (p. 1377)
—Snowboard Standoff Aburto, Jesus et al, illus. (p. 1600)
—Snowboard Standoff Esparza, Andres et al, illus. (p. 1600)
Cieply, Angela. Economy of Colorado. (p. 503)
Ciesa, Mary E. Dina Prima the Ballerina. (p. 440)
Ciesemier, Kali, illus. see Priest, Cherie.
Ciesinka, Izabela, illus. see Chapman, Karean.
Ciesinki, Izabela, illus. see Johnson, Cheryl.
Ciesinska, Izabela, illus. see Bernard, Margaret Mitchell.
Ciesinska, Izabela, illus. see Chapman, Karean.
Ciesinska, Izabela, illus. see Fast, David R.
Ciesinska, Izabela, illus. see Karandeev, Oleg.
Ciesinska, Izabela, illus. see Warren, G. A.
Cifuentes, Carolina. My Family. Snider, Jackie, illus. (p. 1202)
—Weather. Hullinger, C. D., illus. (p. 1869)
—What Time Is It? Calitri, Susan Chapman, illus. (p. 1894)
Cifuentes, Carolina, ed. see Rosa-Mendoza, Gladys.
Cifuentes, Carolina, ed. My Family. Snider, Jackie, illus. (p. 1202)
—Weather. Hullinger, C. D., illus. (p. 1869)
—What Time Is It? Calitri, Susan Chapman, illus. (p. 1894)
Cima, Alessandro V. Pirate Jack. (p. 1362)
Cimarusti, Marie Torres & George, Jean Craighead. Buffalo Are Back. Peterson, Stephanie & Minor, Wendell, illus. (p. 235)
Cimatoribus, Alessandra, illus. see Bloom, Valerie.
Cimatoribus, Alessandra, illus. see Piumini, Roberto & Wilde, Oscar.
Cimatoribus, Alessandra, illus. see Visconti, Guido.
Ciment, James. Encyclopedia of Conflicts since World War II (p. 525)
—Postwar America: An Encyclopedia of Social, Political, Cultural, & Economic History (p. 1388)
Ciment, James, jt. auth. see Ness, Immanuel.
Ciminelli, Marilyn Johnson. Where's My Father? Ciminelli, Matthew Joseph, illus. (p. 1910)
Ciminelli, Matthew Joseph, illus. see Ciminelli, Marilyn Johnson.
Ciminera, Siobhan. Farm Animal Friends. Collection/Jupiterimages Unlimited, illus. (p. 573)
—Stuck on Christmas! Collection/Jupiterimages Unlimited, illus. (p. 1669)
Ciminera, Siobhan, adapted by. Get the Sillies Out! (p. 668)
Ciminera, Siobhan & Faulkner, Keith. Yummy Mystery: A Scratch-and-Sniff Story. (p. 1983)
Ciminera, Siobhan & Rao, Lisa. Hello, Friends! Yoe! Studio Staff, illus. (p. 764)
Ciminera, Siobhan & Testa, Maggie. Dancey Dance. Yoe! Studio Staff, illus. (p. 402)
—Meet OLIVIA. Childrens Books Staff & Rose, Drew, illus. (p. 1121)
—Shuffle Stories. Gordon, David et al, illus. (p. 1571)
—So Yummy! So Yummy! Yoe! Studio Staff, illus. (p. 1602)
Cimino, Michael, jt. auth. see Shyun, James.
Cimino, Nicole C., ed. see Kuhn, Douglas Wolcik.
Cimino, Rodolfo, et al. Uncle Scrooge Clark, John, ed. (p. 1812)
Cimmet, Brian. Delicious Word Searches. (p. 425)
Cimochowski, Anna. PassWord Decoder for Prefix, Root Word & Suffix Meanings. (p. 1327)
—PassWord Decoder for Tricky Letter Teams. (p. 1327)
Cimorelli, Amber. There Are Monsters Here! Galante, Ashley, illus. (p. 1729)
CINAR Animation Staff, illus. see Pleau-Murissi, Marilyn.
CINAR Corporation Staff, illus. see Johnson, Marion.
Cinar, Lisa. Day It All Blew Away. (p. 413)
—Paulina P. (p. 1331)
Cinco, Blyton-Los, jt. auth. see Blyton, Enid.
Cinco Puntos Press Staff, jt. auth. see Weill, Cynthia.
Cindrich, Sharon. Smart Girl's Guide to Style: How to Have Fun with Fashion, Shop Smart, & Let Your Personal Style Shine Through. Laskey, Shannon, illus. (p. 1592)
Cindy, Breckman, ed. see Arlene, Sonday.
Cindy, Huffman, ed. see Matheson, Dawn.
Cindy Lou. Boxes & Bows & Wiggling Toes. (p. 217)
Cinebook. Halloween. Jeffrey, Erica, tr. from FRE. (p. 737)
Cinelli, Lisa, illus. see Bahamon, Claire.
Cinelli, Lisa, illus. see Benson, P. Bryn.
Cinema, Bobby. Princess School. (p. 1405)
Cinema, Cahiers du. Hollywood Interviews. Saada, Nicholas, ed. (p. 789)
Cinema, Cahiers du & Saada, Nicholas, eds. Hollywood Interviews. Flower, John, tr. from FRE. (p. 789)
Cinémathèque, Gaumont, et al. Petit Cinéma - Dance. (p. 1348)
Cinetto, Liliana. Cosquillas en la Nariz. (p. 368)
Cini, Michelle & Bourne, Angela K., eds. Palgrave Advances in European Union Studies. (p. 1320)
Cinotto, Laurie. Itty Bitty Kitty Committee: The Ultimate Guide to All Things Kitten. (p. 900)
Cinque, Maria, jt. auth. see Beck, Alison.
Cinquemani, Romina C., tr. see Gnojewski, Carol.
Cinquemani, Romina C., tr. see Landau, Elaine.
Cintron, Carlos Juan, Sr., ed. De niños a Líderes: Red de Niños. (p. 416)
—Mis Primeros Pasos: Red de Niños. (p. 1150)
Ciocca, Donna. Harley & Homer. (p. 749)
—Harley & Homer for Hire. (p. 749)
—Tavern Tales. (p. 1707)
Ciocca, Gina. Last Year's Mistake. (p. 979)
Ciocchi, Catherine. This Land Is Your Land Morrison, Cathy, illus. (p. 1737)
Ciocchi, Catherine & Morrison, Cathy. Esta Tierra, Es Tu País. Morrison, Cathy, illus. (p. 538)
Cioci, Margie. Season of Thankfulness. (p. 1538)
Ciocon-Heler, Vicky. Paquita-Gamita's Wiggling? (p. 1323)
Cioffi, Ben, illus. see Plantedosi, John J.
Cioffi, Dom. Digby & the Lake Monster. (p. 438)
Cioffi, Erin. Lost Carrot. (p. 1055)
Ciongoli, A. Kenneth & Parini, Jay. Passage to Liberty: The Story of Italian Immigration & the Rebirth of America. (p. 1326)
Cioni, Debra. Bailey & Caboose. (p. 133)
Ciovacco, Justine. Amy Poehler. (p. 66)
—Goats. (p. 687)
—LeBron James: NBA Champion. (p. 987)
—Leonardo Da Vinci (p. 992)
—Meerkats. (p. 1120)
—Rhinoceroses. (p. 1467)
—Saving the Endangered Grizzly Bear. (p. 1517)
—Squirrels. (p. 1637)
Cipriano, Jeri. Alerta Global. (p. 35)
—época Colonial: Set Of 6. (p. 532)
—Global Alert & Alerta Global: 6 English, 6 Spanish Adaptations (p. 684)
—Los indígenas Norteamericanos. (p. 1054)
—Native Americans & Los indígenas Norteamericanos: 6 English, 6 Spanish Adaptations (p. 1234)
—Symbols of Our Country: Set Of 6. (p. 1693)
—Symbols of Our Country: Text Pairs. (p. 1693)
—Three Historical Communities of North America: Set Of 6. (p. 1742)
—Three Historical Communities of North America: Text Pairs. (p. 1742)
—tiempo a Prueba. (p. 1747)
—Weatherworks & el tiempo a Prueba: 6 English, 6 Spanish Adaptations (p. 1870)
Cipriano, Jeri, jt. auth. see Challen, Paul.
Cipriano, Jeri & Trumbauer, Lisa. ¡Los Arboles Son Impresionantes! (p. 1053)
Cipriano, Jeri S. Arithmetricks: More Than 100 Amazing Math Tricks. (p. 98)
—Arithmetricks. (p. 98)
—At the Park (p. 111)
—At the Park. (p. 111)
—Celebrations (p. 285)
—Celebrations. (p. 285)
—Harvest Time (p. 752)
—Harvest Time. (p. 752)
—It's Time! (p. 899)
—Let's Look at Rocks (p. 999)
—Let's Look at Rocks. (p. 999)
—Making a Difference. (p. 1080)
—Miremos Las Rocas. (p. 1149)
Cipriano, Jeri S. & Jackson, Abby. Haciendo Dinero. (p. 735)
Cipriano, Sal. Adventures of Bio Boy: The Best of Season One. (p. 16)
Cipullo, Tom. Thomas of Questionable Fortune. (p. 1739)
Cirafesi-Keszczyk, Diane. Cloudy Christmas Myths to Clear Heavenly Beliefs: A Christian Analogy of the Christmas Season for All Who Are Ready to Learn the Truth about Santa Cla. (p. 335)
Ciraolo, Simona. Hug Me. (p. 824)
Ciravolo, Tish. Everything a Girl Needs to Know Abut Playing Guitar! (p. 544)
Circosta, Jennifer. Many Tails of Luck-shmee. (p. 1089)
Cirella-Mitts, Anne. Candle. (p. 261)
Cirelli, Michael, jt. text see Sitomer, Alan Lawrence.
Ciresi-Abremski, M. Kathleen, illus. see Johnson, Calvin.
Cirillo, Todd, et al. Roxy: The Girl in the Platform Shoes, with the Black Dress On. (p. 1492)
Cirrone, jt. auth. see Cirrone, Dorian.
Cirrone, Dorian. Big Scoop Woodruff, Liza, illus. (p. 183)
—Prom Kings & Drama Queens. (p. 1411)
Cirrone, Dorian & Cirrone. Missing Silver Dollar Woodruff, Liza, illus. (p. 1153)
Cirton, Judy. Candice H. & the Bully. (p. 261)
Cis, Daniel Z. Gino & His Trullo: An Abandoned Dog Who Walked into Paradise. (p. 677)
Cis, Valeria, illus. see Pinson, Isabel.
Cis, Valeria, illus. see Portnoy, Mindy Avra.
Cis, Valeria, illus. see Walter Foster Jr. Creative Team.
Cis, Valeria, illus. see Williams, Brenda.
Cis, Valeria, jt. auth. see Krebs, Laurie.
Cisco Networking Academy Program Staff. Connecting Networks Companion Guide. (p. 358)
Cisner, Naftali. Count with Mendel. Cisner, Naftali, illus. (p. 370)
—Get Ready for Shabbos with Mendel. Cisner, Naftali, illus. (p. 668)
Cisneros, Kevin. Shoelaces: The Secret Art of Fresco Painting. Cadney, Mary, ed. (p. 1568)
Cisneros, Sandra. Hairs. (p. 736)
Cisneros, Sandra & SparkNotes Staff. House on Mango Street. Kestler, Justin & Florman, Ben, eds. (p. 803)
Cissna, Kent, illus. see Eisen, Laura.
Citak, Michael J. Adventures of Leo- & the Curse of the Dreaded Doors. (p. 19)
—Adventures of Leo- & the Treasure Cave. (p. 19)
Citizenship Foundation Staff, jt. auth. see Thorpe, Tony.
Citra, Becky. After the Fire (p. 28)
—Dog Days (p. 461)
—Jeremy & the Enchanted Theater Milne, Jessica, illus. (p. 913)
—Jeremy & the Enchanted Theater. Milne, Jessica, illus. (p. 913)
—Jeremy & the Fantastic Flying Machine Milne, Jessica, illus. (p. 913)
—Jeremy & the Golden Fleece Milne, Jessica, illus. (p. 913)
—Missing (p. 1152)
—Never to Be Told (p. 1243)
—Runaway (p. 1496)
—Sam's Ride Meissner, Amy, illus. (p. 1509)
—Strawberry Moon (p. 1666)
—Whiteout (p. 1914)
Citrin, James M. & Smith, Richard A. 5 Patterns of Extraordinary Careers: The Guide for Achieving Success & Satisfaction. (p. 1992)
Citrin, Michael, jt. auth. see Mack, Tracy.
Citro, Asia. Curious Kid's Science Book: 100+ Creative Hands-On Activities for Ages 4-8. Citro, Asia, photos by. (p. 394)
Cittadino, Kristen, illus. see Russo, Frank M.
Cittadino, Kyle, illus. see Russo, Frank M.
City of Edmonton. Naming Edmonton: From Ada to Zoie. (p. 1228)
Citylit Kids. Write On! (p. 1963)
Ciundziewicki, Lech. Glupcio Zeglarz: Zbior Bajek I Wierszy. (p. 685)
Civan, et al. Haitians, History & Culture. (p. 736)
Civardi, A. First Experiences. (p. 594)
Civardi, Anna. Farm Magnet Book. Cartwright, Stephen, illus. (p. 574)
—Going on a Plane Sticker Book. (p. 692)
—Going to the Doctor Sticker Book. (p. 693)
—New Puppy Sticker Book. (p. 1247)
Civardi, Anne. Action! Movement in Art. (p. 10)
—Cambiarse de Casa. (p. 255)
—Complete Book of First Experiences. Cartwright, Stephen, illus. (p. 352)
—First Experiences. (p. 594)
—Going on a Plane. Bates, Michelle, ed. (p. 692)
—Going to a Party. Watt, Fiona, ed. (p. 693)
—Going to School. Cartwright, Stephen, illus. (p. 693)
—Going to School Sticker Book. (p. 693)
—Going to the Dentist. (p. 693)
—Going to the Dentist. Bates, Michelle, ed. (p. 693)
—Going to the Doctor. (p. 693)
—Going to the Hospital. (p. 693)
—Going to the Hospital. Bates, Michelle, ed. (p. 693)
—Moving House. Bates, Michelle, ed. (p. 1183)
—Moving House Sticker Book. (p. 1183)
—New Baby. Bates, Michelle, ed. (p. 1243)
—New Baby Sticker Book. (p. 1243)
Civiello, Emmanuel, illus. see Mosdi, Thomas, et al.
Civil War Photographers Staff, photos by see Lewis, J. Patrick.
Civitano, Tom, jt. auth. see Bloch, Lyudmila.
Civitella, Mark. Angus the Angler: Snapper Surprise. (p. 75)
Cizmich, Marilyne. Sonia, the Church Cat. (p. 1612)
C.J. Elgert. Elder Brothers & the Padstow Crystals. (p. 508)
cky publications. HaSifronim Sheli Series Two: Hasalat she'aino Salat (p. 752)
Clack, Barbra, illus. see Dromgoole, Glenn.
Clack, Barbra, jt. auth. see Dromgoole, Glenn.
Clack, Cynthia. Doodles the American Hero. (p. 469)
Clack, Karin, jt. auth. see Mathes, Ben.
Claerhout, Paul, illus. see Brehm, David L.
Claflin, Willy. Little Moose Who Couldn't Go to Sleep. Stimson, James, illus. (p. 1032)
—Maynard Moose Tales. (p. 1113)
—Rapunzel & the Seven Dwarfs: A Maynard Moose Tale. Stimson, James, illus. (p. 1439)
—Uglified Ducky. Stimson, James, illus. (p. 1808)
Claiborn, Trevor M. Li'l Missy & Antman: Colors. (p. 1017)
—Monkey & the Forbidden Fruit. (p. 1165)
C.Laird, Elizabeth & Skindzier, Jon. Guilford College College Prowler off the Record. (p. 730)
Clairday, Robynn. Girl's Story: How to Write Your Autobiography. (p. 681)
Claire, Black. Puss in Boots. Eric, Kincaid, illus. (p. 1420)
Claire, Elizabeth. Help Your Buddy Learn English Nichols, Dave, illus. (p. 766)
—Hi! (p. 775)
—New Boy Is Lost! An ESL Picture Novel (p. 1243)
Claire Hamelin Bruyere. Princess Bonnie & the Dragon. Mary Connors, illus. (p. 1403)
Claire, Onge. Caillou Que manque t Il. (p. 251)
Claire, Roxanne St., see St. Claire, Roxanne.
Clairey, Hannah. Return from Stony Lonesome. (p. 1464)
Clairmont, Patsy. 5 Cheesy Stories: About Friendship, Bravery, Bullying, & More Oeltjenbruns, Joni, illus. (p. 1992)
—Basil & Parsley Oeltjenbruns, Joni, illus. (p. 142)
—Sleep Sweet, My Little One. Johannes, Shelley, illus. (p. 1588)
CLAMP. Blood-C Volume 3. Simon, Philip, ed. (p. 200)
—X Clamp (p. 1967)
Clamp. XxxHOLiC Rei 1. (p. 1967)
Clamp, Janet. Adventures of Lilly the Bloodhound & Her Friends: Lilly Gets a New Home & Family. (p. 19)
Clamp, Mike. Shakespeare King Richard II. Gibson, Rex, ed. (p. 1559)
Clamp Staff. Angelic Layer (p. 74)
—Angelic Layer Horn, Carl Gustav, ed. (p. 74)
—Blood-C Simon, Philip, ed. (p. 200)
—Cardcaptor Sakura (p. 265)
—Cardcaptor Sakura Clamp Staff, illus. (p. 265)
—Cardcaptor Sakura Horn, Carl Gustav, ed. (p. 265)
—Cardcaptor Sakura (p. 266)
—Cardcaptor Sakura Onishi, Mika, tr. (p. 266)
—Cardcaptor Sakura Clamp Staff, illus. (p. 266)
—Cardcaptor Sakura: Master of the Clow (p. 266)
—Cardcaptor Sakura. (p. 266)
—Legal Drug (p. 987)
—Magic Knight Rayearth (p. 1072)
—Magic Knight Rayearth Sengupta, Anita, tr. from JPN. (p. 1072)
—Magic Knight Rayearth II (p. 1072)
—Master of the Clow 5. (p. 1103)
—RG Veda (p. 1467)
—RG Veda Clamp Staff, illus. (p. 1467)
—Rg Veda. (p. 1467)
—Suki (p. 1673)
—Tokyo Babylon (p. 1762)
—Wish (p. 1940)
Clamp Staff, illus. see Furukawa, Haruko, tr.
Clamp Staff, illus. see Yoshimoto, Ray, tr.
Clamp Staff, jt. auth. see Mokona.
Clamp Staff & Sugisaki, Yukiru. Lagoon Engine (p. 971)
Clamp Staff, contrib. by. Legend of Chun Hyang (p. 988)
—Magic Knight Rayearth (p. 1072)
Clamp Staff, creator. Angelic Layer (p. 74)
—Cardcaptor Sakura (p. 266)
—Tokyo Babylon (p. 1762)
Clamp Staff, ed. Chobits with Figurine. (p. 309)
—Clover. (p. 335)
—Duklyon: Clamp School Defenders (p. 489)
—Magic Knight Rayearth (p. 1072)
—Suki (p. 1673)
Clampet, Jason, jt. auth. see Chambers, Veronica.
Clampett, Bobby & Brumer, Andy. Impact Zone: Mastering Golf's Moment of Truth. (p. 862)
Clampitt, Ed & Fortier, Robert. Team Dawg Stranger Danger. (p. 1710)
—Team Dawg Trevor's Bully Problem. (p. 1710)
Clampitt, Edward L. Team Dawg It's All about Respect. (p. 1710)
Clampitt, Linda. Tatiana: A Proud Turkey's Tale. (p. 1707)
Clanahan, Mary. Nama Kwa's Garden. Taylor, Jacqui, illus. (p. 1228)
Clanchy, Kate. Our Cat Henry Comes to the Swings. Bird, Jemima, illus. (p. 1308)
Clancy, Charmaine. My Zombie Dog. (p. 1222)
Clancy, Kaycee. Sky Painters. (p. 1587)
Clancy, Michael. Once Around on a Bicycle. (p. 1292)
Clancy, Stephanie. Violet, the Fuzzy Honeybee. (p. 1843)
Clancy, Tom. Red Rabbit. (p. 1454)
Clancy, Tom & Rovin, Jeff. Call to Treason. (p. 254)
Clancy, Tom, et al. Battle Ready (p. 147)
—Death Match. (p. 420)
—Into the Storm: A Study in Command. Pt. 2 (p. 881)
Clanton, Ben. It Came in the Mail. (p. 893)
—Rex Wrecks It! Clanton, Ben, illus. (p. 1467)
—Something Extraordinary. Clanton, Ben, illus. (p. 1609)
—Table Sets Itself. Clanton, Ben, illus. (p. 1694)
Clanton, Ben, illus. see Adderson, Caroline.
Clanton, Ben, illus. see Blevins, Wiley.
Clanton, Ben, jt. auth. see Clanton, Benjamin.
Clanton, Benjamin & Clanton, Ben. Table Sets Itself. Clanton, Ben, illus. (p. 1694)
Clanton, Connie. Boy Who Cried Wolf: The Boy Who Cried Wolf. (p. 219)
Clapin, Jeremy, jt. auth. see Delalandre, Benoît.
Clapp. Eloy the Elk & His Desert Friends. Clapp, ed. (p. 516)
Clapp, Nicholas. Who Killed Chester Pray? A Death Valley Mystery. (p. 1916)
Clapp, Patricia. Jane-Emily: And Witches' Children. (p. 908)
Clapp, Sarah & Varacalli, Lauren. Denison University College Prowler off the Record. (p. 426)
Clapper, Kathryn N. Irma Rangel (p. 888)
Clapper, Nikki Bruno. All Aboard! (p. 41)
—Camel Spiders. (p. 256)
—City Trains. (p. 324)
—Creepy Crawlers. (p. 381)
—Crickets. (p. 382)
—Earthworms. (p. 498)
—Freight Trains. (p. 635)
—High-Speed Trains. (p. 778)
—Learning about Plagiarism. (p. 984)
—Learning about Primary Sources. (p. 984)
—Media Literacy for Kids. (p. 1118)
—Millipedes. (p. 1144)
—Passenger Trains. (p. 1326)
Clar, David, illus. see Decaire, Camaale, ed.
Clar, David Austin, illus. see Davidson, Alice Joyce.
Clar, David Austin, illus. see DeBoer, Jesslyn.
Clar, David Austin, illus. see Donovan, Gail.
Clar, David Austin, illus. see Jensen, Patricia & Demar, Regier.
Clar, David Austin, illus. see Publications International Ltd. Staff, ed.
Clara, Machado Maria, jt. auth. see Machado, Maria Clara.
Clara, Miss, illus. see Gresham, Xanthe.
Clara, Miss, illus. see Hoffman, Mary.
Clara, Miss, illus. see Lowes, Sarah.
Clara Mulholland. Naughty Miss Bunny. (p. 1237)
Clara Roddy-Worsham. Bear Baby Ran a Race. (p. 150)
Clare, Anna. Ed Signals. (p. 503)
—Make You a Man. (p. 1079)
Clare, Caitlen. Rabbit Hash Christmas. Haltermon, Becky, illus. (p. 1429)
Clare, Cassandra. City of Ashes. (p. 323)
—City of Bones: Movie Tie-In Edition. (p. 323)
—City of Bones. (p. 323)
—City of Fallen Angels (p. 323)
—City of Fallen Angels. (p. 323)
—City of Glass. (p. 324)
—City of Heavenly Fire. (p. 324)
—City of Lost Souls (p. 324)

—City of Lost Souls. (p. 324)
—Clockwork Angel. (p. 333)
—Clockwork Prince. (p. 333)
—Clockwork Princess. (p. 333)
—Infernal Devices: Clockwork Angel; Clockwork Prince; Clockwork Princess. (p. 873)
—Mortal Instruments: City of Bones; City of Ashes; City of Glass; City of Fallen Angels; City of Lost Souls. (p. 1176)
—Mortal Instruments: City of Bones; City of Ashes; City of Glass; City of Fallen Angels; City of Lost Souls; City of Heavenly Fire. (p. 1176)
Clare, Cassandra, jt. auth. see Black, Holly.
Clare, Cassandra & Lewis, Joshua. Shadowhunter's Codex. (p. 1558)
Clare, Cassandra, ed. Shadowhunters & Downworlders: A Mortal Instruments Reader. (p. 1558)
Clare, Cassandra, et al. Bane Chronicles. Clare, Cassandra, ed. (p. 136)
Clare, John. Braveheart. (p. 223)
—I Am: The Selected Poetry of John Clare. Bate, Jonathan, ed. (p. 831)
Clare, John, jt. auth. see Leadbeater, Tim.
Clare, John D. Aztec Life. (p. 122)
—Britain 1750-1900. (p. 229)
—Cold War & After. (p. 339)
—Germany, 1918-45. (p. 666)
—Great War. (p. 719)
—Medicine in the Industrial World. (p. 1119)
—Medieval Britain, 1066-1500. (p. 1119)
—Nation of Immigrants. (p. 1231)
—Second World War. (p. 1540)
—Vietnam, 1939-75. (p. 1841)
—World Study after 1900. (p. 1958)
Clare, Mimi St. Fairbluffs of Pennington Island. (p. 562)
Clare, Patricia. Living Green: Saving Our Earth. (p. 1041)
Claremont, Chris. Cyber Force Origins (p. 396)
—God Loves, Man Kills. Anderson, Brent, illus. (p. 689)
—X-Men Forever. (p. 1967)
Claremont, Chris & Austin, Terry. X-Men Silvestri, Marc et al, illus. (p. 1967)
Claremont, Chris & Buscema, John. Marvel Comics Presents: Wolverine. Vol. 1 (p. 1098)
Claremont, Chris & Lopresti, Aaron. Excalibur: Forging the Sword. (p. 547)
Claremont, Chris & Simonson, Louise. X-Tinction Agenda. Lee, Jim et al, illus. (p. 1967)
Claremont, Chris & Wolfman, Marv. Fantastic Four Byrne, John et al, illus. (p. 571)
Claremont, Chris, et al. Alpha Flight. Smith, Paul & Byrne, John, illus. (p. 48)
Claremont, Chris, text. Captain Britain - Volume 1: Birth of a Legend. (p. 263)
Claremont, Heather, illus. see Lundy, Charlotte.
Claret, Albert. Sonar: Ten Years. Caballero, Sergio, ed. (p. 1611)
Clari, Michela. Collins Easy Learning Italian Dictionary. (p. 340)
Claridge, Marit. How to Draw Dinosaurs & Prehistoric Life. Tatchell, Judy, ed. (p. 817)
Clarin, Leopoldo Alas, et al. Cuentos. (p. 389)
Clarizio, Laura. If i Had a Magic Carpet. (p. 853)
—If I Had a Magic Carpet II: Key to Kindness. (p. 853)
—If I Had a Magic Carpet III: Haunted Holidays. (p. 853)
—Traveling Through Time: If I Had a Magic Carpet IV. (p. 1780)
Clark, A. C. Sam's World of Imagination: Sir Sam, Knight of the Realm. (p. 1509)
Clark, Abbie. Way down Yonder in the Paw Paw Patch. Taylor, Jennifer, illus. (p. 1864)
Clark, Admont G. Boy Who Saved a Cape Cod Town: And Other Cape Cod Stories. Fraser, Richard M., illus. (p. 219)
Clark, Alan M., illus. see Lumley, Brian.
Clark, Amy. God's Favorite Color. (p. 691)
—Mom Just Said No! (p. 1161)
Clark, Andy, illus. see Ostrow, Kim.
Clark, Andy, jt. illus. see Bond, Clint.
Clark, Andy S. Heavenly Magic: The Unforgettable Journey of Cassidy, the Valiant. (p. 761)
Clark, Anita. Bible Rhymes from Aa to Zz. (p. 176)
Clark, Ann Nolan. In My Mother's House. Herrera, Velino, illus. (p. 864)
—Little Boy with Three Names: Stories of Taos Pueblo. Lujan, Tonita, illus. (p. 1025)
Clark, Ann Nolan & Harrington, John P. Little Herder in Winter: Haigo Na'nilkaadi' Ya'zhi' Denetsosie, Hoke, illus. (p. 1029)
Clark, Anthony & Whybrow, Ian. Little Wolf's Book of Badness. (p. 1038)
Clark, Aubrey, jt. auth. see Smith, L. J.
Clark, Augusta, et al. C'est a Toi! (p. 288)
Clark, B. Book of Life. (p. 211)
Clark, B. McClemon. Diary of a Reluctant Political Candidate. (p. 435)
Clark, Barbara Hoserman, illus. see Meade, Jean McCurdy.
Clark, Bartholomew, illus. see Carr, Dan.
Clark, Betsy Huhn. Lizzie's Extraordinary Adventure. (p. 1043)
Clark, Betty. Choosing a Career in Real Estate. (p. 310)
Clark, Bill, illus. see Busch, Melinda Kay.
Clark, Bill, illus. see Carr, Dan.
Clark, Bill, illus. see Dietrich, Julie.
Clark, Bill, illus. see Leigh, Susan K.
Clark, Billy C. Champion of Sourwood Mountain. (p. 289)
Clark, Brenda. Spiro & Zinger Rescue the Orphans: Spiro the Shooting Star - Book Three (p. 1629)
—Spiro Goes West: More Adventures of Spiro the Shooting Star. (p. 1629)
Clark, Brenda, illus. see Bourgeois, Paulette & Bourgeois, Paulette.
Clark, Brenda, illus. see Bourgeois, Paulette.
Clark, Brenda, illus. see Jennings, Sharon & Bourgeois, Paulette.
Clark, Brenda, jt. auth. see Bourgeois, Paulette.
Clark, Brenda, jt. auth. see Staunton, Ted.
Clark, Brenda & Commers, Judy. Entrepreneurship. (p. 531)
Clark, Brian D. Stoned off Our Mad Libs. (p. 1653)
Clark, Brian, et al. Annie Mad Libs. (p. 87)
Clark, Bridie. Because She Can. (p. 155)
—Maybe Tonight? (p. 1113)
—You Only Live Once. (p. 1976)
Clark Brown, Jane, illus. see Paterson, Katherine.
Clark, Bruce E. Memories of a Long Life. (p. 1126)
Clark, Carol. Christmas Tree. (p. 316)
—Eternity Express. (p. 539)
Clark, Carson & Clark, Jim. Adventures of Buddy the Beaver: Buddy Explores the Pond. (p. 17)
Clark, Carson & Clark, Jim, photos by. Adventures of Buddy the Beaver: Mystery of the Missing Friends. (p. 17)
Clark, Casey, illus. see Swinson, Joyce Ann.
Clark, Catherine. Alison Rules. (p. 41)
—Banana Splitsville. (p. 136)
—Frozen Rodeo. (p. 645)
—How to Meet Boys. (p. 820)
—Icing on the Lake. (p. 851)
—Love & Other Things I'm Bad At: Rocky Road Trip & Sundae My Prince Will Come. (p. 1059)
—Maine Squeeze. (p. 1077)
—Picture Perfect. (p. 1355)
—So Inn Love. (p. 1602)
Clark, Catherine Anthony. Golden Pine Cone. Guzek, Greta, illus. (p. 695)
Clark, Chap. Next Time I Fall in Love: How to Handle Sex, Intimacy, & Feelings in Dating Relationships. (p. 1249)
Clark, Charles. Islam. (p. 891)
Clark, Cherith & Stokes, Kirstin. Monster Spray. (p. 1168)
Clark, Chris Elliott. Hazel's Secret. (p. 756)
Clark, Christian. Mr. Clark's Awesome Designs Coloring Book. (p. 1184)
Clark, Claire. Calendar. (p. 252)
—How Long Is a Day? (p. 810)
—How Long Is a Month? (p. 810)
—How Long Is a Week? (p. 810)
—How Long Is a Year? (p. 810)
Clark, Claire & Shaskan, Trisha Speed. How Long Is a Day? (p. 810)
—How Long Is a Month? (p. 810)
—How Long Is a Week? (p. 810)
—How Long Is a Year? (p. 810)
Clark, Claire D., jt. auth. see Adams, Dena C.
Clark, Clara. Nellie Bishop. Shine, Andrea, illus. (p. 1240)
Clark, Clara Gillow. Hattie on Her Way. Thompson, John, illus. (p. 753)
—Secrets of Greymoor. (p. 1545)
—Willie & the Rattlesnake King. (p. 1934)
Clark, Connie. Who in the World Was the Unready King? The Story of Ethelred. (p. 1915)
—Who in the World Was the Unready King? The Story of Ethelred. Mickle, Jed, illus. (p. 1915)
Clark, CoraMarie. Emily's Magical Journey with Toothena the Tooth Fairy. Lawton, Val, illus. (p. 519)
Clark, Danell. Daisy. Irwin, April, illus. (p. 400)
Clark, Darrel. Happy Frog. (p. 745)
Clark, David, illus. see Dolenz, Micky.
Clark, David, illus. see Einhorn, Edward.
Clark, David, illus. see Hauth, Katherine B.
Clark, David, illus. see Lasky, Kathryn.
Clark, David, illus. see Polisar, Barry Louis.
Clark, David, illus. see Reisberg, Joanne.
Clark, David, illus. see Shore, Diane Z.
Clark, Debbie. Amberleigh's Christmas Angel: An Adolescent's Story of Love, Loss, & Renewed Hope for the Future. (p. 57)
Clark, Debbie, illus. see Schwaeber, Barbie Heit.
Clark, Dennis, jt. auth. see Gamble, Adam.
Clark, Diane C. & Harcourt, Inc Staff. Kid's Guide to Washington, D. C. Brown, Richard, illus. (p. 954)
Clark, Domini. South Africa: The Land. (p. 1616)
—South Africa: The People. (p. 1616)
—South Africa: The Culture. (p. 1616)
—South Africa - The Culture. (p. 1616)
—South Africa - The Land. (p. 1616)
—South Africa - The People. (p. 1616)
Clark, Don, illus. see DeYoung, Kevin.
Clark, Donna Osborn, illus. see Johnson, Harvell.
Clark, Doris C. Joy Dancing: Upper-torso Liturgical Dance Including the Lord's Prayer, the 23rd Psalm & the Apostles' Creed plus Sunday School Curriculum for Adults with Developmental Disabilities. (p. 929)
Clark, Eleanor. Eleanor Jo: The Farmer's Daughter. (p. 508)
—Katie Sue: Heading West. (p. 945)
—Mary Elizabeth: Welcome to America. (p. 1100)
—Melanie Ann: A Legacy of Love. (p. 1125)
—Sarah Jane: Liberty's Torch. (p. 1514)
—Victoria Grace: Courageous Patriot. (p. 1840)
Clark, Electa. Wildcat, the Seminole: The Florida War. Nicholas, Frank, illus. (p. 1931)
Clark, Elijah Brady, illus. see Robson, Gary D.
Clark, Elizabeth Palmer, illus. see Snedeker, Caroline Dale.
Clark, Emma Chicester, illus. see Lewis, Naomi.
Clark, Emma Chichester. Find a Smile (p. 587)
—Lulu & the Treasure Hunt! Clark, Emma Chichester, illus. (p. 1064)
—Minty & Tink. Clark, Emma Chichester, illus. (p. 1148)
—My Baby Sister. (p. 1196)
—No More Kissing! (p. 1259)
Clark, Emma Chichester, illus. see Ahlberg, Allan.
Clark, Geneva. Murder by Dawn. (p. 1192)
Clark, Georgia. Parched. Gams, Allen, illus. (p. 1324)
Clark, Geri. Finland - Enchantment of the World. (p. 589)
Clark, Gloria. Little Candy Breathing Dragons. (p. 1025)
Clark, Hamish. Mara's Flame. (p. 1091)
Clark, Hannah L. Uncovering Cobbogoth. (p. 1812)
Clark, Harriet. Davy Asks His Dad. Clark, Tim, photos by. (p. 411)
Clark, Hattie Mae. It Happened at a Hanging. (p. 894)
Clark, Henry. Book That Proves Time Travel Happens. (p. 212)
—What We Found in the Sofa & How It Saved the World. (p. 1895)
Clark, Henry Scott. Legionaires: A Story of the Great Raid. (p. 990)
Clark, Henry W., jt. auth. see Appel, Benjamin.
Clark, I. E. Stagecrafters' Handbook: A Guide for Theatre Technicians. (p. 1638)
Clark, Irene, illus. see Bradshaw, Georgine & Wrighton, Charlene.
Clark, Irene, illus. see Wrighton, Charlene & Bradshaw, Georgine.
Clark, Isabelle. Enchanted Forest of Hope. (p. 523)
Clark, Isobel. My Big Book of Words. Tulip, Jenny, illus. (p. 1197)
Clark, J. T. Bare Bones Book of Screenwriting: The Definitive Beginner's Guide to Story, Format & Business. (p. 138)
Clark, Janet. Princesses & the Quest for the Magic Hula Hoop. (p. 1406)
Clark, Janice E. Roscoe Is a RAKster: You Can Be One Too. (p. 1489)
Clark, Janice Stump. Enough Salt & Pepper: A Mischievous Dog Adventure. (p. 531)
—Miss Golden-silk Unties a Tangle. (p. 1151)
Clark, Jay. Edumacation of Jay Baker. (p. 505)
—Finding Mr. Brightside. (p. 588)
Clark, Jeanne B. Second Encounter: With the Snake Named Bully. (p. 1539)
Clark, Jeff. Dad's Masterpiece: The Patricia Masotto Story. (p. 399)
Clark, Jeff, illus. see Thomas, Rich.
Clark, Jerusha. Inside a Cutter's Mind: Understanding & Helping Those Who Self-Injure. (p. 876)
Clark, Jim, jt. auth. see Clark, Carson.
Clark, Jim, jt. photos by see Clark, Carson.
Clark, Joan. Ann Drew Jackson. Clark, Nathan, illus. (p. 85)
—Jackson Whole Wyoming. (p. 904)
—Penny Nichols & the Black Imp. (p. 1338)
—Penny Nichols & the Knob Hill Mystery. (p. 1338)
—Penny Nichols & the Mystery of the Lost Key. (p. 1338)
—Penny Nichols Finds a Clue. (p. 1338)
—Penny Nichols Omnibus - Finds a Clue, Mystery of the Lost Key, Black Imp, & Knob Hill Mystery. (p. 1338)
—Road to Bliss. (p. 1477)
Clark, Joel N., jt. auth. see Batterson, Mark.
Clark, John. Matter & Materials. (p. 1109)
Clark, John, ed. see Artibani, Francesco, et al.
Clark, John, ed. see Barks, Carl & Kinney, Dick.
Clark, John, ed. see Barks, Carl, et al.
Clark, John, ed. see Barks, Carl.
Clark, John, ed. see Barosso, Abramo, et al.
Clark, John, ed. see Block, Shelly, et al.
Clark, John, ed. see Blum, Geoffrey & Barks, Carl.
Clark, John, ed. see Cimino, Rodolfo, et al.
Clark, John, ed. see Connell, Del, et al.
Clark, John, ed. see De Maris, Merrill, et al.
Clark, John, ed. see Erickson, Byron, et al.
Clark, John, ed. see Erickson, Byron.
Clark, John, ed. see Geradts, Evert, et al.
Clark, John, ed. see Gerstein, David.
Clark, John, ed. see Gilbert, Janet, et al.
Clark, John, ed. see Gilbert, Michael T., et al.
Clark, John, ed. see Hamill, Jeff, et al.
Clark, John, ed. see Jensen, Lars, et al.
Clark, John, ed. see Jippes, Daan, et al.
Clark, John, ed. see Kinney, Sarah, et al.
Clark, John, ed. see Klein, Robert, et al.
Clark, John, ed. see Korhonen, Kari, et al.
Clark, John, ed. see Laban, Terry, et al.
Clark, John, ed. see Laban, Terry.
Clark, John, ed. see Langhans, Bob.
Clark, John, ed. see Lustig, John, et al.
Clark, John, ed. see McGreal, Pat, et al.
Clark, John, ed. see O'Connor, Eddie, et al.
Clark, John, ed. see Petrucha, Stefan, et al.
Clark, John, ed. see Pijlnaar, Wilbert, et al.
Clark, John, ed. see Rawson, Dave & Van Horn, William.
Clark, John, ed. see Rosa, Don, et al.
Clark, John, ed. see Rota, Marco & Barks, Carl.
Clark, John, ed. see Salvagnini, Rudy, et al.
Clark, John, ed. see Scarpa, Romano & Block, Pat and Shelly.
Clark, John, ed. see Scarpa, Romano, et al.
Clark, John, ed. see Van Horn, William & Block, Shelly.
Clark, John, ed. see Van Horn, William & Gilbert, Janet.
Clark, John, ed. see Van Horn, William & Rawson, Dave.
Clark, John, ed. see Van Horn, William & Rosa, Don.
Clark, John, ed. see Van Horn, William, et al.
Clark, John, ed. see Van Horn, William.
Clark, John, ed. see Walsh, Bill, et al.
Clark, John & Walker, Richard. Light & Sound. (p. 1014)
Clark, John, ed. Donald Duck Adventures (p. 465)
—Donald Duck Adventures. (p. 465)
—Mickey Mouse Adventures (p. 1136)
—Mickey Mouse Adventures. (p. 1136)
—Mystery of the Old Mansion (p. 1225)
—Uncle Scrooge (p. 1812)
—Uncle Scrooge #337. (p. 1812)
—Uncle Scrooge #338. (p. 1812)
—Uncle Scrooge #339. (p. 1812)
—Walt Disney's Comics & Stories #652. (p. 1855)
Clark, John, III. God's Heartbeat: A Powerful Premise for Leading a Christian Life. (p. 691)
Clark, John O. E. Basics of Electric Charges. (p. 142)
—Basics of Heat. (p. 142)
—Basics of Light. (p. 142)
—Basics of Matter. (p. 142)
—Basics of Mechanics. (p. 142)
Clark, John Philip, Jr. Patient's Resource Book: For Hospital & Home. (p. 1328)
Clark, Johnny C. Poor Poor Ollie. (p. 1383)
Clark, Joyce. Katie. (p. 944)
Clark, Jr. Metrognomes. (p. 1130)
Clark, Judy. I Spy Disney: An ABC Book. (p. 846)
Clark, Julie. 10 Greatest Breakthroughs in Space Exploration. (p. 1993)
—10 Most Essential Chemical Messengers in the Body. (p. 1993)
Clark, Julie Aigner. You Are the Best Medicine. Christy, Jana, illus. (p. 1973)
Clark, Justin, jt. auth. see Clark, Steven.
Clark, Justus L. Expressway. (p. 555)
Clark, K. C., illus. see Tulley, Tara.
Clark, K. M. Beautiful Disaster. (p. 153)
Clark, Karen. Flash Bang Wheee! White, Ian, illus. (p. 602)
—Flash, Bang, Wheee! White, Ian, illus. (p. 602)
Clark, Karen & White, Ian. Flash, Bang, Wheee! Bing, Bang, Boum! (p. 602)
—Flash, Bang, Wheee! Shkreptime, Gjemim Dhe Vershellime! (p. 602)
Clark, Kate Stevenson & Banas, Sharon L. Handling Peer Pressure. (p. 740)
Clark, Katherine. Seagull Sam. Huntington, Amy, illus. (p. 1536)
Clark, Kathy. Choice (p. 309)
—Guardian Angel House (p. 728)
Clark, Katie. Animal Actors. (p. 76)
—Balanced Meals. (p. 133)
—Dairy Group. (p. 400)
—Grandma Drove the Garbage Truck. Huntington, Amy, illus. (p. 708)
—Grandma Drove the Lobsterboat Huntington, Amy, illus. (p. 708)
—Lincoln Memorial: Myths, Legends, & Facts (p. 1018)
—Police Horses. (p. 1380)
—Tour of Your Muscular & Skeletal Systems. Jones, Chris B., illus. (p. 1773)
Clark, Katie, jt. auth. see Wynne, Sarah.
Clark, Katie Lea. Tour of Your Muscular & Skeletal Systems Jones, Chris B., illus. (p. 1773)
Clark, Kevin, jt. auth. see Porter, Rosalie Pedalino.
Clark, Kim, ed. see Heidrich, Delana.
Clark, Kimberly, ed. see Klawitter, Pamela Amick.
Clark, Kristin Elizabeth. Freakboy. (p. 631)
Clark, Kristina. Great Adventures of Ella: The Magic Desk. (p. 713)
Clark, L. D. World According to Coho. (p. 1953)
Clark, Larry, jt. see Feldstein, Sandy.
Clark, Leslie Ann. Peepsqueak! Clark, Leslie Ann, illus. (p. 1335)
—Peepsqueak Wants a Friend! Clark, Leslie Ann, illus. (p. 1335)
Clark, Linda, illus. see Ross, Stewart.
Clark, Lisa. 10 Most Revolting Parasites. (p. 1994)
—Song of Christmas. Dyrud, Chris Wold, illus. (p. 1611)
Clark, Lucinda. View from the Middle of the Road: Where the Greenest Grass Grows Brenda, Baratto, ed. (p. 1841)
Clark, M. H. ABC Menagerie. (p. 3)
—Grandma Is a Superhero. (p. 708)
—I Am... (p. 831)
—I Can... (p. 834)
—I Can Fly? (p. 835)
—No Birthday Cake for Me. Riedler, Amelia, ed. (p. 1257)
—T. L. C. (p. 1694)
Clark, Malcolm. Bounty's Cave. (p. 216)
Clark Mancuso, Jackie. Hudson in Provence: A Paris-Chien Adventure. Clark Mancuso, Jackie, illus. (p. 824)
Clark, Marc. Princess Fables. Hosford, Eric, illus. (p. 1403)
Clark, Margaret. Friends Forever: A Secret Diary by Sara Swan. (p. 638)
—Love Charms. (p. 1059)
—Secret Friends' Stuff. (p. 1540)
Clark, Margaret & Malone, Peter. Classic Treasury of Princess Fairy Tales. (p. 328)
Clark, Margery. Poppy Seed Cakes. (p. 1385)
Clark, Maria. Lousy Luck Lucy. (p. 1059)
Clark, Marian. Benji's Sicarii Sword. (p. 165)
—Friend Forever. (p. 637)
Clark, Marilyn K. Mrs Cratchit's Christmas. (p. 1187)
Clark, Mary. Biographical Sketches of the Fathers of New England. (p. 188)
Clark, Mary, illus. see Baum, L. Frank.
Clark, Mary Cowles, illus. see Baum, L. Frank.
Clark, Mary Higgins. Ghost Ship. Minor, Wendell, illus. (p. 671)
—Magical Christmas Horse. Minor, Wendell, illus. (p. 1074)
Clark, Matthew. SongrrLines: A Beastie Bedtime Dreaming, & Coloring Book. (p. 1611)
Clark, Matthew, illus. see McKeever, Sean.
Clark, Matthew Levi, illus. see King, Seth David.
Clark, Maxine. Build-A-Bear Workshop Furry Friends Hall of Fame: The Official Collector's Guide. (p. 237)
Clark, Mel. Kiss Closed Circuit Rebreather. (p. 961)
Clark, Michelle. Special Gift: Michelle Clark. (p. 1623)
Clark, Nancy Lawrence, ed. Gliders Soaring: The Sport of Motorless Flight with Pioneer Larry Lawrence. (p. 683)
Clark, Nathan, illus. see Clark, Joan.
Clark, Nicole K. Pigment the Rainbow Pig. Clark, Nicole K., illus. (p. 1358)
Clark, Ouida Ouijella. He Planned to Be A Leader: First Drama of Children of the 21st Century. (p. 756)
Clark, Pat. Katz & Dogz Rule. (p. 946)
Clark, Patricia Nikolina. In the Shadow of the Mammoth. LeTourneau, Anthony Alex, illus. (p. 867)
Clark, Paul. Good Wagon. Preston, Graham, illus. (p. 700)
Clark, Paul, jt. auth. see Bush-Retherford, Dody.
Clark, Paul L., jt. auth. see Giuffre, Mary.
Clark, Phil & Wilde, Oscar. Oscar Wilde: Three Plays for Children. (p. 1305)
Clark, Philip. Little Red. (p. 1034)
Clark, Platte F. Bad Unicorn. (p. 132)
—Fluff Dragon. (p. 608)
—Good Ogre. (p. 700)
Clark, Pushman, ed. Adventures of Damion Koehkh, MD: Selected Scripts & Photos from the Series. (p. 17)
Clark, Raymond C., jt. auth. see Egelberg, Arlene.
Clark, Raymond C., jt. auth. see Siebert, Anne.
Clark, Richard & Fehl, Pamela. Career Opportunities in the Visual Arts. (p. 267)
Clark, Ron. Excellent 11: Qualities Teachers & Parents Use to Motivate, Inspire, & Educate Children. No. 11 (p. 547)
Clark, Rosalind. Bruce's Diary: It's a Geriatric Dog's Life. (p. 232)
Clark, Rosalynn. World of Alphabets. (p. 1956)
Clark, Roy Peter. Writing Tools: 50 Essential Strategies for Every Writer. (p. 1965)

C

Clark, Ruth. Airport Mouse Explores on Opening Day. (p. 32)
—Airport Mouse Works the Nightshift. (p. 32)
Clark, Ruth E. Airport Mouse. Jones, Phil, illus. (p. 32)
—Airport Mouse Activity Fun Book 1. Jones, Phil, illus. (p. 32)
—Airport Mouse Becomes a VIP/VIM World Traveler. Jones, Phil, illus. (p. 32)
—Airport Mouse Becomes a VIP/VIM World Traveler Activity Fun Book 4. Jones, Phil, illus. (p. 32)
—Airport Mouse Explores on Opening Day Activity Fun Book 3. Jones, Phil, illus. (p. 32)
—Airport Mouse Works the Night Shift Activity Fun Book 2. Jones, Phil, illus. (p. 32)
—Florida Santa: Is He Real? How Do We Know It? Caterisano, Sarah, illus. (p. 607)
Clark, Sally. Where's My Hug? Corke, Estelle, illus. (p. 1910)
Clark, Sandra. Goldie Is Upside Down. (p. 695)
—My Tears Count Too. (p. 1220)
Clark, Sarah Kartchner. Doctors Then & Now. (p. 459)
—Mind Twisters, Grade 4. (p. 1145)
—Nurses Then & Now. (p. 1273)
—¡En Equipo Con el Sr. Supercoyote! (p. 522)
Clark Sawyer, J. Animal Colors: What They Mean. (p. 77)
—Barn Swallows. (p. 139)
—Holiday Colors: Our Favorite Days. (p. 788)
—Las Ardillas de Tierra de Trece Franjas. (p. 976)
—Las Golondrinas Comunes. (p. 976)
—Las Serpientes de Cascabel de Bandas. (p. 977)
—Los Colores de la Selva Tropical: Hermosos y Brillantes. (p. 1053)
—Los Colores de Las Celebraciones: Nuestros Días Favoritos. (p. 1053)
—Los Colores de Los Animales: Qué Significan. (p. 1053)
—Patterns in the City. (p. 1329)
—Patterns in the Park. (p. 1329)
—Patterns in the Snow. (p. 1329)
—Rain Forest Colors: Bright & Beautiful. (p. 1434)
—Thirteen-Lined Ground Squirrels. (p. 1735)
—Timber Rattlesnakes. (p. 1750)
Clark, Seneca & Giardi, Sandy. Frankie Goes to Fenway: The Tale of the Faithful, Red Sox-Loving Mouse. Decedue, Julie, illus. (p. 629)
—Lily & the Imaginary Zoo Decedue, Julie, illus. (p. 1018)
—Yellowest Yellow Lab. Decedue, Julie, illus. (p. 1970)
Clark, Sherryl. Kim's Fake Cake Bake. McKenzie, Heath, illus. (p. 957)
—Kim's Pet Scoop. McKenzie, Heath, illus. (p. 957)
—Kim's Super Science Day. McKenzie, Heath, illus. (p. 957)
—Kim's Tug of War. McKenzie, Heath, illus. (p. 957)
—Tutu Muy Apretado. Betteo, Patricio, illus. (p. 1799)
Clark Sherryl Staff. Bone Song. (p. 209)
Clark, Sheryl. Asking for Trouble: Prove It!, Take a Hike!, Knock It Off! (p. 106)
Clark, Sondra. 77 Creative Ways Kids Can Serve. (p. 1998)
Clark, Stacy. When the Wind Blows. Sneed, Brad, illus. (p. 1905)
Clark, Stephen. Katahdin a Guide to Baxter State Park & Katahdin. (p. 944)
Clark, Steve, illus. see Sprick, Marilyn & Sprick, Jessica.
Clark, Steve, illus. see Sprick, Marilyn, et al.
Clark, Steven, tr. see Sakurai, Ami.
Clark, Steven & Clark, Justin. Golden Knight #1: The Boy Is Summoned. Gibson, Taylor, illus. (p. 695)
Clark, Stuart. Discovering the Universe. (p. 450)
—Earth (p. 495)
—Project U. L. F. Ludvigsen, Henning, illus. (p. 1410)
Clark, Susan, ed. Echoes of the Lost Boys of Sudan. Friedman, Michael (Myk), illus. (p. 502)
Clark, Terri A. Sleepless. (p. 1589)
Clark, Thomas Curtis, jt. ed. see Gillespie, Esther A.
Clark, Tim, photos by see Clark, Harriet.
Clark, Tim & Kay, Carl. Saying Yes to Japan: How Outsiders Are Reviving a Trillion Dollar Services Market. (p. 1519)
Clark, Todd. Ice Cream Kid: Brain Freeze! (p. 850)
Clark, Tom, jt. auth. see Green, Dan.
Clark, Tracey, jt. auth. see Gilbert, Sara.
Clark, Tracy. Deviate. (p. 432)
—Scintillate. (p. 1529)
Clark, Travis. Alex Rodriguez. (p. 36)
—Portland Trail Blazers. (p. 1386)
—Punk'd. (p. 1417)
—Stressed-Out Guy's Guide: How to Deal. (p. 1667)
—Survivor. (p. 1687)
—Will Ferrell. (p. 1932)
—Yao Ming. (p. 1968)
Clark, Travis & Belfield, Annie. Guys' Guide to Stress. (p. 733)
Clark, Vivienne, et al. Key Concepts & Skills for Media Studies. (p. 950)
Clark, Warren, illus. see Dixon, Norma.
Clark, Warren, illus. see Schendlinger, Mary.
Clark, Warren, illus. see Swanson, Diane.
Clark, Wendy, illus. see Nannini, Randi.
Clark, Wendy S. Troubles with Bubbles. (p. 1790)
Clark, William. Magic Raindrops. (p. 1073)
Clark, Willow. Animal Families (p. 77)
—Asian Dolphins & Other Marine Mammals. (p. 106)
—Bengal Tigers. (p. 164)
—Bikes on the Move. (p. 185)
—Black Widow Spider! (p. 197)
—Boats on the Move. (p. 205)
—Burmese Pythons. (p. 243)
—Bush Babies. (p. 244)
—Camels. (p. 256)
—Cars on the Move. (p. 272)
—Crocodile! (p. 384)
—Dolphins: Life in the Pod. (p. 464)
—Dolphins: Delfines: Life in the Pod: Vida en la Manada. (p. 464)
—Flying Lemurs. (p. 610)
—Gila Monster! (p. 676)
—Gorillas: Life in the Troop. (p. 703)
—Gorillas: Gorilas: Life in the Troop: Vida en la Manada. (p. 703)
—Green Tree Pythons. (p. 722)
—Koalas. (p. 966)
—Lions: Life in the Pride. (p. 1021)
—Lions: Leones: Life in the Pride: Vida en la Manada. (p. 1021)
—Meerkats: Life in the Mob. (p. 1120)
—Meerkats: Suricatas: Life in the Mob: Vida en la Colonia. (p. 1120)
—Motorcycles on the Move. (p. 1180)
—Pandas. (p. 1321)
—Penguins: Life in the Colony. (p. 1337)
—Penguins: Pingüinos: Life in the Colony: Vida en la Colonia. (p. 1337)
—Planes on the Move. (p. 1367)
—Poison Dart Frog! (p. 1377)
—Rattlesnake! (p. 1440)
—Shark! (p. 1561)
—Three-Toed Sloths. (p. 1744)
—Trains on the Move. (p. 1777)
—Transportation Station (p. 1779)
—Tree Kangaroos. (p. 1783)
—True Story of the Civil War. (p. 1793)
—True Story of the Declaration of Independence. (p. 1793)
—True Story of the Emancipation Proclamation. (p. 1793)
—Wolves: Life in the Pack. (p. 1945)
—Wolves: Lobos: Life in the Pack: Vida en la Manada. (p. 1945)
—Yaks. (p. 1968)
Clark, Willow & Rockwood, Leigh. Centipedes & Millipedes Are Gross! (p. 287)
—Salamanders Are Gross! (p. 1504)
—Snails Are Gross! (p. 1596)
—Worms Are Gross! (p. 1961)
Clark, Wook Jin. Megagogo (p. 1124)
Clarke, illus. see Gilson.
Clarke, Alan. IT Skills for Successful Study. (p. 894)
Clarke, Alan, illus. see Cashman, Seamus.
Clarke, Alan, illus. see Dagg, Stephanie.
Clarke, Alan, illus. see Lenihan, Eddie.
Clarke, Angelique. Boomer Explores Annapolis Hunt, Jim, illus. (p. 213)
Clarke, Ann. People Are So Different! Smith, Duncan, illus. (p. 1339)
Clarke, Arthur C. & Lee, Gentry. Rama II. (p. 1437)
Clarke, Ashanti. Michael & the Can of Lemon Spray. Crewe, Robert, illus. (p. 1134)
Clarke, Asiya, illus. see Arif, Amrana.
Clarke, Asiya, illus. see Bokhari, Raana.
Clarke, Barry & Dorling Kindersley Publishing Staff. Amphibian. Brightling, Geoff & Greenaway, Frank, photos by. (p. 65)
Clarke, Benjamin S., illus. see Vincolisi, Marnie.
Clarke, Carol Page. Cuddly Mogs. (p. 389)
Clarke, Cassandra Rose. Assassin's Curse. (p. 107)
—Pirate's Wish. (p. 1364)
—Wizard's Promise. (p. 1943)
Clarke, Cat. Undone. (p. 1817)
Clarke, Catriona. 100 Things for Little Children to Do on a Trip. (p. 1999)
—50 Things to Do on Vacation. Meredith, Samantha, illus. (p. 1997)
—Armor. McKenna, Terry, illus. (p. 99)
—Aztecs - Internet Referenced (Level 2) (p. 122)
—Pirates. McKenna, Terry, illus. (p. 1363)
—Reptiles: Internet-Referenced. (p. 1461)
—Sharks: Information for Young Readers - Level 1. Relf, Adam, illus. (p. 1563)
—Weather: Level 7. Chen, Kuo Kang, illus. (p. 1869)
—Weather. Ibrahim, Nouran, tr. (p. 1869)
—Weather. Slane, Andrea & Chen, Kuo Kang, illus. (p. 1869)
Clarke, Christie. Star Spirit. (p. 1641)
Clarke, Covington. For Valor & Desert Wings. (p. 616)
Clarke, David. Snake Bite: A Novel. (p. 1596)
Clarke, Denise B. Never Go with Strangers! Nunca Vayas Con Extranos. Torres, Rosa, tr. from ENG. (p. 1243)
Clarke, Duncan, jt. auth. see Johnson, Michael.
Clarke, Ella. I Am So Beautiful. (p. 834)
—Snake's Diary by Little Yellow. (p. 1596)
—When I Grow Up (p. 1903)
Clarke, Eva Marie. Shania Twain: Hometown Canadian to International Superstar. (p. 1559)
Clarke, Evelyn. Crisis. (p. 383)
Clarke, George Elliott. Lasso the Wind: Aurelia's Verses & Other Poems Tooke, Susan, illus. (p. 977)
Clarke, Ginjer L. Baby Elephant. Cuddy, Robin & Wummer, Amy, illus. (p. 126)
—Baby Meerkats. Cuddy, Robbin, illus. (p. 127)
—Baby Otter. Cuddy, Robin, illus. (p. 127)
—Black Out! Animals That Live in the Dark. Mueller, Pete, illus. (p. 196)
—Bug Out! The World's Creepiest, Crawliest Critters. Mueller, Pete, illus. (p. 236)
—Cheetah Cubs. Washburn, Lucia, illus. (p. 296)
—Cheetah Cubs, Level 3. Washburn, Lucia, illus. (p. 296)
—Fake Out! Animals That Play Tricks. Mueller, Pete, illus. (p. 565)
—Far Out! Animals That Do Amazing Things. Mueller, Pete, illus. (p. 572)
—Freak Out! Animals Beyond Your Wildest Imagination. Mueller, Pete, illus. (p. 631)
—Giant Lizards. Rothman, Michael, illus. (p. 673)
—Gross Out! Animals That Do Disgusting Things. Mueller, Pete, illus. (p. 725)
—Maxed Out! Gigantic Creatures from the Past. Mueller, Pete, illus. (p. 1112)
—Platypus! Mirocha, Paul, illus. (p. 1370)
—Pouch Babies. Washburn, Lucia, illus. (p. 1389)
—Watch Out! The World's Most Dangerous Creatures. Mueller, Pete, illus. (p. 1861)
Clarke, Gordon. Canada in World War I: Outstanding Victories Create a Nation. (p. 260)
—Major Battles of the War of 1812. (p. 1078)
Clarke, Gordon, jt. auth. see Corporate Contibutor Staff.
Clarke, Gordon, jt. auth. see Crabtree Staff.
Clarke, Graham. Alfred Stieglitz. (p. 37)
Clarke, Greg, illus. see Wolf, Allan.
Clarke, Gus. Cuantos Dias Faltan para Mi Cumpleanos? (p. 388)
Clarke, Harry & Perrault, Charles. Classic Fairy Tales of Charles Perrault. (p. 328)
Clarke, Helene. Why Did the Osprey Poop on my Head? (p. 1923)
Clarke, Henry. Miss Merivale's Mistake. (p. 1151)
Clarke, Herbert. Introduction to Northern California Birds. Ort, Kathleen, ed. (p. 882)
—Introduction to Southern California Birds. Clarke, Herbert, photos by. (p. 882)
Clarke, Isabel. My Big Book of Words. Tulip, Jenny, illus. (p. 1197)
Clarke, J. Erskine. Chatterbox for 1927. (p. 295)
—Chatterbox For 1928. (p. 295)
Clarke, Jacqueline. Alphabet: 30 Instant Centers with Reproducible Templates & Activities That Help Kids Practice Important Literacy Skills-Independently! (p. 49)
—Shoe Box Learning Centers: Alphabet: 30 Instant Centers with Reproducible Templates & Activities That Help Kids Practice Important Literacy Skills-Independently! (p. 1568)
—Shoe Box Learning Centers: Math: 40 Instant Centers with Reproducible Templates & Activities That Help Kids Practice Important Math Skills-Independently! (p. 1568)
—Teaching with Favorite Jan Brett Books: Engaging Activities That Build Essential Reading & Writing Skills & Explore the Themes in These Popular Books. (p. 1710)
—Timothy Has a Bad Day. (p. 1755)
Clarke, Jacqueline A. Moose's Loose Tooth. McNally, Bruce, illus. (p. 1173)
Clarke, Jacqueline & Rhodes, Immacula A. Shoe Box Learning Centers: Counting: 30 Instant Centers with Reproducible Templates & Activities That Help Kids Practice Important Literacy Skills-Independently! (p. 1568)
Clarke, Jane. Amazing Adventures of Batbird. Moon, Cliff, ed. (p. 52)
—Chewy Hughie. McConnell, Sarah, illus. (p. 299)
—Creaky Castle. Fox, Christyan, illus. (p. 378)
—Dancing with the Dinosaurs. Wildish, Lee, illus. (p. 403)
—G. E. M. Parsons, Garry, illus. (p. 651)
—I'm Not Wearing That! Mostyn, David, illus. (p. 859)
—Only Tadpoles Have Tails. Gray, Jane, illus. (p. 1298)
—Plodney Creeper, Supersloth. (p. 1374)
—Prince Albert's Birthday. Chatterton, Martin, illus. (p. 1401)
—Runny Honey. Zlatic, Tomislav, illus. (p. 1497)
—Sherman Swaps Shells. Parker, Ant, illus. (p. 1566)
Clarke, Judith. Al Capsella & Watchdogs. (p. 32)
—Kalpana's Dream. (p. 942)
—Night Train. (p. 1254)
—One Whole & Perfect Day. (p. 1297)
Clarke, Judith & Boyds Mills Press Staff. Starry Nights. (p. 1642)
Clarke, Judith Holmes, illus. see Papademetriou, Lisa.
Clarke, Julie & Kirby-Payne, Ann. Understanding Weight & Depression. (p. 1816)
Clarke, Kathryn. Breakable Vow. (p. 224)
Clarke, Kathryn Ann. Breakable Vow. (p. 224)
Clarke, Kay, et al. Geography for CCEA GCSE. (p. 662)
Clarke, Kevin & Dutton, Demi. Jenny Can't Read: A Story about Dyslexia & Its Effect on Self-Esteem. (p. 913)
Clarke, Lisa Anne. Wishing Wellness: A Workbook for Children of Parents with Mental Illness. Candace, Bonnie & Ellen, illus. (p. 1941)
Clarke, Lizzy. Spirit of the Jaguar. (p. 1628)
Clarke, Lyndia A. Tidy up Tommy. Clarke, Lyndia A., illus. (p. 1747)
Clarke, M. Story of Troy. (p. 1662)
Clarke, Margaret Bruce. Hunter's Marjory. (p. 828)
Clarke, Michael. Story of Troy: The Story of Troy. (p. 1662)
—Story of Troy. (p. 1662)
Clarke, Nadine. Get Bushwise: on Safari Desert, River, Bushveld: A Young Explorer's Guide. (p. 667)
Clarke, Nancy & Muire, Penny. Stormy Hill's Challenge. (p. 1656)
Clarke, Nzingha. Karen Hesse. (p. 943)
Clarke, Nzingha, jt. selected by see Herlihy, Matt.
Clarke, P., jt. auth. see Smith, A.
Clarke, Penny. Arctic. (p. 95)
—Hippos. (p. 781)
—Scary Creatures of the Arctic. (p. 1520)
—Scary Creatures of the City. Baker, Janet et al, illus. (p. 1520)
—Scary Creatures of the Mountains. (p. 1520)
—Scary Creatures of the Rain Forest. (p. 1520)
—Scary Creatures of the Wetlands. (p. 1520)
—Story of the Exploration of Space. Antram, David et al, illus. (p. 1661)
—Wolves. Hersey, Bob, illus. (p. 1944)
Clarke, Peter, ed. see Mumford, Jeanette, et al.
Clarke, Peter, illus. see Barchers, Suzanne.
Clarke, Peter, ed. Collins New Primary Maths - Software 2. (p. 341)
—Software 1. (p. 1606)
Clarke, Phil. Sharks. (p. 1562)
Clarke, Phil, jt. auth. see Robson, Kirsteen.
Clarke, Phillip. Little Book of Dogs & Puppies: Internet-Linked. (p. 1025)
—Mysteries & Marvels of Science - Internet Linked. (p. 1222)
—Planet Earth Facts & Lists - Internet Linked. (p. 1367)
—Seas & Oceans Game Kid Kit. (p. 1538)
—Seas & Oceans Sticker Atlas. Le Rolland, Leonard, illus. (p. 1538)
—Unicorns. Scott, Peter, illus. (p. 1818)
Clarke, Phillip, ed. see Dickins, Rosie.
Clarke, Phillip, ed. see Khan, Sarah.
Clarke, Phillip, ed. see Norman, David.
Clarke, Phillip, jt. auth. see Smith, Alastair.
Clarke, Phillip & Furnival, Keith. Sharks. Scott, Peter David, illus. (p. 1562)
Clarke, Phillip & Khan, Sarah. Animals Sticker Book. Rogers, Kirsteen, ed. (p. 84)
—Facts & Records - Internet Linked: Combined Volume. (p. 561)
Clarke, Phillip & Tudhope, Simon, eds. 100 Rocks & Minerals to Spot. (p. 1998)
Clarke, Phillip, ed. 100 Animals to Spot at the Zoo. McGregor, Malcolm, illus. (p. 1998)
Clarke, Phillip, et al. Usborne Internet-Linked Mysteries & Marvels of Science. Furnival, Keith, illus. (p. 1827)
Clarke, Roger & Wight, Al. Do Mice Eat Rice? (p. 457)
Clarke, Steve. Themes to Inspire. (p. 1728)
—Themes to Inspire for Ks3 Pupil's. (p. 1728)
Clarke, Steve, jt. auth. see Kolka, Diane.
Clarke, Tom E. Puddle Jumper: The Adventures of A Young Flyer in Alaska. (p. 1414)
Clarke, Tony, jt. ed. see Lohan, Tara.
Clarke, Victoria, ed. see Ingram, Roger.
Clarke, Wanda Marie. Butterfly Ball. (p. 247)
Clarke, Zoë. Modern Pentathlon. (p. 1158)
Clarke-Elliott, Mary. Day Ms. Qualbaum Came to Visit. (p. 413)
Clark-Jackson, Joann. Adventures of Hodgi Brigman: Secrets in the Shack-Book One in the Hodgi Brigman Series. (p. 18)
Clarkson, Clay. Our 24 Family Ways Kids Color-In Book: Color-In Book. (p. 1307)
Clarkson, Janet M., illus. see Mothershead, Martha Fulford.
Clarkson, Karen, illus. see Tingle, Tim.
Clarkson, Mark. Battlebots: The Official Guide. (p. 147)
Clarkson, Stephanie. Let's Get Moving with Wenlock & Mandeville! (p. 997)
—Sleeping Cinderella & Other Princess Mix-Ups. Barrager, Brigette, illus. (p. 1589)
Clarrain, Dean. Teenage Mutant Ninja Turtles Adventures Volume 9. (p. 1714)
Clary, Margie Willis. Gullah Alphabet. Brown, Dennis L., illus. (p. 731)
Clasen, Lindsey, jt. auth. see Reeves, Diane Lindsey.
Clasman, Charles David, jt. auth. see Anthony, David.
Class 1-208. Pizza Place Ghost. (p. 1365)
Class, Albert. infallible Dog. (p. 873)
Class, Michael S. Anthony & the Magic Picture Frame: The Story of the Boy Who Traveled into the Past by Stepping into the Picture Frame on His Bedroom Wall & Returned to See His Own Time in A New Light. (p. 89)
Class P3 in Scoil Chiarain Staff. 10 Scary Monsters. (p. 1994)
Class, Virginia Tyree, illus. see Fields, Melissa.
Classic Goosebumps & Stine, R. L. Be Careful What You Wish For. (p. 148)
—Curse of the Mummy's Tomb. (p. 395)
—Haunted Mask. (p. 753)
—Say Cheese & Die! (p. 1518)
Classical Learning Universe. Reading Success: Student Book: Effective Comprehension Strategies Level C. (p. 1446)
—Reading Success: Foundations Student Book: Effective Comprehension Strategies. (p. 1446)
Classroom Complete Press, creator. High Frequency Picture Words, Grades PK-2. (p. 777)
—High Frequency Sight Words, Grades PK-2. (p. 777)
—Sight & Picture Words, Grades PK-2. (p. 1574)
Claude, Jean, illus. see Jantzen, Doug.
Claudette, Jean Leigh. Classified Files: JD & the Missing Treasure. (p. 328)
—Classified Files of Sweet William Farm: JD's Adventures Begin. (p. 328)
—Classified Files of Sweet William Farm: The Adventure Continues. (p. 328)
—Gracie Phizz, Private Detective. (p. 705)
—Mercedes James: On Birdies, Mice, Cookies & Clocks. (p. 1127)
—Mercedes James ~ Shrugs, Hugs & Other Valuable Things. (p. 1127)
Claudia, Kesser. Princess Emily Meets the Leper. (p. 1403)
Claudine Sherels Johnson. Nire Goes to the Color Books Bookstore: Featuring God Is Awesome & Pink Carnation. (p. 1257)
Claudio, Abbado. Yo Sere Director de Orquesta. (p. 1971)
Claudy, C. H. Battle of Base-Ball. Durr, Mark & Mitchem, Gary, eds. (p. 146)
Claughton, Dena, ed. see Lynn, Richard & Nova Blue.
Claus, Fred J. You're Too Small Webb, Sarah, illus. (p. 1982)
Claus, Ingrid. Little Black Traveling Cat: EIGHTY, Six Raccoons & the Big Black Bear. (p. 1024)
Claus, J. Matteson, jt. auth. see Miller, Reagan.
Claus, Matteson. Animals & Deforestation. (p. 82)
Claus, Nancy. Santa's Hat. Ferchaud, Steve, illus. (p. 1513)
—Santa's Prize. Ferchaud, Steve, illus. (p. 1513)
Claus, Rimana. I Want That! Moran, Lyn, illus. (p. 847)
Claus, Santa. Santa Legends Present: The Lost Button. (p. 1513)
—Santa's World: North Pole Series (p. 1513)
Clausen, Andrew. Prince Caspian. (p. 1401)
clausen, audrey. I Think My Little Sister Is Out to Get Me. (p. 846)
Clausen, Kristin. Hank & Frank Encounter the Creatures from Hedgeton. (p. 742)
Clausen-Grace, Nicki. Please Say Please. (p. 1373)
—What Can You Make? (p. 1881)
Clausey, Steeling N. Sinfulnyms. (p. 1578)
Clausman, Rachel. Miriam, Come Sit. (p. 1149)
—Phineas the Talker. (p. 1351)
—Who Made the World? (p. 1917)
Clauson, Marilyn & Drake, Lana. Woody Acorn. Drake, Lana, illus. (p. 1950)
Claussen, Janet, et al. Catholic Connections Handbook for Middle Schoolers. (p. 280)
Claussen-Schoolmeester, Wendy. Police Car Abc's. (p. 1379)
Clave, Israel, tr. see Crouch, Adele.
Clavel, Bernard. Leyendas de Montanas. (p. 1004)
—Leyendas del Mar. (p. 1004)
Claverie, Jean & Chapouton, Anne Marie. Julian. (p. 932)
Clavette, Taylor. Shapeshifter's Mark. (p. 1561)
Clawson, Calvin C. Ride to the Infernal Regions: Yellowstone's First Tourists. Silliman, Lee, ed. (p. 1471)
Clawson, Kevan Kingsley. Raising a Worthy Missionary. (p. 1437)
Clawson, Kevan Kingsley, compiled by. Enhanced Old Testament. (p. 530)

Clawson, Kimberly. Fun O' Licious. Bellomy, Gail, illus. (p. 648)
Clawson, T. Kimmy the Kangaroo Chooses Kindness: Animal Tales. (p. 957)
Clawson, Teresa. Animal Tales, the Collection. (p. 80)
Claxton, Lena & Woo, Alison. Marketing with New Media: A Guide to Promoting Your Small Business Using Websites, E-Zines, Blogs, & Podcasts. (p. 1095)
Clay, Adam. How to Draw Cartoons: An Easy Step-By-Step Guide. (p. 817)
Clay, Amanda. Echo. (p. 502)
Clay, Brittney. B C the Way God Sees You & Me! (p. 122)
Clay, Cliff, illus. see Moore, Mary.
Clay, Dorian. Freddie Loses His Game. (p. 632)
—Freddie Loses His Game. Clay, Dorian, illus. (p. 632)
Clay, Doris, illus. see Robison, Peggy.
Clay, Ian. Coyote Lake. (p. 374)
Clay III, J. Percy. Sampson's Pumpkin Playhouse. (p. 1509)
Clay, Jonathan. At the Basketball Game: Work with Addition & Subtraction Equations. (p. 110)
—At the Basketball Game. (p. 110)
Clay, Josh, illus. see Wheadon, Bill(Beepa) & Wheadon, Bill.
Clay, Joshua, illus. see Furman, Necah Stewart & Huff, Bailey.
Clay, Judith L. Mansfield. "ABE" the Chumsy Angel. (p. 4)
Clay, Julie, illus. see David, Juliet.
Clay, Kathryn. All about Winter Weather. (p. 43)
—Bailando Jazz. Translation Services Staff & Translations.com Staff, trs. from ENG. (p. 132)
—Bailando Tap. Translation Services Staff & Translations.com Staff, trs. (p. 132)
—Ballet Dancing (p. 134)
—Battling for Victory: The Coolest Robot Competitions (p. 147)
—Chickens (p. 300)
—Construction Vehicles. (p. 360)
—Cool Baseball Facts. (p. 362)
—Cool Baseball Facts (Datos Geniales Sobre Béisbol) Strictly Spanish Translation Services Staff, tr. from SPA. (p. 362)
—Cool Football Facts (p. 363)
—Cool Football Facts (Datos Geniales Sobre Fútbol Americano) Strictly Spanish LLC. Staff, tr. from SPA. (p. 363)
—Cool Hockey Facts (p. 363)
—Dance, Dance, Dance (p. 402)
—Farm Dogs (p. 574)
—Farm Machines. (p. 574)
—Girls' Guide to Drawing: Horses, Flowers, Faces, & Other Cool Stuff. (p. 680)
—Girls' Guide to Drawing [LTD Commodities]. (p. 680)
—Goats (p. 687)
—Hip-Hop Dancing (p. 780)
—How to Draw Amazing Letters Martin, Cynthia, illus. (p. 816)
—How to Draw Cool Fashions Nielsen, Julia L., illus. (p. 817)
—How to Draw Cool Kids (p. 817)
—How to Draw Cute Animals Brigman, June, illus. (p. 817)
—How to Draw Faces Timmons, Anne, illus. (p. 817)
—How to Draw Flowers Brigman, June, illus. (p. 817)
—How to Draw Horses Brigman, June, illus. (p. 817)
—How to Draw Mythical Creatures Timmons, Anne, illus. (p. 818)
—Humanoid Robots: Running into the Future (p. 826)
—Jazz Dancing (p. 911)
—Kids' Guide to Sign Language (p. 954)
—My First Guide to Military Vehicles. (p. 1206)
—My First Guide to Robots. (p. 1206)
—Robots at Your Service: From the Factory to Your Home (p. 1481)
—Robots in Risky Jobs: On the Battlefield & Beyond (p. 1481)
—Signing Around Town: Sign Language for Kids Reid, Mick, illus. (p. 1574)
—Signing at Home: Sign Language for Kids Chewning, Randy, illus. (p. 1574)
—Signing at School: Sign Language for Kids Lucas, Margeaux, illus. (p. 1574)
—Signing in My World: Sign Language for Kids Griffo, Daniel, illus. (p. 1574)
—Stegosaurus: Armored Defender Dove, Jason, illus. (p. 1646)
—Tap Dancing (p. 1705)
—Time to Sign: Sign Language for Kids Chewning, Randy et al, illus. (p. 1753)
—Time to Sign. (p. 1753)
—Top 10 Unsolved Mysteries (p. 1768)
—Top 10 Urban Legends (p. 1768)
—World of Robots (p. 1957)
Clay, Kathryn, jt. auth. see Abramovitz, Melissa.
Clay, Kathryn, jt. auth. see Polydoros, Lori.
Clay, Kathryn & Czeskleba, Abby. Datos Geniales Sobre Deportes/Cool Sports Facts. Strictly Spanish LLC. Staff, tr. (p. 409)
Clay, Kathryn & Doyle, Sheri. Farm Animals. (p. 573)
Clay, Kathryn & Polydoros, Lori. Top 10 Unexplained. (p. 1768)
Clay, Kathryn & Shores, Erika L. Cool Robots (p. 364)
Clay, Kathryn, et al. Cool Sports Facts. (p. 364)
—First Graphics: Dinosaurs. Dove, Jason, illus. (p. 595)
Clay Lamberton Elementary School Students. Who Let the Cougars Out? (p. 1916)
Clay, Shenise Tiana. Kids Who Were Left Alone When There Was A Tornado. (p. 955)
Clay, Wil, illus. see Smothers, Ethel Footman.
Claybourne, A. Complete Book of the Human Body. (p. 352)
—Encyclopedia of Planet Earth. (p. 525)
—Introduction to Genes & DNA. (p. 882)
Claybourne, A. & Khanduri, K. Greek Myths: Ulysses & the Trojan War: Mini-Edition. (p. 721)
Claybourne, A. & Larkum, A. Inventor's Portfolio Kit (Bag) (p. 884)
Claybourne, A. & Treays, R. World of Shakespeare. (p. 1957)
Claybourne, A. & Young, Charles A. Treasure Hunting. (p. 1781)
Claybourne, Anna. 100 Deadliest Things on the Planet. (p. 1998)
—100 Most Awesome Things on the Planet. (p. 1998)
—100 Most Dangerous Things on the Planet. (p. 1998)
—100 Most Destructive Natural Disasters Ever. (p. 1998)
—100 Most Disgusting Things on the Planet. (p. 1998)
—100 Most Feared Creatures on the Planet. (p. 1998)
—100 Scariest Things on the Planet. (p. 1999)
—1001Things to Spot in the Town. (p. 2002)
—Accessories for All. (p. 8)
—Adventures of Ulysses. (p. 24)
—Ancient Greece. (p. 69)
—Animal Atlas. Gwinn, Saskia, ed. (p. 76)
—Bedroom Makeover. (p. 156)
—Blackout! Electricity & Circuits (p. 197)
—Can You Tell a Skink from a Salamander? Classification (p. 260)
—Cards, Wrap, & Tags. (p. 266)
—Caves. HL Studios Staff, illus. (p. 282)
—Colony of Ants: And Other Insect Groups (p. 342)
—Compl Bk of the Human Body - Internet Linked. (p. 352)
—Customize Your Clothes. (p. 395)
—Deserts. (p. 429)
—Dolphins (p. 464)
—Don't Kiss the Frog! Princess Stories with Attitude. Burfoot, Ella et al, illus. (p. 467)
—Ear-Splitting Sounds & Other Vile Noises. (p. 492)
—Electric Shocks & Other Energy Evils. (p. 508)
—Electricity. (p. 509)
—Elephant. (p. 511)
—Enciclopedia del Planeta Tierra. (p. 524)
—Extreme Earth. (p. 556)
—Feasts in Ancient Times (p. 579)
—Feel the Noise: Sound Energy (p. 580)
—Forms of Energy (p. 620)
—Glaring Light & Other Eye-Burning Rays. (p. 682)
—Gorilla. (p. 703)
—Greek Myths. Sansom, Fiona, illus. (p. 720)
—Gut-Wrenching Gravity & Other Fatal Forces. (p. 733)
—Healthy Eating: Diet & Nutrition (p. 758)
—Hippo. (p. 781)
—Human Body - Group 1 (p. 825)
—Human Body - Group 1. (p. 825)
—Humpback Whales (p. 827)
—Insects - Weird Wildlife (p. 876)
—Introduction to Genes & DNA. (p. 882)
—Investigating Volcanoes (p. 885)
—Killer Plants & Other Green Gunk. (p. 956)
—Knight Survival Guide. (p. 964)
—Life Processes (p. 1012)
—Light & Dark. (p. 1014)
—Make It Boom! Scott, Kimberly & Dean, Venetia, illus. (p. 1079)
—Make It Change! Scott, Kimberly & Dean, Venetia, illus. (p. 1079)
—Make It Glow! Scott, Kimberly & Dean, Venetia, illus. (p. 1079)
—Make It Grow! Scott, Kimberly & Dean, Venetia, illus. (p. 1079)
—Make It Splash! Scott, Kimberly & Dean, Venetia, illus. (p. 1079)
—Make It Zoom! Scott, Kimberly & Dean, Venetia, illus. (p. 1079)
—Materials. (p. 1104)
—Mental Development: From Birth to Old Age (p. 1126)
—Mountains. (p. 1181)
—Mummies Around the World (p. 1191)
—Octopuses (p. 1278)
—Orcas (p. 1302)
—Pack of Wolves: And Other Canine Groups (p. 1317)
—Pirate Secrets Revealed (p. 1363)
—Plant Secrets: Plant Life Processes (p. 1369)
—Pushes & Pulls. (p. 1420)
—Rats (p. 1440)
—Renaissance. (p. 1460)
—Rhino. (p. 1467)
—Saving the Earth. (p. 1517)
—Science of a Glass of Water: The Science of States of Matter. (p. 1527)
—Science of a Guitar: The Science of Sound. (p. 1527)
—Secrets of Light. (p. 1545)
—Shocking Story of Electricity. Hopgood, Kevin, illus. (p. 1568)
—Sick at Sea? Cure It or Cut It Off! (p. 1572)
—Smelly Farts & Other Body Horrors. (p. 1593)
—Sound. (p. 1615)
—Story of Exploration. McNee, Ian, illus. (p. 1658)
—Story of Inventions. Chisholm, Jane, ed. (p. 1658)
—Story of Science Kid Kit. (p. 1660)
—Surrealism (p. 1686)
—Tiger. (p. 1748)
—Tigers (p. 1749)
—Treasure Hunter's Handbook. (p. 1781)
—What Are the Limits of Organ Transplants? (p. 1880)
—Whiz Kid Science Scott, Kimberly & Dean, Venetia, illus. (p. 1914)
—Who Discovered Natural Selection? (p. 1915)
—Who Split the Atom? (p. 1917)
—World's Most Amazing Coasts (p. 1960)
—World's Most Amazing Deserts (p. 1960)
—World's Most Amazing Volcanoes (p. 1960)
—World's Worst Germs: Microorganisms & Disease (p. 1961)
Claybourne, Anna, jt. auth. see Connolly, Sean.
Claybourne, Anna, jt. auth. see Doherty, Gillian.
Claybourne, Anna, jt. auth. see Guillain, Charlotte.
Claybourne, Anna & Daynes, Katie. Titanic. McNee, Ian, illus. (p. 1757)
Claybourne, Anna & Doherty, Gillian. Peoples of the World. (p. 1340)
Claybourne, Anna & Ganeri, Anita. First Animal Encyclopedia: Seas & Oceans. (p. 593)
Claybourne, Anna & Heinemann Library Staff. Forms of Energy (p. 620)
—World's Most Amazing Coasts (p. 1960)
—World's Most Amazing Deserts (p. 1960)
—World's Most Amazing Volcanoes (p. 1960)
Claybourne, Anna, et al. Explorer Travel Guides. (p. 551)
—Living in the Wild: Sea Mammals. (p. 1041)
Claybourne, Anna, retold by. Jane Eyre. (p. 908)
—Stories from Shakespeare. (p. 1654)
Claybrook-Lucas, Michele. Quilting a Life: Piecing Together Livelihood, Lifestyle, & Life Dreams. (p. 1428)
Claycomb, Norma L., illus. see Hesselbein, Deborah A.
Claycomb, Patty. Learning Circle: A Preschool Teachers Guide to Circle Time. Charner, Kathleen, ed. (p. 985)
Clayden, Julie. Noah. Jolliffe, Angela, illus. (p. 1261)
Clayden, Julie & Jolliffe, Angela. Martha. (p. 1097)
Claydon, Darlene. Most Unusual Whale Tale: The Adventure Begins. (p. 1177)
Clayman, Fillys, illus. see Libritos Mios staff, et al.
Clayton, Christian, illus. see Rice, David & Rice, David Talbot.
Clayton, Colleen. What Happens Next. (p. 1886)
Clayton, Dallas. Awesome Book! Clayton, Dallas, illus. (p. 121)
—Awesome Book of Love! Clayton, Dallas, illus. (p. 121)
—Awesome Book of Thanks! (p. 121)
—Lily the Unicorn. Clayton, Dallas, illus. (p. 1018)
—Make Magic! Do Good! Clayton, Dallas, illus. (p. 1079)
Clayton, Darcy M. Making Mouth Sounds All Day Long. Freeswick, Jill, illus. (p. 1081)
Clayton, David. NASCAR Blast. (p. 1230)
Clayton, Dhonielle, jt. auth. see Charaipotra, Sona.
Clayton, E. Pearl. Adventures of My Heart. (p. 21)
Clayton, Elaine, illus. see Smiley, Jane.
Clayton, Elaine, illus. see Zimmer, Tracie Vaughn.
Clayton, Emily. If my Parents Only Knew... (p. 853)
Clayton, Emma. Roar. (p. 1478)
—Whisper. (p. 1912)
Clayton, Gary E. Economics: Principles & Practices. (p. 502)
Clayton, Gidget & Stoll, Krisit. Road to TeenVision: How to Find Your Passion & Realize Your Dreams. (p. 1477)
Clayton, Henry, illus. see Tobin, Paul.
Clayton, Irene Noda. Hole in the Wall, a Christmas Tale. (p. 788)
Clayton, Kim, illus. see Hetzer, Michael.
Clayton, Lawrence. Amphetamines & Other Stimulants. (p. 65)
—Barbiturates & Other Depressants. (p. 138)
—Coping with a Drug-Abusing Parent. (p. 365)
Clayton, Lew, illus. see Wlodarski, Loran.
Clayton, Lisa. Melvin the Mailman. Clayton, Sean & Spears, Ashley, illus. (p. 1125)
Clayton, Maggie. Create an Impression: Landscaping for Curb Appeal. (p. 378)
Clayton, Marie. Elvis Presley: Unseen Archives. (p. 517)
Clayton, Marie, jt. compiled by see Hill, Tim.
Clayton, Sally. Tales Told in Tents: Stories from Central Asia. Herxheimer, Sophie, illus. (p. 1703)
Clayton, Sally Pomme. Greek Myths. Ray, Jane, illus. (p. 720)
—Persephone. Lee, Virginia, illus. (p. 1344)
Clayton, Sean, illus. see Clayton, Lisa.
Clayton, Stuart. Xtreme Bass. (p. 1967)
CLE, Troy. Marvelous Effect. (p. 1099)
Cle, Troy. Marvelous World; Book 1: The Marvelous World of the Supposedly Soon to be Phenominal Young Mr. Louis Proof Book 1: the Marvelous Effect: the Marvelous Effect (Advanced Limited Collector's Edition) (p. 1099)
—Olivion's Favorites. (p. 1287)
CLE, Troy, jt. auth. see Cle, Troy.
Cle, Troy & CLE, Troy. Marvelous Effect. (p. 1099)
Cleare, John. Epic Climbs. (p. 532)
Clearwater, Linda, illus. see Simon, Mary Manz.
Cleary, B., jt. auth. see Cleary, Beverly.
Cleary, Beverly. Beezus & Ramona. (p. 158)
—Beezus & Ramona. Darling, Louis, illus. (p. 158)
—Beezus & Ramona. Darling, Louis et al, illus. (p. 158)
—Beezus & Ramona. Darling, Louis & Rogers, Jacqueline, illus. (p. 158)
—Beezus & Ramona. Dockray, Tracy & Rogers, Jacqueline, illus. (p. 158)
—Complete Ramona Collection: Beezus & Ramona; Ramona & Her Father; Ramona & Her Mother; Ramona Quimby, Age 8; Ramona Forever; Ramona the Brave; Ramona the Pest; Ramona's World. Dockray, Tracy & Rogers, Jacqueline, illus. (p. 353)
—Ellen Tebbits. (p. 514)
—Ellen Tebbits. Darling, Louis & Dockray, Tracy, illus. (p. 514)
—Emily's Runaway Imagination. (p. 519)
—Emily's Runaway Imagination. Krush, Beth et al, illus. (p. 519)
—Henry & Beezus. (p. 767)
—Henry & Beezus. Darling, Louis et al, illus. (p. 767)
—Henry & Ribsy. Darling, Louis et al, illus. (p. 767)
—Henry & Ribsy Box Set: Henry Huggins, Henry & Ribsy, Ribsy. (p. 767)
—Henry & the Clubhouse. Darling, Louis et al, illus. (p. 767)
—Henry & the Paper Route. Darling, Louis et al, illus. (p. 767)
—Henry Huggins. Darling, Louis, illus. (p. 768)
—Henry Huggins. Darling, Louis et al, illus. (p. 768)
—Jean & Johnny. (p. 911)
—Just for Me: My Ramona Quimby Journal. Rogers, Jacqueline & Parlagreco, Aurora M., illus. (p. 938)
—Mitch & Amy. Marstall, Bob et al, illus. (p. 1155)
—Mitch & Amy. Tiegreen, Alan & Dockray, Tracy, illus. (p. 1155)
—Mouse & the Motorcycle. Darling, Louis et al, illus. (p. 1182)
—Muggie Maggie. (p. 1189)
—Muggie Maggie. Tiegreen, Alan & Dockray, Tracy, illus. (p. 1189)
—Otis Spofford. Darling, Louis & Dockray, Tracy, illus. (p. 1307)
—Querido Senor Henshaw. (p. 1426)
—Ralph Mouse Collection. (p. 1437)
—Ralph S. Mouse. (p. 1437)
—Ralph S. Mouse. Zelinsky, Paul O. et al, illus. (p. 1437)
—Ralph S. Mouse. Zelinsky, Paul O. & Rogers, Jacqueline, illus. (p. 1437)
—Ramona & Her Family. (p. 1438)
—Ramona & Her Father. (p. 1438)
—Ramona & Her Father. Tiegreen, Alan et al, illus. (p. 1438)
—Ramona & Her Father. Tiegreen, Alan & Rogers, Jacqueline, illus. (p. 1438)
—Ramona & Her Mother. (p. 1438)
—Ramona & Her Mother. Tiegreen, Alan et al, illus. (p. 1438)
—Ramona & Her Mother. Tiegreen, Alan & Rogers, Jacqueline, illus. (p. 1438)
—Ramona Collection: Beezus & Ramona, Ramona & Her Father, Ramona the Brave, Ramona the Pest. Vol. 1 Dockray, Tracy & Rogers, Jacqueline, illus. (p. 1438)
—Ramona Collection: Ramona & Her Mother; Ramona Quimby, Age 8; Ramona Forever; Ramona's World. Vol. 2 Dockray, Tracy & Rogers, Jacqueline, illus. (p. 1438)
—Ramona Empieza el Curso. (p. 1438)
—Ramona Empieza el Curso. Bustelo, Gabriela, tr. (p. 1438)
—Ramona Forever. (p. 1438)
—Ramona Forever. Tiegreen, Alan et al, illus. (p. 1438)
—Ramona Forever. Tiegreen, Alan & Rogers, Jacqueline, illus. (p. 1438)
—Ramona la Chinche. Darling, Louis et al, illus. (p. 1438)
—Ramona la Valiente. (p. 1438)
—Ramona Quimby, Age 8. (p. 1438)
—Ramona Quimby, Age 8. Tiegreen, Alan et al, illus. (p. 1438)
—Ramona Quimby, Age 8. Tiegreen, Alan & Rogers, Jacqueline, illus. (p. 1438)
—Ramona the Brave. (p. 1438)
—Ramona the Brave. Tiegreen, Alan et al, illus. (p. 1438)
—Ramona the Pest. (p. 1438)
—Ramona the Pest. Darling, Louis et al, illus. (p. 1438)
—Ramona the Pest. Darling, Louis & Rogers, Jacqueline, illus. (p. 1438)
—Ramona y Su Madre. (p. 1438)
—Ramona y Su Padre. (p. 1438)
—Ramona's World. (p. 1438)
—Ramona's World. Tiegreen, Alan et al, illus. (p. 1438)
—Ramona's World. Dockray, Tracy & Rogers, Jacqueline, illus. (p. 1438)
—Ramona's World. Tiegreen, Alan & Rogers, Jacqueline, illus. (p. 1438)
—Ratoncito de la Moto. (p. 1440)
—Ratoncito de la Moto. Netto, Lydia, tr. (p. 1440)
—Ribsy. Darling, Louis et al, illus. (p. 1469)
—Runaway Ralph. (p. 1496)
—Runaway Ralph. Darling, Louis et al, illus. (p. 1496)
—Sister of the Bride. (p. 1581)
—Socks. (p. 1605)
—Socks. Darwin, Beatrice et al, illus. (p. 1605)
—Socks. Tiegreen, Alan & Dockray, Tracy, illus. (p. 1605)
—Troton Mi Perro. (p. 1789)
—Two Times the Fun. Taylor, Thomas, illus. (p. 1804)
—Viva Ramona. (p. 1846)
Cleary, Beverly & Cleary, B. Fifteen. (p. 584)
—Luckiest Girl. (p. 1062)
Cleary, Brian. Breezier, Cheesier, Newest, & Bluest: What Are Comparatives & Superlatives? Gable, Brian, illus. (p. 226)
—Dollar, a Penny, How Much & How Many? Gable, Brian, illus. (p. 463)
—How Long or How Wide? A Measuring Guide. Gable, Brian, illus. (p. 810)
—Lime, a Mime, a Pool of Slime: More about Nouns. Gable, Brian, illus. (p. 1018)
—Madam & Nun And 1001: What Is a Palindrome? Gable, Brian, illus. (p. 1069)
—Ode to a Commode: Concrete Poems. Rowland, Andy, illus. (p. 1278)
—Slide & Slurp, Scratch & Burp: More about Verbs. Gable, Brian, illus. (p. 1590)
Cleary, Brian P. A-B-a-B-A: A Book of Pattern Play. Gable, Brian, illus. (p. 1)
—A-B-a-B-a-A Book of Pattern Play. Gable, Brian, illus. (p. 1)
—Action of Subtraction. Gable, Brian, illus. (p. 10)
—Apples, Cherries, Red Raspberries: What Is in the Fruits Group? Goneau, Martin, illus. (p. 93)
—Bat Cannot Bat, a Stair Cannot Stare: More about Homonyms & Homophones. Goneau, Martin, illus. (p. 143)
—Black Beans & Lamb, Poached Eggs & Ham: What Is in the Meat & Beans Group? Goneau, Martin, illus. (p. 195)
—Bow-Tie Pasta: Acrostic Poems. Rowland, Andy, illus. (p. 216)
—Breezier, Cheesier, Newest, & Bluest: What Are Comparatives & Superlatives? Gable, Brian, illus. (p. 226)
—Bug in the Jug Wants a Hug. Miskimins, Jason, illus. (p. 236)
—But & for, yet & Nor: What Is a Conjunction? Gable, Brian, illus. (p. 246)
—Butterfly, Flea, Beetle, & Bee: What Is an Insect? Goneau, Martin, illus. (p. 247)
—Catfish, Cod, Salmon, & Scrod: What Is a Fish? Goneau, Martin, illus. (p. 280)
—Chips & Cheese & Nana's Knees: What Is Alliteration? Goneau, Martin, illus. (p. 308)
—Clown in the Gown Drives the Car with the Star. Miskimins, Jason, illus. (p. 335)
—Cool! Whoa! Ah & Oh! What Is an Interjection? Gable, Brian, illus. (p. 364)
—Dearly, Nearly, Insincerely: What Is an Adverb? Gable, Brian, illus. (p. 419)
—Do You Know Dewey? Exploring the Dewey Decimal System. Lew-Vriethoff, Joanne, illus. (p. 458)
—Dollar, a Penny, How Much & How Many? Gable, Brian, illus. (p. 463)
—Dolphin, Fox, Hippo, & Ox: What Is a Mammal? Goneau, Martin, illus. (p. 464)
—Eight Wild Nights: A Family Hanukkah Tale. Udovic, David, illus. (p. 507)
—Feet & Puppies, Thieves & Guppies: What Are Irregular Plurals? Gable, Brian, illus. (p. 580)
—Food Is CATegorical Goneau, Martin, illus. (p. 613)
—Fraction's Goal: Parts of a Whole. Gable, Brian, illus. (p. 627)
—Fraction's Goal - Parts of a Whole. Gable, Brian, illus. (p. 627)
—Frail Snail on the Trail. Miskimins, Jason, illus. (p. 627)
—Ful & -Less, -Er And -Ness: What Is a Suffix? Goneau, Martin, illus. (p. 646)
—Green Beans, Potatoes, & Even Tomatoes: What Is in the Vegetables Group? Goneau, Martin, illus. (p. 721)
—Hairy, Scary, Ordinary: What Is an Adjective? Prosmitsky, Jenya, illus. (p. 736)
—How Long or How Wide? A Measuring Guide. Gable, Brian, illus. (p. 810)

—How Much Can a Bare Bear Bear? Gable, Brian, illus. (p. 811)
—How Much Can a Bare Bear Bear? What Are Homonyms & Homophones? Gable, Brian, illus. (p. 811)
—I & You & Don't Forget Who: What Is a Pronoun? Gable, Brian, illus. (p. 834)
—I & You & Don't Forget Who: What Is a Prounoun? Gable, Brian, illus. (p. 834)
—I'm & Won't, They're & Don't: What's a Contraction? Gable, Brian, illus. (p. 858)
—Laugh Stand: Adventures in Humor. Sandy, John, illus. (p. 980)
—Lazily, Crazily, Just a Bit Nasally: More about Adverbs. Gable, Brian, illus. (p. 981)
—Limericks. Rowland, Andrew, illus. (p. 1018)
—Macaroni & Rice & Bread by the Slice: What Is in the Grains Group? Goneau, Martin, illus. (p. 1067)
—Madam & Nun & 1001: What Is a Palindrome? Gable, Brian, illus. (p. 1069)
—Miss Pell Would Never Misspell & Other Painless Tricks for Memorizing How to Spell & Use Wily Words. Sandy, J. P., illus. (p. 1152)
—Mission of Addition. Gable, Brian, illus. (p. 1153)
—Mrs. Riley Bought Five Itchy Aardvarks & Other Painless Tricks for Memorizing Science Facts. Sandy, J. P., illus. (p. 1187)
—Nice Mice in the Rice. Miskimins, Jason, illus. (p. 1250)
—Oils (Just a Bit) to Keep Your Body Fit: What Are Oils? Goneau, Martin, illus. (p. 1282)
—On the Scale, A Weighty Tale. (p. 1291)
—On the Scale, a Weighty Tale. Gable, Brian, illus. (p. 1291)
—Peaches on the Beaches. Miskimins, Jason, illus. (p. 1332)
—Peanut Butter & Jellyfishes: A Very Silly Alphabet Book. Snyder, Betsy E., illus. (p. 1332)
—Pitch & Throw, Grasp & Know: What Is a Synonym? Gable, Brian, illus. (p. 1364)
—Pre- & Re-, Mis- & Dis- What Is a Prefix? Goneau, Martin, illus. (p. 1393)
—Punctuation Station. Lew-Vriethoff, Joanne, illus. (p. 1417)
—Quirky, Jerky, Extra Perky: More about Adjectives. Gable, Brian, illus. (p. 1428)
—Rainbow Soup: Adventures in Poetry. Layton, Neal, tr. (p. 1436)
—Rhyme & Punishment: Adventures in Wordplay. Sandy, J. P., illus. (p. 1468)
—Run & Hike, Play & Bike: What Is Physical Activity? Goneau, Martin, illus. (p. 1496)
—Run & Hike, Play & Bike: What Is Physical Activity? Goneau, Martin & Gable, Brian, illus. (p. 1496)
—Salamander, Frog, & Polliwog: What Is an Amphibian? Goneau, Martin, illus. (p. 1504)
—Second, a Minute, a Week with Days in It: A Book about Time. Gable, Brian, illus. (p. 1539)
—Six Sheep Sip Thick Shakes: And Other Tricky Tongue Twisters. Mack, Steve, illus. (p. 1582)
—Skin Like Milk, Hair of Silk: What Are Similes & Metaphors? Gable, Brian, illus. (p. 1585)
—Slide & Slurp, Scratch & Burp: More about Verbs. Gable, Brian, illus. (p. 1590)
—Something Sure Smells Around Here: Limericks. Rowland, Andrew, illus. (p. 1610)
—Sparrow, Eagle, Penguin, & Seagull: What Is a Bird? Goneau, Martin, illus. (p. 1622)
—Stop & Go, Yes & No: What Is an Antonym? Gable, Brian, illus. (p. 1653)
—Stop & Go, Yes & No. Gable, Brian, illus. (p. 1653)
—Stop, Drop, & Flop in the Slop. Miskimins, Jason, illus. (p. 1653)
—Straight & Curvy, Meek & Nervy: More about Antonyms. Gable, Brian, illus. (p. 1664)
—Stroll & Walk, Babble & Talk: More about Synonyms. Gable, Brian, illus. (p. 1668)
—Stroll & Walk, Babble & Talk. (p. 1668)
—Super-Hungry Mice Eat Onions & Other Painless Tricks for Memorizing Geography Facts. Sandy, J. P., illus. (p. 1680)
—They're There on Their Vacation. Paillot, Jim, illus. (p. 1732)
—Thing on the Wing Can Sing. Miskimins, Jason, illus. (p. 1732)
—Thumbtacks, Earwax, Lipstick, Dipstick: What Is a Compound Word? Gable, Brian, illus. (p. 1745)
—To Root, to Toot, to Parachute: What Is a Verb? Prosmitsky, Jenya, illus. (p. 1759)
—Tortoise, Tree Snake, Gator, & Sea Snake: What Is a Reptile? Goneau, Martin, illus. (p. 1771)
—Under, over, by the Clover: What Is a Preposition? Gable, Brian, illus. (p. 1813)
—Washing Adam's Jeans & Other Painless Tricks for Memorizing Social Studies Facts. Sandy, J. P., illus. (p. 1859)
—Whose Shoes Would You Choose. Miskimins, Jason, illus. (p. 1922)
—Windows, Rings, & Grapes: A Look at Different Shapes. Gable, Brian, illus. (p. 1936)
—Windows, Rings, & Grapes - A Look at Different Shapes. Gable, Brian, illus. (p. 1936)
—Yogurt & Cheeses & Ice Cream That Pleases: What Is in the Milk Group? Goneau, Martin, illus. (p. 1972)
Cleary, Brian P. & Goneau, Martin. Apples, Cherries, Red Raspberries: What Is in the Fruits Group? (p. 93)
—Black Beans & Lamb, Poached Eggs & Ham: What Is in the Meat & Beans Group? (p. 195)
—Green Beans, Potatoes, & Even Tomatoes: What Is in the Vegetables Group? (p. 721)
—Macaroni & Rice & Bread by the Slice: What Is in the Grains Group? (p. 1067)
—Oils (Just A Bit) to Keep Your Body Fit: What Are Oils? (p. 1282)
—Run & Hike, Play & Bike: What Is Physical Activity? (p. 1496)
—Yogurt & Cheeses & Ice Cream That Pleases: What Is in the Milk Group? (p. 1972)
Cleary, Brian P. & Maday, Alice M. Bug in the Jug Wants a Hug: A Short Vowel Sounds Book. Miskimins, Jason, illus. (p. 236)
—Clown in the Gown Drives the Car with the Star: A Book about Diphthongs & R-Controlled Vowel. Miskimins, Jason, illus. (p. 335)
—Frail Snail on the Trail: Long Vowel Sounds with Consonant Blends. Miskimins, Jason, illus. (p. 627)
—Nice Mice in the Rice: A Long Vowel Sound Book. Miskimins, Jason, illus. (p. 1250)
—Peaches on the Beaches: A Book about Inflectional Endings. Miskimins, Jason, illus. (p. 1332)
—Sounds Like Reading Miskimins, Jason, illus. (p. 1615)
—Stop, Drop, & Flop in the Slop: A Short Vowel Sounds Book with Consonant Blends. Miskimins, Jason, illus. (p. 1653)
—Thing on the Wing Can Sing: Short Vowel Sounds & Consonant Digraphs. Miskimins, Jason, illus. (p. 1732)
—Whose Shoes Would You Choose? A Long Vowel Sounds Book with Consonant Digraphs. Miskimins, Jason, illus. (p. 1922)
Cleary, Brian P. & Nelson, Jennifer K. Apples, Cherries, Red Raspberries: What Is in the Fruits Group? Goneau, Martin, illus. (p. 93)
—Black Beans & Lamb, Poached Eggs & Ham: What Is in the Meat & Beans Group? Goneau, Martin, illus. (p. 195)
—Green Beans, Potatoes, & Even Tomatoes: What Is in the Vegetables Group? Goneau, Martin, illus. (p. 721)
—Macaroni & Rice & Bread by the Slice: What Is in the Grains Group? Goneau, Martin, illus. (p. 1067)
—Yogurt & Cheeses & Ice Cream That Pleases: What Is the Milk Group? Goneau, Martin, illus. (p. 1972)
Cleary, Christopher. Writing on the Wall. (p. 1965)
Cleary, Daniel. My Friend, Fred. Usui, Kanako, illus. (p. 1209)
—Prickles vs. the Dust Bunnies. (p. 1398)
—Stop Bugging Me: That's What Friends Are For. (p. 1653)
Cleary, Jacqueline Rogers. Waiting for William: Letters from Wolfborough New Hampshire. (p. 1853)
Cleary, Janice, illus. see Flanagan, Anne.
Cleary, Jon. Sundowners. (p. 1676)
Cleave, Andrew. Snakes & Reptiles - Pb: A Portrait of the Animal World. (p. 1596)
Cleave, Brenda. Money Tree. (p. 1164)
Cleave, Ryan G. Van, see Van Cleave, Ryan G.
Cleaver, Bill, jt. auth. see Cleaver, Vera.
Cleaver, Vera & Cleaver, Bill. Donde Florecen los Lirios. (p. 466)
Clee, Stephen, jt. auth. see Harte, Lawrence.
Cleef, Henny van. Israeli Table Kitchen. (p. 893)
Cleese, John, jt. auth. see Johnson, Kim Howard.
Cleeves, Frances. Feeding Farm Animals: Use Place Value & Properties of Operation to Add. (p. 580)
—Feeding Farm Animals: Use Place Value & Properties of Operations to Subtract. (p. 580)
Clegg, Dave, illus. see Myers, Janet Nuzum.
Clegg, Holly. Holly Clegg's Trim & Terrific Freezer Friendly Meals: Quick & Healthy Recipes You Can Make in Advance. Humphreys, David, photos by. (p. 789)
Clegg, Maryanne & Bester, Maryanne. Why Dog Is Afraid of Storms. Bester, Shayle, illus. (p. 1924)
Cleland, Jo. Achoo! (p. 9)
—Best Birthday. Dufalla, Anita, illus. (p. 168)
—Clean Hands, Dirty Hands. (p. 330)
—Clean Teeth, Dirty Teeth. (p. 330)
—Fabulous Food. (p. 560)
—Get Moving. (p. 667)
—Getting Your Zzzzs. (p. 670)
—I Can Make Colors. (p. 836)
—I Touch, Sing & Read. (p. 847)
—Jungle in My Yard. Dufalla, Anita, illus. (p. 935)
—Kitty Come Down! Dufalla, Anita, illus. (p. 963)
Cleland, JoAnn. Do You See 3? (p. 458)
—Good Morning, Little Python! (p. 698)
—I Hear, Sing & Read: Sing along, Tune: the Farmer in the Dell. (p. 839)
—I Hear, Sing & Read. (p. 839)
—I Listen. (p. 841)
—I See, Sing & Read. (p. 845)
—I Smell, Sing & Read. (p. 845)
—I Taste, Sing & Read. (p. 846)
—Ladybug, Ladybug, What Are You Doing? (p. 971)
—Searching for Circles. (p. 1537)
—Surviving the Great Chicago Fire. (p. 1687)
Clem, Joseph H. Christmas Movie Trivia Book. (p. 314)
Clem, Margaret H. Elbert ein Swine, Genius Pig. Clem, Margaret H., illus. (p. 508)
—Elbert ein Swine Learns Line Dancing No. 2. Clem, Margaret H., illus. (p. 508)
Clem, Paula. Shrinking Gnome. (p. 1571)
Clem, Stephen C. Moderato Cantabile: Pour la Paration de l'examan de Littérature: Guide de Lecture. (p. 1158)
Clemens, Edgar T. Trail Back: Epic Verse & Poems of The 1800s. (p. 1776)
Clemens, Justin. Black River. (p. 196)
Clemens, Meg, et al. Everything Kids' Math Puzzles Book: Brain Teasers, Games, & Activities for Hours of Fun. (p. 545)
Clemens, Micki. 10 Most Ingenious Fictional Detectives. (p. 1994)
Clemens, Nora & Greenberger, Robert. Discovering the Nature of Energy. (p. 449)
Clemens, Samuel L., jt. auth. see Twain, Mark, pseud.
Clemens, Samuel Langhorne, see Twain, Mark, pseud.
Clemens, Samuel Langhorne, see Twain, Mark, pseud.
Clemens, Samuel Langhorne, tr. see Twain, Mark, pseud.
Clemens, Verla. Andy's Journey Home. (p. 73)
Clemenston, John, illus. see Hughes, Mónica.
Clement, Ben & LoPatin, Norman. Stone's Throw Away. (p. 1653)
Clement, Christine. My Family Reunion: Learning to Recognize Fractions as Part of a Group. (p. 1203)
Clement, Debbie. Red, White, & Blue. (p. 1455)
Clement, Debbie, et al. You're Wonderful. (p. 1982)
Clement, Devyn, illus. see Young, Francis Kerr.
Clement, Edgar, illus. see Cortes Hernandez, Santiago & Cortes, Santiago.
Clement, Edgar, illus. see McGaughrean, Geraldine, et al.
Clement, Emily Gillespie. Bea & the Smart Kids. (p. 149)
Clement, Gary. Great Poochini (p. 718)
—Great Poochini. (p. 718)
—Swimming, Swimming (p. 1691)
Clement, Gary, illus. see Fagan, Cary.
Clement, Gary, illus. see King, Thomas.
Clement, Gary, illus. see Lottridge, Celia Barker.
Clement, Gary, illus. see Lottridge, Celia.
Clement, Gary, illus. see Shepard, Aaron.
Clement, Janet. Jewish Alphabet Rodriguez, Albert G., illus. (p. 917)
Clement, Marilyn, illus. see Bettenberg, Barbie.
Clement, Mark. Kid's Carpenter's Workbook. (p. 953)
Clement, Maryceleste. Mr. Tootles & the Polka-Dot Lollypops. Schexnayder, Paul, illus. (p. 1186)
Clement, Nathan. Big Tractor. (p. 184)
—Drive. Clement, Nathan, illus. (p. 485)
—Job Site. Clement, Nathan, illus. (p. 919)
—Speed. Clement, Nathan, illus. (p. 1624)
Clement, Rod. Olga the Brolga. Clement, Rod, illus. (p. 1285)
Clement, Stacy, illus. see Davis, Rebecca.
Clement-Davies, David. Fell. (p. 581)
—Fire Bringer. (p. 590)
—Sight. (p. 1573)
—Sight. (p. 1574)
—Telling Pool. (p. 1717)
—Telling Pool. Huebsch, Rand, illus. (p. 1717)
Clement-Moore, Rosemary. Hell Week. (p. 763)
—Prom Dates from Hell. (p. 1411)
—Spirit & Dust. (p. 1628)
—Texas Gothic. (p. 1724)
Clements, Andrew. About Average. Elliott, Mark, illus. (p. 5)
—Andrew Clements' School Stories. (p. 72)
—Back to School. (p. 130)
—Because Your Daddy Loves You. Alley, R. W., tr. (p. 155)
—Because Your Daddy Loves You. Alley, R. W., illus. (p. 155)
—Because Your Grandparents Love You. Alley, R. W., illus. (p. 155)
—Because Your Mommy Loves You. Alley, R. W., illus. (p. 155)
—Big Al. Yoshi, illus. (p. 177)
—Big Al & Shrimpy. Kogo, Yoshi, illus. (p. 177)
—Brave Norman. Beier, Ellen, illus. (p. 223)
—Bully Buster. (p. 241)
—Bully Buster. Frazee, Marla & Pedersen, Janet, illus. (p. 241)
—Bully Buster. Pedersen, Janet & Frazee, Marla, illus. (p. 241)
—Dinero para comer. (p. 440)
—Dogku. Bowers, Tim, illus. (p. 462)
—Dolores & the Big Fire: A True Story. Beier, Ellen, illus. (p. 464)
—Extra Credit. Elliott, Mark, illus. (p. 555)
—Fear Itself. Stower, Adam, illus. (p. 579)
—Frindel. (p. 639)
—Frindle. (p. 639)
—Frindle. Selznick, Brian, illus. (p. 639)
—Handiest Things in the World. Jaramillo, Raquel, illus. (p. 740)
—Head of the Class: Frindle - The Landry News - The Janitor's Boy. Selznick, Brian, illus. (p. 756)
—In Harm's Way. Stower, Adam, illus. (p. 863)
—Jacket. (p. 903)
—Jacket. Henderson, McDavid, illus. (p. 903)
—Jake Drake, Class Clown. Pedersen, Janet, illus. (p. 906)
—Jake Drake, Know-It-All. Frazee, Marla & Pedersen, Janet, illus. (p. 906)
—Jake Drake, Know-It-All. Pedersen, Janet & Frazee, Marla, illus. (p. 906)
—Jake Drake, Teacher's Pet. (p. 906)
—Jake Drake, Teacher's Pet. Pedersen, Janet, illus. (p. 906)
—Janitor's Boy. (p. 908)
—Last Holiday Concert. (p. 978)
—Last Holiday Concert. Selznick, Brian, illus. (p. 978)
—Lost & Found. (p. 1054)
—Lost & Found. Elliott, Mark, illus. (p. 1054)
—Lunch Money. (p. 1065)
—Lunch Money. Selznick, Brian, illus. (p. 1065)
—Map Trap. LaMarche, Jim & Andreasen, Dan, illus. (p. 1090)
—Million Dots. Reed, Mike, illus. (p. 1144)
—No Talking. (p. 1260)
—No Talking. Elliott, Mark, illus. (p. 1260)
—Periodico Landry. Selznick, Brian, illus. (p. 1343)
—Report Card. (p. 1461)
—Room One: A Mystery or Two. Elliott, Mark, illus. (p. 1488)
—Room One: A Mystery or Two. Blair, Chris & Elliott, Mark, illus. (p. 1488)
—School Story. (p. 1523)
—Tara & Tiree, Fearless Friends: A True Story. Beier, Ellen, illus. (p. 1706)
—Things Hoped For. (p. 1733)
—Things Not Seen. (p. 1733)
—Things That Are. (p. 1733)
—Troublemaker. (p. 1790)
—Troublemaker. Elliott, Mark, illus. (p. 1790)
—We Hold These Truths. Stower, Adam, illus. (p. 1867)
—We the Children. (p. 1868)
—We the Children. Stower, Adam, illus. (p. 1868)
—Week in the Woods. (p. 1871)
—Whites of Their Eyes. (p. 1914)
—Whites of Their Eyes. Stower, Adam, illus. (p. 1914)
Clements, Becky. Picnic with Friends: Alaska Adventure Bears. (p. 1355)
Clements, Frida, illus. see Earnhardt, Heather L.
Clements, Gillian. Indus Valley City. (p. 872)
—Medieval Castle. (p. 1119)
—Tudor Theatre. (p. 1796)
Clements, J. M. Vikings. (p. 1842)
Clements, Jan, jt. auth. see Windle, Jeanette.
Clements, Jonathan. Chinese Life. (p. 307)
Clements, Kenny, jt. auth. see Facts on File, Inc. Staff.
Clements, Peter. Prosperity, Depression & the New Deal. (p. 1412)
Clements, Richmond. Turning Tiger Special Edition. Finbow, Alexander, ed. (p. 1798)
Clements, Ruth Sypherd, illus. see Tarkington, Booth.
Clementson. Jungle Flowers Gift Wrap (Loos. (p. 935)
Clemesha, David, jt. auth. see Zimmerman, Andrea Griffing.
Clemesha, David, jt. auth. see Zimmerman, Andrea.
Clemesha, David & Zimmerman, Andrea. Fire Engine Man. Clemesha, David & Zimmerman, Andrea, illus. (p. 590)
Cleminson, Katie. Otto the Book Bear. (p. 1307)
Clemont, Lynn C. Angel Children. (p. 73)
Clemson, C. J. Charlie Mcbly & his Curiosity. (p. 293)
—Charlie Mcbly & the Long Walk Home. (p. 293)
Clemson, David, jt. auth. see Clemson, Wendy.
Clemson, Frances, jt. auth. see Clemson, Wendy.
Clemson, Wendy & Clemson, David. Digging for Dinosaurs. (p. 439)
—Firefighters to the Rescue. (p. 591)
—Ocean Giants. (p. 1276)
—Real World Math Blue Level: Dinosaur Dig. (p. 1449)
—Real World Math Blue Level: Firefighters to the Rescue. (p. 1449)
—Real World Math Blue Level: Journey to the Moon. (p. 1449)
—Real World Math Blue Level: Treasure in the Jungle. (p. 1449)
—Real World Math Blue Level: Zookeeper for the Day. (p. 1449)
—Rocket to the Moon. (p. 1483)
—Times Tables! (p. 1754)
—Treasure Hunt in the Jungle. (p. 1781)
—Zookeeper for a Day. (p. 1989)
Clemson, Wendy & Clemson, Frances. Dinosaur Dig. (p. 442)
Clemson, Wendy, et al. Be a Stuntman. (p. 148)
—Extreme Sports: Exciting Real Life Math Activities for Ages 8+ (p. 557)
—Fly a Jumbo Jet: Exciting Real Life Math Suitable for Ages 8+ (p. 609)
—Real World Math Orange Level: Win a Grand Prix. (p. 1449)
—Real World Math Orange Level: Zoo Vet. (p. 1449)
—Solve a Crime: Exciting Real Life Math Suitable for Ages 8+ (p. 1608)
Clendenin, Arlene M. & Clendenin, Bernard S. Adventures of the Yellow Beak Bird & the Flying Cats: Yellow Beak Bird & the Flying Cats. (p. 24)
Clendenin, Bernard S., jt. auth. see Clendenin, Arlene M.
Clendening, John. Animal Shelters. (p. 79)
—Veterinary Hospitals. (p. 1839)
—Wildlife Preserves. (p. 1931)
Clennell, Bobby. Watch Me Do Yoga. (p. 1861)
Clenott, Peter. Devolution. (p. 432)
Cleofas-Moore, Ramona. Tiffany. (p. 1748)
Clerc, Lucille. Flip Fashion. (p. 604)
Clerman, Lisa, jt. auth. see D'Elia, Amy.
Cleveland, Alexandra, et al. Camino al Primer Grado. Franco, Sharon, tr. from ENG. (p. 256)
Cleveland, Don. How Do We Know How the Brain Works. (p. 807)
Cleveland, Donald. How Do We Know How the Brain Works. (p. 807)
—Seven Wonders of Communication. (p. 1555)
Cleveland, Fred, illus. see Grammer, Maurine.
Cleveland, Lance. Splinter Tree. Arant, Bruce, illus. (p. 1630)
Cleveland, Marie. Jason's Giant Dilemma: A Storybook Land Adventure. (p. 910)
—Prowlers in Peril: A Storybook Land Adventure (p. 1413)
Cleveland, Nicole K. Ode to a Fly. (p. 1278)
Cleveland, Rob. Archer & the Sun: A Tale from China. Hoffmire, Baird, illus. (p. 95)
—Bear, the Bat & the Dove: Three Stories from Aesop. Hoffmire, Baird, illus. (p. 151)
—Clever Monkey: A Folktale from West Africa. Hoffmire, Baird, illus. (p. 331)
—Drum: A Folktale from India. Wrenn, Tom, illus. (p. 487)
—Magic Apple: A Middle Eastern Folktale. Hoffmire, Baird, illus. (p. 1071)
Cleveland, Will & Alvarez, Mark. Yo, Millard Fillmore! And All Those Other Presidents You Don't Know. Nation, Tate, illus. (p. 1971)
—Yo, Sacramento! (And All Those Other State Capitals You Don't Know) - Memorize Them All (Forever) in 20 Minutes-Without Trying! Nation, Tate, illus. (p. 1971)
Clevenger, Lee. IncrediBoy: Be Careful What You Wish. (p. 870)
CleverKits, creator. Safari Adventure. (p. 1501)
—Under the Sea. (p. 1814)
Clevinger, Brian. Atomic Robo & the Deadly Art of Science (p. 113)
Clewarth, John. Firestorm Rising. (p. 592)
Cleyet-Merle, Laurence. Animal Stencil Book. (p. 79)
Cleyet-Merle, Laurence, illus. see Sattgast, L. J.
Cleyet-Merle, Laurence, illus. see Sattgast, L. J. & Sattgast, Linda.
Clibbon, Lucy, illus. see Clibbon, Meg & Meg, Merry.
Clibbon, Lucy, illus. see Clibbon, Meg & Meg, Mighty.
Clibbon, Lucy, illus. see Clibbon, Meg, et al.
Clibbon, Lucy, illus. see Clibbon, Meg.
Clibbon, Lucy, illus. see Meg, Magic.
Clibbon, Meg. Ballerina. Clibbon, Lucy, illus. (p. 134)
—Brave Knights. Clibbon, Lucy, illus. (p. 223)
—Cowboy! Clibbon, Lucy, illus. (p. 373)
—Fabulous Fairies. Clibbon, Lucy, illus. (p. 560)
—Fairy Party Book: Magic Meg & Lucy Loveheart. Clibbon, Lucy, illus. (p. 563)
—Imagine You're a Ballerina. Clibbon, Lucy, illus. (p. 861)
—Imagine You're a Princess! Princess Megerella & Princess Lulubelle. Clibbon, Lucy, illus. (p. 861)
—Magical Creatures. Clibbon, Lucy, illus. (p. 1074)
—My Beautiful Ballet Pack. Clibbon, Lucy, illus. (p. 1196)
—Shimmering Mermaids. Clibbon, Lucy, illus. (p. 1566)
—Sparkly Princesses. Clibbon, Lucy, illus. (p. 1622)
—Starry Ballerinas. Clibbon, Lucy, illus. (p. 1642)
—Wicked Pirates. Clibbon, Lucy, illus. (p. 1927)
—Wizard! Clibbon, Lucy, illus. (p. 1942)
Clibbon, Meg & Meg, Merry. Magical Christmas. Clibbon, Lucy, illus. (p. 1074)
Clibbon, Meg & Meg, Mighty. Lots of Love: From Meg & Lucy. Clibbon, Lucy & Loveheart, Lucy, illus. (p. 1057)
Clibbon, Meg, et al. Fairyland Olympics. Clibbon, Lucy, illus. (p. 564)
—My Pretty Pink Fairy Journal. Clibbon, Lucy, illus. (p. 1217)
—My Wicked Pirate Journal. Clibbon, Lucy, illus. (p. 1221)

Clickard, Carrie. Victricia Malicia: Book-Loving Buccaneer. Meyers, Mark, illus. (p. 1840)
Clief, Sylvia Van, jt. auth. see Heide, Florence Parry.
Cliff Road Books Staff & Sweetwater Press Staff, contrib. by. Jokes & Riddles for Kids of All Ages (p. 924)
Cliffe, Kara. Jeff & His Magic Hot Air Balloon. Campbell, Ken, illus. (p. 911)
Cliffe, Susan. Thread of Deceit (p. 1741)
Clifford, Barry. Real Pirates: The Untold Story of the Whydah from Slave Ship to Pirate Ship. Manchess, Gregory, illus. (p. 1448)
Clifford, Caroline, illus. see Coming, Soon.
Clifford, Caroline, illus. see Luetkemeyer, Jenny.
Clifford, Eth. Help! I'm a Prisoner in the Library. Hughes, George, illus. (p. 765)
Clifford, J. Candace, jt. auth. see Clifford, Mary Louise.
Clifford, Jack D. Alien Attack. Daff, Russ, illus. (p. 40)
—Dragon Rock. Daff, Russ, illus. (p. 478)
—Egyptian Treasure Tomb. Daff, Russ, illus. (p. 507)
—Runaway Horses. Daff, Russ, illus. (p. 1496)
Clifford, Jack D. & Daff, Russ. Polar Explorers. (p. 1379)
Clifford, Kathleen & Uy, Megan Black. Great Lives, Vital Lessons: A Character Education Curriculum Resource for Grades 5-8. Bohlin, Karen E. & Lerner, Bernice, eds. (p. 717)
Clifford, Kathryn & Renn, Chantal. George the Sun Safe Superstar. (p. 663)
Clifford, Leah. Touch Menacing. (p. 1772)
—Touch Morbid. (p. 1772)
—Touch Mortal. (p. 1772)
Clifford, Mary Louise & Clifford, J. Candace. Mind the Light, Katie: The History of Thirty-Three Female Lighthouse Keepers. (p. 1145)
Clifford, Mikaela Rae. Live & Love it Up! When Life Gets You Down. (p. 1039)
Clifford, Patricia. Fox Loses a Tooth. (p. 626)
Clifford, Ross. Shiddakovich Adventure. (p. 1566)
Clifford, Tim. American Coins & Bills. (p. 60)
—Energy. (p. 528)
—Paying Without Money. (p. 1331)
—Space. (p. 1618)
Clift, Eva, illus. see Crane, Stephen.
Clift, Eva, illus. see London, Jack.
Clift, Eva, illus. see Pyle, Howard.
Clift, Eva, illus. see Shelley, Mary.
Clift, Eva, illus. see Spyri, Johanna.
Clift, Eva, illus. see Stevenson, Robert Louis.
Clift, Eva, illus. see Swift, Jonathan.
Clift, Eva, tr. see London, Jack.
Clift, Eva, tr. see Pyle, Howard.
Clift, Eva, tr. see Shelley, Mary.
Clift, Eva, tr. see Stevenson, Robert Louis.
Clifton, Chuck & Clifton, Joyce. Crossword Walk with Lewis & Clark. (p. 385)
—Daily Walk with Lewis & Clark - 1804. (p. 400)
—Fundamentals of Freedom Crossword Puzzles - Volume 1. (p. 649)
Clifton, Donald O., jt. auth. see Rath, Tom.
Clifton, Dorinda. Everybody Is Somebody. (p. 543)
—Ginger Bird & the Big Bad Bug with the Hard, Hard Heart. (p. 676)
—Take the Cake. (p. 1697)
Clifton Johnson, illus. see Thoreau, Henry.
Clifton, Joyce, jt. auth. see Clifton, Chuck.
Clifton, Lutricia. Freaky Fast Frankie Joe. (p. 632)
—Immortal Max. Sheban, Chris, illus. (p. 861)
Clifton, Sharon. What My Jesus Needs. (p. 1892)
Clifton, Tom, illus. see Parkhurst, Liz S.
Clifton Wisler, G. All for Texas. (p. 44)
Clifton-Brown, Holly. Annie Hoot & the Knitting Extravaganza. Clifton-Brown, Holly, illus. (p. 87)
Clifton-Brown, Holly, illus. see Castor, Harriet.
Clifton-Brown, Holly, illus. see Hosford, Kate.
Clifton-Brown, Holly, illus. see Miles, Brenda & Patterson, Colleen A.
Clifton-Brown, Holly, illus. see Schiffer, Miriam B.
Climent, Elena. Triste Historia del Sol con Final Feliz. (p. 1787)
Climent, Henry, jt. auth. see Johnson, Julia.
Climent, Paco. Tesoro del Capitan Nemo. (p. 1722)
—Tesoror del Capitan Nemo. (p. 1722)
Climer, Steven Lee. Young of Heart. (p. 1979)
Climo, Liz. Rory the Dinosaur: Me & My Dad. (p. 1488)
—Rory the Dinosaur Gets a Pet. (p. 1488)
Climo, Shirley. Pandora's Gift. (p. 1321)
Climpson, Sue, illus. see Steele, Philip.
Clinch, Karen. Charlie's Misfit Christmas. (p. 293)
—Peek-A-Boo Moon. (p. 1334)
Clinch, Kelly. Soccer Princess. (p. 1603)
Clinch, Mike, et al. Allwedd Daearyddiaeth: Cyfnod Allweddol 3. (p. 48)
Cline, Barbara Jean. Seth's Journey. (p. 1554)
Cline, Bev. Turkey. (p. 1797)
Cline, Crystal. Wings of Faith. (p. 1936)
Cline, Eric H. Ancient World: Civilizations of Africa; Civilizations of Europe; Civilizations of the Americas; Civilizations of the near East & Southwest Asia; Civilizations of Asia & the Pacific Takacs, Sarolta A., ed. (p. 71)
Cline, Eric H. & Rubalcaba, Jill. Ancient Egyptian World. (p. 69)
—Digging for Troy: From Homer to Hisarlik. Brannen, Sarah S., illus. (p. 439)
Cline, Gina. Chimps Use Sticks. Shusterman, Danielle, illus. (p. 306)
Cline, Gina, jt. auth. see Sánchez, Lucía M.
Cline, Gina, jt. auth. see Zorzi, Gina.
Cline, H. R. Baxter's Backyard Adventures. (p. 147)
—Just Mommy & Me. (p. 939)
Cline, Ian, photos by see Ramoutar, Tagore.
Cline, Jeff, illus. see D'Amico, Joan & Drummond, Karen Eich.
Cline, Mike, illus. see Maher, Adele.
Cline, Mike & Yi-Cline, Nancy. Franky Fox's Fun with English Activity Book, Level A1. Yi-Cline, Nancy, ed. (p. 631)
—Franky Fox's Fun with English Level A1. Yi-Cline, Nancy, ed. (p. 631)
—Franky Fox's Fun with English Resource Guide Level A1. (p. 631)
Cline, Renee. Kawndra the Tiger. (p. 946)
Clinedinst, B. West, illus. see Stockton, Frank R.
Clinedinst, B. West, illus. see Stockton, Frank Richard.
Clineff, Jeff. Too Many Kitties. Movshina, Marina, illus. (p. 1766)
Cline-Ransome, Lesa. Benny Goodman & Teddy Wilson: Taking the Stage as the First Black & White Jazz Band in History. Ransome, James E., illus. (p. 165)
—Freedom's School. Ransome, James E., illus. (p. 635)
—Helen Keller: The World in Her Heart. Ransome, James E., illus. (p. 763)
—Just a Lucky So-And-So: The Story of Louis Armstrong. Ransome, James, illus. (p. 937)
—Light in the Darkness: A Story about How Slaves Learned in Secret. Ransome, James E., illus. (p. 1015)
—Major Taylor, Champion Cyclist. Ransome, James E., illus. (p. 1078)
—Quilt Alphabet. Ransome, James E., illus. (p. 1428)
—Satchel Paige. Ransome, James E., illus. (p. 1515)
—Whale Trails, Before & Now. Karas, G. Brian, illus. (p. 1877)
—Words Set Me Free: The Story of Young Frederick Douglass. Ransome, James E., illus. (p. 1952)
—Young Pele: Soccer's First Star. Ransome, James E., illus. (p. 1979)
Clingan, B. V. Great Geese Migration: The Science of Evolution Series for Kids. (p. 716)
Clingan, Darrell, tr. see Ireland, Mary E. & Brandstaedter, German H.
Clinker, Gayle. Very Busy Vizzi. (p. 1837)
Clint, Marc. Aztec Warriors. (p. 122)
Clinton, Ann M. Stevie Inchworm. Canavan, Jean, illus. (p. 1649)
Clinton, Catherine. Hold the Flag High. Evans, Shane W., illus. (p. 788)
—When Harriet Met Sojourner. Evans, Shane W., illus. (p. 1902)
Clinton, Cathryn. Calling. (p. 254)
—Stone in My Hand. (p. 1652)
Clinton, Chelsea. It's Your World: Get Informed, Get Inspired & Get Going! (p. 899)
Clinton, Greg. Fairies. (p. 562)
—Life in Contemporary Texas. (p. 1010)
—Puerto Rico & the Spanish-American War. (p. 1415)
—Texas During Reconstruction. (p. 1724)
Clinton, J. Noel. Prince of Warwood & the King's Key. (p. 1401)
Clinton, Tim. Turn Your Life Around: Break Free from Your Past to a New & Better You. (p. 1798)
Clipston, Amy. Miles from Nowhere (p. 1142)
—Roadside Assistance (p. 1477)
Cliquet, Ronan, et al. Marvel Universe Thor Digest. (p. 1099)
Clish, Lori, illus. see Clish, Marian L.
Clish, Lori, illus. see Staheli, Bee, ed.
Clish, Marian L. Fish Don't Swim in a Tree. Clish, Lori, illus. (p. 598)
—I Wonder What a Fish Would Wish For? Swaim, Mike, illus. (p. 849)
—Wolf's Tale. Anderson, Jan, illus. (p. 1944)
Clissold, Caroline. All about Pirates. (p. 43)
—Dinosaur. (p. 441)
—Extreme Earth. (p. 556)
—Food Around the World. (p. 613)
—Let's Go. (p. 997)
—Out of This World. (p. 1311)
—Wild Animals. (p. 1928)
Clive, Dorman, jt. auth. see Equipo Staff.
Clo, Kathy, illus. see Gordon, Elaine R.
Cloci, Gabriella. Minda's Happily Ever After. (p. 1145)
Clocktowerhill Research & Publishing Group. Loyd & Boyd & the Slug Monster of Webster County. (p. 1061)
Clodd, Edward. Fetish Worship & Idolatry. (p. 583)
—Myths about the Earth & Man. (p. 1227)
Cloke, Rene. Adventures of Tom Thumb. (p. 24)
—Aladdin & His Magical Lamp. (p. 33)
—Cinderella. (p. 320)
—Favourite Bible Stories: Best-Loved Tales from the New Testament. Cloke, Rene, illus. (p. 578)
—Little Red Riding Hood. (p. 1035)
—Little Tin Soldier. (p. 1037)
—My Best Brer Rabbit Stories. (p. 1196)
—My First Picture Book of Nursery Rhymes. (p. 1207)
—Pinocchio. (p. 1360)
—Puss in Boots. (p. 1420)
—Snow White & the Seven Dwarfs. (p. 1600)
—Storytime Classics. (p. 1664)
—Three Little Pigs. (p. 1742)
—Treasury of Traditional Tales. (p. 1783)
—Ugly Duckling. (p. 1808)
Cloke, Rene, illus. see Bishop, Michael.
Cloke, Rene, illus. see Carruth, Jane.
Cloke, Rene, illus. see Wilkin, Wendy.
Cloke, Rene, jt. auth. see Cloke, Rene.
Cloke, Rene, jt. auth. see Traditional.
Cloke, Rene & Cloke, Rene. Woodland Stories. (p. 1949)
Cloke, Renee. Best-Loved Bible Stories: Favourite Tales from the Old Testament. (p. 170)
—Storyland Classics. (p. 1663)
Cloninger, Shirley, jt. auth. see Sievert, Jean.
Clonts, E. M. M., illus. see Hartley, Bob.
Clontz, Jay F. Tiny Star. (p. 1756)
Cloonan, J. S. Samuel T. Wallington: A Squirrelly Mess. (p. 1509)
Close, Chuck & Mouly, Françoise. Chuck Close: Face Book. (p. 318)
Close, Edward. Dinosaur Hunters. (p. 442)
—Endangered Animals. (p. 526)
—What Do We Do with Trash? (p. 1882)
Close, Laura Ferraro. Grey Squirrel. (p. 723)
Close, Laura Ferraro, illus. see StJohn, Amanda.
Close, Laura Ferraro, illus. see York, J.
Close, Rosa. Como a Raposinha Salvou Sua Pele: How the Little Fox Saved Her Coat. Tsibana, Rosana, tr. (p. 350)
Cloud, Deena, contrib. by. Human Body: How It Works Set, 11-Volumes. (p. 825)
Cloud, Megan & Nash, Kevin. Barnard College College Prowler off the Record. (p. 139)
Cloud, Olivia, ed. see Smith, Brenda J.
Cloud, Tanya. Circle of Sisters. (p. 321)
Cloud Tapper, Suzanne. Abolition of Slavery: Fighting for a Free America. (p. 5)
—America as a World Power: From the Spanish-American War to Today. (p. 59)
Cloud Tapper, Suzanne & Tapper, Suzanne Cloud. Cherokee: A Proud People. (p. 298)
Clouette, Katie, illus. see Shakespeare, Nancy.
Clough, Brenda W. Crystal Crown. (p. 387)
Clough, Julie. Dolphin. (p. 464)
—Octopus. (p. 1278)
—Starfish. (p. 1642)
Clough, Lisa. Petal & Poppy. Briant, Ed, illus. (p. 1346)
—Petal & Poppy & the Penguin. Briant, Ed, illus. (p. 1346)
—Petal & Poppy & the Spooky Halloween! Briant, Ed, illus. (p. 1346)
Clough, Peter. Clay in the Classroom. (p. 330)
Clous, Kelly. Liftoff! Book One of the Fire & Flight Series. (p. 1014)
Clout, Susan. Six Week Road Trip. (p. 1583)
Cloutier, Tammy. Firefly Freddie. (p. 592)
Cloutier, Toni Lynn. Word Search USA. (p. 1951)
—World Word Search. (p. 1960)
Clover. Groundhogs & Golfers. (p. 725)
Clover, Forever & Bell, Holly. Forever Clover: Forever Friends Sticker & Activity Book. (p. 619)
Clover, Gordon, illus. see Lawrence, Duane.
Clover, Louise. Bullring Kid & Country Cowboy. (p. 240)
—Bullring Kid & Country Cowboy Level 4 Intermediate. (p. 240)
Clover, Peter. Rescue Riders: Fire Alert. (p. 1462)
—Rescue Riders: Ghost Pony. (p. 1462)
—Rescue Riders: Race Against Time. (p. 1462)
—Sheltie & the Stray. (p. 1565)
—Sheltie in Trouble. (p. 1565)
Cloverfield, James. At Home with Animals. (p. 110)
Clovis, Charlotte. Curious Creatures of the Sea. (p. 392)
Clow, Alexine. Jenny's Dreams. Clow, Alexine, illus. (p. 913)
Clowes, Martin, jt. auth. see Woodford, Chris.
Clown, Pogo the. Ricki Roars. Miller, Richard, illus. (p. 1470)
Cloyd, J. B. Rocks We Use: A Content Area Reader. (p. 1484)
Cloyd, Nancy J. & Wach, Delia Bowman. Teddy Bear's Favorite Pictures: A Quiet Time Sharing Book. Wach, Delia Bowman, illus. (p. 1712)
Cloyd, Suzy. Pippi's Silent Message: Adventures of Suzy Q & You Too. Barham, Timothy E., illus. (p. 1362)
Cloyne, Rachel, illus. see Brothers Grimm, Becky & Brothers Grimm.
Clua, Guillem. Skin in Flames. Lamartina-Lens, Iride & Berardini, Susan, eds. (p. 1585)
Clucas, Richard A. Readings & Cases in State & Local Politics. (p. 1447)
Cluess, Jessica. Shadow Bright & Burning. (p. 1557)
Clugston, Chynna, illus. see Fisch, Sholly & Age, Heroic.
Clulow, Helen. Frog Prince of Barker's Bay. (p. 640)
Clum, James. Koji's Ninja Secrets. (p. 966)
Clunes, Rebecca. Drawing Creepy Crawlies. (p. 481)
—Drawing Dinosaurs. (p. 481)
—Drawing Sea Creatures. (p. 482)
—Drawing Speed Machines. (p. 482)
Cluster, Dick & Hernández, Rafael. History of Havana. (p. 784)
Cluster Springs Elementary School Staff, jt. auth. see Stansberry, Don.
Clute, Tom, jt. auth. see Fritz, Jean.
Clutterbuck, Peter M. Bright Ideas for Managing the Positive Classroom. (p. 228)
Clutton-Brock, Juliet. DK Eyewitness Books: Cat: Cat. (p. 456)
—Dog. (p. 460)
—Horse. (p. 799)
Clyde, Addie M. Sophie the Sofa. (p. 1613)
Clyde, Addie Mae. Charlie the Chair. (p. 293)
Clyde, Bulla, jt. auth. see Robert, Bulla Clyde.
Clydesdale, David T., contrib. by. Acorns to Oaks: Planted, Rooted & Growing in Christ. (p. 9)
—Angel Alert! The Night That Heaven Came Down. (p. 73)
—King of the Jungle: The God of Creation Is Lord of My Heart. (p. 959)
—Little Drummer Boy: Behind the Music. (p. 1027)
Clymer, Susan. There's a Rabbit in My Backpack. (p. 1731)
Clyne, Densey. Secret Life of Caterpillars. (p. 1541)
Clyne, Margaret & Griffiths, Rachel. Let's Make Music. (p. 999)
Clynes, Kate. Ali Baba. Anstey, David, illus. (p. 39)
—Goldilocks & the Three Bears. Daykin, Louise, tr. (p. 696)
—Goldilocks & the Three Bears. Daykin, Louise, illus. (p. 696)
—Little Red Hen & Wheat. (p. 1035)
—Not Again, Red Riding Hood! Daykin, Louise, illus. (p. 1267)
Clynes, Kate & Anstey, David. Ali Baba & the Forty Thieves. (p. 39)
Clynes, Kate, et al. Ali Baba & the Forty Thieves. Holland, Richard, illus. (p. 39)
C.M.M. Life of Many Forms. (p. 1012)
CMSP Projects Staff. Applied Math Concepts: Lines & Perimeters Area & Volume. (p. 93)
—Prealgebra. (p. 1394)
Cneut, Carll, illus. see Johnson, Lindsay Lee.
Cneut, Carll, illus. see Kockere, Geert De.
Cneut, Carll, illus. see Singer, Marilyn.
Cnockaert, Cindy. Magical Stones. (p. 1075)
Co, Alleen, illus. see Manhardt, Laurie Watson.
Co, Miguel, illus. see Bushnell, Jack.
Coach B. God's Animal Tales. (p. 690)
—Kingdom College. (p. 959)
Coach Pedro & Adam-Rita, Susan. 20 Easy Ways to Help Save the Earth. (p. 1995)
Coachman, Mary Kaye. Dance Team. (p. 402)
Coad, John. Green Technology (p. 722)
—Reducing Pollution (p. 1456)
Coakley, Lena. Witchlanders. (p. 1941)
Coakley, Louis C. & Karamanides, Dimitra. Pythagoras: Mathematician & Mystic. (p. 1421)
Coalson, Glo, illus. see Scott, Ann Herbert.
Coan, S. M. Crawlspace Charlie. (p. 377)
Coan, Sharon. Birds & Bugs. (p. 191)
—Changing Weather. (p. 290)
—Good for Me: Love. (p. 698)
—Good for Me: Healthy Food. (p. 698)
—Good for Me: Play & Exercise. (p. 698)
—How Heat Moves (p. 809)
—How Many Toys? (p. 811)
—How Sound Moves. (p. 812)
—Light Makes a Rainbow. (p. 1015)
—Message Received! (p. 1129)
—My Birthday Party. (p. 1198)
—Pushes & Pulls. (p. 1420)
—Shadows. (p. 1558)
—Special Me. (p. 1623)
—What the Sun Can Do. (p. 1894)
—Workers at My School (Foundations Plus) (p. 1952)
—Workers in My City (Foundations Plus) (p. 1952)
—Yo Soy Especial. (p. 1971)
Coan, Sharon, ed. see Crane, Kathy Dickerson.
Coan, Sharon, jt. auth. see Rice, Dona Herweck.
Coast, John & Attenborough, David. Dancing Out of Bali. (p. 403)
Coat, Janik. Hippopposites. (p. 781)
—Rhymoceros. (p. 1468)
Coates, Angel J. Mommy Loves No ! (p. 1162)
Coates, Ashley, jt. auth. see Coates, Kimberly.
Coates, Charmian. Secret Staircase. (p. 1544)
Coates, Dan. Kids' Music Collection (p. 954)
Coates, Diamond Ruth. Cheese & Quackers. (p. 296)
Coates, Doug. Pitching for Success: Character Lessons, the Joe Nuxhall Way. (p. 1364)
Coates, Jan. Hare in the Elephant's Trunk (p. 748)
—King of Keji MacKinnon, Patsy, illus. (p. 959)
—Rocket Man (p. 1482)
Coates, Jan L. Power of Harmony (p. 1389)
Coates, Jennifer. Lizards. (p. 1042)
—Snakes. (p. 1596)
Coates, Jennifer, illus. see Howard-Parham, Pam.
Coates, Julia. Trail of Tears (p. 1776)
Coates, Kathy, illus. see Kaemmerlen, Cathy.
Coates, Kathy, illus. see Knowlton, Laurie Lazzaro.
Coates, Kathy, illus. see Smith, J.
Coates, Kimberly & Coates, Ashley. If I Only Knew How to Tell Time. (p. 853)
Coates, Paul. Tim & the Iceberg Haywood, Ian Benfold, illus. (p. 1750)
Coates, Sean, illus. see Hinton, Cheryl.
Coates, Sue. Rusty: The Lame Reindeer. (p. 1498)
Coates, Theresa. Imaginary Time of Life. (p. 860)
Coates, Tim. Shooting of John F. Kennedy 1963: The Warren Commission. (p. 1568)
Coates-Smith, Renee. Bobby's Secret Is Out. (p. 206)
Coatney, Sharon, jt. auth. see Arnone, Marilyn P.
Coats, J. Anderson. Wicked & the Just. (p. 1927)
Coats, Lucy. Bear's Best Friend. Dyer, Sarah, illus. (p. 151)
—Captain Beastlie's Pirate Party. Mould, Chris, illus. (p. 263)
—Down in the Daisies. Bolam, Emily, illus. (p. 474)
—Hootcat Hill. (p. 796)
—Hound of Hades #2. Bean, Brett, illus. (p. 802)
—Steeds of the Gods #3. Bean, Brett, illus. (p. 1646)
Coats, Sylvia. Thinking as You Play: Teaching Piano in Individual & Group Lessons. (p. 1734)
Coats, Vivian. His Special Love. (p. 781)
—His Star. (p. 781)
—In His Love. (p. 863)
—Safe in His Love. (p. 1502)
Coatsworth, Elizabeth. Away Goes Sally. Sewell, Helen, illus. (p. 120)
—Cat Who Went to Heaven. (p. 278)
—Cat Who Went to Heaven. Vitale, Raoul, illus. (p. 278)
—Door to the North: A Saga of 14th Century America. Chapman, Frederick T., illus. (p. 470)
—Five Bushel Farm. Sewell, Helen, illus. (p. 600)
—Gata Que Se Fue Para el Cielo. (p. 657)
—White Horse. Sewell, Helen, illus. (p. 1913)
—Wonderful Day. Sewell, Helen, illus. (p. 1948)
Coatsworth, Elizabeth Jane. Fair American. Sewell, Helen, illus. (p. 562)
—Forgotten Island. Paull, Grace, illus. (p. 619)
Cobain, Beverly. When Nothing Matters Anymore: A Survival Guide for Depressed Teens. (p. 1904)
Cobalt Illustrations Studio Staff, illus. see Lewis, Elizabeth Foreman.
Cobalt Illustrations Studio Staff, illus. see O'Reilly, Bill.
Cobalt Illustrations Studio Staff, jt. auth. see Low, William.
Cobb, Allan. Cadmium. (p. 250)
—Weather Observation Satellites. (p. 1870)
Cobb, Allan B. Basics of Chemistry. (p. 142)
—Basics of Nonmetals. (p. 142)
—Bionic Human. (p. 190)
—Cell Theory. (p. 286)
—Earth Chemistry. (p. 495)
—First Responders. (p. 596)
—Frequently Asked Questions about Migraines & Headaches. (p. 636)
—Heroin & Your Veins: The Incredibly Disgusting Story. (p. 773)
—How the US Security Agencies Work. (p. 813)
—Looking at the Interdependence of Plants, Animals, & the Environment with Graphic Organizers. (p. 1051)
—Mars. (p. 1096)
—Mexico: A Primary Source Cultural Guide. (p. 1131)
—Scientifically Engineered Food. (p. 1528)
—Skating the X Games. (p. 1584)
—Skating the X-Games. (p. 1584)
—Super Science Projects about Animals in Their Habitats. (p. 1680)
—Super Science Projects about Light & Optics. (p. 1681)
—Super Science Projects about Oceans. (p. 1681)
—Super Science Projects about Sound. (p. 1681)
Cobb, Allan B., et al. Heroin. (p. 773)

C

Cobb, Amy. Dude, Where's My Saxophone? Cattish, Anna, illus. (p. 489)
—First Chair. Cattish, Anna, illus. (p. 593)
—Notes from a Pro. Cattish, Anna, illus. (p. 1267)
—Shredding with the Geeks. Cattish, Anna, illus. (p. 1571)
—Snaring the Trumpet. Cattish, Anna, illus. (p. 1597)
—Swing Vote for Solo. Cattish, Anna, illus. (p. 1691)
Cobb, Annie & Jones, Davy. Ruedas! Jones, Davy, illus. (p. 1494)
Cobb, Bob. Building the Ultimate Bank Advisor: 8 Essential Keys for Unleashing your Maximum Competitive Edge. (p. 239)
Cobb, Carlene. Coping with an Abusive Relationship. (p. 365)
Cobb, Carrie. Day in the Life of Becky the Unfortunate. (p. 413)
Cobb, Daryl. Greta's Magical Mistake. (p. 723)
—Henry Hare's Floppy Socks. (p. 768)
—Mr. Moon. (p. 1185)
—Pirates: Legend of the Snarlyfeet. (p. 1363)
Cobb, Daryl K. Boy on the Hill. (p. 218)
—Count with Daniel Dinosaur. (p. 370)
—Do Pirates Go to School. (p. 457)
Cobb, Debbie. Gracie's Big Adventure... with Augustine the Beaver. Ferchaud, Steve, illus. (p. 705)
Cobb, Josh, jt. illus. see Cobb, Vicki.
Cobb, Judith A. First Gift. Cowper-Thomas, Wendy, illus. (p. 595)
Cobb, Lisa Kaniut. Literary Ideas & Scripts for Young Playwrights (p. 1022)
Cobb, Nyelah. True Identity. (p. 1792)
Cobb, Paul M., tr. see Ibn Munqidh, Usama & ibn Munqidh, Usama.
Cobb, Rebecca. Missing Mommy: A Book about Bereavement. Cobb, Rebecca, illus. (p. 1152)
—Spooky Sums & Counting Horrors. (p. 1631)
—Tongue Twisters to Tangle Your Tongue. (p. 1765)
Cobb, Rebecca, illus. see Blyton, Enid.
Cobb, Shawna. Little Sticker. (p. 1036)
Cobb, Soozi Bruun. Skis for Feet. (p. 1586)
Cobb, Thomas J. Polly & His Frog Tale: Forbidden Meadow (p. 1381)
Cobb, Vicki. I Face the Wind. Gorton, Julia, illus. (p. 838)
—I Fall Down. Gorton, Julia, illus. (p. 838)
—Junk Food. Gold, Michael, photos by. (p. 936)
—On Stage. Gold, Michael, photos by. (p. 1289)
—Perk up Your Ears: Discover Your Sense of Hearing. Lewis, Cynthia, illus. (p. 1343)
—See for Yourself! More Than 100 Amazing Experiments for Science Fairs & School Projects. Klug, Dave, illus. (p. 1546)
—This Place Is Cold. Lavallee, Barbara, illus. (p. 1737)
—This Place Is Wet. Lavallee, Barbara, illus. (p. 1737)
—What's the BIG Idea? Amazing Science Questions for the Curious Kid. (p. 1899)
—What's the Big Idea? Amazing Science Questions for the Curious Kid. (p. 1899)
—Your Body Battles A Broken Bone. (p. 1980)
—Your Body Battles a Broken Bone. Harris, Andrew, illus. (p. 1980)
—Your Body Battles a Cavity. Harris, Andrew, illus. (p. 1980)
—Your Body Battles A Cold. (p. 1980)
—Your Body Battles a Cold. Harris, Andrew, illus. (p. 1980)
—Your Body Battles A Skinned Knee. (p. 1980)
—Your Body Battles a Skinned Knee. Harris, Andrew, illus. (p. 1980)
—Your Body Battles an Earache. (p. 1980)
—Your Body Battles an Earache. Harris, Andrew, illus. (p. 1980)
Cobb, Vicki & Cobb, Josh. Light Action! Amazing Experiments with Optics. (p. 1014)
Cobb, Vicki & Darling, Kathy. We Dare You! Hundreds of Fun Science Experiments, Tricks, & Games You Can Try at Home. (p. 1867)
Cobb, Vicki & Dorling Kindersley Publishing Staff. Harry Houdini: A Photographic Story of a Life. (p. 750)
—Marie Curie. (p. 1093)
Cobb, Vicki & Lavallee, Barbara. This Place Is Wet. (p. 1737)
Cobb, William, Jr. Willie Cobb's Invention: Inventing with a Motive. (p. 1934)
Cobblekids Staff. Making Melody W/Your Heart Pri. (p. 1081)
Cobblestone Publishing, Inc. Staff, jt. auth. see Cricket Books Staff.
Cobblestone Publishing Staff, jt. auth. see Cricket Books Staff.
Coben, Harlan. Found. (p. 624)
—Seconds Away. (p. 1540)
—Shelter (p. 1565)
—Shelter. (p. 1565)
—Woods. (p. 1949)
Coble, Charles. Earth Science. (p. 496)
Coble, Eric. Cinderella Confidential. (p. 320)
—Pecos Bill & the Ghost Stampede. (p. 1334)
Coble, Eric, adapted by. Giver. (p. 681)
Coble, Lynn Bemer, ed. see Lawrence, Donna.
Cobleigh, Carolynn, illus. see Bagert, Brod, ed.
Coblenz, John. Viata Familiei Crestine (Christian Family Living) Brinzei, Daniel, ed. (p. 1839)
Cobley, Jason. Legend of Tom Hickathrift. (p. 989)
Cobot, Meg. All-American Girl. (p. 43)
Coburn, Ann. Alex & the Warrior. (p. 35)
—Alex & the Winter Star. (p. 36)
—Glint. (p. 683)
—Mission 1: Flying Solo. Horne, Sarah, illus. (p. 1153)
—Showtime. Horne, Sarah, illus. (p. 1571)
Coburn, Broughton. Triumph on Everest: A Photobiography of Sir Edmund Hillary. (p. 1788)
Coburn, Claudia. Did the Aardvarks Say "No Ark"? Hoard, Angela, illus. (p. 437)
Coburn, Dylan, illus. see Cheshire, Simon.
Coburn, Jake. Lovesick. (p. 1061)
—Prep. (p. 1395)
Coburn, Jewell Reinhart. Angkat: The Cambodian Cinderella. Flotte, Eddie, illus. (p. 75)
Coburn, Jewell Reinhart & Lee, Tzexa Cherta. Jouanah: A Hmong Cinderella. O'Brien, Anne Sibley, illus. (p. 927)
Cocagne, Marie-Pascale. Big Book of Shapes. Stevens-Marzo, Bridget, illus. (p. 179)
Cocca, Lisa Colozza. Bar Graphs. (p. 137)
—Graphing Story Problems. (p. 711)
—Line Graphs. (p. 1019)
—Pictographs. (p. 1355)
—Pie Graphs. (p. 1356)
—Sleepy Hollow. (p. 1589)
—Tally Charts. (p. 1704)
Cocca, Lisa Colozza, jt. auth. see Miller, Reagan.
Cocca-Leffler, Maryann. Calling All Cats. Cocca-Leffler, Maryann, illus. (p. 254)
—Dog Wash Day. Cocca-Leffler, Maryann, illus. (p. 462)
—Easter Bunny in Training. Cocca-Leffler, Maryann, illus. (p. 499)
—Homemade Together Christmas. Cocca-Leffler, Maryann, illus. (p. 793)
—It's Halloween Night. Cocca-Leffler, Maryann, illus. (p. 897)
—Jack's Talent. Cocca-Leffler, Maryann, illus. (p. 904)
—Janine. Cocca-Leffler, Maryann, illus. (p. 908)
—Mr. Tanen's Ties. Cocca-Leffler, Maryann, illus. (p. 1186)
—Princess for a Day. (p. 1403)
—Princess K. I. M. & the Lie That Grew. Cocca-Leffler, Maryann, illus. (p. 1404)
—Princess Kim & Too Much Truth. (p. 1404)
—Princess Kim & Too Much Truth. Cocca-Leffler, Maryann, illus. (p. 1404)
—Rain Brings Frogs: A Little Book of Hope. Cocca-Leffler, Maryann, illus. (p. 1434)
—Spotlight on Stacey. (p. 1634)
—Theo's Mood: A Book of Feelings. Cocca-Leffler, Maryann, illus. (p. 1729)
—Vacation for Pooch. Cocca-Leffler, Maryann, illus. (p. 1830)
Cocca-Leffler, Maryann, illus. see Buller, Jon, et al.
Cocca-Leffler, Maryann, illus. see Bunting, Eve.
Cocca-Leffler, Maryann, illus. see Knudsen, Michelle.
Cocca-Leffler, Maryann, illus. see Spinelli, Eileen.
Coccia. Adventures of Itsy Bitsy Franny Frog: I Like What I Can Do When I Try! (p. 19)
Coccia, Anthony. Sancho the Snowboarder. (p. 1510)
Coccia, Mina. Mother Nature & Mz Bee. (p. 1178)
Cocciolone, Kathy Roberts, illus. see Hammock, Sarah Owens.
Cochard, David. Legend of Honey Hollow. (p. 988)
Cochard, David, illus. see McNaney, Jeanne.
Cochard, Nadège. Daycare for Connor. Fanny, illus. (p. 415)
—Grandma & Grandpa Visit Connor. Fanny, illus. (p. 708)
Cochran, Bill. Forever Dog. (p. 619)
—Forever Dog. Andreasen, Dan, illus. (p. 619)
—My Parents Are Divorced My Elbows Have Nicknames & Other Fact. Björkman, Steve, illus. (p. 1216)
Cochran, Bruce. First Birthday Bear. (p. 593)
—First Pony: Blue. (p. 596)
—First Pony: Pink. (p. 596)
—It's the Big 1: Blue. (p. 899)
—It's the Big 1: Pink. (p. 899)
Cochran, Cheryl. Mini Message Man & the Great Candy Caper. Cochran, Christina, illus. (p. 1146)
Cochran, Christina, illus. see Cochran, Cheryl.
Cochran, Gayle. Dinner for Six: A set-the-table Fable. Cochran, Paige, illus. (p. 441)
Cochran, Jean M. Farmer Brown & His Little Red Truck. Enos, Daryl, illus. (p. 574)
—If a Monkey Jumps onto Your School Bus. Morris, Jennifer & Morris, Jennifer E., illus. (p. 852)
—Off I Go! Gullens, Lee M., illus. (p. 1279)
—On a Dark, Dark Night. Morris, Jennifer E., illus. (p. 1288)
—Your Tummy's Talking! Gullens, Lee M., illus. (p. 1981)
Cochran, Josh. Inside & Out: New York. Cochran, Josh, illus. (p. 876)
Cochran, Kate & Benchmark Education Co., LLC Staff. Room for Moose. (p. 1488)
—Why Mice Hide. (p. 1925)
Cochran, Matthew. Yagoos Go to Town. (p. 1968)
Cochran, Melinda. Emma the Fire Ant Finds a Friend. (p. 520)
Cochran, Molly. Legacy. (p. 987)
—Poison. (p. 1377)
Cochran, Paige, illus. see Cochran, Gayle.
Cochran, Randy. Critter Golf: The Adventures at Owl's Nest. (p. 384)
—Critter Golf Ii: Chaos at Owl's Nest. (p. 384)
—Critter Golf Iii: The Storm. (p. 384)
Cochran, Rod. Bear Hollow. (p. 150)
Cochran, Sue. God's Abcs: (Spanish) (p. 690)
—God's ABCs. (p. 690)
Cochrane, Gillian. Week at Aunty Betty's. (p. 1871)
Cochrane, Ian. Shian & the Corryvreckan. (p. 1566)
Cochrane, Kelly. Significant Battles of World War II. (p. 1574)
Cochrane, KerryAnn, tr. see Gamache, Line.
Cochrane, Mick. Fitz. (p. 599)
—Girl Who Threw Butterflies. (p. 679)
Cochrane, Pierre. Thunderbolt's Treasure. (p. 1746)
Cockburn, Gerrie L. Why Turtles Have Shells. Cockburn, Ian, ed. (p. 1926)
Cockburn, Ian, ed. see Cockburn, Gerrie L.
Cockcroft, James D. Latinos in Beisbol. (p. 979)
Cockcroft, Jason. Counter Clockwise. (p. 370)
Cockcroft, Jason, illus. see Cotten, Cynthia.
Cockcroft, Jason, illus. see Doherty, Berlie.
Cockcroft, Jason, illus. see McCaughrean, Geraldine.
Cockcroft, Jason, illus. see McGee, Marni.
Cockcroft, Jason, illus. see Riordan, James.
Cockcroft, Jason, illus. see Waddell, Martin.
Cockcroft, Jason, tr. see Riordan, James.
Cockell, Charles & Cockell, Charles S. Space on Earth: Saving Our World by Seeking Others. (p. 1619)
Cockell, Charles S., jt. auth. see Cockell, Charles.
Cockey, Barton M., jt. auth. see Cockey, Elizabeth J.
Cockey, Elizabeth J. & Cockey, Barton M. Drawn to the Land: The Romance of Farming. (p. 482)
Cockrell, Amanda. What We Keep Is Not Always What Will Stay. (p. 1895)
Cockrum, Dave, jt. illus. see Byrne, John.
Cockrum, Dave & Byrne, John. Uncanny X-Men (p. 1811)
Cockrum, James L. Short Boat on a Long River. Sansevero, Tony, illus. (p. 1569)
Cocks, Harry, jt. ed. see Houlbrook, Matt.
Cocks, Heather & Morgan, Jessica. Messy. (p. 1130)
—Spoiled. (p. 1630)
Cocks, Nancy. Fergie Tries to Fly. Marton, Jirina, illus. (p. 582)
—Where, Oh Where, Is Fergie? Marton, Jirina, illus. (p. 1909)
—You Can Count on Fergie. Marton, Jirina, illus. (p. 1974)
Cocks, Nancy & Marton, Jirina. Fergie Cleans Up. (p. 582)
—Fergie Counts His Blessings. (p. 582)
—Fergie Goes to Grandma's. (p. 582)
—Fergie Has a Birthday Party. (p. 582)
—Nobody Loves Fergie. (p. 1262)
Cocoretto. What's That Noise? CHOO! CHOO! Guess the Vehicle! (p. 1899)
—What's That Noise? SNAP! SNAP! Guess the Animal! (p. 1899)
—What's That Noise? TAP! TAP! Guess the Toy! (p. 1899)
—What's That Noise? TOOT! TOOT! Guess the Instrument! (p. 1899)
Cocos, Deborah. Tale One of the Wignuts: The Golden Sprigget of Fritzwitz. (p. 1701)
Cocotos, Tom Nick, illus. see Krieger, Emily.
Cocotos, Tom Nick, illus. see U. S. National Geographic Society Staff.
Cocteau, Jean. Enfants Terribles. (p. 529)
Coddington, Andrew. Ghosts. (p. 672)
Coddon, Karin S. Black Women Activists. (p. 197)
Coddon, Karin S., ed. Black Abolitionists. (p. 194)
Codell, Esmé Raji. Basket Ball. Plecas, Jennifer, illus. (p. 142)
—Fairly Fairy Tales. Chavarri, Elisa, illus. (p. 563)
—It's Time for Preschool! Ramá, Sue, illus. (p. 899)
—Sahara Special. (p. 1503)
—Seed by Seed: The Legend & Legacy of John Appleseed Chapman. Perkins, Lynne Rae, illus. (p. 1547)
—Seed by Seed: The Legend & Legacy of John Appleseed Anniversary. Perkins, Lynne Rae, illus. (p. 1547)
—Vive la Paris. (p. 1846)
Codell, Esmé Raji, illus. see Sudjic, Deyan.
Codor, Richard. Too Many Latkes! Codor, Richard, illus. (p. 1766)
Cody, Christina. Perfectly Imperfect Pumpkin. (p. 1342)
Cody, Jacquelyne. How to Be Happy. (p. 815)
Cody, Matt W. Calvin Klein. (p. 255)
—Peter Stuyvesant. (p. 1347)
Cody, Matthew. Dead Gentlemen. (p. 416)
—Powerless. (p. 1391)
—Super. (p. 1679)
—Villainous. (p. 1842)
—Will in Scarlet. (p. 1932)
Cody, Nancy. Cooking S'More with Nana: An Activity & Cooking Book for Kids. (p. 362)
—Cooking with Nana: Holiday Crafts & Recipes for Kids. (p. 362)
Cody, Sherwin. Four American Poets. (p. 624)
Cody, Tod. Cowboy's Handbook: How to Become a Hero of the Wild West. (p. 374)
Cody, William, jt. auth. see Carrero, Jorge.
Coe, Anne, illus. see Dunphy, Madeleine.
Coe, Catherine. Best Friend Boom. McCafferty, Jan, illus. (p. 169)
—Horse Horror. McCafferty, Jan, illus. (p. 799)
—Showdown at Dawn. McCafferty, Jan, illus. (p. 1571)
Coe, Jara & Hardy, Donna. Jack Meets the New Baby. (p. 903)
Coe, Julie L. Friendship Puzzle: Helping Kids Learn about Accepting & Including Kids with Autism. Brassel, Sondra, illus. (p. 639)
Coe, Kimberly. My Dad Is A Marine. Coe, Kimberly, illus. (p. 1200)
Coe, Layla. At the Art Store: Compare Numbers. (p. 110)
Coe, Les. Space Crew-Zers: Adventures on Dallas Station. (p. 1618)
Coe, Mary. Prince of Betherland. (p. 1401)
Coe, Mary E. Prince of Betherland. (p. 1401)
—Prince of Betherland A Wonderful World of Fantasy. (p. 1401)
—Willy: the Best Christmas Gift Ever. (p. 1934)
—Willy: the Best Christmas Gift Ever a Children's Book. (p. 1934)
Coelho, Alexa & Field, Simon Quellen. Why Is Milk White? & 200 Other Curious Chemistry Questions. (p. 1925)
Coelho, Joseph. Werewolf Club Rules. (p. 1875)
Coelho, Paulo. Veronika beschließt zu sterben. (p. 1837)
—Warrior of the Light: A Manual. (p. 1858)
Coerr, Eleanor. Circus Day in Japan: Bilingual English & Japanese Text. Matsunari, Yumi, tr. (p. 322)
—Josefina Story Quilt. Degen, Bruce, illus. (p. 926)
—Mieko & the Fifth Treasure. (p. 1139)
—S Is for Silver: A Nevada Alphabet. Park, Darcie, illus. (p. 1499)
—Sadako & the Thousand Paper Cranes. Himler, Ronald, illus. (p. 1501)
Coerr Eleanor & Eleanor, Coerr. Sadako y las Mil Grullas de papel. (p. 1501)
Coester, Alfred Lester. Literary History of Spanish America. (p. 1022)
Coetzee, Eirka, et al. Social Science Matters Grade 8 Learner's Book. (p. 1604)
—Social Science Matters Grade 8 Learner's Book Afrikaans Translation. (p. 1604)
Coetzee, Erika, et al. Social Sciences Matters Grade 7 Learner's Book. (p. 1604)
Coetzee, Mark M., et al. Where Art Is Happening - Artcenter/South Florida. (p. 1906)
Coevoet, Sylvie, illus. see Averous, Helene.
Coey, Julia. Animal Hospital: Rescuing Urban Wildlife. (p. 78)
Cofer, Amadeus. Aloha Adventure: The Magic of Imagination on a Rainy Day. (p. 48)
—Friendship Rules: How to Make & Keep Friends (p. 639)
—Mystery of the Golden Pearls: A Halloween Adventure in Clarkesville (p. 1225)
Cofer, Judith Ortiz. Call Me Maria. (p. 254)
Cofer, Judith Ortiz. Ano de Nuestra Revolucion: Cuentos y Poemas. Olazagasti-Segovia, Elena, tr. from ENG. (p. 87)
—Call Me Maria: A Novel in Letters, Poems & Prose. (p. 254)
—If I Could Fly. (p. 852)
—Island Like You. (p. 892)
—Poet Upstairs. Ortiz, Oscar, illus. (p. 1376)
—¡A Bailar! / Let's Dance! Rodriguez, Christina Ann, illus. (p. 1)
Coffee, Karen Lynn. God, Do You Love Me? Hardison, Buist, illus. (p. 688)
Coffee, Kathy. Old Faithful Jellybeans. (p. 1283)
Coffelt, Nancy. Aunt Ant Leaves Through the Leaves: A Story with Homophones & Homonyms. Coffelt, Nancy, illus. (p. 115)
—Aunt Ant Leaves Through the Leaves. Coffelt, Nancy, illus. (p. 115)
—Big, Bigger, Biggest! Coffelt, Nancy, illus. (p. 178)
—Catch That Baby! Nash, Scott, illus. (p. 279)
—Fred Stays with Me! Tusa, Tricia, illus. (p. 632)
—Listen. (p. 1022)
—Pug in a Truck. (p. 1415)
—Uh-Oh, Baby! Nash, Scott, illus. (p. 1808)
Coffelt, Soraya Diase. It's Not about You Mr. Santa Claus: A Love Letter about the True Meaning of Christmas. (p. 898)
Coffen, Matt. Time Well Spent. (p. 1753)
Coffey, Anthony, jt. auth. see Labbe, Jesse.
Coffey, Colleen, tr. see Auld, Mary.
Coffey, Colleen, tr. see Holland, Gini.
Coffey, Colleen, tr. see Macken, JoAnn Early.
Coffey, Durwood, illus. see McDiarmid, Gail S. & McGee, Marilyn S.
Coffey, Ethel. How Meg Changed Her Mind. Schweitzer-Johnson, Betty, illus. (p. 811)
Coffey, Heather Whitman. Almost True Adventures of Coonie Raccoon. (p. 48)
Coffey, Jan. Tropical Kiss. (p. 1789)
Coffey, Joe. Lynnie Leonardson & the Weeping Willow. Selby, Shannon, illus. (p. 1066)
Coffey, Kevin, illus. see Baker, Alison.
Coffey, Kevin, illus. see Canale, Suzie Hearl.
Coffey, Kevin, illus. see French, Mary B.
Coffey, Kevin, illus. see Stotter, Ruth.
Coffey, Kevin, illus. see Weiland, Peter.
Coffey, M. Carol. Zoe Lucky: And the Green Gables' Mystery. (p. 1987)
—Zoe Lucky & the Mystery of the Pink Pearl Necklace. (p. 1987)
Coffey, Michele. Let's Look at Leopards. (p. 999)
—Park Ranger's Day. (p. 1324)
Coffey, Stephen. Rosemary Herbb & the Zodiac Ghosts. (p. 1489)
Coffin, Bill, jt. auth. see Siembieda, Kevin.
Coffin, Marilyn, illus. see Stephenson, Nancy Ann.
Coffin, Rebecca, et al. Binkie & the Firemen: A Lost Puppy Rescued in A Basement Fire Becomes the Firemen's Pet. (p. 188)
Coffin, Rebecca J. Airplanes: The Work They Do & How They Do It. Coffin, Rebecca J. et al, eds. (p. 32)
Coffin, Rebecca J., et al, eds. Boats: The Work They Do & the Way They Do It. (p. 205)
Coffman, Dan. Titu Miata's Spider. (p. 1758)
Coffman, Jan. Common Bond. (p. 349)
Coffman, Patrick, tr. see Judal.
Coffman, Patrick, tr. see Shimizu, Aki.
Coffman, Patrick, tr. from JPN. Vampire Game Judal, illus. (p. 1832)
Coffman, Thomas L. Sarah, a Christmas Story. (p. 1514)
Cofreros, Felipe. Sam's Wish. (p. 1509)
Cofreros, Felipe A. Hungry Frog. (p. 828)
Cogan, John, illus. see Gotsch, Connie.
Cogan, Karen. Pancho Finds A Home. Davidson, Blanche, illus. (p. 1320)
Cogan, Kim, illus. see Shin, Sun Yung.
Cogan, Kim, tr. see Shin, Sun Yung.
Cogancherry, Helen, illus. see Sanders, Scott Russell.
Cogar, Karen S., ed. see Cogar, Tubal U., et al.
Cogar, Tubal U., et al. Journeys of Wobblefoot the Beginning. Cogar, Karen S., ed. (p. 929)
Cogdill, Jill K. Cracker the Crab & the Sideways Afternoon. (p. 375)
Coggan, Donald A. Fundamentals of Industrial Control: Practical Guides for Measurement & Control. (p. 649)
Coggins, Jack. Illustrated Book of Knights. (p. 857)
Coggins, James R. Who's Grace? (p. 1920)
Coghlan, Jo. Switched. (p. 1691)
Coghlan, John, jt. auth. see Ellis, Edward Sylvester.
Cogswell, Jackie Chirco. Super Luke Faces His Bully: GiggleHeart Adventures #2. Johannes, Shelley, illus. (p. 1680)
Cogswell, Matthew, illus. see Coville, Bruce.
Coh, Smiljana. Big Brave Daddy. (p. 179)
—I Have a Brother. (p. 839)
—I Have a Sister. (p. 839)
—Princesses on the Run. (p. 1406)
Coh, Smiljana, illus. see Membrino, Anna.
Cohagan, Carolyn. Lost Children. (p. 1055)
Cohan, George M. & Schwaeber, Barbie. Give My Regards to Broadway. Newsom, Carol, illus. (p. 681)
Cohee, Ron, illus. see Berrios, Frank.
Cohee, Ron, illus. see Drake, Tim.
Cohee, Ron, illus. see Lagonegro, Melissa.
Cohee, Ron, illus. see Smith, Geof.
Cohen, jt. auth. see Williams, Jane.
Cohen, Abe M. Monotheistic Religions: Islam, Christianity & Judaism. (p. 1166)
Cohen, Adam. Perfect Store: Inside EBay. (p. 1342)
Cohen, Alana. All Around Chuggington. (p. 43)
—Big Time Audition. (p. 184)
—Heroes! White, David A., illus. (p. 772)
Cohen, Allen C. Beyond Basic Textiles: Advances the Study of Textiles One Step Further! (p. 173)
Cohen, Allison. Scattered Pieces. (p. 1521)
Cohen, Andrea Joy. Blessing in Disguise: 39 Life Lessons from Today's Greatest Teachers. (p. 199)
Cohen, Barbara. Carp in the Bathtub. (p. 271)
—Molly's Pilgrim. (p. 1161)

—Molly's Pilgrim. Duffy, Daniel Mark & Deraney, Michael J., illus. (p. 1161)
Cohen, Barbara Berkule. Donkey That Couldn't Find His Bray. (p. 466)
Cohen, Barbara S. Forever Friends. Hall, Dorothy Louise, illus. (p. 619)
Cohen, Barry M., jt. auth. see Cohen, Terry Scott.
Cohen, Bernard. Paul Needs Specs. Kelly, Geoff, illus. (p. 1330)
Cohen, Brie, photos by see Cornell, Karl.
Cohen, Brie, photos by see Larson, Jennifer S.
Cohen, Caron Lee. Broom, Zoom! Ruzzier, Sergio, illus. (p. 231)
—Digger Pig & the Turnip. (p. 438)
—Digger Pig & the Turnip. Denise, Christopher, illus. (p. 438)
Cohen, Charles & Seuss, Dr. How the Grinch Stole Christmas! (p. 813)
Cohen, Daniel. Brachiosaurus. (p. 221)
—Bridgestone Science Library (p. 227)
—Diplodocus (p. 445)
—Spinosaurus (p. 1628)
Cohen, Deborah. Seventh Day. Hall, Melanie, illus. (p. 1555)
Cohen, Deborah Bodin. Engineer Ari & the Hanukkah Mishap. Kober, Shahar, illus. (p. 529)
—Engineer Ari & the Passover Rush. Kober, Shahar, illus. (p. 529)
—Engineer Ari & the Rosh Hashanah Ride. Kober, Shahar, illus. (p. 529)
—Engineer Ari & the Sukkah Express. Kober, Shahar, illus. (p. 529)
—Nachshon, Who Was Afraid to Swim: A Passover Story. Jago, illus. (p. 1227)
—Papa Jethro. Dippold, Jane, illus. (p. 1322)
Cohen, Deene, illus. see Benjamin, Ruth.
Cohen, Della. Eleanor Roosevelt: Proud & Tall. (p. 508)
—Whoppers! (p. 1920)
Cohen, Don. Calculus for Young People (p. 252)
Cohen, Donald. Calculus by & for Young People - Ages 7, Yes 7 & Up (CD-ROM) (p. 252)
Cohen, Edythe. Ghetto Garden. (p. 670)
Cohen, Elaine. Super-Duper Cupcakes: Sweet & Easy Cupcake Decorating. (p. 1679)
Cohen, Elly, illus. see Dinn, Philip & Jones, Andy.
Cohen, Eric, jt. auth. see Sandler, Michael.
Cohen, Eta. Eta Choen Violin Method Book (p. 539)
Cohen, Frumi. Magic Flute RELOADED: (play Script) (p. 1072)
—Try a Little Shakespeare. (p. 1794)
Cohen, Greg A., illus. see Rouss, Sylvia A.
Cohen, Hannah, ed. Once upon a Doodle: Fairy-Tale Pictures to Create & Complete. Cooke, Andy, illus. (p. 1292)
Cohen, Hilda Stern & Gilcher, William Harry. Words That Burn Within Me: Faith, Values, Survival Cohen, Werner V. & Rosen, Gail, eds. (p. 1952)
Cohen, Ivan. Beware the Batman Vecchio, Luciano, illus. (p. 173)
Cohen, Ivan & Eltaeb, Gabe. Tattooed Man Trouble! Vecchio, Luciano, illus. (p. 1707)
Cohen, Ivan, et al. Beware the Batman. Vecchio, Luciano & Brizuela, Dario, illus. (p. 173)
—Law & Disorder. Vecchio, Luciano, illus. (p. 981)
—Son of the Man-Bat. Vecchio, Luciano, illus. (p. 1611)
Cohen, Izhar, illus. see Forward, Toby.
Cohen, Jacob. Getting the Most Out of Makerspaces to Build Robots. (p. 669)
Cohen, Jan Barger, illus. see Zucker, Jonny.
Cohen, Jared. Children of Jihad: A Young American's Travels among the Youth of the Middle East. (p. 302)
Cohen, Jeff. Eva & Sadie & the Best Classroom Ever! Allen, Elanna, illus. (p. 540)
—Eva & Sadie & the Worst Haircut EVER! Allen, Elanna, illus. (p. 540)
Cohen, Jerianne. Max A. Million's Birthday Party. (p. 1110)
Cohen, Jesse, photos by see Galvin, Laura.
Cohen, Jessica, tr. see Grossman, David.
Cohen, Jessie, illus. see Galvin, Laura Gates.
Cohen, Jessie, photos by see Galvin, Laura.
Cohen, Jessie, photos by see Lamm, Drew.
Cohen, Jessie, photos by. Flamingo Grows Up. (p. 602)
Cohen, Joan Freeman & Freeman, Jonathan M. In Every Generation: A Model Seder Haggadah. (p. 863)
Cohen, Joel H. Oscar Robertson. (p. 1305)
Cohen, Joshua C. Leverage. (p. 1003)
Cohen, Judith, jt. auth. see Friend, Robyn.
cohen, judith L. & friend, robyn. Future Engineering: The Clean Water Challenge. katz, david A., illus. (p. 651)
Cohen, Judith Love. You Can Be A Chemist. Katz, David A., illus. (p. 1973)
—You Can Be a Woman Animator. (p. 1973)
—You Can Be A Woman Chemist. Katz, David A., illus. (p. 1973)
—You Can Be A Woman Video Game Producer. (p. 1974)
Cohen, Judith Love, jt. auth. see Bozak, Kristin.
Cohen, Judith Love, jt. auth. see Franks, Sharon E.
Cohen, Judith Love, jt. auth. see Friend, Robyn C.
cohen, Judith Love, jt. auth. see friend, robyn C.
Cohen, Judith Love, jt. auth. see Ghez, Andrea Mia.
Cohen, Judith Love & Friend, Robyn. You Can Be A Woman Makeup Artist or Costume Designer (p. 1973)
Cohen, Judith Love & Friend, Robyn C. Clean Sky: The Global Warming Story. Katz, David A., illus. (p. 330)
Cohen, Judy, jt. auth. see Pinto, Mindee.
Cohen, Larry. Barfalloems: Much Grosser Than Poems & Ten Times More Fun. Brizendine, Brad, illus. (p. 139)
Cohen, Laura. Gault Case & Young People's Rights: Debating Supreme Court Decisions. (p. 658)
Cohen, Laurie. Flea Owikids Books Inc. Staff & Quinn, Sarah, trs. (p. 603)
Cohen, Lawrence J. Dragon's Familiar. (p. 479)
Cohen, Leah. Magic Pond: How a Small Flock of Birds Brought Life & Cheer to a Lonely Pond. (p. 1073)
—Sophie. (p. 1613)
Cohen, Lee. Find the Magic: A Rip Squeak Book. (p. 587)
—Find the Magic. (p. 587)
—Surprise Party. Neuville, Loyal de, illus. (p. 1686)
Cohen, Lee, jt. auth. see Golabek, Mona.
Cohen, Leslie. I've Got 5 Dollars! Understanding Addition & Subtraction. (p. 900)
Cohen, Leslie, et al. Jewish Love Stories for Kids: An Anthology of Short Stories. (p. 917)
Cohen, Lester H., ed. see Ramsay, David.
Cohen, Lettie. Lila's New Pet. (p. 1017)
Cohen, Liz Zoller & Dicillo, Mike. My Interactive Point-And-Play 10-Book Library (p. 1211)
Cohen, Lynda, illus. see Jackson, Marjorie.
Cohen, Marina. 3-D Shapes. (p. 1991)
—Cells. (p. 286)
—Changing Cultural Landscapes: How Are People & Their Communities Affected by Migration & Settlement? (p. 290)
—Chasing the White Witch. (p. 294)
—Deserts Inside Out. (p. 429)
—Genetic Engineering. (p. 660)
—Ghost Ride. (p. 671)
—Live It: Cooperation. (p. 1040)
—Live It: Inclusiveness. (p. 1040)
—Mind Gap. (p. 1145)
—Money Problems. (p. 1164)
—Polygons. (p. 1381)
—Probability. (p. 1408)
—What Is Cell Theory? (p. 1889)
—Why We Need Vitamins. (p. 1926)
Cohen, Mary. Mary Cohen's Tuneful Introduction to 2nd Finger Spacing: Easy Well-Known Pieces for Violin. O'Neill, Todd, illus. (p. 1100)
Cohen, Matt. Elizabeth & After: A Novel. (p. 513)
Cohen, Melissa. PuzzlePal Books: Cuddly Cow. Magnayon, Megan Coy, illus. (p. 1421)
—PuzzlePal Books: Dear Dinosaur. Magnayon, Megan Coy, illus. (p. 1421)
Cohen, Melissa, illus. see Magnayon, Megan Coy.
Cohen, Milly. Dulceria de Don Tono. Velazquez, Jose Luis Reyes & Velazquez, Jose Luis Reye, illus. (p. 489)
Cohen, Miriam. Backpack Baby (Spanish/English) Fiol, Maria A., tr. (p. 130)
—Bee My Valentine Himmler, Ronald, illus. (p. 157)
—Bee My Valentine! Himler, Ronald, illus. (p. 157)
—Daddy's Busy Day (p. 399)
—Down in the Subway Greenberg, Melanie Hope, illus. (p. 474)
—Eggy Meggy & Peggy. (p. 506)
—First Grade Takes a Test Himler, Ronald, illus. (p. 595)
—First Grade Takes a Test. (p. 595)
—First Grade Takes a Test (Spanish/English) Himler, Ronald, illus. (p. 595)
—Jim's Dog Muffins Himler, Ronald, illus. (p. 918)
—Layla's Head Scarf Himler, Ronald, illus. (p. 981)
—Liar, Liar, Pants on Fire! Himler, Ronald, illus. (p. 1005)
—Mine! (Spanish/English) A Backpack Baby Story Fiol, Maria A., tr. (p. 1145)
—My Big Brother Himler, Ronald, illus. (p. 1197)
—My Big Brother (Spanish/English) Himler, Ronald, illus. (p. 1197)
—Tough Jim Himler, Ronald, illus. (p. 1772)
—Two Little Mittens Cohen, Miriam, illus. (p. 1804)
—Will I Have a Friend? Himler, Ronald, illus. (p. 1932)
Cohen, Miriam, jt. auth. see Cohen, Morris L.
Cohen, Miriam & Himler, Ronald. examen de primer Grado Himler, Ronald, illus. (p. 547)
Cohen, Morris L. & Cohen, Miriam. Best Friends. (p. 169)
Cohen, Pamela. Ashie: Lost in a Hurricane (p. 106)
Cohen, Pamela June. Ashie: Lost in the Hurricane. Lang, Allison, illus. (p. 106)
Cohen, Paula Marantz. Jane Austen in Scarsdale: Or Love, Death, & the SATs. (p. 908)
—Much Ado about Jessie Kaplan. (p. 1188)
Cohen, Penny L. Tapuchim & Dvash. Polsky, Beanie, illus. (p. 1706)
Cohen, Peter. Boris's Glasses. Sandin, Joan, tr. from SWE. (p. 214)
Cohen, R. G. Place That I Love. Levitas, Alexander, illus. (p. 1365)
Cohen, Rafael. Makoy, the Apache Boy. Balkovek, James, illus. (p. 1083)
Cohen, Rich. Alex & the Amazing Time Machine. Murphy, Kelly, illus. (p. 35)
—Sweet & Low: A Family Story. (p. 1689)
Cohen, Robert Z. Body Piercing & Tattooing: Making Smart Choices. (p. 207)
—Catfish Fishing. (p. 280)
—Discovering the Asante Kingdom. (p. 449)
—Discovering the Empire of Ghana. (p. 449)
—Jewish Resistance Against the Holocaust. (p. 917)
—Stomach & Intestines in Your Body (p. 1652)
—Transylvania: Birthplace of Vampires. (p. 1779)
Cohen, Ron. Bible Survey for High School — Answer Key (p. 176)
—Bible Survey for High School — Student Workbook (p. 176)
—Bible Survey for High School — Study Guide (p. 176)
Cohen, Ronald D., frwd. Folk. (p. 611)
Cohen, Rosalind. Scotland Yard, Us. (p. 1530)
Cohen, Santiago. Yiddish Fish. (p. 1971)
Cohen, Santiago, illus. see Gamble, Adam.
Cohen, Sasha. Sasha Cohen: Autobiography of a Champion Figure Skater. Goedeken, Kathy, illus. (p. 1515)
Cohen, Sasha & Maciel, Amanda. Fire on Ice: Autobiography of a Champion Figure Skater. Goedeken, Kathy, illus. (p. 590)
Cohen, Sheila & Terman Cohen, Sheila. Gaylord Nelson: Champion for Our Earth. (p. 659)
—Mai Ya's Long Journey. (p. 1076)
Cohen, Sheldon, illus. see Davis, Aubrey.
Cohen, Sheldon, illus. see Fischman, Sheila, tr.
Cohen, Sheldon & Drawing Staff. How to Draw & Save Your Planet from Alien Invasion! (p. 816)
Cohen, Sherman. Cartooning: Character Design - Learn the Art of Cartooning Step by Step. (p. 273)
Cohen, Sonia. Gigi. (p. 676)
Cohen, Stephanie. Northeast: Set Of 6. (p. 1265)
—Northeast: Text Pairs. (p. 1265)
Cohen, Steve & Cohen, Steven Martin. Next Stop Hollywood: Short Stories Bound for the Screen. (p. 1249)
Cohen, Steven Martin, jt. auth. see Cohen, Steve.
Cohen, Terry Scott & Cohen, Barry M. Disabled & Challenged: Reach for Your Dreams! (p. 446)
Cohen, Tina. Pesach What & Why? (p. 1345)
Cohen, Tish. Inside Out Girl. (p. 877)
Cohen, Tod, illus. see Kropf, Latifa Berry.
Cohen, Tod, photos by see Danis, Naomi.
Cohen, Tod, photos by see Dietrick, Ellen.
Cohen, Tod, photos by see Kropf, Latifa Berry.
Cohen, Tod, photos by see Topek, Susan Remick.
Cohen, Valerie Mendenhall. Woman on the Rocks: The Mountaineering Letters of Ruth Dyar Mendenhall. (p. 1945)
Cohen, Warren Lee. Dragon Baked Bread. Ssebulime, John, illus. (p. 476)
Cohen, Werner V., ed. see Cohen, Hilda Stern & Gilcher, William Harry.
Cohen, Whitney & Life Lab Science Program Staff. Kids' Garden: 40 Fun Outdoor Activities & Games. Arenson, Roberta, illus. (p. 953)
Cohen-Janca, Irène. Mister Doctor: Janusz Korczak & the Orphans of the Warsaw Ghetto. Quarello, Maurizio A. C., illus. (p. 1155)
Cohen-Spence, Susan. Amazing Adventure Back in Time. Scott, Susan, illus. (p. 52)
Cohlene, Terri. Something Special. Keith, Doug, illus. (p. 1610)
—Won't Papa Be Surprised! Dooling, Michael & Sayles, Elizabeth, illus. (p. 1949)
Cohn. Dream Carver Pb. (p. 483)
Cohn, Amy, ed. see Kellogg, Steven.
Cohn, Ariel. Zoo Box. Steinke, Aron Nels, illus. (p. 1988)
Cohn, Arlen. Firsts. Vasconcellos, Daniel, illus. (p. 598)
Cohn, Brian, jt. auth. see Cohn, Karen.
Cohn, Diana. ¡Sí, Se Puede! Delgado, Francisco, illus. (p. 891)
—¡Sí, Se Puede! Franco, Sharon, tr. from ENG. (p. 891)
—Mr Goethes Garden. Mirocha, Paul, illus. (p. 1185)
—Namaste! Cordova, Amy, illus. (p. 1228)
—Roses for Isabella. Córdova, Amy, illus. (p. 1490)
Cohn, Diana, jt. auth. see Buchmann, Stephen.
Cohn, Diana & Buchmann, Stephen. Bee Tree. Mirocha, Paul, illus. (p. 157)
Cohn, Edith. Spirit's Key. (p. 1629)
Cohn, Jessica. Ancient Chinese. (p. 68)
—Ancient Egyptians. (p. 69)
—Ancient Greeks. (p. 69)
—Ancient Indians. (p. 69)
—Ancient Romans. (p. 70)
—Animator. (p. 84)
—Architect. (p. 95)
—Aztecs. (p. 122)
—BASE Jumping. (p. 140)
—BMX. (p. 204)
—Education & Social Services. (p. 505)
—Electronic Music Scene: The Stars, the Fans, the Music. (p. 509)
—Fashion Buyer. (p. 575)
—Free Running. (p. 634)
—Great Careers with a High School Diploma: Manufacturing & Transportation. (p. 714)
—Hand to Earth: Saving the Environment. (p. 740)
—Hand to Earth Saving the Environment. (p. 740)
—Hand to Heart: Improving Communities. (p. 740)
—Hand to Heart: Improving Communities. (p. 740)
—Hand to Paw: Protecting Animals. (p. 740)
—Hand to Paw - Protecting Animals. (p. 740)
—Medieval Islamic World. (p. 1119)
—Military Machines. (p. 1143)
—Mountain Climbing. (p. 1180)
—Muhammad: Prophet of Islam. (p. 1189)
—Parasite Collector. (p. 1324)
—Pest Control Worker. (p. 1345)
—Poems about Choices (p. 1376)
—Road Cycling. (p. 1476)
—Rodeo. (p. 1484)
—Trucks. (p. 1791)
—What Is Scarcity of Resources? (p. 1890)
Cohn, Jessica & Kuligowski, Stephanie. Fearless! Stunt People. (p. 579)
—Wild Work! Animal Trainers. (p. 1931)
Cohn, Karen & Cohn, Brian. Polar Bear Who Couldn't, Wouldn't Swim. (p. 1379)
Cohn, Marvin. Tell Me A Story Gramps. (p. 1716)
Cohn, Rachel. Beta. (p. 171)
—Cupcake. (p. 392)
—Emergent. (p. 518)
—Shrimp (p. 1571)
—Shrimp. (p. 1571)
—Steps. (p. 1648)
—Two Steps Forward. (p. 1804)
—Very Lefreak. (p. 1838)
—You Know Where to Find Me. (p. 1975)
Cohn, Rachel & Levithan, David. Dash & Lily's Book of Dares. (p. 409)
—Naomi & Ely's No Kiss List. (p. 1229)
—Nick & Norah's Infinite Playlist. (p. 1251)
Cohn, Rachel & Wattenberg, Jane. Gingerbread. (p. 677)
Cohn, Riley. Martin in the Narthex. (p. 1097)
Cohn, Ronald, jt. ed. see Russell, Jesse.
Cohn, Scott, illus. see Rosen, Lucy.
Cohn, Scott M. Daddy Sat on a Duck. (p. 399)
Cohn, Scotti. Animal Partners Bersani, Shennen, illus. (p. 79)
—Avanzando ... de Aquí para Allá: Migraciones Masivas Detwiler, Susan, illus. (p. 118)
—Big Cat, Little Kitty Detwiler, Susan, illus. (p. 180)
—On the Move: Mass Migrations Detwiler, Susan, illus. (p. 1291)
—One Wolf Howls Detwiler, Susan, illus. (p. 1297)
Cohn, Tricia L. Beobi & the Magic Coloring Book ABC First Words. (p. 166)
Cohon, Rhody, jt. auth. see Chatlien, Ruth Hull.
Cohon, Rhody, jt. auth. see Deutsch, Stacia.
Coia, Kristina. Lymeria. (p. 1066)
Coiblon, Shannon Rivers, jt. auth. see Rivers, Francine.
Coil, Carolyn. Becoming an Achiever. (p. 156)
Coil, Kate. Misadventures of a Goth Cheerleader. (p. 1150)
Coiley, John, jt. auth. see Dorling Kindersley Publishing Staff.
Coillen, Lisa P., illus. see Jarrell, Pamela R.
Coiner, Tea Railene. Hear the Song of the Fairies. (p. 759)
Cointe, François, illus. see Jaffé, Laura.
Cointe, François, illus. see Pouilloux, David.
Coipel, Olivier. House of M. (p. 803)
—Siege. (p. 1573)
Coipel, Olivier, illus. see Fraction, Matt.
Coipel, Olivier, illus. see Way, Daniel, et al.
Coipel, Olivier & Donovan, Deric. X-Men: To Serve & Protect. (p. 1967)
Coirault, Christine. My First Book of Learning. (p. 1205)
Coirault, Christine, illus. see Wise, Sue.
Cokal, Susann. Kingdom of Little Wounds. (p. 959)
Coke, Sherrie, illus. see Evangelista, Susan.
Coker, Carla, illus. see Langley, Judy.
Coker, Lauren. Phantom's Lullaby: A Novel. (p. 1349)
Coker, Paddy & Ganderton, Paul. Environmental Biogeography. (p. 532)
Coker, Paul, Jr., illus. see Hahn, Phil.
Coker, Rachel. Chasing Jupiter (p. 294)
—Interrupted: A Life Beyond Words (p. 881)
Coker, Tom. Daredevil Noir. (p. 406)
Coker, Tomm. Avengers Assemble - Science Bros. (p. 118)
Cola, Arthur. Papa & the Gingerbread Man. (p. 1321)
Colak, Mirko & Hickman, Jonathan. Secret Warriors - Night Marquez, David, illus. (p. 1544)
Colakis, Marianthe & Dubose, Gaylan. Excelability in Advanced Latin. (p. 547)
Colan, Gene & Heck, Don. Invincible Iron Man. (p. 885)
Colan, Gene, et al. Guardians of the Galaxy - Tomorrow's Avengers (p. 728)
Colander, David C. Economics. (p. 502)
—Microeconomics. (p. 1136)
Colandro, Lucille. There Was a Cold Lady Who Swallowed Some Snow! (p. 1730)
—There Was a Cold Lady Who Swallowed Some Snow! Lee, Jared, illus. (p. 1730)
—There Was an Old Lady Who Swallowed a Bat! Lee, Jared, illus. (p. 1730)
—There Was an Old Lady Who Swallowed a Bat! Lee, Jared D., illus. (p. 1730)
—There Was an Old Lady Who Swallowed a Bell! (p. 1730)
—There Was an Old Lady Who Swallowed a Bell! Lee, Jared, illus. (p. 1730)
—There Was an Old Lady Who Swallowed a Chick! (p. 1730)
—There Was an Old Lady Who Swallowed a Chick! Lee, Jared, illus. (p. 1730)
—There Was an Old Lady Who Swallowed a Clover! (p. 1730)
—There Was an Old Lady Who Swallowed a Clover. Lee, Jared, illus. (p. 1730)
—There Was an Old Lady Who Swallowed a Frog! Lee, Jared D., illus. (p. 1730)
—There Was an Old Lady Who Swallowed a Sticker Book! Lee, Jared D., illus. (p. 1730)
—There Was an Old Lady Who Swallowed Some Books! Lee, Jared, illus. (p. 1730)
—There Was an Old Lady Who Swallowed Some Books! Lee, Jared D., illus. (p. 1730)
—There Was an Old Lady Who Swallowed Some Leaves! (p. 1730)
—There Was an Old Lady Who Swallowed Some Leaves! Lee, Jared, illus. (p. 1730)
Colangione-B, Christie, illus. see Badavino, Jimmy.
Colarik, Kim, jt. auth. see Athens, Sandra.
Colasanti, Marina. En el Laberinto del Viento y Otros Cuentos. (p. 522)
—Lejos Como Mi Querer y Otros Cuentos. (p. 991)
Colasanti, Susane. All I Need. (p. 44)
—City Love. (p. 323)
—Keep Holding On. (p. 946)
—Now & Forever. (p. 1269)
—So Much Closer. (p. 1602)
—Something Like Fate. (p. 1610)
—Take Me There. (p. 1696)
—Waiting for You. (p. 1853)
—When It Happens. (p. 1903)
Colavecchio, Alan, illus. see Powers, John.
Colbert, Brandy. Pointe. (p. 1377)
Colbert, Catherine McNulty. Downsize Your Parents! Tips for Moving from a 2400 Sq Ft Home into an 800 Sq Ft Home. (p. 474)
Colbert, Christine. But Who Did Jesus Say That He Is? (p. 246)
Colbert, Cory. Sammy the Sea Otter Makes New Friends: Adventures of Sammy the Sea Otter. (p. 1508)
Colbert, David. Abraham Lincoln. (p. 6)
—Anne Frank. (p. 85)
—Benjamin Franklin. (p. 164)
—Martin Luther King Jr. (p. 1097)
—Maya Angelou. (p. 1112)
—Michelle Obama: An American Story. (p. 1135)
—Thomas Edison. (p. 1738)
Colbert, David & Chambers, Mark. Frida Kahlo. (p. 637)
Colbert, Don. Toxic Detective. (p. 1774)
Colbert, June. King of Large. (p. 959)
Colbert, Larry C. Insights from an Out-of-Sight Guy. (p. 878)
Colbert, Nancy A. Firing on Fort Sumter: A Splintered Nation Goes to War. (p. 592)
—Great Society: The Story of Lyndon Baines Johnson. (p. 718)
Colburn, Cherie Foster. Bloomin' Tales: Legends of Seven Favorite Texas Wildflowers. Hein, Joy Fisher, illus. (p. 201)
—Our Shadow Garden. (p. 1310)
Colburn, Kerry, et al. So, You Want to Be Canadian: All about the Most Fascinating People in the World & the Magical Place They Call Home. (p. 1602)
Colby, Carolyn. Penny Penguin: A Baby Penguin's Adventures on the Ice & Snow. Warren, Leonard, illus. (p. 1338)
Colby, Devon English, illus. see Nielsen, Gwyn English.
Colby, Garry, illus. see Fuerst, Jeffrey B.

C

Colby, Garry, illus. see Harrast, Tracy.
Colby, J. Z. Trilogy One. Colby, J. Z. et al, illus. (p. 1786)
Colby, J. Z. & Persons, Katelynn. Flight Training, Kibi & the Search for Happiness. Colby, J. Z. & Powers, Mireille Xioulan, illus. (p. 604)
Colby, Jennifer. Flowers. (p. 608)
—Growing New Plants. (p. 726)
—Healing Plants. (p. 757)
—Plants Need Sunlight. (p. 1370)
—Plants We Eat. (p. 1370)
—Plants We Wear. (p. 1370)
—Trees. (p. 1784)
—What Is a Plant? (p. 1888)
Colby, Rebecca. It's Raining Bats & Frogs. Henry, Steven, illus. (p. 898)
Coldfeather, Suzanne D. Places to Work. (p. 1366)
Coldiron, Deborah. Anglerfish. (p. 75)
—Barracuda. (p. 140)
—Clownfish. (p. 335)
—Coral. (p. 366)
—Crayfish. (p. 377)
—Cuttlefish. (p. 396)
—Eels. (p. 505)
—Jellyfish. (p. 912)
—Lobsters. (p. 1044)
—Manatees. (p. 1086)
—Ocean Sunfish. (p. 1276)
—Octopuses. (p. 1278)
—Piranhas. (p. 1362)
—Sea Horses. (p. 1534)
—Sea Sponges. (p. 1535)
—Sea Urchins. (p. 1536)
—Sharks. (p. 1562)
—Shrimp. (p. 1571)
—Squid. (p. 1636)
—Starfish. (p. 1642)
—Stingrays. (p. 1651)
—Swordfish. (p. 1692)
—Trout. (p. 1790)
—Tuna. (p. 1796)
Coldon, Christine. Emmalynn: Home Tweet Home. (p. 520)
—Emmalynn: Wondrously Magical Christmas Eve. (p. 520)
Coldwell, Andrew, jt. auth. see Kluzek, Stan.
Cole, Al, illus. see Harris, Jane Ellen.
Cole, Alyson, tr. see Schneider, Antonie & Bansch, Helga.
Cole, Amy, illus. see Norton, J. Renae.
Cole, Anjennetta. Cory's Classroom Rules. (p. 368)
Cole, Babette. Animales Me Aterrorizan. (p. 81)
—Hairy Book. Cole, Babette, illus. (p. 736)
—Libro de Etiqueta de Lady Lupina. (p. 1006)
—Libro Tonto. (p. 1007)
—Mama Puso un Huevo. (p. 1084)
—Prince Cinders. (p. 1401)
—Princesa Listilla. (p. 1402)
—Princess Smartypants. (p. 1405)
—Princess Smartypants. Cole, Babette, illus. (p. 1405)
—Princess Smartypants Breaks the Rules. (p. 1405)
—Principe Ceniciento. (p. 1406)
—Problemas con Mi Tio. (p. 1408)
—Slimy Book. (p. 1590)
—Tarzana. (p. 1706)
—Trouble with Dad. (p. 1790)
—Trouble with Gran. (p. 1790)
Cole, Babette, illus. see Larsen, Mylisa.
Cole, Babette, illus. see Rosen, Michael.
Cole, Barbara. Anna & Natalie Himler, Ronald, illus. (p. 85)
Cole, Barbara H. Anna & Natalie Himler, Ronald, illus. (p. 85)
—Wash Day Himler, Ronald, illus. (p. 1859)
Cole, Bethan, et al. Mathematics Assessment Sampler, Grades 6-8: Items Aligned with NCTM's Principles & Standards for School Mathematics. Burrill, John & Collins, Anne M., eds. (p. 1108)
Cole, Bob. Charging Forward: Heart, Team & Eight Seconds, the Boys that Refuse to Lose (p. 291)
—Power Reading: Nail-Biters! 2. Morton, Vivian, illus. (p. 1390)
—Power Reading: Comic Book/Superhero. Ford, David, illus. (p. 1390)
—Power Reading: Comic Book/Time Warp. Ford, David, illus. (p. 1390)
—Power Reading: Classics/Treasure Island. Lee, Joe, illus. (p. 1390)
—Power Reading: Classics/Jungle Book. Connor, Robin, illus. (p. 1390)
—Power Reading: Comic Book/Time Warp 2. Ford, David, illus. (p. 1390)
—Power Reading: Comic Book/Treasure Island. Lee, Joe, illus. (p. 1390)
—Power Reading: Chapter/Sci-Fi/Superhero. Ford, David, illus. (p. 1390)
—Power Reading: Chapter/Sci-Fi/Time Warp. Ford, David, illus. (p. 1390)
—Power Reading: Comic Book/Dr. Little. Sirrell, Terri, illus. (p. 1390)
—Power Reading: Comic Book/Jungle Book. Connor, Robin, illus. (p. 1390)
—Power Reading: Chapter/Sci-Fi/Time Warp 2. Ford, David, illus. (p. 1390)
—Power Reading: Comic Book/Wizard of OZ. Sirrell, Terri, illus. (p. 1390)
—Power Reading: Chapter/Sci-Fi/Dr. Little 2. Ford, David, illus. (p. 1390)
—Power Reading: Chapter/Sci-Fi/Dr. Little. Sirrell, Terri, illus. (p. 1390)
—Power Reading: Chapter Books/Wizard of OZ. Sirrell, Terri, illus. (p. 1390)
Cole, Bob & Sirrell, Terri. Power Reading: Comic Book/Dr. Little 2. (p. 1390)
Cole, Brock. Celine. (p. 286)
—Facts Speak for Themselves. (p. 561)
—Fair Monaco. (p. 562)
—Goats. (p. 687)
—Goats. Cole, Brock, illus. (p. 687)
—Money We'll Save. Cole, Brock, illus. (p. 1164)
Cole, Brock, illus. see Chandra, Deborah & Comora, Madeleine.
Cole, Brock, illus. see Seidler, Tor.
Cole, Bud. Mystery of Little Bear. (p. 1224)
Cole, Burton. Bash & the Chocolate Milk Cows. Lewis, Buddy, illus. (p. 141)
Cole, Carol A. Dama de Los Pingüinos Rogers, Sherry, illus. (p. 401)
—Penguin Lady Rogers, Sherry, illus. (p. 1337)
Cole, Cathleen. Four Seasons Stables: A Saddle Seat Rid. (p. 625)
—Night Mare of Four Seasons Stables. (p. 1253)
Cole, Chandra L. Little Piece of Broken Glass. (p. 1033)
Cole, Charmaine W. Barky, a Very Special Beaver. (p. 139)
Cole, Cora. Adventures of Angel Skylet & Clarence Cloudy. (p. 16)
Cole, Dick, illus. see Reed, Jennifer.
Cole, Diedra. Adventures of Chris & Abby: First Day of School. (p. 17)
Cole, Dina. Are There Alligators at the Equator? An Eddie the Equator Adventure. (p. 96)
—Maggie's Magic Unicorn. (p. 1071)
—Meet Eddie the Equator. (p. 1121)
Cole, Dylan. Other Worldly Adventures of Tyler Washburn: the New Kid. (p. 1306)
Cole, Evelyn. For the Sake of All Others. (p. 616)
Cole, F. Molaumby. (p. 1160)
Cole, Forrest. Tiananmen Square Protests. (p. 1746)
Cole, Frank. Adventures of Hashbrown Winters. (p. 18)
—Hashbrown Winters & the Mashimoto Madness. (p. 752)
—Hashbrown Winters & the Phantom of Pordunce. (p. 752)
Cole, Frank L. Afterlife Academy. (p. 28)
—Guardians of the Finisher's Fury (Guardians 3) (p. 728)
—Hashbrown Winters & Whiz-Tastrophe. (p. 752)
Cole, Gina. Adapt. (p. 11)
Cole, Hana. Hooray! I'm Catholic. Steege, Joanna, illus. (p. 796)
Cole, Hannah. Crocodiles. (p. 384)
Cole, Heidi & Vogl, Nancy. Am I a Color Too? Purnell, Gerald, illus. (p. 51)
Cole, Henry. Big Bug. Cole, Henry, illus. (p. 180)
—Brambleheart. Cole, Henry, illus. (p. 222)
—Jack's Garden. (p. 904)
—Littlest Evergreen. (p. 1039)
—Littlest Evergreen. Cole, Henry, illus. (p. 1039)
—Nest for Celeste: A Story about Art, Inspiration, & the Meaning of Home. Cole, Henry, illus. (p. 1242)
—On Meadowview Street. Cole, Henry, illus. (p. 1289)
—On the Way to the Beach. Cole, Henry, illus. (p. 1292)
—Trudy. Cole, Henry, illus. (p. 1791)
—Unspoken: A Story from the Underground Railroad. Cole, Henry, illus. (p. 1822)
Cole, Henry, illus. see Andrews, Julie & Edwards, Julie Andrews.
Cole, Henry, illus. see Aylesworth, Jim.
Cole, Henry, illus. see Bauer, Marion Dane.
Cole, Henry, illus. see Capucilli, Alyssa Satin.
Cole, Henry, illus. see Chall, Marsha Wilson.
Cole, Henry, illus. see Corbett, Sue.
Cole, Henry, illus. see DeFelice, Cynthia C.
Cole, Henry, illus. see Dempsey, Kristy.
Cole, Henry, illus. see Dorros, Arthur.
Cole, Henry, illus. see Duncan Edwards, Pamela.
Cole, Henry, illus. see Edwards, Julie Andrews.
Cole, Henry, illus. see Edwards, Pamela Duncan.
Cole, Henry, illus. see Fierstein, Harvey.
Cole, Henry, illus. see Geist, Ken.
Cole, Henry, illus. see Greene, Rhonda Gowler.
Cole, Henry, illus. see Helakoski, Leslie.
Cole, Henry, illus. see Hopkins, Jackie Mims.
Cole, Henry, illus. see Krensky, Stephen.
Cole, Henry, illus. see Laminack, Lester L.
Cole, Henry, illus. see Laminack, Lester.
Cole, Henry, illus. see Norman, Kim.
Cole, Henry, illus. see Palatini, Margie.
Cole, Henry, illus. see Perl, Erica S.
Cole, Henry, illus. see Richardson, Justin & Parnell, Peter.
Cole, Henry, illus. see Smith, Roland & Smith, Marie.
Cole, Henry, illus. see Sobel, June.
Cole, Henry, illus. see Tripp, Paul.
Cole, Henry, illus. see Urban, Linda.
Cole, Henry, illus. see Verburg, Bonnie.
Cole, Henry, illus. see Vernick, Audrey.
Cole, Henry, jt. auth. see Capucilli, Alyssa Satin.
Cole, Henry, tr. see Edwards, Pamela Duncan.
Cole, Herbert, illus. see Canton, William.
Cole, Ian. Colors. (p. 344)
Cole, Jack. Plastic Man. (p. 1370)
Cole, Jami. What Wolves Are Wearing. (p. 1895)
Cole, Jeff, illus. see Accord Publishing Staff & Andrews McMeel Publishing, LLC Staff.
Cole, Jeff, jt. auth. see Andrews McMeel Publishing, LLC Staff.
Cole, Jeff & Andrews McMeel Publishing, LLC Staff. Eyeball Animation Drawing Book: Funny Folks Edition. Cole, Jeff, illus. (p. 558)
—Eyeball Animation Drawing Book: Underwater Safari Edition. Cole, Jeff, illus. (p. 558)
Cole, Jeff & Stone, Kate. Stick to It - Toys: A Magnetic Puzzle Book. (p. 1649)
Cole, Jess. Six Swans: A Folktale. (p. 1582)
Cole, Joanna. Asking about Sex & Growing Up: A Question & Answer Book for Kids. Thomas, Bill, illus. (p. 106)
—Asking about Sex & Growing Up: A Question-and-Answer Book for Kids. Thomas, Bill, illus. (p. 106)
—At the Waterworks. Degen, Bruce, illus. (p. 111)
—Dinosaurs. (p. 443)
—Human Body. (p. 825)
—I'm a Big Brother. Kightley, Rosalinda, illus. (p. 858)
—I'm a Big Sister. Kightley, Rosalinda, illus. (p. 858)
—Insects. (p. 875)
—Inside the Human Body. Degen, Bruce, illus. (p. 877)
—Lost in the Solar System. Degen, Bruce, illus. (p. 1056)
—Magic School Bus & the Climate Challenge. Degen, Bruce, illus. (p. 1073)
—Magic School Bus at the First Thanksgiving. Bracken, Carolyn, illus. (p. 1073)
—My Big Boy Potty. Chambliss, Maxie, illus. (p. 1197)
—My Big Girl Potty. Chambliss, Maxie, illus. (p. 1197)
—My Friend the Doctor. Chambliss, Maxie, illus. (p. 1209)
—On the Ocean Floor. Degen, Bruce, illus. (p. 1291)
—Our Solar System. (p. 1310)
—Planet Earth. (p. 1367)
—Polar Animals. (p. 1378)
—Rainforest. (p. 1436)
—Science Fair Expedition. Degen, Bruce, illus. (p. 1526)
—Sea Creatures. (p. 1534)
—Soy un Hermano Mayor. Kightley, Rosalinda, illus. (p. 1618)
—Soy una Hermana Mayor. Kightley, Rosalinda, illus. (p. 1618)
—Volcanoes & Earthquakes. (p. 1849)
—Wild Weather. (p. 1930)
Cole, Joanna, jt. auth. see Calmenson, Stephanie.
Cole, Joanna, jt. auth. see Capeci, Anne.
Cole, Joanna, jt. auth. see Egan, Kate.
Cole, Joanna, jt. auth. see Lane, Jeanette.
Cole, Joanna, jt. auth. see Simon, Jenne.
Cole, Joanna & Calmenson, Stephanie. Yours till Banana Splits: 201 Autograph Rhymes. Tiegreen, Alan, illus. (p. 1982)
Cole, Joanna & Calmenson, Stephanie, eds. Tons of Fun: Over 300 Action Rhymes, Old & New Riddles, Tongue Twisters, & Play Rhymes. Tiegreen, Alan, illus. (p. 1765)
Cole, Joanna & Capeci, Anne. Takes a Moonwalk. Bracken, Carolyn, illus. (p. 1697)
Cole, Joanna & Carson, Mary Kay. Ocean Adventure. (p. 1276)
Cole, Joanna & Jackson, Tom. Magic School Bus Presents: Dinosaurs: A Nonfiction Companion to the Original Magic School Bus Series. Degen, Bruce & Bracken, Carolyn, illus. (p. 1073)
—Magic School Bus Presents: Insects: A Nonfiction Companion to the Original Magic School Bus Series. Degen, Bruce & Bracken, Carolyn, illus. (p. 1073)
—Our Solar System. Degen, Bruce & Bracken, Carolyn, illus. (p. 1310)
—Planet Earth. Degen, Bruce & Bracken, Carolyn, illus. (p. 1367)
—Rainforest. Degen, Bruce & Bracken, Carolyn, illus. (p. 1436)
—Sea Creatures. Degen, Bruce & Bracken, Carolyn, illus. (p. 1534)
—Volcanoes & Earthquakes. Degen, Bruce & Bracken, Carolyn, illus. (p. 1849)
Cole, Joanna & O'Brien, Cynthia. Polar Animals. Degen, Bruce & Bracken, Carolyn, illus. (p. 1378)
Cole, Joanna & Van Horn, William. Ca C'est Chez Moi. (p. 250)
Cole, Joanna, et al. Human Body. Degen, Bruce & Bracken, Carolyn, illus. (p. 825)
—Wild Weather. Degen, Bruce & Bracken, Carolyn, illus. (p. 1930)
Cole, John O. Plugged in to English: English & Language Arts Activities for the Computer Lab. (p. 1374)
Cole, Katelyn. Class Terrarium. (p. 327)
Cole, Kathryn. Never Give Up: A Story about Self-Esteem Leng, Qin, illus. (p. 1243)
—Reptile Flu: A Story about Communication Leng, Qin, illus. (p. 1461)
Cole, Kathryn, ed. see Barclay, Jane.
Cole, Kenneth. Friends & Neighbors: We Love to Learn. Ruebartsch, John, photos by. (p. 638)
Cole, Kresley. Dead of Winter. (p. 417)
—Endless Knight: The Arcana Chronicles Book 2. (p. 527)
—Endless Knight. (p. 527)
—Poison Princess. (p. 1377)
Cole, Kristin & Burns, Adam. Loyola Marymount University College Prowler off the Record. (p. 1061)
Cole, Landry. Season of Faith's Revival. (p. 1538)
Cole, Linda, jt. auth. see Tai, Elise See.
Cole, Lisa. Chessie of the Chesapeake Bay. Cole, Lisa, illus. (p. 298)
Cole, Lois. Spirit of Torenia. (p. 1628)
Cole, Melissa S. Desert. (p. 428)
—Forest. (p. 618)
—Mountain. (p. 1180)
—Rain Forests. (p. 1434)
Cole, Mernie, illus. see Amoroso, Cynthia.
Cole, Mernie, illus. see Klingel, Cynthia Fitterer & Klingel, Cynthia.
Cole, Mernie, illus. see Klingel, Cynthia Fitterer.
Cole, Mernie, illus. see Rosenberg, Pam.
Cole, Mernie Gallagher, illus. see Bader, Bonnie.
Cole, Michael D. Columbia Space Shuttle Disaster: From First Liftoff to Tragic Final Flight. (p. 346)
—Comets & Asteroids: Ice & Rocks in Space. (p. 348)
—Eye on the Universe: The Incredible Hubble Space Telescope. (p. 558)
Cole, Michelle. F. A. T. Chance. (p. 559)
Cole, Molly. Joe & His Strong Purr. (p. 920)
Cole, Myke. Wildsidhe Chronicles: Car Trouble. Bk. 6 (p. 1931)
Cole, Nikki. Princess Hope. (p. 1404)
Cole, Penelope Ann. Magical Matthew. Collier, Kevin Scott, illus. (p. 1074)
Cole, Penelope Anne. Magical Matthew. Collier, Kevin Scott, illus. (p. 1074)
—Magical Mea. Collier, Kevin, illus. (p. 1074)
—Magico Mateo. Collier, Kevin, illus. (p. 1075)
Cole, Peter. Ben Fletcher: The Life & Times of a Black Wobbly: Including Fellow Worker Fletcher's Writings & Speeches. (p. 163)
Cole, Peter, jt. auth. see Ahluwalia, Libby.
Cole, Quinn. Alphabet Puke: Monsters' Medicine A-Z. Eubanks, Charles, illus. (p. 50)
Cole, Raymond A., illus. see Cole, T. M.
Cole, Sarah, illus. see Henry, Sandi.
Cole, Sarah, illus. see Press, Judy.
Cole, Sonja. Booktalking Around the World: Great Global Reads for Ages 9-14. (p. 213)
Cole, Stacey. Fluffy's Very Special Christmas. (p. 608)
Cole, Stephen. Thieves Like Us. (p. 1732)
—Xtreme Hockey. (p. 1967)
Cole, Steve. Z. Rex. (p. 1984)
Cole, Steve, jt. auth. see Chapman, Linda.
Cole, Steve & Takitin, Sarah. Kids' Easy Bike Care: Tune-Ups, Tools & Quick Fixes. (p. 953)
Cole, Swensen, tr. see Pesquès, Nicolas.
Cole, T. M. Slip in Time: The Book of Eventide. Cole, Raymond A., illus. (p. 1590)
Cole, Tayler. Aquamarine. (p. 93)
—Bloodsucking Leeches. (p. 201)
Cole, Tim, tr. see Cole, Véronique.
Cole, Tom Clohosy. Wall. Cole, Tom Clohosy, illus. (p. 1854)
Cole, Trevor, jt. auth. see Marshall Bradley, Fern.
Cole, Véronique. C'est Si Bon d'être un Chaton ! Cole, Véronique, illus. (p. 288)
—Do You Know Your Birds? Cole, Tim, tr. (p. 458)
—So Good to Be a Kitten! Cole, Tim, tr. (p. 1602)
Cole, William. Monster Knock Knocks. (p. 1167)
Cole, William Edward. Cole's Funny Picture Book No. (p. 339)
Colebourn, Craig. Knights of Videnland: Passing the Torch. (p. 964)
Cole-Dai, Phyllis, ed. Book of the World: A Contemporary Scripture. (p. 212)
Colella, Cheryl, jt. auth. see Richmond, Dee.
Colella, O. Animales de la Selva (Jungle Animals) (p. 80)
Colello, Nicholas. Architecture Alphabet. (p. 95)
Coleman, Alice Scovell. Engraved in Stone. Armand, Anjale Renee, illus. (p. 530)
—Spirit of Chatsworth Mansion. (p. 1628)
Coleman, Andrew & Mason, Chris. Clemson University College Prowler off the Record. (p. 331)
Coleman, Ann Marie. Charlie's Christmas Carol. (p. 293)
Coleman, Audrey, illus. see Kotzwinkle, William & Murray, Glenn.
Coleman, Audrey, illus. see Kotzwinkle, William, et al.
Coleman, Candace. Zubie the Lightning Bug - I Want to Remember Your Thoughts. (p. 1990)
Coleman, Charles G. Shining Sword. (p. 1566)
Coleman, Claudia. Yo Yo & the Great Flood. (p. 1971)
Coleman, Courtney S., jt. auth. see Borrelli, Robert L.
Coleman, Dave, jt. auth. see Jacobsen, Wayne.
Coleman, David R. Old Troop, Rainbow Fairies, & the Forget-Me-Now Potion. (p. 1285)
Coleman, Emily. Christmas with Mary, Mom, Dad, & Dee. (p. 316)
Coleman, Evelyn. Circle of Fire. (p. 321)
—Freedom Train. (p. 635)
—Freedom Train. Riley, David, illus. (p. 635)
—Mystery of the Dark Tower. (p. 1225)
—Shadows on Society Hill: An Addy Mystery. Tibbles, Jean-Paul, illus. (p. 1558)
—Shadows on Society Hill. (p. 1558)
Coleman, Janet Wyman. Eight Dolphins of Katrina: A True Tale of Survival. Nascimbene, Yan, illus. (p. 507)
Coleman, Janet Wyman & Warren, Elizabeth V. Baseball for Everyone: Stories from the Great Game. (p. 141)
Coleman, Jason A., jt. auth. see Coleman, Pansy J.
Coleman, Jennifer B. Ready, Set, Motivate! How to Capture Young Readers with Visual Aids (p. 1447)
Coleman, Jerry & Finger, Bill. World's Finest Comics Archives (p. 1960)
Coleman, Jerry, et al. Showcase Presents Superman Swan, Curt, illus. (p. 1571)
Coleman, Joshua. Marriage Makeover: Finding Happiness in Imperfect Harmony. (p. 1096)
Coleman, Ken, jt. auth. see Argueta, José René.
Coleman, Lori. American Saddlebred Horse (p. 63)
Coleman, Lori & Capstone Press Staff. Girls' Soccer: Going for the Goal (p. 680)
Coleman, Lowell T. You Can Do This: 12 Ways to Bring Out the Best in You! (p. 1974)
Coleman, Melvin. B. C. & Phoenicia: A Traditional Folktale. (p. 122)
—Black Fatherhood: A Call from the Heart. (p. 196)
Coleman, Michael. Squabbling Squads! (p. 1636)
Coleman, Michael & Phillips, Mike. Esos Estupidos Ordenadores. Phillips, Mike, tr. (p. 536)
Coleman, Michelle, compiled by. My Pets. (p. 1217)
—Wild Animals. (p. 1928)
Coleman, Miriam. Arkansas: The Natural State. (p. 99)
—Culture & Crafts of India. (p. 391)
—Culture & Crafts of Mexico. (p. 391)
—Earth-Friendly Buildings. (p. 496)
—Earth-Friendly Living. (p. 496)
—Earth-Friendly Transportation. (p. 496)
—Find It: Searching for Information. (p. 587)
—Life of Black Elk. (p. 1011)
—Louisiana: The Pelican State. (p. 1058)
—Mississippi: The Magnolia State. (p. 1154)
—Mujeres en la Politica (Women in Politics) (p. 1189)
—Mujeres en Las Ciencias (Women in Science) (p. 1189)
—Mujeres en Las Fuerzas Armadas (Women in the Military) (p. 1189)
—Nebraska: The Cornhusker State. (p. 1239)
—New Mexico: Land of Enchantment. (p. 1246)
—Oklahoma: The Sooner State. (p. 1283)
—Plan It: Conducting Short-Term & Long-Term Research. (p. 1366)
—Present It: Understanding Contexts & Audiences. (p. 1396)
—Prove It: Gathering Evidence & Integrating Information. (p. 1413)
—Share It: Using Digital Tools & Media. (p. 1561)
—Swimming with Dolphins. (p. 1691)
—Swimming with Manatees. (p. 1691)
—Swimming with Penguins. (p. 1691)
—Swimming with Sea Lions. (p. 1691)
—Swimming with Sea Turtles. (p. 1691)
—Swimming with Sharks. (p. 1691)
—Using the Weather to Learn about Earth. (p. 1828)
—Women in Politics. (p. 1946)
—Women in Science. (p. 1946)
—Women in the Military. (p. 1946)
Coleman, Pansy J. & Coleman, Jason A. Wings of an Angel. (p. 1936)
Coleman, Patricia. What Mama Never Told Me! (p. 1892)
Coleman, Roger. Pope & the Snowman: A Christmas Tale. (p. 1384)

Coleman, Rowan. Film Star. (p. 586)
—Hollywood Star. (p. 789)
—Musical Star. (p. 1194)
—Shooting Star. (p. 1568)
Coleman, Rudoph. Soul Ties. (p. 1614)
Coleman, Ryan. Folli: Children's Book of Characters. (p. 612)
Coleman, Ryan S. Wonderful World of Folli: Milly & Tilly. (p. 1948)
Coleman, Sadie. Biggest Heart Ever. Coleman, Sadie, illus. (p. 185)
Coleman, Tamala J. Donovan's Shoes. (p. 466)
Coleman, William. Cholera. (p. 309)
Coleman, William L. Big Book of Animal Devotions: 250 Daily Readings about God's Amazing Creation (p. 178)
—How, Why, When, Where: A Treasure Chest of Wonderful Bible Facts, Stories, Games! Walles, Dwight, illus. (p. 823)
—Oscar: A Cat's Tale. Amatisto, Brandi, illus. (p. 1305)
Coleman, Wim. Constitution & the Bill of Rights. Perrin, Pat, ed. (p. 359)
Coleman, Wim, jt. auth. see Perrin, Pat.
Coleman, Wim & Perrin, Pat. Alamo: A MyReportLinks.com Book. (p. 33)
—Amazing Erie Canal & How a Big Ditch Opened up the West. (p. 54)
—Colonial Williamsburg: A MyReportLinks.com Book. (p. 342)
—Death of the Good Wizard. (p. 420)
—Follow the Drinking Gourd: Come along the Underground Railroad. Martin, Courtney, illus. (p. 612)
—George Washington: Creating a Nation. (p. 664)
—Iraq in the News: Past, Present, & Future. (p. 887)
—Llorona: Retelling a Mexican Legend. Weber Feeney, Siri, illus. (p. 1043)
—Martin Luther King, Jr. National Historic Site: A MyReportLinks.com Book. (p. 1098)
—My Sprig of Lilac: Remembering Abraham Lincoln. Catalano, Dominic, illus. (p. 1219)
—Racism on Trial: From the Medgar Evers Murder Case to Ghosts of Mississippi. (p. 1432)
—Rebellious Californians & the Brave Struggle to Join the Nation. (p. 1451)
—Runaway Train: Saved by Belle of the Mines & Mountains. Renaud, Joanne, illus. (p. 1496)
—Sequoyah & His Talking Leaves: A Play about the Cherokee Syllabary. Weber Feeney, Siri, illus. (p. 1552)
—Slave's Education in Courage: The Life of Frederick Douglass. Ward, Damian, illus. (p. 1588)
—Steam! Taming the River Monster. Todd, Sue, illus. (p. 1646)
—Transcontinental Railroad & the Great Race to Connect the Nation. (p. 1778)
—What Made the Wild West Wild. (p. 1892)
Coleman, Winfield, illus. see Myers, Tim J.
Coleman-Cunningham, Carol D. Maria Was Touched by an Angel. (p. 1093)
Coleman-Grider, Angelee. Awakening Words: For the Poetically Correct. (p. 120)
Coleman-Grider, Angelee, ed. see Joseph, Annette.
Coleman-Veach, Marti. Balloons in Heaven. (p. 135)
Coleman-Woolslayer, Mary. Biplane & Her Boy. (p. 190)
Cole-McCrea, Candace. Seeing-Eye Dog: A Story of Brotherly Love. (p. 1548)
Coleridge, E. P., tr. see Euripides.
Coleridge, Edward P., tr. see Euripides.
Coleridge, Margaret, jt. auth. see Mills, Nathan.
Coleridge, Samuel Taylor. Rime of the Ancient Mariner. Motter, Dean, ed. (p. 1473)
Coleridge, Samuel Taylor, et al. Coleridge's Poetry & Prose. (p. 339)
Coles, Chantel. Valentina: Lisa's Dream Come True. (p. 1830)
Coles, Diane Taylor. Still Smiling: The Life Story of Bradley Taylor Coles. (p. 1650)
Coles, Jade. Sister Like You. (p. 1581)
Coles, James, illus. see Burns, John.
Coles, Mary, illus. see Peers, Judi.
Coles, Michael Joseph, et al. Land of Caring Bou. Banks, Timothy, illus. (p. 973)
Coles, Robert. Bruce Springsteen's America: The People Listening, a Poet Singing. (p. 232)
—Story of Ruby Bridges. Ford, George, illus. (p. 1659)
Coles, William E., Jr. Compass in the Blood: A Reissue of the Simon & Schuster Original Novel. (p. 352)
Coleson, Julie, jt. auth. see Brimmer, Debi.
Colette, Sidonie-Gabrielle. My Mother's House; & Sido. (p. 1215)
Coletti, Sharon. Everything You Need to Supplement U. S. & State Studies. (p. 546)
—Everything You Need to Teach Africa. (p. 546)
—Everything You Need to Teach Ancient Civilizations. (p. 546)
—Everything You Need to Teach Latin America. (p. 546)
—Everything You Need to Teach Oceania. (p. 546)
—Everything You Need to Teach the Middle East. (p. 546)
—Power of One: A Guide to Service-Learning & Social Science Research. (p. 1389)
Coletti, Sharon, jt. auth. see Corr, Kendra.
Coley, Liz. Pretty Girl-13. (p. 1398)
Coley, Mary McIntyre. Environmentalism: How You Can Make a Difference (p. 532)
Coley, Mike, ed. see Kids, Belly.
Coley, Patrick. Chronicles of Maxwell & His Runaways. (p. 317)
Colfer, Chris. Beyond the Kingdoms. Dorman, Brandon, illus. (p. 174)
—Enchantress Returns. (p. 523)
—Grimm Warning. (p. 724)
—Land of Stories (p. 973)
—Struck by Lightning: The Carson Phillips Journal. (p. 1668)
—Wishing Spell. (p. 1940)
—Wishing Spell. Dorman, Brandon, illus. (p. 1940)
Colfer, Eoin. Airman. (p. 31)
—Arctic Incident. (p. 96)
—Artemis Fowl (p. 103)
—Artemis Fowl: El Mundo Subterráneo. (p. 103)
—Artemis Fowl. (p. 103)
—Artemis Fowl. Feldmann, Claudia, tr. (p. 103)
—Artemis Fowl & the Atlantis Complex. (p. 103)
—Atlantis Complex. (p. 112)
—Benny & Babe. (p. 165)
—Benny & Omar. (p. 165)
—Encuentro en el Artico. (p. 524)
—Eternity Code. (p. 539)
—Half-Moon Investigations. (p. 736)
—Hangman's Revolution. (p. 742)
—Imaginary Fred. Jeffers, Oliver, illus. (p. 860)
—Last Guardian. (p. 978)
—Legend of Spud Murphy. McCoy, Glenn, illus. (p. 988)
—Lost Colony. (p. 1055)
—Opal Deception. (p. 1299)
—Supernaturalist. (p. 1684)
—Time Paradox. (p. 1752)
—Wish List. (p. 1940)
Colfer, Eoin & Colfereoin. Artemis Fowl. (p. 103)
Colfer, Eoin & Donkin, Andrew. Arctic Incident. Rigano, Giovanni, illus. (p. 96)
—Artemis Fowl. Rigano, Giovanni & Lamanna, Paolo, illus. (p. 103)
—Artemis Fowl the Opal Deception Graphic Novel. Rigano, Giovanni & Lamanna, Paolo, illus. (p. 103)
—Eternity Code. Rigano, Giovanni & Lamanna, Paolo, illus. (p. 539)
—Supernaturalist. Rigano, Giovanni & Lamanna, Paolo, illus. (p. 1684)
Colfer, Eoin, et al. Doctor Who - 12 Doctors 12 Stories. (p. 459)
—Doctor Who Anthology. (p. 459)
Colfereoin, jt. auth. see Colfer, Eoin.
Colford, Joseph E., jt. auth. see Cavaiola, Alan.
Colgan, Lynda. Mathemagic! Number Tricks. Kurisu, Jane, illus. (p. 1107)
Colhoun, Sheelah. Elric's Florida Holiday. Cotton, Sue Lynn, illus. (p. 516)
—It's Fun to Feed the Little Lambs. Cotton, Sue Lynn, illus. (p. 897)
ColiaStudios, illus. see Jaffe, Ilene.
Colich, Abby. Drawing Amazing Animals. Calle, Juan & Howard, Colin, illus. (p. 481)
—Drawing Fascinating Animals. Howard, Colin, illus. (p. 481)
—Drawing Ocean Animals. Calle, Juan, illus. (p. 482)
—Drawing Wild Animals. Juta, Jason, illus. (p. 482)
—Drawing Your Pets. Azzalin, Stefano, illus. (p. 482)
—Exploring Materials. (p. 552)
—Glass (p. 682)
—Grace Lin Byers, Michael, illus. (p. 704)
—Metal (p. 1130)
—Mo Willems Byers, Michael, illus. (p. 1157)
—Paper (p. 1322)
—Plastic (p. 1370)
—Protecting Food Chains (p. 1412)
—Rock (p. 1481)
—Rubber (p. 1493)
—Ultimate Girls' Guide to Drawing: Puppies, Polar Bears, & Other Adorable Animals. Howard, Colin, illus. (p. 1809)
—Wilma Mankiller (p. 1934)
—Wood (p. 1949)
Colich, Abby, jt. auth. see Butzer, Anna.
Colin, Beatrice & Pinto, Sara. My Invisible Sister. (p. 1211)
Colin, Jose Juan, tr. see Baca, Ana.
Colin, Jose Juan, tr. see Griswold del Castillo, Richard.
Colin Macfarlane. Hit the Headlines: Exciting Journalism Activities for Improving Writing & Thinking Skills. (p. 785)
Colin, Paul, jt. auth. see Kusmierski, Janet.
Colin, Thompson. How to Live Forever. (p. 820)
Colins, Luke. George Washington Carver (p. 664)
—Mae Jemison (p. 1070)
—Thurgood Marshall (p. 1746)
Colins, Luke & Flynn, Riley. Great African Americans (p. 713)
Colkmire, Lance. Know It, Live It: Helping Kids Embrace Pentecostal Teachings. (p. 965)
Colkmire, Lance, jt. auth. see Kraft, Tamera.
Coll, C., jt. auth. see Coll, L.
Coll, Ivar Da. Bien Vestidos. (p. 177)
—Carlos. Coll, Ivar Da, illus. (p. 270)
—Cinco Amigos. (p. 319)
—Maria Juana. (p. 1093)
—Medias Dulces. (p. 1118)
—Senor Joser Tomillo. (p. 1550)
Coll, Ivar Da, illus. see MacHado, Ana Maria.
Coll, Ivar Da, illus. see Reyes, Yolanda.
Coll, Ivar Da & Da Coll, Ivar. Pies para la Princesa. (p. 1357)
Coll, L. & Coll, C. Beware the Unknown: The Landing. (p. 173)
Coll, Susan. Rockville Pike: A Suburban Comedy of Manners. (p. 1484)
Collander, Hope. Inclined Planes. (p. 869)
Collar, Bill. It;s More Than A Game! Vervoort, Sarah, illus. (p. 897)
Collar, Orpheus, illus. see Riordan, Rick.
Collar, Orpheus, jt. auth. see Riordan, Rick.
Collard, Liz. Secret of Pirate Taz. (p. 1542)
Collard, Sneed B. Sneed B. Collard III's Most Fun Book Ever about Lizards. (p. 1597)
Collard, Sneed B. & Collard, Sneed B., III. Australia's Cane Toads: Overrun! (p. 116)
Collard, Sneed B., III. Abraham Lincoln: A Courageous Leader. (p. 6)
—American Heroes (p. 61)
—B Is for Big Sky Country. Yardley, Joanna, illus. (p. 122)
—Benjamin Franklin: The Man Who Could Do Just about Anything. (p. 165)
—Cesar Chavez: The Farm Workers' Best Friend. (p. 288)
—David Crockett: Fearless Frontiersman. (p. 411)
—Deep-Sea Floor. Wenzel, Gregory, illus. (p. 423)
—Dog 4491. (p. 460)
—Dog Sense (p. 461)
—Double Eagle (p. 472)
—Eleanor Roosevelt: Making the World a Better Place. (p. 508)
—Fire Birds. (p. 590)
—Flash Point (p. 602)
—George Washington: Our First President. (p. 664)
—Governor's Dog Is Missing. (p. 704)
—In the Deep Sea. (p. 865)
—In the Rain Forest Canopy. (p. 867)
—In the Wild. (p. 868)
—Jacob Lawrence: A Painter's Story. (p. 904)
—John Adams: Our Second President. (p. 921)
—John Glenn: Hooked on Flying. (p. 922)
—Lady Bird Johnson: Keeping America Green. (p. 970)
—Many Biomes, One Earth. Needham, James M., illus. (p. 1089)
—On the Coral Reefs. (p. 1290)
—One Night in the Coral Sea. Brickman, Robin, illus. (p. 1296)
—Phillis Wheatley: She Loved Words. (p. 1351)
—Platypus, Probably. Plant, Andrew, illus. (p. 1370)
—Pocket Babies: And Other Amazing Marsupials. (p. 1375)
—Rosa Parks: The Courage to Make a Difference. (p. 1489)
—Sacagawea: Brave Shoshone Girl. (p. 1500)
—Science Adventures (p. 1524)
—Shep: Our Most Loyal Dog. Yardley, Joanna, illus. (p. 1565)
—Sitting Bull: Tatanka-Iyotake. (p. 1582)
—Smart Survivors. (p. 1593)
—Teeth. Saroff, Phyllis V., illus. (p. 1715)
—Thomas Jefferson: Let Freedom Ring! (p. 1739)
—Tough Terminators. (p. 1773)
—World Famous Miles City Bucking Horse Sale. (p. 1955)
Collard, Sneed B., III, jt. auth. see Collard, Sneed B.
Collection/Jupiterimages Unlimited, illus. see Ciminera, Siobhan.
Collective Work Staff, illus. see Melodie.
Colledge, Anne. Falling into Fear. (p. 567)
Colleen Connelly, jt. auth. see Janice Turner.
Colleen Madonna Flood Williams. Bahamas Henderson, James D., ed. (p. 132)
—Ecuador Henderson, James D., ed. (p. 503)
—Jamaica Henderson, James D., ed. (p. 906)
—Suriname Henderson, James D., ed. (p. 1685)
College Board Staff. Official SAT Study Guide: 2016 Edition. (p. 1280)
Collenberger, Chris, illus. see Belle, Deborah A.
Coller, H., illus. see Smith, Evelyn.
Collesano, Melissa J. Phoebe Mckeeby's Garden Apartment. (p. 1350)
Collet, Géraldine. Ah! Spagnol, Estelle Billon, illus. (p. 30)
Collet-Derby, Pierre, illus. see Lynn, Sarah.
Collett, Debra. Reluctant Butterfly. (p. 1458)
Collett, Farrell R., illus. see Luce, Willard.
Collett, Heather, illus. see Birkemoe, Karen.
Collett, Jo & Smith, Lee. Social Science Matters: Grade 4 Learner's Book. (p. 1604)
—Social Science Matters Grade 4 Afrikaans Translation. (p. 1604)
Collett, Jo, et al. Social Sciences Matters: Grade 5 Learner's Book. (p. 1604)
—Social Sciences Matters: Grade 5 Learners Book Affrikaans Translation. (p. 1604)
Collett, Susan. Christmas Dragon. (p. 313)
Collette, Paul & Wright, Robert. Huddles: Playscript. (p. 824)
Colletti, Steve. FITT Golfer. (p. 599)
Colley, Abdoulie, illus. see Sullivan, Marija.
Colley, Jacqui, illus. see De Goldi, Kate.
Collicott, Sharleen. Mildred & Sam. Collicott, Sharleen, illus. (p. 1142)
—Mildred & Sam & Their Babies. Collicott, Sharleen, illus. (p. 1142)
Collicott, Sharleen, illus. see Numeroff, Laura Joffe.
Collict, Joan E. Robot Horse: A Christmas Tale. (p. 1480)
Collicutt, Paul. City in Peril! Collicutt, Paul, illus. (p. 323)
—Indestructible Metal Men. Collicutt, Paul, illus. (p. 870)
—Murder on the Robot City Express. Collicutt, Paul, illus. (p. 1192)
—Rust Attack! Collicutt, Paul, illus. (p. 1498)
Collie, Ashley Jude. Gridiron Greats: 8 of Today's Hottest NFL Stars. (p. 723)
Collie, Devyn. Courageous the Unicorn. (p. 373)
Collier, Andrea King, et al. Black Woman's Guide to Black Men's Health. (p. 197)
Collier, Bruce & Maclachlan, James. Charles Babbage & the Engines of Perfection. (p. 291)
Collier, Bryan. Untitled Collier 2/4. (p. 1823)
—Untitled Collier 3/4. (p. 1823)
—Untitled Collier 4/4 (p. 1823)
—Uptown (p. 1825)
—Uptown Collier, Bryan, illus. (p. 1825)
—Uptown. (p. 1825)
—Uptown. Collier, Bryan, illus. (p. 1825)
Collier, Bryan, illus. see Andrews, Troy.
Collier, Bryan, illus. see Bates, Katharine Lee.
Collier, Bryan, illus. see Giovanni, Nikki.
Collier, Bryan, illus. see Grimes, Nikki.
Collier, Bryan, illus. see Hill, Laban Carrick.
Collier, Bryan, illus. see Hughes, Langston.
Collier, Bryan, illus. see MacLachlan, Patricia.
Collier, Bryan, illus. see Murphy, Claire Rudolf.
Collier, Bryan, illus. see Murray, Diana.
Collier, Bryan, illus. see Perdomo, Willie.
Collier, Bryan, illus. see Price, Hope Lynne.
Collier, Bryan, illus. see Rappaport, Doreen.
Collier, Bryan, illus. see Schotter, Roni.
Collier, Bryan, illus. see Smith, Charles R., Jr.
Collier, Christine. Adventure on Apple Orchard Road. (p. 14)
—Twelve Months of Mystery. (p. 1800)
Collier, Christopher, jt. auth. see Collier, James Lincoln.
Collier, Irene Dea. Chinese Mythology Rocks! Bock, William Sauts, illus. (p. 307)
Collier, James Lincoln. Alexander Hamilton. (p. 36)
—Automobile. (p. 117)
—Christopher Columbus: To the New World. (p. 317)
—Clock. (p. 333)
—Electricity & the Lightbulb. (p. 509)
—George Washington You Never Knew. Copeland, Greg, illus. (p. 665)
—Me & Billy (p. 1115)
—Sitting Bull You Never Knew. (p. 1582)
—Steam Engine. (p. 1646)
—Tecumseh You Never Knew. Copeland, Greg, illus. (p. 1712)
Collier, James Lincoln & Collier, Christopher. My Brother Sam Is Dead. (p. 1199)
Collier, John. Fancies & Goodnights. (p. 570)
—Indians of the Americas. (p. 872)
Collier, John, illus. see Grimes, Nikki.
Collier, Kathy Lynn. Walter S. (Spy) Pigeon Pace, Brittany Lee Ann, illus. (p. 1856)
Collier, Kelly L. Mommy, Why am I Different? (p. 1162)
Collier, Kevin, illus. see Bloomberg, Sandi.
Collier, Kevin, illus. see Byers, James.
Collier, Kevin, illus. see Cole, Penelope Anne.
Collier, Kevin, illus. see Houdek, Andi.
Collier, Kevin, illus. see Jones, Debra M.
Collier, Kevin, illus. see Skordy, Anne Marie.
Collier, Kevin, jt. auth. see Collier, Kristen.
Collier, Kevin Scott. Barthpenn@heaven. Org: The Story of Young Jordan Mink & the Email He Got from Heaven. (p. 140)
—Diligence the Dragon: A Prebiblical Fable. Vol. 1 (p. 440)
—Esther's Channel. (p. 538)
—Hope, the Angelfish. Collier, Kevin Scott, illus. (p. 796)
—Journeys of Hope, a Star Shall Lead Them. (p. 929)
—Journeys of Hope, Pearl of Wisdom. Collier, Kevin Scott, illus. (p. 929)
—Professor Horace, Cryptozoologist. Collier, Kevin Scott, illus. (p. 1409)
—Tales from Kensington Forest. (p. 1701)
Collier, Kevin Scott, illus. see Appel, Cindy.
Collier, Kevin Scott, illus. see Cahill, Bear.
Collier, Kevin Scott, illus. see Cole, Penelope Ann.
Collier, Kevin Scott, illus. see Cole, Penelope Anne.
Collier, Kevin Scott, illus. see Hall, Raelene.
Collier, Kevin Scott, illus. see Houdek, Andrea.
Collier, Kevin Scott, illus. see James, Catherine.
Collier, Kevin Scott, illus. see Lake, Mary.
Collier, Kevin Scott, illus. see Lyle-Soffe, Shari.
Collier, Kevin Scott, illus. see McElligott, Walter Lee.
Collier, Kevin Scott, illus. see Osborne, Jill.
Collier, Kevin Scott, illus. see Rogers, Michelle Elizabeth.
Collier, Kevin Scott, illus. see Shepherd, Donna J.
Collier, Kevin Scott, illus. see Squires, R. L.
Collier, Kevin Scott, jt. auth. see Collier, Kristen.
Collier, Kevin Scott & Collier, Kristen. Dreamchaser. (p. 484)
Collier, Kristen. Joy the Jellyfish. (p. 930)
Collier, Kristen, jt. auth. see Collier, Kevin Scott.
Collier, Kristen & Collier, Kevin. Natalie's Ark. (p. 1230)
Collier, Kristen & Collier, Kevin Scott. Jumbo Shrimp of Dire Straits. (p. 933)
Collier, Kristi. Jericho Walls. (p. 913)
Collier, Lisa. Sara Had Sara. (p. 1514)
Collier, Mary, illus. see Rosa-Mendoza, Gladys.
Collier, Mary, illus. see Schmauss, Judy Kentor.
Collier, Paul H. & O'Neill, Robert John. World War II: The Mediterranean 1940-1945. (p. 1959)
Collier, Peter. Choosing Courage: True Stories of Heroism from Soldiers & Civilians. (p. 310)
Collier, Polly, reader. Pumpkin Book. (p. 1416)
Collier, Robert. Secret of the Ages. (p. 1542)
Collier, Roberta, illus. see Rauenhorst, Linda.
Collier, Sandra. Wake up to Your Dreams. (p. 1853)
Collier, Talina L. Jacob & the Orange. (p. 904)
—Jacob & the Turtle Race. (p. 904)
Collier, Wayne Evans. Grumpy the Grasshopper. Goodman, Larry, illus. (p. 727)
Collier-Morales, Roberta. Where Is Thumbkin? (p. 1909)
Collier-Morales, Roberta, illus. see Bennett, Jeffrey.
Collier-Morales, Roberta, illus. see Dreyer, Nicole E.
Collier-Morales, Roberta, illus. see Halley, Wendy Stofan.
Collier-Morales, Roberta, illus. see Hinkle, Cynthia A.
Collier-Morales, Roberta, illus. see Kesseiring, Mari.
Collier-Thompson, Kristi. Girls' Guide to Dreams. Turchyn, Sandie, illus. (p. 680)
Colligan, Douglas, jt. auth. see Wouk, Henry.
Colligan, L. H. City. (p. 323)
—Drug Dependence. (p. 486)
—Global Warming. (p. 684)
—Measles & Mumps. (p. 1117)
—Mercury. (p. 1127)
—Muscles. (p. 1192)
—Pain Treatments. (p. 1318)
—Sleep Disorders. (p. 1588)
—Tick-Borne Illnesses. (p. 1747)
Colligan, Louise H. Government. (p. 704)
Collin, Francesca, jt. auth. see Stevermer, Caroline.
Collin, Grace. Man of Destiny: The Life of Leopold Sedar Senghor. Bostic, Alex, illus. (p. 1085)
Collin, Marie-Marthe, jt. auth. see Paraire, Philippe.
Collinet, Rob, illus. see Horsfall, Jacqueline.
Collingridge, Richard. When It Snows. Collingridge, Richard, illus. (p. 1903)
Collingridge, Richard, illus. see Gavin, Jamila.
Collings, Julie. Creaturas. (p. 380)
Collings, Matthew. Ron Arad Talks to Matthew Collings about Designing Chairs, Vases, Buildings And... Shafran, Nigel & Davies, Richard, photos by. (p. 1486)
Collington, Peter. Small Miracle. (p. 1592)
Collingwood, Harry. Across the Spanish Main. (p. 9)
—Castaways. (p. 276)
—Cruise of The 'Esmeralda' (p. 386)
—In Search of el Dorado. (p. 864)
—Log of a Privateersman. (p. 1045)
—Log of the 'Flying Fish' (p. 1045)
—Pirate Island: A Story of the South Pacific. (p. 1362)
—Rover's Secret. (p. 1492)
—Strange Adventures of Eric Blackburn. (p. 1664)
—Under the Chilean Flag. (p. 1813)
Collins. Collins French School Dictionary. (p. 340)
—Elementary English Grammar. (p. 510)
Collins, Amanda. Bffl!! or Not??? (p. 174)
Collins, Amanda E. Bffl!! or Not??? (p. 174)
Collins, Amberly, jt. auth. see Collins, Brandilyn.
Collins, Amberly & Collins, Brandilyn. Final Touch (p. 586)
Collins, Andrew. See, Hear, Smell, Taste, & Touch: Using Your Five Senses. (p. 1546)
—Violent Weather: Thunderstorms, Tornadoes, & Hurricanes. (p. 1843)
Collins, Andrew Dawe, illus. see Giangregorio, Anthony.

C

Collins, Anne & Pearson Education Staff. Island for Sale. (p. 892)
Collins, Anne M., ed. see Cole, Bethan, et al.
Collins, Anthony & Kenner, Harold. Rip Power: Reading Gave Him the Strength to Fight Back! (p. 1473)
Collins, Arda. Another Way of Life. Kiplinger Pandy, Lori, illus. (p. 88)
Collins, Barbara G. & Collins, Thomas M. Crisis & Trauma: Developmental-Ecological Intervention. (p. 383)
Collins, Bernard, Jr., illus. see Turner-Barnes, Sandra.
Collins, Bert McLemore. Excitement at Double B Acres. (p. 547)
Collins, Beth. Every Family Is Special. (p. 542)
Collins, Betsy. Raindrops. Cotton, Lisa, illus. (p. 1436)
Collins, Billy. Daddy's Little Boy. (p. 399)
—Voyage. Romagna, Karen, illus. (p. 1850)
Collins, Billy, ed. see Paschen, Elise.
Collins, Billy, jt. auth. see O'Brien, Geoffrey.
Collins, Brandilyn, jt. auth. see Collins, Amberly.
Collins, Brandilyn & Collins, Amberly. Always Watching (p. 51)
—Final Touch (p. 586)
Collins, C. B. Where's My Face? A Simon-the-Cat Tale. Holgren, Anna C., illus. (p. 1910)
Collins, Carleen. Everyone Loves Chocolate. (p. 544)
Collins, Carolyn Strom & Eriksson, Christina Wyss. Inside the Secret Garden: A Treasury of Crafts, Recipes, & Activities. Tudor, Tasha, illus. (p. 877)
—World of Little House. Williams, Garth & Maze, Deborah, illus. (p. 1957)
Collins, Cat. Sleeping Dragons. (p. 1589)
Collins, Charles. Hover for a Day. Seltzer, Jerry, illus. (p. 804)
Collins, Chris. Abc People of the Bible. DeBroeck, Sarah, illus. (p. 3)
—Grow Your Own for Kids. (p. 726)
Collins, Christine. Knight Meets Ole Dragon. (p. 964)
Collins, Christine, ed. see Peirce, Jeremy L.
Collins, Christine, ed. see Thakkar, Vatsal.
Collins, Christine, jt. auth. see Holtje, Bert.
Collins, Christine, jt. auth. see Veague, Heather Barnett.
Collins, Courtney, illus. see Brown, Phoenix.
Collins, Darluniau Mike, jt. auth. see Evans, Gwen.
Collins, Daryl, illus. see O'neal, Katherine Pebley.
Collins, Daryl, illus. see Dahl, Michael.
Collins, Daryll, illus. see Fuerst, Jeffrey B.
Collins, Daryll, illus. see Marks, Melanie.
Collins, Daryll, jt. auth. see Dahl, Michael.
Collins, David Paul. Shanghaied. (p. 1559)
Collins, David R. Clarence Thomas: Fighter with Words Lauve, Celia & Shepherd, Rosalie M., illus. (p. 327)
—Dr. Shinichi Suzuki: Teaching Music from the Heart. (p. 475)
—Huey P. Long: Talker & Doer Smith, Jack K., illus. (p. 824)
—J. R. R. Tolkien. (p. 902)
—Tales for Hard Times: A Story about Charles Dickens. Mataya, David, illus. (p. 1701)
—Washington Irving: Storyteller for a New Nation. (p. 1860)
—Write a Book for Me: The Story of Marguerite Henry. (p. 1963)
Collins, David R., et al. Ishi: The Last of His People. Welch, Kelly, illus. (p. 891)
Collins, Dennis. Happy Hummingbirds. (p. 746)
—Spinley's Spaceship. (p. 1628)
Collins, Diana Sue. Elfin, the Elf. (p. 512)
Collins Dictionaries. Collins School Dictionary & Thesaurus: The World's Favourite Little Dictionaries. (p. 339)
—Collins Primary French Dictionary. (p. 341)
—Collins Primary Illustrated Dictionary: Boost Your Word Power. (p. 341)
—Collins School - Collins French School Dictionary. (p. 341)
—Collins School - Collins Spanish School Dictionary. (p. 341)
—Collins Very First French Words. (p. 341)
Collins Dictionaries & Harpercollins Staff. Collins Primary Dictionaries - Collins Junior Illustrated Thesaurus. (p. 341)
Collins Dictionaries Staff. Collins Cobuild Primary Learnere's Dictionary. (p. 340)
—Collins Primary Illustrated Spanish Dictionary. (p. 341)
—Collins School Dictionary & Thesaurus in Colour. (p. 341)
—Collins Very First French Dictionary. (p. 341)
Collins Dictionary Staff. Collins Spanish School Dictionary. (p. 341)
Collins, Don, illus. see Chambers, Sam T., et al.
Collins, Don, illus. see Chemerka, William R.
Collins, Don, jt. auth. see Chemerka, William R.
Collins, Don, jt. auth. see Wade, Mary Dodson.
Collins Easy Learning. English Ages 9-11. (p. 529)
—Maths Ages 9-11. (p. 1108)
Collins Easy Learning & Collins UK. Maths Ages 6-8. (p. 1108)
Collins Easy Learning & HarperCollins UK Staff. Counting Practice. (p. 371)
—Shapes, Colours & Patterns (p. 1560)
—Telling the Time Practice. (p. 1717)
Collins Easy Learning Staff, jt. auth. see Law, Karina.
Collins Easy Learning Staff & HarperCollins UK Staff. Writing Practice. (p. 1965)
Collins Education. Peter & the Wolf. (p. 1346)
Collins Educational Staff. Amazing Writers. (p. 56)
Collins Educational Staff & Cronick, Mitch. In the Garden. Sharp, Melanie, illus. (p. 866)
Collins Educational Staff & Hambleton, Laura. Bad Bat. (p. 131)
Collins Educational Staff & Harvey, Damian. Dinosaur Rock. Ward, Matt, illus. (p. 442)
Collins Educational Staff & Hawes, Alison. Weather Report. Stojic, Manya, illus. (p. 1870)
Collins Educational Staff & Hughes, Monica. Cars. Moon, Cliff, ed. (p. 271)
Collins Educational Staff & Robinson, Anthony. Lion & the Mouse. Duffy, Ciaran, illus. (p. 1020)
Collins Educational Staff, et al. Buzz & Bingo in the Monster Maze. (p. 248)
—Castles. Moon, Cliff, ed. (p. 277)
—Seasons Scrapbook. (p. 1539)
Collins, Elaine Banks. I Like Dressing Up. Floyd, John, Jr., illus. (p. 841)
—See What I Can Do. Floyd, John, Jr., illus. (p. 1547)
Collins, Elizabeth & Lyon, Abby. Swarthmore College College Prowler off the Record. (p. 1689)
Collins, Ellen. Biography: My Life As a Basset Hound ((p. 188)
Collins, Ellen M. My Book: Fun Favorite Stories. (p. 1198)
Collins, Erica. Aloha Activity Book. Collins, Erica, illus. (p. 48)
Collins, Francis. Boys' Book of Model Aeroplanes: How to Build & Fly Them: with the Story of the Evolution of the Flying Machine. (p. 220)
—Second Boys' Book of Model Aeroplanes. (p. 1539)
Collins, Frank, jt. auth. see Catel, Patrick.
Collins, Harper & Harper Collins / LeapFrog. Paddington Bear. (p. 1317)
Collins, Heather. Hey Diddle Diddle. (p. 774)
—Jack & Jill. (p. 902)
—Little Miss Muffet. (p. 1031)
—Out Came the Sun: A Day in Nursery Rhymes. Collins, Heather, illus. (p. 1310)
—Pat-a-Cake. (p. 1327)
Collins, Heather, illus. see Butts, Ed.
Collins, Heather, illus. see Drake, Jane & Love, Ann.
Collins, Heather, illus. see Love, Ann & Drake, Jane.
Collins, Heather, illus. see Pitt, Steve.
Collins, Heather, illus. see Stinson, Kathy.
Collins, Heather, jt. auth. see Aldis, Dorothy.
Collins, Heather, tr. see Love, Ann & Drake, Jane.
Collins, Izola. Pip, Squeak, & Zoom. (p. 1361)
Collins, Jacob, illus. see Evans, Richard.
Collins, James. Rosa Parks: Not Giving In with Buffalo Bill & Farley's Raiders. Cox, Brian T., illus. (p. 1489)
—Theodore Roosevelt: With Buffalo Bill & Farley's Raiders. Cox, Brian T., illus. (p. 1729)
—Trail of Tears with Buffalo Bill & Farley's Raiders. (p. 1776)
Collins, Janet Ann. Peril of the Sinister Scientist. (p. 1343)
—Secret Service Saint. Ruble, Eugene, illus. (p. 1543)
Collins, John M. New World Champion Paper Airplane Book: Featuring the Guinness World Record-Breaking. (p. 1247)
Collins, Jonathan. Adventures of Mali & Keela: A Virtues Book for Children. Cooper, Jenny, illus. (p. 20)
Collins, Julia B., illus. see Georgiady, Nicholas P., et al.
Collins, Katherine. Neil the Horse: The Complete Comics Stories. Herman, Daniel, ed. (p. 1240)
Collins, Kathleen. Day with the Baker: Learning to Tell Time by Quarter Hours. (p. 415)
—Jesse James: Western Bank Robber. (p. 914)
—Jesse James: Bank Robber of the American West. (p. 914)
—Jesse James: Legendario Bandido del Oeste Americano. (p. 914)
—Jesse James: Bank Robber of the American West / Legendario bandido del oeste Americano. (p. 914)
—Jesse James: Legendario bandido del oeste americano (Jesse James: Bank Robber of the American West) (p. 914)
—Marques de Lafayette: Heroe Frances de la Guerra de Independencia. (p. 1096)
—Marquis de Lafayette: French Hero of the American Revolution. (p. 1096)
—Marquis de Lafayette / el Marques de Lafayette: French Hero of the American Revolution / Héroe francés de la Revolución Estadounidense. (p. 1096)
—Music Math: Exploring Different Interpretations of Fractions. (p. 1193)
—On the Trail with Lewis & Clark: Learning to Use Line Graphs. (p. 1291)
—Our New Fish Tank: Learning to Estimate to the Nearest Ones, Tens, & Hundreds Places. (p. 1309)
—Our New Fish Tank: Learning to Estimate & Round Numbers to the Nearest Ones, Tens, & Hundreds Places. (p. 1309)
—Sojourner Truth: Equal Rights Advocate. (p. 1606)
—Sojourner Truth: Defensora de los derechos Civiles. (p. 1606)
—Sojourner Truth: Equal Rights Advocate / Defensora de los derechos Civiles. (p. 1606)
—Sojourner Truth: Defensora de los derechos civiles (Sojourner Truth: Equal Rights Advocate) (p. 1606)
Collins, Kathleen, jt. auth. see Schimel, Kate.
Collins, Katie. Anatomy Academy: Cells, Muscles & Bones. Bk. 1 (p. 67)
—Anatomy Academy: Respiration, Circulation & Digestion (p. 67)
Collins, Katrina. voice from our Souls. (p. 1848)
Collins, Kelsey, illus. see Slanina, Anne Maro.
Collins, Linda, illus. see Mazur, Gabrielle.
Collins, Lori & Koski, Mary. Learn to Call 911. Brown, Dan, illus. (p. 983)
Collins, Malia. Pele & Poliahu. Peterson Kathleen, illus. (p. 1335)
Collins, Malia & Oszajca, Linda. Santa's Hawaiian Holiday. (p. 1513)
Collins Maps Staff. Collins Grammar, Punctuation & Spelling Dictionary. (p. 340)
Collins Maps Staff, jt. auth. see Royal Observatory Greenwich Staff.
Collins Maps Staff, jt. auth. see Scoffham, Stephen.
Collins Maps Staff & HarperCollins Publishers Ltd. Staff. Children's World Atlas. (p. 304)
Collins, Mark, jt. auth. see Seaworthy, Oscar.
Collins, Mark, et al. Mother Goose's Bedtime Rhymes Scheffler, Axel, illus. (p. 1178)
Collins, Mary. Airborne: A Photobiography of Wilbur & Orville Wright. (p. 31)
Collins, Matt, illus. see Adler, David A. & Adler, Michael S.
Collins, Matt, illus. see Krull, Kathleen.
Collins, Matt, illus. see Lemna, Don.
Collins, Matt, illus. see Macy, Sue.
Collins, Max Allan. Johnny Dynamite. (p. 923)
Collins, Max Allan & Rowan, Dave. Jax Epoch & the Quicken Forbidden: Borrowed Magic. Vol. 1 Beatty, Terry, illus. (p. 910)
Collins, Meg. Twinkle, Twinkle Starry Sky. (p. 1802)
Collins, Michael. Anu & the Blue. (p. 90)
Collins, Mike, illus. see Dickens, Charles.
Collins, Mike, illus. see Matthews, John.
Collins, Mike, jt. auth. see Richards, Justin.
Collins, Nafessa. Mrs. Precious & the Possum. (p. 1187)
Collins, Nancy. All about Tree Crickets. (p. 43)
Collins, Nancy A. After Dark. (p. 28)
—Night Life. (p. 1253)
—Vamps. (p. 1832)
Collins, Nicholas & Woods, Samuel G. Frequently Asked Questions about STDs. (p. 636)
Collins, P. J. Sarah. Sam & Nate Jin, Katherine, illus. (p. 1506)
—Sam & Nate. Jin, Katherine, illus. (p. 1506)
Collins, Pat Lowery. Daughter of Winter. (p. 409)
—Deer Watch. Slonim, David, illus. (p. 423)
—Fattening Hut. (p. 577)
—Hidden Voices: The Orphan Musicians of Venice. (p. 776)
Collins, Paul. Cyberkids: The Knockout, the Great Escape, the Final Countdown. (p. 396)
—Dragonlinks: Book One in the Jelindel Chronicles (Large Print 16pt) (p. 478)
—Lucy & the Red Street Boyz. Bocquée, Christian, illus. (p. 1063)
—Lucy in a Jam. Bocquée, Christian, illus. (p. 1063)
—Lucy, Kung-Fu Queen. Bocquée, Christian, illus. (p. 1063)
—Lucy, the Boss. Bocquée, Christian, illus. (p. 1063)
—Slaves of Quentaris. (p. 1588)
—Spell of Undoing. (p. 1625)
—Swords of Quentaris. (p. 1692)
—Tale of Two Squirrels. (p. 1701)
Collins, Paul, ed. Trust Me! (p. 1793)
Collins, Peggy. In the Garden. (p. 866)
—In the Garden. Collins, Peggy, illus. (p. 866)
Collins, Peggy, illus. see Cretney, Brian.
Collins, Peggy, illus. see Winters, Karl-Lynn & Sherritt-Fleming, Lori.
Collins Powell, Judy, illus. see Howell, Brian.
Collins Publishers Staff. Collins KS3 Revision & Practice - English: All-in-One Revision & Practice. (p. 340)
—Collins KS3 Revision & Practice - French. (p. 340)
—Collins KS3 Revision & Practice - KS3 Science. (p. 340)
—Collins KS3 Revision & Practice - Maths. (p. 340)
—Collins KS3 Revision & Practice - Maths Year 7. (p. 340)
—Collins New Key Stage 3 Revision - French: All-in-One Revision & Practice. (p. 341)
—Collins New Key Stage 3 Revision - Geography. (p. 341)
—Collins New Key Stage 3 Revision - Maths (Advanced) (p. 341)
—Geography. (p. 662)
Collins Publishers Staff & Bodleian Library Staff. Chapter of Kings. (p. 291)
Collins, R. Sea Hole. (p. 1534)
Collins, R. L. Rubber Rulers & Lackadaisical Clocks Simplify Gravity. (p. 1493)
Collins, Rachel. Fiddle Faddle Frog & Piddle Paddle Polliwog. (p. 583)
—Sidney Swallow Sings. (p. 1573)
—Sidney Swallow's Baby Sister. (p. 1573)
—Sidney Swallow's Christmas. (p. 1573)
—Soul Sprouts. (p. 1614)
Collins, Reverie, jt. auth. see Burnett, Frances Hodgson.
Collins, Robert, photos by see Flying Eagle & Whispering Wind.
Collins, Robyn, et al. Prepare to Be a Teen Millionaire: Detailed Examples & Step-By-Step Instructions from Self-Made Millionaires. (p. 1396)
Collins, Ross. Doodleday. Collins, Ross, illus. (p. 469)
—Elephantom. Collins, Ross, illus. (p. 511)
—Medusa Jones. (p. 1120)
—My Amazing Dad. (p. 1196)
Collins, Ross, illus. see Bryant, Ann.
Collins, Ross, illus. see Durant, Alan.
Collins, Ross, illus. see French, Vivian.
Collins, Ross, illus. see Grant, John.
Collins, Ross, illus. see Graves, Sue.
Collins, Ross, illus. see Hodgson, Karen J.
Collins, Ross, illus. see Kelly, Mij.
Collins, Ross, illus. see Mabbitt, Will.
Collins, Ross, illus. see MacRae, Tom.
Collins, Ross, illus. see McAuliffe, Nichola.
Collins, Ross, illus. see Sparkes, Ali.
Collins, Ross, tr. see McAuliffe, Nichola.
Collins, Rudy. Vanessa Owens & the Bond of Sisterhood. (p. 1833)
Collins, Sally J., illus. see Strachan, Linda.
Collins, Sheila. Truffles' Diary: The Encore. (p. 1793)
Collins Smith, Anne, tr. see Constantine, Clélia.
Collins Smith, Anne, tr. see Loisillier, Maud & Morel, Diane.
Collins, Sonny. Mouse Tails. (p. 1182)
Collins, Sophie. How to Love a Werewolf. (p. 820)
Collins Staff. Amazing Women. (p. 56)
—Collins Elt Readers - Amazing Composers. MacKenzie, Fiona, ed. (p. 340)
—Collins ELT Readers - Amazing Leaders (Level 4) MacKenzie, Fiona, ed. (p. 340)
—Collins ELT Readers - Amazing Mathematicians (Level 2) MacKenzie, Fiona, ed. (p. 340)
—Collins Elt Readers - Amazing Philanthropists, Level 3. MacKenzie, Fiona, ed. (p. 340)
Collins Staff, illus. see Thomson, Sarah L.
Collins Staff, jt. auth. see HarperCollins UK Staff.
Collins, Stan. Animal Signs. (p. 79)
—Food Signs. (p. 614)
—School Signs. (p. 1523)
Collins, Stephan. Chronicles of Timothy Tabbis. (p. 317)
Collins, Susan, jt. auth. see Teacher Created Resources Staff.
Collins, Suzanne. Catching Fire. (p. 279)
—En Llamas (p. 522)
—En Llamas. (p. 522)
—Gregor (p. 723)
—Gregor & the Code of Claw. (p. 723)
—Gregor & the Curse of the Warmbloods (p. 723)
—Gregor & the Curse of the Warmbloods. (p. 723)
—Gregor & the Marks of Secret. (p. 723)
—Gregor & the Prophecy of Bane. (p. 723)
—Gregor - The Overlander. (p. 723)
—Hunger Games: Foil Edition. (p. 827)
—Hunger Games. (p. 827)
—Hunger Games. O'Brien, Tim, illus. (p. 827)
—Hunger Games. Fournier, Guillaume, tr. (p. 827)
—Hunger Games Trilogy: The Hunger Games; Catching Fire; Mockingjay. Set (p. 828)
—Hunger Games Trilogy Collection. (p. 828)
—Juegos del Hambre. (p. 931)
—Mockingjay. (p. 1157)
—Sinsajo. (p. 1580)
—When Charlie McButton Lost Power. Lester, Mike, illus. (p. 1901)
—Year of the Jungle. Proimos, James, illus. (p. 1969)
Collins, Suzanne, jt. auth. see Seife, Emily.
Collins, Suzanne, et al. Official Illustrated Movie Companion. (p. 1280)
Collins, Tami, illus. see Bayrock, Fiona.
Collins, Tami, illus. see Glaser, Jason.
Collins, Tami, illus. see Preszler, June.
Collins, Tami, illus. see Richardson, Adele & Richardson, Adele D.
Collins, Tami, illus. see Richardson, Adele D.
Collins, Terry. Ancient China: An Interactive History Adventure (p. 68)
—Assassination of John F. Kennedy: November 22 1963 (p. 107)
—Assassination of Martin Luther King, Jr. April 4 1968 (p. 107)
—Bigfoot & Adaptation (p. 185)
—Bigfoot & Adaptation Mallea, Cristian, illus. (p. 185)
—Buried in Rubble: True Tales of Surviving Earthquakes. (p. 243)
—Buried in Rubble: True Stories of Surviving Earthquakes. Chater, Mack, illus. (p. 243)
—Chew on This! Goldberg, Barry, illus. (p. 299)
—Eagle Eye. (p. 492)
—Elvis: A Graphic Novel Melcher, Michele, illus. (p. 517)
—Escape from Pompeii: An Isabel Soto Archaeology Adventure. (p. 535)
—FBI. Brown, Kelly, illus. (p. 578)
—High-Flying Sam. (p. 777)
—Into the West: Causes & Effects of U. S. Westward Expansion (p. 881)
—John Deere's Powerful Idea: The Perfect Plow. Pearce, Carl, illus. (p. 921)
—King of Pop: The Story of Michael Jackson Byers, Michael, illus. (p. 959)
—Liberty Bascle, Brian, illus. (p. 1005)
—Louis Armstrong: Jazz Legend Pope, Richie, illus. (p. 1058)
—Robert E. Lee: The Story of the Great Confederate General Mallea, Cristian, illus. (p. 1479)
—Spongebob NaturePants (p. 1630)
—Stake a Claim! Nickolas Flux & the California Gold Rush Ginevra, Dante, illus. (p. 1638)
—Tea at the Treedome. (p. 1708)
—True Stories of World War II Kinsella, Pat, illus. (p. 1793)
—Whatever Says Mark: Knowing & Using Punctuation Cox, Russ, illus. (p. 1896)
—Wind Blows. (p. 1935)
—Women's Right to Vote Bascle, Brian, illus. (p. 1946)
—World's Greatest Valentine (p. 1960)
Collins, Terry, jt. auth. see Biskup, Agnieszka.
Collins, Terry, jt. auth. see Gunderson, Jessica.
Collins, Terry, jt. auth. see Raum, Elizabeth.
Collins, Terry, jt. auth. see Weakland, Mark.
Collins, Terry & Schulz, Barbara. Escape from Pompeii: An Isabel Soto Archaeology Adventure (p. 535)
Collins, Terry & Weakland, Mark. Unmasking Monsters with Scooby-Doo! Cornia, Christian et al, illus. (p. 1821)
Collins, Terry, et al. American Graphic. Hayden, Seitu & Kinsella, Pat, illus. (p. 61)
—Building the Great Wall of China: An Isabel Soto History Adventure (p. 239)
—Escape from Pompeii: An Isabel Soto Archaeology Adventure (p. 535)
—Getting to the Bottom of Global Warming: An Isabel Soto Investigation (p. 670)
—Getting to the Bottom of Global Warming: An Isabel Soto Investigation. Schulz, Barbara, illus. (p. 670)
—Mesa Verde Cliff Dwellers: An Isabel Soto Archaeology Adventure (p. 1129)
—Mesa Verde Cliff Dwellers: An Isabel Soto Archaeology Adventure Anderson, Bill, illus. (p. 1129)
—Monster Science. Mallea, Cristian & Gervasio, illus. (p. 1168)
—Nickolas Flux History Chronicles Simmons, Mark, illus. (p. 1251)
—Tracking Bigfoot: An Isabel Soto Investigation (p. 1775)
Collins, Terry Lee, jt. auth. see Weakland, Mark Andrew.
Collins, Terry Lee & Weakland, Mark Andrew. Scooby Doo Unmasks the Truth behind Ghosts. (p. 1529)
—Scooby Doo Unmasks the Truth behind Sea Monsters. (p. 1529)
—Scooby Doo Unmasks the Truth behind Zombies. (p. 1529)
Collins, Thomas M., jt. auth. see Collins, Barbara G.
Collins Thoms, Susan. Noah's Ark. Stoop, Naoko, illus. (p. 1261)
Collins, Tim. Diary of Dorkius Maximus. Pinder, Andrew, illus. (p. 435)
—Diary of Dorkius Maximus in Egypt. Pinder, Andrew, illus. (p. 435)
—Diary of Dorkius Maximus in Pompeii. Pinder, Andrew, illus. (p. 435)
—Fangs a Lot: Final Notes from a Totally Lame Vampire. Pinder, Andrew, illus. (p. 571)
—Notes from a Hairy-Not-Scary Werewolf. Pinder, Andrew, illus. (p. 1267)
—Notes from a Totally Lame Vampire: Because the Undead Have Feelings Too! Pinder, Andrew, illus. (p. 1268)
—Prince of Dorkness: More Notes from a Totally Lame Vampire. Pinder, Andrew, illus. (p. 1401)
—Sneezy Alien Attack. Dreidemy, Joëlle & Bigwood, John, illus. (p. 1597)
—Stinky Space Race. Dreidemy, Joëlle, illus. (p. 1651)
Collins, Tim, jt. auth. see Saslow, Joan M.
Collins, Tim & Maples, Mary Jane. Time Zones 1. (p. 1753)
Collins, Tracy Brown. Babe Ruth. (p. 123)
—Living Through the Great Depression. (p. 1042)

Collins, Tracy Brown & Chuck D. Missy Elliott. (p. 1154)
Collins UK. Collins KS3 Revision & Practice - History: All-in-One Revision & Practice. (p. 340)
—Collins Primary World Atlas. (p. 341)
—English Ages 6-8. (p. 529)
Collins UK, jt. auth. see Collins Easy Learning.
Collins UK, jt. auth. see Ellis, Rob.
Collins UK Publishing Staff. Collins KS3 Revision & Practice - English. (p. 340)
—Collins KS3 Revision & Practice - Science: All-in-One Revision & Practice. (p. 340)
—Collins KS3 Revision & Practice - Science Year 7. (p. 341)
—Collins New Key Stage 3 Revision - Science Year 9. (p. 341)
—English Ages 5-7. (p. 529)
—English Ages 8-10. (p. 529)
—Maths Ages 5-7. (p. 1108)
—Maths Ages 7-9. (p. 1108)
—Maths Ages 8-10. (p. 1108)
—World Atlas. (p. 1954)
Collins UK Publishing Staff, jt. auth. see Ellis, Rob.
Collins UK Staff. English Ages 7-9. (p. 529)
Collins, Wendy Jane. Adventure Door: Book 1 'How it all began' & Book 2 'Return to Courtney Bay' (p. 14)
Collins, Yo Yo. Good As Grape Juice: Growing Better-Not Bitter-Through Adversity (p. 697)
Collins, Yozette Yogi & Jennings, Marlis. Goodnight, Boone. Ziolkowski, Ania, illus. (p. 701)
Collins, Yvonne & Rideout, Sandy. Black Sheep. (p. 196)
—Totally Me: The Teenage Girl's Survival Guide. (p. 1771)
Collins-Donnelly, Kate. Banish Your Body Image Thief: A Cognitive Behavioural Therapy Workbook on Building Positive Body Image for Young People. (p. 136)
—Banish Your Self-Esteem Thief: A Cognitive Behavioural Therapy Workbook on Building Positive Self-Esteem for Young People. (p. 136)
—Starving the Anger Gremlin: A Cognitive Behavioural Therapy Workbook on Anger Management for Young People. (p. 1644)
—Starving the Anxiety Gremlin: A Cognitive Behavioural Therapy Workbook on Anxiety Management for Young People. (p. 1644)
—Starving the Anxiety Gremlin for Children Aged 5-9: A Cognitive Behavioural Therapy Workbook on Anxiety Management. (p. 1644)
—Starving the Stress Gremlin: A Cognitive Behavioural Therapy Workbook on Stress Management for Young People. (p. 1644)
Collins-Matza, Carol. Palindrome Kids. (p. 1320)
Collinson, Clare. Ancient & Classical World 500 BC to AD 600. (p. 67)
—Arts, Society, & Religion. (p. 105)
—Fall. (p. 566)
—First Civilizations to 500 BC. (p. 593)
—Peoples of the East, Southeast, & Plains. (p. 1340)
—Spring. (p. 1634)
—Summer. (p. 1673)
—Winter. (p. 1937)
Collinson, Roger. Butterfingers. (p. 247)
Collins-Philippe, Jane. Sail Away with Me. Beingessner, Laura, illus. (p. 1503)
Collisin, Shauna. Heavenites Learning to Count on God Board Book with audio CD. Nelson, Christine, illus. (p. 761)
Collison, Cathy & Campbell, Janis. G Is for Galaxy: An Out of This World Alphabet. Stacy, Alan, illus. (p. 651)
Collison, Paul, et al. Nelson Modular Science (p. 1241)
Collison, Shauna. Heavenites Angels to Zebras Board Book with Audio CD. Nelson, Christine, illus. (p. 761)
Collister, Linda. Baking with Kids. Wreford, Polly, photos by. (p. 133)
—Cooking with Kids. Davies, Vanessa, photos by. (p. 362)
Colllins, Linda, illus. see Mazur, Gabrielle.
Collmann, Phyllis A. Rose's Heart's Decision. (p. 1490)
Collodi, C. Adventures of Pinocchio. (p. 21)
—Adventures of Pinocchio. Della Chiesa, Carol, tr. (p. 21)
—Pinocchio: the Tale of a Puppet. Carsey, Alice, illus. (p. 1361)
Collodi, Carlo. Adventures of Pinocchio. Lucas, Ann Lawson, tr. from ITA. (p. 21)
—Adventures of Pinocchio. Staino, Franco & Innocenti, Roberto, illus. (p. 21)
—Pinocchio: Candlewick Illustrated Classic. Rose, Emma, tr. from ITA. (p. 1360)
—Pinocchio. Cowley, Joy, ed. (p. 1360)
—Pinocchio. McKowen, Scott, illus. (p. 1360)
—Pinocchio. Carsey, Alice & Greban, Quentin, illus. (p. 1360)
—Pinocchio (illustrated) Brock, Geoffrey, tr. from ITA. (p. 1360)
Collodi, Carlo, jt. auth. see Carsey, Alice.
Collodi, Carlo, jt. auth. see Gonzalez, Jorge.
Collodi, Carlo & Baruzzi, Agnese. Pinocchio: A Cut-Paper Book. Baruzzi, Agnese, illus. (p. 1360)
Collodi, Carlo, et al. Pinocchio & Peter Pan: Selections from Two Classic Children's Novels. Palmer, James, illus. (p. 1360)
Colloredo, Sabino. Apollo. Ferrari, Antongionata, illus. (p. 91)
—Athena. Ferrari, Antongionata, illus. (p. 112)
—Hercules. Ferrari, Antongionata, illus. (p. 769)
—Zeus. Ferrari, Antongionata, illus. (p. 1986)
Collum, Karen. Blow Me a Kiss. Geddes, Serena, illus. (p. 202)
Collura, Mary-Ellen Lang. Winners (p. 1937)
Coll-Vinent, Anna, tr. see Ashbe, Jeanne.
Coll-Vinent, Anna, tr. see Crowther, Kitty & Crowther.
Colman. Pearl Story Book: a Collection of Tales, Original & Selected. (p. 1333)
Colman, Audrey, illus. see Katzwinkle, William, et al.
Colman, Audrey, illus. see Kotzwinkle, William & Murray, Glenn.
Colman, Audrey, illus. see Kotzwinkle, William, et al.
Colman, Michelle Sinclair. Artsy Babies Wear Paint. Dion, Nathalie, illus. (p. 105)
—Beach Babies Wear Shades. Dion, Nathalie, illus. (p. 149)
—Country Babies Wear Plaid. Dion, Nathalie, illus. (p. 372)
—Foodie Babies Wear Bibs. Dion, Nathalie, illus. (p. 614)
—Not That Tutu! Nakata, Hiroe, illus. (p. 1267)
—Rocker Babies Wear Jeans. Dion, Nathalie, illus. (p. 1482)
—Sporty Babies Wear Sweats. Dion, Nathalie, illus. (p. 1633)
—Urban Babies Wear Black. Dion, Nathalie, illus. (p. 1825)
Colman, Penny. Elizabeth Cady Stanton & Susan B. Anthony: A Friendship That Changed the World. (p. 513)
—Thanksgiving: The True Story. (p. 1725)
Colnaghi, Stefania, illus. see Powell, Jillian.
Cologne, Starla, illus. see Schmidt, Kristina Edelkamp.
Coloma, Lester, illus. see Lipp, Frederick J.
Coloma, Lester, tr. see Lipp, Frederick J.
Colombo, Angelo, illus. see Francia, Giada, ed.
Colombo, Angelo, illus. see Francia, Giada.
Colombo, David, illus. see Korty, Carol.
Colón, Daniel, illus. see O'Connor, Jim.
Colon, Danny. Little Caterpillar Who Dreams to Fly. (p. 1026)
Colon De Mejias, Leticia. Dinero the Frog Learns to Save Energy. Tamara, Visco, illus. (p. 440)
Colon, Edie. Good-Bye, Havana! Hola, New York! Colón, Raúl, illus. (p. 697)
Colon, Ernie, illus. see Friedhoffer, Bob.
Colón, Ernie, illus. see Mishkin, Dan.
Colon, Margot McCloskey. Etiqueta para Profesionales. (p. 539)
Colon, Maribel. Night Time All Around. (p. 1254)
Colón, Priscilla, jt. auth. see BrickHouse Education.
Colón, Raúl. Draw! Colón, Raúl, illus. (p. 480)
Colón, Raúl, illus. see Borden, Louise.
Colón, Raúl, illus. see Bradley, Kimberly Brubaker.
Colón, Raúl, illus. see Brown, Monica.
Colón, Raúl, illus. see Burleigh, Robert.
Colón, Raúl, illus. see Colon, Edie.
Colón, Raúl, illus. see Dorros, Arthur.
Colón, Raúl, illus. see Herrera, Juan Felipe.
Colón, Raúl, illus. see Hopkinson, Deborah.
Colón, Raúl, illus. see Johnston, Tony.
Colón, Raúl, illus. see Martínez, Rueben.
Colón, Raúl, illus. see Michelson, Richard.
Colón, Raúl, illus. see Mora, Pat.
Colón, Raúl, illus. see Posada, Jorge.
Colón, Raúl, illus. see Reich, Susanna.
Colón, Raúl, illus. see Shelton, Paula Young.
Colón, Raúl, illus. see Weatherford, Carole Boston.
Colón, Raúl, illus. see Wilson, Karma.
Colón, Raúl, illus. see Winter, Jonah.
Colonial Williamsburg Foundation Staff, jt. auth. see Kostyal, Karen.
Colorado Historical Society Staff, ed. Civil War Scrapbook: I Was There Too! (p. 325)
Colorado, Papa. Nui & Kiwi's Fantastic Adventures. (p. 1270)
Coloring Books for Adults, jt. auth. see Gottesman, Eric.
Coloring Books for Adults, jt. auth. see Noble, Marty.
Coloring Books for Adults, jt. auth. see Snozek, Lee Anne.
Coloring Books for Adults, jt. auth. see Stegenga, Wil.
Coloring Books for Adults, jt. auth. see Wik, John.
Coloring Books for Grownups Staff, jt. auth. see Elder, Jeremy.
Coloring Books Staff, jt. auth. see Bulleman, Curtis David.
Coloring Books Staff, jt. auth. see Crossling, Nick.
Coloring Books Staff, jt. auth. see David, Hop.
Coloring Books Staff, jt. auth. see Donahue, Peter.
Coloring Books Staff, jt. auth. see Dutton, Michael.
Coloring Books Staff, jt. auth. see Elder, Jeremy.
Coloring Books Staff, jt. auth. see Green, John.
Coloring Books Staff, jt. auth. see Laberis, Stephanie.
Coloring Books Staff, jt. auth. see Mazurkiewicz, Jessica.
Coloring Books Staff, jt. auth. see Noble, Marty.
Coloring Books Staff, jt. auth. see O'Toole, Patrick.
Coloring Books Staff, jt. auth. see Petruccio, Steven James.
Coloring Books Staff, jt. auth. see Pomaska, Anna.
Coloring Books Staff, jt. auth. see Rechlin, Ted.
Coloring Books Staff, jt. auth. see Roytman, Arkady.
Coloring Books Staff, jt. auth. see Schmidt, Carol.
Coloring Books Staff, jt. auth. see Skiles, Janet.
Coloring Books Staff, jt. auth. see Soffer, Ruth.
Coloring Books Staff, jt. auth. see Sovak, Jan.
Coloring Books Staff, jt. auth. see Stegenga, Wil.
Coloring Books Staff, jt. auth. see Toufexis, George.
Coloring Books Staff, jt. auth. see Walker, Sylvia.
Coloring Books Staff, jt. auth. see Zourelias, Diana.
Colossal, Eric. Rutabaga: The Adventure Chef. (p. 1498)
—Rutabaga the Adventure Chef (p. 1498)
Colough, Barbara. Tips for JAKS Mathematics Weekly Problem Solving. (p. 1757)
Colozza Cocca, Lisa, jt. auth. see Corporate Contibutor Staff.
Colozza Cocca, Lisa, jt. auth. see Smith, Paula.
Colquhoun, Christine. Pick-a-WooWoo - A Child Called Indigo: Follow your heart, you are Unique! (p. 1354)
—Pick-a-WooWoo - the Little Sparkle in Me: My Sparkle Is A Gift to Feel Hear & See Colquhoun, Christine, illus. (p. 1354)
Colson, A. W., illus. see Glenn, Judith.
Colson, Charles. Fundamentals: Creation vs. Evolution, Real Story Teach Pack. (p. 649)
Colson, Mary. Action Poems (p. 10)
—Albert Einstein & Sir Arthur Eddington. (p. 34)
—Australia (p. 116)
—Being a Makeup Artist. (p. 160)
—Beyoncé: A Life in Music. (p. 173)
—Bigfoot & the Yeti (p. 185)
—Bigfoot & the Yeti King, Chris, illus. (p. 185)
—Charles Darwin & Alfred Russel Wallace. (p. 292)
—Chinese Culture (p. 307)
—Coping with Absent Parents (p. 365)
—Coping with Unemployment (p. 365)
—Crumbling Earth: Erosion & Landslides (p. 386)
—Destroy after Reading: The World of Secret Codes. (p. 431)
—Earth Erupts: Volcanoes. (p. 495)
—Environment (p. 531)
—Fighting AIDS. (p. 585)
—Fighting Polio. (p. 586)
—Forest Furnace: Wild Fires (p. 618)
—France (p. 627)
—Germany (p. 666)
—Get Inventing! (p. 667)
—New Zealand (p. 1249)
—Race to Feed the Hungry. (p. 1431)
—Shaky Ground: Earthquakes. (p. 1559)
—Sports Poems (p. 1633)
—Wales (p. 1853)
—What Happens If the Ozone Disappears? (p. 1886)
—What Happens If the Rain Forests Disappear? (p. 1886)
Colson, Mary, jt. auth. see Ganeri, Anita.
Colson, Mary, jt. auth. see Guillain, Charlotte.
Colson, Mary & Throp, Claire. Digital Music: A Revolution in Music. (p. 439)
Colson, Rob. Motorbikes. (p. 1179)
—Ultimate Survivor Guide for Kids. (p. 1810)
Colson, Rob Scott. Aston Martin. (p. 108)
—BMW. (p. 204)
—Bone Collection: Animals. (p. 208)
—Ferrari. (p. 582)
—Helicopters. (p. 763)
—Jaguar. (p. 905)
—Lamborghini. (p. 972)
—Porsche. (p. 1386)
—Tanks & Military Vehicles. (p. 1705)
—Trucks. (p. 1791)
—Warships. (p. 1859)
Colson, Rob Scott & de la Bédoyère, Camilla. Bone Collection: Skulls. Doyle, Sandra, illus. (p. 208)
Colston, Pati. Perfect Just As I Am: The Story of Me. (p. 1342)
Colt, James P. & Rogers, Marcus K. Cyberpredators. (p. 396)
Colton, Ellie, illus. see Elkins, Stephen.
Colton, Timothy J., ed. see Bailey, Diane.
Colton, Timothy J., ed. see Davidson, Tish.
Colton, Timothy J., ed. see Gelletly, LeeAnne.
Colton, Timothy J., ed. see Heits, Rudolph T.
Colum, Padraic. Adventures of Odysseus & Tales of Troy. (p. 21)
—Adventures of Odysseus & the Tale of Troy. Pogány, Willy, illus. (p. 21)
—Adventures of Odysseus & the Tales of Troy. (p. 21)
—Children of Odin: The Book of Northern Myths. Pogány, Willy, illus. (p. 302)
—Children's Homer: The Adventures of Odysseus & the Tale of Troy. (p. 303)
—Children's Homer: The Adventures of Odysseus & the Tale of Troy. Pogány, Willy, illus. (p. 303)
—Golden Fleece: And the Heroes Who Lived Before Achilles. Pogány, Willy, illus. (p. 694)
—Golden Fleece & the Heroes Who Lived Before Achilles. Pogány, Willy, illus. (p. 694)
—King of Ireland's Son. Pogány, Willy, illus. (p. 959)
—Story of the Golden Fleece. Pogány, Willy, illus. (p. 1661)
Colum, Padraic, jt. auth. see Padraic.
Colum, Padraic & Pogány, Willy. Adventures of Odysseus & the Tale of Troy. (p. 21)
—Children of Odin the Book of Northern Myths. (p. 302)
Columbin, Corey, illus. see Wigden, Susan.
Columbro, Judy. Gift of Rainbows. Scottorosano, Deborah, illus. (p. 675)
—Gift That Grows. Scottorosano, Deborah, illus. (p. 675)
Columbus, Chris & Vizzini, Ned. Battle of the Beasts. (p. 146)
—House of Secrets. (p. 803)
—House of Secrets. Call, Greg, illus. (p. 803)
—House of Secrets: Battle of the Beasts. Call, Greg, illus. (p. 803)
Columbus, Christopher, jt. auth. see Banacloche, Julieta.
Columbus, Curt, jt. auth. see Campbell, Marilyn.
Colver, Anne. Nobody's Birthday. Bileck, Marvin, illus. (p. 1262)
Colville, Lucy & Magninie, Betty. Ombu - A Ghost Story. (p. 1288)
Colvin, Adele. Donkey of Tarsus: His Tales about the Apostle Paul Carmichael, Peyton, illus. (p. 466)
Colvin, Adele Bibb. Donkey's Easter Tale Carmichael, Peyton, illus. (p. 466)
Colvin, Denise. Born in My Heart: A Plane, a Car, & a Train. (p. 214)
Colvin, Denise Marie. Suzy's Big Dream Comes True. (p. 1688)
Colvin, Helen W. Shell Quilt. (p. 1564)
Colvin, L. Living World Encyclopedia. (p. 1042)
Colvin, L. & Speare, E. Living World Encyclopedia. (p. 1042)
Colvin, Layne. Augustus' Bath. (p. 115)
Colvin, S. R. R. Krybosian Stairpath: Magnetic Reversal. (p. 968)
Colwell, Emerson/Mylon, Jr. Fisher Cat. Colwell, Emerson/Mylon, Jr., illus. (p. 598)
Colwell, Todd. Get Real about Relationships: Leader's Guide. (p. 668)
Coman, Carolyn. Big House. Shepperson, Rob, illus. (p. 181)
—Many Stones. (p. 1089)
—Memory Bank. Shepperson, Rob, illus. (p. 1126)
—Sneaking Suspicions. Shepperson, Rob, illus. (p. 1597)
—What Jamie Saw. (p. 1891)
Comaroto, Maryanne. Skinny, Tan & Rich: Unraveling the Myth. (p. 1585)
Combel Editorial Staff. Bella Durmiente. Delclòs, Jordi Vila, illus. (p. 162)
—Musicos de Bremen. Steinmeyer, Petra, illus. (p. 1194)
—Pedrito y el Rey Gloton. Ruiz, Margarita & Ruiz Abello, Margarita, illus. (p. 1334)
—Princesa de Verdad. Ruiz, Margarita & Ruiz Abello, Margarita, illus. (p. 1402)
—Ruisenor. Ruiz, Margarita & Ruiz Abello, Margarita, illus. (p. 1494)
—Vendedora de Fósforos. Ruiz, Margarita & Ruiz Abello, Margarita, illus. (p. 1835)
—Zapatos Bailarines. Ruiz, Margarita & Ruiz Abello, Margarita, illus. (p. 1985)
Combel Editorial Staff, jt. auth. see Andersen, Hans Christian.
Combel Editorial Staff & árabe, Cuento popular. Ali Baba y Los Cuarenta Ladrones. Ruiz, Margarita, illus. (p. 39)
Combel Editorial Staff & catalán, Cuento popular. Castanera. Rius, Maria, illus. (p. 276)
—Ratita Presumida. Curto, Rosa María, illus. (p. 1440)
Combel Editorial Staff & Esopo. Leon y el Raton. (p. 992)
Combel Editorial Staff & Menotti, Gian Carlo. Amahal y los tres Reyes. Ruiz, Margarita, illus. (p. 52)
Combel Editorial Staff & Samaniego, Félix María. Lechera. Póveda Piérola, Mabel, illus. (p. 987)
Combel Editorial Staff, et al. Cuento de la Lechera. Ruiz, Margarita, illus. (p. 389)
—Ricitos de Oro. Espluga, Maria, illus. (p. 1470)
Comber, L. More Oriental Stories. (p. 1174)
—Oriental Stories. (p. 1303)
Combres, Élisabeth & Tanaka, Shelley. Broken Memory: A Novel of Rwanda (p. 230)
Combs, Bradley, illus. see Tuttle, Mark.
Combs, Jan Marie. Forever Garden. (p. 619)
Combs, Jeffery. Psychologically Unemployable: Life on Your Terms. Laut, Phil, ed. (p. 1413)
Combs, Kathy, jt. auth. see Griffin, Kitty.
Combs, Katie. Present Is the Future: A Kids' Christmas Musical about the Gift of Hope. (p. 1396)
Combs, M. Gutter Dreams: Inside My Glass Garden. (p. 733)
Combs, Maggie. How to Analyze the Works of F. Scott Fitzgerald. (p. 814)
—How to Analyze the Works of John Adams. (p. 814)
—Postwar United States. (p. 1388)
Combs, Paul, illus. see Scarff, Ruth.
Combs, Sarah. Breakfast Served Anytime. (p. 225)
Combs, Sharon, jt. auth. see Silveira, Terri.
Comden, Betty & Green, Adolph. What's New at the Zoo? Foster, Travis, illus. (p. 1898)
Comeau, Ceara. Adventures of the Young & Curious. (p. 24)
Comeau, Joey. Ninja-Rella. Lozano, Omar, illus. (p. 1256)
Comeau, Joey & Holmes, Mike. Bravest Warriors Holmes, Mike, illus. (p. 223)
Comeau, Joey, et al. Far Out Fairy Tales. Frampton, Otis et al, illus. (p. 572)
Comeaux, Tom. Molly's Pollywogs. (p. 1161)
Comella, Angels. Hablemos de Dios. (p. 735)
—Let's Talk about God/Hablemos de Dios. Twomey, Lisa A., tr. from SPA. (p. 1001)
Comella, Maria Angeles & Seix, Merce. Tarde con Joan Oro. (p. 1706)
Comelles, Salvador. Cuentame un Cuento Decis, Anne, illus. (p. 389)
Comenole, Bob. Long Night of Clement C. Craggogre: A Christmas Novel. (p. 1047)
Comer, Arthur L., Jr. Beginner's Guide to Successfully Growing Tillandsias - Commonly known as Air Plants. (p. 159)
Comer, Brigitte Renee. Little Hopping Frog. (p. 1029)
Comerford, Lynda B. Rissa Bartholomew's Declaration of Independence. (p. 1475)
Comès, Didier. Lágrimas del Tigre. (p. 971)
Comet, Renee, photos by see Maze, Stephanie, ed.
Comfort, Louise. Fairy Phones Counter Display (p. 563)
Comfort, Louise, illus. see Bateson, Maggie.
Comfort, Louise, illus. see Bruzzone, Catherine & Martineau, Susan.
Comfort, Louise, illus. see Bruzzone, Catherine & Martinneau, Susan.
Comfort, Louise, illus. see Bruzzone, Catherine & Millar, Louise.
Comfort, Louise, illus. see Bruzzone, Catherine, et al.
Comfort, Louise, tr. see Bruzzone, Catherine & Martinneau, Susan.
Comfort, Mike, illus. see Matchette, Katharine E.
Comfort, Philip. Rescued Retriever. (p. 1462)
Comfort, Ray. Scratch & Sniff. Hohnstadt, Cedric, illus. (p. 1532)
—What Your Nose Shows. Hohnstadt, Cedric, illus. (p. 1896)
Comikers. Pen & Ink. (p. 1336)
Coming, Soon. Gospel on Five Fingers: The Story of Mother Theresa Gosselin, Katie & Bono, Ignacio, trs. (p. 703)
Comings, David E. Did Man Create God? Is Your Spiritual Brain at Peace with Your Thinking Brain? (p. 436)
Comino, Sandra. Casita Azul Zeller, Beatriz & Wald, Susana, trs. (p. 276)
Comins, Andy, illus. see Heos, Bridget.
Comins, Andy, illus. see Turner, Pamela S.
Cominskey, Michael J. Number System & Common & Decimal Fractions (p. 1271)
Comire, S. Joshua & Porter, Malcolm. Atlas of Australia & the Pacific. (p. 112)
Comley, Kathlyn. My Sugar Bear. Platt, Robert, illus. (p. 1219)
Comley, Kathryn. Follow God. Lane, Ranae, illus. (p. 612)
—God Made My Hands. Wacker, Ranae, illus. (p. 690)
—Know & Remember all These Things. Lane, Ranae, illus. (p. 965)
—That's How I Found God. Lane, Ranae, illus. (p. 1726)
Commander X. William Cooper: Death of a Conspiracy Salesman! Survivalist! Patriot! Fanatic? (p. 1933)
Commers, Judy, jt. auth. see Clark, Brenda.
Commey, Pusch Komiete. Tofi's Fire Dance: An Extraordinary African Story. (p. 1761)
Common Core Staff, creator. Higher Scores on Reading & Language Arts Standardized Tests, Grade 4. (p. 779)
Common, Gabriel. Demon of Basile High: The Return of Cassius. (p. 426)
Communication Design (Firm) Staff, illus. see Shaskan, Trisha Speed.
Comora, Madeleine. Rembrandt & Titus: Artist & Son. Locker, Thomas, illus. (p. 1459)
Comora, Madeleine, jt. auth. see Arnold, Caroline.
Comora, Madeleine, jt. auth. see Chandra, Deborah.
Comotto, Agustín. Selva Azul. (p. 1550)
Compagnucci, Veronica M. Emily Finds Her Voice. (p. 518)
Compass Point Books, jt. auth. see Skog, Jason.
Compass Point Books Staff. Global Connections (p. 684)
Compass Point Books Staff, jt. auth. see Anderson, Dale.
Compass Point Books Staff, jt. auth. see Basel, Roberta.
Compass Point Books Staff, jt. auth. see Baumgart, Brian.
Compass Point Books Staff, jt. auth. see Burgan, Michael.
Compass Point Books Staff, jt. auth. see Byrne, Paul J.
Compass Point Books Staff, jt. auth. see Cantwell, Rebecca.

C

Compass Point Books Staff, jt. auth. see Cooper, Sharon Katz.
Compass Point Books Staff, jt. auth. see Dargie, Richard.
Compass Point Books Staff, jt. auth. see Englar, Mary.
Compass Point Books Staff, jt. auth. see Haugen, Brenda.
Compass Point Books Staff, jt. auth. see Heinrichs, Ann.
Compass Point Books Staff, jt. auth. see Jones, Caryn Gracey.
Compass Point Books Staff, jt. auth. see McKissack, Lisa Beringer.
Compass Point Books Staff, jt. auth. see Nobleman, Marc Tyler.
Compass Point Books Staff, jt. auth. see Shores, Lori.
Compass Point Books Staff, jt. auth. see Somervill, Barbara A.
Compass Point Books Staff, jt. auth. see Staton, Hilarie.
Compass Point Books Staff, jt. auth. see Stille, Darlene R.
Compass Point Books Staff & Conaway, Judith. Brown V. Board of Education: The Case for Integration (p. 232)
Compendium Inc. Never Quit - Thoughts to Inspire the Will to Win. (p. 1243)
Compendium Inc, creator. My Artwork. (p. 1196)
—My Writing. (p. 1222)
Comperchio, Shheila. Club House & the Gang. (p. 335)
Compere, Janet, illus. see Davidson, Margaret.
Compestine, Vinson, jt. auth. see Compestine, Ying Chang.
Compestine, Ying Chang. Boy Dumplings. Yamasaki, James, illus. (p. 217)
—Crouching Tiger. Nascimbene, Yan, illus. (p. 385)
—D Is for Dragon Dance. Xuan, YongSheng, illus. (p. 397)
—Real Story of Stone Soup. Jorisch, Stéphane, illus. (p. 1449)
—Revolution Is Not a Dinner Party. (p. 1466)
—Runaway Wok: A Chinese New Year Tale. Serra, Sebastia, illus. (p. 1496)
Compestine, Ying Chang & Compestine, Vinson. Secrets of the Terra-Cotta Soldier. (p. 1546)
Compoint, Stéphane. Buried Treasures: Uncovering Secrets of the Past. (p. 243)
Compo-Pratt, Paula. BooBoo & the Land of Mists & Dreams. (p. 210)
Comport, Sally Wern, illus. see Bartlett, Robert Merrill.
Comport, Sally Wern, illus. see Bruchac, Joseph.
Comport, Sally Wern, illus. see Coury, Tina Nichols.
Comport, Sally Wern, illus. see Davis, Gibbs.
Comport, Sally Wern, illus. see Frederick, Heather Vogel.
Comport, Sally Wern, illus. see Hood, Susan.
Comport, Sally Wern, illus. see Levy, Elizabeth.
Comport, Sally Wern, illus. see Malcolm, Jahnna N.
Comport, Sally Wern, illus. see Nickerson, Sara.
Comport, Sally Wern, illus. see Roop, Peter & Roop, Connie.
Comport, Sally Wern, illus. see Stevenson, Robert Louis.
Comport, Sally Wern, illus. see Watkins, Angela Farris.
Compton, Annette, illus. see Sasso, Sandy Eisenberg.
Compton, Brian L., illus. see Lindsey, Ms. Elanna T.
Compton, Carrie. Alaska's Wildlife. Ember, Dave, illus. (p. 34)
Compton, Dawn. Grand Entry. Kollman, Carrie, illus. (p. 707)
—Leave 'Em Standing. (p. 986)
Compton, Donna, illus. see Koenig, Albert.
Compton, Leanne, et al. Jump Start 7 & 8: Health & Physical Education. (p. 934)
Compton, Peggy. Captain Johnnie (p. 264)
Compton, Shanna. Down Spooky: Poems. (p. 474)
Compton, Zella & Swainson, Jess. Ten Rules of Skimming. (p. 1719)
Comrie, Bernard, et al. Atlas of Languages. (p. 112)
Comrie, Margaret S. Heroes of Castle Bretten. (p. 773)
Comstock, Chris, illus. see Susedik, Tina.
Comstock, Eric, jt. auth. see Sadler, Marilyn.
Comtesse, Gavin. Hamish & the Terrible Poo. (p. 739)
Comyns, Barbara. Juniper Tree. (p. 936)
Conahan, Carolyn Digby, illus. see Baum, L. Frank.
Conahan, Carolyn Digby, illus. see Bayrock, Fiona.
Conahan, Carolyn Digby, illus. see Blackaby, Susan.
Conahan, Carolyn Digby, illus. see Kitch, Anne E.
Conahan, Carolyn Digby, illus. see Lund, Deb.
Conahan, Carolyn Digby, illus. see Lund, Deborah.
Conahan, Carolyn Digby, illus. see Norman, Kim.
Conami, Shoko. Shinobi Life (p. 1567)
Conan, Sally Anne. Sleepy Time Blessings. Rutten, Nicole, illus. (p. 1590)
Conant, Susan Sens. Lewis & Clark's Journey of Discovery: A Guide for Young Explorers. Lynn, Rick, illus. (p. 1004)
Conard, Vincent, illus. see Walters, Nicole Y.
Conaway, Jim, illus. see Elkins, Stephen.
Conaway, Judith, jt. auth. see Compass Point Books Staff.
Conboy, Fiona, jt. auth. see Jermyn, Leslie.
Conboy, Fiona & NgCheong-Lum, Roseline. France. (p. 627)
Concannon, Sue, illus. see Ruth, Nick.
Concepcion, Jorge L., creator. Tale of Innovation & Persistence. (p. 1699)
Conceptis Puzzles. Dots! Super Connect-the-Dots Puzzles. (p. 472)
—Sneaky Picture Mazes. (p. 1597)
Concha, López Narváez, jt. auth. see López Narváez, Concha.
Concha, López Narváez, jt. auth. see Narváez, Concha López.
Conchie, Kathryn. I Am a Mole, & I Live in a Hole. Top That Publishing Staff, ed. (p. 832)
Concord, Juliet. I Am Kind. (p. 833)
—I Am Kind / Soy Amable. (p. 833)
Concord, Parker & Hayhurst, Chris. Lungs in 3D. (p. 1066)
Concordia Publishing Staff, ed. One Hundred Bible Stories. (p. 1295)
Concordia International School Shanghai. Stories from Room 113: International Adventures. (p. 1654)
Concordia Publishing House, compiled by. Confirmation Remembered. (p. 357)
Concordia Publishing House, creator. Chosen! Won! Devotions for Teens by Teens. (p. 311)
—Exploring God's Word with Maps. (p. 552)
—Exploring God's Word with Puzzles: Grades 3-8. (p. 552)
—Happy Birthday: God's Blessings to You! (p. 744)
Concordia Publishing House Staff, compiled by. Imagine That! Devotions for Teens by Teens. (p. 861)
Concordia Publishing House Staff, contrib. by. Child's Garden of Prayer. (p. 305)
Concordia Publishing Staff. Story of Easter: Giant Flap Book. (p. 1658)
Cond, Sandie, jt. auth. see Downey, Glen R.
Conde, Carmen. Despertar. (p. 430)
Condé, J. M., illus. see Paine, Albert Bigelow.
Conde, Manuel, illus. see Madonna, Lenae.
Condé, Maryse. Reves Amers. (p. 1466)
Condenzio, John. Cocoa the Witch Cat. (p. 337)
Condenzio, Mary. Mouse & the Star. Long, Paulette Rich, illus. (p. 1182)
—Oliver. (p. 1285)
Conder, Jen, jt. auth. see Griffith, Michelle.
Condi-Babich, Kris. 4Cam. us. (p. 1992)
Condie, Ally. Atlantia. (p. 112)
—Being Sixteen. (p. 161)
—Crossed. (p. 385)
—First Day. (p. 594)
—Freshman for President. (p. 636)
—Juntos. (p. 936)
—Matched. (p. 1104)
—Reached. (p. 1442)
—Reunion. (p. 1465)
—Yearbook. (p. 1969)
Condie, Catherine. Whirl of the Wheel. (p. 1912)
Condon, Bill. Confessions of a Liar, Thief & Failed Sex God. (p. 356)
—Dream Team (p. 484)
—Give Me Truth. (p. 681)
—How to Survive in the Jungle by the Person Who Knows. (p. 822)
—Human Calculator. (p. 826)
—Joker. Smith, Craig, illus. (p. 924)
—No Worries. (p. 1261)
—Pipeline News. (p. 1361)
—Planet Puzzle. (p. 1368)
—Race to the Moon. (p. 1431)
—Riley & the Fantastic Plan. Hopgood, Andrew, illus. (p. 1472)
—Riley & the Treasure. Hopgood, Andrew, illus. (p. 1472)
—Riley Clowns Around. Hopgood, Andrew, illus. (p. 1472)
—Riley Versus the Giant Banana. Hopgood, Andrew, illus. (p. 1472)
—Simple Things. Norling, Beth, illus. (p. 1578)
—Straight Line to My Heart. (p. 1664)
—Time Travelers: The Jungle Goes Bananas, Sherwood Forest Goes to Pieces, the Wild West Goes Crazy. (p. 1753)
Condon, Tom. Sandman: Stories to Read to Children. (p. 1511)
Condra, Estelle. See the Ocean. (p. 1547)
Condra, Janelle. Daily Editing Practice, Grade 1. (p. 399)
Condy, Roy, jt. auth. see Sadu, Itah.
Cone, Breanna. Adventures of Pirate & Black Bart. (p. 21)
Cone, Carl. There's a Season for All. Cone, Carl, illus. (p. 1731)
Cone, Carl, illus. see Shu, Sammy.
Cone, David & Cone, Marina. Adventures of Goose & Oscar: Camping Fun: Camping Fun with Goose & Oscar. (p. 18)
Cone, Marina, jt. auth. see Cone, David.
Cone, Molly. Hello, Hello, Are You There, God? Kaye, Rosalind Charney, illus. (p. 764)
—Hello, Hello, Are You There God?, Grades Preschool-3. Kaye, Rosalind Charney, illus. (p. 764)
Coné, Robert. Candy Bandit Strikes Again! Baker, David, illus. (p. 261)
Cone, Stephanie M. Grandma's Moving In! Sample, Matthew & Sample, Matthew, illus. (p. 709)
Cone, William, illus. see Moore, Clement C.
Conerly, Lawrence. Babies E. Names. (p. 124)
Cones, Harold, et al. Zenith Radio, the Glory Years 1936-1945 (p. 1986)
Conescu, Nancy, ed. see Hagen, Bethany.
Cone-Watson, Arianna. Fooey Fruits & Fickle Foods. (p. 614)
Coney, Malachy, jt. auth. see Lobdell, Scott.
Confalone, Chelsea, jt. auth. see Confalone, Nick.
Confalone, Chelsea & Confalone, Nick. Helicopters. (p. 763)
Confalone, Nick, jt. auth. see Confalone, Chelsea.
Confalone, Nick & Confalone, Chelsea. Ocean Monsters. (p. 1276)
Confederated Salish and Kootenai Tribes Staff. Beaver Steals Fire: A Salish Coyote Story. Sandoval, Sam, illus. (p. 155)
—Bull Trout's Gift: By the Confederated Salish & Kootenai Tribes. (p. 240)
Conford, Ellen. And This Is Laura. (p. 71)
—Annabel the Actress Starring in Camping It Up. Andriani, Renee W., illus. (p. 85)
—Annabel the Actress Starring in Just a Little Extra. Andriani, Renee W., illus. (p. 85)
—Annabel the Actress Starring in the Hound of the Barkervilles. Andriani, Renee W., illus. (p. 85)
—Case for Jenny Archer. Palmisciano, Diane & Brooks, Erik, illus. (p. 273)
—Jenny Archer, Author. Palmisciano, Diane & Brooks, Erik, illus. (p. 913)
—Job for Jenny Archer. Palmisciano, Diane & Brooks, Erik, illus. (p. 919)
—To All My Fans, with Love, From Sylvie. (p. 1758)
—What's Cooking, Jenny Archer? Palmisciano, Diane & Brooks, Erik, illus. (p. 1897)
Conforti, John W., illus. see Evelyn.
Conforti, John W., tr. see Evelyn.
Conforto, Lisa. Very Compromising Adventures of Thumby Blackstone (p. 1837)
Conger, Holli. Cultural Holidays (p. 391)
—Shapes. (p. 1560)
Conger, Holli, illus. see Anderson, Sheila.
Conger, Holli, illus. see Bellisario, Gina.
Conger, Holli, illus. see Bullard, Lisa.
Conger, Holli, illus. see Feldman, Thea.
Conger, Holli, illus. see Gellman, Ellie B.
Conger, Holli, illus. see Koster, Gloria.
Conger, Holli, illus. see Marsico, Katie.
Conger, Holli, illus. see Owens, L. L.
Conger, Holli, illus. see Rustad, Martha E. H.
Conger, Holli, illus. see Rustad, Martha.
Conger, Holli, illus. see Slade, Suzanne.
Conger, Holli, intro. Little Chef. (p. 1026)
Conger, Hollil, illus. see Bullard, Lisa.
Congress (U.S.), Joint Committee on Printing Staff, compiled by. Our Flag. (p. 1308)
Congressional Quarterly, Inc. Staff. CQ's Guide to Current American Government: Fall 2005. (p. 375)
Congreve, William. Comedies. (p. 347)
—Way of the World. Perry, Henry Ten Eyck, ed. (p. 1864)
Coniaris, Anthony M. Nicene Creed for Young People. (p. 1250)
Conigliaro, Phil. Colossal Paper Machines: Make 10 Giant Models That Move! (p. 346)
Coniglio, John. Cat Who Slept All Day: What Happens While the Cat Sleeps. Key, Pamela, illus. (p. 278)
Coniglio, Rebecca Perlman. Lily's Little Life Lessons: Lily's Laces. Mundy, Jen, illus. (p. 1018)
Conklin, Alice. Crown for a Princess. (p. 386)
—Jacob & Caleb's Great Adventure. (p. 904)
Conklin, Barbara Gardner, jt. auth. see Gardner, Robert.
Conklin, Blane. Barack Obama: President of the United States. (p. 137)
—Leaders of the Middle East. (p. 981)
—Modern Middle East. (p. 1158)
Conklin, Jennie Maria. Miss Prudence: A Story of Two Girls' Lives. (p. 1152)
—Miss Prudence A Story of Two Girls' Lives. (p. 1152)
Conklin, Lin. Impact of Belief: Learning to Take Control of Your Life. (p. 862)
Conklin, Paul, photos by see Ashabranner, Brent.
Conklin, Tom. Comprehension Cliffhanger Stories: 15 Action-Packed Stories That Invite Students to Infer, Visualize, & Summarize to Predict the Ending of Each Story. (p. 354)
—Soar! All about Pterosaurs. (p. 1603)
Conklin, Wendy. Amigos Planos Viajan por el Mundo. (p. 65)
—Ancient Civilizations - China - India - Africa - Mesopotamia: All-in-One Resource with Background Information, Map Activities, Simulations & Games, & a Read-Aloud Play to Support Comprehension & Critical Thinking in Social Studies, Grades 5 & Up. (p. 68)
—Battles of the Civil War. (p. 147)
—Benjamin Franklin. (p. 164)
—Christopher Columbus. (p. 316)
—Civil Rights Movement. (p. 325)
—Civil War Leaders. (p. 325)
—Cold War. (p. 339)
—Cold War Leaders. (p. 339)
—Digestion & Using Food. (p. 438)
—DNA. (p. 456)
—Early Congresses. (p. 493)
—Earth's Cycles. (p. 498)
—Eleanor Roosevelt. (p. 508)
—Exploring the New World. (p. 554)
—Life Cycles. (p. 1009)
—Martin Luther King Jr. (p. 1097)
—Mayas, Aztecs, Incas: All-in-One Resource with Background Information, Map Activities, Simulations & Games, & a Read-Aloud Play to Support Comprehension & Critical Thinking in Social Studies. (p. 1113)
—Mayas, Incas, & Aztecs. (p. 1113)
—Moctezuma: Aztec Ruler (p. 1157)
—Robert E. Lee. (p. 1479)
—Rock Cycle. (p. 1482)
—Strategies for Developing Higher-Order Thinking Skills: Grades 6-12. (p. 1666)
—Strategies for Developing Higher-Order Thinking Skills, Grade K-2. (p. 1666)
—Surviving the Wild Backyard. (p. 1687)
—Ulysses S. Grant. (p. 1810)
—Winston Churchill. (p. 1937)
Conklin, Wendy, jt. auth. see Herwick Rice, Dona.
Conklin, Wendy, jt. auth. see Zamosky, Lisa.
Conklin, Wendy & Lee, Gisela. Confucius: Chinese Philosopher (p. 357)
Conkling, Fleur. Bingity-Bangity School Bus. Wood, Ruth, illus. (p. 188)
Conkling, Jon, ed. see Smith, Brian.
Conkling, Keri. Glove of Their Own. Lambiase, Lauren, illus. (p. 685)
Conkling, Neil & Philip, Hilda. Bird's Way of Singing. (p. 192)
Conkling, Philip, jt. ed. see Platt, D. D.
Conkling, Winifred. Passenger on the Pearl: The True Story of Emily Edmonson's Flight from Slavery. (p. 1326)
—Sylvia & Aki. (p. 1692)
Conlan, Craig, illus. see Scott-Cameron, Nancy.
Conlan, Kathy & Canadian Museum of Nature Staff. Under the Ice: A Marine Biologist at Work. (p. 1813)
Conley, Autumn. Colby's Peace. (p. 338)
Conley, Cindy Taylor. For Little Louie Someday. (p. 615)
Conley, Connie. Alphabet Doggie Style. (p. 49)
Conley, Deane W. Angelino & Friends. (p. 74)
—Angelino Courage to Fly. (p. 74)
—Angelino Flies Again. (p. 74)
Conley, Eddie And Uchenna. Team Conley: Elaykim's Life Lessons for the Love of Music. (p. 1710)
Conley, Erin, ed. Dinomite. (p. 441)
—Madcap Mazes. (p. 1069)
—Zany Riddles. (p. 1985)
Conley, Erin Elisabeth. Crush: A Girl's Guide to Being Crazy in Love. (p. 386)
Conley, Erin Elisabeth, et al. Crap: How to Deal with Annoying Teachers, Bosses, Backstabbers, & Other Stuff That Stinks. (p. 376)
Conley, Jennise M. I Think There's a Monster under My Bed! (p. 846)
Conley, Kate. Cuba. (p. 388)
—South Africa. (p. 1616)
Conley, Kate A. Burmilla Cats. (p. 243)
—Joseph Priestly & the Discovery of Oxygen. (p. 926)
—Puerto Rican Americans. (p. 1414)
—Siberian Cats. (p. 1572)
—Turkish Van Cats. (p. 1797)
Conley, Mark W., et al, eds. Meeting the Challenge of Adolescent Literacy: Research We Have, Research We Need. (p. 1124)
Conley, Nia. Ray's School Daze. (p. 1441)
Conley, Robert J. Cherokee. (p. 298)
Conley, Robyn. Automobile. (p. 117)
—Motion Pictures. (p. 1179)
Conley, Stephanie, illus. see Heyman, Carly.
Conleyosb, Dolores. Bitsy's Strange Adventures: Bitsy Meets Miss Maple & Cassie Bitsy's New Friends. (p. 194)
Conliff, Marie. Muddy Tracks. (p. 1189)
Conlin, C. Unternehmen Deutsch: Arbeitsbuch. (p. 1823)
—Unternehmen Deutsch: Lehrbuch, Einsprachig. (p. 1823)
Conlin, Christy Ann & Lee, Jen SookFong. Dead Time & Shelter. (p. 417)
Conlin, Judy. Crissy,the Cross-Eyed Cat. (p. 383)
Conlin, Laura E. Winston's Wild Journeys: Live Outside Your Shell. (p. 1937)
Conlon, Linda L. Not Today. (p. 1267)
Conlon, Mara. Brainiac's Go Green! Activity Book. Klug, David, illus. (p. 222)
—Butterflies & Friends: An Art Activity Book for Adventurous Artists of All Ages. Zschock, Martha, illus. (p. 247)
—Chuggington: Braking Brewster. (p. 318)
—Chuggington - Wilson & the Ice Cream Fair. (p. 318)
—Nutcracker Ballet: A Book, Theater, & Paper Doll Foldout Play Set. Gershman, Jo, illus. (p. 1274)
—Ready, Set, Draw... under the Sea! Steckler, Kerren Barbas, illus. (p. 1447)
—Tonka Picture Clues: Working the Farm. (p. 1765)
Conlon, Mara, adapted by. Bill Hatches an Egg. (p. 186)
—Scratch & Sketch Wizard of Oz: An Art Activity Story Book for Artists on Both Sides of the Rainbow. (p. 1532)
Conlon-McKenna, Marita. Fields of Home. (p. 584)
—Girl Called Blue. (p. 678)
—Under the Hawthorn Tree. (p. 1813)
—Under the Hawthorn Tree. Teskey, Donald, illus. (p. 1813)
—Wildflower Girl. (p. 1931)
Conly, Jane Leslie. Impetuous R., Secret Agent. Leick, Bonnie, illus. (p. 862)
Conn, Alexandra, illus. see Fass, Tara.
Conn, Bruce. Curse of Durgan's Reef. (p. 394)
Conn, Peter. Adoption: A Brief Social & Cultural History. (p. 13)
Conn, Robert. Jesus Christ for Youth Leader (p. 915)
Conn, Robert A. Jesus Christ for Youth (p. 915)
Connally. Instructor's Manual & Test Bank to Accompany Functions Modeling Change. (p. 878)
—Instructor's Resource to Accompany Functions Modeling Change. (p. 878)
—Instructor's Solutions Manual to Accompany Functions Modeling Change. (p. 878)
Connally, Eric, et al. Functions Modeling Change, Test Bank: A Preparation for Calculus. (p. 649)
Connally, Perry L., Sr., illus. see Switzer, Vern.
Connatser, Scott. Excited about Pre-School. (p. 547)
Connaught, illus. see Haynes, M.
Connell, Del, et al. Christmas Parade Clark, John, ed. (p. 315)
Connell, J. Diane. Brain-Based Strategies to Reach Every Learner: Surveys, Questionnaires, & Checklists That Help You Identify Students' Strengths-Plus Engaging Brain-Based Lessons & Activities. (p. 221)
Connell, Jacqueline, illus. see Cook, Maureen McNamee.
Connell, Jane, jt. auth. see Spence, Nancy.
Connell, John. Halos of Fire: Enjoying a Life Filled with the Power of the Holy Spirit. (p. 739)
Connell, Julie. Adventures of Cutie Pie & Mr. Squishy. (p. 17)
Connell, Karen. Adventures of Katie & Sam: A Day to Fly (p. 19)
—Slow Down: The Adventures of Katie & Sam (p. 1591)
Connell, Kate. Hoping for Rain: The Dust Bowl Adventures of Patty & Earl Buckler. (p. 797)
—Servant to Abigail Adams: The Early American Adventures of Hannah Cooper. (p. 1552)
—Thirteen Colonies. (p. 1734)
—Yankee Blue or Rebel Grey? A Family Divided by the Civil War. (p. 1968)
Connell, Kate & Feresten, Nancy. Servant to Abigail Adams: The Early Colonial Adventures of Hannah Cooper. (p. 1552)
Connell, Kate & National Geographic Learning Staff. Dust Bowl Days. (p. 490)
Connell, Kate, et al. Spirit of a New Nation. (p. 1628)
Connell, Richard. Most Dangerous Game. (p. 1177)
Connell, Richard Edward. Most Dangerous Game. (p. 1177)
Connell, Rita S. One Gray Hippo. (p. 1295)
Connell, Rod. Silly Snake Rhymes: And the Real Stuff. (p. 1576)
Connell, Sarah & Nash, Kevin. Bates College College Prowler off the Record. (p. 143)
Connellan, Sue. Special Treasure. (p. 1623)
Connelly, Caitlin & Connelly, Nancy. Annabel Adams & the Puzzling Project. (p. 85)
Connelly, Claire K. Moxie. Jacobs, Joyce M., illus. (p. 1184)
Connelly, Elizabeth Russell. Nicotine= (p. 1251)
—Predatory Drugs = Busted! (p. 1395)
Connelly, Garrett. Construcao Do Tanques Do Ferrocimento. (p. 359)
—Construcción de Tanques de Ferrocemento: Segunda Edición. (p. 359)
—Ferrocement Tank Construction: English Metric Version. (p. 582)
Connelly, Gwen, illus. see Fischer, Carl.
Connelly, Gwen, illus. see Hillert, Margaret.
Connelly, Gwen, illus. see Leon, Carol Boyd.
Connelly, Gwen, illus. see Pankow, Valerie.
Connelly, Gwen, illus. see Schur, Maxine Rose.
Connelly, Jack. Christopher Columbus: Discovering the Americas. (p. 316)
—Discovering Mission Santa Bárbara. (p. 449)
—Ferdinand Magellan: Circumnavigating the Globe. (p. 581)
Connelly, Jack, jt. auth. see Ching, Jacqueline.
Connelly, Luella, jt. auth. see Williams, Rozanne Lanczak.

Connelly, Michael. Chasing the Dime. (p. 294)
—Closers. (p. 334)
—Darkness More Than Night. (p. 408)
—Echo Park. (p. 502)
—Last Coyote; Trunk Music; Angels Flight. (p. 977)
—Lost Light. (p. 1056)
—Narrows. (p. 1229)
Connelly, Nancy, jt. auth. see Connelly, Caitlin.
Connelly, Neil. Miracle Stealer. (p. 1148)
Connelly, Neil O. Alphabet. Thomburgh, Rebecca, illus. (p. 49)
—Colors. Thomburgh, Rebecca, illus. (p. 344)
—Miracle Stealer. (p. 1148)
—Numbers. Thomburgh, Rebecca, illus. (p. 1271)
—Shapes. Thomburgh, Rebecca, illus. (p. 1560)
Connelly, Peg. If the Forest Is Silent, Beware! (p. 854)
—Madman Hunts for Bigfoot. (p. 1070)
Connelly, Peggy. My Quirky, Oddball, Eccentric, Unpredictable Grandma. (p. 1217)
Connelly, Sheila, illus. see Ross Williamson, Hugh.
Connelly, Valerie. Arthur, the Christmas Elf: A Christmas Adventure. (p. 104)
—Goosh Gosh from the Lilac Kitchen & Other Childhood Stories. (p. 702)
Connelly, Wendy. Fiona the Firefly! (p. 589)
Connely, Chris L. & Vaughan, Mark. Alien from Earth. (p. 40)
Connely, Krystal. This Little Light. (p. 1737)
Conner, Bobbi. Unplugged Play: No Batteries. No Plugs. Pure Fun. Patacchiola, Amy, illus. (p. 1822)
Conner, Daniel. Tempest. Martin, Cynthia, illus. (p. 1717)
Conner, Deborah N. Bully Magnet. (p. 241)
Conner, Guy. Elizabeth & Parr. (p. 513)
Conner, Jimmie L. Adventures of Captain Computerman & His Sidekick Mouseman: The Saving of the Toy Websites. (p. 17)
Conner, John. Breaking the Spanish Barrier, Level I (Beginner), Teacher's Edition: The Language Series with All the Rules You Need to Know. Level I (p. 225)
—Breaking the Spanish Barrier, Level I (Beginner), Teacher Test Packet: The Language Series with All the Rules You Need to Know. (p. 225)
—Breaking the Spanish Barrier, Level I (Beginner), Self Learner Special: The Language Series with All the Rules You Need to Know. (p. 225)
—Breaking the Spanish Barrier, Level II (Intermediate), Student Edition: The Language with All the Rules You Need to Know. Level II (p. 225)
—Breaking the Spanish Barrier, Level II (Intermediate) / Teacher's Edition: The Language Series with All the Rules You Need to Know. Level II (p. 225)
—Breaking the Spanish Barrier, Level II (Intermediate), Teacher Test Packet: The Language Series with All the Rules You Need to Know. (p. 225)
—Breaking the Spanish Barrier, Level II (Intermediate), Self Learner Special: The Language Series with All the Rules You Need to Know. (p. 225)
—Breaking the Spanish Barrier, Level III IV AP (Advanced), Answer Key Booklet. (p. 225)
—Breaking the Spanish Barrier, Level III IV AP (Advanced), Teacher Test Packet. (p. 225)
Conner, John & Folts, Cathy. Breaking the Spanish Barrier, Advanced Level / Student Edition: The Language Series with All the Rules You Need to Know. Level III (p. 225)
—Breaking the Spanish Barrier, Advanced Level / Teacher's Edition: The Language Series with All the Rules You Need to Know. (p. 225)
Conner, John, et al. Breaking the French Barrier, Level I (Beginner), Answer Key Booklet: The Language Series with All the Rules You Need to Know. (p. 225)
Conner, John, Jr. Breaking the Spanish Barrier, Level II (Intermediate), Answer Key Booklet: The Language Series with All the Rules You Need to Know. (p. 225)
Conner, John, text. Breaking the Spanish Barrier, Level I (Beginner), Student Edition: The Language Series with All the Rules You Need to Know. (p. 225)
Conner, Kate. 10 Things for Teen Girls. (p. 1994)
—Enough: 10 Things We Should Tell Teenage Girls. (p. 531)
Conner, Mac. Ambrose. (p. 57)
Conner, Paula, illus. see Atkins, Jeannine.
Conner, Sharon Landsberg. Magnetizing Princess: A children's story that uses some of the most powerful tools available, to get more of what you Want. (p. 1076)
Conner, Wendy Simpson. Princess of the Moon. (p. 1404)
—Stuff, Stuff, I Want More Stuff. (p. 1670)
Conners, Beatrice. VeryVery Enchanted Kingdom (p. 1839)
Conners, Cathy. Let's Look at Soil. (p. 999)
Conners, Christine & Conners, Tim. Scout's Deck of Outdoor Recipe Cards. (p. 1532)
Conners, Daryle, jt. auth. see Allen, Elise.
Conners, Lauren. Stuffed Frog in Santa's Sack. (p. 1670)
Conners, Tim, jt. auth. see Conners, Christine.
Conness, Kari. Making Friends. (p. 1081)
Conness, Steven A. George Huck, the Founding of Huckville: The Huck Family Chronicles (p. 663)
Connick, Harry, Jr. Happy Elf. Andreasen, Dan, illus. (p. 745)
Connikie, Yvonne. Fashions of a Decade: The 1960s. (p. 576)
Conno, Gianni de, see De Conno, Gianni.
Connolly, Brian A. Allegheny River Christmas & Other Stories. (p. 46)
—Hawk. (p. 755)
—Wolf Journal: A Novel. (p. 1944)
Connolly, C J. Boomerang. (p. 213)
—Wil, Fitz, & a Flea Named T. (p. 1928)
Connolly, David, tr. see Stamatis, Alexis.
Connolly, Debbie & Danley, Laurie. Passport to Genre: A Literature Enrichment Guide. Mitchell, Judy, ed. (p. 1327)
Connolly, Ed. Summer Dance of the Fireflies. Flynn, Noel, illus. (p. 1674)
Connolly, Faye. Puddle Stomp. (p. 1414)
Connolly, Helen. Field Hockey: Rules, Tips, Strategy, & Safety. (p. 584)
Connolly, John. Book of Lost Things. (p. 211)
—Gates. (p. 658)
Connolly, Kate, tr. see Junge, Alexandra.
Connolly, Kate, tr. see Stamm, Peter & Bauer, Jutta.
Connolly, Lorraine. Bad, Bad Germs - Stay Away!!! (p. 131)
Connolly, MarcyKate. Monstrous. Young, Skottie, illus. (p. 1169)
Connolly, Megan B. Mommy, Mommy! Is This for Me? Mundy, Jen, illus. (p. 1162)
Connolly, Patrick. Adventures of Funny, the Amazing Fish-Bunny. (p. 18)
Connolly, Rachel, jt. auth. see Gendell, Megan.
Connolly, Randy, et al. Poison Ivy, Pets & People: Scratching the Poison Ivy, Oak & Sumac Itch. (p. 1377)
Connolly, Ryan. Tom's Field Trip. (p. 1765)
Connolly, Sean. Alcohol. (p. 35)
—Banks & Banking. (p. 136)
—Book of Potentially Catastrophic Science: 50 Experiments for Daring Young Scientists. (p. 211)
—Book of Totally Irresponsible Science: 64 Daring Experiments for Young Scientists. (p. 212)
—Botticelli. (p. 215)
—Cocaine. (p. 337)
—Communism. (p. 349)
—Democracy. (p. 425)
—Dictatorship. (p. 436)
—Earthquakes. (p. 497)
—Ecstasy. (p. 503)
—Famines & Droughts. (p. 569)
—French Revolution (p. 636)
—Fun on the Farm Joke Book. (p. 648)
—Fundamentalism. (p. 649)
—Getting the Message: Television & Radio. (p. 669)
—Greenpeace. (p. 723)
—Hysterical History Joke Book. (p. 831)
—Inhalants. (p. 874)
—Insurance. (p. 879)
—International Aid & Loans. (p. 880)
—International Red Cross. (p. 880)
—International Trade. (p. 880)
—Jolly Jungle Joke Book. (p. 924)
—Laugh Out Loud: The Silly Spells Joke Book. (p. 980)
—Marijuana. (p. 1094)
—Monarchy. (p. 1163)
—Money & Credit. (p. 1163)
—Money & Credit. (p. 1164)
—Movies & Video. (p. 1183)
—New Testament Miracles. (p. 1247)
—Newspapers & Magazines. (p. 1249)
—Out to Sea Joke Book. (p. 1312)
—Oxfam. (p. 1315)
—Paul Cezanne. (p. 1330)
—Political Messages & Propaganda. (p. 1380)
—Racial & Ethnic Equality. (p. 1432)
—Religious Freedom. (p. 1458)
—Rights at Work. (p. 1472)
—Stock Market. (p. 1651)
—Theocracy. (p. 1729)
—Tobacco. (p. 1760)
—UNICEF. (p. 1818)
—Unicef. (p. 1818)
—United Nations. (p. 1819)
—War. (p. 1857)
—World Health Organization. (p. 1955)
—World War I (p. 1958)
Connolly, Sean, jt. auth. see Barnham, Kay.
Connolly, Sean & Barnham, Kay. Animal Antics Joke Book. (p. 76)
—Funny Food Joke Book. (p. 649)
—Monster Fun Joke Book. (p. 1167)
—Outer Space Joke Book. (p. 1312)
—School's Cool Joke Book. (p. 1524)
—Silly Safari Joke Book. (p. 1576)
Connolly, Sean & Claybourne, Anna. Insurance. (p. 879)
Connolly, Sean & Harris, Joe. Crazy Computers Joke Book. (p. 377)
Connolly, Sean & Michelangelo Buonarroti. Michelangelo. (p. 1135)
Connolly, Sean & Monet, Claude. Claude Monet. (p. 329)
Connolly, Sean & Morgan, Sally. International Aid & Loans. (p. 880)
Connolly, Sean & Pipe, Jim. Banks & Banking. (p. 136)
—International Trade. (p. 880)
—Stock Market. (p. 1651)
Connolly, Timothy. Joy's Journey Home. Sullivan, Mary, illus. (p. 930)
Connolly, Tina. Seriously Wicked. (p. 1552)
Connor, Cathy & O'Haire, Daniel. Roadside Geology of Alaska. (p. 1477)
Connor, Chris, illus. see Farmer, Penelope.
Connor, D. E. L. Spirit Warriors: The Concealing. (p. 1629)
Connor, Daniel. MidSummer Night's Dream. Espinosa, Rod, illus. (p. 1139)
Connor, David. Archie & Billy in Monster Cave. (p. 95)
Connor, James. Surfing Summer. (p. 1685)
—Surfing Summers. (p. 1685)
Connor, Julie, illus. see Hathorn, Libby.
Connor, Leslie. Crunch. (p. 386)
—Miss Bridie Chose a Shovel. Azarian, Mary, illus. (p. 1151)
—Things You Kiss Goodbye. (p. 1734)
—Waiting for Normal. (p. 1853)
Connor, Lexi. B Magical #5: the Chocolate Meltdown. (p. 123)
—Cat-Astrophe. (p. 277)
—Runaway Spell. (p. 1496)
Connor, Michael, illus. see Dawson, Brianóg Brady.
Connor, Michael, illus. see Dawson, Brianog Brady.
Connor, Michael, illus. see Perdue, Gillian.
Connor, Michael, tr. see Dawson, Brianog Brady.
Connor, Naomi. Big Brown Eyes. (p. 180)
—I Am. (p. 831)
—Rainy Day Blues. (p. 1436)
Connor, Patrick M. Tree House. (p. 1783)
Connor, Peyton. Humpty Dumpty's Whole Story. (p. 827)
Connor, Robin, illus. see Cole, Bob.
Connor, Sarah, illus. see Williamson, Karen.
Connors, Bill. Aiden's Aquarium Adventure: Add Within 20. (p. 30)
Connors, Cathy. Let's Look at Soil. (p. 999)
Connors, Clare, ed. see Santora, L. Steven.
Connors, Colleen. Real Princess. (p. 1448)
Connors, Faith Raymond. Love, Midgie. Connors, Tracy D., ed. (p. 1060)
Connors, Jackie, ed. see Carey, Michael.
Connors, Jerrold. Now, Louie! Connors, Jerrold, illus. (p. 1269)
Connors, John. Ten Commandments for protecting Your Million Dollar Idea. (p. 1718)
Connors, Kathleen. Acadia National Park. (p. 7)
—Chameleons. (p. 289)
—Dinosaur Fossils. (p. 442)
—Everglades National Park. (p. 542)
—Geckos. (p. 659)
—Gila Monsters. (p. 676)
—Homophones at Home. (p. 794)
—Human Fossils. (p. 826)
—Iguanas. (p. 856)
—Insect Fossils. (p. 875)
—Komodo Dragons. (p. 966)
—Let's Explore the Great Basin. (p. 996)
—Let's Explore the Midwest. (p. 996)
—Let's Explore the Northeast. (p. 996)
—Let's Explore the Pacific Northwest. (p. 996)
—Let's Explore the Southeast. (p. 996)
—Opposites at the Park. (p. 1301)
—People of the Chesapeake Bay. (p. 1339)
—Petrified Forests. (p. 1348)
—Plants & Animals of the Chesapeake Bay. (p. 1369)
—Punctuation at the Game. (p. 1417)
—Rhyming on the Road. (p. 1468)
—Saying I'm Sorry. (p. 1519)
—Sea Creature Fossils. (p. 1534)
—Snapping Turtles. (p. 1597)
—Synonyms at School. (p. 1693)
—Visiting the Chesapeake Bay. (p. 1845)
—What's It Like to Be the First Lady? (p. 1898)
—What's It Like to Be the President? (p. 1898)
—What's It Like to Be the President's Kid? (p. 1898)
—What's It Like to Live in the White House? (p. 1898)
—What's It Like to Work in the White House? (p. 1898)
Connors, Kathleen & Stevens, Gareth. Contractions at the Zoo. (p. 361)
Connors, Mary, illus. see Edmonds, Lin.
Connors, Mary, illus. see Gatewood, June S.
Connors, Mary, illus. see Heywood, Grand-Mere Geny.
Connors, Paul. Homosexuality. (p. 794)
Connors, Paul G. Homosexuality. (p. 794)
Connors, Stompin' Tom. Hockey Night Tonight Jones, Brenda, illus. (p. 786)
Connors, Thomas, tr. see Fromental, Jean-Luc.
Connors, Tracy D., ed. see Connors, Faith Raymond.
Conoley, Chris. Level Chemistry: Strengthen Your Science, Maths & Quality of Written Communication Skills. (p. 1003)
Conover, Bret, illus. see Nyikos, Stacy.
Conover, Chris. Lion's Share. (p. 1021)
Conover, David & Conover, David, Sr. Once upon an Island. (p. 1293)
Conover, David, Sr., jt. auth. see Conover, David.
conover, ron. Little Charlie Bass: Jennifer Johnson. (p. 1026)
Conover, Sarah. Kindness: A Treasury of Buddhist Tales & Wisdom. Wahl, Valerie, illus. (p. 957)
Conover, Sarah & Crane, Freda, adapted by. Ayay Jamilah: Beautiful Signs: A Treasury of Islamic Wisdom for Children & Parents. (p. 121)
Conquistadore, H. Omni Presents the Universe. West, Jeremy, illus. (p. 1288)
Conrad. Tub People. (p. 1795)
conrad, catherine. Lemonade Stand. (p. 991)
Conrad, Cody And Arnetta. Gerbil & the Arabian Nights: Jamal's Night Trip for Water. (p. 666)
Conrad, Colleen Mullen. Reggie's Place: The Story of How One Boy's Life Made A Difference for Homeless Youth. (p. 1457)
Conrad, David. Burps, Boogers, & Other Body Functions (p. 244)
—Exploring Space (p. 553)
—Gravedad a Nuestro Alrededor. (p. 712)
—Gravity All Around (p. 712)
Conrad, David C. Empires of Medieval West Africa, Revised Edition. (p. 521)
Conrad, Didier, illus. see Ferri, Jean-Yves, et al.
Conrad, Didier, illus. see Ferri, Jean-Yves.
Conrad, Jeffrey, illus. see Random House Staff.
Conrad, Joseph. End of the Tether. (p. 526)
—Lord Jim. Simmons, Allan H. & Stape, J. H., eds. (p. 1052)
—Secret Agent. (p. 1540)
Conrad, Joseph & Snyder, John K., III. Secret Agent. (p. 1540)
Conrad, Lauren. Fame Game. (p. 567)
—Infamous. (p. 873)
—L. A. Candy. (p. 969)
—Lauren Conrad Style. (p. 980)
—Starstruck. (p. 1643)
—Sugar & Spice. (p. 1672)
—Sweet Little Lies. (p. 1690)
Conrad, Lauren, et al. Beauty. (p. 154)
Conrad, Liz. Little Bunny. (p. 1025)
—Little Chick. (p. 1026)
—Little Duck. (p. 1027)
—Little Lamb. (p. 1030)
—Skeleton Shake. (p. 1584)
Conrad, Liz, illus. see Schoenberg, Jane.
Conrad, Perrin Cothran. Ballad of the Shirley T & Other Stories. (p. 134)
Conrad, Peter. Canadian Wartime Prison Escapes: Courage & Daring Behind Enemy Lines. (p. 260)
Conrad, Tim, jt. auth. see Palonen, Jukka.
Conrad, Will, jt. illus. see Deodato, Mike.
Conradie, Elsabé, et al. Study & Master Accounting Grade 10 Learner's Book. (p. 1670)
Conrads, T. J. Traditional Bowhunter's Handbook: History, How-to, & Practical Information for the Traditional Bowhunter. (p. 1776)
Conradt, Shana. Getting Fit with Food: 101 healthy eating Recipes. (p. 669)
Conrique, Samantha. Pod-Poppers. (p. 1375)
Conroe, Lindy. Rockafella Jones & the Hidden Treasure. Riette, Susanne, illus. (p. 1482)
Conroy, Christine. Emma's Memoirs: A Book of Comical Poems & Drawings with Emma as Your Hostess. Conroy, Robert, illus. (p. 520)
—Mama Wants a Llam. (p. 1084)
Conroy, Dennis. Pioneers of the Stillaguamish. (p. 1361)
Conroy, Erin Brown, jt. auth. see Lapham, Thea Rozetta.
Conroy, Jim & Alexander, Basia. Messages from Trees Set 1: A Coloring Book for the Young & Young-At-Heart. (p. 1129)
Conroy, Joseph F. Francais Vivant 1. (p. 627)
—Frissons et Chair de Poule. (p. 639)
Conroy, Kathy. Life Through a Dog's Eyes: The Adventures of Ralph. (p. 1013)
Conroy, Melissa. Grandma Is an Author. Kreloff, Elliot, illus. (p. 708)
Conroy, Robert, illus. see Conroy, Christine.
Conroy, Thom. D Day. (p. 397)
—D-Day. (p. 397)
Conroy, Tim. How to Become a Star Athlete. (p. 815)
Considine, Declan, illus. see Noughton, Barbara.
Consiglio, Joe. Big Billy & the Ice Cream Truck That Wouldn't Stop Simko, Joe, illus. (p. 178)
Consolazio, Pamela A., illus. see Archer, Nick.
Constable, Cathryn. Wolf Princess. (p. 1944)
Constable, John & Noble, Marty. Colour Your Own John Constable Paintings. (p. 346)
Constable, Kate. Taste of Lightning. (p. 1707)
Constable, Lewis, jt. auth. see Farrington, Karen.
Constable, Nick, jt. auth. see Farrington, Karen.
Constans, Gabriel. Skin of Lions. (p. 1585)
Constant, Clare, et al. Experiencing Poetry (p. 549)
Constantin, illus. see Ralph, Gordon & If.
Constantin, Pascale. Little Monster. (p. 1032)
Constantin, Pascale, illus. see Eaton, Jason Carter.
Constantin, Pascale, illus. see Rivers, Francine & Coibion, Shannon Rivers.
Constantin, Pascale, illus. see Rockliff, Mara.
Constantin, Pascale, illus. see Sierra, Judy.
Constantin, Pascale, illus. see Sydor, Colleen.
Constantin, Pascale, jt. auth. see Sydor, Colleen.
Constantine, Adam, illus. see Large, Tori.
Constantine, Cara J. I Can Choose to Be Happy. Barge III, John S., illus. (p. 835)
Constantine, Clélia. Planet of Ludokaa. Élyum Studio, illus. (p. 1367)
—Planet of Music. Smith, Owen & Collins Smith, Anne, trs. (p. 1367)
Constantine, Michael P. Holism Movement: 30 Day Wellness Plan to Balance Your Body, Mind, & Spirit. (p. 789)
Constantine, Robin. Promise of Amazing. (p. 1411)
—Secrets of Attraction. (p. 1545)
Constantinople, Louise T. Adventures of Ralph Ribbit. (p. 22)
Consuegra, Carlos Manuel Diaz, illus. see Tolstoy, Leo.
Consuegra, Claudio & Consuegra, Pamela. Making Jesus My Best Friend: Baptism Preparation for Younger Children (Ages 8-10) (p. 1081)
Consuegra, Pamela, jt. auth. see Consuegra, Claudio.
Consugar, Beth. Swanee Day. Rottinger, Amy, illus. (p. 1688)
Consumer Guide Editors, ed. American Auto: Over 100 Years. (p. 59)
Consumer Reports Magazine Staff. Consumer Reports Guide to Diet, Health & Fitness. (p. 360)
Consumer Reports Staff, ed. see Gordon, Sandra J. & Gordon, Sandra.
Consumer Reports Staff, creator. Used Car Buying Guide 2007. (p. 1827)
Cont Media Staff. Ancient Rome. (p. 70)
Cont Media Staff, ed. Ancient Egyptains. (p. 68)
Conte, Alexander. Snow Storm. (p. 1599)
Conte, Paola, et al. Some Bunny to Talk To: A Story for Children about Going to Therapy. Beeke, Tiphanie, illus. (p. 1609)
Conteh, Gerald. I Still Believe in Santa. (p. 846)
Conteh-Morgan, Jane, illus. see Cricket Magazine Editors.
Conteh-Morgan, Jane, illus. see Gunney, Lynn Tuttle.
Conti, Alexis. One Blue Shoe. Beth, Shannon, illus. (p. 1294)
Conti, Nicolette & Johanson, Paula. Truth about Amphetamines & Stimulants. (p. 1794)
Continental Press Staff. Finish Line for ELLs: English Proficiency Practice: Student Book. (p. 589)
Contreras, Gilbert, illus. see DeRosier, Cher.
Contreras, Kathleen. Braids - Trencitas. Lindmark, Margaret, illus. (p. 221)
Contreras, Kathleen & Lindmark, Margaret. Sweet Memories/Dulces Recuerdos. Lindmark, Margaret, illus. (p. 1690)
Contreras-Freeland, Gina, illus. see Smith, M. a. & Smith, M. A.
Contro, Arturo. Cristiano Ronaldo. (p. 383)
—Cristiano Ronaldo. Benson, Megan, tr. (p. 383)
—Gianluigi Buffon. (p. 673)
—Gianluigi Buffon. Benson, Megan, tr. from SPA. (p. 673)
—Landon Donovan. (p. 974)
—Landon Donovan. Benson, Megan, tr. (p. 974)
—Rafael Marquez. (p. 1433)
—Rafael Marquez. Benson, Megan, tr. from SPA. (p. 1433)
Conure, Lunatico. Tico's Book. Durr, Carol Atkinson, illus. (p. 1747)
Converse, P. J. Subway Girl. (p. 1671)
Conway, Aaron. Alex the Sea Turtle. (p. 36)
Conway, Aaron, illus. see Overland, Sarah.
Conway, Agnes Ethel & Conway, Martin. Book of Art for Young People. (p. 210)
Conway, Agnes Ethel & Conway, William Martin. Book of Art for Young People. (p. 210)
Conway, Beth, jt. auth. see Buchanan, Johnny.
Conway, Celeste. Body Image & the Media. (p. 207)
—Unlovely. (p. 1821)
—When You Open Your Eyes. (p. 1905)

Conway, David. Bedtime Hullabaloo. Fuge, Charles, illus. (p. 157)
—Errol & His Extraordinary Nose. Angaramo, Roberta, illus. (p. 534)
—Great Fairy Tale Disaster. Williamson, Melanie, illus. (p. 716)
—Great Nursery Rhyme Disaster. Williamson, Melanie, illus. (p. 717)
—Lila & the Secret of Rain. Daly, Jude, illus. (p. 1017)
—Shine Moon Shine. Kolanovic, Dubravka, illus. (p. 1566)
Conway, Gerry. Break-Up! Henrique, Paulo, illus. (p. 224)
—Crawling with Zombies. Henrique, Paulo, illus. (p. 377)
—Nancy Drew: Together with the Hardy Boys. Murase, Sho, illus. (p. 1228)
Conway, Gerry, jt. auth. see Edelman, Scott.
Conway, Gerry, jt. auth. see Levitz, Paul.
Conway, Gerry & Lee, Stan. Mighty Thor Buscema, John & Mooney, Jim, illus. (p. 1140)
Conway, Gerry & Wein, Len. Essential Thor Buscema, John et al, illus. (p. 537)
Conway, Gerry, et al. Spider-Man: The Original Clone Saga. Andru, Ross et al, illus. (p. 1626)
—Super-Villain Team-Up. (p. 1682)
Conway, Hollis. Grasshopper: The Hollis Conway Story. (p. 711)
Conway, Jill Ker. Felipe the Flamingo. Millis, Lokken, illus. (p. 581)
Conway, Jill Ker, et al. Flamingo Felipe. Millis, Lokken, illus. (p. 602)
Conway, John Richard. Look at the First Amendment: Freedom of Speech & Religion. (p. 1049)
—Look at the Thirteenth & Fourteenth Amendments: Slavery Abolished, Equal Protection Established. (p. 1049)
—Primary Source Accounts of the Korean War. (p. 1399)
—Primary Source Accounts of World War II. (p. 1399)
—World War I: A MyReportLinks. Com Book. (p. 1958)
Conway, Kathleen E. Journey to the Stars: A Child's Dream. (p. 929)
Conway, Laurence. Sing & Learn! (p. 1579)
Conway, Louise, illus. see Bently, Peter.
Conway, Martin, jt. auth. see Conway, Agnes Ethel.
Conway, Portia. Where My Shoes Have Been (p. 1909)
Conway, Tricia, illus. see Farah, Barbara.
Conway, William Martin, jt. auth. see Conway, Agnes Ethel.
Conyers, Courtney, illus. see Jacobs, Jerry L.
Conyers, Miranda Parbhoo. Daddy Please Don't Cry. (p. 398)
Conyers, Tom. Morse Code for Cats. Litchfield, Judie, ed. (p. 1176)
Coode, Chris, jt. auth. see Gibbons, Lynn.
Coode, Chris & Gibbons, Lynn. Sharks & the World's Scariest Sea Monsters. (p. 1563)
Coogan, Carol, illus. see Welles, Lee.
Cook, Alexandra. Colored Pencils. (p. 343)
Cook, Alison Reeger. Scholar, the Sphinx & the Shades of Nyx. (p. 1521)
Cook, Amy Allgeyer. Iron Bodkin: Lux St. Clare ~ Book One. (p. 888)
Cook, Ande, illus. see Ditchfield, Christin.
Cook, Andrew. Skipper & Tango: In Search for the Golden Egg. (p. 1586)
Cook, Ann, jt. auth. see Blance, Ellen.
Cook, Annabel. Poems for Dad: A Collection of Poetry. (p. 1376)
Cook, Barbara L. Families. Cress, Michelle H., illus. (p. 567)
Cook, Beatrice. Journey with the Spider & Snake to Arizona. Campis, Adrian, Jr., illus. (p. 929)
Cook, Bernadine. Little Fish That Got Away. Johnson, Crockett, illus. (p. 1027)
Cook, Bernard A. Belgium: A History. (p. 161)
Cook, Berty Segal. Linking the ESL Student to the Mainstream. (p. 1019)
Cook, Beryl, jt. auth. see Newman, Nanette.
Cook, Billie Montgomery. Real Deal: A Spiritual Guide for Black Teen Girls. (p. 1448)
Cook, Bob. Is for Anteater! Greenhalgh, Rachel, illus. (p. 889)
Cook, Brian & Tupper, Mark. Brian Cook: An Illini Legend. (p. 226)
Cook, Bridget M., ed. Special Occasions in Lace. (p. 1623)
Cook, Bruce. Parents, Teens & Sex: The Big Talk Book - 10 Steps to Empower Your Teen to Choose the Best-Abstinence until Marriage. (p. 1324)
Cook, Cathy T. Adventures of Rose Bush. (p. 22)
Cook, Cheryl. Kids Prayer Time Series: Lord, Teach me how to pray, Lord, Teach me how to walk by faith, Lord, Teach me how to love others, Lord, Teach me how to take care of the Temple. (p. 955)
—Scripture to Grow On: Character lessons for Kids. (p. 1533)
Cook, Christopher. Washington Irving's The Legend of Sleepy Hollow: A Play in Two Acts. (p. 1860)
—Washington Irving's the Legend of Sleepy Hollow. (p. 1860)
Cook, Christy. I Told My Friend about Jesus. (p. 846)
Cook, Colleen Ryckert. Kentucky: Past & Present. (p. 949)
—Your Career in the Marines. (p. 1980)
Cook Communications Ministries, creator. Bible Crafts for All Seasons. (p. 175)
Cook Communications Staff, et al. Toddlerific: Fun Faith-Builders. (p. 1761)
Cook, Danielle. Letters from Pyggles (p. 1002)
Cook, Darren A., jt. auth. see Mantlo, Mickey A.
Cook, David C. David & the 23rd Psalm (p. 410)
Cook, David C., 3rd. Mary & Martha. (p. 1100)
Cook, David C. Publishing Staff. God Made It Gook: Pencil Fun Book. (p. 689)
Cook, David C. Publishing Staff & Harmon, Jeannie. God's Promise to Abraham. (p. 691)
Cook, David C. Publishing Staff & Tangvald, Christine. Josiah, the Boy King. (p. 927)
Cook, David Fuller, compiled by. Balanced Approach to Long Life & Vitality, Signature Edition: As Used in Fitness, Wellness, Clinical Weight Loss, & Cardiac Rehabilitation Programs. (p. 133)
Cook, David Fuller, ed. Balanced Approach to Long Life & Vitality for Christians: As Used in Fitness, Wellness, Clinical Weight Loss, & Cardiac Rehabilitation Programs. (p. 133)
Cook, Dawn. Lost Truth. (p. 1057)
Cook, Dawn, see Harrison, Kim, pseud.
Cook, Deanna F. Cooking Class: 50 Fun Recipes Kids Will Love to Make (And Eat!) (p. 361)
—Kids' Multicultural Cookbook: Food & Fun Around the World. Kline, Michael P., illus. (p. 954)
—Teddy Bear Doctor: Fix the Boo-Boos & Heal the Ouchies of Your Favorite Stuffed Animals. (p. 1712)
Cook, Debbie. Pete the Poodle. (p. 1346)
Cook, Deena & McIntosh, Cherie. Pinky & Peanut: The Adventure Begins. Scruggs, Trina, illus. (p. 1360)
Cook, Diana. Wink Fish: Nate's Missed Adventure. (p. 1936)
Cook, Diane. Cameroon. (p. 256)
—Cameroon. Rotberg, Robert I., ed. (p. 256)
—Charles Darwin: British Naturalist. (p. 292)
—Henri Toulouse-Lautrec: 19th Century French Painter. (p. 767)
—Michelangelo: Renaissance Artist. (p. 1135)
—Mohandas Gandhi: Spiritual Leader. (p. 1160)
—Mohandas K. Gandi: Spiritual Leader. (p. 1160)
—Pathfinders of the American Frontier. (p. 1328)
—Paul Gaugin: 18th Century French Painter. (p. 1330)
—Paul Gauguin: 18th Century French Painter. (p. 1330)
—Wolfgang Amadeus Mozart: World-Famous Composer. (p. 1944)
Cook, Donald, illus. see Murphy, Frank & Brenner, Martha.
Cook, Donna. Silly Solar System. (p. 1576)
Cook, E. Diann. Andersuns: Jarrell's Sweet Tooth. (p. 72)
Cook, Earl N., tr. see Flett, Julie.
Cook, Eileen. Almost Truth. (p. 48)
—Education of Hailey Kendrick. (p. 505)
—Fourth Grade Fairy. (p. 625)
—Getting Revenge on Lauren Wood. (p. 669)
—Gnome Invasion. (p. 685)
—Remember. (p. 1459)
—Unraveling Isobel. (p. 1822)
—Used to Be: The Education of Hailey Kendrick & Getting Revenge on Lauren Wood. (p. 1827)
—What Would Emma Do? (p. 1895)
—Wishes for Beginners. (p. 1940)
—Year of Mistaken Discoveries. (p. 1969)
Cook, Elizabeth. Achilles: A Novel. (p. 9)
Cook, Elizabeth, jt. auth. see Benton, Michael.
Cook, Esky. Jewish Artwork by Esky: Complete Set of Jewish Graphics. (p. 917)
—Jewish Artwork by Esky: Children, Borders, Hebrew Alphabets. (p. 917)
—Jewish Artwork by Esky: Mitzvot, Animals, Food & Brachot. Whitman, Jonathan, ed. (p. 917)
Cook, Gary. Best Saturday Ever! Sward, Adam, illus. (p. 171)
Cook, Gary W. Stories for Small Angels. (p. 1654)
Cook, Geoff, illus. see Scillian, Devin.
Cook, Gerri. Christmas in the Badlands. (p. 314)
—Penny for Albert. (p. 1338)
—Where the Buffalo Jump. Yu, Chao & Wang, Jue, illus. (p. 1909)
Cook, Gina J. Just a Little Lion: A Little Cheetah Learns the Truth about Little Lions As We Learn the Truth about Little Lies. (p. 937)
Cook, Gladys Emerson. Zoo Animals. (p. 1988)
Cook, Harry. Karate. (p. 943)
Cook, Heidi. Hero Boy. (p. 772)
Cook, Hugh & Miéville, China. Walrus & the Warwolf. Mona, Erik et al, eds. (p. 1855)
Cook, Jacqueline. Little Bear Who Worried Too Much: Suzie Bear Goes to London. (p. 1024)
—Little Bear Who Worried Too Much: Suzie Bear & the Music Festival. (p. 1024)
—Little Bear Who Worried Too Much: Suzie Bear & the Social Studies Test. (p. 1024)
—On to Nationals. (p. 1292)
Cook, James Wyatt. Encyclopedia of Ancient Literature. (p. 524)
—Encyclopedia of Renaissance Literature. (p. 525)
Cook, Jane Hampton. B Is for Baylor. Dobbins, Erin, illus. (p. 122)
—What Does the President Look Like? Ziskie, Adam, illus. (p. 1884)
Cook, Janet. How to Draw Robots & Aliens. Tatchell, Judy, ed. (p. 818)
Cook, Janice. Beau, a Puppy's Tale: A Children's Book Aimed at Helping Kids Overcome Bullies & Gain Self-Esteem. Cook, Janice, illus. (p. 153)
Cook, Jaye E. & Spencer, Lauren. Writing Personal Stories. (p. 1965)
Cook, Jean G. & Jimmie, Elsie. How the Crane Got Its Blue Eyes. (p. 813)
Cook, Jeffrey, illus. see Kelly, Kelley R.
Cook, Jennifer. Ariadne: The Maiden & the Minotaur. (p. 98)
Cook, Jennifer, ed. see Hudson, Phillip.
Cook, Jeremy. Illusion Meets Reality. (p. 857)
—Illusion of Time (p. 857)
—Illusion Stick. (p. 857)
Cook, Jessica & Stephens, Michael. What If Mommy Took a Vacation? (p. 1887)
Cook, Julia. Bad Case of Tattle Tongue. DuFalla, Anita, illus. (p. 131)
—Bubble Wrap Queen. Valentine, Allison, illus. (p. 233)
—Cliques Just Don't Make Cents! DuFalla, Anita, illus. (p. 333)
—D Word: Divorce. Rodgers, Phillip W., illus. (p. 398)
—Decibella & Her 6-Inch Voice. DuFalla, Anita, illus. (p. 421)
—Gas Happens! What to Do When It Happens to You. DuFalla, Anita, illus. (p. 657)
—Hygiene You Stink! DuFalla, Anita, illus. (p. 831)
—I Can't Believe You Said That! De Weerd, Kelsey, illus. (p. 837)
—I Just Want to Do It My Way! De Weerd, Kelsey, illus. (p. 840)
—I Just Want to Do It My Way Audio CD with Book. DeWeerd, Kelsey, illus. (p. 840)
—I'm a Booger... Treat Me with Respect! (p. 858)
—It's Hard to Be a Verb! Hartman, Carrie, illus. (p. 897)
—Making Friends Is an Art! (p. 1081)
—My Mom Thinks She's My Volleyball Coach... but She's Not! (p. 1214)
—My Mouth Is a Volcano! Hartman, Carrie, illus. (p. 1215)
—Peer Pressure Gauge. Dufalla, Anita, illus. (p. 1335)
—Peor Dia de TODA Mi Vida. DeWeerd, Kelsey, illus. (p. 1340)
—Personal Space Camp. (p. 1344)
—Personal Space Camp. Hartman, Carrie, illus. (p. 1344)
—Scoop. Venting, Elisabeth, illus. (p. 1529)
—Sorry, I Forgot to Ask! (p. 1614)
—Sorry I Forgot to Ask! Book with audio CD. (p. 1614)
—Teamwork Isn't My Thing, & I Don't Like to Share! DeWeerd, Kelsey, illus. (p. 1711)
—Tease Monster: (a Book about Teasing vs. Bullying) DuFalla, Anita, illus. (p. 1711)
—Thanks for the Feedback, I Think. De Weerd, Kelsey, illus. (p. 1725)
—Well, I Can Top That! Dufalla, Anita, illus. (p. 1874)
—Worst Day of My Life Ever! Cook, Julia & De Weerd, Kelsey, illus. (p. 1961)
Cook, Julia & Jana, Laura. It's You & Me Against the Pee... & the Poop, Too! DuFalla, Anita, illus. (p. 899)
—Melvin the Magnificent Molar. Valentine, Allison, illus. (p. 1125)
Cook, Julie Kidd. One Is Enough. Iwai, Melissa, illus. (p. 1295)
Cook, Kacy. Nuts (p. 1274)
Cook, Kajsa. Discoveries in the Shriver Family Attic: How a Woman & Her Children Dealt with the Battle of Gettysburg. (p. 448)
Cook, Kajsa C. Untold Story: About the War of 1812. (p. 1823)
Cook, Katie. Friendship Is Magic (p. 639)
—Little Big Benny: The Wicked Itch. (p. 1024)
—Little Big Benny: The Boy Who Didn't Know He Was the Universe. (p. 1024)
—My Little Pony: Friendship Is Magic Part 1: Friendship Is Magic Part 1. (p. 1213)
—My Little Pony: Friendship Is Magic Volume 3: Friendship Is Magic Volume 3. (p. 1213)
—Rarity. Price, Andy, illus. (p. 1439)
Cook, Katie, illus. see King, Trey.
Cook, Katie, illus. see Randolph, Grace, et al.
Cook, Kenneth A. Booktalk & other short Stories. (p. 213)
Cook, Kristi. Eternal. (p. 539)
—Haven. (p. 754)
—Magnolia. (p. 1076)
—Mirage. (p. 1149)
Cook, Laurie, illus. see Mathews, Madge.
Cook, LaVelle. Little Jimmie & the Lord's Prayer. (p. 1029)
Cook, Lisa Broadie. Peanut Butter & Homework Sandwiches. Davis, Jack E., illus. (p. 1332)
Cook, Louis J. & Freedman, Jeri. Brain Tumors. (p. 222)
Cook, Lydia. Make a Mobile: 12 Cool Designs to Press Out & Hang. (p. 1078)
Cook, Lyn. Bells on Finland Street (p. 163)
—Flight from the Fortress (p. 604)
Cook, Lynette R., illus. see Halpern, Paul.
Cook, Makayla. Voice of the Unborn. (p. 1848)
Cook, Malcolm. 101 Youth Soccer Drills for 12 to 16 Year Olds. (p. 2000)
Cook, Marisa. Adventures of Ollie & Ronnie: Litter. (p. 21)
Cook, Marlene. Buster & Ozzie: The Friendship Begins. (p. 245)
Cook, Mauliola. Discover Hawaii's Volcanoes: Birth by Fire. Orr, Katherine, illus. (p. 447)
Cook, Mauliola & Orr, Katherine. Discover His Birth by Fire Volcanoes. (p. 447)
Cook, Maureen McNamee. Is There Magic in the Mountains, Mamma? Connell, Jacqueline, illus. (p. 890)
Cook, Melissa. Anna & the Garden Fairy: Anna's Little Black Bear. (p. 85)
Cook, Michele, jt. auth. see Sandford, John, pseud.
Cook, Michelle. Our Children Can Soar: A Celebration of Rosa, Barack, & the Pioneers of Change. Ford, A. G. et al, illus. (p. 1308)
Cook, Monique, illus. see Marie, K.
Cook, Norman. Sam in the Crimea: A Victorian Adventure Based on the Work of Lord Shaftesbury. (p. 1506)
Cook, Peter. You Wouldn't Want to Be at the Boston Tea Party! Wharf Water You'd Rather Not Drink. Antram, David, illus. (p. 1977)
—You Wouldn't Want to Sail on the Mayflower! A Trip That Took Entirely Too Long. Whelan, Kevin, illus. (p. 1977)
Cook, Peter, illus. see Radford, Megan.
Cook, Peter, photos by see Vandenberg, Maritz.
Cook, Peter & Nash, Kevin. Pomona College College Prowler off the Record. (p. 1382)
Cook, Peter & Salariya, David. Sail on a 19th-Century Whaling Ship! Grisly Tasks You'd Rather Not Do. Antram, David, illus. (p. 1503)
Cook, Peter & Whelan, Kevin. You Wouldn't Want to Sail on the Mayflower! A Trip That Took Entirely Too Long. (p. 1977)
Cook, Philip. Erden: Flame of the Creator. (p. 533)
Cook, Randall D. American Idle: A Full-Length Comic Parody. (p. 61)
Cook, Rebecca. Breeze's Big Day. (p. 226)
Cook, Reginald. Veil. (p. 1834)
Cook, Rhodes. Race for the Presidency: Winning the 2004 Nomination. (p. 1431)
Cook, Robin. Invasion. (p. 883)
Cook, Sally. Good Night Pillow Fight. (p. 700)
Cook, Sally & Charlton, James. Hey Batta Batta Swing! The Wild Old Days of Baseball. MacDonald, Ross, illus. (p. 774)
Cook, Samantha. Darkness Has Fallen. (p. 408)
Cook, Sharon & Sholander, Graciela. Dream It, Do It: Inspiring Stories of Dreams Come True. (p. 483)
Cook, Sherry & Johnson, Martin. Underwater Utley Kuhn, Jesse, illus. (p. 1817)
Cook, Sherry & Johnson, Terri. Andy Acid Kuhn, Jesse, illus. (p. 72)
—Botanist Bert Kuhn, Jesse, illus. (p. 215)
—Colorful Caroline Kuhn, Jesse, illus. (p. 344)
—Density Dan Kuhn, Jesse, illus. (p. 426)
—Ellie Electricity Kuhn, Jesse, illus. (p. 514)
—Friction Fred Kuhn, Jesse, illus. (p. 637)
—Gilbert Gas Kuhn, Jesse, illus. (p. 676)
—Hallie Heat Kuhn, Jesse, illus. (p. 737)
—Inquisitive Inman Kuhn, Jesse, illus. (p. 875)
—Jazzy Jet Kuhn, Jesse, illus. (p. 911)
—Kitchen Chemistry Kal Kuhn, Jesse, illus. (p. 962)
—Mary Motion Kuhn, Jesse, illus. (p. 1101)
—Nosey Nina Kuhn, Jesse, illus. (p. 1266)
—Ollie Oxygen Kuhn, Jesse, illus. (p. 1287)
—Pressure Pete Kuhn, Jesse, illus. (p. 1397)
—Quincy Quake Kuhn, Jesse, illus. (p. 1428)
—Ronnie Rock Kuhn, Jesse, illus. (p. 1487)
—Susie Sound Kuhn, Jesse, illus. (p. 1688)
—Timothy Tornado Kuhn, Jesse, illus. (p. 1755)
—Vinnie Volcano Kuhn, Jesse, illus. (p. 1843)
—Watery William Kuhn, Jesse, illus. (p. 1864)
—X. E. Ecology Kuhn, Jesse, illus. (p. 1967)
—Zany Science Zeke Kuhn, Jesse, illus. (p. 1985)
Cook, Sherry & Terri, Johnson. Yawning Yolanda (p. 1968)
Cook, Sue D., ed. see Knab, Christopher & Day, Bartley F.
Cook, Susan D. Book of Galahad. (p. 211)
Cook, Teri Ann. Adventures of Mrs. Patsy's Farm: A Gift! Is a Gift! Is a Gift! (p. 21)
Cook, Terry. Moose at the Bus Stop. Cook, Terry, illus. (p. 1173)
Cook, Tina H. Lindsey & the Yellow Masterpiece. (p. 1019)
Cook, Tony, jt. auth. see Blance, Ellen.
Cook, Trahern, illus. see Haynie, Rachel.
Cook, Trevor. Experiments with Forces. (p. 549)
—Experiments with Light & Sound. (p. 549)
—Experiments with Plants & Other Living Things. (p. 549)
—Science Lab Set. (p. 1526)
Cook, Trevor, jt. auth. see Henry, Sally.
Cook, Trevor & Henry, Sally. Awesome Experiments: Electricity & Magnetism, Forces, Plants & Living Things, Heat, Materials, Light & Sound. (p. 121)
—Origami: A Step-By-Step Introduction to the Art of Paper Folding. (p. 1303)
Cook, Trevor & Miles, Lisa. Drawing Fantasy Figures. (p. 481)
—Drawing Manga. (p. 482)
—Drawing Pets & Farm Animals. (p. 482)
—Drawing Sports Figures. (p. 482)
—Drawing Vehicles. (p. 482)
—Drawing Wild Animals. (p. 482)
Cook, Trevor M. Experiments with Electricity & Magnetism. (p. 549)
—Experiments with Heat. (p. 549)
—Experiments with States of Matter. (p. 549)
Cook, William. Worth the Wait. Kim, Jeehyun, illus. (p. 1962)
Cookbook Resources, ed. Super Simple Cupcake Recipes. (p. 1681)
Cook-Cottone, Catherine. brain owner's manual for Kids: Helping the feeling & thinking parts work Together. (p. 221)
Cooke, Alistair. Reporting America: The Life of the Nation, 1946 - 2004. (p. 1461)
Cooke, Andrew, et al. Spectrum Year 7 Testmaker. (p. 1624)
Cooke, Andy, illus. see Cohen, Hannah, ed.
Cooke, Andy & Martin, Jean. Resourcemaker. (p. 1463)
—Spectrum Biology Class. (p. 1624)
—Spectrum Physics Class Book. (p. 1624)
—Spectrum Year 9 Testmaker. (p. 1624)
Cooke, Andy & Martin, Jean Ami. Spectrum Chemistry. (p. 1624)
Cooke, Andy, et al. Resourcemaker. (p. 1463)
—Spectrum 8. (p. 1624)
—Spectrum, Key Stage 3. (p. 1624)
—Spectrum Year 8 Testmaker Assessment. (p. 1624)
—Spectrum Year 9. (p. 1624)
Cooke, Arthur O. Flowers of the Farm. (p. 608)
Cooke, Barbara, jt. auth. see Foley, Erin.
Cooke, Barbara, jt. auth. see Kagda, Sakina.
Cooke, Barbara, jt. auth. see Sheehan, Sean.
Cooke, Bev. Feral (p. 581)
Cooke, Bev, illus. see Wrucke, Mary.
Cooke, Brandy. Cupcakes! A Sweet Treat with More Than 200 Stickers. Kramer, Connie, photos by. (p. 392)
—My Valentine. Wilkinson, Annie, illus. (p. 1220)
—What's Following Us? Reasoner, Charles & Reasoner, John, illus. (p. 1897)
Cooke, Bruce. Tubby's Magic Socks. (p. 1795)
Cooke, C. W. Fame: The Cast of Glee. (p. 567)
Cooke, C. W., jt. auth. see Ooten, Tara Broeckel.
Cooke, C. W. & McCormack, Patrick. Pop Star - Fame. (p. 1384)
Cooke, Charlotte, illus. see Gassman, Julie A.
Cooke, Clare. NTC Language Masters for Beginning French Students. (p. 1269)
Cooke, Clare, jt. auth. see Patnicroft, Robert.
Cooke, Darwyn & Grist, Paul. Ego & Other Tails. (p. 506)
Cooke, Darwyn & Stewart, Dave. New Frontier (p. 1244)
Cooke, Elizabeth, jt. auth. see Oplinger, Jon.
Cooke, Eunice Perneel. Awesome Lost & Found Society. (p. 121)
Cooke, Flora J. Nature Myths & Stories for Little Chil. (p. 1236)
Cooke, Jackie. Early Sensory Skills. (p. 494)
Cooke, Jackie & Williams, Diana. Working with Children's Language. (p. 1953)
Cooke, James. Pink Pig in a Boat. (p. 1360)
Cooke, Jim, illus. see Lewis, Patrick J.
Cooke, Jim, tr. see Lewis, Patrick J.
Cooke, Lucy. Little Book of Sloth. Cooke, Lucy, photos by. (p. 1025)
Cooke, Majorie Benton. Bambi. (p. 135)
Cooke, Marjorie Benton. Bambi. (p. 135)
Cooke, Pam. There's a Rainbow in Me. Dustin, Michael, illus. (p. 1731)
Cooke, Tim. 1906 San Francisco Earthquake. (p. 2002)
—After the War. (p. 28)
—Ancient Aztec: Archaeology Unlocks the Secrets of Mexico's Past. (p. 68)
—Ancient Egyptians. (p. 69)
—Ancient Greeks. (p. 69)
—Ancient Romans. (p. 70)
—Aztecs. (p. 122)
—Billy the Kid: A Notorious Gunfighter of the Wild West. (p. 187)
—Blackbeard: A Notorious Pirate in the Caribbean. (p. 197)

—Bombers. (p. 208)
—Bonnie & Clyde: Notorious Outlaws of the Great Depression. (p. 209)
—Butch Cassidy & the Sundance Kid: Notorious Outlaws of the West. (p. 246)
—Causes of the War: 1860-1861. (p. 282)
—Causes of the War. (p. 282)
—Confederacy on the Advance: 1861-1862. (p. 356)
—Exploration of Africa. (p. 550)
—Exploration of Arabia & Asia. (p. 550)
—Exploration of Australasia & the Pacific. (p. 550)
—Exploration of North America. (p. 550)
—Exploration of South America. (p. 550)
—Exploration of the North & South Poles. (p. 550)
—Explore with Henry Hudson. (p. 550)
—Explore with Marco Polo. (p. 550)
—Fighter Planes. (p. 585)
—Government Maps. (p. 704)
—Gulf War on the Front Lines. (p. 731)
—Helicopters. (p. 763)
—Home Front. (p. 792)
—Home Front, 1861-1865. (p. 792)
—Jesse James: A Notorious Bank Robber of the Wild West. (p. 914)
—Key Figures. (p. 950)
—Life on the Front Lines. (p. 1012)
—Magic & Illusions. (p. 1071)
—Maps & Cities. (p. 1090)
—Maps & Exploration. (p. 1090)
—Maps & Navigation. (p. 1090)
—Maps Today. (p. 1090)
—Ned Kelly: A Notorious Bandit of the Australian Outback. (p. 1239)
—Politics of the War: 1861-1865. (p. 1381)
—St. Lawrence River. (p. 1638)
—Submarines. (p. 1671)
—Tanks. (p. 1705)
—Triumph of the Union: 1864-1865. (p. 1788)
—Turning Point, 1863. (p. 1798)
—U. S. Civil War on the Front Lines. (p. 1806)
—US Airborne Forces. (p. 1826)
—US Army Rangers. (p. 1826)
—US Army Special Forces. (p. 1826)
—US Marine Corps. (p. 1826)
—US Navy SEALs. (p. 1826)
—Victorians. (p. 1840)
—Vietnam War on the Front Lines. (p. 1841)
—Vikings. (p. 1842)
—Warships. (p. 1859)
—Weapons & Tactics. (p. 1869)
—World War I on the Front Lines. (p. 1959)
—World War II on the Front Lines. (p. 1959)
Cooke, Tim, jt. auth. see Russell, Henry.
Cooke, Tim, ed. Battles & Campaigns. (p. 147)
—Experience of the War. (p. 548)
—International War. (p. 880)
—Johnson Years 1965-68. (p. 924)
—NAM - The Vietnam War: Causes & Outbreak. (p. 1228)
—NAM - The Vietnam War: Disengagement & Defeat 1969-75. (p. 1228)
—People. (p. 1338)
—Politics. (p. 1380)
—War & U. S. Society. (p. 1857)
—Weapons, Tactics, & Strategy. (p. 1869)
Cooke, Tobias. Secret of the Lost Soul: A Ben Street Mystery. (p. 1542)
Cooke, Tom, illus. see Hayward, Linda, et al.
Cooke, Tom, illus. see Ross, Katharine.
Cooke, Trish. Full, Full, Full of Love. Howard, Paul, illus. (p. 646)
—Look Back! Binch, Caroline, illus. (p. 1049)
—So Much! Oxenbury, Helen, illus. (p. 1602)
Cookie Jar Entertainment Inc Staff. ABC Doodlebops. (p. 3)
—Doodlebops Count to Ten. (p. 469)
—Doodlebops Rock. (p. 469)
—It's a Happy Holiday! (p. 895)
Cookie Jar Publishing Staff. Don't Pull the Rope: Kids' Favorite Rock Band! (p. 468)
Cookie Jar Publishing Staff, creator. Doodlebops: Friends & Favorites. (p. 469)
—Doodlebops: Let's Get on the Bus! (p. 469)
Cooksey, Ashley J. My Mom Is A Super Hero. (p. 1214)
Cookson, Catherine. Hannah Massey. (p. 742)
Cookson, Dave, jt. auth. see Chandler, Simon Cookson.
Cookson, Jan. Ant on the Run. (p. 88)
Cookson, Paul. Crazy Classrooms. Wells, Steve, illus. (p. 377)
—Doodle On! Football Doodles. Boretzki, Anja, illus. (p. 469)
—How to Embarrass Teachers. (p. 819)
—I'd Rather Be a Footballer: The Very Best of Paul Cookson (p. 851)
—Paul Cookson's Joke Shop. (p. 1330)
—Sing That Joke. (p. 1579)
—Unzip Your Lips. (p. 1824)
—Works. (p. 1953)
—Works: Every Poem You Will Ever Need at School. (p. 1953)
Cookson, Paul & Harmer, David. It Came from Outer Space! (p. 893)
—It's Behind You! (p. 896)
Cookson, Paul, et al. Truth about Parents (p. 1794)
Cookson, Paul, et al, selected by. Body Poems & Movement Poems. (p. 207)
Cool, Anna Maria, illus. see Olson, Kay Melchisedech.
Cool, Kim. Cool Road Trips in SW Florida. (p. 364)
—Ghost Stories of Clearwater & St. Petersburg. (p. 671)
Cool, Rebecca, illus. see Mewburn, Kyle.
Cool, Rebecca, illus. see Millard, Glenda.
Cool Springs Press Editors Staff, jt. auth. see Crisp, Marty.
Cool Springs Press Publications Staff, jt. auth. see Kranz, Linda.
Cool Things Press. 75 Cool Things to Color. (p. 1998)
—75 Cool Things to Cut Out. (p. 1998)
Cooley, Joan, et al. Talking Together about Death: A Bereavement Pack for People with Learning Disabilities, Their Carers & Families. (p. 1703)
Cooley, Judy. I Love You More. (p. 843)
—I Want to Be a Mommy. (p. 847)
—Mom Says I Can. (p. 1161)
Coolidge, Olivia E. Hercules & Other Tales from Greek Myths. Lockhart, David, illus. (p. 769)
Coolidge, Susan. Clover. (p. 335)
—Clover. Mcdermot, Jessie, illus. (p. 335)
—Verses. (p. 1837)
—What Katy Did. (p. 1891)
—What Katy Did. Ledyard, Addie, illus. (p. 1891)
—What Katy Did at School. (p. 1891)
Coolidge, Susan & Ledyard, Addie. What Katy Did. (p. 1891)
Coolidge, Susan, et al. Famous Classics for Girls: Heidi, What Katy Did, Black Beauty. Egmont UK Staff, ed. (p. 569)
—Twilight Stories. (p. 1801)
Cooling, Wendy. All the Wild Wonders: Poems of Our Earth. Grobler, Piet, illus. (p. 46)
—Camel Fair. Moon, Cliff, ed. (p. 256)
—Puffin Book of Stories for Eight- Year- Olds. Cooling, Wendy, ed. (p. 1415)
—Puffin Book of Stories for Five-Year-Olds. Cox, Steve, illus. (p. 1415)
—Puffin Book of Stories for Six-Year-Olds. Cox, Steve, illus. (p. 1415)
Cooling, Wendy & Quarto Generic Staff. A Is Amazing: Poems about Feelings. Grobler, Piet, illus. (p. 1)
Cooling, Wendy, ed. Come to the Great World: Poems from Around the Globe. Moxley, Sheila, tr. (p. 347)
Coomber, Suzanne. Magic Sandcastle. (p. 1073)
—Run Away Persimmon. (p. 1496)
—Salt & Pepper. (p. 1505)
Coombes, Patrick. Witch's Assistant. (p. 1941)
Coombs, Bob. Ted P Bear - A Bitter Tale. (p. 1712)
Coombs, Charles. Detective Stories: Young Readers. Geer, Charles H., illus. (p. 431)
—Railroad Stories: Young Readers. Geer, Charles H., illus. (p. 1434)
—Ranch Mystery: Young Readers. Priscilla, Louis, illus. (p. 1438)
—Young Infield Rookie. Geer, Charles H., illus. (p. 1979)
Coombs, Charles Ira. Indoor Sports Stories. Geer, Charles H., illus. (p. 872)
Coombs, Jonathan, illus. see Galindo, Claudia & Pluecker, John.
Coombs, Jonathan, illus. see Galindo, Claudia.
Coombs, Kate. Goodnight Mr. Darcy Board Book Arnold, Alli, illus. (p. 701)
—Runaway Princess. (p. 1496)
—Secret-Keeper. Solomon, Heather M., illus. (p. 1541)
—Tooth Fairy Wars. Parker, Jake, illus. (p. 1768)
—Water Sings Blue: Ocean Poems. So, Meilo, illus. (p. 1863)
Coombs, Kate & Austen, Jane. Goodnight Mr. Darcy: A Babylit Parody (p. 701)
Coombs, Patricia & Burg, Shana. Laugh with the Moon. Coombs, Patricia, illus. (p. 980)
Coombs, Rachel. Year in a Castle. (p. 1969)
Coombs-Richardson, Rita & Meisgeier, Charles H. Connecting with Others, Grades 9-12: Lessons for Teaching Social & Emotional Competence. (p. 358)
Coon, Cyndi. Art That Pops! How to Make Wacky 3-D Creations That Jump, Spin, & Spring! (p. 103)
Coon, Dianne. Nerual's Adventures & the Greatness of Agnes. (p. 1241)
Coon, Helene, jt. auth. see Coon, Thomas.
Coon, Kathy. Dog Intelligence Test: Kathy Coon's Dog Intelligence Test. (p. 461)
Coon, Kathyann. We Are Different. (p. 1865)
Coon, Nora. Teen Dream Jobs: How to Find the Job You Really Want Now! (p. 1713)
Coon, Nora E., ed. It's Your Rite: Girls' Coming-of-Age Stories. Gross-Andrew, Susannah, illus. (p. 899)
Coon, Thomas & Coon, Helene. Two of Our Friends Are Doves. MacMenamin, John, illus. (p. 1804)
Coonan, Candace N. Break of Dawn: Tales from Fadreama: Book 3. (p. 224)
—Darkest Hour: Tales from Fadreama: Book 1. (p. 408)
—Shattered Souls: Tales from Fadreama: Book 4. (p. 1563)
—Where Shadows Linger: Tales from Fadreama: Book 2. (p. 1909)
Cooner, Donna. Can't Look Away. (p. 262)
—Skinny. (p. 1585)
Cooney, Barbara. Miss Rumphius. Cooney, Barbara, illus. (p. 1152)
Cooney, Barbara, illus. see Becker, John E.
Cooney, Barbara, illus. see Bierhorst, John.
Cooney, Barbara, illus. see Godden, Rumer.
Cooney, Barbara, illus. see Horwitz, ElinorLander.
Cooney, Barbara, illus. see McLerran, Alice & Mclerran, Alice.
Cooney, Caroline B. Code Orange. (p. 338)
—Diamonds in the Shadow. (p. 434)
—Enter Three Witches: A Story of MacBeth. (p. 531)
—Enter Three Witches: A Story of Macbeth. (p. 531)
—Face on the Milk Carton. (p. 560)
—Friend at Midnight. (p. 637)
—Goddess of Yesterday. (p. 690)
—Hit the Road. (p. 785)
—If the Witness Lied. (p. 854)
—Janie Face to Face. (p. 908)
—Lost Songs. (p. 1056)
—No Such Person. (p. 1260)
—Ransom of Mercy Carter. (p. 1438)
—Terrorist. (p. 1722)
—They Never Came Back. (p. 1732)
—Three Black Swans. (p. 1741)
—Vampire's Promise. (p. 1832)
—Voice on the Radio. (p. 1848)
—What Janie Found. (p. 1891)
—Whatever Happened to Janie? (p. 1896)
Cooney, Caroline B. & Shakespeare, William. Enter Three Witches: A Story of Macbeth. (p. 531)
Cooney, Doug. Beloved Dearly. DiTerlizzi, Tony, illus. (p. 163)
—I Know Who Likes You. Bernardin, James, illus. (p. 840)
Cooney, Doug, jt. auth. see Matlin, Marlee.
Coons, Anita. Graze, Gaze & Saddle Days. (p. 713)
—What about Me? (p. 1878)
Coons, Dean, illus. see Baum, Roger S.
Coons, Mary. Piglys & the Hundred-Year Mystery. (p. 1358)
Coons, Mary H. Teacher's Classroom Companion: A Handbook for Primary Teachers. Appel, Morgan, illus. (p. 1709)
Coons, Susan. Lighthouse Mouse. (p. 1015)
Coons, Susan Anderson. Ibakon, Gretl & the Stinky,Sticky Dragon (p. 849)
—Lighthouse Mouse Meets Simon the Cat. Sanne, Don, illus. (p. 1015)
Coons, Timothy A. School of Chaos (p. 1523)
Coop, Kay. Gertrude's Moving Day. (p. 667)
Coope, Katy. How to Draw Manga Characters. Coope, Katy, illus. (p. 818)
—How to Draw More Manga. Coope, Katy, illus. (p. 818)
Cooper, Adrian, photos by see Barber, Nicola.
Cooper, Adrian, photos by see Mason, Paul.
Cooper, Adrian, photos by see Pellegrini, Nancy.
Cooper, Afua. My Name Is Henry Bibb: A Story of Slavery & Freedom. (p. 1215)
—My Name Is Phillis Wheatley: A Story of Slavery & Freedom. (p. 1215)
—Red Caterpillar on College Street. Martin, Stephanie, illus. (p. 1453)
Cooper, Alexandra. Spin the Dreidel! Gévry, Claudine, illus. (p. 1627)
Cooper, Alison. Facts about Buddhism. (p. 561)
—Facts about Hinduism. (p. 561)
—Facts about Islam. (p. 561)
—Facts about Judaism. (p. 561)
—Media Power? (p. 1118)
Cooper, Alison & McRae, Anne. Children's Pictorial Atlas of the World. De Luca, Daniela, illus. (p. 304)
Cooper, Amy & Keller, Carolyn. Rochester Institute of Technology College Prowler off the Record: Inside RIT. (p. 1481)
Cooper, Ann Goode. Zebordee Goes to the Races. Jessee, Diana, illus. (p. 1985)
Cooper, Ann Goode & Bowlin, William Harrison. Lawyer Will: The Story of an Appalachian Lawyer. Jessee, Diana, illus. (p. 981)
Cooper, Anne Lloyd, jt. auth. see Davies, Helen Emanuel.
Cooper, Anthony. Bernard the Barnyard Pig. (p. 167)
Cooper, Ashlee B., jt. auth. see Costello, Kim.
Cooper, Barbara. Alan Apostrophe. Raynor, Maggie, illus. (p. 33)
—Christopher Comma. Raynor, Maggie, illus. (p. 317)
—Emma Exclamation Point. Raynor, Maggie, illus. (p. 519)
—Hannah Hyphen-Hyphen. Raynor, Maggie, illus. (p. 742)
Cooper, Barbara & Widdows, Nancy. Knowing Yourself, Knowing Others: A Workbook for Children with Asperger's Disorder, Nonverbal Learning Disorder, & Other Social-Skill Problems. (p. 965)
—Social Success Workbook for Teens: Skill-Building Activities for Teens with Nonverbal Learning Disorder, Asperger's Disorder & Other Social-Skill Problems. (p. 1604)
Cooper, Belinda, tr. see Janisch, Heinz.
Cooper, Bernice Soroka. Little Elf-Frog. (p. 1027)
Cooper, Blair, illus. see Aryal, Aimee.
Cooper, Candy J. P.O.W. (p. 1389)
—Reporting from Iraq: On the Ground in Fallujah. (p. 1461)
—Beach. Cooper, Elisha, illus. (p. 149)
—Bear Dreams. Cooper, Elisha, illus. (p. 150)
—Farm. (p. 573)
—Good Night Walk. (p. 700)
—Homer. Cooper, Elisha, illus. (p. 793)
—Train. (p. 1777)
Cooper, Emmanuel, illus. see Battle, Cleaton D.
Cooper, Floyd. Jump! From the Life of Michael Jordan. Cooper, Floyd, illus. (p. 933)
—Juneteenth for Mazie. Cooper, Floyd, illus. (p. 934)
—Max & the Tag-Along Moon. Cooper, Floyd, illus. (p. 1110)
—Willie & the All-Stars. Cooper, Floyd, illus. (p. 1934)
Cooper, Carylton. Carb-Less for ALL Seasons. (p. 265)
Cooper, Catherine. Golden Acorn. (p. 694)
Cooper, Catherine W. Ukraine. (p. 1808)
Cooper, Chris. Arsenic. (p. 101)
—Basics of Energy & Reactions. (p. 142)
Cooper, Chris & Dorling Kindersley Publishing Staff. Forensic Science. (p. 617)
Cooper, Christina. If I Only Had One Wish. (p. 853)
Cooper, Christopher. Basics of Electric Current. (p. 142)
—Basics of Electronics. (p. 142)
—Basics of Magnetism. (p. 142)
—Basics of Nuclear Physics. (p. 142)
—Basics of Sound. (p. 142)
—Electricity: From Amps to Volts. (p. 509)
—Forces & Motion: From Push to Shove. (p. 617)
—Magnetism: From Pole to Pole. (p. 1076)
—Sound: From Whisper to Rock Band. (p. 1615)
Cooper, Clare. Time Ball. (p. 1751)
Cooper, D. C. Rascal the Baby Squirrel. (p. 1439)
Cooper, Debbie. Ancient Maya: Cultures of the Caribbean & Central America (p. 70)
—Garifuna: Cultures of the Caribbean & Central America (p. 657)
Cooper, Deborah, illus. see Hirschi, Ron.
Cooper, Diana. Angel Cards for Children. (p. 73)
—Angel Colouring Book. Zoutewelle-Morris, Sarah, illus. (p. 73)
—Magical Adventures of Tara & the Talking Kitten. Shannon, Kate, illus. (p. 1074)
—Tara & Her Talking Kitten Meet a Mermaid. Shannon, Kate, illus. (p. 1706)
—Tara & the Talking Kitten Meet a Unicorn. Shannon, Kate, illus. (p. 1706)
—Tara & the Talking Kitten Meet Angels & Fairies. Shannon, Kate, illus. (p. 1706)
Cooper, Dolores Thome. Hands Are Not for Hitting. (p. 741)
—Story of the Knus. (p. 1661)
Cooper, Doris Marie. Ben Bear's Eventful Day. (p. 163)
Cooper, Douglas Anthony. Milrose Munce & the Den of Professional Help. (p. 1144)
Cooper, E. E. Vanished. (p. 1833)
Cooper, Elisha. 8: An Animal Alphabet. (p. 1993)
Cooper, Floyd, illus. see Alexander, Elizabeth & Nelson, Marilyn.
Cooper, Floyd, illus. see Armand, Glenda.
Cooper, Floyd, illus. see Crisler, Curtis L.
Cooper, Floyd, illus. see De Baun, Hillary H.
Cooper, Floyd, illus. see Dempsey, Kristy.
Cooper, Floyd, illus. see Lang, Heather.
Cooper, Floyd, illus. see Mason, Margaret H.
Cooper, Floyd, illus. see Myers, Walter Dean.
Cooper, Floyd, illus. see Perry, M. LaVora.
Cooper, Floyd, illus. see Reynolds, Aaron.
Cooper, Floyd, illus. see Rockwell, Anne F.
Cooper, Floyd, illus. see Sherman, Patrice.
Cooper, Floyd, illus. see Skead, Robert.
Cooper, Floyd, illus. see Smith, Charles R., Jr.
Cooper, Floyd, illus. see Thomas, Joyce Carol.
Cooper, Floyd, illus. see Thomas, Kenneth W. & Thomas, Joyce Carol.
Cooper, Floyd, illus. see Vander Zee, Ruth.
Cooper, Floyd, illus. see Weatherford, Carole Boston.
Cooper, Floyd, illus. see Williams, Karen Lynn.
Cooper, France, illus. see Gifford, Myrna.
Cooper, Frances, illus. see Gifford, Myrna Ross.
Cooper, Frances, illus. see Gifford, Myrna.
Cooper, Gael. Kermeena Kermudgeon Meets Gordon. (p. 949)
—My Name Is Kermeena Kermudgeon. (p. 1215)
Cooper, Gem & Martin, Louise. Fairy Tale Theater — Cinderella. (p. 564)
—Fairy Tale Theater — Little Red Riding Hood. (p. 564)
Cooper, Gene. Who, Who... Who Is Reading My Book? Cooper, Gene, illus. (p. 1919)
Cooper, Gill, illus. see Baxter, Nicola.
Cooper, Gilly Cameron. How the World Began: Creation in Myths & Legends. Ludlow, Patricia, illus. (p. 813)
Cooper, Glenessa. Daddy's Number One Little Girl. Joseph, Patricia, illus. (p. 399)
Cooper, Hayley. Jade Lily. (p. 905)
Cooper, Heather, et al. Jacob Has Cancer: His Friends Want to Help. McMillion, Lindsey, illus. (p. 904)
Cooper, Helen. Delicious! Cooper, Helen, illus. (p. 425)
—Dog Biscuit. (p. 461)
—Historias de Juguetes. (p. 782)
—Pumpkin Soup (p. 1416)
—Pumpkin Soup. (p. 1416)
—Pumpkin Soup. Cooper, Helen, illus. (p. 1416)
—Tatty-Ratty. Cooper, Helen, illus. (p. 1707)
Cooper, Helen & Butterworth, Ian. Pinsiaid o Bupur. Williams, Dylan, tr. from ENG. (p. 1361)
Cooper, Helen Wendy. Vegetarian Vampire: The Lost Fangs. (p. 1834)
—Vegetarian Vampire. (p. 1834)
Cooper, Ilene. Absolutely Lucy #6: Thanks to Lucy. Merrell, David, illus. (p. 7)
—Golden Rule. Swiatowska, Gabi, illus. (p. 695)
—Golden Rule. Swiatowska, Gabi, illus. (p. 695)
—Jack: the Early Years of John F. Kennedy. (p. 903)
—Little Lucy. Kanzler, John, illus. (p. 1031)
—Little Lucy Goes to School. (p. 1031)
—Look at Lucy! Merrell, David, illus. (p. 1048)
—Lucy on the Ball. Merrell, David, illus. (p. 1063)
—Lucy's Holiday Surprise. Fitzgerald, Royce, illus. (p. 1063)
—Lucy's Tricks & Treats. Merrell, David, illus. (p. 1063)
—Woman in the House (and Senate) How Women Came to the United States Congress, Broke down Barriers, & Changed the Country. Baddeley, Elizabeth, illus. (p. 1945)
—Worst Noel: A Novel. (p. 1961)
Cooper, J. Barnyard Friends Discovery Library (p. 140)
Cooper, James Fenimore. Last of the Mohicans. (p. 978)
—Last of the Mohicans. Howell, Troy, illus. (p. 978)
—Last of the Mohicans. Wyeth, N. C., illus. (p. 978)
—Leatherstocking Saga. (p. 986)
—Pathfinder. (p. 1328)
—Pioneers. (p. 1361)
—Ultimo Mohicano. Eric, F. Rowe, illus. (p. 1810)
Cooper, James M., jt. auth. see Borich, Gary D.
Cooper, James M., jt. auth. see Larrivee, Barbara.
Cooper, James M., jt. auth. see Tomlinson, Carol Ann.
Cooper, James M. & Burden, Paul. Classroom Management. (p. 329)
Cooper, Janet Evins. Three Proud Princesses. (p. 1743)
Cooper, Jason. Ants. (p. 90)
—Black Widow Spiders. (p. 197)
—Black Widows. Rourke Publishing Staff, ed. (p. 197)
—Butterflies. (p. 247)
—Camouflage & Disguise. (p. 257)
—Camuflaje y Disfraz. (p. 258)
—Death Valley. (p. 420)
—Department of the Treasury. (p. 427)
—Fishing Spiders. (p. 599)
—Garden Spiders. (p. 656)
—Gilbert the Great Fish. (p. 676)
—Great Whale. (p. 719)
—Honeybee. (p. 794)
—Hormigas. (p. 798)
—Jumping Spiders. (p. 934)
—Jumping Spiders. Rourke Publishing Staff, ed. (p. 934)
—Man Made Wonders (p. 1085)
—Mariposas. (p. 1094)
—Praying Mantises. (p. 1393)
—Sunflower. (p. 1676)
—Tarantulas. (p. 1706)
—Tarantulas. Rourke Publishing Staff, ed. (p. 1706)
—Wolf Spiders. (p. 1944)
Cooper, Jennifer. Guardian Angel. (p. 728)
Cooper, Jenny. Forest Life to Color. (p. 618)
—Rainforest to Color. (p. 1436)
Cooper, Jenny, illus. see Bone, Emily.
Cooper, Jenny, illus. see Bowman, Lucy.
Cooper, Jenny, illus. see Collins, Jonathan.
Cooper, Jenny, illus. see Cullis, Megan.
Cooper, Jenny, illus. see Holden, Pam.
Cooper, Jenny, illus. see Meredith, Susan & Cullis, Megan.
Cooper, Jenny, illus. see Meredith, Susan.
Cooper, John. Dinosaurs. (p. 443)

C

—Greyhound. (p. 723)
—In the Groove: Heroes Start As Kids! Vol. 2 (p. 866)
—Putting on Your Pantos. (p. 1420)
—Season of Rage: Hugh Burnett & the Struggle for Civil Rights. (p. 1538)
Cooper, John A. Dinosaurs. (p. 443)
Cooper, John E. & Smith, P. Athene, trs. Captive Birds in Health & Disease: A Practical Guide for Those Who Keep Gamebirds, Raptors, Parrots, Waterfowl & Other Species. Smith, P. Athene, illus. (p. 264)
Cooper, Joseph, illus. see Moskowitz, Nachama Skolnik.
Cooper, Judith. Many Moons. (p. 1089)
Cooper, Kris A. Noble & Great Ones of the Book of Mormon - Especially for Teens. (p. 1262)
Cooper, Laurette E. Facing Shark Music. (p. 561)
Cooper, Lori. 10,000 House Names & Their Meanings. (p. 2003)
Cooper, Louise. Short & Scary! (p. 1569)
—Short & Spooky! (p. 1569)
Cooper, Lula. How the Penguins Got Their Polka Dots. (p. 813)
Cooper, Lyn Anne. Henry the Prickly Porcupine. (p. 768)
Cooper, Lynne. Alien Invaders. Leick, Bonnie, illus. (p. 40)
Cooper, Marcie. Meet the Teens. (p. 1123)
Cooper, Margaret. Christmas Horse. Bohart, Lisa, illus. (p. 314)
Cooper, Mark A. Fledgling: Jason Steed. (p. 603)
—Revenge: Jason Steed. (p. 1465)
Cooper, Martha, photos by see Chevat, Richie.
Cooper, Martha, photos by see Laredo, Elizabeth.
Cooper, Mary H., ed. see CQ Press Staff.
Cooper, Michael L. Fighting Fire! Ten of the Deadliest Fires in American History & How We Fought Them. (p. 585)
—Hero of the High Seas: John Paul Jones & the American Revolution. (p. 772)
—Jamestown 1607. (p. 907)
Cooper, Michelle. Brief History of Montmaray. (p. 227)
—FitzOsbornes at War. (p. 599)
—FitzOsbornes in Exile. (p. 599)
—Rage of Sheep. (p. 1433)
Cooper, Mimi. Me Versus Bedtime. (p. 1116)
—Me Versus Cooties. (p. 1116)
—Me Versus Snow. (p. 1116)
—Me Versus the Tooth. (p. 1116)
Cooper, Nelle. Princess Lil. (p. 1404)
Cooper, Nicole, illus. see Standish, Joyce, ed.
Cooper, P. King of the Cats. (p. 959)
Cooper, Page. Amigo, Circus Horse. Pitz, Henry, illus. (p. 65)
Cooper, Patrick. tesoro de los reyes de Irlanda. Cuellar, Olga, illus. (p. 1722)
Cooper, Paul, illus. see Niedworok, Claudio O.
Cooper, Paul Fenimore. Tal, His Marvelous Adventures with Noom-Zor-Noom. Reeves, Ruth, illus. (p. 1699)
Cooper, Polly. Adventures of Sir George & His Friends. (p. 23)
Cooper, R., et al. Bahrain. (p. 132)
—Croatia. (p. 384)
Cooper, Robbi, creator. Help! We're Having a Baby: Solicited Advice from Family & Friends. (p. 766)
Cooper, Robert. Light Behind Their Eyes: The Story of Jack & Bunny Rabbit. (p. 1015)
—World of Wonders: Prayers & Pictures. (p. 1958)
Cooper, Robert & Yong, Jui Lin. Bhutan. (p. 174)
Cooper, Robert K. Aprenda a Utilizar el Otro 90% La Mayoria de la Gente Solo Utiliza el 10% de su Potencial. (p. 93)
Cooper, Rose. Gossip from the Girls' Room. (p. 703)
—I Text Dead People. (p. 846)
—Rumors from the Boys' Room. (p. 1495)
—Secrets from the Sleeping Bag. (p. 1544)
Cooper, Ross Gordon. African Birds (p. 27)
—Clarence the Catfish. (p. 327)
—Common Antelope in Africa (p. 349)
—Craig the Crab. (p. 376)
Cooper, Scott. Speak up & Get Along! Learn the Mighty Might, Thought Chop, & More Tools to Make Friends, Stop Teasing, & Feel Good about Yourself. (p. 1623)
Cooper, Sharon, jt. illus. see Kirkby, Joanne.
Cooper, Sharon Katz. Caves & Crevices (p. 282)
—Compost Heap (p. 354)
—Costa Rica ABCs: A Book about the People & Places of Costa Rica Eitzen, Allan, illus. (p. 368)
—Extraordinary Migrations. Leonard, Tom et al, illus. (p. 555)
—Garbage Cans & Landfills (p. 655)
—Gustave Eiffel's Spectacular Idea: The Eiffel Tower. Bock, Janna, illus. (p. 733)
—Horrible Habitats (p. 798)
—Marshes & Pools (p. 1096)
—Milton Hershey's Sweet Idea: A Chocolate Kingdom. Lokus, Rex & Sánchez, Alvaro Iglesias, illus. (p. 1144)
—Rotten Logs & Forest Floors (p. 1490)
—Sewers & Gutters (p. 1555)
—Usar el Carbón, el Petróleo y el Gas (p. 1826)
—Using Air (p. 1828)
—Using Coal, Oil, & Gas (p. 1828)
—Using Plants (p. 1828)
—Using Rocks (p. 1828)
—Using Soil (p. 1828)
—Using Water (p. 1829)
—Venezuela ABCs: A Book about the People & Places of Venezuela Previn, Stacey, illus. (p. 1835)
—When Butterflies Cross the Sky: The Monarch Butterfly Migration. Brunet, Joshua S., illus. (p. 1901)
—When Crabs Cross the Sand: The Christmas Island Crab Migration. Wald, Christina, illus. (p. 1901)
—When Penguins Cross the Ice: The Emperor Penguin Migration. Leonard, Tom, illus. (p. 1904)
—When Whales Cross the Sea: The Gray Whale Migration. Leonard, Tom, illus. (p. 1905)
—Whose Hat Is This? A Look at Hats Workers Wear - Hard, Tall, & Shiny Muehlenhardt, Amy Bailey, illus. (p. 1921)
—Whose Tools Are These? A Look at Tools Workers Use - Big, Sharp, & Smooth Muehlenhardt, Amy Bailey, illus. (p. 1922)
Cooper, Sharon Katz & Compass Point Books Staff. Human Body Systems: Maintaining the Body's Functions Hoffmann, Eric & Hossain, Farhana, illus. (p. 826)
—Periodic Table: Mapping the Elements Hossain, Farhana, illus. (p. 1343)
Cooper, Sharon Katz & Katz Cooper, Sharon. Aristotle: Philosopher, Teacher, & Scientist (p. 98)
Cooper, Sharon Katz, et al. Story Behind the Name. (p. 1656)
Cooper, Simon, illus. see Hay, Sam.
Cooper, Stephanie. Crab the Traveler. (p. 375)
Cooper, Stephanie, illus. see Archambault, John.
Cooper, Stephanie, et al. Children's Year: Seasonal Crafts & Clothes. (p. 304)
Cooper, Susan. Boggart. (p. 207)
—Boggart. Rayyan, Omar & Dillon, Julie, illus. (p. 207)
—Boggart & the Monster. (p. 207)
—Boggart & the Monster. Rayyan, Omar & Dillon, Julie, illus. (p. 207)
—Dark Is Rising. (p. 407)
—Dark Is Rising Sequence: Over Sea, under Stone - The Dark Is Rising - Greenwitch - The Grey King - Silver on the Tree. (p. 407)
—Dark Is Rising Sequence: Over Sea, under Stone; The Dark Is Rising; Greenwitch; The Grey King; Silver on the Tree. Set (p. 407)
—Dawn of Fear. Gill, Margery, illus. (p. 411)
—Ghost Hawk. (p. 670)
—Green Boy. (p. 721)
—Greenwitch. (p. 723)
—Grey King. (p. 723)
—King of Shadows. (p. 959)
—Magician's Boy. Riglietti, Serena, illus. (p. 1075)
—Over Sea, under Stone. (p. 1313)
—Seaward. (p. 1539)
—Silver on the Tree. (p. 1576)
—Victory. (p. 1840)
Cooper, Susan, et al. Haunted. Andersen Press Staff, ed. (p. 753)
Cooper, T. & Glock-Cooper, Allison. Changers Book Two: Oryon. (p. 290)
—Drew. (p. 485)
Cooper, Teri. Meet Simple Signman: His quiet talk counting 1 Thru 10. (p. 1122)
Cooper, Terry, ed. see Dooley, Virginia & Teaching Resources Staff.
Cooper, Terry, ed. see Dooley, Virginia.
Cooper, Terry, ed. see Teaching Resources Staff.
Cooper, Terry, ed. 1st Grade Reading Practice. (p. 1991)
—3rd Grade Reading Practice. (p. 1992)
—Cursive Handwriting Practice. (p. 395)
—Manuscript Handwriting Practice. (p. 1089)
—Reading & Math. (p. 1445)
—Reading & Math, Grade 3. (p. 1445)
—Writing Practice. (p. 1965)
Cooper, Timothy S., jt. auth. see Doty, Richard C.
Cooper, Velyn. Rusty the Rat. (p. 1498)
Cooper, Wade. Animals Around the World. Cooper, Wade, illus. (p. 82)
—Farm Animals. Cooper, Wade, illus. (p. 573)
—Night Creatures. (p. 1253)
—Polar Animals. (p. 1378)
—Starry, Starry Night. (p. 1642)
Cooper, Wendy. My First Ride with Isaiah. Elizabeth Mobley, illus. (p. 1207)
Cooper, William Y. Nakai & the Red Shoes. (p. 1228)
Cooper-Gwaltney, Shannon. Family for Biskuit. (p. 568)
Cooperman, Ben. Cereal for Breakfast Cereal for Lunch. Dishaw, Karen, illus. (p. 287)
Cooperman, Sheila & Gilbert, Sara. Living with Eating Disorders. (p. 1042)
Cooperman, Sheila & Gilbert, Sara Dulaney. Living with Eating Disorders. (p. 1042)
Cooperman, Stephanie. Chien-Shiung Wu: Pioneering Physicist & Atomic Researcher. (p. 301)
Cooperman, Stephanie H. Chien-Shiung Wu: Pioneering Physicist & Atomic Researcher. (p. 301)
Cooper-Perez, Susan. Boone Files: Making of the Boone Clan: 105 Years Frozen in Time. (p. 213)
Coopersmith, Harry, compiled by. New Jewish Songbook. (p. 1245)
Coote, Mark, illus. see Hughes, Mónica.
Coote, Roger. Earth. (p. 494)
Coots, Catherine & Viegas, Jennifer. How Cells Function (p. 805)
Coots, J. Fred. Santa Claus Is Comin' to Town. Kellogg, Steven, illus. (p. 1511)
Coots, J. Fred, jt. auth. see Gillespie, Haven.
Coover, Colleen, jt. illus. see Cruz, Roger.
Coover, Colleen & Tobin, Paul. Adventure Time: The Flip Side. (p. 14)
Coovert, J. P., illus. see Gould, Francesca & Haviland, David.
Coovert, J. P., illus. see Gould, Francesca.
Coovert, J. P., illus. see Greenwald, Tommy.
Coovert, J. P., illus. see Kuhlman, Evan.
Cope, Andrew. Captured! (p. 265)
—Raccoon Rampage. (p. 1430)
—Rocket Rider. (p. 1483)
—Rollercoaster! (p. 1485)
—Spy Dog. Wallace, Tig, ed. (p. 1636)
—Spy Dog Joke Book. (p. 1636)
—Spy Pups - Training School. (p. 1636)
—Superbrain. (p. 1682)
—Teacher's Pet. (p. 1709)
—Unleashed. (p. 1821)
Cope, Andy, et al. Art of Being a Brilliant Teenager. (p. 102)
Cope Bowley, Tonia. From a Street Kid: Stephen Lungu's Incredible Life Journey. Petropouleas, Niko, illus. (p. 641)
Cope, Clifford D. Caleb: The mouse Engineer. (p. 252)
Cope, Dorothy. Day Star: A Love Spirit (p. 414)
Cope, Jane, illus. see Graves, Sue.
Cope, Michele. Linda & Michele: The Search for Snow Creek Circle. (p. 1019)
Cope, Steven R. Crow. (p. 385)
—Crow ! The Children's Poems. (p. 385)
—Crow 2. Baumgardner, Julie, illus. (p. 385)
—Frogville Skits. (p. 641)
Copeland, Colene. Pig That Bethlehem Never Knew. Somerville, Sheila, illus. (p. 1357)
Copeland, Cynthia L. Elin's Island. (p. 513)
Copeland, Cynthia L., illus. see Ubberhall, R.
Copeland, Cynthia L., jt. auth. see Cider Mill Press Staff.
Copeland, David, jt. auth. see Louis, Ron.
Copeland, Deborah Bunch. Who Knew You Were You? (p. 1916)
Copeland, Edna D. & Love, Valerie L. Attention Without Tension: A Teacher's Handbook on Attention Deficit Disorders (ADHD & ADD) Love, Terrence, illus. (p. 114)
Copeland, Eric, illus. see Dorling Kindersley Publishing Staff.
Copeland, Eric, illus. see Mendelson, Edward, ed.
Copeland, Gloria. Go with the Flow Booklet. (p. 687)
Copeland, Greg. Frederick Douglass You Never Knew. (p. 633)
Copeland, Greg, illus. see Collier, James Lincoln.
Copeland, Gregory, illus. see Buckley, James, Jr.
Copeland, Gregory, illus. see Rau, Dana Meachen.
Copeland, Mindy. Halloween Spanish for Young Children. (p. 738)
Copeland, Misty. Firebird. Myers, Christopher, illus. (p. 591)
Copeland, Peter F. Blackbeard & Other Notorious Pirates. (p. 197)
—Columbus Discovers America Coloring Book. (p. 346)
—Daniel Boone Coloring Book. (p. 405)
—George Washington Coloring Book. (p. 664)
—Heroes & Heroines of the American Revolution. (p. 772)
—Historic North American Forts. (p. 782)
—North American Indian Crafts. (p. 1264)
—Scenes of Olde New York Coloring Book. (p. 1521)
—Story of Christopher Columbus. (p. 1657)
—Story of the Alamo Coloring Book. (p. 1660)
—Story of World War II. (p. 1663)
Copeland, Peter F., et al. Big Book of the Old West to Color. (p. 179)
Copeland, Ron G. Caves of Kazoo. (p. 282)
Copeland, Tim. Investigating Romans. (p. 885)
Copelman, Evelyn, illus. see Alden, Raymond MacDonald.
Copenhagen Publishing Company, prod. Shepherd & the Sheep. (p. 1565)
Cope-Robinson, Lyn. Cat Tails. Cope-Robinson, Lyn, illus. (p. 278)
Copes, Liz Pecchi. Whompoo: The First Night. (p. 1920)
Copiel, Olivier, illus. see Johns, Geoff.
Copland, Steve. Just Because. (p. 938)
Coplans, Peta. Spaghetti for Suzy. (p. 1620)
Coplans, Peta & Williams, Dylan. Syniad Da Gwenlli Gwydd. (p. 1693)
Coplestone, Jim, illus. see Anholt, Laurence.
Coplestone, Jim, illus. see Jones, Elisabeth & Jones, Lis.
Coplestone, Jim, jt. auth. see Anholt, Laurence.
Coplestone, Jim, jt. auth. see Coplestone, Lis.
Coplestone, Lis & Coplestone, Jim. Noah's Bed. (p. 1261)
Copmbined, Slide. Discovering Art History. (p. 448)
Copp, Raymond. Carolyn Quimby. Manning, Mary, illus. (p. 271)
Coppage, Merry Ann. Periwinkle Island. Venema, Lisa J. & Garland, Lynn Rockwell, illus. (p. 1343)
Coppard, A. E. Clorinda Walks in Heaven Stories. (p. 333)
Coppard, Yvonne. Bully. (p. 241)
Coppel, Alfred, jt. auth. see Coppel, Alfred Jr.
Coppel, Alfred Jr. & Coppel, Alfred. Peacemaker. (p. 1332)
Coppel, Chris. Far from Burden Dell. (p. 572)
Coppel, Jr., Alfred, jt. auth. see Brackett, Leigh.
Coppendale, Jane. Ultimate Pet Guide. (p. 1809)
Coppendale, Jean. Family Festivals. (p. 568)
—Fire Trucks & Rescue Vehicles. (p. 591)
—Gerbils & Hamsters. (p. 666)
—Guinea Pig. (p. 731)
—Kitten. (p. 962)
—Life & Death. (p. 1007)
—Mice. (p. 1134)
—Party Time. (p. 1326)
—Puppy. (p. 1418)
—Rabbit. (p. 1429)
—Rats. (p. 1440)
—Special Holidays. (p. 1623)
—Tractors & Farm Vehicles. (p. 1775)
—Trucks. (p. 1791)
Coppendale, Jean & Graham, Ian. Cars. (p. 271)
—Great Big Book of Mighty Machines. (p. 714)
Copperwaite, Paul, ed. New Erotica (p. 1244)
Coppin, Cheryl Branch. Everything You Need to Know about Healing from Rape Trauma. (p. 545)
Coppin, Sara, jt. auth. see Beattie, Amy.
Coppini, Clementina. Apasionante Vida de Mujeres Famosas. (p. 91)
Copplestone, Jim, illus. see Jones, Liz.
Coppock, Phil & Bower's 2008-2009 4th Grade Class. Rubber Tuesday. (p. 1493)
Coppola, Angela, photos by see Neuman, Maria & Dorling Kindersley Publishing Staff.
Coppola, Denise. Sammy Beagle's Birthday Party. (p. 1507)
Coppola, Vanessa Rodriguez. Party in a Jar: 16 Kid-Friendly Jar Projects for Parties, Holidays& Special Occasions Roberts, Jennifer, photos by. (p. 1326)
Coppolillo, Rob. Holy Spokes! A Biking Bible for Everyone. (p. 791)
Copter, Steve, illus. see Chilman-Blair, Kim, et al.
Coquillat, Marcela S. Rey Chiquiton. (p. 1467)
Cora, Cat, et al. Cat Cora's Kitchen: Favorite Meals for Family & Friends. (p. 277)
Corace, Jen, illus. see Barnett, Mac.
Corace, Jen, illus. see de Sève, Randall.
Corace, Jen, illus. see Esbaum, Jill.
Corace, Jen, illus. see Lewis, Rose A.
Corace, Jen, illus. see Rosenthal, Amy Krouse.
Corace, Jen, illus. see Rylant, Cynthia & Andersen, Hans Christian.
Coram, Robert. Boyd: The Fighter Pilot Who Changed the Art of War. (p. 220)
Coray, Stacy A., illus. see Hensley, Sarah M.
Corazza, Joe. Frog Prince: A Story about Keeping Your Word. (p. 640)
Corbeil, Jean-Claude & Archambault, Ariane. My First Spanish/English Visual Dictionary. (p. 1208)
Corbeil, Jean-Claude, et al. Milet Bilingual Visual Dictionary: English-Arabic. (p. 1142)
—Milet Bilingual Visual Dictionary. (p. 1142)
Corbera, Gabriel, illus. see Kenny, Michael Daedalus.
Corbett, Barry. Embrace the Pun! (p. 517)
—Gormon: The Sentinel Awakes. Corbett, Barry, illus. (p. 703)
Corbett, Burl N. Coon Tales. (p. 364)
Corbett, CeCe. Please Turn on the Lights! (p. 1373)
Corbett, David. History of Cars. (p. 783)
Corbett, Liza, illus. see Posner, Tina.
Corbett, Pie. Growing Up. (p. 726)
—Machines. (p. 1068)
Corbett, Pie, jt. auth. see Buckton, Chris.
Corbett, Pie, jt. auth. see Palmer, Sue.
Corbett, Pie, jt. auth. see Thomson, Ruth.
Corbett, Pie, et al. Color Poems & Sounds Poems. (p. 343)
Corbett, Pie, et al, selected by. Color Poems & Sounds Poems. (p. 343)
Corbett, Robyn. Kokoye Kiko Yo: Kiko's Coconuts. (p. 966)
Corbett Sampson, Natalie. Game Plan. (p. 654)
Corbett, Sara. Hats off to Hats! (p. 752)
Corbett, Sean. Heat Waves. (p. 760)
Corbett, Steve. What Was Where? Book of Buffalo's Canals: A Field Guide. (p. 1895)
Corbett, Sue. 12 Again. (p. 1994)
—Cornelia Funke. (p. 367)
—Free Baseball. (p. 634)
—Gary Paulsen. (p. 657)
—Jeff Kinney. (p. 912)
—Jennifer L. Holm. (p. 912)
—Kate Dicamillo. (p. 944)
—Last Newspaper Boy in America. (p. 978)
—Rick Riordan. (p. 1470)
—Twelve Days of Christmas in Virginia. Cole, Henry, illus. (p. 1800)
Corbett, Susannah & Roberts, David. One Cool Cat! (p. 1294)
Corbett, W. J. Ark of the People. (p. 99)
—Dragon's Egg & Other Stories. (p. 479)
—Return to the Last Chance Zoo. (p. 1465)
Corbin, Gloria. Maggie the Miniature Schnauzer & Friends: The Valentine's Gift. (p. 1071)
Corbin, Hillam, illus. see McFarren, Kathleen & Graf, Mike.
Corbin, Marissa, illus. see Murray, Barbara.
Corbishley, Mike. Ancient Rome. (p. 70)
—Illustrated Encyclopedia of Ancient Rome. (p. 857)
—Middle Ages. (p. 1137)
Corby, Linda. girl who believed in Fairies. (p. 679)
Corcacas, Maria, photos by see Lanning, Andrea J.
Corchin, Dj. Marching Band Nerds Handbook. Dougherty, Dan, illus. (p. 1091)
Corcoran, Daniel. Iddly Widdly Fiddly Poo! (p. 852)
Corcoran, Jill. Dare to Dream... Change the World. (p. 406)
Corcoran, Mark, illus. see Higgins, Kitty.
Corcoran, Mary K. Circulatory Story. Czekaj, Jef, illus. (p. 321)
—Quest to Digest. Czekaj, Jef, illus. (p. 1426)
Corcoran, Tebra, jt. auth. see Jordano, Kimberly.
Corcorane, Ann. Animals Everywhere. (p. 82)
—Big & Small Animals. (p. 177)
—Circles Everywhere. (p. 321)
—Counting at the Parade. (p. 370)
—Counting to Ten. (p. 371)
—Hot & Cold. (p. 801)
—Measuring. (p. 1117)
—Numbers Are Everywhere (p. 1272)
—Patterns Everywhere! (p. 1329)
—Patterns Everywhere. (p. 1329)
—Sorting (p. 1614)
—Subtracting. (p. 1671)
—Zoo Full of Birds (p. 1989)
Cordeiro, James, illus. see Paniccia, Mark & Cosby, Nathan, eds.
Cordell, Cleo. Senses Bejewelled. (p. 1551)
Cordell, Evie, jt. auth. see Cordell, Ryan.
Cordell, Greg. Doodle Bug: Digging to Reach the Top. Hyun, Jinsun, illus. (p. 469)
Cordell, Matthew. Another Brother. Cordell, Matthew, illus. (p. 87)
—Hello! Hello! Cordell, Matthew, illus. (p. 764)
—Trouble Gum. Cordell, Matthew, illus. (p. 1789)
—Wish. Cordell, Matthew, illus. (p. 1940)
Cordell, Matthew, illus. see Berry, Lynne.
Cordell, Matthew, illus. see Haber, Tiffany Strelitz.
Cordell, Matthew, illus. see Hood, Susan.
Cordell, Matthew, illus. see Jennings, Patrick.
Cordell, Matthew, illus. see Levine, Gail Carson.
Cordell, Matthew, illus. see Lewis, J. Patrick.
Cordell, Matthew, illus. see Meadows, Michelle.
Cordell, Matthew, illus. see Root, Phyllis.
Cordell, Matthew, illus. see Stead, Philip C.
Cordell, Matthew, illus. see Sternberg, Julie.
Cordell, Matthew, illus. see Thompson, Lauren.
Cordell, Matthew, illus. see Vail, Rachel.
Cordell, Matthew, illus. see Vernick, Audrey.
Cordell, Matthew, illus. see Wissinger, Tamera Will & Long, Earlene R.
Cordell, Matthew, illus. see Wissinger, Tamera Will.
Cordell, Ray. Airborne Bunny. (p. 31)
Cordell, Ryan & Cordell, Evie. Two Girls Want a Puppy. Lam, Maple, illus. (p. 1803)
Cordello, Red, et al. Stakeout: Spying & Secret Surveillance. (p. 1638)
Corder, Roger. Red Wine Diet. (p. 1455)
Corder, Zizou. Lion Boy - The Chase. (p. 1020)
—Lionboy: The Truth. (p. 1021)
—Lionboy. (p. 1021)
Cordero, Chris, ed. see Polsky, Milton & Gilead, Jack.
Cordero, Flor de Maria, photos by. M is for Mexico. (p. 1067)
Cordero, Germán Santos. Camino de la Vida. (p. 256)
Cordero, Silvia Jaegar, jt. auth. see Cordero, Silvia Jaeger.

Cordero, Silvia Jaeger & Cordero, Silvia Jaegar. Huevo Azul. Sunset Producciones & Producciones, Sunset, illus. (p. 824)
Cordero-Santiago, Angelita. Curriculum Integrado de pre pre y pre Escolar. (p. 394)
Corderoy, Tracey. Beastly Feast! Artful Doodlers Limited Staff, illus. (p. 152)
—Big Splash! Artful Doodlers Limited Staff, illus. (p. 184)
—Flower in the Snow. Allsopp, Sophie, illus. (p. 607)
—Freaky Funfair (p. 632)
—Grunt & the Grouch. (p. 727)
—Hubble Bubble, Granny Trouble. Berger, Joe, illus. (p. 824)
—I Want My Mommy! Edgson, Alison, illus. (p. 847)
—It's Potty Time! Pedler, Caroline, illus. (p. 898)
—Just Right for Two. Beardshaw, Rosalind, illus. (p. 939)
—Lost Little Penguin Scott, Gavin, illus. (p. 1056)
—Magical Snow Garden. Chapman, Jane, illus. (p. 1075)
—Pick 'n' Mix (p. 1354)
—Shifty Mcgifty & Slippery Sam. Lenton, Steven, illus. (p. 1566)
—Whizz! Pop! Granny, Stop! Berger, Joe, illus. (p. 1914)
Cordery, Stacy A. Alice: Alice Roosevelt Longworth, from White House Princess to Washington Power Broker. (p. 39)
Cordery-Maring, Jeanee. Climbing over Rainbows. (p. 333)
Cordes, Miriam, illus. see Abedi, Isabel.
Cordi, Kevin, jt. auth. see Sima, Judy.
Cordier, Claire. Candy Apple. (p. 261)
—Candy Apple; Dolce Mela. (p. 261)
—Candy Apple; Maçã do Amor. (p. 261)
—Candy Apple; Manzana de Dulce. (p. 261)
—Candy Apple; Pomme d'Amour. (p. 261)
—Candy Apple; Ponm-madousiwo. (p. 261)
—Nobody will hear Me... (p. 1262)
—POLAR BEAR in CENTRAL PARK. (p. 1378)
Cordier, Severine, illus. see de Lambilly, Elisabeth.
Cordier, Séverine & Lacroix, Cynthia, creators. Day at School. (p. 412)
Cordill, Lloyd, jt. auth. see London, Matt.
Cordina, Annette. Sausage Curls. McKenzie, Heath, illus. (p. 1516)
Cordish, Janet Luckey. Dolly Dolphin. Cordish, Janet Luckey, illus. (p. 464)
—First Ice Cream Cone. Cordish, Janet Luckey, illus. (p. 595)
Cordner, Theo, illus. see Farwell, Nick.
Cordone Warner, Debra. Buddy & A Walk in the Woods. (p. 234)
—Busy Day for Baby Duck & Little Boy Blue. (p. 246)
—Henry's Daily Walk. (p. 769)
—I Almost Found Some Dinosaur Bones! (p. 831)
—Pumpkee & the Day of Harvest. (p. 1416)
cordone-warner, debra. Starzzee & A Day of Play. (p. 1644)
Córdova, Amy. Abuelita's Heart. Córdova, Amy, illus. (p. 7)
Córdova, Amy, illus. see Anaya, Rudolfo A.
Córdova, Amy, illus. see Anaya, Rudolfo A. & Anaya, Rudolfo.
Córdova, Amy, illus. see Anaya, Rudolfo.
Córdova, Amy, illus. see Cohn, Diana.
Córdova, Amy, illus. see Lamadrid, Enrique R.
Córdova, Amy, illus. see Lamadrid, Enrique R. & Arellano, Juan Estevan.
Cordova, Amy, illus. see Tafolla, Carmen.
Cordova, Amy & Gollogly, Gene. Talking Eagle & the Lady of Roses: The Story of Juan Diego & Our Lady of Guadalupe. Cordova, Amy, illus. (p. 1703)
Córdova, Ricardo, jt. auth. see Cruz, José Miguel.
Cordova, Sarah. Arch Angel (p. 95)
Cordova, Soledad. Mi libro. Cornejo, Eulalia, illus. (p. 1132)
—Poemas de Perros y Gatos. Graullera, Fabiola, illus. (p. 1376)
Cordova, Zoraida. Savage Blue. (p. 1516)
—Vast & Brutal Sea. (p. 1833)
—Vicious Deep. (p. 1840)
Cordoves, Barbara, pseud & Cordoves, Gladys M. Legend of Zias. Cordoves, Barbara & Cordoves, Gladys M., illus. (p. 989)
Cordoves, Gladys M., jt. auth. see Cordoves, Barbara, pseud.
Cordoza, Sandra Sandlin. Smarticus & the Abc's. (p. 1593)
Cordsen, Carol Foskett. Milkman. Jones, Douglas B., illus. (p. 1143)
Cordwell, Mary Hebert. Dirty-Foot Fairy. (p. 446)
Core, Sarah & Varacalli, Lauren. College of Wooster College Prowler off the Record. (p. 340)
Coren, Alan. Arthur & Bellybutton Diamond. (p. 103)
—Arthur & the Purple Panic. (p. 103)
—Arthur the Kid. (p. 104)
—Arthur's Last Stand. (p. 104)
—Buffalo Arthur. (p. 235)
—Klondike Arthur. (p. 963)
—Railroad Arthur. (p. 1433)
Coren, Michael. C. S. Lewis: The Man Who Created Narnia. (p. 250)
Coren, Stanley. Why Do Dogs Have Wet Noses? (p. 1923)
Corentin, Philippe. Chafl (p. 288)
—Fulanito de Tal. Ros, Rafael, tr. (p. 646)
—Ogro, el Lobo, la Niña y el Pastel. (p. 1280)
—Papa! (p. 1321)
—Papa. (p. 1321)
—¡Papá! (p. 1321)
Corey, Barbara, illus. see Hillert, Margaret.
Corey, Dorothy. You Go Away Paterson, Diane, illus. (p. 1975)
—You Go Away. Fox, Lisa, illus. (p. 1975)
Corey, Joy. Tools of Spiritual Warfare. (p. 1767)
Corey, Melinda. Chronology of 20th-Century America. (p. 317)
Corey, Shana. Barack Obama: Out of Many, One. Bernardin, James, illus. (p. 137)
—Barack Obama: Out of Many, One. (p. 137)
—Here Come the Girl Scouts! Hooper, Hadley, illus. (p. 770)
—James Goes Buzz, Buzz. Courtney, Richard, illus. (p. 907)
—Mermaid Queen: The Spectacular True Story of Annette Kellerman, Who Swam Her Way to Fame, Fortune, & Swimsuit History. Fotheringham, Edwin, illus. (p. 1128)
—Milly & the Macy's Parade. Helquist, Brett, illus. (p. 1144)
—Monster Parade. Terry, Will, illus. (p. 1168)
—Players in Pigtails. Gibbon, Rebecca, illus. (p. 1372)
Corey, Shana & Awdry, Wilbert V. Stuck in the Mud. Courtney, Richard, illus. (p. 1668)
Corey, Victoria, illus. see Archambault, Jeanne.
Corfe, Robert. Deism & Social Ethics: The Role of Religion in the Third Millennium. (p. 424)
Corfee, Stephanie. Creative Doodling & Beyond. (p. 379)
Corfield, Robin Bell, illus. see Waters, Fiona.
Corgliano, K. L. Millie & Me (p. 1144)
—Millie & Me Fourth Grade Field Day. (p. 1144)
Corianne, Strupp. Friends for Keeps. (p. 638)
Corichi, Yadhira, illus. see Hernandez, Ruben.
Coriell, Shelley. Goodbye, Rebel Blue. (p. 701)
—Welcome, Caller, This Is Chloe. (p. 1873)
Corio, Paul, illus. see Matsen, Bradford.
Corirossi, Steven A. Angus & the Hidden Fort. (p. 75)
corjanjamnic. Angels on Earth (p. 75)
Cork, Barbara. Pocket Nature. (p. 1375)
Corke, Estelle. Gingerbread Man. (p. 677)
—Goldilocks & the Three Bears. (p. 696)
Corke, Estelle, illus. see Butterfield, Moira.
Corke, Estelle, illus. see Clark, Sally.
Corke, Estelle, illus. see Daley, Michael J.
Corke, Estelle, illus. see Froeb, Lori C.
Corke, Estelle, illus. see Harrast, Tracy & Readers Digest Childrens Publishing Inc. Staff.
Corke, Estelle, illus. see Harrast, Tracy.
Corke, Estelle, illus. see Rock, Lois & Piper, Sophie.
Corke, Estelle, illus. see Wright, Robin & Costello, Dee.
Corkran, Alice. Down the Snow Stairs: Or, from Goodnight to Goodmorning. Browne, Gordon, illus. (p. 474)
Corlett, Mary Lee. Belle: The Amazing, Astonishingly Magical Journey of an Artfully Painted Lady. Saroff, Phyllis, illus. (p. 162)
—Belle's Wild Ride: The Artful Adventure of a Butterfly & a Cabbie. Cayless, Sophie, illus. (p. 163)
Corlett, William. Bridge in the Clouds. (p. 227)
—Door in the Tree. (p. 470)
—Steps up the Chimney. (p. 1648)
—Tunnel Behind the Waterfall. (p. 1797)
Corley & Vivian Levinge, Suzanne. I've Always Wanted a Monkey. (p. 900)
Corley, Monte, jt. auth. see Nichols, Roy.
Corley, Rob, illus. see McCorkle, Brent & Parker, Amy.
Corley, Rob, illus. see Peterson, Eugene H., tr.
Corley, Rob, illus. see Sorrells, W. A.
Corley, Sandra J. Scrawny Little Tree. (p. 1532)
Corley, Sandra Y. Crochet Detective Case #101: The Case of the Missing Afirican Treasure. (p. 384)
Corley, Suzanne, jt. auth. see Levinge, Vivian.
Corley, Theresa. Journey Home: The Story of Michael Thomas & the Seven Angels. (p. 928)
Corliss, William R. Scientific Anomalies & other Provocative Phenomena. (p. 1528)
Corlyn, Ron. House That Grew. (p. 803)
Cormack, Allan, illus. see Bradford, Karleen.
Cormack, Allan, illus. see Flatt, Lizann.
Cormack, Allan, illus. see Souza, D. M.
Cormack, Kim. Being. (p. 160)
Cormack, Malcolm & Twiggs, Ruth. Tigers & Sails & ABC Tales. (p. 1749)
Corman, Cid. One Man's Moon: Poems by Basho & Other Japanese Poets. (p. 1296)
Corman, Clifford L. & Trevino, Esther. Eukee the Jumpy Jumpy Elephant. DiMatteo, Richard A., illus. (p. 540)
Corman, Dick. Fountain of Age. (p. 624)
—Noah Knows. (p. 1261)
Cormand, Bernat. Barcelona, Tell Us about Gaudi. Kliczkowski, H., ed. (p. 138)
—Barcelona, Tell Us about Yourself. (p. 138)
Cormier, Cindy Mitchell. Don't Look over the Edge. (p. 468)
Cormier, Robert. Chocolate War. (p. 309)
—Fade. (p. 561)
—Frenchtown Summer. (p. 636)
—Guerra Dei Cioccolatini. (p. 728)
—Guerra del Chocolate. (p. 728)
—Heroes. (p. 772)
—I Am the Cheese. (p. 834)
—Rag & Bone Shop. (p. 1433)
—Sindrome de la Ternura. Palmer, Magdalena, tr. (p. 1578)
—Tenderness. (p. 1719)
—We All Fall Down. (p. 1865)
Cormier, Shawn P. Necromancer. (p. 1239)
—NiDemon. (p. 1251)
—Nomadin. (p. 1263)
Corn, Tori. Dixie Wants an Allergy. Cote, Nancy, illus. (p. 455)
—What Will It Be, Penelope? Ceccolini, Danielle, illus. (p. 1895)
Cornejo, Eduardo, illus. see Bravo, Leonor.
Cornejo, Eulalia. Enriqueta. (p. 531)
—Porque Existes Tu. (p. 1386)
Cornejo, Eulalia, illus. see Cordova, Soledad.
Cornejo, Eulalia, illus. see Iturralde, Edna.
Cornejo, Eulalia, illus. see Iturralde, Edna.
Cornejo, Eulalia, illus. see Williams, Ricardo.
Cornejo, Santiago, illus. see Lomba, Ana.
Cornelia Meigs. Master Simon's Garden. (p. 1103)
Cornelison, Reuel, illus. see White, Russ.
Cornelison, Sue. Down by the Bay. (p. 474)
Cornelison, Sue, illus. see Sileo, Frank J.
Cornelison, Sue, illus. see Wilson, Land.
Cornelison, Sue, illus. see Wooden, John, et al.
Cornelison, Sue F. Twelve Days of Christmas in Iowa. (p. 1800)
Cornelison, Sue F., illus. see Wooden, John, et al.
Cornelison, Susan F., illus. see Binkow, Howard.
Cornelison, Susan F., illus. see Wooden, John.
Cornelius, Brad, illus. see Simoneau, D. K.
Cornell, Betty & Van Wagenen, Maya. Betty Cornell's Teen-Age Popularity Guide. (p. 172)
Cornell, Curtis L. Leprechauns, Unicorns, & Mark Kurnan. (p. 993)
Cornell du Houx, Emily, illus. see du Houx, Ramona, et al.
Cornell du Houx, Emily M. D., illus. see Russell, Elaine.
Cornell, George & Henry, Gordon. Ojibwa. (p. 1282)
Cornell, Joseph Bharat, jt. auth. see Muir, John.
Cornell, Karl. Awesome Snacks & Appetizers. Cohen, Brie, photos by. (p. 121)
—Dandy Desserts. Cohen, Brie, photos by. (p. 403)
—Diana Trujillo: Mars Science Lab Engineer. (p. 434)
—Facebook Founder & Internet Entrepreneur Mark Zuckerberg. (p. 560)
—Marvelous Muffins, Breads, & Pancakes. Cohen, Brie, photos by. (p. 1099)
—Minecraft Creator Markus "Notch" Persson. (p. 1146)
—Slurpable Smoothies & Drinks. Cohen, Brie, photos by. (p. 1591)
—Sweet Cookies & Bars. Cohen, Brie, photos by. (p. 1689)
—Terrific Veggies on the Side. Cohen, Brie, photos by. (p. 1721)
—Theoretical Physicist Stephen Hawking. (p. 1729)
—Urban Biologist Danielle Lee. (p. 1825)
Cornell, Karl A. Nitty-Gritty Gardening Book: Fun Projects for All Seasons. Larson, Jennifer S., photos by. (p. 1257)
Cornell, Karl & Anwar, Merry. Cooking the Indonesian Way: Includes Low-Fat & Vegetarian Recipes. (p. 362)
Cornell, Karl & Thomas, Peter. Cooking the Southern African Way. (p. 362)
Cornell, Karl & Turkoglu, Nurcay. Cooking the Turkish Way. (p. 362)
Cornell, Kevin. Mojo the Sock Monkey. (p. 1160)
Cornell, Kevin, illus. see Barnett, Mac & John, Jory.
Cornell, Kevin, illus. see Barnett, Mac.
Cornell, Kevin, illus. see Cronin, Doreen.
Cornell, Kevin, illus. see Reed, Lynn Rowe.
Cornell, Laura, illus. see Cronin, Doreen.
Cornell, Laura, illus. see Curtis, Jamie Lee.
Cornell, Laura, illus. see Komaiko, Leah.
Cornell, Laura, illus. see Newman, Lesléa.
Cornell, Laura, illus. see Robinson, Barbara.
Cornell, Paul & Venditti, Robert. Demon Knights. Chang, Bernard, illus. (p. 426)
Cornell, Teresa Cornell, et al. Follow-the-Directions Art Activities: 20 Easy Seasonal Projects with Step-by-Step Instructions & Templates That Give Kids Practice in Reading & Following Directions. (p. 612)
Cornell-Castle, Violet R. Santa's Elves. (p. 1513)
Corner, Chris, illus. see Casey, Dawn.
Cornerstone Books. Cornerstonia: The Rose River Journey (p. 367)
Cornette, Sylvia. House Across the Lake. (p. 803)
Cornfield, Lynda Ellis. Rocks for Clean Oceans. (p. 1483)
Cornforth, Amy. Flopsy the Flamingo. (p. 606)
Cornia, Christian, illus. see Collins, Terry & Weakland, Mark.
Cornia, Christian, illus. see Slade, Suzanne.
Cornia, Christian, illus. see Weakland, Mark & Collins, Terry.
Cornia, Christian, illus. see Weakland, Mark & Slade, Suzanne.
Cornia, Christian, illus. see Weakland, Mark.
Corniel, Janet. Moving Journal for Kids. (p. 1183)
Cornille, Didier. Who Built That? Modern Houses: An Introduction to Modern Houses & Their Architects. (p. 1914)
—Who Built That? Skyscrapers: An Introduction to Skyscrapers & Their Architects. (p. 1914)
Cornilliat, Francois, tr. see Shaw, Mary.
Cornioley, Pearl Witherington & Atwood, Kathryn J. Code Name Pauline: Memoirs of a World War II Special Agent. (p. 338)
Cornish, Celeste. Voyages of the Starship Sid. (p. 1851)
Cornish, D. M. Foundling. Cornish, D. M., illus. (p. 624)
Cornish, David, illus. see McCleary, Stacey.
Cornish, Geoff. Tanks. (p. 1705)
Cornish, Linda Sowa Young. Pong's Birthday Journey. (p. 1382)
Cornish, Melanie J. & Hubbard, Ben. History of Hip Hop. (p. 784)
Cornman, Sabrina. Lepi's Golden America. Pierce, Kim, illus. (p. 993)
Cornsweet, Tom. Why Is Everything! Doing Science. (p. 1925)
Cornue, Don, illus. see Cardno, Anthony R.
Cornwall, Phyllis. Mind Your Manners Online. (p. 1145)
—Play It Safe Online. (p. 1371)
—Super Smart Information Strategies: Put It All Together. (p. 1682)
—Super Smart Information Strategies: Online Etiquette & Safety. (p. 1682)
Cornwell. Brandherd: Ein Kay-Scarpetta-Roman. (p. 222)
Cornwell, Autumn. Carpe Diem. (p. 271)
Cornwell, Betsy. Mechanica. (p. 1118)
—Tides. (p. 1747)
Cornwell, Brendan W. Aesop in Goudy. (p. 25)
Cornwell, Charles Scott. Bell. (p. 162)
Cornwell, Nicki. Armel's Revenge. Pal, Erika, illus. (p. 99)
Cornwell, Nikki. Christophe's Story. Littlewood, Karin, illus. (p. 317)
Cornwell, Patricia. Unnatural Exposure (p. 1822)
Cornwell, Paul. Only by Failure: The Many Faces of the Impossible Life of Terence Gray. (p. 1298)
Cornwell, R. D. World History in the Twentieth Century. (p. 1955)
Cornwell, T. Bettina, ed. see Rutsky, R. L.
Coro, Edys. Edys' Collection of Short Tales. (p. 505)
Corona, Laurel. War Within a War: Vietnam & the Cold War. (p. 1858)
Corona, Sarah. Misterio del Tiempo Robado. (p. 1155)
Coronado, Jinky, illus. see Cabot, Meg.
Coronado, Mark & Jackson, Dominic. Swamp Life. (p. 1688)
Coronado, Martha Munoz de, see Munoz de Coronado, Martha, ed.
Coronato, Rocco. Jonson Versus Bakhtin: Carnival & the Grotesque. (p. 925)
Coronet Instructional Media (Firm) Staff, contrib. by. Counterpoint Reader: Myth, Magic & Mystery. (p. 370)
Corp, Carey. HALO CHRONICLES: the Guardian. (p. 739)
Corp, Carey & Langdon, Lorie. Destined for Doon (p. 430)
—Doon (p. 470)
Corpi, Lucha. Where Fireflies Dance: Ahi, Donde Bailan Las Luciernagas. Reisberg, Mira, illus. (p. 1907)
Corpi, Lucha & Fields, Lisa. Triple Banana Split Boy/El Nino Goloso. Corpi, Lucha & Fields, Lisa, illus. (p. 1787)
Corporate Contibutor & Perritano, John. Causes of the American Revolution. (p. 282)
—Outcome of the American Revolution. (p. 1312)
Corporate Contibutor & Snedden, Robert. Mechanical Engineering & Simple Machines. (p. 1118)
Corporate Contibutor Staff. Dinosaur Alphabet. (p. 441)
Corporate Contibutor Staff & Aloian, Molly. George Washington: Hero of the American Revolution. (p. 664)
—Phillis Wheatley: Poet of the Revolutionary Era. (p. 1351)
Corporate Contibutor Staff & Clarke, Gordon. Significant Battles of the American Revolution. (p. 1574)
Corporate Contibutor Staff & Colozza Cocca, Lisa. Marquis de Lafayette: Fighting for America's Freedom. (p. 1096)
Corporate Contibutor Staff & Mason, Helen. Life on the Homefront During the American Revolution. (p. 1012)
Corporate Contibutor Staff & Roberts, Steve. King George Iii: England's Struggle to Keep America. (p. 958)
Corporate Contibutor Staff & West, David. Dinosaur Alphabet. (p. 441)
—Dinosaur Colors. (p. 441)
—Dinosaur Numbers. (p. 442)
—Dinosaur Shapes. (p. 442)
Corporate Contributor. Drew Brees. (p. 485)
—Selena Gomez. (p. 1549)
—Steve Nash. (p. 1649)
—Taylor Lautner. (p. 1708)
Corporate Contributor, ed. Diary of a Texas Kid. (p. 435)
Corporate Contributor Staff. Economics of a Video Game. (p. 502)
Corporate Contributor Staff, jt. ed. see Gale Editors.
Corporate Contributor Staff & Flatt, Lizann. Economics of the Super Bowl. (p. 503)
Corporate Contributor Staff & Johnson, Robin. Economics of Making a Movie. (p. 502)
Corporate Contributor Staff & Nixon, James. London 2012: Olympic Venues. (p. 1046)
Corporate Contributor Staff & O'Brien, Cynthia. Climate Maps. (p. 332)
Corporate Contributor Staff & Pegis, Jessica. Political Maps. (p. 1380)
Corporate Contributor Staff & Perl, Sheri. Economics of a Rock Concert. (p. 502)
Corporate Contributor Staff & Rodger, Ellen. Atlas & Globe Skills. (p. 112)
—Physical Maps. (p. 1353)
Corpus, Mary Grace, illus. see Dans, Peter E.
Corr, Christopher. Heaven in a Poem: An Anthology of Poems. (p. 761)
—Map of the World Play Scene. (p. 1090)
—Whole World: PB with CD. (p. 1920)
—Whole World: Fun Eco Activities. (p. 1920)
Corr, Christopher, illus. see Blackstone, Stella.
Corr, Christopher, illus. see Davies, Stephen.
Corr, Christopher, illus. see Ganeri, Anita.
Corr, Christopher, illus. see Hickey, Matt.
Corr, Christopher, illus. see Krebs, Laurie & Blackstone, Stella.
Corr, Christopher, illus. see Krebs, Laurie.
Corr, Christopher, illus. see Mudpuppy Press Staff.
Corr, Christopher, illus. see Samuel, Quentin.
Corr, Christopher, jt. auth. see Blackstone, Stella.
Corr, Christopher, jt. auth. see Davies, Stephen.
Corr, Christopher, jt. auth. see Krebs, Laurie.
Corr, Christopher, jt. auth. see Nanji, Shenaaz.
Corr, Christopher, jt. auth. see Penner, Fred.
Corr, Christopher & Penner, Fred. Whole World. (p. 1920)
—Whole World. Corr, Christopher, illus. (p. 1920)
Corr, Janice. Aussie Time Travellers & the Cave of the Opal Eyed Snake. (p. 116)
Corr, Kendra & Coletti, Sharon. Ancient Greeks: I Think: It's Elementary! (p. 69)
Corrado, Diane. I Wanna Be Purr-Fect! ShowCat. Kanarek, Michael, illus. (p. 847)
Corrain, Lucia. Art of the Renaissance. (p. 102)
Corral, Alberto. Mi Monstruo Burrufu. Sorrentino, Alessandra, illus. (p. 1133)
Corral, Mercedes, tr. see Jacq, Christian.
Corral, Rodrigo, jt. creator see Anthony, Jessica.
Corre, Lorraine. Book #1, Just for Fun. (p. 210)
Correa, Alvaro. Mountain Miracle: A Navtivity Story. Lorenzo, Gloria, illus. (p. 1181)
Correa, Shan. Gaff (p. 652)
Correll, Ann. Ears to Hear. (p. 494)
Correll, Gemma. What I Wore Today. (p. 1887)
Correll, Gemma, illus. see Berry, Lynne.
Correll, Gemma, illus. see Turner, James.
Correll, Stephanie. Newton's Wildlife Adventures: The Old Mill Pond. Knott, Simon, illus. (p. 1249)
Corrette, Keith F., photos by see Mesplay, Gail G.
Corrick, Dave. Louie the Bee: The Insects Prevail. (p. 1058)
Corrick, James, jt. auth. see Corrick, James A.
Corrick, James A. Bloody, Rotten Roman Empire: The Disgusting Details about Life in Ancient Rome (p. 201)
—Civil War & Emancipation. (p. 325)
—Dwayne "The Rock" Johnson. (p. 491)
—Early Middle Ages. (p. 494)
—Gritty, Stinky Ancient Egypt: The Disgusting Details about Life in Ancient Egypt. (p. 724)
—Rough, Stormy Age of Vikings: The Disgusting Details about Viking Life (p. 1491)
Corrick, James A. & Corrick, James. Uniquely Arizona (p. 1818)
Corrick, James A. & Lew, Kristi. Acids & Bases. (p. 9)
Corrick, James A., et al. Disgusting History: The Smelliest, Dirtiest Eras of the Past 10,000 Years. (p. 450)
Corrie, Chad. Seer's Quest: Book One of the Divine Gambit Trilogy (p. 1548)
Corrie, Linda D., jt. auth. see Corrie, William E., 3rd.

C

Corrie, William E., 3rd & Corrie, Linda D. Another Man's Treasure: A Guide to Shadazar. Breed, Jessica & Corrie, Linda D., eds. (p. 88)
—Shades of Earth: Earth History with a Twist Breed, Jessica & Corrie, Linda D., eds. (p. 1557)
Corriel, Michele. Weird Rocks. Bilyeu, Dan, illus. (p. 1872)
Corrigan, Delia Stubbs & Tighe, Elizabeth. Go Team! Mascots of the SEC. (p. 687)
Corrigan, Eireann. Accomplice. (p. 8)
—Believing Game. (p. 162)
—Ordinary Ghosts. (p. 1302)
Corrigan, Jim. 1900s Decade in Photos: A Decade of Discovery. (p. 2002)
—1910s Decade in Photos: A Decade That Shook the World. (p. 2002)
—1920s Decade in Photos: The Roaring Twenties. (p. 2002)
—1930s Decade in Photos: Depression & Hope. (p. 2002)
—1940s Decade in Photos: A World at War. (p. 2002)
—1950s Decade in Photos: The American Decade. (p. 2002)
—1960s Decade in Photos: Love, Freedom, & Flower Power. (p. 2002)
—1970s Decade in Photos: Protest & Change. (p. 2002)
—1980s Decade in Photos: The Triumph of Democracy. (p. 2002)
—1990s Decade in Photos: The Rise of Technology. (p. 2002)
—2000s Decade in Photos: A New Millennium. (p. 2003)
—Alan Turing. (p. 33)
—Business Leaders: Steve Jobs. (p. 245)
—Cargo Planes. (p. 268)
—Causes of the War on Terrorism. (p. 282)
—Causes of World War II. (p. 282)
—Civil War in the West. (p. 325)
—Ethiopia. (p. 539)
—Ethiopia. Rotberg, Robert I., ed. (p. 539)
—Europeans & Native Americans. Johnson, Troy, ed. (p. 540)
—Filipino Immigration. (p. 586)
—General George G. Meade: Victor at Gettysburg. (p. 660)
—General James Longstreet: Lee's "Old War Horse" (p. 660)
—Kazakhstan. (p. 946)
—Kenya. (p. 949)
—Kenya. Rotberg, Robert I., ed. (p. 949)
—Steve Jobs. (p. 1649)
—Supreme Court Justices: The Story of John Marshall. (p. 1685)
—Training. (p. 1777)
—World War II Musteen, Jason R., ed. (p. 1959)
Corrigan, Kathleen. 123 (p. 2000)
—ABC (p. 2)
—My First 123 (p. 1203)
—My First ABC (p. 1204)
—My First Colours (p. 1206)
—My First Shapes (p. 1207)
Corrigan, Patricia. Bringing Science to Life: A Guide from the St. Louis Science Center. (p. 229)
Corrigan, Patrick, illus. see Martin, Bill, Jr., et al.
Corris, Charles R. Donald Ditz & the Red Tiger (p. 465)
Corriveau, Art. 13 Hangmen. (p. 1995)
—How I Got a Life & a Dog. (p. 810)
—How I, Nicky Flynn, Finally Got a Life (And a Dog) (p. 810)
Corriveau, Ron. Agent's Daughter. (p. 29)
Corsaro, Nicola. What Are Sound Waves? (p. 1879)
Corse, Nicole. Power Rangers Samurai: Power Cards. (p. 1390)
Corse, Nicole & Foster, Dara. Pupstyle. (p. 1418)
Corsetto, Danielle. Adventure Time (p. 14)
—Adventure Time - Seeing Red. (p. 14)
—Adventure Time Vol. 2: Pixel Princesses. (p. 15)
—Pixel Princesses Sterling, Zack, illus. (p. 1365)
—Playing with Fire. (p. 1372)
Corsey, Jenny, ed. see Marsh, Carole.
Corso, Bertina, illus. see Corso, Erika.
Corso, Cherie. Crazy Ponytails. (p. 378)
Corso, Erika. Day You Came. Corso, Erika & Corso, Bertina, illus. (p. 415)
Corso, Joseph. Mother Earth Four. (p. 1177)
Corso, Suzanne. Sammy & Sue Go Green Too! (p. 1507)
Cort, Ben. Muddle Ocean: A Magnetic Play Book. (p. 1188)
Cort, Ben, illus. see Bently, Peter.
Cort, Ben, illus. see Freedman, Claire.
Cort, Ben, illus. see Grant, Richard E. & Bently, Peter.
Cort, Ben, illus. see Knapman, Timothy.
Cort, Ben, illus. see Simon, Francesca.
Cort, Ben, illus. see Starr, Ringo, pseud.
Cort, Ben, illus. see Weale, Andrew.
CortA%s, Elena Valencia, tr. see Aranega, Merce.
Cortazar, Alicia Canas, illus. see Martín Anguita, Carmen & Carmen, Martín Anguita.
Cortázar, Julio. Todos Los Fuegos el Fuego. (p. 1761)
Cortes, Eunice, tr. see Andrews-Goebel, Nancy.
Cortes, Eunice, tr. see Bull, Jane.
Cortes, Eunice, tr. see Jenkins, Emily.
Cortes, Eunice, tr. see Krebs, Laurie.
Cortes, Eunice, tr. see Manning, Mick.
Cortes, Eunice & Cortes, Laura. Diego Rana-Pintor. Pilatowski, Boris, illus. (p. 437)
Cortes Hernandez, Santiago & Cortes, Santiago. Hombre Qve Se Convirtio en Toro: Y Otras Historias de la Inquisicion. Clement, Edgar, illus. (p. 791)
Cortes, Laura, jt. auth. see Cortes, Eunice.
Cortes, Mario, illus. see Driscoll, Laura & RH Disney Staff.
Cortes, Mary. Where on Earth Did My Sock Go? (p. 1909)
Cortes, Osvaldo, illus. see Lara, Jose Luis Trueba.
Cortes, Osvaldo, illus. see Trueba, Jose Luis.
Cortes, Paulina, illus. see Baez, Josefina.
Cortés, Ricardo. It's Just a Plant: A Children's Story about Marijuana. (p. 897)
Cortés, Ricardo, illus. see Mansbach, Adam.
Cortes, Ricardo, illus. see Terrell, Heather.
Cortés, Ricardo, jt. auth. see Harris, Devon.
Cortes, Santiago, jt. auth. see Cortes Hernandez, Santiago.
Cortez, Jess S. My Trip to the Harbor. Cortez, Jess S., illus. (p. 1220)
Cortez, Linda. When I Was Little. Shrum, Edgar, illus. (p. 1903)
Cortez, Sarah, ed. Windows into My World: Latino Youth Write Their Lives. (p. 1936)
—You Don't Have a Clue: Latino Mystery Stories for Teens. (p. 1975)
Cortina, Janice. Grandpa Kolbe & the Squirrels. (p. 709)
—Lonely Sixteenth. (p. 1046)
Cortina, Regina & San Román, Sonsoles, eds. Women & Teaching: Global Perspectives on the Feminization of a Profession. (p. 1945)
Cortinas, John. On the Job with a Meteorologist. (p. 1290)
Cortinas, Suzanne. Tale of Red Feather. (p. 1700)
Cortino, Becky. From the Heart: Injecting Healing Humor in the Healthcare Setting. (p. 644)
Cortland, D J. Look at Books: Learning to Count by Tens to 50. (p. 1048)
—Week of Weather: Learning to Collect & Record Data on a Pictograph. (p. 1871)
Cortland, Riley, jt. auth. see Mills, Nathan.
Cortright, Angel. Miss Adventure of Animals & Their Short Stories. (p. 1151)
Cortright, Robert S. Bridging the World. Cortright, Robert S., photos by. (p. 227)
Corts, Enrique, illus. see Nickel, Scott.
Corum, Jaime, illus. see Wilbur, Helen L.
Corum, Stephanie J. Goats with Coats. (p. 688)
Corvaisier, Laurent. Songs in the Shade of the Flamboyant Tree: French Creole Lullabies & Nursery Rhymes (p. 1612)
Corvino, Lucy. Arabian Nights. (p. 94)
Corvino, Lucy, illus. see Alcott, Louisa May.
Corvino, Lucy, illus. see Burnett, Frances Hodgson.
Corvino, Lucy, illus. see Doyle, Arthur.
Corvino, Lucy, illus. see Flinn, Lisa & Younger, Barbara.
Corvino, Lucy, illus. see Hugo, Victor.
Corvino, Lucy, illus. see Kipling, Rudyard.
Corvino, Lucy, illus. see Lofting, Hugh.
Corvino, Lucy, illus. see London, Jack.
Corvino, Lucy, illus. see Montgomery, L. M.
Corvino, Lucy, illus. see Pyle, Howard.
Corvino, Lucy, illus. see Schoonmaker, Frances, ed.
Corvino, Lucy, illus. see Sewell, Anna.
Corvino, Lucy, illus. see Stevenson, Robert Louis.
Corvino, Lucy, illus. see Twain, Mark, pseud.
Corvino, Lucy, illus. see Zamorsky, Tania & Burnett, Frances Hodgson.
Corvino, Lucy, tr. see Flinn, Lisa & Younger, Barbara.
Corwin, Edward S. "Higher Law" Background of American Constitutional Law. (p. 779)
Corwin, Jeff. Great Alaska Adventure! (p. 713)
—Snake-Tacular. Pascoe, Elaine, ed. (p. 1596)
—Whale of a Time! (p. 1877)
—Wild Life: The Authorized Biography. (p. 1929)
—Wild, Wild Southwest! (p. 1930)
—Your Backyard Is Wild. (p. 1980)
Corwin, Jeff, jt. auth. see Dewin, Howard.
Corwin, Jeffrey, contrib. by. World of Primates. (p. 1957)
Corwin, Judith Hoffman. Bright Yellow Flower. (p. 228)
—Kwanzaa Crafts: A Holiday Craft Book. (p. 969)
—Native American Crafts of California, the Great Basin, & the Southwest. (p. 1234)
—Native American Crafts of the Northeast & Southeast. Corwin, Judith Hoffman, illus. (p. 1234)
—Native American Crafts of the Plains & Plateau. (p. 1234)
—Native American Crafts of the Plains & Plateau. Corwin, Judith Hoffman, illus. (p. 1234)
Corwin, Katherine. River of Glass. Jasuna, Aija, illus. (p. 1476)
Corwin, Katherine A. R. Greg the Bearded Dragon & Thomas the Sea Turtle: A Tale of Adventure, Discovery, & Friendship. (p. 723)
Corwin, Lena, illus. see Ronci, Kelli.
Corwin, Stuart, illus. see Corwin, Susan Simon.
Corwin, Susan Simon. Cryptic Cat. Corwin, Stuart, illus. (p. 387)
Cory, Adrian A. On the Eighth Tin. (p. 1290)
Cory, David. Little Jack Rabbit's Favorite Bunny Tales. Day, Maurice, illus. (p. 1029)
Cory, Diane. God & Me! 2: Ages 6-9 (p. 688)
—Gotta Have God 2: Ages 6-9. Heiser, Aline, illus. (p. 704)
Cory, Fanny Y., illus. see Gates, Josephine Scribner.
Cory, Kim Delmar. Home to Mackinac: The Tale of Young Jack Murphy's Discovery of Loyalty, Family, & Forgiveness. Evans, Laura, illus. (p. 793)
—Tending Ben's Garden. (p. 1719)
Cory'S Club Staff. Adventures of Cory: Lessons in Disobedience. (p. 17)
Cosby, Andrew. Mary Scary. (p. 1101)
Cosby, Andrew & Nelson, Michael Alan. X Isle Scott, Greg, illus. (p. 1967)
Cosby, Andrew & Stokes, Johanna. Death Valley Marcellus, Rhoald, illus. (p. 420)
—Savage Brothers. Albuquerque, Rafael, illus. (p. 1516)
Cosby, Bill. Friends of a Feather: One of Life's Little Fables. Cosby, Erika, illus. (p. 638)
Cosby, Braxton/A. Sect: The Windgate. (p. 1546)
Cosby, Erika, illus. see Cosby, Bill.
Cosby, Nate. Cow Boy: A Boy & His Horse. Eliopoulos, Chris, illus. (p. 373)
Cosby, Nathan, jt. ed. see Paniccia, Mark.
Cosby, Sam & Metzger, Clancy. Ceruladons: Blue dreams rain to Tears. (p. 287)
Cosco, Rafaella, illus. see Mackenzie, Carine.
Cosco, Raffaella, illus. see MacKenzie, Carine.
Cosentino, Mike. Atlanta Running Guide. (p. 112)
Cosentino, Ralph. Batman: The Story of the Dark Knight. Cosentino, Ralph, illus. (p. 144)
—Superman: The Story of the Man of Steel. (p. 1683)
—Wonder Woman: The Story of the Amazon Princess. Cosentino, Ralph, illus. (p. 1947)
Cosford, Nina. Dublin. (p. 487)
Cosgrove, Brian & Dorling Kindersley Publishing Staff. Weather. (p. 1869)
Cosgrove, Lee, illus. see Halls, Kelly Milner & Holland, Simon.
Cosgrove, Lee, illus. see Halls, Kelly Milner.
Cosgrove, Lee, illus. see Holland, Simon.
Cosgrove, Stephen. Across a Stream. (p. 9)
—Bee Double Bopp: Respecting Others. Arroyo, Fian, illus. (p. 157)
—Big Bubba Bigg, Jr: Dealing with Bullies. Arroyo, Fian, illus. (p. 180)
—Bigg Family: Getting along with Others. Arroyo, Fian, illus. (p. 185)
—Bugglar Brothers: Consequences of Stealing. Arroyo, Fian, illus. (p. 236)
—Buttermilk. James, Robin, illus. (p. 248)
—Columbus Meets Isabella & Ferdinand. (p. 346)
—Creole. James, Robin, illus. (p. 381)
—Cricket Clickett: Finding Your Talents. Arroyo, Fian, illus. (p. 382)
—Easter Bunnies. Edelson, Wendy, illus. (p. 499)
—Fanny. James, Robin, illus. (p. 571)
—Fiddler T. Bear. Edelson, Wendy, illus. (p. 583)
—Flutterby. James, Robin, illus. (p. 609)
—Flynn "Flea" Flicker: Sticking to the Truth. Arroyo, Fian, illus. (p. 610)
—Frazzle. (p. 631)
—Gabriel Faintheart. Edelson, Wendy, illus. (p. 652)
—Gnome from Nome. James, Robin, illus. (p. 685)
—GrandPa Sam. Edelson, Wendy, illus. (p. 709)
—Grumpling. James, Robin, illus. (p. 727)
—Hickory B. Hopp: Paying Attention. Arroyo, Fian, illus. (p. 775)
—Jalopy. (p. 906)
—Katy Didd Bigg: Standing up for Yourself. Arroyo, Fian, illus. (p. 945)
—Leo the Lop. James, Robin, illus. (p. 992)
—Melody Moth: Practice Makes Perfect. Arroyo, Fian, illus. (p. 1125)
—Mizz Buggly: Doing Your Best. Arroyo, Fian, illus. (p. 1157)
—Morgan & Me. James, Robin, illus. (p. 1175)
—Muffin Dragon. James, Robin, illus. (p. 1189)
—Pickles & the P-Flock Bullies. James, Robin, illus. (p. 1354)
—Pretty, Pretty Prettina. Edelson, Wendy, illus. (p. 1398)
—Sniffles. James, Robin, illus. (p. 1597)
—Snugg N. Flitter: Facing Your Fears. Arroyo, Fian, illus. (p. 1601)
—Storybook Readers Steelhammer, Ilona, illus. (p. 1663)
—Wheedle & the Noodle. James, Robin, illus. (p. 1900)
—Wheedle on the Needle. James, Robin, illus. (p. 1900)
Cosgrove, Stephen, jt. auth. see Penn, Audrey.
Cosgrove, Stephen & Higgins, Kathy. Under Siege. (p. 1813)
Cosgrove, Stephen & Higgins, Kitty. el juicio del pastelero & Tasty Tort Trial. (p. 507)
—Golden Spike. (p. 695)
—Semillas de Estrellamelón Star-Melon Seeds. (p. 1550)
—Star-Melon Seeds. (p. 1640)
—Trivia Pursuit. (p. 1788)
Cosgrove, Stephen & Higgins, Kitty, told to. Tasty Tort Trial. (p. 1707)
Cosimano, Elle. Nearly Found. (p. 1239)
Cosman, Felicia. Osteoporosis: Help Prevent—And Even Reverse—The Disease That Burdens Millions of Women. (p. 1306)
Cosman, Madeline Pelner & Jones, Linda Gale. Handbook to Life in the Medieval World (p. 740)
Cosmic Debris Etc., Inc. Staff, jt. auth. see Gomi, Taro.
Cosmic Debris Etc., Inc. Staff & Chronicle Books Staff. Thumbelina. Max, illus. (p. 1745)
—Wine Deck: 50 Ways to Choose, Serve, & Enjoy Great Wines. Armstrong, E. J., photos by. (p. 1936)
Cosmic Debris Etc., Inc Staff & Streeten, Roz. Rosie Flo's Animals Coloring Book. (p. 1490)
—Rosie Flo's Coloring Book. (p. 1490)
—Rosie Flo's Garden Coloring Book. (p. 1490)
Cosmic Debris Etc., Inc. Staff, et al. Little Giraffe: Finger Puppet Book. (p. 1028)
—Little Lion. (p. 1030)
—Uglydoll School Planner. (p. 1808)
—Worst-Case Scenario Survival Handbook: Middle School. (p. 1961)
Cosmin, Constantin, illus. see Ralph, Gordon & lf.
Cosneau, Géraldine. All Around the World. (p. 44)
Cosner, Jeff, illus. see Lough, Whitney.
Cosper, Andy. Adventures of Drew Kreeger: Book 1. (p. 17)
Coss, Lauren. Let's Sort by Color. (p. 1000)
—Let's Sort by Size. (p. 1000)
—Let's Sort Money. (p. 1000)
—Let's Sort Shapes. (p. 1000)
—Life in Estuaries. (p. 1010)
—Life in Oceans. (p. 1010)
—Life in Ponds. (p. 1011)
—Volcanoes. (p. 1849)
—Weird-But-True Facts about Earth. Petelinsek, Kathleen, illus. (p. 1872)
—Weird-But-True Facts about Scary Things. Gallagher-Cole, Mernie, illus. (p. 1872)
—Weird-But-True Facts about the Human Body. Gallagher-Cole, Mernie, illus. (p. 1872)
—Weird-But-True Facts about Weather. Gallagher-Cole, Mernie, illus. (p. 1872)
Cossi, Olga. Playing Your Heart Out. (p. 1373)
Cosson, J. Easter Traditions Around the World. Chavarri, Elisa, illus. (p. 499)
—Smart Kid's Guide to Feeling Sad or Angry. Rooney, Ronnie, illus. (p. 1592)
—Smart Kid's Guide to Friendships. Rooney, Ronnie, illus. (p. 1592)
—Smart Kid's Guide to Knowing What to Say. Rooney, Ronnie, illus. (p. 1592)
—Smart Kid's Guide to Using the Internet. Rooney, Ronnie, illus. (p. 1593)
—Wishing Traditions Around the World. Chavarri, Elisa, illus. (p. 1940)
Cosson, Jody. Civil War & Reconstruction: 1850-1877. (p. 325)
—George Washington: 1st U. S. President. Soud, illus. (p. 664)
—Sacagawea: Indian Guide. Soud, illus. (p. 1500)
Cosson, Kip. Ned Visits New York. (p. 1239)
Cosson, M. J. Affirmative Action. (p. 26)
—Golden Eagle Migration. (p. 694)
—Harriet Tubman. (p. 749)
—Mystery of the Old Car. (p. 1225)
—Pirate, Big Fist, & Me Garvey, Brann, illus. (p. 1362)
—Rock Art Rebel Garvey, Brann, illus. (p. 1482)
—Salmon Migration. (p. 1505)
—Sherlock Holmes & A Scandal in Bohemia. (p. 1565)
—Sherlock Holmes & the Adventure at the Abbey Grange. (p. 1565)
—Sherlock Holmes & the Adventure of the Blue Gem. (p. 1565)
—Sherlock Holmes & the Adventure of the Dancing Men. (p. 1565)
—Sherlock Holmes & the Adventure of the Speckled Band. (p. 1565)
—Sherlock Holmes & the Adventure of the Sussex Vampire. (p. 1565)
—Three Worlds Meet. (p. 1744)
—Troodon. (p. 1788)
—Your Mission to Mars. (p. 1981)
—Your Mission to Saturn. (p. 1981)
Cosson, M. J., jt. auth. see MacPhail, C.
Cosson, M. J., jt. auth. see Shaw, Murray.
Cossons, Malcolm & Stevens, Neil. Dot to Dot... (p. 472)
Cost, Steve, illus. see Stewart, Maria.
Costa, David. What's the Difference? Frink, Phil, photos by. (p. 1899)
Costa, Jana. Sleeping Beauty. (p. 1589)
Costa, Jana, illus. see Davidson, Susanna.
Costa, Margaret Jull, jt. auth. see Atxaga, Bernardo.
Costa, Maria, illus. see Canetti, Yanitzia & Yanitzia, Canetti.
Costa, Nicoletta. Little Tree That Would Not Share. (p. 1037)
—Olga the Cloud. Costa, Nicoletta, illus. (p. 1285)
Costa, Nicoletta, illus. see Piumini, Roberto & Wilde, Oscar.
Costa, Nicoletta, illus. see Piumini, Roberto, et al.
Costa, Nicoletta, illus. see Piumini, Roberto.
Costa, Patricia Castelao, illus. see Barrie, J. M.
Costa, Paul, jt. auth. see Kelly, John P.
Costa, Rosa & Costa-Pau, Rosa. Delfines. (p. 424)
—Elefantes. (p. 510)
Costa, T. L. Playing Tyler. (p. 1372)
Costain, Meredith. Ancient Egypt. (p. 68)
—Burned. (p. 243)
—Devouring Flames: The Story of Forest Fires. (p. 432)
—Into the Earth: The Story of Caves. (p. 881)
—Kids for Hire. Dale, Rae, illus. (p. 953)
—Life Cycle of Paper. (p. 1009)
—Mammals Great & Small. (p. 1085)
—Native Americans of the Great Plains. (p. 1234)
—Reptiles: Cold-Blooded Creatures. (p. 1461)
—Rock Raps: Five Decades of Popular Music. (p. 1482)
—Spies Revealed. (p. 1627)
—Stella & the Movie Star. McGowan, Shane, illus. (p. 1646)
—Stella & the Pet Parade. McGowan, Shane, illus. (p. 1646)
—Stella, Circus Star. McGowan, Shane, illus. (p. 1647)
—Stella's Got Talent. McGowan, Shane, illus. (p. 1647)
—Trashed. (p. 1780)
—You Wouldn't Want to Be an 18th-Century British Convict! A Trip to Australia You'd Rather Not Take. Antram, David, illus. (p. 1977)
Costain, Meredith, jt. auth. see Irwin, Bindi.
Costales, Amy. Abuelita Full of Life: Abuelita llena de Vida. Avilés, Martha, illus. (p. 7)
—Abuelo Vivia Solo/Grandpa Used to Live Alone. Gama, Esperanza, illus. (p. 7)
—Hello Night/Hola Noche. McDonald, Mercedes, illus. (p. 764)
—Lupe Vargas & Her Super Best Friend/Lupe Vargas y Su Super Mejor Amiga. (p. 1066)
—Sundays on Fourth Street/Los Domingos en la Calle Cuatro. Jerome, Elaine, illus. (p. 1676)
Costantino, Eric. Beeboo Bear Dreamed A Dream. (p. 157)
Costantino, Maria. Fashions of a Decade: The 1930s. (p. 576)
Costanza, Francine. Autumn's Indigo. Petru, Suzin, illus. (p. 118)
Costanza, Stephen. Smudge & the Book of Mistakes: A Christmas Story. (p. 1595)
—Vivaldi & the Invisible Orchestra. Costanza, Stephen, illus. (p. 1846)
Costanza, Stephen, illus. see Gow, Nancy.
Costanza, Stephen, illus. see Noble, Trinka Hakes.
Costanzo, Beth. Day at the Beach. (p. 412)
Costanzo, Charlene, jt. auth. see Costanzo, Charlene A.
Costanzo, Charlene A. & Costanzo, Charlene. Twelve Gifts of Birth. Ackison, Wendy Wassink, illus. (p. 1800)
Costa-Pau, Rosa, jt. auth. see Costa, Rosa.
Costa-Pau, Rosa, jt. auth. see Parramon Staff.
Coste, Marion. Finding Joy. Chen, Yong, illus. (p. 588)
—Hawaiian Bat: Ope'ape'a. Maxner, Pearl, illus. (p. 755)
—Hawaii's Animals Do the Most Amazing Things! Ekmanis, Rena, illus. (p. 755)
—Wild Beach. Gray, Cissy, illus. (p. 1929)
Coste, Twila Robar-De, see Hickman, Pamela.
Costelli, Donna Aka: Az-U-C-It. Meet Silly Sammy. (p. 1122)
Costello, David, illus. see Lambert, Megan Dowd.
Costello, David, illus. see Lambert, Megan.
Costello, David Hyde. I Can Help. Costello, David Hyde, illus. (p. 835)
—Little Pig Joins the Band. Costello, David Hyde, illus. (p. 1033)
Costello, David Hyde, illus. see Lambert, Megan Dowd.
Costello, Dee, jt. auth. see Wright, Robin.
Costello, Dee & Keith, Helen. Build the Bones Whale. Carter, Robin, illus. (p. 238)
Costello, Emily. Realm of the Panther: A Story of South Florida's Forest. (p. 1450)
—Realm of the Panther: A Story of South Florida's Forests. (p. 1450)
—Realm of the Panther: A Story of South Florida's Forests. Siegrist, Wes, illus. (p. 1450)
Costello, Jim, illus. see Lane, Lori & Winsor, Kathy.
Costello, Jim, photos by see Lane, Lori & Winsor, Kathy.
Costello, John H., tr. see Bulychev, Kirill.

Costello, Judi. Gertrude & the Creature. Bouthyette, Valerie, illus. (p. 667)
Costello, Kim & Cooper, Ashlee B. Great Monkeys All Are We. (p. 717)
Costello, Kim & Frank. Dash the Sea Turtle. (p. 409)
Costello, Lou, jt. auth. see Abbott, Bud.
Costello, Rita D., jt. ed. see Rachel, T. Cole.
Costello, Sam. My iPad for Kids. (p. 1211)
Costello, Shawn, illus. see Caraballo, Samuel.
Costello, Shawn, illus. see Fireside, Bryna J.
Costello, Shawn, illus. see Schmauss, Judy Kentor.
Costenoble, Steven R., jt. auth. see Waner, Stefan.
Coster, Charles. Flemish Legends. (p. 603)
Coster, Patience. Animal Rights. (p. 79)
—Euthanasia. (p. 540)
—My Life in Brazil. (p. 1212)
—My Life in France. (p. 1212)
—My Life in Jamaica. (p. 1212)
—Rain & Floods. (p. 1434)
—Smoking. (p. 1594)
—Struggle Against Apartheid. (p. 1668)
Coster, Patience, jt. auth. see Rowe, Percy.
Coster, Patience & Walker, Pamela. New Deal for Women. (p. 1244)
Coster, Simon. My Dinosaur Is More Awesome! (p. 1202)
Costi, Vincent. Planet of the Gargand. Smith, Anne & Smith, Owen, trs. from FRE. (p. 1368)
Costley, Kirk. Custer Brown in Marshmallow Madness. Firpo, Ethan, illus. (p. 395)
Costner, Howard, illus. see Cheng, Haw.
Costner, Howard, illus. see Marvin, Isabel R.
Costolo, Raebeth. 3 W Boys: A Children's Book of Short Stories. (p. 1991)
Cota, Cecilia, illus. see Doddoli, Consuelo.
Cote, Denis. Chemins de Mirlande. (p. 297)
—Descente Aux Enfers. (p. 428)
—Foret aux Cent Perils. Poulin, Stephane, tr. (p. 618)
Côté, Denis. Forêt aux Mille et un Périls Poulin, Stephane, illus. (p. 618)
—Machination du Scorpion Noir. (p. 1068)
Cote, Denis. Parfum de Mystere. (p. 1324)
Côté, Denis. Viaje en el Tiempo. (p. 1839)
Cote, Denis. Yeux d'Emeraude. (p. 1971)
Cote, Denis & Poulin, Stephane, eds. Otages de la Terreur. (p. 1306)
Côté, Geneviève. Bob's Hungry Ghost. (p. 206)
Côté, Genevieve. Me & You. Cote, Genevieve, illus. (p. 1115)
Côté, Geneviève. Mr. King's Things. Côté, Geneviève, illus. (p. 1185)
Cote, Genevieve. Starring Me & You Cote, Genevieve, illus. (p. 1642)
Côté, Geneviève. What Elephant? Côté, Geneviève, illus. (p. 1884)
Cote, Genevieve. Without You. Cote, Genevieve, illus. (p. 1942)
Côté, Geneviève, illus. see Duchesne, Christiane.
Cote, Genevieve, illus. see Fagan, Cary.
Cote, Genevieve, illus. see George, Kallie.
Côté, Geneviève, illus. see Hartt-Sussman, Heather.
Côté, Geneviève, illus. see Leigh, Heather.
Côté, Geneviève, illus. see Lord Tennyson, Alfred.
Cote, Genevieve, illus. see Nielsen-Fernlund, Susin.
Côté, Geneviève, illus. see Renaud, Anne.
Côté, Geneviève, illus. see Simard, Danielle.
Côté, Geneviève, illus. see Wong, Janet S.
Cote, Genevieve, illus. see Wong, Janet S. & Wong, Janet G.
Cote, Genevieve, jt. auth. see Côté, Geneviève.
Cote, Genevieve, tr. see Pelletier, Marthe.
Côté, Geneviève & Cote, Genevieve. Mr. King's Castle. Côté, Geneviève & Cote, Genevieve, illus. (p. 1185)
Côté, Genviève, illus. see Pelletier, Marthe.
Cote, Jenny. Ark, the Reed & the Fire Cloud: The Amazing Tales of Max & Liz Book One (p. 99)
Cote, Keith. Beyond the Game: Living Out Your Faith Every Day with Excellence. Keels, Steve, ed. (p. 174)
Cote, Nancy. It Feels Like Snow. Cote, Nancy, illus. (p. 894)
—Watch the Cookie! Cote, Nancy, illus. (p. 1861)
Cote, Nancy, illus. see Borgo, Lacy Finn.
Cote, Nancy, illus. see Brisson, Pat.
Cote, Nancy, illus. see Callahan, Sean.
Cote, Nancy, illus. see Corn, Tori.
Cote, Nancy, illus. see Glaser, Linda.
Cote, Nancy, illus. see Kimmelman, Leslie.
Cote, Nancy, illus. see Kroll, Virginia.
Cote, Nancy, illus. see Levine, Abby.
Cote, Nancy, illus. see Spelman, Cornelia.
Cote, Richard N. City of Heroes: The Great Charleston Earthquake Of 1886. (p. 324)
—Strength & Honor: The Life of Dolley Madison. (p. 1667)
Cote, Samuel. Journals & Stories: An Experience for Kids. (p. 927)
Côté, Yvonne. Bago the Adventurer: A Star's Help Book 2. (p. 132)
Coteau Books Staff, ed. see Webber, Jennifer Wynne.
Coteau Books Staff, jt. auth. see Bishop, Mary Harelkin.
Coteau Books Staff, jt. auth. see Glaze, Dave.
Coteau Books Staff, jt. auth. see Silverthorne, Judith.
Coteau Books Staff, jt. auth. see Simmie, Lois.
Coteau Books Staff, jt. auth. see Warwaruk, Larry.
Cotes, Everard. Story of Sonny Sahib. (p. 1660)
Cotes, Gilles. OGM et Chant de Mais. Begin, Jean-Guy, illus. (p. 1280)
Cotes Stanley, Marsha, illus. see Miller, Vern.
Cothran, Helen, ed. see Kallen, Stuart A.
Cothran, Helen, ed. see Ruggiero, Adriane.
Cothran, Helen, ed. see Young, Mitchell.
Cothran, Helen, jt. ed. see Burns, Kate.
Cothran, Helen, jt. ed. see Carroll, Jamuna.
Cothran, Helen, jt. ed. see Kallen, Stuart A.
Cothran, Helen, jt. ed. see Torr, James D.
Cothran, Helen, jt. ed. see Weatherly, Myra.
Cothran, Helen & Canini, Mikko, eds. Genetic Engineering. (p. 660)
Cothran, Helen, ed. Do Nuclear Weapons Pose a Serious Threat? (p. 457)
—Water. (p. 1862)
Cothran, Helen, et al, eds. Buddhism. (p. 234)
Cotler, Steve. Cheesie Mack Is Cool in a Duel. McCauley, Adam, illus. (p. 296)
—Cheesie Mack Is Not a Genius or Anything. McCauley, Adam, illus. (p. 296)
—Cheesie Mack Is Not Exactly Famous. Holgate, Douglas, illus. (p. 296)
—Cheesie Mack Is Running Like Crazy! Holgate, Douglas, illus. (p. 296)
—Cheesie Mack Is Sort of Freaked Out. Holgate, Douglas, illus. (p. 296)
Cotner, June. House Blessings: Prayers, Poems, & Toasts Celebrating Home & Family. (p. 803)
Cotner, June, ed. Bless the Beasts: Children's Prayers & Poems about Animals. Waldherr, Kris, illus. (p. 199)
Cotsen, Margit Sperling & Hobbs, Anne Stevenson. Beatrix Potter Collection of Lloyd Cotsen. (p. 153)
Cotta, Susan. I Can Show You I Care: Compassionate Touch for Children. Crawford, Gregory, illus. (p. 836)
Cotta-Flood, Stephanie, illus. see Dahl, Steven.
Cotten, Cynthia. Book Boat's In. Lessac, Frané, illus. (p. 210)
—Snow Ponies. Cockcroft, Jason, illus. (p. 1599)
—This Is the Stable. Bettoli, Delana, illus. (p. 1736)
Cotter, Amelia. Breakfast with Bigfoot. Swinford, Charles, illus. (p. 225)
Cotter, Bill. Beard in a Box. (p. 151)
—Don't Push the Button! (p. 468)
—Hello, Airplane! (p. 763)
Cotter, Charis. Born to Write: The Remarkable Lives of Six Famous Authors. (p. 214)
—Kids Who Rule: The Remarkable Lives of Five Child Monarchs. (p. 955)
—Swallow. (p. 1688)
—Wonder Kids: The Remarkable Lives of Nine Child Prodigies. (p. 1947)
—World Full of Ghosts. Mongeau, Marc, illus. (p. 1955)
Cotter, Eileen. College Writing (p. 340)
Cotter, Emily & Cotter, Jonathan. Emily Learns to Read. (p. 519)
Cotter, Jonathan, jt. auth. see Cotter, Emily.
Cotter, Natasha. Christmas Blessing. (p. 312)
—Pj Is Special. (p. 1365)
Cotterell, Arthur, et al. Eyewitness Travel Guide - Ancient China. Hills, Alan & Brightling, Geoff, photos by. (p. 558)
Cotterill, Colin. Average Alan. (p. 119)
Cottin, Menena. Black Book of Colors. Amado, Elisa, tr. from SPA. (p. 195)
—Libro Negro de los Colores. Amado, Elisa, tr. (p. 1006)
Cottin, Menena, illus. see Orozco, Rebeca.
Cottle, John, jt. auth. see Hirsch, Rebecca E.
Cotton, Anthony, et al. Maths. (p. 1108)
—Oxford International Primary Maths 5. (p. 1315)
—Oxford International Primary Maths, Stage 3. (p. 1315)
Cotton, Connie. Crashing. (p. 376)
Cotton, Jack. Dog's Guide to Life: Lessons from "Moose" (p. 463)
Cotton, Jacqueline S. Polar Bears. (p. 1379)
Cotton, Lisa, illus. see Collins, Betsy.
Cotton, Marie. Animal Olympics & the Stubborn Snowflake. (p. 79)
Cotton, Peter B. When Jungle Jim Comes to Visit Fred the Snake. Lemaire, Bonnie, illus. (p. 1903)
Cotton, Sue Lynn, illus. see Adrian, Mikel.
Cotton, Sue Lynn, illus. see Colhoun, Sheelah.
Cotton, Sue Lynn, illus. see Hattaway, Carol.
Cotton, Sue Lynn, illus. see Howell, Julie Ann.
Cotton, Sue Lynn, illus. see Lang, Kathy.
Cotton, Sue Lynn, illus. see Lostorto, Eric.
Cotton, Sue Lynn, illus. see MacKenzie-Krysko, Claudia & Krysko, Kenneth L.
Cotton, Sue Lynn, illus. see Musick, Stacy.
Cotton, Sue Lynn, illus. see Ringley, Patrick & Brown, Anne Corbett.
Cottone-Kolthoff, Carol, illus. see Christian, Peggy.
Cottrell Boyce, Frank. Astounding Broccoli Boy. (p. 109)
Cottrell, Kim. Izaboo, Izaboo, What Are We to Do. (p. 901)
—Jimmy Has the Bugaloo Zoo Flu. (p. 918)
Cottrell, Laura. Introducing: Honey Gem Sheasby (p. 882)
Cottrell, Leonard. Land of the Pharaohs. Powers, Richard M., illus. (p. 973)
Cottrell, Robert. London: From the Walled City to New Towns. (p. 1046)
Cottrell, Robert C. Czechoslovakia & the Velvet Revolution. Matray, James I., ed. (p. 397)
—South Africa: A State of Apartheid. Matray, James I., ed. (p. 1616)
—Vietnam: The 17th Parallel. (p. 1841)
Cottrell, Stephen. Adventures of Naughty Nora: 14 Fun Stories of Everyday Life for Collective Worship, Assemblies & Storytelling in the Classroom. (p. 21)
Cottrell, Sue. Can I Tell You about Stammering? A Guide for Friends, Family & Professionals. Khan, Sophie, illus. (p. 258)
—Can I Tell You about Stuttering? A Guide for Friends, Family, & Professionals. Khan, Sophie, illus. (p. 258)
Cottrell-Bentley, Lisa M. Wright on Time: Iowa. Bauerle, Tanja, illus. (p. 1963)
—Wright on Time: Minnesota. Bauerle, Tanja, illus. (p. 1963)
—Wright on Time: Collection 1. Bauerle, Tanja, illus. (p. 1963)
Cottrill, Peter, illus. see Zobel-Nolan, Allia.
Cottringer, Anne. Eliot Jones Midnight Superhero. Smith, Alex T., illus. (p. 513)
—Hot Dog. Walker, Katherine, illus. (p. 801)
—Mary Is Scary. Gale, Cathy, illus. (p. 1100)
—Singing It. (p. 1579)
Cotts, Nat. Daddy Yankee. (p. 399)
—Don Omar. (p. 465)
—Pitbull. (p. 1364)
—Young Jeezy. (p. 1979)
Cottswold, Wooley. Rose & the Bald-Headed Elephant. (p. 1489)
Cotugno, Katie. 99 Days. (p. 1998)
—How to Love. (p. 820)
Cotugno, Megan. Investigating Cells (p. 884)
—Measure It! (p. 1117)
—Real World Data (p. 1449)
—Soldiers of the Civil War. (p. 1607)
—Why We Fought - The Civil War Set (p. 1926)
Cotumbeanu, Alexandra, illus. see Carrier, Misty.
Couch, Caroline. Ally Gator & Her Search for a Rainbow (p. 48)
Couch, Crista, illus. see Woo, Melissa.
Couch, Greg, illus. see Hornsby, Ashley.
Couch, Greg, illus. see Krull, Kathleen.
Couch, Greg, illus. see Kunstler, James Howard.
Couch, Greg, illus. see Stauffacher, Sue.
Couch, Greg, jt. auth. see Plourde, Lynn.
Couch, Jack C. Cody's Guide to Oregon's South Coast. (p. 338)
Couch, N. C. Christopher & Weiner, Stephen. Will Eisner Companion: The Pioneering Spirit of the Father of the Graphic Novel. (p. 1932)
Coudakpo, Agrey Emile A. Malignant & a Malignant One & Half: The Story of the Baby Frog & the Vicious Viper. (p. 1083)
Coudray, Philippe. Benjamin Bear in Brain Storms! (p. 164)
—Benjamin Bear in Bright Ideas! (p. 164)
—Benjamin Bear in Fuzzy Thinking. (p. 164)
Coudrille, Jonathon. Farmer Fisher's Russian Christmas. (p. 574)
Coues, Elliott. Citizen Bird Scenes from Bird-Life in Plain English for Beginners. (p. 322)
Coues, Elliott, jt. auth. see Wright, Mabel Osgood.
Coues, Elliott & Wright, Mabel Osgood. Citizen Bird: Scenes from Bird-Life in Plain English for Beginners. (p. 322)
—Citizen Bird: Scenes from Bird-Life in Plain English for Beginners. (p. 322)
Coughlan, Cheryl. Flies. (p. 603)
—Grasshoppers. (p. 711)
—Ladybugs. (p. 971)
Coughlan Publishing Staff, jt. auth. see Hoena, Blake A.
Coughlan Publishing Staff, jt. auth. see Murphy, Patricia J.
Coughlin, Denise. Dragon in My Pocket. Kastan, Bill, illus. (p. 477)
Coughlin, Denise & Pappas, Maria. Petal Pals. (p. 1346)
Coughlin, Jennie Rose. Purple Scarf. Howes, Bryan Arthur, illus. (p. 1419)
Coughlin, Shirley. Beyond the Flood. (p. 174)
—Toby & the Pirates. (p. 1760)
Coughlin, T. Glen. One Shot Away: A Wrestling Story. (p. 1297)
Couillard, Joanly. Royal Tots: Love. (p. 1492)
Coulman, Valerie. Je Suis Ballerine! Duchesne, Christiane, tr. from ENG. (p. 911)
—When Pigs Fly. (p. 1904)
Couloumbis, Akila, jt. auth. see Couloumbis, Audrey.
Couloumbis, Audrey. Getting near to Baby. (p. 669)
—Jake. (p. 905)
—Lexie. Denos, Julia, illus. (p. 1004)
—Maude March on the Run! Or Trouble Is Her Middle Name. (p. 1110)
—Misadventures of Maude March: Or Trouble Rides a Fast Horse. (p. 1150)
—Not Exactly a Love Story. (p. 1267)
—Say Yes. (p. 1519)
Couloumbis, Audrey & Couloumbis, Akila. War Games. (p. 1857)
Coulson, Art. Creator's Game: A Story of Baaga'adowe/Lacrosse. Desjarlait, Robert, illus. (p. 380)
Coulson, Cotton, illus. see Arenstam, Peter, et al.
Coulson, Cotton, photos by see Arenstam, Peter, et al.
Coulson, Cotton, photos by see Bruchac, Margaret M. & Grace, Catherine O'Neill.
Coulson, Cotton, photos by see Grace, Catherine O'Neill & Bruchac, Margaret M.
Coulson, Cotton, photos by see Plimoth Plantation Staff, et al.
Coulson, David, illus. see Highlights for Children Editorial Staff.
Coulson-Staak, Louise. Clarisse the Cow: A Circus Adventure. (p. 327)
Coult, Lucy Alice. Animals at Home. Byrne, Mike, illus. (p. 82)
Coultas, Amanda. Language & Social Contexts. (p. 974)
Coulter, Ann. How to Talk to a Liberal (If You Must) The World According to Ann Coulter. (p. 822)
Coulter, Barbara, jt. auth. see Steck-Vaughn Staff.
Coulter, Catherine. Deception. (p. 421)
—Wizard's Daughter (p. 1943)
Coulter, Catherine, et al. Winging It: A Beginner's Guide to Birds of the Southwest. Dewey, Jennifer Owings, illus. (p. 1936)
Coulter, Laurie. Ballplayers & Bonesetters: One Hundred Ancient Aztec & Maya Jobs You Might Have Adored or Abhorred. Newbigging, Martha, illus. (p. 135)
—Cowboys & Coffin Makers: One Hundred 19th-Century Jobs You Might Have Feared or Fancied. Newbigging, Martha, illus. (p. 374)
—Kings & Carpenters: One Hundred Bible Land Jobs You Might Have Praised or Panned. Newbigging, Mary, illus. (p. 960)
—Secrets in Stone: All about Maya Hieroglyphs. English, Sarah Jane, illus. (p. 1544)
Coulter, Nancy J. When Grandma Went to Heaven. (p. 1902)
Coulter, Shirley. Chemistry. (p. 297)
Coulthard, Emma. Recorder Wizard. (p. 1452)
Coulton, Beth, jt. auth. see Schwartz, Corey Rosen.
Coulton, Mia. All about Danny. Coulton, Mia, photos by. (p. 42)
—At Grandma Ruth's House. Coulton, Mia, photos by. (p. 110)
—Bird Feeder, 6-pack: 6 Copies Palmer, Kate Salley & Palmer, Kate S., illus. (p. 190)
—Carla Tiene Gafas Nuevas. Totire, Valerie et al, illus. (p. 270)
—Carla's New Glasses. Totire, Valerie, illus. (p. 270)
—Circus Fish. Coulton, Mia, photos by. (p. 322)
—Danny & Abby Play Tag. Coulton, Mia, photos by. (p. 405)
—Danny & Bee's Book of Opposites. Coulton, Mia, photos by. (p. 405)
—Danny & Dad Go Shopping. Coulton, Mia, photos by. (p. 405)
—Danny & Heather Share. Coulton, Mia, photos by. (p. 405)
—Danny & the Little Worm. Coulton, Mia, photos by. (p. 405)
—Danny Can Sort. Coulton, Mia, photos by. (p. 405)
—Danny Likes Red. Coulton, Mia, photos by. (p. 406)
—Danny Likes to Help. Coulton, Mia, photos by. (p. 406)
—Danny Paints a Picture. Coulton, Mia, photos by. (p. 406)
—Danny's Big Adventure. Coulton, Mia, photos by. (p. 406)
—Danny's Castle. Coulton, Mia, photos by. (p. 406)
—Danny's Favorite Shapes. Coulton, Mia, photos by. (p. 406)
—Danny's Party. Coulton, Mia, photos by. (p. 406)
—Danny's Rocket. Coulton, Mia, photos by. (p. 406)
—Danny's Special Tree. Coulton, Mia, photos by. (p. 406)
—Danny's Timeline. Coulton, Mia, photos by. (p. 406)
—Danny's Window. Coulton, Mia, photos by. (p. 406)
—Five Danny Dogs. Coulton, Mia, photos by. (p. 600)
—Get down Danny. Coulton, Mia, photos by. (p. 667)
—I Am Danny. Coulton, Mia, photos by. (p. 832)
—Lunch for Baby Elephant. Campbell, D. B., illus. (p. 1065)
—New Home for Fish. Coulton, Mia, photos by. (p. 1245)
—Pirate Fish. Coulton, Mia, photos by. (p. 1362)
—Spy Danny. Coulton, Mia, photos by. (p. 1636)
—Super Danny. Coulton, Mia, photos by. (p. 1679)
Counce, Betty. Baxter's Big Teeth Seay, Dave, illus. (p. 147)
Counce, Paula. Journey Remembered. (p. 928)
Council for Agricultural Science and Technology Staff, contrib. by. Boundless Science for Bountiful Agriculture: Winning Student Essays, 2003. (p. 216)
Councilman, Janet H. Rocky & His Responsible Band of Cowboys (p. 1484)
—Rocky the Respectful Raccoon & His Red Sunglasses. (p. 1484)
Councilman, Janet Harden. Petie the Penguin & the Electric Igloo. (p. 1348)
Counsell, Christine. History & Literacy. (p. 783)
—History & Literacy in Y7: Building the Lesson Around the Text. (p. 783)
Counsell, Michael. Basic Bible Dictionary. (p. 141)
Counter, Marlow, jt. auth. see Counter, Marlow.
Counter, Marlow & Counter, Marlow. Nanook the Penguin. Hilmer, Evelyn, illus. (p. 1229)
Counting Cards Staff. LP-Counting: Level 1 Math. (p. 1061)
Countryman, Jack & Parker, Amy. God's Promises for Boys (p. 691)
—God's Promises for Girls (p. 691)
Counts, Monika. Alabama Countdown to Touchdown. (p. 33)
—Florida Countdown to Touchdown. (p. 607)
—LSU Countdown to Touchdown. (p. 1061)
County Studio Staff. Katie: The Mischievous Kitten. (p. 944)
Coupe, Laurence. Marina Warner. (p. 1094)
Coupe, Peter. Doodle Mania: Oodles of Fun Pictures to Finish! (p. 469)
—Zoodles! Oodles of Animal Pictures to Finish! (p. 1989)
Coupe, Robert. Antiguo Egipto/Acient Egypt. (p. 89)
—Cats of the Wild. (p. 281)
—Dinosaur Hunters. (p. 442)
—Great Wall of China. (p. 719)
—Predators & Prey: Battle for Survival. (p. 1394)
—Vanishing Ice. (p. 1833)
Coupper, Heather. Atlas Visual del Espacio. (p. 113)
Courage, Nick. Loudness: A Novel. (p. 1058)
Courageous $oul, illus. see !Myster?Ous M! & Courageous $Oul.
Courcy, Jon. Scourges: Seeds of Dissent. (p. 1532)
Courl, Kathryn A., illus. see Bentley, Dawn.
Courl, Kathy, illus. see Simon, Mary Manz.
Couric, Katherine, jt. auth. see Couric, Katie.
Couric, Katie. Blue Ribbon Day. Priceman, Marjorie, illus. (p. 203)
—Brand New Kid. (p. 222)
Couric, Katie & Couric, Katherine. Blue Ribbon Day. Priceman, Marjorie, illus. (p. 203)
Courlander, Harold & Herzog, George. Cow-Tail Switch: And Other West African Stories. Chastain, Madye Lee, illus. (p. 373)
Cournoyer, Brittany. Ultimate Betrayals. (p. 1809)
—Ultimate Revelations. (p. 1809)
Cournoyer, Linda. Jethro. (p. 916)
Coursaget, Catherine & Myers, Micheline. Breaking the French Barrier, Advanced Level / Student Edition: The Language Series with All the Rules You Need to Know. Level III (p. 225)
—Breaking the French Barrier, Advanced Level /Teacher's Edition: The Language Series with All the Rules You Need to Know. Level III (p. 225)
—Breaking the French Barrier, Level I (Beginner), Student Edition: The Language Series with All the Rules You Need to Know. Level I (p. 225)
—Breaking the French Barrier, Level I (Beginner), Teacher's Edition Level I. (p. 225)
—Breaking the French Barrier, Level I (Beginner), Teacher Test Packet: The Language Series with All the Rules You Need to Know. (p. 225)
—Breaking the French Barrier, Level II (Intermediate), Student Edition: The Language Series with All the Rules You Need to Know. (p. 225)
—Breaking the French Barrier, Level II (Intermediate), Answer Key Booklet: The Language Series with All the Rules You Need to Know. (p. 225)
—Breaking the French Barrier, Level II (Intermediate), Teacher Test Packet: The Language Series with All the Rules You Need to Know. (p. 225)
—Breaking the French Barrier, Level III IV AP (Advanced), Answer Key Booklet: The Language Series with All the Rules You Need to Know. (p. 225)
—Breaking the French Barrier, Level III IV AP (Advanced), Teacher Test Packet: The Language Series with All the Rules You Need to Know. (p. 225)
CourseCrafters Staff, des. Interactive Storybooks - Fun Time. (p. 879)
—Interactive Storybooks - Let's Go to School! (p. 879)
—Interactive Storybooks - Look at Me! (p. 879)
—Interactive Storybooks - School Time. (p. 879)
—Interactive Storybooks - the Family Home. (p. 879)

C

—Interactive Storybooks - This Is My House. (p. 879)
Court, Georgia. Traitor of Bled. (p. 1777)
Court, Moira, illus. see Owen, Chris.
Court, Rob. How to Draw Christmas Things. (p. 817)
—How to Draw Flowers & Trees. (p. 817)
—How to Draw Halloween Things. (p. 817)
—How to Draw Independence Day Things. (p. 817)
—How to Draw Thanksgiving Things. (p. 818)
—How to Draw Watercraft. (p. 819)
Court, Shirley & Whitlock, Val. Singing Sherlock: A Singing Resource for KS1 & KS2. (p. 1579)
—Singing Sherlock: The Complete Singing Resorce for Primary Schools. Vol. 2 (p. 1579)
Courtauld, Sarah. Bears. Furukawa, Masumi, illus. (p. 151)
—Bugs. Scarpa, Daniel, illus. (p. 237)
—Monkeys Internet-Referenced. (p. 1166)
—On a Pirate Ship. Davies, Benji, illus. (p. 1288)
—Owls: Internet-Referenced. Hussey, Lorna, illus. (p. 1315)
—Queen's Pirate - Francis Drake. Dutrait, Vincent, illus. (p. 1425)
—Story of Art Sticker Book. (p. 1657)
—Story of Slavery. (p. 1660)
Courtauld, Sarah, jt. auth. see Dickens, Rosie.
Courtauld, Sarah & Burniac, Lauren. Perilous Princess Plot. (p. 1343)
Courtauld, Sarah & Davies, Kate. Impressionists Sticker Book. Chiang, Shirley, illus. (p. 862)
Courtauld, Sarah & Dickens, Rosie. Art Coloring Book with Stickers. (p. 101)
Courtenay, Bryce. Power of One. (p. 1389)
Courtenay, Christina. New England Rocks. (p. 1244)
Courtenay, L. A. Space Penguins Cosmic Crash! Davies, James, illus. (p. 1619)
—Space Penguins Galaxy Race! Davies, James, illus. (p. 1619)
—Space Penguins Meteor Madness! Davies, James, illus. (p. 1619)
—Space Penguins Star Attack! Davies, James, illus. (p. 1619)
Courtenay, Lucy. Freda the Fearless. McConnell, Sarah, illus. (p. 632)
—Impossible Island. McConnell, Sarah, illus. (p. 862)
—Matey M'Lad. McConnell, Sarah, illus. (p. 1104)
—Space Penguins. Davies, James, illus. (p. 1619)
—Vague Vagabond. McConnell, Sarah, illus. (p. 1830)
Courtenay, Lucy, jt. auth. see McConnell, Sarah.
Courter, John. Cheetah & the Turtle. (p. 296)
Courtin, Thierry. Decouvre les animaux avec T. (p. 422)
—Decouvre les contraires Avec. (p. 422)
—Decouvre les nombres Avec. (p. 422)
—Decouvre les petits de la Ferme. (p. 422)
—L imagier de T Choupi. (p. 969)
—T choupi fait un bonhomme De. (p. 1693)
—T choupi rentre a l Ecole. (p. 1693)
Courtin, Thierry, illus. see O'Hair, Margaret.
Courtney, Carla. On the Banks of Plum Creek: Reading Comprehension Guide. (p. 1289)
Courtney, Kateri. Welby & the Knobby King. (p. 1873)
Courtney, Richard. Thomas Gets a Snowplow. (p. 1738)
Courtney, Richard, illus. see Awdry, W.
Courtney, Richard, illus. see Awdry, Wilbert V.
Courtney, Richard, illus. see Awdry, Wilbert V. & Awdry, W.
Courtney, Richard, illus. see Awdry, Wilbert V. & Hooke, R. Schuyler.
Courtney, Richard, illus. see Behrens, Janice.
Courtney, Richard, illus. see Carbone, Courtney.
Courtney, Richard, illus. see Corey, Shana & Awdry, Wilbert V.
Courtney, Richard, illus. see Corey, Shana.
Courtney, Richard, illus. see Golden Books Staff.
Courtney, Richard, illus. see Hooke, R. Schuyler.
Courtney, Richard, illus. see Random House.
Courtney, Richard, illus. see RH Disney Staff & Random House Staff.
Courtney, Richard, photos by see Golden Books Staff.
Courtney, Richard H., illus. see Awdry, Wilbert V.
Courtney, Suzanne Gene. Dear Diary: My Brother Died Today. (p. 418)
—Florence Flies Alone: An Alliterative Airline Adventure. (p. 606)
—Rainfrog. (p. 1436)
—Ride to the Stars, a Story for Children about Life, Loss, & Love. (p. 1471)
Courtney, Vicki. Get a Life: Debunking Six Myths in the Quest for Contentment. (p. 667)
—Teenvirtue Confidential: Your Questions Answered about Guys, God, & Getting Older. (p. 1715)
Courtney-Clarke, Margaret, illus. see Angelou, Maya.
Courtright, Anne. Reaching Your Goals: The Ultimate Teen Guide. Raasch, Peg, illus. (p. 1442)
Courtright, Jordan K., jt. auth. see Jensen, Brandi Ann.
Coury, Tina Nichols. Hanging off Jefferson's Nose: Growing up on Mount Rushmore. Comport, Sally Wern, illus. (p. 742)
Cousin. My Friend at School: Big Book: Level C. (p. 1209)
—My Teacher Helps Me. (p. 1220)
Cousineau, Craig S. Skippy & Oaf: The Battle Against Oxygen Radicals. (p. 1586)
—Skippy & Oaf Explore the Battles of the Immune System. (p. 1586)
Cousineau, Kelley, illus. see Harrison, David L.
Cousineau, Normand, illus. see Galloway, Priscilla.
Cousineau-Peiffer, Trisha. Have You Ever Heard of a Rainbow Farm: The Missing Color Kittens. Everett-Hawkes, Bonnie, illus. (p. 754)
—Have You Ever Heard of a Rainbow Farm. Everett-Hawkes, Bonnie, illus. (p. 754)
Cousins. Mausi Spielt. (p. 1110)
Cousins, C. J. Bailey & Friends Have a Party. (p. 133)
Cousins, Dave. 15 Days Without a Head. (p. 1995)
—Waiting for Gonzo. (p. 1852)
Cousins, Kirk. Game Changer (p. 654)
Cousins, Lindsey, jt. auth. see Bredeson, Carmen.
Cousins, Lucy. Alimentos de Maisy. Cousins, Lucy, illus. (p. 41)
—Bedtime Rhymes. (p. 157)
—Count with Maisy, Cheep, Cheep, Cheep! Cousins, Lucy, illus. (p. 370)
—Create with Maisy: A Maisy First Arts-and-Crafts Book. Cousins, Lucy, illus. (p. 378)
—Dónde Vas Maisy? (p. 466)
—Doodle with Maisy. (p. 469)
—Fire Engine. Cousins, Lucy, illus. (p. 590)
—Hooray for Fish! Cousins, Lucy, illus. (p. 796)
—I'm the Best. (p. 860)
—I'm the Best. Cousins, Lucy, illus. (p. 860)
—Jazzy in the Jungle. Cousins, Lucy, illus. (p. 911)
—Juguetes de Maisy. Cousins, Lucy, illus. (p. 932)
—Maisy, Charley, & the Wobbly Tooth. Cousins, Lucy, illus. (p. 1077)
—Maisy Goes Camping. (p. 1077)
—Maisy Goes Camping. Cousins, Lucy, illus. (p. 1077)
—Maisy Goes on a Sleepover. Cousins, Lucy, illus. (p. 1077)
—Maisy Goes on Vacation. (p. 1077)
—Maisy Goes on Vacation. Cousins, Lucy, illus. (p. 1077)
—Maisy Goes Swimming: A Maisy Classic Pop-up Book. Cousins, Lucy, illus. (p. 1077)
—Maisy Goes to Bed: A Maisy Classic Pop-Up Book. Cousins, Lucy, illus. (p. 1077)
—Maisy Goes to Preschool: A Maisy First Experiences Book. Cousins, Lucy, illus. (p. 1077)
—Maisy Goes to the City. (p. 1077)
—Maisy Goes to the City. Cousins, Lucy, illus. (p. 1077)
—Maisy Goes to the Hospital. (p. 1077)
—Maisy Goes to the Hospital. Cousins, Lucy, illus. (p. 1077)
—Maisy Goes to the Library. (p. 1077)
—Maisy Goes to the Library. Cousins, Lucy, illus. (p. 1077)
—Maisy Goes to the Movies: A Maisy First Experiences Book. Cousins, Lucy, illus. (p. 1077)
—Maisy Goes to the Movies. (p. 1077)
—Maisy Goes to the Museum. (p. 1077)
—Maisy Goes to the Museum. Cousins, Lucy, illus. (p. 1077)
—Maisy Grows a Garden. (p. 1077)
—Maisy Learns to Swim. Cousins, Lucy, illus. (p. 1077)
—Maisy Plays Soccer. (p. 1078)
—Maisy Plays Soccer. Cousins, Lucy, illus. (p. 1078)
—Maisy, qué Estás Haciendo? (p. 1078)
—Maisy Te Quiere. (p. 1078)
—Maisy Va de Excursión. (p. 1078)
—Maisy's Amazing Big Book of Learning. (p. 1078)
—Maisy's Amazing Big Book of Words. Cousins, Lucy, illus. (p. 1078)
—Maisy's Animals (Los Animales de Maisy) Cousins, Lucy, illus. (p. 1078)
—Maisy's Band. Cousins, Lucy, illus. (p. 1078)
—Maisy's Birthday Party Sticker Book. Cousins, Lucy, illus. (p. 1078)
—Maisy's Castle: A Maisy Pop-Up & Play Book. Cousins, Lucy, illus. (p. 1078)
—Maisy's Christmas: Sticker Book. Cousins, Lucy, illus. (p. 1078)
—Maisy's Christmas Tree. Cousins, Lucy, illus. (p. 1078)
—Maisy's Clothes/La Ropa de Maisy. Cousins, Lucy, illus. (p. 1078)
—Maisy's Digger: A Go with Maisy Board Book. Cousins, Lucy, illus. (p. 1078)
—Maisy's Fairground: A Maisy Pop-Up-and-Play Book. (p. 1078)
—Maisy's First Clock. Cousins, Lucy, illus. (p. 1078)
—Maisy's First Colors: A Maisy Concept Book. Cousins, Lucy, illus. (p. 1078)
—Maisy's First Numbers: A Maisy Concept Book. Lucy Cousins, illus. (p. 1078)
—Maisy's Pirate Ship: A Pop-Up-and-Play Book. Cousins, Lucy, illus. (p. 1078)
—Maisy's Placemat Doodle Book. Cousins, Lucy, illus. (p. 1078)
—Maisy's Plane. Cousins, Lucy, illus. (p. 1078)
—Maisy's Pool. (p. 1078)
—Maisy's Race Car: A Go with Maisy Board Book. Cousins, Lucy, illus. (p. 1078)
—Maisy's Seaside Adventure Sticker Book. Cousins, Lucy, illus. (p. 1078)
—Maisy's Seasons. Cousins, Lucy, illus. (p. 1078)
—Maisy's Snuggle Book. (p. 1078)
—Maisy's Thanksgiving Sticker Book. Cousins, Lucy, illus. (p. 1078)
—Maisy's Tractor. Cousins, Lucy, illus. (p. 1078)
—Maisy's Train. Cousins, Lucy, illus. (p. 1078)
—Maisy's Valentine Sticker Book. Cousins, Lucy, illus. (p. 1078)
—Maisy's Wonderful Weather Book. (p. 1078)
—Maisy's Wonderful Weather Book. Cousins, Lucy, illus. (p. 1078)
—Maisy's World of Animals: A Maisy First Science Book. Cousins, Lucy, illus. (p. 1078)
—Mejores Amigos de Maisy. (p. 1124)
—Munch Munch, Maisy: A Stroll-Along Book. Cousins, Lucy, illus. (p. 1191)
—Noah's Ark. Cousins, Lucy, illus. (p. 1261)
—Nochebuena de Maisy. (p. 1262)
—Nursery Rhymes. (p. 1273)
—Peck, Peck, Peck. Cousins, Lucy, illus. (p. 1334)
—Pina Place Giocare. (p. 1359)
—Suenos de Colores. (p. 1672)
—Sweet Dreams, Maisy. Cousins, Lucy, illus. (p. 1689)
—Tren de Maisy. (p. 1784)
—Where Are Maisy's Friends? Cousins, Lucy, illus. (p. 1906)
—Where Does Maisy Live? (p. 1907)
—Where Does Maisy Live? Cousins, Lucy, illus. (p. 1907)
—Where Is Maisy? Cousins, Lucy, illus. (p. 1908)
—With Love from Maisy. Cousins, Lucy, illus. (p. 1942)
—Yummy: Eight Favorite Fairy Tales. Cousins, Lucy, illus. (p. 1983)
Cousins, Lucy, jt. auth. see Harris, Robie H.
Cousins, Margaret. Ben Franklin of Old Philadelphia. (p. 163)
Coussens, Penrhyn W. Child's Book of Stories. Smith, Jessie Willcox, illus. (p. 304)
Coute, Ursula T., jt. auth. see Buyer, Robert L.
Coute, Ursula T., jt. auth. see Buyer, Robert.
Couteaud, Cheryl. Monster for Halloween. Couteaud, Cheryl, illus. (p. 1167)
Coutee, Kelly, et al. Eating Disorders Book of Hope & Healing. (p. 501)
Coutellier, Connie, jt. auth. see Low, Mary.
Coutin, Gustavo. When I climb a Tree. (p. 1902)
Coutinho, Lucy M. Rangers of Andor: The Beginning. (p. 1438)
Coutts, Alexandra. Tumble & Fall. (p. 1796)
Coutts, Lisa, illus. see Simons, Moya.
Couvillon, Alice, jt. auth. see Moore, Elizabeth.
Couvillon, Alice & Moore, Elizabeth. Ancient Mounds of Watson Brake: Oldest Earthworks in North America Anderson, Rick, illus. (p. 70)
Couvillon, Jacques. Chicken Dance. (p. 300)
Couwenhoven, Terri. Boys' Guide to Growing Up: Choices & Changes During Puberty. (p. 220)
—Girls' Guide to Growing Up: Choices & Changes in the Tween Years. (p. 680)
Couzens, Dominic & Nurney, David. Color Yourself Smart: Dinosaurs. (p. 343)
covaleski, john. Hacking. (p. 735)
Covan, Jennie, tr. see Gorky, Maxim.
Covas Sadriwalla, Deborah. Top Secret. (p. 1769)
Coveleskie, Sally & Goodrich, Peter. Henry the Steinway Tours the World. Friedman, Laura, illus. (p. 768)
Coveleskie, Sally & Peter, Goodrich. Henry the Steinway a Star Is Born. Friedman, Laura, illus. (p. 768)
Coveleskie, Sally, et al. Henry the Steinway & the Piano Recital. Friedman, Laura, illus. (p. 768)
Covell, David. Rat & Roach Friends to the End. (p. 1440)
Coven, Wanda. Heidi Heckelbeck & the Christmas Surprise. (p. 762)
—Heidi Heckelbeck & the Christmas Surprise. Burris, Priscilla, illus. (p. 762)
—Heidi Heckelbeck & the Cookie Contest. (p. 762)
—Heidi Heckelbeck & the Cookie Contest. Burris, Priscilla, illus. (p. 762)
—Heidi Heckelbeck Casts a Spell. (p. 762)
—Heidi Heckelbeck Casts a Spell. Burris, Priscilla, illus. (p. 762)
—Heidi Heckelbeck Collection: A Bewitching Four-Book Boxed Set: Heidi Hecklebeck Has a Secret; Heidi Heckelbeck Casts a Spell; Heidi Heckelbeck & the Cookie Contest; Heidi Heckelbeck in Disguise. Burris, Priscilla, illus. (p. 762)
—Heidi Heckelbeck Gets Glasses. (p. 762)
—Heidi Heckelbeck Gets Glasses. Burris, Priscilla, illus. (p. 762)
—Heidi Heckelbeck Goes to Camp! (p. 762)
—Heidi Heckelbeck Goes to Camp! Burris, Priscilla, illus. (p. 762)
—Heidi Heckelbeck Has a Secret. (p. 762)
—Heidi Heckelbeck Has a Secret. Burris, Priscilla, illus. (p. 762)
—Heidi Heckelbeck Has a Secret - Heidi Heckelbeck Casts a Spell - Heidi Heckelbeck & the Cookie Contest. Burris, Priscilla, illus. (p. 762)
—Heidi Heckelbeck in Disguise. (p. 762)
—Heidi Heckelbeck in Disguise. Burris, Priscilla, illus. (p. 762)
—Heidi Heckelbeck Is a Flower Girl. Burris, Priscilla, illus. (p. 762)
—Heidi Heckelbeck Is Not a Thief! Burris, Priscilla, illus. (p. 762)
—Heidi Heckelbeck Is Ready to Dance! (p. 762)
—Heidi Heckelbeck Is Ready to Dance! Burris, Priscilla, illus. (p. 762)
—Heidi Heckelbeck Says "Cheese!" Burris, Priscilla, illus. (p. 762)
Cover, Arthur Byron, et al. Buffy the Vampire Slayer: Coyote Moon - Night of the Living Rerun - Portal Through Time. (p. 236)
Coverdale, Linda, tr. see Bujor, Flavia.
Coverdale, Linda, tr. see Hatzfeld, Jean.
Cover-Kwarcinski, Karen. No Time for Tangles. (p. 1260)
Coverly, Dave. Dogs Are People, Too: A Collection of Cartoons to Make Your Tail Wag. (p. 462)
Coverly, Dave, illus. see Tobin, Jim.
Covert, Kim. Ancient Greece: Birthplace of Democracy (p. 69)
—New Mexico. (p. 1246)
—Wisconsin. (p. 1939)
—Wyoming. (p. 1966)
Covert, Kim, et al. Great Civilizations. (p. 714)
Covert, Ralph & Mills, G. Riley. Nutty Nutcracker Christmas. Swain, Wilson, illus. (p. 1274)
Covey, Dominic, creator. Darwin's World: Post Apocalyptic Adventures. (p. 409)
Covey, Dominic, des. Lost City. (p. 1055)
Covey, Ken. Adventures of a Little Boy Named Kenny. (p. 16)
Covey, Richard D., jt. auth. see Pappas, Diane H.
Covey, Richard D. & Pappas, Diane H. I Always Turn off the Light! (p. 831)
—Let's All Be Water-Wise. (p. 994)
—Let's Keep Our Oceans, Rivers, & Lakes Clean. (p. 998)
—Ugh! Don't Be a Litterbug! (p. 1808)
—What Is Global Warming? (p. 1889)
—What's Happening to the Rain Forests? (p. 1897)
Covey, Rosemary Feit, illus. see Porte, Barbara Ann.
Covey, S. K. Road to Rincon (p. 1477)
Covey, Sean. 7 Habits of Happy Kids. (p. 1992)
—7 Habits of Happy Kids. Curtis, Stacy, illus. (p. 1992)
—7 Habits of Happy Kids Collection: Just the Way I Am; When I Grow up; a Place for Everything; Sammy & the Pecan Pie; Lily & the Yucky Cookies; Sophie & the Perfect Poem; Goob & His Grandpa. Curtis, Stacy, illus. (p. 1992)
—Goob & His Grandpa. Curtis, Stacy, illus. (p. 697)
—Just the Way I Am: Habit 1. Curtis, Stacy, illus. (p. 940)
—Lily & the Yucky Cookies. Curtis, Stacy, illus. (p. 1018)
—Place for Everything: Habit 3. Curtis, Stacy, illus. (p. 1365)
—Sammy & the Pecan Pie. Curtis, Stacy, illus. (p. 1507)
—Sophie & the Perfect Poem. Curtis, Stacy, illus. (p. 1613)
—When I Grow Up: Habit 2. Curtis, Stacy, illus. (p. 1903)
Covey, Sean, jt. auth. see Covey, Stephen R.
Covey, Stephen R. & Covey, Sean. 6 Most Important Decisions You'll Ever Make: A Guide for Teens. (p. 1992)
Covi, illus. see Cerda, Alfredo Gomez.
Covleo, Jeff, illus. see Yankee, Kris.
Coville, Bruce. Aliens Ate My Homework: Rod Allbright & the Galactic Patrol. Coville, Katherine, illus. (p. 41)
—Aliens Ate My Homework. (p. 41)
—Aliens Ate My Homework. Coville, Katherine, illus. (p. 41)
—Aliens Stole My Body. Coville, Katherine, illus. (p. 41)
—Always October. (p. 51)
—Diary of a Mad Brownie. (p. 434)
—Dragon of Doom. Coville, Katherine, illus. (p. 477)
—Dragonslayers. (p. 479)
—Evil Elves. Coville, Katherine, illus. (p. 546)
—Goblins on the Prowl. (p. 688)
—I Left My Sneakers in Dimension X. Coville, Katherine, illus. (p. 840)
—I Lost My Grandfather's Brain. (p. 841)
—I Was a Sixth Grade Alien. (p. 848)
—Into the Land of the Unicorns. (p. 881)
—Jennifer Murdley's Toad: A Magic Shop Book. Lippincott, Gary A., illus. (p. 913)
—Jennifer Murdley's Toad. (p. 913)
—Jeremy Thatcher, Dragon Hatcher: A Magic Shop Book. Lippincott, Gary A., illus. (p. 913)
—Jeremy Thatcher, Dragon Hatcher. (p. 913)
—Juliet Dove, Queen of Love. (p. 932)
—Mischief Monster. Coville, Katherine, illus. (p. 1150)
—Monsters of Morley Manor: A Madcap Adventure. (p. 1169)
—Monsters of Morley Manor. (p. 1169)
—Monster's Ring. Coville, Katherine, illus. (p. 1169)
—My Teacher Flunked the Planet. Pierard, John, illus. (p. 1219)
—My Teacher Fried My Brains. Pierard, John, illus. (p. 1220)
—My Teacher Glows in the Dark. Pierard, John, illus. (p. 1220)
—My Teacher Is an Alien. (p. 1220)
—My Teacher Is an Alien. Wimmer, Mike, illus. (p. 1220)
—Naughty Nork. Coville, Katherine, illus. (p. 1237)
—Odds Are Good: An Oddly Enough & Odder Than Ever Omnibus. (p. 1278)
—Search for Snout. Coville, Katherine, illus. (p. 1537)
—Skull of Truth: A Magic Shop Book. Lippincott, Gary A., illus. (p. 1586)
—Skull of Truth. (p. 1586)
—There's an Alien in My Classroom! (p. 1731)
—Thor's Wedding Day: By Thialfi, the Goat Boy. Cogswell, Matthew, illus. (p. 1740)
—Unicorn Treasury: Stories, Poems, & Unicorn Lore. (p. 1818)
—Weeping Werewolf. Coville, Katherine, illus. (p. 1872)
—William Shakespeare's a Midsummer Night's Dream. Nolan, Dennis, illus. (p. 1933)
—Windlord's Horn. (p. 1936)
Coville, Bruce, jt. auth. see Levy, Elizabeth.
Coville, Katherine. Cottage in the Woods. (p. 369)
Coville, Katherine, illus. see Coville, Bruce.
Coville, Katherine, illus. see Levy, Elizabeth & Coville, Bruce.
Coville, Katherine, illus. see San Souci, Robert D.
Covington, Alpha. Place in the Country Where the Animals Live. (p. 1365)
—Sammy Squirrel's Adventure. (p. 1508)
Covington, Emily, illus. see Hassler-Scoop, Jill K., et al.
Covington, Jean. Nanny Planted Love: Color Book. (p. 1229)
—Nanny Planted Love. (p. 1229)
Covington, Nichole. Melinda the Miserable: Eeriness in the Attic. (p. 1125)
Covino, Glenna. Two Boys & a Puppy. (p. 1803)
Covolo, David, illus. see Madison, Ron.
Cowan, Brad V. Skinner's Banks (p. 1585)
—Street Kings (p. 1666)
Cowan, C. C. Amanda's Amazing Adventures: The Case of the Missing Pooch Rashid, Abdul, illus. (p. 52)
Cowan, Caren. No Home on the Range: Diary of an Executive Cowgirl. (p. 1258)
Cowan, Carla Romaine. E-Commerce Careers in Multimedia. (p. 492)
Cowan, Catherine. My Life with the Wave. (p. 1212)
—My Life with the Wave. Buehner, Mark, illus. (p. 1212)
Cowan, Catherine & Buehner, Mark. Mi Vida con la Ola. Rubio, Esther, tr. (p. 1133)
Cowan, Charlotte. Katie Caught a Cold. Bratun, Katy, illus. (p. 945)
—Little Elephant with the Big Earache. Garvin, Elaine, illus. (p. 1027)
—Moose with Loose Poops. Neal, Penelope, illus. (p. 1173)
—Peeper Has a Fever. Banta, Susan, illus. (p. 1335)
—Sadie's Sore Throat. Bratun, Katy, illus. (p. 1501)
Cowan, Dolly. Yeehaw, the Chosen Donkey. (p. 1969)
Cowan, Eric W. Ariadne's Thread: Case Studies in the Therapeutic Relationship. (p. 98)
Cowan, Jennifer. Earthgirl (p. 497)
—Earthgirl. (p. 497)
Cowan, Sarah & Kitchen. Trip to the Beach. (p. 1787)
Coward, Fiona. Swing High, Swing Low. Manna, Giovanni, illus. (p. 1691)
Cowart, Logan. Late October. poho, illus. (p. 979)
Cowcher, Helen. Desert Elephants Cowcher, Helen, illus. (p. 429)
—Jaguar. (p. 905)
—Rainforest. (p. 1436)
—Whistling Thorn. (p. 1912)
Cowdell, Nikki. Bradshaw Vacation. (p. 221)
Cowden, Matt. Emma Mcdougal & the Quest for Father Time. Black, Ilene, illus. (p. 520)
Cowdery, Ray. All American Wonder, Vol 2 (p. 43)
Cowdrey, Richard, illus. see Bauer, Marion Dane.
Cowdrey, Richard, illus. see Brett, Jessica.
Cowdrey, Richard, illus. see Carlstrom, Nancy White.
Cowdrey, Richard, illus. see Fletcher, Ralph J.
Cowdrey, Richard, illus. see Grogan, John & Hill, Susan.
Cowdrey, Richard, illus. see Grogan, John.
Cowdrey, Richard, illus. see Lasky, Kathryn.
Cowdrey, Richard, illus. see Mackall, Dandi Daley.
Cowdrey, Richard, illus. see Salten, Felix.
Cowdrey, Richard, illus. see Walburg, Lori.
Cowdrey, Richard, illus. see Zondervan & Walburg, Lori.
Cowell, Cressida. Cheer up Your Teddy Bear, Emily Brown! (p. 296)

—Complete Book of Dragons: A Guide to Dragon Species. (p. 352)
—Emily Brown & the Elephant Emergency. Layton, Neal, illus. (p. 518)
—Hero's Guide to Deadly Dragons. (p. 773)
—How to Be a Pirate. (p. 814)
—How to Be a Viking. (p. 815)
—How to Betray a Dragon's Hero. (p. 815)
—How to Break a Dragon's Heart. (p. 815)
—How to Cheat a Dragon's Curse. (p. 815)
—How to Cheat a Dragon's Curse. (p. 816)
—How to Cheat a Dragon's Curse. Cowell, Cressida, illus. (p. 816)
—How to Ride a Dragon's Storm. (p. 821)
—How to Seize a Dragon's Jewel. (p. 821)
—How to Speak Dragonese. (p. 821)
—How to Steal a Dragon's Sword. (p. 821)
—How to Train Your Dragon: How to Betray a Dragon's Hero. (p. 822)
—How to Train Your Dragon. (p. 822)
—How to Train Your Dragon: Paperback Gift Set 2. (p. 822)
—How to Train Your Dragon Special Edition: With Brand New Short Stories! (p. 822)
—How to Twist a Dragon's Tale. (p. 822)
—Super Sue at Super School. Ayto, Russell, illus. (p. 1682)
—That Rabbit Belongs to Emily Brown. Layton, Neal, illus. (p. 1726)
—What Shall We Do with the Boo Hoo Baby? Godon, Ingrid, illus. (p. 1893)
Cowell, Cressida, jt. auth. see Layton, Neal.
Cowell, Cressida & Layton, Neal. Emily Brown & the Thing. (p. 518)
Cowen, Carla Romaine. E-Commerce: Careers in Multimedia. (p. 492)
Cowen-Fletcher, Jane. Baby Be Kind. Cowen-Fletcher, Jane, illus. (p. 125)
—Hello, Puppy! Cowen-Fletcher, Jane, illus. (p. 765)
—It Takes a Village. (p. 894)
—My New Puppy. Cowen-Fletcher, Jane, illus. (p. 1216)
—Nell's Elf. Cowen-Fletcher, Jane, illus. (p. 1240)
—Se Necesita Todo un Pueblo. (p. 1534)
Cowen-Fletcher, Jane, illus. see Pandell, Karen.
Cowe-Spigai, Kereth. Valaan. (p. 1830)
Cowey, James. William Snottengrout - Gangor's Reign. (p. 1933)
—William Snottengrout - Quapta's Revenge. (p. 1933)
Cowgur, Eldon, illus. see Storrie, Paul D.
Cowhard, Patricia Ann. B J's Underground Adventure. (p. 123)
Cowherd, Kevin, illus. see Ripken, Cal.
Cowherd, Kevin, jt. auth. see Ripken, Cal, Jr.
Cowhey, Dennis E., illus. see Guzaldo, Jessica.
Cowhey, Dennis R., ed. see Guzaldo, Jessica.
Cowhey, Sharon P. Shy Harold & His Hiding Place (p. 1572)
Cowie, Mabel. Awakenings: 'Neath Ancient Ruins Lie, Book One. Carvajal, Cheryl, ed. (p. 120)
Cowie, Norm. Werewoof. (p. 1875)
Cowing, Sue. Collins Readers - Call Me Drog. (p. 341)
—You Will Call Me Drog. (p. 1976)
Cowing, Sue & Murakami, Jon. My Dog Has Flies: Poetry for Hawaii's Kids. (p. 1202)
Cowlard, Irene. Moriarty's Dream. (p. 1175)
Cowle, Ken. Harold Can't Stand to Be Alone. Dorland, Andrew, illus. (p. 749)
Cowles, Rose, illus. see Harvey, Sarah N.
Cowles, Rose, illus. see Petty, Dini.
Cowles, Rose, illus. see Pohl-Weary, Emily.
Cowles, Rose, illus. see Romanek, Trudee.
Cowles, Rose, illus. see Yes Magazine Editors.
Cowles, Rose, illus. see Yes Magazine Editors.
Cowles, Rose, tr. see Romanek, Trudee.
Cowley. Jigaree's Breakfast (p. 917)
—Meanie's Party. (p. 1116)
—Seven Fat Cats (p. 1554)
—Super Smile Shop. (p. 1682)
Cowley, Joseph. Alice's Adventures in Wonderland by Lewis Carroll: (Adapted by Joseph Cowley) (p. 40)
Cowley, Joy. Agapanthus Hum & the Eyeglasses. Plecas, Jennifer, illus. (p. 29)
—Bedtime Train. Odone, Jamison, illus. (p. 157)
—Chameleon Chameleon. Bishop, Nic, illus. (p. 289)
—Dan & the Parrot. (p. 401)
—Dan's Lost Hat. (p. 406)
—Definitely, Postively, Absolutely No! Big Book. (p. 424)
—Friends: Snake & Lizard. Bishop, Gavin, illus. (p. 638)
—Hungry Giant's Baby. (p. 828)
—Hungry Giant's Shoe. (p. 828)
—Hungry Giant's Shoe Big Book. (p. 828)
—Little Dan. (p. 1026)
—Little Dan Big Book. (p. 1026)
—Meanies in the House. (p. 1116)
—Meanies in the House Big Book. (p. 1116)
—Meanies Night Out. (p. 1116)
—Mrs. WishyWashy & the Big Farm Fair. (p. 1188)
—Mrs. WishyWashy & the Big Tub. (p. 1188)
—Mrs. WishyWashy & the Big Wash. (p. 1188)
—Mrs. WishyWashy & the Big Wash Big Book. (p. 1188)
—Mrs. Wishy-Washy's Farm. Fuller, Elizabeth, illus. (p. 1188)
—Mrs. Wishy-Washy's Tub. (p. 1188)
—Mud Walk. (p. 1188)
—Poor Sore Hungry Giant. (p. 1384)
—Red-Eyed Tree Frog. Bishop, Nic, illus. (p. 1453)
—Smarty No Pants. (p. 1593)
—Smarty Pants & the Talent Show. (p. 1593)
—Smarty Pants at the Circus. (p. 1593)
—Smarty Pants at the Circus Big Book. (p. 1593)
—Snake & Lizard. Bishop, Gavin, illus. (p. 1596)
—Space Aliens in Our School. Ming, Choo Hill, illus. (p. 1618)
—Starbright & the Dream Eater. (p. 1642)
—Stories of the Wild West Gang. Pye, Trevor, illus. (p. 1655)
—Those Yucky Meanies. (p. 1740)
Cowley, Joy, ed. see Barrie, J. M.
Cowley, Joy, ed. see Barrie, James Matthew.
Cowley, Joy, ed. see Brothers Grimm Staff.
Cowley, Joy, ed. see Brothers Grimm.
Cowley, Joy, ed. see Choi, Eun-gyu.
Cowley, Joy, ed. see Choi, Eun-Mi.
Cowley, Joy, ed. see Choi, Na-mi.
Cowley, Joy, ed. see Collodi, Carlo.
Cowley, Joy, ed. see Gam Do, Rin Bo.
Cowley, Joy, ed. see Hsu, Yi Ling.
Cowley, Joy, ed. see Jang, Ki-hwa & Kim, In-sook.
Cowley, Joy, ed. see Jeong, Gu-mi.
Cowley, Joy, ed. see Jeong, Jini.
Cowley, Joy, ed. see Jo, Eun-sook.
Cowley, Joy, ed. see Joo, Mi-hwa.
Cowley, Joy, ed. see Kim, Cecil.
Cowley, Joy, ed. see Kim, Soo-hyeon.
Cowley, Joy, ed. see Kim, Tae-yeon.
Cowley, Joy, ed. see Lee, Mi-Ae.
Cowley, Joy, ed. see Perrault, Charles.
Cowley, Joy, ed. see Yun, Yeo-rim.
Cowley, Joy, contrib. by. Dinosaur Morning. (p. 442)
Cowley, Joy, ed. Insects & Spiders. Do Gam, Rin Bo, illus. (p. 876)
—Insects & Spiders. Gam do, Rin Bo, illus. (p. 876)
Cowley, Katz, illus. see Smith, Craig.
Cowley, Marjorie. Golden Bull. (p. 694)
Cowley, Ray B., illus. see Bourke, Debra.
Cowley, Robert, ed. What Ifs? of American History: Eminent Historians Imagine What Might Have Been. (p. 1887)
Cowley, Stewart & Cox, Greg. Searching for Bigfoot. (p. 1537)
Cowling, Chani. Cookie Baker, Sweet & Sour. (p. 361)
Cowling, Dan. Color Yourself Smart: Geography. Franklin, Mark, illus. (p. 343)
Cowling, Douglas. Vivaldi's Ring of Mystery. Fernandez, Laura & Jacobson, Rick, illus. (p. 1846)
Cowling, Elizabeth. Picasso: Style & Meaning. (p. 1354)
Cowling, Sue, et al, selected by. Giant Poems & Wizzard Poems. (p. 674)
Cowman, Joseph, illus. see Huber, Mike.
Cowman, Joseph, illus. see Worthington, Michelle.
Cowman, L. B., jt. auth. see Ellis, Gwen.
Cowman, L. B. E. Streams in the Desert for Kids: 365 Devotions of God's Awesome Love (p. 1666)
Cowne, Chris, jt. auth. see Sanguedolce, Patty.
Cowne, Joanne, illus. see Morris, Ting & Morris, Neil.
Cowper-Thomas, Wendy. Something Important. (p. 1610)
Cowper-Thomas, Wendy, illus. see Cobb, Judith A.
Cowper-Thomas, Wendy, illus. see Sinex, Roxana Faith.
Cowsar, Susan. Magic Flower. (p. 1072)
Cowsert, Sami. Tammi & Her Dragon. (p. 1704)
Cowsert, Sandra. Continuing Adventures of Tammi & Her Dragon. (p. 361)
Cowsill, Alan. World War One, 1914-1918. Sharma, Lalit Kumar, illus. (p. 1959)
Cox, Alex, illus. see Nobacon, Danbert.
Cox, Amy. Odetta the Octopus Teacher. (p. 1278)
Cox, Birck, illus. see Turkington, Carol & Dover, Jeffrey S.
Cox, Brain T., illus. see Loesch, Joe.
Cox, Brian T., illus. see Collins, James.
Cox, Brian T., illus. see Loesch, Joe.
Cox, Brian T., illus. see Wood, Jill G.
Cox, Buddy. Quicksilver Deep (p. 1427)
Cox, Byron & Berglund, Brad. Gregory Glove. (p. 723)
Cox Cannons, Helen. Clouds (p. 335)
—Rain (p. 1434)
—Snow (p. 1598)
—Sunshine (p. 1677)
—Weather Wise (p. 1870)
—Wind (p. 1935)
Cox, Caroline, jt. auth. see Albala, Ken.
Cox, Caroline, et al. Exploring the Polar Regions, Revised Edition. (p. 554)
Cox, Carolyn. My Very Own Bible. (p. 1221)
—My Very Own Bible Gift. (p. 1221)
Cox, Carolyn, illus. see Box, Su.
Cox, Carolyn, illus. see Rock, Lois.
Cox, Chad, illus. see Reich, J. J.
Cox, Christine. Why the Zero Was Sad? (p. 1926)
Cox, Clinton. Undying Glory: The Story of the Massachusetts 54th Regiment. (p. 1817)
Cox, Daniel J., illus. see Grambo, Rebecca L.
Cox, David. Road to Goonong. Cox, David, illus. (p. 1477)
Cox, David, illus. see Arena, Felice & Kettle, Phil.
Cox, David, illus. see Crew, Gary.
Cox, David, illus. see Gleeson, Libby.
Cox, David, illus. see Pulman, Felicity.
Cox, David, illus. see Walker, Kate.
Cox, Denise L. Ginger Is Adopted (p. 677)
Cox, Dorothy. Oh No! When It's OK to Be Late for School. Cox, Dorothy, illus. (p. 1281)
Cox, Dorothy Ayling. Children's Stories. (p. 304)
Cox, E. J. Adventures of Koen & Katie: The Case of the Masked Bandits. (p. 19)
Cox, Erika. Psychology. (p. 1413)
Cox, Gene. Go Big Red! A History of Leon High School Football 1916-2001. (p. 686)
Cox, Glendyne Dewhurst, illus. see Burton M.Sc., Kathryn Mac. Diarmid.
Cox Gray, Marjorie. Bucky's Adventures. Griffin, Marlin, illus. (p. 234)
Cox, Greg. Bigfoot. (p. 184)
—Riese: Kingdom Falling. (p. 1471)
Cox, Greg, jt. auth. see Cowley, Stewart.
Cox, James. Earth Dogs Don't Speak. (p. 495)
Cox, Janis. Tadeo Turtle. (p. 1695)
Cox, Jason. Puppet. (p. 1417)
Cox, Jessica. It's Time for Bed. (p. 899)
Cox, Joe & Butler-Moore, Nylea L., contrib. by. Grumpy Shepherd. (p. 727)
Cox, Jon. Crazy Man & the Plums. (p. 377)
Cox, Jon, illus. see Washakie, John.
Cox, Joseph J. Grobar & the Mind Control Potion. Becker, Rebecca J., illus. (p. 725)
Cox, Joyce, et al. Microsoft(r) Office Outlook(r) 2007. (p. 1136)
—Microsoft(r) Office Powerpoint(r) 2007 (p. 1136)
—Microsoft(r) Office Word 2007. (p. 1136)
Cox, Judith. Wellness Tree. Rogers, Denny, illus. (p. 1874)
Cox, Judy. Carmen Learns English. Dominguez, Angela, illus. (p. 270)
—Carmen Learns English. Dominguez, Angela N., illus. (p. 270)
—Case of the Purloined Professor Rayyan, Omar, illus. (p. 275)
—Cinco de Mouse-O! Ebbeler, Jeffrey, illus. (p. 319)
—Don't Be Silly, Mrs. Millie! Mathieu, Joe, illus. (p. 467)
—Go to Sleep, Groundhog. Meisel, Paul, illus. (p. 687)
—Happy Birthday, Mrs. Millie! Mathieu, Joe, illus. (p. 745)
—Haunted House, Haunted Mouse. Ebbeler, Jeffrey, illus. (p. 753)
—Mrs. Millie Goes to Philly! Mathieu, Joe, illus. (p. 1187)
—Mystery of the Burmese Bandicoot Rayyan, Omar, illus. (p. 1225)
—Mystery of the Burmese Bandicoot. (p. 1225)
—Nora & the Texas Terror. Haley, Amanda, illus. (p. 1264)
—One Is a Feast for Mouse: A Thanksgiving Tale. Ebbeler, Jeffrey, illus. (p. 1295)
—Pick a Pumpkin, Mrs. Millie! Mathieu, Joe, illus. (p. 1354)
—Puppy Power. Björkman, Steve, illus. (p. 1418)
—Secret Chicken Society. Haley, Amanda, illus. (p. 1540)
—Snow Day for Mouse. Ebbeler, Jeffrey, illus. (p. 1598)
—Ukulele Hayley. Haley, Amanda, illus. (p. 1808)
Cox, Julie. Beginning Face Reading: You CAN Tell a Book by Its Cover. (p. 159)
Cox, Karen. Gwyneira, the Crystal Fairy. (p. 733)
Cox, Karin, jt. auth. see Cox, Miss Karin.
Cox, Kathy Lynn. Far As You See Tales. (p. 572)
Cox, Katie. Learn on the Go Sticker Activity - 123. (p. 983)
Cox, Katie & Make Believe Ideas Staff. Little Hands Animals. (p. 1028)
Cox, Katie, des. Little Hands Colors. (p. 1029)
—Little Hands First Words. (p. 1029)
—Little Hands Trucks. (p. 1029)
Cox, Katie, et al. My Giant Sticker. (p. 1209)
Cox, Kenyon & Edwards, Wallace. Mixed Beasts. Edwards, Wallace, illus. (p. 1156)
Cox, Kim, illus. see McNease, Mitzy.
Cox, Kimberley & Wilde, David. If I Were a Dragon. (p. 853)
Cox, Lisa. Media Muscle: Body Image & the Media for Guys. Warwick, Richard, illus. (p. 1118)
Cox, Lynne. Elizabeth, Queen of the Seas. Floca, Brian, illus. (p. 513)
Cox, M. M. Accidental Mobster. (p. 8)
—Undercover Wiseguy. (p. 1814)
COX, Margaret. Emerald-fire. (p. 517)
—Kiss-diamond. (p. 961)
—Soul-pearl. (p. 1614)
Cox, Marian. Cambridge Checkpoint English Coursebook 8. (p. 255)
—Cambridge Checkpoint English Workbook 8. (p. 255)
Cox, Martyn & Woram, Catherine. Gardening with Kids. Wreford, Polly, photos by. (p. 656)
Cox, Michael. Fitter, Faster, Funnier Football! Everything You Ever Wanted to Know about Football... (p. 599)
—Johnny Catbiscuit & the Stolen Secrets! Dunn, Gary, illus. (p. 923)
—Little Fred Riding Hood. Million, Liz, illus. (p. 1028)
Cox, Michael A. Don't Retire: New Life Stratgeies for Aging Boomers & other Lost Souls. (p. 468)
Cox, Michael & Smedley. Invasion of the Sausage Snatchers. (p. 883)
Cox, Miss Karin & Cox, Karin. Pancakes on Sunday. Acar, Sinan, illus. (p. 1320)
Cox, Mykin. What Every Girl Should Know: A Study in Love, Life, & Faith. (p. 1884)
Cox, Nancy, illus. see Campbell, Jennifer.
Cox, Norma Flora & Flora, Norma Bradshaw. Camp Desoto: A History. (p. 257)
Cox, P. Roxbee. Don't Be a Bully, Billy. (p. 466)
—Who Were the Vikings? (p. 1919)
Cox, Palmer. Brownies: Their Book. Cox, Palmer, illus. (p. 232)
Cox, Paul, illus. see Trachtenberg, Stanley.
Cox, Phil Roxbee. Big Pig on a Dig. Tyler, Jenny, ed. (p. 183)
—Curly's Friends. Cartwright, Stephen, illus. (p. 394)
—Don't Be a Bully, Billy. (p. 466)
—Don't Be Greedy, Graham. Tyler, Jenny, ed. (p. 466)
—Don't Tell Lies, Lucy. (p. 468)
—Fat Cat on a Mat. Tyler, Jenny, ed. (p. 577)
—Frog on a Log. Tyler, Jenny, ed. (p. 640)
—Give That Back, Jack. (p. 681)
—Hen's Pens. Tyler, Jenny, ed. (p. 769)
—Mouse Moves House. Tyler, Jenny, ed. (p. 1182)
—Sam Sheep Can't Sleep. Tyler, Jenny, ed. (p. 1507)
—Shark in the Park. Tyler, Jenny, ed. (p. 1562)
—Ted in a Red Bed. Tyler, Jenny, ed. (p. 1712)
—Ted's Shed. Tyler, Jenny, ed. (p. 1713)
—Toad Makes a Road. Tyler, Jenny, ed. (p. 1759)
—What Were Castles For? (p. 1895)
—Who Were the Romans? (p. 1919)
Cox, Phil Roxbee, ed. see Burgess, Mark.
Cox, Phil Roxbee, jt. auth. see Tudhope, Simon.
Cox, Phil Roxbee & Cartwright, S. Fat Cat on a Mat. (p. 577)
—Fox on a Box. (p. 626)
—Goose on the Loose. (p. 702)
—Rusty's Bone. (p. 1498)
—Sam Sheep Can't Sleep. (p. 1507)
—Ted in a Red Bed. (p. 1712)
—Ted's Shed, Toad Makes a Road, Fat Cat on a Mat & Sam Sheep Can't Sleep. (p. 1713)
—Toad Makes a Road. (p. 1759)
—Wolly's Walk. (p. 1944)
Cox, Phil Roxbee & Cartwright, Stephen. Frog on a Log. (p. 640)
—Goose on the Loose. (p. 702)
—Hen's Pens. (p. 769)
—Mouse Moves House. (p. 1182)
—Shark in the Park. (p. 1562)
—Ted's Shed. (p. 1713)
Cox, Phil Roxbee & Reid, Struan. Who Were the First People? (p. 1919)
—Who Were the First People? Wood, Gerald, illus. (p. 1919)
Cox, Phil Roxbee, ed. Find the Duck. Cartwright, Stephen, illus. (p. 587)
Cox, R. Lonely Wizard Named Wizzy: The Apprentice. (p. 1046)
Cox, Renee K. Sammie Jane Saves Charlie: Cougar's Rescue. (p. 1507)
Cox, Rhonda. Best Friends. Cox, Rhonda, photos by. (p. 169)
—Pigs Peek. Cox, Rhonda, photos by. (p. 1358)
Cox, Richard. Shell Game. (p. 1564)
Cox, Robert & Robins, Jim. Kangaroo Who Couldn't Hop. (p. 942)
Cox, Rosamund Kidman. Wild Animals. (p. 1928)
Cox, Roy. And They Fell Fast Asleep. McCall, Anthony, illus. (p. 71)
Cox, Russ, illus. see Collins, Terry.
Cox, Sarah Webster. Adventures of Willy & Tilly. (p. 24)
Cox, Scott, Sr. Love Your Ego As Your SELF. (p. 1061)
Cox, Stephen Angus. Dare Boys of 1776. (p. 406)
Cox, Steve. Is That You, Alien? Check Inside the Secret Pockets If You Dare. (p. 890)
—Is That You, Monster? Check Inside the Secret Pockets If You Dare! (p. 890)
—Is That You, Wolf? BEWARE! Not a Bedtime Story. (p. 890)
—Seek & You Shall Find. (p. 1548)
Cox, Steve, illus. see Bently, Peter.
Cox, Steve, illus. see Cooling, Wendy.
Cox, Steve, illus. see Ellis, Gwen.
Cox, Steve, illus. see Emmett, Jonathan.
Cox, Steve, illus. see Faurot, Kimberly.
Cox, Steve, illus. see Fine, Anne.
Cox, Steve, illus. see Hodgson, Karen J.
Cox, Steve, illus. see Kroll, Steven.
Cox, Steve, illus. see Lynette, Rachel.
Cox, Steve, illus. see Nolan, Allia Zobel.
Cox, Steve, illus. see Paxton, Tom.
Cox, Steve, illus. see Vantrease, Norma.
Cox, Steve, illus. see Zobel-Nolan, Allia.
Cox, Steven. Justin's Very Own Drum. Saavedra, Anthony, illus. (p. 940)
Cox, Suzy. Dead Girls Detective Agency. (p. 416)
Cox, Tammy Parker. Not So Ordinary Farm. (p. 1267)
Cox, Thomas, illus. see Woelfle, Gretchen.
Cox, Tiffany. Amy, the Frog Who Loved to Sing. (p. 66)
Cox, Tom, illus. see Malocco, Chris & Malocco, Kimberly.
Cox, Tracey M. Angels Do That. Movshina, Marina, illus. (p. 75)
—Arachnabet- an Alphabet of Spiders. (p. 94)
—Liddil Gets Her Light. Ruble, Eugene, illus. (p. 1007)
—Shaping up the Year. Bell, Samantha, illus. (p. 1561)
Cox, Val, illus. see Graves, Judith.
Cox, Val, illus. see Keswick, Kitty.
Cox, Vicki. Betsy Ross: Flag for a New Nation. (p. 172)
—Clarence Thomas. (p. 327)
—History of Third Parties. (p. 785)
—Margaret Sanger. (p. 1092)
—Maya Angelou. (p. 1112)
—Oscar Arias Sanchez: Bringing Peace to Central America. (p. 1305)
Cox, William Drought, ed. see Esten, Sidney R.
Coxall, Darcy. Where Is My Bear? Wittebrood, Menno, illus. (p. 1908)
Cox-Cannons, Helen. Thunder & Lightning (p. 1746)
Coxe, Molly. Benjamin & Bumper to the Rescue. Canine, Craig, ed. (p. 164)
—Wet Hen: A Short Vowel Adventure. (p. 1877)
Coxford, Arthur F., et al. Matematicas Contemporaneas en Contexto Curso 1 Parte A: Un Planteamiento Unificado. (p. 1104)
Coxhead, Averil. Essentials of Teaching Academic Vocabulary. (p. 537)
Coxon, Caroline, jt. auth. see Paren, Liz.
Coxon, Michele. Cat Who Found His Way Home. (p. 278)
—Have You Fed the Cat? (p. 754)
—Have You Fed the Cat? Coxon, Michele, illus. (p. 754)
—Have You Fed the Cat? (Spanish/English) Coxon, Michele, illus. (p. 754)
—Kitten's Adventure (Portuguese/English) (p. 963)
—Kitten's Adventure (Spanish/English) Coxon, Michele, illus. (p. 963)
—Termites on a Stick: A Chimp Learns to Use a Tool Coxon, Michele, illus. (p. 1721)
—Termites on a Stick: A Chimpanzee Learns to Use a Tool Coxon, Michele, illus. (p. 1721)
—Where's My Kitten? (p. 1910)
Coxon, Michele, illus. see McFadden, Patricia.
Coxon, Rachel. Collection of Children's Stories. (p. 339)
Cox-Sands, Angela. Missing Vowel. Piscopo, Samantha, illus. (p. 1153)
Coy, Jason P. Brief History of Germany. (p. 227)
Coy, John. Crackback. (p. 375)
—Eyes on the Goal (p. 558)
—Hoop Genius: How a Desperate Teacher & a Rowdy Gym Class Invented Basketball. Morse, Joe, illus. (p. 795)
—Love of the Game. (p. 1060)
—Take Your Best Shot. (p. 1697)
—Top of the Order. (p. 1769)
—Two Old Potatoes & Me. Fisher, Carolyn, illus. (p. 1804)
Coy, John & Reonegro, Antonio. Around the World. Lynch, Tom, illus. (p. 100)
Coy, Steven. Sandwich: Short Stories & Screenplays by Steven Coy. Sala, Karla, ed. (p. 1511)
Coy, Steven & Dooda, Ian, eds. BOOM! for Real: Anthology of Poetry, Prose, & Pictures (Volume One 2005) (p. 213)
Coyle, Carmela Lavigna. Do Princesses Count? Gordon, Mike & Gordon, Carl, illus. (p. 457)
—Do Princesses Have Best Friends Forever? Gordon, Carl & Gordon, Mike, illus. (p. 457)
—Do Princesses Have Best Friends Forever? Gordon, Mike & Gordon, Carl, illus. (p. 457)
—Do Princesses Make Happy Campers? Gordon, Mike, illus. (p. 457)
—Do Princesses Really Kiss Frogs? Gordon, Mike & Gordon, Carl, illus. (p. 457)
—Do Princesses Scrape Their Knees? (p. 457)

C

—Do Princesses Scrape Their Knees? Keepsake Sticker Doodle Book. Gordon, Mike & Gordon, Carl, illus. (p. 457)
—Do Princesses Wear Hiking Boots? Gordon, Mike & Gordon, Carl, illus. (p. 457)
—Do Superheroes Have Teddy Bears? Gordon, Mike, illus. (p. 457)
—Thank You, Aunt Tallulah! MacPherson, Bruce, illus. (p. 1725)
—Tumbleweed Came Back. Rechin, Kevin, illus. (p. 1796)
Coyle, Charissa B., illus. see Ketchum, Holly.
Coyle, Greg & Allaynalee. Nikki's List of Fun Things to Do Today. (p. 1255)
Coyle, Janeen. Pug with a Plan. (p. 1415)
Coyle, Katie. Vivian Apple at the End of the World. (p. 1846)
—Vivian Apple Needs a Miracle. (p. 1846)
Coyne, Adrian, jt. auth. see Walker, Lisa.
Coyne, Jennifer Tarr. Discovering Women Artists for Children. (p. 450)
Cozens, Gaynor & Thomas, Cheryl Ann. Mathematics Grade 2: New Zambia Basic Education Course. (p. 1108)
—Numeracy Matters Grade 1. (p. 1272)
—Numeracy Matters Grade 1 IsiXhosa. (p. 1272)
—Numeracy Matters Grade 1 Learner's Book isiXhosa Translation. (p. 1272)
—Numeracy Matters Grade 1 Learner's Book Sesotho Translation. (p. 1272)
—Numeracy Matters Grade 1 Sesotho Translation. (p. 1272)
—Numeracy Matters Grade 1 Zambia Basic Education. (p. 1272)
—Numeracy Matters Grade 2: isiXhosa Translation. (p. 1272)
—Numeracy Matters Grade 2 isiXhosa Translation. (p. 1272)
—Numeracy Matters Learner's Book Grade 1. (p. 1272)
Cozzens, Glenn R. How Your Hobby Can Make You Rich! When It's Combined with the Ultimate Business! You Can Finally Take Control of Your Financial Future by Designing Your Life Around Doing What You Love. (p. 823)
Cozzens, Judith H., compiled by. Teen Prayers by Teens. (p. 1713)
Cozzo, Karole. How to Say I Love You Out Loud. (p. 821)
CQ Editors. Historic Documents Index 1972-2002. (p. 782)
CQ Editors, et al. Cq Researcher 2002 (p. 375)
CQ Press Editors. Guide to Current American Government 2004. (p. 730)
CQ Press Staff. Congressional Districts in the 2000s: A Portrait of America (p. 357)
—CQ Researcher 2004 Cooper, Mary H. et al, eds. (p. 375)
CQ Press Staff, ed. see Valelly, Richard M.
CQ Press Staff, creator. Congressional Roll Call 2004 (p. 357)
—Historic Documents Of 2004 (p. 782)
CQ Press Staff, ed. Congressional Roll Call 2002 (p. 357)
—Historic Documents of 2002 (p. 782)
—Understanding Constitutional Issues: Selections from the Cq Researcher (p. 1815)
CQ Products (Firm) Staff. S'more Campfire Fun: Kid's Edition. (p. 1595)
CQ Products Staff. Disgustingly Delicious. (p. 451)
—Fake-Out Food: Wacky Treats to Fool Your Friends! (p. 565)
Cr. Adventures of Jenni & Jake. (p. 19)
Craan, Sheila. I Found a Ses in My Faucet. (p. 838)
—Mr. Ses Attends Stockville Elementary Academy. (p. 1186)
Craats, Rennay. 1910: Canadian Decades. (p. 2002)
—1940: Canadian Decades. (p. 2002)
—1970: Canadian Decades. (p. 2002)
—Arizona. (p. 98)
—Baseball. (p. 140)
—Basketball. (p. 143)
—Black-Footed Ferret. (p. 196)
—Blacksmith: Pioneers of Canada. (p. 197)
—Caring for Your Frog. (p. 269)
—Caring for Your Gecko. (p. 269)
—Caring for Your Snake. (p. 269)
—Cherokee. (p. 298)
—Columbus Day. (p. 346)
—Construction. (p. 359)
—Construction Q & A. (p. 359)
—E. B. White. (p. 491)
—Economy. (p. 503)
—Exploration of North America. (p. 550)
—Fashion. (p. 575)
—For the Love of Baseball. Craats, Rennay & Kissock, Heather, eds. (p. 616)
—For the Love of Karate. Nault, Jennifer & Turner, Kara, eds. (p. 616)
—Foreign Affairs. (p. 617)
—Forgeron: Le Début de la Colonie. Karvonen, Tanjah, tr. from ENG. (p. 619)
—Frog. (p. 639)
—Gecko. (p. 659)
—Gold Rush. (p. 693)
—Illinois. (p. 857)
—Indiana. (p. 871)
—Maasai. (p. 1067)
—Maasai with Code. (p. 1067)
—Magasin Général: Le Début de la Colonie. Karvonen, Tanjah, tr. from ENG. (p. 1071)
—Maryland. (p. 1101)
—Michigan. (p. 1135)
—Natural Landmarks. (p. 1235)
—Navajo. (p. 1237)
—New Hampshire. (p. 1244)
—New Mexico. (p. 1246)
—Ranching. (p. 1438)
—Skateboarding. (p. 1583)
—Snake. (p. 1596)
—Snowboarding. (p. 1600)
—Sports. (p. 1632)
—Trends. (p. 1784)
—United Way. (p. 1820)
—Whooping Cranes. (p. 1920)
Craats, Rennay, jt. auth. see Weigl Publishers Staff.
Craats, Rennay & Gillespie, Katie. Gecko. (p. 659)
Crabapple, Molly, illus. see DePalma, Johnny.
Crabapple, Molly, illus. see Sand, George.
Crabapple, Molly, jt. auth. see DePalma, Johnny.
Crabb, James Anthony. Dinosaur & Dragon Juice Café. (p. 441)
Crabbere, Edna Dookie. American Fudge. (p. 60)
Crabtree, ed. see Bow, James.
Crabtree, ed. see Johnson, Robin.
Crabtree, ed. see Walker, Robert.
Crabtree, Alfred E. Revealing the Thread of the Salt Covenant. (p. 1465)
Crabtree, Andy, illus. see Hastings, Suanne.
Crabtree, Dianne. I Know You & I Love You Too. (p. 840)
—Mel Goes to Camp. (p. 1125)
Crabtree Editor & Miller, Reagan. Sun. (p. 1675)
Crabtree Editors & Donaldson, Chelsea. Planets. (p. 1368)
Crabtree Editors & Miller, Reagan. Moon. (p. 1171)
Crabtree Editors & Romanek, Trudee. Splash It Swimming. (p. 1629)
Crabtree Editors & Stuckey, Rachel. Ride It Bmx. (p. 1471)
Crabtree Editors & Webb, Margaret. Pump It up Cheerleading. (p. 1416)
Crabtree Editors & Wilson, Kyla. Stretch It Yoga. (p. 1667)
Crabtree Editors & Wimbush, Jeff. Stars. (p. 1643)
Crabtree Editors & Winters, Jaime. Carve It Snowboarding. (p. 273)
—Shred It Skateboarding. (p. 1571)
Crabtree, Julie. Crepe Makers' Bond. (p. 381)
—Discovering Pig Magic. (p. 449)
Crabtree, Marc. Meet My Neighbor, the Artist. (p. 1121)
—Meet My Neighbor, the Builder. (p. 1121)
—Meet My Neighbor, the Chef. (p. 1121)
—Meet My Neighbor, the Firefighter. (p. 1121)
—Meet My Neighbor, the Hip-Hop Dancer. (p. 1121)
—Meet My Neighbor, the Librarian. (p. 1121)
—Meet My Neighbor, the News Camera Operator. (p. 1121)
—Meet My Neighbor, the Photographer. (p. 1121)
—Meet My Neighbor, the Taekwondo Master. (p. 1121)
Crabtree, Marc, illus. see Kalman, Bobbie & MacAulay, Kelley.
Crabtree, Marc, illus. see Kalman, Bobbie.
Crabtree, Marc, illus. see MacAulay, Kelley & Kalman, Bobbie.
Crabtree, Marc, illus. see Sjonger, Rebecca & Kalman, Bobbie.
Crabtree, Marc, jt. auth. see Harvey, Joanna.
Crabtree, Marc, photos by see Crossingham, John & Kalman, Bobbie.
Crabtree, Marc, photos by see Crossingham, John.
Crabtree, Marc, photos by see Kalman, Bobbie & MacAulay, Kelley.
Crabtree, Marc, photos by see Kalman, Bobbie.
Crabtree, Marc, photos by see MacAulay, Kelley & Kalman, Bobbie.
Crabtree, Marc, photos by see Sjonger, Rebecca & Kalman, Bobbie.
Crabtree, Marc, photos by see Walker, Niki & Kalman, Bobbie.
Crabtree Publishing Co. Staff, ed. see Miller, Reagan & Berry, Minta.
Crabtree Publishing Co. Staff, ed. see Miller, Reagan & Richardson, Hazel.
Crabtree Publishing Co. Staff & Burns, Kylie. What's Going On? Collecting & Recording Your Data. (p. 1897)
—What's the Problem? How to Start Your Scientific Investigation. (p. 1899)
Crabtree Publishing Co. Staff & Challen, Paul. What Just Happened? Reading Results & Making Inferences. (p. 1891)
—What's Going to Happen? Making Your Hypothesis. (p. 1897)
Crabtree Publishing Co. Staff & Hyde, Natalie. What's the Plan? Designing Your Experiment. (p. 1899)
Crabtree Publishing Co. Staff & Johnson, Robin. What Do We Know Now? Drawing Conclusions & Answering the Question. (p. 1882)
Crabtree Publishing Company Staff. Economics of Entertainment. (p. 502)
Crabtree Publishing Company Staff & Bow, James. Gangs. (p. 655)
—Sex. (p. 1556)
Crabtree Publishing Company Staff & Grell, Marlene. United States: The Land. (p. 1819)
Crabtree Publishing Company Staff & Iorizzo, Carrie. Divorce & Blended Families. (p. 455)
—Eating Disorders. (p. 501)
—Gambling. (p. 654)
Crabtree Publishing Company Staff & Jackson, Tom. Gases & Their Properties. (p. 657)
—Introducing the Periodic Table. (p. 882)
Crabtree Publishing Company Staff & Montgomerie, Adrienne. Metals. (p. 1130)
—Non-Metals. (p. 1263)
Crabtree Publishing Company Staff & Morss, Martha. United States: The People. (p. 1819)
Crabtree Publishing Company Staff & Pegis, Jessica. Bullying. (p. 241)
Crabtree Publishing Company Staff & Rivkin, Jennifer. Physical Bullying. (p. 1353)
—Verbal Bullying. (p. 1836)
Crabtree Publishing Company Staff & Stuckey, Rachel. Cyber Bullying. (p. 396)
Crabtree Publishing Company Staff & Webb, Margaret. Social Bullying. (p. 1604)
Crabtree Publishing Company Staff & Weiss, Lynne. United States: The Culture. (p. 1819)
Crabtree Publishing, compiled by. Exploring Our Solar System Set. (p. 553)
Crabtree Publishing, creator. My Path to Math: Math Concepts Made Simple. (p. 1216)
—Sports Starters. (p. 1633)
Crabtree Publishing Staff, ed. see Berry, Minta.
Crabtree Publishing Staff, ed. see Brennan, Joseph K.
Crabtree Publishing Staff, ed. see Miller, Reagan & Alexander, Carol.
Crabtree Publishing Staff, ed. see Miller, Reagan & Berry, Minta.
Crabtree Publishing Staff, ed. see Miller, Reagan & Boyle, Sarah B.
Crabtree Publishing Staff, ed. see Miller, Reagan & Johnson, Robin.
Crabtree Publishing Staff, ed. see Miller, Reagan & Peppas, Lynn.
Crabtree Publishing Staff, ed. see Miller, Reagan & Richardson, Hazel.
Crabtree Publishing Staff, ed. see Miller, Reagan & Rosen, Suri.
Crabtree Publishing Staff, ed. see Miller, Reagan & Stone, Janet.
Crabtree Publishing Staff, ed. see Miller, Reagan & Walker, Robert.
Crabtree Publishing Staff, ed. see Miller, Reagan.
Crabtree Publishing Staff, ed. see Peppas, Lynn.
Crabtree Publishing Staff, ed. see Richardson, Hazel.
Crabtree, Sally. Magic Train Ride. Esplugas, Sonia, illus. (p. 1074)
—Magic Train Ride. Esplugas, Sonia & Espulgas, Sonia, illus. (p. 1074)
Crabtree Staff. Mustang. (p. 1194)
Crabtree Staff, ed. see Peppas, Lynn.
Crabtree Staff & Aloian, Molly. George Washington: Hero of the American Revolution. (p. 664)
Crabtree Staff & Bow, James. Electrical Engineering & the Science of Circuits. (p. 509)
Crabtree Staff & Clarke, Gordon. Significant Battles of the American Revolution. (p. 1574)
Crabtree Staff & Hyde, Natalie. Understanding Mesoamerican Myths. (p. 1816)
Crabtree Staff & Hynson, Colin. Understanding Indian Myths. (p. 1815)
Crabtree Staff & Johnson, Robin. Take off Track & Field. (p. 1697)
—Takedown Wrestling. (p. 1697)
Crabtree Staff & Kopp, Megan. Understanding Native American Myths. (p. 1816)
Crabtree Staff & Perritano, John. Causes of the American Revolution. (p. 282)
—Outcome of the American Revolution. (p. 1312)
Crabtree Staff & Rivkin, Jennifer. Physical Bullying. (p. 1353)
—Verbal Bullying. (p. 1836)
Crabtree Staff & Roberts, Steve. King George III: England's Struggle to Keep America. (p. 958)
Crabtree Staff & Rooney, Anne. Aerospace Engineering & the Principles of Flight. (p. 25)
Crabtree Staff & Snedden, Robert. Mechanical Engineering & Simple Machines. (p. 1118)
Crabtree Staff & Solway, Andrew. Civil Engineering & the Science of Structures. (p. 324)
Crabtree Staff & Stuckey, Rachel. Cyber Bullying. (p. 396)
Crabtree Staff & Webb, Margaret. Social Bullying. (p. 1604)
Crabtree Staff & Williams, Brian. Understanding Norse Myths. (p. 1816)
Crabtree, Zona Mae. Travelers. (p. 1780)
—White Dove. (p. 1912)
Craddock, Chris. Naked at School: Three Plays for Teens. (p. 1228)
Craddock, Erik. BC Mambo. Craddock, Erik, illus. (p. 147)
—Deep-Space Disco. Craddock, Erik, illus. (p. 423)
—Dragon Boogie. (p. 476)
—Dragon Boogie. Craddock, Erik, illus. (p. 476)
—Ninja Slice. Craddock, Erik, illus. (p. 1256)
—Pirate Palooza. Craddock, Erik, illus. (p. 1362)
—Robot Frenzy. (p. 1480)
—Stone Rabbit #6: Night of the Living Dust Bunnies. Craddock, Erik, illus. (p. 1652)
—Stone Rabbit #8: Robot Frenzy. Craddock, Erik, illus. (p. 1652)
—Superhero Stampede. Craddock, Erik, illus. (p. 1683)
Craddock, Richard S., jt. auth. see Gentry, J. Richard.
Craddock, Sonia. Runaway Gran (p. 1496)
Craddock, T. BIG Team Comic Book. (p. 184)
Craft, Charlotte. King Midas & the Golden Touch. Craft, Kinuko Y., illus. (p. 958)
Craft, Danna, illus. see Harris, Rae Ann & Weintraub, David.
Craft, Dawn. Ethan Green & the GAS Kids: The Case of the Missing Recycling Bin. (p. 539)
Craft, Donna, illus. see Laven, Zp.
Craft, Donna, illus. see McGregor, Janet C.
Craft, Elizabeth. Flavor of the Day. (p. 603)
—I'll Have What He's Having. (p. 856)
—Love Bytes. (p. 1059)
—Make Mine to Go. (p. 1079)
Craft, James. Five Little Honeybees. (p. 600)
Craft, Jerry. Mama's Boyz: Because Learning Shouldn't Stop at 3 o'Clock!: Home Schoolin' (p. 1084)
—Mama's Boyz: What You Need to Succeed!: the Big Picture: the Big Picture. Craft, Jerry, illus. (p. 1084)
Craft, Jerry, illus. see Bass, Patrik Henry.
Craft, Jerry, illus. see Candelario, Margo.
Craft, K. Y., illus. see Craft, Mahlon.
Craft, Kinuko, illus. see Hillert, Margaret.
Craft, Kinuko Y., illus. see Craft, Charlotte.
Craft, Kinuko Y., illus. see Mayer, Marianna.
Craft, Mahlon. Christmas Moon. Craft, K. Y., illus. (p. 314)
Craft, Richard, ed. see Anonymous.
Craft, Sandra. Jesus Whispers in My Ear. (p. 916)
Crafts, Gregory, jt. auth. see Shapiro, Gordon.
Crafts, Hannah. Bondwoman's Narrative. Gates, Henry Louis, Jr., ed. (p. 208)
Cragg, Dan, jt. auth. see Sherman, David.
Cragg, Marcelyn Martin, illus. see Hutchings, Harriet Anne.
Cragg, Richard E. From Hitler to Pearl Harbor. (p. 642)
Cragie. Mysterious Mask. (p. 1223)
Craig, A. & Rosney, C. Science Encyclopedia. (p. 1525)
Craig, Barbara J. Santa's Magical Key. (p. 1513)
Craig, Bobby & Manifold, Delwyn. Learning Adventures of Spot. (p. 985)
Craig, Branden Chapin, illus. see Rehberg, Emily.
Craig, Carol. Floral Fairies Coloring Book. (p. 606)
Craig, Charles, illus. see Wallace, Susan Helen.
Craig, Charlie, illus. see Mohan, Claire Jordan.
Craig, Chris, illus. see McCracken, Connie.
Craig, Colleen. Afrika. (p. 28)
Craig, Dan, illus. see Dasilva, D.
Craig, Dave. Bad Attitude: A Sure Way to Look Rather Silly! (p. 131)
—Cheating: A Sure Way to Become Untrustworthy! (p. 295)
—Lying: A Sure Way to Destroy Your Credibility! (p. 1066)
—Stealing: A Sure Way to Make Life Miserable! (p. 1646)
Craig, David, illus. see Busby, Peter.
Craig, David, illus. see Forrester, Tina, et al.
Craig, David, illus. see Riehle, Mary Ann McCabe.
Craig, David, illus. see Shapiro, Stephen & Forrester, Tina.
Craig, David, illus. see Tanaka, Shelley.
Craig, David, illus. see Trottier, Maxine.
Craig, David, illus. see Weaver, Janice.
Craig, Deborah Anne. Paddle, the Extraordinary Duck. Glueck, Michael Wells, ed. (p. 1317)
Craig, Diane. Giraffe. (p. 677)
—Manatee. (p. 1086)
—Panda. (p. 1320)
—Science History Is No Mystery! (p. 1526)
—Whale Shark. (p. 1877)
Craig, Diane, ed. see Dolphin, Colleen.
Craig, Diane, ed. see Doudna, Kelly.
Craig, Diane, ed. see Hanson, Anders.
Craig, Diane, ed. see Salzmann, Mary Elizabeth.
Craig, Diane, jt. auth. see Hanson, Anders.
Craig, Diane, jt. auth. see Kuskowski, Alex.
Craig, Diane & Doudna, Kelly. No One Slumbers When We Use Numbers! (p. 1259)
Craig, Ellen. Making a Book a Best Seller: Marketing Techniques above & Beyond the Rest. (p. 1080)
Craig, G. Armour, et al. English Literature. (p. 530)
Craig, Gary. I Can Be Anything Creative Activity Book. Craig, Gary, illus. (p. 835)
Craig, Geoffrey & Parkins, Wendy. Slow Living. (p. 1591)
Craig, Helen, illus. see Holabird, Katharine & Grosset and Dunlap Editors.
Craig, Helen, illus. see Holabird, Katharine.
Craig, Helen, illus. see Morrison, Blake.
Craig, Helen, illus. see Pearce, Philippa.
Craig, Helen, jt. auth. see Holabird, Katharine.
Craig, Helen & Holabird, Katharine. Angelina on Stage. (p. 74)
Craig, J. Ann, intro. Children of the Bible: Twelve Stories of Children. (p. 302)
Craig, Janet. Maine: The Pine Tree State. (p. 1077)
Craig, Janet, jt. auth. see Deford, Debra.
Craig, Jenny. I Believe in Genevieve. Edelson, Wendy, illus. (p. 834)
Craig, Joe. Guy's Guide to Sexuality & Sexual Identity in the 21st Century. (p. 733)
—Jimmy Coates: Killer. (p. 918)
—Jimmy Coates: Assassin? (p. 918)
—Jimmy Coates: Assassin? (p. 918)
—Vo-Tech Track to Success in Manufacturing, Mechanics, & Automotive Care. (p. 1847)
Craig, Johnny, et al. Vault of Horror Chabon, Daniel, ed. (p. 1833)
Craig, Jonathan & Light, Bridget. Special Effects Make-Up Artist: The Coolest Jobs on the Planet (p. 1623)
Craig, Joni. Bad Night's Sleep. ALDEN, B. E. A., illus. (p. 132)
—Fish from the Cherryville Grill. (p. 598)
—Shoulder for Oscar. Haddad-Hamwi, Louise, illus. (p. 1570)
Craig, Karen, illus. see Albee, Sarah.
Craig, Karen, illus. see Borkin, Jeff.
Craig, Karen, illus. see Gallo, Tina.
Craig, Karen, illus. see Shaw, Natalie.
Craig, Karen, illus. see Tuchman, Lauryn & Silverhardt, Lauryn.
Craig, Lee, jt. ed. see Kubish, Shelagh.
Craig, Lee A., ed. see Fisher, Chris C. & Brooks, Ronald.
Craig, Lindsey. Dancing Feet! Brown, Marc, illus. (p. 402)
—Farmyard Beat. Brown, Marc, illus. (p. 575)
Craig, Lizabeth. Parasitic Diseases. (p. 1324)
Craig, Lizabeth, jt. auth. see Greenhaven Press Editors.
Craig, Megan, illus. see Aryal, Aimee.
Craig, Michael. Counting Silly Faces: Numbers 21-30. (p. 371)
—Counting Silly Faces: Numbers Fifty-One to Sixty. (p. 371)
—Counting Silly Faces: Numbers Forty-One to Fifty. (p. 371)
—Counting Silly Faces: Numbers Eighty-One to Ninety. (p. 371)
—Counting Silly Faces: Numbers Sixty-One to Seventy. (p. 371)
—Counting Silly Faces: Numbers Seventy-One to Eighty. (p. 371)
—Counting Silly Faces: Numbers Ninety-One to One-Hundred. Craig, Michael, illus. (p. 371)
—Counting Silly Faces Numbers One to Ten: By Michael Richard Craig - Volume One. Craig, Michael, illus. (p. 371)
—Counting Silly Faces Numbers Thirty-One to Forty: Volume Four. (p. 371)
—Professor, the Banker, & the Suicide King: Inside the Richest Poker Game of All Time. (p. 1409)
Craig, Michael, illus. see Carig, Michael.
Craig, Peter. Blood Father. (p. 200)
Craig, Phebe, jt. text see Westine, Katherine.
Craig Quijada, Balinda. Dance for Fun! [Bridge Learning]. (p. 402)
Craig, Sienna R. Sacred Geography: Sonnets of the Himalaya & Tibet. Heebner, Mary D., illus. (p. 1500)
Craig, Tom. Internet: Technology, People, Process. (p. 880)
Craigan, Charles J. Mayuk the Grizzly Bear: A Legend of the Sechelt People. (p. 1113)
Craig-Gaddis, Lora. Elsie & Pooka Stories of the Sabbats & Seasons. (p. 516)
Craighead, Shirley A. Bugling Elk & Sleeping Grizzlies: The Who, What, & When of Yellowstone & Grand Teton National Parks. (p. 237)
Craighill, Lina. Buster Teases Emily. (p. 245)
Craig-Kendall, Ruth. Bobby Pew, That's Who. (p. 206)
Craik, Maria Dinah. Little Lame Prince. (p. 1030)
Crain, Clayton. Venom vs. Carnage. (p. 1836)
Crain, Clayton, illus. see Wells, Zeb.
Crain, Cynthia D. & Lee, Dwight R. Adam Smith. (p. 11)

—John Maynard Keynes. (p. 922)
—Milton Friedman. (p. 1144)
Crain, Dale, illus. see Azzarello, Brian.
Crain, Kira. SEK Statton. (p. 1549)
Crain, Michael. What Catholic Teens Should Know about Retaliation. Larkin, Jean K., ed. (p. 1881)
Crain, Michael A. Babbott & Babboo. (p. 123)
Crain, Sharon. Day the Sun Fell. (p. 414)
Crain, Suzanne L. Remember Me Always: A Remembrance Scrapbook. Howell, Jason W., illus. (p. 1459)
Craine, E. J. Airplane Boys at Belize. (p. 31)
—Airplane Boys at Platinum River. (p. 31)
—Airplane Boys Discover the Secrets of Cuzco. (p. 31)
—Airplane Boys Flying to Amy-Ran Fastness. (p. 31)
—Airplane Boys in the Black Woods. (p. 31)
—Airplane Boys on the Border Line. (p. 31)
—Airplane Boys with the Revolutionists in Bolivia. (p. 31)
Craine, Timothy. Elementary & Intermediate Algebra: A Practical Approach. (p. 510)
Craipeau, Jean-Lou & Dutrieux, Brigitte. Half & Half-Giants of the Ocean: Great Story & Cool Facts. Hyman, Miles & Alibert, Eric, illus. (p. 736)
Craipeau, Jean-Lou & Dutrieux, Julien. Half & Half-Giants of the Ocean: Great Story & Cool Facts. Hyman, Miles & Alibert, Eric, illus. (p. 736)
Crake, A. Alfgar the Dane. (p. 37)
Crake, Augustine David. Alfgar the Dane or the Second Chronicle of Aescendune. (p. 37)
Crall, Mitzi Keen. 100 Smartest Marketing Ideas Ever. (p. 1999)
Cram101 Textbook Reviews Staff. Outlines & Highlights for Cognitive Psychology by Nick Braisby. (p. 1313)
—Outlines & Highlights for College Mathematics for Business, Economics, Life Sciences & Social Sciences by Raymond a Barnett. (p. 1313)
—Outlines & Highlights for Essentials of Business Statistics by Bruce Bowerman. (p. 1313)
—Outlines & Highlights for in Quest of the Stars & Galaxies by Theo Koupelis, Isbn: 9780763766306. (p. 1313)
—Studyguide for Jesus of History Christ of Faith by Zanzig, Isbn 9780884895305. (p. 1670)
Cram101 Textbook Reviews Staff & L. DeVere Burton. Studyguide for Fish & Wildlife: Principles of Zoology & Ecology by L. Devere Burton, Isbn 9781435419636. (p. 1670)
Cramer, illus. see Brunson, Jodi.
Cramer, Cory. Losing Latitude: Death, Dads, & Demons. (p. 1054)
—Losing Latitude Part 4: The Last Place to Run. (p. 1054)
Cramer, Gayle Shaw. Secret of the Dragonfly: A Story of Hope & Promise. Jones, Jan, illus. (p. 1542)
Cramer, Jeffrey S. Thoreau on Freedom: Attending to Man. Vol. 1 (p. 1740)
Cramer, Jon. Ghost! The Adventures of Horace & His Jungle Friends. (p. 670)
Cramer, Kimberley M. Caterpillar's Dream. Bourbois, J. M., illus. (p. 280)
Cramer, Lisa. My Kids Can't Cook Book. (p. 1211)
Cramer, Marcus, jt. auth. see Pateman, Robert.
Crampton, Gertrude. Scuffy the Tugboat: Classic Edition. Gergely, Tibor, illus. (p. 1533)
—Scuffy the Tugboat. Gergely, Tibor, illus. (p. 1533)
—Tootle: Classic Edition. Gergely, Tibor, illus. (p. 1768)
Crampton, Gertrude, et al. Little Golden Book Train Stories. Gergely, Tibor, illus. (p. 1028)
Crampton, Patricia, jt. auth. see Lindgren, Astrid.
Crampton, W. Flags of the World. (p. 602)
Crampton, William. Spotter's Guide to Flags of the World. (p. 1634)
Cranch, Christopher. Last of the Huggermuggers. (p. 978)
Cranch, Christopher Pearse. Three Children's Novels by Christopher Pearse Cranch. Little, Greta D. & Myerson, Joel, eds. (p. 1741)
Cranch, Christopher Pierce. Last of the Huggermuggers. (p. 978)
Crancher, Steve. Dijja Wanna Say Sumfing? A Guide to Estuary English. Wilkes, Ian, ed. (p. 440)
Crandall, Janet. In a Manger. (p. 863)
—Winter on the Farm. (p. 1938)
Crandall, Linda. Kendra the Kat Dreams of Being a Princess. (p. 948)
—Meet Kendra the Kat. (p. 1121)
Crandall, Susan. Road Home. (p. 1476)
Crandell, Bethany. Summer on the Short Bus. (p. 1674)
Crandell, Joyce & Bauer, Susan Wise. Ancient Times: From the Earliest Nomads to the Last Roman Emperor. West, Jeff, illus. (p. 70)
Crandell, Rachel, jt. auth. see Pratt-Serafini, Kristin Joy.
Crandell, Susan. Thinking about Tomorrow: Reinventing Yourself at Midlife. (p. 1734)
Crane, Ben, illus. see Ode, Eric.
Crane, Beverley E. Internet Workshops: 10 Ready-to-Go Workshops for K-12 Educators. (p. 880)
Crane, C. H. Christmas Quest: A Young Boy's Unexpected Christmas Vacation. (p. 315)
Crane, Caprice. Confessions of a Hater. (p. 356)
—Stupid & Contagious. (p. 1670)
Crane, Carol. Brown Mountain Lights: A North Carolina Legend. Wyrick, Monica, illus. (p. 232)
—Christmas Tree Ship. Ellison, Chris, illus. (p. 316)
—D Is for Dancing Dragon: A China Alphabet. Wang, Zong, illus. (p. 397)
—D Is for Dancing Dragon: A China Alphabet. Wang, Zong-Zhou, illus. (p. 397)
—Discover Florida Monroe, Michael Glenn & Monroe Donovan, Jane, illus. (p. 447)
—Discover Texas Stacy, Alan, illus. (p. 448)
—F Is for First State: A Delaware Alphabet. Traynor, Elizabeth, illus. (p. 559)
—Handkerchief Quilt. Palmer, Gary, illus. (p. 740)
—Little Florida. Monroe, Michael Glenn, illus. (p. 1027)
—Little Georgia. Knorr, Laura, illus. (p. 1028)
—Little North Carolina. Brett, Jeannie, illus. (p. 1032)
—Little South Carolina. Monroe, Michael Glenn & Tsairis, Jeannie Brett, illus. (p. 1036)
—Little Texas. Monroe, Michael Glenn, illus. (p. 1037)
—Net Numbers: A South Carolina Numbers Book. Palmer, Gary, illus. (p. 1242)
—P Is for Pilgrim: A Thanksgiving Alphabet. Urban, Helle, illus. (p. 1316)
—Peck of Peaches: A Georgia Number Book. Braught, Mark, illus. (p. 1334)
—Round Up: A Texas Number Book. Stacey, Alan, illus. (p. 1491)
—T Is for Tar Heel: A North Carolina Alphabet. Palmer, Gary, illus. (p. 1693)
—Wright Numbers: A North Carolina Number Book. Palmer, Gary, illus. (p. 1963)
—Y Is for Yellowhammer: An Alabama Alphabet. Burn, Ted, illus. (p. 1968)
Crane, Cheri J. Moment of Truth: A Novel. (p. 1161)
Crane, Cheryl L. Facing Lions, Giants & Other Big Dudes: A Bible Study Workbook on Courage for Ages 6-12. (p. 561)
—Pressing on When the Pressure's On: A Bible Study Workbook on Perseverance for Ages 6-12. (p. 1397)
Crane, Christine E. It's Winter the First Day of Spring on Summer Street. (p. 899)
Crane, Crankey. Horse Book. (p. 799)
Crane, Cynthia A. Divided Lives: The Untold Stories of Jewish-Christian Women in Nazi Germany. (p. 454)
Crane, Devin, illus. see Stern, Beth.
Crane, Eddie, illus. see Bradex, Melissa A.
Crane, Elizabeth J. Armando: The Case of the Missing Tail. (p. 99)
Crane, Ellery Bicknell. Treatment of the Indians by the Colonists. (p. 1783)
Crane, Freda, jt. adapted by see Conover, Sarah.
Crane, Gail. Heartland Legacy: The Art of Jon Crane. (p. 760)
Crane, Gordon. Hattie's Hats. (p. 753)
Crane, John Kenny. Victimless Crimes. (p. 1840)
Crane Johnson, Amy. Home for Pearl Squirrel: Una casa para la ardilla Perla de la Vega, Eida, tr. (p. 792)
Crane, Jordan. Clouds Above. (p. 335)
—Clouds above. (p. 335)
—Keep Our Secrets. (p. 947)
Crane, Jordan, illus. see Dahl, Roald.
Crane, Kathy Dickerson. Phonics - The Gerbil Plays Guitar on the Girafee Klistoff, Lorin & Coan, Sharon, eds. (p. 1351)
Crane, Laura Dent. Automobile Girls at Washington. (p. 117)
Crane, Natalie. I Go to Work as a Teacher. (p. 838)
Crane, Nick. Barefoot Books World Atlas. Dean, David, illus. (p. 139)
Crane, Noelle L. Clever Pug. Crane, Noelle L., illus. (p. 331)
Crane, Peggy Anne. Why Do I Always Have to Stay Home? A Tiny Horse Tale. (p. 1923)
Crane, Phyllis F. Anything but the Most Boring Place on Earth. (p. 91)
Crane, Stephen. Red Badge of Courage: With a Discussion of Self-Esteem. Clift, Eva, illus. (p. 1453)
—Red Badge of Courage. (p. 1453)
—Red Badge of Courage. Akib, Jamel, illus. (p. 1453)
—Red Badge of Courage. Carillo, Fred, illus. (p. 1453)
Crane, Venessa. Duck down Under. (p. 488)
Crane, Walter. Beauty & the Beast, & Other Tales. (p. 154)
—Mr Michael Mouse Unfolds His Tale. (p. 1185)
Crane, Walter, illus. see Beaumont, Jeanne Marie Le Prince De.
Crane, Walter, illus. see Beaumont, Jeanne-Marie Leprince De.
Crane, Walter, illus. see Gould, F. J.
Crane, Walter, illus. see Jacobs, Joseph.
Crane, Walter, et al. Mother Goose's Nursery Rhymes: A Collection of Alphabets, Rhymes, Tales, & Jingles. (p. 1178)
Craner, Ben, tr. I Can Be a Missionary, Too. (p. 835)
Crane-Yvon, Marie, illus. see Laflamme, Essie.
Cranford, Darren, illus. see Moller, Sharon Chickering.
Cranford, Darren, illus. see Rewalt, Nancy E.
Cranford, Darren, illus. see ReWalt, Nancy E.
Cranford, Darren, illus. see Rewalt, Nancy E.
Cranford, Darren, illus. see ReWalt, Nancy E.
Cranford, Darren, illus. see White, Becky.
Crangle, Claudine. Woolfred Does Not Eat Dandelions. (p. 1950)
Crank, Donny, illus. see Kruse, Donald W.
Crann, Jacqueline J. Answers for Xavier: How Did I Get Here Mommy? (p. 88)
Crannell, Karl. John Stark: Live Free or Die. (p. 922)
Cranny-Francis, Anne, et al. Gender Studies: Terms & Debates. (p. 660)
Cranz, Philip. Russian Imperial Guard 1900-1914. (p. 1498)
Crary, Elizabeth. Dealing with Disappointment: Helping Kids Cope When Things Don't Go Their Way. (p. 418)
Crats, Rennay & Rediger, Pat. For the Love of Soccer. Kissock, Heather, ed. (p. 616)
Cratty, Aaron, illus. see Brink, LeeAnn.
Cratzius, Barbara & Thonissen, Uta. Good Morning, Sunshine. (p. 698)
—Good Night, Sleep Tight! (p. 700)
Craughwell, Thomas J. Bible. (p. 175)
Craughwell, Tom. Shakespeare. (p. 1559)
Cravath, Lynne Avril, illus. see Abercrombie, Barbara.
Cravath, Lynne Avril, illus. see Cassels, Jean.
Cravath, Lynne Avril, illus. see Friedman, Laurie.
Cravath, Lynne Avril, illus. see Platt, Kin.
Cravath, Lynne Avril, illus. see Saltz, Gail.
Craven, Georgina. Adventures & Rhymes with Grandmother. (p. 15)
Craven, Josh. Hayrides. Craven, Josh, illus. (p. 756)
Craven, Tracy Leininger. Our Flag Was Still There: The Story of the Star-Spangled Banner. Farnsworth, Bill, illus. (p. 1308)
Craver, Kathleen W. Term Paper Resource Guide to Nineteenth-Century U. S. History (p. 1721)
Craver, Marcella Marino. Chillax! How Ernie Learns to Chill Out, Relax, & Take Charge of His Anger. Pinelli, Amerigo, illus. (p. 305)
—Joey Daring, Caring, & Curious. Lew-Vriethoff, Joanne, illus. (p. 920)
—Shield Up! Pinelli, Amerigo, illus. (p. 1566)
Craw, Gloria. Atlantis Rising. (p. 112)
Crawfird, Donald W. Is This a Test Lord? Prayers, Reflections & Celebrations of a Stroke Survivor, Offering Hope & Healing. (p. 890)
Crawford, Alice, illus. see Domney, Alexis.
Crawford, Alistair. Mario Giacomelli. (p. 1094)
Crawford, Amanda Gandy. Love Your Neighbors. (p. 1061)
Crawford, Andy. Fun with Opposites. Crawford, Andy, photos by. (p. 648)
Crawford, Andy, photos by see Blake, Susannah.
Crawford, Andy, photos by see Lane, Brian, et al.
Crawford, Andy, photos by see Oxlade, Chris.
Crawford, Ann Fears. Barbara Jordan: Breaking the Barriers. (p. 137)
—Keechee: The Witch of the Woods. (p. 946)
—Rosa: A German Woman on the Texas Frontier. Fain, Cheryl, illus. (p. 1488)
Crawford, Bobby, jt. auth. see Ellington, Kyseme Ali.
Crawford, Brent. Carter's Big Break. (p. 272)
—Carter's Unfocused, One-Track Mind. (p. 272)
Crawford, Brittany. I Sit in a Wheelchair but I Will Be Okay! (p. 845)
Crawford, Charlene E. Adventures with Granny in the Garden. (p. 25)
Crawford, Cindy. Drag Racing Basics: Christmas Tree to Finish Line Has Something for All Drag Racing Enthusiasts. (p. 476)
Crawford, Clint. Rag Tag Gang (p. 1433)
Crawford, Dale, illus. see Grandbear the Storyteller.
Crawford, David. Artesia. (p. 103)
—End of the Row. (p. 526)
—Squaring. (p. 1636)
Crawford, David W. Barren Fields. Landes, William-Alan, ed. (p. 140)
Crawford, David W. & Landes, William-Alan. Moments: A Collection of Acting Workshop & Audition Scenes. (p. 1162)
Crawford, Deborah. Tyler the Turtle Is Afraid of the Dark. Balzer, Jeremy, illus. (p. 1805)
Crawford, Deborah & Crawford, Ryan. Pity's Porch. Ballard, Merry, illus. (p. 1365)
Crawford, Deborah Kay. Pity & the Princess. Turner, Aubrey, illus. (p. 1365)
Crawford, Elizabeth, illus. see Lewis, Richard.
Crawford, Elizabeth D., tr. see Jansen, Hanna.
Crawford, Elizabeth D., tr. see Meyer, Kai.
Crawford, F. Marion. Cecilia, a Story of Modern Rome. (p. 283)
—Three Fates. (p. 1742)
Crawford, Georgina. Archie-Parchie-Piddley-Poo. (p. 95)
Crawford, Gerald. Magic in the Mud. (p. 1072)
Crawford, Greg. Super Hero Foods & the Abc's of Nutrition. (p. 1680)
Crawford, Greg, illus. see Otten, Charlotte.
Crawford, Gregory, illus. see Chin, Oliver Clyde.
Crawford, Gregory, illus. see Cotta, Susan.
Crawford, Gregory, tr. see Chin, Oliver Clyde.
Crawford, Hannah. Fight for Light by Hannah Crawford. (p. 585)
—Fight with Darkness. (p. 585)
Crawford, Jaleesa. Teeny Tot. (p. 1715)
Crawford, Jane. Why Can't I Have Everything? Teaching Today's Children to Be Financially & Mathematically Savvy, Grades PreK-2. (p. 1923)
Crawford, Jennifer. No Sand in the House! Tuohy, Hannah, illus. (p. 1260)
Crawford, Joanne. Bilby & the Bushfire. Fielding, Grace, illus. (p. 186)
—Home for Bilby. Fielding, Grace, illus. (p. 792)
Crawford, John. Life in Honeysuckle Valley the Adventur. (p. 1010)
Crawford, John, jt. auth. see Crawford, John R.
Crawford, John R. & Crawford, John. Last True Story I'll Ever Tell: An Accidental Soldier's Account of the War in Iraq. (p. 979)
Crawford, Joyce. Don't Call Me Michael Activity Book. (p. 467)
Crawford, Joyce Holton. Don't Call Me Michael. (p. 467)
—I Dare You Disaster. (p. 837)
—Thumbs up or Thumbs Down. (p. 1745)
Crawford, K., illus. see Allen, Nancy.
Crawford, K. Michael. Batty Malgoony's Mystic Carnivale. (p. 147)
—Munched-up Flower Garden. (p. 1191)
—Mystery of Journeys Crowne-an Adventure Drawing Game. Crawford, K. Michael, illus. (p. 1224)
Crawford, K. Michael, illus. see Allen, Nancy Kelly.
Crawford, Laura. American Revolution from A to Z Hierstein, Judith, illus. (p. 63)
—Benjamin Franklin from A to Z Hierstein, Judith, illus. (p. 165)
—In Arctic Waters Hodson, Ben, illus. (p. 863)
—Pilgrims' Thanksgiving from A to Z Hierstein, Judith, illus. (p. 1359)
—Postcards from Chicago/Postales Desde Chicago. de La Vega, Eida, tr. (p. 1388)
—Postcards from New York City/Postales Desde New York City. de La Vega, Eida, tr. (p. 1388)
—Postcards from Washington D. C./Postales Desde Washington D. C. de La Vega, Eida, tr. (p. 1388)
Crawford, Leslie & Holm, Amy E. Environmental Action. (p. 532)
Crawford, Marc, jt. auth. see Katz, William Loren.
Crawford, Margaret & Kaliski, John. Everyday Urbanism. Chase, John & Crawford, Margaret, eds. (p. 544)
Crawford, Marie. Nutmeg, Ginger & Little Joan. (p. 1274)
Crawford, Mel, illus. see Bedford, Annie North.
Crawford, Mel, illus. see Beecher, Elizabeth.
Crawford, Mel, illus. see Fletcher, Steffi.
Crawford, Mel, illus. see Hill, Monica.
Crawford, Mel, illus. see Verral, Charles Spain.
Crawford, Neil. Journeyers. (p. 929)
Crawford, Philip & Crawford, Philip Charles. Fruit of All Evil. Schoening, Dan, illus. (p. 645)
Crawford, Philip Charles, jt. auth. see Crawford, Philip.
Crawford, Quinton. Moochie the Soochie - Visits the Peace People. (p. 1171)
Crawford, Quinton Douglass. Moochie the Soochie Visits the Peace People. (p. 1171)
Crawford, Ray. Wade & Kayak Fishing on Galveston Bays & Surrounding Areas, 3rd Ed: Honey Holes of Galveston Bay. (p. 1852)
Crawford, Robert, illus. see Bajaj, Varsha.
Crawford, Robert, illus. see Ortakales, Denise.
Crawford, Ruth. Squirrel Boy & Brad: The Storm. (p. 1637)
—Squirrel Boy & Brad: Solve a Mystery. (p. 1637)
—Squirrel Boy & Brad Become Friends. (p. 1637)
Crawford, Ryan, jt. auth. see Crawford, Deborah.
Crawford, Samuel Wylie. Genesis of the Civil War: The Story of Sumter 1860-1861. (p. 660)
Crawford, Shannon Joseph. Halloween War. (p. 739)
Crawford, Sheryl Ann & Harris, Lauren. Human Body: 20 Short, Reproducible Plays That Teach Key Concepts, Expand Vocabulary, & Build Fluency. (p. 825)
Crawford, Sheryl Ann Saunders & Sanderson, Ian. Easy-to-Read Mini-Book Plays (p. 500)
Crawford, Steve. Cold War. (p. 339)
—War on Terror. (p. 1858)
Crawford, Susan. Sea Sprites. (p. 1535)
Crawford, Tammy. Gaby & Her Big Surprise. (p. 652)
Crawford, Teresa. I'm Not Stupid! I'm ADHD! (p. 859)
Crawford, Tracey. Aves (p. 119)
—Bears (p. 151)
—Birds (p. 191)
—Fish (p. 598)
—Frogs (p. 641)
—Monkeys (p. 1165)
—Monos (p. 1166)
—Osos (p. 1306)
—Peces (p. 1333)
—Ranas (p. 1438)
—Serpientes (p. 1552)
—Snakes (p. 1596)
Crawford, Tracie. Bart the Blue Bee. (p. 140)
Crawford, Tynetta. Help Me Carry My Baggage. (p. 765)
Crawford-Haynes, Debra. Bedtime with Julian. (p. 157)
Crawley, Annie, illus. see Newman, Patricia.
Crawley, Annie, jt. auth. see Stierle, Cynthia.
Crawley, Brian. Halloween Math. Beckes, Shirley, illus. (p. 738)
Crawley, Dave. Dog Poems. Petrosino, Tamara, illus. (p. 461)
—Reading, Rhyming, & 'Rithmetic. Callen, Liz, illus. (p. 1446)
Crawley, Oksanna. So, You Be Keon & I'll Be Mahovlich. (p. 1602)
Cray, Jordan. Danger Com 4 Hot Pursuit. (p. 403)
—Dead Man's Hand. (p. 417)
—Firestorm. (p. 592)
—Gemini7. (p. 660)
—Most Wanted. (p. 1177)
—Shadow Man. (p. 1557)
—Shiver. (p. 1567)
—Stalker. (p. 1638)
Cray, Ronda. What's the Matter Cat? (p. 1899)
Crayon, Paula. Angel in My Pocket. (p. 73)
—Mittens in the Attic. (p. 1156)
—Wrong Dog in the Right Bathroom. (p. 1965)
Crays, Lettie L. Timmy the Turtle Learns to Swim. Rollins, Joe, illus. (p. 1755)
Crayton, Lisa A. Student's Guide to Toni Morrison. (p. 1669)
Crayton, Tina. Wolf. (p. 1943)
Crayton, Tina & Burt, Donna. Googinpuffs in Lollipop Land. (p. 702)
Crayton, Tina Anderson. Sniffles: Each Season Brings New Sniffles. (p. 1597)
Crayton, Tina, et al. Meet the Googinpuffs. (p. 1122)
Crayton, Tina Lorice. Lost Sheep. (p. 1056)
Crayton, Tina Lorice (Anderson). Wolf in Sheep's Clothing: The Impostor. (p. 1944)
Craze, Galaxy. Last Princess. (p. 978)
—Tiger, Tiger. (p. 1748)
Craze, Galaxy, jt. auth. see Bomback, Mark.
Creagh, Kelly. Enshadowed: A Nevermore Book. (p. 531)
—Enshadowed. (p. 531)
—Nevermore. (p. 1243)
—Oblivion. (p. 1275)
Creagh, Lachlan, illus. see Irwin, Robert & Wells, Jack.
Creal, Nancy & Taylor, Ann Creal. Lydia Ann & Scraggles: The Adventures of a Girl & Her Dog. Taylor, Ann Creal, illus. (p. 1066)
Creamer, Joan Klatil. Magic Sceptre & Reginald the Rabbit. (p. 1073)
—Magic Sceptre - the Legend of Blue Santa Claus. Creamer, Joan Klatil, illus. (p. 1073)
Crean, Susan. Discover China. (p. 447)
—Discover France. (p. 447)
—Discover Japan. (p. 447)
—Iraq in Our World. (p. 887)
Creanga, Emil & Tudosa, Lucia. Studii Biblice Despre Valorile Crestine. (p. 1669)
Creanga, Ion. Old Man's Daughter & the Old Woman's Daughter / Fata Babei Si Fata Mosneagului. Todd Kaplan, Delia Angelescu, tr. (p. 1284)
Crear, Williadean. Anika & Her New Body. (p. 76)
Crease, Stephanie Stein. Duke Ellington: His Life in Jazz with 21 Activities. (p. 489)
Creasey, Eleanor. On Remembrance Day. (p. 1289)
Creation By Design Staff, creator. Samson & Delilah (p. 1509)
Creation Staff, ed. see Petersen, Dennis R.
Creative Communication Staff, ed. Celebrate! Young Poets Speak Out - Appalachia Spring 2006. (p. 284)
—Celebrate! Young Poets Speak Out - Canada Spring 2006. (p. 284)
—Celebrate! Young Poets Speak Out - Illinois/Indiana Spring 2006. (p. 284)
—Celebrate! Young Poets Speak Out - Michigan Spring 2006. (p. 284)
—Celebrate! Young Poets Speak Out - Midwest Spring 2006. (p. 284)

C

—Celebrate! Young Poets Speak Out - Northeast Spring 2006. (p. 284)
—Celebrate! Young Poets Speak Out - Pennsylvania Spring 2006. (p. 284)
—Celebrate! Young Poets Speak Out - Rocky Mountain Spring 2006. (p. 284)
—Celebrate! Young Poets Speak Out - South Spring 2006. (p. 284)
—Celebrate! Young Poets Speak Out - West Spring 2006. (p. 284)
—Celebrate! Young Poets Speak Out - Wisconsin/Minnesota Spring 2006. (p. 284)
—Celebrating Poetry - East Spring 2006. (p. 285)
—Celebrating Poetry - Midwest Spring 2006. (p. 285)
—Celebrating Poetry - Spring 2006. (p. 285)
—Celebration of Young Poets - California Spring 2006. (p. 285)
—Celebration of Young Poets - Canada Spring 2006. (p. 285)
—Celebration of Young Poets - Heartland Spring 2006. (p. 285)
—Celebration of Young Poets - Illinois/Indiana Spring 2006. (p. 285)
—Celebration of Young Poets - Midwest Spring 2006. (p. 285)
—Celebration of Young Poets - New York Spring 2006. (p. 285)
—Celebration of Young Poets - Ohio Spring 2006. (p. 285)
—Celebration of Young Poets - Pennsylvania Spring 2006. (p. 285)
—Celebration of Young Poets - South Spring 2006. (p. 285)
—Celebration of Young Poets - Wisconsin/Michigan Spring 2006. (p. 285)
Creative Haven, jt. auth. see Crossling, Nick.
Creative Haven, jt. auth. see Noble, Marty.
Creative Haven, jt. auth. see Sluda, Erik.
Creative Haven Staff, jt. auth. see Gaspas, Diane.
Creative Haven Staff, jt. auth. see Hutchinson, Alberta.
Creative Haven Staff, jt. auth. see Montgomery, Kelly.
Creative Haven Staff, jt. auth. see Noble, Marty.
Creative Haven Staff, jt. auth. see Sun, Ming-Ju.
Creative Haven Staff, jt. auth. see Tenben, Peter Von.
Creative Haven Staff, jt. auth. see Weber, Amy.
Creative Haven Staff, jt. auth. see Wik, John.
Creative Illustrations Studio & Good Times At Home LLC, illus. see Moore, Clement C. & Curto Family, The.
Creative Media Applications. Environmental Disasters Set. (p. 532)
—Slavery in the Americas Set. (p. 1588)
Creative Media Applications Staff. Mental Health & Wellness (p. 1126)
Creative Media Applications Staff, contrib. by. American Presidents in World History (p. 62)
—Debatable Issues in U. S. History (p. 420)
—Discovering World Cultures: The Middle East (p. 450)
—Exploring Gun Use in America: The Second Amendment Vol. 1 (p. 552)
—Human Body & the Environment: How Our Surroundings Affect Our Health (p. 825)
—Student's Guide to Earth Science (p. 1669)
Creative Shubrook Staff & Activision Publishing Staff. Book of Elements: Magic & Tech. (p. 211)
Creative Teaching Press Staff. Advantage Math Grade 7: High Interest Skill Building for Home & School (p. 14)
Creative Team at Walter Foster Publishing Staff. 150 Fun Things to Doodle: An Interactive Adventure in Drawing Lively Animals, Quirky Robots, & Zany Doodads. (p. 2000)
—Drawing Animals from a to Z: Learn to Draw Your Favorite Animals Step by Step! (p. 481)
—How to Draw Teenage Mutant Ninja Turtles: Learn to Draw Leonardo, Raphael, Donatello, & Michelangelo Step by Step! (p. 818)
—I Love Cats! Activity Book: Meow-velous stickers, trivia, step-by-step drawing projects, & more for the cat lover in You! Fisher, Diana, illus. (p. 842)
—I Love Dogs! Pup-Tacular Stickers, Trivia, Step-by-Step Drawing Projects, & More for the Dog Lover in You! Fisher, Diana, illus. (p. 842)
—Learn to Draw Angry Birds: Learn to Draw All of Your Favorite Angry Birds & Those Bad Piggies! (p. 983)
—Learn to Draw Angry Birds Drawing Book & Kit: Includes Everything You Need to Draw Your Favorite Angry Birds Characters! (p. 983)
—Legend of Korra: Learn to Draw All Your Favorite Characters, Including Korra, Mako, & Bolin! (p. 988)
—Spongebob Squarepants - The Bikini Bottom Collection. (p. 1630)
Creative Team at Walter Foster Publishing Staff, jt. auth. see Farrell, Russell.
Creative Team of Weldon Owen. 101 Things to Do Before You Grow Up: Fun Activities for You to Check off Your List. (p. 2000)
Creators of the Hit Documentary & Shortz, Will. Wordplay: The Official Companion Book. (p. 1951)
Crebbin, June. Cat for Tom. (p. 278)
—Dog Show. (p. 461)
—Flying Football. Hellard, Susan, illus. (p. 610)
—Please Sit Still. Hellard, Susan, illus. (p. 1373)
—Viaje en Tren. Rubio, Esther, tr. (p. 1839)
Crebbin, June, et al. Spike & the Concert. (p. 1627)
—We See a Cloud. Warren, Celia, illus. (p. 1868)
Cree, Tahara, text. Bonnie the Bee. (p. 209)
Creech, Sharon. Absolutely Normal Chaos. (p. 7)
—Bloomability. (p. 201)
—Boy on the Porch. (p. 218)
—Castle Corona. Diaz, David, illus. (p. 276)
—Chasing Redbird. (p. 294)
—Chasing Redbird. Burckhardt, Marc, illus. (p. 294)
—Fantasma del Tío Roco. (p. 571)
—Fine, Fine School. (p. 589)
—Fine, Fine School. Bliss, Harry, illus. (p. 589)
—Fishing in the Air. (p. 599)
—Fishing in the Air. Raschka, Chris, illus. (p. 599)
—Granny Torrelli Makes Soup. Raschka, Chris, illus. (p. 710)
—Great Unexpected. (p. 719)
—Hate That Cat. (p. 752)
—Heartbeat. (p. 760)
—Love That Dog. (p. 1060)
—Pleasing the Ghost. Schuett, Stacey, illus. (p. 1373)
—Replay. (p. 1461)
—Ruby Holler. (p. 1493)
—Unfinished Angel. (p. 1817)
—Walk Two Moons. (p. 1854)
—Wanderer. Diaz, David, illus. (p. 1856)
Creech, Sharon, et al. Acting Out: Six One-Act Plays! Six Newbery Stars! Chanda, Justin, ed. (p. 10)
Creed, Elizabeth. Millie's Merry Christmas. (p. 1144)
Creed, Frank. Flashpoint. (p. 602)
Creed, Julie. Danny the Dump Truck. Hastings, Ken, illus. (p. 406)
Creek, Chris, illus. see Creek, Lorie.
Creek, Lorie. Who Is This Jesus? A Hidden Picture Book. Creek, Chris, illus. (p. 1916)
Creek, Silent. All the Ice of Afric. (p. 46)
Creel. Perspectives. (p. 1344)
Creel, Ann Howard. Call Me the Canyon: A Love Story. (p. 254)
—Nicki Ben-Ami, Doron, illus. (p. 1251)
—Under a Stand Still Moon. (p. 1813)
Creel, Lori. Emma's Decidedly Grouchy Day. (p. 520)
Creese, S., jt. auth. see Richards, M.
Creese, Sarah. Dinosaurs: I-Explore Reader. (p. 444)
—Extreme Animals: I-Explore Reader. (p. 556)
—Mad about Chicks Lambs & Other Farm Animals. (p. 1068)
—Mad about Insects Spiders & Creepy Crawlies. (p. 1068)
—Mad about Perfect Puppies & Cute Kittens. (p. 1068)
—Mad about Rockets Stars & Outer Space. (p. 1068)
—Mad about Tractors Trucks Digger & Dumpers. (p. 1068)
—Mad about Triceratops T-Rex & Other Dinosaurs. (p. 1068)
Creese, Sarah, jt. auth. see Richards, Mark.
Creevy, Anne. Lets Go Birding, You & Me. (p. 997)
Cregan, Elizabeth R. Building the Future (p. 239)
—Independence & Equality (p. 870)
—Pioneers in Cell Biology (p. 1361)
Cregan, Elizabeth R. & Cregan, Elizabeth R. C. Electromagnetism (p. 509)
—Thomas Edison & the Developers of Electromagnetism (p. 1738)
Cregan, Elizabeth R. & Heinemann Library Staff. Building the Future (p. 239)
—Independence & Equality (p. 870)
Cregan, Elizabeth R. C. All about Mitosis & Meiosis. (p. 43)
—Atom (p. 113)
—Investigating Electromagnetism. (p. 884)
—Investigating the Chemistry of Atoms. (p. 885)
—Marie Curie: Pioneering Physicist (p. 1093)
—Marie Curie: Pioneering Physicist. (p. 1093)
—Pioneers in Cell Biology. (p. 1361)
—Thomas Edison & the Pioneers of Electromagnetism. (p. 1738)
Cregan, Elizabeth R. C., jt. auth. see Cregan, Elizabeth R.
Cregan, Mairin. Old John. Sewell, Helen, illus. (p. 1284)
Cregar, Elyse M. Hanna's Courage: A Story of Love & Betrayal at the Battle of Gettysburg. (p. 743)
Creghan, Brian C. Pauly: The alligator who wore tennis Shoes. (p. 1331)
Crehore, Amy, illus. see Mann, Elizabeth.
Creighton, B. L. Max's Seaworthy Adventure. (p. 1112)
Creighton, Jayne. Sports. (p. 1632)
Creighton, Judith Matlock, et al. Health Education Primer. (p. 758)
—Nutrition Lessons for Kids: (and Their Parents) (p. 1274)
Creighton, Patricia L. Chirpie the Blue Jay: A True Story. (p. 308)
Crelin, Bob. Faces of the Moon. Evans, Leslie, illus. (p. 561)
—There Once Was a Sky Full of Stars. Ziner, Amie, illus. (p. 1730)
Crème, Aurora C., illus. see Arnold, Ginger Fudge.
Cremeans, Robert, illus. see Tiller, Steve.
Cremer, Andrea. Bloodrose. (p. 201)
—Inventor's Secret. (p. 884)
—Nightshade. (p. 1255)
—Rift. (p. 1471)
—Snakeroot. (p. 1596)
—Wolfsbane. (p. 1944)
Cremona, Joseph. Buongiorno Italia! (p. 243)
Crenshaw, Derek, illus. see Acopiado, Ginger.
Crenshaw, Glenda. Friends of the Enchanted Forest: How they Save Christmas. (p. 638)
Crenshaw, Mills. Christmas of 45. (p. 315)
Crenson, Victoria. Horseshoe Crabs & Shorebirds: The Story of a Foodweb Cannon, Annie, illus. (p. 800)
—Horseshoe Crabs & Shorebirds: The Story of a Food Web Cannon, Annie, illus. (p. 800)
Crentsil, Muriel. Germs on My Terms. (p. 667)
Crepeau, Pierre & Hamilton, Garry. Frog Rescue: Changing the Future for Endangered Wildlife. Nguyen, My-Trang, tr. from FRE. (p. 640)
Crespeno, John. Toby: The Mouse Who Lived in a Pumpkin. (p. 1760)
Crespi, Francesca. Ding Dong! Merrily on High. (p. 440)
—Noah's Ark. (p. 1261)
Crespi, Jess. Exploring Ecuador with the Five Themes of Geography. (p. 552)
—Exploring Jamaica with the Five Themes of Geography. (p. 552)
—Exploring Peru with the Five Themes of Geography. (p. 553)
Crespo, Ana. Sock Thief. Gonzales, Nana, illus. (p. 1605)
Cress, J. H. E., ed. see Thucydides.
Cress, Mark. Tercer Reavivamiento Espiritual. (p. 1721)
Cress, Michelle H., illus. see Cook, Barbara L.
Cress, Michelle H., illus. see Mullican, Judy.
Cresse, Peter. Bloody Hand. (p. 201)
Cressey, Pamela J. & Anderson, Margaret J. Alexandria, Virginia. (p. 37)
Cressey, Roger. Talking Giraffe. Cressey, Roger, illus. (p. 1703)
Cressey, Roger, illus. see Winbolt-Lewis, Martin.
Cresswell, Helen. Sophie & the Seawolf. (p. 1613)
Cressy, Judith. Can You Find It, Too? Search & Discover More Than 150 Details in 20 Works of Art. (p. 258)
Cressy, Mike, illus. see Troupe, Thomas Kingsley.
Crestan, David, illus. see Barrette, Melanie.
Creswick, Paul & Wyeth, N. C. Robin Hood. (p. 1479)
Cretan, Gladys Yessayan. Road Map to Wholeness. Jefferson, Robert Louis, illus. (p. 1476)
Cretney, Brian. Tooter's Stinky Wish Collins, Peggy, illus. (p. 1768)
Crevel, Helena, illus. see Poulter, J. R.
Crew, David F. Hitler & the Nazis: A History in Documents. (p. 786)
Crew, Gary. Cat on the Island. Warden, Gillian, illus. (p. 278)
—Memorial. Tan, Shaun, illus. (p. 1125)
—Pig on the Titanic: A True Story. Whatley, Bruce, illus. (p. 1357)
—Saw Doctor. Cox, David, illus. (p. 1518)
—Viewer. Tan, Shaun, illus. (p. 1842)
—Watertower. (p. 1864)
Crew, Hilary S. Women Engaged in War in Literature for Youth: A Guide to Resources for Children & Young Adults. (p. 1945)
Crewe, Megan. Lives We Lost. (p. 1040)
—Worlds We Make. (p. 1961)
Crewe, Robert, illus. see Clarke, Ashanti.
Crewe, Sabrina. Beavers. (p. 155)
—Canadian Coins. (p. 260)
—Canadian Mounties. (p. 260)
—Canadian Symbols. (p. 260)
—colonia de San Agustín. (p. 341)
—FBI & Crimes Against Children. (p. 578)
—History of the FBI. (p. 785)
—In Rivers, Lakes, & Ponds. (p. 864)
—In the Backyard. (p. 865)
—In the Home. (p. 866)
—In the Ocean. (p. 867)
—In Your Body. (p. 868)
—In Your Food. (p. 868)
—Los Angeles. (p. 1053)
—Totem Poles. (p. 1771)
Crewe, Sabrina, jt. auth. see Loveless, Antony.
Crewe, Sabrina, jt. auth. see Uschan, Michael V.
Crewe, Sabrina & Anderson, Dale. Atom Bomb Project. (p. 113)
—Battle of Yorktown. (p. 147)
—Building the Panama Canal. (p. 239)
—Seneca Falls Women's Rights Convention. (p. 1550)
Crewe, Sabrina & Birchfield, D. L. Trail of Tears. (p. 1776)
Crewe, Sabrina & Camper, Anne K. Under the Microscope (p. 1813)
Crewe, Sabrina & Ingram, Scott. 1963 Civil Rights March. (p. 2002)
—Stock Market Crash of 1929. (p. 1651)
—Writing of "The Star-Spangled Banner" (p. 1965)
Crewe, Sabrina & Riehecky, Janet. Colonia de San Agustín. (p. 341)
Crewe, Sabrina & Schaefer, Adam. Triangle Shirtwaist Factory Fire. (p. 1785)
Crewe, Sabrina & Uschan, Michael V. Fiebre del Oro en California. (p. 583)
—Fiebre del oro en California. (p. 583)
—Fort Sumter: The Civil War Begins. (p. 623)
—Lexington & Concord. (p. 1004)
—Lexington y Concord. (p. 1004)
—Oregon Trail. (p. 1303)
—Salem Witch Trials. (p. 1504)
—Scopes "Monkey" Trial. (p. 1530)
—Scottsboro Case. (p. 1532)
Crewe-Jones, Florence, jt. auth. see Malot, Hector.
Crewe-Read, Caroline. Stone Circles. (p. 1652)
Crews, Dana-Susan. Our Daddy's Cancer: How We Helped Him Fight. (p. 1308)
Crews, Deborah Sue. Broken Slippers. (p. 230)
Crews, Donald. Cloudy Day Sunny Day. (p. 335)
—Diez Puntos Negros. Crews, Donald, illus. (p. 437)
—Freight Train. Crews, Donald, illus. (p. 635)
—Freight Train/Tren de Carga. Crews, Donald, illus. (p. 635)
—Ten Black Dots Board Book. Crews, Donald, illus. (p. 1718)
Crews, Donald, illus. see Giganti, Paul.
Crews, Elizabeth, photos by see Mayfield-Ingram, Karen.
Crews, G. Ellen G Goes Fishing. marion, designs & proctor, brian, illus. (p. 514)
Crews, G. S. Adventures of Mercy Saint. (p. 20)
—Ellen G Goes to the Haunted Planetarium. Designs, Marion, photos by. (p. 514)
Crews, Nina. Jack & the Beanstalk. Crews, Nina, illus. (p. 902)
—Neighborhood Mother Goose. Crews, Nina, illus. (p. 1240)
—Neighborhood Sing-Along. Crews, Nina, illus. (p. 1240)
Crexells, Cristina, et al. Plants & Seeds. (p. 1370)
Creyts, Patrick, illus. see Schultz, Joani, et al.
Cribb, Joe & Dorling Kindersley Publishing Staff. Money. (p. 1163)
Cribb, John T. E., Jr., et al. Human Odyssey (p. 826)
Cribben, Patrick & Heinemann Library Staff. Uniquely West Virginia (p. 1818)
Cribbs, Craig. Why People Should Be Like Trees. (p. 1925)
Cribbs, Jack. Adventures of Detective Jack Cribbs: Clarion County Detective. (p. 17)
Cribbs, Randy. Vessel Tinaja: An Ancient City Mystery. (p. 1839)
Cribbs, Randy, jt. auth. see Guinta, Peter.
Cribbs, Randy, narrated by. Tales from the Oldest City: Selected Readings Vol 1. (p. 1702)
Cribbs, W. Randy. One Summer in the Old Town. (p. 1297)
Cribbs, Wayne Randy. Tales from the Oldest City: St. Augustine. (p. 1702)
Crichlow, Ernest, illus. see Sterling, Dorothy.
Crichlow, Giselle. Just Call Me Shaun. (p. 938)
Crichton, John Michael, see Hudson, Jeffrey, pseud & Crichton, Michael.
Crichton, Julie. King & the Queen & the Jelly Bean. Swaim, illus. (p. 958)
—rey y la reina y el frijolito de Goma. Swaim, Ramon, illus. (p. 1467)
Crichton, Michael, jt. auth. see Hudson, Jeffrey, pseud.
Crichton, Michael, see Hudson, Jeffrey, pseud.
Crick Primary School Staff. Summer Time - Inspired by Degas' Beach Scene. (p. 1675)
Crick, Sharon. Maggie. (p. 1071)
—Sounds. (p. 1615)
Crick, Stephanie. Peek-a-Boo Moon. DeFazio, Deborah, illus. (p. 1334)
Crickard, Sarah. John Paul Jones & the Birth of the American Navy. (p. 922)
Cricket Books Staff. Favorite Mother Goose Rhymes. Wenzel, David, illus. (p. 578)
—Ladybug, Ladybug: And Other Favorite Poems. (p. 971)
Cricket Books Staff & Cobblestone Publishing, Inc. Staff. If I Were a Kid in Ancient Egypt: Children of the Ancient World. Sheldon, Ken, ed. (p. 853)
Cricket Books Staff & Cobblestone Publishing Staff. If I Were a Kid in Ancient Greece: Children of the Ancient World. Sheldon, Ken, ed. (p. 853)
Cricket Books Staff & Cobblestone Publishing, Inc. Staff. If I Were a Kid in Ancient Rome: Children of the Ancient World. Sheldon, Ken, ed. (p. 853)
Cricket Magazine Editors. Oink-Oink: And Other Animal Sounds. Conteh-Morgan, Jane, illus. (p. 1282)
Crider. Mike Gonzo & the Almost Invisible Man. (p. 1141)
—Mike Gonzo & the Sewer Monster. (p. 1141)
—Mike Gonzo & the UFO Terror. (p. 1141)
Crider, Darcy R., jt. auth. see Pish, Kathryn.
Crider, Karen. Wisdom of Cheese. (p. 1939)
Crifasi, Georgette. Potpourri of Poetry & Prose for Pre-K. (p. 1388)
Crikelair, Wendy. Poopie Party. (p. 1383)
Crilley, Mark. Akiko Flights of Fancy. (p. 32)
—Autumn. Crilley, Mark, illus. (p. 118)
—Battle for Boach's Keep Vol. 7. (p. 145)
—Brody's Ghost (p. 230)
—Brody's Ghost Volume 4 Edidin, Rachel, ed. (p. 230)
—Brody's Ghost Volume 6. Crilley, Mark, illus. (p. 230)
—Miki Falls: Spring. (p. 1141)
—Miki Falls: Summer. (p. 1141)
—Miki Falls Winter. (p. 1141)
—Spring. Crilley, Mark, illus. (p. 1634)
—Summer. Crilley, Mark, illus. (p. 1673)
—Winter. Crilley, Mark, illus. (p. 1937)
Crilley, Paul. Osiris Curse: A Tweed & Nightingale Adventure. (p. 1305)
Crimi, Carolyn. Boris & Bella. Grimly, Gris, illus. (p. 214)
—Dear Tabby. Roberts, David, illus. (p. 419)
—Henry & the Buccaneer Bunnies. Manders, John, illus. (p. 767)
—Henry & the Crazed Chicken Pirates. Manders, John, illus. (p. 767)
—Louds Move In! Dunnick, Regan, illus. (p. 1058)
—Principal Fred Won't Go to Bed Wu, Donald, illus. (p. 1406)
—Pugs in a Bug. Buscema, Stephanie, illus. (p. 1415)
—Rock 'N' Roll Mole. Munsinger, Lynn, illus. (p. 1482)
—Where's My Mummy? Manders, John, illus. (p. 1910)
Crimi-Trent, Ellen, illus. see Priddy, Roger.
Crimi-Trent, Ellen, jt. auth. see Priddy, Roger.
Crimi-Trent, Ellen & Priddy, Roger. Field Trip. (p. 584)
—School Fair. (p. 1522)
—Schoolies: Chalk Fun. (p. 1524)
—Schoolies - My Fun Activity Box. (p. 1524)
—Super Sticker Book. (p. 1682)
Crimp, Daryl. Crimpy's Cooking for Kids. (p. 382)
—Crimpy's Fishing for Kids. (p. 382)
Crip, illus. see Beka.
Cripe, Daniel Earl. Other Side of Jordan: A Study in the Book of Hebrews. (p. 1306)
Crippa, Luca, et al. Discovery of America. de Pretto, Lorenzo, illus. (p. 450)
Crisalli, Joseph, jt. auth. see Manning, Dennis.
Crisanaz, Catherine M. Best House for Molly. (p. 170)
Criscione, Rachel. How to Draw the Life & Times of Chester A. Arthur. (p. 818)
Criscione, Rachel Damon. Appaloosa. (p. 92)
—Miniature Horse. (p. 1146)
—Morgan. (p. 1175)
—Mustang. (p. 1194)
—Palomino. (p. 1320)
—Quarter Horse. (p. 1422)
Criscon, R. D. How to Draw the Life & Times of Chester A. Arthur. (p. 818)
Criscuolo, Jill. I Want To... Coloring Book. (p. 847)
Crise, Jeff. Little Train That Had No Bell. (p. 1037)
Crisenbery, Casey, illus. see Kelley, Khris.
Crisfield, Deborah & Murphy, Patrick. Winning Soccer for Girls. (p. 1937)
Crisfield, Deborah, et al. Winning Soccer for Girls. (p. 1937)
Crisfield, Deborah W. Soccer Book: Rules, Techniques, & More about Your Favorite Sport! (p. 1603)
Crisler, Curtis L. Tough Boy Sonatas. Cooper, Floyd, illus. (p. 1772)
Crismon, Joy. Chinese Brush Painting. (p. 307)
—Start with Art. (p. 1643)
Crisp, Dan. Ants Go Marching! (p. 90)
—Ants Go Marching. (p. 90)
—Ants Go Marching W/ (p. 90)
—Five Little Men in a Flying Saucer. (p. 600)
—Little Drivers Going Places! (p. 1027)
—Little Drivers Here to Help! (p. 1027)
—Little Drivers to the Rescue! (p. 1027)
—Little Drivers Working Hard! (p. 1027)
—London: A Colourful City. (p. 1046)
—Santa's Missing Reindeer. Crisp, Dan, illus. (p. 1513)
—Trabajo/ Work. (p. 1774)
Crisp, Dan, illus. see Allen, Francesca & Brooks, Felicity.
Crisp, Dan, illus. see Brooks, Felicity & Durber, Matt.
Crisp, Dan, illus. see Dale, Jay.
Crisp, Dan, illus. see Ranson, Erin.
Crisp, Dan, illus. see Smartink Books Staff.
Crisp, Lisa. Stewart & His Fish Tank. (p. 1649)
Crisp, Marty. Everything Cat: What Kids Really Want to Know about Cats. (p. 544)
—Everything Dog: What Kids Really Want to Know about Dogs. (p. 544)
—Everything Dolphin: What Kids Really Want to Know About Dolphins. (p. 544)
—Everything Horse. (p. 545)
—Titanicat. Papp, Robert, illus. (p. 1758)

Crisp, Marty & Cool Springs Press Editors Staff. Everything Cat: What Kids Really Want to Know about Cats. (p. 544)
Crisp, Peter. Mesopotamia: Iraq in Ancient Times. (p. 1129)
Crisp, Victor. Jackie Robinson: Breaking Barriers. (p. 904)
Crispian. Mystery on the Tambo River. (p. 1226)
Crispin, Barbara. City Zoo Blizzard Revue. Houghton, Roswitha, illus. (p. 324)
Crispin, Gerald W. God Speaks Through Dreams: But Who's Listening? Crispin, Gerald W. & Crispin, Vera G., eds. (p. 690)
Crispin, M. Guyle. Holocaust: A Q&A Guide to Help Young Adults Really Understand the Holocaust. (p. 789)
Crispin, Maria Dolores, tr. see Byng, Georgia.
Crispin, Paula. I'm Getting a Baby Sister? (p. 859)
Crispin, Vera G., ed. see Crispin, Gerald W.
Crispino, Enrica. Van Gogh. (p. 1833)
Criss, Lisa. You Can't Teach a Doll How to Fish! (p. 1975)
Crissey, Brian. Loneliest Christmas Tree. Crissey, Noah, illus. (p. 1046)
Crissey, Brian L. Loneliest Christmas Tree. Crissey, Noah, illus. (p. 1046)
Crissey, Noah, illus. see Crissey, Brian L.
Crissey, Noah, illus. see Crissey, Brian.
Crissey, Noah, illus. see Crissey, Pat.
Crissey, Pat. Personal Hygiene? What's That Got to Do with Me? Crissey, Noah, illus. (p. 1344)
Crissy, Pat. Real-World Social Skills Curriculum. (p. 1449)
Crist, Elizabeth. Get Real about Relationships. (p. 668)
Crist, J. J., jt. auth. see Crist, James J.
Crist, James J. Survival Guide for Making & Being Friends. (p. 1686)
—What to Do When You're Cranky & Blue. (p. 1894)
—What to Do When You're Scared & Worried: A Guide for Kids. (p. 1894)
—When Someone You Love Abuses Alcohol or Drugs - a Guide for Kids. (p. 1904)
Crist, James J. & Crist, J. J. Como Superar los Miedos y Preocupaciones. Marti, Nuria, tr. (p. 351)
Crist, James J. & Verdick, Elizabeth. Siblings: You're Stuck with Each Other, So Stick Together. (p. 1572)
Crista, Sciantel. Children's Hour: Four Short Stories. (p. 303)
Cristancho M, Jose Martin, tr. see Kafka, Franz.
Crist-Evans, Craig. Moon over Tennessee: A Boy's Civil War Journal. Christensen, Bonnie, illus. (p. 1172)
Cristnogol, Cymorth, jt. auth. see Harrison, Jean.
Criswell, Ginger. Recycle Michael. (p. 1453)
Criswell, Patti Kelley. Friends: Making Them & Keeping Them. Peterson, Stacy & Watkins, Michelle, illus. (p. 638)
—Smart Girl's Guide: Friendship Troubles. (p. 1592)
—Smart Girl's Guide to Friendship Troubles: Dealing with Fights, Being Left Ou. (p. 1592)
—Smart Girl's Guide to Friendship Troubles: Dealing with Fights, Being Left Out & the Whole Popularity Thing. Martini, Angela, illus. (p. 1592)
—Smart Girl's Guide to Knowing What to Say: Finding the Words to Fit Any Situation. (p. 1592)
—Stand up for Yourself & Your Friends: Dealing with Bullies & Bossiness, & Finding a Better Way. Martini, Angela, illus. (p. 1639)
—What Would You Do? Quizzes about Real-Life Problems. Chobanian, Elizabeth, ed. (p. 1895)
Criswell, Susie G. Nature Through Science & Art. (p. 1236)
Critcher, Chas. Moral Panics & the Media. (p. 1173)
Crites, Elisa Maria. Secrets under the Midnight Sun. (p. 1546)
Critical Thinking Publishing Staff & Husted, Terri. Math Detective A1: Higher-Order Thinking Reading Writing in Mathematics. (p. 1105)
—Math Detective Beginning: Higher-Order Thinking Reading Writing in Mathematics. (p. 1105)
Critical Thinking Publishing Staff, et al. Can You Find Me? K-1: Reading, Math, Science, Social Studies. (p. 259)
—Can You Find Me? PreK: Reading, Math, Science, Social Studies. (p. 259)
Crittenden, Alex. Reading for Real. (p. 1446)
Crittenden, Danielle. Amanda Bright @ Home. (p. 52)
Crittenden, Nina Victor, illus. see Raum, Elizabeth.
Croall, Marie. Ali Baba: Fooling the Forty Thieves [an Arabian Tale]. Hilinski, Clint, illus. (p. 39)
—Finding Nemo: Reef Rescue. Currey, Erica Leigh, illus. (p. 588)
—Finding Nemo: Reef Rescue. Currey, Erica Leigh, illus. (p. 588)
—Sinbad: Sailing into Peril. Hilinski, Clint, illus. (p. 1578)
Croall, Marie P. Ali Baba: Fooling the Forty Thieves. (p. 39)
—Graphic Myths & Legends Sinbad: Sailing into Peril. (p. 711)
—Marwe: Into the Land of the Dead [an East African Legend]. Lago, Ray & Hamilton, Craig, illus. (p. 1100)
—Marwe: Into the Land of the Dead - An East African Folktale. Lago, Ray & Hamilton, Craig, illus. (p. 1100)
—My Boyfriend Is a Monster - Under His Spell. Park, Hyeondo, illus. (p. 1199)
—Psyche & Eros: The Lady & the Monster [A Greek Myth]. Randall, Ron, illus. (p. 1413)
—School of Evil. Carruthers, Sandy, illus. (p. 1523)
—Sinbad: Sailing into Peril. Hilinski, Clint, illus. (p. 1578)
—Under His Spell Park, Hyeondo, illus. (p. 1813)
Croall, Marie P., jt. auth. see Jolley, Dan.
Croall, Marie P. & Jolley, Dan. Agent Mongoose & the Attack of the Giant Insects. Wendt, Matt, illus. (p. 29)
Croce, Carlo P. Mercury. (p. 1127)
Croce, Julia Della & Williams-Sonoma Staff. Pasta. Williams, Chuck, ed. (p. 1327)
Croce, Nicholas. Anthropology: The Study of Humankind. (p. 89)
—Cool Careers Without College for People Who Love Video Games. (p. 363)
—Detectives: Life Investigating Crime. (p. 431)
—Detectives: Life of Investigating Crime. (p. 431)
—History of Film. (p. 784)
Croce, Nicholas, ed. Anarchism, Revolution, & Terrorism. (p. 67)
Croce, Warren. Opposite Day. (p. 1300)
Crocker, Carter & Snyder, Carrie A. Tale of the Swamp Rat. (p. 1700)
Crocker, Carter & Swift, Jonathan. Last of the Gullivers. (p. 978)
Crocker, Mike. It's Not Your Fault. (p. 898)
Crocker, Nancy. Billie Standish Was Here. (p. 187)
Crockett, B. J. Holder - Takaras Transformation. (p. 788)
Crockett, Johns. Click Clack Meuuh. (p. 331)
—Dessin pour Harold. (p. 430)
—Harold et le crayon Rose. (p. 749)
Crockett, Kyle A. Managing Your Weight with Nutrition. Borus, Joshua, ed. (p. 1086)
—Navigating Your School Cafeteria & Convenience Store. Borus, Joshua, ed. (p. 1238)
—Numbers: Calories, BMI, & Portion Sizes. Borus, Joshua, ed. (p. 1272)
—Nutrition & Your Future. Borus, Joshua, ed. (p. 1274)
—Nutrition for Achievement in Sports & Academics. Borus, Joshua, ed. (p. 1274)
Crockett, Linda, illus. see Johnson, Vincent L.
Crockett, Mary, jt. auth. see Rosenberg, Madelyn.
Crockett, Rebecca. Bubblegum Tree. (p. 233)
Crockett, Robert, illus. see Serio, John N., ed.
Crockett, S. D. After the Snow. (p. 28)
—One Crow Alone. (p. 1294)
Crockett, S. R. Surprising Adventures of Sir Toady L. (p. 1686)
Crockett, Sally. Fly Fishing. (p. 609)
Crockett, Sonja Michelle. Meriah Goes to Church. Crockett, Sonja Michelle & Berry, Kenosha, eds. (p. 1127)
Crockett, Tilly. Crockett Tales for Children. (p. 384)
Crockett-Blassingame, Linda. See the Ocean. (p. 1547)
Crofoot, Betty & Arledge, Roo. Battle for the Multiverse - My Genie & Me Series Book 3. (p. 145)
—Great Celebration Ceremony - My Genie & Me Series Book 2. (p. 714)
Crofoot, Nancy. Christmas in the Barn Rawat, Tania, illus. (p. 314)
—Sandy & Mitzi: Off to the Zoo. Rawal, Ishita, illus. (p. 1511)
—Sandy & Mitzi: Their First Adventure Rawat, Tania, illus. (p. 1511)
Crofoot, Nancy L. Off to the Fair: Another Sandy & Mitzi Adventure. (p. 1279)
Croft, Andy. David Beckham. (p. 410)
—Michael Owen. (p. 1134)
Croft, Andy & Basic Skills Agency Staff. Internet. (p. 880)
—Michael Schumacher. (p. 1134)
Croft, Cindy, ed. see Etingoff, Kim.
Croft, Cindy, ed. see Hill, Z. B.
Croft, Cindy, ed. see Waters, Rosa.
Croft, James, illus. see Davies, Nicola.
Croft, James, illus. see Root, Phyllis.
Croft, James Lee, illus. see DePrisco, Dorothea.
Croft, Jennifer. Drugs & the Legalization Debate. (p. 487)
—Everything You Need to Know about Guns in Your Home. (p. 545)
Croft, Laura. Sky Boarders. (p. 1586)
Croft, Malcolm. 5 Seconds of Summer - The Ultimate Fan Book: All You Need to Know about the World's Hottest New Boy Band! (p. 1992)
—One Direction Confidential. (p. 1294)
—One Direction in 3D: Unofficial & Unauthorised. (p. 1294)
Croft, Malcolm, jt. auth. see Cross, Matthew.
Croft, Malcolm & Besley, Preston. 5 Seconds of Summer Confidential: Over 100 Amazing Photographs of the World's Hottest Boy Band. (p. 1992)
Croft, Priscilla. Dealing with Jealousy/Que Hacer con Los Celos. Velazquez De Leon, Mauricio, tr. from ENG. (p. 418)
Croft, Steven. Othello. Beal, Duncan & Jurksaitis, Dinah, eds. (p. 1306)
Croft-Holguin, Leticia. Cancer Starts with C. (p. 261)
Croggon, Alison. Black Spring. (p. 197)
—Crow. (p. 385)
—Naming. (p. 1228)
—Riddle. (p. 1470)
—Singing. (p. 1579)
Croissant-Madden, Gayle. My Wild, Wild Hair! Croissant-Madden, Gayle, illus. (p. 1221)
Croix, Judith Sainte. Everything You Need to Know about Meditation. (p. 545)
Croke, Liam, jt. auth. see Naik, Anita.
Croke, Liam & Naik, Anita. I'm Broke! The Money Handbook. (p. 858)
Croker, Mark. Atlas del Cuerpo Humano. (p. 112)
Croll, Carolyn. Story of Christmas. (p. 1657)
Croll, Carolyn, illus. see DeWitt, Lynda.
Croll, Carolyn, illus. see Fontes, Justine.
Cromarty, J. Pigtail & Chopsticks Man: The Story of J. Hudson Taylor & the China Inland Mission. (p. 1358)
Cromarty, Jim. Great Barrier Reef Adventures. (p. 714)
—Outback Adventures. (p. 1312)
—Sad Little Dog. (p. 1501)
—You Sank My Boat. (p. 1976)
Crommett, Lora. Blue Witch Who Dared to Be Different. (p. 203)
Crompton, Anne Eliot. Merlin's Harp. (p. 1128)
—Percival's Angel. (p. 1341)
Crompton, Laurie Boyle. Adrenaline Crush. (p. 13)
—Blaze (Or, Love in the Time of Supervillains) (p. 199)
—Real Prom Queens of Westfield High. (p. 1448)
Crompton, Lee. 12 Months. (p. 1994)
Crompton, Paul. Remarkable for Short. (p. 1458)
Crompton, Richard. More William. (p. 1175)
Crompton, Richmal. Guillermo Detective. (p. 730)
—Just Jimmy Again. Henry, Thomas, illus. (p. 938)
—Just William As Seen on TV. (p. 940)
—Just William at Christmas. (p. 940)
—Just William's Puzzles. (p. 940)
—Just William's Tricks. (p. 940)
—More William. Henry, Thomas, illus. (p. 1175)
—William at War. (p. 1933)
Crompton, Samuel. Che Guevara: The Making of a Revolutionary. (p. 295)
Crompton, Samuel Etinde. Polio Vaccine: Race for a Cure. (p. 1380)
Crompton, Samuel W. Civil War Musteen, Jason R., ed. (p. 325)
Crompton, Samuel Willard. Alexander the Great. (p. 36)
—Ariel Sharon. (p. 98)
—Boston Tea Party: Colonists Protest the British Government. (p. 215)
—Cyrus the Great. (p. 397)
—Desiderius Erasmus. (p. 429)
—Desmond Tutu: Fighting Apartheid. (p. 430)
—Emanuel Swedenborg. (p. 517)
—Family Values Movement: Promoting Faith Through Action. (p. 569)
—Ferdinand Magellan & the Quest to Circle the Globe. Goetzmann, William H., ed. (p. 582)
—Francis Drake & the Oceans of the World. Goetzmann, William H., ed. (p. 628)
—Gouverneur Morris: Creating a Nation. (p. 704)
—John Adams: American Patriot. (p. 921)
—John Elway. (p. 921)
—Jonathan Edwards. (p. 925)
—Julius Caesar. (p. 932)
—Lewis & Clark. (p. 1004)
—McCulloch V. Maryland: Implied Powers of the Federal Government. (p. 1114)
—Mohawk. (p. 1160)
—Nelson Mandela: Ending Apartheid in South Africa. (p. 1241)
—Peyton Manning. (p. 1349)
—Printing Press. (p. 1407)
—Queen Elizabeth: And England's Golden Age. (p. 1424)
—Raid on Harpers Ferry: John Brown's Rebellion. (p. 1433)
—Repeating Rifle. (p. 1461)
—Robert de la Salle. (p. 1478)
—Scopes Monkey Trial: Debate over Evolution. (p. 1530)
—Sinking of the Bismarck. (p. 1580)
—Sinking of the USS Maine. (p. 1580)
—Sir Edmund Hillary. (p. 1580)
—Sputnik/Explorer I: The Race to Conquer Space. (p. 1635)
—Third Crusade: Richard the Lionhearted vs. Saladin. (p. 1734)
—Thomas More: And His Struggles of Conscience. (p. 1739)
—Thomas Paine & the Fight for Liberty. (p. 1739)
—Troy. (p. 1790)
—Ulysses S. Grant. (p. 1810)
—Wright Brothers: First in Flight. (p. 1963)
Crompton, Samuel Willard, jt. auth. see Hasday, Judy L.
Crompton, Samuel Willard, jt. auth. see Rosier, Paul C.
Crompton, Samuel Williard. Clara Barton. (p. 326)
Cromwell, Daisy. Arthur, the Talking Goat. Paxton, Cameron L., illus. (p. 104)
Cromwell, Danielle, illus. see Young, T. M.
Cromwell, Ellen S. Wiggle-Dee-Dee: A Story about Friendship. (p. 1927)
Cromwell, Sharon. Dred Scott V. Sandford: A Slave's Case for Freedom & Citizenship (p. 484)
—G. I. Joe in World War II. (p. 651)
Crone, Rainers, et al. Drama & Shadows: Photographs, 1945-1950. (p. 480)
Cronick, Mitch. In the Garden. (p. 866)
—In the Garden. Sharp, Melanie, illus. (p. 866)
Cronick, Mitch, jt. auth. see Collins Educational Staff.
Cronin, Ali, jt. auth. see Naik, Anita.
Cronin, Ali & Sayer, Melissa. Making a Difference: The Changing the World Handbook. (p. 1080)
Cronin, Bernie. One Step Ahead: An Adventure in Jordan. (p. 1297)
—We're Coming Home. (p. 1875)
Cronin, Carol Newman. Cape Cod Surprise: Oliver Matches Wits with Hurricane Carol. Cronin, Laurie Ann, illus. (p. 262)
—Oliver's Surprise: A Boy, a Schooner, & the Great Hurricane of 1938. Cronin, Laurie, illus. (p. 1286)
Cronin, Doreen. Barnyard Collection: Click, Clack, Moo & More. Lewin, Betsy, illus. (p. 139)
—Boom Snot Twitty This Way That Way. Liwska, Renata, illus. (p. 213)
—Bounce. Menchin, Scott, illus. (p. 216)
—Busy Day at the Farm. Lewin, Betsy, illus. (p. 246)
—Case of the Weird Blue Chicken: The Next Misadventure. (p. 275)
—Chicken Squad: The First Misadventure. (p. 300)
—Chicken Squad: The First Misadventure. Cornell, Kevin, illus. (p. 300)
—Clic, Clac, Plif, Plaf: Una Aventura de Contar. Lewin, Betsy, illus. (p. 331)
—Clic, Clac, Plif, Plaf: Una Aventura de Contar. Rioja, Alberto Jimenez, tr. from ENG. (p. 331)
—Click, Clack, 123. Lewin, Betsy, illus. (p. 331)
—Click, Clack, ABC. Lewin, Betsy, illus. (p. 331)
—Click, Clack, Boo! A Tricky Treat. Lewin, Betsy, illus. (p. 331)
—Click, Clack, Ho! Ho! Ho! Lewin, Betsy, illus. (p. 331)
—Click, Clack, Moo: Cows That Type. (p. 331)
—Click, Clack, Moo: Cows That Type Lewin, Betsy, illus. (p. 331)
—Click, Clack, Moo: Cows That Type. Lewin, Betsy, illus. (p. 331)
—Click, Clack, Peep! Lewin, Betsy, illus. (p. 331)
—Click, Clack, Quackity-Quack: A Typing Adventure. Lewin, Betsy, illus. (p. 331)
—Click, Clack, Quackity-Quack: An Alphabetical Adventure. Lewin, Betsy, illus. (p. 331)
—Click, Clack, Splish, Splash: A Counting Adventure. Lewin, Betsy, illus. (p. 331)
—Diary of a Fly. (p. 434)
—Diary of a Fly. Bliss, Harry, illus. (p. 434)
—Diary of a Spider. Bliss, Harry, illus. (p. 435)
—Diary of a Worm: Nat the Gnat. Bliss, Harry, illus. (p. 435)
—Diary of a Worm: Teacher's Pet. Bliss, Harry & Nez, John, illus. (p. 435)
—Diary of a Worm. (p. 435)
—Diary of a Worm. Bliss, Harry, illus. (p. 435)
—Dooby Dooby Moo. Lewin, Betsy, illus. (p. 469)
—Dubi Dubi Muu. Jimenez Rioja, Alberto, tr. from ENG. (p. 487)
—Duck for President. Lewin, Betsy, illus. (p. 488)
—Giggle, Giggle, Quack. Lewin, Betsy, illus. (p. 676)
—Jaja Jiji, Cuac. Jimenez, Alberto, tr. from ENG. (p. 905)
—Legend of Diamond Lil. (p. 988)
—Legend of Diamond Lil. Cornell, Kevin, illus. (p. 988)
—M. O. M. (Mom Operating Manual) Cornell, Laura, illus. (p. 1067)
—Nat the Gnat. (p. 1230)
—Pato para Presidente. Lewin, Betsy, illus. (p. 1328)
—Rescue Bunnies. Menchin, Scott, illus. (p. 1462)
—Smick! Medina, Juana, illus. (p. 1593)
—Stretch. Menchin, Scott, illus. (p. 1667)
—Teque, Teque, Muu: Vacas que Escrevem à Máquina. (p. 1721)
—Thump, Quack, Moo: A Whacky Adventure. Lewin, Betsy, illus. (p. 1745)
—Trouble with Chickens. Cornell, Kevin, illus. (p. 1790)
—Wiggle. Menchin, Scott, illus. (p. 1927)
Cronin, Doreen & Jiménez Rioja, Alberto. Pum, Cuac, Muu: Una Loca Aventura. Lewin, Betsy, illus. (p. 1416)
Cronin, Doreen & Lewin, Betsy. Click, Clack, Moo: Cows That Type. (p. 331)
—Click, Clack, Quackity-Quack: An Alphabetical Adventure. (p. 331)
—Click, Clack, Splish, Splash: A Counting Adventure. (p. 331)
Cronin, Doreen & Liwska, Renata. Boom Snot Twitty. (p. 213)
Cronin, Doreen & Simon and Schuster/LeapFrog Staff. Click, Clack, Moo: Cows That Type. Lewin, Betsy, illus. (p. 331)
Cronin, Gaynell. Celebrating the Gospels: A Guide for Parents & Teachers: Activities & Prayers for the Sunday Cycles of A, B, & C. (p. 285)
Cronin, Janet, illus. see Andreae, Giles & World Of Happy Staff.
Cronin, Janet, jt. auth. see Andreae, Giles.
Cronin, Laurie, illus. see Cronin, Carol Newman.
Cronin, Laurie Ann, illus. see Cronin, Carol Newman.
Cronin, M. T. C. Beautiful, Unfinished: Parable, Song, Canto, Poem. (p. 154)
Cronin, Susan L. Gidget Goes Away. (p. 674)
Cronkhite, Lisa. Disconnected. (p. 447)
Cronkite, Walter. Reporter's Life. (p. 1461)
Cronkite, Walter, frwd. Great American Presidents. (p. 713)
Cronn-Mills, Kirstin. Beautiful Music for Ugly Children. (p. 154)
—Collapse! The Science of Structural Engineering Failures (p. 339)
—Transgender Lives: Complex Stories, Complex Voices. (p. 1778)
Cronshaw, Joseph. Podge & Dodge. (p. 1375)
Cronstrom, Kendell & Real Simple Magazine Staff. Real Simple: The Organized Home. (p. 1449)
Crook, Alja Robinson. Origin of the Cahokia Mounds. (p. 1304)
Crook, Connie Brummel. Acts of Courage: Laura Secord & the War of 1812. (p. 10)
—Flight (p. 604)
—Meyers' Creek (p. 1131)
—No Small Victory (p. 1260)
—Perilous Year (p. 1343)
Crook, Jennifer. Mrs. Crook's Kindergarten Sings about the Weather: Musical Colors Series. (p. 1187)
Crook, Lydia. Paper Play. Running Press Staff, ed. (p. 1323)
—Two-Player Big Fun Book: Puzzles & Games for Two to Do! (p. 1804)
Crook, M. J. Village on Crooked Hill. (p. 1842)
Crook, Mackenzie. Ragetti's Secret Diary. (p. 1433)
Crooker, Richard A. Argentina. (p. 97)
—Chile. (p. 305)
—Venezuela. Gritzner, Charles F., ed. (p. 1835)
Crooker, Richard A., jt. auth. see Pavlovic, Zoran.
Crooker, Richard A. & Gritzner, Charles F. Cuba. (p. 388)
Crooks, Andrea Syvrud. Little Truck Without a Load. (p. 1037)
Crooks, Claire V. Engagement et Responsabilisation des Jeunes Autochtones: Trousse D'Outils DestinéE Aux Fournisseurs des Services. (p. 529)
Crooks, Lois. Bird in the Bag. (p. 190)
Croom, Terry. Grandma's Here. (p. 708)
Crosbie, Duncan. Claddagh Ring for Nuala Rutherford, Peter, illus. (p. 326)
—Cool Kid's Field Guide to Dinosaurs. Field, James, illus. (p. 363)
—Find Out about France: Learn French Words & Phrases & about Life in France. Hutchinson, Tim, illus. (p. 587)
—Life in an Irish Castle: The Journal of a 17th Century Castles in Times of Peace & War. Dixey, Kay, illus. (p. 1010)
Crosbie, Duncan & Potter, Tony, compiled by. Irish Jokes. (p. 887)
Crosby. Introduction to Greek. (p. 882)
Crosby, Bobby. Pupkin: Half Puppy Half Pumpkin All Love. (p. 1417)
Crosby, Jeff. Wiener Wolf. Crosby, Jeff, illus. (p. 1927)
Crosby, Jeff, illus. see Curry, Jane Louise & Livy.
Crosby, Jeff, illus. see Davis, David.
Crosby, Jeff, illus. see McDermott, Tom.
Crosby, Jeff, jt. auth. see Jackson, Shelley Ann.
Crosby, Jeff & Asbjornsen, Peter Christen. Rockabilly Goats Gruff. (p. 1482)
Crosby, Jeff & Jackson, Shelley Ann. Little Lions, Bull Baiters & Hunting Hounds: A History of Dog Breeds. Crosby, Jeff & Jackson, Shelley Ann, illus. (p. 1030)
Crosby, Jim. Devotions for the Armchair Quarterback. (p. 432)
Crosby, June. Monster in the Attic. Chapman, Michelle, illus. (p. 1167)
Crosby, Michael T. Sacagawea: Lewis & Clark's Pathfinder. (p. 1500)
Crosby, Sarah. Cindy's Story Hare, Mary Alyce, illus. (p. 321)
Crosby, Sherry. Bad Case of the Grownies. (p. 131)
Crosby, Vernon H. Adventures of Scurry Little: Lost in my Dream. (p. 22)
Crosetto, Alice & Garcha, Rajinder. Death, Loss, & Grief in Literature for Youth: A Selective Annotated Bibliography for K-12. (p. 420)
—Native North Americans in Literature for Youth: A Selective Annotated Bibliography for K-12. (p. 1235)
Crosier, Mike, illus. see Kahan, Alex.

C

Crosier, Mike, illus. see Sneideman, Joshua & Twamley, Erin.
Croskerry, Frank J. Our Land Is the Sky: The Adventures of Jimmy Fastwing. (p. 1309)
Croskery, Mike. Weight Training for a New Body: Over 300 Exercises to Tone, Strengthen, & Build Muscle. (p. 1872)
Crosley, Tiffany Monique. God's Little Bug Garden. (p. 691)
Cross, Alan, jt. auth. see Board, Jon.
Cross, Carrie L. & Iorizzo, Carrie. Crystal Meth. (p. 387)
Cross, Cecil R., II. First Semester. (p. 596)
—Next Semester. (p. 1249)
Cross, Chris, illus. see David, Peter.
Cross, Craig, et al. Questions You Can't Ask Your Mama about Sex. (p. 1426)
Cross, D. A. Cahokia. (p. 251)
Cross, David B., ed. Book of Stories & Study Guide. (p. 212)
Cross, Elsa. Himno de las Ranas. Zacchi, Lucia, illus. (p. 780)
Cross, F. J. Beneath the Banner: Being Narratives of Noble Lives & Brave Deeds. (p. 164)
Cross, Frances. Boy the Witch & the Blobber 1. (p. 219)
—Butternut Blobber & the Blue Jade. (p. 248)
—Marty's Diary. (p. 1098)
—Mystery of the Green Elephant. (p. 1225)
Cross, Gillian. Brother Aelred's Feet. Stevens, Tim, illus. (p. 231)
—Iliad. Packer, Neil, illus. (p. 856)
—Odyssey. Packer, Neil, illus. (p. 1278)
—Sam Sorts It Out. Mier, Colin, illus. (p. 1507)
—Where I Belong. (p. 1908)
Cross, Gillian & Quarto Generic Staff. Roman Beanfeast. Asquith, Ros, illus. (p. 1485)
Cross, James, illus. see Wilkes, Ruth.
Cross, Jenny. Sadie the Ladybug. Bohart, Lisa, illus. (p. 1501)
Cross, Jo Ellen, illus. see Chisolm, Melinda.
Cross, John R. Lamb: PowerPoint Booklet. Mastin, Ian, illus. (p. 972)
Cross, Julie. Tempest. (p. 1717)
—Timestorm: A Tempest Novel. (p. 1754)
—Vortex: A Tempest Novel. (p. 1850)
—Vortex. (p. 1850)
Cross, Julie, jt. auth. see Perini, Mark.
Cross, Kady. Girl in the Steel Corset. (p. 678)
—Girl with the Iron Touch. (p. 679)
—Girl with the Windup Heart. (p. 679)
—Sisters of Blood & Spirit. (p. 1581)
Cross, Ken. Who Is Pat Dump? (p. 1916)
Cross, Kevin, illus. see Jean, April.
Cross, Kyra J. Natalie's Hidden Treasures: The Intruder. (p. 1230)
Cross, Laurie. Down to the Folks: A Visit with Grandpa & Grandma. (p. 474)
Cross, Linda B. Lines from Linda. (p. 1019)
Cross, Luther. Ogres. (p. 1280)
Cross, Matthew & Croft, Malcolm. Cool Astronomy: 50 Fantastic Facts for Kids of All Ages. (p. 362)
Cross, Melissa. Mommy's Princess. (p. 1163)
Cross, Nathaniel & Sommers, Michael A. Understanding Your Right to Bear Arms. (p. 1816)
Cross, Neal, illus. see Sullivan, E. J.
Cross, P. C. Summer Job: A Virgil & Cy Mystery. (p. 1674)
Cross, P. W. Idea Miners: The Lost Lake Dig. (p. 852)
Cross, Ruth Belov. Hansel y Cretel. Pels, Winslow Pinney, illus. (p. 743)
Cross, Sarah. Dull Boy. (p. 489)
Cross, Shauna. Whip It. (p. 1911)
Cross, Steven. Fall of Knight. (p. 566)
—Lazy Daze Inn: A Full-Length Comedy. (p. 981)
Cross, Vince. Club: The Blogs of Abi Goodenough. (p. 335)
Crossan, Sarah. Apple & Rain. (p. 92)
—Breathe. (p. 226)
—One. (p. 1293)
—Resist. (p. 1463)
Crossett, Warren, illus. see Harvey, Jacqueline.
Crossingham, John. Cheerleading. (p. 296)
—Extreme Skateboarding. (p. 556)
—Extreme Sports - No Limits (p. 557)
—Football in Action. (p. 615)
—Futbol Americano en Accion. (p. 650)
—Fútbol Americano en Acción. (p. 650)
—Lacrosse in Action. (p. 970)
—Learn to Speak Music: A Guide to Creating, Performing, & Promoting Your Songs. Kulak, Jeff & Owlkids Books Inc. Staff, illus. (p. 984)
—Natation. (p. 1230)
—Patinetas en Acción. (p. 1328)
—Porristas en Acción. Rouse, Bonna, illus. (p. 1386)
—Spike It Volleyball. (p. 1627)
Crossingham, John, jt. auth. see Dann, Sarah.
Crossingham, John, jt. auth. see Kalman, Bobbie.
Crossingham, John & Bishop, Amanda. Extreme BMX. (p. 556)
Crossingham, John & Dann, Sarah. Basketball. (p. 143)
—Basquetbol en Accion. (p. 143)
—Volleyball. (p. 1849)
Crossingham, John & Kalman, Bobbie. Cadenas Alimentarias de la Costa Marina. (p. 250)
—Ciclo de Vida del Tiburon. (p. 319)
—Éléphants. (p. 511)
—Endangered Pandas. (p. 527)
—Extreme in-Line Skating. (p. 556)
—Extreme Surfing. (p. 557)
—High Flying Martial Arts. (p. 777)
—Judo in Action. (p. 931)
—Judo in Action. Crabtree, Marc, photos by. (p. 931)
—Life Cycle of a Shark. (p. 1009)
—Life Cycle of a Snake. (p. 1009)
—Pandas. (p. 1321)
—Planche à Roulettes Extrême. Briere, Marie-Josee, tr. from ENG. (p. 1366)
—Qué Es la Hibernación? (p. 1423)
—Que Es la Migración? (p. 1423)
—Seals & Sea Lions. (p. 1536)
—Seashore Food Chains. (p. 1538)
—Serpents. (p. 1552)
—Ski Alpin. Briere, Marie-Josee, tr. from ENG. (p. 1584)
—Skiing in Action. (p. 1584)
—Slap Shot Hockey. (p. 1587)
—Spike It Volleyball. (p. 1627)
—Tennis. (p. 1720)
—Track Events in Action. (p. 1775)
Crossingham, John & Rouse, Bonna. Cheerleading in Action. (p. 296)
—Cyclisme. (p. 397)
—Wrestling in Action. (p. 1962)
Crossingham, John, et al. Judo. (p. 931)
—Ratons Laveurs. (p. 1440)
Crossland, Caroline, illus. see Umansky, Kaye.
Crossley, Darry, tr. see Reynolds, Ralph V.
Crossley, David. 123. (p. 2000)
—ABC. (p. 2)
—Baby's First Learning Book: 123. (p. 129)
—First Words. (p. 597)
—On the Farm. (p. 1290)
Crossley, J. N., et al. What Is Mathematical Logic? (p. 1889)
Crossley, Kezzia, illus. see Zielinski, David.
Crossley, Laura C. Three Little Tiger Cubs: A Journey Through the Seasons with a Mom & Her Cubs. (p. 1743)
Crossley-Holland, Kevin. At the Crossing-Places. (p. 111)
—Crossing to Paradise. (p. 385)
—Enchantment: Fairy Tales, Ghost Stories & Tales of Wonder. Chichester Clark, Emma, illus. (p. 523)
—Seeing Stone. (p. 1548)
—Short! A Book of Very Short Stories. (p. 1569)
—Short Too! (p. 1569)
Crossling, Nick. Alhambra Stained Glass Coloring Book. (p. 38)
Crossling, Nick & Coloring Books Staff. Arabic Floral Patterns Coloring Book. (p. 94)
Crossling, Nick & Creative Haven. Creative Haven Alhambra Designs. (p. 379)
Crossman, D. A. Legend of Burial Island: A Bean & Ab Mystery. (p. 988)
Crossman, David. Legend of Burial Island: A Bean & Ab Mystery. (p. 988)
Crossman, Keith, ed. see Lorraine, Florido.
Crosson, Cierra, illus. see Magee, Kanika.
Crosson, Denise D. Mommy's Coming Home from Treatment. Motz, Mike, illus. (p. 1162)
—Mommy's Gone to Treatment. Motz, Mike, illus. (p. 1162)
CrossStaff Publishing, creator. Ten Commandments Movie Coloring Book: Part 1. (p. 1718)
—Ten Commandments Movie Coloring Book, Part 2. (p. 1718)
Crossway Bibles Staff, creator. Children's Bible. (p. 303)
Crosthwaite, Luis Humberto, tr. see Garza, Xavier.
Crosthwaite, Luis Humberto, tr. see Lozano, José.
Croswell, Ken. Lives of Stars. (p. 1040)
Croteau, Marie-Danielle. Fred & the Mysterious Letter. St-Aubin, Bruno, illus. (p. 632)
—Fred & the Mysterious Letter. Cummins, Sarah, tr. from FRE. (p. 632)
—Fred & the Pig Race. Cummins, Sarah, tr. from FRE. (p. 632)
—Grande Aventure d'un Petit Mouton Noir. (p. 707)
—Petite Reine au Nez Rouge. St. Aubin, Bruno, illus. (p. 1348)
—Tresor de Mon Pere. (p. 1785)
—Vent de Liberte. (p. 1836)
Croteau, Marie-Danielle & St. Aubin, Bruno. Des Fantomes Sous la Mer. (p. 427)
Croteau-Fleury, Marie-Danielle. Des Citrouilles pour Cendrillon. (p. 427)
Crothers, Samuel McChord. Children of Dickens. Smith, Jessie Willcox, illus. (p. 302)
Croton, Guy. Rembrandt. (p. 1459)
Crotts, Barbara. Gemini Cricket: John Glenn - First Person to Orbit the Earth. Khory, Emil, illus. (p. 660)
Crotty, Martha. Hong Kong Kitty. Thum, Gwen & Thum, David Ryan, illus. (p. 795)
Crouch, Adele. Creations by Crouch Color Me. Crouch, Adele, illus. (p. 379)
—Dance of the Caterpillars Bilingual Japanese English. Kohl, Carly & Ikeya, Sarah, trs. (p. 402)
—Dance of the Caterpillars Bilingual Korean English. Kim, Seong, tr. (p. 402)
—How the Fox Got His Color. Kim, Seong, tr. (p. 813)
—How the Fox Got His Color Bilingual French English. Rafalli, Yakeen, tr. (p. 813)
—How the Fox Got His Color Bilingual German English. Enderle, Evelyn, tr. (p. 813)
—How the Fox Got His Color Bilingual Greek English. Avrameli, Maria, tr. (p. 813)
—How the Fox Got His Color Bilingual Hungarian English. Sholtes, Andrew, tr. (p. 813)
—How the Fox Got His Color Bilingual Indonesian English. Mukhid, Abdul, tr. (p. 813)
—How the Fox Got His Color Bilingual Italian English. Spera, Massimiliano, tr. (p. 813)
—How the Fox Got His Color Bilingual Japanese English. Spiller, Yuko & Ikeya, Sarah, trs. (p. 813)
—How the Fox Got His Color Bilingual Portuguese English. Kohl, Carly & Clave, Israel, trs. (p. 813)
—How the Fox Got His Color Bilingual Russian English. Lank, Annytsya, tr. (p. 813)
—How the Fox Got His Color Bilingual Spanish English. Retana, Maria, tr. (p. 813)
—How the Fox Got His Color Bilingual Vietnamese English. Kha, Dang, tr. (p. 813)
—Where Hummingbirds Come from Bilingual Chinese English. Hu, Bin, tr. (p. 1907)
—Where Hummingbirds Come from Bilingual French English. Rafalli, Yakeen, tr. (p. 1907)
—Where Hummingbirds Come from Bilingual German English. Enderle, Evelyn, tr. (p. 1907)
—Where Hummingbirds Come from Bilingual Greek English. Avrameli, Maria, tr. (p. 1907)
—Where Hummingbirds Come from Bilingual Hungarian English. Sholtes, Andrew, tr. (p. 1908)
—Where Hummingbirds Come from Bilingual Indonesian English. Mukhid, Abdul, tr. (p. 1908)
—Where Hummingbirds Come from Bilingual Italian English. Spera, Massimiliano, tr. (p. 1908)
—Where Hummingbirds Come from Bilingual Japanese English. Spiller, Yuko & Ikeya, Sarah, trs. (p. 1908)
—Where Hummingbirds Come from Bilingual Korean English. Kim, Seong, tr. (p. 1908)
—Where Hummingbirds Come from Bilingual Portuguese English. Kohl, Carly, tr. (p. 1908)
—Where Hummingbirds Come from Bilingual Russian English. Lank, Annytsya, tr. (p. 1908)
—Where Hummingbirds Come from Bilingual Spanish English. Retana, Maria, tr. (p. 1908)
—Where Hummingbirds Come from Bilingual Vietnamese English. Kha, Dang, tr. (p. 1908)
Crouch, Amie. Feng Shui Workbook for Teens. (p. 581)
Crouch, Cheryl. Super Ace & the Space Traffic Jam Vander Pol, Matt, illus. (p. 1679)
—Troo Makes a Big Splash Zimmer, Kevin, illus. (p. 1788)
—Troo's Big Climb Zimmer, Kevin, illus. (p. 1788)
—Troo's Secret Clubhouse Zimmer, Kevin, illus. (p. 1788)
—Trouble in East Timor. (p. 1789)
Crouch, Cheryl & Vander Pol, Matt. Super Ace & the Mega Wow 3000 (p. 1679)
—Super Ace & the Rotten Robots (p. 1679)
—Super Ace & the Thirsty Planet (p. 1679)
Crouch, Cheryl Lynne. Tennis Shoes Trouble. (p. 1720)
Crouch, Frances, illus. see Dixon, Karen S.
Crouch, Julian, illus. see Gardner, Sally.
Crouch, Karen Hillard, illus. see Moulton, Mark Kimball.
Crouch, Kathryn L. Nibbly Noshers. (p. 1250)
Crouch, Katie. Magnolia League. (p. 1076)
—White Glove War. (p. 1913)
Crouch, Tim. I, Cinna (the Poet) (p. 837)
—I, Shakespeare. (p. 845)
Croucher, Barry, illus. see Whittley, Sarah & Showler, Dave.
Crouse, Donna J. Ruby Ring: The Whispering Cove Kids Club. (p. 1493)
Crouser, Brad. What's My Excuse for Not Being a Christian? 12 Myths of Christianity 12 Myths of Christianity. (p. 1898)
Crout, Brenda. Eliza: A Novel. (p. 513)
Crouth, Julia, illus. see Mills, David.
Crouthamel, Katherine. Animals & Their Habitats. (p. 82)
Crovatto, Lucie, illus. see Sadler, Marilyn.
Crow, A. D. Daisy & Her Shiny Heart. (p. 400)
Crow, Anne & Miller, Arthur. Philip Allan Literature Guide: Death of a Salesman. (p. 1350)
Crow, Bill. Tale of Two Friends. (p. 1700)
Crow, Brock, jt. auth. see Crow, Gary.
Crow, E. J. Eye Pocket. (p. 558)
Crow, Gary & Crow, Brock. JimJim Meets PosterGuy. (p. 918)
Crow, Gary & Crow, Marissa. Success Train. (p. 1672)
—Yes Bank. (p. 1970)
Crow, Heather, illus. see Lockhart, Barbara.
Crow, Jeffrey J., jt. auth. see Bell, John L.
Crow, Joseph Medicine & Viola, Herman. Counting Coup: Becoming a Crow Chief on the Reservation & Beyond. (p. 371)
Crow, Katie, illus. see Carkhuff Jr., Sam.
Crow, Kristyn. Bedtime at the Swamp. Pamintuan, Macky, illus. (p. 156)
—Hello, Hippo! Goodbye, Bird! Bernatene, Poly, illus. (p. 764)
—Middle-Child Blues. Catrow, David, illus. (p. 1137)
—Really Groovy Story of the Tortoise & the Hare. Forshay, Christina, illus. (p. 1450)
—Skeleton Cat. (p. 1584)
—Skeleton Cat. Krall, Dan, illus. (p. 1584)
—Zombelina. Idle, Molly, illus. (p. 1987)
—Zombelina Dances the Nutcracker. Idle, Molly, illus. (p. 1987)
Crow, Kristyn & Aesop. Really Groovy Story of the Tortoise & the Hare. Forshay, Christina, illus. (p. 1450)
Crow, Marilee. Cartwheel Annie. Snider, K. C., illus. (p. 273)
—Does Heaven Get Mail? Snider, K. C., illus. (p. 460)
—Down by the Shore. Roberts, MarySue, photos by. (p. 474)
—Down by the Shore. Roberts, Mary Sue, photos by. (p. 474)
—Pocketful of Manners. Snider, K. C., illus. (p. 1375)
—Short Tale about a Long Tail. Snider, K. C., illus. (p. 1569)
—So Silly. Snider, K. C., illus. (p. 1602)
Crow, Marilee & Foster, Jack. Once There Was a Monster. (p. 1292)
Crow, Marilee & Snider, K. C. Alleycat. (p. 47)
Crow, Marissa, jt. auth. see Crow, Gary.
Crow, Matthew. Brilliant Light of Amber Sunrise. (p. 228)
Crow, Melinda Melton. Brave Fire Truck Thompson, Chad, illus. (p. 223)
—Busy, Busy Train Thompson, Chad, illus. (p. 246)
—Camiones Amigos/Truck Buddies Heck, Claudia M., tr. from ENG. (p. 256)
—Carrera en la Carretera. Heck, Claudia M., tr. (p. 271)
—Drive Along Girouard, Patrick, illus. (p. 485)
—Field Trip for School Bus Thompson, Chad, illus. (p. 584)
—Helpful Tractor Thompson, Chad, illus. (p. 766)
—Let's Paint the Garage! Thompson, Chad, illus. (p. 999)
—Líos en el Lodo. Heck, Claudia M., tr. from ENG. (p. 1021)
—Líos en la Nieve. Heck, Claudia M., tr. from ENG. (p. 1021)
—Little Lizards. Rowland, Andrew, illus. (p. 1030)
—Little Lizard's Big Party Rowland, Andrew, illus. (p. 1030)
—Little Lizard's Big Party. Rowland, Andrew & Rowlands, Andy, illus. (p. 1030)
—Little Lizard's Family Fun Rowland, Andrew, illus. (p. 1030)
—Little Lizard's Family Fun. Rowland, Andrew & Rowlands, Andy, illus. (p. 1030)
—Little Lizard's First Day Rowland, Andrew, illus. (p. 1030)
—Little Lizard's First Day. Rowland, Andrew & Rowlands, Andy, illus. (p. 1030)
—Little Lizard's New Baby Rowland, Andrew, illus. (p. 1030)
—Little Lizard's New Bike. Rowland, Andrew & Rowlands, Andy, illus. (p. 1030)
—Little Lizard's New Friend Rowland, Andrew, illus. (p. 1030)
—Little Lizard's New Pet Rowland, Andrew, illus. (p. 1030)
—Little Lizard's New Shoes Rowland, Andrew, illus. (p. 1030)
—Little Wheels Girouard, Patrick, illus. (p. 1037)
—Long Train Ride Thompson, Chad, illus. (p. 1047)
—Lucky School Bus Thompson, Chad, illus. (p. 1063)
—Mud Mess Rooney, Ronnie, illus. (p. 1188)
—My Two Dogs. Sassin, Eva, illus. (p. 1220)
—Ride & Seek Girouard, Patrick, illus. (p. 1471)
—Road Race Rooney, Ronnie, illus. (p. 1477)
—Rocky & Daisy & the Birthday Party. Sassin, Eva, illus. (p. 1484)
—Rocky & Daisy at the Park Brownlow, Mike, illus. (p. 1484)
—Rocky & Daisy Get Trained Brownlow, Mike, illus. (p. 1484)
—Rocky & Daisy Go Camping Brownlow, Mike, illus. (p. 1484)
—Rocky & Daisy Go Home Brownlow, Mike, illus. (p. 1484)
—Rocky & Daisy Go to the Vet. Sassin, Eva, illus. (p. 1484)
—Rocky & Daisy Take a Vacation. Sassin, Eva, illus. (p. 1484)
—Rocky & Daisy Wash the Van. Sassin, Eva, illus. (p. 1484)
—Snow Trouble Rooney, Ronnie, illus. (p. 1599)
—Tired Trucks Girouard, Patrick, illus. (p. 1757)
—Truck Buddies Rooney, Ronnie, illus. (p. 1791)
—Truck Parade Thompson, Chad, illus. (p. 1791)
—Wonder Wheels. (p. 1947)
Crow, Melinda Melton & Sassin, Eva. Rocky & Daisy Take a Vacation (p. 1484)
Crow, Michael. Stories of Fear. (p. 1655)
Crow, Nosy. Bunny Boo Has Lost Her Teddy: A Tiny Tab Book. (p. 242)
—Can You Say It, Too? Moo! Moo! Braun, Sebastien, illus. (p. 259)
—Can You Say It, Too? Woof! Woof! Braun, Sebastien, illus. (p. 259)
—Flip Flap Farm. Scheffler, Axel, illus. (p. 604)
—Pip & Posy: the Bedtime Frog. Scheffler, Axel, illus. (p. 1361)
—Pip & Posy: the Scary Monster. Scheffler, Axel, illus. (p. 1361)
—Teeny Weeny Looks for His Mommy: A Tiny Tab Book. Ho, Jannie, illus. (p. 1715)
Crow, P. For the Love of Miss Bard. (p. 616)
Crow, Sharon L. Mrs. Titlebomb Drives to Town. (p. 1187)
Crow, Sherry. Library Lightning. Crow, Sherry, ed. (p. 1006)
Crow, Stanford. Lazy Hero Cat of Egypt. Hemmingson, Nancy S., illus. (p. 981)
Crowder, Jack L., et al. Stephanie & the Coyote. Morgan, William, tr. (p. 1648)
Crowder, Melanie. Audacity. (p. 114)
—Nearer Moon. (p. 1239)
—Parched. (p. 1324)
Crowder-Hefner-Montez, Pamela. Twila: Facts Are Facts! Journey One & Journey Two. (p. 1801)
Crowe, Carole. Waiting for Dolphins. (p. 1852)
—Waiting for Dolphins. Chayka, Doug, illus. (p. 1852)
Crowe, Chris. Getting Away with Murder: The True Story of the Emmett till Case. (p. 669)
—Just as Good: How Larry Doby Changed America's Game. Benny, Mike, illus. (p. 937)
—Mississippi Trial 1955. (p. 1154)
Crowe, Duane E. Catfish Annie to the Rescue. Ackison, Wendy Wassink, illus. (p. 280)
Crowe, Ellie. Go to Sleep, Hide & Seek. Wu, Julie, illus. (p. 687)
—Kamehameha: The Boy Who Became a Warrior King. Robinson, Don, illus. (p. 942)
Crowe, Ellie & Fry, Juliet. HOKU the Stargazer: The Exciting Pirate Adventure! Petosa-Sigel, Kristi, illus. (p. 787)
Crowe, Louise, illus. see Steven, Kenneth.
Crowe, Marla. Believability Factor: A Ten-Minute Dramatic Duet. (p. 161)
Crowe, Robert L. Children's Stories for ALmost Everyone. (p. 304)
Crowe, Robert L., jt. auth. see Bradbury, Ken.
Crowe, Sharon. Daniel & the Big Belly Button. (p. 404)
Crowell, Helen, illus. see Pierce, Brian.
Crowell, Knox, illus. see Black, Jessica L. & Mullican, Judy.
Crowell, Knox, illus. see Hensley, Sarah M.
Crowell, Knox, illus. see Howard-Parham, Pam.
Crowell, Knox, illus. see Jarrell, Pamela R.
Crowell, Knox, illus. see Muench-Williams, Heather.
Crowell, Knox, illus. see Williams, Heather L.
Crowell, Knox, jt. auth. see Mullican, Judy.
Crowell, Marcia. Adventures of Little Blackie & Friends. (p. 19)
Crowell, Pers, illus. see Holt, Stephen.
Crowell, Peter Thomas. Haunted Mountain: The Tales of True Adventure, Book Two. (p. 753)
—Silverlance: The Tales of True Adventure. Bk. 1 (p. 1577)
Crowl, Janice. Kili & the Singing Snails. Orme, Harinani, illus. (p. 956)
—Pulelehua & Mamaki. Orme, Harinani, illus. (p. 1415)
Crowl, Jasey. You're COLORing. (p. 1982)
Crowl, Jordan. Ed's Journal: Motivation. (p. 504)
Crowley, Adam A., photos by see Richardson, Kimberly Stanton.
Crowley, Ashley. Officer Panda - Fingerprint Detective. Crowley, Ashley, illus. (p. 1280)
Crowley, Bridget. Step into the Dark. (p. 1648)
Crowley, Cath. Chasing Charlie Duskin. (p. 294)
—Graffiti Moon. (p. 705)
—Little Wanting Song. (p. 1037)
Crowley, Cheryl, illus. see Rieback, Milton.
Crowley Conn, Kathe. Juliette Kinzie: Frontier Storyteller. (p. 932)
Crowley, James. Magic Hour. (p. 1072)
Crowley, Jennifer Brasington. Lyndsay & Lainey Lion: E Is for Dragon. (p. 1066)
—Lyndsay & Lainey Lion: F Is for Dragon. (p. 1066)
Crowley, Jennifer Brasington, ed. Lyndsay & Lainey Lion: D Is for Dragon. (p. 1066)
Crowley, Katherine & Elster, Kathi. Working with You Is Killing Me: Freeing Yourself from Emotional Traps at Work. (p. 1953)
Crowley, Kerry. Smart Thing to Do. (p. 1593)
Crowley, Kieran Mark. Colm & the Ghost's Revenge. (p. 341)
—Colm & the Lazarus Key. (p. 341)
Crowley, Krista. We're on the way to see Daddy-O! (p. 1875)
Crowley, Ned. Nanook & Pryce: Gone Fishing. Day, Larry, illus. (p. 1229)
Crowley, Peter. J T Seavey. (p. 902)
Crowley, Richard J., jt. auth. see Mills, Joyce C.
Crowley, Suzanne. Very Ordered Existence of Merilee Marvelous. (p. 1838)
Crowley, Suzanne, jt. auth. see Crowley, Suzanne Carlisle.

Crowley, Suzanne Carlisle & Crowley, Suzanne. Stolen One. (p. 1652)
Crowley-Ranelli, D. Holiday Island: Santa in a Bathing Suit? (p. 788)
Crown, Adam Adrian. Classical Fencing: The Martial Art of Incurable Romantics. (p. 328)
Crown Peak Publishing. Just Be You. Crown Peak Publishing, illus. (p. 938)
Crownberry, Ethan. Bobby Bumble's Afraid to Fly. (p. 206)
—Fish with a Wish. (p. 598)
—Johnny Jetpack. (p. 923)
—Willies. (p. 1934)
Crowne, Alyssa. Green Princess Saves the Day. Alder, Charlotte, illus. (p. 722)
—Orange Princess Has a Ball. Alder, Charlotte, illus. (p. 1302)
—Pink Princess Rules the School. Alder, Charlotte, illus. (p. 1360)
Crownover, Amy & Crownover, Dean. My Perfect Man Coloring & Activity Book. (p. 1216)
Crownover, Dean, jt. auth. see Crownover, Amy.
Crownover, Rebecca. Texas Farm Girl. Daigle, Brian, illus. (p. 1724)
Crowson, Andrew. Flip Flap Christmas. Crowson, Andrew, illus. (p. 604)
—Flip Flap Fairytale. (p. 604)
—Flip Flap Farm. (p. 604)
—Flip Flap Ocean. (p. 604)
—Flip Flap People. (p. 604)
—Flip Flap Prehistoric. Crowson, Andrew, illus. (p. 604)
—Flip Flap Safari. Crowson, Andrew, illus. (p. 604)
—Flip Flap Spooky. Crowson, Andrew, illus. (p. 604)
Crowson, Andrew, jt. auth. see Askew, Amanda.
Crowther, jt. auth. see Crowther, Kitty.
Crowther, Clare. People. (p. 1338)
Crowther, Jeff, illus. see Ciencin, Scott.
Crowther, Jeff, illus. see Dahl, Michael & Nickel, Scott.
Crowther, Jeff, illus. see Dahl, Michael.
Crowther, Jeff, illus. see Nickel, Scott & Dahl, Michael.
Crowther, John, ed. see Shakespeare, William & SparkNotes Staff.
Crowther, Kitty & Crowther. Scric Scrac Bibib Blub! Coll-Vinent, Anna, tr. (p. 1533)
Crowther, Robert. Deep down under Ground: A Pop-up Book of Amazing Facts & Feats. Crowther, Robert, illus. (p. 423)
—Most Amazing Hide-and-Seek Alphabet Book. Crowther, Robert, illus. (p. 1177)
—Most Amazing Hide-and-Seek Numbers Book. Crowther, Robert, illus. (p. 1177)
—Robert Crowther's Amazing Pop-Up Big Machines. Crowther, Robert, illus. (p. 1478)
—Robert Crowther's Pop-Up Dinosaur ABC. Crowther, Robert, illus. (p. 1478)
—Robert Crowther's Pop-Up House of Inventions: Hundreds of Fabulous Facts about Your Home. Crowther, Robert, illus. (p. 1478)
—Ships: A Pop-Up Book. Crowther, Robert, illus. (p. 1567)
—Soccer: Facts & Stats & the World Cup & Superstars: A Pop-up Book. Crowther, Robert, illus. (p. 1603)
—Trains: A Pop-Up Railroad Book. Crowther, Robert, illus. (p. 1777)
Croy, Anita. Ancient Aztec & Maya. (p. 68)
—Ancient Pueblo: Archaeology Unlocks the Secrets of America's Past. (p. 70)
—Colombia. (p. 341)
—Everyday Life. (p. 543)
—Exploring the Past. (p. 554)
—Guatemala. (p. 728)
—Myths & Legends of Ancient Rome. (p. 1227)
—Myths & Legends of Australia, New Zealand, & Pacific Islands. (p. 1227)
—Myths & Legends of Central & South America. (p. 1227)
—Peru. (p. 1345)
—Solving the Mysteries of Aztec Cities. (p. 1608)
—Titanic: The Search for the Lost Fugitives. Posen, Mick, illus. (p. 1757)
Croy, Anita, jt. auth. see Wright, Anne.
Croy, Anita & Wright, Anne Margaret. Art & Architecture. (p. 101)
Croy, Elden. United States. (p. 1819)
Croyle, Anna. Mandala Stained Glass Pattern Book. (p. 1087)
Croyle, John. Two-Minute Drill to Manhood: What Every Parent Wants Their Son to Be & Their Daughter to Marry. (p. 1804)
Croyle, Paula. Today I'll Be a Princess. Brown, Heather, illus. (p. 1760)
—Who Lives Here? A Lift-The-Flap Book. Brown, Heather, illus. (p. 1916)
Croyle, Paula, jt. auth. see Hannigan, Paula.
Croyle, William, jt. auth. see Jenkins, Missy.
Croza, Laurel. From There to Here James, Matt, illus. (p. 644)
Crozat, Francois, illus. see Chausse, Sylvie.
Croze, Harvey. Africa for Kids: Exploring a Vibrant Continent - 19 Activities. (p. 26)
Crozier, A. J. Technology & the Civil War: Set Of 6. (p. 1711)
—Technology & the Civil War: Text Pairs. (p. 1711)
Crozier, Eric. Let's Make an Opera! - an Entertainment for Young People in Three Acts. (p. 999)
Crozier, Lorna. Lots of Kisses (p. 1057)
—So Many Babies Watson, Laura, illus. (p. 1602)
Crozon, Alain. All Shook Up! (p. 45)
—Who's There? (p. 1921)
Crozrock. Don't Chat about That! A Book of Chat Room Safety Tips for Children. (p. 467)
—Dr Crozrock Says Don't Smoke! (p. 475)
Crubel, Thomas K. Kyanna's Trip to the Zoo (p. 969)
Cruce, Lana. Caring for Your Pet Bird. (p. 269)
Cruden, Alex & Bryfonski, Dedria. End of Apartheid. (p. 526)
Cruden, Alex, ed. Bosnian Conflict. (p. 214)
—Student Movements of The 1960s. (p. 1669)
Cruea, Kim. Adventures Continue for Summer Falls Junior Rangers (p. 15)
—Summer Falls Junior Rangers: The First Adventures. (p. 1674)
Cruella & Birch, Penny. Indecencies of Isabelle. (p. 870)
Cruickshank, Don. Bowling. (p. 216)
—Calgary Flames. (p. 253)
—Canadiens de Montréal: Les Equipes de Hockey du Canada. Karvonen, Tanjah, tr. from ENG. (p. 260)
—Canucks de Vancouver: Les Equipes de Hockey du Canada. Karvonen, Tanjah, tr. from ENG. (p. 262)
—Edmonton Oilers. (p. 504)
—Flames de Calgary: Les Equipes de Hockey du Canada. Karvonen, Tanjah, tr. from ENG. (p. 602)
—Giant Pandas. (p. 673)
—Maple Leafs de Toronto: Les Equipes de Hockey du Canada. Karvonen, Tanjah, tr. from ENG. (p. 1090)
—Montreal Canadiens. (p. 1170)
—Oilers D'Edmonton: Les Equipes de Hockey du Canada. Karvonen, Tanjah, tr. from ENG. (p. 1282)
—Ottawa Senators. (p. 1307)
—Sénateurs D'Ottawa: Les Equipes de Hockey du Canada. Karvonen, Tanjah, tr. from ENG. (p. 1550)
—Toronto Maple Leafs. (p. 1770)
—Vancouver Canucks. (p. 1833)
Cruikshank, Beth & Johnston, Lynn. Farley & the Lost Bone. (p. 573)
Cruikshank, Don. For the Love of Bowling. (p. 616)
Cruikshank, Fran. Tale of the Not-So-Perfect Christmas Tree. Olson, Tom, illus. (p. 1700)
Cruikshank, George, illus. see Brothers Grimm, Becky, et al.
Cruikshank, George, illus. see Landes, William-Alan, ed.
Cruikshank, George, illus. see Paris, John Ayrton.
Cruise, ed. see Yoon, Ae-hae.
Cruise, Robin. Nuclear Disaster at Chernobyl. Taylor, Marjorie, illus. (p. 1269)
Crull, Kim. Castaway Cousins. (p. 276)
Crum, A. M., illus. see Mertz, Alyssa.
Crum, Anna-Maria. Animal Behaviorists: Set Of 6. (p. 76)
—Animal Behaviorists & Conductistas de Animales: 6 English, 6 Spanish Adaptations. (p. 76)
—Math to Build On: Set Of 6. (p. 1107)
—Math to Build on & Matemáticas para Construir: 6 English, 6 Spanish Adaptations. (p. 1107)
—Trackers of Dynamic Earth: Set Of 6. (p. 1775)
—Trackers of Dynamic Earth & Rastreadores de nuestra dinámica Tierra: 6 English, 6 Spanish Adaptations. (p. 1775)
Crum, Anna-Maria, illus. see Cangilla-McAdam, Claudia.
Crum, Anna-Maria, illus. see McAdam, Claudia Cangilla.
Crum, Anna-Maria, illus. see Pease, Elaine.
Crum, Anna-Maria, illus. see Sprick, Jessica.
Crum, Anna-Maria, illus. see Sprick, Marilyn, et al.
Crum, Karen Boyden. Family Angels. (p. 568)
Crum, Nate. Abc. (p. 2)
Crum, Sally. Race to Moonrise Rev. Carlson, Eric S., illus. (p. 1431)
—Race to the River: The Ancient Journey Continues. (p. 1431)
Crum, Shaun, illus. see Ridenour, Melissa.
Crum, Shutta. Dozens of Cousins. Catrow, David, illus. (p. 474)
—Mine! Barton, Patrice, illus. (p. 1145)
—My Mountain Song. (p. 1215)
—Thomas & the Dragon Queen. Wildish, Lee, illus. (p. 1738)
—Thunder-Boomer! Thompson, Carol, illus. (p. 1746)
—Uh-Oh! Barton, Patrice, illus. (p. 1808)
Crum, Shutta & Beder, John. Click! (p. 331)
Crumbaugh, David. Primrose Kids. (p. 1401)
Crumbley, Paul. Student's Encyclopedia of Great American Writers (p. 1669)
Crumley, Daniel Wade. 4 -0n- 4 Flag Football Training Manual: Flag Football. (p. 1992)
Crumly, Billie Lang. Best of Country Living. (p. 170)
Crummel, Susan Stevens. All in One Hour Donohue, Dorothy, illus. (p. 44)
—City Dog, Country Dog Donohue, Dorothy, illus. (p. 323)
—Sherlock Bones & the Missing Cheese Donohue, Dorothy, illus. (p. 1565)
—Ten-Gallon Bart Donohue, Dorothy, illus. (p. 1718)
—Ten-Gallon Bart & the Wild West Show (p. 1718)
—Ten-Gallon Bart Beats the Heat Donohue, Dorothy, illus. (p. 1718)
—Tumbleweed Stew. (p. 1796)
—Tumbleweed Stew. Stevens, Janet, illus. (p. 1796)
Crummel, Susan Stevens, jt. auth. see Stevens, Janet.
Crummel, Susan Stevens & Donohue, Dorothy. City Dog & Country Dog. Donohue, Dorothy, illus. (p. 323)
Crummel, Susan Stevens & Stevens, Janet. Cook-a-Doodle-Doo! (p. 361)
—Plaidypus Lost. Stevens, Janet, illus. (p. 1366)
—Shoe Town. (p. 1568)
Crump, A. K., ed. see Reed, Kevin.
Crump, A. K., ed. Chocolate French: Recipes, Language, & Directions to Francais Au Chocolat. (p. 309)
Crump, Christopher, illus. see Hussey, Charmian.
Crump, Fred, Jr. Brave Toy Soldier. (p. 223)
—Ebonita & the Seven Boyz. (p. 502)
—Little Mermaid. (p. 1031)
—Marigold & the Dragon. (p. 1094)
—Three Kings & a Star. Crump, Fred, Jr., illus. (p. 1742)
—Three Little Brown Piggies. (p. 1742)
Crump, Jennifer. Canada on Fire: The War of 1812. (p. 260)
—Canada under Attack. (p. 260)
—War of 1812: Heroes of a Great Canadian Victory. (p. 1857)
Crump Jr., Fred. Brave Toy Soldier. (p. 223)
—Three Little Brown Piggies. (p. 1742)
Crump, Leslie, illus. see Barbour, Ralph Henry.
Crump, Lil, illus. see Kyi, Tanya Lloyd.
Crump, Marty. Amphibians & Reptiles: An Introduction to Their Natural History & Conservation. (p. 66)
—Mysteries of the Komodo Dragon: The Biggest, Deadliest Lizard Gives up Its Secrets. (p. 1222)
—Mystery of Darwin's Frog. Jenkins, Steve & Rodriguez, Edel, illus. (p. 1224)
Crumpacker, Bunny. Sex Life of Food: When Body & Soul Meet to Eat. (p. 1556)
Crumpler, Rebecca Lee, jt. auth. see Kovatch, Sarah.
Crumpley, Harold William & Crumpley, Joan Irene Beck. Come All Ye Yankee Farmers: An American Family Diary. (p. 347)
Crumpley, Joan Irene Beck, jt. auth. see Crumpley, Harold William.
Crumpton, Nick. Triassic Terrors. Lenkiewicz, Isaac, illus. (p. 1785)
Crunk, Tony. Railroad John & the Red Rock Run Austin, Michael, illus. (p. 1434)
crunkhurn, helen. SH! Listen. (p. 1556)
Crupi, Jaclyn. Theo at the Beach. Verdoux, Aurélia, illus. (p. 1729)
Cruschiform. Full Speed Ahead! (p. 646)
Cruse, Beryl, et al. Bittangabee Tribe: An Aboriginal Story from Coastal New South Wales. (p. 194)
Cruse, Howard. Stuck Rubber Baby. Taggart, B., ed. (p. 1669)
Cruse, Howard, illus. see Shaffer, Jeanne E.
Crush, Chip. Biblical Guesses: Looking at Life Through the Bible. (p. 177)
Crutcher, Anquisha Janea. To Grandma's House I Go. (p. 1759)
Crutcher, Chris. Angry Management. (p. 75)
—Chinese Handcuffs. (p. 307)
—Crazy Horse Electric Game. (p. 377)
—Deadline. (p. 417)
—Ironman. (p. 888)
—King of the Mild Frontier: An Ill-Advised Autobiography. (p. 959)
—Period 8. (p. 1343)
—Running Loose. (p. 1497)
—Sledding Hill. (p. 1588)
—Staying Fat for Sarah Byrnes. (p. 1645)
—Stotan! (p. 1664)
—Whale Talk. (p. 1877)
Crutchfield, Jim, illus. see Sparkman, Winette.
CRUTCHFIELD, Shannon. Arion's Way. (p. 98)
Crutchfield, Tylicia, jt. auth. see Carr, Suzanna.
Cruts, Randy. Dragon's Mist. (p. 479)
Cruttenden, Jamie & Pecsenye, Jessica. University of Pittsburgh College Prowler off the Record. (p. 1821)
Cruz, Abel. Jugultos para Ninos. (p. 932)
Cruz, Alexandra. Abc's Around the World. (p. 4)
Cruz, Amada, contrib. by. Slater Bradley: Don't Let Me Disappear. (p. 1588)
Cruz, Arthur Dela. Nonstop Beauty Vol. 2. (p. 1263)
Cruz, Barbara C. Alvin Ailey: Celebrating African-American Culture in Dance. (p. 51)
Cruz, Bàrbara C. Cesar Chavez: A Voice for Farmworkers. (p. 288)
Cruz, Barbara C. Fight for Latino Civil Rights. (p. 585)
Cruz, Bàrbara C. Triumphs & Struggles for Latino Civil Rights. (p. 1788)
Cruz, Calvin. Bentley Continental GT. (p. 165)
—Bugatti Veyron. (p. 236)
—Chevrolet Corvette Z06. (p. 299)
—Dodge Viper SRT. (p. 460)
—Ferrari 458 Italia. (p. 582)
—Lamborghini Aventador. (p. 972)
—McLaren 12C. (p. 1114)
—Porsche 918 Spyder. (p. 1386)
Cruz, Cheryl, illus. see Hineman, Jonathan.
Cruz, Cheryl, illus. see Lucas, Ian & Medoza, Chris.
Cruz, D. Nina, illus. see Brammer, Ethriam Cash.
Cruz, D. Nina, illus. see Caraballo, Samuel.
Cruz De Jesus, Marta. Chosen: By Nature. (p. 310)
Cruz, E. R., illus. see Twain, Mark, pseud.
Cruz, Ernesto R, illus. see Sohl, Marcia & Dackerman, Gerald.
Cruz, et al. Jonas en Apuros. (p. 925)
Cruz Garcia, Juanita. Yocumal & Juno. (p. 1972)
Cruz, Ginny Wilson. E Is for Ellisville. (p. 492)
Cruz Gonzalez, Jose. Thaddeus & Tila (A Crane & Frog Tale) (p. 1724)
Cruz, Jeffrey Chamba. RandomVeus Volume 1. (p. 1438)
Cruz, José Miguel & Córdova, Ricardo. Cultura política de la democracia en el Salvador 2008: El impacto de la Gobernabilidad. (p. 390)
Cruz, Juan, et al. Jonas Tiene un Problema Muy Gordo. (p. 925)
Cruz, Kelly De La. Super Boy's Adventurous Imagination: Let your imagination Flow. (p. 1679)
Cruz, Maria Colleen. Border Crossing. (p. 213)
Cruz, María Hernández de la, illus. see Endredy, James.
Cruz, María Hernández de la, tr. see Endredy, James.
Cruz, Nardo, illus. see Shelley, Mary & Shelley, Mary.
Cruz, Nardo, illus. see Stevenson, Robert Louis.
Cruz, Ray, illus. see Jaffe, Nina.
Cruz, Ray, illus. see Viorst, Judith.
Cruz, Roger, illus. see Davis, Alan, et al.
Cruz, Roger, illus. see Lobdell, Scott, et al.
Cruz, Roger & Coover, Colleen. X-Men First Class - Volume 2. (p. 1967)
Cruz, Sarah, et al. Bernie Burn: A Storybook about Burn Injury Prevention & Safety in the Home. (p. 167)
Cruz, Stefanie. Delta & Dawn: Mother & Baby Whales' Journey. Toppenberg, Lily, illus. (p. 425)
Cruz, Wilfredo. Charlie's Box: A Story about a Boy & His Magical Box. (p. 293)
Cruzan, Patricia. Max Does It Again. Solly, Gloria D., illus. (p. 1111)
—Molly's Mischievous Dog. (p. 1161)
—Wonder in the Woods. Brewer, Kathaleen, illus. (p. 1947)
Cruzan, Patricia & Solly, Gloria. Molly's Mischievous Dog. (p. 1161)
Cruz-Contarini, Rafael & Rafael, Cruz-Contarini. De la A A la Z con Mozart y la Musica. Salmeron, Rafael & Salmeron Lopez, Rafael, illus. (p. 416)
—Zaranda. (p. 1985)
Cruz-Martinez, George. Wonder of Keys for Kids. Sturgeon, Brad, illus. (p. 1947)
Cryan, Mary Beth. BFF - Farm: Easy-to-Make Models for You & a Friend! (p. 174)
—BFF - Pets: Easy-to-Make Models to Share with Your Best Friend! (p. 174)
—Easy-to-Make Sea Animals Finger Puppets. (p. 500)
—Easy-to-Make Zoo Animals Finger Puppets. (p. 500)
—Make Your Own Masks: Tear Them, Share Them, Color & Wear Them! (p. 1080)
—My Christmas Tree. (p. 1200)
—Paper Shaper Forest Friends: 3-D Crafts to Make & Display. Anton, Carrie, ed. (p. 1323)
—Paper Shapers Chic Boutique: 3-D Crafts to Make & Display. Anton, Carrie, ed. (p. 1323)
—Standups! at Work: 8 Easy-To-Make Models! (p. 1639)
—Standups! Presidents: 8 Easy-To-Make Models! (p. 1639)
Cryan, Michelle. Where Is Baby? (p. 1908)
Cryer, Debby, et al. Active Learning for Fives. (p. 10)
—Active Learning for Ones. (p. 10)
—Active Learning for Threes. (p. 10)
Crysdale, Joy & Second Story Press Staff. Fearless Female Journalists (p. 579)
Crysler, Ian, photos by see Reid, Barbara.
Crystal, Ben, jt. auth. see Crystal, David.
Crystal, Billy. 700 Sundays. (p. 2001)
—Grandpa's Little One. Porfirio, Guy, illus. (p. 710)
—I Already Know I Love You. Sayles, Elizabeth, illus. (p. 831)
Crystal, David & Crystal, Ben. Oxford Illustrated Shakespeare Dictionary. (p. 1315)
Crystal Productions, creator. Principles of Design Posters. (p. 1406)
Crystian, Carol Payne. Ebony Black & The 7. (p. 502)
—Jas & Poetic Lucy. Crystian, Carol Payne, illus. (p. 909)
Crystow, Charisse. Dainty Dee & Lanky Lee. (p. 400)
Csavas, Sally, illus. see Price, Diane J.
Csicsko, David Lee, illus. see Tyler, Michael.
Csotonyi, Julius, illus. see Norman, Kim & American Museum of Natural History Staff.
Csotonyi, Julius, illus. see Stewart, Melissa.
Csotonyi, Julius, illus. see Switek, Brian.
Cua, Marcus Loo. How the Hungry T-Rex Got Fixed. (p. 813)
Cuartas, Jennifer M. Adventures of Delilah Doodle: Mealy Bug Stew. (p. 17)
—So Many Things. (p. 1602)
Cuasay, Alison Taimanglo. Tasi & Matina: The Story of the First Clown Fish. (p. 1706)
Cuban, Mark. Let's Go Mavs! (p. 997)
Cubillas, Roberto, illus. see Pez, Alberto.
Cucca, Vincenzo, illus. see Kesel, Barbara.
Cucchiara, Chris. Lessons from the Gym for Young Adults: 5 Secrets to Being in Control of Your Life. (p. 993)
Cuccia, Louis J. Bottle Tree. (p. 215)
Cuccia, Ronni. Maria & the Monster. (p. 1093)
Cucco, Giuliano, illus. see Miller, John.
Cuchna, Reid. Out of Love (p. 1311)
Cucko, D. Kirsten. If Dinosaurs Were Around Today. (p. 852)
Cudby, Simon. Motocross Exposure. Cudby, Simon, photos by. (p. 1179)
Cudd, Savannah, illus. see Fitzgerald, D. M.
Cuddehe, Judy Link. Heron Chronicles. Cuddehe, Judy Link, illus. (p. 773)
Cuddy, Robbin. All about Drawing Farm & Forest Animals: Learn to Draw More Than 40 Barnyard Animals & Wildlife Critters Step by Step. (p. 42)
—All about Drawing: Farm & Forest Animals. Cuddy, Robin, illus. (p. 42)
—Learn to Draw Cats & Kittens: Step-By-step Instructions for More Than 25 Favorite Feline Friends. (p. 983)
—Learn to Draw Dogs & Puppies: Step-By-Step Instructions for More Than 25 Different Breeds. (p. 983)
—Learn to Draw Forest Animals: Step-By-step Instructions for More Than 25 Woodland Creatures. (p. 983)
—Learn to Draw Forest Animals & Wildlife: Step-by-Step Instructions for 25 Different Woodland Animals. (p. 983)
—Learn to Draw Pets: Step-By-Step Instructions for More Than 25 Cute & Cuddly Animals. (p. 983)
—Learn to Draw Polar Animals: Draw More Than 25 Favorite Arctic & Antarctic Wildlife Critters. (p. 983)
—Learn to Draw Rainforest & Jungle Animals: Step-by-Step Drawing Instructions for 25 Exotic Creatures. (p. 983)
—Learn to Draw Safari Animals: Step-By-step Instructions for More Than 25 Exotic Animals. (p. 983)
—Learn to Draw Sea Creatures. (p. 983)
—Polar Animals: Draw More Than 25 Favorite Arctic & Antarctic Wildlife Critters. (p. 1378)
Cuddy, Robbin, illus. see Clarke, Ginjer L.
Cuddy, Robbin, illus. see Lane, Jeanette & Cole, Joanna.
Cuddy, Robbin, illus. see Phan, Sandy.
Cuddy, Robbin, illus. see Sander, Sonia & Bridwell, Norman.
Cuddy, Robbin, illus. see Torres, Jickie.
Cuddy, Robbin, illus. see Walter Foster Creative Team.
Cuddy, Robin. Learn to Draw Horses & Ponies: Step-by-Step Instructions for More Than 25 Different Breeds. (p. 983)
—Learn to Draw Pets: Step-By-Step Instructions for More Than 25 Cute & Cuddly Animals. (p. 983)
—Learn to Draw Sea Creatures: Step-by-Step Instructions for More Than 25 Ocean Animals. (p. 983)
Cuddy, Robin, illus. see Clarke, Ginjer L.
Cuddy, Robin, illus. see Cuddy, Robbin.
Cuddy, Robin, illus. see Parent, Nancy.
Cuddy, Robin, illus. see Weiss, Ellen.
Cudeyro, Erica M. American History for Young Minds - Volume 1, Looking Towards the Sky, Book 1, the First Airplane. Butler, Lindsay L., illus. (p. 61)
Cudjoe, Dzagbe. Tales My Ghanaian Grandmother Told Me. (p. 1702)
Cudney, Chriss. Brothers Are Here! Preschool Years. (p. 231)
Cue, Harold, illus. see Bartlett, Arthur C.
Cue, Ian J. Renewal: First Encounter. (p. 1460)
Cuellar, Joey, et al. Capcom Fighting Evolution(R) Official Fighter's Guide. (p. 262)
Cuellar, Olga, illus. see Andricain, Sergio.
Cuellar, Olga, illus. see Cooper, Patrick.
Cuellar, Olga, illus. see Hoyos, Hector.
Cuellar, Olga, illus. see Rodriguez, Antonio Orlando.
Cuellar, Olga, illus. see Wang, Gabrielle.
Cuenca, Hector. Cucarachita Martina. (p. 389)
Cuencas, Angel. Dear Mom. (p. 419)
Cuesta, Vivian. It Can Be Done: The Life & Legacy of César Chávez. (p. 893)

C

Cuesy, Silvia. Diario de Mercedes (1844-48) (p. 434)
Cueva, Susana & Shibaja, Calixto. Lita the Hardworking Worm/Lita la Trabajadora. (p. 1022)
Cuevas, Andres Mario Ramirez, illus. see Santillan, Maria Luisa.
Cuevas, Ernesto, illus. see Herrera, Juan Felipe.
Cuevas, Ernesto, jt. illus. see Herrera, Juan Felipe.
Cuevas, Michelle. Beyond the Laughing Sky. Morstad, Julie, illus. (p. 174)
—Confessions of an Imaginary Friend: A Memoir by Jacques Papier. (p. 356)
Cuff. Super Spelling. (p. 1682)
Cuff, Ed. D. City of Thieves. (p. 324)
Cuffaro, Anna. Gatwick Bear & the Secret Plans. Anguissola, Anna, illus. (p. 658)
Cugota, Lluís, et al. Albert Einstein. (p. 34)
Cuillain, Adam. Zak's King Arthur Adventure. (p. 1984)
Cuillain, Adam & Cuillain, Charlotte. Pirates on Holiday. Van Wyk, Rupert, illus. (p. 1364)
Cuillain, Charlotte, jt. auth. see Cuillain, Adam.
Cuillain, Charlotte, jt. auth. see Guillain, Adam.
Cuisenaire Staff. Super Source: Tangrams. (p. 1682)
—Super Source: Geoboards. (p. 1682)
—Super Source: Snap Cubes. (p. 1682)
—Super Source: Pattern Blocks. (p. 1682)
—Super Source: Cuisenaire Rods. (p. 1682)
Culbard, Ian N. J., jt. auth. see Lovecraft, H. P.
Culbertson, James Forrest, illus. see Eakin, Sue, et al.
Culbertson, Jan E. Legend of Dunsmoor Manor. (p. 988)
—Legend of the Lost Tiki. (p. 989)
Culbertson, Ken. Kenny the Guinea. (p. 949)
Culbertson, Kim. Catch a Falling Star. (p. 279)
—Instructions for a Broken Heart. (p. 878)
—Songs for a Teenage Nomad. (p. 1611)
Culen, Konstantin. History of Slovaks in America. Potach, Steven G. & Kopanic, Michael J., eds. (p. 784)
Culham, Ruth. 6 + 1 Traits of Writing: The Complete Guide - Grades 3 & up - Everything You Need to Teach & Assess Student Writing with This Powerful Model. (p. 1992)
—Complete Guide for the Primary Grades. (p. 353)
—Daily Trait Warm-Ups: 180 Revision & Editing Activities to Kick off Writing Time. (p. 400)
—Reproducible Forms for the Writing Traits Classroom, Grade K-2: Checklists, Graphic Organizers, Rubrics, Scoring Sheets & More to Boost Students' Writing Skills in All Seven Traits. (p. 1461)
—Trait Crate, Grade 6: Mentor Texts, Model Lessons, & More to Teach Writing with the 6 Traits. (p. 1777)
—Trait Crate, Grade 7: Mentor Texts, Model Lessons, & More to Teach Writing with the 6 Traits. (p. 1777)
—Trait Crate Grade 8: Mentor Texts, Model Lessons, & More to Teach Writing with the 6 Traits. (p. 1777)
—Trait Crate(r), Kindergarten: Picture Books, Model Lessons, & More to Teach Writing with the 6 Traits. (p. 1777)
—Using Picture Books to Teach Writing with the Traits: Bibliography of More Than 200 Titles with Teacher-Tested Lessons. (p. 1828)
Culham, Ruth & Wheeler, Amanda. 40 Reproducible Forms for the Writing Traits Classroom: Checklists, Graphic Organizers, Rubrics & Scoring Sheets, & More to Boost Students' Writing Skills in All Seven Traits. (p. 1997)
—Literature Response. (p. 1023)
—Writing to Prompts in the Trait-Based Classroom - Content Areas: Prompts That Provide All the Elements Students Need to Start Writing - A Role, Audience, Format, Topic, & Strong Verb. (p. 1965)
Culic, Ned, jt. auth. see Reilly, Carmel.
Culici, Tonia. Kiku Gecko & Rainbow Girl. (p. 956)
Culin, Stewart. Games of the North American Indians. (p. 655)
Culkin-Lawrence, Teresa, illus. see Gervay, Susanne.
Culkin-Lawrence, Teresa, illus. see Murray, Kirsty.
Cull, Selby. Rocks & Minerals. (p. 1483)
Cullagh, Yolanda. Sabina the Beach Fly. (p. 1500)
Cullen, Dave. Big Book of Science. Leeks, David, illus. (p. 179)
—My First Atlas. Leeks, David, illus. (p. 1204)
Cullen, Dave & Williams, Simon. My First Atlas. Leeks, David, illus. (p. 1204)
Cullen, J. Heather. Barbara McClintock. (p. 137)
Cullen, Jim. Imperfect Presidents: Tales of Misadventure & Triumph. (p. 862)
Cullen, Katherine. Earth Science. (p. 496)
—Physics: The People Behind the Science. (p. 1353)
—Science, Technology, & Society: The People Behind the Science. (p. 1528)
Cullen, Katherine E. Marine Science: The People Behind the Science. (p. 1094)
Cullen, Katherine E., jt. auth. see Katherine Cullen, PH D.
Cullen, Katherine, et al. Pioneers in Science Set. (p. 1361)
Cullen, Lyn. I Am Rembrandt's Daughter. (p. 833)
Cullen, Lynn. Dear Mr. Washington. Carpenter, Nancy, illus. (p. 419)
—Diary of Nelly Vandorn. (p. 435)
—Little Scraggly Hair: A Dog on Noah's Ark. Rogers, Jacqueline, illus. (p. 1036)
Cullen, Murray & O'Neill, Susan. Try: Treatment Readiness for Youth at Risk. (p. 1794)
Cullen, Ruth. Brainiac's Giant Book of Gross Outs. (p. 222)
Cullen-DuPont, Kathryn, jt. auth. see Frost-Knappman, Elizabeth.
Cullen-Skowronski, Fiona. Smugglers' Caves. (p. 1595)
Culley, Claire & Phipps, Amy. Paper Cutting: 20 Projects for Friends to Make. (p. 1322)
Cullimore, Stan. Alien Swap. Schon, Nick, illus. (p. 41)
Cullinan, Bernice E. & Wooten, Deborah, eds. Another Jar of Tiny Stars: Poems by More NCTE Award-Winning Poets. (p. 88)
Cullingworth, Phillip. Naptime Adventures with Sleepy Slump: The Kings New Fence. (p. 1229)
Cullis, Megan. Big Book of Big Trains. (p. 179)
—Birds to Color. Cooper, Jenny, illus. (p. 192)
—Butterflies Coloring Book. Cooper, Jenny, illus. (p. 247)
—Essential French Phrases Internet-Referenced. (p. 537)
—See Inside Famous Palaces. (p. 1546)
—Sticker Dressing Heroes. (p. 1650)
Cullis, Megan, jt. auth. see Meredith, Susan.
Cullison, Martha J. Adventures of the Culli Bear Boys. (p. 23)
Cullquipuma, Diana y. Jose, tr. see Elliott, Ruth.
Cullum, A. A. Rugly Puffs: The Bear Detective. (p. 1494)
Cullum, Albert, ed. Geranium on the Windowsill Just Died, but Teacher You Went Right On. (p. 666)
Culotta, Kent, illus. see Ode, Eric.
Culotta, Theodore J. American Railway Association Standard Box Car of 1932. (p. 63)
Culp. Keys to Good Language: Level 3 Test. (p. 950)
—Keys to Good Language: Level 4 Test. (p. 950)
—Keys to Good Language: Level 6 Test. (p. 950)
—Keys to Good Language: Blackline Masters. (p. 950)
—Keys to Good Language. (p. 950)
Culp, Barbara D. Incredible Dream. (p. 869)
Culp, Debbie. Truman Wooley. (p. 1793)
Culp, Jennifer. Call of Duty: Vince Zampella, Grant Collier, & Jason West (p. 254)
—I Have Been Sexually Abused. Now What? (p. 839)
—Neil DeGrasse Tyson. (p. 1240)
—Online Gaming Safety & Privacy. (p. 1298)
—What Are Sedimentary Rocks? (p. 1879)
—What Is a Play? (p. 1888)
Culpepper, Gina G. Felix, jt. auth. see Culpepper, Peter Ryan.
Culpepper, Karen. Homework Monster. (p. 794)
Culpepper, Peter Ryan & Culpepper, Gina G. Felix. Brownie the Lonely Dragon. Make-a-Wish Foundation Staff, ed. (p. 232)
Culpepper, R. B. W. Ellena & the Magic Lamp. (p. 514)
Culpepper, Victoria Lynn Felix, illus. see Culpepper, Peter Ryan & Culpepper, Gina G. Felix.
Culpin, Chris, et al. SHP History. (p. 1571)
—SHP History Year 8. (p. 1571)
Culpin, Christopher. Twentieth Century. (p. 1800)
Culpin, Christopher, jt. auth. see Moore, Ann.
Culturatti Ink, ed. Secrets of the Undercover Gold Digger. (p. 1546)
Culver, Dennis, illus. see Allen, Gregory G.
Culver, Kathy. Things I See When I Open My Eyes. Hauck, Christie, illus. (p. 1733)
Culver, Kathy L. Faith & a Backpack. (p. 565)
—What Will I Be When I Grow Up? (p. 1895)
Culverwell, C. Ellen. Horse Lady. (p. 799)
Culwell, Lori. Dirt. (p. 446)
Cumbaa, Stephen. Bones Book & Skeleton. (p. 209)
—Sea Monsters: A Canadian Museum of Nature Book. Thompson, Margot, illus. (p. 1535)
Cumberbatch, Judith, tr. see Adonis.
Cumberland, Dale. Angel Trap. (p. 74)
Cumberland, Diana. Listen to Your Body: Empowering Children to Be Safe. (p. 1022)
Cumberland, Marcie Hoye. Tree at the Top of the Hill. (p. 1783)
Cumberland, Wendy. Inkwelo Mountain: A Child's Adventure in Kwa Zulu, South Africa. (p. 874)
Cumbie, Patricia. Where People Like Us Live. (p. 1909)
Cumming, Hannah. Cloud. Cumming, Hannah, illus. (p. 334)
—Lost Stars. Cumming, Hannah, illus. (p. 1056)
—Red Boat. Cumming, Hannah, illus. (p. 1453)
Cumming, Peter. Out on the Ice in the Middle of the Bay. Priestley, Alice, illus. (p. 1311)
Cumming, Wendy. How to Soar Like an Eagle When You Are Standing with the Turkeys. (p. 821)
Cummings. Instructor Solutions Manual for Underst Anding Physics. (p. 878)
—Test Bank for Understanding Physics. (p. 1723)
Cummings, Alicia. Adventures of Jayda. (p. 19)
Cummings, Betsy. Real World Careers: Why College Is Not the Only Path to Becoming Rich. (p. 1449)
Cummings, C. R. Boy & the Battleship: The Navy Cadets. (p. 217)
—Cadet Under-Officer: The Army Cadets. (p. 250)
Cummings, David W. How Biddikins & Buddikins Made Santa Claus Work Fast! (p. 805)
Cummings, Diana M. Hardy. Trimp II Mystic Island. (p. 1786)
Cummings, E. E. Fairy Tales. Firmage, George James, ed. (p. 564)
Cummings, Fiona. Party Time. (p. 1326)
Cummings, Jaha F., jt. auth. see Bireda, Martha R.
Cummings, John Michael. Ugly to Start With. (p. 1808)
Cummings, Judy Dodge. Civil War. (p. 325)
—Exploring Polar Regions. (p. 553)
—Macklemore & Ryan Lewis: Grammy-Winning Hip-Hop Duo. (p. 1068)
Cummings, K. M. I Hate Medicine! (p. 839)
Cummings, Karen, et al. Understanding Physics. (p. 1816)
Cummings, Lindsay. Death Code. (p. 420)
—Fires of Calderon. (p. 592)
—Murder Complex. (p. 1192)
—Pillars of Ponderay. (p. 1359)
Cummings, Mag. Fishplates & Frogs. (p. 599)
Cummings, Maris, illus. see Stella, Pilar.
Cummings, Mary. And the Baker's Boy Went to Sea. (p. 71)
Cummings, Matthew. What Is the Legislative Branch? (p. 1890)
Cummings Moore, Thelma Wyatt. Living with a Passion. (p. 1042)
Cummings, Pat. Ananse & the Monster. (p. 67)
—Harvey Moon, Museum Boy. Cummings, Pat, illus. (p. 752)
Cummings, Pat, illus. see Lee, H. Chuku.
Cummings, Pat, illus. see MacDonald, Margaret Read.
Cummings, Pat, illus. see Stroud, Bettye.
Cummings, Phil. Boom Bah! Rycroft, Nina, illus. (p. 213)
Cummings, Priscilla. Autumn Journey Ben-Ami, Doron, illus. (p. 118)
—Beddy Bye in the Bay Ramsey, Marcy Dunn, illus. (p. 156)
—Beetle Boddiker Ramsey, Marcy Dunn, illus. (p. 158)
—Blindsided. (p. 199)
—Cheating for the Chicken Man. (p. 295)
—Chesapeake Rainbow. Aiken, David, illus. (p. 298)
—Face First. (p. 560)
—Journey Back. (p. 927)
—Red Kayak. (p. 1454)
—Santa Claws: The Christmas Crab. Ramsey, Marcy Dunn, illus. (p. 1511)
Cummings, Quasheba Gil. World's First Submarine. (p. 1960)
Cummings, Rhoda & Fisher, Gary. Supera Tus Dificultades de Aprendizaje: Itu Puedes! (p. 1682)
Cummings, Richard. 101 Hand Puppets: A Guide for Puppeteers of All Ages. (p. 1999)
Cummings, Robert. Basketmath: Elementary. (p. 143)
Cummings, Steven, illus. see Westerfeld, Scott & Grayson, Devin.
Cummings, Suzy Lynch. Oh Goodness, Oh Gracious! What Have I Done to my Family? (p. 1280)
Cummings, Terrance, illus. see Stotts, Stuart.
Cummings, Troy. Attack of the Shadow Smashers. (p. 114)
—Charge of the Lightning Bugs. Cummings, Troy, illus. (p. 291)
—Chomp of the Meat-Eating Vegetables. (p. 309)
—Day of the Night Crawlers. (p. 414)
—Eensy Weensy Spider Freaks Out! (p. 505)
—Flurry of the Snombies. (p. 608)
—Giddy-Up, Daddy! (p. 674)
—Notebook of Doom #6: Pop of the Bumpy Mummy (a Branches Book) Cummings, Troy, illus. (p. 1267)
—Notebook of Doom #6: Pop of the Bumpy Mummy (a Branches Book) - Library Edition. (p. 1267)
—Notebook of Doom #7: Flurry of the Snombies (a Branches Book) (p. 1267)
—Notebook of Doom #8: Charge of the Lightning Bugs (a Branches Book) Cummings, Troy, illus. (p. 1267)
—Pop of the Bumpy Mummy. (p. 1384)
—Rise of the Balloon Goons. (p. 1474)
—Whack of the P-Rex. (p. 1877)
Cummings, Troy, illus. see Barton, Chris.
Cummings, Troy, illus. see Griffin, Donna.
Cummings, Troy, illus. see Nesbitt, Kenn.
Cummings, Troy, illus. see Weakland, Mark.
Cummings, W. L. Far West Texas Christmas (p. 572)
Cummins, Amanda Lynn. Wolf: The Untold Story. (p. 1943)
Cummins, Chris. Bigsbie - A Bunny's Tale of Surviving Cancer. (p. 185)
Cummins, Judi, creator. Flying Free Again. (p. 610)
—Ginger & Snoops (p. 676)
—Ginger the Mouse Beagle. (p. 677)
—It's Raining Acorns & Ladybugs. (p. 898)
—What's in My Backyard? (p. 1897)
Cummins, Julia, jt. auth. see Cummins, Julie.
Cummins, Julie. Flying Solo: How Ruth Elder Soared into America's Heart. Laugesen, Malene R., illus. (p. 610)
—Sam Patch: Daredevil Jumper. Austin, Michael Allen, illus. (p. 1507)
—Women Explorers. Harness, Cheryl, illus. (p. 1945)
Cummins, Julie & Cummins, Julia. Women Daredevils: Thrills, Chills, & Frills. Harness, Cheryl, illus. (p. 1945)
Cummins, Lucy Ruth, illus. see Travesty, Shrill.
Cummins, Maria S. Lamplighter. (p. 972)
Cummins, Mimi, jt. auth. see Johnson, Kristin.
Cummins, Molly. Jewel of Fez. (p. 917)
Cummins, Pat, illus. see Winthrop, Elizabeth.
Cummins, Sandy, ed. see Readett, Gerard.
Cummins, Sandy, ed. see Schembra, John.
Cummins, Sandy, ed. see Schuler, Betty Jo.
Cummins, Sandy, ed. see St.Clair, Jennifer.
Cummins, Sarah, tr. see Croteau, Marie-Danielle.
Cummins, Sarah, tr. see Décary, Marie.
Cummins, Sarah, tr. see Flutsztejn-Gruda, Ilona.
Cummins, Sarah, tr. see Langlois, Annie.
Cummins, Sarah, tr. see Langlois, Suzanne.
Cummins, Sarah, tr. see Leblanc, Louise.
Cummins, Sarah, tr. see Lemieux, Jean & Casson, Sophie.
Cummins, Sarah, tr. see Lemieux, Jean.
Cummins, Sarah, tr. see Merola, Caroline.
Cummins, Sarah, tr. see Meunier, Sylvain.
Cummins, Sarah, tr. see Plante, Raymond.
Cummins, Scott, illus. see Morris, Rooster.
Cummiskey, Kristen Marie. Bedtime Is Fun. (p. 157)
Cumpiano, Ina. Quinito's Neighborhood (El Vecindario de Quinito) Ramirez, Jose, illus. (p. 1428)
—Quinito's Neighborhood (El Vecindario de Quinito) Ramírez, José, illus. (p. 1428)
Cumpiano, Ina & Ramirez, Jose. Quinito, Day & Night. (p. 1428)
Cumyn, Alan. After Sylvia. (p. 28)
—Dear Sylvia (p. 419)
—Secret Life of Owen Skye. (p. 1541)
—Tilt. (p. 1750)
Cundiff, Joe. Fly to the Moon on a Witch's Broom. (p. 609)
Cundy, Linda. She Acts Very Different. (p. 1564)
Cunha, Francisco. My Very Own Lighthouse. Leal, Joao, tr. from POR. (p. 1221)
Cunha, Stephen F. Bee. (p. 157)
—How to Ace the National Geographic Bee. (p. 814)
—National Geographic Bee. (p. 1231)
Cunha, Stephen F., jt. auth. see Bockenhauer, Mark H.
Cuniff, Joe, illus. see Wilson, Shannan.
Cunill, Pedro. Venezuela II. (p. 1835)
Cunliffe, April. Willy the Weeping Willow. (p. 1934)
Cunliffe, Ian. I Want to Be a Witch. Cunliffe, Ian, illus. (p. 847)
—Sunny Seaside. Cunliffe, Ian, illus. (p. 1677)
Cunliffe, Ian, illus. see Rusling, Annette.
Cunliffe, John. Postman Pat & the Frog Pie Dinner. (p. 1388)
—Postman Pat & the Beast of Greendale (p. 1388)
—Postman Pat & the Big Surprise. (p. 1388)
—Postman Pat & the Goat's Supper. (p. 1388)
—Postman Pat & the Hole in the Road. (p. 1388)
—Postman Pat & the Mystery Tour. (p. 1388)
—Postman Pat & the Robot. (p. 1388)
—Postman Pat & the Sheep of Many Colours. (p. 1388)
—Postman Pat Follows a Trail. (p. 1388)
—Postman Pat Has the Best Village. (p. 1388)
—Postman Pat Has Too Many Parcels (p. 1388)
—Postman Pat in a Muddle. (p. 1388)
—Postman Pat Makes a Clock. (p. 1388)
—Postman Pat Makes an Aeroplane. (p. 1388)
—Postman Pat Misses the Show. (p. 1388)
—Postman Pat Paints the Ceiling. (p. 1388)
—Postman Pat Surprise Breakfast. (p. 1388)
—Postman Pat Takes a Photo. (p. 1388)
—Postman Pat Takes Flight. (p. 1388)
—Postman Pats Special Delivery Bind. (p. 1388)
Cunliffe, Juliette. Chinese Shar Pei Today. (p. 308)
—Encyclopedia of Dog Breeds. (p. 525)
Cunnane, Kelly. Chirchir Is Singing. Daly, Jude, illus. (p. 308)
—Deep in the Sahara. Hadadi, Hoda, illus. (p. 423)
—For You Are a Kenyan Child. Juan, Ana, illus. (p. 616)
Cunniffe, Kim. Friendly Flower. (p. 638)
Cunning, Concord. Scripture Sleuth 3. (p. 1533)
Cunningham, Alan Blain, compiled by. Goodbye My Good Friend: Memories of Lost Animal Companions & Loved Ones. (p. 701)
Cunningham, Alvin Robert. Washington Is Burning! The War of 1812. (p. 1860)
Cunningham, Andrew, tr. see Kishimoto, Masashi.
Cunningham, Ann. Adventures of Bossie & the Circus. (p. 16)
Cunningham, Ann Elizabeth. Sadie Can Count: A Multi-sensory Book Cunningham, Ann Elizabeth, illus. (p. 1501)
Cunningham, Anna. All Aboard! & Treasure. McClurkan, Rob, illus. (p. 41)
—Bedtime & New School. Sharp, Melanie, illus. (p. 156)
—Stormy Day & Snowy Day. Vagnozzi, Barbara, illus. (p. 1656)
Cunningham, Anna & McClurkan, Rob. Rocket Ship/the Planet. Dunton, Trevor, illus. (p. 1483)
Cunningham, Anne, et al. Literacy Center Grade 1+ Edition. (p. 1022)
—Literacy Center Kindergarten Edition. (p. 1022)
Cunningham, Bob, illus. see Boles, Jim.
Cunningham, Charles E., illus. see Beal, Tracy Lynn.
Cunningham, Chet. Prostate Handbook: What Every Man over Forty Needs to Know about His Prostate. (p. 1412)
Cunningham, D. M. Niles Wormwart, Accidental Villain. (p. 1255)
Cunningham, Darrell. Adventures of Stan: Book One the Awakening. (p. 23)
Cunningham, David L. & Ratto EdM, Linda Lee. Holy Hostage. (p. 791)
Cunningham, Edie. One Day. McInturff, Linda & Brownlie, Ian, illus. (p. 1294)
—Trust & Obey: A Visualized Gospel Song. Anthoine, Leila et al, illus. (p. 1793)
Cunningham, Elaine. Ethan, a Soccer Player for Jesus. Valliant, Kristi, illus. (p. 539)
—Missing in Madagascar. (p. 1152)
Cunningham, Gillie, jt. auth. see Redston, Chris.
Cunningham, Greg P. Journey to Jupiter (p. 928)
Cunningham, Imogen, photos by see Sills, Leslie.
Cunningham, Jesse G., ed. McCarthy Hearings. (p. 1114)
Cunningham, Julia. Burnish Me Bright. (p. 244)
Cunningham, Karen. I See a Bug (p. 845)
Cunningham, Kay. Bucky: The Adventures of the Dinosaur Cowboy. Wilson, Mary Ann, illus. (p. 234)
Cunningham, Kelley. Ultimate How-To-Draw Real Stuff Book. (p. 1809)
Cunningham, Kelley, illus. see Harrison, David L.
Cunningham, Kelley, illus. see Sobel, M., et al.
Cunningham, Kelley, illus. see Spirn, M. S.
Cunningham, Kelley, illus. see Townsend, John.
Cunningham, Kevin. Americas Before 1492. (p. 64)
—Boston Tea Party. (p. 215)
—Bubonic Plague. (p. 233)
—Cell Phones. (p. 286)
—Colas. (p. 338)
—Computer Graphics: From Concept to Consumer. (p. 354)
—Computers. (p. 355)
—Condoleezza Rice. (p. 356)
—Connecticut Colony. (p. 358)
—Contemporary United States. (p. 360)
—Delaware Colony. (p. 424)
—Diseases in History (p. 450)
—Flu. (p. 608)
—Gasoline. (p. 657)
—Georgia Colony. (p. 665)
—HIV/AIDS. (p. 786)
—How Political Campaigns & Elections Work. (p. 812)
—Malaria. (p. 1083)
—Maryland Colony. (p. 1101)
—Massachusetts Colony. (p. 1102)
—Migration from Africa (p. 1141)
—New Hampshire Colony. (p. 1245)
—New Jersey Colony. (p. 1245)
—New York Colony. (p. 1248)
—North Carolina Colony. (p. 1265)
—Nurse. (p. 1273)
—Pandemics. (p. 1321)
—Pencils. (p. 1336)
—Plague. (p. 1366)
—Reading Maps. (p. 1446)
—Rhode Island Colony. (p. 1468)
—Roller Coasters: From Concept to Consumer. (p. 1485)
—Soil. (p. 1606)
—South Carolina Colony. (p. 1616)
—Surviving Droughts & Famines (p. 1687)
—Surviving Tsunamis (p. 1687)
—Teacher. (p. 1709)
—Toys: From Concept to Consumer. (p. 1774)
—Toys. (p. 1774)
—Types of Maps. (p. 1805)
—Video Game Designer. (p. 1841)
—Video Games: From Concept to Consumer. (p. 1841)
—Virginia Colony. (p. 1844)
—Wildfires. (p. 1931)
Cunningham, Kevin & Benoit, Peter. Cheyenne. (p. 299)
—Comanche. (p. 346)
—Inuit. (p. 883)
—Lakota Sioux. (p. 972)
—Navajo. (p. 1237)
—Pueblo. (p. 1414)
—Sioux. (p. 1580)
—Ute. (p. 1829)
—Wampanoag. (p. 1856)
—Zuni. (p. 1990)

Cunningham, Kim Webster, jt. auth. see Webster, Dennis.
Cunningham, Laura. Bay Area Through Time. (p. 147)
Cunningham, Laura S., jt. auth. see Cunningham, Laura Shaine.
Cunningham, Laura Shaine & Cunningham, Laura S. Midnight Diary of Zoya Blume. (p. 1138)
Cunningham, Leisa. Santa All Year Long. (p. 1511)
Cunningham, Mark. Meet Ankylosaurus. (p. 1120)
—Meet Iguanodon. (p. 1121)
—Molly Pitcher. (p. 1161)
Cunningham, Mark, jt. auth. see Madison, Richard.
Cunningham, Mark E. & Zwier, Lawrence. Aftermath of the French Defeat in Vietnam. (p. 28)
Cunningham, Mark E. & Zwier, Lawrence J. End of the Shoguns & the Birth of Modern Japan. (p. 526)
Cunningham, Mary. Curse of the Bayou. (p. 394)
—Cynthias Attic Magicians Castle. (p. 397)
—Magic Medallion. (p. 1072)
—Missing Locket. (p. 1152)
Cunningham, Michael & Briscoe, Connie. Jewels: 50 Phenomenal Black Women over 50. (p. 917)
Cunningham, P. E. Slayer for Hire. (p. 1588)
Cunningham, Patricia. Making Places. (p. 1082)
Cunningham, Patricia M., jt. auth. see Hall, Dorothy P.
Cunningham, Patrick. How to Dazzle at Macbeth. (p. 816)
—How to Dazzle at Romeo & Juliet. (p. 816)
—Mexico. (p. 1131)
Cunningham, Paul, illus. see Dateno, Maria Grace.
Cunningham, Raymond Kelly, Jr. & Shoaf, Molly Spencer. From the Timber to the Prairie: A History of Homer Illinois (p. 644)
Cunningham, Rob, illus. see Sandler, Steve.
Cunningham, Robin. Little Tuatara. (p. 1037)
Cunningham, Ryan. Gary's Gray World. (p. 657)
Cunningham, S. C. Ginormous Joe's Broken Bark. (p. 677)
Cunningham, Sarah. Donkey in the Living Room: A Tradition That Celebrates the Real Meaning of Christmas. Foster, Michael K., illus. (p. 466)
—Donkey in the Living Room Nativity Set: A Tradition That Celebrates the True Meaning of Christmas. Foster, Michael K., illus. (p. 466)
Cunningham, Scott. Scooby-Doo & the Hungry Ghost. Duendes Del Sur Staff, illus. (p. 1529)
Cunningham, Scott, jt. auth. see Pyle, Kevin C.
Cunningham, Sheila S. Willow's Walkabout: A Children's Guide to Boston. Kelleher, Kathie, illus. (p. 1934)
Cunningham, Steven C. Dinosaur Name Poems/Poemas de Nombres de Dinosaurios. Gorospe, Myriam, tr. (p. 442)
Cunningham, Terri Ann. Hillary Hind Hooth Lost Her Tooth. (p. 779)
Cunningham, Thelma. Lisa's Unforgettable Stories. (p. 1022)
CUNNINGHAM, WHO AM I SAUNDA. Who am I? (p. 1914)
Cunningham-Burkhardt, Tobbie. Bullfrog in a Dress. (p. 240)
Cuno, Sabine. Abre, Cierra y Aprende! Caballero, D., tr. (p. 7)
Cunxin, Li. Mao's Last Dancer. (p. 1089)
Cunyus, John G. Path Beyond Suffering: Working the Buddhist Method. (p. 1328)
Cunyus, John Grady, tr. Way of Wisdom: Job, Proverbs, Ecclesiastes, Song of Solomon. (p. 1864)
Cupala, Holly. Don't Breathe a Word. (p. 467)
—Tell Me a Secret. (p. 1716)
Cupolo, Eileen, illus. see Webb, Jane K.
Cupp, Dave, jt. auth. see Minden, Cecilia.
Cupp, Dave & Minden, Cecilia. Television Reporters. (p. 1716)
Cupp, Quentin O. Kidlings of Tiger Island 2. (p. 952)
Cupp, Tonya. Taylor Swift. (p. 1708)
Cupper, Karin. More Adventures from Eidland. (p. 1174)
Cupples, Andrew, et al. Airlock. (p. 31)
Cupples, Pat, illus. see Dickson, Louise.
Cupples, Pat, illus. see Mason, Adrienne.
Cupples, Patricia, illus. see Mason, Adrienne.
Cuqui. Little House Without Windows: A Casinha sem Janelas. (p. 1029)
Curatilo Zieminski, D. Stumbling but Not Falling. (p. 1670)
Curato, Mike. Little Elliot, Big City. Curato, Mike, illus. (p. 1027)
Curatola Knowles, Carmela N. Piano & Laylee & the Cyberbully. (p. 1354)
—Piano & Laylee & the Cyberbully. Lewellen, Emily, illus. (p. 1354)
—Piano & Laylee Go Online. (p. 1354)
—Piano & Laylee Go Online. Lewellen, Emily, illus. (p. 1354)
—Piano & Laylee Learn about Acceptable Use Policies. Lewellen, Emily, illus. (p. 1354)
Curcio Malicia, Jeannette. If the Ladybugs Came to Stay. (p. 854)
Curelli, Augusta, jt. auth. see Wright, Melissa.
Cureton-Heifner, Donna Lynn. Adventures of Itsy & Willy Wabbit: In Search of Lillian the Ladybug. (p. 19)
Curfew, Baron. Around the Houses. (p. 100)
Curham, Siobhan. Dark of the Moon. (p. 408)
—Finding Cherokee Brown. (p. 588)
Curl, Terry J. Abby's Aunt Ate All the Apples. (p. 2)
Curlee, Lynn. Ballpark: The Story of America's Baseball Fields. Curlee, Lynn, illus. (p. 135)
—Capital. Curlee, Lynn, illus. (p. 262)
—Liberty. Curlee, Lynn, illus. (p. 1005)
—Mythological Creatures: A Classical Bestiary. Curlee, Lynn, illus. (p. 1227)
—Parthenon. Curlee, Lynn, illus. (p. 1325)
—Skyscraper. Curlee, Lynn, illus. (p. 1587)
—Trains. Curlee, Lynn, illus. (p. 1777)
Curless, Allan, illus. see Jacques, Brian.
Curley, Andrea, ed. see Dorling Kindersley Publishing Staff.
Curley, Carol, illus. see Sammarco, Teresa
Curley, Marianne. Broken. (p. 230)
—Dark. (p. 407)
—Elegidos. (p. 510)
—Key. (p. 950)
—Old Magic. (p. 1284)
—Oscuridad. (p. 1305)
Curley, Robert. Britannica Guide to Geometry. Hosch, William L., ed. (p. 229)
—Renewable & Alternative Energy. (p. 1460)
—Spy Agencies, Intelligence Operations, & the People Behind Them. Curley, Robert, ed. (p. 1635)
Curley, Robert, contrib. by. Explorers of the Renaissance. (p. 551)
Curley, Robert, ed. 100 Most Influential Inventors of All Time. (p. 1998)
—Britannica Guide to Inventions That Changed the Modern World. (p. 229)
—Complete History of Aviation: From Ballooning to Supersonic Flight. (p. 353)
—Complete History of Ships & Boats: From Sails & Oars to Nuclear-Powered Vessels. (p. 353)
—Computing: From the Abacus to the IPad. (p. 355)
—New Thinking about Pollution. (p. 1247)
—Weapons of Mass Destruction. (p. 1869)
Curlin, Tera. Pat's Mountain (p. 1329)
Curmi, Serena, illus. see Enderle, Judith Ross & Gordon, Stephanie Jacob.
Curnin, V. J. Millie's Magic Wellies. (p. 1144)
Curnow, Bobby. Applejack. Hickey, Brenda, illus. (p. 92)
Curr, Martin. Sharp Claws Learns to Swim. (p. 1563)
currah, ruth. Grandma's Wisdom: In Short Stories Vol 1. (p. 709)
Curran, Abbey & Kaye, Elizabeth. Courage to Compete: Living with Cerebral Palsy & Following My Dreams. (p. 372)
Curran, Bob. Frankenstein & Other Man-Made Monsters. (p. 629)
Curran, Christine Perdan, ed. Metabolic Processes & Energy Transfers: An Anthology of Current Thought. (p. 1130)
Curran, Greg. Homework Helpers Chemistry: Chemistry. (p. 794)
—Physics. (p. 1353)
Curran, John. When I First Saw Santa. (p. 1902)
Curran, Kim. Control. (p. 361)
Curran, M. J, creator. Power Patterns with Professor Jiaozi Jiachong (English/Chinese Version) Real English in the Real World. (p. 1390)
Curran, Steven Earl. Whales used to Fly in the Sky. (p. 1878)
Currant, Gary, illus. see Berry, Ron & Sharp, Chris.
Currant, Gary, illus. see Fuerst, Jeffrey B.
Currant, Gary, illus. see Hall, Pamela.
Curreli, Augusta, illus. see Amadeo, Diana M.
Curreli, Augusta, illus. see Wright, Melissa & Curelli, Augusta.
Curren, Cindy, illus. see Bryan-Brown, Kim.
Currey, Andrew K., illus. see Marranzino, Sami.
Currey, Anna. Albertine. (p. 35)
—Christmas Unicorn. (p. 316)
—Hush-a-Bye, Baby: And Other Nursery Rhymes. (p. 830)
—Pat-a-Cake: And Other Nursery Rhymes. (p. 1327)
—Ring-a-Ring O' Roses: And Other Nursery Rhymes. (p. 1473)
—Truffle Goes to Town. Currey, Anna, illus. (p. 1793)
Currey, Anna, illus. see Donaldson, Julia.
Currey, Anna, illus. see Napoli, Donna Jo.
Currey, Anna, illus. see Shields, Gillian.
Currey, Anna, illus. see Umansky, Kaye & Umansky.
Currey, Anna, illus. see Umansky, Kaye.
Currey, Anna, illus. see Wilson, Karma.
Currey, Anna, jt. illus. see Umansky, Kaye.
Currey, Carolyn Joy, jt. auth. see Thomson, Rachel Starr.
Currey, Erica Leigh, illus. see Croall, Marie.
Curriculum Associates Staff. Ready New York CCLS Common Core Math Instruction 2014: Grade 4. (p. 1447)
Curriculum Associates Staff, ed. Spelling Power Book H. (p. 1625)
Curriculum Committee, jt. auth. see CA HS Speech Association.
Curriculum Corporation. Tai Hao Le! (p. 1695)
Currie, Cherie & O'Neill, Tony. Neon Angel: A Memoir of a Runaway. (p. 1241)
Currie, David P. & Stevos, Joyce L. Constitution: Student Text. (p. 359)
Currie, Justin, illus. see Wolff, Susan.
Currie, Lindsay, jt. auth. see Leaver, Trisha.
Currie, Lisa. Me, You, Us: A Book to Fill Out Together. (p. 1116)
Currie, Philip J. & Koppelhus, Eva B. 101 Questions about Dinosaurs. (p. 1999)
Currie, Robin. Baby Bible 123. (p. 125)
—Baby Bible ABC. (p. 125)
—Baby Bible ABCs Basaluzzo, Constanza, illus. (p. 125)
—Baby Bible Animals Basaluzzo, Constanza, illus. (p. 125)
—Baby Bible Animals. (p. 125)
—Baby Bible Storybook for Boys. Busaluzzo, Constanza, illus. (p. 125)
—Biblia Para los Bebes. (p. 176)
—Biblia para los Bebes el Padre Nuestro: The Lord's Prayer. (p. 176)
Currie, Robin, jt. auth. see David C. Cook Publishing Company Staff.
Currie, Stephen. Adrian Peterson. (p. 13)
—African-American Folklore. (p. 27)
—African-American Inventors. (p. 27)
—African-American Literature. (p. 27)
—Antarctica. (p. 88)
—Australia & the Pacific Islands. (p. 116)
—Birmingham Church Bombing. (p. 192)
—Cheating. (p. 295)
—Cycling. Greenhaven Press Editors, ed. (p. 397)
—Ecosystems. (p. 503)
—Environmentalism in America. (p. 532)
—Escapes from Man-Made Disasters. (p. 535)
—Escapes from Natural Disasters. (p. 535)
—Escapes from Nazi Persecution. (p. 535)
—Escapes from Slavery. (p. 535)
—Goblins. (p. 688)
—Himalayas. (p. 780)
—Hydropower. (p. 831)
—Importance of Evolution Theory. (p. 862)
—Junk Food. (p. 936)
—Medieval Crusades. (p. 1119)
—Medieval Punishment & Torture. (p. 1119)
—Outsourcing America. (p. 1313)
—Panama Canal. (p. 1320)
—Peculiar Institution: Slavery in the Plantation South. (p. 1334)
—Quest for Freedom: The Abolitionist Movement. (p. 1426)
—Religious Oppression. (p. 1458)
—Renaissance. (p. 1460)
—Struggle for Equality: Landmark Court Cases. (p. 1668)
—Tallest Building. (p. 1704)
—West Africa. (p. 1876)
currie, stephen. What Is the Future of Hydropower? (p. 1890)
Currie, Stephen, ed. see Nardo, Don.
Currie, Stephen & National Geographic Learning Staff. Expeditions in the Americas, 1492-1700. (p. 548)
—Missions in Space. (p. 1153)
—Travels to Distant Lands, 1000-1400. (p. 1780)
Currie, Tamicia. Juice & Berries History Adventure: To the Whitehouse! (p. 932)
Currie, Tamicia, adapted by. Juice & Berries History Adventure: Peanut Butter & Sweet Potato Pie. (p. 932)
Curriel, Hector, illus. see Kratz, Marilyn.
Currie-McGhee, L. K. Alicia Keys. (p. 40)
—Biofuels: By Leanne Currie-Mcghee. (p. 188)
—Drug Addiction. (p. 486)
—Miley Cyrus. (p. 1142)
—What Are Sleep Disorders? (p. 1879)
currie-mcghee, leanne. Teenage Alcoholism. (p. 1714)
Currie-McGhee, Leanne. Teenage Drug Abuse. (p. 1714)
Currie-McGhee, Leanne, jt. auth. see George, Charles.
Currie-McGhee, Leanne K. AIDS. (p. 30)
—Brittany & Robbie Bergquist: Cell Phones for Soldiers. (p. 230)
—Emmanuel Osofu Yeboah: Champion for Ghana's Disabled. (p. 520)
—Exercise Addiction. (p. 548)
—Mattie Stepanek: Inspirational Poet. (p. 1110)
—Sexually Transmitted Diseases. (p. 1556)
Currie-McGhee, Leanne K., jt. auth. see Mooney, Carla.
Currier, Alvin Alexsi. Wonderful Life of Russia's Saint Sergius of Radonezh. Glazunova, Nadezda, illus. (p. 1948)
Currier Brileya, Elizabeth. Grandma B. 's Bedtime Stories. (p. 708)
Currier, Katrina Saltonstall. Kai's Journey to Gold Mountain: An Angel Island Story. (p. 941)
Currim, Nazli. Grandma Lives with Us. Tung, Kadhima Ren, illus. (p. 708)
Currington, Rebecca. Winter Fun: Bible-Based Christmas Activities for Kids. (p. 1938)
Curry, Casey. I Remember You Today: An Interactive Picturebook for Children Dealing with the Loss of a Sibling or Parent. (p. 844)
Curry, Cicero. Tickle Man. Ledbetter, John'el, illus. (p. 1747)
Curry, Don, ed. see Meredith Books Staff.
Curry, Don, ed. Crate Escape No. 2. (p. 376)
—DC Heroes Ultimate Color & Activity Set. (p. 415)
—Esape Africa. (p. 534)
—Jungle Fun: Puzzles & Games. (p. 935)
—Madagascar (p. 1069)
Curry, Don L. En Mi Patio. Brown, Erin O'Leary, illus. (p. 522)
—Fall Leaves. Jasinski, Aaron, illus. (p. 566)
—How Do Your Lungs Work? (p. 808)
—How Does Your Brain Work? (p. 809)
—In My Backyard. O'Leary Brown, Erin, illus. (p. 864)
—Take Care of Your Eyes. (p. 1696)
—Take Care of Your Teeth. (p. 1696)
—What Is Mass? (p. 1889)
—What Is Matter? (p. 1889)
—Willie's Word World. Stromoski, Rick, illus. (p. 1934)
Curry, Don L. & O'Leary Brown, Erin. En Mi Patio. O'Leary Brown, Erin, illus. (p. 522)
Curry, Elizabeth & Curry, Judson. Midwest (p. 1139)
Curry, Ella I. Ella's Little Cookbook. (p. 514)
Curry, Erastus S. Pre-Historic Races of America & Other Lands as Disclosed Thru Indian Traditions, Comprehending Also the Origin of Matter & the Formation of the World. (p. 1394)
Curry, Francis X. Just Stories. (p. 940)
Curry, Garrett A., illus. see El Wilson, Barbara.
Curry, Jane Louise. Black Canary. (p. 195)
—Egyptian Box. (p. 506)
—Hold up the Sky: And Other Native American Tales from Texas & The. Watts, James, illus. (p. 788)
Curry, Jane Louise & Livy. Brave Cloelia: Retold from the Account in the History of Early Rome by the Roman Historian Titus Livius. Crosby, Jeff, illus. (p. 223)
Curry, Judi. Moose & the Elk. (p. 1173)
Curry, Judson, jt. auth. see Curry, Elizabeth.
Curry, Kenneth. Chuka & the Drum. (p. 318)
—Fuzzy & the All Bear Band. (p. 651)
—Legend of the Dancing Trees: An African American Folk Tale. (p. 989)
—Mandu & Minka. (p. 1087)
—Priscilla & the Reindeer. (p. 1407)
—Priscilla & the Talking Monkey. (p. 1407)
—Return of Gamalok: The Return of Gamalok. (p. 1464)
—Star & Peanut. (p. 1640)
Curry, Kenneth, et al. Legend of the Dancing Tees Teachers Resource: The Legend of the Dancing Trees. (p. 989)
Curry, Marion. 1000 Facts on Horses. (p. 2001)
—Horse & Pony Basics. (p. 799)
—Horse & Pony Breeds. (p. 799)
—Horse & Pony Care. (p. 799)
—Horse & Pony Competitions. (p. 799)
Curry, Peter. Millie at Home. (p. 1144)
—Millie Goes Driving. (p. 1144)
—Millie Goes Shopping. (p. 1144)
—Millie in the Garden. (p. 1144)
Curry, Peter, illus. see Powell, R.
Curry Smallwood, Yvonne. Transitioning Through Real Teen Life: A Common Sense Guide for Today's Teen. (p. 1778)
Curry, Tom, illus. see Kelley, Ellen A.
Curry, Tom, illus. see Lewis, J. Patrick.
Curry, Tom, illus. see Wojciechowski, Susan.
Cursha Pierce-Lunderman. God's Going Too! His Promises for Kids During Deployments. (p. 691)
Curtain-Phillips, Marilyn. Who Is This Mathematician/Scientist? A Diverse Collection of Biographies. (p. 1916)
Curtatone, Raffaello. Adventures of Mr Greenwood from Jamaic. (p. 20)
Curtayne, Alice. Twenty Tales of Irish Saints. (p. 1801)
Curte, Asia, jt. auth. see Vodicka-Paredes, Lenka.
Curti, Anna M., illus. see Paltro, Piera.
Curtin, Jeremiah. Introduction to Seneca Fiction, Legends, & Myths: With J. N. B. Hewitt. (p. 882)
Curtin, Judi. Alice Again. Fox, Woody, illus. (p. 39)
—Alice in the Middle. Fox, Woody, illus. (p. 39)
—Alice Next Door. Fox, Woody, illus. (p. 39)
—Don't Ask Alice. Fox, Woody, illus. (p. 466)
—Eva & the Hidden Diary. Fox, Woody, illus. (p. 540)
—Eva's Holiday. (p. 541)
—Leave It to Eva. (p. 986)
Curtin, Judi & Meaney, Roisin. See If I Care. (p. 1546)
Curtin, Mallory. There Are Dogs. (p. 1729)
Curtis, Alice. Little Maid of New Orleans. (p. 1031)
—Little Maid of Newport. Price, Hattie Longstreet, illus. (p. 1031)
Curtis, Alice Turner. Frontier Girl of New York. Snyder, Harold E., illus. (p. 644)
—Yankee Girl at Fort Sumter. (p. 1968)
Curtis, Andrea. What's for Lunch? Duivenvoorden, Yvonne, photos by. (p. 1897)
Curtis, Annabelle. Paper People: A Collection of Delightful Paper Characters to Make Yourself. (p. 1322)
Curtis, Bruce, photos by see Krezel, Cindy.
Curtis, Carolyn. I Took the Moon for a Walk. Jay, Alison, illus. (p. 847)
Curtis, Carolyn, jt. auth. see Jay, Alison.
Curtis, Carolyn, et al. Lleve a la Luna a Pasear. Jay, Alison, illus. (p. 1043)
Curtis, Chary. Fancy & Brandy Peacock. (p. 570)
Curtis, Christopher Paul. Bucking the Sarge. (p. 234)
—Bud, Not Buddy. (p. 234)
—Elijah of Buxton. (p. 512)
—Madman of Piney Woods. (p. 1070)
—Mighty Miss Malone. (p. 1140)
—Mr. Chickee's Funny Money. (p. 1184)
—Mr. Chickee's Messy Mission. (p. 1184)
—Watsons Go to Birmingham 1963. (p. 1864)
—Watsons Go to Birmingham—1963. (p. 1864)
Curtis, Christopher Paul & Paul, Curtis Christopher. Elias de Buxton. (p. 512)
Curtis, D. D. Catching Rodeo Fever. (p. 279)
Curtis, Dolores. Rhyming Pretzels. (p. 1468)
Curtis, E., illus. see Varsell, Linda.
Curtis, Eugene G. Nazi Gold in New Hampshire (p. 1238)
Curtis, Gavin. Bat Boy & His Violin. (p. 143)
—Bat Boy & His Violin. Lewis, E. B., illus. (p. 143)
Curtis, Howard, tr. see Izzo, Jean-Claude.
Curtis, Jamie Lee. A Donde Van los Globos? Cornell, Laura, illus. (p. 1)
—Big Words for Little People. Cornell, Laura, illus. (p. 184)
—Boy/Girl Book. Cornell, Laura, illus. (p. 220)
—I'm Gonna Like Me: Letting off a Little Self-Esteem. Cornell, Laura, illus. (p. 859)
—Is There Really a Human Race? Cornell, Laura, illus. (p. 890)
—It's Hard to Be Five: Learning How to Work My Control Panel. Cornell, Laura, illus. (p. 897)
—Jamie Lee Curtis's Books to Grow by Treasury. Cornell, Laura, illus. (p. 907)
—My Brave Year of Firsts: Tries, Sighs, & High Fives. Cornell, Laura, illus. (p. 1199)
—My Mommy Hung the Moon: A Love Story. (p. 1214)
—My Mommy Hung the Moon: A Love Story. Cornell, Laura, illus. (p. 1214)
—Tell Me Again about the Night I Was Born. (p. 1716)
—Today I Feel Silly & Other Moods That Make My Day. Cornell, Laura, illus. (p. 1760)
—When I Was Little: A Four-Year-Old's Memoir of Her Youth. (p. 1903)
Curtis, Jennifer. Scute Salute. (p. 1534)
Curtis, Jennifer Keats. Animal Helpers: Zoos (p. 78)
—Animal Helpers: Aquariums (p. 78)
—Animal Helpers: Sanctuaries (p. 78)
—Animal Helpers: Raptor Centers (p. 78)
—Ayudantes de Animales: Acuarios (p. 121)
—Baby Owl's Rescue Jacques, Laura, illus. (p. 127)
—Camada con Suerte: Cachorros de Lobo Rescatados de un Incendio Forestal. Gomes, John, illus. (p. 255)
—Kali's Story: An Orphaned Polar Bear Rescue Gomes, John, photos by. (p. 942)
—Lucky Litter: Wolf Pups Rescued from Wildfire. Gomes, John, illus. (p. 1062)
—Osprey Adventure. Ramsey, Marcy Dunn, illus. (p. 1306)
—Primate School (p. 1400)
—Saving Squeak: The Otter Tale Ramsey, Marcy Dunn, illus. (p. 1517)
—Seahorses. Wallace, Chad, illus. (p. 1536)
—Squirrel Rescue Jacques, Laura, illus. (p. 1637)
—Turtles in My Sandbox Schongut, Emanuel, illus. (p. 1799)
Curtis, Jennifer Keats & Frederick, J. Adam. Salamander Season Bersani, Shennen, illus. (p. 1504)
Curtis, Jennifer Keats, et al. Temporada de Salamandras. (p. 1718)
Curtis, Jessica Lynn. Papa's New Home. Harmon, Steve, illus. (p. 1322)
Curtis, Jillian M. Little Prince & His Magic Wand. (p. 1033)
Curtis, Joan Scott. Number Fairy. (p. 1271)
Curtis, Kelli. Amber & the Fallen Bridge. (p. 56)
Curtis King, jt. auth. see Tshekeche, Anna.
Curtis King, Anna, illus. see Tshekeche.
Curtis, Marci Lyn. One Thing. (p. 1297)
Curtis, Mary. Little Stinky Gets Ready for School. (p. 1036)
Curtis, Morgan. Second-hand Alligata: A Cajun Tale. (p. 1539)
Curtis, Neil, illus. see Grant, Joan.
Curtis, Neil, jt. auth. see Farrer, Vashti.
Curtis, Philip. Senor Browser y los Afilacerebros. Ross, Tony, illus. (p. 1550)
Curtis, Rebecca S. Charlotte Avery on Isle Royale. (p. 293)
Curtis, S. R. Bandidos Fantasmas. (p. 136)

—Muertos no Hablan. (p. 1189)
—Origen de la Leyenda. (p. 1304)
Curtis, Sarah. Wondrous Flower. (p. 1949)
Curtis, Scotty. Music Room: Syd Finds His Tune. (p. 1193)
Curtis, Shelly. Shellbear's Adventures. (p. 1564)
Curtis, Stacy, illus. see Covey, Sean.
Curtis, Stacy, illus. see Haig, Matt.
Curtis, Stacy, illus. see Katz, Alan.
Curtis, Stacy, illus. see Knudson, Mike & Wilkinson, Steve.
Curtis, Stacy, illus. see Krensky, Stephen.
Curtis, Stacy, illus. see Regan, Dian Curtis.
Curtis, Stacy, illus. see Tocher, Timothy.
Curtis, Stephen, ed. see Manser, Martin H.
Curtis, Suzanne. John Wesley Powell: American Hero. (p. 923)
Curtis, Tony. Gnomes of Genom. (p. 685)
Curtis, Vanessa. Baking Life of Amelie Day. (p. 133)
—Zelah Green: Who Says I'm a Freak? (p. 1986)
Curtis, Vanessa & Quarto Generic Staff. Taming of Lilah May. (p. 1704)
Curtis, Walter J., Sr. History's Master Golfers: The Only Four-Time Champions of the U. S. Open & the Only Four-or-More Time Champions of the British Open. (p. 785)
Curtiss, A. B. Dragons Guard the Zoo. (p. 479)
—Little Chapel That Stood Golino, Mirto, illus. (p. 1026)
Curtiss, A. B., jt. auth. see Curtiss, A. B.
Curtiss, A. B. & Curtiss, A. B. Hanner & the Bullies. Brown, Jason, illus. (p. 743)
Curtiss, A. B. & Lucarelli, Sue. T Bear's Tale. (p. 1693)
Curtiss, Dominique. Where Do I Come From? Hill, Rowland, tr. (p. 1907)
Curtiss, Melody, illus. see Robinson, Kelley.
Curtiss, Phebe A. Christmas Stories & Legends. Curtiss, Phebe A., ed. (p. 315)
Curtiss, Phebe A., ed. Christmas Stories & Legends. (p. 315)
Curto Family, The, jt. auth. see Moore, Clement C.
Curto Family, The & Fischer, Rusty. One Little Christmas Tree. (p. 1295)
Curto, Rosa M. Art from Simple Shapes: Make Amazing Art from 8 Simple Geometric Shapes! Includes a Shape Stencil. (p. 102)
—Draw the Magic Blue Fairy. (p. 481)
—Draw the Magic Green Fairy. (p. 481)
—Draw the Magic Pink Fairy. (p. 481)
—Draw the Magic Red Fairy. (p. 481)
—Fingerprint Drawing: Art Fun at Your Fingertips! (p. 589)
—Fun & Easy Drawing at Sea. (p. 647)
—Fun & Easy Drawing Fantasy Characters. (p. 647)
—Fun & Easy Drawing on the Farm. (p. 647)
—Fun & Easy Drawing Storybook Characters. (p. 647)
Curto, Rosa M., illus. see Candell, Arianna.
Curto, Rosa M., illus. see Jimenez, Nuria & Jimenez, Empar.
Curto, Rosa M., illus. see Moore-Mallinos, Jennifer & Moore-Mallinos, Jennifer.
Curto, Rosa Maria. Draw the Magic Green Fairy. (p. 481)
Curto, Rosa Maria, illus. see Bailer, Darice & Dominguez, Madelca.
Curto, Rosa Maria, illus. see Combel Editorial Staff & catalán, Cuento popular.
Curto, Rosa Maria, illus. see Moore-Mallinos, Jennifer & Moore-Mallinos, Jennifer.
Curto, Rosa Maria, illus. see Roca, Nuria.
Curtsinger, Bill, illus. see Cerullo, Mary M.
Curtsinger, Bill, photos by see Cerullo, Mary M.
Curwood, James Oliver. Baree Son of Kazan. (p. 139)
—Country Beyond. (p. 372)
—Flaming Forest. (p. 602)
Cusack, Bob. Squirming Squirrel. (p. 1637)
Cusack, Dale. Grace & the Drawl. (p. 704)
—Grace & the Revenge of the Drawl. (p. 704)
—Gwen & the Dragon. (p. 733)
Cusack, Elizabeth, illus. see Whitaker, Joan.
Cusack, Geraldine O'Connell. Wrecker's Cove. (p. 1962)
Cush, Don. School of the Future: The Dawning of Aquarius. (p. 1523)
Cushenberry, Lisa. No Tears for Teary. (p. 1260)
Cushing, Christopher. Let's Celebrate! (p. 995)
Cushing, Mims. Sleepover Surprise. Phillips, Alan, illus. (p. 1589)
Cushion, Hazel. Triplet Tales. Platt, Brian, illus. (p. 1787)
Cushman, Amanda, tr. from SON. Zarma Folktales of Niger. (p. 1985)
Cushman, Clare. Supreme Court Decisions & Women's Rights (p. 1684)
Cushman, Clare, et al. Black, White, & Brown: The Landmark School Desegregation Case in Retrospect (p. 197)
Cushman, Doug. Dirk Bones & the Mystery of the Haunted House. (p. 445)
—Dirk Bones & the Mystery of the Haunted House. Cushman, Doug, illus. (p. 445)
—Inspector Hopper's Mystery Year Cushman, Doug, illus. (p. 878)
—Pigmares: Porcine Poems of the Silver Screen. (p. 1358)
—Pigmares: Porcine Poems of the Silver Screen. Cushman, Doug, illus. (p. 1358)
—Space Cat. Cushman, Doug, illus. (p. 1618)
Cushman, Doug, illus. see Calmenson, Stephanie.
Cushman, Doug, illus. see Deàk, Erzsi.
Cushman, Doug, illus. see Franco, Betsy.
Cushman, Doug, illus. see Hazen, Lynn E.
Cushman, Doug, illus. see Markel, Michelle.
Cushman, Doug, illus. see Prelutsky, Jack.
Cushman, Doug, illus. see Regan, Dian Curtis.
Cushman, Doug, illus. see Roberts, Bethany.
Cushman, Doug, illus. see Roth, Carol.
Cushman, Doug, illus. see Sierra, Judy.
Cushman, Doug, illus. see Simon, Seymour & Fauteux, Nicole.
Cushman, Doug, illus. see Strasser, Todd.
Cushman, Doug, illus. see Tegen, Katherine.
Cushman, Doug, illus. see Weeks, Sarah.
Cushman, Doug, illus. see Williams, Jacklyn.
Cushman, Doug, illus. see Wood, Douglas.
Cushman, Doug, illus. see Yorinks, Arthur.
Cushman, Douglas, illus. see Wilson, Karma.
Cushman, Jean. Do You Wanna Bet? Your Chance to Find Out about Probability. Weston, Martha, illus. (p. 458)
Cushman, Jean, et al. Little Golden Book Mommy Stories. Wilkin, Eloise & Meisel, Paul, illus. (p. 1028)
Cushman, Karen. Alchemy & Meggy Swann. (p. 35)
—Aprendiz de Comadrona. (p. 93)
—Catherine, Called Birdy. (p. 280)
—Libro de Catherine. (p. 1006)
—Matilda Bone. (p. 1109)
—Matilda Huesos. (p. 1109)
—Midwife's Apprentice. (p. 1139)
—Will Sparrow's Road. (p. 1932)
Cushner, Susie, photos by see Barber, Mary Corpening, et al.
Cushner, Susie, photos by see Kahate, Ruta.
Cushner, Susie, photos by see Schmidt, Denyse.
Cusick, Dawn. Animal Tongues. (p. 80)
—Cool Animal Names. (p. 362)
—Get the Scoop on Animal Poop: From Lions to Tapeworms: 251 Cool Facts about Scat, Frass, Dung, & More! (p. 668)
—Get the Scoop on Animal Puke! From Zombie Ants to Vampire Bats, 251 Cool Facts about Vomit, Regurgitation, & More! (p. 668)
Cusick, Dawn & National Wildlife Federation Staff. Animals That Make Me Say Ouch! (p. 84)
—Animals That Make Me Say Wow! (p. 84)
Cusick, Dawn & O'Sullivan, Joanne. Animal Eggs: An Amazing Clutch of Mysteries & Marvels. Greenelsh, Susan, illus. (p. 77)
Cusick, John. Wesleyan University College Prowler off the Record. (p. 1876)
Cusick, John M. Cherry Money Baby. (p. 298)
—Girl Parts. (p. 678)
Cusick, N. L. Tales from Grey Squirrel Manor #1 - a Tale of Two Squirrels. (p. 1701)
Cusick, Richie Tankersley. Blood Brothers: The Unseen #3. (p. 200)
—It Begins - Rest in Peace (p. 893)
—Overdue. (p. 1314)
—Shadow Mirror. (p. 1557)
—Someone at the Door. (p. 1609)
—Spirit Walk: Walk of the Spirits & Shadow Mirror. (p. 1629)
—Starstruck. (p. 1643)
—Summer of Secrets. (p. 1674)
—Unseen 1 It Begins. (p. 1822)
—Unseen 2 Rest in Peace. (p. 1822)
—Unseen IV. (p. 1822)
—Unseen Volume 2: Blood Brothers/Sin & Salvation. (p. 1822)
—Walk of the Spirits. (p. 1853)
Cusick-Dickerson, Heidi Haughy, et al. Sonoma: Ultimate Winery Guide. (p. 1612)
Cusimano/Achieve Publications Staff. Achieve: A Visual Memory Program Levels I-IV Levels I-IV (p. 8)
—Achieve: A Visual Memory Program Levels V & VI Levels V & VI (p. 8)
—Auditory Sequential Memory Instructional Workbook: For the Development of Auditory Processing & Listening of Numbers, Letters & Words. (p. 115)
Cusiter, M. & Cusiter, V. Creelman HSC Exam Questions: Chemistry 2008 Edition. (p. 380)
Cusiter, V., jt. auth. see Cusiter, M.
Cussen, Sarah. Those Beautiful Butterflies. Weaver, Steve, illus. (p. 1740)
—Those Enormous Elephants. Weaver, Steve, illus. (p. 1740)
—Those Peculiar Pelicans. Weaver, Steve, illus. (p. 1740)
—Those Perky Penguins. (p. 1740)
—Those Terrific Turtles. Weaver, Steve, illus. (p. 1740)
Cussen, Sarah R. Those Peculiar Pelicans. Weaver, Steve, illus. (p. 1740)
Cussler, Clive. Adventures of Hotsy Totsy. (p. 18)
—Adventures of Vin Fiz. Farnsworth, Bill & W, Farnsworth, illus. (p. 24)
Custard, P. T. Jules the Lighthouse Dog Greer, Ana, illus. (p. 932)
—Kid Canine - Superhero! Custard, P. T. & Pearson, David, illus. (p. 951)
Custard, Stefanie. Story of Baby Moose Joe. (p. 1657)
Custer, Cliff. Gift of Peace: Three Essential Steps to Healing & Happiness. (p. 675)
Custer, Jason. Everyday Monsters. (p. 544)
Custom Curricul Staff. Can I Know What to Believe? (p. 258)
—Can I Really Have a Relationship with God? (p. 258)
—Do I Know What the Bible Says? (p. 457)
—Does God Love You No Matter What? (p. 460)
—Does the Bible Have Any Answers? (p. 460)
—What about Sex, Drugs, And... ? (p. 1879)
—What, Me Holy? (p. 1892)
Custom Curriculum Staff. Can I Really Know Jesus? (p. 258)
Custureri, Mary. Happy Anderson & Connie Clam. Folmsbee, Patricia, illus. (p. 744)
Custureri, Mary C. Meet Happy Anderson. (p. 1121)
Cutbill, Andy. Albie & the Big Race. (p. 35)
—Beastly Feast at Baloddan Hall. (p. 152)
—Cow That Laid an Egg. Ayto, Russell, illus. (p. 373)
—First Week at Cow School. Ayto, Russell, illus. (p. 597)
Cutcher, Jenai. Bob Fosse. (p. 205)
—Feel the Beat! Dancing in Music Videos. (p. 580)
—Gotta Dance! The Rhythms of Jazz & Tap. (p. 704)
Cutchin, Marcia. Feathers: A Jewish Tale from Eastern Europe. (p. 579)
Cutchins, Judy, jt. auth. see Johnston, Ginny.
Cuthand, Beth. Little Duck Sikihpsis. Cuthand, Stan, tr. (p. 1027)
—Sikihpsis. Cuthand, Stan, tr. (p. 1575)
Cuthand, Doug. Askiwina: A Cree World. (p. 106)
Cuthand, Stan, tr. see Cuthand, Beth.
Cuthbert, Jennifer. Adventures of Lollipop. (p. 20)
Cuthbert, Kate. Max the Monster. Hinkler Books Staff, ed. (p. 1111)
Cuthbert, Megan. Africa. (p. 26)
—Europe. (p. 540)
Cuthbert, Megan, jt. auth. see Diemer, Lauren.
Cuthbert, R M. Reindeer. Cuthbert, R M & Vincent, Allison, illus. (p. 1457)
Cuthbertson, creator. French Verb Wheel. (p. 636)
Cuthbertson, Ollie, illus. see Barron's Educational Series & Benton, Lynne.
Cutler, Betty Jackson. Flight of SaraJane. (p. 604)
—Flight of SaraJane. (p. 604)
Cutler, Dave. When I Wished I Was Alone. Cutler, Dave, illus. (p. 1903)
Cutler, Henry T. King Mork. (p. 958)
Cutler, Ivor. Desayuno de Tomas. (p. 428)
—Desayuno de Tomas. Oxenbury, Helen, illus. (p. 428)
Cutler, Jane. Family Dinner. (p. 568)
—My Wartime Summers. (p. 1221)
—Song of the Molimo: A Pygmy at the St. Louis World's Fair. (p. 1611)
—Susan Marcus Bends the Rules. (p. 1688)
Cutler, Nelida Gonzalez, jt. ed. see Garton, Keith.
Cutler, Paris. Planet Cake Clever Creations for Kids. (p. 1367)
Cutler, Stephen. Rally Caps. (p. 1437)
Cutler, Stewart & Galvin, Linda. Get a Grip: Hands-On Christianity. (p. 667)
Cutler, Timothy G. Jockey Hollow Historic Trail: A Five-Mile Adventure for Cub Scouts of All Ages. (p. 919)
Cutler, U. Waldo. Stories of King Arthur & His Knights. (p. 1655)
Cutler, Warren, illus. see Thach, James Otis.
Cutler-Broyles, Teresa. One Eyed Jack. (p. 1294)
Cutnell, John D. Instructor's Resource Guide to Accompany Cutnell Physics. (p. 878)
—Instructor's Resource to Accompany Cutnell Physics. (p. 878)
—Instructor's Solutions Manual to Accompany Physics, Chapters 1-17 (p. 879)
—Test Bank to Accompany Physics. (p. 1723)
Cutnell, John D., jt. auth. see Johnson, Kenneth W.
Cutnell, John D. & Johnson, Steve. Laboratory Manual to Accompany Physics: Annotated Instructor's Edition W/CD (Cutnell) (p. 970)
Cutnell, John D., et al. Physics. (p. 1353)
Cutrer, Elisabeth. Molly's Magic Smile. Sexton, Jessa R., ed. (p. 1161)
Cutrera, Melissa. God's Great Plan. Sample, Matthew II, illus. (p. 691)
Cutri, Julia E. Don't Stir the Tea! (p. 468)
Cutting, Ann, photos by see Gates, Valerie.
Cutting, David. Toy Doctor Sticker Paper Doll. (p. 1774)
Cutting, David, illus. see GIANTmicrobes(r).
Cutting, David A., illus. see Matheson, Anne.
Cutting, Michael. Goosebumps Mixed Floor. (p. 702)
Cutting, Robert. 10 Most Revolutionary Inventions. (p. 1994)
—Falling Star. Ng, Drew, illus. (p. 567)
—Mars Colony. Jeevan, Dhamindra, illus. (p. 1096)
Cuxart, Bernadette. Art Painting on Everyday Items. (p. 102)
—Art Painting with Different Tools. (p. 102)
—Art Painting with Everyday Materials. (p. 102)
—Art Stamping Using Everyday Objects. (p. 103)
—Fantasy Characters: Easy-To-Follow Clay-Making Projects in Simple Steps. (p. 572)
—Modeling Clay Animals: Easy-to-Follow Projects in Simple Steps. (p. 1157)
—Spooky Characters: Easy-To-Follow Clay-Making Projects in Simple Steps. (p. 1631)
Cuxart, Bernadette, illus. see Navarro, Paula & Jimenez, Angels.
Cuxart, Bernardette. Cuentame un Cuento (p. 389)
Cuyler, Margery. 100th Day Worries. Howard, Arthur, illus. (p. 1999)
—Biggest, Best Snowman. (p. 185)
—Biggest, Best Snowman. Hillenbrand, Will, illus. (p. 185)
—Bullies Never Win. (p. 240)
—Bullies Never Win. Howard, Arthur, illus. (p. 240)
—Christmas Snowman. Westerman, Johanna, illus. (p. 315)
—Groundhog Stays up Late. Cassels, Jean, illus. (p. 725)
—Hooray for Reading Day! Howard, Arthur, illus. (p. 796)
—I Repeat, Don't Cheat! Howard, Arthur, illus. (p. 844)
—Jesus Spirin, Gennady, illus. (p. 914)
—Kindness Is Cooler, Mrs. Ruler. Yoshikawa, Sachiko, illus. (p. 957)
—Little Dump Truck. Kolar, Bob, illus. (p. 1027)
—Little School Bus. Kolar, Bob, illus. (p. 1036)
—Monster Mess! Schindler, S. D., illus. (p. 1167)
—Please Say Please! Penguin's Guide to Manners. Hillenbrand, Will, illus. (p. 1373)
—Princess Bess Gets Dressed. Malone, Heather Harms & Malone, Heather, illus. (p. 1403)
—Skeleton for Dinner. Terry, Will, illus. (p. 1584)
—Skeleton Hiccups. Schindler, S. D., illus. (p. 1584)
—Stop Drop & Roll. Howard, Arthur, illus. (p. 1653)
—That's Good! That's Bad! in Washington, DC. Garland, Michael, illus. (p. 1726)
—Tick Tock Clock. Neubecker, Robert, illus. (p. 1747)
Cuyler, Margery & Pearson, Tracey Campbell. Guinea Pigs Add Up. (p. 731)
Cuzik, David, illus. see Lacey, Minna.
Cuzik, David, illus. see Levene, Rebecca.
Cuzik, David, illus. see O'Brien, Eileen.
Cuzzone, Beth. Two Lily Pads & One Froggie Family. (p. 1803)
Cvetkovic, Judith. Mandy & Star's Sheep Ranch Getaway (p. 1087)
Cvetkovic, Judith Lynn. Mandy's Lost Adventure. (p. 1087)
—Special Love for Twelve Border Collies. (p. 1623)
Cyber. Transdimensional War Series. (p. 1778)
CyberConnect2 Staff. Nekki/Link (p. 735)
Cybriwsky, Roman A., jt. auth. see Hirsch, Rebecca E.
Cymru, Addysg Cyfryngau, jt. auth. see Evans, Sian.
Cynthia, A. Sears. World Divided: The Fairy Princess Chronicles - Book 1. (p. 1954)
Cynthia, Arent. Kingdom Tales: the True Stories of Lord Elohim & the Adventures of His Family: Wondrous Beginning. (p. 960)
Cynthia, Rylant. Every Living Thing. (p. 542)
—Henry & Mudge. (p. 767)
Cypess, Leah. Death Marked. (p. 420)
—Death Sworn. (p. 420)
—Mistwood. (p. 1155)
—Nightspell. (p. 1255)
Cyr, Christopher, illus. see Cyr, Liz.
Cyr, James, illus. see Cyr, Liz.
Cyr, Jessica & Keller, Carolyn. Ohio University College Prowler off the Record. (p. 1282)
Cyr, Joe. Magical Trees & Crayons: Great Stories. (p. 1075)
—Shadi, the Shadow Who Wanted to Be Free. Owen, Ramon, illus. (p. 1557)
—Two Happy Stories. Owen, Ramon, illus. (p. 1803)
Cyr, Liz. Pete-O Burrito & the Lucky Stripes. Cyr, Christopher & Cyr, James, illus. (p. 1346)
Cyr, Lynne G. Drako's ABC Adventures as an Iguana. (p. 480)
Cyr, Myriam. Letters of a Portuguese Nun: Uncovering the Mystery Behind a Seventeenth-Century Forbidden Love. (p. 1002)
Cyrus, Kurt. Motor Dog. Gordon, David George, illus. (p. 1179)
—Tadpole Rex. (p. 1695)
—Voyage of Turtle Rex. (p. 1850)
Cyrus, Kurt, illus. see Anderson, M. T.
Cyrus, Kurt, illus. see Bunting, Eve.
Cyrus, Kurt, illus. see Day, Nancy Raines.
Cyrus, Kurt, illus. see Durango, Julia.
Cyrus, Kurt, illus. see Lee, Mark.
Cyrus, Kurt, illus. see Meadows, Michelle.
Cyrus, Kurt, illus. see Paul, Ann Whitford.
Cyrus, Kurt, illus. see Wheeler, Lisa.
Czajak, Paul. Monster Needs a Christmas Tree. Grieb, Wendy, illus. (p. 1168)
—Monster Needs a Costume. Grieb, Wendy, illus. (p. 1168)
—Monster Needs a Party. Grieb, Wendy, illus. (p. 1168)
—Monster Needs His Sleep. Grieb, Wendy, illus. (p. 1168)
—Monster Needs Your Vote. Grieb, Wendy, illus. (p. 1168)
Czajak, Paul & Brothers Hilts Staff. Seaver the Weaver. Hilts, Ben, illus. (p. 1539)
Czarnecki, Stefan. 40 Writing Prompts with Graphic Organizers: Engaging Prompts with Reproducible Organizers That Spark Ideas, Focus Thinking, & Put Students on the Path to Wonderful Writing. (p. 1997)
Czarnota, Jennifer. Blessing Baby & the Heart As Big As the Sky. (p. 199)
Czarnota, Lorna MacDonald. Medieval Tales: That Kids Can Read & Tell. (p. 1119)
Czech, Jan M. Rhino: A MyReportLinks. com Book. (p. 1467)
—Vermont. (p. 1837)
Czech, Jan M., jt. auth. see Katirgis, Jane.
Czekaj, Jef. Austin, Lost in America: A Geography Adventure. Czekaj, Jef, illus. (p. 116)
—Call for a New Alphabet. Czekaj, Jef, illus. (p. 254)
—Cat Secrets. Czekaj, Jef, illus. (p. 278)
—Oink-a-Doodle-Moo. Czekaj, Jef, illus. (p. 1282)
Czekaj, Jef, illus. see Corcoran, Mary K.
Czekaj, Jef, illus. see Mills, J. Elizabeth.
Czernecki, Stefan. How a Baby Begins. (p. 804)
—I Do Not Understand Arf. (p. 837)
—Mystery at Midnight Museum. (p. 1223)
—Paper Lanterns. Czernecki, Stefan, illus. (p. 1322)
—What is a Kiss. (p. 1888)
—Wild Queen. (p. 1930)
Czernecki, Stefan, illus. see Andersen, Hans Christian & White, Mus.
Czernecki, Stefan, illus. see Andersen, Hans Christian.
Czernecki, Stefan, illus. see Hughes, V. I.
Czernecki, Stefan, illus. see McAlister, Caroline.
Czernecki, Stefan, illus. see San Souci, Robert D.
Czernecki, Stefan, illus. see Smith, Emilie & Tejada, Marguerita.
Czerneda, Julie E. Reap the Wild Wind. (p. 1450)
Czerneda, Julie E. & Griessman, Annette. Stardust: Teacher's Resource. (p. 1642)
Czerneda, Julie E., ed. Fantastic Companions (p. 571)
—Polaris: A Celebration of Polar Science Normand, Jean-Pierre, illus. (p. 1379)
Czerneda, Julie, ed. Summoned to Destiny (p. 1675)
Czerniawski, Adam. Invention of Poetry: Selected Poems. Higgins, Iain, tr. from POL. (p. 884)
Czernichowska, Joanna, illus. see Strom, Laura Layton, et al.
Czerw, Nancy Carpenter. Itty & Bitty - On the Road. Berlin, Rose Mary, illus. (p. 900)
Czeskleba, Abby. Cool Basketball Facts (p. 362)
—Cool Basketball Facts (Datos Geniales Sobre Básquetbol) Strictly Spanish Translation Services Staff, tr. from SPA. (p. 362)
—Cool Soccer Facts (p. 364)
—Cool Soccer Facts Saunders-Smith, Gail, illus. (p. 364)
—Cool Soccer Facts (Datos Geniales Sobre Fútbol) Strictly Spanish Translation Services Staff, tr. from SPA. (p. 364)
Czeskleba, Abby, jt. auth. see Clay, Kathryn.
Czeskleba, Abby, jt. auth. see de Winter, James.
Czubinski, Amber, illus. see Czubinski, Robert.
Czubinski, Robert. Many Adventures of Pig Batter: A Day at the Park Czubinski, Amber, illus. (p. 1089)
Czukas, Liz. Ask Again Later. (p. 106)

D

D. Carlo the Mouse/ Book 1: Too Many Rules for One Little Mouse. (p. 270)
—City Kittens & the Old House Cat. (p. 323)
—Good Morning World. (p. 698)
D' Almfras, Pauline H. Pisi the Cat & His Adventures. (p. 1364)
D C Thomson Staff, ed. see Gay, Francis.
D C Thomson Staff, ed. see Hope, David.
D C Thomson Staff, creator. Mandy Annual for Girls. (p. 1087)
D C Thomson Staff, ed. 60 Years of the Beano & the Dandy 2004: Favourites from the Forties. (p. 1992)

—Animals & You Annual 2004. (p. 82)
—Bash Street Kids Annual 2004. (p. 141)
—Best of My Weekly Annual 2004. (p. 170)
—Broons 2004. (p. 231)
—Broons & Oor Wullie 2004: More Classics from the Fifties. (p. 231)
—Bunty Annual for Girls 2004. (p. 243)
—Dandy Annual 2004. (p. 403)
—People's Friend Annual 2004. (p. 1340)
D., Jessie, jt. auth. see _Meli, Ayani.
Da Coll, Ivar. Azucar! Da Coll, Ivar, illus. (p. 122)
—Balada Peluda. (p. 133)
—Hamamelis, Miosotis y el Senor Sorpresa. Da Coll, Ivar, illus. (p. 739)
—Hamamelis y el Secreto. Da Coll, Ivar, illus. (p. 739)
—Jose Tomillo, Maria Juana. Da Coll, Ivar, illus. (p. 926)
—No, No Fui Yo! Da Coll, Ivar, illus. (p. 1259)
Da Coll, Ivar, jt. auth. see Coll, Ivar Da.
Da Costa, Deborah. Hanukkah Moon. Mosz, Gosia, illus. (p. 744)
da Costa, Deborah. Snow in Jerusalem. Hu, Ying-Hwa & Van Wright, Cornelius, illus. (p. 1599)
Da Costa, Simone. Emily Rose's Day at the Farm. (p. 519)
Da Guia, Higina. Pajamas O Pijam. (p. 1319)
Da Pavlova, Chrisi E. Animal Stories from Green Lane Estate: Series Six. (p. 80)
—Animal Stories from Green Lane Estate: Series Four. (p. 80)
—Animal Stories from Green Lane Estate: Series Three. (p. 80)
—Animal Stories from Green Lane Estate Series 5. (p. 80)
Da Puzzo, Allegra & Da Puzzo, Jackson. Cloudy Day. Gauvin, Matthew, illus. (p. 335)
Da Puzzo, Jackson, jt. auth. see Da Puzzo, Allegra.
Da Silva, Rosa. 10 Most Uncontrollable Functions of the Body. (p. 1994)
da Vignola, Giacomo Barozzi. Canon of the Five Orders of Architecture. Leeke, John, tr. from ITA. (p. 261)
da Vinci, Leonardo. Leonardo's Fables & Jests. (p. 992)
Da Vinci, Leonardo, jt. auth. see Noble, Marty.
da Vinci, Leonardo & Benchmark Education Co. Staff. Da Vinci Notebooks. (p. 398)
Da2. Bb Roc & His Adventurous Days. (p. 147)
Dabbert, Dana. Cardboard Village. (p. 265)
Dabbs, Douglas, illus. see Carr, Patrick W.
Dabcovich, Lydia, illus. see Milord, Susan.
Dabell, John. Moon People. (p. 1172)
Dabija, Violeta. Twelve Days of Christmas. (p. 1800)
Dabija, Violeta, illus. see Salas, Laura Purdie.
Dabney, Undra, illus. see Gaffney, Linda.
Dabrio-Martinez, Mutzal. Day the Dinosaurs Came to St. Andrew. (p. 414)
Dabritz, Evelyn. It's Not Easy Being a Pelican. Hoffman, Isobel, illus. (p. 898)
Dabrowski, Kristen. 111 One-Minute Monologues: The Ultimate Monologue Book for Middle School Actors (p. 2000)
—111 One-Minute Monologues. (p. 2000)
—My First Scene Book: 51 One-Minute Scenes about Etiquette. (p. 1207)
—My Second Monologue Book: Famous & Historical People: 100 Monologues for Young Children. (p. 1218)
—My Third Monologue Book: 100 Monologues about Places near & Far. (p. 1220)
—Teens Speak, Girls Ages 13 to 15: Sixty Original Character Monologues. (p. 1715)
—Ten-Minute Plays for Teens: Drama Vol. 9 (p. 1719)
—Ten-Minute Plays for Teens: Comedy. Vol. 8 (p. 1719)
—Ultimate Audition Book for Middle School Actors Volume IV: 111 One-Minute Monologues: the Rich, the Famous, the Historical (p. 1809)
—Ultimate Audition Book for Teens: 111 One-Minute Monologues - Just Comedy! (p. 1809)
—Volume IV for Kids: 10+ Format Comedy. (p. 1850)
—Volume V for Kids: 10+ Format Drama. (p. 1850)
—Volume V for Middle School: 10+ Format Comedy. (p. 1850)
—Volume VII for Middle School: 10+ Format Drama. (p. 1850)
Dabrowski, Kristen, ed. 60 Seconds to Shine: 101 Original One-Minute Monologues for Women Ages 18-25. Vol. 5 (p. 1997)
Dace, Peggy, jt. auth. see Whitaker, Julian M.
Dacey, Bandelin, illus. see Koontz, Robin Michal & Koontz, Robin.
Dacey, Bob, illus. see Bullard, Lisa.
Dacey, Bob, illus. see Gayle, Sharon Shavers & Gayle, Sharon.
Dacey, Bob, illus. see Halfmann, Janet.
Dacey, Bob, illus. see Krensky, Stephen.
Dacey, Bob, illus. see Lakin, Patricia.
Dacey, Bob, illus. see Thomson, Sarah L.
Dacey, Bob, illus. see Winstead, Amy.
Dacey, Bob, tr. see Gayle, Sharon Shavers & Gayle, Sharon.
Dacey, Linda. Strategies to Integrate the Arts in Mathematics (p. 1666)
Dacey, Richard. Spinner McClock & the Christmas Visit. Gillett, Hallie, illus. (p. 1628)
Dachman, Adam. Player Piano Mouse. Julich, Jenniffer, illus. (p. 1372)
Dackerman, Gerald, jt. auth. see Sohl, Marcia.
DaColl, Ivar. Dia de Muertos. (p. 433)
DaCosta, Barbara. Nighttime Ninja. (p. 1255)
Dacquino, V. T. I. M. Pei. (p. 844)
—Louis Pasteur. (p. 1058)
Dacquino, Vin. Max's Glasses. (p. 1112)
Dacus, Bobbie, illus. see Willoughby, Bebe.
D'Adamo, Anthony, illus. see Berg, Jean Horton.
D'Adamo, Francesco. Iqbal: A Novel. Vol. 5 Leonori, Ann, tr. (p. 886)
—Iqbal. Leonori, Ann, tr. from ITA. (p. 886)
—My Brother Johnny. (p. 1199)
D'Adamo, Tony, jt. auth. see Ames, Lee J.
Daddo, Andrew. Goodnight, Me. Quay, Emma, illus. (p. 701)
Daddy, The Bigg. Bed Time Stories to Grandchildren. (p. 156)
Dade, Barbara A. Story Time with Grandm. (p. 1663)
Dade, Raheem, illus. see Ms. G.
Dadey, Debbie. Battle of the Best Friends. Avakyan, Tatevik, illus. (p. 146)
—Danger in the Deep Blue Sea. Avakyan, Tatevik, illus. (p. 403)
—Dream of the Blue Turtle. Avakyan, Tatevik, illus. (p. 483)
—Great Green Gator Graduation. Lucas, Margeaux, illus. (p. 716)
—Lost Princess. Avakyan, Tatevik, illus. (p. 1056)
—Mermaid Tales Sparkling Collection: Trouble at Trident Academy - Battle of the Best Friends - A Whale of a Tale - Danger in the Deep Blue Sea - The Lost Princess. Avakyan, Tatevik, illus. (p. 1128)
—Secret Sea Horse. Avakyan, Tatevik, illus. (p. 1543)
—Slime Wars. Basso, Bill, illus. (p. 1590)
—Tail of Two Sisters. Avakyan, Tatevik, illus. (p. 1695)
—Tale of Two Sisters. Avakyan, Tatevik, illus. (p. 1701)
—Treasure in Trident City. Avakyan, Tatevik, illus. (p. 1781)
—Trouble at Trident Academy. (p. 1789)
—Trouble at Trident Academy. Avakyan, Tatevik, illus. (p. 1789)
—Whale of a Tale. Avakyan, Tatevik, illus. (p. 1877)
Dadey, Debbie, jt. auth. see Dadey, Debby.
Dadey, Debbie, jt. auth. see Jones, Marcia Thornton.
Dadey, Debbie & Dadey, Nathan. Slime Time. Basso, Bill, illus. (p. 1590)
Dadey, Debbie & Jones, Marcia Thornton. Inside the Magic. (p. 877)
—Monsters Don't Scuba Dive. (p. 1169)
—Wrong Side of Magic. (p. 1965)
Dadey, Debbie, et al. Abominable Snowman Doesn't Roast Marshmallows. (p. 5)
Dadey, Debby. Mermaid Tales. (p. 1128)
Dadey, Debby & Dadey, Debbie. Battle of the Best Friends (p. 146)
—Danger in the Deep Blue Sea (p. 403)
—Dream of the Blue Turtle (p. 483)
—Lost Princess (p. 1056)
—Secret Sea Horse (p. 1543)
—Treasure in Trident City (p. 1781)
—Trouble at Trident Academy (p. 1789)
—Whale of a Tale (p. 1877)
Dadey, Nathan, jt. auth. see Dadey, Debbie.
Dael, Do Van. Earth Child. (p. 495)
—Earthly Walk: A Season-Ing Story. (p. 497)
Daene, Tanya. There's a Gorilla in the Library. (p. 1731)
Daff, Russ, illus. see Clifford, Jack D.
Daff, Russ, illus. see Kanner, Robert.
Daff, Russ, illus. see Zocchi, Judith Mazzeo.
Daff, Russ, jt. auth. see Clifford, Jack D.
Daffern, Brian. Prince Albert: The Beast School. Bk. 2 (p. 1401)
—Prince Albert: The Realm Pirates. Bk. 3 (p. 1401)
—Prince Albert in a Can (p. 1401)
Daffney. Birthday Fairy. (p. 192)
Dafydd, Myrddin ap. Brwydr y Brodyr. (p. 233)
—Syniad Da Iawn! (p. 1693)
Dafydd, Myrddin ap & Gwalch, Gwasg Carreg. Mae Modfedd Yn Llawer Mewn Trwyn. (p. 1070)
Dagash, Denise. Lorenzo the Iguana That Walked on Water. (p. 1053)
D'Agata, Tabatha Jean. Ick the Stick: Yes, I Can Read! Nature Series, Book 1. Lineberger, Judy, illus. (p. 851)
—Storm Tunes: Yes, I Can Read! Nature Series, Book 2. Lineberger, Judy, illus. (p. 1656)
Dages, Juliette Garesche. Learning about Virtues: A Guide to Making Good Choices. Dages, Juliette Garesche, illus. (p. 985)
Dagg, Carole Estby. Year We Were Famous. (p. 1969)
Dagg, Stephanie. Big Brother. Clarke, Alan, illus. (p. 179)
Daggers, Ben, tr. see Min, Fang.
Daggett, Irma, illus. see Pighin, Marcel.
Daggett, Wade. Coco's New Friend. (p. 337)
D'Agnese, Joseph. Blockhead: The Life of Fibonacci. (p. 200)
—Blockhead: The Life of Fibonacci. O'Brien, John, illus. (p. 200)
D'Agnese, Joseph & Silbert, Jack. American History Comic Books: 12 Reproducible Comic Books with Activities Guaranteed to Get Kids Excited about Key Events & People in American History. (p. 61)
Dagnino, Arianna. Jesus Christ Cyberstar. (p. 915)
Dagnino, Michelle. Hip Hop from A to Z: A Fresh Look at the Music, the Culture, & the Message. Baldwin, Alisa, illus. (p. 780)
Dagostino, Argus. Belcher Bomb. (p. 161)
—Stop the Lute. (p. 1653)
Daher, Anita. Flight from Big Tangle (p. 604)
—On the Trail of the Bushman (p. 1291)
—Poachers in the Pingos (p. 1374)
—Racing for Diamonds (p. 1432)
—Two Foot Punch (p. 1803)
Dahi, Khetam. Mulberry Tree. (p. 1189)
Dahiméne, Adelheid. Donkeys. Stollinger, Heide, illus. (p. 466)
Dahl, Elisabeth. Genie Wishes. (p. 661)
Dahl, Gina M. Choices, Choices Everywhere! (p. 309)
Dahl, Lisa. Gorm the Viking: The Lost Voyage. (p. 703)
Dahl, M. B. Through the Balustrade. (p. 1745)
Dahl, Michael. Alien Snow (p. 41)
—Alien Snow Glass House Graphics Staff, illus. (p. 41)
—Animal Jokes! (p. 78)
—Animals All Around D'Antonio, Sandra, illus. (p. 82)
—Assistant Vanishes! Weber, Lisa K., illus. (p. 107)
—Attack of the Paper Bats Blanco, Martin, illus. (p. 114)
—Bandera a Cuadros: Un Libro para Contar Sobre Carreras de Autos. Alderman, Derrick & Shea, Denise, illus. (p. 136)
—Bear Says Thank You. Vidal, Oriol, illus. (p. 151)
—Bear Says Thank You Kit. Vidal, Oriol, illus. (p. 151)
—Beast Beneath the Stairs Mofett, Patricia, illus. (p. 152)
—Bell Buzzers: A Book of Knock-Knock Jokes Landmark, Ken & Haugen, Ryan, illus. (p. 162)
—Big Bed for Giraffe. Vidal, Oriol, illus. (p. 178)
—Blood in the Library Kendall, Bradford, illus. (p. 200)
—Blood Shark! Sinkovec, Igor, illus. (p. 200)
—Book That Ate My Brother Kendall, Bradford, illus. (p. 212)
—Book That Dripped Blood Kendall, Bradford, illus. (p. 212)
—Brown (p. 231)
—Brown: Seeing Brown All Around Us. (p. 231)
—Bunches of Buttons: Counting by Tens Trover, Zachary, illus. (p. 241)
—Bunny Eats Lunch Vidal, Oriol, illus. (p. 242)
—Bye-Bye Bottles, Zebra. Vidal, Oriol, illus. (p. 249)
—Cave of the Bookworms Kendall, Bradford, illus. (p. 282)
—Christmas. Ho, Jannie, illus. (p. 312)
—Claws in the Snow Vue, Tou, illus. (p. 330)
—Claws in the Snow Evans, Mark & Vue, Tou, illus. (p. 330)
—Cold Feet Ornia-Blanco, Miguel, illus. (p. 338)
—Creeping Bookends Kendall, Bradford, illus. (p. 381)
—Curtains! A High School Musical Mystery. Prothero, Tiffany, illus. (p. 395)
—Cut, Chop, & Stop: A Book about Wedges Shea, Denise, illus. (p. 396)
—Dark Tower Rising Kovar, Ben, illus. (p. 408)
—Dead Wings Piatti, Federico, illus. (p. 417)
—Death Sentence. Evergreen, Nelson, illus. (p. 420)
—Dictionary of 1,000 Rooms Kendall, Bradford, illus. (p. 436)
—Dinosaur World Yesh, Jeff, illus. (p. 443)
—Do Whales Have Wings? A Book about Animal Bodies. D'Antonio, Sandra, illus. (p. 457)
—Doll That Waved Goodbye: And Other Scary Tales. Bonet, Xavier, illus. (p. 463)
—Downhill Fun: A Counting Book about Winter Ouren, Todd, illus. (p. 474)
—Dragon Cowboy Piatti, Federico, illus. (p. 476)
—Dragon in the Desert Vue, Tou, illus. (p. 477)
—Dragon Theft Auto Rong, Yap Kun, illus. (p. 478)
—Dragon Theft Auto Evans, Mark & Kun Rong, Yap, illus. (p. 478)
—Dragon with the Girl Tattoo Aime, Luigi, illus. (p. 478)
—Dragonblood Spring 2010 (p. 478)
—Duck Goes Potty Vidal, Oriol, illus. (p. 488)
—Dungeon of Seven Dooms (p. 490)
—Eggs & Legs: Counting by Twos Ouren, Todd, illus. (p. 506)
—England: A Question & Answer Book (p. 529)
—Escape from the Pop-Up Prison. Kendall, Bradford, illus. (p. 535)
—Eye in the Graveyard. Molinari, Fernando, illus. (p. 557)
—Eye of the Monster Piatti, Federico, illus. (p. 557)
—Fallen Star Kovar, Ben, illus. (p. 566)
—Fangs in the Mirror Aime, Luigi, illus. (p. 571)
—Fantastic Flexy Frog Baltazar, Art, illus. (p. 571)
—Fast, Faster, Fastest: Animals That Move at Great Speeds Jensen, Brian, illus. (p. 576)
—Frightmares: A Creepy Collection of Scary Stories. Bonet, Xavier, illus. (p. 639)
—From the Garden: A Counting Book about Growing Food. Ouren, Todd, illus. (p. 644)
—Ghost Writer Kendall, Bradford, illus. (p. 672)
—Girl Who Breathed Fire. Piatti, Federico, illus. (p. 679)
—Golden Book of Death. Souleiman, Serg, illus. (p. 694)
—Goodnight Baseball Forshay, Christina E., illus. (p. 701)
—Goodnight Baseball. Forshay, Christina, illus. (p. 701)
—Goodnight Hockey. Forshay, Christina, illus. (p. 701)
—Gran Edificio: Un Libro para Contar Sobre Construcción. Ouren, Todd, illus. (p. 706)
—Guardian of Earth Schoening, Dan, illus. (p. 728)
—Halloween. Ho, Jannie, illus. (p. 737)
—Hello Genius (p. 764)
—Hello Genius Vidal, Oriol, illus. (p. 764)
—Hello Genius. Vidal, Oriol, illus. (p. 764)
—Hippo Says "Excuse Me" Vidal, Oriol, illus. (p. 781)
—Hocus Pocus Hotel Weber, Lisa K., illus. (p. 787)
—Hocus Pocus Hotel. (p. 787)
—Horizontal Man: Finnegan Zwake #1. (p. 798)
—Hot, Hotter, Hottest: Animals That Adapt to Great Heat. Jensen, Brian, illus. (p. 801)
—Huevos y Patas: Cuenta de Dos en Dos. Ouren, Todd, illus. (p. 824)
—If You Were a Noun Gray, Sara, illus. (p. 855)
—If You Were a Palindrome Gray, Sara, illus. (p. 855)
—If You Were a Synonym Gray, Sara, illus. (p. 855)
—If You Were a Verb Gray, Sara, illus. (p. 855)
—If You Were an Adjective Gray, Sara, illus. (p. 855)
—If You Were an Adverb Gray, Sara, illus. (p. 855)
—In One Ear, Out the Other Ornia-Blanco, Miguel, illus. (p. 864)
—Inkfoot Kendall, Bradford, illus. (p. 874)
—It Screams at Night Kun Rong, Yap, illus. (p. 894)
—It Screams at Night Rong, Yap Kun & Kun Rong, Yap, illus. (p. 894)
—Jar of Eyeballs. Sinkovec, Igor, illus. (p. 909)
—Killer App Kendall, Bradford, illus. (p. 956)
—Knock Your Socks Off: A Book of Knock-Knock Jokes Haugen, Ryan & Jensen, Brian, illus. (p. 965)
—Know Your Numbers Ouren, Todd, illus. (p. 965)
—Laff-O-Tronic Animal Jokes! Collins, Daryll et al, illus. (p. 971)
—Laff-O-Tronic Animal Jokes! Holgate, Douglas & Collins, Daryll, illus. (p. 971)
—Laff-O-Tronic Joke Books. Collins, Daryll & Holgate, Douglas, illus. (p. 971)
—Laff-O-Tronic Monster Jokes! Collins, Daryll et al, illus. (p. 971)
—Laff-O-Tronic Monster Jokes! Collins, Daryll & Holgate, Douglas, illus. (p. 971)
—Laff-O-Tronic School Jokes! Collins, Daryll et al, illus. (p. 971)
—Laff-O-Tronic School Jokes! Holgate, Douglas & Collins, Daryll, illus. (p. 971)
—Laff-O-Tronic Sports Jokes! Collins, Daryll et al, illus. (p. 971)
—Laff-O-Tronic Sports Jokes! Holgate, Douglas & Collins, Daryll, illus. (p. 971)
—Last Super Hero Schoening, Dan, illus. (p. 979)
—Lava Crown Kovar, Ben, illus. (p. 980)
—Library of Doom: the Final Chapters. (p. 1006)
—Little Dinos Don't Bite Record, Adam, illus. (p. 1026)
—Little Dinos Don't Hit Record, Adam, illus. (p. 1026)
—Little Dinos Don't Push Record, Adam, illus. (p. 1026)
—Little Dinos Don't Yell Record, Adam, illus. (p. 1026)
—Little Elephant Listens Vidal, Oriol, illus. (p. 1027)
—Little Lion Shares Vidal, Oriol, illus. (p. 1030)
—Little Monkey Calms Down Vidal, Oriol, illus. (p. 1032)
—Little Tiger Picks Up Vidal, Oriol, illus. (p. 1037)
—Lost Page. Evergreen, Nelson, illus. (p. 1056)
—Lots of Ladybugs! Counting by Fives Ouren, Todd, illus. (p. 1057)
—Man Behind the Mask Schoening, Dan, illus. (p. 1085)
—Marshmallow Mermaid. Crowther, Jeff, illus. (p. 1096)
—Missing Fang Piatti, Federico, illus. (p. 1152)
—Monster Hunter Aime, Luigi, illus. (p. 1167)
—Monster Jokes! (p. 1167)
—Monster Street Ornia-Blanco, Miguel, illus. (p. 1168)
—Mouse Says Sorry Vidal, Oriol, illus. (p. 1182)
—Museum Monsters. Schoening, Dan, illus. (p. 1193)
—Nap Time for Kitty Vidal, Oriol, illus. (p. 1229)
—No More Pacifier, Duck. Vidal, Oriol, illus. (p. 1259)
—Old, Older, Oldest: Animals That Live Long Lives Jensen, Brian, illus. (p. 1284)
—On the Launch Pad: A Counting Book about Rockets Alderman, Derrick & Shea, Denise, illus. (p. 1290)
—One Big Building: A Counting Book about Construction Ouren, Todd, illus. (p. 1294)
—Ooze Is It? Sinkovec, Igor, illus. (p. 1299)
—Out the Rear Window Weber, Lisa K., illus. (p. 1311)
—Penguin Says Please. Vidal, Oriol, illus. (p. 1337)
—Phantom on the Phone & Other Scary Tales. Bonet, Xavier, illus. (p. 1349)
—Pig Takes a Bath Vidal, Oriol, illus. (p. 1357)
—Pink: Seeing Pink All Around Us. (p. 1359)
—Pirate. Ho, Jannie, illus. (p. 1362)
—Play Time for Puppy Vidal, Oriol, illus. (p. 1371)
—Poison Pages. Blanco, Martin, illus. (p. 1377)
—Pony Brushes His Teeth Vidal, Oriol, illus. (p. 1382)
—Princess. Ho, Jannie, illus. (p. 1402)
—Prisoners of the Thirteenth Floor Weber, Lisa K., illus. (p. 1407)
—Pull, Lift, & Lower: A Book about Pulleys Shea, Denise, illus. (p. 1415)
—Rats on the Page Kendall, Bradford, illus. (p. 1440)
—Read-It! Joke Books (p. 1443)
—Return of Abracadabra. Weber, Lisa K., illus. (p. 1464)
—Return to the Library of Doom (p. 1465)
—Ruby Raven. (p. 1493)
—School Daze: A Book of Riddles about School Reibeling, Brandon & Nichols, Garry, illus. (p. 1522)
—School Jokes! (p. 1523)
—Scooby Doo Joke Books. Jeralds, Scott, illus. (p. 1529)
—Scooby-Doo Animal Jokes. Jeralds, Scott, illus. (p. 1529)
—Scooby-Doo! Food Jokes! Jeralds, Scott, illus. (p. 1529)
—Scooby-Doo Monster Jokes. Jeralds, Scott, illus. (p. 1529)
—Scooby-Doo on the Go Jokes. Jeralds, Scott, illus. (p. 1529)
—Scooby-Doo's Laugh-Out-Loud Jokes! Jeralds, Scott, illus. (p. 1529)
—Scoop, Seesaw, & Raise: A Book about Levers Shea, Denise, illus. (p. 1529)
—Sea of Lost Books Kendall, Bradford, illus. (p. 1535)
—Skyfall Kovar, Ben, illus. (p. 1587)
—Smashing Scroll Kendall, Bradford, illus. (p. 1593)
—Snack Time for Cow Vidal, Oriol, illus. (p. 1595)
—Spine Tingler. Evergreen, Nelson, illus. (p. 1628)
—Sports Illustrated Kids Bedtime Books. Forshay, Christina E., illus. (p. 1632)
—Sports Jokes! (p. 1632)
—Story Time for Lamb Vidal, Oriol, illus. (p. 1663)
—Stowaway Monster Pellegrino, Richard, illus. (p. 1664)
—Stranger on the Stairs: And Other Scary Tales. Bonet, Xavier, illus. (p. 1665)
—Sugar Hero. Crowther, Jeff, illus. (p. 1673)
—Swift Thief: The Adventure of Velociraptor. Yesh, Jeff, illus. (p. 1690)
—Terror Beach Pellegrino, Richard, illus. (p. 1722)
—Thirteenth Mystery Weber, Lisa K., illus. (p. 1735)
—Thumbs up, Brown Bear. Vidal, Oriol, illus. (p. 1745)
—To Catch a Ghost Weber, Lisa K., illus. (p. 1758)
—Tome Raider. Evergreen, Nelson, illus. (p. 1764)
—Trial of the Amazons Schoening, Dan, illus. (p. 1785)
—Troll Hunters Kovar, Ben, illus. (p. 1788)
—Trouble with Abracadabra Weber, Lisa K., illus. (p. 1790)
—Twist, Dig, & Drill: A Book about Screws Shea, Denise, illus. (p. 1802)
—Twister Trap Kendall, Bradford, illus. (p. 1803)
—Two Heads Are Better Than One Ornia-Blanco, Miguel, illus. (p. 1803)
—Vampire Chapter Kendall, Bradford, illus. (p. 1832)
—Viking Claw. (p. 1842)
—Voice in the Boys' Room & Other Scary Tales. Bonet, Xavier, illus. (p. 1848)
—Werewolf Skin. Sinkovec, Igor, illus. (p. 1875)
—What's Bugging Pamela? Trover, Zachary, illus. (p. 1896)
—White (p. 1912)
—White: Seeing White All Around Us. (p. 1912)
—Wings above the Waves Piatti, Federico, illus. (p. 1936)
—Wizard & the Wormhole Weber, Lisa K., illus. (p. 1942)
—Wolves (p. 1944)
—Word Eater Kendall, Bradford, illus. (p. 1950)
—Worm Tunnel: Finnegan Zwake #2. (p. 1961)
—Zombie in the Library Kendall, Bradford, illus. (p. 1988)
—¡Córrele, Córrele Ciempiés! Cuenta de Diez en Diez. Trover, Zachary, illus. (p. 368)
—¡Montones de Mariquitas! Cuenta de Cinco en Cinco. Ouren, Todd, illus. (p. 1170)
Dahl, Michael, jt. auth. see Loewen, Nancy.
Dahl, Michael, jt. auth. see Nickel, Scott.
Dahl, Michael, jt. auth. see Rollins, Barbara B.
Dahl, Michael, jt. auth. see Ziegler, Mark.
Dahl, Michael & Aime, Luigi. Duel of Dragons (p. 489)
Dahl, Michael & Collins, Daryll. Laff-O-Tronic Joke Books. Holgate, Douglas, illus. (p. 971)
Dahl, Michael & Jensen, Brian. Caliente, Más Caliente, Muy Caliente: Animales Que Se Adaptan a Climas Calientes. Translations.com Staff, tr. (p. 253)
—Frío, Más Frío, Muy Frío: Animales Que Se Adaptan a Climas Fríos. Translations.com Staff, tr. (p. 639)
—Profundo, Más Profundo, Muy Profundo: Animales Que Van a Grandes Profundidades. Translations.com Staff, tr. (p. 1410)

D

—Rápido, Más Rápido, Muy Rápido: Animales Que se Muevan a Grandes Velocidades. Translations.com Staff, tr. from ENG. (p. 1439)
Dahl, Michael & Loewen, Nancy. If You Were a Palindrome Gray, Sara, illus. (p. 855)
Dahl, Michael & Loughridge, Lee. Shrinking City Schigiel, Gregg, illus. (p. 1571)
—Shrinking City. Schigiel, Gregg, illus. (p. 1571)
Dahl, Michael & Moore, Mark. Screaming with Laughter: Jokes about Ghosts, Ghouls, Zombies, Dinosaurs, Bugs, & Other Scary Creatures Haberstroh, Anne & Reibeling, Brandon, illus. (p. 1533)
Dahl, Michael & Nickel, Scott. Dozer Strikes! Jennings, C. S., illus. (p. 474)
—Green Queen of Mean. Crowther, Jeff, illus. (p. 722)
Dahl, Michael & Picture Window Books Staff. If You Were a Synonym Gray, Sara, illus. (p. 855)
Dahl, Michael & Ziegler, Mark. Laughs for a Living: Jokes about Doctors, Teachers, Firefighters, & Other People Who Work Haugen, Ryan & Jensen, Brian, illus. (p. 980)
Dahl, Michael, et al. Everything Kids' Giant Book of Jokes, Riddles, & Brain Teasers. (p. 1134)
—Five Riddles for Robin Schigiel, Gregg, illus. (p. 601)
—Last Son of Krypton. (p. 978)
—Trickster's Bubble Trouble (p. 1786)
—Wise Crackers: Riddles & Jokes about Numbers, Names, Letters, & Silly Words Haugen, Ryan et al, illus. (p. 1940)
Dahl, Regina. Love Is Not Selfish. (p. 1060)
—When Butterflies Fly. (p. 1901)
Dahl, Roald. Agu Trot. Blake, Quentin, illus. (p. 30)
—BFG: A Set of Plays. Walmsley, Jane, illus. (p. 174)
—BFG. (p. 174)
—BFG. Blake, Quentin, illus. (p. 174)
—BFG. Dahl, Roald & Blake, Quentin, illus. (p. 174)
—Boy & Going Solo. Blake, Quentin, illus. (p. 217)
—Brujas. (p. 232)
—Brujas. Blake, Quentin, illus. (p. 232)
—Charlie & the Chocolate Factory. (p. 292)
—Charlie & the Chocolate Factory. Blake, Quentin, illus. (p. 292)
—Charlie & the Chocolate Factory. Brunetti, Ivan & Schindelman, Joseph, illus. (p. 292)
—Charlie & the Great Glass Elevator. (p. 292)
—Charlie & the Great Glass Elevator. Blake, Quentin, illus. (p. 292)
—Charlie und die Schokoladenfabrik. (p. 293)
—Charlie y el Gran Ascensor de Cristal. Sanz, Jesús, tr. (p. 293)
—Charlie y el Gran Ascensor de Cristal. Jacques, Faith, illus. (p. 293)
—Charlie y la Fabrica de Chocolate. (p. 293)
—Charlie y la Fabrica de Chocolate. Sanz, Jesús, tr. (p. 293)
—Charlie y la Fabrica de Chocolate. Jacques, Faith, illus. (p. 293)
—Complete Adventures of Charlie & Mr. Willy Wonka. Blake, Quentin, illus. (p. 352)
—Cretinos. Blake, Quentin, illus. (p. 381)
—Cuentos en Verso para Niños Perversos. Blake, Quentin, illus. (p. 390)
—D Is for Dahl: A Gloriumptious A-Z Guide to the World of Roald Dahl. Blake, Quentin, illus. (p. 397)
—Danny el Campeon del Mundo. Blake, Quentin, illus. (p. 405)
—Danny the Champion of the World. Blake, Quentin, illus. (p. 406)
—Dedo Magico. Marriott, Pat, illus. (p. 422)
—Dedo Magico. Marriott, Pat, illus. (p. 422)
—Doigt Magique. (p. 463)
—Enormous Crocodile. (p. 530)
—Esio Trot. (p. 535)
—Esio Trot. Blake, Quentin, illus. (p. 535)
—Fantastic Mr. Fox. (p. 572)
—Fantastic Mr. Fox. Blake, Quentin, illus. (p. 572)
—George's Marvelous Medicine. (p. 665)
—George's Marvelous Medicine. Blake, Quentin, illus. (p. 665)
—Giraffe & the Pelly & Me. Blake, Quentin, illus. (p. 677)
—James & the Giant Peach: A Play. (p. 906)
—James & the Giant Peach. Blake, Quentin, illus. (p. 906)
—James & the Giant Peach. Crane, Jordan & Burkert, Nancy E., illus. (p. 906)
—James et la Grosse Peche. (p. 907)
—James und der Riesenpfirsich: (Das Buch zum Film) (p. 907)
—James y el Melocoton Gigante. Blake, Quentin, illus. (p. 907)
—Magic Finger. Blake, Quentin, illus. (p. 1072)
—Maravillosa Medicina de Jorge. Blake, Quentin, illus. (p. 1091)
—Matilda. (p. 1109)
—Matilda. Blake, Quentin, illus. (p. 1109)
—Matilda. Blake, Quentin & Terrazzini, Daniela Jaglenka, illus. (p. 1109)
—Minpins. (p. 1148)
—Missing Golden Ticket & Other Splendiferous Secrets. Blake, Quentin, illus. (p. 1152)
—More about Boy: Roald Dahl's Tales from Childhood. Blake, Quentin, illus. (p. 1173)
—More about Boy. Blake, Quentin, illus. (p. 1173)
—Potion Magique de Georges Bouillon. (p. 1388)
—Revolting Rhymes. (p. 1466)
—Roald Dahl Set: Charlie & the Chocolate Factory; Charlie & the Great Glass Elevator; Fantastic Mr. Fox; Danny the Champion of the World; James & the Giant Peach Blake, Quentin, illus. (p. 1478)
—Roald Dahl's Story-Sketcher: Create! Doodle! Imagine! Blake, Quentin, illus. (p. 1478)
—Roald Dahl¿s Whipple-Scrumptious Chocolate Box Blake, Quentin, illus. (p. 1478)
—Scrumdiddlyumptious Sticker Book. Blake, Quentin, illus. (p. 1533)
—Superzorro. Elena, Horacio, illus. (p. 1684)
—Twits. (p. 1803)
—Twits. Blake, Quentin, illus. (p. 1803)
—Umbrella Man & Other Stories. (p. 1810)
—Witches. Blake, Quentin, illus. (p. 1941)
Dahl, Roald, illus. see Top That Publishing Editors, ed.
Dahl, Roald, jt. auth. see Wood, David.
Dahl, Sarah, illus. see Bolte, Mari.
Dahl, Steven. Harold Angel. Cotta-Flood, Stephanie, illus. (p. 749)
Dahlberg, Laurie. Larry Fink. Hemming, Denny, ed. (p. 976)
Dahle, Lele, et al. Monterey Shorts 2: More on the Line Jones, Ken et al, eds. (p. 1170)
Dahle, Stefanie. Lily, the Little Elf Princess. (p. 1018)
Dahlen, Kirsten. Wrong Way Peach Fuzz: A Turtle Tale. (p. 1965)
Dahlen, Noelle. Christmas Cheer! Stained Glass Coloring Book. (p. 313)
—Gone Green Stickers. (p. 697)
—Merry Christmas Tattoos. (p. 1129)
—My Christmas Alphabet Coloring Book. (p. 1200)
—Owls Coloring Book. (p. 1315)
—SPARK — Cool Cats Coloring Book. (p. 1622)
—SPARK - Owls Coloring Book. (p. 1622)
Dahlen, Noelle, jt. auth. see Mazurkiewicz, Jessica.
Dahlen, Noelle & Stickers. Glitter Candy Stickers. (p. 683)
Dahlgren, Leta. Amusement Trains: The Story of Freddy & Flash. Vieira, Sueli, illus. (p. 66)
Dahlgren, Sylvia. Max Profit's Money Guide for Kids: What Young People Need to Know about Finance (p. 1111)
Dahlin, Adam A. Junk Collector School. Sandin, Joan, tr. from SWE. (p. 936)
Dahlman, Tricia, ed. MnCareers 2005. (p. 1157)
Dahlstrom, Halene. Raven Cove Mystery: A Rennie of Alaska Mystery. (p. 1441)
Dahlstrom, Kathryn. Hate Fighters. (p. 752)
—Peppy's Rescue. (p. 1340)
—Street Games. (p. 1666)
—Trapped by an Earthquake. (p. 1779)
Dahlstrom, S. J. Elk Hunt: The Adventure Begins. (p. 513)
—Texas Grit: the Adventures of Wilder Good #2. (p. 1724)
—Wilder & Sunny: the Adventures of Wilder Good #3. (p. 1931)
Dahme, Joanne. Plague. (p. 1366)
Dahms, Theresa V. Pookie & the Rainbow Bridge. (p. 1383)
—Pookie, the Little Caterpillar. (p. 1383)
Dahn Healer School. Home Massage Therapy Book 1: Heal Yourself & Your Loved Ones (p. 792)
Dahnke, Julie. I'm Not Perfect So What? (p. 859)
Dai Zovi, Lonnie. Canti,Ritmi e Rime: Chants, Rhythms & Rhymes for the Italian Classroom. (p. 262)
Daidoji, Yoko, jt. auth. see Winsor, Michael.
Daigh, Rachel. When Shamrocks Smile. (p. 1904)
Daigle, Brian, illus. see Crownover, Rebecca.
Daigle, Casie, illus. see Daigle, Damien.
Daigle, Damien. Fish That Went Roar. Daigle, Casie, illus. (p. 598)
Daigle, Evelyne. World of Penguins. Wright, Genevieve, tr. from FRE. (p. 1957)
Daigle, Stephan, illus. see Charles, Veronika Martenova.
Daigle, Sylvie, illus. see Dube, Jasmine.
Daigneault, Sylvie, illus. see Milway, Katie Smith.
Daiker, John, illus. see Rowles, Chuck, et al.
Dail, Ernestine. Voice in the Night. Gillen, Rosemarie, illus. (p. 1848)
Dail, Maggie. Getting to First Base - Chris Struggles to Read. (p. 669)
Dailey, Allison, jt. illus. see Dailey, Dan.
Dailey, Christopher, ed. see Miner, W. Lawrence, Jr.
Dailey, D. C. Billy the Bully. (p. 187)
—Billy the Bully Educators Edition. (p. 187)
—Mindy the Meanie. (p. 1145)
—Mindy the Meanie Educators Edition. (p. 1145)
Dailey, Dan & Dailey, Allison. Glassigator. (p. 682)
Dailey, Donna. Charles Dickens. (p. 292)
—Tamora Pierce. (p. 1704)
Dailey, Franklyn E., Jr. Triumph of Instrument Flight: A Retrospective in the Century of U. S. Aviation. (p. 1788)
Dailey, Joanna. Catholic Children's Bible Activity Booklet. (p. 280)
—Catholic Children's Bible Leader Guide. (p. 280)
Dailey, Reid. Legend of Ross the Reader: A Story of How a Smart Cowboy Saved the Prairie One Book at a Time. Edgerley, Ross, illus. (p. 988)
—Ross the Reader & the Adventure of the Pirate's Treasure. Edgerley, Ross, illus. (p. 1490)
—Ross the Reader & the Great Balloon Race. Stacy, Alan F., illus. (p. 1490)
Dailey, Victoria, afterword by. Let's Play. (p. 999)
Daily, Don. Classic Treasury of Aesop's Fables. (p. 328)
—Grimms' Fairy Tales. (p. 724)
—Twelve Days of Christmas Cats. Daily, Don, illus. (p. 1800)
Daily, Don, illus. see Grahame, Kenneth.
Daily, Don, illus. see Harris, Joel Chandler, et al.
Daily, Don, illus. see Kipling, Rudyard.
Daily, Don, illus. see Williams, Margery.
Daily, Don, jt. auth. see Williams, Margery.
Daily, Eileen M. Beyond the Written Word: Exploring Faith Through Christian Art. (p. 174)
Daily, Lisa. Beauty. (p. 154)
Daily, Lorrie Ann. Castlewood Twins, the Magic Begins. (p. 277)
Daily Nonpareil Staff, prod. Heroes Remembered. (p. 773)
Daily, Rick, illus. see Thomas, Jesse Lee.
Daily, Steven, jt. auth. see Dirge, Roman.
Dain, Claudia. Courtesan's Daughter. (p. 373)
Daines, Cameron, illus. see Daines, McKay.
Daines, Ellie. Lolly Luck. (p. 1046)
Daines, McKay. Cats of Storm Mountain. Daines, Cameron, illus. (p. 281)
Daintith, Eve, jt. ed. see Owen, Elizabeth.
Daintith, John. Facts on File Dictionary of Chemistry. (p. 561)
Daintith, John & Rennie, Richard. Facts on File Dictionary of Physics. (p. 561)
Daintith, John, ed. Facts on File Dictionary of Organic Chemistry. (p. 561)
Dairman, Tara. All Four Stars. (p. 44)
—Stars of Summer. (p. 1643)
Daisley, Liesel F. Adventures of Lisbeth. (p. 19)
Daisuke, Higuchi, jt. auth. see Higuchi, Daisuke.
Daisy, April. Crazy 8 Diner. (p. 377)
—Lonely Dragon. Daisy, April, illus. (p. 1046)
—Monster's in My Room. Daisy, April, illus. (p. 1169)
Daitch, Richard, jt. auth. see Daitch, Richard W.
Daitch, Richard W. & Daitch, Richard. Northwest Territories (p. 1266)
Daitz, Stephen G., reader. Iliad of Homer (p. 856)
Dajani, Suad Farsakh. Grandma's Stories: A Collection of Six Children's Stories. (p. 709)
Dakers, Diane. Albert Einstein: Forging the Path of Modern Physics. (p. 34)
—Beatles: Leading the British Invasion. (p. 153)
—Calvin Klein: Fashion Design Superstar. (p. 255)
—Carbon Cycle. (p. 265)
—Chris Hadfield: Inspiring New Generations to Explore Space. (p. 311)
—Earth's Cycles. (p. 498)
—Earth's Water Cycle. (p. 498)
—Elie Wiesel: Holocaust Survivor & Messenger for Humanity. (p. 512)
—Green Ways of Getting Around: Careers in Transportation. (p. 722)
—Homecoming (p. 793)
—Nelson Mandela: South Africa's Anti-Apartheid Revolutionary. (p. 1241)
—Nitrogen Cycle. (p. 1257)
—Oprah Winfrey: Media Legend & Inspiration to Millions. (p. 1301)
—Vera Wang: A Passion for Bridal & Lifestyle Design. (p. 1836)
Dakers, John R. Defining Technological Literacy: Towards an Epistemological Framework. (p. 424)
Dakin, Margaret. Secrets of the Flower Fairies. (p. 1545)
Dakins, Todd, illus. see Hoffman, Don.
Dakins, Todd, illus. see Pritchard, Jean.
Dakos, Kalli. Funeral in the Bathroom: And Other School Bathroom Poems. Beech, Mark, illus. (p. 649)
Dakos, Kalli & DesMarteau, Alicia. Our Principal Promised to Kiss a Pig. DiRocco, Carl, illus. (p. 1309)
Dakota, Heather. Emma's Very Busy Week. Panaccione, Nancy, illus. (p. 520)
—Fangs! (p. 571)
—Sharks: Menacing or Misunderstood? (p. 1563)
—Space. Myers, Lawrence E., illus. (p. 1618)
—Tote-Ally You: Design Your Own Purse. (p. 1771)
Dakota, Mahkij, ed. Prism Comics: Your LGBT Guide to Comics (p. 1407)
Dal Bello, Thiago, illus. see Terrell, Brandon.
Dal Chele, Egido Victor, illus. see Mueller, Richard.
Dal Fuoco, Gina. Rachel Carson: Nature's Guardian. (p. 1431)
—Spaceship Earth. (p. 1620)
Dal Lago, Alberto, illus. see Strange, Jason.
Dal Santo, Sandy. I Live on a Colorful Street. (p. 841)
—I See a Zoo up in the Sky. (p. 845)
—My Fantasy Forest. (p. 1203)
Dalager, Stig. David's Story. (p. 411)
Dalal, A. Kamala. India. (p. 870)
Dalal, A. Kamala, jt. auth. see U. S. National Geographic Society Staff.
Dalal, Anita. Ancient India: Archaeology Unlocks the Secrets of India's Past. (p. 69)
—Ancient India: Archaeology Unlocks the Secrets of India's Past. (p. 69)
—Mesoamerican Myths. (p. 1129)
—Native American Myths. (p. 1234)
Dalby, Danny Brooks, illus. see Florie, Christine.
Dalby, Danny Brooks, jt. auth. see Florie, Christine.
Dalby, Elizabeth. Complete Book of Chess. Le Rolland, Leonard, illus. (p. 352)
—Complete Book of Chess (Reduced Format) - Internet Linked. (p. 352)
—First Atlas. (p. 593)
—First Atlas - Internet Linked. (p. 593)
—First Atlas - Internet Linked. Rogers, Kirsteen, ed. (p. 593)
—Mysteries & Marvels of Nature. Tatchell, Judy, ed. (p. 1222)
—Usborne Internet-Linked Complete Book of Chess. (p. 1827)
—World History Sticker Atlas. Larkum, Adam, illus. (p. 1955)
Dalby, Elizabeth, et al. Introduction to Asia. (p. 882)
Dalby, L. Mysteries & Marvels of Nature. (p. 1222)
Daldry, Jeremy. Teenage Guy's Survival Guide. (p. 1714)
Dale, Anna. Magical Mischief. (p. 1075)
—Spellbound. (p. 1625)
Dale, Christine, jt. auth. see Redhead, Janet S.
Dale, David. Tale of St Thomas. (p. 1700)
Dale, Decisive. Determined Dream Cars. (p. 431)
Dale, Elizabeth. Circus Fun! Gausden, Vicki, illus. (p. 322)
—Off to Market. Pal, Erika, illus. (p. 1279)
Dale, Fanny. Golden Rule or Second Series of Househol. (p. 695)
Dale, Jay. Baby Dinosaur Can Play East, Jacqueline, illus. (p. 125)
—Baby Dinosaur Is Hiding East, Jacqueline, illus. (p. 125)
—Baby Dinosaur Is Lost East, Jacqueline, illus. (p. 125)
—Baby Farm Animals (p. 126)
—Bananas in My Tummy Hancock, Anna, illus. (p. 136)
—Big Balloon Meldrum, Ned, photos by. (p. 178)
—Big Box of Bananas Diggory, Nick, illus. (p. 179)
—Big Green Crocodile Hancock, Anna, illus. (p. 181)
—Big Mud Puddle Gulliver, Amanda, illus. (p. 182)
—Birthday Party Robledo, Emilia, illus. (p. 193)
—Birthdays Around the World Zamazing, Cherie, illus. (p. 193)
—Can You See It? Ball, Natalie, illus. (p. 259)
—Captain Ross & the Old Sea Ferry Smith, Graham, illus. (p. 264)
—Carlos & the Puppies Dybing, Michelle, illus. (p. 270)
—Cooking in Class Robledo, Emilia, illus. (p. 362)
—Daisy Wants to Go Riding Draycott, Michelle, illus. (p. 401)
—Dinosaurs Vanzet, Gaston, illus. (p. 443)
—Dress-Up Day Heyworth, Heather, illus. (p. 485)
—Environment Park Meldrum, Ned, photos by. (p. 532)
—Farmer Jill Crisp, Dan, illus. (p. 574)
—Gran & Me Dybing, Michelle, illus. (p. 706)
—Growing Up (p. 726)
—Grumpy Old Bear East, Jacqueline, illus. (p. 727)
—Here I Go Draycott, Michelle, illus. (p. 770)
—I Am Big Gulliver, Amanda, illus. (p. 832)
—I Am in the Park. Dybing, Michelle, illus. (p. 833)
—I Can See It Too! Gulliver, Amanda, illus. (p. 836)
—I Go Up Gulliver, Amanda, illus. (p. 838)
—I Go up & Down. Dybing, Michelle, illus. (p. 838)
—In My Car Kreinberg, Sylvia, photos by. (p. 864)
—Jo & Jess Go to the Dentist Chapman, Katriona, illus. (p. 919)
—Lazy Old Pirates Diggory, Nick, illus. (p. 981)
—Lea Is Hungry Gulliver, Amanda, illus. (p. 981)
—Lea's Birthday Gulliver, Amanda, illus. (p. 986)
—Let's Make a Boat Zamazing, Cherie, illus. (p. 999)
—Letter to Sam Zamazing, Cherie, illus. (p. 1002)
—Little Sam Jackson, Katy, illus. (p. 1036)
—Little Zebra East, Jacqueline, illus. (p. 1038)
—Look at the Animals Fleming, Garry, illus. (p. 1049)
—Make a Monkey Kreinberg, Sylvia, photos by. (p. 1078)
—Min Monkey Hancock, Anna, illus. (p. 1145)
—My Big Sandwich Meldrum, Ned, photos by. (p. 1197)
—My Little Toys (p. 1213)
—My Pets Richards, Kirsten, illus. (p. 1217)
—My Toy Box Kreinberg, Sylvia, photos by. (p. 1220)
—Off You Go! Zamazing, Cherie, illus. (p. 1279)
—Our Baby Everitt-Stewart, Andrew, illus. (p. 1307)
—Our Special Rock Pool Everitt-Stewart, Andrew, illus. (p. 1310)
—Pippa & the Flowers Draycott, Michelle, illus. (p. 1362)
—Shopping for Socks Jackson, Katy, illus. (p. 1569)
—Taking Care of the Ocean (p. 1698)
—To the Moon Dybing, Michelle, illus. (p. 1759)
—Top Ten Birds of Prey: Deadly & Incredible Animals. (p. 1769)
—Two Old Pirates Diggory, Nick, illus. (p. 1804)
—Up & Down Bailey, Martin, illus. (p. 1824)
—Up Here Hancock, Anna, illus. (p. 1824)
—Ways We Go to School (p. 1865)
—What Is the Matter, Mrs. Long? Diggory, Nick, illus. (p. 1890)
—Where Is Carl the Corn Snake? Alder, Charlie, illus. (p. 1908)
—Where Is Molly's Teddy? Jackson, Katy, illus. (p. 1908)
—Who Is under There? Webb, Philip, illus. (p. 1916)
—Zookeeper (p. 1989)
Dale, Jenny. Blossom & Beany. Hellard, Susan, illus. (p. 202)
—Boomerang Bob. Reid, Mick, illus. (p. 213)
—Bubble & Squeak. Hellard, Susan, illus. (p. 233)
—Carrot & Clover. (p. 271)
—Forever Sam. Reid, Mick, illus. (p. 619)
—Hattie & Henry. (p. 752)
—Homeward Bound. Reid, Mick, illus. (p. 794)
—Husky Hero. Reid, Mick, illus. (p. 830)
—Jake's Progress. Reid, Mick, illus. (p. 906)
—Jingle Belle. Reid, Mick, illus. (p. 918)
—Little Star. Reid, Mick, illus. (p. 1036)
—Murphy's Mystery. Reid, Mick, illus. (p. 1192)
—Puppy Express. Reid, Mick, illus. (p. 1418)
—Puppy Power. Reid, Mick, illus. (p. 1418)
—Snowy the Surprise Puppy. Hellard, Susan, illus. (p. 1601)
—Top Dog! Reid, Mick, illus. (p. 1769)
Dale, Jenny & Rowe, Michael. Milly's Triumph. Reid, Mick, illus. (p. 1144)
Dale, Jeremy. Into the Woods. (p. 881)
—Skyward Volume 3: Battle at Three Rivers TP: Battle at Three Rivers TP. (p. 1587)
—Strange Creatures (p. 1665)
Dale, Katie. Little White Lies. (p. 1037)
—Someone Else's Life. (p. 1609)
Dale, Kim. What Am I? (p. 1879)
Dale, Mitzi. Bryna Means Courage. (p. 233)
—Great & Awful Summer (p. 713)
Dale, Monica. Eurhythmics for Young Children: Six Lessons for Spring. (p. 540)
Dale, Penny. Dinosaur Dig! Dale, Penny, illus. (p. 442)
—Dinosaur Rescue! Dale, Penny, illus. (p. 442)
—Dinosaur Zoom! Dale, Penny, illus. (p. 443)
—Ten in the Bed. Dale, Penny, illus. (p. 1718)
Dale, Penny, illus. see Fine, Anne.
Dale, Rae, illus. see Costain, Meredith.
Dale, Rae, illus. see Roy, James.
Dale Seymour Staff. Mathematics: Problem Solving Activities. (p. 1108)
Dale, Shelley, illus. see Quezada, Juan.
Dale, Unity-Joy, illus. see Jay, Caroline & Thomas, Jenni.
Dale, Unity-Joy, illus. see Jay, Caroline.
Dalecki, Linden. Kid B. (p. 951)
Dalena, Antonello, illus. see Bianco, Guillaume.
Dalena, Antonello, illus. see Machetto, Augusto, et al.
Dalena, Antonello, illus. see Rodrigue, Michel & Razzi, Manuela.
Dalena, Antonello, illus. see Rodrigue, Michel.
Dales, Cindy. Autumn's First Easter. (p. 118)
Daleski, Gil. Is God Sad? Kaufman, Shirley, tr. from HEB. (p. 889)
D'Alessandro-Cox, Jayne. Passover Blessing. (p. 1327)
Daley, Debbie. Harp of Elvyth. (p. 749)
Daley, James. Great Horse Stories. (p. 716)
Daley, James Ryan. Jesus Jackson. (p. 915)
Daley, Laurie & Panckridge, Michael. Live Action. (p. 1039)
—On the Whistle. (p. 1292)
—Shielding the Truth. (p. 1566)
Daley, Michael J. Beach Socks Corke, Estelle, illus. (p. 149)
—Pinch & Dash & the Terrible Couch. Yezerski, Thomas F., illus. (p. 1359)
—Pinch & Dash Make Soup. Yezerski, Thomas F., illus. (p. 1359)
—Rat Trap. (p. 1440)
—Space Station Rat. (p. 1620)
Daley, Patrick Allen, et al. Scholastic Read-Aloud Anthology: 35 Short, Riveting Read-Alouds That Build Comprehension, Listening, & Higher-Level Thinking Skills-And Keep Kids on the Edge of Their Seats. (p. 1522)
Daley, Patrick, et al. Amazing Word Power: 100 Words Every 3rd Grader Should Know. (p. 56)
Daley, Pj. Roger & the Giant People: Roger meets Giant People. (p. 1484)
—Roger & the Xmas Elf. (p. 1484)
Daley, Robert. What Color Are You? (p. 1881)
Daley, Sofia. Elephant: From Trunk to Tail. (p. 511)
Daley-Prado, M. Super Heroes Save Christmas! (p. 1680)

Daley-Prado, M. J. Baby Duck Gets A New Grandma. (p. 126)
—Buzz. (p. 248)
—Grandma,What Is Cancer? (p. 709)
—Super Heroes' in: FIND THAT BUNNY!! (p. 1680)
Daley-Prado, M. J., illus. see Adams-Cantrell;, Renee.
Daley-Prado, M. J., illus. see Nestell, Mark.
Dalgleish, Sharon. It's a Mystery. (p. 895)
Dalglish, Alice. coraje de Sarah Noble. (p. 366)
Dalglish, Rich, ed. see LaFleur, James & Massie, Gordon.
Dalglish, Rich, et al. Order of 5ive: The Complete Second Season. (p. 1302)
Dalhaimer Bartkowski, Anna. Maggie Visits Grandpa: A Coloring Adventure. Dalhaimer Bartkowski, Anna, illus. (p. 1071)
D'Alimonte, Dan, jt. auth. see Hutchman, Laurence.
Dalkin, Monika & Hollis, Mignonne. Other Rope Book. (p. 1306)
Dall, Christopher M., illus. see Grant, Susan.
Dall, Jeanette, jt. auth. see Washington, Linda.
Dall, Jeanette & Washington, Linda. God & Me! 2: Ages 10-12 (p. 688)
Dall, John, illus. see H M Bricker & Bricker, Howard Michael.
Dall, Mary Doerfler. Little Hands Create! Art & Activities for Kids Ages 3 to 6. Rakitin, Sarah, illus. (p. 1029)
Dalla, Juliana, tr. see Hathorn, Libby.
Dalla Vecchia, Fabio Marco. Iguanodon. Calvetti, Leonello & Massini, Luca, illus. (p. 856)
d'Allancé, Mireille. Dejame Decorar El Arbol De Navidad. (p. 424)
—Dejame Decorar el Arbol de Navidad. (p. 424)
—No, No Y No! (p. 1259)
—Vaya Rabieta. (p. 1833)
—What a Tantrum. (p. 1878)
d'Allancé, Mireille, et al. Siempre Puedes Contar con Papa. Ros, Rafael & Sarfatti, Esther, trs. (p. 1573)
Dallas, Donald, jt. auth. see Longman Publishing Staff.
Dallas, Justin & Rissman, Rebecca. Fashion Photographer: The Coolest Jobs on the Planet (p. 576)
Dallas, Krissi. Watermark. (p. 1863)
Dallas, Sandra. New Mercies. (p. 1246)
—Quilt Walk. (p. 1428)
—Red Berries, White Clouds, Blue Sky. (p. 1453)
Dallas SCORES Students. Learning Kicks! a Dallas Scores Anthology. (p. 985)
D'Allessandro, Alan. Growing Out of Fear. (p. 726)
Dalley, Kirsten. Encounters with Ufos & Extraterrestrial Life. Pye, Michael, ed. (p. 524)
Dallimore, Jan. Captain Cal & the Giant Straw Morden, Richard, illus. (p. 263)
—Captain Cal & the Great Space Race Morden, Richard, illus. (p. 263)
—Captain Cal & the Robot Army Morden, Richard, illus. (p. 263)
Dallion 7th, David W. Tales of Tura. (p. 1703)
Dalmatian Press Staff. Adam & Eve. (p. 10)
—Alphabet Song Book. (p. 50)
—Birth of a Savior. (p. 192)
—David & Goliath. (p. 410)
—Fuzzy Ducky's Birthday! (p. 651)
—God Bless Me. (p. 688)
—God's Creation. Mendenhall, Cheryl, illus. (p. 691)
—I Know an Old Lady Who Swallow. (p. 840)
—Icky Sticky Anteater. (p. 851)
—Icky Sticky Frog. (p. 851)
—Jonah & the Big Fish. (p. 925)
—Lesson In... Thankfulness: Book to Color with Stickers. (p. 993)
—Little Whale Tale. (p. 1037)
—Maggie Can Count. (p. 1071)
—Maggie's Colorful Garden. (p. 1071)
—Mommy, Is That You? (p. 1162)
—My Family Tree. (p. 1203)
—My Favorite Bible Storybook for Early Readers. (p. 1203)
—My First Nursery Rhymes. (p. 1207)
—My First Prayers: Happy Tale Storybook. (p. 1207)
—My Race into Space! (p. 1217)
—Noah's Ark. (p. 1261)
—On Top of Spaghetti. (p. 1292)
—One Little Sheep. (p. 1295)
—Paint Box Book to Color. (p. 1318)
—Pizza! Pizza! Pizza! (p. 1365)
—Pop & Shine Colors. (p. 1384)
—Pop & Shine Trucks. (p. 1384)
—Pop & Sniff Fruit. (p. 1384)
—Pop & Touch Baby Animals. (p. 1384)
—Say Moo! (p. 1518)
—Star Light, Star Bright. (p. 1640)
—Thanks You, God: Board Book with Plush Toy. (p. 1725)
—To the Rescue! (p. 1759)
—VeggieTale Champs of the Bible. (p. 1834)
—Where's Daddy? (p. 1910)
—You Are Special! Coloring Activity Book with Stickers. (p. 1973)
—Zany Fun! Coloring Activity Book with Stickers. (p. 1985)
Dalmatian Press Staff, adapted by. Black Beauty. (p. 195)
—Heidi. (p. 762)
—Moby Dick. (p. 1157)
—Oliver Twist. (p. 1285)
—Secret Garden. (p. 1541)
Dalmatian Press Staff, ed. Daniel in the Lion's Den. (p. 405)
—God Loves Me. (p. 689)
Dalmus, Linneah. Purspy's Colorful Tale. (p. 1419)
Dalon, Phillip A. Clanwickie: Life High in the Kabalas. (p. 326)
Dalrymple, Farel. Wrenchies. Dalrymple, Farel, illus. (p. 1962)
Dalrymple, Jay. Legend of Tiny O'Liddle. (p. 989)
Dalrymple, Lisa. Explore with James Cook. (p. 550)
—If It's No Trouble... a Big Polar Bear Pratt, Lizz, illus. (p. 853)
Dalrymple, Marilyn. Bartholomew's Buttons. (p. 140)
Dalrymple, Marilyn & Foor, Joan, compiled by. It's Tough Growing Up: Children's Stories of Courage. (p. 899)
Dalton, Alex, illus. see Titan Books Staff, et al.
Dalton, Andrew. New Empire of Malplaquet. Boatfield, Jonny, illus. (p. 1244)
—Temples of Malplaquet. Boatfield, Jonny, illus. (p. 1718)
Dalton, Anna. Examining Oil Spills. (p. 547)
Dalton, Anne. Lenape of Pennsylvania, New Jersey, New York, Delaware, Wisconsin, Oklahoma, & Ontario. (p. 991)
Dalton, Annie. Budding Star: Mission - Rescue a Pop Princess. (p. 234)
—Calling the Shots. (p. 254)
—Cosmic Collection: Three Heavenly Missions in One Book! (p. 368)
—Divine Collection: Three Amazing Missions in One Book! (p. 454)
—Feeling the Vibes: Babysit a Buddha! (p. 580)
—Fighting Fit: Mission - Get into the Gladiator Groove! (p. 585)
—Flying High (p. 610)
—Fogging Over: Mission - Take a Trip down Under. (p. 611)
—Heavenly Collection: Three Amazing Missions in One Book! (p. 761)
—Lilac Peabody & Honeysuckle Hope Griff, illus. (p. 1017)
—Losing the Plot: Mission: Rescue a Teenage Trio! (p. 1054)
—Making Waves: Mission - Foil the Pirates. (p. 1082)
—Winging It: Mission: Enrol at Angel School! (p. 1936)
Dalton, Curt. Dayton Inventions: Fact & Fiction. (p. 415)
Dalton, Dave. Sikhism: Inderjeet's Story. (p. 1575)
Dalton, Denise, et al, texts. Jesus Lives in Us. (p. 915)
Dalton, James. Computer Classroom: Word Processing. (p. 354)
—Computer Classroom. (p. 354)
Dalton, Jane & Fairchild, Lyn. Compassionate Classroom: Lessons That Nurture Wisdom & Empathy. (p. 352)
Dalton, Julie. Counting Money. (p. 371)
—Look & Count. (p. 1048)
—Making Change at the Fair. (p. 1080)
—Patterns Everywhere. (p. 1329)
Dalton, Linda J. Mystery of the Broomstick Horse. (p. 1225)
Dalton, Mar, illus. see Sones, Sonya & Tramer, Ava.
Dalton, Mary Clark. Rainbow's Promise. (p. 1436)
Dalton, Matthew. Next Steve Erwin Cavanaugh, Stacy, illus. (p. 1249)
Dalton, Max, illus. see Ackerman, Peter.
Dalton, Max, jt. auth. see Ackerman, Peter.
Dalton, Michelle. Fifteenth Summer. (p. 584)
—Pulled Under. (p. 1415)
—Sixteenth Summer. (p. 1583)
—Swept Away. (p. 1690)
Dalton, Missouri. Necromancy & You! (p. 1239)
—Vampirism & You! (p. 1832)
Dalton, Nicola. Adventurers - the Mystery of the Magical Crystal. (p. 15)
Dalton, Pamela. Story of Christmas. (p. 1657)
—Under the Silver Moon: Lullabies, Night Songs, & Poems. (p. 1814)
Dalton, Pamela, illus. see Bloomquist, Stephen, ed.
Dalton, Pamela, illus. see Paterson, Katherine.
Dalton, R. M. Sisters' Story: The Legend of Queen Brighton & Sister Jasmine. (p. 1581)
Dalton, Sarah, et al, eds. Encyclopedia of Careers & Vocational Guidance. (p. 525)
Dalton, Sherry A. Do Indians Eat Soup? (p. 457)
—New Day - a New Beginning: All about a Day on the Farm. Whitlatch, Jessica A., illus. (p. 1244)
Dalton, Sommer. While You Sleep. Baker, David, illus. (p. 1911)
Dalton, Susan. Magic Glasses. (p. 1072)
Dalton, William. Little Story, about the Biggest thing that Ever Happened. Kaiser, Lisa, illus. (p. 1037)
D'Aluisio, Faith & Menzel, Peter. What the World Eats. Menzel, Peter, photos by. (p. 1894)
Daly, Catherine. DaDaDa. (p. 398)
—Ghost of Christmas Past. (p. 671)
Daly, Catherine & Leonard, Tom. Whiskers. (p. 1912)
Daly, Catherine R. Too Many Blooms. (p. 1766)
Daly, Cathleen. Emily's Blue Period. Brown, Lisa, illus. (p. 519)
—Prudence Wants a Pet. King, Stephen Michael, illus. (p. 1413)
Daly, Dan, illus. see Brooks, John R.
Daly, Gael. Hopkinton & the Boston Marathon from, a Tp Z. (p. 797)
Daly, James & Zuckerman, Amy. 2030: A Day in the Life of Tomorrow's Kids. Manders, John, illus. (p. 2003)
Daly, Jerald James. Early Snow (the Visions Come) (p. 494)
Daly, John A., jt. auth. see Engleberg, Isa N.
Daly, Joseph M. Strange Town Volume One: The Woods Behind Trevor Malone's House. (p. 1665)
Daly, Jude. Seb & Hamish. Daly, Niki, illus. (p. 1539)
—Sivu's Six Wishes: A Taoist Tale. (p. 1582)
—To Everything There Is a Season. Daly, Jude, illus. (p. 1758)
Daly, Jude, illus. see Buzzeo, Toni.
Daly, Jude, illus. see Conway, David.
Daly, Jude, illus. see Cunnane, Kelly.
Daly, Jude, illus. see Daly, Niki.
Daly, Jude, illus. see Roome, Diana Reynolds.
Daly, Jude, illus. see Stewart, Dianne & Quarto Generic Staff.
Daly, Karen Anne, illus. see Mitchell, Colleen.
Daly, Karen Anne, illus. see Westover, Gail.
Daly, Kathleen. Howdy Doody's Animal Friends. Seiden, Art, illus. (p. 823)
Daly, Kathleen N. Greek & Roman Mythology A to Z. (p. 720)
—Norse Mythology A to Z, Third Edition. (p. 1264)
Daly, Kerry. Finding Feldspar. (p. 588)
Daly, Lisa, illus. see Deluca, Alison.
Daly, Mariah. James Has Diabetes. (p. 907)
Daly, Maureen. Seventeenth Summer. (p. 1555)
Daly, Meghan, illus. see Preza, Jessie.
Daly, Niki. Herd Boy. (p. 769)
—Next Stop—Zanzibar Road! Daly, Niki, illus. (p. 1249)
—Pretty Salma: A Little Red Riding Hood Story from Africa. Daly, Niki, illus. (p. 1398)
—Song for Jamela. Daly, Niki, illus. (p. 1611)
—Thank You, Jackson: How One Little Boy Makes a Big Difference. Daly, Jude, illus. (p. 1725)
—Where's Jamela? (p. 1910)
Daly, Niki, illus. see Daly, Jude.
Daly, Niki, illus. see Gregorowski, Christopher.
Daly, Niki, illus. see Quarto Generic Staff.
Daly, Niki, illus. see Wells, Philip.
Daly, Niki, jt. auth. see Borden, Louise.
Daly, Niki, jt. auth. see Mbanze, Dinah M.
Daly, R. Dale. From Hot Rods to Heaven. (p. 643)
Daly, Ruth. Biltmore Estate. (p. 188)
—Lions. (p. 1021)
—Mandrills. (p. 1087)
—North America. (p. 1264)
—Rosa Parks. (p. 1488)
Daly, Stuart. Army of the Undead. (p. 100)
—Devil's Fire. (p. 432)
—Scourge of Jericho. (p. 1532)
—Wardens. (p. 1858)
Daly, Sue V., illus. see Kristen, Judith.
Daly, Timothy M. Alligators. (p. 47)
—Black Bears. (p. 195)
Damanda, Lori. Story of the Star-Spangled Banner. (p. 1662)
—Story of the "Star-Spangled Banner" (p. 1662)
Damant, Aurore, illus. see Butler, Dori Hillestad.
D'Amario, Patricia, jt. auth. see Bunting, Elaine.
Dambra, Marianne E. Cooking Is Cool: Heat-Free Recipes for Kids to Cook. (p. 362)
Dambrot, Marc. Destined: A Hero's Calling. (p. 430)
Damerau, Diane Deci. Petoskey Stones (p. 1348)
—Qiosha (p. 1422)
Dameron, Ned, illus. see King, Stephen.
Damerum, Kanako, illus. see Davey, Peter.
Damerum, Kanako, illus. see Horowitz, Anthony.
Dames-Johnson, Angela. What's Gerald Done Now? Supermarket Fun. (p. 1897)
Dami, Elisabetta, jt. auth. see Heim, Julia.
Dami, Elisabetta, jt. auth. see Stilton, Geronimo.
Damian, Gabriela Georgeta. Chocolate Tree. (p. 309)
Damiani, AU, Kathleen. Molly O'Brien & the Mark of the Dragon Slayer. (p. 1161)
Damiano, Vinny. Man Named Sam. (p. 1085)
D'Amica, Steve, jt. auth. see D'Amico, Carmela.
D'Amico, Carmela. Ella Sets the Stage. D'Amico, Steven, illus. (p. 514)
D'Amico, Carmela & D'Amica, Steve. Ella the Elegant Elephant. (p. 514)
D'Amico, Carmela & D'Amico, Steven. Ella: The Elegant Elephant. D'Amico, Carmela & D'Amico, Steven, illus. (p. 513)
—Ella Sets Sail. (p. 514)
—Ella Sets the Stage. (p. 514)
—Ella the Elegant Elephant. (p. 514)
D'Amico, Carol. Vince, Boy Prince: And the Secrets of How Anyone Can Become a True Prince (or Princess) Cerniga, Kira, illus. (p. 1842)
D'Amico, Christine. Higgledy-Piggledy: Mabel's World. Bell-Myers, Darcy, illus. (p. 777)
D'Amico, Christy. No Dinner for Tom. Grabowski, Daniel, illus. (p. 1258)
D'Amico, Dee Densmore, illus. see Hanson, Maria.
Damico, Gina. Croak. (p. 384)
—Hellhole. (p. 763)
—Rogue. (p. 1484)
—Scorch. (p. 1530)
D'Amico, Joan, jt. auth. see Drummond, Karen Eich.
D'Amico, Joan & Drummond, Karen Eich. U. S. History Cookbook: Delicious Recipes & Exciting Events from the Past. Cline, Jeff & Cash-Walsh, Tina, illus. (p. 1806)
D'Amico, Joan & Drumond, Karen Eich. US History Cook Book: Delicious Recipes & Exciting Events from the Past. (p. 1826)
D'Amico, Steven, illus. see D'Amico, Carmela.
D'Amico, Steven, illus. see Silverman, Erica.
D'Amico, Steven, jt. auth. see D'Amico, Carmela.
Damien, Alex. Doomsday Club. (p. 470)
Damiron, Anya. Dreamboy. Pino, Pablo, illus. (p. 484)
—Inventor Boy. Pino, Pablo, illus. (p. 884)
—Nino Inventor. Pino, Pablo, illus. (p. 1257)
Damitz, Charlie. Diving for el Corazon. Diefendorf, Cathy, illus. (p. 455)
Damjan, Mischa. Big Red Squirrel & the Little Rhinoceros. Steadman, Ralph, illus. (p. 183)
—Clown Said No. (p. 335)
—False Flamingoes. Steadman, Ralph, illus. (p. 567)
Damm, Antje. Ask Me. (p. 106)
Dammann, Anke. Chester Crumbleberry Dammann, Anke, illus. (p. 298)
D'Ammassa, Don. Encyclopedia of Science Fiction. (p. 525)
Dammer, Mike, illus. see Highlights for Children Staff.
Dammer, Mike, illus. see McAdams Moore, Carol.
Dammier, Patti. Got Carrots? Rescued Horse: The Winter Vacation. (p. 703)
Damon Danielson, illus. see Garnett, Tarreka.
Damon, Duane. Mein Kampf: Hitler's Blueprint for Aryan Supremacy. (p. 1124)
Damon, Duane C. Life in Victorian England. (p. 1011)
Damon, Emma. All Kinds of Beliefs. (p. 44)
—Busytime. Damon, Emma, illus. (p. 246)
Damon, Emma, illus. see Safran, Sheri.
Damon, Sidney. Harold the Orange Juice Boy. (p. 749)
Damone, G. L., 3rd, illus. see Del Bene, Terry A., et al.
Damrell, John. Flooring Family. (p. 606)
Damron, C. Dancer: Tales from a Horse's Heart. (p. 402)
Damron, Dugan. Further Adventures of Old Shorty: Tales of a Midwestern Country Boy (p. 650)
—Old Shorty: Tales of a Midwestern Farm Boy (p. 1284)
Damsch, Manuela. Kochbuch fur Missionare. (p. 966)
Damschroder, Scott. Crazy Carnival Clown We Call Croc. (p. 377)
—Pinky's Rainy Day: Pinky Padooka takes a trip to Imaginationville. Faust, Laurie, illus. (p. 1360)
—Small Dog, Small Dog, Small, Small, Dog. Faust, Laurie, illus. (p. 1592)
Damson, D. A. Dory & Her Long Bedtime Story. (p. 472)
Dan, Houser, illus. see Lee, Newman.
Dan, Joseph & Talmage, Frank, eds. Studies in Jewish Mysticism (p. 1669)
Dana, B. J. Tales of the Sugar Hollow Twins: And Their Very Most Favorite Stories. Bk. 3 (p. 1703)
Dana, Barbara. Emily Dickinson: Fictionalized Biography. (p. 518)
—Spencer & His Friends. (p. 1625)
—Voice of Her Own: Becoming Emily Dickinson. (p. 1848)
Dana, John Cotton, ed. see Prescott, Della.
Dana, Katherine. Family Picture Day. (p. 568)
—Never Invite an Otter to Stay the Night. (p. 1243)
Dana, Kimberly. Lucy & Cecee's How to Survive (and Thrive) in Middle School. (p. 1063)
—Pretty Dolls. (p. 1398)
Dana Kittendorf. Trail of Dreams. (p. 1776)
Dana, Rose. Cruise Ship Nurse. (p. 386)
Dana, Steve, illus. see Emigh, Karen.
Danakas, John. Choice of Colours: The Pioneering African-American Quarterbacks Who Changed the Face of Football. (p. 309)
Danakas, John & Brignall, Richard. Small Town Glory: The Story of the Kenora Thistles' Remarkable Quest for the Stanley Cup (p. 1592)
—Small Town Glory. (p. 1592)
Danalis, John. Dog 37. Danalis, John, illus. (p. 460)
—Riding the Black Cockatoo. (p. 1471)
Danalis, John, illus. see Eaton, Anthony.
Danalis, John, illus. see Risson, Toni.
Danalis, Stella, jt. auth. see Bourke, Nike.
Danby, Aaron. Jazzmin's Jamboree. Martin, M. J., illus. (p. 911)
Danby, Aaron, jt. illus. see Martin, M. J.
Danby, Nicholas. My Aquarium. (p. 1196)
Dance, Jennifer. Paint. (p. 1318)
—Red Wolf. (p. 1455)
Dancer, Audrey & Behrens, Janice. Let's Talk Riding. (p. 1001)
Dancy, Deborah, illus. see Nelson, Marilyn.
Danczyk, Kenneth. Grandpas Farm. (p. 709)
D'Anda, Carlos, illus. see ABDO Publishing Company Staff & Wood, Brian.
D'Anda, Carlos, illus. see Wood, Brian.
Dandan-Albano, Corazon, illus. see Romulo, Liana.
Dandan-Albano, Corazon & Romulo, Liana. Filipino Friends. (p. 586)
Dando, Marc, illus. see Honovich, Nancy.
Dando, William A. Russia. (p. 1498)
Dando-Collins, Stephen. Caesar the War Dog. (p. 250)
—Operation Blue Dragon. (p. 1300)
—Operation Green Parrot. (p. 1300)
—Operation Pink Elephant. (p. 1300)
—Tank Boys. (p. 1705)
D'Andra, Anastasia. In the Shadows: Book 2 Rosegrove Series. (p. 867)
D'Andrade, Hugh, illus. see Gidwitz, Adam, et al.
D'Andrade, Hugh, illus. see Gidwitz, Adam.
D'Andrea, Deborah. Picture Me One: Baby's First Year in Photos. Roush, April, illus. (p. 1355)
—Picture Me Three: Child's Third Year in Photos. Vol. 3 Roush, April, illus. (p. 1355)
—Picture Me Two: Toddler's Second Year in Photos. Vol. 2 Roush, April, illus. (p. 1355)
D'Andrea, Deborah & Borlasca, Hector. Pretend & Play Kitty: With Real Crown You Can Wear! (p. 1398)
—Pretend & Play Superhero. (p. 1398)
D'Andrea, Deborah, concept. Picture Me Bee My Honey. (p. 1355)
D'Andrea, Deborah, creator. Words. (p. 1951)
D'Andrea, Elinor. Olivia the Magical Gourd. (p. 1287)
D'Andrea, Patricia, tr. see Asimov, Isaac & Hantula, Richard.
D'Andrea, Patricia, tr. see Ball, Jacqueline A. & Behrens, Kristen.
D'Andrea, Patricia, tr. see Barenblat, Rachel.
D'Andrea, Patricia, tr. see Chui, Patricia.
D'Andrea, Patricia, tr. see Feeley, Kathleen.
D'Andrea, Patricia, tr. see Holtz, Eric Siegfried.
Dandridge, Gwen. Stone Lions. (p. 1652)
Dane, Dichira A. Pathway of Pebbles. (p. 1328)
Dane, Donna, illus. see Wilmes, Liz & Wilmes, Dick.
Dane, Donna, illus. see Wilmes, Liz, et al.
Dane, Jordan. Crystal Fire. (p. 387)
—In the Arms of Stone Angels. (p. 865)
—Indigo Awakening. (p. 872)
Dane Rehagen. How Katie Got Her Meow. (p. 810)
Danellis, Charles W., ed. Group Theory: Classes, Representation & Connections, & Applications. (p. 725)
Daneman, Meredith. Margot Fonteyn: A Life. (p. 1092)
Danes, E. Music Theory for Beginners. (p. 1193)
Danes, Emma. Music Theory for Beginners. Wood, Gerald, illus. (p. 1193)
Danes, Emma, ed. see O'Brien, Eileen.
Danes, Emma, jt. auth. see Hooper, Caroline.
Danescary, Pollygeist. Have a Claw-Some Howloween: A Creepy-Cool Activity Book. (p. 754)
—Monster High - Happy Howlidays! (p. 1167)
—Monster High - Monster Exchange. (p. 1167)
—Monster High - Pretty Scary Parties: An Activity Journal. (p. 1167)
—Monster High - Too Ghoul for School. (p. 1167)
—Summer Scarecation: An Activity Journal for Ghouls. (p. 1675)
Danesh, H. B. Mysterious Case of the Iws: A Story to Help Children Cope with Death. Breton, Katia, illus. (p. 1223)
Daneshjoo, Gita, tr. see Bednar, Sylvie.
Daneshvari, Gitty. Class Is Not Dismissed! (p. 327)
—Final Exam. (p. 586)
—Ghoulfriends Forever. (p. 673)
—Ghoulfriends Just Want to Have Fun. (p. 673)
—Ghoulfriends 'Til the End. (p. 673)
—Ghouls Rule Boxed Set (p. 673)
—Monster High: Ghoulfriends the Ghoul-It-Yourself Book. (p. 1167)
—School of Fear Gifford, Carrie, illus. (p. 1523)
—School of Fear. (p. 1523)
—Who's That Ghoulfriend? (p. 1921)
Danesi, Marcel. Sudoku: 215 Puzzles from Beginner to Expert. (p. 1672)
Danesi, Marcel, tr. see Cali, Davide.

D

Danford, Dan. May I Help You? Why You Need an Investment Advisor. (p. 1112)
Danforth, Emily M. Miseducation of Cameron Post. (p. 1150)
Danforth, Suzanne. Jack - Family Ties. Van Dijk, Jerianne, illus. (p. 902)
Dangel, Leo. Crow on the Golden Arches: New Poems. (p. 386)
D'Angelo, Elaina R. Magic Book of E (p. 1071)
D'Angelo, Gus. New York ABCs. (p. 1247)
D'Angelo, Louis J. Granger Brothers in Their Own Words: Letters from Home for the US Civil War Battlefield. (p. 710)
Danger, Chris, illus. see Feldman, Thea.
Danger, Jen. Day King Headache Decided. (p. 413)
Dangle, Lloyd. Troubletown: Axis of Trouble: Axis of Trouble. (p. 1790)
Danic, Chantelle. To Smile a Smile. (p. 1759)
Daniel, Alan. Fireside Al's Treasury of Christmas Stories (p. 592)
Daniel, Alan, illus. see Bailey, Linda.
Daniel, Alan, illus. see Carter, Anne Laurel.
Daniel, Alan, illus. see Howe, Deborah & Howe, James.
Daniel, Alan, illus. see Howe, James.
Daniel, Alan, illus. see Lakin, Patricia, et al.
Daniel, Alan, illus. see Lakin, Patricia.
Daniel, Alan, illus. see Naylor, Phyllis Reynolds.
Daniel, Alan, illus. see Shapiro, Deborah & Daniel, Lea.
Daniel, Alan, illus. see Waldron, Kathleen Cook.
Daniel, Andy, et al. Bid-It! Card Game. (p. 177)
—LINX Card Game. (p. 1019)
Daniel, Beverly. Adventures of Madilyn Millicent Middleton-Mew. Daniel, Cindy, ed. (p. 20)
Daniel, Carol, illus. see Jackaman, Philippa.
Daniel, Cindy, ed. see Daniel, Beverly.
Daniel, Claire. Are You Scared, Jacob? Lap Book. Poole, Helen, illus. (p. 97)
—Chick That Wouldn't Hatch. (p. 299)
—Chick That Wouldn't Hatch. Ernst, Lisa Campbell, illus. (p. 299)
—Dylan's Questions Lap Book. Evans, Antony, illus. (p. 491)
—I Can Stay Calm. Patton, Julia, illus. (p. 836)
—I Can Stay Calm Lap Book. Patton, Julia, illus. (p. 836)
—That's Not Fair! Lap Book. Mones, Marc, illus. (p. 1727)
—Winning Attitude. Winborn, Marsha, illus. (p. 1937)
Daniel, Claire & Benchmark Education Co. Staff. True Story of Paul Revere's Ride. (p. 1793)
Daniel, Claire & Ernst, Lisa Campbell. Pollito Que No Queria Salir del Huevo. Flor Ada, Alma & Campoy, F. Isabel, trs. from ENG. (p. 1381)
Daniel, Danielle. Sometimes I Feel Like a Fox (p. 1610)
Daniel, David A. Gone Ice Cream Fishing. (p. 697)
Daniel, Eileen L. Annual Editions: Health 04/05. (p. 87)
Daniel, Eileen L., ed. Taking Sides Health & Society: Clashing Views on Controversial Issues in Health & Society. (p. 1698)
Daniel, Ellen, illus. see Demeritt, Mary Anne.
Daniel Fernandez Memorial Center Projec. Man of Honor: The Story of Daniel Fernandez. (p. 1085)
Daniel, Hale, jt. auth. see LaBrot, Matthew.
Daniel, Jennifer, illus. see Rogers, Simon.
Daniel, Kashya. I Got the Terrible Twos Blues. (p. 838)
Daniel, Lea, illus. see Bailey, Linda.
Daniel, Lea, illus. see Carter, Anne Laurel.
Daniel, Lea, illus. see Lakin, Patricia, et al.
Daniel, Lea, illus. see Lakin, Patricia.
Daniel, Lea, illus. see Waldron, Kathleen Cook.
Daniel, Lea, jt. auth. see Shapiro, Deborah.
Daniel, Liesle. Mittens: A Kitten in Search of Hope. (p. 1156)
Daniel, Marie, jt. auth. see Hall, Dorothy.
Daniel, Martha Ann. Mimi Mouse Meets Roger Rat: A Tail of Bullying. (p. 1145)
Daniel, Mikhal. Children's Picture Prayer Book: Sh'ma, V'ahavta & Shemoneh Esrei. (p. 304)
—Children's Prayer Book: A Messianic Siddur. (p. 304)
Daniel, Noel, ed. see Andersen, Hans Christian.
Daniel, Noel, ed. Treasury of Wintertime Tales. (p. 1783)
Daniel, P. K. Best Golfers of All Time. (p. 170)
—IndyCar Racing. (p. 873)
—Magic vs. Bird in the NCAA Final. (p. 1074)
Daniel, R. F., illus. see Sandage, Charley.
Daniel, Rick, illus. see Van Horn, Stephanie.
Daniel, Robert W. Ultimate Guidebook for Independent Filmmakers' A Unique Fast Track Approach to Making Independent Films in the New Millennium (p. 1809)
Daniel, Susan Spence. House That Wanted a Family. (p. 804)
Daniel, Susanna. Karen Cushman. (p. 943)
—Lois Lowry. (p. 1045)
—Paul Zindel. (p. 1330)
—Paula Fox. (p. 1330)
Daniel, Susanna, jt. auth. see Faulkner, Nicholas.
Daniel, Terry. Loveland's: the Main Event: Tender Stories for Today's Tough Times. (p. 1061)
Daniele, Tammy. I Love You Penelope Rose. (p. 844)
Daniell, G. Dusty & Albert's Beaver Tales. (p. 490)
Daniell, Rosemary. Secrets of the Zona Rosa: How Writing (And Sisterhood) Can Change Women's Lives. (p. 1546)
Danielle, Sara & James, Danielle. Where's Father Christmas? Find Father Christmas & His Festive Helpers in 15 Fun-Filled Puzzles. Bloom, Harry, illus. (p. 1910)
Daniel-Rops, Henri. Golden Legend of Young Saints. (p. 695)
Daniels, Babygirl. 16 1/2 on the Block. (p. 1995)
—Glitter. (p. 683)
Daniels, Bethany. How Farming Has Changed. (p. 809)
Daniels, Cheri & Nicewander, Carol. Shadow Tail Meets the Gang. (p. 1558)
Daniels, Chub, creator. Read Me Now: A Novel. (p. 1443)
Daniels, Darla. Carrie Goes Camping. (p. 271)
—Magic Ring: Summer Vacation in London. (p. 1073)
Daniels, Dominique. Mike & the Bike: Money Doesn't Grow on Trees. (p. 1141)
Daniels, Donna. What Do Monsters Do Tonight? (p. 1882)
Daniels, Gail. Pretty Princess: Words. Daniels, Gail, illus. (p. 1398)
Daniels, Gerald. Sweet Silver: A Quackers Book. (p. 1690)
Daniels, Greg, illus. see McInnes, Dawn Daniels.
Daniels, J. M. Secret of the Little Dutch Doll. (p. 1542)
Daniels, Jake. Do Dragons Burn Their Tongues? (p. 456)
Daniels, Jimmy. Dusty Road. (p. 490)
Daniels, Johanna. What About Claus? (p. 1878)
Daniels, John. Love & Pain. (p. 1059)
Daniels, Julie. Enjoying Dog Agility. (p. 530)
Daniels, Kathryn. Bluestocking Guide - Applying the Clipper Ship Strategy: Based on Richard J. Maybury's Book the Clipper Ship Strategy. Williams, Jane A., ed. (p. 204)
—Bluestocking Guide - Justice: Companion Workbook to Richard J. Maybury's Book Whatever Happened to Justice? Williams, Jane A., ed. (p. 204)
—Bluestocking Guide - the Money Mystery: Based on Richard J. Maybury's book the Money Mystery. Williams, Jane A., ed. (p. 204)
—Common Sense Business for Kids. Williams, Jane A. & Williams, Ann M., eds. (p. 349)
Daniels, Kathryn, ed. see Hess, Karl.
Daniels, Kathryn, ed. see Maybury, Richard J.
Daniels, Kathryn, ed. see Williams, Jane A.
Daniels, Kathryn, jt. ed. see Williams, Jane A.
Daniels, Katie C. Danny's Adventure in Afric. (p. 406)
Daniels, Kimberly. Animal Bible Stories - AbraHAM (p. 76)
—Delivered to Destiny: From Crack Addict to the Military's Fastest Female Sprinter to Pastoring a Diverse & Multicultural Church, Kim's Story of Hope Is for Everyone. (p. 425)
—Libre Para Alcanzar Su Destino: De Haber Sido la Corredora Más Veloz de la Fuerza Militar, Se Tornó en Una Adicta Al Crack, y Ahora Pastorea Una Iglesia Diversa y Multicultural. (p. 1006)
Daniels, Kristine. Floyd & the Irresistible Cookie. (p. 608)
—Floyd & the Mysterious Night Time Noise. (p. 608)
Daniels, Leonard & Orr, Tamra. Web-Based Digital Presentations. (p. 1870)
Daniels, Linda. Friend Called Glen: A Bedtime Story for African-American Girls. Delaney, Janine, illus. (p. 637)
—Friend Called Glen. (p. 637)
—Magic Gazebo. (p. 1072)
Daniels, Lucy. Oscar's Best Friends. (p. 1305)
Daniels, Lucy, jt. auth. see Baglio, Ben M.
Daniels, M. K. Nursery Rhymes & Bible Stories with Eli the Bear. (p. 1273)
Daniels, Marilyn, et al. Toddlers at Play. (p. 1761)
Daniels, Miriam Rs. Bully-Free School. (p. 241)
Daniels, Nicole M. Potpourri in the Wind: Nursery Rhymes from One Kid to Another. (p. 1388)
Daniels, Patricia, et al. Ultimate Bodypedia: An Amazing Inside-Out Tour of the Human Body. (p. 1809)
—Ultimate Body-Pedia: An Amazing Inside-Out Tour of the Human Body. (p. 1809)
Daniels, Peggy. School Violence. (p. 1523)
—Zero Tolerance Policies in Schools. (p. 1986)
Daniels, Peter, et al. Introduction to Human Geography: Issues for the 21st Century (p. 882)
Daniels, Regina, illus. see Auxier, Bryan.
Daniels, Rick. Little Remy: The Little Boy Who Doesn't Want to Go to School. (p. 1035)
—Little Remy. (p. 1035)
Daniels, Sara. Pieces of the Sky. (p. 1356)
Daniels, Sharon. Fifi the Fabulous. (p. 584)
Daniels, Sterling N., 2nd. Yas. Daniels, Sterling N., 2nd, illus. (p. 1968)
Daniels, Susan & Vincent, Seth. Student Bylines: Anthology. Vol. 1 (p. 1669)
Daniels, W. J. Empress Academy: The Secret of Glittershine. (p. 521)
Danielsdottir, Sigrun. Your Body Is Brilliant: Body Respect for Children. Bjarkdottir, Bjork, illus. (p. 1980)
Danielski, A. Nick & Austin Chronicles: The Pirate Ship's Magic & a New Home. (p. 1251)
Danielson, Damon, illus. see Smith, Sherri Graves.
Danielson, Diane K. There Is a Mouse That Is Haunting Our House. (p. 1730)
Danielson, Ethan. Inside Bird Nests. (p. 876)
—Nidos de Aves (Inside Bird Nests) (p. 1251)
—Our Water Experiment. (p. 1310)
Daniewicz, Mark. When Jesus Was A Kid. (p. 1903)
Danilewicz, Jamie, illus. see Petersen, Pat.
Danilo, Roberto. Mylene & the Moon. (p. 1222)
Daning, Tom. Chinese Mythology: The Four Dragons. (p. 307)
—Egyptian Mythology: Osiris & Isis. (p. 507)
—Four Dragons: A Chinese Myth. (p. 624)
—Fun-To-Make Crafts for Halloween. (p. 648)
—Mesoamerican Mythology: Quetzalcoatl. (p. 1129)
—Mitologa China: Los Cuatro Dragones. Obregon, Jose Maria, tr. (p. 1156)
—Mitologa Egipcia: Isis y Osiris. Obregon, Jose Maria, illus. (p. 1156)
—Mitología China: Los Cuatro Dragones. (p. 1156)
—Mitología Egipcia: Isis y Osiris. (p. 1156)
—Mitologia Mesoamericana: Quetzalcóatl. Obregón, José María, illus. (p. 1156)
—Mitologia Romana: Rómulo y Remo. Obregón, José María, illus. (p. 1156)
—Roman Mythology: Romulus & Remus. (p. 1486)
Daning, Tom & Obregón, José María. Mitologia Mesoamericana: Quetzalcóatl. (p. 1156)
—Mitologia Romana: Rómulo y Remo. (p. 1156)
Danioth, David, illus. see Humphrey, Lisa.
Danis, Naomi. It's Tot Shabbat! Cohen, Tod, photos by. (p. 899)
—Splish-Splash, into the Bath! Kreloff, Elliot, illus. (p. 1630)
Daniti, F. X. Being Perfectly Frank with You: Images & Reflections to Enlighten & Renew Your Spirit. (p. 161)
Dankberg, Tracy & Graham, Leland. Math Bridge Enriching Classroom Skills: 6th Grade. Willie, Kirsten et al, eds. (p. 1105)
—Math Bridge Enriching Classroom Skills: 8th Grade. Willie, Kirsten et al, eds. (p. 1105)
Danker, Jennifer Anne, illus. see Martin, Ms. Amalyn Persohn.
Danker, Mervyn. Bingo: The Black & White Dog. Calander, Sydney, illus. (p. 188)
Danko, Dan, jt. auth. see Mason, Tom.
Danko, Dan & Mason, Tom. Brotherhood of Rotten Babysitters. Gott, Barry, illus. (p. 231)
Danks, Fiona & Schofield, Jo. Make It Wild! 101 Things to Make & Do Outdoors. (p. 1079)
—Wild Weather Book: Loads of Things to Do Outdoors in Rain, Wind & Snow. (p. 1930)
Danks, Fiona, et al. Nature's Playground: Activities, Crafts, & Games to Encourage Children to Get Outdoors. (p. 1237)
Danks, Hugh, jt. auth. see Storey Publishing Staff.
Dankyi, Jane Osafoa. Incredible Adventures of Wapi. (p. 869)
Danley, Jerry J. Billy Black Ant's Exciting Adventures. Hilley, Thomas, illus. (p. 187)
Danley, Laurie, jt. auth. see Connolly, Debbie.
Dann, Colin. Animals of Farthing Wood. (p. 83)
—Animals of Farthing Wood. Tettmar, Jacqueline, illus. (p. 83)
Dann, Geoff, illus. see Dorling Kindersley Publishing Staff & Greenaway, Theresa.
Dann, Geoff, illus. see Platt, Richard.
Dann, Geoff, photos by see Dorling Kindersley Publishing Staff & Greenaway, Theresa.
Dann, Kiefer, jt. auth. see Dann, Lucy.
Dann, Lucy & Dann, Kiefer. Loongie, the Greedy Crocodile. Houston, Bronwyn, illus. (p. 1052)
Dann, Penny. Eensy Weensy Spider. (p. 505)
—Me Lees un Cuento, Por Favor? (p. 1116)
—My Big Rainy Day Activity Book. Smee, Nicola, illus. (p. 1197)
Dann, Penny, illus. see Mellor, Jodie.
Dann, Sarah. Beyonce. (p. 173)
—Beyoncé. (p. 173)
—Lindsey Vonn. (p. 1019)
—Play Like a Pro: Soccer Skills & Drills. (p. 1371)
Dann, Sarah, jt. auth. see Crossingham, John.
Dann, Sarah, jt. auth. see Walker, Niki.
Dann, Sarah & Crossingham, John. Baseball. (p. 140)
—Béisbol en Accion. (p. 161)
—Béisbol en Acción. (p. 161)
D'Anna, Cindy. Field Day! (p. 583)
—Field Day! Represent & Interpret Data. (p. 583)
Danna, Mark. Amazing Word Search Puzzles for Kids. (p. 56)
—Clever Word Search Puzzles for Kids. (p. 331)
—Fantastic Word Search Puzzles for Kids. (p. 572)
—Great Word Search Puzzles for Kids. (p. 719)
—Word Searches. (p. 1951)
Danna, Minnie. Miss Poppy & Red Jeans: Adventure to Willie Willie's Garden. Danna Sr., Gerald, illus. (p. 1152)
Danna, Natasha. Any Two Can Be Twindollicious. Dye, Jerel, illus. (p. 90)
Danna Sr., Gerald, illus. see Danna, Minnie.
Danneberg, Julie. Big Test. Love, Judy, illus. (p. 184)
—Family Reminders. Shelley, John, illus. (p. 568)
—Field-Trip Fiasco. Love, Judy, illus. (p. 584)
—First Year Letters. Love, Judy, illus. (p. 598)
—¡Que Nervios! El Primer Dia de Escuela. Mlawer, Teresa, tr. (p. 886)
—John Muir Wrestles a Waterfall. Hogan, Jamie, illus. (p. 922)
—Last Day Blues. Love, Judy, illus. (p. 977)
—Monet Paints a Day. Heimerl, Caitlin, illus. (p. 1163)
—Women Writers of the West: Five Chroniclers of the American Frontier. Vol. 1 (p. 1946)
Danneberg, Julie & Monet, Claude. Monet Paints a Day. Heimerl, Caitlin, illus. (p. 1163)
Dannenbring, Cheryl. My Puppy Gave to Me Kremsner, Cynthia, illus. (p. 1217)
Dannenbring, Cheryl & Hess, Anna. Beaver, Bear, & Snowshoe Hare: Mammal Poems. (p. 154)
—Beaver, Bear, & Snowshoe Hare: Mammal poems. (p. 154)
Dannenbring, McKinsey. Lemon Without the Sour. (p. 991)
Dannenbring-Eichstadt, Lana. Bubble. Harvey, Kathleen, illus. (p. 233)
—Uncle Lon. (p. 1812)
Danner, Maggie, illus. see Waldman, David K.
Danner, Pamela. Andre' Angel in a Poodle Suit. Neuburger, Jenny, illus. (p. 72)
Dannreuther, Charles & Perren, Lew. Political Economy of the Small Firm. (p. 1380)
DANO, Reverend Uncle. Littlest Pumpkin. (p. 1039)
Danowski, Edwin K. Green Turkey & Other Holiday Classics: (for Kids of All Ages & All Seasons Plus Reflections from the Heart -for Those a Little Older) (p. 722)
Danowski, Jeff. Grandma's Necklace. (p. 709)
Danowski, Jeffrey K. Teddy Bear Necklace. (p. 1712)
Danowski, Sonja, illus. see Rosen, Michael J.
Danowski, Sonja, illus. see Suzhen, Fang.
Dans, Peter E. Perry's Baltimore Adventure: A Bird's-Eye View of Charm City. Harrell, Kim, illus. (p. 1344)
—Sergeant Bill & His Horse Bob. Corpus, Mary Grace, illus. (p. 1552)
Dansereau, Diane. Savoir Dire. (p. 1518)
Dansicker, Michael, ed. Kids' Musical Theatre Audition. (p. 954)
—Kid's Theatre Audition Songs - Boys Edition. (p. 955)
Danson, Lesley. Snow White. (p. 1599)
Danson, Lesley, illus. see Goodhart, Pippa & Goodheart, Pippa.
Danson, Lesley, illus. see Law, Felicia.
Danson, Lesley, illus. see Watt, Fiona.
Dant, Jennifer. Everybody Is Important: A Kids' Guide to Our Seven Principles. (p. 543)
—Unitarian Universalism Is a Really Long Name. Carter, Anne, illus. (p. 1818)
Dantat, Dan, illus. see Elya, Susan Middleton.
Dante DiMartino, Michael, jt. auth. see Kanietzko, Bryan.
Dante, Miguel. Evangeline, Alive & Well: A Story of Hope in Haiti. (p. 541)
Danticat, Edwidge. Behind the Mountains. (p. 160)
—Eight Days: A Story of Haiti. Delinois, Alix, illus. (p. 507)
—Mama's Nightingale: A Story of Immigration & Separation. Staub, Leslie, illus. (p. 1084)
D'Antoni, Colleen, illus. see Gibson, Cay.
D'Antonio, Sandra. I've Been Working on the Railroad Owen, Ann, ed. (p. 900)
D'Antonio, Sandra, illus. see Dahl, Michael.
D'Antonio, Sandra, illus. see Qualey, Marsha, ed.
Danyi, Barb. Maker of Heaven & Earth. (p. 1080)
Danzer, Gerald A. Americans: Reconstruction to the 21st Century. (p. 64)
Danzer, Gerald A., et al. Americans: With Atlas by Rand Mcnally. (p. 64)
—Americans: Reconstruction to the 21st Century. (p. 64)
Danzig, Dianne. Babies Don't Eat Pizza: A Big Kids' Book about Baby Brothers & Baby Sisters. Tilley, Debbie, illus. (p. 123)
Danzig, Robert J. There Is Only One You: You Are Unique in the Universe. (p. 1730)
Danziger, Paula. Ámbar en Cuarto y Sin Su Amigo Ross, Tony, illus. (p. 56)
—Amber Brown Goes Fourth. (p. 56)
—Amber Brown Goes Fourth. Ross, Tony, illus. (p. 56)
—Amber Brown Is Feeling Blue. (p. 56)
—Amber Brown Is Green with Envy. (p. 56)
—Amber Brown Is Green with Envy. Ross, Tony, illus. (p. 56)
—Amber Brown Is Not a Crayon. Ross, Tony, illus. (p. 56)
—Amber Brown Is Not a Crayon. (p. 57)
—Amber Brown Sees Red. (p. 57)
—Amber Brown Wants Extra Credit. (p. 57)
—Amber Brown Wants Extra Credit. Ross, Tony, illus. (p. 57)
—Can You Sue Your Parents for Malpractice? (p. 259)
—Cat Ate My Gymsuit. (p. 277)
—Divorce Express. (p. 455)
—Es Dia de Feria, Ambar Dorado. Ross, Tony, illus. (p. 534)
—Forever Amber Brown. (p. 619)
—Get Ready for Second Grade, Amber Brown. (p. 668)
—Get Ready for Second Grade, Amber Brown. Ross, Tony, illus. (p. 668)
—I, Amber Brown. (p. 834)
—I, Amber Brown. Ross, Tony, illus. (p. 834)
—It's a Fair Day, Amber Brown. (p. 895)
—It's a Fair Day, Amber Brown. Ross, Tony, illus. (p. 895)
—It's an Aardvark-Eat-Turtle World. (p. 896)
—It's Justin Time, Amber Brown. Ross, Tony, illus. (p. 897)
—Justo a Tiempo, Ambar Dorado. Ross, Tony, illus. (p. 941)
—Lista para Segundo Grado, Ambar Dorado. Ross, Tony, illus. (p. 1022)
—Orange You Glad It's Halloween, Amber Brown? Ross, Tony, illus. (p. 1302)
—Pistachio Prescription. (p. 1364)
—Que Viaje, Ambar Dorado! Ross, Tony, illus. (p. 1424)
—Remember Me to Harold Square. (p. 1459)
—Second Grade Rules, Amber Brown. Ross, Tony, illus. (p. 1539)
—Segundo Grado Es Increible, Ambar Dorado. Ross, Tony, illus. (p. 1548)
—Thames Doesn't Rhyme with James. (p. 1725)
—There's a Bat in Bunk Five. (p. 1730)
—This Place Has No Atmosphere. (p. 1737)
—What a Trip, Amber Brown. (p. 1878)
—You Can't Eat Your Chicken Pox, Amber Brown. (p. 1974)
—You Can't Eat Your Chicken Pox, Amber Brown. Ross, Tony, illus. (p. 1974)
—¿Seguiremos Siendo Amigos? (p. 1548)
Danziger, Paula & Martin, Ann M. P. S. Longer Letter Later. (p. 1316)
—Snail Mail No More. (p. 1596)
Danziger, Paula & Mazer, Anne. Is Green with Envy. Ross, Tony, illus. (p. 889)
Danziger, Paula, et al. Amber Brown Horses Around. Lewis, Anthony, illus. (p. 56)
—Amber Brown Is on the Move. Lewis, Anthony, illus. (p. 57)
—Amber Brown Is Tickled Pink. Ross, Tony, illus. (p. 57)
Danzinger, Paula. Amber Brown Is Tickled Pink. Ross, Tony, illus. (p. 57)
—Get Ready for Second Grade, Amber Brown. Ross, Tony, illus. (p. 668)
Dao, Cindy. Mama? (p. 1084)
Dapice, Carmine. Lets Rhyme with Time. (p. 1000)
Dapre, Alan & Rooney, Ronnie. Brum Big Town Songs. (p. 232)
d'Aquino, Alfonso. Fauna Mayor. Riglietti, Serena, illus. (p. 577)
Dara Cicciarelli. Sam Loses His Sneaker. Hoke, Jason, illus. (p. 1506)
Daranga, Ana-Maria, illus. see Ionescu, Julian.
Darby, Ada. Skip-Come-A-Lou. (p. 1585)
Darby, Graham. Europe at War, 1939-45. (p. 540)
Darby Hall. Adventures of Tigeret S Meow. (p. 24)
Darby, Jason. Creating Adventure Games for Teens. (p. 378)
—Game Creation for Teens. (p. 654)
Darby, Jean. Martin Luther King Jr. (p. 1097)
Darby, Joel, et al. Milestones. Grant, Lisa, ed. (p. 1142)
Darby, Kim. I Wish I May I Wish I Might. (p. 849)
Darby, Stephania Pierce, jt. auth. see Jones, C. Denise West.
Darby, Stephania Pierce, jt. auth. see Jones, Denise West.
D'Arcy, Brian, ed. see Chatterjee, Debjani & Quarto Generic Staff.
D'Arcy, Brian, jt. auth. see Chatterjee, Debjani.
D'Arcy, Brian, jt. ed. see Chatterjee, Debjani.
Darcy, James, jt. auth. see Ogle, Jennifer.
D'Arcy, Julian Meldon, tr. see Magnason, Andri Snaer.
Darcy, Kate. Winnie Windmill: The Village Fete. (p. 1937)
D'Arcy, Megan. Be Happy. Gawthrop, Shaughn, illus. (p. 148)
Darcy N. Carmichael. Ember's Rising. (p. 517)
D'Arcy, Sean. Freestyle BMX Tricks: Flatland & Air. (p. 635)
—Freestyle Soccer Street Moves: Tricks, Stepovers, Passes. (p. 635)
—Freestyle Soccer Tricks: Tricks, Flick-Ups, Catches. (p. 635)
Darcy-Bérubé, Françoise & Berube, John Paul. Growing up a Friend of Jesus: A Guide to Discipleship for Children. (p. 726)
Darden, Amy. Yesterday Once Again: Guenevere's Quest. (p. 1971)
Darden, Ellington. Bowflex Body Plan: The Power Is Yours. (p. 216)
Darden, Floyd. Drumdee makes a Drum. (p. 487)
Darden, Hunter. Pete's Angel. Vaca, Sally, illus. (p. 1348)
Dardik, Helen, illus. see Klein, Samara Q.
Dardik, Helen, illus. see Pantone.
Darding, Kathy Meismer. Through Mitzy's Eyes: A Dog's Tale. (p. 1745)

Dare, Bill, illus. see Bailey, Helen.
Dare, Danni. Jake Jett: Adventures in Space. (p. 906)
Dare, Sterling. Money Menagerie: A Collection of Wild or Strange Animals. (p. 1164)
Darens, Cat. My Bedtime Angel. Oliver, Julia, illus. (p. 1196)
—My Morning Angel. Oliver, Julia, illus. (p. 1214)
Dargaud Media, illus. see Davis, Jim & Evanier, Mark.
Dargaud Media, illus. see Davis, Jim & Michiels, Cedric.
Dargaud Media, illus. see Davis, Jim.
Dargaud Media Staff, illus. see Berts, Peter, et al.
Dargaud Media Staff, illus. see Davis, Jim & Evanier, Mark.
Dargaud Media Staff, illus. see Davis, Jim & Michiels, Cedric.
Dargaud Media Staff, illus. see Davis, Jim, et al.
Dargaud Media Staff, illus. see Magnat, Julien, et al.
Dargaw, Kate. Who Came First. Oleynikov, Igor, illus. (p. 1914)
Dargento, Beverly. Spot the Dot. (p. 1633)
D'Argenzio, Gertilyn Elinor. What Color Is Your Happiness? (p. 1881)
Dargie, Richard. Ancient Rome. (p. 70)
—Castles under Siege. (p. 277)
—Knights & Castles. (p. 964)
—Look Around a Greek Temple. (p. 1048)
—Rich & Poor in Ancient Rome. (p. 1469)
Dargie, Richard & Compass Point Books Staff. Ancient Greece Health & Disease Hook, Adam, illus. (p. 69)
D'Argo, Laura, illus. see Carson, Mary Kay.
D'Argo, Laura, illus. see Posner, Renee & Quinton, Sasha.
Darhansoff, Liz, jt. auth. see Hirsch, Edward.
Darian-Smith, Kate. Australia, Antarctica, & the Pacific. (p. 116)
D'Ariggo, Jay, illus. see Michelle, Jean.
Darío, Rubén. Ruben Dario Para Niños. (p. 1493)
Dark, Gregory. Susie & the Snow-it-alls. (p. 1688)
Dark Horse Comics Staff & Warner, Christopher S., eds. Dark Horse Heroes (p. 407)
Dark Overlord Media. Rookie: Galactic Football League, Volume One. (p. 1487)
Darke, J. A. Attack of the Mud Creatures. Evergreen, Nelson, illus. (p. 113)
—Grin in the Dark. Evergreen, Nelson, illus. (p. 724)
—Screaming Bridge. Evergreen, Nelson, illus. (p. 1533)
—Tech Fury. Evergreen, Nelson, illus. (p. 1711)
Darkhor, P. H. Silent Being. (p. 1575)
Darlene, Cannon. Dollygal, Peacock, & the Serpent. Mathis, Leslie, illus. (p. 464)
Darling, Angela. Isabella's Spring Break Crush. (p. 891)
—Lauren Likes Charlie: Does He Like Her Too? (p. 980)
—Lauren's Beach Crush. (p. 980)
—Lindsay Likes Nick Crush: Does He Like Her Too? (p. 1019)
—Lindsay's Surprise Crush. (p. 1019)
—Maddie's Camp Crush. (p. 1069)
—Noelle's Christmas Crush. (p. 1262)
—Rachel's Valentine Crush. (p. 1432)
Darling, F. Fraser. Seasons & the Fisherman: A Book for Children. Tunnicliffe, C. F., illus. (p. 1538)
Darling, Fiona. Horse's Curse. (p. 800)
Darling, Harold, jt. ed. see Darling, Sandra.
Darling, Helen. Hide-n-seek Monday. Glickstein, Jennifer, ed. (p. 777)
Darling, Kathy, jt. auth. see Cobb, Vicki.
Darling, Louis, illus. see Cleary, Beverly.
Darling, Lucrecia, jt. auth. see Wickstrom, Lois June.
Darling, Nina. Pet Shop Talk: A Grooming for Max (p. 1345)
Darling, Pollyanna. Heartwood. Chalmers, Kirsty, illus. (p. 760)
Darling, Sandra & Darling, Harold, eds. Golden Rule. (p. 695)
Darling, Tellulah. My Date from Hell. (p. 1201)
—My Life from Hell. (p. 1212)
Darlington, Edgar. Circus Boys on the Mississippi. (p. 322)
Darlington, Edgar B. Circus Boys on the Flying Rings. (p. 322)
Darlington, Edgar B. P. Circus Boys Across Continent or Making the Start in the Sawdust Life. (p. 322)
—Circus Boys Across the Continent. (p. 322)
—Circus Boys in Dixie Land. (p. 322)
—Circus Boys in Dixie Land or Winning the Plaudits of the Sunny South. (p. 322)
—Circus Boys on the Mississippi. (p. 322)
—Circus Boys on the Mississippi or Afloat with the Big Show on the Big River. (p. 322)
—Circus Boys on the Plains or the Young Advance Agents Ahead of the Show. (p. 322)
Darlington, Franklin, jt. auth. see Bill, Alfred Hoyt.
Darman, Peter, ed. Allied Invasion of Europe. (p. 47)
—Attack on Pearl Harbor: America Enters World War II. (p. 114)
—Battle of the Atlantic: Naval Warfare From 1939-1945. (p. 146)
—Holocaust & Life under Nazi Occupation. (p. 789)
—Home Fronts: Allied & Axis Life During World War II. (p. 792)
—World War II Begins. (p. 1959)
Darmani, L. Stories from Africa (p. 1654)
D'Armata, Frank, illus. see Dixon, Chuck.
Darmon, Reed. Made in China. (p. 1070)
Darne, Txell, illus. see de Boer, Joan & De Boer, Joan.
Darneal, June. Cracker's Journey. (p. 375)
Darnell, Cynthia. Cameron Asks, What If... (p. 256)
Darnell, K. L., illus. see Burg, Ann E.
Darnell, K. L., illus. see Noble, Trinka Hakes.
Darnell, K. L., illus. see Schonberg, Marcia.
Darnell, K. L., illus. see Wargin, Kathy-jo.
Darnell, Kate, illus. see Young, Judy Dockrey.
Darnell, Kathey. Billy, the Kid. (p. 187)
Darnell, Melissa. Consume. (p. 360)
—Crave. (p. 376)
Darnell, Regna, jt. auth. see Herr, Melody.
Darnell, Yolanda. Almost There: A Series of Monologues. First Choice Productions Staff, photos by. (p. 48)
—Terror in the Darkness (Confessions of a Stalked Fan) Stengel, Michelle, photos by. (p. 1722)
Daronco, Mickey. Aquí Hay (?) (p. 94)
—Circus in the City: Set Of 6. (p. 322)
—En Un (?) (p. 523)
—Es (?) (p. 534)
—Es De (?) (p. 534)
—Está en Una (?) (p. 538)
—Hay un señor en Un (?) (p. 755)
—Puedo Ver (?) (p. 1414)
—Voy a Tomar (?) (p. 1850)
—Yo Soy (?) (p. 1971)
—¡(?) lo puede Hacer! (p. 1044)
—¿Entró El (?) ? (p. 531)
—¿Es grande Una (?) ? (p. 534)
—¿Estoy en Una (?) ? (p. 538)
—¿Se puede poner En (?) ? (p. 1534)
—¿Será Un (?) ? (p. 1552)
—¿Soy Yo (?) ? (p. 1618)
—¿Voy (?) ? (p. 1850)
Daronco, Mickey & Ohanesian, Diane. Am I in It? Set Of 6. (p. 51)
—Am I Sad? Set Of 6. (p. 51)
—Big Band: Set Of 6. (p. 178)
—Big Clock: Set Of 6. (p. 180)
—Can We Pick It? Set Of 6. (p. 258)
—Game: Set Of 6. (p. 654)
—Home with Mom & Dad. (p. 793)
—Is It Big? Set Of 6. (p. 889)
—Look at Me Now! Set Of 6. (p. 1048)
—Lot to Sell: Set Of 6. (p. 1057)
—More Corn: Set Of 6. (p. 1174)
—My Big Day: Set Of 6. (p. 1197)
—My Pet Pup: Set of 6. (p. 1217)
—My Turn to Fit: Set Of 6. (p. 1220)
—On a Cold Day: Set Of 6. (p. 1288)
—One to Ten: Set Of 6. (p. 1297)
—Play this Game with Me. (p. 1371)
—Two by Two: Set Of 6. (p. 1803)
—What Might I Spy? Set Of 6. (p. 1892)
—Will It Float? Set Of 6. (p. 1932)
Daronco, Mickey & Presti, Lori. Ants & Las Hormigas: 6 English, 6 Spanish Adaptations (p. 90)
—Instrumentos para Medir: Set Of 6. (p. 879)
—Las Hormigas: Set Of 6. (p. 976)
—Measuring Tools & Instrumentos para Medir: 6 English, 6 Spanish Adaptations (p. 1117)
Daronco, Mickey & Priesti, Lori. Measuring Tools. (p. 1117)
Darr, Cynthia G., jt. auth. see Bauld, Jane Scoggins.
Darragh, Aileen, illus. see Slade, Suzanne & Kutner, Laura.
Darragh, Jill. Milly Feather. Gamble, Gael, illus. (p. 1144)
Darragh, Marty & Pitkin, Jo. Women of the Prairie State: 25 Illinois Women You Should Know. Greenleaf, Lisa, illus. (p. 1946)
Darraj, Susan Muaddi. Amy Tan. (p. 66)
—Anna Sui. (p. 85)
—Bashar Al-Assad: President of Syria. Schlesinger, Arthur M., Jr., ed. (p. 141)
—Collapse of the Soviet Union. (p. 339)
—Felipe Calderón. (p. 581)
—Hosni Mubarak. (p. 801)
—Indian Independence Act Of 1947. (p. 871)
—Jackie Robinson. (p. 903)
—Mairead Corrigan & Betty Williams: Partners in Peace in Northern Ireland. (p. 1077)
—Mary Eliza Mahoney & the Legacy of African American Nurses. (p. 1100)
—Oscar de la Renta. (p. 1305)
—Silvio Berlusconi: Prime Minister of Italy. Schlesinger, Arthur M., Jr., ed. (p. 1577)
Darraj, Susan Muaddi & Puller, Meredyth. United Arab Emirates. (p. 1818)
Darrenkamp, Julia Mary, illus. see Orfeo, Christine Virginia.
Darrenkamp, Julia Mary, illus. see Roddy, Lauren S.
Darring, Gerald, jt. auth. see Perrotta, Kevin.
Darrington, Rebecca. Doodletoot- a Happy Little Basset Hound Dog. (p. 470)
Darroch, Jane, ed. see Frey, Lisa A.
Darroch, Jane, illus. see Frey, Lisa A.
Darrow, Geof, illus. see Miller, Frank.
Darrow, Sharon. Trash. (p. 1779)
Darrow, Sharon, jt. auth. see Pettitt, Linda.
D'Arruda, Kim. Day to Play. (p. 414)
Darsana, Nam Aste. Guppie: God's Unified Perfect Plan Inspiring Everyone. (p. 732)
Dart, Allan, ed. SpongeBob SquarePants & Other TV Tunes (p. 1630)
Dart, Lisa, jt. auth. see Sutherland, Keston.
Dartes, Staci, illus. see Smith, Nerissia.
Dartez, C. Jenny Giraffe Discovers the French Quarter. (p. 913)
Dartford, Mark. Bombers. (p. 208)
—Fighter Planes. (p. 585)
—Helicopters. (p. 763)
—Missiles & Rockets. (p. 1152)
—Warships. (p. 1859)
Dartnell, Lewis. Astrobiology: Exploring Life in the Universe. (p. 109)
Dartt, Gina L. Unexpected Ties. (p. 1817)
Darwin, Beatrice, illus. see Cleary, Beverly.
Darwin, Charles. Riverbank. Negrin, Fabian, illus. (p. 1476)
Darwin, Charles, jt. auth. see Schanzer, Rosalyn.
Darwin, Erwin L., illus. see Snell, Roy Judson.
Darwin, Florence Henrietta. Lovers' Tasks. (p. 1061)
Darwin, James M. Way I Want to Be Treated. (p. 1864)
Das, Amrita. Hope Is a Girl Selling Fruit. (p. 796)
Das, Christina. Coo Coo Duckling. (p. 361)
—Munchy Mouse. (p. 1191)
—Oomph-Pa-Pa at the Circus. (p. 1298)
—Red Spotted Balloon. (p. 1455)
—Swinging under the Stars. (p. 1691)
Das Group Staff, illus. see Man-Kong, Mary.
Das Grup, illus. see Depken, Kristen L.
Das, Prodeepta. Day I Remember. (p. 413)
—I Is for India. Das, Prodeepta, illus. (p. 839)
—Prita Goes to India. (p. 1407)
Das, Prodeepta, illus. see Frederick, Malcolm.
Das, Prodeepta, illus. see Kabakov, Vladimir.
Das, Prodeepta, illus. see Naidoo, Beverley.
Das, Prodeepta, photos by see Cheung, Hyechong.
Das, Prodeepta, photos by see Kabakov, Vladimir.
Das, Prodeepta, photos by see Mrowczynska, Agnieszka.
Das, Prodeepta, photos by see Rahman, Urmi & Quarto Generic Staff.
Das, Prodeepta, photos by see Razzak, Shazia.
Das, Prodeepta, photos by see Tossuon, Nevin, et al.
Das, Prodeepta, photos by see Zephaniah, Benjamin.
Das, Prodeepta, photos by. Geeta's Day: From Dawn to Dusk in an Indian Village. (p. 659)
Das, Rasamandala. Hinduism. (p. 780)
Dascher, Helge, tr. see Ricard, Anouk.
Dase, Pam. Hurricane Hunters. (p. 829)
—Tonight's Concert. (p. 1765)
—Tornado Chasers. (p. 1770)
Dasent, G. W. East o' the Sun & West o' the Moon. (p. 498)
Dash Greenspan, Shari, tr. see Fox, Mem.
Dash, Meredith. Calico Cats. (p. 253)
—Columbus Day. (p. 346)
—Dia de Accion de Gracias. (p. 433)
—Dia de la Raza. (p. 433)
—Dia de Los Presidentes. (p. 433)
—Día de Los Veteranos de Guerra. (p. 433)
—Dia de Martin Luther King Jr. (p. 433)
—Dia Del Trabajo. (p. 433)
—Labor Day. (p. 969)
—Maine Coon Cats. (p. 1077)
—Manx Cats. (p. 1089)
—MLK Jr. Day. (p. 1157)
—Persian Cats. (p. 1344)
—Presidents' Day. (p. 1397)
—Scottish Fold Cats. (p. 1532)
—Siamese Cats. (p. 1572)
—Thanksgiving. (p. 1725)
—Veterans Day. (p. 1839)
Dash, Meredith, jt. auth. see ABDO Publishing Company Staff.
Dashiell, Margaret, illus. see Trigg, Roberta.
Dashiell, Melissa. Moosa's Christmas Adventure. (p. 1173)
Dashner, James. 13th Reality Complete Set: The Journal of Curious Letters; the Hunt for Dark Infinity; the Blade of Shattered Hope; the Void of Mist & Thunder. (p. 1995)
—Blade of Shattered Hope. (p. 198)
—Blade of Shattered Hope. Dorman, Brandon, illus. (p. 198)
—Death Cure. (p. 420)
—Door in the Woods. (p. 470)
—Eye of Minds. (p. 557)
—Gift of Ice. (p. 675)
—Hunt for Dark Infinity. Beus, Bryan, illus. (p. 828)
—Iron Empire. (p. 888)
—Journal of Curious Letters. Beus, Bryan, illus. (p. 927)
—Kill Order. (p. 956)
—Maze Runner (p. 1113)
—Maze Runner: Virus Letal. (p. 1113)
—Maze Runner. (p. 1113)
—Maze Runner & the Scorch Trials (p. 1113)
—Maze Runner Trilogy (p. 1113)
—Mutiny in Time. (p. 1194)
—Mutiny in Time (Infinity Ring, Book 1) (p. 1194)
—Rule of Thoughts. (p. 1495)
—Scorch Trials. (p. 1530)
—The Maze Runner - The Scorch Trials - The Death Cure - The Kill Order (p. 1728)
—Void of Mist & Thunder. Dorman, Brandon, illus. (p. 1848)
—War of the Black Curtain. Phipps, Michael, illus. (p. 1857)
Dashney, John. Adventures of Walter the Weremouse ; the Adventures of Mishka the Mousewere. Somerville, Sheila, illus. (p. 24)
DaSilva, Barbara, ed. Roosters. (p. 1488)
—Textiles: Vintage Images of America's Living Past. (p. 1724)
Dasilva, D. Mom Has Left & Gone to Vegas. Craig, Dan, illus. (p. 1161)
Dasilva, Kiko. Moncho y la Mancha. (p. 1163)
DaSilva-Gordon, Maria. Powerful Bones: Keeping Your Skeleton Healthy. (p. 1390)
—Puerto Rico: Past & Present. (p. 1415)
—Top 10 Secrets for Making Money & Even More Money. (p. 1768)
—Your First Year of College: From Classroom to Dorm Room. (p. 1980)
Dass, Sujan. Real Life Is No Fairy Tale. (p. 1448)
Daste, Larry. Alphabet Search: Activity & Coloring Book. (p. 50)
—Easy Gingerbread House Sticker Picture Puzzle. (p. 500)
—Fast Food Stickers. (p. 576)
Daste, Larry, illus. see Jacobs, Frank, ed.
Daste, Larry, jt. auth. see Rubins, Diane Teitel.
Daste, Larry, et al. Hidden Picture Mania. Boddy, Joe, illus. (p. 776)
Daswani, Kavita. Indie Girl. (p. 872)
—Lovetorn. (p. 1061)
Data Notes Staff. Word Mapping for Literacy & Language. (p. 1950)
Dateno, Maria Grace. Braving the Storm Cunningham, Paul, illus. (p. 223)
—Courageous Quest. Cunningham, Paul, illus. (p. 373)
—Danger at Sea. Cunningham, Paul, illus. (p. 403)
—Discovery at Dawn. Cunningham, Paul, illus. (p. 450)
—I Pray the Stations of the Cross. Rchards, Virginia Helen, illus. (p. 844)
—My First Missal. Esquinaldo, Virginia, illus. (p. 1207)
—Mystery of the Missing Jars. Cunningham, Paul, illus. (p. 1225)
—Shepherds to the Rescue Cunningham, Paul, illus. (p. 1565)
—Stations of the Cross for Children. Pompei, Maria Teresa, tr. (p. 1644)
D'Ath, Justin. Pool. (p. 1383)
—Robbie & the Dolphins. Johnson, Jessica, illus. (p. 1478)
—Terrors of Nature. (p. 1722)
Dathini, Desiré. Memez: Songs to Make You Shout & Dance. (p. 1125)
Datlow, Ellen. Wolf at the Door. Windling, Terri, ed. (p. 1943)
Datlow, Ellen, jt. ed. see Windling, Terri.
Datlow, Ellen & Windling, Terri. After (Nineteen Stories of Apocalypse & Dystopia) (p. 28)
—Teeth: Vampire Tales. (p. 1715)
Datlow, Ellen & Windling, Terri, eds. Swan Sister: Fairy Tales Retold. (p. 1688)
Datnow, Claire L. Edwin Hubble: Discoverer of Galaxies. (p. 505)
—Edwin Hubble: Genius Discoverer of Galaxies. (p. 505)
Datsiouk, Andrew. Kristo. (p. 967)
Datta, Aparajita & Manjrekar, Nima. Walk the Rainforest with Niwupah. Ramaswamy, Maya, illus. (p. 1854)
Dattola, Chiara, illus. see Kim, Cecil.
Datz, Jim, illus. see Buzzeo, Toni.
Datz, Margot, illus. see Schaal, Patty.
Dau, John Bul. Lost Boy Lost Girl: Escaping Civil War in Sudan. (p. 1055)
Dau, John Bul & Akech, Martha Arual. Lost Boy, Lost Girl: Escaping Civil War in Sudan. (p. 1055)
Daubenspeck, Julie & Daubenspeck, Vince. May I See the King? Pendergrass, Mark D., illus. (p. 1112)
Daubenspeck, Vince, jt. auth. see Daubenspeck, Julie.
Dauber, Liz, illus. see Hillert, Margaret.
Dauber, Veronica. Mudslide. (p. 1189)
Daubert Standards Committee, et al. Discussions of the Committee on Daubert Standards: Summary of Meetings. (p. 450)
Daubney, Kate, illus. see Dods, Emma.
Daubney, Kate, illus. see Goldsmith, Mike.
D'Aubuisson, Elisabeth. Rainy Days. (p. 1436)
d'Aubuisson, Elisabeth. Rainy Days. (p. 1436)
D'Aubuisson, Elisabeth. Snowy Days. (p. 1601)
d'Aubuisson, Elisabeth. Snowy Days. (p. 1601)
D'Aubuisson, Elisabeth. Sunny Days. (p. 1677)
d'Aubuisson, Elisabeth. Sunny Days. (p. 1677)
D'Aubuisson, Elisabeth. What's the Weather? (p. 1900)
—Windy Days. (p. 1936)
d'Aubuisson, Elisabeth. Windy Days. (p. 1936)
Daudet, Alphonse. Siege of Berlin & Other Stories. (p. 1573)
Daudet, Alphonse, jt. auth. see Daudet, Alphonse.
Daudet, Alphonse & Daudet, Alphonse. Aventuras Prodigiosas de Tartarin de Tarascon. (p. 119)
Dauer, Marty. Harvey's Woods: the Royal Adventures. LaRiccia, Mike, illus. (p. 752)
Daugherty, Deborah Kay. Hair in the Way. (p. 736)
Daugherty, Doug. Boxy: A Tree of the Prairie. Gasal, Ben, illus. (p. 217)
Daugherty, Evan, et al. Snow White & the Huntsman. (p. 1599)
Daugherty, James, illus. see Sandburg, Carl.
Daugherty, Leanna. Climbing by Faith, Not by Sight. (p. 333)
Daugherty, Leo J. Vietnam War. (p. 1841)
Daugherty, Sharleen, ed. Young Voices of Silver City. (p. 1979)
Daugherty, Steven R. & Lewolt, Bruce. Getting A's: Secrets Expert Learners Use to Get Straight A's. (p. 669)
Daughters of St Paul. Stations of Cross Col & Act Bk. (p. 1644)
Daughters of St. Paul Staff. No Place for Defeat. (p. 1259)
Daughters of St. Paul Staff, jt. auth. see Vecchini, Silvia.
Daughters of St. Paul Staff, tr. see Paltro, Piera.
Daughters of St. Paul Staff, contrib. by. Prayers for Young Catholics. (p. 1393)
Daughtrey, Patricia & Benson, Gary. Shanaya & Friends: Litter Bugs Turn Eco H. E. R. O. S. Balkovek, Jim, illus. (p. 1559)
Daughtry, Carolyn Minor. I Am Fearfully & Wonderfully Made ! (p. 833)
D'Aulaire, Edgar Parin, jt. auth. see D'Aulaire, Ingri.
D'Aulaire, Edgar Parin & D'Aulaire, Ingri. D'Aulaires' Book of Norse Myths. (p. 410)
—Ola. (p. 1283)
D'Aulaire, Ingri, jt. auth. see D'Aulaire, Edgar Parin.
D'Aulaire, Ingri & D'Aulaire, Edgar Parin. Abraham Lincoln. (p. 6)
—Aulaires' Book of Trolls. (p. 115)
—Children of the Northlights. (p. 302)
—D'Aulaires' Book of Animals. (p. 410)
—Foxie, the Singing Dog. (p. 626)
—Leif the Lucky. (p. 991)
—Too Big. (p. 1766)
—Two Cars. (p. 1803)
D'Aulaire, Ingri, et al. Terrible Troll-Bird. (p. 1721)
Daunis, Marcia Prosco. Miller's Ben. (p. 1143)
Dauphin, Lili. I Will Fly Again: The Restavek. (p. 848)
Dauphin, Vaya. Greenstone Garden: The Elementals of Aotearoa (p. 723)
D'Aurio, Ariana. Legend of the Rainbow. Gubitosi-D'Aurio, Gina & Gubitosi, Lillian, illus. (p. 989)
Daurio, Ken, jt. auth. see Paul, Cinco.
Dautel, Daniel. Mission to Mount Everest. (p. 1153)
Dauterman, Mary & Antosh, Peter. Dirty Library: Twisted Children's Classics & Folked-Up Fairy Tales. (p. 446)
Dauth, Freya. Zoe & the Albatross. (p. 1987)
Dautremer, Rebecca. Enamorados. (p. 523)
Dautremer, Rébecca, illus. see Lechermeier, Philippe.
Dautremer, Rébecca, illus. see Norac, Carl.
Dautremer, Rebecca, illus. see Weulersse, Odile & Merz, Kathleen.
Dautremer, Rebecca, jt. auth. see Lechermeier, Philippe.
Dauvillier, Loïc, jt. auth. see Dickens, Charles.
Dauvillier, Loïc & Salsedo, Greg. Hidden. Lizano, Marc, illus. (p. 775)
Daval, Josie. Wright Twist. (p. 1963)
Davalos, Felipe, illus. see Elya, Susan Middleton.
Davalos, Felipe, illus. see Flor Ada, Alma & Campoy, F. Isabel.
Davalos, Felipe, illus. see Flor Ada, Alma.
Dávalos, Felipe, illus. see Harshman, Marc.
Davalos, Felipe, illus. see Markle, Sandra & Markle, William.
Davalos, Felipe, illus. see Serrano, Francisco.
Dávalos, Felipe, illus. see Slate, Joseph & Slate.
Davani, Keyvan. SmokeReality. (p. 1594)
D'Avanzo, Maria. Turn & Talk Vocalic R: Bk341. (p. 1797)
Davauer, Nathaniel, illus. see Sauer, Abe.
Dave, jt. auth. see Matt.
Dave & Matt. Yuck's Fart Club. Baines, Nigel, illus. (p. 1983)

D

Dave, Grandpa. Children's Stories Iii. (p. 304)
Dave, Paul. Visions of England: Class & Culture in Contemporary Cinema. (p. 1845)
Dave, Safety. Safety Dave & Daisy Ride the Bus. (p. 1502)
Dave, Vijay, photos by see Jani, Mahendra & Jani, Vandana.
Davenier, Christine, illus. see Andrews, Julie & Hamilton, Emma Walton.
Davenier, Christine, illus. see Andrews, Julie & Walton Hamilton, Emma.
Davenier, Christine, illus. see Andrews, Julie, et al.
Davenier, Christine, illus. see Ashman, Linda.
Davenier, Christine, illus. see Best, Cari.
Davenier, Christine, illus. see Durand, Hallie.
Davenier, Christine, illus. see Eagle, Kim.
Davenier, Christine, illus. see Gray, Karlin.
Davenier, Christine, illus. see Guest, Elissa Haden.
Davenier, Christine, illus. see Holt, Kimberly Willis.
Davenier, Christine, illus. see L'Engle, Madeleine.
Davenier, Christine, illus. see Maccarone, Grace.
Davenier, Christine, illus. see Prelutsky, Jack.
Davenier, Christine, jt. auth. see Johnston, Tony.
Davenport, Andrew. Here Come the Teletubbies. (p. 770)
—Teletubbies (Ce p'Tit Agneau) (p. 1716)
Davenport, Andy, illus. see Dayton, Howard & Dayton, Beverly.
Davenport, Andy, illus. see Hawks, Robb.
Davenport, Chris, illus. see Finley, Danielle.
Davenport, Eddie. Bunnyburg: The Newcomers. (p. 242)
Davenport, Jefferson. Let's Help the Librarian! (p. 998)
—Let's Help the Librarian! Subtract Within 20. (p. 998)
—Our Fishing Trip: Measure Lengths. (p. 1308)
—What Lives in Your Backyard? (p. 1892)
Davenport, Jennifer. Anna Begins. (p. 85)
Davenport, John. Age of Feudalism. (p. 29)
—American Revolution. (p. 63)
—Brief Political & Geographic History of Africa: Where Are... Belgian Congo, Rhodesia, & Kush. (p. 228)
—Brief Political & Geographic History of the Middle East: Where Are... Persia, Babylon, & the Ottoman Empire. (p. 228)
—Juan Ponce de Leon & His Lands of Discovery. Goetzmann, William H., ed. (p. 930)
—Nuremberg Trials. (p. 1273)
—U. S.-Mexico Border. (p. 1806)
Davenport, John, jt. text see Stafford, Mark.
Davenport, John C. Attack on Pearl Harbor: The United States Enters World War II. (p. 114)
—Bolshevik Revolution. (p. 208)
—C. S. Lewis. (p. 250)
—Dante: Poet, Author & Proud Florentine. (p. 406)
—D-Day & the Liberation of France. (p. 397)
—French Revolution & the Rise of Napoleon. (p. 636)
—Internment of Japanese Americans During World War II: Detention of American Citizens. (p. 880)
—Louisiana Territory. Matray, James I., ed. (p. 1059)
—Saladin. (p. 1504)
Davenport, Kathy. Holly's Best Friend. (p. 789)
—Holly's Chocolate Heart. (p. 789)
Davenport, Kelly. Do Hotdogs Grow on Trees? (p. 457)
Davenport, Peter. Unforgettable: Images That Have Changed Our Lives. (p. 1817)
Davenport, Roger. Wanderer. (p. 1856)
Daves-Schneider, Lida, et al. Auf Deutsch! (p. 115)
Davey, Frances. Brief Political & Geographic History of Europe: Where Are... Prussia, Gaul, & the Holy Roman Empire. (p. 228)
Davey, Keith Peter. Squeaks Narrow Squeaks. Frost, Justine, illus. (p. 1636)
Davey, Owen. Foxly's Feast. (p. 626)
—Laika: Astronaut Dog. Davey, Owen, illus. (p. 972)
—Night Knight. Davey, Owen, illus. (p. 1253)
Davey, Peter. Abracadabra Violin (p. 6)
—Abracadabra Violin Hussey, Christopher & Sebba, Jane, eds. (p. 6)
Davi. Chichonazo! (p. 299)
—Senor Simplon. (p. 1550)
Davi, Annou, tr. see Bronson, Tammy Carter.
DaVia, Paul C., jt. auth. see DaVia, Sylvia C.
DaVia, Sylvia C. & DaVia, Paul C. Adventures of Teeny Jeanie. (p. 23)
Davick, Linda. I Love You, Nose! I Love You, Toes! Davick, Linda, illus. (p. 844)
—Say Hello! Davick, Linda, illus. (p. 1518)
Davick, Linda, illus. see Hays, Anna Jane.
Davick, Linda, illus. see Madaras, Lynda.
Davick, Linda, illus. see Schulman, Janet.
Davick, Linda, illus. see Sierra, Judy.
Davick, Linda, jt. auth. see Madaras, Lynda.
Davick, Linda, tr. see Madaras, Lynda.
David. Counting Nifty from One to Fifty. (p. 371)
David, jt. auth. see Aiken, Zora.
David, A. Rosalie. Handbook to Life in Ancient Egypt. (p. 740)
David, Amanda, illus. see Michael.
David, Amor, illus. see Rashad, Girmen.
David And Stephanie Williams. Pajamazon Amazon vs the Goofers Twisters. (p. 1319)
David, Annette, tr. see Alemagna, Beatrice.
David, Beth. Zorena: And the Medallion of Corandu. (p. 1990)
David C. Cook Publishing Company Staff. ABC's. (p. 4)
—Adam & Eve (p. 11)
—Asteroid Alley Games Guide. (p. 108)
—Baby Moses (p. 127)
—Backpack Danglers. (p. 130)
—Beginning. (p. 159)
—Bible Promises. (p. 176)
—Blast off! Preschool Student Book. (p. 198)
—Bread or Stone (p. 224)
—Breakfast on the Beach (p. 225)
—Cc Crafts, Red Book. (p. 283)
—Cc Leader's Guide, Red Book. (p. 283)
—CC Snacks & Games, Red Book. (p. 283)
—Cosmic City Elementary Student Book. (p. 368)
—Crafty Cookin' (p. 376)
—Daniel in the Lion's Den. (p. 405)
—David Giant Fighter. (p. 411)
—David's Friend (p. 411)
—Dive In! Fun Faith Builders (p. 454)
—Elijah, God's Brave Prophet Pack (p. 512)
—Fizz, Foam, & Froth Science Lab. (p. 601)
—Fun & Freaky Science (p. 647)
—God's Fruit. (p. 691)
—Hot Crafts for Cool Kids (p. 801)
—It's a Snap! Fun Faith Builders. (p. 896)
—Jesus & Me: BOZ's Big Book of Bible Fun. (p. 915)
—Jesus Feeds 5000. (p. 915)
—Jonah & the Big Fish. (p. 925)
—Land of Milk & Honey. (p. 973)
—Lazarus Lives (p. 981)
—Learning to Count. (p. 985)
—Let the Children Come (p. 994)
—Lord's Prayer. (p. 1053)
—Manners. (p. 1088)
—Noah & the Floating Zoo. (p. 1261)
—Nursery Rhymes. (p. 1273)
—Ooze & Awes in God's Creations (p. 1299)
—Outer Limits Mission Log Upper Elementary Student Book. (p. 1312)
—Pencil Fun Book: Jesus Is Alive. (p. 1336)
—Pencil Fun Book: Noah Builds an Ark. (p. 1336)
—Pencil Fun Book: Joeseph Saves His Family. (p. 1336)
—Quiet Moment with God Devotional Journal for Teens. (p. 1428)
—Ring, Robe & Shoes (p. 1473)
—Rock the Room Games (p. 1482)
—Samson, God's Strong Man Pack (p. 1509)
—Scripture Pictures - Journey through the Old Testament. (p. 1533)
—Scripture Pictures - Miracles & Parables of Jesus. (p. 1533)
—Shooting Star Drive-in Snack Guide. (p. 1568)
—Spur-of-the-Moment Crafts. (p. 1635)
—Ten Commandments. (p. 1718)
—Twenty-Third Psalm (p. 1801)
—Wise Men Follow the Star (p. 1940)
—X-Perience It! (p. 1967)
David C. Cook Publishing Company Staff & Currie, Robin. Baby Bible Sing & Pray. Busaluzzo, Constanza, illus. (p. 125)
—Baby Bible Storybook for Girls. Busaluzzo, Constanza, illus. (p. 125)
—Stories about Jesus. Busaluzzo, Constanza, illus. (p. 1654)
David C. Cook Publishing Company Staff, creator. Action! Cool Theater. (p. 10)
—Classy, Flashy Bible Dramas. (p. 329)
—Full Tilt Wacky Games. (p. 646)
—Fun Science That Teaches God's Word for Tweeners. (p. 648)
—Game-a-Thon. (p. 654)
—Memory Maker Bible Crafts. (p. 1126)
—More Toddlerific! Faith-Building Activities for Toddlers & Twos. (p. 1175)
—Pretty Quick & Easy Bible Dramas. (p. 1398)
—Score with Scripture Games. (p. 1530)
—Stick'em up Bible Crafts. (p. 1650)
—Through-the-Bible Crafts. (p. 1745)
David, Carole. Averses et Réglisses Noires. Athanassiadis, Kiki, illus. (p. 119)
David, Catrow, illus. see Zweibel, Alan.
David, Charles. Knightscares #2: (Knightscares) (p. 964)
David, Charles, jt. auth. see Anthony, David.
David, Chris, jt. auth. see Magruder, Trula.
David, Christopher. Denholme & the Skeleton Mystery. (p. 426)
David Cook Publishers, creator. God Is My Song. (p. 689)
David, Doyle. Walker Bulldog. (p. 1854)
David, E. L. Christmas Gift. (p. 314)
David, Erica. All Hail the Queen. RH Disney Staff & Robinson, Bill, illus. (p. 44)
—Anna & Elsa #5: the Polar Bear Piper (Disney Frozen) Robinson, William & Legramandi, Francesco, illus. (p. 85)
—Anna & Elsa - A Warm Welcome. RH Disney Staff et al, illus. (p. 85)
—Big Pony Race. Fruchter, Jason, illus. (p. 183)
—Christmas with Krabby Klaws. Martinez, Heather, illus. (p. 316)
—Extreme Rescue: Crocodile Mission. McGee, Warner, illus. (p. 556)
—Great Ice Engine. RH Disney Staff et al, illus. (p. 716)
—Memory & Magic. RH Disney Staff & Robinson, William E., illus. (p. 1126)
—Mr. Peabody & Sherman Big Golden Book (Mr. Peabody & Sherman) Laguna, Fabio & Spaziante, Patrick, illus. (p. 1186)
—Mr. Peabody & Sherman Junior Novelization (Mr. Peabody & Sherman) Random House, illus. (p. 1186)
—Toothless: A Dragon Hero's Story. (p. 1768)
—Warm Welcome RH Disney Staff et al, illus. (p. 1858)
David, Erica, jt. auth. see Random House.
David, Erica, adapted by. Hotel for Dogs. (p. 802)
—How to Pick Your Dragon. (p. 821)
David, Erica & Artifact Group Staff. Good Times! (p. 700)
David, Francois. Cabeza en Las Nubes. Solal, Marc, tr. (p. 250)
David Haugen. Colonists. (p. 342)
—Leaders. (p. 981)
David, Hop & Coloring Books Staff. Surreal Visions Coloring Book. (p. 1686)
David Iii, Paul. Brave Americans. (p. 223)
David, Jack. Abrams Tanks. (p. 7)
—Air Force Air Commandos. (p. 31)
—Apache Helicopters. (p. 91)
—Army Green Berets. (p. 100)
—ATVs. (p. 114)
—AV-8B Harrier Jump Jets. (p. 118)
—B-1B Lancers. (p. 122)
—B-2 Stealth Bombers. (p. 122)
—B-52 Stratofortresses. (p. 122)
—Big Air Skateboarding. (p. 177)
—BMX Racing. (p. 204)
—Caving. (p. 282)
—Choppers. (p. 310)
—Cruisers. (p. 386)
—Dirt Bikes. (p. 446)
—Enduro Motorcycles. (p. 527)
—F-14 Tomcats. (p. 559)
—F-15 Eagles. (p. 559)
—Go-Kart Racing. (p. 686)
—Harley Davidson Motorcycles. (p. 749)
—HH-60 Pave Hawk Helicopters. (p. 775)
—HH-60 Pavehawk Helicopters. (p. 775)
—Indy Cars. (p. 873)
—In-Line Skating. (p. 864)
—Karts. (p. 944)
—Kiteboarding. (p. 962)
—Lowriders. (p. 1061)
—M2A2 Bradleys. (p. 1067)
—Marine Corps Force Recon. (p. 1094)
—Motocross Cycles. (p. 1179)
—Motocross Racing. (p. 1179)
—Moto-X Freestyle. (p. 1179)
—Navy SEALs. (p. 1238)
—Predator Drones. (p. 1394)
—Sport Bikes. (p. 1631)
—Stock Cars. (p. 1651)
—Supercross Racing. (p. 1683)
—Torque: Humvees. (p. 1770)
—Torque: B-1B Lancers. (p. 1770)
—Torque: M2A2 Bradleys. (p. 1770)
—Torque: B-52 Stratofortresses. (p. 1770)
—Torque - Military Machines (p. 1770)
—Touring Motorcycles. (p. 1773)
—Tuner Cars. (p. 1796)
—U-2 Planes. (p. 1805)
—United States Army. (p. 1819)
—United States Coast Guard. (p. 1819)
—United States Marine Corps. (p. 1819)
—United States Navy. (p. 1819)
David, Jamie. Johann Sebastian Humpbach. David, Jamie, illus. (p. 920)
David, Jason, illus. see John, Roberta.
David, Juliet. All Aboard with Noah Allen, Marie, illus. (p. 42)
—Baby Jesus Is Born Prole, Helen, illus. (p. 126)
—Bible Stories Painting Book Abbott, Simon, illus. (p. 176)
—Busy Christmas Stable Pitt, Sarah, illus. (p. 246)
—Candle Bible for Kids Parry, Jo, illus. (p. 261)
—Candle Bible for Kids Board Book Parry, Jo, illus. (p. 261)
—Candle Bible for Toddlers Prole, Helen, illus. (p. 261)
—Candle Bible for Toddlers Carry along Bible Fun. Prole, Helen, illus. (p. 261)
—Candle Day by Day Bible Heyes, Jane, illus. (p. 261)
—Candle Prayers for Toddlers Prole, Helen, illus. (p. 261)
—Candle Prayers for Toddlers & Candle Bible for Toddlers Prole, Helen, illus. (p. 261)
—Christmas Story Parry, Jo, illus. (p. 315)
—Daniel & the Lions' Den Denham, Gemma, illus. (p. 404)
—Dot to Dot Coloring & Stickers Smith, Jan, illus. (p. 472)
—Dot to Dot Coloring & Stickers Bk. 1 Smith, Jan, illus. (p. 472)
—Easter Story Parry, Jo, illus. (p. 499)
—First Christmas Denham, Gemma, illus. (p. 593)
—Follow the Star Prole, Helen, illus. (p. 612)
—God Helps Me Byrne, Mike, illus. (p. 689)
—God Knows Me Byrne, Mike, illus. (p. 689)
—God Loves Me Byrne, Mike, illus. (p. 689)
—Great Flood Parry, Jo, illus. (p. 716)
—Innkeeper Wood, Hannah, illus. (p. 875)
—Learn & Play: Chalkboard Activities. Prole, Helen, illus. (p. 982)
—Lift the Flap Nativity. Denham, Gemma & Ward, Sylvia, illus. (p. 1014)
—Lift the Flap Noah Ward, Sylvia, illus. (p. 1014)
—Lost Sheep Denham, Gemma, illus. (p. 1056)
—Noah & His Boat Denham, Gemma, illus. (p. 1261)
—Noah & His Great Ark Prole, Helen, illus. (p. 1261)
—Noah's Busy Boat Pitt, Sarah, illus. (p. 1262)
—Prayers for Little Girls Clay, Julie, illus. (p. 1393)
—Puddle Pen Bible Stories Martin, Stuart, illus. (p. 1414)
—Puddle Pen Christmas Poole, Helen, illus. (p. 1414)
—Shepherds Wood, Hannah, illus. (p. 1565)
—Stable in Bethlehem. Denham, Gemma & Scott, Richard, illus. (p. 1638)
—Very First Christmas Prole, Helen, illus. (p. 1838)
—Very First Christmas - Changing Pictures Siewert, Pauline, illus. (p. 1838)
—Wise Men Wood, Hannah, illus. (p. 1940)
David, Juliet, jt. auth. see Dowley, Tim.
David, Juliet, jt. auth. see Williamson, Karen.
David, Juliet & Ayliffe, Alex. Easter Story Ellis, Elina, illus. (p. 499)
—My Very First Bible & Prayers Prole, Helen, illus. (p. 1221)
David, Juliet & Dowley, Tim. Time for Bed Bible Stories Pitt, Sarah, illus. (p. 1751)
David, Kate. Murphy & the Magical Hat. (p. 1192)
David, Keren. Almost True. (p. 48)
—Another Life. (p. 88)
—Lia's Guide to Winning the Lottery. (p. 1005)
—When I Was Joe. (p. 1903)
David, Kerens. Almost True. (p. 48)
David, Lawrence. Invasion of the Shag Carpet Creature. Gott, Barry, illus. (p. 883)
—Most Evil Friendly Villain Ever. (p. 1177)
—Terror of the Pink Dodo Balloons. Gott, Barry, illus. (p. 1722)
David, Lawrence, jt. auth. see Wilcox, Brian.
David, Lawrence, ed. Chicken Run: Action-Packed Storybook. Barnes, Tom, photos by. (p. 300)
David, Mark. Crazy Cars: For Crazy Kids. (p. 377)
David, Mark, illus. see Ball, Duncan.
David, Messing, illus. see McCloud, Carol & Martin, Katherine.
David, Patrick. True Story of Noah's Ark. (p. 1793)
David, Peter. Astonishing X-Men. (p. 109)
—Crazy Like a Fox Youngquist, Jeff, ed. (p. 377)
—Essential Web of Spider-Man Mooney, Jim et al, illus. (p. 537)
—Hand in Hand: Part 1. (p. 740)
—Hand in Hand: Part 2. (p. 740)
—Incredible Hunk (p. 869)
—Many Happy Returns. (p. 1089)
—Nothing to Lose. Cross, Chris, illus. (p. 1268)
—Out of the Shadows. Thomas, LeSean, illus. (p. 1311)
—Rock Gods. (p. 1482)
—Sachs & Violens. (p. 1500)
—Spider-Man: The Death of Jean Dewolff. Buckler, Rich & Buscema, Sal, illus. (p. 1626)
—X-Factor - Hell on Earth War (p. 1967)
David, Peter, illus. see Romita, John, Jr.
David, Peter, jt. auth. see Busiek, Kurt.
David, Peter & Lente, Fred Van. Wolverine First Class Set 2. (p. 1944)
David, Peter, et al. Amazing Spider-Man Epic Collection: Ghosts of the Past. Buscema, Sal & Frenz, Ron, illus. (p. 56)
—Cyrano de Bergerac: A Heroic Comedy in Five Acts. (p. 397)
—Return of the Worthy. (p. 1465)
—Wizard Spiderman (p. 1943)
David, R. Joseph & His Brothers. (p. 926)
—Noahs Ark. (p. 1261)
David, Racheli, illus. see Ginsburg, Sara.
David, Racheli, illus. see Levy, Rochel.
David, Racheli, illus. see Paretzky, Leah.
David, Racheli, illus. see Rosenberg, Faigy & Weiss, Esti.
David, Racheli, illus. see Schwartz, Sara Leah.
David, Richard, illus. see Pablo, Norma.
David, Ryan. Magic Raincoat. Benatova, Sibylla, illus. (p. 1073)
David, Sarah B. Reducing Your Carbon Footprint at Home. (p. 1456)
David West. Helicopter. (p. 763)
—Jet Plane. (p. 916)
—Motorcycle. (p. 1179)
—Tank. (p. 1705)
—Train. (p. 1777)
David, Yvonne. Out of the Apple Orchard. (p. 1311)
Daviddi, Evelyn. My Sister Makes Me Happy! My Sister Makes Me Mad! (p. 1218)
Daviddi, Evelyn, illus. see Cali, Davide.
Davidge, Bud. Mummer's Song Wallace, Ian, illus. (p. 1190)
Davidge, James. Driftwood Ellesmere. Palmer, Judd, illus. (p. 485)
—Driftwood Saves the Whales. (p. 485)
—Duchess Ranch of Old John Ware. Prodor, Bob, illus. (p. 488)
—Mathemagick: The Point & the Invisible Hand. Davidge, Jesse, illus. (p. 1107)
Davidge, James & Davidge, Jesse. Mathemagick: The War of Flat & Wonder. (p. 1107)
—Mathemagick: Apples & Origins - Featuring Hypatia of the Wandering Stars. (p. 1107)
Davidge, Jesse, illus. see Davidge, James.
Davidge, Jesse, jt. auth. see Davidge, James.
Davidow, Shelley. Early Readers- Set of Six (p. 494)
—Spirit of the Mountain. (p. 1628)
—Wise Enchanter: A Journey through the Alphabet. Kurzyca, Krystyna Emilia, illus. (p. 1940)
Davids, Paul. Fountain of Youth. Davids, Paul, photos by. (p. 624)
Davids, Stacy B. Hip-Hop Greats (p. 780)
—Strange but True Science (p. 1665)
—Strange but True Weather (p. 1665)
Davids, Tom & Davids, Veronica. Wrestling the ABCs: Creating Character & Fostering Fitness. (p. 1963)
Davids, Veronica, jt. auth. see Davids, Tom.
Davidsen, Keith & Hayes, Drew. Hyena (p. 831)
Davidshofer, Kathleen. Libby's Gift. (p. 1005)
Davidson, Alice Joyce. Christmas Blessings Baby's Holiday Photo Album. Stanley, Mandy, illus. (p. 312)
—My Day with Jesus Clar, David Austin, illus. (p. 1201)
—My Take-Along Bible. Mazille, Capucine, illus. (p. 1219)
—St. Francis & the Animals. Swanson, Maggie, illus. (p. 1638)
—St. Therese: the Little Flower. Swanson, Maggie, illus. (p. 1638)
—We Love You Baby. Lewis, Anthony, illus. (p. 1867)
Davidson, Amy. Abigail Breslin. (p. 5)
—Darren Criss. (p. 409)
—Elle Fanning. (p. 514)
—Keke Palmer. (p. 948)
—Kendall Jenner. (p. 948)
—Rico Rodriguez. (p. 1470)
Davidson, Amy, jt. auth. see Mills, Nathan.
Davidson, Andrew. Discovering Africa's Past. (p. 448)
Davidson, Arden. Playing Hopscotch on a Rubber Roof. (p. 1372)
Davidson, Arnold I., ed. see Foucault, Michel.
Davidson, Arnold I., jt. auth. see Foucault, Michel.
Davidson, Avelyn. Beach Biology. (p. 149)
—Dollars & Sense: Economics & Science. (p. 463)
—Tundras of the World. (p. 1796)
Davidson, Barbara. Billys Most Difficult Choice. (p. 187)
Davidson, Blanche, illus. see Cogan, Karen.
Davidson, Chris, illus. see Koontz, Robin Michal.
Davidson, Chris, illus. see Koontz, Robin.
Davidson, Chris, illus. see Owens, L. L.
Davidson, Dawn, illus. see Stevenson, Paula.
Davidson, Elizabeth W. Cheery: The True Adventures of a Chiricahua Leopard Frog. Hagelberg, Michael, illus. (p. 296)
Davidson, Ellen. When the Third Moon Wanes. (p. 1905)
Davidson, Gary, des. Mesozoic & Cenozoic (p. 1129)
—Paleozoic Era (p. 1319)
Davidson, Halsey. Navy Boys Behind the Big Guns: Or Sinking the German U-Boats. (p. 1238)
—Navy Boys Behind the Big Guns or Sinking the German U-Boats. (p. 1238)
Davidson, James West & Stoff, Michael B. American Nation. (p. 62)
Davidson, Jamie, illus. see Woodsmall, Marilyne.
Davidson, Janice. Inside the White House. (p. 878)
Davidson, Jean. My Daddy Makes the Best Motorcycles in the Whole Wide World, the Harley-Davidson. Hammerquist, Theresa, illus. (p. 1201)

—My Grandma Rides a Harley: She's Cool! Bauknecht, Julie, illus. (p. 1210)
Davidson, Jenny. Explosionist. (p. 554)
Davidson, Jody. Broadway Beginner. (p. 230)
Davidson, Jordan. Rubber Boots: Poetry for Rainy & Not-So-Rainy Days. (p. 1493)
Davidson, Karen Louise. Number Phonics: A Complete Learn-by-Numbers Reading Program for Easy One-on-One Tutoring of Children. (p. 1271)
Davidson, Kay. Becoming a Better Writer Using the Simple 6: Grades 3rd - 6th. (p. 156)
—Simple 6 for K-2 Writers. (p. 1577)
—Writing the Simple 6: A Writing Rubic for Kids. (p. 1965)
Davidson, Kayla Shurley. Daddy's Little Squirrel. (p. 399)
Davidson, Kevin, illus. see Ball, Ann & Will, Julianne M.
Davidson, Kevin, illus. see Leichner, Jeannine Timko.
Davidson L. Haworth. Dragon of Prali. (p. 477)
Davidson, Leigh, ed. see Houts, Amy.
Davidson, Lg. Supernova's Unique Family. (p. 1684)
Davidson, Mannis, jt. auth. see Mannis, Celeste Davidson.
Davidson, Margaret. Five True Dog Stories. (p. 601)
—Louis Braille. Compere, Janet, illus. (p. 1058)
Davidson, Margaret & Wilson, Roger. Neuf Histoires Vraies de Dauphins. (p. 1242)
Davidson, Margot, creator. Stories with a View. (p. 1655)
Davidson, Mary, illus. see Plunkett, Windyann.
Davidson, Mary Richmond. Buffalo Bill: Wild West Showman. Savitt, Sam, illus. (p. 235)
Davidson, MaryJanice, jt. auth. see Alongi, Anthony.
Davidson, MaryJanice & Alongi, Anthony. Silver Moon Elm (p. 1576)
Davidson, Michael. Ready, Teddy, Go! Davidson, Michael, illus. (p. 1447)
Davidson, Michele R. Stowaways to Smith Island: Hayden & Chloe's Enchanted Journey with the Nurses to Maryland's Mysterious Smith Island. Watjen, Laureen, illus. (p. 1664)
Davidson, Mike, et al. Draw What? A Doodling, Drawing, & Coloring Book. (p. 481)
Davidson, Nadine, jt. auth. see Hughes, Mair Wynn.
Davidson, Paul. X-Men Legacy: Aftermath. (p. 1967)
Davidson, Paul, illus. see Spurrier, Simon & Swierczynski, Duane.
Davidson, Paul, illus. see Swanson, Diane.
Davidson, Paul, et al. X-Factor: Hard Labor. (p. 1967)
Davidson, Rebecca Piatt. All the World's a Stage. Lobel, Anita, illus. (p. 46)
Davidson, S. & Daynes, K. Princess Jewelry Kid Kit (Bag) (p. 1404)
Davidson, Simon & Gardner, Julia. What Is Waste? Inquiry Box. (p. 1891)
Davidson, Susanna. Baby & Toddler Treasury. Furukawa, Masumi et al, illus. (p. 124)
—Christmas Carol (Picture Book) (p. 313)
—Cinderella Picture Book. (p. 320)
—Frog Prince. (p. 640)
—Musicians of Bremen. Gordon, Mike & Gordon, Carl, illus. (p. 1194)
—Nursery Rhyme Treasury. Kolanovic, Dubravka, illus. (p. 1273)
—Nutcracker with Music. (p. 1274)
—Princess Handbook. Gordon, Mike, illus. (p. 1404)
—Princess Polly & the Pony. Hill, Dave, illus. (p. 1405)
—See Inside Fairyland. Ligi, Raffaella, illus. (p. 1546)
—Stories of Dolls. Wanert, Amandine, illus. (p. 1655)
—Stories of Magic Ponies. Costa, Jana, illus. (p. 1655)
—Stories of Mermaids. (p. 1655)
—Story of Baby Jesus. (p. 1657)
—Story of Hanukkah. (p. 1658)
—Story of the Nativity. (p. 1661)
—Swan Lake with Music. (p. 1688)
—That's Not My Puppy. (p. 1727)
—Thumbelina. (p. 1745)
—Treasury of Animal Stories. (p. 1782)
—Usborne Stories of Dolls & Fairies. Wanert, Amandine, illus. (p. 1827)
—Whales & Dolphins: Internet-Linked. (p. 1878)
—World of Animals: Internet-Linked. Unwin, Mike, illus. (p. 1956)
Davidson, Susanna, jt. auth. see Lacey, Minna.
Davidson, Susanna & Daynes, Katie. Little Princess Treasury. McNicholas, Shelagh & Cascio, Maria Cristina Lo, illus. (p. 1034)
Davidson, Susanna & Stowell, Louie. My First Fairyland Book. Raffaella, Ligi, illus. (p. 1206)
Davidson, Susanna & Unwin, Mike. Usborne World of Animals. Montgomery, Lee & Jackson, Ian, illus. (p. 1827)
Davidson, Susanna, et al. Usborne Internet-Linked World Atlas of Dinosaurs. Rey, Luis V., illus. (p. 1827)
Davidson, Susanna, retold by. East of the Sun, West of the Moon. (p. 498)
—Goldilocks & the Three Bears (Picture Book) (p. 696)
—Railway Children. (p. 1434)
—Secret Garden (Picture Book) (p. 1541)
Davidson, Susannah. Dinosaur Sticker Atlas. Turnbull, Stephanie, ed. (p. 443)
—Whales & Dolphins. (p. 1878)
—World Atlas of Dinosaurs: Internet-Linked. (p. 1954)
Davidson, Susannah, jt. auth. see Daynes, Katie.
Davidson, Susannah, et al. Whales & Dolphins. Woodcock, John, illus. (p. 1878)
Davidson, Susannah, retold by. Cinderella. (p. 320)
Davidson, Thomas A. Penny Found in Willowbrooke. (p. 1338)
Davidson, Tish. African American Scientists & Inventors. (p. 27)
—African American Scientists & Inventors. Hill, Marc Lamont, ed. (p. 27)
—African Americans in Business. (p. 27)
—African Americans in Business. Hill, Marc Lamont, ed. (p. 27)
—Atlantic: North Carolina, Virginia, West Virginia (p. 112)
—East South-Central States: Kentucky & Tennessee (p. 498)
—Prejudice. (p. 1395)
—School Conflict. (p. 1522)
—Southern New England: Connecticut, Massachusetts, Rhode Island (p. 1617)
—Theocracy. Colton, Timothy J., ed. (p. 1729)
Davidson, William Michael. Dragon Who Pulled Her Scales: The Everwynn Chronicles. (p. 478)
Davidsson, Ashton, illus. see Johnson, Rhonda & Paladin, Frank.
Davie, Brooke N. My Bumblebee Friend. (p. 1199)
Davie, Helen K., illus. see Pfeffer, Wendy & Pfeffer.
Davie, Helen K., illus. see Pfeffer, Wendy.
Davie, Helen K., illus. see Zoehfeld, Kathleen Weidner.
Davie, Jan. Apollo Cafe. (p. 91)
—Arthur's Amulet. (p. 104)
—Nexus Facilitator. (p. 1249)
—Stairway to the Stars. (p. 1638)
Davie, Rob, jt. auth. see Kavanagh, Shannon.
Davies, Adam. Mine All Mine. (p. 1145)
Davies, Aled, ed. see Stowell, Gordon.
Davies, Aled, tr. see Mortensen, Carl Anker.
Davies, Alun Emanuel. Dwy Ochr y Geiniog. (p. 491)
Davies, Andy, et al. Boys' World of Doodles: Over 100 Pictures to Complete & Create. (p. 220)
Davies, Andy Robert, illus. see Heling, Kathryn & Hembrook, Deborah.
Davies, Andy Robert, illus. see Wolf, Sallie.
Davies, Ann. Fun Adding. (p. 647)
—Fun Size. (p. 648)
Davies, Ann & Davies, Gill. One Tiger. (p. 1297)
Davies, Ann & Ne, Harriet. Sum Fun. (p. 1673)
—Teddy Is Yellow. (p. 1712)
—What Time Is It? Asks Elephant. (p. 1894)
Davies, Anna. Followers. (p. 612)
—Wrecked. (p. 1962)
Davies, Aysha & Benchmark Education Co., LLC Staff. Lunch for Patch. (p. 1065)
Davies, Benji. Storm Whale. Davies, Benji, illus. (p. 1656)
Davies, Benji, illus. see Courtauld, Sarah.
Davies, Benji, illus. see John, Jory.
Davies, Benji, illus. see Milbourne, Anna.
Davies, Benji, illus. see Nosy Crow.
Davies, Beth. Batman's Missions. (p. 144)
Davies, Beulah, ed. see Vergo, Peter.
Davies, Bronwen. Scholastic Reader Level 1: Get the Giggles: A First Joke Book. (p. 1522)
Davies, Caroline. Duck. (p. 488)
—Fish. (p. 598)
—Turtle. (p. 1798)
—Whale. (p. 1877)
Davies, Caroline, illus. see Child, Jeremy.
Davies, Caroline & Martin, Sharon. Chwarae Cuddio. (p. 318)
—Cotiau Newydd. (p. 369)
—Y Frech Goch. (p. 1968)
Davies, Caroline, et al. Big & Little. (p. 177)
Davies, Caroline, tr. Hey, Diddle Diddle. (p. 774)
—Humpty Dumpty. (p. 827)
—Little Miss Muffet. (p. 1031)
—Pat-A-Cake. (p. 1327)
Davies, Carolyn. Josef Herman in Wales. (p. 926)
Davies, Carolyn & Bebb, Lynne. Josef Herman in Wales. (p. 926)
Davies, Christie. Dewi the Dragon. (p. 432)
Davies, Christine. Where Art Thou Unicorn. (p. 1906)
Davies, Dalene. Sock Monster's Invade Earth: Hold on to Your Socks! (p. 1605)
Davies, David Stuart. Darlington Substitution Scandal & Sherlock Holmes & the Reichenbach Secret. (p. 409)
Davies, Dilys, jt. auth. see Bhugra, Dinesh K. L.
Davies, Donna. Night of the Candy Creepers. Peters, Rob, illus. (p. 1254)
Davies, Donna M. Bye, Bye Boogeyman. Bailin-Rembar, Jill, ed. (p. 249)
Davies, Elaine, et al. Dysgu Gofalu / Learning to Care. (p. 491)
Davies, Elgan Philip. Cic o'r Smotyn. (p. 318)
Davies, Elgan Philip & Ceredigion, Cymdeithas Lyfrau. Olion Hen Elyn. (p. 1285)
Davies, Florence S., illus. see Schneider, Richard H.
Davies, Gill. 365 Awesome Facts & Records about Everything. McRae, Anne, ed. (p. 2001)
—Brave Little Owl. Twinney, Dick, illus. (p. 223)
—British Colonies. Aronson, Marc, ed. (p. 229)
—Hispanic America 1490s - the Present. Aronson, Marc, ed. (p. 781)
—Hispanic America 1490s- the Present. Aronson, Marc, ed. (p. 781)
—I Won't Do That Today: A Story of Stubbornness. O'Neill, Rachael, illus. (p. 849)
—Illustrated Timeline of Medicine. (p. 858)
—My Nursery Rhyme Pop-up Book. Guile, Gill, illus. (p. 1216)
—Native America 900 BC - the Present. Aronson, Marc, ed. (p. 1234)
—One Wind. (p. 1297)
—Special Wish: A Story of Confidence. O'Neill, Rachael, illus. (p. 1623)
—Ten in a Bed: A Pop-up Counting Book. Guile, Gill, illus. (p. 1718)
—Thirteen Colonies 1584 - 1776. (p. 1734)
—Thirteen Colonies 1584 - 1776. Aronson, Marc, ed. (p. 1734)
Davies, Gill, jt. auth. see Davies, Ann.
Davies, Gill & Freeman, Tina. Friend for Flash. (p. 637)
—Happy Hen. (p. 746)
—Lucy Lamb. (p. 1063)
—Two Naughty Piglets. (p. 1804)
Davies, Gill & Morris, Neil. 365 Awesome Facts & Records about Nature. (p. 2001)
Davies, H. French Dictionary for Beginners Internet-Referenced. (p. 635)
—Spanish Dictionary for Beginners. (p. 1621)
Davies, H. & Holmes, F. French Dictionary for Beginners. (p. 635)
Davies, Hannah & Gunnell, Beth. Pretty Patterns: Beautiful Patterns to Color! (p. 1398)
Davies, Hannah & Ryan, Nellie. Pretty Costumes: Beautiful Costumes to Color! (p. 1398)
Davies, Helen. French Dictionary for Beginners. Irving, Nicole, ed. (p. 635)
—German Dictionary for Beginners. Irving, Nicole, ed. (p. 666)
—Italian Dictionary for Beginners. Irving, Nicole, ed. (p. 894)
—Spanish Dictionary for Beginners. Irving, Nicole, ed. (p. 1621)
Davies, Helen & Iannaco, G. Italian Dictionary for Beginners. (p. 894)
Davies, Helen Emanuel. Siff a Saff: A Straeon Eraill. Maclean, Andrew, illus. (p. 1573)
Davies, Helen Emanuel & Cooper, Anne Lloyd. Torri Gair. (p. 1770)
Davies, Humphrey, tr. see Khoury, Elias.
Davies, Huw. Games Book: How to Play the Games of Yesterday. (p. 654)
Davies, Jacqueline. Bell Bandit. (p. 162)
—Boy Who Drew Birds: A Story of John James Audubon. Sweet, Melissa, illus. (p. 219)
—Candy Smash. (p. 261)
—House Takes a Vacation (p. 803)
—Lemonade Crime. (p. 991)
—Lemonade War. (p. 991)
—Magic Trap. (p. 1074)
—Panda Pants. Hanson, Sydney, illus. (p. 1320)
—Tricking the Tallyman. Schindler, S. D., illus. (p. 1786)
—Where the Ground Meets the Sky (p. 1909)
Davies, James, illus. see Bradman, Tony & Banana, Red.
Davies, James, illus. see Courtenay, L. A.
Davies, James, illus. see Courtenay, Lucy.
Davies, Jean S. Neighborly Notes: From Turn of the Century Small Town Vermont (p. 1240)
Davies, Jocelyn. Beautiful Dark. (p. 153)
—Fractured Light. (p. 627)
—Radiant Sky. (p. 1432)
Davies, Jon. Storm Chasers! on the Trail of Twisters. Rath, Robert, illus. (p. 1655)
Davies, Kate. Little Squeak School. (p. 1036)
—Princess Tales. (p. 1405)
—See under the Sea. (p. 1547)
—Welcome to the Mouse House. (p. 1874)
—What's Physics All About? (p. 1899)
—What's Science All About? (p. 1899)
Davies, Kate, illus. see Giles, Sophie.
Davies, Kate, illus. see Heddle, Rebecca.
Davies, Kate, jt. auth. see Courtauld, Sarah.
Davies, Kate, jt. auth. see Giles, Sophie.
Davies, Kate & Stowell, Louie. Sticker Dressing Pirates. (p. 1650)
Davies, Kate, ed. Old Woman Who Swallowed a Fly. Horne, Sarah, illus. (p. 1285)
Davies, Kathern. Bugs, Bugs, Bugs! Sorensen, Heather, illus. (p. 237)
Davies, Katie. Complete Critter Capers: The Great Hamster Massacre; The Great Rabbit Rescue; The Great Cat Conspiracy; The Great Dog Disaster. Set Shaw, Hannah, illus. (p. 352)
—Elephants: Internet-Referenced. (p. 511)
—Great Cat Conspiracy. Shaw, Hannah, illus. (p. 714)
—Great Dog Disaster. Shaw, Hannah, illus. (p. 715)
—Great Hamster Massacre. Shaw, Hannah, illus. (p. 716)
—Great Rabbit Rescue. Shaw, Hannah, illus. (p. 718)
—Knights Sticker Dressing. (p. 964)
Davies, Lauretta, illus. see Ruckman, Kathleen.
Davies, Leah. Kelly Bear Earth. Davies, Leah, ed. (p. 948)
Davies, Lewis. Tai & the Tremorfa Troll. Acreman, Hayley, illus. (p. 1695)
—Tai, Troll & the Black & White Cow. (p. 1695)
Davies, Margaret Anne. God Made Me. (p. 689)
Davies, Margaret, et al. Y Dewin Diog. (p. 1968)
Davies, Margo. Do You Believe in Santa Claus? (p. 457)
Davies, Matt. Ben Draws Trouble. (p. 163)
—Ben Rides On. (p. 163)
Davies, Matt, illus. see Reynolds, Aaron.
Davies, Michelle, illus. see Griffin, Marcia.
Davies, Mike. Lousy Thinking: Hitching a Ride on a Schoolboy's Mind. (p. 1059)
Davies, Monika. Adaptations. (p. 11)
—Tracking the Weather. (p. 1775)
Davies, Nic, illus. see Reader, Jenny.
Davies, Nicola. Bat Loves the Night: Read & Wonder. Fox-Davies, Sarah, illus. (p. 143)
—Bat Loves the Night. Fox-Davies, Sarah, illus. (p. 143)
—Big Blue Whale. Maland, Nick, illus. (p. 178)
—Deadly! The Truth about the Most Dangerous Creatures on Earth. Layton, Neal, illus. (p. 417)
—Discover Science: Birds. (p. 448)
—Discover Science: Desert. (p. 448)
—Discover Science: Oceans & Seas. (p. 448)
—Dolphin Baby! (p. 464)
—Dolphin Baby! Granström, Brita, illus. (p. 464)
—Escape from Silver Street Farm. McEwen, Katharine, illus. (p. 535)
—Everything You Need to Know about Animals: A First Encylopedia for Budding Zoologists. (p. 545)
—Extreme Animals: The Toughest Creatures on Earth. Layton, Neal, illus. (p. 556)
—I (Don't) Like Snakes. Lozano, Luciano, illus. (p. 837)
—Ice Bear: In the Steps of the Polar Bear. Blythe, Gary, illus. (p. 850)
—Ice Bear with Audio, Peggable: Read, Listen, & Wonder: in the Steps of the Polar Bear. Blythe, Gary, illus. (p. 850)
—Just Ducks! (p. 938)
—Just Ducks! Rubbino, Salvatore, illus. (p. 938)
—Just the Right Size: Why Big Animals Are Big & Little Animals Are Little. Layton, Neal, illus. (p. 940)
—Lion Who Stole My Arm. Wright, Annabel, illus. (p. 1020)
—Oceans & Seas. (p. 1277)
—One Tiny Turtle: Read & Wonder. Chapman, Jane, illus. (p. 1297)
—One Tiny Turtle. Chapman, Jane, illus. (p. 1297)
—Outside Your Window: A First Book of Nature. Hearld, Mark, illus. (p. 1313)
—Poop: A Natural History of the Unmentionable. Layton, Neal, illus. (p. 1383)
—Promise. Carlin, Laura, illus. (p. 1411)
—Rubbish Town Hero. (p. 1493)
—Surprising Sharks: Read & Wonder. Croft, James, illus. (p. 1686)
—Surprising Sharks. Croft, James, illus. (p. 1686)
—Tiny Creatures: The World of Microbes. Sutton, Emily, illus. (p. 1756)
—Welcome to Silver Street Farm. McEwen, Katharine, illus. (p. 1873)
—Whale Boy. (p. 1877)
—What Happens Next? Boutavant, Marc, illus. (p. 1886)
—What Will I Be? Boutavant, Marc, illus. (p. 1895)
—What's Eating You? Parasites — the Inside Story. Layton, Neal, illus. (p. 1897)
—White Owl, Barn Owl: Read & Wonder. Foreman, Michael, illus. (p. 1913)
—White Owl, Barn Owl with Audio, Peggable. Foreman, Michael, illus. (p. 1913)
—Who's Like Me? Boutavant, Marc, illus. (p. 1920)
Davies, Nicola & Lovelock, James. Gaia Warriors. (p. 652)
Davies, Niki. It's Time to Wake up (Niki Davies) (p. 899)
Davies, Norman. No Simple Victory: World War II in Europe, 1939-1945. (p. 1260)
Davies, Pat. Wizard Jasper & the Absent Prince. (p. 1943)
—Wizard Jasper & the Wandering Princess. (p. 1943)
Davies, Peter. Molly's Magic Pencil: The Blue Genie. (p. 1161)
—Molly's Magic Pencil: The Flying Carpet. (p. 1161)
Davies, Rhona. Biblia en un Año para Niños. Piwowarski, Marcin, illus. (p. 176)
—One Year Children's Bible. Piwowarski, Marcin, illus. (p. 1297)
Davies, Richard, photos by see Collings, Matthew.
Davies, Rob. Henhouse High Jinx: Mr. Stevens & Friends. (p. 767)
Davies, Robert, adapted by. Lit a Shuck for Texas: Adapted Louis l'Amour Short Stories Series. (p. 1022)
—Merrano of the Dry Country: Adapted Louis l'Amour Short Story Series. (p. 1128)
—Trail to the West: Adapted Louis l'Amour Short Stories Series. (p. 1776)
Davies, Rocky. Harvey Happy Bee. (p. 752)
Davies, Ross. Andre the Giant. (p. 72)
—Bobo Brazil. (p. 206)
—Wrestling Greats (p. 1962)
Davies, Simon, tr. see Carroll, Lewis, pseud.
Davies, Stephen. Don't Spill the Milk! Corr, Christopher, illus. (p. 468)
—Goggle-Eyed Goats. Corr, Christopher, illus. (p. 692)
—Outlaw. (p. 1312)
—Sophie & the Albino Camel. (p. 1613)
Davies, Stephen & Corr, Christopher. Goggle-Eyed Goats. (p. 692)
Davies, Taffy, illus. see Frewins, Clive & Open Churches Trust Staff.
Davies, Taffy, illus. see Stannard, Russell.
Davies, Tanya. Sarah's Song. (p. 1514)
Davies, Tim. Crystals. (p. 387)
Davies, Timothy, Sr. Polka-Dotted Elephant. (p. 1381)
Davies, Tracy, jt. auth. see Hughes, Mair Wynn.
Davies, Valentine. Miracle on 34th Street. (p. 1148)
—Miracle on 34th Street. dePaola, Tomie, illus. (p. 1148)
Davies, Valerie. Sounds of the Wild: Animals. Pledger, Maurice, illus. (p. 1615)
Davies, Vanessa, photos by see Collister, Linda.
Davies, Vanessa, photos by see Woram, Catherine.
Davies, Will & Lynch, Edward P. Somme Mud: An Australian Teenager in the First World War. (p. 1610)
Daviess, Maria Thompson. Golden Bird. (p. 694)
Davila, Andrew. Prophecies of the Ancient. (p. 1411)
Dávila, Claudia. Luz Sees the Light. Dávila, Claudia, illus. (p. 1066)
Dávila, Claudia, illus. see Becker, Helaine.
Dávila, Claudia, illus. see Humphreys, Jessica Dee & Chikwanine, Michel.
Dávila, Claudia, illus. see Jocelyn, Marthe & Scrimger, Richard.
Dávila, Claudia, illus. see Love, Ann & Drake, Jane.
Dávila, Claudia, illus. see Mason, Adrienne.
Dávila, Claudia, illus. see Weaver, Janice & Wishinsky, Frieda.
Davina. Mr. G - Are You Listening? (p. 1185)
Davio, John, ed. see Arrathoon, Leigh A.
Davio, John, jt. auth. see Arrathoon, Leigh A.
Davis, Adam. Avengers: Age of Ultron: Hulk to the Rescue. (p. 118)
—Captain America: The Winter Soldier. (p. 263)
—Captain America: The Winter Soldier - Falcon Takes Flight. Disney Book Group Staff, illus. (p. 263)
—Captain America: the Winter Soldier - the Movie Storybook. Disney Book Group Staff, illus. (p. 263)
—Guardians of the Galaxy: Rocket & Groot Fight Back. (p. 728)
—Guardians of the Galaxy. (p. 728)
Davis, Adam, jt. auth. see Marvel.
Davis, Adda Leah. Caleb's Song. (p. 252)
Davis, Alan. Avengers Prime. (p. 119)
—Killraven. Davis, Alan, illus. (p. 956)
—Nail. (p. 1227)
—Uncanny X-Men. (p. 1811)
Davis, Alan, illus. see Smith, Raymond R.
Davis, Alan, et al. Mighty Thor/Journey into Mystery: Everything Burns. (p. 1140)
—Road to Onslaught. Cruz, Roger et al, illus. (p. 1477)
Davis, Alan S. Fun Seeker's Las Vegas: The Ultimate Guide to One of the World's Hottest Cities. (p. 648)
Davis, Alexus. Juke Joint. (p. 932)
Davis, Allen, illus. see Kimmel, Eric A.
Davis, Allen, illus. see Lamm, C. Drew.
Davis, Allen, illus. see Lamm, Drew C.
Davis, Allen, illus. see Sherrow, Victoria.
Davis, Amy, illus. see Zellerhoff, Christi.
Davis, Amy & Mandelbaum, Jolie. Michigan State University College Prowler off the Record. (p. 1135)
Davis, Andrea Nicek. Rex Polar Bear. (p. 1467)
Davis, Angie & Davis, Storm. Make That a Table For: A Grizzly Family Story. (p. 1079)
Davis, Anita. Grandma, It's Beautiful. (p. 708)

D

Davis, Anita Price, ed. Praxis II: PLT, Grades K-6 - The Best Test Preparation for the Principles of Learning & Teaching Tests. (p. 1393)
—Praxis II: PLT, Grades 7-12 - The Best Test Preparation for the Principles of Learning & Teaching Tests. (p. 1393)
Davis, Ann. Sunny Von Bunny. (p. 1677)
Davis, Anne. Bud & Gabby. Davis, Anne, illus. (p. 234)
—No Dogs Allowed! Davis, Anne, illus. (p. 1258)
Davis, Anne, jt. auth. see Evans, Alwyn.
Davis, Anne Shirley. No Red Suit for Santa? (p. 1260)
Davis, Anthony. Forgotten Heir. (p. 619)
Davis, Anthony C. I Ain't Lying. (p. 831)
Davis, Ashley. Big Storm. (p. 184)
Davis, Aubrey. Bagels from Benny. Petricic, Dusan, illus. (p. 132)
—Grosse Patate. (p. 725)
—Kishka for Koppel Cohen, Sheldon, illus. (p. 961)
Davis, B. Trouble with Bubbles. (p. 1790)
Davis, Barbara. 404 Deskside Activities for Energetic Kids. (p. 2001)
Davis, Barbara J. Air & Weather. (p. 31)
—Biomes & Ecosystems. (p. 190)
—Conquering England: The Battle of Hastings. (p. 358)
—Earth's Core & Crust. (p. 498)
—Kids' Guide to Aliens (p. 953)
—Kids' Guide to Robots (p. 953)
—Minerals, Rocks, & Soil (p. 1146)
—National Grape Boycott: A Victory for Farmworkers (p. 1233)
—One Million Lost: The Battle of the Somme. (p. 1296)
Davis, Barbara J. & Heinemann Library Staff. Minerals, Rocks, & Soil (p. 1146)
Davis, Barbara J., et al. Hydrogen Fuel. (p. 831)
Davis, Beneta. My Covers. (p. 1200)
Davis, Bertha. Jay's Friend Kitty Brew Jumbo Coloring & Activity Book. Bowman, Todd A., illus. (p. 910)
Davis, Bertha M. Growing up in Mississippi. (p. 726)
—Jay's Friend Kitty Brew. Bowman, Todd A., illus. (p. 910)
Davis, Beth. Sago, A Very Special Service Dog: N/a. Schilling, Deborah, illus. (p. 1503)
Davis, Betsy, illus. see White, Gene.
Davis, Bill, illus. see Paul, Marcy Beller.
Davis, Bonita. Jasmine & the Missing Hat. (p. 910)
Davis, Brandon. Mary the Glary Tree Fairy. (p. 1101)
Davis, Brian. Matthew & Goliath. Wheeler, Ron, illus. (p. 1109)
—Matt's Birthday Blessing. Wheeler, Ron, illus. (p. 1110)
—My Shoes Got the Blues Wheeler, Ron, illus. (p. 1218)
Davis, Bryan. Bones of Makaidos. (p. 209)
—Enoch's Ghost (p. 530)
—From the Mouth of Elijah. (p. 644)
—Last of the Nephilim (p. 978)
—Raising Dragons. (p. 1437)
—Starlighter (p. 1642)
—Tears of a Dragon (p. 1711)
Davis, Buddy. Whale of a Story: Adventures on the High Seas. (p. 1877)
Davis, Buddy, jt. auth. see Ham, Ken.
Davis, Buddy, et al. Buddy Davis' Cool Critters of the Ice Age. (p. 234)
Davis, C. B. Christmas 1948. (p. 312)
Davis, C. Paul & Davis, Paul. I Love You - A Message to You from the Heart of God. (p. 843)
Davis, Calvin Ray. Lunacy Runs Deep: Unleashed. (p. 1065)
Davis, Cameron Christine. Job: A Biography of Job. (p. 919)
—Job. (p. 919)
Davis, Carol Marie. Adventures of Moon Spirit, a Girl from Florida's Past. Davis, Carol Marie, illus. (p. 20)
Davis, Carolina A., illus. see Powell, Richard.
Davis, Caroline. Animals in the Water. (p. 83)
—Animals on the Farm. (p. 83)
—Babies. Davis, Caroline, illus. (p. 123)
—Bugs. Davis, Caroline, illus. (p. 237)
—Diggers. Davis, Caroline, illus. (p. 438)
—First Abc. (p. 592)
—First Animals. (p. 593)
—First Opposites. (p. 596)
—First Pictures. (p. 596)
—First Words. (p. 597)
—Sparkly Farm. Davis, Caroline, illus. (p. 1622)
—Sparkly Garden. Davis, Caroline, illus. (p. 1622)
—Sparkly Ocean. Davis, Caroline, illus. (p. 1622)
—Yum Yum! Davis, Caroline, illus. (p. 1983)
Davis, Caroline, illus. see Baxter, Nicola.
Davis, Caroline, illus. see Emma Treehouse Ltd.
Davis, Caroline, illus. see Engel, Christiane.
Davis, Caroline, illus. see Powell, Richard.
Davis, Caroline, jt. auth. see Powell, Richard.
Davis, Carolyn Findlay. Star for Anana. (p. 1640)
Davis, Catherine. Abby & Alex Feel Their Hearts' Little. (p. 2)
Davis, Catherine, jt. auth. see Billitteri, Thomas J.
Davis, Catherine Baptista, illus. see DeRosa Bodie, Leona.
Davis, Catherine Jennings & Thompson, Traci Shirley. Goodnight Cavaliers. (p. 701)
Davis, Cathy Mackey. Lucky el Perro de la Estación de Bomberos. (p. 1062)
Davis, Cecelia And Andrew. Budgie Tale: Emmit Goes to the Vet. (p. 235)
Davis, Chad L., illus. see Toledo, Leila J.
Davis, Charles. Boating Book for Boys: A Guide to Motor Boating, Sailing, Canoeing & Rowing. (p. 205)
Davis, Charles W., jt. auth. see Umstattd, William D.
Davis, Chasta. Easter Bunny & His Famous Painted Eggs. (p. 499)
—Maggie's Little Strawberry (p. 1071)
Davis, Chip, concept. Mannheim Steamroller Halloween - the World Between (p. 1088)
—Mannheim Steamroller - the Christmas Angel (p. 1088)
Davis, Christina. Teeter Twins in Without a Fight. (p. 1715)
Davis, Christine. For Every Dog an Angel. (p. 615)
—Shelter Dog. Davis, Christine, illus. (p. 1565)
Davis, Christopher Owen, illus. see Adams, Jesse.
Davis, Christy. Newshounds. (p. 1249)
Davis, Cindy. Sammy's Great Adventures. (p. 1508)
Davis, Claire. Cookbook for Young Adults. (p. 361)
Davis, Cristine, jt. auth. see Andrew, Stacy.
Davis, Cristine, jt. auth. see Megill, Colin.
Davis, Cristine, jt. auth. see Smith, Stacy.
Davis, Crystal. School Rhymes. (p. 1523)
Davis, Cynthia. Drink the Rain. (p. 485)
Davis, Cynthia, ed. see Smith, A. Valentine.
Davis, Damian. Digger Field: World Champion (Maybe) (p. 438)
Davis, Dan. Orphan's Promise: A Christmas Story. Davis, Jan, ed. (p. 1305)
Davis, Dan, illus. see McCann, Jesse Leon.
Davis, Dan, illus. see Torres, J.
Davis, Dan, illus. see Weisman, Greg, et al.
Davis, Dan T. Blacksmith's Gift: A Christmas Story. Davis, Jan, ed. (p. 197)
Davis, Dan W., illus. see Wayne, Matt.
Davis, Dana A. Teala & Tony's Adventure to Baby Land. (p. 1710)
Davis, Daniel K. Miles Standish. (p. 1142)
Davis, Daniel M., illus. see McClellan, Sara, ed.
Davis, Daniel M. & Davis, Dawna Jo. Klawberry: Good Girl Bad World. McClellan, Sara, ed. (p. 963)
Davis, Daniel N. Affair's Apology: The Tooth Fairy Speaks. (p. 26)
Davis, Darlene. God Made Everything. (p. 689)
Davis, Darren. Atlas 123S for Superheroes. (p. 112)
—Atlas Gt Planets. (p. 112)
Davis, Darren & Davis, Darren G. ABC's for Superheroes. (p. 4)
Davis, Darren G., jt. auth. see Davis, Darren.
Davis, Darren G., jt. auth. see Wolfman, Marv.
Davis, Darren G. & Larner, Bob. Atlas: Greetings from Earth. (p. 112)
Davis, Darren G. & Misuraca, Thomas J. Maze of the Minotaur. (p. 1113)
Davis, David. Librarian's Night Before Christmas Harris, Jim, illus. (p. 1005)
—Nurse's Night Before Christmas Rice, James, illus. (p. 1273)
—Rock 'n' Roll Dogs Galey, Chuck, illus. (p. 1482)
—Southern Child's Garden of Verses Leonhard, Herb, illus. (p. 1617)
—Southern Mother Goose Leonhard, Herb, illus. (p. 1617)
—Southern Twelve Days of Christmas Camling, Candace, illus. (p. 1617)
—Ten Redneck Babies: A Southern Counting Book Ward, Sue Marshall, illus. (p. 1719)
—Ten Texas Babies Jackson, Shelley & Crosby, Jeff, illus. (p. 1719)
—Texas Aesop's Fables Ward, Sue Marshall, illus. (p. 1724)
—Texas Mother Goose Ward, Sue Marshall, illus. (p. 1724)
—Texas Zeke & the Longhorn Stacy, Alan, illus. (p. 1724)
—Twelve Days of Christmas—In Texas, That Is Camling, Candace, illus. (p. 1800)
Davis, David, jt. auth. see Peck, Jan.
Davis, David Denton. Polly's Promise: A Story about Thriving Rather Than Simply Surviving... Turning Apparent Disability into Gifted Ability. (p. 1381)
Davis, Dawna Jo, jt. auth. see Davis, Daniel M.
Davis, Dayna. All White Dogs Love Mud. Osker, Denise, illus. (p. 46)
Davis, Dean. Dangerous Journey of Sherman the Sheep. (p. 404)
Davis, Deborah L. & Tesler Stein, Mara. Parenting Your Premature Baby & Child: The Emotional Journey. Vol. 1 (p. 1324)
Davis, Deneena. 10 Most Essential Natural Resources. (p. 1994)
Davis, Dennis, illus. see Boyd, Charles F.
Davis, Deon M. Beanie & the Bully. (p. 150)
Davis, Derek and Nikki. T. E. A. the Ered Adventures Presents Skinny Skelley in: Do the Right Thing. (p. 1693)
—T. E. A. the Ered Adventures Presents Skinny Skelley in It's Ok to Be Different. (p. 1693)
Davis, Diane. Something Is Wrong at My House: A Book about Parents' Fighting. Neely, Keith R., illus. (p. 1610)
Davis, Dick, illus. see Keckler, Ben.
Davis, Donald. Don't Kill Santa! Christmas Stories. (p. 467)
—Listening for the Crack of Dawn. (p. 1022)
—Mama Learns to Drive: Stories That Celebrate Mothers. (p. 1084)
—Pig Who Went Home on Sunday: An Appalachian Folktale. Mazzucco, Jennifer, illus. (p. 1357)
—Ride the Butterflies: Back to School with Donald Davis. (p. 1471)
—See Rock City: A Story Journey Through Appalachia. (p. 1547)
—Southern Jack Tales. (p. 1617)
—Thirteen Miles from Suncrest: A Novel. (p. 1735)
Davis, Donna. Martha May Finds a Home. (p. 1097)
Davis, Dorothy W. Robin's Return (p. 1480)
Davis, Edith Kunhardt. Pat the Birthday Bunny (Pat the Bunny) (p. 1327)
Davis, Eleanor. Secret Science Alliance. (p. 1543)
—Secret Science Alliance & the Copycat Crook. Davis, Eleanor, illus. (p. 1543)
—Stinky. (p. 1651)
Davis, Eleanor & Weing, Drew. Flop to the Top! TOON Level 3. (p. 606)
Davis, Elena. Where Do the Balloons Go? Jurinich, Anna, illus. (p. 1907)
Davis, Emily Cleveland. Ancient Americans; The Archaeological Story of Two Continents. (p. 67)
Davis, Erik. Visionary State: A Journey Through California's Spiritual Landscape. Rauner, Michael, photos by. (p. 1845)
Davis, Erin, jt. auth. see Moore, Karen.
Davis, Florence S., illus. see Schneider, Richard H.
Davis, Fredrick. Forms of Energy. (p. 620)
Davis, G. M. You Can Change Almost Anything! Go Challenge the Old Status Quo. (p. 1974)
Davis, Gabriel. Moving Book: A Kids' Survival Guide. Dennen, Sue, illus. (p. 1183)
Davis, Garfield. Little Blue Water Dragon. (p. 1024)
Davis, Gene. Dromedarius & Camela. (p. 485)
Davis, Gerry. Doctor Who & the Cybermen. (p. 459)
—Doctor Who & the Tenth Planet. (p. 459)
Davis, Gibbs. First Kids. Comport, Sally Wern, illus. (p. 595)
Davis, Graeme. Earthquakes. (p. 497)
—Floods. (p. 605)
—Re-Read Harry Potter & the Chamber of Secrets Today! an Unauthorized Guide. (p. 1442)
—Theseus & the Maze of the Minotaur. (p. 1732)
—Unauthorized Harry Potter Quiz Book: 165 Questions Ranging from the Sorcerer's Stone to the Deathly Hallows. (p. 1811)
—Weapons & Gear of the Revolutionary War. (p. 1869)
Davis, Guy. Spring Garden Sticker Storybook. (p. 1635)
Davis, Guy, illus. see Sturm, James.
Davis, Harold. Starrigans of Little Brook Bottom Carter, Dana, illus. (p. 1642)
Davis, Heather. Clearing. (p. 330)
—Ever Changing Summers. (p. 541)
—Lam & the Pickle-Eating Bear. (p. 972)
—Never Cry Werewolf. (p. 1242)
Davis, Helen J. Good Times with Gregory: Airplanes: A Visit to A 747. Davis, Robyn L., illus. (p. 700)
—Good Times with Gregory: Birds: Rescuing a Baby Bird. Davis, Robyn L., illus. (p. 700)
Davis, Holly. Thankful Together. Sokolova, Valerie, illus. (p. 1725)
Davis, Izzy. Croaks at Roaring River (p. 384)
Davis, J. L. What She Wants to Be. (p. 1893)
Davis, Jack, illus. see Petersen, George & Jenkins, J. J.
Davis, Jack, illus. see Simon, Joe.
Davis, Jack E., illus. see Choldenko, Gennifer.
Davis, Jack E., illus. see Cook, Lisa Broadie.
Davis, Jack E., illus. see Esbaum, Jill.
Davis, Jack E., illus. see Fallon, Joe & Scarborough, Ken.
Davis, Jack E., illus. see Grambling, Lois G.
Davis, Jack E., illus. see Greenburg, Dan.
Davis, Jack E., illus. see Harley, Bill.
Davis, Jack E., illus. see Hayles, Marsha.
Davis, Jack E., illus. see Lithgow, John.
Davis, Jack E., illus. see Palatini, Margie.
Davis, Jack E., illus. see Pinkwater, Daniel M.
Davis, Jack E., illus. see Wilson, Karma.
Davis, Jack E., jt. auth. see Lithgow, John.
Davis, Jack E., jt. auth. see Palatini, Margie.
Davis, Jack E. & Palatini, Margie. Bedhead. (p. 156)
Davis, Jacky. Amazing Adventures of Bumblebee Boy. Soman, David, illus. (p. 52)
—Do You Like These Boots? (p. 458)
—Do You Like These Boots? Soman, David, illus. (p. 458)
—Ladybug Girl & the Best Ever Playdate. Soman, David, illus. (p. 971)
—Ladybug Girl Ready for Snow. Soman, David, illus. (p. 971)
Davis, Jacky, jt. auth. see Soman, David.
Davis, Jacky & Soman, David. Ladybug Girl. Soman, David, illus. (p. 971)
—Ladybug Girl & Bingo. Soman, David, illus. (p. 971)
—Ladybug Girl & Bumblebee Boy. Soman, David, illus. (p. 971)
—Ladybug Girl & Her Mama. Soman, David, illus. (p. 971)
—Ladybug Girl & the Big Snow. Soman, David, illus. (p. 971)
—Ladybug Girl & the Bug Squad. Soman, David, illus. (p. 971)
—Ladybug Girl & the Dress-Up Dilemma. Soman, David, illus. (p. 971)
—Ladybug Girl at the Beach. Soman, David, illus. (p. 971)
—Ladybug Girl Book & Doll Set. Soman, David, illus. (p. 971)
—Ladybug Girl Dresses Up! Soman, David, illus. (p. 971)
—Ladybug Girl Feels Happy. Soman, David, illus. (p. 971)
—Ladybug Girl Loves... Soman, David, illus. (p. 971)
—Ladybug Girl Loves... Gift Set. Soman, David, illus. (p. 971)
—Ladybug Girl Makes Friends. Soman, David, illus. (p. 971)
—Ladybug Girl Plays. Soman, David, illus. (p. 971)
—Ladybug Girl Says Good Night. Soman, David, illus. (p. 971)
—Ladybug Girl Visits the Farm. Soman, David, illus. (p. 971)
—Super Catarina y los Super Insectos. Soman, David, illus. (p. 1679)
—Who Can Play? Soman, David, illus. (p. 1914)
Davis, James. Rosetta Stone of God. Klemp, Joan et al, eds. (p. 1490)
Davis, James (Jim) W. Out-takes of 55 Years of Camping (p. 1311)
Davis, Jan, ed. see Davis, Dan T.
Davis, Jan, ed. see Davis, Dan.
Davis, Jason, illus. see Lee, Gia.
Davis, Jeff, illus. see Rosas, Beverly.
Davis, Jenny. U. S. Lawyer-Presidents Coloring & Activity Book. (p. 1806)
Davis, Jenny & Skindzier, Jon. Indiana University College Prowler off the Record. (p. 871)
Davis, Jenny B. U. S. Supreme Court Coloring & Activity Book. (p. 1807)
—U. S. Supreme Court Coloring Book. (p. 1807)
Davis, Jerry & Davis, Katie. Little Chicken's Big Day. Davis, Katie, illus. (p. 1026)
Davis, Jill. First Rule of Little Brothers. McMenemy, Sarah, illus. (p. 596)
Davis, Jim. Fat Cat (p. 577)
—Garfield: Sticht Zu. Goetting, Waltraud & Bartoszko, Alexandra, trs. from ENG. (p. 656)
—Garfield & Co. #7: Home for the Holidays. Ellipsanime Staff & Dargaud Media, illus. (p. 656)
—Garfield Benimmt sich Daneben. Goetting, Waltraud & Bartoszko, Alexandra, trs. from ENG. (p. 656)
—Garfield Blast sich Auf. Goetting, Waltraud & Bartoszko, Alexandra, trs. from ENG. (p. 656)
—Garfield Bleibt sich Treu. Goetting, Waltraud & Bartoszko, Alexandra, trs. from ENG. (p. 656)
—Garfield Caution - Wide Load. (p. 656)
—Garfield Dreht Durch. Goetting, Waltraud & Bartoszko, Alexandra, trs. from ENG. (p. 656)
—Garfield en el Mundo. (p. 656)
—Garfield Fat Cat 3-Pack #9. (p. 656)
—Garfield Gets in a Pickle. (p. 656)
—Garfield Hace Regimen. (p. 656)
—Garfield Halt die Ohren Steif. Goetting, Waltraud & Bartoszko, Alexandra, trs. from ENG. (p. 656)
—Garfield Hangt Ab. Bartoszko, Alexandra, tr. from ENG. (p. 656)
—Garfield Hat Genug. Goetting, Waltraud & Bartoszko, Alexandra, trs. from ENG. (p. 656)
—Garfield Hat Schwein. Bartoszko, Alexandra, tr. from ENG. (p. 657)
—Garfield Haut Rein. Goetting, Waltraud & Bartoszko, Alexandra, trs. from ENG. (p. 657)
—Garfield Hebt Ab. Goetting, Waltraud & Bartoszko, Alexandra, trs. from ENG. (p. 657)
—Garfield ist Spitze. Goetting, Waltraud & Bartoszko, Alexandra, trs. from ENG. (p. 657)
—Garfield Kommt Rum. Goetting, Waltraud & Bartoszko, Alexandra, trs. from ENG. (p. 657)
—Garfield Kratzt die Kurve. Goetting, Waltraud & Bartoszko, Alexandra, trs. from ENG. (p. 657)
—Garfield Lasst nicht Locker. Goetting, Waltraud & Bartoszko, Alexandra, trs. from ENG. (p. 657)
—Garfield Legts Drauf An. Goetting, Waltraud & Bartoszko, Alexandra, trs. from ENG. (p. 657)
—Garfield Nimmt den Mund Voll. Goetting, Waltraud & Bartoszko, Alexandra, trs. from ENG. (p. 657)
—Garfield Nimmt's Leicht. Bartoszko, Alexandra, tr. from ENG. (p. 657)
—Garfield Out to Lunch Davis, Jim, illus. (p. 657)
—Garfield Platzt aus allen Naehten. Bartoszko, Alexandra, tr. from ENG. (p. 657)
—Garfield Riecht den Braten. Bartoszko, Alexandra, tr. from ENG. (p. 657)
—Garfield Se Pasa! (p. 657)
—Garfield Spielt auf Zeit. Goetting, Waltraud & Bartoszko, Alexandra, trs. from ENG. (p. 657)
—Garfield Streicht Ein. Goetting, Waltraud & Bartoszko, Alexandra, trs. from ENG. (p. 657)
—Garfield Waechst & Gegeiht. Bartoszko, Alexandra, tr. from ENG. (p. 657)
—Garfield Will es Wissen. Goetting, Waltraud & Bartoszko, Alexandra, trs. from ENG. (p. 657)
—Garfield y el Deporte. (p. 657)
—Garfield y Sus Amigos. (p. 657)
—Garfield Zeigt die Krallen. Goetting, Waltraud & Bartoszko, Alexandra, trs. from ENG. (p. 657)
—Survival of the Fattest (p. 1686)
Davis, Jim & Evanier, Mark. Catzilla. Ellipsanime Staff & Dargaud Media, illus. (p. 281)
—Garfield. Barker, Gary, illus. (p. 656)
—Garfield & Co. #4: Caroling Capers. Ellipsanime Staff & Dargaud Media, illus. (p. 656)
Davis, Jim & Michiels, Cedric. Garfield Show #1: Unfair Weather. Dargaud Media Staff & Ellipsanime Staff, illus. (p. 657)
—Garfield Show #2: Jon's Night Out. Ellipsanime Staff & Dargaud Media, illus. (p. 657)
—Jon's Night Out. (p. 925)
—Jon's Night Out. Ellipsanime Staff & Dargaud Media, illus. (p. 925)
—Long Lost Lyman. (p. 1047)
—Unfair Weather. Dargaud Media Staff & Ellipsanime Staff, illus. (p. 1817)
Davis, Jim, et al. Game of Cat & Mouse. Dargaud Media Staff & Ellipsanime Staff, illus. (p. 654)
—Garfield: I'll Give You All the Ten Seconds to Get off the Comic Racks! Vol. 2 Barker, Gary, illus. (p. 656)
—Garfield & Co. #6: Mother Garfield. Ellipsanime Staff, illus. (p. 656)
—Secret Agent X Ellipsanime Staff & Dargaud Media Staff, illus. (p. 1540)
Davis, Jimmie. More We Get Together. Church, Caroline Jayne, illus. (p. 1175)
—You Are My Sunshine. Church, Caroline Jayne, illus. (p. 1973)
Davis, Joann. Son Is a Gift. (p. 1611)
—Where Is Butterfly. (p. 1908)
—Where Is Ladybug. (p. 1908)
Davis, John Parke, jt. auth. see Ryan, Carrie.
Davis, John Watson, illus. see Loyola, Mother Mary.
Davis, Jon. Small Blue & the Deep Dark Night. (p. 1591)
Davis, Jon, illus. see Adams, Diane.
Davis, Jon, illus. see Eboch, Chris.
Davis, Jon, illus. see Levis, Caron.
Davis, Jon, illus. see Michalak, Jamie.
Davis, Jon, illus. see Montgomery, Heather L.
Davis Jones, Melanie, et al. School Box: Field Day - 100th Day of School - One Happy Classroom. Molnar, Albert & McKillip Thornburgh, Rebecca, illus. (p. 1522)
Davis, Joyce E. Can't Stop the Shine. (p. 262)
—Fancy the Prancing Horse. (p. 570)
Davis, Julie. Philip the Frog Who Barked Like a Dog. (p. 1350)
Davis, Julie, ed. Best of Animerica Anime & Manga Monthly: The Year's Best Articles. (p. 170)
Davis, K. Walk in the Woods. (p. 1853)
Davis, K. C., jt. auth. see Davis, Kenneth C.
Davis, Kaley, illus. see Richardville, Carol.
Davis, Karen Lyn. Coolmath Algebra (p. 364)
—Coolmath Algebra Part 1. (p. 364)
DAvis, Kate. Raptors of the Rockies: Biology of the Birds of Prey & Species Accounts of the Raptors of the Northern Rockies. (p. 1439)
Davis, Kate, jt. auth. see Giles, Sophie.
Davis, Katherine K., et al. Little Drummer Boy: Sheet. (p. 1027)
Davis, Katheryn, illus. see Kohl, MaryAnn F. & Potter, Jean.
Davis, Kathryn. Girl Who Trod on a Loaf. (p. 679)
—Hell: A Novel. (p. 763)
—Thin Place. (p. 1732)
—Versailles: A Novel. (p. 1837)
Davis, Kathryn Gibbs. Mr. Ferris & His Wheel. Ford, Gilbert, illus. (p. 1185)
Davis, Kathryn Lynn, illus. see Gerver, Jane E.
Davis, Kathryn Lynn, jt. auth. see Davis, Nancy.
Davis, Katie. Curse of Addy McMahon. (p. 394)
—Curse of Addy Mcmahon. (p. 394)
—Kindergarten Rocks! (p. 957)
Davis, Katie, jt. auth. see Davis, Jerry.
Davis, Kauline, et al. Fat Dogs & Coughing Horses. (p. 577)
Davis, Kellie. Sophie, the Great Dane That Nearly Drove My Family Insane. (p. 1613)
Davis, Ken, jt. auth. see Rollans, Scott.

Davis, Kenneth C. Don't Know Much about Abraham Lincoln Shepperson, Rob, illus. (p. 467)
—Don't Know Much about Abraham Lincoln Abraham Lincoln Shepperson, Rob, illus. (p. 467)
—Don't Know Much About American History. (p. 467)
—Don't Know Much About American History. Faulkner, Matt, illus. (p. 467)
—Don't Know Much about Dinosaurs. (p. 467)
—Don't Know Much about Dinosaurs. Martin, Pedro, illus. (p. 467)
—Don't Know Much about George Washington. Shepperson, Rob, illus. (p. 467)
—Don't Know Much about Mummies. (p. 467)
—Don't Know Much about Planet Earth. (p. 467)
—Don't Know Much about Sitting Bull Sitting Bull (p. 467)
—Don't Know Much about Space. (p. 467)
—Don't Know Much about the 50 States. Andriani, Renee, illus. (p. 467)
—Don't Know Much about the American Presidents. (p. 468)
—Don't Know Much about the Bible: Everything You Need to Know about the Good Book but Never Learned. (p. 468)
—Don't Know Much about the Kings & Queens of England. (p. 468)
—Don't Know Much about the Pilgrims. Schindler, S. D., illus. (p. 468)
—Don't Know Much about the Pioneers & Indians. (p. 468)
—Don't Know Much about the Solar System. Martin, Pedro, illus. (p. 468)
—Don't Know Much about Thomas Jefferson. Shepperson, Rob, illus. (p. 468)
—Presidents. Martin, Pedro, illus. (p. 1397)
Davis, Kenneth C. & Davis, K. C. Todo lo Que Hay Que Saber Sobre el Espacio. (p. 1761)
Davis, Kent. Riddle in Ruby. (p. 1470)
Davis, Kerry. Plumple. (p. 1374)
Davis, Kesa Royette. Adventures of Keitly Dee & Geode. (p. 19)
Davis, Kim P., compiled by. My Life, His Mission: A Six Week Challenge to Change the World! True Stories from Students Living on the Edge (p. 1212)
Davis, L. J. Simple Brown Leaf. Victoria, Lisa, illus. (p. 1577)
Davis, L. Mitchell. Tale of Micah Mouse. (p. 1699)
Davis, Lambert, illus. see Bates, Janet Costa.
Davis, Lambert, illus. see Stafford, Liliana.
Davis, Lane. I Swear. (p. 846)
Davis, Laura. No! No! I Won't Be Slow! (p. 1259)
Davis, Laura E., et al, eds. Poetry Inside Out: A Creative Writing Workbook. (p. 1376)
Davis, Lauren & Varacalli, Lauren. Bucknell University College Prowler off the Record. (p. 234)
Davis, Lee. Beware the Last Cousins. (p. 173)
—Darkness Bled. (p. 408)
—Lifesize Animal Opposites Book. (p. 1013)
—Natural Disasters. (p. 1235)
Davis, Linda. Chanukah Story. Taub, Udi, illus. (p. 291)
—Sir Ernest Shackleton. (p. 1580)
Davis, Lindsay Renae. It's Your Turn to Count! (p. 899)
Davis, Lindsey. Body in the Bathhouse. (p. 207)
Davis, Lois. Happy to Be Me. (p. 747)
Davis, Lois A. 5 Silly Elephants. (p. 1992)
Davis, Lowrey. Papa's Storybook. (p. 1322)
Davis, Lucile. Caddo of Texas. (p. 250)
—Charles Lindbergh. (p. 292)
Davis, Lydia. End of the Story. (p. 526)
Davis, Lydia & Ollivant, Alfred. Alfred Ollivant's Bob, Son of Battle: The Last Gray Dog of Kenmuir. Kirmse, Marguerite, illus. (p. 37)
Davis, Lynda S. & Weisel, Kaitlyn E. Christopher James Mcabee & the Wonderful Tree. Trone, Melody Karns, illus. (p. 317)
Davis, Lynn. Alexander Graham Bell. (p. 36)
—George Eastman. (p. 663)
—Henry Ford. (p. 768)
—Samuel Morse. (p. 1509)
—Thomas Edison. (p. 1738)
—Wright Brothers. (p. 1963)
Davis, Lynne, illus. see Elkins, Stephen.
Davis, Maggie Steincrohn. Garden of Whales. O'Connell, Jennifer Barrett, illus. (p. 656)
Davis, Marc. Florence Nightingale: Founder of the Nightingale School of Nursing. (p. 606)
Davis, Marc & Santella, Andrew. Wright Brothers: Inventors & Aviators. (p. 1963)
Davis, Marcia. Teach Your Child to Swim the Gentle Way: With Positive Reinforcement. (p. 1709)
Davis, Marcus, illus. see Watkins, T. a.
Davis, Marilyn. Adelia's Last Name. McBride, Roxie, ed. (p. 12)
—Gazillion Things I Like about Me. (p. 659)
Davis, Mark. Millenium Diet: The Practical Guide for Rapid Weight Loss. (p. 1143)
Davis, Mario. Morning Princess. (p. 1175)
Davis, Marshall L. Og the Magical Green Frog. (p. 1280)
Davis, Marti. Handwriting Helper a Workbook for Teachers & Therapists. (p. 741)
Davis, Martine. There's a Red Hippo at My Door. (p. 1731)
Davis, Mary. Five-Minute Sunday School Activities: Exploring the Bible. (p. 601)
—Five-Minute Sunday School Activities: Jesus' Miracles & Messages. (p. 601)
—Instant Bible Lessons for Toddlers: God Blesses Me. (p. 878)
—Instant Bible Lessons for Toddlers: Growing up for God. (p. 878)
—Instant Bible Lessons for Toddlers: Jesus Is My Friend. (p. 878)
—Instant Bible Lessons for Toddlers: God Takes Care of Me. (p. 878)
—Teaching Children Memory Verses: Ages 2&3. Galey, Chuck & Winn, Chris, illus. (p. 1710)
—Teaching Children Memory Verses: Grades 1&2. Galey, Chuck & Winn, Chris, illus. (p. 1710)
—Teaching Children Memory Verses: Grades 3&4. Galey, Chuck & Winn, Chris, illus. (p. 1710)
Davis, Mary Byrd & Purcell, Arthur H. Weapons of Mass Destruction. (p. 1869)
Davis, Mary J. Five-Minute Sunday School Activities for Preschoolers: Jesus Shows Me. Galey, Chuck, illus. (p. 601)
—Five-Minute Sunday School Activities for Preschoolers: Bible Adventures. Galey, Chuck, illus. (p. 601)
—My Answer Journal: What Kids Wonder about God & the Bible. (p. 1196)
—My Bible Journal: A Journey Through the Word for Kids. (p. 1197)
—My Wisdom Journal: A Discovering of Proverbs for Kids. (p. 1221)
—Teaching Children Memory Verses: Ages 4&5. (p. 1710)
Davis, Mary J., jt. auth. see Legacy Press Staff.
Davis, Mattie Campbell, jt. ed. see Vaughn, Wally G.
Davis, Mehkiyah. Turtle & Ladybug: Best Friends Forever. (p. 1798)
Davis, Melissa. Denny the Duck. (p. 426)
—Remy's First Day of School. Kalpart, illus. (p. 1460)
Davis, Michael Dale. Bumperly Bumper Bee. (p. 241)
Davis, Mike. Land of the Lost Mammoths: A Science Adventure. (p. 973)
—Pirates, Bats, & Dragons. Simpson, William, illus. (p. 1363)
Davis, Milton J. Amber & the Hidden City. (p. 56)
Davis, Mo'ne & Tbd Staff. Mo'Ne - Remember My Name: My Story from First Pitch to Game Changer. (p. 1163)
Davis, Nancy. Halloween Faces. Davis, Nancy, illus. (p. 737)
Davis, Nancy, illus. see Ackerman, Jill.
Davis, Nancy, illus. see Fox, Karen C.
Davis, Nancy, illus. see Gerver, Jane E.
Davis, Nancy, illus. see Graham, Joan Bransfield.
Davis, Nancy & Davis, Kathryn Lynn. First Thanksgiving. Davis, Nancy & Davis, Kathryn Lynn, illus. (p. 597)
—Wake Up! Wake Up! Davis, Nancy & Davis, Kathryn Lynn, illus. (p. 1853)
Davis, Natalie, ed. see Davis, Trevor.
Davis, Nelle, illus. see Gravelle, Karen.
Davis, Oslo, illus. see Lawson, Henry.
Davis, Ozzie. ADV of Frog Man. (p. 13)
—World of Fuzzwald & Friends: Fuzzwald's Three Day Weekend. (p. 1956)
Davis, Pat. Estelle & the Escape from Mars: A Children's Novel By. (p. 538)
Davis, Patricia. Orangutans. (p. 1302)
—Turtles. (p. 1798)
Davis, Paul, jt. auth. see Davis, C. Paul.
Davis, Paul B. Charles Dickens: A Literary Reference to His Life & Work. (p. 292)
Davis, Pauline. Including Children with Visual Impairment in Mainstream Schools: A Practical Guide. (p. 869)
Davis, Peg. After the Storm: A Napoleon & Marigold Adventure. (p. 28)
—Napoleon & Marigold. (p. 1229)
Davis, Penny. Annabel's Yearnings. (p. 85)
Davis, Pollyanna S., tr. see Lee, Betsy B.
Davis, R. Hunt, jt. auth. see Page, Willie F.
Davis, R. I. Men's Costume, Cut & Fashion of the 17th & 18th Century: Patterns for Men's Costumes. Landes, William-Alan, ed. (p. 1126)
—Men's Garments, 1830-1900: A Guide to Pattern Cutting & Tailoring. (p. 1126)
Davis, Rachayl Eckstein, jt. auth. see Schram, Peninnah.
Davis, Rachel. My Life at Mapleleaf Cabin. (p. 1212)
Davis, Rachel, creator. Hero's Stand: An Experience of Self Discovery for Teens. (p. 774)
Davis, Raymond Mace. Sinjin & the Mosaic Garden (p. 1579)
Davis, Rebecca. George Mueller: A Father to the Fatherless. (p. 663)
—God's Special Creation. de Papenbrock, Dervy Romero, tr. (p. 691)
—Jake Riley: Irreparably Damaged. (p. 906)
Davis, Rebecca F. 10, 9, 8 Polar Animals! A Counting Backward Book (p. 1993)
—Flowers & Showers: A Spring Counting Book. (p. 608)
—Playas y Bicicletas: Un Libro para Contar en el Verano. (p. 1372)
Davis, Rebecca F., jt. auth. see Schuette, Sarah L.
Davis, Rebecca F. & Fjelland Davis, Rebecca. Footballs & Falling Leaves: A Fall Counting Book (p. 615)
Davis, Rebecca Fjelland. Beaches & Bicycles: A Summer Counting Book. (p. 149)
—Chasing AllieCat. (p. 294)
—Counting Pets by Twos (p. 371)
—More or Less: A Rain Forest Counting Book (p. 1174)
—Zoo Animals 1, 2, 3 (p. 1988)
Davis, Rebecca Henry. Fanny Crosby: Queen of Gospel Songs. (p. 571)
Davis, Regina & Spencer, Carolyn Royer. Señor Smarty Pantaloons & the Mystery of the Missing Teachers. (p. 1550)
Davis, Render S., et al. Atlanta Walks: A Comprehensive Guide to Walking, Running, & Bicycling Around the Area's Scenic & Historic Locales (p. 112)
Davis, Rhonda L. Faces of Darkness: The Daredevil Friends. (p. 561)
Davis, Rich, illus. see Meister, Cari.
Davis, Richard. Boy Scout & Other Stories for Boys. (p. 218)
—Red Cross Girl & Other Stories. (p. 1453)
Davis, Richard A. Spinner's Secret. (p. 1628)
Davis, Robert J. Right under Your Feet. (p. 1472)
Davis, Robin & Starr, Lara. Wookiee Pies, Clone Scones, & Other Galactic Goodies. (p. 1950)
Davis, Robyn L., illus. see Davis, Helen J.
Davis, Russell G. & Ashabranner, Brent. Choctaw Code. (p. 309)
Davis, Samantha A., jt. auth. see Ziefert, Harriet.
Davis, Samira And Edwina. Nikko & Sierra's Adventures: I Hate Knuckle Sandwiches. (p. 1255)
Davis, Sampson, et al. We Beat the Street: How a Friendship Pact Led to Success. (p. 1866)
Davis, Sarah, illus. see Cheng, Christopher.
Davis, Sarah, illus. see Haas, Jessie.
Davis, Sarah, illus. see MacIver, Juliette.
Davis, Sarah, illus. see Mirabella, Erin.
Davis, Sharon & Patton, Charlene. Baking with Friends: Recipies, Tips & Fun Facts for Teaching Kids to Bake. Beatty, Nicholas, ed. (p. 133)
Davis, Sheila & Williams, Nadia. Claudia & Grammy Lose Weight: A Mississippi Grammy & California Granddaughter Lose Weight. (p. 329)
Davis, Shelley, illus. see White, Gene.
Davis, Shelley L. a. Lee the Bee. (p. 987)
Davis, Shelley L. A., illus. see Reece, Eva.
Davis, Shelley La, illus. see Reece, Eva.
Davis, Spencer W. Charlie Chubby Bubble. (p. 293)
Davis, Stephen, illus. see Chopin, Kate.
Davis, Storm, jt. auth. see Davis, Angie.
Davis, Susan. I'm Adopted, You're Adopted: Welcome to God's Family. (p. 858)
Davis, Susan Burdick. Old Forts & Real Folks. (p. 1283)
Davis, Susan Page. Feather. (p. 579)
—Sarah's Long Ride. (p. 1514)
DAVIS, Tamika. If i knew back then what i know Now. (p. 853)
—Now i Know. (p. 1269)
Davis, Tanita S. Happy Families. (p. 745)
—La Carte. (p. 969)
—Mare's War. (p. 1092)
Davis, Terrance. Mom & Me. (p. 1161)
Davis, Terry. Camping with Dad: The Mystery of Valley Gulch. (p. 257)
Davis, Thomas J. John Calvin. (p. 921)
Davis, Thomas L., jt. auth. see Williams, Jack S.
Davis, Tim. Case of the Purple Diamonds. (p. 275)
Davis, Tim, illus. see Pellowski, Michael J.
Davis, Tim, illus. see Yuen, Dan.
Davis, Tina. Look & Cook: A Cookbook for Children. (p. 1048)
—See & Sew: A Sewing Book for Children. (p. 1546)
—Sow & Grow: A Gardening Book for Children. (p. 1618)
Davis, Toby K. Ever Part of Always: Keely Tucker's First Adventure. (p. 541)
Davis, Todd & Frey, Marc. New Big Book of U. S. Presidents: Fascinating Facts about Each & Every President, Including an American History Timeline. (p. 1243)
Davis, Tony. Are You for Wheel? The Most Amazing Cars Ever. Nagle, Shane, illus. (p. 97)
—Roland Wright: at the Joust. Rogers, Gregory, illus. (p. 1485)
—Roland Wright: Brand-New Page. Rogers, Gregory, illus. (p. 1485)
—Roland Wright: Future Knight. Rogers, Gregory, illus. (p. 1485)
Davis, Trevor. Adventures of Charley Mcchoochoo: Danny & the Whistling Engine. Davis, Natalie, ed. (p. 17)
Davis, Trisha. Wildfire! (p. 1931)
Davis, W. Harry. Changemaker: W. Harry Davis. Sturdevant, Lori, ed. (p. 290)
Davis, Wayne R. Safety & Technique Posters: Set C. (p. 1502)
Davis, Wayne R., jt. auth. see J., Mary.
Davis, Wayne R., jt. auth. see Roberts, Willo Davis.
Davis, Will. Simply for Kids. (p. 1578)
Davis, Will, illus. see Petty, J. T.
Davis, William Michael. Barack Obama: The Politics of Hope. (p. 137)
Davis, Yvonne, illus. see MacDonald, Margaret Read.
Davis, Yvonne LeBrun. Girl Who Wore Too Much: A Folktale from Thailand. (p. 679)
Davis, Yvonne LeBrun, illus. see MacDonald, Margaret Read & Jaeger, Winifred.
Davison, Gary Marvin. Tales from the Taiwanese (p. 1702)
Davison, Marion & Marsh, Audrey. Smoke over Grand Pre. (p. 1594)
Davison, Roz, jt. auth. see Laird, Elizabeth.
Davisson, Vanessa, illus. see Garr, Rebecca.
Davisson, Zack, tr. see Mizuki, Shigeru.
Davis-Swing, Joanna, ed. see Rasinski, Timothy V. & Padak, Nancy.
Davitt Bell, Cathleen. I Remember You. (p. 844)
Davoust, Eugene-Pierre. Resistance? Defendu, Mademoiselle! (p. 1463)
Dawes, Will, illus. see Leigh, Susannah.
Dawkin, Deborah, tr. see Rossland, Ingelin.
Dawkins, Rotha J. Treats & Tales. (p. 1783)
Dawley, Linda. Tooth Fairy's Mistake. (p. 1768)
—Wee Mac. (p. 1871)
Dawley, Sarah, illus. see Doty, Sara.
Dawn, Baumer, illus. see Baldwin, Rich & Jones, Sandie.
Dawn, Endres. I Am Forever in His Hands. (p. 833)
Dawn, Nyrae. Searching for Beautiful. (p. 1537)
Dawn, Nyrae, et al. Out of Play. (p. 1311)
Dawn Phillips, illus. see By Kaleena Ma.
Dawnay, Gabby. London Calls. Barrow, Alex, illus. (p. 1046)
Dawson, Amanda, jt. auth. see Brasch, Nicolas.
Dawson, Arthur, ed. Creek Wisdom: An Ecological History of Sonoma Valley. (p. 380)
Dawson, B. L. Clover's Little Problem. (p. 335)
Dawson, Brianog Brady. Danny's Pesky Pet. Connor, Michael, tr. (p. 406)
Dawson, Brianóg Brady. Pageboy Danny. Connor, Michael, illus. (p. 1318)
Dawson, Christopher B. Treasure in the Mirror. (p. 1781)
Dawson, Delilah, et al. Mr. Satisfaction. (p. 1186)
Dawson, Delilah S. Hit. (p. 785)
—Servants of the Storm. (p. 1552)
Dawson, Diane, illus. see Robbins, Maria Polushkin & Polushkin Robbins, Maria.
Dawson, Donna, jt. auth. see Peters, Laura.
Dawson, Donna & Peters, Laura. Annuals for Alberta. (p. 87)
—Best Garden Plants for Alberta (p. 169)
Dawson, Dorothy M. Email on a Special Journey. (p. 517)
Dawson, Dylan. Tinkertoy Building Manual: Graphic Instructions for 37 World-Famous Designs. Steimle, Robert, illus. (p. 1756)
Dawson, Emily C. Airplanes. (p. 32)
—Animal Clothing. (p. 77)
—Birds & Trees. (p. 191)
—City. (p. 323)
—Cooking. (p. 361)
—Holidays & Celebrations. (p. 788)
—How Animals Find Water. (p. 804)
—How Animals Sleep. (p. 804)
—How Bees Make Honey. (p. 805)
—My Bones. Alberini, Teresa, illus. (p. 1198)
—Ocean Animals. (p. 1276)
—Push & Pull. (p. 1420)
—Town Leaders. (p. 1773)
—Trains. (p. 1777)
—Weddings Around the World. (p. 1871)
—Where Animals Live. (p. 1906)
—Zoo. (p. 1988)
Dawson, Eugene T. Little Valerie Wants to Grow Taller. (p. 1037)
Dawson, Gerrit Scott. Responding to Our Call: Participant's Book. (p. 1463)
Dawson, Ian. Greek & Roman Medicine. (p. 720)
—Prehistoric & Egyptian Medicine. (p. 1395)
—Renaissance Medicine. (p. 1460)
—What Is History? (p. 1889)
Dawson, Ian, ed. see Scarboro, Dale.
Dawson, Ian, jt. auth. see Richardson, Jane.
Dawson, Ian & Walsh, Ben. Essential Struggle for Peace in Northern Ireland Students Book. (p. 537)
Dawson, Ian & Wilson, Maggie. SHP History (p. 1571)
—SHP History: A Schools History Project Course for Year 7. (p. 1571)
Dawson, Ian, et al. SHP History Elearning Activities. (p. 1571)
Dawson, Imogen. Food & Feasts with the Aztecs. (p. 613)
Dawson, Isabel, illus. see Gipson, Morrell, ed.
Dawson, J. M. Bug, Bug, Where's the Bug? Hoofnagle, Therese, illus. (p. 236)
Dawson, James. Hollow Pike. (p. 789)
—This Book Is Gay. (p. 1735)
Dawson, James Phillip. I Am. (p. 831)
—In the Days of Peleg. (p. 865)
—Land of Promise. (p. 973)
—Why Believe. (p. 1922)
Dawson, Janine, illus. see Matthews, Penny.
Dawson, Janine, illus. see Odgers, Darrel & Odgers, Sally.
Dawson, Janine, illus. see Odgers, Darrel & Sally.
Dawson, Janine, illus. see Odgers, Sally & Odgers, Darrel.
Dawson, Janine, illus. see Prior, Natalie Jane.
Dawson, Janine, illus. see Prior, Natalie.
Dawson, Janine, illus. see Urdahl, Catherine.
Dawson, Jennifer. Silly Sally Sue. (p. 1576)
Dawson, JoAnn. Willie to the Rescue. (p. 1934)
Dawson, JoAnn S. Lady's Big Surprise. (p. 971)
—Star of Wonder. (p. 1641)
Dawson, Joy. Intimate Friendship with God: Through Understanding the Fear of the Lord. (p. 881)
—Maggie, the Color-Blind Cow: A loving heart—that didn't see Color. (p. 1071)
Dawson, Kai, jt. auth. see LeBaron, Sarah.
Dawson, Kai, jt. auth. see Rossi, Regine.
Dawson, Kate & Glucksman, Jodi, compiled by. Over the Moon: The Broadway Lullaby Project. (p. 1314)
Dawson, Kathy, jt. auth. see Prior, Natalie Jane.
Dawson, Ken, illus. see James, Gilmory.
Dawson, Kenneth M. & Dawson, Sheryl N. Job Search: Achieve Your Better Job... Better Pay... Better Life!: the Total System. (p. 919)
Dawson, Liz, illus. see Blackwood, Melissa & Monaghan, Stephen.
Dawson, Mary, et al. Snow Poems & Star Poems. (p. 1599)
Dawson, Mary, et al, selected by. Snow Poems & Star Poems. (p. 1599)
Dawson, Mike. Growing up Yanomamö: Missionary Adventures in the Amazon Rainforest. Pintor, Ruben, illus. (p. 727)
Dawson, Ouida Foster. Wait. (p. 1852)
Dawson, Paola. Dancing Dream. (p. 402)
Dawson, Patricia. Adventures of Farmer Bill. (p. 18)
—Doctor's Job. (p. 459)
—Electrician's Job. (p. 509)
—Ninjas: Masters of Stealth & Secrecy. (p. 1256)
—Samurai: Warlords of Japan. (p. 1509)
Dawson, Patricia A. Asia Through the Ages: Early History to European Colonialism. (p. 106)
—First Peoples of the Americas & the European Age of Exploration. (p. 596)
Dawson, Peg & Guare, Richard. Smart but Scattered: The Revolutionary "Executive Skills" Approach to Helping Kids Reach Their Potential. (p. 1592)
Dawson, Peter. Desert Drive: A Western Quintet. (p. 429)
Dawson, Peter, jt. auth. see Goldsack, Gaby.
Dawson, Piper. Adventures of Fenway & Becc. (p. 18)
Dawson, Robert. Bees. (p. 157)
Dawson, Sandy, photos by see Pierce, Paul.
Dawson, Scott, illus. see Rosenstock, Barb.
Dawson, Scott, illus. see Tarshis, Lauren.
Dawson, Sheldon, illus. see Delaronde, Deborah L.
Dawson, Sheldon, illus. see Howell, Lauren.
Dawson, Sheryl N., jt. auth. see Dawson, Kenneth M.
Dawson, Stephanie Mara. best recess Ever. (p. 171)
Dawson, Stephen, jt. auth. see Shryer, Donna.
Dawson, Ted. Dinosaur Digs (p. 442)
Dawson, Ted, illus. see Korb, Rena B.
Dawson, Ted, illus. see Korb, Rena.
Dawson, Willow. Lila & Ecco's Do-It-Yourself Comics Club. Dawson, Willow, illus. (p. 1017)
—Wolf-Birds. (p. 1943)
Dawson, Willow, illus. see Becker, Helaine.
Dawson, Willow, illus. see Hughes, Susan.
Dawson, Willow, illus. see Wishinsky, Frieda.
Day, Alexandra. Carl & the Baby Duck. (p. 269)
—Carl & the Kitten. (p. 269)
—Carl & the Puppies. Day, Alexandra, illus. (p. 269)
—Carl & the Sick Puppy. (p. 269)
—Carl at the Dog Show Day, Alexandra, illus. (p. 269)
—Carl's Christmas. (p. 270)
—Carl's Halloween. Day, Alexandra, illus. (p. 270)
—Carl's Sleepy Afternoon. Day, Alexandra, illus. (p. 270)
—Carl's Snowy Afternoon. Day, Alexandra, illus. (p. 270)
—Carl's Summer Vacation. Day, Alexandra, illus. (p. 270)
—Fairy Dogfather. Day, Alexandra, illus. (p. 563)
—Frank & Ernest. (p. 628)
—Frank & Ernest Play Ball. (p. 628)

D

Day, Alexandra, illus. see Edens, Cooper.
Day, Amelia. Olivia's Ocean Adventure: Understand Place Value. (p. 1287)
—Olivia's Ocean Adventure. (p. 1287)
Day, Andrew, illus. see LeFrak, Karen.
Day, Andrew, illus. see Wiley, Thom.
Day, Bartley F., jt. auth. see Knab, Christopher.
Day, Betsy, illus. see Check, Laura.
Day, Betsy, illus. see Osteen, Victoria.
Day, Betsy, illus. see Press, Judy.
Day, Betsy, tr. see Check, Laura.
Day, Bruce, illus. see Stegall, Kim.
Day, Cansarra, jt. auth. see Yusuf, Hanna S.
Day, Caroline, illus. see Watt, Fiona.
Day, Chuck. Jacksonville Football History. (p. 904)
Day, David. Rey de los Bosques. Brown, Ken, illus. (p. 1467)
Day, Deborah A. Mindful Messages Mentoring Workbook: Healing Thoughts for the Hip & Hop Descendants from the Motherland Patterson, L. Kahlil, ed. (p. 1145)
—Mindful Messages Mentoring Workbook: Healing Thoughts for the Hip & Hop Descendants from the Motherland. Patterson, L. Kahlil, ed. (p. 1145)
Day, Ed D. Why Dogs Bark: & Other Tall Tales. Scott, Sarah C., illus. (p. 1924)
Day, Holly. Shakira. (p. 1559)
Day, J. David. Canyonlands National Park Favorite Jeep Roads & Hiking Trails. Day, J. David, photos by. (p. 262)
Day, Jan & Mason, Janeen. Kissimmee Pete & the Hurricane (p. 962)
—Kissimmee Pete, Cracker Cow Hunter (p. 962)
—Pirate Pink & Treasures of the Reef (p. 1363)
—World's Greatest Explorer (p. 1960)
Day, Janet, jt. see Jacobson, John.
Day, Jeff. Don't Touch That! The Book of Gross, Poisonous, & Downright Icky Plants & Critters. (p. 469)
Day, Jeff, illus. see Boritzer, Etan.
Day, Jon. Arswyd Mawr! Yr Anhygoel A'r Anesboniadwy. (p. 101)
—Supernatural. (p. 1684)
Day, Jonathan. Politics of Navigation: Globalisation, Music & Composition. (p. 1381)
Day, K. Silver Bullet: Tour of the Universe. (p. 1576)
Day, Karen. Million Miles from Boston. (p. 1144)
—No Cream Puffs. (p. 1258)
Day, Kathleen. Sweet Song of Rainbow Bird. (p. 1690)
Day, Larry, illus. see Beller, Susan Provost.
Day, Larry, illus. see Busch, Miriam.
Day, Larry, illus. see Crowley, Ned.
Day, Larry, illus. see Fradin, Dennis Brindell.
Day, Larry, illus. see Jurmain, Suzanne Tripp.
Day, Larry, illus. see Kay, Verla.
Day, Larry, illus. see Morris, Richard T.
Day, Larry, illus. see Spinner, Stephanie.
Day, Larry, illus. see Thompson, Gare.
Day, Larry, illus. see Winters, Kay.
Day, Larry, jt. auth. see Fradin, Dennis Brindell.
Day, Laura. Welcome to Your Crisis: How to Use the Power of Crisis to Create the Life You Want. (p. 1874)
Day, Linda S. Grandma's Magic Scissors: Paper Cutting from A to Z. (p. 709)
Day, Linda S., ed. see Butterworth, MyLinda.
Day, Linda S., illus. see Darby, Joel, et al.
Day, Linda S., illus. see Zern, Linda L.
Day, Linda S., jt. auth. see Butterworth, MyLinda.
Day, Linda S., jt. auth. see Day, Robert O.
Day, Lisa. Penelope Desiree Montclair, Age 11 (and Countin'!) (p. 1336)
—Penelope Desiree Montclair, Age 9 (Pert' near a Double Digit) (p. 1336)
Day, Lucille. Chain Letter. Dworkin, Doug, illus. (p. 288)
Day, Margery, illus. see Burrows, Jennifer S.
Day, Maria. Perfect Butterfly. (p. 1341)
Day, Martin. Animal Parables. Day, Martin & Evans, Jamie, illus. (p. 79)
Day, Maurice, illus. see Cory, David.
Day, Maurice, illus. see LeCron, Helen Cowles.
Day, Meredith & Adams, Colleen. Primary Source Investigation of Women's Suffrage. (p. 1400)
Day, Meredith & Augustyn, Adam. Lacrosse & Its Greatest Players (p. 970)
Day, Meredith, ed. Revolution & Independence in Latin America. (p. 1466)
Day, Nancy. Way down below Deep Sheldon, David, illus. (p. 1864)
Day, Nancy Raines. Fairy Childs Busy Week. (p. 563)
—On a Windy Night. Bates, George, illus. (p. 1288)
—What in the World? Sets in Nature. Cyrus, Kurt, illus. (p. 1887)
Day, Ralph M. Peter Porcupine One Quill. (p. 1347)
Day, Reed B. Two Families: A History of the Lives & Times of the Families of Isaac Newton Day & Lucilla Caroline Blachly 1640-1940. (p. 1803)
Day, Rob, illus. see Loewen, Nancy.
Day, Rob, illus. see Whiting, Jim & Loewen, Nancy.
Day, Robert O. & Day, Linda S. There's a Frog on a Log in the Bog. Day, Linda S., illus. (p. 1730)
Day, Roger P., jt. auth. see House, Peggy.
Day, Shirley. Luna & the Big Blur: A Story for Children Who Wear Glasses. Morris, Don, illus. (p. 1065)
Day, Sunnie. Sunnie & Her Peeps. (p. 1677)
Day, Susan. Astro's Adventures. the Great Escape. (p. 109)
—Cognitive Behavioral Theory: Used with ... Day-Theory & Design in Counseling & Psychotherapy. (p. 338)
Day, Susie. My Invisible Boyfriend. (p. 1211)
—Serafina67 - "Urgently Requires Life" (p. 1552)
Day, Thomas Fleming. Voyage of Detroit (p. 1850)
Day, Todd. Never Play Checkers with a Leapfrog. Preston, Halsey, illus. (p. 1243)
Day, Tracy. Silver Lining: Book the First of the Kadnohkka Grey Series. (p. 1576)
Day, Trevor. Body Bugs! Uninvited Guests on Your Body (p. 207)
—Body Bugs! [Scholastic]: Uninvited Guests on Your Body. (p. 207)
—Genetics: Investigating the Function of Genes & the Science of Heredity. (p. 661)
—Lakes & Rivers. Garratt, Richard, illus. (p. 972)
—Life in the Crusher: Mysteries of the Deep Oceans (p. 1011)
—Oceans. Garratt, Richard, illus. (p. 1277)
—Oceans & Beaches (p. 1277)
—Pets Parents Hate! Animal Life Cycles (p. 1348)
—Pets Parents Hate! [Scholastic]: Animal Life Cycles. (p. 1348)
—Taiga (p. 1695)
—Taiga. Garratt, Richard, illus. (p. 1695)
Day, Trevor, rev. Genetics. (p. 660)
Day, Williamson. Pretorius Stories. (p. 1398)
Dayal, Jyothsna. Forest Friends: Description of Different Forest & Farm Animals. (p. 618)
Dayal, Mala. Ramayana in Pictures. Joshi, Jagdish, illus. (p. 1437)
Dayan, Linda Marcos. Monstruo Graciopeo. Nepomniachi, Leonid, illus. (p. 1169)
Daybell, Chad. Aaronic Priesthood: Seven Principles That Will Make This Power a Part of Your Daily Life. Murray, Rhett E., illus. (p. 2)
—Book of Mormon Numbers. Bonham, Bob, illus. (p. 211)
Daybell, Chad & Daybell, Tammy. Tiny Talks: Volume 4: the Family. Vol. 4 (p. 1756)
Daybell, Chad G. Baptism: Entering the Path to Eternal Life. (p. 137)
—Prophet in Palmyra. Priddis, C. Michael, illus. (p. 1411)
Daybell, Tammy, jt. auth. see Daybell, Chad.
Day-Bivins, Pat. Bullies Beware! Larkins, Mona & Anderson, Jan, illus. (p. 240)
Daykin, Louise. Goldilocks & the Three Bears. (p. 696)
Daykin, Louise, illus. see Clynes, Kate.
Daykin, Louise, tr. see Clynes, Kate.
Daykin, Louise, tr. Goldilocks & the Three Bears. (p. 696)
Daykin, Rachmiel, tr. see Fuchs, Menucha.
Day-MacLeod, Deirdre. Career Building Through Blogging. (p. 266)
—States of Central Mexico. (p. 1644)
—States of Northern Mexico. (p. 1644)
—Viruses & Spam. (p. 1844)
Dayn, Penelope, illus. see Dyan, Penelope.
Daynes, K. Adventures of Sinbad the Sailor. (p. 23)
Daynes, K., jt. auth. see Davidson, S.
Daynes, K. M. Race Cars II. (p. 1430)
Daynes, Katie. 1001 Things to Spot in the Sea. (p. 2002)
—1001 Things to Spot in the Sea. Gower, Teri, illus. (p. 2002)
—1001 Things to Spot in the Sea Sticker Book. (p. 2002)
—Adolf Hitler. (p. 13)
—Cars. Larkum, A., illus. (p. 271)
—Chocolate. Larkum, Adam, illus. (p. 309)
—Cleopatra. (p. 331)
—Enormous Turnip. Overwater, Georgien, illus. (p. 531)
—Fabulous Story of Fashion. Mistry, Nilesh, illus. (p. 560)
—Farm Animals. Fox, Christyan, illus. (p. 573)
—Firefighters. Fox, Christyan, illus. (p. 591)
—Flip Flap Airport. (p. 604)
—Flip Flap Farm. (p. 604)
—Jack & the Beanstalk. Mounter, Paddy, illus. (p. 902)
—Living in Space. Wray, Zoe & Fox, Christyan, illus. (p. 1041)
—Living in Space. Fox, Christyan & Pang, Alex, illus. (p. 1041)
—Look Inside a Farm. (p. 1049)
—Marie Antoinette. Mistry, Nilesh, illus. (p. 1093)
—Questions & Answers. (p. 1426)
—Revealing Story of Underwear. Mistry, Nilesh, illus. (p. 1465)
—See Inside Ancient Rome. Hancock, David, illus. (p. 1546)
—See Inside Castles. Hancock, David, illus. (p. 1546)
—See Inside Space. Allen, Peter, illus. (p. 1546)
—See Inside Weather & Climate IR. (p. 1546)
—See Inside Your Body. King, Colin, illus. (p. 1546)
—Stinking Story of Garbage. Mayer, Uwe, illus. (p. 1651)
—Story of Toilets, Telephones & Other Useful Inventions. Larkum, Adam, illus. (p. 1662)
—Toilets, Telephones & Other Useful Inventions. (p. 1762)
—Trucks. (p. 1791)
—Vietnam War. (p. 1841)
—Winston Churchill. Tomlins, Karen, illus. (p. 1937)
Daynes, Katie, jt. auth. see Claybourne, Anna.
Daynes, Katie, jt. auth. see Davidson, Susanna.
Daynes, Katie & Allen, Peter. See Inside Planet Earth - Internet Referenced. (p. 1546)
Daynes, Katie & Davidson, Susannah. Ballet Treasury. (p. 135)
Daynes, Katie & Irving, N. Easy French. (p. 500)
Daynes, Katie & King, Colin. Tu Cuerpo: Conoce Por Dentro. (p. 1795)
Daynes, Katie & Watt, Fiona, eds. Baby Scrapbook. (p. 128)
Daynes, Katie & Wray, Zoe. Life in Space. Fox, Christyan & Pang, Alex, illus. (p. 1011)
Daynes Katie, et al. Firefighters. Fox, Christyan, illus. (p. 591)
Daynes, Katie, retold by. Pinocchio. (p. 1360)
—Sinbad. (p. 1578)
Da-Young Im, Linda, illus. see Roberts, Deborah.
DaySpring Greeting Card Staff. Really Woolly Bedtime Prayers (p. 1450)
Dayspring Staff. Holy Bible (p. 791)
Dayton, Beverly, jt. auth. see Dayton, Howard.
Dayton, Connor. Asphalt Pavers. (p. 107)
—Balers. (p. 134)
—Cherry Pickers. (p. 298)
—Choppers. (p. 310)
—Columbus Day: Día de la Raza. Alamán, Eduardo, tr. from ENG. (p. 346)
—Columbus Day. (p. 346)
—Cool Bikes. (p. 362)
—Cool Bikes/Motos Cool. Alaman, Eduardo, tr. (p. 362)
—Cranes. (p. 376)
—Crystals. (p. 387)
—Cultivators. (p. 390)
—Denny Hamlin. (p. 426)
—Denny Hamlin. Alaman, Eduardo, tr. (p. 426)
—Desert Animals. (p. 428)
—Dirt Bikes. (p. 446)
—Dirt Bikes. Alaman, Eduardo, tr. (p. 446)
—Forest Animals. (p. 618)
—Fossils. (p. 623)
—Garbage Trucks. (p. 655)
—Gemstones. (p. 660)
—Greg Biffle. (p. 723)
—Greg Biffle. Alaman, Eduardo, tr. (p. 723)
—Harvesters. (p. 752)
—Hearing. (p. 759)
—Independence Day: Día de la Independencia. Alamán, Eduardo, tr. from ENG. (p. 870)
—Independence Day. (p. 870)
—Jackhammers. (p. 903)
—Jamie Mcmurray. (p. 907)
—Jamie Mcmurray. Alaman, Eduardo, tr. (p. 907)
—Jeff Burton. (p. 911)
—Jeff Burton. Alaman, Eduardo, tr. (p. 911)
—Kasey Kahne. (p. 944)
—Kasey Kahne. Alaman, Eduardo, tr. (p. 944)
—Kobe Bryant: NBA Scoring Sensation. (p. 966)
—Kyle Busch. (p. 969)
—Kyle Busch. Alaman, Eduardo, tr. (p. 969)
—Labor Day: Día Del Trabajo. Alamán, Eduardo, tr. from ENG. (p. 969)
—Labor Day. (p. 969)
—Martin Luther King Jr. Day: Natalicio de Martin Luther King Jr. Alamán, Eduardo, tr. from ENG. (p. 1098)
—Martin Luther King Jr. Day. (p. 1098)
—Memorial Day: Día de Los Caídos. Alamán, Eduardo, tr. from ENG. (p. 1125)
—Memorial Day. (p. 1125)
—Milking Machines/[text by Connor Dayton]. (p. 1143)
—Minerals. (p. 1146)
—Motorcycles: Made for Speed (p. 1180)
—Mountain Animals. (p. 1180)
—Planters. (p. 1369)
—Prairie Animals. (p. 1392)
—Presidents' Day: Día de Los Presidentes. Alamán, Eduardo, tr. from ENG. (p. 1397)
—Presidents' Day. (p. 1397)
—Rock Formations. (p. 1482)
—Rocks & Minerals (p. 1483)
—Sight. (p. 1573)
—Street Bikes. (p. 1666)
—Street Bikes/Motos de Calle. Alaman, Eduardo, tr. (p. 1666)
—Street Sweepers. (p. 1667)
—Superbikes. (p. 1682)
—Superbikes. Alaman, Eduardo, tr. (p. 1682)
—Thanksgiving: Día de Accion de Gracias. Alamán, Eduardo, tr. from ENG. (p. 1725)
—Thanksgiving. (p. 1725)
—Touch. (p. 1772)
—Tractors. (p. 1775)
—Tricks with Bikes. (p. 1786)
—Tricks with Bikes/Trucos con la Moto. Alaman, Eduardo, tr. from ENG. (p. 1786)
—Tundra Animals. (p. 1796)
—Veterans Day: Día de Los Veteranos. Alamán, Eduardo, tr. from ENG. (p. 1839)
—Veterans Day. (p. 1839)
—Volcanic Rocks. (p. 1848)
—Water. (p. 1862)
—Wetland Animals. (p. 1877)
Dayton, Dorothy. Legend of Farmer Will. (p. 988)
Dayton, Doug. Total Market Domination: 10 Steps for Supercharging Your Sales & Marketing. (p. 1771)
Dayton, Howard & Dayton, Beverly. ABC's of Handling Money God's Way. (p. 4)
—ABC's of Handling Money God's Way. Davenport, Andy, illus. (p. 4)
—Secret of Handling Money God's Way. (p. 1542)
—Secret of Handling Money God's Way. Davenport, Andy, illus. (p. 1542)
Dayton, Melissa, illus. see Manhardt, Laurie Watson.
Dayton, Melissa, illus. see Watson Manhardt, Laurie.
Dayton, Tyler, illus. see Garcia, Emerald.
Daywalt, Drew. Day the Crayons Came Home. Jeffers, Oliver, illus. (p. 414)
—Day the Crayons Quit. Jeffers, Oliver, illus. (p. 414)
D.B., Wach, et al. Teddy Bear Guardians of the Rain Forest. (p. 1712)
DC. DC Super Friends Heroes to the Rescue: Book & 3-D Playset. (p. 415)
—Team of Heroes. (p. 1710)
DC Artists Staff, illus. see Reader's Digest Editors.
DC Comics Staff. Batman Jumbo Color & Activity Book. Meredith Books Staff et al, eds. (p. 144)
—Bizarro Comics. (p. 194)
—DC Super Heroes Storybook Collection. (p. 416)
—Justice League Flip Clips. (p. 940)
—Return of Superman. Kahan, Bob, ed. (p. 1464)
—Superman: Flying into Action. (p. 1683)
—Superman. (p. 1683)
—Superman Returns: The Official Movie Guide. (p. 1683)
—Team up with Batman! (p. 1710)
DC Comics Staff, illus. see Bright, J. E.
DC Comics Staff, illus. see Lemke, Donald B., et al.
DC Comics Staff, illus. see Sonneborn, Scott.
DC Comics Staff, illus. see Weissburg, Paul.
DC Comics Staff, jt. auth. see Fox, Gardner.
DC Comics Staff, jt. creator see Kane, Bob.
DC Comics Staff & Reinhart, Matthew. DC Super Heroes: The Ultimate Pop-Up Book. (p. 416)
DC Comics Staff & Waid, Mark. Divided We Fall. (p. 454)
DC Comics Staff, contrib. by. Seven Soldiers of Victory (p. 1555)
DC Comics Staff, creator. Batgirl. (p. 143)
—Greatest Stories Ever Told. (p. 720)
—Hawkman. (p. 755)
—House of Mystery (p. 803)
—Robin Archives (p. 1479)
—Superman Cover to Cover. (p. 1683)
—War Games. (p. 1857)
DC Comics Staff, ed. Archives. (p. 95)
DC Comics Staff, et al. Death of Superman. Kahan, Bob, ed. (p. 420)
DC Justice League, D. C. Justice. DC Justice League Draw It! (p. 415)
D'Costa, Jasmine. Real Justice: Branded a Baby Killer: The Story of Tammy Marquardt. (p. 1448)
D'Costa, Jean. Sprat Morrison. (p. 1634)
D'Cruz, Anna-Marie. Do It Yourself Projects! Set. (p. 457)
—Make Your Own Books. (p. 1079)
—Make Your Own Masks. (p. 1080)
—Make Your Own Musical Instruments. (p. 1080)
—Make Your Own Puppets. (p. 1080)
—Make Your Own Purses & Bags. (p. 1080)
—Make Your Own Shoes & Slippers. (p. 1080)
Ddlewis. Adventurers. (p. 15)
de Alarcón, Pedro Antonio & Alarcón Ariza, Pedro Antonio de. Sombrero de Tres Picos. (p. 1608)
de Alba, Arlette, tr. see Wax, Wendy A.
de Alba, Arlette, tr. Musica en Casa: Libro de Cuentos. (p. 1194)
—Winnie Pooh Tesoros para Llevar. (p. 1937)
de Alba, Laura, tr. Caritas Felices. (p. 269)
De Alessi, O. B, jt. auth. see Richards, Chip.
De Almeida, Guilherme, et al. Galileo Galilei. (p. 653)
De Anda, Diane. Day without Sugar / un día sin Azúcar. Baeza Ventura, Gabriela, tr. (p. 415)
—Kikiriki / Quiquiriquí. Hernández, Karina, tr. from ENG. (p. 955)
—Patchwork Garden. Ventura, Gabriela Baeza, tr. (p. 1328)
De Angel, M., illus. see Olson, Lute.
De Angel, Miguel. Let's Go, Patriots! (p. 997)
De Angel, Miguel, illus. see Aryal, Aimee.
De Angel, Miguel, illus. see Beamer, Cheryl & Beamer, Frank.
De Angel, Miguel, illus. see Dooley, Vince.
De Angel, Miguel, illus. see Dye, Pat.
De Angel, Miguel, illus. see Edwards, Pat & Edwards, LaVell.
De Angel, Miguel, illus. see Stabler, Ken.
De Angeli, Marguerite. Door in the Wall. (p. 470)
de Angeli, Marguerite. Elin's Amerika. (p. 513)
De Angelis, Gina. Motion Pictures: Making Cinema Magic. (p. 1179)
De Angelis, Gina & Bianco, David J. Computers: Processing the Data. (p. 355)
De Angelis, Maurizio, illus. see Hartman, Eve & Meshbesher, Wendy.
De Angelis, Maurizio, illus. see Hartman, Eve, et al.
De Angelis, Maurizio, illus. see Latham, Donna & Heinemann Library Staff.
De Angelis, Maurizio, illus. see Latham, Donna.
De Angelis, Maurizio, illus. see Rand, Casey & Heinemann Library Staff.
De Angelis, Maurizio, illus. see Rand, Casey.
De Angelis, Therese. Blackout! Cities in Darkness. (p. 197)
—New Mexico. (p. 1246)
De Angelis, Therese & DeAngelis, Therese. Navajo: Weavers of the Southwest (p. 1237)
De Aragon, Ray J. Dodo the Bird & Other Stories. Calles, Rosa M., illus. (p. 460)
De Arazoza, Ralph. Technology: At Your Service. (p. 1711)
de Atauri, Ines, ed. see Twain, Mark, pseud.
de Atauri, Juan Diaz, ed. see Twain, Mark, pseud.
De Audrade, Norma. Frog, the Princess, the Purpurine, & the Silk Threads. (p. 640)
de Balincourt, Jules. Personal Survival Doom Buggy: Users Manual & Equipment Guide (artist Book) (p. 1344)
De Ballon, N. V., contrib. by. Alphabet Dot to Dot. (p. 49)
De Bats, M., jt. auth. see Graham, H. P.
De Baun, Hillary H. Last Stop Before Heaven. Cooper, Floyd, illus. (p. 978)
De Bear, Tedrick & Rizzi, Trefoni Michael. Teddy's Travels: America's National Parks. (p. 1713)
De Beaumont, Leprince. Belle et la Bete. (p. 162)
de Beer, Hans, illus. see Romanelli, Serena.
de Beer, Hans, see de Beer, Hans, pseud.
de Beer, Hans, pseud. Ahoy There, Little Polar Bear. (p. 30)
—Kleiner eisbar wohin fahrst Du. (p. 963)
—Lars & His Friends: Board Book & Doll. (p. 976)
—Little Polar Bear. (p. 1033)
—Little Polar Bear & the Big Balloon. Lanning, Rosemary, tr. from GER. (p. 1033)
—Little Polar Bear & the Reindeer. (p. 1033)
—Little Polar Bear & the Submarine. (p. 1033)
—Little Polar Bear & the Whales. (p. 1033)
—Little Polar Bear Finds a Friend. de Beer, Hans, illus. (p. 1033)
—Little Polar Bear Lars & the Husky Pup. (p. 1033)
de Beer, Hans, pseud & Bos, Burny. Ollie the Elephant Tuff Book. (p. 1287)
De Bella, Pablo, illus. see Molina, Maria I.
de Bernières, Louis & Bassett, Jennifer. Red Dog. (p. 1453)
de Bie, Ceciel. My Brother Vincent Van Gogh. Williams, Kate, tr. (p. 1199)
De Bie, Erik Scott. Ghostwalker. (p. 673)
De Blumenthal, Verra X. K. Folk Tales from the Russian. (p. 611)
De Boer, Joan, jt. auth. see de Boer, Joan.
de Boer, Joan & De Boer, Joan. Sultan & the Mice. Dame, Txell, illus. (p. 1673)
De Boer, Michel, illus. see Howat, Irene.
De Bonneval, Gwen. William & the Lost Spirit. Smith, Anne, tr. (p. 1933)
de Bourgoing, Pascale, jt. auth. see Broutin, Christian.
De Bourgoing, Pascale, jt. auth. see Jeunesse, Gallimard.
De Bourgoing, Pascale, jt. auth. see Kniffe, Sophie.
De Bourgoing, Pascale, jt. auth. see Perols, Sylvaine.
De Bourgoing, Pascale, et al. On the Seashore. Houbre, Gilbert, illus. (p. 1291)
de Bree, Alexander. Casting Dragon (p. 276)
De Bruin, Sandra. Patient's Medical Log. (p. 1328)
de Brun, Brendan Joseph, illus. see de Brun, Kieran Christopher.
de Brun, Kieran Christopher. Talking Llama: la Llama Que Habla. de Brun, Brendan Joseph, illus. (p. 1703)
de Brunhoff, Jean. Babar & Zephir. de Brunhoff, Jean, illus. (p. 123)
—Classic Tales of Babar. (p. 328)
de Brunhoff, Laurent. Anniversaire de Babar. (p. 87)

—B Is for Babar: An Alphabet Book. (p. 122)
—Babar & the Ghost. (p. 123)
—Babar & the Wully-Wully. (p. 123)
—Babar dans l'Ile aux Oiseaux. (p. 123)
—Babar et la Vieille Dame. (p. 123)
—Babar et le Wouly-Wouly. (p. 123)
—Babar et ses Amis a la Ferme. (p. 123)
—Babar et ses Amis a la Fete. (p. 123)
—Babar et ses Amis a la Maison. (p. 123)
—Babar et ses Amis au Spectacle. (p. 123)
—Babar et ses Amis en Foret. (p. 123)
—Babar et ses Amis en Vacances. (p. 123)
—Babar et ses Amis Font les Courses. (p. 123)
—Babar et ses Amis Visitent le Royaume. (p. 123)
—Babar in Famiglia. (p. 123)
—Babar les 500 Premiers Mots. (p. 123)
—Babar on Paradise Island. (p. 123)
—Babar pour Chaque Soir de la Semaine. (p. 123)
—Babar Raconte Flore Reporter. (p. 123)
—Babar Raconte Halte a la Pollution. (p. 123)
—Babar Raconte la Course a la Lune. (p. 123)
—Babar Raconte l'Affaire de la Couronne. (p. 123)
—Babar Raconte l'Arrivee du Bebe Elephant. (p. 123)
—Babar Raconte le Fantome. (p. 123)
—Babar Raconte le Meilleur Ami des Elephants. (p. 123)
—Babar Raconte le Pianiste. (p. 123)
—Babar Raconte le Plus Beau Cadeau du Monde. (p. 123)
—Babar Raconte Que la Fete Continue. (p. 123)
—Babar Raconte un Diner Chez Rataxes. (p. 123)
—Babar Raconte Zephir Fait le Singe. (p. 123)
—Babar the Magician. (p. 123)
—Babar Visits Another Planet. (p. 123)
—Babar's ABC. (p. 123)
—Babar's Birthday Surprise. (p. 123)
—Babar's Book of Color. (p. 123)
—Babar's Counting Book. (p. 123)
—Babar's Little Girl. (p. 123)
—Babar's Museum of Art. (p. 123)
—Babar's USA. (p. 123)
—Babar's Yoga for Elephants. (p. 123)
—Meet Babar & His Family. (p. 1120)
—Re Babar. (p. 1441)
—Roi Babar. (p. 1485)
—Storia de Babar l'elefantino. (p. 1654)
de Brunhoff, Laurent, jt. auth. see Rose, Phyllis.
de Brunhoff, Laurent & Rose, Phyllis. Babar & His Family. (p. 123)
—Babar Comes to America. (p. 123)
—Babar's Celesteville Games. (p. 123)
de Bruno, Oanna. Cuentos de Dragones para Ninos. (p. 389)
De Camp, Alison. My near-Death Adventures (99% True!) (p. 1215)
de Camp, L. Sprague. Years in the Making: The Time Travel Stories of L. Sprague de Camp. Olson, Mark L., ed. (p. 1969)
de Campi, Alex. Agent Boo Fuijkschot, Edo, illus. (p. 29)
De Campi, Alex. Kat & Mouse (p. 944)
—Kat & Mouse Manfredi, Frederica, illus. (p. 944)
de Campi, Alex. Kat & Mouse. Manfredi, Federica, illus. (p. 944)
De, Campialex. Kat & Mouse Manfredi, Federica, illus. (p. 944)
De Capua, Sarah. Andrew Carnegie. (p. 72)
—Armenia in Pictures. (p. 99)
—Being a Governor. (p. 160)
—California. (p. 253)
—California. Risco, Eida del, tr. from ENG. (p. 253)
—Cherokee. (p. 298)
—Cheyenne. (p. 299)
—Choctaw. (p. 309)
—Comanche. (p. 346)
—Como Nos Orientamos? (p. 351)
—Iroquois. (p. 888)
—Making a Law. (p. 1080)
—Massachusetts. (p. 1102)
—Menominee. (p. 1126)
—Nueva York: New York. (p. 1270)
—Nueva York. (p. 1270)
—Paying Taxes. (p. 1331)
—Running for Public Office. (p. 1497)
—Sandra Day O'Connor. (p. 1511)
—Serving on a Jury. (p. 1553)
—Shawnee. (p. 1563)
—Shoshone. (p. 1569)
—Tlingit. (p. 1758)
—True Book - Civics: Serving on a Jury. (p. 1792)
—Voting. (p. 1850)
De Capua, Sarah & DiPiazza, Francesca. Finland in Pictures. (p. 589)
De Castro, Ines E. Teddy Bear Faeries. De Castro, Ines E., illus. (p. 1712)
de Cervantes, Miguel. Don Quijote. Svetlin, illus. (p. 465)
—Don Quijote de La Mancha: Leer y Aprender. (p. 465)
—Don Quijote de la Mancha: Leer y Aprender. (p. 465)
—Don Quijote de la Mancha. Saez, Fernando, illus. (p. 465)
—Novelas Ejemplares. (p. 1268)
de Cervantes, Miguel & Brook, Henry. Don Quixote: From the Story by Miguel de Cervantes Saavedra. (p. 465)
De Chabaneix, Hortense, jt. auth. see Laffon, Martine.
De Charleroy, Charles, Jr. Roger's Lion. Knight, Vanessa, illus. (p. 1484)
De Conno, Gianni. Poemas a la Luna/ Poems to the Moon. (p. 1376)
de Coronado, Martha Munoz, see Munoz de Coronado, Martha, ed.
De Costa, Batrice. Boetry: The Poetic Soul of a Bahamian. (p. 207)
de Cumptich, Roberto de Vicq, see De Vicq de Cumptich, Roberto.
de Diaz, Rosario Ahumada. Juguemos a Leer: Libro de Lectura. (p. 932)
—Juguemos con Letras: Ejercicios de Iniciacion a la Escritura. (p. 932)
De Dios, Susana, illus. see Keane, Jerome.
De Duve, Catherine. Hello Matisse: Get to Know Matisse Through Stories, Games & Draw-It-Yourself Fun. (p. 764)
de Duve, Catherine. Hello Rousseau: Get to Know Rousseau through Stories, Games & Draw-It-Yourself Fun. (p. 765)
de', Elda, tr. see Hillert, Margaret.
De felice, Cynthia. Devil's Bridge. (p. 432)
—Light on Hogback Hill. (p. 1015)
—Lostman's River. (p. 1057)
—Strange Night Writing of Jessamine Colter. (p. 1665)
De Fombelle, Timothée. Prince Without a Kingdom. (p. 1401)
—Toby Alone. Ardizzone, Sarah, tr. from FRE. (p. 1760)
—Toby & the Secrets of the Tree. Ardizzone, Sarah, tr. from FRE. (p. 1760)
—Vango: Between Sky & Earth. (p. 1833)
de Fontaine, Jean. Fables. (p. 559)
De Fonte', Desiree. Gaining the Heart of a Man: A Story of Hope & Forgiveness. (p. 652)
De Fonté, Desiree. Jazzy: A Story of Love. (p. 911)
—Zach: A Story of Obedience. (p. 1984)
De Gante, Guillermo, illus. see Estrada, E. Gabriela Aguileta.
de Garis, Nina. Cambridge Checkpoints VCE Economics 2004-2005. (p. 255)
De Gasztold, Carmen B. & Godden, Rumer. Creatures' Choir. (p. 380)
De Gieter, Lucien. Evil Mummies. Spear, Luke, tr. from FRE. (p. 546)
—Imhotep's Transformation. Spear, Luke, tr. from FRE. (p. 861)
—Rameses' Revenge. Spear, Luke, tr. from FRE. (p. 1438)
—Tutankhamun: The Assassinated Pharaoh. (p. 1799)
de Giorgi, Sergio, illus. see Holmes, Andy.
De Giorgi, Sergio, illus. see Salas, Laura Purdie.
De Giorgi, Sergio, jt. auth. see Ashburn, Boni.
De Goede, Marieke. International Political Economy & Poststructural Politics. (p. 880)
De Goldi, Kate. 10 PM Question. (p. 1994)
—Clubs. Colley, Jacqui, illus. (p. 335)
De Golyer, Blu. Adventures of Captain Greenspud. (p. 17)
de Gonzales, Angelica Villagran, tr. see Shah, Idries.
De Graaf, A. M. Dios Crea al Mundo. (p. 445)
—Noe y el Arca. (p. 1262)
—Primera Navidad (The First Christmas) (p. 1400)
—Torre de Babel. (p. 1770)
De Graaf, Anne. Best of the Classics: Retold for Today's Children. (p. 171)
—Little Children's Bible Storybook. Montero, Jose Perez, illus. (p. 1026)
—Son of a Gun. (p. 1611)
De Graaf, Anne, jt. auth. see Dickens, Charles.
De Gramont, Nina. Every Little Thing in the World. (p. 542)
De Grift Stevenson, Fanny Van & Stevenson, Robert Louis. Dynamiter. (p. 491)
de Groot, Bob. Clifton Vol. 6: Kidnapping. (p. 332)
de Groot, Bob & Morris Publishing Company Staff. One-Armed Bandits (p. 1293)
de Groot, Jan. Boy in War (p. 218)
de Guzman, Jennifer, ed. see Weisman, Greg.
de Guzman, Magdalena, tr. see Robles, Anthony D. & Children's Book Press Staff.
De Haas, Rick. Peter & the Seal. (p. 1346)
—Peter & the Winter Sleepers. (p. 1346)
de Hamel, Christopher. Book: A History of the Bible. (p. 210)
de Hartog, Arnold, jt. auth. see Strelitski, Mies.
de Harven, Emile. Gefahrliche Wege. (p. 659)
—Suivez la Piste. (p. 1673)
De Haven, Amanda. Queen Elizabeth's Travel. (p. 1424)
De Haven, Tom. Orphan's Tent. (p. 1305)
de Heer, Margreet. Science. (p. 1524)
de Heriz, Enrique, tr. see Paolini, Christopher.
De Horna, Luis, illus. see Ende, Michael.
De Horna, Luis, illus. see varios & Varios.
De Horne, George. Pixie O'Shaughnessy. (p. 1365)
—Pixie O'shaughnessy. (p. 1365)
de Hugo, Pierre. Fish Underwater. de Hugo, Pierre, illus. (p. 598)
—Polar Bears. de Hugo, Pierre, illus. (p. 1379)
de, Iriarte Tomás, jt. auth. see Iriarte, Tomas De.
De Jenkins, Lyll Becerra, see Becerra de Jenkins, Lyll.
de Jesus Alvarez, Maria, illus. see White, Amy.
de Jesus, Eloisa D., tr. see Robles, Anthony D.
de Jesus, Eloisa D., tr. see Robles, Anthony D. & Children's Book Press Staff.
De Jesus, Opal. Magical Purple-Blue Frog Pagona, Aurora, illus. (p. 1075)
De Jong, Riet M. W. I. Little Freebie & All His Friends. (p. 1028)
De Jonge, Alex, tr. see Sue, Eugene.
De Kelaita, Jade. Harry the Hippopotamus' Journey to Find His Hat. (p. 751)
De Kinder, Jan. Red. (p. 1453)
De Klerk, Judith. Illustrated Maths Dictionary for Australian Schools. (p. 857)
de Klerk, Roger. Foxy Learns Colors. (p. 626)
—Foxy Learns Shapes. (p. 626)
—Foxy Learns to Add. (p. 626)
—Foxy Learns to Tell Time. (p. 626)
de Klerk, Roger, illus. see Andrews, Jackie.
De Kockere, Geert. Piglet Bo Can Do Anything! Van Hemeldonck, Tineke, illus. (p. 1358)
De Kockere, Geert & Dom, An. Dragon Fire. Van Hemeldonck, Tineke, illus. (p. 477)
De Koning, Lezanne. Magic of Nature. (p. 1073)
De La B, et al. Discover Germany. (p. 447)
De La Bedoyere C. Why Why Why Cant Penguins Fly. (p. 1926)
de la Bédoyere, Camilla. 3-D Explorer: Human Body. (p. 1991)
De la Bédoyère, Camilla. Acorn to Oak Tree. (p. 9)
—Action Files: Sharks. (p. 10)
—Balancing Work & Play. (p. 133)
—Big Cats. (p. 180)
—Biggest & Smallest. (p. 185)
—Birds of Prey. (p. 191)
—Caterpillar to Butterfly. (p. 279)
—Coral Reef. (p. 366)
de la Bédoyere, Camilla. Could a Penguin Ride a Bike? And Other Questions. Bitskoff, Aleksei, illus. (p. 369)
De la Bédoyère, Camilla. Deadly Creatures. (p. 417)
—Deadly Predators. (p. 418)
—Deep Ocean. (p. 423)
—Discover Germany. (p. 447)
—Discovery of DNA. (p. 450)
—Dogs & Puppies. (p. 462)
—Egg to Bee. (p. 506)
—Egg to Chicken. (p. 506)
—Egg to Penguin. (p. 506)
—Elephants. (p. 511)
—Fastest & Slowest. (p. 576)
—Fearsome Reptiles: Danger! Take Care as You Discover the World's Deadliest Reptiles. (p. 579)
—France. (p. 627)
—Fry to Sea Horse. (p. 646)
—Great White Shark. (p. 719)
—Hammerhead Shark. (p. 739)
de la Bédoyere, Camilla. Horses & Ponies. (p. 800)
De la Bédoyère, Camilla. Human Body. (p. 825)
—Joey to Kangaroo. (p. 920)
—Lifecycles Caterpillar to Butterfly SchoIBC SS. (p. 1013)
—Lifecycles Egg to Chicken SchoIBC SS. (p. 1013)
—Mini Monsters: Danger! Watch Your Step as You Explore the World's Most Gruesome Creepy Crawlies. (p. 1146)
—Monkeys & Apes. (p. 1166)
—Nocturnal Animals. (p. 1262)
—Oceans. (p. 1277)
—Penguins. (p. 1337)
—Personal Hygiene & Sexual Health. (p. 1344)
—Plants. (p. 1369)
—Pup to Shark. (p. 1417)
—Rainforests. (p. 1436)
—Scary Sharks: Danger! (p. 1520)
—Science of a Piece of Paper: The Science of Materials. (p. 1527)
—Seed to Sunflower. (p. 1547)
—Smartest & Silliest. (p. 1593)
—Snakelet to Snake. (p. 1596)
—Strongest & Weakest. (p. 1668)
—Tadpole to Frog. (p. 1695)
—Tiger Shark. (p. 1748)
—Why Why Why Are Orang-Utans So Hairy? (p. 1926)
—Why Why Why... Are Orangutans So Hairy? (p. 1926)
—Why Why Why... Can't Penguins Fly? (p. 1926)
—Why Why Why Did Dinosaurs Lay Eggs? (p. 1926)
—Why Why Why... Were Dinosaurs Scaly? (p. 1926)
—Wild Animals. (p. 1928)
—Wild Life of Bears (p. 1929)
—Wild Life of Big Cats (p. 1929)
—Wild Life of Frogs (p. 1929)
—Wild Life of Lizards (p. 1929)
—Wild Life of Penguins (p. 1929)
—Wild Life of Sharks (p. 1929)
De La Bédoyère, Camilla. Wild Side (p. 1930)
de la Bédoyère, Camilla, jt. auth. see Colson, Rob Scott.
De la Bédoyère, Camilla, jt. auth. see De la Bédoyère, Guy.
De la Bédoyère, Camilla, jt. auth. see Ripley Entertainment Staff.
De la Bédoyère, Camilla & Ripley's Believe It or Not Editors. Wild Animals: Fun, Facts, & Frights... (p. 1928)
De la Bédoyère, Camilla, et al. Human Body: Fun, Facts, & Goo... Its All about Your Body with a Ripley Twist! (p. 825)
De la Bédoyère, Guy. First Polio Vaccine. (p. 596)
De la Bédoyère, Guy & De la Bédoyère, Camilla. Discovery of Penicillin. (p. 450)
—First Computers. (p. 593)
—First Polio Vaccine. (p. 596)
de la Bretesche, Genevieve, jt. auth. see Scholastic, Inc. Staff.
De La Concha, Bertha Ruiz, tr. see Hager, Jenna Bush.
De La Cour, Gary. Counting in the Snow. (p. 371)
de La Cour, Gary, illus. see Studio Mouse Staff.
de La Cour, Gary, et al. Twinkle Twinkle: And Other Sleepy-Time Rhymes. (p. 1802)
—Wheels on the Bus. (p. 1901)
De La Cruz, Erin Harris, illus. see Morrison, Kevin.
De La Cruz, Melissa. Angels on Sunset Boulevard. (p. 75)
—Ashley Project. (p. 106)
—Ashleys. (p. 106)
—Au Pairs. (p. 114)
—Beach Lane. (p. 149)
—Birthday Vicious. (p. 193)
—Blue Bloods. (p. 202)
—Crazy Hot. (p. 377)
—Fresh off the Boat. (p. 636)
—Gates of Paradise. (p. 658)
—Isle of the Lost. (p. 893)
—Jealous? (p. 911)
—Lost in Time. (p. 1056)
—Masquerade. (p. 1102)
—Misguided Angel. (p. 1150)
—Revelations. (p. 1465)
—Ring & the Crown. (p. 1473)
—Skinny-Dipping. (p. 1585)
—Social Order. (p. 1604)
—Sun-Kissed. (p. 1676)
De la Cruz, Melissa & Johnston, Michael. Frozen. (p. 645)
—Stolen: Heart of Dread. Bk. 2 (p. 1652)
De La Fuente, Mary, illus. see Horowitz, Alena Netia.
de la Fuente, Pilar, illus. see Fernandez, Alberto.
De La Garza, Amanda. Biomass: Energy from Plants & Animals. (p. 189)
De La Garza, David. Great, Great, Great Chicken War. (p. 716)
De La Garza, Felipe de Jesús. Quince días de Las Matemáticas. (p. 1428)
De La Hoya, Oscar. Super Oscar. Montejo, Andrea, tr. (p. 1680)
De La Hoya, Oscar & Shulman, Mark. Super Oscar. (p. 1680)
De la Hoz, Cindy, ed. see Weber, Ken.
de la Jara, Fatima. Castaño. (p. 276)
—Drago. (p. 476)
—Limoneros y Naranjos. (p. 1018)
—Olivo. (p. 1287)
—Olmo. (p. 1287)
—Palmera. (p. 1320)
De La Llata, Lorenza. Awaking the Mighty. (p. 120)
de la Mare, Walter. Rhymes & Verses: Collected Poems for Young People. Blaisdell, Elinore, illus. (p. 1468)
—Three Mulla-Mulgars. (p. 1743)
De la Mora, Maribel. Andrés Chupadedos. (p. 72)
—Andrés Chupadedos CD. (p. 72)
—baston de la Reina. (p. 143)
De La Mora, Maribel, Sr. Andrés Chupadedos. Editorial Cultural, ed. (p. 72)
De La Paz, Myrna J. Abadeha: The Philippine Cinderella. Tang, Youshan, illus. (p. 2)
de la Paz, Myrna J. Abadeha: The Philippine Cinderella. Tang, Youshan, illus. (p. 2)
De la Peña, Matt. Ball Don't Lie. (p. 134)
—Curse of the Ancients. (p. 394)
—Eternity. (p. 539)
—Hunted. (p. 828)
—I Will Save You. (p. 848)
—Last Stop on Market Street. Robinson, Christian, illus. (p. 978)
—Living. (p. 1040)
—Mexican WhiteBoy. (p. 1131)
—Mexican Whiteboy. (p. 1131)
—Nation's Hope: The Story of Boxing Legend Joe Louis. (p. 1234)
—Nation's Hope: The Story of Boxing Legend Joe Louis. Nelson, Kadir, illus. (p. 1234)
—We Were Here. (p. 1868)
De La Ramee, Louise. Bimbi. (p. 188)
De La Ramee, Louise & Ouida. Bimbi. (p. 188)
—Nurnberg Stove. (p. 1273)
De la Torre, Cristina, tr. see Deedy, Carmen Agra.
De La Torre, Roberto, illus. see Jenkins, Paul.
De La Torre, Roberto & Checchetto, Marco. Shadowland - Daredevil. (p. 1558)
de la Vega, Eida, ed. see Garrett, Winston.
De La Vega, Eida, ed. see Gibbs, Maddie.
de la Vega, Eida, ed. see Kidde, Rita.
de la Vega, Eida, ed. see Peters, Elisa & Eida, de la Vega.
de la Vega, Eida, ed. see Peters, Elisa.
de la Vega, Eida, tr. see Alexander, Emmett.
de la Vega, Eida, tr. see Allen, Nancy Kelly.
de la Vega, Eida, tr. see Brunell, Heather.
de la Vega, Eida, tr. see Crane Johnson, Amy.
de La Vega, Eida, tr. see Crawford, Laura.
de la Vega, Eida, tr. see Falwell, Cathryn.
de la Vega, Eida, tr. see Gagne, Tammy.
de la Vega, Eida, tr. see Gibson, Karen.
de La Vega, Eida, tr. see Heling, Kathryn & Hembrook, Deborah.
de la Vega, Eida, tr. see Heling, Kathryn, et al.
de la Vega, Eida, tr. see Hinman, Bonnie.
de la Vega, Eida, tr. see Hinman, Christmas.
de la Vega, Eida, tr. see Hoppey, Tim.
de la Vega, Eida, tr. see Huggins-Cooper, Lynn.
de la Vega, Eida, tr. see James, Simon.
de la Vega, Eida, tr. see Jarkins, Sheila.
de La Vega, Eida, tr. see Jeffers, Dawn.
de la Vega, Eida, tr. see Johnson, Amy Crane.
de la Vega, Eida, tr. see Levy, Janice.
de la Vega, Eida, tr. see McGrath, Liz & Quick, Barbara.
de la Vega, Eida, tr. see Murcia, Rebecca Thatcher.
de la Vega, Eida, tr. see O'Hara, Nicholas.
de la Vega, Eida, tr. see O'Neill, Alexis.
de la Vega, Eida, tr. see Orr, Tamra.
de la Vega, Eida, tr. see Phillips, Larissa.
de la Vega, Eida, tr. see Polette, Keith.
de la Vega, Eida, tr. see Rockhill, Dennis.
de la Vega, Eida, tr. see Scholl, Elizabeth.
de la Vega, Eida, tr. see Sherman, Patrice & Murica, Rebecca Thatcher.
de la Vega, Eida, tr. see Smith, J. D.
de la Vega, Eida, tr. see Thatcher Murcia, Rebecca.
de la Vega, Eida, tr. see Tracy, Kathleen.
de La Vega, Eida, tr. see Weatherford, Carole Boston.
de La Vega, Eida, tr. Celebratin with Me/Celebra Conmigo (p. 284)
de la Vega, Eida, tr. from ENG. Estela en el Mercado de Pulgas. Sanchez, Enrique O., illus. (p. 538)
de la Vega, Pablo, tr. see Bloor, Edward.
De Lafayette, Madame. Princess de Montpensier. (p. 1403)
de Lambana, Martha Lucia Martinez. Grafias 1: Escritura Asociativa Script: Afianzamiento. 1 (p. 705)
—Grafias 2: Escritura Asociativa Script: Transicion. 2 (p. 705)
—Grafias 3: Escritura Asociativa Script: Afianzamiento. 3 (p. 705)
—Grafias 4: Escritura Asociativa Script: Ejercitacion. 4 (p. 705)
—Grafias 5: Escritura Asociativa Script: Intermedio. 5 (p. 705)
—Grafias 6: Escritura Asociativa Script: Avanzada. 6 (p. 705)
—Grafias K: Escritura Asociativa Script: Aprestamiento. (p. 705)
de Lambilly, Elisabeth. Gandhi: His Life, His Struggles, His Words. Cordier, Severine, illus. (p. 655)
de Lambilly-Bresson, Elisabeth. Animales de la Casa. (p. 80)
—Animales de la Charca. (p. 80)
—Animales de la Granja. (p. 80)
—Animales de la Noche. (p. 80)
—Animales de Vivos Colores. (p. 81)
—Animales del Desierto. (p. 81)
—Animales Marinos. (p. 81)
—Animales Nos Cuentan Su Vida (Animal Show & Tell) (p. 81)
—Animales Sorprendentes. (p. 81)
—Animals at the Pond. (p. 82)
—Animals in Polar Regions. (p. 83)
—Animals in the Desert. (p. 83)
—Animals in the Field. (p. 83)
—Animals in the Forest. (p. 83)
—Animals in the Garden. (p. 83)
—Animals in the Jungle. (p. 83)
—Animals of the Mountains. (p. 83)

—Animals of the Night. (p. 83)
—Animals on the Farm. (p. 83)
—Baby Animals. (p. 124)
—Colorful Animals. (p. 344)
—Crias de Animales. (p. 382)
—Sea Animals. (p. 1534)
—Unusual Animals. (p. 1823)
De Las Casas, Dianne. Blue Frog: The Legend of Chocolate Stone-Barker, Holly, illus. (p. 202)
de Las Casas, Dianne. Cajun Cornbread Boy Gentry, Marita, illus. (p. 252)
De Las Casas, Dianne. Cinderellaphant Jolet, Stefan, illus. (p. 320)
—Dinosaur Mardi Gras Gentry, Marita, illus. (p. 442)
de Las Casas, Dianne. Gigantic Sweet Potato Gentry, Marita, illus. (p. 676)
De Las Casas, Dianne. House That Santa Built Stone-Barker, Holly, illus. (p. 804)
—House That Witchy Built Stone-Barker, Holly, illus. (p. 804)
De Las Casas, Dianne. Little Read Hen Stone-Barker, Holly, illus. (p. 1034)
—Madame Poulet & Monsieur Roach Gentry, Marita, illus. (p. 1069)
—Mama's Bayou Stone-Barker, Holly, illus. (p. 1084)
De Las Casas, Dianne. There's a Dragon in the Library Gentry, Marita, illus. (p. 1730)
De Las Casas, Dianne & Eliana, Kid. Cool Kids Cook: Fresh & Fit Lisette, Soleil, illus. (p. 363)
De Laurentiis, Giada. Hawaii! #6. Gambatesa, Francesca, illus. (p. 755)
—Hong Kong! (p. 795)
—Hong Kong! #3. Gambatesa, Francesca, illus. (p. 795)
—Naples! (p. 1229)
—Naples! Gambatesa, Francesca, illus. (p. 1229)
—New Orleans! (p. 1246)
—New Orleans! #4. Gambatesa, Francesca, illus. (p. 1246)
—Paris! (p. 1324)
—Paris! Gambatesa, Francesca, illus. (p. 1324)
—Paris! No. 2. Gambatesa, Francesca, illus. (p. 1324)
—Rio de Janeiro! #5. Gambatesa, Francesca, illus. (p. 1473)
de le Bédoyère, Camilla. Egg to Penguin. (p. 506)
De Leeuw, Cateau. Fear in the Forest. Vosburgh, Leonard, illus. (p. 579)
De Leiris, Lucia, illus. see Grady, Monica, et al.
De Leon, Aya, et al. Como Sacar Quitar los Idiotas del Gobierno: El Guia Anti-Politico No Aburrido al Poder. Wimsatt, William Upski et al, eds. (p. 351)
De Leon, Mauricio Velzaquez, tr. see Feldman, Heather.
De Leon, Mauricio Velzaquez, tr. see Johnston, Marianne.
De Leon, Mauricio Velzaquez, tr. see Kirkpatrick, Rob.
De Leon, Mauricio Velzaquez, tr. see Obregon, Jose Maria.
De Leon, Mauricio Velzaquez, tr. see Zuravicky, Orli.
De Lesseps, Ferdinand Zoticus. Oceanology: The True Account of the Voyage of the Nautilus. Steer, Dugald A. & Hawkins, Emily, eds. (p. 1277)
de Lint, Charles. Blue Girl. (p. 202)
De Lint, Charles. Cats of Tanglewood Forest. (p. 281)
de Lint, Charles. Cats of Tanglewood Forest. Vess, Charles, illus. (p. 281)
—Dingo. (p. 440)
—Harp of the Grey Rose. (p. 749)
—Memory & Dream. (p. 1126)
—Seven Wild Sisters: A Modern Fairy Tale. Vess, Charles, illus. (p. 1555)
—Wild Wood. (p. 1930)
—Wolf Moon. (p. 1944)
De Lint, Charles, jt. auth. see de Lint, Charles.
de Lint, Charles & De Lint, Charles. Waifs & Strays. (p. 1852)
De Lolme, Jean Louis. Constitution of England. (p. 359)
De Long, Janice, jt. auth. see De Long, Robert.
De Long, Robert & De Long, Janice. Redwall Study Guide. (p. 1456)
De Long, Ron, et al. Dream-Makers Mathematics: Art & Mathematics. De Long, Ron et al, eds. (p. 483)
—Dream-Makers Principles of Art & Design: Art & Design. De Long, Ron et al, eds. (p. 483)
—Dream-Makers Science: Art & Science. De Long, Ron et al, eds. (p. 483)
De Lopez, Jacqueline Salazar. Little Hands, Busy Minds. (p. 1029)
De Lorenzo, Dawn. Peanut Butter & Jelly Possibilities: Youthful Inspirations. (p. 1332)
de los Heros, Luis, jt. auth. see Wilson, Elizabeth.
De Los Heros, Luis & Wilson, Elizabeth. Chifa Chi's Little Adventure in New York City. (p. 301)
de los reyes Cruz, Cheryl, illus. see Brisland, Toni.
De Los Santos, Elizabeth G. Secret House. (p. 1541)
de los Santos, Marisa & Teague, David. Connect the Stars. (p. 357)
—Saving Lucas Biggs. (p. 1517)
De Luca, Daniela. Ben the Beaver. (p. 163)
—Buster the Kangaroo. (p. 245)
—Celia the Tiger. (p. 286)
—Harry the Wolf. (p. 751)
—Josh the Anteater. (p. 926)
—Lizzie the Elephant. (p. 1043)
—Meyers Bunter Weltatlas fuer Kinder. (p. 1131)
De Luca, Daniela, illus. see Cooper, Alison & McRae, Anne.
De Luca, Daniela, illus. see McRae, Anne.
De Luca, Daniela, illus. see Morris, Neil.
De Lucia, Joseph. Andy Ore's Magical Christmas Story: Santa's Gift. (p. 73)
—Christmas Angel. (p. 312)
De Lucio-Brock, Anita, illus. see Herrera, Juan Felipe.
De Macedo, Joao. How to Be a Surfer. (p. 815)
de Maeyer, Gregie & Vanmechelen, Koen. Juul. (p. 941)
De Magalhaes, Roberto Carvalho. Claude Monet. (p. 329)
—Paul Gauguin. (p. 1330)
de Marcken, Gail, illus. see Brumbeau, Jeff.
de Marcken, Gail, illus. see Cary, Bob.
de Marcken, Gail, illus. see Maccarone, Grace.
De Marco, Arielle, illus. see Degarmo, Serena.
De Marco, Clare. Freddy's Teddy. (p. 633)
—Mad Scientist Next Door. (p. 1069)
De Marco, Tony. Jackie Robinson. (p. 903)
de Mariaffi, Elisabeth. Eat It Up! Lip-Smacking Recipes for Kids. Stephens, Jay, illus. (p. 501)
—Eat It Up! Lip-Smacking Recipes for Kids. Manale, Steven Charles et al, illus. (p. 501)
De Maris, Merrill, et al. Walt Disney's Comics & Stories Clark, John, ed. (p. 1855)
de Mariscal, Blanca Lopez. Harvest Birds: Los Pajaros de la Cosecha. Flores, Enrique, illus. (p. 751)
De Matos, Isabel Freire. Carta de Delke. Saez, Sofia, illus. (p. 272)
—Carta de Monica. Saez, Sofia, illus. (p. 272)
—Pececito Magico. Torres, Walter, illus. (p. 1333)
de Maupassant, Guy. Contes du jour et de la nuit (p. 360)
—Mon Oncle Jules et Autres Nouvelles (p. 1163)
—Necklace. Kelley, Gary, illus. (p. 1239)
De Medeiros, J. Pulleys. (p. 1415)
De Medeiros, James. Al Gore. (p. 32)
—Anacondas. (p. 66)
—Dolphins. (p. 464)
—Justin Timberlake. (p. 940)
—Kayaking. (p. 946)
—Migration North. (p. 1141)
—Parthenon. (p. 1325)
—Pulleys. (p. 1415)
—Slavery. (p. 1588)
De Medeiros, M. Screws. (p. 1533)
De Medeiros, Michael. Barack Obama. (p. 137)
—Chaparral. (p. 291)
—Chaparrals. (p. 291)
—Common Sense. (p. 349)
—Gorillas. (p. 703)
—Marc Brown: My Favorite Writer. (p. 1091)
—Mountain Biking. (p. 1180)
—NBA. (p. 1238)
—Orangutans. (p. 1302)
—Polar Bears. (p. 1379)
—Screws. (p. 1533)
—Steve Nash. (p. 1649)
De Medeiros, Michael & Banting, Erinn. Wheels & Axles. (p. 1900)
De Michel. What's an Egg Got to Do with It? A Dozen Adventures with God for Grades 4-6. (p. 1896)
de Monfreid, Dorothée, illus. see Girard, Franck.
De Monfreid, Henry. Hashish: A Smuggler's Tale. Bell, Helen Buchanan, tr. from FRE. (p. 752)
de Montaigne, Michel. Selected Essays. (p. 1549)
De Montignie, Leon, illus. see Klein, Peter.
De Monvel, Maurice Boutet, see Boutet de Monvel, Maurice.
De Moratin, Leandro Fernandez, tr. see Shakespeare, William.
de Moüy, Iris. Naptime Tanaka, Shelley, tr. from FRE. (p. 1229)
De Munnik, Hema. Bhole: Adventures of a Young Yogi. (p. 174)
De Muth, Roger, illus. see Ziefert, Harriet.
De Nijs, Erika. Dentist's Job. (p. 427)
de Nijs, Erika. Teacher's Job. (p. 1709)
de Niles, Anita & Myrick, Gladys, eds. Manual de Estrellas: Alumna (p. 1088)
de Oaxaco, Jesus, illus. see Weill, Cynthia.
De Palma, Toni. Devil's Triangle. (p. 432)
—Under the Banyan Tree. (p. 1813)
de, Paola Tomie, jt. auth. see dePaola, Tomie.
De Paolo, Tom. Paddy Platypus & the Ring-Tail Squatteroo. (p. 1317)
de Papenbrock, Dervy Romero, tr. see Davis, Rebecca.
De Paulis, M. Rene. Bed & Bisket Gang: Everybody's Different. (p. 156)
De Pauw, Linda Grant. In Search of Molly Pitcher. (p. 864)
de Pennart, Geoffroy & Pennart, Geoffroy De. Sofia, la Vaca Que Amaba la Musica. (p. 1605)
De Pennington, Joanne. Modern America: The USA, 1865 to the Present. (p. 1158)
de Perez, Ursula S., jt. auth. see de Sturtz, Maria Ester H.
de Pinna, Simon. Chemical Reactions. (p. 297)
—Transfer of Energy. (p. 1778)
de Polonia, Nina, illus. see Pierce, Kelly.
de Posada, Isabel Corpas. Planeacion Estrategica para Parejas. (p. 1367)
de Posada, Joachim & Singer, Ellen. Don't Eat the Marshmallow... Yet! The Secret to Sweet Success in Work & Life. (p. 467)
—Don't Gobble the Marshmallow Ever! (p. 467)
De Posadas Mane, Carmen. Senor Viento Norte. (p. 1550)
De Pree, Julia K. Body Story. (p. 207)
de Pretto, Lorenzo, illus. see Crippa, Luca, et al.
De Quevedo, Francisco, see Quevedo, Francisco de.
De Regniers, Beatrice Schenk. Little Sister & the Month Brothers Tomes, Margot, illus. (p. 1036)
—What Did You Put in Your Pocket? (p. 1882)
de Rham, Mickey. Hey Bossie, You're a Spokescow! Gusterson, Leigh, illus. (p. 774)
De Roma, Giuseppino. Francis of Assisi. (p. 628)
De Roo, Peter. History of America Before Columbus, According to Documents & Approved Authors. (p. 783)
de Saint-Exupéry, Antoine. Day with the Little Prince. (p. 415)
—Friends of the Little Prince. (p. 638)
—Le Petit Prince: Avec les dessins de l'auteur. (p. 981)
—Little Prince. (p. 1033)
—Little Prince. Howard, Richard, tr. (p. 1033)
—Little Prince. Howard, Richard, tr. from FRE. (p. 1033)
—Petit Prince. (p. 1348)
—Petit Prince Graphic Novel. Sfar, Joann, illus. (p. 1348)
—Piccolo Principe. (p. 1354)
—Principito. (p. 1406)
De Salvia, Maria Siponta. Michelangelo. (p. 1135)
de Salvia, Maria Siponta. Paul Gauguin. (p. 1330)
De San Martin, Juan Zorrilla. Tabare. (p. 1694)
De Saulles, Tony, illus. see Arnold, Nick.
De Saulles, Tony, jt. auth. see Arnold, Nick.
De Saulles, Tony, tr. see Arnold, Nick, et al.
De Saulnier, Gia Volterra. Journey to Jazzland. Zieroth, Emily, illus. (p. 928)
De Sede, Gerard & de Sede, Sophie. Accursed Treasure of Rennes-le-Chateau. Kersey, W.T. & Kersey, R.W., trs. from FRE. (p. 8)
de Sede, Sophie, jt. auth. see De Sede, Gerard.
De Segur, Comtesse & Willard, J. H. Story of a Donkey. (p. 1657)
De Segur, Condesa. Memorias de un Asno. (p. 1126)
de Sena, Carla Cristina R. G., et al, eds. Children Map the World: Selections from the Barbara Petchenik Children's World Map Competitions. (p. 302)
De Sena, Joseph. Butterfly & the Bunny's Tail. Anfuso, Dennis, illus. (p. 247)
—Little Sammy Sunshine & the Frightful Forest. (p. 1036)
—Love Bug & the Light of Love. (p. 1059)
—Mrs. Mouse & the Golden Flower. (p. 1187)
De Serres, Michelle. Gecko Ball. (p. 659)
de Seve, Karen & Castaldo, Nancy F. National Geographic Kids Mission: Polar Bear Rescue: All about Polar Bears & How to Save Them. (p. 1232)
de Sève, Peter, illus. see de Sève, Randall.
de Sève, Peter, illus. see Gleeson, Brian.
de Sève, Peter, illus. see Jinks, Catherine.
de Sève, Randall. Duchess of Whimsy. de Sève, Peter, illus. (p. 487)
—Mathilda & the Orange Balloon. Corace, Jen, illus. (p. 1108)
de Seve, Randall. Peanut & Fifi Have a Ball. Schmid, Paul, illus. (p. 1332)
—Toy Boat. Long, Loren, illus. (p. 1774)
de Sève, Randall. Toy Boat. Long, Loren, illus. (p. 1774)
de Sève, Randall, et al. Mi Barco/Toy Boat. Long, Loren, illus. (p. 1132)
de Silva, Eugenie. Adventures of Princess Eugenie. (p. 22)
De Silva, Matheu. Accidental Snake Thief. (p. 8)
De Silva, Nisansa, jt. auth. see Dicker, Katie.
De Silva-Nijkamp, Tineke. Samaya: The Deaf Baby Elephant. Maters, Ingrid, illus. (p. 1507)
De Smet, Catherine. Corbusier: Architect of Books (p. 366)
De Smet, Marian. Anna's Tight Squeeze. Meijer, Marja, illus. (p. 85)
De Smet, Marian & Meijer, Marja. Encerrada: Anna's Tight Squeeze. Pacheco, Laura Emilia, tr. (p. 523)
De, Soham, illus. see Robinson, Lorna.
de Sosa, Linda. I'm Not Crazy: A Workbook for Teens with Depression & Bipolar Disorder. (p. 859)
De Soto, Ben, illus. see Chachas, George & Wojtak, James.
de Souza, Michael, jt. auth. see Webster, Genevieve.
de Souza, Philip & Langley, Andrew. History News: the Roman News. (p. 783)
De Spiegeleer, Chantal, illus. see Van Hamme, Jean.
De Sterck, Goedele, tr. see Heide, Iris van der.
De Sterck, Goedele, tr. see Van Haeringen, Annemarie.
De Sturtz, Mari. God Gave Me. (p. 688)
—God Is. (p. 689)
—Living for Jesus. (p. 1041)
de Sturtz, Maria Ester. Desde Belén (From Bethlehem) (p. 428)
de Sturtz, Maria Ester H. Milagros en la Biblia. Fernandez, Lucia, illus. (p. 1142)
de Sturtz, Maria Ester H. & de Perez, Ursula S. Manos a la Obra: La Iglesia Celebra, Bilingual Level 1. (p. 1088)
de Sturtz, Marie Ester H. Por Las Aguas De la Biblia (God & Water in the Bible) (p. 1385)
—Por Las Aguas De La Biblia (God & Water in the Bible) - Bilingual. (p. 1385)
—Reyes y Profetas (Kings & Prophets) (p. 1467)
—Reyes y profetas (Kings & Prophets) - Bilingual. (p. 1467)
De Tagyos, Paul Rátz, illus. see Rostoker-Gruber, Karen.
De Tagyos, Paul Ratz, illus. see Speck, Katie.
De Tagyos, Paul Ratz, illus. see Wright, Maureen.
De Tagyos, Paul Rátz, jt. auth. see Speck, Katie.
de, Toledo Salvador, jt. auth. see Toledo, Salvador de.
de Trevino, Elizabeth Borton. I, Juan de Pareja. (p. 839)
—I, Juan de Pareja. (p. 840)
—Nacar, the White Deer: A Story of Old Mexico. (p. 1227)
De Ulloa, Leanor Alvarez, see Ulloa, Justo.
de Unamuno, Miguel, see Unamuno, Miguel de.
De Uribe, Maria L. Senorita Amelia (Miss Amelia) (p. 1550)
De Valdenebro, Eladio. Tono y el Bosque. (p. 1765)
—Tono y los Animales Cautivos. (p. 1765)
De Valera, Sinead. Magic Gifts: Classic Irish Fairytales. (p. 1072)
De Valor, Diana. Great Adventures of Sea Worthy with the I Can Crew: The Treasure of Captain Blue Beard. (p. 713)
de Vega, Lope, see Vega, Lope de.
De Velasco, Miguel Martin Fernandez. Pabluras y Gris. (p. 1317)
De Velasco, Miguel Martin Fernandez & Martin Fernández deelasco, Miguel, V. Pabluras. (p. 1317)
De Vere, Felice. Sexual Strategy. (p. 1556)
De Vicq de Cumptich, Roberto. Counting Insects. (p. 371)
de Vigan, Delphine. No & Me. Miller, George, tr. from FRE. (p. 1257)
De Villiers Family Staff. Purple Spot Sickness. De Villiers Family Staff, illus. (p. 1419)
De Villiers, Les. Africa 2004. (p. 26)
de Villiers, Les. Africa 2004. (p. 26)
—Africa 2005 (p. 26)
De Villiers, Les, text. Africa 2005 (p. 26)
De Vine, Ginger. Cameron the Charming Chimpanzee. (p. 256)
de Vos, Gail. Storytelling for Young Adults: A Guide to Tales for Teens (p. 1664)
De Vos, Philip. Carnival of the Animals. Grobler, Piet, illus. (p. 270)
de Vosjoli, Philippe. Land Hermit Crabs. (p. 973)
de Vries, Anke. Raf. Dematons, Charlotte, illus. (p. 1433)
De Vries, Anne. New Children's Bible. Apps, Fred, illus. (p. 1244)
De Vries, Bruce, illus. see Hasselbring, Janet.
de Vries, Maggie. Big City Bees Benoit, Renné, illus. (p. 180)
—Fraser Bear: A Cub's Life. Benoit, Renné, illus. (p. 631)
De Vries, Maggie. Somebody's Girl (p. 1609)
de Vries, Maggie. Tale of a Great White Fish: A Sturgeon Story. Benoit, Renné, illus. (p. 1699)
de Vries, Marloes, illus. see Eissler, Trevor.
De Waard, E. John, jt. auth. see De Waard, Nancy.
De Waard, Nancy & De Waard, E. John. Science Challenge Level 2: 190 Fun & Creative Brainteasers for Kids (p. 1525)
De Walschburger, Ute B. Leyendas de Nuestra America. (p. 1004)
De Weerd, Kelsey, illus. see Cook, Julia.
de Winter, James. Amazing Tricks of Real Spies (p. 56)
De Winter, James. Amazing Tricks of Real Spies. (p. 56)
—Discovering Lost Cities & Pirate Gold. (p. 449)
de Winter, James. How to Catapult a Castle: Machines That Brought down the Battlements (p. 815)
de Winter, James, jt. auth. see De Winter, James.
de Winter, James & Czeskleba, Abby. Secrets of Sport: The Technology That Makes Champions (p. 1545)
De Winter, James & de Winter, James. Amazing Tricks of Real Spies (p. 56)
—Discovering Lost Cities & Pirate Gold (p. 449)
De Witt, Peter. Toaster Pond. (p. 1760)
De Young, Sandy. Kasey's Poodle Skirt. (p. 944)
De Zayas, Alfred-Maurice. Terrible Revenge: The Ethnic Cleansing of the East European Germans. (p. 1721)
Deach, Carol, illus. see Britain, Lory.
Deacon, Alexis. Cheese Belongs to You! Schwarz, Viviane, illus. (p. 296)
—I Am Henry Finch. Schwarz, Viviane, illus. (p. 833)
—Place to Call Home. Schwarz, Viviane, illus. (p. 1365)
Deacon, Alexis, illus. see Hoban, Russell.
Deacon, Carol. Manualidades Divertidas. (p. 1089)
Deacon, Melissa. Chicken Pox? (p. 300)
—I Have a Monkey in My Tub! (p. 839)
Deady, Kathleen W. Ancient Egypt: Beyond the Pyramids (p. 68)
—Colorado. (p. 343)
—Costa Rica. (p. 368)
—Iceland. (p. 851)
—Massachusetts Bay Colony. (p. 1102)
—Mississippi. (p. 1154)
—New Hampshire Colony. (p. 1245)
—Ohio. (p. 1281)
—Rhode Island Colony. (p. 1468)
—Rwanda. (p. 1499)
—Salvador: A Question & Answer Book (p. 1506)
—Utah. (p. 1829)
Deady, Kathleen W., jt. auth. see Dubois, Muriel L.
Deady, Kathleen W. & Dubois, Muriel L. Ancient China: Beyond the Great Wall. (p. 68)
Deagan, Rachel. Prophecy. (p. 1411)
Deák, Erzsi. Pumpkin Time! Cushman, Doug, illus. (p. 1416)
Deak, Gloria. Kissing Skunks. Nathan, Cheryl, illus. (p. 962)
Deak, JoAnn. Your Fantastic, Elastic Brain: Stretch It, Shape It. O'Malley, Judy, ed. (p. 1980)
Deak, JoAnn & Deak, Terrence. Owner's Manual for Driving Your Adolescent Brain. Harrison, Freya, illus. (p. 1315)
Deak, Mike. Magical Land of Kallamazoo. (p. 1074)
Deak, Terrence, jt. auth. see Deak, JoAnn.
Deal, Darlene. Play with Your Food & Learn How to Eat Right: Nutritional Book about Fruits & Vegetables. (p. 1372)
Deal, David, photos by see Henry, Debra.
Deal, James Robert. What to Serve A Goddess When She Comes for Dinner: A Theology of Food. (p. 1894)
Deal, L. Kate. Boxcar Children. (p. 216)
Deal, Linda. Boredom Solution: Understanding & Dealing with Boredom. (p. 214)
Deal, Paul. Lighting Candles. (p. 1015)
Deal, Sarah E. Spotless Ladybug. (p. 1633)
Dealey, Erin. Deck the Walls: A Wacky Christmas Carol. Ward, Nick, illus. (p. 421)
—Goldie Locks Has Chicken Pox. (p. 695)
—Goldie Locks Has Chicken Pox. Wakiyama, Hanako, illus. (p. 695)
—Little Bo Peep Can't Get to Sleep. Wakiyama, Hanako, illus. (p. 1025)
Dealia, Yancey. Cardinal Nest: Where the Life Cycle Begins. Ted, Hood, Jr., photos by. (p. 266)
Deal-Trainor, Carol. Marilee: A Manatee's First Journey to the Springs. (p. 1094)
Deamer, Gaye. Clay Aiken: Everything You've Ever Wanted to Know about the New Singing Sensation. (p. 330)
DeAmicis, Bonita. Multiple Intelligences Made Easy: Strategies for Your Curriculum. (p. 1190)
Dean, Arlan. Crossing the Delaware: George Washington & the Battle of Trenton. (p. 385)
—Mathematical Thinking Ideas Procedures. (p. 1107)
—Mormon Pioneer Trail: From Nauvoo, Illinois to the Great Salt Lake, Utah. (p. 1175)
—Old Spanish Trail: From Santa Fe, New Mexico to Los Angeles, California. (p. 1284)
—Oregon Trail: From Independence, Missouri to Oregon City, Oregon. (p. 1303)
—Overland Trail: From Atchison, Kansas to Ft. Bridger, Wyoming. (p. 1314)
—Overland Trail: From Atchison, Kansas, to Fort Bridger, Wyoming. (p. 1314)
—Santa Fe Trail: From Independence, Missouri to Santa Fe, New Mexico. (p. 1511)
—Wilderness Road: From the Shenandoah Valley to the Ohio River. (p. 1931)
—Wilderness Trail: From the Shenandoah Valley to the Ohio River. (p. 1931)
—With All My Might: Cochise & the Indian Wars. (p. 1942)
Dean, Barbara. Rattalia's Birthday Stories. (p. 1440)
Dean, Carla, ed. see Rell, G.
Dean, Carol. Hen House: A True Story of Growing up on a Maine Farm. Dunn, Sandy, illus. (p. 767)
Dean, Carolee. Comfort. (p. 348)
—Forget Me Not. (p. 619)
—Take Me There. (p. 1696)
Dean, Cynthia A. Michelle Wie: She's Got the Power! (p. 1135)
—Rock Climbing: Making It to the Top. (p. 1482)
Dean, David, illus. see Crane, Nick.
Dean, David, illus. see McElwain, Sarah & O'Neal, John H.
Dean, David, illus. see Moverley, Richard.

Dean, David, illus. see St John, Lauren & St. John, Lauren.
Dean, Debbie. Time with God. (p. 1753)
Dean, Denise. Under Tommy's Bed: A Tommy Maloney Book. (p. 1814)
Dean, James. Cavecat Pete. (p. 282)
—Cavecat Pete. Dean, James, illus. (p. 282)
—Construction Destruction. (p. 359)
—Construction Destruction. Dean, James, illus. (p. 359)
—Five Little Pumpkins. Dean, James, illus. (p. 600)
—I Love My White Shoes. (p. 842)
—Old MacDonald Had a Farm. Dean, James, illus. (p. 1284)
—Pete at the Beach. (p. 1346)
—Pete at the Beach. Dean, James, illus. (p. 1346)
—Pete the Cat & the Bad Banana. Dean, James, illus. (p. 1346)
—Pete the Cat - Rock On, Mom & Dad! Dean, James, illus. (p. 1346)
—Pete the Cat's Big Doodle & Draw Book. Dean, James, illus. (p. 1346)
—Pete the Cat's Super Cool Reading Collection. Dean, James, illus. (p. 1346)
—Pete the Cat's Train Trip. (p. 1346)
—Pete the Cat's Train Trip. Dean, James, illus. (p. 1346)
—Pete's Big Lunch. (p. 1348)
—Pete's Big Lunch. Dean, James, illus. (p. 1348)
—Play Ball! (p. 1371)
—Play Ball! Dean, James, illus. (p. 1371)
—Rock on, Mom & Dad! Dean, James, illus. (p. 1482)
—Sing-Along Story Collection. Dean, James, illus. (p. 1579)
—Too Cool for School. (p. 1766)
—Twinkle, Twinkle, Little Star. (p. 1802)
—Twinkle, Twinkle, Little Star. Dean, James, illus. (p. 1802)
—Valentine's Day Is Cool. (p. 1830)
—Wheels on the Bus. Dean, James, illus. (p. 1901)
Dean, James, illus. see Holub, Joan.
Dean, James, illus. see Litwin, Eric.
Dean, James, jt. auth. see Dean, Kim.
Dean, James, jt. auth. see Litwin, Eric.
Dean, James & Dean, Kimberly. Big Easter Adventure. Dean, James & Dean, Kimberly, illus. (p. 181)
—First Thanksgiving. Dean, James, illus. (p. 597)
—Pet for Pete. Dean, James, illus. (p. 1345)
—Pete the Cat & His Magic Sunglasses. Dean, James, illus. (p. 1346)
—Pete the Cat & the Bedtime Blues. Dean, James, illus. (p. 1346)
—Pete the Cat & the New Guy. Dean, James, illus. (p. 1346)
—Pete the Cat's Groovy Guide to Life. Dean, James, illus. (p. 1346)
—Too Cool for School. Dean, James & Dean, Kimberly, illus. (p. 1766)
Dean, Jan & Stevens, Roger. Penguin in Lost Property. (p. 1337)
Dean, Janice. Freddy the Frogcaster. (p. 633)
—Freddy the Frogcaster & the Big Blizzard. (p. 633)
—Freddy the Frogcaster & the Huge Hurricane. (p. 633)
Dean, Jennings, jt. auth. see Vazquez, Ana Maria.
Dean, Jessica Casey, jt. auth. see Mott, A. S.
Dean, Karen. Kitty Kate's Tea Party. Dean, Karen, illus. (p. 963)
Dean, Kim & Dean, James. Big Easter Adventure. (p. 181)
Dean, Kimberly. Going Deep. (p. 692)
—High School Reunion. (p. 778)
Dean, Kimberly, jt. auth. see Dean, James.
Dean Kleven Studios, illus. see Joyce, Bridget & Furman, Eric.
Dean, Lani. One Misty Morning. Cassidy, Al, illus. (p. 1296)
Dean, Linda Greene. Wally Rooster's Big Move: A Blackberry Lane Book. (p. 1855)
—Wally Rooster's Calling You! A Blackberry Lane Book. (p. 1855)
Dean, Marshall, jt. auth. see Marbury, Stephon.
Dean, Myers Walter. Bad Boy: A Memoir. (p. 131)
—Fast Sam, Cool Clyde, & Stuff. (p. 576)
—Monster. (p. 1166)
—Scorpions. (p. 1530)
Dean, Nancy. Discovering Voice: Lessons to Teach Reading & Writing of Complex Text. (p. 450)
Dean, Natalia. Dream. (p. 483)
Dean, Nicholas. Snow Squall: The Last American Clipper Ship (p. 1599)
Dean, Pamela. Hidden Land. (p. 776)
—Secret Country. (p. 1540)
—Whim of the Dragon. (p. 1911)
Dean, Patricia. When America Was Young. (p. 1901)
Dean, Patricia Gayle. Tig Is Not Sad. (p. 1748)
—Will Dolli, the Un-Fish, Get Her Wish? (p. 1932)
—Wind: God Is Like That. (p. 1935)
Dean, Ramsey. Riding on a Beam of Light: Albert Einstein. Hamdan, Noah, illus. (p. 1471)
Dean, Richard B. Bear & the Ox. (p. 150)
Dean, Ruth, jt. auth. see Thomson, Melissa.
Dean, Sara. Puppy Who Found a Boy Hacker, Randy, illus. (p. 1418)
Dean, Sheila Anne. Read on Target Parent. (p. 1443)
Dean, Sheri. Flag Day. (p. 601)
—Flag Day (Día de la Bandera) (p. 602)
—Flag Day (Día de la Bandera) (p. 602)
—Fourth of July. (p. 625)
—Fourth of July (Cuatro de Julio) (p. 625)
—Martin Luther King, Jr. Day. (p. 1098)
—Memorial Day. (p. 1125)
—Memorial Day (Día de Los Caídos) (p. 1126)
—Presidents' Day. (p. 1397)
—Presidents Day/día de los Presidentes. (p. 1397)
—Thanksgiving. (p. 1725)
—Thanksgiving/Día de Acción de Gracias. (p. 1726)
Dean, Tina, ed. see Wood, Francis Eugene.
Dean Van Scoyoc, Andrea. Graveyard katie & her Pals. (p. 712)
Dean, Venetia, illus. see Claybourne, Anna.
Dean, Venitia, illus. see Graves, Robert.
Dean, Venitia, illus. see Rowell, Rebecca.
Dean Wafstet, Cindi. Wings of Light. (p. 1936)
Dean, Walter. How Leo the Lion Learned to Roar. (p. 810)
—How Leo the Lion Learned to Roar Student/ Teacher Workbook. (p. 810)
Dean, Zoey. Blonde Ambition. (p. 200)
—Tall Cool One. (p. 1704)
DeAnda, Diane. Monster in the Mattress & Other Stories: El Monstruo en el Colchón y Otros Cuentos. (p. 1167)
Deane, Charles, ed. see Bradford, William.
Deane, Elvis. Pistachio the Tyrant. (p. 1364)
Deane, Nancy Lou. Meg's Secret. (p. 1124)
Deane-Pratt, Ade. Electrical Gadgets. (p. 509)
—Musical Instruments. (p. 1194)
—Sensors. (p. 1551)
—Simple Machines. (p. 1577)
DeAngelis, Gina. Greece (p. 720)
—Mexico (p. 1131)
—Virginia. (p. 1844)
DeAngelis, Jason, ed. see Yamazaki, Kore.
DeAngelis, Therese. Women's Rights on the Frontier. (p. 1947)
—Women's Rights on the Frontier. Harrington, A. Page, ed. (p. 1947)
DeAngelis, Therese, jt. auth. see De Angelis, Therese.
DeAngelis, Therese, jt. auth. see Roppelt, Donna J.
DeAngelo, Frank T. Greetings from the President: A Memoir of WWII. (p. 723)
DeAngelo, Jeremy. Out Crowd. (p. 1310)
DeAnguelo Hout, Sarah, illus. see Anderson, Steven.
Deans, Karen. Playing to Win: The Story of Althea Gibson. Brown, Elbrite, illus. (p. 1372)
—Swing Sisters: The Story of the International Sweethearts of Rhythm. Cepeda, Joe, illus. (p. 1691)
Deans, Nora L., ed. see Tinsley, P. S.
Deans, Sis Boulos. Racing the Past. (p. 1432)
Deanthony, Dylan. Show a Soldier You Care! Understand the Relationship Between Multiplication & Division (p. 1570)
Dearborn, Dorothy, jt. auth. see Watts, Ana Dearborn.
Dearborn, Sabrina. Barefoot Book of Blessings: From Many Faiths & Cultures. Whelan, Olwyn, illus. (p. 139)
Dearborne, Hilary. Heavy & Light: Describe & Compare Measurable Attributes. (p. 761)
Dearborn-Watts/Dearborn, Ana/Dorothy. Pouliche Princesse Louise. (p. 1389)
Dearen, Patrick. When the Sky Rained Dust. (p. 1905)
Dearing, Kate & Lyon, Abby. Tulane University College Prowler off the Record. (p. 1796)
Dearing, Ruth. Tommy & the Hiccups. (p. 1764)
Dearle, Anne Crofton. Ginger Cat. (p. 677)
Dearling, Robert. Encyclopedia of Musical Instruments (p. 525)
Dearmer, Mabel. Child's Life of Christ. (p. 305)
Dearth, Carol. Cooking Class: A Chef's Step-by-Step Guide to Stress-Free Dinner Parties That Are Simply Elegant! (p. 361)
DeArville, J. It's Kambri Time! (p. 897)
Deary, T. Twist of the Knife. (p. 1802)
Deary, Terry. Blood-Curdling Box Brown, Martin, illus. (p. 200)
—Boy Who Cried Horse Flook, Helen, illus. (p. 219)
—Esa Deplorable Segunda Guerra Mundial. (p. 534)
—Esa Espantosa Primera Guerra Mundial. (p. 534)
—Esos Asombosos Egipcios. (p. 536)
—Esos Degolladores Celtas. (p. 536)
—Esos Fabulosos EE.UU. (p. 536)
—Esos Increibles Incas. (p. 536)
—Esos Indomitos Irlandeses. (p. 536)
—Esos Ruidos Revolucionarios. (p. 536)
—Esos Siniestros Castillos y Sus Nobles Caballeros. (p. 536)
—Esos Supergeniales Griegos. (p. 536)
—Fire Thief. (p. 591)
—Historical Tales Flook, Helen, illus. (p. 783)
—Walking Shadows. (p. 1854)
—War Game. (p. 1857)
Deas, Jason. Camp Timber View. (p. 257)
Deas, Mike. Dalen & Gole: Scandal in Port Angus (p. 401)
Deas, Mike, illus. see Helmer, Marilyn.
Deas, Mike, illus. see McClintock, Norah.
Deas, Mike, illus. see O'Donnell, Liam.
Deas, Rich, illus. see Johnston, Tony.
Deas, Richard F., illus. see Johnston, Tony.
Deas, Robert, illus. see Shakespeare, William.
Deas, Stephen. Thief-Taker's Apprentice: With a Sword, Comes Blood... (p. 1732)
—Warlock's Shadow. (p. 1858)
Deasey, Kevin, illus. see Porrata, Mayra.
Deasy, H. H. P. In Tibet & Chinese Turkestan: Being the Record of Three Years' Exploration. (p. 868)
Deats, Adam, jt. auth. see BradyGames Staff.
Deaver, Julie, jt. auth. see Deaver, Julie Reece.
Deaver, Julie Reece. Night I Disappeared. (p. 1253)
Deaver, Julie Reece & Deaver, Julie. Say Goodnight, Gracie. (p. 1518)
Deaville, Dawnie Reynolds. A-Z of Being a Girl of God. (p. 2)
Deb, Capone. Dumplings are Delicious Learning & Activity Guide. Stan, Jaskiel, illus. (p. 490)
Debacque, Pascal. Create Your Own Mandalas — Fantasy. (p. 378)
—Create Your Own Mandalas — Nature. (p. 378)
Debaer-Levoy, Carole. Story of Candyland. (p. 1657)
Debbie, Gibler. Roxy's Big Adventure. (p. 1492)
Debbie Lamb & Michelle Villa. Luis Discovers the Lab N Earth. (p. 1064)
DeBear, Kirsten. Toby & Tutter Therapy Dogs. Dwight, Laura, photos by. (p. 1760)
Debecker, Benoit & Benoît, Debecker. Primera Navidad de los Animales. (p. 1400)
Debeer, Kristen. I Believe in You: A Mother's Message to Her Son with Learning Differences. Santy, Elizabeth & Fisher, Jessie, illus. (p. 834)
DeBellis, Aaron. Bee's C's (p. 158)
DeBellis, Thea. Miss Anne & Her Doll Collection. (p. 1151)
Debenham, A., jt. auth. see Middlewood, G.
DeBerry, Virginia & Grant, Donna. Better Than I Know Myself. (p. 172)
Debesay, Samson. Cubby, the Lionsheep: Son, you are a lion, live like One! (p. 388)
Debi Rogers, illus. see Summer Rogers Martin.
DeBlasio, Allison, jt. auth. see Marsocci, Joey.
Deblinger, Esther, jt. auth. see Stauffer, Lori.
Debnam, Mio. Animalympics, 5 BK Set. (p. 84)
Debney, John, jt. auth. see Scelsa, Greg.
DeBoard, Will. Building a Stock Car. (p. 238)
DeBoer, Jesslyn. First Easter Clar, David Austin, illus. (p. 594)
DeBold, Carol, jt. auth. see Kaplan, Andrew.
Debon, Nicolas. Four Pictures by Emily Carr (p. 625)
—Strongest Man in the World (p. 1668)
Debon, Nicolas, illus. see Carter, Anne Laurel.
Debon, Nicolas, illus. see DeMers, Dominique & Demers, Dominique.
Debon, Nicolas, illus. see Fagan, Cary.
Debon, Nicolas, illus. see McPherson, Stephanie Sammartino.
Debon, Nicolas, illus. see Pendziwol, Jean E.
Debon, Nicolas, illus. see Pilegard, Virginia Walton.
Debon, Nicolas, illus. see Scandiffio, Laura.
Debon, Nicolas, illus. see Sydor, Colleen.
Debon, Nicolas, illus. see Zemlicka, Shannon.
DeBonis, Todd DeBonis. SwordMaster of Ashland -Book One- (p. 1692)
Debono, Angelo. Magic in You. (p. 1072)
Deboo, Ana. Clownfish & Other Saltwater Aquarium Fish. (p. 335)
Deborah, Allwright, illus. see Victoria, Roberts.
Deborah, Brown Armes, illus. see Brown, Paul Henry.
Deborah, Ellis. Breadwinner. (p. 224)
Deborah Strandberg, Rebecca Reynolds and. Trammler Triplet Tales #2 - HIDDEN in TIME. (p. 1778)
—Trammler Triplet Tales Advente #4 MYSTERIOUS ABBY. (p. 1778)
—Trammler Triplet Tales-Adventure #3 SEEKING the SOURCE. (p. 1778)
Deborah Sue. All Things Remembered. (p. 46)
Deborah Wanda. Wanda's Wittle Wunders. (p. 1856)
Deborah, Wiles. Freedom Summer. (p. 635)
Debose, Alison. Lenny & Di in the Frog & the Fly. (p. 991)
Debowski, Sharon. Grape Escape: Call 9-1-1, the Grapes Are on the Run! Fonseca-Hughes, Sarah, illus. (p. 710)
Debowski, Sharon. Snowman, the Owl, & the Groundhog. (p. 1601)
Debra Maymon. Debra Meets Her Best Friend in Kindergarten. Richa Kinra, illus. (p. 421)
Debram, Mio. Kidsgo Hong Kong: Tell Your Parents. Willis, Tania, illus. (p. 955)
—Kidsgo London: Tell Your Parents. Willis, Tania, illus. (p. 955)
DeBray, Sherry. Teacher's Gift. Cauthen, Tommy, illus. (p. 1709)
DeBrecht, Katharine. Help! Mom! There Are Liberals under My Bed! Hummel, Jim, illus. (p. 765)
Debrock, Guy. Process Pragmatism: Essays on a Quiet Philosophical Revolution. (p. 1408)
DeBroech, Sarah, illus. see Reyes, Cameron.
DeBroech, Sarah, illus. see Van Tassel, Mary A.
DeBroeck, Sarah, illus. see Atwater, Jillene.
DeBroeck, Sarah, illus. see Bailey, Leslie J.
DeBroeck, Sarah, illus. see Cardoso, Kelly.
DeBroeck, Sarah, illus. see Collins, Chris.
DeBroeck, Sarah, illus. see Lynch, Lauren Boehm.
DeBroeck, Sarah, illus. see Saupé, Rick.
DeBruyn, Ardyth. Chosen Sister. (p. 311)
Debruzzi, Jeremy. Minnesota Fish Tail. (p. 1147)
Decaen, Rose, ed. see Gibson, Cay.
Decaire, Camela, illus. see Anton, Carrie, ed.
Decaire, Camela, jt. ed. see Magruder, Trula.
Decaire, Carmale, ed. Girls & Their Horses. Clar, David, illus. (p. 679)
DeCandido, Keith R. A., et al. Alien Spotlight (p. 41)
DeCapua, Sarah. Malawi in Pictures. (p. 1083)
—Sandra Day O'Connor. (p. 1511)
—Wilderness Road (p. 1931)
DeCapua, Sarah, jt. auth. see Lindop, Edmund.
DeCarlo, Dan. Archie - The Best of Dan Decarlo (p. 95)
DeCarlo, Jacqueline. Fair Trade & How It Works. (p. 562)
DeCarlo, Mike, illus. see Wrecks, Billy.
DeCarlo, Mike, et al. Captain Boomerang's Comeback! (p. 263)
—Master of Mirrors! (p. 1103)
—Shell Shocker Doescher, Erik, illus. (p. 1564)
DeCarmelo, Marie. Little Christmas Story. (p. 1026)
DeCarolis, Lisa. Alexander Hamilton: Federalist & Founding Father. (p. 36)
deCarufel, Laura. Learn to Speak Fashion: A Guide to Creating, Showcasing, & Promoting Your Style. Kulak, Jeff & Owlkids Books Inc. Staff, illus. (p. 984)
Decary, Marie. Adam et le Raton Dessinateur. Beshwathy, Steve, illus. (p. 11)
—Adam's Tropical Adventure. Beshwaty, Steve, illus. (p. 11)
Décary, Marie. Adam's Tropical Adventure. Cummins, Sarah, tr. from FRE. (p. 11)
Decary, Marie. Combats des Chocolats. Brignaud, Pierre, illus. (p. 346)
—Rose Neon Series. Brignaud, Pierre, illus. (p. 1489)
Decedue, Julie, illus. see Clark, Seneca & Giardi, Sandy.
Decenciere, Isabelle, illus. see Binder, Betsy.
DeCesare, Ruth. Songs for the German Class. (p. 1612)
Decis, Anne, illus. see Abril, Paco & Francisco, Abril Berán.
Decis, Anne, illus. see Canetti, Yanitzia & Yanitzia, Canetti.
Decis, Anne, illus. see Comelles, Salvador.
Decis, Anne, illus. see Mainé, Margarita.
Deck, Upper. Dinosaur King Blister. (p. 442)
—Dinosaur King Starter. (p. 442)
Decker, C. B., illus. see Levy, Janice.
Decker, C. B., illus. see Rostoker-Gruber, Karen & Isaacs, Ronald H.
Decker, Celia A., jt. auth. see Ryder, Verdene.
Decker, Celia Anita. Children the Early Years: Teaching Package Teacher's Resource Portfolio. (p. 303)
—Children the Early Years. (p. 303)
Decker, Cynthia, illus. see Punter, Russell.
Decker, Elizabeth. Mystery of Belle Jardin. (p. 1224)
Decker, Jacqueline, illus. see Bull, Webster.
Decker, Janet M., et al. Anthrax. (p. 89)
—Mononucleosis. (p. 1166)
Decker, Jeni. Far from Happy. (p. 572)
Decker, Lori. Princess Allie, the Littlest Hero. (p. 1402)
Decker, Peter R. Utes Must Go! American Expansion & the Removal of a People (p. 1829)
Decker, Rick S. Ricky's Adventures: Scrapbook Memories. (p. 1470)
Decker, Robert. Spanish Word Games: 56 Word Games & Puzzles for Building Vocabulary. (p. 1621)
Decker, Suzan Tyler. Johnny Green & the Little Green Man. (p. 923)
Decker, Tim. Punk Ethic. Decker, Tim, illus. (p. 1417)
Decker, Timothy. For Liberty: The Story of the Boston Massacre. (p. 615)
—Run Far, Run Fast. (p. 1496)
Decker, Wendy. Bedazzling Bowl. (p. 156)
Decker, William. Growing Flowers. (p. 726)
—Songs That Honor America. (p. 1612)
Decker-Ahmed, Stasia. Weirder the Better. (p. 1873)
Deckert, Tempany, jt. auth. see Bancks, Tristan.
Deckker, Zilah. Ancient Rome: Archaeology Unlocks the Secrets of Rome's Past. (p. 70)
—Brazil. (p. 224)
—Poland. (p. 1378)
Deckker, Zilah Quezado, jt. auth. see U. S. National Geographic Society Staff.
Declare Yourself Staff. Declare Yourself: Speak. Connect. Act. Vote. More Than 50 Celebrated Americans Tell You Why. (p. 422)
DeClements, Barthe. Fourth Grade Wizards. (p. 625)
—Nothing's Fair in Fifth Grade. (p. 1268)
Declements, Barthe, jt. auth. see DeClements, Barthe.
DeClements, Barthe & Declements, Barthe. Sixth Grade Can Really Kill You. (p. 1583)
Declercq, Al, et al. Bemida: A Michigan Sailing Legend. Miles, David, illus. (p. 167)
Declus, Jennifer. What Might I Find in a Geyser. Kalasea, illus. (p. 1892)
—What Might I Find in a Rainforest. Kalasea, illus. (p. 1892)
—What Might I Find in a Swamp. Kalasea, illus. (p. 1892)
—What Might I Find in a Tidepool. Kalasea, illus. (p. 1892)
—What Might I Find on a Pond. Kalasea, illus. (p. 1892)
Decola, Diane. Butterfly. (p. 247)
Deconnick, Kelly Sue. Captain Marvel - Down. (p. 264)
—In Pursuit of Flight Vol. 1 Rios, Emma, illus. (p. 864)
DeCoster, Miles. Uccello Rosso: Paintings by Miles Decoster. (p. 1807)
DeCristofano, Carolyn Cinami. Big Bang! The Tongue-Tickling Tale of a Speck That Became Spectacular. Carroll, Michael, illus. (p. 178)
—Black Hole Is Not a Hole. Carroll, Michael, illus. (p. 196)
—Sun & the Moon. Morley, Taia, illus. (p. 1676)
DeCristoforo, Jennifer. Lucky Bamboo Book of Crafts: Over 100 Projects & Ideas Celebrating Chinese Culture DeCristoforo, Jennifer, illus. (p. 1062)
Decter, Ed. Expedition to Pine Hollow. Yuen, Sammy, Jr. & Yuen Jr., Sammy, illus. (p. 548)
—VIP Lounge. (p. 1843)
Decter, Ed & Burns, Laura J. Hot Mess. (p. 802)
Dede, Vivian Hughes. Elizabeth's Christmas Story. Morris, Susan, illus. (p. 513)
Dedering, Victoria, illus. see Written By Susan J. Perry; Illustrated B.
DeDomenico, Elizabeth Marie. Saint John Vianney: A Priest for All People. Hatke, Ben, illus. (p. 1503)
Dedomenico, Elizabeth Marie. Saint Martin de Porres: Humble Healer. Alfano, Wayne, illus. (p. 1503)
DEE and AMA, The Toybox Grannies. Katie & Savannah - Special Edition. (p. 944)
Dee, Barbara. Just Another Day in My Insanely Real Life. (p. 937)
—Solving Zoe. (p. 1608)
—This Is Me from Now On. (p. 1736)
—Trauma Queen. (p. 1780)
Dee, Carole. Bully Returns to Margaret. (p. 241)
Dee, Carolyn. Tree Who Couldn't Choose. (p. 1784)
Dee, Debbie. Underground Witch. (p. 1815)
Dee, Gabrielle. Planting a Community Garden: Reason with Shapes & Their Attributes (p. 1369)
Dee, Janet. Practical Guide to Everyday Health & Well Being. (p. 1392)
Dee, Joan. Bertie. (p. 168)
Dee, Kati, illus. see Rogers-Busboom, Kimberly.
Dee, Katya. Orna Puella (p. 1304)
Dee, Nora. Making Circle Graphs. (p. 1080)
Dee, Stacy, jt. auth. see Prm, Katherine.
Deebs, Tracy. Doomed. (p. 470)
—Tempest Rising. (p. 1717)
—Tempest Unleashed. (p. 1717)
Deebs, Tracy, jt. auth. see Childs, Tera Lynn.
Deebs, Tracy & Adams, Ivy. Doomed. (p. 470)
Deedrick, Tami. Construction Workers Help (p. 360)
—Teachers Help (p. 1709)
Deedrick, Tami & Ready, Dee. Our Community Helpers (p. 1308)
Deeds, Christopher. Light & Color: What We See. (p. 1014)
Deedy, Carmen Agra. 14 Cows for America González, Thomas, illus. (p. 1995)
—14 Vacas para América González, Thomas, illus. (p. 1995)
—14 Vacas para América De la Torre, Cristina, tr. from ENG. (p. 1995)
—Colchón de Plumas para Ágata De la Torre, Cristina, tr. from ENG. (p. 338)
—Library Dragon White, Michael P., illus. (p. 1006)
—Martina the Beautiful Cockroach Austin, Michael, illus. (p. 1098)
—Martina the Beautiful Cockroach: A Cuban Folktale Austin, Michael, illus. (p. 1098)
—Martina the Beautiful Cockroach. (p. 1098)
—Martina una Cucarachita Muy Linda: Un Cuento Cubano Austin, Michael, illus. (p. 1098)
—Martina una Cucarachita Muy Linda: Un Cuento Cubano. De la Torre, Cristina, tr. (p. 1098)
—Return of the Library Dragon White, Michael P., illus. (p. 1464)

D

Deedy, Carmen Agra & Wright, Randall. Cheshire Cheese Cat: A Dickens of a Tale Moser, Barry, illus. (p. 298)
Deegan, J. E. When I Was a Little Guy. (p. 1903)
Deeks, Graham. Ratrigues & the Invisible Intelligence. (p. 1440)
Deekster, Deek. Ozzie Rozzie. (p. 1316)
Deeley, Patrick. Mo Mhadra Beoga. Fagan, Martin, illus. (p. 1157)
—Snobby Cat. Feeney, Tatyana, illus. (p. 1598)
Deem, James M. 3 NBs of Julian Drew. (p. 1991)
—Auschwitz: Voices from the Death Camp. (p. 116)
—Bodies from the Ash: Life & Death in Ancient Pompeii. (p. 206)
—Bodies from the Bog. (p. 206)
—Bodies from the Ice: Melting Glaciers & the Recovery of the Past. (p. 206)
—Faces from the Past: Forgotten People of North America. (p. 561)
—Kristallnacht: The Nazi Terror That Began the Holocaust. (p. 967)
—Millard Fillmore: A MyReportLinks.com Book. (p. 1143)
—Primary Source Accounts of the Mexican-American War. (p. 1399)
—Primary Source Accounts of the Revolutionary War. (p. 1399)
—Prisoners of Breendonk: Personal Histories from a World War II Concentration Camp. (p. 1407)
—Salvador: A MyReportLinks.com Book. (p. 1506)
—Vikings: A MyReportLinks. com Book. (p. 1842)
Deem, Saltofi Anne. Myrtle Teachable Moments Series (p. 1222)
Deen, David, illus. see Weiss, Bobbi & Weiss, David.
Deen, Janet. Princess of the Bride. (p. 1404)
Deen, Marilyn. Big, Bigger, Biggest (p. 178)
—Divided By (p. 454)
—Dollars & Cents (p. 463)
—Finding Patterns (p. 588)
—From 1 To 100 (p. 641)
—Measure by Measure (p. 1117)
—Odd & Even (p. 1278)
—Odd or Even. (p. 1278)
—Right Place (p. 1472)
—Share & Be Fair (p. 1561)
—Taking Shape (p. 1698)
—Tiling Shapes (p. 1750)
—Wonder Readers: Mathematics. (p. 1947)
Deen, Paula. Paula Deen's Cookbook for the Lunch-Box Set. Mitchell, Susan, illus. (p. 1330)
—Paula Deen's My First Cookbook. Mitchell, Susan, illus. (p. 1330)
Deen, Roderick. My Favorite Entrepreneurs. (p. 1203)
Deen, Ron. Annabelle Rides Her Bike on an Iowa Farm. (p. 85)
Deep-Jones, Liz. Lucy Zeezou's Glamour Game. (p. 1063)
—Lucy Zeezou's Goal. (p. 1063)
Deer, Ada E., Intro. Indians of North America. (p. 872)
Deere, John. Barney Backhoe's Big Idea. Running Press Staff, ed. (p. 139)
—Johnny Tractor & the Hide-and-Seek Cat. Running Press Staff, ed. (p. 923)
Deere, John, jt. auth. see Dorling Kindersley Publishing Staff.
Deere, John & Berg, Ron. Corey Combine & the Great Big Mess. Running Press Staff, ed. (p. 367)
Deere, John & Hill, Dave. Johnny Tractor Saves the Parade. Running Press Staff, ed. (p. 923)
Deering, Freemont B. Border Boys Across the Frontier. (p. 213)
Deering, Leta. Patriotic Samáand the Mendez Twins at the Alamo. (p. 1329)
Dees, Leighanne, illus. see Burgard, Anna Marlis.
Dees, Russell L., tr. see Zeruneith, Keld.
Deese, Teut, tr. see Burke, David.
Deesing, Jim, illus. see Hawkins, Colin.
Defabio, Richard Bryan. Magic Spoon. (p. 1073)
DeFalco, Julie, ed. see Guzaldo, Jessica.
Defalco, Tom. Spider-Man: The Ultimate Guide. (p. 1626)
—Spider-Man: The Complete Alien Costume Saga. Bk. 1 Leonardi, Rick et al, illus. (p. 1626)
—Thor: The Lost Gods. (p. 1739)
—Thor: Black Galaxy Saga. Frenz, Ron, illus. (p. 1739)
Defalco, Tom, jt. auth. see Stern, Roger.
Defalco, Tom & McDaniel, Scott. Green Goblin: A Lighter Shade of Green. Kobasic, Kevin et al, illus. (p. 722)
Defalco, Tom & Michelinie, David. Ghost Rider Death Race! (p. 671)
DeFalco, Tom, et al. Monsters (p. 1168)
Defalco, Tom, et al. Spider-Man: The World's Greatest Super Hero. (p. 1626)
—Spider-Man - Complete Ben Reilly Epic Bagley, Mark et al, illus. (p. 1626)
—Thor Epic Collection: War of the Pantheons. Frenz, Ron et al, illus. (p. 1739)
DeFatta Barattini, Kathryn. I Live in Shreveport-Bossier! by Louise E. Ana, Ladybug. (p. 841)
DeFazio, Deborah, illus. see Crick, Stephanie.
Defelice, Bonnie, illus. see Defelice, Jennie & Landry, Jennifer.
DeFelice, Bonnie, illus. see DeFelice, Jennie & Landry, Jennifer.
DeFelice, Cynthia. Fort. (p. 623)
—Ghost & Mrs. Hobbs. (p. 670)
—Ghost of Cutler Creek. (p. 671)
—Wild Life. (p. 1929)
Defelice, Cynthia & DeFelice, Cynthia C. Under the Same Sky. (p. 1814)
DeFelice, Cynthia C. Apprenticeship of Lucas Whitaker. (p. 93)
—Ghost of Cutler Creek. (p. 671)
—Ghost of Fossil Glen. (p. 671)
—Missing Manatee. (p. 1152)
—Nelly May Has Her Say. Cole, Henry, illus. (p. 1240)
—One Potato, Two Potato. U'Ren, Andrea, illus. (p. 1296)
—Signal. (p. 1574)
DeFelice, Cynthia C., jt. auth. see Defelice, Cynthia.
Defelice, Jennie & Landry, Jennifer. Adventures of Zsa Zsa & Gabby Lou a Country Harvest. (p. 24)
—Adventures of Zsa Zsa & Gabby Lou in New Orleans. Defelice, Bonnie, illus. (p. 24)
DeFelice, Jennie & Landry, Jennifer. Adventures of Zsa-Zsa & Gabby-Lou: Dangers at the Seashore. DeFelice, Bonnie, illus. (p. 24)
Defenbaugh, David, illus. see Lluch, Alex A.
Defenbaugh, David, illus. see Lluch, Alex.
Defense Department Staff, jt. ed. see U.S. Defense Dept.
DeFerle, Steph. After the Rain King. (p. 28)
Deferle, Steph. Ghost Rider: The Final Journey on the Underground Railroad. (p. 671)
Deffenbaugh, David & McFarland, Bill. Strength for the Journey: A daily devotional Guide. Waldroop, Wista, ed. (p. 1667)
Deffenbaugh, Dena, illus. see Reid, Demetra.
Defilippis, Nunzio, jt. auth. see Weir, Christina.
DeFilippis, Nunzio & Weir, Christina. Amazing Agent Luna Omnibus 1. Shiei, illus. (p. 52)
Defilippis, Nunzio & Weir, Christina. Avalon Chronicles Volume 1: Once in a Blue Moon. (p. 118)
—Avalon Chronicles Volume 2 HC. (p. 118)
—Play Ball. (p. 1371)
DeFilippis, Nunzio & Weir, Christina. Three Strikes. (p. 1744)
DeFilippis, Nunzio, et al. Skinwalker. (p. 1585)
DeFilippo, Lauren Frances. Dance with Me, Please. (p. 402)
DeFilippo, Steve. Growing up Nicely! Grammy Helps Adam Grow up & Develop Social Skills & Moral Values. (p. 727)
Deflitch, Jennifer L. Delia the Dragonfly's Grand Adventures: Delia Goes to Washington D. C. (p. 425)
—Where Do You Go? (p. 1907)
Defoe, Daniel. Aventuras de Robinson Crusoe. (p. 119)
—Journal of the Plague Year: Written by a Citizen Who Continued All the While in London. (p. 927)
—Journal of the Plague Year. (p. 927)
—Robinson Crusoe: The Complete Story of Robinson Crusoe. (p. 1480)
—Robinson Crusoe: With a Discussion of Resourcefulness. Landgraf, Kenneth, illus. (p. 1480)
—Robinson Crusoe. (p. 1480)
—Robinson Crusoe. Akib, Jamel, illus. (p. 1480)
—Robinson Crusoe. Cabrera, Eva, illus. (p. 1480)
—Robinson Crusoe. McKowen, Scott, illus. (p. 1480)
—Robinson Crusoe. Elphinstone, Katy, illus. (p. 1480)
—Robinson Crusoe Level 4. (p. 1480)
—Robinson Crusoe Level 4 Intermediate. (p. 1480)
—Storm. Hamblyn, Richard, ed. (p. 1655)
Defoe, Daniel & McVeagh, John. Defoe's Review, 1704-13 (p. 424)
Defoe, Daniel & Perry, John Jasiel. Atalantis Major. (p. 111)
Defoe, Daniel, et al. Robinson Crusoe: The Complete Story of Robinson Crusoe. (p. 1480)
DeFord, Deborah H. African Americans During the Civil War. Schwarz, Philip, ed. (p. 27)
—American Revolution. (p. 63)
—Civil War. (p. 325)
—Life under Slavery. Schwarz, Philip, ed. (p. 1013)
—Steam Engine. (p. 1646)
Deford, Debra & Craig, Janet. Nevada: The Silver State. (p. 1242)
DeFord, Diane. Chief Sitting Bull. (p. 301)
—Harriet Tubman. (p. 749)
—Sacagawea. (p. 1500)
Deford, Ted. Po & the Gang: In Two Big Adventures. (p. 1374)
Deforges, Regine. Bicyclette Bleue (p. 177)
Defosse, Rosana Curiel. Santiago & the Fox of Hatsune. Barradas, Leticia, illus. (p. 1513)
—Santiago en el Mundo de me de la Gana. Barradas, Leticia, illus. (p. 1513)
—Santiago en el Pantano. Barradas, Leticia, illus. (p. 1513)
—Santiago y el talisman de la Luz. Barradas, Leticia, illus. (p. 1513)
—Santiago y los Dobraks. Barradas, Leticia, illus. (p. 1513)
DeFrancesco, B. J. Rising above Global Warming. Myers, Shari, illus. (p. 1475)
DeFranco, Robert, jt. auth. see Lyga, Barry.
Defrange, Tom. Tinker Tale: Celebrating Differences. (p. 1756)
DeFreitas, Henrietta. Henratty Mortimer: The Meerville Myth. (p. 767)
—Henratty Mortimer: Chapter One - Oscar's Birthday. (p. 767)
—Henratty Mortimer: We Were Only Strawberry Picking. (p. 767)
—Henratty Mortimer Presents: Poppy the Most Beautiful Worm. (p. 767)
DeFries, Cheryl L. Bald Eagle: A MyReportLinks. com Book. (p. 133)
—Leif Eriksson: Viking Explorer of the New World. (p. 991)
—Seven Natural Wonders of the United States & Canada: A MyReportLinks. com Book. (p. 1554)
—What Are the 7 Natural Wonders of the United States? (p. 1879)
DeGaetano, Gloria. Parenting Well in a Media Age: Keeping Our Kids Human. (p. 1324)
DeGaetano, Steve. Welcome Aboard the Disneyland Railroad! The Complete Disneyland Railroad Reference Guide. Nirattisai, Preston, illus. (p. 1873)
DeGarmo, John & DeGarmo, Kelly. Different Home: A New Foster Child's Story. (p. 438)
DeGarmo, Kelly, jt. auth. see DeGarmo, John.
Degarmo, Serena. Penny Sue the Pure Hearted. De Marco, Arielle, illus. (p. 1338)
Degelman, Charles, et al. Active Citizenship Today Field Guide. (p. 10)
Degen, Bruce. Degen Picture Book. (p. 424)
—I Gotta Draw. Degen, Bruce, illus. (p. 838)
—I Said, Bed! Degen, Bruce, illus. (p. 845)
—Jamberry. (p. 906)
—Jamberry. Degen, Bruce, illus. (p. 906)
—Nate Likes to Skate. (p. 1230)
—Snow Joke. (p. 1599)
—Snow Joke. Degen, Bruce, illus. (p. 1599)
—Time of the Dinosaurs. (p. 1752)
Degen, Bruce, illus. see Beech, Linda Ward.
Degen, Bruce, illus. see Calmenson, Stephanie.
Degen, Bruce, illus. see Carlstrom, Nancy White.
Degen, Bruce, illus. see Coerr, Eleanor.
Degen, Bruce, illus. see Cole, Joanna & Jackson, Tom.
Degen, Bruce, illus. see Cole, Joanna & O'Brien, Cynthia.
Degen, Bruce, illus. see Cole, Joanna, et al.
Degen, Bruce, illus. see Cole, Joanna.
Degen, Bruce, illus. see Nixon, Joan Lowery.
Degen, Bruce, illus. see Simon, Jenne & Cole, Joanna.
Degenhardt, Scott. Surviving Death Anderson, ed. (p. 1687)
deGennaro, Sue, illus. see Wilson, Tony.
DeGeorge, Dennis A. 30 Days 'Til Proz@k. (p. 1996)
DeGezelle, Terri. City Council. (p. 323)
—City Mayor. (p. 323)
—Cómo Cuidar Mis Manos y Pies. Saunders-Smith, Gail, ed. (p. 350)
—Ellis Island. (p. 514)
—Exploring Fall (p. 552)
—Exploring Spring (p. 553)
—Exploring Summer (p. 553)
—Exploring the Seasons. (p. 554)
—Exploring Winter (p. 554)
—Franklin D. Roosevelt y la Gran Depresión (p. 630)
—Great Seal of the United States. (p. 718)
—Let's Play Baseball! (p. 1000)
—Pentagon. (p. 1338)
—Rosa Parks & the Civil Rights Movement (p. 1489)
—Rosa Parks y el Movimiento por los Derechos Civiles. (p. 1489)
—Serving on a Jury. (p. 1553)
—Street Sweepers (p. 1667)
—Susan B. Anthony y el Movimiento por los Derechos de la Mujer. (p. 1688)
—Taking Care of My Eyes (p. 1698)
—Taking Care of My Hair (p. 1698)
—Taking Care of My Hands & Feet (p. 1698)
—Taking Care of My Teeth (p. 1698)
—Thomas Jefferson Memorial. (p. 1739)
—U. S. Capitol. (p. 1806)
—Voting in Elections. (p. 1850)
—Your Bones. (p. 1980)
—Your Brain. (p. 1980)
—Your Heart. (p. 1980)
—¡Vamos a Jugar Al Béisbol! (Let's Play Baseball!) (p. 1831)
DeGezelle, Terri & Andrews, Melodie. Ellis Island. (p. 515)
DeGezelle, Terri & Capstone Press Staff. Cómo Cuidar Mi Piel. Saunders-Smith, Gail, ed. (p. 350)
—Cómo Cuidar Mis Ojos. Saunders-Smith, Gail, ed. (p. 350)
DeGezelle, Terri, et al. Deportes y Actividades. (p. 427)
—Mighty Machines. (p. 1140)
—Mighty Machines: Construction (6 book Set) [NASCO]. (p. 1140)
Deghand, Tim, illus. see Feyh, Janelle.
Degman, Lori. 1 Zany Zoo. Jack, Colin, illus. (p. 1991)
—Cock-A-Doodle-Oops! Zemke, Deborah, illus. (p. 337)
Degman-Reed, Ruth. Blake the Snake Had a Bellyache. (p. 198)
Degn, Bibi. My Horse, My Friend: Hands-On Ttouch Training for Kids. Joseph, Lilliana, tr. (p. 1211)
Degnan, Robert W. Fife's Lessons: The Tao of Cool. (p. 584)
DeGoede, Jeannette. Tulip Fairy's Holiday. (p. 1796)
DeGorsky, Gregory J. Christmas Pirate. DeGorsky, Jon, ed. (p. 315)
DeGorsky, Jon, ed. see DeGorsky, Gregory J.
DeGraaf, Rebecca L., ed. see DeGraaf, Rob L.
DeGraaf, Rebecca L., photos by see DeGraaf, Rob L.
DeGraaf, Rob L. Fat Tire Favorites: South Florida off-Road Bicycling. DeGraaf, Rob L. & DeGraaf, Rebecca L., eds. (p. 577)
Degrado, Louis Paul. Questors' Adventures: The Round House & the Moaning Walls. (p. 1426)
DeGraff, Patti Jo. RD Maye & the Gold Locket. (p. 1441)
DeGrand, David, illus. see Kloepfer, John.
DeGrand, Ned, illus. see Kloepfer, John.
DeGrasse, Samantha. Taber Is Beautiful. McPherson, Melinda, illus. (p. 1694)
DeGraw, Aleine. Alexander Hamilton: American Statesman. (p. 36)
—Alexander Hamilton: Estadista Estadounidense. (p. 36)
—Alexander Hamilton: American Statesman / Estadista Estadounidense. (p. 36)
—Alexander Hamilton: Estadista estadounidense (Alexander Hamilton: American Statesman) (p. 36)
DeGreen, Keith. Emerging Markets: Why & How you absolutely-positively-should invest Now! (p. 518)
DeGregorio, Linda. Ned the Banana. (p. 1239)
DeGrie, Eve. Opposites. Rose, Drew, illus. (p. 1300)
deGroat, Diane. Ants in Your Pants, Worms in Your Plants! Gilbert Goes Green. deGroat, Diane, illus. (p. 90)
—April Fool! Watch Out at School! deGroat, Diane, illus. (p. 93)
—Brand-New Pencils, Brand-New Books. deGroat, Diane, illus. (p. 222)
—Gilbert & the Lost Tooth. (p. 676)
—Gilbert & the Lost Tooth. deGroat, Diane, illus. (p. 676)
—Gilbert, the Surfer Dude. (p. 676)
—Gilbert, the Surfer Dude. deGroat, Diane, illus. (p. 676)
—Good Night, Sleep Tight, Don't Let the Bedbugs Bite! deGroat, Diane, illus. (p. 700)
—Happy Birthday to You, You Belong in a Zoo. deGroat, Diane, illus. (p. 745)
—Jingle Bells, Homework Smells. deGroat, Diane, illus. (p. 918)
—Last One in Is a Rotten Egg! (p. 978)
—Last One in Is a Rotten Egg! deGroat, Diane, illus. (p. 978)
—Mother, You're the Best! (But Sister, You're a Pest!) deGroat, Diane, illus. (p. 1178)
—No More Pencils, No More Books, No More Teacher's Dirty Looks! deGroat, Diane, illus. (p. 1259)
—Trick or Treat, Smell My Feet (p. 1786)
—Trick or Treat, Smell My Feet. deGroat, Diane, illus. (p. 1786)
deGroat, Diane, illus. see Bate, Lucy.
deGroat, Diane, illus. see Drummond, Ree.
deGroat, Diane, illus. see Gilson, Jamie.
deGroat, Diane, illus. see Rotner, Shelley.
DeGroat, Harry De W. & Firman, Sidney G. Iroquois Arithmetics for School & Life Book: Grades Five & Six. (p. 888)
—Iroquois Arithmetics for School & Life Book: Grades Seven & Eight. (p. 888)
DeGross, Monalisa. Donavan's Double Trouble. Bates, Amy, illus. (p. 466)
Degruy, David. As the Sparks Fly Upward: The Jimmy & Johnny Adventure Stories. (p. 105)
Deguchi, Ryusei, illus. see Akahori, Satoru.
Dehart, Andy, ed. see Brusha, Joe.
DeHart, Jessica C. Girl's Guide to Living a Brilliant Life! (p. 680)
DeHart, Leslie Marie. Paloma: The Lilly Fairy (p. 1320)
DeHaven, Brad. Currency of the Future: When You Know This, You Control Your Destiny (p. 394)
Dehesa, Germán. Adiós a Las Trampas. (p. 12)
Dehesa, Juana Ines. Rebel Doll. (p. 1450)
Dehesa, Juana Inés, tr. see Bernard, Fred & Roca, François.
Dehghanpisheh, Corine. Buddy's Dream. Dehghanpisheh, Corine, illus. (p. 235)
—Can We Play Again? Dehghanpisheh, Corine, illus. (p. 258)
Dehm, Debbie. Animal Stories of the Desert. (p. 80)
Dehoratius. Follow Your Fates Exile of Aeneas. (p. 612)
DeHoratius, Ed. Journey of Odysseus. Delandro Hardison, Brian, illus. (p. 928)
—Wrath of Achilles. (p. 1962)
Deich, Cheri Bivin. Messy Monkey Tea Party. Genth, Christina, illus. (p. 1130)
Deifell, Tony. Seeing Beyond Sight. (p. 1548)
Deighton, Jo, adapted by. Ali Baba & the Forty Thieves: Traditional Stories:Cinderella: The Elves & the Shoemaker. (p. 39)
—Bacbouc the Lazy Tailor: Traditional Stories:Beauty & the Beast: The Red Shoes. (p. 129)
—Codadad & His Brothers: Traditional Stories:The Grocer, the Student & the Elf: The Ugly Duckling. (p. 338)
—Fisherman & the Wicked Genie: Traditional Stories:The Shepherdess & the Chimney Sweep: Seven with One Blow. (p. 599)
—Scheherezade Presents. (p. 1521)
Deighton-O'Flynn, Heather, et al. Kiwi Phonics: Level 3: Complex Code Riley, Larry, illus. (p. 963)
—Kiwi Phonics: Level 2: Consonant Clusters Riley, Larry, illus. (p. 963)
—Kiwi Phonics: Level 1: Basic Vowels & Consonants Riley, Larry, illus. (p. 963)
Deike, Ruth. Stone Wall Secrets Teacher's Guide: Exploring Geology in the Classroom. (p. 1653)
Deinard, Jenny. How to Draw Illinois's Sights & Symbols. (p. 817)
—How to Draw Indiana's Sights & Symbols. (p. 817)
—How to Draw Iowa's Sights & Symbols. (p. 817)
—How to Draw Kansas's Sights & Symbols. (p. 817)
—How to Draw Kentucky's Sights & Symbols. (p. 817)
—How to Draw Louisiana's Sights & Symbols. (p. 818)
—How to Draw Maine's Sights & Symbols. (p. 818)
—How to Draw Maryland's Sights & Symbols. (p. 818)
—How to Draw Massachusetts's Sights & Symbols. (p. 818)
—How to Draw Michigan's Sights & Symbols. (p. 818)
Deines, Ann, ed. Wilbur & Orville Wright: A Handbook of Facts. (p. 1928)
Deines, Brian, illus. see Fitz-Gibbon, Sally.
Deines, Brian, illus. see Highway, Tomson.
Deines, Brian, illus. see Hundal, Nancy.
Deines, Brian, illus. see Innes, Stephanie & Endrulat, Harry.
Deines, Brian, illus. see Kaldor, Connie & Campagne, Carmen.
Deines, Brian, illus. see MacGregor, Roy.
Deines, Brian, jt. auth. see Fitz-Gibbon, Sally.
Deines, Donna. Remarkable Red Rock: A Timothy Adventure. (p. 1459)
—Spirits from the Past. (p. 1629)
Deisadze, Zaur, illus. see Brezinova, Ivona.
Deisadze, Zaur, illus. see Haxhia, Miranda.
Deiser, Donald. Egg Money. (p. 506)
Deisher, Kathleen E. Beyond the Gloesmur: In the Gloesmur Scrolls. Deisher, Kathleen E., illus. (p. 174)
Deisler, Veronica, jt. auth. see Ambrose, Marylou.
Deiss, A. Sullivan Girls & the Mystery of Moonhouse. (p. 1673)
Deiss, A. G. Meet Ella-Bella. (p. 1121)
Deiss, A. G. & Emi. Sad Tale of Emmaline Austin, Monkey-Girl. (p. 1501)
Deitch, Jeffrey, ed. Fractured Figure. (p. 627)
Deitch, JoAnne Weisman, ed. Voting in America. (p. 1850)
Deiters, Erika & Deiters, Jim. African Community in America. (p. 27)
—Chinese Community in America. (p. 307)
—French Community in America. (p. 635)
—Italian Community in America. (p. 894)
—Mexican Community in America. (p. 1131)
Deiters, Jim, jt. auth. see Deiters, Erika.
Deitz Shea, Pegi, jt. auth. see Shea, Pegi Deitz.
DeJesus, Edward. Makin' It: The Hip-Hop Guide to True Survival. (p. 1080)
DeJesus, Melissa. Sokora Refugees (p. 1606)
DeJesus, Melissa, illus. see Segamu.
DeJesus, Melissa, illus. see Tregay, Sarah.
DeJesus, Robert, illus. see Yourgrau, Barry.
Dejohn. Return of SF. (p. 1464)
DeJohn. Return of SF. (p. 1464)
DeJohn, Marie, illus. see Brown, Fern.
DeJohn, Marie, illus. see Ellsworth, Mary Ellen.
DeJohnette-Harvin, Yvonne. Bed Time Blues. (p. 156)
DeJong Artman, Catherine, illus. see Wales, Dirk.
DeJong, Meindert. Colina Que Canta. (p. 339)
—Gata Casi Blanca. (p. 657)
—Wheel on the School. (p. 1900)
Dekel, Amir. Grandma Birdie's Red String. Jacob, Sona &, illus. (p. 708)
DEKELB-RITTENHOUSE, Diane. Immortal Longings. (p. 861)
DeKeyser, Stacy. Brixen Witch. Nickle, John, illus. (p. 230)
—Jump the Cracks. (p. 934)

—Wampanoag. (p. 1856)
Dekker, James. Scum (p. 1534)
Dekker, James C. Impact (p. 862)
—Scum (p. 1534)
Dekker, Joanne. Off Kilter. (p. 1279)
Dekker, Ted. Lost Books Collectors Box Set: Chose; Infidel; Renegade; Chaos; Lunatic; Elyon (p. 1055)
DeKlyen, Chuck, jt. auth. see Schwiebert, Pat.
DeKnight, Cathy, illus. see Brown, Stacia Bradley.
DeKock, Paul & Yount, David. Next Step. (p. 1249)
Del Adelman, Garry. Civil War Kids 150: Fifty Fun Things to Do, See, Make, & Find. (p. 325)
del, Amo Javier, jt. auth. see del Amo, Javier.
del Amo, Javier & del, Amo Javier. Nino Que Pinto el Mundo. (p. 1257)
Del Amo, Montserrat. Abrazo del Nilo. (p. 7)
—Fuego y el Oro. (p. 646)
—Nudo. (p. 1270)
—Patio de Corredor. (p. 1328)
Del Amo, Montserrat & Amo, Montserrat del. Piedra y el Agua. (p. 1357)
Del Angel, Varinia. Juego de Pelota Mixteca. Leon, Gabriela, illus. (p. 931)
Del Bene, Terry A., et al. Interrupted Journey's: Wyoming's Haunted Historic Trails. Damone, G. L., 3rd, illus. (p. 881)
del Carmen, Maria & Hurtado, Bobadilla. Jovenes en Crisis: Guia de valores para padres y Adolescentes. (p. 929)
del Conte, Mia, illus. see Benjamin, Matthew C.
Del George, Dana. Queen of Fire & the King of Ice. (p. 1425)
Del Greco, Marjorie. Special Time with Grandm: The Snow Fort. (p. 1623)
del Hierro, K. Riding Polluto. (p. 1471)
Del Mar, David Peterson, jt. auth. see Peterson del Mar, David.
Del Moral, S., tr. Animales. (p. 80)
—Colores. (p. 344)
—Contrarios. (p. 361)
—Formas. (p. 620)
Del Moral, Susana. Agua Por Todas Partes. Zaidi, Nadeem, illus. (p. 30)
—Baby Da Vinci, Mi Cuerpo. Zaidi, Nadeem, illus. (p. 125)
—Casa de Violet. Zaidi, Nadeem, illus. (p. 273)
—Como Me Siento. Zaidi, Nadeem, illus. (p. 351)
—Juego de las Formas. Zaidi, Nadeem, illus. (p. 931)
—Las Rimas de Bard: Un Libro con Ventanas. Zaidi, Nadeem, illus. (p. 977)
—Mundo A Mi Alrededor: El Cielo. Zaidi, Nadeem, illus. (p. 1191)
—Paseo Por la Selva. Zaidi, Nadeem, illus. (p. 1326)
—Que Flota? Un Libro para Banarse y Disfrutar. Zaidi, Nadeem, illus. (p. 1423)
Del Moral, Susana, tr. Sr. Cuadrado. (p. 1637)
del Moral Zavariz, Susana. Donde Viven? (p. 466)
del Moral Zavariz, Susana & Zaidi, Nadeem. Concurso: Un Libro con Espejos. (p. 355)
Del Negro, jt. auth. see Del Negro, Janice M.
Del Negro, Janice M. Passion & Poison: Tales of Shape-Shifters, Ghosts, & Spirited Women Natale, Vince, illus. (p. 1327)
Del Negro, Janice M. & Del Negro. Willa & the Wind Solomon, Heather M., illus. (p. 1932)
Del Riego, Erica. Heart of Life. (p. 759)
Del Rio, Adam. Teo en Palo Verde/Teo en Palo Verde. Ill, Noel, illus. (p. 1720)
del Rio, Ana Maria. Historia de Manu (Manu's Story) Cardemil, Carmen, illus. (p. 782)
del Rio, Tania. Sabrina the Teenage Witch: the Magic Within 1. (p. 1500)
del Risco, Elda, tr. see Ericsson, Annie Beth & Christian, Cheryl.
Del Risco, Elda, tr. see Hillert, Margaret.
Del Risco, Elda, tr. see Hnatov, Catherine.
Del Risco, Elda, tr. see Jeffers, Dawn.
del Risco, Elda, tr. see Pan, Hui-Mei.
Del Risco, Elda, tr. see Solomon, Sharon.
Del Risco, Elda, tr. see Wellington, Monica.
del Risco, Elda, tr. What's in My Toybox? (Spanish/English) Un libro de formas/A Book of Shapes (p. 1898)
Del Rosario, Michael, ed. see Sanchez, Alex.
Del Russo, John William, Sr., illus. see Godsey, J. P.
Del Toro, Gladys. Mutation of Black Cat (p. 1194)
del Toro, Guillermo & Kraus, Daniel. Trollhunters. Murray, Sean, illus. (p. 1788)
Del Toro, Mark, illus. see Fitzgibbon, Diana.
del Valle, Clara J., photos by see Ames, Heidi L.
Del Vecchio, Gene. Pearl of Anton (p. 1333)
Del Vecchio, Gene, jt. auth. see del Vecchio, Gene.
del Vecchio, Gene & Del Vecchio, Gene. Sword of Anton (p. 1692)
dela Pena, Alba. Tales of Gorba the Crafty Giant of Loomsville. (p. 1702)
DeLa Vega, Timothy T., et al. 200 Years of Surfing Literature: An Annotated Bibliography. (p. 2001)
Delaborde, Gilles, photos by see Tracqui, Valérie.
Delaby, Phillipe, jt. auth. see Dufaux, Jean.
Delace Wofford Canada. Smiles for God from a Sunflower & You. (p. 1594)
Delacre, Lulu. Alicia Afterimage. (p. 40)
—Arrorro Mi Nino: Latino Lullabies & Gentle Games (p. 101)
—How Far Do You Love Me? (p. 809)
—How Far Do You Love Me? Delacre, Lulu, illus. (p. 809)
—Rafi & Rosi. (p. 1433)
—Rafi & Rosi. Delacre, Lulu, illus. (p. 1433)
—Salsa Stories. (p. 1505)
—Salsa Stories. Delacre, Lulu, illus. (p. 1505)
Delacre, Lulu, illus. see Marti, José & José, Marti.
Delacre, Lulu, jt. auth. see Gonzalez, Lucia M.
Delacre, Lulu & Swanson, Katharine. Jay & Ben. Delacre, Lulu, illus. (p. 910)
DeLaCroix, Alice. Best Horse Ever. Himler, Ronald, illus. (p. 170)
—How to Survive a Totally Boring Summer. Fisher, Cynthia, illus. (p. 821)
Delafontaine, Ariane. Prince des Montagnes. (p. 1401)
Delafosse, Claude. Haus. (p. 754)
—Let's Look at Archimboldo's Portraits. Delafosse, Claude, illus. (p. 998)
Delafosse, Claude, jt. auth. see Broutin, Christian.
Delafosse, Claude, jt. auth. see Equipo Staff.
Delafosse, Claude, jt. auth. see Grant, Donald.
Delafosse, Claude, jt. auth. see Jeunesse, Gallimard.
Delafosse, Claude, jt. auth. see Krawczyk, Sabine.
Delafosse, Claude & Broutin, Christian. Let's Look at the Jungle. Broutin, Christian, illus. (p. 999)
Delafosse, Claude & Krawczyk, Sabine. Let's Look at the Circus. Krawczyk, Sabine, illus. (p. 999)
—Let's Look at the Zoo at Night. Krawczyk, Sabine, illus. (p. 999)
—Plantas. Barroso, Paz, tr. (p. 1369)
Delafosse, Claude & Mettler, Réne. Maus. (p. 1110)
—Vogel. (p. 1847)
Delafosse, Claude & Valat, Pierre-Marie. Let's Look at Building Sites by Night. Valat, Pierre-Marie, illus. (p. 998)
Delafosse, Claude, et al. Let's Look at Life below the City. (p. 999)
DeLage, Charlene, illus. see Blackaby, Susan.
Delage, Kristi, illus. see Hanson, Sandy.
Delahunty, Andrew. Barron's First Thesaurus. (p. 140)
—Oxford Pocket School Dictionary. (p. 1315)
Delainey, James, illus. see Campbell, Marjorie Wilkins.
Delalandre, Benoît & Clapin, Jeremy. My Multicultural Atlas. (p. 1215)
Delalandre, Benoit & Oakes, Terry. Classic Tales of Horror: A Pop-Up Book. Oakes, Terry, illus. (p. 328)
DeLallo, Laura. Arctic Wolf: The High Arctic. (p. 96)
—Hammered by a Heat Wave! (p. 739)
Delamain, Catherine & Spring, Jill. Developing Baseline Communication Skills. (p. 431)
—Speaking, Listening & Understanding: Games for Young Children. (p. 1623)
—Understanding & Using Spoken Language: Games for 7 to 9 Year Olds. (p. 1815)
DeLance, Michael. Beyond Mere Mortals. (p. 174)
DeLand, M. Maitland. Baby Santa & the Lost Letters. (p. 128)
—Baby Santa's Worldwide Christmas Adventure. Wilson, Phil, illus. (p. 128)
—Busy Bees at Work & Play. (p. 245)
—Busy Bees on Broadway. Martin, Lyn, illus. (p. 245)
—Great Katie Kate Discusses Diabetes. (p. 716)
—Great Katie Kate Offers Answers about Asthma. (p. 716)
—Great Katie Kate Tackles Questions about Cancer. (p. 716)
Delande, J., ed. see Moore, P.D.
Delandro Hardison, Brian, illus. see DeHoratius, Ed.
DeLaney, Edgar Azell. Magical Hammock. DeLaney, Edgar Azell, illus. (p. 1074)
Delaney, Janine, illus. see Daniels, Linda.
Delaney, Joseph. Attack of the Fiend. Arrasmith, Patrick, illus. (p. 113)
—Clash of the Demons. Arrasmith, Patrick, illus. (p. 327)
—Coven of Witches. Arrasmith, Patrick, illus. (p. 373)
—Curse of the Bane. Arrasmith, Patrick, illus. (p. 394)
—Fury of the Seventh Son. Arrasmith, Patrick, illus. (p. 650)
—Ghost Prison. (p. 671)
—Grimalkin the Witch Assassin Bk. 9 Arrasmith, Patrick, illus. (p. 724)
—Grimalkin the Witch Assassin. Arrasmith, Patrick, illus. (p. 724)
—I Am Alice Arrasmith, Patrick, illus. (p. 832)
—Last Apprentice: Seventh Son: Book 1 & Book 2. (p. 977)
—Last Apprentice: Rage of the Fallen. Bk. 8 Arrasmith, Patrick, illus. (p. 977)
—Last Apprentice: Revenge of the Witch Bk. 1 Arrasmith, Patrick, illus. (p. 977)
—Last Apprentice - I Am Alice Arrasmith, Patrick, illus. (p. 977)
—Last Apprentice - Slither (p. 977)
—Last Apprentice: the Spook's Bestiary: The Guide to Creatures of the Dark. Heller, Julek, illus. (p. 977)
—Lure of the Dead. Arrasmith, Patrick, illus. (p. 1066)
—New Darkness. (p. 1244)
—Night of the Soul Stealer (p. 1254)
—Night of the Soul Stealer Bk. 3. Arrasmith, Patrick, illus. (p. 1254)
—Rage of the Fallen Arrasmith, Patrick, illus. (p. 1433)
—Revenge of the Witch Arrasmith, Patrick, illus. (p. 1466)
—Rise of the Huntress Arrasmith, Patrick, illus. (p. 1475)
—Rise of the Huntress Bk. 7 Arrasmith, Patrick, illus. (p. 1475)
—Seventh Son (p. 1555)
—Slither. (p. 1590)
—Spook's Bestiary: The Guide to Creatures of the Dark. Heller, Julek, illus. (p. 1631)
—Spook's Tale & Other Horrors. (p. 1631)
—Spook's Tale - And Other Horrors. (p. 1631)
—Spook's Tale-And Other Horrors. (p. 1631)
—Wrath of the Bloodeye. (p. 1962)
Delaney, Kate, jt. auth. see Albee, Sarah.
Delaney, Lawrence. Detective Sniffer & the Mysterious Case of the Sphinx's Beard. Sager, Michelle, illus. (p. 431)
DeLaney, Lynn, ed. see Rothschild Moellers, Marcia.
Delaney, Mark. Pepperland (p. 1340)
Delaney, Michael. Obi: Gerbil on a Mission. (p. 1275)
—Obi, Gerbil on the Loose! (p. 1275)
Delaney, Molly. My Sister. (p. 1218)
Delaney, Molly, illus. see Athey, Victoria.
Delaney, Molly, illus. see Christopher, Matt.
Delaney, Molly, illus. see Olsen, Jan Z.
Delaney, Molly, illus. see Williams, Rozanne Lanczak.
Delaney, Ned. Two Strikes, Four Eyes. (p. 1804)
Delaney, Sally & Richards, Wendy. How Do You Say That in French? 1000 Words & Phrases for Kids. Galloway, Ruth, illus. (p. 808)
DeLange, Alex Pardo, illus. see Bertrand, Diane Gonzales.
Delange, Alex Pardo, illus. see Lachtman, Ofelia Dumas.
Delano, Jamie. Original Sins. Kahan, Bob, ed. (p. 1304)
Delano, Marfe Ferguson. American Heroes. (p. 61)
—Cielo. (p. 319)
—Desierto. (p. 429)
—Explore My World Baby Animals. (p. 550)
—Explore My World Butterflies. (p. 550)
—Explore My World Clouds. (p. 550)
—Explore My World Frogs. (p. 550)
—Genius: A Photobiography of Albert Einstein. (p. 661)
—Genius. (p. 661)
—Helen's Eyes: A Photobiography of Annie Sullivan, Helen Keller's Teacher. (p. 763)
—Inventing the Future: A Photobiography of Thomas Alva Edison. (p. 883)
Delano, Marfe Ferguson, jt. auth. see U. S. National Geographic Society Staff.
Delano, Poli. When I Was a Boy Neruda Called Me Policarpo: A Memoir Higgins, Sean, tr. from SPA. (p. 1903)
Delanssay, Cathy, illus. see Agin, Élodie, et al.
Delanssay, Cathy, illus. see Galliez, Roxane Marie.
Delanssay, Cathy, illus. see Hanna, Virginie.
Delany, Shannon. 13 to Life. (p. 1995)
—Destiny & Deception: A 13 to Life Novel. (p. 431)
—Rivals & Retribution: A 13 to Life Novel. (p. 1475)
—Stormbringer. (p. 1656)
—Weather Witch. (p. 1870)
Delany, Shannon, jt. auth. see Redgrave, Saoirse.
Delany, Shannon & Redgrave, Saoirse. Secrets & Shadows: A 13 to Life Novel. (p. 1544)
DeLap, Mark. Little Acorn (p. 1023)
Delaporte, Bérengère. My Beastly Book of Twisted Tales: 150 Ways to Doodle, Scribble, Color & Draw. (p. 1196)
Delaronde, Deborah L. Duck's Bay. Dawson, Sheldon, illus. (p. 488)
—Rabbits' Race. McCoy, Virginia, illus. (p. 1430)
Delashmit, Margaret V. Thief! (p. 1732)
Delashmutt, Amy. Hello, Cy! Torgeson, Sarah, illus. (p. 763)
Delaware, Steven S. Art & Culture of the Medieval World. (p. 101)
Delaware, Steven S., et al. Art & Culture of the Medieval World. (p. 101)
Delawrence, T. M. Millie: M. C. E. (Mail Carrier Extraordinaire) In. (p. 1144)
DelBello, Melissa P., jt. ed. see Geller, Barbara.
Delclos, Jordi V., illus. see Puerto, Carlos.
Delclòs, Jordi Vila, illus. see Combel Editorial Staff.
Delco, Bobby. Lil Mack Jr. (p. 1017)
Delcoglin, Gwen. Bella's Umbrella. Delcoglin, Nathan, illus. (p. 162)
Delcoglin, Nathan, illus. see Delcoglin, Gwen.
Delderfield, Angela, illus. see Moseley, Sophia.
Delduce, Karen Blanchard. Poodles in the Park: A Poodle Party. (p. 1383)
Delea, Pattie. Wisdom for Young Hearts Volume 1 Wisdom's Foundation. DeLea, Ray and Daniella, ed. (p. 1939)
—Wisdom for Young Hearts Volume 2 - Applications of Wisdom. Gammage, Dana, illus. (p. 1939)
DeLea, Ray and Daniella, ed. see Delea, Pattie.
Delehanty, Hugh, jt. auth. see Jackson, Phil.
Delehanty, Joan M., illus. see Bruce, David.
Delehanty, Joan M., illus. see Silvano, Wendi.
Delena Deatherage. Beginning of People's Chicken. Joe Kent, illus. (p. 159)
DeLeon, Angelo, ed. Summary of U. S. Supreme Court Decisions for Correctional Services. (p. 1673)
deLeon Diaz, Rosa, et al. Big Keep Books-Spanish Caption Books: Dinosaurios; Camiones; ¿Qué Es lo Que Veo?; el Tráfico; Globos; la Granja deLeon Diaz, Rosa et al, trs. (p. 182)
De'Leon, Lunden. Oops Loops. (p. 1299)
Delessert, Etienne. Glass. Delessert, Etienne, illus. (p. 682)
—Hungry for Numbers. (p. 828)
—Moon Theater. (p. 1172)
—Night Circus. Delessert, Etienne, illus. (p. 1253)
—Spartacus the Spider. (p. 1622)
—Was an Apple Pie. Delessert, Etienne, illus. (p. 1859)
—Yok-Yok Delessert, Etienne, illus. (p. 1972)
Delessert, Etienne, illus. see Frisch, Aaron.
Delessert, Etienne, illus. see Henry, O.
Delessert, Etienne, illus. see Highet, Alistair.
Delessert, Etienne, illus. see Ionesco, Eugène.
Delessert, Etienne, illus. see Kirkpatrick, Patricia.
Delessert, Etienne, illus. see Marshall, Rita.
Delessert, Etienne, illus. see Wilde, Oscar.
Delessert, Etienne, creator. Full Color. (p. 646)
Delezenne, Christine. Torrie & the Firebird. Delezenne, Christine, illus. (p. 1770)
Delezenne, Christine, illus. see Hutchins, Hazel.
Delezenne, Christine, illus. see Johansen, K. V.
Delezenne, Christine, illus. see Plante, Raymond.
Delf, Brian, illus. see Kemp, Richard.
Delgado, Alvin. Spirit of the Gang. (p. 1628)
Delgado, Ben & Benchmark Education Co., LLC Staff. Big Bus. (p. 180)
Delgado, Diana, tr. see Thompson, Kate.
Delgado, Francisco. Enano y un Gigante. Gonzalez, Santiago, illus. (p. 523)
Delgado, Francisco, illus. see Byrd, Lee Merrill.
Delgado, Francisco, illus. see Cohn, Diana.
Delgado, Josep Francesc. Nima, El Sherpa. (p. 1255)
Delgado, Linda D. Hijab-Ez Friends. (p. 779)
—Saying Goodbye. (p. 1519)
—Stories. (p. 1654)
—Visitors. (p. 1845)
Delgado, Luis Cabrera. Catalina la Maga. (p. 278)
—Maritimi Quiere Ser Escritora. Cardemil, Carmen, illus. (p. 1094)
Delgado, Ricardo. Age of Reptiles Omnibus. (p. 29)
Delgato, Carolyn A. Jiggy & his Hiccups (p. 917)
Delgatto, Laurie, ed. Hey, God! What Now? Biblical Assurance for Life's Questions. (p. 774)
—She Said ... He Said ... Teens Speak Out on Life & Faith. (p. 1564)
—Teens Speak on Family Matters: Truth, Tension, Trials, Triumphs. (p. 1715)
Delhohne, Jean-Philippe. Visit to Another Planet. (p. 1845)
D'Elia, Amy & Clerman, Lisa. Dreams Come True: A story about the blessing of Adoption. (p. 484)
D'Elia, Una. Painting in the Renaissance. (p. 1318)
Delibero, Bob. Petrucchio. (p. 1348)
DeLibero, Nicholas & Benchmark Education Co. Staff. Cadence of War. (p. 250)
Delibes, Miguel. Camino. (p. 256)
—Cinco Horas con Mario. (p. 319)
—Cuentos. (p. 389)
Delibes, Miguel, et al. Parientes Lejanos: Cuentos de Animales. (p. 1324)
Delice, Shelly Meredith, illus. see Zuckerman, Heather.
Deling, Bjorn, jt. auth. see Sander, Hedda.
Delinois, Alix, illus. see Danticat, Edwidge.
Delinois, Alix, illus. see Myers, Walter Dean.
Delinois, Alix, illus. see Woelfle, Gretchen.
Delioglu, Mustafa, illus. see Finke, Margot.
Delios, Kim, photos by see Magabala Books Staff.
Delios, Louis & Sharma, Vicky. Tomorrow Will Be a New Day. (p. 1765)
Delisa, Patricia, illus. see Flaxman, Andrew.
Delisi, Don. Junk Pyle. (p. 936)
Delisle, Anne-Claire, illus. see Rivard, Émilie & Quinn, Sarah.
Delisle, Annette Gonzalez. Nettey Loves Shoeboxes. Leyva, Juan Camilo, illus. (p. 1242)
Delisle, Carolynne E. Nonna & Grandp. (p. 1263)
Delisle, James R. & Schultz, Robert. If I'm So Smart, Why Aren't the Answers Easy? Advice from Teens on Growing up Gifted. (p. 853)
Delisle, Jim, jt. auth. see Galbraith, Judy.
Delisle, Kathryn H., illus. see Frrich, Lewandowski & Riccards, Michael.
Delisle, Shel. Dolphin Girl. (p. 464)
Deliso, Chris & Dorling Kindersley Publishing Staff. Playtime with Sophie. (p. 1373)
Delittle, Cathy. Hamster Cheeks. Milicevic, Adam, illus. (p. 739)
Deliz, Osdila O., ed. see Ronnholm, Ursula O.
Delk, Cheryl L. College Oral Communication (p. 340)
—College Oral Communication. (p. 340)
Delk, Chrissy, illus. see Nelson, O. T.
Dell, Bella. Rosie the Robin. (p. 1490)
Dell, Christy. Three Pirate Brothers & the Lost Princess. (p. 1743)
Dell, Helen Sue. Thinker's Pizza Cookbook. (p. 1734)
Dell, J. A. Gateways of Knowledge: An Introduction to the Study of the Senses. (p. 658)
Dell, Jacob J. & Dell, Rachel E. Piece of Notre Dame: A pictorial guide to the University of Notre Dame, leading you on an insightful tour of the often unnoticed, yet beautifully crafted details of Campus. Wilson, Robin M., ed. (p. 1356)
Dell, John, illus. see Morrison, Grant & DeMatteis, J. M.
Dell, Pamela. American Quarter Horses. (p. 63)
—Ancient Egypt (p. 68)
—Apache Resistance: Causes & Effects of Geronimo's Campaign. (p. 91)
—Appaloosas. (p. 92)
—Arabians. (p. 94)
—Benedict Arnold: From Patriot to Traitor. (p. 164)
—Blood in the Water: A Story of Friendship During the Mexican War. (p. 200)
—Cause & Effect: American Indian History (p. 282)
—Clydesdales. (p. 336)
—Gavilan: A Story of Hollywood During the McCarthy ERA. (p. 658)
—Half-Breed: A Story of Two Boys During the Klondike Gold Rush. (p. 736)
—Last Battle: Causes & Effects of the Massacre at Wounded Knee. (p. 977)
—Man on the Moon: How a Photograph Made Anything Seem Possible (p. 1085)
—Mapping the Sky. (p. 1090)
—Mississippi. (p. 1154)
—Mustangs. (p. 1194)
—Paintball for Fun! (p. 1318)
—Przewalski's Horses. (p. 1413)
—Queen Noor. (p. 1425)
—Rain Forest Plants (p. 1434)
—Shaky Bones: A Story of the Harlem Renaissance. (p. 1559)
—Shetland Ponies. (p. 1566)
—Show Me the Continents: My First Picture Encyclopedia (p. 1570)
—Show Me the Continents. (p. 1570)
—Show Me the U. S. Presidency: My First Picture Encyclopedia (p. 1570)
—Stamping for Fun! (p. 1639)
—Tag-along Tay: A Story about Annie Oakley & Buffalo Bill's Wild West Show. (p. 1695)
—Thoroughbreds. (p. 1740)
—Undertaker: Life of the Dead Man (p. 1816)
—World War I Timeline (p. 1959)
—You Can't Read This! Why Books Get Banned (p. 1975)
Dell, Pamela, jt. auth. see Dell, Pamela J.
Dell, Pamela, jt. auth. see Wooster, Patricia.
Dell, Pamela & Delmar, Peter. Science of Military Vehicles (p. 1527)
Dell, Pamela & Raatma, Lucia. Science of Soldiers (p. 1527)
Dell, Pamela J. How Animals Move. (p. 804)
Dell, Pamela J. & Dell, Pamela. Why Do Tigers Have Stripes? A Book about Camouflage (p. 1924)
Dell, Pamela Jain. Ancient Egypt (p. 68)
Dell, Rachel E., jt. auth. see Dell, Jacob J.
Dell, Scott O. Isola Dei Delfini Blu. (p. 893)
Della Chiesa, Carol, tr. see Collodi, C.
Dellaira, Ava. Love Letters to the Dead. (p. 1060)
Dellapenna, Joseph W., jt. auth. see Higgins, Melissa.
Dellar, Hugh, jt. auth. see Walkley, Andrew.
Della-Rovere, Cynthia, illus. see Langley, Andrew.
Dellas, Melanie & Woodworth, John. Pat-A-Cake, Pat-a-Cake... We Made a Mistake! Sun, Antuanette, illus. (p. 1327)
Dellasega, Cheryl. Nugrl90 LaPierre, Karina, illus. (p. 1270)
Dellasega, Cheryl & Sourcebooks, Inc Staff. Girl's Friendship Journal. (p. 680)
DelleCava, Karen. Closer Look. (p. 334)
Dell'edera, Werther, illus. see Azzarello, Brian, et al.
Dellicurti, Dana. Christopher's Little Blue Backpack. (p. 317)
—Joey's First Day at School. (p. 920)
Dellinger, Annetta. Adopted & Loved Forever. McDonnell, Janet, illus. (p. 13)

D

Dellinger, Hampton. Thanks for Nothing: How Willie & Abe Saved Thanksgiving. (p. 1725)
Dellinger, Robert. Mitchell's Peak: A Novel of Discovery. (p. 1155)
Dellolio, Kristina. Penelope's Tea Party Oh No Where's Kangaroo. (p. 1336)
Dell'orco, Antonio. Wolf Lion & Whistle: Two Children's Stories. (p. 1944)
Dell'Oro, Suzanne Paul. Let's Look at Earthworms. (p. 998)
Delmain, Judy. Andy Beane & the Catkins' Tale. (p. 73)
Delmar, Natasha, illus. see Shah, Idries.
Delmar, Pete. U. S. Army Green Berets: The Missions. (p. 1806)
—Vehicles of the Civil War (p. 1834)
Delmar, Pete, jt. auth. see Grayson, Robert.
Delmar, Pete & Grayson, Robert. American Special Ops. (p. 63)
Delmar, Peter, jt. auth. see Dell, Pamela.
delMazo, Deborah. No Cookies for Christmas: The Story of Grandma's Missing Package. Horsfall, Jacqueline, ed. (p. 1258)
Delmege, Sarah. Pink Pages. (p. 1360)
Delmonte, Ellis. Miracle Girl. (p. 1148)
DelMonte, Joan. Plonk Goes the Weasel. (p. 1374)
Delmouzos, Alexandros, et al. Alfavitario: A Greek Alphabet Book for Children. (p. 37)
Delo, Ken. Ugly Little Christmas Tree. (p. 1808)
DeLoach, Kathleen. Daniel's World. Best, Cathy, illus. (p. 405)
—Monde de Daniel: Un livre sur les enfants Handicapés. Best, Cathy, illus. (p. 1163)
—Mundo de Daniel: Un libro sobre niños Minusválidos. Best, Cathy, illus. (p. 1191)
Deloach, Pam. Shauna's Frog. (p. 1563)
Deloache, Shawn, illus. see Chilman-Blair, Kim & Hersov, Kate.
deLoache, Shawn, illus. see Chilman-Blair, Kim.
DeLoache, Shawn, jt. auth. see Chilman-Blair, Kim.
deLoache, Shawn, jt. auth. see Chilman-Blair, Kim.
Delonas, Sean, illus. see Snell, Gordon.
DeLong, Jessica Rena. My Reflection: A Story of Wonder & Discovery. (p. 1217)
DeLong, Lucianne. Mrs. Mumford's Missing. Richoll, Stephanie, illus. (p. 1187)
—Tall Southern Tale. Ungureanu, Dan Paul, illus. (p. 1704)
—Whiskers Takes a Walk: A Possum Squat Tale. Ungureanu, Dan Paul, illus. (p. 1912)
DeLong, Ron. Crayola Dream-Makers: Dreams You Can Count On. DeLong, Ron, ed. (p. 377)
—Crayola (R) Dream-Makers (R) 11: Drawing on Character. DeLong, Ron, ed. (p. 377)
—Dream-Makers Visual Arts & Science: Dreams & Explorations. Brown-McCracken, Janet & Chastain, Donna, eds. (p. 483)
—Dream-Makers Visual Arts & Social Studies: Dreams that Support a Changing World. Brown-McCracken, Janet & Chastain, Donna, eds. (p. 483)
DeLong, Ron & Brown-McCracken, Janet. Crayola Dream-Makers Supporting Creativity Beyond the Classroom: 18 Standards-Based Activities/Lessons for after-School Programs & Other Groups. Thomas, Tavy, ed. (p. 377)
DeLong, Ron, ed. Dream-Makers: Visual Art & Literacy (p. 483)
DeLorge, Jaqueline. Gilfinton under the Sea. (p. 676)
Deloria, Vine, Jr. Evolution, Creationism, & Other Modern Myths: A Critical Inquiry. (p. 546)
—God Is Red: A Native View of Religion. (p. 689)
—Indians of the Pacific Northwest: From the Coming of the White Man to the Present Day. (p. 872)
DeLorme Map Staff. New York Atlas & Gazetteer. (p. 1247)
Delors, Catherine. Mistress of the Revolution. (p. 1155)
Delosh, Diana Ting, illus. see Brott, Wayne.
Delp, Marie. Patches & his Garden Staff. (p. 1328)
Delp, Randy. Ugly Bug & the Beautiful Butterfly. (p. 1808)
Delpech, Sylvie, ed. see Quarto Generic Staff.
Delpech, Sylvie & Frances Lincoln Editors. Klimt: With More Than 60 Reusable Stickers! (p. 963)
Delpech, Sylvie & Leclerc, Caroline, eds. Henri Matisse. (p. 767)
Delporte, Peyo, et al. Smurfs & the Howlibird. Peyo, illus. (p. 1595)
Delporte, Yvan. Purple Smurf Peyo, illus. (p. 1419)
—Purple Smurfs. Peyo, illus. (p. 1419)
—Smurf King. Peyo, Peyo, illus. (p. 1595)
—Smurfs & the Magic Flute. Peyo, illus. (p. 1595)
Delporte, Yvan, jt. auth. see Peyo, Peyo.
Delporte, Yvan, jt. auth. see Peyo.
Delrio, Martin, jt. auth. see Case, Nikki.
DelRisco, Elda, tr. see Farmer, Jacqueline.
DelRisco, Elda, tr. see Wade, Mary Dodson.
Delrose, Julian. Feeding Time at the Farm: Use Place Value & Properties of Operation to Subtract. (p. 580)
—Feeding Time at the Farm: Use Place Value & Properties of Operations to Subtract. (p. 580)
—Feeding Time at the Farm. (p. 580)
Delrusso, Diana. Pages, the Book-Maker Elf. Schwab, Jordan, illus. (p. 1318)
Delsante, Vito. Babe Ruth. Martínez, Andrés Vera, illus. (p. 123)
Delsi, Dawna, illus. see Glupker, Dianne.
Delsi, Dawna, jt. auth. see Glupker, Dianne.
Delsol, Wendy. Flock. (p. 605)
—Frost. (p. 644)
—Stork. (p. 1655)
Delta, Penelope. Secrets of the Swamp. Bobick, Ruth, tr. (p. 1546)
Delton, Judy. Angel Bites the Bullet. Weber, Jill, illus. (p. 73)
Delton, Judy, jt. auth. see Judy Delton Family Trust Staff.
Delton, Judy & Pee Wee Scouts Staff. Peanut-Butter Pilgrims. Tiegreen, Alan, illus. (p. 1332)
Deltoro, Antonio. Plaza. Ochoa, Francisco, illus. (p. 1373)
Deluc, Yves & Ruck. Prisunic. (p. 1407)
Deluca, Alison. Christmas O'Clock: A Collection. Daly, Lisa, illus. (p. 315)
DeLuca, Doreen, jt. auth. see Napoli, Donna Jo.
Deluca, Laura. Demon. (p. 426)
DeLuca, Laura. Destiny. (p. 430)
Deluca, Laura. Flora & the Silver Coins. Manni, Mia (Maio), illus. (p. 606)
—Hyde. (p. 831)
DeLuca-Acconi, Robin, jt. auth. see Moss, Wendy L.
DeLuise, Dom & Brown, Tim. No Place Like Home. (p. 1260)
DeLuise, Dom & Carter, Derek. Pouch Potato. (p. 1389)
Deluna, Alicia C. Tippy Gets a Friend. (p. 1757)
Delval, Marie-Hélène. Animals of the Bible. Fronty, Aurélia, illus. (p. 83)
—Bible for Young Children. Götting, Jean-Claude, illus. (p. 175)
—'Ecole des Geants. (p. 502)
—Elephants est toujours Conten. (p. 512)
—Hippopo va se Baigner. (p. 781)
—Images of God. Nascimbeni, Barbara, illus. (p. 860)
—Lili et Mistigri jouent a Cache. (p. 1017)
—Psalms for Young Children. Arno, illus. (p. 1413)
—Voici les trois freres Ours. (p. 1848)
Delvaux, Nancy, jt. auth. see Legrand, Martine.
Demado. En Avant: Enhanced Online Edition. (p. 522)
—En Route: Enhanced Online Edition. (p. 522)
—Se Allez, Viens! En Route! (p. 1534)
DeMalo, Alison. Tyler, the tiniest Tiger. (p. 1805)
DeMalo, Katie. Big Charles. (p. 180)
DeMakas, Meg, jt. auth. see Grandfield, Meg.
Demallie, Howard R. Behind Enemy Lines: A Young Pilot's Story. (p. 160)
Demand, Carlo. Airplanes of World War I Coloring Book. (p. 32)
—Classic Racing Cars of the World Coloring Book. (p. 328)
Demar, Regier, jt. auth. see Jensen, Patricia.
Demar, Regier, jt. auth. see Woodruff, Liza.
DeMarco, Julie Reece, jt. auth. see Reece, Colleen L.
DeMarco, Kathleen, jt. auth. see Van Cleve, Kathleen.
Demarco, Lisa. Unusual Tales of Matilda Marmalade. (p. 1823)
DeMarco, Neil. Vietnam, 1939-75. (p. 1841)
—World Study after 1900. (p. 1958)
DeMarco, Neil & Aylett, J. F. Cold War & After. (p. 339)
Demarco, Stacey. Goddesses & Sirens. Manton, Jimmy, illus. (p. 690)
—Gods & Titans. Manton, Jimmy, illus. (p. 690)
DeMarco, Tony. Ed McCaffrey: Catching a Star. (p. 503)
Demarest, Chris L. Alpha Bravo Charlie: The Military Alphabet. Demarest, Chris L., illus. (p. 48)
—Arabic Picture Dictionary. (p. 94)
—Arlington: The Story of Our Nation's Cemetery. Demarest, Chris L., illus. (p. 99)
—Firefighters A to Z. Demarest, Chris L., illus. (p. 591)
—Hurricane Hunters! Riders on the Storm. Demarest, Chris L., illus. (p. 829)
—Mayday! Mayday! A Coast Guard Rescue. Demarest, Chris L., illus. (p. 1113)
—My Blue Boat. (p. 1198)
Demarest, Chris L., illus. see Maguire, Gregory.
Demarest, Chris L., illus. see Stamper, Judith Bauer & Stamper, Judith.
Demarest, Chris L., illus. see Stamper, Judith Bauer.
Demarest, Chris L., illus. see Thomas, Patricia.
Demarest, Chris L., illus. see Ziefert, Harriet.
Demarest, Chris L. & Mayer, Bill. All Aboard! A Traveling Alphabet. (p. 41)
Demarest, Jeannie. My Best Friend Troubles. (p. 1196)
DeMari, Donna, jt. auth. see Chester, Laura.
Demarie, Teresa, ed. see McLaren, Keir.
deMarin, Layne. Amazon Adventure (p. 56)
—Built from Stone (p. 240)
—Desert Seasons. (p. 429)
—Everybody Moves (p. 543)
DeMarin, Layne. Look & Learn. (p. 1048)
deMarin, Layne. Look & Learn. (p. 1048)
—Moon Book (p. 1172)
—Oh Baby! (p. 1280)
—Oranges: from Fruit to Juice. (p. 1302)
—Save the Animals (p. 1516)
—To Fly in the Sky (p. 1759)
—Too Much Snow (p. 1767)
—Too Much Snow! (p. 1767)
—What Scientists Do (p. 1893)
—Wonder Readers: Science. (p. 1947)
DeMaris, Sheri-Lynn. Macro Magic for Kids & Parents: Taking the Mystery Out of Macrobiotic Cooking. (p. 1068)
Demars, Sue. Jesus Loves You More. (p. 916)
Demarte, Lisa Marie. I Can See. (p. 836)
Demartino, Damian, jt. auth. see Teer, Robert.
Demas, Corinne. Always in Trouble. Jones, Noah Z., illus. (p. 51)
—Everything I Was. (p. 545)
—Halloween Surprise. Alley, R. W., illus. (p. 739)
—Here Comes Trouble! Jones, Noah, illus. (p. 770)
—Here Comes Trouble! Jones, Noah Z., illus. (p. 770)
—Middle Grade Novel. (p. 1137)
—Pirates Go to School. Manders, John, illus. (p. 1363)
—Returning to Shore. (p. 1465)
—Saying Goodbye to Lulu. Hoyt, Ard, illus. (p. 1519)
—Two Christmas Mice. Roth, Stephanie, illus. (p. 1803)
—Valentine Surprise. Alley, R. W., illus. (p. 1830)
DeMascio, William. Don't Forget to Visit the Moon. (p. 467)
DeMasque, Catherine. Quest of the White Stag. (p. 1426)
Dematons, Charlotte. Holland. (p. 789)
—Holland & a Thousand Things about Holland. (p. 789)
—Yellow Balloon. (p. 1970)
Dematons, Charlotte, illus. see de Vries, Anke.
DeMatte, Darcey, illus. see Assunto, Cecelia.
Dematteis, Heidi Gestvang. Sisters Are Forever. (p. 1581)
DeMatteis, J. M. Imaginalis. (p. 860)
Dematteis, J. M. Puppet, the Professor, & the Prophet. Ploog, Mike, illus. (p. 1417)
DeMatteis, J. M. Stardust Kid. Ploog, Mike, illus. (p. 1642)
DeMatteis, J. M., jt. auth. see Giffen, Keith.
DeMatteis, J. M., jt. auth. see Morrison, Grant.
DeMatteis, J. M. & Kleid, Neil, texts. Spider-Man: Kraven's Last Hunt. (p. 1626)
DeMatteis, J. M., et al. Son of the Goblin. (p. 1611)
DeMauro, Lisa. Theodore Roosevelt the Adventurous President. (p. 1729)
—Thomas Edison A Brilliant Inventor. (p. 1738)
DeMauro, Lisa & Time for Kids Editors. Theodore Roosevelt: The Adventurous President. (p. 1729)
Dembar Greene, Jacqueline. Speak up, Tommy! Melmon, Deborah, illus. (p. 1623)
Dember-Paige, Judith. Sana Sonrisa Para Toda La Vida: Nicol Visita el Consultorio de la Dentista. (p. 1510)
—Smile Wide Look Inside. (p. 1594)
Dembicki, Carol & Dembicki, Matt. Mr. Big: A Tale of Pond Life. (p. 1184)
Dembicki, Matt. Xoc: The Journey of a Great White. (p. 1967)
Dembicki, Matt, jt. auth. see Dembicki, Carol.
Dembicki, Matt, ed. Wild Ocean: Sharks, Whales, Rays, & Other Endangered Sea Creatures. (p. 1930)
Dembinski, Chris. Maxi the Taxi. (p. 1112)
Dembkoski, Kacey. Believe. (p. 161)
Dembo, Jaiden. Finding Strider. (p. 588)
Dembo, Margot, tr. see Fest, Joachim C.
Dembowski, Jill, jt. auth. see Patterson, James.
Demby, Kyri. Lori Biscuit, the Musical Detective: The Escape of Fortissimo. (p. 1053)
—Simon the Self Control Seal: Demby's Playful Parables. (p. 1577)
—Simon the Self Control Seal. (p. 1577)
Demcak, Andrew. Ghost Songs. (p. 671)
DeMedeiros, James. Touch. (p. 1772)
DeMeo, Kimberly F. One Little Egg. (p. 1295)
Demeo, Kristen. Sounds Like This ... (p. 1615)
Demeritt, Dwight B., Jr. Maine Made Guns & Their Makers. (p. 1077)
Demeritt, Mary Anne. Twilight Ride of the Pink Fairy. Daniel, Ellen, illus. (p. 1801)
Demers, Aimee, jt. auth. see Hichs, Donald E.
DeMers, Barbara. Willa's New World. (p. 1933)
Demers, David & Demers, Lee Ann. My Grandpa Loves Trains: A Storybook for Preschoolers. Demers, David, photos by. (p. 1210)
—My Grandpa Loves Trains: A Picture Storybook for Preschoolers. Demers, David, photos by. (p. 1210)
Demers, Dominique. Old Thomas & the Little Fairy. (p. 1285)
—Today, Maybe Grimard, Gabrielle, illus. (p. 1760)
Demers, Dominique, jt. auth. see DeMers, Dominique.
DeMers, Dominique & Demers, Dominique. Every Single Night Debon, Nicolas, illus. (p. 543)
Demers, Karen. Adventuresome Antics of Taf, Tif, Tobe, Tiggy, Princess & Toby. (p. 25)
—My Love of the Animals in the Town of St Jovite: Our Beautiful Laurentians. (p. 1213)
Demers, Lee Ann, jt. auth. see Demers, David.
Demers, Roxanna. Rusty Bucket Kids, A Behind the Scenes Look at the Rusty Bucket Kids, Lincoln, Journey To 16. Eason, D. M., illus. (p. 1498)
Demery, Ramona. Hey, Little Bird: Verses for Children. (p. 774)
Demeter, Brian. Pedro & the Coyote. (p. 1334)
Demetrios, Heather. Blood Passage. (p. 200)
—Exquisite Captive. (p. 555)
—I'll Meet You There. (p. 856)
—Something Real. (p. 1610)
Demetris, Alex, illus. see Demetris, Jean.
Demetris, Jean. Grandma's Box of Memories: Helping Grandma to Remember. Demetris, Alex, illus. (p. 708)
Demi. Columbus Demi, illus. (p. 346)
—Conference of the Birds. (p. 356)
—Empty Pot. Demi, illus. (p. 521)
—Fantastic Adventures of Krishna. Demi, illus. (p. 571)
—Florence Nightingale. Demi, illus. (p. 606)
—Genghis Khan (p. 661)
—Girl Who Drew a Phoenix. Demi, illus. (p. 679)
—Great Voyages of Zheng He. (p. 719)
—Greatest Power. Demi, illus. (p. 720)
—Hungry Coat: A Tale from Turkey. Demi, illus. (p. 828)
—Jesus. Demi, illus. (p. 914)
—Joan of Arc (p. 919)
—Legend of Saint Nicholas. Demi, illus. (p. 988)
—Magic Pillow. Demi, illus. (p. 1073)
—Marco Polo (p. 1092)
—Pandas & Their Chopsticks: And Other Animal Stories. (p. 1321)
—Rumi: Persian Poet, Whirling Dervish (p. 1495)
—Saint Francis of Assisi. (p. 1503)
—Tutankhamun (p. 1799)
Demi, illus. see Jain, Manoj.
Demi, illus. see James, J. Alison.
Demi, illus. see Spivak, Dawnine.
Demi & Demi Staff. Boy Who Painted Dragons. Demi & Demi Staff, illus. (p. 219)
—Su Dongpo. (p. 1670)
Demi, Barbara. Muhammad. Demi, Barbara, illus. (p. 1189)
Demi Staff. Happy, Happy Chinese New Year! (p. 745)
Demi Staff, jt. auth. see Demi.
Demi Staff & Marshall Cavendish Corporation Staff. Alexander the Great (p. 36)
DeMicco, Michelle, illus. see Bendt, Valerie.
Demick, Nancy. It Began As an Ordinary Day. (p. 893)
DeMico, Judy. Bus Trip Johnson, Catherine LeAnn, illus. (p. 244)
DeMille, Katherine. I Wish Daddy Was Here. (p. 848)
DeMille, Nelson. Up Country. (p. 1824)
Demilly, Christian. Pop Art. (p. 1384)
Deming, Lynette. Day in Matthews Shoes. (p. 413)
Demirel, Ruhi, et al. Abu Bakr As-Siddiq. (p. 7)
—Uthman Ibn Affan. (p. 1829)
Demirel, Selçuk, illus. see Fagan, Cary.
DeMitchell, Terri A. Portsmouth Alarm. (p. 1387)
—You Will Come Back - the First in the Olde Locke Beach Mysteries. (p. 1976)
Demitri, Alyssa. I See Shapes. (p. 845)
Demme, Tina, jt. auth. see Chambers, Cindy.
Demmers, Justina, illus. see Mele, Leo.
Demming, Karen, illus. see Brannon, Pat.
DeMolay, Jack. Amityville: La casa encantada (Ghosts in Amityville:the Haunted House) (p. 65)
—Amityville: La Casa Encantada. Obregón, José María, tr. from ENG. (p. 65)
—Atlántida: El Misterio de la Ciudad Perdida. Obregón, José María, tr. from ENG. (p. 112)
—Atlántida: El misterio de la ciudad perdida (Atlantis:the Mystery of the Lost City) (p. 112)
—Atlantis: The Mystery of the Lost City. (p. 112)
—Bermuda Triangle: The Disappearance of Flight 19. (p. 167)
—Bigfoot: A North American Legend. (p. 184)
—Bigfoot: La Leyenda del Hombre-Monstruo. Obregón, José María, tr. (p. 184)
—Bigfoot: La Leyenda del hombre-monstruo (A North American Legend) (p. 184)
—Ghosts in Amityville: The Haunted House. (p. 672)
—Loch Ness Monster: Scotland's Mystery Beast. (p. 1044)
—Monstruo del Lago Ness: Una Misteriosa Bestia en Escocia. Obregón, José María, tr. from ENG. (p. 1169)
—monstruo del lago Ness: Una misteriosa bestia en Escoci (the Loch Ness Monster: Scotland's Mystery Beast) (p. 1169)
—Ovnis: El caso Roswell (UFO: the Roswell Incidents) (p. 1314)
—Ovnis: El Caso Roswell. Obregón, José María, tr. from ENG. (p. 1314)
—Triángulo de las Bermudas: La Desaparicíon del Vuelo 19. Obregón, José María, tr. (p. 1785)
—Triángulo de las Bermudas: La desaparición del vuelo 19 (the Bermuda Triangle:the Disappearance of Flight 19) (p. 1785)
—UFOs: The Roswell Incident. (p. 1808)
Demolin, G. Blaue Hexe. (p. 198)
DeMonfreid, Dorothée. Dark Night. Stahlberg, Whitney, tr. from FRE. (p. 408)
Demong, Todd, illus. see Gallardo, Adam.
Demonia, Lori. Leah's Voice. (p. 982)
—Leah's Voice. Turchan, Monique, illus. (p. 982)
DeMonte, Joe. Lucy & the Magic Factory. (p. 1063)
deMontignie, Leon, illus. see Klein, Peter.
DeMoss, Nancy Leigh. Place of Quiet Rest: Finding Intimacy with God Through a Daily Devotional Life. (p. 1365)
Demps, Rhonda R. Angel I Left Behind. (p. 73)
Dempsey, Kristy. Dance Like Starlight: One Ballerina's Dream. Cooper, Floyd, illus. (p. 402)
—Me with You. Denise, Christopher, illus. (p. 1116)
—Mini Racer. Stevens-Marzo, Bridget, illus. (p. 1146)
—Surfer Chick. Cole, Henry, illus. (p. 1685)
Dempsey, Sheena. Bruno & Titch. Dempsey, Sheena, illus. (p. 232)
—Bye-Bye Baby Brother! (p. 249)
Dempsey, Tami. We Are a Champion! (p. 1865)
Dempski, Seth. Natalie's Nature Walk: Represent & Interpret Data. (p. 1230)
Dempster, Al, illus. see Barrie, J. M. & RH Disney Staff.
Demski, James, Jr., illus. see Jones, Christianne C.
Demski, James, Jr., illus. see Manushkin, Fran.
Demund, Tom. From Slave to Superstar of the Wild West: The Awesome Story of Jim Beckwourth. (p. 643)
Demuth, Patricia. What Was Pearl Harbor? (p. 1895)
Demuth, Patricia Brennan. Those Amazing Ants. Schindler, S. D., illus. (p. 1740)
—What Was D-Day? Kenyon, David Grayson & Anderson, Scott, illus. (p. 1894)
—What Was Ellis Island? (p. 1894)
—What Was Ellis Island? McVeigh, Kevin & Groff, David, illus. (p. 1894)
—What Was Pearl Harbor? Mantha, John & Tomkinson, Tim, illus. (p. 1894)
—Where Is the Great Wall? (p. 1909)
—Where Is the Great Wall? Groff, David & Hoare, Jerry, illus. (p. 1909)
—Who Is Bill Gates? Hammond, Ted & Harrison, Nancy, illus. (p. 1915)
—Who Was Galileo? (p. 1918)
—Who Was Galileo? O'Brien, John & Harrison, Nancy, illus. (p. 1918)
—Who Was Laura Ingalls Wilder? (p. 1918)
Demuth, Patricia Brennan, jt. auth. see Brennan, Patricia.
DeMuth, Robert R. Grandpa's Treasures. (p. 710)
Den Ouden, Marijke, jt. auth. see Sanmugam, Devagi.
Den Uyl, Paul. Holland Fire Department: The First Fifty Years 1867-1916. (p. 789)
Dena. Happi Baby, Happi Mommy. (p. 744)
Dena, Anael. Colores. (p. 344)
—Contrarios. (p. 361)
—Los Numbers. (p. 1054)
DeNaro, Rose. Incredible, Unforgettable Adventures of Jaxby. (p. 869)
Denaro, Sal, illus. see Stratten, Lou.
DeNault, Shiri, illus. see McBride, Linda Ray.
Denby, Neil, jt. auth. see Thomas, Peter, Jr.
Dencer, Christine. Misty. Meserve, Jessica, illus. (p. 1155)
Denchfield, Nick. Charlie Chick Parker, Ant, illus. (p. 293)
—Penelope the Piglet. Parker, Ant, illus. (p. 1336)
Denchfield, Nick & Sharp, Anne. Pop-up Minibeast Adventure. (p. 1384)
Dendinger, Roger. Guatemala. (p. 728)
Dendinger, Roger E. & Gritzner, Charles F. Honduras. (p. 794)
Dendrites, Waymore. Branton's Blossoms. (p. 222)
Dendy, Christina. Bringing Home the Constitution: Defining Moments in Canadian History. (p. 229)
—Underground Railroad: Defining Moments in Canadian History. (p. 1815)
Dendy, Leslie, jt. auth. see Boring, Mel.
Denecke, Edward J., Jr. & Long, Lynette. Painless Earth Science. (p. 1318)
Deneen, Brendan. Rudolph the Red-Nosed Reindeer: the Island of Misfit Toys. Kambadais, George, illus. (p. 1494)
Denega, Danielle. Graduation Day. Johnson, Jay, illus. (p. 705)
Denega, Danielle, jt. auth. see Denega, Danielle M.
Denega, Danielle & Bridwell, Norman. Pumpkin Patch Puppy. (p. 1416)
Denega, Danielle M. & Denega, Danielle. Skulls & Skeletons: True-Life Stories of Bone Detectives. (p. 1586)

Denenberg, Barry. Lincoln Shot: A President's Life Remembered. Bing, Christopher, illus. (p. 1018)
—Nelson Mandela: No Easy Walk to Freedom. (p. 1241)
—Titanic Sinks! Experience the Titanic's Doomed Voyage in This Unique Presentation of Fact & Fiction. (p. 1758)
—True Patriot: The Journal of William Thomas Emerson, a Revolutionary War Patriot. (p. 1792)
—When Will This Cruel War Be Over? Diary of Emma Simpson, Gordonsville, Virginia 1864. (p. 1905)
—When Will This Cruel War Be Over? The Diary of Emma Simpson, Gordonsville, Virginia 1864. (p. 1905)
Denenberg, Dennis & Roscoe, Lorraine. 50 American Heroes Every Kid Should Meet. (p. 1997)
Denetdale, Jennifer. Long Walk: The Forced Navajo Exile. (p. 1047)
Denetsosie, Hoke, illus. see Clark, Ann Nolan & Harrington, John P.
Deneulin, Séverine. Capability Approach & the Praxis of Development. (p. 262)
Deneux, Xavier. Colours. (p. 346)
—My Animals. Deneux, Xavier, illus. (p. 1196)
—My Circus. (p. 1200)
—Numbers. (p. 1271)
—Opposites. (p. 1300)
—Shapes. (p. 1560)
—TouchThinkLearn: Farm. (p. 1772)
—TouchThinkLearn: Vehicles. (p. 1772)
Deneux, Xavier, illus. see Bus, Sabrina.
Denffer, Ahmad Von. Islam for Children. (p. 891)
Denger, Monique. Who Colored the Rainbow, Mimi? (p. 1915)
Dengler-McKerchar, Rosemarie. Australia's History in Rhyme - Part 19: Gold Fever. (p. 116)
Dengo, Monica. Pick up Your Pen: The Art of Handwriting. (p. 1354)
Denham, Bill. Windshield Reflections. (p. 1936)
Denham, Brian, jt. auth. see Dunn, Joeming.
Denham, Caitlin, illus. see Mooney, Carla.
Denham, Gemma, illus. see David, Juliet.
Denham, Joyce. Dragon Slayers: Essential Training Guide for Young Dragon Fighters. Snure, Roger, illus. (p. 478)
—Saint Francis of Assisi. Temporin, Elena, illus. (p. 1503)
—Stories of the Saints. Stevens, Judy, illus. (p. 1655)
—Study Guide for Dragon Slayers. (p. 1670)
Denham, M. Nonna & the Great Horse Rescue. (p. 1263)
Denice, Sonia. Chow-E-Chowz: Saved by a Whistle. (p. 311)
Denim, Sue & Pilkey, Dav. Dumb Bunnies. (p. 489)
DeNinno, Joanne & Gill, Kim. Question Challenge Card Game Fun Sheets. (p. 1426)
Denis, Erik & LeBlanc, Natalie. Bubble. (p. 233)
Denis, Florencia, illus. see Ryan, Ann Marie.
Denis, Kasey. Henry the Hippo. (p. 768)
Denis, Stephane, illus. see Lee, Ingrid.
Denis, Toni. How Do the Children Pray? Olds, Irene, illus. (p. 807)
Denisch, Anna. Jack the Clown. (p. 903)
Denise, Anika. Baking Day at Grandma's. Denise, Christopher, illus. (p. 133)
—Bella & Stella Come Home. Denise, Christopher, illus. (p. 162)
Denise, Carolyn. I Am Tan! Chatterji, Somnath, illus. (p. 834)
—I Can Do It Myself! Chatterji, Somnath, illus. (p. 835)
Denise, Christopher, illus. see Cohen, Caron Lee.
Denise, Christopher, illus. see Dempsey, Kristy.
Denise, Christopher, illus. see Denise, Anika.
Denise, Christopher, illus. see Elliott, David.
Denise, Christopher, illus. see Floyd, Lucy.
Denise, Christopher, illus. see Jacques, Brian.
Denise, Christopher, illus. see Lewis, J. Patrick.
Denise, Christopher, illus. see McGhee, Alison.
Denise, Christopher, illus. see Milord, Susan.
Denise, Christopher, illus. see Wells, Rosemary.
Denise, Myla. Dawn: Diary of a Poet. (p. 411)
Denise, Susan Denise. Little Lazy Lizard. (p. 1030)
Denis-Huot, Christine & Denis-Huot, Michel. Cheetah. (p. 296)
Denis-Huot, Michel, jt. auth. see Denis-Huot, Christine.
Denison, Susan, illus. see Quarles, Pamela.
DeNivo, Jennifer. Sneaky Sam. (p. 1597)
DeNize, Anne, jt. auth. see Potter, Anne.
Denk, James, ed. see Tharp, Barbara, et al.
Denk, Mary. Anna's Million Dollar Cow. (p. 85)
Denkhaus, Henry. Anna & the Magical Horse - Henry the Hobo - the Pond. (p. 85)
Denlinger, Dennis. Muscle N' Bone: New Discovery Can Help or Prevent Neck Pain, Back Pain, Foot Pain & More. (p. 1192)
Denlinger, Sam, illus. see Dixon, Amy.
Denman, Gregory. Mathematics: Strategies for Explaining Thinking. (p. 1108)
Denman, K. L. Agent Angus (p. 29)
—Battle of the Bands (p. 146)
—Cache: (Stuff We All Get) (p. 250)
—Destination Human (p. 430)
—Me, Myself & Ike (p. 1116)
—Mirror Image (p. 1149)
—Perfect Revenge (p. 1342)
—Rebel's Tag (p. 1451)
—Revanche Parfaite (p. 1465)
—Shade (p. 1556)
—Spiral (p. 1628)
—Stuff We All Get (p. 1670)
Denman, K. L. & Fernández, Queta. Guerra de las Bandas (p. 728)
Denman, Michael, illus. see Fogle, Robin.
Denman, Michael, illus. see Fraggalosch, Audrey.
Denman, Michael, illus. see Galvin, Laura Gates.
Denman, Michael, illus. see Grey, Chelsea Gillian.
Denman, Michael, illus. see Sommer, Carl.
Denman, Michael L., illus. see Galvin, Laura Gates.
Denman, Michael L., illus. see Grey, Chelsea Gillian.
Denman, Michael L., illus. see Sommer, Carl.
Denman, Michael L., illus. see Suen, Anastasia.
Denman, Michael L., illus. see Tourville, Amanda Doering.
Denman, Michael L., tr. see Galvin, Laura Gates.
Denmark, Evangeline, jt. auth. see Paul, Donita K.
Denmark, Thomas, illus. see Torpie, Kate.
Denmark-Allen, Eva. I Was, I Am, I Will Be! - Yo Fui! Yo soy! Yo Sere! (p. 848)
Dennard, Deborah. Alligators & Crocodiles. Dewey, Jennifer Owings, illus. (p. 47)
—Apes & Monkeys. McGee, John F., illus. (p. 91)
—Bullfrog at Magnolia Circle. Kest, Kristin, illus. (p. 240)
—Chimpanzees. McGee, John F., illus. (p. 306)
—Gorillas. McGee, John F., illus. (p. 703)
—Hedgehog Haven: A Story of a British Hedgerow Community. (p. 761)
—Hedgehog Haven: The Story of an English Hedgerow Community. Hynes, Robert, illus. (p. 762)
—Hurry up, Hedgehog! Hynes, Robert, illus. (p. 830)
—Koala Country: A Story of an Australian Eucalyptus Forest. (p. 966)
—Koala Country: A Story of an Australian Eucalyptus Forest. McKinnon, James, illus. (p. 966)
—Lemur Landing: A Story of a Madagascan Dry Tropical Forest. Kest, Kristin, illus. (p. 991)
—Lizards. Dewey, Jennifer Owings, illus. (p. 1042)
—Reptiles: Explore the Fascinating Worlds of Alligators & Crocodiles, Lizards, Snakes, Turtles. Dewey, Jennifer Owings, tr. (p. 1461)
—Snakes. Dewey, Jennifer Owings, illus. (p. 1596)
—Turtles. Dewey, Jennifer Owings, illus. (p. 1798)
Dennard, Deborah & Kest, Kristin. Lemur Landing: A Story of a Madagascan Dry Tropical Forest. (p. 991)
Dennard, Susan. Darkness Strange & Lovely. (p. 408)
—Something Strange & Deadly. (p. 1610)
—Strange & Ever After. (p. 1664)
Denne, B. Amazing Magic Tricks. (p. 55)
—First Encyclopedia of Seas & Oceans. (p. 594)
—First Encyclopedia of Seas & Oceans II. (p. 594)
Denne, B. & Irving, N. Easy Spanish. (p. 500)
Denne, Ben. Amazing Magic Tricks Kid Kit. (p. 55)
—First Encyclopedia of Seas & Oceans. (p. 594)
—Flags Sticker Atlas. (p. 602)
—Magia Para Todos. (p. 1071)
—Magic Tricks to Make & Do. (p. 1074)
Denne, Ben, jt. auth. see O'Brien, Eileen.
Denne, John, photos by see Herrera, Nicholas.
Dennen, Sue, illus. see Davis, Gabriel.
Dennett, Kathleen. 4 Corners Mystery. (p. 1992)
Dennett, Preston E., jt. auth. see Guiley, Rosemary Ellen.
Denney, Cathie. Adventurous Lamb. (p. 25)
Denney, John Michael. Phoebe's Turf. (p. 1351)
Denning, Richard. Catacombs of Vanaheim. (p. 278)
Denning, Troy. Tempest. (p. 1717)
Dennis, Brian, et al. Nubs: The True Story of a Mutt, a Marine & a Miracle. (p. 1269)
Dennis, Chantal. Sammy the Mouse. (p. 1508)
Dennis, Cindy. Lo Mas Importante / the Most Important Thing. (p. 1044)
—Most Important Thing. (p. 1177)
Dennis, David M., photos by see Cussen, Sarah.
Dennis, Jamie. Mister's Backyard Adventures. (p. 1155)
Dennis, Jane, illus. see Oliver, Chad.
Dennis, Jen. Snoozy Sam. (p. 1598)
Dennis, John. Heroes of Literature: English Poets, a B. (p. 773)
Dennis, Kathryn, jt. auth. see Mahle, Melissa.
Dennis, Latasha F. Prince Ifekoya Finds Courage! (p. 1401)
Dennis, Mary L. Preparing for the PSSA in Reading & Writing Grade 11. (p. 1396)
Dennis, Matthew, jt. auth. see Heiligman, Deborah.
Dennis, Nadine, illus. see Stafford, Mary.
Dennis, Penny Ruth. How I Learn My ABC's Through Sights & Sounds Around Me. (p. 810)
Dennis, Peter. Adventures of King Arthur. (p. 19)
—Castle. (p. 276)
Dennis, Peter, illus. see Bruce, Julia.
Dennis, Peter, illus. see Everett, Felicity & Reid, Struan.
Dennis, Peter, illus. see Harris, Nicholas.
Dennis, Peter, illus. see Harris, Nicolas.
Dennis, Peter, illus. see Masters, Anthony.
Dennis, Peter, jt. auth. see Harris, Nicholas.
Dennis, Peter, jt. auth. see Murrell, Deborah Jane.
Dennis, Peter & Rawson, Christopher. Treasure Island. (p. 1781)
Dennis, Rainey. Passport 2 Purity. (p. 1327)
Dennis, Robert. Gingerbread Bear. Lyon, Tammie, illus. (p. 677)
Dennis, Sandra L. King of New Hearts. (p. 959)
Dennis, Sarah. Cinderella: A Cut-Paper Book. (p. 320)
Dennis, Stacy Terrell. My Guardian Angel Is So Real: My True Encounter with Angels & Demons. (p. 1210)
Dennis, Tammy D., illus. see Thompson, Debra.
Dennis, Trevor. Book of Books: The Bible Retold. (p. 211)
Dennis, Vernelle T. Murray Resource Directory & Career Guide to Historically Black Colleges & Universities Black College & Career Guide Third Edition. (p. 1192)
Dennis, Wesley, illus. see Henry, Marguerite.
Dennis, Wesley, illus. see Robertson, Keith.
Dennis, Yvonne Wakim & Addasi, Maha. Kid's Guide to Arab American History. (p. 953)
Dennis, Yvonne Wakim & Hirschfelder, Arlene. Kid's Guide to Native American History: More Than 50 Activities. (p. 953)
Dennison, Amy, et al, as told by. Our Dad Died: The True Story of Three Kids Whose Lives Changed. (p. 1308)
Dennison, John A. & Johnson, Charles D. Technical Illustration: Techniques & Applications. (p. 1711)
—Technical Illustration Techniques & Applications: Teaching Package PowerPoint Presentations Site License. (p. 1711)
—Technical Illustration Techniques & Applications: Teaching Package Powerpoint Presentations Individual License. (p. 1711)
Dennison, Matt. Building with Blocks: Work with 11-19 to Gain Foundations for Place Value. (p. 239)
Denniston, David. American Paint Horse (p. 62)
Denny, Elizabeth. Jenneli's Dance Auchter, Chris, illus. (p. 912)
Denny, Joe. Triune: Jimmy's Escape. (p. 1788)
—Triune 2: Journey to the Unknown. (p. 1788)
Denny, Roz & Watt, Fiona. Cooking for Beginners. (p. 361)
Denofsky, Howard. Sillyishis, Beanie & the Hobblebobs. (p. 1576)
DeNomme, Donna & Proctor, Tina. Ophelia's Oracle: Discovering the Healthy, Happy, Self-aware, & Competant Girl in the Mirror. (p. 1300)
Denos, Julia, illus. see Ashburn, Boni.
Denos, Julia, illus. see Cardillo, Margaret.
Denos, Julia, illus. see Castellucci, Cecil.
Denos, Julia, illus. see Couloumbis, Audrey.
Denos, Julia, illus. see Denton, P. J.
Denos, Julia, illus. see Hest, Amy.
Denos, Julia, illus. see McNamara, Margaret.
Denos, Julia, illus. see Merchant, Peter.
Denos, Julia, illus. see Perl, Erica S.
Denos, Julia, illus. see Strong, Cynda.
Denou, Violeta. Teo y Sus Amigos. (p. 1720)
Denshire, Jayne. Exercise. (p. 548)
—Hygiene. (p. 831)
—Nutrition. (p. 1274)
—Rest & Sleep. (p. 1464)
—Staying Safe. (p. 1645)
—Well-Being. (p. 1874)
Denslow, Heather. Ainslie's Smile. (p. 30)
Denslow, W. W. Denslow's Mother Goose. (p. 426)
Denslow, W. w. Denslow's One Ring Circus. (p. 426)
Denslow, W. W., illus. see Baum, L. Frank.
Denslow, W. W., jt. auth. see Baum, L. Frank.
Denslow, W. W., jt. auth. see Moore, Clement C.
Denslow, W. W., jt. auth. see Noble, Marty.
Denslow, W. W., jt. auth. see West, Paul.
Densmore, Don. Tongue Twister Experiments Student Workbook. Evans, Andrew, illus. (p. 1765)
Dent, Grace, jt. auth. see Dent, Grace.
Dent, Grace & Dent, Grace. Diva Without a Cause. (p. 454)
Dent, Jenny. Adventures of Hoppy the Gnome. (p. 18)
—Giant Jigsaw Puzzle: Democratic Committee Assignments in the Modern House. (p. 673)
—God Loves Us All. (p. 689)
—Great Teachers. (p. 718)
—Hoppy's Christmas Book. (p. 797)
—Spiritual Teachings for Children. (p. 1629)
—Story of Hoppy's Friend Pickle. (p. 1658)
—Where Is Heaven? (p. 1908)
Dent, Josh. Hot Chips & Sauce. (p. 801)
Dent, Sabrina. Proverbs Kids Fun Activity Book. (p. 1413)
Dent, Sue. Forever Richard. (p. 619)
—Never Ceese: Can Two Who Were Wronged Make It Right? (p. 1242)
Dent, Valeda. Wowie Howie's Amazin' Adventure: Time to Save! (p. 1962)
Denton, Carolyn, jt. auth. see Hasbrouck, Jan.
Denton, Dawn. Betzy the Bumblebee. (p. 173)
—Last Leaf. (p. 978)
—Oliver the Toad. (p. 1285)
—Ruby & Rocket. (p. 1493)
Denton, Gill. Mysterious Case of Spying & Espionage: Techniques & Tales of Master Spies. (p. 1223)
Denton, Graham, jt. auth. see Carter, James.
Denton, Ivan, jt. auth. see Sargent, Dave.
Denton, Kady MacDonald. Child's Treasury of Nursery Rhymes. (p. 305)
Denton, Kady MacDonald, illus. see Becker, Bonny.
Denton, Kady MacDonald, illus. see Heidbreder, Robert.
Denton, Kady MacDonald, illus. see Hutchins, Hazel J.
Denton, Kady MacDonald, illus. see Hutchins, Hazel.
Denton, Kady MacDonald, illus. see Little, Jean.
Denton, Kady MacDonald, illus. see Masurel, Claire.
Denton, Kady MacDonald, illus. see Scanlon, Liz Garton.
Denton, Kady MacDonald, illus. see Wadham, Tim.
Denton, Kady MacDonald, illus. see Wishinsky, Frieda.
Denton, Kady MacDonald, jt. auth. see Gibson, Betty.
Denton, Kiwi. Freddie's Magical Glasses (p. 633)
Denton, Lynette Harris. Christmas Greetings, My Little Friend. (p. 314)
Denton, P. J. Girls Against Boys. Denos, Julia, illus. (p. 679)
—Keeping Secrets. Denos, Julia, illus. (p. 947)
—Pony Party! Denos, Julia, illus. (p. 1382)
Denton, Shannon, illus. see Niz, Xavier & Niz, Xavier W.
Denton, Shannon E., illus. see Englar, Xavier & Niz, Xavier W.
Denton, Shannon E., illus. see Niz, Xavier & Niz, Xavier W.
Denton, Shannon Eric. Boxcar Children: A Graphic Novel Dubisch, Mike, illus. (p. 216)
Denton, Shannon Eric & Warner, Gertrude Chandler. Amusement Park Mystery Dubisch, Mike, illus. (p. 66)
—Boxcar Children. Dubisch, Michael, illus. (p. 216)
—Castle Mystery Dubisch, Mike, illus. (p. 277)
Denton, Shannon, et al. Komikwerks Presents Nuts & Bolts (p. 966)
—Zapt! (p. 1985)
Denton, Terry. Eye of Ulam. (p. 558)
—Golden Udder. Denton, Terry, illus. (p. 695)
—It's True! Pigs Do Fly. Denton, Terry, illus. (p. 899)
—Minotaur's Maze. (p. 1148)
—Obelisk of Eeeno. (p. 1275)
—Summer in the City. Denton, Terry, illus. (p. 1674)
—Thrillseekers. Denton, Terry, illus. (p. 1744)
—Ultimate Wave. Denton, Terry, illus. (p. 1810)
—Wombat & Fox: Tales of the City. Denton, Terry, illus. (p. 1945)
—Wooden Cow. Denton, Terry, illus. (p. 1949)
Denton, Terry, illus. see Carthew, Mark & Rosen, Michael.
Denton, Terry, illus. see Dubosarsky, Ursula.
Denton, Terry, illus. see Griffiths, Andy.
Denton, Terry, illus. see Tulloch, Richard.
Dentone, Odie. House Without a Family. (p. 804)
—Spat the Cat. (p. 1622)
Denton-Rinzler, Denise. Small Minds. (p. 1592)
—Wishing Jewel. (p. 1940)
DeNucci, Corinne, illus. see Denucci, Sharon.
DeNucci, Corinne, illus. see DeNucci, Sharon.
DeNucci, Sharon. Ava Goes to Africa. DeNucci, Corinne, illus. (p. 118)
Denucci, Sharon. Ava Goes to Alask: Grammie & the Gecko Series. (p. 118)
—Grammie & the Gecko. DeNucci, Corinne, illus. (p. 706)
Denver, John. Ancient Rhymes, a Dolphin Lullaby: With Audio CD & Score. Canyon, Christopher, illus. (p. 70)
—Ancient Rhymes, a Dolphin Lullaby. Canyon, Christopher, illus. (p. 70)
—For Baby (For Bobbie) Mason, Janeen, illus. (p. 615)
—Grandma's Feather Bed. Canyon, Christopher, illus. (p. 708)
—John Denver's Grandma's Feather Bed. Canyon, Christopher, illus. (p. 921)
—John Denver's Sunshine on My Shoulders. Canyon, Christopher, illus. (p. 921)
—Sunshine on My Shoulders. Canyon, Christopher, tr. (p. 1678)
Denzer, Barbara. Kids Guide to Petiquette: The Inside Scoop on Pet Behavior. (p. 953)
Denzer, Barbara & Denzer, Missy. Crazy Kids Guide to Cooking for Your Pet: Recipes, Jokes, Pet Care Tips & Fun Things to Do with Your Pet Featuring the Back Bones of Character. Rodriguez, Manny, illus. (p. 377)
Denzer, Missy, jt. auth. see Denzer, Barbara.
Deodato, Mike. Marvel Art of Mike Deodato. (p. 1098)
Deodato, Mike, illus. see Brubaker, Ed.
Deodato, Mike & Conrad, Will. Eyes of the Dragon (p. 558)
Deogratias Simba. Mystery Door. (p. 1224)
Deol, Gunleen. Sleepover Disaster. (p. 1589)
DePalma, Johnny. Raindrop Keeper: (Limited Edition Hardcover) Crabapple, Molly, illus. (p. 1436)
—Raindrop Keeper. Crabapple, Molly, illus. (p. 1436)
DePalma, Johnny & Crabapple, Molly. Once upon a Christmas Tree - A Holiday Fairy Tale. (p. 1292)
DePalma, Mary Newell. Bow-Wow Wiggle Waggle. (p. 216)
—Grand Old Tree. (p. 707)
—Nutcracker Doll. (p. 1274)
—Perfect Gift. (p. 1342)
—Uh-Oh! (p. 1808)
DePalma, Mary Newell, illus. see MacDonald, Margaret Read.
DePalma, Mary Newell, illus. see Molski, Carol.
DePalma, Mary Newell, illus. see Spinelli, Eileen.
DePalma, Vanessa. This Is My Body: A Safety for Little Girls. Depalma, Victoria, illus. (p. 1736)
Depalma, Victoria, illus. see DePalma, Vanessa.
Depandi, Giuliana. Think Like a Guy: How to Get a Guy by Thinking Like One. (p. 1734)
dePaola, Tomie. 26 Fairmount Avenue (p. 1996)
—26 Fairmount Avenue. dePaola, Tomie, illus. (p. 1996)
—Adelita: A Mexican Cinderella Story. dePaola, Tomie, illus. (p. 12)
—Birds of Bethlehem. dePaola, Tomie, illus. (p. 191)
—Brava, Strega Nona! A Heartwarming Pop-Up Book. dePaola, Tomie et al, illus. (p. 223)
—Charlie Needs a Cloak. (p. 293)
—Cloud Book. (p. 334)
—Days of the Blackbird: A Tale of Northern Italy. dePaola, Tomie, illus. (p. 415)
—For the Duration: The War Years dePaola, Tomie, illus. (p. 616)
—Four Friends at Christmas. dePaola, Tomie, illus. (p. 625)
—Four Friends in Autumn. dePaola, Tomie, illus. (p. 625)
—Four Friends in Summer. dePaola, Tomie, illus. (p. 625)
—Here We All Are. (p. 770)
—Hermanita de Tommy. (p. 771)
—I'm Still Scared: A 26 Fairmount Avenue Book. (p. 860)
—I'm Still Scared. (p. 860)
DePaola, Tomie. In a Small Kingdom. (p. 863)
dePaola, Tomie. Jack. dePaola, Tomie, illus. (p. 902)
—Jamie O'Rourke & the Big Potato. (p. 907)
—Joy to the World: Christmas Stories & Songs. dePaola, Tomie, illus. (p. 930)
—Joy to the World: Tomie's Christmas Stories. dePaola, Tomie, illus. (p. 930)
—Let the Whole Earth Sing Praise. dePaola, Tomie, illus. (p. 994)
—Little Grunt & the Big Egg: A Prehistoric Fairy Tale. (p. 1028)
—Little Grunt & the Big Egg: A Prehistoric Fairy Tale. dePaola, Tomie, illus. (p. 1028)
DePaola, Tomie. Look & Be Grateful. (p. 1048)
dePaola, Tomie. Meet the Barkers: Morgan & Moffat Go to School. (p. 1122)
—Meet the Barkers: Morgan & Moffat Go to School. dePaola, Tomie, illus. (p. 1122)
—Miracles of Jesus. (p. 1149)
—More Mother Goose Favorites. dePaola, Tomie, illus. (p. 1174)
—Mother Goose Favorites. dePaola, Tomie, illus. (p. 1178)
—My First Angels. (p. 1204)
—My First Bible Stories. (p. 1204)
—My First Chanukah. dePaola, Tomie, illus. (p. 1206)
—My First Christmas. dePaola, Tomie, illus. (p. 1206)
—My First Christmas Carols. (p. 1206)
—My First Easter. dePaola, Tomie, illus. (p. 1206)
—My First Halloween. (p. 1206)
—My First Legends: The Story of Bluebonnet. (p. 1207)
—My First Mother Goose. (p. 1207)
—My First Passover. dePaola, Tomie, illus. (p. 1207)
—My First Songs. (p. 1208)
—My First Thanksgiving. (p. 1208)
—My Mother Is So Smart. dePaola, Tomie, illus. (p. 1214)
—Nana Upstairs & Nana Downstairs. (p. 1228)
—Now One Foot, Now the Other. (p. 1269)
—Now One Foot, Now the Other. dePaola, Tomie, illus. (p. 1269)
—On My Way. (p. 1289)
—Pascual & the Kitchen Angels. dePaola, Tomie, illus. (p. 1326)
—Stagestruck. dePaola, Tomie, illus. (p. 1638)
—Strega Nona. dePaola, Tomie, illus. (p. 1667)
—Strega Nona Does It Again. dePaola, Tomie, illus. (p. 1667)
—Strega Nona Takes a Vacation. dePaola, Tomie, illus. (p. 1667)
—Strega Nona's Gift. dePaola, Tomie, illus. (p. 1667)
—Strega Nona's Harvest. (p. 1667)
—Strega Nona's Harvest. dePaola, Tomie, illus. (p. 1667)

D

—Things Will Never Be the Same. (p. 1734)
—Things Will Never Be the Same. dePaola, Tomie, illus. (p. 1734)
—Tomie's Baa Baa Black Sheep & Other Rhymes. dePaola, Tomie, illus. (p. 1764)
—Tomie's Three Bears & Other Tales. dePaola, Tomie, illus. (p. 1764)
—Trouble in the Barkers' Class. dePaola, Tomie, illus. (p. 1790)
—What a Year: A 26 Fairmount Avenue Book (p. 1878)
—What a Year: A 26 Fairmount Avenue Book. (p. 1878)
—What a Year. dePaola, Tomie, illus. (p. 1878)
dePaola, Tomie, illus. see Davies, Valentine.
dePaola, Tomie, illus. see Frith, Margaret.
dePaola, Tomie, illus. see Hale, Sarah Josepha.
dePaola, Tomie, illus. see MacLachlan, Patricia.
dePaola, Tomie, illus. see Madrigal, Antonio Hernandez.
dePaola, Tomie, illus. see Moore, Clement C.
dePaola, Tomie, illus. see Oliver, Lin.
dePaola, Tomie, illus. see Pandell, Karen.
dePaola, Tomie, illus. see Ward, Cindy.
dePaola, Tomie & de, Paola Tomie. Oliver Button Es una Nena. (p. 1285)
DePaolo, Daniel, illus. see Allen, Katy C.
Department of Chamorro Affairs, Division of Research, Publication and Training Staff. I Manfayi: Who's Who in Chamorro History. Vol. I (p. 844)
—I Manfayi: Who's Who in Chamorro History. Vol. II (p. 844)
Department of Labor Staff, jt. auth. see JIST Works, Inc. Staff.
DePaulo, Dorothy, illus. see McClelland, Pam.
DePauw, Sandra A., illus. see Gehret, Jeanne.
Depew, C. S. Tell Me Why. (p. 1717)
Depew, Lanette. Bridge Spanning Time. (p. 227)
Depew, Robert, illus. see Friden, Chris.
DePew, Robert, illus. see Speregen, Devra Newberger & Running Press Staff.
DePietro, Frank. Central American Immigrants. (p. 287)
—Central American Immigrants. Limón, José E., ed. (p. 287)
—Cuban Americans. (p. 388)
—Cuban Americans. Limón, José E., ed. (p. 388)
—Latino American Cuisine. (p. 979)
—Latino American Cuisine. Limón, José E., ed. (p. 979)
—Latino Americans & Immigration Laws. (p. 979)
—Latino Americans & Immigration Laws. Limón, José E., ed. (p. 979)
—Latino Americans & Religion. (p. 979)
—Latino Americans & Religion. Limón, José E., ed. (p. 979)
—Latino Arts in the United States. Limón, José E., ed. (p. 979)
—Latino Migrant Workers. (p. 979)
—Latino Migrant Workers. Limón, José E., ed. (p. 979)
—Mexican Americans. (p. 1131)
—Mexican Americans. Limón, José E., ed. (p. 1131)
—South American Immigrants. (p. 1616)
—South American Immigrants. Limón, José E., ed. (p. 1616)
—Spain Arrives in the Americas. (p. 1620)
—Spain Arrives in the Americas. Limón, José E., ed. (p. 1620)
Depinet, Linda. God Just Needed Another Angel. Depinet, Linda, illus. (p. 689)
DePino, Catherine S. Blue Cheese Breath & Stinky Feet: How to Deal with Bullies. Matthews, Bonnie, illus. (p. 202)
Depisco, Dorothea. Beetle Bugs Party: A Counting Book. Parry, Jo, illus. (p. 158)
Depken, Kristen & Depken, Kristen L. One, Two... Boo! Gévry, Claudine, illus. (p. 1297)
Depken, Kristen L. Barbie in a Mermaid Tale 2. Golden Books Staff, illus. (p. 138)
—Castle Caper. Cartobaleno, illus. (p. 276)
—Coloring Fun with Pocoyo (Pocoyo) Golden Books, illus. (p. 344)
—Dragon Hiccups. Burch, Benjamin, illus. (p. 477)
—Dream Closet. (p. 483)
—Driving School. (p. 485)
—Driving School (Disney/Pixar Cars) RH Disney Staff, illus. (p. 485)
—Fairytale Magic. (p. 565)
—Fairytale Magic (Dora the Explorer) Random House & Miller, Victoria, illus. (p. 565)
—Good Night, Pocoyo (Pocoyo) Random House Staff, illus. (p. 700)
—Happy Easter, Pocoyo! (p. 745)
—Here Comes Peter Cottontail. (p. 770)
—Here Comes Peter Cottontail (Peter Cottontail) Karl, Linda, illus. (p. 770)
—I Can Be a Baby Doctor. (p. 835)
—I Can Be... a Baby Doctor (Barbie) Das Grup, illus. (p. 835)
—I Can Be a Gymnast. (p. 835)
—I Can Be a Gymnast (Barbie) (p. 835)
—Island of the Lost Horses (Dora & Friends) Aikins, David, illus. (p. 892)
—Julius Jr. Super Deluxe Pictureback (Julius Jr.) Golden Books, illus. (p. 933)
—Let's Go to the Circus! (Pocoyo) (p. 997)
—Little Lost Dolphin. (p. 1031)
—Merry Christmas, Pocoyo (Pocoyo) Random House, illus. (p. 1129)
—Merry Christmas, Woody. (p. 1129)
—Merry Christmas, Woody (Disney/Pixar Toy Story) RH Disney Staff, illus. (p. 1129)
—Open the Door & Explore! (Julius Jr.) Random House, illus. (p. 1299)
—Party Central (Disney/Pixar Monsters University) RH Disney Staff, illus. (p. 1326)
—Pearl Princess. (p. 1333)
—Pit Crew Pups. Jackson, Mike, illus. (p. 1364)
—Pocoyo & Friends (Pocoyo) Random House Staff, illus. (p. 1375)
—Pocoyo Dance (Pocoyo) Random House Staff, illus. (p. 1375)
—Poky Little Puppy. (p. 1378)
—Princess & the Popstar. Golden Books, illus. (p. 1403)
—Roaring Adventure (Disney/Pixar Toy Story) RH Disney Staff & Holtsclaw, Josh, illus. (p. 1478)
—Rubble to the Rescue! (Paw Patrol) Jackson, Mike, illus. (p. 1493)
—Rudolph the Red-Nosed Reindeer. Karl, Linda, illus. (p. 1494)
—Toys That Go Bump in the Night (Disney/Pixar Toy Story) RH Disney Staff, illus. (p. 1774)
—Wally's Best Friends. Random House, illus. (p. 1855)
—We Love to Dance! (p. 1867)
—We Love to Dance! (Dora & Friends) Aikins, David, illus. (p. 1867)
—Where's Woody? (Disney/Pixar Toy Story) RH Disney Staff, illus. (p. 1911)
—Wild West Showdown! RH Disney Staff, illus. (p. 1930)
—Woody's White Christmas. Random House Disney Staff, illus. (p. 1950)
Depken, Kristen L., jt. auth. see Depken, Kristen.
Depken, Kristen L., jt. auth. see Random House Staff.
Depken, Kristen L., jt. auth. see RH Disney Staff.
Depken, Kristen L. & Jackson, Kathryn. Tawny, Scrawny Lion. DiCicco, Sue, illus. (p. 1707)
Depken, Kristen L. & Schurr, Cathleen. Shy Little Kitten. DiCicco, Sue, illus. (p. 1572)
Depner, Mary. Smart Monologues: Vocabulary Building Monologues for Teens & Young Adults. (p. 1593)
Depner, Stefan. Aunt Francy the Ant Book II. (p. 115)
DePorter, Vince, illus. see Banks, Steven.
Depp, Laurie & Easton, Tom. Secrets, Lies & Videotape. (p. 1545)
Depper, Hertha, illus. see Hillert, Margaret.
Depperschmidt, Dustin & Andrea. Adventures of Dax: The Golden Hammer. (p. 17)
Depratto, Marcel, illus. see Sanschagrin, Joceline.
Depre, Mickey. Garden Whimsy Applique. (p. 656)
Depree, Helen. Foundations: Early Emergent Teacher Guide. (p. 624)
—Foundations: Upper Emergent Teacher Guide. (p. 624)
—Foundations: Early Emergent Records of Reading Behavior. (p. 624)
—Foundations: Upper Emergent Records of Reading Behavior. (p. 624)
—Foundations: Upper Emergent - Upper Emergent - Complete Kit (p. 624)
—Foundations: Upper Emergent - Student Book Set - 1 Each of 16 Titles (p. 624)
—Foundations: Early Emergent - Student Book Set - 1 Each of 16 Titles. (p. 624)
—Foundations: Upper Emergent - Lesson Plan Set - 1 Each of 16 Lesson Plans (p. 624)
—Foundations: Early Emergent - Lesson Plan Set - 1 Each of 16 Lesson Plans. (p. 624)
—Foundations Upper Emergent Guided Reading Kit 1. (p. 624)
—Upper Emergent Guided Reading: Lesson Plans. (p. 1825)
—Upper Emergent Guided Reading: Student Books. (p. 1825)
DePree, Julia K. Body Story. (p. 207)
DePrince, Elaine, jt. auth. see DePrince, Michaela.
DePrince, Erik, illus. see Tedesco, Ann & Alimonti, Frederick.
DePrince, Michaela & DePrince, Elaine. Ballerina Dreams: From Orphan to Dancer. Morrison, Frank, illus. (p. 134)
—Taking Flight: From War Orphan to Star Ballerina. (p. 1698)
DePrisco, Dorothea. Apple. Taxali, Gary, illus. (p. 92)
—Bluebird's Nest. Parry, Jo, illus. (p. 204)
—Country Mouse & City Mouse. (p. 372)
—Dinosaur Dance. (p. 441)
—Lemon. Taxali, Gary, illus. (p. 991)
—Little School of Fish. Gévry, Claudine, illus. (p. 1036)
—Lullaby & Good Night: Music & Lights. (p. 1064)
—Maximus the Monster Roars NO! (p. 1112)
—Meet Gator: A Picture Clues Touch & Feel Book. Croft, James Lee, illus. (p. 1121)
—Mini Snowbears Winter Day. (p. 1146)
—One Little Sheep. (p. 1295)
—Orange. Taxali, Gary, illus. (p. 1301)
—Pear. Taxali, Gary, illus. (p. 1332)
—Peek-A-Boooo Who? A Lift-the-Flap & Sound Book. Hedgecock, Lucie, illus. (p. 1335)
—Pig-a-Boo! A Farmyard Peekaboo Book. Runnells, Patricia & Runnells, Treesha, illus. (p. 1357)
—Randall Reindeer's Naughty & Nice Report. Reagan, Susan, illus. (p. 1438)
—Smithsonian Discover: Earth. (p. 1594)
—Snowbear's Winter Day: A Winter Wonder Book. Fehlau, Dagmar, illus. (p. 1600)
—Tub-A-Tub. (p. 1795)
—Who's in the Jungle? Gilvan-Cartwright, Chris, illus. (p. 1920)
—Who's in the Ocean? Gilvan-Cartwright, Chris, illus. (p. 1920)
—Who's on the Farm? Gilvan-Cartwright, Chris, illus. (p. 1921)
—Willie & Buster Take the Train. Ansley, Frank, illus. (p. 1934)
DePrisco, Dorothea & McKendry, Sam. I'm a Big Kid Now. (p. 858)
Deprisco Wang, Dorothea. I Love You Little One. Eriksen, Tone, illus. (p. 843)
—My Baby. Gevry, Christine, illus. (p. 1196)
Depucci, Diana M. Lady Stutz, Chris, illus. (p. 970)
der Heide, William van, see van der Heide, William.
Der Manuelian, Peter. Hieroglyphs from A to Z: A Rhyming Book with Ancient Egyptian Stencils for Kids. (p. 777)
Deraney, Michael J., illus. see Cohen, Barbara.
DeRaymond, Devaki, illus. see Dietz, Kamala.
Derbez, Eugenio. Lonjito Moco y Sus Amigos. (p. 1047)
Derby, jt. auth. see Derby, Sally.
Derby, Katy. 10 Most Daring Escapes. (p. 1993)
Derby, Kenneth. Top Ten Ways to Ruin the First Day of 5th Grade. (p. 1769)
Derby, Sally. Jump Back, Paul: The Life & Poems of Paul Laurence Dunbar. Qualls, Sean, illus. (p. 934)
—Kyle's Island. (p. 969)
—No Mush Today Tadgell, Nicole, illus. (p. 1259)
—Sunday Shopping Strickland, Shadra, illus. (p. 1676)
—Whoosh Went the Wind! (p. 1920)
Derby, Sally & Burrowes, Adjoa J. My Steps. (p. 1219)
Derby, Sally & Derby. Two Fools & a Horse: An Original Tale Rayevsky, Robert, illus. (p. 1803)
Derby, Sarah, illus. see Kezar, Wanda.
Derbyshire, Katy, tr. see Reh, Rusalka.
Derdowski, Chad. All Robots Must Die: Nacho-Geddon. (p. 45)
Derejko-Vlinikka, Jennifer. Marko & the Monster. (p. 1095)
Derek the Ghost Staff. Monsters on the March. Fischer, Scott M., illus. (p. 1169)
—Northern Frights. Fischer, Scott M., illus. (p. 1265)
—Scary School. Fischer, Scott M., illus. (p. 1520)
Derenge, Garett. Adventures of Iggy the Iguana. (p. 19)
Derenne, Juliette, illus. see Cadic, Olivier & Gheysens, Francois.
Dereske, Jo. Index to Murder. (p. 870)
Derezinski, Amelia. Star Turns: Dancing on Broadway. (p. 1641)
—Twyla Tharp. (p. 1804)
Derezinzki, Amelia. Star Turns: Dancing on Broadway. (p. 1641)
Dergachov, Oleg. Yellow Elves. Andryczyk, Mark, tr. from UKR. (p. 1970)
Dergachov, Oleg, des. Hand. (p. 740)
Dérib, illus. see Job.
Dérib, jt. auth. see Job.
Dérib & Jeffrey, Erica. Yakari & Great Eagle. (p. 1968)
Derib, et al. Yakari & the White Buffalo. (p. 1968)
Derico, Laura. All God's Bugs. Smith, Matt, illus. (p. 44)
—Prayers for a Child's Day. Allen, Joy, illus. (p. 1393)
Derico, Laura Ring. All God's Bugs. Smith, Matt, illus. (p. 44)
—Easter Surprises. Harris, Phyllis, illus. (p. 499)
—Jesus Lives! the Easter Story. Krum, Ronda, illus. (p. 915)
Derig, Betty. Roadside History of Idaho. (p. 1477)
Derig, Betty & Fuller, Margaret. Wild Berries of the West. (p. 1929)
Derington, Nick, illus. see Biskup, Agnieszka.
Derington, Nick, illus. see Sohn, Emily.
Deriso, Christine Hurley. Right-Under Club: Second Stage. (p. 1472)
—Talia Talk. (p. 1703)
—Then I Met My Sister. (p. 1729)
—Thirty Sunsets. (p. 1735)
Derkazarian, Susan. Dairy. (p. 400)
—Fruits & Vegetables. (p. 645)
—You Have Head Lice! (p. 1975)
—You Have Healthy Bones! (p. 1975)
Derke, Connie Butterfield. Mommy Has 1 Foot: Learning about Numbers - Learning about People. Smith, Tracy, illus. (p. 1162)
Derkez, Linda. Chip's Sharing Day. Doehring, Phoebe, illus. (p. 308)
Derkins, Susie. Immune System. (p. 861)
—Irish Republican Army. (p. 888)
—Legionnaire's Disease. (p. 990)
—Meltdown at Three Mile Island. (p. 1125)
Derkow-Disselbeck, Barbara & Kirsch, Dieter. Anna, Schmidt und Oskar (p. 85)
Derks, Scott. Working Americans 1880-2003: At War. (p. 1952)
Derksen, Barbara Ann. Alexis Learns to Trust: Shih-Tzu Puppy Adventures. (p. 37)
—Scruffles Finds a Home. (p. 1533)
Derner, Seth, jt. auth. see Reardon, Mark.
Dernoot, Peter R. Van, see Van Dernoot, Peter R.
DeRoche, Ed, et al. Character: A Guide for Middle Grade Students. (p. 291)
Deroche, Ed, et al. Character: A Guide for Middle Grade Students. (p. 291)
Derolf, Shane. Crayon Box That Talked. (p. 377)
Derom, Dirk. Pigeon & Pigeonette. Verroken, Sarah, illus. (p. 1357)
Derome, Pierre-André, illus. see Gauthier, Gilles.
Derome, Pierre-Andre, jt. auth. see Gauthier, Gilles.
Derome, Pierre-Andre, tr. see Gauthier, Gilles.
Derong, Gary. Milwaukee Brewers. (p. 1144)
—Milwaukee Bucks. (p. 1145)
DeRoo, John, ed. see James, Will.
DeRosa Bodie, Leona. One Is Fun. Davis, Catherine Baptista, illus. (p. 1295)
DeRosa, Dee, illus. see Hall, Kirsten.
DeRosa, Nancy. Lazy Robert. Verona Publishing, illus. (p. 981)
DeRose, Kim, illus. see Garfield, Yvette & Azima, Cricket.
DeRosier, Cher. Pea & the Grape. DeRosier, Cher & Cerone, Sal, illus. (p. 1331)
—Plight of the Jelly Bean. Contreras, Gilbert, illus. (p. 1374)
DeRosier, Melissa, jt. auth. see Brightwood, Laura.
DeRouin, Edward M. North Shore Line - Interurban Freight. (p. 1265)
Derovan, David. Israeli Culture in Perspective. (p. 893)
Derr, Louise Barrett. Experiencing Bible Science: An Activity Book for Children. (p. 548)
—Experiencing Bible Science. (p. 548)
Derrick, David G., Jr. Animals Don't, So I Won't! (p. 82)
—I'm the Scariest Thing in the Jungle! (p. 860)
—Play with Your Food. (p. 1372)
—Sid the Squid: And the Search for the Perfect Job. (p. 1572)
Derrick Patricia. Beaser the Bear's Rocky Mountain Christmas. Hoch, Doug, illus. (p. 152)
Derrick, Patricia. Dody the Dog Has a Rainbow. Martinez, J-P Loppo, illus. (p. 460)
—Farley the Ferret of Farkleberry Farm. Martinez, J-P Loppo, illus. (p. 573)
—Mr. Walrus & the Old School Bus. Martinez, J-P Loppo, illus. (p. 1187)
—Rickity & Snickity at the Balloon Fiesta. Martinez, J-P Loppo, illus. (p. 1470)
—Riley the Rhinoceros. Martinez, J-P Loppo, illus. (p. 1472)
—Sly the Dragonfly. Martinez, J-P Loppo, illus. (p. 1591)
Derrick, Patricia & O'Neil, Shirley. Rathbone the Rat. Martinez, J-P Loppo, illus. (p. 1440)
Derrick, Patricia & Sibbett, Joyce. Montgomery the Moose Can Shake His Caboose. Martinez, J-P Loppo, illus. (p. 1170)
Derrick, Paul. Learning the Night Sky. (p. 985)
d'Errico, Camilla & Sanders, Scott. Camilla d'Errico's Burn. d'Errico, Camilla, illus. (p. 256)
Derryberry, Larry. Vampire Snacks. (p. 1832)
Dershowitz, Yosef, illus. see Weinbach, Shaindel.
Derstine, Charlene, illus. see Martin, Mary.
Derstine, Elise Hofer, jt. auth. see Ajmera, Maya.
Derting, Kimberly. Body Finder. (p. 207)
—Dead Silence. (p. 417)
—Desires of the Dead. (p. 430)
—Essence. (p. 536)
—Last Echo. (p. 977)
—Offering: A Pledge Novel. (p. 1279)
—Offering. (p. 1279)
—Pledge. (p. 1373)
—Replaced. (p. 1461)
—Taking. (p. 1697)
Deru, Myriam, illus. see Grimm, Jacob, et al.
deRubertis, Barbara. Alexander Anteater's Amazing Act. Alley, R. W., illus. (p. 36)
—Bobby Baboon's Banana Be-Bop. Alley, R. W., illus. (p. 206)
—Coleccion para Kate (A Collection for Kate) Fiammenghi, Gioia, illus. (p. 339)
—Corky Cub's Crazy Caps. Alley, R. W., illus. (p. 367)
DeRubertis, Barbara. Cuenta con Pablo: Math Matters en Espanol. Thornburgh, Rebecca, illus. (p. 389)
deRubertis, Barbara. Deena y su centavo de la Suerte. Holub, Joan & Fisher, Cynthia, illus. (p. 422)
—Deena Y Su Centavo de la Suerte; Deena's Lucky Penny. (p. 422)
—Dilly Dog's Dizzy Dancing. Alley, R. W., illus. (p. 440)
Derubertis, Barbara. Eddie Elephant's Exciting Egg-Sitting. (p. 503)
deRubertis, Barbara. Eddie Elephant's Exciting Egg-Sitting. Alley, R. W., illus. (p. 503)
Derubertis, Barbara. Frances Frog's Forever Friend. (p. 627)
deRubertis, Barbara. Frances Frog's Forever Friend. Alley, R. W., illus. (p. 627)
Derubertis, Barbara. Gertie Gorilla's Glorious Gift. (p. 667)
deRubertis, Barbara. Gertie Gorilla's Glorious Gift. Alley, R. W., illus. (p. 667)
Derubertis, Barbara. Hanna Hippo's Horrible Hiccups. (p. 742)
deRubertis, Barbara. Hanna Hippo's Horrible Hiccups. Alley, R. W., illus. (p. 742)
Derubertis, Barbara. Izzy Impala's Imaginary Illnesses. (p. 901)
deRubertis, Barbara. Izzy Impala's Imaginary Illnesses. Alley, R. W., illus. (p. 901)
Derubertis, Barbara. Jeremy Jackrabbit's Jumping Journey. (p. 913)
deRubertis, Barbara. Jeremy Jackrabbit's Jumping Journey. Alley, R. W., illus. (p. 913)
—Kylie Kangaroo's Karate Kickers. Alley, R. W., illus. (p. 969)
—Lana Llama's Little Lamb. Alley, R. W., illus. (p. 972)
DeRubertis, Barbara. Let's Celebrate Columbus Day. Sperling, Thomas, illus. (p. 995)
—Let's Celebrate Constitution Day. (p. 995)
—Let's Celebrate Earth Day. (p. 995)
—Let's Celebrate Independence Day. (p. 995)
—Let's Celebrate Labor Day. (p. 995)
deRubertis, Barbara. Let's Celebrate Martin Luther King, Jr. Day. (p. 995)
DeRubertis, Barbara. Let's Celebrate Martin Luther King, Jr. Day. Griffith, Gershom, illus. (p. 995)
deRubertis, Barbara. Let's Celebrate Martin Luther King, Jr. Day. Griffith, Gershom, illus. (p. 995)
DeRubertis, Barbara. Let's Celebrate Presidents' Day: George Washington & Abraham Lincoln. Griffith, Gershom, illus. (p. 995)
—Let's Celebrate Thanksgiving Day. Sperling, Thomas, illus. (p. 995)
deRubertis, Barbara. Let's Celebrate Thanksgiving Day. Sperling, Thomas, illus. (p. 995)
DeRubertis, Barbara. Let's Celebrate Veterans Day. (p. 995)
deRubertis, Barbara. Maxwell Moose's Mountain Monster. Alley, R. W., illus. (p. 1112)
—Nina Nandu's Nervous Noggin. Alley, R. W., illus. (p. 1256)
—Oliver Otter's Own Office. Alley, R. W., illus. (p. 1285)
—Polly Porcupine's Painting Prize. Alley, R. W., illus. (p. 1381)
—Quentin Quokka's Quick Questions. Alley, R. W., illus. (p. 1425)
—Rosie Raccoon's Rock & Roll Raft. Alley, R. W., illus. (p. 1490)
Derubertis, Barbara. Sammy Skunk's Super Sniffer. Alley, R. W., illus. (p. 1508)
deRubertis, Barbara. Sammy Skunk's Super Sniffer. Alley, R. W., illus. (p. 1508)
Derubertis, Barbara. Tessa Tiger's Temper Tantrums. Alley, R. W., illus. (p. 1723)
deRubertis, Barbara. Tessa Tiger's Temper Tantrums. Alley, R. W., illus. (p. 1723)
Derubertis, Barbara. Umma Ungka's Unusual Umbrella. Alley, R. W., illus. (p. 1810)
deRubertis, Barbara. Umma Ungka's Unusual Umbrella. Alley, R. W., illus. (p. 1810)
Derubertis, Barbara. Victor Vicuna's Volcano Vacation. Alley, R. W., illus. (p. 1840)
deRubertis, Barbara. Victor Vicuna's Volcano Vacation. Alley, R. W., illus. (p. 1840)
Derubertis, Barbara. Walter Warthog's Wonderful Wagon. Alley, R. W., illus. (p. 1856)
deRubertis, Barbara. Walter Warthog's Wonderful Wagon. Alley, R. W., illus. (p. 1856)
Derubertis, Barbara. Xavier Ox's Xylophone Experiment. Alley, R. W., illus. (p. 1967)
deRubertis, Barbara. Xavier Ox's Xylophone Experiment. Alley, R. W., illus. (p. 1967)
—Yoko Yak's Yakety Yakking. Alley, R. W., illus. (p. 1972)
Derubertis, Barbara. Zachary Zebra's Zippity Zooming. Alley, R. W., illus. (p. 1984)
deRubertis, Barbara. Zachary Zebra's Zippity Zooming. Alley, R. W., illus. (p. 1984)
deRubertis, Barbara, jt. auth. see deRubertis, Barbara.
deRubertis, Barbara & DeRubertis, Barbara. Alexander Anteater's Amazing Act. Alley, R. W., illus. (p. 36)
—Bobby Baboon's Banana Be-Bop. Alley, R. W., illus. (p. 206)
—Corky Cub's Crazy Caps. Alley, R. W., illus. (p. 367)
—Dilly Dog's Dizzy Dancing. Alley, R. W., illus. (p. 440)
—Eddie Elephant's Exciting Egg-Sitting. Alley, R. W., illus. (p. 503)
—Frances Frog's Forever Friend. Alley, R. W., illus. (p. 627)

—Gertie Gorilla's Glorious Gift. Alley, R. W., illus. (p. 667)
—Hanna Hippo's Horrible Hiccups. Alley, R. W., illus. (p. 742)
—Izzy Impala's Imaginary Illnesses. Alley, R. W., illus. (p. 901)
—Jeremy Jackrabbit's Jumping Journey. Alley, R. W., illus. (p. 913)
—Kylie Kangaroo's Karate Kickers. Alley, R. W., illus. (p. 969)
—Lana Llama's Little Lamb. Alley, R. W., illus. (p. 972)
—Maxwell Moose's Mountain Monster. Alley, R. W., illus. (p. 1112)
—Nina Nandu's Nervous Noggin. Alley, R. W., illus. (p. 1256)
—Oliver Otter's Own Office. Alley, R. W., illus. (p. 1285)
—Polly Porcupine's Painting Prizes. Alley, R. W., illus. (p. 1381)
—Quentin Quokka's Quick Questions. Alley, R. W., illus. (p. 1425)
—Rosie Raccoon's Rock & Roll Raft. Alley, R. W., illus. (p. 1490)
—Sammy Skunk's Super Sniffer. Alley, R. W., illus. (p. 1508)
—Tessa Tiger's Temper Tantrums. Alley, R. W., illus. (p. 1723)
—Umma Ungka's Unusual Umbrella. Alley, R. W., illus. (p. 1810)
—Victor Vicuna's Volcano Vacation. Alley, R. W., illus. (p. 1840)
—Walter Warthog's Wonderful Wagon. Alley, R. W., illus. (p. 1856)
—Xavier Ox's Xylophone Experiment. Alley, R. W., illus. (p. 1967)
—Yoko Yak's Yakety Yakking. Alley, R. W., illus. (p. 1972)
—Zachary Zebra's Zippity Zooming. Alley, R. W., illus. (p. 1984)
deRubertis, Barbara & Roser, Nancy. Let's Read Together: Resource Guide. (p. 1000)
DeRungs, Tina, illus. see Oksanen, Sue & Zeisler, Riley.
Derwent, Lavinia. Return to Sula Rush. Peter, illus. (p. 1465)
—Song of Sula (p. 1611)
—Sula (p. 1673)
Derzipilski, Kathleen. Indiana. (p. 871)
Derzipilski, Kathleen & Hantula, Richard. Indiana. (p. 871)
Derzipilski, Kathleen & Hudson, Amanda. Arizona. (p. 98)
Des Chenes, Elizabeth, ed. see Friedman, Lauri S.
Des Chenes, Elizabeth, ed. see Metcalf, Tom.
Des Chenes, Elizabeth, jt. ed. see Bily, Cynthia A.
Des Chenes, Elizabeth, jt. ed. see Egendorf, Laura K.
Des Chenes, Elizabeth, jt. ed. see Friedman, Lauri S.
Des Chenes, Elizabeth, jt. ed. see Langwith, Jacqueline.
Des Chenes, Elizabeth, jt. ed. see Rosenthal, Beth.
Des Chenes, Elizabeth, ed. Internet. (p. 880)
—Natural Gas. (p. 1235)
—Pollution. (p. 1381)
Des Forges, Roger V. & S., John. Asian World, 600-1500. (p. 106)
Des Fosses, John. Cat Lottery. (p. 278)
Desai, Naina. Fun Jungle. (p. 648)
Desaix, Deborah Durland, illus. see Ruelle, Karen Gray.
DeSaix, Deborah Durland & Ruelle, Karen Gray. Peter's War. DeSaix, Deborah Durland, illus. (p. 1347)
Desalle, Nicole. I Am Clean, Healthy. (p. 832)
—Safe at Home. (p. 1502)
—Safe at Play. (p. 1502)
—Safe at School. (p. 1502)
DeSalle, Rob. Brain: A 21st Century Look at a 400 Million Year Old Organ. Wynne, Patricia, illus. (p. 221)
Desannoy, Margot. Alex & the Amazing Dr. Frankenslime. (p. 35)
DeSantis, Debi. Bunch of Giggles & Hugs. (p. 241)
DeSantis, Susan, illus. see Kesselring, Susan.
DeSantis, Susan, illus. see Moncure, Jane Belk.
Desarthe, Agnes, jt. auth. see Ponti, Claude.
Desaulniers, Kristi. Northern America. Gritzner, Charles F., ed. (p. 1265)
Desautels, Denise. Marathonienne. Chronopoulos, Maria, illus. (p. 1091)
Desautels, Jodi. There Were Always Noises. (p. 1730)
Desautels, Stacie, illus. see Betts, McKenzie Leigh.
Desberg, Stephen & Marini, Enrico. Escorpión: La Cruz de Pedro. (p. 535)
—Escorpión: El Secreto del Papá (p. 535)
—Escorpión: La Marca del Diablo (p. 535)
—In the Name of the Father. (p. 866)
Desbordes, Astrid. Edmond, the Moonlit Party. Boutavant, Marc, illus. (p. 504)
Desbordes, Astrid & Martin, Pauline. Daydreams of a Solitary Hamster. (p. 415)
Descamps, Luc. Dark Numbers. (p. 408)
Descartes, Rene. Discurso del Metodo: Seguido de la Busqueda de la Verdad Mediante la Luz Natural. Florian S, Victor, tr. (p. 450)
Desch, Sandra Lee. Erika Flowers. Seeds of Grace. Phipps, Catherine Wood, illus. (p. 533)
DESCHAMPS, NICHOLA, jt. auth. see Equipo Staff.
Desclot, Miquel. Snow White. Blanch, Ignasi, illus. (p. 1599)
Desclouds, Rick. Jackie, Luther, & I. (p. 903)
—My Year with the ESL Boys. (p. 1222)
Descola, Philippe. Diversité des Natures, Diversité des Cultures. (p. 454)
Descoteaux, Chad. Once upon A Crime Syndicate: A mafia fairy Tale. (p. 1292)
Desenfants, Millie. Long Ago Sally. (p. 1046)
Deseret Book Company Staff, contrib. by. Story to Tell: The Classic Book of Virtues for Children. (p. 1663)
Desetta, Al, ed. see Youth Communication.
Desetta, Al, jt. ed. see Educators for Social Responsibility Staff.
Desharnais, Margo, illus. see Katris Gonis, Theofania.
DeShazer, Dennis & Green, Jon, creators. Music Is for Children: Kit B Advanced (p. 1193)
DeShazo, Sharon B., illus. see Jones, Alice Eley.
Deshmukh, Manisha. Chinu's Day Out. (p. 308)
Deshone, Jerry Michael. Bear in Mind. (p. 151)
DeShong, Molly, et al. Which One Doesn't Belong? Fd163. (p. 1911)
Deshpande, Sanjay. In Defense of the Realm: Graphic Novel. Sharma, Lalit Kumar, illus. (p. 863)
Deshpande, Shashi. 3 Novels. (p. 1991)
DeSica, Melissa. Gecko & Mosquito. (p. 659)
DeSica, Melissa, illus. see Kakugawa, Frances.
Design Eye Publishing, Ltd., et al. Amazing Automata — Dinosaurs! (p. 53)
—Amazing Automata — Pirates! (p. 53)
Design, Mada, illus. see Matheis, Mickie.
Designs, Marion, photos by see Crews, G. S.
Desimini, Lisa, illus. see Aida, Arlene.
Desimini, Lisa, illus. see Annino, J G.
Desimini, Lisa, illus. see Annino, Jan Godown.
Desimini, Lisa, illus. see Gifford, Peggy.
Desimini, Lisa, illus. see Lewis, J. Patrick.
DeSimone, Corkey Hay. Planet Hue. DeSimone, Corkey Hay, illus. (p. 1367)
DeSimone, Suzanne, illus. see Kilodavis, Cheryl.
DeSio, Delores. Annie's Journey Through the Golden Door (p. 87)
Desio, Delores. Legend of Ruby O'Grady: Grandma Was A Hippie. (p. 988)
DeSio, Delores . Up a Tree with Mary Mcphee: A Mystery for Children. (p. 1824)
Desir, C. Fault Line. (p. 577)
Desira, Angela, illus. see Sinclair, Mehded Maryam.
Desisti, Sam F. Paco & Angelina Stories (p. 1317)
Desisto, Allie, jt. auth. see Goldstein, Sam.
Desjardins, Dawn. Leopold's Long Awaited Leap Year Birthday. (p. 993)
Desjardins, Margaret M. Murky, Quirky, Beserky Math. Bohart, Lisa, illus. (p. 1192)
Desjardins, Vincent, illus. see Furstinger, Nancy.
Desjarlait, Robert, illus. see Coulson, Art.
Deskcube, illus. see Stevens, A. P.
Deskins, Charlotte H. Tales from Poplar Hollow. Allen, Dana K., illus. (p. 1701)
Deskov, Vladimir, ed. see Ives, Bob.
Deslauriers, Anne. Fee Dentiste. Begin, Jean-Guy, illus. (p. 580)
Desmarais, Kathleen. History Odyssey, Early Modern (level Two) (p. 783)
Desmarattes, J. Lyonel. Atali. (p. 111)
—Lakòl Medam Yo. (p. 972)
DesMarteau, Alicia, jt. auth. see Dakos, Kalli.
Desmarteau, Claudine, jt. auth. see Larrondo, Valérie.
Desmazieres, Sandra. Emma & Her Friends: A Book about Colors. (p. 519)
—Emma y Sus Amigos: Un Libro Sobre los Colores. (p. 520)
Desmet, Sara. Scared Silly. Desmet, Sara, illus. (p. 1519)
Desmet, Wendy. My Dad Is Different. (p. 1201)
Desmoinaux, Christel, illus. see Pearlman, Bobby.
Desmoineaux, Christel, illus. see Hanna, Virginie.
Desmond, Elisabeth. God s Little Adventures Destiny & Dillon. (p. 690)
Desmond, Hillary, illus. see Beall, Kirsten.
Desmond, Jenni. Eric, the Boy Who Lost His Gravity. (p. 533)
—Red Cat, Blue Cat. (p. 1453)
Desmond, Jenni, creator. Blue Whale. (p. 203)
Desmond, Ray. Great Natural History Books & Their Creators. (p. 717)
Desnick, Chaim. Little Room. Zwebner, Janet, illus. (p. 1036)
Desnos, Robert. Voyage in Burgundy. Sanders, Todd & Taeger, Oonagh, trs. (p. 1850)
Desonie, Dana. Atmosphere: Air Pollution & Its Effects. (p. 113)
—Biosphere: Ecosystems & Biodiversity Loss. (p. 190)
—Climate. (p. 332)
—Geosphere: The Land & Its Uses. (p. 665)
—Humans & the Natural Environment. (p. 826)
—Hydrosphere: Freshwater Systems & Pollution. (p. 831)
—Oceans: How We Use the Seas. (p. 1277)
—Our Fragile Planet Set, 8-Volumes. (p. 1308)
—Polar Regions: Human Impacts. (p. 1379)
DeSosa-Rocha, Darla. Olympos the Selfish Squirrel. (p. 1288)
Desoto, Ernestine. Sugar Bear Story. (p. 1672)
deSouza, Sabrina. Catarbie Conspiracy: Book 1 of the Houkura Series. Lindsey, Michael, illus. (p. 278)
DeSpain, Christine. And Please Take the Banana off Your Head. (p. 71)
DeSpain, Pleasant. Dancing Turtle: A Folktale from Brazil. Boston, David, illus. (p. 403)
—Eleven Nature Tales: A Multicultural Journey. Shlichta, Joe, illus. (p. 512)
—Eleven Turtle Tales: Adventure Tales from Around the World. (p. 512)
—Emerald Lizard: Fifteen Latin American Tales to Tell in English & Spanish. (p. 517)
—Magic Pot: Story Cove. Wrenn, Tom, illus. (p. 1073)
—Sweet Land of Story: Thirty-Six American Tales to Tell. (p. 1690)
—Tales of Cats Bell, Don, tr. (p. 1702)
—Tales of Enchantment Bell, Don, tr. (p. 1702)
—Tales of Heroes Bell, Don, illus. (p. 1702)
—Tales of Holidays Bell, Don, illus. (p. 1702)
—Tales of Insects Bell, Don, illus. (p. 1702)
—Tales of Nonsense & Tomfoolery Bell, Don, illus. (p. 1702)
—Tales of Tricksters: Books of Nine Lives Bell, Don, illus. (p. 1703)
—Tales of Tricksters. Bell, Don, illus. (p. 1703)
—Tales of Wisdom & Justice Bell, Don, illus. (p. 1703)
—Tales to Frighten & Delight Bell, Don, tr. (p. 1703)
—Thirty-Three Multicultural Tales to Tell. Shlichta, Joe, illus. (p. 1735)
Despeyroux, Denise. Big Book of Vampires. Falcone, Fernando, illus. (p. 179)
Despeyroux, Denise & Poe, Edgar Allen. Dark Graphic Tales by Edgar Allan Poe. Serratosa, Miquel, illus. (p. 407)
Desplanche, Vincent, illus. see Larousse Mexico Staff, ed.
Desplechin, Mar. Verte. (p. 1837)
Després, Geneviève, illus. see Itani, Frances.
Despres, Genevieve, illus. see MacGregor, Roy.
Desputeaux, Helene, illus. see Douglas, Ann.
Desputeaux, Helene, illus. see Munsch, Robert & Kusugak, Michael.
Desputeaux, Helene, illus. see Munsch, Robert.
Desrocher, Jack. Health Zone (p. 758)
Desrocher, Jack, illus. see Doeden, Matt.
Desrocher, Jack, illus. see Donovan, Sandy.
Desrocher, Jack, illus. see Johnson, Rebecca L.
Desrocher, Jack, illus. see Leder, Jane Mersky & Donovan, Sandy.
Desrocher, Jack, illus. see Nelson, Sara Kirsten.
Desrochers, Diane O. Little Tree That Would Be Great. Boucher, Julie, illus. (p. 1037)
DesRochers, Diane O., jt. auth. see Zwald, John.
Desrochers, Lisa. Last Rite. (p. 978)
—Original Sin. (p. 1304)
—Personal Demons. (p. 1344)
Desrosiers, Sylvie. Aimez-Vous la Musique? Sylvestre, Daniel, illus. (p. 30)
—Hocus Pocus. Simard, Rémy, illus. (p. 787)
—Mais Qui Va Trouver le Tresor? (p. 1077)
—Qui Veut Entrer dans la Legende? Sylvestre, Daniel, illus. (p. 1427)
Desrosiers, Sylvie & Franson, Leanne. Je Suis Thomas. (p. 911)
DesRosiers, Trisha, illus. see Stokes, Brenda.
Dessen, Macl. Elephant Seals. (p. 511)
—Let's Go Snorkeling! Use Place Value Understanding. (p. 997)
—Look Out for the Mosquito! (p. 1050)
Dessen, Sarah. Along for the Ride. (p. 48)
—Dreamland. (p. 484)
—How to Deal: Someone Like You & That Summer. (p. 816)
—How to Deal. (p. 816)
—Just Listen. (p. 939)
—Keeping the Moon. (p. 947)
—Lock & Key. (p. 1045)
—Moon & More. (p. 1171)
—Saint Anything. (p. 1503)
—Someone Like You. (p. 1609)
—That Summer. (p. 1726)
—This Lullaby. (p. 1737)
—Truth about Forever. (p. 1794)
—What Happened to Goodbye. (p. 1885)
Desso, Karen. Early Learning Reading Games: Levels A-D. (p. 493)
DeStefano, Anthony. Little Star. Elliott, Mark, illus. (p. 1036)
DeStefano, Lauren. Burning Kingdoms. (p. 244)
—Curious Tale of the In-Between. (p. 394)
—Fever (p. 583)
—Fever. (p. 583)
—Fiebre. (p. 583)
—Perfect Ruin. White, Teagan, illus. (p. 1342)
—Sever. (p. 1555)
—Wither (p. 1942)
—Wither. (p. 1942)
Destefano, Merrie, jt. auth. see Berry, Bob.
DeStefano, Stephen, illus. see Tanguay, Dave.
DeStefano, Susan. Symbols of America. (p. 1693)
Destiny, A. & Berne, Emma Carlson. Sunset Ranch. (p. 1677)
Destiny, A. & Hapka, Catherine. Lessons in Love (p. 993)
Destiny, A. & Helms, Rhonda. Never Too Late. (p. 1243)
—Portrait of Us. (p. 1386)
—Sparks in Scotland. (p. 1622)
Destiny, A. & Kahler, A. R. Love Is in the Air. (p. 1060)
Destiny, A. & Lenhard, Elizabeth. Our Song. (p. 1310)
Destiny Images Staff, illus. see Burstein, John.
DeStout, Carole. My Dad Wears Striped Pajamas. Heath, Paul Reaves, illus. (p. 1201)
Destra, Ronald. Hoppy the Frog. (p. 797)
DeStrulle, Arlene & Johnson, Tora. Guide to Freshwater Animals Without Backbones. Sayre, Tamara, illus. (p. 730)
DeTellis, Luc. Who's There: 101 Knock Knock Jokes for Kids. (p. 1921)
—Who's There Again? 101 More Knock Knock Jokes for Kids. (p. 1921)
Deters, Kevin. Care Bears Sing & Play: Follow-the-Lights Piano Songbook. (p. 266)
Detlefsen, Lisl H. Time for Cranberries. Henry, Jed, illus. (p. 1751)
Detmold, Edward J., illus. see Kipling, Rudyard.
Detmold, Maurice, illus. see Kipling, Rudyard.
Dettman, Eileen. Determo: The true story of a very clever North Carolina red Squirrel. (p. 431)
Dettman, Eric. Any Day Friends. (p. 90)
Detweiler, Katelyn. Immaculate. (p. 861)
Detwiler, Susan. Fine Life for a Country Mouse. Detwiler, Susan, illus. (p. 589)
Detwiler, Susan, illus. see Cohn, Scotti.
Detwiler, Susan, illus. see Kay, Helen.
Detwiler, Susan, illus. see Perry, Phyllis J.
Deubreau, Sharon. Heather & Avery & the Magic Kite. Pileggi, Steve, illus. (p. 760)
Deuchars, Marion. Draw Paint Print Like the Great Artists. (p. 481)
—Let's Make More Great Placemat Art. (p. 999)
—Let's Make Some Great Art. (p. 999)
—Let's Make Some Great Fingerprint Art. (p. 999)
Deucher, Sybil, jt. auth. see Wheeler, Opal.
Deuker, Carl. Gym Candy. (p. 733)
—Heart of a Champion. (p. 759)
—High Heat. (p. 777)
—Night Hoops. (p. 1253)
—On the Devil's Court. (p. 1290)
—Swagger. (p. 1688)
Deuker, Carl & Perry, Thomas. Runner. (p. 1497)
Deutch, Yvonne. Animals Everywhere: A Pop-Up Adventure. Woodward, Jonathan, illus. (p. 82)
Deutsch, Barry. Hereville: How Mirka Got Her Sword. (p. 771)
—Hereville: How Mirka Met a Meteorite. (p. 771)
Deutsch, Barry & Hansen Literary Agency Staff. Hereville: How Mirka Got Her Sword. (p. 771)
Deutsch, David. In Search of the Little People. (p. 865)
Deutsch, Jessica. Downhill Skiing for Fun! (p. 474)
Deutsch, Neil. Rose & the Pelican. (p. 1489)
Deutsch, Stacia. Book of Life Movie Novelization. (p. 211)
—Disney Fairies - Legend of the Neverbeast: The Chapter Book. (p. 451)
—Disney Fairies: the Pirate Fairy: the Chapter Book. (p. 451)
—Mean Ghouls. (p. 1116)
—Rotten Apple #1: Mean Ghouls. (p. 1490)
Deutsch, Stacia, adapted by. Cloudy with a Chance of Meatballs 2 Movie Novelization. (p. 335)
Deutsch, Stacia & Cohon, Rhody. Bell's Breakthrough. Wenzel, David, illus. (p. 163)
—Ben Franklin's Fame. Francis, Guy, illus. (p. 163)
—Carlos Mencia. (p. 270)
—Disney's Dream. Wenzel, David, illus. (p. 453)
—Hot Pursuit: Murder in Mississippi. Orback, Craig, illus. (p. 802)
—In the Stars. (p. 867)
—Jermaine Dupri. (p. 913)
—John B. Herrington. (p. 921)
—King's Courage. Wenzel, David, illus. (p. 960)
—Life of a Star: Set Of 6. (p. 1011)
—Life of a Star: Text Pairs. (p. 1011)
—Lincoln's Legacy. Wenzel, David, illus. (p. 1019)
—Lucky Phoo. (p. 1063)
—Martin Lawrence. (p. 1097)
—Sacagawea's Strength. Wenzel, David T. & Wenzel, David, illus. (p. 1500)
—Samuel L. Jackson. (p. 1509)
Deutsch, Stacia & Hargreaves, Roger. Mr. Men Little Miss Guide to Life. (p. 1185)
Deutsch, Tehilla. Dollars & Sense. Zimmer, Glenn, illus. (p. 463)
Deutsch/Cohon. Disney's Dream. Wenzel, David, illus. (p. 453)
—Lincoln's Legacy. Wenzel, David, illus. (p. 1019)
Devadasan, Rashmi Ruth. Kumari Loves a Monster: Kumariyin Ratcaca Katalan. Shyam, illus. (p. 968)
Devaney, Adam. What? (p. 1878)
—When? (p. 1901)
—Where? (p. 1906)
—Who? (p. 1914)
Devaney, Adam, illus. see Adams, Michelle Medlock.
Devaney, Adam, illus. see Reasoner, Charles.
Devaney, Sherri. Ripped from the Headlines: The Death Penalty. (p. 1474)
Devaney, Sherri, et al. Barack Obama. (p. 137)
Devant, Jourdan. Little Ladybug. (p. 1030)
Devantier, Alecia T., jt. auth. see Turkington, Carol A.
Devantier, Alecia T. & Turkington, Carol. Extraordinary Jobs in Health & Science. (p. 555)
Devantier, Alecia T. & Turkington, Carol A. Extraordinary Jobs with Animals. (p. 555)
Devard, Nancy, illus. see Joy, N.
Devard, Nancy, illus. see Scholastic, Inc. Staff & Hooks, Gwendolyn.
Devard, Nancy, illus. see Scholastic, Inc. Staff & Taylor-Butler, Christine.
Devargas, Casey Anthony. Kindergarten Treasure. (p. 957)
Developed in Association with the Gallup Organization Staff, ed. see Hernandez, Roger E.
Developed in Association with the Gallup Organization Staff, ed. see Marcovitz, Hal.
Developed in Association with the Gallup Organization Staff, ed. see Owens, Peter.
Developed in Association with the Gallup Organization Staff, ed. see Snyder, Gail.
Developmental Studies Center Staff. AfterSchool KidzMath 3-6 Games. (p. 29)
Deveny, Mary Alice. Pockets: Book: Nonfiction_Juvenile Sweetman, Gary W., photos by. (p. 1375)
Dever, Joe. Caverns of Kalte. (p. 282)
Deverell, Christine. Pop-up Pets. Deverell, Richard & King, Chris, illus. (p. 1384)
Deverell, Richard, illus. see Deverell, Christine.
Deverell, Richard, illus. see Jones, Graham.
Deverell, Richard & King, Chris. Sparkly Sea. (p. 1622)
Devereux, Cecily, ed. see Montgomery, L. M.
Devereux, Jan. Poe the Crow. Devereux, Jan, ed. (p. 1375)
Devernois, Elsa. Vez Mas. Gay, Michel, illus. (p. 1839)
Devers, Joe. Dungeons of Torgar. (p. 490)
Devers, Mark. Turtles. (p. 1798)
Devers, William J., III, et al. Every Teacher's Thematic Booklist. (p. 543)
deVet, L. J. Teddy's Christmas Wish. Zabarylo-Duma, Ewa, illus. (p. 1713)
Deveze, Winky. Hewitch. Neate, Andy, illus. (p. 774)
Devi, Chandra, jt. auth. see Ma, Jyoti.
Devi, Dulari. Following My Paint Brush. (p. 612)
Devillers, Edith, tr. see Papillon, Margaret.
DeVillers, Julia. Cleared for Takeoff. Pooler, Paige, illus. (p. 330)
—How My Private Personal Journal Became a Bestseller. (p. 811)
—Liberty Porter, First Daughter. Pooler, Paige, illus. (p. 1005)
—New Girl in Town. Pooler, Paige, illus. (p. 1244)
DeVillers, Julia, jt. auth. see Bryan, Sabrina.
DeVillers, Julia & Roy, Jennifer. Double Feature. (p. 473)
—Triple Trouble. (p. 1787)
DeVillers, Julia & Roy, Jennifer Rozines. Double Feature. (p. 473)
—Take Two. (p. 1697)
—Times Squared. (p. 1754)
—Trading Faces. (p. 1776)
—Trading Faces. Smith, Alison, illus. (p. 1776)
Devillier, Christy. Betsy Ross. (p. 172)
—Chameleons. (p. 289)
—Clara Barton. (p. 326)
DeVillier, Christy. Corythosaurus. (p. 368)
DeVillier, Christy. Davy Crockett. (p. 411)
DeVillier, Christy. Deinonychus. (p. 424)
DeVillier, Christy. Helen Keller. (p. 762)
DeVillier, Christy. Molly Pitcher. (p. 1161)
—Nathan Hale. (p. 1231)
—Spinosaurus. (p. 1628)
DeVillier, Christy. Styracosaurus. (p. 1670)
DeVillier, Christy. Troodon. (p. 1788)
Devillier, Christy & ABDO Publishing Company Staff. Dinosaurs Set 3 (p. 445)
DeVince, James, ed. see Lewis, Carolyn.
DeVince, James, jt. auth. see Lewis, Carolyn.
Devine, Eric. Dare Me. (p. 406)
—Press Play. (p. 1397)
—Tap Out. (p. 1705)

D

Devine, Ginger. Hooray for the Circus: A Story of Sam the Lamb. (p. 796)
—Missing Goose Egg: A Sam the Lamb Mystery. (p. 1152)
—Missing Pencils: A Sam the Lamb Mystery. (p. 1152)
Devine, Mary A. Float Plan: Study Guide for Use with Takashi's Voyage. (p. 605)
Devine, Monica. Carry Me Mama Paquin, Pauline, illus. (p. 271)
—Hanna Bear's Christmas Cassidy, Sean, illus. (p. 742)
—Kayak Girl. Dwyer, Mindy, illus. (p. 946)
Devine, Robert. Barney of the Serengeti. (p. 139)
DeVita, James. Silenced: A Novel. (p. 1575)
—Silenced. (p. 1575)
Devita, James, jt. auth. see DeVita, James.
DeVita, James & Devita, James. Silenced. (p. 1575)
DeVito, Anthony T., illus. see Lucia, Doriane.
DeVito, Carlo. Encyclopedia of International Organized Crime. (p. 525)
DeVito, Michael A., ed. see Smith, Brian.
Devlin, Harry, illus. see Devlin, Wende.
Devlin, Ivy. Low Red Moon. (p. 1061)
Devlin, Jane V. Hattie the Bad. Berger, Joe, illus. (p. 753)
Devlin, Wende. Cranberry Halloween. Devlin, Harry, illus. (p. 376)
—Cranberry Thanksgiving. Devlin, Harry, illus. (p. 376)
—Old Black Witch! Devlin, Harry, illus. (p. 1283)
DeVoe, James E. Daydreamer: The Adventures of Dylan Lawson & His Unbridled Imagination. (p. 415)
DeVogt, Rindia M. Tommy Hare & the Color Purple Trogdon, Kathryn, illus. (p. 1765)
Devol, Laura. To Be a Frog. Boone, Patti, illus. (p. 1758)
Devoles, Margaret. My Aunt Calls Me Saree. (p. 1196)
DeVoogd, Glenn, jt. auth. see McLaughlin, Maureen.
DeVore & Sons, creator. African American Family Heirloom Bible-KJV. (p. 27)
Devore, David, jt. auth. see Tessie.
Devore, David Y. Tessie, ed. Happy Birthday to Me. (p. 745)
DeVore, Janna. Ballerina Cookbook (p. 134)
Devore, Janna. Ballerina Cookbook. (p. 134)
DeVore, Sheryl, et al. Birding Illinois (p. 191)
DeVorkin, David, jt. auth. see Weitekamp, Margaret A.
Devorsine, Sally. Now I Know... That I Wouldn't Be Who I Think I Am, Without Other People. (p. 1269)
—Now I Know... That Silly Hopes & Fears Will Just Make Wrinkles on My Face. (p. 1269)
—Now I Know... That We All Have a Jewel Inside Us, Somewhere. (p. 1269)
DeVos, Janie. How High Can You Fly? Rejent, Renee, illus. (p. 809)
—Path Winds Home. Marsh, Nancy, illus. (p. 1328)
DeVoss, Joyce A. & Andrews, Minnie F. School Counselors as Educational Leaders. (p. 1522)
DeVries, Catherine. Adventure Bible for Toddlers (p. 14)
—Adventure Bible Storybook Madsen, Jim, illus. (p. 14)
DeVries, Catherine & Zondervan Publishing Staff. All Aboard with Noah! Pulley, Kelly, illus. (p. 42)
DeVries, Douglas. Enticed by Gold. (p. 531)
—Head Butting. (p. 756)
DeVries, John, contrib. by. Flower of the Holy Night: An Easy-to-Sing, Easy-to-Stage Christmas Musical for Children. (p. 607)
DeVries, Mike, jt. auth. see Burns, Jim.
DeVries, Mike & Murphy, Troy. Exodus: The Sacred Journey. (p. 548)
DeVries, Mike, et al. Acts: Face of the Fire. (p. 10)
Devries, Rachel. Teeny Tiny Tino's Fishing Story. (p. 1715)
Dew, Rachel. Big Bunny Bed. (p. 180)
Dew, Robb Forman. Fortunate Lives. (p. 623)
—Time of Her Life. (p. 1752)
Dewan, Ted, illus. see Masson, Sophie.
Dewan, Ted, jt. auth. see Parker, Steve.
Dewane, Patrick Ryan. What If the Rain Were Bugs? Konecny, John, illus. (p. 1887)
Dewar, Bob, illus. see Laing, Robin.
Dewar, Ken, illus. see Shea, Kevin.
Dewdney, Anna. Grumpy Gloria. Dewdney, Anna, illus. (p. 727)
—Llama Llama & the Bully Goat. (p. 1043)
—Llama Llama - Birthday Party! Dewdney, Anna, illus. (p. 1043)
—Llama Llama Easter Egg. Dewdney, Anna, illus. (p. 1043)
—Llama Llama Gram & Grandpa. (p. 1043)
—Llama Llama Holiday Drama. (p. 1043)
—Llama Llama Home with Mama. (p. 1043)
—Llama Llama Hoppity-Hop. (p. 1043)
—Llama Llama I Love You. (p. 1043)
—Llama Llama Jingle Bells. Dewdney, Anna, illus. (p. 1043)
—Llama Llama Mad at Mama. (p. 1043)
—Llama Llama Mad at Mama. Dewdney, Anna, illus. (p. 1043)
—Llama Llama Misses Mama. (p. 1043)
—Llama Llama Nighty-Night. (p. 1043)
—Llama Llama Red Pajama (p. 1043)
—Llama Llama Red Pajama. (p. 1043)
—Llama Llama Red Pajama. Dewdney, Anna, illus. (p. 1043)
—Llama Llama Time to Share. (p. 1043)
—Llama Llama Trick or Treat. Dewdney, Anna, illus. (p. 1043)
—Llama Llama Wakey-Wake. (p. 1043)
—Llama Llama's Little Library. (p. 1043)
—Nelly Gnu & Daddy Too. (p. 1240)
—Nobunny's Perfect. (p. 1262)
—Nobunny's Perfect. Dewdney, Anna, illus. (p. 1262)
—Zippity-Zoom. (p. 1987)
Dewdney, Anna, illus. see Christopher, Matt.
Deweerd, Jamison. Priceless. (p. 1398)
DeWeerd, Kelsey, illus. see Cook, Julia.
DeWeerd, Kelsey, illus. see McCumbee, Stephie.
Dewees, Jacob. Great Future of America & Africa; an Essay Showing Our Whole Duty to the Black Man Consistent with Our Own Safety & Glory. (p. 716)
Deweese, Susan, illus. see Beck, Bev.
DeWeese, Susan, illus. see Breece, Beverly.
Dewees-Gilger, Connie. Isla Saves Egypt. Bouthyette, Valerie, illus. (p. 891)
Dewey, Ariane, illus. see Beaumont, Karen.
Dewey, Ariane, illus. see Bruchac, Joseph & Bruchac, James.
Dewey, Ariane, illus. see Howard, Reginald.
Dewey, Ariane, illus. see Shannon, George.
Dewey, Ariane, illus. see Sharmat, Mitchell.
Dewey, Ariane, illus. see Sierra, Judy.
Dewey, Ariane, jt. auth. see Aruego, Jose.
Dewey, Ariane & Aruego, Jose. Splash! (p. 1629)
Dewey, Jennifer Owings. Clem: The Story of a Raven. Dewey, Jennifer Owings, illus. (p. 330)
—Shaman & the Water Serpent. Yazzie, Benton, illus. (p. 1559)
—Zozobra! The Story of Old Man Gloom. Fleming, Jeanie Puleston, illus. (p. 1990)
Dewey, Jennifer Owings, illus. see Coulter, Catherine, et al.
Dewey, Jennifer Owings, illus. see Dennard, Deborah.
Dewey, Jennifer Owings, tr. see Dennard, Deborah.
Dewey, Ralph. Dewey's Gospel Balloon Routines (p. 432)
Dewey, Simon, illus. see Dickens, Charles.
Dewey, Simon, illus. see Dobson, Cynthia Lund.
Dewhirst, Robert E. Encyclopedia of the United States Congress. (p. 525)
Dewhurst, Carin. Nutcracker. Howland, Naomi, illus. (p. 1274)
DeWildt, Jim, illus. see Lewis, Anne Margaret.
Dewin, Howard. Lab to the Rescue! (p. 969)
—Star Is Born. (p. 1640)
Dewin, Howard & Barba, M. J. Scooby-Doo! A to Z Ultimate Joke Book. (p. 1529)
Dewin, Howard & Corwin, Jeff. Habitat Is Where It's At! A Sticker Book Experience. (p. 734)
Dewin, Howard, told to. Dog: Dogs Rule Cats Drool. (p. 460)
—Dog: Why Do Dogs Love to Sniff?: The Do's & Don'ts of the Dogs. (p. 460)
Dewin, Howie. Why Are Dogs' Noses Wet? And Other True Facts. (p. 1922)
DeWire, Elinor. Florida Lighthouses for Kids. (p. 607)
DeWitt, Becky. Destiny's Closet: Circle of Friends. (p. 431)
DeWitt, Becky. Destiny's Closet: The Wonder School. (p. 431)
—Destiny's Closet. (p. 431)
DeWitt, Fowler. Contagious Colors of Mumpley Middle School. Montalvo, Rodolfo, illus. (p. 360)
Dewitt, Kenny, illus. see Gosule, Bette & Longmire, Lynda.
Dewitt, Levi, illus. see Wright, Mary.
DeWitt, Lockwood. Dig It! Hixson, Bryce, illus. (p. 438)
DeWitt, Lynda. What Will the Weather Be? Croll, Carolyn, illus. (p. 1895)
DeWitt, Nancy, illus. see Beck, Mary Giraudo.
Dewitt, Robert. I Want to Be As Strong As Milo. (p. 847)
DeWolf, Holly, illus. see Mercer, Gerald.
Dewolfe, Jeannee'. Adventures of Billy Chicken Toes & the Wolf: Add Your Own Art Children's Books. (p. 16)
DeWoskin, Rachel. Blind. (p. 199)
Dewyea, Glenn, illus. see Dohr, Robert.
Dexter, Emma, et al. Vitamin D: New Perspectives in Drawing. (p. 1846)
Dey, Frederic Van Re. Magic Story. (p. 1073)
Dey, Joy M. Agate: What Good Is a Moose? Johnson, Nikki, illus. (p. 29)
Dey, Lorraine. Rainforest Party / Fiesta en el bosque Tropical. (p. 1436)
Dey, Lorraine, illus. see Bilderback Abel, Mary & Borg, Stan W.
Dey, Lorraine, illus. see Malone, Margaret Gay.
Dey, Romi, illus. see Dobkin, Bonnie.
Deyes, Alfie. Pointless Book 2: Continued by Alfie Deyes Finished by You. (p. 1377)
DeYoe, Aaron. Biggest, Baddest Book of Ghosts. (p. 185)
—Moons. (p. 1173)
—Planets. (p. 1368)
—Space Travel. (p. 1620)
DeYoe, Aaron, illus. see Parnell, Robyn.
DeYoe, Katie, illus. see Parnell, Robyn.
deYonge, Sandra. Last Bit Bear: A Fable. (p. 977)
DeYoung, Anita. Thank God the Pelican. (p. 1725)
DeYoung, Kevin. Biggest Story: How the Snake Crusher Brings Us Back to the Garden. Clark, Don, illus. (p. 185)
Dezago, Todd. Casper & the Spectrals TP. (p. 276)
—Perhapanauts Volume 00: Dark Days TP: Dark Days TP. (p. 1343)
Dezakin, Akin, illus. see Hagen, Oddmund.
DeZearn, Cee Bradford. Freckle Face, Freckle Face. (p. 632)
Dezső, Andrea, illus. see Koertge, Ron.
D'Ghent, Laurie. Dryer Sheet Fairy. (p. 487)
Dhade, Sukhdev Kaur. Robin with the Red Hat (p. 1480)
D'hamers, Heidi, illus. see Richards, Dawn.
Dhami, Narinder. Bindi Babes. (p. 188)
—Monster under the Stairs. Spoor, Mike, illus. (p. 1168)
—Samosa Thief. Blundell, Tony, illus. (p. 1508)
DHANJAL, Meena. Mattie Has Wheels: Traveling on a Plane. (p. 1110)
Dhar, Lisa Jane. Aisha Goes in Search of Colour. Zulkifi, Azhari, illus. (p. 32)
Dharkar, Anuja, ed. see Underwood, Dale & Aho, Kirsti.
Dharkar, Anuja & Tapley, Scott. Digital Narrative Project for Macromedia Flash MX 2004: Communicating Information & Ideas in Science & Other Disciplines. Aho, Kirsti & McCain, Malinda, eds. (p. 439)
Dharma, A. M. Teacher Resource Guide Set: Teacher Resource Guide boxed with 12 Jataka Tales. (p. 1709)
Dharma Publishing. Hunter & the Quail: The Story about the Power of Cooperation. (p. 828)
Dharma Publishing Staff. Fish King: A Story about the Power of Goodness. (p. 598)
—Golden Foot: A Story about Unselfish Love. (p. 694)
—Great Gift & the Wish-Fulfilling Gem: A Story about the Wish to Help Others. (p. 716)
—Heart of Gold: The Story about the Power of Generosity. (p. 759)
—King Who Understood Animals: A Story about Using Knowledge Wisely. (p. 959)
—Monkey King: A Story about Compassion & Leadership. (p. 1165)
—Power of a Promise: A Story about the Power of Keeping Promises. (p. 1389)
—Proud Peacock: A Story about Humility. (p. 1412)
—Rabbit Who Overcame Fear: A Story about Wise Action. (p. 1429)
—Spade Sage: The Story about Finding Happiness. (p. 1620)
—Three Wise Birds: A Story about Wisdom & Leadership. (p. 1744)
—Value of Friends: A Story about Helping Friends in Need. (p. 1831)
—Wise Ape Teaches Kindness: A Story about the Power of Positive Actions. (p. 1939)
Dharmarajan, Geeta. Magic Raindrop. Thapar, Bindia, illus. (p. 1073)
Dheensaw, Cleve, jt. auth. see Whitfield, Simon.
D'Heur, Valérie, illus. see Bourguignon, Laurence.
Dhilawala, Sakina. Armenia. (p. 99)
Dhilawala, Sakina, jt. auth. see Bassis, Volodymyr.
Dhilawala, Sakina, jt. auth. see Sheehan, Patricia.
Dhillon, Natasha C. History of Western Architecture. (p. 785)
Dhillon, Natasha C. & Lim, Jun. Socrates: The Father of Ethics & Inquiry. (p. 1605)
Dhillon, Natasha C., ed. History of Western Architecture. (p. 785)
DHP, Inc. Staff, ed. see Twenstrup, Norm.
Di Bartolo, Jim, illus. see Jordan, Devin.
Di Bartolo, Jim, illus. see Taylor, Laini.
Di Bartolo, Jim, jt. auth. see White, Kiersten.
Di Bella, Brenda. I'm up to Big Things. (p. 860)
Di Benedetto, Angelo. How the Donkeys Came to Haiti & Other Folk Tales. (p. 813)
Di Cagno, Gabriella. Michelangelo. (p. 1135)
Di Certo, Joseph J. Saga of the Pony Express. (p. 1502)
di Chiara, Francesca. Sun & the Wind. (p. 1676)
Di Donato, Robert, et al. Deutsch: Na Klar! (p. 431)
—Deutsch: Na Klar! An Introductory German Course. (p. 431)
Di Fabbio, Nancy. Midnight Magic: Be Careful What You Wish For! (p. 1139)
Di Fiore, Mariangela. Elephant Man. Hodnefjeld, Hilde, illus. (p. 511)
Di Fiori, Larry, illus. see Evans, Douglas.
Di Franco, Aaron. Pacific Region Goggans, Janice W., ed. (p. 1317)
Di Franco, Armand L. Gloves. (p. 685)
di Gaudesi, Andrea Ricciardi, illus. see Hipp, Andrew.
Di Gennaro, Andrea, illus. see Carew-Miller, Anna.
Di Giacomo, Kris, illus. see Burgess, Matthew.
Di Giacomo, Kris, illus. see Escoffier, Michaël.
Di Giacomo, Kris, illus. see Saudo, Coralie.
Di Giandomenico, Carmine, illus. see Fraction, Matt.
Di Gregorio, Robert & Schauer, S. Ava the Adventurer: Ava in India. (p. 118)
Di Luzio-Poitras, Linda & Poitras, Bruno. Kitchi's New Year's Resolution. (p. 962)
Di Marco, Audrey, illus. see Kolar, Marsha.
Di Nunzio, Mario R. Theodore Roosevelt (p. 1729)
Di Pasquale, Emanuel, et al. Cartwheel to the Moon: My Sicilian Childhood. (p. 273)
Di Piazza, Francesca. Malaysia in Pictures. (p. 1083)
—Zimbabwe in Pictures. (p. 1986)
Di Salle, Rachel, jt. auth. see Warwick, Ellen.
Di Salvo, Roberto, illus. see Tobin, Paul.
Di Santo, Melina. Mel & her Magic Journey. (p. 1125)
Di Stante, Melanie. Purple Card for Papa: When Cancer Is in the Family. (p. 1419)
Di Stiso, Robin Rountree. Cyber Monsters. (p. 396)
Di Vecchio, Jerry Anne & Kirkman, Françoise Dudal. You've Got Recipes: A cookbook for a Lifetime. (p. 1982)
Di Vito, Andrea, illus. see Dixon, Chuck.
Di Vito, Andrea, illus. see Gage, Christos & Grummett, Tom.
Di Vito, Andrea, illus. see Gage, Christos.
Di Vito, Andrea, illus. see Priest, Christopher.
Di Vito, Andrea, illus. see Sumerak, Marc.
Di Vito, Andrea, illus. see Wong, Clarissa S.
Di Vito, Andrea, jt. auth. see Rogers, John.
Di Vito, Andrea & Gurihiru Staff. Wolverine Comic Reader 1. (p. 1944)
di Vries, Maggie. Hunger Journeys. (p. 828)
—Rabbit Ears. (p. 1429)
Diaco, Paula Tedford, ed. see Hipp, Helen C.
Diagana, Susan. Princess Aminata & the Apple Tree. (p. 1402)
Diagram Group Staff. Biology: An Illustrated Guide to Science. (p. 189)
—Chemistry: An Illustrated Guide to Science. (p. 297)
—Earth Science: An Illustrated Guide to Science. (p. 496)
—Environment: An Illustrated Guide to Science. (p. 532)
—Human Body on File (p. 825)
—Life on Earth Set (p. 1012)
—Marine Science: An Illustrated Guide to Science. (p. 1094)
—Physics: An Illustrated Guide to Science. (p. 1353)
—Science Visual Resources Set. (p. 1528)
—Space & Astronomy: An Illustrated Guide to Science. (p. 1618)
—Weather & Climate: An Illustrated Guide to Science. (p. 1869)
Diagram Group Staff, contrib. by. Facts on File Earth Science Handbook. (p. 561)
—First Humans. (p. 595)
—Human Physiology on File. (p. 826)
Diagram Group Staff, creator. Facts on File Physics Handbook. (p. 561)
Diakite, Baba Wague. Gift from Childhood: Memories of an African Boyhood (p. 675)
Diakité, Baba Wagué, illus. see Badoe, Adwoa.
Dial Whitmore, Courtney. Candy Making for Kids. (p. 261)
Diamand, Emily. Flood & Fire. (p. 605)
—Raiders' Ransom. (p. 1433)
Diamant, Vlasta. This Really Happened. (p. 1737)
Diamond, Charlotte. Slippery Fish in Hawaii. Aardema, John, illus. (p. 1590)
Diamond, Cheryl. Model: A Memoir. (p. 1157)
Diamond, Claudia. Children of Ancient Greece. (p. 302)
—What's under the Sea? (p. 1900)
Diamond, Claudia C. Gorilla Families. (p. 703)
Diamond, Corinna. Mystical Manifestations of Morgan. (p. 1226)
Diamond, Donna. Shadow. Diamond, Donna, illus. (p. 1557)
Diamond, Donna, illus. see Kudlinski, Kathleen V.
Diamond, Donna, illus. see Paterson, Katherine.
Diamond, Donna, illus. see Shlasko, Robert.
Diamond, Donna, illus. see Wersba, Barbara.
Diamond, Eileen. Everyday Songbook: 29 Bright & Happy Songs & Activities for Children. (p. 544)
—Let's Make Music Fun! Songs to Sing, Action Songs, Rounds & Songs with Percussion Instruments. (p. 999)
Diamond, Jared. Third Chimpanzee for Young People: On the Evolution & Future of the Human Animal. (p. 1734)
Diamond, Jeremy. REV!-Alation! Habjan, Peter & Duhaney, Rich, illus. (p. 1465)
Diamond, Judy, ed. Virus & the Whale: Exploring Evolution in Creatures Small & Large. (p. 1844)
Diamond, Kathryn. Day I Almost Drowned: A Child's near-Death Experience. (p. 413)
—Rachel's Magic Swing. (p. 1432)
Diamond, Laura. Endure. (p. 527)
—Shifting Pride. (p. 1566)
Diamond, Lorraine. I Want a Camel for a Pet (p. 847)
Diamond, Marie Josephine, jt. auth. see Boucquey, Thierry.
Diamond, Mark. 6 Tricks to Student Narrative Writing Success: An Easy Guide for Students, Teachers & Parents. (p. 1992)
Diamond, Nicola, jt. auth. see Marrone, Mario.
Diamond, Patrick, ed. New Labour's Old Roots: Revisionist Thinkers in Labour's History 1930-1997. (p. 1246)
Diamond, Shendl. True Story of Critter Angels by Yani. (p. 1793)
Diamond, Susan. Social Rules for Kids-the Top 100 Social Rules Kids Need to Succeed. (p. 1604)
Diana, illus. see Carmen, Indigo.
Diana, Bocco, ed. Don't Turn the Lights On. (p. 469)
Diana Cox, illus. see Laverty, Neil.
Diane Bogdan. Twigs Is a Poet! (p. 1801)
Diane Lair, Lair & Lair, Diane. Miss Muggles: The Comical Dog. (p. 1151)
Diane O'Connell. People Person: The Story of Sociologist Marta Tienda. (p. 1339)
Diane, Rachel And Rebecca Sall. Mother Earth's Message. (p. 1177)
Dias, Christina & Abreu, Aline. O Misterio Da Bola Castanho-Avermelhada. (p. 1274)
Dias, Denise. Burton & Isabelle Pipistrelle: Out of the Bat Cave. Winterhalt, Tara, illus. (p. 244)
Dias, Joe, photos by see Roberts, Angela.
Dias, Ron, illus. see Korman, Justine.
Dias, Ron, illus. see RH Disney Staff.
Dias, Ron, illus. see Slater, Teddy.
Dias, Ron, illus. see Teitelbaum, Michael & Golden Books Staff.
Dias, Suzy, jt. auth. see Guerra, Miguel.
Diaz Caballero, Jose Juan, ed. see Torres Batista, Nellilud.
Diaz, Cassandra, illus. see Wooding, Chris.
Diaz, Cynthia. Sunny & Cubby's Real Life: ... Venturing Through Darkness. (p. 1677)
Diaz, David. Sharing the Seasons: A Book of Poems. (p. 1561)
Diaz, David, illus. see Alexander, Elizabeth.
Diaz, David, illus. see Andrews-Goebel, Nancy.
Diaz, David, illus. see Bernier-Grand, Carmen T.
Diaz, David, illus. see Bernier-Grand, Carmen.
Diaz, David, illus. see Brown, Margaret Wise.
Diaz, David, illus. see Brown, Monica & Dominguez, Adriana.
Diaz, David, illus. see Cabral, Len.
Diaz, David, illus. see Charest, Emily MacLachlan & MacLachlan, Patricia.
Diaz, David, illus. see Creech, Sharon.
Diaz, David, illus. see Feliciano, Jose.
Diaz, David, illus. see Flor Ada, Alma & Campoy, F. Isabel.
Diaz, David, illus. see Jackson, Jill & Miller, Sy.
Diaz, David, illus. see Krull, Kathleen.
Diaz, David, illus. see Novesky, Amy.
Diaz, David, illus. see Orozco, Jose-Luis.
Diaz, David, illus. see Schmidt, Gary D.
Diaz, David, illus. see Soto, Gary.
Diaz, David, illus. see Thomas, Joyce Carol.
Diaz, David, illus. see Weeks, Sarah.
Diaz, Diego, illus. see Bullard, Lisa.
Diaz, Enrique Perez. Letters from Alain. (p. 1002)
—Pelusos, Cuentos Policiacos. Martinez, Enrique, illus. (p. 1336)
Diaz, Francesca, illus. see Diaz, James.
Diaz, Francesca, jt. auth. see Diaz, James.
Diaz, Gabriel, illus. see Bernard, Teko & Wilson, Wayne L.
Diaz, Gloria Cecilia. Botella Azul. (p. 215)
—Valle de los Cocuyos. (p. 1830)
Diaz, Gloria Cecilia, jt. auth. see Diaz, Gloria Cecilia.
Diaz, Gloria Cecilia & Diaz, Gloria Cecilia. Bruja de la Montana. (p. 232)
Diaz Granados, Jose Luiz. Cuentos y Leyendas de Colombia. (p. 390)
Diaz, Inmaculada & Inmaculada, Diaz. Miguel y la Cabra Traidora. (p. 1141)
Diaz, Irene, illus. see Marr, Melissa.
Diaz, James. Popigami: When Everyday Paper Pops! Diaz, Francesca, illus. (p. 1384)
Diaz, James, jt. auth. see Carter, David A.
Diaz, James & Diaz, Francesca. Making Colors: A Pop-Up Book. (p. 1080)
—Making Shapes: A Pop-Up Book. (p. 1082)
Diaz, James & Gerth, Melanie. Numbers: Learning Fun for Little Ones! (p. 1272)
Diaz, Joanne Ruelos. Animals All Day! Mendez, Simon, illus. (p. 82)
—Animals by the Seashore Mendez, Simon, illus. (p. 82)
—Animals in the Rain Forest Mendez, Simon, illus. (p. 83)
—Animals on the African Savanna Mendez, Simon, illus. (p. 83)
—Animals on the Farm Mendez, Simon, illus. (p. 83)

Diaz, Juan R. Amaneciendo en la Adolescencia: Comprendiendo la Adolescencia (p. 52)
—Amaneciendo en Ti: Una guia vivencial para el cuerpo, la mente y el Espiritu (p. 52)
Díaz, Junot. Drown. (p. 486)
Diaz, Karen R. & O'Hanlon, Nancy. IssueWeb: A Guide & Sourcebook for Researching Controversial Issues on the Web (p. 893)
Diaz, Katacha. Badger at Sandy Ridge Road. Kest, Kristin, illus. (p. 132)
Diaz, Katacha. Badger at Sandy Ridge Road. Kest, Kristin, illus. (p. 132)
Diaz, Katacha. Carolina's Gift: A Story of Peru. Landolt, Gredna, illus. (p. 270)
—Wild Horse Country. Casale, Paul, illus. (p. 1929)
Diaz, Katacha & Bosson, Jo-Ellen. Wild Horse Country. Casale, Paul, illus. (p. 1929)
Díaz, Lorenzo, tr. see Peyo.
Díaz, Lorenzo, tr. see Tolkien, J. R. R., et al.
Diaz, Luis. Dream. (p. 483)
Diaz, Mariano. Adventures of KCTMJ: Kitty, China, Tina, & Mary Jane. (p. 19)
Díaz, Maritza. Little God in Me. (p. 1028)
Díaz, Miguelina. Lonely Shape. (p. 1046)
Diaz, Natalia & Owens, Melissa. Ticket Around the World. Smith, Kim, illus. (p. 1747)
Díaz, Nelbaliz. Laura y Su Caja de Sorpresas. (p. 980)
Diaz, Olimpia, ed. Oraciones y Guias: Para Jovenes Catolicos. (p. 1301)
Díaz, Raquel, illus. see Sánchez Beras, César.
Diaz, S. Jemmy & the Little Spider of Hope. (p. 912)
Diaz, Stephanie. Extraction. (p. 555)
—Rebellion. (p. 1451)
Diaz, T. Richard. Little Growler, Big Heart. (p. 1028)
Diaz Viana, Luis, et al. Romancero. (p. 1486)
Diaz, Viviana, illus. see Houran, Lori Haskins.
Diaz, Wendy Umm Uthman. Nuestros Oficios. (p. 1270)
Diaz-Cubero, Jose H. Practicas de Ortografia: 2 Grado. (p. 1392)
—Practicas de Ortografia: 3 Grado. (p. 1392)
—Practicas de Ortografia: 5 Grado. (p. 1392)
—Practicas de Ortografia: 6 Grado. (p. 1392)
Díaz-Pimienta, Alexis. Cuentos Clasicos en Verso. (p. 389)
Dibani, Robyn. People in My Life. (p. 1339)
DiBattista, Mary Ann & Finn, Sandra J. Puddinhead Story. Bresnahan, Patrick, illus. (p. 1414)
Dibben, Colin. Flight. (p. 604)
Dibble, Traci. Bats. (p. 144)
—Brown Bears. (p. 231)
—Brown Bears. Dibble, Traci, illus. (p. 231)
—Caterpillars Love to Eat. (p. 280)
—Cobras. (p. 336)
—Cobras. Dibble, Traci, illus. (p. 336)
—Leopards. (p. 993)
—Wolves. (p. 1944)
Dibble, Traci, illus. see Johnson, Gee, et al.
Dibble, Traci, illus. see Zorzi, Gina & Cline, Gina.
Dibble, Traci, jt. auth. see Washington, Joi.
Dibble, Traci, jt. auth. see Zorzi, Gina.
Dibble, Traci & Sánchez, Lucía M. Cobras. (p. 337)
—Leopardos: Leopards. (p. 993)
Dibble, Traci & Sanchez, Lucia M. Leopardos (Leopards) (p. 993)
—Lobos: Wolves. (p. 1044)
Dibble, Traci & Sánchez, Lucía M. MurciéLagos: Bats. (p. 1192)
Dibble, Traci & Sanchez, Lucia M. Murciélagos (Bats) (p. 1192)
Dibble, Traci & Sánchez, Lucía M. Osos Pardos. (p. 1306)
Dibble, Traci & Washington, Joi. Wolves. Washington, Joi, illus. (p. 1944)
DiBenedetto, Barbara, jt. auth. see Richardson, Ellis.
DiBenedetto, Salvatore. Christian the Fish: Who am I? (p. 312)
DiBiase, Judy, illus. see Bochinski, Julianne Blair.
Dibinga, Omekongo. G. R. O. W. Towards Your Greatness!: 10 Steps to Living Your Best Life. (p. 651)
Dibinga, Omekongo, ed. Poems from the Future: Poetic Reflections from the Next Generation. (p. 1376)
Dibley, Glin, illus. see Ficocelli, Elizabeth.
Dibley, Glin, illus. see Freeman, Martha.
Dibley, Glin, illus. see Raczka, Bob.
Dibley, Glin, illus. see Rosenswelg, Jay B. & Repka, Janice.
DiCamillo, Kate. Because of Winn-Dixie. (p. 155)
—Cane Piú Brutto del Mondo. (p. 261)
—Despereaux. Basil, Timothy, illus. (p. 430)
—Essential Kate DiCamillo Collection. (p. 537)
—Flora & Ulysses: The Illuminated Adventures. (p. 606)
—Flora & Ulysses: The Illuminated Adventures. Campbell, K. G., illus. (p. 606)
—Francine Poulet Meets the Ghost Raccoon: Tales from Deckawoo Drive, Volume Two. Van Dusen, Chris, illus. (p. 627)
—Gracias a Winn-Dixie. (p. 705)
—Great Joy. Ibatoulline, Bagram, illus. (p. 716)
—Leroy Ninker Saddles Up. (p. 993)
—Leroy Ninker Saddles Up. Van Dusen, Chris, illus. (p. 993)
—Louise, the Adventures of a Chicken. Bliss, Harry, illus. (p. 1058)
—Magician's Elephant. (p. 1075)
—Magician's Elephant. Tanaka, Yoko, illus. (p. 1075)
—Mercy Watson Fights Crime. Van Dusen, Chris, illus. (p. 1127)
—Mercy Watson Fights Crime. DiCamillo, Kate & Van Dusen, Chris, illus. (p. 1127)
—Mercy Watson Goes for a Ride. Van Dusen, Chris, illus. (p. 1127)
—Mercy Watson Thinks Like a Pig. Van Dusen, Chris, illus. (p. 1127)
—Mercy Watson to the Rescue. Van Dusen, Chris, illus. (p. 1127)
—Mercy Watson to the Rescue. DiCamillo, Kate & Van Dusen, Chris, illus. (p. 1127)
—Miraculous Journey of Edward Tulane. Ibatoulline, Bagram, illus. (p. 1149)
—Princess in Disguise. Van Dusen, Chris, illus. (p. 1404)
—Something Wonky This Way Comes. Van Dusen, Chris, illus. (p. 1610)
—Tale of Despereaux: Being the Story of a Mouse, a Princess, Some Soup & a Spool of Thread (p. 1699)
—Tale of Despereaux: Being the Story of a Mouse, a Princess, Some Soup & a Spool of Thread. (p. 1699)
—Tale of Despereaux: Being the Story of a Mouse, a Princess, Some Soup & a Spool of Thread. Ering, Timothy B., illus. (p. 1699)
—Tale of Despereaux: Being the Story of a Mouse, a Princess, Some Soup & a Spool of Thread. Ering, Timothy Basil, illus. (p. 1699)
—Tale of Despereaux Student Packet. (p. 1699)
—Tiger Rising. (p. 1748)
—Tiger Rising. Sheban, Chris, illus. (p. 1748)
DiCamillo, Kate, jt. auth. see Alexander, Carol.
DiCamillo, Kate, jt. auth. see White, E. B.
DiCamillo, Kate & Candlewick Press Staff. Tale of Despereaux: Glow-in-the-Dark Sticker Book. (p. 1699)
DiCamillo, Kate & Ering, Timothy Basil. Tale of Despereaux: Being the Story of a Mouse, a Princess, Some Soup & a Spool of Thread. (p. 1699)
DiCamillo, Kate & McGhee, Alison. Best Friends Forever. (p. 169)
—Best Friends Forever. Fucile, Tony, illus. (p. 169)
—Bink & Gollie. (p. 188)
—Bink & Gollie. Fucile, Tony, illus. (p. 188)
—Bink & Gollie: Best Friends Forever. Fucile, Tony, illus. (p. 188)
—Bink & Gollie - The Completely Marvelous Collection. Fucile, Tony, illus. (p. 188)
—Bink & Gollie - Two for One. Fucile, Tony, illus. (p. 188)
—Two for One. (p. 1803)
—Two for One. Fucile, Tony, illus. (p. 1803)
DiCamillo, Kate & Van Dusen, Chris. Princess in Disguise. Van Dusen, Chris, illus. (p. 1404)
DiCampli, Nicki, jt. auth. see Humphries, Jennifer.
Dice, Elizabeth A. & Matters, Print. Christmas & Hanukkah. (p. 312)
—Western & Chinese New Year's Celebrations. (p. 1876)
Dicello, Bob. Juni B. Small, Jan, illus. (p. 935)
DiCerto, Joseph J. Wall People: In Search of a Home. (p. 1854)
Dicerto, Mike. Ghost of Winter Joy. (p. 671)
DiCianni, Ron. Praying with the Presidents: One Nation's Legacy of Prayer. (p. 1393)
DiCianni, Ron, illus. see Alcorn, Randy.
DiCianni, Ron, illus. see Eareckson Tada, Joni & Jensen, Steve.
DiCianni, Ron, illus. see Lucado, Max.
Dicicco, Joe. Planet Baseball, Dominican Republic Edition, Volume 1: Making the Play Jimenez, Ruben D., tr. (p. 1367)
—Planet Baseball, Japanese Edition, Volume 1: Making the Play Jimenez, Ruben D., tr. (p. 1367)
—Planet Baseball, Puerto Rico: Volume 1, Making the Play Jimenez, Ruben D., tr. (p. 1367)
DiCicco, LeeAnn, illus. see Reader's Digest Editors & Froeb, Lori C.
DiCicco, Sue. 1, 2, 3 in the Sea. DiCicco, Sue, illus. (p. 1990)
—1, 2 at the Zoo. DiCicco, Sue, illus. (p. 1990)
—Feelings. DiCicco, Sue, illus. (p. 580)
—Manners. DiCicco, Sue, illus. (p. 1088)
—Peek-a-Boo Baby. (p. 1334)
—Princess Potty Time. (p. 1405)
—Santa's Elves ABC. (p. 1513)
Dicicco, Sue. Scholastic Reader Level 1: Funny Bunnies: Morning, Noon, & Night. (p. 1522)
DiCicco, Sue. Superhero Potty Time. (p. 1683)
—Totally Monster: Best Friends. (p. 1771)
—Totally Monster: Feelings. (p. 1771)
—Totally Monster: Manners. (p. 1771)
—You Are My Work of Art. (p. 1973)
DiCicco, Sue, illus. see Depken, Kristen L. & Jackson, Kathryn.
DiCicco, Sue, illus. see Depken, Kristen L. & Schurr, Cathleen.
DiCicco, Sue, illus. see Golden Books.
DiCicco, Sue, illus. see Posner-Sanchez, Andrea.
DiCicco, Sue, illus. see Reader's Digest Editors & Froeb, Lori C.
DiCicco, Sue, illus. see RH Disney Staff & Posner-Sanchez, Andrea.
DiCicco, Sue, illus. see RH Disney Staff & Teitelbaum, Michael.
DiCicco, Sue, illus. see Teitelbaum, Michael & Golden Books Staff.
DiCicco, Sue, illus. see Teitelbaum, Michael.
DiCicco, Sue & Mawhinney, Art. Diego y los Dinosaurios. (p. 437)
—Diego's Great Dinosaur Rescue. (p. 437)
Dicillo, Mike, jt. auth. see Cohen, Liz Zoller.
Dick, Beth-Ann. Henry the Hart Room Hamster. (p. 768)
Dick, Debra. Zoo Haiku. (p. 1989)
Dick, Everett. Sod-House Frontier. (p. 1605)
Dick, Judy. Chanukah. (p. 291)
—Our Community. (p. 1308)
—Sacred Time: The Jewish Calendar & Life Cycle. (p. 1500)
—Seder Activity Book. Dick, Judy, illus. (p. 1546)
Dick, Peggy, illus. see Gressman, Carylee Anne.
Dick, Philip K. Gun. (p. 731)
—Nick & the Glimmung. (p. 1251)
—Philip K. Dick - Five Novels of the 1960s & 70s: Martian Time-Slip - Dr. Bloodmoney - Now Wait for Last Year - Flow My Tears, The Policeman Said - A Scanner Darkly. Lethem, Jonathan, ed. (p. 1350)
Dick, Regina Frances, illus. see Scarfi, Margaret Rose.
Dick, William & Scott, Laurie. Mastery for Strings (p. 1103)
Dickason, Chris, illus. see Moore, Gareth.
Dicken-Bradshaw, Mark. I Am Adopted: Finding My Forever Family. (p. 832)
Dickens, Charles. Annotated Christmas Carol: A Christmas Carol in Prose. Leech, John, illus. (p. 87)
—Bleak House. (p. 199)
—Campanas. (p. 257)
—Charles Dickens/A Christmas Carol. Lo Famia, Jon, illus. (p. 292)
—Child 's History of England. (p. 301)
—Child?s History of England. (p. 301)
—Child's History of England (p. 305)
—Child's History of England: With Original Engravings. (p. 305)
—Child's History of England: With Original Engravings - Primary Source Edition. (p. 305)
—Child's History of England: England from the Ancient Times, to the Reign of Henry the Fifth. (p. 305)
—Child's History of England: England from the Reign of Henry the Sixth to the Revolution Of 1688. (p. 305)
—Child's History of England: England from the Ancient Times, to the Reign of Henry the Fifth - Primary Source Edition. (p. 305)
—Child's History of England. (p. 305)
—Child's History of England. Townsend, F. H., illus. (p. 305)
—Child's History of England V1: England from the Ancient Times to the Reign of Henry the Fifth (1854) (p. 305)
—Christmas Carol. (p. 313)
—Christmas Carol: Being a Ghost Story of Christmas. (p. 313)
—Christmas Carol: Prestwick House Literary Touchstone Edition. (p. 313)
—Christmas Carol Laurel Associates Inc. Staff & Saddleback Educational Publishing Staff, eds. (p. 313)
—Christmas Carol. (p. 313)
—Christmas Carol. Bryant, Clive, ed. (p. 313)
—Christmas Carol. Howell, Keith, tr. (p. 313)
—Christmas Carol. Kelly, Richard, ed. (p. 313)
—Christmas Carol. Lynch, P. J., illus. (p. 313)
—Christmas Carol. Andrews, Gary, illus. (p. 313)
—Christmas Carol. Blake, Quentin, illus. (p. 313)
—Christmas Carol. McKowen, Scott, illus. (p. 313)
—Christmas Carol. Donnelly, Karen, illus. (p. 313)
—Christmas Carol. Helquist, Brett, illus. (p. 313)
—Christmas Carol. Innocenti, Roberto, illus. (p. 313)
—Christmas Carol. Sanchez Almara, Dono & Almara, Dono Sanchez, illus. (p. 313)
—Christmas Carol & the Remembrance of Mugby. Meyrand, Estelle, illus. (p. 313)
—Christmas Carol - Spotlight Edition. (p. 313)
—Christmas Carol the Graphic Novel - Original Text: British Edition. Collins, Mike et al, illus. (p. 313)
—Cricket on the Hearth. (p. 382)
—David Copperfield. (p. 410)
—David Copperfield, Level 3. (p. 410)
—Great Expectations: The Graphic Novel. (p. 715)
—Great Expectations: And Related Readings. (p. 715)
—Great Expectations. (p. 715)
—Great Expectations. Geary, Rick, illus. (p. 715)
—Great Expectations. Freeberg, Eric, illus. (p. 715)
—Great Expectations. Donnelly, Karen, illus. (p. 715)
—Great Expectations & Hard Times. (p. 715)
—Hard Times. (p. 748)
—Hard Times. Donnelly, Karen, illus. (p. 748)
—Historia de dos Ciudades. (p. 782)
—Illustrated Stories from Dickens. Ablett, Barry, illus. (p. 858)
—Life of Our Lord: The Story of Jesus Told by Charles Dickens. (p. 1012)
—Life of Our Lord: Written for His Children During the Years 1846 To 1849. (p. 1012)
—Life of Our Lord: Illustrated 200th Anniversary Edition. Dewey, Simon, illus. (p. 1012)
—Little Dorrit. (p. 1027)
—Mr. Pickwick's Promise. Landes, William-Alan, ed. (p. 1186)
—Nicolas Nickleby. (p. 1251)
—Oliver Twist. (p. 1285)
—Oliver Twist. (p. 1285)
—Oliver Twist. Ablett, Barry, illus. (p. 1285)
—Oliver Twist. Andreasen, Dan, illus. (p. 1285)
—Oliver Twist. Belli, Alfredo, illus. (p. 1285)
—Oliver Twist. McKowen, Scott, illus. (p. 1285)
—Oliver Twist. Donnelly, Karen, illus. (p. 1285)
—Oliver Twist. Volpari, Daniela, illus. (p. 1285)
—Oliver Twist. Morgan, Richard & Fennell, Tracy, illus. (p. 1285)
—Oliver Twist: With a Discussion of Honesty. (p. 1286)
—Oliver Twist. (p. 1286)
—Oliver Twist. Johnson, Cynthia Brantley, ed. (p. 1286)
—Oliver Twist & Other Classic Tales. Thorne, Jenny, illus. (p. 1286)
—Quentin Blake's a Christmas Carol. Blake, Quentin, illus. (p. 1425)
—Tale of Two Cities: A Classic Retelling. (p. 1700)
—Tale of Two Cities. (p. 1700)
—Timeless Classics Low Level: Great Expectations (p. 1754)
Dickens, Charles, jt. auth. see Imbernón, Maite.
Dickens, Charles, jt. auth. see Tavner, Gill.
Dickens, Charles & Dauvillier, Loïc. Oliver Twist. (p. 1286)
Dickens, Charles & De Graaf, Anne. Best of Charles Dickens' Classics. Montero, Jose Perez, illus. (p. 170)
Dickens, Charles & Fischer, Chuck. Christmas Carol: A Pop-Up Book. (p. 313)
Dickens, Charles & Hawksley, L. Dickens. Tale of Two Cities. (p. 1700)
Dickens, Charles & Mahony, J. Child's History of England. (p. 305)
Dickens, Charles & Sims, L. Christmas Carol. (p. 313)
Dickens, Charles & Sims, Lesley. Christmas Carol. (p. 313)
Dickens, Charles, et al. Budget of Christmas Tales. (p. 235)
—Child's History of England. (p. 305)
—Christmas Books & Stories. (p. 313)
Dickens, Christina, illus. see Hunt, James.
Dickens, Earl, illus. see Benanti, Carol.
Dickens, Frank. Albert Herbert Hawkins: The Naughtiest Boy in the World. Dickens, Frank, illus. (p. 34)
—Fly Away Peter. Steadman, Ralph, illus. (p. 609)
Dickens, Lydia. Little Donkey Nico / el Burrito Nico. (p. 1027)
Dickens, Monica. House at World's End. (p. 803)
—Spring Comes to World's End. (p. 1635)
—Summer at World's End. (p. 1673)
—World's End in Winter. (p. 1960)
Dickens, Ned. By a Thread Ross, Graham, illus. (p. 249)
Dickens, R., jt. auth. see Harvey, G.
Dickens, Rosie. Children's Book of Art: Internet Linked. (p. 303)
—Famous Paintings: Internet-Linked. (p. 569)
—Impressionists. Blackwood, Freyda, illus. (p. 862)
—Introduction to Modern Art - Internet Linked. (p. 882)
—My First Art Sticker Book. Ballesteros, Carles, illus. (p. 1204)
—My Very First Art Coloring Book with Stickers. (p. 1221)
Dickens, Rosie, jt. auth. see Courtauld, Sarah.
Dickens, Rosie & Courtauld, Sarah. My Very First Art Book. Gordan, Gus, illus. (p. 1221)
Dickens, Rosie, et al. Usborne Book of Art. (p. 1827)
Dickens, Sara Jo. Karner's Quest for Blue Lupine. Nancy, Scheibe, illus. (p. 944)
Dickenson, Ben. Hollywood's New Radicalism: War, Globalisation & the Movies from Reagan to George W. Bush. (p. 789)
Dicker, K. I Belong to the Muslim Faith. Azizi, Z., photos by. (p. 834)
Dicker, Katie. AIDS & HIV. (p. 30)
—Chickens. (p. 300)
—Cows. (p. 374)
—Ducks. (p. 488)
—Forces & Motion. (p. 617)
—Goats. (p. 687)
—Horses. (p. 800)
—Light. (p. 1014)
—Missing! (p. 1152)
—Mysterious Creatures. (p. 1223)
—Mysterious Messages. (p. 1223)
—Mysterious Places. (p. 1223)
—Pigs. (p. 1358)
—Properties of Matter. (p. 1411)
—Sheep. (p. 1564)
—Turkeys. (p. 1797)
—Unsolved Crimes. (p. 1822)
—Visitors from Space. (p. 1846)
—You Can Draw Birds! Saunders, Mike, illus. (p. 1974)
—You Can Draw Cats! Saunders, Mike, illus. (p. 1974)
—You Can Draw Exotic Pets! Saunders, Mike, illus. (p. 1974)
—You Can Draw Fish! Saunders, Mike, illus. (p. 1974)
—You Can Draw Horses! Saunders, Mike, illus. (p. 1974)
Dicker, Katie & Azizi, Zoha. I Belong to the Muslim Faith. (p. 834)
Dicker, Katie & De Silva, Nisansa. I Belong to the Buddhist Faith. (p. 834)
Dicker, Katie & Dilkes, Sam. I Belong to the Christian Faith. (p. 834)
Dicker, Katie & Johnson, Jinny. Cavalier King Charles Spaniel. (p. 282)
—Collie. (p. 340)
—Doberman Pinscher. (p. 458)
—Great Dane. (p. 715)
—Miniature Schnauzer. (p. 1146)
—Rottweiler. (p. 1491)
—Siberian Husky. (p. 1572)
Dicker, Katie & Perihar, Amar Singh. I Belong to the Sikh Faith. (p. 834)
Dicker, Katie & Sheldon, Sam. I Belong to the Jewish Faith. (p. 834)
Dicker, Katie & Vekaria, Alka. I Belong to the Hindu Faith. (p. 834)
Dickerhof-Kranz, Susanne, tr. see McDonnell, Patrick.
Dickerson, Brookie. My Name Is JJ: JJ & the Witch of Vineyard Street. (p. 1215)
Dickerson, Jennifer. Mini Flower Loom Crafts: 18 Super Simple Projects. (p. 1146)
Dickerson, Joy E. Pack & Go. (p. 1317)
Dickerson, Karle. Forgotten Filly. (p. 619)
Dickerson, Melanie. Fairest Beauty (p. 562)
—Healer's Apprentice (p. 757)
—Huntress of Thornbeck Forest (p. 829)
—Princess Spy (p. 1405)
Dickerson, Sharon. Jessica & the Tangle Monster. (p. 914)
Dickerson, Theophilus L. Artisans & Artifacts of Vanished Races. (p. 104)
Dickerson, Tim. Napping with Daddy. (p. 1229)
Dickert, Sheryl, illus. see Phillips, Betty Lou & Herndon, Roblyn.
Dickey, Eric Jerome. Thieves' Paradise. (p. 1732)
Dickey, Eric Wayne. Alex the Ant Goes to the Beach. Paccia, Abbey, illus. (p. 36)
Dickey, Janet. Anyone's Guess Jr: Who's a Fraidy Kat? (p. 91)
Dickey, R. A. Knuckleball Ned. Bowers, Tim, illus. (p. 965)
Dickie, Lisa, jt. auth. see Edwards, Ron.
Dickins, R. Bugs. (p. 237)
Dickins, Rosie. Art Treasury. Butler, Nicola, illus. (p. 103)
—Bugs. (p. 237)
—Illustrated Pirate Stories IR. (p. 857)
—Introduction to Art - Internet Linked. Chisholm, Jane, ed. (p. 882)
—London Sticker Book. Clarke, Phillip, ed. (p. 1046)
—Story of Rome. Gower, Teri, illus. (p. 1659)
—Usborne First Book of Art. Hopman, Philip, illus. (p. 1827)
—Usborne the Children's Book of Art: Internet Linked. Armstrong, Carrie, ed. (p. 1827)
—William Shakespeare - Internet Referenced. (p. 1933)
Dickins, Rosie & Ball, Karen. Leonardo Da Vinci. Unzner, Christa, illus. (p. 992)
Dickins, Rosie & Griffith, Mari. Introduction to Art: Internet-Linked. (p. 882)
Dickins, Rosie & McCafferty, Jan. Drawing Faces. (p. 481)
Dickins, Rosie & Pratt, Leonie. Horse & Pony Treasury. Sims, Lesley, ed. (p. 799)
Dickins, Rosie & Sims, Lesley. Aesop's Stories for Little Children. (p. 26)
Dickins, Rosie, et al. Usborne Introduction to Art: In Association with the National Gallery, London. (p. 1827)
—Usborne Introduction to Modern Art. (p. 1827)
Dickins, Rosie, retold by. Illustrated Stories from Shakespeare. (p. 858)

D

Dickinson, Asa Don. Good Cheer Stories Every Child Should Know. (p. 697)
Dickinson, Asa Don & Dickinson, Helen Winslow, eds. Patriotic Stories Every Child Should Know. (p. 1329)
Dickinson, Asa Don & Skinner, Ada M. Children's Book of Christmas Stories. (p. 303)
Dickinson, Becky. Gardening Year. (p. 656)
Dickinson, Darol. Fillet of Horn II. (p. 586)
Dickinson, Donald J. Bird's Eye View of the Civil War in Loudon County & Campbell's Station, TN: A Book for Children. (p. 191)
Dickinson, Emily. My Letter to the World & Other Poems. Arsenault, Isabelle, illus. (p. 1211)
Dickinson, Emily, jt. auth. see Berry, S. L.
Dickinson, Gill. Creative Crafts for Kids. (p. 379)
Dickinson, Gill & Lowe, Jason. Crafts for Kids: Birthdays - Easter - Halloween - Christmas - Mother's Day - Thanksgiving - And More... (p. 376)
Dickinson, Helen Winslow, jt. ed. see Dickinson, Asa Don.
Dickinson, Mary & Charlotte. Alex's Bed. (p. 37)
Dickinson, Peter. Blue Hawk. (p. 203)
—Chuck & Danielle. (p. 318)
—Earth & Air: Tales of Elemental Creatures. (p. 495)
—Emma Tupper's Diary. (p. 520)
—Eva. (p. 540)
—Ropemaker. (p. 1488)
—Ropemaker. Andrew, Ian, illus. (p. 1488)
Dickinson, Peter, jt. auth. see McKinley, Robin.
Dickinson, Rachel. Great Pioneer Projects. Braley, Shawn, illus. (p. 717)
—Tools of the Ancient Romans: A Kid's Guide to the History & Science of Life in Ancient Rome. (p. 1767)
Dickinson, Rebecca. Over in the Hollow. Britt, Stephanie, illus. (p. 1313)
Dickinson, Rebecca, illus. see Berkes, Marianne.
Dickinson, Richard, jt. auth. see Royer, France.
Dickinson, Tom. Bob's Secret Hideaway. (p. 206)
Dickison, Forrest. Sword of Abram. (p. 1692)
Dickler, Katie. You Can Draw Dogs! Saunders, Mike, illus. (p. 1974)
Dickman, Jacqueline Rosett. God's Little Lake: Max & Me (p. 691)
—Rebecca & Mom: Friends Forever (p. 1450)
Dickman, Jean M. Santa in Space. (p. 1512)
Dickman, Michael, illus. see Banerjee, Timir.
Dickmann, Nancy. Alimentos de la Granja. (p. 41)
—Animales de la Granja. (p. 80)
—Año Nuevo Chino (p. 87)
—Apple's Life (p. 93)
—Bean's Life (p. 150)
—Bee's Life (p. 158)
—Butterfly's Life (p. 248)
—Centipedes (p. 287)
—Chicken's Life (p. 300)
—Chinese New Year (p. 307)
—Christmas (p. 312)
—Dairy. (p. 400)
—Diwali (p. 455)
—Dog's Life (p. 463)
—Easter (p. 499)
—Energy from Nuclear Fission: Splitting the Atom. (p. 528)
—Estaciones en la Granja. (p. 538)
—Exploring Beyond the Solar System. (p. 551)
—Exploring Comets, Asteroids, & Other Objects in Space. (p. 551)
—Exploring Planet Earth & the Moon. (p. 553)
—Exploring the Inner Planets. (p. 554)
—Exploring the Outer Planets. (p. 554)
—Exploring the Sun. (p. 554)
—Farm Animals (p. 573)
—Farm Machines (p. 574)
—Food from Farms (p. 613)
—Fracking: Fracturing Rock to Reach Oil & Gas Underground. (p. 626)
—Frog's Life (p. 641)
—Fruits. (p. 645)
—Galileo: Conqueror of the Stars. (p. 653)
—Grains. (p. 705)
—Hanukkah (p. 743)
—Janucá (p. 908)
—Jobs on a Farm (p. 919)
—Las Plantas de la Granja (p. 977)
—Louis Pasteur: Germ Destroyer. (p. 1058)
—Máquinas de la Granja. (p. 1091)
—Mount Everest (p. 1180)
—Mundo de la Granja (p. 1191)
—Navidad (p. 1237)
—Oak Tree's Life (p. 1274)
—Pascua (p. 1326)
—Penguin's Life (p. 1337)
—Plants on a Farm (p. 1370)
—Protein. (p. 1412)
—Rachel Carson: Environmental Crusader. (p. 1431)
—Ramadan & Id-Ul-Fitr (p. 1437)
—Ramadán y el Eid Al-Fitr (p. 1437)
—Seasons on a Farm (p. 1538)
—South Pole (p. 1617)
—Sunflower's Life (p. 1676)
—Trabajos en la Granja. (p. 1774)
—Turtle's Life (p. 1799)
—Vegetables. (p. 1834)
—Vida de la Abeja (p. 1840)
—Vida de la Manzana (p. 1840)
—Vida de la Mariposa (p. 1840)
—Vida de la Rana (p. 1840)
—Vida de la Tortuga (p. 1840)
—Vida del Frijol. (p. 1840)
—Vida del Girasol. (p. 1840)
—Vida del Perro. (p. 1840)
—Vida del Pingüino. (p. 1840)
—Vida del Pollo. (p. 1840)
—Vida del Roble. (p. 1840)
—Watch It Grow (p. 1861)
—World of Farming (p. 1956)
—¡Mira Cómo Crece! (p. 1148)
Dickow, Cheryl. All Things Girl: Friends, Fashion & Faith Journal. (p. 46)
—All Things Girl. (p. 46)
Dicks, Terrance. Day of the Daleks. (p. 414)
—Doctor Who & the Loch Ness Monster. (p. 459)
—Three Doctors - Doctor Who. (p. 1742)
Dickson, Benjamin, jt. auth. see Wilson, Sean Michael.
Dickson, Bill. David & Goliath. (p. 410)
Dickson, Bill, illus. see Blair, Eric, et al.
Dickson, Bill, illus. see Blair, Eric.
Dickson, Bill, illus. see Dwire, Joyann.
Dickson, Bill, illus. see Petach, Heidi.
Dickson, Bill, illus. see Wildman, Dale.
Dickson, Darnell G. Small Town, Big Dreams: A Dane Jordan Sports Novel. (p. 1592)
Dickson, Diane. 3 Things That Might Have Happened. (p. 1991)
—Daisy & the Dust Angel. (p. 400)
Dickson, Gary. Children's Crusade: Medieval History, Modern Mythistory. (p. 303)
Dickson, John. Children Learning Math. (p. 302)
Dickson, John & Pasquali, Elena. Mrs. Noah's Vegetable Ark. Lavis, Steve, illus. (p. 1187)
Dickson, Julie A. Girl from the Shadows. (p. 678)
Dickson, Kari, tr. see Holt, Anne.
Dickson, Kari, tr. see Lunde, Stein Erik.
Dickson, Keith D. World War II Almanac Facts on File, Inc. Staff, ed. (p. 1959)
Dickson, Kristin & Pecsenye, Jessica. Trinity University Texas College Prowler off the Record. (p. 1787)
Dickson, Louise. Disappearing Magician. Cupples, Pat, illus. (p. 446)
Dickson, Robert. Sam Ferret Mysteries. (p. 1506)
Dickson, Sue. Sing, Spell, Read & Write: On Track. (p. 1579)
—Sing, Spell, Read & Write: All Aboard. (p. 1579)
Dickson, Vivian. To Be a Bean. (p. 1758)
—To Be a Bird. Grandelis, Leiah, illus. (p. 1758)
Dickstein, Leslie, jt. auth. see Time for Kids Editors.
Dicmas, Courtney. Great Googly Moogly. Dicmas, Courtney, illus. (p. 716)
—Harold Finds a Voice. Dicmas, Courtney, illus. (p. 749)
—Home Tweet Home. (p. 793)
—Wild Bath Time! (p. 1929)
—Wild Bedtime! (p. 1929)
—Wild Mealtime! (p. 1929)
—Wild Playtime! (p. 1930)
DiConsiglio, John. Bad Breath: A Deadly Fungus Becomes Airborne. (p. 131)
—Bitten! Mosquitoes Infect New York. (p. 194)
Diconsiglio, John. Blood Suckers! Deadly Mosquito Bites. (p. 200)
DiConsiglio, John. Francisco Pizarro: Destroyer of the Inca Empire. (p. 628)
—Mad Cow! Tracking down Killer Cattle. (p. 1069)
—Mexican-American War (p. 1131)
—Reporting Live. (p. 1461)
—Superbugs (p. 1682)
Diconsiglio, John. There's a Fungus among Us! True-Life Cases! (p. 1730)
—There's a Fungus among Us! True Stories of Killer Molds. (p. 1730)
—True Confessions: Real Stories about Drinking & Drugs. (p. 1792)
DiConsiglio, John. Vietnam: The Bloodbath at Hamburger Hill. (p. 1841)
Diconsiglio, John. When Birds Get Flu & Cows Go Mad! How Safe Are We? (p. 1901)
DiConsiglio, John. Young Americans: Tales of Teenage Immigrants. (p. 1978)
DiConsiglio, John, jt. auth. see Price, Sean Stewart.
DiConsoglio, John. Franklin Pierce. (p. 630)
Dictionary, Oxford, ed. Oxford Children's Rhyming Dictionary. (p. 1315)
—Oxford First Rhyming Dictionary. (p. 1315)
Didier, Dominique A. Moray Eel. (p. 1173)
—Sea Anemone. (p. 1534)
Didio, Dan, ed. see Anderson, Murphy, et al.
Didio, Dan, ed. see Bridwell, E. Nelson, et al.
Didio, Dan, ed. see Willingham, Bill, et al.
Didling, Alisha Anne. Alisha, Her Blankie & the Surprise! (p. 41)
DiDomenico, Allison. You Can Do It, Fiona! (p. 1974)
Didur, Dean, jt. auth. see Peters, Laura.
Diederich, Ellen Jean. Where's Petunia? (p. 1910)
Diedrich, Ann Goshia. Randal the Flannel Camel. (p. 1438)
Diedrich, John. Clydesdale Horse (p. 336)
Diedrick, Noah. Submarines: Use Place Value Understanding & Properties of Operations to Perform Multi-Digit Arithmetic. (p. 1671)
Diefendorf, Cathy, illus. see Damitz, Charlie.
Diefendorf, Cathy, illus. see O'Donnell, Liam.
Diego, John & Benchmark Education Co., LLC Staff. Go Slow, Go Fast. (p. 687)
—Grace & Ace. (p. 704)
Diego, Marene. Hyper Spin (p. 831)
Diego, Rapi. Sapo Hechizado. (p. 1514)
Diego, Rapi, illus. see Ferré, Rosario.
Diego, Rapi, illus. see Foreman, Michael.
Dieguez Dieguez, Remedios, tr. see Farquharson, Polly.
Dieguez Dieguez, Remedios, tr. see Seth, Vikram.
Diehl, Bill. Hungry Bunny. (p. 828)
Diehl, Jean Heilprin. Loon Chase Freeman, Kathryn S., illus. (p. 1052)
—Three Little Beavers Morrison, Cathy, illus. (p. 1742)
Diehl, Matt. My So-Called Punk: Green Day, Fall Out Boy, the Distillers, Bad Religion - How Neo-Punk Stage-Dived into the Mainstream. (p. 1219)
Diehl, Nichole, illus. see Lo, Monica.
Diehn, Andi. Explore Poetry! With 25 Great Projects. Stone, Bryan, illus. (p. 550)
—Technology: Cool Women Who Code. (p. 1711)
Dieker, Wendy. Cranes. (p. 376)
—Ducks. (p. 488)
—Pigs. (p. 1358)
—Tractors. (p. 1775)
—Turkeys. (p. 1797)
Dieker, Wendy Strobel. Sheep. (p. 1564)
Diemberger, Jana, illus. see McCaughrean, Geraldine.
Diemer, Lauren. Cows. (p. 374)
—Flags. (p. 602)
—Guggenheim Museum. (p. 729)
—Igloos. (p. 856)
—Igloos or les Igloos [Check Which Translator Used]: Les Emblèmes Canadiens. McMann, Julie, tr. from ENG. (p. 856)
—Jaguars. (p. 905)
—Natural Landmarks. (p. 1235)
—Rose Bowl. (p. 1489)
—Sears Tower. (p. 1538)
—Squirrels. (p. 1637)
—Squirrels. Hudak, Heather C., ed. (p. 1637)
Diemer, Lauren, jt. auth. see Wearing, Judy.
Diemer, Lauren & Cuthbert, Megan. Abraham Lincoln. (p. 6)
Diemer, Lauren & Kissock, Heather. Prince William & Kate Middleton. (p. 1401)
Diemer, Sarah. Dark Wife. (p. 408)
Dieneman, Debbie, illus. see Wolos-Fonteno, Mary, et al.
Diep, Bridgette. Trip Through Cambodia. Vaing, Jocelang, illus. (p. 1787)
Dierbeck, Lisa. One Pill Makes You Smaller: A Novel. (p. 1296)
Dierenfeldt, Jane. Grammy's Curtain Calls Hanawalt, Josh, illus. (p. 706)
—Time for Everything. Hanawalt, Josh, illus. (p. 1751)
Diersch, Sandra. Ceiling Stars (p. 283)
—False Start (p. 567)
—No Contact (p. 1258)
—Play On (p. 1371)
Diersch, Sandra & London, Gerri. Skin Deep (p. 1585)
Diersch, Sandra & Moreira, Carol. Ceiling Stars (p. 283)
Diesen, Deborah. Hide & Seek, Pout-Pout Fish. Hanna, Dan, illus. (p. 777)
—Not Very Merry Pout-Pout Fish. Hanna, Dan, illus. (p. 1267)
—Picture Day Perfection. Santat, Dan, illus. (p. 1355)
—Pout-Pout Fish. Hanna, Dan, illus. (p. 1389)
—Pout-Pout Fish Book & CD Storytime Set. (p. 1389)
—Pout-Pout Fish Goes to School. Hanna, Dan, illus. (p. 1389)
—Pout-Pout Fish in the Big-Big Dark. Hanna, Dan, illus. (p. 1389)
—Pout-Pout Fish Tank. Hanna, Dan, illus. (p. 1389)
—Smile, Pout-Pout Fish. Hanna, Dan, illus. (p. 1594)
Dieter, Debra. Lightning & Mikey. (p. 1016)
Dieterichs, Shelley. Let's Color Together — Fabulous Fairies. (p. 995)
Dieterichs, Shelley, illus. see Gerver, Jane E.
Dieterichs, Shelley, illus. see Hoffmann, Sara E.
Dieterichs, Shelley, et al. Fabulous Fairies Coloring Book. (p. 560)
Dieterle, Amber. Will You Miss Me? (p. 1932)
Dieterman, Nicole. Child's View of War: A Collection of Poems by Nicole Dieterman. (p. 305)
Diethelm, Laurie, ed. Occupational Guidance, Unit 1I (p. 1275)
—On the Job: A Work Skills Development Program. (p. 1290)
Dietl, Erhard. Andres y Su Nuevo Amigo. (p. 72)
—Veces Quisiera Ser un Tigre. (p. 1834)
Dietrich, Andrea, illus. see Toynton, Ian.
Dietrich, David. Revenge of the Lucky Thirteen. (p. 1466)
Dietrich, Julie. David & His Friend, Jonathan. Ramsey, Marcy, illus. (p. 410)
—Tiny Baby Moses. Clark, Bill, illus. (p. 1756)
Dietrich, Julie & Fernández, Cecilia. niño Moisés (Tiny Baby Moses) - Bilingual. (p. 1257)
Dietrich, Sean. Hansel & Gretel: The Graphic Novel (p. 743)
Dietrich, Sean, illus. see Andersen, Hans Christian & Capstone Press Staff.
Dietrich, Sean, illus. see Andersen, Hans Christian & Stone Arch Books Staff.
Dietrich, Sean, illus. see Capstone Press Staff.
Dietrich, Sean, illus. see Stone Arch Books (Firm : Afton, Minn.) Staff.
Dietrich, Sean, creator. Industriacide. (p. 872)
Dietrick, Ellen. It's Israel's Birthday! Cohen, Tod, photos by. (p. 897)
Dietrick, Robin C., ed. see Takemori, Lianne K.
Dietz, Irene Andrighetti. Clariss, Did You Do This? (p. 327)
Dietz, Kamala. Who Has Seen the Sun: A Yoga Activity & Coloring Book. DeRaymond, Devaki, illus. (p. 1915)
Dietz, Mike, illus. see Gutman, Dan.
Dietz, Stephanie Kelly. Under the Blinking Light. (p. 1813)
Dietze, Jurgen, jt. auth. see Barth, Katrin.
Diez, Dalia Alvarado, illus. see Dreser, Elena.
Diez, Lola, tr. see Holm, Jennifer L.
Diez-Luckie, Cathy. Dinosaurs on the Move: Movable Paper Figures to Cut, Color, & Assemble. (p. 445)
Diez-Luckie, Cathy, illus. see Ford, Carolyn.
Diez-Luckie, Cathy, illus. see Hill, Merle Roddy.
Diffenderfer, David W. Adventures of Boo & Fred. (p. 16)
Diffily, Deborah, jt. auth. see Carr, Karen.
Diffily, Deborah & Sassman, Charlotte. Teaching Effective Classroom Routines: Establish Structure in the Classroom to Foster Children's Learning-From the First Day of School & All Through the Year. (p. 1710)
DiFiori, Larry, illus. see Albee, Sarah & Sesame Street Staff.
DiGenti, Victor. Windrusher. (p. 1936)
DiGerolamo, Tony. Wildsidhe Chronicles: The Undercover Dragon. Bk. 5 (p. 1931)
Digest Readers Staff & Bright, J. E. Batman Stand-Up Mover. (p. 144)
Diggins, Julia E. String, Straightedge & Shadow: The Story of Geometry. Diggins, Julia E. & Bell, Corydon, illus. (p. 1667)
Diggins, Matthew. Andrew & the Secret Gallery. Diggins, Matthew, illus. (p. 72)
Diggle, Andy. Shadowland. (p. 1558)
Diggle, Andy, et al. Silent Dragon. (p. 1575)
Diggle, Daniel James, illus. see Diggle, David Mark.
Diggle, David Mark. Annie: A Small Ant with Some Big Questions. Preuss, Sarah Louise, illus. (p. 86)
—Barbara: A Sssslithering Adventure of Self Discovery. Diggle, Daniel James, illus. (p. 137)
—Bella: Shares Her Sticky Plan. Preuss, Sarah Louise, illus. (p. 162)
—Brian: Eats Himself Smarter. Diggle, Daniel James, illus. (p. 226)
—Douglas: Pays the Price for Not Paying Attention. Preuss, Sarah Louise, illus. (p. 473)
—Enjoy the Ride: 10 Metaphors to Teach Children Through Their Own Imagination. (p. 530)
—Ewan: From Bullied to Superhero in One Afternoon. Diggle, Daniel James, illus. (p. 547)
—Frederick: Thinking Makes Breathing Easy. Diggle, Daniel James, illus. (p. 633)
—George & Toby: Won't Have A Baaa of Bed Wetting. Diggle, Daniel James, illus. (p. 663)
—Lilly: The Crazy Little Van. Preuss, Sarah Louise, illus. (p. 1017)
—Malana: Learns When Enough Is Enough. Preuss, Sarah Louise, illus. (p. 1083)
—Melanie: Honestly Finds Herself Out of Her Depth. Diggle, Daniel James, illus. (p. 1125)
—Paco: The High-Performance Penguin. Preuss, Sarah Louise, illus. (p. 1317)
—Reggie: Learns to Roll with It. Preuss, Sarah Louise, illus. (p. 1457)
—Sally: And Her Singing Stage Debut. Preuss, Sarah Louise, illus. (p. 1505)
—Samantha: One Finger, One Nose, A Whole Lot of Bugs. Preuss, Sarah Louise, illus. (p. 1507)
—Sammy: Leaves His Mark. Diggle, Daniel James, illus. (p. 1507)
Diggory, Nick, illus. see Dale, Jay.
Diggory, Nikki. Inventor Nikola Tesla. (p. 884)
—Jacob Counts Down: Understanding Subtraction. (p. 904)
Diggory, Nikki, jt. auth. see Mills, Nathan.
Diggory, Terence. Encyclopedia of the New York School Poets. (p. 525)
Diggs, Dylan. Palladium: Trust No One. (p. 1320)
—Palladium: Second Contact. (p. 1320)
—Palladium. (p. 1320)
Diggs, Linda. Gwynepe Slew the Dragon Almost. Hanna, Ellen & Steier, John, eds. (p. 733)
Diggs, Taye. Chocolate Me! Evans, Shane W., illus. (p. 309)
DiGiacomo, Kris, illus. see Escoffier, Michaël.
Digman, Kristina, jt. auth. see Naslund, Gorel Kristina.
Dignan, James, illus. see Zawacki, Neil.
DiGuardo, Maggie & Leventis, Kelly. Celly. (p. 286)
Diienno, Trish, illus. see Ireland, Charles E.
Dilulio, John J., Jr., jt. auth. see Wilson, James Q.
Dijkstra, Lida. Little Mouse. Grobler, Piet, illus. (p. 1032)
Dike, Diane. Gracie Comes Home: The Adventures of Gracie & Diane. Grasso, Craig A. & Grasso, Samantha A., illus. (p. 705)
DiLiberto, Frank. Gypsy Kids: Diary & Writing Journal. (p. 734)
—Gypsy Kids: The Adventures of Colby Myers & Mark Howard. (p. 734)
Dilkes, D. H. Beans, Nuts, & Oils. (p. 150)
—Bread & Grains. (p. 224)
—Fruit. (p. 645)
—I See Circles. (p. 845)
—I See Ovals. (p. 845)
—I See Rectangles. (p. 845)
—I See Squares. (p. 845)
—I See Stars. (p. 845)
—I See Triangles. (p. 845)
—Meat & Fish. (p. 1118)
—Milk & Dairy. (p. 1143)
—Vegetables. (p. 1834)
Dilkes, Sam, jt. auth. see Dicker, Katie.
Dilks, Christabelle. Argentina. (p. 97)
Dill, Bonnie. Brain Quest Grade 1 Reading. (p. 221)
—Brain Quest Grade 2 Reading. (p. 222)
Dill, Margo L. Finding My Place: One Girl's Strength at Vicksburg. (p. 588)
Dill, Mark. Maddie & Me: Go to the Zoo. (p. 1069)
Dill, Melanie, et al. 31 Verses - The Bible: Every Teenager Should Know. (p. 1996)
Dill, Pamela Wescovich. Katrina's Rainbow: The Miracle of the Storm Crosses. (p. 945)
Dillard, Mark. Journey Through the Asteroid Belt (p. 928)
Dillard, Mary Gregory. Days of My Youth. (p. 415)
—Finding Betsyanna. (p. 588)
—Jeepers Creepers! The Squirrels Are Coming. (p. 911)
Dillard, Sarah. Extraordinary Warren: A Super Chicken. Dillard, Sarah, illus. (p. 555)
—First Day at Zoo School. Dillard, Sarah, illus. (p. 594)
Dillard, Sarah, illus. see Aboff, Marcie & Shaskan, Trisha Speed.
Dillard, Sarah, illus. see Aboff, Marcie.
Dillard, Sarah, illus. see Auerbach, Annie.
Dillard, Sarah, illus. see Blaisdell, Molly.
Dillard, Sarah, illus. see Feldman, Thea.
Dillard, Sarah, illus. see Larson, Beverly.
Dillard, Sarah, illus. see Runnells, Treesha.
Dillard, Sarah, illus. see Shaskan, Trisha Speed.
Dillard, Sarah, illus. see Wax, Wendy.
Dillard, Sheri. Roman Gladiators. (p. 1485)
—Viking Warriors. (p. 1842)
—What's Great about Delaware? (p. 1897)
—What's Great about Oklahoma? (p. 1897)
—What's Great about West Virginia? (p. 1897)
Dillard, Tara & Williamson, Don. Best Garden Plants for Georgia. (p. 169)
Dille, John F. & Nowlan, Philip Francis. Buck Rogers in the 25th Century: the Complete Newspaper Dailies Volume 4: The Complete Newspaper Dailies Volume 4. (p. 234)
Dillemuth, Julie. Lucy in the City: A Story about Spatial Thinking. Wood, Laura, illus. (p. 1063)
Diller, Howard, jt. auth. see Smith, Jill.
Diller, Janelle. Mystery of the Ballerina Ghost. Turner, Adam, illus. (p. 1225)
Dilley, Kristi. Squiggy the Squirrel Meets Wallis the Woodpecker. Dilley, Kristi, illus. (p. 1637)

Dilley, Nichole. George Washington's Journey of Faith. (p. 665)
Dilley, Ray. Brian's Lighthouse. (p. 227)
Dilliard, Tara, jt. auth. see Williamson, Don.
Dillies, Lyn. Your Vote Is Magic! (p. 1981)
Dillingham, Charlene, illus. see Roach, Hesta.
Dillingham, Jeffrey & Dillingham, Laurie. Bella the Bumblebee. (p. 162)
Dillingham, Laurie, jt. auth. see Dillingham, Jeffrey.
Dillingham, Mike. Rivers Book Two: Through the Eyes of a Blind Sled Dog. (p. 1476)
Dillingham Pierson, Clara. Among the Farmyard People. (p. 65)
—Among the Forest People. (p. 65)
—Among the Meadow People. (p. 65)
—Among the Night People. (p. 65)
—Among the Pond People. (p. 65)
—Clara Dillingham Pierson's Complete among the People Series. (p. 326)
Dillman, Jennifer, illus. see Gow, Kailin.
Dillman, Shanley Chris. Black Pond. (p. 196)
Dillon, Diane, illus. see Bach, Alice & Exum, J. Cheryl.
Dillon, Diane, illus. see Bradbury, Ray.
Dillon, Diane, illus. see Brown, Margaret Wise.
Dillon, Diane, illus. see Fox, Mem.
Dillon, Diane, illus. see Hamilton, Virginia.
Dillon, Diane, illus. see Haugaard, Erik Christian.
Dillon, Diane, illus. see Hearn, Michael Patrick.
Dillon, Diane, illus. see Mathis, Sharon Bell.
Dillon, Diane, illus. see McKissack, Patricia C.
Dillon, Diane, illus. see Musgrove, Margaret.
Dillon, Diane, illus. see Paterson, Katherine.
Dillon, Diane, illus. see Rawlings, Marjorie Kinnan.
Dillon, Diane, jt. auth. see Dillon, Leo.
Dillon, Doug. Brief Political & Geographic History of Asia: Where Are... Saigon, Kampuchea, & Burma. (p. 228)
—St. Augustine. (p. 1637)
—Stepping off a Cliff [the St. Augustine Trilogy: The St. Augustine Trilogy: Book II. (p. 1648)
—We Visit Venezuela. (p. 1868)
Dillon, Eilis. Island of Horses. (p. 892)
—Lost Island. Kennedy, Richard, illus. (p. 1056)
Dillon, Elena. Breathe. (p. 226)
—Crushing. (p. 387)
Dillon, Elizabeth. Forgetful Lucy Goes to the Ranch. (p. 619)
Dillon, Eric. Peer Pressure. (p. 1335)
Dillon, Eric, ed. Obesity. (p. 1275)
Dillon, Jana. Lucky O'Leprechaun in School Dillon, Jana, illus. (p. 1063)
Dillon, Julia, ed. see Burden, Peter.
Dillon, Julie, illus. see Cooper, Susan.
Dillon, Kadi. Babies in the Barnyard (p. 124)
Dillon, Katherine V., ed. see Ugaki, Matome.
Dillon, Kimberly M. Ghosts of Wolf Creek. (p. 673)
Dillon, Leo, illus. see Bach, Alice & Exum, J. Cheryl.
Dillon, Leo, illus. see Bosak, Susan V.
Dillon, Leo, illus. see Bradbury, Ray.
Dillon, Leo, illus. see Brown, Margaret Wise.
Dillon, Leo, illus. see Fox, Mem.
Dillon, Leo, illus. see Hamilton, Virginia.
Dillon, Leo, illus. see Haugaard, Erik Christian.
Dillon, Leo, illus. see Hearn, Michael Patrick.
Dillon, Leo, illus. see Mathis, Sharon Bell.
Dillon, Leo, illus. see McKissack, Patricia C.
Dillon, Leo, illus. see Musgrove, Margaret.
Dillon, Leo, illus. see Paterson, Katherine.
Dillon, Leo, illus. see Rawlings, Marjorie Kinnan.
Dillon, Leo & Dillon, Diane. If Kids Ran the World. Dillon, Leo & Dillon, Diane, illus. (p. 853)
—Rap a Tap Tap: Here's Bojangles - Think of That! (p. 1438)
Dillon, Patrick. Story of Britain from the Norman Conquest to the European Union. Lynch, P. J., illus. (p. 1657)
—Story of Buildings: From the Pyramids to the Sydney Opera House & Beyond. Biesty, Stephen, illus. (p. 1657)
Dillon, Paul, illus. see Polette, Nancy.
Dillon, Preston, jt. auth. see Rinne, Teresa.
Dillon, Sally Pierson. Champions of the King: The Story of the Apostles. (p. 289)
—Exile of the Chosen: God's Heroes from Solomon to Malachi. (p. 548)
Dillon, Steve, illus. see Ennis, Garth.
Dillon, Steve, illus. see Morrison, Grant.
Dillon, Susan. Addiction & Subtraction: Dozens of Leveled Practice Pages to Improve Students' Speed & Accuracy with Math Facts. (p. 11)
Dillon-Butler, Marybeth. Myrtle the Hurdler: And Her Pink & Purple Polka-Dotted Girdle. Messing, David, illus. (p. 1222)
Dillon-Hreha, Denise. Wedding of Q & U. (p. 1871)
Dillsworth-Swift, Tammy. Bermuda Triangle & the Lost Island. (p. 167)
Dilmore, Don. Danny's Red Jacket. (p. 406)
DiLorenzo, Michael A. Bows, Does & Bucks! An Introduction to Archery Deer Hunting. Julich, Jenniffer, illus. (p. 216)
DiLorenzo, Michael A. & Julich, Jennifer. Adventures with Jonny: Road Trip to the Parks. (p. 25)
DiLorenzo, Michael & Julich, Jennifer. Adventures with Jonny: Ice Fishing! The Coolest Sport on Earth - A Parent & Child Ice Fishing Adventure & Guide. (p. 25)
Dilpickles, Emily. Catman. (p. 280)
Dils, Tracey E. Around the Moon 1,2,3: A Space Counting Book. (p. 100)
—Down in the Jungle 1,2,3: A Rainforest Counting Book. (p. 474)
—Down on the Farm 1,2,3: A Farm Counting Book. (p. 474)
—Falling Leaves 1,2,3: A Farm Counting Book. (p. 567)
—My Pet & Me, 1,2,3: A Pets Counting Book. (p. 1217)
—Under the Sea 1,2,3: An Ocean Counting Book. (p. 1814)
Dilworth, Kristopher, ed. see Adkins, Linda.
Dilz, Ric. My Dad Could do Anything! (p. 1200)
—My Grandma Could do Anything! (p. 1210)
—My Grandma Could do Anything in Hawaii! (p. 1210)
—My Grandma Could do Anything in the Great Outdoors! (p. 1210)
DiMaggio, Brian K. Jasper. (p. 910)
Dimarcello, Pete. Panic at the Pool. Harpan, Gaile, ed. (p. 1321)
DiMarcello, Pete, jt. auth. see Harpan, Gaile.
DiMarco, Carol. Alchemy. (p. 35)
—Magical Child. (p. 1074)
DiMarco, Carol & Bowman, Sharon. Tale of Two Kingdoms. (p. 1700)
DiMarco, Hayley. God Girl Journey: A 30-Day Guide to a Deeper Faith. (p. 688)
—Idol Girls: What's Your Obsession? (p. 852)
—Mean Girls: Facing Your Beauty Turned Beast. (p. 1116)
—Mean Girls Gone: A Spiritual Guide to Getting Rid of Mean. (p. 1116)
Dimarco, Tony. Three Keys. Mallette, Dania, illus. (p. 1742)
DiMare, Loren Spiotta, et al. Rockwell: A Boy & His Dog. Miller, Cliff, illus. (p. 1484)
Dimari. I See a Healthy Me! (p. 845)
Dimartino, Catherine. Early American Alliances. (p. 493)
Dimartino, Konietzko, et al. Legend of Korra. (p. 988)
DiMartino, Michael Dante. Legend of Korra. (p. 988)
Dimartino, Michael Dante, jt. auth. see Kanietzko, Bryan.
DiMartino, Michael Dante, jt. auth. see Konietzko, Bryan.
DiMartino, Michael Dante, jt. auth. see Yang, Gene Luen.
DiMartino, Michael Dante, jt. creator see Kanietzko, Bryan.
DiMartino, Michael Dante & Konietzko, Bryan. Avatar: The Last Airbender. (p. 118)
DiMartino, Michael Dante & Konietzko, Bryan, creators. Avatar. (p. 118)
—Avatar: the Last Airbender, Chapter 4. (p. 118)
Dimatteo, Richard, illus. see Sirotowitz, Sandi, et al.
DiMatteo, Richard A., illus. see Corman, Clifford L. & Trevino, Esther.
DiMatteo, Richard A., illus. see Parker, Roberta N.
DiMatteo, Richard A., illus. see Parker, Roberta N. & Parker, Harvey C.
DiMatteo, Richard A., illus. see Sirotowitz, Sandi, et al.
DiMatteo, Richard A., illus. see Zentall, Sydney & Goldstein, Sam.
DiMaulo, Michael A. Maggie's Window (p. 1071)
diMauro, Laurie & Grant, Tim, eds. Ethics. (p. 539)
diMauro, Laurie & Grant, Tina, eds. Ethics. (p. 539)
Dimaya, Emerson, illus. see Bowen, Carl & Poe, Edgar Allen.
Dimbylow, Jube, illus. see Norton Kreider, Barbara.
Dimensions for Living Staff. Personal Prayers for Children. (p. 1344)
Dimitri, Simona, illus. see Bird, Helen.
Dimitri, Simona, illus. see Brooks, Felicity.
Dimitri, Simona, illus. see Milbourne, Anna.
Dimitriadis, Nick, illus. see Vollmer, Cheryl.
Dimopoulos, Elaine. Material Girls. (p. 1104)
DiMotta, Michael J., illus. see Bekoff, Marc.
Dimpel, Matt. War of the Serpent Swords. (p. 1857)
Dimplechin, Lord Reginald. Does a Wuzz. (p. 460)
—McKenzie Was Here. (p. 1114)
Din, Anne Bar, tr. see Marcos, Subcomandante.
Dina, Madalina, illus. see Hodgson, Karen J.
Dinaberg, Leslie. Spider Life. (p. 1626)
—Volcanoes. (p. 1849)
—Women in Charge. (p. 1945)
Dinan, Robert S. Drug Free Teen: The Ultimate Guide for Parents, Teens, Teachers & Friends. (p. 486)
Dinardo, Jeff. Bunny & Bird Are Best Friends: Making New Friends. Ho, Jannie, illus. (p. 242)
—Klink & Klank: Accepting Differences. Paillot, Jim, illus. (p. 963)
—Mr. Mouse's Motel: Helping Others. Lubach, Peter, illus. (p. 1185)
—Sunrise Band: Cooperating. Palen, Debbie, illus. (p. 1677)
—Worm & Farmer Maguire: Teamwork/Working Together. Joven, John, illus. (p. 1961)
Dinbergs, Holly Smith. Bowling Buddies. Foye, Lloyd, illus. (p. 216)
—Hair Scare. Stewart, Chantal, illus. (p. 736)
Dindar, Kubra, illus. see Ochs, Tom.
Dineen, Jacqueline. Elephants. (p. 511)
—Grizzly Bears. (p. 724)
—Lions. (p. 1021)
Dineen, Kaite. What Santa Wants You to Know: A Story of Santa's Love for Jesus (p. 1893)
Dineen, Tom, illus. see Bryant, John E.
Dineen, Tom, illus. see Schneider, Elaine Ernst.
Diner, Hasia R. Encyclopedia of American Women's History (p. 524)
Dines, Carol. Queen's Soprano. (p. 1425)
Dinesen, Isak. Cuento del Joven Marinero. Lago, Angela, illus. (p. 389)
Ding, Sean. Monkey Ming & the Dream Team. (p. 1165)
—Zediogram. (p. 1985)
Ding, Yuhui Andrew. Warrior Soul. (p. 1859)
Dingle, Adrian. How to Make a Universe with 92 Ingredients: An Electrifying Guide to the Elements. (p. 820)
Dingle, Adrian, jt. auth. see Basher, Simon.
Dingle, Adrian & Basher, Simon. Periodic Table: Elements with Style! Basher, Simon, illus. (p. 1343)
Dingle, Adrian, et al. Basher Science: the Complete Periodic Table: All the Elements with Style! Basher, Simon, illus. (p. 141)
Dingle, Charles A. Popey's Secret. (p. 1384)
Dingler, Jay. Infinite Odyssey. Lafan, Algie, illus. (p. 873)
Dingles, Molly. Black as a Bat. Velez, Walter, illus. (p. 195)
—Black as a Bat/Negro como un Murcielago. Velez, Walter, illus. (p. 195)
—Blue as a Blueberry. Velez, Walter, illus. (p. 202)
—Blue as a Blueberry/Azul como un Arandano. Velez, Walter, illus. (p. 202)
—Blue as a Blueberry/Bleu comme un Bleuet. Velez, Walter, illus. (p. 202)
—Brown as an Acorn. Velez, Walter, illus. (p. 231)
—Brown as an Acorn/Marrón como una Bellota. Velez, Walter, illus. (p. 231)
—Crescent Kitchen: Cocina de Medialuna. Brodie, Neale, illus. (p. 381)
—Crescent Kitchen. Brodie, Neale, illus. (p. 381)
—Diamond Downhill. Dobson, Len, illus. (p. 434)
—Diamond Downhill/Cuesta abajo en forma de Rombo. Dobson, Len, illus. (p. 434)
—Gray as a Dolphin. Velez, Walter, illus. (p. 713)
—Gray as a Dolphin/Gris como un Delfin. Velez, Walter, illus. (p. 713)
—Green as a Frog. Velez, Walter, illus. (p. 721)
—Green as a Frog/Verde como una Rana. Velez, Walter, illus. (p. 721)
—Green as a Frog/Vert comme une Grenouille. Velez, Walter, illus. (p. 721)
—Number 1 What Grows in the Sun?/Número 1 Qué crece en el Sol? Wallis, Rebecca, illus. (p. 1271)
—Number 10 Where Is the Hen? Wallis, Rebecca, illus. (p. 1271)
—Number 10 Where Is the Hen?/Número 10 en dónde está la Gallina? Wallis, Rebecca, illus. (p. 1271)
—Number 2 Let's Go to the Zoo! Wallis, Rebecca, illus. (p. 1271)
—Number 2 Let's Go to the Zoo!/Número 2 Vamos al Zoologico! Wallis, Rebecca, illus. (p. 1271)
—Number 3 What's in the Sea? (p. 1271)
—Number 3 What's in the Sea? Wallis, Rebecca, illus. (p. 1271)
—Number 3 What's in the Sea?/Número 3 Qué hay en el Mar? Wallis, Rebecca, illus. (p. 1271)
—Number 4 Shop at the Store! Wallis, Rebecca, illus. (p. 1271)
—Number 4 Shop at the Store!/Número 4 Vamos de compras a la Tienda! Wallis, Rebecca, illus. (p. 1271)
—Number 5 Let's Go for a Drive! Wallis, Rebecca, illus. (p. 1271)
—Number 5 Let's Go for a Drive!/Número 5 Vamos a viajar en Coche! Wallis, Rebecca, illus. (p. 1271)
—Number 6 What Can We Mix? Wallis, Rebecca, illus. (p. 1271)
—Number 6 What Can We Mix ? Wallis, Rebecca, illus. (p. 1271)
—Number 6 What Can We Mix?/Número 6 Qué podemos Mezclar? Wallis, Rebecca, illus. (p. 1271)
—Number 7 Stars in the Heaven. Wallis, Rebecca, illus. (p. 1271)
—Number 7 Stars in the Heaven/Número 7 Estrellas en el Cielo. Wallis, Rebecca, illus. (p. 1271)
—Number 8 Let's Stay up Late! Wallis, Rebecca, illus. (p. 1271)
—Number 8 Let's Stay up Late!/Número 8 Vamos a quedarnos en vela hasta muy Noche! Wallis, Rebecca, illus. (p. 1271)
—Number 9 Dress up to Dine! Wallis, Rebecca, illus. (p. 1271)
—Number 9 Dress up to Dine!/Número 9 Vestirse con elegancia para Cenar! Wallis, Rebecca, illus. (p. 1271)
—On Christmas Eve. Wallis, Rebecca, illus. (p. 1288)
—On Easter Morning. Wallis, Rebecca, illus. (p. 1288)
—Orange as a Pumpkin. Velez, Walter, illus. (p. 1301)
—Orange as a Pumpkin/Anaranjado como una Calabaza. Velez, Walter, illus. (p. 1301)
—Orange as a Pumpkin/Orange comme une Citrouille. Velez, Walter, illus. (p. 1301)
—Oval Opera: Ópera de óvalos. Brodie, Neale, illus. (p. 1313)
—Oval Opera. Brodie, Neale, illus. (p. 1313)
—Pink as a Piglet. Velez, Walter, illus. (p. 1359)
—Pink as a Piglet/Rosa como un Cerdito. Velez, Walter, illus. (p. 1359)
—Purple as a Plum. Velez, Walter, illus. (p. 1419)
—Purple as a Plum/Morado como una Ciruela. Velez, Walter, illus. (p. 1419)
—Purple as a Plum/Violet comme une Prune. Velez, Walter, illus. (p. 1419)
—Rectangle Ranch. Dobson, Len, illus. (p. 1452)
—Rectangle Ranch/Rancho Rectangular. Dobson, Len, illus. (p. 1452)
—Red as a Fire Truck. Velez, Walter, illus. (p. 1453)
—Red as a Fire Truck/Rojo como un camion de Bomberos. Velez, Walter, illus. (p. 1453)
—Red as a Firetruck/Rouge comme un camion de Pompiers. Velez, Walter, illus. (p. 1453)
—Seaside Circles. Brodie, Neale, illus. (p. 1538)
—Seaside Circles/Círculos a la orilla del Mar. Brodie, Neal, illus. (p. 1538)
—Seaside Circles/Círculos a la orilla del Mar. Brodie, Neale, illus. (p. 1538)
—Star Ship: Barco de Estrellas. Brodie, Neale, illus. (p. 1641)
—Star Ship. Brodie, Neale, illus. (p. 1641)
—Sweet Hearts: Dulce Corazón. Brodie, Neale, illus. (p. 1689)
—Sweet Hearts. Brodie, Neale, illus. (p. 1689)
—Town Squares. Brodie, Neale, illus. (p. 1773)
—Town Squares/Cuadrados en la Plaza. Brodie, Neale, illus. (p. 1773)
—Triangle Trail: Sendero de Triángulos. (p. 1785)
—Turquoise as a Parakeet. Velez, Walter, illus. (p. 1798)
—Turquoise as a Parakeet/Turquesa como un Periquito. Velez, Walter, illus. (p. 1798)
—White as a Seashell. Velez, Walter, illus. (p. 1912)
—White as a Seashell/Blanco como una concha Marina. Velez, Walter, illus. (p. 1912)
—Yellow as a Lemon. Velez, Walter, illus. (p. 1970)
—Yellow as a Lemon/Amarillo como un Limon. Velez, Walter, illus. (p. 1970)
—Yellow as a Lemon/Jaune comme un Citron. Velez, Walter, illus. (p. 1970)
Dingman, April Gholson. Even Cowgirls Comb Their Hair. (p. 541)
Dingman, Matthew. Very Different Animal from Mars. (p. 1837)
Dingrando, Laurel, et al. Chemistry: Matter & Change. (p. 297)
Dingus, Lowell, et al. Dinosaur Eggs Discovered! Unscrambling the Clues. (p. 442)
Dingwall, Cindy. Bible Banquets with Kids. (p. 175)
—Bible Verse Fun with Kids: 300+ Ideas & Activities to Help Children Learn & Live Scripture. (p. 176)
Dingwell, Carson. Rory of Cain's Mountain. (p. 1488)
Dini, Paul. Men of Steel Burchett, Rick & Austin, Terry, illus. (p. 1126)
Dinkles, jt. auth. see Atkinson, Joelle.
Dinn, Philip & Jones, Andy. Peg Bearskin. Cohen, Elly, illus. (p. 1335)
Dinneen, John. Practical Joker's Handbook. (p. 1392)
—Practical Joker's Handbook 2. Maddison, Lucy, illus. (p. 1392)
Dinnen, Marie, jt. auth. see Christian Focus Publications (CFP) Staff.
Dinnison, Kris. You & Me & Him. (p. 1973)
Dinola, Jack. Two Squirrels & a Mouse: A Christmas Story. (p. 1804)
Dinolfo, Louann S. Calico Kite. (p. 253)
Dinosaurs, jt. auth. see Whelon, Chuck.
Dinsdale, Christopher. Betrayed: The Legend of Oak Island. (p. 172)
—Broken Circle. (p. 230)
—Emerald Key. (p. 517)
—Stolen Away. (p. 1652)
Di-Nsteins, The Albert. No Reading Allowed. (p. 1260)
Dintiman, George Blough. Speed Improvement for Young Athletes: How to Sprint Faster in Your Sport in 30 Workouts. (p. 1624)
DiNubile, Nicholas A. & Patrick, William. Framework: Your 7-Step Program for Healthy Muscles, Bones, & Joints. (p. 627)
Dinzeo, Paul. Sheamus. (p. 1564)
—Spartans. (p. 1622)
Diocese of San Bernardino Staff. My Quinceanera Student Bk: Bilingual Formation Program & Remembrance Book. (p. 1217)
Dion. Chess with Butterflies. (p. 298)
—Fishing with Balloons. (p. 599)
Dion, Elayne. Brass Button. (p. 222)
Dion, L. M. Opposites of My Jewish Year. Olson, Julie, illus. (p. 1301)
Dion, Nathalie, illus. see Beker, Jeanne.
Dion, Nathalie, illus. see Colman, Michelle Sinclair.
Dion, Nathalie, illus. see Samoun, Abigail.
Dion, Nathalie, jt. auth. see Schroeder, Lisa.
Dionne, Deanna, illus. see Blankenship, Julianna.
Dionne, Erin. Models Don't Eat Chocolate Cookies. (p. 1158)
—Moxie & the Art of Rule Breaking: A 14-Day Mystery. (p. 1184)
—Notes from an Accidental Band Geek. (p. 1268)
—Ollie & the Science of Treasure Hunting. (p. 1287)
—Total Tragedy of a Girl Named Hamlet. (p. 1771)
Dionne, Nina, illus. see Tomaszewski, Suzanne Lyon.
Diorio, Al. Bobby Darin: The Incredible Story of an Amazing Life. (p. 206)
DiOrio, Ariel. Mystery of the Missing Menorahs: A Hanukkah Humdinger! (p. 1225)
Diorio, Mary Ann L. Student's Guide to Herman Melville. (p. 1669)
—Student's Guide to Mark Twain. (p. 1669)
—Student's Guide to Nathaniel Hawthorne. (p. 1669)
DiOrio, Rana, jt. auth. see Little Pickle Press.
Diouf, Sylviane. Bintou's Braids. Evans, Shane, illus. (p. 188)
DiPalma, Emilio & Chetkowski, Emily DiPalma. Just a Kid: A Guard at the Nuremberg Trials. (p. 937)
DiPiazza, Francesca. Friend Me! Six Hundred Years of Social Networking in America. (p. 637)
—Remaking the John: The Invention & Reinvention of the Toilet. (p. 1458)
—Slovakia in Pictures. (p. 1591)
Dipiazza, Francesca. Turkey in Pictures. (p. 1797)
—When Did George Washington Fight His First Military Battle? And Other Questions about the French & Indian War. (p. 1901)
DiPiazza, Francesca, jt. auth. see De Capua, Sarah.
DiPiazza, Francesca Davis. Algeria in Pictures. (p. 38)
—Bolivia in Pictures. (p. 208)
—Chile in Pictures. (p. 305)
—Democratic Republic of Congo in Pictures. (p. 426)
—Kuwait in Pictures. (p. 968)
—Mali in Pictures. (p. 1083)
—Morocco in Pictures. (p. 1176)
—New Zealand in Pictures. (p. 1249)
—Salvador in Pictures. (p. 1506)
—When Did George Washington Fight His First Military Battle? And Other Questions about the French & Indian War. (p. 1901)
—Yemen in Pictures. (p. 1970)
DiPiero, Josh. Tickets for the Talent Show: Use Place Value Understanding & Properties of Operations to Add & Subtract. (p. 1747)
Dipietro, Frances. Eagle & Dolphin: We Are Wonderfully Made. (p. 492)
Dipietro, Kara, jt. auth. see Fleming, Vicki.
Dipinto, Michael J. Princess Mermaid & the Missing Sea Shells. Marsh, Bobbie, illus. (p. 1404)
Dipper, F. D. & Dipper, Frances. Misterios de los Oceanos. (p. 1155)
Dipper, Frances, jt. auth. see Dipper, F. D.
Dippold, Jane, illus. see Bennett, Donna I.
Dippold, Jane, illus. see Cohen, Deborah Bodin.
Dippold, Jane, illus. see Galbraith, Kathryn Osebold.
Dippold, Jane, illus. see Suen, Anastasia.
Dippold, Jane, illus. see Trent, Shanda.
Dippold-Brady, Melissa. Florida Fossils for Kids. (p. 607)
DiPrimio, Pete. Ancient Rome. (p. 70)
—Ancient Sparta. (p. 70)
—Drew Brees. (p. 485)
—Dwyane Wade. (p. 491)
—Eli Manning. (p. 512)
—Jeremy Lin. (p. 913)
—Judicial Branch. (p. 931)
—Sphinx. (p. 1626)
—Tom Brady. (p. 1762)
—We Visit Iran. (p. 1868)
—World of CrossFit. (p. 1956)
DiPrince, Dawn. Twisting Arms: Teaching Students How to Write to Persuade. (p. 1803)
DiPrince, Dawn, jt. auth. see Thurston, Cheryl Miller.
DiPucchio, Kelly. Alfred Zector, Book Collector. Pamintuan, Macky, illus. (p. 37)
—Clink. Myers, Matthew, illus. (p. 333)

D

—Crafty Chloe. Ross, Heather, illus. (p. 376)
—Dinosnores. Goembel, Ponder, illus. (p. 445)
—Dog Days of School. Biggs, Brian, illus. (p. 461)
—Dress-Up Mess-Up. Ross, Heather, illus. (p. 485)
—Everyone Loves Bacon. Wight, Eric, illus. (p. 544)
—Gaston. Robinson, Christian, illus. (p. 657)
—Gilbert Goldfish Wants a Pet. Shea, Bob, illus. (p. 676)
—Grace for President. Pham, LeUyen, illus. (p. 704)
—Monster Makeovers. Pham, LeUyen, illus. (p. 1167)
—One Little, Two Little, Three Little Children. Lundquist, Mary, illus. (p. 1296)
—Zombie in Love. Joseph, Robin & Campbell, Scott, illus. (p. 1988)
—Zombie in Love 2 + 1. Campbell, Scott, illus. (p. 1988)
Direct Access. Ultimate Betrayal of street Life. (p. 1809)
Direen, William. Coma. (p. 346)
Dirge, Roman & Daily, Steven. It Ate Billy on Christmas. Dirge, Roman, illus. (p. 893)
Dirksing, Donna. First Stage: A Collection of Musical Plays for Children's First Performances Arranged with Orff Instruments for Grades 1-3. (p. 597)
DiRocco, Carl, illus. see Berglin, Ruth.
DiRocco, Carl, illus. see Braver, Vanita.
DiRocco, Carl, illus. see Chase, L. P.
DiRocco, Carl, illus. see Dakos, Kalli & DesMarteau, Alicia.
DiRocco, Carl, illus. see Haddon, Jean.
Diroma, Joseph. Pinuccio. Jones, Bob, illus. (p. 1361)
Dirr, Karen, illus. see Hage, Mike.
Dirst, Tracy. Adventures of Pixie & Pete: They Meet. (p. 21)
DiRubbio, Jennifer, illus. see Berkes, Marianne.
DiRubbio, Jennifer, illus. see Fredericks, Anthony D.
DiRubbio, Jennifer, tr. see Fredericks, Anthony D.
DiSalle, Zanita. Sofia's Pink Balloon. (p. 1605)
DiSalvo, Len, illus. see Weck, Peter.
DiSalvo, Len, illus. see Weck, Thomas & Weck, Peter.
DiSalvo-Ryan, DyAnne. Sloppy Copy Slipup. (p. 1591)
DiSalvo-Ryan, DyAnne, illus. see Stier, Catherine.
Disbray, Samantha. Warumungu Picture Dictionary. (p. 1859)
Disbro, Laura M. Adventures with Miss Lol: The Magic Paper Ride. (p. 25)
Disbrow, Sheri. Math Warm-Ups: Developing Fluency in Math. (p. 1107)
—Math Warm-Ups, Grade 2. (p. 1107)
Dischler, Patricia. Patty Cake Kids & the Lost Imagination Cap. (p. 1329)
—Tea Party Celebrations! (p. 1708)
Discovery Channel. Discovery Channel Sharkopedia: The Complete Guide to Everything Shark. (p. 450)
Discovery Channel (Firm) Staff, contrib. by. Mythbusters. (p. 1227)
Discovery Education Staff, creator. DE Science Techbook for Colorado - Grade 5. (p. 416)
—DE Science Techbook for National - Grades 3-5: Earth Science. (p. 416)
Dise, Molly. Fun at the Zoo! (p. 647)
—Math Hike. (p. 1106)
DiSesa, Verdi J. Chester County Hospital Heart Book: An Every Person's Guide to a Healthy Heart. Shoemaker, Eleanor B., ed. (p. 298)
Dishaw, Karen, illus. see Cooperman, Ben.
Disher, Garry. Flaminio, el Piano. (p. 602)
DiSiena, Laura Lyn & Eliot, Hannah. Chickens Don't Fly: And Other Fun Facts. Oswald, Pete, illus. (p. 300)
Disiena, Laura Lyn & Eliot, Hannah. Chickens Don't Fly. (p. 300)
DiSiena, Laura Lyn & Eliot, Hannah. Did You Know? Hippos Can't Swim; Chickens Don't Fly; Rainbows Never End; Trains Can Float. Oswald, Pete & Spurgeon, Aaron, illus. (p. 437)
Disiena, Laura Lyn & Eliot, Hannah. Dinosaurs Live On! (p. 445)
DiSiena, Laura Lyn & Eliot, Hannah. Dinosaurs Live On! And Other Fun Facts. Spurgeon, Aaron, illus. (p. 445)
—Hippos Can't Swim: And Other Fun Facts. Oswald, Pete, illus. (p. 781)
Disiena, Laura Lyn & Eliot, Hannah. Hippos Can't Swim. (p. 781)
DiSiena, Laura Lyn & Eliot, Hannah. Rainbows Never End: And Other Fun Facts. Oswald, Pete, illus. (p. 1436)
—Saturn Could Sail: And Other Fun Facts. Oswald, Pete & Spurgeon, Aaron, illus. (p. 1515)
Disiena, Laura Lyn & Eliot, Hannah. Saturn Could Sail. (p. 1515)
DiSiena, Laura Lyn & Eliot, Hannah. Trains Can Float: And Other Fun Facts. Oswald, Pete & Spurgeon, Aaron, illus. (p. 1777)
Disner, R. M. Angel Feather. (p. 73)
Disney. Big Bear, Little Bear. (p. 178)
—Big Hero 6 8x8. (p. 181)
—Big Hero 6 Deluxe Step into Reading. (p. 181)
—Big Hero 6 Step into Reading. (p. 181)
—Brave Firefighters. (p. 223)
—Disney Fairies: Pixie Hollow Reading Adventures. (p. 451)
—Disney Frozen - Anna's Act of Love. (p. 451)
—Disney Jake & the Never Land Pirates Yo Ho! Let's Go! (p. 451)
—Disney Pixar Inside Out Funbook. (p. 452)
—Disney Princess: Adventure under the Sea. (p. 452)
—Dusty to the Rescue. (p. 490)
—Friend for Merida. (p. 637)
—Frozen. (p. 645)
—Frozen - Anna's Icy Adventure. (p. 645)
—Frozen Cinestory, Volume 1. (p. 645)
—Inside Out #2. (p. 877)
—Inside Out 8x8 Pictureback. (p. 877)
—Inside Out Junior Novel. (p. 877)
—Journey into the Mind. (p. 928)
—Land of Oz. (p. 973)
—Monsters University Junior Novelization. (p. 1169)
—Mother's Love. (p. 1179)
—Rapunzel's Royal Wedding/Belle's Royal Wedding. (p. 1439)
—Scaring Lessons. (p. 1520)
—Sofia Takes the Lead. (p. 1605)
Disney / LeapFrog, jt. auth. see Disney.
Disney & Disney / LeapFrog. Disney Princess: Les aventures D'Ariel. (p. 452)
—World of Cars: L'escapade Nocturne. (p. 1956)
Disney & Fox, Jennifer. Meet Nyx the Scout Fairy. (p. 1121)
Disney & Sisler, Celeste. Disney Fairies: Meet Tinker Bell. (p. 451)
—Disney Fairies: Pixie Hollow Bake Off. (p. 451)
Disney & Studiomouse Staff. Give a Dog a Bone: Mother Goose. (p. 681)
Disney Animators Staff, illus. see Reader's Digest Editors & Miller, Sara.
Disney Art Archives Staff. Race & Rescue. (p. 1430)
Disney Artists Staff. Disney Pixar Cars 2 3-D Movie Theater. (p. 452)
Disney Artists Staff, illus. see Stierle, Cynthia.
Disney Baby Staff. Disney Planes Dusty Saves the Day! Storybook & Projector. (p. 452)
Disney Baby Staff & Disney Book Group Staff. Cozy Baby. Disney Storybook Artists Staff, illus. (p. 375)
Disney Book Club Staff. Disney Junior Music Player Storybook. (p. 451)
—Disney Planes Built for Speed. (p. 452)
—Disney Sofia the First Becoming a Princess: Storybook & Amulet Necklace. (p. 453)
—Pirates of the Caribbean - On Stranger Tides: Six Sea Chanties - An Original Graphic Novel Anthology. (p. 1364)
Disney Book Club Staff, illus. see Castro, Nachie.
Disney Book Group. Descendants: Mal's Diary. Disney Storybook Art Team, illus. (p. 428)
—Descendants: Mal's Spell Book. Disney Storybook Art Team, illus. (p. 428)
—Doc Mcstuffins a Dragon's Best Friend. Disney Storybook Art Team, illus. (p. 459)
—Frozen 5-Minute Frozen Stories. Disney Storybook Art Team, illus. (p. 645)
—Frozen Arendelle Adventures: Purchase Includes Mobile App for iPone & iPad! Disney Storybook Art Team, illus. (p. 645)
—Mickey Mouse Clubhouse Mickey's Halloween. Disney Storybook Art Team, illus. (p. 1136)
—Palace Pets: Pumpkin the Puppy for Cinderella. (p. 1319)
—World of Reading: Doc Mcstuffins Peaches Pie, Take a Bath! Level Pre-1. Disney Storybook Art Team, illus. (p. 1957)
—World of Reading: Sheriff Callie's Wild West Callie Asks for Help: Level Pre-1. Disney Storybook Art Team, illus. (p. 1957)
—World of Reading Star Wars Rebels Kanan's Jedi Training: Level 2. (p. 1957)
Disney Book Group Staff. 5-Minute Disney*Pixar Stories. (p. 1992)
—5-Minute Marvel Stories. (p. 1992)
—5-Minute Minnie Tales. Disney Storybook Artists Staff, illus. (p. 1992)
—5- Minute Palace Pets Stories. (p. 1992)
—5-Minute Snuggle Stories. Disney Storybook Artists Staff, illus. (p. 1992)
—5-Minute Spider-Man Stories. Disney Book Group Staff, illus. (p. 1992)
—5-Minute Spooky Stories. Disney Storybook Artists Staff & Disney Storybook Art Team, illus. (p. 1992)
—Aladdin Read-Along Storybook & CD. Disney Storybook Artists Staff, illus. (p. 33)
—Amazing Spider-Man 2 Movie Storybook. Disney Book Group Staff, illus. (p. 56)
—Avengers: a Mighty Sticker Book. (p. 118)
—Avengers: Earth's Mightiest Heroes!: Hulk Versus the World. (p. 119)
—Becoming Spider-Man. (p. 156)
—Belle: The Mysterious Message. Disney Storybook Artists Staff, illus. (p. 162)
—Brave. (p. 223)
—Captain Jake & the Never Land Pirates the Great Never Sea Conquest. Disney Storybook Art Team, illus. (p. 264)
—Chimpanzee: Oscar & Freddy. (p. 306)
—Cinderella. Disney Storybook Artists Staff, illus. (p. 320)
—Color Our World. Disney Storybook Artists Staff, illus. (p. 343)
—Colors All Around. Disney Storybook Artists Staff, illus. (p. 345)
—Disney 5-Minute Fairy Tales. Disney Storybook Artists Staff, illus. (p. 451)
—Disney Baby Baby Animals. Disney Storybook Art Team, illus. (p. 451)
—Disney Baby My First Words. Disney Storybook Art Team & Houston, Lauren, illus. (p. 451)
—Disney Bedtime Favorites. Disney Storybook Artists Staff & Disney Book Group Staff, illus. (p. 451)
—Disney Junior 5-Minute Sofia the First & Friends Stories. Disney Storybook Art Team, illus. (p. 451)
—Disney Junior Storybook Collection. Disney Storybook Art Team, illus. (p. 451)
—Disney Mickey & Minnie. Disney Storybook Artists Staff, illus. (p. 451)
—Disney Princess (p. 452)
—Disney Princess Cookbook. Disney Storybook Art Team, illus. (p. 452)
—Disney Princess Dear Princess. Disney Storybook Artists Staff & Disney Storybook Art Team, illus. (p. 452)
—Disney Princess Read-and-Sing - Cinderella. Disney Storybook Artists Staff, illus. (p. 453)
—Disney Storybook Collection. Disney Storybook Art Team, illus. (p. 453)
—Disney*Pixar Storybook Collection. Disney Storybook Art Team, illus. (p. 453)
—Doc Mcstuffins Dad's Favorite Toy. Disney Storybook Art Team, illus. (p. 459)
—Doc Mcstuffins Helping Hands. Disney Storybook Artists Staff & Disney Storybook Art Team, illus. (p. 459)
—Doc Mcstuffins Training Army Al. Disney Storybook Art Team, illus. (p. 459)
—Dusty's Big Job. Disney Storybook Art Team, illus. (p. 490)
—Easter Egg Hunt. (p. 499)
—Elsa's Gift. Disney Storybook Artists Staff, illus. (p. 516)
—Enchanting Tale. (p. 523)
—Finding Nemo. (p. 588)
—Fly-and-Drive Read-Along Storybook. Disney Storybook Artists Staff & Disney Storybook Art Team, illus. (p. 609)
—Follow That Sound! Disney Storybook Artists Staff, illus. (p. 612)
—Frozen Read-Along Storybook & CD. Disney Storybook Artists Staff, illus. (p. 645)
—Gravity Falls: Pining Away. (p. 712)
—Gravity Falls Once upon a Swine. Disney Storybook Artists Staff & No New Art Needed, illus. (p. 712)
—Gravity Falls Pining Away. Disney Storybook Artists Staff & Disney Storybook Art Team, illus. (p. 712)
—Greatest Battles. (p. 719)
—Guess Who! Disney Storybook Artists Staff, illus. (p. 729)
—Haunted Clubhouse. (p. 753)
—I Love You! Disney Storybook Artists Staff, illus. (p. 843)
—Inside Out Box of Mixed Emotions. (p. 877)
—Inside Out - Driven by Emotions. Disney Storybook Art Team, illus. (p. 877)
—Inside Out - Sadly Ever After? Purchase Includes Disney Ebook! (p. 877)
—Inside Scoop. Peake, Marilyn, ed. (p. 877)
—Iron Man vs. Titanium Man. Disney Storybook Artists Staff, illus. (p. 888)
—Jake & the Never Land Pirates Skull Rock. Disney Storybook Artists Staff & Disney Storybook Art Team, illus. (p. 905)
—Junior Encyclopedia of Animated Characters. Disney Storybook Art Team, illus. (p. 936)
—Lady & the Tramp. Disney Storybook Art Team, illus. (p. 970)
—Little Mermaid Read-Along Storybook & CD. Disney Storybook Artists Staff, illus. (p. 1031)
—Lost at Sea. (p. 1055)
—Magical Christmas. (p. 1074)
—Meeska Mooska-Tales. Disney Storybook Art Team, illus. (p. 1120)
—Meet the Cars. (p. 1122)
—Merry Christmas Cookbook. Disney Storybook Artists Staff, illus. (p. 1128)
—Mickey & Friends Mickey's Spooky Night: Purchase Includes Digital App! Disney Storybook Artists Staff & Disney Storybook Art Team, illus. (p. 1136)
—Mickey Mouse Clubhouse Choo Choo Express. (p. 1136)
—Mickey Saves Santa. Disney Storybook Artists Staff, illus. (p. 1136)
—Minnie & Daisy Best Friends Forever Doodle Book: Over 100 Doodle Pages! 5 Sticker Scenes! 21 Character Stencils 43 Stickers! Disney Storybook Artists Staff, illus. (p. 1147)
—Minnie Bow-Toons Trouble Times Two: Purchase Includes Digital App! - Design Bows with Minnie! Disney Storybook Artists Staff & Disney Storybook Art Team, illus. (p. 1147)
—Minnie Busy Bow-Tique. Disney Storybook Artists Staff & Disney Storybook Art Team, illus. (p. 1147)
—Minnie Easter Bonnet Parade. Disney Storybook Art Team, illus. (p. 1147)
—Minnie's Fashion & Fun. Disney Storybook Artists Staff, illus. (p. 1148)
—Nursery Rhymes. (p. 1273)
—Palace Pets: Berry the Bunny for Snow White. Disney Storybook Art Team, illus. (p. 1319)
—Palace Pets: Summer the Kitten for Rapunzel. (p. 1319)
—Palace Pets: Teacup the Pup for Belle. (p. 1319)
—Part of Their World. Disney Storybook Artists Staff, illus. (p. 1325)
—Perfect Princess Christmas. Disney Storybook Artists Staff, illus. (p. 1342)
—Perry Speaks! (p. 1344)
—Peter Pan Read-Along Storybook & CD. Disney Storybook Art Team, illus. (p. 1347)
—Planes - Fire & Rescue. Disney Storybook Art Team, illus. (p. 1367)
—Pretty in Pink. Disney Storybook Artists Staff, illus. (p. 1398)
—Pretty Princess Puzzles. Disney Storybook Art Team, illus. (p. 1398)
—Princess Adventure Stories. Disney Storybook Artists Staff, illus. (p. 1402)
—Princess Bedtime Stories. Disney Storybook Artists Staff, illus. (p. 1403)
—Rapunzel: A Day to Remember. (p. 1439)
—Reading Adventures Cars Level 1 Boxed Set. Disney Storybook Artists Staff, illus. (p. 1445)
—Ready to Be a Princess. Disney Storybook Art Team, illus. (p. 1447)
—Royal Friends: A Princess Book & Magnetic Play Set. Disney Storybook Art Team, illus. (p. 1492)
—Royal Kittens: A Palace Pets Book & Magnetic Play Set. (p. 1492)
—Royal Slumber Party. Disney Storybook Art Team, illus. (p. 1492)
—Royal Treasury. Disney Storybook Artists Staff & Disney Storybook Art Team, illus. (p. 1492)
—Sheriff Callie's Wild West - The Cat Who Tamed the West. Disney Storybook Art Team, illus. (p. 1565)
—Sleeping Beauty. Disney Storybook Artists Staff & Disney Storybook Art Team, illus. (p. 1589)
—Sleepy-Time Fun. (p. 1590)
—Sofia the First a Magical Match. Disney Storybook Art Team, illus. (p. 1605)
—Sofia the First Royal Prep Academy. Disney Storybook Artists Staff & Disney Storybook Art Team, illus. (p. 1605)
—Sofia the First S Is for Sofia. Disney Storybook Art Team, illus. (p. 1605)
—Sofia the First Sofia's Princess Adventures: Board Book Boxed Set. Disney Storybook Art Team, illus. (p. 1605)
—Sofia's Cup of Tea. Disney Storybook Art Team, illus. (p. 1605)
—Star Wars: Ewoks Join the Fight, Level 1. (p. 1641)
—Star Wars Rebels. (p. 1641)
—Star Wars: Return of the Jedi Read-Along Storybook & CD. (p. 1642)
—Story of Iron Man, Level 2. (p. 1658)
—Story of Spider-Man (Level 2) (p. 1660)
—Story of the Avengers, Level 2. (p. 1660)
—Tangled. Disney Storybook Art Team, illus. (p. 1705)
—Tangled. Disney Storybook Artists Staff, illus. (p. 1705)
—Teen Beach 2. (p. 1713)
—Teen Beach Movie. (p. 1713)
—These Are the Avengers Level 1 Reader. (p. 1731)
—This Is Iron Man. (p. 1736)
—This Is Spider-Man, Level 1. (p. 1736)
—This Is Thor. (p. 1736)
—This Is Wolverine Level 1 Reader. (p. 1737)
—Thumper Finds a Friend. Disney Storybook Artists Staff & Disney Storybook Art Team, illus. (p. 1746)
—Tiara Time. Disney Storybook Art Team, illus. (p. 1747)
—Tinker Bell & the Pirate Fairy. Disney Storybook Art Team, illus. (p. 1755)
—Toy Story. (p. 1774)
—Toy Story Storybook Collection. (p. 1774)
—Walt Disney's Classic Storybook (Volume 3) Disney Storybook Artists Staff & Disney Storybook Art Team, illus. (p. 1855)
—Wildcats Boxed Set Disney Press Staff, ed. (p. 1931)
—Wolverine vs. Sabretooth. (p. 1944)
—Wonderful World of Animals. (p. 1948)
—World of Reading Disney Storybook Art Team, illus. (p. 1957)
—World of Reading: Sofia the First Riches to Rags: Level 1. Disney Storybook Art Team, illus. (p. 1957)
—World of Reading Star Wars Rescue from Jabba's Palace: Level 2. (p. 1957)
—World of Reading This Is Captain America: Level 1. Disney Book Group Staff, illus. (p. 1957)
Disney Book Group Staff, illus. see Behling, Steve.
Disney Book Group Staff, illus. see Candau, Brittany.
Disney Book Group Staff, illus. see Castro, Nachie.
Disney Book Group Staff, illus. see Davis, Adam.
Disney Book Group Staff, illus. see Higginson, Sheila Sweeny.
Disney Book Group Staff, illus. see Macri, Thomas.
Disney Book Group Staff, illus. see Marvel Press Staff & Palacios, Tomas.
Disney Book Group Staff, illus. see Marvel Press Staff, et al.
Disney Book Group Staff, illus. see Palacios, Tomas.
Disney Book Group Staff, illus. see Scollon, Bill.
Disney Book Group Staff, illus. see Thomas, Rich, Jr. & Siglain, Michael.
Disney Book Group Staff, illus. see Thomas, Rich.
Disney Book Group Staff, jt. auth. see Amerikaner, Susan.
Disney Book Group Staff, jt. auth. see Auerbach, Annie.
Disney Book Group Staff, jt. auth. see Baer, Jill.
Disney Book Group Staff, jt. auth. see Bergen, Lara.
Disney Book Group Staff, jt. auth. see Bryant, Megan.
Disney Book Group Staff, jt. auth. see Burton, Tim.
Disney Book Group Staff, jt. auth. see Cars.
Disney Book Group Staff, jt. auth. see Disney Baby Staff.
Disney Book Group Staff, jt. auth. see Disney Press Staff.
Disney Book Group Staff, jt. auth. see Disney Princess Staff.
Disney Book Group Staff, jt. auth. see Driscoll, Laura.
Disney Book Group Staff, jt. auth. see Feldman, Thea.
Disney Book Group Staff, jt. auth. see Glass, Calliope.
Disney Book Group Staff, jt. auth. see Hapka, Catherine, pseud.
Disney Book Group Staff, jt. auth. see Hapka, Cathy, pseud.
Disney Book Group Staff, jt. auth. see Hicks, Barbara Jean.
Disney Book Group Staff, jt. auth. see Higginson, Sheila Sweeny.
Disney Book Group Staff, jt. auth. see Kelman, Marcy.
Disney Book Group Staff, jt. auth. see LaRose, Melinda.
Disney Book Group Staff, jt. auth. see Loggia, Wendy.
Disney Book Group Staff, jt. auth. see Marsoli, Lisa Ann.
Disney Book Group Staff, jt. auth. see Marvel Book Group Staff.
Disney Book Group Staff, jt. auth. see Marvel Books Staff.
Disney Book Group Staff, jt. auth. see Marvel Press Group.
Disney Book Group Staff, jt. auth. see Murray, Kiel.
Disney Book Group Staff, jt. auth. see Nathan, Sarah.
Disney Book Group Staff, jt. auth. see O'Ryan, Ellie.
Disney Book Group Staff, jt. auth. see Peterson, Scott.
Disney Book Group Staff, jt. auth. see Richards, Kitty.
Disney Book Group Staff, jt. auth. see Ritchey, Kate.
Disney Book Group Staff, jt. auth. see Scollon, William.
Disney Book Group Staff, jt. auth. see Scott, Denise.
Disney Book Group Staff, jt. auth. see Valentino, Serena.
Disney Book Group Staff, jt. auth. see Wong, Clarissa.
Disney Book Group Staff, photos by see Fletcher, Charlie.
Disney Book Group Staff & Auerbach, Annie. Monsters, Inc. Storybook Collection. (p. 1169)
Disney Book Group Staff & Bergen, Lara. Tangled Ever After. Disney Storybook Artists Staff, illus. (p. 1705)
Disney Book Group Staff & Brooke, Samantha. Gravity Falls Happy Summerween! / the Convenience Store... of Horrors! (p. 712)
Disney Book Group Staff & Disney Storybook Artists Staff. Doc Mcstuffins Time for Your Checkup! (p. 459)
Disney Book Group Staff & Disney Storybook Art Team. Meet the Planes. Disney Storybook Artists Staff, illus. (p. 1123)
Disney Book Group Staff & DiTerlizzi, Tony. Adventures of Luke Skywalker, Jedi Knight. McQuarrie, Ralph, illus. (p. 20)
Disney Book Group Staff & Donnelly, Jennifer. Deep Blue. (p. 422)
Disney Book Group Staff & Driscoll, Laura. Thumper & the Noisy Ducky. Disney Storybook Art Team, illus. (p. 1746)
Disney Book Group Staff & Dworkin, Brooke. World of Reading: Thor This Is Thor: Level 1. Disney Book Group Staff & Semeiks, Val, illus. (p. 1957)
Disney Book Group Staff & Fry, Jason. Rebel in the Ranks. (p. 1450)
Disney Book Group Staff & Glass, Calliope. Dusty's Great Race. Disney Storybook Artists Staff, illus. (p. 490)
Disney Book Group Staff & Gold, Gina. Minnie a Walk in the Park, Level 1. Disney Storybook Artists Staff, illus. (p. 1147)
—World of Reading: Minnie Hocus Bow-Cus! Level 1. Disney Storybook Artists Staff, illus. (p. 1957)

Full bibliographic information is available on the Title Index page number referenced in parentheses at the end of each entry

Disney Book Group Staff & Green, Rico. Cinderella: A Night at the Ball. Disney Storybook Art Team & Disney Book Group Staff, illus. (p. 320)
—Cinderella Kindness & Courage, Level 2. (p. 320)
—Descendants: Junior Novel. Disney Storybook Art Team, illus. (p. 428)
Disney Book Group Staff & Hapka, Catherine. Me & Our Mom. Disney Storybook Art Team, illus. (p. 1115)
—Sofia the First. Lee, Grace, illus. (p. 1605)
—Sofia the First the Enchanted Feast. Disney Storybook Artists Staff & Lee, Grace, illus. (p. 1605)
—Sofia the First the Enchanted Science Fair. Disney Storybook Artists Staff, illus. (p. 1605)
Disney Book Group Staff & Hapka, Cathy. Sofia the First the Royal Games. Disney Storybook Artists Staff, illus. (p. 1605)
Disney Book Group Staff & Heddle, Jennifer. Ezra & the Pilot, Level 2. (p. 559)
—World of Reading Star Wars Rebels. (p. 1957)
Disney Book Group Staff & Hicks, Barbara Jean. Frozen an Amazing Snowman. Disney Storybook Artists Staff & Mosqueda, Olga, illus. (p. 645)
Disney Book Group Staff & Hidalgo, Pablo. New Hero. Rebels Animation Team, illus. (p. 1245)
Disney Book Group Staff & Higginson, Sheila Sweeny. Doc Mcstuffins a Very Mcstuffins Christmas. Disney Storybook Artists Staff & Disney Storybook Art Team, illus. (p. 459)
—Doc Mcstuffins Bunny in a Basket. Disney Storybook Art Team, illus. (p. 459)
—Doc Mcstuffins Doc's Big Book of Boo-Boos. Disney Storybook Artists Staff, illus. (p. 459)
—Doc Mcstuffins Doctor's Helper: Purchase Includes Disney EBook! Disney Storybook Artists Staff, illus. (p. 459)
—Henry Hugglemonster Daddo in Charge. Disney Storybook Art Team, illus. (p. 768)
—Henry Hugglemonster Pet Party. Disney Storybook Artists Staff & Disney Storybook Art Team, illus. (p. 768)
—Henry Hugglemonster Welcome to Roarsville. Disney Storybook Artists Staff, illus. (p. 768)
—Minnie: Minnie's Costume Contest. Disney Storybook Artists Staff, illus. (p. 1147)
—Minnie: Minnie's Valentine. Disney Storybook Artists Staff, illus. (p. 1147)
—Minnie Wishing on a Bow. Disney Storybook Artists Staff, illus. (p. 1148)
—My Huggy Valentine. Disney Storybook Art Team, illus. (p. 1211)
Disney Book Group Staff & Kelman, Marcy. All Hands on Hooks. Disney Storybook Art Team, illus. (p. 44)
—Animal ABCs. Disney Storybook Art Team, illus. (p. 76)
—Doctor Bag. Disney Storybook Art Team, illus. (p. 459)
—Minnie's Purse. Disney Storybook Artists Staff, illus. (p. 1148)
—Sofia the First Sofia's Purse. Disney Storybook Artists Staff, illus. (p. 1605)
Disney Book Group Staff & Kogge, Michael. Ezra's Duel with Danger. (p. 559)
—Rebellion Begins. (p. 1451)
—Rebels Droids in Distress. (p. 1451)
—Rise of the Rebels. (p. 1475)
Disney Book Group Staff & LaRose, Melinda. Jake & the Never Land Pirates - Winter Never Land. Disney Storybook Art Team, illus. (p. 905)
—World of Reading: Jake & the Never Land Pirates Surfin' Turf: Level 1. Disney Storybook Artists Staff, illus. (p. 1957)
Disney Book Group Staff & Lewis, Kevin. Hide & Hug Olaf: A Fun Family Experience! Disney Storybook Art Team & Mosqueda, Olga, illus. (p. 776)
Disney Book Group Staff & Littlefield, Cynthia. Minnie & Friends Cookbook. Disney Storybook Art Team, illus. (p. 1147)
Disney Book Group Staff & Macri, Thomas. Kree-Skrull War. Bachs, Ramon, illus. (p. 967)
—These Are the X-Men Level 1. Disney Storybook Artists Staff & Bachs, Ramon, illus. (p. 1731)
Disney Book Group Staff & Marsoli, Lisa Ann. Frozen Sing-Along Storybook. Disney Storybook Artists Staff, illus. (p. 645)
—World of Reading: Sofia the First the Missing Necklace: Level Pre-1. Disney Storybook Art Team, illus. (p. 1957)
Disney Book Group Staff & Miller, Bryan Q. Disney Comics Tomorrowland. Jones, Kelley, illus. (p. 451)
Disney Book Group Staff & O'Ryan, Ellie. Platypus Power! (p. 1370)
Disney Book Group Staff & Peterson, Scott. Meet the Marvel Super Heroes: Includes a Poster of Your Favorite Super Heroes! (p. 1123)
Disney Book Group Staff & Richards, Kitty. Lost Tiara. Disney Storybook Art Team & Studio Iboix Staff, illus. (p. 1056)
Disney Book Group Staff & Ritchey, Kate. Huey, Dewey, & Louie's Rainy Day Adventure. Loter, Inc. Staff, illus. (p. 824)
—Mickey & Friends Goofy's Sledding Contest. Disney Storybook Art Team, illus. (p. 1136)
Disney Book Group Staff & Rusu, Meredith. Star Wars Rebels Always Bet on Chopper: Level 1. (p. 1641)
—Star Wars Rebels: the Inquisitor's Trap. (p. 1642)
Disney Book Group Staff & Rusu, Meredith L. Disney Princess Sleeping Beauty Read-Along Storybook & CD. (p. 453)
—Star Wars - Rebels. (p. 1641)
Disney Book Group Staff & Ryals, Lexi. Crush Crazy. (p. 386)
—Jessie Livin' the Life. (p. 914)
Disney Book Group Staff & Schaefer, Elizabeth A. Chopper Saves the Day. (p. 310)
Disney Book Group Staff & Scollon, Bill. Sofia the First: a Royal Mouse in the House. Lee, Grace, illus. (p. 1605)
—Walt Disney: Drawn from Imagination. Disney Storybook Artists Staff, illus. (p. 1855)
Disney Book Group Staff & Scollon, William. Jake & the Never Land Pirates Battle for the Book. Disney Storybook Art Team, illus. (p. 905)
—Mickey Mouse Clubhouse a Goofy Fairy Tale. Disney Storybook Art Team, illus. (p. 1136)
Disney Book Group Staff & Siglain, Michael. Escape from Darth Vader, Level 1. Disney Book Group Staff & Roux, Stephane, illus. (p. 534)
Disney Book Group Staff & Stephens, Leigh F. Attack of the Ferb Snatchers! (p. 113)
Disney Book Group Staff & Thomas, Rich. Amazing Spider-Man: An Origin Story. (p. 55)
—Happy Holidays! From Avengers: Featuring the Voice of Stan Lee. Lim, Ron & Rosenberg, Rachelle, illus. (p. 746)
Disney Book Group Staff & Thornton, Randy. Star Wars: a New Hope Read-Along Storybook & CD. Rood, Brian, illus. (p. 1641)
Disney Book Group Staff & Ward, Jessica. Friends on Ice. Disney Storybook Art Team et al, illus. (p. 638)
Disney Book Group Staff & Weinberg, Jennifer Liberts. World of Reading: Doc Mcstuffins Blame It on the Rain: Level 1. Disney Storybook Artists Staff & Disney Storybook Art Team, illus. (p. 1957)
Disney Book Group Staff & Wilsdon, Christina. Wonderful World of Sharks. (p. 1948)
Disney Book Group Staff & Windham, Ryder. Ezra's Gamble. (p. 559)
Disney Book Group Staff, et al. Curse of Maleficent: The Tale of a Sleeping Beauty. Disney Storybook Artists Staff & Kole, Nicholas, illus. (p. 394)
—Disney Christmas Storybook Collection. Disney Storybook Artists Staff, illus. (p. 451)
—Doc Mcstuffins Boo to You! Disney Storybook Artists Staff, illus. (p. 459)
—Gravity Falls - Dipper's & Mabel's Guide to the Unknown & Nonstop Fun! (p. 712)
—It's a Small World. Chou, Joey, illus. (p. 896)
—Layout & Background. (p. 981)
—Minnie Minnie's Winter Bow Show. Disney Storybook Artists Staff, illus. (p. 1148)
—Sofia the First the Curse of Princess Ivy: Purchase Includes Disney EBook! Lee, Grace, illus. (p. 1605)
—World of Reading: Doc Mcstuffins Brave Dragon: Level Pre-1. Disney Storybook Artists Staff, illus. (p. 1957)
—Zeb to the Rescue, Level 1. (p. 1985)
Disney Doc McStuffins, Disney Doc. Disney Doc Mcstuffins Movie Theater Storybook & Movie Projector. (p. 451)
Disney, ed. Big Learning Superstar: Read & Sing. (p. 182)
Disney Editions, creator. Birnbaum's Disney Cruise Line. (p. 192)
Disney Enterprises Inc. Staff, jt. auth. see RH Disney Staff.
Disney Enterprises Inc. Staff, creator. Caritas Felices. (p. 269)
—Disney Caritas Felices: Simba. (p. 451)
—Disney's Lilo & Stitch Time for Fun! Bath Time Bubble Book. (p. 453)
Disney Enterprises Staff, ed. Cars Stuck on Stories. (p. 272)
Disney, et al. World of Cars: Tractor Tipping. (p. 1956)
Disney Frozen, Disney. Disney Frozen Music Player Storybook. (p. 451)
Disney Frozen Staff. Disney Frozen Movie Theater: Storybook & Movie Projector. (p. 451)
Disney Global Artists Staff, illus. see Winskill, John.
Disney Inside Out, Disney Inside. Disney Pixar Inside Out Joy's Journey. (p. 452)
—So Many Feelings: Riley's World Inside & Out. (p. 1602)
Disney Junior Staff. Disney Doc Mcstuffins: All Better! (p. 451)
—Disney Doc Mcstuffins CarryAlong Play Book. (p. 451)
—Disney Doc Mcstuffins Guess Who, Doc! (p. 451)
Disney Mickey Mouse Clubhouse, Disney Mickey. Disney Mickey Mouse Clubhouse: Schoolhouse Fun: A,B,Cs And 1, 2, 3s. (p. 452)
Disney Mickey Mouse Clubhouse, ed. Clubhouse ABCs: Mickey Mouse Clubhouse. (p. 335)
Disney Minnie, Disney. Disney Minnie - My Colorful Closet. (p. 452)
Disney Minnie Mouse Staff. Disney Minnie. (p. 452)
—Disney Minnie Mouse Flutter Bow Fun. (p. 452)
Disney Modern Publishing & Greenwald, Todd J., creators. Wizards of Waverly Place: A Day in the Life. (p. 1943)
Disney, Pixar Cars, ed. Red Light, Green Light: Action Opposites. (p. 1454)
—Rhymes on the Go. (p. 1468)
Disney Pixar Staff. Big Monsters on Campus. (p. 182)
—Go Sulley! (p. 687)
—Increíbles: Gran Colección Disney. (p. 870)
—Monsters University Roooar! (p. 1169)
—Nemo's Big Race. (p. 1241)
—Rescue Mater: And Other Tall Tales. (p. 1462)
Disney Pixar Staff, jt. auth. see RH Disney Staff.
Disney Planes, Disney. Disney Planes Fire & Rescue: to the Rescue: Build 6 Planes That Really Fly! (p. 452)
Disney Press. Ant-Man: Small World, Big Problems. (p. 88)
—Avengers: The New Team. (p. 118)
—Avengers: Battle with Ultron. (p. 118)
—Awesome Guy to the Rescue! / Bella's Big Break. (p. 121)
—Callie Asks for Help. (p. 254)
—Doc Mcstuffins: Dad's Favorite Toy. (p. 459)
—Miles from Tomorrowland: Who Stole the Stellosphere? (p. 1142)
—Peaches Pie, Take a Bath! (p. 1332)
—Sofia the First: Riches to Rags. (p. 1605)
—Star Wars: Ewoks Join the Fight. (p. 1641)
—Star Wars Rebels: TIE Fighter Trouble. (p. 1641)
—Star Wars Rebels: Always Bet on Chopper. (p. 1641)
—Star Wars Rebels: Hera's Phantom Flight. (p. 1641)
—Star Wars Rebels: Kanan's Jedi Training. (p. 1641)
Disney Press Staff. Cinderella. (p. 320)
—Doc Mcstuffins: Training Army Al. (p. 459)
—Droids in Distress. (p. 485)
—Gravity Falls: Once upon a Swine. (p. 712)
—Inquisitor's Trap. (p. 875)
—Kiss the Frog. (p. 961)
—Rescue from Jabba's Palace. (p. 1462)
—Sabine's Art Attack. (p. 1500)
—School's Out. (p. 1524)
—Sheriff Callie's Wild West: Toby Braves the Bully. (p. 1565)
—Sheriff Callie's Wild West: Peck's Trail Mix Mix-Up. (p. 1565)
—Star Wars: Use the Force! (p. 1641)
—Star Wars: Escape from Darth Vader. (p. 1641)
—Valley of Vipers. (p. 1831)
Disney Press Staff, ed. see Disney Book Group Staff.
Disney Press Staff, illus. see Flake, Sharon G.
Disney Press Staff & Disney Book Group Staff. 5-Minute Princess Stories. Disney Storybook Artists Staff, illus. (p. 1992)
—Best School Day Ever. (p. 171)
—Cars 2. (p. 272)
—Cars Storybook Collection. Disney Storybook Art Team, illus. (p. 272)
—Forever Friends. (p. 619)
—Furry Friends! Disney Storybook Artists Staff, illus. (p. 650)
—Lion King. (p. 1020)
—Princess Mix & Match. (p. 1404)
—Road Trip. Disney Storybook Art Team, illus. (p. 1477)
—Thumper's Furry Friends. (p. 1746)
Disney Press Staff, ed. Mickey's New Friend. (p. 1136)
—Pirates of the Caribbean 3: Swann. (p. 1364)
Disney Press Staff, et al. Across the 2nd Dimension. (p. 9)
—Hello, World! Disney Storybook Artists Staff, illus. (p. 765)
Disney Princess, Disney. Disney Princess - Bibbity-Bobbity-Boo! (p. 452)
—Disney Princess Once upon a Castle: Hidden Stories. (p. 453)
Disney Princess Staff. Disney Princess Sparkling Beauty: Twinkling Lights Mirror. (p. 453)
—Movie Theater: Storybook & Movie Projector(r). (p. 1183)
Disney Princess Staff, adapted by. Princess Enchanted Palace: Storybook & Play Castle. (p. 1403)
Disney Princess Staff & Disney Book Group Staff. Ariel: The Birthday Surprise. Cagol, Andrea & Studio Iboix Staff, illus. (p. 98)
Disney Princess Staff, et al. Disney Princess Carry along Treasury. (p. 452)
Disney, Princesses, ed. ClubHouse ABCs. (p. 335)
—Snow White, My Best Friends Audio Tales: Disney. (p. 1600)
Disney Publishing Creative Development (Firm) Staff, et al, contrib. by. Learn to Draw Disney/Pixar Toy Story: Featuring Favorite Characters from Toy Story 2 & Toy Story 3! (p. 983)
Disney Publishing Staff. Arts & Crafts Day. (p. 104)
—Big Bug Hunt. (p. 180)
—Blow, Wind, Blow. (p. 202)
—I Spy Shapes. (p. 846)
—My Favorite Season. (p. 1203)
—Piglet's Night Lights. (p. 1358)
—Playing Pirates. (p. 1372)
—Rainbow Colors. (p. 1435)
—Sense of Fun. (p. 1551)
—What's That Sound? (p. 1899)
—Where Is Your Home? (p. 1909)
—Wonders of Water. (p. 1949)
Disney Publishing Staff & Studiomouse Staff. Panda Cub Explores. (p. 1320)
Disney Read-Along. 101 Dalmatians (Live Action). (p. 1999)
Disney, Sofia the First. Disney Guess Who, Sofia! (p. 451)
Disney Sofia the First, Disney Sofia. Disney Sofia the First Movie Theater Storybook & Movie Projector. (p. 453)
—Disney Sofia the First: Please & Thank You: Your Guide to Becoming the Perfect Princess! (p. 453)
—Disney Sofia the First: Where Is My Tiara? (p. 453)
Disney Staff. 101 Dalmatians. (p. 1999)
—Aladdin. (p. 33)
—Bambi. (p. 135)
—Beauty & the Beast. (p. 154)
—Belle et la Bete. (p. 162)
—Disney Doc Mcstuffins Happy to Be Healthy! (p. 451)
—Disney Fairies - Mensajes Misteriosos. (p. 451)
—Dumbo. (p. 489)
—Little Mermaid. (p. 1031)
—Rox & Rouky. (p. 1492)
—Sleeping Beauty. (p. 1589)
—Snow White & the Seven Dwarfs. (p. 1600)
—Sol Que Desaparecio. (p. 1606)
—Stories to Tell a Three Year Old. (p. 1655)
—Story of Clarabelle Cow. (p. 1657)
—Story of Pluto the Pup. (p. 1659)
—Winnie the Pooh. (p. 1937)
Disney Staff, jt. contrib. by see Modern Publishing Staff.
Disney Staff & Posner-Sanchez, Andrea. Bambi's Hide-and-Seek. Mones, Isidre, illus. (p. 135)
Disney Staff & Rodriguez, Robert, creators. Spy Kids 2: The Island of Lost Dreams. (p. 1636)
Disney Staff & Schooley, Bob. Monkey Fist Strikes. (p. 1165)
Disney Staff, contrib. by. Write, Slide & Learn Disney Mickey Mouse Clubhouse: Colors & Shapes. (p. 1964)
—Write, Slide & Learn Disney Pixar Cars: Numbers. (p. 1964)
—Write, Slide & Learn Disney Princess: Spelling. (p. 1964)
—Write, Slide & Learn Disney Winnie the Pooh: ABC. (p. 1964)
Disney Staff, creator. Bambi. (p. 135)
—Chicken Little. (p. 300)
—Kim Possible: The New Ron & Mind Games. (p. 956)
—Search Begins. (p. 1537)
Disney Staff, et al, creators. Monkey Fist Strikes & Attack of the Killer Be. (p. 1165)
Disney Staff, prod. Cine-Manga: Magic Train & Grubby Longjohn's Olde Tyme Revue Vol. 9. (p. 321)
—Sparring & Charring. (p. 1622)
Disney Storybook Art Team. Cinderella: The Great Mouse Mistake. (p. 320)
—Legend of the Neverbeast. (p. 989)
—Monsters, Inc. (p. 1169)
—Royal Lessons. (p. 1492)
Disney Storybook Art Team, illus. see Bryant, Megan & Disney Book Group Staff.
Disney Storybook Art Team, illus. see Disney Book Group Staff & Driscoll, Laura.
Disney Storybook Art Team, illus. see Disney Book Group Staff & Green, Rico.
Disney Storybook Art Team, illus. see Disney Book Group Staff & Hapka, Catherine.
Disney Storybook Art Team, illus. see Disney Book Group Staff & Higginson, Sheila Sweeny.
Disney Storybook Art Team, illus. see Disney Book Group Staff & Kelman, Marcy.
Disney Storybook Art Team, illus. see Disney Book Group Staff & LaRose, Melinda.
Disney Storybook Art Team, illus. see Disney Book Group Staff & Lewis, Kevin.
Disney Storybook Art Team, illus. see Disney Book Group Staff & Littlefield, Cynthia.
Disney Storybook Art Team, illus. see Disney Book Group Staff & Marsoli, Lisa Ann.
Disney Storybook Art Team, illus. see Disney Book Group Staff & Richards, Kitty.
Disney Storybook Art Team, illus. see Disney Book Group Staff & Ritchey, Kate.
Disney Storybook Art Team, illus. see Disney Book Group Staff & Scollon, William.
Disney Storybook Art Team, illus. see Disney Book Group Staff & Ward, Jessica.
Disney Storybook Art Team, illus. see Disney Book Group Staff & Weinberg, Jennifer Liberts.
Disney Storybook Art Team, illus. see Disney Book Group Staff.
Disney Storybook Art Team, illus. see Disney Book Group.
Disney Storybook Art Team, illus. see Disney Press Staff & Disney Book Group Staff.
Disney Storybook Art Team, illus. see Glass, Calliope & Disney Book Group Staff.
Disney Storybook Art Team, illus. see Glass, Calliope.
Disney Storybook Art Team, illus. see Hapka, Catherine, pseud & Disney Book Group Staff.
Disney Storybook Art Team, illus. see Hapka, Cathy, pseud & Disney Book Group Staff.
Disney Storybook Art Team, illus. see Hapka, Cathy, pseud, et al.
Disney Storybook Art Team, illus. see Higginson, Sheila Sweeny & Disney Book Group Staff.
Disney Storybook Art Team, illus. see Kelman, Marcy & Disney Book Group Staff.
Disney Storybook Art Team, illus. see LaRose, Melinda & Disney Book Group Staff.
Disney Storybook Art Team, illus. see Larsen, Kirsten, et al.
Disney Storybook Art Team, illus. see Lettrick, Robert.
Disney Storybook Art Team, illus. see Loggia, Wendy & Disney Book Group Staff.
Disney Storybook Art Team, illus. see Marsoli, Lisa Ann & Disney Book Group Staff.
Disney Storybook Art Team, illus. see Nathan, Sarah & Disney Book Group Staff.
Disney Storybook Art Team, illus. see Peterson, Scott & Disney Book Group Staff.
Disney Storybook Art Team, illus. see Ritchey, Kate & Disney Book Group Staff.
Disney Storybook Art Team, illus. see Scollon, William & Disney Book Group Staff.
Disney Storybook Art Team, illus. see Scott, Denise & Disney Book Group Staff.
Disney Storybook Art Team, illus. see Valentino, Serena & Disney Book Group Staff.
Disney Storybook Art Team, illus. see Zappa, Ahmet & Muldoon Zappa, Shana.
Disney Storybook Art Team, illus. see Zappa, Ahmet & Zappa, Shane Muldoon.
Disney Storybook Art Team, jt. auth. see Disney Book Group Staff.
Disney Storybook Art Team Staff, illus. see Posner-Sanchez, Andrea & Julius, Jessica.
Disney Storybook Art Team Staff, illus. see Scollon, William, et al.
Disney Storybook Artists, illus. see Posner-Sanchez, Andrea.
Disney Storybook Artists Staff. Brave. (p. 223)
—Cars. (p. 272)
—Disney Mickey Mouse Clubhouse Movie Theater: Storybook & Movie Projector. (p. 451)
—Enchanted Princesses Drawing Book & Kit: Includes Everything You Need to Draw Your Favorite Disney Princesses! (p. 523)
—Fabulous Fashions: Learn to Draw Minnie, Daisy, & Their Favorite Fashions & Accessories - Step by Step! (p. 560)
—Favorite Fairies: Learn to Draw the Magical World of Tinker Bell, Silver Mist, Rosetta, & All of Your Favorite Disney Fairies! (p. 578)
—Finding Nemo. (p. 588)
—Learn to Draw Disney I Pixar Cars. (p. 983)
—Learn to Draw Disney Phineas & Ferb: Featuring Candace, Agent P, Dr. Doofenshmirtz, & Other Favorite Characters from the Hit Show! (p. 983)
—Learn to Draw Disney Villains: Featuring Favorite Villains, Including Captain Hook, Cruella de Vil, Jafar, & Others! (p. 983)
—Learn to Draw Disney's Enchanted Princesses: Learn to Draw Ariel, Cinderella, Belle, Rapunzel, & All of Your Favorite Disney Princesses! (p. 983)
—Learn to Draw Disney's Frozen: Featuring Anna, Elsa, Olaf, & All Your Favorite Characters! (p. 983)
—Learn to Draw Disney's Phineas & Ferb Drawing Book & Kit: Includes Everything You Need to Draw Candace, Agent P, & Your Other Favorite Characters from the Hit Show! (p. 983)
—Learn to Draw Disney's Planes: Featuring Dusty Crophopper, Skipper Riley, Ripslinger, el Chupacabra, & All Your Favorite Characters! (p. 983)
—Learn to Draw Disney's the Little Mermaid: Learn to Draw Ariel, Sebastian, Flounder, Ursula, & Other Favorite Characters Step by Step! (p. 983)
—Learn to Draw Mickey Mouse & His Friends. (p. 983)
—Learn to Draw Winnie the Pooh: Featuring Tigger, Eeyore, Piglet, & Other Favorite Characters of the Hundred Acre Wood! (p. 984)
—Learn to Draw Your Favorite Disney/Pixar Characters: Featuring Woody, Buzz Lightyear, Lightning Mcqueen, Mater, & Other Favorite Characters. (p. 984)

D

—Palace Pets: Featuring Pumpkin, Beauty, Treasure, Blondie & All of Your Favorite Princesses' Pets! (p. 1319)
—Rapunzel's Dream: Storybook with Musical Hairbrush. (p. 1439)
—Tangled, Rapunzel's Adventures: Storybook with Music Player. (p. 1705)
—Toy Story. (p. 1774)
—Your Favorite Disney Pixar Characters. (p. 1980)
Disney Storybook Artists Staff, illus. see Amerikaner, Susan & Disney Book Group Staff.
Disney Storybook Artists Staff, illus. see Auerbach, Annie & Disney Book Group Staff.
Disney Storybook Artists Staff, illus. see Auerbach, Annie.
Disney Storybook Artists Staff, illus. see Baer, Jill & Disney Book Group Staff.
Disney Storybook Artists Staff, illus. see Bazaldua, Barbara & Bergen, Lara.
Disney Storybook Artists Staff, illus. see Bazaldua, Barbara.
Disney Storybook Artists Staff, illus. see Bergen, Lara & Disney Book Group Staff.
Disney Storybook Artists Staff, illus. see Berrios, Frank & RH Disney Staff.
Disney Storybook Artists Staff, illus. see Bobowicz, Pamela.
Disney Storybook Artists Staff, illus. see Chambers, Whittaker, tr.
Disney Storybook Artists Staff, illus. see Disney Baby Staff & Disney Book Group Staff.
Disney Storybook Artists Staff, illus. see Disney Book Group Staff & Bergen, Lara.
Disney Storybook Artists Staff, illus. see Disney Book Group Staff & Disney Storybook Art Team.
Disney Storybook Artists Staff, illus. see Disney Book Group Staff & Glass, Calliope.
Disney Storybook Artists Staff, illus. see Disney Book Group Staff & Gold, Gina.
Disney Storybook Artists Staff, illus. see Disney Book Group Staff & Hapka, Catherine.
Disney Storybook Artists Staff, illus. see Disney Book Group Staff & Hapka, Cathy.
Disney Storybook Artists Staff, illus. see Disney Book Group Staff & Hicks, Barbara Jean.
Disney Storybook Artists Staff, illus. see Disney Book Group Staff & Higginson, Sheila Sweeny.
Disney Storybook Artists Staff, illus. see Disney Book Group Staff & Kelman, Marcy.
Disney Storybook Artists Staff, illus. see Disney Book Group Staff & LaRose, Melinda.
Disney Storybook Artists Staff, illus. see Disney Book Group Staff & Macri, Thomas.
Disney Storybook Artists Staff, illus. see Disney Book Group Staff & Marsoli, Lisa Ann.
Disney Storybook Artists Staff, illus. see Disney Book Group Staff & Scollon, Bill.
Disney Storybook Artists Staff, illus. see Disney Book Group Staff & Weinberg, Jennifer Liberts.
Disney Storybook Artists Staff, illus. see Disney Book Group Staff, et al.
Disney Storybook Artists Staff, illus. see Disney Book Group Staff.
Disney Storybook Artists Staff, illus. see Disney Press Staff & Disney Book Group Staff.
Disney Storybook Artists Staff, illus. see Disney Press Staff, et al.
Disney Storybook Artists Staff, illus. see Driscoll, Laura & Disney Book Group Staff.
Disney Storybook Artists Staff, illus. see Feldman, Thea & Disney Book Group Staff.
Disney Storybook Artists Staff, illus. see Feldman, Thea.
Disney Storybook Artists Staff, illus. see Glass, Calliope & Disney Book Group Staff.
Disney Storybook Artists Staff, illus. see Hamilton, Tisha.
Disney Storybook Artists Staff, illus. see Hands, Cynthia.
Disney Storybook Artists Staff, illus. see Hapka, Catherine, pseud & Disney Book Group Staff.
Disney Storybook Artists Staff, illus. see Hapka, Cathy, pseud & Disney Book Group Staff.
Disney Storybook Artists Staff, illus. see Hapka, Cathy, pseud, et al.
Disney Storybook Artists Staff, illus. see Hicks, Barbara Jean & Disney Book Group Staff.
Disney Storybook Artists Staff, illus. see Higginson, Sheila Sweeny & Disney Book Group Staff.
Disney Storybook Artists Staff, illus. see Higginson, Sheila Sweeny, et al.
Disney Storybook Artists Staff, illus. see Higginson, Sheila Sweeny.
Disney Storybook Artists Staff, illus. see Jordan, Apple & RH Disney Staff.
Disney Storybook Artists Staff, illus. see Kelman, Marcy & Disney Book Group Staff.
Disney Storybook Artists Staff, illus. see Kelman, Marcy.
Disney Storybook Artists Staff, illus. see Lagonegro, Melissa & RH Disney Staff.
Disney Storybook Artists Staff, illus. see LaRose, Melinda & Disney Book Group Staff.
Disney Storybook Artists Staff, illus. see Marsoli, Lisa Ann & Disney Book Group Staff.
Disney Storybook Artists Staff, illus. see McCafferty, Catherine, et al.
Disney Storybook Artists Staff, illus. see Murray, Kiel & Disney Book Group Staff.
Disney Storybook Artists Staff, illus. see O'Ryan, Ellie & Disney Book Group Staff.
Disney Storybook Artists Staff, illus. see Posner-Sanchez, Andrea.
Disney Storybook Artists Staff, illus. see Random House Disney Staff.
Disney Storybook Artists Staff, illus. see Random House Editors & Posner-Sanchez, Andrea.
Disney Storybook Artists Staff, illus. see Random House Editors & RH Disney Staff.
Disney Storybook Artists Staff, illus. see Reader's Digest Staff & Miller, Sara.
Disney Storybook Artists Staff, illus. see RH Disney Staff & Hands, Cynthia.
Disney Storybook Artists Staff, illus. see RH Disney Staff & Peymani, Christine.
Disney Storybook Artists Staff, illus. see RH Disney Staff & Scollon, Bill.
Disney Storybook Artists Staff, illus. see RH Disney Staff & Smiley, Ben.
Disney Storybook Artists Staff, illus. see RH Disney Staff & Wooster, Devin Ann.
Disney Storybook Artists Staff, illus. see RH Disney Staff.
Disney Storybook Artists Staff, illus. see Richards, Kitty & RH Disney Staff.
Disney Storybook Artists Staff, illus. see Ritchey, Kate & Disney Book Group Staff.
Disney Storybook Artists Staff, illus. see Scollon, Bill.
Disney Storybook Artists Staff, illus. see Scollon, William & Disney Book Group Staff.
Disney Storybook Artists Staff, illus. see Scollon, William & Parent, Nancy.
Disney Storybook Artists Staff, illus. see Scollon, William, et al.
Disney Storybook Artists Staff, illus. see Thomas, Rich, Jr.
Disney Storybook Artists Staff, illus. see Valentino, Serena & Disney Book Group Staff.
Disney Storybook Artists Staff, illus. see Walter Foster Creative Team.
Disney Storybook Artists Staff, jt. auth. see Froeb, Lori C.
Disney Storybook Artists Staff, jt. auth. see Lombardi, Kristine.
Disney Storybook Artists Staff, jt. auth. see Reader's Digest Staff.
Disney Storybook Artists Staff, jt. illus. see Disney Book Group Staff.
Disney Storybook Artists Staff, jt. illus. see Mawhinney, Art.
Disney Storybook Artists Staff & Reader's Digest Staff. Disney Princess Music Player Storybook. (p. 453)
Disney Storybook Artists Staff & Thammavongsa, Christine. Little Mermaid. (p. 1031)
Disney Storybook Artists Staff, contrib. by. Disney/Pixar Cars: Learn to Draw. (p. 453)
—Learn to Draw Disney/Pixar Brave. (p. 983)
—Learn to Draw Plus Disney Pixar Toy Story: Featuring Favorite Characters from Toy Story 2 & Toy Story 3! (p. 983)
—Princess Adventure Stories. (p. 1402)
—Princess Songs. (p. 1405)
Disney Storybook Artists Staff, ed. Celebrated Characters Collection: Including Your Disney/Pixar Favorites! (p. 284)
—Disney Lilo & Stitch Drawing Book & Kit. (p. 451)
—Disney/Pixar Cars Drawing Book & Kit. (p. 453)
—Disney/Pixar Finding Nemo Drawing Book & Kit. (p. 453)
—Learn to Draw Disney's - Favorite Princesses: Featuring Tiana, Cinderella, Ariel, Snow White, Belle, & Other Characters! (p. 983)
Disney Storybook Artists Staff, et al. Disney's the Lion King. (p. 453)
Dispenzio, Michael A. Map Mania: Discovering Where You Are & Getting to Where You Aren't. Garbot, Dave, illus. (p. 1090)
DiSpirito, Rocco, et al. Rocco's Italian-American: More Than 150 Recipes from Rocco & Mama. (p. 1481)
Diss-Braden, Karen. My Name Is PugzzyWawa! (p. 1215)
Dissler, Erica, illus. see Wood, David.
Distefano, Matthew. Homework Helpers: Biology. (p. 794)
Distler, Christine A. Pegasus: The Introduction. (p. 1335)
DiSunno, Rebecca, et al. Jeremy Goes to Camp Good Grief. (p. 913)
Ditama, Bow. Mahoromatic (p. 1076)
—Mahoromatic: Automatic Maiden: The Misato Residence's Maid (p. 1076)
Ditama, Bow, illus. see Nakayama, Bunjuro.
DiTaranto, Cynthia A. Kristmas Karol the Nigerian Dwarf Goat. (p. 967)
Ditchfield, Christin. Bible Heroes. Cook, Ande, illus. (p. 175)
—Bible Stories of Boys & Girls. Smath, Jerry, illus. (p. 176)
—Bono. (p. 209)
—Christian Teacher's Guide to the Lion, the Witch & the Wardrobe, Grades 2 - 5. (p. 312)
—Clara Barton: Founder of the American Red Cross. (p. 326)
—Condoleezza Rice: America's Leading Stateswoman. (p. 356)
—Crow. (p. 385)
—Freedom of Speech. (p. 634)
—Johnny Appleseed. (p. 923)
—Knowing Your Civil Rights. (p. 965)
—Lewis & Clark Expedition. (p. 1004)
—Louisa May Alcott: Author of Little Women. (p. 1058)
—Memorial Day. (p. 1125)
—Northeast Indians (p. 1265)
—Oil. (p. 1282)
—Plateau Indians (p. 1370)
—Soil. (p. 1606)
—Spanish Missions. (p. 1621)
—Story Behind Plastic (p. 1656)
—Story Behind Soap (p. 1656)
—Story Behind Water (p. 1656)
—Story Behind Wool (p. 1656)
—Tennis. (p. 1720)
—Wood. (p. 1949)
Ditchfield, Lily K. & Zielski, Julie A. Witches That Saved the Dogs. (p. 1941)
DiTerlizzi, Angela. Baby Love. Hughes, Brooke Boynton, illus. (p. 127)
—Say What? Chou, Joey, illus. (p. 1518)
—Some Bugs. Wenzel, Brendan, illus. (p. 1609)
DiTerlizzi, Angela, jt. auth. see DiTerlizzi, Tony.
DiTerlizzi, Angela, jt. auth. see Greenburg, Dan.
DiTerlizzi, Tony. Battle for Wondla. (p. 145)
—Battle for WondLa. DiTerlizzi, Tony, illus. (p. 145)
—G Is for One Gzonk! An Alpha-Number-Bet Book. DiTerlizzi, Tony, illus. (p. 651)
—Hero for WondLa (p. 772)
—Hero for WondLa. (p. 772)
—Hero for WondLa. DiTerlizzi, Tony, illus. (p. 772)
—Jimmy Zangwow's Out-of-This-World Moon-Pie Adventure. DiTerlizzi, Tony, illus. (p. 918)
—Kenny & the Dragon. (p. 949)
—Kenny & the Dragon. DiTerlizzi, Tony, illus. (p. 949)
—Search for Wondla. (p. 1537)
—Search for WondLa. DiTerlizzi, Tony, illus. (p. 1537)
—Ted. (p. 1712)
—Ted. DiTerlizzi, Tony, illus. (p. 1712)
DiTerlizzi, Tony, illus. see Cooney, Doug.
DiTerlizzi, Tony, illus. see Howitt, Mary.
DiTerlizzi, Tony, illus. see Johnston, Tony.
DiTerlizzi, Tony, illus. see Stoker, Bram.
DiTerlizzi, Tony, jt. auth. see Black, Holly.
DiTerlizzi, Tony, jt. auth. see Disney Book Group Staff.
DiTerlizzi, Tony & Black, Holly. Care & Feeding of Sprites. DiTerlizzi, Tony, illus. (p. 266)
—Field Guide. DiTerlizzi, Tony, illus. (p. 583)
—Ironwood Tree. (p. 888)
—Ironwood Tree. DiTerlizzi, Tony, illus. (p. 888)
—Lucinda's Secret DiTerlizzi, Tony, illus. (p. 1062)
—Lucinda's Secret. (p. 1062)
—Nixie's Song. DiTerlizzi, Tony, illus. (p. 1257)
—Nixies Song - A Giant Problem - The Wyrm King Set DiTerlizzi, Tony, illus. (p. 1257)
—Notebook for Fantastical Observations. DiTerlizzi, Tony, illus. (p. 1267)
—Wrath of Mulgarath. (p. 1962)
DiTerlizzi, Tony & DiTerlizzi, Angela. Big Fun! DiTerlizzi, Tony, illus. (p. 181)
—Uh-Oh Sick! DiTerlizzi, Tony, illus. (p. 1808)
—Wet Friend! DiTerlizzi, Tony, illus. (p. 1877)
—Yummy Trip! DiTerlizzi, Tony, illus. (p. 1983)
DiTerlizzi, Tony, et al. Anteojo Asombroso. (p. 89)
—Arbol Metálico. Abreu, Carlos, tr. (p. 94)
—Libro Fantástico. Abreu, Carlos, tr. (p. 1006)
—Mapa Perdido. (p. 1090)
Ditewig, Diann, illus. see Kretzmann, Jane.
Ditko, Mark Shawn. Zen Guide to InRoads Essentials. (p. 1986)
Ditko, Steve, illus. see Lee, Stan, et al.
Ditko, Steve, illus. see Rude, Steve.
Ditko, Steve, jt. illus. see Kirby, Jack.
Ditko, Steve, jt. illus. see Romita, John.
Ditmars, Maribeth R. Bald-Headed Princess: Cancer, Chemo, & Courage. (p. 134)
DiTocco, Robyn & DiTocco, Tony. Atlas' Revenge: Another Mad Myth Mystery. (p. 113)
—Hero Perseus: A Mad Myth Mystery. (p. 772)
DiTocco, Tony, jt. auth. see DiTocco, Robyn.
Ditta-Donahue, Gina. Josh's Smiley Faces: A Story about Anger. Blake, Anne Catharine, illus. (p. 926)
Dittler, William F., ed. Spiritual & spectacular Yellowstone National Park. (p. 1629)
Dittman, Jeffery. Jungle Heroes. (p. 935)
Dittmar, Gordie Cheney. Message for Natalie. (p. 1129)
Dittmer, Cherie. Angel Angel. (p. 73)
Dittmer, Cherie Pless. Angel! Angel! (p. 73)
Dittmer, Lori. Future of Medicine. (p. 651)
—Future of Transportation. (p. 651)
—Heart Disease. (p. 759)
—HIV/AIDS. (p. 786)
—Parkinson's Disease. (p. 1325)
—Story of the Orlando Magic. (p. 1661)
—Story of the San Francisco 49ers. (p. 1662)
—Story of the St. Louis Rams. (p. 1662)
—Story of the Tennessee Titans. (p. 1662)
Dittrich, Dennis, illus. see Frender, Sam & Schiffmiller, Robin.
Dittrich, Melissa Joy. Family Flower. (p. 568)
Dittrich, Tina, jt. auth. see Morrison, Kathy.
Dittrich, Tina & Morrison, Kathryn. Stellaluna: An Study of Birds & Bats. (p. 1647)
Dittrick, A. L., as told by. Once upon A Christmas: The 4th Wiseman. (p. 1292)
Dittus, Jade Moon, illus. see Andrew-Kollmann, Marcia.
Divakaruni, Chitra Banerjee. Conch Bearer. (p. 355)
—Grandma & the Great Gourd: A Bengali Folktale. Waters, Susy Pilgrim, illus. (p. 708)
—Mirror of Fire & Dreaming. (p. 1149)
DiVencenzo, Maria T. Scariest Dream Ever. Martin, Alixandra, illus. (p. 1520)
—Star of Christmas. Verstraete, Elaine S., illus. (p. 1640)
DiVencenzo, Roberto. First Male Born. (p. 596)
DiVenuto, John. Scruffy Hawk & Freddy Ferret. (p. 1533)
Divenuto, John. Scruffy Hawk & Freddy Ferret. (p. 1533)
Diver, Bradford B. Van, see Van Diver, Bradford B.
Diver, Lucas. Austin Mahone: Famous Pop Singer & Songwriter. (p. 116)
—Katy Perry: Famous Pop Singer & Songwriter. (p. 946)
—One Direction: Popular Boy Band. (p. 1294)
—Pop Bios. (p. 1384)
—Ross Lynch: Disney Channel Actor. (p. 1490)
—Rowan Blanchard: Star of Girl Meets World. (p. 1492)
—Zendaya: Disney Channel Actress. (p. 1986)
Diver, Lucienne. Fangtabulous. (p. 571)
DIVINCENZO, Sofia & Yoselem, jt. auth. see Garcia Orihuela, Luis.
DIVINCENZO, Yoselem G., illus. see Robles Echeverria, Maria De Jesus & ALONSO CURIEL, Jorge David.
Divine, J. J. Light & the Shadow: Adventures in Sacred Geometry. (p. 1014)
Divine, Jill. Wicked Rabbit. (p. 1927)
Divine, L. Cold as Ice. (p. 338)
—Culture Clash. (p. 391)
—Drama High - Pushin' (p. 480)
—Drama High - Second Chance. (p. 480)
—Fight (p. 585)
—Fight. (p. 585)
—Frenemies. (p. 636)
—Holidaze. (p. 789)
—Hustlin' (p. 830)
—Keep It Movin' (p. 947)
—Lady J. (p. 971)
Divine, Miss Jill. alien who came to Tea. (p. 41)
—Miles Smiles. (p. 1142)
Diviny, Sean. Halloween Motel. Rocco, Joe, illus. (p. 738)
DiVito, Andrea, illus. see Dixon, Chuck.
DiVito, Anna. Annie Oakley Saves the Day. DiVito, Anna, illus. (p. 87)
DiVito, Anna, illus. see Goldsmith, Howard.
DiVito, Anna, illus. see Holub, Joan.
DiVito, Anna, illus. see Merchant, Peter.
Dix, Catherine R. Rosetta Stones. (p. 1490)
Dix, Colton. Popcorn Sale: Understand Place Value. (p. 1384)
Dix, Steph, illus. see Bruzzone, Catherine, et al.
Dixey, Kay, illus. see Crosbie, Duncan.
Dixit, Rama, illus. see Walker, Peter Lancaster.
Dixon, Amy. Marathon Mouse. Denlinger, Sam, illus. (p. 1091)
—Sophie's Animal Parade. Wish, Katia, illus. (p. 1613)
Dixon, Andy. Dragon Quest. Brooks, Felicity, ed. (p. 477)
—Mision en el Planeta Paradiso. (p. 1150)
—Star Quest. Brooks, Felicity, ed. (p. 1641)
—Sword Quest. Brooks, Felicity, ed. (p. 1692)
Dixon, Ann. Waiting for Noel: An Advent Story. Graham, Mark, illus. (p. 1853)
Dixon, Bob. Holiday Bunny. (p. 788)
—Rooty the Tree Troll. (p. 1488)
Dixon, Carol, illus. see Brooks, Karl.
Dixon, Carol, illus. see Pope, Ellen Dittman.
Dixon, Carol, illus. see Wilson, Rock.
Dixon, Chuck. Blood Red Sea. Epting, Steve & D'Armata, Frank, illus. (p. 200)
—Brath. DiVito, Andrea et al, illus. (p. 223)
—Crux Epting, Steve et al, illus. (p. 387)
—Dragon's Wake Johnson, Jeff et al, illus. (p. 479)
—Gladiator Triumphant Di Vito, Andrea et al, illus. (p. 682)
—Haunted Zhumar Johnson, Jeff et al, illus. (p. 754)
—Perdition's Gate Eaglesham, Dale et al, illus. (p. 1341)
—Resurrection Cariello, Sergio et al, illus. (p. 1464)
—Sigil Eaton, Scot et al, illus. (p. 1574)
—Silken Ghost. Rosado, Will et al, illus. (p. 1575)
—Strangers in Atlantis Epting, Steve et al, illus. (p. 1665)
—Walls of Zhumar. Johnson, Jeff et al, illus. (p. 1855)
—Way of the Rat Traveler (p. 1864)
Dixon, Chuck, jt. auth. see Hama, Larry.
Dixon, Chuck, jt. auth. see Truman, Timothy.
Dixon, Chuck & Kwapisz, Gary. Civil War Adventure: Book One. (p. 325)
Dixon, Chuck, et al. Knightfall: Broken Bat Vol. 1 (p. 964)
—Knightfall: Who Rules the Night Pt. 2 Kahan, Bob, ed. (p. 964)
—Knights End (p. 964)
—Year One. (p. 1969)
Dixon, Corey, illus. see McLaurin, Corey F.
Dixon, Dallas L. Little Boys Run. Little Boys Play. Williams, Nancy E., ed. (p. 1025)
—Shelby's Collection Day. Williams, Nancy E., ed. (p. 1564)
—Shelby's Shoes. Williams, Nancy E., ed. (p. 1564)
Dixon, Danielle. Project: Purest. (p. 1410)
Dixon, Darla. What Really Happened During the Middle Ages: A Collection of Historical Biographies (p. 1893)
—What Really Happened in Ancient Times: A Collection of Historical Biographies (p. 1893)
Dixon, Darla, illus. see Johnson, Terri.
Dixon, Debra, illus. see White, Kate.
Dixon, Debra Spina, illus. see Mullarkey, Lisa.
Dixon, Debra Spina, illus. see Wheeler, Annie.
Dixon, Dougal. Agustinia & Other Dinosaurs of Central & South America Weston, Steve & Field, James, illus. (p. 30)
—Aletopelta & Other Dinosaurs of the West Coast Weston, Steve & Field, James, illus. (p. 35)
—Big Book of Dinosaur Questions & Answers. Ticktock Media, Ltd. Staff, ed. (p. 179)
—Deltadromeus & Other Shoreline Dinosaurs Field, James & Weston, Steve, illus. (p. 425)
—Diceratops & Other Horned Dinosaurs Weston, Steve & Field, James, illus. (p. 435)
—Dinosaur Explorer (p. 442)
—Dinosaur Find Field, James & Weston, Steve, illus. (p. 442)
—Dinosaur Find Weston, Steve & Field, James, illus. (p. 442)
—Dromaeosaurus & Other Dinosaurs of the North Weston, Steve & Field, James, illus. (p. 485)
—Ice Age. (p. 850)
—Maiasaura & Other Dinosaurs of the Midwest Weston, Steve & Field, James, illus. (p. 1076)
—My First Book of Dinosaurs. (p. 1205)
—Neovenator & Other Dinosaurs of Europe Weston, Steve & Field, James, illus. (p. 1241)
—Ornithomimus & Other Fast Dinosaurs Weston, Steve & Field, James, illus. (p. 1304)
—Saltopus & Other First Dinosaurs Weston, Steve & Field, James, illus. (p. 1506)
—Scutellosaurus & Other Small Dinosaurs Weston, Steve & Field, James, illus. (p. 1534)
—Triceratops & Other Forest Dinosaurs Field, James & Weston, Steve, illus. (p. 1785)
—Tsintaosaurus & Other Duck-Billed Dinosaurs. Weston, Steve & Field, James, illus. (p. 1795)
Dixon, Dougal, jt. auth. see Macnair, Patricia.
Dixon, Dougal & Boyds Mills Press Staff. Clams All Year. (p. 326)
Dixon, Dougal & Picture Window Books Staff. Tyrannosaurus & Other Dinosaurs of North America Weston, Steve & Field, James, illus. (p. 1805)
Dixon, Douglas. Discovering Dinosaurs: An Exciting Guide to Prehistoric Creatures. (p. 449)
Dixon, Edna, jt. auth. see Cartwright, Stan.
Dixon, Ellen B., jt. auth. see Nadeau, Kathleen G.
Dixon, Franklin W. Bayport Buccaneers. (p. 147)
—Best of the Hardy Boys(r) Classic Collection: The House on the Cliff; The Ghost on Skeleton Rock; The Sting of the Scorpion (p. 171)
—Bicycle Thief. Burroughs, Scott, illus. (p. 177)
—Blown Away. (p. 202)
—Boardwalk Bust (p. 205)
—Burned. (p. 243)
—Camping Chaos. (p. 257)
—Comic con Artist. (p. 348)

—Dangerous Transmission. (p. 404)
—Death & Diamonds. (p. 420)
—Deprivation House. (p. 427)
—Double Down. (p. 472)
—Double Jeopardy. (p. 473)
—Extreme Danger. (p. 556)
—Farming Fear. (p. 574)
—Feeding Frenzy. (p. 580)
—Figure in Hiding Laune, Paul, illus. (p. 586)
—Fossil Frenzy. (p. 623)
—Foul Play. (p. 624)
—Great Escape. Burroughs, Scott, illus. (p. 715)
—Hardy Boys Collector's Boxed Set. (p. 748)
—Haunted. (p. 753)
—Hazed. (p. 756)
—Hidden Harbor Mystery Gretter, J. Clemens, illus. (p. 775)
—Hidden Mountain. (p. 776)
—House Arrest. (p. 803)
—Hurricane Joe. (p. 829)
—In Plane Sight. (p. 864)
—Kickoff to Danger. (p. 951)
—Kidnapped at the Casino. (p. 952)
—Line of Fire. (p. 1019)
—Martial Law. (p. 1097)
—Motocross Madness. (p. 1179)
—Mummy's Curse. (p. 1191)
—Murder at the Mall. (p. 1192)
—Murder House. (p. 1192)
—Mystery of the Black Rhino. (p. 1225)
—No Way Out. (p. 1261)
—One False Step. (p. 1295)
—Operation: Survival. (p. 1300)
—Passport to Danger. (p. 1327)
—Pushed. (p. 1420)
—Rocky Road. (p. 1484)
—Running on Fumes. (p. 1497)
—Running on Fumes. (p. 1497)
—Secret of the Soldier's Gold. (p. 1543)
—Ship of Secrets. (p. 1567)
—Sinister Sign Post. (p. 1579)
—Skin & Bones. (p. 1585)
—Speed Times Five. (p. 1624)
—Thrill Ride. (p. 1744)
—Thrill Ride. (p. 1744)
—Top Ten Ways to Die. (p. 1769)
—Training for Trouble. (p. 1777)
—Trick-or-Trouble. (p. 1786)
—Trouble in Paradise. (p. 1789)
—Trouble in Warp Space. (p. 1790)
—Wanted. (p. 1856)
—Warehouse Rumble. (p. 1858)
—Wreck & Roll. (p. 1962)
Dixon, Franklin W., jt. auth. see Keene, Carolyn.
Dixon, Franklin W. & Frost, Michael. Double Trouble. (p. 473)
Dixon, Franklin W. & Keene, Carolyn. Bonfire Masquerade. (p. 209)
Dixon, Franklin W. & Walker, Jeff. Mystery of the Black Rhino. (p. 1225)
—Passport to Danger. (p. 1327)
—Secret of the Soldier's Gold. (p. 1543)
—Typhoon Island. (p. 1805)
Dixon, Gary, illus. see Papaj, Dana.
Dixon, Greg. Paradigms of Suffering: Torturous Awakening. (p. 1323)
Dixon, Heather. Entwined. (p. 531)
—Illusionarium. (p. 857)
Dixon, John. Phoenix Island. (p. 1351)
Dixon, Joseph I. Jack Craig P. I., the Cuban Affair. (p. 903)
Dixon, Joyce Ann. Katie's Tree House. (p. 945)
—Witches' Cat. (p. 1941)
Dixon Jr., John T. Mommy, What Is a POW/MIA? (p. 1162)
Dixon, Karen S. Alexander the Moose. Crouch, Frances, illus. (p. 36)
Dixon, Karin, tr. see Schelvis, Jules.
Dixon, Ken. Cobweb Jack & the Sacred Khunjar. (p. 337)
Dixon, Kirstie. Pickles Helps a Friend. (p. 1354)
Dixon, Laura Emily. Talking to a Child with Bone Marrow Disease. (p. 1703)
Dixon, Linda A. Cupcakes for Cristina! (p. 392)
Dixon, Louisa. What Did I Do Today? (p. 1882)
Dixon, Louisa & Boshers, Martha. What Did I Do Today? For Young Writers. (p. 1882)
Dixon, Margaret Davis. Don't Go Fishing with a Caterpillar! (p. 467)
Dixon, Miranda. God Is Enormous! (p. 689)
Dixon, Nehemiah F., illus. see Gross, Carmen.
Dixon, Norma. Focus on Flies (p. 610)
—In Deep with the Octopus (p. 863)
—Lowdown on Earthworms. (p. 1061)
—Lowdown on Earthworms Clark, Warren, illus. (p. 1061)
Dixon, Philip. Knights & Castles. (p. 964)
Dixon, Rachel, illus. see Fritz, Jean.
Dixon, Ronald. Adventures of Nip & Dip, on a Dog Named Duffy. (p. 21)
Dixon, Steve. Out of the Shadows. (p. 1311)
Dixon, Tennessee, illus. see Blanc, Esther Silverstein & Eagle, Godeane.
Dixon, Thomas. From Passions to Emotions: The Creation of a Secular Psychological Category. (p. 643)
Dixon, Tiffany. Everyone Is Special. (p. 544)
Dixon, Tom, et al. And Fork: 100 Designers, 10 Curators, 10 Good Designs. Hancock, Robert, tr. (p. 71)
Dixon, Virginia. What Happened to Willie? Thomas, Tim, illus. (p. 1885)
Dixon-Engel, Tara & Jackson, Mike. Neil Armstrong: One Giant Leap for Mankind. (p. 1240)
Dixon-McCoy, Niyoka. Little Boy Like Me. (p. 1025)
Dj Caz. Spiders & Cupcakes. (p. 1627)
Djeli, Moses, jt. auth. see Yanique, Tiphanie.
Djilimand, Shira Yehudit. Secret of the Ruined Castle: And Other Stories. (p. 1543)
DK. Star Wars Rebels: Heroes of Lothal. (p. 1641)
DK Spanish Staff. DK Workbooks: Spelling, First Grade: Spelling, First Grade. (p. 456)
DKSmith. My Inner Child. (p. 1211)
D'Lacey, Chris. Dark Fire. (p. 407)
d'Lacey, Chris. Dark Fire. (p. 407)
—Dark Inheritance. (p. 407)
D'Lacey, Chris. Fire Ascending. (p. 590)
d'Lacey, Chris. Fire Ascending. (p. 590)
—Fire Eternal. (p. 590)
—Fire Star. (p. 590)
—Fire Within. (p. 591)
—Fire World. (p. 591)
—Frankin's Bear. Taylor, Thomas, illus. (p. 630)
—Gauge. (p. 658)
—Gruffen. (p. 727)
D'Lacey, Chris. Icefire. (p. 851)
d'Lacey, Chris. Icefire. d'Lacey, Chris, illus. (p. 851)
—Snail Patrol. Reeve, Philip, illus. (p. 1596)
D'Lacey, Chris. UFiles #1: a Dark Inheritance. (p. 1807)
d'Lacey, Chris. UFiles #2: Alexander's Army. (p. 1807)
d'Lacey, Chris, jt. auth. see d'Lacey, Jay.
D'Lacey, Chris & Caldey, Vincent. Good Clean Edge. (p. 697)
d'Lacey, Jay & d'Lacey, Chris. Rain & Fire. (p. 1434)
Dlin, Doug, ed. see Bevard, Robby, et al.
Dlin, Doug, jt. auth. see Perry, Fred.
Dlugolecki, Michele. Mr. Mish Mosh & His Wash. (p. 1185)
Dlugos, Josephine. Josie's Red Shoes. (p. 927)
Dlugos, Pamela J. Messages from Heaven: Be a Shining Star. Dlugos, Pamela J., illus. (p. 1129)
Dmaples. Big Dog, Little Puppy. (p. 181)
Dmitriev, Sergei, illus. see Uralskaia, Valeria, et al.
DNA Productions Staff, ed. Jimmy Neutron (p. 918)
Do, Elisa Shipon-Blum. Understanding Katie: A Day in the Life Of. Salus, Diane, illus. (p. 1815)
Do Gam, Rin Bo, illus. see Cowley, Joy, ed.
Do Gooder Press. PS 238 VII Daughters Sons & Shrink-Rays. (p. 1413)
Do, Kim-Thu, tr. see Zhang, Song Nan & Zhang, Hao Yu.
Do, Kim-Thu, tr. from ENG. Tang Monk Disciples Monkey King: English/Vietnamese. Ma, Wenhai, illus. (p. 1705)
Doak, Melissa J., jt. auth. see Miller, Reagan.
Doak, Robin. Conflicts in Iraq & Afghanistan. (p. 357)
—Empire of the Islamic World, Revised Edition. (p. 521)
—Genetic Disorders: Set Of 6. (p. 660)
—Genetic Disorders: Text Pairs. (p. 660)
—Maryland, 1634-1776. (p. 1101)
—South Carolina, 1540-1776. (p. 1616)
Doak, Robin S. Amelia Earhart (p. 58)
—Arctic Peoples (p. 96)
—Barack Obama. (p. 137)
—Black Tuesday: Prelude to the Great Depression (p. 197)
—Dian Fossey: Friend to Africa's Gorillas (p. 434)
—Dolores Huerta: Labor Leader & Civil Rights Activist (p. 464)
—Eleanor Roosevelt (p. 508)
—Harriet Tubman. (p. 749)
—Hawaii: The Aloha State. (p. 755)
—Hillary Clinton. (p. 779)
—Homeland Security. (p. 793)
—Hudson: Henry Hudson Searches for a Passage to Asia (p. 824)
—Investigating Hauntings, Ghosts, & Poltergeists (p. 884)
—James A. Garfield. (p. 906)
—Jane Goodall: Chimpanzee Protector (p. 908)
—John Tyler. (p. 923)
—Kate Middleton: Dutchess of Cambridge. (p. 944)
—Kate Middleton. (p. 944)
—Korean War. (p. 967)
—Liberia (p. 1005)
—Malala Yousafzai. (p. 1083)
—Mark Zuckerberg. (p. 1095)
—Martin Van Buren. (p. 1098)
—Michelle Obama (p. 1135)
—National Intelligence. (p. 1233)
—New Jersey, 1609-1776. (p. 1245)
—Phillis Wheatley: Slave & Poet (p. 1351)
—Phonograph. (p. 1352)
—Pope Leo X: Opponent of the Reformation (p. 1384)
—Smith: John Smith & the Settlement of Jamestown (p. 1594)
—Subarctic Peoples (p. 1671)
—Zebulon Pike: Explorer & Soldier. (p. 1985)
Doak, Robin S., jt. auth. see Housel, Debra J.
Doak, Robin S., jt. auth. see Macceca, Michael L.
Doak, Robin S. & McConville, Brendan. New Jersey, 1609-1776. (p. 1245)
Doak, Robin S., et al. Confederate General: Stonewall Jackson (p. 356)
—Extraordinary Women (p. 555)
—Women in Conservation (p. 1945)
Doak, Robin Santos. California, 1542-1850. (p. 253)
—Conflicts in Iraq & Afghanistan. (p. 357)
—Fighting for American Values: 1941-1985. Overmyer-Velazquez, Mark, ed. (p. 585)
—Georgia 1521-1776. (p. 665)
—Georgia, 1521-1776. (p. 665)
—Indian Americans. (p. 871)
—Slave Rebellions. Schwarz, Philip, ed. (p. 1588)
—Struggling to Become American: 1899-1940. Overmyer-Velazquez, Mark, ed. (p. 1668)
Doan, Catriona Le May, see Le May Doan, Catriona.
Doan, Donna. Henry the Homeschool Hamster. (p. 768)
Doan, Janet Mailan. Monster Stole My Chickens! (p. 1168)
Doan, Laura, jt. ed. see Garrity, Jane.
Doan, Lisa. Jack & the Wild Life. Stevanovic, Ivica, illus. (p. 902)
—Jack at the Helm. Stevanovic, Ivica, illus. (p. 902)
—Jack the Castaway. Stevanovic, Ivica, illus. (p. 903)
Doan, Nicholas. Fat Rabbit Farm: Big T's Big Adventure. (p. 577)
Doane, Beth. From the Jungle: Stories & Original Art from Children Living in Rainforests. (p. 644)
Doane, Nancy L. Indian Doctor Book. (p. 871)
Doane, Pelagie, illus. see Sutton, Margaret.
Dob, Bob, illus. see Basye, Dale E.
Dobbin, Rob, tr. see Kotzwinkle, William & Murray, Glenn.
Dobbin, Robert, ed. see Epictetus & Dobbin, Robert F.
Dobbin, Robert, tr. see Epictetus & Dobbin, Robert F.
Dobbin, Robert F., jt. auth. see Epictetus.
Dobbins, Erin, illus. see Cook, Jane Hampton.
Dobbins, Jan. Driving My Tractor. Sim, David, illus. (p. 485)
—Driving My Tractor Puzzle. Sim, David, illus. (p. 485)
—Farmer's Life for Me. Hullska-Beith, Laura, illus. (p. 574)
Dobbins, Jan & Bernal, Natalia. Vivamos la Granja! Huliska-Beith, Laura, illus. (p. 1846)
Dobbins, Jan & Songs, Steve. Driving My Tractor. Sim, David, illus. (p. 485)
Dobbs, Steve & Miller, Jane. Statistics 1. (p. 1644)
—Statistics 2 (International) (p. 1644)
Dobbyn, Nigel. Creating Science Fiction Comics. (p. 379)
Dobbyn, Nigel, illus. see Shakespeare, William.
Dobeck, Maryann. Circling the Sun. (p. 321)
—Volcanoes Nature's Awesome Power: Set Of 6. (p. 1849)
—Volcanoes: Nature's Awesome Power & Volcanes: 6 English, 6 Spanish Adaptations: el poder asombroso de la Naturaleza. (p. 1849)
Dobel, Jean-Marc, et al. Planet of the Bubble Gob. Smith, Anne Collins & Smith, Owen, trs. from FRE. (p. 1367)
Dobell, Darcy. Oyster Who Looked at the Sky. (p. 1316)
Dobell, Steve. Child's Book of Prayer. (p. 304)
Dobelmann, Collene L., ed. see Geiser, Traci Ferguson.
Dober, Jim. Hickory Woods Adventures: Waiting for A Bubble. (p. 775)
Dobi, Rob, illus. see Simon, Leslie & Kelley, Trevor.
Dobinson, Tony. Crossing. (p. 385)
Dobkin, Bonnie. Crazy Pizza Day. Dey, Romi, illus. (p. 378)
—Great Bug Hunt. Dunnington, Tom, illus. (p. 714)
Dobler, Shirley Jean, illus. see Pierce, Mary E.
Dobrescu, Irina, illus. see Bruder Grimm Staff.
d'Obrin, Felix, illus. see Franks, T. S.
Dobrina, Elena. Beaver Kid's Adventures. (p. 154)
Dobry, Beth. Why Ronald Fell Apart. (p. 1925)
Dobson. Holt Science Spectacular: Physical Science. (p. 791)
Dobson, Andrew. Formera (p. 620)
—So, You're a Cartoonist? Learning Curve. (p. 1602)
Dobson, Carol Anne. Freedom. (p. 634)
Dobson, Christina. Pizza Counting. Holmes, Matthew, illus. (p. 1365)
Dobson, Clive. Wind Power: 20 Projects to Make with Paper. (p. 1935)
Dobson, Clive, illus. see Hughes, Susan.
Dobson, Clive, illus. see Zonta, Pat.
Dobson, Cynthia Lund. I'm Trying to Be Like Jesus. Dewey, Simon, illus. (p. 860)
Dobson, Danae. Let's Talk! Good Stuff for Girlfriends about God, Guys, & Growing Up. (p. 1001)
Dobson, Donna. Timmy's First Adventure. (p. 1755)
Dobson, James C. Life on the Edge: The Next Generation's Guide to a Meaningful Future. (p. 1012)
—Preparing for Adolescence: How to Survive the Coming Years of Change. (p. 1396)
—Romantic Love: How to Be Head over Heels & Still Land on Your Feet. (p. 1486)
Dobson, Jill. Last Ship. (p. 978)
Dobson, Jolie. Bang Bang Plink Plink. (p. 136)
—Beep Beep Choo Choo. (p. 157)
—Ring Ring Pop Pop. (p. 1473)
—Snap Snap Woof Woof. (p. 1597)
Dobson, Len, illus. see Dingles, Molly.
Dobson, Leonard. This Little Piggy Went to Market. (p. 1737)
Dobson, Phil, illus. see Sanderson, Ana.
Dobson, S. Gaston, illus. see Green, Richard L., et al, eds.
Dobson, Shirley. God Answers Prayer: Coloring Book. (p. 688)
—God Cares for Me Coloring Book. (p. 688)
—God Helps Me Share: Coloring Book about Abigail & David. (p. 689)
—God Made the World Coloring Book: 100-Unit Counter Merchandiser. (p. 690)
—God Made the World Coloring Book. (p. 690)
—God's Little Helper Coloring Book. (p. 691)
—God's Ten Best Coloring Book 50-Unit Merch. (p. 692)
—Jesus Takes Care of Me Coloring Book: A Read-to-Me Bible Story Coloring Book about Jesus' Feeding 5,000 People. (p. 916)
Dobson, Shirley, contrib. by. God Gives Me Joy Coloring Book. (p. 688)
—God's Ten Best: The Ten Commandments Comic & Activity Book. (p. 692)
Dobson, Starr. My Goat Gertrude Dodwell, Dayle, illus. (p. 1210)
—My Goat Gertrude (pb) Dodwell, Dayle, illus. (p. 1210)
Dobyns, Stephen. Best Words, Best Order: Essays on Poetry. (p. 171)
Docalavich, Heather. Antidepressants & Psychology: Talk Therapy vs. Medication. (p. 89)
—Antiterrorism Policy & Fighting Fear Russett, Bruce, ed. (p. 89)
—Denmark. (p. 426)
—Economic Globalization & Sustainable Development Russett, Bruce, ed. (p. 502)
—Future of Antidepressants: The New Wave of Research. (p. 651)
—Future of Antidepressants: the New Wave of Research. (p. 651)
—History, Structure, & Reach of the Un Russett, Bruce, ed. (p. 785)
—Hungary. (p. 827)
—Netherlands. (p. 1242)
—Slovenia. (p. 1591)
—Sweden. (p. 1689)
—un & the Global Marketplace: Economic Developments. (p. 1810)
Docalavich, Heather & Indovino, Shaina C. Czech Republic. Bruton, John, ed. (p. 397)
—Denmark. Bruton, John, ed. (p. 426)
—Netherlands. Bruton, John, ed. (p. 1242)
—Poland. Bruton, John, ed. (p. 1378)
—Sweden. Bruton, John, ed. (p. 1689)
Docalavich, Heather & Indovino, Shaina Carmel. Croatia. (p. 384)
—Czech Republic. (p. 397)
—Denmark. (p. 426)
—Hungary. (p. 827)
—Latvia. (p. 980)
—Lithuania. (p. 1023)
—Netherlands. (p. 1242)
—Poland. (p. 1378)
—Slovakia. (p. 1591)
—Slovenia. (p. 1591)
—Sweden. (p. 1689)
Docampo, Valeria, illus. see Flanagan, Liz.
Docampo, Valeria, illus. see Flannigan, Liz.
Docampo, Valeria, illus. see Flor Ada, Alma.
Docampo, Valeria, illus. see Kimmel, Eric A.
Docampo, Valeria, illus. see Kingsbury, Karen.
Docampo, Valeria, illus. see Lestrade, Agnès de & Frank-McNeil, Julia.
Docampo, Valeria, illus. see Lynn, Sarah.
Docampo, Valeria, illus. see Morton, Carlene.
Docampo, Valeria, illus. see Primavera, Elise.
Docampo, Valeria, illus. see Slater, Dashka.
Docampo, Valeria, illus. see Stout, Shawn K.
Docampo, Valeria, jt. auth. see Flor Ada, Alma.
Docampo, Valeria, jt. auth. see Stout, Shawn K.
Docherty, Helen. Snatchabook. Docherty, Helen, illus. (p. 1597)
Docherty, Thomas. Big Scary Monster. Docherty, Thomas, illus. (p. 183)
—Little Boat. Docherty, Thomas, illus. (p. 1025)
—To the Beach. Docherty, Thomas, illus. (p. 1759)
—Wash-A-Bye Bear. Docherty, Thomas, illus. (p. 1859)
Docherty, Thomas, illus. see Gutzschhahn, Uwe-Michael.
Dockery, Amanda, illus. see Payne, M. D.
Dockery, Amie, jt. auth. see Tenney, Tommy.
Dockery, Jonathan. Children of the Apocalypse. (p. 302)
Dockery, Kevin. Future Weapons. (p. 651)
Dockery, L. D. Michael Monkey Saves the Day. (p. 1134)
—Multiplication Song Book. (p. 1190)
Dockery, Marie F. Three Billy Goats Gruff Find Jesus & the Three Little Souls. (p. 1741)
Dockray, Tracy. Lost & Found Pony. Dockray, Tracy, illus. (p. 1054)
—My Life Story. Dockray, Tracy, illus. (p. 1212)
Dockray, Tracy, illus. see Cleary, Beverly.
Dockray, Tracy, illus. see Estes, Allison & Stark, Dan.
Dockray, Tracy, illus. see Janni, Rebecca.
Dockray, Tracy, illus. see Manushkin, Fran.
Dockray, Tracy, illus. see O'Hair, Margaret.
Dockray, Tracy Arah, jt. illus. see Howard, Linda.
Dockrey, Donna. Tell Me about A Place Called Heaven. (p. 1716)
Dockrey, Karen. Vital Skills: How to Build Strong Friendships. (p. 1846)
Dockrey Young, Judy, jt. auth. see Young, Richard.
Dockrey Young, Richard & Young, Judy Dockrey. 1492, New World Tales. (p. 2002)
Dockter, Debra. Deadly Design. (p. 417)
Dockter, Toni. Percy & the Plod. (p. 1341)
Docktor, Irv, illus. see Appel, Benjamin & Clark, Henry W.
Doctor McGougain. Stevie's Dreams: Doctor Mcgougain. (p. 1649)
Doctor, Ronald M., jt. auth. see Kahn, Ada P.
Doctorick, Jonathan & Gohari, Omid. Duquesne University College Prowler off the Record. (p. 490)
Doctoroff, Tom. Billions: Selling to the New Chinese Consumer. (p. 187)
Doctorow, Cory. For the Win. (p. 616)
—Homeland. (p. 793)
—In Real Life. Wang, Jen, illus. (p. 864)
—Little Brother. (p. 1025)
—Pirate Cinema. (p. 1362)
Dodd, Anne Elizabeth. Angel of Winter. (p. 74)
Dodd, Anne Westcott. Story of the Sea Glass. Owens, Mary Beth, illus. (p. 1662)
Dodd, Christina. Back to School Mom (p. 130)
—Thigh High. (p. 1732)
Dodd, Emma. Always. Dodd, Emma, illus. (p. 51)
—Best Bear (p. 168)
—Cinderelephant. Dodd, Emma, illus. (p. 320)
—Dog's Farmyard Friends. (p. 462)
—Dog's Colorful Day: A Messy Story about Colors & Counting. (p. 462)
—Dog's Colorful Day: A Messy Story about Colors & Counting. Dodd, Emma, illus. (p. 462)
—Everything. Dodd, Emma, illus. (p. 544)
—Forever. Dodd, Emma, illus. (p. 619)
—Foxy. Dodd, Emma, illus. (p. 626)
—Foxy in Love. (p. 626)
—Foxy in Love. Dodd, Emma, illus. (p. 626)
—Go to Bed. Dodd, Emma, illus. (p. 687)
—I Am Small. Dodd, Emma, illus. (p. 833)
—I Love Bugs. Dodd, Emma, illus. (p. 842)
—Lots of Love. Dodd, Emma, illus. (p. 1057)
—Meow Said the Cow. Dodd, Emma, illus. (p. 1127)
—More & More. Dodd, Emma, illus. (p. 1174)
—When I Grow Up. Dodd, Emma, illus. (p. 1902)
—When You Were Born. Dodd, Emma, illus. (p. 1905)
Dodd, Emma, illus. see Andreae, Giles.
Dodd, Emma, illus. see Borden, Louise.
Dodd, Emma, illus. see Nilsen, Anna.
Dodd, Emma, illus. see Reidy, Hannah.
Dodd, Emma, illus. see Slingsby, Janet.
Dodd, Emma, illus. see Smith, Kath.
Dodd, Emma & Nosy Crow Staff. Baby & Me. Dodd, Emma, illus. (p. 124)
Dodd, Joseph D., illus. see Belknap, Jodi P. & Montgomery, Tamara.
Dodd, Kelly. Gregarious Gabby & Her Gabbyful Life: Moving Day. (p. 723)
Dodd, Lynley. Gold Star First Readers (p. 694)
—Hairy Maclary's Caterwaul Caper. Dodd, Lynley, illus. (p. 736)
—Hairy Maclary's Showbusiness. Dodd, Lynley, illus. (p. 736)
—Schnitzel Von Krumm, Dogs Never Climb Trees. (p. 1521)
—Slinky Malinki Catflaps. Dodd, Lynley, illus. (p. 1590)
—Slinky Malinki, Open the Door. (p. 1590)
—Zachary Quack Minimonster. Dodd, Lynley, illus. (p. 1984)

D

Dodd, Marion. Mystic by the A,B, Sea. Dodd, Marion, illus. (p. 1226)
Dodd, Melissa. Santa Sheds (p. 1513)
Dodd, Sarah J. Bible Stories for Little Angels. Kolanovic, Dubravka, illus. (p. 176)
—Christmas Stories for Little Angels. Kolanovic, Dubravka, illus. (p. 315)
Dodd, Sarah J. & Kolanovic, Dubravka. Christmas Stories for Little Angels. (p. 315)
Dodd, Susan. Dreaming the Dreams That Only Cats Can Dream. (p. 484)
Dodd-Carlile, Vowery. Multicultural Legends & Tales. (p. 1190)
—Pot Full of Tales. (p. 1388)
Doddoli, Consuelo. Punto y Rayo: Los Puntos Cardinales y Los Mapas. Cota, Cecilia, illus. (p. 1417)
Dodds, Dayle Ann. Full House: An Invitation to Fractions. Carter, Abby, illus. (p. 646)
—Great Divide: A Mathematical Marathon. Mitchell, Tracy, illus. (p. 715)
—Minnie's Diner: A Multiplying Menu. Manders, John, illus. (p. 1148)
—Teacher's Pets. Hafner, Marylin, illus. (p. 1709)
Dodds, John Thomas. Sneaky Twitch of an Itch. (p. 1597)
Dodds, Keshawn. Menzuo: The Calling of the Sun Prince. (p. 1127)
Dodds, Robert. Murrian. (p. 1192)
Dodds, Sherril. Dance on Screen: Genres & Media from Hollywood to Experimental Art. (p. 402)
Dodds, Terry. Complete Package: Intermediate Level. (p. 353)
—Descriptive Writing: Advanced Level. (p. 428)
—Descriptive Writing: Intermediate Level. (p. 428)
—Expository Writing: Advanced Level. (p. 554)
—Expository Writing: Intermediate Level. (p. 554)
—High-Performance Writing: A Structured Approach. (p. 778)
—High-Performance Writing: a Structured Approach: Report Writing. (p. 778)
—High-Performance Writing: a Structured Approach: Writer's Guide. (p. 778)
—High-Performance Writing: a Structured Approach: Complete Package. (p. 778)
—High-Performance Writing: a Structured Approach: Narrative Writing. (p. 778)
—High-Performance Writing: a Structured Approach: Practical Writing. (p. 778)
—High-Performance Writing: a Structured Approach: Expository Writing. (p. 778)
—High-Performance Writing: a Structured Approach: Persuasive Writing. (p. 778)
—High-Performance Writing: a Structured Approach: Descriptive Writing. (p. 778)
—Narrative Writing: Advanced Level. (p. 1229)
—Narrative Writing: Intermediate Level. (p. 1229)
—Persuasive Writing: Advanced Level. (p. 1344)
—Persuasive Writing: Intermediate Level. (p. 1344)
—Report Writing: Advanced Level. (p. 1461)
—Report Writing: Intermediate Level. (p. 1461)
—Writer's Guide: Advanced Level. (p. 1964)
—Writer's Guide: Intermediate Level. (p. 1964)
Dodee, jt. auth. see Dodee.
Dodee & Dodee. That Big Old Round Orange Thing: A Mrs. Tockalocka Adventure. (p. 1726)
Doder, Joshua. Dog Called Grk. (p. 461)
—Grk: Operation Tortoise. (p. 724)
—Grk Smells a Rat. (p. 725)
—Grk Takes Revenge. (p. 725)
—Time Traveler's Guide to Shakespeare's London. (p. 1753)
—Timetraveller's Guide to Saxon & Viking London. (p. 1754)
Dodge, Andrew. Exploring Capitol Hill: A Kid's Guide to the U. S. Capitol & Congress. Wasniewski, Matthew, ed. (p. 551)
Dodge, Barbara A., illus. see Siwak, Brenda S.
Dodge Cummings, Judy. American Revolution: Experience the Battle for Independence. Casteel, Tom, illus. (p. 63)
Dodge, Jim. Fup. (p. 650)
Dodge, Louis. Everychild: A Story Which the Old May Interpret to the Young A. (p. 543)
Dodge, Mary Mapes. Hans Brinker, or the Silver Skates. (p. 743)
—Hans Brinker, or the Silver Skates. Kopito, Janet Baine, ed. (p. 743)
—Hans Brinker or the Silver Skates A Story of Life in Holland. Doggett, Allen B., illus. (p. 743)
—Hans Brinker; or, the Silver Skates (Dod. (p. 743)
—Po No Kah an Indian Tale of Long Ago. (p. 1374)
—PoNoKah an Indian Tale of Long Ago. (p. 1382)
—Rhymes & Jingles. (p. 1468)
Dodgson, Charles Lutwidge, see Carroll, Lewis, pseud.
Dodgson, Y. K. Day the Horse Was Free. T. W. Zimmerman, illus. (p. 414)
—Day the Horse Was Free. Zimmerman, T. W., illus. (p. 414)
Dods, Emma. Wow! Surprising Facts about the Human Body. Aspinall, Marc, illus. (p. 1962)
—Zoo. Daubney, Kate, illus. (p. 1988)
Dods, Emma, jt. auth. see Kingfisher Editors.
Dodson, Bert. Helping Santa: My First Christmas Adventure with Grandma. Dodson, Bert, illus. (p. 766)
—Super Grandpa. (p. 1680)
Dodson, Bert, illus. see Christopher, Matt.
Dodson, Bert, illus. see Krisher, Trudy.
Dodson, Bert, illus. see Lange, Willem.
Dodson, Bert, illus. see Paine, Walter.
Dodson, Bert, illus. see Reynolds, Cynthia Furlong.
Dodson, Bert, illus. see Schwartz, David M.
Dodson, Bert, illus. see Stryer, Andrea Stenn.
Dodson, Bert, illus. see Wallis, Ginger.
Dodson, Bert, illus. see Winter, Jonah.
Dodson, Emma. Speckle the Spider. Dodson, Emma, illus. (p. 1624)
—Very Important Idea. (p. 1838)
—Very Important Idea. Dodson, Emma, illus. (p. 1838)
Dodson, Emma, illus. see Powell, Jillian.
Dodson, Emma, illus. see Voake, Steve.
Dodson, Emma & Woodward, John. Wow, I Didn't Know That! Surprising Facts about Animals. Aspinall, Marc, illus. (p. 1962)
Dodson, Kris. YES Book: Your Emergency Safety Handbook (p. 1970)
Dodson, Merilee. Kids from Critter Cove. Gregor, Terri, illus. (p. 953)
Dodson, Misty. Flightless Flip. (p. 604)
Dodson, Peter. Pterosaurs up Close: Flying Reptiles. Bindon, John, illus. (p. 1414)
Dodson, Peter & Library Association Staff. Diplodocus up Close: Long-Necked Dinosaur. Marshall, Todd & Bindon, John, illus. (p. 445)
—Stegosaurus up Close: Plated Dinosaur. Marshall, Todd et al, illus. (p. 1646)
—Triceratops up Close: Horned Dinosaur. Marshall, Todd & Fields, Laura, illus. (p. 1786)
—Tyrannosaurus Rex up Close: Meat-Eating Dinosaur. Marshall, Todd et al, illus. (p. 1805)
—Velociraptor up Close: Swift Dinosaur. Fields, Laura & Walters, Bob, illus. (p. 1835)
Dodson, Shon. All I Need. (p. 44)
Dodson, Terry, illus. see Fraction, Matt.
Dodson, Terry, illus. see Mackie, Howard, et al.
Dodson, Terry, illus. see Millar, Mark & Santoro, Frank.
Dodson, Terry & Land, Greg. X-Men: Nation X. (p. 1967)
Dodson Wade, Mary. All Around Texas: Regions & Resources (p. 43)
—People of Texas (p. 1339)
—Texas History (p. 1724)
—Texas Native Peoples (p. 1724)
—Uniquely Texas (p. 1818)
Dodson Wade, Mary, jt. auth. see Bredeson, Carmen.
Dodson Wade, Mary, jt. auth. see Stewart, Mark.
Dodwell, Dayle, illus. see Dobson, Starr.
Doe, Charles J., ed. see Stretton, Hesba.
Doe, Cheyenne. Kitty Kats. (p. 963)
Doe, Jayne, et al. Jon & Jayne's Guide to Making Friends & Getting the Guy (Or Girl) (p. 924)
Doe, Juan, jt. illus. see Haspiel, Dean.
Doeden, Matt. Adele: Soul Music's Magical Voice. (p. 12)
—Air Show Jets. (p. 31)
—Aircraft Carriers. (p. 31)
—All about Baseball. (p. 42)
—All about Basketball. (p. 42)
—All about Football. (p. 42)
—All about Hockey. (p. 42)
—All about Sports. (p. 43)
—Anatomy of a Dragon. Mayer, Jonathan, illus. (p. 67)
—At Battle in World War II: An Interactive Battlefield Adventure. (p. 110)
—Aviones Caza. Ferrer, Martin Luis Guzman, tr. from ENG. (p. 120)
—Aztecs: Life in Tenochtitlan. Hiti, Samuel, illus. (p. 122)
—Basketball Legends in the Making (p. 143)
—Battle of the Alamo Barnett, Charles et al, illus. (p. 146)
—Battle of the Alamo Barnett, Charles, III & Miller, Phil, illus. (p. 146)
—Berlin Wall: An Interactive Modern History Adventure (p. 167)
—Best of Pro Baseball (p. 170)
—Best of Pro Basketball (p. 170)
—Best of Pro Football (p. 170)
—Best of Pro Ice Hockey (p. 170)
—BMX Freestyle (p. 204)
—Boa Constrictors (p. 205)
—Boston Tea Party Barnett III, Charles & Hoover, Dave, illus. (p. 215)
—Boston Tea Party Barnett, Charles, III & Hoover, Dave, illus. (p. 215)
—Cal Ripken, Jr. (p. 252)
—Camionetas Monster Trucks/Monster Trucks. (p. 256)
—Can You Survive a Global Blackout? An Interactive Doomsday Adventure. Nathan, James, illus. (p. 259)
—Can You Survive a Virus Outbreak? An Interactive Doomsday Adventure. (p. 259)
—Can You Survive Extreme Mountain Climbing? An Interactive Survival Adventure (p. 259)
—Can You Survive in the Special Forces? An Interactive Survival Adventure (p. 259)
—Can You Survive the Desert? An Interactive Survival Adventure (p. 259)
—Can You Survive the Jungle? An Interactive Survival Adventure. (p. 259)
—Can You Survive the Wilderness? An Interactive Survival Adventure (p. 259)
—Carey Price. (p. 268)
—Central African Republic in Pictures. (p. 287)
—Chinese: Life in China's Golden Age. Hiti, Sam, illus. (p. 307)
—Choppers. (p. 310)
—Civil War: An Interactive History Adventure (p. 325)
—Civil War [Scholastic]: An Interactive History Adventure. (p. 325)
—College Football Championship: The Fight for the Top Spot. (p. 340)
—Combat Sports. (p. 346)
—Conflict Resolution Smarts: How to Communicate, Negotiate, Compromise, & More. (p. 357)
—Copperheads (p. 366)
—Cottonmouths (p. 369)
—Crazy Cars. (p. 377)
—Custom Cars. (p. 395)
—Dale Earnhardt Jr. (p. 401)
—Darkness Everywhere: The Assassination of Mohandas Gandhi. (p. 408)
—Deadly Venomous Animals. (p. 418)
—Destroyers (p. 431)
—Dirt Bikes. (p. 446)
—Doug Flutie. (p. 473)
—Dragon Behavior Mayer, Jonathan, illus. (p. 476)
—Dragon Legends (p. 477)
—Dragon Life Mayer, Jonathan, illus. (p. 477)
—Dragonatomy Mayer, Jonathan, illus. (p. 478)
—Dragons in Mythology (p. 479)
—Dragsters (p. 479)
—Dwyane Wade: Basketball Superstar (p. 491)
—Eat Right! How You Can Make Good Food Choices. (p. 501)
—Eat Right! How You Can Make Good Food Choices. Desrocher, Jack, illus. (p. 501)
—Ejército de EE. UU. (p. 507)
—Enduro Racing (p. 527)
—Fighter Planes (p. 585)
—Finding Out about Coal, Oil, & Natural Gas. (p. 588)
—Finding Out about Geothermal Energy. (p. 588)
—Finding Out about Hydropower. (p. 588)
—Finding Out about Nuclear Energy. (p. 588)
—Finding Out about Solar Energy. (p. 588)
—Finding Out about Wind Energy. (p. 588)
—Floods (p. 605)
—Football Legends in the Making (p. 615)
—Football's Greatest Defenders (p. 615)
—Football's Greatest Quarterbacks (p. 615)
—Fuegos Arrasadores. (p. 646)
—Fuerza Aérea de EE. UU.) (p. 1806)
—Garter Snakes (p. 657)
—George Washington: Leading a New Nation. Martin, Cynthia, illus. (p. 664)
—George Washington: Dirigiendo una Nueva Nación. Martin, Cynthia, illus. (p. 664)
—GoPro Inventor Nick Woodman. (p. 702)
—Greatest Baseball Records. (p. 719)
—Greatest Basketball Records. (p. 719)
—Greatest Hockey Records. (p. 720)
—Green Day: Keeping Their Edge. (p. 721)
—Gun Control: Preventing Violence or Crushing Constitutional Rights? (p. 732)
—Helicópteros Militares. Ferrer, Martin Luis Guzman, tr. from ENG. (p. 763)
—Hindenburg Disaster Erwin, Steve et al, illus. (p. 780)
—How to Survive a Flood (p. 821)
—Human Travel to the Moon & Mars: Waste of Money or Next Frontier? (p. 826)
—Humvees Saunders-Smith, Gail, ed. (p. 827)
—Hurricanes. (p. 830)
—Impact: The Story of the September 11 Terrorist Attacks. (p. 862)
—Inundaciones/Floods (p. 883)
—Jeff Gordon (p. 911)
—Jeremy Lin: Basketball Superstar. (p. 913)
—Jimmie Johnson (p. 918)
—John Sutter & the California Gold Rush Barnett, Charles, III et al, illus. (p. 923)
—Johnny Depp: Hollywood Rebel. (p. 923)
—Kasey Kahne (p. 944)
—Kevin Durant: Basketball Superstar (p. 950)
—Kevin Harvick (p. 950)
—Lady Gaga: Pop's Glam Queen. (p. 970)
—Lance Armstrong. (p. 973)
—Laos in Pictures. (p. 975)
—Legalized Gambling: Revenue Boom or Social Bust? (p. 988)
—Life as a Ninja: An Interactive History Adventure. (p. 1008)
—Life as a Samurai: An Interactive History Adventure. (p. 1008)
—Life as a Samurai. (p. 1008)
—Lowriders. (p. 1061)
—Malala Yousafzai: Shot by the Taliban, Still Fighting for Equal Education. (p. 1083)
—Marked Man: The Assassination of Malcolm X. (p. 1095)
—Matt Kenseth (p. 1109)
—Miguel Cabrera: Baseball Superstar (p. 1141)
—Military Helicopters (p. 1143)
—Miz: Pro Wrestling Superstar (p. 1156)
—Mohandas Gandhi. (p. 1160)
—Monster Trucks (p. 1168)
—Motocross Freestyle (p. 1179)
—Motorcycles (p. 1179)
—NASCAR Behind the Scenes (p. 1230)
—NASCAR Fan Experience (p. 1230)
—Oregon Trail: An Interactive History Adventure. (p. 1303)
—Outrageous Football Rivalries. (p. 1313)
—Peyton Manning. (p. 1349)
—Phil Kessel. (p. 1350)
—Play Football Like a Pro: Key Skills & Tips (p. 1371)
—Prince William & Kate: A Royal Romance. (p. 1401)
—Put on Your Thinking Cap: And Other Expressions about School. (p. 1420)
—Rattlesnakes (p. 1440)
—Real-World Dragons Pellegrino, Rich, illus. (p. 1449)
—Safety Smarts: How to Manage Threats, Protect Yourself, Get Help, & More. (p. 1502)
—Salem Witch Trials: An Interactive History Adventure (p. 1504)
—Samuel Adams: Patriot & Statesman. Smith, Tod G. et al, illus. (p. 1509)
—Semitrucks (p. 1550)
—Shaun White. (p. 1563)
—Sidney Crosby: Hockey Superstar. (p. 1573)
—Sinking of the Titanic Barnett, Charles, III et al, illus. (p. 1580)
—Sinking of the Titanic Barnett, Charles, III & Miller, Phil, illus. (p. 1580)
—Skateboarding (p. 1583)
—Snowboarding (p. 1600)
—Snowmobiles (p. 1601)
—SpaceX & Tesla Motors Engineer Elon Musk. (p. 1620)
—Sports Car Racing. (p. 1632)
—Sports Cars. (p. 1632)
—Stars of Basketball (p. 1643)
—Stars of Hockey (p. 1643)
—Stay Fit! How You Can Get in Shape. (p. 1645)
—Steve Jobs: Technology Innovator & Apple Genius. (p. 1649)
—Steven Stamkos. (p. 1649)
—Stick Out Like a Sore Thumb: And Other Expressions about Body Parts. (p. 1649)
—Stock Cars (p. 1651)
—Stock Cars. (p. 1651)
—Submarines. (p. 1671)
—Supercross (p. 1683)
—Superstar Athletes. (p. 1684)
—Tanks (p. 1705)
—Tanques/Tanks. Ferrer, Martin Luis Guzman, tr. from ENG. (p. 1705)
—Theoretical Physicist Brian Greene. (p. 1729)
—Thomas Jefferson: Great American Purcell, Gordon & Beatty, Terry, illus. (p. 1739)
—Thunderstorms. (p. 1746)
—Tiger Woods. (p. 1749)
—Tim Tebow: Football Superstar. (p. 1750)
—Todoterrenos. (p. 1761)
—Tom Brady: Unlikely Champion. (p. 1762)
—Tom Brady. (p. 1762)
—Tony Dungy. (p. 1766)
—Tools & Treasures of Ancient Egypt. (p. 1767)
—Tools & Treasures of Ancient Greece. (p. 1767)
—Tools & Treasures of Ancient Mesopotamia. (p. 1767)
—Tools & Treasures of Ancient Rome. (p. 1767)
—Tools & Treasures of the Ancient Maya. (p. 1767)
—Tornadoes. (p. 1770)
—Track & Field. (p. 1775)
—Tractores Agrícolas. (p. 1775)
—Trapped in a Canyon! Aron Ralston's Story of Survival (p. 1779)
—Trenes. (p. 1784)
—U. S. Air Force. (p. 1806)
—U. S. Air Force [Scholastic]. (p. 1806)
—U. S. Army. (p. 1806)
—U. S. Army [Scholastic]. (p. 1806)
—U. S. Coast Guard. (p. 1806)
—U. S. Marine Corps (p. 1806)
—U. S. Navy (p. 1807)
—Volleyball. (p. 1849)
—Wayne Gretzky. (p. 1865)
—Weapons of Ancient Times. (p. 1869)
—Weapons of the American Indians (p. 1869)
—Weapons of the Civil War. (p. 1869)
—Weapons of the Cold War (p. 1869)
—Weapons of the Middle Ages. (p. 1869)
—Weapons of the Modern-Day (p. 1869)
—Weapons of the Revolutionary War. (p. 1869)
—Weapons of the Vikings (p. 1869)
—Weapons of World War I. (p. 1869)
—Weapons of World War II. (p. 1869)
—Whistleblowers. (p. 1912)
—Whistle-Blowers: Exposing Crime & Corruption. (p. 1912)
—Wildfires (p. 1931)
—Will Smith: Box Office Superstar. (p. 1932)
—Will Smith. (p. 1932)
—Willie Mays. (p. 1934)
—Wilt Chamberlain. (p. 1935)
—World of Dragons. Mayer, Jonathan & Pellegrino, Rich, illus. (p. 1956)
—World Series: Baseball's Biggest Stage. (p. 1958)
—World's Fastest Animals (p. 1960)
—World's Greatest Baseball Players (p. 1960)
—World's Greatest Basketball Players (p. 1960)
—World's Greatest Football Players (p. 1960)
—World's Greatest Soccer Players (p. 1960)
—World's Greatest Sports Stars (p. 1960)
—Yao Ming. (p. 1968)
—You Choose: Survival. (p. 1975)
Doeden, Matt, jt. auth. see Burgan, Michael.
Doeden, Matt, jt. auth. see Hoena, Blake.
Doeden, Matt, jt. auth. see Lassieur, Allison.
Doeden, Matt, jt. auth. see Wacholtz, Anthony.
Doeden, Matt & Capstone Press Editors. Lost at Sea! Tami Oldham Ashcroft's Story of Survival (p. 1055)
—Motocicletas. Saunders-Smith, Gail, ed. (p. 1179)
Doeden, Matt & Capstone Press Staff. Autos de Carreras. Saunders-Smith, Gail, ed. (p. 117)
—Camiones Con Tráiler. Saunders-Smith, Gail, ed. (p. 256)
—Camionetas Monstruo. Saunders-Smith, Gail, ed. (p. 256)
—Nostradamus (p. 1266)
—Stonehenge (p. 1653)
—Trains Saunders-Smith, Gail, ed. (p. 1777)
—Tugboats Saunders-Smith, Gail, ed. (p. 1796)
Doeden, Matt & Hoena, Blake. War in Afghanistan: An Interactive Modern History Adventure (p. 1857)
Doeden, Matt & Penn, Jim. Can You Survive the Jungle? An Interactive Survival Adventure (p. 259)
Doeden, Matt & Savage, Jeff. Eli Manning. (p. 512)
Doeden, Matt & Schuh, Mari. Sport Stars (p. 1631)
Doeden, Matt & Stewart, Mark. Peyton Manning. (p. 1349)
Doeden, Matt & Wacholtz, Anthony. Superstar Athletes. (p. 1684)
Doeden, Matt, et al. Aircraft Carriers (p. 31)
—Fighter Planes (p. 585)
—Hockey Superstars. (p. 787)
—Pro Wrestling Superstars (p. 1408)
—Sports Rivalries. (p. 1633)
Doeden, Matthew. Advances in Genetics: Set Of 6. (p. 13)
—Advances in Genetics: Text Pairs. (p. 13)
Doehring, Aurora, illus. see Bernstein, Jordan.
Doehring, Phoebe, illus. see Derkez, Linda.
Doell, Glenn. Creative Coloring Books: The What If. . . series. (p. 379)
Doerfler-Dall, Mary. Hands on Faith: 66 Projects, Activities & Crafts for Children. (p. 741)
Doerflinger, Marion, jt. auth. see Lux, Josephine Kei.
Doering, Amanda. Cats ABC: An Alphabet Book (p. 281)
—Cinco de Mayo: Day of Mexican Pride (p. 319)
—Homes Around the World ABC: An Alphabet Book (p. 793)
—Insults Aren't Funny: What to Do about Verbal Bullying. Shin, Simone, illus. (p. 879)
—Kwanzaa: African American Celebration of Culture Williams, Robert, illus. (p. 969)
—Martin Luther King, Jr. Day: Honoring a Civil Rights Hero (p. 1098)
—Sometimes Jokes Aren't Funny: What to Do about Hidden Bullying. Shin, Simone, illus. (p. 1610)
Doering, Amanda & Knox, Barbara. Rain Forest ABC: An Alphabet Book (p. 1434)
Doering, Amanda F. & Higgins, Melissa. No More Bullies. Shin, Simone, illus. (p. 1259)
Doering, Jennie Spray. Beach Riddles. Pica, Steve, illus. (p. 149)
Doering, Kimber, illus. see Moody, Gloria.
Doering Tourville, Amanda. Community Helper Mysteries. (p. 350)

—Manners in the Lunchroom. Lensch, Chris, illus. (p. 1088)
—Manners on the School Bus Lensch, Chris, illus. (p. 1088)
—Manners with a Library Book Lensch, Chris, illus. (p. 1088)
—My Friend Has ADHD Sorra, Kristin, illus. (p. 1209)
—My Friend Has ADHD [Readers World]. Sorra, Kristin, illus. (p. 1209)
—My Friend Has Autism Sorra, Kristin, illus. (p. 1209)
—My Friend Has Autism [Readers World]. Sorra, Kristin, illus. (p. 1209)
—My Friend Has down Syndrome Sorra, Kristin, illus. (p. 1209)
—My Friend Has down Syndrome [Readers World]. Sorra, Kristin, illus. (p. 1209)
—My Friend Has Dyslexia Sorra, Kristin, illus. (p. 1209)
—My Friend Has Dyslexia [Readers World]. Sorra, Kristin, illus. (p. 1209)
—Pledge of Allegiance. Ouren, Todd, illus. (p. 1373)
—Transportation in the City Thompson, Jeffrey, illus. (p. 1779)
—United States Flag. Ouren, Todd, illus. (p. 1819)
—Visit to the Police Station Thompson, Jeffrey, illus. (p. 1845)
Doerr, Bonnie J. Island Sting Britt, Joanna & Edwards, Laurie J., illus. (p. 892)
—Kenzie's Key. Aberle, Xylena Apotheloz, illus. (p. 949)
—Stakeout. Edwards, Laurie J. & Britt, Joanna, illus. (p. 1638)
Doerr, Joe Francis. Order of the Ordinary. (p. 1302)
Doerrfeld, Cori. Little Bunny Foo Foo: The Real Story. (p. 1025)
—Matilda in the Middle. (p. 1109)
—Penny Loves Pink. (p. 1338)
Doerrfeld, Cori, illus. see Broach, Elise.
Doerrfeld, Cori, illus. see Emerson, Carl.
Doerrfeld, Cori, illus. see Jones, Christianne C.
Doerrfeld, Cori, illus. see Loewen, Nancy.
Doerrfeld, Cori, illus. see Meister, Cari.
Doerrfeld, Cori, illus. see Rustad, Martha E. H.
Doerrfeld, Cori, illus. see Shields, Brooke.
Doery, Marya, illus. see Robinson, Virginia.
Doescher, Erik, illus. see Bright, J. E.
Doescher, Erik, illus. see DeCarlo, Mike, et al.
Doescher, Erik, illus. see Kupperberg, Paul, et al.
Doescher, Erik, illus. see Lemke, Donald B., et al.
Doescher, Erik, illus. see Mason, Jane B., et al.
Doescher, Erik, illus. see Sautter, Aaron.
Doescher, Erik, illus. see Saxon, Victoria.
Doescher, Erik, illus. see Shealy, Dennis & Random House Staff.
Doescher, Erik, illus. see Simonson, Louise, et al.
Doescher, Erik, illus. see Sonneborn, Scott, et al.
Doescher, Erik, illus. see Sutton, Laurie S., et al.
Doescher, Erik, illus. see Wrecks, Billy.
Doft, Tony. Nostradamus. (p. 1266)
Dog Artlist Collection Staff. Dog from Arf! Arf! to Zzzzzz. Dog Artlist Collection Staff, illus. (p. 461)
Dogan, Nakia C. My Daddy Is My Hero. (p. 1201)
Dogar, Sharon. Annexed. (p. 86)
Doggett, Al, illus. see Edwards, Helen L.
Doggett, Allen B., illus. see Dodge, Mary Mapes.
Doggett, Sue, ed. see Howie, Vicki.
Doggett, Sue, ed. see Lockett, Eve.
Doggett, W. Kirk, illus. see Phillips, Carey R. & Johannen, Kevin C.
Doghouse Press Inc. Staff, ed. see Silkman, Anne.
Dogi, Fiametta, illus. see Jewitt, Kathryn.
Dogi, Fiametta, jt. auth. see Jewitt, Kathryn.
Dogi, Fiammetta, illus. see Hipp, Andrew.
Dogi, Fiammetta, illus. see Riggs, Kate.
Dogi, Fiammetta, illus. see Ganeri, Anita.
Dogi, Fiammetta, illus. see McRae, Anne & Agosta, Loredana.
Dogi, Fiammetta, illus. see Williams, Brian & Egan, Vicky.
Dogiakis, Helen. Captain Terry the Pirate Cow's Adventure to Greece. (p. 264)
—Captain Terry the Pirate Cow's Adventure to Italy. (p. 264)
Dogliani, Daniela, illus. see Maidment, Stella.
Dohanish, Jason, illus. see O'Shea, Pauleen.
Doherty, Ann, illus. see Doherty, Vrinda & Valmiki.
Doherty, Barbara, jt. auth. see Jaffe, Charlotte.
Doherty, Berlie. Coconut Comes to School. Bates, Ivan, illus. (p. 337)
—Company of Ghosts. (p. 351)
—Jack the Giant Killer. (p. 903)
—Nutcracker. Beck, Ian, illus. (p. 1273)
—Oxford Book of Bible Stories. Cockcroft, Jason, illus. (p. 1315)
—Treason. (p. 1781)
Doherty, Berlie & Varios Autores. Cuentos Magicos. (p. 390)
Doherty, Brian. Search-a-Words. (p. 1537)
Doherty, Catherine, illus. see Durkin, Shawn.
Doherty, Catherine, illus. see Jennings, Sharon.
Doherty, Catherine, illus. see Kropp, Paul.
Doherty, Catherine, illus. see Muirine, Jennifer.
Doherty, Catherine, illus. see Varrato, Tony.
Doherty, Catherine, jt. auth. see Durkin, Shawn.
Doherty, Catherine, jt. auth. see Kropp, Paul.
Doherty, Craig A. California Indians. Facts on File, Inc. Staff, ed. (p. 253)
—Great Basin Indians. Facts on File, Inc. Staff, ed. (p. 714)
—Northwest Coast Indians. Facts on File, Inc. Staff, ed. (p. 1266)
—Southwest Indians. Facts on File, Inc. Staff, ed. (p. 1618)
—Subarctic Peoples. Facts on File, Inc. Staff, ed. (p. 1671)
Doherty, Craig A. & Doherty, Katherine M. Arctic Peoples. (p. 96)
—Connecticut. (p. 357)
—Delaware. (p. 424)
—Georgia. (p. 665)
—Maryland. (p. 1101)
—Massachusetts (p. 1102)
—New Hampshire. (p. 1244)
—New Jersey (p. 1245)
—New York (p. 1247)
—North Carolina (p. 1264)
—Northeast Indians. (p. 1265)
—Pennsylvania (p. 1337)
—Plateau Indians. (p. 1370)
—Rhode Island. (p. 1468)
—South Carolina. (p. 1616)
—Southeast Indians. (p. 1617)
—Thirteen Colonies Set. (p. 1735)
—Virginia. (p. 1844)
Doherty, Dave. There Once Was a Place Called P.O.P. (p. 1730)
Doherty, Diane. Trapped Inside Myself. (p. 1779)
Doherty, Edith J. S. Primary Independent. (p. 1399)
Doherty, Edith J. S. & Evans, Louise C. How to Develop Your Own Curriculum Units. (p. 816)
Doherty, Ellen. Ellis Island: Set Of 6. (p. 515)
—Ellis Island. (p. 515)
—Mondo & Gordo Weather the Storm: Set Of 6. (p. 1163)
—William's Journal. (p. 1934)
—William's Journal: Set Of 6. (p. 1934)
Doherty, Gillian. 1001 Animales Que Buscar. (p. 2001)
—1001 Animals, Farm, Town & Long Ago. (p. 2001)
—1001 Animals to Spot. (p. 2001)
—1001 Cosa Que Buscar En Pueblos y Ciudades. (p. 2002)
—1001 Cosas Que Buscar en el Psia de las Hadas. Gower, Teri, illus. (p. 2002)
—1001 MonsterThings to Spot. (p. 2002)
—1001 Things to Spot in Fairyland. Gower, Teri, illus. (p. 2002)
—1001 Things to Spot Long Ago. (p. 2002)
—1001 Things to Spot Long Ago. Gower, Teri, illus. (p. 2002)
—1001 Things to Spot Long Ago. Brooks, Felicity, ed. (p. 2002)
—1001 Things to Spot on the Farm. (p. 2002)
—1001 Wizard Things to Spot. Gower, Teri, illus. (p. 2002)
—Aves. (p. 119)
—Birds: Internet -Linked. (p. 191)
—Birds. (p. 191)
—Encyclopedia of World Geography: With Complete World Atlas. (p. 525)
—Encyclopedia of World Geography II (Reduced) (p. 526)
—Fairyland Jigsaw Bk. Gower, Teri, illus. (p. 564)
—Rainy Day. (p. 1436)
—Stencil Book. (p. 1647)
—Stories of Dragons. Milbourne, Anna, ed. (p. 1655)
—Stories of Wizards. Edwards, Linda, illus. (p. 1655)
Doherty, Gillian, ed. see Milbourne, Anna.
Doherty, Gillian, ed. see Stowell, Louie & Pearcey, Alice.
Doherty, Gillian, jt. auth. see Amery, Heather.
Doherty, Gillian, jt. auth. see Brocklehurst, Ruth.
Doherty, Gillian, jt. auth. see Claybourne, Anna.
Doherty, Gillian, jt. auth. see Usborne Books Staff.
Doherty, Gillian, jt. ed. see Tyler, Jenny.
Doherty, Gillian & Claybourne, Anna. Encyclopedia of World Geography Internet Linked. (p. 526)
—Peoples of the World. (p. 1340)
—Pueblos Del Mundo - Internet Linked. (p. 1414)
Doherty, Gillian, ed. First Stories from the Bible. Field, Mandy & Pearson, Maria, illus. (p. 597)
—Usborne Advent Nativity Book. Allman, Howard, photos by. (p. 1827)
Doherty, Gillian, et al. Usborne Big Book of Things to Spot. Gower, Teri, illus. (p. 1827)
Doherty, Glen. Eddie's Christmas Surprise. (p. 503)
—Magic Sucker or How Love Really Works. (p. 1073)
Doherty, Heather, jt. auth. see Wilson, Norah.
Doherty, Katherine M., jt. auth. see Doherty, Craig A.
Doherty, Kieran. Voyageurs, Lumberjacks & Farmers: Pioneers of the Midwest. (p. 1851)
Doherty, Meghan. How Not to Be a Dick: An Everyday Etiquette Guide. (p. 811)
Doherty, Patrick. Waves of Grace. Ordaz, Frank, illus. (p. 1864)
Doherty, Paul & Cassidy, John. Magia Magnetica. (p. 1071)
Doherty, Paula, illus. see Godfrey, Jan, et al.
Doherty, Paula, illus. see Godfrey, Jan.
Doherty, Paula, illus. see Harrast, Tracy.
Doherty, Paula, illus. see Reasoner, Charles.
Doherty, Vrinda & Valmiki. Prince Rama of the Solar Dynasty: Prince in Exile, the Journey Begins. Pt. 1 Doherty, Ann, illus. (p. 1401)
Dohlke, Nora. Wonderful Adventures of Ozzie Sea Otter (Spanish) Stearns, Forest, illus. (p. 1948)
—Wonderful Adventures of Ozzie the Sea Otter. Stearns, Forest, illus. (p. 1948)
—Wonderful Adventures of Ozzie the Sea Otter (Book & CD) Stearns, Forest, illus. (p. 1948)
Dohr, Robert. Pumpkin Se. Dewyea, Glenn, illus. (p. 1416)
Doig, James, ed. Devil of the Marsh & Other Stories. (p. 432)
Doige, Jay, jt. auth. see Doige, Vania.
Doige, Vania & Doige, Jay. Lost Souls: The Story of Hakiki. (p. 1056)
Dojeiji, Mony, jt. auth. see Agraso, Alberto.
Dokas, Dara. Saving Shadow Duverne, Evelyne, illus. (p. 1517)
Dokas, Dara, jt. auth. see Dokas, Dara Sanders.
Dokas, Dara Sanders & Dokas, Dara. Muriel's Red Sweater. Pons, Bernadette, illus. (p. 1192)
Dokey, Cameron. Beauty Sleep: A Retelling of Sleeping Beauty. (p. 154)
—Before Midnight: A Retelling of Cinderella. (p. 158)
—Belle: A Retelling of Beauty & the Beast. (p. 162)
—Golden: A Retelling of Rapunzel. (p. 694)
—How Not to Spend Your Senior Year. (p. 811)
—Kissed: Belle; Sunlight & Shadow; Winter's Child. (p. 961)
—Once: Before Midnight; Golden; Wild Orchid. (p. 1292)
—Storyteller's Daughter: A Retelling of the Arabian Nights. (p. 1664)
—Sunlight & Shadow: Her Love Is Trapped Between Night & Day.... (p. 1677)
—Truth & Consequences. (p. 1794)
—Wild Orchid: A Retelling of the Ballad of Mulan. (p. 1930)
—World Above. (p. 1953)
—Zack's Story Orback, Craig, illus. (p. 1984)
Dokey, Cameron & Burge, Constance M. Truth & Consequences. (p. 1794)
Doktorski, Jennifer Salvato. Famous Last Words. (p. 569)
—How My Summer Went up in Flames. (p. 811)
—Summer after You & Me. (p. 1673)
Dolamore, Jaclyn. Between the Sea & Sky. (p. 173)
—Dark Metropolis. (p. 407)
—Glittering Shadows. (p. 684)
—Magic under Glass. (p. 1074)
—Magic under Stone. (p. 1074)
Dolan, Amy, illus. see Adams, Mark.
Dolan, Edward F. Careers in the U. S. Air Force. (p. 268)
—Careers in the U. S. Army. (p. 268)
—Careers in the U. S. Coast Guard. (p. 268)
—Careers in the U. S. Marine Corps. (p. 268)
—George Washington. (p. 664)
—Military Service (p. 1143)
Dolan, Ellen M. Thomas Alva Edison: American Inventor & Businessman. (p. 1737)
Dolan, Elys. Nuts in Space. Dolan, Elys, illus. (p. 1274)
—Weasels. Dolan, Elys, illus. (p. 1869)
Dolan, Graham. On the Line: The Story of the Greenwich Meridian. (p. 1290)
Dolan, Hannah. Lego Ninjago the Visual Dictionary. (p. 990)
Dolan, Hannah, jt. auth. see Dorling Kindersley Publishing Staff.
Dolan, Hannah, jt. auth. see Taylor, Victoria.
Dolan, Penny. At the End of the Garden. (p. 111)
—At the End of the Garden. Impey, Martin, illus. (p. 111)
—Great Chapatti Chase. Suad, Laura, illus. (p. 714)
—Joey the Juggler Robert, Bruno, illus. (p. 920)
—Little Troll. Smith, Lisa, illus. (p. 1037)
—Lola Fanola Robert, Bruno, illus. (p. 1045)
—Lovely Duckling. (p. 1061)
—Plip & Plop. Smith, Lisa, illus. (p. 1374)
—Princess Rani Robert, Bruno, illus. (p. 1405)
Dolan, Richard M. & Zabel, Bryce. Project Disclosure: Revealing Government Secrets & Breaking the Truth Embargo (p. 1410)
Dolan, Sean. Adolf Eichmann: Engineer of Death. (p. 13)
—Everything You Need to Know about Cults. (p. 545)
Dolan, Sean J. Helen Keller. (p. 762)
—Minnesota. (p. 1147)
Dolan, Stan. Decision 2 for AQA. (p. 421)
Dolbear, Emily. How Did That Get to My Table? Ketchup. (p. 806)
—How Did That Get to My Table? Pasta. (p. 806)
—How Did That Get to My Table? Pumpkin Pie. (p. 806)
Dolbear, Emily J. Bald Eagles. (p. 133)
Dolbear, Emily J., jt. auth. see Flanagan, Alice K.
Dolbear, Emily J. & Benoit, Peter. Iroquois. (p. 888)
—Timucua. (p. 1755)
Dolbeck, Andrew. Fever Jenny (p. 583)
Dolber, Wendy. Guru Next Door: A Teacher's Legacy. (p. 732)
Dolby, Jan, illus. see Grant, Joyce.
Dolby, Karen. Dragon in the Cupboard. (p. 477)
—Incredible Dinosaur Expedition. Haw, Brenda, illus. (p. 869)
—Oranges & Lemons: Rhymes from Past Times. (p. 1302)
—Spooks' Surprise. Marks, Alan, illus. (p. 1631)
Dolby, Karen & Fischel, Emma. Chocolate Island. (p. 309)
—Molly's Magic Carpet. (p. 1161)
—Spooks' Surprise. (p. 1631)
Dolby, Tom. Secret Society. (p. 1544)
—Trust. (p. 1793)
Dolce, Ellen, illus. see Kennedy, Dana & Wilson, Etta.
Dole, Mayra L. Birthday in the Barrio. Pedlar, Elaine & Tonel, illus. (p. 192)
—Drum, Chavi, Drum! Tonel, illus. (p. 487)
—Toca, Chavi, Toca! Tonel, illus. (p. 1760)
Dole, Mayra Lazara. Down to the Bone. (p. 474)
Dole Nutrition Institute Staff. Dole Counting Book. (p. 463)
Dolenz, Ami. Harold & Agatha: The Mysterious Jewel. (p. 749)
Dolenz, Micky. Gakky Two-Feet. Clark, David, illus. (p. 652)
Doles, Sean Patrick. All Saints Day: A New Orleans Football Fairy Tale (p. 45)
—Saving Mr. Bingle: A New Orleans Christmas Fairy Tale. (p. 1517)
Dolezal, Robert. Birds in Your Backyard: A Bird Lover's Guide to Creating a Garden Sanctuary. (p. 191)
Dolheguy, Heather. Meg & Mr Biggs - the Magic Cat. (p. 1124)
Dolk, Maarten, jt. auth. see Fosnot, Catherine Twomey.
Doll, Nancy L. Buddee the Bugger & Me: Told by Mac (p. 234)
Doll, Susan. Elvis Presley: With Profiles of Muddy Waters & Mick Jagger. (p. 517)
Dollak, Nicholas. Jenna of Erdovon: The Philosopher's Egg. (p. 912)
Dollak, Nicholas, illus. see McClear, Preston.
Dollar, Creflo A. Breaking Out of Trouble: God's Failsafe System for Overcoming Adversity. (p. 225)
—In the Presence of God: Find Answers to the Challenges of Life. (p. 867)
—Live Without Fear: Learn to Walk in God's Power & Peace. (p. 1040)
—Love, Live, & Enjoy Life: Uncover the Transforming Power of God's Love. (p. 1060)
—Not Guilty: Experience God's Gift of Acceptance & Freedom. (p. 1267)
—Walking in the Confidence of God in Troubled Times. (p. 1854)
Dollar, Diane, illus. see Garretson, Jerri.
Dollar, Diane A., illus. see Garretson, Jerri.
Dollenmayer, David B. & Hansen, Thomas S. Neue Horizonte: Introductory German: Text with Multimedia CD-ROM. (p. 1242)
Doller, Trish. Devil You Know. (p. 432)
—Something Like Normal. (p. 1610)
—Where the Stars Still Shine. (p. 1909)
Dolnick, Irene. Kurt, Gert, Jazmine, & Bagel. (p. 968)
Dolphin, Colleen. Adventurous to Zealous: All about Me from A to Z. (p. 25)
—Advisories to Zero Degrees: Weather from A to Z. (p. 25)
—Alcatraz to Zanzibar: Famous Places from A to Z. (p. 35)
—Angles to Zeros: Mathematics from A to Z. (p. 75)
—April Fools' Day to Z Day: Holidays from A to Z. (p. 93)
—Armadillos to Zorillas: Animals from A to Z. (p. 99)
—Armpits to Zits: The Body from A to Z. Craig, Diane, ed. (p. 100)
—Casual Cows. (p. 277)
—Clucky Chickens. (p. 335)
—Cool Exercise: Healthy & Fun Ways to Get Your Body Moving. (p. 363)
—Gleeful Goats. (p. 683)
—Happy Horses. (p. 746)
—Ice Hockey by the Numbers. (p. 850)
—It's E! (p. 896)
—Leaping Lily: A Story about Georgia. Doucet, Bob, illus. (p. 982)
—Playful Pigs. (p. 1372)
—Rocky's Outdoor Adventure: A Story about Colorado. Doucet, Bob, illus. (p. 1484)
—Signs of Autumn. (p. 1574)
—Signs of Spring. (p. 1574)
—Signs of Summer. (p. 1574)
—Signs of Winter. (p. 1574)
—Soccer by the Numbers. (p. 1603)
—Super Sheep. (p. 1681)
—Volleyball by the Numbers. (p. 1849)
Dolphin, Laurie. Our Journey from Tibet. Johnson, Nancy Jo, photos by. (p. 1309)
Dolsingh, Kanisha. Once upon a Time: In London Town with Minnie Drew. (p. 1293)
Dolson, Carol Bland. Hattie & the Higgledy-Piggledy Hedge. Rabon, Elaine Hearn, illus. (p. 752)
Dom, An, jt. auth. see De Kockere, Geert.
Domain Public Staff. Tall Book of Mother Goose. Ivanov, Aleksey & Ivanov, Olga, illus. (p. 1704)
—Three Billy Goats Gruff. Kliros, Thea, illus. (p. 1741)
—Three Little Pigs. Kliros, Thea, illus. (p. 1742)
Domaine, Helena. Robotics. (p. 1480)
Doman, Glenn. Nose Is Not Toes. (p. 1266)
Doman, Mary Kate. Airplanes. (p. 32)
—Big Military Machines. (p. 182)
—Big Trucks. (p. 184)
—Cool Cars. (p. 363)
—Earthmovers & Diggers. (p. 497)
—Rescue Vehicles. (p. 1462)
—Tragedy at the Triangle: Friendship in the Tenements & the Shirtwaist Factory Fire. (p. 1776)
Doman, Regina. Angel in the Waters. Hatke, Ben, illus. (p. 73)
—Mi Angelito en Las Aguas. Hatke, Ben, illus. (p. 1132)
Dombek, Jeff. Caveman Art Teacher. Dombek, Jeff, illus. (p. 282)
—How the Oysters Saved the Bay (p. 813)
Dombey, Elizabeth. Beautiful Ballerinas. McNicholas, Shelagh, illus. (p. 153)
Dombey, Elizabeth & Muldrow, Diane. How Do Penguins Play? Walker, David, illus. (p. 807)
Domblewski, Carol. Citizens Who Made a Difference: Set Of 6. (p. 323)
—Citizens Who Made a Difference: Text Pairs. (p. 323)
—Uniquely Massachusetts (p. 1818)
Domboski, Brian, jt. auth. see Kaminsky, Kristy.
Dombrower, Jan. Getting to Know Your Emotional Needs. Sorba, Richard, illus. (p. 670)
Domeier, Renee, ed. see Peralas, Jorge.
Domeij, Scoti, jt. auth. see Arthur, Kay.
Domeij, Scoti & Kuhn, Pamela J. Favorite Bible Heroes: Grades 1&2. Galey, Chuck, illus. (p. 578)
D'Omellas, Veronica, tr. see Werlin, Nancy & WERLIN, NANCY.
Domenico, Kelly Di. Women Scientists Who Changed the World. (p. 1946)
Domeniconi, David. Golden Numbers: A California Number Book. Carroll, Pam, illus. (p. 695)
—M Is for Majestic: A National Parks Alphabet. Carroll, Pam, illus. (p. 1067)
—M Is for Masterpiece: An Art Alphabet. Bullas, Will, illus. (p. 1067)
Domergue, Agnes, illus. see Charrier, Lisa.
Domi, illus. see Argueta, Jorge.
Domi, illus. see Liano, Dante, et al.
Domi, illus. see Mora, Pat.
Domi, illus. see Ramirez, Antonio.
Domi, illus. see Ramírez, Antonio.
Domi, illus. see Sanroman, Susana.
Domi, Carlos, illus. see Menchú, Rigoberta & Liano, Dante.
Domi, Carlos, illus. see Mora, Pat.
Domiano, Gloria. Ship Shapes: Identify & Describe Shapes. (p. 1567)
Dominado, Guia. Fear of Max. (p. 579)
Domingo, Roger. Eye Openers & Show Stoppers in the Bible. (p. 558)
Domingo, Vernon. South Africa. (p. 1616)
Domingos, Fernanda Feitosa Rosas. O Jardim / the Garden. (p. 1274)
Dominguez, Adriana, jt. auth. see Brown, Monica.
Dominguez, Adriana, jt. auth. see Mora, Pat.
Domínguez, Adriana, tr. Dora y la Aventura de Cumpleaños. Roper, Robert, illus. (p. 471)
Dominguez, Angel, illus. see Wainwright, Jen.
Dominguez, Angela. Knit Together. (p. 964)
—Let's Go, Hugo! (p. 997)
—Maria Tenía una Llamita. Dominguez, Angela, illus. (p. 1093)
—Santiago Stays. (p. 1513)
Dominguez, Angela, illus. see Cox, Judy.
Dominguez, Angela, illus. see Flor Ada, Alma.
Dominguez, Angela, illus. see Medina, Meg.
Dominguez, Angela, illus. see Sacre, Antonio.
Dominguez, Angela N., illus. see Cox, Judy.
Dominguez, Angela N., illus. see Krull, Kathleen.
Dominguez, Domitila, illus. see Marcos, Subcomandante.
Dominguez, Elaudy. Mountain Mystery. (p. 1181)
Domínguez, José A. Mamerto: A Children's Story. (p. 1084)
Dominguez, Madelca, jt. auth. see Bailer, Darice.
Dominguez, Manuel, tr. see Satrapi, Marjane.
Dominguez, Maria, illus. see Ortiz, Raquel M. & Ventura, Gabriela Baeza.
Dominguez, Oliver, illus. see Kelly, David A.
Dominguez, Oliver, illus. see Rusch, Elizabeth.
Dominguez, Ramon Garcia. Grillo del Tercer Milenium. (p. 724)
—Pirana en mi Banera. (p. 1362)
Dominguez, Richard, illus. see Biskup, Agnieszka & Sohn, Emily.
Dominguez, Richard, illus. see O'Donnell, Liam & Barnett III, Charles.

D

Dominguez, Richard, illus. see O'Donnell, Liam & Barnett, Charles, III.
Dominguez, Richard, illus. see O'Donnell, Liam.
Dominguez, Richard, illus. see Olson, Kay Melchisedech.
Dominguez, Richard, illus. see Olson, Nathan.
Dominguez, Stephanie, illus. see Glatzer, Jenna.
Dominic, Sister M. Little Nellie of Holy God 1903-1908. Vianney, M. John, illus. (p. 1032)
Dominie Press Staff. Aesop's Fables. (p. 25)
Domino, Connie. Law of Attraction: Develop Irresistible Attraction. (p. 981)
Dominquez, Amalia. Busy, Busy Butterfly. (p. 246)
—Happy, Hopping Frog. (p. 746)
Dominquez, Richard, illus. see Biskup, Agnieszka & Sohn, Emily.
Dominquez, Richard, illus. see Krohn, Katherine E.
Dominy, Amy Fellner. Audition & Subtraction. (p. 115)
—Matter of Heart. (p. 1109)
—OyMG. (p. 1316)
Domiteaux, Diane & Wallis, Karen. Washoe Seasons of Life: A Native American Story. (p. 1860)
Domitrovich, Michael, jt. auth. see Machado, Eduardo.
Domm, Jeffrey, illus. see Tobin, Deborah.
Domm, Jeffrey C., illus. see Domm, Kristin Bieber.
Domm, Kristin Bieber. Atlantic Puffin: Little Brother of the North Domm, Jeffrey C., illus. (p. 112)
—Eagle of the Sea Domm, Jeffrey C., illus. (p. 492)
Domnauer, Teresa. Cornerstones of Freedom, Third Series: the Lewis & Clark Expedition. (p. 367)
—I'm a Writer! (and I Didn't Even Know It), Grade 1: Crunchies. (p. 858)
—Lewis & Clark Expedition. (p. 1004)
—Life in the West. (p. 1011)
—Peculiar Pets. (p. 1334)
—Skeletal System. (p. 1584)
—Westward Expansion. (p. 1876)
Domnauer, Teresa & Kenah, Katharine. Incredible Edibles. (p. 869)
—Ultimate Sports. (p. 1810)
Domney, Alexis. Splish, Splat! Crawford, Alice, illus. (p. 1630)
Domogala, Sophia Z. Buzzin' with Kindness. (p. 249)
Domoney, Cathy. Madeleine, Maddy & Midge: Positive Thinking for Children. (p. 1070)
Dompieri, Patricia Lynn. Lemon Bee & Other Peculiar Tales. (p. 991)
Dompierre, Judith. Body & Body Functions. (p. 207)
—Gulp (p. 731)
—I See Pigs Everywhere. (p. 845)
—Jennie's Search for Colors & Numbers. (p. 912)
—Little Bear's & Friend's Summer Trip. (p. 1024)
—Read It Whichever Direction You Want. (p. 1443)
—Rhymes the Size of Dimes (p. 1468)
—Strange Passions. (p. 1665)
—Unleashing Fruits & Vegetables. (p. 1821)
Dompierre, Judith E. Jennie's New Adventure Looking for Letters. (p. 912)
—Jennie's Search for Colors & Numbers. (p. 912)
—Little Bear's & Friend's Summer Trip. (p. 1024)
—No More Than Four of a Kind. (p. 1259)
—Read It Whichever Direction You Want. (p. 1443)
—Strange Passions. (p. 1665)
—Unleashing Fruits & Vegetables. (p. 1821)
—Wow, What's That? (p. 1962)
Domschke, Angelika, illus. see Atticus, C. J.
Don, Freeman. Corduroy. (p. 366)
Don, Katherine. Nujood Ali & the Fight Against Child Marriage. (p. 1270)
—Real Courage: The Story of Harper Lee. (p. 1448)
Don, Lari. First Aid for Fairies & Other Fabled Beasts. (p. 592)
—Hungry Wolf: A Story from North America. Williamson, Melanie, illus. (p. 828)
—Masha & the Bear: A Story from Russia. Williamson, Melanie, illus. (p. 1102)
—Never Trust a Tiger: A Story from Korea. Williamson, Melanie, illus. (p. 1243)
—Tortoise's Gift: A Story from Zambia. Williamson, Melanie, illus. (p. 1771)
Don, Lari & James, Cate. Breaking the Spell: Stories of Magic & Mystery from Scotland. James, Cate, illus. (p. 225)
Don, Lari, et al. Little Red Riding Hood. Chauffrey, Celia, illus. (p. 1035)
Don Nardo. Trial of Galileo. (p. 1785)
Donaera, Patrizia, illus. see Beckett-Bowman, Lucy.
Donaera, Patrizia, illus. see Helbrough, Emma.
Donaera, Patrizia, illus. see Krum, Atticus.
Donaera, Patrizia, illus. see Meredith, Sue.
Donaera, Patrizia, illus. see Milbourne, Anna.
Donaghe, Ronald L. Uncle Sean. (p. 1812)
Donaghey, Reese. Telling the Truth. (p. 1717)
Donaghy, Thomas J. Angels All Around Us. (p. 75)
—Celebrating Mass. (p. 285)
—Joyful Prayers. (p. 930)
—My Golden Book of Saints. (p. 1210)
—My Golden Children's Bible. (p. 1210)
—My Golden Christmas Book. (p. 1210)
—New Catholic Children's Bible. (p. 1244)
Donaher, D. F. & Bibleco. Biblemania: The Old Testament Magazine. (p. 176)
Donaher, D F. & Bibleco. Daniel & the Lions. (p. 404)
Donahue, Bill. Grandma Wentworth's Children's Storybooks, Volume One. (p. 708)
Donahue, Jill L., et al. Chuckle Squad: Jokes about Classrooms, Sports, Food, Teachers, & Other School Subjects Haugen, Ryan et al, illus. (p. 318)
Donahue, Jill Lynn. Being Considerate. Previn, Stacey, illus. (p. 161)
—Dad's Shirt Lee, Jisun, illus. (p. 399)
—Ser Honesto. Previn, Stacey, illus. (p. 1552)
Donahue, Jill Lynn & Small, Mary. Way to Be! How to Be Brave, Responsible, Honest, & an All-Around Great Kid Previn, Stacey, illus. (p. 1864)
Donahue, Jill Urban. Cómo Contener el Fuego. Masheris, Bob, illus. (p. 350)
—Contain the Flame: Outdoor Fire Safety Masheris, Bob, illus. (p. 360)
—Juega Con Cuidado. Masheris, Bob, illus. (p. 931)
—Wendell the Worrier Spence, Thomas, illus. (p. 1875)
Donahue, Jim, illus. see Bishop, Karen C.
Donahue, Laurie. God's Plan My Response. Rittenhouse, Ralph, ed. (p. 691)
—Mr. Blue a Job for You. Bryan, Hintz, illus. (p. 1184)
Donahue, Laurie & Phillips, Paul. Lord's Supper... Let's Get Ready! Palmer, Scott, illus. (p. 1053)
Donahue, Laurie & Rittenhouse, Ralph. God... Should I Be Baptized? (p. 690)
Donahue, Linda, illus. see Johnston, Camille.
Donahue, Mary R. & Thornburgh, Gail. What's My Job? Helping Children Navigate the Rough Waters of Separation & Divorce. (p. 1898)
Donahue, Peter. 3-D Mazes—Robots. (p. 1991)
—All Aboard! Trains Stained Glass Coloring Book. (p. 42)
—Build a Poster Coloring Book — ABC & 123. (p. 238)
—Cars & Trucks Stained Glass Coloring Book. (p. 272)
—Classic Arabian Nights Stained Glass Coloring Book. (p. 327)
—Construction Site Super Sticker Book. (p. 360)
—Cool Cars & Trucks Stained Glass Jr. Coloring Book. (p. 363)
—Farm & Zoo. (p. 573)
—Mustache Doodle Book. (p. 1194)
—Not-Your-Average Superhero Mazes. (p. 1267)
—Not-Your-Average Superhero Stickers. (p. 1267)
—Robot Mazes. (p. 1480)
—Shiny Robot Stickers. (p. 1567)
—Spot the Differences Picture Puzzles for Kids. (p. 1633)
—Things That Fly Stained Glass Coloring Book. (p. 1733)
—Things That Go Coloring Book: Cars, Trucks, Planes, Trains & More! (p. 1733)
—What to Doodle? Jr. - Superheroes & Robots! (p. 1894)
Donahue, Peter & Coloring Books Staff. Mix & Match ROBOTS. (p. 1156)
—Robot Buddies Stained Glass Coloring Book. (p. 1480)
Donahue, Peter & Wright, Blanche Fisher. Real Mother Goose Stained Glass Coloring Book. (p. 1448)
Donahue, Peter, et al. Mix & Match FANTASY CREATURES. (p. 1156)
Donahue, Shari Faden. Zebra-Striped Whale Alphabet Book. Thalamus, illus. (p. 1985)
Donaki & Rosenberry, Donald. Spectacular Journey. Rosenberry, Akiko & Rosenberry, Susan, illus. (p. 1624)
Donald, jt. auth. see Wojahn, Rebecca Hogue.
Donald, David R. Gogo's Song. (p. 692)
—I Am Thabek. (p. 834)
—Tikoloshe & the Three Fox Cubs. (p. 1750)
Donald, Diana. My Special Angel: A Bedtime Story. Polito, Mike, illus. (p. 1219)
Donald, et al. Justin's Angel. (p. 940)
Donald, George Mac. Cross Purposes. (p. 385)
Donald, Margaret. Eli the Elephant: A Tsunami Story. Grant, Sophia & Noble, Stuart, illus. (p. 512)
—Tipsy: The Hurricane Hero. (p. 1757)
Donald, Rhonda Lucas. Animal Rights: How You Can Make a Difference (p. 79)
—Deep in the Desert Neidigh, Sherry, illus. (p. 423)
—Dino Tracks Morrison, Cathy, illus. (p. 441)
—Dino Treasures Morrison, Cathy, illus. (p. 441)
—Life on Other Planets. (p. 1012)
Donald W. Ballard. Disneyland Hotel 1954-1959: The Little Motel in the Middle of the Orange Grove. (p. 453)
Donaldson, Babette. Emma Lea's First Tea Party. Van Dijk, Jerianne, illus. (p. 520)
—Emma Lea's Magic Teapot. Van Dijk, Jerianne, illus. (p. 520)
Donaldson, Chelsea. Canadian Biographies. (p. 260)
—Chris Hadfield (p. 311)
—Christine Sinclair (p. 312)
—Hayley Wickenheiser (p. 755)
—Planets. (p. 1368)
—Robert Munsch (p. 1479)
Donaldson, Chelsea, jt. auth. see Crabtree Editors.
Donaldson, Chelsea, jt. auth. see Sutoski, Jennifer.
Donaldson, Connie & Polinko, Les. Ganorch under the Porch. Polinko, Les, illus. (p. 655)
Donaldson, Jennifer, illus. see Pesout, Christine.
Donaldson, Joan. On Viney's Mountain. (p. 1292)
—Secret of the Red Shoes. Ettinger, Doris, illus. (p. 1543)
Donaldson, Julia. Animal Music. Sharratt, Nick, illus. (p. 78)
—Animals in School. Parsons, Gary & Richards, Lucy, illus. (p. 83)
—Bombs & Blackberries: A World War Two Play. Dupasquier, Philippe, illus. (p. 208)
—Charlie Cook's Favorite Book. Scheffler, Axel, illus. (p. 293)
—Chocolate Mousse for Greedy Goose Sharratt, Nick, illus. (p. 309)
—Fish Who Cried Wolf. Scheffler, Axel, illus. (p. 598)
—Follow the Swallow. Smy, Pam, illus. (p. 612)
—Freddie & the Fairy George, Karen, illus. (p. 632)
—Giants & the Joneses. Swearingen, Greg, illus. (p. 674)
—Goat Goes to Playgroup. Sharratt, Nick, illus. (p. 687)
—Gold Star for Zog. Scheffler, Axel, illus. (p. 694)
—Grufalo. Scheffler, Axel, illus. (p. 727)
—Gruffalo. (p. 727)
—Gruffalo. Scheffler, Axel, illus. (p. 727)
—Gruffalo (Al Gharfoul) Fouda, Nadia, tr. (p. 727)
—Gruffalo Theatre Scheffler, Axel, illus. (p. 727)
—Gruffalo's Child. Scheffler, Axel, illus. (p. 727)
—Highway Rat. Scheffler, Axel, illus. (p. 779)
—Hippo Has a Hat Sharratt, Nick, illus. (p. 781)
—Hippo Has a Hat. Sharratt, Nick, illus. (p. 781)
—Night Monkey, Day Monkey. Richards, Lucy, illus. (p. 1253)
—One Mole Digging a Hole Sharratt, Nick, illus. (p. 1296)
—One Mole Digging a Hole. Sharratt, Nick, illus. (p. 1296)
—One Ted Falls Out of Bed. Currey, Anna, illus. (p. 1297)
—Play Time: A Selection of Plays by the Best Selling Author of the Gruffalo. (p. 1371)
—Princess Mirror-Belle & the Flying Horse Monks, Lydia, illus. (p. 1404)
—Princess Mirror-Belle & the Magic Shoes Monks, Lydia, illus. (p. 1404)
—Princess Mirror-Belle Collection Monks, Lydia, illus. (p. 1404)
—Quick Brown Fox Cub. (p. 1427)
—Room on the Broom. Scheffler, Axel, illus. (p. 1488)
—Room on the Broom Big Activity Book. Scheffler, Axel, illus. (p. 1488)
—Room on the Broom Board Book. Sheffler, Axel, illus. (p. 1488)
—Scarecrows' Wedding. Scheffler, Axel, illus. (p. 1519)
—Sharing a Shell Jigsaw Book. Monks, Lydia, illus. (p. 1561)
—Shuffle & Squelch. Sharratt, Nick, illus. (p. 1571)
—Snail & the Whale. Scheffler, Axel, illus. (p. 1595)
—Spiffiest Giant in Town. Scheffler, Axel, illus. (p. 1627)
—Spinderella. Pichon, Liz, illus. (p. 1628)
—Stick Man. Scheffler, Axel, illus. (p. 1649)
—Superworm. Scheffler, Axel, illus. (p. 1684)
—Swallows & Spiders. Ursell, Martin & Pichon, Liz, illus. (p. 1688)
—Tabby McTat: The Musical Cat. Scheffler, Axel, illus. (p. 1694)
—Toddle Waddle. Sharratt, Nick, illus. (p. 1761)
—What the Ladybug Heard. Monks, Lydia, illus. (p. 1893)
—Where's My Mom? Scheffler, Axel, illus. (p. 1910)
—Wriggle & Roar! Sharratt, Nick, illus. (p. 1963)
—Wriggle & Roar! Rhymes to Join in With. Sharratt, Nick, illus. (p. 1963)
—Wrong Kind of Bark. Parsons, Garry, illus. (p. 1965)
Donaldson, Julia & Axworthy, Anni. Mermaid & the Octopus. (p. 1128)
Donaldson, Julia & Richards, Lucy. Quick Brown Fox Cub. (p. 1427)
Donaldson, Julia & Walker, Sholto. Pot of Gold. (p. 1388)
Donaldson, Leo. Toby's Big Surprise. (p. 1760)
Donaldson, Madeline. Africa. (p. 26)
—Antarctica. (p. 88)
—Asia. (p. 106)
—Australia. (p. 116)
—Deadly Bloody Battles. (p. 417)
—Europe. (p. 540)
—Iran. (p. 886)
—Ireland. (p. 887)
—Italy. (p. 894)
—North America. (p. 1264)
—Pakistan. (p. 1319)
—Pirates, Scoundrels, & Scallywags. (p. 1364)
—Richard Nixon. (p. 1469)
—Ruby Bridges. (p. 1493)
—South America. (p. 1616)
—Spain. (p. 1620)
—Thailand. (p. 1724)
—Turkey. (p. 1797)
—United Kingdom. (p. 1818)
—Venus & Serena Williams. (p. 1836)
—Venus & Serena Williams. (p. 1836)
Donaldson, Norman. Life Begins. (p. 1008)
Donaldson, Olivia. Influenza. (p. 873)
—Malaria. (p. 1083)
Donaldson, Stephanie, jt. auth. see Walton, Sally.
Donaldson, Stephen R. Fatal Revenant: The Last Chronicles of Thomas Covenant. (p. 577)
Donaldson, Sue, et al. GCSE Leisure & Tourism (Double Award) (p. 659)
Donaldson, Terry, et al, creators. Lord of the Rings Tarot Gravity Feed Counter Display. (p. 1052)
Donaldson, Valeria. My Electricity Experiments. (p. 1202)
Donaldson-Forbes, Jeff. Jacques Cartier. (p. 905)
—Jacques Marquette & Louis Jolliet. (p. 905)
—Salle. (p. 1505)
DoNascimento, Nicole. Lucky Nickel. Molitor, Sherrie, illus. (p. 1063)
Donatelli, Jen Jones. Sean Diddy Combs: A Biography of a Music Mogul. (p. 1536)
Donati, Giuliana, illus. see Caviezel, Giovanni.
Donati, Paolo, jt. auth. see Wilkinson, Philip.
Donato, Cindy. Monsters! Monsters! (p. 1169)
Donato, Dona, jt. auth. see Kobert, Michael Gilead.
Donato, Janice, illus. see Barclay, Jane.
Donato, Michael A., illus. see Metaxas, Eric.
Donato, Michael A., illus. see Milord, Susan.
Donavan, Barbara A. Body Systems: Set of 6: Respiratory & Circulatory. (p. 207)
Donbavand, Tommy. Attack of the Trolls. (p. 114)
—Blood of the Witch: Book 2. Cartoon Saloon, illus. (p. 200)
—Blood of the Witch. (p. 200)
—Claw of the Werewolf Cartoon Saloon Staff, illus. (p. 330)
—Claw of the Werewolf: Book 6. Cartoon Saloon, illus. (p. 330)
—Cyber Shock. Gibbons, Alan & Packer, Natalie, eds. (p. 396)
—Fang of the Vampire: Book 1. Cartoon Saloon, illus. (p. 571)
—Fang of the Vampire. Cartoon Saloon Staff, illus. (p. 571)
—Flame of the Dragon. Donbavand, Tommy, illus. (p. 602)
—Flesh of the Zombie Cartoon Saloon Staff, illus. (p. 603)
—Flesh of the Zombie: Book 4. Cartoon Saloon, illus. (p. 603)
—Heart of the Mummy Cartoon Saloon Staff, illus. (p. 759)
—Heart of the Mummy: Book 3. Cartoon Saloon, illus. (p. 759)
—Hunger of the Yeti. Donbavand, Tommy, illus. (p. 828)
—Invasion of the Normals. (p. 883)
—Rampage of the Goblins. Donbavand, Tommy, illus. (p. 1438)
—Scream Street: Attack of the Trolls (Book #8) (p. 1533)
—Scream Street: Invasion of the Normals (Book #7) (p. 1533)
—Scream Street - Terror of the Nightwatchman. (p. 1533)
—Secret of the Changeling. Donbavand, Tommy, illus. (p. 1542)
—Skull of the Skeleton Cartoon Saloon Staff, illus. (p. 1586)
—Skull of the Skeleton: Book 5. Cartoon Saloon, illus. (p. 1586)
—Terror of the Nightwatchman. (p. 1722)
—Wolf. (p. 1943)
Donbavand, Tommy & Harpercollins Staff. Our Head Teacher Is a Super-Villain. Mosedale, Julian, illus. (p. 1309)
Donbo, Koge. Di Gi Charat (p. 433)
—Di Gi Charat. Morimoto, Mari, tr. (p. 433)
—Di Gi Charat Theater (p. 433)
—Pita-Ten (p. 1364)
—Pita-Ten Rymer, Nan, tr. from JPN. (p. 1364)
Donbo, Koge, jt. auth. see Punch Monkey Staff.
Donbo, Koge, creator. Pita-Ten (p. 1364)
Donegan, Luz, jt. auth. see Donegan, Noel.
Donegan, Noel & Donegan, Luz. Hot-Headed Bassoon. (p. 801)
—Noisy Blue Drum. (p. 1263)
—Sad Little Violin. (p. 1501)
Donegan, Patricia. Haiku: Learn to Express Yourself by Writing Poetry in the Japanese Tradition. (p. 735)
Donehey, Jennifer Caulfield, illus. see Flaherty, Kathleen Marion.
Donelly, Joe & Donnelly, Joe. Jack Flint y el Arpa de las Estaciones. Gurqui, Montserrat & Sabate, Hernan, trs. (p. 903)
Donelly, Karen. American Women Pilots of World War II. (p. 64)
—Coping with Lyme Disease. (p. 365)
Donenfeld, Deborah. Baby 123. (p. 124)
—Baby ABC. (p. 124)
Doner, Kim, illus. see Griffis, Molly.
Doner, Kim, illus. see Schwartz, David & Schwartz, David M.
Doner, Kim, illus. see Scillian, Devin.
Doner, Kim, jt. auth. see Cast, P. C.
Donev, Mary, jt. auth. see Kline, Trish.
Doney. Gorrion Muy Preocupado. (p. 703)
Doney, Meryl. Festivals. (p. 582)
—How the Bible Came to Us: The Story of the Book That Changed the World. (p. 812)
—Masks. (p. 1102)
—Paper Crafts. (p. 1322)
—Puppets. (p. 1417)
—Toys. (p. 1774)
—Very Worried Sparrow. Hansen, Gaby, illus. (p. 1839)
—Whisker's Great Adventure. (p. 1912)
Doney, Meryl & Geldart, William. Ears & the Secret Song. (p. 494)
Donfrancesco, Anna. Keepers of the Dream. (p. 947)
Dong Chen, Wei. Band of Brothers. Peng, Chao, illus. (p. 136)
—Battle of Red Cliffs. Liang, Xiao Long, illus. (p. 146)
—Dual. Peng, Chao, illus. (p. 487)
—Expulsion of Sun Wu. Peng, Chao, illus. (p. 555)
—Fanning the Flames. Peng, Chao, illus. (p. 571)
—Fight to the Death. Peng, Chao, illus. (p. 585)
—Fortunate Sons. Long Liang, Xiao, illus. (p. 623)
—Golden Temple. Peng, Chao, illus. (p. 695)
—Journey Ends. Peng, Chao, illus. (p. 928)
—Lost Children. Peng, Chao, illus. (p. 1055)
—Masters & Disciples. Peng, Chao, illus. (p. 1103)
—Realm of Infant King. Peng, Chao, illus. (p. 1450)
—Seven Sisters. Peng, Chao, illus. (p. 1554)
—Stolen Kingdom. Peng, Chao, illus. (p. 1652)
—Treasures of Mt Kings. Peng, Chao, illus. (p. 1782)
—Trust & Temptation. Peng, Chao, illus. (p. 1793)
—Wagers & Vows. Liang, Xiao Long, illus. (p. 1852)
—War of Words. Long Liang, Xiao, illus. (p. 1858)
Dong Chen, Wei & Peng, Chao. Bane of Heaven. (p. 136)
—Birth of Stone Monkey. (p. 192)
—Enemies & New Friend. (p. 527)
—Journey to the West. (p. 929)
—Sacred Tree. (p. 1500)
—Three Trials. (p. 1744)
Dong, Haidan. Of Trouble & Trickery. (p. 1279)
Dong, Li. Tuttle Learner's Chinese-English Dictionary. (p. 1799)
Dong-Seong, Kim, illus. see Tae-Jun, Lee, et al.
Dongweck, James. Dragon Cant. Baker, Joe, illus. (p. 476)
—Goblin's Story. Bixby, Sean, illus. (p. 688)
Doniger, Nancy, illus. see Raczka, Bob.
Doninck, Sebastiaan Van, illus. see Moser, Lisa.
Donivee, Martin. Snow White & the Seven Menehune. (p. 1600)
Donkin, Andrew, jt. auth. see Colfer, Eoin.
Donlan, Leni. Benjamin Franklin: A Life Well Lived (p. 164)
—Cherokee Rose: The Trail of Tears (p. 298)
—Following Freedom: The Underground Railroad (p. 612)
—George Washington: Revolution & the New Nation (p. 664)
—How Did This Happen Here? Japanese Internment Camps (p. 806)
—Mathew Brady: Photographing the Civil War (p. 1108)
—Strike It Rich in Cripple Creek: Gold Rush (p. 1667)
—Working for Change: The Struggle for Women's Right to Vote (p. 1952)
Donley, Jan. Side Door. (p. 1573)
Donley, Shawn. UEA Elf Workers Union Handbook: Department of Elfand Security. (p. 1807)
Donlon, Bridget. Got Milk? How? Chelsey, Emily, illus. (p. 703)
Donlon, Diane Youngblood. Balancing on a Rock. (p. 133)
—Like a Cat: Creep, Sleep, Pounce, & Peek . . . Suhr, James W., illus. (p. 1016)
—Tippee Tippee Tiptoe. Suhr, James W., illus. (p. 1757)
Donlon, Eleanor, ed. see Bollendorf, Robert F. & Makely, William.
Donn, Don, jt. auth. see Donn, Lin.
Donn, Lin & Donn, Don. Ancient & Medieval Africa. (p. 67)
Donna, Gelsinger, ed. In My Father's Garden. (p. 864)
Donnan, Hastings, jt. auth. see Wilson, Thomas M.
Donnanna. Jamie & the Cheesy Foot Monster. (p. 907)
Donne, John. Air & Angels. (p. 31)
Donnell, Annie Hamil. Three Young Knights. (p. 1744)
Donnell, Annie Hamilton. Four Girls & A Compact. (p. 625)
—Four Girls & a Compact. (p. 625)
—Three Young Knights. (p. 1744)
—Three Young Knights & Miss Theodosia's Heartstrings. (p. 1744)
Donnell, Frances. Goblins Will Be Seen: When It's Time for Halloween. Hebert, Catherine, ed. (p. 688)
Donnell, Kerri, jt. auth. see Levy, Janey.
Donnelly, James, jt. auth. see Gorey, Edward.
Donnelly, Jenifer, illus. see Garcia, Tom & Naga, Karun.
Donnelly, Jennifer. Deep Blue. (p. 422)
—Humble Pie. Gammell, Stephen, illus. (p. 826)
—Northern Light. (p. 1265)
—Revolution. (p. 1466)
—Rogue Wave. (p. 1485)
—Winter Rose. (p. 1938)
Donnelly, Jennifer, jt. auth. see Disney Book Group Staff.
Donnelly, Joe. Jack Flint & the Dark Ways: Lunatics & Luck. (p. 903)
—Spellbinder's Curse. (p. 1625)

Donnelly, Joe, jt. auth. see Donelly, Joe.
Donnelly, Karen. Bill of Rights. (p. 186)
—Biomes of the Past & Future. (p. 190)
—Biomes of the Past & the Future. (p. 190)
—Cruzan V. Missouri: The Right to Die. (p. 387)
—Deacon Jones. (p. 416)
—Droughts of the Past & the Future. (p. 486)
—Floods of the Past & the Future. (p. 606)
—Ice Ages of the Past & the Future. (p. 850)
—Leprosy (Hansen's Disease) (p. 993)
—Rising Temperatures of the Past & Future. (p. 1475)
—Rising Temperatures of the Past & the Future. (p. 1475)
—Storms of the Past & the Future. (p. 1656)
Donnelly, Karen, illus. see Dickens, Charles.
Donnelly, Karen, illus. see MacPhail, C.
Donnelly, Karen, illus. see Moore, Alan & Tavner, Gill.
Donnelly, Karen, illus. see Tavner, Gill & Dickens, Charles.
Donnelly, Karen, illus. see Ure, Jean.
Donnelly, Karen, illus. see Van Vleet, Carmella.
Donnelly, Karen J. Coping with Dyslexia. (p. 365)
—Coping with Lyme Disease. (p. 365)
—Cruzan v. Missouri: The Right to Die. (p. 387)
—Droughts of the Past & the Future. (p. 486)
—Everything You Need to Know about Lyme Disease. (p. 545)
—Floods of the Past & Future. (p. 606)
—Ice Ages of the Past & the Future. (p. 850)
—Storms of the Past & the Future. (p. 1656)
Donnelly, Liza. End of the Rainbow. Donnelly, Liza, illus. (p. 526)
Donnelly, Matt. George W. Bush. (p. 663)
Donnelly, Patrick. Best NBA Centers of All Time. (p. 170)
—Best NBA Forwards of All Time. (p. 170)
Donnelly, S. E., jt. auth. see MacDonald, Fiona.
Donnelly, Shannon. Eleanor Roosevelt. Wolek, Guy, illus. (p. 508)
Donner, Andrea, ed. What Pets Teach Us: Life's Lessons Learned from Our Best Friends. (p. 1892)
Donner, Brad, photos by see Grollman, Earl A. & Johnson, Joy.
Donner, Candie. American Girl: Meet Kaya Lapbook. Kinney, Cyndi, ed. (p. 61)
—American Girl: Meet Molly Lapbook. Kinney, Cyndi, ed. (p. 61)
—American Girl: Assembled: Meet Kaya Lapbook. Kinney, Cyndi, ed. (p. 61)
—American Girl: Assembled: Meet Molly Lapbook. Kinney, Cyndi, ed. (p. 61)
—Apologia Worldview: Who Am I Lapbook. Kinney, Cyndi, ed. (p. 92)
—Apologia Worldview: Assembled: Who Am I Lapbook. Kinney, Cyndi, ed. (p. 92)
—Apologia Worldview: 'Who Is My Neighbor? Lapbook. Kinney, Cyndi, ed. (p. 92)
—Apologia Worldview: Assembled: 'Who Is My Neighbor? Lapbook. Kinney, Cyndi, ed. (p. 92)
—Easter Activity Book. Kinney, Cyndi, ed. (p. 499)
Donner, Rebecca. Burnout. (p. 244)
Donnier, Christine, jt. auth. see Barbara, Diane.
Donnini, Joy. Story of Ruby Lee: 2nd Edition. (p. 1659)
Donnio, Sylviane. I'd Really Like to Eat a Child. (p. 851)
Donobo, Koge. Pita-Ten (p. 1364)
Donofrio, Antonio R. & Donofrio, Beatrice Batnag. G-String Cordilleran Revelries: Fairy Tales Retold for Centuries to Teach Life's Family Values & Basic Reading Skills with Simple Magic Tricks & I. (p. 651)
Donofrio, Beatrice Batnag, jt. auth. see Donofrio, Antonio R.
Donofrio, Beverly. Mary & the Mouse, the Mouse & Mary. McClintock, Barbara, illus. (p. 1100)
—Where's Mommy? McClintock, Barbara, illus. (p. 1910)
D'Onofrio, J. J., jt. auth. see Riseman, Daniel.
D'Onofrio, Sister Alice Marie. Woofs, Whiskers, & Wags: Tales of Rocky's Brave Heart. (p. 1950)
Donoghue, Stella. Lift & Learn 123. Snaith, Andy, photos by. (p. 1014)
Donohoe, Kitty & Warstler, Pasqua Cekola. Bunyan & Banjoes: Michigan Songs & Stories. Warstler, Pasqua Cekola, illus. (p. 243)
Donohue, D. M. My Morning Prayer: A Gift from God. (p. 1214)
Donohue, Dorothy, illus. see Bauer, Marion Dane.
Donohue, Dorothy, illus. see Carr, Jan.
Donohue, Dorothy, illus. see Crummel, Susan Stevens.
Donohue, Dorothy, jt. auth. see Crummel, Susan Stevens.
Donohue, Laurie. To the Core: Granola Crumble. (p. 1759)
Donohue, Moira Rose. Alfie the Apostrophe Adinolfi, JoAnn, illus. (p. 37)
—Christopher Columbus. (p. 316)
—Christopher Newport. (p. 317)
—Henry Hudson. (p. 768)
—Jacques Cartier. (p. 905)
—John Cabot. (p. 921)
—Juan Ponce de León. (p. 930)
—L. Douglas Wilder. (p. 969)
—Maggie L. Walker. (p. 1071)
—Penny & the Punctuation Bee Law, Jenny, illus. (p. 1338)
Donohue, Moira Rose, jt. auth. see National Geographic Kids Staff.
Donohue, Moira Rose & Scott, Clarke C. Arthur R. Ashe, Jr. (p. 104)
Donoso, Marcela, illus. see Lazaro, Georgina.
Donovan, Amy. Birds of Prey. (p. 191)
Donovan, Amy & Shafran, Michael. My First Pocket Guide Birds of Prey. Emmett, Jennifer, ed. (p. 1207)
Donovan, Anna. Dragon's Tale. (p. 479)
—Emma Says Boo. Fox, Woody, illus. (p. 520)
—Emma Says Oops! Fox, Woody, illus. (p. 520)
Donovan, Barabara. Numbers Everywhere: A Content Area Reader-math. (p. 1272)
Donovan, Barbara A. Body Systems: Respiratory & Circulatory: Text Pairs. (p. 207)
—It's All Matter (p. 896)
—Move It! (p. 1183)
—World of Animals (p. 1956)
Donovan, Barbara A. & Capstone Press Staff. It's All Matter (p. 896)
—Move It! (p. 1183)
—World of Animals (p. 1956)
Donovan, Dan. Christmas Tail! (p. 316)
—Holiday Tails! (p. 788)
Donovan, Dawn. Nosey Rosie. (p. 1266)
Donovan, Derec, illus. see Bedard, Tony.
Donovan, Deric, jt. illus. see Coipel, Olivier.
Donovan, Gail. 100th Day Fun. Clar, David Austin, illus. (p. 1999)
—In Memory of Gorfman T. Frog. Pedersen, Janet, illus. (p. 864)
—!Listos... Ya! Clar, David Austin, illus. (p. 1022)
—Waffler. (p. 1852)
Donovan Guntly, Jenette, jt. auth. see Burch, Regina G.
Donovan, Jane. Just Perfect! (p. 939)
Donovan, Jane Monroe. Small, Medium & Large. Donovan, Jane Monroe, illus. (p. 1592)
Donovan, Jane Monroe, illus. see Brennan-Nelson, Denise.
Donovan, Jane Monroe, illus. see Sewell, Anna.
Donovan, John. I'll Get There. It Better Be Worth the Trip: 40th Anniversary Edition. (p. 856)
Donovan, Kevin. Billy & His Friends Rescue a Baby Bear. (p. 187)
—Billy & His Friends Rescue Betsy Bear. (p. 187)
—Billy & His Friends Tame a Wild Wolf. (p. 187)
Donovan, Kim. St Viper's School for Super Villains. the Big Bank Burglary. Bean, Izzy, illus. (p. 1638)
Donovan, Kyle. CurBee Races the NasBee 500: The Do'Bees. (p. 392)
—HoniBee Loses Her Voice: The Do'Bees. (p. 795)
—Introducing the Do'Bees. (p. 882)
Donovan, Kyle, Sr. CurBee Races the NasBee 500: The Do'Bees. (p. 392)
—Introducing the Do'Bees: The Do'Bees. (p. 882)
Donovan, Lois. Winds of l'Acadie. (p. 1936)
Donovan, Michelle O. Joshua, Helmut, & Bethlehem. (p. 927)
Donovan, Patrick, jt. auth. see Scully, Michael.
Donovan, Patrick J., jt. auth. see Scully, Michael.
Donovan, Patte, illus. see Rooney, Thomas L.
Donovan, Rebecca. Barely Breathing (p. 139)
—Breathing Series: Books 1 And 2 (p. 226)
—Out of Breath (p. 1311)
—Reason to Breathe (p. 1450)
Donovan, Robin Michelle. Christmas Rescue. (p. 315)
—Tales from the North Pole: A Christmas Flight. (p. 1702)
Donovan, Sandra. African American Experience. (p. 27)
—Budgeting Smarts: How to Set Goals, Save Money, Spend Wisely, & More. (p. 235)
—Deadliest Destinations. (p. 417)
—Hispanic American Experience. (p. 781)
—Job Smarts: How to Find Work or Start a Business, Manage Earnings, & More. (p. 919)
—Middle Eastern American Experience. (p. 1137)
—Military/Dictators. (p. 1143)
—Teen Wise Guide to Time Management. (p. 1714)
—Thrift Shopping: Discovering Bargains & Hidden Treasures. (p. 1744)
Donovan, Sandra, jt. auth. see Nelson, Robin.
Donovan, Sandra & Donovan, Sandy. Did President Grant Really Get a Ticket for Speeding in a Horse-Drawn Carriage? And Other Questions about U. S. Presidents. (p. 436)
—Teens in Thailand (p. 1715)
Donovan, Sandy. Bat in Its Cave. (p. 143)
—Beaver in Its Lodge. (p. 154)
—Bob the Alien Discovers the Dewey Decimal System Haake, Martin, illus. (p. 205)
—Bored Bella Learns about Fiction & Nonfiction Hernandez, Leeza, illus. (p. 214)
—Budgeting. (p. 235)
—Communication Smarts: How to Express Yourself Best in Conversations, Texts, E-Mails, & More. (p. 349)
—Cool BMX Racing Facts (p. 362)
—Cool Skateboarding Facts (p. 364)
—Cool Stock Car Racing Facts (p. 364)
—Deadly Danger Zones. (p. 417)
—Derek Jeter. (p. 427)
—Derek Jeter (Revised Edition) (p. 427)
—Does It Really Take Seven Years to Digest Swallowed Gum? And Other Questions You've Always Wanted to Ask. (p. 460)
—Does My Voice Count? A Book about Citizenship. (p. 460)
—Fox in Its Den. (p. 626)
—Hawk & Drool: Gross Stuff in Your Mouth. Slack, Michael H., illus. (p. 755)
—How Can I Deal with Bullying? A Book about Respect. (p. 805)
—Hypatia: Mathematician, Inventor, & Philosopher (p. 831)
—Karl & Carolina Uncover the Parts of a Book Mullan, Michael, illus. (p. 943)
—Keep Your Eye on the Ball: And Other Expressions about Sports. (p. 947)
—Lance Armstrong. (p. 973)
—Lethal Leaders & Military Madmen. (p. 994)
—Media: From News Coverage to Political Advertising. (p. 1118)
—Movies & TV Top Tens. (p. 1183)
—Music & Theater Top Tens. (p. 1193)
—Pingpong Perry Experiences How a Book Is Made Christoph, James, illus. (p. 1359)
—Protecting America: A Look at the People Who Keep Our Country Safe. (p. 1412)
—Rumble & Spew: Gross Stuff in Your Stomach & Intestines. Slack, Michael H., illus. (p. 1495)
—Running for Office: A Look at Political Campaigns. (p. 1497)
—Snake in Its Burrow. (p. 1596)
—Special Interests: From Lobbyists to Campaign Funding. (p. 1623)
—Sports Top Tens. (p. 1633)
—Stay Clear! What You Should Know about Skin Care. (p. 1645)
—Stay Clear! What You Should Know about Skin Care. Desrocher, Jack, illus. (p. 1645)
—Technology Top Tens. (p. 1712)
—Teens in Morocco (p. 1715)
—Teens in South Korea (p. 1715)
—Triple H: At the Top of His Game (p. 1787)
—U. S. Naval Special Warfare Forces. (p. 1807)
—Until the Cows Come Home: And Other Expressions about Animals. Blecha, Aaron, illus. (p. 1823)
—USA TODAY(r) Teen Wise Guides: Time, Money, & Relationships: Spring 2012 New Releases. (p. 1826)
—Volunteering Smarts: How to Find Opportunities, Create a Positive Experience, & More. (p. 1850)
—When Is It My Turn? A Book about Fairness. (p. 1903)
—Zoe Kravitz: X-Men's Amazing Angel. (p. 1987)
Donovan, Sandy, jt. auth. see Donovan, Sandra.
Donovan, Sandy, jt. auth. see Leder, Jane Mersky.
Donovan, Sandy, jt. auth. see Nelson, Robin.
Donovan, Stacey. Who I Am Keeps Happening. (p. 1915)
Donovan, Star. Gappy's Great Escape: Book Five of the Young Vampire Adventures. (p. 655)
Donovan, Sue. Istanbul, Once Constantinople. (p. 893)
Donovan, Tristan. Feral Cities: Adventures with Animals in the Urban Jungle. (p. 581)
Donploypetch, Jintanan. Mystery of the Maya. Pornkerd, Vorrarit & Yaweera, Sasiprapa, illus. (p. 1225)
Donploypetch, Jintanan, illus. see Wallace, Jim.
DonRauf & Vescia, Monique. Virtual Apprentice: Actor. (p. 1844)
Dontell, Susan L. Sassafras in What Is Metamorphosis? Andrews, Luke, illus. (p. 1515)
Dony, John. Henderson the Hedgehog. (p. 767)
—Leah's Lions. (p. 982)
Donze, Lisa, illus. see Kessel, Joyce K.
Donzelli, Janine. I Am Like You, & You Are Like Me. (p. 833)
Doo, DooLee. 4D Stories. (p. 1992)
Doo, Robin, jt. auth. see Le Gall, Frank.
Dooda, Ian, jt. ed. see Coy, Steven.
Doodle. Most Amazing Drawing, Doodle, Colouring, Sketchbook in the World. (p. 1177)
Doodle, Nanny. Divorced at Six. (p. 455)
Doodle Pictures Studio Staff, jt. auth. see Landers, Ace.
Doodlemum & Smith, Justine. My Mummy Says. Stevens, Angie, illus. (p. 1215)
Doodler, Todd H. Bear, Do You Wear Underwear? (p. 150)
—Bear in Underwear - Color & Draw. Sami, illus. (p. 151)
—Color & Draw Bear in Underwear Activity Kit: Includes Activity Book, Crayons, & Stickers in a Carryall Case! (p. 342)
—Honey Bear's Blue Bathing Suit. (p. 794)
—One Potato, Two Potato. Doodler, Todd H., illus. (p. 1296)
—Peas on Earth. (p. 1333)
—Rawr! Doodler, Todd H., illus. (p. 1441)
—Super Fly: The World's Smallest Superhero! (p. 1680)
—Super Rawr! (p. 1680)
—Veggies with Wedgies. Doodler, Todd H., illus. (p. 1834)
—Zoo I Drew. (p. 1989)
Doodler, Todd H., illus. see Goldman, Todd.
Doodler, Todd H., illus. see Ziefert, Harriet.
Doolan, Catherine. Drochla Gruaige. Kelly, Maeve, illus. (p. 485)
Dooley, Angela, jt. auth. see Rigby, Ed.
Dooley, Audrey, jt. auth. see Childress, Gavin.
Dooley, Caroline, jt. auth. see Perkins, David.
Dooley, Dimingo. Color of God. (p. 343)
Dooley, Larry. Peanut Butter & Monster Sandwich. Grzelak, Kyle, illus. (p. 1332)
Dooley, Norah. Everybody Brings Noodles. Thornton, Peter J., illus. (p. 543)
—Everybody Cooks Rice. Thornton, Peter J., illus. (p. 543)
Dooley, Sarah. Wilfred & Harold's Dinner Party Disaster . (p. 1932)
Dooley, Vince. How 'Bout Them Dawgs! De Angel, Miguel, illus. (p. 805)
Dooley, Virginia. Reading & Math. Cooper, Terry, ed. (p. 1445)
Dooley, Virginia & Teaching Resources Staff. Reading & Math Jumbo. Cooper, Terry, ed. (p. 1445)
Dooley, Virginia, et al. Amazing Word Power: 100 Words Every 5th Grader Should Know. (p. 56)
Doolin, Jimmy. Day the Circus Came to My Backyard. (p. 414)
Dooling, Michael. Great Horse-Less Carriage Race. Dooling, Michael, illus. (p. 716)
—Young Thomas Edison. Dooling, Michael, illus. (p. 1979)
Dooling, Michael, illus. see Cohlene, Terri.
Dooling, Michael, illus. see Giblin, James Cross.
Dooling, Sandra. James Madison. (p. 907)
—Japanese Internment: Defining Moments in Canadian History. (p. 909)
—Last Spike in CPR: Defining Moments in Canadian History. (p. 978)
Doolittle, Bev, illus. see Maclay, Elise.
Doolittle, Eva M. Old Fairy Tales Anew. Telielska, M. Magdalena, illus. (p. 1283)
—Silver Letters. (p. 1576)
Doolittle, John H. Dr. DooRiddles A1: Associative Reasoning Activities. (p. 475)
—Dr. DooRiddles A2: Associative Reasoning Activities. (p. 475)
—Dr. DooRiddles A3: Associative Reasoning Activities. (p. 475)
—Dr. DooRiddles B1: Associative Reasoning Activities. (p. 475)
—Dr. DooRiddles C1: Associative Reasoning Activities. (p. 475)
—Dr. Funster's Creative Thinking Puzzlers A1: Creative Problem-Solving Fun. (p. 475)
Doolittle, John H. & Doolittle, Tracy A. Dr. DooRiddles B2: Associative Reasoning Activities. (p. 475)
Doolittle, Joyce, ed. Playhouse: Six Fantasy Plays for Children (p. 1372)
Doolittle, Linda C. It's a Dog's Life. (p. 895)
Doolittle, Michael, illus. see Goodman, Susan E.
Doolittle, Michael, photos by see Goodman, Susan E.
Doolittle, Michael J., illus. see Goodman, Susan E.
Doolittle, Sara. Lillie's Smile. Locke, Margo, illus. (p. 1017)
Doolittle, Tracy A., jt. auth. see Doolittle, John H.
Doonan, Gladys & Sorensen, Rebekah M. Crown Him King! A Christmas Program. (p. 386)
Dooney, Michael, jt. auth. see Lawson, Jim.
Doors, Mason. I T I P. (p. 846)
Doose, Heidi. As the Sun Said Goodnight. (p. 105)
Dopffer, Guillaume. 1000 First Words in French. Lacome, Susie, illus. (p. 2001)
Doppert, Monika, illus. see Kurusa.
Dopson, Jennifer. Life Goes On. (p. 1010)
Dor, George Vincent. Sit. (p. 1581)
Dora the Explorer, Dora the. Dora the Explorer: Sing with Dora! (p. 471)
Dora the Explorer Publishing Staff. Dora the Explorer Dora Loves Easter! A HUGS Book. (p. 471)
—Dora the Explorer Holidays Are for Hugs: A Hugs Book. (p. 471)
—Rockin' Maraca Adventure: Storybook with Maracas. (p. 1483)
Dorado, Steve, illus. see Guillain, Charlotte.
Dorais, Katherine M. Revolutionary War & a Few Things More. (p. 1466)
Doran, Colleen. Coda (p. 338)
—Distant Soil: the Gathering TP: The Gathering TP. (p. 453)
Doran, Colleen, illus. see Lyga, Barry.
Doran, David, illus. see Ferry, Therese.
Doran, Fran, illus. see Melton, Marcia.
Doran, Joe. SeeDEGA Method: C Double Excellent Guitar Arranging. (p. 1547)
Doran, Mary. Easy in, Not So Easy Out: A Quinton Quarter Adventure. (p. 500)
—Quinton Quarter Story: A Quinton Quarter Adventure. (p. 1428)
—What a Disaster: A Quinton Quarter Adventure. (p. 1878)
Dorankamp, Michelle, illus. see Greene, Carol.
Dorantes, Kathleen. Princess So-Wise. (p. 1405)
Dorato, A. P. Arthur, Donna, & the Magic Crown of Tiabora. (p. 103)
Dordick, Barry. Macaroni on the Moon. Amado, Defne, illus. (p. 1067)
Doré, Gustave, illus. see Brabourne, Edward Hugessen Knatchbull-Hugessen.
Doré, Gustave, illus. see Moers, Walter.
Doré, Gustave, illus. see Raspe, Rudolf Erich.
Doré, Gustavo, illus. see Perrault, Charles & Perrault, Charles.
Doreen Norberg. Soldier's Dog. (p. 1607)
Dorémus, Gaëtan, illus. see Gillot, Laurence & Sebaoun, Elisabeth.
Dorémus, Gaëtan, creator. Bear Despair. (p. 150)
Doremus, Gaetan, creator. Coyote Run. (p. 374)
Doremus, Robert. Albert Einstein. (p. 34)
—Sacagawea. (p. 1500)
Doremus, Robert, illus. see Winders, Gertrude Hecker.
Doren, Greg Van. Obleo. (p. 1275)
Dorenda W. Madkins. Sammy's Battle with the L-I-E Word. (p. 1508)
Dorenkamp, Michelle. Bear Went over the Mountain. Dorenkamp, Michelle, illus. (p. 151)
Dorenkamp, Michelle, illus. see Bohnet, Eric.
Dorenkamp, Michelle, illus. see Busch, Melinda Kay.
Dorenkamp, Michelle, illus. see Fryar, Jane L.
Dorenkamp, Michelle, illus. see Miller, Claire.
Dorenkamp, Michelle, illus. see Schkade, Jonathan.
Dorenkamp, Michelle, illus. see Sonberg, Caryn.
Dorenkamp Repa, Michelle, illus. see Hovland, Stephenie.
Dorfman, Craig. I Knew You Could! A Book for All the Stops in Your Life. Ong, Cristina, illus. (p. 840)
Dorfman, Elsa, photos by. No Hair Day. (p. 1258)
Dorfman, Janet. Wright Brothers. (p. 1963)
Dorfman, Joaquin. Long Wait for Tomorrow. (p. 1047)
Dorfman, Leo, et al. Robin the Boy Wonder (p. 1480)
Dorfmueller, Daniel P., jt. auth. see Brown, Walter C.
Dorian, Camille, jt. auth. see Shifrine, Moshe.
Dorian, Judith. Tiny Little Door. Dorian, Judith, illus. (p. 1756)
D'Orlo, Wayne. Al Sharpton. (p. 33)
Dorion. Melanie Bluelake's Dream. (p. 1125)
Dorion, Betty, jt. auth. see Dorion, Betty F.
Dorion, Betty F. & Dorion, Betty. Whose Side Are You On? (p. 1922)
Dorion, Christiane. Are We Running Out of Energy? (p. 96)
—Earth's Garbage Crisis. (p. 498)
—How the Weather Works: A Hands-On Guide to Our Changing Climate. Young, Beverley, illus. (p. 813)
—How the World Works: A Hands-On Guide to Our Amazing Planet. Young, Beverley, illus. (p. 813)
—Pollution. (p. 1381)
Dorisann. Blasting Ogres. (p. 198)
Dorisi-Winget, Dianna. Pythons. (p. 1422)
—Snow Leopards (p. 1599)
Dorismond, Joanne R. Day in New York with Beatrice & Duke. (p. 413)
Dorismond, Marie L. Island Called Haiti. (p. 892)
Dorison, Guillaume, et al. Planet of the Firebird. Fayolle, Diane & Benoit, Jérôme, illus. (p. 1367)
—Planet of Wind. Fayolle, Diane & Benoit, Jérôme, illus. (p. 1368)
Dorison, Xavier. Emerald Maze Lauffray, Mathieu, illus. (p. 517)
—Lady Vivian Hastings. Saincantin, Jerome, tr. from FRE. (p. 971)
—Long John Silver Vol. 4: Guiana-Capac. Lauffray, Mathieu, illus. (p. 1047)
—Neptune: Long John Silver. Vol. 2 Lauffray, Mathieu, illus. (p. 1241)
—Sanctum. (p. 1510)
Dorison, Xavier & Nury, Fabian. Spooks. Ross, C., illus. (p. 1631)
Dorison, Xavier & Nury, Fabien. Santero: Spooks. Vol. 3 Rossi, Christian, illus. (p. 1513)
Dority, Victoria & Andes, Mary Lou. Saint Frances Xavier Cabrini: Cecchina's Dream. Kiwak, Barbara, illus. (p. 1503)
Dorland, Andrew, illus. see Cowle, Ken.
Dorling, Anna, et al. One Shining Day. Fairhurst, Carol, illus. (p. 1296)

D

Dorling Kindersley Publishing Staff. 10 Minutes a Day: Math Grade 5. (p. 1993)
—10 Minutes a Day: Decimals, Fourth Grade: Decimals, Fourth Grade. (p. 1993)
—10 Minutes a Day: Fractions, Fourth Grade: Fractions, Fourth Grade. (p. 1993)
—10 Minutes a Day Math, Grade 2. (p. 1993)
—10 Minutes a Day - Math, Grade 4. (p. 1993)
—10 Minutes a Day: Multiplication, Third Grade. (p. 1993)
—10 Minutes a Day - Phonics, Grade K. (p. 1993)
—10 Minutes a Day: Problem Solving, Fourth Grade: Problem Solving, Fourth Grade. (p. 1993)
—10 Minutes a Day: Problem Solving, Third Grade: Problem Solving, Third Grade. (p. 1993)
—10 Minutes a Day - Spelling. (p. 1993)
—10 Minutes a Day Spelling, Grade 4. (p. 1993)
—10 Minutes a Day: Vocabulary, Fourth Grade. (p. 1993)
—100 People Who Made History. (p. 1998)
—1000 Inventions & Discoveries. (p. 2001)
—ABC. (p. 2)
—ABC - Fun Flaps, Plus Touch & Feel! (p. 3)
—Adventure Guide. (p. 14)
—Adventures of Brer Rabbit & Friends. Copeland, Eric, illus. (p. 17)
—Adventures of C-3PO. (p. 17)
—Ahsoka in Action! (p. 30)
—Ahsoka in Action!, Level 1. (p. 30)
—Airplanes. (p. 32)
—All about Everything. (p. 42)
—Amazing Battles! (p. 54)
—Amazing Giant Dinosaurs. (p. 54)
—Amazing Giant Sea Creatures. (p. 54)
—Amazing Giant Wild Animals. (p. 54)
—Amazing Visual Math. (p. 56)
—Amazon. (p. 56)
—Ancient Egypt. (p. 68)
—Angry Birds. (p. 75)
—Angry Birds Star Wars II. (p. 75)
—Angry Birds - Transformers. (p. 75)
—Animal. (p. 76)
—Animal Alphabet. (p. 76)
—Animal Antics. (p. 76)
—Animal Book. (p. 77)
—Animal Colors. (p. 77)
—Animal Counting. (p. 77)
—Animal Face Book. (p. 77)
—Animals. (p. 81)
—Animals. Quasha, Jennifer, ed. (p. 81)
—Arms & Armor. (p. 100)
—Attack of the Clones. (p. 113)
—Aztec, Inca & Maya. (p. 122)
—Baby Animals. (p. 124)
—Baby Animals - Touch & Feel. (p. 124)
—Baby Baa Baa! (p. 125)
—Baby Beep! Beep! (p. 125)
—Baby Cheep! Cheep! (p. 125)
—Baby Colors! (p. 125)
—Baby Faces! (p. 126)
—Baby Faces Peekaboo! (p. 126)
—Baby First Words! (p. 126)
—Baby Go! Go! Go! (p. 126)
—Baby Hide & Seek! (p. 126)
—Baby Loves Peekaboo! Quasha, Jennifer, ed. (p. 127)
—Baby Peekaboo! (p. 127)
—Baby Pets! (p. 127)
—Baby Roar! Roar! (p. 127)
—Baby Talk: 6 Giant Flasp for Baby to Flip. (p. 128)
—Baby Tractor! (p. 128)
—Baby What's That? (p. 128)
—Baby Woof Woof! (p. 128)
—Ballet. (p. 134)
—Bathtime. (p. 144)
—Bathtime Peekaboo! (p. 144)
—Batman's Missions. (p. 144)
—Bedtime. (p. 156)
—Beep! Beep! (p. 157)
—Beware the Inquisitor. (p. 173)
—Big Book of Crafts & Activities. (p. 179)
—Big Busy Book - Words. (p. 180)
—Big Cats. (p. 180)
—Big Dump Truck. (p. 181)
—Big Girls Use the Potty! (p. 181)
—Big Hero 6. (p. 181)
—Big Idea Science Book. (p. 181)
—Birthday. (p. 192)
—Blast Off! (p. 198)
—Blast Off!, Pre-Level 1. (p. 198)
—Bounty Hunters for Hire, Level 2. (p. 216)
—Boys' Noisy Potty Book. (p. 220)
—Boys' Potty Time. (p. 220)
—Brain Attack! (p. 221)
—Brain Wars. (p. 222)
—Brickmaster: Fight the Power of the Snakes. (p. 227)
—Brickmaster: Battle for the Stolen Crystals. (p. 227)
—Brickmaster. (p. 227)
—Brickmaster - The Quest for Chi. (p. 227)
—Brickmaster - Treasure Hunt in Heartlake City. (p. 227)
—Bugs: Over 60 Reusable Full Color Stickers. (p. 237)
—Bugs. (p. 237)
—Build Your Own Adventure. (p. 238)
—Bunny. (p. 242)
—Busy Home: Let's Look & Learn! (p. 246)
—Butterfly & Moth. (p. 247)
—Can You Spot a Jedi? (p. 259)
—Careers. (p. 267)
—Cars. (p. 271)
—Cars: Character Encyclopedia. (p. 272)
—Cars 2. (p. 272)
—Castles & Knights. (p. 277)
—Cat. (p. 277)
—Celebrations Around the World. (p. 285)
—Character Encyclopedia. (p. 291)
—Chicago. (p. 299)
—Children's Book of Art: An Introduction to the World's Most Amazing. (p. 303)
—Children's Book of Magic. (p. 303)
—Children's Book of Mythical Beasts & Magical Monsters. (p. 303)
—Children's Book of Philosophy. (p. 303)
—Children's Encyclopedia of American History. (p. 303)
—Children's Illustrated Dictionary. (p. 303)
—Children's World Atlas. (p. 304)
—Christmas. (p. 312)
—Christmas Peekaboo! (p. 315)
—Christmas - Pop-Up Peekaboo! (p. 312)
—Chug Chug Tractor. (p. 318)
—Civil War. (p. 325)
—Climate Change. (p. 332)
—Clone Wars. (p. 333)
—Clone Wars - Forces of Darkness, Level 3. (p. 333)
—Cock-a-Doodle-Doo! - Farm. (p. 337)
—Color Illusions. (p. 342)
—Colorful Days. (p. 344)
—Colorful World. (p. 344)
—Colors. (p. 344)
—Colors & Shapes. (p. 345)
—Complete Children's Cookbook. (p. 352)
—Computer Coding. (p. 354)
—Cook It: Learn to Cook 100 Easy Recipes. (p. 361)
—Cookbook for Girls. (p. 361)
—Cuddly Animals. (p. 389)
—Dance. (p. 402)
—Danger! (p. 403)
—Did You Know? Amazing Answers to the Questions You Ask. (p. 437)
—Diggers & Dumpers. Parsons, Jayne, ed. (p. 439)
—Dinosaur! (p. 441)
—Dinosaurs. (p. 443)
—Dinosaurs & Other Prehistoric Life. (p. 444)
—Dinosaurs Eye to Eye. (p. 444)
—Disney Frozen: Ultimate Sticker Collection. (p. 451)
—Disney Frozen. (p. 451)
—Disney Frozen Factivity Fun READERLINK. (p. 451)
—Disney Infinity. (p. 451)
—Disney Infinity Character Encyclopedia. (p. 451)
—Disney Pixar. (p. 452)
—Disney Pixar Character Encyclopedia. (p. 452)
—Disney Pixar Inside Out: the Essential Guide: The Essential Guide. (p. 452)
—Disney Planes. (p. 452)
—Disney Planes Fire & Rescue: the Essential Guide: The Essential Guide. (p. 452)
—DK Adventures: a Trip Through the Body: A Trip Through the Body. (p. 455)
—DK Adventures: Bug Hunters. (p. 455)
—DK Adventures: Secrets of the Cave: Secrets of the Cave. (p. 455)
—DK Adventures: Star Wars: Jedi Battles: Star Wars: Jedi Battles. (p. 455)
—DK Adventures: Star Wars: Sith Wars: Star Wars: Sith Wars. (p. 455)
—DK Eyewitness Books: Animal: Animal. (p. 456)
—DK Eyewitness Books: Civil War: Civil War. (p. 456)
—DK Eyewitness Books: the Amazon: The Amazon. (p. 456)
—DK Eyewitness Books: Universe: Universe. (p. 456)
—DK Eyewitness Travel Guide: Boston: Boston. (p. 456)
—DK Readers L0: Nighttime Animals: Nighttime Animals. (p. 456)
—DK Readers L0: Snakes Slither & Hiss: Snakes Slither & Hiss. (p. 456)
—DK Readers L0: Weather: Weather. (p. 456)
—DK Readers L2: Star Wars Rebels: Beware the Inquisitor: Star Wars Rebels: Beware the Inquisitor. (p. 456)
—DK Readers L3: LEGO DC Comics Super Heroes: Batman's Missions: LEGO DC Comics Super Heroes: Batman's Missions. (p. 456)
—DK Readers L3: Rocket Science: Rocket Science. (p. 456)
—DK Workbooks: Geography, First Grade: Geography, First Grade. (p. 456)
—DK Workbooks: Geography, Kindergarten: Geography, Kindergarten. (p. 456)
—DK Workbooks: Geography, Pre-K: Geography, Pre-K. (p. 456)
—DK Workbooks: Geography, Second Grade: Geography, Second Grade. (p. 456)
—DK Workbooks: Geography, Third Grade: Geography, Third Grade. (p. 456)
—DK Workbooks: Spelling, Kindergarten: Spelling, Kindergarten. (p. 456)
—DK Workbooks: Spelling, Pre-K: Spelling, Pre-K. (p. 456)
—DK Workbooks: Spelling, Second Grade: Spelling, Second Grade. (p. 456)
—DK Workbooks: Spelling, Third Grade: Spelling, Third Grade. (p. 456)
—Don't Wake the Zillo Beast! (p. 469)
—Doodlepedia. (p. 469)
—Duck & Friends. (p. 488)
—Early Humans. (p. 493)
—Early People. (p. 494)
—Earth. (p. 494)
—Enchanted. (p. 523)
—Encyclopedia of Science. (p. 525)
—Even Droids Need Friends! (p. 541)
—Everything You Need to Know about Bugs. (p. 545)
—Everything You Need to Know about Frogs & Other Slippery Creatures. (p. 545)
—Everything You Need to Know about Sharks: And other creatures of the Deep. (p. 546)
—Everything You Need to Know about Snakes. (p. 546)
—Extra Math Practice: Fifth Grade: Fifth Grade. (p. 555)
—Extra Math Practice: First Grade: First Grade. (p. 555)
—Extra Math Practice: Fourth Grade: Fourth Grade. (p. 555)
—Extra Math Practice: Kindergarten: Kindergarten. (p. 555)
—Extra Math Practice: Second Grade: Second Grade. (p. 555)
—Extra Math Practice: Third Grade: Third Grade. (p. 555)
—Eyes, Nose, Toes Peekaboo! (p. 558)
—Eyewitness - Animal. (p. 558)
—Eyewitness Explorer: Nature Ranger: Nature Ranger. (p. 558)
—Eyewitness Explorer: Night Sky Detective: Night Sky Detective. (p. 558)
—Eyewitness - Gandhi. (p. 558)
—Eyewitness - Science. (p. 558)
—Eyewitness Travel Guide - German. (p. 559)
—Eyewitness Travel Guide - Italian Phrase Book. (p. 559)
—Eyewitness Travel Guide Phrase Books - Latin-American Spanish. (p. 559)
—Eyewitness Travel Guide - Spanish. (p. 559)
—Eyewitness Travel Guides - German: Pronunciation, Food, Shopping, Time Numbers, Everyday Phrases, Mini Dictionary. (p. 559)
—Eyewitness Travel Guides Phrase Book French. (p. 559)
—Eyewitness - Wonder of the World. (p. 558)
—Fairies Encyclopedia. (p. 563)
—Farm: Lego Ville. (p. 573)
—Farm. (p. 573)
—Farm Animals. (p. 573)
—Farm Friends. (p. 574)
—Farm - Little Hide & Seek. (p. 574)
—Farm Tractor. (p. 574)
—Fashion. (p. 575)
—Fashion Book. (p. 575)
—Feel & Find Fun: Building Site: Building Site. (p. 580)
—Feel Farm Animals. (p. 580)
—Finding Nemo. (p. 588)
—Fire Engine. (p. 590)
—Fire Truck. (p. 591)
—First Animal Encyclopedia. (p. 593)
—First Earth Encyclopedia. (p. 594)
—First Encyclopedia. (p. 594)
—First Human Body Encyclopedia. (p. 595)
—First Nature Encyclopedia. (p. 596)
—First Science Encyclopedia. (p. 596)
—First Words. (p. 597)
—Flaptastic - Animals. (p. 602)
—Flaptastic Colors. (p. 602)
—Flaptastic - First Words. (p. 602)
—Fluffy Animals. (p. 608)
—Frozen. (p. 645)
—Garden Friends, Pre-Level 1. (p. 656)
—Geography: a Visual Encyclopedia: A Visual Encyclopedia. (p. 662)
—Get Ready for School - Color Match Games. (p. 668)
—Get Ready for School: I'm Ready for School: I'm Ready for School. (p. 668)
—Girls' Noisy Potty Book. (p. 680)
—Girl's Potty Time. (p. 680)
—Glow in the Dark Ocean Creatures. (p. 685)
—Happy Birthday! (p. 744)
—Happy Birthday Sophie! (p. 745)
—Help Your Kids with Computer Coding. (p. 766)
—Help Your Kids with Music. (p. 766)
—Heroes of Lothal. (p. 773)
—Heroes Unite! (p. 773)
—Hide & Seek - Farm. (p. 776)
—Hide & Seek First Words. (p. 776)
—Hide & Seek - Things That Go. (p. 776)
—History Year by Year. (p. 785)
—Hoppity Hop Peekaboo! (p. 797)
—Horse. (p. 799)
—Horses. (p. 800)
—Horses & Ponies. (p. 800)
—How Animals Work. (p. 805)
—How People Lived. (p. 812)
—How Things Work Encyclopedia. (p. 814)
—How To... Ballet. (p. 814)
—How to Be a Genius. (p. 814)
—How to Play the Recorder. (p. 821)
—How To... Soccer. (p. 821)
—Human Body. (p. 825)
—Ideas That Changed the World. (p. 852)
—Italian Pharse Book. (p. 856)
—In the Park. (p. 867)
—Incredible Math Games Book. (p. 869)
—Inside Out. (p. 877)
—It Can't Be True? (p. 893)
—Japanese Phrase Book. (p. 909)
—Jedi Battles. (p. 911)
—Jedi in Training. (p. 911)
—Jungle Animals. (p. 935)
—Kitten. (p. 962)
—Knowledge Encyclopedia. (p. 965)
—Language Arts: Learn & Explore. (p. 974)
—Language Arts, 1st Grade. (p. 974)
—Language Arts, 3rd Grade. (p. 974)
—Language Arts, Grade Pre-K. (p. 974)
—Language Arts - Learn & Explore. (p. 974)
—Lard Vader's Villains. (p. 975)
—Leaf it to Cubs. (p. 982)
—Lego Friends: The Adventure Guide. (p. 990)
—LEGO Legends of Chima. (p. 990)
—LEGO Legends of Chima - Character Encyclopedia. (p. 990)
—LEGO Minifigure Ultimate Sticker Collection. (p. 990)
—LEGO Ninja, Go! (p. 990)
—LEGO Ninjago: Character Encyclopedia. (p. 990)
—Lego - Rescue: Lego Ville. (p. 990)
—Lego Star Wars. (p. 990)
—LEGO Star Wars Character Encyclopedia: Updated & Expanded: Updated & Expanded. (p. 990)
—Lego Star Wars in 100 Scenes. (p. 990)
—LEGOÂ(r) City Factivity Fun READERLINK. (p. 991)
—LEGO(r) Star Wars Minifigures Ultimate Sticker Collection. (p. 990)
—Let's Get Counting! (p. 996)
—Let's Go Riding! (p. 997)
—Life Like Mine: How Children Live Around the World. (p. 1011)
—Little Hide & Seek Animals. (p. 1029)
—Little Hide & Seek Pets. (p. 1029)
—Little Hide & Seek Words. (p. 1029)
—Look Closer Ocean. (p. 1049)
—Make Your Own Gifts. (p. 1079)
—Mammals. (p. 1085)
—Marvel the Avengers. (p. 1099)
—Marvel the Avengers Factivity Fun READERLINK. (p. 1099)
—Masters of the Force. (p. 1103)
—Math Grade 1. (p. 1106)
—Math Grade 2. (p. 1106)
—Math Grade 3. (p. 1106)
—Math Grade K. (p. 1106)
—Math Grade Pre-K. (p. 1106)
—Mealtime. (p. 1116)
—Meet the Rebels. (p. 1123)
—Meet Unikitty! (p. 1123)
—Megadoodle. (p. 1124)
—Merriam-Webster Children's Dictionary. (p. 1128)
—Mind Benders. (p. 1145)
—Mommy & Me Bake. (p. 1162)
—Muppets Character Encyclopedia. (p. 1191)
—My Art Book. (p. 1196)
—My First 123. (p. 1203)
—My First ABC. (p. 1204)
—My First Animals: Let's Squeak & Squawk! (p. 1204)
—My First Animals. (p. 1204)
—My First Baby Animals: Let's Find Our Favorites! (p. 1204)
—My First Body Board Book. Rosoff, Iris, ed. (p. 1205)
—My First Colors: Let's Learn Them All! (p. 1206)
—My First Colors. (p. 1206)
—My First Dictionary. (p. 1206)
—My First Dinosaur Board Book. Landis, Beth, ed. (p. 1206)
—My First Doodle Fun! Hands-On Fun with a Wipe-Clean Pen! (p. 1206)
—My First Encyclopedia. (p. 1206)
—My First Farm: Let's Get Working! (p. 1206)
—My First Farm Board Book. Curley, Andrea, ed. (p. 1206)
—My First Number Board Book. Ward, Kristin, ed. (p. 1207)
—My First Things That Go: Let's Get Moving! (p. 1208)
—My First Things That Go Board Book. Wilson, Hannah & Sirett, Dawn, eds. (p. 1208)
—My First Trucks. (p. 1208)
—My First Trucks & Diggers. (p. 1208)
—My First Words. (p. 1208)
—My Little Picture Bible. Mayo, Diana, illus. (p. 1212)
—Mysteries of the Jedi. (p. 1222)
—New Children's Encyclopedia. (p. 1244)
—Nighttime Animals. (p. 1255)
—Noisy Animal Peekaboo! (p. 1262)
—Noisy Digger Peekaboo! (p. 1263)
—Noisy Peekaboo! Baa! Baa! (p. 1263)
—Noisy Peekaboo! - Choo! Choo! (p. 1263)
—Noisy Peekaboo! Vroom! Vroom! (p. 1263)
—Noisy Peekabook - Toot! Toot! (p. 1263)
—Number Crunch. (p. 1271)
—Number Memory Games. (p. 1271)
—Numbers. (p. 1271)
—Number's Let's Get Counting! (p. 1272)
—Obi-Wan Kenobi Jedi Knight. (p. 1275)
—OBI-Wan Kenobi Jedi Knight, Level 3. (p. 1275)
—Ocean. (p. 1276)
—Ocean: a Visual Encyclopedia: A Visual Encyclopedia. (p. 1276)
—Oceans. (p. 1277)
—Optical Illusions. (p. 1301)
—Outdoor Crafts. (p. 1312)
—Park. (p. 1324)
—Passover. (p. 1327)
—Peekaboo Sophie! (p. 1335)
—Pets. (p. 1348)
—Petting Zoo. (p. 1349)
—Phantom Menace, Level 2. (p. 1349)
—Pirate Glow-in-the-Dark. (p. 1362)
—Playtime. (p. 1373)
—Playtime Peekaboo! (p. 1373)
—Pocket Genius: Dogs: Dogs. (p. 1375)
—Ponies. (p. 1382)
—Ponies & Horses. (p. 1382)
—Pop-Up Peekaboo! - Colors. (p. 1384)
—Pop-Up Peekaboo! - Meow! (p. 1384)
—Pop-Up Peekaboo! - Playtime. (p. 1384)
—Portuguese Phrase Book. (p. 1387)
—Predator. (p. 1394)
—Pull the Tab - Animals. (p. 1415)
—Puppies & Kittens. (p. 1418)
—Puppy. (p. 1418)
—Rain Forest. (p. 1434)
—Rainbow Colors Peekaboo! (p. 1435)
—Rebel Power! (p. 1451)
—Reptiles. (p. 1461)
—Revenge of the Sith. (p. 1466)
—Roar! Roar! (p. 1478)
—Rocks & Minerals. (p. 1483)
—Science: Facts at Your Fingertips. (p. 1524)
—Science. (p. 1524)
—Science, Grade 1. (p. 1526)
—Science, Grade 2. (p. 1526)
—Science Grade 3. (p. 1526)
—Science, Grade Pre-K: Learn & Experience. (p. 1526)
—Science Kit (p. 1526)
—Secrets of the Cave. (p. 1545)
—Secrets of the Rebels. (p. 1545)
—Shakespeare. (p. 1559)
—Shapes. (p. 1560)
—Sharkpedia. (p. 1562)
—Sharks. (p. 1562)
—Sharks: Open Your Eyes to a World of Discovery. (p. 1563)
—Sharks, Dolphins, & Other Sea Creatures. (p. 1563)
—Sith Wars. (p. 1582)
—Skylanders Universe Chronicles. (p. 1587)
—Smithsonian Geography. (p. 1594)
—Smithsonian Super Nature Encyclopedia. (p. 1594)
—Sophie Pop-Up Peekaboo! (p. 1613)
—Sophie's Busy Day. (p. 1613)
—Space: A Visual Encyclopedia. (p. 1618)
—Space. (p. 1618)
—Spanish English Bilingual Visual Dictionary. (p. 1621)
—Spanish Language Learner. (p. 1621)
—Spanish Picture Dictionary. Wilson, Hannah & Ferris, Julie, eds. (p. 1621)
—Spelling Games. (p. 1625)

—Spider-Man: Inside the World of Your Friendly Neighborhood Hero. (p. 1626)
—Spider-Man. (p. 1626)
—Splish! Splash! (p. 1630)
—Sports Car. (p. 1632)
—Spot the Bug. (p. 1633)
—Squeaky Baby Bath: Baby Animals: Baby Animals. (p. 1636)
—Squeaky Baby Bath: Colors: Colors. (p. 1636)
—Star Wars: Sith Wars. (p. 1641)
—Star Wars: Jedi Battles. (p. 1641)
—Star Wars Character Encyclopedia. (p. 1641)
—Star Wars Factivity Fun READERLINK. (p. 1641)
—Star Wars Rebels. (p. 1641)
—Star Wars Rebels - Fight the Empire! (p. 1641)
—Stars & Planets: Glow in the Dark. (p. 1643)
—Sticker Encyclopedia - Animals. (p. 1650)
—Sticker Encyclopedia - Dinosaurs. (p. 1650)
—Sticker Encyclopedia Space. (p. 1650)
—Story of the Titanic. Noon, Steve, illus. (p. 1662)
—Summer Adventures. (p. 1673)
—Super Heroes - Ready for Action! (p. 1680)
—Super Human Encyclopedia. (p. 1680)
—Super Shark Encyclopedia. (p. 1681)
—Super-Villains. (p. 1682)
—Tangled. (p. 1705)
—The Clone Wars Character Encyclopedia. (p. 1728)
—The Solar System & Beyond. (p. 1728)
—Things That Go! (p. 1733)
—Things That Go. (p. 1733)
—Total Tractor! (p. 1771)
—Touch & Feel 123. (p. 1772)
—Touch & Feel: Animal Library: Animal Library. (p. 1772)
—Touch & Feel Christmas. (p. 1772)
—Touch & Feel Pets. (p. 1772)
—Toys. (p. 1774)
—Tractor. (p. 1775)
—Tractors. (p. 1775)
—Transportation. (p. 1779)
—Trip Through the Body. (p. 1787)
—Truck. (p. 1791)
—Trucks & Other Things That Go. (p. 1791)
—True or False? (p. 1792)
—Ultimate Dinosaurs. (p. 1809)
—Ultimate Factivity Collection - Bugs. (p. 1809)
—Ultimate Factivity Collection: LEGO City: LEGO City. (p. 1809)
—Ultimate Factivity Collection: Star Wars: Star Wars. (p. 1809)
—Ultimate Sticker Book - Presidents. (p. 1810)
—Ultimate Sticker Collection: LEGO Spooky! LEGO Spooky! (p. 1810)
—Ultimate Sticker Collection: LEGO Star Wars: Mighty Minifigures: LEGO Star Wars: Mighty Minifigures. (p. 1810)
—Universe. (p. 1820)
—Visual Encyclopedia of Dinosaurs. (p. 1846)
—Volcanoes. (p. 1849)
—Washington, D. C. (p. 1859)
—Whales & Dolphins. (p. 1878)
—What Am I? Truck. (p. 1879)
—What Do You Believe? (p. 1883)
—Wheelie Baby: Truck & Friends. (p. 1900)
—When on Earth? (p. 1904)
—Where to Go When. Rosendo, Joseph, ed. (p. 1910)
—Who Am I? Baby Animals. (p. 1914)
—Who Am I? Cuddly Animals. (p. 1914)
—Who Am I? Farm Animals. (p. 1914)
—Who Saved the Galaxy? (p. 1917)
—Wild Animals. (p. 1928)
—Winnie the Pooh. (p. 1937)
—Wonder of the World. (p. 1947)
—Woodcarving. (p. 1949)
—Woodwork: A Step-by-Step Photographic Guide to Successful Woodworking. (p. 1950)
—Woodworking. (p. 1950)
—Woof! Woof! (p. 1950)
—World War II: Visual Encyclopedia. (p. 1959)
—Yoda Bird's Heroes. (p. 1972)
Dorling Kindersley Publishing Staff, ed. see Ardley, Neil.
Dorling Kindersley Publishing Staff, ed. see Beecroft, Simon.
Dorling Kindersley Publishing Staff, ed. see Papastavrou, Vassili.
Dorling Kindersley Publishing Staff, ed. see Parker, Steve.
Dorling Kindersley Publishing Staff, ed. see Stone, Tanya Lee.
Dorling Kindersley Publishing Staff, ed. see Taylor, Paul.
Dorling Kindersley Publishing Staff, jt. auth. see Ardley, Neil.
Dorling Kindersley Publishing Staff, jt. auth. see Arthur, Alex.
Dorling Kindersley Publishing Staff, jt. auth. see Atkins, Jill.
Dorling Kindersley Publishing Staff, jt. auth. see Ball, Johnny.
Dorling Kindersley Publishing Staff, jt. auth. see Beecroft, Simon.
Dorling Kindersley Publishing Staff, jt. auth. see Bender, Lionel.
Dorling Kindersley Publishing Staff, jt. auth. see Bingham, Caroline.
Dorling Kindersley Publishing Staff, jt. auth. see Bos, Samone.
Dorling Kindersley Publishing Staff, jt. auth. see Bridgman, Roger.
Dorling Kindersley Publishing Staff, jt. auth. see Brown, Laaren.
Dorling Kindersley Publishing Staff, jt. auth. see Bull, Jane.
Dorling Kindersley Publishing Staff, jt. auth. see Buller, Laura.
Dorling Kindersley Publishing Staff, jt. auth. see Bussell, Darcey.
Dorling Kindersley Publishing Staff, jt. auth. see Chambers, Catherine E.
Dorling Kindersley Publishing Staff, jt. auth. see Chambers, Catherine.
Dorling Kindersley Publishing Staff, jt. auth. see Ching, Jacqueline.
Dorling Kindersley Publishing Staff, jt. auth. see Clarke, Barry.
Dorling Kindersley Publishing Staff, jt. auth. see Cobb, Vicki.
Dorling Kindersley Publishing Staff, jt. auth. see Cooper, Chris.
Dorling Kindersley Publishing Staff, jt. auth. see Cosgrove, Brian.
Dorling Kindersley Publishing Staff, jt. auth. see Cribb, Joe.
Dorling Kindersley Publishing Staff, jt. auth. see Deliso, Chris.
Dorling Kindersley Publishing Staff, jt. auth. see Dougall, Alastair.
Dorling Kindersley Publishing Staff, jt. auth. see Foreman, Niki.
Dorling Kindersley Publishing Staff, jt. auth. see Fortey, Jacqueline.
Dorling Kindersley Publishing Staff, jt. auth. see Gardner, Charlie.
Dorling Kindersley Publishing Staff, jt. auth. see Garrett, Leslie.
Dorling Kindersley Publishing Staff, jt. auth. see Gifford, Clive.
Dorling Kindersley Publishing Staff, jt. auth. see Gold, Maya.
Dorling Kindersley Publishing Staff, jt. auth. see Greenwood, Elinor.
Dorling Kindersley Publishing Staff, jt. auth. see Griffey, Harriet.
Dorling Kindersley Publishing Staff, jt. auth. see Grindley, Sally.
Dorling Kindersley Publishing Staff, jt. auth. see Hackett, Jane.
Dorling Kindersley Publishing Staff, jt. auth. see Hammond, Richard.
Dorling Kindersley Publishing Staff, jt. auth. see Hammond, Tim.
Dorling Kindersley Publishing Staff, jt. auth. see Hester, Beth Landis.
Dorling Kindersley Publishing Staff, jt. auth. see Hester, Elizabeth.
Dorling Kindersley Publishing Staff, jt. auth. see Hornby, Hugh.
Dorling Kindersley Publishing Staff, jt. auth. see Jenner, Caryn.
Dorling Kindersley Publishing Staff, jt. auth. see Kelly, Neil.
Dorling Kindersley Publishing Staff, jt. auth. see King, David C.
Dorling Kindersley Publishing Staff, jt. auth. see Krensky, Stephen.
Dorling Kindersley Publishing Staff, jt. auth. see Langley, Myrtle.
Dorling Kindersley Publishing Staff, jt. auth. see Last, Shari.
Dorling Kindersley Publishing Staff, jt. auth. see Lipkowitz, Daniel.
Dorling Kindersley Publishing Staff, jt. auth. see Lock, Deborah.
Dorling Kindersley Publishing Staff, jt. auth. see Mack, Lorrie.
Dorling Kindersley Publishing Staff, jt. auth. see Malam, John.
Dorling Kindersley Publishing Staff, jt. auth. see Margeson, Susan.
Dorling Kindersley Publishing Staff, jt. auth. see Mattern, Joanne.
Dorling Kindersley Publishing Staff, jt. auth. see Matthews, Rupert.
Dorling Kindersley Publishing Staff, jt. auth. see Morimoto, Masaharu.
Dorling Kindersley Publishing Staff, jt. auth. see Mound, Laurence.
Dorling Kindersley Publishing Staff, jt. auth. see Murdoch, David.
Dorling Kindersley Publishing Staff, jt. auth. see Murray, Stuart.
Dorling Kindersley Publishing Staff, jt. auth. see Neuman, Maria.
Dorling Kindersley Publishing Staff, jt. auth. see Newmark, Ann.
Dorling Kindersley Publishing Staff, jt. auth. see O'Donnell, Liam.
Dorling Kindersley Publishing Staff, jt. auth. see Parker, Steve.
Dorling Kindersley Publishing Staff, jt. auth. see Patendaude, Jeremy.
Dorling Kindersley Publishing Staff, jt. auth. see Pinnington, Andrea.
Dorling Kindersley Publishing Staff, jt. auth. see Platt, Richard.
Dorling Kindersley Publishing Staff, jt. auth. see Polin, C. J.
Dorling Kindersley Publishing Staff, jt. auth. see Santillana.
Dorling Kindersley Publishing Staff, jt. auth. see Scagell, Robin.
Dorling Kindersley Publishing Staff, jt. auth. see Seabrook, Heather.
Dorling Kindersley Publishing Staff, jt. auth. see Sebag-Montefiore, Hugh.
Dorling Kindersley Publishing Staff, jt. auth. see Simblet, Sarah.
Dorling Kindersley Publishing Staff, jt. auth. see Simkins, Kate.
Dorling Kindersley Publishing Staff, jt. auth. see Sirett, Dawn.
Dorling Kindersley Publishing Staff, jt. auth. see Smith, Penny.
Dorling Kindersley Publishing Staff, jt. auth. see Steele, Philip.
Dorling Kindersley Publishing Staff, jt. auth. see Stock, Lisa.
Dorling Kindersley Publishing Staff, jt. auth. see Stone, Tanya Lee.
Dorling Kindersley Publishing Staff, jt. auth. see Taylor, Victoria.
Dorling Kindersley Publishing Staff, jt. auth. see van Rose, Susanna.
Dorling Kindersley Publishing Staff, jt. auth. see Wallace, Daniel.
Dorling Kindersley Publishing Staff, jt. auth. see Weeks, Marcus.
Dorling Kindersley Publishing Staff, jt. auth. see Whitelaw, Ian.
Dorling Kindersley Publishing Staff, jt. auth. see Wishinsky, Frieda.
Dorling Kindersley Publishing Staff, jt. auth. see Woodward, John.
Dorling Kindersley Publishing Staff, jt. auth. see Yorke, Jane.
Dorling Kindersley Publishing Staff & Adams, Simon. Soldier. (p. 1607)
Dorling Kindersley Publishing Staff & Amos, Ruth. Decepthogs Versus Autobirds. (p. 421)
—Race for Chi. (p. 1430)
—Race for Chi, Level 3. (p. 1430)
—Robot Birds in Disguise. (p. 1480)
—Tribes of Chima, Level 2. (p. 1785)
Dorling Kindersley Publishing Staff & Baker, Nick. Bug Zoo. (p. 236)
Dorling Kindersley Publishing Staff & Ball, Johnny. Why Pi? (p. 1925)
Dorling Kindersley Publishing Staff & Beecroft, Simon. Ackbar's Underwater Army, Level 3. (p. 9)
—Anakin in Action! (p. 66)
—Chewbacca & the Wookiee Warriors. (p. 299)
—Chewbacca & the Wookiee Warriors, Level 2. (p. 299)
—Clone Wars - Jedi Adventures. (p. 333)
—Clone Wars, Level 3: Yoda in Action! (p. 333)
—Even Droids Need Friends. (p. 541)
—LEGO Monster Fighters: Meet the Monsters. (p. 990)
—LEGO Monster Fighters: Watch Out, Monsters About! (p. 990)
—Luke Skywalker's Amazing Story. (p. 1064)
—Meet the Monsters. (p. 1123)
—R2-D2 & Friends. (p. 1429)
—R2-D2 & Friends, Level 2. (p. 1429)
—Revenge of the Sith. (p. 1466)
—Watch Out for Jabba the Hutt!, Level 1. (p. 1861)
—Watch Out, Monsters About! (p. 1861)
Dorling Kindersley Publishing Staff & Bray, Adam. DK Adventures: Star Wars: What Makes a Monster? Star Wars: What Makes a Monster? (p. 455)
—Into Battle! (p. 881)
—Star Wars Rebels the Visual Guide. (p. 1642)
—What Makes a Monster? (p. 1892)
Dorling Kindersley Publishing Staff & Buller, Laura. Great Panda Tale. (p. 717)
—Pirate Attack! (p. 1362)
Dorling Kindersley Publishing Staff & Chambers, Catherine. Dinosaur Hunters. (p. 442)
Dorling Kindersley Publishing Staff & Chambers, Catherine E. DK Adventures: Dinosaur Hunters: Dinosaur Hunters. (p. 455)
Dorling Kindersley Publishing Staff & Charing, Douglas. Judaism. (p. 930)
Dorling Kindersley Publishing Staff & Chrisp, Peter. One Million Things: A Visual Encyclopedia. (p. 1296)
Dorling Kindersley Publishing Staff & Colley, John. Train. (p. 1777)
Dorling Kindersley Publishing Staff & Deere, John. Big Book of Tractors. (p. 179)
Dorling Kindersley Publishing Staff & Dolan, Hannah. Lego Movie - Essential Guide. (p. 990)
—LEGO Ninjago Visual Dictionary. (p. 990)
—Phantom Menace. (p. 1349)
Dorling Kindersley Publishing Staff & Dowsett, Elizabeth. Attack of the Clones. (p. 113)
—Attack of the Clones, Level 2. (p. 113)
—Revenge of the Sith. (p. 1466)
—Revenge of the Sith, Level 3. (p. 1466)
Dorling Kindersley Publishing Staff & East Dubowski, Cathy. Ahsoka in Action! (p. 30)
—Masters of the Force. (p. 1103)
Dorling Kindersley Publishing Staff & Fentiman, David. Lego Movie. (p. 990)
—Star Wars Rebels - Fight the Empire. (p. 1641)
Dorling Kindersley Publishing Staff & Forbeck, Matt. Battle Against Ultron. (p. 145)
Dorling Kindersley Publishing Staff & Foreman, Niki. DK Readers L3: Snappy Crocodile Tale: Snappy Crocodile Tale. (p. 456)
—Snappy Crocodile Tale. (p. 1597)
Dorling Kindersley Publishing Staff & Fry, Jason. Star Wars - The Secret Life of Droids. (p. 1641)
Dorling Kindersley Publishing Staff & Fullman, Joseph. Ancient Civilizations. (p. 68)
Dorling Kindersley Publishing Staff & Gamlin, Linda. Evolution. (p. 546)
Dorling Kindersley Publishing Staff & Gersh, Camilla. Frogs & Toads. (p. 641)
Dorling Kindersley Publishing Staff & Goldsmith, Mike. How to Be a Math Genius. (p. 814)
Dorling Kindersley Publishing Staff & Graham-Dixon, Andrew. Art: Over 2,500 Works from Cave to Contemporary. (p. 101)
Dorling Kindersley Publishing Staff & Grau, Andre. Dance. (p. 402)
Dorling Kindersley Publishing Staff & Greenaway, Theresa. Jungle - DK Eyewitness Books. Dann, Geoff, illus. (p. 934)
Dorling Kindersley Publishing Staff & Hall, Alvin D. Show Me the Money. (p. 1570)
Dorling Kindersley Publishing Staff & Harper, Benjamin. Feel the Force! (p. 580)
Dorling Kindersley Publishing Staff & Hastings, Selina. Children's Illustrated Bible. (p. 303)
Dorling Kindersley Publishing Staff & Hibbert, Clare. Boba Fett Jedi Hunter, Level 2. (p. 205)
—Clone Troopers in Action. (p. 333)
—Clone Wars - Jedi Heroes. (p. 333)
—Tatooine Adventures. (p. 1707)
—Tatooine Adventures, Level 1. (p. 1707)
Dorling Kindersley Publishing Staff & Hunt, Paul. Things That Go. (p. 1733)
Dorling Kindersley Publishing Staff & Ibbs, Katharine. DK Children's Cookbook. Shooter, Howard, photos by. (p. 455)
Dorling Kindersley Publishing Staff & Kent, Lindsay. Adventures of Han Solo, Level 2. (p. 18)
—The Adventures of Han Solo. (p. 1728)
—Ultimate Duels, Level 4. (p. 1809)
Dorling Kindersley Publishing Staff & Khatreja, Himani. DK Readers L2: LEGO Star Wars: Free the Galaxy. (p. 456)
Dorling Kindersley Publishing Staff & Langley, Andrew. Medieval Life. (p. 1119)
Dorling Kindersley Publishing Staff & Last, Shari. DK Readers L1: the LEGO Movie: Meet Unikitty! The LEGO Movie: Meet Unikitty! (p. 456)
—Let's Mix! (p. 999)
—Meet the Heroes. (p. 1122)
—Meet the Heroes, Level 2. (p. 1122)
—Meet the Mixels. (p. 1123)
—The Adventures of C-3PO. (p. 1728)
Dorling Kindersley Publishing Staff & Lipkowitz, Daniel. Character Encyclopedia. (p. 291)
—Dark Side. (p. 408)
—LEGO Ideas Book. (p. 990)
—Yoda Chronicles. (p. 1972)
Dorling Kindersley Publishing Staff & Lippincott, Kristen. Eyewitness Books - Astronomy. (p. 558)
Dorling Kindersley Publishing Staff & Lock, Deborah. African Adventure. (p. 26)
—DK Adventures: Terrors of the Deep: Terrors of the Deep. (p. 455)
—Emperor Penguins, Level 2. (p. 521)
—Terrors of the Deep. (p. 1722)
Dorling Kindersley Publishing Staff & Mack, Lorrie. Big Babies, Little Babies. (p. 177)
Dorling Kindersley Publishing Staff & Manning, Matthew. Iron Man: The Ultimate Guide to the Armored Super Hero. (p. 888)
Dorling Kindersley Publishing Staff & Manning, Matthew K. Wolverine. (p. 1944)
Dorling Kindersley Publishing Staff & March, Julia. Chima Power Up! (p. 306)
—Heroes into Battle. (p. 773)
—Power Up! (p. 1390)
Dorling Kindersley Publishing Staff & Matthews, Rupert. Battle in the Air. (p. 146)
Dorling Kindersley Publishing Staff & Mitton, Jacqueline. Moon. (p. 1171)
Dorling Kindersley Publishing Staff & Murdoch, David S. North American Indian. (p. 1264)
Dorling Kindersley Publishing Staff & Murphy, Patricia J. DK Readers L3: Hope for the Elephants: Hope for the Elephants. (p. 456)
—Hope for the Elephants. (p. 796)
Dorling Kindersley Publishing Staff & Nahum, Andrew. Flight. (p. 604)
Dorling Kindersley Publishing Staff & O'Hara, Scarlett. Angry Birds: Path to the Pork Side. (p. 75)
—Angry Birds: Darth Swindle's Secrets. (p. 75)
—Darth Swindle's Secrets. (p. 409)
—Path to the Pork Side. (p. 1328)
Dorling Kindersley Publishing Staff & Parachute Press Staff, creators. Farm ABC. (p. 573)
Dorling Kindersley Publishing Staff & Parachute Press Staff. Tractor. (p. 1775)
Dorling Kindersley Publishing Staff & Parker, Steve. Fish. (p. 598)
Dorling Kindersley Publishing Staff & Pearson, Nicole. My First Halloween Board Book. (p. 1206)
Dorling Kindersley Publishing Staff & Platt, Richard. Spy. (p. 1635)
Dorling Kindersley Publishing Staff & Putnam, James. Mummy. (p. 1191)
Dorling Kindersley Publishing Staff & Ring, Susan. Mammals (p. 1085)
Dorling Kindersley Publishing Staff & Saunders, Catherine. Brain Attack! (p. 221)
—Brain Wars. (p. 222)
—Darth Maul Sith Apprentice. (p. 409)
—Legendary Yoda. (p. 989)
—Legendary Yoda, Level 3. (p. 989)
—Lego Friends - Let's Go Riding! (p. 990)
—Let's Go Riding!, Level 2. (p. 997)
—Summer Adventures. (p. 1673)
—Summer Adventures, Level 3. (p. 1673)
Dorling Kindersley Publishing Staff & Scott, Heather. Stand Aside - Bounty Hunters! (p. 1639)
Dorling Kindersley Publishing Staff & Smith, Alison. Sewing Book: Clothes - Home Accessories - Best Tools - Step-by-Step Techniques - Creative Projects. (p. 1556)
Dorling Kindersley Publishing Staff & Snider, Brandon T. DC Comics Ultimate Character Guide. (p. 415)
Dorling Kindersley Publishing Staff & Stamps, Caroline. How to ... Horseback Riding. (p. 814)
Dorling Kindersley Publishing Staff & Stock, Lisa. Battle for Naboo. (p. 145)
Dorling Kindersley Publishing Staff & Stone, Caroline. Islam. (p. 891)
Dorling Kindersley Publishing Staff & Taylor, Victoria. Around Town, Level 1. (p. 101)
—On the Farm. (p. 1290)
—Ready for Action! (p. 1447)
—Super-Villains Level 2. (p. 1682)
—Super-Villians. (p. 1682)
Dorling Kindersley Publishing Staff & Unicef, India Country Office. A School Like Mine: A Unique Celebration of Schools Around the World. (p. 1)

D

Dorling Kindersley Publishing Staff & Vorderman, Carol. Math Dictionary. (p. 1105)
Dorling Kindersley Publishing Staff & Walker, Richard. Human Body. (p. 825)
Dorling Kindersley Publishing Staff & Wallace, Daniel. Battle for the Galaxy. (p. 145)
—Spider-Man Character Encyclopedia. (p. 1626)
Dorling Kindersley Publishing Staff & Wilkinson, Philip. Myths & Legends: Stories Gods Heroes Monsters. (p. 1227)
Dorling Kindersley Publishing Staff & Windham, Ryder. Star Wars: the Ultimate Visual Guide: The Ultimate Visual Guide. (p. 1642)
Dorling Kindersley Publishing Staff & Winston, Robert. Utterly Amazing Science. (p. 1829)
Dorling Kindersley Publishing Staff & Woodward, John. Horses: The Ultimate Treasury. (p. 800)
Dorling Kindersley Publishing Staff, creator. Aircraft. (p. 31)
—Baby Says Peekaboo! (p. 128)
—Bedtime Peekaboo! (p. 157)
—Butterflies. (p. 247)
—Cars. (p. 271)
—Castle & Knight. (p. 276)
—Dog. (p. 460)
—Grow It Cook It. (p. 726)
—Kitten: More Than 60 Reusable Full Colos Stickers. (p. 962)
—My First Spanish Body Board Book/Mi Primer Libro del Cuerpo. (p. 1208)
—Puppy. (p. 1418)
—Reptile. (p. 1461)
—Train. (p. 1777)
—Ultimate Sticker Book - Jungle. (p. 1810)
Dorling Kindersley Publishing Staff, ed. Baby Animals. (p. 124)
—Buenas Noches, Bebe! / Good Night, Baby! (p. 235)
—Buenos Dias, Bebe! (p. 235)
—Bulldozer. (p. 240)
—Clone Wars. (p. 333)
—Dangerous Dinosaurs. (p. 404)
—Digger. (p. 438)
—Doodlepedia Wow. (p. 469)
—Farm. (p. 573)
—Hanukkah. (p. 743)
—Noisy Farm. (p. 1263)
—Princess. (p. 1402)
—Shark & Whale. (p. 1562)
—Space. (p. 1618)
—Star Wars. (p. 1641)
—Truck. (p. 1791)
—WWE Triple H. (p. 1966)
—WWE Undertaker. (p. 1966)
Dorling Kindersley Publishing Staff, et al. Character Encyclopedia. (p. 291)
—Clone Wars - Pirates... & Worse. (p. 333)
—First Atlas. (p. 593)
—Jungle Adventure. (p. 935)
—Jungle Adventures. (p. 935)
—Planets in Peril. (p. 1368)
—Visual Dictionary. (p. 1846)
—WWE Ultimate Superstar Guide. (p. 1966)
Dormal, Alexis, illus. see Roques, Dominique.
Dorman, Brandon. Pirates of the Sea! Dorman, Brandon, illus. (p. 1364)
—Santa's Stowaway. Dorman, Brandon, illus. (p. 1513)
—Slippery Map. (p. 1590)
Dorman, Brandon, illus. see Beck, Glenn, et al.
Dorman, Brandon, illus. see Berger, Melvin & Berger, Gilda.
Dorman, Brandon, illus. see Berkeley, Jon.
Dorman, Brandon, illus. see Bird, Betsy.
Dorman, Brandon, illus. see Bode, N. E.
Dorman, Brandon, illus. see Boylan, Jennifer Finney.
Dorman, Brandon, illus. see Buehner, Caralyn.
Dorman, Brandon, illus. see Colfer, Chris.
Dorman, Brandon, illus. see Dashner, James.
Dorman, Brandon, illus. see Finn, Perdita.
Dorman, Brandon, illus. see Hale, Bruce.
Dorman, Brandon, illus. see Haydon, Elizabeth.
Dorman, Brandon, illus. see Jonell, Lynne.
Dorman, Brandon, illus. see Kennedy, Emma.
Dorman, Brandon, illus. see Mull, Brandon.
Dorman, Brandon, illus. see Murray, Marjorie Dennis & Murray, Marjorie D.
Dorman, Brandon, illus. see Murray, Marjorie Dennis.
Dorman, Brandon, illus. see Nelson, Wendy Watson.
Dorman, Brandon, illus. see Prelutsky, Jack.
Dorman, Brandon, illus. see Riley, J. D.
Dorman, Brandon, illus. see Snyder, Laurel.
Dorman, Brandon, illus. see Tegen, Katherine Brown.
Dorman, Brandon, illus. see Thornley, Rebecca Gundersen.
Dorman, Clive, jt. auth. see Dorman, Helen.
Dorman, Clive & Dorman, Helen. Okomi Enjoys His Outings Hutchings, Tony, illus. (p. 1283)
—Okomi Goes Fishing Hutchings, Tony, illus. (p. 1283)
—Okomi Wakes up Early Hutchings, Tony, illus. (p. 1283)
—Okomi Wanders Too Far Hutchings, Tony, illus. (p. 1283)
Dorman, Daniel, illus. see Theisen, Sue.
Dorman, Genie. Bubble Monster. (p. 233)
Dorman, Helen, jt. auth. see Dorman, Clive.
Dorman, Helen & Dorman, Clive. Okomi & the Tickling Game Hutchings, Tony, illus. (p. 1283)
—Okomi Climbs a Tree Hutchings, Tony, illus. (p. 1283)
—Okomi Plays in the Leaves Hutchings, Tony, illus. (p. 1283)
—Okomi, the New Baby. Hutchings, Tony, illus. (p. 1283)
Dorman, Jennifer. Are Women Paid Fairly? (p. 96)
Dorman, Robert L. Oklahoma: Past & Present. (p. 1283)
Dormer, Cindy. Hold That Thought for Kids: Capturing Precious Memories Through Fun Questions, Images & Conversations. (p. 788)
Dormer, Frank W. Socksquatch. Dormer, Frank W., illus. (p. 1605)
—Sword in the Stove. (p. 1692)
Dormer, Frank W., illus. see Ries, Lori, et al.
Dormer, Frank W., illus. see Ries, Lori.
Dormer, Frank W., illus. see Trine, Greg.
Dorn, Owen A. Ruth: A Love Story. (p. 1498)
Dorn, Susy. Canternos en Español Song-Book: Spanish Learning Song-Book for Children. Carbajal, Diego, illus. (p. 262)
—Sal y Pimienta Song-Book: Spanish Learning Song-Book for Children. Carbajal, Diego, illus. (p. 1504)
Dornan, Dave. Tree Talkers: A Christmas Story Swope, Brenda, illus. (p. 1783)
Dornan, Rae. Sunbuddy Fables. (p. 1676)
Dornbush, Jennifer. Picadilly Children's Ballet: A Ferda & Felicity Big Apple Adventure. (p. 1354)
Dornemann, Volker, illus. see Rumpf, Wolfgang.
Dornemann, Volker, jt. auth. see Rumpf, Wolfgang.
Dorner, Nancy L. Crackerjack the Christmas Cat. Alphenaar, Pamela L., illus. (p. 375)
Dorner, V. K. Little Lambs & the Rainbow Zebra. (p. 1030)
Dornfeld, Margaret. Bats. (p. 144)
—Vermont. (p. 1837)
Dornfeld, Margaret & Hantula, Richard. Wisconsin. (p. 1939)
Dornfeld, Margaret & Hart, Joyce. Maine. (p. 1077)
Dornfest, Asha. Front Page 2003 for Dummies(r). (p. 644)
Doro, Ann. Missing Canary. (p. 1152)
Doron. Look in the Mirror. (p. 1049)
—Look in the Mirror... (p. 1049)
Dorothy Disanto-Morrell. Dorotea & Friends Visit the Hospital. (p. 471)
Dorothy, Grandma. Magic, Mystery, Adventure: Wild Animals Talk to Us. (p. 1072)
Dorpinghaus, Penny. Fear Balls & Button Wads. (p. 579)
Dorr, Shay. Khloe Dutch! (p. 951)
Dorrian, James G., contrib. by. Lullabys for Starry Nights. (p. 1064)
Dorricott, Jean. Science & Religion. (p. 1525)
Dörrie, Doris, jt. auth. see Dorrie, Doris.
Dorrie, Doris & Dörrie, Doris. Luisa Quiere Ser Princesa. Kaergel, Julia, illus. (p. 1064)
Dorrie, Roxanne. Venus & Serena Williams: The Smashing Sisters (p. 1836)
Dorris, Donna & Parker, Martha. Test Prepartation Guide for AAPA 303, Annuity Systems & Administration. (p. 1723)
Dorris, Michael. Morning Girl. (p. 1175)
—Sees Behind Trees. (p. 1548)
—Tainos. Escrivá, Viví, illus. (p. 1696)
Dorris, Peggy. Dragon. Knox, Dahk, ed. (p. 476)
Dorros, Arthur. Abuelo. Colón, Raúl, illus. (p. 7)
—City Chicken. (p. 323)
—City Chicken. Cole, Henry, illus. (p. 323)
—Isla. (p. 891)
—Julio's Magic. (p. 932)
—Julio's Magic. Grifalconi, Ann, illus. (p. 932)
—Mama & Me. Gutierrez, Rudy, illus. (p. 1084)
—Papá & Me. Gutierrez, Rudy, illus. (p. 1321)
Dorros, Arthur, illus. see Branley, Franklyn M.
Dorset, Skylar. Boy with the Hidden Name. (p. 220)
—Girl Who Never Was. (p. 679)
Dorsey, Angela. Abandoned. (p. 2)
—Autumn in Snake Canyon. (p. 118)
—Autumn of Angels. (p. 118)
—Fighting Chance. (p. 585)
—Horse Angel Comic: Rough Diamond. (p. 799)
—Horse Angel Comic - the Desert King. (p. 799)
—Silver Dream. (p. 1576)
—Spring of Secrets. (p. 1635)
—Spring of the Poacher's Moon. (p. 1635)
—Summer of Desperate Races. (p. 1674)
—Summer of Wild Hearts. (p. 1674)
—Time Thief. (p. 1752)
—Winter of Sinking Waters. (p. 1938)
—Winter of the Crystal Dances. (p. 1938)
—Winter of the Whinnies Brigade. (p. 1938)
Dorsey, Angela & Miller, Marina. Sun Catcher. (p. 1676)
—Sun Chaser. (p. 1676)
Dorsey, C. Unsacred Gift. (p. 1822)
Dorsey, Colleen. Epic Rubber Band Crafts: Totally Cool Gadget Gear, Never Before Seen Bracelets, Awesome Action Figures, & More! (p. 532)
—Super Sands! Awesome Activities for Sands Alive! And Kinetic Sand. (p. 1680)
—Totally Awesome Rubber Band Jewelry: Make Bracelets, Rings, Belts & More with Rainbow Loom(r), Cra-Z-Loom & FunLoom. (p. 1771)
Dorsey, Kathleen. Building Vocabulary with Familiar Songs: A Unique & Fun Way to Motivate Students to Play with Language & Enrich Their Vocabulary. (p. 239)
Dorsey, Maggie. My Hero, My Dad, the Nurse. (p. 1211)
Dorsey, Maggie Thurmond. My Hero, My Dad the Nurse Knocked Out Cancer. (p. 1211)
D'Orso, Michael. Eagle Blue: A Team, a Tribe, & a High School Basketball Season in Arctic Alaska. (p. 492)
Dortch, Chris, et al. Greatest Rivalries in Sports. (p. 720)
Dos Anjos, Charles, jt. auth. see Shealy, Larry.
Dos Santos, Julie. Aircraft. (p. 31)
—Diggers. (p. 439)
—Trucks. (p. 1791)
Dos Santos, Lisa. Grandpa's Bridge. (p. 709)
dos Santos, Steven. Culling. (p. 390)
—Sowing. (p. 1618)
Doscher, E. L. M. S. Emmy Sue & the Blue Moo. Doscher, Susan, illus. (p. 520)
Doscher, Melissa. Yale University College Prowler off the Record. (p. 1968)
Doscher, Susan, illus. see Doscher, E. L. M. S.
Doss, Andrea, illus. see Bell, Lucy.
Doss, Carson. Ramblings of a Grandfather. (p. 1437)
Doss, Jessi. Percy the Uncolorful Peacock (p. 1341)
Dossantos, Laurie Staples. Adventures of Stormy. (p. 23)
Dostis, Isaac & Haddad Ikonomopoulos, Marcia. Ten Gold Medals: Glory or Freedom. (p. 1718)
Dostoevsky, Fyodor. Crime & Punishment - Literary Touchstone Edition. (p. 382)
—Crimen y Castigo. (p. 382)
—Fiodor Mijailovich Dostoievsky. Acosta, Patricia, illus. (p. 589)
Dostoevsky, Fyodor, ed. Crimen y Castigo. (p. 382)
DOT. My Grandkids Need to Go Home! (p. 1210)
Doti Chavez, Caryn. Invisible Isabelle... As Told by Jimmy Pizzelli. Gillen, Rosemarie, illus. (p. 885)
Doti, James. Jimmy Finds His Voice. Mertins, Lisa, illus. (p. 918)
Dotlich, Rebecca Kai. Bella & Bean. Leijten, Aileen, illus. (p. 162)
—Digger the Dinosaur. (p. 438)
—Digger the Dinosaur. Gynux, illus. (p. 438)
—Digger the Dinosaur & the Cake Mistake. (p. 438)
—Digger the Dinosaur & the Cake Mistake. Gynux, illus. (p. 438)
—In the Spin of Things: Poetry of Motion. Dugan, Karen, illus. (p. 867)
—Mama Loves. Brown, Kathryn, illus. (p. 1084)
—Peanut & Pearl's Picnic Adventure. Alley, R. W., illus. (p. 1332)
—What Is Science? Yoshikawa, Sachiko, illus. (p. 1890)
—When Riddles Come Rumbling: Poems to Ponder. Dugan, Karen, illus. (p. 1904)
Dotlich, Rebecca Kai, jt. auth. see Yolen, Jane.
Dotson, Dolores. This Is Your Seasin: Where You Will Find Rest for Your Soul. (p. 1737)
Dotson, Jacob. React & Rise Up (p. 1442)
Dotson, Kyt. Specter in the Spectacles. (p. 1624)
Dotson-Lewis, B. L. Appalachia: Spirit Triumphant. (p. 92)
D'Ottavi, Francesca. Isis & Osiris (p. 891)
D'Ottavi, Francesca, illus. see Bell, Michael & Quie, Sarah.
D'Ottavi, Francesca, illus. see Evans, Lynette.
D'Ottavi, Francesca, illus. see Griswood, John, ed.
D'Ottavi, Francesca, illus. see Kuhtz, Cleo & Martell, Hazel.
D'Ottavi, Francesca, illus. see Matthews, Rupert & Van Pelt, Todd.
D'Ottavi, Francesca, illus. see Morris, Neil & Morris, Ting.
D'Ottavi, Francesca, illus. see Scurman, Ike & Malam, John.
D'Ottavi, Francesca, illus. see Yomtov, Nel.
D'Ottavi, Francesca, illus. see Yomtov, Nelson.
Dotterweich, Kass. What Catholic Teens Should Know about Divorce. Larkin, Jean, ed. (p. 1881)
Dotterweich, Kass P. 25 Stories for Sharing Faith with Teens: Making Connections. Cannizzo, Karen A., ed. (p. 1996)
Dotts, M. Franklin, ed. see Halverson, Delia Touchton.
Dotty, Zens, illus. see Rolling, Greg.
Doty, Eldon. Truth & Rumors (p. 1794)
Doty, Eldon, illus. see Burgan, Michael.
Doty, Eldon, illus. see Montgomery, Heather L.
Doty, Eldon, illus. see Price, Sean Stewart.
Doty, Eldon, illus. see Shores, Lori.
Doty, Eldon, illus. see Spengler, Kremena T.
Doty, Eldon, illus. see Wooster, Patricia.
Doty, Eldon C., illus. see Pearson, Mary E.
Doty, Jean Slaughter. Can I Get There by Candlelight? (p. 258)
—Gabriel. (p. 652)
—If Wishes Were Horses. (p. 854)
—Summer Pony. Sanderson, Ruth, illus. (p. 1674)
—Valley of the Ponies. (p. 1831)
—Winter Pony. Sanderson, Ruth, illus. (p. 1938)
Doty, Kathryn Adams. Wild Orphan. (p. 1930)
Doty, Linda. Hydrangea Hill: A New Home for Amy Manchester. (p. 831)
—In Search of the Robin. (p. 865)
Doty, M. Surviving High School. (p. 1687)
Doty, Mariel. Different Kind of Princess: Pictures of You. (p. 438)
Doty, Richard C. & Cooper, Timothy S. Exempt from Disclosure: UFOs, Aliens, Rick Doty, Mj12, Area 51/S4, LANL Reverse Engineering in the Z-Division, Crystal Rectangle (p. 548)
Doty, Sara. You Are Special Little Bee. Dawley, Sarah, illus. (p. 1973)
Doubilet, David. Fish Face. (p. 598)
—Water Light Time. (p. 1863)
Doubilet, David, jt. auth. see Hayes, Jennifer.
Doubleday, Dorothy, illus. see Minarik, Else Holmelund.
Doubleday, Russell. Stories of Inventors. (p. 1655)
Doucet, Alexandra. Going to a Horse Show: Equestrian Showing. (p. 693)
Doucet, Bob. Cat Craze (p. 277)
—Fact & Fable: State Stories (p. 561)
Doucet, Bob, illus. see Abdo, Kenny.
Doucet, Bob, illus. see Dolphin, Colleen.
Doucet, Bob, illus. see Gaarder-Juntti, Oona.
Doucet, Bob, illus. see Hanson, Anders.
Doucet, Bob, illus. see Hengel, Katherine.
Doucet, Bob, illus. see Roberts, G. Gregory.
Doucet, Bob, illus. see Salzmann, Mary Elizabeth.
Doucet, Bob, illus. see Scheunemann, Pam.
Doucet, Bob, illus. see Tuminelly, Nancy.
Doucet, Patricia. Adventures of Blackie & Brownie. (p. 16)
Doucet, Sharon Arms. Fiddle Fever. (p. 583)
Doucette, Christina. Gordon's Treasure! A Sparkle Cove Adventure. (p. 702)
Doucette, Constance, illus. see Ballard, Lisa.
Doud, Guy Rice. Stuff You Gotta Know: Straight Talk on Real Life. (p. 1670)
Doudna, Kelly. Any Day but Today! (p. 90)
—Are Buses Big? (p. 96)
—Art from the Mart. (p. 102)
—Baby African Animals (p. 124)
—Balloons Go up, up, up! (p. 135)
—Bashful Ball Pythons. Nobens, C. A., illus. (p. 141)
—Billy Goat Can Float. (p. 187)
—Boys & Girls Around the World: Set of 6. (p. 220)
—Boys & Girls Around the World. (p. 220)
—Bret & His Pet. (p. 226)
—Bride & the Slide. (p. 227)
—Can You Fly? (p. 259)
—Cheeky Chinchillas. Nobens, C. A., illus. (p. 295)
—Clothing Around the World. (p. 334)
—Crab Cakes. Haberstroh, Anne, illus. (p. 375)
—Crook Can Cook! (p. 384)
—Culture Around the World. (p. 391)
—Dip the Chip. (p. 445)
—Dip the Chip! (6-pack) (p. 445)
—Doggie Pants. Haberstroh, Anne, illus. (p. 462)
—Emma & Eddie. (p. 519)
—Et As in Jet. (p. 539)
—Eva & Ethan. (p. 540)
—Fay & Felix. (p. 578)
—Flock on the Dock. (p. 605)
—Flora & Floyd. (p. 606)
—Fran & Fred. (p. 627)
—Frisky Ferrets. Craig, Diane, ed. (p. 639)
—Gail & Gary. (p. 652)
—Gina & George. (p. 676)
—Give It a Try! (p. 681)
—Gladys & Glen. (p. 682)
—Goat Cheese. Haberstroh, Anne, illus. (p. 687)
—Goose Down. Haberstroh, Anne, illus. (p. 702)
—Grace & Grant. (p. 704)
—Grant's Aunts from France. (p. 710)
—Gwen the Hen. (p. 733)
—Hannah & Henry. (p. 742)
—Hidden Hermit Crabs. (p. 775)
—Hilarious Hedgehogs. Nobens, C. A., illus. (p. 779)
—Homing Pigeon. Chawla, Neena, illus. (p. 794)
—Honestly! Craig, Diane, ed. (p. 794)
—Id As in Squid. (p. 851)
—Ida & Ike. (p. 851)
—If You Prefer, I'll Use a Thermometer! (p. 854)
—Ig As in Pig. Marx, Monica, ed. (p. 855)
—Ill As in Grill. (p. 856)
—I'll Use a Hand Lens with My Friends! (p. 856)
—Ill Use Information for My Explanation! (p. 856)
—Im on a Roll with Variable Control! (p. 859)
—In As in Twin. (p. 863)
—India & Iggy. (p. 871)
—Ip As in Ship. (p. 886)
—Is It a Party? (p. 889)
—Is the TV On? (p. 890)
—It As in Sit. (p. 893)
—It Is Cloudy. (p. 894)
—It Is My Hat. (p. 894)
—It Is Raining. (p. 894)
—It Is Snowing. (p. 894)
—It Is Stormy. (p. 894)
—It Is Sunny. (p. 894)
—It Is Windy. (p. 894)
—It's a Baby African Elephant! (p. 895)
—It's a Baby Baboon! (p. 895)
—It's a Baby Beaver! (p. 895)
—It's a Baby Black Bear! (p. 895)
—It's a Baby Cheetah! (p. 895)
—It's a Baby Chimpanzee! (p. 895)
—It's a Baby Gazelle! (p. 895)
—It's a Baby Giraffe! (p. 895)
—It's a Baby Gray Wolf! (p. 895)
—It's a Baby Hippopotamus! (p. 895)
—It's a Baby Kangaroo! (p. 895)
—It's a Baby Lion! (p. 895)
—It's a Baby Lynx! (p. 895)
—It's a Baby Meerkat! (p. 895)
—It's a Baby Moose! (p. 895)
—It's a Baby Mustang! (p. 895)
—It's a Baby Opossum! (p. 895)
—It's a Baby Prairie Dog! (p. 895)
—It's a Baby Raccoon! (p. 895)
—It's a Baby Red Fox! (p. 895)
—It's a Baby Rhinoceros! (p. 895)
—It's a Baby Skunk! (p. 895)
—It's a Baby White-Tailed Deer! (p. 895)
—It's a Baby Wildebeest! (p. 895)
—It's a Baby Zebra! (p. 895)
—It's a Date, Let's Investigate! (p. 895)
—It's an Event When We Experiment! (p. 896)
—It's K ! (p. 897)
—It's My Mission to Make a Definition! (p. 897)
—It's My Pleasure to Measure the Treasure! (p. 897)
—It's Not Too Late, Let's Communicate! (p. 898)
—It's T ! (p. 899)
—It's Time to Dance, We Can Use a Balance! (p. 899)
—Jelly Bean Machine. (p. 912)
—Jellyfish Role. Chawla, Neena, illus. (p. 912)
—Jump from the Stump. (p. 934)
—Just Make Some Art! (p. 939)
—Keep Your Cool! (p. 947)
—Kid's Book of Simple Everyday Science. (p. 952)
—Kids' Book of Simple Machines: Cool Projects & Activities That Make Science Fun! (p. 952)
—Kids' Book of Simple Machines. (p. 952)
—Knead with Speed, Chef Mead! (p. 964)
—Lamb Chops. Chawla, Neena, illus. (p. 972)
—Lana de la Oveja. Chawla, Neena, illus. (p. 972)
—Let's Add Bills. (p. 994)
—Let's Add Coins. (p. 994)
—Let's Add Money. (p. 994)
—Let's Be Kids & Measure Liquids! (p. 994)
—Let's Subtract Bills. (p. 1000)
—Let's Subtract Coins. (p. 1000)
—Let's Subtract Money. (p. 1000)
—Look Your Best! (p. 1050)
—Mermaid Parade. (p. 1128)
—Mischievous Mosquitoes. (p. 1150)
—Moe's Toes Froze. (p. 1160)
—My Brother, My Sister. (p. 1199)
—My House Is Big! (p. 1211)
—Orejas del Conejo. Nobens, C. A., illus. (p. 1303)
—Ow As in Crow. (p. 1314)
—Pack Rat. Chawla, Neena, illus. (p. 1317)
—Parrot Crackers. Haberstroh, Anne, illus. (p. 1325)
—Peinado Del Gallo. Haberstroh, Anne, illus. (p. 1335)
—Penguin Suit. Chawla, Neena, illus. (p. 1337)
—People Around the World. (p. 1339)
—Pin in the Bin. (p. 1359)
—Play Fair! (p. 1371)
—Rabbit Ears. Nobens, C. A., illus. (p. 1429)
—Rabbit Ears. Nobens, Cheryl A., illus. (p. 1429)
—Rascally Rabbits. (p. 1439)
—Rata Coleccionista. Chawla, Neena, illus. (p. 1440)

—Religions Around the World. (p. 1458)
—Right on Time! (p. 1472)
—Rooster Combs. Haberstroh, Anne, illus. (p. 1488)
—Running Rats. (p. 1497)
—School Around the World. (p. 1522)
—Sheep Is Asleep. (p. 1564)
—She'll Use a Ruler So You Won't Fool Her! (p. 1564)
—Snake Charmer. (p. 1596)
—Sound Words. (p. 1615)
—Speak Up! (p. 1622)
—Splish Splash. (p. 1630)
—Squeak from My Cheek. (p. 1636)
—Squirrel Hollow. Chawla, Neena, illus. (p. 1637)
—Stand Up! (p. 1639)
—Super Simple Science (p. 1681)
—Super Simple Things to Do with Balloons: Fun & Easy Science for Kids. (p. 1681)
—Super Simple Things to Do with Bubbles: Fun & Easy Science for Kids. (p. 1681)
—Super Simple Things to Do with Plants: Fun & Easy Science for Kids. (p. 1681)
—Super Simple Things to Do with Temperature: Fun & Easy Science for Kids. (p. 1681)
—Super Simple Things to Do with Water: Fun & Easy Science for Kids. (p. 1681)
—There Are Ants down There! (p. 1729)
—Tick Tock. (p. 1747)
—To the Camp! (p. 1759)
—Tweet Fleet. (p. 1800)
—Tweet Fleet (6-pack) (p. 1800)
—Universe. (p. 1820)
—Up the Path. (p. 1824)
—Use Your Eye, Let's Classify! (p. 1827)
—Was That Fun? (p. 1859)
—We Are Wise, Let's Hypothesize! (p. 1866)
—We Can Jump! (p. 1866)
—We Go to the Park. (p. 1867)
—We Have the Nerve, Now Let's Observe! (p. 1867)
—When Can You Play Again? (p. 1901)
Doudna, Kelly, jt. auth. see ABDO Publishing Company Staff.
Doudna, Kelly, jt. auth. see Beck, Esther.
Doudna, Kelly, jt. auth. see Craig, Diane.
Doudna, Kelly, jt. auth. see Pederson, Bridget.
Dougall, Alastair & Dorling Kindersley Publishing Staff. Spider-Man. (p. 1626)
Dougall, Edwin. T. V. Tangle. (p. 1694)
Dougan, Michael, jt. auth. see Dougan, Michael B.
Dougan, Michael B. & Dougan, Michael. Uniquely Arkansas (p. 1818)
Dougherty, Brandi. Friendship Experiment. (p. 639)
—Littlest Christmas Star. Richards, Kirsten & Rescek, Sanja, illus. (p. 1039)
—Littlest Elf. Richards, Kirsten, illus. (p. 1039)
—Littlest Elf. Richards, Kristen, illus. (p. 1039)
—Littlest Pilgrim. Richards, Kristen, illus. (p. 1039)
—Valentine's Day Disaster. (p. 1830)
Dougherty, Charles L., illus. see Betz, Eva K.
Dougherty, Charles L., illus. see McHugh, Michael.
Dougherty, Chris. I Must Become Less: Making More Room in. (p. 844)
Dougherty, Dan, illus. see Corchin, Dj.
Dougherty, Denis. Michael Vick. (p. 1135)
Dougherty, Jane L. Pig Party. (p. 1357)
Dougherty, John. Bansi O'Hara & the Bloodline Prophecy. (p. 136)
—Bansi O'Hara & the Edges of Halloween. (p. 136)
—Niteracy Hour. (p. 1257)
Dougherty, Karla. Jealousy: Triumphing over Rivalry & Envy. (p. 911)
Dougherty, Kristen M. Kiki B. Mamus: A Year without Mom. (p. 955)
Dougherty, Martin. Most Amazing Weapons of War (p. 1177)
—Secrets of Martial Arts Masters. (p. 1545)
Dougherty, Martin, jt. auth. see Scholastic, Inc. Staff.
Dougherty, Martin J. Air Warfare. (p. 31)
—Aircraft. (p. 31)
—Land Warfare. (p. 974)
—Most Amazing Weapons of War (p. 1177)
—Sea Warfare. (p. 1536)
—Secrets of Martial Arts Masters (p. 1545)
—Weapons & Technology. (p. 1869)
Dougherty, Mary. Life Adventures with Fossy. (p. 1007)
Dougherty, Meghan. Rise of the Undead Redhead. Bimbach, Alece, illus. (p. 1475)
—Woe of Jade Doe. Bimbach, Alece, illus. (p. 1943)
Dougherty, Mike, jt. ed. see Kallas, Randi.
Dougherty, Rachel, illus. see Gunderson, Jessica.
Dougherty, Rachel, illus. see Peaslee Levine, Martha.
Dougherty, Steve. Attack on Pearl Harbor: World War II Strikes Home in the USA. (p. 114)
—Idi Amin. (p. 852)
—Justin Timberlake. (p. 940)
—Pearl Harbor: The U. S. Enters World War II. (p. 1333)
Dougherty, Steven. Idi Amin. (p. 852)
—Pearl Harbor: The U. S. Enters World War II. (p. 1333)
Dougherty, Terri. Admiral David Farragut: "Full Speed Ahead!" (p. 13)
—Anatomy of a Flood (p. 67)
—Anatomy of a Hurricane (p. 67)
—Anatomy of a Tornado (p. 67)
—Ben Stiller. (p. 163)
—Daniel Radcliffe. (p. 405)
—Freedom of Expression & the Internet. (p. 634)
—Ichiro Suzuki. (p. 851)
—Illinois. (p. 857)
—Jennifer Lopez. (p. 913)
—Raven-Symoné. (p. 1441)
—Salma Hayek. (p. 1505)
—Search for the Titanic: Finding the Ship's Watery Grave (p. 1537)
—Sexually Transmitted Diseases. (p. 1556)
—Titanic's Crew: Working Aboard the Great Ship (p. 1758)
—Tobey Maguire. (p. 1760)
—Tyra Banks. (p. 1805)
—Worst Hurricanes of All Time. (p. 1961)
—Worst Tornadoes of All Time (p. 1961)
—Worst Tsunamis of All Time (p. 1961)
Dougherty, Terri, jt. auth. see Sievert, Terri.
Dougherty, Terri & Gale Editors. Epilepsy. (p. 532)
Dougherty, Terri & Hillstrom, Kevin. Brett Favre. (p. 226)
Dougherty, Terri & Leavitt, Amie Jane. Disasters. (p. 447)
Dougherty, Terri & Sievert, Terri. 300 Heroes: The Battle of Thermopylae (p. 2001)
—America's Deadliest Day: The Battle of Antietam. (p. 64)
—Girls' Skateboarding: Skating to Be the Best. (p. 680)
—Mongol Warriors (p. 1164)
—Raising the Flag: The Battle of Iwo Jima. (p. 1437)
—World Collides: The Battle of Gallipoli (p. 1954)
Dougherty, Terri & Wacholtz, Anthony. Worst Floods of All Time (p. 1961)
Dougherty, Terri, et al. Sports Debate: A Rip-Roaring Game of Either-Or Questions. (p. 1632)
—Titanic Perspectives (p. 1758)
Dougherty, Terry. Rob Dyrdek's Fantasy Factory. (p. 1478)
Doughten, Naconda K. Sunny's Good Heart. (p. 1677)
Doughty, Clare, illus. see Hayler, Kate.
Doughty, Rebecca, illus. see Rosenthal, Amy Krouse.
Doughty, Rebecca, illus. see Ziefert, Harriet & Harriet, Ziefert.
Douglas, Alan. Afloat: Or Adventures on Watery Trails. (p. 26)
Douglas, Allen, illus. see Holt, Christopher.
Douglas, Allen, illus. see Hunter, Erin.
Douglas, Ana, illus. see Douglas, Bettye.
Douglas, Ann. Baby Science: How Babies Really Work! Desputeaux, Helene, illus. (p. 128)
Douglas, Atom. Mathew's Space Ship. (p. 1108)
Douglas, Babette. Amazing Grace. Rockwell, Barry, illus. (p. 54)
—Blue Wise. Johnson, John, illus. (p. 203)
—Curly Hare Gets It Straight. Williams, Ted, illus. (p. 394)
—Falcon Eddie. Johnson, John, illus. (p. 565)
—Kiss a Me: A Little Whale Watching. Rockwell, Barry, illus. (p. 961)
—Kiss a Me Goes to School. Rockwell, Barry, illus. (p. 961)
—Kiss a Me to the Rescue. Rockwell, Barry, illus. (p. 961)
—Larkspur: And His Wooden Nose. Johnson, John, illus. (p. 975)
—Lyon Bear. Johnson, John, illus. (p. 1066)
—Miss Evonne: And the Mice of Nice! Johnson, John, illus. (p. 1151)
—Noreen: The Real King of the Jungle. Johnson, John, illus. (p. 1264)
—Oscarpus. Rockwell, Barry, illus. (p. 1305)
—Rosebud. (p. 1489)
—Squirt: The Magic Cuddlefish. Williams, Ted, illus. (p. 1637)
Douglas, Bettye. Portrait of a People: The Bettye Douglas Forum, Inc. Multicultural Resource Book. Douglas, Bettye, ed. (p. 1386)
—Safari Oklahoma Presents: God Bless America Historical. Douglas, Garbrielle, illus. (p. 1502)
—Safari Oklahoma Presents: The Magic of Christmas Around the World. Douglas, Bettye, ed. (p. 1502)
Douglas, Donna. Miss Donna's Mulberry Acres Farm. Balzer, Gayle Susan, illus. (p. 1151)
Douglas, Eileen. Rachel & the Upside down Heart. (p. 1431)
Douglas, Erin. Get That Pest! Yee, Wong Herbert, illus. (p. 668)
—Get That Pest! / ¡Agarren a Ése! Campoy, F. Isabel & Flor Ada, Alma, trs. (p. 668)
Douglas, Erin & Yee, Wong Herbert. Get That Pest! (p. 668)
Douglas, Gabrielle & Burford, Michelle. Grace, Gold & Glory: My Leap of Faith (p. 704)
—Raising the Bar (p. 1437)
Douglas, Garbrielle, illus. see Douglas, Bettye.
Douglas, George, jt. auth. see Taylor, Ronald J.
Douglas, H. I. Voyage to the Stars: David's First Adventure. (p. 1850)
Douglas, Heather. Jesus loves the little Children: The Adventures of Katie & Gideon. (p. 916)
Douglas, Helen. After Eden. (p. 28)
Douglas, Janine, illus. see Wicke, Ed.
Douglas, Jozua. Dinosaurs. van Rheenen, Barbara, illus. (p. 443)
Douglas, Kathleen. Johnny, the Unaware Angel. (p. 923)
Douglas, Keith Cartoon Man, illus. see St. Pierre, Todd-Michael.
Douglas, L. B. Looking for Moemoe: Love Is never far Away. (p. 1051)
Douglas, Lisa Jo. Active Animals A Thru Z. (p. 10)
Douglas, Lloyd G. American Flag. (p. 60)
—Bald Eagle. (p. 133)
—Crab. (p. 375)
—Jellyfish. (p. 912)
—Kelp. (p. 948)
—Liberty Bell. (p. 1005)
—My Ears. (p. 1202)
—My Eyes. (p. 1202)
—My Legs & Feet. (p. 1211)
—My Mouth. (p. 1215)
—Statue of Liberty. (p. 1645)
—White House. (p. 1913)
Douglas, Lola, jt. auth. see Simmons, Cari.
Douglas, Margaret. Spirit of Meradoon. (p. 1628)
Douglas, Marianne. How to Deal When Your Middle Name Is Stress: Real Teens - Real Advice. (p. 816)
Douglas, Marjory Stoneman & Milkweed Editions Staff. Alligator Crossing. Nicholson, Trudy, illus. (p. 47)
Douglas, Murray & Irvine, Chippy. Brunschwig & Fils up Close: From Grand Rooms to Your Rooms. (p. 232)
Douglas, Paul & Spieler, Marlena. Tennis: Breaks down the Subject into 101 Easy-to-Grasp Tips. (p. 1720)
Douglas, Punchye. Safari Oklahoma Presents: Thanksgiving History Coloring Book. (p. 1502)
—Safari Oklahoma Presents Operation Safe 2000: Halloween Coloring Book. (p. 1502)
Douglas, Punchye, illus. see Douglas, Bettye.
Douglas, Rachel. "You're a Meany!" Drewes, Dan, illus. (p. 1982)
Douglas, Rich. Secret of the Dogs. (p. 1542)
Douglas, Ryke. Tock a Tick. (p. 1760)
Douglas, Ryke Leigh. Big Wheel. (p. 184)
—Molly the Trolley & Bud. (p. 1161)
—Sam's Surprise. (p. 1509)
Douglas, Tasha K. God's Beautiful Daughter: Discover the Love of Your Heavenly Father (p. 691)
Douglas, Vannick, illus. see Shinno, Stephanie.
Douglas, Vincent. Complete Book of the Alphabet, Grades Preschool-1. (p. 352)
—Everything for Early Learning. (p. 544)
—Everything for Early Learning, Grade Preschool Vol. 1. (p. 544)
—Florida Test Prep, Grade 4. Spectrum Staff, ed. (p. 607)
Douglas, Vincent & Blevins, Wiley. Money (p. 1163)
Douglas, Vincent, et al. California Test Practice, Grade 3. (p. 253)
—Florida Test Prep, Grade 4. (p. 607)
—Illinois Test Prep, Grade 3. (p. 857)
—New York Test Prep, Grade 6. (p. 1248)
—Numbers & Counting. (p. 1272)
—Texas Test Prep, Grade 3. (p. 1724)
Douglas, Vincent, et al, adapted by. Money. (p. 1163)
Douglas-Hobbs, Kathy. Kobe & the Rescue Adventure. (p. 966)
Douglass, Ali, illus. see Flaherty, Somer & Kollmer, Jen.
Douglass, E. Squirrel Friends Adventures: The Monster & the Great Storm. (p. 1637)
Douglass, Jackie Leatherbury, jt. auth. see Douglass, John.
Douglass, John & Douglass, Jackie Leatherbury. Shells. Peterson, Roger Tory, ed. (p. 1565)
Douglass, Mary E. Unusually Happy Bear. (p. 1823)
Douglass, Sara. Starman. (p. 1642)
Douglass, Susan L. Ramadan. Reeves, Jeni, illus. (p. 1437)
Douglass Thom, Kara. Dancer Girl M. C's Story: One Step at a Time. Seatter, Pamela, illus. (p. 402)
—Gymnastics Girl Maya's Story: Becoming Brave. Seatter, Pamela, illus. (p. 734)
—Soccer Girl Cassie's Story: Teamwork Is the Goal. Seatter, Pamela, illus. (p. 1603)
Doupe, Pauline Wood. My Arctic Circle of Friends. Fawcett, Vicki, illus. (p. 1196)
Dousias, Spiro, illus. see Maher, Mickie Brandt.
Doust, Jon & Spillman, Ken. Magwheel Madness. (p. 1076)
Douthat, Ross Gregory. Privilege: Harvard & the Education of the Ruling Class. (p. 1408)
Douthit, George. Boy Who Slept with Bears. (p. 219)
Douthwaite, Gina, et al. Farm Poems & Seasons Poems. (p. 574)
Douthwaite, Gina, et al, selected by. Farm Poems & Seasons Poems. (p. 574)
Douthwaite, Wendy. Orange Pony. (p. 1302)
Doutrive, Kaleb D. Funny Chaps. (p. 649)
Dove, Debra. Fur Flew. (p. 650)
Dove, Jane. Tourism & Recreation. (p. 1773)
Dove, Jason, illus. see Bolte, Mari.
Dove, Jason, illus. see Clay, Kathryn, et al.
Dove, Jason, illus. see Clay, Kathryn.
Dove, Jason, illus. see Hammer, Sheila.
Dove, Jason, illus. see Kolpin, Molly.
Dove, Jonathon, jt. auth. see Middleton, Alasdair.
Dove, Karen. Gift for Santa. (p. 675)
Dove, Rita, frwd. Multicultural Voices. (p. 1190)
Dove, S. R. Gabriel the First Christmas Dragon (p. 652)
Dover. Animals Activities Dover Chunky Book. (p. 82)
—At the Zoo Activities Dover Chunky Book. (p. 111)
—Bugs Activities Dover Chunky Book. (p. 237)
—Dinosaurs Activities Dover Chunky Book. (p. 444)
—Dover Digital Design Source #6: Spiders, Insects & Crustaceans. (p. 473)
—Dover's Greatest Clips CD-ROM & Book: Volume II. (p. 473)
—Friendly Lion Tattoos. (p. 638)
—Friendly Monkey Tattoos. (p. 638)
—Geometric Stained Glass Coloring Book: Deluxe Edition with 48 Stained Glass Sheets. (p. 662)
—KNUX — Knuckle Tattoos for Boys. (p. 966)
—KNUX — Knuckle Tattoos for Girls. (p. 966)
—Moustache Stickers. (p. 1182)
—On the Go Activities Dover Chunky Book. (p. 1290)
—Spot the Differences (p. 1633)
—Spot the Differences: Art Masterpiece Mysteries. Bk. 4 (p. 1633)
Dover, A. T., jt. auth. see Noble, Marty.
Dover & Hourglass Press, Hourglass. Art Smart: Spot the Details & Find Out the Facts! (p. 103)
Dover & Printworks KMG Staff. Sea Life Field Guide. (p. 1534)
Dover & Tattoos. Moustache Tattoos: For Your Face or Finger! (p. 1182)
Dover, et al. Christmas Treasury. Price, Margaret Evans et al, illus. (p. 316)
Dover, Ilana. Talking MacHine: The Story of Alexander Graham Bell. (p. 1703)
Dover, Jeffrey S., jt. auth. see Turkington, Carol.
Dover Publications Inc. Staff. Create Your Own Animal Sticker Pictures: 12 Scenes & over 300 Reusable Stickers. (p. 378)
—Design Discovery Coloring Book. (p. 429)
Dover Publications Inc. Staff, jt. auth. see Levy, Barbara Soloff.
Dover Publications Inc. Staff, jt. auth. see Weller, Alan.
Dover Publications Inc. Staff, creator. Shiny Rainbow Stars Stickers. (p. 1567)
Dover Staff. Art Masterpieces to Color: 60 Great Paintings from Botticelli to Picasso. (p. 102)
—Big Book of Nature Stencil Designs. (p. 179)
—Birthday Bash: Silly Sticker Story. (p. 192)
—Circus Surprise: Silly Sticker Story. (p. 322)
—Create Your Own Action Sticker Pictures: 12 Scenes & over 300 Reusable Stickers. (p. 378)
—Listen & Color: Favorite Poems for Children. Kliros, Thea, illus. (p. 1022)
—Spectacular Scales & Nifty Notes Tattoos. (p. 1624)
—Wild Animals. (p. 1928)
Dover Staff & Printworks KMG Staff. Dinosaurs Field Guide. (p. 444)
Dover Staff & Radtke, Becky. Girls on the Go Mazes. (p. 680)
Dovey, Belinda. Alphabet Adventures. (p. 49)
Dovidija-Budney, Elizabeth. My Little Red Mittens. (p. 1213)
Dow, Carrie. Morning, Miss Moo: (story of an ornery Cat) (p. 1175)
Dow, Christopher. Dead Detective. (p. 416)
—Devil of a Time. (p. 432)
Dow, Danica, jt. illus. see Dow, Kathy.
Dow, Jill, jt. auth. see Bellamy, David.
Dow, Kathy & Dow, Danica. Low-Down Dirty Words. (p. 1061)
Dow, S. B., illus. see Heinze, Monica Bacon.
Dow, S. B., illus. see Hilgendorf, L. B.
Dow, S. B., illus. see Otukile, Mpho.
Dow, Suzanne. Bike Race. (p. 185)
Doward, Jan S. Grandpa's Furry & Feathered Friends: Meet Stubbytail, Hop-Hops, & All Other Birds & Animals at Grandpa's Place. (p. 709)
—Sweeeet! God's Awesome Plan for You. (p. 1689)
Dowd, Olympia. Young Dancer's Apprenticeship: On Tour with the Moscow City Ballet. (p. 1978)
Dowd, Siobhan. Bog Child. (p. 207)
—London Eye Mystery. (p. 1046)
—Solace of the Road. (p. 1606)
—Swift Pure Cry. (p. 1690)
Dowd, Tara. No More Boogers Book. (p. 1259)
Dowd, Tom, jt. auth. see Peter, Val J.
Dowdeswell, Evelyn, et al. Scott of the Antarctic. (p. 1531)
Dowding, Philippa. Gargoyle at the Gates. (p. 657)
—Gargoyle in My Yard. (p. 657)
—Myles & the Monster Outside. (p. 1222)
—Strange Gift of Gwendolyn Golden. (p. 1665)
Dowdle, Mary, illus. see Friedman, Lise.
Dowdle, Mary, photos by see Friedman, Lise.
Dowds, Alan. High-Speed Superbikes. (p. 778)
Dowdy, Linda Cress. All Kinds of Kisses. Lamont, Priscilla, illus. (p. 45)
Dowdy, Penny. Animal Cells. (p. 77)
—Battle of Vimy Ridge: Defining Moments in Canadian History/Graphic Novels. (p. 147)
—Body Math. (p. 207)
—British North America Act: Defining Moments in Canadian History/Graphic Novels. (p. 230)
—Cross Country & Endurance. (p. 385)
—Dressage. (p. 485)
—Estimation. (p. 538)
—Famous Five: Defining Moments in Canadian History/Graphic Novels. (p. 569)
—Fractions. (p. 626)
—Geometry. (p. 662)
—Graphing. (p. 711)
—Measurement. (p. 1117)
—Money. (p. 1163)
—Nature Math. (p. 1236)
—October Crisis: Defining Moments in Canadian History/Graphic Novels. (p. 1277)
—Place Value. (p. 1366)
—Plant Cells. (p. 1368)
—Time. (p. 1750)
Dowdy, Penny, jt. auth. see Knowlton, MaryLee.
Dowdy, Penny & Becker, Ann. Subtraction. (p. 1671)
Dowell, Brandy, jt. auth. see Edwards, Amanda.
Dowell, F. M. C. Little Palace. (p. 1033)
Dowell, Frances O'Roark. Blasts Off! McDaniels, Preston, illus. (p. 198)
—Chicken Boy. (p. 300)
—Chicken Boy. Krause, George, photos by. (p. 300)
—Erupts! McDaniels, Preston, illus. (p. 534)
—Falling In. (p. 567)
—Kind of Friends We Used to Be. (p. 957)
—Phineas L. Macguire... Blasts Off! McDaniels, Preston, illus. (p. 1351)
—Phineas L. Macguire... Erupts! McDaniels, Preston, illus. (p. 1351)
—Phineas L. MacGuire... Gets Slimed! McDaniels, Preston, illus. (p. 1351)
—Sam the Man & the Chicken Plan. (p. 1507)
—Second Life of Abigail Walker. (p. 1539)
—Secret Language of Girls. (p. 1541)
—Shooting the Moon. (p. 1568)
—Sound of Your Voice, Only Really Far Away. (p. 1615)
—Ten Miles Past Normal. (p. 1719)
—Where I'd Like to Be. (p. 1908)
Dowell, Krista. Lord Pa & Lady Moffy. (p. 1052)
Dowell, Larry, illus. see Hannah, Martha.
Dowell, Lori. Be a Paleontologist. (p. 148)
Dowell, Ruth I. Move over, Mother Goose! Finger Plays, Action Verses & Funny Rhymes. Charner, Kathleen, ed. (p. 1183)
Dowell, Vivian "Vee". I'm Da Muva, Said Miss Bossy. Huntley, Doris, illus. (p. 858)
Dower, Laura. Beast with 1000 Eyes. Schlafman, Dave, illus. (p. 152)
—Curse of the Lake Monster. (p. 395)
—For Girls Only: Everything Great about Being a Girl. (p. 615)
—Give Me a Break. (p. 681)
—On the Case. (p. 1290)
—Return of Mega Mantis Schlafman, Dave, illus. (p. 1464)
—Sunny & the Secret Passage. (p. 1677)
—Sunny & the Snowy Surprise. (p. 1677)
—Sunny to the Rescue. (p. 1677)
—Sunny to the Rescue. Gurney, John Steven, illus. (p. 1677)
—They Came from Planet Q. Schlafman, Dave, illus. (p. 1732)
—Three's a Crowd. (p. 1744)
DOWLAND, MELANIE, jt. auth. see Equipo Staff.
Dowler, Pattie. Suzie Squirrel & the Disappearing Pies. (p. 1688)
Dowley, jt. auth. see Pohle.
Dowley, Coco, illus. see Rylant, Cynthia.
Dowley, Ruth. Hard Rock. (p. 748)
Dowley, T. Viaje Maravilloso. (p. 1839)
Dowley, Tim. Bible Animal Stencil Book (p. 175)
—Casa Llena de Gente. (p. 273)

D

—Changing Picture Bible Stories Martin, Stuart, illus. (p. 290)
—Kregel Pictorial Guide to the Tabernacle Parry, Alan, illus. (p. 967)
—My First Story Bible Langton, Roger, illus. (p. 1208)
—My First Story of Christmas. Langton, Roger, illus. (p. 1208)
—My First Story of Easter. Langton, Roger, illus. (p. 1208)
—My First Story of Jesus. Langton, Roger, illus. (p. 1208)
—Noah & His Big Boat. (p. 1261)
—Noah's Ark Pop-Up. Martin, Stuart, illus. (p. 1261)
—Paul's Travels (p. 1331)
—Pop-Up Bible Adventures. Moseley, Dudley, illus. (p. 1384)
—Solomon's Temple Model Pohle, Peter, illus. (p. 1608)
—Stories from the Bible: With Over 50 Flaps to Open Vol. 2 Kochnez, Jane & Kochnevitz, Jane, illus. (p. 1654)
—Viaje Especial del Burrito - Donkey's Special Ride. (p. 1839)
Dowley, Tim, jt. auth. see David, Juliet.
Dowley, Tim & Bewley, Robert. Look Inside the Bible - Life of Jesus Rabou, John, illus. (p. 1049)
Dowley, Tim & Bishop, Veronica. Casa Llena de Gente. (p. 273)
Dowley, Tim & David, Juliet. Candle Pop-Up Bible Atlas Nicholls, Paul, illus. (p. 261)
—Story of Easter Whitlow, Steve, illus. (p. 1658)
Dowley-Wise, Justine. Pig Called Harriet. (p. 1357)
Dowling, Iris. Christmas Program Ideas. (p. 315)
Dowling, Iris Gray. Change of Hats. Bouthyette, Valerie, illus. (p. 290)
—Pony for My Birthday. Bouthyette, Valerie, illus. (p. 1382)
Dowling, Jane, ed. see Kelman, Louise & Kelman, Suzanne.
Dowling, Joni. Friends Forever. (p. 638)
Dowling, June. Twas the Eve Before All Saints. (p. 1799)
Dowling, Lucy. Why Why Why... Do Bees Make Honey? (p. 1926)
—Why Why Why... Do Clocks Have Hands? (p. 1926)
—Why Why Why... Do Lizards Stick to Walls? (p. 1926)
—Why Why Why... Do People Want to Explore? (p. 1926)
—Why Why Why... Does the Earth Spin Round? (p. 1926)
—Why Why Why... Were Vikings So Fierce? (p. 1926)
Dowling, Paul. Night Journey. (p. 1253)
Dowling, Victor J., illus. see Villiers, Alan.
Down, Alan. Beowulf: An Anglo-Saxon Epic. (p. 166)
Down, Alan, illus. see Barkow, Henriette.
Down, Dale. Adventures of Dennis the Dimetrodon. (p. 17)
Down, David. Archaeology Book. (p. 95)
Down, Hayley & Make Believe Ideas Staff. My Easter Basket. Ede, Lara, illus. (p. 1202)
Down, Heather. Cartes Postales de L'Espace: L'Histoire de Chris Hadfield. Garon, Pierre, tr. (p. 272)
—Deadly Distance. (p. 417)
—Postcards from Space: The Chris Hadfield Story. (p. 1388)
Down, Heather, text. Postcards from Space: The Chris Hadfield Story. (p. 1388)
Down, Reg. Lost Lagoon. (p. 1056)
—Magic Knot: And other Tangles. (p. 1072)
—Starry Bird: An Easter Tale. (p. 1642)
Down, Susan. Muhammad Ali: The Greatest. (p. 1189)
—Theodore Weld: Architect of Abolitionism. (p. 1729)
Down, Susan Brophy. Legally Green: Careers in Environmental Law. (p. 988)
—Muhammad Ali: The Greatest. (p. 1189)
Downard, Barry. Carla's Famous Traveling Feather & Fur Show. Downard, Barry, illus. (p. 270)
—Race of the Century. Downard, Barry, illus. (p. 1431)
Downer, Alan S., ed. see Ibsen, Henrik.
Downer, Alan S., tr. see Ibsen, Henrik.
Downer, Ann. Books of the Keepers. (p. 212)
—Dragon of Never-Was. Rayyan, Omar, illus. (p. 477)
—Glass Salamander. (p. 682)
—Hatching Magic. (p. 752)
—Hatching Magic. Rayyan, Omar, illus. (p. 752)
—Shark Baby Bersani, Shennen, illus. (p. 1562)
—Smart & Spineless: Brainy Without a Backbone. (p. 1592)
—Spellkey. (p. 1625)
—Tiburoncito Bersani, Shennen, illus. (p. 1747)
—Wild Animal Neighbors: Sharing Our Urban World. (p. 1928)
DOWNER, ANN, jt. auth. see Downer, Ann.
Downer, Ann & DOWNER, ANN. Dragones y Magia. Martinez, Catalina, tr. (p. 478)
Downer, Anna. Elephant Talk: The Surprising Science of Elephant Communication. (p. 511)
Downer, Deborah A. Classic American Ghost Stories: 200 Years of Ghost Lore from New England, the Mid-Atlantic, the Great Plains, the South, & the Pacific Northwest. (p. 327)
Downer, Denise. Soul Mates. Frampton, Otis, illus. (p. 1614)
—Tombstone Twins: Soul Mates Frampton, Otis, illus. (p. 1764)
—Tombstone Twins Package: Soul Mates. Frampton, Otis, illus. (p. 1764)
Downer, Jim, jt. auth. see Hughes, Ted.
Downer, Maggie, illus. see Blyton, Enid.
Downer, Maggie, illus. see Frantz, Jennifer.
Downer, Romeo, illus. see Callender, Simone.
Downes, Alice. Lucy & the Magic Loom: A Rainbow Loomer's Adventure Story. (p. 1063)
Downes, Alice & Hargreaves, Roger. Little Miss Splendid & the Beast. (p. 1032)
Downes, Belinda. Baby Days: A Quilt of Rhymes & Pictures. Downes, Belinda, illus. (p. 125)
Downes, Kit. Zal & Zara & the Great Race of Azamed. (p. 1984)
Downes, Patrick. Come Home, Angus. Kulikov, Boris, illus. (p. 347)
—Fell of Dark. (p. 581)
Downey, Autumn, illus. see Stephenson, Wendy.
Downey, Dagney, illus. see Brown, Jordan D.
Downey, Fairfax. Famous Horses of the Civil War. Chapman, Frederick T., illus. (p. 569)
Downey, Glanville. Aristotle, Dean of Early Science. (p. 98)
Downey, Glen. Escape from East Berlin. Lingas, Leo, illus. (p. 535)
—Gladiators. (p. 682)
—Ice Journey. Brucker, Glenn, illus. (p. 850)
—Miracle Men. Brennan, Anthony, illus. (p. 1148)
—Rebel Prince. Okum, David, illus. (p. 1451)
Downey, Glen R. 10 Greatest Sports Showdowns. (p. 1993)
—10 Most Decisive Battles. (p. 1993)
—10 Most Extreme Jobs. (p. 1994)
—10 Most Memorable TV Moments. (p. 1994)
—10 Most Remarkable Writers. (p. 1994)
—10 Most Revolutionary Military Inventions. (p. 1994)
—10 Most Shocking Sports Scandals. (p. 1994)
—10 Most Significant Documents in History. (p. 1994)
—10 Most Unforgettable NASCAR Moments. (p. 1994)
—10 Smartest Animals. (p. 1994)
Downey, Glen R. & Cond, Sandie. 10 Coolest Flying Machines. (p. 1993)
Downey, Glen R. & Malara, Maria. 10 Hottest Hollywood Cars. (p. 1993)
Downey, Jen Swann. Ninja Librarians: The Accidental Keyhand. (p. 1256)
Downey, Joni J. Will You Be My Friend? —We Really Are No Different. Brudos, Susan E., illus. (p. 1932)
Downey, Lisa, illus. see Fisher, Doris.
Downey, Lisa, illus. see Karwoski, Gail Langer.
Downey, Lisa, illus. see Pierce, Terry.
Downey, Lisa & Fox, Kathleen. Pirates of Plagiarism. Downey, Lisa, illus. (p. 1364)
Downey, Lynn. Flea's Sneeze. Firehammer, Karla, illus. (p. 603)
Downey, Matthew T. American History 1 (Before 1865) (p. 61)
—American History 1, Before 1865. (p. 61)
—American History 2 (After 1865) (p. 61)
—American History 2 (after 1865) - Softcover Student Text Only. (p. 61)
Downey, Matthew T. & Pettit, Jenny. Discover Colorado: Its People, Places, & Times. (p. 447)
Downey, Michael. Digging Deep: Fostering the Spirituality of Young Men. (p. 439)
Downey, Roma, jt. auth. see Burnett, Mark.
Downey, Tika. Biggest Snowball. (p. 185)
—California: The Golden State. (p. 253)
—Delaware: The First State. (p. 424)
—Florida: The Sunshine State. (p. 606)
—History of Zero: Exploring Our Place-Value Number System. (p. 785)
—How the Arabs Invented Algebra: The History of the Concept of Variables. (p. 812)
—Indiana: The Hoosier State. (p. 871)
—Massachusetts: The Bay State. (p. 1102)
—New Jersey: The Garden State. (p. 1245)
—New York: The Empire State. (p. 1247)
—Tennessee: The Volunteer State. (p. 1720)
—Texas: The Lone Star State. (p. 1724)
—Tracks in the Snow. (p. 1775)
—Washington: The Evergreen State. (p. 1859)
Downey, William, illus. see Simon, Seymour.
Downham, Jenny. Before I Die. (p. 158)
—You Against Me. (p. 1972)
Downie, Christopher, illus. see Nadimi, Suzan.
Downie, David. David & Jacko. Seroya, Tea, illus. (p. 410)
—David & Jacko. Ivanova, Kalina, tr. (p. 410)
—David & Jacko. Tatsi, Andreanna, tr. (p. 410)
—Horrible Stories My Dad Told Me. M, Akiko, tr. (p. 798)
—Horrible Stories My Dad Told Me. Seroya, Tea, illus. (p. 798)
—Horrible Stories My Dad Told Me. Ivanova, Kalina, tr. (p. 798)
—Horrible Stories My Dad Told Me. Nanevich, Julia, tr. (p. 798)
—Horrible Stories My Dad Told Me. Nanevych, Julia, tr. (p. 798)
—Horrible Stories My Dad Told Me. Tatsi, Andreanna, tr. (p. 798)
Downie, John, jt. auth. see Downie, Mary Alice.
Downie, Mary Alice. Pioneer Alphabet. Gerber, Mary Jane, illus. (p. 1361)
Downie, Mary Alice & Downie, John. Alison's Ghosts (p. 41)
Downie, Mary Alice & Rawlyk, George. Chanson pour l'Acadie. Lorioz, Jacques Loïc, tr. from ENG. (p. 290)
Downie, Mary Alice & Zola, Mequido. How the Devil Got His Cat & Other Multicultural Folktales for Children. Gilliland, Jillian Hulme, illus. (p. 813)
Downing, Brian M. Paths of Glory: Social Change in America from the Great War to Vietnam. (p. 1328)
Downing, David. Aftermath & Remembrance. (p. 28)
—Colombia. (p. 341)
—Conflicts of the Middle East. (p. 357)
—Debate about Terrorist Tactics. (p. 421)
—Geography & Resources of the Middle East. (p. 662)
—Governments & Leaders of the Middle East. (p. 704)
—History of the Middle East. (p. 785)
—Malcolm X. (p. 1083)
—Nazi Death Camps. (p. 1238)
—Origins of the Holocaust. (p. 1304)
Downing, David & Cavendish, Marshall. Afghanistan. (p. 26)
Downing, David & Marshall Cavendish Corporation Staff. Iran. (p. 886)
Downing, David & Thorpe, Yvonne. Zimbabwe. (p. 1986)
Downing, Erin. Best Friends (until Someone Better Comes Along) (p. 169)
—Dancing Queen. (p. 403)
—Drive Me Crazy. (p. 485)
—For Soccer-Crazy Girls Only. (p. 616)
—Funny Thing about Love: Dancing Queen; Prom Crashers; Drive Me Crazy. (p. 650)
—Kiss It. (p. 961)
Downing, Johnette. Amazon Alphabet Downing, Johnette, illus. (p. 56)
—Fifolet Lindsey, Jennifer, illus. (p. 584)
—Louisiana, the Jewel of the Deep South Marshall, Julia, illus. (p. 1059)
—Macarooned on a Dessert Island Wald, Christina, illus. (p. 1067)
—My Aunt Came Back from Louisiane (p. 1196)
—There Was an Old Lady Who Swallowed Some Bugs (p. 1730)
—Why the Crawfish Lives in the Mud Downing, Johnette, illus. (p. 1926)
—Why the Oyster Has the Pearl Hill, Bethanne, illus. (p. 1926)
—Why the Possum Has a Large Grin Wald, Christina, illus. (p. 1926)
Downing, Johnette, jt. auth. see Kadair, Deborah.
Downing, Johnette & Kadair, Deborah Ousley. Today Is Monday in Louisiana (p. 1760)
Downing, Julie. All the Ways I Love You (bilingual Edition) (p. 46)
—Lullaby & Good Night: Songs for Sweet Dreams. (p. 1064)
—Night Before Christmas. Downing, Julie, illus. (p. 1252)
—Where Is My Mommy? Downing, Julie, illus. (p. 1908)
—White Snow, Blue Feather. (p. 1913)
Downing, Julie, illus. see Burk, Rachelle.
Downing, Julie, illus. see Chancellor, Deborah.
Downing, Julie, illus. see Feder, Jane.
Downing, Julie, illus. see Gherman, Beverly.
Downing, Julie, illus. see Helldorfer, M. C.
Downing, Julie, illus. see Hoffman, Mary.
Downing, Julie, illus. see Metzger, Steve.
Downing, Julie, illus. see Park, Linda Sue.
Downing, Julie, illus. see Piggy Toes Press Staff.
Downing, Julie, illus. see Wang, Dorothea DePrisco & Imperato, Teresa.
Downing, Lee. My Organ Buddies. (p. 1216)
Downing, Sybil, ed. see Barker, Jane Valentine.
Downing, Sybil, jt. auth. see Barker, Jane Valentine.
Downing, Sybil & Barker, Jane Valentine. Happy Harvest. (p. 746)
—Magic, Mystery, & Monsters. (p. 1072)
—Mesas to Mountains. (p. 1129)
Downing, Todd. Filmmaking. (p. 586)
Downs, Braden, illus. see Holthaus, Abbey.
Downs, Dorothy. Patchwork: Seminole & Miccosukee Art & Activities. (p. 1328)
Downs, Downs. Explore Bible People: 52 Bible Lessons for Ages 4-6. (p. 550)
Downs, Jay & Downs, Jeanie. Flutterfly. (p. 609)
Downs, Jeanie, jt. auth. see Downs, Jay.
Downs, Mike. Noisy Airplane Ride. Gordon, David, illus. (p. 1262)
—You See a Circus, I See... McGrory, Anik, illus. (p. 1976)
Downs, Pamela. Colorado Today: Influences from Many Cultures. (p. 343)
Downs Webb, Michelle. What Color Is Love? (p. 1881)
Downtain, C.J. 1 2 3 Count with Me. (p. 1990)
Downtown Bookworks Inc. Staff & Turgeon, Carolyn. Next Full Moon. (p. 1249)
Downtown Bookworks Inc. Staff & Wolf, Laurie Goldrich. Boy-Made: Green & Groovy. (p. 218)
Downtown Bookworks Inc. Staff, et al. Shark-Tastic! (p. 1562)
Dowsett, Elizabeth, jt. auth. see Dorling Kindersley Publishing Staff.
Dowson, Anthony & Morris, Keith E. J. Fun & Games: 100 Sport-Related Activities for Ages 5-16. (p. 647)
Dowson, Jonas. Meteor Man. (p. 1130)
Dowson, Nick. North: The Amazing Story of Arctic Migration. Benson, Patrick, illus. (p. 1264)
—Tigress Chapman, Jane, illus. (p. 1749)
—Tigress: Read & Wonder. Chapman, Jane, illus. (p. 1749)
—Tigress: Read, Listen & Wonder. Chapman, Jane, illus. (p. 1749)
—Tracks of a Panda: Read & Wonder. Rong, Yu, illus. (p. 1775)
—Tracks of a Panda. Rong, Yu, illus. (p. 1775)
Dowson, Thomas A. Archaeology of Art. (p. 95)
Dowswell. Military Aircraft (p. 1142)
Dowswell, P. Secret Agent Spy. (p. 1540)
—True Survival Stories. (p. 1793)
Dowswell, P., jt. auth. see Fleming, F.
Dowswell, Paul. Auslander. (p. 116)
—Dictatorship. (p. 436)
—Eleven Eleven. (p. 512)
—Escape. (p. 534)
—First Encyclopedia of Animals. (p. 594)
—First Encyclopedia of Space. (p. 594)
—First World War - Internet Referenced. (p. 597)
—Genetic Engineering. (p. 660)
—Little Encyclopedia of Animals. (p. 1027)
—Mi Primera Enciclopedia del Espacio. (p. 1133)
—Powder Monkey: Adventures of a Young Sailor. (p. 1389)
—Prison Ship: Adventures of a Youn Sailor. (p. 1407)
—Second World War. (p. 1540)
—Second world war - internet Linked. Le, Leonard Rolland, illus. (p. 1540)
—Story of Second World War. (p. 1660)
—Story of the First World War. (p. 1661)
—Survival. (p. 1686)
—True Escape Stories. (p. 1792)
—True Escape Stories. Tyler, Jenny, ed. (p. 1792)
—True Everest Adventures. Woodcock, John, illus. (p. 1792)
—True Polar Adventures. Woodcock, John, illus. (p. 1792)
—True Stories of Heroes. (p. 1792)
—True Stories of Sea Adventures. (p. 1792)
—True Stories of the First World War. (p. 1793)
—True Stories of the Second World War. (p. 1793)
—Usborne Little Book of Animals. (p. 1827)
—Usborne Little Encyclopedia of Space. Bines, Gary & Hancock, David, illus. (p. 1827)
—War Stories. (p. 1858)
Dowswell, Paul, ed. see Rogers, Kirsteen.
Dowswell, Paul, jt. auth. see Allan, Tony.
Dowswell, Paul & Allen, Troy. Ghosts. (p. 672)
Dowswell, Paul & Fleming, Fergus. Spies. (p. 1627)
—True Adventures Collection. (p. 1791)
—True Spy Stories. (p. 1792)
Dowswell, Paul & Greenwood, Susan. Amazing World of Witches: Discover the Spellbinding History of Witches, Wizardry, Magic & Mystery. (p. 56)
Dowswell, Paul & Hachette Children's Books Staff. Western Front in World War One. (p. 1876)
Dowswell, Paul & Harvey, Gill. True Adventure Stories. (p. 1791)
Dowswell, Paul, et al. World Wars: An Introduction to the First & Second World Wars. Chisholm, Jane, ed. (p. 1959)
Doxey, Heidi. Jane Journals at Pemberley Prep: Liam Darcy, I Loathe You. (p. 908)
—Tiny Talks (p. 1756)
—Tiny Talks, Vol. 14. (p. 1756)
—Tiny Talks, Volume 15. (p. 1756)
Doyel, Ginger, illus. see Silvermetz, Marcia A.
Doyen, Denise. Once upon a Twice. (p. 1293)
—Once upon a Twice. Moser, Barry, illus. (p. 1293)
—Pomegranate Witch. Moser, Barry, illus. (p. 1382)
D'Oyen, Fatima. Islamic Manners. Zulkifli, Azhar, illus. (p. 892)
D'Oyen, Fatima M. & Chachi, Abdelkader. In the Prophet's Garden: A Selection of Ahadith for the Young. (p. 867)
Doyle, Adam, illus. see Theule, Larissa.
Doyle, Alfreda C. Alfreda's Reader's Theatre: Dialogues. (p. 37)
—Alfreda's Reader's Theatre: Comedy Club. (p. 37)
—Alfreda's Reader's Theatre: Public Transportation. (p. 37)
—Missing Sugar Beet. (p. 1153)
—Story Time Literacy Coach: Literacy, Storytelling & Rhyme. (p. 1663)
Doyle, Alfreda C., ed. see Story Time Staff.
Doyle, Arthur. #07 Sherlock Holmes & the Redheaded League. Rohrbach, Sophie & Morrow, Jt, illus. (p. 1992)
—#08 Sherlock Holmes & the Adventure at the Copper Beeches. Rohrbach, Sophie & Morrow, Jt, illus. (p. 1993)
—#09 Sherlock Holmes & the Adventure of the Six Napoleons. Rohrbach, Sophie & Morrow, Jt, illus. (p. 1993)
—#10 Sherlock Holmes & the Boscombe Valley Mystery. Rohrbach, Sophie & Morrow, Jt, illus. (p. 1994)
—Adv of the Devils Foot. (p. 13)
—Adventures & the Memoirs of Sherlock Holmes. McKowen, Scott, illus. (p. 15)
—Adventures of Sherlock Holmes: With a Discussion of Curiosity. Butterfield, Ned, tr. (p. 22)
—Adventures of Sherlock Holmes. (p. 22)
—Adventures of Sherlock Holmes. Corvino, Lucy, illus. (p. 22)
—Boys' Sherlock Holmes. Haycraft, Howard, ed. (p. 220)
—Chien des Baskerville. (p. 301)
—Crime of the Congo. (p. 382)
—Desert Drama: Being the Tragedy of the Korosko. (p. 429)
—Extraordinary Cases of Sherlock Holmes. (p. 555)
—Hound of the Baskervilles. (p. 802)
—Hound of the Baskervilles. Harvey, Bob, illus. (p. 802)
—Hound of the Baskervilles. Kumar, Vinod, illus. (p. 802)
—Hound of the Baskervilles. Pérez, Daniel et al, illus. (p. 802)
—Perro de los Baskerville. Pareja, Alejandro, ed. (p. 1343)
—Refugees: A Tale of Two Continents. (p. 1456)
—Sabueso de Los Baskerville Ferran, Adriana & Ferran, Daniel, illus. (p. 1500)
—Sherlock Holmes: The Hound of the Baskervilles. (p. 1565)
—Sherlock Holmes. (p. 1565)
—Sherlock Holmes & a Scandal in Bohemia. Rohrbach, Sophie, illus. (p. 1565)
—Sherlock Holmes & the Adventure at the Abbey Grange. Rohrbach, Sophie, illus. (p. 1565)
—Sherlock Holmes & the Adventure of Black Peter. Rohrbach, Sophie & Morrow, J. T., illus. (p. 1565)
—Sherlock Holmes & the Adventure of the Blue Gem. Rohrbach, Sophie, illus. (p. 1565)
—Sherlock Holmes & the Adventure of the Cardboard Box. Rohrbach, Sophie & Morrow, J. T., illus. (p. 1565)
—Sherlock Holmes & the Adventure of the Dancing Men. Rohrbach, Sophie, illus. (p. 1565)
—Sherlock Holmes & the Adventure of the Sussex Vampire. Rohrbach, Sophie, illus. (p. 1565)
—Sherlock Holmes & the Adventure of the Three Garridebs. Rohrbach, Sophie & Morrow, J. T., illus. (p. 1565)
—Sherlock Holmes & the Boscombe Valley Mystery. Rohrbach, Sophie & Morrow, J. T., illus. (p. 1565)
—Sherlock Holmes & the Case of the Hound of the Baskervilles. Vogel, Malvina G., ed. (p. 1565)
—Sherlock Holmes & the Gloria Scott. Rohrbach, Sophie & Morrow, J. T., illus. (p. 1565)
—Sherlock Holmes & the Three Garridebs. Rohrbach, Sophie & Morrow, J. T., illus. (p. 1565)
—Study in Scarlet & Other Sherlock Holmes Adventures. (p. 1670)
Doyle, Arthur, jt. auth. see Bevins, Pegi.
Doyle, Arthur, jt. auth. see Brenchley, Chaz.
Doyle, Arthur & Saddleback Educational Publishing Staff, eds. Hound of the Baskervilles (p. 802)
Doyle, Arthur, et al. Arthur Conan Doyle. Pomplun, Tom, ed. (p. 103)
Doyle, Beverly, illus. see Batten, Mary.
Doyle, Beverly, illus. see St. Pierre, Stephanie.
Doyle, Beverly J., illus. see Batten, Mary.
Doyle, Bill. Attack of the Shark-Headed Zombie. Altman, Scott, illus. (p. 114)
—Big Foot in the End Zone. Lee, Jared, illus. (p. 181)
—Mysteries: 15 Suspenseful Stories That Guide Students to Infer, Visualize, & Summarize to Predict the Ending of Each Story. (p. 1222)
—Space Explorer's Guide to Mars— in 3-D! (p. 1619)
—Space Explorer's Guide to the Universe. Labat, Yancey C., illus. (p. 1619)
—Trapped! The 2031 Journal of Otis Fitzmorgan. (p. 1779)
—Werewolf at Home Plate. Lee, Jared D., illus. (p. 1875)
—Zombie at the Finish Line. Lee, Jared, illus. (p. 1988)
Doyle, Bill H. Behind Enemy Lines: Under Fire in the Middle East. (p. 160)
—Behind Enemy Lines. (p. 160)
—Betrayed! The 1977 Journal of Zeke Moorie. (p. 172)
—Stampede of the Supermarket Slugs. Altman, Scott, illus. (p. 1639)
Doyle, Brian. Angel Square (p. 74)
—Boy O'Boy (p. 218)
—Covered Bridge. (p. 373)
—Easy Avenue (p. 500)
—Hey, Dad! (p. 774)
—Mary Ann Alice (p. 1100)
—Mary Ann Alice. (p. 1100)
—Pure Spring (p. 1419)
—Saints Passionate & Peculiar: Brief Exuberant Essays for Teens. (p. 1504)
—Spud in Winter (p. 1635)
—Spud Sweetgrass (p. 1635)
—Uncle Ronald (p. 1812)
—Up to Low (p. 1824)
—You Can Pick Me up at Peggy's Cove. (p. 1974)

Doyle, Catherine. Vendetta. (p. 1835)
Doyle, Celia. Lizzie's Dream. (p. 1043)
Doyle, Christopher. Amazing Tales & Strange Stories of the Bible. (p. 56)
—Story of Easter. Haysom, John, illus. (p. 1658)
Doyle, Edwina Ann. Bless Mark. (p. 199)
Doyle, Eugenie. Many Hands: A Farm Prepares for Winter. Stadtlander, Becca, illus. (p. 1089)
Doyle, Evan Brain, jt. auth. see Becker-Doyle, Eve.
Doyle, Garry, jt. auth. see Rowe, Barry.
Doyle, Helen. Rainbow Pals. (p. 1435)
Doyle, James. I Wish I Knew That: Geography: Cool Stuff You Need to Know. (p. 848)
—Young Scientist's Guide to Defying Disasters with Skill & Daring: Includes 20 Experiments for the Sink, Bathtub & Backyard Brozyna, Andrew, illus. (p. 1979)
—Young Scientist's Guide to Faulty Freaks of Nature Brozyna, Andrew, illus. (p. 1979)
—Young Scientist's Guide to Faulty Freaks of Nature: Including 20 Experiments for the Sink, Bathtub & Backyard (Large Print 16pt) (p. 1979)
Doyle, Kelly. 1880-1900 (Events That Changed the World) (p. 2002)
—Is Gun Ownership a Right? (p. 889)
Doyle, Kevin. Aircraft Carriers. (p. 31)
Doyle, Laura. Entregada Pero no Sometida: The Surrendered Wife. (p. 531)
Doyle, Laura, jt. auth. see Doyle, Mick.
Doyle, Malachy. Albert & Sarah Jane. Parry, Jo, illus. (p. 34)
—Big Pig. Bendall-Brunello, John, illus. (p. 183)
—Get Happy. Uff, Caroline, illus. (p. 667)
—Hair Scare. Allen, Jonathan, illus. (p. 736)
—Horse. Rinaldi, Angelo, illus. (p. 799)
—King Donal's Secret. Watson, Richard, illus. (p. 958)
—Little Chick & the Secret of Sleep. McLean, Gill, illus. (p. 1026)
—Long Gray Norris. (p. 1047)
—Rory's Lost His Voice. Semple, David, illus. (p. 1488)
—Snuggle Sandwich. Millward, Gwen, illus. (p. 1601)
—Spooky Soccer. Parsons, Gary, illus. (p. 1631)
—Tales from Old Ireland. Sharkey, Niamh, illus. (p. 1701)
DOYLE, Malachy. Too Noisy! Vere, Ed, illus. (p. 1767)
Doyle, Malachy & Black, Jeremy. Get Happy. Uff, Caroline, illus. (p. 667)
Doyle, Malachy & Jones, Jac. Changeling. (p. 290)
Doyle, Malachy & Philpot, Graham. Jack the Giant-Killer. (p. 903)
Doyle, Malachy & Sharkey, Niamh. Tales from Old Ireland. (p. 1701)
Doyle, Malachy, et al. Owain A'r Mynydd. (p. 1314)
Doyle, Malacy. Barefoot Book of Fairy Tales. Ceccoli, Nicoletta, illus. (p. 139)
Doyle, Marissa. Betraying Season. (p. 172)
—Courtship & Curses. (p. 373)
Doyle, Mary K. Saint Theodora & Her Promise to God. Velikan, Phil, illus. (p. 1504)
Doyle, Mick & Doyle, Laura. My Rhyming Abc. (p. 1217)
Doyle, Ming, illus. see Smith, Cynthia Leitich.
Doyle, Oliver. Strange Mysteries of the Unexplained. (p. 1665)
Doyle, Patrick H. T. Edgar Font's Hunt for a House to Haunt: Adventure One: the Castle Tower Lighthouse. (p. 504)
—Edgar Font's Hunt for a House to Haunt: Adventure Three: the Flint Island Treehouse. (p. 504)
—Edgar Font's Hunt for a House to Haunt: Adventure Two: the Fakersville Power Station. Doyle, Patrick H. T., illus. (p. 504)
Doyle, Renee, illus. see Jones, Jen.
Doyle, Richard. Fairyland Notebook. (p. 564)
—Jack the Giant Killer. Doyle, Richard, illus. (p. 903)
Doyle, Richard & Noble, Marty. Fairyland Stained Glass Coloring Book. (p. 565)
Doyle, Roddy. Brilliant. Hughes, Emily, illus. (p. 228)
—Greyhound of a Girl. (p. 723)
—Her Mother's Face. Blackwood, Freya, illus. (p. 769)
Doyle, Sandra, illus. see Colson, Rob Scott & de la Bédoyère, Camilla.
Doyle, Sheldon. Purple Mountain's Majesty. (p. 1419)
Doyle, Sheri. Cows (p. 374)
—Horses (p. 800)
—Pigs (p. 1358)
—Understanding Egyptian Myths. (p. 1815)
—What Is a Noun? (p. 1888)
—What Is a Preposition? (p. 1888)
—What Is a Pronoun? (p. 1888)
Doyle, Sheri, jt. auth. see Clay, Kathryn.
Doyle, Sheri, jt. auth. see Fandel, Jennifer.
Doyle, Sheri & Fandel, Jennifer. Parts of Speech. (p. 1325)
Doyle, Sheri & Saunders-Smith, Gail. What Is a Noun? (p. 1888)
Doyle, Teresa J. Dream Box: Big Dreams for Little Sleepers. (p. 483)
Doyle, V. L. & Rohm, Robert. Four Friends Find Fun. Zulewski, Timothy, illus. (p. 625)
Doyle, Warren. Book 1 a Walking Adventure to Mt. Bartle Frere. (p. 210)
Doyle, William. Tell Me a Story Please: Read-Aloud Short Stories for Children & the Young at Heart. (p. 1716)
Doyle, Winifred, jt. auth. see Summer, Deborah.
Dozier, Ashlyn, illus. see Dozier, Kim.
Dozier, Ashlyn McCauley, illus. see Dozier, Kim.
Dozier, Brendan, photos by see Titzer, Robert C.
Dozier, Dolly, ed. see Willard, Hugh.
Dozier, Kamilah. Monster Named Fear. (p. 1168)
Dozier, Kim. Backwards Wizard. Dozier, Ashlyn McCauley & Dozier, Makenna Joy, illus. (p. 130)
—Confused Tooth Fairy. Dozier, Ashlyn & Dozier, Makenna Joy, illus. (p. 357)
—Ear-Less Kingdom. Dozier, Ashlyn McCauley, illus. (p. 492)
—Forgetful Princess. Dozier, Ashlyn McCauley, illus. (p. 619)
—Where's Dwight Dragon. Dozier, Ashlyn McCauley, illus. (p. 1910)
Dozier, Lisa, photos by see Titzer, Robert C.
Dozier, Makenna Joy, illus. see Dozier, Kim.
Dozier, Mike. Little Inchworm with the Big Dream. (p. 1029)
—Zack & the Bean Stalk. (p. 1984)
Dozois, Gardner. Best of the Best, Volume 2: 20 Years of the Best Short Science Fiction Novels Dozois, Gardner, ed. (p. 170)
DPWW, ed. High School Musical Actors' Biography. (p. 778)
Dr. Seuss Enterprises Staff. Hop on Pop. (p. 796)
Dr. Seuss Enterprises Staff & Perkins, Al. Nose Book. Mathieu, Joe, illus. (p. 1266)
Drachman, Eric. Bad Rats. Muscarello, James, illus. (p. 132)
—Ellison the Elephant. Muscarello, James, illus. (p. 515)
—Frog Thing. Muscarello, James, illus. (p. 640)
—It's Me! Isabelle, Decenciere, illus. (p. 897)
—Leo the Lightning Bug. Muscarello, James, illus. (p. 992)
Dracker, Pune. Doll & Teddy Bear Activity Book. Bart, Kathleen & Hofmann, Ginnie, illus. (p. 463)
Draeger, Manuela. In the Time of the Blue Ball. Evenson, Brian, tr. (p. 867)
Drage, Robyn, illus. see O'Brien, Duncan.
Draggoo, Karen. Snow Angels. (p. 1598)
Dragland. Simon Jesse's Journey. (p. 1577)
Drago, Ty. Queen of the Dead. Williams, Eric L., illus. (p. 1425)
—Undertakers: The Rise of the Corpses. (p. 1817)
Dragon, Laura. Hurricane Boy (p. 829)
Dragonblood, A. Whispering V: Children of the Others Collection. (p. 1912)
Dragonheart, Jesse C. Y. When I Grow Up. (p. 1902)
Dragonwagon, Crescent. All the Awake Animals Are Almost Asleep. McPhail, David, illus. (p. 45)
—And Then It Rained ... And Then the Sun Came Out... Greenseid, Diane, illus. (p. 71)
—Bat in the Dining Room Schindler, S. D., illus. (p. 143)
Dragony, Barbara, illus. see Frankford, Marilyn.
Dragotta, Nick, jt. auth. see Hickman, Jonathan.
Dragotta, Nick, jt. illus. see Bobillo, Juan.
Dragotta, Nick & Hickman, Jonathan. Death of Spider-Man Fallout. Pichelli, Sara, illus. (p. 420)
Dragotta, Nick, et al. Captain America: Forever Allies. (p. 263)
—Marvel Zombies Return. (p. 1099)
Dragovich, Joe. Empty Hook. (p. 521)
Drahos, Peter. Global Intellectual Property Rights: Knowledge, Access & Development. Drahos, Peter & Mayne, Ruth, eds. (p. 684)
Drainville, Beth, illus. see O'Connor, Jane.
Drake, Aaron, jt. auth. see Drake, Jennifer.
Drake, Aaron & Drake, Jennifer. A-B-C & 1-2-3 Travel Coloring Book. (p. 1)
Drake, Arnold, jt. auth. see Arneson, Donald.
Drake, Arnold, et al. Boris Karloff Tales of Mystery Archives Volume 6. (p. 214)
Drake, Carol. 10 Best Movies from Books. (p. 1993)
—10 Most Incredible Ancient Wonders. (p. 1994)
Drake, Christina M. Milo the Monkey. (p. 1144)
Drake, David. Kidd's Grand Adventure. (p. 952)
—Master of the Cauldron. (p. 1103)
Drake, Emily. Curse of Arkady. (p. 394)
Drake, Ensign Robert L. Boy Allies with Uncle Sams Cruisers. (p. 217)
Drake, Ernest. Dragonology: The Complete Book of Dragons. Steer, Dugald A., ed. (p. 478)
—Dragonology Handbook: A Practical Course in Dragons. Steer, Dugald A., ed. (p. 478)
—Monsterology: The Complete Book of Monstrous Creatures. Steer, Dugald A., ed. (p. 1168)
—Monsterology Handbook: A Practical Course in Monsters. Steer, Dugald A., ed. (p. 1168)
Drake, Gertrude, ed. Latin Readings. (p. 979)
—More Latin Readings. (p. 1174)
—More Latin Readings, Grades 9-12. (p. 1174)
Drake, Gwasg Addysgol, jt. auth. see Williams, Alwena.
Drake, Jane, jt. auth. see Love, Ann.
Drake, Jane & Love, Ann. Alien Invaders: Species That Threaten Our World. Thurman, Mark, illus. (p. 40)
—Cool Woods: A Trip Around the World's Boreal Forest. Kiss, Andrew, illus. (p. 364)
—Get Outside: The Kids Guide to Fun in the Great Outdoors. Collins, Heather, illus. (p. 668)
—Pandemic Survival: It's Why You're Alive. Slavin, Bill, illus. (p. 1321)
—Snow Amazing: Cool Facts & Warm Tales. Thurman, Mark, illus. (p. 1598)
Drake, Jennifer, jt. auth. see Drake, Aaron.
Drake, Jennifer & Drake, Aaron. Travel Fun with Towty: A Color & Activity. (p. 1780)
Drake, Jennifer & Feltham, Sarah. Scotty's Postcards from Rome. (p. 1532)
Drake, Karen. Please Be Quiet! Jones, Aaron, illus. (p. 1373)
Drake, Lana, jt. auth. see Clauson, Marilyn.
Drake, Michael. Growing Books: My Inside Is Outside. (p. 726)
Drake, Michelle. Walking with God: The Young Person's Prayer Diary. Knapp, Cheryl, illus. (p. 1854)
Drake, Paula. How to Make a Snow Day: The Official Rules & Regulations. (p. 820)
Drake, R. C. Let's Find a Toy for Moo Moo the Mutdog. (p. 996)
Drake, Robert L. Boy Allies at Jutland: Or, the Greatest Naval Battle of History. (p. 217)
—Boy Allies at Jutland. (p. 217)
—Boy Allies under the Sea. (p. 217)
—Boy Allies under Two Flags. (p. 217)
—Boy Allies with the Victorious Fleet. (p. 217)
—Boy Allies with the Victorious Fleets. (p. 217)
—Boy Allies with Uncle Sams Cruisers. (p. 217)
—Boy Scouts of the Eagle Patrol. (p. 218)
Drake, Rudy. Dushan (p. 490)
Drake, Stephen. Vancouver Canucks. (p. 1833)
Drake, Tim. From an Angel in a Dream, the Story of Saint Joseph, Marys Husband: De un Angel en un Sueño, la Historia de San José, Esposo de María. Alvarado, Tomas, tr. (p. 641)
—Santos Valientes de los Caballeros de Columbus. Alvarado, Tomas, tr. (p. 1513)
Drake, W. H., Jr., illus. see Kipling, Rudyard.
Drakeford, Luther D. Quiet Please. (p. 1428)
Drakeford, Philippa, illus. see Weatherhead, Yvonne.
Drakulic, Slavenka. Frida's Bed. Pribichevich-Zoric, Christina, tr. from CRO. (p. 637)
Dramer, Kim. Chinese. (p. 307)
Dran, Ruth. Little Peninsula. Katz, Avi, illus. (p. 1033)
Drane, John Wanzer. Sassafras & Chicory. (p. 1515)
Dranger, Joanna Rubin, jt. auth. see Brundin, Anders.
Dranoel, Elttem. Elttem Dranoel: Judgement Day. (p. 516)
—Elttem Dranoel:Judgement Day. (p. 516)
Dransfield, Don, jt. auth. see Dransfield, Robert.
Dransfield, Robert. Statistics Made Easy. (p. 1644)
Dransfield, Robert & Dransfield, Don. Key Ideas in Economics. (p. 950)
Drape, Kaitlin, illus. see Finally, Lil Rose.
Drapeau, Patti. Making It Work: A Practical Guide to Planning, Managing, & Implementing Differentiated Instruction to Meet the Needs of All Learners. (p. 1081)
Draper, Adrian. Chili Peppers in Oatmeal. (p. 305)
Draper, Allison Stark. Assassination of Malcolm X. (p. 107)
—Boston Massacre: Five Colonists Killed by British Soldiers. (p. 215)
—Boston Tea Party: Angry Colonists Dump British Tea. (p. 215)
—Choosing a Career in the Pulp & Paper Industry. (p. 310)
—Clothing, Costumes & Uniforms Throughout American History (p. 334)
—Coping with Natural Disasters. (p. 365)
—Earth. (p. 494)
—Historical Atlas Of Egypt. (p. 782)
—Historical Atlas of Egypt. (p. 782)
—Historical Atlas of Syria. (p. 783)
—Hydropower for the Future: New Ways of Turning Water into Energy. (p. 831)
—Hydropower of the Future: New Ways of Turning Water into Energy. (p. 831)
—India: A Primary Source Cultural Guide. (p. 870)
—Mission San Fransisco de Solano. (p. 1153)
—Mission San Juan Bautista. (p. 1153)
—Pastor André Trocmé: Spiritual Leader of the French Village le Chambon. (p. 1327)
—Pastor Andre Trocme: Spiritual Leader of the French Village, Le Chambon. (p. 1327)
—Start of the American Revolutionary War: Paul Revere Rides at Midnight. (p. 1643)
—Trail Riding: Have Fun, Be Smart. (p. 1776)
—Vasco da Gama: The Portuguese Quest for a Sea Route from Europe to India. (p. 1833)
—What People Wore During the American Revolution. (p. 1892)
—What People Wore During the Civil War. (p. 1892)
—What People Wore in Early America. (p. 1892)
—What People Wore on Southern Plantations. (p. 1892)
Draper, Allison Stark, jt. auth. see Levin, Judy.
Draper, Catheryne. Algebra Game Linear Graphs: Cooperative Learning Activities. (p. 38)
—Algebra Game: Quadratic Equations: Cooperative Learning Activities. (p. 38)
Draper, Diane E. Expressions from the Experience: Christian Poetry & Short Inspirations. (p. 555)
Draper, Edythe, ed. Awesome Words: Daily Bible Readings for Teens. (p. 121)
Draper, Jimmy. We Believe: Living in the Light of God's Truth. (p. 1866)
Draper, Judith. My First Horse & Pony Show & Games. (p. 1206)
Draper, Judith & Roberts, Matthew. My First Horse & Pony Book: From Breeds & Bridles to Jophpurs & Jumping. (p. 1206)
Draper, Melissa J. Holly the Christmas Collie. Kravanek, J. Elise, illus. (p. 789)
Draper, Penny. Day of the Cyclone Sapergia, Barbara, ed. (p. 414)
—Graveyard of the Sea (p. 712)
—Ice Storm! (p. 850)
—Peril at Pier Nine (p. 1343)
—Red River Raging (p. 1455)
—Terrible Roar of Water (p. 1721)
—Terror at Turtle Mountain (p. 1722)
Draper, Polly. Cry Wolff. (p. 387)
Draper, Richard, illus. see Everett, Felicity & Reid, Struan.
Draper, Richard, illus. see Parker, Steve.
Draper, Rochelle. Stone Wall Dragon. Draper, Rochelle, illus. (p. 1653)
Draper, Rohan. Sunny & Mayo. (p. 1677)
Draper, Sharon M. Backyard Animal Show. Watson, Jesse Joshua, illus. (p. 130)
—Battle of Jericho. (p. 146)
—Birthday Storm. (p. 193)
—Buried Bones Mystery. Watson, Jesse Joshua, illus. (p. 243)
—Copper Sun. (p. 365)
—Copper Sun. (p. 366)
—Darkness Before Dawn. (p. 408)
—Double Dutch. (p. 472)
—Fire from the Rock. (p. 590)
—Forged by Fire. (p. 619)
—Just Another Hero. (p. 937)
—Lost in the Tunnel of Time. Watson, Jesse Joshua, illus. (p. 1056)
—November Blues. (p. 1268)
—Out of My Mind. (p. 1311)
—Panic. (p. 1321)
—Sassy - Little Sister Is Not My Name! (p. 1515)
—Shadows of Caesar's Creek. Watson, Jesse Joshua, illus. (p. 1558)
—Silver Secret. (p. 1577)
—Space Mission Adventure. Watson, Jesse Joshua, illus. (p. 1619)
—Stars & Sparks on Stage. Watson, Jesse Joshua, illus. (p. 1643)
—Stella by Starlight. (p. 1647)
—Tears of a Tiger. (p. 1711)
Draper, Sharon M. & Bascoul, Eric. Battle of Jericho. (p. 146)
Draper, Tricia. Bobby Bear Learns to Be a Cowboy. Babinski, Michael, illus. (p. 206)
Drashner, Diane, illus. see Richter, Bernd & Richter, Susan.
Draught Associates. Visual Aid Doodling Book for Creative Kids. (p. 1846)
Draus, Naudia Burtwell. My Grandma Wears A Number: How One Girl Survived World War Ii. (p. 1210)
Draven, Shelly, illus. see Baldwin, Christy.
Drawhorn, Barbara. Maddie Waaa! (p. 1069)
Drawing Staff, jt. auth. see Cohen, Sheldon.
Drawing Staff, jt. auth. see Giannotta, Andres Bernardo.
Drawing Staff, jt. auth. see Green, John.
Drawing Staff, jt. auth. see Levy, Barbara Soloff.
Drawing Staff, jt. auth. see Tallarico, Tony, Sr.
Drawing Staff, jt. auth. see Tallarico, Tony.
Drawson, Blair. Flying Dimitri (p. 609)
—Mary Margaret's Tree. (p. 1100)
Drawson, Blair, illus. see Hovey, Kate.
Drawson, Blair, illus. see Oberman, Sheldon.
Draxler, Hans-Dieter, et al. Unterwegs - Kursbuch: Lehrwerk fur die Mittelstufe (p. 1823)
Draxlir, A. T. Flower. (p. 607)
Dray, Matt. Dougal, the Garbage Dump Bear. Dray, Matt, illus. (p. 473)
Dray, Philip. Yours for Justice, Ida B. Wells: The Daring Life of a Crusading Journalist Alcorn, Stephen, illus. (p. 1982)
Draycott, Michelle, illus. see Dale, Jay.
Drayer, Lee. Misadventures of Pal & Samantha: As Pal, the Dog, Tells It. (p. 1150)
Drayton, Adrienne, illus. see Day, Deborah A.
Drayton, Bill, frwd. Be a Changemaker: How to Start Something That Matters. (p. 148)
Drayton, Marta, illus. see Frender, Gloria.
Draze, Dianne. Attribute Block - Thinking Activities - Sequences. (p. 114)
—First Time Analogies. (p. 597)
—Inventions, Inventors & You. (p. 884)
—Junior Literature Companion. (p. 936)
—Loose Caboose & Other Math Mysteries. (p. 1052)
—Math-a-Logic. (p. 1105)
—Red Hot Root Words: Mastering Vocabulary with Prefixes, Suffixes & Root Words. Bk. 1 (p. 1454)
Drazman, Jenya, tr. see Berger, Barry W.
Dreadfuls, Penny, ed. see Gerard, Kevin.
DreamWorks. Kung Fu Panda: Po's Tasty Training. (p. 968)
DreamWorks / LeapFrog, jt. auth. see DreamWorks.
DreamWorks & DreamWorks / LeapFrog. Kung Fu Panda: L'Entrainement Gourmand. (p. 968)
DreamWorks Animation Creative Team, jt. auth. see Walter Foster Jr. Creative Team.
DreamWorks Animation Staff. Shrek 2. (p. 1571)
DreamWorks Animation Staff, jt. contrib. by see Scholastic, Inc. Staff.
Dreamworks How to Train Your Dragon, Dreamworks How. DreamWorks How to Train Your Dragon 2: Draw-It Dragons. (p. 484)
—Dreamworks How to Train Your Dragon 2: Time to Race! (p. 484)
DreamWorks Staff. DreamWorks Turbo Need for Speed! Storybook & Picture Viewer. (p. 484)
—DreamWorks Turbo Racing Team. (p. 484)
Dreany, E. Joseph, illus. see Fletcher, Steffi.
Dreany, E. Joseph, illus. see Stevenson, Augusta.
Dreany, E. Joseph, illus. see Verral, Charles Spain.
Drechsler, Lawrence. Pirates. (p. 1363)
Dredge, Kath. Living 4 God: Learning from the Lives of William Tyndale, John Newton, David Brainerd, Eric Liddell. (p. 1040)
Dredge, Richard. World's Fastest Cars: The Fastest Road & Racing Cars on Earth. (p. 1960)
Drees, Allen, ed. see Evanger, Brent.
Dreher, Gidge. Gus, Scruffy, Clara & Friends. (p. 732)
Dreher, Patrick, tr. see Zink, Rui.
Dreher, Ruth. Ralph the Red Engine. (p. 1437)
Drehsen, Britta. Flip-O-Saurus. Ball, Sara, illus. (p. 605)
Dreidemy, Joëlle, illus. see Bailey, Gerry.
Dreidemy, Joëlle, illus. see Collins, Tim.
Dreidemy, Joëlle, illus. see Forde, Patricia & Agnew, Kate.
Dreidemy, Joëlle, illus. see Forde, Patricia.
Dreidemy, Joëlle, illus. see Gale, Emily.
Dreidemy, Joëlle, illus. see Goodhart, Pippa.
Dreidemy, Joëlle, illus. see Hiranandani, Veera.
Dreidemy, Joëlle, illus. see Jones, Marcia Thornton & Dadey, Debbie.
Dreidemy, Joëlle, illus. see Marlow, Layn.
Dreidemy, Joëlle, illus. see North, Laura.
Dreidemy, Joëlle, illus. see Patchett, Fiona.
Dreidemy, Joëlle, illus. see Smallman, Steve.
Dreidmy, Joelle, illus. see Fine, Anne.
Dreier, David. Baseball: How It Works (p. 140)
—Be a Storm Chaser. (p. 148)
—Electrical Circuits: Harnessing Electricity Schultz, Ashlee, illus. (p. 508)
Dreier, David & Dreier, David Louis. Baseball: How It Works. (p. 140)
Dreier, David L. Science of Baseball with Max Axiom, Super Scientist. Aranda, Tom, illus. (p. 1527)
Dreier, David L. & Hoena, Blake. Science of Sports with Max Axiom. Cacau, Caio, illus. (p. 1527)
Dreier, David Louis. Be a Storm Chaser. (p. 148)
—Forces & Motion. (p. 617)
Dreier, David Louis, jt. auth. see Dreier, David.
Dreier, Ted, jt. auth. see Morton, Jane.
Dreiling, Christy. Holes in My Socks. (p. 788)
Dreis, Stella, illus. see Hahn, Daniel.
Dreisbach, Kristin Wolf. Winston the Duck & His Big Orange Bill. Dreisbach, Kristin Wolf & Foreman, Austin Lee, illus. (p. 1937)
Dreissigacker Martin, Susan. Princess Stephanie Stories: The Road Trip & the New School. (p. 1405)
Dreistadt, Jessica R. Ashley & Tiana. (p. 106)
Dreliozis, Nick. Forever in Your Debt: A Christian's Guide to Health, Happiness & Contentment. (p. 619)
Drella, Michele. Laberinto de Graci. (p. 969)
—Mazing Grace. (p. 1113)
Drescher, Daniela. Elves' Big Adventure (p. 517)
—In the Land of Elves (p. 866)
—In the Land of Fairies (p. 866)
—Little Fairy's Christmas (p. 1027)
—What's Hiding in There? (p. 1897)

D

Drescher, Fran. Cancer Schmancer. (p. 260)
Drescher, Heather, illus. see Stephens, Edna Cucksey, et al.
Drescher, Henrick, illus. see Metaxas, Eric.
Drescher, Henrik. Love the Beastie: A Spin-and-Play Book. (p. 1060)
—Pat the Beastie: A Pull-and-Poke Book. Drescher, Henrik, illus. (p. 1327)
—Simon's Book. (p. 1577)
—Strange Appearance of Howard Cranebill. (p. 1664)
Drescher, Henrik, illus. see Harris, Joel Chandler.
Drescher, Henrik, illus. see Sierra, Judy.
Drescher, Henrik, illus. see Tyson, Leigh Ann.
Dreser, Elena. Secreto del Sauce. Diez, Dalia Alvarado, illus. (p. 1544)
Dreske, Erin, jt. auth. see Raffaelli, Sean.
Dresner, Hal. Amazing Menorah of Mazeltown. Shapiro, Neil, illus. (p. 55)
Dress, Robert, illus. see Banks, Steven.
Dress, Robert, illus. see Thompson, Kate.
Dress, Robert, illus. see Willson, Sarah.
Dressel, Toni Ankeney. Sophie Smiles (p. 1613)
Dressen-McQueen, Stacey, illus. see Fleming, Candace.
Dressen-McQueen, Stacey, illus. see Hopkins, Lee Bennett.
Dressler, Craig. Kids' Bible Poems. (p. 952)
Dressler, Isidore. Algebra I. (p. 38)
—Geometry: Revised. (p. 662)
Drevitch, Gary. Asia. (p. 106)
—Presidents FYI. (p. 1397)
Drew, Alejandrina. Abra Cadabra, Patas de Cabra: A Spanish, English Story for Young Readers. Satcher, David & Ford, Richard, trs. (p. 6)
Drew And Hilary McSherry. Terrance the Trapezoid. (p. 1721)
Drew, Benjamin, illus. see Drew, Joyce.
Drew, David. Caterpillar Diary. (p. 279)
—Mystery Monsters: A Game for Two or More Players. (p. 1224)
Drew, Ellie. Partnering with Spirit: Homer's Journey. (p. 1325)
Drew, Jane Myers. Where Were You When I Needed You Dad? A Guide for Healing Your Father Wound. (p. 1910)
Drew, Jon. Matt's Field Day: Represent & Interpret Data. (p. 1110)
Drew, Joyce. Grandma's Adventures with Benjamin. Drew, Benjamin, illus. (p. 708)
Drew, Keith. Branding Online. (p. 222)
Drew, Mary E. C. One Common Country for One Common People. (p. 1294)
Drew, Nancy, jt. auth. see Keene, Carolyn.
Drew, Naomi. Kids' Guide to Working Out Conflicts: How to Keep Cool, Stay Safe, & Get Along. (p. 954)
Drew, Rosa, et al. K-2 Resource Book 4 Set (p. 941)
Drew, Ursula & Watson, Stephanie. Conquering Bulimia. (p. 358)
Drew-Brook, Deborah, illus. see Bradford, Karleen.
Drew-Brook, Deborah, illus. see Souza, D. M.
Drewe, James, jt. auth. see Jennings, Madeleine.
Drewery, Melanie. Grumble Rumble Mumbler. Smits, Josh, illus. (p. 727)
Drewes, Dan, illus. see Douglas, Rachel.
Drewes, Dan, illus. see Manderly, Lorin.
Drewes, Dan, illus. see Seykora, Teresa.
Drewes, Dan, illus. see Wimberly, Nikisha.
Drewett, Jim. How to Improve at Tennis. (p. 820)
Drewett, Jim, jt. auth. see Morgan, Paul.
Drewett, Jim & Martin, Ashley. How to Improve at Karate. (p. 820)
Drews, Judith. Ava: Magnetic Dress-up Doll. (p. 118)
—Lucas: Magnetic Dress-up Doll. (p. 1062)
—Zoo's Grand Opening: An ABC & Counting Book. (p. 1990)
Drews, Judith, illus. see Lüftner, Kai.
Drexler, Sam, jt. auth. see Alshalabi, Firyal M.
Drexler, Sam & Shelby, Fay. Murder in Bozeman. (p. 1192)
Dreyer, Ellen. Band of Brave Men: The Story of the 54th Massachusetts Regiment. (p. 136)
—Glow Stone (p. 685)
—Grow, Tree, Grow! Swanson, Maggie, tr. (p. 726)
—Speechless in New York. Huerta, Catherine, illus. (p. 1624)
—Starfishers to the Rescue. (p. 1642)
Dreyer, Kira. My New Bedroom: Estimate Lengths in Standard Units. (p. 1216)
Dreyer, Laura, illus. see Scherm, Deedra.
Dreyer, Nicole. Easter Stranger. (p. 499)
Dreyer, Nicole E. Joseph's Christmas Story. Ebert, Len, illus. (p. 926)
—Lost Coin. Collier-Morales, Roberta, illus. (p. 1055)
—Parable of the Talents. Morris, Susan, illus. (p. 1323)
—Peter's Easter Story. Motoyama, Keiko, illus. (p. 1347)
Dreyer, ZoAnn. Living with Cancer. (p. 1042)
Dreyfuss, Katy. Reflexology Deck: 50 Healing Techniques. Shavell, Lauren, illus. (p. 1456)
Drez, Jennifer & Bumstead, Robin. Goodnight Cowtown. Voight, Lisa, illus. (p. 701)
Drez, Ronald J. Remember D-Day: The Plan, the Invasion, Survivor Stories. (p. 1459)
Dries, L. M. H. Stella & the Rocks. (p. 1646)
—Tales & Adventures of Hopper the Frog: Strangers. (p. 1701)
—Tales & Adventures of Hopper the Frog: The First Day of School. (p. 1701)
—Tales & Adventures of Hopper the Frog: The Trip Across the Lily Pond. (p. 1701)
Driesel, Amy. Why Gretchen Can't Spell. (p. 1925)
Driessen, Anita, illus. see Hebler, Michael.
Driessen, Elizabeth, illus. see Allen, Nancy Kelly.
Driftin' Aarong. Claude Henry, the Iditarod Mouse ~3: The Great Castaway Adventure. (p. 329)
Driggs, Howard R. When Grandfather Was a Boy. Hales, J. Rulon, illus. (p. 1902)
Drinkard, Lawson. Riding on a Range: Western Activities for Kids. Lee, Fran, illus. (p. 1471)
Drinnon, Sheila. Cuddles. (p. 389)
Drion, Donna. Stop & Look at God's Word. (p. 1653)
—Stop & Look at God's World. (p. 1653)
—Stop & Look at Yourself. (p. 1653)
Drischel, Candy L. Restless with the Dark Moon Rising. (p. 1464)
Driscoll, Amanda. Duncan the Story Dragon. (p. 490)
—Wally Does Not Want a Haircut. (p. 1855)
Driscoll, Christ. And God Blessed the Irish: The Story of Patrick. Kelley, Patrick, illus. (p. 71)
Driscoll, Colleen. Piper the Elf Trains Santa. Dumm, Brian, illus. (p. 1362)
Driscoll, James R. Brighton Boys with the Flying Corps. (p. 228)
—Brighton Boys with the Submarine Fleet. (p. 228)
Driscoll, Laura. Apples: And How They Grow. Smith, Tammy, illus. (p. 92)
—Blast off Kid! Thornburgh, Rebecca McKillip, illus. (p. 198)
—Chico del Despegue. Ramirez, Alma, tr. from ENG. (p. 301)
—Chico Del Despegue (the Blast-off Kid) (p. 301)
—Count off, Squeak Scouts! Melmon, Deborah, illus. (p. 369)
—Dance to the Rescue. Aikins, Dave, illus. (p. 402)
—Do Dolphins Really Smile? Wald, Christina, illus. (p. 456)
—George Washington Carver: The Peanut Wizard. Weber, Jill, illus. (p. 664)
—Lila the Fair. Sims, Blanche, illus. (p. 1017)
—Mickey's Birthday. (p. 1136)
—Mousy Mess. Melmon, Deborah, illus. (p. 1182)
—My Brother, the Knight. Smath, Jerry, illus. (p. 1199)
—Real Heroes Don't Wear Capes. (p. 1448)
—Real Heroes Don't Wear Capes. Wummer, Amy, illus. (p. 1448)
—Sally's Big Save. Wummer, Amy, illus. (p. 1505)
—Slow down, Sara! O'Rourke, Page Eastburn, illus. (p. 1591)
—Super Specs. Gott, Barry, illus. (p. 1682)
—Thumper Goes A-Thumpin' Tyminski, Lori, illus. (p. 1746)
—Titanic: The Story Lives On! (p. 1757)
—Titanic: The Story Lives On! Kayganich, Bob, illus. (p. 1757)
—We Are Twins. (p. 1866)
—We Are Twins. Campion, Pascal, illus. (p. 1866)
—Where Is Baby Jaguar? Mangano, Tom & Miller, Victoria, illus. (p. 1908)
Driscoll, Laura, jt. auth. see Disney Book Group Staff.
Driscoll, Laura, jt. auth. see Scotton, Rob.
Driscoll, Laura & Disney Book Group Staff. I Love You, My Bunnies. Tyminski, Lori et al, illus. (p. 844)
—Mickey's Birthday. Disney Storybook Artists Staff, illus. (p. 1136)
—Thumper Finds an Egg. Tyminski, Lori et al, illus. (p. 1746)
—Thumper's Fluffy Tail. Tyminski, Lori & Vallorani, Giorgio, illus. (p. 1746)
Driscoll, Laura & Rey, H. A. Curious George at the Baseball Game. Hines, Anna Grossnickle, illus. (p. 393)
Driscoll, Laura & RH Disney Staff. Smash Trash! Cortes, Mario et al, illus. (p. 1593)
Driscoll, Laura, et al. Curious George at the Baseball Game. Hines, Anna Grossnickle, illus. (p. 393)
Driscoll, Michael. Child's Introduction to the Night Sky: The Story of the Stars, Planets & Constellations - And How You Can Find Them in the Sky. Hamilton, Meredith, illus. (p. 305)
Driscoll, Roger K. Echo Mccool, Outlaw Through Time. (p. 502)
Driskell, Cheryl. Child & Youth Reiki Program: Mount Kurama & the Emerald Lake. (p. 301)
Driskill, Qwo-Li. Walking with Ghosts: Poems. (p. 1854)
Driver, Audrey, illus. see Takara, Kathryn Waddell.
Driver, Stephanie Schwartz. Understanding the Declaration of Independence. (p. 1816)
Driver, Stephanie Schwartz, ed. see Childs, William R.
Driver, Stephanie Schwartz & Garcia, Rachel. I Wish I Knew That Science: Cool Stuff You Need to Know. (p. 849)
Driver, Stephanie Schwartz, ed. Personal Finance: A Guide to Money & Business. (p. 1344)
Driza, Debra. Mila 2.0. (p. 1142)
Drobeck, Ronald D. My Name Is Prince Albert. (p. 1215)
Drogo, Susette. Five Blessings. Lukas, Mary, illus. (p. 600)
Droham, Michele Ingber, jt. auth. see Katirgis, Jane.
Drohan, Michele Ingber, jt. auth. see Katirgis, Jane.
Droll, jt. auth. see Kroll, Steven.
Dromgoole, Glenn. Good Night Cowboy. Clack, Barbra, illus. (p. 699)
—Good Night Little Texan. Clack, Barbra, illus. (p. 699)
—What Puppies Teach Us: Life's Lessons Learned from Our Little Friends. (p. 1893)
Dromgoole, Glenn & Clack, Barbra. Good Night Cowgirl. Clack, Barbra, illus. (p. 699)
Dronet, Sandra, et al. Kings Don't Spit. (p. 960)
Droney, John, illus. see Kline, Trish & Donev, Mary.
Droney, Susan K. Stalker. Winton, Byron, illus. (p. 1638)
Dronsfield, Paul. Bob-Alongs - Colors: Bath Books That Float. (p. 205)
—Bulldozer. (p. 240)
—Concrete Mixer. (p. 355)
—Digger. (p. 438)
—Dump Truck. (p. 489)
Dronsfield, Paul, illus. see Top That Publishing Staff, ed.
Dronsfield, Paul, illus. see Trowell, Michelle.
Dronzek, Laura, illus. see Griffith, Helen V.
Dronzek, Laura, illus. see Henkes, Kevin.
Dronzek, Laura, illus. see Rowand, Phyllis.
Dronzek, Laura, illus. see Shannon, George & Shannon.
Dronzek, Laura, illus. see Shannon, George.
Droop, Constanza. Que? Como? Por Que?: Las Estaciones del Ano. Caballero, D., tr. (p. 1423)
Droop, Constanza, illus. see Krenzer, Rolf.
Droop, Constanza, illus. see Langen, Annette.
Drost, Joost & Bayley, Sydney. Therapeutic Groupwork with Children. (p. 1729)
Drotar, illus. see Clapp.
Drotleff, David J., illus. see Snedeker, Erin.
Drouhard, Brianne. Billie the Unicorn. (p. 187)
Drouin, Julie Saint-Onge, illus. see Lefrancois, Viateur.
Drouin, Matthew. Web Hosting & Web Site Development: A Guide to Opportunities. (p. 1870)
Drouin, Véronique. Île D'Aurélie. (p. 856)
Droujkova, Maria, jt. auth. see McManaman, Yelena.
Drown, Eleanor J., illus. see Kraemer, Lillian Rosa.
Drozd, Jerzy, illus. see Mishkin, Dan.
Dru Tecco, Betsy. Food for Fuel: The Connection Between Food & Physical Activity. (p. 613)
Drubbel, Bart. 21st Century Webster's International Encyclopedia: 10 Volume Box Set (p. 1996)
—21st Century Webster's International Encyclopedia: Standard Edition. (p. 1996)
Drucker, Susan, illus. see Francis, Lee DeCora.
Druckman, Joan, illus. see Druckman, Michael.
Druckman, Michael. Memory Emory & His Hiding Places. Druckman, Joan, illus. (p. 1126)
Druckman, Mike, jt. auth. see Masterson, Carla.
Druckmann, Neil, jt. auth. see Hicks, Faith Erin.
Druery, Donna Michelle. What Mama Said. (p. 1892)
Druett, Joan. Watery Grave. (p. 1864)
Druitt, Tobias. Corydon & the Siege of Troy. (p. 368)
Drum, Emily. Happy Trails Horse Ranch. (p. 747)
Drumlin, Sam. Dolphins: Los Delfines. Alamán, Eduardo, tr. from ENG. (p. 464)
—Dolphins. (p. 464)
—Harp Seals: Las Focas de Groenlandia. Alamán, Eduardo, tr. from ENG. (p. 749)
—Harp Seals. (p. 749)
—Manatees: Los Manatíes. Alamán, Eduardo, tr. from ENG. (p. 1086)
—Manatees. (p. 1086)
—Orcas: Las Orcas. Alamán, Eduardo, tr. from ENG. (p. 1302)
—Orcas. (p. 1302)
—Sea Otters: Las Nutrias Marinas. Alamán, Eduardo, tr. from ENG. (p. 1535)
—Sea Otters. (p. 1535)
—Walruses: Las Morsas. Alamán, Eduardo, tr. from ENG. (p. 1855)
—Walruses. (p. 1855)
Drummond, Allan. Energy Island: How One Community Harnessed the Wind & Changed Their World. Drummond, Allan, illus. (p. 528)
Drummond, Allan, illus. see Borden, Louise & Borden, Louise W.
Drummond, Allan, illus. see Borden, Louise W.
Drummond, James H. Marketing's 10 Deadly Sins(and how to avoid Them) (p. 1095)
Drummond, Karen Eich, jt. auth. see D'Amico, Joan.
Drummond, Karen Eich & D'Amico, Joan. Coming to America Cookbook: Delicious Recipes & Fascinating Stories from America's Many Cultures. (p. 348)
Drummond, Karona. Along Came You (p. 48)
Drummond, Nancy. Wright to Machu Picchu. (p. 1963)
Drummond Publishing Group Editors, ed. Youth Soccer Unleashed: A Parent's & Player's Guide to the Fundamentals of the Game. (p. 1982)
Drummond, Ree. Charlie & the Christmas Kitty. deGroat, Diane, illus. (p. 292)
—Charlie & the New Baby. deGroat, Diane, illus. (p. 292)
—Charlie Goes to School. deGroat, Diane, illus. (p. 293)
—Charlie Goes to the Doctor. (p. 293)
—Charlie Plays Ball. deGroat, Diane, illus. (p. 293)
—Charlie the Ranch Dog: Where's the Bacon? deGroat, Diane, illus. (p. 293)
—Charlie the Ranch Dog: Charlie's Snow Day. deGroat, Diane, illus. (p. 293)
—Charlie the Ranch Dog: Charlie's New Friend. deGroat, Diane, illus. (p. 293)
—Charlie the Ranch Dog: Charlie Goes to the Doctor. deGroat, Diane, illus. (p. 293)
—Charlie the Ranch Dog: Stuck in the Mud. deGroat, Diane & Whipple, Rick, illus. (p. 293)
—Charlie the Ranch Dog. (p. 293)
—Charlie the Ranch Dog. deGroat, Diane, illus. (p. 293)
—Charlie the Ranch Dog - Charlie's Snow Day. deGroat, Diane, illus. (p. 293)
—Charlie the Ranch Dog - Stuck in the Mud. deGroat, Diane & Whipple, Rick, illus. (p. 293)
—Charlie's New Friend. (p. 293)
—Charlie's Snow Day. (p. 293)
—Stuck in the Mud. (p. 1669)
Drummond, Sarah. Raven & the Red Ball. (p. 1441)
Drummond, V. H., illus. see Sleigh, Barbara.
Drummond-Hay, Fran, ed. see Dunkley, Cheryl.
Drumond, Karen Eich, jt. auth. see D'Amico, Joan.
Drury, Richard S. Flightlines. (p. 604)
Druschel, Bob, illus. see Janacone, Matt.
Dry, Roland. Pied Piper. (p. 1356)
Dry, Roland, illus. see Barkow, Henriette.
Dryhurst, Dinah, illus. see Nesbit, E.
Dryhurst, Dinah, tr. see Nesbit, E.
Dryland, David. Fibromyalgia Cure. Scarpaci, Mark, ed. (p. 583)
Drzewiecki, Paul, illus. see Gould, Carol.
Drzewiecki, Paul, illus. see Hiris, Monica.
Drzewiecki, Paul, illus. see Hoenecke, Karen.
D'shindia, Albert. Fable Musical. (p. 559)
D'souza, Maris, illus. see Amarsingh, Bahia.
D'Souza, Mel, illus. see Hall, Noelle.
D'souza, Nadine. Revenge of the Puppets. Rajvanshi, Ayush, illus. (p. 1466)
Dtpolk. Shoes & the Laces. Barge III, John, illus. (p. 1568)
Du Bois, Crystal L. God Made My Butt Big. (p. 690)
—Where Are My Socks? (p. 1906)
du Bois, William Pène. Twenty-One Balloons. du Bois, William Pène, illus. (p. 1801)
du Bois, William Pène, illus. see Godden, Rumer.
Du Bouchet, Paule. Franz Schubert Voake, Charlotte, illus. (p. 631)
—Prince Orpheus. Negrin, Fabian, tr. from FRE. (p. 1401)
du Bouchet, Paule, jt. auth. see Khoury, Marielle D.
Du Bouchet, Paule & Khoury, Marielle D. Henry Purcell Voake, Charlotte, illus. (p. 768)
Du Chaillu, Paul. World of the Great Forest: How Animals, Birds, Reptiles & Insects Talk, Think, Work & Live. Knight, C. R., illus. (p. 1957)
Du Houx, E. M. Cornell, illus. see Barry, Holly, et al.
Du Houx, E. M. Cornell, illus. see Kroner, David & Du Houx, Ramona.
Du Houx, E. M. Cornell, illus. see Ouilette, K. T. Valliere-Denis.
du Houx, Emily, illus. see Halter, Loretta.
du Houx, Emily, illus. see Haque, Mary Baca.
du Houx, Emily C., illus. see Hoffmann, Burton R.
du Houx, Ramona, illus. see Levesque, Dawn Renee.
Du Houx, Ramona, jt. auth. see Kroner, David.
du Houx, Ramona, et al. Manitou, a Mythological Journey in Time. du Houx, Ramona & Cornell du Houx, Emily, illus. (p. 1087)
Du Jardin, Rosamond. Man for Marcy. (p. 1085)
—Marcy Catches Up. (p. 1092)
—Young & Fair. (p. 1978)
Du Lac, Leo J. Dogfish on the Moon: Santa Claus & the Flying Carpet 2. Baker, David, illus. (p. 462)
—Moon Fruit & the Dragons: Santa Claus & the Flying Carpet 3. Washington, Victoria, ed. (p. 1172)
Du Plessis, Claire. Rebit's Rainbow. (p. 1451)
du Plessis, David, jt. auth. see Greaves, Nick.
Du Pont, Brittany, illus. see Oehmichen, Ariel.
Du Pont, Brittany, illus. see Schmidt, Shawntay.
Du Puy, William Atherton & Nelson, Edward William. Our Animal Friends & Foes. (p. 1307)
Du, Sharon & Li, Oswald. Word Whirlpool. (p. 1951)
Duane, Daniel, jt. auth. see Waters, Alice.
Duane, Diane. Deep Wizardry. (p. 423)
—High Wizardry (p. 778)
—Wizard Alone. (p. 1942)
—Wizard of Mars Bk. 9. (p. 1943)
—Wizards at War Bk. 8. (p. 1943)
—Wizard's Holiday. (p. 1943)
Duarte, Gustavo. Monsters! & Other Stories. Hahn, Sierra, ed. (p. 1169)
Duarte, Pamela, illus. see Golden Books Staff.
Duarte, Pamela, illus. see Golden Books.
Duarte, Pamela, illus. see Man-Kong, Mary.
Duarte, Pamela, illus. see Random House Staff.
Duarte, Pamela, illus. see Reader's Digest Editors & Lombardi, Kristine.
Duarte, Pamela, illus. see Reader's Digest Editors.
Duarte, Pamela, illus. see Reader's Digest Staff & Lombardi, Kristine.
Duarte, Pamela, illus. see Reader's Digest Staff & London, Olivia.
Duarte, Pamela, illus. see Silk, Courtney.
Dubac, Debra, illus. see Brown, Tricia.
Dubay, Tayloe, ed. see Muller, Seth.
Dubbs, Chris. Space Dogs: Pioneers of Space Travel. (p. 1619)
Dube, Jasmine. Gratelle au Bois Mordant. (p. 712)
—Tu N'es Plus Seul, Nazaire. Daigle, Sylvie, illus. (p. 1795)
Dubé, Jean-Claude. Chevalier de Montmagny: First Governor of New France. Rapley, Elizabeth, tr. from FRE. (p. 298)
Dube, Pierrette. How to Become a Perfect Knight in Five Days. Hamel, Caroline, illus. (p. 815)
—How to Become a Perfect Princess in Five Days. Melanson, Luc, illus. (p. 815)
Dube, Tory. Trixi, a Shmoop & a Monster. Vasilevsky, Marina, illus. (p. 1788)
Dube, Tory Lee. Trixi, a Shmoop & a Monster. (p. 1788)
Dubel, Dorothy. Magical Shoes of Santa's Elves(c). (p. 1075)
Duberstein, John. Velvet Revolution: Vaclav Havel & the Fall of Communism. (p. 1835)
Dubin, Jill, illus. see Berkes, Marianne.
Dubin, Jill, illus. see Metzger, Steve.
Dubin, Jill, illus. see Mishica, Clare.
Dubin, Jill, illus. see Parker, David.
Dubin, Lawrence. Santa's Big Red Hat. (p. 1513)
Dubin, Shawn, jt. auth. see LaFleur, John.
Dubinski, Lisa. Gift to Give & Coloring Book. (p. 675)
Dubinsky, Lon, ed. see Sale, Carolyn.
Dubisch, Michael, illus. see Denton, Shannon Eric & Warner, Gertrude Chandler.
Dubisch, Michael, illus. see Warner, Gertrude Chandler.
Dubisch, Michael, illus. see Worley, Rob M. & Warner, Gertrude Chandler.
Dubisch, Mike. Haunted Cabin Mystery. (p. 753)
—Mike's Mystery (p. 1141)
—Mystery Ranch. (p. 1226)
—Pizza Mystery. (p. 1365)
—Surprise Island. (p. 1686)
—Tree House Mystery. (p. 1783)
Dubisch, Mike, illus. see Denton, Shannon Eric & Warner, Gertrude Chandler.
Dubisch, Mike, illus. see Denton, Shannon Eric.
Dubisch, Mike, illus. see Warner, Gertrude Chandler.
Dubisch, Mike, illus. see Worley, Rob M. & Warner, Gertrude Chandler.
Dubisch, Mike & Bloodworth, Mark. Amusement Park Mystery. (p. 66)
Dubison, Valentine. Willington Woods. (p. 1934)
Dubke, Karon. Pet Parrots up Close. (p. 1345)
Dubke, Karon, et al. Pets up Close. (p. 1348)
Duble, Kathleen Benner. Bravo Zulu, Samantha! (p. 224)
—Hearts of Iron. (p. 760)
—Madame Tussaud's Apprentice: An Untold Story of Love in the French Revolution. (p. 1069)
—Phantoms in the Snow. (p. 1349)
—Pilot Mom. Marks, Alan, illus. (p. 1359)
—Quest. (p. 1426)
—Sacrifice. (p. 1500)
Dublin, Angela. Banjo Bongo Bugs Greatest Adventures: By Angela Dublin. (p. 136)
Dublin, Anne. Baby Experiment: A Novel (Large Print 16pt) (p. 126)
—Baby Experiment. (p. 126)
—Bobbie Rosenfeld: The Olympian Who Could Do Everything (p. 206)
—Dynamic Women Dancers (p. 491)
—June Callwood: A Life of Action (p. 934)
—Stealing Time. (p. 1646)
Dublin, Anne & Second Story Press Staff. Orphan Rescue (p. 1304)
Dubner, Stephen J. Boy with Two Belly Buttons. Niemann, Christoph, illus. (p. 220)

Dubofsky, Melvyn. Industrialism & the American Worker, 1865-1920. Eisenstadt, Abraham S. & Franklin, John Hope, eds. (p. 873)
Dubois & Fuller, Barbara. Germany. (p. 666)
DuBois, Claude, illus. see Van Den Abeele, Veronique.
Dubois, Claude K. Nouille Vivante. (p. 1268)
DuBois, Claude K., illus. see Norac, Carl.
Dubois, Claude K., jt. auth. see Norac, Carl.
Dubois, Gérard, illus. see Gingras, Charlotte.
Dubois, Gérard, illus. see Schubert, Leda.
DuBois, J., et al. Cultures of the World - Group 7 (p. 391)
DuBois, Jill & Nevins, Debbie. South Korea. (p. 1617)
Dubois, Jill & Nevins, Debbie. South Korea. (p. 1617)
DuBois, Jill & Rosh, Mair. Israel. (p. 893)
DuBois, Jill, et al. Israel. (p. 893)
DuBois, Juli. Happiness of Being Me: An A-Z Owners Manual Zitnak, Allison Day, illus. (p. 744)
Dubois, Laurent, et al. Slave Revolution in the Caribbean, 1789-1804: A Brief History with Documents. (p. 1588)
Dubois, Liz Goulet. What Does a Seed Need? (p. 1884)
Dubois, Liz Goulet, illus. see Rouss, Sylvia A.
Dubois, Liz Goulet, tr. see Rouss, Sylvia A.
Dubois, Marie. Village Children, an Introduction to the Art of Painting Children & Their Stories. (p. 1842)
Dubois, Marie Thérèse, jt. auth. see Wilson-Timmons, Karen.
Dubois, Muriel L. Alaska Facts & Symbols. (p. 34)
—Ancient Rome: A Mighty Empire (p. 70)
—Connecticut Colony. (p. 358)
—Cuba: A Question & Answer Book (p. 388)
—Delaware Colony. (p. 424)
—Liberia: A Question & Answer Book (p. 1005)
—Maryland Facts & Symbols. (p. 1101)
—New Jersey Colony. (p. 1245)
—Peru: A Question & Answer Book (p. 1345)
—Rosa Parks. (p. 1488)
—To My Countrywomen: The Life of Sarah Josepha Hale. (p. 1759)
—U. S. House of Representatives. (p. 1806)
—U. S. Presidency. (p. 1807)
—Virginia. (p. 1844)
Dubois, Muriel L., jt. auth. see Brown, Jonatha A.
Dubois, Muriel L., jt. auth. see Deady, Kathleen W.
Dubois, Muriel L. & Brown, Jonatha A. Michigan. (p. 1135)
Dubois, Muriel L. & Deady, Kathleen W. Ancient China: Beyond the Great Wall (p. 68)
Dubois, Muriel L., et al. Great Civilizations. (p. 714)
Dubois, Philippe J. Birds of the World: 365 Days. (p. 192)
Dubois, Ricardo. Ghost Squirrel. (p. 671)
Dubois, Rikki Marie-José Grenier. Muffy Was Fluffy. (p. 1189)
Dubos, Delphine. Planet of Tear-Eaters. Smith, Anne & Smith, Owen, trs. from FRE. (p. 1367)
—Planet of Wind. Burrell, Carol Klio, tr. (p. 1368)
Dubosarsky, Ursula. Golden Day. (p. 694)
—Looming Lamplight. Denton, Terry, illus. (p. 1052)
—Perplexing Pineapple. Denton, Terry, illus. (p. 1343)
—Terrible Plop. Joyner, Andrew, illus. (p. 1721)
—Tibby's Leaf. Bray, Peter, illus. (p. 1747)
—Word Snoop. Riddle, Tohby, illus. (p. 1951)
Dubose, Gaylan, jt. auth. see Colakis, Marianthe.
DuBose, Judy. Santa's Count down 'Til Christmas. (p. 1513)
Dubose, Sarah. Uncharted Waters. (p. 1811)
DuBosque, Doug, illus. see Joyce, Susan.
Dubovik, Ludmila, ed. see AZ Books Staff.
Dubovoy, Silvia. Turquesita. (p. 1798)
Dubovoy, Silvia & Silvia, Dubovoy. color de la amistad. (p. 342)
Dubovoy, Silvia, et al. olor de la esperanza. (p. 1287)
Dubowski, Cathy East. Clara Barton: I Want to Help! (p. 326)
—Rosa Parks: Don't Give In! (p. 1489)
—Shark Attack! (p. 1562)
Dubowski, Cathy East & Pascal, Janet. Who Was Maurice Sendak? Marchesi, Stephen & Harrison, Nancy, illus. (p. 1919)
Dubowski, Mark. Discovery in the Cave. Barnard, Bryn, illus. (p. 450)
—DK Readers L3: Titanic: The Disaster That Shocked the World! (p. 456)
—Superfast Boats. (p. 1683)
—Superfast Cars. (p. 1683)
—Superfast Motorcycles. (p. 1683)
—Superfast Planes. (p. 1683)
—Superfast Trains. (p. 1683)
Dubravka, Kolanovic, jt. auth. see McCaughrean, Geraldine.
Dubreuil, Robert. Daniel & the Harmonica. Eisenstadter, Dave, ed. (p. 404)
Dubros, Aaron. Would'a Could'a Should'a. (p. 1962)
Dubrovin, Barbara. Fantasy Fair: Bright Stories of Imagination. Dubrovin, Barbara, illus. (p. 572)
Dubrow, Terry J. & Adderly, Brenda D. Acne Cure: The Nonprescription Plan That Shows Dramatic Results in As Little As 24 Hours. (p. 9)
Dubrule, Jackie. Kelli, God & New York. Baker, David, illus. (p. 948)
—Little John, God, & the Circus. Swope, Brenda, illus. (p. 1029)
—Miranda, God & the Park. Swope, Brenda, illus. (p. 1149)
Dubuc, Marianne. Animal Masquerade. Dubuc, Marianne, illus. (p. 78)
—In Front of My House. Ghione, Yvette, tr. from FRE. (p. 863)
—Sea. (p. 1534)
Dubuc, Marianne & Ghione, Yvette. Bus Ride. (p. 244)
Dubuc, Marianne, creator. Lion & the Bird. (p. 1019)
Dub-u-el. Zoom-Zoom & Slo-Poke. (p. 1989)
Dubuisson, Rachelle. Tree of Life: Meet the Solomons. (p. 1783)
Duburke, Randy. Little Mister. (p. 1032)
DuBurke, Randy, illus. see George, Olivia.
DuBurke, Randy, illus. see Hubbard, Crystal.
Duburke, Randy, illus. see McKissack, Patricia C., et al.
DuBurke, Randy, illus. see Omololu, Cynthia Jaynes.
DuBurke, Randy, illus. see Scholastic, Inc. Staff & George, Olivia.
DuBurke, Randy, jt. auth. see Neri, G.
Dubuvoy, Silvia, et al. Murmullos de la Selva. Tsuda, Efrain Rodriguez, illus. (p. 1192)
Duby, Marjorie. From Caravels to the Constitution: Puzzles Trageting Historical Themes That Reinforce Logic & Problem-Solving Skills. Armstrong, Bev, illus. (p. 642)
Dubya, Jay. Eighteen Story Gingerbread House. (p. 507)
Dubyn, Bj. Thrilling & Dynamic Adventures of Barbara Ann, Her Kid Brother, Billy, Jr , & Manfred the Magnificent, Their Parrot. (p. 1744)
Ducatteau, Florence. Day at the Museum. Peten, Chantal, illus. (p. 412)
Duce, Gillian. Magic & Mayhem. (p. 1071)
Duchamp, L. Timmel. Grand Conversation: Volume 1 in the Conversation Pieces Series. Vol. 1 (p. 707)
Ducharme, Huguette. Enquete Tres Speciale. Caron, Romi, illus. (p. 531)
Ducharme, P. J. Adventures of Jungle Foot Rot (p. 19)
Duchateau, illus. see Follet, René.
Duchéne, Mique. Mystery of Foo & the Great Chasm. (p. 1224)
Duchene-Marshall, Michele A. Charley Finds A Family. Marshall, Alan David, ed. (p. 292)
—Shirley's Red Satin Shoes. Marshall, Alan David, ed. (p. 1567)
Duchesne, Christiane. Edmond et Amandine. (p. 504)
—W Is for Wapiti! An Alphabet Songbook. Côté, Geneviève, illus. (p. 1851)
Duchesne, Christiane, jt. auth. see Ziskind, Hélio.
Duchesne, Christiane, tr. see Coulman, Valerie.
Duchesne, Lucie, tr. see Beech, Linda Ward.
Duchesne, Lucie, tr. see Marzollo, Jean.
Duchesne, Lucie, tr. see Nadler, Beth.
Duchess of Northumberland Staff, jt. auth. see Wood, Maryrose.
Duchess of York Staff, jt. auth. see Ferguson, Sarah.
Duchess of York Staff & Ferguson, Sarah. Ballerina Rosie. Goode, Diane, illus. (p. 134)
Ducie, Joe. Rig. (p. 1471)
Duck Egg Blue & Autumn Publishing. Press-Out & Make Dolly Dressing — Fashionable Friends. (p. 1397)
Duck Egg Blue (Firm) Staff, illus. see Hewett, Angela.
Duck Egg Blue (Firm) Staff & Autumn Publishing Staff. Press-Out & Make Dolly Dressing — Princesses. (p. 1397)
Duck, Phillip Thomas. Dirty South. (p. 446)
Ducker Signs Plus, illus. see Wilson, Elaine Moody.
Duckers, John. Amazing Adventures of the Silly Six. (p. 52)
Duckett, Brenda. Casey's Shadow. (p. 275)
—Giggling Purple Dragon. (p. 676)
—Jeffrey & the blue Monkey. (p. 912)
—Summit Lane. (p. 1675)
Duckett, Richard & Loane, Cormac. Team Brass Repertoire: French Horn: French Horn. (p. 1710)
Ducklow, Tony. Summer of the Crows: Not Your Typical Boy Meets Crow Story. (p. 1674)
Duckro, Rebecca S. Adventures of Charlie KeeperTechnobrat. (p. 17)
Duckworth, Jeffrey, illus. see Wise-Douglas, Terri.
Duckworth, Katie. Education. (p. 505)
—Health. (p. 757)
Duckworth, Liz. Amanda's Spider Surprise: A Bible Memory Buddy Book about Being Brave. Harrington, David, illus. (p. 52)
Duckworth, Michael. Voodoo Island. Oxford University Press Staff & Bassett, Jennifer, eds. (p. 1850)
Duckworth, Michelle, illus. see Fischer, Kelly.
Duckworth, Ruth, illus. see Seco, Nina S. & Pilutik, Anastasia D.
Ducommon, Barbara, illus. see Purkapile, Susan.
Ducommun, Barbara, illus. see Purkapile, Susan & Peck, Amy.
Ducommun, Debbie, jt. auth. see Ducommun, Debbiee.
Ducommun, Debbiee & Ducommun, Debbie. Complete Guide to Rat Training: Tricks & Games for Rat Fun & Fitness (p. 353)
Ducornet, Rikki, illus. see Gander, Forrest.
Ducote, Billie Seaon. Adventures of Artie Eco Part One: The Problem with Greed Ducote, Billie Seaon, illus. (p. 16)
—Adventures of Artie Eco Part Two: The Problem with Greed Artie Eco Goes to Dirtyville Ducote, Billie Seaon, illus. (p. 16)
duCray, Belle Crow, illus. see Sullivan, Ayn Cates.
Ducrest, Olivier, illus. see Sarn, Amélie & Trouillot, Virgile.
Ducy, George, illus. see Ms. Sue.
Dudar, Judy. I Spy a Bunny Rudnicki, Richard, illus. (p. 846)
—I Spy a Bunny (pb) Rudnicki, Richard, illus. (p. 846)
Dudash, C. Michael, illus. see Rinaldi, Ann.
Duddle, Johnny, illus. see Thompson, Kate.
Duddle, Jonny. Gigantosaurus. Duddle, Jonny, illus. (p. 676)
—King of Space. Duddle, Jonny, illus. (p. 959)
—Pirate Cruncher. Duddle, Jonny, illus. (p. 1362)
—Pirates Next Door. (p. 1363)
Duddle, Jonny, illus. see London, C. Alexander.
Duddle, Jonny, illus. see Newsome, Richard.
Duddle, Jonny, illus. see Sinden, David, et al.
Duddle, Jonny, illus. see Thompson, Kate.
Dude, Rosanna Eubank. Natalia's Favorite Color. Eubank, Patricia Reeder, illus. (p. 1230)
Dudek, Mike. Fairytale of the Morley Dog. (p. 565)
Dudek, V. A. Soldiers of Fate. (p. 1607)
Duden. Kennst du Das? Das ABC. (p. 949)
—Kennst du Das? Lastwagen. (p. 949)
Duden, Jane. Avalanche! The Deadly Slide. (p. 118)
—Why Do Bears Sleep All Winter? [Chicago]: A Book about Hibernation. (p. 1923)
Duden, Jane, jt. auth. see Englar, Mary.
Duder, Tessa. Carpet of Dreams. Wilson, Mark, illus. (p. 271)
—Is She Still Alive? (p. 890)
—Margaret Mahy: A Writer's Life: A Literary Portrait of New Zealand's Best-Loved Children's Author. (p. 1092)
—Story of Sir Peter Blake. (p. 1660)
Duder, Tessa, ed. Book of Pacific Lullabies. Hagin, Sally, illus. (p. 211)
—Down to the Sea Again: True Sea Stories for Young Newzealanders. (p. 474)
Dudgeon, Laura, jt. auth. see Dudgeon, Pat.
Dudgeon, Pat & Dudgeon, Laura. Lilli & Her Shadow. (p. 1017)
Dudley, Blanche R. Siggy & the Bullies. (p. 1573)
—Siggy's Parade: Helping Kids with Disabilities Find Their Strengths. (p. 1573)
Dudley, Cathy D. Toddler Theology: Childlike Faith for Everyone. (p. 1761)
Dudley, David L. Cy in Chains. (p. 396)
Dudley, Dick, illus. see Hulme, Joy N.
Dudley Gold, Susan. Women's Rights Movement & Abolitionism. (p. 1947)
Dudley, Joshua. Lost in Oz: Rise of the Dark Wizard. (p. 1055)
Dudley, Joyce. Justice Served. (p. 940)
Dudley, Karen. Giant Pandas with Code. (p. 674)
Dudley, Linda. Aunt Linda's Mommy & Me Book. (p. 115)
Dudley, Linda S. Aunt Linda's Shape Book. Neal, Jill Faith, illus. (p. 115)
Dudley, Marie Luther. Tennessee Ocean Frogs. Primm, Patricia, illus. (p. 1720)
Dudley, Maywill. Story of Little Red Riding Hood. (p. 1659)
Dudley, Peter, illus. see Ford, Sally.
Dudley, Rebecca. Hank Has a Dream. Dudley, Rebecca, photos by. (p. 742)
Dudley, Sean. Who's Afraid of the Pumpkin Man??? (p. 1920)
Dudley, William. Antidepressants. (p. 89)
—Biofuels. (p. 188)
—Environment. (p. 531)
—Great Depression. (p. 715)
—How Should the U. S. Proceed in Iraq? (p. 812)
—Human Rights. (p. 826)
—Reconstruction. (p. 1452)
—Social Justice: Opposing Viewpoints. (p. 1604)
—Synthetic Drug Addiction. (p. 1693)
—Unicorns. (p. 1818)
Dudley, William, ed. Environment. (p. 531)
—Freedom of Speech. (p. 634)
Dudney, Emma Mae. Runaway. (p. 1496)
Dudok de Wit, Michael, illus. see Theo.
Due, Kirsten L. Bearen Bear & the Bunbury Tales. Berends, Jenny, illus. (p. 151)
Due, Noel. Created for Worship: From Genesis to Revelation to You. (p. 378)
Duebber, Carol. Praise Power for Kids. (p. 1393)
Duebbert, Harold F., ed. Wildfowling in Dakota 1873-1903: Old-Time Duck & Goose Shooting on the Dakota Prairies. (p. 1931)
Dueck, Adele. Nettie's Journey (p. 1242)
—Racing Home (p. 1432)
Duehl, Kristine. Where Do I Live? Castronovo, Katy, illus. (p. 1907)
Duenas, Ana Maria, jt. auth. see Echerique, Alfredo Bryce.
Duendes del Sur, illus. see McCann, Jesse Leon.
Duendes Del Sur Staff, illus. see American Bible Society Staff.
Duendes Del Sur Staff, illus. see Balaban, Mariah.
Duendes Del Sur Staff, illus. see Cunningham, Scott.
Duendes Del Sur Staff, illus. see Gelsey, James.
Duendes Del Sur Staff, illus. see Herman, Gail.
Duendes Del Sur Staff, illus. see Howard, Kate.
Duendes Del Sur Staff, illus. see McCann, Jesse Leon.
Duendes Del Sur Staff, illus. see Sander, Sonia.
Duendes Del Sur Staff, illus. see Simon, Mary Manz.
Duendes Del Sur Staff, jt. auth. see Gelsey, James.
Duendes Del Sur Staff, jt. auth. see Howard, Kate.
Duendes Del Sur Staff, jt. contrib. by see Scholastic, Inc. Staff.
Duer, William. My Daddy Works in Heaven. (p. 1201)
Duerksen, Carol, et al. Short Tales. (p. 1569)
Duerr Berrick, Jill. Good Parents or Good Workers? How Policy Shapes Families' Daily Lives. Fuller, Bruce & Duerr Berrick, Jill, eds. (p. 700)
Duerr, Doug. Adventures of Jazz & Elliott: The Love Ness Monster. (p. 19)
—Adventures of Jazz & Elliott: Danielle goes to the Magical Land of Roop-E-Doo. (p. 19)
Duersch, Gretchen, ed. see McInnes, Lisa.
Duesler, Cheney. Other Side. (p. 1306)
Duey, K. & Bale, K. A. Salvados! Terremoto. (p. 1506)
—Salvados! Titanic. (p. 1506)
Duey, Kathleen. Arthur. Epstein, Eugene, illus. (p. 103)
—Arthur. Gould, Robert, photos by. (p. 103)
—Castle Avamir. Rayyan, Omar, illus. (p. 276)
—Ella the Baby Elephant: A Baby Elephant's Story. Gurin, Lara, illus. (p. 514)
—Following Magic. Tang, Sandara, illus. (p. 612)
—Full Moon. Tang, Sandara, illus. (p. 646)
—Journey Home. Rayyan, Omar, illus. (p. 928)
—Korow: A Baby Chimpanzee's Story. Gurin, Lara, illus. (p. 967)
—Lara & the Moon-Colored Filly (p. 975)
—Leo: A Baby Lion's Story. Gurin, Lara, illus. (p. 991)
—Leo the Lion - Book & Dvd. Gurin, Laura, illus. (p. 992)
—Leonardo Epstein, Eugene, illus. (p. 992)
—Leonardo. Epstein, Eugene, illus. (p. 992)
—Margret & Flynn 1875. (p. 1092)
—Mountains of the Moon. Rayyan, Omar, illus. (p. 1181)
—Nanuq: A Baby Polar Bear's Story. Gurin, Lara, illus. (p. 1229)
—Pony Express: Time Soldiers Book #7. (p. 1382)
—Rex. (p. 1467)
—Rex. Epstein, Eugene, illus. (p. 1467)
—Rex 2. Epstein, Eugene, illus. (p. 1467)
—Rex2. Epstein, Eugene, illus. (p. 1467)
—Sacred Scars Rayyan, Sheila, illus. (p. 1500)
—Samurai (p. 1509)
—Samurai. Epstein, Eugene, illus. (p. 1509)
—Silence & Stone. Tang, Sandara, illus. (p. 1575)
—Silver Bracelet. Rayyan, Omar, illus. (p. 1576)
—Skin Hunger. (p. 1585)
—Sunset Gates. Rayyan, Omar, illus. (p. 1677)
—Tahi: A Baby Dolphin's Story. Gurin, Lara, illus. (p. 1695)
—Time Soldiers Epstein, Eugene, illus. (p. 1752)
—Time Soldiers - Mummy. Epstein, Eugene, illus. (p. 1752)
—Time Soldiers - Patch. (p. 1752)
—Time Soldiers - Patch. Epstein, Eugene, illus. (p. 1752)
—True Heart. Rayyan, Omar, illus. (p. 1792)
—Wishes & Wings. Tang, Sandara, illus. (p. 1940)
Duey, Kathleen, jt. auth. see Berry, Rob.
Duey, Kathleen, jt. auth. see Big Guy Books Staff.
Duey, Kathleen, jt. auth. see Gould, Robert.
Duey, Kathleen & Bale, Karen A. Earthquake: San Francisco 1906. (p. 497)
—Fire: Chicago 1871. (p. 590)
—Flood: Mississippi 1927. (p. 605)
—Titanic: April 1912. (p. 1757)
Duey, Kathleen & Gould, Robert. Rex. Windler-Cheren, Victoria, tr. (p. 1467)
—Rex 2. Epstein, Eugene, illus. (p. 1467)
—Rex2. Epstein, Eugene, illus. (p. 1467)
Duey, Kathleen & Grosset and Dunlap Staff. Katie & the Mustang (p. 944)
Duey, Kathleen, et al. Katie & the Mustang. (p. 944)
DuFalla, Anita. Sumac & the Magic Lake. (p. 1673)
DuFalla, Anita, illus. see Butler, Dori Hillestad.
DuFalla, Anita, illus. see Cleland, Jo.
DuFalla, Anita, illus. see Cook, Julia & Jana, Laura.
DuFalla, Anita, illus. see Cook, Julia.
DuFalla, Anita, illus. see Fox, Laura.
Dufalla, Anita, illus. see Greve, Meg.
DuFalla, Anita, illus. see Hord, Colleen.
DuFalla, Anita, illus. see Howard, Annabelle.
DuFalla, Anita, illus. see Picou, Lin.
DuFalla, Anita, illus. see Pugliano-Martin, Carol.
Dufalla, Anita, illus. see Reed, Jennifer.
DuFalla, Anita, illus. see Robertson, Jean.
Dufalla, Anita, illus. see Romer, Ruth.
DuFalla, Anita, illus. see Shells, Christine M.
DuFalla, Anita, illus. see Steinkraus, Kyla.
DuFalla, Anita, illus. see Totilo, Rebecca Park.
Dufalla, Anita, illus. see Williams, Sam.
Dufaux, Jean. Rapaces. Marini, Enrico, illus. (p. 1439)
—Siobhan. Rosinski, Grzegorz, illus. (p. 1580)
Dufaux, Jean, jt. auth. see Marini, Enrico.
Dufaux, Jean & Delaby, Philippe. Conquerors: Swords of Rome. Vol. 1 (p. 358)
Dufey, Alexandra, illus. see Apostoll, Andrea, ed.
Duff, Hilary. Devoted: An Elixir Novel. (p. 432)
—Devoted. (p. 432)
—Elixir. (p. 513)
—True: An Elixir Novel. (p. 1791)
Duff, Hilary & Allen, Elise. Elixir. (p. 513)
Duff, Jc. Tornado Watch. (p. 1770)
Duff, Justin. Alex Goes Apple Picking. (p. 36)
—Big Boy. (p. 179)
—Wishing Well. (p. 1941)
Duff, Leo, illus. see Maddern, Eric & Quarto Generic Staff.
Duff, Ms. Michelle Ann. Five Cats, One Dog, a Motorcycle & a Lady in a Hot Pink Jacket. (p. 600)
Duffek, Kim Kanoa, illus. see Hanson, Jonathan.
Duffett-Smith, James. Curious Robot on Mars! Straker, Bethany, illus. (p. 394)
—Stella & Steve Travel Through Space! Straker, Bethany, illus. (p. 1646)
Duffey, Betsy. Boy in the Doghouse. (p. 218)
Duffey, Gary. Windows. (p. 1936)
Duffield, J. W. Bert Wilson in the Rockies. (p. 168)
Duffield, Katy. Chad Hurley, Steve Chen, Jawed Karim: You Tube Creators. (p. 288)
—Farmer McPeepers' Milk Cows. Gray, Steve, illus. (p. 574)
—Poltergeists. (p. 1381)
Duffield, Katy S. California History for Kids: Missions, Miners, & Moviemakers in the Golden State, Includes 21 Activities. (p. 253)
—Earth's Biomes. (p. 498)
Duffield, Neil. Plays for Youth Theatres & Large Casts. Duffield, Neil, ed. (p. 1373)
Duffield, W. J. Radio Boys in the Thousand Islands. (p. 1433)
Duffield, Wendell. Chasing Lava: A Geologist's Adventures at the Hawaiian Volcano Observatory (p. 294)
Duffield, Wendell A. What's So Hot about Volcanoes? Black, Bronze, illus. (p. 1899)
Duffour, Jean-Pierre, illus. see Surget, Alain & Hirsinger, Julien.
Duffy, Beth. Anthropology for Children. (p. 89)
—Sociology for Youth. (p. 1605)
Duffy, Betsy Smeltzer. I Am Beautiful Because... I Am Creative. (p. 832)
Duffy, Carol Ann. Gift. Ryan, Rob, illus. (p. 674)
—Princess's Blankets. Hyde, Catherine Ryan, illus. (p. 1406)
—Queen Munch & Queen Nibble. Monks, Lydia, illus. (p. 1425)
—Tear Thief. Ceccoli, Nicoletta, illus. (p. 1711)
Duffy, Carol Ann & Ryan, Rob. Gift. Ryan, Rob, illus. (p. 674)
Duffy, Carol Ann & Stevenson, Juliet. Tear Thief. Ceccoli, Nicoletta, illus. (p. 1711)
Duffy, Chris, ed. see Various Authors.
Duffy, Chris, ed. Nursery Rhyme Comics: 50 Timeless Rhymes from 50 Celebrated Cartoonists. Chast, Roz & Feiffer, Jules, illus. (p. 1273)
Duffy, Ciaran, illus. see Collins Educational Staff & Robinson, Anthony.
Duffy, Cr. Return of the Dark Star. (p. 1464)
Duffy, Daniel Mark, illus. see Cohen, Barbara.
Duffy, Jacqueline Ann. Dillon the Dog Finds His Family. (p. 440)
Duffy, James. Desaparecida. (p. 428)
Duffy, James E. Auto Electricity & Electronics. (p. 117)
—Modern Automotive Technology: Teaching Package Instructor's Resource Binder. (p. 1158)
—Modern Automotive Technology: Teaching Package Powerpoint Presentations Site License. (p. 1158)
—Modern Automotive Technology. (p. 1158)
Duffy, James E., jt. auth. see Johanson, Chris.
Duffy, Jo. Fallen Angels. Gammill, Kerry et al, illus. (p. 566)
Duffy, Joe & Zeck, Mike. Punisher: Circle of Blood. (p. 1417)
Duffy, Kate & McRedmond, Sarah. Fit Kids Cookbook. Bagley, Pat, illus. (p. 599)

D

Duffy, Lois. Zillah's Gift. (p. 1986)
Duffy, Martin. Peg Leg Gus. (p. 1335)
Duffy, Shannon. Awakening. (p. 120)
Duffy, Tanya. Bonkers. (p. 209)
Dufilho, Rhonda. Talking with Tomahachie: An Introduction to Sign Language for Kids. (p. 1704)
Dufner, Annette. Rise of Adolf Hitler. (p. 1474)
Duforu, Sebastian, illus. see Bornemann, Elsa.
Dufosse, Christophe. School's Out. Whiteside, Shaun, tr. from FRE. (p. 1524)
Dufresne, Didier, et al. Solamente un Poco de Gripe. Vinent, Julia, tr. (p. 1606)
Dufresne, Michele. I Can Fly. (p. 835)
Dufris, William, reader. Case of the Climbing Cat. (p. 273)
Dufton, Jo S., jt. auth. see Johnson, Liliane.
Dugan, Alan, illus. see Butcher, A D.
Dugan, Christine. 180 Days of Language for First Grade. (p. 2000)
—180 Days of Language for Kindergarten. (p. 2000)
—Between the Wars. (p. 173)
—Defying Gravity! Rock Climbing. (p. 424)
—Final Lap! Go-Kart Racing. (p. 586)
—From Rags to Riches. (p. 643)
—Hang Ten! Surfing. (p. 742)
—Julius Caesar: Roman Leader (p. 933)
—Landscape by Design. (p. 974)
—Living in Space. (p. 1041)
—Marcha Hacia Delante. (p. 1091)
—Muchas Manos Ayudan. (p. 1188)
—Rome (p. 1486)
—Sense of Art. (p. 1551)
—Space Exploration. (p. 1619)
—Where Does Your Money Go? (p. 1907)
Dugan, Christine & Lane, Chloe. Pack It Up: Surface Area & Volume. (p. 1317)
Dugan, David J. Missing Prince of Distria. (p. 1153)
Dugan, Ellen. Elements of Witchcraft: Natural Magick for Teens. (p. 511)
Dugan, Joanne. 123 Nyc: A Counting Book of New York City. (p. 2000)
—ABC Nyc: A Book about Seeing New York City. (p. 3)
Dugan, Karen. Always Blue for Chicu. Dugan, Karen, illus. (p. 51)
—Ms. April & Ms. Mae: A Fable. (p. 1188)
Dugan, Karen, illus. see Blankenship, LeeAnn.
Dugan, Karen, illus. see Dotlich, Rebecca Kai.
Dugan, Karen, illus. see Lankford, Mary D.
Dugan, Karen, illus. see Mattern, Joanne & Brandt, Keith.
Dugan, Karen, illus. see Wadsworth, Ginger.
Dugan, Kyle. CIC for Older Youth & Young Adults: Choosing to be on Pilgrimage. (p. 318)
Dugan, Michael. Life's a Riot! (p. 1013)
Dugas, Lisa, jt. ed. see Lewis, David.
Duggan, Gerry. Batman: Arkham Manor Vol. 1. (p. 144)
—Nova Baldeon, David, illus. (p. 1268)
Duggan, Janet. Christmas Story As Told by Assellus the Christmas Donkey. Robertson, Catherine, illus. (p. 315)
Duggan, John M. Action-Packed Book of Adventure Doodles: 187 Fun & Exciting Drawings You Can Finish Yourself. (p. 10)
—Doodle Book: 187 Fun Drawings You Can Finish Yourself. (p. 469)
Duggan, Kevin, illus. see Keenan, Sheila.
Duggan, Laurie. Mangroves. (p. 1087)
Duggan, Michael. IPad Action Gaming for Teens. (p. 886)
Duggan, Micheal, illus. see Soto, Manuel.
Duggan, Olive. Spy Kitties Create a Better World. (p. 1636)
Duggan, Paul. Deux Squelettes au Téléphone. Sylvestre, Daniel, illus. (p. 431)
Dugger, Elizabeth L. & Kanell, Beth. Darkness under the Water. (p. 409)
Duggins, Peat, illus. see Homan, Michael.
Duggins, Shirley, jt. auth. see Pez, Christine.
Duggleby, John. Revolution: The Story of John Lennon. (p. 1466)
—Uh Huh! The Story of Ray Charles. (p. 1808)
Duggleby, Ross, jt. auth. see Duggleby, Sue.
Duggleby, Sue & Duggleby, Ross. Adjectives. (p. 13)
—Narrative. (p. 1229)
—Prepositions. (p. 1396)
—Sequencing. (p. 1552)
—Verbs. (p. 1836)
Dugin, Andrei. Dragon Feathers. Dugina, Olga, illus. (p. 477)
Dugina, Olga, illus. see Dugin, Andrei.
Duguay, Kathleen. Andy Finds a Home. (p. 73)
Duguë, Georges, Jr., tr. see Jameson, Steven.
Duhaime, Edmund. Discipline Required. (p. 447)
Duhamel, Megan. Earth. (p. 494)
—Space. (p. 1618)
Duhaney, Rich, illus. see Diamond, Jeremy.
Duhatschek, Marty. I Hate Christmas: A Christmas Comedy in Three Acts. (p. 838)
Duhgam, P. Island Hopping with Anancy. (p. 892)
Duhig, Lee. Draw Dinosaurs! (p. 480)
Duhn, Jo. Casey & the Crab: The Gruesome Green Goo. (p. 275)
—Casey & the Crab Ii: Trinidad Tomayo's Treasure. (p. 275)
Duignan, Brian. History of Western Ethics. (p. 785)
Duignan, Brian, ed. 100 Most Influential Philosophers of All Time. (p. 1998)
—Britannica Guide to the World's Most Influential People (Print/eBook Combo Set) (p. 229)
—Thinkers & Theories in Ethics. (p. 1734)
Duis, Laura, illus. see Groce, Michelle.
Duivenoorden Mitic, Trudy. Ernie Coombs: Mr Dressup (p. 534)
Duivenvoorden, Yvonne, photos by see Curtis, Andrea.
DuJardin, Judy, jt. auth. see DuJardin, Rosamond.
DuJardin, Rosamond. Boy Trouble. (p. 219)
—Class Ring. (p. 327)
—One of the Crowd. (p. 1296)
—Practically Seventeen: A Tobey Heydon Story. (p. 1392)
—Real Thing. (p. 1449)
—Senior Prom. (p. 1550)
—Someone to Count On. (p. 1609)
—Wait for Marcy. (p. 1852)
—Wedding in the Family. (p. 1871)
DuJardin, Rosamond & DuJardin, Judy. Junior Year Abroad. (p. 936)
Duk, Lor. Firestorm Heart: A Dragon Friend Story. (p. 592)
Duke, Barbara, illus. see Scholastic, Inc. Staff & Barnes, Derrick D.
Duke, James A., jt. auth. see Foster, Steven.
Duke Jones, JoEllen. Adventures of Shelby the Puppy Angel: A New Baby in the House. (p. 22)
—Adventures of Shelby, the Puppy Angel: Sasha's Parents Get a Divorce. (p. 22)
—Adventures of Shelby, the Puppy Angel. (p. 22)
Duke, Kate. In the Rainforest. Duke, Kate, illus. (p. 867)
—Ready for Pumpkins. (p. 1447)
Duke, Kate, illus. see Baker, Barbara.
Duke, Marion, illus. see LeFroy, Joy & Frylinck, Diana.
Duke, Marion, illus. see Polizzotto, Carolyn & Spinks, Sarah.
Duke, Mave Lough, jt. auth. see Lough, Erin.
Duke, Nell K. & Bennett-Armistead, V. Susan. Reading & Writing Informational Text in the Primary Grades: Research-Based Practices. (p. 1445)
Duke, Nell K., et al. Beyond Bedtime Stories: A Parent's Guide to Promoting Reading Writing, & Other Literacy Skills from Birth to 5. (p. 173)
—Engaging Families in Children's Literacy Development: A Guide for Leading Successful Workshops, Including Ready-to-Show Videos * Step-by-Step Plans & Schedules * Easy-to-Prepare Workshop Activities * Read-Aloud Trade Book Pack. (p. 529)
Duke, Salvacion Corpus. Curriculum Based English-Spanish Work Text I: Taller Gramática Española I Basado en un Plan de Estudios 2012. (p. 394)
Duke, Sharon, jt. auth. see Napoles, Ann.
Duke, Shirley. Animal Science. (p. 79)
—Earth & the Role of Water. (p. 495)
—Enterprise Stem. (p. 531)
—Environmental Disasters. (p. 532)
—Forces & Motion at Work. (p. 617)
—Money Counts. (p. 1164)
—Nervous System. (p. 1241)
—Science Lab: Gases. (p. 1526)
—Skyscrapers & Towers. (p. 1587)
—STEM Jobs in Music. (p. 1647)
—STEM Jobs with Animals. (p. 1647)
—Step-by-Step Experiments with the Water Cycle. Ostrom, Bob, illus. (p. 1647)
—Unthinkable. (p. 1823)
—What's the Place Value? (p. 1899)
Duke, Shirley Smith. Infections, Infestations, & Disease. (p. 873)
—No Bows! Mattheson, Jenny, illus. (p. 1257)
—Nuclear Power. (p. 1270)
—You Can't Wear These Genes. (p. 1975)
Duke, Shirley. Erosion. (p. 534)
—Hypothesis, Theory, Law. (p. 831)
—Waves of Light & Sound. (p. 1864)
Dukes, Alicia. Ms. Mabel's Fables. (p. 1188)
Dukes, Dorothy. Coloring Book. (p. 344)
—Kg - 2nd Grade Basic Math Elements. (p. 951)
Dukes, Janet Walton. Harold & Tyler: Bravery. Dukes, Jazalyn D., ed. (p. 749)
Dukes, Jazalyn D., ed. see Dukes, Janet Walton.
Dukes, LeRoy. Chill Street Gang. (p. 305)
Dukes, LeRoy L. Christmas on Chill Street. (p. 315)
Dukes, Martin. Worm Winds of Zanzibar. (p. 1961)
Dukoff, K. D. If I Had A Wish. Graham, C. E., illus. (p. 853)
Dukovich, Amanda J. Star Named Little One (Boy) Pride, Matthew, illus. (p. 1640)
—Star Named Little One (Girl) Pride, Matthew, illus. (p. 1640)
Duksta, Laura. I Love You More. Keesler, Karen, illus. (p. 843)
—I Love You More Padded Board Book. Keesler, Karen, illus. (p. 843)
—Te Quiero Más. Keesler, Karen, illus. (p. 1708)
—You Are a Gift to the World. Turner, Dona, illus. (p. 1973)
Dulac, Edmund. Sleeping Beauty & Other Fairy Tales. (p. 1589)
Dulac, Edmund, illus. see Andersen, Hans Christian.
Dulac, Edmund, illus. see Menges, Jeff A., ed.
Dulac, Edmund, illus. see Stawell, Rodolph.
Dulany, Joseph P. Burial of the Outlaw Emmitt Dalton & Other Stories My Father Told Me: And other stories my father told Me. (p. 243)
Dulemba, Elizabeth. Soap, Soap, Soap. (p. 1603)
—Soap, Soap, Soap/Jabon, Jabon, Jabon. (p. 1603)
Dulemba, Elizabeth, illus. see Polette, Keith.
Dulemba, Elizabeth O. Soap Soap Soap. Dulemba, Elizabeth O., illus. (p. 1603)
Dulemba, Elizabeth O., illus. see Hollon, Frank Turner, et al.
Dulemba, Elizabeth O., illus. see Spain, Susan Rosson.
Dulemba, Elizabeth O., illus. see Ting, Renee.
Duley, Wayla C. Strawberry Soup & Other Crazy Things. (p. 1666)
Dulin, Amber. Wilma the Waitress & the Waffle House. (p. 1934)
Dulin, Dorothy, illus. see Smith, Laura Rountree.
Duling, Astrid. Guinea Pigs Twiggy & Molly. (p. 731)
Duling, Jean Saunders. Marco Island A-Z: A Coloring Book for You. Duling, Jean Saunders, ed. (p. 1092)
Dull, Dennis Stanley. Baby Basics & Beyond: ABC's, 123's & Shapes. Dull, Dennis Stanley, illus. (p. 125)
Dullaart, Alberta M. Snowy Black & White. (p. 1601)
Dultz, Dorothy. Stories for Dreamers. Margolis, Al, illus. (p. 1654)
Dumas, Alexandre. Barbie & the Three Musketeers: A Junior Novelization. Choi, Allan, illus. (p. 138)
—Count of Monte Cristo. (p. 369)
—Man in the Iron Mask (p. 1085)
—Man in the Iron Mask Laurel Associates Inc. Staff & Saddleback Educational Publishing Staff, eds. (p. 1085)
—Man in the Iron Mask. (p. 1085)
—Man in the Iron Mask. Howell, Troy, illus. (p. 1085)
—Man in the Iron Mask. Rogers, Jacqueline, tr. from FRE. (p. 1085)
—Three Musketeers (p. 1743)
—Three Musketeers Laurel Associates Inc. Staff & Saddleback Educational Publishing Staff, eds. (p. 1743)
—Three Musketeers. (p. 1743)
—Three Musketeers. Akib, Jamel, illus. (p. 1743)
—Three Musketeers. Green, John, illus. (p. 1743)
—Three Musketeers. Tayal, Amit, illus. (p. 1743)
—Three Musketeers. Dunn, Robert, illus. (p. 1743)
—Three Musketeers. Pevear, Richard, tr. (p. 1743)
—Three Musketeers. Ruben, Ruben, illus. (p. 1743)
—Three Musketeers. Helquist, Brett, illus. (p. 1743)
—Three Musketeers. Hochman, Eleanor, tr. from FRE. (p. 1743)
—Tres Mosqueteros. (p. 1784)
—Women's War. Buss, Robin, ed. (p. 1947)
Dumas, Alexandre, jt. ed. see Dumas, Alexandre.
Dumas, Alexandre & Dumas, Alexandre, eds. Dama de las Camelias. (p. 401)
Dumas, Bianca & Ross, D. J. Uniquely Utah (p. 1818)
Dumas, Kim Foster. Gator Gets a Nose Bleed. (p. 658)
Dumas Lachtman, Ofelia. Looking for la Unica. (p. 1051)
Dumas, Ryan, illus. see Perkins, T J.
Dumas, Willam. Pisim Finds Her Miskinow. Paul, Leonard, illus. (p. 1364)
Dumble, Carol. R U My Friend? (p. 1429)
Dumbleton, Mike. Cat. Smith, Craig, illus. (p. 277)
—Meet Douglas Mawson. (p. 1121)
—Muddled-Up Farm Murphy, Jobi, illus. (p. 1188)
—Santa's Outback Secret. Jellett, Tom, illus. (p. 1513)
—Santa's Secret. Jellett, Tom, illus. (p. 1513)
—Watch Out for Jamie Joel. (p. 1861)
Dumesnil, Phil & Sanchez, Asa. Woollyhoodwinks: Vs. the Dark Patch. Root, Jeff & Runcorn, Scott, illus. (p. 1950)
Dumin, Jennifer. Wolfie & Freddie: the New Puppy. (p. 1944)
Dumit, Sharon & Nowak, Jeffrey. Cool Science Matters with Molly Cool & Atom: A - Air. (p. 364)
Dumm, Brian, illus. see Driscoll, Colleen.
Dumm, Brian, illus. see Higgins, Nadia.
Dumm, Brian Caleb. Meet Your Community Workers (p. 1123)
Dumm, Brian Caleb, illus. see Gunderson, Jessica.
Dumm, Brian Caleb, illus. see Kenney, Karen L.
Dumm, Brian Caleb, illus. see Kenney, Karen Latchana.
Dumm, Brian Caleb, illus. see Kesselring, Mari.
Dumm, Brian Caleb, illus. see Troupe, Thomas Kingsley.
Dummies Press Staff, et al. Rabbits for Dummies(r). (p. 1430)
Dummies Technical Press Staff, et al. IBS Cookbook for Dummies(r). (p. 850)
Dumon Tak, Bibi, jt. auth. see Tak, Bibi Dumon.
DuMont, Brianna. Famous Phonies: Legends, Fakes, & Phonies Who Changed History. (p. 569)
Dumont, C. & Lacoursiere, Suzanne. Jesus: A Story of Love. Merola, Caroline, tr. from FRE. (p. 914)
Dumont, Claire & Lacoursiere, Suzanne. Jesus Gives Us Peace: The Sacrament of Reconciliation. Larocque, Gisele, tr. from FRE. (p. 915)
Dumont, Daniel, illus. see Gauthier, Bertrand.
Dumont, Jean-François. Chickens Build a Wall. (p. 300)
Dumont, Jean-François, illus. see Mathews, Leslie.
Dumont, Madeleine, illus. see Averous, Helene.
Dumont, Naomi K. Mr. Kitty & the Magical Island. (p. 1185)
Dumont, Thora & Malone, Janet. Nemeth Reference Sheets. (p. 1241)
Dumont, Virginie, et al. Enredos de Familia. Boucher, Michel, illus. (p. 531)
Dumortier, Marjorie. Zoe & Her Zany Animals. (p. 1987)
Dumortier, Marjorie, illus. see Bowman, Donna H.
Dumortier, Marjorie, illus. see Harvey, Damian.
Dunagan, Cindy. Journaling Toward Moral Excellence Volume Four for Young Adults: A Character Building Workbook of 100 Thought-Provoking Questions to Help the Young Discover the Value of Moral Strength. (p. 927)
—Journaling Toward Moral Excellence Volume One for Young Writers. (p. 927)
—Journaling Toward Moral Excellence Volume Three for Teenagers: A Character Building Workbook of 100 Thought-Provoking Questions to Help the Young Discover the Value of Moral Strength. (p. 927)
—Journaling Toward Moral Excellence Volume Two for Pre-Teens: A Character Building Workbook of 100 Thought-Provoking Questions to Help the Young Discover the Value of Moral Strength. Vol. 2 (p. 927)
Dunagan, Jennifer. Santana's Harrowing Halloween. Hines, Marcel, illus. (p. 1513)
Dunagan, Ted. Yellow Watermelon. (p. 1970)
Dunagan, Ted M. Secret of the Satilfa. (p. 1543)
Dunaway, Nancy, illus. see Morrison, Lillian.
Dunbar, Eddie. Lake Merritt & Greater Oakland Insects. (p. 972)
Dunbar, Eddie, photos by. Insects of Wente Scout Reservation: Mendocino County, California. (p. 876)
Dunbar, Fiona. Chocolate Wishes. (p. 309)
—Truth Cookie. (p. 1794)
Dunbar, Geoff, illus. see Ardagh, Philip.
Dunbar, Geoff & Ardagh, Philip. High in the Clouds. (p. 777)
Dunbar, Helene. These Gentle Wounds. (p. 1731)
—What Remains. (p. 1893)
Dunbar, Joyce. Chick Called Saturday. Granström, Brita, illus. (p. 299)
—Do Dare Duck. Massey, Jane, illus. (p. 456)
—Oddly. Benson, Patrick, illus. (p. 1278)
—Pat-A-Cake Baby. Dunbar, Polly, illus. (p. 1327)
—Puss Jekyll Cat Hyde. Barton, Jill, illus. (p. 1420)
—Spring Rabbit. Varley, Susan, illus. (p. 1635)
—Tell Me Something Happy Before I Go to Sleep. Gliori, Debi, illus. (p. 1716)
Dunbar, Joyce & Gliori, Debi. Muy Chiquitin. Gliori, Debi, illus. (p. 1195)
Dunbar, Katherine, ed. Antidepressants. (p. 89)
Dunbar, Paul Laurence. Howdy, Honey, Howdy. (p. 823)
—In Old Plantation Days. (p. 864)
—Life & Works of Paul Laurence Dunbar. (p. 1008)
—Lyrics of Love & Laughter. (p. 1067)
—Lyrics of Sunshine & Shadow. (p. 1067)
—Lyrics of the Hearthside. (p. 1067)
—Paul Lawrence Dunbar Collection (p. 1330)
Dunbar, Paula J. Ruby's Rainbow: A Story of Acadia National Park. (p. 1494)
Dunbar, Polly. Arthur's Dream Boat. Dunbar, Polly, illus. (p. 104)
—Doodle Bites: A Tilly & Friends Book. Dunbar, Polly, illus. (p. 469)
—Goodnight, Tiptoe. Dunbar, Polly, illus. (p. 701)
—Hello, Tilly. Dunbar, Polly, illus. (p. 765)
—Here's a Little Poem: A Very First Book of Poetry. (p. 771)
—Penguin. Dunbar, Polly, illus. (p. 1336)
—Pretty Pru: A Tilly & Friends Book. Dunbar, Polly, illus. (p. 1398)
Dunbar, Polly, illus. see Almond, David.
Dunbar, Polly, illus. see Dunbar, Joyce.
Dunbar, Polly, illus. see Ely, Lesley.
Dunbar, Polly, illus. see Mahy, Margaret.
Dunbar, Polly, jt. auth. see Ely, Lesley.
Dunbar, Polly, tr. see Ely, Lesley.
Duncalf, Joanne. Zookeeper's Menagerie. (p. 1989)
Duncan, Al. Rescue Dog. Panse, Sonal, illus. (p. 1462)
Duncan, Alexandra. Salvage. (p. 1506)
—Sound. (p. 1615)
Duncan, Alice Faye. Honey Baby Sugar Child. Keeter, Susan, illus. (p. 794)
Duncan, Andrew. Failure of Conservatism in Modern British Poetry. (p. 562)
—Imaginary in Geometry. (p. 860)
—Origins of the Underground: British Poetry Between Apocryphon & Incident Light, 1933-79. (p. 1304)
Duncan, Andrew & Allen, Tim, eds. Don't Start Me Talking: Interviews with Contemporary Poets. (p. 468)
Duncan, Aubrey. Understanding God's Sabbath: A Decision to Make. (p. 1815)
Duncan, Barbara, ed. Origin of the Milky Way & Other Living Stories of the Cherokee. Standingdeer, John, Jr. & Goshorn, Shan, illus. (p. 1304)
Duncan, Beverly, illus. see Goodman, Susan E.
Duncan, Billy. Haunting Good Time (p. 754)
Duncan, Brenda. Reese - the Dog Who Almost Ruined Christmas. (p. 1456)
Duncan, Caroline, jt. auth. see McLean, Linda.
Duncan, Christa. Story of the H Brothers. (p. 1661)
Duncan, Courtney B. Just Fly. (p. 938)
Duncan, Cynthia L. Kids Say Such Silly Things. (p. 955)
Duncan, David A. Dude, Where's Your Helmet? (p. 489)
Duncan, Denis & Barclay, William. Marching Orders: Daily Readings for Younger People. (p. 1092)
Duncan Edwards, Pamela. Honk! Cole, Henry, illus. (p. 795)
Duncan, Frances. When Mother Lets Us Garden: A Book for Little Folk Who Want to Make Gardens. (p. 1904)
Duncan, George T., Jr. Walking with God, Intimately: As Your Father. (p. 1854)
Duncan Gurley, Ann. Esbe's Halo. (p. 534)
Duncan, Hall F. Those Tires Have Got to Go! (p. 1740)
Duncan, James Carl. Lucy — the Colt That Went to the Belmont Stakes. (p. 1063)
Duncan, Jasmin. Unicorn Legacy. (p. 1818)
Duncan, Jenni. Helping Children Cope with Divorce. (p. 766)
Duncan, Jennifer. Frontier Spirit: The Brave Women of the Klondike. (p. 644)
Duncan, Jodi. Happy Flowers. (p. 745)
Duncan, John. UFOs. (p. 1807)
Duncan, John & Saddleback Educational Publishing Staff. UFO's (p. 1808)
Duncan, Karen, illus. see Robb, Jackie & Stringle, Berny.
Duncan, Karen & Issa, Kate Hannigan. Good Fun! Book: 12 Months of Parties That Celebrate Service. LeTourneau, Anthony Alex, illus. (p. 698)
Duncan, Kathryn, jt. auth. see Brown, Tiffanie.
Duncan, Leonard C. Greek Roots J-Ology. Bigelow, Holly, illus. (p. 721)
Duncan, Lizzy, jt. auth. see Iggulden, Conn.
Duncan, Lois. Daughters of Eve. (p. 410)
—Debutante Hill. (p. 421)
—Don't Look Behind You (p. 468)
—Don't Look Behind You. (p. 468)
—Down a Dark Hall. (p. 474)
—Gift of Magic. (p. 675)
—Hotel for Dogs. (p. 802)
—I Know What You Did Last Summer. (p. 840)
—Killing Mr. Griffin. (p. 956)
—Locked in Time. (p. 1045)
—Movie for Dogs. (p. 1183)
—Stranger with My Face. (p. 1665)
—Summer of Fear. (p. 1674)
—Third Eye. (p. 1734)
Duncan, Michelle. Middle Shmiddle. (p. 1138)
Duncan, Randy. Miranda & Her Pand. (p. 1149)
Duncan, S. L. Revelation of Gabriel Adam. (p. 1465)
—Salvation of Gabriel Adam. (p. 1506)
Duncan, Sandy Frances. Gold Rush Orphan. (p. 694)
Duncan, Sarah. Nice Girls Do. (p. 1250)
Duncan, Shannon. Present Moment Awareness: A Simple, Step-by-Step Guide to Living in the Now. (p. 1396)
Duncan, Sharyn. Mouse House & other Stories: You Are the Artist. (p. 1182)
Duncan, Shirley, ed. see Bernard, Margaret Mitchell.
Duncan, Stacy Lin. Chicken & Dumplings. (p. 300)
Duncan, Tisha Admire. Myrtle the Blue Eyed Turtle: A My Dirty Cat Mutt Adventure. (p. 1222)
Duncan, Vicky, jt. auth. see Garth, Richard.
Duncan-Goetz, Betty. Squiggle the Wiggle Worm. (p. 1637)
Duncan-Pauley, Chadney. Bull's Paradise. (p. 241)
Duncklee, John. Manchado & His Friends Manchado Y Sus Amigos. (p. 1086)
Dundon, Adamarie. Niklas Rogers: The Adventure Begins. (p. 1255)
Dundy, Melanie Richardson. Westward Ho with Ollie Ox! (p. 1876)
DuneCraft & Soffer, Ruth. DuneCraft Weird & Wacky Plantlife. (p. 490)
Dungan, Julia, illus. see Gomes, Julie.
Dungey, Thomas, illus. see Meek, Jeffrey/K.

Dungworth, Richard, et al. Usborne Book of Famous Lives. (p. 1827)
Dungy, Lauren, jt. auth. see Dungy, Tony.
Dungy, Tony. You Can Do It! Bates, Amy June, illus. (p. 1974)
Dungy, Tony & Dungy, Lauren. Go, Jade, Go! Newton, Vanessa Brantley, illus. (p. 686)
—Here Comes the Parade! Newton, Vanessa Brantley, illus. (p. 770)
—Justin & the Bully. (p. 940)
—Justin & the Bully. Newton, Vanessa Brantley, illus. (p. 940)
—Missing Cupcake Mystery. (p. 1152)
—Missing Cupcake Mystery. Newton, Vanessa Brantley, illus. (p. 1152)
—Ruby's New Home. Newton, Vanessa Brantley, illus. (p. 1493)
—Team Stays Together! Newton, Vanessa Brantley, illus. (p. 1710)
—You Can Be a Friend. Mazellan, Ron, illus. (p. 1973)
Dunham Akiyama, Laine, illus. see Stewart, Whitney.
Dunham, Bandhu Scott. We Like to Invent! Stark, Ryan, illus. (p. 1867)
Dunham, Kelli. Boy's Body Book: Everything You Need to Know for Growing up You. (p. 220)
—Girls Body Book: Everything You Need to Know for Growing up YOU. Tallardy, Laura, illus. (p. 679)
—Girl's Body Book: Everything You Need to Know for Growing up You. (p. 679)
—Girl's Body Book: Everything You Need to Know for Growing up You! Tallardy, Laura, illus. (p. 679)
Dunham, Montrew. Abner Doubleday: Boy Baseball Pioneer Underdown, Harold D., ed. (p. 5)
—Mahalia Jackson: Gospel Singer & Civil Rights Champion Underdown, Harold D., ed. (p. 1076)
Dunham, Terri Hoover. Legend of Papa Noel: A Cajun Christmas Story. Knorr, Laura, illus. (p. 988)
Dunham, Wendy. My Name Is River. (p. 1215)
Dunigan, Anne, ed. see Thrasher, Amanda M.
Dunivan, Dennis W. Escape from Communist Heaven. (p. 534)
Dunkell, Barbara & Broyles, Janell. Frequently Asked Questions about Hate Crimes. (p. 636)
Dunkin, Beth. Cabin Woolgathering. (p. 250)
Dunkle, Clare B. Close Kin. (p. 333)
—Hollow Kingdom. (p. 789)
—House of Dead Maids. Arrasmith, Patrick, illus. (p. 803)
—In the Coils of the Snake. (p. 865)
—Sky Inside. (p. 1586)
—Walls Have Eyes. (p. 1855)
Dunkle, Clare B., jt. auth. see Dunkle, Elena.
Dunkle, Elena & Dunkle, Clare B. Elena Vanishing. (p. 511)
Dunkleberger, Amy. So You Want to Be a Film or TV Director? (p. 1602)
—So You Want to Be a Film or TV Screenwriter? (p. 1602)
—Student's Guide to Arthur Miller. (p. 1669)
—Write a Mystery in 5 Simple Steps. (p. 1963)
Dunkleburger, Amy, jt. auth. see Svitil, Torene.
Dunklee, Annika. My Name Is Elizabeth! Forsythe, Matthew, illus. (p. 1215)
Dunkley, Andrew, photos by see Blake, Peter.
Dunkley, Cheryl. Torment at Play. Drummond-Hay, Fran, ed. (p. 1769)
Dunkwu, Jude. Tortoise Tales Niki the Tortoise & the Birds: Why the Tortoise's Shell Is Cracked. (p. 1771)
Dunlap, jt. auth. see Grosset.
Dunlap Cather, Katherine. Boyhood Stories of Famous Men. (p. 220)
Dunlap, Hope, illus. see Browning, Robert.
Dunlap Inc. Staff, jt. auth. see Grosset.
Dunlap, Jennifer, jt. auth. see Privateer, Mark.
Dunlap, Jim. Sam Snake Says. Holland, Kathy, illus. (p. 1507)
Dunlap, Joan, illus. see Bennett, Marcia.
Dunlap, Julie & Lorbiecki, Marybeth. John Muir & the Stickeen: An Icy Adventure with a No Good Dog. Farnsworth, Bill, illus. (p. 922)
Dunlap, Julie & Olmsted, Frederick Law. Parks for the People: The Life of Frederick Law Olmsted. (p. 1325)
Dunlap, Shiree, jt. auth. see Burncrot, Curt.
Dunlap, Sonya. Responza the Bull Learns the Ropes of Friendship. Snider, Sharon, illus. (p. 1464)
Dunlap, Sonya K. Responza the Bull Learns the Ropes. (p. 1463)
Dunlap, Susanne. Academie. (p. 7)
—Anastasia's Secret. (p. 67)
—In the Shadow of the Lamp. (p. 867)
—Musician's Daughter. (p. 1194)
Dunlavey, Rob, illus. see Appelt, Kathi.
Dunlavey, Rob, illus. see Rose, Caroline.
Dunlavey, Rob, illus. see Sheehan, Kevin.
Dunleavy, Deborah. Jumbo Book of Drama. Kurisu, Jane, tr. (p. 933)
Dunlop, Cliff. Flights of Fancy: An Anthology. (p. 604)
Dunlop, Ed. Escape to Liechtenstein. (p. 535)
—Incredible Rescues. Halverson, Tom, illus. (p. 869)
—Search for the Silver Eagle. Halverson, Tom, illus. (p. 1537)
—Sherlock Jones: The Missing Diamond. (p. 1565)
—Sherlock Jones: The Assassination Plot. (p. 1565)
—Sherlock Jones: The Phantom Airplane. (p. 1566)
—Sherlock Jones: The Willoughby Bank Robbery. (p. 1566)
Dunlop, Graham. Military Economics, Culture & Logistics in the Burma Campaign, 1942-1945 (p. 1143)
Dunlop, Jenna & Morganelli, Adrianna. Minerals. (p. 1146)
Dunlop, Jenna & Zronik, John. Salt. (p. 1505)
Dunlop-Kahren, Anne, ed. see Barcus, Dawn.
Dunmore, Helen. Deep. (p. 422)
—Ingo. (p. 874)
—Tara's Tree House. Littlewood, Karin, illus. (p. 1706)
—Tide Knot. (p. 1747)
Dunn, Anthony. Completely Magi-CaLL: The TRUE Secrets of Magic: A Study of the Magician's Art. Gunther, Chat, photos by. (p. 353)
Dunn, Ben. Heaven Sent. (p. 761)
—How to Draw Manga. (p. 818)
—How to Draw Steampunk Supersize TP. (p. 818)
—Ninja High School (p. 1256)
—Warrior Nun Areala (p. 1858)
Dunn, Ben, illus. see Barrie, J. M.
Dunn, Ben, illus. see Dunn, Joe.
Dunn, Ben, illus. see Dunn, Joeming & Warner, Gertrude Chandler.
Dunn, Ben, illus. see Dunn, Joeming W.
Dunn, Ben, illus. see Dunn, Joeming.
Dunn, Ben, illus. see Dunn, Rebecca.
Dunn, Ben, illus. see Goodwin, Vincent.
Dunn, Ben, illus. see Pyle, Howard.
Dunn, Ben, illus. see Warner, Gertrude Chandler.
Dunn, Ben, illus. see Wells, H. G.
Dunn, Ben, jt. auth. see Dunn, Joeming W.
Dunn, Ben, jt. auth. see Dunn, Joeming.
Dunn, Ben, jt. illus. see Dunn, Joeming W.
Dunn, Ben, jt. illus. see Dunn, Joeming.
Dunn, Ben & Mallette, Herb. Ninja High School (p. 1256)
Dunn, Ben, et al, contrib. by. How to Draw Manga (p. 818)
Dunn, Brian, tr. see Mashima, Hiro.
Dunn, Carole, jt. auth. see Lowry, Patrick.
Dunn, Carolyn. Pie Went By. (p. 1356)
Dunn, Carolyn, jt. auth. see Berk, Ari.
Dunn, Carrie. Gracie Goes to Grandma's (p. 705)
Dunn, Catherine. Oscar & Solomon. (p. 1305)
Dunn, Claire Ross, jt. auth. see Schlegel, Elfi.
Dunn, David H., jt. auth. see Emmett, Jonathan.
Dunn, Dennis L. Johnny Bear. (p. 923)
Dunn, Dinah. Haunted Prisons. (p. 753)
Dunn, Edward Grieves. Crinkles Academy for Wizards. (p. 383)
Dunn, Gary, illus. see Cox, Michael.
Dunn, Gary, illus. see Sage, Alison.
Dunn, Herb. Jackie Robinson. Henderson, Meryl, illus. (p. 903)
Dunn, Hunter S. Winter's Dream. Ellis, Joey, illus. (p. 1938)
Dunn, James. ABC London. Slater, Kate, illus. (p. 3)
—ABC UK. Bate, Helen, illus. (p. 3)
Dunn, James & Quarto Generic Staff. ABC London. Slater, Kate, illus. (p. 3)
Dunn, Jeremy K. Ray Lewis. (p. 1441)
Dunn, Jill. Littering Is for Losers. Hill, Bodhi, illus. (p. 1023)
Dunn, Joe. Abraham Lincoln. Espinosa, Rod, illus. (p. 6)
—Anne Frank. (p. 85)
—Bombing of Pearl Harbor. Wight, Joseph & Espinosa, Rod, illus. (p. 208)
—California Gold Rush. Dunn, Ben, illus. (p. 253)
—Jackie Robinson. Espinosa, Rod, illus. (p. 903)
—Miracle on Ice. Dunn, Ben, illus. (p. 1148)
—Moon Landing. Espinosa, Rod et al, illus. (p. 1172)
—Titanic. (p. 1757)
—Underground Railroad. (p. 1814)
—Wright Brothers. Dunn, Ben, illus. (p. 1963)
Dunn, Joeming. Barack Obama: 44th U. S. President. Espinosa, Rod, illus. (p. 137)
—Cask of Amontillado. (p. 276)
—Eyes: A Graphic Novel Tour. Espinosa, Rod, illus. (p. 558)
—Fall of the Berlin Wall. (p. 566)
—Graphic Adventures: The Human Body Espinosa, Rod, illus. (p. 710)
—Kidneys: A Graphic Novel Tour. Espinosa, Rod, illus. (p. 952)
—Lighthouse Mystery. Dunn, Ben, illus. (p. 1015)
—Liver: A Graphic Novel Tour. Espinosa, Rod, illus. (p. 1040)
—Lungs: A Graphic Novel Tour. Espinosa, Rod, illus. (p. 1066)
—Macbeth. Hutchinson, David, illus. (p. 1067)
—Mountain Top Mystery Dunn, Ben, illus. (p. 1181)
—Raven. (p. 1441)
—Romeo & Juliet. Espinosa, Rod, illus. (p. 1486)
—Thomas Jefferson. Espinosa, Rod, illus. (p. 1738)
—Woodshed Mystery. Dunn, Ben, illus. (p. 1950)
Dunn, Joeming & Denham, Brian. Dolly: The 1st Cloned Sheep. (p. 464)
—Shamu: The 1st Killer Whale in Captivity. (p. 1559)
Dunn, Joeming & Dunn, Ben. Albert II: The 1st Monkey in Space. (p. 34)
—Bicycle Mystery. (p. 177)
—Bill Clinton: 42nd U. S. President. (p. 186)
—Cher Ami: WWI Homing Pigeon. (p. 297)
—Houseboat Mystery. (p. 804)
—Laika: The 1st Dog in Space. (p. 972)
—Mystery in the Sand (p. 1224)
—Richard Nixon: 37th U. S. President. (p. 1469)
—Ronald Reagan: 40th U. S. President. (p. 1486)
Dunn, Joeming & Espinosa De Santayana, Rodrigo De. Ulysses S. Grant: 18th U. S. President. (p. 1810)
Dunn, Joeming & Espinosa, Rod. Brain: A Graphic Novel Tour. Espinosa, Rod, illus. (p. 221)
—Heart: A Graphic Novel Tour. Espinosa, Rod, illus. (p. 759)
—John Adams: 2nd U. S. President. (p. 921)
Dunn, Joeming & Warner, Gertrude Chandler. Lighthouse Mystery Dunn, Ben, illus. (p. 1015)
—Mountain Top Mystery Dunn, Ben, illus. (p. 1181)
—Mystery in the Sand Dunn, Ben, illus. (p. 1224)
—Woodshed Mystery Dunn, Ben, illus. (p. 1950)
Dunn, Joeming W. Amelia Earhart. Dunn, Ben, illus. (p. 58)
—Booker T. Washington. Allen, Chris, illus. (p. 212)
—Building the Transcontinental Railroad. Espinosa, Rod, illus. (p. 239)
—Cesar Chavez. Espinosa, Rod, illus. (p. 288)
—Clara Barton. Espinosa, Rod, illus. (p. 326)
—Custer's Last Stand. Smith, Tim, illus. (p. 395)
—George Washington Carver. Allen, Chris, illus. (p. 664)
—Gettysburg. Dunn, Ben, illus. (p. 670)
—Martin Luther King, Jr. Allen, Chris, illus. (p. 1097)
—Oregon Trail. Smith, Tim, illus. (p. 1303)
—Pony Express. Martin, Cynthia, illus. (p. 1382)
—Reaching the North Pole. Espinosa, Rod, illus. (p. 1442)
—Sacagawea. Espinosa, Rod, illus. (p. 1500)
—Salem Witch Trials. Martin, Cynthia, illus. (p. 1504)
Dunn, Joeming W., illus. see Warner, Gertrude Chandler.
Dunn, Joeming W. & Dunn, Ben. Armistice Day. (p. 99)
—D-Day. Dunn, Joeming W. & Dunn, Ben, illus. (p. 397)
—Fallujah. (p. 567)
—Tet Offensive. (p. 1723)
Dunn, John M. Birth of Modern India. Greenhaven Press Editors, ed. (p. 192)
—Constitution & Founding of America. (p. 359)
—Life in Castro's Cuba. (p. 1010)
—Prohibition. (p. 1410)
Dunn Jr., Howard Alfred, illus. see Dunn, Layne.
Dunn, Judy. Little Duck. Dunn, Phoebe, photos by. (p. 1027)
—Little Rabbit. Dunn, Phoebe, photos by. (p. 1034)
Dunn, Judy, photos by see Dunn, Phoebe, illus.
Dunn, Justine. Hey! There's Science in My Literature! Grades 1-2. Radtke, Becky, illus. (p. 774)
—Hey! There's Social Studies in My Literature! Grades 1-2. Radtke, Becky, illus. (p. 774)
Dunn, Karen Lewit. Saturday Night Pizza. (p. 1515)
—Technology & Natural Disasters. (p. 1711)
—Visiting Grandma. (p. 1845)
—What's the Problem? (p. 1899)
—What's the Solution? (p. 1899)
Dunn, Kevin Ikim. In Search of Yourself Word Search Puzzles: Explorations into the Black Experience. Sedalia, Rajan, illus. (p. 865)
Dunn, Layne. Light of the Moon. Dunn Jr., Howard Alfred, illus. (p. 1015)
Dunn, Mark. Age Altertron (p. 29)
Dunn, Mark, jt. auth. see Turner, Dona.
Dunn, Mary. Garter Snakes (p. 657)
—My Adventure at a Concert Hall. (p. 1195)
—My Adventure at a Flower Farm. (p. 1195)
—My Adventure at an Artist's Studio: Where You Create the Story. (p. 1195)
—My Adventure at Pompeii. (p. 1195)
—My Adventure at Stonehenge. (p. 1195)
—My Adventure Building the Eiffel Tower. (p. 1195)
—My Adventure in a Mohawk Village. (p. 1195)
—My Adventure in the Southeast: Advanced My Adventure. (p. 1195)
—My Adventure on a Dinosaur Dig. (p. 1195)
—My Adventure with Mozart. (p. 1195)
—My Adventure with Rembrandt. (p. 1195)
Dunn, Mary R. California Condors. (p. 253)
—Capybaras (p. 265)
—Copperheads (p. 366)
—Dream Jobs (p. 483)
—Fireflies (p. 592)
—Hedgehogs (p. 762)
—I Want to Be a Ballet Dancer. (p. 847)
—I Want to Be a Chef. (p. 847)
—I Want to Be a Fashion Designer. (p. 847)
—I Want to Be in Musicals. (p. 848)
—I Want to Make Movies. (p. 848)
—I Want to Write Books. (p. 848)
—Llamas (p. 1043)
—Look at Earth. (p. 1048)
—Look at Mars. (p. 1048)
—Look at Mercury. (p. 1048)
—Look at Venus. (p. 1049)
—Opossums (p. 1300)
—Ospreys. (p. 1306)
—Owls (p. 1315)
—Piranhas (p. 1362)
—Porcupines (p. 1386)
—Pygmy Marmosets (p. 1421)
—Quiero Hacer Películas. (p. 1428)
—Quiero Ser Chef. (p. 1428)
—Quiero Ser Diseñador de Modas. (p. 1428)
—Rattlesnakes (p. 1440)
—Spider Monkeys (p. 1626)
—Tamarin Monkeys (p. 1704)
—Toucans (p. 1772)
—Turkey Vultures. (p. 1797)
Dunn, Mary R., jt. auth. see Gillenwater, Chadwick.
Dunn, Mary R., jt. auth. see Higgins, Melissa.
Dunn, Mary R., jt. auth. see Johnson, J. Angelique.
Dunn, Mary R. & Alamán, Eduardo. Quiero Trabajar en Los Musicales. (p. 1428)
Dunn, Mary R. & Hill, Melissa. Birds of Prey. (p. 191)
Dunn, Matthew. Day One. (p. 414)
—Spy Trade: A Spycatcher Novella. (p. 1636)
Dunn, Michael P. What's the Big Secret? (p. 1899)
Dunn, Nora. Kebo's Big Adventures: Life Is What You Make It. (p. 946)
Dunn, Opal. Number Rhymes to Say & Play! Gon, Adriano, illus. (p. 1271)
Dunn, Paul. Why Bird. (p. 1922)
Dunn, Phoebe. Big Treasury of Little Animals. Dunn, Phoebe, illus. (p. 184)
—Guess Who I Am... (p. 729)
—Little Duck. Dunn, Judy, photos by. (p. 1027)
—Little Kitten. (p. 1030)
Dunn, Phoebe, photos by see Dunn, Judy.
Dunn, Phoebe, photos by. Little Puppy. (p. 1034)
Dunn, Rebecca. Hamlet. Dunn, Ben, illus. (p. 739)
Dunn, Richard, jt. auth. see Barksdale, Miechel.
Dunn, Richard, jt. auth. see Gunn, Barbara.
Dunn, Richard & Sprick, Jessica. Whales: Read Well Level K Unit 18 Storybook. Koontz, Robin Michal, illus. (p. 1878)
Dunn, Robert. Littlest Bunny in Michigan: An Easter Adventure. (p. 1039)
—Littlest Bunny in Rhode Island: An Easter Adventure. (p. 1039)
Dunn, Robert, illus. see Alcott, Louisa May.
Dunn, Robert, illus. see Dumas, Alexandre.
Dunn, Robert, illus. see Jacobs, Lily.
Dunn, Robert, illus. see Jessell, Tim.
Dunn, Robert, illus. see Smallman, Steve.
Dunn, Robert, illus. see Ziarnik, Natalie.
Dunn, Robert A., illus. see Jacobs, Lily.
Dunn, S. K., compiled by. Just Joking! 1001 Jokes to Crack You Up. (p. 938)
Dunn, Sandy, illus. see Dean, Carol.
Dunn, Todd. We Go Together! Sakamoto, Miki, illus. (p. 1867)
Dunnahoe, Hugh, illus. see Oh! Suzannah.
Dunn-Dern, Lisa. Dr. Duncan Dog on Duty! Yomtob, Andrea, illus. (p. 475)
Dunne, Amy. Secret Lies. (p. 1541)
Dunne, Colin. Werewolf. (p. 1875)
Dunne, Kathleen, illus. see Williams, Rozanne Lanczak.
Dunne, Kevin, photos by see Knowlden, Martin.
Dunne, Steve. Fool's Gold. (p. 614)
Dunne, Tom, illus. see Pliscou, Lisa.
Dunn-Georgiou, Elisha. Everything You Need to Know about Organic Foods. (p. 545)
Dunnick, Regan, illus. see Brennan, Eileen.
Dunnick, Regan, illus. see Crimi, Carolyn.
Dunnick, Regan, illus. see Root, Phyllis.
Dunnick, Regan, illus. see Shaskan, Kathy.
Dunnier, Tina, illus. see Fisher, Meaghan.
Dunnier, Tina, illus. see Wehrman, Tom.
Dunning, Joan. Seabird in the Forest: The Mystery of the Marbled Murrelet. Dunning, Joan, illus. (p. 1536)
Dunning, John Harris & Singh, Nikhil. Salem Brownstone: All along the Watchtowers. Singh, Nikhil, illus. (p. 1504)
Dunning, Lisa. Restless Spirits-Utah's Small Town Ghosts. (p. 1464)
Dunning, Rebecca. Real-Life Princess. Rohman, Stefanie & Ritchie, Mary, eds. (p. 1448)
Dunningham, Jo, illus. see Sullivan, Kathryn.
Dunnington, Gwenyth. Second Chance: Girl with the Heart of a Dragon. (p. 1539)
Dunnington, Tom, illus. see Dobkin, Bonnie.
Dunnington, Tom, illus. see Hamsa, Bobbie.
Dunnington, Tom, illus. see Punnett, Dick.
Dunnion, Kristyn. Big Big Sky Hopkinson, Nalo, ed. (p. 178)
—Mosh Pit (p. 1176)
Dunphy, Catherine. Caitlin (p. 252)
Dunphy, Lorraine F. Australian Fairy Tale. (p. 116)
Dunphy, Madeleine. At Home with the Gopher Tortoise: The Story of a Keystone Species. Rothman, Michael, illus. (p. 110)
—Here Is Antarctica. Leonard, Tom, illus. (p. 770)
—Here Is the African Savanna. Leonard, Tom, illus. (p. 770)
—Here Is the Arctic Winter. Robinson, Alan James, illus. (p. 770)
—Here Is the Coral Reef. Leonard, Tom, illus. (p. 770)
—Here Is the Southwestern Desert. Coe, Anne, illus. (p. 770)
—Here Is the Tropical Rain Forest. Rothman, Michael, illus. (p. 770)
—Here Is the Wetland. McLoughlin, Wayne, illus. (p. 770)
—Peregrine's Journey: A Story of Migration. Kest, Kristin, illus. (p. 1341)
Dunrea, Olivier. BooBoo. (p. 210)
—Gansi y Gerti/Gossie & Gertie Bilingual Board Book. (p. 655)
—Gemma & Gus. (p. 660)
—Gideon: It's Play Time, Not Naptime! (p. 674)
—Gideon. (p. 674)
—Gideon & Otto: Best Friends, Lost & Found. (p. 674)
—Gideon & Otto. (p. 674)
—Gossie. (p. 703)
—Gossie & Friends: A First Flap Book. Dunrea, Olivier, illus. (p. 703)
—Gossie & Friends Sticker Fun. (p. 703)
—Gossie & Gertie. (p. 703)
—Gossie & Gertie. Dunrea, Olivier, illus. (p. 703)
—Gossie & Gertie Padded Board Book. (p. 703)
—Gossie & Gertie (Reader) (p. 703)
—Gossie Padded Board Book. (p. 703)
—Gossie Plays Hide & Seek. Wilcox, Mary, ed. (p. 703)
—Gossie (Reader) (p. 703)
—Gus. (p. 732)
—Hanne's Quest. (p. 743)
—It's Snowing! Dunrea, Olivier, illus. (p. 898)
—Jasper & Joop: A Perfect Pair: One Tidy, One Messy. (p. 910)
—Jasper & Joop. (p. 910)
—Merry Christmas, Ollie! (p. 1129)
—Old Bear & His Cub. Dunrea, Olivier, illus. (p. 1283)
—Oli/Ollie Bilingual Board Book. (p. 1285)
—Ollie. (p. 1287)
—Ollie. Dunrea, Olivier, illus. (p. 1287)
—Ollie (Reader) (p. 1287)
—Ollie the Stomper. (p. 1287)
—Ollie the Stomper (Reader) (p. 1287)
—Ollie's Easter Eggs. (p. 1287)
—Ollie's Easter Eggs Board Book. (p. 1287)
—Ollie's Halloween. (p. 1287)
—Peedie. (p. 1334)
Dunrea, Olivier, illus. see Brenner, Barbara.
Dunsany, Lord. Glittering Gate. (p. 684)
—Gods of the Mountain. (p. 691)
—Golden Doom. (p. 694)
—Lost Silk Hat. (p. 1056)
Dunsany, Taylor. Little Witch Who Lost Her Broom & Other Stories. (p. 1038)
Dunseith, Peter. Bird of Heaven: The Story of a Swazi Sangoma. (p. 190)
Dunshee, Gloria. Will & the Red Ball. (p. 1932)
Dunshee, Gloria Fjare. Will & the Magic Snowman. (p. 1932)
Dunsmore, Roger, ed. see Charlo, Victor A.
Dunsmuir, Tom. You Can't Milk a Dancing Cow. Jones, Brian T., illus. (p. 1975)
Dunstan, David, illus. see Cuthbert, Kate.
Dunstan, David, illus. see Tovey, Peter.
Dunstan, Simon. Entebbe: The Most Daring Raid of Israel's Special Forces. (p. 531)
Dunston, Marc. Magic of Giving Cantrell, Katie, illus. (p. 1073)
Duntemann, Jeff. Jeff Duntemann's Drive-By Wi-Fi Guide. (p. 911)
Dunton, Jamie. Fish & the Coin. (p. 598)
Dunton, Lese. Betsy & the Golden Room. (p. 172)
Dunton, Trevor, illus. see Cunningham, Anna & McClurkan, Rob.
Dunton, Trevor, illus. see Shipton, Paul.
Duntze, Dorothee, illus. see Brothers Grimm.
Duntze, Dorothee, illus. see Grimm, Jacob & Grimm, Wilhelm K.
Duntze, Dorothee, illus. see Grimm, Jacob & Grimm, Wilhelm.
Dunwoodie, Helen. Dogspell. (p. 463)
Duopress Labs Staff. Hello, Ocean Friends. (p. 764)
Dupasquier, Philippe. Aeropuerto (The Airport) Ibeas Delgado, Juan Manuel, tr. (p. 25)
—Blue. Dupasquier, Philippe, illus. (p. 202)
—Estacion de Ferrocarril. (p. 538)
—Obra. (p. 1275)

D

Dupasquier, Philippe, illus. see Bradman, Tony.
Dupasquier, Philippe, illus. see Donaldson, Julia.
Dupasquier, Philippe, illus. see Fine, Anne.
DuPaul, George J. & Stoner, Gary. Assessing a D H D in the Schools. (p. 107)
Dupernex, Alison. Start to Knit. (p. 1643)
Dupeyron, Sarah. ABC's of Vermont Coloring Book. (p. 4)
Duplaix, Georges & Golden Books Staff. Merry Shipwreck. Gergely, Tibor, illus. (p. 1129)
Dupler, Douglas. Constructing a Life Philosophy. (p. 359)
DuPlessis, Rachel Blau. Drafts: Drafts 39-57, Pledge, with Draft, Unnumbered - Précis. (p. 476)
Dupon-Martinez, Christopher, illus. see Carson, Shonette.
DuPont, Brittany, illus. see Silvola, Liz.
Dupont, Ellen. United States Justice System. (p. 1819)
Dupont, Lindsay Harper, illus. see Harper, Jessica.
Dupont, Matthew. As I Look in Your Eyes. Gutierez, Francisco & Renteria, Justin, illus. (p. 105)
DuPrau, Jeanne. Car Trouble. (p. 265)
—City of Ember: The Graphic Novel. Asker, Niklas, illus. (p. 323)
—City of Ember. (p. 323)
—City of Ember Deluxe Edition: The First Book of Ember. (p. 323)
—Diamond of Darkhold. (p. 434)
—People of Sparks. (p. 1339)
—Prophet of Yonwood. (p. 1411)
Duprau, Jeanne & Middaugh, Dallas. City of Ember: The Graphic Novel. (p. 323)
Dupré, Judith. De las pirámides a los Rascacielos. (p. 416)
—From Pyramids to Skyscrapers & de las pirámides a los Rascacielos: 6 English, 6 Spanish Adaptations (p. 643)
—Magic Passport. (p. 1073)
Dupre, Kelly, illus. see Ahmed, Said Salah.
Dupre, Kelly, illus. see Jackson, Leona Novy.
Dupre, Kelly, illus. see Krensky, Stephen.
Dupre, Kelly, illus. see Peterson, Sheryl.
DuPree, Ben & Skindzier, Jon. Reed College College Prowler off the Record. (p. 1456)
Dupree, Bruce, illus. see McManis, Margaret.
Dupree, J. And S. Cat Tales: The Travel Adventures of Blue Boo & Sambootoo. (p. 278)
Dupuis, Lynda. Au Pied de la Lettre: Manuel de Lecture de Vocabulaire d'Expression Orale et Ecrite. (p. 114)
Dupuy, Diane. Little Girl Who Did... What?!!! Stockelbach, Ed, illus. (p. 1028)
Dupuy, Trevor Nevitt. Military History of Civil War Land Battles. Fisher, Leonard Everett, illus. (p. 1143)
Dupuy, W. Story of Poppy's Frankentoe (p. 1659)
Duque, Olga, tr. see Gillis, Jennifer Blizin.
Duquennoy, Jacques. Las Cataratas del Niagara. Duquennoy, Jacques, illus. (p. 976)
—Little Ghost Party. (p. 1028)
Duquet, Guy J., illus. see Waters, George T.
Duquin, Judy. Rusty. (p. 1498)
Duracell and the National Center for Missing & Exploited Children (NCMEC), creator. Great Tomato Adventure: A Story about Smart Safety Choices. (p. 718)
Duran, Eduardo. Buddha in Redface. (p. 234)
Durán, Ivy Adriana, ed. see Durán, Oscar Manuel.
Duran, Magdalena. Jewel of Friendship. (p. 917)
—Joya de la Amistad. (p. 930)
Durán, Oscar Manuel. Mama Cuentame un Cuento. Durán, Ivy Adriana, ed. (p. 1084)
Durán, Rosa Dopazo. Galeon de Manila: Los Objetos Que Llegaron de Oriente. Alvarez, Diego, illus. (p. 653)
Duran, Teresa. Fabulame un Fabula. Espluga, Maria, illus. (p. 559)
Duran, Teresa, illus. see Tort, Pep & Josep, Tort.
Duranceau, Suzanne, illus. see Ashby, Ruth.
Duranceau, Suzanne, illus. see Weeks, Sarah.
Durand, Delphine. Bob & Co. (p. 205)
—My House. Adams, Sarah, tr. from FRE. (p. 1211)
Durand, Delphine, illus. see Amato, Mary.
Durand, Delphine, illus. see Chandler, Susan.
Durand, Delphine, illus. see Root, Phyllis.
Durand, Delphine, illus. see Rosenthal, Amy Krouse.
Durand, Élodie, illus. see Feuchter, Anke.
Durand, Hallie. Catch That Cookie! (p. 279)
—Catch That Cookie! Small, David, illus. (p. 279)
—Dessert First. Davenier, Christine, illus. (p. 430)
—Just Desserts. Davenier, Christine, illus. (p. 938)
—Mitchell Goes Bowling. Fucile, Tony, illus. (p. 1155)
—Mitchell Goes Driving. (p. 1155)
—Mitchell Goes Driving. Fucile, Tony, illus. (p. 1155)
—Mitchell's License. Fucile, Tony, illus. (p. 1155)
—No Room for Dessert. Davenier, Christine, illus. (p. 1260)
Durand, Stephane & Poyet, Guillaume. Winged Migration: The Junior Edition. Wharry, David, tr. (p. 1936)
Durango, Julia. Angels Watching over Me. Kleven, Elisa, illus. (p. 75)
—Cha-Cha Chimps. Taylor, Eleanor, illus. (p. 288)
—Go-Go Gorillas. Taylor, Eleanor, illus. (p. 686)
—Leveller. (p. 1003)
—Pest Fest. Cyrus, Kurt, illus. (p. 1345)
—Sea of the Dead. (p. 1535)
—Under the Mambo Moon. VandenBroeck, Fabricio, illus. (p. 1813)
—Walls of Cartagena. Pohrt, Tom, illus. (p. 1855)
Durango, Julia, jt. auth. see Park, Linda Sue.
Durango, Julia & Trupiano, Katie Belle. Dream Away. Goldstrom, Robert, illus. (p. 483)
Durant, Alan. Billy Monster's Daymare. Collins, Ross, illus. (p. 187)
—Dear Santa Claus. Cabban, Vanessa, illus. (p. 419)
—Dear Tooth Fairy. Cabban, Vanessa, illus. (p. 419)
—Doing the Double. (p. 463)
—Gamer Mason, Sue, illus. (p. 654)
—Humpty Dumpty's Great Fall. Heming, Leah-Ellen, illus. (p. 827)
—I Love You Little Monkey. (p. 843)
—I Love You, Little Monkey. McEwen, Katharine, illus. (p. 843)
—If You Go Walking in Tiger Wood. Boon, Debbie, illus. (p. 854)
—Little Bo-Peep's Missing Sheep. Heming, Leah-Ellen, illus. (p. 1025)
—Little Miss Muffet's Big Scare. Heming, Leah-Ellen, illus. (p. 1032)
—Old Mother Hubbard's Stolen Bone. Heming, Leah-Ellen, illus. (p. 1284)
—Spider Mcdrew & the Egyptians: Band 12. Hopman, Philip, illus. (p. 1626)
—Spider's Big Match. Hopman, Philip, illus. (p. 1627)
—Teeth. Scratchmann, Max, illus. (p. 1715)
—That's Not Right! McEwen, Katharine, illus. (p. 1727)
—That's Not Right. McEwen, Katharine, illus. (p. 1727)
Durant, Alan, jt. auth. see Cassidy, Anne.
Durant, Alan & Lucas, Kath. Bird Flies South. (p. 190)
Durant, Alan & Walker, Sholto. Buzz & Bingo in the Starry Sky. (p. 248)
Durant, Michael J. & Hartov, Steven. In the Company of Heroes. (p. 865)
Durant, Michael J., et al. Night Stalkers: Top Secret Missions of the U. S. Army's Special Operations Aviation Regiment. (p. 1254)
Durant, Penny Raife. Sniffles, Sneezes, Hiccups, & Coughs: Level 2. (p. 1597)
Durant, Sybrina, ed. see Johnson, Sandi, et al.
Durant, Sybrina, ed. see Johnson, Sandi.
Durant, Sybrina, et al. Legend of the Blue Unicorn: Return of the Dragons Johnson, Britt, ed. (p. 989)
Durante, Dianne. Internationalism. (p. 880)
Duras, Marguerite. Hiroshima Mon Amour (p. 781)
—Pluie d'Ete. (p. 1374)
Durben, Toni. Grandpa Isn't Grandpa Anymore. Mulholland, Bailey, illus. (p. 709)
Durber, Matt. Backyard. Litchfield, Jo, illus. (p. 130)
—First ABC. (p. 592)
—First Colors. Allman, Howard & MMStudios, photos by. (p. 593)
Durber, Matt, jt. auth. see Brooks, Felicity.
Durber, Matt & Brooks, Felicity. Muddy Hippo. Wells, Rachel, illus. (p. 1188)
Durber, Matt & Jones, Stephanie. First Picture Nature. MMStudios, photos by. (p. 596)
Durbin, Amanda. Tree Houses & Treasures. (p. 1783)
Durbin, Frederic S. Star Shard. (p. 1641)
Durbin, Gail. Our Pets. (p. 1309)
—Under the Ground. (p. 1813)
Durbin, William. Blackwater Ben. (p. 198)
—Darkest Evening. (p. 408)
—Until the Last Spike: The Journal of Sean Sullivan, a Transcontinental Railroad Worker, Nebraska & Points West 1867. (p. 1823)
—Until the Last Spike: The Journal of Sean Sullivan, a Transcontinental Railroad Worker, Nebraska & Points West, 1867. (p. 1823)
Durden, Angela K. Heroes Need Practice, Too! Hohn, Tracy, illus. (p. 773)
Durden, Robert F. Life of Carter G. Woodson: Father of African-American History. (p. 1011)
Durden, Robert Franklin. Life of Carter G.Woodson: Father of African-American History. (p. 1011)
Durden-Nelson, Mae. I Just Called Her Momma. (p. 840)
Dureke, Angel, jt. auth. see Dureke, Chidinma.
Dureke, Chidinma & Dureke, Angel. Arts, Poems & Stories of the Heart. (p. 105)
Dureke, Jottn O. Z - the Goodluck Bird. Dureke, Jottn O., tr. (p. 1984)
Durell, Charles Pend. Lights off Shore or Sam & the Outlaws. (p. 1016)
Duren, Sheila Gregory. Pepper's Great Move! (p. 1340)
Durfee, Jim. Something for Teenagers & Those Who Love Them. (p. 1610)
Durgan, Lori Origer. Little Scrub Lady. (p. 1036)
Durham, Felicity. Storyboards. (p. 1663)
Durham, Kathryn. Mom, Can You Buy Me This? Richard Gets a Job (p. 1161)
Durham, Lilly, illus. see Powell, Opal.
Durham, Paul. Fork-Tongue Charmers. Antonsson, Petur, illus. (p. 620)
—Luck Uglies. Antonsson, Petur, illus. (p. 1062)
Durham, Roy. Andre the Squirrel & the Christmas Gift. Tandoc, Melissa, illus. (p. 72)
Durham, Victor G. Submarine Boys & the Spies: Dodging the Sharks of the Deep. (p. 1671)
—Submarine Boys & the Spies. (p. 1671)
—Submarine Boys for the Flag: Deeding Their Lives to Uncle Sam. (p. 1671)
—Submarine Boys for the Flag. (p. 1671)
—Submarine Boys Lightning Cruise. (p. 1671)
—Submarine Boys' Lightning Cruise: The Young Kings of the Deep. (p. 1671)
—Submarine Boys on Duty. (p. 1671)
—Submarine Boys Trial Trip. (p. 1671)
Durica, Karen. "Animals You See... a to Z. (p. 84)
Durick, Agnes York. Baby Bear, Mother Bear, Father Bear. Durick, Agnes York, illus. (p. 125)
Durie, Sally, illus. see Wendling, Peter.
Duriez, Marcel Ray. Many Adventures of Cuddles: Tobey, Pandora & Cuddles. (p. 1089)
Duris, Joan & Jones, Gillian. B Is for Berkshires. (p. 122)
Durk, Jim, illus. see Awdry, W.
Durk, Jim, illus. see Awdry, Wilbert V.
Durk, Jim, illus. see Brooke, Samantha.
Durk, Jim, illus. see Fisch, Sarah & Bridwell, Norman.
Durk, Jim, illus. see Fisch, Sarah.
Durk, Jim, illus. see Golden Books Staff.
Durk, Jim, illus. see Golden Books.
Durk, Jim, illus. see Kosara, Victoria.
Durk, Jim, illus. see Marsoli, Lisa Ann.
Durk, Jim, illus. see Onish, Liane B.
Durkee, Noura. Fall of the Giant. Durkee, Noura, illus. (p. 566)
—King, the Prince & the Naughty Sheep. Durkee, Noura, illus. (p. 959)
—Yunus & the Whale. Durkee, Noura, illus. (p. 1983)
Durkin, Chris, ed. see Head, Jeff.
Durkin, Kath & Maidment, Stella. Paint It! (p. 1318)
Durkin, Mary Jane. Shabby Little Princess. (p. 1556)
Durkin, Shawn. Stealing Home. Doherty, Catherine, illus. (p. 1646)
Durkin, Shawn & Doherty, Catherine. Shola's Game: A Novel. (p. 1568)
Durland, Maud, illus. see Renaud, Anne.
Durman, Laura. Castle Life. (p. 277)
—Knights. (p. 964)
—Siege. (p. 1573)
Durman, Laura, jt. auth. see Bauman, Amy.
Durmush, F. Ayshe, an Anatolian Tale. (p. 121)
Durnell, Marilyn F., jt. auth. see Wile, Jay L.
Durnil, Lari. Tale of Two Sisters. (p. 1701)
Duro, Karin L., jt. auth. see Behnke, Alison.
Durocher, Amelia. 3 Steps to Happy: Stop, Snap & Smile. (p. 1991)
Duroux, Mary. Rain Flower. Briggs, Karen, illus. (p. 1434)
Durr, Carol Atkinson, illus. see Conure, Lunatico.
Durr, Mark, ed. see Claudy, C. H.
Durrah, Jolan. Adventure in Borneo: The True Story of One Man's Quest to Find the Bornean Peacock Pheasant. (p. 14)
Durrant, George D. Sam's Christmas Wish. Burr, Dan, illus. (p. 1509)
—Seven Years Old & Preparing for Baptism. (p. 1555)
—Shakespeare's Best Work: A Novel of Unexpected Family Ties & Uncommon Faith. (p. 1559)
Durrant, Geraldine. Pirate Gran. Forshall, Rose, illus. (p. 1362)
—Twinbane: an Appalling True History. (p. 1802)
Durrant, Lynda, jt. auth. see Oelschlager, Vanita.
Durrant, Sabine. Cross Your Heart, Connie Pickles. (p. 385)
Durrell, Gerald. Toby the Tortoise. (p. 1760)
Durrell, Julie, illus. see Parker, David.
Durrell, Julie, illus. see Stockstill, Gloria McQueen.
Durrell, Julie, illus. see Wing, Natasha.
Durrett, Deanne. Arizona. (p. 98)
—Oklahoma. (p. 1282)
—Right to Vote. (p. 1472)
Durrie, Karen. Al Baloncesto. (p. 32)
—Al Béisbol. (p. 32)
—Al Fútbol. (p. 32)
—Al Hockey. (p. 32)
—Alabama: The Yellowhammer State. (p. 33)
—Alaska: The Last Frontier. (p. 34)
—Arizona: The Grand Canyon State. (p. 98)
—Arkansas: The Natural State. (p. 99)
—Artes. (p. 103)
—Artes Marciales. (p. 103)
—Arts. (p. 104)
—Baseball. (p. 140)
—Basketball. (p. 143)
—California: The Golden State. (p. 253)
—Colorado: Colorful Colorado. (p. 343)
—Connecticut: The Constitution State. (p. 358)
—Delaware: The First State. (p. 424)
—District of Columbia: The Nation's Capital. (p. 454)
—Diversión. (p. 454)
—Florida: The Sunshine State. (p. 606)
—Football. (p. 614)
—Fun. (p. 647)
—Fútbol Americano. (p. 650)
—Georgia: The Peach State. (p. 665)
—Gran Tiburón Blanco. (p. 707)
—Hawaii. (p. 755)
—Health. (p. 757)
—Hearing. (p. 759)
—Hockey. (p. 786)
—I Am a Camel. (p. 832)
—I Am a Great White Shark. (p. 832)
—I Am a Grizzly Bear. (p. 832)
—I Am a Lion. (p. 832)
—I Am a Penguin. (p. 832)
—I Am an Alligator. (p. 832)
—Idaho: The Gem State. (p. 852)
—Illinois: The Prairie State. (p. 857)
—León. (p. 992)
—Martial Arts. (p. 1097)
—Oso Gris. (p. 1305)
—Pingüino. (p. 1359)
—Safety. (p. 1502)
—Salud. (p. 1506)
—Seguridad. (p. 1548)
—Sight. (p. 1574)
—Smell. (p. 1593)
—Soccer. (p. 1603)
—Taste. (p. 1707)
—Touch. (p. 1772)
—Yo Soy el Caimán. (p. 1971)
—Yo Soy un Camello. (p. 1971)
Durso, Diana T. Did You Know That's Not My Name? (p. 437)
Durst, Beverly. Fairly Identical. (p. 563)
Durst, Sarah Beth. Chasing Power. (p. 294)
—Conjured. (p. 357)
—Drink, Slay, Love. (p. 485)
—Enchanted Ivy. (p. 523)
—Ice. (p. 850)
—Vessel. (p. 1839)
Durston, George. Boy Scouts' Victory. (p. 219)
Durual, Christophe, illus. see Grimm, Jacob, et al.
Dusablon, David. Dee Dee's First Shot Spoerl, Amber, illus. (p. 422)
—Dentist Spoerl, Amber, illus. (p. 426)
Duse Sr, Phillip M. Phil Duse Exposes Government Quack Silliness to Us Law-Abiding Citizens. (p. 1350)
Dusek, Cheryl. Maybe One Day: What Do You Want to Be? (p. 1113)
Dusek, Jiri & Pasala, Jan. All Around the Town. (p. 44)
—All Around the Zoo. (p. 44)
Dusek, Jiri & Pisala, Jan. Space Atlas. Tuma, Tomas, illus. (p. 1618)
Dusek, Jiri, et al. World Atlas. Hikadova, Katerina et al, illus. (p. 1954)
Dusen, Chris Van, see DiCamillo, Kate & Van Dusen, Chris.
Dusen, Chris Van, see Van Dusen, Chris.
Dusikova, Maja, illus. see Grimm, J. & W.
Dusikova, Maja, illus. see Lagerloeff, Selma.
Dusikova, Maja, illus. see Mohr, Joseph.
Dusikova, Maja, illus. see Schneider, Antonie.
Dusikova, Maja, jt. auth. see Salten, Felix.
Dusikova, Maja & Spyri, Johanna. Heidi. Dusikova, Maja, illus. (p. 762)
Dussling, Deborah, illus. see Dussling, Jennifer.
Dussling, Jennifer. Bugs! Bugs! Bugs! (p. 237)
—Deadly Poison Dart Frogs. (p. 417)
—Fair Is Fair! Palmisciano, Diane, illus. (p. 562)
—Giant Squid: Mystery of the Deep. Johnson, Pamela, illus. (p. 674)
—Gotcha! Nez, John, illus. (p. 704)
—If the Shoe Fits: Nonstandard Units of Measurement. Dussling, Deborah, illus. (p. 854)
—In a Dark, Dark House. Jones, Davy, illus. (p. 863)
—Lo Justo Es Justo; Fair Is Fair. (p. 1044)
—Misterio del Arco Iris. Ramirez, Alma B., tr. from ENG. (p. 1155)
—Misterio Del Arco Iris (the Rainbow Mystery) Gott, Barry, illus. (p. 1155)
—One Little Flower Girl. Bynum, Janie, illus. (p. 1295)
—Picky Peggy. Adams, Lynn, tr. (p. 1355)
—problema de 100 Libras: Math Matters en Espanol. Thornburgh, Rebecca, illus. (p. 1408)
—Whatcha Got? Wummer, Amy, illus. (p. 1896)
—Which Way, Wendy? Thornburgh, Rebecca McKillip, illus. (p. 1911)
Dussling, Jennifer, jt. auth. see Royston, Angela.
Dussling, Jennifer A. Lo Justo Es Justo! Palmisciano, Diane, illus. (p. 1044)
—Longest Yawn. Sims, Blanche, illus. (p. 1047)
Dussling, Susanna. Sunny & her Cochlear Implants. (p. 1677)
Dussutour, Olivier, jt. auth. see Guéry, Anne.
Dustin, Michael, illus. see Cooke, Pam.
Dustman, Jeanne. American Culture. (p. 60)
—Cultures Around the World (p. 391)
Dutchak, Shelly, illus. see Sterner, Nathan.
Dutcher, David. Feebie Brainiac & the Lysis Virus. (p. 580)
Dutcher, Kieren, illus. see Wu, Faye-Lynn.
DuTemple, Lesley A. Colosseum. (p. 346)
—Hoover Dam. (p. 796)
—R Is for Raccoon. (p. 1429)
—Taj Mahal. (p. 1696)
DuTemple, Leslie A. One Little Balsam Fir: A Northwoods Counting Book. Robinson, Susan, illus. (p. 1295)
Dutertre, Charles, illus. see Philippo, Sophie.
Duthaluru, Vidhya. Michael's Field Trip. (p. 1135)
Duthie, Marion. Adventures of Pussy Whoosie. (p. 22)
Dutka, Pamela. Madame Cecil's Swamp. (p. 1069)
Dutkiewicz, Michal, illus. see McNamara, Pat & Turner, Gary.
Dutrait, Vincent, illus. see Courtauld, Sarah.
Dutrait, Vincent, illus. see Jones, Rob Lloyd.
Dutrieux, Brigitte, jt. auth. see Craipeau, Jean-Lou.
Dutrieux, Julien, jt. auth. see Craipeau, Jean-Lou.
Dutson, Shelly. Jingle Jangle Jungle Jeepers. Christenson, Maren, illus. (p. 918)
Dutt, Arjun & Varacalli, Lauren. Claremont Mckenna College College Prowler off the Record. (p. 326)
Dutta, Arup Kumar. Boy Who Became King. Arya, Viki, illus. (p. 219)
Dutta, Kunal, jt. text see Lemmens, Riske.
Dutta-Yean, Tutu & Maire, Lucy Bedoya. Twelve Treasures of the East: Legends & Folk Tales from Asia. Dutta-Yean, Tutu, ed. (p. 1800)
Dutto, Lisa M., jt. auth. see Pearson, Jean W.
Dutton, Christopher, jt. auth. see Dutton, Christopher.
Dutton, Christopher & Dutton, Christopher. Rubear of Algonquin Park: The Story of a Very Courageous Bear. (p. 1493)
Dutton, Demi, jt. auth. see Clarke, Kevin.
Dutton, John. Tiger's Island. Dutton, John, illus. (p. 1749)
Dutton, Louise. Wishing Moon. (p. 1940)
Dutton, Maude Barrows. Tortoise & the Geese & Other Fables of Bidpai. Smith, E. Boyd, illus. (p. 1771)
Dutton, Michael. Amazing Carbon Footprint Facts. (p. 54)
—Amusement Park Science Activity Book. (p. 66)
—Exploring Ecosystems! An Environmentally Friendly Coloring Book. (p. 552)
—Fantastic Facts! Tantalizing Trivia from Around the World! (p. 571)
—Water Cycle Coloring Book. (p. 1862)
—Zombies Stained Glass Coloring Book. (p. 1988)
Dutton, Michael & Coloring Books Staff. Habitats Coloring Book. (p. 735)
Dutton, Michael & Roytman, Arkady. 3-D Coloring Book—Vampires & Zombies. (p. 1991)
Dutton, Mike, illus. see Newman, Lesléa.
Dutwin, Phyllis. Health Occupations. (p. 758)
Duty, William. Boomtown: Darkpit Mountain & the Princess Three (p. 213)
Duufek, Kim Kanoa, illus. see Hanson, Jonathan.
Duval, Alex. Bloodlust. (p. 201)
—Bloodlust - Initiation. (p. 201)
—Ritual. (p. 1475)
—Vampire Beach 2 - Ritual - Legacy. (p. 1832)
Duval, Kathy. Take Me to Your BBQ. McCauley, Adam, illus. (p. 1696)
—Three Bears' Christmas. Meisel, Paul, illus. (p. 1741)
—Three Bears' Halloween. Meisel, Paul, illus. (p. 1741)
Duvall, Deborah L. How Medicine Came to the People: A Tale of the Ancient Cherokees. Jacob, Murv, illus. (p. 811)
—How Rabbit Lost His Tail: A Traditional Cherokee Legend. Jacob, Murv, illus. (p. 812)
—Rabbit & the Fingerbone Necklace. Jacob, Murv, illus. (p. 1429)
—Rabbit & the Wolves. Jacob, Murv, illus. (p. 1429)
—Rabbit Goes Duck Hunting: A Traditional Cherokee Legend. Jacob, Murv, illus. (p. 1429)
—Rabbit Goes to Kansas. Jacob, Murv, illus. (p. 1429)
—Rabbit Plants the Forest. Jacob, Murv, illus. (p. 1429)
Duvall, Deborah L., text. Rabbit & the Bears. (p. 1429)
Duvall, Lori. Creekbank Mystery. (p. 380)

Duvall, Maggie. Smallest Panda. (p. 1592)
DuVall, Nell. Summer Day. Weltner, Dave, illus. (p. 1674)
Duvall, Sheila Marie. I See Fun. (p. 845)
Duvernay, Sharon. My Alphabet Book: Mi Libro Alfabeto Flash Cards. (p. 1196)
Duverne, Evelyne, illus. see Dokas, Dara.
Duverne, Evelyne, illus. see McKerley, Jennifer Guess.
Duviols, Jean-Paul, ed. see Guinnard, Auguste.
Duvoisin, Roger. Petunia. (p. 1349)
—Petunia, Beware! Duvoisin, Roger, illus. (p. 1349)
—Veronica on Petunia's Farm. (p. 1837)
Duvoisin, Roger, illus. see Fatio, Louise.
Duvoisin, Roger & Moore, Clement C. Night Before Christmas. (p. 1252)
Duxfield, Philip. Se. (p. 1534)
Duyvis, Corinne. Otherbound. (p. 1306)
Düzakin, Akin, illus. see Orbeck-Nilssen, Constance.
Duzan, Clytice C. Granny & the Kitten. (p. 710)
—Granny, Read Me A Story: A Collection of Children's Stories. (p. 710)
—I Wannabe A... (p. 847)
—Now What? (p. 1269)
—Sammy's Picture Book. (p. 1508)
—Sylvester & the Hole. (p. 1692)
Dver, Alyssa. When Whizzly Wanders. (p. 1905)
Dvok, Eduard & Dvorák, Eduard. Bobek, the Cat with a Pompon Tail. Dvorák, Jaroslav, illus. (p. 206)
Dvorak, Antonin. Dances for Solo Piano. Buechner, Sara Davis, ed. (p. 402)
Dvorak, Denise L. Clarence the Carousel Horse. (p. 327)
Dvorák, Eduard, jt. auth. see Dvok, Eduard.
Dvorák, Jaroslav, illus. see Dvok, Eduard & Dvorák, Eduard.
Dvorkin, Aaron, jt. auth. see Abramson, Susan.
Dwamena, Kwame, jt. auth. see Meyrick, Caroline.
Dwan, Ann. Wishing Away. (p. 1940)
Dweck, Joey. Losing for Good. (p. 1054)
Dwek, Victoria, jt. auth. see Schapira, Leah.
Dwell Studio Staff. Color & Count Placemats. (p. 342)
—Count. (p. 369)
—Good Morning, Toucan. (p. 698)
—Goodnight, Owl. (p. 701)
—Hello Dinosaur. (p. 763)
—Kitty in Squares. (p. 963)
—Look. (p. 1047)
—Puppy in Circles. (p. 1418)
—What's Inside? Neighborhood. (p. 1898)
Dwell Studio Staff, jt. auth. see Sami.
Dwell Studio Staff & Blue Apple Staff. Eat. (p. 501)
—Go. (p. 685)
—Touch & Feel Town. (p. 1772)
Dwell Studio Staff & Forss, Sarah. Alphabet Wall Cards. (p. 50)
Dwight, Laura. Brothers & Sisters (p. 231)
—We Can Do It! Dwight, Laura, photos by. (p. 1866)
Dwight, Laura, photos by see Christian, Cheryl.
Dwight, Laura, photos by see DeBear, Kirsten.
Dwire, Joyann. What Kind of Cow Are You? Being Content with How God Made You. Dickson, Bill, illus. (p. 1891)
Dworkin, Brooke, jt. auth. see Disney Book Group Staff.
Dworkin, Doug, illus. see Dyan, Lucille.
Dworkin, Motoko. Year in Japan: Folktales, Songs & Art for the Classroom. (p. 1969)
Dworsky, D. Wayne. Carpenter of Auguliere. (p. 271)
Dwyer, Carol. Cursive Writing. (p. 395)
Dwyer, Chelly. Blackfoot. (p. 197)
Dwyer, Corinne, illus. see Wielkiewicz, Richard M.
Dwyer, Cynthia. Can You See Me Now? Schuepbach, Lynnette, illus. (p. 259)
—Four-Eyed Philip. Schuepbach, Lynnette, illus. (p. 624)
Dwyer, Helen. Cognitive Development. (p. 338)
—Early Modern World, 1492 to 1783. (p. 494)
—Earthquakes. (p. 497)
—Floods. (p. 605)
—Middle Ages, 600 to 1492. (p. 1137)
—Peoples of the Southwest, West, & North. (p. 1340)
—Tsunamis! (p. 1795)
—Volcanoes! (p. 1849)
—Warfare, Economy, & Technology. (p. 1858)
Dwyer, Helen & Birchfield, D. L. Ojibwe History & Culture. (p. 1282)
Dwyer, Helen & Stone, Amy M. Creek History & Culture. (p. 380)
—Oneida History & Culture. (p. 1298)
Dwyer, Helen & Stout, Mary. Aztec History & Culture. (p. 122)
—Cree History & Culture. (p. 380)
Dwyer, Helen & Stout, Mary A. Hopi History & Culture. (p. 797)
Dwyer, Helen, ed. History of Psychology. (p. 784)
—Individual & Society. (p. 872)
—Intellectual Development. (p. 879)
Dwyer, Jacqueline. Fruits. (p. 645)
Dwyer, Joe & Levison, Doug. Daniel - the Miracle Beagle: A Story for Young Readers. (p. 404)
Dwyer, Judy. Novel Activities. (p. 1268)
—Storybook Starters. (p. 1663)
Dwyer, Kerry. Rhett's Colorful Campus Tour- Boston University A-Z. (p. 1467)
Dwyer, Kevin & Dwyer, Shawnae. Blue Baboon. Harman, Micah, illus. (p. 202)
Dwyer, Kieron, illus. see Gruenwald, Mark.
Dwyer, Mary. Barnyard Bash. Dwyer, Michael, illus. (p. 139)
Dwyer, Megan & Campbell, Meredith. Amazon Heart: Coping with Breast Cancer Warrior Princess Style. (p. 56)
Dwyer, Michael, illus. see Dwyer, Mary.
Dwyer, Mindy. Alaska's Sleeping Beauty. Dwyer, Mindy, illus. (p. 34)
—Alaska's Snow White & Her Seven Sled Dogs. (p. 34)
—Coyote in Love: The Story of Crater Lake. (p. 374)
—Just Close Your Eyes. (p. 938)
—Salmon Princess: An Alaska Cinderella Story. (p. 1505)
—Sweet Dreams, Polar Bear. (p. 1689)
Dwyer, Mindy, illus. see Devine, Monica.
Dwyer, Mindy, illus. see Laverde, Arlene.
Dwyer, Mindy, illus. see Thalcker, Karen.
Dwyer, Mindy, jt. auth. see Thalacker, Karen.
Dwyer, Shawnae, jt. auth. see Dwyer, Kevin.
Dyan, Penelope. Abraham Lincoln Was Here! a Kid's Guide to Washington D C. Weigand, John D., photos by. (p. 7)
—Adam. (p. 10)
—Animal Rescue, Book 1, Seals, Sea Lions & Elephant Seals, Oh My! Weigand, John D., photos by. (p. 79)
—Animal Rescue, Book 2, Hanauma Bay, Hawaii. Weigand, John D., photos by. (p. 79)
—Apple a Day! a Kid's Guide to Julian, Californ. Weigand, John D., photos by. (p. 92)
—Arianna's Shoes. Dyan, Penelope, illus. (p. 98)
—Around Corners—A Kid's Guide to Malaga, Spain. Weigand, John D., photos by. (p. 100)
—Ba-Ba-Ba-Bad—The Story of One Mean Moose. Dyan, Penelope, illus. (p. 123)
—Bake a Cake, Make Two—and Let Them Eat Cake. Dyan, Penelope, illus. (p. 133)
—Baylee's Giraffes! Sometimes Only a Giraffe Will Do. Dyan, Penelope, illus. (p. 147)
—Beaching It! a Kid's Guide to la Jolla, California. Weigand, John, photos by. (p. 149)
—Beatitudes Are Attitudes. (p. 153)
—Ben's Adventures—Proof Positive That Boys Will Be Boys. Dyan, Penelope, illus. (p. 165)
—Beyond the Trees! a Kid's Guide to Lake Tahoe, Us. Weigand, John D., photos by. (p. 174)
—Big Clock! a Kid's Guide to Munich, Germany. Weigand, John D., photos by. (p. 180)
—Big Mikey & Me Workbook. (p. 182)
—Big Mikey & Me Workbook. Dyan, Penelope, illus. (p. 182)
—Blake the Cat & His Very Loose Tooth! Dyan, Penelope, illus. (p. 198)
—Book for Girls about Being a Girl. (p. 210)
—Bubble Trouble—for Boys Only (r). Dyan, Penelope, illus. (p. 233)
—Bunny Love! a Book about Home & Bunnies. Dyan, Penelope, illus. (p. 242)
—By the Bay! a Kid's Guide to San Diego, California. Weigand, John D., photos by. (p. 249)
—By the Sea—A Kid's Guide to Valletta, Malt. Weigand, John D., photos by. (p. 249)
—Cabbages & Kings—A Kid's Guide to Tallinn, Estoni. Weigand, John D., photos by. (p. 250)
—Carousel. Dyan, Penelope, illus. (p. 271)
—Cat Named Blake. Weigand, John D., photos by. (p. 278)
—Changes! Dyan, Penelope, illus. (p. 290)
—Christmas Flamingo. Dyan, Penelope, illus. (p. 314)
—Christmas Is—A Time to Remember, to Smile & to Share. Dyan, Penelope, illus. (p. 314)
—Classy Nancy—A One of a Kind Girl. Dyan, Penelope, illus. (p. 329)
—Color Your Life! a Kid's Guide to Lisbon, Portugal. Weigand, John D., photos by. (p. 343)
—Comeback Kids, Book 12, the Redwood Forest. Weigand, John D., photos by. (p. 347)
—Comeback Kids, Book 8, the Antioch Burrowing Owl. Weigand, John D., photos by. (p. 347)
—Comeback Kids — Book 9 — the Barbary Macaques of Gibraltar. Weigand, John D., photos by. (p. 347)
—Comeback Kids—Book 10—The American Bison. Weigand, John, photos by. (p. 347)
—Comeback Kids—Book 11—The Wild Mustangs. Weigand, John D., photos by. (p. 347)
—Courtney's Beach. Dyan, Penelope, illus. (p. 373)
—Cruisin' 4 Fun! a Kid's Guide to Santa Cruz, Californ. Weigand, John, photos by. (p. 386)
—Day an Elephant Flies! Dyan, Penelope, illus. (p. 412)
—Dear God, Thank-You! Dyan, Penelope, illus. (p. 419)
—Did You Call? (p. 437)
—Do You Know Juneau? a Kid's Guide to Juneau, Alaska. Weigand, John D., photos by. (p. 458)
—Don't Wake up the Bear! Dyan, Penelope, illus. (p. 469)
—Easter Eggs & Bunny Wishes. (p. 499)
—Eileen Green the Recycling Queen. Dyan, Penwlope, illus. (p. 507)
—Endangered—the Peninsular Bighorn Sheep. Weigand, John D., photos by. (p. 526)
—Eve. Dyan, Penelope, illus. (p. 541)
—Even More of My Life As I Know It. (p. 541)
—Fat Rat, Fat Cat—Because Cats & Rats Are Also People. Dayn, Penelope, illus. (p. 577)
—Fish That Got Away—for Boys Only(r). Dyan, Penelope, illus. (p. 598)
—Flying High in the Sky—for Boys Only. Weigand, John D., photos by. (p. 610)
—For Boys Only! No Girls Allowed! (p. 615)
—For the Matterhorn's Face, Zermatt Is the Place, a Kid's Guide to Zermatt, Switzerland. Weigand, John D., photos by. (p. 616)
—Frugal Frannie—and the Big Room Cleaning Day. Dyan, Penelope, illus. (p. 645)
—Fun in the Sun! a Kids' Guide to Santa Barbara, Californ. Weigand, John D., photos by. (p. 648)
—Gabriela's Dogs—Because Happiness Really Is a Warm Puppy! Dyan, Penelope, illus. (p. 652)
—Gettin' Dirty! for Boys Only R. Dyan, Penelope, illus. (p. 668)
—Girl Named Dot. Dyan, Penelope, illus. (p. 678)
—Go Far Star Car—Even Though Cars Are Not People. Dyan, Penelope, illus. (p. 686)
—Go Run, Have Fun—Because Everyone Likes Fun. Dyan, Penelope, illus. (p. 687)
—Go to Rat House, Go to Cat House—Even Though Houses Are Not People. Dyan, Penelope, illus. (p. 687)
—Gold Rush! a Kid's Guide to Techatticup Gold Mine, Eldorado Canyon, Nevad. Weigand, John D., photos by. (p. 694)
—Good Luck Chuck! Dyan, Penelope, illus. (p. 698)
—Good Night! Dyan, Penelope, illus. (p. 699)
—Grandma's Suitcase—Where a Kid Can Always Find a Surprise! Dyan, Penelope, illus. (p. 709)
—Great Grandma Is Getting Old. Dyan, Penelope, illus. (p. 716)
—Hair We Are! Dyan, Penelope, illus. (p. 736)
—Halfway to the Stars! a Kid's Guide to San Francisco. Weigand, John D., photos by. (p. 737)
—Hangin' Loose! a Kid's Guide to Oahu, Hawaii. Weigand, John D., photos by. (p. 742)
—Happy Birthday! a Book about Birthdays, Dreams & Wishes. Dyan, Penelope, illus. (p. 744)
—Happy Birthday Usa! Dyan, Penelope, illus. (p. 745)
—Hatchling, the Story of Stegi Stegosaurus. Dyan, Penelope, illus. (p. 752)
—Hello Doctor! Dyan, Penelope, illus. (p. 763)
—Helping Hands. (p. 766)
—High on a Hill! a Kid's Guide to Innsbruck, Austri. Weigand, John D., photos by. (p. 778)
—Hooray 4 Five! Dyan, Penelope, illus. (p. 795)
—Hoppy Easter! (p. 797)
—Hoppy Go Lucky Little Easter Bunny. (p. 797)
—Hush! (p. 830)
—I Am a Monster! Dyan, Penelope, illus. (p. 832)
—I Am Eight! Dyan, Penelope, illus. (p. 832)
—I Am the Moon. (p. 834)
—I Am There! Dyan, Penelope, illus. (p. 834)
—I Am Three! Dyan, Penelope, illus. (p. 834)
—I Can't Stand the Rain! Dyan, Penelope, illus. (p. 837)
—I Did It, & I Hid It! a Book about Taking Responsibility. Dyan, Penelope, illus. (p. 837)
—I Like Football—for Boys Only(r). Dyan, Penelope, illus. (p. 841)
—I Love You! Dyan, Penelope, illus. (p. 843)
—I Remember Still, a Kid's Guide to Seville, Spain. Weigand, John D., photos by. (p. 844)
—If You Snooze! Dyan, Penelope, illus. (p. 854)
—In Gracie's Yard! Dyan, Penelope, illus. (p. 863)
—In My Attic. Dyan, Penelope, illus. (p. 864)
—Introducing Fabulous Marie, a Girl with a Good Head on Her Shoulders. Dyan, Penelope, illus. (p. 882)
—Island Style! a Kid's Guide to Coronado, California. Weigand, John D., photos by. (p. 892)
—It's Hot, Hot, Hot! a Kid's Guide to Hawaiian Volcanoes National Park. Weigand, John D., illus. (p. 897)
—It's Magic! a Kid's Guide to Monterey, California. Weigand, John D., photos by. (p. 897)
—It's Medieval! a Kid's Guide to Nuremberg, Germany. Weigand, John D., photos by. (p. 897)
—It's Nice to Be Gone When You're in Milan, a Kid's Guide to Milan, Italy. Weigand, John D., photos by. (p. 897)
—Jordan's Hair—the Big Dilemm. Dyan, Penelope, illus. (p. 925)
—Jump Frog, Funny Frog—Because Frogs Are Funny. Dyan, Penelope, illus. (p. 934)
—Just Look Out the Window! Dyan, Penelope, illus. (p. 939)
—Kingdom of York, a Kid's Guide to York, Uk. Weigand, John D., photos by. (p. 960)
—Kona Forevermore—A Kid's Guide to Kona Hawaii. Weigand, John D., photos by. (p. 967)
—Ladies First, Please! a Kid's Most Important & Fun Guide to Good Manners. Dyan, Penelope, illus. (p. 970)
—Last Mustang. (p. 978)
—Let It Snow! a Kid's Guide to Regensburg, Germany. Weigand, John D., photos by. (p. 994)
—Life in the Pits. Dyan, Penelope, illus. (p. 1011)
—Life Is a Dream! Dyan, Penelope, illus. (p. 1011)
—Little Hospital Book. Quinn, Courtney, illus. (p. 1029)
—Little Miss Chris & the Incredible Red Shoes. Dyan, Penelope, illus. (p. 1031)
—Lot o' Granada, a Kid's Guide to Granada, Spain. Weigand, John D., photos by. (p. 1057)
—Lot of Snot, a for Boys Only Book. Dyan, Penelope, illus. (p. 1057)
—Lovely Libby. Dyan, Penelope, illus. (p. 1061)
—Marco Polo Was Here! a Kid's Guide to Venice, Italy. Weigand, John D., photos by. (p. 1092)
—Mermaids & Wishes for Tails Like Fishes. Dyan, Penelope, illus. (p. 1128)
—Mikey & Me & the Bees, the Continuing Story of a Girl & Her Dog. Dyan, Penelope, illus. (p. 1141)
—Mikey & Me & the Fly—the Continuing Story of a Girl & Her Dog. Dyan, Penelope, illus. (p. 1141)
—Mikey & Me & the Frogs—the Continuing Story of a Girl & Her Dog. Dyan, Penelope, illus. (p. 1141)
—Mikey & Me & the Se. (p. 1141)
—Mikey & Me & the Spider—the Continuing Story of a Girl & Her Dog. Dyan, Penelope, illus. (p. 1141)
—Mikey & Me & the Valentines—the Continuing Story of a Girl & Her Dog. Dyan, Penelope, illus. (p. 1141)
—Molly Moose Is on the Loose. Dyan, Penelope, illus. (p. 1161)
—Movin' on! a Kid's Guide to Skagway, Alaska. Weigand, John D., photos by. (p. 1183)
—Musical Family—Sometimes a Song Says It All. Dyan, Penelope, illus. (p. 1194)
—My Life As I Know It—Part Iv. (p. 1212)
—My Mother Always Says. Dyan, Penelope, illus. (p. 1214)
—My Two Cents Worth! (p. 1220)
—My Valentines. (p. 1221)
—New Bag! Dyan, Penelope, illus. (p. 1243)
—New Shoes for Hand Me down Rose. Dyan, Penelope, illus. (p. 1247)
—New York! New York! a Kid's Guide to New York City. Weigand, John D., photos by. (p. 1248)
—Nose by Any Other Name Is Still a Nose! Dyan, Penelope, illus. (p. 1266)
—Off to School. Dyan, Penelope, illus. (p. 1279)
—Oh Victoria! a Kid's Guide to Victoria, Bc. Canada. Weigand, John D., photos by. (p. 1281)
—Oh Vienna! a Kid's Guide to Vienna, Austri. Weigand, John D., photos by. (p. 1281)
—Olympic Gold—Because Everyone Loves a Winner! Dyan, Penelope, illus. (p. 1287)
—On the Hill! a Kid's Guide to Melk, Austri. Weigand, John D., photos by. (p. 1290)
—On the Way to Rome — a Kid's Guide to Civitavecchia, Italy. Weigand, John D., photos by. (p. 1292)
—One Big Hole in the Ground, a Kid's Guide to Grand Canyon, Us. Weigand, John D., photos by. (p. 1294)
—Out of Deepest Africa—Another of Ben's Big Adventures—for Boys Only (r). Dyan, Penelope, illus. (p. 1311)
—Over a Bridge! a Kid's Guide to Budapest, Hungary. Weigand, John D., photos by. (p. 1313)
—Over Dover—A Kid's Guide to Dover, Uk. Weigand, John D., photos by. (p. 1313)
—Over the Edge, a Kid's Guide to Niagara Falls, Ontario, Canad. Weigand, John D., photos by. (p. 1314)
—Pass the Gas! for Boys Only(r). (p. 1326)
—Pink Patti Pinkerton. Dyan, Penelope, illus. (p. 1360)
—Place of Tales— a Kid's Guide to Canterbury, Kent, England. Weigand, John, photos by. (p. 1365)
—Rain in Spain—A Kid's Guide to Barcelona, Spain. Weigand, John D., photos by. (p. 1435)
—Reindeer & Mermaids, a Kid's Guide to Helsinki Finland. Weigand, John D., photos by. (p. 1457)
—Respect! Dyan, Penelope, illus. (p. 1463)
—Road to Hilo! a Kid's Guide to Hilo, Hawaii. Weigand, John D., illus. (p. 1477)
—Rockin' the Rock, a Kid's Guide to the Rock of Gibraltar. Weigand, John D., photos by. (p. 1483)
—Royal Residence—A Kid's Guide to Windsor Castle. Weigand, John D., photos by. (p. 1492)
—See You 2-Maui—A Kid's Guide to Maui, Hawaii. Weigand, John D., photos by. (p. 1547)
—Shoes & Ships & Sealing Wax—A Kids's Guide to Warnemünde, Germany. Weigand, John D., photos by. (p. 1568)
—Smile! Dyan, Penelope, illus. (p. 1593)
—Smile Seattle! a Kid's Guide to Seattle, Washington. Weigand, John D., photos by. (p. 1594)
—Some Bunny Loves You! (p. 1609)
—Someone's Getting Married! (p. 1609)
—Spend a Day in Old Pompeii, a Kid's Travel Guide to Ancient Pompeii, Italy. Weigand, John D., photos by. (p. 1625)
—Squeaky Wheel Gets to Greece—A Kid's Guide to Athens, Greece. Weigand, John D., photos by. (p. 1636)
—Steam Train! All the Way to Canterbury, England. Weigand, John D., photos by. (p. 1646)
—Step in Time—A Kid's Guide to Ephesus, Turkey. Weigand, John D., photos by. (p. 1648)
—Sticks—Because Sticks Are Also People. Dyan, Penelope, illus. (p. 1650)
—Sticks—the for Boys Only Version—Because Sticks Are Also People. Dyan, Penelope, illus. (p. 1650)
—Story of Snagatooth—Who Is Commonly Known As the Tooth Fairy. Dyan, Penelope, illus. (p. 1660)
—Summer Surfs the Olympic Trials. (p. 1675)
—Sunny Side! Dyan, Penelope, illus. (p. 1677)
—Surfing on Summer's Wave: The Second Book in the Surfer Girl Series. (p. 1685)
—Surfing on Summer's Wave. (p. 1685)
—Surfing Sixteen. (p. 1685)
—Surfing Through Springtime & Swimming. (p. 1685)
—Take a Dam Tour! a Kid's Guide to Hoover Dam, Nevad. Weigand, John D., photos by. (p. 1696)
—Tammy's Left Shoe—As Opposed to Her Right. Dyan, Penelope, illus. (p. 1704)
—Ted E Bearæs Most Unfortunate Experience to Date. Dyan, Penelope, illus. (p. 1712)
—Teeth! Dyan, Penelope, illus. (p. 1715)
—That Fat Elephant—Because Everyone Likes Elephants. Dyan, Penelope, illus. (p. 1726)
—That Fat Rat Family—Because All Families Aren't Rats. Dyan, Penelope, illus. (p. 1726)
—There Are Bees in My Trees! Dyan, Penelope, illus. (p. 1729)
—There Are No Ants in My Pants! for Boys Only(r). Dyan, Penelope, illus. (p. 1729)
—There's a Chicken in My Kitchen! Dyan, Penelope, illus. (p. 1730)
—There's a Flea in My Te. Dyan, Penelope, illus. (p. 1730)
—There's a Racoon in My House! Dyan, Penelope, illus. (p. 1731)
—There's a Skunk in My Trunk. Dyan, Penelope, illus. (p. 1731)
—There's a Teddy Bear in My Heart! Dyan, Penelope, illus. (p. 1731)
—There's an Alligator in My Closet! Dyan, Penelope, illus. (p. 1731)
—There's No Business Like Bartholomew Bunny's Business. Dyan, Penelope, illus. (p. 1731)
—This Is Sweden—A Kid's Guide to Stockholm, Swedem. Weigand, John D., photos by. (p. 1736)
—This Is the House George Built! a Kid's Guide to Mount Vernon. Weigand, John D., photos by. (p. 1736)
—This Means War! for Boys Only. Dyan, Penelope, illus. (p. 1737)
—Thou Shalt Not Covet! Dyan, Penelope, illus. (p. 1740)
—Thousand Stars. Dyan, Penelope, illus. (p. 1740)
—Three Strikes—Doesn't Really Mean You Are Out. Dyan, Penelope, illus. (p. 1744)
—To See or Not to See—the Story of Kourtney's Glasses. Dyan, Penelope, illus. (p. 1759)
—Today I Am 4! Dyan, Penelope, illus. (p. 1760)
—Today I Am Two! I Am Two Years Old Today! Dyan, Penelope, illus. (p. 1760)
—Tony Pickleloni, a Boy Full of Baloney. Dyan, Penelope, illus. (p. 1766)
—Totems & More! a Kid's Guide to Ketchikan, Alaska. Weigand, John D., photos by. (p. 1772)
—Turkish Delight—A Kid's Guide to Istanbul, Turkey. Weigand, John D., photos by. (p. 1797)
—VanCouver's Song — a Kid's Guide to Vancouver, Bc, Canada. Weigand, John, photos by. (p. 1833)
—Vita Mccafee Mckay, Cat Rescuer. Dyan, Penelope, illus. (p. 1846)
—Walk the Renaissance Walk—A Kid's Guide to Florence, Italy. Weigand, John D., photos by. (p. 1854)
—Warrior Mouse of Forest Hollow. (p. 1858)
—Warrior Mouse of Forest Hollow. Quinn, Courtney, illus. (p. 1858)
—Water & Blood—A Kid's Guide to St Petersburg, Russi. Weigand, John D., photos by. (p. 1862)

D

—What Happens in Vegas a Kid's Guide to Las Vegas, Nevad. Weigand, John D., photos by. (p. 1886)
—What Is a Telephant? Dyan, Penelope, illus. (p. 1888)
—What Is Truth? Dyan, Penelope, illus. (p. 1891)
—When in Rome, a Kid's Guide to Rome. Weigand, John, photos by. (p. 1903)
—When Touching Is Bad. Dyan, Penelope, illus. (p. 1905)
—Where Is London Bridge? a Kid's Guide to London. Weigand, John D., photos by. (p. 1908)
—Where Is Lucy? Dyan, Penelope, illus. (p. 1908)
—White Elephant No One Wants. Dyan, Penelope, illus. (p. 1912)
—Who Cut the Cheese? a for Boys Only Book. Dyan, Penelope, illus. (p. 1915)
—Who Deserves a Giant Chocolate Chip Cookie? Dyan, Penelope, illus. (p. 1915)
—Who's the Fairest of Them All? Dyan, Penelope, illus. (p. 1921)
—Why Angels Sing! Dyan, Penelope, illus. (p. 1922)
—Why Lie? the Truth Is Easier to Remember! (p. 1925)
—Woolly Bully! Dyan, Penelope, illus. (p. 1950)
—Work It Out! Dyan, Penelope, illus. (p. 1952)
—Yesterday's Rain— a Kid's Guide to Kauai, Hawaii. Weigand, John D., photos by. (p. 1971)
—You Are Okay! Dyan, Penelope, illus. (p. 1973)
—Yummy Solvang! a Kid's Guide to Solvang, Californi. Weigand, John D., photos by. (p. 1983)
—¡Hola Córdoba! a Kid's Guide to Córdoba, Spain. Weigand, John D., photos by. (p. 787)
—¡Hola Madrid! a Kid's Guide to Madrid, Spain. Weigand, John D., photos by. (p. 787)
Dyan, Penelope, illus. see Dyan, Peneope.
Dyan, Penelope, jt. auth. see Hillan, Pam.
Dyan, Penelope, jt. auth. see Hillan, Pamela.
Dyan, Penelope, photos by see Weigand, John D.
Dyan, Penelope, creator. For Love of Pete! The Story of the Boy Who Played the Taps on Iwo Jima. (p. 615)
—Surfer Girl. (p. 1685)
—Sweet Lorraine. (p. 1690)
Dyan, Peneope. Bunny Ears. Dyan, Penelope, illus. (p. 242)
Dyan, Penwlope, illus. see Dyan, Penelope.
D'yans, Masha. Razzle-Dazzle Ruby. D'yans, Masha, illus. (p. 1441)
D'Yans, Masha, illus. see Teachers Writers Collaborative, ed.
Dyas, Amy. Robins of St Lawrence Church. (p. 1480)
Dyas, Mecca. Busy Bee Who Me? (p. 245)
Dybacz, Carol. Tanner (p. 1705)
Dybing, Michelle, illus. see Dale, Jay.
Dybvik, Tina. Cute Clothes for the Crafty Fashionista (p. 396)
—Sadie's Seed Adventures: Learning about Seeds Record, Adam, illus. (p. 1501)
—Space Cowboy Caleb & the Night Sky Round-Up: Learning about the Night Sky Record, Adam, illus. (p. 1618)
—Trendy Jewelry for the Crafty Fashionista (p. 1784)
Dybvik, Tina & Meister, Cari. Take It Outside. Record, Adam, illus. (p. 1696)
Dybwad, G. L. & Bliss, Joy V. White City Recollections: The Illustrated 1893 Diary of Friend Pitts Williams' Trip to the World's Columbian Exposition. (p. 1912)
Dychtwald, Ken, et al. Gideon's Dream: A Tale of New Beginnings. Zaboski, Dave, illus. (p. 674)
Dyck, Noel & Archetti, Eduardo P., eds. Sport, Dance & Embodied Identities. (p. 1631)
Dyckman, Ame. Boy & Bot. Yaccarino, Dan, illus. (p. 217)
—Wolfie the Bunny. OHora, Zachariah, illus. (p. 1944)
Dyckman, Ame & Campbell, K. G. Tea Party Rules. (p. 1708)
Dycus, Warren. Monyum Bay - Time Travel. (p. 1171)
Dye, Jerel, illus. see Danna, Natasha.
Dye, Karen. Just Beweeve! ...Through the Eyes of a Child! (p. 938)
Dye, Pat. War Eagle! De Angel, Miguel, illus. (p. 1857)
Dye, Stephen. Kid's Guide to GPS - How It Works & How It's Used: Engineering Adventures with the Global Positioning System. (p. 953)
Dye, Troy & Kelesides, Tom. Goblin Chronicles 01A. (p. 688)
—Goblin Chronicles #1B. (p. 688)
—Goblin Chronicles #2A. (p. 688)
—Megamind: Bad, Blue, Brilliant. Vol. 2 (p. 1124)
—Puss in Boots Movie Prequel: the Sword Master of Rancho Castillo: The Sword Master of Rancho Castillo. (p. 1420)
Dyen, Don, illus. see Olivas, Daniel.
Dyer, Alan. Mission to the Moon. (p. 1153)
—Space. (p. 1618)
Dyer, Ann. Zyoga, the Yoga Sleep Ritual (p. 1990)
Dyer, Bob, jt. auth. see Vizquel, Omar.
Dyer, Brooke, illus. see Modugno, Maria.
Dyer, Brooke, illus. see Rosenthal, Amy Krouse.
Dyer, Brooke, illus. see Wilson, Karma.
Dyer, Brooke, illus. see Yolen, Jane & Stemple, Heidi E. Y.
Dyer, Brooke, illus. see Yolen, Jane & Stemple, Heidi Elisabet Y.
Dyer, Dorothy & Lloyd, Glynis. English Matters Grade 8 Learner's Pack. (p. 530)
—Reading Matters Grade 8. (p. 1446)
Dyer, Hadley. Potatoes on Rooftops: Farming in the City. (p. 1388)
—Watch This Space: Designing, Defending & Sharing Public Spaces. Ngui, Marc, illus. (p. 1861)
Dyer, Hadley, jt. auth. see Kalman, Bobbie.
Dyer, Hadley & Kalman, Bobbie. Fishing in Action. (p. 599)
—Fourmis. Briere, Marie-Josee, tr. from ENG. (p. 625)
—Life Cycle of an Ant. (p. 1009)
—Pêche. (p. 1334)
Dyer, Heather. Girl with the Broken Wing. Bailey, Peter, illus. (p. 679)
—Tina & the Penguin. Levert, Mireille, illus. (p. 1755)
Dyer, Howard Wayne. Itty Bitty Bear. (p. 900)
Dyer, Jane, illus. see Appelt, Kathi.
Dyer, Jane, illus. see Beaumont, Karen.
Dyer, Jane, illus. see Birdsall, Jeanne.
Dyer, Jane, illus. see Fox, Mem.
Dyer, Jane, illus. see Goss, Gary.
Dyer, Jane, illus. see Krauss, Ruth.
Dyer, Jane, illus. see Krull, Kathleen.
Dyer, Jane, illus. see Modugno, Maria.
Dyer, Jane, illus. see Rosenthal, Amy Krouse.
Dyer, Jane, illus. see Spinelli, Eileen.
Dyer, Jane, illus. see Willard, Nancy.
Dyer, Jane, illus. see Yolen, Jane.
Dyer, Jane, jt. auth. see Lloyd-Jones, Sally.
Dyer, Jill. Plant of the Zorks. (p. 1369)
Dyer, K. C. Facing Fire. (p. 561)
—Ms. Zephyr's Notebook. (p. 1188)
—Shades of Red: An Eagle Glen Trilogy Book. (p. 1557)
—Walk Through a Window. (p. 1854)
Dyer, Kevin. Monster under the Bed: A Play for Children. (p. 1168)
Dyer, Mary E. Secret Whispers. (p. 1544)
Dyer, Saje, et al. Good-Bye, Bumps! Talking to What's Bugging You. (p. 697)
Dyer, Sarah. Mrs. Muffly's Monster. (p. 1187)
—Princess for a Day: A Clementine & Mungo Story. Dyer, Sarah, illus. (p. 1403)
Dyer, Sarah, illus. see Coats, Lucy.
Dyer, Sarah, tr. see Kyung-ah, Choi.
Dyer, Sarah, tr. Snow Drop (p. 1599)
Dyer, Summer, jt. auth. see Dyer, Wayne W.
Dyer, Wayne W. I Am: Why Two Little Words Mean So Much. (p. 831)
—It's Not What You've Got! Lessons for Kids on Money & Abundance. Budnick, Stacy Heller & Heller Budnick, Stacy, illus. (p. 898)
Dyer, Wayne W. & Dyer, Summer. 10 Secrets for Success & Inner Peace for Teens. (p. 1994)
Dyer, Wayne W. & Tracy, Kristina. Incredible You! 10 Ways to Let Your Greatness Shine Through. Siegel, Melanie, illus. (p. 869)
—No Excuses! How What You Say Can Get in Your Way. Budnick, Stacy Heller, illus. (p. 1258)
—Unstoppable Me! 10 Ways to Soar Through Life. Budnick, Stacy Heller, illus. (p. 1823)
—¡Eres Increíble! 10 Formas de Permitir Que Tu Grandeza Brille a Traves de Ti. Siegel, Melanie, illus. (p. 533)
Dyer-Groves, Beverly E. Spooky Nights on the Island. (p. 1631)
Dyess, Hal. Night the Rabbits Dance: An Easter Story. (p. 1254)
Dyke, Jan Van, see Van Dyke, Jan.
Dyke, Sylvie. "Descant" Recorder Music Made Easy - Just for Little Fingers! (p. 428)
—Piano Music Made Easy. (p. 1354)
Dykema, Marjorie. Ella's Joy: Signs of Joy. Helsom, Geoff, illus. (p. 514)
Dykema, Owen W., jt. ed. see Dykema, Owen Wood.
Dykema, Owen Wood & Dykema, Owen W., eds. Warbird History Part II: Fighter, Attack & Support Aircraft of WWII. (p. 1858)
Dykes, John S., illus. see Gutman, Dan.
Dykes, Tami J. Being Too Small Is Big Enough. (p. 161)
Dykstra, Danell. Man Who Invented the Ferris Wheel: The Genius of George Ferris. (p. 1086)
Dykstra, Mary. Iowa. (p. 886)
—South Carolina. (p. 1616)
Dylan, Bob. Blowin' in the Wind. Muth, Jon J., illus. (p. 202)
—Forever Young. Rogers, Paul, illus. (p. 619)
—If Dogs Run Free. Campbell, Scott, illus. (p. 852)
—Man Gave Names to All the Animals. Arnosky, Jim, illus. (p. 1085)
Dymock, Christina. Young Chefs. (p. 1978)
Dymock, Melissa. Sliding in the Snow: Winter Activities for Kids Lee, Frances Cook, illus. (p. 1590)
Dymond, Detta, ed. see Dymond, Kenneth.
Dymond, Kenneth. Guide to the CMMI: Interpreting the Capability Maturity Model Integration. Dymond, Detta, ed. (p. 730)
Dynamo. Googly Eyes: Leo Lion's Noisy Roar! (p. 702)
—Googly Eyes: Goodnight, Benjy Bunny! (p. 702)
—Googly Eyes: Fluffy Kitten Goes Exploring! (p. 702)
—Googly Eyes: Flipper the Seal Makes a Discovery! (p. 702)
Dynamo Limited Staff, illus. see Bolte, Mari.
Dynamo Limited Staff, illus. see Meadows, Daisy.
Dynamo Limited Staff, illus. see Scholastic, Inc. Staff & Steele, Michael Anthony.
Dyne, Edith Van. Aunt Jane's Nieces on Vacation. (p. 115)
Dynyel. Windy the Winged Unicorn. (p. 1936)
Dyro, Janniche. Forever Dancing. (p. 619)
Dyrud, Chris Wold, illus. see Clark, Lisa.
Dyrud, Chris Wold, illus. see Loulan, Joann & Worthen, Bonnie.
Dyrud, Loiell O. & Furman, Leola Dyrud. Each for the Other, All for Christ: Missionaries to Madagascar Rev. Amos & Ovidie Dyrud. (p. 492)
Dysinger, Stephen. William. Dysinger, Stephen, illus. (p. 1933)
Dyson, Edward. Missing Link. (p. 1152)
Dyson, Janet. Illustrated Children's Stories from the New Testament: All the Classic Bible Stories Retold with More Than 700 Beautiful Illustrations, Maps & Photographs. (p. 857)
Dyson, Janet, jt. auth. see Parker, Victoria.
Dyson, Kyree, jt. auth. see Turner, Tracie.
Dyson, Laurence. Journey to the Moon (p. 929)
Dyson, Marianne, jt. auth. see Bredeson, Carmen.
Dyson, Marianne J. Home on the Moon: Living on a Space Frontier. (p. 792)
—Space Station Science. Klug, Dave, illus. (p. 1620)
Dyson, Marianne J., jt. auth. see Aldrin, Buzz.
Dyson, Marianne J., jt. auth. see Khan, Hena.
Dyson, Nikki. 1,000 Things to Eat. (p. 2001)
Dyson, Nikki, illus. see Fliess, Sue.
Dyson, Tony. Crystal Wand. (p. 387)
Dyssegaard, Elisabeth Kallick, tr. see Bergstrom, Gunilla.
Dyssegaard, Elisabeth Kallick, tr. see Bergström, Gunilla.
Dyssegaard, Elisabeth Kallick, tr. see Edvall, Lilian.
Dyssegaard, Elisabeth Kallick, tr. see Eriksson, Eva E.
Dyssegaard, Elisabeth Kallick, tr. see Eriksson, Eva.
Dyssegaard, Elisabeth Kallick, tr. see Lindahl, Inger.
Dyssegaard, Elisabeth Kallick, tr. see Lindenbaum, Pija.
Dyssegaard, Elisabeth Kallick, tr. see Lindgren, Astrid.
Dyssegaard, Elisabeth Kallick, tr. see Lindgren, Barbro & Lindgren, B. L.
Dyssegaard, Elisabeth Kallick, tr. see Lindgren, Barbro.
Dzama, Marcel, illus. see Might Be Giants Staff, et al.
Dzidrums, Christine. Cutters Don't Cry. Allison, Elizabeth, ed. (p. 396)
—Fair Youth: Emylee of Forest Springs. Lopez, Lyle & Dzidrums, Joseph, illus. (p. 562)
—Idina Menzel: Broadway Superstar. (p. 852)
—Kelly Clarkson: Behind Her Hazel Eyes. (p. 948)
—Mike Trout: Baseball Sensation. Dzidrums, Joseph, photos by. (p. 1141)
—Missy Franklin: Swimming Sensation. (p. 1154)
—Princess Dessabelle: Tennis Star. Muths, Tohn Fayette, illus. (p. 1403)
—Princess Dessabelle Makes a Friend. Muths, Tohn, illus. (p. 1403)
—Timmy Adopts a Girl Dog. Lopez, Lyle & Dzidrums, Joseph, illus. (p. 1754)
—Timmy & the Baseball Birthday Party. Lopez, Lyle, illus. (p. 1754)
—Yuna Kim: Ice Queen. Rendon, Leah, ed. (p. 1983)
Dzidrums, Christine & Rendon, Leah. Jennie Finch. Dzidrums, Joseph, photos by. (p. 912)
—Joannie Rochette: Canadian Ice Princess. Allison, Elizabeth, ed. (p. 919)
—Matt Kemp: True Blue Baseball Star. (p. 1109)
Dzidrums, Joseph, illus. see Dzidrums, Christine.
Dzidrums, Joseph, photos by see Dzidrums, Christine & Rendon, Leah.
Dzidrums, Joseph, photos by see Dzidrums, Christine.
Dziedzic, Nancy. Family Violence (p. 569)
Dziedzic, Nancy & Naff, Clayton Farris. Malaria. (p. 1083)
Dziekan, Jennifer Ellen. Wishing Bear. (p. 1940)
Dziekan, Michal, illus. see Smith, Clete Barrett.
Dziengel, Sharon, et al, eds. Ice Age Trail Companion Guide - 2004. (p. 850)
Dzuver, Leo, et al. How to Get a Girlfriend. (p. 820)
Dzwonik, Cristian, jt. auth. see Klutz Editors.

E

E. C. CASWELL, jt. auth. see Wells, Carolyn.
E Hinton, Susan, jt. auth. see Hinton, Susan E.
E Llamas, Melissa Ann. I Came from Your Tummy, Too! Right Mom? (p. 834)
E. O., Monalisa. Dan & Derrick's Prayer to the Troops. (p. 401)
E. S. Townsend. Secrets of Marsh House. (p. 1545)
E. Taylor, Marcia. Orientation Business English Lev 1. (p. 1303)
E. Vigil, Janet. Perfect You. (p. 1342)
E. Z. Writer. I Think I'll Be a Doctor: I Know What to Do. (p. 846)
E.A. Budd. Stella Saves the Game. Lucas, Diane, illus. (p. 1647)
Eachus, Jennifer, illus. see McBratney, Sam.
Eaddy, Susan. Poppy's Best Paper. Bonnet, Rosalinde, illus. (p. 1385)
Eaddy, Susan, illus. see Galvin, Laura Gates.
Eaddy, Susan, illus. see Hubbell, Patricia.
Eade, Oliver. Terminus. (p. 1721)
Eadie, Inger Sommer, illus. see Siefker, Eunice.
Eadie, John. Lectures on the Bible to the Young. (p. 987)
Eadon, Jack E. Gigolo on the Row. (p. 676)
Eagan, Colin & Varacalli, Lauren. Davidson College College Prowler off the Record. (p. 411)
Eagan, Mary. Alexee's Animals from A-Z King, Cheryl, illus. (p. 37)
—Chelsea & the Swan. (p. 297)
Eagan, Robynne. Kid Concoctions, Creations & Contraptions. Tom, Darcy & Mathis, Teresa, illus. (p. 951)
Eagen, Rachel. Biography of Bananas. (p. 189)
—Biography of Sugar. (p. 189)
—Body Care Chemistry. (p. 207)
—Buzz off, Flies! (p. 248)
—Cutting & Self-Injury. (p. 396)
—Environmental Chemistry. (p. 532)
—Flood & Monsoon Alert! (p. 605)
—Nascar. (p. 1230)
—Ponce de Leon: Exploring Florida & Puerto Rico. (p. 1382)
—Rats Around Us. (p. 1440)
—Suicide. (p. 1673)
Eager, Edward. Half Magic. (p. 736)
—Half Magic. Bodecker, N. M., illus. (p. 736)
Eager, Michiko, illus. see Wigglesworth, Penny.
Eagland, Jane. Wild Song. (p. 1930)
—Wildthorn. (p. 1931)
—World Within: A Novel of Emily Bronte. (p. 1959)
Eagle, Cameron, illus. see Hartelius, Margaret A.
Eagle, Cameron, illus. see Tallarico, Tony & Tallarigo, Tony.
Eagle, Godeane, jt. auth. see Blanc, Esther Silverstein.
Eagle, Golden. Father Sun & Luis the Lizard. (p. 577)
—It's Good to Laugh at Yourself (Coyote Medicine. (p. 897)
—It's Good to Shed Your Skin (Snake Medicine) (p. 897)
—It's Okay to Cry (Frog Medicine) (p. 898)
—Owl Who Lives in My House. (p. 1315)
—You Can Play All Day If You Know the Way: Otter Medicine. (p. 1974)
—You've Got to Know When to Lead. (p. 1982)
Eagle, Joy, illus. see Ballock-Dixon, Saige J. & Medina, Sylvia M.
Eagle, Joy, illus. see Medina, Sylvia M. & B alloxk-Dixon, Saige J.
Eagle, Joy, illus. see Medina, Sylvia M. & Ballock-Dixon, Saige J.
Eagle, Kin. It's Raining, It's Pouring. Davenier, Christine & Gilbert, Rob, illus. (p. 898)
Eagle, Kin. Humpty Dumpty. (p. 827)
Eagle, Mike, illus. see Weisberg, Barbara & Haley, Alex.
Eagle, Rita. Farina & the Baby. (p. 573)
—Sniffy the Beagle. Rasmussen, Gerry, illus. (p. 1597)
Eaglehouse, Carolyn. Magic of Milky Way Farm. (p. 1073)
Eagleman, Robert. Cards: Heart of the Underdog. (p. 266)
Eaglesham, Dale. What If? (p. 1887)
Eaglesham, Dale, illus. see Brubaker, Ed.
Eaglesham, Dale, illus. see Dixon, Chuck.
Eaglesham, Dale, illus. see Rucka, Greg, et al.
Eagleson, Holly, jt. auth. see Vranich, Belisa.
Eagleton, Terry. Myths of Power: A Marxist Study of the Brontës. (p. 1227)
Eaker Weil, Bonnie. Can We Cure & Forgive Adultery? (p. 258)
Eakin, Sue, et al. Louisiana: The Land & Its People Culbertson, James Forrest, illus. (p. 1058)
Eakins, Bonny Mae. Wonder Island. Eakins, Bonny Mae & Hoffbauer, Wyng, illus. (p. 1947)
Eakle, Janice. 3 A's & 3 B's All the Way to Z Eakle, Tayah, illus. (p. 1991)
Eakle, Tayah, illus. see Eakle, Janice.
Ealy, Gerald, jt. auth. see Ealy, Gerald.
Ealy, Gerald & Ealy, Gerald. I Made a Wish to Be a Fish. (p. 844)
Eamer, Claire. Before the World Was Ready: Stories of Daring Genius in Science. Boothroyd, Sa, illus. (p. 158)
—Lizards in the Sky: Animals Where You Least Expect Them. (p. 1043)
—Spiked Scorpions & Walking Whales: Modern Animals, Ancient Animals, & Water. (p. 1627)
—Super Crocs & Monster Wings: Modern Animals' Ancient Past. (p. 1679)
—World in Your Lunch Box: The Wacky History & Weird Science of Everyday Foods. Boothroyd, Sa, illus. (p. 1956)
Eames, Brian. Dagger Quick. (p. 399)
—Dagger X. (p. 399)
Eames, Marion. Baner Beca. (p. 136)
Eanes, Jim. Elvis in Virginia. (p. 517)
Eareckson Tada, Joni. I'll Be with You Always. Nelson, Craig, illus. (p. 856)
—You've Got a Friend. Meyer, Jeff, illus. (p. 1982)
Eareckson Tada, Joni & Jensen, Steve. Meanest Teacher. (p. 1116)
—Mission Adventure. (p. 1153)
—Tell Me the Promises. DiCianni, Ron, illus. (p. 1716)
Eareckson Tada, Joni & Wolgemuth, Bobbie. Christmas Carols for a Kid's Heart Martinez, Sergio, illus. (p. 313)
Earhart, Kristin. Buttercup Mystery. (p. 247)
—Buttercup Mystery. Geddes, Serena, illus. (p. 247)
—Fancy. Alba, Elisabeth, illus. (p. 570)
—Great Reef Games. (p. 718)
—Hide & Go Fetch. (p. 776)
—Magic School Bus Fixes a Bone. Bracken, Carolyn, illus. (p. 1073)
—Puppy Powers #1: a Wishbone Come True. (p. 1418)
—Puppy Powers #2: Wag, You're It! (p. 1418)
—Puppy Powers #3: Take a Bow-Wow. (p. 1418)
—Puppy Powers #4: Hide & Go Fetch. (p. 1418)
—Race the Wild #1: Rain Forest Relay. (p. 1431)
—Race the Wild #2: Great Reef Games. (p. 1431)
—Rain Forest Relay. (p. 1434)
—Roscoe & the Pony Parade. Gurney, John Steven, illus. (p. 1489)
—Starlight. Andreasen, Dan, illus. (p. 1642)
—Take a Bow-Wow. (p. 1696)
—Wag, You're It! (p. 1852)
—Welcome Home! (p. 1873)
—Welcome Home! Geddes, Serena, illus. (p. 1873)
—Wishbone Come True. (p. 1940)
Earhart, Kristin, ed. Life-Size Zoo: From Tiny Rodents to Gigantic Elephants, an Actual Size Animal Encyclopedia. Fukuda, Toyofumi, photos by. (p. 1013)
Earhart, Kristin, et al. Magic School Bus & the Butterfly Bunch. Bracken, Carolyn, illus. (p. 1073)
—Magic School Bus Inside a Volcano. Bracken, Carolyn, illus. (p. 1073)
Earl, Archie William, Sr. Inside Scoop on American Colleges & Universities. (p. 877)
Earl, C. F. Alicia Keys. (p. 40)
—Black Eyed Peas. (p. 196)
—Building a Business in the Virtual World. Madrian, Brigitte, ed. (p. 238)
—Business Funding & Finances. Madrian, Brigitte, ed. (p. 245)
—Dr. Dre. (p. 475)
—Drake. (p. 479)
—Flo Rida. (p. 605)
—Green Berets. (p. 721)
—Hip-Hop: A Short History. (p. 780)
—Jay-Z. (p. 910)
—Kanye West. (p. 943)
—Lil' Wayne. (p. 1017)
—Ludacris. (p. 1063)
—Marketing Your Business. Madrian, Brigitte, ed. (p. 1095)
—Superstars of Hip Hop: T-Pain. (p. 1684)
—T. I. (p. 1693)
—Timbaland. (p. 1750)
—What Does It Mean to Be an Entrepreneur? Madrian, Brigitte, ed. (p. 1884)
—World's Best Soldiers. (p. 1960)
Earl, C. F., jt. auth. see Hill, Z. B.
Earl, C. F. & Hill, Z. B. Rihanna. (p. 1472)
—Superstars of Hip Hop - T-Pain. (p. 1684)
Earl, C. F. & Vanderhoof, Gabrielle. Army Rangers. (p. 100)
Earl, Cheri, jt. auth. see Walton, Rick.
Earl, Cheri Pray, jt. auth. see Williams, Carol Lynch.
Earl, Cheri Pray & Williams, Carol Lynch. Rescue Begins in Delaware. Oliphant, Manelle, illus. (p. 1462)
—Secret in Pennsylvania. (p. 1541)
Earl, David G. Koala Koala, I'm Not a Bear, I'm a Koala. Gentry, T. Kyle, illus. (p. 966)
Earl, Esther, et al. This Star Won't Go Out: The Life & Words of Esther Grace Earl. (p. 1737)
Earl, Janice. Jan Has a Doll. Tusa, Tricia, illus. (p. 907)
Earl, Sari. Benjamin O. Davis, Jr: Air Force General & Tuskegee Airmen Leader. (p. 165)

—George Washington: Revolutionary Leader & Founding Father. (p. 664)
Earl, Sari & Watson, Stephanie. Under Pressure: Handling the Stresses of Keeping Up. (p. 1813)
Earle, Erin. Surprise Party! (p. 1686)
—Surprise Party! Shapes & Their Attributes. (p. 1686)
Earle, Joan Zuber, mem. Children of Battleship Row: Pearl Harbor 1940-1941. (p. 302)
Earle, Sylvia A. Coral Reefs. (p. 366)
—Coral Reefs. Matthews, Bonnie, illus. (p. 366)
Earlenbaugh, Dennis, illus. see Senuta, Michael.
Earley, Catherine. Jesus Loves Me for Me. (p. 915)
—Outside Fun Earley, Catherine, ed. (p. 1313)
Earley, Catherine M. God Makes Beautiful Things. Earley, Catherine M., ed. (p. 690)
Earley, Chris. Weird Birds. (p. 1872)
—Weird Frogs. (p. 1872)
Earley, Chris, jt. auth. see Earley, Chris G.
Earley, Chris G. Caterpillars: Find - Identify - Raise Your Own. (p. 279)
—Dragonflies: Find - Identify - Raise Your Own. (p. 478)
—Sparrows & Finches of the Great Lakes Region & Eastern North America. (p. 1622)
Earley, Chris G. & Earley, Chris. Warblers of the Great Lakes Region & Eastern North America. (p. 1858)
Earley, Chris G. & McCaw, Robert. Birds A to Z. McCaw, Robert, photos by. (p. 191)
Earls, J S. Realm Unseen: Hard Cover. (p. 1450)
—Realm Unseen. (p. 1450)
Earls, J. S., ed. see Lee, Young Shin & Rogers, Buddy.
Earls, J. S., ed. see Rogers, Bud & Lee, Young Shin.
Earls, Nick. 48 Shades of Brown. (p. 1997)
—After January. (p. 28)
—After Summer. (p. 28)
Early, Alan. Arthur Quinn & Hell's Keeper. (p. 104)
—Arthur Quinn & the Fenris Wolf. (p. 104)
—Arthur Quinn & the World Serpent. (p. 104)
Early Bird Books Staff. Chase. (p. 294)
—Going Camping. (p. 692)
—Going Fishing: Step 2, Level C. (p. 692)
—Race. (p. 1430)
Early, Bobbi. Tiny Life in a Puddle. (p. 1756)
Early, Gerald Lyn. Ralph Ellison: Invisible Man. (p. 1437)
Early, Kelly. Something for Nothing. Sherman, Shandel, illus. (p. 1610)
Early Macken, JoAnn. Mail Carriers. Andersen, Gregg, photos by. (p. 1077)
—Mail Carriers / Carteros. Andersen, Gregg, photos by. (p. 1077)
—Read, Recite, & Write Limericks. (p. 1443)
—Read, Recite, & Write Narrative Poems. (p. 1443)
—Read, Recite, & Write Nursery Rhymes. (p. 1443)
—Read, Write, & Recite Free Verse Poetry. (p. 1444)
—Teachers. Andersen, Gregg, photos by. (p. 1709)
—Teachers / Maestros. Andersen, Gregg, photos by. (p. 1709)
Early Macken, JoAnn, jt. auth. see Macken, JoAnn Early.
Early, Sandy. Tell Tanner Tales: We're Adopted! (p. 1717)
Early, Theresa S. New Mexico. (p. 1246)
Earnest, Peter. Real Spy's Guide to Becoming a Spy. Harper, Suzanne, illus. (p. 1449)
Earnhardt, Crystal. Race to Victory Lane. (p. 1431)
Earnhardt, Donna W. & Castellani, Andrea. Being Frank. (p. 161)
Earnhardt, Heather L. Wandering Goose: A Modern Fable of How Love Goes. Clements, Frida, illus. (p. 1856)
Earnhart, Jeanine, illus. see Schiller, Dawn.
Earnhart, Shirley J. Ludwig the Lift. (p. 1064)
Earp-Bridgmon, Krista D. Adventures of Jim-Bob: A Bearography. (p. 19)
Easer, Katherine. Vicious Little Darlings. (p. 1840)
Easey, Chris, illus. see Thompson, Kimberly.
Eash, Sara. Adeline. (p. 12)
Easler, Kris, illus. see Katz, Alan.
Easley, Maryann. Warriors Daughter. (p. 1859)
Easley, Michael F. Look Out, College, Here I Come! (p. 1049)
Easley, Sheila. Abbott Celebrates a Birthday. (p. 2)
Easley, Terriana. Bubbles & Elie: A Party for Elie. (p. 233)
Eason, Alethea. Hungry. (p. 828)
Eason, D. M., illus. see Demers, Roxanna.
Eason, D. M., illus. see Willard, Hugh.
Eason, Sarah. Chin up, Charlie: Be Brave. (p. 306)
—Come Clean, Carlos: Tell the Truth. (p. 347)
—Dinosaurs: Discover the Awesome Lost World of the Dinosaur. Field, James, illus. (p. 444)
—Don't Play Dirty, Gertie: Be Fair. (p. 468)
—Drawing Baby Animals. (p. 481)
—Drawing Baby Animals. Santillan, Jorge, illus. (p. 481)
—Drawing Dinosaurs. Santillan, Jorge, illus. (p. 481)
—Drawing Dragons. Santillan, Jorge, illus. (p. 481)
—Drawing Fairies, Mermaids, & Unicorns. Santillan, Jorge, illus. (p. 481)
—Drawing Knights & Castles. Santillan, Jorge, illus. (p. 482)
—Drawing Pirates & Pirate Ships. Santillan, Jorge, illus. (p. 482)
—Hand It over, Harry: Don't Steal. (p. 740)
—How Does a Car Work? (p. 808)
—How Does a Helicopter Work? (p. 808)
—How Does a High-Speed Train Work? (p. 808)
—How Does a Jet Plane Work? (p. 808)
—How Does a Powerboat Work? (p. 808)
—How Does a Rocket Work? (p. 808)
—Learn to Draw. Santillan, Jorge, illus. (p. 983)
—Save the Orangutan. Geeson, Andrew & Veldhoven, Marijke, illus. (p. 1516)
—Save the Panda. Geeson, Andrew & Veldhoven, Marijke, illus. (p. 1516)
—Save the Polar Bear. Geeson, Andrew & Veldhoven, Marijke, illus. (p. 1517)
—Save the Tiger. Geeson, Andrew & Veldhoven, Marijke, illus. (p. 1517)
Eason, Sarah, jt. auth. see Mason, Paul.
Eason, Sarah, jt. auth. see Santillan, Jorge.
Eason, Sarah, ed. Animals & Humans. (p. 82)
—Ecology. (p. 502)
—Evolution. (p. 546)
—Plants & Microorganisms. (p. 1370)
—Reproduction & Genetics. (p. 1461)
East, Bob. Tommy Cat & the Giant Chickens. East, Matt, illus. (p. 1764)
—Tommy Cat & the Haunted Well (p. 1764)
East, Cathy. Anna Sewell's Black Beauty. Wald, Christina, illus. (p. 85)
East Dubowski, Cathy, jt. auth. see Dorling Kindersley Publishing Staff.
East, Helen & Maddern, Eric. Spirit of the Forest: Tree Tales from Around the World. Marks, Alan, illus. (p. 1628)
East, Jacqueline. Easter Hop. (p. 499)
—Learn Good Habits with Jessica: Above All, Don't Behave Like Zoe! (p. 983)
—Learn Good Manners with Charles: Above All, Don't Behave Like Trevor! (p. 983)
—No Quiero comer Eso! (p. 1260)
—Peter Cottontails Busy Day. (p. 1346)
—Princess Palace: A Three-Demensional Playset. (p. 1405)
—Town Mouse & the Country Mouse. (p. 1773)
East, Jacqueline, illus. see Barritt, Margaret.
East, Jacqueline, illus. see Beardsley, Martyn.
East, Jacqueline, illus. see Box, Su.
East, Jacqueline, illus. see Dale, Jay.
East, Jacqueline, illus. see Elliot, Rachel.
East, Jacqueline, illus. see Ghigna, Charles.
East, Jacqueline, illus. see Giles, Sophie, et al.
East, Jacqueline, illus. see Holden, Pam.
East, Jacqueline, illus. see Llewellyn, Claire.
East, Jacqueline, illus. see Shoshan, Beth.
East, Jacqueline, illus. see Taylor, Dereen.
East, Jacqueline, illus. see Williams, Becky.
East, Jacqueline, illus. see Zobel-Nolan, Allia.
East, Jacqueline, et al. Hickory Dickory Dock: And Other Silly-Time Rhymes. (p. 775)
East, Jaqueline. Tengo Miedo a la Oscuridad. (p. 1720)
East, Kathy & Thomas, Rebecca L. Across Cultures: A Guide to Multicultural Literature for Children (p. 9)
East, Matt, illus. see East, Bob.
East, Mike, et al. Global Issues: Project Organizer, No. 3 Lelievre, Barclay, ed. (p. 684)
East, Nick, illus. see Mongredien, Sue.
East, Stella, illus. see Trottier, Maxine.
East, Vastine. I Swam with an Angel. (p. 846)
Eastabrooks, Linda. Willie's New Home. (p. 1934)
Eastaway, Rob & Wyndham. Why Do Buses Come in Threes? (p. 1923)
Eastburn, Lynsi. Miranda's Calling. (p. 1149)
Eastcott, John, photos by see Momatiuk, Yva.
Easter, Dennis, illus. see Kirkland, Jane.
Easter, Julie. My Military Dad. (p. 1214)
Easter, Paige, illus. see Augustine, Peg & Flegal, Daphna.
Easterling, Anne S. Ozzie the Great Christmas Crocodile. (p. 1316)
Easterling, Doris. Family Vacation. (p. 569)
Easterling, Lisa. Clothing (p. 334)
—Families (p. 567)
—Games (p. 654)
—Music (p. 1193)
—Schools (p. 1524)
Easterling, Lisa & Mayer, Cassie. Escuelas (p. 535)
—Familias (p. 567)
—Juegos (p. 931)
Eastham, Chad. Truth about Breaking Up, Making Up, & Moving On (p. 1794)
—Truth about Guys: One Guy Reveals What Every Girl Should Know (p. 1794)
Eastham, Chad, et al. Guys Are Waffles, Girls Are Spaghetti (p. 733)
Eastland, Chris, jt. auth. see Bleiman, Andrew.
Eastley, Melanie, illus. see Fraser, Jennifer.
Eastman, Brett, jt. auth. see Fields, Doug.
Eastman, Brock, jt. auth. see Eastman, Brock D.
Eastman, Brock D. & Eastman, Brock. Taken. (p. 1697)
Eastman, Charles A. Indian Scout Craft & Lore. (p. 871)
Eastman, Charles A. & Eastman, Elaine Goodale. Raccoon & the Bee Tree. Susan, Turnbull, illus. (p. 1430)
—Wigwam Evenings: 27 Sioux Folk Tales. (p. 1928)
Eastman, Curtis. Extreme Talk Youth Devotional. (p. 557)
Eastman, Dianne, illus. see Bowers, Vivien.
Eastman, Dianne, illus. see Helmer, Marilyn.
Eastman, Dianne, illus. see Nicolson, Cynthia Pratt.
Eastman, Dianne, illus. see Thomas, Lyn.
Eastman, Elaine Goodale, jt. auth. see Eastman, Charles A.
Eastman, Gail. Anna's Home by the River: A Children's History of Anaheim. Bates, Bob, illus. (p. 85)
Eastman, Kevin B., jt. auth. see Waltz, Tom.
Eastman, Kevin B. & Laird, Peter. Teenage Mutant Ninja Turtles (p. 1714)
Eastman, Kevin B. & Waltz, Tom. Sins of the Fathers. (p. 1580)
—Teenage Mutant Ninja Turtles Volume 1: Change Is Constant: Change Is Constant. (p. 1714)
—Teenage Mutant Ninja Turtles Volume 2: Enemies Old, Enemies New: Enemies Old, Enemies New. (p. 1714)
Eastman, Linda Sue. Leathercraft. (p. 986)
Eastman, P. D. Aaron Has a Lazy Day. (p. 2)
—Aaron Is Cool. (p. 2)
—Aaron Loves Apples & Pumpkins. (p. 2)
—Alphabet Book. (p. 49)
—Are You My Mother? (p. 97)
—Big Blue Book of Beginner Books. (p. 178)
—Big Dog ... Little Dog: A Bedtime Story. (p. 181)
—Go, Dog. Go! (p. 686)
—Go, Dog. Go! Eastman, P. D., illus. (p. 686)
—Mejor Nido. Mlawer, Teresa, tr. from ENG. (p. 1124)
—My Nest Is Best. (p. 1216)
—Red, Stop! Green, Go! An Interactive Book of Colors. (p. 1455)
—Ve, Perro, Ve! Perdomo, Adolfo Perez, tr. (p. 1834)
Eastman, P. D. & Eastman, Tony. Big Dog... Little Dog. Eastman, P. D. & Eastman, Tony, illus. (p. 181)
Eastman, P. D. & Frith, Michael. Little Red Box of Bright & Early Board Books. (p. 1034)
Eastman, P. D., et al. Big Red Book of Beginner Books. (p. 183)
Eastman, Peter. Fred & Ted Go Camping. (p. 632)
—Fred & Ted Like to Fly. (p. 632)
—Fred & Ted Like to Fly. Eastman, Peter, illus. (p. 632)
—Fred & Ted's Road Trip. (p. 632)
Eastman, Peter, et al. Big Purple Book of Beginner Books. (p. 183)
Eastman, Seth, jt. auth. see Lorbiecki, Marybeth.
Eastman, Tony, jt. auth. see Eastman, P. D.
Easton, Kelly. Aftershock. (p. 29)
—Outlandish Adventures of Liberty Aimes. Swearingen, Greg, illus. (p. 1312)
—Place for Elijah. Friar, Joanne H., illus. (p. 1365)
—To Be Mona. (p. 1758)
—Walking on Air. (p. 1854)
Easton, Marilyn. Big & Little. (p. 177)
—Eris to the Rescue. (p. 533)
—New Girl in Town. (p. 1244)
Easton, Marilyn, illus. see Scholastic, Inc. Staff.
Easton, Marilyn J. & Scholastic, Inc. Staff. Power Rangers Samurai: the New Ranger. (p. 1390)
Easton, Samantha, jt. auth. see Greive, Bradley Trevor.
Easton, Susan, illus. see Trooboff, Rhoda.
Easton, T. S. Boys Don't Knit. (p. 220)
Easton, Tom. Seven Second Delay. (p. 1554)
Easton, Tom, jt. auth. see Depp, Laurie.
Easton, W. G., illus. see Farrow, George Edward.
Eastridge, Jim. Gregory & the Moon. (p. 723)
Eastwick, Ivy O. Some Folks Like Cats: And Other Poems. Maass, Mary Kurnick, illus. (p. 1609)
Eastwood, John, illus. see King-Smith, Dick.
Eastwood, John, illus. see Lindsay, Elizabeth.
Eastwood, Kay. Life in a Castle. (p. 1010)
—Life of a Knight. (p. 1011)
—Medieval Society. (p. 1119)
—Places of Worship in the Middle Ages. (p. 1366)
—Women & Girls in the Middle Ages. (p. 1945)
Eather, Jenny. Maths Dictionary for Kids. (p. 1108)
Eaton, Anthony. Fireshadow. (p. 592)
—Girl in the Cave. Danalis, John, illus. (p. 678)
—New Kind of Dreaming. (p. 1245)
—Nightpeople. (p. 1255)
Eaton, Connie Clough. Birds, Flowers & Butterflies Stained Glass Pattern Book. (p. 191)
—Easy Victorian Florals Stained Glass Pattern Book. (p. 500)
Eaton, Deborah. Canciones de Monstruos. Translations.com Staff, tr. from ENG. (p. 261)
Eaton, Deborah J. My Wild Woolly. Karas, G. Brian, illus. (p. 1221)
Eaton, Gordon J. Piebald & the Parade of Small Animals. (p. 1356)
Eaton, Jason Carter. Facttracker. Constantin, Pascale, illus. (p. 561)
—How to Train a Train. Rocco, John, illus. (p. 822)
Eaton, Kait. I Want to Be A... Fairy. Enright, Amanda, illus. (p. 847)
Eaton, Katherine B. Daily Life in the Soviet Union (p. 400)
Eaton, Kay A. Gleason & the Dewdrop's Dream. (p. 682)
—Gleason, the Christmas Giraffe. (p. 682)
Eaton, Kelly Toole. Kellina Makes Her Dreams Come True. (p. 948)
—Kitten Trouble. (p. 962)
Eaton, Maxwell, III. Andy Also. (p. 72)
—Birds vs. Bunnies. (p. 192)
—Flying Beaver Brothers & the Crazy Critter Race. (p. 609)
—Flying Beaver Brothers & the Evil Penguin Plan. (p. 609)
—Flying Beaver Brothers & the Fishy Business. (p. 609)
—Flying Beaver Brothers & the Hot Air Baboons. (p. 609)
—Mystery. (p. 1223)
—Okay, Andy! Eaton, Maxwell, III, illus. (p. 1282)
—Two Dumb Ducks. (p. 1803)
Eaton, Scot. DoomWar. (p. 470)
Eaton, Scot, illus. see Dixon, Chuck.
Eaton, Scot, illus. see Jurgens, Dan.
Eaton, Scot, illus. see Nimoy, Leonard.
Eaton, Scot & Epting, Steve. Captain America by Ed Brubaker - Volume 4. (p. 263)
Eaton, Seymour. Roosevelt Bears Travels Adventures. (p. 1488)
Eaton, Walter Pricha. Peanut Cub Reporter: A Boy Scout's Life. (p. 1332)
Eaton, Walter Prichard. Boy Scouts in the White Mountains: the Story of a Long Hike. Merrill, Frank T., illus. (p. 218)
Eaves, Ed, illus. see Bateson, Maggie.
Eaves, Ed, illus. see Hart, Caryl.
Eaves, Ed, illus. see Whybrow, Ian.
Eaves, Edward, illus. see Whybrow, Ian.
Eaves, G. L. Operation Tiger. (p. 1300)
Eaves, Victor Caleb. Vee's the Chapters of Expudict: Book One. (p. 1834)
Ebanks, Timall. Caymanian Heritage Series: Christmas Time. (p. 282)
Ebbeler, Jeff, illus. see Chapman, Kelly.
Ebbeler, Jeff, illus. see Gunderson, Jessica Sarah.
Ebbeler, Jeff, illus. see Gunderson, Jessica.
Ebbeler, Jeff, illus. see Shulimson, Sarene.
Ebbeler, Jeff, illus. see Slater, David Michael.
Ebbeler, Jeff, illus. see Suen, Anastasia.
Ebbeler, Jeffrey. Click! (p. 331)
—Jingle Bells. (p. 918)
—Jingle Bells - Musical. (p. 918)
Ebbeler, Jeffrey, illus. see Adler, David A.
Ebbeler, Jeffrey, illus. see Bellisario, Gina.
Ebbeler, Jeffrey, illus. see Cox, Judy.
Ebbeler, Jeffrey, illus. see Gerber, Carole.
Ebbeler, Jeffrey, illus. see Hill, Leonard.
Ebbeler, Jeffrey, illus. see Hill, Susanna Leonard.
Ebbeler, Jeffrey, illus. see Lear, Edward.
Ebbeler, Jeffrey, illus. see Levins, Sandra.
Ebbeler, Jeffrey, illus. see Orshoski, Paul.
Ebbeler, Jeffrey, illus. see Sheth, Kashmira.
Ebbeler, Jeffrey, illus. see Shulimson, Sarene.
Ebbeler, Jeffrey, illus. see Solheim, James.
Ebbeler, Jeffrey, illus. see Suen, Anastasia.
Ebbeler, Jeffrey, illus. see Troupe, Thomas Kingsley.
Ebbeler, Jeffrey, jt. auth. see Troupe, Thomas Kingsley.
Ebbers, Susan M. Jamie's Journey: The Savvy Traveler. Godbey, Cory, illus. (p. 907)
Ebbesmeyer, Joan, jt. auth. see Polette, Nancy.
Ebbing, Darrell. Essential General Chemistry. (p. 537)
—Essentials of General Chemistry. (p. 537)
—Student Solutions Manual: Used with ...Ebbing-Essentials of General Chemistry. (p. 1669)
Ebbitt, Carolyn Q. Extra-Ordinary Princess. (p. 555)
Ebel, Julia Taylor. Picture Man. Canter, Idalia, illus. (p. 1355)
Ebel, Julia Taylor, Jr. Hansi & the Ice Man. Canter, Idalia, illus. (p. 743)
Ebel, Sherry. Cassie's Magic Doors. (p. 276)
—Cassie's Magic Doors the Butterfly Garden. (p. 276)
Ebeling, Vicki. Winners Group. (p. 1937)
Ebeltoft, Christine. Koo & Jay in the Rainforest. (p. 967)
Eben Field, Jon & Field, Jon Eben. Dealing with Drugs Inhalants & Solvents. (p. 418)
Eberbach, Andrea, illus. see Louthain, J. A.
Eberhard, Phyllis Lunde Brees. Little Miss Neat-As-A-Pin. Jacoby, Nickolina Dye, illus. (p. 1032)
Eberhardt, Nancy Chapel, jt. auth. see Chapel, Jamie Moore.
Eberhart, Donald G., illus. see Fraggalosch, Audrey M.
Eberhart, Donald G., jt. auth. see Fraggalosch, Audrey.
Eberhart, Nancy. Adventures of Granny: Granny Goes to the Zoo. Pyers, Kelsey, illus. (p. 18)
—Anabelle's Wish. Pyers, Kelsey, illus. (p. 66)
Eberle, Dina P. Mice Next Door (p. 1134)
Eberle, Irmengarde. Benjamin Franklin, Man of Science: A First Biography. Gillette, Henry S., illus. (p. 165)
Eberle, Melissa. Fricka the Flying Frog. (p. 637)
Eberly, Chelsea. Barbie Fall 2014 DVD Step into Reading. (p. 138)
—Mater & the Little Tractors. (p. 1104)
—Mater & the Little Tractors. RH Disney Staff, illus. (p. 1104)
—Surf Princess. (p. 1685)
—Surf Princess. Random House Staff, illus. (p. 1685)
Ebers, Georg. Greylock. (p. 723)
—Question. (p. 1426)
Ebersol, Schuyler J. Hidden World (p. 776)
Ebersole, Rene. Gorilla Mountain: The Story of Wildlife Biologist Amy Vedder. (p. 703)
Ebert, Anne, illus. see Caballero, D., tr.
Ebert, Len, illus. see Albee, Sarah.
Ebert, Len, illus. see Allen, Kathy.
Ebert, Len, illus. see Dreyer, Nicole E.
Ebert, Len, illus. see Graver, Jane.
Ebert, Len, illus. see Grimm, Jacob & Grimm, Wilhelm K.
Ebert, Len, illus. see Mortensen, Lori.
Ebert, Len, illus. see Mullins, Patty Rutland.
Ebert, Len, illus. see Rosenfeld, Dina.
Ebert, Len, illus. see Standard Publishing Staff.
Ebert, Len, illus. see Wedeven, Carol.
Ebert, Len, illus. see Wilde, Oscar.
Ebert, Len, illus. see Wilsdon, Christina.
Ebert, Roey, illus. see Wasson, E. & Strausser, A.
Eberts, Marge, jt. auth. see Riley, James.
Ebertsch, Ted, illus. see Barden, Laura.
Eberz, Robert, illus. see Scotton, Rob.
Ebia, Iris. Get up & Go! (p. 668)
—When the Wind Blows What Is That Noise? (p. 1905)
Ebie, Mora. Going to the Zoo in Hawaii. (p. 693)
—Little Mouse's Hawaiian Christmas Present. Braffet, Holly, illus. (p. 1032)
Ebin, Matthew. Wonderfully Ridiculous Alphabet Book. (p. 1948)
Ebina, Hiro. Joy to the World! Warabe, Kimika, illus. (p. 930)
Ebiringa, Chudy. The, Adventures of Ella at Bulukutu Stream. (p. 1728)
Ebl, Donna. Adventures of Salamander Sam. (p. 22)
Ebner, Abra. Ladybird, Ladybird. (p. 971)
Ebner, Aviva. Earth Science Experiments. (p. 496)
—Engineering Science Experiments. (p. 529)
—Environmental Science Experiments. (p. 532)
—Forensic Science Experiments. (p. 617)
—Health Science Experiments. (p. 758)
—Junior Science Experiments on Filetrade; Set, 4-Volumes. (p. 936)
—Physical Science Experiments. (p. 1353)
Ebner, Louise M. Learning English with the Bible (p. 985)
Eboch, Chris. Amazing Feats of Mechanical Engineering. (p. 54)
—Chaco Canyon. (p. 288)
—Ghost on the Stairs. (p. 671)
—Green Movement. (p. 722)
—Knight in the Shadows. (p. 964)
—Magnets in the Real World. (p. 1076)
—Riverboat Phantom. (p. 1476)
—Science Measurements: How Heavy? How Long? How Hot? Davis, Jon, illus. (p. 1526)
Eboch, M. M. 12 Biggest Breakthroughs in Energy Technology. (p. 1994)
—12 Biggest Breakthroughs in Transportation Technology. (p. 1994)
—History of Film. (p. 784)
—History of Television. (p. 784)
—Jesse Owens: Young Record Breaker. Henderson, Meryl, illus. (p. 914)
—Milton Hershey: Young Chocolatier. Henderson, Meryl, illus. (p. 1144)
Ebon Research Systems Staff. Dare to Be: Roberto Clemente. (p. 406)
—Dare to Be: Luis Munoz Marion. Vol. 4 (p. 406)
—Dare to Be: Lessons in the Life of Esperanza. Vol. 2 (p. 406)
—Dare to Be... A Hero: Cesar Chavez. Vol. 3 (p. 406)
Ebong, Ima, jt. auth. see Polyansky, Nikita.
Ebrey, Patricia Buckley. China: A Cultural, Social, & Political History. (p. 306)
Eburne, Tim. Zebra Stripes: A Tail of Personal Branding. (p. 1985)
Ebwelleson, Nelson. Helpless King. (p. 766)
Eby, Wes. Coban Treasure Hunt. (p. 336)
—Jungle Jeopardy. (p. 935)

E

E.C Drury Life Skills Class, et al. Viral Avenger: Adventures at Auld College. (p. 1844)
E.C., Nanci. I Just Might! Meade, Gregory S., illus. (p. 840)
Eccles, Jane, illus. see Li, Amanda.
Eccles, Jane, illus. see Phinn, Gervase.
Eccleston, Linda. When I Grow Up, I Want to Be a Supreme Court Justice: A Young Person's Guide to Understanding the Supreme Court of the United States. (p. 1903)
Eccleston, Linda M. When I Grow Up, I Want to Be President: A Young Persons Guide to Understanding the Presidency of the United States. (p. 1903)
Echaore-McDavid, Susan. Career Opportunities in Education & Related Services. (p. 267)
—Career Opportunities in Law Enforcement, Security, & Protective Services. (p. 267)
Echaore-McDavid, Susan, jt. auth. see McDavid, Richard A.
Echaore-McDavid, Susan & McDavid, Richard. Agriculture, Food & Natural Resources. (p. 30)
Echerique, Alfredo Bryce & Duenas, Ana Maria. Goig. Roederer, Charlotte, illus. (p. 692)
Echeverri, Catalina. There's a Dinosaur in My Bathtub. (p. 1730)
Echeverri, Catalina, illus. see Rose, Lisa.
Echeverria, Angel. Walking with a Psychopath. (p. 1854)
Echeverria Gyorkos, Charmaine, illus. see Echeverria-Bis, Olivia.
Echeverria, Jessica. Dora y el Dia lluvioso. Savitsky, Steven, illus. (p. 471)
Echeverria, Jessica, jt. auth. see Paz, Veronica.
Echeverria-Bis, Olivia. EGGbees. Echeverria Gyorkos, Charmaine, illus. (p. 506)
Echeverrma, Esteban. Matadero la Cautiva. (p. 1104)
EchoHawk, Terry. Call Me Little Echo Hawk. (p. 254)
Echols, Jean C. Animal Defenses. Bevilacqua, Carol, illus. (p. 77)
Echols, Jennifer. Biggest Flirts. (p. 185)
—Boys Next Door. (p. 220)
—Endless Summer: The Boys Next Door; Endless Summer. (p. 527)
—Ex Games. (p. 547)
—Going Too Far. (p. 693)
—Love Story. (p. 1060)
—Most Likely to Succeed. (p. 1177)
—One That I Want. (p. 1297)
—Perfect Couple. (p. 1341)
—Such a Rush. (p. 1672)
Echols, Jennifer, jt. auth. see Hapka, Catherine, pseud.
Echols, Larry. When the Eagles Fly. (p. 1904)
Echols, Tim. Real Citizenship. (p. 1448)
Eck, Bernhard, illus. see Martin, Ivonne.
Eck, Ed. Baseball in the American League West Division. (p. 141)
—Baseball in the National League Central Division. (p. 141)
—Baseball in the National League West. (p. 141)
—Baseball in the National League West Division. (p. 141)
Eck, Edward. Baseball in the American League West Division. (p. 141)
Eck, Kristin. Animales en Mi Casa. (p. 81)
—Animals in My House. (p. 83)
—Bicycle Stunt Riding: Check It Out. (p. 177)
—Colores en Mi Casa. (p. 344)
—Colors in My House. (p. 345)
—Drafting the Constitution: Weighing Evidence to Draw Sound Conclusions. (p. 476)
—Formas en Mi Casa. (p. 620)
—Hide & Seek Animals. (p. 776)
—Hide & Seek Clothes. (p. 776)
—Hide & Seek Food. (p. 776)
—Hide & Seek Toys. (p. 777)
—Hide-and-Seek Animals. (p. 776)
—Hide-and-Seek Clothes. (p. 776)
—Hide-and-Seek Food. (p. 776)
—Hide-and-Seek Toys. (p. 777)
—Opposites in My House. (p. 1301)
—Opuestas en mi Casa. (p. 1301)
—Shapes in My House. (p. 1560)
—Wakeboarding: Check It Out. (p. 1853)
Eck, Michael. Internet: Inside & Out. (p. 880)
Eck, Thomas Van. Tarsiers in the Dark. (p. 1706)
Eckart, Edana. Bottlenose Dolphin. (p. 215)
—California Condor. (p. 253)
—Cheetah. (p. 296)
—I Can Go Camping. (p. 835)
—I Can Go Hiking. (p. 835)
—Koala. (p. 966)
—Monarch Butterfly. (p. 1163)
—Watching the Moon. (p. 1861)
—Watching the Seasons. (p. 1861)
—Watching the Sun. (p. 1861)
—Watching the Weather. (p. 1861)
—Watching the Wind. (p. 1861)
Eckdahl, Judith & Eckdahl, Kathryn. Collection of Street Games. O'Regan, Lucy, ed. (p. 340)
Eckdahl, Kathryn, jt. auth. see Eckdahl, Judith.
Eckel, Jessie. Boys' Coloring Book. (p. 220)
—Doodle Dolls: Over 300 Outfits to Design & Decorate. (p. 469)
—Doodle Dolls. (p. 469)
—Girls' Coloring Book. (p. 680)
—How to Be a Princess in 7 Days or Less. (p. 814)
—Vacation Coloring Book. (p. 1829)
Eckel, Jessie, illus. see Brunelle, Lynn.
Eckel, Marc Thomas. Stan the Snowman's Plan for a Summer Tan. (p. 1639)
Eckelberg, Aimie. Walk the Walk. (p. 1854)
Ecker, Catherine, jt. auth. see Bick, Margaret.
Ecker, Rebecca. Miss Emmalou Strain & the Hunt for Hermie. (p. 1151)
Eckerson, Margaret, illus. see Jepson, Edgar.
Eckert, Charles, photos by see Chu, C. K.
Eckert, Sharon, jt. auth. see Leimbach, Judy.
Eckhardt, Jason C. Legend of the China Poblana. (p. 989)
Eckhardt, Jason C., illus. see Bennett, Marcia Allen.
Eckhardt, Jason C., illus. see Komechak, Marilyn Gilbert.
Eckhardt, Jason C., illus. see Law, Janice.
Eckhardt, Jason C., jt. auth. see Bennett, Marcia Allen.
Eckl, Joseph J. & Eckl, Theresa R. What Is It All About? Eckl-Shear, Veronica, illus. (p. 1889)
Eckl, Theresa R., jt. auth. see Eckl, Joseph J.
Eckler, Rebecca. Rotten Apple. (p. 1490)
Eckles, Alice. My Life as a Flower: Color, Fragrance. Chapters 1&2 (p. 1212)
Eckl-Shear, Veronica, illus. see Eckl, Joseph J. & Eckl, Theresa R.
Ecklund, Faith & Case, Carrie L. Our Friends in Chairs with Wheels. (p. 1308)
Eckman, Edie. I Can Knit. (p. 836)
Eckmann, Sabine & Koepnick, Lutz P. Window - Interface. (p. 1936)
Eckroat, Laura W. Red Goes to Kindergarten. (p. 1454)
—Simpler Time. (p. 1578)
—Went Out to Get a Donut - Came Home with a Muffin. (p. 1875)
Ecks. Riddle in the Middle. (p. 1470)
Eckstein, David & Brown, Greg. Have Heart. (p. 754)
Eckstein, Joe, illus. see Caron, Susie.
Eckstein, Joe, illus. see Eckstein, Kristen.
Eckstein, Kristen. Ultimate Friend Book: More Than Your Average Address Book for Kids. Eckstein, Joe, illus. (p. 1809)
—Ultimate Friend Book: More Than Your Average Address Book for Teens. Eckstein, Joe, illus. (p. 1809)
Eckstrom, Nathaniel, illus. see Lee, Spider.
Ecob, Simon, illus. see Oliver, Martin.
Ecob, Simon, illus. see Stride, Lottie & Oliver, Martin.
Economy, Peter. We Both Read-New Car Design. (p. 1866)
Ecton, Anne Massey. Passing Through Camelot. (p. 1326)
Ecton, Emily. Boots & Pieces. (p. 213)
—Curse of Cuddles McGee. (p. 394)
—Night of the Living Lawn Ornaments. (p. 1254)
—Project Jackalope. (p. 1410)
Ed. Fat Man, Fat Man. (p. 577)
(ed.), Chambers. Chambers Junior Illustrated Dictionary. (p. 289)
(Ed.), Chambers. Mini School Thesaurus. (p. 1146)
EDC Publishing, creator. Rocks & Fossils Kid Kit. (p. 1483)
EDCON Publishing Group Staff. Classic Children's Tales. (p. 328)
—Jack & the Beanstalk - The Stubborn Witch - Rapunzel - Betsy - The Magic Bus. (p. 902)
—Little Toot - The Story of White Satin - Five Peas in a Pod - Rumpelstiltskin - The Little Magic Pot. (p. 1037)
—Sports Math Complete Program. (p. 1633)
—Surprise Pies - Snow White & Rose Red - The Emperor's New Clothes - The Three Bears - The Mixed up Family - A Valentine Story. (p. 1686)
Eddie Ree Stolinski, Ree Stolinski & Stolinski, Eddie Ree. Prayer Closet. (p. 1393)
Eddings, David & Eddings, Leigh. Crystal Gorge. (p. 387)
Eddings, Leigh, jt. auth. see Eddings, David.
Eddleman, Peggy. Escape One Danger - Jump into Another.... (p. 535)
—Sky Jumpers: Book 1. (p. 1586)
—Sky Jumpers. (p. 1586)
—Sky Jumpers: Escape One Danger - Jump into Another. Bk. 1 (p. 1587)
—Sky Jumpers Book 2: the Forbidden Flats. (p. 1587)
Eddy, Catherine J. Sandbox Sandshoes. Krupnek, Joann J., illus. (p. 1511)
Eddy, Claudia. Boone: The Cat Who Could Stand on His Head. (p. 213)
Eddy, Daniel. Walter's Tours in the East: Walter in Je. (p. 1856)
Eddy, Dawn. Good Knight & an Ordinary Day. (p. 698)
Eddy, Mary Baker. Big with Blessings. (p. 184)
Eddy, Olivia. Hatchling. (p. 752)
Eddy, Olympia. Mysterious View. (p. 1223)
Eddy, Randon T. DILLO the Coloring Book. (p. 440)
Eddy, Randon T., illus. see Miller, Kyle Linda.
Eddy, Susan. Cesar Chavez. (p. 288)
—Mother Teresa. (p. 1178)
Ede, Lara. Bible Stories for Boys. (p. 176)
—Bible Stories for Girls. (p. 176)
—Press-Out & Play Busy Farm. (p. 1397)
—Press-Out & Play Fairy Land. (p. 1397)
—Press-Out & Play Pampered Pets. (p. 1397)
Ede, Lara, illus. see Boon, Fiona, ed.
Ede, Lara, illus. see Boon, Fiona.
Ede, Lara, illus. see Down, Hayley & Make Believe Ideas Staff.
Edeburn, Andrew, ed. see Edeburn, Carl.
Edeburn, Carl. Sturgis: The Story of the Rally. Edeburn, Andrew, ed. (p. 1670)
Edelfield, Bruce & Moosa, Tracey J. Drug Abuse. (p. 486)
Edelman, Lana. School Friends. (p. 1523)
Edelman, Marian W., jt. auth. see Edelman, Marian Wright.
Edelman, Marian Wright & Edelman, Marian W. I Can Make a Difference: A Treasury to Inspire Our Children. Moser, Barry, illus. (p. 836)
Edelman, Scott & Conway, Gerry. Marvel Masterworks: Captain Marvel. Vol. 5 Broderick, Pat, illus. (p. 1099)
Edelmann, Heinz, illus. see Gardner, Charlie.
Edelson, Madelyn. Proud Beech: A Long Island Folk Tale. Tucker, Diane, illus. (p. 1412)
Edelson, Stephen B. & Mitchell, Deborah. What Your Doctor May Not Tell You about Autoimmune Disorders: The Revolutionary Drug-Free Treatments for Thyroid Disease, Lupus, MS, Ibd, Chronic Fatigue, Rheumatoid Arthritis & Other Diseases. (p. 1896)
Edelson, Wendy, illus. see Ban Breathnach, Sarah.
Edelson, Wendy, illus. see Child, Lydia Maria.
Edelson, Wendy, illus. see Cosgrove, Stephen.
Edelson, Wendy, illus. see Craig, Jenny.
Edelson, Wendy, illus. see McGranaghan, John.
Edelson, Wendy, illus. see Pingry, Patricia A.
Edelson, Wendy, illus. see Pingry, Patricia A. & Urbano, Aide.
Edelstein, Judy & Howe, Katherine. Money Matters: How to Become a Smart Consumer. (p. 1164)
Edelstein, June. Big Snow & la Nevada: 6 English, 6 Spanish Adaptations (p. 184)
—Fossils. (p. 623)
—Los Fósiles: Set Of 6. (p. 1054)
—Nevada: Set Of 6. (p. 1242)
Edelstein, Rachell, illus. see Licht, S.
Edelstein, Terese, tr. see Spillebeen, Geert.
Eden, Alexandra. Duchess to the Rescue: A Bones & the Duchess Mystery. (p. 488)
—Holy Smoke: A Bones & the Duchess Mystery. (p. 791)
Eden, Cynthia, et al. Secrets Volume 18 Dark Passions - the Secrets Collecion Vol. 18. (p. 1546)
—Secrets Volume 21 Primal Heat - the Secrets Collection: The Best in Women's Erotic Romance. Vol. 21 (p. 1546)
Eden, David. Potter's Wheel Story & Activity Book. Eden, David, illus. (p. 1388)
Eden Odyssey D20 Staff. Waysides: The Book of Taverns. (p. 1865)
Eden, Paul E. Helicopters. (p. 763)
—Weird & Wonderful Aircraft. (p. 1872)
Edens, Cooper. Classic Western Stories: The Most Beloved Stories. (p. 328)
—Edens Picture Book Day, Alexandra, illus. (p. 504)
Edens, Cooper, jt. auth. see Barrie, J. M.
Edens, Cooper & Kehl, R. Put on a Happy Face. (p. 1420)
Edens, Cooper, compiled by. Big Book of Little. (p. 179)
Edens, Cooper, et al. Alice's Adventures in Wonderland. (p. 40)
Eder, Enelle. Create & Take Bible Crafts: Special Days. (p. 378)
—Create & Take Bible Crafts: Exploring Nature. (p. 378)
—Create & Take Bible Crafts: Parables & Miracles. (p. 378)
—Create & Take Bible Crafts: Animals of the Bible. (p. 378)
—Create & Take Bible Crafts: Old Testament Heroes. (p. 378)
Eder, Tamara. Mammals of California. (p. 1085)
—Mammals of Ontario (p. 1085)
Edgar, Barrie, illus. see Trotter, Bob.
Edgar, John. Footprints of Famous Men Biography for. (p. 615)
Edgar, Kathleen J. Mission San Diego de Alcala. (p. 1153)
—Mission San Francisco de Asis. (p. 1153)
—Mission San Miguel Arcangel. (p. 1153)
Edgar, Kathleen J., jt. auth. see Bigelow, Barbara C.
Edgar, Kathleen J., jt. auth. see Edgar, Susan E.
Edgar, Kathleen J., jt. auth. see Gall, Susan B.
Edgar, Kathleen J. & Edgar, Susan E. Mission San Carlos Borromeo Del Rio Carmelo. (p. 1153)
—Mission San Diego de Alcala. (p. 1153)
—Mission San Francisco de Asis. (p. 1153)
—Mission San Miguel Arcangel. (p. 1153)
Edgar, Kathleen J., et al. Compassion. (p. 352)
—Courage. (p. 372)
—Determination. (p. 431)
—Discovering Mission San Carlos Borromeo Del Carmelo. (p. 449)
—Discovering Mission San Juan Capistrano. (p. 449)
—Imagination. (p. 860)
—Responsibility. (p. 1463)
—Vision. (p. 1844)
Edgar, M. G. Treasury of Poems for Children. Pogány, Willy, illus. (p. 1783)
Edgar, Robert. Tom Tuff to the Rescue. Sharp, Todd, illus. (p. 1764)
Edgar, Sherra G. Bar Graphs. (p. 137)
—Egypt. (p. 506)
—Graphing Story Problems. (p. 711)
—Ireland. (p. 887)
—Israel. (p. 893)
—Kenya. (p. 949)
—Large Animal Veterinarian. (p. 975)
—Line Graphs. (p. 1019)
—Pictographs. (p. 1355)
—Pie Graphs. (p. 1356)
—Tally Charts. (p. 1704)
—What's Great about Idaho? (p. 1897)
—What's Great about Kentucky? (p. 1897)
Edgar, Susan E., jt. auth. see Edgar, Kathleen J.
Edgar, Susan E. & Edgar, Kathleen J. 50 American Women of Courage & Vision. (p. 1997)
Edgar, Val. How to Be Brilliant at Christmas Time. (p. 815)
—How to Be Brilliant at Word Puzzles. (p. 815)
—How to Sparkle at Christmas Time. (p. 821)
Edge, A. M. Frankie Feinstein & the Fenworld Thief-Takers. (p. 629)
Edge, Christopher. Black Crow Conspiracy. (p. 195)
—Shadows of the Silver Screen. (p. 1558)
—Twelve Minutes to Midnight. (p. 1800)
Edge, Elizabeth, illus. see Henderson, Patti & Golden Books Staff.
Edge, Jason Joseph. Find the Tree Find the Morel. (p. 587)
Edge, Laura B. Hilary Duff: Celebrity with Heart. (p. 779)
Edge, Laura B. & Edge, Laura Bufano. From Jazz Babies to Generation Next: The History of the American Teenager. (p. 643)
Edge, Laura Bufano. Hilary Duff: Celebrity with Heart. (p. 779)
—Laura Bush: Portrait of a First Lady. (p. 980)
—Locked Up: A History of the U.S. Prison System. (p. 1045)
—Steven Spielberg: Director of Blockbuster Films. (p. 1649)
—We Stand As One: The International Ladies Garment Workers' Strike, New York, 1909. (p. 1868)
—Wild West Dreams. (p. 1930)
Edge, Laura Bufano, jt. auth. see Edge, Laura B.
Edge, Raymond S. S the Iconic Gentleman's Activity Book. (p. 1499)
Edgecombe, Jane. Fly Away Home. Martin, Stuart, illus. (p. 609)
—Whoops! (p. 1920)
Edgehill, S. D. To Honor Thy Mother. (p. 1759)
Edgell, Ernest. Cowbears of Texas: The Hero. Haycraft, Marilynn J., illus. (p. 373)
Edgemon, Darcie. Seamore, the Very Forgetful Porpoise. Seibold, J. Otto, illus. (p. 1536)
Edgerley, Ross, illus. see Dailey, Reid.
Edgers, Geoff. Who Is Stan Lee? (p. 1916)
—Who Is Stan Lee? Laznicka, Mike et al, illus. (p. 1916)
—Who Was Elvis Presley? O'Brien, John, illus. (p. 1918)
—Who Was Elvis Presley? O'Brien, John & Harrison, Nancy, illus. (p. 1918)
—Who Were the Beatles? Tageau, Jerry, illus. (p. 1919)
—Who Were the Beatles? Tugeau, Jeremy, illus. (p. 1919)
Edgerton, Les. Surviving Little League: For Players, Parents, & Coaches. (p. 1687)
Edgerton, Martha. Civility Matters: Anna Moves to the Big City. (p. 326)
Edgeworth, Maria. Bracelets or Amiability & Industry Rewarded. (p. 221)
—Moral Tales, by Maria Edgeworth Embellished with Original Designs, by Darley. (p. 1173)
—Parents Assistance or Stories for Child. (p. 1324)
—Parent's Assistant; or, Stories for Children. (p. 1324)
—Rosamond: With Other Tales. by Maria Edgeworth. (p. 1489)
—Tomorrow. (p. 1765)
Edghill, Rosemary, jt. auth. see Lackey, Mercedes.
Edgin, Brenda. Little Winston & his Big Adventures in Natchez: Down in the Bayou. (p. 1038)
—Little Winston & his Big Adventures in Natchez: New Home near the Woods. (p. 1038)
Edginton, Ian. Sojourn: The Sorcerer's Tale Land, Greg et al, illus. (p. 1606)
Edgren, David. Kingdom Scroll. (p. 960)
—Lamb Scroll. (p. 972)
—Serpent Scroll. (p. 1552)
Edgren, Elizabeth. Little Tree's Mightiest Deed. Penk, Kathryn, illus. (p. 1037)
Edgson, Alison. Elves & the Shoemaker. (p. 517)
—Emperor's New Clothes. (p. 521)
—Magician's Apprentice. (p. 1075)
—Three Billy Goats Gruff. (p. 1741)
Edgson, Alison, illus. see Corderoy, Tracey.
Edgson, Alison, illus. see Jennings, Linda.
Edgson, Alison, illus. see Peters, Andrew Fusek.
Edgson, Alison, illus. see Peters, Andrew.
Edgson, Alison, illus. see Powell-Tuck, Maudie.
Edgson, Alison, illus. see Ritchie, Alison.
Edgson, Alison, illus. see Rusling, Annette.
Edgson, Alison, et al. Hansel & Gretel. (p. 743)
Edgson, Allison, illus. see Keith, Donna.
Edicare, ed. see Tullet, Hervé.
Edicare Staff, ed. see Tullet, Hervé.
Ediciones B (Firm) Staff & Outhwaite, Ida Rentoul. Magia de las Hadas. (p. 1071)
Edick, Grant. Space Station. (p. 1620)
Edidin, Rachel, ed. see Crilley, Mark.
Edidin, Rachel, ed. see Hicks, Faith Erin.
Edidin, Rachel, ed. see Nicolle, Malachai.
Ediger, Max. Caleb & Shalev. (p. 252)
Edimat Libros, ed. see Van Gool, A, et al.
Eding, Bob, illus. see Loop, Mary Ann.
Eding, June. Who Was Queen Elizabeth? Harrison, Nancy & Harrison, illus. (p. 1919)
Edinger, Monica. Africa Is My Home: A Child of the Amistad. Byrd, Robert, illus. (p. 26)
Edison, Erin. Abraham Lincoln (p. 6)
—Básico Sobre el Tiempo. Strictly Spanish, LLC., tr. (p. 142)
—Blow It Up! (p. 202)
—Clara Barton. (p. 326)
—Clouds (p. 335)
—Crush It! (p. 386)
—Destruction. (p. 431)
—Favorite Designer Dogs (p. 578)
—Florence Nightingale (p. 606)
—Franklin D. Roosevelt (p. 630)
—George Washington (p. 664)
—Great Women in History (p. 719)
—Harriet Tubman. (p. 749)
—Helen Keller (p. 762)
—Jane Goodall. (p. 908)
—John F. Kennedy (p. 921)
—Knock It Down! (p. 965)
—Lightning (p. 1015)
—Marie Curie (p. 1093)
—Pocahontas. (p. 1375)
—Rain (p. 1434)
—Rosa Parks (p. 1488)
—Sally Ride (p. 1505)
—Shred It! (p. 1571)
—Snow (p. 1598)
—Sunlight (p. 1677)
—Susan B. Anthony (p. 1687)
—Weather Basics. (p. 1870)
—Wind (p. 1935)
—You'll Love Chiweenies (p. 1977)
—You'll Love Puggles (p. 1978)
Edison, Erin, jt. auth. see Lee, Sally.
Edison, Erin & Saunders-Smith, Gail. Lluvia. Strictly Spanish LLC. Staff, tr. from ENG. (p. 1043)
—Luz del Sol. Strictly Spanish LLC. Staff, tr. from ENG. (p. 1066)
—Nieve/Snow. Strictly Spanish LLC. Staff, tr. (p. 1252)
—Nubes. Strictly Spanish LLC. Staff, tr. from ENG. (p. 1269)
—Relámpagos. Strictly Spanish LLC. Staff, tr. from ENG. (p. 1457)
—Viento. Strictly Spanish LLC. Staff, tr. from ENG. (p. 1841)
Edison, Richard E. Trouble on the Blue Planet. Santillan, Mariano, illus. (p. 1790)
Edison-Clark, Gina. Amone's Daddies! Newkirk, Errol Q., illus. (p. 101)
—I Just Want My Daddy! Newkirk, Errol Q., illus. (p. 840)
Edith, Nesbit, jt. auth. see Nesbit, E.
Editions Phidal Staff. Radical Rides Super Sticker Book. (p. 1432)
Editions Phidal Staff, ed. Senses. (p. 1551)
Editora Campamocha, Sr. Word: Prosa y Poesia Politica. (p. 1950)
Editorial Barsa Planeta, Inc. Staff. Enciclopedia Hispanica. (p. 524)
—Libro Del Ano 2007 (p. 1006)
—Panorama 2004. (p. 1321)
—Panorama 2004 - Suplemento Especial Multimedia. (p. 1321)

—Panorama 2005. (p. 1321)
—Panorama 2005 - Suplemento Especial Multimedia. (p. 1321)
Editorial Barsa Planeta Staff. Gran Enciclopedia Hispanica 2008. (p. 706)
Editorial Cultural, ed. see De La Mora, Maribel, Sr.
Editorial El Antillano. Tai Juega Pelota. Editorial El Antillano, ed. (p. 1695)
—Tai va de Pesca. Editorial El Antillano, ed. (p. 1695)
Editorial, Equipo. Mis 365 Mejores Adivinanzas. Aubert, Elena G., illus. (p. 1149)
Editorial JUCUM, tr. see Benge, Janet & Benge, Geoff.
Editorial Portavoz Staff. Manual de Exploracion (p. 1088)
Editors of Kingfisher. Who's That? Playing. (p. 1921)
Editors of Klutz, jt. auth. see Chorba, April.
Editors of Time for Kids Magazine, Editors of. Awesome Animal Kingdom (p. 120)
Editors of Time Magazine. TIME Your Body. (p. 1753)
Edles, Philip. Benny the Penny & the Big Secret. (p. 165)
Edleson, Wendy, illus. see Pingry, Patricia A.
Edley, Joe. 10-Minute Bananagrams! (p. 1993)
Edley, Joe, et al. Bananagrams! For Kids. (p. 136)
—Bananagrams! The Official Book. (p. 136)
Edlund, Ben, et al. Tales of the Vampires. Matthews, Brett, illus. (p. 1703)
Edmaier, Bernhard. Earthsong Postcards. (p. 498)
Edmaier, Bernhard & Jung-Hüttl, Angelika. Patterns of the Earth. Edmaier, Bernhard, photos by. (p. 1329)
Edman Lamote, Lisa. Booklet Goes to the Doctor. Wilson, Alisha, illus. (p. 212)
—Day Out for Opus. Wilson, Alisha, illus. (p. 414)
—Don't Judge a Book by Its Cover. Wilson, Alisha, illus. (p. 467)
Edminister, David. Pork Chop. (p. 1386)
Edmiston, Rachel. Buddy Finds A Home. (p. 234)
Edmond, Wally. Cuddles the Chocolate Cow & Friends. Melinda, Sheffler, illus. (p. 389)
Edmonds, Lin. Jaden & the Terrible Terrible Toad. (p. 905)
—Patric the Pony & the Flash of Lightning. (p. 1328)
—Patric the Pony & the Golden Salamander. (p. 1328)
—Patric the Pony & the Race for Freedom. (p. 1328)
—Patric the Pony & the Shining Star. (p. 1328)
—Patric the Pony Finds a Friend. Connors, Mary, illus. (p. 1328)
Edmonds, Mark. Ghost of Scootertrash Past: Memories & Rants of a Longrider. (p. 671)
Edmonds, Walter D. Matchlock Gun. (p. 1104)
Edmonds, Wayne. Mi Gato. (p. 1132)
Edmondson, Brad, illus. see Edmondson, Frank.
Edmondson, Frank. Mr. Frank's Magic School Bus: Rainbow's End Adventure Edmondson, Brad, illus. (p. 1185)
—Mr. Frank's Magic School Bus: Rainbow's End Adventure. Edmondson, Brad, illus. (p. 1185)
Edmondson, J. R. Jim Bowie: Frontier Legend, Alamo Hero. (p. 917)
Edmondson, Jacqueline. Venus & Serena Williams: A Biography (p. 1836)
Edmondson, Nathan. Activity Volume 3. (p. 10)
—Black Widow - The Finely Woven Thread (p. 197)
—Light TP. (p. 1015)
—Where Is Jake Ellis? TP. (p. 1908)
—Who Is Jake Ellis? (p. 1916)
Edmonson, Tim, illus. see Fudge, Benjamin.
Edmonston, Phil & Sawa, Maureen. Car Smarts: Hot Tips for the Car Crazy. Sauve, Gordon, illus. (p. 265)
Edmonton Natural History Club. Nature Walks & Sunday Drives 'Round Edmonton Ross, Gary, illus. (p. 1236)
Edmund, Neo, jt. auth. see Silver Dragon Books Staff.
Edmunds, Kate. Dry Bones. (p. 487)
—Dry Bones W/ (p. 487)
Edmunds, Kirstie, illus. see Haber, Tiffany Strelitz.
Edmunds, Kirstie, illus. see Lakin, Patricia.
Edmunds, Kirstie, illus. see Vernick, Audrey.
Edmundson, Chris, jt. auth. see Long, Greg.
Edom, H. Science Activities (p. 1524)
Edom, H., jt. auth. see Butterfield, M.
Edom, H. & Sims, L. Starting Riding. (p. 1644)
Edom, Helen. Science with Plants. Abel, Simone, illus. (p. 1528)
Edom, Helen, ed. see Heddle, Rebecca.
Edom, Helen & Katrak, N. Starting Ballet - Internet Linked. (p. 1644)
Edom, Helen & Osborne, Mike. Starting Soccer. Young, Norman, illus. (p. 1644)
Edquist, Patrick. Zombie Penguins of the Antarctic. (p. 1988)
Edrington, Greg Q., illus. see Caprio-Scalera, Jill.
Edsall, Steven, illus. see Prince-Stokes, Cathy.
Edsall, Susan. Into the Blue: A Father's Flight & a Daughter's Return. (p. 881)
Edson, Allen. Goose Monkeys Are Real. (p. 702)
Edson, Anharad, illus. see Vaughan, Kathryn Mademann.
Edson, Ann & Insel, Eunice. Reading Maps, Globes, Charts, Graphs. (p. 1446)
Edson, Ann & Schwartz, Allan A. Read & Solve Math Problems (p. 1442)
Eduar, Gilles, illus. see London, Jonathan.
Educa Vision, Inc., Staff. Papiyon. (p. 1323)
Education and More Staff. Tri-Puzzles for Genesis (p. 1785)
Education Development Center, Inc, Inc. Lenses on Learning Series: Facilitator's Package. (p. 991)
Education Pub Staff. Code Cards. (p. 338)
Educational Adventures, creator. Blazin' Hot: Picture Book (Spanish) 9x9. (p. 199)
—Blazin' Hot: Coloring/Activity Book (Spanish) w/ Snipe. (p. 199)
—Cool by the Pool: Picture Book (Spanish) 9x9. (p. 362)
—Cool by the Pool: Coloring/Activity Book (Spanish) w/ Snipe. (p. 362)
—Danger Alert: Picture Book (Spanish) 9x9. (p. 403)
—Danger Alert: Coloring/Activity Book (Spanish) w/ Snipe. (p. 403)
—Free Wheelin' Picture Book (Spanish) w/ Snipe. (p. 634)
—Free Wheelin' Coloring/Activity Book (English) w/ Snipe. (p. 634)
—Poison Patrol: Picture Book (Spanish) 9x9. (p. 1377)
—Poison Patrol: Coloring/Activity Book (Spanish) w/ Snipe. (p. 1377)
—Street Smarts: Coloring/Activity Book (Spanish) w/ Snipe. (p. 1666)
—Street Smarts: Picture Book (Spanish) 9x9. (p. 1667)
Educational Solutions Staff & Gattegno, Caleb. Primary 3. (p. 1399)
Educational Staff. Skills in Reading (p. 1585)
Education.com. Adventures in Writing: A Workbook of Imagination & Writing. (p. 16)
—All Sorts of Science: A Workbook Full of Science Fun Facts. (p. 45)
—All That Math: A Workbook of Basic Operations & Small Numbers. (p. 45)
—Alphabet? Alphabet! A Workbook of Uppercase Letters & Beginning Sounds. (p. 49)
—Celebrate the Seasons: A Workbook of Seasons, Holidays, Weather, & Time. (p. 284)
—Count It: A Workbook of Patterning, Counting, & Addition. (p. 369)
—Creatures & Counting: A Workbook of Counting, Sorting, & Discovery. (p. 380)
—Earth & Sky: A Workbook of Science Facts & Math Practice. (p. 495)
—Fun with Nature: A Workbook of Natural Science Topics. (p. 648)
—History & Me: A Workbook of Historic Figures & Family Research. (p. 783)
—Let's Go Outside! A Workbook of Plants, Animals, & the Outdoors. (p. 997)
—Math Mania: A Workbook of Whole Numbers, Fractions, & Decimals. (p. 1106)
—Number Roundup: A Workbook of Place Values & Number Strategies. (p. 1271)
—Nursery Rhymes & More: A Workbook of Letter Tracing, Letter Recognition, & Rhymes. (p. 1273)
—Tell Me a Story: A Workbook of Story Pages & Activities. (p. 1716)
—Wonderful Words: A Workbook of Spelling, Bit by Bit. (p. 1948)
—Write Away: A Workbook of Creative & Narrative Writing Prompts. (p. 1963)
—Write It Your Way: A Workbook of Reading, Writing, & Literature. (p. 1963)
—Your World of Words: A Workbook of Books & Words. (p. 1981)
Educators for Social Responsibility Staff & Desetta, Al, eds. Courage to Be Yourself: True Stories by Teens about Cliques, Conflicts, & Overcoming Peer Pressure. (p. 372)
Edupress, creator. My Story Book: Primary. (p. 1219)
Edvall, Lilian. Rabbit Who Couldn't Find His Daddy. Gimbergsson, Sara, illus. (p. 1429)
—Rabbit Who Didn't Want to Go to Sleep. Dyssegaard, Elisabeth Kallick, tr. from SWE. (p. 1429)
Edward, Aaron, illus. see Edward, Judy.
Edward Eggleston. Queer Stories for Boys & Girls. (p. 1425)
Edward, Herman. Pink Floyd. (p. 1360)
Edward, J. P. Bobby & Buddy Friends for Life. Hose, Ryan, illus. (p. 206)
—Outsider. (p. 1313)
—Truckin with Rocky (p. 1791)
Edward J Russell Elementary School Students, illus. see Bacon, Joy.
Edward, Judy. Calvin Can - Be Happy. Edward, Aaron, illus. (p. 255)
Edward, Justine. Shine. (p. 1566)
Edward, Linda, illus. see O'Brien, Eileen.
Edward S. Ellis. Cave in the Mountain: A Sequel to in the Pecos Country by Lieut. R. H. J. (p. 282)
Edward Stratemeyer. Rover Boys on Treasure Isle: Or - the Strange Cruise of the Steam Yacht. (p. 1491)
Edwardes, Dan. Parkour. (p. 1325)
Edwardes, Marian, tr. see Grimm, Jacob & Grimm, Wilhelm.
Edwards, Adrianna, jt. auth. see Edwards, Ron.
Edwards, Amanda & Dowell, Brandy. Land of the Tooth Fairy. (p. 973)
Edwards, Amelia. Carousel Colors (p. 271)
—It's Good Enough to Eat! (p. 897)
—Name That Dinosaur. Jirankova-Limbrick, Martina, illus. (p. 1228)
—Playground Friends (p. 1372)
—Treasure Hunt. (p. 1781)
Edwards, Andrew. Powder Hills. (p. 1389)
Edwards, Andrew & Thornton, Fleur. John Bunyan: The Story of How a Hooligan & Soldier Became a Preacher, Prisoner & Famous Writer. (p. 921)
—Wilberforce: an Activity Book: 24 Ready to Use Lesson Plans. (p. 1928)
—William Carey: The Story of a Country Boy & Shoe Mender Whose Big Dreams Took Him to India. (p. 1933)
Edwards, Anfrew & Edwards, Fleur. Footsteps of the past: C S Lewis: The story of one of the world's most famous authors who sold over a hundred million Books. (p. 615)
Edwards, Ann. How to Sunday School Guide Curriculum Workshop for Preschool Lead. (p. 821)
Edwards, Antonio. Script the Strong Ant. (p. 1533)
Edwards, Asasimone. What's a Mimi-Saurus? (p. 1896)
Edwards, Becky. My First Day at Nursery School. Flintoft, Anthony, illus. (p. 1206)
Edwards, Becky & Armitage, David. My Brother Sammy Is Special. Armitage, David, illus. (p. 1199)
Edwards, Bruce H., jt. auth. see Larson, Ron.
Edwards, Carol. Firefly Who Asked Why. (p. 592)
—Jacy Faces Evil: Jacy's Search for Jesus Book III. Frey, Daniel J., illus. (p. 905)
—Jacy Meets Betsy: Jacy's Search for Jesus Book 2. Frey, Daniel, illus. (p. 905)
—Jacy's Search for Jesus Frey, Daniel J., illus. (p. 905)
Edwards, Caroline. Who Took Poppy's Skates? (p. 1917)
Edwards, Cedric, illus. see Wheeler, Tonika Yvonne.
Edwards, Chris. Jovenes Patinadores en Linea. (p. 929)
Edwards, Christine. Charmed Enchanted Book. (p. 294)
Edwards, Cindi. Imagination Rocks. Bruner, Justine, illus. (p. 860)
Edwards, Clint. Show Me Community Helpers: My First Picture Encyclopedia (p. 1570)
Edwards, Cory & Edwards, Todd. Hoodwinked! The True Story of Red Riding Hood. (p. 795)
Edwards, Cory, et al. Hoodwinked! The True Story of Little Red Riding Hood. (p. 795)
Edwards, David. Choice of Poets. (p. 309)
Edwards, David, jt. auth. see Strack, Jay.
Edwards, Deborah. Madie Gets a New Home. (p. 1070)
Edwards, Diane. Norwegian Rosemaling for Young People. (p. 1266)
Edwards, Dianna. It's Not Easy Being Patou - Book One. (p. 898)
—Meet Patou. (p. 1122)
—My Journal & Drawings. (p. 1211)
—When Niki Got Sick (p. 1904)
—Why Can't Everything Just Stay the Same? Book Three. (p. 1923)
Edwards, Dorothy. More Naughty Little Sister Stories. Hughes, Shirley, illus. (p. 1174)
—My Naughty Little Sister. Hughes, Shirley, illus. (p. 1215)
—My Naughty Little Sister's Friends. Hughes, Shirley, illus. (p. 1215)
—When My Naughty Little Sister Was Good. Hughes, Shirley, illus. (p. 1904)
Edwards, Elizabeth Marshall. How Parker James Got the Monsters Out from under His Bed. (p. 811)
—How the Fairies Came to Live at Allie's House. (p. 813)
Edwards, Emyr. O Achos y Mab Bychan: Casgliad o Ddramâu I Blant Ar Gyfer y Nadolig. (p. 1274)
Edwards, Ethan. All-Star Players (p. 45)
—Meet Albert Pujols: Baseball's Power Hitter. (p. 1120)
—Meet Derek Jeter: Baseball's Superstar Shortstop. (p. 1120)
—Meet Derek Jeter: Captain of the New York Yankees. (p. 1120)
—Meet Kevin Garnett: Basketball's Big Ticket. (p. 1121)
—Meet LaDainian Tomlinson: Football's Fastest Running Back. (p. 1121)
—Meet Ladainian Tomlinson: Football's Fastest Running Back. (p. 1121)
—Meet Steve Nash: Basketball's Ultimate Team Player. (p. 1122)
—Meet Tom Brady: Football's Famous Quarterback. (p. 1123)
Edwards, Eve. Lacey Chronicles #2: the Queen's Lady. (p. 970)
—Lacey Chronicles #3: the Rogue's Princess. (p. 970)
Edwards, Felicity. Spider King. (p. 1626)
Edwards, Fleur, jt. auth. see Edwards, Anfrew.
Edwards, Fran. Lord's Prayer. (p. 1053)
Edwards, Frank, illus. see Bianchi, John.
Edwards, Frank B. Bug Bianchi, John, illus. (p. 236)
—Robert Munsch: Portrait of an Extraordinary Canadian (p. 1479)
Edwards, Frank B., jt. auth. see Bianchi, John.
Edwards, Gabrielle I. & Hunter, G. Scott. Biology: The Living Environment. (p. 189)
Edwards, Gail & Saltman, Judith. Picturing Canada: A History of Canadian Children's Illustrated Books & Publishing. (p. 1356)
Edwards, Gareth. Never Ask a Dinosaur to Dinner. Parker-Rees, Guy, illus. (p. 1242)
Edwards, Garth. #01 Shipwrecked! Stasyuk, Max, illus. (p. 1991)
—#02 Trolls of Sugar Loaf Wood. Stasyuk, Max, illus. (p. 1991)
—#03 King of the Castle. Stasyuk, Max, illus. (p. 1991)
—#04 Magic Boots. Stasyuk, Max, illus. (p. 1992)
—#05 Blue Wizard. Stasyuk, Max, illus. (p. 1992)
—Blue Wizard. Stasyuk, Max, illus. (p. 203)
—King of the Castle. Stasyuk, Max, illus. (p. 959)
—Magic Boots. Stasyuk, Max, illus. (p. 1071)
—Trolls of Sugar Loaf Wood. Stasyuk, Max, illus. (p. 1788)
Edwards, Garth & Stasyuk, Maz. Secrets of Mercy Hall. (p. 1545)
Edwards, Garth & Statyuk, Max. Heroes of Mercy Hall. (p. 773)
Edwards, Gary, ed. see Taylor, Tom.
Edwards, Glenna S. Rainbow Bed: A child's perspective on coping with Grief. (p. 1435)
Edwards, Gunvor, illus. see Sebba, Jane.
Edwards, Hazel. Duty Free. (p. 491)
—Fake ID. (p. 565)
—Plato the Platypus Plumber (Part-Time) Petropoulos, John, illus. (p. 1370)
—Stalker. (p. 1639)
Edwards, Hazel & Alexander, Goldie. Talking about Illnesses. (p. 1703)
—Talking about the Dangers of Taking Risks. (p. 1703)
—Talking about What You Eat. (p. 1703)
—Talking about Your Weight. (p. 1703)
Edwards, Hazel & Anketell, Christine. DuckStar & Cyberfarm. Goss, Mini, illus. (p. 488)
—Operatic Duck & Duck on Tour. Goss, Mini, illus. (p. 1300)
Edwards, Hazel & Kennedy, Ryan. F2M: The Boy Within. (p. 559)
Edwards, Hazel, et al. Duckstar / Cyberfarm. (p. 488)
—Operatic Duck / Duck on Tour. (p. 1300)
—River Boy. Rawlins, Donna, illus. (p. 1475)
Edwards, Helen L. Clara's Imagination. Doggett, Al, illus. (p. 326)
Edwards, Hilma Lloyd. Y Mabin-OD-I. (p. 1968)
Edwards, Jaimi. Silly Sock. (p. 1576)
Edwards, Jamee-Marie. But I Am a Cat! (p. 246)
Edwards, Jane Taylor. Ching-Ching the Snoopy Schnauzer. (p. 308)
Edwards, Janet. Earth Flight. (p. 496)
—Earth Girl. (p. 496)
—Earth Star. (p. 497)
Edwards, Jason. Will Allen & the Great Monster Detective: Chronicles of the Monster Detective Agency Volume 1. Friedman, Jeffrey, illus. (p. 1932)
Edwards, Jean E. Adventure Tales: For Kids Who Want to Become Better Readers. (p. 14)
Edwards, Jean Pearce. Little Jean's War. (p. 1029)
Edwards, Jeannell. New House for Jennie. (p. 1245)
Edwards, Jeff, illus. see Oxlade, Chris.
Edwards, Jo. Go Figure. (p. 686)
—Love Undercover. (p. 1060)
Edwards, Josephine Cunnington. Children Can Be Taught. (p. 302)
Edwards, Josh. Pull-Out David & Goliath Embleton Hall, Chris, illus. (p. 1415)
—Pull-Out Jonah & the Big Fish Embleton-Hall, Chris, illus. (p. 1415)
Edwards, Judith. Abolitionists & Slave Resistance: Breaking the Chains of Slavery. (p. 5)
—At the Top of the Mountain: The Adventures of Will Ryan & the Civilian Conservation Corps, 1936-38, Book III. (p. 111)
—History of the American Indians & the Reservation. (p. 784)
—Invasion on the Mountain: The Adventures of Will Ryan & the Civilian Conservation Corps 1933. (p. 883)
—Journey of Lewis & Clark in United States History. (p. 928)
—Plymouth Colony & the Pilgrim Adventure in American History. (p. 1374)
—Trouble on the Mountain: The Adventures of Will Ryan & the Civilian Conservation Corps, 1934-35. (p. 1790)
—Vladamir Lenin & the Russian Revolution. (p. 1846)
Edwards, Judith, jt. auth. see Petrikowski, Nicki Peter.
Edwards, Julie Andrews. Last of the Really Great Whangdoodles. (p. 978)
—Little Bo in London Cole, Henry, illus. (p. 1024)
—Mandy. Westerman, Johanna, illus. (p. 1087)
Edwards, Julie Andrews, jt. auth. see Andrews, Julie.
Edwards, Julie Andrews & Hamilton, Emma Walton. Dragon: Hound of Honor. (p. 476)
Edwards, Karen. Christopher Reeve: A Real-Life Superhero. (p. 317)
—Idaho. (p. 851)
—Idaho: The Gem State. (p. 852)
Edwards, Karl, illus. see Williams, Rozanne Lanczak.
Edwards, Karl Newsom. Fly! (p. 609)
Edwards, Kasey. OMG! That's Not My Baby. (p. 1288)
Edwards, Katie. Myths & Monsters: Secrets Revealed. Mendez, Simon, illus. (p. 1227)
Edwards, Ken, illus. see Bak, Jenny.
Edwards, Ken, illus. see Simon-Kerr, Julia.
Edwards, Kris. Santa Paws on Christmas Island. (p. 1513)
Edwards, Latoya, jt. auth. see Edwards, Tanille.
Edwards, Laurie J. Rihanna. (p. 1472)
Edwards, Laurie J., illus. see Doerr, Bonnie J.
Edwards, Laurie J., et al. U*X*L Encyclopedia of Native American Tribes (p. 1829)
Edwards, LaVell, jt. auth. see Edwards, Pat.
Edwards, Leo. Andy Blake's Comet Coaster. Salg, Bert, illus. (p. 73)
—Jerry Todd & the Rose-Colored Cat. (p. 913)
—Poppy Ott Hits the Trail. Salg, Bert, illus. (p. 1385)
Edwards, Linda, illus. see Amery, Heather, ed.
Edwards, Linda, illus. see Amery, Heather.
Edwards, Linda, illus. see Brocklehurst, Ruth.
Edwards, Linda, illus. see Doherty, Gillian.
Edwards, Linda, illus. see Maskell, Hazel.
Edwards, Linda Carol, et al. Music: A Way of Life for the Young Child. (p. 1193)
Edwards, Linda M. Emma & Topsy's Story: The Art of Loving & Letting Go. Maher, Bob, illus. (p. 519)
Edwards, Linda McMurry. George Washington Carver: The Life of the Great American Agriculturist. (p. 664)
Edwards, Lori. Fire Fawn. (p. 590)
Edwards, M. J. Dontayan. (p. 469)
Edwards, Mark. Gang Book 1 the Saint's Bones. (p. 655)
Edwards, Mark, illus. see Martinez, Kathleen & Edwards, Sue.
Edwards, Mark, et al. Connecting Science Pupil Handbook. (p. 358)
Edwards, Marnie. Magical Mix-Ups: Birthdays & Bridesmaids. Hodgkinson, Leigh, illus. (p. 1075)
—Magical Mix-Ups: Friends & Fashion. Hodgkinson, Leigh, illus. (p. 1075)
—Magical Mix-Ups: Spells & Surprises. Hodgkinson, Leigh, illus. (p. 1075)
—Pets & Parties. Hodgkinson, Leigh, illus. (p. 1348)
Edwards, Mat, illus. see Hunter, Nick.
Edwards, Mat, illus. see McCurry, Kristen.
Edwards, Meinir Wyn. Dic Penderyn. Wade, Gini, illus. (p. 435)
—Maelgwn, King of Gwynedd. Wade, Gini, illus. (p. 1070)
—Red Bandits of Mawddwy. Wade, Gini, illus. (p. 1453)
—Rhys & Meinir. Wade, Gini, illus. (p. 1468)
—Welsh Folk Stories. Tomos, Morgan, illus. (p. 1874)
—Welsh Tales in a Flash: Cantre'r Gwaelod. Wade, Gini, illus. (p. 1875)
Edwards, Melvin Neal. Blakee the Bald Eagle. (p. 198)
—Goodee the Rabbit. (p. 701)
—Sticks & Stones. (p. 1650)
Edwards, Michelle. Alef-Bet. Edwards, Michelle, illus. (p. 35)
—Chicken Man. (p. 300)
—Pa Lia's First Day: A Jackson Friends Book. (p. 1316)
—Pa Lia's First Day. (p. 1316)
—Papa's Latkes. Gustavson, Adam & Schuett, Stacey, illus. (p. 1322)
—Stinky Stern Forever: A Jackson Friends Book. (p. 1651)
—Stinky Stern Forever. (p. 1651)
—Zero Grandparents. (p. 1986)
Edwards, Mike. Key Ideas in Media. (p. 950)
Edwards, Miriam. Start to Quilt. (p. 1643)
Edwards, Myrtice J. Dirty Sally. (p. 446)
Edwards, Nancy. Mom for Mayor. Chesworth, Michael D., illus. (p. 1161)
Edwards, Neil. Spider-Man: Season One. (p. 1626)
—Warriors Three: Dog Day Afternoon. (p. 1859)
Edwards, Neil, illus. see Parker, Jeff, et al.
Edwards, Neil & Pierfederici, Mirco. Dark Avengers: Masters of Evil. (p. 407)
Edwards, Nicholas. Adventures of Santa Paws. (p. 22)
—Dog Whisperer: Storm Warning. (p. 462)
—Dog Whisperer: the Ghost. (p. 462)

E

Edwards, Nicholas & White, Ellen Emerson. Rescue. (p. 1462)
Edwards, Nick, illus. see Kloepfer, John.
Edwards, Nicola. Bullying. (p. 241)
—Cereals. (p. 287)
—Divorce. (p. 455)
—Domestic Violence. (p. 465)
—Eating Disorders. (p. 501)
—Flowers. (p. 608)
—Friend. (p. 637)
—Fruits. (p. 645)
—Leaves. (p. 986)
—My Friend Has Allergies. (p. 1209)
—My Friend Has Dyslexia. (p. 1209)
—My Friend Has Dyspraxia. (p. 1209)
—My Friend Is Blind. (p. 1209)
—Parent. (p. 1324)
—Pet. (p. 1345)
—Racism. (p. 1432)
—Sibling. (p. 1572)
—Trees. (p. 1784)
—Vegetables. (p. 1834)
—Voice. (p. 1847)
Edwards, Nicola, ed. see Carter, Andrew.
Edwards, Pamela Duncan. B Is for Big Ben: An England Alphabet. Rose, Melanie, illus. (p. 122)
—Bus Ride That Changed History: The Story of Rosa Parks. Shanahan, Danny, illus. (p. 244)
—Clara Caterpillar. (p. 326)
—Clara Caterpillar. Cole, Henry, illus. (p. 326)
—Dinosaur Sleepover. Allwright, Deborah, illus. (p. 443)
—Dinosaur Starts School Allwright, Deborah, illus. (p. 443)
—Gigi & Lulu's Gigantic Fight. Cole, Henry, tr. (p. 676)
—Grumpy Morning. (p. 727)
—Jack & Jill's Treehouse. Cole, Henry & Bond, Felicia, illus. (p. 902)
—Leprechaun's Gold. Cole, Henry, illus. (p. 993)
—Livingstone Mouse II. (p. 1042)
—McGillycuddy Could! (p. 1114)
—McGillycuddy Could! Porter, Sue, illus. (p. 1114)
—Mixed-up Rooster. Lloyd, Megan, illus. (p. 1156)
—O Is for Old Dominion: A Virginia Alphabet. Howell, Troy, illus. (p. 1274)
—Princess Pigtoria & the Pea. Cole, Henry, illus. (p. 1405)
—Roar! A Noisy Counting Book. Cole, Henry, illus. (p. 1478)
—Teddy Bear Hide-and-Seek. Birkett, Georgie, illus. (p. 1712)
—Wacky Wedding: A Book of Alphabet Antics. (p. 1852)
—Why the Stomach Growls. Taylor, Bridget Starr, illus. (p. 1926)
—Worrywarts. Cole, Henry, illus. (p. 1961)
—Wrong Way Rooster. (p. 1965)
Edwards, Pat & Edwards, LaVell. Hello, Cosmo! De Angel, Miguel, illus. (p. 763)
Edwards, Paul, illus. see Haworth, Margaret.
Edwards, Paul M. Korean War Almanac. (p. 967)
Edwards, R. Katie King's Journal. (p. 945)
—Modwl Chwech. (p. 1160)
Edwards, R. G. Eafin Lokdore & the Altar of the Sun Book II. (p. 492)
—Eafin Lokdore & the Magician's Lost Medallion: Book I of the Eafin Lokdore Trilogy. (p. 492)
Edwards, Rebecca, illus. see Richardson, Duncan.
Edwards, Richard. Forest Child. Malone, Peter, illus. (p. 618)
Edwards, Roberta. Barack Obama: United States President. Call, Ken, illus. (p. 137)
—Barack Obama: Presidente de Estados Unidos. Call, Ken, illus. (p. 137)
—Best Friends: The True Story of Owen & Mzee. Schwartz, Carol, illus. (p. 169)
—Emperor Penguins. Schwartz, Carol, illus. (p. 520)
—Flight of the Butterflies. Kayganich, Bob, illus. (p. 604)
—Hail to the Chiefs (p. 735)
—Michelle Obama: Mom-in-Chief. Call, Ken, illus. (p. 1135)
—Michelle Obama: Primera Dama y Primera Mama. Call, Ken, illus. (p. 1135)
—Polar Bears: In Danger. Johnson, Pamela, illus. (p. 1379)
—Who Is Barack Obama? Harrison, Nancy & O'Brien, John, illus. (p. 1915)
—Who Is Jane Goodall? (p. 1916)
—Who Is Jane Goodall? Marchesi, Stephen et al, illus. (p. 1916)
—Who Was George Washington? (p. 1918)
—Who Was George Washington? Kelley, True & Harrison, Nancy, illus. (p. 1918)
—Who Was Leonardo da Vinci? Kelley, True, illus. (p. 1918)
—Who Was Neil Armstrong? Harrison, Nancy & Marchesi, Stephen, illus. (p. 1919)
—Who Was Paul Revere? Harrison, Nancy & O'Brien, John, illus. (p. 1919)
—¿Quién Fue el Rey Tut? (Who Was King Tut?) Kelley, True, illus. (p. 1427)
Edwards, Roberta, jt. auth. see Schwartz, Carol.
Edwards, Ron & Dickie, Lisa. Diamonds & Gemstones. (p. 434)
Edwards, Ron & Edwards, Adrianna. Coal. (p. 336)
Edwards, Ron & Gladstone, James. Gold. (p. 693)
Edwards, Ron, et al. Oil & Gas. (p. 1282)
Edwards, Roy. Mathemateg Cynradd Caergrawnt (p. 1107)
—Modwl Chwech. (p. 1160)
—Modwl Pump. (p. 1160)
—School Mathematics Project 11-16 (p. 1523)
Edwards, Roy, et al. Mathemateg Cynradd Caergrawnt. (p. 1107)
Edwards, S. Neil. My Dog, Digger. (p. 1202)
Edwards, Sal A. Forever Family: Living in the Big House. (p. 619)
Edwards, Sherri L. Sally the Platypus. (p. 1505)
Edwards, Sonia. Noson y Llygaid Llachar. (p. 1266)
Edwards, Stuart. Dragon Jack. (p. 477)
Edwards, Sue, jt. auth. see Martinez, Kathleen.
Edwards, Sue Bradford. Ancient Maya. (p. 69)
Edwards, Susan Denise. Computer Science Student Activity Book. (p. 355)
Edwards, Tanille. Jordan & Justine's Weekend Adventures Tm: Go Go Green. (p. 925)
Edwards, Tanille & Edwards, Latoya. Jordan & Justine's Weekend Adventures: Plants. Pts. 1-2 (p. 925)
—Jordan & Justine's Weekend Adventures Tm: Plantas Partes 1 y 2 Spanish Language Version. (p. 925)
Edwards, Todd, jt. auth. see Edwards, Cory.
Edwards, Tommy Lee, illus. see Sudduth, Brent.
Edwards, W M. Booger Boogie. (p. 210)
—Island Potty Party. (p. 892)
Edwards, W M, illus. see Friedlander, Tim.
Edwards, W M, illus. see Thiel, Annie.
Edwards, Wallace. Alphabeasts. Edwards, Wallace, illus. (p. 48)
—Cat's Pajamas. Edwards, Wallace, illus. (p. 281)
—Extinct Files: My Science Project. Edwards, Wallace, illus. (p. 555)
—Monkey Business. Edwards, Wallace, illus. (p. 1165)
—Painted Circus: P. T. Vermin Presents a Mesmerizing Menagerie of Trickery & Illusion Guaranteed to Beguile & Bamboozle the Beholder. Edwards, Wallace, illus. (p. 1318)
—Uncle Wally's Old Brown Shoe (p. 1812)
—Unnatural Selections (p. 1822)
Edwards, Wallace, illus. see Suzuki, David & Vanderlinden, Kathy.
Edwards, Wallace, jt. auth. see Cox, Kenyon.
Edwards, Wayne. Ali & the Magic Ball. Golden, Rayna, illus. (p. 39)
Edwards, William. Joey Bear's First Day of School. (p. 920)
Edwards, William M., illus. see Thiel, Annie & Fanning, Tena.
Edwards, William M., illus. see Thiel, Annie.
Edwards, Wysteria. Bethany Bubbles Makes a Mistake. Abbott, Jason, illus. (p. 171)
Edwards-Hammond, Arlene. Keys, Please? Please Keys? (p. 950)
Edwardson, Debby Dahl. My Name Is Not Easy (p. 1215)
—Whale Snow. Patterson, Annie, illus. (p. 1877)
Edwardson, Treva Jean. Froggy Fun. (p. 641)
Edwards-Tomdio, Stacy. Alexia Goes to School! Oladimeji, Solomon, illus. (p. 37)
Edwards-Wright, Tracy. Feasting on Fruit God's Way: The Fruit of the Spirit. (p. 579)
—Meet Angel & All Her Friends. Shekailo, Pamela, illus. (p. 1120)
Edwin, Kimberly, illus. see Ford, Carole S.
Ee, Susan. Angelfall (p. 74)
—Angelfall. (p. 74)
—World After (p. 1953)
EEBOO Staff, creator. Circus Animals' Adventures Write Me a Story - #WSADV. (p. 322)
Eeckhout, Emmanuelle. There's No Such Thing As Ghosts! Eeckhout, Emmanuelle, illus. (p. 1731)
Eedle, Arthur. Full Cycle. (p. 646)
Efaw, Amy. After. (p. 28)
—Battle Dress. (p. 145)
Effe Team, jt. auth. see Stewart, Kathy.
Effie Mae Shearin. Cleopatra: Glory to Her Race. (p. 331)
Effinger, George Alec. Exile Kiss. (p. 548)
Efflandt, Lisa M. My Grandma Is with God Today. (p. 1210)
Effle, Sandy. New Comings of What's Next. (p. 1244)
Effler, Jim, illus. see Nagda, Ann Whitehead.
Efimova, Tatiana, ed. see AZ Books Staff.
Egan, Caroline, illus. see RH Disney Staff & Depken, Kristen L.
Egan, Caroline LaVelle, illus. see Glass, Calliope & Disney Book Group Staff.
Egan, Caroline LaVelle, illus. see Reader's Digest Staff.
Egan, Catherine. Bone, Fog, Ash & Star (p. 208)
—Shade & Sorceress: The Last Days of Tian Di Bk. 1 (p. 1556)
—Unmaking (p. 1821)
Egan, Cecilia. Hey Diddle Diddle: The Story. McAllan, Marina, illus. (p. 774)
—Humpty Dumpty: The Story. McAllan, Marina, illus. (p. 827)
—Little Miss Muffet: The Story. McAllan, Marina, illus. (p. 1032)
Egan, Danielle & Egan, R. Danielle. Dancing for Dollars & Paying for Love: The Relationships Between Exotic Dancers & Their Regulars. (p. 403)
Egan, Erin. Hottest Race Cars. (p. 802)
—Smokin' Open-Wheel Race Cars. (p. 1594)
Egan, Jennifer, jt. auth. see Jeannine.
Egan, Jill. Hillary Rodham Clinton. (p. 779)
—Maya Angelou: A Creative & Courageous Voice. (p. 1112)
Egan, Jill & Stewart, Rhea A. How Video Game Designers Use Math. (p. 823)
Egan, Joseph, jt. auth. see Fendler, Donn.
Egan, Kate. Divergent Official Illustrated Movie Companion. (p. 454)
—Evil Comes in Pairs. Merkel, Joe F., illus. (p. 546)
—Hunger Games - Catching Fire. (p. 828)
—Kate & Nate Are Running Late! Yaccarino, Dan, illus. (p. 944)
Egan, Kate, adapted by. World's Apart. (p. 1960)
Egan, Kate & Cole, Joanna. Magic School Bus Fights Germs. Bracken, Carolyn, illus. (p. 1073)
Egan, Kate & Lane, Mike. Disappearing Magician. Wight, Eric, illus. (p. 446)
—Great Escape. Wight, Eric, illus. (p. 715)
—Incredible Twisting Arm Wight, Eric, illus. (p. 869)
—Vanishing Coin. Wight, Eric, illus. (p. 1833)
Egan, Kate, et al. World of the Hunger Games. (p. 1957)
Egan, R. Danielle, jt. auth. see Egan, Danielle.
Egan, Tim. Dodsworth in London. Egan, Tim, illus. (p. 460)
—Dodsworth in New York. (p. 460)
—Dodsworth in Paris. Egan, Tim, illus. (p. 460)
—Dodsworth in Tokyo. (p. 460)
—Dodsworth in Tokyo. Egan, Tim, illus. (p. 460)
—Metropolitan Cow. (p. 1130)
Egan, Timothy, jt. auth. see Ingold, Jeanette.
Egan, Tracie. Cynthia Ann Parker: Comanche Captive. (p. 397)
—Cynthia Ann Parker: Comanche Captive / Cautiva de los Comanches. (p. 397)
—Cynthia Ann Parker: Cautiva de los Comanches. Gonzalez, Tomas, tr. (p. 397)
—Cynthia Ann Parker: Cautiva de los comanches (Cynthia Ann Parker: Comanche Captive) (p. 397)
—Field Hockey. (p. 584)
—Francisca Alavez, the Angel of Goliad. (p. 628)
—Francisca Alvarez: El angel de Goliad. (p. 628)
—Francisca Alvarez: The Angel of Goliad. (p. 628)
—Francisca Alvarez: The Angel of Goliad / el ángel de Goliad. (p. 628)
—Francisca Alvarez: El ángel de Goliad (Francisca Alvarez: the Angel of Goliad) (p. 628)
—George Washington: Padre de la Patria. (p. 664)
—George Washington: The Father of the American Nation. (p. 664)
—George Washington: Padre de la patria (George Washington: Father of the American Nation) (p. 664)
—How a Bill Becomes a Law. (p. 804)
—John Paul Jones: American Naval Hero. (p. 922)
—John Paul Jones: Heroe de la Marina Estadounidense. (p. 922)
—John Paul Jones: American Naval Hero / Héroe de la marina Estadounidense. (p. 922)
—John Paul Jones: Héroe de la marina estadounidense (John Paul Jones: American Naval Hero) (p. 922)
—John Paul Jones. (p. 922)
—President & the Executive Branch. (p. 1396)
—Skin Cancer: Current & Emerging Trends in Detection & Treatment. (p. 1585)
—Water Polo: Rules, Tips, Strategy, & Safety. (p. 1863)
—Water Polo. (p. 1863)
—Weapons of Mass Destruction & North Korea. (p. 1869)
Egan, Tracie, jt. auth. see Zahensky, Kenneth.
Egan, Vicky, jt. auth. see Williams, Brian.
Egar, Joann. Caillou: Sometimes Moms Get Angry. Brignaud, Pierre, illus. (p. 251)
Egart, Patricia. Alley Learns Something New. (p. 47)
Egbert, Charles. Story of Princess Olivia: Wherein an Optimistic Slip of a Girl Brings Sunshine into the Lives of Her Royal Parents, the Whiny King & the ... & His Magical Minion, the Mischi. (p. 1659)
Egbert, Corey, illus. see Chabot, Shersta.
Egbert, Corey, illus. see Hall, Annalisa.
Egbert, Corey, illus. see Parker, Lehua.
Egbert, Elaine. Nature in a Nutshell. (p. 1236)
Egea, Marcelo. Sobe, the Cat That Thinks He's a Dog. (p. 1603)
Egelberg, Arlene & Clark, Raymond C. How & Why Folktales: From Around the World. Braun, Chuck, illus. (p. 804)
Egendorf, Laura K. Censorship. (p. 286)
—Free Speech. (p. 634)
—Girls & Sports. (p. 679)
—Immigration. (p. 861)
—Islam in America. (p. 891)
—Organ Donation. (p. 1303)
—Performance Enhancing Drugs. (p. 1343)
—Sexually Transmitted Diseases. (p. 1556)
—Should the U. S. Do Business with China? (p. 1570)
—Steroids. (p. 1649)
Egendorf, Laura K., jt. auth. see Haugen, David M.
Egendorf, Laura K. & Des Chenes, Elizabeth, eds. Smoking. (p. 1594)
Egendorf, Laura K., ed. Advertising. (p. 25)
Eger, Caroline Ruth, illus. see Wadsworth, Wallace.
Egermeier, Elsie. Egermeier's ABC Bible Storybook: Favorite Stories Adapted for Young Children. Rhodes, Karen, ed. (p. 506)
Egermeier, Elsie E. Egermeier's ABC Bible Storybook: Favorite Stories Adapted for Young Children. Rhodes, Karen, ed. (p. 506)
Eggen, Paul D., jt. auth. see Main, June.
Eggen, Paul D. & Main, June. Developing Critical Thinking through Science: Hands-on Physical Science. Bk. 2 (p. 431)
Egger, Virginie, illus. see Austen, Catherine.
Eggerich, Emerso. Amor y Respeto. (p. 65)
Eggerling, Kristin J. Breath of Wilderness: The Life of Sigurd Olson. (p. 225)
Eggers, James, illus. see Patten, Lewis B.
Eggers, Jeanette S. Grandmas Don't Rollerskate. (p. 708)
—Grandmas Don't Tilt-A-Whirl(r). (p. 708)
Eggers-Pierola, Costanza. Connections & Commitments: Reflecting Latino Values in Early Childhood Programs. (p. 358)
Eggins, Heather & MacDonald, Ranald. Scholarship of Academic Development. (p. 1521)
Egginton, Jane. Pick Your Brains about the USA. Williams, Caspar, illus. (p. 1354)
Eggleston, Edward. Hoosier Schoolboy. (p. 796)
—Mr. Blake's Walking Stick. (p. 1184)
—Schoolmaster's Stories for Boys & Girls. (p. 1524)
—Stories of Great Americans for Little Americans. (p. 1655)
—Stories of Great Americans for Little Americans (Yesterday's Classics) (p. 1655)
Eggleston, George Cary. Big Brother: A Story of Indian War. (p. 179)
Eggleston, Jerry. Musings & Mirth of a Muddled Mind. (p. 1194)
Eggleston, Margaret. Fireside Stories for Girls in Their Teen. (p. 592)
Eggleston, Rhonda. Ladies of the Ironhorse: The Voices of Those Who Wait at Home. (p. 970)
Eggleton. Sail Blu Nf Chimpanzees. (p. 1503)
—Sail Blu Nf Fantastic Frogs. (p. 1503)
Eggleton, Bob, illus. see de Camp, L. Sprague.
Eggleton, Bob, illus. see Plumridge, Marianne.
Eggleton, Grace. Children's Stories My Mother Wrote. (p. 304)
Eggleton, Hazel. Ghost of Widdecot Manor. (p. 671)
Eggleton, Jill. Amazing Machine: 6 Small Books. Kieley, Rob, illus. (p. 55)
—Amazing Machine. Kieley, Rob, illus. (p. 55)
—Bertha & the Beeman: 3-in-1 Package. (p. 168)
—Bertha & the Beeman. (p. 168)
—Big Bill's Bed. Matijasevich, Astrid, illus. (p. 178)
—Big Red Comes to Stay. Cammell, Sandra, illus. (p. 183)
—Billy Mcbrown. Pye, Trevor, illus. (p. 187)
—Bird Is a Bird. Chambers, Brent, illus. (p. 190)
—Brave Mouse Taylor, Clive, illus. (p. 223)
—Bubble Trouble: 6 Small Books. Webb, Philip, illus. (p. 233)
—Bubble Trouble: Big Book Only. Webb, Philip, illus. (p. 233)
—Bubble Trouble: 3-in-1 Package. Webb, Philip, illus. (p. 233)
—Bully Cat & Fat Cat. (p. 241)
—Clown's Pants. Smith, Craig, illus. (p. 335)
—Clown's Party. Smith, Craig, illus. (p. 335)
—Creatures of the Extreme. (p. 380)
—Crumpet, the Cat: Big Book Only. Hawley, Kelvin, illus. (p. 386)
—Crumpet, the Cat: 3-in-1 Package. Hawley, Kelvin, illus. (p. 386)
—Dad & the Bike Race. McGrath, Raymond, illus. (p. 398)
—Davy D's Dog: 6 Small Books. Gibson, Dave, illus. (p. 411)
—Davy D's Dog: Big Book Only. Gibson, Dave, illus. (p. 411)
—Davy D's Dog: 3-in-1 Package. Gibson, Dave, illus. (p. 411)
—Deep Ocean. (p. 423)
—Dream Catcher. (p. 483)
—Elephant Is Stuck! 6 Small Books. (p. 511)
—Elephant Is Stuck! Big Book Only. (p. 511)
—Elephant Is Stuck! 3-in-1 Package. (p. 511)
—Eye of the Law. (p. 557)
—Fact or Fiction? (p. 561)
—Fearless Phil: 6 Small Books. McGrath, Raymond, illus. (p. 579)
—Fearless Phil: Big Book Only. McGrath, Raymond, illus. (p. 579)
—Fearless Phil: 3-in-1 Package. McGrath, Raymond, illus. (p. 579)
—Fire. Pye, Trevor, illus. (p. 590)
—Flea & Big Bill. Matijasevich, Astrid, illus. (p. 603)
—Flea Goes Out! Matijasevich, Astrid, illus. (p. 603)
—Giant's Ice Cream: Big Book Only. Hawley, Kelvin, illus. (p. 674)
—Giant's Ice Cream: 3-in-1 Package. Hawley, Kelvin, illus. (p. 674)
—Granny Groggin: Big Book Only. (p. 710)
—Granny Groggin: 3-in-1 Package. (p. 710)
—Ice-Cream Machine. Pye, Trevor, illus. (p. 850)
—Idea Seed. (p. 852)
—Invasive Species. (p. 883)
—Living to Tell the Tale. (p. 1042)
—Mickey Maloney's Missing Bag. Pye, Trevor, illus. (p. 1136)
—Mrs. Mcfee. Webb, Philip, illus. (p. 1187)
—Mystery of Missing Big Wig. (p. 1224)
—Nomads. (p. 1263)
—Rabbit & Rooster's Ride: 6 Small Books. Taylor, Clive, illus. (p. 1429)
—Rabbit & Rooster's Ride: Big Book Only. Taylor, Clive, illus. (p. 1429)
—Rabbit & Rooster's Ride: 3-in-1 Package. Taylor, Clive, illus. (p. 1429)
—Right to Survive. (p. 1472)
—Robber Fox: 3-in-1 Package. (p. 1478)
—Sailor Sam in Trouble. Storey, Jim, illus. (p. 1503)
—Sky Bridge. (p. 1586)
—Tony's Dad. Hawley, Kelvin, illus. (p. 1766)
—Treasures. (p. 1782)
—Turtle's Trouble. Cammell, Sandra, illus. (p. 1799)
—Up to the Challenge. (p. 1824)
—Where Are You, Mouse? McGrath, Raymond, illus. (p. 1906)
—Wonder of the Wind. (p. 1947)
Eghdam, Tara. My Little Mici. (p. 1212)
Egielski, Richard. Itsy Bitsy Spider. Egielski, Richard, illus. (p. 900)
—Saint Francis & the Wolf. Egielski, Richard, illus. (p. 1503)
—Sleepless Little Vampire. (p. 1589)
—Sleepless Little Vampire. Egielski, Richard, illus. (p. 1589)
—Slim & Jim. (p. 1590)
—Slim & Jim. Egielski, Richard, illus. (p. 1590)
Egielski, Richard, illus. see Broach, Elise.
Egielski, Richard, illus. see Brown, Margaret Wise & Brown.
Egielski, Richard, illus. see Brown, Margaret Wise.
Egielski, Richard, illus. see LaRochelle, David.
Egielski, Richard, illus. see Winter, Jonah.
Egielski, Richard, illus. see Yorinks, Arthur.
Egitim, Hasan, illus. see Ergün, Erol.
Eglin, Lorna. Boy of Two Worlds. (p. 218)
—Girl of Two Worlds. (p. 678)
Eglitis, Anna, jt. auth. see Brim, Warren.
Eglseder, Bonnie Bryan. Birthday Puzzle. (p. 193)
Egmont. Thunderbirds (p. 1746)
Egmont Books Staff, jt. auth. see Hergé.
Egmont Staff, jt. auth. see Thomas The Tank Engine.
Egmont UK. Christmas Doodle & Colouring Book. (p. 313)
Egmont UK, ed. see Stevenson, R. L.
Egmont UK, Egmont. Peekaboo! Farm. (p. 1335)
—Peekaboo! Jungle. (p. 1335)
Egmont UK, Egmont & Big Blue Bubble Inc. Staff. My Singing Monsters - Design Your Own Monster. (p. 1218)
Egmont Uk Limited Staff. Toy Story 3 My First Little Library. (p. 1774)
Egmont UK Staff. My Singing Monsters Downloaded. (p. 1218)
Egmont UK Staff, ed. see Coolidge, Susan, et al.
Egmont UK Staff, jt. auth. see Big Blue Bubble Inc., Big Blue.
Eguiguren, A. R., illus. see Jones, Thomas Rumsey.
Eguiguren, India J., illus. see Jones, Thomas Rumsey.
Ehlers, Sabine. Hawaiian Stories for Boys & Girls. (p. 755)
Ehlert, Lois. Boo to You! Ehlert, Lois, illus. (p. 210)
—Eating the Alphabet: Fruits & Vegetables from A to Z. (p. 501)
—Eating the Alphabet. (p. 501)
—Growing Vegetable Soup. (p. 727)
—Hands: Growing up to Be an Artist. (p. 741)
—In My World. (p. 864)
—Lazo a la Luna. Prince, Amy, tr. (p. 981)
—Leaf Man. (p. 982)
—Lots of Spots. Ehlert, Lois, illus. (p. 1057)
—Moon Rope: A Peruvian Folktale. (p. 1172)
—Nuts to You! (p. 1274)
—Oodles of Animals. (p. 1298)
—Pie in the Sky. (p. 1356)
—Planting a Rainbow: Lap-Sized Board Book. (p. 1369)

—Planting a Rainbow. Ehlert, Lois, illus. (p. 1369)
—RRRalph. Ehlert, Lois, illus. (p. 1493)
—Scraps Book: Notes from a Colorful Life. Ehlert, Lois, illus. (p. 1532)
—Sembrar Sopa de Verduras. (p. 1550)
—Snowballs. (p. 1600)
—Wag a Tail. (p. 1852)
Ehlert, Lois, illus. see Archambault, John & Martin, Bill, Jr.
Ehlert, Lois, illus. see Fyleman, Rose.
Ehlert, Lois, illus. see Martin, Bill, Jr.
Ehlert, Lois, illus. see Martin, Bill, Jr. & Archambault, John.
Ehlert, Lois, illus. see Martin, Bill, Jr. & Sampson, Michael.
Ehlert, Lois, illus. see Martin, Bill, Jr., et al.
Ehlin, Gina. Emma & Friends: Emma's Airport Adventure. Ayzenberg, Nina, illus. (p. 519)
—Emma & Friends; Emma Rescues Cali. Ayzenberg, Nina, illus. (p. 519)
—Emma's Airport Adventure. Ayesenberg, Nina, illus. (p. 520)
Ehlke, Paul. Clouds: Science Information in American Sign Language: A Paws Science Adventure. (p. 335)
Ehren, Michael. They Sleep Too: An A-Zzz Animal Sleeping Patterns. (p. 1732)
Ehren, Michael J. They Sleep Too: A to Zzzz Sleeping Patterns of Animals (and More) (p. 1732)
Ehrenberg, Pamela. Ethan, Suspended. (p. 539)
—Tillmon County Fire. (p. 1750)
Ehrenclou, Martine. Critical Conditions: The Essential Guide to Get Your Loved One Out Alive. (p. 383)
Ehrenfreund, Pascale, et al, eds. Astrobiology: Future Perspectives. (p. 109)
Ehrenhaft, Daniel. 10 Things to Do Before I Die. (p. 1994)
—After Life. (p. 28)
—Drawing a Blank: Or How I Tried to Solve a Mystery, End a Feud, & Land the Girl of My Dreams. Ristow, Trevor, illus. (p. 481)
—Friend Is Not a Verb. (p. 637)
—Last Dog on Earth. (p. 977)
Ehrenhaft, Daniel, ed. see Melissa, De La Cruz, et al.
Ehrenhaft, Daniel, jt. auth. see Levithan, David.
Ehrenreich, Barbara. Bait & Switch: The (Futile) Pursuit of the American Dream. (p. 133)
Ehrhardt, Karen. This Jazz Man. Roth, R G, illus. (p. 1737)
—This Jazz Man. Roth, R. G., illus. (p. 1737)
Ehrich, Meghen, jt. auth. see Kinney, Monica.
Ehrler, Brenda. Aprender a Ser Tu Mismo; Comienza en Tu Interior: Recuperacion y Cura Para los Seres Queridos de Personas Adictas a Sustancias. Casas, Marisol Perez, tr. from SPA. (p. 93)
Ehrlich, Amy. Girl Who Wanted to Dance. Walsh, Rebecca, illus. (p. 679)
—Joyride. (p. 930)
—Rachel: The Story of Rachel Carson. Minor, Wendell, illus. (p. 1431)
—Wild Swans. Jeffers, Susan, illus. (p. 1930)
—With a Mighty Hand: The Story in the Torah. Nevins, Daniel, illus. (p. 1942)
Ehrlich, Amy, jt. auth. see Jeffers, Susan.
Ehrlich, Amy, ed. When I Was Your Age: Original Stories about Growing Up. Vol. 2 (p. 1903)
—When I Was Your Age: Original Stories about Growing Up. Vols. I & II (p. 1903)
Ehrlich, Carl S. Judaism. (p. 930)
Ehrlich, Esther. Nest. (p. 1242)
Ehrlich, Fred, jt. auth. see Ziefert, Harriet.
Ehrlich, Gretel. Early Morning at the Bird Cafe. (p. 494)
Ehrlich, Paul. Living with Allergies. (p. 1042)
Ehrlich, Paul M. Living with Allergies. (p. 1042)
Ehrlich, Robert, et al. Physics Matters: An Introduction to Conceptual Physics. (p. 1353)
Ehrlichman, Wes, jt. auth. see BradyGames Staff.
Ehrman, M. K. Living with Diabetes. (p. 1042)
Ehrman, Mark. Just Chill: Navigating Social Norms & Expectations. (p. 938)
Ehrmann, Johanna. Life of a Colonial Wigmaker. (p. 1011)
Ehrmann, Max. Desiderata: Words to Live By. Tauss, Marc, illus. (p. 429)
Ehrmantraut, Brenda. Hope Weavers. Magnuson, Diana, illus. (p. 797)
—I Want One Too! Short, Robbie, illus. (p. 847)
—Night Catch. Wehrman, Vicki, illus. (p. 1253)
Eichelberger, Jennifer, illus. see McClain, Jennie.
Eichenberg, Fritz, illus. see White, T. H.
Eicher, Jerry S. Dream for Hannah. (p. 483)
Eichler, Darlene. Where's the Kitty. Wyles, Betty, illus. (p. 1911)
Eichler, Ken. Swift Eagle's Dangerous Journey (p. 1690)
—Swift Eagle's Odyssey with the Buffalo. (p. 1690)
—Swift Eagle's Vision Quest (p. 1690)
—Swift Eagle's Wagon Train Adventure (p. 1690)
Eichlin, Lisa. Bravest Boy I Ever Knew. (p. 223)
Eick, Jean. Concrete Mixers. (p. 355)
—Easter Crafts. Petelinsek, Kathleen, illus. (p. 499)
Eick, Jean, jt. auth. see Berendes, Mary.
Eickhoff, Kim, et al. Bamboo Zoo: Meet Lester Panda & his Friends! (p. 135)
Eid, Alain. 1000 Photos of Minerals & Fossils. Viard, Michel, illus. (p. 2001)
Eid, Diab. Maido's Story: The Secret of the Engraved Spear. (p. 1077)
Eid, Jean-Paul, illus. see Chartrand, Lili.
Eid, Jean-Paul, illus. see Wishinsky, Frieda.
Eida, de la Vega, jt. auth. see Peters, Elisa.
Eide, Brock, jt. auth. see Eide, Fernette.
Eide, Brock & Eide, Fernette. Mislabeled Child: Looking Beyond Behavior to Find the True Sources - And Solutions - For Children's Learning Challenges. (p. 1150)
Eide, Fernette, jt. auth. see Eide, Brock.
Eide, Fernette & Eide, Brock. Mislabeled Child: How Understanding Your Child's Unique Learning Style Can Open the Door to Success. (p. 1150)
Eide, Scott M. Chicago Bob & the Case of the Missing Elephant. (p. 299)
Eidelberg, Martin & Cass, Claire. Edmond Lachenal & His Legacy. Ben-Yosef, Yoni, photos by. (p. 504)
Eiden, T. J. Little Guine. (p. 1028)
Eidenbuller, Bernd & Reisinger, Manfred. Beaded Lizards & Gila Monsters: Captive Care & Husbandry. (p. 149)
Eifrig, Kate. I'll Be a Pirate: World of Discovery II. Graves, Dennis, illus. (p. 856)
—Scary Monster. Graves, Dennis, illus. (p. 1520)
Eikum, John. 4th Dimension & Beyond: Imagining Worlds with 0, 1, 2, 3, 4 Dimensions & More. (p. 1992)
Eiland, Marie, jt. auth. see Triplett, Donald.
Eileen, Angela, jt. auth. see Eileen, Pamela.
Eileen, Pamela & Eileen, Angela. No Wrong Turns. (p. 1261)
Eiler, John H., jt. auth. see Miller, Debbie S.
Eilers, Roxanne. Chocolate Brown Coat (p. 309)
Eilrich, Dinah Kay. Teeny Tessie's Big Baking Adventure. (p. 1715)
Eimann, Céline, illus. see Morgan, Anne.
Eimann, Céline, tr. see Morgan, Anne.
Eimer, Patricia & Buchanan, Andria. Evanescent: Freedom Only Waits So Long... (p. 541)
—Everlast. (p. 542)
—Infinity. (p. 873)
Einarson, Earl. Moccasins. Einarson, Earl, illus. (p. 1157)
Einfeld, Aaron, illus. see Einfeld, C.
Einfeld, C. Neverdark. Einfeld, Aaron, illus. (p. 1243)
Einfeld, Jann. Afghanistan. (p. 26)
—Living in Imperial China. (p. 1041)
Einfeld, Jann, ed. see Burns, Jann.
Einfeld, Jann, ed. Afghanistan. (p. 26)
—Indonesia. (p. 872)
—Is Islam a Religion of War or Peace? (p. 889)
Einhard, et al. Two Lives of Charlemagne. Ganz, David, ed. (p. 1804)
Einhorn, Edward. Fractions in Disguise: A Math Adventure. Clark, David, illus. (p. 627)
—Living House of Oz. Shanower, Eric, illus. (p. 1041)
—Very Improbable Story. Gustavson, Adam, illus. (p. 1838)
Einhorn, Kama. 240 Vocabulary Words Kids Need to Know, Grade 1: 24 Ready-to-Reproduce Packets That Make Vocabulary Building Fun & Effective. (p. 2001)
—All about Me: 40 Fun Reproducible Activities That Guide Children to Share about Themselves in Pictures. (p. 42)
—Explosive Story of Fireworks! Guidera, Daniel, illus. (p. 554)
—Letter of the Week Flip Chart: Write-On/Wipe-Off Activity Pages That Introduce Each Letter from A to Z. (p. 1002)
—Number of the Week Flip Chart: Lively, Interactive Acvtive Pages That Teaches Each Number from 0 to 30. (p. 1271)
—Olivia Imagines: A Carryalong Treasury. (p. 1286)
Einhorn, Nicholas. Abracadabra! Cool Magic Tricks with Cards. (p. 6)
—Alakazam! Sensational Magic Tricks with Silk, Thimbles, Paper, & Money. (p. 33)
—Close-Up Magic. (p. 334)
—Presto Change-O! Jaw-Dropping Magic with Dinner Table Objects. (p. 1397)
—Stand-up Magic & Optical Illusions. (p. 1639)
—Stunts, Puzzles, & Stage Illusions. (p. 1670)
Einon, D. Juegos para Aprender. (p. 931)
Einon, Dorothy. Brain Games for Preschoolers: More Than 200 Brain-Boosting Activities for 2-5s. (p. 221)
Einspruch, Andrew. Analyzing Data in the Jungle Park Case (p. 67)
—Consumer Sense. (p. 360)
—Currency. (p. 394)
—DNA Detectives. (p. 456)
—Life on a Space Station. (p. 1012)
—Managing Money. (p. 1086)
—Migration: Animals on the Move. (p. 1141)
—Money System. (p. 1164)
—Mysteries of the Universe: How Astronomers Explore Space. (p. 1222)
—Number Patterns at My Lemonade Stand (p. 1271)
—Overpopulation. (p. 1314)
—Rain Forest Habitats. (p. 1434)
—Reducing Waste. (p. 1456)
—Smart Shopping. (p. 1593)
—Treading Lightly on the Earth. (p. 1781)
—Using Decimals to Plan Our Vacation (p. 1828)
—Using Energy at Home & School. (p. 1828)
—Using Energy to Get Around. (p. 1828)
—Using Water. (p. 1829)
—Wired World. (p. 1939)
Einstein, Albert & Born, Max. Born-Einstein Letters, 1916-1955: Friendship, Politics & Physics in Uncertain Times. (p. 214)
Einstein, Ann, ed. see Norman, Penny.
Einstein, Susan, illus. see Wong, Stephen.
Eirheim, Jeanne, tr. see Salinas, Veronica.
Eirienne, Arielle. You Behind the Mascara: A Growing-up Guide for Teenage Girls. (p. 1973)
Eirug Wyn. Powdwr Rhech! (p. 1389)
Eisan, Daniel. Lonely Peach. (p. 1046)
Eisbruch, Emily. Curious Kids Activity Guide to Michigan. (p. 394)
Eisby, Lizzy, illus. see Osterbach, Batya Kirshenbaum.
Eischen, Michael. Clever Pheasant. Peterson, Mark, ed. (p. 331)
Eisele. Hip Hip Hooray. (p. 780)
Eisele & Hanlon. Hip Hip Hooray. (p. 780)
—Hip Hip Hooray Starter. (p. 780)
Eisele, Barbara. Curious Cozy. (p. 392)
—Miss Thistle & Friends. (p. 1152)
Eiselein, Gregory, ed. see Alcott, Louisa May.
Eiseman, Joan. Ricardo & the Fisherman. Eiseman, Joan, illus. (p. 1469)
Eisen, Andrew R., ed. Treating Childhood Behavioral & Emotional Problems: A Step-by-Step, Evidence-Based Approach. (p. 1783)
Eisen, Laura. Clouds for Breakfast. Cissna, Kent, illus. (p. 335)
—Nubes para Desayunar. Cissna, Kent, illus. (p. 1269)
Eisen, Nancy, illus. see Peck, Judith.
Eisenberg, Azriel. Fill a Blank Page: A Biography of Solomon Schechter. (p. 586)
Eisenberg, Azriel & Robinson, Jessie B. My Jewish Holidays. (p. 1211)
Eisenberg, Deborah. Twilight of the Superheroes: Stories. (p. 1801)
Eisenberg, Kristy. When I Grow Up. Joslin, Irene, illus. (p. 1902)
Eisenberg, Lisa, jt. auth. see Hall, Katy, pseud.
Eisenberg, Rebecca & Frailey, Cheris. Webber Functional Communication Games: Gb146. (p. 1870)
Eisenberg, Rebecca & Kjesbo, Rynette. Cool in School Communication Game: Gb362. Lefebvre, Patrick, photos by. (p. 363)
Eisenberg, Serge, illus. see Soler, Michael.
Eisenfeld, Candice, illus. see Robbins, Neal.
Eisenkraft, Arthur & Kirkpatrick, Larry D. Quantoons: MetaphysicalIllustrations by Tomas Bunk. Bunk, Tomas, illus. (p. 1422)
Eisenpreis, Bettijane. Coping: A Young Woman's Guide to Breast Cancer Prevention. (p. 365)
Eisenring, Rahel Nicole, illus. see Schuler, Christoph.
Eisenson, Adam. Hope. (p. 796)
Eisenstadt, Abraham S., ed. see Dubofsky, Melvyn.
Eisenstadt, Abraham S., ed. see Levering, Ralph B.
Eisenstadt, Abraham S., ed. see Martin, James Kirby & Lender, Mark Edward.
Eisenstadt, Abraham S., ed. see Newmyer, R. Kent.
Eisenstadt, Abraham S., ed. see Wright, Donald R.
Eisenstadter, Dave, ed. see Dubreuil, Robert.
Eisenstark, Reyna. Baseball's Stars: The Negro League. (p. 141)
Eisenstark, Reyna, jt. auth. see Books, D. W. J.
Eisenstark, Reyna & Friedenthal, Lora. Progressivism. (p. 1410)
Eisenstein, Ann. Fallen Prey, a Sean Gray Junior Special Agent Mystery. Waugh, Leslie, ed. (p. 566)
Eisenstein, Ann E. Hiding Carly, a Sean Gray Junior Special Agent Mystery. (p. 777)
Eisikowitz, Michal, jt. auth. see Leon, Sarah.
Eisinger, Justin, jt. auth. see Byerly, Kenny Sternin.
Eisinger, Justin, jt. auth. see Rau, Zachary.
Eisinger, Justin & Simon, Alonzo, eds. Ben Here Before Beavers, Ethen, illus. (p. 163)
Eismann, Sheila F. & Putz, Ali F. Christmas Tin. Richardson, Cathie, illus. (p. 316)
Eisner, Fern. Saba's Room. (p. 1499)
Eisner, Will. Best of the Spirit. (p. 171)
—Fagin el Judio. Abuli, Enrique Sanchez, tr. (p. 562)
—Last Knight: An Introduction to Don Quixote. (p. 978)
—Spirit (p. 1628)
—Spirit: January 7 - June 24, 1945. (p. 1628)
—Spirit: July 7-December 29, 1946. Vol. 3 (p. 1628)
—Spirit. (p. 1628)
—Spirit Archives (p. 1628)
—Spirit Archives. (p. 1628)
—Sundiata: A Legend of Africa. (p. 1676)
Eisner, Will, illus. see Melville, Herman.
Eisner, Will, jt. auth. see Eisner, Will.
Eisner, Will & Eisner, Will. Last Knight: An Introduction to Don Quixote. (p. 978)
—Princess & the Frog. Eisner, Will, illus. (p. 1402)
—Sheena: Queen of the Jungle. Vol. 3 (p. 1564)
—Spirit (p. 1628)
—Spirit Archives. (p. 1628)
Eisner, Will & Melville, Herman. Moby Dick. (p. 1157)
Eisner, Will & Miller, Frank. Eisner/Miller. Brownstein, Charles, ed. (p. 507)
Eissler, Trevor. 4,962,571. Chung, Ruth, illus. (p. 2003)
—That 17th Hat. de Vries, Marloes, illus. (p. 1726)
Eitan (tchernov), Ora, illus. see Sschweiger-dmiel, Izhak.
Eitner-England, Lita. Bullmina the Courageous Bulldog to the Rescue. (p. 240)
Eitzen, Allan, illus. see Cooper, Sharon Katz.
Eitzen, Allan, illus. see Eitzen, Ruth.
Eitzen, Allan, illus. see McCourt, Lisa.
Eitzen, Allan, illus. see Moore, Ruth Nulton.
Eitzen, Allan, illus. see Navillus, Nell.
Eitzen, Allan, illus. see Suen, Anastasia.
Eitzen, Allan, illus. see Vernon, Louise A.
Eitzen, Ruth. Tara's Flight. Eitzen, Allan, illus. (p. 1706)
Ejanda, Maria Y. Basil & Emmanuel. (p. 142)
Ejaz, Khadija. Lionel Messi. (p. 1021)
—Meet Our New Student from India. (p. 1122)
—Persian Empire. (p. 1344)
—Recipe & Craft Guide to India. (p. 1451)
—We Visit Oman. (p. 1868)
Ejersbo, Jakob & Liberman, W. L. Mr. X & the Circle of Death. (p. 1187)
Ejsing, Jesper. Jarvis: the Sorcerer's Apprentice: The Sorcerer's Apprentice. (p. 909)
Ekberg, Jodi & Lisman, Jaclyn. Adventures of Cain & Frankie: The Husky Brothers - the Beginning. (p. 17)
Ekberg, Nancy. What Kind of War Was It, Anyhow? Reynolds, Rhonda, tr. (p. 1891)
Eke, Vincent. Turtle's Shell. (p. 1799)
Ekeland, Ivar. Cat in Numberland. O'Brien, John, illus. (p. 278)
Ekholm, Jan. Little Red Rascal. (p. 1035)
Eklund, Håkan, illus. see Cadeau, Michelle.
Ekman, Joseph Anthony. Kids Ultimate Online Homework Resource Guide 2004. (p. 955)
Ekman, Paul & Friesen, Wallace V. Unmasking the Face: A Guide to Recognizing Emotions from Facial Expressions. (p. 1821)
Ekmanis, Rena, illus. see Coste, Marion.
Eko-Burgess, Carrie, illus. see Meltzer, Lynn.
Ekster, Carol Gordon. Before I Sleep I Say Thank You. Rojas, Mary, illus. (p. 158)
Ekuni, Kaori. Twinkle Twinkle. Shimokawa, Emi, tr. from JPN. (p. 1802)
El Amin, Khalid Hamid, jt. auth. see Swarabi, Fatma Abdulla.
El Fisgsn, illus. see Villoro, Juan.
El Hamamsy, Salwa, jt. auth. see Pateman, Robert.
El Nabli, Dina. Danica Patrick. (p. 404)
—Henry Ford - Putting the World on Wheels. Time for Kids Editors, ed. (p. 768)
—Time for Kids - Henry Ford: Putting the World on Wheels. Time for Kids Editors, ed. (p. 1751)
El Wakil, Mohamed, illus. see Hamed, Maissa.
El Wilson, Barbara. Sugarfootn' in the South with Brer' Rabbit: How Handclapping Got Started in the Church Sugarfootstrade; Tattle-Tales Series. Curry, Garrett A., illus. (p. 1673)
Elahe. Story of Earth. (p. 1658)
El-Ahraf, Amer, ed. see Alexan, Julie.
Elaine & Shaun Turner. Owen's Train Ride. (p. 1314)
Elaine, Rachel. Seth & John (hardback) (p. 1554)
—Thoughts for Thought: Meditations, Musings & Poems for the Inner Life. (p. 1740)
Elaine Vanier. Crystal Lights: Awaken the Power. (p. 387)
Elam, Brock, illus. see Puccinelli, Joanne.
Elam Jr., Richard M. Young Visitor to Mars. Geer, Charles, illus. (p. 1979)
Elam, Keir & Mooney, Sinead. Samuel Beckett. (p. 1509)
Elasky, Kathy Sue. What Is a Family? (p. 1888)
Elayne. Entrance of the Theotokos into the Temple. Gillis, Bonnie, illus. (p. 531)
Elborough, Travis. Highwayman, Outlaws & Bandits of London. (p. 779)
—Rebels, Traitors & Turncoats of London. (p. 1451)
Elchgar, Yasmin. Noonoo the Doctor. (p. 1264)
Elda, Dorry, jt. auth. see Elda, Doug.
Elda, Dory, jt. auth. see Elda, Doug.
Elda, Doug & Elda, Dorry. Lyrical Earth Science: Geology. Raskauskas, Sally, illus. (p. 1067)
Elda, Doug & Elda, Dory. Lyrical Earth Science: Geology. Raskauskas, Sally, illus. (p. 1067)
Elden, Christian, illus. see Breisacher, Cathy.
Elder, Elizabeth. When I'm with You. Mansmann, Leslie, illus. (p. 1903)
Elder, Harold, illus. see Foley, Betsy, ed.
Elder, Jennifer. Autistic Planet. Elder, Jennifer & Thomas, Marc, illus. (p. 117)
—Different Like Me: My Book of Autism Heroes. Elder, Jennifer & Thomas, Marc, illus. (p. 438)
Elder, Jeremy. ComicQuest ZOMBIES UNLEASHED. (p. 348)
—Creative Haven Steampunk Devices Coloring Book. (p. 379)
—Dragons Activity Book. (p. 478)
—Hot Rod Tattoos Stained Glass Coloring Book. (p. 802)
—Japanese Tattoo Art Stained Glass Coloring Book. (p. 909)
—Manga Mazes. (p. 1087)
—Monsters Destroyed My City! Mazes. (p. 1169)
—Monsters Destroyed My City! Stained Glass Coloring Book. (p. 1169)
—Monsters Destroyed My City! Sticker Activity Book. (p. 1169)
—My Skateboard Sticker Activity Book. (p. 1218)
—Neon Lights Stained Glass Coloring Book. (p. 1241)
—Pinball Mazes Activity Book: Can You Top the High Score? (p. 1359)
—Race Against the Clock! Secret Agent. (p. 1430)
—Sci-Fi Stained Glass Coloring Book. (p. 1524)
—Space Agent. (p. 1618)
Elder, Jeremy & Coloring Books for Grownups Staff. In the Wild Stained Glass Coloring Book. (p. 868)
Elder, Jeremy & Coloring Books Staff. Steampunk Stained Glass Coloring Book. (p. 1646)
Elder, Josh. Scribblenauts Unmasked - A DC Comics Adventure. Archer, Adam, illus. (p. 1533)
Elder, Joshua & Joshua, Elder. Mail Order Ninja (p. 1077)
Elder, Laurel, jt. auth. see Greene, Steven.
Eldin, Peter. Great Box of Magic. (p. 714)
Eldon, Dorry, jt. auth. see Eldon, Doug.
Eldon, Doug & Eldon, Dorry. Lyrical Earth Science: Geology. Raskavskas, Sally, illus. (p. 1067)
Eldred, Delmer. Cubby & Scotty. (p. 388)
Eldred, Margaret, jt. auth. see Beisswenger, Iffer.
Eldred, Tim. Grease Monkey. (p. 713)
Eldredge, Ernie, illus. see Sullivan, E. J.
Eldredge, Ernie, illus. see Sullivan, Ellen.
Eldredge, John. Salvaje de Corazón: Descubramos el Secreto Del Alma Masculina (p. 1506)
Eldredge, Larry, illus. see Moore, Clement C.
Eldredge, Larry, illus. see Sullivan, E. J.
Eldredge, Richard, jt. auth. see Smith Bresciani, Cathleen.
Eldridge, Alison & Eldridge, Stephen. American Flag: An American Symbol. (p. 60)
—Bald Eagle: An American Symbol. (p. 133)
—Coolest Inventor: Willis Haviland Carrier & His Air Conditioner. (p. 364)
—Investigate Club Drugs. (p. 884)
—Liberty Bell: An American Symbol. (p. 1005)
—Mount Rushmore: An American Symbol. (p. 1180)
—Statue of Liberty: An American Symbol. (p. 1645)
—White House: An American Symbol. (p. 1913)
Eldridge, Courtney. Ghost Time. (p. 672)
Eldridge, Crystal, illus. see LaPoint, Crystal Godfrey.
Eldridge, David. Hollywood's History Films. (p. 789)
Eldridge, Jim. Invisible Assassin: The Malichea Quest. (p. 885)
—Last Enemy: The Malichea Quest. (p. 977)
—Lethal Target: The Malichea Quest. (p. 994)
Eldridge, Jim, illus. see Anastasio, Dina.
Eldridge, Jim, illus. see Shone, Rob.
Eldridge, Jim, illus. see Spinner, Stephanie.
Eldridge, Les. Santa's Cat. Eldridge, Les & Casey, James, illus. (p. 1513)
Eldridge, Marion, illus. see Adams, Michelle Medlock.
Eldridge, Marion, illus. see Piernas-Davenport, Gail.
Eldridge, Marion, illus. see Rothenberg, B. Annye.
Eldridge, Sherrie. Forever Fingerprints: An Amazing Discovery for Adopted Children. Williams, Rob, illus. (p. 619)
Eldridge, Stephen. Logan! Rising Star Logan Lerman. (p. 1045)
—Trace Evidence: Dead People Do Tell Tales. (p. 1774)
Eldridge, Stephen, jt. auth. see Eldridge, Alison.
Eldridge, VonDa. Wiggles the Worm. (p. 1928)
Eldridge-Murray, Lauren, illus. see Burns, Ian.
Ele, Delores. Horse Bones: The Adventures of Daisy & Maisy. (p. 799)
Eleanor, Coalson. Simon Says Run. (p. 1577)

Eleanor, Coerr. Sadako & the Thousand Paper Cranes. (p. 1501)
Eleanor, Coerr, jt. auth. see Coerr Eleanor.
Eleanor Gates. Poor Little Rich Girl. (p. 1383)
Eleanor Hallowell Abbott. White Linen Nurse. (p. 1913)
Eleanor Russell Brown. Mary Warin's Rats: A Time Warp Adventure. (p. 1101)
Electra, Agnes. Medical School for Children: Part I. (p. 1118)
Elefritz, Erin. My Pet Dinosaur. Rolf, Heidi, illus. (p. 1217)
Elejalde, Eliana, illus. see Graziani, Maria.
Elementary, Rock Spring. Roadrunners Writing Rocks! (p. 1477)
Elena, Antonio E. Santa, see Santa Elena, Antonio E.
Elena, Horacio, illus. see Dahl, Roald.
Elena, Horacio, illus. see Vecchione, Glen.
Elena, Horacio, tr. see Vecchione, Glen.
Elena, Horacio & Ramos, Pilar. Largo Dia. (p. 975)
Eleniak, Erika. What Do You Do, If You Lose Your Lalabaloo? Monroe, Daniel, illus. (p. 1883)
Elerding, Louise. You've Got Manners! Table Tips from A to Z for Kids of All Ages. (p. 1982)
—You've Got Respectful Manners! Tactful Tips from A to Z for Kids of All Ages. (p. 1982)
—You've Got Social Manners! Party Pointers from A to Z for Kids of All Ages. (p. 1982)
Elerya. One Step Higher: Piano Paradise Book II (p. 1297)
Eleven. Spirit Comes to Earth: Renewing Your Heart's Mission. Eleven, illus. (p. 1628)
Eley, Kitt. Cindy Lou. (p. 321)
Elfakir, Mahamad Ali. Blueberry Bubble Gum. (p. 204)
Elferr, Aluney. Lives Discolored: How Paul Was Lost to Drugs. (p. 1040)
Elfezzani, Thierry, illus. see Branford, Henrietta.
Elffers, Joost & Freymann, Saxton. How Are You Peeling? Foods with Moods. (p. 805)
Elfgren, Sara B. & Strandberg, Mats. Circle: The Engelsfors Trilogy—Book 1. (p. 321)
—Circle. (p. 321)
—Fire: The Engelsfors Trilogy Book II. (p. 590)
Elfman, Eric, jt. auth. see Shusterman, Neal.
Elford, Jole Shack. William Harvey & the Mechanics of the Heart. (p. 1933)
Elgar, Rebecca. Is That an Elephant over There? (p. 890)
—Where's My Dinner? (p. 1910)
Elgert, C. J. Elder Brothers & the Dragon's Portal. (p. 508)
—Elder Brothers & the Padstow Crystals. (p. 508)
Elgin, Kathleen, illus. see Pallister, John C.
Elgin, Kathy. Egyptian Myths. Sansom, Fiona, illus. (p. 507)
—Elizabethan England. Woolf, Alex, ed. (p. 513)
—France. (p. 627)
—India. (p. 870)
—Italy. (p. 894)
—Roman Myths. Sansom, Fiona, illus. (p. 1486)
—Spain. (p. 1620)
Elgin, Kathy, jt. auth. see Bailey Publishing Staff.
Elgin, Wade. Martin's Imagination. (p. 1098)
Elhart, James L. Automobiles & America's Dream Builders. (p. 117)
El-Hewie, Mohamed F. Essentials of Weightlifting & Strength Training. (p. 537)
Eliana, Kid, jt. auth. see De Las Casas, Dianne.
Elías, Annette, tr. see Estice, Rose Mary & Fried, Mary.
Elías, Annette, tr. see Libritos Mios staff, et al.
Elias, Joseph. Dictionary for Children: Arabic-Arabic. (p. 436)
Elias, Josie, jt. auth. see Elias, Marie Louise.
Elias, Josie, jt. auth. see Pateman, Robert.
Elias, Josie, jt. auth. see Sheehan, Sean.
Elias, Josie, jt. auth. see Yin, Saw Myat.
Elias, Keith James. Friendly Dragons & the Secrets of K-star: Kids Learning the Wisdom of Money Management. (p. 637)
Elias, Marie Louise & Elias, Josie. Barbados. (p. 137)
Elias, Megan & Feeley, Kathleen. Illinois. (p. 857)
Elias, Megan J. Stir It Up: Home Economics in American Culture. (p. 1651)
Eliasen, Lorena, ed. see Swallow, Pamela C.
Eliasen, Lorena, ed. see Swallow, Pamela Curtis.
Eliason, Mike & Kelley, K. C. Firefighter (p. 591)
Eliason, Scott. Andy's Magic Marble. (p. 73)
Eliaszevich, Esteban, jt. auth. see Sad, Elizabeth Levy.
Elig, Jennifer. Cat's Life: La Vida de un Gato. (p. 281)
—One Lord, Two People — un Señor, Dos Personas: A Bible Counting Book — una Biblia para Contar. (p. 1296)
Elin Hirschman, Jessica & Bright, Bonnie. Tangle Tower. Bright, Bonnie, illus. (p. 1705)
Eliopulis, Chris & Sumerak, Marc, texts. Franklin Richards: Son of a Genius Ultimate Collection - Book 1. (p. 630)
Eliopoulos, Chris. Does a Great Job Eliopoulos, Chris, illus. (p. 460)
—Mr. Puzzle. Eliopoulos, Chris, illus. (p. 1186)
—Mr. Puzzle Super Collection! Eliopoulos, Chris, illus. (p. 1186)
—No Instructions Needed Eliopoulos, Chris, illus. (p. 1258)
—Okie Dokie Donuts: Open for Business! Open for Business! (p. 1282)
—Perfect Fit Eliopoulos, Chris, illus. (p. 1341)
—Piece by Piece Eliopoulos, Chris, illus. (p. 1356)
—Yo Gabba Gabba: Gabba Ball: Gabba Ball. (p. 1971)
Eliopoulos, Chris, illus. see Cosby, Nate.
Eliopoulos, Chris, illus. see Lemke, Donald B.
Eliopoulos, Chris, illus. see Mandel, Peter.
Eliopoulos, Chris & Caramagna, Joe. Marvel Universe Ultimate Spider-Man Volume 4. (p. 1099)
Eliopoulos, Christopher, illus. see Meltzer, Brad.
Eliopulos, Nick & Random House Staff. DC Super Friends: Flying High. Wallace, Loston et al, illus. (p. 415)
Eliopulos, Nick, et al. Hero Story Collection. (p. 772)
Eliot, Chip & Lewman, David. Funny-Side Up! A SpongeBob Joke Book. (p. 650)
Eliot, Ethel. Little House in the Fairy Wood. (p. 1029)
Eliot, Ethel Cook. House above the Trees. (p. 803)
—House on the Edge of Things. (p. 803)
—Little House in the Fairy Wood. (p. 1029)
Eliot, George. Mill on the Floss. (p. 1143)
—Silas Marner. (p. 1575)
Eliot, Hannah. Glasses to Go. Roode, Daniel, illus. (p. 682)
—Sweet Treats. Ingham, Julie, illus. (p. 1690)
Eliot, Hannah, jt. auth. see Disiena, Laura Lyn.
Eliot, Hannah, jt. auth. see DiSiena, Laura Lyn.
Eliot, Hannah, jt. auth. see Disiena, Laura Lyn.
Eliot, Hannah, jt. auth. see DiSiena, Laura Lyn.
Eliot, Hannah, jt. auth. see Disiena, Laura Lyn.
Eliot, Jan. First Collection of the Syndicated Cartoon Strip (p. 593)
—Not So Picture Perfect. (p. 1267)
—Road Kill in the Closet No. 4. (p. 1476)
—You Can't Say Boobs on Sunday: The Second Collection of the Syndicated Cartoon Stone Soup. No. 2 (p. 1975)
Eliot, Margaret. Cat & Tiger Go to the Seaside. (p. 277)
Eliott, Lisa J. Adventures of Derby Doodle. (p. 17)
Elisabeth, Megan. Star's Journey from Twinkle to Shine. (p. 1643)
Elise, Christy. Beez Take Flight. (p. 158)
Eliseev, Sergey, illus. see Holmes, Andy.
Eliseev, Sergey, illus. see Larsen, Carolyn.
Elish, Dan. Attack of the Frozen Woodchucks. Call, Greg, illus. (p. 113)
—Battle of Gettysburg. (p. 146)
—Black Sox Scandal of 1919. (p. 197)
—Edmund Hillary: First to the Top. (p. 504)
—Extreme Mountain Biking. (p. 556)
—Franklin Delano Roosevelt. (p. 630)
—Galaxies. (p. 653)
—Insight. (p. 878)
—Jackie Robinson. (p. 903)
—James Madison. (p. 907)
—John Quincy Adams. (p. 922)
—Kaleidoscope Space Gorup 2 (p. 942)
—Louis Armstrong & the Jazz Age. (p. 1058)
—Manhattan Project. (p. 1087)
—NASA. (p. 1230)
—Plays. (p. 1373)
—Prius. (p. 1407)
—Satellites. (p. 1515)
—School for the Insanely Gifted. (p. 1523)
—Screenplays. (p. 1533)
—Sun. (p. 1675)
—Theodore Roosevelt. (p. 1729)
—U. S. Supreme Court. (p. 1807)
—Vermont. (p. 1837)
—Washington, D. C. (p. 1860)
—Watergate Scandal. (p. 1863)
Elish, Dan, jt. auth. see Brown, Jason Robert.
Elish, Dan & Ayer, Eleanor. Colorado. (p. 343)
Elish, Dan & Benjamin, Daniel. American Life & Movies from the Ten Commandments to Twilight. (p. 62)
Elish, Dan & Fitzgerald, Stephanie. New York. (p. 1247)
Elish, Dan & Horn, Robert. 13: The Complete Book & Lyrics of the Broadway Musical the Applause Libretto Library. (p. 1994)
Elisha, . & Elyssa. I Love Me: Self-Esteem in Seven Easy Steps. (p. 842)
Elissa, Barbara, jt. auth. see Savedoff, Barbara E.
Elissa Grodin. Everyone Counts: A Citizens' Number Book. Juhasz, Victor, illus. (p. 544)
Elissa, Grodin. N Is for Nutmeg: A Connecticut Alphabet. Brookfield, Maureen, illus. (p. 1227)
Ellum, Don, jt. auth. see Ellum, Jeanne.
Ellum, Jeanne & Ellum, Don. Raising a Daughter: Parents & the Awakening of a Healthy Woman. (p. 1437)
Elizabeth Anne Biddle. Girl Called Nothing: A Tale of Cambodia. (p. 678)
Elizabeth, Annelise, jt. auth. see Elizabeth, Julie.
Elizabeth Arkward Newton. Little Boy Who Wished God Had Not Given Him a Brain: Big Momma Books. (p. 1025)
Elizabeth, Julie & Elizabeth, Annelise. Take Care of Our Friend, Baby Dog. (p. 1696)
Elizabeth, Lauren. Far from Forgotten. (p. 572)
—Looks of an Angel. (p. 1051)
Elizabeth Mobley, illus. see Cooper, Wendy.
Elizabeth, Neering, ed. see Lee, Newman.
Elizabeth, Shelby. Dabby's Pond. (p. 398)
Elizabeth, Stevens. Can I Keep Him. (p. 258)
Elizabeth Tarquinio Sciulli. Butterfly Milk. (p. 248)
Elizalde, Marcelo, illus. see Metzger, Joanna.
Elizalde, Marcelo, illus. see Tompert, Ann.
Elk, Ronit. Surprise at Dancing Fields. (p. 1685)
Elkeles, Simone. Better Than Perfect. (p. 172)
—Chain Reaction. (p. 288)
—How to Ruin a Summer Vacation. (p. 821)
—How to Ruin My Teenage Life. (p. 821)
—How to Ruin Your Boyfriend's Reputation. (p. 821)
—Leaving Paradise. (p. 986)
—Perfect Chemistry. (p. 1341)
—Return to Paradise. (p. 1465)
—Rules of Attraction. (p. 1495)
—Wild Cards. (p. 1929)
Elkerton, Andy, illus. see Bryant, Ann.
Elkerton, Andy, illus. see John, Louise.
Elkerton, Andy, illus. see Moore, Suse.
Elkerton, Andy, illus. see Punter, Russell.
Elkerton, Andy, illus. see Rosa-Mendoza, Gladys.
Elkerton, Andy, illus. see Watt, Fiona.
Elkhatib, Tristan & Anthony. Determined Cow. (p. 431)
Elkhouly, Mona Henri. Take Me along Series: How It All Started. (p. 1696)
Elkin, Matthew. 20 Fun Facts about Centipedes. (p. 1995)
Elkin, Matthew, jt. auth. see Chiger, Arielle.
Elkind, Samuel. Improvisation, Theatre Games & Scene Handbook. (p. 862)
—Scenes for Acting & Directing. (p. 1521)
Elkington, John. Pirates of the Gayoso Bayou. (p. 1364)
Elkins, Caroline. Imperial Reckoning: The Untold Story of Britain's Gulag in Kenya. (p. 862)
Elkins, Christy. Seedling Heart. (p. 1547)
—Sir Stinks-A-Lot. (p. 1580)
Elkins, Dov Peretz. Seven Delightful Stories for Every Day. (p. 1554)
—Seven Delightful Stories for Every Day. Smekhov, Zely, illus. (p. 1554)
Elkins, J. Theron. You Are the Pea, & I Am the Carrot. Lemaitre, Pascal, illus. (p. 1973)
Elkins, Stephen. 100 Bible Stories 100 Bible Songs (p. 1998)
—100 Devotions, 100 Bible Songs (p. 1998)
—100 Prayers, 100 Praise Songs (p. 1998)
—100 Ways to Know God Loves Me, 100 Songs to Love Him Back (p. 1999)
—Bible Blessings. Colton, Ellie, illus. (p. 175)
—Bible Prayer Collection: 30 Life Changing Prayers from the Bible for Children. Colton, Ellie, illus. (p. 176)
—Bible Prayers. Colton, Ellie, illus. (p. 176)
—Bible Promises. Colton, Ellie, illus. (p. 176)
—Bible Verses. Colton, Ellie, illus. (p. 176)
—Ebony & Ivory: Discovering 10 Keys to Racial Harmony. Reisch, Jessie, illus. (p. 502)
—First Steps in Faith: Beginning Lessons of God's Love. Colton, Ellie, illus. (p. 597)
—First Steps in Prayer. Colton, Ellie, illus. (p. 597)
—First Steps in the Bible: A Child's Walk with God Begins Here! (p. 597)
—First Steps to God: Beginning Lessons of God's Love. Colton, Ellie, illus. (p. 597)
—Just Like Jesus Bible Storybook. (p. 939)
—Know God, No Fear. Reisch, Jessie, illus. (p. 965)
—Little Dongs for Little Souls: Sharing God's Love. Davis, Lynne, illus. (p. 1027)
—Little Songs for Little Souls: God Cares for Me. Davis, Lynne, illus. (p. 1036)
—Little Songs for Little Souls: I Can Praise the Lord. Davis, Lynne, illus. (p. 1036)
—Little Songs for Little Souls: I Can Be Happy in Jesus. Davis, Lynne, illus. (p. 1036)
—LullaBible: A Musical Treasury for Mother & Baby. (p. 1064)
—LullaBible: A Musical Treasury for Mother & Baby. Colton, Ellie, illus. (p. 1064)
—Lullabible Storybook. Ellie, Colton, illus. (p. 1064)
—Lullabies for Babies. Colton, Ellie, illus. (p. 1064)
—My LullaBible A to Z Promise Book. Colton, Ellie, illus. (p. 1213)
—My Sing-Along Bible: 50 Easy-Read Stories + 50 Fun Bible Songs. Reagan, Susan, illus. (p. 1218)
—Read 'n' See DVD Bible O'Connor, Tim, illus. (p. 1443)
—Snuggle Time Devotions That End with a Hug! Jones, Mark, illus. (p. 1601)
—Special Times Bible Prayers for Toddlers. Reagan, Susan Joy, illus. (p. 1623)
—Special Times Bible Promises for Toddlers. Reagan, Susan Joy, illus. (p. 1623)
—Special Times Bible Rhymes for Toddlers. (p. 1623)
—Special Times Bible Stories for Toddlers. (p. 1623)
—Stories That End with a Prayer. Menck, Kevin, illus. (p. 1655)
—Tell Me about Baptism. (p. 1716)
—Tell Me about Church. (p. 1716)
—Tell Me about Faith. (p. 1716)
—Tell Me about Grace. (p. 1716)
—Tell Me about Praise & Worship. (p. 1716)
—Tell Me about Prayer. (p. 1716)
—Tell Me about Salvation. (p. 1716)
—Tell Me about the Bible. (p. 1716)
—Ultimate Travel Time Bible. Conaway, Jim, illus. (p. 1810)
—Word & Song Bible. (p. 1950)
—Word & Song Bible. O'Connor, Tim, illus. (p. 1950)
—Word & Song Songbook: The Old Testament. Vol. 1 (p. 1950)
—Word & Song Songbook: The New Testament. Vol. 2 (p. 1950)
Elkins-Tanton, Linda T. Uranus, Neptune, Pluto, & the Outer Solar System. (p. 1825)
Elkorek, Alexander. Twelve Bright Trumpets. (p. 1800)
Elkorek, Alexander, illus. see Snedeker, Caroline Dale.
Elkus, Julie. Cuando Mi Mama Me Lee/When My Mama Reads to Me. Fagin, Cristina, tr. from ENG. (p. 388)
Ell, Flynn J. Golden Metis. LaLonde, Deanna L., illus. (p. 695)
Ella, Peter Leo. Class Party on the Big Yellow School Bus. Ella, Peter Leo, illus. (p. 327)
Ella, Peter Leo, illus. see Bala, Edward.
Ella, Rhys. Kato & the Fountain of Wrinkles. (p. 945)
Ellams, Victoria, illus. see Whitley-Kinzett, Sara.
Elledge, Kristine. Big Ear. (p. 181)
Ellefson, D. R. Willie Woolly Wiggle Worm. (p. 1934)
Ellen, Chantal. Reason for the Season. Pierre-Louis, Phillip, illus. (p. 1450)
Ellen, Connie. Marvel Mansion Gang. (p. 1098)
ELLEN E. FREWER, tr. see Verne, Jules.
Ellen, Kleiner, ed. see Saranam, Sankara.
Ellen Koski, Rachel, ed. see Singlehurst, Naomi.
Ellen, Raskin. Westing Game. (p. 1876)
Ellenbogen, Keith, illus. see Montgomery, Sy.
Ellenport, Craig. Ladainian Tomlinson: All-Pro on & off the Field. (p. 970)
Ellens, Brenda L. Duckling Pond. (p. 488)
Eller, Angie. Modest Princess. (p. 1159)
Eller, Jerod R., illus. see West, Stephen Earl.
Eller, Jon, ed. see Bradbury, Ray.
Eller, Sydney, illus. see McCord, Joseph Lennon.
Eller, Sylvia Klope. Squirrel Who Hitchhiked to Atlanta. (p. 1637)
Eller, Tracy & Mason, Joan. Cousins & Kinship. (p. 373)
Ellerbe, Kevin. Ralphy & the Woman in the White Coat. (p. 1437)
Ellermeyer, Deborah & Rowell, Judith. Perfect Poems for Teaching Sight Words: Delightful Poems, Research-Based Lessons, & Instant Activities That Teach the Top High-Frequency Words. (p. 1342)
Ellermeyer, Deborah & Rowell, Judy. Ancient Civilizations Reader's Theater: Develop Reading Fluency & Text Comprehension Skills. Vol. 2246 Hults, Alaska, ed. (p. 68)
Ellerson, Terryann. Rappin' Tappin Alphabet. (p. 1439)
Ellery, Amanda. If I Had a Dragon. Ellery, Tom, illus. (p. 853)
—If I Were a Jungle Animal. Ellery, Tom, illus. (p. 853)
Ellery, Amanda, illus. see Mlawer, Teresa.
Ellery, Tom, illus. see Ellery, Amanda.
Ellery, Tom, illus. see Mlawer, Teresa.
Ellie. Bengal & Sengal. (p. 164)
Ellie, Colton, illus. see Elkins, Stephen.
Elliff, Tom. Come Home to the Heart of God: Building Life on the 7 Pillars God. (p. 347)
Ellig, Janice Reals & Morin, William J. Lo que Sabe Toda Mujer que Triunfa. (p. 1044)
Ellingsworth, Colleen, illus. see Farrell, Connie.
Ellington, Charlotte Jane. Dancing Leaf. (p. 403)
Ellington, Kyseme Ali & Crawford, Bobby. I'mpossible: ChessLife Strategies for Children & Young Adults. (p. 862)
Elliot, David. Henry's Map. Elliot, David, illus. (p. 769)
—Henry's Stars. Elliot, David, illus. (p. 769)
Elliot, David, illus. see Jacques, Brian.
Elliot, David, illus. see Kerr, Donald.
Elliot, Gertrude, illus. see Hurd, Edith Thacher & Brown, Margaret Wise.
Elliot, Henry. Frederick Douglass: From Slavery to Statesman. (p. 633)
—Harriet Beecher Stowe: The Voice of Humanity in White America. (p. 749)
—John Muir: Protecting & Preserving the Environment. (p. 922)
Elliot, Jane & King, Colin. Children's Encyclopedia. (p. 303)
Elliot, Jane & King, Colin, eds. Children's Encyclopedia. (p. 303)
Elliot, Jessie. Girls Dinner Club. (p. 680)
—Girls' Dinner Club. (p. 680)
Elliot, Joseph, jt. auth. see Elster, Charles Harrington.
Elliot, K. & Gimmell, K. Piano Course Book 1. (p. 1354)
Elliot, Lee, photos by see Brown, Ayanna.
Elliot, Marion. Crafty Fun with Paper! 50 Fabulous Papercraft Projects to Make Yourself. (p. 376)
—Recycled Craft Projects for Kids: 50 Fantastic Things to Make from Junk, Shown. (p. 1453)
Elliot, Mark, illus. see Norwich, Grace.
Elliot, Mark, illus. see Presnall, Judith Janda.
Elliot, Rachel. Elephant. East, Jacqueline, illus. (p. 511)
—Elephant Who Was Scared. Bendall-Brunello, John, illus. (p. 511)
—Monkey. East, Jacqueline, illus. (p. 1164)
—Seek & Find Fairy: Find a Charm Book. Regan, Lisa, illus. (p. 1548)
—Seek & Find Princess: Find a Charm Book. Regan, Lisa, illus. (p. 1548)
—Who Is New York's Prettiest Princess? Spenceley, Annabel, illus. (p. 1916)
Elliot, Rebecca, illus. see Benjamin, A. H.
Elliot, Rebecca, illus. see Elliott, Rebecca.
Elliot, Rebecca, illus. see Hubery, Julia.
Elliott, Alan. Willy the Texas Longhorn Ford, Stephanie, illus. (p. 1934)
Elliott, Ann. GypsyBridge Friends: The Gift. (p. 734)
—GypsyBridge Friends: The Vine. (p. 734)
—GypsyBridge Friends: The Surprise. (p. 734)
Elliott, Catherine & Quinn, Frances. AS Law. (p. 105)
Elliott, Cathy. Can You Guess What It Is? (p. 259)
—How Much Does It Weigh? (p. 811)
Elliott, Chris. Shroud of the Thwacker. Andersen, Amy Elliott, illus. (p. 1571)
Elliott, Craig. Craig Elliott Sketchbook. (p. 376)
—Racer Buddies: Rematch at Richmond. (p. 1431)
—Racer Buddies-Opening Day at Daytona. William, Harper, illus. (p. 1431)
Elliott, Dan, et al. David's Shield. (p. 411)
Elliott, David. And Here's to You! Cecil, Randy, illus. (p. 71)
—Cool Crazy Crickets Club. Meisel, Paul, illus. (p. 363)
—Cool Crazy Crickets to the Rescue. Meisel, Paul, illus. (p. 363)
—Evangeline Mudd & the Golden-Haired Apes of the Ikkinasti Jungle. Wesson, Andrea, illus. (p. 541)
—Finn Throws a Fit! Ering, Timothy Basil, illus. (p. 589)
—In the Sea. (p. 867)
—In the Wild. (p. 868)
—In the Wild. Meade, Holly, illus. (p. 868)
—Knitty Kitty. Denise, Christopher, illus. (p. 965)
—Nobody's Perfect. Zuppardi, Sam, illus. (p. 1262)
—On the Farm. Meade, Holly, illus. (p. 1290)
—On the Wing. Stadtlander, Becca, illus. (p. 1292)
—One Little Chicken: A Counting Book. Long, Ethan, illus. (p. 1295)
—This Orq. (He Cave Boy.) Nichols, Lori, illus. (p. 1737)
—What the Grizzly Knows. Grafe, Max, illus. (p. 1893)
—Wuv Bunnies from Outers Pace. Long, Ethan, illus. (p. 1966)
Elliott, David, illus. see Jacques, Brian.
Elliott, David, jt. auth. see Elliott, Ruth.
Elliott, Edward, adapted by. 99 Poems. (p. 1998)
Elliott, Emilia. Patricia. (p. 1328)
Elliott, Eric. Dear Miss Karana. (p. 419)
Elliott, George. Boy Who Loved Bananas. Krystoforski, Andrej, illus. (p. 219)
Elliott, Jane & King, Colin. Children's Encyclopedia. (p. 303)
Elliott, Jeff, illus. see Gatz, Krissandra.
Elliott, Jenny. Save Me. (p. 1516)
Elliott, John, illus. see Marchione, Margherita.
Elliott, John C. Ri Ra: An Adventure Begins. (p. 1469)
Elliott, Joyce L., illus. see Rodriguez, Cindy L.
Elliott, Julia. Where Did God Come From? Elliott, Julia, illus. (p. 1906)
Elliott, Karen. Kid's Box Level 3 Language Portfolio. (p. 952)
Elliott, Kate, pseud. Court of Fives. (p. 373)
Elliott, Kevin, jt. auth. see Carter, Nikki.
Elliott, L. M. Across a War-Tossed Sea. (p. 9)
—Annie, Between the States. (p. 86)
—Da Vinci's Tiger. (p. 398)
—Give Me Liberty. (p. 681)
—Under a War-Torn Sky. (p. 1813)
Elliott, Laura. 13 on Halloween. (p. 1995)
Elliott, Laura Malone. Annie, Between the States. (p. 86)
—Give Me Liberty. (p. 681)
—Hunter's Best Friend at School. Munsinger, Lynn, illus. (p. 828)
—String of Hearts. Munsinger, Lynn, illus. (p. 1667)
—Thanksgiving Day Thanks. Munsinger, Lynn, illus. (p. 1726)
Elliott, Leia Mae, jt. auth. see Jamison, Jo Lynn.
Elliott, Linda. When Little Pinkie Gets Her Wings. Switzer, Bobbi, illus. (p. 1903)
Elliott, Luke, illus. see Henkel, Pat.

Full bibliographic information is available on the Title Index page number referenced in parentheses at the end of each entry

Elliott, Lynne. Children & Games in the Middle Ages. (p. 302)
—Clothing in the Middle Ages. (p. 334)
—Exploration in the Renaissance. (p. 550)
—Food & Feasts in the Middle Ages. (p. 613)
—Medieval Medicine & the Plague. (p. 1119)
—Medieval Towns, Trade, & Travel. (p. 1119)
—Renaissance in Europe. (p. 1460)
Elliott, M. G. Magic Wheel: And the Adventures of Ding-How, Ah-So, & Mi-Tu. (p. 1074)
Elliott, Marc. House at the End of the Tracks. (p. 803)
Elliott, Mark, illus. see Carson, Mary Kay.
Elliott, Mark, illus. see Chew, Elizabeth V.
Elliott, Mark, illus. see Clements, Andrew.
Elliott, Mark, illus. see DeStefano, Anthony.
Elliott, Mark, illus. see Fishman, Cathy Goldberg.
Elliott, Mark, illus. see Haddix, Margaret Peterson.
Elliott, Mark, illus. see Hanson, Warren.
Elliott, Mark, illus. see Levine, Gail Carson.
Elliott, Mark, illus. see Wallace, Sandra Neil.
Elliott, Mark, jt. auth. see Pateman, Robert.
Elliott, Mel. Color Me Swoon: The Beefcake Activity Book for Good Color-Inners As Well As Beginners. (p. 343)
Elliott, Naneki. Angels on the Bench: Conversations with Cora on the Afterlife. (p. 75)
Elliott, Ned & Somerville, Charles C. F Is for Football. Somerville, Charles C., illus. (p. 559)
Elliott, Neil, illus. see Bentel, Erica & Bentel Family Trust Staff.
Elliott, Nick, tr. see Berner, Rotraut Susanne.
Elliott, Odette. My Big Brother JJ. Aggs, Patrice, illus. (p. 1197)
—Sammy Goes Flying. McIntyre, Georgina, illus. (p. 1508)
Elliott, Patricia. Pale Assassin. (p. 1319)
Elliott, R. Kenley. Stories from a Kentucky Boy. (p. 1654)
Elliott, Rachel. Hippo Who Was Happy. (p. 781)
—Tiger Who Was Angry. Bendall-Brunello, John, illus. (p. 1748)
—Zebra Who Was Sad. Bendall-Brunello, John, illus. (p. 1985)
Elliott, Rebecca. Eva Sees a Ghost. (p. 540)
—Eva's Treetop Festival Elliott, Rebecca, illus. (p. 541)
—Just Because. (p. 938)
—Last Tiger. Elliot, Rebecca, illus. (p. 979)
—Last Tiger. Elliott, Rebecca, illus. (p. 979)
—Missing Jack. Elliott, Rebecca, illus. (p. 1152)
—Owl Diaries #2: Eva Sees a Ghost (a Branches Book) (p. 1315)
—Owl Diaries #2: Eva Sees a Ghost (a Branches Book) - Library Edition. (p. 1315)
—Painless Grammar. (p. 1318)
—Sometimes. Elliott, Rebecca, illus. (p. 1610)
—Zoo Girl. Elliott, Rebecca, illus. (p. 1989)
Elliott, Rebecca, illus. see Baxter, Nicola.
Elliott, Rebecca, illus. see Foster, Karen & Law, Felicia.
Elliott, Rebecca, illus. see Foster, Karen.
Elliott, Rebecca, illus. see Goodings, Christina.
Elliott, Rebecca, illus. see Law, Felicia.
Elliott, Rebecca, illus. see Munton, Gill.
Elliott, Rebecca, illus. see Nesbitt, Kenn.
Elliott, Rebecca, illus. see Pearce, Clemency.
Elliott, Rebecca, illus. see Studio Mouse Staff.
Elliott, Rebecca, illus. see Top That Publishing Staff, ed.
Elliott, Rebecca, illus. see Wang, Margaret.
Elliott, Rebecca, jt. auth. see Koontz, Robin Michal.
Elliott, Rebecca, et al. Five Little Monkeys: And Other Counting Rhymes. (p. 600)
—Poles & Oceans Lodge, Ali, illus. (p. 1379)
Elliott, Rick. He Watches over Me: The Story of Creation. (p. 756)
Elliott, Rob. Laugh-Out-Loud Animal Jokes for Kids. (p. 980)
—Laugh-Out-Loud Doodles for Boys. Hawkins, Jonny, illus. (p. 980)
—Laugh-Out-Loud Doodles for Girls. Hawkins, Jonny, illus. (p. 980)
—More Laugh-Out-Loud Jokes for Kids. (p. 1174)
Elliott, Robert B. Inventing Flight A Construction Handbook for the Classroom: The Toothpick Airforce. (p. 883)
Elliott, Ruth. Little Blossom Culiquipuma, Diana y. Jose, tr. (p. 1024)
—Night Princess Elliott, Ruth, illus. (p. 1254)
—See What You're Looking At. Elliott, Ruth, illus. (p. 1547)
Elliott, Ruth & Elliott, David. Richest Kid in the Poor House. Elliott, Ruth, illus. (p. 1470)
Elliott, Ruth C. Basic English Grammar. (p. 141)
—Basic English Skills Book One. (p. 141)
—Basic English Skills Kindergarten. (p. 141)
Elliott, Sharon M., jt. auth. see Grant, Elaine Y.
Elliott, Sherria L. My Shaking Eyes. Moore, Sasha & Tilak, Brian, illus. (p. 1218)
Elliott, Sherry. Great Veiled Pearl. (p. 719)
Elliott, Stacey "Sissy". What Kind of Bread Does a Monkey Eat ? (p. 1891)
Elliott, Stephen. Looking Forward to It: Or, How I Learned to Stop Worrying & Love the American Electoral Process. (p. 1051)
Elliott, Tommy. I Don't Want To: Go to School. (p. 838)
Elliott, Tori, illus. see Rhodes, Lou.
Elliott, Wade. What Will You Do Today? (p. 1895)
Elliott, Zetta. Ship of Souls. (p. 1567)
Elliott, Zetta & Strickland, Shadra. Bird. (p. 190)
Ellipsanime Staff, illus. see Berts, Peter, et al.
Ellipsanime Staff, illus. see Davis, Jim & Evanier, Mark.
Ellipsanime Staff, illus. see Davis, Jim & Michiels, Cedric.
Ellipsanime Staff, illus. see Davis, Jim, et al.
Ellipsanime Staff, illus. see Davis, Jim.
Ellipsanime Staff, illus. see Magnat, Julien, et al.
Ellis, Althia Melody, ed. see Hinton, Cheryl.
Ellis, Amanda & Block, Maggie. Jwenlapaix in the Bateyes. (p. 941)
Ellis, Amy, illus. see Ferry, Francis.
Ellis, Amy, des. Looking at Myself I. (p. 1051)
—Looking at Myself I Answer Folder. (p. 1051)
Ellis, Amy, rev. Major-Minor Finder: College to Career Planner. (p. 1078)
Ellis, Andy. When Lulu Went to the Zoo. Ellis, Andy, illus. (p. 1903)
Ellis, Andy, illus. see Baglio, Ben M.
Ellis, Andy, illus. see Leeson, Christine.
Ellis, Ann Dee. End or Something Like That. (p. 526)
—This Is What I Did. (p. 1736)
ELLIS, B. J. Mrs. Morgan's Adventures with Aliens. (p. 1187)
Ellis, Barbara A. Eggs Are Talking: Book 2. (p. 506)
Ellis, Barbara C. Brain Quest Black History. (p. 221)
Ellis, Belinda. Baby See-A-Shape Colors. (p. 128)
—Baby See-A-Shape Things That Go! (p. 128)
—Giant See-a-Shape My Giant ABC Book. (p. 674)
—Touch & Learn: Fairy Tale ABC. (p. 1772)
—Tractor. (p. 1775)
Ellis, Benjamin. Walaboo-Kies. (p. 1853)
Ellis, Brendan, illus. see Carville, Declan.
Ellis, Brian. Web at Dragonfly Pond. Maydak, Michael S., illus. (p. 1870)
Ellis, Carol. African American Activists. (p. 26)
—African American Activists. Hill, Marc Lamont, ed. (p. 26)
—African American Artists. (p. 26)
—African American Artists. Hill, Marc Lamont, ed. (p. 26)
—Apes. (p. 91)
—Hamsters & Gerbils. (p. 740)
—Kendo. (p. 948)
—Landmark Hip-Hop Hits. (p. 974)
—Leopards. (p. 993)
—New Orleans Voodoo. (p. 1246)
—Vaccines. (p. 1830)
—Wrestling. (p. 1962)
Ellis, Carol, jt. auth. see Ellis, Carole.
Ellis, Carol & Grayson, Robert. Drug Cartels & Smugglers. (p. 486)
Ellis, Carole & Ellis, Carol. Judo & Jujitsu. (p. 931)
Ellis, Carson. Home. (p. 791)
Ellis, Carson, illus. see Meloy, Colin.
Ellis, Carson, illus. see Rylant, Cynthia.
Ellis, Carson, illus. see Snicket, Lemony, pseud & Stookey, Nathaniel.
Ellis, Carson, illus. see Stewart, Trenton Lee.
Ellis, Catherine. Cars & Trucks. (p. 272)
—Cars & Trucks/Autos y Camiones. (p. 272)
—Cars & Trucks/Autos y Camiones. Brusca, Maria Cristina, tr. from ENG. (p. 272)
—Helicopters. (p. 763)
—Helicopters/Helicópteros. (p. 763)
—Helicopters/Helicópteros. Brusca, Maria Cristina, tr. (p. 763)
—Key Figures of World War II. (p. 950)
—Mega Military Machines (p. 1124)
—Planes. (p. 1367)
—Planes/Aviones. (p. 1367)
—Planes/Aviones. Brusca, Maria Cristina, tr. (p. 1367)
—Ships. (p. 1567)
—Ships/Barcos. (p. 1567)
—Ships/Barcos. Brusca, Maria Cristina, tr. (p. 1567)
—Submarines. (p. 1671)
—Submarines/Submarinos. (p. 1671)
—Submarines/Submarinos. Brusca, Maria Cristina, tr. from ENG. (p. 1671)
—Tanks. (p. 1705)
—Tanks/Tanques. (p. 1705)
—Tanks/Tanques. Brusca, Maria Cristina, tr. from ENG. (p. 1705)
Ellis, Catherine & Roberts, Jeremy. Adolf Hitler. (p. 13)
Ellis, Catherine, ed. Key Figures of World War II. (p. 950)
Ellis, Christina, illus. see Joyce, William.
Ellis, Colette. Credo: I Believe. Avakoff, Caroline, ed. (p. 380)
—Following Christ. (p. 612)
Ellis, David. In the Company of Liars. (p. 865)
Ellis, Debi. Just Dance. (p. 938)
Ellis, Deborah. Breadwinner. (p. 224)
—Breadwinner Trilogy. (p. 224)
—Cat at the Wall (p. 277)
—Children of War: Voices of Iraqi Refugees (p. 303)
—Ciudad de Barro. (p. 324)
—Company of Fools (p. 351)
—Heaven Shop (p. 761)
—I Am a Taxi (p. 832)
—Jakeman (p. 906)
—Kids of Kabul: Living Bravely Through a Never-Ending War (p. 954)
—Looks Like Daylight (p. 1051)
—Lunch with Lenin (p. 1065)
—Moon at Nine (p. 1171)
—Mud City (p. 1188)
—Mud City. (p. 1188)
—No Ordinary Day (p. 1259)
—No Ordinary Day. (p. 1259)
—No Safe Place. (p. 1260)
—Off to War: Voices of Soldiers' Children (p. 1279)
—Our Stories, Our Songs: African Children Talk about AIDS (p. 1310)
—Parvana's Journey (p. 1326)
—Parvana's Journey. (p. 1326)
—Sacred Leaf (p. 1500)
—Three Wishes: Palestinian & Israeli Children Speak (p. 1744)
—We Want You to Know: Kids Talk about Bullying (p. 1868)
Ellis, Deborah & Reed, Fred. We Want You to Know: Kids Talk about Bullying (p. 1868)
Ellis, Deborah & Walters, Eric. Bifocal (p. 177)
Ellis, Deborah, ed. Three Wishes: Palestinian & Israeli Children Speak. (p. 1744)
Ellis, Diane. How Smart Is God? (p. 812)
Ellis, Dianne. Rusty Rumble & His Smelly Socks. (p. 1498)
—Rusty Rumble's Day at the Beach. (p. 1498)
Ellis, Edward S. Boy Patriot. (p. 218)
—Life of Kit Carson: Hunter, Trapper, Guide, Indian Agent & Colonel U. S. A. (p. 1012)
Ellis, Edward Sylvester. Life of Kit Carson: The Life of Kit Carson. (p. 1012)
—Through Forest & Fire. (p. 1744)
—Two Boys in Wyoming: A Tale of Adventure (Northwest Series No. 3) (p. 1803)
Ellis, Edward Sylvester & Coghlan, John. Camp in the Mountains. (p. 257)
—Hunters of the Ozark. (p. 829)
Ellis, Elina, illus. see David, Juliet & Ayliffe, Alex.
Ellis, Erin A. Great Horror Movie Villains Paper Dolls: Psychos, Slashers & Their Unlucky Victims! (p. 716)
Ellis, Gerry, illus. see Kane, Karen.
Ellis, Gerry, photos by see Kane, Karen.
Ellis, Greg. Baby's First 1-2-3 in Hawaii. (p. 129)
Ellis, Gwen. Bible Adventures. Cox, Steve, illus. (p. 175)
—Christmas Flower. Hansen, Clint, illus. (p. 314)
—First Christmas Pichon, Liz, illus. (p. 593)
—Flor de Pascua. Hansen, Clint, illus. (p. 606)
—I Can Learn Bible Stories. Regan, Dana, illus. (p. 836)
—My Little Learner Bible. (p. 1212)
—Read & Share (p. 1442)
—Read & Share Bible: More Than 200 Best-Loved Bible Stories Smallman, Steve, illus. (p. 1442)
—Read & Share: the Story of Easter (p. 1442)
—Read & Share Toddler Bible (p. 1442)
—Story of Easter Smallman, Steve, illus. (p. 1658)
Ellis, Gwen & Cowman, L. B. Streams in the Desert(r) for Kids: 366 Devotions to Bring Comfort (p. 1666)
Ellis, Helen. What Curiosity Kills. (p. 1881)
Ellis, Jan Davey, illus. see Jackson, Ellen B.
Ellis, Jane, jt. auth. see Jones, Alan.
Ellis, Jason. Long Journey to Sincerity. (p. 1047)
Ellis, Jesse. Kyle Learns Baseball. (p. 969)
—My Pal Willie: Willie Gets a Home. (p. 1216)
Ellis, Jessica, illus. see Walters, David.
Ellis, Joey, illus. see Dunn, Hunter S.
Ellis, Julie. Flags of the World. (p. 602)
—Lizzie's Hidden Message (p. 1043)
—New Neighbors. Lewis, Naomi C., illus. (p. 1246)
—Pythagoras & the Ratios: A Math Adventure. Peacock, Phyllis Hornung, illus. (p. 1421)
—What's Your Angle, Pythagoras? Hornung, Phyllis, illus. (p. 1900)
Ellis, Julie & Nickel, Adam. Giant's Causeway. (p. 674)
Ellis, Julie & Stewart, Christen. Lizzie's Hidden Message. (p. 1043)
Ellis, Kat. Blackfin Sky. (p. 197)
Ellis, Kathryn. Joey Jeremiah (p. 920)
Ellis, Kathy. Mrs. Upside down & Her House. (p. 1188)
Ellis, Kevin L., jt. auth. see Lyon, Nathan W.
Ellis, Kiersten. Do Planets Hang on Strings? (p. 457)
Ellis, Kiersten R. Do Planets Hang on Strings? (p. 457)
Ellis, Kim. Bernard & His Dad. (p. 167)
Ellis, Latoya. Dancing Christmas Tree. (p. 402)
Ellis, Leanne Statland. Tree Huggers. (p. 1783)
—Ugly One. (p. 1808)
Ellis, Libby. Midge & Max's Scavenger Hunt. Jonason, Dave, illus. (p. 1138)
—Ziggy the Zebra. Yoon, Salina, illus. (p. 1986)
Ellis, Libby, illus. see Nelson, Esther & Hirsch, Davida.
Ellis, M. Henderson. Petra K & the Blackhearts: A Novel. (p. 1348)
Ellis, Madelynne. Passion of Isis. (p. 1327)
Ellis, Mark & Campbell, Ruth. Words. (p. 1951)
Ellis, Mark, et al. Professional English. (p. 1409)
Ellis, Mark Richard. Granddad Tales. (p. 707)
Ellis, Martyn, jt. auth. see Martin, Rosa Maria.
Ellis, Martyn & Martin, Rosa Maria. Aventura Nueva. (p. 119)
Ellis, Marvie. Keisha's Doors: An Autism Story. Bk. 1 (p. 948)
—Tacos Anyone? (p. 1695)
—Tacos Anyone?: An Autism Story Book. Bk. 2 (p. 1695)
Ellis, Mary. Dick & His Cat. (p. 435)
Ellis, Melissa Martin, photos by see Van Gruisen, Janette van de Geest, et al.
Ellis, Melody A. Unexpected Hero. (p. 1817)
Ellis, Paula. Arizona Activity Book Nitzsche, Shane, illus. (p. 98)
—Minnesota Activity Book (p. 1147)
—Texas Activity Book Nitzsche, Shane, illus. (p. 1724)
—Yellowstone & Grand Teton Activity Book. Nitzsche, Shane, illus. (p. 1970)
—Yosemite Activity Book Nitzsche, Shane, illus. (p. 1972)
Ellis, Paula J. There's a Fish Inside My Bathroom Scales. (p. 1730)
Ellis, Peter Berresford, see Tremayne, Peter, pseud.
Ellis, Ralph. Love & the Abyss: An Essay on Finitude & Value. (p. 1059)
Ellis, Rene'. Billy Bob the Bullfrog from Marshy Bog. (p. 187)
Ellis, Rich, illus. see Kneece, Mark & Serling, Rod.
Ellis, Richard E. Andrew Jackson (p. 72)
Ellis, Rob & Collins UK. Edexcel GCSE Maths - Higher Practice Book: Use & Apply Standard Techniques. (p. 504)
Ellis, Rob & Collins UK Publishing Staff. Collins GCSE Maths - AQA GCSE Maths Higher Practice Book: Use & Apply Standard Techniques. (p. 340)
Ellis, Roger. Complete Audition Book for Young Actors: A Comprehensive Guide to Winning by Enhancing Acting Skills. (p. 352)
—More Scenes & Monologs from the Best New Plays: An Anthology of New Dramatic Writing from Professionally-Produced Plays (p. 1174)
Ellis, Roland. Cyfres Cled: Castell Marwolaeth Boenus AC Erchyll. (p. 397)
Ellis, Rosemary, et al. Sugar Solution Cookbook: More Than 200 Delicious Recipes to Balance Your Blood Sugar Naturally. (p. 1673)
Ellis, Sarah. Baby Project (p. 127)
—Ben over Night LaFave, Kim, illus. (p. 163)
—Big Ben. LaFave, Kim, illus. (p. 178)
—Odd Man Out (p. 1278)
—Queen's Feet Petricic, Dusan, illus. (p. 1425)
—Several Lives of Orphan Jack St-Aubin, Bruno, illus. (p. 1555)
Ellis, Sarah, ed. see McPhail, David.
Ellis, Sarah, jt. auth. see Page, P. K.
Ellis, Sarah, jt. auth. see Pearson, S.
Ellis, Sarah & Suzuki, David. Salmon Forest. Lott, Sheena, illus. (p. 1505)
Ellis, Scott. Our Fun Dad. (p. 1308)
Ellis, Sherry. That Mama Is a Grouch. (p. 1726)
Ellis, Sophia L. Through the Eyes of Tre. (p. 1745)
Ellis, Stacy. Wiccan ABC Book for Babies. (p. 1927)
Ellis, Susan E., creator. Aliens among Us: A Book of Insect Portraits. (p. 41)
Ellis, Timothy Craig. Centennial History of Loray Baptist Church, Gastonia, North Carolina, 1905-2005. (p. 287)
—Three Tales. (p. 1744)
Ellis, Toni T. Baby Girl's Mirror. (p. 126)
Ellis, Tonya. Sophie Washington: Queen of the Bee. (p. 1613)
Ellis, Warren. Cure (p. 392)
—Doom 2099: The Complete Collection by Warren Ellis. Klein, David et al, illus. (p. 470)
—Iron Man: Armor Wars. Kurth, Steve, illus. (p. 888)
—Leaving the 20th Century (p. 986)
—Orbiter. (p. 1302)
—Planetary Omnibus. (p. 1368)
—Secret. (p. 1540)
—Switchblade Honey. (p. 1691)
—Thunderbolts by Warren Ellis & Mike Deodato Ultimate Collection. (p. 1746)
Ellis, Warren & Guice, Jackson. New Maps of Hell. (p. 1246)
Ellison, Chris, illus. see Crane, Carol.
Ellison, Chris, illus. see Mackall, Dandi Daley.
Ellison, Chris, illus. see Raven, Margot Theis.
Ellison, Chris, illus. see Riehle, Mary Ann McCabe.
Ellison, Chris, illus. see Scillian, Devin & Young, Judy.
Ellison, Chris, illus. see Scillian, Devin.
Ellison, Chris, illus. see Stiegemeyer, Julie.
Ellison, Chris, illus. see Young, Judy.
Ellison, Connie, ed. see Annie's Staff.
Ellison, Elizabeth Stow. Flight. (p. 604)
Ellison, Harlan. Troublemakers. (p. 1790)
—Vic & Blood: The Continuing Adventures of a Boy & His Dog. (p. 1840)
Ellison, James W. & Atchison, Doug. Akeelah & the Bee. (p. 32)
Ellison, Jesse Andrews, jt. auth. see Nunez, Ralph da Costa.
Ellison, Joy D. Carol & Connie. (p. 270)
Ellison, Kate. Curse Girl. (p. 394)
Ellison, Laura. Hard Rock, Hard Times: Coming of Age in Butte Montana, 1911-1917. (p. 748)
Ellison, Nancy, photos by see American Ballet Theatre Staff, et al.
Ellison, Penny. Daisy the Dancing Flower. (p. 400)
Ellison, Renee. Character Traits Coloring Book pages PDF Files. (p. 291)
Ellison, Sheila & Gray, Judith. 365 Smart after-School Activites: TV-Free Fun Anytime for Kids Ages 7-12. (p. 2001)
Ellison, Sheila, ed. If Women Ruled the World: How to Create the World We Want to Live In. (p. 854)
Ellison, Virginia H. Winnie-the-Pooh Cookbook. Shepard, Ernest H., illus. (p. 1937)
Ellis-Ritter, Karen, jt. auth. see Ritter, Joshua.
Elliston, Beth. Baby Book as told by ME! the Big Sister. (p. 125)
Ellis-Wright, Norma. I Love to Look. (p. 843)
Ellithorpe, Chris, illus. see Callella, Trisha.
Ellithorpe, Chris, illus. see Harding, Davilla.
Elroy, James. Black Dahlia. (p. 195)
Ells, Marcia Louise. Glips, Snodagers & Wallywogs. Ells, Marcia Louise, illus. (p. 683)
Ellsberry, Sharon. Spaniel Family Goes to the State Fair. Espinosa, Chris, illus. (p. 1620)
Ellse, Mark & Honeywill, Chris. Fields, Forces & Synthesis. (p. 584)
—Mechanics & Radioactivity. (p. 1118)
—Waves & Our Universe. (p. 1864)
Ellse, Mark, et al. Electricity & Thermal Physics. (p. 509)
Ellsworth, Geoff. Palazzo con Elephante. (p. 1319)
Ellsworth, Loretta. In a Heartbeat. (p. 863)
—Shrouding Woman. (p. 1571)
—Unforgettable. (p. 1817)
Ellsworth, Mark R. Bolds of a Feather (p. 207)
—Capped for Courage. (p. 263)
—Grawnma Becky's Bread. (p. 713)
Ellsworth, Mary Ellen. Gertrude Chandler Warner & the Boxcar Children. DeJohn, Marie, illus. (p. 667)
Ellsworth, Nick. Twinkle the Tooth Fairy. White, Michelle, illus. (p. 1802)
Ellsworth, Theo. Eyes of War. (p. 558)
Ellwand, David, ed. see Tagg, Christine.
Ellwand, David, jt. auth. see Ellwand, Ruth.
Ellwand, David, photos by see Tagg, Christine.
Ellwand, David, photos by. Old MacDonald Had a Farm. (p. 1284)
Ellwand, Ruth & Ellwand, David. Mystery of the Fool & the Vanisher. Ellwand, David, illus. (p. 1225)
Ellwell, Tristan, illus. see Datlow, Ellen.
Ellwood, Nancy. Lance Armstrong: With a Discussion of Determination. (p. 973)
Ellynby, Christy. 24th Room: The Vale Legend. (p. 1996)
Elman, Natalie Madorsky & Kennedy-Moore, Eileen. Unwritten Rules of Friendship: Simple Strategies to Help Your Child Make Friends. (p. 1824)
Elman, Robert. Nature. (p. 1236)
Elmer, Robert. Beyond Corista (p. 173)
—Candy Bombers (p. 261)
—Life Behind the Wall: Candy Bombers, Hidden Bunkers, & Smugglers Treasure (p. 1008)
—Trion Rising (p. 1787)
Elmer, Robert, jt. auth. see McCusker, Paul.
Elmer, Robert, jt. auth. see Viguié, Debbie.
Elmokadem, Shirley. Serena & The Moor's Last Sigh. (p. 1552)
Elmore, Amber. Betsy Beansprout Adventure Guide. Short, Kasey, illus. (p. 172)
—Betsy Beansprout Camping Guide. Hickey, Josh, illus. (p. 172)
Elmore, Barbara. Saviors of the Bugle. (p. 1518)
Elmore, Larry, illus. see Young, Louise O.
Elmore, Larry, illus. see Young, Louise.
Elmore, Larry, jt. auth. see Young, Louise O.
Elmore, Wanda M. & Elmore, Wardon O. Mr. Fix, Design It, Carry It with You, My Dadee & Me. (p. 1185)
Elmore, Wardon O., jt. auth. see Elmore, Wanda M.
Elon, Amos. Pity of It All: A Portrait of the German-Jewish Epoch, 1743-1933. (p. 1365)

E

Elora, Grace. Bear Cubs. (p. 150)
—Bunnies. (p. 242)
—Dinosaur Fossils. (p. 442)
—Foals. (p. 610)
—Kittens. (p. 963)
—Piglets. (p. 1358)
—Puppies. (p. 1417)
Elovitz Marshall, Sylvia A. & Marshall, Linda. Mitzvah Magician. Engel, Christiane, illus. (p. 1156)
Elpel, Thomas J. Shanleya's Quest: A Botany Adventure for Kids Ages 9 - 99 Brown, Gloria Dean, illus. (p. 1559)
Elphick, Jonathan, et al. Encyclopedia of Animals. (p. 524)
Elphinstone, Katy, illus. see Defoe, Daniel.
Elphinstone, Katy, illus. see Melville, Herman.
Elrazky, Sumaiyah, jt. auth. see Anderson, Melissa.
Elrod, Julie. Splitting Hares. (p. 1630)
Elsammak, Ariane, illus. see Hamilton, Martha & Weiss, Mitch.
Elsby, Lizzy, illus. see Osterbach, Batya.
Elschner, Geraldine. Little Hippo: A Children's Book Inspired by Egyptian Art. Klauss, Anja, illus. (p. 1029)
—Where Is the Frog? A Children's Book Inspired by Claude Monet. Girel, Stephane, illus. (p. 1909)
Elschner, Geraldine & Nille, Peggy. Cat & the Bird: A Children's Book Inspired by Paul Klee. (p. 277)
Elsdale, Bob & PQ Blackwell, Ltd. Staff. Mom, I'm a Lucky Duck. (p. 1161)
Else, Barbara. Queen & the Nobody Boy: Hodie's Journey (in Five Parts All about Bad Choices) Broad, Sam, illus. (p. 1424)
—Traveling Restaurant: Jasper's Voyage in Three Parts. (p. 1780)
Elsen, Janis A., illus. see Nees, Diane L.
Elser, Smoke & Brown, Bill. Packin' in on Mules & Horses. (p. 1317)
Elshof, Phyllis Ten, et al. What Cancer Cannot Do: Stories of Courage (p. 1881)
Elsmore, Warren. Brick Wonders: Ancient, Modern, & Natural Wonders Made from LEGO. (p. 227)
Elsner, Alan. Guarded by Angels: How My Father & Uncle Survived Hitler & Cheated Stalin. (p. 728)
Elsohn Ross, Michael. Mama's Milk. Wolff, Ashley, illus. (p. 1084)
Elsom, Clare, illus. see Guillain, Charlotte & Mason, Paul.
Elsom, Clare, illus. see Guillain, Charlotte.
Elsom, Clare, illus. see Irwin, Kate.
Elsom, Clare, illus. see Katschke, Judy.
Elsom, Clare, illus. see Mason, Paul.
Elsom, Clare, illus. see Smith, Justine.
Elsom, Clare, jt. auth. see Smith, Justine.
Elson, Maya Mackowiak. Mystery of the Pirate Bell. (p. 1226)
Elson, Richard, illus. see Abnett, Dan.
Elson, William H. Elson Readers (p. 516)
—Elson Readers, Book 5. (p. 516)
Elson, William H. & Keck, Christine M. Elson Readers - Book V. (p. 516)
Elson, William H., et al. Elson Readers (p. 516)
—Elson Readers, Book Eight (p. 516)
Elster, Charles Harrington. Test of Time: A Novel Approach to the SAT & ACT. (p. 1723)
Elster, Charles Harrington & Elliot, Joseph. Tooth & Nail: A Novel Approach to the SAT. (p. 1768)
Elster, Jean Alicia. Colored Car. (p. 343)
—I'll Do the Right Thing. Tadgell, Nicole, illus. (p. 856)
—Who's Jim Hines? (p. 1920)
Elster, Jean Alicia, ed. see McMickle, Marvin Andrew.
Elster, Kathi, jt. auth. see Crowley, Katherine.
Elston, Ashley. Rules for Breaking. (p. 1495)
—Rules for Disappearing. (p. 1495)
Elston, Heidi. George H. W. Bush. (p. 663)
—Snakes: Level 1. (p. 1596)
—Snakes Eat & Grow: Level 2. (p. 1596)
—Snakes in the Desert: Level 3. (p. 1597)
Elston, Heidi M. D. Buffaloes: Level 1. Keimig, Candice, illus. (p. 236)
—Buffaloes Eat & Grow: Level 2. Keimig, Candice, illus. (p. 236)
—Buffaloes on the Prairie: Level 3. Keimig, Candice, illus. (p. 236)
—Calvin Coolidge. (p. 255)
—Chester Arthur. (p. 298)
—Harry S. Truman. (p. 751)
—Jimmy Carter. (p. 918)
—John Adams. (p. 921)
—John Quincy Adams. (p. 922)
—Millard Fillmore. (p. 1143)
—Thomas Jefferson. (p. 1739)
—Warren G. Harding. (p. 1858)
—William H. Harrison. (p. 1933)
—Zachary Taylor. (p. 1984)
Elston, James W., illus. see Simonson, Louise.
Eltaeb, Gabe, jt. auth. see Cohen, Ivan.
Elting, Mary, jt. auth. see Folsom, Michael.
Elton, Candice, jt. auth. see Elton, Richard.
Elton, Candice & Elton, Richard. My Family Album. (p. 1202)
—My Vacation Album: Includes: Reusable Camera, Film, Batteries & Glue Stick. Lee, Fran, illus. (p. 1220)
Elton, Richard, jt. auth. see Elton, Candice.
Elton, Richard & Elton, Candice. Every Kid Needs a Rubber Band Launcher. (p. 542)
Elton, Sarah. Starting from Scratch: What You Should Know about Food & Cooking Kulak, Jeff & Owlkids Books Inc. Staff, illus. (p. 1644)
Eltoukhy, G. N. Fattopia a C: The Tablet Legacy. (p. 577)
Eltoukhy, G.N. 12 Enchanted Kindles for Bedtime Lullabies: Don't Live in Darkness Sorry for Failed Life , You Must Try the Unwritten. (p. 1994)
—Princess & the Enchanted Pegasus. (p. 1402)
—Sheherazade Chronicles of the Fairy Tales. (p. 1564)
Elum, Deborah, ed. see Page, Brenda.
Elvgren, Jennifer. Josias, Hold the Book. Tadgell, Nicole, illus. (p. 927)
—Whispering Town. Santomauro, Fabio, illus. (p. 1912)
Elwell, Ellen Banks. Toddler's Songbook. Elwell, Ellen Banks & Turk, Caron, illus. (p. 1761)
Elwell, Ellen Banks & Turk, Caron. Toddler's Songbook. (p. 1761)
Elwell, Jake & Ross, Jeffrey Ian. Cybercrime. (p. 396)
Elwell, Maggie. My Mom, the Coconut MacHine. (p. 1214)
Elwell, Peter. Most Remarkable Bear. Elwell, Peter, illus. (p. 1177)
Elwell, Peter, illus. see Bauer, Marion Dane.
Elwell, Sharon. Caught in the Middle: Reflections of a Middle School Teacher. (p. 282)
—Jeremy & the Wappo. Gentry, Debra, illus. (p. 913)
Elwell, Susan. Madigan's Discoveries: Book One - the Magic of Transformation. (p. 1070)
Elwell, Telva & Kelley, Barbara. Eliasense Misses the Train. Elwell, Telva, illus. (p. 514)
Elwell, Tristan, illus. see Pearson, Ridley.
Elwick, Elissa. Princess & the Sleep Stealer. Elwick, Elissa, illus. (p. 1403)
Elwood, Danielle. I Love Me, I Love You. (p. 842)
Elwood, Taty. Perfect Gift / el Mejor Regalo. (p. 1342)
Elworthy, Antony, illus. see Hawes, Alison.
Elworthy, Antony, illus. see Pym, Tasha.
Elworthy, Antony, illus. see Shipton, Paul.
Elworthy, Antony, photos by see Pym, Tasha.
Ely, Alex. Destiny at Dawn. (p. 431)
Ely, Dave, illus. see Kremer, Kevin R.
Ely, Dave, illus. see Kremer, Kevin.
Ely, Dave, illus. see Pohl, Dora & Kremer, Kevin.
Ely, Jennifer W. Mommy Teach Me to Read: Pre-Reader Series 1. (p. 1162)
Ely, Kosa. Peaceable Forest: India's Tale of Kindness to Animals. Johansson, Anna, illus. (p. 1332)
Ely, Lesley. Looking after Louis. Dunbar, Polly, tr. (p. 1050)
Ely, Lesley & Dunbar, Polly. Measuring Angels. Dunbar, Polly, illus. (p. 1117)
Ely, Lesley, et al. Cuidando a Louis. (p. 390)
Ely, Lisa, jt. auth. see Glassman, Michael.
Ely, Lisa & Glassman, Michael. Kinder Gardens: Autumn Fun (p. 957)
—Kinder Gardens: Growing Inspiration for Children (p. 957)
Ely, Paul, illus. see Hulme, Joy N.
Ely, Scott. Elephant Mountains (p. 511)
Elya, Susan Middleton. Al fin en Casa. Davalos, Felipe, illus. (p. 32)
—Bebé Goes Shopping. Salerno, Steven, illus. (p. 155)
—Fire! Fuego! Brave Bomberos. Santat, Dan, illus. (p. 590)
—Fire! ¡Fuego! Brave Bomberos. Dantat, Dan & Santat, Dan, illus. (p. 590)
—Home at Last. Dávalos, Felipe, illus. (p. 792)
—Little Roja Riding Hood. Guevara, Susan, illus. (p. 1036)
—Madre Goose: Nursery Rhymes for Niños. Martinez-Neal, Juana, illus. (p. 1070)
—Oh No, Gotta Go! Karas, G. Brian, illus. (p. 1281)
—Say Hola to Spanish at the Circus. Lopez, Loretta, illus. (p. 1518)
—Say Hola to Spanish, Otra Vez (Again!) Lopez, Loretta, illus. (p. 1518)
Elyssa, jt. auth. see Elisha, .
Élyum Studio, illus. see Adrien, Gilles & Broders, Alain.
Élyum Studio, illus. see Bick, Ilsa J.
Élyum Studio, illus. see Bidaud, Agnès.
Élyum Studio, illus. see Cerami, Matteo, et al.
ÉLyum Studio, illus. see Constantine, Clélia.
Élyum Studio, illus. see Costi, Vincent.
Élyum Studio, illus. see Dubos, Delphine.
Élyum Studio, illus. see Gaudin, Thierry.
ÉLyum Studio, illus. see Loisillier, Maud & Morel, Diane.
ÉLyum Studio, illus. see Magnet, Julien.
Élyum Studio, illus. see N'Leh, Anne-Claire.
Élyum Studio Staff, illus. see Benedetti, Hervé & Robin, Nicolas.
Élyum Studio Staff, illus. see Benedetti, Hervé, et al.
Élyum Studio Staff, illus. see Dubos, Delphine.
Elzaurdia, Paco. Cuauhtemoc Blanco. (p. 388)
—Rafael Marquez. (p. 1433)
Elzaurdia, Sharon, illus. see Hillert, Margaret.
Elzbieta. Mimi's Scary Theater: A Play in Nine Scenes for Seven Characters & an Egg. Elzbieta & Hawcock, David, illus. (p. 1145)
Elzina, Philda. Purple Is the Magic Colour. (p. 1419)
em, est. Red Blinds the Foolish. (p. 1453)
Emam, Ruby, tr. see Beh-Rang, Samad.
Eman, Leisa M. Pugsley's Imagination. (p. 1415)
Emanuel, Effie Ann. Charles Chameleon. (p. 292)
—Penguin Party (p. 1337)
Emanuel, Effie Ann, illus. see Phillips, Cynthia.
Emanuel, Lora. Puppy Tree Swope, Brenda, illus. (p. 1418)
Emanuele, Patricia. Coping with Aggression. (p. 365)
—Everything You Need to Know about Epilepsy. (p. 545)
Embacher, Eric. Stowed Away (p. 1664)
—Will Smith: The Funny, Funky, & Confident Fresh Prince. (p. 1932)
Ember, Dave, illus. see Compton, Carrie.
Ember, Kathi, illus. see Burch, Regina G.
Ember, Kathi, illus. see Burch, Regina G. & Donovan Guntly, Jenette.
Ember, Kathi, illus. see Krensky, Stephen.
Ember, Kathi, illus. see Mehlhaff, Christine.
Ember, Kathi, illus. see Miller, Pat.
Ember, Kathi, illus. see Nolan, Janet.
Emberley, Adrian, jt. auth. see Emberley, Rebecca.
Emberley, Barbara. One Wide River to Cross. Emberley, Barbara, ed. (p. 1297)
—Story of Paul Bunyan. Emberley, Ed, illus. (p. 1659)
Emberley, Barbara & Ed, illus. see Branley, Franklyn M.
Emberley, Ed. Bye-Bye, Big Bad Bullybug! Emberley, Ed, illus. (p. 249)
—Ed Emberley's Complete Funprint Drawing Book. (p. 503)
—Ed Emberley's Drawing Book of Trucks & Trains. Emberley, Ed, illus. (p. 503)
—Ed Emberley's Fingerprint Drawing Book. Emberley, Ed, illus. (p. 503)
—Ed Emberley's Picture Pie: A Cut & Paste Drawing Book. Emberley, Ed, illus. (p. 503)
—Nighty Night, Little Green Monster. (p. 1255)
—Where's My Sweetie Pie? (p. 1910)
—Wing on a Flea. (p. 1936)
Emberley, Ed, illus. see Emberley, Barbara.
Emberley, Ed, illus. see Emberley, Rebecca & Emberley, Adrian.
Emberley, Ed, illus. see Emberley, Rebecca.
Emberley, Ed, jt. auth. see Emberley, Rebecca.
Emberley, Ed, jt. auth. see LBCL.
Emberley, Ed & Emberley, Rebecca. Chicken Little. Emberley, Ed, illus. (p. 300)
—Red Hen. Emberley, Ed, illus. (p. 1454)
Emberley, Edward R. Ed Emberley's Big Green Drawing Book. (p. 503)
—Ed Emberley's Big Green Drawing Book. Emberley, Edward R., illus. (p. 503)
—Ed Emberley's Big Purple Drawing Book. Emberley, Edward R., illus. (p. 503)
—Ed Emberley's Drawing Book - Make a World: Learn to Draw the Ed Emberley Way! Emberley, Edward R., illus. (p. 503)
—Ed Emberley's Drawing Book of Animals. Emberley, Edward R., illus. (p. 503)
—Ed Emberley's Drawing Book of Faces. Emberley, Edward R., illus. (p. 503)
—Ed Emberley's Drawing Book of Weirdos. (p. 503)
—Ed Emberley's Great Thumbprint Drawing Book. Emberley, Edward R., illus. (p. 503)
Emberley, Edward R., jt. auth. see Emberley, Rebecca.
Emberley, Michael, illus. see Bottner, Barbara.
Emberley, Michael, illus. see Harris, Robie H.
Emberley, Michael, illus. see Harris, Robie H. & Cousins, Lucy.
Emberley, Michael, illus. see Hoberman, Mary Ann.
Emberley, Michael, illus. see Lloyd-Jones, Sally.
Emberley, Michael, jt. auth. see Hoberman, Mary Ann.
Emberley, Rebecca. Ant & the Grasshopper. Emberley, Ed, illus. (p. 88)
—Crocodile & the Scorpion. Emberley, Ed, illus. (p. 384)
—My Big Book of Spanish Words. (p. 1197)
—My City/ Mi Ciudad. (p. 1200)
—My Garden/ Mi Jardin. (p. 1209)
—My Numbers (Mis Numeros) (p. 1216)
—My Opposites (Mis Opuestos) (p. 1216)
—My Room/Mi Cuarto. (p. 1217)
—My School/Mi Escuela. (p. 1218)
Emberley, Rebecca, ed. see Sayres, David.
Emberley, Rebecca, illus. see Sayres, David.
Emberley, Rebecca, jt. auth. see Emberley, Ed.
Emberley, Rebecca & Emberley, Adrian. There Was an Old Monster! Emberley, Ed, illus. (p. 1730)
Emberley, Rebecca & Emberley, Ed. Ant & the Grasshopper. (p. 88)
—Chicken Little. (p. 300)
—If You're a Monster & You Know It... Emberley, Ed, illus. (p. 855)
—Lion & the Mice. (p. 1020)
—Mice on Ice. (p. 1134)
—Ten Little Beasties. Emberley, Rebecca & Emberley, Ed, illus. (p. 1719)
Emberley, Rebecca & Emberley, Edward R. Lion & the Mice. Emberley, Rebecca & Emberley, Edward R., illus. (p. 1020)
—Mice on Ice. Emberley, Rebecca & Emberley, Edward R., illus. (p. 1134)
Embleton-Hall, Chris, illus. see Edwards, Josh.
Embleton-Hall, Chris, illus. see Williamson, Karen.
Embry, Eugene, ed. see Goodall, Barry, Jr.
Embry, Stacey, illus. see Jones, Bryan E.
Emch, Christiana M. Donut Cat's Bakery. (p. 469)
—Rainbow Girl, Make a Joyful Noise. (p. 1435)
EMC-Paradigm Publishing Staff. Discovering Literature: Resource. (p. 449)
—Discovering Literature: Vocabulary Resource. (p. 449)
Emde, Nicole. Alabaster the Albino Alligator. (p. 33)
Emecz, Steve, ed. see Morgan, Bernard.
Emel Alp Sari, illus. see Poulter, J. R.
Emeott, Bill. How to Sunday School Guide Curriculum Workshop for Children's Lead. (p. 821)
Emerald Books, creator. Heroes of History - Maps of the United States Workbook: A Reproducible Workbook & Curriculum Guide. (p. 773)
Emerick, Becky. Duncan's Journey: A Little Lamb's Adventure through the Twenty-Third Psalm. (p. 490)
Emerick, Yahiya. Puedo Colorear Mi Mundo Musulman: Libro para Colorear. Meehan, Patricia, illus. (p. 1414)
Emerling, Dorothy, illus. see Fourment, Tiffany & Glanniny, Gary.
Emerling, Dorothy, illus. see Fourment, Tiffany.
Emerling, Dorothy, illus. see McKnight, Diane.
Emerson, Alice. Betty Gordon at Boarding School. (p. 172)
—Betty Gordon in Washington. (p. 172)
Emerson, Alice B. Betty Gordon at Boarding School: The Treasure of Indian Chasm. (p. 172)
—Betty Gordon in Washington. (p. 172)
—Ruth Fielding at Snow Camp: Or, Lost in the Backwoods. (p. 1498)
—Ruth Fielding at Snow Camp or Lost in the Backwoods. (p. 1498)
—Ruth Fielding at the War Front. (p. 1498)
—Ruth Fielding in the Red Cross or Doing. (p. 1498)
—Ruth Fielding on Cliff Island: Or the Old Hunter's Treasure Box. (p. 1498)
—Ruth Fielding on the St. Lawrence or the. (p. 1498)
Emerson, Carl. Cold Winter Day Doerrfeld, Cori, illus. (p. 339)
—Falling Freddy the Fainting Goat. Trover, Zachary, illus. (p. 567)
—Monster Boy - 6 Titles Levin, Lon, illus. (p. 1166)
—Monster Boy & the Classroom Pet. Levin, Lon, illus. (p. 1166)
—Monster Boy & the Halloween Parade. Levin, Lon, illus. (p. 1166)
—Monster Boy & the Scary Scouts. Levin, Lon, illus. (p. 1166)
—Monster Boy at the Library. Levin, Lon, illus. (p. 1166)
—Monster Boy's Art Project. Levin, Lon, illus. (p. 1166)
—Monster Boy's Field Trip. Levin, Lon, illus. (p. 1166)
—Monster Boy's First Day of School. Levin, Lon, illus. (p. 1166)
—Monster Boy's Gym Class. Levin, Lon, illus. (p. 1166)
—Monster Boy's School Lunch. Levin, Lon, illus. (p. 1166)
—Monster Boy's Soccer Game. Levin, Lon, illus. (p. 1166)
—Monster Boy's Valentine. Levin, Lon, illus. (p. 1166)
—Nosy Arnie the Anteater. Trover, Zachary, illus. (p. 1266)
—Opie the Opossum Wakes Up. Trover, Zachary, illus. (p. 1300)
—Sally the Salamander's Lost Tail. Trover, Zachary, illus. (p. 1505)
—Speed up, Sammy the Tree Sloth! Trover, Zachary, illus. (p. 1624)
—What Are You, Patty? A Platypus Tale. Trover, Zachary, illus. (p. 1880)
Emerson, Charles P. & Betts, George Herbert. Living at Our Best, Book: Habits of Right Living Series. (p. 1040)
Emerson, Charles Phillips, et al. Habits for Health, Book: Habits of Right Living Series. (p. 735)
Emerson, Darcie. One Sock. (p. 1297)
Emerson, Hunt, illus. see Wilson, Sean Michael & Dickson, Benjamin.
Emerson, Joan. Itty Bitty Animals. (p. 900)
—Itty-Bitty Animals. (p. 900)
—Stinky Bugs. (p. 1651)
—Stinky Bugs, Level 2. (p. 1651)
Emerson, Judy. Franklin D. Roosevelt Saunders-Smith, Gail, ed. (p. 630)
—John F. Kennedy Saunders-Smith, Gail, ed. (p. 921)
—Theodore Roosevelt (p. 1729)
—Theodore Roosevelt. Saunders-Smith, Gail, ed. (p. 1729)
Emerson, Kevin. Breakout. (p. 225)
—Carlos Is Gonna Get It. (p. 270)
—Dark Shore. (p. 408)
—Encore to an Empty Room. (p. 524)
—Exile. (p. 548)
—Far Dawn. (p. 572)
—Fellowship for Alien Detection. (p. 581)
—Lost Code. (p. 1055)
Emerson, Kim & Antebi, Marcus. Skydiver's Survival Guide Second Edition. Mazur, Danielle, ed. (p. 1587)
Emerson, Oliver Farrar, ed. see Johnson, Samuel.
Emerson, Ralph Waldo. Essays: First Series. Vol. 2 (p. 536)
—Essays: Second Series. Vol. 3 (p. 536)
—Representative Men: Seven Lectures - Including. (p. 1461)
Emerson, Ralph Waldo, jt. auth. see Keyes, Charlotte E.
Emerson, Roger. Cover Your Sneeze, Please! A Short Musical Play about Kids' Healthy Habits. (p. 373)
—Sing 6-7-8! 50 Ways to Improve Your Elementary or Middle School Choir. (p. 1578)
Emerson, Scott. Case of the Cat with the Missing Ear: From the Notebooks of Edward R. Smithfield, D. V. M. Mullett, Viv, illus. (p. 273)
Emerson, Sharon. Zebrafish. Reynolds, Peter H. & Kurilla, Renee, illus. (p. 1985)
Emerson, Zelda. Tweens Santa Surprise: How to Explain Santa to Pre-Teens. Emerson, Zelda, illus. (p. 1799)
Emerson-Stonnell, Sharon. Number Systems. (p. 1271)
Emert, Phyllis. Pottery. (p. 1388)
Emert, Phyllis, ed. Michelangelo. (p. 1135)
Emert, Phyllis Raybin. Art in Glass. (p. 102)
—Attorneys General: Enforcing the Law. (p. 114)
—Marc Chagall. Greenhaven Press Editors, ed. (p. 1091)
—World War II: The European Theater. (p. 1959)
Emert, Sarah. Chanler & Friends: Backyard Camping. (p. 290)
Emery, Airin. Dance Divas: The Dance Series (Book #2) (p. 402)
—Tap In: The Dance Series (Book #3) (p. 1705)
—Triple Threats: The Dance Series (Book #4) (p. 1787)
Emery, Anne. Dinny Gordon, Freshman. (p. 441)
—Dinny Gordon Junior. (p. 441)
—Dinny Gordon Senior. (p. 441)
—Dinny Gordon Sophomore. (p. 441)
—Senior Year. Krush, Beth, illus. (p. 1550)
—Sorority Girl. (p. 1614)
Emery, Bruce Maynard. Fingerstyle Guitar from Scratch. (p. 589)
Emery, Jennifer, illus. see Fletcher, Ralph.
Emery, Jennifer, illus. see O'Keefe, Susan Heyboer.
Emery, Jennifer, illus. see Ross, Kathy.
Emery, Jennifer, illus. see Ruurs, Margriet.
Emery, Jennifer, illus. see Smalley, Ruth Ann.
Emery, Joanna. Brothers of the Falls. Erickson, David, illus. (p. 231)
—Caring for a Colony: The Story of Jeanne Mance. Thompson, Allister, ed. (p. 269)
Emery, R. G. T-Quarterback. (p. 1694)
Emery, Thomas, illus. see Sherman, M. Zachary.
Emery, Thomas J., illus. see Sherman, M. Zachary.
Emigh, Karen. Bookworm: Discovering Idioms, Sayings & Expressions. Dana, Steve, illus. (p. 213)
—Herman's Hiding Places: Discovering up, in, under & Behind. (p. 771)
—Who Took My Shoe? Dana, Steve, illus. (p. 1917)
Emilio, Urberuaga, illus. see Lindo, Elvira.
Emily, Bolam, illus. see Tiger Tales Staff, ed.
Emily, Katelyn. Treasure-Trove Tales at the Gazebo. (p. 1782)
Emily Reed-Guildin, jt. auth. see Emily Reed-Guildin, Reed-Guildin.
Emily Reed-Guildin, Reed-Guildin & Emily Reed-Guildin. Sarah & Sammi's Playhouse Bedroom. (p. 1514)
Emily Rose Townsend. Arctic Foxes [Scholastic]. (p. 96)
—Penguins [Scholastic]. (p. 1337)
—Polar Bears [Scholastic]. (p. 1379)
—Seals [Scholastic]. (p. 1536)
Emin, Rebecca. When Dreams Come True. (p. 1902)
Emina, Peter. Lyra & the Adventure of the Flying Fish. Ridley, Alice, illus. (p. 1066)
Eminger, Cleta. Snow Lady's Wish. (p. 1599)
Emison, Patricia A. & Feldman Emison, Chloë. Growing with the Grain: Dynamic Families Shaping History from Ancient Times to the Present. (p. 727)
Emlyn, Non ap. Hamddena: Llawlyfr i Athrawon. (p. 739)
—Hamddena - Llyfr 1 Lefel 3/4. (p. 739)
—Hamddena - Llyfr 2 Lefel 4/5. (p. 739)
—Hamddena - Llyfr 3 Lefel 5/6. (p. 739)
—Hamddena - Llyfr 4 Lefel 6/7. (p. 739)

Emm, David. Madison Meets the Minister. Bedrick, Jeff, illus. (p. 1070)
Emma Chiarenza, jt. auth. see Annmarie.
Emma Treehouse Ltd. My Babies. Davis, Caroline, illus. (p. 1196)
—My Friends. Davis, Caroline, illus. (p. 1209)
—My Pets. Davis, Caroline, illus. (p. 1217)
—My Toys. Davis, Caroline, illus. (p. 1220)
Emmanuel, Linda. Angel Children: I Love Who I Am. (p. 73)
Emmaus. Emmaus Coordinator's Manual. (p. 520)
Emmel, Richard. Louisa. (p. 1058)
Emmeluth, Donald. Antibiotics. (p. 89)
—Fifth Disease. (p. 584)
—Influenza. (p. 873)
—Nicotine. (p. 1251)
—Plague, Second Edition. (p. 1366)
Emmeluth, Donald, et al. Staphylococcus aureus Infections. (p. 1640)
Emmendorfer, Marianne. Feather Collection. (p. 579)
Emmer, E. R. Dolphin Project. (p. 464)
—Me, Minerva & the Flying Flora. Huerta, Catherine, illus. (p. 1116)
Emmer, Rae. Band: Banda. (p. 136)
—Band. (p. 136)
—Band / Banda. (p. 136)
—Cheerleading: Porristas. (p. 296)
—Cheerleading / Porristas. (p. 296)
—Chorus: Coro. (p. 310)
—Chorus. (p. 310)
—Chorus / Coro. (p. 310)
—Community Service: Servicio Comunitario. (p. 350)
—Community Service. (p. 350)
—Community Service / Servicio Comunitario. (p. 350)
—Drama Club: Club de Teatro. (p. 480)
—Drama Club. (p. 480)
—Drama Club / Club de Teatro. (p. 480)
—School Newspaper: Periodico Escolar. (p. 1523)
—School Newspaper. (p. 1523)
—School Newspaper / Periódico Escolar. (p. 1523)
Emmer, Rick. Bigfoot: Fact or Fiction? (p. 184)
—Giant Anaconda & Other Cryptids: Fact or Fiction? (p. 673)
—Kraken: Fact or Fiction? (p. 967)
—Loch Ness Monster: Fact or Fiction? (p. 1044)
—Megalodon: Fact or Fiction? (p. 1124)
—Mokele-Mbembe: Fact or Fiction? (p. 1160)
—Virus Hunter. (p. 1844)
Emmerich, Anne Catherine. Dolorous Passion of Our Lord Jesus Christ. (p. 464)
Emmerich, Michael, tr. see Takahashi, Genichiro.
Emmerson, Michael, illus. see Meister, Carl.
Emmerson-Hicks, J., jt. auth. see Harvest House Publishers.
Emmet, Laura. Julie Trent & the Lightning. (p. 932)
—Julie Trent & the Tempest. (p. 932)
Emmett, Jennifer, ed. see Donovan, Amy & Shafran, Michael.
Emmett, Jennifer, ed. see Howell, Catherine.
Emmett, Jonathan. Best Gift of All. Cabban, Vanessa, illus. (p. 170)
—Conjuror's Cookbook: Goblin Stew. Vol. I (p. 357)
—Conjuror's Cookbook: Serpent Soup. Vol. II (p. 357)
—Conjuror's Cookbook: Ghostly Goulash. Vol. III (p. 357)
—Foxes in the Snow Harry, Rebecca, illus. (p. 626)
—Let's Read! Monsters: An Owner's Guide. Oliver, Mark, illus. (p. 1000)
—Santa Trap Bernatene, Poly, illus. (p. 1513)
—This Way, Ruby! Harry, Rebecca, illus. (p. 1737)
—Through the Heart of the Jungle. Gomez, Elena, illus. (p. 1745)
—Treasure of Captain Claw. Cox, Steve, illus. (p. 1782)
Emmett, Jonathan & Dunn, David H. Princess & the Pig. Bernatene, Poly, illus. (p. 1403)
—Wanda Wallaby Finds Her Bounce. Chambers, Mark, illus. (p. 1856)
Emmett, Jonathan & Reed, Nathan. What Friends Do Best. (p. 1884)
Emmitt, Randy. Butterflies of the Carolinas & Virginias. Emmitt, Randy, photos by. (p. 247)
Emond, Stephen. Bright Lights, Dark Nights. (p. 228)
—Happyface. (p. 747)
—Winter Town. (p. 1938)
Emory, Kb. Tyler Tales: What Is My Color/ Different Families. (p. 1805)
Emoto, Masaru. Secret of Water: For the Children of the World. (p. 1543)
Empson, Jo. Never Ever. Empson, Jo, illus. (p. 1242)
—Rabbityness. Empson, Jo, illus. (p. 1430)
Emroca Flores, Jose, illus. see Wallace, Rich.
Emshwiller, Carol. Mister Boots. (p. 1155)
—Mount. (p. 1180)
Emslie, Peter, illus. see Weinberg, Jennifer & RH Disney Staff.
Emura. W Juliet. (p. 1851)
—W Juliet. Emura, illus. (p. 1851)
—W Juliet. Flanagan, William, tr. from JPN. (p. 1851)
eMusic, Tom, ed. see Barrie, J. M.
Emzer, Counselor. Day Before Summer Vacation. (p. 412)
—Duane, You Must be Insane. (p. 487)
Enander, Glen. Elisabeth Schussler Fiorenza. (p. 513)
Encarnacion, Elizabeth. Cat's Cradle & Other Fantastic String Figures: Over 20 String Games. [BURST] Includes DVD & 2 Strings. (p. 281)
—Girls' Guide to Campfire Activities. (p. 680)
—Sports Stadiums. (p. 1633)
Encarnacion, Elizabeth, ed. see Longfellow, Henry Wadsworth.
Encarnacion, Elizabeth, ed. see Santore, Charles & Potter, Beatrix.
Encarnacion, Liz, ed. see Williams, Margery.
Encybrita. Looking at an Angle Mic 2006 G. (p. 1050)
—Packages & Polygons Mic 2006. (p. 1317)
—Revisiting Numbers Mic 2006 G. (p. 1466)
Encyclopaedia Britannica. Britannica Student Encyclopedia 2012 (p. 229)
Encyclopaedia Britannica, ed. American Presidency. (p. 62)
Encyclopaedia Britannica, Inc. Staff. Britannica Illustrated Science Library Series (18 Title Series) (p. 229)
Encyclopaedia Britannica, Inc. Staff, compiled by. Arts. (p. 104)
—Beginning of the Food Chain. (p. 159)
—Brigham Young. (p. 228)
—Britannica Illustrated Science Library: Birds (p. 229)
—Britannica Illustrated Science Library: Plants (p. 229)
—Britannica Illustrated Science Library: Climate (p. 229)
—Britannica Illustrated Science Library: Mammals (p. 229)
—Britannica Illustrated Science Library: Universe (p. 229)
—Britannica Illustrated Science Library: Volcanoes (p. 229)
—Britannica Illustrated Science Library: Human Body (p. 229)
—Britannica Illustrated Science Library: Technology. (p. 229)
—Britannica Illustrated Science Library: Invertebrates. (p. 229)
—Britannica Illustrated Science Library: Rocks & Minerals (p. 229)
—Britannica Illustrated Science Library: Fish & Amphibians (p. 229)
—Britannica Illustrated Science Library: Space Exploration (p. 229)
—Britannica Illustrated Science Library: Energy & Movement. (p. 229)
—Britannica Illustrated Science Library: Evolution & Genetics (p. 229)
—Britannica Illustrated Science Library: Reptiles & Dinosaurs (p. 229)
—Britannica Illustrated Science Library Print: Ecology. (p. 229)
—Britannica Illustrated Science Library Print: Environment. (p. 229)
—Britannica Math in Context Test & Practice Generator with Examview Assessment Suite. (p. 229)
—Cinderella. (p. 320)
—Discover English with Ben & Bella: Series 1: Outdoors. (p. 447)
—Discover English with Ben & Bella: Series 6: Shopping. (p. 447)
—Discover English with Ben & Bella: Series 4: at the Zoo. (p. 447)
—Discover English with Ben & Bella: Series 5: on the Farm. (p. 447)
—Discover English with Ben & Bella: Series 2 : Going Places. (p. 447)
—Discover English with Ben & Bella: Series 3 : in the Circus. (p. 447)
—Emcyclopaedia Britannica Children's Learning Suite 2007. (p. 517)
—Exploring Space. (p. 553)
—Familiar Tales Around the World. (p. 567)
—Food Plants. (p. 614)
—Hansel & Gretel. (p. 743)
—How Many Teeth? (p. 811)
—How the Elephant Got His Trunk. (p. 813)
—I Wish Daddy Didn't Drink So Much. (p. 848)
—If Your Parents Drink. (p. 855)
—Learn & Explore: Earth's Changing Environment. (p. 982)
—Learning about Our Bodies. (p. 984)
—Legends, Myths & Folktales. (p. 990)
—Legends, Myths, & Folktales. (p. 990)
—My First Britannica (p. 1206)
—My First Britannica: Africa. (p. 1206)
—My First Britannica: Plants. (p. 1206)
—My First Britannica: Mammals. (p. 1206)
—My First Britannica: The Americas. (p. 1206)
—My First Britannica: People in History. (p. 1206)
—My First Britannica: Reference Guide & Index. (p. 1206)
—My First Britannica: Asia, Australia, & New Zealand. (p. 1206)
—My First Britannica: Birds, Insects, Reptiles, & Aquatic Life. (p. 1206)
—My First Britannica: A Captivating 13-Volume Reference Set for Children 6-11 Years Set (p. 1206)
—My Little Foster Sister. (p. 1212)
—Planet Earth. (p. 1367)
—Rapunzel. (p. 1439)
—Respiratory System. (p. 1463)
—Rumpelstiltskin. (p. 1495)
—Science & Nature. (p. 1525)
—Sleeping Beauty. (p. 1589)
—Space Exploration. (p. 1619)
—Tales Around the World. (p. 1701)
—Technology & Inventions. (p. 1711)
—Views of Africa. (p. 1842)
—Views of Asia & Australia. (p. 1842)
—Views of Europe. (p. 1842)
—Views of the Americas. (p. 1842)
—What Happens to a Hamburger? (p. 1886)
—Wildlife Wonders. (p. 1931)
Encyclopaedia Britannica Publishers. Britannica Student Encyclopaedia (p. 229)
Encyclopaedia Britannica Publishers, Inc. Staff. Britannica Illustrated Science Library (p. 229)
Encyclopaedia Britannica Publishers, Inc. Staff, ed. Britannica's Student Atlas. (p. 229)
Encyclopaedia Britannica Publishers, Inc. Staff. Creatures of the Waters. (p. 380)
—Earth's Changing Environment. (p. 498)
—Food Plants. (p. 614)
—Math in Context. (p. 1106)
—Math in Context: Operations. (p. 1106)
—Math in Context: Reallotment. (p. 1106)
—Math in Context: Ups & Downs. (p. 1106)
—Math in Context: More or Less. (p. 1106)
—Math in Context: Number Tools. (p. 1106)
—Math in Context: Algebra Rules! (p. 1106)
—Math in Context: Second Chance. (p. 1106)
—Math in Context: Take a Chance. (p. 1106)
—Math in Context: Fraction Times. (p. 1106)
—Math in Context: Ratios & Rates. (p. 1106)
—Math in Context: Facts & Factors. (p. 1106)
—Math in Context: Made to Measure. (p. 1106)
—Math in Context: Building Formulas. (p. 1106)
—Math in Context: Dealing with Data. (p. 1106)
—Math in Context: Great Predictions. (p. 1106)
—Math in Context: It's All the Same. (p. 1106)
—Math in Context: Picturing Numbers. (p. 1106)
—Math in Context. (p. 1106)
—My First Britannica. (p. 1206)
Encyclopaedia Britannica Publishers, Inc. Staff, contrib. by. My First Britannica: An Engaging 13-Volume Thematic Reference Set for Grades 2-5 (p. 1206)
—Religions Around the World. (p. 1458)
Encyclopaedia Britannica Publishers, Inc. Staff. Remarkable People in History. (p. 1459)
—Views of Africa. (p. 1842)
—Views of Asia & Australia. (p. 1842)
—Views of Europe. (p. 1842)
—Views of the Americas. (p. 1842)
Encyclopedia Britannica Staff, creator. Birds. (p. 191)
—Energy & Movement. (p. 528)
—Invertebrates. (p. 884)
—Mammals. (p. 1085)
—Plants, Algae, & Fungi. (p. 1369)
—Reptiles & Dinosaurs. (p. 1461)
—Universe. (p. 1820)
End, Jackie, jt. auth. see Rosen, Wendy.
End the Clutter ETC. Computer & Internet Basics Step-by-Step. (p. 354)
Endacott, C. R. Afflatus. (p. 26)
Ende, Debra. Making Sense of Asperger's: A Story for Children. Guthridge, Bettina, illus. (p. 1082)
Ende, Michael. Dragon y la Mariposa. De Horna, Luis, illus. (p. 478)
—Historia Interminable. (p. 782)
—Historia Interminable. Quadflieg, Roswitha, tr. (p. 782)
—Historia Interminable. Quadflieg, Roswitha & Sáenz, Miguel, trs. (p. 782)
—Momo. Ende, Michael, illus. (p. 1163)
—Norberto Nucagorda Wittenberg, Stella, illus. (p. 1264)
—Tranquila Tragaleguas: La Tortuga Cabezota. Asensio, Agusti, illus. (p. 1778)
Ende, Michael & Fushubert, Annegert. Tragasuenos. (p. 1776)
Ende, Michael & Michael, Ende. Largo Camino Hacia Santa Cruz. Kehn, Regina, illus. (p. 975)
Endelman, David, illus. see Scaglione, Joanne & Small, Gail.
Enderle, Dotti. Aesop's Opposites: Interactive Aesop Fables. Mitchell, Judy, ed. (p. 26)
—Beyond the Grave: An Up2U Mystery Adventure. Uhles, Mary, illus. (p. 174)
—Book 13: Yo Ho No! (p. 210)
—Book 14: Plop! (p. 210)
—Book 15: Rock & Roll! (p. 210)
—Book 16: Abracadabra! (p. 210)
—Book 17: Grow a Ghost! (p. 210)
—Book 18: Spaced Out! (p. 210)
—Clawed! An Up2U Horror Adventure. To, Vivienne, illus. (p. 330)
—Cotton Candy Catastrophe at the Texas State Fair Galey, Chuck, illus. (p. 369)
—Crosswire. (p. 385)
—Fat Stock Stampede at the Houston Livestock Show & Rodeo Galey, Chuck, illus. (p. 577)
—Ghost Detectors Volume 1: Let the Specter-Detecting Begin, Books 1-3. McWilliam, Howard, illus. (p. 670)
—Gingerbread Man Superhero! Kulka, Joe, illus. (p. 677)
—Granny Gert & the Bunion Brothers Kulka, Joe, illus. (p. 710)
—Grow a Ghost! McWilliam, Howard, illus. (p. 726)
—Hidden Gentry, T. Kyle, illus. (p. 775)
—Library Gingerbread Man. Madden, Colleen M., illus. (p. 1006)
—Spaced Out! McWilliam, Howard, illus. (p. 1620)
—Storytime Discoveries: Earth Science. (p. 1664)
—Storytime Discoveries: Biological Science. (p. 1664)
—Storytime Discoveries: Math. Ginger Illustrations Staff, illus. (p. 1664)
Enderle, Dotti & Sansum, Vicki. Grandpa for Sale. Gentry, T. Kyle, illus. (p. 709)
Enderle, Evelyn, tr. see Crouch, Adele.
Enderle, Judith Ross & Gordon, Stephanie Jacob. Smile, Principessa! Curmi, Serena, illus. (p. 1594)
Enderlein, Cheryl L. Christmas Around the World. (p. 312)
—Christmas in England (p. 314)
—Christmas in Mexico (p. 314)
—Christmas in Sweden (p. 314)
—Christmas in the Philippines (p. 314)
Enderlein, Cheryl L. & Manning, Jack. Christmas Around the World. (p. 312)
Enderlin, Darlene C. Pathways of Hermie. (p. 1328)
Enderlin, Lisa. Dad, There's a Bear in the Pool!!! (p. 398)
Enders, Genie. Don't Call Me Hefty Holly. (p. 467)
Endersby, Frank, illus. see Baxter, Nicola & Birkinshaw, Marie.
Endersby, Frank, illus. see Brown, Janet Allison.
Endersby, Frank, illus. see Butler, M. Christina.
Endersby, Frank, illus. see Lloyd-Jones, Sally.
Endersby, Frank, illus. see Rivers-Moore, Debbie.
Endersby, Frank, illus. see Yemm, Catherine.
Endersly, Frank, illus. see Bowman, Crystal.
Endich, Roberta. Media Literacy: Activities for Understanding the Scripted World (p. 1118)
Endicott, Megan. In the Hall of the Mountain King. (p. 866)
Endle, Kate. What Is Green? A Colors Book by Kate Endle. (p. 1889)
—Who Hoo Are You? An Animals Book by Kate Endle. (p. 1915)
Endle, Kate, illus. see Babypants, Caspar & Ballew, Chris.
Endle, Kate, illus. see Babypants, Caspar.
Endle, Kate, illus. see Larsen, Andrew.
Endle, Kate, illus. see Lendroth, Susan.
Endle, Kate, illus. see Sayre, April Pulley.
Endle, Kate, illus. see Wiley, Thom.
Endoh, Minari. Dazzle (p. 415)
—Dazzle Endoh, Minari, illus. (p. 415)
—Dazzle. (p. 415)
Endraske, Jackie. Dudley. (p. 489)
Endredy, James. Journey of Tunuri & the Blue Deer: A Huichol Indian Story. Cruz, María Hernández de la & López, Casimiro de la Cruz, trs. (p. 928)
Endres, Hollie. Cats. (p. 280)
—Dogs. (p. 462)
—Ducks. (p. 488)
—Geese. (p. 659)
—Mountain Biking. (p. 1180)
—Prairies. (p. 1393)
—Rabbits. (p. 1429)
—Rock Climbing. (p. 1482)
—Snowboarding. (p. 1600)
—Turkeys. (p. 1797)
—Wakeboarding. (p. 1853)
—Wetlands. (p. 1877)
Endres, Hollie, jt. auth. see Endres, Hollie J.
Endres, Hollie J. Fair Share. (p. 562)
—Farm (p. 573)
—Healthy Foods (p. 758)
—Helping at School (p. 766)
—How Much Money? (p. 811)
—Letter Bb: What Animals Do Set (p. 1002)
—Letter Cc: Food Set (p. 1002)
—Letter Dd: Things I Can Do Set (p. 1002)
—Letter Ee: Things That Are Alike Set (p. 1002)
—Letter Gg: The World Around You Set (p. 1002)
—Letter Hh: Homes Set (p. 1002)
—Letter Kk: Animals Set (p. 1002)
—Letter Mm: People Who Help Us Set (p. 1002)
—Letter Nn: At the Grocery Store Set (p. 1002)
—Letter Rr Maps. Set, 6 vols. (p. 1002)
—Letter Ss: Spring & Summer Set (p. 1002)
—Letter Tt: Magnets Set (p. 1002)
—Letter Vv: Sink or Float? Set (p. 1002)
—Letter Ww: The Ocean Set (p. 1002)
—Letter Xx: Things I Can See Set (p. 1002)
—Letter Yy: All about Me! Set (p. 1002)
—Our Red-White-and-Blue Holidays (p. 1309)
—Push & Pull. (p. 1420)
—Trip to the Repair Shop (p. 1787)
—Wetlands. (p. 1877)
—What Computers Do. (p. 1881)
Endres, Hollie J., jt. auth. see Schaefer, Lola M.
Endres, Hollie J. & Capstone Press Editors. Letter Ll: A Trip to the Repair Shop (p. 1002)
Endres, Hollie J. & Capstone Press Staff. Letter Bb: What Animals Do (p. 1002)
—Letter Cc: Food (p. 1002)
—Letter Dd: Things I Can Do (p. 1002)
—Letter Ee: Things That Are Alike (p. 1002)
—Letter Ff: The Farm (p. 1002)
—Letter Gg: The World Around You (p. 1002)
—Letter Hh: Homes (p. 1002)
—Letter Jj: Helping at School (p. 1002)
—Letter Kk: Animals (p. 1002)
—Letter Mm: People Who Help Us (p. 1002)
—Letter Nn: At the Grocery Store (p. 1002)
—Letter Pp: Healthy Foods (p. 1002)
—Letter Rr: Maps (p. 1002)
—Letter Ss: Spring & Summer (p. 1002)
—Letter Tt: Magnets (p. 1002)
—Letter Vv: Sink or Float? (p. 1002)
—Letter Ww: The Ocean (p. 1002)
—Letter Xx: Things I Can See (p. 1002)
—Letter Yy: All about Me! (p. 1002)
—Our Red-White-and-Blue Holidays. (p. 1309)
Endres, Hollie J. & Catala, Ellen. Nuestros Cinco Sentidos. (p. 1270)
Endres, Hollie J. & Endres, Hollie. Scientists Try, Try Again. (p. 1529)
Endres, Patrick J., photos by see Gill, Shelley.
Endres, Patrick J., photos by see Miller, Debbie S.
Endres, Sharlene Duggan, illus. see Schmitt, Nannette Toups.
Endrulat, Harry, jt. auth. see Innes, Stephanie.
Endrulat, Harry, et al. Adventures of Franklin & Friends: A Collection of 8 Stories. (p. 18)
—Franklin & the Best Friend Problem. (p. 630)
—Franklin Feels at Home. (p. 630)
—Franklin's Christmas Spirit. (p. 631)
Endsaff, Najoud & Rooney, Anne. Retail Careers. (p. 1464)
Endsley, Kezia. How to Do Great Online Research. (p. 816)
—Michelle Obama: 44th First Lady & Health & Education Advocate. (p. 1135)
—Website Design. (p. 1870)
Endsley, Kezia, et al. Inventors of Computer Technology. (p. 884)
Enea, Paul J. Letters to My Granddaughter. (p. 1002)
Eneas, Celeste. My Body, My Temple. (p. 1198)
Enersen, Adele. Vincent & the Night. (p. 1842)
—When My Baby Dreams. Enersen, Adele, illus. (p. 1904)
—When My Baby Dreams of Fairy Tales. Enersen, Adele, illus. (p. 1904)
Eng, Loman & Eng, Petula. Collecting American Belleek (p. 339)
Eng, Paul & Tok, Stephanie. Kungfu for Kids. (p. 968)
Eng, Petula, jt. auth. see Eng, Loman.
Engdahl, Sharon & Engdahl, Terry. Evolution of Creation: A Children's Primer on the Evolution of God's Creation (p. 547)
Engdahl, Sylvia. Amendment XIV: Equal Protection. (p. 58)
—Amendment XXVI — Lowering the Voting Age. (p. 58)
—Amendments XVIII & XXI: Prohibition & Repeal. (p. 58)
—Animal Welfare. (p. 80)
—Assisted Suicide. (p. 107)
—Blogs. (p. 200)
—Bolshevik Revolution. Greenhaven Press Editors, ed. (p. 208)
—Challenger Disaster. Greenhaven Press Editors, ed. (p. 289)
—Chronic Fatigue Syndrome. (p. 317)
—Driving. Greenhaven Press Staff, ed. (p. 485)
—Elderly. Gale Editors, ed. (p. 508)
—Enchantress from the Stars. (p. 523)
—Espionage & Intelligence. Greenhaven Press Editors, ed. (p. 536)
—Far Side of Evil. (p. 572)
—Forensic Technology. Gale Editors, ed. (p. 617)
—Free Press. (p. 634)
—Internet Activism. Greenhaven Press Editors, ed. (p. 880)

E

—John F. Kennedy Assassination. Gale Editors, ed. (p. 921)
—Medical Rights. (p. 1118)
—Meningitis. (p. 1126)
—Mental Health. (p. 1126)
—Mobile Apps. Greenhaven Press Editors & Gale Editors, eds. (p. 1157)
—Neurodegenerative Disorders. Greenhaven Press Editors, ed. (p. 1242)
—Obesity. Greenhaven Press Staff, ed. (p. 1275)
—Online Social Networking. (p. 1298)
—Prescription Drugs. (p. 1396)
—Prohibition. (p. 1410)
—Taxation. (p. 1707)
—This Star Shall Abide. (p. 1737)
—War. (p. 1857)
—Welfare. (p. 1874)
Engdahl, Sylvia, jt. auth. see Young, Mitch.
Engdahl, Sylvia, ed. Alternative Therapies. (p. 50)
—Apollo 11 Moon Landing. (p. 91)
—Dissociative Disorders. (p. 453)
Engdahl, Sylvia Louise. Domestic Wiretapping. (p. 465)
Engdahl, Sylvia Louise, ed. Domestic Wiretapping. (p. 465)
Engdahl, Terry, jt. auth. see Engdahl, Sharon.
Engebretson, Don & Williamson, Don. Annuals for Minnesota & Wisconsin. (p. 87)
—Best Garden Plants for Minnesota & Wisconsin. (p. 169)
—Gardening Month by Month in Minnesota & Wisconsin (p. 656)
—Perennials for Minnesota & Wisconsin. (p. 1341)
—Tree & Shrub Gardening for Minnesota & Wisconsin (p. 1783)
Engebretson, Erika. Pounce. (p. 1389)
Engebretson, Monica fall. Lucky: Based on a true Story. (p. 1062)
Enge-Grandbois, Kathryn L. Suzy Q: Book 2. (p. 1688)
—Suzy Q. (p. 1688)
Engel, Amy. Book of Ivy. (p. 211)
Engel, Barbara, et al. From Ur to Eternity: The Historical Adventures of the Jewish People. (p. 644)
Engel, Christiane. Knick Knack Paddy Whack. (p. 964)
—Knick Knack Paddy Whack. Songs, Steve, illus. (p. 964)
—Knick Knack Paddy Whack. Engels, Christiane, illus. (p. 964)
—Little Green Helpers Grow! (p. 1028)
—Recycle! (p. 1452)
—Shimmery Dinkies - Ring Ring! Davis, Caroline, illus. (p. 1566)
—We Are Moving: Louis & Bobo. Engel, Christiane, illus. (p. 1865)
Engel, Christiane, illus. see Bowman, Crystal, et al.
Engel, Christiane, illus. see Elovitz Marshall, Sylvia A. & Marshall, Linda.
Engel, Christiane, illus. see Green, Jen.
Engel, Christiane, illus. see Marshall, Linda Elovitz.
Engel, Christiane & Songs, Steve. Knick Knack Paddy Whack. Engel, Christiane, illus. (p. 964)
Engel, Cynthia. Granny's Garden. (p. 710)
Engel, Gerhard, jt. auth. see Heyens, Gudrun.
Engel, Margaret, jt. auth. see Hodges, Henry.
Engel, Natalie. Marely & Me - Meet Marley. (p. 1092)
—Meet Marley. (p. 1121)
Engel, Robert, jt. auth. see Petty, Angel Bishop.
Engel, Steve. Tracks Count: A Guide to Counting Animal Prints. Petersen, Alexander, illus. (p. 1775)
Engel, Tonya, illus. see Bernier-Grand, Carmen T.
Engel, Wolfgang, ed. see St-Laurent, Sebastien.
Engelbert, Jo Anne, tr. see Serrano, Francisco.
Engelbrecht, Edward A., jt. ed. see Pawlitz, Gail E.
Engelbrecht, Edward A. & Pawlitz, Gail E., eds. Christmas Story: Drawn Directly from the Bible. (p. 315)
—Easter Story: Drawn Directly from the Bible. (p. 499)
Engelbreit, Mary. Baby Booky: Honey Bunny. Engelbreit, Mary, illus. (p. 125)
—Blessings of Friendship Treasury (p. 199)
—Fun & Games with Ann Estelle. (p. 647)
—Mary Engelbreit's A Merry Little Christmas: Celebrate from A to Z. Engelbreit, Mary, illus. (p. 1100)
—Mary Engelbreit's a Merry Little Christmas: Celebrate from A to Z. Engelbreit, Mary, illus. (p. 1100)
—Mary Engelbreit's Mother Goose: One Hundred Best-Loved Verses. Engelbreit, Mary, illus. (p. 1100)
—Mary Engelbreit's Mother Goose. Engelbreit, Mary, illus. (p. 1100)
—Mary Engelbreit's Nursery & Fairy Tales Collection. Engelbreit, Mary, illus. (p. 1100)
—Mary Engelbreit's Nutcracker. Engelbreit, Mary, illus. (p. 1100)
—Mary Engelbreit's Paper Dolls: Fun with Ann Estelle & Mikayla. (p. 1100)
—Nursery Tales: A Treasury of Children's Classics. Engelbreit, Mary, illus. (p. 1273)
—Queen of Christmas. Engelbreit, Mary, illus. (p. 1425)
—Queen of Easter. Engelbreit, Mary, illus. (p. 1425)
—Queen of Halloween. Engelbreit, Mary, illus. (p. 1425)
—Queen of Hearts. Engelbreit, Mary, illus. (p. 1425)
—Queen of the Class. Engelbreit, Mary, illus. (p. 1425)
—Twelve Timeless Treasures. Engelbreit, Mary, illus. (p. 1800)
Engelbreit, Mary, illus. see Burnett, Frances Hodgson.
Engelbreit, Mary, illus. see Moore, Clement C.
Engelbrite, Eve. Arithmability: Addition & Subtraction of Whole Numbers: Dyscalculia Workbook. (p. 98)
Engelhardt. Efficient Use of School Build. (p. 505)
Engelhardt, Lisa O. Making Good Choices: Just for Me Book. Fitzgerald, Anne, illus. (p. 1081)
Engelhart, Ann, illus. see Welborn, Amy.
Engelhart, Ann Kissane, illus. see Welborn, Amy.
Engelhart, Margaret S., jt. auth. see Kurelek, William.
Engelhart, Steve, jt. auth. see Simonson, Louise.
Engelman Berner, Beth. Finding Fairyland: A Picture Riddle Book. Riggs, Jenna, illus. (p. 588)
Engelman, Beth. Kite Race. (p. 962)
Engelman, Peter G. Magic, Malice & Murder. (p. 1072)
Engelmann, Owen, jt. auth. see Engelmann, Siegfried.
Engelmann, Richard. Deathblow in Darrabadesh: Oliver Millbrook. (p. 420)
Engelmann, Siegfried. Reading Mastery Level 5. (p. 1446)
—Reading Mastery - Level 6 Textbook. (p. 1446)
Engelmann, Siegfried & Bruner, Elaine C. Reading Mastery. (p. 1446)
Engelmann, Siegfried & Engelmann, Owen. Funnix Beginning Math. (p. 649)
—Funnix Beginning Math Workbook. (p. 649)
Engels, Christiane, illus. see Engel, Christiane.
Engelsgjerd, Marc, jt. auth. see Snyder, R. Bradley.
Engen, Harvey & Engen, Shirley. Goldie the Kitten: A Basic Reading Vocabulary Book. (p. 696)
Engen, Shirley, jt. auth. see Engen, Harvey.
Engfer, Lee. Cubans in America. (p. 388)
—Desserts Around the World: Culturally Authentic Foods Including Low-Fat & Vegetarian Recipes. (p. 430)
—Desserts Around the World. (p. 430)
—Wilma Rudolph: Olympic Track Star Martin, Cynthia & Timmons, Anne, illus. (p. 1934)
Engholm, Evelyn. Ted & Danny's Secret. (p. 1712)
Engineering is Elementary Team. Aisha Makes Work Easier: An Industrial Engineering Story. (p. 32)
—Javier Builds a Bridge: A Civil Engineering Story. (p. 910)
—Kwame's Sound: An Acoustical Engineering Story. (p. 968)
—Leif Catches the Wind: A Mechanical Engineering Story. (p. 991)
—Mariana Becomes a Butterfly: An Agricultural Engineering Story. (p. 1093)
—Michelle's MVP Award: A Chemical Engineering Story. (p. 1135)
—Reminder for Emily: An Electrical Engineering Story. (p. 1460)
—Saving Salila's Turtle: An Environmental Engineering Story. (p. 1517)
—Yi Min's Great Wall: A Materials Engineering Story. (p. 1971)
England, Brooke. Guardian Fairies. (p. 728)
England, Don. God, Are You Really There? (p. 688)
—Old Billy, the Bike. Scardina, Tom, illus. (p. 1283)
England, Donald, illus. see Watt, Mike.
England, Kathryn. Grandfather's Wrinkles. McFarland, Richard, illus. (p. 707)
England, Linda. 3 Kids Dreamin' Schutzer, Dena, illus. (p. 1991)
—Old Cotton Blues. Flavin, Teresa, illus. (p. 1283)
England, Nora. Witches of Dorkdom. (p. 1941)
England, Paul. Knights of Bonalia. (p. 964)
England, Tamara, ed. see Casanova, Mary.
England, Tamara, ed. see Kurtz, Jane.
England, Tamara, ed. see Tripp, Valerie.
England, Tamara, ed. see Yep, Laurence.
England, Victoria. Top 10 Worst Things about Ancient Egypt. Antram, David, illus. (p. 1768)
—Top 10 Worst Things about Ancient Greece. Antram, David, illus. (p. 1768)
—Top 10 Worst Things about Ancient Rome. Antram, David, illus. (p. 1768)
Englandar, Anrenee. Dear Diary, I'm Pregnant: Ten Real Life Stories. (p. 418)
Englander, Karen, tr. see Kurusa.
England-Lord, Susan. Adventures of Andrew: Breezy's Day Out. (p. 16)
Englar, Mary. Apache: Nomadic Hunters of the Southwest (p. 91)
—Bosnia-Herzegovina in Pictures. (p. 214)
—Cherokee & Their History (p. 298)
—Cheyenne: Hunter-Gatherers of the Northern Plains (p. 299)
—Chief Joseph, 1840-1904. (p. 301)
—Dutch Colonies in America. (p. 490)
—Ethiopia: A Question & Answer Book (p. 539)
—Fall of Saigon. (p. 566)
—French Colonies in America. (p. 635)
—Grand Duchess Anastasia Romanov (p. 707)
—Guatemala: A Question & Answer Book (p. 728)
—Illustrated Timeline of U. S. Presidents Epstein, Len, illus. (p. 858)
—Marie Antoinette, Queen of France (p. 1093)
—Nefertiti of Egypt (p. 1240)
—Pancho Villa: Rebel of the Mexican Revolution (p. 1320)
—Pilgrims & the First Thanksgiving McDonnell, Peter, illus. (p. 1358)
—Pueblo: Southwestern Potters (p. 1414)
—Queen Rania of Jordan (p. 1425)
—September 11 (p. 1551)
—Southwest Indians: Daily Life in the 1500s. (p. 1618)
—Tet Offensive. (p. 1723)
—Turkey. (p. 1797)
—Union General & 18th President: Ulysses S. Grant (p. 1818)
—Vietnam: A Question & Answer Book (p. 1841)
—Worst Earthquakes of All Time (p. 1961)
Englar, Mary & Capstone Press Staff. Lebanon: A Question & Answer Book (p. 986)
Englar, Mary & Compass Point Books Staff. Battle of Bunker Hill (p. 146)
Englar, Mary & Duden, Jane. Sieur de la Salle (p. 1573)
—Why Do Bears Sleep All Winter? A Book about Hibernation (p. 1923)
Englar, Mary & Vander Hook, Sue. Confederate Commander: General Robert E. Lee (p. 356)
Englar, Mary, et al. Epic Disasters. (p. 532)
Englar, Mary L. September 11 (p. 1551)
Englar, Xavier & Niz, Xavier W. Mystery of the Roanoke Colony Denton, Shannon E., illus. (p. 1226)
Englart, Mindi. Televison Show. (p. 1716)
Engle, Dawn A. Ella's Golden Heart Goes to Camp. (p. 514)
Engle, Dawn D. Ella's Golden Hearts. (p. 514)
Engle, Janice. Rainbows Stories & Poetry for Children. (p. 1436)
Engle, Jason, illus. see Stowell, Louie.
Engle, Jenny, illus. see Palmore, Julie.
Engle, Margarita. Drum Dream Girl: How One Girl's Courage Changed Music. López, Rafael, illus. (p. 487)
—Firefly Letters: A Suffragette's Journey to Cuba. (p. 592)
—Hurricane Dancers: The First Caribbean Pirate Shipwreck. (p. 829)
—Lightning Dreamer: Cuba's Greatest Abolitionist. (p. 1016)
—Mountain Dog. Ivanov, Aleksey & Ivanov, Olga, illus. (p. 1180)
—Orangutanka. Kurilla, Renee, illus. (p. 1302)
—Poet Slave of Cuba: A Biography of Juan Francisco Manzano. Qualls, Sean, illus. (p. 1376)
—Silver People: Voices from the Panama Canal. (p. 1576)
—Summer Birds: The Butterflies of Maria Merian. Paschkis, Julie, illus. (p. 1674)
—Surrender Tree: Poems of Cuba's Struggle for Freedom. (p. 1686)
—Tiny Rabbit's Big Wish. Walker, David, illus. (p. 1756)
—Tropical Secrets: Holocaust Refugees in Cuba. (p. 1789)
—When You Wander: A Search-and-Rescue Dog Story. Morgan, Mary, illus. (p. 1905)
—Wild Book. (p. 1929)
Engle, Stephen Douglas. Civil War: The Siege of Vicksburg & Other Western Battles, 1861-July 1863. O'Neill, Robert, ed. (p. 325)
Englebaugh, Debi. Integrating Art & Language Arts Through Children's Literature (p. 879)
Engleberg, Isa & Raimes, Ann. Pocket Keys for Speakers. (p. 1375)
Engleberg, Isa N. & Daly, John A. Presentations in Everyday Life: Strategies for Effective Speaking. (p. 1396)
Englehart, Steve. Batman - Dark Detective. (p. 144)
—Jurassic Park: Dark Cargo!: Vol. 6. (p. 937)
—Jurassic Park: Aftershocks!: Vol. 5. (p. 937)
—Jurassic Park: Gods vs. Men!: Vol. 10. (p. 937)
—Jurassic Park: Raptors Attack!: Vol. 7. (p. 937)
—Jurassic Park: Animals vs. Man!: Vol. 8. (p. 937)
—Jurassic Park: Animals vs. Gods!: Vol. 9. (p. 937)
Englehart, Steve, jt. auth. see Simonson, Walter.
Englehart, Victoria. Whose Shoes? (p. 1922)
Engleheart, Phil, illus. see Sunderland, Margot & Pickering, Ken.
Engleman, Dennis. Holloween Town. (p. 789)
Engler, Jerry. Highly Embellished Truth & Some Poetry Just Folks Three. (p. 779)
Engler, L. S. 10: Nine Stories to Read Before You Die!!!!!:29. (p. 1993)
Engler, Lori, illus. see Kennedy, Geno.
Engler, Michael. Elephantastic! Tourlonias, Joëlle, illus. (p. 511)
Engler, Zoe. Lonely Starfish (p. 1046)
Englert, June Scott. My Story by Jake (p. 1219)
English, Billie Joan, jt. auth. see Calhoun, Sharon Cooper.
English, Carolyn B. Grandpa & the Orange Bowl. (p. 709)
English, D. N. Downtown Wanderings & Memories. (p. 474)
English, David. Confessions of a Dedicated Englishman (p. 356)
English, Edward D. Encyclopedia of the Medieval World (p. 525)
English Heritage Staff. My Life as a Knight. (p. 1212)
—My Life as a Princess. (p. 1212)
English, Jill, jt. auth. see Schultz, Shelley.
English, June. Anglican Young People's Dictionary. (p. 75)
—Let's Talk Tails. Regan, Dana, illus. (p. 1001)
English, Karen. Birthday Blues. Freeman, Laura, illus. (p. 192)
—Dog Days. Freeman, Laura, illus. (p. 461)
—Francie. (p. 627)
—Nadia's Hands. Weiner, Jonathan, illus. (p. 1227)
—Newsy News Newsletter. Freeman, Laura, illus. (p. 1249)
—Nikki & Deja: Substitute Trouble. Freeman, Laura, illus. (p. 1255)
—Nikki & Deja. Freeman, Laura, illus. (p. 1255)
—Skateboard Party: The Carver Chronicles, Book Two. Freeman, Laura, illus. (p. 1583)
—Wedding Drama. Freeman, Laura, illus. (p. 1870)
English, Keri. Zo's Debut. (p. 1990)
English, Melissa. Caution: Why You Need to Think about Careers NOW! (p. 282)
—Molly Mccreary, There's Something in the Garden! (p. 1160)
English, Sarah Jane, illus. see Coulter, Laurie.
English, Sarah Jane, illus. see Coulter, Lavrie.
English, Travis. Knights of Paris. (p. 964)
English-Hawke, Kiri. Handkerchief Map. (p. 740)
Englund, Frederick, jt. auth. see Mills, Nathan.
Englund, Jonathon, illus. see Brett, James.
Engman, Camilla, illus. see Salinas, Veronica.
Engram, Teta. Baxter & the Sidewalk Alligator. Holland, Lisa Tomms, illus. (p. 147)
Engvick, William. Lullabies & Night Songs. Sendak, Maurice, illus. (p. 1064)
Enik, Ted. Sticks 'N Stones 'N Dinosaur Bones. Newland, g. f., illus. (p. 1650)
Enik, Ted, illus. see Brooke, Susan Rich & Seuss, Dr.
Enik, Ted, illus. see Lane, Jeanette, et al.
Enik, Ted, illus. see O'Connor, Jane.
Enik, Ted, illus. see Stem, J. David, et al.
Enik, Ted, illus. see Trimble, Tonya.
Enlwaye, Olu O. Adventures of Jabi-Jabi II: The Return of the King Fly 2nd in the series of adventures of the King Fly Jabi-Jabi. (p. 19)
—Country Bully & the City Bully: A Children's Book. (p. 372)
Enloe, Rochelle, jt. auth. see Enloe, Tim.
Enloe, Rochelle & Enloe, Tim. Kid-Power! How Kids Can Get the Holy Spirit's Power! (p. 951)
Enloe, Tim, jt. auth. see Enloe, Rochelle.
Enloe, Tim & Enloe, Rochelle. (Bengali) Kid Power! the Holy Spirit's Super Power for Kids! (p. 164)
Enna, Bruno. Double Duck. Soffritti, Donald, illus. (p. 472)
Ennis, Brenda. Secret of Sleeveen. (p. 1542)
Ennis, Garth. All Hell's A-Coming. (p. 44)
—Ancient History. Kahan, Bob, ed. (p. 69)
—ERF. (p. 533)
—Preacher - Gone to Texas Kahan, Bob, ed. (p. 1394)
—Pride & Joy. (p. 1398)
—Rage in Arkham. (p. 1433)
—Salvation. (p. 1506)
—Until the End of the World. (p. 1823)
Ennis, Garth & Fabry, Glen. Dead or Alive. (p. 417)
Ennis, Garth, et al. Enemy Ace: War in Heaven. (p. 527)
Ennis, Kristin. Keep a Poem in Your Pocket. (p. 946)
Ennis, Pat. Becoming a Young Woman Who Pleases God: A Teen's Guide to Discovering Her Biblical Potential. (p. 156)
Ennis, Robert & Millman, Jason. Cornell Critical Thinking Test Level Z. (p. 367)
Ennis, Ryan R. September Surprise: A Story about Kids & Autism. (p. 1551)
—Thursday Surprise: A Story about Kids & Autism. Stroud, Brenda, illus. (p. 1746)
Ennis, Tom R. Stranger & the Three Little Children. (p. 1665)
Eno, Laura. My Enchanted Life. (p. 1202)
Enock, Charles Reginald. Secret of the Pacific: A Discussion of the Origin of the Early Civilizations of America, the Toltecs, Aztecs, Mayas, Incas, & Their Predecessors; & the Possibilities of Asiatic Influence Thereon. (p. 1542)
Enos, Barbara. When George Stopped Talking. Kinney, Jo Hannah, illus. (p. 1902)
Enos, Daryl, illus. see Cochran, Jean M.
Enos, Deanna. Wooden Garden of Romano Gabriel (p. 1949)
Enos, Joel. Parallel Paradox. Brown, Alan, illus. (p. 1324)
Enos, Joel, ed. Bravest Warriors: the Search for Catbug. Brown, Alan et al, illus. (p. 223)
Enos, K. D. Chronicles of Artci: Children of the Dead. (p. 317)
Enos, Randall, illus. see Heinz, Brian.
Enos, Randall, illus. see Pinczes, Elinor J.
Enos, Solomon, illus. see Armitage, Kimo.
Enria, Samantha, illus. see Panzieri, Lucia & Maccarone, Grace.
Enright, Amanda, illus. see Eaton, Kait.
Enright, Amanda, illus. see Foster, Juliana.
Enright, Amanda, illus. see O'Brien, Melanie.
Enright, Amanda, illus. see Rustad, Martha E. H.
Enright, Amanda, illus. see Wharton, Ellie.
Enright, Amanda, illus. see Williamson, Karen.
Enright, Cheri. Riley & Me. (p. 1472)
Enright, D. J. By-Blows: Uncollected Poems. (p. 249)
Enright, Dominique, et al. How to Be the Best at Everything. Barnes, Samantha & Wingate, Philippa, eds. (p. 815)
Enright, Elizabeth. Four-Story Mistake. Enright, Elizabeth, illus. (p. 625)
—Gone-Away Lake. Krush, Beth & Krush, Joe, illus. (p. 697)
—Saturdays. Enright, Elizabeth, illus. (p. 1515)
—Spiderweb for Two: A Melendy Maze. Enright, Elizabeth, illus. (p. 1627)
—Then There Were Five. Enright, Elizabeth, illus. (p. 1729)
—Thimble Summer. (p. 1732)
—Thimble Summer. Enright, Elizabeth, illus. (p. 1732)
Enright, Maginel Wright, illus. see Baum, L. Frank, et al.
Enright, Robert D. Rising above the Storm Clouds: What It's Like to Forgive. Finney, Kathryn Kunz, illus. (p. 1475)
Enright, Vicky, illus. see Allen, Susan & Lindaman, Jane.
Enright, Vicky, illus. see Haddon, Jean.
Enright, Vicky, illus. see Ross, Kathy.
Enright, Vicky, tr. see Haddon, Jean.
Enright, Walter J., illus. see Warren, Maude Radford.
Enrique, Luque Muñoz. Fiódor Dostoievski. (p. 589)
Enrique, Sanchez, illus. see Ofelia, Dumas Lachtman.
Enriquez, Jose. Saving the Mango Farm. (p. 1517)
Enriquez, Lucy Rivas. Dj's Lullaby: A Mother's Love Song. (p. 455)
Enroc Illustrations, illus. see Thrasher, Jenny & Thrasher, Phil.
Ensaff, Najoud, et al. Retail Careers. (p. 1464)
Enslow, Brian. Counting Ants 1-2-3. (p. 370)
—Counting Bees 1-2-3. (p. 370)
—Counting Butterflies 1-2-3. (p. 371)
—Counting Ladybugs 1-2-3. (p. 371)
—Fall Colors. (p. 566)
—My Body. (p. 1198)
—My Ears. (p. 1202)
—My Eyes. (p. 1202)
—My Hands & Feet. (p. 1210)
—My Mouth. (p. 1215)
—My Nose. (p. 1216)
—Spring Colors. (p. 1635)
—Summer Colors. (p. 1674)
—Winter Colors. (p. 1938)
Ensor, Andrew. Luke Carter & the Sword of Kings. (p. 1064)
Ensor, Barbara. Cinderella (As If You Didn't Already Know the Story) Ensor, Barbara, illus. (p. 320)
Ensor, Brad. If My Grandpa Were President. (p. 853)
Ensor, Rod. Getting It. (p. 669)
Entin, Cindy. Marines. Boldman, Craig, illus. (p. 1094)
—My First Counting Book: Coast Guard. (p. 1206)
—My First Counting Book: Firefighters. Boldman, Craig, illus. (p. 1206)
—My First Counting Book: Marines. (p. 1206)
—My First Counting Book: Police. Boldman, Craig, illus. (p. 1206)
Entin, Cindy, jt. auth. see Press, Applesauce.
Entin, Cindy, jt. auth. see Press, Cider Mill.
Entinger, Chad. Deaf Boy Meets Jesus. Schofield-Farmer, Twila, illus. (p. 418)
Entrekin, Allison Weiss. For the Love of Dogs: An A-to-Z Primer for Dog Lovers of All Ages. Anderson, Mark, illus. (p. 616)
Entwistle, Charles. Promise. (p. 1411)
Envionrment Canada Staff. Oil, Water & Chocolate Mousse. (p. 1282)
Environmental Protection Agency (US), ed. see American Cancer Society Staff.
Enwezor, Okwui, et al. Life & Afterlife in Benin. Adjovi, Benoit et al, photos by. (p. 1007)
Enyagotailak, Darla, jt. auth. see Willett, Mindy.
Enyancha. Legends of the Garden: Faeries & Herbs: A Child's Activity Book for Exploring the Worlds of Faeries & Herbs. (p. 990)
Enyart, Helen R. Barney on Fred's Funny Farm. (p. 139)
Enyi, Patricia Nmukoso. Marcus the Magician: At the Beach. (p. 1092)
Enz, Tammy. Amazing Story of Cell Phone Technology: Max Axiom STEM Adventures (p. 56)
—Amazing Story of Cell Phone Technology. Pop Art Properties Staff, illus. (p. 56)
—Batmobiles & Batcycles: The Engineering Behind Batman's Vehicles (p. 144)
—Batplanes & Batcopters: The Engineering Behind Batman's Wings (p. 144)

—Behind the Double Doors: Exploring the Secrets of a Hospital. (p. 160)
—Behind the Racks: Exploring the Secrets of a Shopping Mall (p. 160)
—Beyond the Bars: Exploring the Secrets of a Police Station. (p. 174)
—Build It: Invent New Structures & Contraptions (p. 238)
—Build It Yourself (p. 238)
—Build Your Own Car, Rocket, & Other Things That Go (p. 238)
—Build Your Own Fort, Igloo, & Other Hangouts Haus, Estudio, illus. (p. 238)
—Build Your Own Fort, Igloo, & Other Hangouts. (p. 238)
—Build Your Own Mini Golf Course, Lemonade Stand, & Other Things to Do (p. 238)
—Build Your Own Periscope, Flashlight, & Other Useful Stuff (p. 238)
—Dynamic Planet: Exploring Changes on Earth with Science Projects. (p. 491)
—Engineering a Totally Rad Skateboard with Max Axiom, Super Scientist Pop Art Studios, illus. (p. 529)
—Engineering a Totally Rad Skateboard with Max Axiom, Super Scientist Pop Art Studios Staff, illus. (p. 529)
—Harness It: Invent New Ways to Harness Energy & Nature (p. 749)
—Hidden Worlds (p. 776)
—Invent It. (p. 883)
—Liquid Planet: Exploring Water on Earth with Science Projects. (p. 1021)
—Repurpose It: Invent New Uses for Old Stuff (p. 1462)
—Super Cool Construction Activities with Max Axiom. Baez, Marcelo, illus. (p. 1679)
—Super Cool Mechanical Activities with Max Axiom. Baez, Marcelo, illus. (p. 1679)
—Terrific Tale of Television Technology: Max Axiom STEM Adventures (p. 1721)
—Terrific Tale of Television Technology. Pop Art Properties Staff, illus. (p. 1721)
—Under the Lights: Exploring the Secrets of a Sports Stadium (p. 1813)
—Zoom It: Invent New Machines That Move (p. 1989)
Enz, Tammy, jt. auth. see Biskup, Agnieszka.
Enz, Tammy & Biskup, Agnieszka. Batman Science (p. 144)
—Max Axiom Science & Engineering Activities. Baez, Marcelo, illus. (p. 1111)
—STEM Adventures. Pop Art Properties Staff, illus. (p. 1647)
Enz, Tammy, et al. Discover Earth Science. (p. 447)
—Graphic Science & Engineering in Action. Baez, Marcelo, illus. (p. 711)
Enzoe, Pete, jt. auth. see Willett, Mindy.
Enzor, Norman. Yoyo King: Second Edition. (p. 1982)
Eoff, Linda King. Country Morning. (p. 372)
—Pitter Patter: God's Little Drops of Rain. (p. 1364)
Eone. Peppa Pig: Peppa Goes Swimming. (p. 1340)
Eone, François René, illus. see Scholastic, Inc. Staff.
Epelbaum, Anna V. Moscow - Chicago, Further- Everywhere. (p. 1176)
—Selected Works. (p. 1549)
Epelbaum, Mariano, illus. see Braun, Eric.
Epelbaum, Mariano, illus. see Flor Ada, Alma.
Epelbaum, Mariano, illus. see Kesselring, Mari.
Ephraim, Shelly Ephraim, illus. see Jacobs, Laurie A.
Ephron, Delia. Frannie in Pieces. Beckerman, Chad, illus. (p. 631)
—Girl with the Mermaid Hair. (p. 679)
Epictetus & Dobbin, Robert F. Discourses & Selected Writings. Dobbin, Robert, ed. (p. 447)
Epner, Paul. Herbert Hilligan & His Magical Adventure. Kuon, Vuthy & Nguyen, Duke, illus. (p. 769)
—Herbert Hilligan & His Magical Lunchbox. Kuon, Vuthy & Nguyen, Duke, illus. (p. 769)
—Herbert Hilligan's Lone Star Adventure. Kuon, Vuthy & Nguyen, Duke, illus. (p. 769)
—Herbert Hilligan's Prehistoric Adventure. Kuon, Vuthy & Nguyen, Duke, illus. (p. 769)
—Herbert Hilligan's SeaWorld Adventure. Reed, Bill, illus. (p. 769)
—Herbert Hilligan's Tropical Adventure. Kuon, Vuthy & Nguyen, Duke, illus. (p. 769)
—There's a Dachshund in My Bed! Reed, Bill, illus. (p. 1730)
Epner, Paul & Kuon, Vuthy. Herbert Hilligan's Prehistoric Adventure. (p. 769)
Eppard, Jon. Aircraft. (p. 31)
—Big Cats. (p. 180)
—Dogs. (p. 462)
—Horses. (p. 800)
—Manga. (p. 1087)
—Monsters. (p. 1168)
Eppehimer, Trevor. Protestantism. (p. 1412)
Epperson, James F. Causes of the Civil War. (p. 282)
Epperson, Kathy. Belly Thumpers. (p. 163)
—Mermaids. (p. 1128)
Eppie, Maria. Gone Wild. (p. 697)
Eppler, Jamie. Suzy & the Sewing Room Adventure: It's about Time. (p. 1688)
—Suzy & the Sewing Room Mystery. (p. 1688)
Epps, Lawrence. Stomping on Toad Stools. (p. 1652)
Epps, S. Emmanuel & Robateau, Lisa. Bubble Brain: Story Time Rhymes That Build the Mind. (p. 233)
Epps, SArah, illus. see Giordano, Jean.
Epstein, Adam Jay & Jacobson, Andrew. Circle of Heroes. (p. 321)
—Familiars. (p. 567)
—Familiars. Chiu, Bobby, illus. (p. 567)
—Palace of Dreams. Phillips, Dave, illus. (p. 1319)
—Secrets of the Crown. (p. 1545)
—Starbounders: Rebellion. Vol. 2 (p. 1642)
—Starbounders. McClellan, David, illus. (p. 1642)
Epstein, Alex. Circle Cast (p. 321)
—Crafty TV Writing: Thinking Inside the Box. (p. 376)
Epstein, Brad. Arizona Diamondbacks 101: My First Team-Board-Book. (p. 98)
—Baltimore Orioles 101. (p. 135)
—Chicago White Sox 101. (p. 299)
—Chicago White Sox ABC. (p. 299)
—Colorado Rockies 101: My First Team-Board-Book. (p. 343)
—Florida Marlins 101: My first Team-board-book. (p. 607)
—Kansas City Royals 101: My First Team-Board-Books. (p. 943)
—Los Angeles Angels of Anaheim 101: My First Team-Board-Book. (p. 1053)
—Miami Marlins 101. (p. 1134)
—Minnesota Twins 101: My first Team-board-book. (p. 1147)
—New York Giants 101. (p. 1248)
—New York Jets 101. (p. 1248)
—New York Mets 101. (p. 1248)
—New York Mets ABC. (p. 1248)
—New York Yankees 101. (p. 1248)
—Philadelphia Eagles 101. (p. 1350)
—Philadelphia Phillies 101: My First Team-Board-Book. (p. 1350)
—Pittsburgh Pirates 101. (p. 1364)
—San Diego Padres 101: My first Team-board-book. (p. 1510)
—Seattle Mariners 101: My First Team-Board-Book. (p. 1539)
—St. Louis Cardinals ABC. (p. 1638)
—Tampa Bay Rays 101: My first Team-board-book. (p. 1704)
—Texas Rangers 101. (p. 1724)
—Washington Nationals 101. (p. 1860)
Epstein, Brad M. Arizona Cardinals 101: My First Team-Board-Book. (p. 98)
—Arizona State University 101: My First Text-Board-Book. (p. 99)
—Army 101: My First Text-Board-Book. (p. 100)
—Atlanta Braves 101: My First Team-Board-Book. (p. 112)
—Auburn Tigers 123: My first counting Book. (p. 114)
—Auburn University 101: My First Text-Board-Book. (p. 114)
—Barack Obama 101. (p. 137)
—Boston 101. (p. 215)
—Boston Red Sox 101: My First Team-Board-Book. (p. 215)
—Boston Red Sox 101. (p. 215)
—Chicago 101: My first City-board-book. (p. 299)
—Chicago Bears 101. (p. 299)
—Chicago Cubs 101: My First Team-Board-Book. (p. 299)
—Chicago White Sox 101: My First Team-Board-Book. (p. 299)
—Clemson University 101: My First Text-Board-Book. (p. 331)
—Columbia University 101: My First Text-Board-Book. (p. 346)
—Cornell University 101: My First Text-Board-Book. (p. 367)
—Dallas Cowboys 101. (p. 401)
—Dartmouth College 101. (p. 409)
—Detroit Tigers 101: My First Team-Board-Book. (p. 431)
—Florida 101. (p. 606)
—Florida State University 101: My First Text-Board-Book. (p. 607)
—Green Bay Packers 101. (p. 721)
—Indianapolis Colts 101. (p. 871)
—Iowa State University 101: My First Text-Board-Book. (p. 886)
—Kansas State Univ 101: My First Text-Board-Book. (p. 943)
—Los Angeles 101: My first City-board-book. (p. 1053)
—Los Angeles Dodgers 101: My First Team-Board-Book. (p. 1053)
—Louisiana State University 101: My First Text-Board-Book. (p. 1059)
—Miami Dolphins 101. (p. 1133)
—Michigan State University 101: My First Text-Board-Book. (p. 1135)
—Milwaukee Brewers 101: My First Team-Board-Book. (p. 1144)
—Minn Vikings 101. (p. 1147)
—Nebraska 101. (p. 1239)
—New England Patriots 101. (p. 1244)
—New Orleans Saints 101. (p. 1246)
—New York 101. (p. 1247)
—New York Mets 101: My First Team-Board-Book. (p. 1248)
—North Carolina State University 101: My First Text-Board-Book. (p. 1265)
—Ohio State 101. (p. 1281)
—Oklahoma State University 101: My First Text-Board-Book. (p. 1283)
—Penn State University 101: My First Text-Board-Book. (p. 1337)
—Pittsburgh Steelers 101. (p. 1365)
—Purdue University 101: My First Text-Board-Book. (p. 1419)
—San Diego Chargers 101. (p. 1510)
—San Francisco 49ers 101. (p. 1510)
—San Francisco Giants 101. (p. 1510)
—St Louis Rams 101. (p. 1638)
—Stanford 101. (p. 1639)
—Stanford University 101: My First Text-Board-Book. (p. 1639)
—UCLA 101: My First Text-Board-Book. (p. 1807)
—University of Alabama 101. (p. 1820)
—University of Alabama Crimson Tide 123: My First Counting Book. (p. 1820)
—University of Arkansas 101: My First Text-Board-Book. (p. 1820)
—University of California, Berkeley 101: My First Text-Board-Book. (p. 1820)
—University of Florida 101: My First Text-Board-Book. (p. 1820)
—University of Georgia 101: My First Text-Board-Book. (p. 1820)
—University of Georgia Bulldogs 123: My First Counting Book. (p. 1820)
—University of Illinois 101: My First Text-Board-Book. (p. 1820)
—University of Iowa 101: My First Text-Board-Book. (p. 1820)
—University of Iowa Hawkeyes 123: My First Counting Book. (p. 1820)
—University of Kansas 101: My First Text-Board-Book. (p. 1820)
—University of Kentucky 101: My First Text-Board-Book. (p. 1820)
—University of Michigan 101: My First Text-Board-Book. (p. 1820)
—University of Mississippi 101: My First Text-Board-Book. (p. 1820)
—University of Nebraska 101: My First Text-Board-Book. (p. 1821)
—University of North Carolina 101: My First Text-Board-Book. (p. 1821)
—University of Notre Dame 101: My First Text-Board-Book. (p. 1821)
—University of Notre Dame Fighting Irish 123: My First Counting Book. (p. 1821)
—University of Oklahoma 101: My First Text-Board-Book. (p. 1821)
—University of Pennsylvania 101. Michaelson Entertainment Staff, ed. (p. 1821)
—University of South Carolina 101: My First Text-Board-Book. (p. 1821)
—University of Tennessee 101: My First Text-Board-Book. (p. 1821)
—University of Texas at Austin 101: My First Text-Board-Book. (p. 1821)
—University of Texas Longhorns 123: My First Counting Book. (p. 1821)
—University of Washington 101: My First Text-Board-Book. (p. 1821)
—University of Wisconsin 101: My First Text-Board-Book. (p. 1821)
—Usc 101: My First Text-Board-Book. (p. 1827)
—USC 123: My First Counting Book. (p. 1827)
—Washington 101. (p. 1859)
—Washington D. C. 101: My first City-board-book. (p. 1860)
—Washington Redskins 101. (p. 1860)
—Washington State University 101: My First Text-Board-Book. (p. 1860)
—Yale 101: My First Text-Board-Book. (p. 1968)
epstein, brad M. & lee-Epstein, michael. Pittsburgh Steelers Doodle Playbook: For kids & Fans. (p. 1365)
epstein, brad M., et al. Dogs ABC: My First Alphabet Book. (p. 462)
Epstein, Diane & Sullivan, Abigail. Three Nearsighted Mice. (p. 1743)
Epstein, Dwayne. Adam Sandler. (p. 11)
—Connie's Secret. Miller, Fujiko, illus. (p. 358)
—Denzel Washington. (p. 427)
—Hillary Clinton. (p. 779)
—Nancy Pelosi. (p. 1229)
Epstein, Estelle Pottern. I Heard My Father's Voice. (p. 839)
Epstein, Eugene, illus. see Duey, Kathleen & Gould, Robert.
Epstein, Eugene, illus. see Duey, Kathleen.
Epstein, Eugene, illus. see Gould, Robert & Duey, Kathleen.
Epstein, Eugene, illus. see Gould, Robert.
Epstein, Eugene, photos by see Duey, Kathleen.
Epstein, Gabriela, illus. see Lammers, Elizabeth A. & McKinney, Dan.
Epstein, Len. Presidents Facts & Fun Activity Book. (p. 1397)
Epstein, Len, illus. see Blackaby, Susan.
Epstein, Len, illus. see Englar, Mary.
Epstein, Len, illus. see Jones, Christianne C.
Epstein, Len, illus. see Kalz, Jill.
Epstein, Len, illus. see Schmauss, Judy Kentor.
Epstein, Len, illus. see Wooster, Patricia.
Epstein, Lori, photos by see Kostyal, Karen.
Epstein, Robin. Choose or Lose: How to Pick a Winner. (p. 310)
—First Pajama Party: Slumberrific Six. (p. 596)
—Great Outdoors: Take a Hike. (p. 717)
—Growing up Groovy: An Out of This World Adventure. (p. 726)
—Pranks a Lot: The Girls vs. the Boys. (p. 1393)
—Rock & Roll: Divas Supreme. (p. 1481)
—Sleepover Surprise: A Twin-Sational Birthday. (p. 1589)
Epstein, Robin, jt. auth. see Borgenicht, David.
Epstein, Seymour, jt. auth. see Sederman, Marty.
Epstein, Sylvia & Migron, Hagit. How the Rosh Hashanah Challah. (p. 813)
Epting, Steve. Death of Captain America: The Burden of Dreams. Vol. 2 (p. 420)
—Fantastic Four (p. 571)
Epting, Steve, illus. see Brubaker, Ed.
Epting, Steve, illus. see Dixon, Chuck.
Epting, Steve, illus. see Hama, Larry, et al.
Epting, Steve, illus. see Hickman, Jonathan & Dragotta, Nick.
Epting, Steve, jt. illus. see Eaton, Scot.
Epting, Steve, et al. X-Men: Age of Apocalypse Prelude. (p. 1967)
Equipo Lexicográfico Everest, jt. auth. see Equipo Staff.
Equipo Staff. 1000 Preguntas y Respuestas. (p. 2001)
—365 Cuentos, uno para Cada Dia. (p. 2001)
—Atlas Enciclopedico Paises de America. (p. 112)
—Blanca Nieves. (p. 198)
—Dicionario Inicial Everest. Jorge, Gutiérrez Sahagún, illus. (p. 435)
—Encuentros. (p. 524)
—Escuela Infantil. (p. 535)
—Este No es Mi Conejito. (p. 538)
—Everest Diccionario Cima de la Lengua Espanola. (p. 542)
—Gran Aventura de las Palabras. (p. 706)
—Gusto. (p. 733)
—Libro de la Selva y Cuatro Cuentos Mas. (p. 1006)
—Nuevo Atlas Escolar Everest. (p. 1270)
—Olfato. (p. 1285)
—Pinocho y Cuatro Cuentos Mas. (p. 1361)
—Tiburones. (p. 1747)
Equipo Staff & Andrew, Charman. Dodo Desaparecio. (p. 460)
Equipo Staff & Brian, Williams. 22 de Noviembre De: Asesinatodel Presidente Kennedy. (p. 1996)
—Paises del Mundo. (p. 1319)
Equipo Staff & Clive, Dorman. Amaso la Masa. (p. 52)
—Me Hago un Sandwich. (p. 1116)
—Te Envio Una Postal. (p. 1708)
—¡Mira Que Macedonia! (p. 1148)
Equipo Staff & Delafosse, Claude. Oido. (p. 1282)
—Tacto. (p. 1695)
—Telefono y los Medios de Communicación. (p. 1716)
Equipo Staff & DESCHAMPS, NICHOLA. Mi Primer Libro de Los Números. (p. 1133)
Equipo Staff & DOWLAND, MELANIE. Mi Primer Libro de Dinosaurios. (p. 1133)
Equipo Staff & Equipo Lexicográfico Everest. Everest Diccionario Practico de Sinonimos y Antonimos. (p. 542)
—Everest Diccionario Practico Ilustrado de la Lengua Espanola. (p. 542)
—Mi Primer Diccionario. (p. 1133)
Equipo Staff & Gómez Cerdá, Alfredo. Animales. (p. 80)
Equipo Staff & Hands, Gill. Darwin. (p. 409)
Equipo Staff & Joly, Dominique. Montaña. (p. 1170)
Equipo Staff & Josephine, Paker. Iautas Tienen Agujeros. (p. 980)
Equipo Staff & LE GRECCO, SILVIA. Mi Primer Libro de la Granja. (p. 1133)
Equipo Staff & Mercedes, Neuschäfer Carlón. Draki, el Pequeño Dragon. (p. 480)
Equipo Staff & Messenger, Norman. Cabezas. (p. 250)
Equipo Staff & WARDLEY, RACHEL. Mi Primer Libro de Los Animales. (p. 1133)
Equipo Staff, et al. Atlas Geografico Universal. (p. 112)
—Manuel y Didi y el Gato de Nieve. (p. 1089)
Erazo, Carlos. Butterfly & Scorpions: Story of a First Love. (p. 247)
—Venganza Injusta. (p. 1835)
Erb, Diane. Enemy Cat: A Companion to the Growing Erbs Series. Koski, Rozanne, illus. (p. 527)
Erb, Greg & Oremland, Jason. Return of King Doug. (p. 1464)
Erb Iii, Walter J. Junior's Fishpond: A Financial Fable. (p. 936)
Erb, Sharlyne. hug from Daddy. (p. 824)
Ercilla, Alonso de. Araucana. (p. 94)
Ercolini, David, illus. see Lewis, Kevin.
Erdel, Peter, ed. 150 American Folk Songs to Sing Read & Play. (p. 2000)
Erdelji, Darka, illus. see Malone, Beni & White, Marian Frances.
Erdman, Loula G. Wind Blows Free. (p. 1935)
Erdman, Loula Grace. Good Land. (p. 698)
Erdman, Marjory. Little Pumpkins. (p. 1034)
Erdogan, Buket, illus. see Knowlton, Laurie Lazzaro.
Erdogan, Buket, illus. see Thompson, Lauren & Jackson, Livia.
Erdogan, Buket, illus. see Thompson, Lauren.
Erdogan, Buket, illus. see Wilson, Karma.
Erdogan, Faith, tr. see Hambleton, Laura.
Erdogan, Fatih. Ece Ve Efe Ile Türkçe. Hambleton, Laura, illus. (p. 502)
Erdogan, Fatih, tr. see Mycek-Wodecki, Anna.
Erdreich, Sarah. Cults. Espejo, Roman, ed. (p. 390)
Erdrich, jt. auth. see Erdrich, Louise.
Erdrich, Heid E. Mother's Tongue. (p. 1179)
Erdrich, Lise, illus. see Fifield, Lisa.
Erdrich, Liselotte, jt. auth. see Buffalohead, Julie.
Erdrich, Louise. Chickadee. Erdrich, Louise, illus. (p. 299)
—Game of Silence. (p. 654)
—Porcupine Year. Erdrich, Louise, illus. (p. 1386)
Erdrich, Louise & Erdrich. Game of Silence. (p. 654)
Eremeyev, Margarita, illus. see Merrick, Laurie K.
Erford, Bradley. Counselor's Guide to Clinical, Personality, & Behavioral Assessment. (p. 369)
Ergün, Erol. All-Merciful Master: The Beautiful Names of God. Egitim, Hasan, illus. (p. 45)
Ergun, Erol. All-Merciful Master. (p. 45)
—Generous Bestower. (p. 660)
—Hearer & the Seer of All. (p. 759)
—Supreme Ruler. (p. 1685)
Erguner, Kudsi. Journeys of a Sufi Musician. Mayers, Annette Courtenay, tr. from FRE. (p. 929)
Erhard, Lorie. Mama's Many Hats. Kalis, Jennifer, illus. (p. 1084)
Eric Carle Museum of Picture Book Art Staff. Artist to Artist: 23 Major Illustrators Talk to Children about Their Art. Gauch, Patricia Lee et al, eds. (p. 104)
Eric, F. Rowe, illus. see Cooper, James Fenimore.
Eric, F. Rowe, illus. see Haggard, H. Rider.
Eric, Kincaid, illus. see Claire, Black.
Eric, Whitfield, illus. see Showstack, Richard.
Erica, Bertram. Beyond Sunday School: Knowing God Series. (p. 174)
—Spirit Heroes & the Dean of Deceit. (p. 1628)
Erich, James. Dreams of Fire & Gods: Gods [Library Edition]. (p. 484)
—Seidman [Library Edition]. (p. 1548)
Erichsen, Rachael. Jessica Hedgehog Becomes Rich. (p. 914)
Erichson, Carey & Gurstien, Shari. Willie Learns a Lesson. (p. 1934)
Ericka Grogan, jt. auth. see Paul Ahrens-Gray.
Erickes, Leonard. Red Dragon Ryan Learns How to Fly. (p. 1453)
—Things We Should All Know about Dragons. (p. 1734)
Ericksen, Barb, illus. see Ormondroyd, Edward.
Ericksen, Barbara, illus. see Ormondroyd, Edward.
Erickson, Amelia. My First Airplane Trip: Solve Problems Involving Measurement (p. 1204)
Erickson, Arnold. Stories to Be Shared. (p. 1655)
Erickson, Byron. World of the Dragon Lords. Clark, John, ed. (p. 1957)
Erickson, Byron, et al. Mickey Mouse Adventures Clark, John & Kolberg, Sue, eds. (p. 1136)
—Walt Disney's Comics Clark, John, ed. (p. 1855)
—Walt Disney's Comics & Stories #686. Clark, John, ed. (p. 1855)
Erickson, C. J. Lovet Legend (p. 1061)
Erickson, Carol. Not a Used Dog, at All. (p. 1266)
Erickson, Carolly. To the Scaffold: The Life of Marie Antoinette. (p. 1759)
Erickson, Christian. Biz4Kids Business Start-up Kit BABY-SITTING. (p. 194)
—Biz4Kids Business Start-up Kit NEIGHBORHOOD BUSINESSES. (p. 194)
Erickson, Christian, creator. Biz4KidsBusiness Start-up Guide - Lawn Care. (p. 194)
Erickson, David, illus. see Bohlmann, Katharine.
Erickson, David, illus. see Emery, Joanna.
Erickson, David, illus. see Henley, Karyn.
Erickson, David, illus. see Knudsen, Shannon.

E

Erickson, David L., illus. see Henley, Karyn.
Erickson, Gina Clegg, jt. auth. see Foster, Kelli C.
Erickson, Jenny. My Favorite Advent & Christmas Activity Book. (p. 1203)
—My Favorite Bible. (p. 1203)
Erickson, John & Willard, Carolyn. Color Analyzers: Investigating Light & Color. Erickson, John & Klofkorn, Lisa, illus. (p. 342)
Erickson, John, et al. Electric Circuits: Inventive Physical Science Activities. (p. 508)
Erickson, John R. Big Question. Holmes, Gerald L., illus. (p. 183)
—Case of the Black-Hooded Hangmans. Holmes, Gerald L., illus. (p. 273)
—Case of the Blazing Sky. Holmes, Gerald L., illus. (p. 273)
—Case of the Booby-Trapped Pickup. Holmes, Gerald L., illus. (p. 273)
—Case of the Burrowing Robot. Holmes, Gerald L., illus. (p. 273)
—Case of the Car-Barkaholic Dog. Holmes, Gerald L., illus. (p. 273)
—Case of the Coyote Invasion. Holmes, Gerald L., illus. (p. 273)
—Case of the Deadly Ha-Ha Game. Holmes, Gerald L., illus. (p. 274)
—Case of the Dinosaur Birds. Holmes, Gerald L., illus. (p. 274)
—Case of the Double Bumblebee Sting. Holmes, Gerald L., illus. (p. 274)
—Case of the Falling Sky. Holmes, Gerald L., illus. (p. 274)
—Case of the Fiddle-Playing Fox. Holmes, Gerald L., illus. (p. 274)
—Case of the Halloween Ghost. Holmes, Gerald L., illus. (p. 274)
—Case of the Haystack Kitties. Holmes, Gerald L., illus. (p. 274)
—Case of the Hooking Bull. Holmes, Gerald L., illus. (p. 274)
—Case of the Kidnapped Collie. Holmes, Gerald L., illus. (p. 274)
—Case of the Measled Cowboy. Holmes, Gerald L., illus. (p. 274)
—Case of the Midnight Rustler. Holmes, Gerald L., illus. (p. 274)
—Case of the Missing Bird Dog. Holmes, Gerald L., illus. (p. 274)
—Case of the Missing Cat. Holmes, Gerald L., illus. (p. 274)
—Case of the Monkey Burglar. Holmes, Gerald L., illus. (p. 274)
—Case of the Most Ancient Bone. Holmes, Gerald L., illus. (p. 274)
—Case of the Mysterious Voice. Holmes, Gerald L., illus. (p. 274)
—Case of the Night-Stalking Bone Monster. Holmes, Gerald L., illus. (p. 274)
—Case of the One-Eyed Killer Stud Horse. Holmes, Gerald L., illus. (p. 274)
—Case of the Perfect Dog. Holmes, Gerald L., illus. (p. 274)
—Case of the Raging Rottweiler. Holmes, Gerald L., illus. (p. 275)
—Case of the Saddle House Robbery. Holmes, Gerald L., illus. (p. 275)
—Case of the Secret Weapon. Holmes, Gerald L., illus. (p. 275)
—Case of the Shipwrecked Tree. Holmes, Gerald L., illus. (p. 275)
—Case of the Swirling Killer Tornado. Holmes, Gerald L., illus. (p. 275)
—Case of the Tender Cheeping Chickies. Holmes, Gerald L., illus. (p. 275)
—Case of the Three Rings. Holmes, Gerald L., illus. (p. 275)
—Case of the Tricky Trap. Holmes, Gerald L., illus. (p. 275)
—Case of the Twisted Kitty. Holmes, Gerald L., illus. (p. 275)
—Case of the Vampire Cat. Holmes, Gerald L., illus. (p. 275)
—Case of the Vampire Vacuum Sweeper. Holmes, Gerald L., illus. (p. 275)
—Case of the Vanishing Fishhook. Holmes, Gerald L., illus. (p. 275)
—Curse of the Incredible Priceless Corncob. Holmes, Gerald L., illus. (p. 395)
—Disappearance of Drover. Holmes, Gerald L., illus. (p. 446)
—Drover's Secret Life. Holmes, Gerald L., illus. (p. 486)
—Dungeon of Doom. Holmes, Gerald L., illus. (p. 490)
—Every Dog Has His Day. Holmes, Gerald L., illus. (p. 542)
—Faded Love. Holmes, Gerald L., illus. (p. 562)
—Fling. Holmes, Gerald L., illus. (p. 604)
—Garbage Monster from Outer Space. Holmes, Gerald L., illus. (p. 655)
—Ghost of Rabbits Past. Holmes, Gerald L., illus. (p. 671)
—Hank Cowdog 50. Holmes, Gerald L., illus. (p. 742)
—Hank the Cowdog & Monkey Business. Holmes, Gerald L., illus. (p. 742)
—It's a Dog's Life. Holmes, Gerald L., illus. (p. 895)
—Let Sleeping Dogs Lie. Holmes, Gerald L., illus. (p. 994)
—Lost in the Blinded Blizzard. Holmes, Gerald L., illus. (p. 1055)
—Lost in the Dark Unchanted Forest. Holmes, Gerald L., illus. (p. 1055)
—Moonlight Madness. Holmes, Gerald L., illus. (p. 1172)
—Mopwater Files. Holmes, Gerald L., illus. (p. 1173)
—Murder in the Middle Pasture. Holmes, Gerald L., illus. (p. 1192)
—Original Adventures of Hank the Cowdog. Holmes, Gerald L., illus. (p. 1304)
—Phantom in the Mirror. Holmes, Gerald L., illus. (p. 1349)
—Quest for the Great White Quail. Holmes, Gerald L., illus. (p. 1426)
—Return of the Charlie Monsters. Holmes, Gerald L., illus. (p. 1464)
—Secret Laundry Monster Files. Holmes, Gerald L., illus. (p. 1541)
—Slim's Good-Bye. Holmes, Gerald L., illus. (p. 1590)
—Wounded Buzzard on Christmas Eve. Holmes, Gerald L., illus. (p. 1962)
Erickson, John R. & Holmes, Gerald L. Case of the Prowling Bear. (p. 275)
Erickson, John R., et al. AfterSchool KidzScience: Earth & Space Science: Sunlight Science Kit. (p. 29)
Erickson, Justin. Alien Abductions. (p. 40)
Erickson, Karen. MEville to WEville Unit 1: Unit 1 ME (p. 1130)
Erickson, Mary. My Wee Book of Rhymes. (p. 1221)
Erickson, Mary Ellen. First Day of School. (p. 594)
—Snowstorm. (p. 1601)
—What Happened to the Deer? Peanut Butter Club Mysteries. (p. 1885)
—Who Jinxed the CG Ranch? (p. 1916)
Erickson, Melissa. When the Tooth Fairy Comes... Erickson, Melissa, illus. (p. 1905)
Erickson, Patricia. Little Christmas Tree. (p. 1026)
—Shiny New Shoes. (p. 1567)
Erickson, Paul. Daily Life on a Southern Plantation. Gabbey, Terry, illus. (p. 400)
—Pier at the End of the World Martinez, Andrew, photos by. (p. 1357)
Erickson, Rick. Royal Delft: A Guide to de Porceleyne Fels (p. 1492)
Erickson, Robert. Fluke Family Hero: Book Two in the Saga of Maynerd Dumsted. (p. 608)
Erickson, Russell. Toad for Tuesday. (p. 1759)
Erickson, Sharon. Opposites. Ready, D. M., illus. (p. 1300)
Erickson, Terri, illus. see Hawkins, Al.
Erickson, Timothy Ronald. Death's Whisper Recoil Erickson, Timothy Ronald, illus. (p. 420)
Ericksson, Ashe, jt. auth. see Mellor, Corinne.
Ericson, Emma. I Collect Bugs! Understanding Addition. (p. 837)
—Who Was Kit Carson? (p. 1918)
Ericson, Emma, jt. auth. see Mills, Nathan.
Ericson, Helen. Harriet Spies Again. (p. 749)
Ericson, Helen & Fitzhugh, Louise. Harriet Spies Again. (p. 749)
Ericson, Kristi. Huger. (p. 825)
Ericson, Lisa, illus. see Ericson, Nora.
Ericson, Nora. Dill & Bizzy: An Odd Duck & a Strange Bird. Ericson, Lisa, illus. (p. 440)
Ericsson, Annie Beth, illus. see Christian, Cheryl.
Ericsson, Annie Beth & Christian, Cheryl. ¿Que hay en mi Jardin? (Spanish/English) Un libro de colores/A Book of Colors. del Risco, Eida, tr. (p. 1424)
Ericsson, Jennifer A. Whoo Goes There? Kitchen, Bert, illus. (p. 1920)
Ericsson, Jennifer A., jt. auth. see Blair, Beth L.
Eriksen, Craig A. Nollie Gnome & Friends: 1. Return from Holiday. (p. 1263)
Eriksen, Kathryn E. Walk with the Master: A Biblical Adventure of Canine Proportions. (p. 1854)
Eriksen, Thomas Hylland. Engaging Anthropology: The Case for a Public Presence. (p. 529)
Eriksen, Tone, illus. see Deprisco Wang, Dorothea.
Eriksen, Valanee. Christmas Bells & Hero's Tails. (p. 312)
Eriksen, Steven. House of Chains. (p. 803)
—Memories of Ice. (p. 1126)
—Midnight Tides. (p. 1139)
Eriksson, Christina Wyss, jt. auth. see Collins, Carolyn Strom.
Eriksson, Eva. Molly Goes Shopping. Dyssegaard, Elisabeth Kallick, tr. from SWE. (p. 1160)
Eriksson, Eva, illus. see Holmberg, Bo R.
Eriksson, Eva, illus. see Lagercrantz, Rose.
Eriksson, Eva, illus. see Lindgren, Barbro.
Eriksson, Eva, illus. see Stark, Ulf.
Eriksson, Eva, illus. see Wagner, Anke.
Eriksson, Eva E. Crash Course for Molly. Dyssegaard, Elisabeth Kallick, tr. from SWE. (p. 376)
Eriksson, Kjell. Princess of Burundi. Segerberg, Ebba, tr. from SWE. (p. 1404)
Erin, Audrey. Visit the Lincoln Memorial. (p. 1845)
Erin, Bethany. Wind & the Blows. (p. 1935)
Erin, Clemmer. How Did I Get You? (p. 806)
Erin, K. c. Blueberry Pie: The Adventures of Blueberry Bear & Her Friends. Sloane, Roxy, illus. (p. 204)
—Carnival. (p. 270)
Ering, Timothy B., illus. see DiCamillo, Kate.
Ering, Timothy Basil. Almost Fearless Hamilton Squidlegger. Ering, Timothy Basil, illus. (p. 48)
—Necks Out for Adventure! The True Story of Edwin Wiggleskin. Ering, Timothy Basil, illus. (p. 1239)
—Story of Frog Belly Rat Bone. Ering, Timothy Basil, illus. (p. 1658)
Ering, Timothy Basil, illus. see Blumenthal, Deborah.
Ering, Timothy Basil, illus. see DiCamillo, Kate.
Ering, Timothy Basil, illus. see Elliott, David.
Ering, Timothy Basil, illus. see Losure, Mary.
Ering, Timothy Basil, illus. see Nelson, Marilyn.
Ering, Timothy Basil, illus. see Rapp, Adam.
Ering, Timothy Basil, illus. see Wood, Nancy.
Ering, Timothy Basil, jt. auth. see DiCamillo, Kate.
Erinn, Banting. Wheels & Axles. (p. 1900)
Erker, Robert, illus. see Pohlmann-Eden, Bernd.
Erkert, A. & Erkert, Andrea. Islas de Relajacion. (p. 892)
Erkert, Andrea, jt. auth. see Erkert, A.
Erkocak, Sahin, illus. see Kalz, Jill.
Erkocak, Sahin, illus. see Meister, Cari.
Erlandson, Nick. Duncan & the Bone Tree (p. 490)
Erlbach, Arlene. Middle School Survival Guide. Flook, Helen, illus. (p. 1138)
Erlbach, Arlene & Erlbach, Herb. Fun Mother's Day Crafts. (p. 648)
—Fun Thanksgiving Day Crafts. (p. 648)
—Fun Valentine's Day Crafts. (p. 648)
Erlbach, Arlene & Erlbach, Herbert. Fun Mother's Day Crafts. (p. 648)
—Fun Thanksgiving Day Crafts. (p. 648)
—Mother's Day Crafts. (p. 1178)
—Thanksgiving Day Crafts. Ponte, June, illus. (p. 1726)
—Valentine's Day Crafts. (p. 1830)
Erlbach, Herb, jt. auth. see Erlbach, Arlene.
Erlbach, Herbert, jt. auth. see Erlbach, Arlene.
Erlbruch, Wolf. Duck, Death & the Tulip. (p. 488)
—Miracle of Bears. Reynolds, Michael, tr. from GER. (p. 1148)
Erlbruch, Wolf, illus. see Holzwarth, Werner.
Erlbruch, Wolf, jt. auth. see Holzwarth, Werner.
Erlbruch, Wolf & Holzwarth, Werner. Story of the Little Mole Who Knew It was None of His Business: Plop Up Edition. (p. 1661)
Erlic, Lily. Grasslands. (p. 712)
—Lois Lowry. (p. 1045)
—Louis Sachar. (p. 1058)
Erlich, Arty. Vegie Adventure. (p. 1834)
Erlich, Bev. Pink Roses Everywhere. (p. 1360)
Erlich, Esther, illus. see Kliman, Susie.
Erlings, Fridrik. Boy on the Edge. (p. 218)
—Fish in the Sky. (p. 598)
Erne, Monica. Fantazzzmia: Where Dreams Come From. (p. 572)
Ernest Boehnert. Great Alphabet Reminder Book. (p. 713)
Ernest, Brother. Angel of the Poor: A Story of Mother Emmelie Gamelin. Jagodits, Carolyn Lee, illus. (p. 74)
Ernest, Edward. Child's First Book. (p. 304)
Ernestine. Town Girl. (p. 1773)
Erno, Jeff. You Belong with Me. (p. 1973)
—You Belong with Me [Library Edition]. (p. 1973)
Ernsperger, Lori & Stegen-Hanson, Tania. Just Take a Bite: Easy, Effective Answers to Food Aversions & Eating Challenges! (p. 940)
Ernst, Carol. Messages to the Heart. (p. 1129)
Ernst, Cindy Kathleen. Sunny the Sunflower. (p. 1677)
Ernst, Clara, illus. see Madan, Fredric C.
Ernst, Clara, illus. see Mingo, Norman.
Ernst, Howard R., jt. auth. see Sabato, Larry J.
Ernst, Jackie. Many Different Colors. (p. 1089)
Ernst, Kathleen. Caroline Takes a Chance. (p. 270)
—Caroline's Secret Message. (p. 270)
—Changes for Caroline. (p. 290)
—Clues in the Shadows. Tibbles, Jean-Paul, illus. (p. 336)
—Danger at the Zoo: A Kit Mystery. Tibbles, JeanPaul, illus. (p. 403)
—Ghosts of Vicksburg. (p. 673)
—Highland Fling. (p. 779)
—Midnight in Lonesome Hollow: A Kit Mystery. (p. 1139)
—Midnight in Lonesome Hollow: A Kit Mystery. Tibbles, Jean-Paul, illus. (p. 1139)
—Retreat from Gettysburg. (p. 1464)
—Runaway Friend. Tibbles, Jean-Paul, illus. (p. 1496)
—Surprise for Caroline. (p. 1685)
—Trouble at Fort la Pointe. (p. 1789)
—Whistler in the Dark. (p. 1912)
Ernst, Lisa Campbell. Gingerbread Girl. Ernst, Lisa Campbell, illus. (p. 677)
—Gingerbread Girl Goes Animal Crackers. Ernst, Lisa Campbell, illus. (p. 677)
—Goldilocks Returns. Ernst, Lisa Campbell, illus. (p. 696)
—How Things Work in the House. (p. 814)
—Round Like a Ball! Ernst, Lisa Campbell, illus. (p. 1491)
—Snow Surprise. (p. 1599)
—Sylvia Jean, Scout Supreme. Ernst, Lisa Campbell, illus. (p. 1692)
—Sylvia Jean, the Drama Queen. (p. 1692)
—This Is the Van That Dad Cleaned. Ernst, Lisa Campbell, illus. (p. 1736)
—Turn-Around, Upside-Down Alphabet Book. Ernst, Lisa Campbell, illus. (p. 1797)
—Wake up, It's Spring! Ernst, Lisa Campbell, illus. (p. 1853)
Ernst, Lisa Campbell, illus. see Daniel, Claire.
Ernst, Lisa Campbell, illus. see Medearis, Angela Shelf.
Ernst, Lisa Campbell, illus. see Moran, Alex.
Ernst, Lisa Campbell, jt. auth. see Daniel, Claire.
Ernst, Lisa Campbell & Blue Apple Staff. How Things Work - In the Yard. (p. 814)
Ernst, Lyle, jt. auth. see Sigafus, Kim.
Ernt, Clara, illus. see Mingo, Norman.
Eroglu, Aysin D., illus. see Shaskan, Trisha Speed.
Eros, Keith, jt. auth. see Fox, Paula.
Erps, Yitzy. Tell Me a Tale: 8 Great Stories. (p. 1716)
Errico, Daniel. Journey of the Marmabill. Turrill, Tiffany, illus. (p. 928)
—Journey of the Noble Gnarble. Turrill, Tiffany, illus. (p. 928)
Errico, Jessica / C. Grandpa's Magical Accordion. Star, Brenda, illus. (p. 710)
Errington, Rachael, illus. see Blackhurst, Rebecca.
Erroll, Mark. I Am Honest. (p. 833)
—I Am Honest / Soy Honesto. (p. 833)
Erskine, Gary, illus. see Hama, Larry.
Erskine, Gary, illus. see Morrison, Grant.
Erskine, Gary, illus. see White, Steve.
Erskine Hirko, Holly, tr. see Sand, George.
Erskine, Kathryn. Absolute Value of Mike. (p. 7)
—Badger Knight. (p. 132)
—Mockingbird. (p. 1157)
—Quaking. (p. 1422)
—Seeing Red. (p. 1548)
Erskine, Kevin L. Derek's Dream Team (p. 427)
Erskine-Levinson, Robin. McGill University College Prowler off the Record. (p. 1114)
Ersoz, Isabella. Mad Mysterious Mansion: Izzy & Daisy. Ersoz, Sahin, illus. (p. 1069)
Ersoz, Sahin, illus. see Ersoz, Isabella.
Ersoz, Sahin, illus. see Lebost, Diana.
Erte. Erte Fashions Coloring Book. Noble, Marty, ed. (p. 534)
Ertekin, Betul. I Love My Prophet: This World I Love. (p. 842)
—Thank You God: This World I Love. (p. 1725)
—This World I Love Coloring & Activity Book. (p. 1737)
Ertle-Rickard, Stephen. Astronaut. (p. 109)
—Deep Sea Dive. (p. 423)
—Drag Race. (p. 476)
—Fighter Pilot. (p. 585)
—Formula 1: Life at the Edge. (p. 620)
—Powerboat Race. (p. 1390)
—Sky Dive. (p. 1586)
—Stunt Man. (p. 1670)
Ertner, Jim, jt. auth. see Lederer, Richard.
Ertner, Jim & Lederer, Richard. Super Funny Animal Jokes. (p. 1680)
—Wild & Wacky Animal Jokes. (p. 1928)
Ervin, C. H. Hummingbird,Hummingbird. (p. 826)
Ervin, Imogene. Charlie & Chu Chu's Day of Adventure. Ervin, Keith, illus. (p. 292)
—Rainey Days. (p. 1436)
Ervin, Keith, illus. see Ervin, Imogene.
Ervin, Pamela. Sebastian. (p. 1539)
Ervin, Randy. Maycroft From 232nd. (p. 1113)
Ervin, Robert Edgar. John Hunt Morgan Raid of 1863. (p. 922)
Ervin, Wendy. Boo Boo. (p. 209)
—Boo-Boo & the Crazy Old Goat/ Boo-Boo & the Wild Turkeys: Flip Book. (p. 209)
Erwert, Scott, illus. see Gray, Amy.
Erwin, J. L., illus. see Orr, Andy.
Erwin, Kay. Sheepdog's Christmas. (p. 1564)
Erwin, Steve, illus. see Anderson, Jameson.
Erwin, Steve, illus. see Biskup, Agnieszka, et al.
Erwin, Steve, illus. see Braun, Eric.
Erwin, Steve, illus. see Burgan, Michael & Hoena, Blake A.
Erwin, Steve, illus. see Burgan, Michael.
Erwin, Steve, illus. see Doeden, Matt.
Erwin, Steve, illus. see Friedman, Michael Jan, et al.
Erwin, Steve, illus. see Gunderson, Jessica Sarah & Gunderson, Jessica.
Erwin, Steve, illus. see Miller, Connie Colwell.
Erwin, Steve, illus. see Niz, Xavier W., et al.
Erwin, Steve, illus. see Niz, Xavier, et al.
Erwin, Steve, illus. see Sautter, Aaron.
Erwin, Steve, illus. see Sohn, Emily & Barnett II, Charles.
Erwin, Steve, illus. see Sohn, Emily.
Erwin, Vicki Berger. Elizabeth Bryan Mysteries Set (p. 513)
Erwin, Wesley. Boundary Waters ABC Kemp, Kathie, illus. (p. 216)
Esbaum, Jill. Angry Birds Playground: Animals - An Around-the-World Habitat Adventure. (p. 75)
—Angry Birds Playground - Animals: An Around-the-World Habitat Adventure. (p. 75)
—Animal Groups. Lanting, Frans, illus. (p. 78)
—Apples for Everyone. (p. 93)
—Cherry Blossoms Say Spring. (p. 298)
—Everything Spring. (p. 545)
—Explore My World Nighttime. (p. 550)
—Explore My World Penguins. (p. 550)
—Explore My World Snow Leopards. (p. 550)
—I Am Cow, Hear Me Moo! Gordon, Gus, illus. (p. 832)
—I Hatched! Corace, Jen, illus. (p. 838)
—Seed, Sprout, Pumpkin, Pie. (p. 1547)
—Stanza. Davis, Jack E., illus. (p. 1640)
—Tom's Tweet. Stone, Kyle M. & Santat, Dan, illus. (p. 1765)
—Winter Wonderland. (p. 1938)
Esbaum, Jill, jt. auth. see National Geographic Editors.
Esbaum, Jill, jt. auth. see National Geographic Kids Staff.
Esbensen, Barbara Juster. Playful Slider: The North American River Otter. Brown, Mary Barrett, illus. (p. 1372)
—Swing Around the Sun. Chee, Cheng-Khee et al, illus. (p. 1691)
—Who Is Calling? (p. 1915)
Esbenshade, Richard S. & Nevins, Debbie. Hungary. (p. 827)
Esberger, Trudi. Boy Who Lost His Bumble. Esberger, Trudi, illus. (p. 219)
Escalante, Travis. Henry the Little Sailboat & the Happy Harbor. (p. 768)
—Story of Rocks & Balloons. (p. 1659)
Escalera, Manuel Silva. Cassandrita y Los Sabios: De Los 10 Mandamientos y Filosofia. (p. 276)
Escandell, Victor. Wonderful World of Animals: Doodle Art Book. (p. 1948)
Escandell, Victor (ALEHOP), jt. auth. see Cabre, Jordi.
Escardo Bas, Mercè. Tres Cerditos. Joan, Pere, illus. (p. 1784)
Eschbach, Andrea & Eschbach, Markus. How to Speak Horse: A Horse-Crazy Kid's Guide to Reading Body Language, Understanding Behavior, & Talking Back with Simple Groundwork Lessons. (p. 821)
Eschbach, Markus, jt. auth. see Eschbach, Andrea.
Eschberger, Beverly. Elephants in the City of Light: An Elephant Family Adventure. Gower, Jim, illus. (p. 512)
—Elephants in the Land of Enchantment: An Elephant Family Adventure. Gower, Jim, illus. (p. 512)
—Elephants Tour England: An Elephant Family Adventure. Gower, Jim, illus. (p. 512)
—Elephants Visit London: An Elephant Family Adventure. Gower, Jim, illus. (p. 512)
Escher, Jill. Boneyville Dogs - Scuba Dogs. (p. 209)
Escher, M. C., illus. see Born, Mark Alan.
Eschler, Linda. Strawberry Fairies & the Secret of Mystery Island. (p. 1666)
—Strawberry Fairies Save Sandcastle Island. (p. 1666)
Esckilsen, Erik E. Last Mall Rat. (p. 978)
Escobar, Antonio Rocha, illus. see Anza, Ana Luisa.
Escobar, Antonio Rocha, illus. see Garcia, Juan Carlos Quezadas, et al.
Escobar, Arturo, jt. ed. see Ribeiro, Gustavo Lins.
Escobar, Gabe. Turkeys in the Moonlight. (p. 1797)
Escobar, Melba. Siete Mejores Cuentos Rabes. Neira, Muyi, illus. (p. 1573)
Escobar, Michael, jt. auth. see MacDonald, Daniel.
Escoffier, Michaël. Brief Thief. Di Giacomo, Kris, illus. (p. 228)
—Day I Lost My Superpowers. Di Giacomo, Kris, illus. (p. 413)
—Mammoth in the Fridge. (p. 1085)
—Me First! Di Giacomo, Kris, illus. (p. 1115)
—Rabbit & the Not-So-Big-Bad Wolf. DiGiacomo, Kris, illus. (p. 1429)
—Take Away the A. Di Giacomo, Kris, illus. (p. 1696)
Escott, Colin, et al. Hank Williams: The Biography. (p. 742)
Escott, Esther, illus. see Escott, Jamison.
Escott, Ian, illus. see Hartman, Eve, et al.
Escott, Ian, illus. see Rand, Casey & Heinemann Library Staff.
Escott, Ian, illus. see Rand, Casey.
Escott, Jamison. Clockmaker of Mullen. Escott, Esther, illus. (p. 333)
Escott, John & Falkner, John Meade. Moonfleet. (p. 1172)

Escott, John & Henry, O. One Thousand Dollars & Other Plays, Level 2. Oxford University Press Staff & West, Clare, eds. (p. 1297)
Escott, John & Pearson Education Staff. Ghost of Genny Castle. (p. 671)
Escott, John & Pearson Longman Staff. Hannah & the Hurricane. (p. 742)
Escott, Maria. Green Anole Meets Brown Anole, a Love Story. Wigal, Mike, illus. (p. 721)
Escriva, Ana Lopez, illus. see Alonso, Fernando & Fernando, Alonso.
Escriva, Ana Lopez, illus. see Naylor, Phyllis Reynolds.
Escriva, Ana Lopez, illus. see Pacheco, Miguel Angel.
Escrivá, Victoria Pérez. ¡Achís! Ranucci, Claudia, illus. (p. 9)
—¡Cataplof! Cosas, Cositas Y Cacharros. Ranucci, Claudia, illus. (p. 278)
—¡Splash! Ranucci, Claudia, illus. (p. 1629)
Escrivá, Viví, illus. see Ada, Alma Flor, et al.
Escrivá, Viví, illus. see Dorris, Michael.
Escrivá, Viví, illus. see Flor Ada, Alma & Campoy, F. Isabel.
Escrivá, Viví, illus. see Flor Ada, Alma.
Escrivá, Viví, illus. see Guy, Ginger Foglesong.
Escrivá, Viví, illus. see Puncel, Maria.
Escudero, Antonio. Revolucion Industrial. (p. 1466)
Esdaile, Leslie, see Banks, L. A., pseud.
Esdaille-Richardson, Eudora. Malcolm & the Money Tree. Williams, Christopher, illus. (p. 1083)
EsDesignStudio, illus. see Bates, Delphine Branon.
Esenwa, Anthony. Jaja, King of Opobo. (p. 905)
Esham, Barbara. If You're So Smart, How Come You Can't Spell Mississippi? Esham, Barbara, illus. (p. 855)
—Last to Finish: A Story about the Smartest Boy in Math Class. Gordon, Mike, illus. (p. 979)
—Stacey Coolidge's Fancy Smancy Cursive Handwriting. Gordon, Mike, illus. (p. 1638)
Esham, Barbaraa. Mrs. Gorski, I Think I Have the Wiggle Fidgets. Gordon, Mike, illus. (p. 1187)
Eshbach, Charles. Twig's Guide to My Old Growth Forest. (p. 1801)
Eshbach, Karen, jt. auth. see Shertzer, Twilene.
Eshed, Tina. Adventures of Bunzy: The Beginning. (p. 17)
Eshelman, Priscilla. When Annabelle Moved to the Big City. (p. 1901)
Esherick, Donald, ed. see Bonnice, Sherry & Hoard, Carolyn.
Esherick, Donald, ed. see Bonnice, Sherry.
Esherick, Donald, ed. see Brinkerhoff, Shirley.
Esherick, Donald, ed. see Esherick, Joan.
Esherick, Donald, ed. see Libal, Autumn.
Esherick, Donald, ed. see Libal, Joyce.
Esherick, Donald, ed. see Vitale, Ann.
Esherick, Joan. Balancing Act: A Teen's Guide to Managing Stress. (p. 133)
—Brain Injury. Albers, Lisa et al, eds. (p. 221)
—Breaking down Barriers: Youth with Physical Challenges. (p. 225)
—Criminal Psychology & Personality Profiling. Noziglia, Carla Miller & Siegel, Jay A., eds. (p. 382)
—Dead on Their Feet: The Health Effects of Sleep Deprivation in Teens (p. 417)
—Diet & Your Emotions: The Comfort Food Falsehood. (p. 437)
—Drug - & Alcohol-Related Health Issues. McDonnell, Mary Ann & Forman, Sara, eds. (p. 486)
—Drug Therapy & Mood Disorders. (p. 487)
—Drug Therapy & Sleep Disorders. (p. 487)
—Dying for Acceptance: A Teen's Guide to Drug- & Alcohol-Related Health Issues. (p. 491)
—Emotions & Eating. Garcia, Victor, ed. (p. 520)
—FDA & Psychiatric Drugs: How a Drug Is Approved. (p. 578)
—FDA & Psychiatric Drugs: How a Drug Is Approved. McDonnell, Mary Ann & Esherick, Donald, eds. (p. 578)
—Guaranteed Rights: The Legislation that Protects Youth with Special Needs. (p. 728)
—Guaranteed Rights: The Legislation That Protects Youths with Special Needs. (p. 728)
—How a Drug Is Approved: The FDA & Psychiatric Drugs. (p. 804)
—Journey Toward Recovery: Youth with Brain Injury. (p. 929)
—Laws That Protect Youth with Special Needs. Albers, Lisa et al, eds. (p. 981)
—Looking & Feeling Good in Your Body. Garcia, Victor, ed. (p. 1050)
—Managing Stress. Bridgemohan, Carolyn & Forman, Sara, eds. (p. 1086)
—Mood Disorders. McDonnell, Mary Ann & Esherick, Donald, eds. (p. 1171)
—No More Butts: Kicking the Tobacco Habit. (p. 1259)
—Physical Challenges. Albers, Lisa et al, eds. (p. 1353)
—Prisoner Rehabilitation: Success Stories & Failures. (p. 1407)
—Prozac: North American Culture & the Wonder Drug. (p. 1413)
—Prozac: North American Culture & the Wonder Drug. (p. 1413)
—Silent Cry: Teen Suicide & Self-Destructive Behaviors. (p. 1575)
—Sleep Deprivation & Its Consequences. Bridgemohan, Carolyn & Forman, Sara, eds. (p. 1588)
—Sleep Disorders. McDonnell, Mary Ann & Esherick, Donald, eds. (p. 1588)
—Smoking-Related Health Issues. (p. 1595)
—Smoking-Related Health Issues. McDonnell, Mary Ann & Forman, Sara, eds. (p. 1595)
—Suicide & Self-Destructive Behaviors. McDonnell, Mary Ann & Forman, Sara, eds. (p. 1673)
—Women in the World of Africa. (p. 1946)
Esherick, Joan, frwd. Drug Therapy & Sleep Disorders. (p. 487)
Eshleman, Catherine, et al. Perry Passyflyer. (p. 1344)
Eshleman, William & Kimball, Paige. Prank & Pray You Get Away! over 60 Fun Jokes to Play on Your Sibling. (p. 1393)
Esiri, Allie & Kelly, Rachel, eds. IF: A Treasury of Poems for Almost Every Possibility. Lawton, Natasha, illus. (p. 852)
Eskandani, Shadi, tr. see Akbarpour, Ahmad.
Eske, Aaron & Nash, Kevin. University of Nebraska College Prowler off the Record. (p. 1821)
Eskeland, N. L. Menace in the Walls: A Summer Project Turns Treacherous. (p. 1126)
Eskeland, N. L., jt. auth. see Bailey, N. C.
Eskelin, Neil, jt. auth. see Hartness, Jim.
Eskelsen, Emily Warner, jt. auth. see Johnson, Ned.
Eskridge, Ann E. Slave Uprisings & Runaways: Fighting for Freedom & the Underground Railroad. (p. 1588)
Eskye, Tony. Adventures of Fojo the Frog. (p. 18)
Eslami, Mansour. Senior Design Experience: Lessons for Life, Second Edition, Revised & Expanded. (p. 1550)
Eslinger, Sara. Quick Learn: Meaningful Symbols & Imagery That Makes Bible Verse Learning Easy & Fun. (p. 1427)
Esmaili, Roza. Zagros & Nature Force: Coloring Book. Sun Rise Illustration and Computer Animation Staff, illus. (p. 1984)
Esola, Mike. Diary of a Dinosaur: The Attack of Benny. (p. 434)
Esopo. Leon y la Zorra. (p. 992)
—Zorra Se Pasa de Lista. (p. 1990)
Esopo, jt. auth. see Combel Editorial Staff.
Esopo, jt. auth. see Uribe, Veronica.
Esopo, et al. Fábulas y Sus Buenas Moralejas. (p. 559)
ESP International Ltd. Garfield It's All about Math: Ages 6-7 Years. (p. 657)
—Garfield It's All about Spelling & Vocabulary Grade/Year One. (p. 657)
ESP International Ltd, creator. Garfield It's All about Colors, Shapes & Time. (p. 657)
—Garfield It's All about Letters & Words. (p. 657)
—Garfield It's All about Numbers & Counting. (p. 657)
—Garfield It's All about Reading & Phonics. (p. 657)
Espadaler, Rosa, illus. see Stranaghan, Crystal J.
Espaillat, Rhina P., tr. see Alvarez, Julia.
Esparra, Lydia. Heaven Is All Around You. Esparra, Veronica, illus. (p. 761)
Esparra, Veronica, illus. see Esparra, Lydia.
Esparz, Esther LaMadrid. Rocking Horse Rhymes. (p. 1483)
Esparza, Andres, illus. see Ciencin, Scott & Cano, Fernando.
Esparza, Andres, illus. see Ciencin, Scott & Maese, Fares.
Esparza, Andres, illus. see Ciencin, Scott, et al.
Esparza, Andres, illus. see Kreie, Chris & Maese, Fares.
Esparza, Andres, illus. see Maese, Fares & Shakespeare, William.
Esparza, Andres, illus. see Sonneborn, Scott.
Esparza, Andres, illus. see Tulien, Sean & Maese, Fares.
Esparza, Bob, photos by see Haab, Rachel.
Esparza, Carolyn. Parenting Business: Hindsight Is 20/20. (p. 1324)
Esparza, Thomas, Jr., prod. Esther's Playhouse, 2 Disk Set. (p. 538)
—Esther's Playhouse, Disk 1. (p. 538)
Esparza-Vela, Mary. Bearly Learning about Water. Morris, Alexander, illus. (p. 151)
—Lucky's Lick. Prouix, Denis, illus. (p. 1063)
—Smiling Burro. Motz, Mike, illus. (p. 1594)
Esparza- Vela, Mary. You Can't Take the Dinosaur Home. Motz, Mike, illus. (p. 1975)
Espejo, Roman. Adaptation & Climate Change. (p. 11)
—Are Natural Disasters Increasing? (p. 96)
—Behavioral Disorders. Greenhaven Press Editors & Gale Editors, eds. (p. 160)
—Bioterrorism. (p. 190)
—Can Glacier & Icemelt Be Reversed? Greenhaven Press Editors, ed. (p. 258)
—Can Glacier & Icemelt Be Reversed? Greenhaven Press Editors & Gale Editors, eds. (p. 258)
—Cars in America. (p. 272)
—Celebrity Culture. (p. 285)
—Cell Phones in Schools. Greenhaven Press Editors, ed. (p. 286)
—Cell Phones in Schools. Greenhaven Press Editors & Gale Editors, eds. (p. 286)
—Chemical Dependency. (p. 297)
—Civil Liberties (p. 324)
—Civil Liberties. (p. 324)
—Community Policing. Greenhaven Press Editors, ed. (p. 350)
—Community Policing. Greenhaven Press Editors & Gale Editor, eds. (p. 350)
—Consumerism. (p. 360)
—Culture of Beauty. (p. 391)
—Custody & Divorce. (p. 395)
—Do Infectious Diseases Pose a Threat? Greenhaven Press Editors, ed. (p. 457)
—Does the World Hate the U. S. ? (p. 460)
—Fashion Industry. (p. 575)
—Film Industry. (p. 586)
—Has Technology Increased Learning? (p. 752)
—How Does Advertising Impact Teen Behavior? (p. 808)
—Hurricane Katrina. (p. 829)
—Privacy. (p. 1407)
—Sexting. (p. 1556)
—Should Vaccinations Be Mandatory? Gale, G., ed. (p. 1570)
—Smartphones. (p. 1593)
—Teen Smoking. Greenhaven Press Editors, ed. (p. 1714)
—Tobacco & Smoking. (p. 1760)
—Tobacco & Smoking. Greenhaven Press Editors, ed. (p. 1760)
—Transgender People. (p. 1778)
—Urban America. (p. 1825)
—User-Generated Content. (p. 1828)
—Voter Fraud. (p. 1850)
—What Is Humanity's Greatest Challenge? (p. 1889)
—What Is the Future of Higher Education? Greenhaven Press Staff, ed. (p. 1890)
—What Is the Future of the Music Industry? (p. 1890)
—What Is the Impact of Automation? (p. 1890)
—What Is the Impact of Tourism? (p. 1890)
—What Is the Impact of Twitter? Greenhaven Press Editors, ed. (p. 1890)
Espejo, Roman, ed. see Erdreich, Sarah.
Espejo, Roman & Mur, Cindy. Drug Testing. (p. 487)
Espejo, Roman, ed. AIDS. (p. 30)
—Alcohol. (p. 35)
—Bioterrorism. (p. 190)
—Eating Disorders. (p. 501)
—How Does Advertising Impact Teen Behavior. (p. 808)
Espeland, Pamela. Knowing Me, Knowing You: The I-Sight Way to Understand Yourself & Others. (p. 965)
Espeland, Pamela, ed. see Gootman, Marilyn E.
Espeland, Pamela, ed. see Lewis, Barbara A.
Espeland, Pamela & Verdick, Elizabeth. Doing & Being Your Best: The Boundaries & Expectations Assets. (p. 463)
—Dude, That's Rude! (Get Some Manners) Mark, Steve, illus. (p. 489)
—Helping Out & Staying Safe: The Empowerment Assets. (p. 766)
—Knowing & Doing What's Right: The Positive Values Assets. (p. 965)
—Loving to Learn: The Commitment to Learning Assets. (p. 1061)
—Making Choices & Making Friends: The Social Competencies Assets. (p. 1080)
—People Who Care about You: The Support Assets. (p. 1340)
—Proud to Be You: The Positive Identity Assets. (p. 1413)
—See You Later, Procrastinator! (p. 1547)
—Smart Ways to Spend Your Time: The Constructive Use of Time Assets. (p. 1593)
Espenel, Gwenael. Children's Bookshelf. (p. 303)
Espenson, Jane & Bell, Brad. Husbands. Hahn, Sierra, ed. (p. 830)
Espenson, Jane, et al. Predators & Prey Jeanty, Georges & Madsen, Michelle, illus. (p. 1394)
Esperanza, Charles George. Red, Yellow, Blue, & a Dash of White, Too! (p. 1455)
Esperanza, Charles George, illus. see Grossinger, Tania.
Esperanzate-Buenafe, Norma. You Don't Have to Like It. (p. 1975)
Esperon, Maria Garcia. Copo de Algodon. Rivero, Marcos Almada, illus. (p. 365)
Esphyr, Slobodkina & Slobodkina. Caps for Sale: A Tale of a Peddler, Some Monkeys & Their Monkey Business. (p. 263)
Espina, Vito, illus. see Rawlings, John S.
Espinal, Rosario, jt. auth. see Morgan, Jana.
Espinola, Nicole, illus. see Webb, Mack H., Jr.
Espinos, J. Asi Vivian los Romanos. (p. 106)
Espinosa, Albert. Mundo Azul: Ama Tu Caos. (p. 1191)
Espinosa, Chris, illus. see Ellsberry, Sharon.
Espinosa, Chris & Rawlett, Robert. Rocket Megabyte's Texas Adventure. Espinosa, Chris, illus. (p. 1483)
Espinosa De Santayana, Rodrigo De, jt. auth. see Dunn, Joeming.
Espinosa, Frank. Journey to the Hidden Sea (p. 929)
—Rocketo: The Journey to the Hidden Sea. (p. 1483)
Espinosa Guerra, Julio. Poesia Del Siglo Xx en Chile la; antologia. (p. 1376)
Espinosa, Leo, illus. see Rozier, Lucy Margaret.
Espinosa, Marta Catalina Vanni. Testigos 25 D - Y Mas. (p. 1723)
Espinosa, Nuri, illus. see Róman, Pedro.
Espinosa, Patrick, photos by see Marrewa, Jennifer.
Espinosa, Rod. American Revolution. (p. 63)
—Battle of the Alamo. Espinosa, Rod, illus. (p. 146)
—Benjamin Franklin. Espinosa, Rod, illus. (p. 164)
—Boston Tea Party. Espinosa, Rod, illus. (p. 215)
—Courageous Princess: Beyond the Hundred Kingdoms. Vol. 1 Espinosa, Rod, illus. (p. 373)
—Courageous Princess Pocket Manga. (p. 373)
—George Washington. Espinosa, Rod, illus. (p. 664)
—I Hunt Monsters. (p. 839)
—Lewis & Clark. Espinosa, Rod, illus. (p. 1004)
—Patrick Henry. Espinosa, Rod, illus. (p. 1329)
—The Unremembered Lands. Espinosa, Rod, illus. (p. 1728)
Espinosa, Rod, illus. see Connor, Daniel.
Espinosa, Rod, illus. see Dunn, Joe.
Espinosa, Rod, illus. see Dunn, Joeming W.
Espinosa, Rod, illus. see Dunn, Joeming.
Espinosa, Rod, illus. see Leroux, Gaston.
Espinosa, Rod, illus. see Melville, Herman.
Espinosa, Rod, illus. see Shakespeare, William.
Espinosa, Rod, jt. auth. see Dunn, Joeming.
Espinosa, Rod, et al. How to Draw Manga Supersize (p. 818)
Espinoza, Aaron. Muchacho de la Musica Feliz: The Boy with Happy Music. (p. 1188)
Espinoza, Carlota D. God Made a Very Big Big Bang! Espinoza, Gabbi & EspinoZa, Carlota D., illus. (p. 689)
EspinoZa, Carlota D., illus. see Espinoza, Carlota D.
Espinoza, Gabbi, illus. see Espinoza, Carlota D.
Espinoza, Olivia G. Jay-Dylan's Cat & Fish. (p. 910)
Espinoza, Ramon, illus. see Hoppey, Tim.
Espinoza, Romina. Freedom of my Eyes. (p. 634)
Espinoza, Vicki. Donnie Dollar. (p. 466)
Esplanie, Kevin. Counting Pennies: Number Names & Count Sequence. (p. 371)
Espluga, Maria. I Am a Ballerina. (p. 831)
—I Am a Farmer. (p. 832)
—I Am a Sailor. (p. 832)
—I Am an Astronaut. (p. 832)
—I, Astronaut: Yo, Astronauta. (p. 834)
—I, Ballerina: Yo, Bailarina. (p. 834)
—I, Farmer: Yo, Campesino. (p. 838)
—I, Sailor: Yo, Marinero. (p. 845)
Espluga, Maria, illus. see Bailer, Darice & Dominguez, Madelca.
Espluga, Maria, illus. see Combel Editorial Staff, et al.
Espluga, Maria, illus. see Duran, Teresa.
Esplugas, Sonia, illus. see Crabtree, Sally.
ESPN Staff. ESPN Book (p. 536)
Esposito, Ralph. Ghost Detectives & Silverton's Treasure. (p. 670)
Esposito, Tony. Vagabond Penguin. (p. 1830)
Espriella, Leopoldo Berdella De La. Koku-Yo, Mensajero del Sol. Riano, Carlos, illus. (p. 966)
—Travesuras del Tio Conejo. Torres, Nora Estela, illus. (p. 1781)
Esprit, Keisha. Serena Goes to School. (p. 1552)
Espulgas, Sonia, illus. see Crabtree, Sally.
Esquenazi, Martha E., jt. ed. see Cabrera, Mirna Y.
Esquinaldo, Virginia. My Book of Prayers. (p. 1199)
—What Did Baby Jesus Do? Esquinaldo, Virginia, illus. (p. 1882)
Esquinaldo, Virginia, illus. see Dateno, Maria Grace.
Esquinaldo, Virginia, illus. see Glavich, Mary Kathleen.
Esquinaldo, Virginia, tr. see Glavich, Mary Kathleen.
Essama, Molly Jane. Prince & the Three Ugly Hags. (p. 1401)
Esselman, Mary D. & Vélez, Elizabeth Ash. Kiss Off: Poems to Set You Free. (p. 961)
Esseltine, Christopher R. Caleb's Quest. (p. 252)
Essence, Angel. Amazing Adventures of Callie the Cat: The Long Night. (p. 52)
Esseveld, Nelson, jt. auth. see Seghetti, Nancy.
Essig, Helena & Perez, Victoria. Angela's Angel. (p. 74)
Estadella, Pere, jt. auth. see Ros, Jordina.
Este, James, illus. see Williams, Rose.
Esteban, Angel. Pablo, Pablo en Busca del Sol. (p. 1316)
Esteban, Angel, et al. Grumete de Colon. (p. 727)
Estefan, Gloria & Garland, Michael. Noelle's Treasure Tale: A New Magically Mysterious Adventure. (p. 1262)
Estefanía, Oscar, tr. see Scott, Jerry & Borgman, Jim.
Estela, Linda. Lilly Camara Catches Heat. (p. 1017)
Estelle, Carrie. Molly Loves Her Sister. (p. 1160)
Estellon, Pascale. Color-Play Coloring Book. (p. 343)
—It's about Time: Untangling Everything You Need to Know about Time (p. 896)
—Photo Finish. (p. 1352)
—Picture This. (p. 1356)
Estellon, Pascale, jt. auth. see Chronicle Books Staff.
Esten, Sidney R. Bird Stamps of All Countries, with a Natural History of Each Bird. Cox, William Drought, ed. (p. 190)
Estep, Jennifer. Crimson Frost. (p. 383)
—Dark Frost. (p. 407)
—Killer Frost. (p. 956)
—Midnight Frost. (p. 1138)
—Touch of Frost. (p. 1772)
Estep, Joanna. Roadsong (p. 1477)
Estep, Lorena. Puddles on the Floor. Thayne, Tamira Ci, illus. (p. 1414)
Estergren, Fred B. Tale of a Dog Called Sunshine (p. 1699)
Esterman, Sophia, illus. see Park, Margaret.
EsterSonia. Sissi My Story - My life with my loving Owners. (p. 1581)
Estes, Allison & Stark, Dan. Izzy & Oscar. Dockray, Tracy, illus. (p. 901)
Estes, Angie. Chez Nous. (p. 299)
Estes, Don. Willy: The Little Jeep Who Wanted to Be a Fire Truck. Garrison, Sue, illus. (p. 1934)
—Willy & Friends traveling through the Seasons: The continuing story of Willy the little fire Jeep. Glass, Eric, illus. (p. 1934)
Estes, Eleanor. Alley. Ardizzone, Edward, illus. (p. 47)
—Curious Adventures of Jimmy McGee. O'Brien, John A., illus. (p. 392)
—Ginger Pye (p. 677)
—Hundred Dresses. Slobodkin, Louis, illus. (p. 827)
—Miranda the Great. Ardizzone, Edward, illus. (p. 1149)
—Tunnel of Hugsy Goode. Ardizzone, Edward, illus. (p. 1797)
Estes, Jhon H. Living with Big Foot (p. 1042)
Estes-Hill, Katrina. My Imagination. Kwong, Alvina, illus. (p. 1211)
Esteve, Laura, tr. see Haab, Rachel.
Esteve, Laura, tr. see Klutz Editors & Dzwonik, Cristian.
Estevis, Anne. Chicken Foot Farm. (p. 300)
—Down Garrapata Road. (p. 474)
Esther Cravens Schwalger. Not Too Close. Eve Cravens Nawahine, illus. (p. 1267)
Estice, Rose Mary & Fried, Mary. Big Keep Books- Spanish Emergent Reader 1: Mira como Juego; ¡Curitas!; Los Animales del Zoológico; Construyendo una Casa; la Alberca; ¡Agua y Jabón!; Me Visto; Mi Gato Elías, Annette, tr. (p. 182)
Estigarribia, Diana. Learing about Rocks, Weathering, & Erosion with Graphic Orgainzers. (p. 982)
—Learning about Rocks, Weathering, & Erosion with Graphic Organizers. (p. 984)
—Learning about the Effects of Natural Events with Graphic Organizers. (p. 985)
—Learning about Weather with Graphic Organizers. (p. 985)
—Moose. (p. 1173)
—Smithsonian National Zoological Park. (p. 1594)
Estill, Amy, illus. see Mathisen, Michael.
Estill, Linda. Flowers Made Simple: How to Arrange Flowers Just for the Fun of It. (p. 608)
Estrada, Altamira Perea. Abecedario Muy Sabroso. (p. 4)
Estrada, Dimas, Jr., ed. Strange Case of Dr. H. H. Holmes. (p. 1665)
Estrada, E. Gabriela Aguileta. Espejo en el Agua. De Gante, Guillermo, illus. (p. 536)
Estrada, Gabriela Aguileta. Conspiracion de Las Tias. Campos F, Angel, illus. (p. 359)
Estrada, Ixchel, illus. see Olivera, Martin Bonfil.
Estrada, Ixchel, illus. see Otero, Armando Lenero.
Estrada, Jorge Antonio. Isla de los Pollos. Luna, Margarita, illus. (p. 891)
Estrada Michel, Rafael, tr. Diario de Lupita. (p. 434)
Estrada, Pau. Pedro's Burro. Estrada, Pau, illus. (p. 1334)
Estrada, Pau, illus. see Andersen, Hans Christian.
Estrada, Pau, illus. see Boada, Francesc & Andersen, Hans Christian.
Estrada, Pau, illus. see Boada, Francesc.
Estrada, Pau, illus. see Capucilli, Alyssa Satin.
Estrada, Pau, illus. see Fern, Tracey E.
Estrada, Pau, illus. see Grimm, Jacob & Grimm, Wilhelm K.
Estrada, Pau, illus. see Joles, Alonso Sennell.
Estrada, Pau, illus. see McGrath, Barbara Barbieri & Alderman, Peter.
Estrada, Pau & Capucilli, Alyssa Satin. Pedro's Burro. Estrada, Pau, illus. (p. 1334)
Estrada, Ric, illus. see Pappas, Diane H. & Covey, Richard D.
Estrada, Ric, jt. auth. see Ames, Lee J.
Estrada, Xinia M. Pluma en Silencio. (p. 1374)

E

Estrin, James, photos by see Thompson, Lauren & Ferrara, Joanne.
Estrin, Leibel. Rabbi Riddle Says... Look Who Dropped in for Yom Tov. Sears, Dovid, illus. (p. 1429)
Estudio Haus, illus. see Yasuda, Anita.
Esty, Amos. Liberator: The Story of William Lloyd Garrison. (p. 1005)
—Plessy V. Ferguson. (p. 1374)
—Unbound & Unbroken: The Story of Frederick Douglass. (p. 1811)
Eswar, Smrithi. Naboola Island. (p. 1227)
Eszterhas, Suzi. Eye on the Wild: Lion. (p. 558)
—Eye on the Wild: Cheetah. (p. 558)
—Gorilla. (p. 703)
Eszterhas, Suzi, photos by see Quarto Generic Staff.
Eszterhas, Suzi, photos by. Cheetah. (p. 296)
—Elephant. (p. 511)
—Eye on the Wild: Lion. (p. 558)
—Gorilla. (p. 703)
—Tiger. (p. 1748)
ETA Cuisenaire Staff. Hands-On-Standards, Common Core Edition, Teacher's Resource Guide, Grade 1: Book. (p. 741)
ETA/Cuisenaire Staff. At the Beach. (p. 110)
—Ben's Bath. (p. 165)
—I See. (p. 845)
—Snap Cubes. (p. 1597)
—Super Source: Tangrams. (p. 1682)
—Super Source: Pattern Blocks. (p. 1682)
—Super Source: Cuisenaire Rods. (p. 1682)
—Tangrams. (p. 1705)
Etcheberry-Morton, Mary Jean. Oui Oui Oui of the Pyrenees. (p. 1307)
Etchison, Denise. Kids! Picture Yourself Making Jewelry. (p. 952)
Eterno-Harris, Jacqueline. Be'Be: A Very Special Friendship. Cagle, Eddie, illus. (p. 155)
Eterovich-Boynar, Janine. Those Mean Bugs Are Going to Get Me, Mommy! (p. 1740)
Ethan, Eric. Black Widow Spiders. (p. 197)
—Brown Recluse Spiders. (p. 232)
—Diamonds. (p. 434)
—Emeralds. (p. 518)
—Funnel Web Spiders. (p. 649)
—Hobo Spiders. (p. 786)
—Opals. (p. 1299)
—Rubies. (p. 1493)
—Sapphires. (p. 1514)
—Tarantulas. (p. 1706)
—Turquoise. (p. 1798)
—Yellow Sac Spiders. (p. 1970)
Ethel Cook Eliot. Little House in Fairy Wood. (p. 1029)
Etheredge, Laura. Historic Palestine, Israel, & the Emerging Palestinian Autonomous Areas Edited by Laura S. Etheredge. (p. 782)
—Iran. (p. 886)
—Iraq. (p. 887)
—Persian Gulf States: Kuwait, Qatar, Bahrain, Oman, & the United Arab Emirates. (p. 1344)
—Saudi Arabia & Yemen. (p. 1516)
—Syria, Lebanon, & Jordan. (p. 1693)
Etheredge, Laura S., ed. Egypt. (p. 506)
—Islamic History. (p. 891)
Etheridge, Judy. Olivia's Wish. (p. 1287)
Etheridge, Katy, jt. auth. see Villaloz, ChiChi.
Etheridge, William, III. Heart on Fire Trilogy: Runda. (p. 760)
Etherly, L. D. When I Fall Asleep. (p. 1902)
—When I Fall Asleep. Velarde, Chase, illus. (p. 1902)
—Winter Arrives This Summer. (p. 1938)
Ethier, Vicki. I Know My Nana Rosa Is an Alien. Ethier, Vicki, illus. (p. 840)
—Papa & the Hen. Ethier, Vicki, illus. (p. 1321)
Ethington, Rebecca. Through Glass Omni 1: Omnibus Books 1-3. (p. 1744)
Etienne, Doris. Jewels of Sofia Tate. (p. 917)
Etienne, Sara Wilson. Harbinger. (p. 747)
Etingoff, Kim. Abusing Over-the-Counter Drugs: Illicit Uses for Everyday Drugs. Henningfield, Jack E., ed. (p. 7)
—All Around Good Habits. (p. 43)
—Building a Healthy Diet with the 5 Food Groups. Prock, Lisa Albers, ed. (p. 238)
—Bully on Campus & Online. Stephens, Ronald, ed. (p. 241)
—Concentration. (p. 355)
—Confidence. (p. 356)
—Corn. (p. 367)
—Cyprus. (p. 397)
—Dairy Products. (p. 400)
—Decisions, Decisions: Vegetarianism, Breakfasts, & Beyond. Borus, Joshua, ed. (p. 421)
—Diet Myths: Sorting Through the Hype. Borus, Joshua, ed. (p. 437)
—Drugs & Alcohol. Stephens, Ronald, ed. (p. 487)
—Eating Out: How to Order in Restaurants. Borus, Joshua, ed. (p. 501)
—Eggs. (p. 506)
—Embarrassment, Shame, & Guilt. Croft, Cindy, ed. (p. 517)
—Farmed Fish. (p. 574)
—Fear & Anxiety. Croft, Cindy, ed. (p. 579)
—Gunman on Campus. Stephens, Ronald, ed. (p. 732)
—Hand-Eye Coordination. (p. 740)
—Handling Peer Pressure. (p. 740)
—Harry Truman: From Farmer to President. (p. 751)
—Healthy Alternatives to Sweets & Snacks. Borus, Joshua, ed. (p. 758)
—Healthy Fast Foods. Borus, Joshua, ed. (p. 758)
—How to Read Food Product Labels. Borus, Joshua, ed. (p. 821)
—Howling at the Moon: Vampires & Werewolves in the New World. (p. 824)
—Ivy Queen. (p. 901)
—Jennifer Aniston: From Friends to Films. (p. 912)
—Jennifer Aniston. (p. 912)
—Junior Martial Arts (p. 936)
—Methamphetamines: Unsafe Speed. (p. 1130)
—Navigating Cyberspace. Stephens, Ronald, ed. (p. 1238)
—Portugal. (p. 1387)
—Science of the Beast: The Facts Behind the Fangs. (p. 1527)
—T. I. (p. 1693)
—Understanding Nutrition: A Gateway to Physical & Mental Health (p. 1816)
—Women in Chemistry. Lee-Karlon, Ann, ed. (p. 1945)
—Women in Medicine. Karlon, Ann Lee, ed. (p. 1946)
—Women Who Built Our Scientific Foundations. Lee-Karlon, Ann, ed. (p. 1946)
Etingoff, Kim & Indovino, Shaina C. Greece. (p. 720)
—Portugal. Bruton, John, ed. (p. 1387)
Etingoff, Kim & Indovino, Shaina Carmel. Cyprus. (p. 397)
—Greece. (p. 720)
Etlinger, Rebecca. To Be Me. (p. 1758)
Etringer, Kathy. Mrs. E's Extraordinary Number Activities. Mitchell, Judy & Sussman, Ellen, eds. (p. 1187)
Ets, Marie Hall. Just Me. Ets, Marie Hall, illus. (p. 939)
Etshied, Karl Jeffrey. Eggplant Rufus: Amused Indifference on a Stupid Planet. (p. 506)
Ettinger, Charles, illus. see Blackwell, Nancy.
Ettinger, Charles, illus. see Sharpe, Charlotte.
Ettinger, Dorris, illus. see Price, Matt.
Ettinger, Roseann. 40s & 50s Popular Jewelry (p. 1997)
Ettinger, Steve, jt. auth. see Active Spud Press.
Ettling, Tali. Max's Amazing Adventure. (p. 1112)
Ettlinger, Doris, illus. see Adams, Michelle Medlock.
Ettlinger, Doris, illus. see Baglio, Ben M.
Ettlinger, Doris, illus. see Cameron, Eileen.
Ettlinger, Doris, illus. see Donaldson, Joan.
Ettlinger, Doris, illus. see Goodman, Susan E.
Ettlinger, Doris, illus. see Hall, Becky.
Ettlinger, Doris, illus. see Jackson, Ellen.
Ettlinger, Doris, illus. see Knowlton, Laurie Lazzaro, et al.
Ettlinger, Doris, illus. see Layne, Deborah & Layne, Stephen L.
Ettlinger, Doris, illus. see Layne, Steven L.
Ettlinger, Doris, illus. see Layne, Steven L. & Layne, Deborah Dover.
Ettlinger, Doris, illus. see Layne, Steven L., et al.
Ettlinger, Doris, illus. see Michelson, Richard.
Ettlinger, Doris, illus. see Noble, Trinka Hakes.
Ettlinger, Doris, illus. see Peacock, Carol Antoinette.
Ettlinger, Doris, illus. see Redmond, Shirley Raye.
Ettlinger, Doris, illus. see Stier, Catherine.
Ettlinger, Doris, illus. see Young, Judy.
Ettlinger, Doris, jt. auth. see Redmond, Shirley Raye.
Etulain, Richard W., jt. auth. see Riley, Glenda.
Etzel. Marketing: Student Study Guide. (p. 1095)
Etzel, Laurie Hopkins, jt. auth. see Thurston, Cheryl Miller.
Etzel, Michael J., et al. Marketing with Powerweb. (p. 1095)
Etzell, Amy K. Back & Forth Journal: Written & Passed Between Parent & Child. (p. 130)
Eubank, Bill, ed. see Perliger, Arie.
Eubank, Lorie. How Does Your Garden Grow? (p. 809)
Eubank, Patricia Reeder. ABCs of Easter. (p. 4)
—ABCs of Halloween. Eubank, Patricia Reeder, illus. (p. 4)
—Countdown to Christmas. (p. 370)
—Halloween 123s. Eubank, Patricia Reeder, illus. (p. 737)
—Leprechaun's Big Pot of Gold. Eubank, Patricia Reeder, illus. (p. 993)
—Princess & the Snarls. Eubank, Patricia Reeder, illus. (p. 1403)
—Seaman's Journal. (p. 1536)
—Valentine ABCs. Eubank, Patricia Reeder, illus. (p. 1830)
Eubank, Patricia Reeder, illus. see Dude, Rosanna Eubank.
Eubank, Patti Reeder. Count Your Blessings! (p. 370)
—Just Where You Belong. (p. 940)
Eubank, Patti Reeder, tr. ABCs of Halloween. (p. 4)
Eubank, William L., jt. auth. see Weinberg, Leonard.
Eubanks, Charles, illus. see Cole, Quinn.
Eubanks, Holly L. Through the Eye of the Needle: Answer Key. (p. 1745)
—Through the Eye of the Needle. (p. 1745)
Eubanks, Jacquelyn R. Last Summer. McTyre, Robert E., ed. (p. 979)
Eubanks, Sandra. Carina the Angel. (p. 269)
Eubanks, Toni. Let's Celebrate! Girl Scout Ceremonies. (p. 995)
Eubanks, Toni & Lombardi, Janet. Let's Play! (p. 999)
Eubanks-Adkison, Eufa. When the Moon Was Born Spinks, Stefphany (Snider), illus. (p. 1905)
Eudes-Pascal, Elisabeth, illus. see Meunier, Sylvain.
Eudes-Pascal, Elisabeth, illus. see Poulin, Andree.
Eudes-Pascal, Elisabeth, illus. see Poulin, Andrée.
Eudes-Pascal, Elisabeth, illus. see Rabley, Stephen.
Eudes-Pascal, Elisabeth, tr. see Meunier, Sylvain.
Eudy, P. D. PB & J Delight. (p. 1331)
Eugenia, Maria, illus. see Johnston, Jan.
Eugenio, Johnny. Lil Jordan's 9 Holes of Fear. (p. 1017)
—Lil' Jordan's 9 Holes of Fear. (p. 1017)
Eugster, Rachel. Pocket Mommy. Goldsmith, Tom, illus. (p. 1375)
Eugster, Rachel & Lassieur, Allison. Trade & Commerce in the Early Islamic World. (p. 1776)
Eugster, Rachel & Whiting, Jim. Role of Religion in the Early Islamic World. (p. 1485)
Eulalie. Buds, Blossoms, & Leaves: Eulalie's Collected Poems. (p. 235)
Eulate, Ana. Cuerpo de Nube. (p. 390)
—Life Is Beautiful! (p. 1011)
—Little Cloud Lamb. (p. 1026)
—Sky of Afghanistan. (p. 1587)
Eulberg, Elizabeth. Better off Friends. (p. 172)
—Lonely Hearts Club. (p. 1046)
—Prom & Prejudice. (p. 1411)
—Revenge of the Girl with the Great Personality. (p. 1466)
—Take a Bow. (p. 1696)
—We Can Work It Out. (p. 1866)
Eulo, Elena Yates. Great Receiver. (p. 718)
Eun, Lee. Antique Gift Shop (p. 89)
Eun-Ha, Jo. Bijoux Sang-Sun, Park, illus. (p. 185)
—Bijoux Lee, Seung-Ah, tr. from KOR. (p. 185)
Eun-Jeong, Kim. Zippy Ziggy (p. 1987)
—Zippy Ziggy Seung-Man, Hwang, illus. (p. 1987)
Eunjoo, Jang, jt. auth. see Lindeen, Mary.
Eurich, Kevin. Waterbury: The other love of My Life. (p. 1863)
Euripides. Andromache. Landes, William-Alan, ed. (p. 72)
—Cyclops. Landes, William-Alan, ed. (p. 397)
—Euripides' Hippolytos. Roy, Indrapramit, illus. (p. 540)
—Hecuba. Landes, William-Alan, ed. (p. 761)
—Hippolytus. Landes, William-Alan, ed. (p. 781)
—Medea. Wodhull, Michael, tr. from GRE. (p. 1118)
—Suppliants. Landes, William-Alan, ed. (p. 1684)
Euripides, jt. auth. see Sofocles.
Euripides & Burian, Peter. Euripides - Helen. (p. 540)
European Commission Staff, contrib. by. May Day: Young Literature from the Ten New Member States of the European Union. (p. 1112)
European Language Institute Staff. Espanol en Crucigramas (p. 536)
Eustace, Robert & Meade, L. T. Master of Mysteries. Walton, J. Ambrose, illus. (p. 1103)
Eustache, Harold. Shuswap Journey. (p. 1572)
Eutsey, Nicole. Real Mccoy Drops Knowledge on Millennium Youth. (p. 1448)
—Real Wiz Mccoy. (p. 1449)
Euvremer, Teryl, illus. see Steig, William.
Evan, Frances Y. Forgotten Flag: Revolutionary Struggle in Connecticut. (p. 619)
Evan, Kelsey L. Starshine. (p. 1643)
Evangelical Press Staff & Scrimshire, Hazel. God's Little Giants: A Colouring Book. (p. 691)
Evangelista, Beth. Gifted. (p. 675)
Evangelista, Colette. My Autism. Stone, Diane, illus. (p. 1196)
Evangelista, Gloria. In Search of the Perfect Pumpkin. Shea, Shawn, illus. (p. 865)
Evangelista, Kate. Til Death. (p. 1750)
Evangelista, Mauro, illus. see Baum, L. Frank.
Evangelista, Mauro, illus. see Carroll, Lewis, pseud.
Evangelista, Susan. Tommy's New Shell Coke, Sherrie, illus. (p. 1765)
Evanger, Brent. Elusive Foe. Drees, Allen, ed. (p. 516)
Evanier, Mark. Born Orphans Vol. 1 (p. 214)
—Hollywood Hero (p. 789)
Evanier, Mark, jt. auth. see Davis, Jim.
Evan-Moor. Art for All Seasons: Grades 1-4. (p. 102)
—Basic Math Skills Grade 1. (p. 142)
—Basic Math Skills, Grade 4. (p. 142)
—Basic Phonics Skills, Level A: Grades PreK-K. (p. 142)
—Basic Phonics Skills, Level B: Grades K-1. (p. 142)
—Basic Phonics Skills, Level C: Grades 1-2. (p. 142)
—Basic Phonics Skills, Level D: Grades 2-3. (p. 142)
—Daily Geography Practice Grade 1. (p. 399)
—Daily Paragraph Editing Grade 2. (p. 400)
—Early Learning Centers, Grades PreK-K. (p. 493)
—Easy File Folder Reports Grades 3-6. (p. 500)
—English / Spanish Science Activities, Grades 1-3. (p. 529)
—Geography Centers, Grades 1-2. (p. 662)
—Hands-on Science-20 Themes: Grades 1-3. (p. 741)
—History Pockets: Moving West, Grades 4-6. (p. 785)
—History Pockets: Ancient Egypt, Grades 4-6+ (p. 785)
—History Pockets: Colonial America, Grades 4-6. (p. 785)
—History Pockets: Ancient Civilizations, Grades 1-3. (p. 785)
—History Pockets: Life in Plymouth Colony, Grades 1-3. (p. 785)
—Hot Topics, High-Interest Reading: Sets A, B, & C (Classroom Set) (p. 802)
—Literacy Centers, Grades 2-3. (p. 1022)
—Maps of the USA, Grades 1-6. (p. 1090)
—Math Centers, Grades 2-3. (p. 1105)
—Never-Bored Kid Book 2, Ages 6-7 (p. 1242)
—Never-Bored Kid Book, Ages 5-6. (p. 1242)
—Phonics Centers Level A, Grades PreK-K. (p. 1352)
—Phonics Centers Level B, Grades K-1. (p. 1352)
—Phonics Centers, Level C, Grades 1-2. (p. 1352)
—Readers' Theater, Grade 1. (p. 1444)
—Science Centers, Grades 1-2. (p. 1525)
—Science Centers Grades PreK-K. (p. 1525)
—Skill Sharpenerd Reading Grade 3. (p. 1585)
—Skill Sharpeners, Math, Grade 1. (p. 1585)
—Skill Sharpeners Math, Grade 2. (p. 1585)
—Skill Sharpeners Math, Grade PreK. (p. 1585)
—Skill Sharpeners Reading, Grade 1. (p. 1585)
—Skill Sharpeners, Reading, Grade 6. (p. 1585)
—Skill Sharpeners Reading, Grade PreK. (p. 1585)
—Skill Sharpeners, Spell & Write, Grade 1. (p. 1585)
—Skill Sharpeners Spell & Write, Grade 2. (p. 1585)
—Skill Sharpeners Spell & Write Grade PreK. (p. 1585)
—Spanish / English Early Learning Activities, Grades PreK-1. (p. 1620)
—Spanish / English Read & nderstand Science Grades 4-6. (p. 1620)
—Spanish / English Read & Understand, Grade 1. (p. 1620)
—Spanish/English Read & Understand Nonfiction: Grades 4-6. (p. 1622)
—US Facts & Fun, Grades 1-3. (p. 1826)
—Vocabulary Centers, Grades 1-2. (p. 1847)
—World Reference Maps & Forms, Grades 3-6. (p. 1958)
—Writing Centers, Grades 1-2. (p. 1964)
—Writing Centers Grades 2-3. (p. 1964)
Evan-Moor & McFarren, Kathleen. History Pockets: Explorers of North America, Grades 4-6. (p. 785)
Evan-Moor, ed. Daily Academic Vocabulary, Grade 2. (p. 399)
Evan-Moor Educational Publishers. At the Park: Grades 1-3. (p. 111)
Evan-Moor Educational Publishers, creator. At-Home Tutor Math, Grade 2. (p. 110)
—Reading Informational Text, Grade 2: Common Core Mastery. (p. 1446)
—Reading Informational Text, Grade 5. (p. 1446)
—Reading Paired Text, Grade 4: Common Core Mastery. (p. 1446)
—Text-Based Writing Nonfiction, Grade 2: Common Core Mastery. (p. 1724)
Evan-Moor, Kare. History Pockets: Native Americans, Grades 1-3. (p. 785)
Evan-Moor Staff. How to Do Science Experiments with Children: Grades 2-4. (p. 816)
Evanoff, Corrine R., jt. auth. see Riggs, Jon.
Evanovich, Alex & Evanovich, Janet. Troublemaker. (p. 1790)
Evanovich, Janet, jt. auth. see Evanovich, Alex.
Evanovsky, Dennis & Kos, Eric J. Lost San Francisco. (p. 1056)
Evans, Alfreda. Little Boy in Blue. (p. 1025)
Evans, Alfreda Lockett. Little Boy in Blue. (p. 1025)
Evans, Allan, jt. ed. see Mitchell, Mark.
Evans, Alwyn & Davis, Anne. Pumpkin in Hollow Countdown. Capelle, Joanna, illus. (p. 1416)
Evans, Alwyn, et al. Monty's Tale. (p. 1170)
Evans, Amina Marix, tr. see Bersma, Danielle & Visscher, Marjoke.
Evans, Amina Marix, tr. see Purperhart, Helen.
Evans, Andrew, illus. see Densmore, Don.
Evans, Andy. Three to Go Mario! Morgan-Magee, Mary, ed. (p. 1744)
Evans, Angela. Lovely Swing up High. (p. 1061)
—Monster Can Be Friendly. (p. 1166)
Evans, Ann. Cry Danger. (p. 387)
Evans, Anthony, jt. auth. see McDonald, Meinir.
Evans, Antony, illus. see Daniel, Claire.
Evans, Antony, illus. see Garcia, Ellen.
Evans, Antony, illus. see Giachetti, Julia.
Evans, Antony, illus. see Linde, Barbara M.
Evans, Antony, illus. see Sparks, Stacey.
Evans, Arthur. Palace of Minos 4 Volume Set in 7 Pieces: A Comparative Account of the Successive Stages of the Early Cretan Civilization As Illustrated by the Discoveries at Knossos. (p. 1319)
Evans, Arthur V. Grzimek's Student Animal Life Resource: Crustaceans, Mollusks & Segmented Worms. Harris, Madeline S. et al, eds. (p. 728)
Evans, Arthur V., et al. Grzimek's Student Animal Life Resource (p. 728)
—Student Animal Life Resource (p. 1669)
Evans, Ashley Putnam. Princess Prissypants Goes to Spain. Ferguson, Martha-Elizabeth, illus. (p. 1405)
Evans, Audrey. Lena. (p. 991)
Evans, Barbara Greene. Oscar, the Inquisitive Spider. Greene, Kelly Evelyn, illus. (p. 1305)
Evans, Betty A. World's Greatest Possum Trainer. (p. 1960)
Evans, Betty J. Three Young Wild Cats. Bucher, Barbara Latini, illus. (p. 1744)
Evans, Bill. It's Raining Fish & Spiders. (p. 898)
Evans, Brad. Bishop Museum Color & Activity Book. (p. 193)
Evans, Brian, jt. auth. see Potts, Will.
Evans, C, jt. auth. see Johnson, S.
Evans, C & Millard, A. Greek Myths & Legends. (p. 721)
Evans, C. S. Sleeping Beauty. Rackham, Arthur, illus. (p. 1589)
Evans, Cambria. Bone Soup. (p. 209)
Evans, Cambria, illus. see Schoenberg, Jane.
Evans, Cambria, illus. see Underwood, Deborah.
Evans, Carol, jt. auth. see Christensen, Gerda.
Evans, Carol Wolfe. No Thank You Bite Williams, G. L., illus. (p. 1260)
Evans, Carolyn, jt. auth. see McCarthy, Jenna.
Evans, Carolyn, et al. Maggie Malone Gets the Royal Treatment. (p. 1071)
Evans, Casey, illus. see Krinsky, Ed.
Evans, Cathy. Halo & the Rainbows. (p. 739)
Evans, Catrin & Evans, Guto. Oli Olew. (p. 1285)
—Peiriant y Tywydd. (p. 1335)
Evans, Chadrick Michael, illus. see Evans, Rhonda Boone.
Evans, Charlene & Spence, Robert. Read to Me Bo. (p. 1443)
Evans, Charlotte. Historia (Enciclopedias Everst Internacional) (p. 782)
Evans, Charlotte & Charlotte, Evans. Enciclopedia de la Historia (p. 523)
Evans, Cheryl, ed. see Meredith, Susan.
Evans, Cheryl, ed. see Unwin, Mike.
Evans, Cheryl, jt. auth. see Johnson, Sue.
Evans, Cheryl & Millard, Anne. Greek Myths & Legends. Matthews, Rodney, illus. (p. 721)
Evans, Cheryl & Smith, Lucy. Acting & Theatre. Evans, Cheryl, ed. (p. 9)
Evans, Christopher. Aliens & UFOs. (p. 41)
Evans, Clay Bonnyman. Winter Witch. Bender, Robert, illus. (p. 1938)
Evans, Colin. Crime Scene Investigation. (p. 382)
—New York Police Department. (p. 1248)
—Trials & the Courts. (p. 1785)
Evans, Connie. Sasha & Babushka: A Story of Russia. Schpitalnik, Vladimir, illus. (p. 1515)
Evans, Connie, jt. auth. see Shpitalnik, Vladimir.
Evans, Cordelia. Bet on It. Reel FX Inc. Staff, illus. (p. 171)
—Christmas in Glendragon. HIT Entertainment Staff, illus. (p. 314)
—Dragon Race! Style Guide Staff, illus. (p. 478)
—Olivia & Grandma's Visit. Johnson, Shane L., illus. (p. 1286)
—Olivia & the Easter Egg Hunt. (p. 1286)
—Olivia & the Fancy Party. (p. 1286)
—OLIVIA & the Fancy Party. Johnson, Shane L., illus. (p. 1286)
—Olivia Helps the Tooth Fairy. (p. 1286)
—Olivia Takes Ballet: From the Fancy Keepsake Collection. Spaziante, Patrick, illus. (p. 1287)
Evans, Cordelia, adapted by. Jewel of Glendragon. (p. 917)
—Santa's Little Helper. (p. 1513)
Evans, Cornelia, jt. auth. see Shpitalnik, Vladimir.
Evans, Cornelia & Shpitalnik, Vladimir. Sasha & Babushka: A Story of Russia. (p. 1515)
Evans, Courtney. Percy the Penguin (p. 1341)
Evans, D. D. Pixie Eden. (p. 1365)
Evans, D. L. & Sinclair, Valerie. How Rolly Robot Saved the Starbabies (p. 812)
Evans, D. R. Palindor. (p. 1320)
Evans, Dan C. High Peaks Paradigm Shift: A Canine Agent Teabo Adventure (p. 778)
Evans, David. Years of Liberalism & Fascism: Italy 1870-1945. (p. 1969)
Evans, David & Williams, Claudette. Air & Flying. (p. 31)
—Living Things. (p. 1042)
—Make It Change. (p. 1079)

—Seasons & Weather. (p. 1538)
Evans, Diane. Daisy MacSnow, P. I. The Napa Valley Scottish Fold Detective. (p. 400)
Evans, Douglas. Anta Claus of Antarctica. (p. 88)
—Bedbugs. (p. 156)
—Bradley's Odyssey. (p. 221)
—Captain John Paul Jellyfish. (p. 264)
—Cozy up to the Whiteboard. (p. 375)
—Del & Estelle: A Story of Two Pigeons. (p. 424)
—Mouth Moths: More Classroom Tales. Di Fiori, Larry, illus. (p. 1182)
—MVP. Shelley, John, illus. (p. 1195)
—Pixels: Journey to the Bottom of the Desk. (p. 1365)
—Sh! (p. 1556)
—Specials Book 1: Special Assignment. (p. 1623)
—Specials Book 2: Special Effects. (p. 1624)
—Substitute of Last Resort. (p. 1671)
—Twists. (p. 1803)
—Twists2. (p. 1803)
—VR Solution. (p. 1851)
Evans, Dustin. Costume Craziness. (p. 368)
—Dinosaur Drama. (p. 442)
—Medieval Mess. (p. 1119)
—Raging Robots. (p. 1433)
Evans, Dustin, illus. see Specter, Baron.
Evans, Florence Adéle. Alice's Adventures in Pictureland: A Tale Inspired by Lewis Carroll's Wonderland. (p. 39)
Evans, Fran, illus. see Francis, Marnie, et al.
Evans, Fran, illus. see Matthews, Cerys.
Evans, Freddi Williams. Hush Harbor: Praying in Secret. Banks, Erin, illus. (p. 830)
Evans, Freddi Williams, jt. auth. see Williams Evans, Freddi.
Evans, G. Blakemore, ed. see Shakespeare, William.
Evans, G. Keith. Appearances: The Art of Class. (p. 92)
Evans, Gabriel, illus. see Frantz, Donna.
Evans, Gabriel, illus. see Kyle, Bradley.
Evans, Gabriel, illus. see Lee, Patricia Mary.
Evans, Gabriel, illus. see Nicholl, Jacqueline.
Evans, Gabriel, illus. see Nicoll, Jacqueline.
Evans, Glen & Farberow, Norman L. Encyclopedia of Suicide. (p. 525)
Evans, Guto, jt. auth. see Evans, Catrin.
Evans, Gwen & Collins, Darluniau Mike. Delyth a'r Ffair Haf. (p. 425)
Evans, Gwydion, et al. Ar Dîm Duw: Cyfres o Sesiynau Sydd Yn Defnyddio Byd Chwaraeon I Son Am y Ffydd Gristnogol. (p. 94)
—Gemau Gwirion! (p. 659)
Evans, Henry. Bogie Does Hollywood - the Ride! (p. 207)
—Cubeworld: An Adventure in Solid Geometry. (p. 389)
Evans, Hestia. Mythology. Steer, Dugald A., ed. (p. 1227)
—Mythology Handbook: An Introduction to the Greek Myths. Steer, Dugald A., ed. (p. 1227)
Evans, Hilda Clark. Karbee the Kangaroo Says. (p. 943)
Evans, Hubert. Bear Stories. La Fave, Kim, illus. (p. 151)
—Silversides: The Life of a Sockeye. La Fave, Kim, illus. (p. 1577)
Evans, Hubert R. Forest Friends: Stories of Animals, Fish, & Birds, West of the Rockies. (p. 618)
Evans, Jamie, illus. see Day, Martin.
Evans, Jan. Repetitive Rhonda: A Coloring Book. (p. 1461)
—Repetitive Rhonda. (p. 1461)
Evans, Jane. How Are You Feeling Today Baby Bear? Exploring Big Feelings after Living in a Stormy Home. (p. 805)
Evans, Jean. Rhymes & Stories. (p. 1468)
Evans, Jeffery. Starweaver's Retreat. (p. 1644)
Evans, Jermaine W. Adventures of Orden: The Sock Bandit. (p. 21)
Evans, John D. Cut. (p. 395)
Evans, Joseph. Trinity Awakening. (p. 1786)
Evans, Joyce, illus. see Hume, Margaret Anne.
Evans, June P. Michael in Paris. (p. 1134)
Evans, K. D. Corey, the Little Purple Shopping Cart. (p. 367)
Evans, Karen, jt. auth. see Urmston, Kathleen.
Evans, Karen & Urmston, Kathleen. Thanksgiving. Kaeden Corp. Staff, ed. (p. 1725)
Evans, Kate. Weird Weather: Everything You Didn't Want to Know about Climate Change but Probably Should Find Out (p. 1873)
Evans, Keri. Yo Banana Boy! A Book of Palindromes. (p. 1971)
Evans, Kevin, illus. see Sutliff, Jamie.
Evans, Kevin C., illus. see Sutliff, Jamie.
Evans, Kevin, et al. Edexcel GCSE Maths Foundation Student Book. (p. 504)
—Homework (p. 794)
—Maths Frameworking. (p. 1108)
—Maths Frameworking - Pupil Book 3. 1. (p. 1108)
—New Maths Frameworking - Year 7. (p. 1246)
—Practice Book - Year 9. (p. 1392)
Evans, Kirsti. Something Different about Dad: How to Live with Your Asperger's Parent. Swogger, John-Gordon, illus. (p. 1609)
Evans, Kristina. Best Easter Prize. Wallace, John, illus. (p. 169)
Evans, Laneta Fullenwiley. Life Plays: A Collection of Real Life Dramas. Wiggins, L. J. & Evision Staff, eds. (p. 1012)
Evans, Latonya, adapted by. Jack & the Beanstalk. (p. 902)
Evans, Laura, illus. see Cory, Kim Delmar.
Evans, Laura, illus. see Panagopoulos, Janie Lynn.
Evans, Leah Beth. Different Kind of Hero. Gedrich, Colleen, illus. (p. 438)
Evans, Len. Yr Enillwyr. (p. 1982)
Evans, Lesli. But All My Friends Smoke: Cigarettes & Peer Pressure. (p. 246)
—Transport Math. (p. 1779)
Evans, Leslie. You Have to Be Smart If You're Going to Be Tall/Tienes Que Ser Inteligente Si Vas a Ser Alta. (p. 1975)
Evans, Leslie, illus. see Bulion, Leslie.
Evans, Leslie, illus. see Crelin, Bob.
Evans, Leslie, illus. see Gerber, Carole.
Evans, Leslie, illus. see Gold-Vukson, Marji.
Evans, Lezlie. Can You Count Ten Toes? Count to 10 in 10 Different Languages. Roche, Denis, illus. (p. 258)
—Can You Greet the Whole Wide World? 12 Common Phrases in 12 Different Languages. Roche, Denis, illus. (p. 259)
Evans, Linda, jt. auth. see Greenley, Amanda.
Evans, Lisa, illus. see Light, John.
Evans, Lisa M. Rich Man's Song. Evans, Lisa M., illus. (p. 1469)
Evans, Lissa. Horten's Incredible Illusions: Magic, Mystery & Another Very Strange Adventure. (p. 801)
—Horten's Miraculous Mechanisms: Magic, Mystery, & a Very Strange Adventure. (p. 801)
Evans, Loralee. King's Heir. (p. 960)
Evans, Lory. One-Page Math Games: 30 Super-Easy, Super-Fun, Reproducible Games for Seatwork, Centers, Homework, & More! (p. 1296)
Evans, Louise C., jt. auth. see Doherty, Edith J. S.
Evans, Lucas. Year of Happy Holidays. (p. 1969)
Evans, Lynette. Bee Life. (p. 157)
—Bug Life. D'Ottavi, Francesca, illus. (p. 236)
—Camp Extreme. (p. 257)
—Extreme Sports. (p. 557)
—Move Your Bones. (p. 1183)
—Whose Egg? A Lift-The-Flap Book. Troughton, Guy, illus. (p. 1921)
—Whose Nest? Troughton, Guy, illus. (p. 1921)
Evans, M. J. Behind the Mist. (p. 160)
Evans, Margaret. Tale of Rainbow's End. (p. 1700)
Evans, Margaret, illus. see Shorty.
Evans, Mari. Dear Corinne, Tell Somebody! Love, Annie: A Book about Secrets. (p. 418)
—Dear Corinne, Tell Somebody! Love, Annie. (p. 418)
—I'm Late: The Story of Laneese & Moonlight & Alisha Who Didn't Have Anyone of Her Own. (p. 859)
Evans, Marion, Anna Baraitser. Home Number One. (p. 792)
Evans, Mark, illus. see Dahl, Michael.
Evans, Mark, ed. Just War Theory: A Reappraisal. (p. 940)
Evans, Mary. Cats! Cats! Cats! Kovalcik, Terry, illus. (p. 281)
—Good Pets (p. 700)
Evans, Mary & Landes, William-Alan. How to Make Historic American Costumes. Brooks, Elizabeth et al, illus. (p. 820)
Evans, Meg, et al. Mirai: Course Book Stage 1 (p. 1149)
Evans, Melvyn, illus. see Poitier, Anton.
Evans, Michael. Over in the Meadow. (p. 1313)
—Poggle & the Birthday Present. Evans, Michael, illus. (p. 1376)
—Poggle & the Treasure. Evans, Michael, illus. (p. 1376)
Evans, Michael & Wichman, David. Adventures of Medical Man: Kids' Illnesses & Injuries Explained. Williams, Gareth, illus. (p. 20)
Evans, Michael E. EncourageMINT: A Wealth of Daily Inspiration, Encouraging You to Become Who God Says You Are — in Him. (p. 524)
Evans, Michelle D. I Don't Belong in the Jungle. (p. 837)
Evans, Moana & Pecsenye, Jessica. Harvey Mudd College College Prowler off the Record. (p. 752)
Evans, Nate, jt. auth. see Numeroff, Laura Joffe.
Evans, Nate & Brown, Stephanie Gwyn. Bang! Boom! Roar! A Busy Crew of Dinosaurs. Santoro, Christopher, illus. (p. 136)
—Dinosaur ABC. Santoro, Christopher, illus. (p. 441)
Evans, Nate & Evans, Vince. Beast Friends Forever: Meet the Beast. (p. 152)
—Beast Friends Forever: The Super Swap-O Surprise! (p. 152)
Evans, Nicola, illus. see Rider, Cynthia.
Evans Ogden, Lesley J. Forces & Motion. (p. 617)
—Properties of Matter. (p. 1411)
Evans, Olive. Secrets of the Forest: Playscript. (p. 1545)
—Thrift Store Bears. Woolley, Patricia, illus. (p. 1744)
Evans, Olivia, jt. auth. see AZ Books Staff.
Evans, Pamela. Tina Queen of the Dragons. (p. 1755)
Evans, Patricia, ed. see Goff, John.
Evans, Renee Call, jt. auth. see Perucca, Nancy Call.
Evans, Renee Call & Perucca, Nancy Call. Multiplication Camp. Perucca, Nancy Call, illus. (p. 1190)
Evans, Rhonda Boone. Johnny Lumpkin Wants a Friend. Evans, Chadrick Michael, illus. (p. 923)
—Thanksgiving with the Lumpkins. (p. 1726)
Evans, Richard. Battle of the Ampere. (p. 146)
—Christmas Candle. Collins, Jacob, illus. (p. 313)
—Dance. Linton, Jonathan, illus. (p. 402)
—Electrifying Michael Vey (p. 509)
—Hunt for Jade Dragon. (p. 828)
—Michael Vey Books One & Two: The Prisoner of Cell 25; Rise of the Elgen. (p. 1135)
—Prisoner of Cell 25. (p. 1407)
—Rise of the Elgen. (p. 1474)
—Spyglass: A Book about Faith. Linton, Jonathan, illus. (p. 1636)
—Tower: A Story of Humility. Linton, Jonathan, illus. (p. 1773)
Evans, Richard & Wilburg, Dale. Patunia Peacock: And Her Flair Weather Friend. (p. 1330)
Evans, Robert C. Student's Encyclopedia of Great American Writers (p. 1669)
Evans, Robert J. Dorothy's Mystical Adventures in Oz. (p. 472)
Evans, Robin. Cymru A'r Byd: Pecyn Lluniau a Llyfr Athrawon. (p. 397)
Evans, Rose-Marie. Unexpected Adventure at East Haddam High. (p. 1817)
Evans, Rosemary R. Adventures of the Little Prince. Taylor, Erin, illus. (p. 23)
—Little Princesses Magial Party. Taylor, Erin, illus. (p. 1034)
Evans, Rowena, illus. see Boer, Paula.
Evans, Rusty. Bible, a Story to Read & Color. (p. 175)
Evans, Ruth Todd. Panda Who Would Not Eat. Evans, Ruth Todd, illus. (p. 1320)
Evans, S. Annetje. Sour Little Lemon Tree. (p. 1616)
Evans, Sally. Sea Treasure. Richardson, Linda, illus. (p. 1535)
Evans, Sarah. Moose, the Flea, the Fly. (p. 1173)
Evans, Shane, illus. see Brown, Tameka Fryer.
Evans, Shane, illus. see Diouf, Sylvianne.
Evans, Shane W. Olu's Dream. Evans, Shane W., illus. (p. 1287)
—Travelin' Man. (p. 1780)
—Underground: Finding the Light to Freedom. Evans, Shane W., illus. (p. 1814)
—We March. Evans, Shane W., illus. (p. 1867)
Evans, Shane W., illus. see Clinton, Catherine.
Evans, Shane W., illus. see Diggs, Taye.
Evans, Shane W., illus. see Jordan, Deloris.
Evans, Shane W., illus. see Peete, Holly Robinson & Peete, Ryan Elizabeth.
Evans, Shane W., illus. see Pinkney, Andrea Davis.
Evans, Shane W., illus. see Rappaport, Doreen.
Evans, Shane W., illus. see Smith, Charles R., Jr.
Evans, Shane W., illus. see Smith, Hope Anita.
Evans, Shane W., illus. see Washington, Donna L.
Evans, Shane W., illus. see Whitehead, Kathy.
Evans, Shane W., illus. see Winter, Jonah.
Evans, Sherri, illus. see Helbig-Miller, Theresa.
Evans, Sian & Cymru, Addysg Cyfryngau. Gweithgareddau Dylunio a Thechnoleg CA1/2. (p. 733)
Evans, Stephanie. Steven James: I Just Can't Pay Attention. (p. 1649)
Evans, Steve, illus. see Mumford, Jeanette, et al.
Evans, Toby Sally. Chakra Labyrinth Cards. (p. 288)
Evans, Tony. Kid's Guide to the Armor of God. (p. 954)
Evans, Vince, jt. auth. see Evans, Nate.
Evans, Wynne, illus. see Tourville, Jacqueline.
Evans, Yvette Kemp. If I Take a Shower. (p. 853)
Evans, Zoe. Bevan vs. Evan: And Other School Rivalries. Barrager, Brigette, illus. (p. 173)
—Confessions of a Wannabe Cheerleader. Barrager, Brigette, illus. (p. 356)
—Holiday Spirit. Barrager, Brigette, illus. (p. 788)
—Pyramid of One. Barrager, Brigette, illus. (p. 1421)
—Revenge of the Titan. Barrager, Brigette, illus. (p. 1466)
Evans-Martin, F. Fay. Down Syndrome. (p. 474)
—Nervous System. (p. 1241)
Evatt, Harriet. Mystery of the Alpine Castle. (p. 1225)
—Secret of the Old Coach Inn. Stone, David, illus. (p. 1542)
Evdokimoff, Natasha. Kentucky. (p. 949)
—Missouri. (p. 1154)
—Pennsylvania. (p. 1337)
—Volleyball. (p. 1849)
Eve Cravens Nawahine, illus. see Esther Cravens Schwalger.
Eve, Helen. Boarding School Girls. (p. 205)
—Stella: A Novel. (p. 1646)
Eve, Lealand, illus. see Herman, Alison & Grossman, Lynne.
Eve, Lealand, illus. see Weigman, Matthew.
Eveland, Keith, illus. see Thoresen, Susan Werner.
Eveleigh, Victoria. Joe & the Hidden Horseshoe. (p. 920)
—Joe & the Lightning Pony. (p. 920)
—Joe & the Race to Rescue. (p. 920)
—Katy's Pony Surprise. (p. 946)
Evelyn. Lucy the Elephant & Sami the Mouse: A Bedtime Story. Conforti, John W., tr. (p. 1063)
—Lucy the Elephant & Sami the Mouse: The Birthday Party. Conforti, John W., illus. (p. 1063)
Evelyn Gill Hilton. Kidnapped by Pirates: Based on the true story of a fourteen year-old boy, Charles Tilton, who was kidnapped alone from an Amer. (p. 952)
Evelyn, Gilmer. Maggie the Beagle & the Wolves. (p. 1071)
Evens, Kevin C., illus. see Sutliff, Jamie.
Evensen, Rachelle. Finn's Marching Band: A Story of Counting, Colors, & Playing Together. (p. 589)
Evenson, Brian, tr. see Draeger, Manuela.
Evenson, Wallace. Bible Dates - From Adam to Christ. (p. 175)
Evento, Susan. Connecticut. Hamilton, Harriet, tr. (p. 357)
—Mary McLeod Bethune. (p. 1101)
—Mighty Hippopotamus. (p. 1140)
—Nueva Jersey. Hamilton, Harriet, tr. from ENG. (p. 1270)
—Sitting Bull. (p. 1582)
—Your Dream Vacation High Beginning Book with Online Access. (p. 1980)
Evento, Susan & Jaffe, Elizabeth Dana. World's Deadliest Creatures. (p. 1960)
Evento, Susan & Meredith Books Staff. Vet Emergencies 24/7. (p. 1839)
Evento, Susan & Vargus, Nanci Reginelli. New Jersey. (p. 1245)
Evento, Susan, et al. World's Deadliest Creatures. (p. 1960)
Evenwel, Patricia L., illus. see Barry, Todd J.
Everall, Nayera, jt. auth. see Rogers, Kirsteen.
Everard, John, tr. see Hermes, Trismegistus.
Everburg, R. S. Audrika's Magic. (p. 115)
Everest. Adivina, Adivinanza. Quesada, Maria Fe, illus. (p. 12)
Everest, D. D. Archie Greene & the Magician's Secret. (p. 95)
Everett, Anita. Abc Adventures Continued: D e F G. (p. 3)
Everett, Clare. Henrietta - a Rabbit's Tale of Summer Time Fun. (p. 767)
Everett, F. Burglar's Breakfast. (p. 243)
Everett, Felicity. Make Your Own Jewelry. (p. 1080)
Everett, Felicity, ed. see Gibson, Ray.
Everett, Felicity & Rawson, Christopher. Stories of Princes & Princesses. (p. 1655)
Everett, Felicity & Reid, Struan. Usborne Book of Explorers. Dennis, Peter & Draper, Richard, illus. (p. 1827)
Everett, George W. G. W. Frog & the Circus Lion. (p. 652)
—G. W. Frog & the Haunted House in Misty Meadows. (p. 652)
—G W Frog & the Pickle-Barrel Time MacHine. (p. 652)
—G. W. Frog & the Pumpkin Patch Bandit. (p. 652)
Everett Hale, Edward. Last of the Peterkins with Others of the. (p. 978)
Everett, J. H. & Scott-Waters, Marilyn. Haunted Histories: Creepy Castles, Dark Dungeons, & Powerful Palaces. (p. 753)
—Haunted Histories: Creepy Castles, Dark Dungeons, & Powerful Palaces. Everett, J. H. & Scott-Waters, Marilyn, illus. (p. 753)
Everett, Lawrence. Ghosts & Legends of Southeastern Ohio & Beyond: Tales of Legends, Hauntings & the Unexplained (p. 672)
Everett McNeil. Cave of Gold: A Tale of California In '49. (p. 282)
Everett, Melissa. Baa, Baa, Black Sheep. Imodraj, illus. (p. 123)
—Diddle Diddle Dumpling. Imodraj, illus. (p. 437)
—Hey Diddle Diddle. Manning, Mary, illus. (p. 774)
—I Wish I Was a Little. Paiva, Johannah Gilman, ed. (p. 849)
—Jack & Jill. Imodraj, illus. (p. 902)
—One, Two, Buckle My Shoe. Morgan, Christopher, illus. (p. 1297)
—Owl & the Kitty Cat. Kummer, Mark, illus. (p. 1314)
—Pat-A-Cake. Kummer, Mark, illus. (p. 1327)
—Rain, Rain, Go Away. Wendel, Carrie, illus. (p. 1435)
—Rock-A-Bye Baby. Wendel, Carie, illus. (p. 1481)
—Rock-A-Bye Baby. Wendel, Carrie, illus. (p. 1481)
—Twinkle, Twinkle, Little Star. Pasishnychenko, Oksana, illus. (p. 1802)
Everett, Mikaela. Unquiet. (p. 1822)
Everett-Camplin, Helen. Grandad's Magic Gadgets. (p. 707)
—Two Worlds Level 4 Intermediate Book with CD-ROM & Audio CD Pack. (p. 1804)
Everette, Maureen C., jt. auth. see Moon, Catherine R.
Everett-Green, Evelyn. Heroine of France. (p. 773)
—Tom Tufton's Travels. (p. 1764)
Everett-Hawkes, Bonnie, illus. see Cousineau-Peiffer, Trisha.
Everett-Hawkes, Bonnie, illus. see Maher, Liam.
Evergreen, Nelson, illus. see Capstone Press Staff.
Evergreen, Nelson, illus. see Dahl, Michael.
Evergreen, Nelson, illus. see Darke, J. A.
Evergreen, Nelson, illus. see Hulme-Cross, Benjamin.
Evergreen, Nelson, illus. see Stone Arch Books Staff.
Evergreen, Nelson, illus. see Strange, Jason.
Everhart, Adelaide, illus. see Stein, Evaleen.
Everhart, Loretta Jean. Math Vitamins: Daily Dose for Students Learning How to Solve Word Problems. (p. 1107)
Everheart, Chris. Demolition Day Arcana Studio Staff, illus. (p. 426)
—Hidden Face of Fren-Z (p. 775)
—Mixed Signals Arcana Studio Staff, illus. (p. 1156)
—Nuclear Distraction (p. 1269)
—Prep Squadron (p. 1395)
—Shadow Cell Scam (p. 1557)
—Storm Surge Arcana Studio Staff, illus. (p. 1656)
—Teen Agent Arcana Studio Staff, illus. (p. 1713)
Everheart, Chris, et al. Toys of Terror (p. 1774)
Everidge, Channing, illus. see Spady, Angie.
Everitt, Anne. Hush Little Baby. Flowerpot Press, ed. (p. 830)
Everitt, Betsy, illus. see Moran, Alex.
Everitt-Stewart, Andrew, illus. see Dale, Jay.
Everitt-Stewart, Andy, illus. see Baxter, Nicola.
Everitt-Stewart, Andy, illus. see Burlingham, Abi.
Everitt-Stewart, Andy, illus. see Nash, Sarah.
Everly, Nita. Early Social Behavior Books Can You Be a Friend? (p. 494)
—Early Social Behavior Books Can you Be Polite? (p. 494)
—Early Social Behavior Books Can You Listen with Your Eyes? (p. 494)
—Early Social Behavior Books Can You Share? (p. 494)
—Early Social Behavior Books Can You Take Turns? (p. 494)
—Early Social Behavior Books Can You Talk to Your Friends. (p. 494)
—Early Social Behavior Books Can You Tell How Someone Feels? (p. 494)
—Early Social Behavior Books Can You Use a Good Voice? (p. 494)
—Early Social Behavior Books Can You Use Your Words? (p. 494)
—Early Social Behavior Books Set (12) (p. 494)
Evers, Alf. Treasure of Watchdog Mountain: The Story of a Mountain in the Catskills. Yanow-Schwartz, Jo & Schwartz, Arthur, eds. (p. 1782)
Evers, Betty Jo. Alphabet: Instant Manipulatives That Teach Each Letter of the Alphabet. (p. 49)
Evers, Charlotte & Welbourne, Dave. Britain 1783-1851: From Disaster to Triumph? (p. 229)
Evers, Charlotte, et al. Britain, 1851-1918: A Leap in the Dark? (p. 229)
Evers, June V. Mazes & Connect the Dots: Volume 1: Horses! (p. 1113)
—Wonderful Life of Lola: A Day at the Beach. (p. 1948)
Evershed-Martin, Susanna, ed. see Lancaster, Gwen, et al.
Eversole, Barbara. Adventures of Zorro. (p. 24)
—My Name Is Zorro. (p. 1215)
Eversole, Linda L. Discover Intensive Phonics for Yourself: Parent Involvement Pack. (p. 447)
Eversole, Robyn. East Dragon, West Dragon. Campbell, Scott, illus. (p. 498)
Everson, Andy, illus. see Bouchard, David.
Everson, Chance. Beginnings: Tales of the Mandrasaurs, Volume the Second. Vol. 2 Geary, Steve, illus. (p. 160)
—Discoveries: Tales of the Mandrasaurs, Volume the Third. Geary, Steve, illus. (p. 448)
—Forever & a Day: Tales of the Mandrasaurs, Volume the First. Vol. 1 Geary, Steve, illus. (p. 619)
—Verlin's Magical Blunder: Tales of the Mandrasaurs, Volume the Seventh. Geary, Steve, illus. (p. 1837)
Everson, Hobart G. Rosie Robin: The Bird Who Loved People Kelly, Judy, illus. (p. 1490)
Everson, Lowell, jt. auth. see Grier, Gene.
Everson, Michael, jt. auth. see Carroll, Lewis, pseud.
Everson, Michael, jt. auth. see Harris, J. Henry.
Everson, Michael, jt. auth. see Sewell, Byron W.
Everson, Mya, illus. see Jacobsen, Annie.
Everstine, Andrew D. Seth: A Visitor's Pass. (p. 1554)
Evert, J. Pure Love. (p. 1419)
Evert, Jeffrey. Tree That Didn't Want to Be. (p. 1783)
Evert, Laura. Planets, Moons, & Stars. Garrow, Linda, illus. (p. 1368)
Evert, Laura & Lynch, Wayne. Birds of Prey. (p. 191)
Evert, Lori. Christmas Wish. Breiehagen, Per, illus. (p. 316)
—Christmas Wish. Breiehagen, Per, photos by. (p. 316)
—Tiny Wish. Breiehagen, Per, illus. (p. 1757)

E

Everything, Eva. What Does the Moon Smell Like? 151 Astounding Science Quizzes. (p. 1884)
Eves, Sue. Hic. (p. 775)
—Quiet Woman & the Noisy Dog. Busby, Ailie, illus. (p. 1428)
Evetts-Secker, Josephine. Barefoot Book of Father & Daughter Tales. Cann, Helen, illus. (p. 139)
—Mother & Daughter Tales. Cann, Helen, illus. (p. 1177)
Evision Staff, ed. see Evans, Laneta Fullenwiley.
Evlin, Frances. Ginger Gold. (p. 677)
Evrard, Gaetan, illus. see Anderson, Jill, ed.
Evry, Philip, jt. auth. see Canwell, Peter.
Evslin, Bernard. Trojan War. (p. 1788)
Ewald, Jenny, jt. ed. see Fleming, Sean.
Ewald, Thomas. Christian Reader's Theater. Flint, Russ, illus. (p. 312)
—Spiritual Practices: Biblical Disciplines for Living the Greatest Commandment. (p. 1629)
Ewald, Thomas & Carson-Dellosa Publishing Staff. Five-Minute Sermons for Children: 56 Invitations to Grow in Grace. (p. 601)
Ewald, Thomas C. Fruit of the Spirit: Developing Powerful Attributes That Help Kids Be More Like Jesus! (p. 645)
—God-Given Gifts, Grades 3 - 6: Skits & Activities to Identify & Nurture Spiritual Gifts in Children. (p. 688)
—New Testament Take-Home Bible Stories, Grades Preschool - 2: Easy-to-Make, Reproducible Mini-Books That Children Can Make & Keep. (p. 1247)
—Old Testament Take-Home Bible Stories, Grades Pk - 2: Easy-to-Make, Reproducible Mini-Books That Children Can Make & Keep. (p. 1285)
Ewaldsen, Joan O. Beside the Still Waters. (p. 168)
—Emma. (p. 519)
—Janet. (p. 908)
—Jessica. (p. 914)
—Linka. (p. 1019)
—Samantha. (p. 1507)
Ewan, Ann. Brondings' Honour. (p. 230)
—Firedrake. (p. 591)
Ewanits, Tara, photos by see Haitz, Rochelle.
Ewart, Claire. Fossil. Ewart, Claire, illus. (p. 623)
Ewart, Claire, illus. see Marston, Elsa.
Ewart, Claire, illus. see Miller, Peggy Reiff.
Ewart, Claire, illus. see Shahegh, Mahvash.
Ewart, Francesca, et al. There's a Hamster in My Pocket! Bate, Helen, illus. (p. 1731)
Ewart, Franzeska G. Speak up, Spike. Oliver, Mark, illus. (p. 1623)
Ewart, Franzeska G. & Quarto Generic Staff. Sita, Snake-Queen of Speed. Bate, Helen, illus. (p. 1582)
Ewashen, Julie. Life in the Arctic with Nina & Nikita. (p. 1011)
Ewell, Katherine. Dear Killer. (p. 419)
Ewen, Caroline, illus. see Hassall, Angela.
Ewen, David. Leonard Bernstein: A Biography for Young People. (p. 992)
Ewers, Brenda. Hedy & Howie Enjoy Easter. (p. 762)
—Hedy & Howie Planting a Garden: Succeed with Rocco's 4 R's. (p. 762)
—Hedy & Howie's 4th of July Party: The Rising of a Man. (p. 762)
—Hedy & Howie's 4th of July Party. (p. 762)
—Hedy & Howie's Christmas Tree: Reclaiming One's Self Through Memory & Forgiveness. (p. 762)
—Hedy & Howie's Christmas Tree (hardcover) (p. 762)
—Hedy & Howie's Halloween Adventure: America Is Falling. (p. 762)
—Hedy & Howie's Thanksgiving Trip: A Journey Out of Darkness. (p. 762)
—Hedy & Howie's Thanksgiving Trip. (p. 762)
Ewers, Hans Heinz. Spider. (p. 1626)
Ewers, Joe. Pied Piper: A Tale about Promises. (p. 1356)
Ewers, Joe, illus. see Albee, Sarah.
Ewers, Joe, illus. see Allen, Constance & Albee, Sarah.
Ewers, Joe, illus. see Schoberle, Cecile.
Ewert, Marcus. 10,000 Dresses. Ray, Rex, illus. (p. 2003)
—Mummy Cat. Brown, Lisa, illus. (p. 1191)
Ewing, Amy. Jewel. (p. 916)
—White Rose. (p. 1913)
Ewing, Carolyn, jt. auth. see Treselt, Alvin.
Ewing, Deborah. Secret Celebrity. (p. 1540)
Ewing, Drew & Burns, Adam. St Louis University College Prowler off the Record: Inside Saint Louis. (p. 1638)
Ewing, Frances. Barkley's Bones. (p. 139)
—Erin's Dance. (p. 533)
Ewing, Jack. Monkeys Are Made of Chocolate: Exotic & Unseen Costa Rica. (p. 1166)
Ewing, John. Adventures of Rennie & Bodger (p. 22)
Ewing, John, illus. see Florido, Lorraine.
Ewing, John, illus. see Lorraine, Florido.
Ewing, Juliana Horatia. Brothers of Pity & Other Tales of Beasts & Men. (p. 231)
—Brownies & Other Tales. (p. 232)
—Flat Iron for a Farthing. Wheelhouse, M. V., illus. (p. 603)
—Great Emergency & Other Tales. (p. 715)
—Jackanapes, Daddy Darwin's Dovecot & Other Stories. Caldecott, Randolph, illus. (p. 903)
—Mary's Meadow: And Other Tales of Fields & Flowers. (p. 1101)
—Mary's Meadow & Other Tales of Fields & Flowers. (p. 1101)
—Melchior's Dream & Other Tales. (p. 1125)
—Miscellanea. (p. 1150)
—Old-Fashioned Fairy Tales. (p. 1283)
—Peace Egg & Other Tales. (p. 1331)
—Six To. (p. 1582)
—Six to Sixteen. (p. 1583)
—Story of A Short Life. (p. 1657)
—Verses for Children & Songs for Music. (p. 1837)
—We & the World. (p. 1865)
Ewing, Lynne. Daughters of the Moon (p. 410)
—Daughters of the Moon: Volume Two. (p. 410)
—Lure. (p. 1066)
—Motown Anthology. (p. 1180)
Ewing, Nancy Nelson. Journey to Virtue Planet: An Inter-Active Storybook. (p. 929)
Ewing, Richard, illus. see Wizner, Jake.
Ewing, Sherm. Ranch: A Modern History of the North American Cattle Industry. Greer, Daniel, ed. (p. 1438)
Ewing, Susan. Cats! Train Your Owner! Cider Mill Press Staff, ed. (p. 281)
—Lucky Hares & Itchy Bears: And Other Alaskan Animals. Blessing, Marlene, ed. (p. 1062)
—Ten Rowdy Ravens. Zerbetz, Evon, illus. (p. 1719)
Exelby, Kathy. My Dog Harpo: The Biggest Kid I Know. Wall Darby, Colleen, illus. (p. 1202)
Exeter, Donna. Love Juice. (p. 1060)
Exley, Helen. Giggles: A Jokebook. (p. 676)
Expert Book Reviews. Rush Revere & the First Patriot. (p. 1498)
Exploratorium Staff. Exploralab. (p. 550)
Extranjeros, jt. auth. see Peregrinos.
Exum, J. Cheryl, jt. auth. see Bach, Alice.
Eyckerman, Merel. Ant & the Grasshopper. (p. 88)
Eyheramonno, Jèoelle, tr. see Perrault, Charles & Perrault, Charles.
Eynon, Bob & Wen, Dref. Crwydro'r Mor Mawr. (p. 387)
Eyolfson, Norman, illus. see Richler, Mordecai.
Eyre, David. Breaking the Blood. Kalahele, Imaikalani, illus. (p. 225)
—Lumpy Poi & Twisting Eels. Kalahele, Imaikalani, illus. (p. 1065)
—Rise of a King. (p. 1474)
—Sacred Awa Piercing Spears. Kalahele, Imaikalani, illus. (p. 1500)
—White Rainbow Black Curse. (p. 1913)
Eyre, David & Kalahele, Imaikalani. Floating Islands. (p. 605)
Eyre, Jane. Creatures of the New Jersey Pine Barrens Coloring Book Eyre, Jane, illus. (p. 380)
Eyre, Jane, illus. see Beraducci, Deborah.
Eyre, Lindsay. Best Friend Battle. Santoso, Charles, illus. (p. 169)
Eyres, John. Shown' Ya the Ropes: A Young Adult's Resource Guide to Navigate Life. (p. 1571)
Eyres, Rose. Amazing Adventures at Pencil Point. (p. 52)
Eystad, Janet Lynn. What I Got into Last Summer. (p. 1886)
Eyuboglu, Melisa. Angel in a Bubble. (p. 73)
EZ Comics, ed. James A. Baker, III: The Authorised Comic Book Biography. (p. 906)
Ez, Daniel, jt. auth. see Hern.
Eze-Offormezie, Ngozika. Invitation from the Fairy. (p. 886)
Ezirim, E. C. Jet Black & the Ebony Knights. (p. 916)
Ezozo, Wanda. According to the Book of Genesis Nursery Rhyme. (p. 8)
Ezpeleta, Laurie. Lucky Dog. Glenn, Melissa, illus. (p. 1062)
Ezrin, Amy, tr. see Francia, Giada, ed.

F

F. S. Creations. Exam View Pro: Test Development Software. (p. 547)
F, Stacey, ed. see Groeneweg, Nicole.
F., Warner, jt. auth. see Bodleian Library Staff.
Faas, Linde, illus. see Lootens, Ann.
Faassen, Louis, illus. see Dymond, Kenneth.
Fabamwo, Tolulope. Gift from Daddy: The Lara Series. (p. 675)
Fabbella, Teresa. Forever Friends. Giaquinta, Maria, illus. (p. 619)
Fabbretti, Valerio, illus. see Fields, Jan.
Fabbretti, Valerio, illus. see Hashimoto, Daniel & Richardville, Mandy.
Fabbretti, Valerio, illus. see Sadar, Albin.
Fabbri, Daniele, illus. see Aboff, Marcie.
Fabbri, Daniele, illus. see Adamson, Thomas K.
Fabbri, Daniele, illus. see Heos, Bridget.
Fabbri, Daniele, illus. see Kalz, Jill.
Fabbri, Daniele, illus. see Korba, Joanna & Benchmark Education Co., LLC.
Fabbri, Daniele, illus. see Mayesky & Kalz, Jill.
Fabbri, Daniele, illus. see Meister, Cari.
Fabbri, Daniele, illus. see Shand, Jennifer.
Fabbri, Freddie, jt. auth. see Kasko, John.
Faber and Faber Staff. Clarinet Basics. (p. 327)
Faber, David & Kitchen, James D. Because of Romek: A Holocaust Survivor's Memoir (p. 155)
Faber, David & Kurson, Ken. Faber Report: CNBC's the Brain Tells You How Wall Street Really Works & How You Can Make It Work for You. (p. 559)
Faber, David, et al. Because of Romek: A Holocaust Survivor's Memoir. (p. 155)
Faber, Harold. Airplane. (p. 31)
—Samuel de Champlain, Explorer of Canada. (p. 1509)
Faber, Laurie, jt. auth. see Saunders, Nicholas.
Faber, Nancy & Faber, Randall. BigTime Kids' Songs: Level 4. (p. 185)
—ShowTime Rock 'n Roll: Level 2A. (p. 1571)
Faber, Randall, jt. see Faber, Nancy.
Faber, Rudy, illus. see Kudlinski, Kathleen V.
Faber, Sharon. How to Teach Reading When You're Not a Reading Teacher. (p. 822)
Faber, Toni Tuso. Poodle Tales: Book One. Rudd, Benton, illus. (p. 1383)
—Poodle Tales: Book Six. Rudd, Benton, illus. (p. 1383)
—Poodle Tales: Book Ten. Rudd, Benton, illus. (p. 1383)
—Poodle Tales: Book Two. Rudd, Benton, illus. (p. 1383)
—Poodle Tales: Book Five. Rudd, Benton, illus. (p. 1383)
—Poodle Tales: Book Four. Rudd, Benton, illus. (p. 1383)
—Poodle Tales: Book Nine. Rudd, Benton, illus. (p. 1383)
—Poodle Tales: Book Eight. Rudd, Benton, illus. (p. 1383)
—Poodle Tales: Book Seven. Rudd, Benton, illus. (p. 1383)
—Poodle Tales: Book Three. Rudd, Benton, illus. (p. 1383)
—Poodle Tales: Book Twelve. Rudd, Benton, illus. (p. 1383)
Fabian, Cynthia. Can't & Able: An Inspirational Story. Stevens, Daniel, illus. (p. 261)
—Orchestra in Our Brain: The Story of a Child with Epilepsy. Stevens, Daniel, illus. (p. 1302)
Fabian, Gabriella, illus. see Morrison, Julia.
Fabian, Ingrid. Black Arabian Foal. (p. 195)
Fabiancic, Miriam, tr. see Marin, Cheech.
Fabiano, Antonino. Egmont Passage: Tale of the Dreamcatcher. (p. 506)
Fabiny, Sarah. Snoop Dogg Mad Libs. (p. 1598)
—Who Is Gloria Steinem? (p. 1915)
—Who Is Gloria Steinem? Hergenrother, Max & Harrison, Nancy, illus. (p. 1915)
—Who Was Beatrix Potter? Lacey, Mike & Harrison, Nancy, illus. (p. 1918)
—Who Was Frida Kahlo? (p. 1918)
—Who Was Frida Kahlo? Hoare, Jerry, illus. (p. 1918)
—Who Was Rachel Carson? (p. 1919)
—Who Was Rachel Carson? Putra, Dede & Harrison, Nancy, illus. (p. 1919)
Fabiny, Sarah, jt. auth. see Alligator Books Staff.
Fabiyi, Jan Goldin. Where Shabbat Lives. Ramá, Sue, illus. (p. 1909)
Fable, Aesop. Tortoise & the Hare. (p. 1771)
Fable Vision Studios Staff, illus. see New York Hall of Science Staff.
Fables, Aesops, jt. auth. see Huusmann, Thomas-Bo.
FableVision. Spf 40. Reynolds, Peter H., illus. (p. 1625)
FableVision Staff. Spf 40. Reynolds, Peter H., illus. (p. 1625)
FableVision Studios Staff. Zebrafish. FableVision Studios Staff & Reynolds, Peter H., illus. (p. 1985)
Fabre, J. Henri. Animal Life in Field & Garden. (p. 78)
Fabre, Jean Henri. Secret of Everyday Things. Bicknell, Florence Constable, tr. (p. 1542)
—Story Book of Science. (p. 1656)
—Wonder Book of Chemistry. (p. 1947)
Fabrega, Marta, illus. see Moore-Malinos, Jennifer.
Fabrega, Marta, illus. see Moore-Mallinos, Jennifer & Roca, Nuria.
Fabrega, Marta, illus. see Moore-Mallinos, Jennifer, et al.
Fabrega, Marta, illus. see Moore-Mallinos, Jennifer.
Fabrega, Marta, illus. see Pollack, Pam & Belviso, Meg.
Fabrega, Marta, jt. auth. see Moore-Mallinos, Jennifer.
Fabregat, Antonio-Manuel. Cuentos de Mi Escuela. (p. 390)
Fabrick, Harriet. Furello Journeys: Furello Questions. (p. 650)
Fabrikant, Amy. When Kayla Was Kyle. Levine, Jennifer, illus. (p. 1903)
Fabris, Judith. Money...Cool! Brolin, Carol, illus. (p. 1164)
Fabrizio, Anthony. Last Forest (p. 977)
Fabrizio, T. L. Natalie Bean. (p. 1230)
Fabry, Chris, jt. auth. see Jenkins, Jerry B.
Fabry, Chris & Jenkins, Jerry B. Haunted Waters. (p. 754)
Fabry, Glen, jt. auth. see Ennis, Garth.
Fabry, Glenn, jt. auth. see Carey, Mike.
Fabul, J. C., illus. see Tullen, Sean & Poe, Edgar Allen.
Facchini, Fiorenzo. Day with Homo Erectus: Life 400,000 Years Ago. Baldanzi, Alessandro, illus. (p. 415)
—Day with Homo Sapiens: Life 15,000 Years Ago. (p. 415)
—Day with Neanderthal Man: Life 70,000 Years Ago. Baldanzi, Alessandro, illus. (p. 415)
Faccini, Enrico, illus. see Jensen, Lars, et al.
Facer, Dirk. BCS Breakthrough: Utah's Historic 2004 Season. (p. 147)
Facey, La-Toya S. Brielle-Elaine Tries to Fit In! (p. 228)
Facey, Paulet. Annie & the Washpan of Ripe Bananas. (p. 86)
—Tom-Tom & the Punch Bowl of Irish Moss. (p. 1764)
Fach, Gernot, illus. see Feigin, Misha.
Facia Kromah. Leah Toppings: The New Experience. (p. 982)
Faciana, Michelle. Snickers' Day Out. (p. 1597)
Facio, Sebastian, illus. see Hoena, Blake A.
Facio, Sebastian, jt. auth. see Stevenson, Robert L.
Fackelmayer, Regina & Unzner, Christa. Gifts. (p. 675)
Facklam, Margery. Only a Star. Carpenter, Nancy, illus. (p. 1298)
Facklam, Margery & Thomas, Peggy. New York: The Empire State. Messer, Jon, illus. (p. 1247)
Facklam, Paul, illus. see Thomas, Peggy.
Fackler, David. Governing the Centennial State. (p. 704)
Fackrell, Caitlin & Lyon, Abby. Lewis & Clark College College Prowler off the Record. (p. 1004)
Fackrell, David. Princess, the Collection (p. 1405)
Fact Families Staff. LP-Fact Families: Level 1 Math. (p. 1061)
Factor. Language Works Jelly Plate. (p. 975)
Factor, Eric. W-Aah-tch Out Witch. (p. 1851)
Factor, Judith, ed. Pearl Workbook for 6th Grade: Mosdos Press Literature Series. (p. 1333)
Facts On File, Inc. English. (p. 529)
—Food. (p. 612)
—Library & Information Science. (p. 1005)
—Publishing. (p. 1414)
—Radio. (p. 1432)
—Television. (p. 1716)
Facts on File, Inc. Staff. Adventure. (p. 14)
—Animals. (p. 81)
—Art. (p. 101)
—Career Skills Library: Research & Information Management, Third Edition. (p. 267)
—Computers. (p. 355)
—Construction. (p. 359)
—Discovering Careers for Your Future: Radio & Television. (p. 449)
—Environment. (p. 531)
—Facts on File Encyclopedia of Health & Medicine (p. 561)
—Fashion. (p. 575)
—Health. (p. 757)
Facts On File, Inc. Staff. Maps on File. (p. 1090)
Facts on File, Inc. Staff. Math. (p. 1104)
—Math on File Set. (p. 1106)
—Movies. (p. 1183)
—Nature. (p. 1236)
—Performing Arts. (p. 1343)
—Science. (p. 1524)
—Space Exploration. (p. 1619)
—Timelines on File. (p. 1754)
—Top Careers for Economics Graduates. (p. 1769)
—Transportation. (p. 1779)
—Writing. (p. 1964)
Facts on File, Inc. Staff, ed. see Dickson, Keith D.
Facts on File, Inc. Staff, ed. see Doherty, Craig A.
Facts on File, Inc. Staff & Clements, Kenny. Encyclopedia of Birds (p. 525)
Facts on File, Inc. Staff, contrib. by. Top Careers for Art Graduates. (p. 1769)
Facts on File, Inc. Staff, ed. Fashions of a Decade (p. 576)
—Invasive Species Set (p. 883)
—Nature Walk (p. 1236)
—Science in Focus (p. 1526)
Facts on File, Inc. Staff, et al. World History on File (p. 1955)
—World History on File Chapman, Victoria L. & Lindroth, David, eds. (p. 1955)
Fadl, Khaled Abou El. Introducing Islam (p. 882)
Faerber, Jay. Distant Relatives (p. 453)
—In Sickness & in Health (p. 865)
—Near Death Volume 2 TP. (p. 1239)
—Noble Causes (p. 1262)
Faerber, Jay, et al. Universal Heroes. (p. 1820)
Fafalios, Chris, jt. auth. see Hartman, Tony.
Fafoutakis, Anne. Enchanted Talisman & Other Stories for Children of All Ages. (p. 523)
Fagan, Cary. Big Swim (p. 184)
—Book of Big Brothers Melanson, Luc, illus. (p. 211)
—Boy in the Box: Master Melville's Medicine Show. (p. 218)
—Danny, Who Fell in a Hole. (p. 406)
—Directed by Kaspar Snit. (p. 445)
—Ella May & the Wishing Stone. Cote, Genevieve, illus. (p. 514)
—Fortress of Kaspar Snit. (p. 623)
—Jacob Two-Two on the High Seas. Petricic, Dusan, illus. (p. 904)
—Mr. Karp's Last Glass Demirel, Selçuk, illus. (p. 1185)
—Mr. Zinger's Hat. Petricic, Dusan, illus. (p. 1187)
—My New Shirt. Petricic, Dusan, illus. (p. 1216)
—Oy, Feh, So? Clement, Gary, illus. (p. 1316)
—Ten Lessons for Kaspar Snit. (p. 1718)
—Ten Old Men & a Mouse. Clement, Gary, illus. (p. 1719)
—Thing-Thing. Debon, Nicolas, illus. (p. 1732)
Fagan, Dave, jt. auth. see Hanna, Kevin.
Fagan, Deirdre. Critical Companion to Robert Frost: A Literary Reference to His Life & Work. (p. 383)
Fagan, Martin, illus. see Deeley, Patrick.
Fagan, Martin, illus. see Ghlinn, Aine Ni.
Fagan, Martin, illus. see Jenkins, Amanda & Benchmark Education Co., LLC.
Fagan, Martin, illus. see O'Connor, Finbar.
Fagan, Martin, illus. see Turnage, Cyndy.
Fagan, Nikki. Foxy & Wolfy: What Kind of Friend Is This? (p. 626)
Faghih, Parisa. Sign of Green Stars. (p. 1574)
Fagin, Cristina, tr. see Elkus, Julie.
Fagles, Robert, ed. see Homer.
Fagles, Robert, tr. see Homer.
Fagles, Robert & Homer. Iliad. Rouse, W. H. D. & Rouse, W. H. D., trs. from GEC. (p. 856)
Faglia, Matteo. Feliz Cumpleanos, Tengo 1. Rinaldo, Luana, illus. (p. 581)
Faguy, Peter & Boleyn-Fitzgerald, Miriam. Biodiversity. (p. 188)
—Ending & Extending Life. (p. 527)
Faherty, Sara. Welfare Reform. (p. 1874)
Fahey, Effie. Patience of Dearing Bay. (p. 1328)
Fahey, Kathleen. Challenger & Columbia. (p. 289)
—Rio Grande. (p. 1473)
Fahiner, Paul. Dog & Cat. Chambliss, Maxie, illus. (p. 460)
Fahl. Concrete Principles. (p. 355)
Fahl, Thomas P. Concrete Principles: Answer Key. (p. 355)
Fahringer, Sarah, illus. see Thompson, Kathy.
Fahy, Davene. Charlie, Who Couldn't Say His Name. Inouye, Carol, illus. (p. 293)
Fahy, Davene & Mueller, Dagmar H. Anthony Best: A Picture Book about Asperger's. Inouye, Carol, illus. (p. 89)
Fahy, Thomas. Sleepless. (p. 1589)
—Unspoken. (p. 1822)
Fahy, Thomas, jt. auth. see Fahy, Thomas Richard.
Fahy, Thomas Richard & Fahy, Thomas. Sleepless. (p. 1589)
Faidley, Warren, Jr. How to Survive Any Storm: Severe Weather Handbook. (p. 821)
Faidutti, Bruno. Terra: Game. (p. 1721)
Faiella, Grabam. England: A Primary Source Cultural Guide. (p. 529)
Faiella, Graham. Mesoamerican Mythology. (p. 1129)
—Moby Dick & the Whaling Industry of the 19th Century. (p. 1157)
—Moby Dick & the Whaling Industry of the Nineteenth Century. (p. 1157)
—Spain: A Primary Source Cultural Guide. (p. 1620)
—Technology of Mesopotamia. (p. 1712)
Faigen, Anne G. New World Waiting. (p. 1247)
Fain, Cheryl, illus. see Crawford, Ann Fears.
Fain, Shawn. What a Body Needs. (p. 1878)
Fain, Yakov. Java Programming for Kids. (p. 910)
Faine, Edward Allan. Bebop Babies. (p. 155)
—More Little Ned Stories. (p. 1174)
Fair, Barbara A. Children Following the Teachings of Jesus: An Activity Book for Kids. (p. 302)
Fair, Chuck. Steven Sockeye Salmon. (p. 1649)
Fair, Patricia Anne, illus. see Legrand, H J, III.
Fair, Sherry. Best Parade Day: Spatz. Rutland, Jarrett, illus. (p. 171)
Fair, Sherry W. Scratching Sound: Spatz. Rutland, Jarrett, illus. (p. 1532)
Fair, Theodora. Allarinth the Star King. (p. 46)
Fairall, Barbara, tr. see Kyber, Manfred.
Fairbairn, Lee-Anne. Oh, Deer! Christmas Magic: If You Believe Dreams Do Really Come True. (p. 1280)
—Osiepnal Hono e Krismas. (p. 1305)
Fairbanks, Anne. 100 Multiplication Practice Worksheets Arithmetic Workbook with Answers: Reproducible Timed Math Drills: Multiplying Multidigit Numbers. (p. 1998)
—100 Subtraction Practice Worksheets Arithmetic Workbook with Answers: Reproducible Timed Math Drills: Subtracting Multidigit Numbers. (p. 1999)

Full bibliographic information is available on the Title Index page number referenced in parentheses at the end of each entry

—Addition Facts Practice Worksheets Arithmetic Workbook with Answers: Reproducible Timed Math Drills: Adding the Numbers 0-20. (p. 12)
—Division Facts Practice Worksheets Arithmetic Workbook with Answers: Reproducible Timed Math Drills: Dividing by the Numbers 0-12. (p. 455)
—Multiplication Facts Practice Worksheets Arithmetic Workbook with Answers: Reproducible Timed Math Drills: Multiplying the Numbers 0-12. (p. 1190)
—Subtraction Facts Practice Worksheets Arithmetic Workbook with Answers: Reproducible Timed Math Drills: Subtracting the Numbers 0-20. (p. 1671)
Fairbanks, Charles. Note of Army & Prison Life 1862-1865. (p. 1267)
Fairbanks, George R. History & Antiquities of the City of St. Augustine, Florida, Founded 1565. (p. 783)
Fairbanks, George R. George Rainsford. History of Florida from Its Discovery by Ponce de Leon, in 1512, to the Close of the Florida War, In 1842 (p. 784)
Fairbanks, Letitia. Princess April Morning-Glory: What Kind of a World Would You Create, If You Had to Do Three Dood Deeds to Make Ii Home Again? Fairbanks, Letitia, illus. (p. 1403)
Fairbanks, Mark, illus. see Pinto, Mindee & Cohen, Judy.
Fairchild, Dianne. Are You There? Fairchild, Vincent, illus. (p. 97)
Fairchild, Lyn, jt. auth. see Dalton, Jane.
Fairchild, Simone. Plight of Queen Bee. (p. 1374)
—Plight of the Queen Bee. Key, Pamela, illus. (p. 1374)
—Queen Bee's Midnight Caper Key, Pamela Marie, illus. (p. 1424)
Fairchild, Vincent, illus. see Fairchild, Dianne.
Fairchild-Lenyo, Mary. When Winston Wins. Vigil, Cristina, illus. (p. 1905)
Faircloth, Carson. Games. (p. 654)
Faircloth, Harry W. My First Bus Ride. Anderson, Billie Ann, illus. (p. 1206)
Faircloth, Jimmy. Catch the Wave. (p. 279)
Faircloth, M. L. Seana's New Accessory. Margolis, Al, illus. (p. 1537)
—Shawn's Book about Grandfathers. (p. 1563)
—When Will I See Aunt Carole? Ray, Michael, illus. (p. 1905)
Fairclough, Chris, illus. see Chancellor, Deborah.
Fairclough, Chris, photos by see Garrington, Sally.
Fairclough, Chris, photos by see Green, Jen.
Fairclough, Chris, photos by see Humphrey, Paul.
Fairclough, Chris, photos by see Shirley, Rebekah Joy.
Faires, J. Douglas, jt. ed. see Wells, David M.
Fairfield, J. S. Cunning Foe: Faulkil. (p. 392)
Fairfield, Lesley. Tyranny. (p. 1805)
Fairfield Middle School. Poetry 2006 by 6th Grade Students of Fairfield Middle School. (p. 1376)
Fairgray, Richard & Jones, Terry. Gorillas in Our Midst. (p. 703)
Fairhurst, Carol, illus. see Dorling, Anna, et al.
Fairhurst, Joanne. Archie & the Red Wool. Fairhurst, Joanne, illus. (p. 95)
Fairley, Melissa. Ding! Dong! Harland, Jackie, illus. (p. 440)
—Superstar Pocket Activity Fun & Games: Games & Puzzles, Fold-Out Scenes, Patterned Paper, Stickers! (p. 1684)
Fairley, Melissa & Brown, Jonatha A. Massachusetts. (p. 1102)
Fairley, Melissa & Rose, Malcolm. Super Spy: Unmask the Double Agent! (p. 1682)
Fairley, Peter. Electricity & Magnetism. (p. 509)
Fairlie, Emily. Lost Treasure of Tuckernuck. Caparo, Antonio Javier, illus. (p. 1057)
—Magician's Bird. (p. 1075)
—Magician's Bird. Caparo, Antonio Javier, illus. (p. 1075)
Fairman, Jennifer, illus. see Beck, Paul.
Fairman, Jennifer, illus. see Johnson, Rebecca L.
Fairman, Jennifer, et al. Human Body: Take a Three-Dimensional Look Inside the Human Body! (p. 825)
Fairview Elementary Students. Wildcat Tales: A Fairview Family Collection. (p. 1931)
Fairweather, Eileen. French Letters: The Life & Loves of Miss Maxine Harrison. (p. 636)
Fairwell, Kay, ed. see Barber, Jacqueline.
Fairy, Meg, illus. see Ives, Bob.
Faison, Ashley Starr & Ackerman, Bettie Bennett. Garden of Hope: A Story about the Hospice Experience. (p. 656)
Faith First Development Team, creator. Faith First Grade 6. (p. 565)
Faith, Susan. Purple Puppy. Offner, Naomi, illus. (p. 1419)
Faith, Virginia T., jt. auth. see Walley, Judith L.
Faithe, Emil. Natural Q's: Tips the Help You Achieve Optimum Health. (p. 1235)
Faithgirlz!, jt. auth. see Bokram, Karen.
Faithgirlz! and Girls' Life Magazine Editors, ed. see Zondervan Publishing Staff.
Faithgirlz! and Girls' Life Magazine Editors, jt. auth. see Bokram, Karen.
Fajardo, Anika. Dish on Food & Farming in Colonial America (p. 451)
Fajardo, Renee & Ruby, Carl. Chili Today, Hot Tamale & Other Tummy Tales. Fajardo, Renee & Ruby, Carl, eds. (p. 305)
—Ole Posole & Other Tummy Tales. Fajardo, Renee, ed. (p. 1285)
Fajerman, Deborah. How to Speak Moo! (p. 821)
Fajnland, Leibel. Big Small or Just One Wall: A Book about Shuls. Rosenfeld, D. L., ed. (p. 184)
Fakhrid-Deen, Tina. Let's Get This Straight: The Ultimate Handbook for Youth with LGBTQ Parents. (p. 997)
Fakhruddin, Hasan. Physics Demos & Hands-ons. (p. 1353)
Fakkema, Julie Ann. Water Is a Wonderful Thing. (p. 1863)
Falango, Marcy. Rescue. (p. 1462)
Falardeau, Marco. Adventures of Mega Mini Man. (p. 20)
Falcao, Linda. AMERICA SERVES Student Journal - High School Edition. (p. 59)
Falco, Joanna. Diana, the Angel, & the Holy Grail. (p. 434)
Falcó, Roberto, tr. see O'Hare, Mark.
Falcó, Roberto, tr. see Scott, Jerry & Borgman, Jim.
Falcon, David. Weather or Not? LaGrange, Tiffany, illus. (p. 1870)
Falcon, Jonah. Thirteen. (p. 1734)
Falcon Press International. Desta & King Solomon's Coin of Magic & Fortune: And king solomon's coinof of magic & Fortune (p. 430)
Falcone, Brent. Journey. (p. 927)
Falcone, David A. Adventures of Miss Aiden in Dinoland. (p. 20)
Falcone, Fernando, illus. see Despeyroux, Denise.
Falcone, Karen. Tales from Falmac Farm. Frake, Barbara, illus. (p. 1701)
Falcone, L. M. Midnight Curse. (p. 1138)
—Walking with the Dead. (p. 1854)
Falcone, L. M. & Wahl, Charis. Devil, the Banshee & Me. (p. 432)
Falcone, Paul. 96 Great Interview Questions to Ask Before You Hire (p. 1998)
Falconer, C. J. Where Is Kitty? (p. 1908)
Falconer, Ian. Olivia. (p. 1286)
—Olivia. Mlawer, Teresa, tr. (p. 1286)
—Olivia. Falconer, Ian, illus. (p. 1286)
—Olivia. High, Amy, tr. from ENG. (p. 1286)
—Olivia Alphabet Flash Cards. (p. 1286)
—Olivia & the Fairy Princesses. Falconer, Ian, illus. (p. 1286)
—Olivia... & the Missing Toy. Falconer, Ian, illus. (p. 1286)
—Olivia Cuenta. (p. 1286)
—Olivia fait son Cirque. (p. 1286)
—Olivia Forma una Banda. Mlawer, Teresa, tr. from ENG. (p. 1286)
—Olivia Forms a Band. Falconer, Ian, illus. (p. 1286)
—Olivia Goes to Venice. Falconer, Ian, illus. (p. 1286)
—Olivia Helps with Christmas. Falconer, Ian, illus. (p. 1286)
—Olivia Lacing Cards. (p. 1286)
—Olivia Matching Game. (p. 1287)
—Olivia Paper Doll Play Set. (p. 1287)
—Olivia sait Compter. (p. 1287)
—Olivia Saves the Circus. (p. 1287)
—Olivia Saves the Circus. Falconer, Ian, illus. (p. 1287)
—Olivia va a Venecia. (p. 1287)
—Olivia y el Juguete Desaparecido. Mlawer, Teresa, tr. from ENG. (p. 1287)
—Olivia y Las Princesas. (p. 1287)
—Teatro Olivia: Swan Lake; Romeo & Juliet; Turandot. Falconer, Ian, illus. (p. 1711)
Falconer, Ian, illus. see Mlawer, Teresa, tr.
Falconer, Ian & Jordom, Deloris M. Dream Big: Starring Olivia. (p. 483)
Falconer, Ian & Simon & Schuster Audio Firm Staff. Olivia Collection: Olivia; Olivia Saves the Circus; Olivia... & the Missing Toy; Olivia Forms a Band; Olivia Helps with Christmas; Olivia Goes to Venice; Olivia & the Fairy Princesses. Falconer, Ian, illus. (p. 1286)
Falconer, Ian & Simon and Schuster/LeapFrog Staff. Olivia. (p. 1286)
Falconer, Ian, et al. Olivia & Her Great Adventures. Osterhold, Jared & Johnson, Shane L., illus. (p. 1286)
Falconer, Kieran & Quek, Lynette. Peru. (p. 1345)
Falconer, Mary. Spotted Sheep with the Worthless Wool. (p. 1634)
Falconer, Shelley & White, Shawna. Stones, Bones & Stitches: Storytelling Through Inuit Art. (p. 1653)
Falconi, Maria Inés. Hasta el Domingo. (p. 752)
Falewee, Samantha. Stowaway aboard Noah's Ark. (p. 1664)
Falick, Melanie. Kids Knitting. Nicholas, Kristin, illus. (p. 954)
Falini, Nancy Patin. Gluten-Free Friends: An Activity Book for Kids. (p. 685)
Falk, Barbara Bustetter & Hyman, Helen Kandel. Don't Park on the Roof. (p. 468)
Falk, Cathy, jt. auth. see Miteff, Deb.
Falk, Cathy Kennerson, illus. see Kennerson, Vern.
Falk, Connie J. Gold Stars & Daydreams. (p. 694)
Falk, Daniel, jt. auth. see Falk, Kristi.
Falk, Elizabeth Sullivan. Freedom's Fire. Wang, Qi Z., illus. (p. 635)
—Lettie's North Star. Wolf, Elizabeth, illus. (p. 1003)
Falk, Elsa. Akio & the Moon Goddess. Kraynak, George, illus. (p. 32)
—Fire Canoe. Frankenberg, Robert, illus. (p. 590)
Falk, Emily. 78 Things they Didn't Teach You in School: But You Do Need to Know. (p. 1998)
Falk, Jennifer & Morgan. Heart Daddy for Chrissie. (p. 759)
Falk, John H., et al. Bubble Monster: And Other Science Fun. (p. 233)
Falk, Karen. Tacianna & the Endless Ball of String. (p. 1694)
Falk, Kristi & Falk, Daniel. Eartha Gets Well. Peters, Rob, illus. (p. 497)
Falk, Laine. Let's Talk about Opposites, Morning to Night. Michael, Joan & Larsen, Eric, illus. (p. 1001)
—Let's Talk Riding. (p. 1001)
—Let's Talk Tae Kwon Do. (p. 1001)
—Meet President Barack Obama. (p. 1122)
—Meet President Barack Obama. Childrens Press Staff, ed. (p. 1122)
—Meet President John McCain. (p. 1122)
—This Is the Way We Eat Our Food. (p. 1736)
—This Is the Way We Go to School. (p. 1736)
—We Are Citizens. (p. 1865)
—What Is Mount Rushmore? (p. 1890)
—What's in Washington, D. C. ? (p. 1898)
Falk, Laine, jt. auth. see Miller, Amanda.
Falk, Liane. Spots. (p. 1634)
Falk, Nicholas. Troggle the Troll. Lowe, Tony, illus. (p. 1788)
Falk, Nick. Battle for the Golden Egg. Flowers, Tony, illus. (p. 145)
—Eaten Alive! Flowers, Tony, illus. (p. 501)
—First Bite. Flowers, Tony, illus. (p. 593)
—Race for the Shogun's Treasure. Flowers, Tony, illus. (p. 1431)
—Shadow Shifter. Flowers, Tony, illus. (p. 1558)
—Werewolves Beware! Flowers, Tony, illus. (p. 1875)
Falk, Nick & Flowers, Tony. Pterodactyl Stole My Homework: Saurus Street 2 (Large Print 16pt) (p. 1413)
—Tyrannosaurus in the Veggie Patch: Saurus Street 1 (Large Print 16pt) (p. 1805)
Falk, Peter Hastings, ed. see Baron, Lynne Pauls.
Falk, Wendy, ed. see Anderson, Henry Morgan.
Falken, L. C., jt. auth. see McCue, Lisa.
Falken, Linda. Puzzling Places. (p. 1421)
Falken, Linda & Metropolitan Museum of Art Staff. Can You Find It? America: Search & Discover More Than 150 Details in 20 Works of Art. (p. 258)
Falken, Linda & The Metropolitan Museum of Art, The Metropolitan. Noah's Ark. (p. 1261)
—Puzzling Cats. (p. 1421)
—Puzzling Dogs. (p. 1421)
Falkenhain, John Mark. I Don't Want to Go to Church: Turning the Struggle into a Celebration. Alley, R. W., illus. (p. 838)
Falkenrath, Barbara. Danny Finds His Special Gift. (p. 405)
Falkenstern, Lisa. Dragon Moves In (p. 477)
Falkenstern, Lisa, illus. see Ward, Jennifer.
Falki, Pamela Marie. Perfect Christmas Tree: Petrie & Toby's Holiday Adventure. (p. 1341)
Falkner, Brian. Assault (Recon Team Angel #1) (p. 107)
—Battlesaurus: Rampage at Waterloo. (p. 147)
—Brain Jack. (p. 221)
—Ice War (Recon Team Angel #3) (p. 851)
—Maddy West & the Tongue Taker Bixley, Donovan, illus. (p. 1070)
—Northwood (p. 1266)
—Northwood Bixley, Donovan, illus. (p. 1266)
—Project. (p. 1410)
—Task Force. (p. 1706)
—Task Force (Recon Team Angel #2) (p. 1706)
—Tomorrow Code. (p. 1765)
Falkner, John Meade. Moonfleet: A Classic Tale of Smuggling. Marks, Alan, illus. (p. 1172)
—Moonfleet. (p. 1172)
Falkner, John Meade, jt. auth. see Escott, John.
Falkoff, Michelle. Playlist for the Dead. (p. 1373)
Fall, Brandon, illus. see Man-Kong, Mary.
Fall, Brandon, illus. see Michelle, Tanya.
Fall, Brandon, illus. see Noll, Tom.
Fall, G. Everything You Need to Know about Juvenile Arthritis. (p. 545)
Fall, Guy. Everything You Need to Know about Juvenile Arthritis. (p. 545)
Falla, Lynne. World of the Weeples: Sophie & the Weeples. (p. 1957)
Faller, Regis. Adventures of Polo. Faller, Regis, illus. (p. 21)
—Polo & the Dragon. Faller, Regis, illus. (p. 1381)
Falletta, Bernadette. We Love to Read Stories Coloring Book & Word Search Puzzles. (p. 1867)
Falletta, Bernadette, jt. auth. see Gasparro, Marie.
Falletta, Bernadette & Gasparro, Marie. Reflections of the Dog That Learned English. (p. 1456)
Falletta, Bernadette & Lewis, Marla. We Love to Read Stories & Songs. (p. 1867)
Falligant, Erin. Braving the Lake. Studios, Arcana, illus. (p. 223)
—Into the Spotlight. Studios, Arcana, illus. (p. 881)
—Surprise Find. Studios, Arcana, illus. (p. 1685)
Falligant, Erin, ed. see Peterson, Stacy.
Falligant, Erin & American Girl Editors, eds. Stand up for Yourself Journal: Quizzes & Questions to Help You Stand Strong Against Bullying. Martini, Angela, illus. (p. 1639)
Falligant, Erin, ed. 3-D Studio. Laskey, Shannon, illus. (p. 1991)
—Clutter Control: Tips & Crafts to Organize Your Bedroom, Backpack, Locker, Life. McGuinness, Tracy, illus. (p. 336)
—Just Mom & Me: The Tear-Out, Punch-Out, Fill-Out Book of Fun for Girls & Their Moms. Peterson, Stacy, illus. (p. 939)
—School & Earth Smarts Planner. Blasutta, Mary Lynn, illus. (p. 1522)
Falligant, Erin, et al, eds. Is This Normal? Girls Questions, Answered by the Editors of the Care & Keeping of You. Bendell, Norm, illus. (p. 890)
Fallin, Rachel. Little Blessings. (p. 1024)
Fallon, A. Robin's Nest Is Best. (p. 1480)
Fallon, Jennifer. Wolfblade. (p. 1944)
Fallon, Jimmy. Your Baby's First Word Will Be DADA. Ordóñez, Miguel, illus. (p. 1980)
Fallon, Joe & Scarborough, Ken. Halfway Hank. Davis, Jack E., illus. (p. 737)
Fallon, Karla. Rainforest Moon. (p. 1436)
Fallon, Kathy Reilly & Pellegrino, Frank. Heavenly Skies & Lullabies: Illustrated Songbook & CD. Kelly, Becky, illus. (p. 761)
Fallon, Kevin A. Rest in Peas: What Does that Mean? (p. 1464)
Fallon, Leigh. Carrier of the Mark. (p. 271)
—Shadow of the Mark. (p. 1557)
Fallon, Lisa, illus. see Kaminski, Tom.
Fallon, Michael. How to Analyze the Works of Andy Warhol. (p. 814)
—How to Analyze the Works of Georgia O'Keeffe. (p. 814)
—Who Are These People? Coping with Family Dynamics. (p. 1914)
Falloon, Jane, jt. auth. see Andersen, Hans Christian.
Fallows, Ralph. Ralphie's after-School Adventure. (p. 1437)
Falls, C. B. ABC Book. (p. 3)
Falls, Kat. Dark Life. (p. 407)
—Inhuman. (p. 874)
—Rip Tide. (p. 1473)
Fals, Mary. Chosen Colt. (p. 310)
Falsetto, Rita. Cat's Furry Tale. (p. 281)
Falter, Laury. Birthright. (p. 193)
—Residue. (p. 1463)
—Savior. (p. 1518)
Falvo, David C. Passport to Mathematics Practice Workbook: Book 1. (p. 1327)
Falwell, Cathryn. Butterflies for Kiri (p. 247)
—Butterflies for Kiri. Falwell, Cathryn, illus. (p. 247)
—David's Drawings. (p. 411)
—Dibujos de David. de La Vega, Eida, tr. from ENG. (p. 435)
—Feast for 10 Falwell, Cathryn, illus. (p. 579)
—Gobble, Gobble. Falwell, Cathryn, illus. (p. 688)
—Mystery Vine. Falwell, Cathryn, illus. (p. 1226)
—Pond Babies Falwell, Cathryn, illus. (p. 1382)
—Rainbow Stew Falwell, Cathryn, illus. (p. 1436)
—Scoot! Falwell, Cathryn, illus. (p. 1529)
—Shape Capers: Shake a Shape. (p. 1560)
—Shape Capers: Shake a Shape. Falwell, Cathryn, illus. (p. 1560)
—Turtle Splash! Countdown at the Pond. Falwell, Cathryn, illus. (p. 1798)
—Word Wizard. (p. 1951)
Falzon, Adrienne. What Is an Angel? Salzberg, Helen, illus. (p. 1888)
Fama, Angela, photos by see Werker, Kim Piper & Werker, Kim.
Fama, Elizabeth. Monstrous Beauty. (p. 1169)
—Plus One. (p. 1374)
Fambro, Sonja Grimsley. Santa Spent the Night with Me! (p. 1513)
—When Santa Goes to Church. (p. 1904)
Fambrough, Kay. Buzzard in A Birdbath. (p. 248)
Famighetti, Robert, et al. How Do Hybrid Cars Work? (p. 807)
—How Do Islands Form? (p. 807)
—How Do Plants Get Food? (p. 807)
—How Do Refrigerators Work? (p. 807)
—How Does a Spacecraft Reach the Moon? (p. 808)
—Why Do Lights Turn On? (p. 1923)
—Why Do Ships Float? (p. 1924)
Families of Templeton Elementary, creator. Tales from Templeton: Families Writing Together (p. 1701)
Family, jt. auth. see Monin, Luke.
FamilyLife Publishing, creator. What God Wants for Christmas. (p. 1884)
Famous, Howard B. Bobby Bear & Other Stories. (p. 206)
Famularo, Joe. Chiara's Bite of the Big Apple: A Happy Book. (p. 299)
—Taco/Fatso: The Story of a Fat Dog, Too Fat to Fly. (p. 1695)
Fan, Daphne. Money Champ: Teaching Kids about Money Management. (p. 1164)
Fan, Nancy Y. Sword Quest. Rioux, Jo-Anne, illus. (p. 1692)
Fan, Nancy Yi. Sword Mountain. (p. 1692)
—Sword Quest. Rioux, Jo-Anne, illus. (p. 1692)
—Swordbird. (p. 1692)
—Swordbird. Zug, Mark, illus. (p. 1692)
Fan, Nancy Yi, jt. auth. see Zug, Mark.
Fan, Terry, illus. see Rundell, Katherine.
Fancher, Joseph. Sydney's Travels Through Dreamland Part. (p. 1692)
Fancher, Lou, illus. see Bohrer, Maria.
Fancher, Lou, illus. see George, Jean Craighead.
Fancher, Lou, illus. see Hanson, Warren.
Fancher, Lou, illus. see Hill, Karen.
Fancher, Lou, illus. see Keillor, Garrison.
Fancher, Lou, illus. see Krull, Kathleen.
Fancher, Lou, illus. see Larson, Deborah Jo.
Fancher, Lou, illus. see Mora, Pat, et al.
Fancher, Lou, illus. see Oppel, Kenneth.
Fancher, Lou, illus. see Osborne, Mary Pope.
Fancher, Lou, illus. see Palatini, Margie.
Fancher, Lou, illus. see Panahi, H. L.
Fancher, Lou, illus. see Paolilli, Paul & Brewer, Dan.
Fancher, Lou, illus. see Rusch, Elizabeth.
Fancher, Lou, illus. see Salten, Felix.
Fancher, Lou, illus. see Smucker, Anna.
Fancy, Colin, et al. Dydy Crocodeilod Ddim yn Glanhau eu Dannedd. (p. 491)
Fancy, Robin Lyn & Welch, Vala Jeanne. My Filipino Word Book: English - Tagalog - Ilokano. Gasmen, Imelda Fines, ed. (p. 1203)
Fandangleman, Rupert. Comparing Creatures. (p. 352)
Fandangleman, Rupert, jt. auth. see Rissman, Rebecca.
Fandel, Jennifer. Alexander Graham Bell & the Telephone Tucker, Keith, illus. (p. 36)
—Beethoven's Fifth Symphony. (p. 158)
—CM Punk: Straight Edge Heel (p. 336)
—Collect Your Thoughts: Organizing Information. (p. 339)
—Endangered Plants. (p. 527)
—Endangered Trees & Shrubs. (p. 527)
—Ferdinand Magellan. (p. 581)
—Frank Lloyd Wright. (p. 628)
—Golden Gate Bridge. (p. 694)
—Jim Thorpe: Greatest Athlete in the World Whigham, Rod, illus. (p. 918)
—Keats, Shakespeare, & Other Wordsmiths. (p. 946)
—Light Bulb. (p. 1015)
—Louis Pasteur. (p. 1058)
—Martin Luther King, Jr. (p. 1097)
—Martin Luther King, Jr: Great Civil Rights Leader Bascle, Brian, illus. (p. 1098)
—Metaphors, Similes, & Other Word Pictures. (p. 1130)
—Metric System. (p. 1130)
—Pablo Picasso. (p. 1316)
—Picture Yourself Writing Nonfiction: Using Photos to Inspire Writing (p. 1356)
—Postage Stamp. (p. 1387)
—Puns, Allusions, & Other Word Secrets. (p. 1417)
—Rhyme, Meter, & Other Word Music. (p. 1468)
—Rock Climbing. (p. 1482)
—Rudolf Nureyev. (p. 1494)
—Skateboarding. (p. 1583)
—Snowboarding. (p. 1600)
—Statue of Liberty. (p. 1645)
—Voices in Poetry: William Shakespeare. (p. 1848)
—What Is a Conjunction? (p. 1888)
—What Is a Verb? (p. 1888)
—What Is an Adjective? (p. 1888)
—William Shakespeare. (p. 1933)
—You Can Write. (p. 1974)
—You Can Write a Terrific Opinion Piece (p. 1974)
—You Can Write a Terrific Opinion Piece. (p. 1974)
—You Can Write an Amazing Journal. (p. 1974)
—You Can Write Awesome Stories (p. 1974)
—You Can Write Cool Poems (p. 1974)
Fandel, Jennifer, jt. auth. see Doyle, Sheri.
Fandel, Jennifer & Doyle, Sheri. Parts of Speech. (p. 1325)
Fandel, Jennifer & Fields, Jan. You Can Write. (p. 1974)
Fandel, Jennifer & Milgrom, Al. George Eastman & the Kodak Camera Purcell, Gordon, illus. (p. 663)
—George Eastman & the Kodak Camera Purcell, Gordon & Milgrom, Al, illus. (p. 663)

F

Fandel, Jennifer & Miller, Connie Colwell. Thorns, Horns, & Crescent Moons: Reading & Writing Nature Poems Burkes-Larrañaga, Dustin et al, illus. (p. 1740)
Fandel, Jennifer & Saunders-Smith, Gail. What Is a Conjunction? (p. 1888)
—What Is a Verb? (p. 1888)
—What Is an Adjective? (p. 1888)
Fandel, Jennifer, et al. Louis Pasteur & Pasteurization Wilson, Keith, illus. (p. 1058)
—Louis Pasteur & Pasteurization Wilson, Keith et al, illus. (p. 1058)
—Poet in You Smith, Simon et al, illus. (p. 1376)
—Pro Wrestling Stars. (p. 1408)
—Trust, Truth, & Ridiculous Goofs: Reading & Writing Friendship Poems Smith, Simon et al, illus. (p. 1793)
Fandex Family Field Guides Staff, ed. see Vaughan, Carolyn.
Fane, Judy B. Paddy the Pelican Survives the Storm. Alden, Carol, illus. (p. 1317)
Fanelli, Sara. Onion's Great Escape. (p. 1298)
Fanelli, Sara, illus. see Collodi, Carlo.
Fang, Irving. Alphabet to Internet: Mediated Communication in Our Lives. (p. 50)
Fang, Jade, illus. see Accord Publishing Staff.
Fang, Katherine. Sinnoh Hall of Fame Handbook (p. 1580)
Fanger, Rolf. Benjamin Bunny Learns to Fly. (p. 164)
Fanger, Rolf & Moltgen, Ulrike. Moonbeam Bear. (p. 1172)
Fangorn. Little Horrors. (p. 1029)
Fangorn, illus. see Jacques, Brian.
Fankford, Ronald, Jr. What Is the Future of the U. S. Economy? Lankford, Ronnie D., ed. (p. 1890)
Fanlo, Africa, illus. see O'Callaghan, Elena.
Fann, Linsey. Puppy Love. Abdulai, David, ed. (p. 1418)
Fanney, Robert. Luthiel's Song: Dreams of the Ringed Vale. (p. 1066)
Fannin, Cole. Gene Autry & the Golden Stallion. Hampton, John, illus. (p. 660)
Fanning, Kieran. Code Crackers: Trapdoor to Treachery. (p. 338)
—Code Crackers: Voyage to Victory. (p. 338)
Fanning, Kim M. Beyond the Island: The Journey of a Boy. (p. 174)
Fanning, Meghan. Mrs. Kisses. Judah, Nathan, illus. (p. 1187)
Fanning, Mick & Baker, Tim. Surf for Your Life: Grommets' Edition. (p. 1685)
Fanning, Tena, jt. auth. see Thiel, Annie.
Fannon, Chris, illus. see Guiffre, William A.
Fannon, Paul, et al. Mathematics Higher Level for the IB Diploma Option Topic 9 Calculus. (p. 1108)
—Mathematics Higher Level for the IB Diploma Option Topic 10 Discrete Mathematics. (p. 1108)
—Mathematics Higher Level for the IB Diploma Option Topic 7 Statistics & Probability. (p. 1108)
Fannoun, Kathy. Our Loving Grandparents. (p. 1309)
Fanny, illus. see Cochard, Nadège.
Fanny, illus. see Cochard, Nadège.
Fanny, illus. see Cochard, Nadége.
Fanny, Nanny. New Girl in Town: A Children's Book. Fanny, Nanny, illus. (p. 1244)
—Touch the Stars: A Children's Book. Nanny Fanny, illus. (p. 1772)
Fant, Donna. Scotty's Dream: Book & CD. Axford, Elizabeth C., ed. (p. 1532)
Fantasia, Kathryn. Pass It On. Flanagan, Jeff, illus. (p. 1326)
Fantaskey, Beth. Buzz Kill. (p. 248)
—Ishbel Feeney, Star Girl Reporter. (p. 891)
—Jekel Loves Hyde. (p. 912)
—Jessica Rules the Dark Side. (p. 914)
—Jessica's Guide to Dating on the Dark Side. (p. 914)
Fantastik, B. Save the Sleepless Slumbernots! Valentine, M. K., illus. (p. 1517)
Fantich, Susanna. Cat's Tale. (p. 281)
Fantín de Bellocq, Constanza, tr. see Montgomery, L. M.
Fapojuwo, Fapojuwo. And that's Alright! (A Book of Encouragement for Children) (p. 71)
Fapojuwo, Moyo Bukola. Kemi Shows You How to Be A Healthy Kid. (p. 948)
Fara, Patricia, jt. auth. see Reid, Struan.
Faraday, Daniel, jt. auth. see Mills, Nathan.
Faraday, L. Winifred, jt. auth. see Carroll, Lewis, pseud.
Faragher, Nick & Kernaghan, Eileen. Wild Talent: A Novel of the Supernatural. (p. 1930)
Farago, Andrew. Teenage Mutant Ninja Turtles: The Ultimate Visual History. (p. 1714)
Farah, Barbara. Parabola O Jednom Mostu: Parable of the Bridge. (p. 1323)
—Parabola O Jednom Mostu. Conway, Tricia, illus. (p. 1323)
Farah, Najwa Kawar. Chicken Licken. (p. 300)
farahay, m. l. BUTTERFLY, the BEE & the SPIDER. (p. 248)
—BUTTERFLY, the BEE & the SPIDER, Sc3. (p. 248)
Farahay, Michael L. Butterfly, The Bee & The Spider. Farahay, Naomi E., ed. (p. 248)
Farahay, Naomi E., ed. see Farahay, Michael L.
Farb, Carolyn. Lucas Comes to America. (p. 1062)
Farber, E. S. Fish Finelli (Book 1) Seagulls Don't Eat Pickles. Beene, Jason, illus. (p. 598)
—Fish Finelli (Book 2) Operation Fireball. Beene, Jason, illus. (p. 598)
—Operation Fireball. Beene, Jason, illus. (p. 1300)
Farber, Erica. Fish Finelli: Seagulls Don't Eat Pickles. Beene, Jason, illus. (p. 598)
—Kooky Campout. Scarry, Huck, illus. (p. 967)
—Richard Scarry's Readers (Level 1): Get That Hat! Scarry, Huck, illus. (p. 1469)
—Richard Scarry's Readers (Level 1): Snow Dance. Scarry, Huck, illus. (p. 1469)
—Richard Scarry's Readers (Level 2): One, Two, AH-CHOO! Scarry, Huck, illus. (p. 1469)
—Richard Scarry's Readers (Level 3): Spooky Campout. Scarry, Huck, illus. (p. 1469)
Farber, Erica, jt. auth. see Scarry, Richard.
Farberow, Norman L., jt. auth. see Evans, Glen.
Farbs, C. Olympic Ice Skating. (p. 1287)
Fardell, John. Day Louis Got Eaten. Fardell, John, illus. (p. 413)
—Jeremiah Jellyfish Flies High! Fardell, John, illus. (p. 913)
—Manfred the Baddie. Fardell, John, illus. (p. 1087)
Fardon, John. 1000 Things You Should Know about Ancient History. (p. 2001)
—1000 Things You Should Know about Modern History. (p. 2001)
—1000 Things You Should Know about Plants. (p. 2001)
Fare, Dennis & Cacciatore, Mark G. PARCC ELA/ Literacy Assessments, Grades 6-8. (p. 1324)
—PARCC ELA/Literacy Assessments, Grades 9-12. (p. 1324)
Farenhorst, Christine. Amazing Stories from Times Past: Devotions for Children & Families. Mitchell, Steven, illus. (p. 56)
—Cup of Cold Water: The Compassion of Nurse Edith Cavell. (p. 392)
—Wings Like a Dove: The Courage of Queen Jeanne D'Albret. (p. 1936)
Fares, Laura. Glow: The Duck with the Golden Ring. (p. 685)
Farese, Lois Schneider, et al. Sports & Entertainment Marketing. (p. 1632)
Farfan, Flores & Antonio, Jose. Axolotl: El Ajolote. Celestino, Cleofas Ramirez, illus. (p. 121)
Farge, John La, see La Farge, John.
Farge, Oliver La, see La Farge, Oliver.
Fargo, Donna. You Are in My Thoughts & Prayers. (p. 1973)
Fargo, Lisa J., illus. see Santora, L. Steven.
Fargo, Todd, illus. see Brady, Bill & Brady, Laurie.
Fargo, Todd, illus. see Bryant, Louella.
Fargo, Todd, illus. see Mammay, Judith.
Fargo, Todd, illus. see Plucker, Sheri.
Fargo, Todd, illus. see Scott, Rosanna.
Farhat, Michael. Adventures of the Eastside Pigs: Produced by Funnybook Factory. Chan, Carol, ed. (p. 23)
Faria, Joseph D. Statue of Liberty & Ellis Island: A MyReportLinks.com Book. (p. 1645)
Faria, N. K. Little Smart Rabbit & the Greedy Wolf: Finding Carrots. (p. 1036)
Faria, Rosana, illus. see Cottin, Menena.
Faria, Rosana, illus. see MacHado, Ana Maria.
Faria, Rosana, illus. see Pantin, Yolanda.
Farias, Carolina, illus. see Griffith, Gretchen.
Farias, Carolina, illus. see Johnson, J. Angelique.
Farias Diaz-Noriega, Juan, jt. auth. see Farias, Juan.
Farias, Juan. A la Sombra del Maestro. Gaban, Jesus, illus. (p. 1)
—Hijo del Jardinero. (p. 779)
Farias, Juan, jt. auth. see Farias, Juan.
Farias, Juan, tr. see Casalderrey, Fina & Casalderrey Fraga, Xosefa.
Farias, Juan & Farias Diaz-Noriega, Juan. Caminos de la Luna. (p. 256)
Farias, Juan & Farias, Juan. Cosas de Pablo. (p. 368)
Farias, Juan & Juan, Farias. Nino Que Vino Con el Viento. (p. 1257)
—Por Tierras de Pan Llevar. Alonso, Juan Ramon, illus. (p. 1386)
Farias, Susan Norberg, illus. see MacGregor, Cynthia.
Faricy, Patrick, illus. see Gregory, Kristiana.
Faricy, Patrick, illus. see Hopkinson, Deborah.
Faricy, Patrick, illus. see Kennedy, Robert F., Jr.
Faricy, Patrick, illus. see Patrick, Jean L. S.
Faricy, Patrick, illus. see Stanley, George E.
Farina, Kathy, illus. see Washington, Kathy.
Farina, Marcella, jt. auth. see Folse, Keith S.
Farina von Buchwald, Martin & Prado Farina, Gabriela. Joy of Giving. Avendano, Dolores, illus. (p. 929)
Farinango, Maria Virginia & Resau, Laura. Queen of Water. (p. 1425)
Faris, Eva, illus. see Stephenson, Nancy.
Faris, Stephanie. 25 Roses. (p. 1996)
—30 Days of No Gossip. (p. 1996)
Farish, Catherine, jt. auth. see Mornard, Germaine.
Farish, Terry. Alleyway. (p. 47)
—Either the Beginning or the End of the World. (p. 507)
—Good Braider (p. 697)
Fariss, Michelle, illus. see Becker, Curt.
Farizan, Sara. If You Could Be Mine. (p. 854)
—Tell Me Again How a Crush Should Feel. (p. 1716)
Farjeon, Eleanor. Little Bookroom. Ardizzone, Edward, illus. (p. 1025)
Farjeon, Eleanor & Farjeon, Herbert. Kings & Queens. Thornycroft, Rosalind, illus. (p. 960)
Farjeon, Eleanor & Harvey, Anne. Blackbird Has Spoken: Selected Poems for Children. (p. 197)
Farjeon, Herbert, jt. auth. see Farjeon, Eleanor.
Farkas, Bart. Starfleet Academy: Exclusive Game Strategy Guide. (p. 1642)
Farkas, Bart G. Way of the Samurai 2 Official Strategy Guide. (p. 1864)
Farkas, Steven E. Annie Pooh, Princess Pup: How Annie Pooh was lost, was found, & became Princess Pup. (p. 87)
—Annie Pooh, Princess Pup, Monkey Shines. (p. 87)
Farkle, Sandy. Day the Gummies Wrecked: Square Bears Race the Fakers. (p. 414)
Farley, Andrew, illus. see Bentley, Sue.
Farley, Andrew, illus. see Chapman, Linda.
Farley, Brianne. Ike's Incredible Ink. Farley, Brianne, illus. (p. 856)
Farley, C. J. Game World. (p. 654)
Farley, Camille. Emma Just Wants to be Cool! (p. 519)
—Hayden Just Loves to Learn. (p. 755)
Farley, Christina. Gilded (p. 676)
Farley, Colby King. Warm Familiar Feeling. (p. 1858)
Farley, Donna. Ravens of Fame: A Tale of Saint Cuthbert. (p. 1441)
Farley, Jan. Fleur, a Lonely Pocket Mouse. (p. 603)
—Fleur & Cedarick: Book Two in Fleur Series. (p. 603)
—Griffin & Griseld: Book 3 in the Fleur Series. (p. 724)
Farley, Jason, illus. see Bannister, Barbara.
Farley, John, jt. auth. see Sazaklis, John.
Farley, Katherine, illus. see Powell, Amy.
Farley, Rick, illus. see Jacobs, Lana.
Farley, Rick, illus. see Rosen, Lucy.
Farley, Rick, illus. see Sazaklis, John & Roberts, Jeremy.
Farley, Rick, illus. see Stein, Erin K.
Farley, Rick, illus. see Teitelbaum, Michael.
Farley, Rick, illus. see Vivinetto, Gina.
Farley, Robin. Adventures of MIA. Ivanov, A. & Ivanov, O., illus. (p. 20)
—Mia: The Sweetest Valentine. (p. 1133)
—Mia: Time to Trick or Treat! (p. 1133)
—Mia & the Big Sister Ballet. (p. 1133)
—Mia & the Big Sister Ballet. Ivanov, Olga & Ivanov, Aleksey, illus. (p. 1133)
—Mia & the Daisy Dance. (p. 1133)
—Mia & the Daisy Dance. Ivanov, Olga & Ivanov, Aleksey, illus. (p. 1133)
—Mia & the Dance for Two. Ivanov, Olga & Ivanov, Aleksey, illus. (p. 1133)
—Mia & the Girl with a Twirl. (p. 1133)
—Mia & the Girl with a Twirl. Ivanov, Olga & Ivanov, Aleksey, illus. (p. 1133)
—Mia & the Tiny Toe Shoes. (p. 1133)
—Mia & the Tiny Toe Shoes. Ivanov, Aleksey & Ivanov, Olga, illus. (p. 1133)
—Mia & the Too Big Tutu. Ivanov, Aleksey & Ivanov, Olga, illus. (p. 1133)
—Mia Dances Back to School! Ivanov, Olga & Ivanov, Aleksey, illus. (p. 1133)
—Mia Jazzes It Up! (p. 1133)
—Mia Jazzes It Up! Ivanov, Olga & Ivanov, Aleksey, illus. (p. 1133)
—Mia Sets the Stage. (p. 1133)
—Mia Sets the Stage. Ivanov, Olga & Ivanov, Aleksey, illus. (p. 1133)
—Mia - The Snow Day Ballet. Ivanov, Olga & Ivanov, Aleksey, illus. (p. 1133)
—Mia's Nutcracker Ballet. Ivanov, Olga & Ivanov, Aleksey, illus. (p. 1134)
—Sweetest Valentine. Ivanov, Aleksey & Ivanov, Olga, illus. (p. 1690)
—Time to Trick or Treat! Ivanov, Olga & Ivanov, Aleksey, illus. (p. 1753)
Farley, Steve. Black Stallion & the Lost City. (p. 197)
Farley, Steven. Black Stallion & the Shape-Shifter. (p. 197)
Farley, Terri. Desert Dancer. (p. 429)
—Free Again. (p. 634)
—Heartbreak Bronco. (p. 760)
—Phantom Stallion Box Set: The Wild One; Mustang Moon; Dark Sunshine. Call, Greg, illus. (p. 1349)
—Phantom Stallion - Wild Horse Island: The Shining Stallion. Bk. 2 (p. 1349)
—Rain Forest Rose Bk. 3. (p. 1434)
—Seven Tears into the Sea. (p. 1555)
—Wild at Heart: Mustangs & the Young People Fighting to Save Them. Farlow, Melissa, photos by. (p. 1928)
—Wild Honey No. 22. (p. 1929)
—Wild One. (p. 1930)
Farley, Walter. Black Stallion. Ward, Keith, illus. (p. 197)
—Black Stallion Adventures! (p. 197)
—Black Stallion & Flame. (p. 197)
—Black Stallion Challenged! (p. 197)
—Little Black, a Pony: Liishzhiin Yazhi. Carr, Elsie, tr. (p. 1024)
Farlow, Melissa, photos by see Farley, Terri.
Farman, Ella, et al. Lill's Travels in Santa Claus Land, & Other Stories. (p. 1017)
Farman, John. Roundhead & Cavaliers. (p. 1491)
—Shockingly Short History Of Absolutely Everything. (p. 1568)
Farmer, Andy. Father's Guide to Raising Girls. (p. 577)
Farmer, Bonnie. Abc Letters in the Library. (p. 3)
—Oscar Lives Next Door: A Story Inspired by Oscar Peterson's Childhood. Lafrance, Marie, illus. (p. 1305)
Farmer, Christopher. King Who Lost His Crown. (p. 959)
Farmer, Craig. Watson: Family. (p. 1864)
—Watson: School. (p. 1864)
—Watson: Values. (p. 1864)
—Watson: Everyday. (p. 1864)
Farmer, Emily. Jimmie Johnson: NASCAR Driver. (p. 918)
Farmer, Jacqueline. Apples. Tildes, Phyllis Limbacher, illus. (p. 92)
—Calabazas. DelRisco, Eida, tr. from ENG. (p. 252)
—O Christmas Tree: Its History & Holiday Traditions. Friar, Joanne, illus. (p. 1274)
—Pumpkins. Tildes, Phyllis Limbacher, illus. (p. 1416)
—Valentine Be Mine. Halsey, Megan & Addy, Sean, illus. (p. 1830)
Farmer, Jonathan, photos by see Levithan, David.
Farmer, Libby, illus. see Miner, Ann.
Farmer, Merry. Balloons for Bella. (p. 135)
Farmer, Nancy. Ear, the Eye & the Arm. (p. 492)
—Ear, the Eye, & the Arm. (p. 492)
—House of the Scorpion. (p. 803)
—Islands of the Blessed. (p. 892)
—Islands of the Blessed. Foster, Jon, illus. (p. 892)
—Land of the Silver Apples. (p. 973)
—Land of the Silver Apples. Sardinha, Rick, illus. (p. 973)
—Lord of Opium. (p. 1052)
—Sea of Trolls. (p. 1535)
Farmer, Penelope. Charlotte Sometimes. Connor, Chris, illus. (p. 293)
Farmer, Selina, illus. see Gotthardt, Katherine.
Farmer, Suzanne, illus. see Pitkethly, Maggie.
Farmer, Tom. Once upon a Daydream: The Story of Patrick & the Clumsy Camel. (p. 1292)
Farmer, Zoe. Practice Makes Perfect. Farmer, Zoe, illus. (p. 1392)
Farmer, Zoe, illus. see Bellis, Jill.
Farmer, Zoe, illus. see Kimmons, Janet M.
Farndon, J. Astronomy. (p. 109)
Farndon, John. 1000 Things You Should Know about Wild Animals. (p. 2001)
—Archeology. (p. 95)
—Children's Atlas. (p. 303)
—Electricity: An Investigation. (p. 509)
—Experimenting with Chemistry. (p. 549)
—Experimenting with Physics. (p. 549)
—Experimenting with Science (p. 549)
—Exploring Nature: Butterflies & Moths. (p. 552)
—Eyewitness Books - Oil. (p. 558)
—Flowers. (p. 608)
—Fruits. (p. 645)
—Great Scientists. (p. 718)
—History of Civilization Illustrated History Encyclopedia: The Great Landmarks in the Development of Mankind. (p. 783)
—How Things Work. (p. 814)
—Planet Earth. (p. 1367)
—Questions & Answers Science & Nature. (p. 1426)
—Roots. (p. 1488)
—Science & Technology. (p. 1525)
—Space. (p. 1618)
—Special Forces. (p. 1623)
—Stems. (p. 1647)
—Story of Science & Technology. (p. 1660)
—Stuff You Need Know! (p. 1670)
—Stuff You Need to Know! (p. 1670)
—What Do We Know about Stars & Galaxies? (p. 1882)
—Wild Animals. (p. 1928)
Farndon, John & Graham, Ian. Discovering Science. (p. 449)
Farndon, John & Riley, Peter D. Volcanoes & Earthquakes & Other Facts about Planet Earth: Bulletpoints. (p. 1849)
Farndon, John & Walshaw, Rodney. Exploring Science: Planet Earth Continents Oceans Climate Geology. (p. 553)
Farndon, John & Woolf, Alex. Great Scientists. (p. 718)
Farnell, Chris. Mark II. (p. 1095)
Farnes, Catherine. Slide. (p. 1590)
—Snowblind. (p. 1600)
Farnette, Cherrie, et al. Graphic Organizers for Reading. Grayson, Cary, ed. (p. 711)
Farnol, Jeffery. Money Moon. (p. 1164)
Farnsley, Kathleen. This Little Piggy Named Pony. (p. 1737)
Farnsworth, Bill. Great Stone Face. (p. 718)
Farnsworth, Bill, illus. see Acheson, Alison.
Farnsworth, Bill, illus. see Adler, David A.
Farnsworth, Bill, illus. see Ammon, Richard.
Farnsworth, Bill, illus. see Avi.
Farnsworth, Bill, illus. see Bailer, Darice.
Farnsworth, Bill, illus. see Bruchac, Joseph.
Farnsworth, Bill, illus. see Castrovilla, Selene.
Farnsworth, Bill, illus. see Craven, Tracy Leininger.
Farnsworth, Bill, illus. see Cussler, Clive.
Farnsworth, Bill, illus. see Dunlap, Julie & Lorbiecki, Marybeth.
Farnsworth, Bill, illus. see Flowers, Pam.
Farnsworth, Bill, illus. see High, Linda Oatman.
Farnsworth, Bill, illus. see Hill, Susan & Sewell, Anna.
Farnsworth, Bill, illus. see Hopkinson, Deborah.
Farnsworth, Bill, illus. see Randall, Alison L.
Farnsworth, Bill, illus. see Rubin, Susan Goldman.
Farnsworth, Bill, illus. see Sneve, Virginia Driving Hawk.
Farnsworth, Bill, illus. see Strohmeier, Lenice & Strohmeier.
Farnsworth, Bill, illus. see Van Steenwyk, Elizabeth.
Farnsworth, Bill, illus. see Vander Zee, Ruth & Sneider, Marian.
Farnsworth, Bill, illus. see Wade, Mary Dodson.
Farnsworth, Bill, illus. see Wise, Bill.
Farnsworth, Bill, illus. see Worthington, Heather Hill.
Farnsworth, Bill, illus. see Young, Judy.
Farnsworth, Bill, jt. auth. see Bruchac, Joseph.
Farnsworth, Bill, jt. auth. see Flowers, Pam.
Farnsworth, Bill, tr. see Flowers, Pam.
Farnsworth, Dewey. Americas Before Columbus. (p. 64)
Farnsworth, Frances. Cubby in Wonderland. (p. 388)
Farnsworth, Frances Joyce. Tike & Tiny in the Tetons. (p. 1749)
Farnsworth, Scott & Hoyt, Peggy R. Like a Library Burning. (p. 1017)
Farnsworth, Vesta J. House We Live in or the Making of the Body. (p. 804)
Farnsworth-Simpson, Patricia Ann. Flick the Karate Pig. (p. 603)
—Stories to Thrill & Delight. (p. 1655)
Farnsworth-Simpson., Patricia Ann. Twinkles Fairy Story. (p. 1802)
Farnsworth-Simpson, Patricia Ann. Wonderful Butterbee Angel's. (p. 1948)
Farnworth, Lauren. Little Zombie. (p. 1038)
Farnworth, Michael M. Sinister Mr. Pickle & the Fickle He Got the Mcwickles Into. (p. 1579)
Farooqi, Imran A. Spell of the Witch-Queen. (p. 1625)
Farquhar, George, et al. Beaux' Strategem. (p. 154)
Farquhar, Ginny, jt. auth. see Butcher, Alice.
Farquhar, Jackie, et al. Try This at Home: Planet-Friendly Projects for Kids. (p. 1794)
Farquharson, Alex, et al. Isa Genzken. Gaskins, Matthew D., tr. (p. 890)
Farquharson, Alexander, illus. see Sutcliffe, Jane.
Farquharson, Jerome. Playtime to Bedtime: Memories That Last Forever... (p. 1373)
Farquharson, Polly. Green Line. (p. 722)
—Linea Verde. Dieguez Dieguez, Remedios, tr. (p. 1019)
Farr, Dan. Mr. Finnegan's Giving Chest. (p. 1185)
Farr, James. Xombie Journal. (p. 1967)
Farr Kelley, Barbara. Prayer in the Dark. (p. 1393)
Farr, Michael. Job Search Basics, Third Edition. (p. 919)
Farr, Michael & Pavlicko, Marie A. Young Person's Guide to Getting & Keeping a Good Job, Third Edition. (p. 1979)
Farr, Rich, illus. see Feurer, Paige.
Farr, Richard. Emperors of the Ice: A True Story of Disaster & Survival in the Antarctic, 1910-13. (p. 521)
Farrant, Natasha. After Iris. (p. 28)
—Following Flora. (p. 612)
—What We Did for Love: Resistance, Heartbreak, Betrayal. (p. 1895)
Farrar, Amy. ADHD. (p. 12)
—Global Warming. (p. 684)
Farrar, F. W. Eric, or, Little by Little. (p. 533)
Farrar, Frederic William. Eric; or, Little by Little. (p. 533)
Farrar, Greg, photos by see Kehret, Peg.
Farrar, John, jt. auth. see Zemtsov, Ilya.
Farrar, Josh. Rules to Rock By. (p. 1495)
—Song for Bijou. (p. 1611)

Farrar, Sid. Year Comes Round: Haiku Through the Seasons. Plume, Ilse, illus. (p. 1969)
Farrar-Hunter, Patricia A., jt. auth. see Johnson, Stephen R.
Farre, Lluis. Grey Boy. Willis, Judith, tr. from CAT. (p. 723)
Farré, Lluís, jt. auth. see Farre, Lluis.
Farre, Lluis & Farré, Lluís. Leyenda de San Jorge. Canals, Mercè, illus. (p. 1004)
Farrel, Bill & Farrel, Pam. First Five Years: Make the Love Investment That Lasts a Lifetime. (p. 595)
Farrel, Pam, jt. auth. see Farrel, Bill.
Farrell, Bill. Walter's Pond: The True Story of Three Brothers Who Went Fishing for Trouble. Julich, Jenniffer, illus. (p. 1856)
Farrell, Connie. Sam's Harvest Party Ellingsworth, Colleen, illus. (p. 1509)
Farrell, Courtney. Build It Green. (p. 238)
—Children's Rights. (p. 304)
—Construir Casas Verdes. (p. 360)
—Green Jobs. (p. 722)
—Gulf of Mexico Oil Spill. (p. 731)
—Human Trafficking. (p. 826)
—Mental Disorders. (p. 1126)
—Methane Energy. (p. 1130)
—Mexican Drug War. (p. 1131)
—Plants Out of Place. (p. 1370)
—Save the Planet: Keeping Water Clean. (p. 1516)
—Save the Planet: Using Alternative Energies. (p. 1516)
—Terror at the Munich Olympics. (p. 1722)
—World Population. (p. 1958)
Farrell, Dan, illus. see Phelan, Thomas W. & Schonour, Sarah Jane.
Farrell, Darren. Doug-Dennis & the Flyaway Fib. (p. 473)
—Thank You, Octopus. (p. 1725)
Farrell, Eric L. & Holmes, Will, Jr. Seeking Solace: In a Time of Distress. (p. 1548)
Farrell, Fiona. Pop-Up Book of Invasions. (p. 1384)
Farrell, Helen, ed. see Gioffre, Rosalba, et al.
Farrell, James T. Young Lonigan. (p. 1979)
Farrell, John. Dear Child. Manning, Maurie J., illus. (p. 418)
Farrell, Liam. Goldilocks the Babysitter from Hell. (p. 696)
—Return of the Big Bad Wolf. Myler, Terry, illus. (p. 1464)
—True Story of the Three Little Pigs & the Big Bad Wolf. (p. 1793)
—True Story of the Three Little Pigs & the Big Bad Wolf. Myler, Terry, illus. (p. 1793)
Farrell, Lynne. Bennie's Forever Gift. (p. 165)
Farrell, Mary. Computer Programming for Kids. (p. 355)
Farrell, Mary Cronk. Pure Grit: How American World War II Nurses Survived Battle & Prison Camp in the Pacific. (p. 1419)
Farrell, Mia. Exploring African-American Culture Through Crafts. (p. 551)
—Exploring Asian Cultures Through Crafts. (p. 551)
—Exploring Latino Cultures Through Crafts. (p. 552)
—Exploring Middle Eastern Cultures Through Crafts. (p. 552)
—Exploring Native American Cultures Through Crafts. (p. 552)
Farrell, Michael. Ode Ode. (p. 1278)
Farrell, Robert. Alien Log. (p. 41)
Farrell, Robert E., Jr. Alien Log. (p. 41)
Farrell, Russell. Horses & Ponies: Step-by-Step Insructions for 25 Different Breeds. (p. 800)
Farrell, Russell, illus. see Walter Foster Creative Team.
Farrell, Russell & Creative Team at Walter Foster Publishing Staff. I Love Horses! Giddy-Up Great Stickers, Trivia, Step-by-Step Drawing Projects, & More for the Horse Lover in You! Fisher, Diana, illus. (p. 842)
Farrell, Russell & Fisher, Diana. All about Drawing Sea Creatures & Animals. (p. 42)
Farrell, Russell & Mueller, Peter. All about Horses & Pets. (p. 42)
Farrell, Steve. What Do You Do on a Rainy Day? Bendoly, Lynne, illus. (p. 1883)
Farrell, Tish. Be a Creative Writer. (p. 148)
—Kenya. (p. 949)
—Write Your Own Fantasy Story (p. 1964)
—Write Your Own Historical Fiction Story (p. 1964)
—Write Your Own Mystery Story (p. 1964)
—Write Your Own Realistic Fiction Story (p. 1964)
—Write Your Own Science Fiction Story (p. 1964)
Farrell-Whelan, Max. Something Fishy Aboard the Red Herring: Can You Catch the Killer? (p. 1609)
Farrelly, Linda. Elliot's Amazing Adventures Number 1. Farrelly, Linda & Hopkins, Simon, illus. (p. 514)
Farren, Rick. Eliza's Wish. (p. 513)
—Grandpa & the Pirate. (p. 709)
—Secret of the Lighthouse. (p. 1542)
Farrens, Brian & Shakespeare, William. King Lear. Allen, Chris, illus. (p. 958)
Farrer, Vashti. Fearsome Creatures. Webb, Melissa, illus. (p. 579)
Farrer, Vashti & Curtis, Neil. Mr. Noah & the Cats. (p. 1186)
Farrey, Brian. Grimjinx Rebellion. Helquist, Brett, illus. (p. 724)
—Shadowhand Covenant. Helquist, Brett, illus. (p. 1558)
—Vengekeep Prophecies. Helquist, Brett, illus. (p. 1835)
—With or Without You. (p. 1942)
Farrington, Karen. Cool Kid's Field Guide to Global Warming. Woollatt, Sue, illus. (p. 363)
Farrington, Karen & Constable, Lewis. Exploring the Magic World of Harry Potter: An Unauthorized Fact Book. (p. 554)
Farrington, Karen & Constable, Nick. Build Your Own Steam Locomotive: A Complete, Easy-to-Assemble Model. Osborne, Graham, illus. (p. 238)
Farrington, S. Kip, Jr. Bill, the Broadbill Swordfish. (p. 187)
Farrington, Teresa, illus. see Huxman, K. D.
Farrington Wilson, Lynda. Autistic? How Silly Is That! I Don't Need Any Labels at All. (p. 117)
—Squirmy Wormy: How I Learned to Help Myself. (p. 1637)
Farris, Cary Bob. Pig & the Pearl. (p. 1357)
Farris, Cat, illus. see Reger, Rob & Huehner, Mariah.
Farris, Christine King. March On! The Day My Brother Martin Changed the World. Ladd, London, illus. (p. 1091)
—My Brother Martin: A Sister Remembers Growing up with the Rev. Dr. Martin Luther King Jr. Soentpiet, Chris K., illus. (p. 1199)
Farris, D. & Brookes, Kate. Activators Cartooning. (p. 10)
Farris, John & King, Stephen. The Ransome Women - The Things They Left Behind. McBain, Ed, ed. (p. 1728)
Farris, Judy. Mr Boo Bear. Farris, Michael, illus. (p. 1184)
Farris, Katherine, jt. auth. see Hendry, Linda.
Farris, Kim, illus. see Cantrell, Pete.
Farris, Michael, illus. see Farris, Judy.
Farrow, Clare, jt. auth. see Yue, Gui.
Farrow, Clare, jt. auth. see Yue, Guo.
Farrow, G. & Farrow, George. Mysterious Shin Shira. (p. 1223)
Farrow, G. E., jt. auth. see Farrow, G. e.
Farrow, G. e. & Farrow, G. E. Wallypug in London. (p. 1855)
Farrow, George, jt. auth. see Farrow, G.
Farrow, George Edward. Mysterious Shin Shira. Easton, W. G., illus. (p. 1223)
Farrow, Nancy L. Lucas & Leroy Schoonmaker, Christina, illus. (p. 1062)
Farrow, Stephanie, ed. Blue Wolf & Friends Storybook (p. 203)
Farruggia, M. E. Lost Memories. (p. 1056)
Farseth, Erik. American Rock: Guitar Heroes, Punks, & Metalheads. (p. 63)
Farshtey, Greg. American Revolution. (p. 63)
—Attack of the Crocodiles. (p. 113)
—Beware of the Wolves. (p. 173)
—Challenge of Samukai. Henrique, Paulo, illus. (p. 289)
—Cole - Ninja of Earth. (p. 339)
—Collision Course (p. 341)
—Collision Course. (p. 341)
—Danger in the Outlands. (p. 404)
—Destiny of Doom. (p. 431)
—Discos de Poder. (p. 447)
—Doom Box. (p. 470)
—Face Off: Makuro's Secret Guidebook. Scholastic, Inc. Staff, illus. (p. 560)
—Fire & Ice. (p. 590)
—Gorillas Gone Bananas (p. 703)
—Gorillas Gone Bananas. (p. 703)
—Jay - Ninja of Lightning (p. 910)
—Kai - Ninja of Fire (p. 941)
—Kingdom of the Snakes. (p. 960)
—Kingdom of the Snakes. Lee, Paul & Yates, Jolyon, illus. (p. 960)
—"Kingdom of the Snakes" Lee, Paul & Yates, Jolyon, illus. (p. 960)
—Legion of Darkness. (p. 990)
—Lego DC Superheroes. (p. 990)
—LEGO DC Superheroes Guidebook. (p. 990)
—LEGO Hero Factory: Faceoff! Makuro's Secret Guidebook. (p. 990)
—LEGO Legends of Chima: Fire & Ice. Ameet Studio, Ameet, illus. (p. 990)
—LEGO Legends of Chima: Danger in the Outlands (Chapter Book #5) Ameet Studio Staff, illus. (p. 990)
—Lego Ninjago Official Guide. (p. 990)
—LEGO(r) Ninjago - It All Begins Here: With "The Challenge of Samukai" & "The Mask of the Sensei" (p. 990)
—Mask of the Sensei. (p. 1102)
—Mask of the Sensei. Henrique, Paulo, illus. (p. 1102)
—"Mask of the Sensei" Henrique, Paulo, illus. (p. 1102)
—Mirror World. (p. 1149)
—Ninjago #9. (p. 1256)
—Rise of the Serpentine. (p. 1475)
—Rise of the Serpentine. Henrique, Paulo & Lee, Paul, illus. (p. 1475)
—Robot Rampage. (p. 1480)
—Stone Cold. (p. 1652)
—Stone Cold. Yates, Jolyon, illus. (p. 1652)
—Tomb of the Fangpyre. (p. 1764)
—Tomb of the Fangpyre. Henrique, Paulo & Yates, Jolyon, illus. (p. 1764)
—Warrior Within. Ameet Studio Staff, illus. (p. 1859)
—Warriors of Stone. (p. 1859)
—Warriors of Stone. Yates, Jolyon, illus. (p. 1859)
—Way of the Ninja. (p. 1864)
Farshtey, Greg, jt. auth. see Lipkowitz, Daniel.
Farshtey, Greg, jt. auth. see Scholastic, Inc. Staff.
Farshtey, Greg & Bolinaga Irasuegui, Iñigo. Misterio de Metru Nui. Perez, Mercedes Dominguez, tr. (p. 1155)
Farshtey, Greg & Lee, Paul. Lego Ninjago Special Edition #2: With Rise of the Serpentine & Tomb of the Fangpyre. Yates, Jolyon, illus. (p. 990)
Farshtey, Greg & Lipkowitz, Daniel. LEGO(r) Minifigure Year by Year: A Visual History. (p. 990)
—Lego(r) Minifigure Year by Year: A Visual History. (p. 990)
Farshtey, Greg & Scholastic, Inc. Staff. Zane - Ninja of Ice. (p. 1984)
Farshtey, Greg & Yates, Jolyon. Comet Crisis. (p. 348)
—LEGO Ninjago #11: Comet Crisis. (p. 990)
—Lego Ninjago Special Edition #3: With Kingdom of the Snakes & Warriors of Stone. (p. 990)
—Phantom Ninja. (p. 1349)
Faruqi, Reem. Lailah's Lunchbox Lyon, Lea, illus. (p. 972)
Farwell, Nick. Minecraft. Burlinson, James & Cordner, Theo, illus. (p. 1146)
—Minecraft: Redstone Handbook (Updated Edition) An Official Mojang Book. (p. 1146)
Faryon, Cynthia J. Real Justice: Guilty of Being Weird: The Story of Guy Paul Morin (p. 1448)
—Sentenced to Life at Seventeen: The Story of David Milgaard (p. 1551)
Fasbinder, George, illus. see Fasbinder, Susie.
Fasbinder, Susie. Boy Who Loves Weather. Fasbinder, George & Jones, Bill, illus. (p. 219)
—I Want to Dress Up. (p. 848)
Faschi, Silvia, illus. see McLean, Linda.
Fashenpour, David R. Snowflake Evolution: A Journey to Aldebaran. (p. 1600)
Fasick, Tracy. Reading Response Road Maps: Comprehension-Boosting Reproducibles for 50 Favorite Picture Books That Guide Children to Stop & Think as They Read. (p. 1446)
Fass, Amanda L. Farm Friends. Swope, Brenda, illus. (p. 574)
Fass, Gertrude. Love among the Centralians. Landes, William-Alan, ed. (p. 1059)
Fass, Tara. Turtlebird's Double Dip Shuffle. Conn, Alexandra, illus. (p. 1798)
Fassio, Dan & Burns, Adam. Washington & Lee University College Prowler off the Record. (p. 1859)
Fassler, Larry. Como Defender Tus Cargos Federales: Manual Para Acusados Arrestados Por los Federales. (p. 350)
Fast, April. Iran: The People. (p. 886)
—Iraq: The Land. (p. 887)
—Iraq: The Culture. (p. 887)
—Iraq - The Culture. (p. 887)
—Iraq - The Land. (p. 887)
—Iraq - The People. (p. 887)
Fast, April, jt. auth. see Hughes, Susan.
Fast, April & Richter, Joanne. Iran - The Land. (p. 886)
Fast, David R. Doctor Dave's Dragon Tales. Ciesinska, Izabela, illus. (p. 459)
Fast, Gerald R., jt. auth. see Hankes, Judith E.
Fast, Howard. Freedom Road. (p. 635)
Fast, Julie A. & Preston, John D. Take Charge of Bipolar Disorder: A 4-Step Plan for You & Your Loved Ones to Manage the Illness & Create Lasting Stability. (p. 1696)
Fast, Suellen M. America's Daughters. Fast, Suellen M., photos by. (p. 64)
—Golden-Brown Baby Bear & the Three Sisters. Serman, Gina L., ed. (p. 694)
Fastback Romance Staff. Mystery Fastbacks (p. 1224)
—Romance Fastbacks (p. 1486)
Fastje, Shanaya B. Mystery School: Monday Sleepover Disaster. (p. 1226)
—Mystery School. (p. 1226)
Fata, Heather. Pledge of Allegiance. (p. 1373)
Fath, Teresa. Train Track Trolley & the Bell Dogs. (p. 1777)
Fatio, Louise. Doll for Marie. Duvoisin, Roger, illus. (p. 463)
—Happy Lion. Duvoisin, Roger, illus. (p. 746)
Fattah, Hala & Caso, Frank. Iraq. (p. 887)
Fattah, Hala Mundhir, et al. Brief History of Iraq. (p. 227)
Fatus. Story Tree Gift Wrap (Loose) (p. 1663)
Fatus, Sophie. Hen, a Chick & a String Guitar. (p. 767)
—Here We Go Round the Mulberry Bush. (p. 771)
—"Monkey business" (The Story Tree) (p. 1165)
—Story Tree Artist Card Portfolio. (p. 1663)
—"Tray-bla, tray-bla, cum qua, kimo" (The Story Tree) (p. 1781)
Fatus, Sophie, illus. see Baptiste, Baron.
Fatus, Sophie, illus. see Flor Ada, Alma.
Fatus, Sophie, illus. see Lumley, Jemima & Penner, Fred.
Fatus, Sophie, illus. see Lumley, Jemima.
Fatus, Sophie, illus. see Lupton, Hugh.
Fatus, Sophie, illus. see MacDonald, Margaret Read.
Fatus, Sophie, illus. see McQuinn, Anna.
Fatus, Sophie, illus. see Parnell, Fran.
Fatus, Sophie, illus. see Penner, Fred.
Fatus, Sophie, illus. see Roberts, Sheena & Horn, Sandra Ann.
Fatus, Sophie, illus. see Weston, Carrie.
Fatus, Sophie, illus. see Williams, Brenda & Barefoot Books Staff.
Fatus, Sophie, illus. see Williams, Brenda.
Fatus, Sophie, illus. see Ziefert, Harriet & Davis, Samantha A.
Fatus, Sophie, illus. see Ziefert, Harriet.
Fatus, Sophie, jt. auth. see Kalish, Leah.
Fatus, Sophie, jt. auth. see Mcdonald, Jill.
Fatus, Sophie, jt. auth. see McQuinn, Anna.
Fatus, Sophie, jt. auth. see Parnell, Fran.
Fatus, Sophie, jt. auth. see Williams, Brenda.
Fatus, Sophie & Barefoot Books. My Big Barefoot Book of Wonderful Words. Fatus, Sophie, illus. (p. 1197)
Fatus, Sophie & Penner, Fred. Here We Go Round the Mulberry Bush. Fatus, Sophie, illus. (p. 771)
Fatus, Sophie, et al. Yoga Pretzels: 50 Fun Yoga Activities for Kids & Grownups. Fatus, Sophie, illus. (p. 1972)
Fauchald, Nick. Batter Up! You Can Play Softball Rooney, Ronnie, illus. (p. 145)
—Funky Chicken Enchiladas: And Other Mexican Dishes Rooney, Ronnie, illus. (p. 649)
—Holy Guacamole! And Other Scrumptious Snacks. Peterson, Rick, illus. (p. 791)
—Keep on Rollin' Meatballs: And Other Delicious Dinners. Peterson, Rick, illus. (p. 947)
—Kids Dish Peterson, Rick, illus. (p. 953)
—On-the-Go Schwarmas: And Other Middle-Eastern Dishes. Rooney, Ronnie, illus. (p. 1290)
—Puffy Popovers: And Other Get-Out-of-Bed Breakfasts. Peterson, Rick, illus. (p. 1415)
—Roly-Poly Ravioli: And Other Italian Dishes Rooney, Ronnie, illus. (p. 1485)
—Wrap-N-Bake Egg Rolls: And Other Chinese Dishes. Rooney, Ronnie, illus. (p. 1962)
Fauche, Xavier, jt. auth. see Léturgie, Jean.
Faucher, Wayne, illus. see Johns, Geoff.
Faucheux, Guy N. & Faucheux, Wallace P. Cajun Comiques Historic Louisiana: An Illustrated History for Kids of All Ages. (p. 252)
Faucheux, Wallace P., jt. auth. see Faucheux, Guy N.
Faul, Nicole. Great Animal Race & Trap the Angry Elephant Finds a Friend. (p. 713)
Faul, Pamela. Tc's Big Game. (p. 1708)
Faulconer, Charlotte. Green Button Wish. (p. 721)
Faulconer, Maria Fasal. Mom for Umande. Hartung, Susan Kathleen, illus. (p. 1161)
Faulconer, Nancy, creator. Living with Children & Horses: A Parent's Guide to Natural Horsemanship & Children. (p. 1042)
Faulconer-Lippert, Gwin, jt. auth. see Hines, Erin.
Faulk, Michelle. Case of the Flesh-Eating Bacteria: Annie Biotica Solves Skin Disease Crimes. (p. 274)
—Case of the Infected Tick: Annie Biotica Solves Circulatory System Disease Crimes. (p. 274)
—Case of the Rusty Nail: Annie Biotica Solves Nervous System Disease Crimes. (p. 275)
—Case of the Sneezy Popcorn: Annie Biotica Solves Respiratory System Disease Crimes. (p. 275)
—Case of the Undercooked Burger: Annie Biotica Solves Digestive System Disease Crimes. (p. 275)
—Gun Crimes: Dead People Do Tell Tales. (p. 732)
Faulk, Richard. Next Big Thing: A History of the Boom-Or-Bust Moments That Shaped the Modern World. (p. 1249)
Faulk, Terry. Joe the Roadside Crow. (p. 920)
Faulkerson, Jeffery A. It's Good to Be Golden: The Stranger in the Shadows. (p. 897)
Faulkerson, President & CEO Jeffery, Founder. IT's GOOD to BE GOLDEN: Golden Innovations. (p. 897)
—IT's GOOD to BE GOLDEN: the Story of Henry the Heart. (p. 897)
Faulkner, Danny. Universe by Design. (p. 1820)
Faulkner, Deborah. Two Magic Blankets from Granny Hannah with Love. (p. 1804)
Faulkner, Georgene. Flying Ship: Fairy Tales from the World Over. Richardson, Frederick & Becker, Charlotte, illus. (p. 610)
—Gingerbread Boy: Fairy Tales from the World Over. Winter, Milo & Becker, Charlotte, illus. (p. 677)
—Little Red Hen & the Fox: Fairy Tales from the World Over. Winter, Milo & Becker, Charlotte, illus. (p. 1034)
—Red Cross Stories for Children. (p. 1453)
—Snow Maiden: Fairy Tales from the World Over. Richardson, Frederick & Becker, Charlotte, illus. (p. 1599)
—Squeaky & the Scare Box: Fairy Tales from the World Over. Richardson, Frederick & Becker, Charlotte, illus. (p. 1636)
Faulkner, Keith. Charlie Chimp's Christmas: A Pop-up Extravaganza of Festive Friends. Lambert, Jonathan, illus. (p. 293)
—Flip-Flap Math: Flip the Flpas to Check Your Answers! Irish, Martin, illus. (p. 604)
—Maths Machine: A Fun New Way to Do Maths! Tyger, Rory, illus. (p. 1108)
—Mummy's Little Monkey! Smith, Eric, illus. (p. 1191)
—Who's Home? McEwan, Joseph, illus. (p. 1920)
Faulkner, Keith, jt. auth. see Ciminera, Siobhan.
Faulkner, Keith & Holmes, Stephen. Animal ? Math. Faulkner, Keith & Holmes, Stephen, illus. (p. 76)
Faulkner, Keith & Tyger, Rory. Time's Up! Faulkner, Keith & Tyger, Rory, illus. (p. 1754)
Faulkner, Matt. Gaijin: American Prisoner of War. (p. 652)
—My First Book of Bedtime Prayers. Faulkner, Matthew & Faulkner, Matt, illus. (p. 1205)
—Taste of Colored Water. (p. 1707)
—Taste of Colored Water. Faulkner, Matt, illus. (p. 1707)
Faulkner, Matt, illus. see Anderson, Laurie Halse.
Faulkner, Matt, illus. see Bunting, Eve.
Faulkner, Matt, illus. see Davis, Kenneth C.
Faulkner, Matt, illus. see Hagen, Carol L.
Faulkner, Matt, illus. see Schnitzlein, Danny.
Faulkner, Matt, illus. see Shapiro, Karen Jo.
Faulkner, Matt, illus. see St. George, Judith.
Faulkner, Matt, jt. auth. see St. George, Judith.
Faulkner, Matthew, illus. see Faulkner, Matt.
Faulkner, Michael H. Pearl Necklace: Miss Kitty Mysteries. (p. 1333)
Faulkner, Nicholas & Daniel, Susanna. Lois Lowry. (p. 1045)
Faulkner, Nicholas & Sherman, Josepha. Ear in 3D. (p. 492)
—Soccer: Girls Rocking It. (p. 1603)
Faulkner, Nicholas & Williams, Kara. Conquering Diet Drug Abuse. (p. 358)
Faulkner, Rebecca. Crystals (p. 387)
—Fossils (p. 623)
—Igneous Rock (p. 856)
—Metamorphic Rock (p. 1130)
—Minerals (p. 1146)
—Sedimentary Rock (p. 1546)
—Soil (p. 1606)
Faulkner, Rhiannon. Talking about Grief, with Brian & the Faulkner Fairies. (p. 1703)
Faulkner, Shirley. Rusty's First Day of School. (p. 1498)
Faulkner, Stacey, ed. see Callella, Kim & Williams, Rozanne Lanczak.
Faulkner, Stacey, ed. see Callella, Kim.
Faulkner, Stacey, ed. see Callella, Trisha.
Faulkner, Stacey, ed. see Cernak, Kim & Williams, Rozanne Lanczak.
Faulkner, Stacey, ed. see Cernak, Kim.
Faulkner, Stacey, ed. see Cernek, Kim & Williams, Rozanne Lanczak.
Faulkner, Stacey, ed. see Cernek, Kim.
Faulkner, Stacey, ed. see Leto, Frank & Scelsa, Greg.
Faulkner, Stacey, ed. see Lubben, Amy & Williams, Rozanne Lanczak.
Faulkner, Stacey, ed. see Scelsa, Greg & Debney, John.
Faulkner, Stacey, ed. see Scelsa, Greg.
Faulkner, Stacey, ed. see Shiotsu, Vicky.
Faulkner, Stacey, ed. see Smith, Laura R. & Fearis, J. S.
Faulkner, Stacey, ed. see Williams, Rozanne Lanczak.
Faulkner, Stacey, jt. auth. see Williams, Rozanne Lanczak.
Faulks, Rebecca Rachel. Curtains Ate My Grandma. (p. 395)
Faundez, Anne. Animals in Danger. (p. 83)
—Cloak for Swallow (p. 333)
—Day the Rains Fell. Littlewood, Karin, illus. (p. 414)
—Imaginary Creatures (p. 860)
—One, Two, Buckle My Shoe. (p. 1297)
—Sea Ceatures. (p. 1534)
—Sing a Song of Sixpence (p. 1578)
—Teddy's Birthday. (p. 1713)
—Tiddalik the Frog. (p. 1747)
—When I'm a Grown-Up. (p. 1903)
Faundez, Anne, ed. Little Red Riding Hood. (p. 1035)
Faundez, Anne, et al. QEB Start Reading Multipack (6 Titles) Paperback (p. 1422)
Faure, Florence, illus. see Spilsbury, Richard.
Faure, Florence, jt. auth. see Hunter, Nick.
Faurot, Kimberly. Mother Goose Rhyme Time Animals. Cox, Steve, illus. (p. 1178)
—Mother Goose Rhyme Time Night. Cox, Steve, illus. (p. 1178)

F

—Mother Goose Rhyme Time People. Cox, Steve, illus. (p. 1178)
Fauroux, et al. Las Desgracias De Marcelo, El Mochuelo. (p. 976)
Fauske, Tore. Sid. (p. 1572)
Faust, Andrea. Pennies from Heaven: The Legend of the Penny. (p. 1337)
Faust, Anke, illus. see Sansone, Adele.
Faust, Daniel R. After Earth: Living on a Different Planet. (p. 28)
—Cambio Climático: Los Gases de Efecto Invernadero y la Capa de Ozono. Obregón, José María, illus. (p. 255)
—Career As an FBI Special Agent. (p. 266)
—Collision Course: Asteroids & Earth. (p. 341)
—Desastres Ecológicos: Los Derrames de Petróleo y el Medio Ambiente = Sinister Sludge: Oil Spills & the Environment. (p. 428)
—Energy Crisis: The Future of Fossil Fuels. (p. 528)
—Global Warming: Greenhouse Gases & the Ozone Layer. (p. 684)
—Más Allá de la Tierra: Vivir en Otro Planeta. (p. 1101)
—Sinister Sludge: Oil Spills & the Environment. (p. 1579)
Faust, Daniel R. & Obregón, José María. Crisis Energética: El Futuro de Los Combustibles Fósiles. (p. 383)
Faust Editors. Faust 2. (p. 577)
Faust Kalscheur, Jann, jt. auth. see Smith, Lynn.
Faust, Laurie. New Home for Honey. (p. 1245)
Faust, Laurie, illus. see Damschroder, Scott.
Faust, Laurie A., illus. see Beadle, David M.
Faust, Laurie A., illus. see Chan, Paul D.
Faust, Laurie A., illus. see Greer, Tom C.
Faust, Laurie A., illus. see Solomon, Michelle & Pereira, Lavinia.
Faust, Laurie A., illus. see The Library Fairy.
Fauteux, Nicole, jt. auth. see Simon, Seymour.
Fautsch, Jackie, illus. see Watson, Gayle.
Favereau, Beatrice, illus. see Allgeier, Steve.
Favole, Robert. Monday Redux. (p. 1163)
Favor, Lesli J. Eukaryotic & Prokaryotic Cell Structures: Understanding Cells with & Without a Nucleus. (p. 540)
—Eva Perón. (p. 540)
—Everything You Need to Know about Growth Spurts & Delayed Growth. (p. 545)
—Food as Foe: Nutrition & Eating Disorders. (p. 613)
—Historical Atlas of America's Manifest Destiny. (p. 782)
—Italy: A Primary Source Cultural Guide. (p. 895)
—Weighing In: Nutrition & Weight Management. (p. 1872)
—Women Doctors & Nurses of the Civil War. (p. 1945)
Favor, Lesli J., jt. auth. see Merchant, Raina G.
Favor, Lesli J. & Freed, Kira. Food As Foe: Nutrition & Eating Disorders. (p. 613)
Favor, Lesli J. & Massie, Elizabeth. Weighing In: Nutrition & Weight Management. (p. 1872)
Favor, Leslie. Everything You Need to Know about Growth Spurts & Delayed Growth. (p. 545)
—Women Doctors & Nurses of the Civil War. (p. 1945)
Favorite Brand Name Recipes Editors, ed. Party Cakes. (p. 1326)
Favorite, Deborah. Tush People. Arinsberg, Norman, illus. (p. 1799)
Favre, Malika, jt. auth. see Pow, Tom.
Favreau, Marie-Claude, illus. see Bertouille, Ariane.
Favreau, Marie-Claude, illus. see Plante, Raymond.
Favrotto, Robert. Cat-Astrophe. (p. 277)
Fawbert, Malcolm. Tales from Thimble Hall Mrs Stopper's Bottle. (p. 1702)
Fawbush, Karla Winther, et al. C'est a Toi! (p. 288)
—C'est a Toi! French Grammar & Vocabulary Exercises (p. 288)
Fawcett, Cheryl & Newman, Robert C. Kids' Questions about Church & the Future. Mazellan, Ron, illus. (p. 955)
—Kids' Questions about God & Jesus. Mazellan, Ron, illus. (p. 955)
—Kids' Questions about Sin & Salvation. (p. 955)
—Kids' Questions about the Bible & Creation. (p. 955)
Fawcett, Jack & Rimes, Raleigh. Dinosaurology. (p. 443)
Fawcett, Katie Pickard. To Come & Go Like Magic. (p. 1758)
Fawcett, Louise & Serrano, Monica. Regionalism & Governance in the Americas: Continental Drift. (p. 1457)
Fawcett, Vicki, illus. see Doupe, Pauline Wood.
Fawkes, Ray. Better House Trap (p. 172)
—Possessions Volume 2: The Ghost Table GN. (p. 1387)
Fax, Mondo. Slam Dunk Small Claims: Laugh Your Way to A Small Claims Win (p. 1587)
Fay, David, illus. see Rushing, John Alan.
Fay, Gail. Battles of the Civil War (p. 147)
—Malcolm X (p. 1083)
—Malcolm X Oxford Bible Staff, illus. (p. 1083)
—Pocahontas (p. 1375)
—Secrets of Mesa Verde: Cliff Dwellings of the Pueblo (p. 1545)
—Using Money (p. 1828)
Fay, Gail, et al. Archaeological Mysteries (p. 95)
Fay, Keith. What's in a Cave? (p. 1897)
Fay, Martha. Rome: 50 Adventures on Foot. (p. 1486)
Fay, Nancy Cartnick. I Wanted a Puppy - Not Fish! (p. 848)
Fay, Nicole. Andy & Armadillo Are Astronauts. (p. 72)
—Brittney & Beario Become Ballerinas. (p. 230)
Faye. Jazzy Shoes. (p. 911)
Faye, Charlet. Chilling Adventures of Marshall McCaw. (p. 305)
Faye, Hannah. Halos' Magic. (p. 739)
Faye, Joanne & Whaley, Stacey Lynn. Conversations with Kids Ages 3 to 6. (p. 361)
Faye Morningstar. Little Dream Athe: The Sand Prince. (p. 1027)
Fayette Writers Guild, contrib. by. Go with Us: Prose & Poetry by Fayette Writers Guild. (p. 687)
Fayetteville Elementary, Students & Staf. Memories of Fayetteville Elementary School. (p. 1126)
Fayman, Corey Lynn. Desert City Diva. (p. 428)
Fayolle, Diane, illus. see Dorison, Guillaume, et al.
Fayon, Robinson. Attitude Change: Kenny's Story. (p. 114)
Fazenbaker, Jo Ann. Daisy & Duke (p. 400)
Fazio, Maria R. Block Party! (p. 200)
Fazio, Michael, illus. see Kopley, Richard.
Fazio, Nicole. Journey of the Sea Glass (p. 928)
Fazio, Nicole, illus. see Hersey, Suzanne Buzby.
Fazio, Nicole, illus. see Villa, Elisabeth.
Fazzi, Cindy. How to Draw Ireland's Sights & Symbols. (p. 817)
—How to Draw Pakistan's Sights & Symbols. (p. 818)
—How to Draw Peru's Sights & Symbols. (p. 818)
—How to Draw the Philippines's Sights & Symbols. (p. 819)
FC and A Publishing Staff, jt. auth. see Wood, Frank K.
Fea, Kenneth Hugh. Astronomy & Beginning Astrophysics. (p. 109)
Fead, Beverlye Hyman, et al. Nana, What's Cancer? Bersani, Shennen, illus. (p. 1228)
Feagan, Robert. Arctic Thunder. (p. 96)
—Mystery at Shildii Rock. (p. 1224)
—Napachee. (p. 1229)
Feagins, Sistah L. E. T. M. E. TELL'YA Bernadine. Hakim & Terrance Shadow Mystery ! (p. 736)
Fear, E. G. Just a Medium Size Frog. (p. 937)
Fear, Sharon, retold by. Sleeping Beauty. (p. 1589)
Fearing, Mark. Dilly Dally Daisy. (p. 440)
—Great Thanksgiving Escape. Fearing, Mark, illus. (p. 718)
Fearing, Mark, illus. see Asher, Sandy.
Fearing, Mark, illus. see Federle, Tim.
Fearing, Mark, illus. see LaRochelle, David.
Fearing, Mark, illus. see McNamara, Margaret.
Fearing, Mark, illus. see Perry, John.
Fearing, Mark, illus. see Shannon, George.
Fearing, Mark & Rummel, Tim. Earthling! (p. 497)
—Earthling. (p. 497)
Fearis, J. S., jt. auth. see Smith, Laura R.
Fearn, Katrina. First Dot-To-Dot Dinosaurs. (p. 594)
—First Dot-To-Dot Pirates. (p. 594)
Fearn, Katrina, illus. see Gilpin, Rebecca.
Fearn, Katrina, illus. see Watt, Fiona & Gilpin, Rebecca.
Fearn, Katrina, illus. see Watt, Fiona.
Fearn, Katrina, jt. auth. see Brooks, Felicity.
Fearn, Laura. Usborne Stories from Shakespeare. Temporin, Elena, illus. (p. 1827)
Fearne, Peter. My Week with Father Christmas. (p. 1221)
Fearn-Lange, Melissa. Beehive Adventures. (p. 157)
Fearnley, Jan. Billy Tibble Moves Out! Fearnley, Jan, illus. (p. 187)
—Light-Fingered Larry. (p. 1015)
—Mr Wolf & the Enormous Turnip. Fearnley, Jan, illus. (p. 1187)
—Mr Wolf's Pancakes. (p. 1187)
—Special Something. (p. 1623)
Fearnley, Jan, illus. see Willis, Jeanne.
Fearns, Georgie & Buster Books Staff. Colour in Kate: Pretty Pictures of the Divine Duchess to Colour & Complete. Fearns, Georgie, illus. (p. 346)
—Dress up One Direction. Fearns, Georgie, illus. (p. 485)
Fearon, Globe. Environmental Science : Energy. (p. 532)
Fearon Globe Staff, ed. see Shakespeare, William.
Fearon, Merrill, illus. see Hamilton, Jen, ed.
Fearon Staff. Biology. (p. 189)
—Chamber of Horrors. (p. 289)
—Crime & Detection: Skillchecks (p. 382)
—Dracula. (p. 476)
—Environmental Science. (p. 532)
—Fearon's Biology. (p. 579)
—Gulliver's Travels. (p. 731)
—Phantom of the Opera. (p. 1349)
Fearon Staff & Janus. Under Western Skies. (p. 1814)
Fears, Melissa. Thank God It's Sunday. (p. 1725)
Feasel, PaPa. Bloop Bloop. Lewis, Robert, illus. (p. 202)
Feasey, Don. Therapy: Intimacy Between Strangers. (p. 1729)
Feasey, Steve. Blood Wolf: Wereling Book #3. (p. 200)
—Dark Moon. (p. 407)
—Mutant City. (p. 1194)
—Wereling. (p. 1875)
Feaster, Raven Joye Raye. Merrileggs of Macon County. (p. 1128)
Feather, Tami Flaming. Wondrous World of Home. Porter, Tammy, illus. (p. 1949)
FeatherHill, Annaha. Little Britches. (p. 1025)
Featherstone, Mark. Computer Games Designer: The Coolest Jobs on the Planet (p. 354)
Feazell, Matt. Amazing Cynicalman Feazell, Matt, illus. (p. 54)
—Amazing Cynicalman. (p. 54)
Fecher, Sarah. Animales Salvajes: Wild Animals. (p. 81)
Fecher, Sarah & Oliver, Clare. Freaky Facts about Natural Disasters. Anderson, Jill, ed. (p. 632)
Fechner, Maggie. Growing Up Gracie. (p. 726)
Fedatova, Marina. 12 Elves: A New Christmas Tradition. (p. 1994)
Fedderesen, Jill. Very Best Friend There Ever Could Be. Sabanski, Helen, illus. (p. 1837)
Feder, Aliza & Sofer, Rochel. We Need to Talk. (p. 1867)
Feder, Debbie, jt. auth. see Kelly, Kathy.
Feder, Jane. Little Kitty. Schwartz, Amy, illus. (p. 1030)
—Little Puppy. Schwartz, Amy, illus. (p. 1034)
—Spooky Friends. (p. 1631)
—Spooky Friends. Downing, Julie, illus. (p. 1631)
—Spooky Friends, Level 2. Downing, Julie, illus. (p. 1631)
Feder, Joel A. Kokomo Superhero. (p. 966)
—Kokomo's Halloween Adventure. (p. 966)
—Legend of Sidney Snowflake. (p. 988)
Feder, Joshua B. Pirates. (p. 1363)
Federation of Ontario Naturalists, jt. auth. see Hickman, Pamela.
Federer, Jessica Joy. Bobby Bacteria & Friends: Inside UR Body Books Presents. (p. 206)
Federici, Diane Marie. Christmas Stocking. (p. 315)
Federico, Julie. Bad Guys: A Students/Teachers Guide to School Safety & Violence Prevention. (p. 131)
Federico, Julie K. Anger Is Okay Violence Is NOT. (p. 75)
—Friends Are Wonderful. (p. 638)
Federle, Tim. Better Nate Than Ever. (p. 172)
—Five, Six, Seven, Nate! (p. 601)
—Tommy Can't Stop! Fearing, Mark, illus. (p. 1764)
Fedhar. Como Dibujar Personajes Magicos. Fedhar, illus. (p. 350)
Fedi Hagan, Suzanne. Kiwi the Chameleon. (p. 963)
Fedigan-Linton, Katherine V., illus. see Froimowitz, Michael P.
Fedorchek, Robert M., jt. tr. see Castroviejo, Concha.
Fedorko, Jamie. Charles Barkley. (p. 291)
—Kevin Garnett. (p. 950)
Fedorov, Valentin, illus. see Herman, Mark & Apter, Ronnie, trs.
Fedorovich, Debbie. Adventures of Sheila the Therapy Dog. (p. 22)
Fedoruk, Dennis, prod. Bilingual Baby - Flashcard Set - French. (p. 186)
—Bilingual Baby - Flashcard Set - Italian. (p. 186)
—Bilingual Baby - Flashcard Set - Japanese. (p. 186)
Fedotova, Marina, illus. see Guest, Elissa Haden.
Fedunkiw, Marianne. Inventing the Radio. (p. 883)
Fedyszyn, Kirra. Molly Brown. (p. 1160)
—Molly Pitcher. (p. 1161)
Fee, Deb. Life & Times of Sir Ear Alot. (p. 1008)
Fee, J. M. Amazing Adventures of Phineas Screwdriver. (p. 52)
Fee, Jim, illus. see Long, Mark A.
Feehan, Christine. Dangerous Tides. (p. 404)
—Oceans of Fire. (p. 1277)
—Predatory Game. (p. 1395)
Feehan, Mary Edward. Mary's Rainbow. (p. 1101)
Feehan-Vileria, Elaine. Legend of Old Mr. Clarke. (p. 988)
Feek, Cathy, illus. see Richardson, Dick.
Feeley, Kathleen. Illinois. Porras, Carlos & D'Andrea, Patricia, trs. from ENG. (p. 857)
Feeley, Kathleen, jt. auth. see Elias, Megan.
Feeley, Kathleen, et al. Nueva York. (p. 1270)
Feeley, Lisa. SpendRight: Need to Know Money Basics from A to Z: the Smart Start for Students. (p. 1625)
Feelings, Muriel L. Moja Means One: A Swahili Counting Book. Feelings, Tom, illus. (p. 1160)
Feelings, Tom, illus. see Feelings, Muriel L.
Feelings, Tom, illus. see Lester, Julius.
Feely, Eliza. Peka-Boo - The Smallest Bird in All the World. Feely, Eliza, illus. (p. 1335)
Feely, Jenny. Forest. (p. 618)
—Looking after Baby Animals. (p. 1050)
Feely, Maria Luisa, tr. see Andersen, Hans Christian & Capstone Press Staff.
Feeney, Betsy Franco, illus. see Lavin, Christine.
Feeney, Kathryn, ed. see Lavin, Christine & Franco-Feeney, Betsy.
Feeney, Kathy. Alabama. (p. 33)
—Caring for Your Ferret (p. 269)
—Caring for Your Gerbil (p. 269)
—Marco Polo: Explorer of China. (p. 1092)
—Rhode Island Facts & Symbols. (p. 1468)
—Sharp Shooters. Underwood, Kay Povelite, illus. (p. 1563)
—Sleep Well: Why You Need to Rest. (p. 1588)
—Tennessee Facts & Symbols. (p. 1720)
—Those Amazing Alligators. Weaver, Steve, illus. (p. 1740)
Feeney, Rik. Cheerleading Conditioning for Back Hands. (p. 296)
Feeney, Siri, illus. see Mead, Maggie.
Feeney, Siri Weber, illus. see Allen, Kathy.
Feeney, Siri Weber, illus. see Mortensen, Lori.
Feeney, Stephanie. Sun & Rain: Exploring Seasons in Hawai'i. (p. 1676)
Feeney, Tatyana. Little Frog's Tadpole Trouble. (p. 1028)
—Little Owl's Orange Scarf. (p. 1033)
—Small Bunny's Blue Blanket. (p. 1592)
—Small Elephant's Bathtime. (p. 1592)
Feeney, Tatyana, illus. see Deeley, Patrick.
Feeney, Tatyana, jt. auth. see Ní Mhurchú, Caitríona.
Fefie, Flora, jt. auth. see Johnson, Sandi.
Feher, Joseph & Kane, Herb K. Hawai'i. (p. 755)
Fehl, Pamela. Business & Construction. (p. 244)
—Communication, Education, & Travel. (p. 349)
—Environment & Natural Resources. (p. 532)
—Law, Government, & Public Safety. (p. 981)
—Science. (p. 1524)
Fehl, Pamela, jt. auth. see Clark, Richard.
Fehlau, Dagmar, illus. see Bunting, Eve.
Fehlau, Dagmar, illus. see DePrisco, Dorothea.
Fehlau, Dagmar, illus. see Hopkins, Lee Bennett.
Fehlbaum, Beth. Big Fat Disaster. (p. 181)
—Hope in Patience. (p. 796)
Fehler, Gene. Beanball. (p. 150)
—Cutoff Play. (p. 396)
—Forced Out. (p. 617)
—Never Blame the Umpire (p. 1242)
Fehling, Leslie, illus. see Ridenour, Melissa Harker.
Fehr, Sheryl. Luke Helps Out. (p. 1064)
Fehr, Signe. Mama Always Comes Back. (p. 1084)
Fehrenbach, Heather. Go to Sleep Dinosaurs. (p. 687)
Fehrenbach, T. R. Lone Star: The Story of Texas. (p. 1046)
Fei, Kanara. Kalani's Wish. (p. 941)
Fei, Wang, illus. see Sellier, Marie.
Feierabend, John. First Steps in Music Vocal Development Kit. (p. 597)
Feierabend, John M. Book of Beginning Circle Games: Let's Make a Circle. (p. 211)
—Book of Call & Response. Caton, Tim, illus. (p. 211)
—Book of Children's Song Tales. Caton, Tim, illus. (p. 211)
—Book of Echo Songs. Caton, Tim, illus. (p. 211)
—Book of Finger Plays & Action Songs. (p. 211)
—Book of Pitch Exploration: Can Your Voice Do This? (p. 211)
—Book of Song Dances. (p. 211)
—Book of Song Tales for Upper Grades. (p. 211)
—Book of Songs & Rhymes with Beat Motions: Let's Clap Our Hands Together. (p. 211)
—Oh, in the Woods. (p. 1280)
—Other Day I Met a Bear. Miller, Julia Love, illus. (p. 1306)
—Pitch Exploration Pathways. (p. 1364)
—Pitch Exploration Stories. (p. 1364)
—Tailor & the Mouse. McGann, James, illus. (p. 1695)
Feierabend, John M. & Kahan, Jane. Book of Movement Exploration: Can You Move Like This? (p. 211)
Feierabend, John M. & Poulin, Ashley. Risseldy, Rosseldy. (p. 1475)
Feiffer, Jules. Bark, George. (p. 139)
—By the Side of the Road. (p. 249)
—Daddy Mountain. (p. 398)
—House Across the Street. Feiffer, Jules, illus. (p. 803)
—I'm Not Bobby! Feiffer, Jules, illus. (p. 859)
—Room with a Zoo. Feiffer, Jules, illus. (p. 1488)
—Rupert Can Dance. Feiffer, Jules, illus. (p. 1497)
Feiffer, Jules, illus. see Duffy, Chris, ed.
Feiffer, Jules, illus. see Feiffer, Kate.
Feiffer, Jules, illus. see Heide, Florence Parry.
Feiffer, Jules, illus. see Juster, Norton.
Feiffer, Jules, illus. see Kobliner Shaw, Beth & Shaw, Jacob.
Feiffer, Jules, illus. see Lowry, Lois.
Feiffer, Kate. But I Wanted a Baby Brother! Goode, Diane, illus. (p. 246)
—Double Pink. Ingman, Bruce, illus. (p. 473)
—Henry the Dog with No Tail. Feiffer, Jules, illus. (p. 768)
—My Mom Is Trying to Ruin My Life. Goode, Diane, illus. (p. 1214)
—My Side of the Car. Feiffer, Jules, illus. (p. 1218)
—No Go Sleep! Feiffer, Jules, illus. (p. 1258)
—President Pennybaker. Goode, Diane, illus. (p. 1397)
—President Pennybaker. Glasser, Robin Preiss & Goode, Diane, illus. (p. 1397)
—Problem with the Puddles. Tusa, Tricia, illus. (p. 1408)
—Signed by Zelda. (p. 1574)
—Which Puppy? Feiffer, Kate & Feiffer, Jules, illus. (p. 1911)
—Wild, Wild Inside: A View from Mommy's Tummy! Hulliska-Beith, Laura, illus. (p. 1930)
Feigenbaum, Aaron. American Alligators: Freshwater Survivors. (p. 59)
—Emergency at Three Mile Island. (p. 518)
—Hindenburg Disaster. (p. 780)
Feigh, Alison. I Can Play It Safe. Logan, Laura, illus. (p. 836)
Feigin, Misha. Last Word in Astronomy. Zengin-Karaian, Victoria & Zengin-Karaian, Alex, eds. (p. 979)
Feil, Denise J. Praze B. a Growing, Loving Day: Forgiveness & Responsibility. Feil, Denise J., illus. (p. 1393)
Feil, Hila. Blue Moon. (p. 203)
Feiler, Bruce. Abraham: A Journey to the Heart of Three Faiths. (p. 6)
—Walking the Bible: An Illustrated Journey for Kids Through the Greatest Stories Ever Told. Meret, Sasha, tr. (p. 1854)
Fein, E. How to Draw Nevada's Sights & Symbols. (p. 818)
—How to Draw New York's Sights & Symbols. (p. 818)
—How to Draw Oklahoma's Sights & Symbols. (p. 818)
—How to Draw Puerto Rico's Sights & Symbols. (p. 818)
—How to Draw Utah's Sights & Symbols. (p. 819)
—How to Draw West Virginia's Sights & Symbols. (p. 819)
Fein, Ellen & Schneider, Sherrie. All the Rules: Time-Tested Secrets for Capturing the Heart of Mr. Right. (p. 46)
Fein, Eric. D-Day: The Battle of Normandy (p. 397)
—Fisherman & the Genie Garcia, Eduardo, illus. (p. 599)
—High Noon: Wild Bill Hickok & the Code of the Old West. (p. 778)
—Impossible Victory: The Battle of Stalingrad. (p. 862)
—Mystery at Manzanar: A WWII Internment Camp Story Hartman, Kurt, illus. (p. 1223)
—Outnumbered: Davy Crockett's Final Battle at the Alamo. (p. 1313)
—U. S. Congress Bascle, Brian, illus. (p. 1806)
—USS Greeneville Submarine Disaster: When Disaster Strikes! (p. 1829)
—USS Greeneville Submarine Disaster. (p. 1829)
—Vehicles of World War II (p. 1834)
—Weapons, Gear, & Uniforms of the Civil War (p. 1869)
—Weapons, Gear, & Uniforms of World War I (p. 1869)
Fein, Eric & Fuentes, Benny. Skateboard Breakdown Sandoval, Gerardo, illus. (p. 1583)
—Wild Pitch Sandoval, Gerardo, illus. (p. 1930)
Fein, Eric & Loughridge, Lee. My Frozen Valentine Schigiel, Gregg, illus. (p. 1209)
Fein, Eric, et al. Catwoman's Halloween Heist (p. 281)
—Maker of Monsters (p. 1080)
—Parasite's Power Drain McManus, Shawn, illus. (p. 1324)
—War Vehicles. (p. 1858)
Feinberg, Jennifer. Chi. (p. 299)
Feinberg, Margaret. Text Messages from God for Girls Only. (p. 1724)
Feinberg, Margaret & Gillespie, Natalie. Text Messages from God for Guys Only. (p. 1724)
—Text Messages from God for Kids. (p. 1724)
Feinberg, Xeth, illus. see Reiss, Mike.
Feinglass, Arthur. Lonesome Dreidel: A Chanukah Adventure. Florendo, R. M., illus. (p. 1046)
Feinman, Anthony & Hall, Andrew. Escape in a Dirigible: Or to Make the World Safe for Tea. Feinman, Anthony et al, illus. (p. 535)
Feinman, Larry J. Malpractice. (p. 1084)
Feinman, Myke, photos by see Feinman, Anthony & Hall, Andrew.
Feinmann, Jane. Everything a Girl Needs to Know about Her PeriodS. (p. 544)
Feinstein, Barbara & Cavanaugh, Catherine. New Volunteerism: A Community Connection. (p. 1247)
Feinstein, Edward. Tough Questions Jews Ask: A Young Adult's Guide to Building a Jewish Life. (p. 1772)
Feinstein, John. Change-Up. (p. 290)
—Cover-Up. (p. 373)
—Foul Trouble. (p. 624)
—Last Shot - Mystery at the Final Four. (p. 978)
—Open: Inside the Ropes at Bethpage Black. (p. 1299)
—Punch: One Night, Two Lives, & the Fight That Changed Basketball Forever. (p. 1416)
—Rush for the Gold: Mystery at the Olympics. (p. 1498)
—Sixth Man (the Triple Threat, 2) (p. 1583)
—Vanishing Act: Mystery at the U. S. Open. (p. 1833)
—Walk On. (p. 1853)
—Walk on (the Triple Threat, 1) (p. 1854)
Feinstein, Stephen. 1900s. (p. 2002)
—1900s from Teddy Roosevelt to Flying Machines. (p. 2002)
—1910s. (p. 2002)
—1910s from World War I to Ragtime Music. (p. 2002)
—1920s. (p. 2002)
—1920s from Prohibition to Charles Lindbergh. (p. 2002)

—1930s. (p. 2002)
—1930s from the Great Depression to the Wizard of Oz. (p. 2002)
—1940s. (p. 2002)
—1940s from World War II to Jackie Robinson. (p. 2002)
—1950s. (p. 2002)
—1950s from the Korean War to Elvis. (p. 2002)
—1960s. (p. 2002)
—1960s from the Vietnam War to Flower Power. (p. 2002)
—1970s. (p. 2002)
—1970s from Watergate to Disco. (p. 2002)
—1980s. (p. 2002)
—1980s from Ronald Reagan to MTV. (p. 2002)
—1990s. (p. 2002)
—1990s from the Persian Gulf War to Y2K. (p. 2002)
—2000s. (p. 2003)
—Alaska: A MyReportLinks.com Book. (p. 33)
—Alexander Graham Bell: The Genius Behind the Phone. (p. 36)
—Ancient Mesopotamia: A Myreportlinks. com Book. (p. 70)
—Barack Obama. (p. 137)
—Bighorn Sheep: Help Save This Endangered Species! (p. 185)
—California Native Peoples (p. 253)
—California Plants & Animals (p. 253)
—Captain Cook: Great Explorer of the Pacific. (p. 264)
—Chimpanzee: Help Save This Endangered Species! (p. 306)
—Chris Rock. (p. 311)
—Colin Powell. (p. 339)
—Colorado: A MyReportLinks.com Book. (p. 343)
—Columbus: Opening up the New World. (p. 346)
—Decades of the 20th Century (p. 421)
—Denzel Washington. (p. 427)
—Discover Ancient Mesopotamia. (p. 447)
—Do You Wonder about Sex & Sexuality? (p. 458)
—Earth: A MyReportLinks. com Book. (p. 495)
—Florida: A MyReportLinks.com Book. (p. 606)
—Hawai'i Volcanoes National Park: Adventure, Explore, Discover. (p. 755)
—Incredible African-American Jazz Musicians. (p. 869)
—Inspiring African-American Civil Rights Leaders. (p. 878)
—Jaguar: Help Save This Endangered Species! (p. 905)
—Johannes Gutenberg: The Printer Who Gave Words to the World. (p. 920)
—Jupiter: A Myreportlinks. com Book. (p. 937)
—LeBron James. (p. 986)
—Lee Sobre Abraham Lincoln/Read about Abraham Lincoln. (p. 987)
—Lee Sobre Cesar Chavez. (p. 987)
—Lee sobre Martin Luther King, Jr. (p. 987)
—Lee Sobre Sacagawea/Read about Sacagawea. (p. 987)
—Lee Sobre Tiger Woods/Read about Tiger Woods. (p. 987)
—Louis Pasteur: The Father of Microbiology. (p. 1058)
—Mae Jemison. (p. 1070)
—Marco Polo: Amazing Adventures in China. (p. 1092)
—Mars: A Myreportlinks. com Book. (p. 1096)
—Minnesota: A MyReportLinks.com Book. (p. 1147)
—Moon: A MyReportLinks. com Book. (p. 1171)
—Muhammad Ali. (p. 1189)
—Oprah Winfrey. (p. 1301)
—Pacific States (p. 1317)
—Queen Latifah. (p. 1424)
—Read about Abraham Lincoln. (p. 1442)
—Read about Amelia Earhart. (p. 1442)
—Read about Annie Oakley. (p. 1442)
—Read about Benjamin Franklin. (p. 1442)
—Read about Cesar Chavez. (p. 1442)
—Read about Crazy Horse. (p. 1442)
—Read about George Washington Carver. (p. 1442)
—Read about Geronimo. (p. 1442)
—Read about Harriet Tubman. (p. 1442)
—Read about Helen Keller. (p. 1442)
—Read about Jackie Robinson. (p. 1442)
—Read about Johnny Appleseed. (p. 1442)
—Read about Martin Luther King, Jr. (p. 1442)
—Read about Neil Armstrong. (p. 1442)
—Read about Sacagawea. (p. 1442)
—Read about Tiger Woods. (p. 1442)
—Read about Walt Disney. (p. 1442)
—Rhode Island: A MyReportLinks.com Book. (p. 1468)
—Saturn: A MyReportLinks.com Book. (p. 1515)
—Savion Glover. (p. 1518)
—Sexuality & Teens: What You Should Know about Sex, Abstinence, Birth Control, Pregnancy, & STDs. (p. 1556)
—Sun: A Myreportlinks. com Book. (p. 1675)
—Uniquely California (p. 1818)
—Utah: A MyReportLinks. Com Book. (p. 1829)
—Venus: A MyReportLinks. com Book. (p. 1836)
—Washington: A MyReportLinks.com Book. (p. 1859)
—Will Smith. (p. 1932)
—Wynton Marsalis. (p. 1966)
—Wyoming: A MyReportLinks.com Book. (p. 1966)
—Yosemite National Park: Adventure, Explore, Discover. (p. 1972)
Feinstein, Stephen, jt. auth. see Taylor, Charlotte.
Feinstein, Stephen & Heinemann Library Staff. California Native Peoples (p. 253)
—California Plants & Animals (p. 253)
—Uniquely California. (p. 1818)
Feinstein, Stephen & Library. Conserving & Protecting Water: What You Can Do. (p. 359)
—Solving the Air Pollution Problem: What You Can Do. (p. 1608)
Feinstein, Stephen C., frwd. Holocaust. (p. 789)
Feinstein-Whittaker, Marjorie & Sikorski, Lorna D. MIAE - Mastering Idioms of American English: Volume 1 Front Vowels (p. 1133)
—MIAE - Mastering Idioms of American English: Volume 2 /r/-colored Vowels & Diphthongs (p. 1133)
Feirer, John L., jt. auth. see Feirer, Mark D.
Feirer, Mark D. & Feirer, John L. Carpentry & Building Construction. (p. 271)
Feisel, Keith. Safe in My Daddy's Arms. (p. 1502)
Feister, Tom, illus. see Vaughan, Brian K.
Feit, Maureen. Letters & Laughs from a to Z. (p. 1002)
Fekany Lee, Kimberly. Cell Scientists: Discovering How Cells Work. (p. 286)
Fekete, Lucy, illus. see Heeney, Bronwyn.
Felber, Bill. Horse in War. (p. 799)
Feld, Ellen F. Annie: The Mysterious Morgan Horse. (p. 86)
—Blackjack: Dreaming of a Morgan Horse (p. 197)
—Rusty: The High-Flying Morgan Horse. (p. 1498)
—Shadow: The Curious Morgan Horse. (p. 1557)
Feld, Paul E. Sailing Through Life. (p. 1503)
Felden, Georgia. When Jesus Hired Santa. (p. 1903)
Felder, Deborah G. 100 American Women Who Shaped American History. (p. 1998)
Felder, Elsa Nelly. Obras de Teatro Infantil. (p. 1275)
Felder, Monica. Juggling Colors. (p. 932)
Feldgus, Eileen G. & Cardonick, Isabell. Kid Writing: A Systematic Approach to Phonics, Journals, & Writing Workshop. (p. 952)
Feldhahn, Cathy J. Nosam. (p. 1266)
Feldhahn, Shaunti. For Women Only: What You Need to Know about the Inner Lives of Men. (p. 616)
Feldhahn, Shaunti & Rice, Lisa A. For Young Women Only: What You Need to Know about How Guys Think. (p. 616)
Feldick, Les. Questions & Answers from the Bible. (p. 1426)
Feldkamp, Jim And Cate. Adventures of Tommy & Clara on Mount Catherine. (p. 24)
Feldman Emison, Chloë, jt. illus. see Emison, Patricia A.
Feldman, Eve B. Animals Don't Wear Pajamas: A Book about Sleeping. (p. 82)
—Billy & Milly, Short & Silly. Mourning, Tuesday, illus. (p. 187)
Feldman, Heather. Columbia: The First Space Shuttle. (p. 346)
—Copperheads. (p. 366)
—Coral Snakes. (p. 366)
—Dennis Tito: The First Space Tourist. (p. 426)
—Dennis Tito, the First Space Tourist. (p. 426)
—Derek Jeter: Estrella del Béisbol (Baseball's Best) (p. 427)
—Derek Jeter: Baseball's Best / Estrella del Béisbol. (p. 427)
—Derek Jeter, Baseball's Best/Estrella del Beisbol. De Leon, Mauricio Velzaquez, tr. (p. 427)
—Hulk Hogan: Campeón de Lucha Libre (Wrestling Pro) (p. 825)
—King Snakes. (p. 959)
—Marion Jones: World Class Runner. (p. 1094)
—Marion Jones: Atleta de Categoría Internacional (World-Class Runner) (p. 1094)
—Mia Hamm: Soccer Superstar. (p. 1133)
—Mia Hamm: Soccer/Soccer Superstar/Superestrella del Fútbol. (p. 1133)
—Mia Hamm: Superestrella del Fútbol Soccer (Soccer Superstar. (p. 1133)
—Mia Hamm, Soccer Superstar/Superestrella del Futbol Soccer. De Leon, Mauricio Velzaquez, tr. (p. 1133)
—Milk Snakes. (p. 1143)
—Skylab: The First American Space Station. (p. 1587)
—Sputnik: The First Satellite. (p. 1635)
—Valentina Tereshkova: The First Woman in Space. (p. 1830)
—Venus Williams: Tennis Champion. (p. 1836)
—Venus Williams: Campeona de Tenis (Tennis Champion) (p. 1836)
—Venus Williams: Tennis Champion / Campeona de Tenis. (p. 1836)
—Venus Williams, Tennis Champion/Campeona del Tenis. De Leon, Mauricio Velzaquez, tr. (p. 1836)
—Wayne Gretzky: Hockey Star. (p. 1865)
—Yuri Gagarin: The First Man in Space. (p. 1983)
Feldman, Jane. We Love Ballet! (p. 1867)
Feldman, Jean. Action Alphabet Lap Book. (p. 10)
—Birdies Lap Book. (p. 191)
—Color Train Lap Book. (p. 343)
—Dinosaur Boogie Lap Book. (p. 441)
—Dr Jean Variety Pack. (p. 475)
—Five Little Monkeys Lap Book. (p. 600)
—Hands-On Art: More Than 100 Delightful, Skill-Building Ideas & Activities for Early Learners. (p. 741)
—Highway Letters, Numbers & Shapes: PreK-1. (p. 779)
—I Know an Old Lady Who Swallowed A One Lap Book. (p. 840)
—May There Always Be Sunshine Lap Book. (p. 1112)
—My Hands on My Head Lap Book. (p. 1210)
—My Mother Is A Baker Lap Book. (p. 1214)
—Nursey Rhyme Rally Lap Book. (p. 1273)
—Puppets & Storytime: More Than 100 Delightful, Skill-Building Ideas & Activities for Early Learners. (p. 1417)
—Reading & Writing: More Than 100 Delightful, Skill-Building Ideas & Activities for Early Learners. (p. 1445)
—Rules Rap Lap Book. (p. 1495)
—Science & Math: More Than 100 Delightful, Skill-Building Ideas & Activities for Early Learners. (p. 1525)
—Sing along & Read along with Dr. Jean All-in-One Pack (with Lap Books) (p. 1578)
—Twinkle Friends Lap Book. (p. 1802)
Feldman, Jean & Karapetkova, Holly. I Know an Old Lady. (p. 840)
—Mulberry Bush. (p. 1189)
Feldman, Jean R. & Karapetkova, Holly. Addition Pokey (Tune, Hokey Pokey) Lap Book. (p. 12)
—Arms Are for Hugging (Tune, the Girl I Left Behind Me) Lap Book. (p. 100)
—Basic Needs (Lap Book) (p. 142)
—Chant & Write (Tune, Sound off Cadence) Lap Book. (p. 290)
—Continents Together (Tune, He's Got the Whole World in His Hands) Lap Book. (p. 361)
—Deck the Room (Tune, Deck the Halls) Lap Book. (p. 421)
—Earth Day (Tune, Clap Your Hands Together) Lap Book. (p. 495)
—Eat Green! (Lap Book) (p. 501)
—Five Senses (Lap Book) (p. 601)
—Found a Penny (Tune, Found a Peanut) Lap Book. (p. 624)
—Fraction Pizza (Tune, He's Got the Whole World in His Hands) (p. 626)
—Good Bye, Friends (Tune, Buffalo Gal) Lap Book. (p. 697)
Feldman, Jody. Gollywhopper Games: The New Champion. Jamieson, Victoria, illus. (p. 697)
—Gollywhopper Games. (p. 697)
—Gollywhopper Games. Jamieson, Victoria, illus. (p. 697)
—Gollywhopper Games - Friend or Foe. Jamieson, Victoria, illus. (p. 697)
—Gollywhopper Games - The New Champion. Jamieson, Victoria, illus. (p. 697)
—Seventh Level. (p. 1555)
Feldman, Julie, creator. No Diet Diet: Healthy Meals in 5 Minutes. (p. 1258)
Feldman, Karen. Glorious Wings. (p. 685)
Feldman, Luke, illus. see Andersen, Hans Christian & Capstone Press Editors.
Feldman, Luke, illus. see Andersen, Hans Christian & Stone Arch Books Staff.
Feldman, Luke, illus. see Chin, Amanda.
Feldman, Luke, illus. see Stone Arch Books Staff.
Feldman, Luke & Chin, Amanda. Chaff n' Skaffs: Mai & the Lost Moskivvy. Feldman, Luke, illus. (p. 288)
Feldman, Rachel S. Little Tree. (p. 1037)
—Pink Blanket. (p. 1359)
Feldman, Reynold & Rumi, M. Jan. WisingUp: A Youth Guide to Good Living. (p. 1941)
Feldman, Roseann & Walker, Sally M. Put Inclined Planes to the Test. (p. 1420)
—Put Levers to the Test. (p. 1420)
—Put Pulleys to the Test. (p. 1420)
—Put Screws to the Test. (p. 1420)
—Put Wedges to the Test. (p. 1420)
—Put Wheels & Axles to the Test. (p. 1420)
Feldman, Roseann, et al. Put Inclined Planes to the Test. (p. 1420)
—Put Levers to the Test. (p. 1420)
—Put Pulleys to the Test. (p. 1420)
—Put Screws to the Test. (p. 1420)
—Put Wedges to the Test. (p. 1420)
—Put Wheels & Axles to the Test. (p. 1420)
Feldman, Ruth Tenzer. Fall of Constantinople. (p. 566)
—How Congress Works: A Look at the Legislative Branch. (p. 806)
—Ninth Day. (p. 1257)
Feldman, Sarah. Incredible, Edible Plants: Set Of 6. (p. 869)
—Incredible, Edible Plants. (p. 869)
—Symmetry in Our World: Set Of 6. (p. 1693)
—Symmetry in Our World. (p. 1693)
—Twisters: Set Of 6. (p. 1803)
Feldman, Steven. Dinner Time in Maine: The Adventures of Bob D. Lobsta. (p. 441)
Feldman, Thea. Adventure in the Park. Ward, April, illus. (p. 14)
—Animales Migratorios: Por Tierra. (p. 81)
—Backyard Pirates. Conger, Holli, illus. (p. 131)
—Dedan Saves the Day. (p. 422)
—First Foil Poetry Love Berg, Michelle, illus. (p. 595)
—Fun Around the Town. (p. 647)
—Hello, Farm! (p. 763)
—Hooray for Palace Pets! Disney Storybook Artists Staff, illus. (p. 796)
—Katya's Busy Morning. (p. 946)
—Kingfisher Readers L1: Animal Colors. (p. 960)
—Kingfisher Readers L1: Ladybugs. (p. 960)
—Kingfisher Readers L1: Time. (p. 960)
—Migrating Animals of the Land. (p. 1140)
—Milla's Big Day. (p. 1142)
—My Day of Ballet. Mayberry, Maranda, illus. (p. 1201)
—My Magnetic Opposites: Big & Little: Best Friends. Dillard, Sarah, illus. (p. 1214)
—Princess Party. (p. 1405)
—Rudolph the Red-Nosed Reindeer - The Classic Story. Madrid, Erwin, illus. (p. 1494)
—Safe & Sound Animal Defenses. (p. 1502)
—Seasons. (p. 1538)
—Stella: The Dog with the Big Heart. Danner, Chris, illus. (p. 1646)
—Tembo Takes Charge. (p. 1717)
—Things That Go. (p. 1733)
—Visit to the Farm. Trasler, Janee, illus. (p. 1845)
Feldman, Thea, ed. see Wilson, Hannah.
Feldman, Thea, jt. auth. see Llewellyn, Claire.
Feldman, Thea, jt. auth. see Oxlade, Chris.
Feldman, Thea, jt. auth. see Stones, Brenda.
Feldman, Thea, jt. compiled by see Bennett, Elizabeth.
Feldman, Thea & American Museum of Natural History Staff. Insects in Action: (Level 1) (p. 876)
—Insects in Action. (p. 876)
—Snakes up Close! (p. 1597)
—Strangest Animals: (Level 2) (p. 1665)
Feldman, Thea & Auerbach, Annie. Snow Family: A Winter's Tale. Alderson, Lisa, illus. (p. 1599)
Feldman, Thea & Disney Book Group Staff. Mickey's Halloween Treat. Disney Storybook Artists Staff, illus. (p. 1136)
Feldman, Thea & Ganeri, Anita. Creepy Crawlies. (p. 381)
Feldman, Thea & Oxlade, Chris. Cars. (p. 271)
Feldman, Thea & Steele, Philip. Arctic & Antarctic. (p. 96)
Feldman, Thea & Stones, Brenda. Trucks. (p. 1791)
Feldman, Thea & Upton, Rachael. Scare-ific Secrets. (p. 1519)
Feldman, Thea, ed. Secrets of Auradon Prep. (p. 1545)
Feldman, Thea, et al. Harry Cat & Tucker Mouse: Harry to the Rescue! (p. 750)
—Harry Cat & Tucker Mouse: Starring Harry. Ivanov, Aleksey et al, illus. (p. 750)
—Harry Cat & Tucker Mouse: Tucker's Beetle Band. Ivanov, Aleksey & Ivanov, Olga, illus. (p. 750)
Feldmann, Claudia, tr. see Colfer, Eoin.
Feldmann, Roseann, jt. auth. see Walker, Sally M.
Feldmeier Sims, Julie, illus. see Zimmerman, Kathleen.
Feldstein, Al. Weird Science. (p. 1872)
Feldstein, Al, jt. auth. see Gaines, William M.
Feldstein, Sandy. Rhythm Party Guide. (p. 1468)
Feldstein, Sandy & Clark, Larry. Antiphony. (p. 89)
—Antiphony - conductor's Score. (p. 89)
—Arietta - Clarinet/Bass Clarinet Solo w/ Piano Acc. w/ CD. (p. 98)
—Arietta - Flute/Oboe Solo w/ Pianio Acc & CD. (p. 98)
—Arietta - Horn in F Solo w/ Piano Acc. w/ CD. (p. 98)
—Arietta - Tenor Sax Solo w/ Piano Acc. w/ CD. (p. 98)
—Arietta - Trombone/Bariton/Bassoon Solo w/ Piano Acc. W/CD. (p. 98)
—Arietta - Trumpet/Baritone Solo w/ Piano Acc. W/CD. (p. 98)
—Arietta - Tuba Solo w/Piano Acc. w/ CD. (p. 98)
—Arietta- Keyboard Percussion Solo w/ Piano Acc. W/CD. (p. 98)
—Arrietta - Alto Sax/Bari Sax Solo w/ Piano Acc. w/ CD. (p. 101)
—Bacarolle - Flute/Oboe Solo with Piano Acc. W/CD. (p. 129)
—Bacarolle - Tenor Sax Solo with Piano Acc. W/CD. (p. 129)
—Barbara Allen - Alto Sax/Bari. Sax Solo with Piano Acc. W/CD. (p. 137)
—Barbara Allen - Clarinet/Bass Clarinet Solo with Piano Acc. W/CD. (p. 137)
—Barbara Allen - Flute/Oboe Solo with Piano Acc. W/CD. (p. 137)
—Barbara Allen - Horn in F Solo with Piano Acc. W/CD. (p. 137)
—Barbara Allen - Keyboard Percussion Solo with Piano Acc. W/CD. (p. 137)
—Barbara Allen - Tenor Sax Solo with Piano Acc. W/CD. (p. 137)
—Barbara Allen - Trombone/Baritone/Bassoon Solo with Piano Acc. W/CD. (p. 137)
—Barbara Allen - Tuba Solo with Piano Acc. W/CD. (p. 137)
—Barcarolle - Alto Sax. /Bari. Sax Solo with Piano Acc. (p. 138)
—Barcarolle - Clarinet/Bass Clarinet Solo with Piano Acc. (p. 138)
—Barcarolle - Keyboard Percussion Solo with Piano Acc. (p. 138)
—Barcarolle - Snare Drum Solo with Piano Acc. (p. 138)
—Barcarolle -Trombone/Baritone/Bassoon Solo with Piano Acc. (p. 138)
—Barcarolle - Tuba Solo with Piano Acc. (p. 138)
—Barcarolle-Trumpet/Baritone Solo with Piano Acc. (p. 138)
—Christmas Suprise. (p. 315)
—Christmas Suprise - Conductor Score. (p. 315)
—Christmas Toyland. (p. 316)
—Christmas Toyland - conductor's Score. (p. 316)
—Fafare Minuet - Keyboard Percussion Solo with Piano Acc. W/CD. (p. 562)
—Fanfare & Minuet -Flute/Oboe Solo with Piano Acc. W/CD. (p. 570)
—Fanfare Minuet - Alto Sax/Bari. Sax Solo with Piano Acc. W/CD. (p. 570)
—Fanfare Minuet - Clarinet/Bass Clarinet Solo with Piano Acc. (p. 570)
—Fanfare Minuet - Horn in F Solo with Piano Acc. (p. 570)
—Fanfare Minuet - Snare Drim Solo with Piano Acc. (p. 571)
—Fanfare Minuet - Tenor Sax Solo with Piano Acc. (p. 571)
—Fanfare Minuet - Trombone/Baritone/Basson Solo with Piano Acc. (p. 571)
—Fanfare Minuet -Trumpet/Baritone Solo with Piano Acc. (p. 571)
—Fanfare Minuet - Tuba Solo with Piano Acc. W/CD. (p. 571)
—Festival Chorale & March. (p. 582)
—Fifers. (p. 584)
—Fifers - Alto Sax. /Bari. Sax Solo with Piano Acc. (p. 584)
—Fifers - Clarinet/Bass Clarinet Solo with Piano Acc. W/CD. (p. 584)
—Fifers - Flute/Oboe Solo with Piano Acc. (p. 584)
—Fifers - Horn in F Solo with Piano Acc. (p. 584)
—Fifers - Keyboard Percussion Solo with Piano Acc. (p. 584)
—Fifers - Snare Drum Solo with Piano Acc. W/CD. (p. 584)
—Fifers - Tenor Sax. Solo with Piano Acc. (p. 584)
—Fifers - Trombone/Baritone/Bassoon Solo with Piano Acc. (p. 584)
—Fifers - Tuba Solo with Piano Acc. (p. 584)
—Honor March. (p. 795)
—Horn in F Solo with Piano Acc. (p. 798)
—Jupiter. (p. 937)
—Jupiter - Conductor's Score. (p. 937)
—Outback Rhapsody. (p. 1312)
—Outback Rhapsody - Conductor's Score. (p. 1312)
—Scherzando - Alto Sax/Bari. Sax Solo with Piano Acc. W/CD. (p. 1521)
—Scherzando - Flute Solo with Piano Acc. w/CD. (p. 1521)
—Scherzando -Horn in F Solo with Piano Acc. W/CD. (p. 1521)
—Scherzando - Keyboard Percussion Solo with piano acc. W/CD. (p. 1521)
—Scherzando - Snare Drum Solo with Piano Acc. W/CD. (p. 1521)
—Scherzando Tenor Sax Solo with Piano Acc. W/CD. (p. 1521)
—Scherzando - Trombone/Baritone/Bassoon Solo with Piano Acc. W/CD. (p. 1521)
—Scherzando -Trumpet/Baritone Solo with Piano Acc. w/ CD. (p. 1521)
—Scherzando - Tuba Solo with Piano Acc. W/CD. (p. 1521)
—Schezando - Clarinet/Bass Clarinet Solo with Piano Acc. W/CD. (p. 1521)
—Sensational Snare - Snare Drum Solo with Piano Acc. W/cd. (p. 1551)
—Sentinel. (p. 1551)
—Sentinel - conductor's Score. (p. 1551)
—Snarendipity - Snare Drum Solo with Piano Acc. W/CD. (p. 1597)
—Sonatina - Alto Sax/Bari. Sax Solo with Piano Acc. W/CD. (p. 1611)
—Sonatina - Clarinet/Bass Clarinet Solo with Piano Acc. W/CD. (p. 1611)
—Sonatina - Flute/Oboe Solo with Piano Acc. W/CD. (p. 1611)
—Sonatina - Horn in F Solo with Piano Acc. W/CD. (p. 1611)
—Sonatina - Keyboard Percussion Solo with Piano Acc. W/CD. (p. 1611)
—Sonatina - Snare Drum Solo with Piano Acc. W/CD. (p. 1611)
—Sonatina - Tenor Sax Solo with Piano Acc. W/CD. (p. 1611)
—Sonatina - Trombone/Baritone/Bassoon Solo with Piano Acc. W/CD. (p. 1611)
—Sonatina - Trumpet/Baritone Solo with Piano Acc. W/CD. (p. 1611)
—Sonatina - Tuba Solo with Piano Acc. W/CD. (p. 1611)

F

—Variations on a Theme by Greig -Flute Solo w/Piano Acc. W/CD. (p. 1833)
—Variations on a Theme by Greig - Alto Sax/Bari. Sax Solo with Piano Acc. W/CD. (p. 1833)
—Variations on a Theme by Greig - Clarinet/Bass Clarinet Solo with Piano Acc. W/CD. (p. 1833)
—Variations on a Theme by Greig - Keyboard Percussion Solo with Piano Acc. W/CD. (p. 1833)
—Variations on a Theme by Greig - Snare Drum Solo with Piano Acc. W/CD. (p. 1833)
—Variations on a Theme by Greig - Trombone/Baritone/Basson Solo with Piano Acc. W/CD. (p. 1833)
—Variations on a Theme by Greig - Trumpet/Baritone Solo with Piano Acc. W/CD. (p. 1833)
—Variations on a Theme by Greig - Tuba Solo with Piano Acc. W/CD. (p. 1833)
—Variations on the theme by Greig - Horn in F Solo with Piano Acc. W/CD. (p. 1833)
—Variations on a theme by Greig- Tenor Sax Solo with Piano Acc. W/CD. (p. 1833)
Feldstein, Sandy & Firth, Vic. Vic Firth/SandyFeldstein Percussion Series - complete Score. (p. 1840)
Felicia, Phyllis. I Count for Something. (p. 837)
Feliciano, Jose. Feliz Navidad: Two Stories Celebrating Christmas. Diaz, David, illus. (p. 581)
Feliciano, Luis. Adventures of the Three Angels. (p. 23)
Feliciano, Maria Inez. Meximan. (p. 1131)
Felico, Dina. Nathaniel & His Best Friend. (p. 1231)
Felin, M. Sindy. Touching Snow. (p. 1772)
Felipe, Juaristi, jt. auth. see Juaristi, Felipe.
Felipe, Nersys. Cuentos de Guane (Stories of Guane) (p. 390)
Felix, Emmanuel. Propos du Vaudou Haitien. (p. 1412)
Felix, Erica. Jay-Bee & Me. (p. 910)
Felix, Erica Lynn. Brother & Sisterly Love. (p. 231)
Félix, José María, tr. see Melville, Herman.
Felix, Monique. Alphabet. Felix, Monique, illus. (p. 49)
—Colors. Felix, Monique, illus. (p. 344)
—Mouse Book: the Valentine. Felix, Monique, illus. (p. 1182)
—Numbers. Felix, Monique, illus. (p. 1271)
—Rumor. (p. 1495)
—Wind. (p. 1935)
Felix, Monique, illus. see Bartlett, T. C.
Felix, Monique, illus. see Lewis, J. Patrick.
Felix, Monique, illus. see Oppenheim, Shulamith.
Felix, Monique, illus. see Wahl, Jan.
Felix, Monique, illus. see Williams, Margery & Bianco, Margery Williams.
Felix, Monique, illus. see Williams, Margery.
Felix, Monique, creator. Mouse Books: the Boat. (p. 1182)
—Mouse Books: the Opposites. (p. 1182)
Felix, Rebecca. Abyssinians. (p. 7)
—Are You a Ewe? (p. 97)
—Big, Bigger, Biggest. (p. 178)
—Can You Be a Bee? (p. 258)
—Fisherman & His Wife. Petelinsek, Kathleen, illus. (p. 599)
—Ghosts: The Truth Behind History's Spookiest Spirits. (p. 672)
—Good Manners with Your Friends. (p. 698)
—Good Manners with Your Siblings. (p. 698)
—Heavy, Heavier, Heaviest. (p. 761)
—How's the Weather in Fall? (p. 824)
—How's the Weather in Fall?/Rebecca Felix. (p. 824)
—How's the Weather in Summer? (p. 824)
—International Adoption. (p. 880)
—Keeping Cool in Summer. (p. 947)
—Little Mermaid. Petelinsek, Kathleen, illus. (p. 1031)
—Long, Longer, Longest. (p. 1047)
—Maine Coons. (p. 1077)
—New Gnu Knew. (p. 1244)
—Northeast. (p. 1265)
—Pair of Pears. (p. 1318)
—Persians. (p. 1344)
—Ragdolls. (p. 1433)
—Rows of Roses. (p. 1492)
—Short, Shorter, Shortest. (p. 1569)
—Siamese. (p. 1572)
—Small, Smaller, Smallest. (p. 1592)
—Southeast. (p. 1617)
—Southwest. (p. 1617)
—Sphynx. (p. 1626)
—Tall, Taller, Tallest. (p. 1704)
—They Won One! (p. 1732)
—Visiting the Beach in Summer. (p. 1845)
—We Celebrate Christmas in Winter. (p. 1866)
—We Celebrate Halloween in Fall. (p. 1866)
—We Celebrate Hanukkah in Winter. (p. 1866)
—We Celebrate Independence Day in Summer. (p. 1866)
—We Celebrate Kwanzaa in Winter. (p. 1867)
—We Celebrate Thanksgiving in Fall. (p. 1867)
—We Harvest Apples in Fall. (p. 1867)
—We Harvest Pumpkins in the Fall. (p. 1867)
—We See Snowflakes in Winter. (p. 1868)
—West. (p. 1876)
—What Do Animals Do in Fall? (p. 1882)
—What Do Animals Do in Summer? (p. 1882)
—What Do Bees Do in Summer? (p. 1882)
—What Do People Do in Fall? (p. 1882)
—What Do People Do in Summer? (p. 1882)
—What Happens to Leaves in Fall? (p. 1886)
—What Happens to Plants in Summer? (p. 1886)
—What's Great about Alaska? (p. 1897)
—What's Great about Louisiana? (p. 1897)
—What's Great about Nevada? (p. 1897)
—What's Great about Oregon? (p. 1897)
—What's Great about Rhode Island? (p. 1897)
—What's Great about South Carolina? (p. 1897)
—What's Great about Utah? (p. 1897)
—What's Great about Wyoming? (p. 1897)
Feliz, Guido, jt. ed. see Arancibia, Janet.
Feliz, Guido, jt. ed. see Fisher, Tammy.
Felker, Linda, et al. What If? (p. 1887)
Felkner, Myrtle. Really Really Really Holy Night. (p. 1450)
Fell, Amy. Two Terrible Eaters. (p. 1804)
Fell, H. Granville, illus. see Nesbit, E.
Fell, Jenny, illus. see Nuttall, Neil & Hawkins, Andy, eds.
Fell, K. Dragon Stones. (p. 478)
Fellag, Linda Robinson. English for Academic Success (p. 530)
Fellag, Linda Robinson, jt. auth. see Avery, John D.
Feller, Bob. Hello, Slider! (p. 765)
Feller, Robyn M. Everything You Need to Know about Peer Pressure. (p. 545)
Fellers, Cody, illus. see Fellers, Tina.
Fellers, Tina. Toby & the Alien: In the Adventures of the Unusual Toys Fellers, Cody, illus. (p. 1760)
Fellows, Fred, jt. auth. see Sohn, Emily.
Fellows, Frederick, jt. auth. see Sohn, Emily.
Fellows, Leonard, jt. auth. see Bragdon, Allen D.
Fellows, Sarah. Misty's Big Idea! (p. 1155)
Fellows, Stan, illus. see Rosen, Michael J.
Fells, Maureen. Adventures of Petey: Or a Schnauzer's Wish. (p. 21)
Fellure, Kathy Boyd. Mr Snowman Ate Our Picnic Lunch. (p. 1186)
Felmang, Romano, illus. see Jeffrey, Gary.
Felsen, Henry Gregor. Crash Club. Welch, Holly Felsen, ed. (p. 376)
—Fever Heat. Welch, Holly Felsen, illus. (p. 583)
—Henry Gregor Felsen Street Rod Collection. Welch, Holly Felsen, illus. (p. 768)
—Rag Top. Felsen, Holly, illus. (p. 1433)
—Road Rocket. (p. 1477)
Felsen, Holly, illus. see Felsen, Henry Gregor.
Felsenfeld, Daniel, jt. auth. see Getzinger, Donna.
Felsing, Dean E. New Orleans or Sunk! (p. 1246)
Felstead, Cathie, illus. see Peters, Lisa Westberg & Peters.
Felstead, Cathie, illus. see Schaefer, Lola M.
Felstead, Cathie, illus. see Sebba, Jane.
Felstead, Cathie, illus. see Shapiro, Jody Fickes.
Felt, Jeremy, jt. auth. see Williams, Jason.
Felten, Ross, illus. see Maggiore, Lisa.
Felter, illus. see Leslie, Emma.
Felter and Gunston, illus. see Leslie, Emma.
Feltes Taylor, Kimberly, jt. auth. see Chaikin, Stacey.
Feltes, Tess, illus. see Glaser, Linda.
Feltes, Tess, illus. see Jango-Cohen, Judith.
Feltham, Sarah, jt. auth. see Drake, Jennifer.
Felton, Amanda, jt. auth. see Felton, Carol.
Felton, Carol & Felton, Amanda. Where's Harley? O'Rourke, Page Eastburn, illus. (p. 1910)
Felton, Harold W. Horse Named Justin Morgan. Fisher, Leonard Everett, illus. (p. 799)
Felton, Jerilyn E. Master's Companion: A Christian Midrash. (p. 1103)
Felton, Richard, illus. see Williams, Lorraine.
Felts, C. C. My Best Friend Mommy. (p. 1196)
Felts, Shirley, illus. see Kendall, Carol & Li, Yao-Wen.
Femia, Vincent J. Possible Dream: How the 2004 Red Sox Reversed History. (p. 1387)
Femiano, Robert. Dr. Funster's Quick Thinks Math C1: Fun Math Brain Teasers. (p. 475)
Femrite, Barbara, creator. Praying with Passion: Life-Changing Prayers For Those Who Walk in Darkness (p. 1393)
Fenderson, David, illus. see Fenderson, Shani.
Fenderson, Shani. Mommy, Why Is the Sky So Blue? Fenderson, David, illus. (p. 1162)
Fendler, Donn & Egan, Joseph. Lost on a Mountain in Maine. (p. 1056)
Fendler, Donn & Plourde, Lynn. Lost Trail: Nine Days Alone in the Wilderness Bishop, Ben, illus. (p. 1056)
Fenech, Liza, illus. see Laberje, Reji.
Fénelon, Marie Jirlande. Two Best Friends & the Old Lady. (p. 1803)
Feng, Katherine, illus. see Ryder, Joanne.
Feng, Katherine, photos by see Ryder, Joanne.
Fenichel Asher, Sandra. Too Many Frogs! (p. 1766)
Fenly, Leigh, jt. auth. see Welsh, Anne Marie.
Fenn, G. Manville. Brownsmith's Boy. (p. 232)
—Rajah of Dah. (p. 1437)
—Young Robin Hood. (p. 1979)
Fenn, George. Marcus the Young Centurion. (p. 1092)
—Rajah of Dah. (p. 1437)
—Yussuf the Guide or the Mountain Bandits: Being the Strange Story of the Travels in Asia Minor of Burne the Lawyer, Preston the Professor, & Lawren. Schönberg, John, illus. (p. 1983)
Fenn, George Manvill. Young Robin Hood. (p. 1979)
Fenn, George Manville. Yussuf the Guide or the Mountain Bandits: Being the Strange Story of the Travels in Asia Minor of Burne the Lawyer, Preston the Professor, & Lawrenc. Schönberg, John, illus. (p. 1983)
Fenne, Edwin, jt. auth. see Poehlmann, Jeffrey.
Fenne, Edwin & Poehlmann, Jeffrey. Those Amazing Dogs : at the Pirate Bay: Book Four of the Those Amazing Dogs Series. Morales, Carlos, illus. (p. 1740)
—Those Amazing Dogs Book Three: at the Arctic Circle: Book Three of the Those Amazing Dogs Series. Morales, Carlos, illus. (p. 1740)
—Those Amazing Dogs Book Two: in the Viking Volcano: Book Two of the Those Amazing Dogs Series. Morales, Carlos, illus. (p. 1740)
—Those Amazing Dogs : on the Coral Island: Book Five of the Those Amazing Dogs Series. Morales, Carlos, illus. (p. 1740)
—Those Amazing Dogs:African River Adventure. Morales, Carlos, illus. (p. 1740)
Fennell, BreAnn. Play? Yay! (p. 1370)
Fennell, Clare, illus. see Paratore, Coleen.
Fennell, Emerald. Creeper. (p. 381)
—Shiverton Hall. (p. 1567)
Fennell, Haywood. Coota & the Magic Quilt. (p. 365)
Fennell, Kristen & Petruccelli, Jessica. World of Hope: Written by Hope's Parents Laurie & Mike. (p. 1956)
Fennell, Tracy, illus. see Dickens, Charles.
Fennell, Tracy, illus. see Ganeri, Anita.
Fenner, Carol. Snowed in with Grandmother Silk. Harvey, Amanda, illus. (p. 1600)
—Yolonda's Genius. (p. 1972)
Fenner, M. On My Block: Learning the BL Sound. (p. 1289)
Fenner, Matthew. Pod of Dolphins. (p. 1375)
—Pod of Dolphins / una Manada de Delfines. (p. 1375)
Fennewald, Joseph Grant, illus. see Matherly, Ashley Page.
Fenoughty, Charles, illus. see Hamley, Dennis.
Fenske, Jonathan. Guppy Up! (p. 732)
—Guppy Up! Fenske, Jonathan, illus. (p. 732)
—Love Is in the Air. (p. 1060)
—Love Is in the Air. Fenske, Jonathan, illus. (p. 1060)
—Love Is in the Air (HC) Fenske, Jonathan, illus. (p. 1060)
—Pig, a Fox, & a Box. Fenske, Jonathan, illus. (p. 1357)
—Woodward & Mctwee. Fenske, Jonathan, illus. (p. 1950)
Fenstermacher, Mary Wisham. Pablo Visits the Ocean. (p. 1317)
Fenstermaker, Rosanne. Mystery of the White Circle K Ranch. (p. 1226)
Fente, et al. Curso Intensivo de Espanol: Ejercicios Practicos: Nivel de Iniciacion y Elemental. (p. 395)
Fentiman, David. Lego Movie. (p. 990)
Fentiman, David, jt. auth. see Dorling Kindersley Publishing Staff.
Fenton, Corinne, jt. auth. see King, Corinne.
Fenton, Geleta. Joel's Adventure at Sea. Siniard, Ricky, illus. (p. 920)
Fenton, Joe. Boo! Fenton, Joe, illus. (p. 209)
—What's under the Bed? Fenton, Joe, illus. (p. 1900)
Fenton, Karen B. It's Raining Outside & I'm Gonna Be Bored! Roth, Stacy Schulstrom, illus. (p. 898)
Fenton, Kate. Vanity & Vexation: A Novel of Pride & Prejudice. (p. 1833)
Fenton, Mary Frances, illus. see Appelhof, Mary, et al.
Fenton, Paul. Modern Sculpture (p. 1159)
Fenton, Sue Fenton, creator. Professor Mel T. Lingual's Coloring Book of Signs: Promoting Language Study & Cultural Awareness. (p. 1409)
Fenton, Tanya. Three Silly Chickens. Fenton, Tanya, illus. (p. 1743)
Fentz, Mike, illus. see Nickel, Scott.
Fentz, Mike, illus. see Teitelbaum, Michael.
Fenwick, Carol. Jenell & the Berry Thicket Village. (p. 912)
—Jennell & the Horse in the Enchanted Valley. (p. 912)
Fenwick, Margaret. Lonnie the Lost Lamb. (p. 1047)
—Stella's Hair. (p. 1647)
Fenwick, Nellie. Gracie & God's Great Ten: How One Girl Learned to Make Good Choices. (p. 705)
Fenwick, Ray, illus. see Fleming, Candace.
Fenzel, J. Ryan. Descending from Duty. (p. 428)
Fequiere, Marie A. Devil Rain & the Bearded Child of the Desert. (p. 432)
Ferber, Elizabeth, jt. auth. see Franklin, Lynn C.
Ferber, Kevin S., jt. auth. see Hansen, Mark.
Ferchaud, Steve. Glen Robbie: A Scottish Fairy Tale. (p. 683)
—Man Who Spoke with Cats. (p. 1086)
Ferchaud, Steve, illus. see Claus, Nancy.
Ferchaud, Steve, illus. see Cobb, Debbie.
Ferdenzi, Til, jt. auth. see Berra, Lawrence Yogi.
Ferdowsi. Rostam: Tales from the Shahnameh. (p. 1490)
ferdowsi. Rostam & Sohrab: Tales from the Shahnameh. (p. 1490)
Ferenc, Bill, illus. see Glaser, Rebecca.
Ferenic, Bill, illus. see Glaser, Rebecca.
Ferer, Whitney H. Owl Who Thinks He Is an Eagle. McCaslin, Anna, illus. (p. 1315)
Feresten, Nancy, ed. see Heiligman, Deborah.
Feresten, Nancy, jt. auth. see Connell, Kate.
Fereyra, Lucas, illus. see Matthews, Alex.
Fergus, Cristin, jt. auth. see Fergus, Cristin L.
Fergus, Cristin L. & Fergus, Cristin. Dylan's Story: Overcoming Autism, a Childhood Epidemic. (p. 491)
Fergus, Maureen. Exploits of a Reluctant (but Extremely Goodlooking) Hero. (p. 549)
—InvisiBill. Petricic, Dusan, illus. (p. 885)
—Ortega. (p. 1305)
—Recipe for Disaster. (p. 1451)
Ferguson. 150 Great Tech Prep Careers, Second Edition. (p. 2000)
—Advertising & Marketing. (p. 25)
—Animal Care. (p. 77)
—Archeology. (p. 95)
—Art. (p. 101)
—Aviation. (p. 119)
—Biology. (p. 189)
—Business Managers. (p. 245)
—Careers in Focus: Energy. (p. 267)
—Careers in Focus: Animation. (p. 267)
—Careers in Focus: Automotives. (p. 267)
—Careers in Focus: Electronics. (p. 267)
—Careers in Focus: Armed Forces. (p. 267)
—Careers in Focus: Comic Books & Graphic Novels. (p. 267)
—Careers in Focus: Entrepreneurs, Third Edition. (p. 267)
—Careers in Focus: Retail. (p. 268)
—Careers in Focus: Geology. (p. 268)
—Careers in Focus: Forensics. (p. 268)
—Careers in Focus: Mechanics. (p. 268)
—Careers in Focus: Government. (p. 268)
—Careers in Focus: Meteorology. (p. 268)
—Careers in Focus: Oceanography. (p. 268)
—Careers in Focus: Personal Services. (p. 268)
—Careers in Focus: Telecommunications. (p. 268)
—Careers in Focus: Mathematics & Physics. (p. 268)
—Careers in Focus: Nonprofit Organizations. (p. 268)
—Careers in Focus: Landscaping & Horticulture. (p. 268)
—Careers in Focus - Nursing. (p. 268)
—Careers in Focus - Politics. (p. 268)
—Clerks & Administrative Workers. (p. 331)
—Coaches & Fitness Professionals. (p. 336)
—Computer & Video Game Design. (p. 354)
—Computers. (p. 355)
—Construction. (p. 359)
—Design. (p. 429)
—Discovering Careers for Your Future: Library & Information Science. (p. 449)
—Discovering Careers for Your Future Set, 24-Volumes. (p. 449)
—Education. (p. 505)
—Ferguson Career Resource Guide Set, 5-Titles: 10-Volumes. (p. 582)
—Geriatric Care. (p. 666)
—Journalism. (p. 927)
—Law. (p. 981)
—Library & Information Science. (p. 1005)
—Medical Technicians & Technologists. (p. 1118)
—Physicians. (p. 1353)
—Social Work. (p. 1605)
—Sports. (p. 1632)
—Teaching. (p. 1709)
—Technicians. (p. 1711)
—Therapists. (p. 1729)
—What Can I Do Now: Business & Finance. (p. 1880)
Ferguson, Addy. Antibullying Clubs. (p. 89)
—Are You a Bully? (p. 96)
—Bullying with Words: Teasing, Name-Calling, & Rumors. (p. 241)
—Group Bullying: Exclusion & Ganging Up. (p. 725)
—How to Deal with an Adult Bully. (p. 816)
—Online Bullying. (p. 1298)
—What to Do When You Are Bullied for Being Different. (p. 1894)
—What to Do When Your Brother or Sister Is a Bully. (p. 1894)
—What to Do When Your Friends Are Bullies. (p. 1894)
—What You Can Do to Stop Bullying. (p. 1896)
Ferguson, Adrian. Hamburger Man: Resurrection. (p. 739)
Ferguson, Alane. Angel of Death. (p. 73)
—Christopher Killer. (p. 317)
Ferguson, Alane, jt. auth. see Skurzynski, Gloria.
Ferguson, Alane & Skurzynski, Gloria. Deadly Waters. (p. 418)
—Escape from Fear: A Mystery in Virgin Islands National Park. (p. 535)
—Running Scared. (p. 1497)
Ferguson, Alex. Tiggie: A Story of Good & Evil Written for Young People. (p. 1749)
Ferguson, Amanda. American Women of the Vietnam War. (p. 64)
—Attack Against the U. S. Embassies in Kenya & Tanzania. (p. 113)
—Attack on U. S. Servicemen in Saudi Arabia on June 25, 1996. (p. 114)
—SAS: British Special Air Service. (p. 1515)
Ferguson, Ann M. Fine New Home for Young James Madison. (p. 589)
Ferguson, B. Renee', jt. auth. see Ferguson, Royce.
Ferguson, Beth. Digestive System. (p. 438)
Ferguson, Brinker, jt. auth. see Kuechenmeister, Mary.
Ferguson, C. Brent, illus. see Carella, C. J., et al.
Ferguson, Chad. Stuff for the Hunt. (p. 1670)
Ferguson, Chaveevah Banks. What the Heart Remembers. (p. 1893)
Ferguson, Chaveevah Banks, illus. see Barbatti, Joyce.
Ferguson, Chaveevah Banks, illus. see Hickey, Joshalyn M.
Ferguson, Christopher L. Southerners at Rest: Confederate Dead at Hollywood Cemetery. (p. 1617)
Ferguson, creator. Architecture & Building. (p. 95)
—Earth Science. (p. 496)
—Engineering. (p. 529)
—Internet. (p. 880)
—Public Safety. (p. 1414)
—Space Exploration. (p. 1619)
—Transportation. (p. 1779)
Ferguson, C.S. Tale of Two Fairies: The Secret of the Spider's Web. (p. 1700)
Ferguson, Don. Winnie the Pooh's A to ZZZZ. Wakeman, Bill & Langley, Bill, illus. (p. 1937)
Ferguson, Donald. Chums of Scranton High. (p. 318)
—Chums of Scranton High at Ice Hockey. (p. 318)
—Chums of Scranton High on the Cinder Pat. (p. 318)
—Chums of Scranton High on the Cinder Path. (p. 318)
—Chums of Scranton High, or, Hugh Morgan's Uphill Fight. (p. 318)
—Chums of Scranton High Out for the Pennant, or, in the Three Town League. (p. 318)
Ferguson, Dwayne. Ghost Ranch: The Legend of Mad Jake (p. 671)
—Mess at Loch Ness. (p. 1129)
Ferguson, Gloria. Fair Money. (p. 562)
—What Season Is It? Weir, Carrie & Weir, Nolet, illus. (p. 1893)
Ferguson, J. M. Bubbles the Little Pig (p. 233)
Ferguson, Jamianne. Lost in Past Remembrence. (p. 1055)
Ferguson, Jennifer. Unwanted Litter. (p. 1823)
Ferguson, John, illus. see Goulis, Julie.
Ferguson, John B. Cindy Before. (p. 321)
Ferguson, John E. & Allport, Alan. Immigration Policy. (p. 861)
Ferguson, John E. & Ferguson, John E., Jr. Right to Die. (p. 1472)
Ferguson, John E., et al. Gun Control. (p. 732)
Ferguson, John E., Jr., jt. auth. see Ferguson, John E.
Ferguson, John H., illus. see Goulis, Julie.
Ferguson, Lee, illus. see Lemke, Donald.
Ferguson, Linda. Ollie Ollie Ox in Free. Patti, Sheila, illus. (p. 1287)
Ferguson, M. J. Mirror in the Box: A Children's Story & a Parable. (p. 1149)
Ferguson, Marfe Delano. Sea Monsters: A Prehistoric Adventure. (p. 1535)
Ferguson, Marfe Delano, jt. auth. see Richards, Mose.
Ferguson, Margaret R., ed. Executive Branch of State Government: People, Process, & Politics (p. 548)
Ferguson, Martha-Elizabeth, illus. see Evans, Ashley Putnam.
Ferguson, Olivia & Haugen, Hayley Mitchell. Is Childhood Becoming Too Sexualized? (p. 889)
Ferguson, Olivia, et al. Is Childhood Becoming Too Sexualized? (p. 889)
Ferguson, Peter, illus. see Bauer, Marion Dane.
Ferguson, Peter, illus. see Bode, N. E.
Ferguson, Peter, illus. see Buckley, Michael.
Ferguson, Peter, illus. see Kelly, Katy.

Ferguson, Peter, illus. see MacHale, D. J.
Ferguson, Peter, illus. see McKenzie, Riford.
Ferguson, Peter, illus. see Newman, Lesléa.
Ferguson, Peter, illus. see Wells, Rosemary, et al.
Ferguson, Peter, jt. auth. see Buckley, Michael.
Ferguson Publishing. Encyclopedia of Careers & Vocational Guidance, 16th Edition, 5-Volume Set (p. 525)
Ferguson Publishing Staff. Animal Careers. (p. 77)
—Animation. (p. 84)
—Career Discovery Encyclopedia. (p. 266)
—Careers in Focus: Business. (p. 267)
—Education. (p. 505)
—Environment. (p. 532)
—Film. (p. 586)
—Journalism. (p. 927)
—Law. (p. 981)
—Nursing. (p. 1273)
—Radio & Television. (p. 1432)
—Safety & Security. (p. 1502)
—Science. (p. 1524)
—Sports. (p. 1632)
—Travel & Tourism. (p. 1780)
Ferguson Publishing Staff, contrib. by. Careers in Focus. (p. 267)
Ferguson Publishing Staff, creator. Art. (p. 101)
—Careers in Focus. (p. 267)
—Cosmetology. (p. 368)
—Engineering. (p. 529)
—Exploring Tech Careers. (p. 553)
—Fashion. (p. 575)
—Food. (p. 612)
—Manufacturing. (p. 1089)
—Public Relations. (p. 1414)
Ferguson, R. L. Mouse Queen: The Dead Queen's Daughter. Wilson, P. M., ed. (p. 1182)
Ferguson, Rebecca. Role of the Individual. (p. 1485)
Ferguson, Royce & Ferguson, B. Renee'. Mi Me. (p. 1132)
Ferguson, Sally. What Will I Be When I Grow Up? (p. 1895)
Ferguson, Sarah. Tea for Ruby. Glasser, Robin Preiss, illus. (p. 1708)
Ferguson, Sarah, jt. auth. see Duchess of York Staff.
Ferguson, Sarah & Duchess of York Staff. Little Red's Autumn Adventure. Williams, Sam, illus. (p. 1035)
—Little Red's Christmas Story. Williams, Sam, illus. (p. 1035)
—Little Red's Summer Adventure. Williams, Sam, illus. (p. 1035)
Ferguson, Scott. Itty Bitty It. Rudd, Benton, illus. (p. 900)
Ferguson, Sinclair. Jesus Teaches Us How to Be Good. (p. 916)
—Jesus Teaches Us How to Be Happy. (p. 916)
—Jesus Teaches Us How to Pray. (p. 916)
Ferguson, Sinclair B. Big Book of Bible Truths Apps, Fred, illus. (p. 179)
—Big Book of Bible Truths 2. Apps, Fred, illus. (p. 179)
—Big Book of Questions & Answers: A Family Devotional Guide to the Christian Faith. (p. 179)
—Big Book of Questions & Answers about Jesus: A Family Guide to Jesus' Life & Ministry. (p. 179)
—Plan: How God Got the World Ready for Jesus. Ruta, Angelo, illus. (p. 1366)
Ferguson, Suzanie P. Ferris, Color & Activity Book: Libro de Colorear & Actividad. (p. 582)
—Ferris Give Thanks. (p. 582)
Ferguson, Tamara, illus. see Hairston, Angelica.
Ferguson, Terrence. Stuttering Sammie: I'm Just Like You, I Just Repeat Some Letters or Words When I Talk. (p. 1670)
Ferguson, The Duchess of York, Sarah, The Duchess of York. Tea for Ruby. Glasser, Robin Preiss, illus. (p. 1708)
Ferguson, Tina. Day I Disappeared. (p. 413)
Ferguson, Walter F. Speed Learning: The Quest for Excellence. (p. 1624)
Ferguson-Jones, Philip, illus. see Leonard, Wendy.
Fergusson, Ian K., jt. auth. see Bright, Michael.
Feria, Humberto. Mi Amigo Gumaro. (p. 1132)
Ferin, Margery. Eyewitnesses at Calvary. (p. 559)
—Joy to the World: Christmas Poetry & Short Stories. (p. 930)
Fermin, Jose D. 1904 World's Fair: The Filipino Experience. (p. 2002)
Fern, Ella. Questions & Answers about World History. (p. 1426)
Fern, Fanny. Little Ferns for Fanny's Little Friends by the Author of Fern Leaves. (p. 1027)
Fern, Jim, jt. auth. see Carey, Mike.
Fern, Tracey E. Barnum's Bones: How Barnum Brown Discovered the Most Famous Dinosaur in the World. Kulikov, Boris, illus. (p. 139)
—Buffalo Music. Castillo, Lauren, illus. (p. 235)
—Dare the Wind: The Record-Breaking Voyage of Eleanor Prentiss & the Flying Cloud. McCully, Emily Arnold, illus. (p. 406)
—Pippo the Fool. Estrada, Pau, illus. (p. 1362)
Fernandes, Eugenie. Difficult Day. (p. 438)
—Kitten's Autumn. Fernandes, Eugenie, illus. (p. 963)
—Kitten's Spring. Fernandes, Eugenie, illus. (p. 963)
—Kitten's Summer. Fernandes, Eugenie, illus. (p. 963)
—Kitten's Winter. Fernandes, Eugenie, illus. (p. 963)
Fernandes, Eugenie, illus. see Hoce, Charley.
Fernandes, Eugenie, illus. see Milway, Katie Smith.
Fernandes, Eugenie, illus. see Peetoom, Laura.
Fernandes, Eugenie, illus. see Spinelli, Eileen.
Fernandes, Eugenie, illus. see Suzuki, David.
Fernandes, Eugenie, illus. see Walters, Eric.
Fernandes, Kim. Gifts to Make with Crayola Model Magic (p. 676)
Fernandes, Kim, illus. see Burton, Katherine.
Fernandes, Matthew, illus. see Wyatt, Valerie.
Fernandes, Roger, illus. see McNutt, Nan.
Fernandez, A. & Fernandez, Q. Hooray for My Ears. (p. 796)
—Hooray for My Eyes. (p. 796)
—Hooray for My Hands. (p. 796)
—Hooray for My Nose. (p. 796)
—Hooray for My Taste. (p. 796)
Fernandez, Alberto. Halloween Story: A frightfully delightful tale by a 5-year-old, for other little monsters Everywhere. de la Fuente, Pilar, illus. (p. 738)
—Halloween Story: A frightfully-delightful tale, by a 5-year-old, for other little monsters, Everywhere. de la Fuente, Pilar, illus. (p. 738)
Fernandez, Alexa. Darn Baby! (p. 409)
Fernandez, Amy. Puppies: A Guide to Caring for Your Puppy. Francais, Isabelle, photos by. (p. 1418)
Fernandez, Amy, jt. auth. see Marrone, Marc.
Fernandez, Amy, jt. auth. see Morrone, Marc.
Fernández, Bernardo. Soy el Robot. Betteo, Patricio, illus. (p. 1618)
Fernandez, Carina, illus. see Giacomo, Renee San.
Fernández, Cecilia. Buen Samaritano. (p. 235)
—Jesus Alimenta a los 5000. (p. 915)
—Jesus y los Niños. (p. 916)
—Jesús y Zaqueo. (p. 916)
—Jonás y el Pez. (p. 925)
—Nacimiento de Moisés. (p. 1227)
Fernández, Cecilia, ed. see Truitt, Gloria.
Fernández, Cecilia, jt. auth. see Dietrich, Julie.
Fernández, Cecilia, jt. auth. see Skipworth, Kelly.
Fernández, Cecilia Fau. Dios Me Escucha: Oraciones en Rima para Ninos. Kroeger, Vanesa, illus. (p. 445)
Fernandez, Cesar. bibliobus Magico. Torres, Marina, illus. (p. 177)
Fernandez, David R. Lady Godiva & the Legend of the Black Rose. (p. 970)
Fernández de Lizardi, José Joaquín. Periquillo Samiento. (p. 1343)
Fernandez de Lizardi, Jose Joaquin. Quijotita y su Prima. Michelotti, Graciela, ed. (p. 1428)
Fernández de Moratín, Leandro. Si de la Ninas. (p. 1572)
Fernández de Oviedo y Valdés, Gonzalo. Bestiario de Indias. (p. 171)
Fernandez, Diana. Little Chickadee: A True Backyard Story. (p. 1026)
Fernandez, Elizabeth. Screenwriting & Directing for Secondary Schools. (p. 1533)
Fernandez, Eugenia. Astria & the Missing Prince. (p. 109)
Fernandez, Francisco. Arca de Noé. Osorio, Sergio, illus. (p. 95)
—Creacion. Osorio, Sergio, illus. (p. 378)
—Jonas. Osorio, Sergio, illus. (p. 925)
—Milagros de Jesus. Osorio, Sergio, illus. (p. 1142)
—Moises. Osorio, Sergio, illus. (p. 1160)
Fernandez, Giselle. Gigi & the Birthday Ring. Petersen, Sheli, illus. (p. 676)
Fernández, Jesús, et al. Curso Intensivo de Espanol: Niveles Intermedio y Superior: Clave. (p. 395)
—Curso Intensivo de Espanol: Niveles Elemental e Intermedio: Clave. (p. 395)
Fernandez, Joy C. Rockman. (p. 1483)
Fernandez, Joyce. Little Bird - Pajarito. (p. 1024)
Fernandez, Joyce & Marsh, Laura. Eins Is One. (p. 507)
—Eins und Zwei are One & Two. (p. 507)
—et Deux are One & Two. (p. 539)
—Is One. (p. 889)
—Um Is One. (p. 1810)
—y Dos are One & Two. (p. 1968)
Fernandez, Laura, illus. see Cowling, Douglas.
Fernandez, Laura, illus. see Jacobson, Rick.
Fernandez, Laura, illus. see Trottier, Maxine.
Fernandez, Leandro. Punisher. (p. 1417)
Fernandez, Leire Amigo, tr. see Wells, Rosemary & Rosemary, Wells.
Fernandez, Leo, illus. see Jones, Bruce.
Fernandez, Linda. Holiday Journey of Ppin & Sassha. (p. 788)
Fernandez, Lucia, illus. see de Sturtz, Maria Ester H.
Fernandez, Luciana, illus. see Repun, Graciela.
Fernandez, Maria Angulo, tr. see Scott, Michael & Scott, Michael.
Fernandez, Maria Xose, illus. see Caccamo, Pepe.
Fernandez, Martina. Jellybean: Jellybean Finds a Home. (p. 912)
Fernández, Mayra. Colores de Mi Mundo (Rainbow Kids) (p. 344)
Fernandez, Mayte. Secrets of Your Guardian Angels. (p. 1546)
Fernandez, Melanie, jt. auth. see Green, Rayna.
Fernandez, Nacho. nueva era del sueno vol. 2: Los desiertos del Norte: The New Age of Dreams vol. 2: the Deserts of the North. (p. 1270)
Fernández, Pablo, illus. see Pescetti, Luis María.
Fernández Paz, Agustín, jt. auth. see Paz, Agustín Fernández.
Fernandez, Q., jt. auth. see Fernandez, A.
Fernández, Queta, jt. auth. see Denman, K. L.
Fernández, Queta, jt. auth. see Goobie, Beth.
Fernández, Queta, jt. auth. see Hillert, Margaret.
Fernández, Queta, jt. auth. see Kyi, Tanya Lloyd.
Fernández, Queta, jt. auth. see Ryan, Darlene.
Fernández, Queta, tr. see Hillert, Margaret.
Fernández, Queta, tr. see Janovitz, Marilyn.
Fernández, Queta, tr. see Mora, Pat.
Fernández, Queta, tr. see Roth, Carol.
Fernandez, Rafael. Diego's Family Christmas. McGee, Warner, illus. (p. 437)
Fernandez, Raul, illus. see Bedard, Tony.
Fernandez, Texanna. My Mighty Mother. (p. 1214)
Fernandez-Pacheco, Miguel. Dos Anos con Leonardo. (p. 472)
Fernando, Almena, jt. auth. see Almena, Fernando.
Fernando, Alonso, jt. auth. see Alonso, Fernando.
Fernando, Jill. Chronicles of Drizzlemania. (p. 317)
Ferne, Catherine. B Sounds. (p. 123)
—C Sounds. (p. 250)
—D Sounds. (p. 398)
—G Sounds. (p. 651)
—K Sounds. (p. 941)
—P Sounds. (p. 1316)
—T Sounds. (p. 1694)
Fernley, Fran. I Wrote on All Four Walls: Teens Speak Out on Violence. (p. 849)
Ferns, Kevin, illus. see Haydon, David J.
Fernstrom, Madelyn H. & Spiker, Ted. Runner's Diet: The Ultimate Eating Plan That Will Make Every Runner (and Walker) Leaner, Faster, & Fitter. (p. 1497)
Ferone, Jen. Number Fun with Riley. Spang, Janine, photos by. (p. 1271)
Ferraiolo, Jack D. Big Splash. (p. 184)
—Quick Fix. (p. 1427)
—Sidekicks. (p. 1573)
Ferran, Adriana, illus. see Doyle, Arthur.
Ferran, Adriana, illus. see Stevenson, Robert L. & Facio, Sebastian.
Ferran, Alexandri, et al. Agatha Christie. (p. 29)
Ferran, Daniel, illus. see Doyle, Arthur.
Ferran, Daniel, illus. see Shakespeare, William.
Ferrándiz, Elena. Media Naranja. (p. 1118)
—Mis Primeras 1000 Palabras/My First 1,000 Words. (p. 1150)
Ferrando, Carol, illus. see Sullivan, Maureen.
Ferrante, Joanne. R. G.'s on Vacation! (p. 1429)
—Where Do the Christmas Trees Go? (p. 1907)
Ferrante, Marguerite A., jt. auth. see Aranda, Margaret.
Ferrara, Brian. Crowpsey / Rufus & Cleveland. Knudtsen, Ken, illus. (p. 386)
Ferrara, Cos. Anna Comstock: A Love Affair with Nature. (p. 85)
—Babe Didrikson Zaharias: Outcast & Hero. (p. 123)
—Mary Cassatt: The Life & Art of a Genteel Rebel. (p. 1100)
Ferrara, Eduardo, illus. see Jacobson, Ryan.
Ferrara, Eduardo, illus. see Terrell, Brandon.
Ferrara, Gin. I'm Not Afraid of Snakes. (p. 859)
Ferrara, Jerry. Rock-O File. (p. 1482)
Ferrara, Joanne, jt. auth. see Thompson, Lauren.
Ferrara, Madeleine, illus. see Keusal, Eugene L.
Ferrara-Lester, Lisa. Sky's the Limit. (p. 1587)
Ferrari, Antongionata, illus. see Colloredo, Sabino.
Ferrari, Antongionata, illus. see Panzieri, Lucia.
Ferrari, G. m. Lake, Sky, Dragonfly. (p. 972)
Ferrari, Michael. Born to Fly. (p. 214)
Ferrari, Vincent. Blogosfear. (p. 200)
Ferraris, Zoë. Galaxy Pirates: Hunt for the Pyxis. (p. 653)
Ferraro, Bonita. Be a Good Citizen: A Content Area Reader-Social Studies. (p. 148)
—Rules All Around: A Content Area Reader-health. (p. 1495)
Ferraro Close, Laura. Farmer in the Dell. (p. 574)
—Little Boy Blue. (p. 1025)
Ferraro Close, Laura, illus. see Plourde, Lynn.
Ferraro, Damiano, jt. auth. see Fiset, Pierre.
Ferraro, Lynn. Joey Discovers Astronomy. Leslie, Melissa, illus. (p. 920)
—Joey's Day of Discovery. Leslie, Melissa, illus. (p. 920)
Ferraro, Maureen. Sugar & Els: The Mystery. (p. 1672)
Ferraro-Oster, Margaret, illus. see Messinger, Midge.
Ferraz, Thiago, illus. see Grimm, Jacob, et al.
Ferré, Rosario. Medio Pollito. (p. 1120)
—Sapita Sabia y Otros Cuentos. Diego, Rapi, illus. (p. 1514)
—Sombrero Magico. (p. 1608)
Ferreira, Ann Devine, jt. auth. see Ferreira, Bailey.
Ferreira, Ann Devine & Bailey. Hi I'm Bailey & I'm Getting A New Special Family. (p. 775)
Ferreira, Bailey & Ferreira, Ann Devine. Bailey Enjoys His First Holiday Season. (p. 133)
Ferreira, Charity. Ice Cream Treats: Easy Ways to Transform Your Favorite Ice Cream into Spectacular Desserts. Beisch, Leigh, photos by. (p. 850)
Ferreira, Melissa, illus. see Harley, Bill.
Ferreiro, Carmen. Mad Cow Disease. Alcamo, I. Edward, ed. (p. 1069)
Ferreiro, Natalia, jt. auth. see Kraselsky, Rebeca.
Ferrell, Annie K. Benny the Burro Bears His Burden. (p. 165)
Ferrell, Claudine L. In the Valley of the Grizzly. (p. 867)
Ferrell, David L. Pecos Bill. (p. 1334)
Ferrell, Deen. Cryptic Spaces: Book One. (p. 387)
Ferrell, Miralee. Horse for Kate. (p. 799)
Ferrell, Nancy Warren. Battle of the Little Bighorn in United States History. (p. 146)
Ferrell, Sean. I Don't Like Koala. Santoso, Charles, illus. (p. 837)
Ferren, Stella. 5 Great Little Read-A-Loud Stories for Grandparents. (p. 1992)
Ferrenburg, Susie, illus. see Snyder, Sandy.
Ferrer, Al, ed. see Buckley, James.
Ferrer, Al, ed. see Burgan, Michael.
Ferrer, Al, ed. see Gigliotti, Jim.
Ferrer, Al, ed. see Marini, Matt.
Ferrer, Al, ed. see Peterson, Brian C.
Ferrer, Al, ed. see Walters, John.
Ferrer, Caridad. When the Stars Go Blue. (p. 1905)
Ferrer, Caridad, et al. Prom Ever After: Haute Date Save the Last Dance Prom & Circumstance. (p. 1411)
Ferrer, Isabel, illus. see Kurusa, Monika.
Ferrer, María, tr. see Gaiman, Neil & Pratchett, Terry.
Ferrer, María, tr. see Gaiman, Neil.
Ferrer, María, tr. see Ozawa, Tadashi.
Ferrer, María, tr. see Spiegelman, Art.
Ferrer, María, tr. Cómo Dibujar Manga: Color. Vol. 6 (p. 350)
—Cómo Dibujar Manga: Chicas Guapas. Vol. 7 (p. 350)
Ferrer, María, tr. from JPN. Cómo Dibujar Manga: Personajes. Vol. 1 (p. 350)
—Cómo Dibujar Manga: El Cuerpo Humano. Vol. 4 (p. 350)
—Cómo Dibujar Manga: Aplicación y Práctica. Vol. 3 (p. 350)
—Tecnicas (p. 1712)
Ferrer, Martin Luis Guzman, tr. see Adamson, Thomas K.
Ferrer, Martin Luis Guzman, tr. see Bullard, Lisa.
Ferrer, Martin Luis Guzman, tr. see DeGezelle, Terri & Capstone Press Staff.
Ferrer, Martin Luis Guzman, tr. see DeGezelle, Terri.
Ferrer, Martin Luis Guzman, tr. see Doeden, Matt & Capstone Press Editors.
Ferrer, Martin Luis Guzman, tr. see Doeden, Matt & Capstone Press Staff.
Ferrer, Martin Luis Guzman, tr. see Doeden, Matt.
Ferrer, Martin Luis Guzman, tr. see Lindeen, Carol K. & Capstone Press Editors.
Ferrer, Martin Luis Guzman, tr. see Lindeen, Carol K. & Capstone Press Staff.
Ferrer, Martin Luis Guzman, tr. see Lindeen, Carol K., et al.
Ferrer, Martin Luis Guzman, tr. see Marks, Jennifer L. & Bruning, Matt.
Ferrer, Martin Luis Guzman, tr. see Olson, Nathan.
Ferrer, Martin Luis Guzman, tr. see Riehecky, Janet & Capstone Press Staff.
Ferrer, Martin Luis Guzman, tr. see Schuette, Sarah L. & Capstone Press Staff.
Ferrer, Martin Luis Guzman, tr. see Williams, Linda D.
Ferrer, Sean Hepburn. Audrey Hepburn, an Elegant Spirit: A Son Remembers. (p. 115)
Ferreras, Alberto, jt. auth. see Hines, Chrissie.
Ferreri, Della Ross. Huggle Wuggle Bedtime Snuggle. (p. 825)
—Star of the Show. Weinstock, Tony, illus. (p. 1641)
Ferrett, Russell. Builders of the Past. (p. 238)
—Great Cities of the World. (p. 714)
—Ice Ages: When the World Chills Out. (p. 850)
Ferri, Francesca. Cucu—Te veo! Mascotas. Ferri, Francesca, illus. (p. 389)
—Good Night, Teddy. (p. 700)
—Peek-A-Boo. (p. 1334)
—Peek-A-Boo Jungle. (p. 1334)
—Peek-a-Boo Pets. Ferri, Francesca, illus. (p. 1334)
—Peek-a-Boo Polar Bear & Friends (p. 1334)
—Peek-A-Boo Sea. (p. 1334)
Ferri, Francesca, illus. see Hellier, Catherine.
Ferri, Giuliano. Illustrated Stories from Aesop. (p. 858)
Ferri, Giuliano, illus. see Gray, Luli.
Ferri, Giuliano, illus. see Grün, Anselm, et al.
Ferri, Giuliano, illus. see Hao, K. T.
Ferri, Giuliano, illus. see Jackson, Antonia.
Ferri, Giuliano, illus. see Kim, Byung-Gyu & Hao, K. T.
Ferri, Giuliano, illus. see McCarthy, Michael.
Ferri, Giuliano, illus. see Spinelli, Eileen.
Ferri, Guiliano, illus. see Kimmel, Elizabeth Cody.
Ferri, Jean-Yves. Asterix & the Picts. Conrad, Didier, illus. (p. 108)
Ferri, Jean-Yves, et al. Asterix & the Picts. Conrad, Didier, illus. (p. 108)
Ferriell, Phil. Bernie Bocks Makes the Team. (p. 167)
Ferrier, Charlotte. Home for Little Fish. Hirashima, Jean, illus. (p. 792)
Ferrier, Florian, et al. Wake up, Spring. Ferrier, Katherine, illus. (p. 1853)
Ferrier, George S. Bo-Peep of the Isles. (p. 205)
Ferrier, Katherine, illus. see Ferrier, Florian, et al.
Ferrier, Paul Eugene. Kavaldo & His Diamond Pills. Gettys, Allan, illus. (p. 946)
Ferrigno, Angela, illus. see Jane, Sarah.
Ferrill, Christi. Adventures of Max & Bloom: Alphabet Gifts. (p. 20)
Ferrin, Wendy Wakefield. Germs on Their Fingers! Tono, Lucia, tr. (p. 667)
—Grandmother's Alligator: Burukenge Wa Nyanya. Mwangi, Simmon, tr. (p. 709)
Ferris, Aimee. Girl Overboard. (p. 678)
Ferris, Carole Anne, illus. see Johnson, Joanne Gail.
Ferris, Diane J. Weather Watcher. (p. 1870)
Ferris, Jean. Love among the Walnuts. (p. 1059)
—Of Sound Mind. (p. 1279)
—Once upon a Marigold: Part Comedy, Part Love Story, Part Everything-but-the-kitchen-Sink. (p. 1293)
—Once upon a Marigold. (p. 1293)
—Thrice upon a Marigold: A Royal Kidnapping Caper. (p. 1744)
—Twice upon a Marigold. (p. 1801)
Ferris, Jeri Chase. Demanding Justice: A Story about Mary Ann Shadd Cary. Smith, Kimanne, illus. (p. 425)
—Noah Webster & His Words. Kirsch, Vincent X., illus. (p. 1261)
Ferris, Julie, ed. see Dorling Kindersley Publishing Staff.
Ferris, Julie Alfriend. Badges, Egg Salad, & Green Jackets: The Masters a to Z. (p. 132)
Ferris, Margaret Ann. Bart the Batronaut. Gove, Frank Stanley, illus. (p. 140)
Ferris, Susan. Mom's Backyard Zoo. Rood, Phil, illus. (p. 1163)
Ferrisi, Kevin. Kids Can Too. (p. 953)
Férriz, Ramón Gónzalez. Franz Kafka -el miedo a la Vida. (p. 631)
Ferro, Beatriz. Arriba el Telon. (p. 101)
Ferro, Jeffrey. Sexual Misconduct & the Church. (p. 1556)
Ferro, Ursula. Tanny's Meow. Huff, Ariella, illus. (p. 1705)
Ferron, Joanne. Luis Saves the Llama. (p. 1064)
Ferrone, John M. Gus & the Golden Dragon. Ferrone, John M., illus. (p. 732)
—Gus & the Pirate Treasure. Ferrone, John M., illus. (p. 732)
—Margo & the Secret Pond. Ferrone, John M., photos by. (p. 1092)
—Margo & the Trail Ride. Ferrone, John M., photos by. (p. 1092)
—Margo Goes on Safari. Ferrone, John M., illus. (p. 1092)
Ferry, Ann. Cozy the Pine Tree & Swaylee the Elm in Featherwood Forest (p. 375)
—Dollop the Cloud & Dee the Bee. Swope, Brenda, illus. (p. 464)
—Gusty the Cloud & Streakie the Snail. Swope, Brenda, illus. (p. 733)
Ferry, Beth. Land Shark. Mantle, Ben, illus. (p. 974)
—Stick & Stone. Lichtenheld, Tom, illus. (p. 1649)
Ferry, Francis. Job-O E: Elementary. Ellis, Amy, illus. (p. 919)
Ferry, Joe. History of African American Social Clubs. (p. 783)
Ferry, Joseph. American Flag: The Story of Old Glory. Moreno, Barry, ed. (p. 60)
—Jefferson Memorial: A Monument to Greatness. Moreno, Barry, ed. (p. 912)
—Jefferson Memorial. (p. 912)
—Maria Goeppert Mayer. (p. 1093)
—Star-Spangled Banner: Story of Our National Anthem. Moreno, Barry, ed. (p. 1641)
—Thomas Jefferson. (p. 1739)
—Vietnam Veterans Memorial: Remembering a Generation & a War. Moreno, Barry, ed. (p. 1841)
—Vietnam Veterans Memorial. (p. 1841)

—Vietnamese Immigration. (p. 1841)
Ferry, Joseph, jt. auth. see Marcovitz, Hal.
Ferry, Monica. Search & Rescue Specialist & Careers in FEMA. (p. 1537)
Ferry, Pasqual. Ultimate X-Men Fantastic Four. (p. 1810)
Ferry, Pasqual, jt. illus. see Kubert, Andy.
Ferry, Pasqual, et al. A+X=Awesome (p. 121)
Ferry, Sharon. Granddad Bud: A Veterans Day Story. (p. 707)
Ferry, Steven. Martin Van Buren. (p. 1098)
Ferry, Suzanne Sumner. Corinna the Christmas Elf. (p. 367)
Ferry, Therese. Feed My Lambs. (p. 580)
—Where Is God? Doran, David, illus. (p. 1908)
Fershee, Joshua P. Energy Law: A Context & Practice Casebook. (p. 528)
Fertig, Dennis. Something Rotten at Village Market. McMahon, Bob, tr. (p. 1610)
—Sylvia Earle: Ocean Explorer (p. 1692)
Fertig, Michael P. Musical Mystery Scooby Doo! McKee, Darren, illus. (p. 1194)
Fertig, Todd. Missionaries' Daughter. (p. 1153)
Ferut, Michael. Gettysburg. (p. 670)
—RMS Queen Mary. (p. 1476)
—St. Louis Cemetery No. 1. (p. 1638)
—Winchester Mystery House. (p. 1935)
Fessahaye, Miss Mehret. Layla the Animals' Friend. (p. 981)
Fesseha, Zewditu. Lakech One: Amharic Ethiopian Script. Mammo, Rebecca et al, eds. (p. 972)
Fessler, Bob. Hey! You Aren't the Boss of Me! (p. 775)
Fessler, Jennifer. Precious Is Worried. (p. 1394)
Fest, Joachim C. Inside Hitler's Bunker: The Last Days of the Third Reich. Dembo, Margot, tr. (p. 876)
Festante, Dom. Computer Applications Student Activity Book. Matthews, Douglas L., ed. (p. 354)
Feterl, Bill, illus. see Cartwright, Nancy & Jones, Joanna.
Fetherston, Catherine, illus. see Hernandez, Regina.
Fett, Ruth E. Goldilocks & the Three Bears: Baxter Bee Teaches about Respect. (p. 696)
Fetter, James, illus. see Fetter, Jim.
Fetter, Jim. Raven, the Kitty Cat, & the Mouse. Fetter, James, illus. (p. 1441)
—Raven, the Kitty Cat & the Mouse. the Hot Air Balloon. (p. 1441)
Fetter-Vorm, Jonathan, jt. auth. see Kelman, Ari.
Fettig, Jamie. Creator's Manual for Your Body. (p. 380)
Fettig, Pamela. Leelah at the Lake. Strecker, Darren, illus. (p. 987)
Fetty, Margaret. Chimpanzees. (p. 306)
—Fire Horses. (p. 590)
—Helen Keller: Break down the Walls! (p. 763)
—Miniature Schnauzer: Whiskers. (p. 1146)
—Parrots. (p. 1325)
—Sea Lions. (p. 1534)
—Seizure-Alert Dogs. (p. 1548)
—Show Horses. (p. 1570)
—Yorkshire Terrier: Tiny but Tough. (p. 1972)
Fetty, Margaret & Jasinski, Diane. Three Cheers for August: Prek-K. (p. 1741)
Fetty, Margaret & Jasinski, Diane, eds. Three Cheers for December: PreK-K. (p. 1741)
—Three Cheers for February. (p. 1741)
—Three Cheers for January. (p. 1741)
Fetty, Margaret, ed. Ultimate Book of Second Grade Skills: Grade 2. Hierstein, Judy & Boyer, Lyn, illus. (p. 1809)
Fetz, Ingrid, illus. see Fox, Paula.
Fetzer, Erin. Sonday System Readers - 6a-10c Breckman, Cindy, ed. (p. 1611)
Fetzer, James H. Evolution of Intelligence: Are Humans the Only Animals with Minds? Num. 63 (p. 547)
Feucht, Jon. Tan Car. (p. 1704)
Feuchter, Anke. Felix from Berlin. Durand, Élodie, illus. (p. 581)
Feuer, Bonnie. Goliath's Secret. Platt, Sharai, illus. (p. 696)
Feuerbach, Jennifer. Chef Philip Has Autism. Wroth, Dean, illus. (p. 297)
Feurer, Paige. And Then It Rained on Malcolm. Farr, Rich, illus. (p. 71)
Feuti, Norman. Pretending You Care: The Retail Employee Handbook. (p. 1398)
Feutl. Rescue at Fort Edmonton: Teacher's Guide. (p. 1462)
Feutl, Rita. Bike Thief (p. 185)
—Rescue at Fort Edmonton (p. 1462)
Feutl, Rita, jt. auth. see Waldman, Debby.
Few, Cyndi. My Family Loves Me: For My Grandson, Talon. (p. 1203)
Few, Valerie. Filbert & Friends. (p. 586)
Fewer, Patrick W. Sammy the Snow Snake: Christmas Rain. (p. 1508)
—Sammy the Snow Snake: A Halloween Haunting Yukon Style. (p. 1508)
Fey, David. Whitetail. (p. 1914)
Fey, Jaki. Last Goose Concert. Hubenthal, Dayna, illus. (p. 978)
Fey, Sid & Vitello, Kathy. Being Game: For the Love of Your Life. (p. 161)
Feyder, Linda, jt. ed. see Chavez, Denise.
Feyer, Diane Le, illus. see Stortz, Diane.
Feyh, Alexa, illus. see Feyh, Janelle.
Feyh, Janelle. Does God Have a Remote Control? Feyh, Alexa & Deghand, Tim, illus. (p. 460)
Feyyaz. F Prinzip (p. 559)
Fforde, Jasper. Eye of Zoltar. (p. 558)
—Last Dragonslayer. (p. 977)
—Song of the Quarkbeast: The Chronicles of Kazam, Book 2. (p. 1611)
—Song of the Quarkbeast. (p. 1611)
ffoulkes, Joy. Kitty Kangaroo. (p. 963)
Ffrench-Davis, Ricardo. Reforming Latin America's Economies: After Market Fundamentalism. (p. 1456)
FHM Magazine Staff. FHM Women: The Exclusive Collection. Fletcher, Brekke & Hecht, Randi, eds. (p. 583)
Fhur, Ute, et al. Abeja. Fhur, Ute et al, trs. (p. 4)
Fiala, Émilie, illus. see Curtiss, Dominique.
Fiammenghi, Gioia, illus. see deRubertis, Barbara.
Fiammenghi, Gioia, illus. see Parker, David.
Fiammenghi, Gioia, illus. see Smith, Robert Kimmel.
Fiammenghi, Gioia, illus. see Williams Aber, Linda.
Fiani, M. Cat Named Monkey. (p. 278)
Fianko, Sandra. Sunnie Meets the Bears. (p. 1677)
Ficarra, Katy. Legend of El. (p. 988)
Fichera, Liz. Hooked. (p. 795)
—Played. (p. 1372)
Fichtelberg, Susan. Encountering Enchantment: A Guide to Speculative Fiction for Teens (p. 524)
Fichthorn, Ashley. Big E, Meet Zeke, Your New Brother. Moise, Nahomie, illus. (p. 181)
Fick, Dean K. Lakeside & Marblehead Railroad (p. 972)
Fickey, Brenda. Beckoning Shadows (p. 156)
—Echoing Silence. (p. 502)
—Whispering Darkness. (p. 1912)
Ficklin, Jonene H. Garden Gate. (p. 656)
—Orinoco Intrigue. (p. 1304)
Ficklin, Sherry D. Losing Logan. (p. 1054)
Ficklin, Sherry D. & Jolley, Tyler H. Extracted. (p. 555)
Fickling, Phillip. Fillmore & Geary Take Off! Shulman, Mark, illus. (p. 586)
Fickling, Phillip, illus. see Shulman, Mark.
Ficocelli, Elizabeth. Child's Guide to First Holy Communion. Blake, Anne Catharine, illus. (p. 305)
—Child's Guide to Reconciliation. Blake, Anne Catharine, tr. (p. 305)
—Child's Guide to the Rosary. Blake, Anne Catharine, illus. (p. 305)
—Child's Guide to the Seven Sacraments. Blake, Anne Catharine, illus. (p. 305)
—Imitation of Christ for Children: A Guide to Following Jesus. Sabatino, Chris, illus. (p. 861)
—Kid Tea Dibley, Glin, illus. (p. 951)
—Kid Tea. Dibley, Glin, illus. (p. 951)
—Where Do Deacons Come From? Wirrenga, Shannon, illus. (p. 1907)
—Where Do Priests Come From? Wirrenga, Shannon, illus. (p. 1907)
Fiddick, Calay. Fortieth Horse. Levy, Shaun & Jamieson, Eden, illus. (p. 623)
Fiddy, Samantha Lane, illus. see Lin, Kelly Jenkins.
Fidge, Louis. Premier English Quick Tests. (p. 1395)
—Premier Maths Quick Tests. (p. 1395)
Fidler, Julie Anne. Adventures in Holy Matrimony: For Better or the Absolute Worst. (p. 15)
Fidler, Kathleen. Boy with the Bronze Axe. (p. 220)
—Flash the Sheepdog. (p. 602)
Fidler, Mark. Blaze of the Great Cliff. (p. 198)
—Pond Puckster. (p. 1382)
—Two Faced Forward. (p. 1803)
Fiebelkorn, Claire, jt. auth. see Bond, Janice.
Fiebelkorn, Ian. Staying Alive! How Animals Stay Safe. (p. 1645)
Fieber, Valerie. Three Caterpillars & a Lost Toy. (p. 1741)
Fiebiger, John, illus. see Hand, Reuben.
Fiedler, Christamaria. Verano de los Animales. Kessler, Siglint, illus. (p. 1836)
Fiedler, Joseph Daniel, illus. see Hayes, Joe.
Fiedler, Joseph Daniel, illus. see McKissack, Fredrick L. & McKissack, Patricia C.
Fiedler, Julie. Boas. (p. 205)
—Bulldogs. (p. 240)
—Cobras. (p. 337)
—Doberman Pinschers. (p. 459)
—German Shepherd Dogs. (p. 666)
—Great Danes. (p. 715)
—How to Deal with Anger. (p. 816)
—How to Deal with Insults. (p. 816)
—Learning about Food Chains & Food Webs with Graphic Organizers. (p. 984)
—Learning about Force & Motion with Graphic Organizers. (p. 984)
—Learning about Heat & Temperature with Graphic Organizers. (p. 984)
—Mambas. (p. 1084)
—Pit Bulls. (p. 1364)
—Pythons. (p. 1422)
—Rattlesnakes. (p. 1440)
—Rottweilers. (p. 1491)
—Vipers. (p. 1844)
Fiedler, Lisa. Green-Eyed Monster. (p. 721)
—Mouseheart. (p. 1182)
—Mouseheart. To, Vivienne, illus. (p. 1182)
Fiedler, Lisa, illus. see Reisfeld, Randi & Bell, Taryn.
Fiedler, Lisa & Wallach, Anya. Showstopper. (p. 1571)
Fiegenschuh, Emily, illus. see Hess, Nina.
Fiegenschuh, Emily, illus. see Qitsualik, Rachel A.
Fiegenschuh, Emily, illus. see Qitsualik-Tinsley, Rachel & Qitsualik-Tinsley, Sean.
Fiegenshuh, Emily, illus. see Banerjee, Anjali.
Fiegenshuh, Emily, illus. see Ransom, Candice.
Fiehn, Terry, et al. Citizenship Studies for Key Stage 4 & GCSE. (p. 323)
Field, Andrea R. Heat. (p. 760)
—Matter. (p. 1109)
Field, Andrea R., ed. Heat. (p. 760)
—Matter. (p. 1109)
—Science of Physics. (p. 1527)
Field, Brett. Screno Magic Medieval Collision. (p. 1533)
Field, Conrad. Alaska Ocean ABCs. Field, Conrad, illus. (p. 34)
Field, Elaine. Sounds (Cuddly Cuffs with Hang Tag) (p. 1615)
—Toys (Cuddly Cuffs W/Hang Tag) Finn, Rebecca, illus. (p. 1774)
Field, Elaine, illus. see Bedford, David.
Field, Ellen. Merry Ham-Ham Christmas. Haefele, Steve, illus. (p. 1129)
Field, Eugene. Christmas Tales & Christmas Verse. (p. 316)
—Christmas Tales & Christmas Verse. Storer, Florence, illus. (p. 316)
—Dibdin's Ghost. (p. 435)
—Little Book of Western Verse. (p. 1025)
—Love Songs of Childhood. (p. 1060)
—Love Songs of Children. (p. 1060)
—Lullaby Land: Songs of Childhood. (p. 1064)
—Lullaby Land: Songs of Childhood. Robinson, Charles, illus. (p. 1064)
—Profitable Tales. (p. 1410)
—Second Book of Verse. (p. 1539)
—Songs & Other Verse. (p. 1611)
—Sugar-Plum Tree & Other Verses: Includes a Read-and-Listen. Peat, Fern Bisel, illus. (p. 1673)
—With Trumpet & Drum. (p. 1942)
Field, Jacob & Grant, R. J. Superstars of History. Basher, Simon, illus. (p. 1684)
Field, James, illus. see Crosbie, Duncan.
Field, James, illus. see Dixon, Dougal & Picture Window Books Staff.
Field, James, illus. see Dixon, Dougal.
Field, James, illus. see Eason, Sarah.
Field, James, illus. see Jeffrey, Gary.
Field, James, illus. see Shone, Rob.
Field, James, illus. see Turnbull, Stephen & Tulloch, Coral.
Field, James, illus. see Turnbull, Stephen.
Field, James, illus. see West, David.
Field, James, jt. illus. see Shone, Rob.
Field, James, jt. illus. see Weston, Steve.
Field, James & Weston, Steve. Iguanodon & Other Leaf-Eating Dinosaurs (p. 856)
Field, Jenepher. Cloth Covered Notebook: That Was My Mother's Story. (p. 334)
Field, Jim, illus. see Bently, Peter.
Field, Jim, illus. see Bright, Rachel.
Field, Jim, illus. see Robinson, Michelle.
Field, Jim, illus. see Watt, Fiona.
Field, Jon Eben. Cleaning Chemistry. (p. 330)
—Kitchen Chemistry. (p. 962)
—Medicine Cabinet Chemistry. (p. 1119)
—Scurrying Cockroaches. (p. 1534)
Field, Jon Eben, jt. auth. see Eben Field, Jon.
Field, Jon Eben, jt. auth. see Rodger, Ellen.
Field, Jon Eben & Hoena, Blake. Mythology: Begin Your Quest for Facts, Photos, & Fun Fit for Gods & Goddesses. (p. 1227)
Field, Mandy, illus. see Doherty, Gillian, ed.
Field, Mandy, jt. auth. see Milbourne, Anna.
Field, Matthew S. Father Like a Tree. Hedderich, Tom, illus. (p. 577)
—Three Pigs, Business School, & Wolf Hash Stew. Hedderich, Tom, illus. (p. 1743)
Field, Nancy & Karasov, Corliss. Discovering Wolves. Hunkel, Cary, illus. (p. 450)
Field, Nancy H. Discovering Sharks & Rays. Maydak, Michael S., illus. (p. 449)
Field, Rachel. Oración para los Niños. Romay, Alexis, tr. (p. 1301)
—Prayer for a Child: Lap Edition. Jones, Elizabeth Orton, illus. (p. 1393)
—Prayer for a Child. Jones, Elizabeth Orton, illus. (p. 1393)
Field, Randi. Gulf States of Mexico. (p. 731)
—Mexico's Gulf States. (p. 1131)
Field, Shelly. Career Opportunities in Advertising & Public Relations. (p. 267)
—Career Opportunities in Casinos & Casino Hotels, Second Edition. (p. 267)
—Career Opportunities in Radio. (p. 267)
—Career Opportunities in the Sports Industry. (p. 267)
—Ferguson Career Coach (p. 582)
—Ferguson Career Coach: Managing Your Career in Education. (p. 582)
—Ferguson Career Coach: Managing Your Career in Law Enforcement. (p. 582)
—Ferguson Career Coach: Managing Your Career in the Art Industry. (p. 582)
—Ferguson Career Coach: Managing Your Career in the Music Industry. (p. 582)
—Ferguson Career Coach: Managing Your Career in the Sports Industry. (p. 582)
—Ferguson Career Coach: Managing Your Career in the Computer Industry. (p. 582)
—Ferguson Career Coach: Managing Your Career in the Health Care Industry. (p. 582)
—Managing Your Career in Education. (p. 1086)
—Managing Your Career in the Health Care Industry. (p. 1086)
—Managing Your Career in Theater & Performing Arts. (p. 1086)
—Managing Your Career in Theater & the Performing Arts. (p. 1086)
Field, Shelly & Orange County Association Staff. Career Opportunities in the Retail & Wholesale Industry, Second Edition. (p. 267)
Field, Simon Quellen, jt. auth. see Coelho, Alexa.
Field, Susan, illus. see Leavy, Una.
Field, Tom. Secrets in the Shadows: The Art & Life of Gene Colan. (p. 1545)
Fielder, Barbara L. Missy, the Kitty, Plays Hide & Go Seek. (p. 1154)
—Missy, the Kitty, Visits the Veterinarian. (p. 1155)
—Treats for Missy, the Kitty. (p. 1783)
Fielder, Barbara L. & Broady, Brianna. Missy, the Kitty, Learns about Sharing. (p. 1154)
—Missy, the Mischievous Kitty. (p. 1155)
—Missy, the Patriotic Kitty. (p. 1155)
Fielder, Geraint. Life Lines: Sane Meditations for a Mad World. (p. 1011)
Fielder, John, photos by. Do You See What I See? (p. 458)
Fielder, Scott. 10 Greatest 21st Century Innovations. (p. 1993)
Fieldhouse, Vicky, illus. see Richards, Katherine.
Fielding, Beth. Animal Baths: Wild & Wonderful Ways Animals Get Clean! Greenelsh, Susan, illus. (p. 76)
—Animal Colors: A Rainbow of Colors from Animals Around the World. (p. 77)
—Animal Colors. (p. 77)
Fielding, Grace, illus. see Crawford, Joanne.
Fielding, Grace, illus. see McRobbie, Narelle.
Fielding, Jonathan E., ed. Annual Review of Public Health (p. 87)
Fielding, Sarah. Governess or the Little Female Academy. (p. 704)
—Governess, or, the Little Female Academy. (p. 704)
Fielding-Lowe, Thea. Hey Auntie, What Color Is God? (p. 774)
Fieldler, Julie. How to Deal with Teasing. (p. 816)
Field-Ridley, Jenan. Adam & Eve Make a Big, Big Mistake: Bible Stories for Caribbean Children. (p. 11)
Fields, April, jt. auth. see Ball, Willow.
Fields, B. H., jt. auth. see Bortz, Fred.
Fields, B. H. & Bortz, Fred. Understanding Neutrons. (p. 1816)
—Understanding Photons. (p. 1816)
—Understanding Quarks. (p. 1816)
Fields, Bryan W. Lunchbox & the Aliens. Atteberry, Kevan, illus. (p. 1065)
Fields, Carole Ruth, photos by see Watt, D. Alison.
Fields, Cassidy. Disaster Lake. (p. 446)
Fields, Doug. Creative Times with God: Discovering New Ways to Connect with the SAVIOR. (p. 380)
Fields, Doug & Eastman, Brett. Starting: To Go Where God Wants You to Be - 6 Small Group Sessions on Beginning Life Together (p. 1644)
—Surrendering Your Life to Honor God (p. 1686)
Fields, Doug, et al. Connecting Your Heart to Others: 6 Small Group Sessions on Fellowship (p. 358)
—Growing to Be Like Jesus: 6 Small Group Sessions on Discipleship (p. 726)
Fields, Frever. Frumpy McDoogle: And the Legend of the Ruby Toad. (p. 646)
Fields, J. Choosing a Career as a Nurse-Midwife. (p. 310)
Fields, Jan. Big City Blues: Back to Wonderland. Altmann, Scott, illus. (p. 180)
—Calm Before the Storm: A Night in Sleepy Hollow. Altmann, Scott, illus. (p. 254)
—Chase the Chupacabra. Brundage, Scott, illus. (p. 294)
—Emerald Dragon. (p. 517)
—Facing a Frenemy. (p. 561)
—Ghost Light Burning: An Up2U Mystery Adventure. Fabbretti, Valerio, illus. (p. 671)
—Hack Attack: A Trip to Wonderland. Altmann, Scott, illus. (p. 735)
—Hunt for Sewer Gators. Brundage, Scott, illus. (p. 828)
—Lightning Strikes Twice: Escaping Great Expectations. Altmann, Scott, illus. (p. 1016)
—Meri Mercer Doesn't Lie, Mostly. (p. 1127)
—Novel Nightmare: The Purloined Story. Altmann, Scott, illus. (p. 1268)
—Really New School: An Up2U Action Adventure. To, Vivienne, illus. (p. 1450)
—Search for Bigfoot. Brundage, Scott, illus. (p. 1537)
—Tame Tahoe Tessie. Brundage, Scott, illus. (p. 1704)
—Tattletale Traitor. (p. 1707)
—Terrible Twin Mania. (p. 1721)
—Trapped in Stormy Seas: Sailing to Treasure Island. Altmann, Scott, illus. (p. 1779)
—Wellspring of Magic. (p. 1874)
—You Can Write Excellent Reports (p. 1974)
—You Can Write Great Letters & E-Mails (p. 1974)
Fields, Jan, jt. auth. see Fandel, Jennifer.
Fields, Jennifer. Choosing a Career as a Nurse-Midwife. (p. 310)
Fields, Joyce. Dear Bully: A Collection of Poems about Bullying. (p. 418)
Fields, Julianna. First-Generation Immigrant Families. (p. 595)
—Foster Families. (p. 624)
—Gay & Lesbian Parents. (p. 659)
—Kids Growing up Without a Home. (p. 953)
—Multiracial Families. (p. 1190)
Fields, Karl. Odd Job Squad. (p. 1278)
Fields, Kim, ed. see Heskett, Tracie.
Fields, Laura, illus. see Dodson, Peter & Library Association Staff.
Fields, Lisa, illus. see Allen, Nancy Kelly.
Fields, Lisa, illus. see Gonzales Bertrand, Diane.
Fields, Lisa, illus. see Ludwig, Trudy.
Fields, Lisa, illus. see Price, Mara & Ventura, Gabriela Baeza.
Fields, Lisa, illus. see Solomon, Sharon.
Fields, Lisa, jt. auth. see Corpi, Lucha.
Fields, Melissa. Auntie Silly & the Crazy Cousins Day Parade Class, Virginia Tyree, illus. (p. 115)
Fields, Randy. Vital Skills: How to Do Servant Evangelism. (p. 1846)
Fields, Sadie & Tango Books Staff. Book of Roman Pop-Up Board Games. Maddison, Kevin, illus. (p. 211)
Fields, T. S. Missing in the Mountains. (p. 1152)
Fields, Teesue H., jt. auth. see Carducci, Bernardo J.
Fields, Terri. Burro's Tortillas Rogers, Sherry, illus. (p. 244)
—Los Más Peligrosos Jacques, Laura, illus. (p. 1054)
—Most Dangerous Jacques, Laura, illus. (p. 1177)
—Most Dangerous Jacques, Laura, illus. (p. 1177)
—One Good Deed. Melmon, Deborah, illus. (p. 1295)
Fields, Timothy J. Indelible Ink: Adventures of a Baby Boomer. (p. 870)
Fields, Trisha A. Eggbert, the Hero. (p. 506)
Fields-Meyer, Ezra. E-Mergency. Lichtenheld, Tom, illus. (p. 492)
Fienberg, Anna. Figaro & Rumba & the Crocodile Cafe. King, Stephen Michael, illus. (p. 585)
—Horrendo's Curse: The Graphic Novel. Simard, Remy, illus. (p. 798)
—Madeline the Mermaid. James, Ann, illus. (p. 1070)
—Minton Goes! Underwater & Home at Last. Gamble, Kim, illus. (p. 1148)
—Power to Burn. (p. 1390)
Fienberg, Anna & Fienberg, Barbara. Once Tashi Met a Dragon. Gamble, Kim, illus. (p. 1292)
—Tashi & the Dancing Shoes. Gamble, Kim, illus. (p. 1706)
—Tashi & the Forbidden Room. Gamble, Kim, illus. (p. 1706)
—Tashi & the Golem. Gamble, Kim, illus. (p. 1706)
—Tashi & the Haunted House. Gamble, Kim, illus. (p. 1706)
—Tashi & the Mixed-up Monster. Gamble, Kim, illus. (p. 1706)
—Tashi & the Phoenix. Gamble, Kim, illus. (p. 1706)
—Tashi & the Royal Tomb. Gamble, Kim, illus. (p. 1706)
—Tashi & the Stolen Bus. Gamble, Kim, illus. (p. 1706)
—Tashi Collection Gamble, Kim, illus. (p. 1706)
—Tashi Lost in the City. Gamble, Kim, illus. (p. 1706)

—There Once Was a Boy Called Tashi. Gamble, Kim, illus. (p. 1730)
Fienberg, Barbara, jt. auth. see Fienberg, Anna.
Fieneig, Annette, illus. see Meinderts, Koos.
Fierstein, Harvey. Sissy Duckling. Cole, Henry, illus. (p. 1581)
Fierstein, Marcy. Smoke Mountain Adventure: Pop Top & Tab, the Ecology Explorers. (p. 1594)
Fiest, Bill. Halo Repair: A Nudge toward Wholeness. (p. 739)
Fife, Bruce, ed. see Hackbarth, Judith A.
Fife, Bruce, ed. see Saenger, Diana.
Fife, Jay, illus. see Kennedy, Kevin.
Fife, Stephen, et al. eds. One on One: Playing with a Purpose - Monologues for Kids 7-14. (p. 1296)
Fife, Wayne. Doing Fieldwork: Ethnographic Methods for Research in Developing Countries & Beyond. (p. 463)
Fifer, Barbara. Going along with Lewis & Clark. (p. 692)
Fifield, Kim, illus. see Dunkley, Cheryl.
Fifield, Lisa. Bears Make Rock Soup. Erdrich, Lise, illus. (p. 152)
Fiford, Tanya. Children under the Bed. (p. 303)
—How to Bake Grandm. (p. 814)
—Robin & the Pocket Dragon. (p. 1479)
Figg, Non, illus. see Gilpin, Rebecca.
Figg, Non, illus. see Pratt, Leonie & Stowell, Louie.
Figg, Non, illus. see Watt, Fiona.
Figg, Non, illus. see Watt, Fiona.
Figg, Non Et Al, illus. see Watt, Fiona.
Figglehorn, Fred & Fisher, J. J. Fred-Tastically Funny Jokes. (p. 632)
Figiel, Lisa. Another Bird in Our Nest. (p. 87)
—Swimming Is Fun! (p. 1691)
Figley, Marthy Rhodes. Clara Morgan & the Oregon Trail Journey. Orback, Craig, illus. (p. 326)
Figley, Marthy Rhodes & Figley, Marty Rhodes. Prison-Ship Adventure of James Forten, Revolutionary War Captive. Hammond, Ted & Carbajal, Richard, illus. (p. 1407)
Figley, Marty Rhodes. Emily & Carlo. Stock, Catherine, illus. (p. 518)
—John Greenwood's Journey to Bunker Hill. (p. 922)
—John Greenwood's Journey to Bunker Hill. Orback, Craig, illus. (p. 922)
—Night the Chimneys Fell. Marshall, Felicia, illus. (p. 1254)
—Prairie Adventure of Sarah & Annie, Blizzard Survivors. Hammond, Ted & Carbajal, Richard, illus. (p. 1392)
—Prairie Adventure of Sarah & Annie, Blizzard Survivors. Hammond, Ted & Carbajal, Richard Pimentel, illus. (p. 1392)
—President Lincoln, Willie Kettles, & the Telegraph Machine. (p. 1397)
—President Lincoln, Willie Kettles, & the Telegraph Machine. Riley, David, illus. (p. 1397)
—Prisoner for Liberty. Orback, Craig, illus. (p. 1407)
—Prison-Ship Adventure of James Forten, Revolutionary War Captive. Hammond, Ted & Carbajal, Richard, illus. (p. 1407)
—Saving the Liberty Bell. Lepp, Kevin, tr. (p. 1517)
—Saving the Liberty Bell. Lepp, Kevin, illus. (p. 1517)
—Schoolchildren's Blizzard. Haas, Shelly O., illus. (p. 1523)
—Washington Is Burning. Orback, Craig, illus. (p. 1860)
—Who Was William Penn? And Other Questions about the Founding of Pennsylvania. (p. 1919)
Figley, Marty Rhodes, jt. auth. see Figley, Marthy Rhodes.
Figley, Mary Rhodes. Prisoner for Liberty. (p. 1407)
Figorito, C. Go Far in the Car: Learning the AR Sound. (p. 686)
—In the City: Learning the Soft C Sound. (p. 865)
Figorito, Christine. How Leaves Change Color. (p. 810)
—Lungs in Your Body. (p. 1066)
—Real Facts about Rivers. (p. 1448)
Figorito, Juliet. Banded Sea Snake: Serpiente Marina Rayada. (p. 136)
—Banded Sea Snake. (p. 136)
—How We Use Globes. (p. 823)
Figorito, M. Matt Kenseth. (p. 1109)
Figorito, Marcus. Dime's Busy Day. (p. 440)
—Ellis Island: Welcome to America. (p. 515)
—Friction & Gravity: Snowboarding Science. (p. 637)
—Let's Play Basketball! Learning Addition Facts to 10. (p. 1000)
—Matt Kenseth. (p. 1109)
—Tara Takes the Train. (p. 1706)
Figtree, Dale. Eat Smarter: The Smarter Choice for Healthier Kids. (p. 501)
Figueras, Ligaya, jt. ed. see Travis, Joelle.
Figueras, Ligaya, ed. En Plena Vista Level 1. Hazan, Maurice, illus. (p. 522)
Figueras, Nuria. Trenzas del Abuelo. Olmos, Roger, illus. (p. 1784)
Figueredo, D. H. Mundo Nuevo. (p. 1191)
—Road to Santiago. Torrecilla, Pablo, illus. (p. 1477)
Figueroa, Acton. Julio Iglesias & Enrique Iglesias. (p. 932)
—Mississippi: The Magnolia State. (p. 1154)
—So Not the Drama. (p. 1602)
—Spider-Man 2: Everyday Hero. Vasquez, Ivan & Redondo, Jesus, illus. (p. 1626)
—Washington, D. C. (p. 1859)
Figueroa, Ephraim. Prince of Belverdere & Other Poems. (p. 1401)
Figueroa, Juanita Kimberly. Kendra Gives a Birthday Party. (p. 948)
Figueroa, M. A. & Figueroa, P. A. Melissa & the Magic Pen. Barnoski, Karel, illus. (p. 1125)
Figueroa, P. A., jt. auth. see Figueroa, M. A.
Figueroa, Robert, jt. ed. see Harding, Sandra.
Figuerola & Alonso. Sal, Caracol. (p. 1504)
—Tengo Tres Ovejas. (p. 1720)
Figuerola, Malte. Deportes. (p. 427)
—Estaciones del Ano. (p. 538)
Figurska, A. B. Island of Harklitt. (p. 892)
Fikse, Julia. Harrowing Tale of Lost Sonnet. (p. 750)
Fil, illus. see Charest, Jocelyne.
Fil, illus. see Tremblay, Marc.
Fil and Julie Staff, illus. see Kaldor, Connie.
Fil et, Julie, illus. see Meunier, Sylvain & Lapierre, Steeve.

Filakosky, Sandra. Star the Mermaid. Anderson, Susan, illus. (p. 1641)
Filali, Lisa. Faith Team 1: Taking Briar Falls. (p. 565)
Filaretos, William. Potion of Time: A Story of Demetrius. (p. 1388)
Filaski, Scott R. Sara's Daily Jog. (p. 1514)
Filasky, Gail. Mrs. Dishes. (p. 1187)
Filbin, Sandra A. Enchanted World: A Tooth Fairy's Tale. (p. 523)
Filella, Nacho, et al. Cumpleaños. (p. 392)
—Juegos. (p. 931)
—Los Disfraces. (p. 1053)
—Nieve. (p. 1252)
Filer, Patricia & Fulton, Cathy. Welcome to the Greenland: A Children's Activity Guide to the Birthplace of Seattle. (p. 1874)
Filgate, Leonard, illus. see Yost-Filgate, Susan.
Filice, Annette, illus. see Graf, Mike.
Filigenzi, Courtney & Bersani, Shennen. Let My Colors Out. Bersani, Shennen, illus. (p. 994)
Filion, Pierre. Pikolo's Night Voyage. Tibo, Gilles, illus. (p. 1358)
Filipak, Cheryl. Sylvie & Sean. (p. 1693)
Filipak, Christine & Vargo, Joseph. Madame Endora's Fortune Cards. (p. 1113)
Filipek, Nina. Animals. O'Toole, Jeanette, illus. (p. 81)
—Cinderella. O'Toole, Jeanette, illus. (p. 320)
—Colors. O'Toole, Jeanette, illus. (p. 344)
—Counting. O'Toole, Jeanette, illus. (p. 370)
—Gingerbread Man. O'Toole, Jeanette, illus. (p. 677)
—Goldilocks & the Three Bears. O'Toole, Jeanette, illus. (p. 696)
—Three Little Pigs. O'Toole, Jeanette, illus. (p. 1742)
—Words. O'Toole, Jeanette, illus. (p. 1951)
Filipek, Nina & Andersen, Hans Christian. Ugly Duckling. O'Toole, Jeanette, illus. (p. 1808)
Filipek, Steele, jt. auth. see Filipek, Steele Tyler.
Filipek, Steele Tyler & Filipek, Steele. Race Car Drivers: Start Your Engines! (p. 1430)
Filipetto, Celia, tr. see Nix, Garth.
Filipi, Carmen. Marvelous Fountain: And other stories my grandma told Me. Long, Dave, illus. (p. 1099)
Filipina, Monika, illus. see Rocklin, Joanne.
Filippello, Michael. In a Place Called Barrontippeny. (p. 863)
Filippello, Mike. Miratambo Moonsong. (p. 1149)
Filippi, Alessio, tr. see Burke, David.
Filippi, Denis Pierre, et al. Muse. (p. 1192)
Filippis, Dina De. Mrs Nguyen's Garden. (p. 1187)
Filippucci, Laura Francesca, illus. see High, Linda Oatman.
Filippucci, Laura Francesca, illus. see Young, Judy.
Filipski, J. W., photos by see Boyds Mills Press Staff.
Filipski, J. W., photos by see Hails, Kelly Milner.
Filipski, J. W., photos by see Highlights for Children Editorial Staff.
Filipski, J. W., photos by see Ross, Kathy.
Filius, Charles A., jt. auth. see Rowe, W. W.
Filkins, Allison J. Amazings. (p. 56)
Fillbach Brothers. Star Wars: Clone Wars Adventures. (p. 1641)
Fillion, Susan. Miss Etta & Dr. Claribel: Bringing Matisse to America. (p. 1151)
—Pizza in Pienza. Fillion, Susan, illus. (p. 1365)
Fillis, Ian & Rentschler, Ruth. Creative Marketing: An Extended Metaphor for Marketing in the New Age. (p. 379)
Fillisetti, Celeste. Just a Dream. (p. 937)
Fillmore, Charles. Prosperity: Spiritual Secrets to an Abundant Life. (p. 1412)
Film Ideas Staff, creator. Little Scientist: Here I Am! Camouflage. (p. 1036)
Filmer, Mary, et al. Farmer Frank: Educational Fire Safety, Poetry & Story Colouring Book. (p. 574)
Filoche, Eric. Hey ! We're Talking about Ourselves ! (p. 774)
Filson, Anne Holmes. Welsh Borderlands: Reflections Afoot. (p. 1874)
Fimbres, Lorraine. Gingerbread Princess. (p. 677)
Finally, Lil Rose. Slowpoke the Turtle & Company. Drape, Kaitlin, illus. (p. 1591)
Finbarr, Desmond. Big Book of Bible Fish Tales. Gévry, Claudine, illus. (p. 178)
Finbow, Alexander, ed. see Clements, Richmond.
Finch. Growing Trees. (p. 726)
Finch, Annie. Encyclopedia of Scotland. (p. 525)
Finch, David. Breakout (p. 225)
—Disassembled. (p. 446)
Finch, David, illus. see Bendis, Brian Michael.
Finch, David, illus. see Youngquist, Jeff, ed.
Finch, David, jt. illus. see Kubert, Adam.
Finch, Donna. Amanda the Panda & the Band. Bolund, Inna, illus. (p. 52)
—Amanda the Panda's ABCs: Amanda the Panda. Bolund, Inna, illus. (p. 52)
—Big Dig: The Continuing Adventures of Brandy the Golden Retriever. (p. 181)
—Brandy & Big Dig: Brandy the Golden Retriever: Author's Version. Plante, Beth, illus. (p. 222)
—Brandy & the Mascot: Brandy the Golden Retriever: Author's Version. Plant, Beth, illus. (p. 222)
—Brandy & the Rapids Plante. Plante, Beth, illus. (p. 222)
—Brandy & the Rapids: Brandy, the Golden Retriever. Plante, Beth, illus. (p. 222)
—Crazy, Cockeyed, Contest Between Peanut Brittle & Petit Four: Pandora Puckett. Bolund, Inna, illus. (p. 377)
—Perpetual, Purposeful, Pointing of Pandora Puckett's Pointer, Peanut Brittle: Pandora Puckett. Bolund, Inna, illus. (p. 1343)
—Very Panda Christmas: Amanda the Panda a Very Panda Christmas. Bolund, Inna, illus. (p. 1838)
—Victoria Finch, the Poodle That's Not a Dog!! Victoria Finch, a True Story. Bolund, Inna, illus. (p. 1840)
Finch, Donna, ed. see Bulakh, Nadia.
Finch, Donna L. Delectable, Deducible, Detectiving of Pandora Puckett: Pandora Puckett. (p. 424)
Finch, Kate. Big Surprise. (p. 184)
—Calling All Pets! (p. 254)
—Nose for Trouble. (p. 1266)

—On with the Show! Gurney, John Steven, illus. (p. 1292)
—On with the Show! Gurney, John Steven, illus. (p. 1292)
—Pet Hotel #1: Calling All Pets! Gurney, John Steven & Jessell, Tim, illus. (p. 1345)
—Pet Hotel #2: a Big Surprise. Gurney, John Steven & Jessell, Tim, illus. (p. 1345)
—Pet Hotel #3: a Nose for Trouble. Gurney, John Steven & Jessell, Tim, illus. (p. 1345)
—Pet Hotel #4: on with the Show! Gurney, John Steven & Jessell, Tim, illus. (p. 1345)
Finch, Keith. Poppy Cat's Garden. Jones, Lara, illus. (p. 1385)
Finch, Keith Andrew, illus. see Marsoli, Lisa Ann.
Finch, Mary. Little Red Hen & the Ear of Wheat. (p. 1034)
—Three Billy Goats Gruff. Arenson, Roberta, illus. (p. 1741)
—Tres Chivitos Gruff. Arenson, Roberta, illus. (p. 1784)
Finch, Mary, jt. auth. see Arenson, Roberta.
Finch, Mary & Barefoot Books. Princess of the Springs. Peluso, Martina, illus. (p. 1405)
Finch, Mary & Messing, Debra. Little Red Hen. Slater, Kate, illus. (p. 1034)
Finch, Mary & Slater, Kate. Gallinita Roja. Slater, Kate, illus. (p. 653)
Finch, Richard F. How to Air Condition ANY Corvair Vehicle. (p. 814)
Finch, Sharon. Stinker & Ralph Adventures: An Introduction to Ralph. (p. 1651)
Finch, Spencer. United States Geography: 10 Color Transparencies, Mini-Lessons, & Activities That Teach Essential Map Skills. (p. 1819)
—World Geography. (p. 1955)
Finch, Susan M. Dino Manners: Some Prehistoric Lessons Featuring Our Friends from the Cretaceous Period. Seda, Alison, illus. (p. 441)
Fincher, Cecilia. Chandra's Adventure. (p. 289)
Fincher, David. Story: An Interwoven Gospel. (p. 1656)
Fincher, Kathryn Andrews, illus. see Carlson, Melody.
Fincher, Kathy. Baby's First Christmas. (p. 129)
—Catholic's Baby's First Prayer Book. (p. 280)
Fincher, Kathy, illus. see Waller, Steven H.
Fincher, Sally. Studying Programming. (p. 1670)
Fincher, Judy. Miss Malarkey Leaves No Reader Behind. O'Malley, Kevin, illus. (p. 1151)
—Miss Malarkey's Field Trip. O'Malley, Kevin, illus. (p. 1151)
—Testing Miss Malarkey. (p. 1723)
—Testing Miss Malarkey. O'Malley, Kevin, illus. (p. 1723)
Fincher, John & O'Malley, Kevin. Congratulations, Miss Malarkey! O'Malley, Kevin, illus. (p. 357)
Findlay, Andrew. Roddy & the Magic Mattress. (p. 1484)
Findlay, Chris. Ae Sma Voice. (p. 25)
Findlay, Diane. Digging into Dewey. (p. 439)
Findlay, Jamieson. Blue Roan Child. (p. 203)
Findlay, Lisa. Puss in Boots. Bowers, Tim, illus. (p. 1420)
Findlay, Lisa & Swift, Jonathan. Gulliver in Lilliput. Caparó, Antonio Javier, illus. (p. 731)
Findlay, Jessica. Thunderela. (p. 1746)
Findlay, Kelly, illus. see Nicholson, Lorna Schultz.
Findlay, Ron J., jt. auth. see Gorman, Carol.
Findlay, Violet. Easy Reader Biographies: Harriet Tubman: Follow the North Star. (p. 500)
—Sea Turtles. (p. 1535)
—Sight Word Wheels: Reproducible Patterns for Hands-On Wheels That Teach the First 25 Sight Words. (p. 1574)
—Word Family Bingo Ladders: Fun-and-Easy Reproducible Games That Teach Kids the Top 25 Word Families. (p. 1950)
Findlay, William. Observations on the Two Sons of Oil: Containing a Vindication of the American Constitutions, & Defending the Blessings of Religious Liberty & Toleration, Against the Illiberal Strictures of the Rev. Samuel B. Wylie. (p. 1275)
Findling, John E., ed. see ABC-CLIO Inc. Staff, Inc.
Findon, Joanne. Auld Lang Syne: The Story of Scotland's Most Famous Poet, Robert Burns Nasmith, Ted, illus. (p. 115)
Fine, Anne. Big Red Balloon. Pankhurst, Kate, illus. (p. 183)
—Billy y el Vestido Rosa. Dupasquier, Philippe, illus. (p. 187)
—Countdown. (p. 370)
—Diary of a Killer Cat. Cox, Steve, illus. (p. 434)
—Hole in the Road. (p. 788)
—Interview with Anne Fine. (p. 881)
—Jamie & Angus Stories. Dale, Penny, illus. (p. 907)
—Jamie & Angus Together. Dale, Penny, illus. (p. 907)
—Press Play. Dreidmy, Joelle, illus. (p. 1397)
—Ruggles. Brown, Ruth, illus. (p. 1494)
Fine, Arnold & Spielman, Howard. Too Many Toys. (p. 1767)
Fine, Aron, illus. see Wilson, Barbara.
Fine, Debra. Beyond Texting: The Fine Art of Face-to-Face Communication for Teenagers. (p. 174)
—Fine Art of Small Talk: How to Start a Conversation, Keep It Going, Build Networking Skills - And Leave a Positive Impression! (p. 588)
Fine, Dvm. Too Many Pets & Not Enough Homes! (p. 1767)
Fine, Edith Hope. Bajo la Luna de Limon. (p. 133)
—Cricket at the Manger. Pels, Winslow, illus. (p. 382)
—Martin Luther King, Jr: Champion of Civil Rights. (p. 1098)
—Rosa Parks: Civil Rights Hero. (p. 1489)
—Under the Lemon Moon. Moreno, Rene King, illus. (p. 1813)
Fine, Edith Hope & Halpin, Angela Demos. Water, Weed, & Wait. Madden, Colleen M., illus. (p. 1863)
Fine, Edith Hope & Josephson, Judith Pinkerton. Armando & the Blue Tarp School Sosa, Heman, illus. (p. 99)
—Armando y la Escuela de Lona Azul. Sosa, Heman, illus. (p. 99)
Fine, Howard, illus. see Bardhan-Quallen, Sudipta.
Fine, Howard, illus. see Hale, Bruce.
Fine, Howard, illus. see Lund, Deb.
Fine, Howard, illus. see Palatini, Margie.
Fine, Jill. Chunnel: The Building of a 200-Year-Old Dream. (p. 318)
—Mayan Writing in Mesoamerica. (p. 1113)
—Sahara: World's Largest Desert. (p. 1503)
—Sahara: El Desierto Mas Grande del Mundo. (p. 1503)
—Sahara: El desierto más grande del mundo (the Sahara: World's Largest Desert) (p. 1503)
—Transcontinental Railroad: Tracks Across America. (p. 1778)

—Writing in Ancient Egypt. (p. 1965)
—Writing in Ancient India. (p. 1965)
—Writing in Ancient Mesopotamia. (p. 1965)
—Writing in Ancient Phoenicia. (p. 1965)
Fine, Karen. Veggiesaurus Lex. (p. 1834)
Fine, Maureen. My Two Shepherds in the Garden: A Lesson in Listening. (p. 1220)
Fine, Sarah. Fractured. (p. 627)
—Of Dreams & Rust. (p. 1279)
—Of Metal & Wishes. (p. 1279)
—Sanctum. (p. 1510)
—Sanctum. (p. 1510)
Fine, Sarah, jt. auth. see Jury, Walter.
Fine, Steve, illus. see Charlton, Dennis.
Fine, Susan, jt. auth. see Bardin, Matt.
Finell, S. Life's Amusement Park: A Whimsical Perspective on the Rides of Life! (p. 1013)
Fineman, Kelly Ramsdell. At the Boardwalk. Armino, Monica, illus. (p. 110)
Finer, Kim Renee. Smallpox. (p. 1592)
Finer, Susie, jt. auth. see Burke, Betty.
Fineran, John J., 3rd, ed. Traditional Siamese & Classic Siamese Cat: A Complete History of the Breed. (p. 1776)
Finger, Bill, jt. auth. see Cameron, Don.
Finger, Bill, jt. auth. see Coleman, Jerry.
Finger, Bill & Fox, Gardner. Batman Chronicles. (p. 144)
Finger, Bill, et al. Dynamic Duo. (p. 491)
Finger, Brad. 13 Art Movements Children Should Know. (p. 1994)
—13 Modern Artists Children Should Know. (p. 1995)
—13 Photos Children Should Know. (p. 1995)
Finger, Bradley. 13 American Artists Children Should Know. (p. 1994)
Finger, Mary E. Charlotte Bakeman Has Her Say. Batti, Kimberly Rose, illus. (p. 293)
Finger, Matthew, illus. see Trent, John.
Fingeroth, Danny. Backstage at an Animated Series. (p. 130)
—Democracy's Signature: Benjamin Franklin & the Declaration of Independence. (p. 425)
—Spider-Man & His Avenging Friends. (p. 1626)
—U.S. Supreme Court. Martin, Cynthia, illus. (p. 1807)
Fingeroth, David. Age of the Avengers. (p. 29)
Finifrock, Jacob E. & Spencer, Melinda. Multiplicity: Lesson Planning Guide. (p. 1190)
Finikakos, Kelly. Paws. (p. 1331)
Fink, Charles. Light Show: Reflection & Absorption. (p. 1015)
Fink, Connie. Helena Hippo & the Magic Ballet Slippers. (p. 763)
Fink, Courtney. Wings, Shells, & Fur: Surviving in the Wild. (p. 1936)
Fink, Jeri & Paltrowitz, Donna. Gizmo's Tall Twisters. (p. 681)
—Mathew's Tangled Trails. (p. 1108)
Fink, Jeri, et al. Gizmo Tales: Working Dogs. (p. 681)
Fink, Larry, photos by see Dahlberg, Laurie.
Fink, Mark. Stepping Up. (p. 1648)
—Summer I Got a Life. (p. 1674)
Fink, Sam. Declaration of Independence: The Words That Made America. Fink, Sam, illus. (p. 422)
Fink, Thad. I Want You to Know, Son. Robert, J. Martin, illus. (p. 848)
Finkbeiner, Betty Ladley. Pepper's Forever Home. (p. 1340)
Finke, M. e. Taconi & Claude: Double Trouble. (p. 1695)
Finke, Margot. Kangaroo Clues. Delloglu, Mustafa, illus. (p. 942)
—Mama Grizzly Bear. Swan, Gloria, illus. (p. 1084)
—Ruthie & the Hippo's Fat Behind. Snider, K. C., illus. (p. 1499)
Finkel, Sidney. Sevek & the Holocaust: The Boy That Refused to Die. (p. 1554)
Finkelman, Paul. Constitution. (p. 359)
Finkelman, Paul & Lesh, Bruce A. Milestone Documents in American History: Exploring the Primary Sources That Shaped America (p. 1142)
Finkelstein, Chaim. Burksfield Bike Club, Book 2: Lost & Found. Jennings, R. W., illus. (p. 243)
Finkelstein, Jeff, illus. see Korngold, Jamie S.
Finkelstein, Jeff, photos by see Korngold, Jamie S.
Finkelstein, Jeff, photos by see Korngold, Jamie.
Finkelstein, Norman H. Jewish Comedy Stars: Classic to Cutting Edge. (p. 917)
—Remember Not to Forget: A Memory of the Holocaust. Hokanson, Lois A Hokanson, Lars, illus. (p. 1459)
—Three Across: The Great Transatlantic Air Race Of 1927. (p. 1741)
Finkelstein, Ruth. Guess-the-Ending Mitzvah Book. Lazewnik, Sara, illus. (p. 729)
—Mendel the Mouse. (p. 1126)
—Thankyou Twins. Rubenstein, Reva, illus. (p. 1726)
Fink-Martin, Patricia A., jt. auth. see Martin, Patricia A. Fink.
Finlay, Lizzie. Buri & the Marrow. (p. 243)
—Little Croc's Purse. (p. 1026)
Finlay, Lizzie, illus. see Barkow, Henriette.
Finlay, Lizzie, illus. see Kimpton, Diana.
Finlay, Lizzie, illus. see Mills, David.
Finlay, Lizzie, illus. see Mills, David.
Finlay, Roger T. Wonder Island Boys: The Tribesmen. (p. 1947)
—Wonder Island Boys: Exploring the Island. (p. 1947)
—Wonder Island Boys: The Mysteries of the Caverns. (p. 1947)
Finlay, Roger Thompson. Wonder Island Boys: Conquest of the Savages. (p. 1947)
—Wonder Island Boys: Treasures of the Island. (p. 1947)
Finlay, Steven. Consumer Credit Fundamentals. (p. 360)
Finlayson, Linda. Adventure & Faith: Volume 1. (p. 14)
—Wilfred Grenfell: The Arctic Adventurer. (p. 1932)
Finlayson, Luke, illus. see Breed, Simon & Butterfield, Moira.
Finlayson, Luke, illus. see Jones, Gareth P.
Finlayson, Reggie. Nelson Mandela. (p. 1240)
Finlayson, Reggie & Rivera, Sheila. Postal Carrier. (p. 1387)
Finley, Danielle. Confronting a Bully Davenport, Chris, illus. (p. 357)
Finley, Leah. Ms T. (p. 1188)

F

—One & Only Mr C. (p. 1293)
Finley, Lou. How to Do Nothin' (p. 816)
Finley, Martha. Christmas with Grandma Elsie (p. 316)
—Christmas with Grandma Elsie. (p. 316)
—Elsie & Her Loved Ones (p. 516)
—Elsie & Her Namesakes (p. 516)
—Elsie & the Raymonds (p. 516)
—Elsie at Home (p. 516)
—Elsie at Home. (p. 516)
—Elsie at Ion (p. 516)
—Elsie at the World's Fair (p. 516)
—Elsie at the Worlds Fair. (p. 516)
—Elsie at the World's Fair. (p. 516)
—Elsie at Viamede (p. 516)
—Elsie Dinsmore (p. 516)
—Elsie Dinsmore. (p. 516)
—Elsie in the South (p. 516)
—Elsie Yachting with the Raymonds (p. 516)
—Elsie's Children (p. 516)
—Elsie's Friends at Woodburn (p. 516)
—Elsie's Girlhood (p. 516)
—Elsie's Girlhood. (p. 516)
—Elsie's Holiday at Roselands. (p. 516)
—Elsie's Holidays at Roselands (p. 516)
—Elsie's Journey on Inland Waters (p. 516)
—Elsie's Kith & Kin (p. 516)
—Elsie's Kith & Kin. (p. 516)
—Elsie's Motherhood (p. 516)
—Elsie's Motherhood. (p. 516)
—Elsie's New Relations (p. 516)
—Elsie's New Relations. (p. 516)
—Elsie's Vacation & after Events (p. 516)
—Elsie's Vacation & after Events. (p. 516)
—Elsie's Widowhood (p. 516)
—Elsie's Winter Trip (p. 516)
—Elsie's Womanhood (p. 516)
—Elsie's Womanhood. (p. 516)
—Elsie's Young Folks (p. 516)
—Elsie's Young Folks. (p. 516)
—Grandmother Elsie (p. 709)
—Holidays at Roselands. (p. 788)
—Two Elsies. (p. 1803)
Finley, Mary L., ed. Candy Wrapper. (p. 261)
Finley, Mary Peace. Meadow Lark. (p. 1116)
Finley, Mavion, ed. see Bumcrot, Curt, et al.
Finley, Shawn, illus. see Joyce, Bridget & Furman, Eric.
Finley, Thomas Murray. Alphabet City. (p. 50)
Finley, Thomas Murray, illus. see Kernan, Martin James.
Finley, Toiya Kristen. Russell Simmons. (p. 1498)
Finley, Ucal P. Proper Place for Boogers. Stroud, Brenda D., illus. (p. 1411)
Finn, Ann-Marie. Captain Kieron. Finn, Ann-Marie, illus. (p. 264)
Finn, Ann-Marie, illus. see Worthington, Michelle.
Finn, Caitlin. Harold the Misfit. (p. 749)
Finn, Carrie. Comportamiento y Modales en el Patio de Juegos. Lensch, Chris, illus. (p. 354)
—Comportamiento y Modales en la Biblioteca. Lensch, Chris, illus. (p. 354)
—Kids Talk about Bullying Muehlenhardt, Amy Bailey, illus. (p. 955)
—Kids Talk about Fairness Muehlenhardt, Amy Bailey, illus. (p. 955)
—Manners at School Lensch, Chris, illus. (p. 1088)
—Manners at School [Scholastic]. Lensch, Chris, illus. (p. 1088)
—Manners at the Table. Lensch, Chris, illus. (p. 1088)
—Manners in Public. Lensch, Chris, illus. (p. 1088)
—Manners in the Library. Lensch, Chris, illus. (p. 1088)
—Manners on the Playground. Lensch, Chris, illus. (p. 1088)
—Manners on the Telephone. Lensch, Chris, illus. (p. 1088)
Finn, Carrie & Picture Window Books Staff. Good Manners: At Play, Home, & School Lensch, Chris, illus. (p. 698)
—Manners on the Playground Lensch, Chris, illus. (p. 1088)
Finn, Carrie, et al. Manners on the Telephone Lensch, Chris, illus. (p. 1088)
Finn, Cheryl. Beanstalk's Basics for Piano (p. 150)
Finn, Cheryl & Morris, Eamonn. Beanstalk's Basics for Piano: Lesson Book Preparatory. Bk. A (p. 150)
—Beanstalk's Basics for Piano: Lesson Book Preparatory Book. Bk. B (p. 150)
Finn, Christine, illus. see Barden, Christine H., et al.
Finn, Daniel. Call down Thunder. (p. 254)
Finn, Felicity. Jeremy & the Aunties (p. 913)
Finn, Francis J. Claude Lightfoot: Or How the Problem Was Solved. (p. 329)
—Ethelred Preston: Or the Adventures of a Newcomer. (p. 539)
—That Football Game: And What Came of It. (p. 1726)
Finn, Isobel. Mariquita Perezosa. (p. 1094)
—Very Lazy Ladybug. Tickle, Jack, illus. (p. 1838)
Finn, Isobel & Tickle, Jack. Very Lazy Ladybug. (p. 1838)
Finn, J. D., jt. auth. see Austen, Chuck.
Finn, Jason. Gift of the Realm. (p. 675)
Finn, Jenny, illus. see Watt, Marg.
Finn, K. C. Leighton's Summer. (p. 991)
—Mind's Eye. (p. 1145)
Finn, Katie. Broken Hearts, Fences & Other Things to Mend. (p. 230)
—Revenge, Ice Cream, & Other Things Best Served Cold. (p. 1465)
—Unfriended. (p. 1817)
—What's Your St@tus? (p. 1900)
Finn, Mark. Scouts: Drafted! Drafted! (p. 1532)
Finn, Mary. Belladonna. (p. 162)
Finn McCool The Magic Leprechaun Cat. Irish Holiday Fairy Tales: Volume 1. (p. 887)
Finn, N. K., ed. see Stevens, A. P.
Finn, Perdita. Crashing the Party. Dorman, Brandon, illus. (p. 376)
—Going for the Gold. (p. 692)
—Mane Event. (p. 1087)
—Monster High - Haunted. (p. 1167)
—Rainbow Rocks. (p. 1436)
—Stealing the Show. Moran, Mike, illus. (p. 1646)
Finn, Perdita & HarperCollins Publishers Ltd. Staff. Alvin & the Chipmunks - The Squeakquel. (p. 51)
Finn, Rebecca. Jolly Snowman. (p. 924)
—Little Bunny. (p. 1025)
—Little Ducky. (p. 1027)
—Little Kitty. (p. 1030)
—Little Puppy. (p. 1034)
—Rudy Learns to Fly (p. 1494)
—Sammy the Snowman! (p. 1508)
—Santa's Day. (p. 1513)
—Sparkle the Fairy. (p. 1622)
Finn, Rebecca, illus. see Baxter, Nicola, ed.
Finn, Rebecca, illus. see Baxter, Nicola.
Finn, Rebecca, illus. see Field, Elaine.
Finn, Rebecca, illus. see Greenwall, Jessica.
Finn, Rebecca, illus. see Patchett, Fiona.
Finn, Rebecca, illus. see Prasadam, Smriti.
Finn, Rebecca, illus. see Sterling Children's, Sterling.
Finn, Rebecca, illus. see Sterling Publishing Co., Inc. Staff.
Finn, Rebecca, jt. illus. see Richards, Lucy.
Finn, Sandra J., jt. auth. see DiBattista, Mary Ann.
Finnan, Gary. Hector: At Ground Level a Very Simple Love Story. (p. 761)
Finnan, Kristie. Mommy's High Heel Shoes. Achilles, Pat, illus. (p. 1162)
Finne, Stephanie. American Curl Cats. (p. 60)
—Balinese Cats. (p. 134)
—Beagles. (p. 150)
—Collies. (p. 340)
—Dachshunds. (p. 398)
—Devon Rex Cats. (p. 432)
—Exotic Shorthair Cats. (p. 548)
—Golden Retrievers. (p. 695)
—How Political Parties Work. (p. 812)
—Old English Sheepdogs. (p. 1283)
—Oriental Shorthair Cats. (p. 1303)
—Russian Blue Cats. (p. 1498)
—Yorkshire Terriers. (p. 1972)
Finnegan, Amy. Not in the Script. (p. 1267)
Finnegan, Delphine. Lady & the Tramp. (p. 970)
Finnegan, Delphine, jt. auth. see Capozzi, Suzy.
Finnegan, Evelyn M. My Little Friend Goes to a Baseball Game. Houghton, Diane R., illus. (p. 1212)
—My Little Friend Goes to the Dentist. Houghton, Diane R., illus. (p. 1212)
—My Little Friend Goes to the Zoo. Bruno, Margaret Farrell, illus. (p. 1212)
Finnell, Cyndy, illus. see Argo, Sandi & Argo, Kaitlyn.
Finnell-Acosta, B. C., illus. see Pwob.
Finnemore, John. Jack Haydons Quest. (p. 903)
Finneron, Karyn A. Susu of the Frufru. Provencher, Annemarie, illus. (p. 1688)
Finney, Eric, et al. Shopping Poems & Food Poems. (p. 1569)
Finney, Eric, et al, selected by. Shopping Poems & Food Poems. (p. 1569)
Finney, Jefferson. Clever Dog. Hopper, Pegge, illus. (p. 331)
Finney, Kathryn. Little Louie. (p. 1031)
Finney, Kathryn Kunz, illus. see Enright, Robert D.
Finney, Pat, jt. auth. see Wade, Mary Dodson.
Finney, Patricia. I, Jack. Bailey, Peter, illus. (p. 839)
—Jack & Rebel, the Police Dog. (p. 902)
Finney, Ruth. Prayer for Momma. (p. 1393)
Finney, Shad. Princess Nap. (p. 1404)
Finney, Simone, illus. see Beckler, Bruce.
Finney, Susan. Independent Reading Activities That Keep Kids Learning ... While You Teach Small Groups: 50 Engaging Reproducible Activity Sheets, Management Strategies, & Tips for Differentiating Instruction That Help Kids Build Key Reading Strategies Independently. (p. 870)
Finneyfrock, Karen. Starbird Murphy & the World Outside. (p. 1642)
—Sweet Revenge of Celia Door. (p. 1690)
Finnie, Virginia. Hey Warrior Kids! Grab Your Slingshot! (p. 774)
Finnigan, Joan. Witches, Ghosts & Loups-Garous. (p. 1941)
Finnigan, Mary C. Our Family Trees. (p. 1308)
Finnigan, Michael. They Did You Can: How to Achieve Whatever You Want in Life with the Help of Your Sporting Heroes. (p. 1732)
Finnis, Anne & Bond, Denis. It's a Boy/Girl Thing! The Truth... in Their Own Words. (p. 895)
Fino, Roberto, illus. see McMillan, Dawn.
Finotti, M. C. Treasure of Amelia Island. (p. 1782)
Finsterbusch, Kurt. Annual Editions: Social Problems 04/05. (p. 87)
Finton, Nancy. Ecosystems. (p. 503)
—Explore the Solar System! (p. 550)
—Wonders of Water. (p. 1949)
Finzi, Arna. At Baba's House. (p. 110)
Fiol, Maria, tr. see Starr, Meg.
Fiol, Maria A., tr. see Christian, Cheryl.
Fiol, Maria A., tr. see Cohen, Miriam.
Fiol, María A., tr. see Galdone, Paul.
Fiol, Maria A., tr. see Grossman, Rena.
Fiol, Maria A., tr. see Jordan, Helene J.
Fiol, Maria A., tr. see Star Bright Books.
Fiol, Maria A., tr. see Starr, Meg.
Fiol, Maria A., tr. see Udry, Janice May & Udry, Janice M.
Fiol, María A., tr. see Zion, Gene.
Fiol, Maria A., tr. Eating the Rainbow (Spanish/English) (p. 501)
—Las Familias (p. 976)
—Llevame (p. 1043)
—Que Sabroso Arco Iris! (p. 1424)
Fiona Fox Staff, ed. see Montgomery, L. M.
Fiona Fox Staff & Giles, Sophie. 365 Bedtime Stories. (p. 2001)
Fiona Fox Staff, ed. Bible for Children. Biro, Val, illus. (p. 175)
—Railway Children. (p. 1434)
—Secret Garden. (p. 1541)
—Swiss Family Robinson. (p. 1691)
—Tales from the Arabian Nights. (p. 1701)
Fiore, C. A. Young Heros of the Civil War. (p. 1978)
Fiore, Carmen Anthony. Young Heroes of the Civil War. (p. 1978)
Fiore, Keith M. Leni the Pug: The Comet Christmas Caper. Sacui, Alexandru, illus. (p. 991)
Fiore, Kelly. Taste Test. (p. 1707)
Fiore, Kelly, et al. Just Like the Movies. (p. 939)
Fiore, Peter, jt. auth. see Cheney, Lynne.
Fiore, Peter M., illus. see Borden, Louise, et al.
Fiore, Peter M., illus. see Cheney, Lynne.
Fiore, Peter M., illus. see Schnur, Steven.
Fiore, Rob, illus. see Zakarin, Debra Mostow.
Fiorella, Christina. My Boy Kyle. (p. 1199)
—My Brother Adam. (p. 1199)
—Timothy's New School Worries. (p. 1755)
Fiorelli, June Estep. Fannie Lou Hamer: A Voice for Freedom. (p. 571)
Fiorelli, Lalo. Hidden Splendors of the Yucatan. (p. 776)
Fiorentino, Al, illus. see Weil, Ann.
Fiorentino, Fabrizio, illus. see Bedard, Tony.
Fiori, Natalie. Lobsters in Seacliff. (p. 1044)
Fiorin, Fabiano, illus. see Benjamin, A. H.
Fiorin, Fabiano, illus. see Frith, Alex.
Fiorin, Fabiano, illus. see Harrison, Paul.
Fiorin, Fabiano, illus. see Punter, Russell.
Fiorin, Fabiano, illus. see Rooney, Anne.
Fiorin, Fabiano, illus. see Stowell, Louie.
Fiorin, Fabiano, illus. see Watt, Fiona.
Fiorini, Nancy, illus. see Walsh, Maria Elena.
Firdausi. Epic of Kings: Hero Tales of Ancient Persia. (p. 532)
Firdawsi, jt. auth. see Schomp, Virginia.
Fire, jt. auth. see Bates.
Firebrace, Francis, illus. see Marshall, James Vance.
Firefly Books Staff. Bedtime. (p. 156)
Firefly Books Staff & Worek, Michael. My Little Book of Cars. (p. 1212)
Firehammer, Karla, illus. see Downey, Lynn.
FireHydrant Creative Studios, ed. see Waerea, James.
Firely, G. M. Raindrop. Holmes, Joshua D., illus. (p. 1436)
Firenze, Inklink, illus. see Bingham, Jane.
Firenze, Inklink, illus. see Chandler, Fiona, et al.
Firenze, Inklink, illus. see Helbrough, Emma.
Firenze, Inklink, illus. see Heywood, Rosie.
Firenze, Inklink, illus. see Hopkins, Andrea.
Fireside, Bryna J. Choices for the High School Graduate. (p. 309)
—Private Joel & the Sewell Mountain Seder. Costello, Shawn, illus. (p. 1407)
—Trial of the Police Officers in the Shooting Death of Amadou Diallo: A Headline Court Case. (p. 1785)
Firestone, Mary. Astrobiologist. (p. 109)
—Earning Money (p. 494)
—Liberty Bell Skeens, Matthew, illus. (p. 1005)
—Lincoln Memorial Skeens, Matthew, illus. (p. 1018)
—Nintendo: The Company & Its Founders. (p. 1257)
—Our American Flag Skeens, Matthew, illus. (p. 1307)
—Our U. S. Capitol Skeens, Matthew, illus. (p. 1310)
—Pyrotechnician. (p. 1421)
—Saving Money. (p. 1517)
—Seti Science. (p. 1554)
—State Governor. (p. 1644)
—State Judicial Branch. (p. 1644)
—Statue of Liberty Skeens, Matthew, illus. (p. 1645)
—Top 50 Reasons to Care about Elephants: Animals in Peril. (p. 1768)
—Top 50 Reasons to Care about Giant Pandas: Animals in Peril. (p. 1768)
—Top 50 Reasons to Care about Rhinos: Animals in Peril. (p. 1769)
—Volcanologist. (p. 1849)
—What Is Money? (p. 1889)
—What's the Difference Between a Frog & a Toad? Bandelin, Debra et al, illus. (p. 1899)
—White House Skeens, Matthew, illus. (p. 1913)
—Wireless Technology. (p. 1939)
Firestone, Mary & Picture Window Books Staff. Liberty Bell Skeens, Matthew, illus. (p. 1005)
Firestone, Mary, et al. Celebrate America: A Guide to America's Greatest Symbols. Skeens, Matthew, illus. (p. 283)
Firmage, George James, ed. see Cummings, E. E.
Firman, Sidney G., jt. auth. see DeGroat, Harry De W.
Firmin, Hannah, illus. see Rock, Lois.
Firmin, Peter, illus. see Amery, Heather.
Firmston, Kim. Schizo (p. 1521)
Firos, Daphne, illus. see McKay, Chelsea.
Firos, Daphne, illus. see Penn, M. W.
Firouz, Anahita. In the Walled Gardens: A Novel. (p. 867)
Firpo, Ethan, illus. see Costley, Kirk.
Firsova, Yuliya, illus. see Zilber, Jeremy.
First Baby Staff. BabyFirst My Feelings: A Look at Me Book. (p. 128)
—Where Is the Acorn? (p. 1909)
First Choice Productions Staff, photos by see Darnell, Yolanda.
First Discovery Staff. Atlas of the Earth. (p. 113)
First Discovery Staff & Mettler, René. Jungle. Mettler, René, illus. (p. 934)
First Discovery Staff & Millet, Claude. Castle. (p. 276)
First Discovery Staff & Peyrols, Sylvaine. Farm Animals. (p. 573)
First Fairy Tales Staff. Tres Chivos Testarudos. (p. 1784)
First, Rachel. Add It Up! Fun with Addition. (p. 11)
—Count It! Fun with Counting & Comparing. (p. 369)
—Measure It! Fun with Length & Distance. (p. 1117)
—Subtract It! Fun with Subtraction. (p. 1671)
—Weigh It! Fun with Weight. (p. 1872)
—What's It Worth? Fun with Coins & Bills. (p. 1898)
Firth, Alex. What's Chemistry All About? (p. 1896)
—What's Happening to Me? Meredith, Susan, ed. (p. 1897)
Firth, Alex & Lacey, Minna. Big Book of Big Sea Creatures. (p. 179)
Firth, Barbara, illus. see Waddell, Martin.
Firth, Barbara, illus. see Wallace, Karen.
Firth, Charlotte & Venkatesh, Katherine. Language Disorder (p. 975)
Firth, Melissa. Behind the Scenes at a Movie Set. (p. 160)
—Behind the Scenes at a Music Video. (p. 160)
—Behind the Scenes at a Play. (p. 160)
Firth, Norma. Tasha a Fraidy Cat. (p. 1706)
Firth, Rachel. Astronomy - Internet Linked. (p. 109)
—Dinosaurs. (p. 443)
—Dinosaurs - Internet Linked. (p. 444)
—First Encyclopedia of Science. (p. 594)
—Julius Caesar. (p. 932)
—Knights. (p. 964)
—Knights & Armor. Gaudenzi, Giacinto & Montgomery, Lee, illus. (p. 964)
—Los Caballeros - Internet Linked. Gaudenzi, Giacinto, illus. (p. 1053)
—Usborne Little Encyclopedia of Science: Internet-Linked. Hancock, David, illus. (p. 1827)
Firth, Rachel & Sims, Leslie B. Illustrated Classics for Boys. (p. 857)
Firth, Vic, jt. auth. see Feldstein, Sandy.
Firtha, Gizella. Spookybrooke. (p. 1631)
Firtl, Mary Meehan, illus. see Zuber, Diane C.
Fisanick, Christina. 1800-1820 (Events That Changed the World) (p. 2002)
—Animal Welfare. (p. 80)
—Child Birth. (p. 301)
—Debt. (p. 421)
—Debt. Greenhaven Press Editors, ed. (p. 421)
—Ecoarchitecture. (p. 502)
—Events that Changed the World - 1800-1820. (p. 541)
—Is Selling Body Parts Ethical? (p. 889)
—Issues in Adoption (p. 893)
—Working Women. (p. 1953)
Fisanick, Christina, jt. ed. see Greenhaven Press Editors.
Fisanick, Christina, ed. Working Women. (p. 1953)
Fisanick, Nick, ed. Ethics of Capital Punishment. (p. 539)
Fisch, Sarah. Little Flower Seed. Roper, Robert, illus. (p. 1027)
—Skating with Friends. Durk, Jim, illus. (p. 1584)
—Smallest Snowman. Durk, Jim, illus. (p. 1592)
Fisch, Sarah & Bridwell, Norman. Backpack Puppy. Durk, Jim, illus. (p. 130)
—Little Blue Easter Egg. Goldberg, Barry, illus. (p. 1024)
—Lots of Love. Johnson, Jay B., illus. (p. 1057)
Fisch, Sholly. April Fools Brizuela, Dario, illus. (p. 93)
—Challenge of the Super Friends Brizuela, Dario, illus. (p. 289)
—DC Super Friends. (p. 415)
—Hungry for Power Brizuela, Dario, illus. (p. 828)
—Just My Luck Brizuela, Dario, illus. (p. 939)
—Monkey Business McKenny, Stewart & Moy, Phil, illus. (p. 1165)
—Mr. Peabody & Sherman. (p. 1186)
—Nothing to Fear McKenny, Stewart & Moy, Phil, illus. (p. 1268)
—Scooby-Doo in Fangs, but No Fangs! (p. 1529)
—Scooby-Doo! Team-Up. Brizuela, Dario, illus. (p. 1529)
—Teen Titans Go! Hernandez, Lea, illus. (p. 1714)
—Wanted - The Super Friends. McKenny, Stewart & Moy, Philip, illus. (p. 1856)
Fisch, Sholly, jt. auth. see Stone Arch Books.
Fisch, Sholly & Age, Heroic. Happy Birthday, Superman! Bone, J., illus. (p. 745)
—Season of Light Brizuela, Dario, illus. (p. 1538)
—Who Is the Mystery Bat-Squad? Clugston, Chynna, illus. (p. 1916)
Fisch, Sholly & Ottolini, Horacio. Dinosaur Round-Up Brizuela, Dario & Staton, Joe, illus. (p. 442)
Fisch, Sholly & Wolfram, Amy. Teen Titans Go! Vol. 1: Party, Party! (p. 1714)
Fisch, Sholly, et al. All-New Batman: the Brave & the Bold. (p. 45)
—Bottle of the Planets. (p. 215)
—Bride & the Bold. (p. 227)
—Clobbered by Clayface! (p. 333)
—Manhandled by Manhunters! (p. 1087)
—Starro & the Pirates (p. 1642)
—That Holiday Feeling. (p. 1726)
—Through the Looking Glass! (p. 1745)
Fisch, Teri, ed. see Burch, Regina G.
Fisch, Teri L., ed. see Burch, Regina G.
Fisch, Teri L., ed. see Callella, Trisha.
Fisch, Teri L., ed. see Jordano, Kimberly & Corcoran, Tebra.
Fischel, Ana. Twelve Quests - Book 2, a Dragon's Tooth. (p. 1800)
—Twelve Quests - Book 3, the Pied Piper's Flute. (p. 1800)
—Twelve Quests - Book 4, Rapunzel's Hair. (p. 1800)
—Twelve Quests - Book 5, a Firebird's Feather. (p. 1800)
—Twelve Quests - Book 6, the Enchanted Harp. (p. 1800)
Fischel, Emma. Hans Christian Andersen. Ward, Nick, illus. (p. 743)
—Land of the lost Teddies. Howarth, Daniel, illus. (p. 973)
—Midnight Ghosts. Kern, Adrienne, illus. (p. 1138)
—William Shakespeare. Remphry, Martin, illus. (p. 1933)
Fischel, Emma, jt. auth. see Dolby, Karen.
Fischell, Emma. Northern Europe. (p. 1265)
Fischer, Amelia S. E. Roo's Cat Tales: The Cat Who Didn't Know First in a Series. (p. 1488)
Fischer, Carl. Days of Faith: Student Planner & Assignment Book/Intermediate Teacher Supplement. (p. 415)
—Days of Faith: Student Planner & Assignment Book 2004-2005. Connelly, Gwen & Holmberg, Ansgar, illus. (p. 415)
—Days of Faith: Assignment Book & Student Planner/Intermediate Grades 2005-2006. Holmberg, Ansgar & Connelly, Gwen, illus. (p. 415)
—Days of Faith Assignment Book & Student Planner. Homberg, Ansgar, illus. (p. 415)
—Days of Faith Student Planner & Assignment Guide Teacher Guide. (p. 415)
—Together in Jesus: First Eucharist Certificate. (p. 1762)
—Together in Jesus: First Reconciliation Certificate. (p. 1762)
Fischer, Chuck. Christmas Around the World. (p. 312)
—Great American Houses & Gardens: A Pop-up Book. Fischer, Chuck, illus. (p. 713)
Fischer, Chuck, jt. auth. see Dickens, Charles.
Fischer, David. Heir to Oswyn. (p. 762)

—Roberto Clemente. (p. 1479)
Fischer, Ellen. If an Armadillo Went to a Restaurant. Wood, Laura, illus. (p. 852)
—Latke, the Lucky Dog. Beeke, Tiphanie, illus. (p. 980)
Fischer, Ellen, jt. auth. see Balsley, Tilda.
Fischer, Gerhard. Planning a Connected Curriculum. (p. 1368)
Fischer, Hans. Pitschi. (p. 1364)
Fischer, Jackie & Fischer, Jackie Moyar. Egg on Three Sticks. (p. 506)
Fischer, Jackie Moyar, jt. auth. see Fischer, Jackie.
Fischer, James. Banking Basics. (p. 136)
—Business & Ethics. Madrian, Brigitte, ed. (p. 244)
—Computer Math. (p. 355)
—Earning Money: Jobs. (p. 494)
—Game Math. (p. 654)
—Keeping Your Business Organized: Time Management & Workflow. Madrian, Brigitte, ed. (p. 948)
—Planning for Your Education. (p. 1368)
—Power to Do Good: Money & Charity. (p. 1390)
—Starting a Business: Creating a Plan. (p. 1644)
—Starting a Business: Creating a Plan. Madrian, Brigitte, ed. (p. 1644)
—Time Math. (p. 1752)
Fischer, Jean. Christmas Prayers for Bedtime. (p. 315)
Fischer, Jean & Thomas Nelson Publishing Staff. Star for Me Steele-Morgan, Alexandra, illus. (p. 1640)
Fischer, Jeff. Johnny Appleseed. (p. 923)
Fischer, Joanie, ed. see Head, Jeff.
Fischer, JoAnn. Our Teacher Is A Fish! (p. 1310)
Fischer, John J. Escape from Korea. Lee, James V., ed. (p. 535)
Fischer, Julie, jt. auth. see Piazzola, Amy.
Fischer, Kelly. Moon Throws a Birthday Party. Duckworth, Michelle, illus. (p. 1172)
—Most Beautiful Color of All. Duckworth, Michelle, illus. (p. 1177)
Fischer, Laura. Life in New Amsterdam. (p. 1010)
—Life on the Trail of Tears. (p. 1012)
Fischer, P. J. Grandma & Her Chocolate Labrador. (p. 708)
Fischer, Rita, jt. auth. see Moon, Keri.
Fischer, Rusty. Vamplayers. (p. 1832)
—Weapons of the West. (p. 1869)
—Zombies Don't Cry. (p. 1988)
Fischer, Rusty, jt. auth. see Curto Family, The.
Fischer, Sandi, illus. see Hoyt, Charlene.
Fischer, Sara, jt. auth. see Klebanow, Barbara.
Fischer, Scott M. Jump! Fischer, Scott M., illus. (p. 933)
Fischer, Scott M., illus. see Burroughs, Edgar Rice.
Fischer, Scott M., illus. see Derek the Ghost Staff.
Fischer, Scott M., illus. see Greenburg, Dan & DiTerlizzi, Angela.
Fischer, Scott M., illus. see Greenburg, Dan.
Fischer, Scott M., illus. see Johnson, Angela.
Fischer, Scott M., illus. see McCaughrean, Geraldine.
Fischer, Scott M., illus. see Michelson, Richard.
Fischer, Shan, illus. see Layne, Casey & Jordan, Cedar.
Fischer, Stephen David & Caroll, Joseph. Science Detective A1: Higher-Order Thinking Reading Writing in Science. (p. 1525)
—Science Detective Beginning: Higher-Order Thinking Reading Writing in Science. (p. 1525)
Fischman, Sheila, tr. from FRE. Flying Canoe. Oberman, Sheldon & Cohen, Sheldon, illus. (p. 609)
Fiscus, James. Coping with Growth Spurts & Delayed Growth. (p. 365)
—Suez Crisis. (p. 1672)
Fiscus, James W. Iraqi Insurgents: Iraqi Resistance to America after the Defeat of Saddam Hussein. (p. 887)
—Meet King Kong. (p. 1121)
—Suez Crisis. (p. 1672)
Fiscus, Jim. Careers in the Fashion Industry. (p. 268)
—Coping with Growth Spurts & Delayed Growth. (p. 365)
Fiset, Pierre & Ferraro, Damiano. Gopher's Christmas Adventure. (p. 702)
Fish, Gale. Hooty Learns to Fly. (p. 796)
Fish, Lori Flying. One Shining Starfish. Fish, Lori Flying, illus. (p. 1297)
Fish, Mister. Snerfy Cat Meets Prancy Finch. (p. 1597)
Fish, Sandra Palmer. Peace by Piece. (p. 1331)
—S E W for Peace. (p. 1499)
Fish, Simon. Alphabet Madness. (p. 49)
—Silly Shapes. (p. 1576)
Fish, Thomas R. & Ober, Jillian. Lucky Dogs, Lost Hats, & Dating Don'ts: Hi-Lo Stories about Real Life. (p. 1062)
Fishback, Jere M. Tyler Buckspan. (p. 1805)
Fishbein, Susie. Kosher by Design Kids in the Kitchen. Uher, John, photos by. (p. 967)
Fishbone, Greg. Penguins of Doom. (p. 1337)
Fishburne, Melody. Three Little Faeries in the Baby Lady Bug Adventure (p. 1742)
Fishel, Dennis. Russell's Revenge (p. 1498)
Fisher, Aileen. Do Rabbits Have Christmas? Fox-Davies, Sarah, illus. (p. 457)
Fisher, Allen. Gravity. (p. 712)
Fisher, Ann Richmond. Explorers of the New World Time Line. Mitchell, Judy & Lindeen, Mary, eds. (p. 551)
—Seasons to Celebrate: January to Summer. (p. 1539)
Fisher, Anne. Look What Brains Can Do! (p. 1050)
Fisher, Barbara. Nobody's Lion. Huismann, Duane, illus. (p. 1262)
Fisher, Barry. Doryman's Day (p. 472)
Fisher, Beverly. Level One Workbook: Getting Started (p. 1003)
—Mental Toughness for Personal Fitness: Workbook for Life (p. 1126)
—Mental Toughness for Weight Management: Workbook for Life. (p. 1126)
Fisher, Blake J., jt. auth. see Augspurger, Eric K.
Fisher, Bonnie, illus. see Whitlow, Crystal K.
Fisher, BreeAnn & Venti, Debra. Night after Christmas. (p. 1252)
Fisher, Brittany J. un-Famous Pigs. (p. 1811)
Fisher, C. R. Adventures of Sam Fisher: It's Ruff to Be A Puppy. (p. 22)
Fisher, Carla Dawn. Summer Bridge Reading Activities: 1st to 2nd. (p. 1674)
—Summer Bridge Reading Activities: 2nd to 3rd. (p. 1674)
Fisher, Carla Dawn & Hobbs, Julia Ann. Summer Bridge Reading Activities: 3rd to 4th. (p. 1674)
Fisher, Carolyn. Snow Show. (p. 1599)
—Twisted Tale. (p. 1802)
Fisher, Carolyn, illus. see Coy, John.
Fisher, Carolyn, illus. see Jenson-Elliott, Cindy.
Fisher, Carolyn, illus. see Perlman, Willa.
Fisher, Catherine. Circle of Stones. (p. 321)
—Corbenic. (p. 366)
—Darkhenge. (p. 408)
—Darkwater. (p. 409)
—Door in the Moon. (p. 470)
—Ghost Box. (p. 670)
—Incarceron. (p. 868)
—Incarceron. November, S., ed. (p. 868)
—Oracle Betrayed. (p. 1301)
—Relic Master Part 1. (p. 1458)
—Relic Master Part 2. (p. 1458)
—Sapphique. (p. 1514)
—Scarab. (p. 1519)
—Slanted Worlds. (p. 1587)
—Snow-Walker. (p. 1599)
—Sphere of Secrets. (p. 1626)
Fisher, Catherine, jt. auth. see Fisher, Catherine.
Fisher, Catherine & Fisher, Catherine. Ghost Box. (p. 670)
Fisher, Catherine, et al. Incarceron. (p. 868)
Fisher, Chris. Third & Long. (p. 1734)
Fisher, Chris, illus. see Castor, Harriet.
Fisher, Chris, illus. see French, Vivian.
Fisher, Chris, illus. see Henderson, Kathy.
Fisher, Chris, illus. see Phinn, Gervase.
Fisher, Chris C. & Brooks, Ronald. Reptiles & Amphibians of Canada. Craig, Lee A. et al, eds. (p. 1461)
Fisher, Cynthia, illus. see DeLaCroix, Alice.
Fisher, Cynthia, illus. see deRubertis, Barbara.
Fisher, Cynthia, illus. see Griswold, Melissa.
Fisher, Cynthia, illus. see Lawlor, Laurie.
Fisher, Cynthia, et al. Human Resource Management. (p. 826)
Fisher, D. H., ed. see Fisher, Pat.
Fisher, D. H., photos by see Fisher, Pat.
Fisher, Daniel, ed. 638 Potential Paper Cuts: 638 Pages of Stories by Sixth-Grade Students of Berkshire Middle School. (p. 2001)
Fisher, David. Cool Jump-Rope Tricks You Can Do! A Fun Way to Keep Kids 6 to 12 Fit Year-'Round. (p. 363)
Fisher, David & Fisher, David Dayan. Puppy School. (p. 1418)
Fisher, David Dayan, jt. auth. see Fisher, David.
Fisher, Deborah. Just When I Needed You: True Stories of Adults Who Made a Difference in the Lives of Young People. Hong, Kathryn L., ed. (p. 940)
Fisher, Diana. Animals: Step-by-Step Instructions for 26 Captivating Creatures. (p. 81)
—Art of Rock Painting. (p. 102)
—Insects: Step-by-Step Instructions for 26 Creepy Crawlies. (p. 875)
—Learn to Draw Cats & Kittens. (p. 983)
—Learn to Draw Insects. (p. 983)
—Learn to Draw Reptiles & Amphibians. (p. 983)
—Modeling Dynamic Systems: Lessons for a First Course. Fisher, Diana, ed. (p. 1157)
—Reptiles & Amphibians: Step by Step Instructions for 29 Reptiles & Amphibians. (p. 1461)
—Rockin' Crafts: Everything You Need to Become a Rock-Painting Craft Star! (p. 1483)
—Watch Me Draw a Boy's Adventure. (p. 1861)
—Watch Me Draw a Magical Fairy World. (p. 1861)
—Watch Me Draw Dinosaurs. (p. 1861)
—Watch Me Draw Disney's Little Einsteins Amazing Missions. (p. 1861)
—Watch Me Draw Favorite Pets. (p. 1861)
—Watch Me Draw the Zoo. (p. 1861)
—Watch Me Draw Things Girls Love. (p. 1861)
Fisher, Diana, illus. see Creative Team at Walter Foster Publishing Staff.
Fisher, Diana, illus. see Farrell, Russell & Creative Team at Walter Foster Publishing Staff.
Fisher, Diana, illus. see Fitzgerald, Stephanie.
Fisher, Diana, illus. see Foster, Walter, ed.
Fisher, Diana, illus. see Razo, Rebecca J.
Fisher, Diana, illus. see Walter Foster Creative Team.
Fisher, Diana, illus. see Winterberg, Jenna.
Fisher, Diana, jt. illus. see Farrell, Russell.
Fisher, Diana & Shelly, Jeff. All about Dinosaurs & Reptiles. (p. 42)
Fisher, Donna R. Hewitt Early Readers: Level I Haidle, Elizabeth, illus. (p. 774)
—Hewitt Early Readers: Level II Haidle, Elizabeth, illus. (p. 774)
Fisher, Doris. Army Camels: Texas Ships of the Desert Buckner, Julie, illus. (p. 100)
—Happy Birthday to Whooo? A Baby Animal Riddle Book Downey, Lisa, illus. (p. 745)
Fisher, Doris, jt. auth. see Sneed, Dani.
Fisher, Doris & Gibbs, D. L. Bowling Alley Adjectives Chandler, Jeff, illus. (p. 216)
—Bowling Alley Adjectives. Angle, Scott & Chandler, Jeff, illus. (p. 216)
—Grammar All-Stars: Parts of Speech Angle, Scott, illus. (p. 706)
—Hole-in-One Adverbs. Angle, Scott, illus. (p. 788)
—Hole-in-One Adverbs. Chandler, Jeff, illus. (p. 788)
—Home Run Verbs. Angle, Scott & Roper, Robert, illus. (p. 792)
—Slam dunk Pronouns Angle, Scott, illus. (p. 1587)
—Slam Dunk Pronouns. Chandler, Jeff, photos by. (p. 1587)
—Tennis Court Conjunctions. Rose, Drew, illus. (p. 1720)
—Touchdown Nouns. Angle, Scott, illus. (p. 1772)
Fisher, Doris & Sneed, Dani. día Non Lee, Karen, illus. (p. 433)
—Mi día Par Lee, Karen, illus. (p. 1132)
—My Even Day Lee, Karen, illus. (p. 1202)
—One Odd Day Lee, Karen, illus. (p. 1296)
Fisher, Dorothy. Understood Betsy. (p. 1816)
Fisher, Dorothy Canfield. Understood Betsy. (p. 1816)
—Understood Betsy - Illustrated. Williamson, Ada C., illus. (p. 1816)
Fisher, Douglas & Glencoe McGraw-Hill Staff. Journey Across Time: World History - Active Reading & Note-Taking Guide. (p. 927)
Fisher, Douglas & McGraw-Hill Book Company Staff. American Vision, Modern Times, Active Reading & Note-Taking Guide. (p. 63)
—Glencoe World Geography, Active Reading Note-Taking Guide. (p. 683)
—World & Its People: Eastern Hemisphere, Active Reading Note-Taking Guide. (p. 1953)
Fisher, Douglas & McGraw-Hill - Jamestown Education Staff. World History. (p. 1955)
Fisher, Douglas & McGraw-Hill Staff. American Journey: Reconstruction to the Present. (p. 62)
—American Journey to World War 1, Active Reading Note-Taking Guide Student Workbook. (p. 62)
—American Republic since 1877: Active Reading Note-Taking Guide. (p. 63)
—American Vision Active Reading Note-Taking Guide: Student Workbook. (p. 63)
—Civics Today: Citizenship, Economics, & You - Active Reading Note-Taking Guide. (p. 324)
—Glencoe World History. (p. 683)
—World & Its People. (p. 1953)
Fisher, Douglas & McGraw-Hill-Glencoe Staff. American Republic to 1877. (p. 63)
Fisher, Douglas W., illus. see Fisher, Phyllis Mae Richardson.
Fisher, Edward J. Little Girl with the Magic Shoes: And Other Delights. (p. 1028)
Fisher, Eve. Best Is yet to Be. (p. 170)
Fisher, G. W., illus. see Malbrough, Page.
Fisher, Gary, jt. auth. see Cummings, Rhoda.
Fisher, George Park. Reformation. (p. 1456)
Fisher, Hans, tr. see Weber, Ilse.
Fisher Hein, Joy, illus. see Foster Colburn, Cherie.
Fisher Hein, Joy, illus. see Wade, Mary Dodson.
Fisher, Henry. ABC Dreams. Fisher, Henry, illus. (p. 3)
—When I Dream of ABC. (p. 1902)
Fisher, Henry, illus. see Moore, Clement C.
Fisher Hill Staff. Health Easy to Read. (p. 758)
Fisher, J. D. Book & the Blade: Awakening. (p. 210)
Fisher, J. J., jt. auth. see Figglehorn, Fred.
Fisher, James C. Oh No! My Shoe! (p. 1281)
Fisher, Jane Smith. On the Air! (p. 1289)
Fisher, Jeff, illus. see Adler, David A.
Fisher, Jeffrey. Birds Notecards. (p. 191)
Fisher, Jen. Ms. Mcbostrich Buys an Ostrich. (p. 1188)
Fisher, Jessie, illus. see Debeer, Kristen.
Fisher, Jude. Senor de los Anillos: Las Dos Torres. Torres, Estela Gutierrez, tr. (p. 1550)
Fisher, Judy. Alpha & Omega. (p. 48)
Fisher, Julie, photos by see Heath, Alan & Bainbridge, Nicki.
Fisher, Karianne M. Pup Named Moose. (p. 1417)
Fisher, Karianne Marie. In a Land Called Hogeye (p. 863)
Fisher, Karin, adapted by. Fish, Fox, & Then Some: Seven Aesop's Fables Retold Using One-syllable Words for the Barton Reading & Spelling System. (p. 598)
—Pig, Pig, & Pig: The Classic Fable of the Three Little Pigs, Retold in One-syllable Words. (p. 1357)
Fisher, Kathleen. English Reading & Spelling for the Spanish Speaker Book 2 (p. 530)
Fisher, Kathleen S. English Reading Comprehension for the Spanish Speaker Book 1. (p. 530)
Fisher, Ken, creator. Wizard Card Game. (p. 1942)
Fisher, Kimball. Finding the Baby Jesus. (p. 588)
Fisher, Leonard Everett. Gods & Goddesses of Ancient China. (p. 690)
—William Tell. Fisher, Leonard Everett, illus. (p. 1933)
Fisher, Leonard Everett, illus. see Dupuy, Trevor Nevitt.
Fisher, Leonard Everett, illus. see Felton, Harold W.
Fisher, Leonard Everett, illus. see Kimmel, Eric A.
Fisher, Leonard Everett, illus. see Morris, Richard B.
Fisher, Leonard Everett, illus. see Wood, James Playsted.
Fisher, Leonard Everett, jt. auth. see Rogasky, Barbara.
Fisher, Lillian M. Feathers in the Wind. (p. 579)
Fisher, Linda C. Runaway Will. (p. 1496)
—Will of Her Own. (p. 1932)
Fisher, Maire & Beautement, Tiah, eds. Follow the Road. (p. 612)
Fisher, Margaret E., et al. Street Law: A Course in Practical Law. (p. 1666)
Fisher, Marianne, illus. see Oliveri, Lisa L.
Fisher, Marilyn Anne. Pony Tales. (p. 1383)
Fisher, Martha. ABC Book of Bible People. (p. 3)
—Bible Numbers. (p. 175)
—Bible Time. (p. 176)
—Dictionary of Bible Animals. (p. 436)
Fisher, Martha, et al. Children of the New Testament. (p. 302)
Fisher, Meaghan. Giuseppe's Famous Pizza Pies. Barrett, Diana, illus. (p. 681)
—I Love Ladybugs! Mathieu, Middy, illus. (p. 842)
—Mousekabitz. Dunnier, Tina, illus. (p. 1182)
Fisher, Michael. Visions of Mughal India: An Anthology of European Travel Writing. (p. 1845)
Fisher, Nancy. Take Your Students on a Cruise: Paul's Journeys Lesson Guide. Witte, Carol, ed. (p. 1697)
Fisher, Nell, illus. see Augustine, Peg.
Fisher, Nick. Living with a Willy: The Inside Story (p. 1042)
Fisher, Pam. Pammy the Pig. (p. 1320)
Fisher, Pat. Favor I Owe the World. Fisher, D. H., ed. (p. 577)
—Walk a Mile in Our Shoes. Fisher, D. H., ed. (p. 1853)
Fisher, Patrica A. I Want to Live. Fisher, Patrica A., ed. (p. 848)
Fisher, Phyllis Mae Richardson. Chrissy (#1 in the 1989 Family Friends Paper Doll Set) (p. 311)
—Janae, #3 in the 1989 Family Friends Paper Doll Set (p. 907)
—Melly, #2 in the 1989 Family Friends Paper Doll Set (p. 1125)
—Natasha, an International Friends Paper Doll from Russia. (p. 1230)
—Rueben & Rachel's Paper Doll Coloring Book. (p. 1494)
—Tess, an International Friends Paper Doll from Africa. (p. 1722)
—Twiglet the Little Christmas Tree. Fisher, Phyllis Mae Richardson & Fisher, Douglas W., illus. (p. 1801)
—Twiglet's Coloring Book. (p. 1801)
Fisher, Richard W. Mastering Essential Math Skills, Book One: Grades 4 And 5: 20 Minutes a Day to Success. (p. 1103)
Fisher, Rick. Unknown Heroes. (p. 1821)
Fisher, Robert, et al. Gato Que Encontró a Dios. (p. 658)
Fisher, Rusty. Littlest Vampire's Story. (p. 1039)
—Littlest Werewolf's Story. (p. 1039)
—Littlest Witch's Story. (p. 1039)
—Littlest Zombie's Story. (p. 1039)
Fisher, Ruth, tr. see Weber, Ilse.
Fisher, Sam. Scare Scape. (p. 1519)
—Scare Scape. Bosma, Sam, illus. (p. 1519)
—The Midnight Door. (p. 1728)
Fisher, Sandy. Adventures of CJ & Angel; the Scary Helicopter Ride. (p. 17)
Fisher, Sean, illus. see Bucher, Heatherly & Menking, Amanda.
Fisher, Stacey, jt. auth. see Paner, Amy.
Fisher, Stacey & Paner, Amy, Illustrator. No Nuts for Nutty. (p. 1259)
"Fisher" Suedmeyer, Paul A. 12 Eternals on the Great Voyage. (p. 1994)
Fisher, Suzanne Woods & Kinsinger, Mary Ann. Surprise for Lily. (p. 1685)
Fisher, Tammy & Feliz, Guido, eds. Cuaderno de la Margarita Tomo 1 (p. 387)
—Manual de la consejera de Margaritas Tomo 2 (p. 1088)
Fisher, Tammy, ed. Cuaderno de la Margarita Tomo 3 Acosta, Olivia & Bogarin, Abigail, trs. (p. 387)
Fisher, Teresa. Croc on the Rock. (p. 384)
—Poland. (p. 1378)
Fisher, Terri. Adventures of Grandma Terri: Grandma Terri's Hospital Visit. (p. 18)
Fisher, Tina Mollie. Pig's Big Adventure. (p. 1358)
Fisher, Todd, illus. see Schwartz, Jean.
Fisher, Valorie. Ellsworth's Extraordinary Electric Ears: And Other Amazing Alphabet Anecdotes. Fisher, Valorie, illus. (p. 515)
—Everything I Need to Know Before I'm Five. Fisher, Valorie, illus. (p. 545)
—I Can Do It Myself. Fisher, Valorie, illus. (p. 835)
—My Big Sister. Fisher, Valorie, photos by. (p. 1197)
Fisher, Valorie, illus. see Gifford, Peggy.
Fisher, Valorie, photos by see Gifford, Peggy.
Fisher, Verna. Explore Colonial America! 25 Great Projects, Activities, Experiments. Stone, Bryan, illus. (p. 550)
Fisher, Vicki. Ketsai: What Shape Is a Friend? (p. 949)
Fisher, Vicki M. Cambio: The Best Blue Butterfly. (p. 255)
Fisher, Vicky. Bonsai Warriors. (p. 209)
Fisher, W. A., jt. auth. see Candy, T. M.
Fisher Wright, Blanche. Real Mother Goose. (p. 1448)
Fisher-Johnson, Paul, illus. see Hoena, B. A.
Fisher-Price. Fisher-Price Little People Let's Imagine at the Zoo. (p. 599)
—Fisher-Price Little People Let's Imagine on the Farm. (p. 599)
—Who's on the Farm? (p. 1921)
Fisher-Price Little People. Fisher-Price Little People Let's Imagine at School! (p. 598)
Fisher-Price Little People, Fisher-Price Little. Fisher-Price Little People Planes, Cars, Trucks & Trains! (p. 599)
Fisher-Price Little People Staff. Santa's Helpers. (p. 1513)
Fisher-Price Staff. Fisher-Price Little People What Do People Do? Lift-The-Flap. (p. 599)
Fisher-Price Staff & Little People of America, Inc Staff. Who's New at School? (p. 1920)
—Who's New at the Zoo? (p. 1920)
Fisher-Shumpert, Sharon Y. Sadie's Hero. (p. 1501)
Fishkin, Rebecca Love. Dance: A Practical Guide to Pursuing the Art (p. 402)
—English Colonies in America. (p. 529)
—Heroes of the Holocaust (p. 773)
—Singing: A Practical Guide to Pursuing the Art (p. 1579)
—Vehicles of the Iraq War (p. 1834)
Fishman, Cathy Goldberg. Car Wash Kid. Gott, Barry, illus. (p. 265)
—Hanukkah. Young, Mary O'Keefe, illus. (p. 743)
—On Hanukkah. Hall, Melanie W., illus. (p. 1289)
—On Sukkot & Simchat Torah. Hall, Melanie, illus. (p. 1289)
—Passover. Reeves, Jeni, illus. (p. 1327)
—Passover. Marshall, Ann & Reeves, Jeni, illus. (p. 1327)
—When Jackie & Hank Met Elliott, Mark, illus. (p. 1903)
Fishman, Cathy Goldberg & Hall, Melanie W. On Passover. (p. 1289)
Fishman, Jon. Andrew Mccutchen. (p. 72)
—Blake Griffin. (p. 198)
—Colin Kaepernick. (p. 339)
—Derrick Rose. (p. 427)
—Dustin Pedroia. (p. 490)
—Russell Wilson. (p. 1498)
Fishman, Jon M. Abby Wambach. (p. 2)
—Andrew Luck. (p. 72)
—Andrew McCutchen. (p. 72)
—Anthony Davis. (p. 89)
—Blake Griffin. (p. 198)
—Bryce Harper. (p. 233)
—Carmelo Anthony. (p. 270)
—Clayton Kershaw. (p. 330)
—Dez Bryant. (p. 433)
—James Harden. (p. 907)
—John Wall. (p. 923)
—Kevin Love. (p. 950)
—Lesean McCoy. (p. 993)
—Mariano Rivera. (p. 1093)
—Miguel Cabrera. (p. 1141)
—Mikaela Shiffrin. (p. 1141)
—Mike Trout. (p. 1141)
—Robert Griffin III. (p. 1479)

F

—Russell Wilson. (p. 1498)
—Stephen Curry. (p. 1648)
—Tim Howard. (p. 1750)
Fishman, Linda Charles. Little Girl Who Loves Colors: Book Four of Grandma's Girls. (p. 1028)
—Little Girl Who Loves Make Believe: Book 2 of Grandma's Girls. (p. 1028)
—Little Girl Who Loves Music: Book Three of Grandma's Girls. (p. 1028)
Fishman, Seth. Dark Water. (p. 408)
—Well's End. (p. 1874)
Fisk, Cindy. Hooga Booga Presents the Little Pumpkin. Fisk, David, illus. (p. 795)
—Melvin Pickles. Fisk, David, illus. (p. 1125)
Fisk, David, illus. see Fisk, Cindy.
Fisk, Katie. Flying with the Angels. (p. 610)
Fisk, Nicholas. Flip Side. (p. 605)
—Trillions. (p. 1786)
Fisk, Pauline. Midnight Blue. (p. 1138)
Fisk, Scott. Herman the Homeless Hermit Crab. (p. 771)
Fiske, Dwight. Without Music. (p. 1942)
Fiske, James. Belgians to the Front. (p. 161)
Fison, J. E. Shark Frenzy! (p. 1562)
Fison, Julie. Counterfeit Love. (p. 370)
—Lust & Found. (p. 1066)
—Tall, Dark & Distant. (p. 1704)
Fisscher, Tiny. RUBY & MAGIC TWIG. (p. 1493)
—RUBY & the LION. (p. 1493)
Fiszer, Edward P. Thoughts to Inspire: Daily Messages for Young People. (p. 1740)
Fitch, Jada, jt. auth. see Kim, Melissa.
Fitch, Janet. Paint It Black. (p. 1318)
—White Oleander. (p. 1913)
Fitch, Michele. When Lizzi & Kathryn Get Together. (p. 1903)
Fitch, Rik, illus. see Tysseland, Elsie.
Fitch, Sheree. If I Had a Million Onions Yayo, illus. (p. 853)
—Kisses Kisses Baby-O! HildaRose, illus. (p. 962)
—Mabel Murple Smith, Sydney, illus. (p. 1067)
—Night Sky Wheel Ride Yayo, illus. (p. 1254)
—One More Step (p. 1296)
—Peek-a-Little Boo Watson, Laura, illus. (p. 1335)
—Pocket Rocks Flook, Helen, illus. (p. 1375)
—Sleeping Dragons All Around Nidenoff, Michele, illus. (p. 1589)
—There Were Monkeys in My Kitchen Smith, Sydney, illus. (p. 1730)
—There Were Monkeys in My Kitchen. (p. 1730)
—There's a Mouse in My House! (p. 1731)
—Toes in My Nose: And Other Poems Smith, Sydney, illus. (p. 1761)
Fitch, Sheree, jt. auth. see Fitzpatrick, Deanne.
Fitchett, Jilda, 4th. Aunt Molly's Transition—Seeing Death in A New Light. (p. 115)
Fite, Ramona. Boy & His God. Monick, Susie, illus. (p. 217)
Fithian, Catherine. Magical Merry-Go-Round. (p. 1075)
Fitterling, Michael, illus. see Newcomer, Mary Jane, et al.
Fitterling, Michael A., illus. see Optic, Oliver, pseud.
Fitterman, Lisa. Super Kids: Ordinary Kids Who Have Done Extraordinary Things. Scarpulla, Caren, illus. (p. 1680)
Fittes, Francine. Craft Lacing Madness. (p. 375)
Fittleworth, George. Your Lungs. (p. 1981)
—Your Muscles. (p. 1981)
—Your Stomach. (p. 1981)
Fitts, Leticia. Black Legacy Learning Series: African American Sheroes & Heroes. (p. 196)
Fitts, Seth, illus. see Tietjen, Amy.
Fitzcharles, Michael S. Greatness of God. (p. 720)
Fitzer, Robin. Summer Stories. (p. 1675)
Fitzgerald, Anita, illus. see Fitzgerald, Kevin.
Fitzgerald, Anne, illus. see Engelhardt, Lisa O.
Fitzgerald, Anne, illus. see Geisen, Cynthia.
Fitzgerald, Anne, illus. see Menéndez-Aponte, Emily.
Fitzgerald, Anne, illus. see Mundy, Linus.
Fitzgerald, Anne, illus. see Mundy, Michaelene.
Fitzgerald, Anne, illus. see Wigand, Molly.
Fitzgerald, Brendan & Burns, Adam. Hofstra University College Prowler off the Record. (p. 787)
Fitzgerald, Brian. Fighting the Vietnam War (p. 586)
—Korean War: America's Forgotten War Fitzgerald, Brian, illus. (p. 967)
—Under Fire in World War II (p. 1813)
Fitzgerald, Brian, illus. see Mannion, Mary.
Fitzgerald, Brian, illus. see Ziefert, Harriet & Texas Tenors Staff.
Fitzgerald, Brian, jt. auth. see King, David C.
Fitzgerald, Caroline. Animal Kingdom Goes to New York. (p. 78)
Fitzgerald, D. M. True Story of the Big Red Onion. Cudd, Savannah, illus. (p. 1793)
FitzGerald, Dawn. Getting in the Game. (p. 669)
—Soccer Chick Rules. (p. 1603)
—Vinnie & Abraham. Stock, Catherine, illus. (p. 1843)
Fitzgerald, Denise. Tear'n Erin's Christmas Tree. (p. 1711)
FitzGerald, Edward. Rubaiyat of Omar Khayyam: First & Fifth Editions. (p. 1493)
FitzGerald, Edward, tr. see Barca, Pedro Calderon de la.
FitzGerald, Edward, tr. see Khayyam, Omar.
Fitzgerald, Edward F. Bank's Bandits. (p. 136)
FitzGerald, Elizabeth. Cursive First: An Introduction to Cursive Penmanship. (p. 395)
Fitzgerald, F. Scott. Bernice Bobs Her Hair & Other Stories. (p. 167)
—Curious Case of Benjamin Button & Other Jazz Age Stories. (p. 392)
—Great Gatsby. Kalda, Sam, illus. (p. 716)
—Great Gatsby. Bloom, Harold Ron, ed. (p. 716)
Fitzgerald, Gerald, illus. see Uhlberg, Myron.
Fitzgerald, Gyleen Xavier. Dream: A Magical Journey in Colourful Stitches. (p. 483)
FitzGerald, Helen. Deviant. (p. 432)
Fitzgerald, Holly. Reading Comprehension, Grades 1-2. (p. 1445)
—Reading Comprehension, Grades 3 - 4. (p. 1445)
Fitzgerald, J. Rupert, the Sturdy Oak Tree: Who thought he was a little better than the other Trees. (p. 1497)
Fitzgerald, Jennifer, illus. see Yerrid, Gable.
FitzGerald, Jerry. Dragon Hunt Card Game. (p. 477)
Fitzgerald, Joanne. Este Soy Yo y lo Que Me Rodea Fitzgerald, Joanne, illus. (p. 538)
—This Is Me & Where I Am (p. 1736)
—Yum! Yum!! (p. 1983)
Fitzgerald, Joanne, illus. see Scharer, Niko.
Fitzgerald, John. Great Brain. (p. 714)
Fitzgerald, John D. Brave Buffalo Fighter. (p. 223)
—Great Brain. (p. 714)
—Great Brain. Mayer, Mercer, illus. (p. 714)
—Me & My Little Brain. Mayer, Mercer, illus. (p. 1115)
—More Adventures of the Great Brain. (p. 1174)
—More Adventures of the Great Brain. Mayer, Mercer, illus. (p. 1174)
Fitzgerald, Josephine. Christ, Our Burden Bearer. Skorackiji, Olga et al, eds. (p. 311)
Fitzgerald, Joslin. Escaping Princess & a Runaway Prince. (p. 535)
—Kute Karing Kids Klub. (p. 968)
Fitzgerald, June. Squeaky: The Little Mouse Who Didn't Listen. (p. 1636)
Fitzgerald, Kevin. Dancing in the Moonlight. Fitzgerald, Anita, illus. (p. 403)
—EGG-Cellent Adventure. Fitzgerald, Anita, illus. (p. 506)
Fitzgerald, Laura Marx. Under the Egg. (p. 1813)
Fitzgerald, Laurie. My Dog Wears Shoes & Her Name Is Maggie Mae. (p. 1202)
Fitzgerald, Lee. Goods & Services. (p. 701)
—My Birthday Surprise: Understanding Subtraction. (p. 1198)
—Pennies! (p. 1337)
—Quarters! (p. 1423)
Fitzgerald, Linda, creator. Stellar: The Teeniest, Tiniest Star in the WHOLE Universe! (p. 1647)
Fitzgerald, Mary. Jodie Has Jagged Edges. (p. 919)
—Samson's Best Friend. (p. 1509)
Fitzgerald, Matt. Complete Triathlon Book: The Training, Diet, Health, Equipment, & Safety Tips You Need to Do Your Best. (p. 353)
Fitzgerald, Michael Oren, jt. ed. see Schuon, Catherine.
Fitzgerald, Paula. ABCs of How I Love You! (p. 4)
Fitzgerald, Paula, jt. auth. see Barry, Ron.
Fitzgerald, Royce, illus. see Abbott, Tony & Jessell, Tim.
Fitzgerald, Royce, illus. see Cooper, Ilene.
Fitzgerald, Royce, illus. see Markey, Kevin.
Fitzgerald, Sami & Caryn. Fish Sticks, Books & Blue Jeans. (p. 598)
Fitzgerald, Sarah Moore. Back to Blackbrick. (p. 130)
Fitzgerald, Stephanie. Children of the Holocaust (p. 302)
—Civil War Timeline (p. 326)
—Little Rock Nine: Struggle for Integration (p. 1036)
—Magical Fairy World: A Step-by-Step Drawing & Story Book. Fisher, Diana, illus. (p. 1074)
—Mary Walker: Civil War Surgeon & Feminist (p. 1101)
—New Deal: Rebuilding America. (p. 1244)
—Pearl Harbor: Day of Infamy Fitzgerald, Stephanie, illus. (p. 1333)
—Reconstruction: Rebuilding America after the Civil War (p. 1452)
—Split History of the Battle of Gettysburg. (p. 1630)
—Split History of the Civil War: A Perspectives Flip Book (p. 1630)
—Struggling for Civil Rights (p. 1668)
—What Is Texture? (p. 1890)
Fitzgerald, Stephanie, jt. auth. see Altman, Linda Jacobs.
Fitzgerald, Stephanie, jt. auth. see Bjorklund, Ruth.
Fitzgerald, Stephanie, jt. auth. see Burgan, Michael.
Fitzgerald, Stephanie, jt. auth. see Elish, Dan.
Fitzgerald, Stephanie, jt. auth. see King, David C.
Fitzgerald, Stephanie & Burgan, Michael. Perspective Flip Books. (p. 1344)
—Perspectives Flip Books. (p. 1344)
Fitzgerald, Stephanie & Heinemann Library. Struggling for Civil Rights (p. 1668)
Fitzgerald, Stephanie, et al. Perspective Flip Books. (p. 1344)
—Perspectives Flip Books. (p. 1344)
—War Timelines (p. 1858)
—Wind Power. (p. 1935)
Fitzgerald, Tamsin. Hip-Hop & Urban Dance (p. 780)
Fitzgerald, Theresa R. Math Dictionary for Kids: The Essential Guide to Math Terms, Strategies, & Tables. (p. 1105)
Fitzgerald, Walter L. HIPAA Security Handbook for Community Pharmacy. (p. 780)
Fitzgerald-Rodriguez, Mary. 20 Foxes. (p. 1995)
Fitzgibbon, Diana. Somewhere in Texas. Gonzales, Diana, ed. (p. 1610)
Fitzgibbon, Monty, jt. auth. see Twist, Clint.
Fitz-Gibbon, Sally. En la Granja del Tio Juan Deines, Brian, illus. (p. 522)
—Lizzie's Storm Wood, Muriel, illus. (p. 1043)
—On Uncle John's Farm Deines, Brian, illus. (p. 1292)
—Two Shoes, Blue Shoes, New Shoes! Zaman, Farida, illus. (p. 1804)
Fitz-Gibbon, Sally & Deines, Brian. En la Granja del Tio Juan (p. 522)
Fitzgugh, Percy Keese. Tom Slade with the Boys over There. (p. 1763)
Fitzhugh, Isaiah C., jt. auth. see Better-Fitzhugh, Nicole.
Fitzhugh, Keese Percy. Roy Blakely, Pathfinder. (p. 1492)
—Roy Blakely- Pathfinder. (p. 1492)
—Tom Slade at Temple Camp. (p. 1763)
—Tom Slade's Double Dare. (p. 1763)
Fitzhugh, Louise. Harriet l Espionne. (p. 749)
—Harriet the Spy. (p. 749)
—Long Secret. (p. 1047)
Fitzhugh, Louise, jt. auth. see Ericson, Helen.
Fitzhugh, Louise, jt. auth. see Gold, Maya.
Fitzhugh, Percy. Tom Slade on Mystery Trail. (p. 1763)
Fitzhugh, Percy K. Pee Wee Harris on the Trail. (p. 1334)
—Pee-Wee Harris. (p. 1334)
—Roy Blakeley. (p. 1492)
—Roy Blakeley on the Mohawk Trail. (p. 1492)
—Roy Blakeley's Adventures in Camp. (p. 1492)
—Tom Slade: Motorcycle Dispatch Bearer. (p. 1763)
—Tom Slade Boy Scout of the Moving Pictur. (p. 1763)
—Tom Slade on Mystery Trail. (p. 1763)
—Tom Slade with the Boys over There. (p. 1763)
—Tom Slade with the Flying Corps. (p. 1763)
—Tom Slade's Double Dare. (p. 1763)
Fitzhugh, Percy Keese. Pee-Wee Harris & Roy Blakeley's Adventures in Camp. (p. 1334)
—Pee-Wee Harris on the Briny Deep. Barbour, H. S., illus. (p. 1334)
—Roy Blakeley. (p. 1492)
Fitzhugh, Steve. Who Will Survive: The Teenager's Ultimate Struggle for Survival. (p. 1919)
Fitzl, Richelle Kristi. Grandma's Garden. (p. 708)
Fitzmartin, Elisa D. God's Silent Soldier. (p. 691)
Fitzmaurice, Gabriel. G. F. Woz Ere. MacDonald, Stella, illus. (p. 651)
—I'm Proud to Be Me: Poems for Children & Their Parents. Phelan, Nicky, illus. (p. 859)
Fitzmaurice, Gabriel & Macdonald, Stella. Splat: And Other Great Poems. Phelan, Nicky, illus. (p. 1629)
Fitzmaurice, John. Miracles from Maddie. Cedar, Emily, illus. (p. 1149)
Fitzmaurice, Kathryn. Destiny, Rewritten. (p. 431)
—Diamond in the Desert. (p. 434)
—Year the Swallows Came Early. (p. 1969)
Fitzpatrick, Anne. Amazon River. (p. 56)
—Automobile. (p. 117)
—Baroque Period: Movements in Art. (p. 140)
—Baroque Period. (p. 140)
—Brain. (p. 221)
—Collies. (p. 340)
—Computer. (p. 354)
—Electricity. (p. 509)
—Heart. (p. 759)
—Late Modernism: Movements in Art. (p. 979)
—Late Modernism. (p. 979)
—Mother Teresa. (p. 1178)
—Muscles. (p. 1192)
—Poodles. (p. 1383)
—Renaissance: Movements in Art. (p. 1460)
—Renaissance. (p. 1460)
Fitzpatrick, Anne, tr. Grand Canyon. (p. 707)
Fitzpatrick, Audrey, illus. see Little, Robert.
Fitzpatrick, Becca. Complete Hush, Hush Saga: Hush, Hush; Crescendo; Silence; Finale. (p. 353)
—Crescendo. (p. 381)
—Finale. (p. 587)
—Hush, Hush Ruiz, Derek, ed. (p. 830)
—Hush, Hush. (p. 830)
—Silence. (p. 1575)
FitzPatrick, Bill. Action Principles: Little Gold Book. (p. 10)
—Catholic Action Principles: Creating Positive Conversations. (p. 280)
—Catholic Action Principles, Spanish Edition. (p. 280)
—Shaolin Action Principles. (p. 1560)
FitzPatrick, Bill, ed. Women on Success. (p. 1946)
Fitzpatrick, Brad. Theodore Roosevelt. (p. 1729)
Fitzpatrick, Brad, illus. see Loewen, Nancy.
Fitzpatrick, Brad, illus. see Meachen Rau, Dana.
Fitzpatrick, Deanne & Fitch, Sheree. Singly Skipping Along (p. 1579)
Fitzpatrick, Deb. 90 Packets of Instant Noodles. (p. 1998)
—Have You Seen Ally Queen? (p. 754)
Fitzpatrick, Heather. Chuck: The Chicken That Thought He Was a Duck. (p. 318)
Fitzpatrick, Huntley. Boy Most Likely To. (p. 218)
—My Life Next Door. (p. 1212)
—What I Thought Was True. (p. 1887)
Fitzpatrick, Jim. Skateboarding. (p. 1583)
—Snowboarding. (p. 1600)
—Surfing. (p. 1685)
Fitzpatrick, Joe. I Am So Awesome. Kummer, Mark, illus. (p. 834)
—Raggedy Snowman. Flowerpot Press, ed. (p. 1433)
Fitzpatrick, Julia, tr. see Brill, Marlene Targ.
Fitzpatrick, Julia, tr. see Mitchell, Melanie.
Fitzpatrick, Julia, tr. see Nelson, Robin.
Fitzpatrick, Julia, tr. see Wadsworth, Ginger.
Fitzpatrick, Marie-Louise. Silly Baby. (p. 1575)
—There. Fitzpatrick, Marie-Louise, illus. (p. 1729)
Fitzpatrick, Marie-Louise, illus. see McAllister, Angela.
Fitzpatrick, Meg, illus. see Friederich, Uve.
Fitzpatrick, Michelle Rene. Noelia's Garden: Children of the Light. (p. 1262)
Fitzpatrick, Tom & Grogan, Jerry. All about Gaelic Football. (p. 42)
Fitzpatrick-Hale-Herself, Donna Marie. Snake & Mouse: Ryan's birthday Tea. (p. 1596)
Fitzrandolph, Joyce. Learn to Paint with the Alexander Brush Club. (p. 984)
Fitzs, jt. auth. see Whiteford.
Fitzsimmons, Christy. Krissy & the Indians Steckler, Megan, illus. (p. 967)
Fitzsimmons, Jim. Prince, the Fairy & the Fouly. (p. 1401)
Fitzsimmons, Jim, jt. auth. see Whiteford, Rhona.
Fitzsimmons, Jim & Whiteford, Rhona. English Tests. (p. 530)
—Maths Tests. (p. 1108)
Fitzsimmons, Kakie. Anna Goes Hiking: Discover Hiking & Explore Nature. (p. 85)
—Bur Bur Throws Out the First Pitch: An Exciting Baseball Experience. VanDeWeghe, Lindsay & Bohnet, Christopher, illus. (p. 243)
—Bur Bur's Boating ABC's: Learn the Most Amazing Things with the ABCs of Boating! (p. 243)
—Bur Bur's Fishing Adventure: An Exciting Fishing Adventure. VanDeWeghe, Lindsay & Bohnet, Christopher, illus. (p. 243)
Fitzsimmons, Kakie, jt. auth. see Pastel, JoAnne.
Fitzsimons, Cecilia. 50 Nature Projects for Kids: Fun-Packed Outdoor & Indoor Things to Do & Make. (p. 1997)
Fitzsimons, Morgan. Saving Sleepy Walter: Fitztown Fairies Tale. Nuñez, Veronica, illus. (p. 1517)
Fiumara, Sebastian. Thor: The Trials of Loki. (p. 1739)
Five Mile Press Staff. Lord of the Rings - The Return of the King Jigsaw Book. (p. 1052)
—Renaissance Artists. (p. 1460)
Five Mile Press Staff, illus. see Mappin, Jennifer.
Fix, Alexandra. Energy (p. 528)
—Food (p. 612)
—Glass (p. 682)
—Metal (p. 1130)
—Paper (p. 1322)
—Plastic (p. 1370)
—Water (p. 1862)
Fix, John D. Astronomy: Journey to the Cosmic Frontier with Essential Study Partner. (p. 109)
Fix, Natalie. Graphing Death Valley: Represent & Interpret Data (p. 711)
Fixico, Donald L., ed. Treaties with American Indians: An Encyclopedia of Rights, Conflicts, & Sovereignty (p. 1783)
Fixman, Jennifer. Make a Difference with Miss Jenny. (p. 1078)
—Science Songs with Miss Jenny. (p. 1528)
Fixmer, Elizabeth. Down from the Mountain. (p. 474)
—Saint Training (p. 1504)
Fiz. George & the Treasure Box Mysteries. (p. 663)
Fjelland Davis, Rebecca. Medusa Tells All: Beauty Missing, Hair Hissing Gilpin, Stephen, illus. (p. 1120)
Fjelland Davis, Rebecca, jt. auth. see Davis, Rebecca F.
Flack, Annie. Mysteries of the Lake. (p. 1222)
Flack, Judy. We're Having a Baby: A Story for Jack. (p. 1875)
Flack, Marjorie, illus. see Heyward, DuBose.
Flack, Sophie. Bunheads. (p. 242)
Flackett, Jennifer, jt. auth. see Levin, Mark.
Fladd, Jane. 1-2-3 Jump! (p. 1990)
Flagg, Phyllis. Five Fun Plays for Christian Kids: Including Two Christmas Plays. (p. 600)
Flaggert, Candy. Ok, Said Carrie Katherine Chipka, Sandy, illus. (p. 1282)
Flaherty, Dan. Fulcrum. (p. 646)
Flaherty, Finn. Flowerpot. (p. 608)
Flaherty, Kathleen Marion. Octopus Named Mom. Donehey, Jennifer Caulfield, illus. (p. 1278)
Flaherty, Liz. Action Numeracy: Bikes. (p. 10)
—Cooking up a Storm. (p. 362)
Flaherty, Louise & Christopher, Neil. Country of Wolves Perez, Ramon, illus. (p. 372)
Flaherty, Michael. Electricity & Batteries. (p. 509)
Flaherty, Michael, jt. auth. see Richards, Jon.
Flaherty, Mildred. Great Saint Patrick's Day Flood. (p. 718)
Flaherty, Patrick. Follow the Arrow: A Collection of Quotes in Support of Brotherhood, Cheerfulness, & Service As Demonstrated by Members of the Order of the Arrow, Boy Scouts of America. (p. 612)
—Why Scouting? A Collection of Thoughts & Stories about Our Family's Experiences with the Boy Scout Program. McLaughlin, Pat, ed. (p. 1925)
Flaherty, Patrick F. & Harper, Steven. Life's Lessons from Dad: Quotes for Life Book Series. McLaughlin, Patrick, ed. (p. 1013)
Flaherty, Patrick J. Camping Challenge: Card Game for Campers. (p. 257)
Flaherty, Patti O. Frogs Divide & Conquer. (p. 641)
—Tricia Turtle Learns about School. (p. 1786)
—Trisha Turtle Learns about School. (p. 1787)
Flaherty, Somer & Kollmer, Jen. Girl in a Fix: Quick Beauty Solutions (and Why They Work) Douglass, Ali, illus. (p. 678)
Flaherty, Tom, photos by see Bowyer, Clifford B.
Flahive, Lynn, jt. auth. see Lanza, Janet.
Flahive, Lynn K., jt. auth. see Lanza, Janet R.
Flahive, Lynn K. & Lanza, Janet. 100% Curriculum Vocabulary Grades K-5. (p. 1998)
Flake, Sharon. Unstoppable Octobia May. (p. 1823)
Flake, Sharon G. Bang! (p. 136)
—Begging for Change. (p. 159)
—Money Hungry. Disney Press Staff, illus. (p. 1164)
—Pinned. (p. 1360)
—Skin I'm In. (p. 1585)
—Skin I'm In. Disney Press Staff, illus. (p. 1585)
—You Don't Even Know Me: Stories & Poems about Boys. (p. 1975)
Flaker, Tracey. Around the Corner: Gwenever's Quest. (p. 100)
Flam, Chanie. By Myself. (p. 249)
—Erev Shabbos. (p. 533)
—Good Night. (p. 699)
—Happy Birthday (p. 744)
—Make Believe. (p. 1079)
—Shoe, Shoe. (p. 1568)
Flamand, D. G. Honesty Plays Baseball. (p. 794)
—Lealtad en la Granja / Loyalty at the Farm: La Serie Buena. (p. 982)
—Little Cloud & His New Friends. (p. 1026)
—Mr. Fanover & the Hummingbird. (p. 1185)
—Old Druid & the Pursuit of Happiness. (p. 1283)
—Sophia at a Royal Wedding. (p. 1613)
—Sophia Crosses the Ocean with Christopher Columbus. (p. 1613)
—Sophia Goes to the Moon. (p. 1613)
—Swim & the Bubble Show: Swim the Octopus Series. (p. 1690)
—Thousand Rainbows. (p. 1740)
—Tommy & the Bees: Tommy & the Magic Dictionary Series. (p. 1764)
—Tommy & the Butterflies: Tommy & the Magic Dictionary Series. (p. 1764)
—Tommy & the Musical Instruments. (p. 1764)
—Tommy & the Trees. (p. 1764)
—Tommy & the Whales: Tommy & the Magic Dictionary Series. (p. 1764)
Flambaum, Andrew, jt. auth. see Flambaum, Victor.
Flambaum, Victor & Flambaum, Andrew. How to Make a Big Bang: A Cosmic Journey. (p. 820)
Flamburis, Georgia M. How Karis' Kitten Got Its Name. (p. 810)
Flamini, Lorella. Growing in Love: Virtues for Little Ones. (p. 726)
—Thank You Dear God! Prayers for Little Ones. (p. 1725)
Flamini, Lorella, illus. see Prestofilippo, Mary Nazarene, tr.

Flamini, Lorella, illus. see Prestofillopo, Mary Nazarene, tr.
Flammang, James M. Cargo Ships. (p. 268)
—Larry Page & Sergey Brin. (p. 976)
—Space Travel. (p. 1620)
Flammang, James M. & Green, Robert. Cars. (p. 271)
Flammer, JoAnn. Last Wish. (p. 979)
—Pukeweed Soup. (p. 1415)
Flamming, James A., jt. auth. see Publications International Ltd. Staff.
Flanagan, Alice K. Buffalo Soldiers. (p. 236)
—Cats: The Sound of Short A. (p. 281)
—Play Day: The Sound of Long A. (p. 1371)
—Pueblos. (p. 1414)
—Shawnee. (p. 1563)
—Women of the Union (p. 1946)
Flanagan, Alice K. & Dolbear, Emily J. Discovering Today's Library. (p. 450)
Flanagan, Anne. Come to Jesus: A Kids' Book for Eucharistic Adoration. Cleary, Janice, illus. (p. 347)
—Family Saints Col/Act Bk. (p. 568)
—Miracles of Jesus Act/Col Bk. (p. 1149)
—Saints of America Col/Act Bk. (p. 1504)
Flanagan, Anne J. Jesus Walks with Us: Activity Book. (p. 916)
Flanagan, Anne J., jt. auth. see Moran, Mary Y.
Flanagan, Artie & Licari, Peter J. Birth of Buzzard Baby (p. 192)
Flanagan, Caitlin. To Hell with All That: Loving & Loathing Our Inner Housewife. (p. 1759)
Flanagan, Cara. Research Methods for AQA 'A' Psychology: An Activity-Based Approach. (p. 1462)
Flanagan, Cara, jt. auth. see Cardwell, Mike.
Flanagan, Cara & Cardwell, Mike. Psychology AS: The Exam Companion for Aqa 'A. (p. 1413)
—Psychology AS. (p. 1413)
Flanagan, Cara, et al. Psychology A2: The Teachers' Companion for AQA 'A. (p. 1413)
Flanagan, James. Stories Heard Around the Lunchroom. (p. 1654)
Flanagan, Jeff, illus. see Fantasia, Kathryn.
Flanagan, Jim. School of Scary Stories. (p. 1523)
Flanagan, John. Battle for Skandia. (p. 145)
—Burning Bridge (p. 244)
—Burning Bridge. (p. 244)
—Emperor of Nihon-Ja (p. 520)
—Emperor of Nihon-Ja. (p. 520)
—Erak's Ransom (p. 533)
—Halt's Peril (p. 739)
—Halt's Peril. (p. 739)
—Hunters. (p. 828)
—Icebound Land (p. 851)
—Icebound Land. (p. 851)
—Invaders. (p. 883)
—Kings of Clonmel (p. 960)
—Lost Stories. (p. 1056)
—Outcasts. (p. 1312)
—Royal Ranger. (p. 1492)
—Ruins of Gorlan (p. 1494)
—Scorpion Mountain. (p. 1530)
—Siege of Macindaw (p. 1573)
—Slaves of Socorro. (p. 1588)
—Sorcerer of the North (p. 1614)
—Sorcerer of the North. (p. 1614)
Flanagan, John A. Slaves of Socorro. (p. 1588)
Flanagan, Liz. Oni & the Eagle. Docampo, Valeria, illus. (p. 1298)
Flanagan, Liz, et al. Dara's Clever Trap: A Story from Cambodia. Peluso, Martina, illus. (p. 406)
Flanagan, Logan, jt. auth. see C., Brandi.
Flanagan, Timothy. Reconstruction: A Primary Source History of the Struggle to Unite the North & South after the Civil War. (p. 1452)
Flanagan, William, tr. see Emura.
Flanagan, William, tr. see Urushibara, Yuki.
Flanary, Sarah. Bob the Bird Chirps Out Against Bullying. (p. 205)
Flanders, Aaron. Balloon Animals. (p. 135)
—Balloon Cartoons & Other Favorites. (p. 135)
—Balloon Hats & Accessories. (p. 135)
Flanders, Ralph E. Locomotive Building: The Construction of a Steam Engine for Railway Use. (p. 1045)
Flanery, Alicia & Stephenson, Caitlin. Wow: We Wrote a Book! (p. 1962)
Flanigan, Gertrude, et al. Finger Hockey: No Poke Checking! (p. 589)
Flannagan, J. S. & Newton, H. L. Magnificent Magnifying Lens. (p. 1076)
Flannery, Tim. We Are the Weather Makers: The History of Climate Change. (p. 1866)
Flannery, William Davis. Calculus Without Tears: Easy Lessons for Learning Calculus for Students from the 4th Grade up - Constant Velocity Motion Vol. 1 (p. 252)
Flannigan, Liz. Cara & the Wizard Docampo, Valeria, illus. (p. 265)
—Starlight Grey. Docampo, Valeria, illus. (p. 1642)
Flash Kids Editors. Addition Activities: Grade 1 (Flash Skills) (p. 12)
—Alphabet Activities: Grade PreK-K (Flash Skills) (p. 49)
—Alphabet Puzzles & Games: Grade Pre-K-K (Flash Skills) (p. 50)
—Colors & Shapes: Grade Pre-K-K (Flash Skills) (p. 345)
—Cursive Writing: Around the World in 26 Letters. Christoph, Jamey, illus. (p. 395)
—Division Activities: Grade 3 (Flash Skills) (p. 455)
—Fraction Activities: Grade 3 (Flash Skills) (p. 626)
—Letter Dot-to-Dot. (p. 1002)
—Main Idea: Grade 3 (Flash Skills) (p. 1077)
—Math Drills: Grade 1 (Flash Skills) (p. 1105)
—Math Drills: Grade 2 (Flash Skills) (p. 1105)
—Math Drills: Grade 3 (Flash Skills) (p. 1106)
—Multiplication Activities: Grade 3 (Flash Skills) (p. 1190)
—My First Book of Tracing. (p. 1205)
—Number Activities: Grade Pre-K-K (Flash Skills) (p. 1271)
—Number Dot-to-Dot, Grade Pre-K-K. (p. 1271)
—Number Puzzles & Games: Grade Pre-K-K (Flash Skills) (p. 1271)
—Phonics Blends: Grade 1 (Flash Skills) (p. 1352)
—Phonics Vowels: Grade 1 (Flash Skills) (p. 1352)
—Place Value: Grade 1 (Flash Skills) (p. 1366)
—Place Value: Grade 2 (Flash Skills) (p. 1366)
—Problem Solving: Grade 2 (Flash Skills) (p. 1408)
—Reading Comprehension: Grade 2 (Flash Skills) (p. 1445)
—Ready for School: Grade Pre-K-K (Flash Skills) (p. 1447)
—Sight Words: Grade 1 (Flash Skills) (p. 1574)
—Sight Words: Grade 2 (Flash Skills) (p. 1574)
—Subtraction Activities: Grade 1 (Flash Skills) (p. 1671)
—Time & Money: Grade 1 (Flash Skills) (p. 1751)
—Vocabulary for the Gifted Student Grade 1 (for the Gifted Student) Challenging Activities for the Advanced Learner. (p. 1847)
—Writing Skills: Grade 2 (Flash Skills) (p. 1965)
Flash Kids Editors & Mack, Steve. Coloring. (p. 344)
—Cutting & Pasting. (p. 396)
—Letters. (p. 1002)
—Mazes. (p. 1113)
—Numbers. (p. 1271)
—Tracing. (p. 1775)
Flash Kids Editors, ed. Print Writing: A Creepy-Crawly Alphabet. Reese, Brandon, illus. (p. 1407)
Flash Kids Editors, Flash Kids, ed. Subtraction Cards. (p. 1671)
Flass, E. C., illus. see Gates, Josephine Scribner.
Flasterstein, Ran. Care Bears Lullaby: A Night Light Book. Moore, Saxton, illus. (p. 266)
Flatau, Susie Kelly, jt. auth. see McConnell, Kathleen.
Flath, Camden. 21st-Century Counselors: New Approaches to Mental Health & Substance Abuse. (p. 1996)
—Careers in Green Energy: Fueling the World with Renewable Resources. (p. 268)
—Freelance & Technical Writers: Words for Sale. (p. 635)
—Kids with Special Needs: IDEA (Individuals with Disabilities Education Act) (p. 955)
—Media in the 21st Century: Artists, Animators, & Graphic Designers. (p. 1118)
—Social Workers: Finding Solutions for Tomorrow's Society. (p. 1605)
—Therapy Jobs in Educational Settings: Speech, Physical, Occupational & Audiology. (p. 1729)
—Tomorrow's Enterprising Scientists: Computer Software Designers & Specialists. (p. 1765)
Flath, Camden, jt. auth. see Chastain, Zachary.
Flath, Camden, jt. auth. see Stewart, Sheila.
Flath, Camden, told to. Kids with Special Needs: IDEA (Individuals with Disabilities Education Act) (p. 955)
Flather, Lisa, illus. see French, Vivian.
Flathers, Sean. 'Twas a Shepherd's First Christmas. (p. 1799)
Flatley, Paula Chorman. Olivia's Tree Palmer, Kimmy, illus. (p. 1287)
Flatow, Norbert. What Next Big Guy? (p. 1892)
Flatt, Andy. Penny Wise Finds Out about Borrowing - Pupil's Book: Penny Is Ten & Wants to Know What Money Is All about & Why Grown-Ups Make Such a Fuss about It. (p. 1338)
Flatt, Lizann. Arts & Culture in the Early Islamic World. (p. 105)
—Cities & Statecraft in the Renaissance. (p. 322)
—Counting on Fall. Barron, Ashley & Owlkids Books Inc. Staff, illus. (p. 371)
—Early Islamic Empires. (p. 493)
—How to Write Realistic Fiction. (p. 823)
—India. (p. 870)
—Legacy of the War of 1812. (p. 987)
—Life in a Farming Community. (p. 1010)
—Life in a Forestry Community. (p. 1010)
—Life in a Suburban City. (p. 1010)
—Life in an Industrial City. (p. 1010)
—Nature Treasury: A First Look at the Natural World. Cormack, Allan et al, illus. (p. 1236)
—Religion in the Renaissance. (p. 1458)
—Shaping up Summer. Barron, Ashley, illus. (p. 1561)
—Sizing up Winter. Barron, Ashley & Owlkids Books Inc. Staff, illus. (p. 1583)
—Sorting Through Spring. Barron, Ashley, illus. (p. 1614)
—Underground Railroad. (p. 1814)
Flatt, Lizann, jt. auth. see Corporate Contributor Staff.
Flaubert, Gustave. Madame Bovary. (p. 1069)
Flavelle, Alix. Mapping Our Land: Community Mapping Handbook. (p. 1090)
Flavin, Dick. Red Sox Rhymes: Verses & Curses by Fenway Park's Poet Laureate. (p. 1455)
Flavin, Pamela. Alphabet of Saints for Young People. (p. 49)
Flavin, Teresa. Blackhope Enigma. (p. 197)
—Crimson Shard. (p. 383)
—Shadow Lantern. (p. 1557)
Flavin, Teresa, illus. see Borden, Louise & Kroeger, Mary Kay.
Flavin, Teresa, illus. see Bruchac, Joseph.
Flavin, Teresa, illus. see England, Linda.
Flavin, Teresa, illus. see Simon, Norma.
Flavius, Brother. Father of the American Cavalry: A Story of Brigadier General Casimir Pulaski. Jagodits, Carolyn Lee, illus. (p. 577)
Flaxenwick, Dim. Dobbin, Our Favourite Pony: Dobbin & the Little Red Squirrel. (p. 458)
Flaxma, Jessica, jt. auth. see Hall, Kirsten.
Flaxman, Andrew. Little Red Riding Hood: The Classic Grimm's Fairy Tale. Delisa, Patricia, illus. (p. 1035)
Flaxman, Jessica & Hall, Kirsten. Who Says? Becker, Wayne, illus. (p. 1917)
Flay, Linda. Abimbaboomb: Has a Secret... (p. 5)
Flebotte, Morrigan, jt. auth. see Burke, Sandra.
Fleck, Denise. Don't Judge a Book by Its Cover. Chin, Lili, illus. (p. 467)
Fleck, Joseph. River Rat: The Storm Treasure. (p. 1476)
—River Rat: The Barnacle & the Bracelets. (p. 1476)
Flecker, Katie, jt. auth. see Pattyn, Denny.
Fleecs, Tony, illus. see Kesel, Barbara.
Fleecs, Tony, illus. see Lindsay, Ryan K.
Fleemin, Sandy, jt. auth. see Carroll, Lewis, pseud.
Flegal, Daphna. Arrival Activities from A to Z. (p. 101)
—Sing Alleluia! An Easter Story for Children. Snyder, Suzanne, illus. (p. 1578)
—Sing & Say: Bibles Verses for Children. (p. 1579)
Flegal, Daphna, jt. auth. see Augustine, Peg.
Flegal, Daphna & Munger, Nancy. Rock-a-Bye Church Is a Special Place. (p. 1481)
Flegal, Daphna & Smith, Betsi H. Sing & Say Bible Verses for Children. Jones, Robert S., illus. (p. 1579)
Flegal, Daphna, ed. More Sign & Say. Jones, Robert S., illus. (p. 1175)
Flegal, Eric & Pecsenye, Jessica. UCLA College Prowler off the Record: Inside University of California Los Angeles. (p. 1807)
Flegal, Gary L. In Wisdom & Stature: Young Men Growing in God. (p. 868)
Flegg, Aubrey. In the Claws of the Eagle Vol. 3. (p. 865)
—Wings over Delft (p. 1936)
Flegg, Aubrey M. Rainbow Bridge. (p. 1435)
Flegg, Jim, jt. auth. see Chandler, David.
Flegg, Jim, jt. auth. see Parker, Steve.
Fleischer, Barbara R. Adventures of Scooby, Charlie, & Fluffy. (p. 22)
Fleischer, Jayson. Bald Eagles. Johnson, Gee, illus. (p. 133)
—Bats & Birds. Rupp, Kristina, illus. (p. 145)
—These Are Wolves. Washington, Joi, illus. (p. 1731)
Fleischer, Jayson, jt. auth. see Johnson, Gee.
Fleischer, Jayson, jt. auth. see Washington, Joi.
Fleischer, Jayson & Lynch, Michelle. Gorilla Family. Rupp, Kristina, illus. (p. 703)
Fleischer, Michael. Original Encyclopedia of Comic Book Heroes: Featuring Wonder Woman. (p. 1304)
Fleischer-Camp, Dean, jt. auth. see Slate, Jenny.
Fleischman, Bill. Dale Earnhardt JR. (p. 401)
—Jimmie Johnson. (p. 918)
Fleischman, Carol. Nadine, My Funny & Trusty Guide Dog Ford, Stephanie, illus. (p. 1227)
Fleischman, John. Black & White Airmen: Their True History. (p. 195)
—Phineas Gage: A Gruesome but True Story about Brain Science. (p. 1351)
Fleischman, Marcia C. Angels Everywhere. (p. 75)
Fleischman, Paul. Animal Hedge. Ibatoulline, Bagram, illus. (p. 78)
—Birthday Tree. Root, Barry, illus. (p. 193)
—Breakout. (p. 225)
—Brunolandia. Hawkes, Kevin, illus. (p. 232)
—Dateline: Troy. Frankfeldt, Gwen & Morrow, Glenn, illus. (p. 409)
—Dunderheads. (p. 490)
—Dunderheads. Roberts, David, illus. (p. 490)
—Dunderheads Behind Bars. Roberts, David, illus. (p. 490)
—Eyes Wide Open: Going Behind the Environmental Headlines. (p. 558)
—Glass Slipper, Gold Sandal: A Worldwide Cinderella. Paschkis, Julie, illus. (p. 682)
—Graven Images. Ibatoulline, Bagram, illus. (p. 712)
—Joyful Noise: Poems for Two Voices. Beddows, Eric, illus. (p. 930)
—Matchbox Diary. Ibatoulline, Bagram, illus. (p. 1104)
—Seedfolks. Pedersen, Judy, illus. (p. 1547)
—Seek. (p. 1548)
—Sidewalk Circus. Hawkes, Kevin, illus. (p. 1573)
—Weslandia. (p. 1876)
—Weslandia. Hawkes, Kevin, illus. (p. 1876)
—Whirligig. (p. 1912)
—Zap: A Play. (p. 1985)
Fleischman, Paul, jt. auth. see Frankfeldt, Gwen.
Fleischman, Sid. 13th Floor: A Ghost Story. Sís, Peter, illus. (p. 1995)
—Bandit's Moon. Smith, Jos. A., illus. (p. 136)
—Disappearing Act. (p. 446)
—Dream Stealer. Sís, Peter, illus. (p. 484)
—Entertainer & the Dybbuk. (p. 531)
—Escape! The Story of the Great Houdini. (p. 534)
—Ghost in the Noonday Sun. Sís, Peter, illus. (p. 671)
—Giant Rat of Sumatra. Hendrix, John, illus. (p. 674)
—Gran Rata de Sumatra. Lara, David, illus. (p. 707)
—Jim Ugly. Smith, Jos. A., illus. (p. 918)
—Maravillosa Granja de McBroom. Blake, Quentin, illus. (p. 1091)
—Midnight Horse. Sís, Peter, illus. (p. 1138)
—Niño de los Azotes. (p. 1257)
—Sir Charlie: Chaplin, the Funniest Man in the World. (p. 1580)
—Trouble Begins at 8: A Life of Mark Twain in the Wild, Wild West. (p. 1789)
—Whipping Boy. (p. 1912)
—Whipping Boy. Sís, Peter, illus. (p. 1912)
—White Elephant. McGuire, Robert, illus. (p. 1912)
Fleischmann, Tomas. Lolli's Apple. (p. 1046)
Fleischner, Jennifer. Nobody's Boy. (p. 1262)
Fleisher, Michael, jt. auth. see O'Neil, Denny.
Fleisher, Michael L. Original Encyclopedia of Comic Book Heroes - Featuring Batman (p. 1304)
Fleisher, Paul. Brain Food: 100+ Games That Make Kids Think. (p. 221)
—Desert Food Webs. (p. 429)
—Desert Food Webs in Action. (p. 429)
—Early Bird Food Webs. (p. 493)
—Early Bird Food Webs. (p. 493)
—Evolution. (p. 546)
—Forest Food Webs. (p. 618)
—Forest Food Webs in Action. (p. 618)
—Gases, Pressure, & Wind: The Science of the Atmosphere. (p. 657)
—Grassland Food Webs. (p. 712)
—Grassland Food Webs in Action. (p. 712)
—Lake & Pond Food Webs. (p. 972)
—Lake & Pond Food Webs in Action. (p. 972)
—Lightning, Hurricanes, & Blizzards: The Science of Storms. (p. 1016)
—Neptune. (p. 1241)
—Ocean Food Webs in Action. (p. 1276)
—Parasites: Latching on to a Free Lunch. (p. 1324)
—Tundra Food Webs. (p. 1796)
—Tundra Food Webs. Schultz, Gary, photos by. (p. 1796)
—Tundra Food Webs in Action. (p. 1796)
—Vapor, Rain, & Snow: The Science of Clouds & Precipitation. (p. 1833)
—Venus. (p. 1836)
—Weatherwise (p. 1870)
—Webs of Life - Group 2 (p. 1870)
Fleishman, Seymour, illus. see Van Riper, Guernsey, Jr.
Fleming. Famous Americans Series: Martin Luther King. (p. 569)
Fleming, Alice. Frederick Douglass: From Slave to Statesman. (p. 633)
—Martin Luther King, Jr. A Dream of Hope. (p. 1098)
Fleming, Alice Mulcahey. Frederick Douglass: From Slave to Statesman. (p. 633)
Fleming, Bryn. Cassie & Jasper to the Rescue. (p. 276)
—Jasper & Willie: Wildfire. (p. 910)
Fleming, Candace. Amelia Lost: The Life & Disappearance of Amelia Earhart. (p. 58)
—Ben Franklin's Almanac: Being a True Account of the Good Gentleman's Life. (p. 163)
—Big Cheese for the White House: The True Tale of a Tremendous Cheddar. Schindler, S. D., illus. (p. 180)
—Boxes for Katje. Dressen-McQueen, Stacey, illus. (p. 217)
—Bulldozer's Big Day. Rohmann, Eric, illus. (p. 240)
—Clever Jack Takes the Cake. Karas, G. Brian, illus. (p. 331)
—Fabled Fifth Graders of Aesop Elementary School. (p. 559)
—Fabled Fourth Graders of Aesop Elementary School. (p. 559)
—Family Romanov: Murder, Rebellion, & the Fall of Imperial Russia. (p. 568)
—Gator Gumbo: A Spicy-Hot Tale. Lambert, Sally Anne, illus. (p. 658)
—Go Sleep in Your Own Bed. Rohmann, Eric, illus. (p. 687)
—Great & Only Barnum: The Tremendous, Stupendous Life of Showman P. T. Barnum. Fenwick, Ray, illus. (p. 713)
—Imogene's Last Stand. Carpenter, Nancy, illus. (p. 862)
—Lincolns: A Scrapbook Look at Abraham & Mary. (p. 1019)
—Lowji Discovers America. (p. 1061)
—Muncha! Muncha! Muncha! (p. 1191)
—Muncha! Muncha! Muncha! Karas, G. Brian, illus. (p. 1191)
—Nam! Nam! Nam! Schmidt, Alejandra, tr. from ENG. (p. 1228)
—Oh, No! Rohmann, Eric, illus. (p. 1281)
—On the Day I Died: Stories from the Grave. (p. 1290)
—Our Eleanor: A Scrapbook Look at Eleanor Roosevelt's Remarkable Life. (p. 1308)
—Papa's Mechanical Fish. Kulikov, Boris, illus. (p. 1322)
—Seven Hungry Babies. Yelchin, Eugene, illus. (p. 1554)
—Tippy-Tippy-Tippy, Hide! Karas, G. Brian, illus. (p. 1757)
—Tippy-Tippy-Tippy, Splash! Karas, G. Brian, illus. (p. 1757)
—Westward Ho, Carlotta! Catrow, David, illus. (p. 1876)
—Who Invited You? Booth, George, illus. (p. 1915)
Fleming, Celestine. Winkey. (p. 1936)
Fleming, Christine. Art As Science. (p. 101)
Fleming, Christopher, illus. see Long, Tyler.
Fleming, Chula. Spooky Old Tree (p. 1631)
Fleming, David. Charlie Blue Berry Fipple Berry. (p. 292)
—Saturday Boy. (p. 1515)
Fleming, Denise. 5 Little Ducks. (p. 1992)
—Alphabet under Construction. Fleming, Denise, illus. (p. 50)
—Barnyard Banter. Fleming, Denise, illus. (p. 139)
—Buster Goes to Cowboy Camp. Fleming, Denise, illus. (p. 245)
—Cow Who Clucked. (p. 373)
—Cow Who Clucked. Fleming, Denise, illus. (p. 373)
—Everything Book. Fleming, Denise, illus. (p. 544)
—First Day of Winter. Fleming, Denise, illus. (p. 594)
—Go, Shapes, Go! Fleming, Denise, illus. (p. 687)
—In the Small, Small Pond. Fleming, Denise, illus. (p. 867)
—In the Tall, Tall, Grass. (p. 867)
—Lunch. (p. 1065)
—Pumpkin Eye. (p. 1416)
—Pumpkin Eye. Fleming, Denise, illus. (p. 1416)
—Shout! Shout It Out! Fleming, Denise, illus. (p. 1570)
—Sleepy, Oh So Sleepy. Fleming, Denise, illus. (p. 1590)
—UnderGROUND. Fleming, Denise, illus. (p. 1814)
Fleming, Diana Trucks, illus. see Calvert, Ellen Hasenecz.
Fleming, F. & Dowswell, P. Shock Horror History! (p. 1568)
Fleming, Fergus, jt. auth. see Dowswell, Paul.
Fleming, Garry. Animals of the World. (p. 83)
—Dinosaurs of the World. (p. 445)
—Dragon Chronicles Jigsaw Book: The Lost Journals of the Great Wizard, Septimus Agorius. (p. 476)
Fleming, Garry, illus. see Dale, Jay.
Fleming, Garry, illus. see Giulieri, Anne.
Fleming, Geronda. Among the Fairies. (p. 65)
Fleming, Ian. Chitty Chitty Bang Bang. Berger, Joe, illus. (p. 308)
Fleming, Jeanie Puleston, illus. see Dewey, Jennifer Owings.
Fleming, Jeanie Puleston, photos by see Dewey, Jennifer Owings.
Fleming, Jesse, jt. illus. see Matsunaga, Judd.
Fleming, Jesse, photos by see Matsunaga, Judd, illus.
Fleming, Jessica & Burns, Adam. Texas Christian University College Prowler off the Record. (p. 1724)
Fleming, K. C. What If? (p. 1887)
Fleming, Kate & Baldwin, Patricia. Teaching Literacy Through Drama: Creative Approaches. (p. 1710)
Fleming, Kye, illus. see Bunny, Hull.
Fleming, Kye, illus. see Hull, Bunny.
Fleming, Ligia Morales. Very Special Princess. (p. 1838)
Fleming, Lucy, illus. see Wallace, Nancy K.
Fleming, Maria. 20 Sing-Along Mini-Books for Emergent Readers: Sweet & Simple Stories That Can Be Sung to the Tunes of Favorite Children's Songs. (p. 1995)
—Bug Book. Swift, Gary, illus. (p. 236)
—Five Shiny Apples. Sexton, Brenda, illus. (p. 601)
—Mini-Book of the Week: 40 Easy-to-Read Mini-Books on Fiction & Nonfiction Topics for Every Week of the School Year. (p. 1146)
—Six Cheers for Ladybug. Chambliss, Maxie, illus. (p. 1582)
Fleming, Maria & Charlesworth, Liza. Chicken in the City. Kennedy, Kelly, illus. (p. 300)

Fleming, Maria & Franco, Betsy. Poem of the Month Flip Chart: 12 Joyful Read-Aloud Poems with Skill-Building Lessons & Writing Springboards. (p. 1375)
Fleming, Maria & Scholastic Canada Ltd. Staff. 30 Mice Are Very Nice. Borlasca, Hector, illus. (p. 1996)
Fleming, Matthew. Nukie Fairy. (p. 1270)
Fleming, Michael, illus. see Gerber, Carole.
Fleming, Michael, illus. see Klimo, Kate.
Fleming, Michael, illus. see Sadler, Marilyn.
Fleming, Sally. Ferocious Fangs. Underwood, Kay Povelite, illus. (p. 582)
—Rapid Runners. Underwood, Kay Povelite, illus. (p. 1439)
Fleming, Sean & Ewald, Jenny, eds. To Catch a Mall Thief. (p. 1758)
Fleming, Theresa. Going Home with Jesus Fleming, Yvonne B., illus. (p. 692)
Fleming, Thomas. King of Prussia & a Peanut Butter Sandwich. (p. 959)
Fleming, Vicki & Dipietro, Kara. North Woods Numbers. (p. 1265)
Fleming, Yvonne B., illus. see Fleming, Theresa.
Flemins, Allan D., jt. auth. see Viverito, Philip J.
Flemmer, Chip. Out of Texas (p. 1311)
Flemming, Denise. Buster. (p. 245)
Flemming, Laraine E. Reading Matters. (p. 1446)
—Words Matter. (p. 1951)
Flemmings, Tyrone. Home Schooled Boss. (p. 793)
Flener, Bettie D. Sidney's Bedtime Stories. Flener, Sheila S., illus. (p. 1573)
Flener, Sheila S., illus. see Flener, Bettie D.
Flensted, Christian, et al. Counting Chickens. (p. 371)
Flentge, Paul. Path of the Wolf. (p. 1328)
Fles, Barthold, tr. see Salten, Felix.
Flesher, Vivienne. Alfred's Nose. Flesher, Vivienne, illus. (p. 38)
Flesher, Vivienne, illus. see MacHale, D. J.
Flesich, Matt, compiled by. Long Way from Henry Street: A Collection of Stories Written by School Nurses. (p. 1047)
Fletcher, Alan. Anteaters to Zebras. (p. 89)
Fletcher, Alan, et al. Picturing & Poeting. (p. 1356)
Fletcher, Alice. Abe & Abby's First Journey: A Tale about Twin Camels. (p. 4)
Fletcher, Ann L. Angora Rabbits, the Complete Owner's Guide, Includes English, French, Giant, Satin & German Breeds. Care, Breeding, Wool, Farming, Lifespan, Colors. (p. 75)
Fletcher, Anthony. Elizabethan Village: Illustrated from Contemporary Sources. (p. 513)
Fletcher, Archibald Lee. Boy Scouts in Northern Wilds. (p. 218)
Fletcher, Ashlee. My Dog, My Cat. (p. 1202)
—My Dog, My Cat. Fletcher, Ashlee, illus. (p. 1202)
Fletcher, B. R. Long Haired Yellow Bellies. (p. 1047)
Fletcher, Barbara. Rose on the River: Level U (p. 1489)
Fletcher, Betty & Harvest House Publishers Staff. My Very Own Bible. Police, Lou, illus. (p. 1221)
Fletcher, Bob, illus. see Lewis, Alan K.
Fletcher, Brekke, ed. see FHM Magazine Staff.
Fletcher, Brent L. Interactive Stories & Life Lessons with Children. (p. 879)
Fletcher, Charlie. Stoneheart. Disney Book Group Staff, photos by. (p. 1653)
Fletcher, Chris. Rock Tales. Harrison, Harry, illus. (p. 1482)
Fletcher, Christine. Ten Cents a Dance. (p. 1718)
Fletcher, Christopher. Guardian Angel. (p. 728)
Fletcher, Corina. Playbook Farm. Teckentrup, Britta, illus. (p. 1372)
—Playbook Pirates. Teckentrup, Britta, illus. (p. 1372)
—Small Smaller Smallest. Marshall, Natalie, illus. (p. 1592)
—Up down Across. Marshall, Natalie, illus. (p. 1824)
Fletcher, Corina, jt. illus. see Roberts, David.
Fletcher, Dacia. Clifton the Cloud & the Land of Rainbows. (p. 332)
Fletcher, Donna. Sweet Baby Heather: Day at the Zoo. (p. 1689)
Fletcher, J. Exploring the Life, Myth, & Art of Ancient Egypt. (p. 554)
Fletcher, J. S. Scarhaven Keep. (p. 1520)
Fletcher, Janet. Four Seasons Pasta. Pearson, Victoria, photos by. (p. 625)
Fletcher, Jessica & Bain, Donald. Maine Mutiny. (p. 1077)
Fletcher, Jessica, et al. Dying to Retire. (p. 491)
—Question of Murder. (p. 1426)
—Three Strikes & You're Dead. (p. 1744)
Fletcher, Lyn, illus. see Shepherd, Jodie.
Fletcher, Marty, jt. auth. see Scherer, Glenn.
Fletcher, Marty & Scherer, Glenn. Florida Panther: Help Save This Endangered Species! (p. 607)
—Green Sea Turtle: Help Save This Endangered Species! (p. 722)
—Snow Leopard: Help Save This Endangered Species! (p. 1599)
Fletcher, Melinda. Dancing Pyjamas. (p. 403)
Fletcher, Pamela. Who Is Freddy Farlittle? (p. 1915)
Fletcher, Perry. Why Snakes Don't Have Legs. (p. 1926)
Fletcher, Ralph. Flying Solo. (p. 610)
—How to Write Your Life Story. Nagy, Ian, illus. (p. 823)
—Marshfield Dreams: When I Was a Kid. (p. 1096)
—Moving Day. Emery, Jennifer, illus. (p. 1183)
—Spider Boy. (p. 1626)
—Writer's Notebook: Unlocking the Writer Within You. (p. 1964)
Fletcher, Ralph, jt. auth. see Fletcher, Ralph J.
Fletcher, Ralph J. Guy-Write: What Every Guy Writer Needs to Know. (p. 733)
—Sandman. Cowdrey, Richard, illus. (p. 1511)
—Writing Kind of Day: Poems for Young Poets. (p. 1965)
Fletcher, Ralph J. & Fletcher, Ralph. Hello, Harvest Moon. Kiesler, Kate, illus. (p. 764)
Fletcher, Robert A. Jeeps at War. Naples, Thomas R. et al, eds. (p. 911)
Fletcher, Rusty, illus. see Beveridge, Amy.
Fletcher, Rusty, illus. see Bowman, Crystal.
Fletcher, Rusty, illus. see George, Olivia.
Fletcher, Rusty, illus. see Head, Heno.
Fletcher, Rusty, illus. see Weil, Ann.
Fletcher, Rusty, illus. see Williams, Rozanne Lanczak.
Fletcher, Sarah. Historia de Jesus (My Stories about Jesus) Historias del Nuevo Testamento. (p. 782)
Fletcher, Sheila. Is It Flexible or Rigid? (p. 889)
Fletcher, Steffi. Gene Autry. Crawford, Mel, illus. (p. 660)
—Lone Ranger. Dreany, E. Joseph, illus. (p. 1046)
Fletcher, Susan. Alphabet of Dreams. (p. 49)
—Ancient, Strange, & Lovely. (p. 70)
—Dadblamed Union Army Cow. Root, Kimberly Bulcken, illus. (p. 398)
—Falcon in the Glass. (p. 565)
—Flight of the Dragon Kyn. (p. 604)
—Sign of the Dove. (p. 1574)
—Walk Across the Sea. Jakesevic, Nenad, illus. (p. 1853)
Fletcher, Terri. Scrumpy's Educational Kid Songs. (p. 1533)
Fletcher, Victoria A. Tweetie Bug's Blessing: A Story of Adoption. (p. 1800)
—You Just Have to Believe. (p. 1975)
Flett, Julie. Li Yiiboo Miyo-Waapamik LII Seer: L'Alfabet Di Michif. (p. 1004)
—Wild Berries. Cook, Earl N., tr. (p. 1929)
Flett, Julie, illus. see Jameson, Catherine.
Flett, Julie, illus. see Miki, Roy & Miki, Slavia.
Flett, Julie, illus. see Van Camp, Richard.
Fletter, Sharon Sofia. My Guardian Angel. Fletter, Sharon Sofia, illus. (p. 1210)
Fleur, Thornton, jt. auth. see Andrew, Edwards.
Fleuriel, Allison. Are You Done Sleeping? (p. 97)
Fleury, Barbara. Runaway Deer. (p. 1496)
Fleury, Kevin. Mummies. (p. 1190)
Fleury, Mike Stevenson. Natural Disaster 2222. (p. 1235)
Fleury, Rick & Staehr, Linda. Rainbows for Buckeroo. (p. 1436)
FLH Students & Lutz, Suzanne. Many Voices: Where Dreams Take Flight III. (p. 1089)
Flickinger, Amanda, jt. auth. see Flickinger, Joie.
Flickinger, Gary L. Where the Hell Are the Light Bulbs? (p. 1909)
Flickinger, Joie & Flickinger, Amanda. Clutch the Trucking Cat. (p. 336)
Fliess, Sue. Dress for Me! Laughead, Mike, illus. (p. 484)
—Gluten-Free Birthday for Me! Morris, Jennifer, illus. (p. 685)
—How to Be a Pirate. Dyson, Nikki, illus. (p. 814)
—How to Be a Superhero. Dyson, Nikki, illus. (p. 815)
—Hug Book. Kennedy, Anne, illus. (p. 824)
—I'm a Ballerina! Chou, Joey, illus. (p. 858)
—Let's Build! (p. 994)
—Robots, Robots Everywhere! Staake, Bob, illus. (p. 1481)
—Shoes for Me! Laughead, Mike, illus. (p. 1568)
—Tons of Trucks. Snyder, Betsy E., illus. (p. 1765)
—We're Getting a Pet! Christy, Jana, illus. (p. 1875)
Flight, B. I. Lonely Winds. (p. 1046)
Flikkema, Elizabeth. Make the World a Better Place! My Sharing Time, Talent & Treasure Activity Book. Olsen, Christian, illus. (p. 1079)
Flinders, Benjamin. Excalibur: Traveling Trunk Adventure 3. (p. 547)
Flinn. Symbols Speak. (p. 1693)
Flinn, Alex. Beastly. (p. 152)
—Bewitching: The Kendra Chronicles. (p. 173)
—Bewitching: Beastly Was Just One of Her Curses. (p. 173)
—Breaking Point. (p. 225)
—Breathing Underwater. (p. 226)
—Cloaked. (p. 333)
—Diva. (p. 454)
—Fade to Black. (p. 562)
—Kiss in Time. (p. 961)
—Mirrored. (p. 1149)
—Nothing to Lose. (p. 1268)
—Towering. (p. 1773)
Flinn, Eugene. Trixie Triphammer's Magical Christmas. (p. 1788)
Flinn, Frank K. Encyclopedia of Catholicism. (p. 525)
Flinn, Hannah, illus. see Albuquerque, Blossom.
Flinn, Lias. Unwrapping the Christmas Creche. (p. 1824)
Flinn, Lisa. Unwrapping the Christmas Creche. (p. 1824)
Flinn, Lisa, jt. auth. see Younger, Barbara.
Flinn, Lisa & Younger, Barbara. Christmas Garland. Corvino, Lucy, tr. (p. 314)
—Sharing God's Love in Children's Church: A Year's Worth of Programs for Children Ages 3-7. (p. 1561)
Flint, Ann. Charlotte's Curtain Call. (p. 293)
Flint, David. Europe. (p. 540)
—Focus on Germany. (p. 610)
Flint, Garrison. Butler Did It! A Raymond Masrters Mystery. (p. 247)
—Case of the Twisted Twins Murders: A Raymond Masters Mystery. (p. 275)
—Sanity in Search of Peter Alexander. (p. 1511)
Flint, Norman. Rag & Bone: Visit London. (p. 1433)
Flint, Russ, illus. see Ewald, Thomas.
Flint, Russ, illus. see Sharp, Anna Layton.
Flint, Scott. Waking the Tiger Within: How to Be Safe from Crime on the Street, at Home, on Trips, at Work, & at School. (p. 1853)
Flint, Shamini. Ten. (p. 1718)
Flint, Stacie, illus. see Atlas, Ron.
Flintham, Thomas. Thomas Flintham's Book of Mazes & Puzzles. Flintham, Thomas, illus. (p. 1738)
Flintham, Thomas, illus. see Litton, Jonathan.
Flintham, Thomas, illus. see VIZ Media Staff.
Flinthart, Dirk, jt. auth. see Anderson, Judith.
Flinthart, Dirk, jt. auth. see Staunton, Joseph.
Flintman, Thomas, illus. see Adams, Tom.
Flintoft, Anthony, illus. see Edwards, Becky.
Flint-Warren, Cathrine. To Dance with the Yellow Butterfly. (p. 1758)
Flipp Sports, des. Albert Pujols - Sports Action Flipp Book. (p. 34)
Flippen, David. Where Is It? (p. 1908)
—Where Is It? Identify & Describe Shapes. (p. 1908)
Flipper, Henry Ossian. Colored Cadet at West Point-Autobiography of Lieut. Henry Ossian Flipper, U. S. A. (p. 343)
Flippin, Ian, jt. auth. see McGee, Robert S.
Flippin, Tan. Vital Truth Stewardship Responsibility Isnt it My Stuff. (p. 1846)
Flitcroft, Jean. Chupacabra. (p. 318)
—Loch Ness Monster. (p. 1044)
—Pacific Giants. (p. 1317)
Floca, Brian. Five Trucks. Floca, Brian, illus. (p. 601)
—Frightful Story of Harry Walfish. Floca, Brian, illus. (p. 639)
—Hinky-Pink: An Old Tale. (p. 780)
—Lightship. (p. 1016)
—Lightship. Floca, Brian, illus. (p. 1016)
—Locomotive. Floca, Brian, illus. (p. 1045)
—Moonshot: The Flight of Apollo 11. Floca, Brian, illus. (p. 1173)
—Racecar Alphabet. Floca, Brian, illus. (p. 1431)
Floca, Brian, illus. see Avi.
Floca, Brian, illus. see Cox, Lynne.
Floca, Brian, illus. see Greenberg, Jan & Jordan, Sandra.
Floca, Brian, illus. see Hopkinson, Deborah.
Floca, Brian, illus. see Hurwitz, Johanna.
Floca, Brian, illus. see Lakin, Patricia.
Floca, Brian, illus. see MacLachlan, Patricia.
Floca, Brian, illus. see Messner, Kate.
Floca, Brian, illus. see Wheeler, Lisa.
Flockhart, Dan. Fantasy Baseball & Mathematics: Student Workbook. (p. 572)
—Fantasy Basketball & Mathematics: Student Workbook. (p. 572)
—Fantasy Football & Mathematics: Student Workbook. (p. 572)
Flodin, Louise E. Sherman the Frog Meets the Snow Princess. (p. 1566)
Flodin, Mickey. Kids' Pocket Signing Guide. (p. 955)
—Signing for Kids. (p. 1574)
Floen, Douglas. Knowing Noah: The Adventures of a Mouse Who Could Read. (p. 965)
Floerchinger, Jeremy, illus. see Floerchinger, Lori Liddic.
Floerchinger, Lori Liddic. Ocean of Dreams. Floerchinger, Jeremy, illus. (p. 1276)
Floersch, Chris. Mr Charlie. (p. 1184)
Floeter, Nell, illus. see Wood, David.
Floherty, John Joseph & McGrady, Mike. Whirling Wings: The Story of the Helicopter. (p. 1912)
Flohr, John W. & Trollinger, Valerie L. Music in Elementary Education. (p. 1193)
Flohr, Perel, tr. see Rotman, Risa.
Flood, Bo. Soldier Sister, Fly Home. (p. 1607)
Flood, C. J. Infinite Sky. (p. 873)
Flood, Heather. Mousey Mousey & the Witches' Revenge. (p. 1182)
Flood, Nancy Bo. Cowboy Up! Ride the Navajo Rodeo. Sonnemair, Jan, illus. (p. 374)
—Hogan That Great-Grandfather Built. Yazzie, Peterson, illus. (p. 787)
—Navajo Year, Walk Through Many Seasons: Activities for Learning & Exploring. Ruffenach, Jessie E., ed. (p. 1237)
—Navajo Year, Walk Through Many Seasons. Whitethorne, Billy, illus. (p. 1237)
—Sand to Stone: And Back Again. Kuyper, Tony, photos by. (p. 1510)
—Warriors in the Crossfire. (p. 1859)
—Water Runs Through This Book. (p. 1863)
Flood, Raymond & Wilson, Robin. Great Mathematicians. (p. 717)
Flood, Robert. Creating RFPs for IP Telephony Communication Systems: PBX, IP Telephony, & IP Centrex System & Services. (p. 378)
Flood, Tim. Dreams of a Ball in Flight: Stories from the Bottom of the Cup. (p. 484)
Flood, Tony. Jody Richards & the Secret Potion. (p. 919)
Flood Williams, Colleen Madonna. Mexican Art & Architecture. (p. 1131)
Flood Williams, Colleen Madonna, jt. auth. see Williams, Colleen Madonna Flood.
Flood Williams, Colleen Madonna, et al. Festivals of Mexico. (p. 582)
Flook, Helen, illus. see Adderson, Caroline.
Flook, Helen, illus. see Deary, Terry.
Flook, Helen, illus. see Erlbach, Arlene.
Flook, Helen, illus. see Fitch, Sheree.
Flook, Helen, illus. see Hopkins, Audrey.
Flook, Helen, illus. see Horrocks, Anita.
Flook, Helen, illus. see Wallace, Karen & Mackey, James.
Flook, Helen, illus. see Wallace, Karen.
Flook, Helen, illus. see White, Wendy.
Floor, Guus, illus. see Anderson, Dale & Goff, Elizabeth Hudson.
Floor, Guus, illus. see Brown, Jonatha A. & Goff, Elizabeth Hudson.
Floor, Guus, illus. see Goff, Elizabeth Hudson, et al.
Floor, Guus, illus. see Uschan, Michael V. & Goff, Elizabeth Hudson.
Flor Ada, Alma. Bajo las Palmas Reales. (p. 133)
—Celebra el Ano Nuevo Chino con la Familia Fong. (p. 283)
—Celebra el Cinco de Mayo con un Jarabe Tapatio. Gomez, Marcela & Silva, David, illus. (p. 283)
—Celebra el Cuatro de Julio con Campeon, el Gloton. Mazali, Gustavo, illus. (p. 283)
—Celebra el Dia de Accion de Gracias con Beto y Gaby. Rueda, Claudia, illus. (p. 283)
—Celebra el Dia De3 San Patricio con Samantha y Lola. Lavandeira, Sandra, illus. (p. 283)
—Celebra el Halloween y el Dia de Muertos con Cristina y Su Conejito Azul. Martinez, Ivanova, illus. (p. 283)
—Celebra el Mardi Gras con Joaquin, Arlequin. (p. 283)
—Celebra Hanukkah con un Cuento de Bubbe. (p. 283)
—Celebra la Navidad y el Dia de Los Reyes Magos con Pablo y Carlitos. Torres, Walter, illus. (p. 283)
—Celebra un Powwow con Sandy Starbright. Alvarez, Maria Jesus, illus. (p. 283)
—Celebrate a Powwow with Sandy Starbright. Alvarez, Maria Jesus, illus. (p. 283)
—Celebrate Chinese New Year with the Fong Family. Castro, Mima, illus. (p. 283)
—Celebrate Christmas & Three Kings Day with Pablo & Carlitos. Torres, Walter, illus. (p. 283)
—Celebrate Fourth of July with Champ, the Scamp. Mazali, Gustavo, illus. (p. 283)
—Celebrate Halloween & the Day of the Dead with Cristina & Her Blue Bunny. Martinez, Ivanova, illus. (p. 283)
—Celebrate Hanukkah with Bubbe's Tales. Hayes, Joe & Franco, Sharon, trs. (p. 283)
—Celebrate Kwanzaa with Boots & Her Kittens. Docampo, Valeria, illus. (p. 284)
—Celebrate Mardi Gras with Joaquin. Nobati, Eugenia, illus. (p. 284)
—Celebrate Martin Luther King, Jr. Day with Mrs. Park's Class. Weiss, Monica, illus. (p. 284)
—Celebrate Thanksgiving Day with Beto & Gaby. Hayes, Joe & Franco, Sharon, trs. (p. 284)
—Daniel y Su Mascota. Karas, G. Brian, illus. (p. 405)
—Daniel's Mystery Egg. Karas, G. Brian, illus. (p. 405)
—Daniel's Pet. (p. 405)
—Daniel's Pet. Karas, G. Brian, illus. (p. 405)
—Dear Peter Rabbit. Tryon, Leslie, illus. (p. 419)
—En Alas del Condor. (p. 522)
—Extra! Extra! Fairy-Tale News from Hidden Forest. Tryon, Leslie, illus. (p. 555)
—Eyes of the Jaguar. Davalos, Felipe, illus. (p. 558)
—Gathering the Sun. (p. 658)
—Golden Cage. (p. 694)
—I Love Saturdays y Domingos. Savadier, Elivia, illus. (p. 843)
—Kite. (p. 962)
—Me Encantan los Saturdays y los Domingos. Savadier, Elvia, illus. (p. 1115)
—Misterioso Huevo de Daniel. Flor Ada, Alma, tr. from ENM. (p. 1155)
Flor Ada Alma. My Name Is Maria Isabel. (p. 1215)
Flor Ada, Alma. Ojos del Jaguar. (p. 1282)
—One More Friend. Fatus, Sophie, illus. (p. 1296)
—Quiero Ayudar! Dominguez, Angela, illus. (p. 1428)
—Rose with Wings. Zubizarreta, Rosa, tr. (p. 1489)
—Surprise for Mother Rabbit. (p. 1685)
—Three Golden Oranges. Cartwright, Reg, illus. (p. 1742)
—Unicorn of the West. (p. 1818)
—Unicorn of the West (Spanish Edition) (p. 1818)
—Vuelo de los Colibries. Jacobson, Judith, illus. (p. 1851)
—Where the Flame Trees Bloom. (p. 1909)
—With Love, Little Red Hen. Tryon, Leslie, illus. (p. 1942)
Flor Ada, Alma, tr. see Avery, Kristin.
Flor Ada, Alma, tr. see Baker, Keith.
Flor Ada, Alma, tr. see Butler, Andrea.
Flor Ada, Alma, tr. see Cabral, Len.
Flor Ada, Alma, tr. see Daniel, Claire & Ernst, Lisa Campbell.
Flor Ada, Alma, tr. see Douglas, Erin.
Flor Ada, Alma, tr. see Forbes, Chris.
Flor Ada, Alma, tr. see Fox, Mem.
Flor Ada, Alma, tr. see Greene, Inez.
Flor Ada, Alma, tr. see Guthrie, Woody.
Flor Ada, Alma, tr. see Krull, Kathleen.
Flor Ada, Alma, tr. see Lester, Helen.
Flor Ada, Alma, tr. see McPhail, David.
Flor Ada, Alma, tr. see Min, Laura.
Flor Ada, Alma, tr. see Mora, Pat.
Flor Ada, Alma, tr. see Moran, Alex.
Flor Ada, Alma, tr. see Most, Bernard.
Flor Ada, Alma, tr. see Murphy, Mary.
Flor Ada, Alma, tr. see Parks, Carmen.
Flor Ada, Alma, tr. see Prap, Lila.
Flor Ada, Alma, tr. see Rohmer, Harriet.
Flor Ada, Alma, tr. see Stevens, Janet & Crummel, Susan Stevens.
Flor Ada, Alma & Campoy, F. Isabel. Anton Pirulero. (p. 90)
—Brocha y Pincel. (p. 230)
—Caballete. (p. 250)
—Celebrate St. Patrick's Day with Samantha & Lola. Hayes, Joe & Franco, Sharon, trs. (p. 284)
—Chuchurumbe. (p. 318)
—Colecciones de Libros de la Biblioteca: El Papalote. (p. 339)
—Colecciones de Libros de la Biblioteca: Un Sillon Para Mi Mama. (p. 339)
—Colecciones de Libros de la Biblioteca: Lucita Regresa a Oaxaca. (p. 339)
—Colecciones de Libros de la Biblioteca: El Coraje de Sarah Noble. (p. 339)
—Dreaming Fish. (p. 484)
—Evaluacion de Destrezas del Lenguaje y Escritura Ediciones del Maestro: Language Skills & Writing Assessment. (p. 540)
—Evaluacion de Destrezas del Lenguaje y Escritura Ediciones del Maestro: Language Skills & Writing Assessment Teacher's Editions. (p. 540)
—Flying Dragon. (p. 609)
—Happy Birthday, Little Red Riding Hood! (p. 745)
—Laughing Crocodiles. (p. 980)
—Lienzo y Papel. (p. 1007)
—Mambru. (p. 1084)
—Muu, Moo! Rimas de Animales - Animal Nursery Rhymes. Escrivá, Viví, illus. (p. 1195)
—On the Wings of the Condor. Davalos, Felipe et al, illus. (p. 1292)
—Pimpon. (p. 1359)
—Semilla de Luz. Dávalos, Felipe, illus. (p. 1550)
—Tales Our Abuelitas Told: A Hispanic Folktale Collection. Davalos, Felipe et al, illus. (p. 1703)
—Ten Little Puppies/Diez Perritos. Wensell, Ulises, illus. (p. 1719)
—Yes! We Are Latinos. Diaz, David, illus. (p. 1970)
—¡Muu, Moo! Rimas de Animales. Escrivá, Viví, illus. (p. 1195)
Flor Ada, Alma & Campoy, F. Isabel, contrib. by. Azul y Verde. (p. 122)
—Blue & Green. (p. 202)
—Caminos. (p. 256)
—Pasos. (p. 1326)
—Paths. (p. 1328)
—Sonrisas. (p. 1613)
—Steps. (p. 1648)
—Voces. (p. 1847)
—Voices. (p. 1848)

Flor Ada, Alma & Docampo, Valeria. Celebra Kwanzaa con Botitas y Sus Gatitos. Docampo, Valeria, illus. (p. 283)
Flor Ada, Alma & Weiss, Mónica. Celebra el Día de Martin Luther King, Jr. con la Clase de la Sra. Park. Weiss, Mónica, illus. (p. 283)
Flor Ada, Alma & Zubizarreta, Gabriel M. Con Cariño, Amalia. (p. 355)
—Dancing Home. (p. 403)
—Love, Amalia. (p. 1059)
—Nacer Bailando (Dancing Home) (p. 1227)
Flor Ada, Alma & Zubizarreta, Rosalma, trs. Uncle Nacho's Hat Reisberg, Mira, illus. (p. 1812)
Flor Ada, Alma, tr. Take-Home Package: Complete Package. (p. 1696)
Flora, B. David. Angel's Day on Earth. Alexander, Johnna A., illus. (p. 75)
Flora, James, creator. Day the Cow Sneezed. (p. 414)
—Kangaroo for Christmas. (p. 942)
Flora, Norma Bradshaw, jt. auth. see Cox, Norma Flora.
Flora, Sherrill B. Alphabet: Signs, Letters, Sounds. (p. 49)
—Building Essential Vocabulary: Reproducible Photo Cards, Games, & Activities to Build Vocabulary in Any Language. Anderson, Julie, illus. (p. 239)
Florea, Jesse, jt. auth. see Arterburn, Stephen.
Florea, Jesse, jt. auth. see Smiley, Bob.
Florea, Jesse, jt. auth. see Yorkey, Mike.
Florea, Jesse & Whiting, Karen. One Year Devotions for Active Boys. (p. 1297)
Florea, Jesse, et al. One Year Father-Daughter Devotions. (p. 1298)
Floreen, Tim. Willful Machines. (p. 1933)
Florek, Amy. Silly Beulah! (p. 1575)
Florence, Amy. Big God Cares for a Little Me. (p. 181)
Florence, Annette R. Peanut the Cat Tells His Tale. (p. 1332)
Florence, Debbi Michiko. China: Over 40 Activities to Experience China - Past & Present. Caputo, Jim, illus. (p. 306)
—Japan. Caputo, James, illus. (p. 908)
Florence John Keller. Meet My Pets. (p. 1121)
Florence, Leigh Anne. Adoption. Asher, James, illus. (p. 13)
—Dog House Divided. (p. 461)
—Mr. Dogwood Goes to Washington. Asher, James, illus. (p. 1184)
—Welcomes a Dad Asher, James, illus. (p. 1874)
Florence, Melanie. Jordin Tootoo: The Highs & Lows in the Journey of the First Inuit to Play in the NHL (p. 925)
Florence, Nancy L. Harold the Goat. (p. 749)
Florence, Ronald. Lawrence & Aaronsohn: T. E. Lawrence, Aaron Aaronsohn, & the Seeds of the Arab-Israeli Conflict. (p. 981)
Florence, Sarah. Pilgrim Foods & Recipes. (p. 1358)
Florence, Sylvia & Keller, Carolyn. James Madison University College Prowler off the Record. (p. 907)
Florence, Tyler. Tyler Makes a Birthday Cake! Frazier, Craig, illus. (p. 1805)
—Tyler Makes Spaghetti! Frazier, Craig, illus. (p. 1805)
Florence, Tyler & Frazier, Craig. Tyler Makes Pancakes! Florence, Tyler & Frazier, Craig, illus. (p. 1805)
Florendo, R. M., illus. see Feinglass, Arthur.
Flores, Brenda, jt. auth. see Fremont, Victoria.
Flores, Carolyn Dee. Canta, Rana, Canta. Rosales-Yeomans, Natalia, tr. from SPA. (p. 262)
Flores, Carolyn Dee, illus. see Caravantes, Peggy.
Flores, Carolyn Dee, illus. see Saldana, Rene.
Flores, Catty, illus. see Hugo, Victor.
Flores, Cory. Bugs on Parade: A Counting Book. (p. 237)
Flores, Debra, et al. Reading Comprehension 1-3: Activities for Understanding. Jennett, Pamela, ed. (p. 1445)
Flores, Eileen. To All a Good Knight. (p. 1758)
Flores, Enrique. Forajidos: Historia y Poesia en Siete Corridos Mexicanos. Sada, Margarita, illus. (p. 616)
Flores, Enrique, illus. see de Mariscal, Blanca Lopez.
Flores, Heyliana, illus. see Chimal, Monica Genis.
Flores, Joe, illus. see Dankberg, Tracy & Graham, Leland.
Flores, Joe, illus. see Ledbetter, Darril & Graham, Leland.
Flores, Joe, illus. see Moore, Jennifer, et al.
Flores, Joe, illus. see Moore, Jennifer.
Flores, Justin, illus. see Schwinn, Ruth E.
Flores, Kim. Gamma Glamma. (p. 655)
Flores, Lupita, illus. see Manzur, Vivian Mansour & Mansour, Vivian.
Flores, Martha, illus. see Foreman, Michael.
Flores, Mina. Growth of the American City: Immigrants & Migrants Travel for Work. (p. 727)
Flores, Valeria. ¿Como Se Metieron Ahi?/How'd They Get in There? (p. 351)
Flores-Galbis, Enrique. 90 Miles to Havana. (p. 1998)
Flores-Hanson, Lourdes, ed. see Camarena, Cathy & Ruff, Gloria B.
Flores-Scott, Patrick. Jumped In. (p. 934)
Florez, Anastacio. Keeper. (p. 947)
Florian, Douglas. Autumnblings. Florian, Douglas, illus. (p. 118)
—Comets, Stars, the Moon, & Mars: Space Poems & Paintings. (p. 348)
—Dinothesaurus: Prehistoric Poems & Paintings. Florian, Douglas, illus. (p. 445)
—How to Draw a Dragon. Florian, Douglas, illus. (p. 816)
—Laugh-Eteria. Florian, Douglas, illus. (p. 980)
—Lizards, Frogs, & Polliwogs. (p. 1043)
—Mammalabilia. (p. 1085)
—Pig Is Big on Books. (p. 1357)
—Pig Is Big on Books. Florian, Douglas, illus. (p. 1357)
—Poem Depot: Aisles of Smiles. (p. 1375)
—Poem Runs: Baseball Poems & Paintings. Jones, Noah, illus. (p. 1376)
—Poetrees. Florian, Douglas, illus. (p. 1376)
—See for Your Self. Florian, Douglas & Taplinger, Lee, photos by. (p. 1546)
—Shiver Me Timbers! Pirate Poems & Paintings. Neubecker, Robert, illus. (p. 1567)
—UnBEElievables: Honeybee Poems & Paintings. Florian, Douglas, illus. (p. 1811)
Florian, Douglas, jt. auth. see Lewis, J. Patrick.
Florian, Melanie. Day with Mommy. Florian, Melanie, illus. (p. 415)
Florian, Mélanie, illus. see Giulieri, Anne.
Florian, Mélanie, illus. see Martin, Molly.
Florian, Melanie, illus. see Rennert, Laura Joy.
Florian, Mlanie, illus. see Spinelli, Eileen.
Florian S, Victor, tr. see Descartes, Rene.
Florida-James, Mark. Berlin Wolf. (p. 167)
Florido, Lorraine. Hugo the Punk. Shami, Susan, ed. (p. 825)
Florie, Christine. Lara Ladybug. Dalby, Danny Brooks, illus. (p. 975)
Florie, Christine & Dalby, Danny Brooks. Mariquita Lara. Dalby, Danny Brooks, illus. (p. 1094)
Florman, Ben, ed. see Cisneros, Sandra & SparkNotes Staff.
Florman, Ben, ed. see Hesse, Hermann & SparkNotes Staff.
Florman, Ben, ed. see Wilde, Oscar & SparkNotes Staff.
Flory, Alan. God Made Me! (p. 689)
Flory, Jane. Too Little Fire Engine. Flory, Jane, illus. (p. 1766)
Flory, Neil. Short Giraffe. (p. 1569)
Florzak, Douglas, jt. auth. see Morris, Paris.
Flotte, Eddie, illus. see Coburn, Jewell Reinhart.
Flotz, Katherine Haeger. Pebble in My Shoe: A Memoir. (p. 1333)
Flounders, Anne. Cars. (p. 271)
—Corps of Discovery. Leon, Karen, illus. (p. 368)
—Friends in the Wild. (p. 638)
—Getting from Here to There. (p. 669)
—Growing Good Food. (p. 726)
—Healthy Trees, Healthy Planet. (p. 759)
—Power for the Planet. (p. 1389)
—Reducing Waste. (p. 1456)
Flounders, Anne, ed. see Butler, Dori Hillestad.
Flournoy, L. Diana, illus. see Love, Mary A.
Flower, Amanda. Andi under Pressure (p. 72)
—Andi under Pressure: An Andi Boggs Novel. (p. 72)
Flower, Graham Jessie. Grace Harlowe's Junior Year at High School: Or Fast Friends in the Sororities. (p. 704)
—Grace Harlowe's Overland Riders on the Great American Desert. (p. 704)
—Grace Harlowe's Return to Overton Campus. (p. 704)
—Grace Harlowe's Second Year at Overton College. (p. 704)
—Grace Harlowe's Senior Year at High School. (p. 704)
—Grace Harlowe's Sophomore Year at High School: The Record of the Girl Chums in Work & Athletics. (p. 704)
Flower, Jessie Graham. Grace Harlowe's Return to Overton Campus. (p. 704)
—Grace Harlowe's Second Year at Overton Campus. (p. 704)
—Grace Harlowe's Sophomore Year at High School. (p. 704)
—Grace Harlowe's Third Year at Overton College. (p. 704)
Flower, John, tr. see Cinema, Cahiers du & Saada, Nicholas, eds.
Flower, John, tr. see Cinema, Cahiers du.
Flower, Miri. Paint Book: Loads of Things You Can Make or Do with Paint. (p. 1318)
—Pencil Book: Loads of Things You Can Make or Do with a Pencil. (p. 1336)
Flowerpot Press, ed. see Bridge, George.
Flowerpot Press, ed. see Everitt, Anne.
Flowerpot Press, ed. see Fitzpatrick, Joe.
Flowerpot Press, ed. see Gardiner, Lisa.
Flowerpot Press, ed. see Gardner, Lisa.
Flowerpot Press, ed. see Kennelly, Sean & Carpenter, Dan.
Flowerpot Press, ed. see Kennelly, Sean.
Flowerpot Press, ed. see Lafond, Pascale.
Flowerpot Press, ed. see Mathison, Anne.
Flowerpot Press, ed. see Nickel, Scott.
Flowerpot Press, contrib. by. Sockheadz: Party. (p. 1605)
—Sockheadz: Picnic. (p. 1605)
—Sockheadz: Shapes. (p. 1605)
—Sockheadz: Counting. (p. 1605)
—Sockheadz: First Words. (p. 1605)
—Sockheadz: Hide & Seek. (p. 1605)
—Sockheadz: 5 Little Sockheadz. (p. 1605)
Flowerpot Press, creator. Animals Coloring Book. (p. 82)
—Dinosaurs Coloring Book. (p. 444)
—Ghosts & Goblins Coloring Book. (p. 672)
—Monsters Coloring Book. (p. 1169)
—Princesses Coloring Book. (p. 1406)
—Trick-Or-Treat Coloring Book. (p. 1786)
—Wacky Witch Coloring Book. (p. 1852)
Flowerpot Press, ed. Child's Book of Prayers: Good Night, Dear God. (p. 304)
Flowers, Arthur. I See the Promised Land: A Life of Martin Luther King, Jr. Chitrakar, Manu, illus. (p. 845)
Flowers, Audrey X. Rhymes of the Times II. (p. 1468)
Flowers, Elizabeth. Butterfly George. (p. 247)
Flowers, Fran. Rosita: The Journey Home. (p. 1490)
Flowers, Halim A. Buried Alive: Dead Men Do Talk! (p. 243)
Flowers, Natasha. Sammy the Snail. (p. 1508)
Flowers, Pam. Big-Enough Anna. Farnsworth, Bill, tr. (p. 181)
—Big-Enough Anna. Farnsworth, Bill, illus. (p. 181)
—Douggie: The Playful Pup Who Became a Sled Dog Hero. Van Zyle, Jon, illus. (p. 473)
—Douggie: The Playful Pup Who Became a Sled Dog Hero. Zyle, Jon Van, illus. (p. 473)
—Ordinary Dogs, Extraordinary Friendships: Stories of Loyalty, Courage, & Compassion. (p. 1302)
—Ordinary Dogs, Extraordinary Friendships: Stories of Loyalty, Courage, & Compassion. Baskin, Jason, illus. (p. 1302)
Flowers, Pam & Farnsworth, Bill. Ellie's Long Walk: The True Story of Two Friends on the Appalachian Trail. (p. 514)
Flowers, Tony, illus. see Falk, Nick.
Flowers, Tony, jt. auth. see Falk, Nick.
Floyd, Amy. Little Perspective: Gardening with Grandma & Grandpa. (p. 1033)
Floyd, Belinda D. Going to America. (p. 693)
Floyd, Brandi. Alex's Choice. (p. 37)
Floyd, Claire, illus. see Wines, Michael P.
Floyd, Donyell. Curious Child. (p. 392)
Floyd, Gina. Can Daddy Stay Home & Play? Scott, Judy, illus. (p. 258)
Floyd, Jackie. American Endurance Rides: The Ultimate Guide. (p. 60)
Floyd, Jamie. Spring Flower. (p. 1635)
Floyd, John, Jr., illus. see Collins, Elaine Banks.
Floyd, John, Jr., illus. see Heath, Beverly C.
Floyd, John, Jr., illus. see Lewis, Bisa.
Floyd, John, Jr., illus. see Mims, Melanie.
Floyd, Kara. Olivia West vs. Middle School: Round One. (p. 1287)
Floyd, Lucretia X., tr. see Alvarez Quintero, Serafin & Alvarez Quintero, Joaquin.
Floyd, Lucy. Conejo y Tortuga van a la Escuela. Ada, Alma Flora & Campoy, F. Isabel, trs. (p. 356)
—Place for Nicholas. McPhail, David, illus. (p. 1365)
—Rabbit & Turtle Go to School. (p. 1429)
—Rabbit & Turtle Go to School. Denise, Christopher, illus. (p. 1429)
Floyd, Thomas L. & Buchla, David M. Science of Electronics - Digital. (p. 1527)
Fluck, Jonathan. T-Bot & Peabody Explore the Zoo. (p. 1693)
Fluckiger, Jay D. & Fluckiger, W. Lynn, creators. How to Escape the Bondage of Debt: A Guide to Personal Fiscal Responsibility. (p. 819)
Fluckiger, Kory. Mylands. (p. 1222)
Fluckiger, W. Lynn, jt. creator see Fluckiger, Jay D.
Fluet, Connie. Day in the Life of a Nurse (p. 413)
Flugge, Klaus. Letters to Klaus. (p. 1002)
Fluharty, Jeff & McAndrew, Kelly. I Can't Talk Now, I'm Busy Writing Nothing. (p. 837)
Fluharty, Kristi & Fluharty, T. Lively. Fool Moon Rising. Fluharty, Kristi & Fluharty, T. Lively, illus. (p. 614)
Fluharty, Linda Cunningham. Civil War - West Virginia: Union Lives Lost. (p. 325)
Fluharty, T. Lively, illus. see Sproul, R. C.
Fluharty, T. Lively, jt. auth. see Fluharty, Kristi.
Flusfeder, David. John the Pupil. (p. 923)
Flutsztejn-Gruda, Ilona. When Grownups Play at War: A Child's Memoir Cummins, Sarah, tr. from FRE. (p. 1902)
Fluttert, Pam. Until Today (p. 1823)
Flying Eagle & Whispering Wind. Atlantis Motherland. Nelson, Emist, illus. (p. 112)
Flying Frog Pub, creator. ABC Fun with Elmo & Friends. (p. 3)
—Big & Small Fun with Elmo & Friends. (p. 177)
—Color Fun with Elmo & Friends. (p. 342)
—Counting Fun with Elmo & Friends. (p. 371)
—Hey Diddle Diddle. (p. 774)
—Itsy Bitsy Spider. (p. 900)
—Mary Had a Little Lamb. (p. 1100)
—Rock-A-Bye, Baby. (p. 1481)
—This Little Piggy. (p. 1737)
—Twinkle, Twinkle, Little Star. (p. 1802)
Flying Frog Publishing, ed. Farm Animals. (p. 573)
—Gigantic Paper Planes. (p. 676)
—Gigantic Sky Cruising Paper Planes. (p. 676)
—Jungle Animals. (p. 935)
—Ocean Animals. (p. 1276)
—Safari Animals. (p. 1501)
Flynn, Andy. New York State's Mountain Heritage: Adirondack Attic 2. (p. 1248)
—New York State's Mountain Heritage: Adirondack Attic 1. Vol. 1 (p. 1248)
Flynn, Brendan. Andrew Mccutchen: National League MVP. (p. 72)
—Kevin Durant: NBA Mvp. (p. 950)
—Miguel Cabrera: MVP & Triple Crown Winner. (p. 1141)
—Seattle Seahawks: Super Bowl Champions. (p. 1539)
Flynn, C. T. System of Universes: Ancient Harmony & Modern Science. (p. 1693)
Flynn, Cam & Benchmark Education Co., LLC Staff. Mark Sees the Stars. (p. 1095)
—Paul Takes a Walk. (p. 1330)
Flynn, Caren. Exceptional Elvis. (p. 547)
Flynn, Claire E. Running with the Bulls. (p. 1497)
—Trip to the Sun. (p. 1787)
—Water World: Earth's Water Cycle. (p. 1863)
—Why Plants Need Light. (p. 1925)
Flynn, Dale Bachm. Very Special Athlete. Soltero, Emilio, illus. (p. 1838)
Flynn, Dave. Nick & the Old Man of the Mountain. (p. 1251)
Flynn, Ian. Mega Man 2: Time Keeps Slipping. (p. 1124)
—Mega Man 3: Return of Dr. Wily. Bates, Ben, illus. (p. 1124)
—Mega Man 4: Spiritus Ex Machina. (p. 1124)
—Mega Man 5: Rock of Ages. Norton, Mike, illus. (p. 1124)
Flynn, Ian & Sonic Scribes Staff. Best of Sonic the Hedgehog. (p. 170)
—Complete Sonic the Hedgehog Comic Encyclopedia. (p. 353)
—Darkest Storm. (p. 408)
—Knuckles the Echidna Archives Spaziante, Patrick Spaz, illus. (p. 965)
—Knuckles - The Echidna Archives (p. 965)
—Sonic Genesis. (p. 1612)
—Sonic Genesis. Spaziante, Patrick, illus. (p. 1612)
—Sonic Select (p. 1612)
—Sonic Select Spaziante, Patrick Spaz, illus. (p. 1612)
—Sonic the Hedgehog Archives. Spaziante, Patrick Spaz, illus. (p. 1612)
—Sonic the Hedgehog Archives 17. (p. 1612)
—Sonic the Hedgehog Archives 18. Spaziante, Patrick, illus. (p. 1612)
—Sonic the Hedgehog: Legacy Vol. 2. (p. 1612)
—Sonic Universe 2: 30 Years Later. (p. 1612)
—Sonic Universe 3: Knuckles Returns. (p. 1612)
Flynn, Ian & Spaziante, Patrick. Let the Games Begin. (p. 994)
Flynn, Ian, et al. Shadow Saga. (p. 1558)
Flynn, James. From Egg to Lizard. (p. 642)
—Water. (p. 1862)
Flynn, James J. Air. (p. 31)
Flynn, Jean. Annie Oakley: Sharpshooter & Entertainer. (p. 87)
—Henry B. Gonzalez: Rebel with a Cause. (p. 767)
—Texas Women Who Dared to Be First. (p. 1724)
Flynn, Jim. Tampa Bay Buccaneers. (p. 1704)
Flynn, John L. Jovian Dilemma. (p. 929)
Flynn, Lesley, et al. Children's Phonology Sourcebook. Stewart, Carolyn, illus. (p. 304)
Flynn, Lisa. Yoga for Children: 200+ Yoga Poses, Breathing Exercises, & Meditations for Healthier, Happier, More Resilient Children. (p. 1972)
Flynn, M. H. Shadow City Ghost Hunters: The Mystery of Mapleshade Manor. Vol. 1 (p. 1557)
Flynn, Matthew J. China Contested: Western Powers in East Asia. (p. 306)
Flynn, Michael. Mutasia: The Wacky World of Figley Finch the Endless Caverns. (p. 1194)
Flynn, Michael, jt. auth. see Allyn, Daisy.
Flynn, Mike. Infinity Explained (p. 873)
—Outer Space Explained (p. 1312)
—Science of Survival: The Ultimate Survival Guide. (p. 1527)
Flynn, Nancy. Jeaneology: Crafty Ways to Reinvent Your Old Blues. Macklin, Karen, ed. (p. 911)
Flynn, Noa. Inhalants & Solvents: Sniffing Disaster. (p. 874)
—Who. (p. 1914)
—Youth with Eating Disorders: When Food Is an Enemy. (p. 1982)
Flynn, Noel, illus. see Connolly, Ed.
Flynn, Pat. Alex Jackson: Closing Out. (p. 36)
—Alex Jackson: Dropping In. (p. 36)
—To the Light. Stewart, Chantal, illus. (p. 1759)
Flynn, Riley. American Indian Homes. (p. 62)
—Bessie Coleman (p. 168)
—Booker T. Washington (p. 212)
—Martin Luther King Jr (p. 1097)
—Plank Houses. (p. 1368)
—Wickiups. (p. 1927)
Flynn, Riley, jt. auth. see Collins, Luke.
Flynn, S. E. That Night. (p. 1726)
Flynn, Samantha, illus. see Seymour, Mary Sue.
Flynn, Tom, jt. auth. see Hitchcock, S. C.
Flynn, Vinny, jt. ed. see Michalenko, Seraphim.
Flynn, Warren. Different Voices. (p. 438)
—Return Ticket. (p. 1465)
Flynn, Wes. Horned Toads Are Not Toads! (p. 798)
Flynn, Wesley, jt. auth. see Mills, Nathan.
Flyte, Tabitha. Coming Round the Mountain. (p. 348)
FMS Students. Poetry by 6th Grade Students of FMS. (p. 1376)
Foa, Edna B. Effective Treatments for PTSD: Practice Guidelines from the International Society for Traumatic Stress Studies. Foa, Edna B. et al, eds. (p. 505)
Foa, Emma. Edward Hopper. (p. 505)
Foa, Eugenie. Boy Life of Napoleon: Afterwards Emperor of the French. (p. 218)
—Boy Life of Napoleon Afterwards Emperor of the French. (p. 218)
Foard, Judith P. Senior Year. (p. 1550)
Foard, Sheila Wood. Diego Rivera. (p. 437)
Foccroulle, Luc. Bertha & the Frog Choir. Masson, Annick, illus. (p. 168)
Foce, Natalia C., tr. see Mackenzie, Carine.
Foce, Natalia, tr. from ENG. Daniel, el Principe que Oraba Apps, Fred, illus. (p. 405)
—Grandes Verdades para Niños Pequeños. (p. 707)
—Historia de Pablo — Viajes de Aventura Apps, Fred, illus. (p. 782)
—Jesus el Milagroso. Anderson, Jeff, illus. (p. 915)
—Jesus Maestro. Anderson, Jeff, illus. (p. 916)
—Jesus Narrador. Anderson, Jeff, illus. (p. 916)
—Jesus Niño. Anderson, Jeff, illus. (p. 916)
—Jesus Salvador. Anderson, Jeff, illus. (p. 916)
—Jesus Sanador. Anderson, Jeff, illus. (p. 916)
—Nacimiento de Jesús: El Niño Prometido Apps, Fred, illus. (p. 1227)
—Plan de Rescate: La Historia de Noe Apps, Fred, illus. (p. 1366)
—Resurrección: Jesús Está Vivo Apps, Fred, illus. (p. 1464)
—Samuel, el Niño que Escuchaba. Apps, Fred, illus. (p. 1509)
—Saúl — el Milagro en el Camino Apps, Fred, illus. (p. 1516)
Fochesato, Giorgio, illus. see Brennan, Sarah Rees.
Fochtman, Omra Jo, illus. see Masterson, Carla Jo.
Födl, Lee Edward. Kendra Kandlestar & the Box of Whispers. (p. 948)
Fodi, Lee Edward. Kendra Kandlestar & the Box of Whispers. Fodi, Lee Edward, illus. (p. 948)
—Kendra Kandlestar & the Crack in Kazah. (p. 948)
—Kendra Kandlestar & the Crack in Kazah. Fodi, Lee Edward, illus. (p. 948)
Födi, Lee Edward. Kendra Kandlestar & the Door to Unger. (p. 948)
Fodi, Lee Edward. Kendra Kandlestar & the Search for Arazeen. (p. 948)
—Kendra Kandlestar & the Shard from Greeve. (p. 948)
—Kendra Kandlestar & the Shard from Greeve. Fodi, Lee Edward, illus. (p. 948)
Födi, Lee Edward, illus. see Hicks, Kyra E.
Fodi, Lee Edward, illus. see Tara, Stephanie L.
Fodi, Lee Edward, illus. see Tara, Stephanie Lisa.
Fodi, Lee Edward, illus. see Tara, Stephanie.
Foehner, Ashley & Irving, Washington. Washington Irving's Rip Van Winkle. Locker, Thomas, illus. (p. 1860)
Foehner, Ashley P., jt. auth. see Locker, Thomas.
Foekel, Alessandra, jt. auth. see Funke, Julie Ann.
Foelker, Rita. Erase Una Vez Galileo Galilei. Abs, Renata, illus. (p. 533)
Foerster, Leland. Californios: Photographs & Stories about the Descendents of the Mission Era in Baja California, Mexico (p. 253)
Fog City Press Staff, contrib. by. Elephants. (p. 511)
—Helicopters. (p. 763)
Fogarty, Alexandria, jt. illus. see Little Airplane Productions.
Fogarty, Laura. I Can Do Anything! (p. 835)
Fogarty, Mignon. Grammar Girl Presents the Ultimate Writing Guide for Students. Haya, Erwin, illus. (p. 706)
Fogarty, Paula. Slave of the Lamp. (p. 1588)
Fogden, Katherine, photos by see Simermeyer, Genevieve.
Fogel, Seymour, illus. see Lloyd, Hugh.

F

Fogelberg, Ellen, et al. Integrating Literacy & Math: Strategies for K-6 Teachers. (p. 879)
Fogelin, Adrian. Anna Casey's Place in the World. (p. 85)
—Big Nothing. (p. 183)
—My Brother's Hero (p. 1199)
—Real Question (p. 1448)
—Sister Spider Knows All (p. 1581)
—Some Kind of Magic (p. 1609)
—Sorta Sisters (p. 1614)
—Sorta Sisters Fogelin, Adrian, illus. (p. 1614)
—Summer on the Moon (p. 1674)
Föger, Regina. Butterfly Letter: A Tale about Life after Life. (p. 248)
Fogerty, Ramona. Come to Galapagos at Sea to See. Hayden, Seitu, illus. (p. 347)
—Compensating & Combining Sensations to Read: Teaching the Learning Disabled Child. (p. 352)
—Froggie Sang Tenor. Nurullah, Seitu, illus. (p. 640)
—Prince, Labino, & Chrecas from State Parkway. (p. 1401)
—Stories That Increase Reading Fluency: Improving Word Recognition & Comprehension. (p. 1655)
Fogg, K. L. Diamondback Cave: A Novel. (p. 434)
—Serpent Tide. (p. 1552)
—Widow's Revenge: A Novel. (p. 1927)
Fogg, Paul. He Leads Me. (p. 756)
—I Know That God Loves Me. (p. 840)
—Jesus Said. (p. 916)
Fogg, Scott. Power Skits for Youth & Young Adults: 25 Faith-Awakening, Disciple-Making Drama Presentations. (p. 1390)
Foggo, Cheryl. Dear Baobab Leng, Qin & Second Story Press Staff, illus. (p. 418)
—I Have Been in Danger Hotchkiss, Conrad & Graham, Heather, illus. (p. 839)
Fogle, Janice. Lucky Ones. (p. 1063)
Fogle, Llynda & González, Althea. Friendship Place. (p. 639)
Fogle, Llynda, et al. Pond Full of Feelings. Bicking, Judy, illus. (p. 1382)
Fogle, Robin. Baby Moses Coloring Book. (p. 127)
—Bible Story Hidden Pictures: Coloring & Activity Book. Johnson, Paul, illus. (p. 176)
—Bible Story Hidden Pictures: Coloring & Activity Book. Denman, Michael, illus. (p. 176)
—Christmas Story. (p. 315)
—Daniel & the Lions' Den Coloring Book. (p. 404)
—David & Golaith Coloring Book. (p. 410)
—Easter Story Coloring Book. (p. 499)
—Itty-bitty Bible Activity Book, Love. (p. 900)
—Itty-bitty Bible Activity Book, the Legend of the Candy Cane. (p. 900)
—Legend of the Candy Cane. (p. 989)
—My Favorite Bible Stories Color-by-number. (p. 1203)
—Shepherd Boy's Christmas. (p. 1565)
Fogle, Robin, ed. see Stoddard, Jeffery.
Fogleman, Laurie. Jimmy, What Are You Eating?! (p. 918)
Foglia, Auttem. Big Picture. (p. 183)
Foglia, Pasquale. Diccionario Illustrado de Electricaa Moderna. (p. 435)
—Electricidad Basica. (p. 509)
—Experimentos DC-AC para Electricidad Basica. (p. 549)
—Experimentos Semiconductores y Circuitos Electronicos. (p. 549)
—Semiconductores y Circuitos Electronicos. (p. 1550)
—Tecnologia Digital. (p. 1712)
Foglia, Por Pasquale. Experimentos de Tecnologia Digital. (p. 549)
Fogliani, Phil. Sparky the Dragon Goes to School. (p. 1622)
—Sparky the Dragon Learns to Brush His Teeth. (p. 1622)
—Sparky the Dragon Learns to Clean Up. (p. 1622)
Fogliano, Julie. And Then It's Spring. (p. 71)
—And Then It's Spring. Stead, Erin E., illus. (p. 71)
—If You Want to See a Whale. Stead, Erin E., illus. (p. 854)
Foglio, Kaja & Foglio, Phil. Agatha Heterodyne & the Airship City: A Gaslamp Fantasy with Adventure, Romance & Mad Science. (p. 29)
—Agatha Heterodyne & the Heirs of the Storm. (p. 29)
Foglio, Phil, jt. auth. see Foglio, Kaja.
Fogorty, Renee. Fair Skin Black Fella. (p. 562)
Fogwill, Joyce Graham. Bubs the Bumblebee & Her Most Unfortunate Fortunate Adventure. (p. 234)
—Bubs the Bumblebee & the Spider's Web. (p. 234)
Fokina, N. N., et al. Lipidnyi Sostav Midii Mytilus Edulis L. Belogo Moria: Vliianie Nekotorykh Faktorov Sredy Obitaniia. (p. 1021)
Folan, Karyn Langhorne & Langan, Paul. Breaking Point. (p. 225)
Foland, Andrew Dean. Energy. (p. 528)
Foland, Janice. Tork's Hope Journey. (p. 1769)
Folch, Sergio, illus. see Gels, Patricia.
Foldvary-Anderson, Carol. 3-D Coloring Book—Hearts. (p. 1991)
—Heart to Heart Stained Glass Coloring Book. (p. 760)
—Hearts & Roses Stained Glass Coloring Book. (p. 760)
—Words of Love Stained Glass Coloring Book. (p. 1951)
Foley, Alyssa Christine. Secret at Half Past Noon: A Christmas Story. (p. 1540)
Foley, Betsy, ed. Green Bay Area in History & Legend. Elder, Harold, illus. (p. 721)
Foley, Colin. Who Was Louis Armstrong? (p. 1918)
Foley, E., et al. Cultures of the World: Group 10 (p. 391)
Foley, Elizabeth. Remarkable. (p. 1458)
Foley, Elizabeth, jt. auth. see Foley, Lizzie K.
Foley, Erin & Cooke, Barbara. Costa Rica. (p. 368)
Foley, Erin & Hapipi, Rafiz. Salvador. (p. 1506)
Foley, Erin & Jermyn, Leslie. Dominican Republic. (p. 465)
—Ecuador. (p. 503)
Foley, Greg. Don't Worry Bear. Foley, Greg, illus. (p. 469)
—Good Luck Bear. (p. 698)
—I Miss You Mouse. (p. 844)
—Purple Little Bird. Foley, Greg, illus. (p. 1419)
—Thank You Bear. Foley, Greg, illus. (p. 1725)
—Thank You Bear Board Book. Foley, Greg, illus. (p. 1725)
—Willoughby & the Lion. Foley, Greg, illus. (p. 1934)
—Willoughby & the Moon. Foley, Greg, illus. (p. 1934)
Foley, James. Danny & the Blue Cloud: Coping with Childhood Depression. Ng-Benitez, Shirley, illus. (p. 405)
Foley, Jeanne. Shooting Two: A Story of Basketball & Friendship. (p. 1568)
Foley, Jonathan. My Very First Adventure. (p. 1221)
Foley, Lizzie K. & Foley, Elizabeth. Remarkable. (p. 1458)
Foley, Marlena. Family Game Night: Poker for Kids! (p. 568)
Foley, Mark. Trivial Matters for Children. (p. 1788)
Foley, Monica. Four of Us. (p. 625)
Foley, Niki, illus. see Random House Staff.
Foley, Patrick. Morning Rituals. (p. 1175)
Foley, Ronan, jt. auth. see Bowden, Rob.
Foley, Ryan. Stolen Hearts: The Love of Eros & Psyche. (p. 1652)
—Stolen Hearts: The Love of Eros & Psyche. Banerjee, Sankha, illus. (p. 1652)
—Treasured Thief. Nagar, Sachin, illus. (p. 1782)
Foley, Sue. Tyrone: A Turtle Tale. Kobak, Carrie, illus. (p. 1805)
Foley, Tim. American Presidents Sticker Book. (p. 62)
—Literary Greats Paper Dolls. (p. 1022)
Foley, Tim, illus. see Anderson, Kirsten.
Foley, Tim, illus. see Buckley, James, Jr.
Foley, Tim, illus. see Medina, Nico.
Foley, Tim, illus. see Pascal, Janet B.
Foley, Tim, illus. see Pascal, Janet.
Foley, Tim, illus. see St. George, Judith.
Foley, Tim, illus. see Yomtov, Nel.
Foley, Tim, illus. see Yomtov, Nelson.
Foley, Virginia C. I Think I Hear Sleigh Bells. (p. 846)
Folgueira, Rodrigo. Bob the Dog. Bernatene, Poly, illus. (p. 205)
—Ribbit! Bernatene, Poly, illus. (p. 1469)
Foli, Gianluca, illus. see Cali, Davide.
Folk, Bertha. Counting with Miss Purse. (p. 372)
Folk Tale Staff. Gingerbread Man. Rodriguez, Beatrix, illus. (p. 677)
Folkard, Charles, illus. see Murray, M. A., tr.
Folkerts, Jason, illus. see Meierhenry, Mark V. & Volk, David.
Folklore. Jack & the Robbers. (p. 902)
—Two Strangers. (p. 1804)
—Two Strangers Director's Guide. (p. 1804)
Follen, Eliza Lee. Pedler of Dust Sticks. (p. 1334)
—Talkative Wig. (p. 1703)
—What the Animals Do & Say. (p. 1893)
Follestad, Catherine. I Dream That I May One Day Be. (p. 838)
—I Think That I Would Like to Be... (p. 846)
—Itty Bitty Kitty. (p. 900)
—Itty Bitty Kitty & the Mystery at Reflection Pond. (p. 900)
Follet, René. Fascinating Madame Tussaud. Duchateau, illus. (p. 575)
Follett, C. B. & Terris, Susan, eds. RUNES, A Review of Poetry: Storm. (p. 1497)
—Runes, a Review of Poetry: Memory. (p. 1497)
—RUNES, A Review of Poetry: Signals. (p. 1497)
Follett, Dave, jt. auth. see Graf, Mike.
Follett, David. Genetis. (p. 661)
Follett, Katherine. Energy Sources for the 21st Century. (p. 528)
—One Giant Leap. (p. 1295)
Follett, Katherine, jt. auth. see Blackwood, Gary L.
Follett, Katherine, jt. auth. see Gottfried, Ted.
Follett, Ross C. Beebear 2. Sievers, Lee, illus. (p. 157)
Folliard, Kevin. Christmas Terror Tales: Stories to Enjoy from October Through December. Molloy, J., illus. (p. 316)
Folloni, Larry. My Way: The Memoirs of Coach Larry Folloni. Michael, Folloni, ed. (p. 1221)
Folmer, A. P. Fabulous Rainy Day Fun Book. (p. 560)
Folmsbee, Judi. Bubba, the Busy Beaver. Benton, Marilyn, illus. (p. 233)
Folmsbee, Patricia, illus. see Custureri, Mary.
Folmsbee, Paul. Flight of the Feathered Serpent. (p. 604)
Folse, Keith S. & Farina, Marcella. College Vocabulary (p. 340)
Folsom, Franklin. Red Power on the Rio Grande. (p. 1454)
Folsom, Michael & Elting, Mary. Q Is for Duck: An Alphabet Guessing Game. Kent, Jack, illus. (p. 1422)
Folsom, Ralph, jt. auth. see Haughwout, Pixie.
Folts, Cathy, jt. auth. see Conner, John.
Foltyn, Sue. Mayzeemioletu. (p. 1113)
Foltz, Joanna "Gwen". Owl Tree. (p. 1315)
Foltz, Linda Lee. Kids Helping Kids Break the Silence of Sexual Abuse. (p. 954)
Foltz, Sharon Terpstra. Jan Napjus & the Ghost. Foltz, Susan Convery, illus. (p. 907)
Foltz, Susan Convery, illus. see Foltz, Sharon Terpstra.
Folz, Alexandra. Indigo's Bracelet. (p. 872)
Fond du Lac Head Start. Story of Manoomin. (p. 1659)
Fonda, Jane. Being a Teen: Everything Teen Girls & Boys Should Know about Relationships, Sex, Love, Health, Identity & More. (p. 160)
Fonder, Toni. Science of Sound. (p. 1527)
Fondo de Cultura Económica (Mexico) Staff, creator. Despertar del Jaguar (p. 430)
Fone, Ann. Elf-help for Giving the Gift of You. (p. 512)
Fonner, Deborah K. Extra Ordinary Day. VonBokel, Jan, illus. (p. 555)
Fonseca, Chris J. Meet Bear. (p. 1120)
Fonseca, Christine. 101 Success Secrets for Gifted Kids: The Ultimate Handbook. (p. 2000)
Fonseca, Mireya (Adaptación), adapted by. NEREO -el anciano del Mar. (p. 1241)
Fonseca, Pedro Luis. Jasmine & Pupulo in the Forest (asi) (p. 910)
Fonseca-Hughes, Sarah, illus. see Debowski, Sharon.
Fontaine, Catherine Silliman. Have a Not for Christmas ... & Always. (p. 754)
Fontaine, Elizabeth. Eagle Peak. (p. 492)
Fontaine, La, jt. auth. see Valeri, Maria Eulàlia.
Fontaine, Nadine. More Than Anything in the World. (p. 1175)
Fontaine, Renee. Boy in the Hoodie. Margolis, Al, illus. (p. 218)
Fontana, Kathryn Dalla. Happy Birthday, Ruby. (p. 745)
Fontana, Lynn & Hoge, Patricia, eds. Education Station Reading Anthology, Volume One: A-B (p. 505)
—Education Station Reading Anthology, Volume Two. (p. 505)
—Education Station Reading, Volume One: C-E: Student Resource Book. (p. 505)
Fontana, Ugo, illus. see Bechstein, Ludwig.
Fontane. Effi Briest. (p. 505)
Fontanel, Beatrice. Tristan e Iseo. (p. 1787)
Fontanez, Edwin. En esta hermosa Isla. Fontanez, Edwin, illus. (p. 522)
—Hadas, Sirenas y Sapos: Un ramito de poemas Encantados. Fontanez, Edwin, illus. (p. 735)
—On This Beautiful Island. Fontanez, Edwin, illus. (p. 1292)
Fontany, Elena. Other Worlds Than This. (p. 1306)
Fonte, Mary Roessler & Hoppe, Jessica. Big Green Gorilla. Verhoosky, Michele, illus. (p. 181)
Fontenot Landry, Julie, jt. auth. see Fontenot, Mary Alice.
Fontenot, Martha Leonard. Grandma Liza's Rainbow Cake. (p. 708)
Fontenot, Mary Alice. Clovis Crawfish & Bertile's Bon Voyage Blazek, Scott R., illus. (p. 335)
—Clovis Crawfish & Echo Gecko Buckner, Julie Dupre, illus. (p. 335)
—Clovis Crawfish & His Friends Graves, Keith, illus. (p. 335)
—Clovis Crawfish & Michelle Mantis Blazek, Scott R., illus. (p. 335)
—Clovis Crawfish & Petit Papillon Graves, Keith, illus. (p. 335)
—Clovis Crawfish & Silvie Sulphur Buckner, Julie Dupre, illus. (p. 335)
Fontenot, Mary Alice & Fontenot Landry, Julie. Clovis Crawfish & the Twin Sister Butler, Julie Dupre & Buckner, Julie Dupre, illus. (p. 335)
Fontes, Justine. Barbie - A Fairy Secret. Mattel Barbie Staff, illus. (p. 138)
—Barbie in the Pink Shoes. (p. 138)
—Barbie the Princess & the Popstar. Mattel & Ulkutay Design Group Staff, illus. (p. 138)
—Barbie the Princess & the Popstar. Mattel Barbie Staff & Ulkutay Design Group, illus. (p. 138)
—Benito Runs. (p. 164)
—Black Meets White. Waring, Geoff, illus. (p. 196)
—Cheerios Action Park Adventure. (p. 296)
—Cheerios Count to 100. Croll, Carolyn, illus. (p. 296)
—Clean up, Grumpy Bunny. (p. 330)
—Crisis in Crittertown. (p. 383)
—Daniel el Descortes: Rude Ralph. Jordan, Charles, illus. (p. 405)
—Deadly Drive. (p. 417)
—Dia Que Jordan Se Enfermo: Jordan's Silly Sick Day. Lee, Jared, illus. (p. 433)
—Henry's Turn. Hefferan, Rob, illus. (p. 769)
—Jordan's Silly Sick Day. Lee, Jared, tr. (p. 925)
—Please Say Please, Grumpy Bunny! McQueen, Lucinda, illus. (p. 1373)
—Pledge of Allegiance. (p. 1373)
—Rude Ralph: A Rookie Reader. Jordan, Charles, illus. (p. 1494)
—Showdown in Crittertown. (p. 1571)
—Toy Trouble. Hefferan, Rob, illus. (p. 1774)
Fontes, Justine, jt. auth. see Fontes, Ron.
Fontes, Justine, jt. creator see Fontes, Ron.
Fontes, Justine & Fontes, Ron. Atalanta: The Race Against Destiny. Yeates, Thomas, illus. (p. 111)
—Casebook: Bigfoot. (p. 275)
—Casebook: Atlantis. (p. 275)
—Casebook: Vampires. (p. 275)
—Casebook: Werewolves. (p. 275)
—Casebook: The Bermuda Triangle. (p. 275)
—Casebook: Ghosts & Poltergeists. (p. 275)
—Casebook: The Loch Ness Monster. (p. 275)
—Casebook: UFOs and/or Alien Encounter. (p. 275)
—Delaware: The First State. (p. 424)
—Delaware, the First State. (p. 424)
—Demeter & Persephone: Spring Held Hostage. Kurth, Steve & Schulz, Barbara, illus. (p. 425)
—Demeter & Persephone: Spring Held Hostage. Schulz, Barbara & Kurth, Steve, illus. (p. 425)
—Fifth Musketeer. Meconis, Dylan, illus. (p. 584)
—Israel. (p. 893)
—Kenya - A-Z. (p. 949)
—Sunjata: Warrior King of Mali [A West African Legend]. Carruthers, Sandy, illus. (p. 1677)
—West Virginia: The Mountain State. (p. 1876)
—Wyoming: The Equality State. (p. 1966)
—Wyoming. (p. 1966)
Fontes, Justine & Jordan, Charles. Daniel el Descortés. Jordan, Charles, illus. (p. 405)
Fontes, Justine & Korman, Justine. Lion King. Golden Books Staff et al, illus. (p. 1020)
Fontes, Justine Korman & Fontes, Ron. Abraham Lincoln: Lawyer, Leader, Legend. (p. 6)
Fontes, Ron. Proteins. (p. 1412)
—Rachel Carson. (p. 1431)
Fontes, Ron, jt. auth. see Fontes, Justine Korman.
Fontes, Ron, jt. auth. see Fontes, Justine.
Fontes, Ron & Fontes, Justine. Atalanta. (p. 111)
—Captured by Pirates. (p. 265)
—Captured by Pirates. Witt, David, illus. (p. 265)
—Demeter & Persephone. (p. 425)
—Trojan Horse: The Fall of Troy - A Greek Legend. Purcell, Gordon & Schulz, Barbara, illus. (p. 1788)
—Trojan Horse. (p. 1788)
Fontes, Ron & Fontes, Justine, creators. Ron & Justine Fontes Present Tales of the Terminal Diner. (p. 1486)
Fontes, Ron & Justine. Sunjata: Warrior King of Mali. (p. 1677)
Fontes, Ron, et al. Trojan Horse: The Fall of Troy. Purcell, Gordon, illus. (p. 1788)
Fonticharo, Kristin. Getting Around Online. (p. 669)
Fontichiaro, Kristin. Blog It! (p. 200)
—Find Out Firsthand: Using Primary Sources. (p. 587)
—Speak Out! Creating Podcasts & Other Audio Recordings. (p. 1622)
—Super Smart Information Strategies: Go Straight to the Source. (p. 1681)
—Super Smart Information Strategies: Podcasting 101. (p. 1682)
—Understanding & Creating Infographics. Petelinsek, Kathleen, illus. (p. 1815)
Fontichiaro, Kristin, jt. auth. see Johnson, Emily.
Fontichiaro, Kristin, jt. auth. see Rodgers, Emily Puckett.
Fontichiaro, Kristin, jt. auth. see Roslund, Samantha.
Fontichiaro, Kristin, jt. auth. see Severance, Charles R.
Fontichiaro, Kristin, jt. auth. see Truesdell, Ann.
Fontichiaro, Kristin & Thomas, AnnMarie P. Squishy Circuits. (p. 1637)
Fontichiaro, Kristin & Truesdell, Ann. Learning & Sharing with a Wiki. Petelinsek, Kathleen, illus. (p. 985)
Fontinalis. Far Shore. (p. 572)
Fontova, Humberto. Exposing the Real Che Guevara: And the Useful Idiots Who Idolize Him. (p. 554)
Fontus, Fritz. Plus Haut Plus Loin Avec le Christ. (p. 1374)
Food and Agriculture Organization of the United Nations. Forests Challenge Badge. (p. 618)
—Soils Challenge Badge. (p. 1606)
—Youth Guide to Biodiversity. (p. 1982)
—Youth Guide to Forests. (p. 1982)
—YUNGA Water Challenge Badge. (p. 1983)
Foon, Dennis. Dirt Eaters. (p. 446)
—Freewalker. (p. 635)
—Keeper's Shadow. (p. 947)
—Kindness. (p. 957)
—Mirror Game. (p. 1149)
—Rick: The Rick Hansen Story. (p. 1470)
—Skud (p. 1586)
—War. (p. 1857)
Foor, Joan, jt. compiled by see Dalrymple, Marilyn.
Football, Virginia. How the Fox Saved the People. Wedzin, James, illus. (p. 813)
Football, Virginia & Mantla, Rosa. How the Fox Got His Crossed Legs. Siemens, Mary, tr. (p. 813)
Foote, Dan, illus. see Hayford, Jack W.
Foote, Dan, illus. see Moores, Katie.
Foote, David, illus. see Blume, Lesley M.
Foote, David, illus. see Blume, Lesley M. M.
Foote, Marilyn. Puddinhead & the Chalkboard. (p. 1414)
—Puddinhead's Daddy. (p. 1414)
—Puddinhead's Sister, Zirah. (p. 1414)
Foote, Samuel. Great Panjandrum Himself. (p. 717)
Foote, Tracy. My Potty Reward Stickers for Boys: 126 Boy Stickers & Chart to Motivate Toilet Training. (p. 1217)
—My Potty Reward Stickers for Boys: 126 Boy Potty Training Stickers & Chart to Motivate Toilet Training. (p. 1217)
—My Potty Reward Stickers for Girls: 126 Girl Stickers & Chart to Motivate Toilet Training. (p. 1217)
—My Potty Reward Stickers for Girls: 126 Girl Potty Training Stickers & Chart to Motivate Toilet Training. (p. 1217)
Foott, Jeff, photos by see León, Vicki.
Foppiano, Steve. Time Tells. (p. 1752)
Foraker, Doreen, ed. see Zimmerman, Brian.
Foran, Jill. Buddha Day. (p. 234)
—Buildings. (p. 239)
—Caring for Your Dog. (p. 269)
—Caring for Your Dog. Marshall, Diana & Nault, Jennifer, eds. (p. 269)
—Caring for Your Guinea Pig. (p. 269)
—Caring for Your Hamster. Marshall, Diana & Nault, Jennifer, eds. (p. 269)
—Caring for Your Rabbit. (p. 269)
—Caring for Your Rabbit. Marshall, Diana & Nault, Jennifer, eds. (p. 269)
—Christmas. (p. 312)
—Dinosaurs. (p. 443)
—Dog. (p. 460)
—Dr. Seuss. (p. 475)
—Guinea Pig. (p. 731)
—Hamster. (p. 739)
—Hanukkah. (p. 743)
—Hawai'i. (p. 755)
—Herbivores. (p. 769)
—Homesteading. (p. 794)
—Idaho. (p. 851)
—Independence Day. (p. 870)
—Independence Day with Code. (p. 870)
—Maine. (p. 1077)
—Mardi Gras. (p. 1092)
—Martin Luther King Jr. Day. (p. 1098)
—Martin Luther King, Jr. Day. (p. 1098)
—Mississippi. (p. 1154)
—Native-American Life. (p. 1234)
—Nebraska. (p. 1239)
—North Carolina. (p. 1264)
—Oktoberfest. (p. 1283)
—Petite école: Le Début de la Colonie. Karvonen, Tanjah, tr. from ENG. (p. 1348)
—Powwow. (p. 1391)
—Rabbit. (p. 1429)
—School House: Pioneers of Canada. (p. 1523)
—Search for the Northwest Passage. (p. 1537)
—Statues & Monuments. (p. 1645)
—Vermont. (p. 1837)
—Vie de Famille: Le Début de la Colonie. Karvonen, Tanjah, tr. from ENG. (p. 1841)
Foran, Jill & Gillespie, Katie. Guinea Pig. (p. 731)
Foran, Racquel. Developing Nations' Debt. (p. 431)
—Knights. (p. 964)
—North Korea. (p. 1265)
—Organ Transplants. (p. 1303)
—Robotics: From Automatons to the Roomba. (p. 1480)
—South Korea. (p. 1617)
Forastieri, María Inés. Juan Bobo. (p. 930)
Forbeck, Matt, jt. auth. see Dorling Kindersley Publishing Staff.
Forberg, Ati, illus. see Uchida, Yoshiko.
Forbes, A. S. Public Safety & Law Enforcement. (p. 1414)
Forbes, Anne. Dragonfire (p. 478)
—Underground City. (p. 1814)
Forbes, Ashley. Pet Preacher. Forbes, Ashley, illus. (p. 1345)
Forbes, Charlotte. Those Amazing Engineers. Pillion, Dean, illus. (p. 1740)

Forbes, Charlotte, jt. auth. see Forbes, Charlotte.
Forbes, Charlotte & Forbes, Charlotte. Those Amazing Scientists. Pillion, Dean, illus. (p. 1740)
Forbes, Chris. Tronco de Arbol Flor Ada, Alma, tr. (p. 1788)
Forbes, Claire. Ancient Peoples. (p. 70)
Forbes, Dawn Hickok. Loose Pieces Make Very Special Families. (p. 1052)
Forbes, Dillon. Careful Enough? (p. 268)
Forbes, E. & Baby Lifeline Staff. Mum Is... (p. 1190)
Forbes, Earl E. Mustang Man. (p. 1194)
Forbes, Esther. Johnny Tremain. (p. 923)
—Johnny Tremain. McCurdy, Michael, illus. (p. 923)
Forbes, Esther Hoskins. Johnny Tremain: Illustrated American Classics. (p. 923)
—Johnny Tremain: Illustrated American Classics Set (p. 923)
—Johnny Tremain. (p. 923)
Forbes, Harriet H. Creative Movement for 3-5 Year Olds: A Complete Curriculum Including 35 Lesson Plans, Dance Notations, Illustrations, Music & Poetry Suggestions Plus Detailed Prop Designs. Barr, Kristen, illus. (p. 380)
Forbes, J. L. Under the Faithful Watch of the River Hawk. Forbes, Justin, illus. (p. 1813)
Forbes, Jake T. Return to Labyrinth (p. 1465)
Forbes, Jake T., ed. see Hyung, Min-Woo.
Forbes, Jake T., ed. see Kamijyo, Akimine.
Forbes, Jake T. & Jake, T. F. Return to Labyrinth Shurei, Kouyu, illus. (p. 1465)
Forbes, Jake T., ed. Tokyopop Manga Sampler: 2002. (p. 1762)
Forbes, Jeff Donaldson. Everything You Need to Know about Sexual Identity. (p. 546)
Forbes, Justin, illus. see Forbes, J. L.
Forbes, Robert. Let's Have a Bite! A Banquet of Beastly Rhymes. Searle, Ronald, illus. (p. 998)
Forbes, Robert L. Beast Friends Forever. Searle, Ronald, illus. (p. 152)
—Beastly Feasts! A Mischievous Menagerie in Rhyme. Searle, Ronald, illus. (p. 152)
Forbes, Ross E., photos by see Forbes, Harriet H.
Forbes, Scott, jt. auth. see Kids Can Press Staff.
Forbush, Kyle. Alaska's Wild Animals Coloring Book. Forbush, Lisa, illus. (p. 34)
—Balto: The Dog Hero. Forbush, Lisa, illus. (p. 135)
—Sourdoughs' Five Children. Forbush, Lisa, illus. (p. 1616)
—Who Is Alaska's Favorite Bear? Forbush, Lisa, illus. (p. 1915)
Forbush, Kyle, jt. auth. see Forbush, Kyle.
Forbush, Kyle & Forbush, Kyle. Is for Alaska - an ABC Book. Forbush, Lisa, illus. (p. 889)
Forbush, Lisa, illus. see Forbush, Kyle & Forbush, Kyle.
Forbush, Lisa, illus. see Forbush, Kyle.
Forcada, Adiela, illus. see Olesen, Demetria Vassiliou.
Forche, Carolyn A. Colors Come from God ... Just Like Me! (p. 345)
Forchuk Skrypuch, Marsha, jt. auth. see Skrypuch, Marsha Forchuk.
Ford, A. G., illus. see Abdul-Jabbar, Kareem & Obstfeld, Raymond.
Ford, A. G., illus. see Cannon, Nick & Carey, Mariah.
Ford, A. G., illus. see Cook, Michelle.
Ford, A. G., illus. see Harris, Teresa E.
Ford, A. G., illus. see Hopkinson, Deborah.
Ford, A. G., illus. see Javaherbin, Mina.
Ford, A. G., illus. see King, Martin Luther, III.
Ford, A. G., illus. see Neri, G.
Ford, A. G., illus. see Robinson, Sharon.
Ford, A. G., illus. see Shabazz, Ilyasah.
Ford, A. G., illus. see Tutu, Desmond.
Ford, A. G., illus. see Winter, Jonah.
Ford, Adam B. Jam-Bo, Litta-Girl, & the Bullies. Huddleston, Courtney, illus. (p. 906)
—Six Sisters & Their Flying Carpets. Abbott, Kristin, illus. (p. 1582)
Ford, Alexandra Victoria. Legacy of the Magi. (p. 987)
Ford, Anne. Davy Crockett. Vosburgh, Leonard, illus. (p. 411)
Ford, Ansley Watson & Holt, Denver W. Snowy Owls: Whoo Are They? Bohman, Jennifer White, illus. (p. 1601)
Ford, Barbara. Paul Revere: American Patriot. (p. 1330)
Ford, Barbara E. Tangrams: The Magnificent Seven Piece Puzzle. (p. 1705)
Ford, Bernette. Ballet Kitty: Christmas Recital. Williams, Sam, illus. (p. 134)
—No More Biting for Billy Goat! Williams, Sam, illus. (p. 1259)
—No More Blanket for Lambkin! Williams, Sam, illus. (p. 1259)
—No More Bottles for Bunny! Williams, Sam, illus. (p. 1259)
—No More Diapers for Ducky! Williams, Sam, illus. (p. 1259)
—No More Pacifier for Piggy! Williams, Sam, illus. (p. 1259)
Ford, Bernette, jt. auth. see Ford, Bernette G.
Ford, Bernette G. First Snow. Braun, Sebastien, illus. (p. 596)
—Hurry Up! Kindert, Jennifer C., illus. (p. 830)
—Princess Puppy. Williams, Sam, illus. (p. 1405)
Ford, Bernette G. & Ford, Bernette. First Snow. Braun, Sebastien, illus. (p. 596)
Ford, Brian. Marshmallows & Bikes: Teaching Children (and Adults) Personal Finance. (p. 1096)
Ford, Brian Nelson. Marshmallows & Bikes: Teaching Children (and Adults) Personal Finance. (p. 1096)
Ford, Carin T. Abraham Lincoln: The 16th President. (p. 6)
—African-American Soldiers in the Civil War: Fighting for Freedom. (p. 27)
—American Civil War: An Overview. (p. 60)
—Battle of Gettysburg & Lincoln's Gettysburg Address. (p. 146)
—Benjamin Franklin: Inventor & Patriot. (p. 165)
—Civil War's African-American Soldiers Through Primary Sources. (p. 326)
—Clara Barton: Brave Nurse. (p. 326)
—Daring Women of the Civil War. (p. 407)
—Dr. Seuss: Best-Loved Author. (p. 475)
—Duke Ellington: I Live with Music. (p. 489)
—Emancipation Proclamation, Lincoln, & Slavery Through Primary Sources. (p. 517)
—Franklin D. Roosevelt: The 32nd President. (p. 630)
—George Eastman: The Kodak Camera Man. (p. 663)
—George Gershwin: American Musical Genius. (p. 663)
—George Washington: The First President. (p. 664)
—Henry Ford: The Car Man. (p. 768)
—Jackie Robinson: Hero of Baseball. (p. 904)
—Jackie Robinson: All I Ask Is That You Respect Me as a Human Being. (p. 904)
—John F. Kennedy: The 35th President. (p. 921)
—Laura Ingalls Wilder: Real-Life Pioneer of the Little House Books. (p. 980)
—Levi Strauss: The Man Behind Blue Jeans. (p. 1004)
—Lincoln, Slavery, & the Emancipation Proclamation. (p. 1018)
—Lincoln's Gettysburg Address & the Battle of Gettysburg Through Primary Sources. (p. 1019)
—Muhammad Ali: I Am the Greatest. (p. 1189)
—Overview of the American Civil War Through Primary Sources. (p. 1314)
—Paul Revere: Patriot. (p. 1330)
—Paul Robeson: I Want to Make Freedom Ring. (p. 1330)
—Pocahontas: American Indian Princess. (p. 1375)
—Ray Charles: I Was Born with Music Inside Me. (p. 1441)
—Robert Fulton: The Steamboat Man. (p. 1479)
—Roberto Clemente: Baseball Legend. (p. 1479)
—Sacagawea: Meet an American Legend. (p. 1500)
—Slavery & the Underground Railroad: Bound for Freedom. (p. 1588)
—Thomas Jefferson: The Third President. (p. 1739)
—Underground Railroad & Slavery Through Primary Sources. (p. 1815)
—Walt Disney: Meet the Cartoonist. (p. 1855)
—Women of the Civil War Through Primary Sources. (p. 1946)
—Wright Brothers: Heroes of Flight. (p. 1963)
Ford, Carol A. & Bowers, Elizabeth Shimer. Living with Sexually Transmitted Diseases. (p. 1042)
Ford, Carole S. Freddie the Fox & Peter the Cheetah. Edwin, Kimberly, illus. (p. 632)
—Timothy Turtle & Sammy Scallop. Edwin, Kimberly, illus. (p. 1755)
Ford, Carolyn. Paper Bag. Diez-Luckie, Cathy, illus. (p. 1322)
Ford, Carrie Elizabeth. Anonymous. (p. 87)
Ford, Christina, illus. see Lawrence, Ava.
Ford, Christine, jt. auth. see Holland, Trish.
Ford, Christopher. Epic Doodle Ford, Christopher, illus. (p. 532)
—Wrath of Zozimos Ford, Christopher, illus. (p. 1962)
Ford, Corri. Have a Little Faith. (p. 754)
—My Daddy Is Just My Daddy to Me. (p. 1201)
Ford, D. Vincent. Transformation: the Missing Piece: Changing Your Life, Your Workplace, Your Church, & Your City. (p. 1778)
Ford, David, illus. see Cole, Bob.
Ford, Emily, illus. see Haluska, David.
Ford, Ford Madox. Queen Who Flew. (p. 1425)
Ford, Gabrielle & Thomson, Sarah. Gabe & Izzy: Speaking up for America's Bullied. (p. 652)
—Gabe & Izzy: Standing up for America's Bullied. (p. 652)
Ford, George, illus. see Coles, Robert.
Ford, George, illus. see Greenfield, Eloise.
Ford, George, jt. auth. see Greenfield, Eloise.
Ford, Gilbert, illus. see Bolden, Tonya.
Ford, Gilbert, illus. see Bosch, Pseudonymous.
Ford, Gilbert, illus. see Davis, Kathryn Gibbs.
Ford, Gilbert, illus. see Springstubb, Tricia.
Ford, H. J., illus. see Lang, Andrew, ed.
Ford, H. J., illus. see Lang, Andrew.
Ford, H. J., illus. see Lang, Leonora Blanche.
Ford, H. J., jt. auth. see Lang, Andrew.
Ford, Harry & Barnham, Kay. Outer Space. (p. 1312)
Ford, Henry J., illus. see Lang, Andrew, ed.
Ford, J. One in Four. (p. 1295)
Ford, Jayme. Adventures of Glop-A-Lopikins. (p. 18)
—Adventures of Glop-A-Lopikins & the Pink Castle. (p. 18)
Ford, Jean. Allergies & Asthma. Bridgemohan, Carolyn & Forman, Sara, eds. (p. 46)
—Antidepressants & the Critics: Cure-Alls or Unnatural Poisons? (p. 89)
—Breathe Easy! A Teen's Guide to Allergies & Asthma. (p. 226)
—Coping with Moods. Bridgemohan, Carolyn & Forman, Sara, eds. (p. 365)
—Explosives & Arson Investigation. Noziglia, Carla Miller & Siegel, Jay A., eds. (p. 554)
—Forensics in American Culture. (p. 617)
—Forensics in American Culture. Noziglia, Carla Miller & Siegel, Jay A., eds. (p. 617)
—Growth & Development. Forman, Sara, ed. (p. 727)
—Health Issues Caused by Obesity. Garcia, Victor, ed. (p. 758)
—Latino Cuisine & Its Influence on American Foods: The Taste of Celebration. (p. 979)
—Right on Schedule! A Teen's Guide to Growth & Development. (p. 1472)
—Surviving the Roller Coaster: A Teen's Guide to Coping with Moods. (p. 1687)
Ford, Jean & Libal, Autumn. No Quick Fix: Fad Diets & Weight-Loss Miracles. Garcia, Victor, ed. (p. 1260)
Ford, Jean Otto. Rural Crime & Poverty: Violence, Drugs, & Other Issues. (p. 1497)
—Teens Who Make a Difference in Rural Communities: Youth Outreach Organizations & Community Action. (p. 1715)
Ford, Jerry Lee, Jr. Scratch 2. 0 Programming for Teens. (p. 1532)
—XNA 3. 1 Game Development for Teens. (p. 1967)
Ford, Jessie. My Birdie Puzzle Book. (p. 1198)
—My Bunny Puzzle Book. (p. 1199)
Ford, John C. Cipher. (p. 321)
Ford, June. Jeff Burton. (p. 911)
Ford, Juwanda G. Shop Talk. Hoston, Jim, illus. (p. 1568)
Ford, Juwanda G., jt. auth. see Scholastic, Inc. Staff.
Ford, Kate, illus. see Burton, Neil.
Ford, Kate, illus. see Hughes, Colin & Wade, Winnie.
Ford, Kate, illus. see Laurence, Jo.
Ford, Kate, illus. see Yates, Irene Dorothy.
Ford, Kate, illus. see Yates, Irene.
Ford, Kate, jt. auth. see Yates, Irene Dorothy.
Ford, Katherine. Barney & Becca: Backyard Buddies. (p. 139)
—Forgotten King. (p. 619)
Ford, Laura. Buster Brown & Tige in Misfit Heroes. (p. 245)
Ford, Linda. Daddy for Christmas. (p. 398)
Ford, Lorry. Goodnight Red: A Lesson in Courage. (p. 701)
—Goodnight Red: A Lesson in Courage. (p. 701)
Ford, Lynne E. Encyclopedia of Women & American Politics. (p. 525)
Ford, Martin. Fishing. (p. 599)
Ford, Michael. Dale Earnhardt, Jr. (p. 401)
—Legacy of Blood. (p. 987)
—You Wouldn't Want to Be a Greek Athlete! (Revised Edition) (p. 1976)
Ford, Michael & Salariya, David. You Wouldn't Want to Be a Greek Athlete! Races You'd Rather Not Run. Antram, David, illus. (p. 1976)
Ford, Michael Curtis. Birth of a Warrior. (p. 192)
Ford, Michael Thomas. Suicide Notes. (p. 1673)
—Z. (p. 1983)
Ford, Mindi. Mommy Says: A preemie Story. (p. 1162)
Ford, Nick. Jerusalem under Muslim Rule in the Eleventh Century: Christian Pilgrims under Islamic Government. (p. 914)
—Niccolo Machiavelli: Florentine Statesman, Playwright, & Poet. (p. 1250)
—Niccolò Machiavelli: Florentine Statesman, Playwright, & Poet. (p. 1250)
Ford, Nicole. Mooshi the Camel. (p. 1173)
Ford, Richard, tr. see Drew, Alejandrina.
Ford, Robert. Adventures of Hit the Road Jack. (p. 18)
Ford, Rodney. Choo Train. (p. 310)
Ford, Ron. Buzz Gets Lost. (p. 248)
—Cindy's Backyard Circus. (p. 321)
—circo de Cindy (Cindy's Backyard Circus) (p. 321)
—What Do You See? (p. 1883)
Ford, RoShawn T. Marty & the Magical Christmas Tree. (p. 1098)
Ford, Sally. Bungee down Under. Dudley, Peter, illus. (p. 242)
Ford, Sandy Lee. Gullah, the Nawleans Cat Meets Katrina. (p. 731)
Ford, Sharon Lea. Pages of Lost Time. (p. 1318)
Ford, Shelby Ann. Shelby & the Deer. (p. 1564)
Ford, Stephanie, illus. see Elliott, Alan.
Ford, Stephanie, illus. see Fleischman, Carol.
Ford, Stephanie, illus. see Vogl, Mark.
Ford, Stephanie A., illus. see Pittman, Rickey E.
Ford, Sylvia & Sigmon, Cheryl. Just-Right Writing Mini-Lessons, Grades 2-3: Mini-Lessons to Teach Your Students the Essential Skills & Strategies They Need to Write Fiction & Nonfiction. (p. 939)
Ford, Vikke. Angel Anya's Adventures: Anya's Magic Heart. (p. 73)
Ford, Xander, jt. auth. see St. Pierre-Ford, Hillary.
Ford, Yvonne, illus. see Marsh, Carole.
Forde, Catherine. Fat Boy Swim. (p. 577)
—Slippy. (p. 1590)
—Sugarcoated. (p. 1673)
—Tug of War. (p. 1796)
Forde, Patricia. Hedgehogs Do Not Like Heights. Dreidemy, Joëlle, illus. (p. 762)
—Witches Do Not Like Bicycles. Dreidemy, Joëlle, illus. (p. 1941)
Forde, Patricia & Agnew, Kate. Frogs Do Not Like Dragons. Dreidemy, Joëlle & Jones, Anna, illus. (p. 641)
Forde, Winston. Airborne Soldiers. (p. 31)
Fordham, Glenda. Greatest Stock Car Races: Triumphs & Tragedies of Yesterday & Today. (p. 720)
—Hottest Stock Car Drivers: Today's Greatest Superstars. (p. 802)
—Women Racers: The Fastest Drivers on the Circuit. (p. 1946)
Fordham, Glenda J. Formula One Drivers. (p. 620)
Fordham, Henrietta. Healthy Food for Young Children Inernet-Referenced. (p. 758)
Fordham, Kate. Me & My Kitten. (p. 1115)
Fordham, Walter. Ilian. Krizmanic, Tatjana, illus. (p. 856)
Fordyce, Deborah. Afghanistan. (p. 26)
—Welcome to Morocco. (p. 1873)
Fordyce, Deborah & Kazem, Halima. Welcome to Afghanistan. (p. 1873)
Fore, Elizabeth, illus. see Wilson, Douglas.
Foreign Policy Research Institute Staff, ed. Growth & Influence of Islam in the Nations of Asia & Central Asia (p. 727)
—Modern Middle East Nations & Their Strategic Places in the World (p. 1158)
Foreign Service Institute Staff. Amharic (p. 65)
—Fula (p. 646)
—Languages of Africa: Swahili (p. 975)
—Yoruba (p. 1972)
Foreman, jt. auth. see Morpurgo, Michael.
Foreman, A., illus. see Smith, C. Michelle.
Foreman, Austin Lee, illus. see Dreisbach, Kristin Wolf.
Foreman, Colin. Moment Comes. Colin Foreman. (p. 1161)
Foreman, Gabe, illus. see Thran, Nick.
Foreman, Jack. Say Hello. Foreman, Michael, illus. (p. 1518)
Foreman, Jack & Foreman, Michael. Say Hello. (p. 1518)
Foreman, Michael. Can't Catch Me! (p. 262)
—Cat & Canary. (p. 277)
—Cat & Dog. Foreman, Michael, illus. (p. 277)
—Chicken Licken. (p. 300)
—Classic Christmas Tales. (p. 328)
—Classic Fairy Tales. (p. 328)
—Fortunately, Unfortunately. Foreman, Michael, illus. (p. 623)
—Friends. Foreman, Michael, illus. (p. 638)
—Hola, Mundo. (p. 787)
—I Love You, Too! Foreman, Michael, illus. (p. 844)
—Jardin del Nino: Una Historia de Esperanza. Diego, Rapi & Flores, Martha, illus. (p. 909)
—Lorito Pelon. Diego, Rapi & Flores, Martha, illus. (p. 1053)
—Newspaper Boy & Origami Girl! (p. 1249)
—Newspaper Boy & Origami Girl! Foreman, Michael, illus. (p. 1249)
—Norman's Ark. Foreman, Michael, illus. (p. 1264)
—Oh! If Only... Foreman, Michael, illus. (p. 1280)
—One World. (p. 1297)
—Scraps. (p. 1532)
—Seal Surfer. Foreman, Michael, illus. (p. 1536)
—Seeds of Friendship. Foreman, Michael, illus. (p. 1548)
—Superfrog! Foreman, Michael, illus. (p. 1683)
—Superfrog & the Big Stink! Foreman, Michael, illus. (p. 1683)
—War Boy: A Wartime Childhood. (p. 1857)
—War Game (Special 100th Anniversary of WW1 Ed.) (p. 1857)
—Wonder Goal! Foreman, Michael, illus. (p. 1947)
Foreman, Michael, illus. see Barrie, J. M.
Foreman, Michael, illus. see Baum, L. Frank.
Foreman, Michael, illus. see Borden, Louise.
Foreman, Michael, illus. see Carroll, Lewis, pseud.
Foreman, Michael, illus. see Charters, Janet.
Foreman, Michael, illus. see Davies, Nicola.
Foreman, Michael, illus. see Foreman, Jack.
Foreman, Michael, illus. see Jones, Terry.
Foreman, Michael, illus. see Morpurgo, Michael & Foreman.
Foreman, Michael, illus. see Morpurgo, Michael.
Foreman, Michael, illus. see Piers, Helen.
Foreman, Michael, illus. see Smiley, Sophie.
Foreman, Michael, illus. see Stevenson, Robert Louis.
Foreman, Michael, illus. see Turnbull, Ann.
Foreman, Michael, jt. auth. see Foreman, Jack.
Foreman, Michael, jt. auth. see Grindley, Sally.
Foreman, Michael, jt. auth. see Paul, Anthony.
Foreman, Michael, jt. auth. see Smiley, Sophie.
Foreman, Michael, jt. tr. see Jones, Terry.
Foreman, Niki. Deadly Dinosaurs. (p. 417)
—Shark Reef. (p. 1562)
Foreman, Niki, jt. auth. see Dorling Kindersley Publishing Staff.
Foreman, Niki & Dorling Kindersley Publishing Staff. Shark Reef. (p. 1562)
Foreman, Wilmoth & Boyds Mills Press Staff. Summer of the Skunks. (p. 1674)
Foresman, Timothy. Last Little Polar Bear: A Global Change Adventure Story. Laura Lee, Cundiff, illus. (p. 978)
Forest, A. K. Time Struggle 1: The Wolves of Odin. (p. 1752)
Forest, Anne. My Lemonade Stand: Represent & Interpret Data. (p. 1211)
—Our Family Album. (p. 1308)
Forest, Chris. What You Need to Know about Cancer. (p. 1896)
Forest, Christopher. Ancient Egyptian Gods & Goddesses (p. 69)
—Biggest Battles of the Revolutionary War (p. 185)
—Brazil. (p. 224)
—Crude, Unpleasant Age of Pirates: The Disgusting Details about the Life of Pirates (p. 386)
—Dollar Bill in Translation: What It Really Means. (p. 463)
—Gangs & Gangsters: Stories of Public Enemies. (p. 655)
—Kids' Guide to Collecting Stuff (p. 953)
—Kids' Guide to Sports Ethics (p. 954)
—Kids' Guide to the Constellations (p. 954)
—Play Soccer Like a Pro: Key Skills & Tips (p. 1371)
—Present What You Know: Sharing Information (p. 1396)
—Pyramids of Ancient Egypt (p. 1421)
—Rebellious Colonists & the Causes of the American Revolution. (p. 1451)
—Robot Competitions. (p. 1480)
—Robots in Space (p. 1481)
—Secret American People: From Secret Societies to Secret Agents (p. 1540)
—Side-By-Side Basketball Stars: Comparing Pro Basketball's Greatest Players (p. 1573)
—This Book Is History: A Collection of Cool U. S. History Trivia (p. 1735)
—World's Wackiest History. (p. 1961)
Forest, Christopher & Wegner, Jennifer Houser. Pyramids of Ancient Egypt (p. 1421)
Forest, Christopher, et al. Ancient Egyptian Civilization. (p. 68)
—Library of Weird. (p. 1006)
—Robots. (p. 1481)
—Story of the American Revolution. (p. 1660)
Forest, Crista, illus. see Fraggalosch, Audrey.
Forest, Crista, illus. see Swinburne, Stephen R.
Forest, G. Daddy's Different: A Look at Brain Injury Through a Child's Eyes. (p. 399)
Forest, Heather. Baker's Dozen. Gaber, Susan, illus. (p. 133)
—Big Quiet House: A Yiddish Folktale. (p. 183)
—Big Quiet House: A Yiddish Folktale from Eastern Europe. Greenstein, Susan, illus. (p. 183)
—Contest Between the Sun & the Wind: An Aesop's Fable. Gaber, Susan, illus. (p. 360)
—Stone Soup. (p. 1652)
—Wisdom Tales from Around the World. (p. 1939)
—Woman Who Flummoxed the Fairies. Gaber, Susan, illus. (p. 1945)
Forest, Jim. Saint Nicholas & the Nine Gold Coins. Andrejev, Vladislav, illus. (p. 1504)
—Silent As a Stone: Mother Maria of Paris & the Trash Can Rescue. Pancheshnaya, Dasha, illus. (p. 1575)
Forest Service (U.S.), Northeastern Area State and Private Forestry, ed. see Burzynski, Roberta.
Forester, MaMa Eagle. Young Eagle, Pretty Flower. Spears, Ashley E., illus. (p. 1978)
Forester, Victoria. Girl Who Could Fly. (p. 679)
Forest-Flier, Nancy, tr. see Matti, Truus.
Forest-Flier, Nancy, tr. see Westera, Marleen.
Forey, Martin. Maurice Minor's Incredible Adventure: A Children's Book for Grown-Ups. (p. 1110)
Forey, Pamela. Wild Flowers of the United States & Canada. (p. 1929)
Forgan, James W. Teaching Problem Solving Through Children's Literature (p. 1710)
Forgas, Christine. After Dark. Forgas-Davis, Melissa, illus. (p. 28)
Forgas-Davis, Melissa, illus. see Forgas, Christine.
Forgensi, David. Midas the Bee: David Forgensi. (p. 1137)
—Tish, of a Dish, for a Fish. (p. 1757)
Forgensi, David A. This Fish, That Fish, Even a Hat Fish. (p. 1735)
Forges, Roger V. Des, see Des Forges, Roger V.
Forget, Thomas. Beastie Boys. (p. 152)
—Creation of Captain America. (p. 379)
—Rolling Stones. (p. 1485)
Forget, Tom. Art Spiegelman. (p. 103)

F

Forgey, Winchester. Chronicle of the Bent Nail. (p. 317)
Forgey, Winchester V. Deleted. (p. 424)
Forgue, Raymond E., jt. auth. see Garman, E. Thomas.
Forhan, Mary C., jt. auth. see Forhan, Mary C.
Forhan, Mary C. & Forhan, Mary C. Introduction to Letter Sounds: Fun, Active, Multisensory. (p. 882)
Forian, Rosemary Talucci. My Own Angel. (p. 1216)
Forier, Elise. We Both Read-Endangered Animals: Level 2. (p. 1866)
—We Both Read-Endangered Animals. (p. 1866)
Forlati, Anna, illus. see Pajalunga, Lorena V.
Forler, Nan. Bird Child. Thisdale, Francois, illus. (p. 190)
—Winterberries & Apple Blossoms: Reflections & Flavors of a Mennonite Year. Snyder, Peter Etril, illus. (p. 1938)
Forlini, Gary. Grammar & Composition. (p. 706)
Forlini, Victoria, ed. Batman Begins Stencil Activity Book. (p. 144)
—Bible Big Color & Activity Book with Stickers. (p. 175)
—Bible Ultimate Color & Activity Book with Paints. (p. 176)
Forman, Gayle. I Was Here. (p. 848)
—If I Stay. (p. 853)
—If I Stay Collection (p. 853)
—Just One Day. (p. 939)
—Just One Year. (p. 939)
—Sisters in Sanity. (p. 1581)
—Where She Went. (p. 1909)
Forman, Lillian. Assisted Suicide. (p. 107)
—Stem Cell Research. (p. 1647)
Forman, Lillian E. Albert Einstein: Physicist & Genius. (p. 34)
—Diamond Trade. (p. 434)
—Genetically Modified Foods. (p. 660)
—Health Care Reform. (p. 758)
Forman, M. L. Adventurers Wanted, Book 1: Slathbog's Gold. (p. 15)
—Adventurers Wanted, Book 2: The Horn of Moran. (p. 15)
—Adventurers Wanted, Book 3: Albrek's Tomb. (p. 15)
—Adventurers Wanted, Book 4: Sands of Nezza. (p. 15)
—Adventures Wanted, Book 3: Albrek's Tomb. (p. 25)
Forman, Mark. Horn of Moran. (p. 798)
—Slathbog's Gold. (p. 1588)
Forman, Ruth. Young Cornrows Callin Out the Moon. Bayoc, Cbabi, illus. (p. 1978)
Forman, Sara, ed. see Bauchner, Elizabeth.
Forman, Sara, ed. see Esherick, Joan.
Forman, Sara, ed. see Ford, Jean.
Forman, Sara, ed. see Hovius, Christopher.
Forman, Sara, ed. see Hunter, Miranda & Hunter, William.
Forman, Sara, ed. see Lange, Donna.
Forman, Sara, ed. see Libal, Autumn.
Forman, Sara, ed. see Simons, Rae.
Formaro, Amanda. Button Mania: Buttons, Bottlecaps, & Beyond! (p. 248)
—Paper Fun Mania. (p. 1322)
Formato, Vicki. Jayson: The True Story of a 20 Year Old Blue Jay. (p. 910)
Formelio, Lorri, illus. see Starling, Landa.
Formento, Alison. These Bees Count! Snow, Sarah, illus. (p. 1731)
—These Rocks Count! Snow, Sarah, illus. (p. 1732)
—This Tree Counts! Snow, Sarah, illus. (p. 1737)
Formento, Alison Ashley. Twigs. (p. 1801)
Formichelli, Linda & Martin, W. Eric. Timekeeping: Explore the History & Science of Telling Time with 15 Projects. Carbaugh, Sam, illus. (p. 1754)
Formichelli, Linda, et al. Timekeeping: Explore the History & Science of Telling Time with 15 Projects. Carbaugh, Samuel, illus. (p. 1754)
Formosa, Natasha, illus. see Rate, Kristina.
Fornari, Giuliano. Panoramas Human Body. (p. 1321)
Fornaro, Claire. Puppy Factory Guide to Dog Care: The Absolute to the Zany of Dog Care. (p. 1418)
Forney, Ellen. Monkey Food: The Complete I was Seven in '75 Collection. Forney, Ellen, illus. (p. 1165)
Forney, Ellen, illus. see Alexie, Sherman.
Forney, Lane. Super Power Teens. (p. 1680)
—Super Power Teens 2: A Blast from the Past. (p. 1680)
Forni, P. M. Choosing Civility: The Twenty-Five Rules of Considerate Conduct. (p. 310)
Forrest. Sign of Blood. (p. 1574)
Forrest, A. S., illus. see Marshall, H. E.
Forrest, Amber, illus. see Ludvik, Elizabeth.
Forrest, C. L. Ant King's Adventure. (p. 88)
Forrest, Chris, illus. see Miller, Paula.
Forrest, Genevieve, illus. see Harper, Julie-Ann.
Forrest, George. Echoes with a Western Air. (p. 502)
Forrest, Grace Metzger, illus. see Barnes, Brenda J.
Forrest, Grace Metzger, illus. see Dixon, Dallas L.
Forrest, Helen, et al, eds. Barron's Children's English-Chinese/Chinese-English Dictionary. (p. 140)
Forrest, James, illus. see Sprecher, John.
Forrest, Nancy, illus. see Boritzer, Etan.
Forrestal, Elaine. Rainbow Jackets. Thompson, Sharon, illus. (p. 1435)
Forrester, Anne Marie, illus. see Monaghan, Patricia & Managhan, Patricia.
Forrester Baldy, Sherri, illus. see Capitelli, Yvonne.
Forrester, Emma. Uncle Arthur's Art Studio. Nunn, Paul E., illus. (p. 1811)
Forrester, Izola L. Kit of Greenacre Farm. (p. 962)
Forrester, Kate, illus. see Parr, Maria.
Forrester, Margaret. Cat Who Decided: The Almost True Story of an Edinburgh Cat. (p. 278)
Forrester, Sandra. Leo & the Lesser Lion. (p. 992)
Forrester, Tina, jt. auth. see Shapiro, Stephen.
Forrester, Tina, et al. Hoodwinked: Deception & Resistance. Craig, David, illus. (p. 795)
Forrey, B. J. Basketball's My Favorite. (p. 143)
Forsberg, Victoria. Little Irma Shirley & the Wand of Better: City Adventures. (p. 1029)
Forschmiedt, Jodi, jt. auth. see Shryer, Donna.
Forsey, Chris, illus. see Ganeri, Anita.
Forsey, Chris, illus. see Jeffrey, Gary.
Forsey, Chris, illus. see Shone, Rob.
Forsey, Christopher, illus. see Jeffrey, Gary.
Forshall, Rose, illus. see Durrant, Geraldine.
Forshaw, Andy, illus. see Lloyd, Christopher.
Forshaw, John, illus. see Popper, Garry.
Forshaw, Louise, illus. see Bateson, Maggie.
Forshay, Christina, illus. see Crow, Kristyn & Aesop.
Forshay, Christina, illus. see Crow, Kristyn.
Forshay, Christina, illus. see Dahl, Michael.
Forshay, Christina E., illus. see Dahl, Michael.
Forsheit, Lewis M. Loving Math: Advanced Problems with Solutions, Applications & Comments. (p. 1061)
Forss, Ian, illus. see Holl, Robert.
Forss, Ian, illus. see Perez, Marlene.
Forss, Sarah, jt. auth. see Dwell Studio Staff.
Forss, Sarah, jt. auth. see Werner, Sharon.
Forss, Sarah & Werner, Sharon. Bugs by the Numbers. (p. 237)
Forssberg, Manne. Sex for Guys Lundin, Maria, tr. from SWE. (p. 1556)
Forstater, Mathew. Trailblazers in Economics (p. 1776)
Forstchen, William R., jt. auth. see Gingrich, Newt.
Forster, Elborg, tr. see Cohen, Hilda Stern & Gilcher, William Harry.
Forster, Imogen, tr. see Calza, Gian Carlo.
Forster, John, jt. auth. see Chapin, Tom.
Forster, Kate. Beauty & the Beat. (p. 154)
—Head over High Heels. (p. 756)
—Piece of Cake. (p. 1356)
—Twice upon a Time. (p. 1801)
—Unlucky Break. (p. 1821)
Forster, Miriam. City of a Thousand Dolls. (p. 323)
Forster, Pamela R. Honor Your Father & Mother: The Fifth Commandment for Little Ones. (p. 795)
Forsyth, Adrian. Exploring the World of Insects: The Equinox Guide to Insect Behaviour. (p. 554)
Forsyth, Amy, tr. see Mashima, Hiro.
Forsyth, Amy, tr. see Tsuda, Masami.
Forsyth, C. A. & Forsyth, Christine. Adrenaline High (p. 13)
—Two on One (p. 1804)
Forsyth, Christine. Two on One (p. 1804)
Forsyth, Christine, jt. auth. see Forsyth, C. A.
Forsyth, Elizabeth, jt. auth. see Hyde, Margaret O.
Forsyth, Elizabeth H., jt. auth. see Hyde, Margaret O.
Forsyth, Fiona. Augustus: The First Emperor. (p. 115)
—Cicero: Defender of the Republic. (p. 318)
Forsyth, Frederick. Afghan. (p. 26)
Forsyth, Gail. Dogs, Flags & Their Countries of Origin: Activity, Coloring & Learning Book. (p. 462)
Forsyth, Robert, illus. see Morley, Margaret Warner.
Forsythe, Amanda J. Contabulous Adventures of M E. (p. 360)
Forsythe, Demming. Ten Little Menehunes: A Hawaiian Counting Book. (p. 1719)
Forsythe, Gary & Kee, Ed, creators. Crazy Praise, Volume 4: Unison. (p. 378)
Forsythe, Matthew, illus. see Dunklee, Annika.
Forsythe, Matthew, illus. see Lehrhaupt, Adam.
Fort, Gary W. Mom, I Love Spaghetti. Schultz, Michael, illus. (p. 1161)
Fort, Holli, et al. Teachers' Favorites Fun Activities for Fall! Hamblin, George, illus. (p. 1709)
Fort, Jean Jacobs. Trouble. (p. 1789)
Forte, Bruno & Tarzia, Antonio. My Prayers: To God with Love & Joy. (p. 1217)
Forte, Helen, illus. see Bell, Barbara.
Forte, Imogene. Arts & Crafts. (p. 104)
—Box Bonanza. (p. 216)
—Crayons & Markers. (p. 377)
—Holidays & Special Days. (p. 788)
—Nature Crafts. (p. 1236)
—Paper Capers. (p. 1322)
—Punctuation Power. Norris, Jill, ed. (p. 1417)
—Puppet Parade. (p. 1417)
—Ready to Learn: Words & Vocabulary. (p. 1447)
—Ready to Learn Alphabet & Beginning Sounds. Bosarge, Charlotte, ed. (p. 1447)
—Ready to Learn Beginning Math. (p. 1447)
—Ready to Learn Beginning Reading. (p. 1447)
—Ready to Learn Beginning Science. (p. 1448)
—Ready to Learn Following Directions. (p. 1448)
—Ready to Learn Shapes & Colors. (p. 1448)
—Ready to Learn Time & Money. Harvey, Gayle, illus. (p. 1448)
—Science Fun. (p. 1526)
Forte, Imogene & Frank, Marjorie. U. S. History BASIC/Not Boring 6-8+ Inventive Exercises to Sharpen Skills & Raise Achievement. Quinn, Anna, ed. (p. 1806)
Forte, Imogene & Schurr, Sandra. Standards-Based Language Arts Graphic Organizers & Rubrics. Bosarge, Charlotte, ed. (p. 1639)
—Standards-Based Math Graphic Organizers & Rubrics. Bosarge, Charlotte, ed. (p. 1639)
—Standards-Based Science Graphic Organizers & Rubrics. (p. 1639)
—Standards-Based Social Studies Graphic Organizers & Rubrics. Borsage, Charlotte, ed. (p. 1639)
Forte, Imogene, et al. Read about It DM: Primary-Comprehension. Frank, Marjorie, ed. (p. 1442)
Forte, Joseph. At the Window. (p. 111)
Forte, Joyce. Brave Little Girl. (p. 223)
—Lost Leprechaun (p. 1056)
Forte, Lauren. Olivia Goes to the Library. (p. 1286)
—Olivia Helps Mother Nature. (p. 1286)
Forte, Mark. Bug Eyes & the Sacred Scrolls: A Sir Frederick Stone Mystery. Bk. 1 (p. 236)
Forte, Virginia. History of Western Painting. (p. 785)
Forten, Charlotte. Diary of Charlotte Forten: A Free Black Girl Before the Civil War (p. 435)
Fortenberry, Julie, illus. see Bunting, Eve.
Fortenberry, Julie, illus. see Korngold, Jamie S.
Fortenberry, Julie, illus. see Korngold, Jamie.
Fortenberry, Julie, illus. see Roosa, Karen.
Fortescue, Madeleine. Animals Undercover: Camouflage. (p. 84)
—Deadly Animal Poisons. (p. 417)
—Super Skin: Spines, Quills, & Plates. (p. 1681)
Fortescue, W. J. Drummer's Coat. (p. 487)
Fortey, Jacqueline & Dorling Kindersley Publishing Staff. Great Scientists. (p. 718)
Forthun, Angela. Joozu! Activities for Beginners. (p. 925)
Fortier, Natali, illus. see Moncomble, Gerard & Van den Dries, Sidonie.
Fortier, Robert, jt. auth. see Clampitt, Ed.
Fortier-Durand, Ghislaine, tr. see Bernard, Fred & Roca, François.
Fortin, Francois, ed. Sports: The Complete Visual Reference. (p. 1632)
Fortman, Susie. Lakota's Alphabet Walk. (p. 972)
Fortner, Tama. God Is Always Good: Comfort for Kids Facing Grief, Fear, or Change Vasylenko, Veronica, illus. (p. 689)
Fortnum, Peggy, illus. see Bond, Michael.
Fortnum, Rebecca. Contemporary British Women Artists: In Their Own Words. (p. 360)
Forton-Barnes, Therese. Zaki & Venus. (p. 1984)
Fortuna, Lorna. When God Spoke to Trees. (p. 1902)
Fortunado, Hector. Jose's Hardware Store: Understand Place Value. (p. 926)
—Jos's Hardware Store: Understand Place Value. (p. 927)
Fortunato, Mike. Later Gator, in a While Crocodile. (p. 979)
Fortune, Emil. Root. (p. 1488)
Fortune, Eric, illus. see Howe, James.
Fortune, Eric, illus. see Kirov, Erica.
Fortune, Eric, illus. see Ursu, Anne.
Fortune, Kim. Aggie & Sterling Find a Family: The Tale of Two Rescue Schnauzers. (p. 29)
Fortune, Leslie, illus. see Nordquist, Donna M.
Fortune, Tracy. Kaila's Garden. (p. 941)
Forty, Sandra. Wonders of the World. (p. 1949)
Forward, Max, illus. see Lee, Lucas Taekwon.
Forward, Toby. Christmas Mouse. Brown, Ruth, illus. (p. 314)
—Dragonborn. (p. 478)
—Fireborn. (p. 591)
—Quayside Cat. Brown, Ruth, illus. (p. 1423)
—Wolf's Story: What Really Happened to Little Red Riding Hood. Cohen, Izhar, illus. (p. 1944)
Forward, Valerie. Bird Land. (p. 190)
Forzy, Nicolas. AlphaNumeric. (p. 50)
Fosberry, Jennifer. Isabella: Girl on the Go. Litwin, Mike, illus. (p. 891)
—Isabella: Star of the Story. Litwin, Mike, illus. (p. 891)
—My Name Is Not Alexander. Litwin, Mike, illus. (p. 1215)
—My Name Is Not Isabella: Just How Big Can a Little Girl Dream? Litwin, Mike, illus. (p. 1215)
—My Name Is Not Isabella. Litwin, Mike, illus. (p. 1215)
Fosburgh. Bella Arabella. (p. 162)
Fosgitt, Jay P. Dino Duck: Prehysterical: Prehysterical. (p. 441)
—Little Green Men. (p. 1028)
—Little Green Men: Small Package, Big Fun! GN: Small Package, Big Fun! GN. (p. 1028)
Fosha, Kent. Cat Who Wanted to Moo. (p. 278)
Fosina, Mickie. Kitten Girls Are Scaredy Cats. (p. 962)
Fosnot, Catherine Twomey. Bunk Beds & Apple Boxes: Early Number Sense. (p. 242)
—Field Trips & Fund-Raisers: Introducing Fractions. (p. 584)
—Measuring for the Art Show: Addition on the Open Number Line. (p. 1117)
Fosnot, Catherine Twomey, jt. auth. see Cameron, Antonia.
Fosnot, Catherine Twomey, jt. auth. see Jacob, Bill.
Fosnot, Catherine Twomey, jt. auth. see Lent, Patricia.
Fosnot, Catherine Twomey & Dolk, Maarten. Exploring Soda Machines, Grades 3-5: A Context for Division. (p. 553)
—Multiplication & Division Minilessons, Grades 3-5. (p. 1190)
—Turkey Investigations, Grades 3-5: A Context for Multiplication. (p. 1797)
Foss, Dawn. Christmas Love. (p. 314)
Foss, Timothy, illus. see Yomtov, Nel.
Foss, Timothy, illus. see Yomtov, Nelson.
Foss, William O., jt. auth. see Bergaust, Erik.
Fossati, Mike. Fishing the Golden Waters of the Texas Gulf Coast. (p. 599)
Fosse, Mika. Garage People. (p. 655)
Fossey, Kevin. Buddhism. (p. 234)
Fossey, Robert. Little Armstrong. (p. 1023)
Fossey, Wietse, illus. see Baeten, Lieve.
Foster, Alan Dean. Star Trek Logs Five & Six (p. 1641)
Foster, Angela. Grandma's Story: the Singing Mouse. Foster, Angela, illus. (p. 709)
Foster, Bennett. Pot Luck: A Western Quintet. (p. 1388)
Foster, Beverly & Foster, Stacy Lynn. Early Articulation Roundup! Bk305. Ink, Bruce & Schwartz, Marty, illus. (p. 493)
Foster, Brad W., illus. see Bolte, Mari.
Foster, Brett, ed. see Bloom, Harold.
Foster, Brett, jt. ed. see Bloom, Harold.
Foster, Brett & Marcovitz, Hal. Rome. (p. 1486)
Foster, Bryan. Wild Logging: Sustainable Forestry among Western Woodlot Owners. Foster, Peggy, illus. (p. 1929)
Foster, Cass. Sixty-Minute Shakespeare: Taming of the Shrew. (p. 1583)
Foster, Cassandra. Do You Know Us? A Collection of Short Stories. (p. 458)
—Good Story: A Collection of Short Short Stories. (p. 700)
Foster, Chad. Dear God: Thank-You Notes to God from Baby Boys & Girls. (p. 419)
Foster, Charles. Story of the Gospel. (p. 1661)
Foster, Christa Simone, jt. auth. see Foster, Sonia Clark.
Foster, Claudie. Princess Vanilla of the Amazon Jungle. (p. 1406)
Foster Colburn, Cherie. Bloomin' Tales: Seven Favorite Wildflower Legends. Fisher Hein, Joy, illus. (p. 201)
Foster, D. S. Stone Heart. Lewis, Jesse, illus. (p. 1652)
Foster, Dara. Now You See It! Puppies & Kittens 2. (p. 1269)
—Now You See It! Pupstyle Red Carpet Pups. Foster, Dara, photos by. (p. 1269)
—Pupstyle Sticker Book. (p. 1418)
Foster, Dara, jt. auth. see Corse, Nicole.
Foster, Darlene. Amanda in England: The Missing Novel. (p. 52)
Foster Dorantes, Andrea & Foster, Laura. Don't Lick the Mailbox. (p. 468)
Foster, Doris. Learn the Alphabet with the Spirit. (p. 983)
Foster, Dylan. My Friend Sammy. (p. 1209)
Foster, Elizabeth. Tutoring, Learning by Doing: A Handbook for Middle Grade Tutors. (p. 1799)
Foster, Elizabeth Vincent. Lyrico: The Only Horse of His Kind. Buba, Joy, illus. (p. 1067)
Foster, Evelyn. Alan & the Animals. (p. 33)
—Elves & the Trendy Shoes. Venturini, Claudia, illus. (p. 517)
Foster, Frank, illus. see Taylor, Paula.
Foster, Genevieve. World of William Penn. (p. 1957)
—Year of the Horseless Carriage, 1801. (p. 1969)
Foster, Greg & Quattro, Jacquelyn. Razor the Vampire! Binns, Chris, illus. (p. 1441)
Foster, Hal, jt. auth. see Francis, Mark.
Foster, Hal & Murphy, John Cullen. Queen of the Amazons (p. 1425)
Foster, Jack, illus. see Harrah, Judith.
Foster, Jack, illus. see Helixon, Tracy Schuldt.
Foster, Jack, illus. see Kennedy, J. Aday.
Foster, Jack, illus. see Lyle-Soffe, Shari.
Foster, Jack, illus. see Reed, Jennifer Bond.
Foster, Jack, illus. see Schreiber, Hannah & Hartsock, Conner.
Foster, Jack, illus. see Stemke, Kathy.
Foster, Jack, illus. see Sullivan, Candida.
Foster, Jack, illus. see Tucker, Susan K.
Foster, Jack, jt. auth. see Crow, Marilee.
Foster, Jack, jt. auth. see Kennedy, J. Aday.
Foster, Jack, jt. auth. see Shepherd, Donna J.
Foster, Jackie. Land of Anear (p. 973)
Foster James, Helen. Little America. (p. 1023)
Foster, Janet, illus. see Robinson, George.
Foster, Jeff, jt. auth. see Angwin, Fiona.
Foster, Jennifer L. Puppy with the White Paw. (p. 1418)
Foster, Jesse, et al. Night Before Christmas in Africa Christodoulou, Jean, illus. (p. 1253)
Foster, Jessica & Pecsenye, Jessice. University of South Carolina College Prowler off the Record. (p. 1821)
Foster, Jo. Great Exhibition Mission Vol. 3 Anderson, Scoular, illus. (p. 715)
—Why Would a Dog Need a Parachute? Questions & Answers about the Second World. (p. 1927)
Foster, Jo, jt. auth. see Turner, Tracey.
Foster, John. Dinosaur Poems. Paul, Korky, illus. (p. 442)
—Fantastic Football Poems. Paul, Korky, illus. (p. 571)
—Football Fever. (p. 615)
—I've Got a Poem for You. (p. 900)
—Llinynnau. (p. 1043)
—Marathon. (p. 1091)
—Poetry Chest. (p. 1376)
—See You Later, Escalator: Rhymes for the Very Young. (p. 1547)
Foster, John, illus. see Baity, Cameron & Zelkowicz, Benny.
Foster, John, jt. auth. see Wright, Philip Lee.
Foster, John & Mellor, Robin. Alphabet Poems & Number Poems. (p. 50)
Foster, John & Mellor, Robin, selected by. Alphabet Poems & Number Poems. (p. 50)
Foster, John & Stewart, Peter. Llinynnau. (p. 1043)
Foster, John & Williams, Brenda. Animal Poems & Family Poems. (p. 79)
Foster, John & Williams, Brenda, selected by. Animal Poems & Family Poems. (p. 79)
Foster, John, compiled by. Completely Crazy Poems. (p. 353)
Foster, John, et al. Body Poems & Movement Poems. (p. 207)
—Transportation Poems & Senses Poems. (p. 1779)
Foster, John, et al, selected by. Transportation Poems & Senses Poems. (p. 1779)
Foster, John L. Dragon Poems. Paul, Korky, illus. (p. 477)
Foster, John L., compiled by. Really Rude Rhymes. (p. 1450)
—Seriously Scary Poems. (p. 1552)
Foster, Jon, illus. see Farmer, Nancy.
Foster, Jonathan, illus. see Spiritworks.
Foster, Juliana. Christmas Book - How to Have the Best Christmas Ever. (p. 313)
—Girls' Book: How to Be the Best at Everything. Wingate, Philippa, ed. (p. 679)
Foster, Karen. Atlas of Africa QTA Media Staff et al, illus. (p. 112)
—Atlas of Africa. Elliott, Rebecca et al, illus. (p. 112)
—Atlas of Australia QTA Media Staff et al, illus. (p. 112)
—Atlas of Australia. Elliott, Rebecca et al, illus. (p. 112)
—Atlas of Europe QTA Media Staff et al, illus. (p. 112)
—Atlas of Europe. Elliott, Rebecca et al, illus. (p. 112)
—Atlas of North America QTA Media Staff et al, illus. (p. 112)
—Atlas of North America. Elliott, Rebecca et al, illus. (p. 112)
—Atlas of South America QTA Media Staff et al, illus. (p. 113)
—Atlas of South America. Elliott, Rebecca et al, illus. (p. 113)
—Atlas of the Poles & Oceans QTA Media Staff et al, illus. (p. 113)
—Atlas of the Poles & Oceans Elliott, Rebecca et al, illus. (p. 113)
Foster, Karen, jt. auth. see Bailey, Gerry.
Foster, Karen & Law, Felicia. Kids' World Atlas: A Young Person's Guide to the Globe. Elliott, Rebecca et al, illus. (p. 955)
Foster, Kate, ed. Nice & Pretty. (p. 1250)
Foster, Kathryn Joy. Always Room for One More. (p. 51)
Foster, Katy. Most Important Job. (p. 1177)
Foster, Kelli C. & Erickson, Gina Clegg. Get Ready... Get Set... Read! Russell, Kerri G., illus. (p. 668)
Foster, Kia. Tom & Rondy. (p. 1762)
Foster, Kimberly. Dolphin up a Tree! (p. 464)
Foster, L. L., pseud. Awakening. (p. 120)
—Servant - The Acceptance: Destiny Can't be Denied. (p. 1552)
Foster, Laura, jt. auth. see Foster Dorantes, Andrea.
Foster, Leila Merrell. Africa (p. 26)
—Antártida (p. 89)

—Asia (p. 106)
—Benjamin Franklin: Statesman & Inventor. (p. 165)
—Europa (p. 540)
—Puerto Rico. (p. 1415)
Foster, Leila Merrell, jt. auth. see Fox, Mary Virginia.
Foster, Linda. United States Naval Academy: Annapolis. Miller, Roger, photos by. (p. 1819)
Foster, Lisa. 5 Little Tomatoes. (p. 1992)
Foster, Lori, see Foster, L. L., pseud.
Foster, Lorri, jt. auth. see Gitchel, Sam.
Foster, Marilyn. Moon Tricks. Vega, Alison, illus. (p. 1172)
Foster, Martha S. Ginger Box. Geer, Charles, illus. (p. 677)
Foster, Matthew. Gateway. (p. 658)
Foster, Michael K., illus. see Cunningham, Sarah.
Foster, Mike, jt. auth. see Gross, Craig.
Foster, Patience. Pocket Scientist. (p. 1375)
Foster, Patricia. Where Did You Come from, Tiny Drop? (p. 1906)
Foster, Peggy, illus. see Foster, Bryan.
Foster, Rick, jt. auth. see Hicks, Greg.
Foster, Robert L. Fort Zion. (p. 623)
Foster, Ron. I Like Rain. (p. 841)
—I Like Snow! (p. 841)
Foster, Ron, illus. see Joseph, O'Day E.
Foster, Ron, illus. see O'Day, Joseph E.
Foster, Ronnie D. One Day As A Lion: True Stories of the Vietnam War. Freudiger, Victoria, ed. (p. 1294)
Foster, Ruth. High Frequency Word Practice. (p. 777)
—Nonfiction Reading Comprehension - Science. (p. 1263)
—Nonfiction Reading Comprehension - Science, Grade 3. (p. 1263)
—Nonfiction Reading Comprehension - Social Studies, Grades 1-2. (p. 1263)
—Social Studies, Grade 3. (p. 1604)
—Take Five Minutes - Fascinating Facts about Geography. (p. 1696)
Foster, Sheilagh. Mr Coyote Visits the Robson Valley. (p. 1184)
Foster, Shelly L. Deadly Choices. (p. 417)
—Disturbing the Piece. (p. 454)
Foster, Simon. Global Concerns. (p. 684)
Foster, Sonia Clark & Foster, Christa Simone. Polka-Dot Girl. (p. 1381)
Foster, Stacy Lynn, jt. auth. see Foster, Beverly.
Foster, Steven & Duke, James A. Peterson Field Guide to Medicinal Plants & Herbs of Eastern & Central North America, Third Edition. (p. 1347)
Foster, T. E., jt. auth. see Foster, T. e.
Foster, T. e. & Foster, T. E. In These Veins. (p. 868)
Foster, Teresa, illus. see Watson, Carol & Moyle, Philippa.
Foster, Thelma Louise Elisher. Brand New House. (p. 222)
Foster, Thomas. Travel Buddies: Robby & Sammy Visit China. (p. 1780)
Foster, Thomas C. How to Read Literature Like a Professor: For Kids. (p. 821)
—How to Read Literature Like a Professor for Kids. (p. 821)
Foster, Tim & Foster, Tina. Abap the Ambulance in Happy to Help! (p. 2)
Foster, Tina, jt. auth. see Foster, Tim.
Foster, Travis. I Can Doodle - Dots. (p. 835)
—I Can Doodle - Rhymes. (p. 835)
Foster, Travis, illus. see Comden, Betty & Green, Adolph.
Foster, Travis, illus. see Ziefert, Harriet.
Foster, Trista, photos by see Reynolds, Loralyn & Caldwell, Christiana Marie Melvin.
Foster, Walter, ed. Cats & Kittens. Fisher, Diana, illus. (p. 281)
Foster, William, illus. see Lear, Edward.
Foster, William H. Kim & Jones Investigations: Welcome to Elm City. Simpson, Howard, illus. (p. 956)
Foster-Fell, Jeremy, ed. see O'Laughlin, Ann.
Foston, Desirae. Hawaiian Hiatus of Herkimer Street. Foston, Desirae, illus. (p. 755)
Foston, Rebera E. Beyond a Reasonable Doubt. (p. 173)
—New Day. (p. 1244)
—No Crown, No Cross. (p. 1258)
—No Forwarding Address. (p. 1258)
—Pictures of the Wedding. (p. 1356)
—Sweet Memories. (p. 1690)
—When You Have Been Alone. (p. 1905)
—While You Were Gone. (p. 1911)
—You Don't Live on My Street. (p. 1975)
Fosyth, Rebekah & Burns, Adam. Rose-Hulman Institute of Technology College Prowler off the Record. (p. 1489)
Foth, Horst. Traumreisen. (p. 1780)
Fotheringham, Ed, illus. see Ryan, Pam Muñoz.
Fotheringham, Edwin, illus. see Corey, Shana.
Fotheringham, Edwin, illus. see Hamburg, Jennifer.
Fotheringham, Edwin, illus. see Kerley, Barbara.
Fotheringham, Edwin, illus. see Ryan, Pam Muñoz.
Fotheringham, Juanita. Little Ranch on the Side. (p. 1034)
Foti, Anthony J., illus. see Gunderson, Jessica.
Foti, Anthony J., illus. see Terrell, Brandon.
Fotolia, photos by see Apsley, Brenda.
Fotos, Jay, illus. see Beranek, Adam & Beranek, Christian.
Fotso, Serge. Hungry Little Cat. Woods, Michele, illus. (p. 828)
—Little Girl & the Lost Bag. Woods, Michele, illus. (p. 1028)
Fouberg, Erin Hogan & Hogan, Edward Patrick. Ireland. (p. 887)
Fouberg, Erin Hogan & Hogan, Edward Patrick, trs. Norway. (p. 1266)
Foucault, Michel. Hermeneutics of the Subject: Lectures at the Collège de France 1981-1982. Davidson, Arnold I. et al, eds. (p. 771)
Foucault, Michel & Davidson, Arnold I. Psychiatric Power. Lagrange, Jacques et al, eds. (p. 1413)
Fouda, Nadia, tr. see Donaldson, Julia.
Fougere, Isabelle. Tell Me Why? (p. 1717)
Foulke, Nancy, illus. see McCabe, Lauren A.
Foulkes, Fiona, illus. see Hunnisett, Jean.
Foulks, Denine. Jimmy Pfeiffer Dragonmeyer. (p. 918)
Foundation for Human Development Inc. Staff. Making Change: An Introduction to Managing Your Money. (p. 1080)
—Spending Wisely. (p. 1625)
Foundation for ZHuman Development Staff. Saving Wisely. (p. 1518)
Fountain, Bill. Raven: The Sleeping Glass Heart. (p. 1441)
Fountain, John, illus. see Phillips, Leigh Hope.
Fountain, Teresa Fowler. From the Manger... to the Cross. (p. 644)
Fountas, Irene C., jt. auth. see Pinnell, Gay Su.
Fountas, Irene C. & Pinnell, Gay Su. Leveled Books, K-8: Matching Texts to Readers for Effective Teaching. (p. 1003)
Four, Melissa. Snowflake Friends: A Magnetic Playbook. (p. 1600)
Fourie, Amanda. Daddy Bird's Lousy Night. (p. 398)
Fourment, Tiffany. My Water Comes from the Rocky Mountains. Emerling, Dorothy, illus. (p. 1221)
—My Water Comes from the San Juan Mountains. (p. 1221)
Fourment, Tiffany & Gianniny, Gary. My Water Comes from the San Juan Mountains. Emerling, Dorothy, illus. (p. 1221)
Fournel, Kelly. Native Women of Courage (p. 1235)
Fourniea, Stephanie. Are You a Monster When You Eat. (p. 97)
Fournier, Chantal. Silent Words. Lajeunesse, Nicolas, illus. (p. 1575)
Fournier, Elizabeth. Sailboat Dreams: Monkey Island. (p. 1503)
Fournier, Guillaume, tr. see Collins, Suzanne.
Fournier, Guillaume, tr. see Westerfeld, Scott.
Fournier, Kevin Mark. Sandbag Shuffle. (p. 1511)
Fournier, Laure, illus. see Mcclure, Gillian.
Fournier, Laure, illus. see Zacharias, Ravi.
Fournier, Martin. Adventures of Radisson 2: Back to the New World. (p. 22)
Fourstar, Jerome & Blue Talk, Richard. How the Morning & Evening Stars Came to Be: And Other Assiniboine Indian Stories. (p. 813)
Fourstar, Jerome, et al. How the Summer Season Came: And Other Assiniboine Indian Stories. (p. 813)
Foust, Cindy. Elephant emma Lou. (p. 511)
—Harry, harry Hippo. (p. 750)
—Kristy Kangaroo. (p. 968)
—Louis Lion. (p. 1058)
Foust, Cindy G. Austin Alligator: I'll See You Guys Later. Revoir, Joyce, illus. (p. 116)
—Benny Bear: Having A Baby Sister Isn't Fair. Revoir, Joyce, illus. (p. 165)
Foutz, Andrea. Friendships & Smiles. (p. 639)
Fowler, C. A. Bramblefrost Fairies. (p. 222)
Fowke, Bob & Fowke, Robert. Anglo-Saxons. (p. 75)
Fowke, Gerard. Montezuma Mounds: Explored by N. D. McEvers, Montezuma, Ill., John M. Wulfing, St. Louis, Mo., David I. Bushnell, St. Louis, Mo. (p. 1170)
Fowke, Robert. Ancient Greeks. (p. 69)
—Romans in Britain. (p. 1486)
—Vikings. (p. 1842)
—What They Don't Tell You about Planet Earth. (p. 1894)
Fowke, Robert, jt. auth. see Barber, N.
Fowke, Robert, jt. auth. see Fowke, Bob.
Fowkes, Charlie, illus. see Jarman, Julia.
Fowle, Patz. Remember When... (p. 1459)
Fowler, Allan. Sound-a-Likes: Homonyms & Phonics Cafferata, Sue, illus. (p. 1615)
Fowler, Allan, jt. auth. see Rockwell, Lizzy.
Fowler, Blair, jt. auth. see Fowler, Elle.
Fowler, Charlie, photos by see Fowler Hicks, Ginny.
Fowler, Claire, illus. see Talhah, Abu & Books, Greenbird.
Fowler, Elizabeth, illus. see Whitby, Rozene.
Fowler, Elle & Fowler, Blair. Beneath the Glitter. (p. 164)
—Where Beauty Lies. (p. 1906)
Fowler, Ethan & Fowler, Mardene. Brushed Back: The Story of Trevor Bullock. (p. 232)
Fowler, Faith, illus. see Goguen, Martha.
Fowler, Frank. Broncho Rider Boys with Funston at Vera Cruz: Or, Upholding the Honor of the Stars & Stripes. (p. 230)
Fowler, Gene. Texas Storms: Stories of Raging Weather in the Lone Star State (p. 1724)
Fowler, Gloria. New York Board Book. (p. 1247)
Fowler, Gloria, jt. auth. see Andersen, Hans Christian.
Fowler, Gloria & Heo, Min. Come with Me to Paris. (p. 347)
Fowler Hicks, Ginny. Mountain Star: A Story about a Mountaineer That Will Teach You How to Draw a Star! Fowler, Charlie, photos by. (p. 1181)
Fowler, Jane & Newlon, Stephanie. Quick & Creative Reading Response Activities: More Than 60 Sensational Make-and-Learn Activities to Help Kids Respond Meaningfully to What They Read. (p. 1427)
Fowler, Jim, illus. see Brown, Tricia.
Fowler, Jim, illus. see Fowler, Susi Gregg.
Fowler, Josefine A. What's the Point? (a book about multiple meaning Words) (p. 1899)
Fowler, Josephine A. Lilly's Faith. (p. 1017)
Fowler, Josh. Indiana Pacers. (p. 871)
Fowler, Leona. I Don't Want to Be Grumpy Anymore! Martins, Ann-Kathrin & Fowler, Romana, illus. (p. 838)
Fowler, Mardene, jt. auth. see Fowler, Ethan.
Fowler, Marie. Long Shot. (p. 1047)
Fowler, Orval Ray. Wally Gumper & Family Travel & Adventures: In Search of the Stones. (p. 1855)
Fowler, Richard, illus. see Wood, David.
Fowler, Romana, illus. see Fowler, Leona.
Fowler, Rosamund, illus. see Williams, Brenda.
Fowler, Rosamund, jt. auth. see Williams, Brenda.
Fowler, Susi Gregg. Arctic Aesop's Fables: Twelve Retold Tales. Fowler, Jim, illus. (p. 95)
Fowler, Will. Children's History of Weapons: Ancient & Modern. (p. 303)
—Counterterrorism in West Africa: The Most Dangerous SAS Assault. (p. 370)
—Exploring History: Ancient Weapons. (p. 552)
—Modern Weapons & Warfare. (p. 1159)
—Story of Ancient Weapons. (p. 1657)
—Story of Modern Weapons & Warfare. (p. 1659)
Fowles, John. French Lieutenant's Woman. (p. 636)
Fowles, Shelley, illus. see Jungman, Ann & Quarto Generic Staff.
Fowles, Shelley, illus. see Laird, Elizabeth & Quarto Generic Staff.
Fowley-Doyle, Moïra. Accident Season. (p. 8)
Fowlie, Wallace, ed. French Stories / Contes Français. (p. 636)
Fox, Adrienne. Starstruck. (p. 1643)
Fox, Alex. Windsock Wesley & His Wild & Wonderful Weather MacHine, Living in Cloud. Bazzoni, Lainie M. A., illus. (p. 1936)
Fox, Andrew, jt. auth. see Skewes, John.
Fox, Annie. Be Confident in Who You Are Kindt, Matt, illus. (p. 148)
—Real Friends vs. the Other Kind. Kindt, Matt, illus. (p. 1448)
Fox, Arthur B. Pittsburgh During the American Civil War 1860-1865. (p. 1364)
Fox Busters Ltd. Staff, jt. auth. see King-Smith, Dick.
Fox, Carol White, jt. auth. see Fox, Robin C.
Fox, Carrie, ed. see Gamble, Amy.
Fox, Charles Philip, photos by see Campbell, Sam.
Fox, Christyan, illus. see Clarke, Jane.
Fox, Christyan, illus. see Daynes Katie, et al.
Fox, Christyan, illus. see Daynes, Katie & Wray, Zoe.
Fox, Christyan, illus. see Daynes, Katie.
Fox, Christyan, illus. see Fox, Diane.
Fox, Christyan, illus. see Howell, Laura.
Fox, Christyan, illus. see Meredith, Susan, et al.
Fox, Christyan, illus. see Milbourne, Anna.
Fox, Christyan, illus. see Punter, Russell.
Fox, Christyan, illus. see Starke, Katherine & Watt, Fiona.
Fox, Christyan, illus. see Stowell, Louie.
Fox, Christyan, illus. see Treays, Rebecca.
Fox, Christyan, illus. see Turnbull, Stephanie.
Fox, Christyan, jt. auth. see Fox, Diane.
Fox, Christyan & Fox, Diane. Enzo the Racing Car. Fox, Christyan & Fox, Diane, illus. (p. 532)
—Monty the Rally Car. Fox, Christyan & Fox, Diane, illus. (p. 1170)
Fox, Culpeo S. Fox & the Crow. (p. 626)
Fox, Dave, illus. see Guarente, Gabe.
Fox, Debbie. Fun in the Sun: A Kid's Guide to Indian River County... & Beyond! (p. 648)
Fox, Diane. Cat, the Dog, Little Red, the Exploding Eggs, the Wolf, & Grandma. Fox, Christyan, illus. (p. 278)
—Rain or Shine. Fox, Christyan, illus. (p. 1435)
—Red or Blue. Fox, Christyan, illus. (p. 1454)
Fox, Diane, jt. auth. see Fox, Christyan.
Fox, Diane & Fox, Christyan. Tyson the Terrible. Fox, Diane, illus. (p. 1805)
Fox, Donna L. Salem's Birthday. (p. 1504)
—Willie the Toad. (p. 1934)
Fox, Erin. Butterfly's Dream. (p. 248)
Fox, Frances Margaret. Flowers & Their Travels. Funk, Clotilde Embree, illus. (p. 608)
—Little Bear at Work & at Play. (p. 1024)
—Washington D C , the Nation's Capital: Romance, Adventure, Achievement. Vincent, Andrew M. & Higgie, Will K., illus. (p. 1860)
Fox, Gaines. Go Fly a Kite: A Juvenile Adventure Novel. (p. 686)
Fox, Gardner. Atom - Archives (p. 113)
—Golden Age Flash Archives Mayer, Sheldon & Gaines, M. C., eds. (p. 694)
—Golden Age Hawkman (p. 694)
—Golden Age Sandman. (p. 694)
—Hawkman. (p. 755)
—Justice League of America. (p. 940)
—Justice League of America. Sekowsky, Mike, illus. (p. 940)
Fox, Gardner, jt. auth. see Binder, Otto.
Fox, Gardner, jt. auth. see Broome, John.
Fox, Gardner, jt. auth. see Finger, Bill.
Fox, Gardner & Broome, John. Elongated Man. Infantino, Carmine & Giella, Joe, illus. (p. 516)
Fox, Gardner & DC Comics Staff. Justice League of America. Kahan, Bob, ed. (p. 940)
Fox, Gardner & O'Neil, Dennis. Justice League of America (p. 940)
Fox, Gardner & Sherman, Howard. Golden Age Doctor Fate. (p. 694)
Fox, Gardner, et al. All Star Comics Archives. Meyer, Sheldon, ed. (p. 45)
—Hereby Elects. (p. 771)
—Justice League of America Sachs, Bernard & Anderson, Murphy, illus. (p. 940)
Fox, Helen. Eager. (p. 492)
Fox, Hugh. Wobbley Zombies. (p. 1943)
Fox, Janet. Faithful. (p. 565)
—Sirens. (p. 1580)
Fox, Janet S. Get Organized Without Losing It. (p. 667)
Fox, Jeannine. Feeding Penny Pig. (p. 580)
Fox, Jennifer. Meet Optimus Prime. (p. 1121)
—Meet the Boxtrolls. (p. 1122)
—My Little Pony: Hearts & Hooves. (p. 1213)
—Team of Heroes. (p. 1710)
—Teen Titans Go!: Brain Food. (p. 1714)
Fox, Jennifer, jt. auth. see Disney.
Fox, Jennifer, jt. auth. see LAIKA.
Fox, Jennifer, jt. auth. see Sisler, Celeste.
Fox, Julie. Ugly As a Toad. Chamberlain-Pecorino, Sarah, illus. (p. 1808)
Fox, Karen C. Older Than the Stars. Davis, Nancy, illus. (p. 1285)
Fox, Kate & Read, Abigail. Dear Mom: A Journal All about You Written by Me. (p. 419)
Fox, Kathleen. Book Is Just Like You! All about the Parts of a Book. Wallace, John, illus. (p. 210)
Fox, Kathleen, jt. auth. see Downey, Lisa.
Fox, Kristine M., jt. auth. see Quaglia, Russell.
Fox, L. B. Adventures of Marky, Slash & Levy. (p. 20)
Fox, Lara. My Summer on the Shelf. (p. 1219)
Fox, Laura. Stan the Timid Turtle: Helping Children Cope with Fears about School Violence. DuFalla, Anita, illus. (p. 1639)
Fox, Lauren. I Did It! I Promise! (p. 837)
Fox, Lee. 10 Little Hermit Crabs. McG, Shane, illus. (p. 1993)
Fox, Lee White. Toby Erdrich & the Golden Eclipse. Selyov, Trebor E., ed. (p. 1760)
Fox, Lisa, illus. see Baxter, Nicola.
Fox, Lisa, illus. see Corey, Dorothy.
Fox, Lisa, illus. see McCombs, Margi.
Fox, Lisa, illus. see Rivers-Moore, Debbie.
Fox, Lucy. Keeper of the Enchanted Pool. (p. 947)
Fox, Martha Capwell. Swimming. (p. 1691)
—Vatican City. (p. 1833)
Fox, Mary, jt. auth. see Perez, Claire M.
Fox, Mary, jt. auth. see Perez, Claire.
Fox, Mary Virginia. Australia (p. 116)
—Australia y Oceanía. (p. 116)
—Colombia (p. 341)
—Costa Rica (p. 368)
—Norteamérica (p. 1264)
—Scheduling the Heavens: The Story of Edmond Halley. (p. 1521)
—Suramérica (p. 1685)
—Treasure of the Revolution. Cary, illus. (p. 1782)
—Visit to Costa Rica. (p. 1845)
Fox, Mary Virginia & Foster, Leila Merrell. North America (p. 1264)
Fox, Matthew, jt. auth. see Wilson, Lois Miriam.
Fox, Matys. To Speak of Many Things. (p. 1759)
Fox Mazer, Norma. Saturday, the Twelfth of October. (p. 1515)
Fox, Mem. Baby Bedtime. (p. 125)
—Diez Deditos de Las Manos y Diez Deditos de Los Pies / Ten Little Fingers & Ten Little Toes Bilingual Board Book. Oxenbury, Helen, illus. (p. 437)
—Goblin & the Empty Chair. Dillon, Leo & Dillon, Diane, illus. (p. 688)
—Good Night, Sleep Tight. Horacek, Judy, illus. (p. 700)
—Harriet, You'll Drive Me Wild! (p. 750)
—Harriet, You'll Drive Me Wild! Frazee, Marla, illus. (p. 750)
—Hello Baby! Jenkins, Steve, illus. (p. 763)
—Let's Count Goats! Thomas, Jan, illus. (p. 995)
—Magic Hat. Tusa, Tricia, illus. (p. 1072)
—Noam Mechapes Zichronot. Dash Greenspan, Shari, tr. from ENG. (p. 1262)
—Sleepy Bears. (p. 1589)
—Straight Line Wonder. (p. 1664)
—Tell Me about Your Day Today. Stringer, Lauren, illus. (p. 1716)
—Ten Little Fingers & Ten Little Toes. Oxenbury, Helen, illus. (p. 1719)
—Ten Little Fingers & Ten Little Toes Lap Board Book. Oxenbury, Helen, illus. (p. 1719)
—Time for Bed: Lap-Sized Board Book. Dyer, Jane, illus. (p. 1751)
—Time for Bed. (p. 1751)
—Time for Bed. Dyer, Jane, illus. (p. 1751)
—Time for Bed (Es Hora de Dormir) Dyer, Jane, illus. (p. 1751)
—Two Little Monkeys. Barton, Jill, illus. (p. 1804)
—Whoever You Are. Staub, Leslie, illus. (p. 1919)
—Whoever You Are (Quienquiera Que Seas) Flor Ada, Alma & Campoy, F. Isabel, trs. (p. 1919)
—Yoo-Hoo, Ladybug! Ljungkvist, Laura, illus. (p. 1972)
Fox, Mem, jt. auth. see Horacek, Judy.
Fox, Mem, jt. auth. see Meyers, Susan.
Fox, Mem & Horacek, Judy. Where Is the Green Sheep? (p. 1909)
—Where Is the Green Sheep? Big Book. Horacek, Judy, illus. (p. 1909)
—Where Is the Green Sheep? (¿Dónde Está la Oveja Verde?) Horacek, Judy, illus. (p. 1909)
Fox, Michael J. Lucky Man: A Memoir. (p. 1063)
Fox, Nancy. Hide & Seek, No Ticks Please. Seward, Daniel, illus. (p. 777)
Fox, Nathan, illus. see Keenan, Sheila.
Fox, Nita. Captain Benjamin Dale. Wallace, Andrea, illus. (p. 263)
Fox, Paul, jt. ed. see Bloom, Harold.
Fox, Paula. Cometa Rota. (p. 348)
—danza de los esclavos. (p. 406)
—Gus Cara de Piedra. (p. 732)
—Habitacion de Mauricio. (p. 734)
—How Many Miles to Babylon? (p. 811)
—Likely Place. (p. 1017)
—Maurice's Room. Fetz, Ingrid, illus. (p. 1110)
—Portrait of Ivan. (p. 1386)
—Slave Dancer. (p. 1588)
—Stone-Faced Boy. (p. 1652)
—Traces. Kuskin, Karla, illus. (p. 1775)
Fox, Paula & Eros, Keith. Slave Dancer. (p. 1588)
Fox, Peter. April. (p. 93)
Fox, Peter, photos by see Hutnick, Theresa & Phillips, Karen.
Fox, R. J. Stuart & His Incredibly Obnoxious Magical Book: Soccer (p. 1668)
Fox, Rebecca, illus. see Smallwood, Sally & Jones, Bryony.
Fox, Robert J. Prayer Book for Young Catholic. (p. 1393)
Fox, Robin C. & Fox, Carol White. Traveling Adventures of the Robin & the Fox Around the World We Go! A Cruise Through the Mediterranean. (p. 1780)
Fox, Ruth M. Bible, in Story, from the Beginning. (p. 175)
Fox, Sabrina. Who Can Help Me Sleep? Rothan, Ann, illus. (p. 1914)
FOX, SABRINA, jt. auth. see Fox, Sabrina.
Fox, Sabrina & FOX, SABRINA. ¿Quién Puede Ayudarme a Dormir? Rothan, Ann & Pérez Galván, Ana, trs. (p. 1427)
Fox, Stephen. Kim the Frog. Bowman, Brent, illus. (p. 957)
Fox, Suzanne G. Meriwether Lewis & William Clark: The Corp of Discovery & the Exploration of the American Frontier. (p. 1127)
Fox, Tamar. No Baths at Camp. Vasquez, Natalia, illus. (p. 1257)
Fox, Tamsin. My Alphabet Book the ABC. (p. 1196)
Fox, Tim & Mehta, Sonia. 101 Things You Should Know about Math. (p. 2000)
Fox, Tom, et al. Cite It Right: The SourceAid Guide to Citation, Research, & Avoiding Plagiarism. (p. 322)
Fox, Tom Paul, illus. see Anderson, Georgia Lee.

F

Fox, Valerie P. Deefa: Seek the Vixen. (p. 422)
Fox, Will. Bertie Bolt. Fox, Will, illus. (p. 168)
—Billy Brush. Fox, Will, illus. (p. 187)
—Hector Hacksaw. Fox, Will, illus. (p. 761)
—Molly Mallet. Fox, Will, illus. (p. 1160)
—Peggy Peg. Fox, Will, illus. (p. 1335)
—Rusty Nail. Fox, Will, illus. (p. 1498)
—Sally Screw. Fox, Will, illus. (p. 1505)
—Spiky Saw. Fox, Will, illus. (p. 1627)
—Suzy Scissors. Fox, Will, illus. (p. 1688)
—Twisty Drill. Fox, Will, illus. (p. 1803)
Fox, Woody, illus. see Curtin, Judi.
Fox, Woody, illus. see Donovan, Anna.
Fox, Woody, illus. see Reddin, Brian.
Fox, Woody, jt. auth. see Wood, Steve.
Fox-Davies, Sarah, illus. see Davies, Nicola.
Fox-Davies, Sarah, illus. see Fisher, Aileen.
Fox-Davies, Sarah, illus. see Howker, Janni.
Fox-Davies, Sarah, illus. see Riel, Jörn & Mason, John.
Foxlee, Karen. Anatomy of Wings. (p. 67)
—Ophelia & the Marvelous Boy. (p. 1300)
Fox-Lee, Kyme, jt. auth. see Fox-Lee, Susan.
Fox-Lee, Kyme & Fox-Lee, Susan. What Are Parents? Jennings, Randy, illus. (p. 1879)
Fox-Lee, Susan, jt. auth. see Fox-Lee, Kyme.
Fox-Lee, Susan & Fox-Lee, Kyme. "What Are Parents?" Jennings, Randy, illus. (p. 1879)
Foxley, Janet. Muncle Trogg. (p. 1191)
—Muncle Trogg. O'Kif, illus. (p. 1191)
Foxley Leach, Deba. Grant Wood: The Artist in the Hayloft. (p. 710)
Foxman, Paul. Worried Child: Recognizing Anxiety in Children & Helping Them Heal. (p. 1961)
Fox-Parrish, et al. Ghost Cats of the Tetons. (p. 670)
—Ghost Cats of the Tetons: Book 2. (p. 670)
—Ghost Cats of the Tetons: Book 3: New Horizons. (p. 670)
Fox-Smith, Angela. Clock-Mess Monster. (p. 333)
Foxton, David. Sepia & Song. (p. 1551)
Foxworthy, Jeff. Dirt on My Shirt: Selected Poems. Björkman, Steve, illus. (p. 446)
—Dirt on My Shirt. Björkman, Steve, illus. (p. 446)
—Hide!!! Björkman, Steve, illus. (p. 776)
—Silly Street. Björkman, Steve, illus. (p. 1576)
Foxx, Darla J. Alexis Mcdougal starring in... Secrets Are Confidential Business!!! A sequel to Alexis Mcdougal starring in... the Day I Met My New Special Friend. (p. 37)
—Alexis Mcdougal starring in the Day I Met My New Special Friend. (p. 37)
Foxx, Teralene S., jt. auth. see Carlisi, Alison.
Foxxe, Ellen. Rising Seas: Shorelines under Threat. (p. 1475)
Foxxe, Ellen, ed. Size, Composition, & Surface Features of the Planets Orbiting the Sun: An Anthology of Current Thought. (p. 1583)
Foy, Debbie. Civil-Rights Activists. (p. 324)
—Medical Pioneers. (p. 1118)
—Musicians. (p. 1194)
—Simon Cowell: Global Music Mogul. (p. 1577)
Foy, Denis, illus. see Gallina, Danielle.
Foy, Don. Israel. (p. 893)
Foye, Lloyd, illus. see Arena, Jacqueline.
Foye, Lloyd, illus. see Dinbergs, Holly Smith.
Foye, Lloyd, illus. see Mullins, Julie.
Foyt, Victoria. Virtual Life of Lexie Diamond. (p. 1844)
Fra, Irene, illus. see García-Castellano, Ana.
Fra, Irene, illus. see Montes, Juan Mari & Montes Gonzalo, Juan Mari.
Frabetti, Carlo. Magia Mas Poderosa. (p. 1071)
Fraction, Matt. Annotated Mantooth! (p. 87)
—Defenders by Matt Fraction - Volume 2. Dodson, Terry & Pierfederici, Mirco, illus. (p. 423)
—Mighty Thor: Fraction - Coipel. Marvel Comics Staff & Coipel, Olivier, illus. (p. 1140)
—My Monsters Di Giandomenico, Carmine et al, illus. (p. 1214)
Fractions Cards Staff. LP-Fractions: Level 2 Math. (p. 1061)
Fractured Pixels Staff, illus. see Universal Books (Panama) Staff & King, Trey.
Frader, Laura L. Industrial Revolution: A History in Documents. (p. 872)
Fradin, Dennis, jt. auth. see Fradin, Dennis Brindell.
Fradin, Dennis, jt. auth. see Fradin, Judy.
Fradin, Dennis B. Underground Railroad. (p. 1814)
Fradin, Dennis B. & Fradin, Judith Bloom. Saving. (p. 1517)
Fradin, Dennis Brindell. Alamo. (p. 33)
—Battle of Gettysburg. (p. 146)
—Battle of Yorktown. (p. 147)
—Bill of Rights. (p. 186)
—Boston Massacre. (p. 215)
—Boston Tea Party. (p. 215)
—California Gold Rush. (p. 253)
—Custer's Last Stand. (p. 395)
—Declaration of Independence. (p. 422)
—Emancipation Proclamation. (p. 517)
—First Lunar Landing. (p. 596)
—Founders: The 39 Stories Behind the U. S. Constitution. McCurdy, Michael, illus. (p. 624)
—Jamestown, Virginia. (p. 907)
—Let It Begin Here! Lexington & Concord - First Battles of the American Revolution. Day, Larry, illus. (p. 994)
—Louisiana Purchase. (p. 1058)
—Mayflower Compact. (p. 1113)
—Montgomery Bus Boycott. (p. 1170)
—Nicolaus Copernicus: The Earth Is a Planet. von Buhler, Cynthia, tr. (p. 1251)
—September 11, 2001. (p. 1551)
—Signers: The 56 Stories Behind the Declaration of Independence. McCurdy, Michael, illus. (p. 1574)
—Stamp Act of 1765. (p. 1639)
—Tell Us a Tale, Hans! The Life of Hans Christian Andersen. von Buhler, Cynthia, illus. (p. 1717)
—Trail of Tears. (p. 1776)
—Turning Points in History (p. 1798)
—Turning Points in U. S. History - Group 2 (p. 1798)
—U. S. Constitution. (p. 1806)
—Underground Railroad. (p. 1814)
—Who Was Ben Franklin? O'Brien, John, illus. (p. 1918)
—Who Was Thomas Jefferson? Harrison, Nancy & O'Brien, John, illus. (p. 1919)
—¿Quién Fue Tomás Jefferson? (Who Was Thomas Jefferson?) O'Brien, John, illus. (p. 1427)
Fradin, Dennis Brindell, jt. auth. see Fradin, Judith Bloom.
Fradin, Dennis Brindell, jt. auth. see Fradin, Judith.
Fradin, Dennis Brindell, jt. auth. see Fradin, Judy.
Fradin, Dennis Brindell & Day, Larry. Let It Begin Here! Lexington & Concord - First Battles of the American Revolution. (p. 994)
Fradin, Dennis Brindell & Fradin, Dennis. Who Was Thomas Jefferson? (p. 1919)
Fradin, Dennis Brindell & Fradin, Judith Bloom. 5,000 Miles to Freedom: Ellen & William Craft's Flight from Slavery. (p. 2003)
—Borrowing. (p. 214)
—Earning. (p. 494)
—Hurricane Katrina. (p. 829)
—Investing. (p. 885)
—Irish Potato Famine. (p. 888)
—Price of Freedom: How One Town Stood up to Slavery. Velasquez, Eric, illus. (p. 1398)
—Spending. (p. 1625)
—Zora! The Life of Zora Neale Hurston. (p. 1990)
Fradin, Dennis Brindell & Fradin, Judy. Tsunamis. (p. 1795)
Fradin, Judith & Fradin, Dennis Brindell. Volcanoes. (p. 1849)
Fradin, Judith Bloom, jt. auth. see Fradin, Dennis B.
Fradin, Judith Bloom, jt. auth. see Fradin, Dennis Brindell.
Fradin, Judith Bloom & Fradin, Dennis Brindell. Hurricanes. (p. 830)
—Lewis & Clark Expedition. (p. 1004)
—Salem Witch Trials. (p. 1504)
Fradin, Judith Bloom, et al. Earthquakes. (p. 497)
Fradin, Judy, jt. auth. see Fradin, Dennis Brindell.
Fradin, Judy & Fradin, Dennis. Tornado! The Story Behind These Twisting, Turning, Spinning, & Spiraling Storms. (p. 1770)
Fradin, Judy & Fradin, Dennis Brindell. Droughts. (p. 486)
—Tsunamis. (p. 1795)
Fradkin, Irving & Arruda, Gilda. Developing Mind: A Workbook for Today's Youth. (p. 431)
Fradon, Ramona. Dinosaur That Got Tired of Being Extinct. (p. 443)
Fraga, Mana F., jt. auth. see Perera, Hilda.
Fragasso, Ruth Ann (Reichner). Little Boy Who Ate Like a Bird. (p. 1025)
Frager, Ray. Baltimore Orioles. (p. 135)
—Dallas Mavericks. (p. 401)
—LSU Tigers. (p. 1061)
—New Jersey Nets. (p. 1245)
—Oklahoma City Thunder. (p. 1283)
—Pittsburgh Pirates. (p. 1364)
—Washington Wizards. (p. 1860)
Fraggalosch, Audrey. Land of the Wild Llama: A Story of the Patagonian Andes. Denman, Michael & Huiett, William J., illus. (p. 973)
—Land of the Wild Llama: A Story of the Patagonian Andes, Including 10" Toy. Denman, Michael & Huiett, William J., illus. (p. 973)
—Let's Explore, Moose! Forest, Crista, illus. (p. 996)
—Trails above the Tree Line: A Story of a Rocky Mountain Meadow. Bond, Higgins, illus. (p. 1776)
Fraggalosch, Audrey & Eberhart, Donald G. Grizzly Bear Family. (p. 724)
Fraggalosch, Audrey M. Grizzly Bear Family. Eberhart, Donald G., illus. (p. 724)
Fraggalosch, Crista, illus. see Fraggolosch, Audrey.
Fraggolosch, Audrey. Land of the Wild Llama: A Story of the Patagonian Andes. (p. 973)
—Northern Refuge: A Story of a Canadian Boreal Forest. Fraggalosch, Crista, illus. (p. 1266)
Fragoso, Sarah. Paleo Pals: Jimmy & the Carrot Rocket Ship. (p. 1319)
Fragoza, Samuel. Josh & the Sock Army. (p. 926)
Frahm, Paul, illus. see St Jean, Catherine Avery.
Frahm, Paul, illus. see St. Jean, Catherine.
Frahm, Randy. Deer Hunting. (p. 423)
—Duck Hunting. (p. 488)
Fraiberg, Jordanna. In Your Room. (p. 868)
—Our Song. (p. 1310)
Frail, Edward J. First Gospel. (p. 595)
Frailey, Cheris, jt. auth. see Eisenberg, Rebecca.
Fraillon, Z. Creeped Out. (p. 381)
—Locked In. Swingler, Simon, illus. (p. 1045)
—Monstrum House Bind-Up. (p. 1169)
—Sucked Under. (p. 1672)
—Taken Over. (p. 1697)
Fraillon, Zana. When No-One's Looking: On the Farm. Masciullo, Lucia, illus. (p. 1904)
Frainier, Tamara, jt. auth. see Merilatt, James.
Fraioli, James O. Polar Ice Expedition: With Jean-Michel Cousteau. (p. 1379)
Frake, Barbara, illus. see Falcone, Karen.
Frakes, Clint, ed. see Vili, Fane.
Frakes, Jack. Acting for Life: A Textbook on Acting (p. 10)
Frakes, Robert M. Writing for College History. (p. 1964)
Fraley, Patty. Fear at Night: To Matthew. (p. 579)
—One Day I Will Grow Up. (p. 1294)
—One Day I Will Grow Up. Worrell, Nicole, illus. (p. 1294)
Fralin, Alfred G. & Szeps-Fralin, Christiane. Francais Vivant 1. (p. 627)
—Francais Vivant 2. (p. 627)
Fralin, Alfred G., et al. Francais Vivant 3. (p. 627)
Frame, Andrew Graham. Stein: The Chipmunk Who Became an Engineer. (p. 1646)
—Stein: The Chipmunk Who Succeeds by Brain Power. (p. 1646)
Framestore, illus. see Weston, Robert Paul.
Framingham Community Charter School Grade Students. Rainforest Exhibits: How We Learned about Designing & Creating an Authentic Biome. (p. 1436)
Framke, Jilly. Prayer Power: With Nehemiah the Praying Mantis. (p. 1393)
Framncavillo, John O. Godfather's Boyscout Memories. (p. 690)
Frampton, Callie, jt. auth. see Mills, Nathan.
Frampton, Caytie. Bernard's Winter Nap. (p. 167)
Frampton, Colleen Mesler. Margret's Morning. (p. 1093)
Frampton, David. Beastie ABC. Frampton, David, illus. (p. 152)
—Mr. Ferlinghetti's Poem. Frampton, David, illus. (p. 1185)
—Whole Night Through: A Lullaby. Frampton, David, illus. (p. 1920)
—Whole Night Through. Frampton, David, illus. (p. 1920)
Frampton, David, illus. see Grimes, Nikki.
Frampton, David, illus. see Mora, Pat.
Frampton, Otis. Red Riding Hood, Superhero. Frampton, Otis, illus. (p. 1455)
Frampton, Otis, illus. see Comeau, Joey, et al.
Frampton, Otis, illus. see Downer, Denise.
Francais, Isabelle, photos by see Fernandez, Amy.
Francavilla, Francesco. Man Without Fear: Urban Jungle. Vol. 1 (p. 1086)
Francavilla, Francesco, illus. see Clencin, Scott.
France, Anatole. Man Who Married a Dumb Wife. Landes, William-Alan, ed. (p. 1086)
France, Mark, illus. see Stanley, Dean.
France, Richard. Joshua Stories: Book 1 - New School, New Friends. (p. 927)
Frances, Barbara. Lottie's Adventure: A Kidnapping Unraveled. (p. 1057)
Frances, Dee. Pink Milk Sea Coloring Book. (p. 1360)
—Pink Milk Sea Coloring Book. Patrick, Scot, illus. (p. 1360)
Frances, Dee, ed. Short Stories, Puzzles & More: 1998 Edition. (p. 1569)
Frances, Ethel & Miller, Marcia. Tales from a Tail Wagging Dog. Starr, Joyce, ed. (p. 1701)
Frances Holloway. Turtle That Lived in the Sand. (p. 1798)
Frances, Janie. Krissy the Littlest Ladybug. (p. 967)
Frances Lincoln Editors, jt. auth. see Delpech, Sylvie.
Frances Lincoln Staff, ed. Treasury of Prayers. Weatherill, Steve, illus. (p. 1783)
Frances, Nelle. Ben, His Helmet & Hats Off. Ambroz, Mark, illus. (p. 163)
—Ben, His Helmet & the Crashing Cymbals. Ambroz, Mark, illus. (p. 163)
—Ben, His Helmet & the Too Tight Hair. Ambroz, Mark, illus. (p. 163)
Francesc Bargada Studios Staff & Staff, Di I. Around the World in 80 Bucks. (p. 100)
Francesca, Sieglinde de. Donsy of Gnomes. (p. 466)
Franceschelli, Christopher. Alphablock. Peskimo, illus. (p. 50)
—Big Green Square. (p. 181)
—Dinoblock. Peskimo, illus. (p. 441)
—Oliver. (p. 1285)
—Red Apple, Yellow Banana & the Blue Cockatoo: An Alphabet Adventure. (p. 1453)
Franceschelli, Christopher, jt. auth. see Parot, Annelore.
Franceschelli, Christopher & Peskimo. Countablock. (p. 370)
Francesco, D'Adamo. Iqbal. (p. 886)
Franchino, Vicky. Animal Architects. (p. 76)
—Animal Brainiacs. (p. 77)
—Animal Camouflage. (p. 77)
—Animal Mash-Ups. (p. 78)
—Animal Migrations. (p. 78)
—Arctic Foxes. (p. 96)
—Black Mambas. (p. 196)
—Brazil. (p. 224)
—Droughts. (p. 486)
—Experiment with Soil. (p. 549)
—Genetically Modified Foods. (p. 660)
—Germany. (p. 666)
—Gorillas. (p. 703)
—How Did They Build That? Bridge. (p. 806)
—How Did They Build That? Skyscraper. (p. 806)
—It's Cool to Learn about Countries: Turkey. (p. 896)
—It's Cool to Learn about the United States Northeast. (p. 896)
—Jaguars. (p. 905)
—Motorcycles. (p. 1179)
—Northeast. (p. 1265)
—Philippines. (p. 1350)
—Roberto Clemente. (p. 1479)
—Scorpions. (p. 1530)
—Sea Turtles. (p. 1535)
—Spider Monkeys. (p. 1626)
—Super Cool Science Experiments: Soil. (p. 1679)
—Tarantulas. (p. 1706)
—Tigers. (p. 1749)
—Tigers - Nature's Children. (p. 1749)
Francia, Giada. Alex & Penny in China Jigsaw Book. (p. 35)
—Alex & Penny in Egypt Jigsaw Book. (p. 35)
—Alex & Penny's Italy Jigsaw Book. Colombo, Angelo, illus. (p. 35)
—Alex & Penny's Wild West Jigsaw Book. Colombo, Angelo, illus. (p. 35)
—In the Wild West on MacKenzie's Trail. McCloskey, Erin, ed. (p. 868)
Francia, Giada, ed. Ballooning over Italy: An Extraordinary Voyage Packed with Games & Fantastic Adventures; Special Agents. Ezrin, Amy, tr. (p. 135)
Franciere, Arlette, tr. see Beissel, Henry.
Francillon, R. E. Gods & Heroes: An Introduction to Greek Mythology (Yesterday's Classics) (p. 690)
Francine, Gerstein, jt. auth. see Fromer, Liza.
Francine Ngardab, Riches, illus. see Pitt, Tamina & Terri, Janke.
Franciosa, John F. Little Johnny Lion. (p. 1029)
Franciosi, Pete. Dusty Wants A Kitty. (p. 490)
Francis. More Saints of the Eucharist. (p. 1174)
Francis, Aidan. Prince Fielder: Home-Run King. (p. 1401)
Francis, Amber Rose, illus. see Blackmore, Charlotte Lozano.
Francis, Amy. Has Child Behavior Worsened? Greenhaven Press Editors, ed. (p. 752)
—Local Food Movement. (p. 1044)
—Road Rage. Greenhaven Press Editors, ed. (p. 1477)
—U. S. Policy on Cuba. (p. 1807)
—Vegetarianism. (p. 1834)
—Wind Farms. (p. 1935)
Francis, Amy M. Why Is Daddy Different? Dealing with Huntington's Disease. (p. 1925)
Francis, Andre. Cultural Instruments: Big Book: Level R. Group 1. (p. 391)
Francis, Anwen. Siani Shetland. (p. 1572)
Francis, Azra Daniel. Grampa's Stories. (p. 706)
—Grandpa's Stories. (p. 710)
Francis, Barbara. Are You Misusing Other People's Words? What Plagiarism Is & How to Avoid It. (p. 97)
—Other People's Words: What Plagiarism Is & How to Avoid It. (p. 1306)
Francis, Bill, jt. auth. see Mills, Nathan.
Francis, Claudette. Jesus Is Risen: An Easter Play for Children. (p. 915)
Francis, Claudia Elizabeth Ruth. Island Issues. (p. 892)
Francis, Dale. Quelbe Method: Music Fundamentals in Quelbe Ensembles. (p. 1425)
Francis, Daniel. Far West: The Story of British Columbia. (p. 572)
Francis, David. Spiritual Gifts a Practical Guide to How God Works Through You. (p. 1629)
Francis, David, illus. see Watts, Frances.
Francis, Dick. Break In. (p. 224)
Francis, Doris, et al. Secret Cemetery. (p. 1540)
Francis, Dorothy Brenner. Courage on the Oregon Trail. (p. 372)
Francis, Elizabeth. Fishing on Father's Day. (p. 599)
Francis, Eugenia. Ensene a Su Hijo: Las Tablas de Multiplicar (Written in Spanish) (p. 531)
Francis, G. W. Electrostatic Experiments: An Encyclopedia of Early Electrostatic Experiments, Demonstrations, Devices, & Apparatus. Jefimenko, Oleg D., ed. (p. 510)
Francis, Gill. Chambers Language Builder. (p. 289)
Francis, Guy, illus. see Bostrom, Kathleen Long.
Francis, Guy, illus. see Deutsch, Stacia & Cohon, Rhody.
Francis, Guy, illus. see Hale, Bruce.
Francis, Guy, illus. see Ikids Staff.
Francis, Guy, illus. see Jones, Marcia Thornton & Dadey, Debbie.
Francis, Guy, illus. see Kehoe, Tim.
Francis, Guy, illus. see Kurtz, Chris.
Francis, Guy, illus. see Mills, Claudia.
Francis, Guy, illus. see Pace, Anne Marie.
Francis, Guy, illus. see Perry, Phyllis Jean.
Francis, Guy, illus. see Ryder, Joanne.
Francis, Guy, illus. see Soderberg, Erin.
Francis, Guy, illus. see Teitel, Linda & Teitel, Linda Phillips.
Francis, Guy, illus. see Teitel, Linda Phillips.
Francis, Isabelle. New York City: Yesterday & Today: Understand Properties of Multiplication (p. 1248)
Francis, Jamaine. Adventures of Pb & Brown Bear: Lost & Found. (p. 21)
Francis, James. Visit the Liberty Bell. (p. 1845)
Francis, Jamie, illus. see deLeon Diaz, Rosa, et al.
Francis, Jan. Animal Tales. (p. 80)
Francis, Jan, jt. auth. see Baxter, Nicola.
Francis, JennaKay. Ferry Boat. Woodward II, Ed, illus. (p. 582)
—Michael's Safari. Howarth, Craig, illus. (p. 1135)
Francis, Jim. Great NASCAR Champions. (p. 717)
—History of NASCAR. (p. 784)
—Stock Car Secrets. (p. 1651)
Francis, Jo. Diego Goes to the Beach: Represent & Solve Addition Problems. (p. 437)
Francis, John, illus. see Cheshire, Gerard.
Francis, John, illus. see Franklin, Carolyn.
Francis, John, illus. see Glover, Harry.
Francis, John, illus. see MacLaine, James.
Francis, John, illus. see Mugford, Simon.
Francis, John, illus. see Stonehouse, Bernard. & Bertram, Esther.
Francis, Lauren, illus. see Yoxen, Jackie.
Francis, Lee DeCora. Kunu's Basket: A Story of Indian Island Drucker, Susan, illus. (p. 968)
Francis, Lilian. Supper Dance. (p. 1684)
Francis, Mark & Foster, Hal. Pop. (p. 1384)
Francis, Marnie, et al. Green Isles of the Ocean. Evans, Fran et al, illus. (p. 722)
Francis, Matthew. Where the People Are: Language & Community in the Poetry of W. S. Graham. (p. 1909)
Francis, Melissa. Bite Me! (p. 194)
Francis, Melissa Mckenzie. Love Sucks! (p. 1060)
Francis, Michael H. Yellowstone Memories: 30 Years of Photographs & Stories. (p. 1970)
Francis, Michael Harlowe, photos by see Wilkinson, Todd.
Francis, Nina. Rosemary's Story. (p. 1489)
Francis, Pauline. Sam Stars at Shakespeare's Globe. Tattersfield, Jane, illus. (p. 1507)
Francis, Pauline & Alcott, Louisa May. Little Women. (p. 1038)
Francis, Pauline & Burnett, Frances Hodgson. Secret Garden. (p. 1541)
Francis, Pauline & London, Jack. White Fang. (p. 1912)
Francis, Pauline & Verne, Jules. Journey to the Center of the Earth. (p. 929)
Francis, Pauline & Wyndham, John. Day of the Triffids. (p. 414)
Francis, Pauline, retold by. Call of the Wild. (p. 254)
—Count of Monte Cristo. (p. 369)
—Kidnapped. (p. 952)
—Mark of Zorro. (p. 1095)
—Phantom of the Opera. (p. 1349)
—Treasure Island. (p. 1781)
—Turn of the Screw. (p. 1797)
—White Fang. (p. 1912)
Francis, Peter, illus. see Keene, Carolyn.
Francis, Richard E., jt. auth. see R.D.Haire.
Francis, Sandra. Gerald R. Ford. (p. 666)
—Rutherford B. Hayes. (p. 1499)
Francis, Stella M. Campfire Girls in the Allegheny Mountains. (p. 257)

Francis, Suzanne. Ancient Animals. (p. 67)
—Dangerous & Deadly Toxic Animals. (p. 404)
—Europe. (p. 540)
—Extreme Dinos. (p. 556)
—How to Survive When (You Think) There's Nothing to Do. (p. 822)
—On the Prowl: Animal Hunters. (p. 1291)
—Planes: Fire & Rescue the Junior Novelization (Disney Planes: Fire & Rescue) RH Disney Staff, illus. (p. 1367)
—Prehistoric Hunters. (p. 1395)
—Protecting Your Room, Your Stuff & Your Secrets. (p. 1412)
Francis, Suzanne, et al. Spy by Night: Stealth & Secrets after Dark. (p. 1636)
Francis, Taneah. Momma's Little Talk with Mia. (p. 1162)
Francis-Bala, Sundari. Olly Jolly Says - Count Your Blessings. (p. 1287)
Francisco, Abril Berán, jt. auth. see Abril, Paco.
Francisco, Manny, illus. see Romero, Victor Eclar.
Francisco, Ruth. Secret Memoirs of Jacqueline Kennedy Onassis. (p. 1542)
Francisco, Wendy, illus. see Carlson, Melody.
Francisco, Wendy, illus. see Hansen, Janis.
Francisco, Wendy, illus. see Hopkins, Mary Rice.
Francis-Harris, Annabel. Other Side of the Forest. (p. 1306)
Franck, Charlotte. Little Rhymes for Quiet Times. Garvin, Sheri, illus. (p. 1035)
Franck, Herman. Winnie & Thunderose: An Illustrated Story about Friendship. (p. 1937)
Franck, Irene M. & Brownstone, David M. Frontier America (p. 644)
—Riches of the Earth (p. 1470)
Franckowiak, Jon. When I Grow up I Want to be a Nittany Lion. (p. 1903)
Franco, illus. see Baltazar, Art.
Franco, jt. auth. see Art Baltazar Comic Book Staff.
Franco, jt. auth. see Baltazar, Art.
Franco, Betsy. Bees, Snails, & Peacock Tails: Patterns & Shapes... Naturally. Jenkins, Steve, illus. (p. 158)
—Counting Our Way to the 100th Day! Salerno, Steven, illus. (p. 371)
—Counting Poems Flip Chart: 20 Playful Poems That Teach Numbers, Counting, & More. (p. 371)
—Curious Collection of Cats. Wertz, Michael, illus. (p. 392)
—Double Play: Monkeying Around with Addition. Cushman, Doug, illus. (p. 473)
—Funny Fairy Tale Math, Grades 3-4: 15 Rib-Tickling Reproducible Stories with Companion Word Problems That Build Key Math Skills & Concepts. (p. 649)
—Going to Grandma's Farm. (p. 693)
—Messing Around on the Monkey Bars: And Other School Poems for Two Voices. Hartland, Jessie, illus. (p. 1130)
—Metamorphosis: Junior Year. Franco, Tom & Franco, Betsy, illus. (p. 1130)
—Pond Circle. Vitale, Stefano, illus. (p. 1382)
—Riddle Poem of the Day: 180 Guess-Me Poems to Build Phonemic Awareness. (p. 1471)
—Spectacular Selection of Sea Critters: Concrete Poems. Wertz, Michael, illus. (p. 1624)
—Summer Beat. Middleton, Charlotte, illus. (p. 1673)
—Why the Frog Has Big Eyes. (p. 1926)
—Zero Is the Leaves on the Tree. Arihara, Shino, illus. (p. 1986)
Franco, Betsy, jt. auth. see Fleming, Maria.
Franco, Betsy & Franco-Feeney, Betsy. Birdsongs. Jenkins, Steve, illus. (p. 192)
—Why the Frog Has Big Eyes. Kim, Joung Un, illus. (p. 1926)
Franco, Betsy & Salerno, Steven. Mathematickles! (p. 1107)
Franco, Betsy, ed. Falling Hard: 100 Love Poems by Teenagers. (p. 567)
Franco, Eloise. Little Stories. Bredius, Rein, illus. (p. 1037)
—Young Look. (p. 1979)
Franco, Fabiola. Concierto Siniestro. (p. 355)
—Concierto Siniestro Kit. (p. 355)
—Novio Robado. (p. 1268)
Franco, Franco. Dino-Mike! Franco, Franco, illus. (p. 441)
Franco, Karen. Just Hold My Hand. (p. 938)
Franco, Liliana & Bacha, Antoine. Cogito: The Dream. Pt. 2 (p. 338)
—Cogito: The Separation. Pt. 1 (p. 338)
—Cogito: Antoine & Liliana, the Separation. Pt. 1 Franco, Liliana, illus. (p. 338)
Franco, Mauricio, illus. see Mzjica, Elisa.
Franco, Nick. Are You Ready to Paint? (p. 97)
Franco, Paula, illus. see Bolte, Mari.
Franco, Paula, illus. see Jones, Jen.
Franco, Paula, illus. see Morgan, Alex.
Franco, Paula, illus. see Mullarkey, Lisa.
Franco, Sharon, tr. see Argueta, Jorge.
Franco, Sharon, tr. see Byrd, Lee Merrill.
Franco, Sharon, tr. see Cleveland, Alexandra, et al.
Franco, Sharon, tr. see Cohn, Diana.
Franco, Sharon, tr. see Flor Ada, Alma & Campoy, F. Isabel.
Franco, Sharon, tr. see Flor Ada, Alma.
Franco, Tom, illus. see Franco, Betsy.
Francoeur, Christine Marie. Adventures of Jimmy Su: The South Pole. (p. 19)
Franco-Feeney, Betsy, jt. auth. see Franco, Betsy.
Franco-Feeney, Betsy, jt. auth. see Lavin, Christine.
Franco-Feeney, Betsy, jt. auth. see Meachen Rau, Dana.
François, André, illus. see Harris, Isobel.
Francois, Betsy. Horse Who Thinks She's a Cat. (p. 800)
Francois, Jethro. Wondrous Butterfly. (p. 1949)
François, Marie B. My busy day / Jounen m trè Chaje. (p. 1199)
Francois, Rose Darlie. Little Miss Daring Evelynne. (p. 1031)
—Sixteen Eggs & the Frying Pan Clock. (p. 1583)
—When You least Expect It. (p. 1905)
Francois, Saragine. Invisible Blanket. (p. 885)
—White Gorilla & the Three Chimpanzees a Day from the Zoo. (p. 1913)
Francoise. Fanchette & Jeannot: A Little Story with Pictures. (p. 570)
Françoise. Jeanne-Marie Counts Her Sheep. (p. 911)
Francour, Kathleen. Friends Forever. (p. 638)
Francour, Kathleen, illus. see Book Company Staff.
Francour, Kathleen, photos by see Appel, Dee.
Francq, Philippe, illus. see Van Hamme, Jean.
Frandsen, Newell. Out of Town on a Rail. (p. 1311)
Frandsen, Rebekah. Return to Health. (p. 1465)
Franfou, illus. see Burke, Christina.
Franfou Studio, illus. see Atkins, Aimee.
Franfou Studio, illus. see Labuda, Scott A.
Frangiosa, Simon J. Adventures of Tom: Tom's First Day. (p. 24)
Frangouli, Rena, illus. see Papaloizos, Theodore C.
Franjelica. Two Little Memory Collectors. (p. 1804)
Frank, jt. auth. see Costello, Kim.
Frank Alvarado Madrigal. Las Increíbles Aventuras Del Pollito Pío Pío: The Incredible Adventures of Pew Pew, the Little Chicken. (p. 976)
Frank Alvarado Madrigal, jt. auth. see Frank Alvarado Madrigal, Alvarado Madrig.
Frank Alvarado Madrigal, Alvarado Madrig & Frank Alvarado Madrigal. Las Increíbles Aventuras Del Patito Kuak Kuak: The Incredible Adventures of Kuack Kuack, the Little Duck. (p. 976)
Frank, Andrew K. Seminole. (p. 1550)
Frank, Anne. Diary of a Anne Frank. (p. 434)
Frank, Arnold L. Fear of God: A Forgotten Doctrine. Garrett, Desta, ed. (p. 579)
Frank, Church & Barnas, Aloura. Epic Adventures of Whiz Grass & Poot Berry. (p. 532)
Frank, Connie. Sadie & the Night Sky (p. 1501)
Frank, Dave, illus. see Shankman, Ed.
Frank, David. Kids & Sites of Kalamazoo. (p. 952)
Frank, Diana Crone, ed. see Andersen, Hans Christian, et al.
Frank, E. R. Dime. (p. 440)
—Friction. (p. 637)
—Wrecked. (p. 1962)
Frank, Hannah. Ballet Shoes. (p. 134)
—If I Had Three Wishes. (p. 853)
—Train to Baker Street. (p. 1777)
Frank, Hillary. I Can't Tell You. (p. 837)
Frank, Janet & Golden Books Staff. Daddies. Gergely, Tibor, illus. (p. 398)
Frank, Jeffrey Crone, ed. see Andersen, Hans Christian, et al.
Frank, John. Lend a Hand: Poems About Giving. Ladd, London, illus. (p. 991)
—Toughest Cowboy: Or How the Wild West Was Tamed. Pullen, Zachary, illus. (p. 1773)
Frank, John & Pullen, Zachary. Toughest Cowboy: Or How the Wild West Was Tamed. Pullen, Zachary, illus. (p. 1773)
Frank, Katherine. Lucie Duff Gordon: A Passage to Egypt. (p. 1062)
Frank, Lisa. Magical World! Giant Coloring & Activity Book. (p. 1075)
Frank, Lucy. Just Ask Iris. (p. 938)
—Lucky Stars. (p. 1063)
—Two Girls Staring at the Ceiling. (p. 1803)
Frank, Marjorie. Geography Mysteries. Bullock, Kathleen, illus. (p. 662)
—Math Conundrums. MacKenzie, Joy, ed. (p. 1105)
—Vocabulary Escapades. MacKenzie, Joy, ed. (p. 1847)
Frank, Marjorie, ed. see Forte, Imogene, et al.
Frank, Marjorie, jt. auth. see Forte, Imogene.
Frank, Marjorie & Norris, Jill. Graphic Organizers for Math. Bullock, Kathleen, illus. (p. 711)
—Interactive Grammar & Usage Lessons - Sentences, Grades 6-9. Grayson, Cary, ed. (p. 879)
—Word Meaning. Grayson, Cary, ed. (p. 1950)
—Word Structure. Grayson, Cary, ed. (p. 1951)
Frank, Mary Kate. Carrie Underwood. (p. 271)
—Rihanna. (p. 1472)
Frank, Michael. Government in Action. (p. 704)
Frank, Michael, ed. see Benanti, Carol.
Frank, Nicole, jt. auth. see Whyte, Harlinah.
Frank, Nicole & Berg, Elizabeth. United States. (p. 1819)
Frank, Nicole & Lord, Richard A. Germany. (p. 666)
Frank, Pat. Little Warriors. (p. 1037)
Frank, Paul, jt. auth. see Chronicle Books Staff.
Frank, Penny. Adam & Eve. (p. 11)
—David & Goliath. (p. 410)
—Good News for Everyone. (p. 699)
—In the Beginning. (p. 865)
—Jesus on Trial. (p. 916)
—Jesus the Teacher. (p. 916)
—Let My People Go! (p. 994)
—Nueva Familia de Rut. (p. 1270)
—Princess & the Baby. (p. 1402)
—Story of the Good Samaritan. (p. 1661)
—When Zacchaeus Met Jesus. Morris, Tony, illus. (p. 1906)
Frank, Penny & Allsopp, Sophie. First Christmas. (p. 593)
—First Easter. (p. 594)
Frank, Remkiewicz, illus. see Kline, Suzy.
Frank, Remkiewicz, illus. see London, Jonathan.
Frank, Rochelle. So What, Saw-Whet? Gast, Linda, photos by. (p. 1602)
Frank, Samuel, jt. auth. see Le Verrier, Renee.
Frank, Sarah. Filipinos in America. (p. 586)
Frank, Sharon, ed. see Annie's.
Frank, Sharon, ed. see Weglarz, Lynn.
Frank, Thomas, jt. auth. see Yates, Gene.
Frank, Thomas C. What's the Matter with Kansas? How Conservatives Won the Heart of America. (p. 1899)
Frank, Vincent. Six Pack. (p. 1582)
Frank, Vivien & Jaffe, Deborah. Make a Book: Six Different Books to Make, Write, & Illustrate. (p. 1078)
Frankau, Gilbert. One of Us: A Novel in Verse. (p. 1296)
Frankcom, Nicholas. Monivong Hit. (p. 1164)
Franke, Alfe. Julianne Hough. (p. 932)
—Miranda Lambert. (p. 1149)
Franke, Kristina & Leberer, Sigrid. Bunny Kindergarten. (p. 242)
Franke, Livia. Kathleen Battle: American Soprano. (p. 944)
Frankel, Alana, jt. auth. see Publications International Ltd. Staff.
Frankel, Alona. Mi Bacinica y Yo (para El) (p. 1132)
—Mi Bacinica y Yo (para Ella) (p. 1132)
—Once upon a Potty - Boy. Frankel, Alona, illus. (p. 1293)
—Once upon a Potty — Boy. (p. 1293)
—Once upon a Potty — Girl. (p. 1293)
—Once upon a Potty - - Girl. Frankel, Alona, illus. (p. 1293)
—Once upon a Potty Sound Book for Girls. Publications International Ltd. Staff, ed. (p. 1293)
Frankel, Bethenny. Cookie Meets Peanut. Roode, Daniel, illus. (p. 361)
Frankel, Erin. Dare! (p. 406)
—Dare! Heaphy, Paula, illus. (p. 406)
—Nobody! A Story about Overcoming Bullying in Schools. Heaphy, Paula, illus. (p. 1262)
—Nobody! a Story about Overcoming Bullying in Schools. (p. 1262)
—Tough! Heaphy, Paula, illus. (p. 1772)
—Weird! Heaphy, Paula, illus. (p. 1872)
Frankel, Fred. Good Friends Are Hard to Find: Help Your Child Find, Make, & Keep Friends. Wetmore, Barry, illus. (p. 698)
Frankel, Jordana. Ward. (p. 1858)
Frankel, Karen. Projects about Ancient Rome. (p. 1410)
Frankel, Laurie, et al. Funny Bunnies. (p. 649)
—Writing Is Nothing More Than a Guided Dream. (p. 1965)
Frankel, Rachel E., as told by. Twinkle Becomes a Real Tooth Fairy. (p. 1802)
Frankel, Valerie. Henry Potty & the Pet Rock: An Unauthorized Harry Potter Parody. (p. 768)
Frankenberg, Robert, illus. see Falk, Elsa.
Frankenberg, Robert, illus. see Mowat, Farley.
Frankenberger, Elizabeth. Crushes, Creeps & Classmates: A Girl's Guide to Getting along with Boys. (p. 387)
Frankenhuyzen, Gijsbert van, illus. see Frankenhuyzen, Robbyn Smith van.
Frankenhuyzen, Gijsbert van, illus. see Raven, Margot Theis.
Frankenhuyzen, Gijsbert van, illus. see Robinson, Jill & Bekoff, Marc.
Frankenhuyzen, Gijsbert van, illus. see Smith, Roland & Smith, Marie.
Frankenhuyzen, Gijsbert van, illus. see Strother, Ruth.
Frankenhuyzen, Gijsbert van, illus. see Swain, Gwenyth.
Frankenhuyzen, Gijsbert van, illus. see Wargin, Kathy-jo.
Frankenhuyzen, Robbyn Smith van. I Love You Just Enough. Frankenhuyzen, Gijsbert van, illus. (p. 843)
Frankeny, Frankie, photos by see Brennan, Georgeanne.
Frankeny, Frankie, photos by see Hellmich, Mittie.
Frankfeldt, Gwen, illus. see Fleischman, Paul.
Frankfeldt, Gwen & Fleischman, Paul. Dateline - Troy. Frankfeldt, Gwen & Morrow, Glenn, illus. (p. 409)
Frankford, Marilyn. My Tiger Cat. Kaeden Corp. Staff, ed. (p. 1220)
Franklin. Franklin & the Gecko Games. (p. 630)
—Franklin in the Stars. (p. 630)
—Franklin's Spaceship. (p. 631)
—Franklin's Ups & Downs. (p. 631)
Franklin, Benjamin. Experiments & Observations on Electricity. (p. 549)
Franklin, Carl J. North American Box Turtles: Natural History & Captive Maintenance. Killpack, David C., illus. (p. 1264)
Franklin, Carolyn. Big Cats. (p. 180)
—How to Draw Big Cats. (p. 817)
—Prehistoric Animals. Francis, John, illus. (p. 1395)
—Scary Dinosaurs. (p. 1520)
Franklin, Carolyn, illus. see Kant, Tanya.
Franklin, Carolyn, illus. see Stewart, David.
Franklin, Carolyn & Stewart, David. Ocean Life. Franklin, Carolyn, illus. (p. 1276)
—Rain Forest Animals. Franklin, Carolyn, illus. (p. 1434)
Franklin, Cathy. Magical Ballet Shoes: A Pinta & Polly Story Watkins, Tammy, illus. (p. 1074)
—Pinta & Polly Go to the Moon Poole, Tracy, illus. (p. 1361)
Franklin, Deborah. Annette's Christmas Gift. (p. 86)
Franklin, E. Joan. I Eat & I Grow. (p. 838)
Franklin, Emily. Last Night at the Circle Cinema. (p. 978)
Franklin, Emily, jt. auth. see Halpin, Brendan.
Franklin, Ian. Adjectives. (p. 13)
—Basic Sequences. (p. 142)
—Basic Verbs: In Simple Settings (p. 142)
—Categories. (p. 279)
—Cause & Effect. (p. 282)
—Daily Living. (p. 400)
—Early Actions. (p. 493)
—Early Objects. (p. 494)
—Early Opposites. (p. 494)
—Early Sequences. (p. 494)
—Emotions. (p. 520)
—Everyday Objects. (p. 544)
—Food. (p. 612)
—Fun Pictures. (p. 648)
—Guess What? (p. 729)
—Home. (p. 791)
—Indoor Sounds. (p. 872)
—Match Up. (p. 1104)
—More Categories: (Colours, Patterns & Shapes) (p. 1174)
—Objects & Owners. (p. 1275)
—Occupations. (p. 1275)
—Odd One Out. (p. 1278)
—Outdoor Sounds. (p. 1312)
—Possessions. (p. 1387)
—Prepositions. (p. 1396)
—Problem Solving. (p. 1408)
—Simple Sequences. (p. 1578)
—Snack Time. (p. 1595)
—Social Situations. (p. 1604)
—Transport & Vehicles. (p. 1779)
—Verb Tenses. (p. 1836)
—What's Added? (p. 1896)
—What's Different? (p. 1897)
—What's Inside? (p. 1898)
—What's Missing? (p. 1898)
Franklin, J. E. Coming to the Mercy Seat. (p. 348)
Franklin, John Hope, ed. see Dubofsky, Melvyn.
Franklin, John Hope, ed. see Levering, Ralph B.
Franklin, John Hope, ed. see Martin, James Kirby & Lender, Mark Edward.
Franklin, John Hope, ed. see Newmyer, R. Kent.
Franklin, John Hope, ed. see Wright, Donald R.
Franklin, Joseph & Wilson, Antoine. S. E. Hinton. (p. 1499)
Franklin, Kathleen. Uncle Holly saves Christmas. (p. 1811)
Franklin, Kent. Exploring Earth & Space Systems. (p. 552)
Franklin, Kirk. How Do Alligators Praise the Lord? Carrier, Jason, illus. (p. 806)
Franklin, Kristine L. Dove Song. (p. 473)
Franklin, Linda. Into the Pumpkin (p. 881)
Franklin, Liz. Cooking Italian with Kids. (p. 362)
Franklin, Lynn C. & Ferber, Elizabeth. Mundo de la Adopcion: Reflexiones Sobre una Experiencia de la Vida Real. (p. 1191)
Franklin, Mark, illus. see Cowling, Dan.
Franklin McKinley School District Staff. Rap a Middle School Advisory Program. (p. 1438)
Franklin, Miles. My Brilliant Career. (p. 1199)
Franklin, Miriam Spitzer. Extraordinary. (p. 555)
Franklin, Rob. Acorn Warriors: Book One: the Dragonnade. (p. 9)
Franklin, Shawna. Catching Achoo. (p. 279)
Franklin, Shirley A. Emma's Fantastique Word Play. (p. 520)
—Lupita's Quinciner: A Celebration to Remember. (p. 1066)
Franklin, Teil L. Ameelia's Adventures: Ameelia's First Play. (p. 57)
Franklin, Theresa. Don't Forget Daddy. (p. 467)
Franklin, Tony, VIII. Victor's Victory: From Tragedy to Victory - A Legacy & Lessons You'll Never Forget. (p. 1840)
Franklin, Virgil. Story of Sacagawea. (p. 1659)
Franklin, Watts, jt. auth. see Beres, D. B.
Franklin Watts & Scholastic, Inc. Staff, contrib. by. Population 1.3 Billion: China Becomes a Super Superpower. (p. 1385)
Franklin Watts, contrib. by. Wait Skates! & Other Funny Stories. (p. 1852)
Franklin, Yvonne. Charcas. (p. 291)
—Desiertos. (p. 429)
—Océanos. (p. 1277)
—Pantanos. (p. 1321)
—Selvas. (p. 1550)
—Selvas Lluviosas. (p. 1550)
Franklin, Yvonne, jt. auth. see Rice, William.
Frank-McNeil, Julia, jt. auth. see Lestrade, Agnès de.
Frankowski, Leo, jt. auth. see Frankowski, Leo A.
Frankowski, Leo A. & Frankowski, Leo. Boy & His Tank. (p. 217)
Frankowski, Leo & Olsen, Rodger. Lord Conrad's Crusade. (p. 1052)
Franks, Alison. On My Feet! (p. 1289)
Franks, C. J., illus. see Sullivan, Ellen & Moore, Clement C.
Franks, Gary L. Bridges at the Foot of the Rapids: An Illustrated History of Maumee-Perrysburg River Crossings & Construction of the 2002 Fort Meigs Memorial Bridge. (p. 227)
Franks, Gene. Pencil Drawing. (p. 1336)
Franks, Katie. Ashley Tisdale. (p. 106)
—Bees up Close. (p. 158)
—Bees up Close / Las Abejas. (p. 158)
—Bees up Close/Las Abejas. Sanz, Pilar, tr. from ENG. (p. 158)
—Choppers. (p. 310)
—Cool Bikes. (p. 362)
—Cool Bikes/Motos Cool. (p. 362)
—Corn up Close. (p. 367)
—Corn up Close / el Maiz. (p. 367)
—Corn up Close/el Maiz. Sanz, Pilar, tr. from ENG. (p. 367)
—Dirt Bikes. (p. 446)
—Drake Bell & Josh Peck. (p. 479)
—Dream Jobs (p. 483)
—Dylan & Cole Sprouse. (p. 491)
—Elephants. (p. 511)
—I Want to Be a Baseball Player. (p. 847)
—I Want to Be a Basketball Player. (p. 847)
—I Want to Be a Movie Star. (p. 847)
—I Want to Be a Race Car Driver. (p. 847)
—I Want to Be a Supermodel. (p. 847)
—Kangaroos. (p. 942)
—Kid Stars! (p. 951)
—Lions. (p. 1021)
—Miley Cyrus. (p. 1142)
—Miranda Cosgrove. (p. 1149)
—Owls up Close. (p. 1315)
—Owls up Close / Los Buhos. (p. 1315)
—Owls up Close/Los Buhos. Sanz, Pilar, tr. from ENG. (p. 1315)
—Pandas. (p. 1321)
—Penguins. (p. 1337)
—Quiero Ser Beisbolista. (p. 1428)
—Quiero Ser Piloto de Carreras. (p. 1428)
—Sea Lions. (p. 1534)
—Spiders up Close. (p. 1627)
—Spiders up Close / Las Aranas. (p. 1627)
—Spiders up Close/Las Aranas. Sanz, Pilar, tr. from ENG. (p. 1627)
—Street Bikes. (p. 1666)
—Street Bikes/Motos de Calle. (p. 1666)
—Sunflowers up Close. (p. 1677)
—Sunflowers up Close / Los Girasoles. (p. 1677)
—Sunflowers up Close/Los Girasoles. Sanz, Pilar, tr. from ENG. (p. 1677)
—Superbikes. (p. 1682)
—Tricks with Bikes. (p. 1786)
—Tricks with Bikes/Trucos con la Moto. (p. 1786)
—Turtles up Close. (p. 1799)
—Turtles up Close / Las Tortugas. (p. 1799)
—Turtles up Close/Las Tortugas. Sanz, Pilar, tr. from ENG. (p. 1799)
—Zac Efron. (p. 1984)
Franks, Lucinda. Timeless: Love, Morgenthau, & Me. (p. 1754)
Franks, Melissa. Warped! An Adventure Through Time: A What-a-saur? Bk. 1 (p. 1858)

Franks, Sharon E. & Cohen, Judith Love. You Can Be A Woman Oceanographer. Katz, David Arthur, illus. (p. 1974)
Franks, T. S. ZZ Dogs. d'Obrin, Felix, illus. (p. 1990)
Frankston, Evan. Mountains & Valleys: What's the Difference? (p. 1181)
Franquin, André. Spirou & Fantasio Vol. 5: The Marsupilami Thieves. (p. 1629)
Fransen, Mi-sA-lê. Scampi the Scallop. (p. 1519)
Fransisco, Tina, illus. see Golden Books.
Fransisco, Wendy, illus. see Hansen, Janis.
Franskevich, Ala, compiled by. Underwater World. (p. 1817)
Franson, Leanne, illus. see Adler, David A.
Franson, Leanne, illus. see Nayer, Judy.
Franson, Leanne, illus. see Packard, Mary, ed.
Franson, Leanne, illus. see Packard, Mary.
Franson, Leanne, illus. see Pawagi, Manjusha.
Franson, Leanne, illus. see Pearce, Jacqueline.
Franson, Leanne, illus. see Roberts, Ken.
Franson, Leanne, illus. see Wishinsky, Frieda & Griffiths, Dean.
Franson, Leanne, illus. see Wishinsky, Frieda.
Franson, Leanne, jt. auth. see Desrosiers, Sylvie.
Fransoy, Monse, illus. see Perrault, Charles.
Frantz, Donna. Silly Gilly Gil - Gay L-U-V. Evans, Gabriel, illus. (p. 1576)
Frantz, Jennifer. Color & Iron-Ons Book. Middleton, Gayle, illus. (p. 342)
—Lion, the Witch & the Wardrobe: Tea with Mr. Tumnus. Downer, Maggie, illus. (p. 1020)
Frantz, Jennifer, jt. auth. see HarperCollins Publishers Ltd. Staff.
Frantz, Jennifer, adapted by. Narnia: Welcome to Narnia. (p. 1229)
Frantz, Kevin. Yes, Santa Claus, There Is a Virginia: The True Story of Santa's First Computerized Christmas. Velarde, Chase, illus. (p. 1970)
Frantz, Rosemary. Bible Men & Women from A to Z: Rhymes, Questions & Activities. (p. 175)
Franz, Del. My Max Score AP U. S. Government & Politics: Maximize Your Score in Less Time. (p. 1214)
Franz, Hübner, jt. auth. see Hubner, Franz.
Franz, Jim. World Without Faces. (p. 1959)
Franz, Kevin. Into the Hidden Lands: A Castle Rose Adventure. Stigler, Marilyn, illus. (p. 881)
—Princess Sisters & the Underwater City. Stigler, Marilyn, illus. (p. 1405)
Franzen, Lenore. Anger. (p. 75)
—Fear. (p. 579)
—Happiness. (p. 744)
—Sadness. (p. 1501)
—Statues of Easter Island. (p. 1645)
—Venus Williams. (p. 1836)
Franzen, Sean, photos by see Schindel, John.
Franzese, Nora Tapp, illus. see Wigden, Susan.
Fraser, Afton, jt. auth. see Smith, Miriam.
Fraser, Alison & Lyon, Abby. Princeton University College Prowler off the Record. (p. 1406)
Fraser, B. Beth. Consider This Before Having a Child: Seeds for Thought Before Having a Child. (p. 359)
Fraser, Betty, illus. see Hoberman, Mary Ann.
Fraser, Betty, illus. see Lowery, Lawrence F.
Fraser, Chelsea Curtis. Around the World in Ten Days. (p. 101)
Fraser, Christine Marion. Rhanna. (p. 1467)
Fraser, Diane L. Play Dancing: Discovering & Developing Creativity in Young Children. (p. 1371)
Fraser, Fil. Alberta's Camelot: Culture & the Arts in the Lougheed Years. Vol. 1 (p. 35)
Fraser, Frank. Bearista: A Grand Adventure. Fraser, Frank, illus. (p. 151)
—Bible Amigos: Five Loaves, Two Fish, & One Big Hat. (p. 175)
—Bible Amigos: Jonah & the Bear. (p. 175)
Fraser, Ian. Life with Mammoth Fraser, Mary Ann, illus. (p. 1013)
—Meet Mammoth Fraser, Mary Ann, illus. (p. 1121)
Fraser, Janine M. Mariposa de Abdullah. (p. 1094)
Fraser, Jennifer. Scott the Starfish - an Unexpected Adventure! Eastley, Melanie, illus. (p. 1531)
Fraser, Jess. Jungle Jingles. (p. 935)
—Legend of the Cosmic Cowboy. (p. 989)
Fraser, Jess, illus. see Fraser, Lynne.
Fraser, Jess, illus. see Wright, Bill, Sr.
Fraser, Kara-Anne, illus. see Reed, Janet.
Fraser, Kay, illus. see Stevens, Eric.
Fraser, Kay, jt. auth. see Bracken, Beth.
Fraser, Kevin, illus. see Bahz, Kahanni.
Fraser, Lynne. Henry's New Home. Fraser, Jess, illus. (p. 769)
Fraser, Mark. Marco: A Novel for Kids That Depicts the Value of Family, Faith, Focus & Teamwork. (p. 1092)
Fraser, Mary Ann. Heebie-Jeebie Jamboree. (p. 762)
—I. Q. Goes to the Library. Fraser, Mary Ann, illus. (p. 844)
—I. Q., It's Time. Fraser, Mary Ann, illus. (p. 844)
—No Yeti Yet. (p. 1261)
—Pet Shop Follies. (p. 1345)
—Pet Shop Lullaby. Fraser, Mary Ann, illus. (p. 1345)
Fraser, Mary Ann, illus. see Bunting, Eve.
Fraser, Mary Ann, illus. see Fraser, Ian.
Fraser, P. J. Mouse with the Torch (p. 1182)
Fraser, Richard M., illus. see Clark, Admont G.
Fraser, Robert. Ben Okri. (p. 163)
Fraser, Sigmund, illus. see Wallace, Jazey.
Fraser, Tara Lynn. My Kitty. (p. 1211)
Fraser, Theresa. Billy Had to Move: A Foster Care Story. Walton, Alex, illus. (p. 187)
—Billy Had to Move. Walton, Alex, illus. (p. 187)
Fraser, W. A. Gold Wolf. (p. 694)
—Outcasts. (p. 1312)
Fraser-Allen, Johnny, illus. see Lilly, Evangeline.
Frashier, Giva. Bogey the Golf Bug. (p. 207)
Frasier, Anne, pseud. Play Dead (p. 1371)
Frasier, Debra. Fabulous Fair Alphabet. Frasier, Debra, illus. (p. 560)
—Miss Alaineus: A Vocabulary Disaster. Frasier, Debra, illus. (p. 1151)
—On the Day You Were Born. (p. 1290)
—Spike: Ugliest Dog in the Universe. Frasier, Debra, illus. (p. 1627)
Frassetto, Michael. Encyclopedia of Barbarian Europe: Society in Transformation (p. 525)
Frater, Glynis. Business & Communication Systems. (p. 244)
Frati, Dorothy. Friendly Bubbles. (p. 637)
Fraticelli, Damin, jt. auth. see Schuff, Nicolás.
Frattini, Stephane. Face-to-Face with the Cat. Klein, Jean-Louis & Hubert, Marie-Luce, illus. (p. 560)
—Tushes & Tails! (p. 1799)
Frattini, Stéphane. Who's Looking at You? (p. 1920)
Fraustino, Lisa Rowe. Hole in the Wall. (p. 788)
Fraustino, Lisa Rowe, ed. Don't Cramp My Style: Stories about That Time of the Month. (p. 467)
Fravel, Gale. Fellsmere the Pirate, Chipley's Adventure. Fravel, Harold, illus. (p. 581)
Fravel, Harold, illus. see Fravel, Gale.
Frawley, Georgia, jt. auth. see Frawley, Ken.
Frawley, Keith, illus. see Urey, Gary.
Frawley, Keith, jt. illus. see Marlet, Nico.
Frawley, Ken & Frawley, Georgia. Play-Along Songs: Musical Activities for Children. Vol. 1 (p. 1371)
Frayre, A. R. Shannon Cabbage-Head. (p. 1559)
Frazao, Catia, illus. see Guatemala, Anne.
Frazee, Marla. Boot & Shoe. Frazee, Marla, illus. (p. 213)
—Boss Baby. Frazee, Marla, illus. (p. 215)
—Couple of Boys Have the Best Week Ever. (p. 372)
—Hush, Little Baby: A Folk Song with Pictures. (p. 830)
—Roller Coaster. (p. 1485)
—Roller Coaster. Frazee, Marla, illus. (p. 1485)
—Santa Claus the World's Number One Toy Expert. (p. 1511)
—Santa Claus - The World's Number One Toy Expert. (p. 1511)
—Walk On! A Guide for Babies of All Ages. Frazee, Marla, illus. (p. 1853)
—Why Did the Chicken Cross the Road? (p. 1923)
Frazee, Marla, illus. see Clements, Andrew.
Frazee, Marla, illus. see Fox, Mem.
Frazee, Marla, illus. see Hoberman, Mary Ann.
Frazee, Marla, illus. see Meyers, Susan & Fox, Mem.
Frazee, Marla, illus. see Meyers, Susan.
Frazee, Marla, illus. see Pennypacker, Sara.
Frazee, Marla, illus. see Rylant, Cynthia.
Frazee, Marla, illus. see Scanlon, Liz Garton.
Frazee, Marla, illus. see Silverman, Erica.
Frazee, Marla, illus. see Smith, Linda.
Frazee, Marla, jt. auth. see Ray, Mary Lyn.
Frazee, Randy. Believe Storybook: Think, Act, Be Like Jesus Adams, Steve, illus. (p. 162)
Frazee, Randy, jt. auth. see Willard, Dallas.
Frazel, Ellen. Adders. (p. 11)
—American Quarter Horse. (p. 62)
—Appaloosa Horse. (p. 92)
—Bow Hunting. (p. 216)
—Bull Snakes. (p. 240)
—Clydesdale Horse. (p. 336)
—Deep Sea Fishing. (p. 423)
—Ethiopia. (p. 539)
—Honduras. (p. 794)
—Kraits. (p. 967)
—Madagascar. (p. 1069)
—Spanish Mustang. (p. 1621)
—Tiger Snakes. (p. 1748)
—Wrestling. (p. 1962)
Frazer, James George. Native Races of America; A Copious Selection of Passages for the Study of Social Anthropology. (p. 1235)
Frazer, Rebecca. Barbie Loves Pets. An, Jiyoung, illus. (p. 138)
—Egg-Cellent Easter! (p. 506)
—Egg-Cellent Easter! (Barbie) Riley, Kellee, illus. (p. 506)
—Secret Hearts. An, Jiyoung, illus. (p. 1541)
Frazetta, Frank. Telling Stories: The Classic Comic Art of Frank Frazetta. Mason, Edward G., ed. (p. 1717)
Frazier. Time Zones. (p. 1753)
Frazier, Angie. Eternal Sea. (p. 539)
—Everlasting. (p. 542)
—Mastermind Plot. (p. 1103)
—Midnight Tunnel: A Suzanna Snow Mystery. (p. 1139)
Frazier, April, jt. auth. see Babour Staff.
Frazier, Bessie. Decisions: A Teenage Play. (p. 421)
Frazier, Craig. Lots of Dots. (p. 1057)
—Stanley Goes Fishing. (p. 1640)
—Stanley Goes for a Drive. (p. 1640)
—There Is a Monkey in My Drawers! (p. 1729)
Frazier, Craig, illus. see Florence, Tyler.
Frazier, Craig, illus. see Frazier, Daniele.
Frazier, Craig, illus. see Lyon, George Ella.
Frazier, Craig, jt. auth. see Florence, Tyler.
Frazier, Daniele. Tiny Brown Seed. Frazier, Craig, illus. (p. 1756)
Frazier, Donna, jt. auth. see Love, Roger.
Frazier, Ian. Fish's Eye: Essays about Angling & the Outdoors. (p. 599)
Frazier, James J., illus. see Frazier, Jeffrey R.
Frazier, Jan Scott, tr. see Aki, Katsu.
Frazier, Janet. Case of the Theme Park Cry. (p. 275)
Frazier, Janet L. Mysterious Mall Disappearance: P. K. Mystery Series # 2. (p. 1223)
Frazier, Jeffrey R. Pennsylvania Fireside Tales Volume V: Origins & Foundations of Pennsylvania Mountains Folktales, Legends, & Folklore. Vol. V Frazier, James J., illus. (p. 1338)
Frazier, Keith. Together Forever in Harmony. (p. 1762)
Frazier, Kelly. Red Sock Christmas. Matthes, Justice, illus. (p. 1455)
Frazier, Laurence. Cranky the Rooster. (p. 376)
Frazier, Laverne & Bishop, Elaine. Where Are My Wings? (p. 1906)
Frazier, Neta Lohnes. Stout-Hearted Seven: Orphaned on the Oregon Trail. (p. 1664)
Frazier, Sundee T. Brendan Buckley's Sixth-Grade Experiment. (p. 226)
—Brendan Buckley's Universe & Everything in It. (p. 226)
—Other Half of My Heart. (p. 1306)
Frazin, Julian. Little Dab of Paint. Schirmer, Susan, illus. (p. 1026)
Freberg, Laura A. Study Guide: Used with ... Freberg-Discovering Biological Psychology. (p. 1670)
Frechette, Carole. In the Key of Do. Ouriou, Susan, tr. (p. 866)
—In the Key of Do. Ouriou, Susan, tr. from FRE. (p. 866)
Frechette, Ellen. Trade & Industry. (p. 1776)
Fred. Cast Away on the Letter A. Fred, illus. (p. 276)
Fred, illus. see Kutner, Richard, tr.
Fred, Anthony. Fred & Anthony Meet the Heinie Goblins from the Black Lagoon. Primavera, Elise, illus. (p. 632)
Freddie. Rooster's Story. (p. 1488)
Frederick, Cynthia. Gray Beetle. (p. 713)
Frederick, Daniel R. & Loe, Deborah M. Prelude to Latin: First Steps. (p. 1395)
—Prelude to Latin: Third Steps. (p. 1395)
—Prelude to Latin: Second Steps. (p. 1395)
Frederick Edward Pitts. Tale of the Hummingpotomus: The Flight for Life. (p. 1700)
Frederick, Guy. 101 Best Magic Tricks. Anderson, Doug, illus. (p. 1999)
Frederick, H. J. Timber Howligan Secret Agent Cat. Wilkins, Wendy H., illus. (p. 1750)
Frederick, Heather Vogel. Black Paw. (p. 196)
—Complete Mother-Daughter Book Club Collection: The Mother-Daughter Book Club; Much Ado about Anne; Dear Pen Pal; Pies & Prejudice; Home for the Holidays; Wish You Were Eyre. (p. 353)
—Dear Pen Pal (p. 419)
—Education of Patience Goodspeed. (p. 505)
—For Your Paws Only. (p. 616)
—For Your Paws Only. Comport, Sally Wern, illus. (p. 616)
—Goldwhiskers. (p. 696)
—Hide-and-Squeak. Payne, C. F., illus. (p. 777)
—Home for the Holidays. (p. 792)
—Little Women Christmas. Ibatoulline, Bagram, illus. (p. 1038)
—Mother-Daughter Book Club. (p. 1177)
—Mother-Daughter Book Club Collection: The Mother-Daughter Book Club; Much Ado about Anne; Dear Pen Pal; Pies & Prejudice, Home for the Holidays. (p. 1177)
—Much Ado about Anne. (p. 1188)
—Once upon a Toad. (p. 1293)
—Pies & Prejudice. (p. 1357)
—Voyage of Patience Goodspeed. (p. 1850)
—Wish You Were Eyre. (p. 1940)
Frederick, J. Adam, jt. auth. see Curtis, Jennifer Keats.
Frederick, John. Flying Hat. (p. 610)
Frederick, Julia C. & Tarver, H. Micheal. History of Venezuela. (p. 785)
Frederick, Malcolm. Kamal Goes to Trinidad. Das, Prodeepta, illus. (p. 942)
Frederick Marryat. Children of the New Forest. (p. 302)
Frederick, Melissa. With a Dream (p. 1942)
Frederick, Milner. Douglas Brain. (p. 473)
Frederick, Rachel. I'm Going to Be a Pilot! (p. 859)
Frederick, Robin, ed. see Weiner, Brian.
Frederick, Sara. History of the Cincinnati Bengals. (p. 784)
Frederick, Sarah, illus. see Mahony, Mary.
Frederick, Shane. Alexander Ovechkin. (p. 36)
—Badminton for Fun! (p. 132)
—Best of Everything Football Book (p. 170)
—Best of Everything Hockey Book (p. 170)
—Boxing. (p. 217)
—Football: The Math of the Game (p. 615)
—Gamers Unite! The Video Game Revolution (p. 654)
—Hockey: The Math of the Game. (p. 786)
—Hockey Legends in the Making (p. 786)
—John Tavares. (p. 923)
—Jonathan Toews: Hockey Superstar (p. 925)
—Kids' Guide to Sports Media (p. 954)
—NBA: a History of Hoops: the Story of the Los Angeles Lakers. (p. 1238)
—NBA: a History of Hoops: the Story of the Miami Heat. (p. 1238)
—NBA: a History of Hoops: the Story of the Milwaukee Bucks. (p. 1238)
—NBA: a History of Hoops: the Story of the New Orleans Pelicans. (p. 1238)
—NBA: a History of Hoops: the Story of the San Antonio Spurs. (p. 1238)
—Side-By-Side Football Stars: Comparing Pro Football's Greatest Players (p. 1573)
—Side-By-Side Hockey Stars: Comparing Pro Hockey's Greatest Players (p. 1573)
—Six Degrees of Sidney Crosby: Connecting Hockey Stars. (p. 1582)
—Speed Training for Teen Athletes: Exercises to Take Your Game to the Next Level (p. 1624)
—Stamina Training for Teen Athletes: Exercises to Take Your Game to the Next Level (p. 1639)
—Story of the Los Angeles Lakers. (p. 1661)
—Story of the Miami Heat. (p. 1661)
—Story of the Milwaukee Bucks. (p. 1661)
—Story of the New Orleans Pelicans. (p. 1661)
—Story of the New York Knicks. (p. 1661)
—Story of the San Antonio Spurs. (p. 1662)
—Technology of Football (p. 1712)
—Technology of Hockey (p. 1712)
—Track & Field. (p. 1775)
—Trap & Skeet Shooting for Fun! (p. 1779)
—Ultimate Collection of Pro Football Records (p. 1809)
—Ultimate Collection of Pro Hockey Records (p. 1809)
—Ultimate Collection of Pro Hockey Records 2015 (p. 1809)
—Ultimate Guide to Pro Football Teams (p. 1809)
—Ultimate Guide to Pro Hockey Teams (p. 1809)
—Ultimate Guide to Pro Hockey Teams 2015 (p. 1809)
—Who's Who of Pro Hockey: A Guide to the Game's Greatest Players. (p. 1921)
Frederick, Shane, jt. auth. see Adamson, Thomas K.
Frederick, Shane, jt. auth. see Scheff, Matt.
Frederick, Shane & Wacholtz, Anthony. Hockey: The Math of the Game (p. 786)
Frederick, Shane, et al. For the Record. (p. 616)
—High-Tech Sports. (p. 778)
Frederick, Sharrol. Pickles Play Baseball. (p. 1354)
Frederick, Susan. Miss Callie Lallie's Mouse Tales. Walter, J., illus. (p. 1151)
Frederick-Frost, Alexis, illus. see Anderson, Maxine & Berkenkamp, Lauri.
Frederick-Frost, Alexis, illus. see Anderson, Maxine.
Fredericks, Anthony D. A Is for Anaconda: A Rainforest Alphabet. Regan, Laura, illus. (p. 1)
—American Folklore, Legends, & Tall Tales for Readers Theatre (p. 60)
—Around One Cactus: Owls, Bats, & Leaping Rats. DiRubbio, Jennifer, tr. (p. 100)
—Around One Log: Chipmunks, Spiders, & Creepy Insiders. DiRubbio, Jennifer, illus. (p. 100)
—Clever Camouflagers. (p. 331)
—Desert Night Desert Day. Spengler, Kenneth J., illus. (p. 429)
—I Am the Desert. Reisch, Jesse, illus. (p. 834)
—In One Tidepool: Crabs, Snails, & Salty Tails. DiRubbio, Jennifer, illus. (p. 864)
—Mountain Night Mountain Day. Spengler, Kenneth, illus. (p. 1181)
—Near One Cattail: Turtles, Logs, & Leaping Frogs. DiRubbio, Jennifer, illus. (p. 1239)
—On One Flower: Butterflies, Ticks & a Few More Icks. DiRubbio, Jennifer, illus. (p. 1289)
—P Is for Prairie Dog: A Prairie Alphabet. Bowles, Doug, illus. (p. 1316)
—Simple Nature Experiments with Everyday Materials. Zweifel, Frances, illus. (p. 1578)
—Tsunami Quilt: Grandfather's Story. Yee, Tammy, illus. (p. 1795)
—Under One Rock: Bugs, Slugs, & Other Ughs. DiRubbio, Jennifer, illus. (p. 1813)
—Weird Walkers. (p. 1872)
Fredericks, Anthony D. & Bongaman. African Legends, Myths, & Folktales for Readers Theatre (p. 27)
Fredericks, Anthony D. & Lynott, Vicky. Write to Comprehend: Using Writing as a Tool to Build Reading Comprehension. (p. 1964)
Fredericks, Carrie. Amendment XIV: Due Process. (p. 58)
—Amendment XIX: Grating Women the Right to Vote. (p. 58)
—Autism. (p. 117)
—Breast Cancer. (p. 225)
—Parkinson's Disease. (p. 1325)
Fredericks, Eleanor. Adventures of Tyler the Dinosaur Fredericks, Rob, illus. (p. 24)
Fredericks, Karen, illus. see Wyatt, Valerie.
Fredericks, Mariah. Crunch Time. (p. 386)
—Girl in the Park. (p. 678)
—Head Games. (p. 756)
—Life. Watkins, Liselotte, illus. (p. 1007)
—Love. Watkins, Liselotte, illus. (p. 1059)
—Season of the Witch. (p. 1538)
Fredericks, Rob, illus. see Fredericks, Eleanor.
Frederickson, A. Experimentos Sencillos con la Naturaleza. (p. 549)
Frederiksen, Barbara. Rippen Ricky Loves the Game: A Book of Perseverance. (p. 1474)
Fredette, Nathalie, jt. auth. see Bernard, Yves.
Fredlein, Paul, jt. auth. see Fredlein, Shumang.
Fredlein, Paul & Fredlein, Shumang. Ni Hao: Simplified Character Edition (p. 1250)
—Ni Hao: Simplified Character Edition 2 (p. 1250)
—Ni Hao: Traditional Character Edition 1 (p. 1250)
—Ni Hao: Traditional Character Edition. Vol. 2 (p. 1250)
—Ni Hao. (p. 1250)
Fredlein, Shumang, jt. auth. see Fredlein, Paul.
Fredlein, Shumang & Fredlein, Paul. Ni Hao (p. 1250)
—Ni Hao: Traditional Character Edition (p. 1250)
—Ni Hao: Traditional Character Edition. Vol. 3 (p. 1250)
Fredley, Nichole. Sirius (p. 1581)
Fredo, Sophia E. Girls of Oak Court: Death at Whitford Pond. (p. 680)
Fredrich, Volker. Rechtschreibtraining fuer die 1. Klasse. (p. 1451)
—Rechtschreibtraining fuer die 1. und 2. Klasse. (p. 1451)
Fredrickson, Anne. Baseball Brothers. (p. 141)
Fredriksen, John C. Chronology of American History (p. 317)
—Civil War Almanac. (p. 325)
Free, jt. auth. see Shrubshall.
Free Jenna Staff, ed. see Bloom, Jan.
Free, Margaret, jt. auth. see Treadwell, Harriette Taylor.
Free Spirit Publishing. Character in Sports: Quotes, Prompts, & Stories about Being Your Best—On & off the Field. (p. 291)
—Classroom Warm-Ups: Quick & Meaningful Activities for All Grades. (p. 329)
—Kids & Nature: Easy Ways to Love & Learn about the Outdoors. (p. 952)
—Questions & Quotes for Girls. (p. 1426)
Free Spirit Publishing & Stein, Deborah Jiang. Guy Talk. (p. 733)
—Quotes & Quotables. (p. 1429)
Free Spirit Publishing Staff, jt. auth. see Lewis, Barbara A.
Free Spirit Publishing Staff & Stein, Deborah Jiang. Fingerplays & Rhymes. (p. 589)
—Kids' Attitude. (p. 952)
—Math. (p. 1104)
—More Feelings. (p. 1174)
Free, Zaccai. Mbutu's Mangos. Vasudevan, Vidya, illus. (p. 1114)
Freeberg, Eric. Animal Stories. (p. 79)
—Ballet Stories. (p. 135)
—Greek Myths. (p. 720)
Freeberg, Eric, illus. see Dickens, Charles.
Freeberg, Eric, illus. see Grimm, Jakob & Grimm, Wilhelm K.
Freeberg, Eric, illus. see Homer.
Freeberg, Eric, illus. see Melville, Herman.
Freeberg, Eric, illus. see Namm, Diane.
Freeberg, Eric, illus. see Verne, Jules.

Freeberg, Jane. Scallop Christmas. Sheckels, Astrid, illus. (p. 1519)
Freeborn, Andrew J. Colorways: For Days. (p. 346)
Freed, Christina. Sophie's Cross. (p. 1613)
Freed, Crissy. Child Within. (p. 301)
Freed, Herb. Sing & Learn Spanish. (p. 1579)
Freed, Kira. Surviving Hurricane Katrina. (p. 1687)
—Surviving Pearl Harbor. (p. 1687)
—Surviving the 2011 Japanese Earthquake & Tsunami. (p. 1687)
Freed, Kira, jt. auth. see Favor, Lesli J.
Freed, Margaret, illus. see Winters-Johnson, Diane.
Freed, marie. Kitty Cat Kids. (p. 963)
Freedman, Anne. Touched by Love. Malone, Susan Mary & Meister, Christine, eds. (p. 1772)
Freedman, Bill. Boy Who Wanted to Marry His Dog. (p. 219)
Freedman, Claire. Aliens in Underpants Save the World. Cort, Ben, illus. (p. 41)
—Aliens Love Panta Claus. Cort, Ben, illus. (p. 41)
—Benjamin Bear Stencil Book Smallman, Steve, illus. (p. 164)
—Candle Prayers for Kids Parry, Jo, illus. (p. 261)
—Christmas Angels Yerrill, Gail, illus. (p. 312)
—Cuddle Bear. Scott, Gavin, illus. (p. 389)
—Cuddle for Little Duck. Pedler, Caroline, illus. (p. 389)
—Dinosaurs Love Underpants. Cort, Ben, illus. (p. 445)
—Dragon Jelly. Hendra, Sue, illus. (p. 477)
—Good Night, Sleep Tight! Tyger, Rory, illus. (p. 700)
—Goodnight, Sleep Tight! Tyger, Rory, illus. (p. 701)
—Gooseberry Goose. Cabban, Vanessa, illus. (p. 702)
—Kiss Goodnight: A Collection of Lullabies (p. 961)
—Little Bear's Special Friend. Kolanovic, Dubravka, illus. (p. 1024)
—Magical Christmas. Yerrill, Gail, illus. (p. 1074)
—Monster of the Woods! Julian, Russell, illus. (p. 1168)
—Monster of the Woods!/By Claire Freedman & Russell Julian. Julian, Russell, illus. (p. 1168)
—Monstersaurus! Cort, Ben, illus. (p. 1169)
—Monstersaurus. Cort, Ben, illus. (p. 1169)
—My First Book of Prayers Atkins, Alison, illus. (p. 1205)
—My Precious Little Bear. Scott, Gavin, illus. (p. 1217)
—New Kid in Town Stephenson, Kristina, illus. (p. 1245)
—Night-Night, Emily! Massey, Jane, tr. (p. 1253)
—Night-Night, Emily! Massey, Jane, illus. (p. 1253)
—One Magical Day Macnaughton, Tina, illus. (p. 1296)
—One Winter's Night. Mendez, Simon, illus. (p. 1297)
—Oops-a-Daisy! Hansen, Gaby, illus. (p. 1299)
—Pirates Love Underpants. Cort, Ben, illus. (p. 1363)
—Silly Dilly Duckling. Chapman, Jane, illus. (p. 1575)
—Spider Sandwiches. Hendra, Sue, illus. (p. 1626)
—Where Snowflakes Fall. Macnaughton, Tina, illus. (p. 1909)
—You're My Little Bunny. Scott, Gavin, illus. (p. 1982)
Freedman, Claire & Cabban, Vanessa. Gooseberry Goose. (p. 702)
Freedman, Claire & Scott, Gavin. Cuddle Bear. (p. 389)
Freedman, Claire, et al. Me & My Mommy: By My Side, Little Panda/Just for You!/Big Bear, Little Bear/the Most Precious Thing/Little Bear's Special Wish/My Mommy & Me. Tyger, Rory et al, illus. (p. 1115)
—My Little Box of Christmas Stories: One Winter's Night/Hurry, Santa!/a Magical Christmas/the Gift of Christmas/the Special Christmas Tree/the Christmas Bear. Mendez, Simon & Warnes, Tim, illus. (p. 1212)
Freedman, Deborah. Blue Chicken. (p. 202)
—By Mouse & Frog. Freedman, Deborah, illus. (p. 249)
—Story of Fish & Snail. (p. 1658)
Freedman, Georgene. Olive Tree. (p. 1285)
Freedman, Jeri. America Debates Civil Liberties & Terrorism. (p. 59)
—America Debates Privacy Versus Security. (p. 59)
—America Debates Stem Cell Research. (p. 59)
—Armenian Genocide. (p. 99)
—Autism. (p. 117)
—Being a Leader: Organizing & Inspiring a Group. (p. 160)
—Brain Cancer: Current & Emerging Trends in Detection & Treatment. (p. 221)
—Career Building Through Skinning & Modding. (p. 266)
—Careers in Child Care (p. 267)
—Careers in Computer Science & Programming. (p. 267)
—Careers in Computer Support. (p. 267)
—Careers in Emergency Medical Response Teams' Search & Rescue Units. (p. 267)
—Careers in Human Resources. (p. 268)
—Careers in the Emergency Medical Response Team's Search & Rescue Unit. (p. 268)
—Dream Jobs in Sports Management & Administration. (p. 483)
—Genetically Modified Food: How Biotechnology Is Changing What We Eat. (p. 660)
—Grasslands: Sweeping Savannas. (p. 712)
—Grasslands: Sweeping Savannahs. (p. 712)
—Hepatitis B. (p. 769)
—Hillary Rodham Clinton: Profile of a Leading Democrat. (p. 780)
—Historical Villages. (p. 783)
—Intellectual Property. (p. 879)
—Iowa: Past & Present. (p. 886)
—Land Formation: The Shifting, Moving, Changing Earth: The Creation of Mountains. (p. 973)
—Life As a Pioneer on the Oregon Trail. (p. 1008)
—Louisiana: Past & Present. (p. 1058)
—Lymphoma: Current & Emerging Trends in Detection & Treatment. (p. 1066)
—Massachusetts: Past & Present. (p. 1102)
—Online Safety. (p. 1298)
—Ovarian Cancer: Current & Emerging Trends in Detection & Treatment. (p. 1313)
—Primary Source History of the Colony of Massachusetts. (p. 1400)
—Professional Wrestling: Steroids in & Out of the Ring. (p. 1409)
—Robots Through History. (p. 1481)
—Software Development. (p. 1606)
—Special Ops: Air Commandos (p. 1623)
—Step-By-Step Guide to Becoming a Leader at School & on the Job. (p. 1647)
—Tay-Sachs Disease. (p. 1707)
—U. S. Economic Crisis. (p. 1806)
—U.S. Auto Industry: American Carmakers & the Economic Crisis. (p. 1826)
—Warsaw Ghetto & Uprising. (p. 1859)
—What Is a Technical Text? (p. 1888)
—Women in the Workplace: Wages, Respect, & Equal Rights. (p. 1946)
—Your Career in the Air Force. (p. 1980)
Freedman, Jeri, jt. auth. see Cook, Louis J.
Freedman, Jeri, ed. Applications & Limitations of Taxonomy (in Classification of Organisms) An Anthology of Current Thought. (p. 93)
Freedman, Leora. Parachuting: A Novel (p. 1323)
Freedman, Lew. All about Amelia Earhart. (p. 42)
—Boston Red Sox. (p. 215)
—Seattle Mariners. (p. 1539)
Freedman, Paula J. My Basmati Bat Mitzvah. (p. 1196)
Freedman, Russell. Abraham Lincoln & Frederick Douglass: The Story Behind an American Friendship. (p. 6)
—Angel Island: Gateway to Gold Mountain. (p. 73)
—Babe Didrikson Zaharias: The Making of a Champion. (p. 123)
—Because They Marched: The People's Campaign for Voting Rights That Changed America. (p. 155)
—Becoming Ben Franklin: How a Candle-Maker's Son Helped Light the Flame of Liberty. (p. 156)
—Boston Tea Party. Malone, Peter, illus. (p. 215)
—Children of the Great Depression. (p. 302)
—Freedom Walkers: The Story of the Montgomery Bus Boycott. (p. 635)
—In Defense of Liberty: The Story of America's Bill of Rights. (p. 863)
—Lafayette & the American Revolution. (p. 971)
—Voice That Challenged a Nation: Marian Anderson & the Struggle for Equal Rights (p. 1848)
—Voice That Challenged a Nation: Marian Anderson & the Struggle for Equal Rights. (p. 1848)
—War to End All Wars: World War I. (p. 1858)
—Washington at Valley Forge. (p. 1859)
—Who Was First? Discovering the Americas. (p. 1918)
Freedman, Sally. Miriam's Journey. (p. 1149)
Freedman, Sharon. Hey Guys: A Story about Going to Day Camp. Nelson, Megan, illus. (p. 774)
Freedman, Zelda. Rosie's Dream Cape. Bevilacqua, Silvana, illus. (p. 1490)
Freel, Mirle, illus. see O'Toole-Freel, Judy.
Freeland, Claire A.B., jt. auth. see Toner, Jacqueline B.
Freeland, Claire A.B. & Toner, Jacqueline B. What to Do When Mistakes Make You Quake: A Kid's Guide to Accepting Imperfection. McDonnell, Janet, illus. (p. 1894)
Freeland, Devon, illus. see Smith, M. a. & Smith, M. A.
Freeland, Kent. Odyssey to Iowa. (p. 1279)
Freeman, Aaron & Rosenzweig, Sharon. Comic Torah: Reimagining the Good Book. (p. 348)
—Comic Torah: Reimagining the Very Good Book. Rosenzweig, Sharon, illus. (p. 348)
Freeman, Angela, illus. see Angelo, Tony.
Freeman, Arnetta L. Play Brelyn Play, Dance Angels Dance. (p. 1371)
Freeman, Charles. Rise of the Nazis. (p. 1475)
—Why Did the Rise of the Nazis Happen? (p. 1923)
Freeman, Chip. Why, Daddy, Why Are There Stars in the Sky? Perry, Lee Ann, illus. (p. 1923)
Freeman, Chris W. & Hunt, Korey. So... I Survived the Zombie Apocalypse & All I Got Was This Podcast. Chabon, Daniel, ed. (p. 1602)
Freeman, Christopher. Drawing Stars & Building Polyhedra. (p. 482)
Freeman, Claire. One Magical Morning. Ho, Louise, illus. (p. 1296)
Freeman Clark, Judith. Gilded Age. (p. 676)
Freeman, Dallas. Mirth & Misery: Memoirs of a Midwestern Maverick. (p. 1149)
Freeman, David. Batty Bat. Beers, Robert Lee, illus. (p. 147)
—Scarecrow. Beers, Robert Lee, illus. (p. 1519)
—Whispery Witch. Beers, Robert Lee, illus. (p. 1912)
Freeman, David, et al. Guided Comprehension: Grade 4. (p. 730)
—Guided Comprehension: Grade 5. (p. 730)
Freeman, Deborah, jt. auth. see Walker, Joyce MacKichan.
Freeman, Diana, jt. auth. see Bursiem, Diana.
Freeman, Don. Beady Bear: With the Never-Before-Seen Story Beady's Pillow. (p. 149)
—Christmas Is Here, Corduroy! (p. 314)
—Corduroy. (p. 366)
—Corduroy. Freeman, Don, illus. (p. 367)
—Corduroy Book & Bear. (p. 367)
—Corduroy Goes to the Doctor. McCue, Lisa, illus. (p. 367)
—Corduroy's Day. McCue, Lisa, illus. (p. 367)
—Corduroy's Fourth of July. McCue, Lisa, illus. (p. 367)
—Earl the Squirrel. Freeman, Don, illus. (p. 492)
—Fly High, Fly Low. Freeman, Don, illus. (p. 609)
—Gregory's Shadow. Freeman, Don, illus. (p. 723)
—Halloween Is Here, Corduroy! McCue, Lisa & Kong, Emilie, illus. (p. 738)
—Happy Hanukkah, Corduroy. McCue, Lisa, illus. (p. 745)
—Manuelo the Playing Mantis. (p. 1089)
—Pocket for Corduroy (p. 1375)
—Quiet! There's a Canary in the Library. (p. 1428)
—Spring Is Here, Corduroy! McCue, Lisa, illus. (p. 1635)
Freeman, Don, illus. see Zuckerman, Linda.
Freeman, Don & Freeman, Roy. One More Acorn. (p. 1296)
Freeman, Don & Hennessy, B. G. Corduroy Lost & Found. Wheeler, Jody, illus. (p. 367)
Freeman, Don & McCue, Lisa. Corduroy Series Boxed Set: Corduroy; A Pocket for Corduroy; Corduroy's Busy Street; Corduroy Goes to the Doctor; Corduroy's Day; Corduroy's Party Freeman, Don & McCue, Lisa, illus. (p. 367)
Freeman, Dorothy Rhodes. St. Patrick's Day. (p. 1638)
Freeman, Dorothy Rhodes & MacMillan, Dianne M. Kwanzaa. (p. 969)
Freeman, Emily. God Bless Your Way: A Christmas Journey. Burr, Dan, illus. (p. 688)
—When Hope Is Gone. (p. 1902)
Freeman, Faith L. Beyond the Magic Waterfall. (p. 174)
Freeman, Gary. Motocross. (p. 1179)
Freeman, Gary, jt. auth. see Bentman, Jonathan.
Freeman, Gayle. Football Friends. (p. 615)
Freeman, Greg. Legend of Booga Bearia: Land of the. (p. 988)
Freeman, Gregory A. Forgotten 500: The Untold Story of the Men Who Risked All for the Greatest Rescue Mission of World War II. (p. 619)
Freeman, J. Miller. Creak in the Night - Mystery of the Crypts. Lavender, Todd, illus. (p. 378)
Freeman, Joe Nathan. Adventures of BG: The Importance of Self-Esteem. (p. 16)
Freeman, Jonathan M., jt. auth. see Cohen, Joan Freeman.
Freeman, Julie, illus. see Weisenfluh, C. C.
Freeman, Kathie. Catwalk: A Feline Odyyssey. (p. 281)
Freeman, Kathryn. Gerry Giraffe: Adventures in Eden. (p. 667)
Freeman, Kathryn S., illus. see Diehl, Jean Heilprin.
Freeman, Kaye. Bible Covenants. (p. 175)
Freeman, Ken. I Hope You Know: A Message from Dad. (p. 839)
Freeman, Kim. Bible Plays for Kids: A Visual Look at the Bible! (p. 176)
Freeman, Laura. Here We Go Looby Loo. Freeman, Laura, illus. (p. 771)
Freeman, Laura, illus. see English, Karen.
Freeman, Laura, illus. see Hooks, Bell.
Freeman, Laura, illus. see York, J.
Freeman, Laurence. Simple Way: The Path of Christian Meditation. (p. 1578)
Freeman, Lisa. Honey Girl. (p. 794)
Freeman, Lisa Show. Colors of God. (p. 345)
Freeman, Lisa Shows. Counting with God: Number Stories from the Bible. (p. 372)
Freeman, Maggie. Castles. (p. 277)
Freeman, Maggie & Murray, Pat. Building High. Moon, Cliff, ed. (p. 239)
Freeman, Marcia S. Catfish & Spaghetti. Stock, Rose, illus. (p. 280)
—Dozen Cousins: Exploring the Number 12. (p. 474)
—Fire Engines [Scholastic]. (p. 590)
—How Muscles & Bones Hold You Up: A Book about Models. (p. 811)
—Let's Look at Rocks. (p. 999)
—Measuring Our World. (p. 1117)
—More Ice Cream: Words for Math Comparisons. (p. 1174)
—Multiply by Hand: The Nines Facts. (p. 1190)
—My Sister Is in Third Grade: Putting Numbers in Order. (p. 1218)
—Police Cars [Scholastic]. (p. 1380)
Freeman, Marcia S., ed. see Schaefer, Adam R.
Freeman, Marcia S., jt. auth. see Mitten, Luana.
Freeman, Martha. 1,000 Reasons Never to Kiss a Boy. (p. 2001)
—Case of Diamond Dog Collar. (p. 273)
—Case of the Bug on the Run: First Kids Mystery #6. (p. 273)
—Case of the Bug on the Run. (p. 273)
—Case of the Diamond Dog Collar. (p. 274)
—Case of the Missing Dinosaur Egg. (p. 274)
—Case of the Missing Dinosaur Egg. Dibley, Glin, illus. (p. 274)
—Case of the Piggy Bank Thief: First Kids Mystery #4. (p. 274)
—Case of the Piggy Bank Thief. (p. 274)
—Case of the Rock 'N' Roll Dog. (p. 275)
—Case of the Rock 'n' Roll Dog. (p. 275)
—Case of the Ruby Slippers. (p. 275)
—Fourth-Grade Weirdo. (p. 625)
—Mrs. Wow Never Wanted a Cow. Salerno, Steven, illus. (p. 1188)
—Orphan & the Mouse. McPhail, David, illus. (p. 1304)
—Secret Cookie Club. (p. 1540)
—Spy Wore Shades. (p. 1636)
—Strudel's Forever Home. (p. 1668)
—Trouble with Twins. Smith, Cat Bowman, illus. (p. 1790)
—Who Is Stealing the 12 Days of Christmas? (p. 1916)
—Who Stole Grandma's Million-Dollar Pumpkin Pie? (p. 1917)
—Who Stole Halloween? (p. 1917)
—Who Stole New Year's Eve? (p. 1917)
—Who Stole Uncle Sam? (p. 1917)
Freeman, Marty. Children of Character. (p. 302)
Freeman, Melissa & Mathison, Sandra. Researching Children's Experiences. (p. 1463)
Freeman, Melita. Knight of Lord Greengate's Castle. Freeman, Melita, illus. (p. 964)
Freeman, Meryl. Voyages of Galley Cat. (p. 1851)
Freeman, Mike, photos by see Miles, Lisa.
Freeman, Mike, photos by see Woolley, Alan.
Freeman, Mylo. Every Girl Is a Princess. Freeman, Mylo, illus. (p. 542)
—Princess Arabella's Birthday. (p. 1403)
Freeman, Pamela. Castings Trilogy. (p. 276)
Freeman, Patricia, illus. see Stevens, Sherri.
Freeman, Philip. Heroes of Olympus. Willis, Drew, illus. (p. 773)
Freeman, R. Gregory. Carpenter's Tale: The Mystery of Kidron Valley. (p. 271)
Freeman, Richard. Legend of Booga Bearia. (p. 988)
Freeman, Roy, jt. auth. see Freeman, Don.
Freeman, Shannon. Accident. (p. 8)
—High School High (p. 778)
—High School High. (p. 778)
—Listed. (p. 1022)
—Port in Pieces. (p. 1386)
—Taken (p. 1697)
—Traumatized. (p. 1780)
Freeman, Suzanne. Cuckoo's Child. (p. 389)
Freeman, T. R., illus. see Vipont, Elfrida.
Freeman, Tina. Ten Little Monkeys. (p. 1719)
Freeman, Tina, illus. see Twinn, A.
Freeman, Tina, jt. auth. see Davies, Gill.
Freeman, Tina, tr. Ten Little Monkeys Jumping on the Bed. (p. 1719)
Freeman, Tor. Ambrose Goes for Gold. (p. 57)
—Olive & the Bad Mood. Freeman, Tor, illus. (p. 1285)
—Olive & the Big Secret. Freeman, Tor, illus. (p. 1285)
—Olive & the Embarrassing Gift. Freeman, Tor, illus. (p. 1285)
Freeman, Troy, illus. see Brodland, Rita, ed.
Freeman, Trudy. Shaggy Nick. (p. 1558)
Freeman, Yusuf, photos by see Whetung, James.
Freeman-Hines, Laura. If You're Happy & You Know It. (p. 855)
Freer, Dave. Cuttlefish. (p. 396)
—Steam Mole. (p. 1646)
Freer, Echo. Magenta Goes Green: The Capers of a Campsite Queen! (p. 1071)
—Magenta in the Pink: The Dramas of a Disaster-Prone Diva. (p. 1071)
—Magenta Orange: The Trials of a Teenage Temptress. (p. 1071)
—Shades of Magenta: Holiday Havoc with a Hazardous Heroine. (p. 1557)
Freer, Ida. Panama Girl. (p. 1320)
Freer, Ulli. Speakbright Leap Passwood: New & Selected Poems. (p. 1623)
Frees, Jessie Lynch. Jackie Winquackey & Her 43 Cats Go to Hollywood. Gebr, Jaroslav, illus. (p. 904)
Freese, Joan. Ballroom Dancing (p. 135)
—Desfile de Patrones. (p. 429)
—Desfile de Patrones. McKinley, Kay, photos by. (p. 429)
—Diversion con Dobles en la Granja. (p. 454)
—Diversión con Dobles en la Granja. (p. 454)
—Doubles Fun on the Farm. (p. 473)
—Hip-Hop Dancing (p. 780)
—Patterns on Parade. McKinley, Kay, photos by. (p. 1329)
—TABLAS y GRÁFICAS de Cosas Saludables. (p. 1694)
—Tablas y Graficas de Cosas Saludables. (p. 1694)
—Tables & Graphs of Healthy Things. (p. 1694)
—Using Math to Make Party Plans. (p. 1828)
—Using Math to Make Party Plans. Andersen, Gregg, photos by. (p. 1828)
—Vamos a Planear una Fiesta con Matemáticas. (p. 1831)
—Vamos A Planear una Fiesta Con Matematicas. Andersen, Gregg, photos by. (p. 1831)
Freese, Susan M. Bees to Trees: Reading, Writing, & Reciting Poems about Nature. Westberg, Jan, illus. (p. 158)
—Buses to Books: Reading, Writing, & Reciting Poems about School. Westberg, Jan, illus. (p. 244)
—Carrots to Cupcakes: Reading, Writing, & Reciting Poems about Food. Westberg, Jan, illus. (p. 271)
—Craigslist: The Company & Its Founder. (p. 376)
—Fashion. (p. 575)
—Fireworks to Fruitcake: Reading, Writing, & Reciting Poems about Holidays. Westberg, Jan, illus. (p. 592)
—Guppies to Puppies: Reading, Writing, & Reciting Poems about Pets. Westberg, Jan, illus. (p. 732)
—Nicknames to Nightmares: Reading, Writing, & Reciting Poems about Me. Westberg, Jan, illus. (p. 1251)
—Nuclear Weapons. (p. 1270)
Freese, Thomas & Riddell, Fran. Halloween Sleepwalker (p. 738)
Freese, Thomas, reader. Fog Swirler & 11 Other Ghost Stories. (p. 611)
—Shaker Ghost Stories from Pleasant Hill, KY Audio Book/cd. (p. 1558)
Freestone, Annie. Little Mars Rovers. (p. 1031)
Freeswick, Jill, illus. see Clayton, Darcy M.
Frehner, Brian, jt. see Smith, Sherry L.
Frei, George, et al. Warhol - Paintings & Sculpture, 1964-1969: The Andy Warhol Catalogue Raisonne Vol. 2,Set (p. 1858)
Freidman, Mel. Blue Moon Effect. Smith, Eric, illus. (p. 203)
Freigruber, Amy Elizabeth. At the Top of the Toboggan Hill. (p. 111)
Freijeiro, Antonio Blanco, see Blanco Freijeiro, Antonio.
Freimark, Lew. Soccer Tales: Legend of the Shoelace Monster. (p. 1603)
Freire, Carolina. Panama. (p. 1320)
Freisager, Katrin, photos by see Seals, David.
Freischlad, Roland, tr. see Sixtus, Albert.
Freisinger, Vickie. Reno Does Chores (p. 1460)
Freistadt, Margo. Kate Spade. (p. 944)
Freitag, Charles, illus. see Aumann, Jane & Ladage, Cindy.
Freitag, Fred. On Hills & Meadows by the River. (p. 1289)
Freitas, Donna. Gold Medal Summer. (p. 693)
—Gold Medal Winter. (p. 693)
—Survival Kit. (p. 1686)
—Tenderness of Thieves. (p. 1719)
Frelinghuysen Eighth Grade Storytellers Staff. Flash Before My Eyes. (p. 602)
Fremes, Ruth & Carteron, Nancy Lee. Body Out of Balance: Understanding the Treating Sjogren's Syndrome. (p. 207)
Fremon, David K. Great Depression in United States History. (p. 715)
—Internment of Japanese Americans in United States History. (p. 880)
—Jim Crow Laws & Racism in United States History. (p. 917)
—Salem Witchcraft Trials in United States History. (p. 1504)
—Schindler, Wallenberg, Miep Gies: The Holocaust Heroes. (p. 1521)
—Watergate Scandal in United States History. (p. 1863)
Fremont, Eleanor. Big Day at School. Lennicx, Michael, illus. (p. 180)
—Picture Me As a Dinosaur. (p. 1355)
Frémont, John Charles. Defence of Lieut. Col. J. C. Fremont. (p. 423)
Fremont, Victoria. Quick Crossword Puzzles. (p. 1427)
Fremont, Victoria & Flores, Brenda. All Around the World Search-a-Word Puzzles. (p. 44)
Fremont, Victoria, et al. Nutcracker. (p. 1273)
Fremont-Barnes, Gregory. Rescue at the Iranian Embassy: The Most Daring SAS Raid. (p. 1462)
Fremont-Barnes, Gregory & Ryerson, Richard A., eds. American Revolutionary War: A Student Encyclopedia (p. 63)
—Encyclopedia of the American Revolutionary War: A Political, Social, & Military History (p. 525)
French. Consumer Mathematics. (p. 360)
French, Alice, see Thanet, Octave, pseud.
French, Allen. Story of Rolf: A Viking Adventure. (p. 1659)
—Story of Rolf & the Viking Bow. (p. 1659)

F

French, Cathy. Cells & Las Células: 6 English, 6 Spanish Adaptations. (p. 286)
—Compramos (?) (p. 354)
—Él Está en El (?) (p. 507)
—En La (?) (p. 522)
—(?) está en el árbol. (p. 538)
—Esta (?) está en el Agua. (p. 537)
—Este (?) es un Hogar. (p. 538)
—Fast Athletes. (p. 576)
—From Axes to Zippers: Simple Machines & Del hacha al Cierre: 6 English, 6 Spanish Adaptations: Las máquinas Simples. (p. 642)
—Fuimos a Ver (?) (p. 646)
—Hay (?) (p. 755)
—Jobs up High. (p. 919)
—Make a Necklace. (p. 1078)
—Make a Paper Airplane & Haz un avión de Papel: 6 English, 6 Spanish Adaptations. (p. 1078)
—Make a Safety Puppet. (p. 1078)
—Make an Animal Mobile. (p. 1079)
—Make an Animal Mobile & Haz un móvil de Animales: 6 English, 6 Spanish Adaptations. (p. 1079)
—Make an Island. (p. 1079)
—Make an Island & Haz una Isla: 6 English, 6 Spanish Adaptations. (p. 1079)
—Me gusta Mi (?) (p. 1116)
—Mi (?) (p. 1132)
—Mi Mamá Es (?) (p. 1132)
—Mi papá Tenia (?) (p. 1133)
—Mira (?) (p. 1148)
—Nos gusta El (?) (p. 1266)
—Nos Gustan (?) (p. 1266)
—People Who Keep You Safe. (p. 1340)
—People Who Use Magnets at Work. (p. 1340)
—Snap, Crackle, & Flow & Chasquea, cruje y Fluye: 6 English, 6 Spanish Adaptations. (p. 1597)
—Using Numbers at Work. (p. 1828)
—Vemos (?) (p. 1835)
—Ven a Ver (?) (p. 1835)
—You Can Make a Memory Scrapbook. (p. 1974)
—You Can Make a Timer. (p. 1974)
—¿Puedes (?) ? (p. 1414)
French, Cindy. Loud Roar. (p. 1057)
French, David, illus. see Pierro, Rita.
French, Diana, ed. see Thay, Edrick.
French, Fiona. Paradise: With Words from the King James Bible. (p. 1323)
French, Fiona, illus. see Walsh, Jill Paton.
French, Holly. One Direction. (p. 1294)
French, Jackie. Big Burps, Bare Bums & Other Bad-Mannered Blunders: 365 Tips on How to Behave Nicely. (p. 180)
—Box Full of Phaeries, Phreddes & Fruit Vane, Mitch, illus. (p. 216)
—Camel Who Crossed Australia. (p. 256)
—Christmas Wombat. Whatley, Bruce, illus. (p. 316)
—Day I Was History. Booth, Christina, illus. (p. 413)
—Diary of a Baby Wombat. Whatley, Bruce, illus. (p. 434)
—Diary of a Wombat. Whatley, Bruce, illus. (p. 435)
—Dog Who Loved a Queen. (p. 462)
—Emily & the Big Bad Bunyip. Whatley, Bruce, illus. (p. 518)
—Flesh & Blood. (p. 603)
—Goat That Sailed the World. (p. 687)
—How High Can a Kangaroo Hop? Whatley, Bruce, illus. (p. 809)
—Josephine Wants to Dance. Whatley, Bruce, illus. (p. 926)
—Macbeth & Son. (p. 1068)
—My Auntie Chook the Vampire Chicken. (p. 1196)
—My Dad the Dragon. King, Stephen Michael, illus. (p. 1201)
—My Dog the Dinosaur. King, Stephen Michael, illus. (p. 1202)
—My Gran the Gorilla. King, Stephen Michael, illus. (p. 1210)
—My Mum the Pirate. King, Stephen Michael, illus. (p. 1215)
—My Pa the Polar Bear. (p. 1216)
—My Uncle Gus the Garden Gnome. King, Stephen Michael, illus. (p. 1220)
—One Big Wacky Family. (p. 1294)
—One Perfect Day. Bray, Peter, illus. (p. 1296)
—Pete the Sheep. Whatley, Bruce, illus. (p. 1346)
—Phaery Named Phredde & Other Stories to Eat with a Banana. Vane, Mitch, illus. (p. 1349)
—Phredde & a Frog Named Bruce & Other Stories to Eat with a Watermelon. Vane, Mitch, illus. (p. 1353)
—Phredde & the Purple Pyramid: A Story to Eat with a Passionfruit. Vane, Mitch, illus. (p. 1353)
—Phredde & the Vampire Footy Team. (p. 1353)
—Phredde & the Zombie Librarian: And Other Stories to Eat with a BloodPlum. Vane, Mitch, illus. (p. 1353)
—Rose for the Anzac Boys. (p. 1489)
—Secret World of Wombats. Whatley, Bruce, illus. (p. 1544)
—Tom Appleby, Convict Boy. (p. 1762)
—Too Many Pears! Whatley, Bruce, illus. (p. 1767)
—Too Many Pears! (Japanese/English) Whatley, Bruce, illus. (p. 1767)
—Too Many Pears! (Portuguese/English) (p. 1767)
—Too Many Pears! (Spanish/English) Whatley, Bruce, illus. (p. 1767)
—Valley of Gold. (p. 1831)
French, Jackie, jt. auth. see French, Jackie.
French, Jackie, jt. auth. see Sullivan, Bryan.
French, Jackie & French, Jackie. Hitler's Daughter. (p. 786)
French, Jackie & Whatley, Bruce. Shaggy Gully Times. (p. 1558)
French, Jackie, et al. Pete the Sheep. (p. 1346)
French, James Austin. Truth Gems for Teacher & Student. (p. 1794)
French, Jennifer. Fidgets. (p. 583)
French, Jennifer Pratt. Hoot Owl Shares the Dawn (p. 796)
French, John L. Criminal Investigations Set, 14-Volumes. (p. 382)
French, Joyce. Popcorn Tree. Hansen, Paisley, illus. (p. 1384)
French, Karen. Dr. Frenchy's Pet Training from a to Z: A Fun, Colorful, Stimulating Alphabet Pattern Book. (p. 475)
French, Karen Lea. Dr. Frenchy's Bible ABCs. (p. 475)
French, Kathy. Cells: Set Of 6. (p. 286)
—From Axes to Zippers Simple Machines: Set Of 6. (p. 642)
—Snap, Crackle, & Flow: Set Of 6. (p. 1597)
—Your Nervous System: Set Of 6. (p. 1981)
French, Lisa S. Eco-Pig Gott, Barry, illus. (p. 502)
—Planet Called Home: Eco-Pig's Animal Protection. Gott, Barry, illus. (p. 1367)
—Terrible Trash Trail: Eco-Pig Stops Pollution. Gott, Barry, illus. (p. 1721)
—What Does It Mean to Be Green? Eco-Pig Explains Living Green. Gott, Barry, illus. (p. 1884)
—Who Turned up the Heat? Eco-Pig Explains Global Warming. Gott, Barry, illus. (p. 1918)
French, Lloyd C. On the Job with an Explorer. (p. 1290)
French, Maci. My Best Day Ever. (p. 1196)
French, Martin. Stompin' at the Savoy: The Story of Norma Miller. (p. 1652)
French, Martin, illus. see Gourse, Leslie.
French, Mary. Animal Gazetteer. (p. 78)
French, Mary B. Bear-Ly There with Compass. Coffey, Kevin, illus. (p. 151)
French, Matt. Uncolored Book for You to Color (p. 1812)
French, Michael, jt. auth. see Kidder, Tracy.
French, Moira. Swingewood Stories. (p. 1691)
French, Nicci. Land of the Living. (p. 973)
—Memory Game. (p. 1126)
French, Peter, photos by see Talaro, Theresa.
French, Phyllis, illus. see Peifer, Meighan.
French, Renee. Barry's Best Buddy. (p. 140)
—Soap Lady. French, Renee, illus. (p. 1603)
French, Renee, illus. see Olson, Martin.
French, S. Terrell. Operation Redwood. (p. 1300)
French, Sarah. Summer Friends. (p. 1674)
French, Simon. My Cousin's Keeper. (p. 1200)
—Where in the World (p. 1908)
—Where in the World. (p. 1908)
French, Tana. In the Woods. (p. 868)
French, Vivian. Alegre Roger y el Tesoro Submarino. Solana, María T., tr. (p. 35)
—Bag of Bones: The Second Tale from the Five Kingdoms. Collins, Ross, illus. (p. 132)
—Caribou Journey. Flather, Lisa, illus. (p. 269)
—Caterpillar Caterpillar: Read & Wonder. Voake, Charlotte, illus. (p. 279)
—Caterpillar, Caterpillar. Voake, Charlotte, illus. (p. 279)
—Cave-Baby & the Mammoth. Williams, Lisa, illus. (p. 282)
—Down in the Jungle. Young, Selina, illus. (p. 474)
—Flight of Dragons: The Fourth Tale from the Five Kingdoms. Collins, Ross, illus. (p. 604)
—Growing Frogs. Bartlett, Alison, illus. (p. 726)
—Growing Frogs Big Book: Read & Wonder Big Book. Bartlett, Alison, illus. (p. 726)
—Heart of Glass: The Third Tale from the Five Kingdoms. Collins, Ross, illus. (p. 759)
—Henny Penny. Windham, Sophie, illus. (p. 767)
—I Love You, Grandpa. Kubick, Dana, illus. (p. 843)
—If I Were an Alien. Williams, Lisa, illus. (p. 853)
—Kitten with No Name. Young, Selina, illus. (p. 962)
—Ladybird Ladybird. Young, Selina, illus. (p. 971)
—Morris the Mouse Hunter. (p. 1176)
—Mountain Mona: Band 09/Gold. Fisher, Chris, illus. (p. 1181)
—Music of Zombies. Collins, Ross, illus. (p. 1193)
—Pig in Love. Archbold, Tim, illus. (p. 1357)
—Polly's Pink Pajamas. Heap, Sue, illus. (p. 1381)
—Princess Bethany & the Lost Piglet. (p. 1403)
—Princess Charlotte & the Enchanted Rose. Gibb, Sarah, illus. (p. 1403)
—Princess Georgia & the Shimmering Pearl. Gibb, Sarah, illus. (p. 1404)
—Princess Katie & the Silver Pony. Gibb, Sarah, illus. (p. 1404)
—Princess Leah & the Golden Seahorse. (p. 1404)
—Princess Lindsey & the Fluffy Guinea Pig. (p. 1404)
—Princess Mia & the Magical Koala at Diamond Turrets. (p. 1404)
—Princess Parade - Christmas Special 2007. Gibb, Sarah, illus. (p. 1405)
—Princess Ruby & the Enchanted Whale. (p. 1405)
—Princess Sarah & the Silver Swan. Gibb, Sarah, illus. (p. 1405)
—Robe of Skulls: The First Tale from the Five Kingdoms. Collins, Ross, illus. (p. 1478)
—Singing to the Sun. Morris, Jackie, illus. (p. 1579)
—Snow Dragon. Fisher, Chris, illus. (p. 1599)
—Story of Christmas. Chapman, Jane, illus. (p. 1657)
—T. Rex: r. Bartlett, Alison, illus. (p. 1694)
—T. Rex: Read & Wonder. Bartlett, Alison, illus. (p. 1694)
—T. Rex with Audio, Peggable: Read, Listen & Wonder. Bartlett, Alison, illus. (p. 1694)
—Tiara Club at Ruby Mansions: Princess Lauren & the Diamond Necklace. No. 5 (p. 1746)
—Yucky Worms. (p. 1983)
—Yucky Worms. Ahlberg, Jessica, illus. (p. 1983)
French, Vivian & Melling. Iggy Pig's Skippy Day. (p. 856)
French, Vivian & Terry, Michael. Ellie & Elvis. (p. 514)
Frender, Gloria. Learning to Learn: Strengthening Study Skills & Brain Power. Drayton, Marta, illus. (p. 986)
Frender, Sam & Schiffmiller, Robin. Brotherly Feelings: Me, My Emotions, & My Brother with Asperger's Syndrome. Dittrich, Dennis, illus. (p. 231)
Frenette, Bethany. Burn Bright. (p. 243)
—Dark Star. (p. 408)
Frenette, Cynthia, illus. see Werker, Kim Piper & Werker, Kim.
Frenette, Liza. Dead End. Gillis, Jane, illus. (p. 416)
Frenetti, Jackson. Flags of the World: Develop Understanding of Fractions & Numbers (p. 602)
Frenkel, Karen A. Light & Sound Technology: Text Pairs. (p. 1014)
—Listening to Sound: Set Of 6. (p. 1022)
—Listening to Sound: Text Pairs. (p. 1022)
—Looking at Light: Set Of 6. (p. 1051)
—Looking at Light: Text Pairs. (p. 1051)
Frenkel, Yetti. Big, Blue Lump. Frenkel, Yetti, illus. (p. 178)
—Libby & the Cat. Frenkel, Yetti, illus. (p. 1005)
—Trudy & the Captain's Cat. Frenkel, Yetti, illus. (p. 1791)
Frenkel, Yetti, illus. see Hodgkins, Fran.
Frenz, Ron, illus. see David, Peter, et al.
Frenz, Ron, illus. see Defalco, Tom, et al.
Frenz, Ron, illus. see Defalco, Tom.
Frenz, Ron, illus. see Slott, Dan & Busiek, Kurt.
Frenz, Ron, illus. see Welvaert, Scott R. & Welvaert, Scott R.
Frenz, Ron & Nauck, Todd. Thunderstrike: Youth in Revolt. (p. 1746)
Frenz, Ron, et al. Fantastic Four: The World's Greatest Comics Magazine. (p. 571)
Frere, John H., tr. see Aristophanes.
Frere, Mary, ed. Old Deccan Days or, Hindoo Fairy Legends Current in Southern Indi. (p. 1283)
Freschet, Gina. Beto & the Bone Dance. Freschet, Gina, illus. (p. 171)
Freshman, Floris R., illus. see James, Larry W.
Freshman, Wendy & Jansson, Kristin. Making History: Have a Blast with 15 Crafts. (p. 1081)
Freshwater Fishing Magazine Staff, et al. Trout Fishing Tactics. (p. 1790)
Fretczak-Rodak, Monika, illus. see Miedzybrodzka, Wiktoria.
Fretland VanVoorst, Jennifer. Performance-Enhancing Risks: The Science of Steroids (p. 1343)
Fretland VanVoorst, Jenny. Animal Classification. (p. 77)
—Ecosystems. (p. 503)
—Homing Pigeons. (p. 794)
—Pig Detectives. (p. 1357)
—Seeing-Eye Dogs. (p. 1548)
—Shapes in the City. (p. 1560)
—Shapes on the Farm. (p. 1561)
—Therapy Cats, Dogs, & Rabbits. (p. 1729)
Fretwell, Holly. Sky's Not Falling! Why It's Ok to Chill about Global Warming. (p. 1587)
Fretz, Denette. Conrad & the Cowgirl Next Door Barretta, Gene, illus. (p. 358)
Freud, Sally. Caged. (p. 251)
Freudenrich, Craig C. Growth & Development of Specialized Cells, Tissues, & Organs: An Anthology of Current Thought. (p. 727)
Freudentha, H. Digging Numbers: Math/Context. (p. 439)
—Pattern & Figures: Math/Context. (p. 1329)
—Powers of Ten: Math Context. (p. 1391)
—Re-Allotment: Math/Context. (p. 1441)
—Re-Allotment Math/Context. (p. 1441)
Freudenthal. Expressions & Formulas. (p. 555)
—Graph Equations. (p. 710)
—Growth. (p. 727)
—Insights into Data. (p. 878)
—Patterns & Symbols. (p. 1329)
—Percentage Sense. (p. 1341)
—Reflections on Numbers. (p. 1456)
—Triangles & Patchwork. (p. 1785)
—Ways to Go. (p. 1865)
Freudiger, Victoria, ed. see Foster, Ronnie D.
Freudiger, Victoria, ed. see White, Elga Haymon.
Freund, Kelly J. Patches. (p. 1328)
Freund, Lisa. Seven Natural Wonders: Set Of 6. (p. 1554)
—Seven Natural Wonders & Las siete maravillas naturales del Mundo: 6 English, 6 Spanish Adaptations. (p. 1554)
Freund, William C. Cookie That Saved My Family, Mikle, Toby, illus. (p. 361)
Frevert, Darshell. Myst. (p. 1222)
Frevert, Patricia. Sunday & Every Day: My Little Book of Unitarian Universalism. (p. 1676)
Frew, Katherine. Gladiators: Battling in the Arena. (p. 682)
Frewer, Ellen E., tr. see Verne, Jules.
Frewin Jones, Allan. Mole & Beverley Miller. (p. 1160)
—Starship. (p. 1643)
—Thunderbolt. (p. 1746)
Frewins, Clive & Open Churches Trust Staff. Be a Church Detective: A Young Person's Guide to Old Churches. Davies, Taffy, illus. (p. 148)
Frey, Ben, illus. see McQuinn, Anna.
Frey, Ben, illus. see Winters, Kari-Lynn.
Frey, Bob. Guide to Seldom Seen Animals. (p. 730)
Frey, Cathy. Muttin's Puttins. (p. 1195)
Frey, Christopher. Double Jeopardy: A Workbook for Treating Juvenile Male Sex Offenders/Substance Abusers. (p. 473)
Frey, Daniel, illus. see Edwards, Carol.
Frey, Daniel J. Jacy's Coloring & Activity Book. (p. 905)
Frey, Daniel J., illus. see Edwards, Carol.
Frey, Hildegard G. Camp Fire Girls at Camp Keewaydin: Or, Paddles Down. (p. 257)
—Camp Fire Girls at School or the Woleho Weavers. (p. 257)
—Camp Fire Girls Do Their Bit. (p. 257)
—Camp Fire Girls Go Motoring: Or along the Road That Leads the Way. (p. 257)
—Camp Fire Girls Go Motoring. (p. 257)
—Camp Fire Girls in the Maine Woods: Or the Winnebagos Go Camping. (p. 257)
Frey, Hildegard Gertrude. Camp Fire Girls Do Their Bit: Or over the Top with the Winnebagos. (p. 257)
Frey, James & Johnson-Shelton, Nils. Calling. (p. 254)
—Endgame #2. (p. 527)
—Endgame: Sky Key. (p. 527)
—Endgame - The Calling. (p. 527)
—The Complete Training Diaries. (p. 1728)
Frey, Lisa A. Story of Monet & Renoir. Frey, Lisa A. & Darroch, Jane, eds. (p. 1659)
Frey, Marc, jt. auth. see Davis, Todd.
Frey, Rebecca Joyce. Fundamentalism. (p. 649)
—Genocide & International Justice. (p. 661)
Frey, Wendy. Citizen Heroes. (p. 323)
Freyburger, Nancy. Case of the Hiccuping Clown. (p. 274)
Freymann, Saxton, illus. see Schachner, Judy.
Freymann, Saxton, jt. auth. see Elffers, Joost.
Freymann-Weyr, Garret. After the Moment. (p. 28)
—French Ducks in Venice. McGuire, Erin, illus. (p. 635)
—Stay with Me. (p. 1645)
Freyou, Lerin. Adventures of Piston the Puppy: A Journey Through the Alphabet as Piston Discovers the World Around Him. (p. 21)
Freysinger, Karen. Adventures of Countess Pigula Her Royal Imagination. Freysinger, Karen, illus. (p. 17)
freysinger, karen. Adventures of Countess Pigula up, up & Away. freysinger, karen, illus. (p. 17)
Freytag, Lorna. My Humongous Hamster. Freytag, Lorna, illus. (p. 1211)
—My Humongous Hamster Goes to School. Freytag, Lorna, illus. (p. 1211)
Friar, Christine. Anansi & the Scarecrow. (p. 67)
Friar, Joanne, illus. see Farmer, Jacqueline.
Friar, Joanne, illus. see Heinz, Brian J.
Friar, Joanne, illus. see Heller, Maryellen.
Friar, Joanne, illus. see Helmso, Candy Grant.
Friar, Joanne, illus. see O'Brien, Claudia Moore.
Friar, Joanne H., illus. see Easton, Kelly.
Frias, Miriam Rocio. Cuentos para Ninos Buenos - Relatos Reafirman Valores Humanos. (p. 390)
Fribley, Kara, jt. auth. see Hoffert, Kara.
Frick, Ivi. Hunting with Great Horned Owls. (p. 829)
Frick, Lisa. "Evie" the Little Jack Russell with Brown Around Her Eyes. (p. 546)
Frick, Sheila M. & Kawar, Mary. Core Concepts in Action. (p. 367)
Fricke, Paul. Night of the Bedbugs. (p. 1253)
Fricker, Steve, illus. see Ganeri, Anita.
Frid, Colt & Frid, Randy. Demons at the Door. (p. 426)
Frid, Randy, jt. auth. see Frid, Colt.
Friday, Anita. Twins. Branman, Liz, illus. (p. 1802)
Friday, Arthur, illus. see Barrie, J. M.
Friday, Kisha. Three Fuzzy Little Bees. (p. 1742)
Friday, Mary Ellen. It's a Bad Day. (p. 895)
Friday, Megan. Green Crafts: Become an Earth-Friendly Craft Star, Step by Easy Step! (p. 721)
—Pet Crafts: Everything You Need to Become Your Pet's Craft Star! (p. 1345)
Friday, Stormy. Signal's Airport Adventure. Saroff, Phyllis, illus. (p. 1574)
Friddell, Claudia. Goliath: Hero of the Great Baltimore Fire. Howell, Troy, illus. (p. 696)
Friddle-Ponder, Alma. Bicycle Unit Study Part 1. (p. 177)
—Bicycle Unit Study Part 1 Reading Enhanced Edition. (p. 177)
—Bicycle Unit Study Parts 1 & 2 Comprehensive Edition. (p. 177)
—Chile Pepper Unit Study Comprehensive Edition. (p. 305)
—Chile Pepper Unit Study Graphic Edition. (p. 305)
—Chile Pepper Unit Study Reading Enhanced Edition. (p. 305)
Fridell, Pat, illus. see Kassirer, Sue.
Fridell, Ron. Cruzan V. Missouri & the Right to Die Debate: Debating Supreme Court Decisions. (p. 387)
—Dictatorship. (p. 436)
—Earth-Friendly Energy. (p. 496)
—Environmental Issues. (p. 532)
—Forensic Science. (p. 617)
—Gideon V. Wainwright: The Right to Free Counsel. (p. 674)
—Military Technology. (p. 1143)
—Military Techonology. (p. 1143)
—Miranda Law: The Right to Remain Silent. (p. 1149)
—Prisoners of War. (p. 1407)
—Privacy vs. Security: Your Rights in Conflict. (p. 1407)
—Protecting Earth's Water Supply. (p. 1412)
—Religious Fundamentalism. (p. 1458)
—Seven Wonders of Transportation. (p. 1555)
—Sports Technology. (p. 1633)
—Spy Technology. (p. 1636)
—U. S. v. Eichman: Flag-Burning & Free Speech. (p. 1807)
Fridell, Ron & Walsh, Patricia. Araña (p. 94)
—Calabaza (p. 252)
—Gusano de Seda (p. 732)
—Pumpkin (p. 1416)
—Silkworm (p. 1575)
—Spider (p. 1626)
—Tortuga (p. 1771)
—Turtle (p. 1798)
Fridell, Ron, et al. Pumpkin (p. 1416)
—Silkworm (p. 1575)
—Spider (p. 1626)
—Turtle (p. 1798)
Friden, Chris. Bathtime with Bubbles. (p. 144)
—Bathtime with Bubbles. Zapater Oliva, Carlos & Depew, Robert, illus. (p. 144)
—Bedtime Safari. (p. 157)
—Bedtime Safari. Otoshi, Kathryn & Ciccarelli, Gary, illus. (p. 157)
—Pajamatime with P.J. Zapater Oliva, Carlos & Glazier, Garth, illus. (p. 1319)
—Sleepytime with Rory. (p. 1590)
—Sleepytime with Rory. Zapater Oliva, Carlos & Glazier, Garth, illus. (p. 1590)
—Toothtime with Chomper. (p. 1768)
—Toothtime with Chomper. Rodriguez Braojos, Alberto et al, illus. (p. 1768)
Friden, Chris & Rodriguez Braojos, Alberto. Storytime with Paige. Jaraiz, David, illus. (p. 1664)
Fridman, Sashi. Doll Maker's Gift. Schiffman, Jessica, illus. (p. 463)
—Great Friday Clean-up (French Flap) Salem, Iosi, illus. (p. 716)
—Great Friday Clean-up (Hard Cover) Salem, Iosi, illus. (p. 716)
—Last Pair of Shoes. Seva, illus. (p. 978)
Frie, Robert R. & Zahradnik, Kristen M. Windy Wildwood: The Secret in the Attic. (p. 1936)
Friebert, Judith M. Flying Cats: Oliver & Jimmy. (p. 609)
Fried, Alyssa & Seaman, Jim. Penn State College Prowler off the Record: Inside Pennsylvania State University. (p. 1337)
Fried, Amelie. Is Grandpa Wearing a Suit? Gleich, Jacky, illus. (p. 889)
Fried, Caren Loebel. Legend of the Gourd. (p. 989)
Fried, Ellen. Stars & Galaxies. (p. 1643)
—What's the Chance? (p. 1899)
Fried, Janice, illus. see Abraham, Michelle Shapiro.
Fried, Leah. Where Is Shimmele? Ruppaport, Aviva, tr. from HEB. (p. 1909)
Fried, Mark, tr. see Marques, Jesus Velasco, et al, eds.
Fried, Mary, jt. auth. see Estice, Rose Mary.

Fried, Miriam. My Jelly Bean Book. (p. 1211)
Fried, Scott. My Invisible Kingdom: Letters from the Secret Lives of Teens. (p. 1211)
Friedberg, Adrienne. Hospitality & Personal Care. (p. 801)
Friedenthal, Lora, jt. auth. see Eisenstark, Reyna.
Friedenthal, Lora & Kavanaugh, Dorothy. Religions of Africa. Ojakorotu, Victor & Rotberg, Robert I., eds. (p. 1458)
Friederich, Uve. World of Bridgett & Emily. Fitzpatrick, Meg & Ravenhill, John A., illus. (p. 1956)
Friedericy Dolls. Into the Woods: Favorite Fairy Tales from the World of Friedericy Dolls. Greer, Rob, photos by. (p. 881)
Friedes, Harriet, jt. auth. see Bates, Kenneth.
Friedhoffer, Bob. Everything You Need for Simple Science Fair Projects: Grades 3-5. Colon, Ernie, illus. (p. 545)
—Everything You Need for Winning Science Fair Projects: Grades 5-7. Colon, Ernie, illus. (p. 545)
—More Scientific American Winning Science Fair Projects. (p. 1174)
Friedhoffer, Bob & Tocci, Salvatore. Scientific American Science Fair Projects (p. 1528)
Friedl, Natalie. Help Me Pray Today. (p. 765)
Friedl, Peter, illus. see Holland, Stephanie.
Friedlaender, Linda, jt. auth. see Wallace, Nancy Elizabeth.
Friedland, Joyce, ed. see Alexander, Carol & DiCamillo, Kate.
Friedland, Joyce, ed. see Alexander, Carol.
Friedland, Joyce, ed. see Christopher, Garrett & McDonald, Megan.
Friedland, Joyce, ed. see Christopher, Garrett.
Friedland, Joyce, ed. see Kirsch, Suzanne.
Friedland, Joyce, ed. see Kleinman, Estelle.
Friedland, Joyce, ed. see Searl, Duncan, et al.
Friedland, Joyce, ed. see Searl, Duncan.
Friedland, Joyce, ed. see Stevens, Garrett.
Friedland, Joyce, ed. Cool Zone with Pain & the Great One: Novel-Ties Study Guide. (p. 364)
—Ender's Game: Novel-Ties Study Guide. (p. 527)
—Hunger Games: Novel-Ties Teachers Study Guide. (p. 828)
—Lizzie Bright & the Buckminster Boy: Novel-Ties Study Guide. (p. 1043)
—Rules: Novel-Ties Study Guide. (p. 1495)
—Turtle in Paradise: Novel-Ties Study Guide. (p. 1798)
Friedland, Katy & Shoemaker, Maria K. Art Museum Opposites. (p. 102)
—Is for Art Museum. (p. 889)
Friedland, Katy & Shoemaker, Maria K. A Is for Art Museum. (p. 1)
Friedlander, Mark P. Outbreak: Disease Detectives at Work. (p. 1312)
Friedlander, Mark P., Jr. Innovators in Action! Leonardo Da Vinci Gets a Do-Over. Sakprayoonpong, Worachet Boon, illus. (p. 875)
Friedlander, Randolyn, illus. see Marsh, Carole.
Friedlander, Tim. I Like Me Dance! Edwards, W M, illus. (p. 841)
Friedle, Patricia J., jt. auth. see Alsheimer, Jeanette E.
Friedman, Aimee. Novel Idea. (p. 1268)
—Sea Change. (p. 1534)
—Year My Sister Got Lucky. (p. 1969)
Friedman, Andy. Future Blues. (p. 651)
Friedman, Becky. Daniel Goes to School. (p. 405)
—Daniel Visits the Doctor. (p. 405)
—Daniel's New Friend. (p. 405)
—Welcome to the Neighborhood! (p. 1874)
—Welcome to the Neighborhood! Style Guide Staff & Garwood, Gord, illus. (p. 1874)
Friedman, Brett, jt. auth. see Friedman, Michael.
Friedman, C. S. Dreamwalker. (p. 484)
Friedman, Caitlin. How Do You Feed a Hungry Giant? A Munch-and-Sip Pop-Up Book. Nielsen, Shaw, illus. (p. 808)
Friedman, Carol. Nicky the Jazz Cat. (p. 1251)
—Nicky the Jazz Cat. Friedman, Carol, illus. (p. 1251)
Friedman, D. Dina. Escaping into the Night. (p. 535)
Friedman, Darlene. Star of the Week: A Story of Love, Adoption, & Brownies with Sprinkles. Roth, Roger, illus. (p. 1641)
Friedman, Debbie. Lullaby. Bubar, Lorraine, illus. (p. 1064)
Friedman, Estelle. Ben Franklin. Caraway, James, illus. (p. 163)
Friedman, Hal, jt. auth. see Patterson, James.
Friedman, Hannah. Everything Sucks: Losing My Mind & Finding Myself in a High School Quest for Cool. (p. 545)
Friedman, Ian C. Education Reform. (p. 505)
—Freedom of Speech & the Press. (p. 634)
—Latino Athletes. (p. 979)
—Manny Ramirez. (p. 1088)
Friedman, J. S. Casablanca. Beatrice, Chris, illus. (p. 273)
—In the Beginning. Beatrice, Chris, illus. (p. 865)
—Micetro of Moscow. Beatrice, Chris, illus. (p. 1134)
Friedman, Jeffrey, illus. see Edwards, Jason.
Friedman, Joe. Boobela & the Belching Giant. Childs, Sam, illus. (p. 210)
—Boobela, Worm & Potion Power. Childs, Sam, illus. (p. 210)
Friedman, Judith, illus. see St. Jean, Alan.
Friedman, Judith, illus. see Williams, Christopher.
Friedman, Kinky. Curse of the Missing Puppet Head. (p. 395)
Friedman, Laura, illus. see Coveleskie, Sally & Goodrich, Peter.
Friedman, Laura, illus. see Coveleskie, Sally & Peter, Goodrich.
Friedman, Laura, illus. see Coveleskie, Sally, et al.
Friedman, Laura, et al. Let's Talk Basketball. (p. 1001)
—Let's Talk Soccer. (p. 1001)
Friedman, Lauri S. Abortion. (p. 5)
—Addiction. Haugen, David M., ed. (p. 11)
—Animal Rights. (p. 79)
—Athletes & Drug Use. (p. 112)
—BP Oil Spill. Greenhaven Press Editors, ed. (p. 220)
—Censorship. (p. 286)
—China. (p. 306)
—Crime. (p. 382)
—Cyberbullying. (p. 396)
—Death Penalty. (p. 420)
—Democracy. (p. 425)
—Discrimination. (p. 450)
—Drug Abuse. (p. 486)
—Drunk Driving. Nasso, Christine & Des Chenes, Elizabeth, eds. (p. 487)
—Eating Disorders. (p. 501)
—Endangered Species. (p. 527)
—Fossil Fuels. (p. 623)
—Garbage & Recycling. (p. 655)
—Genetic Engineering. (p. 660)
—Michael Dell. (p. 1134)
—Nuclear Power. (p. 1270)
—Nuclear Weapons & Security. (p. 1270)
—Obesity. (p. 1275)
—Oceans. (p. 1277)
—Organic Food & Farming. (p. 1303)
—Pandemics. (p. 1321)
—Patriot Act. (p. 1329)
—Prisons. Des Chenes, Elizabeth, ed. (p. 1407)
—Recycling. (p. 1453)
—School Shootings. (p. 1523)
—Smoking. (p. 1594)
—Stem Cell Research. (p. 1647)
—Steroids. (p. 1649)
—Terrorism. (p. 1722)
—Weapons of Mass Destruction. (p. 1869)
—Web 2. 0. (p. 1870)
Friedman, Lauri S., ed. see Scherer, Lauri S.
Friedman, Lauri S., ed. see Watkins, Heidi.
Friedman, Lauri S. & Des Chenes, Elizabeth, eds. Discrimination. (p. 450)
—Drug Abuse. (p. 486)
Friedman, Lauri S. & Scherer, Lauri S., eds. Underage Drinking. (p. 1814)
Friedman, Lauri S., ed. Body Image. (p. 207)
—Bullying. (p. 241)
—Eating Disorders. (p. 501)
—Endangered Species. (p. 527)
—Environmentalism. (p. 532)
—Gay Marriage. (p. 659)
—Gays in the Military. (p. 659)
—Genetic Engineering. (p. 660)
—Global Warming. (p. 684)
—Sexual Orientation. (p. 1556)
—Stem Cell Research. (p. 1647)
Friedman, Lauri S., et al. Dangerous Dues: What You Need to Know about Gangs (p. 404)
Friedman, Laurie. Back to School, Mallory. Schmitz, Tamara, illus. (p. 130)
—Back-to-School Rules. Murfin, Teresa, illus. (p. 130)
—Campfire Mallory. (p. 257)
—Campfire Mallory. Kalis, Jennifer, illus. (p. 257)
—Can You Say Catastrophe? (p. 259)
—Clases Otra Vez, Mallory. Anaya, Josefina, tr. from ENG. (p. 327)
—Happy Birthday, Mallory! Schmitz, Tamara, illus. (p. 745)
—Happy New Year, Mallory! (p. 746)
—Happy New Year, Mallory! Kalis, Jennifer, illus. (p. 746)
—Heart to Heart with Mallory. (p. 760)
—Heart to Heart with Mallory. Pollak, Barbara, illus. (p. 760)
—Honestly, Mallory! (p. 794)
—Honestly, Mallory! Pollak, Barbara, illus. (p. 794)
—I'm Not Afraid of This Haunted House. Murfin, Teresa, illus. (p. 859)
—In Business with Mallory. Pollak, Barbara, illus. (p. 863)
—Love, Ruby Valentine. Cravath, Lynne Avril, illus. (p. 1060)
—Mallory & Mary Ann Take New York. Kalis, Jennifer, illus. (p. 1083)
—Mallory Goes Green! Kalis, Jennifer, illus. (p. 1083)
—Mallory in the Spotlight. Kalis, Jennifer, illus. (p. 1083)
—Mallory McDonald, Super Snoop. Kalis, Jennifer, illus. (p. 1083)
—Mallory on Board. (p. 1083)
—Mallory on Board. Pollak, Barbara, illus. (p. 1083)
—Mallory on the Move. Schmitz, Tamara, tr. (p. 1083)
—Mallory on the Move. Schmitz, Tamara, illus. (p. 1083)
—Mallory vs. Max. Schmitz, Tamara, illus. (p. 1083)
—Mallory's Guide to Boys, Brothers, Dads, & Dogs. Kalis, Jennifer, illus. (p. 1084)
—Mallory's Super Sleepover. Kalis, Jennifer, illus. (p. 1084)
—Oh Boy, Mallory. Kalis, Jennifer, illus. (p. 1280)
—Play It Again, Mallory. Kalis, Jennifer, illus. (p. 1371)
—Red, White, & True Blue Mallory. Kalis, Jennifer, illus. (p. 1455)
—Ruby Valentine & the Sweet Surprise. Avril, Lynne, illus. (p. 1493)
—Ruby Valentine Saves the Day. Avril, Lynne, illus. (p. 1493)
—Step Fourth, Mallory! Kalis, Jennifer, illus. (p. 1647)
—Thanksgiving Rules. Murfin, Teresa, illus. (p. 1726)
—Three's Company, Mallory! Kalis, Jennifer, illus. (p. 1744)
—Too Good to Be True. (p. 1766)
Friedman, Laurie B. Birthday Rules. Murfin, Teresa, illus. (p. 193)
—Change Is in the Air, Mallory. Kalis, Jennifer, illus. (p. 290)
—Game Time, Mallory! Kalis, Jennifer, illus. (p. 654)
—Love or Something Like It. (p. 1060)
—Mallory McDonald, Baby Expert. Kalis, Jennifer, illus. (p. 1083)
—Not What I Expected. Shaloshvili, Natasha, illus. (p. 1267)
—Truth & Kisses. (p. 1794)
Friedman, Lise. Becoming a Ballerina: A Nutcracker Story. Dowdle, Mary, illus. (p. 156)
Friedman, Lita. Mary Robinson: Fighter for Human Rights. (p. 1101)
Friedman, Mark. America's Struggle with Terrorism. (p. 64)
—Democratic Process. (p. 425)
—What Does It Do? Combine. (p. 1884)
—What Does It Do? Windmill. (p. 1884)
Friedman, Mark & Benoit, Peter. Apache. (p. 91)
Friedman, Mark D. Genocide (p. 661)
—Human Rights (p. 826)
Friedman, Matthew. Tic-Tac-Math: 50 Reproducible, Leveled Game Sheets That Kids Can Use Independently or in Small Groups to Practice Important Math Skills. (p. 1747)
Friedman, Maya. Three Falafels in My Pita. Mack, Steve, illus. (p. 1742)
Friedman, Mel. Africa. (p. 26)
—Algebra & Functions Workbook. (p. 38)
—Ancient China. (p. 68)
—Antarctica. (p. 88)
—Australia & Oceania. (p. 116)
—California Gold Rush. (p. 253)
—China. (p. 306)
—Geometry. (p. 662)
—Iraq. (p. 887)
—Mystery of the Backlot Banshee: A ClueFinders Mystery Adventure. (p. 1225)
—Number & Operations. (p. 1271)
—Oregon Trail. (p. 1303)
Friedman, Mel, jt. auth. see Weiss, Ellen.
Friedman, Mel, et al. Castillo para Gatitos. Adams, Lynn, illus. (p. 276)
Friedman, Michael. Cell Communication: Understanding How Information Is Stored & Used in Cells. (p. 286)
—Settlement Houses: Improving the Social Welfare of America's Immigrants. (p. 1554)
Friedman, Michael & Friedman, Brett. Cell Communication: Understanding How Information Is Stored & Used in Cells. (p. 286)
—Settlement Houses: Improving the Social Welfare of America's Immigrants. (p. 1554)
Friedman, Michael Jan, et al. Convergence. Erwin, Steve et al, illus. (p. 361)
Friedman, Michael (Myk), illus. see Clark, Susan, ed.
Friedman, Michelle. Close Your Eyes. (p. 334)
Friedman, Michelle S. Everything You Need to Know about Schizophrenia. (p. 546)
Friedman, Nick. Mike Piazza. (p. 1141)
Friedman, Pamela. Activités d'Halloween. Bauer, Larry, illus. (p. 10)
Friedman, Pamela & Bauer, Larry. Activites de Fin d'Annee Scolaire. (p. 10)
Friedman, Randee & Lander, Donna, eds. New Rabbi Joe Black Songbook: Selected Songs from Aleph Bet Boogie, Everybody's Got A Little Music, Leave A Little Bit Undone, Sabbatical. (p. 1247)
Friedman, Richard D., jt. auth. see Heppermann, Christine.
Friedman, Richard D., jt. auth. see Kenney, Karen Latchana.
Friedman, Robert S., jt. auth. see Tolle, Eckhart.
Friedman, Robin. Importance of Wings. (p. 862)
—Nothing. (p. 1268)
—Silent Witness: A True Story of the Civil War. Nivola, Claire A., illus. (p. 1575)
Friedman, Rosalind. Hannukah Holiday. (p. 743)
Friedman, Samantha & Matisse, Henri. Matisse's Garden. Amodeo, Cristina, illus. (p. 1109)
Friedman, Sarah & Gohari, Omid. Bryn Mawr College College Prowler off the Record. (p. 233)
Friedman, Stanley. I, Dinosaur. (p. 837)
—Quantum Outlaws. (p. 1422)
—Quantum Prisoner. (p. 1422)
Friedman-Brunt, Elyse. Conflict Resolution in American History, Gr. 8: Lessons from the Past, Lessons for Today. Chandler, Terrence, illus. (p. 357)
—Conflict Resolution in American History, Grade 8: Lessons from the Past, Lessons for Today. Chandler, Terrence, illus. (p. 357)
Friedmann, Frank. I Was Wrong, but God Made Me Right. (p. 848)
Friedmann, Patty. Taken Away. (p. 1697)
Friedrich, Eliza. Play Pray & Hooray. (p. 1371)
Friedrich, Joachim. Disappearing Bio Teacher. (p. 446)
Friedrich, Mike. Hawkeye. Heck, Don & Byrne, John, illus. (p. 755)
—Phantom Stranger. (p. 1349)
Friedrich, Mike, et al. Essential Iron Man - Volume 5. Tuska, George et al, illus. (p. 537)
Friedrich, Richard, ed. see Mahan, Asa & Hills, Aaron Merritt.
Friedrich, Richard, ed. see Mahan, Asa.
Friedrich, Richard M., ed. see Mahan, Asa.
Friel, John P., et al, eds. Exploring the World of Aquatic Life (p. 554)
Friel, Maeve. Broomstick Collection Reed, Nathan, illus. (p. 231)
—Charlie's Story (p. 293)
—Charming or What? (p. 294)
—Last Task. Reed, Nathan, illus. (p. 979)
—Moonlight Mischief. Reed, Nathan, illus. (p. 1172)
—Watch-in-Train: Spelling Trouble. Vol. 2 (p. 1861)
—Witch Switch. (p. 1941)
Friend, Albert Lewis, Sr. Innocent 28 Years Old Forgotten in Prison. (p. 875)
Friend, Alison. Freddy & Frito & the Clubhouse Rules. Friend, Alison, illus. (p. 633)
Friend, Alison, illus. see Haas, Jessie.
Friend, Alison, illus. see Kumin, Maxine.
Friend, Alison, illus. see Root, Phyllis.
Friend, Amanda. Lisa & Laura: African Safari Park Adventure. (p. 1021)
Friend, Bonnie, illus. see Waxman, Melanie Brown.
Friend, Catherine. Eddie the Raccoon: Brand New Readers. Yee, Wong Herbert, illus. (p. 503)
—Perfect Nest. Manders, John, illus. (p. 1342)
—When Night & Day Meet. (p. 1904)
Friend, David Michael, illus. see Low, Alice.
Friend, David Michael, illus. see Petty, J. T.
Friend, David Michael, tr. see Low, Alice.
Friend, Gaythel & Miller, Dalton. Mystery of the Green Box. (p. 1225)
Friend, Gaythel Boggs & Miller, Dalton. Foundation of a Clown (p. 624)
Friend, Larry. Icy the Iceberg. Makis, Sidney, illus. (p. 851)
—Squirrelly the Squirrel & Starlett. (p. 1637)
Friend, Natasha. Bounce. (p. 216)
—For Keeps. (p. 615)
—My Life in Black & White. (p. 1212)
—Perfect. (p. 1341)
Friend, Peter. What's the Matter, Aunty May? Joyner, Andrew, illus. (p. 1899)
Friend, R. Down on Friendly Acres Set 1: Books #1-4 (p. 474)
—R. Friend - Hats off to Heroes. (p. 1429)
—Time Out at Home. (p. 1752)
friend, robyn, jt. auth. see cohen, judith L.
Friend, Robyn, jt. auth. see Cohen, Judith Love.
Friend, Robyn & Cohen, Judith. Electricity & You: Be Smart, Be Safe. Katz, David, illus. (p. 509)
Friend, Robyn C. Women of Apollo. Katz, David Arthur, illus. (p. 1946)
Friend, Robyn C., jt. auth. see Cohen, Judith Love.
Friend, Robyn C. & cohen, Judith Love. Clean City: The Green Construction Story. (p. 330)
friend, robyn C. & Cohen, Judith Love. Clean Planet: The Solar Power Story. Katz, David A., illus. (p. 330)
friend, robyn C. & cohen, Judith Love. Clean Planet: The Solar Power Story. katz, david A., illus. (p. 330)
Friend, Robyn C. & Cohen, Judith Love. Cleaner Port, A Brighter Future: The Greening of the Port of Los Angeles. Katz, David Arthur, illus. (p. 330)
Friend, Ronda. R. Friend Swallows Her Pride. (p. 1429)
Friend, Sandra. Exploring Planet Earth (p. 553)
Friend, Shirley. Lucy a Special Ragdoll. (p. 1063)
Friendly, Aunt. Todos Pueden Ayudar. Greendyk, William, tr. from ENG. (p. 1761)
Friends General Conference (U.S.), Religious Education Committee Staff, contrib. by. Lives That Speak: Stories of Twentieth-Century Quakers. (p. 1040)
Friends of Congaree Swamp Staff, jt. contrib. by see Carolinas' Nature Photographers Association Staff.
Frierson, Natasha. Teaching the Abc's W/ the Bible. (p. 1710)
Friese, Diane, et al. Terrible Terrible Terra. (p. 1721)
Friese, Diane Lynn, et al. Martoose, the Pampered Mouse: A Story of Love & Friendship. Friese, Diane Lynn, illus. (p. 1098)
Friesel, Uwe. Tim, the Peacemaker. Wilkon, Jozef, illus. (p. 1750)
Friesen, Anni, illus. see Unrau, Adela.
Friesen, Christi. Under the Sea. (p. 1814)
Friesen, Gayle. For Now. (p. 616)
—Isabel Factor. (p. 890)
Friesen, Helen Lepp. Chimpanzees. (p. 306)
—Fishing. (p. 599)
—Growing a Pumpkin. (p. 726)
—India. (p. 870)
—Maple Syrup. (p. 1090)
—Needs in Nature. (p. 1239)
—Oklahoma: The Sooner State. (p. 1283)
—Oregon: The Beaver State. (p. 1303)
—Pennsylvania: The Keystone State. (p. 1338)
—Puerto Rico: Isle of Enchantment. (p. 1415)
—Rhode Island: The Ocean State. (p. 1468)
—Scaly & Scary. (p. 1519)
—Tio Sam. (p. 1757)
—Uncle Sam with Code. (p. 1812)
—Uses of Light. (p. 1828)
—Vermont: The Green Mountain State. (p. 1837)
—Who Lives Here? (p. 1916)
Friesen, Jonathan. Jerk, California. (p. 913)
—Last Martin (p. 978)
—Mayday. (p. 1113)
—Rush. (p. 1497)
Friesen, Ray. Cheese Related Mishap & Other Stories. (p. 296)
—Fairy Tales I Just Made Up: Snarky Bedtime Stories for Weirdo Children. Liew, Sonny et al, illus. (p. 564)
—Lookit! (p. 1051)
—Pirate Penguin vs Ninja Chicken Volume 1: Troublems with Frenemies: Troublems with Frenemies. (p. 1362)
—RQW (p. 1493)
—RQW Comics #1-4 Collection. (p. 1493)
—Yarg! & Other Stories. (p. 1968)
Friesen, Ray, illus. see Osborn, Linda.
Friesen, Wallace V., jt. auth. see Ekman, Paul.
Friesen, Wayne, illus. see Henry, LaTosha.
Friesen-Wood, Judy. Aloha Cheerio. (p. 48)
Friesner, Esther. Deception's Princess. (p. 421)
—Spirit's Chosen. (p. 1629)
Friesner, Esther, jt. auth. see Friesner, Esther M.
Friesner, Esther & Friesner, Esther M. Nobody's Princess. (p. 1262)
—Nobody's Prize. (p. 1262)
Friesner, Esther M. Deception's Pawn. (p. 421)
—Sphinx's Princess. (p. 1626)
—Sphinx's Queen. (p. 1626)
—Spirit's Bride. (p. 1629)
—Spirit's Princess. (p. 1629)
Friesner, Esther M., jt. auth. see Friesner, Esther.
Friesner, Esther M. & Friesner, Esther. Temping Fate. (p. 1718)
Friesner, Esther M., et al. Cthulhu & the Coeds or Kids & Squids. (p. 387)
Friestad, Kathleen M., et al. Kids' Book of Weather Forecasting. Kline, Michael, illus. (p. 952)
—Kids' Book of Weather Forecasting. Friestad, Kathleen M. & Kline, Michael, illus. (p. 952)
Friester, Paul. Owl Howl. Goossens, Philippe, illus. (p. 1315)
Friester, Paul & Goossens, Philippe. Owl Howl. (p. 1315)
Frieter, Paul & Goossens, Philippe. Owl Howls Again! (p. 1315)
Frieyro, Alicia, tr. see Hurley, Tonya.
Frigon, Kerry, photos by see Ferguson, Gloria.
Friis, Karen, illus. see Jonas-Simpson, Christine.
Frillman, K. Country Stars: The Road Less Traveled. (p. 372)
Frink, Amy M. My Dream Pillow. (p. 1202)
Frink, Phil, photos by see Costa, David.
Frink-Hunter, Chene I. Grandma Died & Mommy Really, Really Cried: Death - Dying. Robertson, Michael, illus. (p. 708)
Frino, Lucy & Williams, Melanie. Kid's Box Level 2 Teacher's Book. (p. 952)
Frino, Michael G. Welcome to Waycool School: Where Learning Is Fun & Lessons are Learned by Everyone! (p. 1874)

F

Frino Ph. D., Michael G. Waycool School Takes the Bus. (p. 1865)
Fripp, Deborah & Fripp, Michael. Naya & Nathan. Fripp, Jean, ed. (p. 1238)
—Naya & the Haunted Shipwreck. Fripp, Jean, ed. (p. 1238)
Fripp, Jean, ed. see Fripp, Deborah & Fripp, Michael.
Fripp, Jean, jt. auth. see Valeska, John.
Fripp, Jean, jt. auth. see Valeska, Jon.
Fripp, Michael, jt. auth. see Fripp, Deborah.
Frippiat, Stéphanie, jt. auth. see Genechten, Guido van.
Frippiat, Stéphanie, jt. auth. see van Genechten, Guido.
Frisaro, Joe. Peyton Manning: Passing Legacy. (p. 1349)
—Reggie Miller: From Downtown. (p. 1457)
Frisch, Aaron. Aaron Rodgers. (p. 2)
—Adrian Peterson. (p. 13)
—Albert Einstein. (p. 34)
—Albert Pujols. (p. 34)
—Atlanta Hawks. (p. 112)
—Baltimore Orioles. (p. 135)
—Baltimore Ravens. (p. 135)
—Bees. (p. 157)
—Boston Celtics. (p. 215)
—Boston Red Sox. (p. 215)
—Bulldozers. (p. 240)
—Butterflies. (p. 247)
—Chicago Bears. (p. 299)
—Chicago Bulls. (p. 299)
—Chicago White Sox. (p. 299)
—Christmas. (p. 312)
—Coral Reefs. (p. 366)
—Cranes. (p. 376)
—Dallas Cowboys. (p. 401)
—Dark Fiddler: The Life & Legend of Nicolo Paganini. Kelley, Gary, illus. (p. 407)
—Denver Broncos. (p. 427)
—Detroit Pistons. (p. 431)
—Diggers. (p. 439)
—Dump Trucks. (p. 489)
—Easter. (p. 499)
—Edgar Allan Poe. (p. 504)
—Edgar Allan Poe. Kelley, Gary, illus. (p. 504)
—Florida Marlins. (p. 607)
—Frogs. (p. 641)
—Ghosts. (p. 672)
—Golden State Warriors. (p. 695)
—Green Bay Packers. (p. 721)
—History of the Chicago Bears. (p. 784)
—History of the Detroit Lions. (p. 785)
—History of the Minnesota Vikings. (p. 785)
—History of the Oakland Raiders. (p. 785)
—History of the Tennessee Titans. (p. 785)
—Houston Rockets. (p. 804)
—Indianapolis Colts. (p. 871)
—Jesse James. (p. 914)
—Justin Bieber. (p. 940)
—Kansas City Chiefs. (p. 943)
—Katy Perry. (p. 946)
—Koalas. (p. 966)
—Lady Gaga. (p. 970)
—Ladybugs. (p. 971)
—Lakes. (p. 972)
—Lebron James. (p. 986)
—Lions. (p. 1021)
—Lonely Pine. Delessert, Etienne, illus. (p. 1046)
—Los Angeles Dodgers. (p. 1053)
—Los Angeles Lakers. (p. 1053)
—Miami Dolphins. (p. 1133)
—Miami Heat. (p. 1133)
—Milwaukee Bucks. (p. 1145)
—Minnesota Twins. (p. 1147)
—Mummies. (p. 1190)
—New England Patriots. (p. 1244)
—New Orleans Saints. (p. 1246)
—New York Giants. (p. 1248)
—New York Islanders. (p. 1248)
—New York Jets. (p. 1248)
—New York Knicks. (p. 1248)
—New York Yankees. (p. 1248)
—Night on the Range. Sheban, Chris, illus. (p. 1254)
—Oakland Raiders. (p. 1274)
—Oakland Raiders. (p. 1275)
—Oklahoma City Thunder. (p. 1283)
—Philadelphia 76ers. (p. 1350)
—Philadelphia Phillies. (p. 1350)
—Pirates at the Plate. Summers, Mark, illus. (p. 1363)
—Pittsburgh Steelers. (p. 1364)
—Pittsburgh Steelers. (p. 1365)
—Portland Trail Blazers. (p. 1386)
—Prairies. (p. 1393)
—Rivers. (p. 1476)
—Sacramento Kings. (p. 1500)
—San Antonio Spurs. (p. 1510)
—San Francisco 49ers. (p. 1510)
—San Francisco Giants. (p. 1510)
—Seedlings: Bees. (p. 1547)
—Seedlings: Bulldozers. (p. 1547)
—Seedlings: Butterflies. (p. 1547)
—Seedlings: Cranes. (p. 1547)
—Seedlings: Diggers. (p. 1547)
—Seedlings: Dump Trucks. (p. 1547)
—Seedlings: Frogs. (p. 1547)
—Seedlings: Ladybugs. (p. 1547)
—St. Louis Cardinals. (p. 1638)
—St. Louis Rams. (p. 1638)
—Story of Nike. (p. 1659)
—Story of Sony. (p. 1660)
—Story of the Baltimore Ravens. (p. 1660)
—Story of the Dallas Mavericks. (p. 1660)
—Story of the Indiana Pacers. (p. 1661)
—Story of the Los Angeles Clippers. (p. 1661)
—Story of the Phoenix Suns. (p. 1662)
—Story of the Portland Trail Blazers. (p. 1662)
—Story of the Washington Wizards. (p. 1662)
—Tampa Bay Buccaneers. (p. 1704)
—Taylor Swift. (p. 1708)
—That's Spooky: Ghosts. (p. 1727)
—That's Spooky: Mummies. (p. 1727)
—That's Spooky: Vampires. (p. 1727)
—That's Spooky: Werewolves. (p. 1727)
—That's Spooky: Witches. (p. 1727)
—That's Spooky: Zombies. (p. 1727)
—Toronto Blue Jays. (p. 1770)
—Tundra. (p. 1796)
—Vampires. (p. 1832)
—Washington Redskins. (p. 1860)
—Washington Wizards. (p. 1860)
—Werewolves. (p. 1875)
—Wetlands. (p. 1877)
—Witches. (p. 1941)
—Zombies. (p. 1988)
Frisch, Aaron & Bodden, Valerie. Big Time: Aaron Rodgers. (p. 184)
—Big Time: Adrian Peterson. (p. 184)
—Big Time: Lebron James. (p. 184)
Frisch, Aaron & Gilbert, Sara. Story of McDonald's. (p. 1659)
Frisch, Carlienne A. Everything You Need to Know about Getting a Job. (p. 545)
—Money Matters: A Teen Guide to the Economics of Divorce. (p. 1164)
—When a Friend Has a Drug Problem. (p. 1901)
—Wyoming. (p. 1966)
Frisch, Joy. Bulldogs. (p. 240)
—Ground Sloths. (p. 725)
—Retrievers. (p. 1464)
Frisch, Nate. Badlands National Park. (p. 132)
—Big Bend National Park. (p. 178)
—Death Valley National Park. (p. 420)
—Everglades National Park. (p. 542)
—Grand Canyon National Park. (p. 707)
—Grand Teton National Park. (p. 707)
—Great Smoky Mountains National Park. (p. 718)
—NBA: a History of Hoops: the Story of the Brooklyn Nets. (p. 1238)
—NBA: a History of Hoops: the Story of the Cleveland Cavaliers. (p. 1238)
—NBA: a History of Hoops: the Story of the Dallas Mavericks. (p. 1238)
—NBA: a History of Hoops: the Story of the Golden State Warriors. (p. 1238)
—NBA: a History of Hoops: the Story of the Houston Rockets. (p. 1238)
—NBA: a History of Hoops: the Story of the Indiana Pacers. (p. 1238)
—NBA: a History of Hoops: the Story of the Memphis Grizzlies. (p. 1238)
—NBA: a History of Hoops: the Story of the Phoenix Suns. (p. 1238)
—NFL Today: Atlanta Falcons. (p. 1249)
—NFL Today: Carolina Panthers. (p. 1249)
—NFL Today: Denver Broncos. (p. 1250)
—NFL Today: Detroit Lions. (p. 1250)
—NFL Today: Houston Texans. (p. 1250)
—NFL Today: Jacksonville Jaguars. (p. 1250)
—NFL Today: Kansas City Chiefs. (p. 1250)
—NFL Today: Oakland Raiders. (p. 1250)
—NFL Today: Philadelphia Eagles. (p. 1250)
—NFL Today: St. Louis Rams. (p. 1250)
—NFL Today: Tampa Bay Buccaneers. (p. 1250)
—Preserving America: Death Valley National Park. (p. 1396)
—Preserving America: Everglades National Park. (p. 1396)
—Preserving America: Great Smoky Mountains National Park. (p. 1396)
—Preserving America: Yellowstone National Park. (p. 1396)
—Preserving America: Yosemite National Park. (p. 1396)
—Rocky Mountain National Park. (p. 1484)
—Story of the Atlanta Falcons. (p. 1660)
—Story of the Brooklyn Nets. (p. 1660)
—Story of the Carolina Panthers. (p. 1660)
—Story of the Chicago Bulls. (p. 1660)
—Story of the Cleveland Cavaliers. (p. 1660)
—Story of the Dallas Mavericks. (p. 1660)
—Story of the Denver Broncos. (p. 1660)
—Story of the Detroit Lions. (p. 1660)
—Story of the Golden State Warriors. (p. 1661)
—Story of the Houston Rockets. (p. 1661)
—Story of the Houston Texans. (p. 1661)
—Story of the Indiana Pacers. (p. 1661)
—Story of the Jacksonville Jaguars. (p. 1661)
—Story of the Kansas City Chiefs. (p. 1661)
—Story of the Memphis Grizzlies. (p. 1661)
—Story of the Oakland Raiders. (p. 1661)
—Story of the Philadelphia Eagles. (p. 1662)
—Story of the Phoenix Suns. (p. 1662)
—Story of the St. Louis Rams. (p. 1662)
—Story of the Tampa Bay Buccaneers. (p. 1662)
—Story of the Toronto Raptors. (p. 1662)
—Yellowstone National Park. (p. 1970)
—Yosemite National Park. (p. 1972)
Frisch, Wilhelmine. Storks of Lillegaard. Jauss, Anne Marie, illus. (p. 1655)
Frisch-Schmoll, Joy. Arctic Shrews. (p. 96)
—Before & After. (p. 158)
—Brushes with Greatness: Portraits. (p. 233)
—Brushes with Greatness: Still Lifes. (p. 233)
—Exploring Opposites. (p. 553)
—Gravity. (p. 712)
—In & Out. (p. 863)
—Magnetism. (p. 1075)
—Motion & Movement. (p. 1179)
—Near & Far. (p. 1238)
—Temperature. (p. 1717)
—Top & Bottom. (p. 1769)
Frisch-Schmoll, Joy & Higgins, Melissa. Ice Age Animals. (p. 850)
Frish, Aaron. Voices in Poetry: Edgar Allan Poe. (p. 1848)
Frishman Co., ed. Standardized Test Prep (p. 1639)
Frisk, Maria, illus. see Perkins, Nicole.
Friskey, Margaret. Surprise on Wheels. Patton, Lucia, illus. (p. 1686)
—True Book of Birds We Know. Pistorius, Anna, illus. (p. 1792)
Fristoe, Teresa. Ollie the Anteater Saves the Day. (p. 1287)
Fritchman, Reta. Spring Praise. (p. 1635)
Frith, Alex. 100 Things to Know about Science. (p. 1999)
—Big Book of Dinosaurs Internet Referenced. Fiorin, Fabiano, illus. (p. 179)
—Forensic Science. Chen, Kuo Kan et al, illus. (p. 617)
—Lift the Flap Picture Atlas. (p. 1014)
—Look Inside Trains. (p. 1049)
—See Inside Science. (p. 1546)
—See Inside the World of Dinosaurs. Scott, Peter, illus. (p. 1546)
—Submarines II. (p. 1671)
—Travel Pocket Puzzle Book. (p. 1780)
—What's Math All About? (p. 1898)
Frith, Alex, ed. see Brook, Henry.
Frith, Alex & King, Colin. See Inside Inventions IR. (p. 1546)
—See Inside Your Head. (p. 1546)
—See under the Ground. (p. 1547)
Frith, Alex & Lacey, Minna. See Inside Math - Internet Referenced. (p. 1546)
Frith, Barbara, jt. auth. see Carroll, Lewis, pseud.
Frith, Lilla. Jason's Talking Computer: Book Three. (p. 910)
Frith, Margaret. Frida Kahlo: The Artist Who Painted Herself. dePaola, Tomie, illus. (p. 637)
—Who Was Franklin Roosevelt? Harrison, Nancy & O'Brien, John, illus. (p. 1918)
—Who Was Louis Braille? (p. 1918)
—Who Was Louis Braille? Anderson, Scott & Squier, Robert, illus. (p. 1918)
—Who Was Thomas Alva Edison? O'Brien, John, illus. (p. 1919)
—Who Was Thomas Alva Edison? O'Brien, John A. et al, illus. (p. 1919)
—Who Was Woodrow Wilson? Thomson, Andrew & Harrison, Nancy, illus. (p. 1919)
Frith, Michael, jt. auth. see Eastman, P. D.
Frith, Sherry. Sticky Icky Booger Bugs. (p. 1650)
Frits, Mary Ann, ed. Trendy Tops. (p. 1784)
Fritz, Barbara & Metzger, Martina, eds. New Issues in Regional Monetary Coordination: Understanding North-South & South-South Arrangements. (p. 1245)
Fritz, Betty. Bang Bang Bang, Hammers in the Morning. (p. 136)
—Bang Bang Bang... Hammers in the Morning. (p. 136)
Fritz, Greg. God Made You Special. (p. 690)
—God Made You Special! Reed, Lisa, illus. (p. 690)
Fritz, Jean. Alexander Hamilton - The Outsider. (p. 36)
—Bunny Hopwell's First Spring. Dixon, Rachel, illus. (p. 242)
—Double Life of Pocahontas. (p. 473)
—Homesick: My Own Story. Tomes, Margot, illus. (p. 793)
—Lost Colony of Roanoke. Talbott, Hudson, illus. (p. 1055)
—Will You Sign Here, John Hancock? Hyman, Trina Schart, illus. (p. 1932)
Fritz, Jean & Clute, Tom. Champion Dog Prince Tom. (p. 289)
Fritz, Julie. My Mother Is an Astronaut. (p. 1214)
Fritz, Kathleen Cheney, illus. see Lewis, Anne Margaret.
Fritz, Kevin. Newf & the Dane. (p. 1249)
Fritz, Laura. Poodle on a Noodle. (p. 1383)
Fritz, Roger. Power of a Positive Attitude: Discovering the Key to Success. (p. 1389)
Fritz, Ronald, illus. see Gabriel, Nat & Ramirez, Alma.
Fritz, Sandy. Genomics & Cloning. (p. 661)
—Nanotechnology: Invisible Machines. (p. 1229)
—Robotics & Artificial Intelligence. (p. 1481)
Fritz, Siegfried, illus. see Iverson, Gregory.
Fritz, Siegfried, illus. see Iverson, Gregry.
Fritz, William J. Roadside Geology of the Yellowstone Country. (p. 1477)
Fritzsche, Peter. Golden Hamsters. (p. 694)
Frizzell, Colin. Chill (p. 305)
—Just J (p. 938)
Frizzell, Sally Parker. Adventures in the Secret Valley. (p. 15)
Frodsham, Ken. Mobile Phone of Jeremy Bone. (p. 1157)
Froeb, Lori. Child's Book of Parables. Mironey, Tracy, illus. (p. 304)
—I Am Daisy. Lemay, Violet, illus. (p. 832)
—I Am Daisy, Level 2. Lemay, Violet, illus. (p. 832)
—I Am McKinley, Level 2. Sakamoto, Miki, illus. (p. 833)
—I Am Nibbles, Level 2. Lyon, Tammie, illus. (p. 833)
Froeb, Lori, ed. see Wallace, Daniel.
Froeb, Lori & Brown, Jo. Zoo! A Big Fold-Out Counting Book. (p. 1988)
Froeb, Lori C. Amazing Human Machine: Book with Acetate Body System Cards. (p. 54)
—Boat Noah Built. Sakamoto, Miki, illus. (p. 205)
—Build My Own Mighty Machines: Construct 3 Amazing Machines! (p. 238)
—Build My Own Rescue Machines: Construct 3 Amazing Machines! (p. 238)
—Butterphants & Elefties. Rinaldo, Luana, illus. (p. 248)
—Colors All Around. (p. 345)
—Farm Friends. SI Artists Staff, illus. (p. 574)
—Fisher Price Little People Noah & the Animals. SI Artists Staff, illus. (p. 599)
—God's Creation Rinaldo, Luana, illus. (p. 691)
—Noah & the Animals. Corke, Estelle, illus. (p. 1261)
—Noah's Ark Rinaldo, Luana, illus. (p. 1261)
Froeb, Lori C., jt. auth. see Reader's Digest Editors.
Froeb, Lori C., jt. auth. see Reader's Digest Staff.
Froeb, Lori C. & Disney Storybook Artists Staff. Cinderella's Shining Moment. (p. 320)
Froeb, Lori C. & Weiss, Ellen. Let's Go to the Farm (Vamos a la Granja) Artists, S. I., illus. (p. 997)
—Let's Go to the Zoo! Artists, S. I., illus. (p. 998)
Froeb, Lori C., ed. My First Bedtime Bible Stories. Jones, Anna, illus. (p. 1204)
Froeber, Sarah & Mosher, Kim. Pelican & Pelicant. (p. 1335)
Froemming, Kaylee. My Mama's Hair Is Everywhere: It just won't go Away!! (p. 1214)
Froese, Dorothy Cheever. Captain Rhino's Progress: An Allegory of the Workplace. (p. 264)
Froggatt, Sarah H. E. Leopard Spots: How the Clouded Leopard Got Her Spots. (p. 993)
Froh, Joanne. Imagine This! Plagens, Frances, illus. (p. 861)
Frohlich, Anja. Animals in the Outhouse. Kiss, Gergely, illus. (p. 83)
Fröhlich, Lorenz, illus. see Andersen, Hans Christian.
Frohlichstein, Jack. Mathematical Fun, Games & Puzzles. (p. 1107)
Frohmuth, Shawn. Wiblet. (p. 1927)
Frohnapfel-Krueger, Lisa. Does Outsourcing Harm America? (p. 460)
—Teen Pregnancy & Parenting. Gale Editors, ed. (p. 1713)
Frohnen, Bruce. American Republic. (p. 63)
Froimowitz, Michael P. Electrum. Fedigan-Linton, Katherine V., illus. (p. 510)
Froissart, Benedicte. Uncle Henry's Dinner Guests. (p. 1811)
Froley, Margaux. Escape Theory. (p. 535)
—Hero Complex. (p. 772)
Froman, Annabelle. Beezeur. (p. 158)
Froman, Craig. Passport to the World: Your a to z guided Tour. (p. 1327)
Froman, Nan. What's That Bug? Everyday Insects & Their Really Cool Cousins. Mulock, Julian, illus. (p. 1899)
Fromental, Jean-Luc. 365 Penguins. Jolivet, Joëlle, illus. (p. 2001)
—Oops! Connors, Thomas, tr. from FRE. (p. 1298)
—Rapido's Next Stop. Jolivet, Joëlle, illus. (p. 1439)
Fromer, Liza & Francine, Gerstein. My Noisy Body. Weissmann, Joe, illus. (p. 1216)
Fromer, Liza & Gerstein, Francine. My Achy Body. Weissmann, Joe, illus. (p. 1195)
—My Healthy Body. Weissmann, Joe, illus. (p. 1210)
—My Itchy Body. Weissmann, Joe, illus. (p. 1211)
—My Messy Body. Weissmann, Joe, illus. (p. 1214)
—My Stretchy Body. Weissmann, Joe, illus. (p. 1219)
Fromm, Megan. Accuracy in Media (p. 8)
—Digital Content Creation (p. 439)
—Gathering & Sharing Digital Information (p. 658)
—Privacy & Digital Security (p. 1407)
—Understanding Advertising & Monetization (p. 1815)
—Why the News Matters (p. 1926)
Frommer, Abbey C. New Fight: (Sequel to the Nix) (p. 1244)
Frommer, Julia. Happiness Is Yours. (p. 744)
Fromowitz, Lori. Louisa May Alcott. (p. 1058)
Fronczak, Blaine. Haley Helps at School: Use Place Value & Properties of Operations to Add. (p. 736)
—Haley Helps at School. (p. 736)
Fronczak, Emerson. There's a Food Chain in Your Garden! (p. 1730)
—Who Works at My School? (p. 1919)
Frongia, Daniela, illus. see Nazeer, Tasnim & Publishing, Greenbirdbooks Childrens.
Frongia, Daniela, illus. see Orcutt, Cherie.
Frongia, Daniela, illus. see Stevens, Elizabeth.
Front, Charles, illus. see Sleigh, Barbara.
Fronte, Kathy. Bella's Bow Tie Bears: Three Magnificent Tales of Adventure, Dreams & Magic. (p. 162)
Frontiera, Deborah. Eric & the Enchanted Leaf: A Night with Echo. Scott, Korey, illus. (p. 533)
Frontiera, Deborah K. Eric & the Enchanted Leaf: The First Adventure Scott, Korey, illus. (p. 533)
—Eric & the Enchanted Leaf / Eric y la Hoja Encantada: A Visit with Canis Lupis / una Visita con Canis Lupis. Santillan-Cruz, Silvia R., tr. (p. 533)
—New South Dairy Colony 50. (p. 1247)
—Re-Creation of Roacheria. (p. 1441)
—To Build a Tunnel. (p. 1758)
Fronty, Aurélia, illus. see Delval, Marie-Hélène.
Fronty, Aurélia, illus. see Krebs, Laurie.
Fronty, Aurélia, illus. see Lechermeier, Philippe.
Fronty, Aurélia, illus. see Lerasle, Magdeleine.
Fronty, Aurélia, illus. see Serres, Alain.
Fronty, Aurélia, illus. see Smith, Chris.
Frood, Earle. Wabasca Adventure. (p. 1851)
Frosch, Mary, ed. Coming of Age in America: A Multicultural Anthology. (p. 348)
Froseth, James O. Alto Saxophone Home Helper First Lessons at School & at Home. (p. 50)
—Baritone BC Home Helper First Lessons at School & at Home. (p. 139)
—Bassoon Home Helper First Lessons at School & at Home. (p. 143)
—Clarinet Home Helper First Lessons at School & at Home. (p. 327)
—Horn in F Home Helper First Lessons at School & at Home. (p. 798)
Frossard, Claire. Emma's Journey. Frossard, Etienne, photos by. (p. 520)
Frossard, Claire, illus. see Renoult, Armelle.
Frossard, Etienne, photos by see Frossard, Claire, illus.
Frost, Abigail, jt. auth. see Mulherin, Jennifer.
Frost, Adam. Awesome Book of Awesomeness. Bramall, Dan, illus. (p. 121)
—Run! The Elephant Weighs a Ton! Chambers, Mark, illus. (p. 1496)
Frost, Adam, ed. see Shakespeare, William.
Frost, Adam, illus. see Grindley, Sally.
Frost, Adriana. Making Things Move: Force & Motion. (p. 1082)
Frost, Andrew David. Magician & the Priestess. (p. 1075)
Frost, Brian. Vintage Soper: God Faith Society. (p. 1843)
Frost, C. Amethyst. Dismal Thoughts. (p. 451)
—Mourning under the Bridge. (p. 1181)
Frost, Catherine, tr. see Bussagli, Marco.
Frost, Daniel, tr. from SPA. You, Them, & the Others. (p. 1976)
Frost, Heather. Guardians. (p. 728)
Frost, Helen. Allosaurus. Hughes, Jon, illus. (p. 47)
—Arctic Hares (p. 96)
—Betsy Ross (p. 172)
—Betsy Ross. Saunders-Smith, Gail, ed. (p. 172)
—Caribou (p. 269)
—Chimpanzees [Scholastic]. (p. 306)
—Crossing Stones. (p. 385)
—Diamond Willow. (p. 434)
—Fog Saunders-Smith, Gail, ed. (p. 611)
—Gorillas [Scholastic]. (p. 703)
—Hidden. (p. 775)

—John F. Kennedy (p. 921)
—Keesha's House. (p. 948)
—Monarch & Milkweed. Gore, Leonid, illus. (p. 1163)
—Parrots [Scholastic]. (p. 1325)
—Praying Mantises. (p. 1393)
—Puffins (p. 1415)
—Room 214: a Year in Poems. (p. 1488)
—Sabertooth Cat. Hughes, Jon, illus. (p. 1499)
—Sabertooth Cat [Scholastic]. Hughes, Jon, illus. (p. 1499)
—Salt: A Story of Friendship in a Time of War. (p. 1505)
—Snow Saunders-Smith, Gail, ed. (p. 1598)
—Snowy Owls (p. 1601)
—Snowy Owls [Scholastic]. (p. 1601)
—Stegosaurus Hughes, Jon, illus. (p. 1646)
—Step Gently Out. Lieder, Rick, photos by. (p. 1648)
—Sweep up the Sun. Lieder, Rick, illus. (p. 1689)
—Thurgood Marshall. Saunders-Smith, Gail, ed. (p. 1746)
—Tigers [Scholastic]. (p. 1749)
—Tiranosaurio Rex. Hughes, Jon, illus. (p. 1757)
—Tree Frogs [Scholastic]. (p. 1783)
—Triceratops Hughes, Jon, illus. (p. 1785)
—Tyrannosaurus Rex Saunders-Smith, Gail, ed. (p. 1805)
—Woolly Mammoth. Hughes, Jon, illus. (p. 1950)
—Woolly Mammoth [Scholastic]. Hughes, Jon, illus. (p. 1950)
Frost, Helen & Rustad, Martha E. H. All about Pets. (p. 43)
Frost, Helen & Schuh, Mari C. Vegetable Group (p. 1834)
Frost, Helen, et al. Dinosaurs & Prehistoric Animals. (p. 444)
Frost, J. Old Hickory. (p. 1284)
Frost, James Bernard. World Leader Pretend. (p. 1956)
Frost, Jayson. Picking Pears: Count to Tell the Number of Objects. (p. 1354)
—Science of Dams. (p. 1527)
Frost, Justine, illus. see Davey, Keith Peter.
Frost, Laurie. Philip Pullman's His Dark Materials: The Definitive Guide. (p. 1350)
Frost, Lesley. Mr Bothers. Cassetta, Andrea, illus. (p. 1184)
Frost, Lulu. Moonlight Tooth Fairy. Brown, Lorna, illus. (p. 1173)
Frost, Mark. Alliance: The Paladin Prophecy Book 2. (p. 47)
—Alliance. (p. 47)
—Grand Slam: Bobby Jones, America, & the Story of Golf. (p. 707)
—Paladin Prophecy (p. 1319)
—Rogue: The Paladin Prophecy Book 3. (p. 1485)
—Second Objective. (p. 1539)
Frost, Melissa. Dating Tutor. (p. 409)
Frost, Michael. Killer Mission. (p. 956)
—Movie Mission: Book Two in the Deathstalker Trilogy. (p. 1183)
Frost, Michael, illus. see Keene, Carolyn.
Frost, Michael, jt. auth. see Dixon, Franklin W.
Frost, Michael, jt. auth. see Kain, P. G.
Frost, Michael, jt. auth. see Keene, Carolyn.
Frost, Michael, jt. auth. see Pascal, Francine.
Frost, Michael, photos by see Glines, Abbi.
Frost, Michael, photos by see Humphrey, Mary.
Frost, Michael, photos by see Keene, Carolyn.
Frost, Michael, photos by see Reynolds, Jason.
Frost, Michael, photos by see Schaefer, Lola M.
Frost, Michael, photos by see Tabby, Abigail.
Frost, Michael, photos by. Private Killer (p. 1407)
Frost, Randall. Globalization of Trade. (p. 685)
Frost, Robert. Cow in Apple Time. Yeagle, Dean, illus. (p. 373)
—Prayer in Spring. Moses, Grandma, illus. (p. 1393)
—Runaway. Lang, Glenna, illus. (p. 1496)
—Stopping by Woods on a Snowy Evening. Jeffers, Susan, illus. (p. 1654)
Frost, Robert Temple. Long Trip Home: Stand up Paddleboard Fantasy. (p. 1047)
Frost, Shelley. I See Kindness Everywhere. (p. 845)
—Kids Guide to Movie Making: How Kids Can Produce & Direct Their Own Movies That Audiences Will Love. (p. 953)
Frost, Simon & Atha, Anthony. Fitness for Young People Step-By-Step. (p. 599)
Frostick, Richard. Sound Beginnings. (p. 1615)
Frost-Knappman, Elizabeth & Cullen-DuPont, Kathryn. Women's Suffrage in America: An Eyewitness History. (p. 1947)
Frothingham, Octavius Brook. Stories of the Patriarchs. (p. 1655)
Frothingham, Octavius Brooks. Boston Unitarianism, 1820-1850: A Study of the Life & Work of Nathaniel Langdon Frothingham. (p. 215)
—Recollections & Impressions, 1822-1890. (p. 1452)
Frotuna, Stan, told to. U Got 2 Pray. (p. 1805)
Froud, Brian. Chelsea Morning. (p. 297)
Froud, Wendy, illus. see Windling, Terri.
Frrich, Lewandowski & Riccards, Michael. It's Christmas Again! Delisle, Kathryn H., illus. (p. 896)
Fruchter, Jason. Daniel Goes Out for Dinner. (p. 405)
—Daniel's First Sleepover. (p. 405)
—Friends Help Each Other. (p. 638)
Fruchter, Jason, illus. see Beinstein, Phoebe.
Fruchter, Jason, illus. see Cecil, Lauren.
Fruchter, Jason, illus. see David, Erica.
Fruchter, Jason, illus. see Golden Books Staff.
Fruchter, Jason, illus. see Golden Books.
Fruchter, Jason, illus. see Lewman, David.
Fruchter, Jason, illus. see McCann, Jesse Leon.
Fruchter, Jason, illus. see Miller, Mona.
Fruchter, Jason, illus. see Posner-Sanchez, Andrea.
Fruchter, Jason, illus. see Random House Staff.
Fruchter, Jason, illus. see Random House.
Fruchter, Jason, illus. see Reader's Digest Editors.
Fruchter, Jason, illus. see Reader's Digest Staff & Froeb, Lori C.
Fruchter, Jason, illus. see Reader's Digest Staff & Roe, David.
Fruchter, Jason, illus. see Reader's Digest Staff.
Fruchter, Jason, illus. see Ricci, Christine.
Fruchter, Jason, illus. see Santomero, Angela C.
Fruchter, Jason, illus. see Silverhardt, Lauryn.
Fruchter, Jason, illus. see Testa, Maggie.
Fruchter, Jason, jt. illus. see Style Guide Staff.
Fruchter, Yaakov. Best of Olomeinu - Series 2: Stories for All Year 'Round. (p. 170)
Frueh, Pamela. Me & My Best Cousin Joy. (p. 1115)
—Who Loves Pugs? (p. 1916)
Frueh, Stacy. Jonah Gets into a Good Book. (p. 925)
—Jonah's Weird, but Totally Cool Field Tr. (p. 925)
Fruge, William. Lewis & Clark: A Journey West. (p. 1004)
Fruisen, Catherine Myler. My Mother's Pearls. (p. 1215)
Fruisen, Catherine Myler, illus. see Maconie, Robin.
Fruisen, Catherine Myler, illus. see Wallace, Paula S.
Fry & Hooper. Little Books of the Bible Stories from the Old Testament. (p. 1025)
Fry, Christopher. Djomi Dream Child. Sarago-Kendrick, Delphine, illus. (p. 455)
Fry, Debbie. Donkeywise & Otherwise: The Story of Daisy Doo & Dudley Duz. (p. 466)
Fry, Edward B. Reading Drills. (p. 1445)
—Skimming & Scanning. (p. 1585)
Fry, Erin. Arthur Ashe Against the Odds. (p. 103)
—Benefactor (p. 164)
—Earth Fast Changes: Set Of 6. (p. 496)
—Earth: Fast Changes: Text Pairs. (p. 496)
—Losing It (p. 1054)
—Power of Friendship. (p. 1389)
—Secrets of the Book (p. 1545)
Fry, Gail Bennett. Thinking Out Loud. (p. 1734)
Fry, Gerald W. Association of Southeast Asian Nations. (p. 107)
Fry, Jason. Complete Saga. (p. 353)
—Darth Maul: Shadow Conspiracy. (p. 409)
—Edge of the Galaxy. Balmet, Jean-Paul, illus. (p. 504)
—Jupiter Pirates: Hunt for the Hydra. (p. 937)
—Jupiter Pirates: Hunt for the Hydra. (p. 937)
—Servants of the Empire. (p. 1552)
Fry, Jason, jt. auth. see Beecroft, Simon.
Fry, Jason, jt. auth. see Disney Book Group Staff.
Fry, Jason, jt. auth. see Dorling Kindersley Publishing Staff.
Fry, Jason, jt. auth. see Scholastic, Inc. Staff.
Fry, Jason, jt. auth. see Windham, Ryder.
Fry, Jason & Windham, Ryder. Switching Gears. (p. 1692)
Fry, Jenny & Award, Anna. Ultimate Book of Questions & Answers. (p. 1809)
Fry, Juliet, jt. auth. see Crowe, Ellie.
Fry, Michael. Chronicles of Time Part 1: Trevor Trubble & the Time Machine. (p. 317)
—Odd Squad Bully Bait. Fry, Michael, illus. (p. 1278)
—Odd Squad King Karl. Fry, Michael, illus. (p. 1278)
—Zero Tolerance. Fry, Michael, illus. (p. 1986)
Fry, Michael & Jackson, Bradley. Naughty List. Fry, Michael, illus. (p. 1237)
Fry, Sonali. Bang! Clang! (p. 136)
—Eloise Takes a Trip. Bracken, Carolyn, illus. (p. 516)
—I'm a Little Vampire. Rescek, Sanja, illus. (p. 858)
—Itsy Bitsy Pumpkin. Rescek, Sanja, illus. (p. 900)
—Let's Read About— George W. Bush. Heyer, Carol, illus. (p. 1000)
—Under the Sea. Blanco, Migy, illus. (p. 1814)
Fry, Sonali & Knight, Hilary. Eloise Goes to the Beach. Lyon, Tammie Speer & Lyon, Tammie, illus. (p. 516)
Fry, Stella. Grandpa's Garden. Jago & Moxley, Sheila, illus. (p. 709)
—Grandpa's Garden. (p. 710)
Fry, Stella & Moxley, Sheila. Grandpa's Garden. Moxley, Sheila, illus. (p. 710)
Fry, Stephen, jt. auth. see Ardizzone, Edward.
Fry, Stephen, jt. auth. see Lihoreau, Tim.
Fryar, Jane L. Easter Day Surprise. Dorenkamp, Michelle, illus. (p. 499)
—Hero of Faith - Katharina Von Bora. (p. 772)
—Jesus Enters Jerusalem. Dorenkamp, Michelle, illus. (p. 915)
Fryar, Jane L. & Varvaris, Cathy. Jesus, Can I Talk with You? A Prayer Journal for Kids. (p. 915)
Fryar, Jane L., ed. My Christmas Bible: King James Version. (p. 1200)
—My Christmas Bible. (p. 1200)
Fryd, Hallie. Scandalous! 50 Shocking Events You Should Know About. (p. 1519)
Frydenborg, Kay. Animal Therapist. (p. 80)
—Chocolate: Sweet Science & Dark Secrets of the World's Favorite Treat. (p. 309)
—Wild Horse Scientists. (p. 1929)
Frye, Curtis D. Microsoft(r) Office Excel(r) 2007 (p. 1136)
Frye, Dennis E. Antietam Revealed: The Battle of Antietam & the Maryland Campaign as You Have Never Seen It Before. (p. 89)
Frye, Karen. Flake (p. 602)
Frye, Keith. Roadside Geology of Virginia. Alt, David & Hyndman, Donald W., eds. (p. 1477)
Frye, Mark. School Shooter: In His Own Words. (p. 1523)
Frye, Paige, illus. see Billin-Frye, Paige.
Frye, Paige Billin, illus. see Aboff, Marcie.
Frye, Timea Csonka. Wishing Star: Lost in the Woods. (p. 1940)
Fryer, Danny. Ultimate Stag Night Kit: How to Prepare for & Survive the Biggest Night of Your Life. (p. 1810)
Fryer, Jane Eayre. Mary Frances First Aid Book 100th Anniversary Edition: A Childrens Story-Instruction First Aid Book with Home Remedies Plus Bonus Patterns for Child's Nurse Cap & Apron. (p. 1100)
—Mary Frances Garden Book: Adventures among the Garden People. (p. 1100)
—Mary Frances Knitting & Crocheting Book 100th Anniversary Edition: A Childrens Story-Instruction Book with Doll Clothes Patterns for American Girl & Other 18-Inch Dolls. (p. 1100)
—Mary Frances Sewing Book 100th Anniversary Edition: A Childrens Story-Instruction Sewing Book with Doll Clothes Patterns for American Girl & Other 18-Inch Dolls. (p. 1100)
Fryer, Janice & Peterson, Valerie. Cookie Craft: Baking & Decorating Techniques for Fun & Festive Occasions. (p. 361)
Fryer, Mary Beacock. Bold, Brave, & Born to Lead: Major General Isaac Brock & the Canadas. (p. 208)
—Champlain: Peacemaker & Explorer. (p. 289)
—Escape: Adventures of a Loyalist Family. (p. 534)
Fryer, Paul. Don't Be So... Hirst, Damien, illus. (p. 467)
Fryer, Samantha. Sorcerer's Tale. (p. 1614)
Frylinck, Diana, jt. auth. see LeFroy, Joy.
Frystak, Timothy D. Jackie Robinson: With Profiles of Satchel Paige & & Branch Rickey. (p. 904)
Fu, Jennifer, jt. auth. see Ma, Hermione.
Fu, Shelley. Hoyi the Archer & other Classic Chinese Tales. Abboreno, Joseph F. & Fu, Sherwin, illus. (p. 824)
—Treasury of Chinese Folk Tales: Beloved Myths & Legends from the Middle Kingdom. Yee, Patrick, illus. (p. 1782)
Fu, Sherwin, illus. see Fu, Shelley.
Fu, Zhiying. Handing down the Light: The Biography of Venerable Master Hsing Yun. (p. 740)
Fuchs, A. P. Hand I've Been Dealt: A Collection of Poetry & Song Streams of Thought & Reflection. (p. 740)
—Magic Man. (p. 1072)
Fuchs, Bernie, illus. see Heinz, Brian.
Fuchs, Gerd. Charly, el Ratón Cazagatos. Bofinger, Manfred, tr. (p. 294)
Fuchs, Kaitlyn, illus. see Sack, Nancy.
Fuchs, Menucha. Best Gift of All. (p. 170)
—Chatzkel, Mendel & Me: An adventure Story. Daykin, Rachmiel, tr. from HEB. (p. 295)
—Flying Invitation. (p. 610)
—Hide & Go Sleep. (p. 776)
—Just a Pinch. (p. 937)
—Little Helpers. (p. 1029)
—Menucha V'Simcha Series #11: All Aboard! Hass, Estie, illus. (p. 1127)
—Most Beautiful Picture in the World. (p. 1177)
—Picky Eater & Other Stories. (p. 1355)
Fuchs, Michael. Keniff & Kieff. (p. 948)
Fuchs-Rice, Dwayne. Shades of Ember. (p. 1557)
—Troika. (p. 1788)
Fucíková, Renata, illus. see Puccini, Giacomo.
Fucile, Tony. Let's Do Nothing! Fucile, Tony, illus. (p. 995)
Fucile, Tony, illus. see DiCamillo, Kate & McGhee, Alison.
Fucile, Tony, illus. see Durand, Hallie.
Fudge, Benjamin. Enrique Speaks with His Hands. Edmonson, Tim, illus. (p. 531)
Fudge, Keith. Rainy Day Discovery. (p. 1436)
Fudoli, Melissa, jt. auth. see Mills, Nathan.
Fuenmayor, Morella, illus. see Barbot, Daniel.
Fuenmayor, Morella & popular, Tradición. Estaba la Pájara Pinta. (p. 538)
Fuente, Claudia Luna, jt. auth. see Fuentes, Claudia Luna.
Fuentes, Benny, illus. see Bowen, Carl.
Fuentes, Benny, jt. auth. see Bowen, Carl.
Fuentes, Benny, jt. auth. see Ciencin, Scott.
Fuentes, Benny, jt. auth. see Fein, Eric.
Fuentes, Benny, jt. auth. see Hoena, Blake A.
Fuentes, Benny, jt. auth. see Stevens, Eric.
Fuentes, Benny, jt. auth. see Terrell, Brandon.
Fuentes, Benny, jt. auth. see Verne, Jules.
Fuentes, Benny, jt. auth. see Wyss, Johann D.
Fuentes, Benny, jt. auth. see Yomtov, Nel.
Fuentes, Benny & Hoena, Blake A. Sack Attack! Sandoval, Gerardo, illus. (p. 1500)
Fuentes, Benny & Stoker, Bram. Dracula Ocampo Ruiz, Jose Alfonso & Smith, Tod, illus. (p. 476)
—Dracula Ruiz, Jose Alfonso Ocampo & Smith, Tod, illus. (p. 476)
Fuentes, Carlos. Aura. (p. 116)
Fuentes, Claudia Luna & Fuente, Claudia Luna. Frutos del Sol. Siller, Germin, illus. (p. 646)
Fuentes, José. Paisaje del eco/EchoLandscape. (p. 1319)
—Paisaje infantil/Children Landscape. (p. 1319)
Fuentes, Mikel, illus. see Calaf, Monica.
Fuentes, Peggy Jo. Boogoos, the Calico Kitty. (p. 210)
Fuentes Silva, Andrea, tr. see Browne, Anthony.
Fuerst, Jeff. Lion & the Rabbit: A Fable from India. (p. 1020)
Fuerst, Jeffrey B. A-Hunting We Will Go. Greenhead, Bill, illus. (p. 1)
—At the Comma Store. Knuvers, Onno, illus. (p. 111)
—Baa Baa Black Sheep Sells Her Wool. (p. 123)
—Bear Goes over the Mountain. (p. 150)
—Bear Went over the Mountain. Oliver, Mark, illus. (p. 151)
—Bingo. Greenhead, Bill, illus. (p. 188)
—Bingo, Come Home! Greenhead, Bill, illus. (p. 188)
—Chuck, Woodchuck, Chuck! Greenhead, Bill, illus. (p. 318)
—Feeding Time at the Zoo: Lap Book. (p. 580)
—Going Places: Lap Book. (p. 692)
—Hickory Dickory Dock; or, Go, Mouse, Go! (p. 775)
—Hot Cross Buns for Everyone. Abbott, Jason, illus. (p. 801)
—Hunting We Will Go. (p. 829)
—Itsy Bitsy Spider Climbs Again. (p. 900)
—Itsy Bitsy Spider. Collins, Daryll, illus. (p. 900)
—Jack B. Nimble Jumps. Colby, Garry, illus. (p. 902)
—Jack Be Nimble. Colby, Garry, illus. (p. 902)
—Lazy Mary. Kelley, Gerald, illus. (p. 981)
—Lazy Mary Gets Up. Kelley, Gerald, illus. (p. 981)
—Look at it Go! Lap Book. (p. 1048)
—Lunch with Little Miss Muffet. (p. 1065)
—Miss Mary Mack & the Jumping Elephants. Workman, Terry, illus. (p. 1151)
—Old Gray Mare. Currant, Gary, illus. (p. 1283)
—Old Gray Mare IS What She Used to Be. Currant, Gary, illus. (p. 1283)
—Old MacDonald. Greenhead, Bill, illus. (p. 1284)
—Old MacDonald's Noisy Farm. (p. 1284)
—Old Woman Who Lived in a Shoe. Greenhead, Bill, illus. (p. 1285)
—Party Time with Old King Cole. (p. 1326)
—Peter Piper Picks & Pickles Peppers. (p. 1347)
—Peter Pumpkin Eater. Greenhead, Bill, illus. (p. 1347)
—Peter Pumpkin Eater Loses His Appetite. Greenhead, Bill, illus. (p. 1347)
—Pies for Simple Simon. Ledger, Bill, illus. (p. 1357)
—Run, Three Blind Mice! Walker, Sholto, illus. (p. 1496)
—Simple Simon. Ledger, Bill, illus. (p. 1578)
—Sing a Song of Sixpence, the King's Special Pie. (p. 1578)
—Sorting at My Desk: Lap Book. (p. 1614)
—Three Blind Mice. Walker, Sholto, illus. (p. 1741)
—Visiting Grandma: Lap Book. (p. 1845)
—Wishing on a Bright Star. (p. 1940)
—Woman Who Lived in a Shoe. Greenhead, Bill, illus. (p. 1945)
Fuerst, Jeffrey B., jt. auth. see Geiger, Beth.
Fuerst, Jeffrey B. & Benchmark Education Co., LLC. Robert Louis Stevenson's Treasure Island: My Sea Adventure Israel Hands. Hondru, Ovi, illus. (p. 1479)
Fuert, L. A., illus. see Burroughs, John.
Fuertes, Gloria. 4 Poemas de Gloria Fuertes y Una Calabaza Vestida de Luna. Aguilar, Jose, illus. (p. 1992)
—Abecedario - Don Hilario (Don Hillario's Alphabet) (p. 4)
—Acertijos, Chistes y Canciones: Chupachus. Menéndez, Margarita, tr. (p. 8)
—Cuentos de Animales: La Pata Mete la Pata. (p. 389)
—Cuentos de Humor: Un Pulpo en un Garaje. (p. 390)
—Cuentos de Risa: El Perro Picatoste. Gabán, Jesús, tr. (p. 390)
—Cuentos Para 365 Dias. (p. 390)
—Diccionario Estrafalario. (p. 435)
—Gran Libro de los Animales. (p. 706)
—Poesia No Es un Cuento. (p. 1376)
—Poesias para Todos los Dias: Versos Fritos. Solana, Javier, tr. (p. 1376)
—Poesias, Rimas y Disparates: Pienso Mesa y Digo Silla. (p. 1376)
Fuertes, Gloria & Gabán, Jesús. Antología. Gabán, Jesús, tr. (p. 89)
Fuertes, Gloria & Torcida, María Luisa. Poesías de Animales: La Selva en Verso. Torcida, María Luisa, tr. (p. 1376)
Fuertes, Louis Agassiz, illus. see Burgess, Thornton W.
Fuertes, Louis Agassiz, illus. see Wright, Mabel Osgood & Coues, Elliott.
Fuertes, Louis Agassiz, jt. auth. see Burgess, Thornton W.
Fugarino, Gloria J. Gabby's Special Day. (p. 652)
Fugate, Alonzo. Pumpkin Guts. (p. 1416)
Fugate, Francis L. & Fugate, Roberta B. Roadside History of New Mexico. (p. 1477)
Fugate, Roberta B., jt. auth. see Fugate, Francis L.
Fuge, Charles. I Know a Rhino. (p. 840)
Fuge, Charles, illus. see Casey, Dawn.
Fuge, Charles, illus. see Churchill, Vicki & McAllister, Angela.
Fuge, Charles, illus. see Conway, David.
Fuge, Charles, illus. see McBratney, Sam.
Fuge, Charles, illus. see Tagg, Christine.
Fuge, Charles, jt. auth. see Churchill, Vicki.
Fuge, Charles, jt. auth. see Churchill, Vicky.
Fuge, Charles, jt. auth. see Kelly, Mij.
Fuge, L. M. When Courage Came to Call. (p. 1901)
Fuggle, Debbie. Two Little Fir Trees. (p. 1804)
Fuglestad, R. A., illus. see Acopiado, Ginger.
Fuhr, Ute. Castle under Seige. Sautai, Raoul, illus. (p. 277)
—Let's Look at Castles. Sautai, Raoul, illus. (p. 998)
Fuhr, Ute & Allaire, Caroline. Let's Look at the Rainforest. Sautai, Raoul, illus. (p. 999)
Fuhr, Ute & Sautai, Raoul. Earth's Surface. (p. 498)
—Let's Look for Lost Treasure. (p. 999)
—Life below the City. (p. 1008)
—Woods & Forests. (p. 1949)
Fuhr, Ute, et al. Indios. Fuhr, Ute & Sautai, Raoul, trs. (p. 872)
Fuhr, UteSautai & Allaire, Caroline. Let's Look at the Ocean Depths. Sautai, Raoul, illus. (p. 999)
Fuhrer, David & Silbermintz, Marvin. Backwords: The Secret Language of Talking Backwards ... & More Incredible Games, Stunts & Mind-Bending Word Fun! (p. 130)
Fuhriman, Raphael Scott, illus. see Oakes, Krista Ralston.
Fuhua, Liu, et al. Chinese Paradise 3 (p. 307)
—Chinese Paradise. (p. 307)
Fuijkschot, Edo, illus. see de Campl, Alex.
Fujieda, Toru, creator. Dragon Girl (p. 477)
—Dragon Girl. (p. 477)
Fujii, Hideaki. Innovators. (p. 875)
—Lbx - Artemis Begins. (p. 981)
—LBX: World Battle, Vol. 6. (p. 981)
Fujii, Jason, photos by see Sabado, Joe, illus.
Fujii, Jocelyn. Pono the Dog That Dreams. Burns, Donna, illus. (p. 1382)
Fujikawa, Brian. Adventures of Bibole, Ri: The CURSE of the WEREMOUSE. (p. 16)
—Adventures of Bibole, Rivol & Michelle: The French Fry Caper. (p. 16)
Fujikawa, Gyo. Are You My Friend Today? (p. 97)
—Baby Animals. Fujikawa, Gyo, illus. (p. 124)
—Child's Book of Poems. (p. 304)
—Fairy Tales & Fables. (p. 564)
—Gyo Fujikawa's A to Z Picture Book. (p. 734)
—Let's Play. (p. 999)
—Mother Goose. (p. 1177)
—Oh, What a Busy Day. (p. 1281)
—Sleepy Time. (p. 1590)
—Sunny Books - Four-Favorite Tales Fujikawa, Gyo, illus. (p. 1677)
—Ten Little Babies. Fujikawa, Gyo, illus. (p. 1718)
Fujikawa, Gyo, illus. see Moore, Clement C.
Fujikawa, Gyo, illus. see Stevenson, Robert Louis.
Fujikawa, Kimiko, tr. see Milky, D. J. & Kujiradov, Misaho.
Fujikawa, Kimiko, tr. see Milky, D. J., et al.
Fujima, Takuya. Deus Vitae (p. 431)
Fujimoto, Makoto, jt. auth. see KidsLabel Staff.
Fujimoto, Yoshie. Ninjas & Goblins. (p. 1256)
Fujinari, Yuuki. Ugly Duckling's Love Revolution (p. 1808)
—Ugly Duckling's Love Revolution. (p. 1808)
Fujisaki, Ryu. Hoshin Engi Fujisaki, Ryu, illus. (p. 801)
—Sennin World War. Fujisaki, Ryu, illus. (p. 1550)
—Waqwaq Fujisaki, Ryu, illus. (p. 1857)
Fujisawa, Tohru. GTO: Great Teacher Onizuka (p. 728)
Fujishima, Kosuke. Hand in Hand. (p. 740)
—Mystery Child. (p. 1224)
—Mystery Child. Lewis, Dana & Smith, Toren, trs. (p. 1224)
—Oh My Goddess! (p. 1280)
—Oh My Goddess! Lewis, Dana & Smith, Toren, trs. from JPN. (p. 1280)
—Oh My Goddess! Volume 14. (p. 1280)

F

—Oh My Goddess! Volume 43. Horn, Carl Gustav, ed. (p. 1280)
—Oh My Goddess Volume 8. (p. 1280)
—Oh My Goddess Volume 9. (p. 1281)
—Phantom Racer. (p. 1349)
Fujishima, Kosuke, jt. auth. see Lewis, Dana.
Fujita, Artur, illus. see Lee, Tony.
Fujita, Goro, illus. see Richards, C. J.
Fujita, Goro, illus. see Sauer, Tammi.
Fujita, Kazuhiro, jt. auth. see Tamura, Mitsuhisa.
Fujita, Maki. Platinum Garden (p. 1370)
Fujita, Mikiko, illus. see Umezawa, Rui.
Fujita, Rima. Save the Himalayas. (p. 1516)
Fujiwara, Hiroko, illus. see Ochiai, Midori & Oyama, Shigeki.
Fujiwara, Kim, illus. see Harris, Carol Gahara.
Fuka, Vladimir, illus. see Mahler, Zdenek.
Fukami, Yuko, tr. see Akahori, Satoru.
Fukami, Yuko, tr. see Yoshizaki, Mine.
Fuks, Menuhah & Tager, Gavriella. Smile with Avigayil #1: Avigayil & the Little Student. Haas, Esti, illus. (p. 1594)
—Smile with Avigayil #2: Avigayil & the Black Cat. Haas, Esti, illus. (p. 1594)
Fukuda, Andrew. Hunt. (p. 828)
—Prey. (p. 1398)
—Trap. (p. 1779)
Fukuda, Toyofumi, photos by see Earhart, Kristin, ed.
Fukui, Isamu. Truancy. (p. 1791)
—Truancy City. (p. 1791)
—Truancy Origins. (p. 1791)
Fukumoto, Jan. It's Hard Not to Stare: Helping Children Understand Disabilities. Huff, Tim, illus. (p. 897)
Fukuoka, Aki, illus. see Rippin, Sally.
Fulan. New Millennium Poems. (p. 1246)
Fulbeck, Kip. Part Asian - 100% Hapa. (p. 1325)
Fulbright, Jeannie. Exploring Creation with Botany. Wile, Jay L., ed. (p. 552)
—Exploring Creation with Zoology 1: The Flying Creatures of Day Five. Wile, Jay L., ed. (p. 552)
—Exploring Creation with Zoology 3: Land Animals of the Sixth Day. Wile, Jay L., ed. (p. 552)
Fulcher, Dean L. Grand Island Adventure. (p. 707)
Fulcher, Roz. Be Good to Your Body: Healthy Eating & Fun Recipes. (p. 148)
—Mind Your Manners! (p. 1145)
—Science Around the House: Simple Projects Using Household Recyclables. (p. 1525)
Fulcher, Roz, illus. see Galvin, Laura Gates.
Fulcher, Roz, illus. see Scelsa, Greg.
Fulcher, Roz & Activity Books. Be Good to Your Body—Learning Yoga. (p. 148)
Fulco, Haley, illus. see Hudson, Marilyn A.
Fulcomer, Betty. My Friend Kate Is a Forest Ranger (p. 1209)
Fulghum Bruce, Debra, see McIlwain, Harris H. & Bruce, Debra Fulghum.
Fulk, David. Raising Rufus. (p. 1437)
Fulla, Monserrat, jt. auth. see Hao, K. T.
Fuller, Abigail, jt. auth. see Wollman, Neil.
Fuller, Audrey. Twintastic Adventures of TJ & Taylor: TJ Gets a Haircut. (p. 1802)
Fuller Baldwin, Fran, illus. see Wollman, Neil & Fuller, Abigail.
Fuller, Barbara. Germany. (p. 666)
—Greece. (p. 720)
Fuller, Barbara, jt. auth. see Dubois.
Fuller, Barbara, jt. auth. see Kohen Winter.
Fuller, Barbara & Nevins, Debbie. Great Britain. (p. 714)
Fuller, Barbara & Vossmeyer, Gabriele. Germany. (p. 666)
Fuller, Bob. Costume Trunk. (p. 368)
—Lauren & the Leaky Pail. Fuller, Bob, illus. (p. 980)
Fuller, Bruce, ed. see Duerr Berrick, Jill.
Fuller, Carl, illus. see Pepin, Rebecca.
Fuller, Charlie, ed. Crime & Detection (p. 382)
Fuller, Dawn. Looper: Bullying. (p. 1052)
Fuller, Donna Jo. Stock Market. (p. 1651)
Fuller, E., illus. see Webster, S.
Fuller, Elizabeth, illus. see Cowley, Joy.
Fuller, Fanny, tr. see Andersen, Hans Christian.
Fuller, Harvey. Tommy & the Island. Fuller, Harvey, illus. (p. 1764)
Fuller, James. Lefty & Righty Move to the Land of Oz: The Adventures of Lefty, Vol. 5. (p. 987)
—Lefty & Righty's Sunny Vacation in Oz: The Adventures of Lefty, Vol. 3. (p. 987)
—Lefty Goes Jousting in Oz: The Adventures of Lefty, Vol. 4. (p. 987)
—Lefty Visits Oz: The Adventures of Lefty: Vol. 1. (p. 987)
Fuller, Jeff C. Zirium Tales: The Shadow King. (p. 1987)
Fuller, Jeremy, illus. see Grindley, Sally.
Fuller, Jill. Springtime Addition. (p. 1635)
—Toy Box Subtraction. (p. 1774)
Fuller, Kathleen. Secrets Beneath (p. 1544)
—Summer Secret (p. 1675)
Fuller, Kimberly. H a Carter. (p. 734)
Fuller, Laurie, illus. see Kobert, Michael Gilead & Donato, Dona.
Fuller, Margaret, jt. auth. see Derig, Betty.
Fuller, Mary. Tattletale, Tattletail. (p. 1707)
Fuller, Mildred. Stairway to My Dreams. (p. 1638)
Fuller, Niki. Cat from M-31. (p. 278)
Fuller, R. Buckminster. Grunch of Giants. (p. 727)
Fuller, Rachel. All Kinds of Festivals. (p. 44)
—Look at Me! (p. 1048)
—My New Baby. (p. 1216)
—Waiting for Baby. (p. 1852)
—You & Me. (p. 1973)
Fuller, Rachel, illus. see Safran, Sheri.
Fuller, Sandy F., jt. auth. see Mainor, Carol L.
Fuller, Sandy F., jt. auth. see Mainor, Carol.
Fuller, Sandy Fergus. Moon Loon. (p. 1172)
Fuller, Sandy Ferguson. Moon Loon. (p. 1172)
—My Cat, Coon Cat Brett, Jeannie, illus. (p. 1200)
Fuller, Sandy Ferguson, illus. see Zimet, Sara Goodman.
Fuller, Stephanie. Sunny Day for Millie. (p. 1677)
Fuller, Steve, illus. see Neusner, Dena & Running Press Staff.
Fuller, Sue. Rocks & Minerals. (p. 1483)
Fuller, Susan. Grandma's Wisdom: Secure in His Love, Faith & Joy. (p. 709)
Fuller, Suzy. Andrew Discovers A Cottontail. (p. 72)
Fuller, Taneka. Taylor's Strawberry. Torey Fuller, illus. (p. 1708)
Fuller, Thomas E., jt. auth. see Strickland, Brad.
Fuller, Veronica. Heart of a Princess: Princess Amari. (p. 759)
—Heart of a Princess: Princess Lady Bug B. (p. 759)
Fullerton, Alma. In the Garage (p. 866)
—Libertad (p. 1005)
Fulleylove, John, illus. see Baikie, James.
Fullick, Ann. Adaptation & Competition (p. 11)
—Body Systems & Health (p. 207)
—Rebuilding the Body: Organ Transplantation (p. 1451)
—Test Tube Babies: In Vitro Fertilization (p. 1723)
—Why Do My Ears Pop? Hearing (p. 1924)
Fullman, Joe. Ancient Chinese. (p. 68)
—Ancient Greeks. (p. 69)
—Coin & Rope Tricks. (p. 338)
—Mind Tricks. (p. 1145)
—Sleight of Hand. (p. 1590)
Fullman, Joe & Tremaine, John. Card Tricks. (p. 265)
—Coin & Rope Tricks. (p. 338)
—Sleight of Hand. (p. 1590)
Fullman, Joseph, jt. auth. see Dorling Kindersley Publishing Staff.
Fullwood, Millie. Daddy's Not Afraid of the Dark. (p. 399)
Fullwood, Millie F. Bright Star. (p. 228)
Fullwood, Ron. Power of Mischief: Military Industry Executives Are Making Bush Policy & the Country Is Paying the Price. (p. 1389)
Fulmer, Jeffrey. My Imagination Kit. Pickering, Jimmy, tr. (p. 1211)
Fulmer, Patrick, illus. see Holt, Madeline.
Fultion, T. C. Jan the Cleaning Lady. (p. 907)
Fulton, Cathy, jt. auth. see Filer, Patricia.
Fulton, Kelly. Larry the Lonely Lionfish. (p. 976)
Fulton, Parker, illus. see Mueller, Doris.
Fulton, Roger & Carpenter, Michael. 25 Short Hikes & Interesting Walks in the Lake George, NY Region. (p. 1996)
Fulton, Stephen (Abdul-Hakeem). 110 Islamic Poems for Children. (p. 2000)
Fulton-Keats, Louise. Best Ever Birthday: Recipes Inspired by Margaret Fulton. Mackintosh, Michelle, illus. (p. 169)
Fulton-Vengco, Aletha. Crocodile Farm in the City. (p. 384)
—Felicidad & Her Pen Pal Kamar. (p. 581)
—Felicidad's Sidewalk Art. (p. 581)
Fultz, Steven D. Adventures of the Barnyard Detectives: Where's Mr. Peacock (p. 23)
Fulves, Karl. Big Book of Magic Tricks. (p. 179)
—More Self-Working Card Tricks: 88 Fool-Proof Card Miracles for the Amateur Magician. (p. 1174)
—Self-Working Paper Magic: 81 Foolproof Tricks. (p. 1549)
Fulvimari, Jeffrey, illus. see Ciccone, Madonna L. & Madonna.
Fulvimari, Jeffrey, illus. see Madonna, pseud.
Fulvimari, Jeffrey, jt. auth. see Madonna, pseud.
Fumarola, Mario. Wasn't it only Yesterday. (p. 1860)
Fumizuki, Kou. Ai Yori Aoshi (p. 30)
—Ai Yori AoshiTM Nibley, Alethea & Nibley, Athena, trs. from JPN. (p. 30)
Funari Willever, Lisa. Nicky Fifth on 32 Dandelion Court. (p. 1251)
Funari-Willever, Lisa. Theres A Kid under My Bed (Cj) (p. 1731)
Funari-Willever, Lisa, jt. auth. see Willever, Lisa.
Funaro, Gregory. Alistair Grim's Odditorium. (p. 41)
Funderburg, April. Soul Snatcher. (p. 1614)
Fundora, Yolanda V., illus. see Moolenaar Bernier, Ashley-Ruth.
Fundora, Yolanda V., illus. see Perez, Annette.
Fundora, Yolanda V., illus. see Picayo, Mario.
Fung, Jane, ed. see Onish, Liane.
Funk, Bev. Wool E. Woola. (p. 1950)
Funk, Clotilde Embree, illus. see Fox, Frances Margaret.
Funk, Clotilde Embree, illus. see Moore, Margaret & Moore, John Travers.
Funk, Constance J. Holy as Thou. (p. 791)
Funk, Debbie, illus. see Holzer, Angela.
Funk, Hermann, et al. Geni@l: Deutsch Fremdsprache fuer Jugendliche - Learning Glossary German-English. (p. 661)
—geni@l B1: Zertifikatsniveau. (p. 661)
—genial. A1 Intensivtrainer: Deutsch als Fremdsprache für Jugendliche. (p. 661)
—genial. A2 Testheft mit CD: Deutsch als Fremdsprache für Jugendliche. (p. 661)
Funk, Jack. Outside, the Women Cried: The Story of the Surrender by Chief Thunderchild's Band of Their Reserve near Delmas, Saskatchewan 1908. (p. 1313)
Funk, Lynda. Snake, the Humming Bird & Me. (p. 1596)
Funk, Michele Housholder. Adventures of Pete & Max: And the Lost Sock. (p. 21)
Funk, Rachel. Christabelle in the Museum of Time. (p. 311)
Funk, Tara. Newton & His Laws. (p. 1249)
—Objects in Motion. (p. 1275)
—Three Laws of Motion. (p. 1742)
Funke, Cornelia. Corazón De Tinta. Blanco, Rosa Pilar, tr. from GER. (p. 366)
—Dragon Rider. (p. 478)
—Emma & the Blue Genie. Latsch, Oliver, tr. from GER. (p. 519)
—Fearless. (p. 579)
—Ghost Knight. (p. 671)
—Igraine the Brave. Bell, Anthea, tr. (p. 856)
—Inkdeath. (p. 874)
—Inkheart. Bell, Anthea, tr. (p. 874)
—Inkheart Trilogy Boxed Set: Inkheart, Inkspell, Inkdeath. (p. 874)
—Inkspell. (p. 874)
—Inkspell. Bell, Anthea, tr. (p. 874)
—Inkspell. Bell, Anthea, tr. from GER. (p. 874)
—Princesa Isabella. (p. 1402)
—Reckless. (p. 1451)
—Reckless. Latsch, Oliver, tr. (p. 1451)
—Thief Lord. (p. 1732)
—Thief Lord. Birmingham, Christian, illus. (p. 1732)
—Viaje con Sorpresa. Alonso, Maria, tr. (p. 1839)
Funke, Julie Ann & Foekel, Alessandra. Conner's Cubbyhole. (p. 358)
Funke, Peggy, illus. see Johnson, Gerald J. J.
Funke, Teresa R. Doing My Part. (p. 463)
—V for Victory. (p. 1829)
Funkhouser, Judy Cooke. Little Green Seldom Seen Mobile Mouse House. (p. 1028)
Funkhouser, Patricia A. Dripps -. Little Star's Dream. (p. 1036)
Funkhouser, Sandi. DoorKeeper: In the King's Presence. (p. 470)
Funko. World of Pop! (p. 1957)
Funnell, Pippa. Solo the Super Star. (p. 1608)
Funnell, Sonja, illus. see Anderson, Henry Morgan.
Funny, Ania. Power of Ania to Change the World of Bullying. (p. 1389)
Funny Faces Staff, jt. auth. see Toms, Kate.
Funston, Sylvia. Kids' Horse Book. (p. 954)
Fuoco, Gina Dal. Earth (p. 494)
—Rachel Carson: Renowned Marine Biologist & Environmentalist (p. 1432)
Fuqua, J. Scott. Secrets of the Greaser Hotel. (p. 1545)
Fuqua, Jonathon. Medusa's Daughter. (p. 1120)
Fuqua, Jonathon Scott. Darby. (p. 406)
—King of the Pygmies. (p. 959)
—Medusa's Daughter. Parke, Steven, illus. (p. 1120)
—Reappearance of Sam Webber. (p. 1450)
Fuqua, Nell & Jankowki, Dan. U. S. Presidents: Feats & Foul-Ups. Saunders, Zina, illus. (p. 1807)
Fur, Emil, illus. see Vujadinovic, Nenad.
Fur, George, Sr. Little Things. (p. 1037)
Furåker, Bengt. Sociological Perspectives on Labor Markets. (p. 1605)
Furbee, Mary Rodd. Anne Bailey: Frontier Scout. (p. 85)
—Outrageous Women of Civil War Times. (p. 1313)
—Shawnee Captive: The Story of Mary Draper Ingles. (p. 1563)
—Wild Rose: Nancy Ward & the Cherokee Nation. (p. 1930)
Furber, Rosemary. What You See Is What You Get. (p. 1896)
Furbush, Helen. Lying Awake. McCroskey, Christine, illus. (p. 1066)
Furchgott, Eve, illus. see Kruger, Malia.
Furcron, Bertha Phillips. No Half, No Step, Just a Whole. Hendrick, Betty Acey, illus. (p. 1258)
Furedi, Judith. Dear John: Letters from a Fan in New York City: An Interactive Book. (p. 419)
Furey, Hester. Body Piercing & Tattoos. (p. 207)
Furfur, Christopher. How Should I Care for My Doggy? (p. 812)
—Rebecca & the Great Goat Getaway. Artigas, Alexandra, illus. (p. 1450)
Furgang, Adam. Adapting to Intense Storms. (p. 11)
—Carbonated Beverages: The Incredibly Disgusting Story. (p. 265)
—Noble Gases. (p. 1262)
—Rhode Island: Past & Present. (p. 1468)
—Rick Riordan. (p. 1470)
—Salty & Sugary Snacks: The Incredibly Disgusting Story. (p. 1506)
—Searching Online for Image, Audio, & Video Files. (p. 1538)
—Snap & Share: Exploring the Potential of Instagram & Other Photo & Video Apps (p. 1597)
Furgang, Adam, jt. auth. see Furgang, Kathy.
Furgang, Kathy. Building Bridges: Set Of 6. (p. 239)
—Building Bridges & Construcción de Puentes: 6 English, 6 Spanish Adaptations. (p. 239)
—Careers in Digital Animation. (p. 267)
—Cooking Contest: Set Of 6. (p. 361)
—Cooking Contest. (p. 361)
—Declaration of Independence & Benjamin Franklin of Pennsylvania. (p. 422)
—Declaration of Independence & Richard Henry Lee of Virginia. (p. 422)
—Declaration of Independence & Roger Sherman of Connecticut. (p. 422)
—Defeating School Violence. (p. 423)
—Dream Jobs in Sports Law. (p. 483)
—Ending Hunger & Homelessness Through Service Learning (p. 527)
—Fact or Fib? A Challenging Game of True or False. (p. 561)
—Fact or Fib? 2: A Challenging Game of True or False. (p. 561)
—Finding Fossils & en busca de Fósiles: 6 English, 6 Spanish Adaptations. (p. 588)
—Frequently Asked Questions about Sports Injuries. (p. 636)
—Great Green Forest: Set Of 6. (p. 716)
—Happy Summer Day & un día feliz de Verano: 6 English, 6 Spanish Adaptations. (p. 746)
—Having Healthful Habits: Set Of 6. (p. 755)
—Having Healthful Habits & Tener hábitos Sanos: 6 English, 6 Spanish Adaptations. (p. 755)
—How the Stock Market Works. (p. 813)
—Kilauea: Hawaii's Most Active Volcano. (p. 956)
—Krakatoa: History's Loudest Volcano. (p. 967)
—Math Fun at the Fair: Set Of 6. (p. 1106)
—Math Fun at the Fair. (p. 1106)
—Measuring Length: Set Of 6. (p. 1117)
—Measuring Length. (p. 1117)
—Mount Pelee: The Biggest Volcano Eruption of the 20th Century. (p. 1180)
—Mount Vesuvius: Europe's Mighty Volcano of Smoke & Ash. (p. 1180)
—My Brain. (p. 1199)
—My Ears. (p. 1202)
—My Eyes. (p. 1202)
—My Heart. (p. 1210)
—My Lungs. (p. 1213)
—My Nose. (p. 1216)
—National Geographic Kids Everything Money: A Wealth of Facts, Photos, & Fun! (p. 1232)
—National Geographic Kids Everything Weather: Facts, Photos, & Fun That Will Blow You Away. (p. 1232)
—National Geographic Readers: Wildfires. (p. 1233)
—Nature in Focus: Set Of 6. (p. 1236)
—Nature in Focus & Enfoque en la Naturaleza: 6 English, 6 Spanish Adaptations. (p. 1236)
—Netiquette: A Student's Guide to Digital Etiquette. (p. 1242)
—Ninth Amendment: Rights Retained by the People. (p. 1257)
—On the Move: Green Transportation. (p. 1291)
—Paul Bunyan & Paul Bunyan (Spanish) 6 English, 6 Spanish Adaptations. (p. 1330)
—Paul Bunyan (Spanish) Set Of 6. (p. 1330)
—Pizza Parts: Set Of 6. (p. 1365)
—Pizza Parts. (p. 1365)
—Rainbow Party: Set Of 6. (p. 1435)
—Rainbow Party. (p. 1435)
—Rainbow Party & una fiesta de Colores: 6 English, 6 Spanish Adaptations. (p. 1435)
—Saving the Bald Eagles: Set Of 6. (p. 1517)
—Saving the Bald Eagles. (p. 1517)
—Saving the Bald Eagles & ¡Salvemos al águila cabeza Blanca! 6 English, 6 Spanish Adaptations. (p. 1517)
—Science Measuring Tools: Set Of 6. (p. 1526)
—Science Measuring Tools & Instrumentos para medir en Ciencias: 6 English, 6 Spanish Adaptations. (p. 1526)
—Seat on the Bus: Set Of 6. (p. 1539)
—Seventh Amendment: The Right to a Jury Trial. (p. 1555)
—Shrimp Joins the Team: Set Of 6. (p. 1571)
—Shrimp Joins the Team & Chaparro se une al Equipo: 6 English, 6 Spanish Adaptations. (p. 1571)
—Tambora: A Killer Volcano from Indonesia. (p. 1704)
—Throne for the King: Set Of 6. (p. 1744)
—Throne for the King & un trono para el Rey: 6 English, 6 Spanish Adaptations. (p. 1744)
—Understanding Economic Indicators: Predicting Future Trends in the Economy. (p. 1815)
—Unlucky Stanley: Set Of 6. (p. 1821)
—Unlucky Stanley. (p. 1821)
—Unlucky Stanley & Stanley no tiene Suerte: 6 English, 6 Spanish Adaptations. (p. 1821)
—Water All Around: Set Of 6. (p. 1862)
—Water All Around. (p. 1862)
—Wendy the Water Drop: Set Of 6. (p. 1875)
—What Will the Weather Be? Set Of 6. (p. 1895)
—Where Does Your Garbage Go? & ¿Adónde va la Basura? 6 English, 6 Spanish Adaptations. (p. 1907)
—Working with Electricity & Magnetism: Set Of 6. (p. 1953)
—Working with Electricity & Magnetism & Trabajar con la electricidad y el Magnetismo: 6 English, 6 Spanish Adaptations. (p. 1953)
Furgang, Kathy, jt. auth. see Benchmark Education Co., LLC Staff.
Furgang, Kathy, jt. auth. see Brocker, Susan.
Furgang, Kathy, jt. auth. see U. S. National Geographic Society Staff.
Furgang, Kathy, jt. auth. see Wassner, Sarah.
Furgang, Kathy & Furgang, Adam. Dream Jobs in Stadium & Sports Facility Operations. (p. 483)
—Leonardo DiCaprio: Environmental Champion. (p. 992)
—On the Move: Green Transportation. (p. 1291)
—Understanding Budget Deficits & the National Debt. (p. 1815)
Furgang, Kathy & Gatta, Frank. Understanding Your Right to Privacy. (p. 1816)
Furgang, Kathy, told to. Paul Bunyan: Set Of 6. (p. 1330)
Furie, Matt. Night Riders. (p. 1254)
Furie, Peter. Numchuks' Curse. (p. 1272)
Furi-Perry, Ursula. Constitutional Law for Kids: Discovering the Rights & Privileges Granted by the U. S. Constitution. (p. 359)
—Going to Court: An Introduction to the U.S. Justice System. (p. 693)
Furlong, C. T. Killer Strangelets. (p. 956)
Furlong, Frank. Before We Were. (p. 159)
—Not Yet: Poems for Kids Five & Up. (p. 1267)
—Pop Pop's Magic Chair. (p. 1384)
Furlong, Michelle. Don't Take Monkeys Home to Lunch. Schrader, Mark, illus. (p. 468)
Furlong, Paul. Emma & Skylark. (p. 519)
Furlong, Reynolds Cynthia. S Is for Star: A Christmas Alphabet. Carroll, Pam, illus. (p. 1499)
Furman, A. I. Everygirls Romance Stories. Furman, A. L., ed. (p. 544)
Furman, A. L., ed. see Furman, A. I.
Furman, A. L., ed. Horse Stories: Young Readers. Geer, Charles, illus. (p. 800)
—Indian Stories. Geer, Charles, illus. (p. 871)
—Pioneer Stories: Young Readers. Geer, Charles, illus. (p. 1361)
—Teenage Frontier Stories. Prezio, Victor, illus. (p. 1714)
—Wild Life Stories: Young Readers. Geer, Charles, illus. (p. 1929)
Furman, Ben. Sam's Quest. (p. 1509)
—Sam's Quest for the Crimson Crystal. (p. 1509)
Furman, Elina. Washington, D. C. (p. 1860)
Furman, Eric. Sesame Street: Elmo (Giant First Play-a-Sound) (p. 1553)
Furman, Eric, jt. auth. see Joyce, Bridget.
Furman, Eric & Mangano, Tom. Good Manners for Me & You: Play a Sound Book. (p. 698)
Furman, Leola Dyrud, jt. auth. see Dyrud, Loiell O.
Furman, Necah Stewart & Huff, Bailey. Lucy Swan's Circle. Clay, Joshua, illus. (p. 1063)
Furman, Simon. Dangerous Dangers of the Deep. (p. 404)
—Dragon Down. (p. 477)
—Dragons: Riders of Berk - Volume 4 - The Stowaway (p. 479)
Furman, Simon, jt. auth. see Titan Comics Staff.
Furman, Simon & Titan Comics Staff. The Legend of Ragnarok (p. 1728)
Furness-Smith, Martin, ed. see Adds, John, et al.
Furniss. Spacecraft 6-Pack. (p. 1620)
Furniss, Alice. Happiest Mommy Ever. (p. 744)
Furniss, Harry, illus. see Carroll, Lewis, pseud.
Furniss, Harry, jt. auth. see Carroll, Lewis, pseud.

Furnival, Keith, illus. see Clarke, Philip, et al.
Furnival, Keith, illus. see Howell, Laura.
Furnival, Keith, illus. see Tatchell, Judy.
Furnival, Keith, jt. auth. see Clarke, Phillip.
Furr, L. David. Hoops & Me. Simonton, Tom, illus. (p. 795)
Furraway, Bec. Matthew's Family Moves / Robert's Family Moves. (p. 1110)
—Sarah Meets a Bully. (p. 1514)
Furrow, Elena, jt. auth. see Napoli, Donna Jo.
Furrow, Rebecca. You Grew in My Heart: An Adoption Story. (p. 1975)
Fursenko, A. A., et al, eds. Technological Innovation Activities. (p. 1711)
Furst, Lilian R. Random Destinations: Escaping the Holocaust & Starting Life Anew. (p. 1438)
Furstinger, Nancy. African Elephants. (p. 27)
—Alligators. (p. 47)
—American Shorthair Cats. (p. 63)
—Cones. (p. 356)
—Cubes. (p. 389)
—Cylinders. (p. 397)
—Davy Crockett. (p. 411)
—Everglades: The Largest Marsh in the United States. (p. 542)
—Everglades. (p. 542)
—Giant Pandas. (p. 674)
—Great White Shark. (p. 719)
—Great White Shark Paperback. (p. 719)
—Helper Robots. (p. 766)
—Henry Bergh: America's First Animal Advocate. Desjardins, Vincent, illus. (p. 767)
—Maine Coon Cats. (p. 1077)
—Prisms. (p. 1407)
—Pyramids. (p. 1421)
—Robots in Space. (p. 1481)
—Say It with Music: The Story of Irving Berlin. (p. 1518)
—Sea Turtles. (p. 1535)
—Siamese Cats. (p. 1572)
—Spheres. (p. 1626)
—Sphynx Cats. (p. 1626)
—Women & Leadership. (p. 1945)
Furstinger, Nancy & Pipe, Sheryl L. Kids Making a Difference for Animals. (p. 954)
Furth, Robin, jt. auth. see Macgregor, Kinley, pseud.
Furtney, Charles S. Tryconnel: An Antebellum Adventure along the C & O Canal. (p. 1795)
Furuhata, Noriko, tr. see Asamiya, Kia.
Furukawa, Haruko, tr. from JPN. Rg Veda Clamp Staff, illus. (p. 1467)
Furukawa, Masumi. Ugly Duckling. (p. 1808)
Furukawa, Masumi, illus. see Bewley, Elizabeth.
Furukawa, Masumi, illus. see Choi, SeoYun.
Furukawa, Masumi, illus. see Courtauld, Sarah.
Furukawa, Masumi, illus. see Davidson, Susanna.
Furukawa, Masumi, illus. see Goodings, Christina.
Furukawa, Masumi, illus. see Shepherd, Jodie.
Furukawa, Masumi, illus. see Taplin, Sam.
Furuya, Michael. Keoni's Special Gift. (p. 949)
Furuya, Michael, illus. see Matsumoto, Lisa.
Furuya, Usamaru. Short Cuts Furuya, Usamaru, illus. (p. 1569)
Furuyama, Kan & Taniguchi, Jiro. Samurai Legend. Pannone, Frank, ed. (p. 1510)
Fury, David Arthur. Maureen O'Sullivan: No Average Jane. Kopplin, Carolin, ed. (p. 1110)
Fuschia. China Doll's Charm. (p. 306)
Fusco, John. Little Monk & the Mantis: A Bug, a Boy, & the Birth of a Kung Fu Legend. Lugo, Patrick, illus. (p. 1032)
Fusco, Kimberly Newton. Beholding Bee. (p. 160)
—Tending to Grace. (p. 1720)
—Wonder of Charlie Anne. (p. 1947)
Fusek Peters, Andrew. Talkative Tortoise. (p. 1703)
Fusek Peters, Andrew, jt. auth. see Peters, Polly.
Fusek Peters, Andrew & Peters, Polly. Poems with Attitude. (p. 1376)
Fusek Peters, Andrew, compiled by. Poems about Earth. (p. 1376)
Fushimi, Tsukasa. Oreimo Volume 4. Jefferson, Jemiah, ed. (p. 1303)
Fushubert, Annegert, jt. auth. see Ende, Michael.
Fuson, Robin Densmore. Rosita Valdez: And the Giant Sea Turtle. (p. 1490)
Fuss, Kevin. Brothers Geek. (p. 231)
Fussell, Bonnie. More Than a Stove. Sadler, Dale, illus. (p. 1175)
Fussell, Sandy. Monkey Fist. (p. 1165)
—Owl Ninja. James, Rhian Nest, illus. (p. 1315)
—Samurai Kids #1: White Crane. James, Rhian Nest, illus. (p. 1509)
—Samurai Kids #2: Owl Ninja. James, Rhian Nest, illus. (p. 1510)
—Samurai Kids #4: Monkey Fist. James, Rhian Nest, illus. (p. 1510)
—Shaolin Tiger. James, Rhian Nest, illus. (p. 1560)
—White Crane. James, Rhian Nest, illus. (p. 1912)
Futaba, Aoi. Level C (p. 1003)
Futaki, Attila, illus. see Riordan, Rick & Venditti, Robert.
Futaki, Attila, illus. see Venditti, Robert & Riordan, Rick.
Futch, Dorothy R. All about Life: A Collection of Children Stories. (p. 42)
Futers, Kevin P. Adventures of the Billy Goats Gruff. (p. 23)
Futran, Eric, illus. see Allen, Kathryn Madeline.
Futran, Eric, photos by see Allen, Kathryn Madeline.
Futran, Eric, photos by see Thomas, Shelley Moore.
Futrell, Edgar Vernell. Twiddle de, the Talking Parrot. (p. 1801)
Futterer, Kurt. Emile. Gray, Bronwen et al, trs. from GER. (p. 518)
Futterer, Ralf, illus. see Futterer, Kurt.
Futterweit, Walter & Ryan, George. Patient's Guide to PCOS: Understanding & Reversing Polycystic Ovary Syndrome. (p. 1328)
Fuzy, Jim. Internet Adventure with Safari Sam. Melvin, Anita Flannery, illus. (p. 880)
Fydler, Chrissy. Mew Mew's Tale. (p. 1130)
Fyfe, Connie. Grandma's Christmas Candy. (p. 708)
Fyfe, H. B., jt. auth. see Fyfe, H. b.
Fyfe, H. b. & Fyfe, H. B. Outbreak of Peace. (p. 1312)
Fyffe, Brian. Christmas Counting: Count & Create with 42 Holiday Stickers. (p. 313)
Fyffe, Brian, illus. see Mackall, Dandi Daley.
Fyffe, Daniel. Indoor Percussion Ensembles & Drum Corps. (p. 872)
Fyke, Laurie & Sinclair, Kerrie. Jolly Songs (US Print Letters) Book & CD. Stephen, Lib, illus. (p. 924)
Fyleman, Rose. Mice. Ehlert, Lois, illus. (p. 1134)
Fyne, Olga. Jerry & Sherry. (p. 913)
—My Shadow Is a Copycat. (p. 1218)
—Squirrel Race. (p. 1637)
Fyne, Olga M. Be Satisfied with Who You Are. Mathis, Leslie, illus. (p. 149)
—My Abc Animal Book of Rhymes & Jingles. (p. 1195)
—You Can't Teach an Old Dog New Tricks Because. (p. 1975)

G

G & G Wilcox. Tex, the Little Caterpillar from Texas. (p. 1723)
G., Ashley R., illus. see Green, Melissa J. & G., Melissa J.
G. D. My Mom Says I Can. (p. 1214)
G. de la Parra, John & Rahimi, Joey. Cooper Union College Prowler off the Record. (p. 365)
G!, Holly, illus. see Golliher, Bill.
G., Judi. Mercury the Mitzvah Dog. (p. 1127)
G., Melissa J., jt. auth. see Green, Melissa J.
G. Nadel, H. Eternal. (p. 539)
Gaab, Carol. Felipe Alou: From the Valleys to the Mountains. (p. 581)
Gaag, Nikki Van Der. Focus on Afghanistan. (p. 610)
Gaard, Betty. Jericho Ride. (p. 913)
Gaarder, Jostein. Christmas Mystery. Rokkan, Elizabeth, tr. (p. 314)
—Orange Girl. (p. 1301)
—Orange Girl. Anderson, James, tr. from NOR. (p. 1301)
Gaarder-Juntti, Oona. Buster's Trip to Cape Cod: A Story about Massachusetts. Doucet, Bob, illus. (p. 245)
—It's C! (p. 896)
—It's D! (p. 896)
—It's L! (p. 897)
—It's N! (p. 897)
—It's O! (p. 898)
—It's S! (p. 898)
—It's Y! (p. 899)
—Shapes at Home. (p. 1560)
—Shapes at School. (p. 1560)
—Shapes in Food. (p. 1560)
—Shapes in Nature. (p. 1560)
—Shapes in Sports. (p. 1560)
—Shapes on a Farm. (p. 1561)
—What in the World Is a Green Garden? (p. 1887)
—What in the World Is a Green Home? (p. 1887)
—What in the World Is Green Energy? (p. 1888)
—What in the World Is Green Food? (p. 1888)
—What in the World Is Green Transportation? (p. 1888)
—What Lives in Antarctica? (p. 1891)
—What Lives in Coral Reefs? (p. 1891)
—What Lives in Streams & Rivers? (p. 1891)
—What Lives in the Arctic? (p. 1891)
—What Lives in the Desert? (p. 1891)
—What Lives in the Forest? (p. 1891)
—What Lives in the Ocean? (p. 1891)
—What Lives in the Prairie? (p. 1891)
—What Lives in the Rain Forest? (p. 1891)
—What Lives in the Savanna? (p. 1891)
—What Lives in the Tundra? (p. 1891)
Gaarder- Juntti, Oona. What Lives in the Wetlands? (p. 1892)
Gaash, Elisheva, illus. see Beckerman, Menucha.
Gaban, Jesus, illus. see Alberti, Rafael.
Gaban, Jesus, illus. see Alonso, Manuel L. & Alonso Gómez, Manuel L.
Gaban, Jesus, illus. see Bornemann, Elsa.
Gaban, Jesus, illus. see Farias, Juan.
Gabán, Jesús, illus. see Fuertes, Gloria.
Gabán, Jesús, jt. auth. see Fuertes, Gloria.
Gabán, Jesús, tr. see Fuertes, Gloria.
Gabb, Deirdre. 12 Inches off the Ground. (p. 1994)
Gabbay, Benjamin. Wingheart: Luminous Rock. (p. 1936)
Gabbert, Rosalie M. Mr. Bee Man: Story of Lorenzo Lorraine Langstroth Father of American Beekeeping. Jarkins, Sheila, illus. (p. 1184)
Gabbey, Terry, illus. see Erickson, Paul.
Gabbi & Somaschini. Los Oceanos. (p. 1054)
Gabbitas, Jay. Smell in the Air. (p. 1593)
Gabel, Claudia. Friends Close, Enemies Closer. (p. 638)
—In or Out. (p. 864)
—Loves Me, Loves Me Not. (p. 1061)
Gabel, Claudia, jt. auth. see Shakespeare, William.
Gabel, Claudia & Klam, Cheryl. Elusion. (p. 516)
—Etherworld. (p. 539)
Gabel, Deborah Boudreau, illus. see Alossa, Janet M.
Gabel, Frank. Sam's Summer Job: Relate Area to Multiplication & to Addition (p. 1509)
Gabel, Ngareta. Oh Hogwash, Sweet Pea! Rainforth, Hannah, tr. (p. 1280)
Gabel, Stacey. Bulldozers Dig a Pond. (p. 240)
—It's Time to Combine. Neuman, Richard, illus. (p. 899)
—New Blue Tractor. Neuman, Richard, illus. (p. 1243)
Gaber, Susan. Little Red Hen: An Old Fable. (p. 1034)
Gaber, Susan, illus. see Forest, Heather.
Gaber, Susan, illus. see Greene, Rhonda Gowler.
Gaber, Susan, illus. see Henson, Heather.
Gaber, Susan, illus. see Macken, JoAnn Early.
Gaber, Susan, illus. see Martin, Jacqueline Briggs.
Gaber, Susan, illus. see Root, Phyllis.
Gable, Brian, illus. see Burns, Diane L., et al.
Gable, Brian, illus. see Cleary, Brian P.
Gable, Brian, illus. see Cleary, Brian.
Gabler, Michael, illus. see Boosel, Brian D.
Gabolinsc, George. Not Again. (p. 1266)
Gabolinscy, Jack. Do Not Disturb. Cashmore-Hingley, Michael, illus. (p. 457)
Gabolinscy, Jack & Harrison, Brian. Not Again. (p. 1266)
Gabolinscy, Jack & Oppatt, Karen. Danny's Dream. (p. 406)
Gabourel, Harriet. True to Her Faith: A Story of France at the Time of the Huguenots. (p. 1793)
Gabretti, Tisa. Number Zoo (p. 1271)
Gabridge, Pat. Den of Iniquity: A Ten-Minute Comedy Duet. (p. 426)
—Flying the Friendly Skies: A Ten-Minute Dramatic Duet. (p. 610)
—Invisible Husband: A Ten-Minute Dramatic Duet. (p. 885)
—It's a Girl! A Ten-Minute Comedy Duet. (p. 895)
—Measuring Matthew: A Ten-Minute Comedy Duet. (p. 1117)
—Phoenix Funeral Draft 3: A Ten-Minute Comedy Duet. (p. 1351)
Gabridge, Patrick. Sky Is Falling: A One-Act Comedy Play. (p. 1586)
Gabriel, Andrea. My Favorite Bear. (p. 1203)
—My Favorite Bear. Gabriel, Andrea, illus. (p. 1203)
—Wandering Woolly (p. 1856)
Gabriel, Andrea, illus. see Blomgren, Jennifer.
Gabriel, Andrea, illus. see Hensel, Boots.
Gabriel, Andrea, illus. see Lindsey, Marta.
Gabriel, Andrea, illus. see Townsend, Dana E.
Gabriel, Camila. I Can Do It! Io Puedo Hacer! Levine, Robyn, illus. (p. 835)
Gabriel, Elizabeth P. & Gabriel, Pamela P. Ziccah Blows Her Horn. (p. 1986)
Gabriel, Evette, illus. see Scotto, Michael.
Gabriel, Faith K. Nifty Thrifty Animal Crafts. Ponte, June, illus. (p. 1252)
Gabriel, Joseph, jt. auth. see Morton, David L.
Gabriel Jr., Carl L. Jester's Quest: Book One. (p. 914)
Gabriel, Karolys, jt. auth. see Gabriel, Paola.
Gabriel, Luke. Hoover Dam. (p. 796)
—Mount Rushmore. (p. 1180)
Gabriel, Nat. Bubble Trouble. Nez, John, tr. (p. 233)
—Bubble Trouble. Nez, John, illus. (p. 233)
—Sam Y Sus Cuadrados de Zapatos (Sam's Sneaker Squares) (p. 1507)
Gabriel, Nat & Ramirez, Alma. Sam y Sus Cuadrados de Zapatos. Fritz, Ronald, illus. (p. 1507)
Gabriel, Pamela P., jt. auth. see Gabriel, Elizabeth P.
Gabriel, Paola & Gabriel, Karolys. Misterio del Colmillo. (p. 1155)
Gabriel, Philip, tr. see Komatsu, Narumi & Suzuki, Ichiro.
Gabriel, Richard A. Empires at War: A Chronological Encyclopedia from Sumer to the Persian Empire (p. 521)
Gabriel, Thora. Chessie Bligh & the Scroll of Andelthor. (p. 298)
Gabriele, Ben. Tale of a Whale Named Snow. (p. 1699)
Gabriele, Joseph. First Days of the Dinosaurs: Text Edition. Hurst, Margaret, illus. (p. 594)
Gabriell, Chantal T., jt. auth. see Alexander-Heaton, Susanne.
Gabrielov, Julia, illus. see Leibovici, Danielle.
Gabrielson, Brian, jt. auth. see Gabrielson, Ernest.
Gabrielson, Curt. Kinetic Contraptions: Build a Hovercraft, Airboat, & More with a Hobby Motor. (p. 958)
—Stomp Rockets, Catapults, & Kaleidoscopes: 30+ Amazing Science Projects You Can Build for Less Than $1. (p. 1652)
—Tinkering: Kids Learn by Making Stuff. (p. 1756)
Gabrielson, Ernest & Gabrielson, Brian. Home in Ithaca: A novel of Ancient Greece & Troy. (p. 792)
Gabrill, Alexandra, illus. see Iakovos-Dalalakis, Helen.
Gaby, Hansen, illus. see Jane, Johnson.
Gac-Artigas, Alejandro. Yo, Alejandro - Bilingual: My/Our Story - Mi/Nuestra Historia. Gac-Artigas, Priscilla, tr. (p. 1971)
Gac-Artigas, Priscilla, tr. see Gac-Artigas, Alejandro.
Gace, Mariah, illus. see Bale, Mary.
Gache, Stephen Vance. Real Mother Goose Coloring Book. Wright, Blanche Fisher, illus. (p. 1448)
Gachot, Lynn. Cohn-Gee's Prayers. (p. 338)
—June-Ah-Vee's Blessing. (p. 934)
Gackenbach, Dick. Harry & the Terrible Whatzit. (p. 750)
Gadd, Ken. Applied Science. (p. 93)
Gadd, Maxine. Faeries & Other Fantastical Folk. (p. 562)
Gadd, Maxine, illus. see Zimmerman, Diana S.
Gaddi, Rosalie. Austin's Airplane Adventure: Solve Problems Involving Measurement. (p. 116)
—Day at Work with a Chemist. (p. 412)
Gaddis, Alisha, ed. Teen Boys Comedic Monologues That Are Actually Funny. (p. 1713)
Gaddis, Susan. Family Discipleship Manual: Prayer. No. 3 (p. 568)
—Family Discipleship Manual: Christian Service. No. 4 (p. 568)
—Family Discipleship Manual: Relationship with Jesus. No. 1 (p. 568)
—Raising up the Next Generation. (p. 1437)
Gaddis, William. Agape Agape. (p. 29)
Gaddy, Kathi. Do Snakes Wear Shoes? Hollis, Tyler, illus. (p. 457)
Gadeberg, Jeanette. Brave New Girls: Creative Ideas to Help Girls Be Confident, Healthy, & Happy. (p. 223)
Gadeselli, Natalie, illus. see Philips, Lyn D.
Gadot, A. S. First Gift. Lafrance, Marie, illus. (p. 595)
—Tower of Babel. Rébora, Cecilia, illus. (p. 1773)
Gadra, Jessica, illus. see McRoberts, Eddison.
Gadri, Stephen Awudi. Revealed Myths about Trokosi Slavery: Human Rights Violations. (p. 1465)
Gadsby, Maggie. Owl Be Home for Christmas. (p. 1315)
Gadson, Cynthia. Big Bully Bob. (p. 180)
—Dad Had Issues. Lindsey, Maurice, illus. (p. 398)
—Mom Had a Problem. Lindsey, Maurice, illus. (p. 1161)
—Show Me! Teach Me! Guide Me! Poetry Through a Child's Perspective. Lindsey, Maurice, illus. (p. 1570)
Gadson, Denise. Penelope's World Famous Cookies. (p. 1336)
Gadtan Jean Louis, Rosley, illus. see Beach, Linda M.
Gaenssien, Robert E. Blood, Bugs, & Plants. (p. 200)
Gaerber, Karl. Messed up Life of Sheldon: The Way to Rock Puke. (p. 1129)
Gaertner, Connie. Wake-Up Calls. (p. 1853)
Gaestel, Tiffany & Benchmark Education Co. Staff. Science of Sleep & Dreams. (p. 1527)
Gaetan-Beltran, Daniel. Titanic. (p. 1757)
Gaetz, Dayle. Catriona le May Doan: La Plus Rapide des Patineuses. (p. 280)
Gaetz, Dayle Campbell. Alberta Alibi (p. 35)
—Barkerville Gold (p. 139)
—Crossbow (p. 385)
—No Problem (p. 1260)
—No Problem. (p. 1260)
—Sea Dog Meissner, Amy, illus. (p. 1534)
—Sea Dog. Meissner, Amy, illus. (p. 1534)
—Something Suspicious in Saskatchewan (p. 1610)
—Spoiled Rotten (p. 1630)
—Spoiled Rotten. (p. 1630)
Gaff, Jackie. George Washington: The Life of an American Patriot. (p. 664)
—Hernan Cortes: The Life of a Spanish Conquistador. (p. 771)
—I Wonder Why Horses Wear Shoes. (p. 849)
—I Wonder Why the Sahara Is Cold at Night. (p. 849)
—Looking at Earth: How Does It Change? (p. 1050)
—Looking at Growing Up: How Do People Change? (p. 1050)
—Looking at Solids, Liquids, & Gases: How Does Matter Change? (p. 1051)
Gaff, Jackie, jt. auth. see West, David.
Gaffney, Ellen. Wings for a Flower. Gaffney, Ellen, illus. (p. 1936)
Gaffney, K. Ollie the Octopus. (p. 1287)
Gaffney, Linda. My Daddy Does GOOD Things, Too! Dabney, Undra & Goettling, Nickalas, illus. (p. 1201)
Gaffney, Michael. Time-Life Programa de Aprendizaje Infantil (Time-Life Early Learning Program) (p. 1752)
Gaffney, Perri. Resurrection of Alice. (p. 1464)
Gaffney, Sean. Larryboy & the Sinister Snow Day (p. 976)
Gaffney, Sean Kevin & Activity Books. AREA 51 UFO Maintenance & Repair Manual Activity Book. (p. 97)
Gaffney, Timothy R. Storm Scientist: Careers Chasing Severe Weather. (p. 1656)
Gaffney, Timothy R., jt. auth. see Way, Jennifer L.
Gafney & Beers. Essential Math Skills. (p. 537)
Gag, Flavia, illus. see Travers, Georgia.
Gág, Wanda. ABC Bunny. (p. 3)
—Funny Thing. (p. 650)
—Gone Is Gone: Or the Story of a Man Who Wanted to Do Housework. Gág, Wanda, illus. (p. 697)
—Millions of Cats. Gág, Wanda, illus. (p. 1144)
—Nothing at All. (p. 1268)
—Snippy & Snappy. (p. 1598)
—Snow White & the Seven Dwarfs. (p. 1600)
Gág, Wanda, illus. see Grimm, Wilhelm K. & Grimm, Jacob.
Gág, Wanda, tr. see Grimm, Wilhelm K. & Grimm, Jacob.
Gág, Wanda, et al. More Tales from Grimm. Gág, Wanda, illus. (p. 1175)
Gage, Amy Glaser & McIntyre, Connie. Upside Downside Inside Out: Poems about Being a Kid. Gage, Amy Glaser & McIntyre, Connie, illus. (p. 1825)
Gage, Brian. Burn, Christmas! Burn!! Petersen, Jeff, illus. (p. 243)
—Saddest Little Robot. Otoshi, Kathryn, tr. (p. 1501)
Gage, Christos. Avengers Academy: Final Exams. Di Vito, Andrea, illus. (p. 118)
—Avengers Academy - Permanent Record McKone, Mike, illus. (p. 118)
—Spider-Man & the Fantastic Four. Alberti, Mario, illus. (p. 1626)
—What You Want, Not What You Need. Allie, Scott & Hahn, Sierra, eds. (p. 1896)
—Wonderland Allie, Scott & Hahn, Sierra, eds. (p. 1948)
Gage, Christos, illus. see Jackson, Dan.
Gage, Christos & Grummett, Tom. Avengers Academy: Final Exams. Di Vito, Andrea, illus. (p. 118)
Gage, Christos & Isaacs, Christos. Buffy: Season Ten Volume 2 - I Wish. (p. 236)
Gage, James, illus. see Smith, Patty.
Gage, Kathryn. Wow, I'm a Big Brother. (p. 1962)
—Wow, I'm a Big Sister. (p. 1962)
Gage, Nicholas. Place for Us: A Greek Immigrant Boy's Odyssey to a New Country & An Unknown Father. (p. 1365)
Gage, Richard L., tr. see Ikeda, Daisaku & Gorbachev, Mikhail.
Gage, Wilson. Wild Goose Tale. Rounds, Glen, illus. (p. 1929)
Gagen, Miscese. Right Track Reading Lessons: A Highly Effective Step-by-Step Direct Systematic Phonic Program. (p. 1472)
Gaggiotti, Lucia, illus. see Butterworth, Chris.
Gaggiotti, Lucia, illus. see Butterworth, Christine.
Gagliano, Eugene. C Is for Cowboy: A Wyoming Alphabet. Guy, Susan, illus. (p. 250)
—My Teacher Dances on the Desk. Mai-Wyss, Tatjana, illus. (p. 1219)
—V Is for Venus Flytrap: A Plant Alphabet. Traynor, Elizabeth, illus. (p. 1829)
Gagliano, Eugene M. Four Wheels West: A Wyoming Number Book. Guy, Sue, illus. (p. 625)
—Little Wyoming. Urban, Helle, illus. (p. 1038)
Gagliardi, Gary, jt. auth. see Sun-Tzu.
Gagliardi, Tina. Don't Forget the Knight Light. Girouard, Patrick, illus. (p. 467)
—Dragonpox. Girouard, Patrick, illus. (p. 478)
—Fire-Breathers' Academy. Girouard, Patrick, illus. (p. 590)
—Fire-Breathers' Science Fair. Girouard, Patrick, illus. (p. 590)
—Golden Dragon. Girouard, Patrick, illus. (p. 694)
—Last One Is a Rotten Egg. Girouard, Patrick, illus. (p. 978)
—School Survival: Keeping Your Cool at School. (p. 1523)
Gagliardo, Lucy, illus. see Salmansohn, Pete & Kress, Stephen W.
Gagne, Eric & Brown, Greg. Eric Gagne: Break Barriers. (p. 533)
Gagne, Michel. Saga of Rex. (p. 1502)
Gagne, Tammy. Aaron Rodgers. (p. 2)

—Abyssinian Cats. (p. 7)
—Adele. (p. 12)
—African Dance Trends. (p. 27)
—All about Animals. (p. 42)
—Australian Shepherds (p. 116)
—Beagles (p. 150)
—Black Bears. (p. 195)
—Bloodhounds (p. 201)
—Boxers (p. 217)
—Brazilian Cultures in Perspective. (p. 224)
—Bulldogs (p. 240)
—Care for a Pet Hedgehog. (p. 266)
—Care for a Racing Pigeon. (p. 266)
—Care for a Wolfdog. (p. 266)
—Celts of the British Isles. (p. 286)
—Cheetahs (p. 296)
—Chihuahuas. (p. 301)
—Colin Kaepernick. (p. 339)
—Crocodile. (p. 384)
—Crocodile Paperback. (p. 384)
—Crocodiles: Built for the Hunt. (p. 384)
—Darius Rucker. (p. 407)
—Day by Day with Bindi Sue Irwin. (p. 412)
—Day by Day with Calvin Johnson. (p. 412)
—Day by Day with Elena Delle Donne. (p. 412)
—Day by Day with Justin Bieber. (p. 412)
—Day by Day with Manny Machado. (p. 412)
—Day by Day with Mia Hamm. (p. 412)
—Day by Day with Shaun White. (p. 412)
—Debby Ryan. (p. 421)
—Dividend Stock Strategy for Teens. (p. 454)
—Dog Care: Feeding Your Pup a Healthy Diet & Other Dog Care Tips (p. 461)
—Dustin Pedroia. (p. 490)
—Elephants. (p. 511)
—Evolution of Government & Politics in Greece. (p. 547)
—Evolution of Government & Politics in Italy. (p. 547)
—Evolution of Government & Politics in Venezuela. (p. 547)
—Geckos. (p. 659)
—German Shepherds (p. 666)
—Great Danes (p. 715)
—Hope Solo. (p. 796)
—Immigration in the United States. (p. 861)
—Incredible Military Weapons. (p. 869)
—Investment Options for Teens. (p. 885)
—Jack Russell Terriers (p. 903)
—Jaguars (p. 905)
—Kesha. (p. 949)
—Kid's Guide to the Voting Process. (p. 954)
—Life on Reservations. (p. 1012)
—Lions (p. 1021)
—LL Cool J. (p. 1043)
—Manx Cats. (p. 1089)
—Mike Trout. (p. 1141)
—Military Dogs (p. 1142)
—Most Adorable Animals in the World. (p. 1177)
—Most Endangered Animals in the World. (p. 1177)
—Mutts (p. 1195)
—Nile River. (p. 1255)
—Persian Cats. (p. 1344)
—Pointers: Loyal Hunting Companions (p. 1377)
—Police Dogs (p. 1380)
—Poodles (p. 1383)
—Power of the States. (p. 1390)
—Pugs (p. 1415)
—Rattlesnakes. (p. 1440)
—Retrievers: Loyal Hunting Companions (p. 1464)
—Roy Halladay. (p. 1492)
—Scottish Fold Cats. (p. 1532)
—Sharks: Built for the Hunt. (p. 1562)
—Sloth Bears. (p. 1591)
—Snakes: Built for the Hunt. (p. 1596)
—Spaniels: Loyal Hunting Companions (p. 1620)
—Spectacled Bears. (p. 1624)
—Strangest Animals in the World. (p. 1665)
—Sun Bears. (p. 1676)
—Take Care of the Earth Every Day. (p. 1696)
—Teen Guide to Buying Bonds. (p. 1713)
—Teen Guide to Buying Goods & Services. (p. 1713)
—Teen Guide to Earning Income. (p. 1713)
—Teen Guide to Protecting & Insuring Assests. (p. 1713)
—Teen Guide to Safe-Haven Savings. (p. 1713)
—Teen Guide to Saving & Investing. (p. 1713)
—Trends in Martial Arts. (p. 1784)
—Ways to Help Chronically Ill Children: A Guide to Giving Back. (p. 1865)
—We Visit Madagascar. (p. 1868)
—We Visit Mexico. (p. 1868)
—We Visit South Africa. (p. 1868)
—What It's Like to Be America Ferrara. de la Vega, Eida, tr. from ENG. (p. 1891)
—What It's Like to Be Cameron Diaz. (p. 1891)
—What It's Like to Be Oscar de la Hoya. (p. 1891)
—What It's Like to Be Pele. de la Vega, Eida, tr. (p. 1891)
—What Its Like to Be Sonia Sotomayor. de la Vega, Eida, tr. from SPA. (p. 1891)
—Will. I. am. (p. 1932)
—Working Animals of the World. (p. 1952)
—Yorkshire Terriers (p. 1972)
—Your Guide to Becoming a United States Citizen. (p. 1980)
Gagne, Tammy, jt. auth. see Palika, Liz.
Gagne, Tammy, et al. Big Cats. (p. 180)
—Hunting Dogs: Loyal Hunting Companions. (p. 829)
Gagnon, Céleste, illus. see Jennings, Sharon, et al.
Gagnon, Celeste, illus. see Jennings, Sharon.
Gagnon, Celeste, illus. see Sadler, Judy Ann & Sadler, Judy.
Gagnon, Celeste, jt. creator see Ghione, Yvette.
Gagnon, Celeste, et al, adapted by. Franklin & the Tin Flute. (p. 630)
Gagnon, Cileste, illus. see Sadler, Judy Ann & Sadler, Judy.
Gagnon, Gail Ann. Rainbows & Peaches: Aliyah's Story. (p. 1436)
Gagnon, Lauren. Exeter Alphabet: Learning about Exeter from A to Z. (p. 548)
Gagnon, Mary. Are Those Your Shoes? (p. 96)
Gagnon, Michelle. Don't Let Go. (p. 468)
—Don't Turn Around. (p. 469)
—Strangelets. (p. 1665)
Gagoh, Lydia Akpene. Ese, the Little Boy Who Loved to Dance. (p. 535)
Gahala, Estella. En Espanol! (p. 522)
—¡En Espanol! (p. 522)
Gahala, Estella, et al. En Espanol! (p. 522)
Gahng, Hwa-kyeong, illus. see Joo, Mi-hwa.
Gahng, In, illus. see Jeong, Jini.
Gaia, Kerry-Anne. Fairy Love Heart Story Time & Songs: Love Fairies & the Talking Tree. (p. 563)
Gaichies, Sarah. Angela & the Prince. (p. 74)
—Mirabelle the Lost Kitten. (p. 1148)
Gaido, Peter, jt. auth. see Jaffe, Marc.
Gaidouk, Ekaterina. Adventures of Chi-Chi the Chinchill. (p. 17)
Gaiewski, Maria Louise. Only by Chance (p. 1298)
Gail, Becky. How the Little White Monkey Became a Woman. (p. 813)
Gail, Cornelia. Juvey. (p. 941)
—My Testimony Before & after Grace: Before Grace. Gail, Cornelia, ed. (p. 1220)
Gail, Gibbons. Frogs. (p. 641)
Gail, Ginnie. Great Pigeon Race. Griffin, Don, illus. (p. 717)
Gail, Margaret. Moggie Grows up, 1939-1945. (p. 1160)
Gail, Stewart B. Teenage Dropouts. (p. 1714)
Gailliard, Jason, illus. see Lipp, Frederick J.
Gailliard, Jason, illus. see Lipp, Frederick.
Gailliard, Jason, tr. see Lipp, Frederick J.
Gaiman, Neil. Blueberry Girl. (p. 204)
—Blueberry Girl. Vess, Charles, illus. (p. 204)
—Chu's Day. (p. 318)
—Chu's Day. Rex, Adam, illus. (p. 318)
—Chu's Day at the Beach. Rex, Adam, illus. (p. 318)
—Chu's Day Board Book. Rex, Adam, illus. (p. 318)
—Chu's First Day of School. Rex, Adam, illus. (p. 318)
—Chu's First Day of School Board Book. Rex, Adam, illus. (p. 318)
—Coraline (p. 366)
—Coraline: Reading Group Guide. McKean, Dave, illus. (p. 366)
—Coraline. (p. 366)
—Coraline. McKean, Dave, illus. (p. 366)
—Coraline. Russell, P. Craig, illus. (p. 366)
—Coraline Graphic Novel. Russell, P. Craig, illus. (p. 366)
—Coraline Novela Grafica. Isern, Carol, tr. (p. 366)
—Crazy Hair. (p. 377)
—Crazy Hair. McKean, Dave, illus. (p. 377)
—Dangerous Alphabet. Grimly, Gris, illus. (p. 404)
—Day I Swapped My Dad for Two Goldfish. McKean, Dave, illus. (p. 413)
—Día Que Cambié a Mi Padre por dos Peces de Colores. Ferrer, María, tr. from ENG. (p. 433)
—Endless Nights. (p. 527)
—Fortunately, the Milk. (p. 623)
—Fortunately, the Milk. Young, Skottie, illus. (p. 623)
—Gaiman Mid Grade Novel. (p. 652)
—Graveyard Book (p. 712)
—Graveyard Book. (p. 712)
—Graveyard Book. McKean, Dave, illus. (p. 712)
—Graveyard Book. McKean, Dave, illus. (p. 712)
—Hansel & Gretel. Mattotti, Lorenzo, illus. (p. 743)
—Instructions. Vess, Charles, illus. (p. 878)
—Libro del Cementerio. (p. 1006)
—Lobos de la Pared. McKean, Dave, illus. (p. 1044)
—M Is for Magic. (p. 1067)
—M Is for Magic. Kristiansen, Teddy, illus. (p. 1067)
—Mirrormask. McKean, Dave, illus. (p. 1149)
—Odd & the Frost Giants. Helquist, Brett, illus. (p. 1278)
—Sleeper & the Spindle. Riddell, Chris, illus. (p. 1588)
—Unnatural Creatures: Stories Selected by Neil Gaiman. (p. 1822)
—Wolves in the Walls. McKean, Dave, illus. (p. 1945)
—Worlds' End Kahan, Bob, ed. (p. 1960)
Gaiman, Neil, tr. see Amano, Yoshitaka.
Gaiman, Neil & Pratchett, Terry. Buenos Presagios. Ferrer, María, tr. from ENG. (p. 235)
Gaiman, Neil & Reaves, Michael. Interworld. (p. 881)
Gaiman, Neil & Russell, P. Craig. Graveyard Book Graphic Novel. Russell, P. Craig, illus. (p. 712)
Gaiman, Neil, et al. Death: The Time of Your Life. Kahan, Bob, ed. (p. 420)
—Eternity's Wheel. (p. 539)
—Silver Dream. (p. 1576)
Gainer, Cindy. I'm Like You, You're Like Me: A Book about Understanding & Appreciating Each Other. Sakamoto, Miki, illus. (p. 859)
Gainer, Shannon. When I Die, Will You Cry? (p. 1902)
Gaines, Ann. Christopher Paul Curtis. (p. 317)
—Jim Bowie: Legendary Hero of the Alamo. (p. 917)
—Kids Top 10 Pet Dogs. (p. 955)
—Kids Top 10 Pet Reptiles & Amphibians. (p. 955)
—Kids Top 10 Small Mammal Pets. (p. 955)
—Mississippi. (p. 1154)
Gaines, Ann, jt. auth. see Gaines, Ann Graham.
Gaines, Ann & Steinitz, Andy. North Carolina. (p. 1264)
Gaines, Ann & Waring, Kerry Jones. Mississippi. (p. 1154)
Gaines, Ann Graham. Ace Your Internet Research. (p. 8)
—Border Patrol Agent & Careers in Border Protection. (p. 214)
—Britney Spears. (p. 230)
—Famous Finishes. (p. 569)
—George Washington. (p. 664)
—Hawaii. (p. 755)
—J. K. Rowling. (p. 901)
—James K. Polk. (p. 907)
—James Madison. (p. 907)
—Jim Bowie: Legendary Hero of the Alamo. (p. 917)
—John Adams. (p. 921)
—Kenny Irwin JR. (p. 949)
—Kentucky. (p. 949)
—Kids Top 10 Pet Dogs. (p. 955)
—Kids Top 10 Pet Reptiles & Amphibians. (p. 955)
—Kids Top 10 Small Mammal Pets. (p. 955)
—Master the Library & Media Center. (p. 1103)
—Mississippi. (p. 1154)
—Richard M. Nixon. (p. 1469)
—Special Agent & Careers in the FBI. (p. 1623)
—Theodore Roosevelt. (p. 1729)
—Thomas Jefferson. (p. 1739)
—Top 10 Dogs for Kids. (p. 1768)
—Top 10 Reptiles & Amphibians for Kids. (p. 1768)
—Top 10 Small Mammals for Kids. (p. 1768)
—Ulysses S. Grant. (p. 1810)
—William Henry Harrison. (p. 1933)
Gaines, Ann Graham & Gaines, Ann. Vicente Fox: The Road to the Mexican Presidency. (p. 1840)
Gaines, Ann Graham & Majors, Reggie. Hip-Hop Scene: The Stars, the Fans, the Music. (p. 780)
Gaines, Ernest J. Autobiography of Miss Jane Pittman: And Related Readings. (p. 117)
—Long Day in November. (p. 1047)
Gaines, Isabel & Milne, A. A. Pooh's Leaf Pile. Rigol, Francesc, illus. (p. 1383)
Gaines, Jena. Haitian Immigration. (p. 736)
Gaines, M. C., ed. see Fox, Gardner.
Gaines, Miriam. Grandfathers Love Pie. (p. 707)
Gaines, Pat. O. O. Octopus: Sheriff of Blue Ribbon Sound. (p. 1274)
Gaines, Richard Marshall. When Bears Attack! (p. 1901)
—When Sharks Attack! (p. 1904)
—When Tigers Attack! (p. 1905)
Gaines, William M. & Feldstein, Al. Shock Suspenstories (p. 1568)
Gainey, Gary. Bonds. Gillen, Rosemarie, illus. (p. 208)
Gainor, Chris. History of Canadians in Space: The People & Stories Behind Canada's Role in the Explorations of Space. (p. 783)
Gainsley, Margaret. Faerie of Kalla. (p. 562)
Gair, Angela. How to Draw Anything: A Complete Guide. (p. 816)
Gair, Cyhoeddiadau'r, jt. auth. see Mackenzie, Carine.
Gaisey, Christopher, illus. see Auerbach, Annie.
Gait, Darlene, illus. see Léger, Diane Carmel.
Gait, Darlene, illus. see Pinkney, Jeff.
Gait, Darlene, illus. see Spalding, Andrea & Scow, Alfred.
Gaither, Doug. Lonely Mare (p. 1046)
Gajadin, Chitra. Amal & the Letter from the King. (p. 52)
Gajewski, Lois. Benny, the Stubborn Bubble. (p. 165)
Gal, Dakota. Jaffy Gaffy. (p. 905)
Gal, Laszlo, illus. see Katz, Welwyn Wilton.
Gal, Laszlo, illus. see Shaw-MacKinnon, Margaret.
Gal, Susan. Day by Day. (p. 412)
—Into the Outdoors. (p. 881)
—Night Lights. (p. 1253)
Gal, Susan, illus. see Newman, Lesléa.
Gal, Susan, illus. see Plourde, Lynn.
Galan, Alvaro. Billy Bully. Simpson, Steve, illus. (p. 187)
Galan, Ana. iQué Cosas Dice Mi Abuela! (p. 886)
Galan, Christian. I'm Learning Japanese! A Language Adventure for Young People. Lerot-Calvo, Florence, illus. (p. 859)
Galán, Johnn. Luis Tejada -Vida Breve, Crítica Crónica. (p. 1064)
Galang, M. Evelina. Angel de la Luna & the 5th Glorious Mystery. (p. 73)
Galan-Robles, Francisco, illus. see Harrar, Frank W.
Galant, Debra. Rattled. (p. 1440)
Galante, Ashley, illus. see Cimorelli, Amber.
Galante, Cecilia. Be Not Afraid. (p. 149)
—Hershey Herself. (p. 774)
—Little Wings #2: Be Brave, Willa Bean! Valiant, Kristi, illus. (p. 1037)
—Little Wings #5: Willa Bean to the Rescue! Valiant, Kristi, illus. (p. 1038)
—One & Only Willa Bean. Valiant, Kristi, illus. (p. 1293)
—Summer of May. Carpenter, Tad, illus. (p. 1674)
—Sweetness of Salt. (p. 1690)
—Willowood. (p. 1934)
Galante, Izzy. He Speaks Through Dreams: Awakening. (p. 756)
Galante, Studio, illus. see Heywood, Rosie.
Galantino, Joanne. Fair Claire Hare. (p. 562)
Galardi Mils, Judith A. Judi Galardi's Thrae Back Atcha! (p. 930)
Galas, Judith C. & Nelson, Richard E. Power to Prevent Suicide: A Guide for Teens Helping Teens. (p. 1390)
Galashan, Kathy. Robots. (p. 1481)
—Skate Boarding. (p. 1583)
—Starting a Band. (p. 1644)
Galaska, Taylor, illus. see Paglia, Rhonda.
Galassi, Isabel. I Want (p. 847)
—Love My Nana. (p. 1060)
Galasso, Marina. I Wish. (p. 848)
Galat, Joan Marie. Black Holes & Supernovas (p. 196)
—Branching Out: How Trees Are Part of Our World. (p. 222)
—Dot to Dot in the Sky: Stories in the Planets. (p. 472)
—Stories of the Moon Bennett, Lorna, illus. (p. 1655)
—Stories of the Planets Bennett, Lorna & Yu, Chao, illus. (p. 1655)
—Stories of the Zodiac Bennett, Lorna, illus. (p. 1655)
Galat, Joan Marie, jt. auth. see Bennett, Lorna.
Galbraith, Alison L., illus. see Kelly, Sharon L. C. M.
Galbraith, Bree. Once upon a Balloon Malenfant, Isabelle, illus. (p. 1292)
Galbraith, Judy. Survival Guide for Gifted Kids. (p. 1686)
Galbraith, Judy & Delisle, Jim. Gifted Teen Survival Guide: Smart, Sharp, & Ready for (Almost) Anything. (p. 675)
Galbraith, Julie. Stable Ground: The Riding Series #1. (p. 1638)
Galbraith, Kathryn O. Boo, Bunny! Mack, Jeff, illus. (p. 209)
—Boo, Bunny! Board Book. Mack, Jeff, illus. (p. 209)
—Planting the Wild Garden Halperin, Wendy, illus. (p. 1369)
—Planting the Wild Garden Halperin, Wendy Anderson, illus. (p. 1369)
—Sparky & Tidbit. Kelley, Gerald, illus. (p. 1622)
—Two Bunny Buddies. Cepeda, Joe, illus. (p. 1803)
—Where Is Baby? Butler, John, illus. (p. 1908)
Galbraith, Kathryn Osebold. Arbor Day Square Moore, Cyd, illus. (p. 95)
—Traveling Babies. Dippold, Jane, illus. (p. 1780)
Galchefski, Christina, compiled by. Coloring the Pieces of Luzerne County (p. 344)
Galchus, Sarah. Charleston Red. (p. 292)
Galdone, Joanna C., jt. auth. see Galdone, Paul.
Galdone, Paul. Cinderella. (p. 320)
—Elves & the Shoemaker. (p. 517)
—Folk Tale Classics Treasury. (p. 611)
—Gingerbread Boy Galdone, Paul, illus. (p. 677)
—Gingerbread Boy. (p. 677)
—Gingerbread Boy Big Book. (p. 677)
—Henny Penny. (p. 767)
—Jack & the Beanstalk. (p. 902)
—Little Red Hen. (p. 1034)
—Little Red Hen. Galdone, Paul, illus. (p. 1034)
—Rumpelstiltskin. (p. 1495)
—Three Bears. (p. 1741)
—Three Bears Big Book. (p. 1741)
—Three Billy Goats Gruff Galdone, Paul, illus. (p. 1741)
—Three Billy Goats Gruff. (p. 1741)
—Three Little Kittens Galdone, Paul, illus. (p. 1742)
—Three Little Kittens. (p. 1742)
—Three Little Pigs Galdone, Paul, illus. (p. 1742)
—Tres Chivitos Gruff. Fiol, María A., tr. (p. 1784)
Galdone, Paul, illus. see Titus, Eve.
Galdone, Paul & Galdone, Joanna C. Three Little Pigs. (p. 1742)
Galdone, Paul & Lear, Edward. Owl & the Pussycat. (p. 1314)
Galdós, Benito Pérez. Tristana. Jull Costa, Margaret, tr. from FRE. (p. 1787)
Galè. Bwlng Btnks Bell Btms 2 (p. 249)
—Junior Worldmark Encyclopedia of Foods & Recipes of the World (p. 936)
—Junior Worldmark Encyclopedia of the Nations (p. 936)
—Middle East Conflict: Almanac. (p. 1137)
—Middle East Conflict: Biographies. (p. 1137)
—Middle East Conflict: Primary Sources. (p. 1137)
—Middle East Conflict Reference Library (p. 1137)
—U-X-L Encyclopedia of Native American Tribes (p. 1807)
Gale, ed. see Bily, Cynthia A.
Gale, ed. see Cartlidge, Cherese.
Gale, ed. see Haerens, Margaret.
Gale, ed. see Haugen, David M.
Gale, ed. see Langwith, Jacqueline.
Gale, ed. see Merino, Noel.
Gale, ed. see Naff, Clay Farris.
Gale, ed. see Nardo, Don.
Gale, ed. see Scherer, Lauri S.
Gale, A. G., ed. see Gerdes, Louise I.
Gale, A. G., ed. see Langwith, Jacqueline.
Gale, A. G., ed. see Thompson, Tamara.
Gale, Anthony, ed. see Gerdes, Louise I.
Gale, Audra. Adventures of Buddy & Me. (p. 17)
Gale, Bob & Grayson, Devin K. Batman: No Man's Land, Vol. 1 Maleev, Alexander et al, illus. (p. 144)
Gale, Cathy, illus. see Cottringer, Anne.
Gale, Cathy, illus. see Puttock, Simon.
Gale Cengage Learning, ed. Junior Worldmark Encyclopedia of the States: 4 Volume Set. (p. 936)
Gale, Debra. Halloween Tripper. (p. 739)
Gale, ed. Encyclopedia of World Biography 1999 Supplement. (p. 525)
Gale Editor, ed. see Espejo, Roman.
Gale Editor, ed. see McDonald, John.
Gale Editor, ed. see Merino, Noël.
Gale Editor & Greenhaven Press Editors, eds. Roger Federer. (p. 1484)
Gale Editor & MacKay, Jennifer, eds. Electric Cars. (p. 508)
Gale Editor & Redmond, Shirley Raye, eds. Golem. (p. 696)
Gale Editor, ed. Christmas Carol: The Graphic Novel. (p. 313)
—Hypnosis. (p. 831)
—Jennifer Hudson. (p. 912)
—Junior Worldmark Encyclopedia of the States: 4 Volume Set (p. 936)
—Katy Perry. (p. 946)
—Romeo & Juliet: The Graphic Novel. (p. 1486)
Gale Editors, ed. see Berlatsky, Noah.
Gale Editors, ed. see Chalk, Frank.
Gale Editors, ed. see Engdahl, Sylvia.
Gale Editors, ed. see Espejo, Roman.
Gale Editors, ed. see Frohnapfel-Krueger, Lisa.
Gale Editors, ed. see Gerdes, Louise I.
Gale Editors, ed. see Gillard, Arthur.
Gale Editors, ed. see Haerens, Margaret.
Gale Editors, ed. see Haugen, David M.
Gale Editors, ed. see Hay, Jeff.
Gale Editors, ed. see Henningfeld, Diane Andrews.
Gale Editors, ed. see Hiber, Amanda.
Gale Editors, ed. see Hina, Paul & Hina, Sarah.
Gale Editors, ed. see Immell, Myra.
Gale Editors, ed. see Langwith, Jacqueline.
Gale Editors, ed. see Lankford, Ronald D.
Gale Editors, ed. see Merino, Noel.
Gale Editors, ed. see Merino, Noel.
Gale Editors, ed. see Merino, Noël.
Gale Editors, ed. see Merino, Noël.
Gale Editors, ed. see Merino, Noël.
Gale Editors, ed. see Miller, Debra A.
Gale Editors, ed. see Riggs, Thomas.
Gale Editors, ed. see Scherer, Lauri S.
Gale Editors, ed. see Stewart, Gail B.
Gale Editors, ed. see Thompson, Tamara.
Gale Editors, ed. see Ullmann, Carol.
Gale Editors, jt. auth. see Dougherty, Terri.
Gale Editors, jt. auth. see Mooney, Carla.
Gale Editors, jt. ed. see Greenhaven Press Editors.
Gale Editors & Carnagie, Julie L., eds. World Religions (p. 1958)
Gale Editors & Corporate Contributor Staff, eds. Junior Worldmark Encyclopedia of World Cultures (p. 936)

Gale Editors & Immell, Myra. Japan's 2011 Natural Distaster & Nucular Meltdown. (p. 909)
Gale Editors & Merino, Noël. Urban Sprawl. (p. 1825)
Gale Editors & Miller, Debra A. Immigration. (p. 861)
Gale Editors & Wilson, Sean Michael. Canterville Ghost: The Graphic Novel. (p. 262)
Gale Editors, ed. Worldmark Conflict & Diplomacy: 2 Volume Set (p. 1960)
Gale, Emily. Girl Out Loud. (p. 678)
—Just Josie & the Number 7. Byrne, Mike, illus. (p. 938)
—Just Josie & the Perfect Day. Byrne, Mike, illus. (p. 938)
—My Explosive Diary. Dreidemy, Joëlle, illus. (p. 1202)
—My Super-Spy Diary. (p. 1219)
Gale, Eric Kahn. Bully Book. (p. 241)
—Zoo at the Edge of the World. Nielson, Sam, illus. (p. 1988)
Gale, G., ed. see Espejo, Roman.
Gale, G., ed. see Hillstrom, Kevin.
Gale, G., ed. see Schier, Helga.
Gale, G., ed. see Thompson, Tamara.
Gale, G., ed. see Williams, Mary E.
Gale, John E. Speedyread: A Phonics-Based Reading & Spelling Program. (p. 1625)
Gale, Paul. Lisek's Great Adventure. (p. 1022)
Gale Research Inc Staff, contrib. by. Global Events: Milestone Events Throughout History. (p. 684)
Gale Research Staff. Grzimek's Animal Life Encyclopedia (p. 728)
—Grzimek's Animal Life Encyclopedia: Cumulative Index (p. 728)
—Industrial Revolution: Biographies. (p. 872)
—Industrial Revolution: Primary Sources. (p. 872)
Gale Research Staff, ed. see Haerens, Margaret.
Gale, Riana, et al. Artistic Expressions of a Child. (p. 104)
Gale, Trevor, et al. Engaging Teachers. (p. 529)
Galeano, Eduardo. Mitos de Memoria del Fuego. (p. 1156)
Galeano, Jose Daniel, illus. see Ramirez, Paul & Ramirez, Matthew.
Galeano, Jose Daniel Oviedo, illus. see Walchle, Donna Douglas.
Galeano, Tomomi, tr. see Rose, Imogen.
Galego, Ane M., illus. see Whittle, J. Robert & Sandilands, Joyce.
Galenorn, Yasmine. Dragon Wytch. (p. 478)
—Flight from Death. (p. 604)
Galens, Judy, et al. UXL Newsmakers. (p. 1829)
Galer, Chris. Ross Gang. (p. 1490)
Galer, Christa, jt. auth. see Galer, Jeffrey.
Galer, Jeffrey & Galer, Christa. Big Red Barn. Galer, Jeffrey, illus. (p. 183)
Galera Staff. Cuervo y la Raposa (Raven & the Fox) (p. 390)
—Liebre y la Tortuga. (p. 1007)
Galeron, Henri. Parrots. Galeron, Henri, illus. (p. 1325)
Galeron, Henri, illus. see Jeunesse, Gallimard & De Bourgoing, Pascale.
Galeron, Henri, illus. see Jeunesse, Gallimard, et al.
Galeron, Henri, illus. see Prunier, James.
Galeron, Henri, tr. see Prunier, Jameâs, et al.
Galeron, Henri, et al. My First Encyclopedia of Dinosaurs. (p. 1206)
—Perro. Galeron, Henri & Barroso, Paz, trs. (p. 1343)
Gales, Rick. Granny Puckerlips: Keepin' It Real with Kindness & Respect. (p. 710)
Galey, Chuck, illus. see Davis, David.
Galey, Chuck, illus. see Davis, Mary J.
Galey, Chuck, illus. see Davis, Mary.
Galey, Chuck, illus. see Domelj, Scot & Kuhn, Pamela J.
Galey, Chuck, illus. see Enderle, Dotti.
Galey, Chuck, illus. see Ivey, Randall.
Galey, Chuck, illus. see Kittinger, Jo S.
Galey, Chuck, illus. see Kittinger, Jo S., et al.
Galey, Chuck, illus. see Layne, Steven L.
Galey, Chuck, illus. see Little, Robert.
Galey, Chuck, illus. see Pearson, Mary R. & Kuhn, Pamela J.
Galey, Chuck, illus. see Pelfrey, Wanda B. & Kuhn, Pamela J.
Galey, Chuck, illus. see Sanders, Nancy I. & Kuhn, Pamela J.
Galfas, Stephan, jt. auth. see Mashonee, Jana.
Galford, Ellen. Festivals. (p. 582)
—Hatshepsut: The Princess Who Became King. (p. 752)
—Julius Caesar: The Boy Who Conquered an Empire. (p. 933)
—Religious Costumes. (p. 1458)
Gali, Merce, jt. auth. see Gil, Carmen.
Galiano, Dean. Clouds, Rain & Snow. (p. 335)
—Electric & Magnetic Phenomena. (p. 508)
—Fourth Amendment: Unreasonable Search & Seizure. (p. 625)
—Nebraska. Brusca, Maria Cristina, tr. (p. 1239)
—North Carolina. (p. 1264)
—North Carolina/Carolina del Norte. Brusca, Maria Cristina, tr. from ENG. (p. 1265)
—Thunderstorms & Lightning. (p. 1746)
—Wisconsin. Brusca, Maria Cristina, tr. from ENG. (p. 1939)
—Wyoming. Brusca, Maria Cristina, tr. from ENG. (p. 1966)
Galiano, Nicole. Choosing a Career in the Pharmacy & in the Pharmaceutical Sciences. (p. 310)
Galindo, Alejandro, illus. see Bertrand, Diane Gonzales & Ventura, Gabriela Baeza.
Galindo, Claudia. It's Bedtime, Cucuy!/A la Cama, Cucuy. Pluecker, John, tr. from ENG. (p. 896)
Galindo, Claudia & Pluecker, John. Do You Know the Cucuy? Conoces Al Cucuy? Coombs, Jonathan, illus. (p. 458)
Galindo, Felipe, illus. see Nikola-Lisa, W.
Galindo, Mary Sue. Icy Watermelon/Sandia Fria. Rodriguez Howard, Pauline & Howard, Pauline Rodriguez, illus. (p. 851)
Galindo, Renata. Cherry Thief. Galindo, Renata, illus. (p. 298)
Galindo-Leal, Carlos. De dos mundos = of Two Worlds: Las ranas, sapos y salamandras de la Peninsula de Yucatán, México = the Frogs, Toads & Salamanders of the Yucatan Peninsula, Mexico. Arreola Alemón, Roberto, illus. (p. 416)
Galioto, Annette. Gordon Ramsay. (p. 702)
Galjanic, Lisa. When Bees Win. Hope, Michelle, illus. (p. 1901)
—When Caterpillars Grow Up. Hope, Michelle, illus. (p. 1901)
—When Fish Are Mean. Hope, Michelle, illus. (p. 1902)
—When Flowers Dance. Hope, Michelle, illus. (p. 1902)
—When Leaves Die. Hope, Michelle, illus. (p. 1903)
—When Series 6 Volume Set (p. 1904)
—When Squirrels Try. Hope, Michelle, illus. (p. 1904)
Galkin, Simon, illus. see Ransome, Arthur.
Galko, Francine. Classifying Invertebrates (p. 328)
—Classifying Nonflowering Plants (p. 328)
Galko, Francine & Heinemann Library Staff. Classifying Flowering Plants Blake, Jo, illus. (p. 328)
—Classifying Invertebrates (p. 328)
—Classifying Nonflowering Plants (p. 328)
Gall, Allan R. Of Mouse & Magic. (p. 1279)
Gall, Chris. Awesome Dawson. (p. 121)
—Dinotrux. (p. 445)
—Dinotrux. Gall, Chris, illus. (p. 445)
—Dinotrux Dig the Beach. (p. 445)
—Dinotrux Go to School. (p. 445)
—Dog vs. Cat. (p. 462)
—Meet the Dinotrux. (p. 1122)
—NanoBots. (p. 1229)
—Revenge of the Dinotrux. (p. 1465)
—Revenge of the Dinotrux. (p. 1466)
—Substitute Creacher. (p. 1671)
Gall, Chris, illus. see Bates, Katharine Lee.
Gall, Chris, illus. see Stein, Peter.
Gall, Susan B., jt. auth. see Gall, Timothy L.
Gall, Susan B. & Edgar, Kathleen J. Junior Worldmark Encyclopedia of Foods & Recipes of the World (p. 936)
Gall, Susan B., ed. Junior Worldmark Encyclopedia of Physical Geography (p. 936)
Gall, Timothy. Lincoln Library of Shapers of Society: 101 Men & Woman Who Shaped the World. (p. 1018)
Gall, Timothy L. & Gall, Susan B. Junior Worldmark Encyclopedia of the States (p. 936)
—Junior Worldmark Encyclopedia of the States. (p. 936)
—Junior Worldmark Encyclopedia of World Cultures. (p. 936)
Galla, Jessica. Not Just Babies Are Adopted (p. 1267)
Galla, Nicole. Water & Ice. (p. 1862)
Gallacher, Marcie. Amaryllis Lilies. (p. 52)
Gallagher, Aileen. Hepatitis. (p. 769)
—Japanese Red Army. (p. 909)
—Muckrakers: American Journalism During the Age of Reform. (p. 1188)
—Prince Henry the Navigator: Pioneer of Modern Exploration. (p. 1401)
Gallagher, Belinda. Why Why Why... Are There Schools in the Sea? (p. 1926)
—Why Why Why... Did Romans Race to the Circus? (p. 1926)
—Why Why Why... Were the Pyramids Built? (p. 1926)
Gallagher, Belinda, ed. see Parker, Steve.
Gallagher, Belinda, ed. see Williams, Brian.
Gallagher, Belinda & Maccuish, Isla, eds. 100 Best-Loved Nursery Rhymes. (p. 1998)
Gallagher, Belinda, ed. Mix & Match: Six Fun Scenes to Search & Find. (p. 1156)
—Nursery Treasury: Best-Loved Nursery Rhymes, Fairytales & First Poems. (p. 1273)
Gallagher, Brendan & Gallagher, Debbie. Protecting Ancient Heritage. (p. 1412)
—Protecting Earth's History: Brendan & Debbie Gallagher. (p. 1412)
—Protecting Ecosystems: Brendan & Debbie Gallagher. (p. 1412)
—Protecting Human Masterpieces. (p. 1412)
—Protecting the Human Story. (p. 1412)
—Protecting Threatened Animals. (p. 1412)
Gallagher, Brian. Friend or Foe. (p. 637)
—Secrets & Shadows: Two Friends in a World at War. (p. 1544)
—Stormclouds: New Friends. Old Differences. (p. 1656)
—Taking Sides: A Boy, a Girl, a Nation Torn Apart. (p. 1698)
Gallagher, Brigid. Langston Hughes (p. 974)
—Langston Hughes Oxford Bible Staff, illus. (p. 974)
—Sonia Sotomayor (p. 1612)
Gallagher, Carole M. Little ABC Phonics Workbook. (p. 1023)
Gallagher, Debbie. Alligators & Crocodiles. (p. 47)
—Ants. (p. 90)
—Bees. (p. 157)
—Butterflies. (p. 247)
—Families (p. 567)
—Family Celebrations. (p. 568)
—Family Homes. (p. 568)
—Family Meals. (p. 568)
—Family Members. (p. 568)
—Family Responsibilities. (p. 568)
—Family Stories. (p. 568)
—Flies. (p. 603)
—Ladybugs. (p. 971)
—Pandas. (p. 1321)
—Parrots. (p. 1325)
—Penguins. (p. 1337)
—Seals & Sea Lions. (p. 1536)
—Snakes. (p. 1596)
—Spiders. (p. 1626)
Gallagher, Debbie, jt. auth. see Gallagher, Brendan.
Gallagher, Debbie & Smart Apple Media Staff. City & Country Homes. (p. 323)
—Mud, Grass, & Ice Homes. (p. 1188)
—Palaces, Mansions & Castles. (p. 1319)
—Portable Homes. (p. 1386)
Gallagher, Derek, text. Ancient Dwellings of the Southwest. (p. 68)
Gallagher, Diana G. Advice about Family: Claudia Cristina Cortez Uncomplicates Your Life. Garvey, Brann, illus. (p. 25)
—Advice about Friends: Claudia Cristina Cortez Uncomplicates Your Life. Garvey, Brann, illus. (p. 25)
—Advice about Friends. Garvey, Brann, illus. (p. 25)
—Advice about School: Claudia Cristina Cortez Uncomplicates Your Life. Garvey, Brann, illus. (p. 25)
—Advice about Work & Play: Claudia Cristina Cortez Uncomplicates Your Life. Garvey, Brann, illus. (p. 25)
—Bad Luck Bridesmaid: The Complicated Life of Claudia Cristina Cortez Garvey, Brann, illus. (p. 132)
—Beach Blues: The Complicated Life of Claudia Cristina Cortez Garvey, Brann, illus. (p. 149)
—Beware! The Complicated Life of Claudia Cristina Cortez Garvey, Brann, illus. (p. 173)
—Boy Trouble: The Complicated Life of Claudia Cristina Cortez. Garvey, Brann, illus. (p. 219)
—Camp Can't: The Complicated Life of Claudia Cristina Cortez Garvey, Brann, illus. (p. 257)
—Dance Trap: The Complicated Life of Claudia Cristina Cortez Garvey, Brann, illus. (p. 402)
—Doggone Dog Juarez, Adriana & Puglisi, Adriana, illus. (p. 462)
—Friends Forever? The Complicated Life of Claudia Cristina Cortez Garvey, Brann, illus. (p. 638)
—Great Kitten Challenge Juarez, Adriana & Puglisi, Adriana, illus. (p. 716)
—Guilty! The Complicated Life of Claudia Cristina Cortez Garvey, Brann, illus. (p. 730)
—Haunted Love (p. 753)
—Hired or Fired? The Complicated Life of Claudia Cristina Cortez Garvey, Brann, illus. (p. 781)
—Homecoming (p. 793)
—Mice Capades Juarez, Adriana & Puglisi, Adriana, illus. (p. 1134)
—Monica & the Bratty Stepsister Canga, C. B, illus. (p. 1164)
—Monica & the Crushworthy Cowboy (p. 1164)
—Monica & the Doomed Dance (p. 1164)
—Monica & the School Spirit Meltdown (p. 1164)
—Monica & the Sweetest Song (p. 1164)
—Monica & the Unbeatable Bet (p. 1164)
—Monica & the Weekend of Drama (p. 1164)
—Monica & the Worst Horse Ever (p. 1164)
—New Firsts (p. 1244)
—No-Sneeze Pet Juarez, Adriana & Puglisi, Adriana, illus. (p. 1260)
—Party! The Complicated Life of Claudia Cristina Cortez Garvey, Brann, illus. (p. 1326)
—Pet Friends Forever (p. 1345)
—Pet Store Pet Show Puglisi, Adriana, illus. (p. 1345)
—Pool Problem: The Complicated Life of Claudia Cristina Cortez Garvey, Brann, illus. (p. 1383)
—Problem Pup Puglisi, Adriana, illus. (p. 1408)
—Sold! The Complicated Life of Claudia Cristina Cortez Garvey, Brann, illus. (p. 1607)
—Tested (p. 1723)
—Vote! The Complicated Life of Claudia Cristina Cortez Garvey, Brann, illus. (p. 1850)
—Whatever! The Complicated Life of Claudia Cristina Cortez Garvey, Brann, illus. (p. 1896)
Gallagher, Diana G. & Burge, Constance M. Trickery Treat. (p. 1786)
Gallagher, Diane Shugrue, et al. Lives of Service: Stories from the Peace Corps. (p. 1040)
Gallagher, Fred, et al. Megatokyo (p. 1124)
Gallagher, Gary W., jt. auth. see O'Neill, Robert John.
Gallagher, Heather Marie & Vlahutin, Peter. Teen, Sex, & Chastity: Straight Talk, Real Issues Art of Choosing Well. (p. 1714)
Gallagher, James. Beatles. (p. 153)
Gallagher, Jim. Causes of the Iraq War. (p. 282)
—Daniel Morgan: Fighting Frontiersman. (p. 405)
—Hassled Guy's Guide: How to Deal. (p. 752)
—Tiger Woods. (p. 1749)
—US-Led Wars in Iraq, 1991-Present Musteen, Jason R., ed. (p. 1826)
Gallagher, Jim & Kavanaugh, Dorothy. Guys' Guide to Conflict. (p. 733)
Gallagher, Kathleen, jt. auth. see Sheffield, Stephanie.
Gallagher, Liz. My Not-So-Still Life. (p. 1216)
Gallagher, M. Witch Wolf? the Curse. (p. 1941)
Gallagher, Mary. Legend of Lisnashee. (p. 988)
—Mulhern Twins. (p. 1189)
Gallagher, Mary, illus. see Nelson, Julie.
Gallagher, Mary Collins. Ginny Morris & Dads New Girlfriend. Martin, Whitney, illus. (p. 677)
—Nine Is Not an Even Number. Martin, Whitney, illus. (p. 1256)
Gallagher, Maureen & Hiesberger, Jean Marie. Take Ten: Daily Bible Reflections for Teens. (p. 1697)
Gallagher, Michael. South Africa. (p. 1616)
—X-Men, Magneto's Master Plan. Severin, Marie, illus. (p. 1967)
—X-Men, Scourge of the Savage Land. Severin, Marie, illus. (p. 1967)
Gallagher, Mike. Sabrina Animated. Manak, Dave, illus. (p. 1500)
Gallagher, Mike, et al. Sonic Select Spaziante, Patrick Spaz, illus. (p. 1612)
—Sonic the Hedgehog Archives (p. 1612)
—Sonic the Hedgehog Archives. Pellerito, Mike, ed. (p. 1612)
Gallagher, R., et al. Addysg Gorfforol Trwy Ddiagramau: Llawlyfr Adolygu TGAU. (p. 12)
Gallagher, S. Saelig, illus. see Schotter, Roni.
Gallagher, Sarah, jt. ed. see Malinowska-Sempruch, Kasia.
Gallagher, Tara. 100 Greatest Moments in Irish History. Bailey, Hannah, illus. (p. 1998)
Gallagher, Toni. Twist My Charm - The Popularity Spell. (p. 1802)
Gallagher-Bolos, Joan, et al. Teaching Inquiry-Based Chemistry: Creating Student-Led Scientific Communities. (p. 1710)
Gallagher-Cole, Mernie, illus. see Amoroso, Cynthia.
Gallagher-Cole, Mernie, illus. see Blackaby, Susan.
Gallagher-Cole, Mernie, illus. see Coss, Lauren.
Gallagher-Cole, Mernie, illus. see Garstecki, Julia.
Gallagher-Cole, Mernie, illus. see Higgins, Nadia.
Gallagher-Cole, Mernie, illus. see Holub, Joan.
Gallagher-Cole, Mernie, illus. see Klein, Adria F.
Gallagher-Cole, Mernie, illus. see Klingel, Cynthia Fitterer & Klingel, Cynthia.
Gallagher-Cole, Mernie, illus. see Klingel, Cynthia Fitterer.
Gallagher-Cole, Mernie, illus. see Lynette, Rachel.
Gallagher-Cole, Mernie, illus. see Moncure, Jane Belk.
Gallagher-Cole, Mernie, illus. see Owings, Lisa.
Gallagher-Cole, Mernie, illus. see Pearson, Yvonne.
Gallagher-Cole, Mernie, illus. see Ringstad, Arnold.
Gallagher-Cole, Mernie, illus. see Rosenberg, Pam.
Gallagher-Cole, Mernie, illus. see Simons, Lisa M. Bolt.
Gallagher-Cole, Mernie, illus. see Worsham, Adria F.
Gallagher-Cole, Mernie, illus. see Zee, Amy Van.
Gallagher-Cole, Mernie, jt. auth. see Klein, Adria F.
Gallais, Celia, jt. auth. see Lecreux, Michele.
Galland, Nicole. Stepdog. (p. 1648)
Gallant, Dany, jt. see Campagne, Michelle.
Gallant, Mark D. Christmas at Wildwood Farm. (p. 312)
Gallant, R. Stephen. Advance to Adventure, Volume 1: Through the River & Fire. (p. 13)
Gallard, Bette. Streaks & Cuckoos. (p. 1666)
Gallardo, Adam. 100 Girls: Vol 1: the First Girl Vol. 1 Demong, Todd, illus. (p. 1998)
—100 Girls. Demong, Todd, illus. (p. 1998)
—Gear School (p. 659)
—Gear School Sandoval, Sergio & Peris, Nuria, illus. (p. 659)
Gallardo, Adam J. Zombified. (p. 1988)
—Zomburbia. (p. 1988)
Gallardo, Edward. Simpson Street & Other Plays. (p. 1578)
Gallardo, Mary. Tiny Little Raindrop. (p. 1756)
Gallardo, Yuri, ed. Houses & Apartments under 1000 Square Feet. (p. 804)
Gallardo-Walker, Gloria. Ka-Lunk! Wallis, Angie, illus. (p. 941)
Gallart, Dolors, tr. see Pullman, Philip.
Gallart, Gemma, tr. see Lewis, C. S.
Gallart Iglesias, Maria Dolores, tr. see Pullman, Philip.
Gallas, G. E., illus. see Latta, Sara.
Gallaudet, Thomas. Child's Book on Repentance. (p. 304)
—Child's Book on the Fall of Man. (p. 304)
—Child's Book on the Soul. (p. 304)
Gallaudet, Thomas H. Scripture Biography for the Young: Vol. 2 - Joseph. (p. 1533)
—Scripture Biography for the Young: The History of Josiah. (p. 1533)
—Scripture Biography for the Young: Vol. 3 - Moses Part 1. (p. 1533)
—Scripture Biography for the Young: Vol. 4 - Moses Part 2. (p. 1533)
—Scripture Biography for the Young: Vol. 1 - Adam to Jacob. (p. 1533)
—Scripture Biography for the Young: Vol. 5 - Joshua & Judges. (p. 1533)
Gallavotti, Barbara. Cuerpo Humano en Acción. (p. 390)
—Human Body in Action. Shapiro, Brett, tr. from ITA. (p. 825)
—Vida en la Tierra. (p. 1840)
Gallaway, Kate, jt. auth. see Witt, Joe.
Gallaz, Christophe. Rose Blanche. Innocenti, Roberto, illus. (p. 1489)
Gallaz, Christophe, jt. auth. see Innocenti, Roberto.
Gallego Garcia, Laura. Retorno a la Isla Blanca. (p. 1464)
Gallego Garcia, Laura, jt. auth. see Gallego García, Laura.
Gallego Garcia, Laura & Bellm, Dan. Legend of the Wandering King. (p. 989)
Gallego Garcia, Laura & Gallego García, Laura. Valle de Los Lobos. (p. 1830)
Gallego Garcia, Laura & Peden, Margaret Sayers. Valley of the Wolves. (p. 1831)
Gallego Garcia, Laura, et al. Hijas de Tara. (p. 779)
Gallego, James, illus. see Posner-Sanchez, Andrea.
Gallego, James, illus. see Random House.
Gallego, Laura, et al. Leyenda Del Rey Errante. (p. 1004)
—Llamada de Los Muertos. (p. 1043)
Gallego, Mercedes. Más Allá de la Batalla: Una Corresponsal de Guerra en Irak. (p. 1101)
Gallegos, Annette, jt. auth. see Gallegos, Rick.
Gallegos, Benito, illus. see Gerard, Kevin.
Gallegos, Bryan. Ghost Train. (p. 672)
Gallegos, Eligio Stephen. Nothing Is Nothing. (p. 1268)
Gallegos, Gary L. Wandering Schoolgirl. (p. 1856)
Gallegos, Jacqueline C. Night the Princesses Danced. (p. 1254)
Gallegos, Lauren, illus. see Cerrito, Dana.
Gallegos, Lauren, illus. see Lang, Diane.
Gallegos, Lauren, illus. see Thayer, Robert Scott.
Gallegos, Manuel. Mi Primer Teatro. (p. 1133)
Gallegos, Michael. Mommy Do You Love Me? (p. 1162)
—Three Royal Horses. (p. 1743)
Gallegos, Rick & Gallegos, Annette. Born with a Broken Heart: Congenital Heart Disease. (p. 214)
Gallegos, Yuliana. Mi Sueno de America/My American Dream. Baeza, Georgina, tr. (p. 1133)
Gallemore, M. H. Annie & the Mermaid. (p. 86)
Gallenkamp, Charles, jt. auth. see Meyer, Carolyn.
Gallenkamp, Kirk Charles. Pages in Tyme: The River's Journey. (p. 1318)
Gallenson, Ann, illus. see Dharkar, Anuja & Tapley, Scott.
Gallenson, Ann, illus. see Underwood, Dale & Aho, Kirsti.
Gallery, Philip D. Can You Find Jesus? Introducing Your Child to the Gospels. Harlow, Janet, illus. (p. 258)
—Can You Find Saints? Introducing Your Child to Holy Men & Women. Harlow, Janet L., tr. (p. 259)
Gallery, Philip D. & Harlow, Janet L. Can You Find Followers of Jesus? Introducing Your Child to the Disciples. (p. 258)
Galleschi, M. Lucrezia, ed. see Bussagli, Marco.
Gallet, Karl, illus. see Mistretta, Jay.
Gallet, Ryan, illus. see Mistretta, Jay Francis.
Galletti, Barbara. Baltimore Symphony Chorus Retrospective. (p. 135)
Galli, Stanley W., illus. see Moody, Ralph.
Gallico, Paul. Abandoned. (p. 2)
—Snow Goose & Other Stories. (p. 1599)
Gallienne, Richard Le, see Le Gallienne, Richard.
Galliez, Roxane Marie. Earth Has Caught Cold. Lhomme, Sandrine, illus. (p. 496)
—Farewell Sadness. Lhomme, Sandrine, illus. (p. 573)
—Give Me Moon. Delanssay, Cathy, illus. (p. 681)
Galliker, Leslie. Joint Replacements. (p. 924)
—Native American Wars on the Western Frontier (1866-1890) Musteen, Jason R., ed. (p. 1234)

G

Gallina, Danielle. Dear God, Are There Any Flies in Heaven? Foy, Denis, illus. (p. 419)
Gallina, Jill, jt. auth. see Gallina, Michael.
Gallina, Jill & Gallina, Michael. Dino Soaring! A Prehistoric Musical Adventure for Cross-Curricular Fun in the Classroom. (p. 441)
—Green Machine Team: A Mini-Musical to Recycle, Replenish, & Renew! (p. 722)
—Happy, the High-Tech Snowman: A One-Act Musical. (p. 747)
—Kitty Cat Capers. (p. 963)
—Oceans of Fun. (p. 1277)
—Rhythm Band Strikes AGAIN! (p. 1468)
—Sing Me a Story: Classic Stories Throughout Time Come to Life in Song & Rhyme. (p. 1579)
—Snoozy Snowflake: Singin' & Swingin' at the K-2 Chorale Series. (p. 1598)
Gallina, Michael, jt. see Gallina, Jill.
Gallina, Michael & Gallina, Jill. Sing & Play about the USA! (p. 1579)
Gallinger, Jared, illus. see Spencer, Betty.
Gallippi, Marisa. Flower Kisser. (p. 607)
Gallivan, Susan. Return of Mr Jeffries. (p. 1464)
Gallo, Anjie R. Story, the Explanation, the Integration: A Woman's Journey through Karma. (p. 1663)
Gallo, Diane. William Wolf & the Three Little Kids: A Tale of a Playground Bully. (p. 1933)
Gallo, Donald. On the Fringe: Stories. Gallo, Donald & Gallo, Donald R., eds. (p. 1290)
Gallo, Donald R. First Crossing: Stories about Teen Immigrants. Gallo, Donald R., ed. (p. 594)
—No Easy Answer. (p. 1258)
Gallo, Donald R., ed. see Gallo, Donald.
Gallo, Donald R., compiled by. What Are You Afraid Of? Stories about Phobias. (p. 1880)
Gallo, Donald R., ed. Owning It: Stories about Teens with Disabilities. (p. 1315)
Gallo, Lisa. Picnic Adventure. Thomas, Laura, illus. (p. 1355)
Gallo, Tina. Behold the Power of Gargamel! Riley, Kellee, illus. (p. 160)
—Brava OLIVIA. Rose, Drew, illus. (p. 223)
—Cinderella: A Wheel-Y Silly Fairy Tale. Scott, Kimberley, illus. (p. 320)
—Day of the Dragon Egg. (p. 414)
—Gabba Land Band. Craig, Karen, illus. (p. 652)
—Huzzah for Spring! HIT Entertainment Staff, illus. (p. 830)
—Let's Put on a Show! Style Guide Staff, illus. (p. 1000)
—Lettuce In! And Other Knock-Knock Jokes. Chollat, Emilie, illus. (p. 1003)
—Mike the Knight & the Good Deed. (p. 1141)
—OLIVIA & the Christmas Party. Rose, Drew, illus. (p. 1286)
—Olivia & the Puppy Wedding. (p. 1286)
—OLIVIA & the Puppy Wedding. Spaziante, Patrick, illus. (p. 1286)
—OLIVIA in the Park. Rose, Drew, illus. (p. 1286)
—Olivia Plays Soccer. (p. 1287)
—OLIVIA Plays Soccer. Osterhold, Jared, illus. (p. 1287)
—Olivia Wishes on a Star. (p. 1287)
—Po's Secret Move. (p. 1387)
—Three Little Pigs: A Wheel-Y Silly Fairy Tale. Bryne, Kelly, illus. (p. 1743)
—Where's My Valentine? (p. 1910)
Gallo, Tina, jt. auth. see Rao, Lisa.
Gallo, Tina, adapted by. Kung Fu Road Trip. (p. 968)
—Mike the Knight & the Good Deed. (p. 1141)
—Po Who Cried Ghost. (p. 1374)
—Triple Trophy Triumph. (p. 1787)
Gallo, Tina & S. I. International Staff. Let's Go, Go, Go! (p. 997)
Gallow, Robyn, illus. see Johnson, Maggie & Wintgens, Alison.
Galloway, Amy, illus. see Morton, Machel.
Galloway, Dorian P. Why Pammie's So Small. (p. 1925)
Galloway, Emily Ledford. Nimby the Cloud. (p. 1256)
Galloway, Fhiona. 123 Counting Sticker Book. (p. 2000)
—ABC Alphabet Sticker Book. (p. 3)
—Busy Day Sticker Book. (p. 246)
Galloway, Fhiona, illus. see Litton, Jonathan.
Galloway, Ginger. Jasper. Zemke, Deborah, illus. (p. 910)
Galloway, Priscilla. Aleta y la Reina: Una Historia de la Antigua Grecia. (p. 35)
—Archers, Alchemists, & 98 Other Medieval Jobs You Might Have Loved or Loathed. Newbigging, Martha, illus. (p. 95)
—Atalanta: La Corredora Mas Veloz del Mundo. (p. 111)
—Atalante: La Coureuse la Plus Rapide au Monde. Cousineau, Normand, illus. (p. 111)
Galloway, Priscilla, compiled by. Too Young to Fight: Memories from Our Youth During World War II (p. 1767)
Galloway, Ruth. Clumsy Crab. Galloway, Ruth, illus. (p. 336)
—Fidgety Fish. Galloway, Ruth, illus. (p. 583)
—Smiley Shark. Galloway, Ruth, illus. (p. 1594)
—Tickly Octopus. Galloway, Ruth, illus. (p. 1747)
—Very Fidgety Fish. Galloway, Ruth, illus. (p. 1838)
Galloway, Ruth, illus. see Bright, Paul.
Galloway, Ruth, illus. see Delaney, Sally & Richards, Wendy.
Galloway, Shannon. Little Pig That Was Afraid of the Mud. Woodard, Dana, illus. (p. 1033)
Galloway, Tammy. I Am Healed: Praying God's Word for Children. (p. 833)
Galloway, Tella. Servant of the King. (p. 1552)
Galloway, Teresa A. Tiny Star Birth of a Soul. (p. 1756)
Gallucci, Susie. Believe I-Can. Sellers, Amy, illus. (p. 161)
—Dream I-Can. Sellers, Amy, illus. (p. 483)
Gallup, Alec, et al. Winning the White House 2008: The Gallup Poll, Public Opinion, & the Presidency. (p. 1937)
Gallup, Zd. Nap Time at the Beach. (p. 1229)
Galluzzi, Edward. Twelve upon a Time. Bock, Adam, illus. (p. 1800)
Galluzzo, Madeline, illus. see Story, Rita.
Galmez, Griselda. Candelaria. Wernicke, Maria, illus. (p. 261)
Galouchko, Annouchka, illus. see Trottier, Maxine.
Galouchko, Annouchka Gravel, illus. see Charles, Veronika Martenova.
Galpine, Louise. Timeline History (p. 1754)
Galson, Evelyn Arena. Unhappy Spud: The Window to Aunt Evie's World. (p. 1817)
Galsterer, Lynne, illus. see Haller, Reese.
Galsworthy, John. Little Man: A Farcical Morality in Three Scenes. Landes, William-Alan, ed. (p. 1031)
—Strife. Landes, William-Alan, ed. (p. 1667)
Galt, Kim. Dancing Trees. (p. 403)
Galus, Pamela J. Science Fair Projects, Grades 5-8: An Inquiry-Based Guide. Armbrust, Janet, illus. (p. 1526)
Galusha, Carol. Same Birthday. (p. 1507)
Galvani, Anouchka. Craft Lacing Mania. (p. 375)
Galvani, Maureen, illus. see Holzer, David.
Galveston, Louise. By the Grace of Todd. (p. 249)
—In Todd We Trust. (p. 868)
Galvez, Daniel, illus. see Rodriguez, Luis J.
Galvez, Jason. I Am Loved Right Where I Am. (p. 833)
Galvin, Jennifer. My Catholic Advent & Christmas Activity Book. (p. 1200)
—My Catholic Lent & Easter. (p. 1200)
—My Catholic School Holiday: Reproducible Sheets for Home & School. Galvin, Jennifer, illus. (p. 1200)
Galvin, Kathleen M., et al. Basics of Speech: Learning to Be a Competent Communicator. (p. 142)
Galvin, Larry J. Pythagoras Solution. (p. 1421)
Galvin, Laura. Baby Dolphin's Busy Day. (p. 126)
—Baby Duck Gets Lost. (p. 126)
—Baby Koala & Mommy. (p. 127)
—Baby Pig Time to Play. (p. 127)
—Big Wide World. (p. 184)
—Elephant & Mommy. Cohen, Jesse, photos by. (p. 511)
—I Love My Mommy. (p. 842)
—I Love My Sister. (p. 842)
—New Baby Giraffe. Cohen, Jessie, photos by. (p. 1243)
—Oh Where, Oh Where Has My Little Dog Gone? Villnave, Erica Pelton, illus. (p. 1281)
—Peep ad the Big Wide World - Discovery. (p. 1335)
—Pooh & Friends Colors & Shapes. (p. 1383)
—River Otter at Autumn Lane. Leeper, Christopher, illus. (p. 1476)
Galvin, Laura, jt. auth. see Galvin, Laura G.
Galvin, Laura & McCune, Jamie. I Love My Pet. (p. 842)
Galvin, Laura G. & Galvin, Laura. I Love My Mommy (with Download) (p. 842)
Galvin, Laura Gates. ABCDEarth. (p. 3)
—Alphabet of African Animals. Denman, Michael et al, illus. (p. 49)
—Alphabet of African Animals. Leeper, Christopher J. et al, illus. (p. 49)
—Alphabet of Animals. Kest, Kristin, illus. (p. 49)
—Alphabet of Ocean Animals. Petruccio, Steven James et al, illus. (p. 49)
—Alphabet of Space. Bond, Higgins, illus. (p. 50)
—Angry, Brave & Cheerful: An Alphabet of Feelings. 123 Sesame Street, ed. (p. 75)
—Ankylosaurus Fights Back. Chesterman, Adrian, illus. (p. 84)
—Baby Dolphins Busy Day. (p. 126)
—Baby Dolphin's Busy Day. (p. 126)
—Baby Duck Gets Lost. (p. 126)
—Baby Koala & Mommy. (p. 127)
—Baby Lamb Finds a Friend. (p. 127)
—Baby Penguin Waddles. (p. 127)
—Baby Pig Time to Play. (p. 127)
—Baby Polar Bear Learns to Swim. (p. 127)
—Best Book of Pooh, Ever: Reading to Grow. (p. 168)
—Black Bear Cub at Sweet Berry Trail. (p. 195)
—Black Bear Cub at Sweet Berry Trail. Nelson, Will, illus. (p. 195)
—Bumblebee at Apple Tree Lane. Kest, Kristin, illus. (p. 241)
—Bumblee at Apple Tree Lane. Kest, Kristin, illus. (p. 241)
—Chirp's Colors. (p. 308)
—Deer Mouse at Old Farm Road. (p. 423)
—First Look at Aircraft. Eaddy, Susan, illus. (p. 596)
—First Look at Dinosaurs. Pindroh, Paula, illus. (p. 596)
—First Look at Farm Animals. Fulcher, Roz, illus. (p. 596)
—First Look at Rescue Vehicles. Eaddy, Susan, illus. (p. 596)
—First Look at Trucks. Eaddy, Susan, illus. (p. 596)
—First Look at Zoo Animals. Fulcher, Roz, illus. (p. 596)
—Handy Manny: 1,2,3 Amigos. Parisi, Anthony, ed. (p. 742)
—Handy Manny Counting on Friends. (p. 742)
—Human Body A to Z. MacDonald, Judy, illus. (p. 825)
—I Love My Brother. Oughton, Taylor, illus. (p. 842)
—I Love My Daddy. (p. 842)
—I Love My Family. (p. 842)
—I Love My Planet Earth. (p. 842)
—I Love My Sister. Oughton, Taylor et al, illus. (p. 842)
—If Cookie Had a Cookie. Wood, Damian, illus. (p. 852)
—If I Were a Bird. (p. 853)
—Iguanodon's Escape. (p. 856)
—Is That You, Piglet? (p. 890)
—I've Been Working on the Railroad. Brown, Dan, illus. (p. 900)
—Judy the Elephant. Denman, Michael & Huiett, William, illus. (p. 931)
—Judy the Elephant. Denman, Michael L. & Huiett, William J., trs. (p. 931)
—Kakuda the Giraffe. Denman, Michael & Huiett, William, illus. (p. 941)
—Kakuda the Giraffe. Denman, Michael L. & Huiett, William J., trs. (p. 941)
—Learning Pack - First Concepts. (p. 985)
—Magical Bedtime Stories. (p. 1074)
—Mickey Mouse Clubhouse Fun with Numbers & Shapes. (p. 1136)
—Mickey Mouse Clubhouse Teamwork: Let's Do It Together. (p. 1136)
—Musical Fun: Colors & Patterns. Williams, Tracee, ed. (p. 1194)
—Musical Safari - Little Einsteins. (p. 1194)
—My First Cookbook: Family Fun in the Kitchen. (p. 1206)
—My First Garden. (p. 1206)
—My First Pet. Schwaeber, Barbie Helt & Halpenny, Karen, eds. (p. 1207)
—My First Trip to the Farm. Rabe, Tish, ed. (p. 1208)
—Norman the Lion. Leeper, Christopher, illus. (p. 1264)
—Oh Where, Oh Where Has My Little Dog Gone? Villnave, Erica Pelton, illus. (p. 1281)
—Peep Animal Homes: Why do You Live Here? (p. 1335)
—PEEP Seasons. (p. 1335)
—Peep's Nature. (p. 1335)
—Peep's Shapes. (p. 1335)
—Pooh & Friends Exercise. (p. 1383)
—Pooh & Friends Weather Pack. (p. 1383)
—Poohs 1-10. (p. 1383)
—Pooh's Counting Fun. (p. 1383)
—Princess ABCs. (p. 1402)
—Princess Counting Fun. Parisi, Anthony, ed. (p. 1403)
—Princess Family Matters. (p. 1403)
—Quack's Masterpiece. (p. 1422)
—Quack's Opposites. (p. 1422)
—River Otter at Autumn Lane. Leeper, Christopher, illus. (p. 1476)
—River Otter at Autumn Lane. Leeper, Christopher J., illus. (p. 1476)
—Take-with-Me Alphabet. (p. 1697)
—Take-with-Me Numbers. (p. 1697)
—Tamarin's Mealtime. Cohen, Jessie, illus. (p. 1704)
—Tiger Cub See-and-Do. Cohen, Jessie, illus. (p. 1748)
—Tracing 123s. (p. 1775)
—What Am I? A Guessing Game. (p. 1879)
—What's That Sound? (p. 1899)
—When Will I Fly? (p. 1905)
—Where Do I Live? (p. 1907)
—Who Am I? (p. 1914)
—Winnie the Pooh Bedtime ABCs. (p. 1937)
Galvin, Laura Gates, jt. auth. see Soundprints Staff.
Galvin, Laura Gates, jt. auth. see Twin Sister Productions Staff.
Galvin, Laura Gates, jt. auth. see Twin Sister Produtions.
Galvin, Laura Gates & Luther, Jacqueline. Read-A-Picture Collection: First Stories for Family Reading. (p. 1442)
Galvin, Laura Gates & Odierno, Lisa. Puppy Explores. (p. 1418)
Galvin, Laura Gates & Smithsonian Institution Staff. Armadillo at Riverside Road (Armadillo en la calle Riverside) (p. 99)
Galvin, Laura Gates & Soundprints Editorial Staff. Animals A to Z. Schwaeber, Barbie H. & Williams, Tracee, eds. (p. 82)
Galvin, Laura Gates & Studio Mouse Editorial. Animals & Nature. (p. 82)
—Cinderella: Dreams Do Come True. (p. 320)
—Cinderella & Belle: Kindness Counts. Williams, Tracee, ed. (p. 320)
Galvin, Laura Gates & Studio Mouse Staff. At the Farm. (p. 111)
—Best Friends. (p. 169)
—Disney Marie A Is for Adorable: A Fabulous Alphabet. Schwaeber, Barbie H., ed. (p. 451)
—Pooh & Friends Exercise. (p. 1383)
—Write-with-Me Alphabet. Giblin, Brian E., ed. (p. 1964)
Galvin, Laura Gates & Studiomouse Staff. Hungry T-Rex. Carr, Karen, illus. (p. 828)
Galvin, Laura, told to. I Love My Mommy. (p. 842)
Galvin, Linda, jt. auth. see Cutler, Stewart.
Galvin, Matthew. Clouds & Clocks: A Story for Children Who Soil. (p. 335)
Galvin, Michael M. B. & Speakman, Peter. Rebels of the Lamp (p. 1451)
Gam Do, Rin Bo. Insects & Spiders. Cowley, Joy, ed. (p. 876)
—What Lives in the Sea? Marine Life. Cowley, Joy, ed. (p. 1891)
Gam do, Rin Bo, illus. see Cowley, Joy, ed.
Gama, Esperanza, illus. see Costales, Amy.
Gamache, Holley. Adventures of Murray the Mouse: Murray's First Adventure. (p. 21)
Gamache, Line. Hello, Me Pretty. Cochrane, KerryAnn, tr. from FRE. (p. 764)
Gamage, Ken, illus. see Payne, Trip.
GAMAGO. GAMAGO Yeti & Friends Place Mats. (p. 654)
Gambassi, Rod. Boy Who Wanted to be a Dancer. Brownlee, Kelly Jackson, illus. (p. 219)
Gambatesa, Francesca, illus. see De Laurentiis, Giada.
Gambill, Henrietta. Seven Special Days. (p. 1555)
Gambini, Josephine. Poetino Piccolino Saves the Day. Stafford, Jordan, illus. (p. 1376)
Gambino, Alisha Ann Guadalupe, illus. see Zepeda, Gwendolyn & Ventura, Gabriela Baeza.
Gambino, Dolores. Flutter the Butterfly Who Found a Home with Jesus. (p. 609)
Gambino, Karlie. Cottonmouth: Serpiente Boca de Algodón. (p. 369)
—Cottonmouth. (p. 369)
—Float of Crocodiles. (p. 605)
—Float of Crocodiles / una Manada de Cocodrilos. (p. 605)
Gamble, Adam. Buenas Noches, California. Kelly, Cooper, illus. (p. 235)
—Buenas Noches, Estados Unidos. Chan, Suwin, illus. (p. 235)
—Buenas Noches, Nueva York. Veno, Joe & Jasper, Mark, illus. (p. 235)
—Good Night America. Chan, Suwin, illus. (p. 699)
—Good Night Arizona. Veno, Joe & Hansen, Red, illus. (p. 699)
—Good Night Atlanta. Veno, Joe, illus. (p. 699)
—Good Night Baby Jesus. (p. 699)
—Good Night Beach. Kelly, Cooper, illus. (p. 699)
—Good Night Boston. Veno, Joe, illus. (p. 699)
—Good Night California. Kelly, Cooper, illus. (p. 699)
—Good Night Cape Cod. Andert, John, illus. (p. 699)
—Good Night Chicago. Veno, Joe, illus. (p. 699)
—Good Night Country Store. Rosen, Anne & Jasper, Mark, illus. (p. 699)
—Good Night Georgia. Rosen, Anne & Veno, Joe, illus. (p. 699)
—Good Night Hawaii. Veno, Joe, illus. (p. 699)
—Good Night Lake. Kelly, Cooper, illus. (p. 699)
—Good Night Los Angeles. Kelly, Cooper, illus. (p. 699)
—Good Night Maine. Chan, Suwin, illus. (p. 699)
—Good Night Michigan. Rosen, Anne, illus. (p. 699)
—Good Night Minnesota. Veno, Joe, illus. (p. 699)
—Good Night Montana. (p. 699)
—Good Night Montreal. Kelly, Cooper, illus. (p. 699)
—Good Night Nantucket. Rosen, Anne, illus. (p. 699)
—Good Night New Hampshire. Rosen, Anne, illus. (p. 699)
—Good Night New York City. Veno, Joe, illus. (p. 699)
—Good Night North Carolina. Rosen, Anne, illus. (p. 699)
—Good Night North Pole. Jasper, Mark, illus. (p. 699)
—Good Night Ohio. Jasper, Mark, illus. (p. 700)
—Good Night Philadelphia. Kelly, Cooper, illus. (p. 700)
—Good Night Rhode Island. Rosen, Anne, illus. (p. 700)
—Good Night San Diego. Kelly, Cooper, illus. (p. 700)
—Good Night San Francisco. Cohen, Santiago, illus. (p. 700)
—Good Night Tennessee. Veno, Joe, illus. (p. 700)
—Good Night Texas. Veno, Joe & Kelly, Cooper, illus. (p. 700)
—Good Night Virginia. Veno, Joe, illus. (p. 700)
—Good Night Washington, DC. Veno, Joe, illus. (p. 700)
—Good Night World. Kelly, Cooper, illus. (p. 700)
—Good Night Zoo. Kelly, Cooper, illus. (p. 700)
Gamble, Adam, jt. auth. see Adams, Megan Weeks.
Gamble, Adam, jt. auth. see Bouse, Susan.
Gamble, Adam, jt. auth. see Jasper, Mark.
Gamble, Adam, jt. auth. see Steere, Jay.
Gamble, Adam & Adams, David J. Good Night Canada. Kelly, Cooper, illus. (p. 699)
Gamble, Adam & Clark, Dennis. Good Night New Jersey. Veno, Joe, illus. (p. 699)
Gamble, Adam & Jasper, Mark. Buenas Noches, Florida. (p. 235)
—Buenas Noches, Texas. (p. 235)
—Count to Sleep Florida. Veno, Joe, illus. (p. 370)
—Count to Sleep Michigan. Veno, Joe, illus. (p. 370)
—Count to Sleep Wisconsin. Veno, Joe, illus. (p. 370)
—Good Night Alabama. Veno, Joe, illus. (p. 699)
—Good Night Alaska. Kelly, Cooper, illus. (p. 699)
—Good Night Brooklyn. (p. 699)
—Good Night Central Park. Palmer, Ruth, illus. (p. 699)
—Good Night Christmas. Kelly, Cooper, illus. (p. 699)
—Good Night Daddy. Kelly, Cooper, illus. (p. 699)
—Good Night Delaware. Jasper, Mark, illus. (p. 699)
—Good Night Dinosaur. Kelly, Cooper, illus. (p. 699)
—Good Night Florida. Veno, Joe & Hansen, Red, illus. (p. 699)
—Good Night Illinois. (p. 699)
—Good Night Indiana. (p. 699)
—Good Night Iowa. (p. 699)
—Good Night Maryland. Veno, Joe et al, illus. (p. 699)
—Good Night Massachusetts. (p. 699)
—Good Night Mermaids. Chan, Suwin, illus. (p. 699)
—Good Night Mississippi. Veno, Joe, illus. (p. 699)
—Good Night Missouri. Veno, Joe, illus. (p. 699)
—Good Night Nebraska. (p. 699)
—Good Night Nevada. Rosen, Anne & Veno, Joe, illus. (p. 699)
—Good Night New Mexico. Palmer, Ruth, illus. (p. 699)
—Good Night Pennsylvania. (p. 700)
—Good Night Pirate Ship. Kelly, Cooper, illus. (p. 700)
—Good Night Pittsburgh. Palmer, Ruth, illus. (p. 700)
—Good Night Planes. Kelly, Cooper, illus. (p. 700)
—Good Night Race Cars. Veno, Joe, illus. (p. 700)
—Good Night Toronto. Veno, Joe & Kelly, Cooper, illus. (p. 700)
—Good Night Twin Cities. Palmer, Ruth, illus. (p. 700)
—Good Night Utah. Rosen, Anne & Hart, Jason, illus. (p. 700)
—Good Night Washington State. Veno, Joe & Kelly, Cooper, illus. (p. 700)
—Good Night Yellowstone. Kelly, Cooper, illus. (p. 700)
Gamble, Adam & Kelly, Cooper. Good Night Farm. Kelly, Cooper, illus. (p. 699)
Gamble, Adam & Mackey, Bill. Good Night Colorado. Rosen, Anne, illus. (p. 699)
Gamble, Adam, et al. Good Night Kentucky. (p. 699)
—Good Night Mountains. (p. 699)
—Good Night New Orleans. Kelly, Cooper, illus. (p. 699)
—Good Night South Carolina. (p. 700)
Gamble, Amy. U. S. Government & Presidents, Grades 3 - 5. Fox, Carrie, ed. (p. 1806)
Gamble, Donna Tabacchi. Games to Go. (p. 655)
Gamble, Gael, illus. see Darragh, Jill.
Gamble, Isobel. Quien Hay? (p. 1427)
Gamble, Jasper, et al. Good Night New York State. Jasper, Mark, illus. (p. 699)
—Good Night Wisconsin. Jasper, Mark & Kelly, Cooper, illus. (p. 700)
Gamble, Kent, illus. see Berman, Len.
Gamble, Kim, illus. see Fienberg, Anna & Fienberg, Barbara.
Gamble, Kim, illus. see Fienberg, Anna.
Gamble, Kim, illus. see Shepard, Aaron.
Gamble, Nikki. Tap & Jazz (p. 1705)
Gamble, Paul. Draw Horrible Pictures. (p. 480)
—Draw Horrible Stuff: A Step-by-Step Guide to Drawing All Things Yucky! (p. 480)
—Draw Scary Pictures. (p. 481)
—Draw Weird Pictures. (p. 481)
Gamble, Penel, illus. see Tayleur, Karen.
Gamble, Rev. Vivian T. I Think All the Time... Ummm. (p. 846)
—Just to Be Myself. (p. 940)
Gamble, Robin. Samphire Tides. (p. 1509)
Gamble, Shanae. God's Dogs go to Heaven: Christian myths & Fables. (p. 691)
Gamble, Shunté. Day I Dressed the Big Boy Way. (p. 413)
Gamblin, Rose Tooley. Baby Moses. (p. 127)
—Birthday Party. (p. 193)
—King David. (p. 958)
Gamblin, Rose Tooley & Hernández, Oscar. Bill's Lunch: El Almuerzo de Bill. (p. 187)
—Esther, the Brave Queen. (p. 538)
—Joash, the Boy King. (p. 919)
—Queen of Sheba. (p. 1425)
Gamboa, Norma & Soberon, Cecilia. Literatura para el Jardin de Ninos (Literature for Young Children) (p. 1023)
Gamboa, Ricardo, illus. see Silvano, Wendi.
Gambordella, Ted. Black Belt in A Box. (p. 195)
Gambrell, Louise Vaughn. Red Angels. (p. 1453)

G

Gamer, Ron. Hidden Chance: Secrets of the Hermit's Hideaway. (p. 775)
—One Last Chance: Trapped by a Blowdown. (p. 1295)
—Wild Chance: Whitewater Awakening. (p. 1929)
Games, Incbandal, jt. auth. see Chiba, Tomohiro.
Gamlin, Jim. Lucky Nickel: The Story of Nickel the Sea Turtle. (p. 1063)
Gamlin, Linda. Evolution. (p. 546)
Gamlin, Linda, jt. auth. see Dorling Kindersley Publishing Staff.
Gamma Jan. Something Really Important. (p. 1610)
Gammage, Dana, illus. see Delea, Pattie.
Gammage, Karen S. Nutty & Buddy. (p. 1274)
Gammel, Stephen, illus. see Bonwill, Ann.
Gammelgaard, Leslie, illus. see Marlow, Susan K.
Gammell, Stephen. More Scary Stories to Tell in the Dark. (p. 1174)
—Mudkin. Gammell, Stephen, illus. (p. 1189)
Gammell, Stephen, illus. see Ackerman, Karen.
Gammell, Stephen, illus. see Bowen, Anne.
Gammell, Stephen, illus. see Donnelly, Jennifer.
Gammell, Stephen, illus. see Gauch, Patricia Lee.
Gammell, Stephen, illus. see Haseley, Dennis.
Gammell, Stephen, illus. see Johnston, Tony.
Gammell, Stephen, illus. see Lyon, George Ella.
Gammell, Stephen, illus. see Sierra, Judy.
Gammill, Kerry, illus. see Duffy, Jo.
Gammon, Bob. Orange Polar Bears Don't Cry. (p. 1302)
Gammon, Shana B. Great State Cookbook: Recipes from Around the Country-for Kids. (p. 718)
Gamonal, Dulce. Diego from Madrid. Audouin, Laurent, illus. (p. 437)
Gamoran, Emanuel, jt. ed. see Schwarz, Jacob David.
Gamow, George. Mr Tompkins Learns the Facts of Life. (p. 1186)
Gampert, John, illus. see McKay, Sindy.
Gamson, Alyse, jt. auth. see Baron, Charlie.
Gamwell, Calvert, jt. auth. see Lee Bates, Katharine.
Gamze-Pendergrast, Marla. China in Colors (p. 306)
Gan & Kohen, Elizabeth. Spain. (p. 1620)
Gan, Jessie Low. How Giraffe Got Spots. (p. 809)
Gana, Joyce Ache. Adventures of Santeh Angum: Kayaking in Carriacou Tyrell Bay Mangrove. (p. 22)
Ganchinello, Sheena. Tim Westergren & Pandora. (p. 1750)
Ganchy, Sally. Career As a Cosmetologist. (p. 266)
—Mark Martin: NASCAR Driver. (p. 1095)
—Reducing Your Carbon Footprint at Home. (p. 1456)
—Taylor Hicks. (p. 1708)
Ganchy, Sally & Isler, Claudia. Understanding Your Right to Free Speech. (p. 1816)
Gander, Forrest. Blue Rock Collection. Ducornet, Rikki, illus. (p. 203)
Ganderton, Paul, jt. auth. see Coker, Paddy.
Gandhi, Arun & Hegedus, Bethany. Be the Change: A Grandfather Gandhi Story. Turk, Evan, illus. (p. 149)
—Grandfather Gandhi. Turk, Evan, illus. (p. 707)
Gandhi, Arun, et al. 411. Mack, David et al, illus. (p. 2001)
Gandhi, Mahatma, et al. My Early Life: An Illustrated Story. (p. 1202)
Gandhi, Mohandas & YKids Staff. Gandhi. (p. 655)
Gandolfi, Claudine. Night Before Christmas dot.com. Barbas, Kerren, illus. (p. 1253)
—Night Before Dog-Mas. Anagost, Karen, illus. (p. 1253)
—Scratch & Sketch Vikings: An Art Activity Book for Legendary Artists & Explorers of All Ages. Zschock, Martha Day, illus. (p. 1532)
Gandolfo, Giora. Sheep. (p. 1564)
Gandy, Deborah A. Squeaky Little Mouse Named Rainbow. (p. 1636)
Gandy, Meg, illus. see Johnson, Alaya Dawn.
Gandy, Meg, illus. see Johnson, Alaya.
Gane, Declan. So You Want to Be Captain? Top Tips from Sporting Heroes. (p. 1602)
Ganeri, Anita. Action Words: Verbs (p. 10)
—Alexander the Great: The Life of a King & Conqueror. (p. 36)
—Anaconda (p. 66)
—Ancient Egypt: The Complete Homework Solution. (p. 68)
—Ancient Maya. Ganeri, Anita & Forsey, Chris, illus. (p. 69)
—Animal Atlas. (p. 76)
—Animal Life Cycles (p. 78)
—Arabian Oryx (p. 94)
—Around the World: A Colorful Atlas for Kids. Corr, Christopher, illus. (p. 100)
—Australia. Isik, Semur, illus. (p. 116)
—Bactrian Camel (p. 131)
—Brass Instruments. (p. 222)
—Brazil: A Benjamin Blog & His Inquisitive Dog Guide Isik, Semur, illus. (p. 224)
—Buddhism. (p. 234)
—Buddhist. (p. 234)
—Buddhist Festivals Through the Year. (p. 234)
—Buddhist Stories. (p. 234)
—Buddhist Vihara. Mukhida, Zul & Card, Vanessa, illus. (p. 234)
—Bunny's Guide to Caring for Your Rabbit Peterson, Rick, illus. (p. 243)
—Butterflies & Caterpillars. Axworthy, Ani, illus. (p. 247)
—Butterflies & Caterpillars. Axworthy, Ann, illus. (p. 247)
—Canada. Isik, Semur, illus. (p. 260)
—Canyon Hunters (p. 262)
—Capybara (p. 265)
—Cats & Kittens. Axworthy, Ani, illus. (p. 281)
—Celebrating Birth Around the World. (p. 284)
—Celebrating Weddings Around the World. (p. 285)
—China: A Benjamin Blog & His Inquisitive Dog Guide Isik, Semur, illus. (p. 306)
—Chinese Myths & Legends (p. 307)
—Christian Festivals Through the Year. (p. 311)
—Christian Stories. Phillips, Rachael, illus. (p. 312)
—Christmas Story. (p. 315)
—Cliff Climbers (p. 332)
—Como Funcionan los Animales. Fricker, Steve, illus. (p. 351)
—Como Funcionan los Huesos y Otras Partes del Cuerpo. Fricker, Steve & Holder, John, illus. (p. 351)
—Country Guides, with Benjamin Blog & His Inquisitive Dog Isik, Semur, illus. (p. 372)
—Cultures & Customs. (p. 391)
—Day & Night (p. 412)
—Demons & Ghouls. West, David, illus. (p. 426)
—Describing Words: Adjectives, Adverbs, & Prepositions (p. 428)
—Dinosaurs. Dogi, Fiammetta, illus. (p. 443)
—Divali Story. (p. 454)
—DK Readers L2: Eruption!: the Story of Volcanoes: Eruption!: the Story of Volcanoes. (p. 456)
—Dogs (p. 462)
—Drums & Percussion Instruments. (p. 487)
—Ducks & Ducklings. Axworthy, Ani, illus. (p. 488)
—Easter Story. Phillips, Rachael, illus. (p. 499)
—Egypt: A Benjamin Blog & His Inquisitive Dog Guide Isik, Semur, illus. (p. 506)
—England. Isik, Semur, illus. (p. 529)
—Ese Tiempo Borrascoso. (p. 535)
—Esos Desesperantes Desiertos. (p. 536)
—Esos Destructores Terremotos. (p. 536)
—Esos Inmensos Oceanos. (p. 536)
—Esos Turbulentos Rios. (p. 536)
—Esos Violentos Volcanes. (p. 536)
—Exploring Asia (p. 551)
—Exploring Coasts: A Benjamin Blog & His Inquisitive Dog Investigation (p. 551)
—Exploring Coral Reefs: A Benjamin Blog & His Inquisitive Dog Investigation (p. 551)
—Exploring Deserts: A Benjamin Blog & His Inquisitive Dog Investigation (p. 552)
—Exploring Habitats, with Benjamin Blog & His Inquisitive Dog (p. 552)
—Exploring Mountains: A Benjamin Blog & His Inquisitive Dog Investigation (p. 552)
—Exploring Rain Forests: A Benjamin Blog & His Inquisitive Dog Investigation (p. 553)
—Exploring Rivers: A Benjamin Blog & His Inquisitive Dog Investigation (p. 553)
—Exploring South America (p. 553)
—Fearsome Forces of Nature (p. 579)
—Fennec Fox (p. 581)
—First Animal Encyclopedia. (p. 593)
—First Animal Encyclopedia Rainforests. (p. 593)
—Flip the Flaps: Things That Go! Humphries, Tudor, illus. (p. 605)
—Focus on Turkey. (p. 611)
—Food Chains (p. 613)
—France: A Benjamin Blog & His Inquisitive Dog Guide Isik, Semur, illus. (p. 627)
—From Bean to Bean Plant (p. 642)
—From Candle to Quartz Clock. (p. 642)
—From Caterpillar to Butterfly (p. 642)
—From Egg to Chicken (p. 642)
—From Egg to Spider (p. 642)
—From Puppy to Dog (p. 643)
—From Seed to Apple (p. 643)
—From Seed to Sunflower (p. 643)
—From Tadpole to Frog (p. 643)
—Funny Stories: Writing Stories (p. 650)
—Germany. Isik, Semur, illus. (p. 666)
—Getting to Grips with Grammar. (p. 669)
—Ghosts & Other Specters. West, David, illus. (p. 672)
—Gila Monster (p. 676)
—Gladiators & Ancient Rome. (p. 682)
—Gods & Goddesses. (p. 690)
—Goldfish (p. 695)
—Goldie's Guide to Caring for Your Goldfish Peterson, Rick, illus. (p. 696)
—Grouping Words: Sentences (p. 725)
—Guinea Pigs (p. 731)
—Guru Granth Sahib & Sikhism. (p. 732)
—Haj Story. (p. 736)
—Hamsters (p. 740)
—Harriet Tubman: The Life of an African-American Abolitionist. Shone, Rob, illus. (p. 750)
—Harsh Habitats (p. 751)
—Hearing. (p. 759)
—Hibernation (p. 775)
—Hindi (p. 780)
—Hindu Festivals Through the Year. (p. 780)
—Hindu Stories. Phillips, Rachael, illus. (p. 780)
—How the Ancient Romans Lived. (p. 812)
—How the Aztecs Lived. (p. 812)
—Howler Monkey (p. 823)
—Human Body. (p. 825)
—Hunt for Food. (p. 828)
—I Can Write! (p. 837)
—I Can Write. (p. 837)
—I Can Write Instructions (p. 837)
—I Can Write Journals & Narratives (p. 837)
—I Can Write Letters & E-Mails (p. 837)
—I Can Write Poems (p. 837)
—I Can Write Reports (p. 837)
—I Can Write Stories (p. 837)
—I Have a Dream: Martin Luther King, Jr. & the Fight for Equal Rights. (p. 839)
—I Wonder Why Camels Have Humps: And Other Questions about Animals. (p. 849)
—I Wonder Why the Sea Is Salty: And Other Questions about the Oceans. (p. 849)
—I Wonder Why the Wind Blows. (p. 849)
—India: A Benjamin Blog & His Inquisitive Dog Guide Isik, Semur, illus. (p. 870)
—India. (p. 870)
—Indian Subcontinent. (p. 871)
—Inside & Out Guide to Animals (p. 876)
—Introducing Antarctica (p. 882)
—Introducing Asia (p. 882)
—Introducing Australia (p. 882)
—Introducing South America (p. 882)
—Islamic Stories Wallis, Rebecca, illus. (p. 892)
—Islamic Stories. Phillips, Rachael, illus. (p. 892)
—Italy. Isik, Semur, illus. (p. 894)
—Jaguar (p. 905)
—Japan: A Benjamin Blog & His Inquisitive Dog Guide Isik, Semur, illus. (p. 909)
—Jewish Festivals Through the Year. (p. 917)
—Jewish Stories. (p. 917)
—Joining Words: Conjunctions (p. 924)
—Journals & Narratives. (p. 927)
—King Arthur's Tale. (p. 958)
—Kings & Queens: The History of the British Monarchy. (p. 960)
—Kitty's Guide to Caring for Your Cat Peterson, Rick, illus. (p. 963)
—Lemur (p. 991)
—Lifesize: Ocean. Jackson-Carter, Stuart, illus. (p. 1013)
—Lifesize: Rainforest: See Rainforest Creatures at Their Actual Size. Jackson-Carter, Stuart, illus. (p. 1013)
—Lluvia. (p. 1043)
—Macaw (p. 1067)
—Martin Luther King's I Have a Dream Speech. (p. 1098)
—Meerkat (p. 1120)
—Mesoamerican Myth: A Treasury of Legends, Art, & History. (p. 1129)
—Mexico: A Benjamin Blog & His Inquisitive Dog Guide Isik, Semur, illus. (p. 1131)
—Mother Teresa's Alms Bowl. Noyes, Leighton & Radford, Karen, illus. (p. 1178)
—Mother Teresa's Alms Bowl. Radford, Karen & Noyes, Leighton, illus. (p. 1178)
—Mummies & Ancient Egypt. (p. 1191)
—Muslim Festivals Through the Year. (p. 1194)
—My Pop-Up World Atlas. Waterhouse, Stephen, illus. (p. 1217)
—Mystery Stories: Writing Stories (p. 1226)
—Naming Words: Nouns & Pronouns (p. 1228)
—Nibble's Guide to Caring for Your Hamster Peterson, Rick, illus. (p. 1250)
—Nieve (Snow) (p. 1252)
—Norse Myths & Legends (p. 1264)
—Ocean Divers (p. 1276)
—On Expedition with Lewis & Clark. (p. 1288)
—Orangutan (p. 1302)
—Orangutan. (p. 1302)
—Passover Story. Phillips, Rachael, illus. (p. 1327)
—Peculiar Plants (p. 1334)
—Pharaohs, Heros & Thieves: More Real-Life Tales from Ancient Egypt. (p. 1350)
—Pianos & Keyboards. (p. 1354)
—Piranha (p. 1362)
—Plant Life Cycles (p. 1369)
—Poison Dart Frog (p. 1377)
—Protecting Ocean Habitats. (p. 1412)
—Protecting Polar Regions. (p. 1412)
—Punctuation: Commas, Periods, & Question Marks (p. 1416)
—Qur'an & Islam. Fennell, Tracy, illus. (p. 1429)
—Rabbits (p. 1430)
—Rain. (p. 1434)
—Rainforests. Bull, Peter, illus. (p. 1436)
—Ramayana & Other Hindu Texts. (p. 1437)
—Record-Breaking Earth. (p. 1452)
—Red Kangaroo (p. 1454)
—Remembering the Dead Around the World. (p. 1460)
—Reports. (p. 1461)
—Republic of Ireland. Isik, Semur, illus. (p. 1462)
—Roadrunner (p. 1477)
—Ruff's Guide to Caring for Your Dog Peterson, Rick, illus. (p. 1494)
—Russia. Isik, Semur, illus. (p. 1498)
—Scary Stories: Writing Stories (p. 1520)
—Scorpion (p. 1530)
—Scorpion Set (p. 1530)
—Scotland. Isik, Semur, illus. (p. 1530)
—Season to Season (p. 1538)
—Shaky Ground. (p. 1559)
—Sight. (p. 1574)
—Sikh Festivals Throughout The Year. (p. 1574)
—Sikh Stories. Phillips, Rachael, illus. (p. 1574)
—Smell. (p. 1593)
—Snow. (p. 1598)
—Sol. (p. 1606)
—Something Old, Something New: Recycling (p. 1610)
—South Africa: A Benjamin Blog & His Inquisitive Dog Guide Isik, Semur, illus. (p. 1616)
—Spain. Isik, Semur, illus. (p. 1620)
—Stringed Instruments. (p. 1667)
—Sunshine. (p. 1677)
—Super Active Tennis. (p. 1679)
—Survival in the Jungle. (p. 1686)
—Tarantula (p. 1706)
—Taste. (p. 1707)
—Tell Me Where Is the Top of the World? And More about Planet Earth. (p. 1717)
—Tipitaka & Other Buddhist Texts. (p. 1757)
—Top Ten Events That Changed the World. (p. 1769)
—Top Ten Explorers That Changed the World. (p. 1769)
—Top Ten Leaders That Changed the World. (p. 1769)
—Touch. (p. 1772)
—United States of America. Isik, Semur, illus. (p. 1819)
—Viento. (p. 1841)
—Volcanes y terremotos/Earthquakes & Volcanoes. (p. 1848)
—Volcanoes in Action. (p. 1849)
—What's the Big Idea? Religion. (p. 1899)
—Wild Weather (p. 1930)
—Wind. (p. 1935)
—Wind Instruments. (p. 1935)
—Winnie's Guide to Caring for Your Horse or Pony Peterson, Rick, illus. (p. 1937)
—World's Most Amazing Islands (p. 1960)
—World's Most Amazing Rivers (p. 1960)
—Writing Stories. (p. 1965)
Ganeri, Anita, jt. auth. see A&C Black Staff.
Ganeri, Anita, jt. auth. see Bull, Peter.
Ganeri, Anita, jt. auth. see Camerena, Rebecca.
Ganeri, Anita, jt. auth. see Champion, Neil.
Ganeri, Anita, jt. auth. see Claybourne, Anna.
Ganeri, Anita, jt. auth. see Feldman, Thea.
Ganeri, Anita, jt. auth. see Hughes, Monica.
Ganeri, Anita, jt. auth. see Jeffrey, Gary.
Ganeri, Anita, jt. auth. see Oxlade, Chris.
Ganeri, Anita, jt. auth. see Petty, Kate.
Ganeri, Anita, jt. auth. see Shone, Rob.
Ganeri, Anita, jt. auth. see West, David.
Ganeri, Anita & Anita, Ganeri. Camellos Tienen Jorobas. (p. 256)
Ganeri, Anita & Bailey, Gerry. Mother Teresa's Alms Bowl. (p. 1178)
Ganeri, Anita & Colson, Mary. Turbulent Planet (p. 1797)
Ganeri, Anita & Heinemann Library Staff. Cats (p. 280)
—Dogs (p. 462)
—Goldfish (p. 695)
—Guinea Pigs (p. 731)
—Hamsters (p. 740)
—Rabbits (p. 1430)
—World's Most Amazing Islands (p. 1960)
Ganeri, Anita & Johnson, Jinny. What's It Like to Be... Bee? Sanzi, Desiderio, illus. (p. 1898)
—What's It Like to Be... Dragonfly? Sanzi, Desiderio, illus. (p. 1898)
Ganeri, Anita & Levete, Sarah. Life in the Rain Forest (p. 1011)
Ganeri, Anita & Oxlade, Chris. Down the Drain: Conserving Water (p. 474)
—Introducing Continents. (p. 882)
Ganeri, Anita & Peterson, Rick. Pets' Guides. (p. 1348)
Ganeri, Anita & West, David. Creatures of Myths & Legends. (p. 380)
—Curse of King Tut's Tomb & Other Ancient Discoveries. (p. 394)
—Dinosaurs. (p. 443)
—Heroes of Myths & Legends. (p. 773)
—Lost in the Bermuda Triangle & Other Mysteries. (p. 1055)
—Outlaws & Villains from History. (p. 1312)
—Sinking of the Titanic & Other Shipwrecks. (p. 1580)
—Supernatural Creatures. (p. 1684)
Ganeri, Anita, et al. Crumbling Earth: Erosion & Landslides (p. 386)
—Cuerpo Humano. Rioja, Alberto Jimenez & Jimenez Rioja, Alberto, trs. (p. 390)
—Earth Erupts: Volcanoes (p. 495)
—Forest Furnace: Wild Fires (p. 618)
Ganerif, Anita. I Wonder Why the Sea Is Salty. (p. 849)
Ganesan, C. T. Fun with Maths. (p. 648)
Ganeshram, Ramin. Stir It Up! (p. 1651)
—Stir It Up! A Novel. (p. 1651)
Gang Jin, Hong, et al. China Scene: An Advanced Chinese Multimedia Course. (p. 307)
Gang, Jobie, illus. see Shealeya, Mildred.
Gang, MinJeong, illus. see Choi, Jeongim.
Gangelhoff, Gene, illus. see Gangelhoff, Jeanne M. & Belk, Bradford.
Gangelhoff, Jeanne M. & Belk, Bradford. Walk Through the Minnesota Zoo. Gangelhoff, Gene, illus. (p. 1854)
Gangemi, Alicia, jt. auth. see Jones, Ashton.
Gangemi, Alphia. Hunting with Wolves. (p. 829)
Gangemi, Angelo. Black Mamba. (p. 196)
—Black Mamba / Mamba Negra. (p. 196)
—Where Does Electricity Come From? (p. 1907)
Ganges, Montse. Cooper, Flying Dog. Urberuaga, Emilio, illus. (p. 365)
—Cooper, King of Cushion Island. Urberuaga, Emilio, illus. (p. 365)
—Fly Hunter. Urberuaga, Emilio, illus. (p. 609)
—King of Cushion Island. Urberuaga, Emilio, illus. (p. 958)
—Meet Cooper. Urberuaga, Emilio, illus. (p. 1120)
Ganges, Montse & Urberuaga, Emilio. Meet Cooper. (p. 1120)
Gangloff, Hope, illus. see Stamper, Judith Bauer & Bauer-Stamper, Judith.
Gangloff, Hope, illus. see Stamper, Judith Bauer.
Gangwer, Rosalie M. & Heffernan, Mary A., texts. Jesus Loves Us. (p. 916)
Gann, Marjorie, jt. auth. see Willen, Janet.
Gann, Marjorie & Willen, Janet. Five Thousand Years of Slavery. (p. 601)
Gannett, Barbara. Count Your Money: A Content Area Reader-math. (p. 370)
Gannett, Ruth Chrisman, illus. see Gannett, Ruth Stiles.
Gannett, Ruth Stiles. Dragons of Blueland. Gannett, Ruth Chrisman, illus. (p. 479)
—Elmer & the Dragon. Gannett, Ruth Chrisman, illus. (p. 515)
—My Father's Dragon. Gannett, Ruth Chrisman, illus. (p. 1203)
Gannij, Joan. Elusive Moose. Beaton, Clare, illus. (p. 516)
—Hidden Hippo. Beaton, Clare, illus. (p. 775)
Gannij, Joan & Beaton, Clare. Hidden Hippo. (p. 775)
Gannij, Joan & Grannij, Joan. Elusive Moose. (p. 516)
Gannon, Gretchen. Rince: The Fairytale of Irish Dance. (p. 1473)
Gannon, Joe. Fun & Games: How to Play More Than 70 of the World's Greatest Games for Two or More Players. (p. 647)
Gannon, Michael B. Blood, Bedlam, Bullets, & Badguys: A Reader's Guide to Adventure/Suspense Fiction (p. 200)
Gannon, Ned, illus. see Addasi, Maha.
Gannon, Ned, illus. see Meyer, Jane G.
Gannon, Ned, jt. auth. see Meyer, Jane G.
Gannon, Nicholas. Doldrums. (p. 463)
Gannon, Patty. Desdemona & the Eggs. (p. 428)
Ganny, Charlee. Chihuawolf: A Tail of Mystery & Horror. Slater, Nicola, illus. (p. 301)
Gano, Debra. Beauty's Secret. Pitre, Dawn, illus. (p. 154)
Ganser, Sara. Weekend Getaway. (p. 1871)
Ganske, Kathy. Mindful of Words: Spelling & Vocabulary Explorations 4-8. (p. 1145)
Gansle, Sherry. Oops, a Curious Horse Big Book. Light, Carol, illus. (p. 1299)
—Oops, a Curious Horse Little Book. Light, Carol, illus. (p. 1299)
—Oops, a Curious Horse Story Book Reader. Light, Carol, illus. (p. 1299)
Gansworth, Eric L. If I Ever Get Out of Here. (p. 853)
Gant, Gene. Battle for Jericho [Library Edition]. (p. 145)
—Lessons on Destroying the World. (p. 994)

—Thunder in His Head [Library Edition]. (p. 1746)
Gant, Linda G. Readers Are Leaders. Gant, Linda G., illus. (p. 1444)
Gant, Robert. My Big Box of Addition & Subtraction. (p. 1197)
—My Big Box of Letters. (p. 1197)
—My Big Box of Numbers. (p. 1197)
—My Big Box of Reading. (p. 1197)
Ganter, Amy Kim. Sorcerers & Secretaries Volume 1. (p. 1614)
Gantos, Jack. Best in Show for Rotten Ralph. Rubel, Nicole, illus. (p. 170)
—Dead End in Norvelt. (p. 416)
—Desire Lines. (p. 430)
—Follower. (p. 612)
—From Norvelt to Nowhere. (p. 643)
—Hole in My Life. (p. 788)
—I Am Not Joey Pigza. (p. 833)
—Jack Adrift: Fourth Grade Without a Clue. (p. 902)
—Joey Pigza Loses Control. (p. 920)
—Joey Pigza Swallowed the Key. (p. 920)
—Key That Swallowed Joey Pigza. (p. 950)
—Love Curse of the Rumbaughs. (p. 1059)
—Nine Lives of Rotten Ralph. Rubel, Nicole, illus. (p. 1256)
—Nueva Fuerza de Jack. (p. 1270)
—Practice Makes Perfect for Rotten Ralph. Rubel, Nicole, illus. (p. 1392)
—Rotten Ralph Feels Rotten. Rubel, Nicole, tr. (p. 1490)
—Rotten Ralph Feels Rotten. Rubel, Nicole, illus. (p. 1490)
—Rotten Ralph Helps Out. (p. 1490)
—Rotten Ralph Helps Out. (p. 1490)
—Rotten Ralph Helps Out. Rubel, Nicole, illus. (p. 1490)
—Rotten Ralph's Rotten Family. Rubel, Nicole, illus. (p. 1490)
—Three Strikes for Rotten Ralph. Rubel, Nicole, illus. (p. 1744)
—What Would Joey Do? (p. 1895)
Gantry, Chris. Underwater Orchestra. Burns, Theresa, illus. (p. 1817)
Gantschev, Ivan, illus. see Aoki, Hisako.
Gantschev, Ivan, illus. see Poppenhager, Nicole.
Gantt, Amy, illus. see Mravetz, Pete.
Gantt, Patricia. Student's Encyclopedia of Great American Writers. (p. 1669)
Gantt-Smith, Michelle. Little Feet Goes to the Barbershop. (p. 1027)
Ganz, Cristina Milián, illus. see Otero, Eduardo A.
Ganz, David, ed. see Einhard, et al.
Ganz, David, tr. see Einhard, et al.
Ganz, Nancy. Numbers: A Commentary for Children. (p. 1272)
Ganz, Yaffa. Adventures of Jeremy & Heddy Levi. Katz, Avi, illus. (p. 19)
—Four in One: Four Favorites. Klineman, Harvey, illus. (p. 625)
—Raise a Rabbit, Grow a Goose. Klineman, Harvey, illus. (p. 1436)
—Travels & Tales of Dr. Emanuel J. Mitzva. (p. 1780)
Ganzer, Diane. Patrick the Wayward Setter: A Christmas Miracle. (p. 1329)
—Summer School Blues. (p. 1675)
Ganzer, Diane & St. Croix, Sammy. Adventures of a Kitten Named Raspberry & Other Tales. (p. 16)
—Llama Tails: Ricky's Adventure. Ganzer, Theresa, illus. (p. 1043)
Ganzer, Diane & Swanson, Christopher. Called to Serve. (p. 254)
Ganzer, Theresa, illus. see Ganzer, Diane & St. Croix, Sammy.
Ganz-Schmitt, Sue. Even Superheroes Get Diabetes. Chambers-Goldberg, Micah, illus. (p. 541)
—Planet Kindergarten: 100 Days in Orbit. Prigmore, Shane, illus. (p. 1367)
—Planet Kindergarten. (p. 1367)
—Planet Kindergarten. Prigmore, Shane, illus. (p. 1367)
Gao, Charlie. Children City & Teacher Town. (p. 302)
Gaona, Gloria. Dominic & His Turtle Michael Angelo. (p. 465)
Gapaillard, Laurent, illus. see Wahl, Jan.
Gapanowicz, Delores. Finchley House Mystery. (p. 587)
Garafalo, Beatrice, illus. see Addino, Victoria.
Garamella, Joyce Orchard, illus. see Whyte, Donna.
Garant, Andre J. Circus Kids. (p. 322)
—Elite Eight. (p. 513)
—Jake's Tree House. (p. 906)
Garassino, Alessandro. Plantas. (p. 1369)
—Vida. (p. 1840)
Garavini, Daniela, ed. Goose: History, Folklore, Ancient Recipes. (p. 702)
Garaway, Margaret K. Old Hogan Coloring Book. (p. 1284)
Garay, Erin. Angel Birthdays. Abbott, Kristin, illus. (p. 73)
Garay, Luis, illus. see Amado, Elisa.
Garay, Luis, illus. see Argueta, Jorge.
Garay, Luis, illus. see Montejo, Victor.
Garay, Martha. Little Siblings' Magic World: Book One. (p. 1036)
Garay, Nicole, illus. see Moreno Winner, Ramona.
Garbani, Tony, jt. auth. see Smith, Jodene Lynn.
Garbe, Suzanne. Ghostly Encounters (p. 672)
—Ghosts of Alcatraz & Other Hauntings of the West (p. 672)
—Ghosts of Gettysburg & Other Hauntings of the East (p. 672)
—Killer Jobs: History's Most Dangerous Jobs. (p. 956)
—Living Earth: Exploring Life on Earth with Science Projects. (p. 1040)
—Secrets of Machu Picchu: Lost City of the Incas (p. 1545)
—Threatening Skies: History's Most Dangerous Weather (p. 1741)
—World's Craziest Records. (p. 1960)
—Worst Avalanches of All Time (p. 1961)
—Worst Volcanic Eruptions of All Time (p. 1961)
—Worst Wildfires of All Time (p. 1961)
Garbe, Suzanne, jt. auth. see Chandler, Matt.
Garbe, Suzanne, et al. Dangerous History. (p. 404)
—Epic Disasters. (p. 532)
Garber, James, jt. auth. see Garber, James J.
Garber, James J. & Garber, James. Harmony in Healing: The Theoretical Basis of Ancient & Medieval Medicine. (p. 749)
Garber, S. David, ed. see Travis, Lucille.
Garbot, Dave. Crazy, Zany Cartoon Characters: Learn to Draw 20 Weird, Wacky Characters! (p. 378)
—Crazy, Zany Cartoon Characters. (p. 378)
—Fairy Tale Fun: Learn to Draw More Than 20 Cartoon Princesses, Fairies, & Adventure Characters. (p. 564)
—Fairy Tale Fun. (p. 564)
—Furry & Feathered Friends: Learn to Draw More Than 20 Cute Cartoon Critters. (p. 650)
—Furry & Feathered Friends. (p. 650)
—Mean 'n' Messy Monsters: Learn to Draw 25 Spooky, Kooky Monsters! (p. 1116)
—Mean 'n' Messy Monsters. (p. 1116)
Garbot, Dave, illus. see Dispenzio, Michael A.
Garbot, Dave, illus. see Grant, Ron & Ovadia, Ron.
Garbot, Dave, illus. see Hale, Bruce.
Garbot, Dave, illus. see Mandell, Muriel.
Garbot, Dave, illus. see Murray, Carol.
Garbot, Dave, illus. see Wax, Wendy.
Garbowska, Agata, et al. Gandy & Parker Escape the Zoo: An Illustrated Adventure. Garbowska, Agata, illus. (p. 655)
Garbus, Julia. Brown vs the Board of Education Trial. Greenhaven Press Staff, ed. (p. 232)
—Eating Disorders. Greenhaven Press Staff, ed. (p. 501)
—UXL Money: Making Sense of Economics & Personal Finance. (p. 1829)
Garbus, Julie. Mexico. Greenhaven Press Staff, ed. (p. 1131)
Garbutt, Chris, illus. see Moses, Brian.
Garbutt, Lisa, illus. see Martz, Sandra, ed.
Garces Iii, Joseph Louis. Garrett the Firefighter. Abercrombie, Bethaney, illus. (p. 657)
—Tyler the Cowpoke. (p. 1805)
Garces, Victor Gabriel. Living Conditions of the Indigenous Populations in American Countries. (p. 1040)
Garcha, Rajinder, jt. auth. see Crosetto, Alice.
Garcha, Rajinder & Russell, Patricia Yates. World of Islam in Literature for Youth: A Selective Annotated Bibliography for K-12. (p. 1957)
Garchik, Leah. San Francisco: The City's Sights & Secrets. (p. 1510)
Garcia, Adam. Inside Submarines: Use Place Value Understanding & Properties of Operations to Perform Multi-Digit Arithmetic (p. 877)
Garcia Aguilar, Eduardo. Voltaire -el festín de la Inteligencia. (p. 1849)
Garcia, Alaycia. Roxy & Chopper Visit the Animal Shelter. Carter, Kelly, illus. (p. 1492)
Garcia, Alfredo. Erase una Vez Entre los Chibchas. (p. 533)
Garcia, Alice Cook. Bella's Dreams. (p. 162)
Garcia, Aurora. Cinco de Mayo (p. 319)
Garcia, Aurora C. Cinco de Mayo (p. 319)
Garcia, Aurora Colon. Cinco de Mayo. (p. 319)
Garcia, Camille Rose, illus. see Brothers Grimm, Becky, et al.
Garcia, Camille Rose, illus. see Carroll, Lewis, pseud.
Garcia Castellano, Ana. Marcela. Maier, Ximena, illus. (p. 1091)
Garcia, Cecelia & Adams, James. Healing with Medicinal Plants of the West: Cultural & Scientific Basis for Their Use. (p. 757)
García, César Fernández. No, No y No. Sales, Jordi, illus. (p. 1259)
Garcia, Cindy Booth. Rat-a-Tat-Tat Not That! (p. 1440)
Garcia, Cristina. Dog Who Loved the Moon. Serra, Sebastia, illus. (p. 462)
Garcia, Cristina. Dreams of Significant Girls. (p. 484)
Garcia, Cristina. Dreams of Significant Girls. (p. 484)
—I Wanna Be Your Shoebox. (p. 847)
Garcia, Cynthia, illus. see Litz, Amanda.
Garcia, David. Don't Awaken Love Before the Time: Why Young People Lose When They Date. (p. 466)
García Dávila, Sandra. Antepasados Para Ninos. (p. 89)
Garcia de la Viuda, Miriam, tr. see Anastasio, Antonio.
Garcia de Ortiz, Lic. Rosalinda, tr. see Plante, Patty.
García Díaz, José, tr. see Montgomery, L. M.
Garcia Dominguez, Ramon. Niño Gol. Urberuaga, Emilio, illus. (p. 1257)
Garcia, Doris Ortiz. As Many Children as the Stars. (p. 105)
García Echeverría, Olga. Falling Angels: Cuentos y Poemas. (p. 566)
Garcia Echeverria, Olga, ed. see Bautista, Gladys, et al.
Garcia Echeverria, Olga Angelina, ed. see Ortiz, Teresa, et al.
Garcia, Edgar Allan. Pais de Los Juguetes. Jacome, Mauricio, illus. (p. 1319)
Garcia, Eduardo, illus. see Bowen, Carl.
Garcia, Eduardo, illus. see Fein, Eric.
Garcia, Eduardo, illus. see Jacobson, Ryan.
Garcia, Eduardo, illus. see Johnson, Lauren.
Garcia, Eduardo, illus. see Maddox, Jake.
Garcia, Eduardo, illus. see Shakespeare, William.
Garcia, Elizabeth. Viaje de Lucita. Tanchez, Plinio, illus. (p. 1839)
Garcia, Ellen. Are You Listening, Jack? Patton, Julia, illus. (p. 97)
—Are You Listening, Jack? Lap Book. Patton, Julia, illus. (p. 97)
—Be Honest, Jess Lap Book. Mones, Marc, illus. (p. 148)
—Be Patient, Maddie Lap Book. Patton, Julia, illus. (p. 149)
—Charlie Is Responsible Lap Book. Mones, Marc, illus. (p. 293)
—Day I Felt Sad. Poole, Helen, illus. (p. 413)
—Day I Felt Sad Lap Book. Poole, Helen, illus. (p. 413)
—I Am a Star! Lap Book. Evans, Antony, illus. (p. 832)
—I Can Make a Plan. Evans, Antony, illus. (p. 836)
—I Can Make a Plan Lap Book. Evans, Antony, illus. (p. 836)
Garcia, Ellen & Benchmark Education Co. Staff. Where There's No Such Thing As Worry & Other African American Folktales. (p. 1909)
Garcia, Eloisa, tr. see Byte Me! P.
Garcia, Emerald. My Dog & My Dad. Dayton, Tyler, illus. (p. 1202)
Garcia, Emma. Tap Tap Bang Bang. (p. 1705)
—Tip Tip Dig Dig. (p. 1757)
—Toot Toot Beep Beep. (p. 1767)
Garcia, Emmett, jt. auth. see Garcia, Emmett Shkeme.
Garcia, Emmett Shkeme. Sister Rabbit's Tricks. Pringle, Victoria, illus. (p. 1581)
Garcia, Emmett Shkeme & Garcia, Emmett. Coyote & the Sky: How the Sun, Moon, & Stars Began. Pringle, Victoria, illus. (p. 374)
Garcia, Geronimo, illus. see Sáenz, Benjamin Alire.
Garcia, Gloria. Los Animales. (p. 1053)
—Magia. (p. 1071)
—Navidad. (p. 1237)
—Universo. (p. 1821)
Garcia, Gretel, jt. auth. see Torrijos, Eduardo.
Garcia, Heather. Brocc O'Li. (p. 230)
Garcia, Helena, illus. see Welsh, Anne Marie & Fenly, Leigh.
Garcia, Helena, illus. see Welsh, Anne Marie & Tuchman, Laura.
Garcia, Humberto, illus. see Lozano, Juan Antonio.
Garcia Iii, Joe. Dragon Boogers. (p. 476)
Garcia, James. Cinco de Mayo: A Mexican Holiday about Unity & Pride. (p. 319)
Garcia, Jeffrey. Santa Claus & the Molokai Mules. (p. 1511)
Garcia, Jesus E. Tim & Ann's First Day at the Beach. (p. 1750)
Garcia, Jesus, et al. Creating America: A History of the United States. (p. 378)
—Creating America: Beginnings Through World War I. (p. 378)
—Creating America: A History of the United States: with Atlas by Rand Mcnally. (p. 378)
—Creating America: A History of the United States: Beginnings Through Reconstruction (p. 378)
—Creating America: Beginnings Through World War I: A History of the United States. (p. 378)
—McDougal Littell Creating America: A History of the United States (p. 1114)
Garcia, Joan. Footsteps of Angels. (p. 615)
Garcia, Jolanda, jt. auth. see Lassiter, Erin.
Garcia, Jose Enrique. Pueblo Llamado Pan y Otros Cuentos Infantiles. (p. 1414)
Garcia, Joseph. Sign with Your Baby - ASL Baby Sign Language Complete Learning Kit (DVD Edition) How to Communicate with Infants Before They Can Speak. (p. 1574)
Garcia, Joy. My Paper Ruler: A Garcia Hands-on Learn-about Book. (p. 1216)
Garcia, Juan. Neil Armstrong: First Man on the Moon. (p. 1240)
Garcia, Juan Carlos Quezadas, et al. Videocasetera YA No Esta a Dieta. Escobar, Antonio Rocha, illus. (p. 1841)
Garcia, Juan F., illus. see Hildebrand, Jens.
Garcia, Juliet. Joshua's Abc Book. (p. 927)
Garcia, Justine Marie. While You Were Gone Year Two. Robin, Gulack, illus. (p. 1911)
Garcia, Kami. Unbreakable. (p. 1811)
Garcia, Kami & Stohl, Margaret. Beautiful Chaos. (p. 153)
—Beautiful Creatures. (p. 153)
—Beautiful Creatures Complete Collection: Beautiful Creatures - Beautiful Darkness - Beautiful Chaos - Beautiful Redemption. (p. 153)
—Beautiful Creatures Complete Paperback Collection: Beautiful Creatures; Beautiful Darkness; Beautiful Chaos; Beautiful Redemption. (p. 153)
—Beautiful Darkness. (p. 153)
—Beautiful Redemption. (p. 154)
—Dangerous Creatures. (p. 404)
—Dangerous Deception. (p. 404)
Garcia, Katherine. Jojo & the Tule Tree. (p. 924)
Garcia, Lisa. Tree of Life: From the Garden of Eden to the New Jerusalem. (p. 1783)
Garcia, Lizbeth. 101 Ways to Burn Fat on the Ball: Lose Weight with Fun Cardio & Body-Sculpting Moves! (p. 2000)
García Lorca, Federico. Bodas de Sangre. (p. 206)
—Canciones (1921-1924) (p. 261)
—Canciones y Poemas para Ninos. (p. 261)
García Lorca, Federico, jt. auth. see García Lorca, Federico X.
García Lorca, Federico & Aguilar, José. 4 Poemas de Lorca y un Viaje a Nueva York. (p. 1992)
García Lorca, Federico X & García Lorca, Federico. Federico Garcia Lorca para Ninos. Canas, Alicia, illus. (p. 580)
García, Luis. Johan Santana. (p. 920)
Garcia, Luis, jt. auth. see Lara, Enrique.
Garcia, Manuel. Black Widow: Kiss or Kill. (p. 197)
Garcia, Marc Khayam. Color Me & My Pals: The Adventures of Billy Butterfly' Coloring Book. (p. 342)
Garcia, Marc Khayam, illus. see Lehnert, R. B.
Garcia, Maria. Aventuras de Connie y Diego. (p. 119)
Garcia, Marina. Dali Para Ninos. (p. 401)
Garcia, Marina & Sola, Emilio. Misterio Velazquez: Diego Rivera. (p. 1155)
Garcia, Marina, et al. Mateo de Paseo por el Museo. (p. 1104)
—Mateo de Paseo Por el Museo Del Prado. (p. 1104)
García Márquez, Gabriel. Gabriel García Márquez's One Hundred Years of Solitude. Bloom, Harold, ed. (p. 652)
—Maria dos Prazeres. (p. 1093)
—Senor muy Viejo con unas Alas Enormes. (p. 1550)
—Siesta del Martes. (p. 1573)
Garcia, Mary. Play with Me: Togetherness Time for Your Preschooler & You. (p. 1371)
—Play with Me: Togetherness Time for Your Preschooler & You: St. Valentine's Day. (p. 1371)
Garcia, Michael. Maxwell Lear's Book. (p. 1112)
Garcia, Mike D., jt. auth. see Rice, David.
Garcia, Molly. G. G. The Diary fo a Space Case. (p. 651)
Garcia, Nasario. Grandma Lale's Tamales: A Christmas Story. Aragon, Dolores, illus. (p. 708)
—Grandpa Lolo & Trampa: A Story of Surprise & Mystery = Abuelito Lolo y Trampa: Un Cuento de Sorpresa y Misterio. Montoya, Jeremy, illus. (p. 709)
—Grandpa Lolo's Navajo Saddle Blanket: La Tilma de Abuelito Lolo. Moeller, Richard, illus. (p. 709)
—Rattling Chains & Other Stories for Children/Ruido de Cadenas y Otros Cuentos para Ninos. Mora, Giovanni, illus. (p. 1440)
—Talking Lizard: New Mexico's Magic & Mystery. Montoya, Jeremy, illus. (p. 1703)
Garcia, Nasario, tr. see Anaya, Rudolfo.
Garcia, Norma Lee. Day with Smiles. (p. 415)
Garcia Ordaz, Daniel. You Know What I'm Sayin'? Poetry Drama. (p. 1975)
GARCIA ORIHUELA, Luis, illus. see Garcia Orihuela, Luis & DIVINCENZO, Sofia & Yoselem.
Garcia Orihuela, Luis & DIVINCENZO, Sofia & Yoselem. Army of Words. GARCIA ORIHUELA, Luis, illus. (p. 100)
Garcia, Patricio, illus. see Ortega, Cristina.
Garcia, R. M. Steamer Trunk Adventures #1: The Trunk & the Tortoise. (p. 1646)
Garcia, Rachel, jt. auth. see Driver, Stephanie Schwartz.
Garcia, Rachel Byard, et al. I Wish I Knew That: Science: Cool Stuff You Need to Know. (p. 849)
Garcia, Ramon. Por Todos los Dioses! (Greek Myths Retold) (p. 1386)
—Soloman. (p. 1608)
Garcia, Randolph. Steamer Trunk Adventures #2: The Ghosts of Machu Picchu. (p. 1646)
Garcia, Richard. Espiritus de Mi Tia Otilia. (p. 536)
Garcia Sanchez, J. L. Nino Gigante (The Giant Child) (p. 1257)
Garcia, Sarah Rafael, jt. auth. see Alaniz, Valeria.
Garcia, Tom & Naga, Karun. Daddy's Heroes: Gibby's Homer: the 1988 World Series. Donnelly, Jenifer, illus. (p. 399)
Garcia, Tracy J. Eli Whitney. (p. 512)
—Thomas Edison. (p. 1738)
Garcia, Victor, ed. see Esherick, Joan.
Garcia, Victor, ed. see Ford, Jean & Libal, Autumn.
Garcia, Victor, ed. see Ford, Jean.
Garcia, Victor, ed. see Hunter, William.
Garcia, Victor, ed. see Libal, Autumn.
Garcia, Victor, ed. see Sanna, Ellyn.
Garcia, Victor Manuel Gut, illus. see Ochoa, Minerva.
Garcia, Victor Manuel Gut, illus. see Parada, Enrique.
Garcia, Victor Manuel Gutierrez, illus. see Parada, Enrique.
Garcia, Victoria. I Imagine Things Because I Picture Myself There: Imagino Cosas... Porque Pienso Que Estoy Ah. (p. 839)
García-Castellano, Ana. Inventores de Cuentos. Fra, Irene, illus. (p. 884)
Garcia-Martinez, Julia, jt. auth. see Pacheco, Maria.
Garcia-Webb, Peter. Aeron. (p. 25)
Gard, Carolyn. Attack on the Pentagon on September 11 2001. (p. 114)
—Attack on the Pentagon on September 11, 2001. (p. 114)
—Attacks on the World Trade Center: February 26, 1993, & September 11, 2001. (p. 114)
—Cool Careers Without College for People Who Love to Sell Things. (p. 363)
—French & Indian War: A Primary Source History of the Fight for Territory in North America. (p. 635)
—French Indian War. (p. 635)
Gard, Don. Adventures of Beezer. Giancanelli, Candace, illus. (p. 16)
Garda, Imran. Thunder That Roars. (p. 1746)
Gardam, Jane. Hollow Land. (p. 789)
Garde, Dora, tr. see Stine, R. L.
Garde, Ruth, jt. auth. see Aakeson, Kim Fupz.
Gardeazabal, Gustavo Alvarez. Condores No Entierran Todos los Dias. (p. 356)
Garden, Jo, illus. see Munro, Fiona & Phillipson, Fiona.
Garden, Jo, illus. see Munro, Fiona.
Garden, Nancy. Annie on My Mind. (p. 87)
—Case of the Stolen Scarab. (p. 275)
—Case of the Vanishing Valuables. (p. 275)
—Endgame. (p. 527)
—Untitled Garden. (p. 1823)
Garden, Randa Sue. Penny the Penguin. (p. 1338)
Gardener, Amanda & Sealey, Nanlie. Butterfly Pavilion. (p. 248)
—Freddy the White Flamingo. (p. 633)
Gardener, Ryan. Thank You God for Making the Sun. (p. 1725)
Gardiner, C. Pirate Betty of Wigan. (p. 1362)
Gardiner, John, jt. auth. see Gardiner, John Reynolds.
Gardiner, John Reynolds. General Butterfingers. Smith, Cat Bowman & Smith, Catharine Bowman, illus. (p. 660)
—Stone Fox. (p. 1652)
—Stone Fox. Sewall, Marcia, illus. (p. 1652)
—Stone Fox. Sewall, Marcia & Hargreaves, Greg, illus. (p. 1652)
Gardiner, John Reynolds & Gardiner, John. Alto Secreto. (p. 50)
Gardiner, Lindsey, illus. see Grindley, Sally.
Gardiner, Lindsey, illus. see Huggins, Peter.
Gardiner, Lindsey, illus. see Langston, Laura.
Gardiner, Lindsey, illus. see Oram, Hiawyn.
Gardiner, Lindsey, illus. see Ormerod, Jan.
Gardiner, Lindsey, jt. auth. see Ormerod, Jan.
Gardiner, Lisa. Big Dreams. Flowerpot Press, ed. (p. 181)
—Catastrophic Colorado! The History & Science of Our Natural Disasters. (p. 278)
—Creatures Great & Small. Flowerpot Press, ed. (p. 380)
—Farm Animals. Flowerpot Press, ed. (p. 573)
—In the Garden. Flowerpot Press, ed. (p. 866)
—Jesus Loves Me. Flowerpot Press, ed. (p. 915)
—People. Flowerpot Press, ed. (p. 1339)
—Things That Work. Flowerpot Press, ed. (p. 1733)
Gardiner, Lisa, illus. see Kelley, Lynn.
Gardiner, Lisa M., illus. see Paiva, Johannah Gilman, ed.
Gardiner, Meghan, et al. Green Thumb Theatre Anthology. Green Thumb Theatre Staff, ed. (p. 722)
Gardiner, Nancy, illus. see Macy, Tana.
Gardiner, Paul D. Project Management: A Strategic Planning Approach. (p. 1410)
Gardner, Adrian. F-14 Tomcat. (p. 559)
Gardner, Alecia. Peachy Penelope. (p. 1332)
Gardner, Alicia. We Are Different, We Are the Same. (p. 1865)
Gardner, Alison. Passport to Paris. (p. 1327)
Gardner, April B. Mao: Boy of Stone. (p. 1089)
Gardner, Carol. Princess Zelda & the Frog. Young, Shane, photos by. (p. 1406)

Gardner, Charlie. Beatles Yellow Submarine. Edelmann, Heinz, illus. (p. 153)
Gardner, Charlie & Dorling Kindersley Publishing Staff. Farm Peekaboo! King, Dave, photos by. (p. 574)
Gardner, Colin. Pythagorean Triangle Properties & Attributes Samples (Enlarged), As Independently Discovered by Colin Gardner, Physicist: Pythagorean triples are everwhere, & have an application in nearly every math lesson(6th grade thru College. (p. 1421)
Gardner, David, illus. see Allegra, Mike.
Gardner, David, et al. Geography, 11-14. (p. 662)
Gardner, David Knill, et al. Geography. (p. 662)
Gardner, Del-Rio. Promise Fulfilled. (p. 1411)
Gardner, Dianne Lynn. Rubies & Robbers. (p. 1493)
Gardner, Faith. Perdita. (p. 1341)
Gardner, Faye. Billy Buck Green Fit: An Angry First Grade Boy. (p. 187)
Gardner, Faye, et al. Shopping in the 1940s. (p. 1569)
Gardner, Graham. Inventing Elliot. (p. 883)
—Santa Beacon. LeBlanc, Nancy, illus. (p. 1511)
Gardner, (Grandpa). Starting School. (p. 1644)
Gardner, Harvey. Fun in Fall: Work with Addition & Subtraction Equations. (p. 648)
Gardner, Jane. Animal Science Lewin, Russ, ed. (p. 79)
Gardner, Jane P. African Wild Dogs. (p. 28)
—Car Science Lewin, Russ, ed. (p. 265)
—Computer Science Lewin, Russ, ed. (p. 355)
—Environmental Science. (p. 532)
—Fashion Science Lewin, Russ, ed. (p. 576)
—Fennec Foxes. (p. 581)
—Food Science Lewin, Russ, ed. (p. 614)
—Gray Foxes. (p. 713)
—Health Science Lewin, Russ, ed. (p. 758)
—Jackals. (p. 903)
—Music Science Lewin, Russ, ed. (p. 1193)
—Photo Science Lewin, Russ, ed. (p. 1353)
—Physics: Investigate the Forces of Nature. Carbaugh, Samuel, illus. (p. 1353)
—Sports Science Lewin, Russ, ed. (p. 1633)
—Take a Closer Look at Your Brain. (p. 1696)
—Take a Closer Look at Your Muscles. (p. 1696)
—Timber & Forest Products (p. 1750)
—Travel Science Lewin, Russ, ed. (p. 1780)
Gardner, Jane P., et al. Geography Book: From the Grand Canyon to the Great Barrier Reef - Explore the World! (p. 662)
Gardner, Julia, jt. auth. see Davidson, Simon.
Gardner, Kay. Maths Dictionary. (p. 1108)
Gardner, L. S. From Bobcat to Wolf: The Story of Den Seven, Pack Four. Stevens, illus. (p. 642)
Gardner, Laurien. Plain Jane: A Novel of Jane Seymour (p. 1366)
Gardner, Lindsey, et al. Pan Fydd Popi a Macs yn Fawr. (p. 1320)
Gardner, Lisa. Things That Go. Flowerpot Press, ed. (p. 1733)
Gardner, Louise. Five Little Easter Eggs. (p. 600)
—Old MacDonald. (p. 1284)
Gardner, Louise, illus. see Maccarone, Grace.
Gardner, Louise, illus. see Powell, Richard.
Gardner, Louise, et al. Old MacDonald & Other Sing-along Rhymes. (p. 1284)
Gardner, Luci, jt. auth. see Jaffe, Amy V.
Gardner, Lyn. Out of the Woods. (p. 1311)
Gardner, Lyn, jt. auth. see Grey, Mini.
Gardner, Marjory, illus. see Alexander, Goldie.
Gardner, Marjory, illus. see Wallace, Jessica.
Gardner, Mark L. Fort Union National Monument. (p. 623)
Gardner, Martin. Martin Gardner's Science Magic: Tricks & Puzzles. (p. 1097)
—Mental Magic: Surefire Tricks to Amaze Your Friends. Sinclair, Jeff, illus. (p. 1126)
—Mind-Boggling Word Puzzles. Myers, V. G., illus. (p. 1145)
Gardner, Martin, jt. auth. see Thayer, Ernest L.
Gardner, Martin & Nye, Russel B. Wizard of Oz & Who He Was. (p. 1943)
Gardner, Paul, jt. auth. see Nguyen, Hoang.
Gardner, Richard, jt. auth. see Schab, Lisa.
Gardner, Richard, jt. auth. see Shore, Hennie.
Gardner, Rita, illus. see MacDonald, Bernell.
Gardner, Robert. Ace Your Math & Measuring Science Project: Great Science Fair Ideas. (p. 8)
—Ace Your Science Project Using Chemistry Magic & Toys: Great Science Fair Ideas. (p. 8)
—Air: Green Science Projects for a Sustainable Planet. (p. 31)
—Astronomy Experiments in Your Own Observatory. (p. 109)
—Astronomy Projects with an Observatory You Can Build. (p. 109)
—Atoms & Molecules Experiments Using Ice, Salt, Marbles, & More: One Hour or Less Science Experiments. (p. 113)
—Bicycle Science Fair Projects. (p. 177)
—Bicycle Science Projects: Physics on Wheels. (p. 177)
—Chemistry Experiments in Your Own Laboratory. (p. 297)
—Chemistry Projects with a Laboratory You Can Build. (p. 297)
—Chemistry Science Fair Projects Using Acids, Bases, Metals, Salts, & Inorganic Stuff. (p. 297)
—Chemistry Science Fair Projects Using Inorganic Stuff. LaBaff, Tom & LaBaff, Stephanie, illus. (p. 297)
—Crime Lab 101: 25 Different Experiments in Crime Detection. (p. 382)
—Dazzling Science Projects with Light & Color. LaBaff, Tom, illus. (p. 415)
—Desert Experiments: 11 Science Experiments in One Hour or Less. (p. 429)
—Earth's Cycles: Great Science Projects about the Water Cycle, Photosynthesis, & More. (p. 498)
—Earth-Shaking Science Projects about Planet Earth. LaBaff, Tom, illus. (p. 497)
—Easy Genius Science Projects with Chemistry: Great Experiments & Ideas. (p. 500)
—Easy Genius Science Projects with Electricity & Magnetism: Great Experiments & Ideas. (p. 500)
—Easy Genius Science Projects with Light: Great Experiments & Ideas. (p. 500)
—Easy Genius Science Projects with the Human Body: Great Experiments & Ideas. (p. 500)
—Easy Genius Science Projects with Weather: Great Experiments & Ideas. (p. 500)
—Electricity & Magnetism Experiments Using Batteries, Bulbs, Wires, & More: One Hour or Less Science Experiments. (p. 509)
—Electricity & Magnetism Science Fair Projects, Revised & Expanded Using the Scientific Method. LaBaff, Stephanie & LaBaff, Tom, illus. (p. 509)
—Electricity & Magnetism Science Fair Projects Using Batteries, Balloons, & Other Hair-Raising Stuff. (p. 509)
—Energizing Science Projects with Electricity & Magnetism. LaBaff, Tom, illus. (p. 528)
—Energy: Green Science Projects about Solar, Wind, & Water Power. (p. 528)
—Energy Experiments Using Ice Cubes, Springs, Magnets, & More: One Hour or Less Science Experiments. (p. 528)
—Experimenting with Plants Science Projects. (p. 549)
—Experimenting with Sound Science Projects. (p. 549)
—Far-Out Science Projects about Earth's Sun & Moon. LaBaff, Tom, illus. (p. 572)
—Far-Out Science Projects with Height & Depth: How High Is up? How Low Is Down? (p. 572)
—Forces & Motion Science Fair Projects, Revised & Expanded Using the Scientific Method. LaBaff, Tom & LaBaff, Stephanie, illus. (p. 617)
—Forces & Motion Science Fair Projects Using Water Balloons, Pulleys, & Other Stuff. (p. 617)
—Forensic Science Experiments in Your Own Crime Lab. (p. 617)
—Forensic Science Projects with a Crime Lab You Can Build. (p. 617)
—Genetics & Evolution Science Fair Projects: Using Skeletons, Cereal, Earthworms, & More. (p. 661)
—Genetics & Evolution Science Fair Projects, Revised & Expanded Using the Scientific Method. LaBaff, Stephanie, illus. (p. 661)
—Grasslands Experiments: 11 Science Experiments in One Hour or Less. (p. 712)
—Heavy-Duty Science Projects with Weight: How Much Does It Weigh? (p. 761)
—How Big Is Big? Science Projects with Volume. (p. 805)
—How Fast Is Fast? Science Projects with Speed. (p. 809)
—How Heavy Is Heavy? Science Projects with Weight. (p. 809)
—How High Is High? Science Projects with Height & Depth. (p. 809)
—How Hot Is Hot? Science Projects with Temperature. (p. 809)
—How Quick Is Quick? Science Projects with Time. (p. 812)
—Human Body Experiments Using Fingerprints, Hair, Muscles, & More: One Hour or Less Science Experiments. (p. 825)
—It's about Time! Science Projects: How Long Does It Take? (p. 896)
—Jazzy Science Projects with Sound & Music. LaBaff, Tom, illus. (p. 911)
—Light, Sound, & Waves Science Fair Projects: Using Sunglasses, Guitars, CDs, & Other Stuff. (p. 1015)
—Light, Sound, & Waves Science Fair Projects, Revised & Expanded Using the Scientific Method. (p. 1015)
—Melting, Freezing, & Boiling Science Projects with Matter. (p. 1125)
—Meteorology Experiments in Your Own Weather Station. (p. 1130)
—Meteorology Projects with a Weather Station You Can Build. (p. 1130)
—Physics Experiments in Your Own Light Box. (p. 1353)
—Physics of Sports Science Projects. (p. 1353)
—Physics of Toys & Games Science Projects. (p. 1353)
—Physics Projects with a Light Box You Can Build. (p. 1353)
—Planet Earth Science Fair Projects, Revised & Expanded Using the Scientific Method. LaBaff, Stephanie & LaBaff, Tom, illus. (p. 1367)
—Planet Earth Science Fair Projects Using the Moon, Stars, Beach Balls, Frisbees, & Other Far-Out Stuff. (p. 1367)
—Rain Forest Experiments: 10 Science Experiments in One Hour or Less. (p. 1434)
—Really Hot Science Projects with Temperature: How Hot Is It? How Cold Is It? (p. 1450)
—Recycle: Green Science Projects for a Sustainable Planet. (p. 1452)
—Science Behind Magic Science Projects. (p. 1525)
—Science Fair Projects about the Properties of Matter Using Marbles, Water, Balloons, & More. Tom, LaBaff, illus. (p. 1526)
—Science Fair Projects about the Properties of Matter, Revised & Expanded Using the Scientific Method. LaBaff, Stephanie, illus. (p. 1526)
—Sensational Science Projects with Simple Machines. LaBaff, Tom, illus. (p. 1551)
—Simple Machine Experiments Using Seesaws, Wheels, Pulleys, & More: One Hour or Less Science Experiments. (p. 1577)
—Sizzling Science Projects with Heat & Energy. LaBaff, Tom, illus. (p. 1583)
—Smashing Science Projects about Earth's Rocks & Minerals. LaBaff, Tom, illus. (p. 1593)
—Soil: Green Science Projects for a Sustainable Planet. (p. 1606)
—Solids, Liquids, & Gases Experiments Using Water, Air, Marbles, & More: One Hour or Less Science Experiments. (p. 1608)
—Solids, Liquids, & Gases Science Projects. (p. 1608)
—Sound Experiments in Your Own Music Lab. (p. 1615)
—Sound Projects with a Music Lab You Can Build. (p. 1615)
—Split-Second Science Projects with Speed: How Fast Does It Go? (p. 1630)
—Stellar Science Projects about Earth's Sky. LaBaff, Tom, illus. (p. 1647)
—Super Science Projects about Earth's Soil & Water. LaBaff, Tom, illus. (p. 1681)
—Super-Sized Science Projects with Volume: How Much Space Does It Take Up? (p. 1681)
—Taiga Experiments: 12 Science Experiments in One Hour or Less. (p. 1695)
—Temperate Forest Experiments: 8 Science Experiments in One Hour or Less. (p. 1717)
—Temperate Forest Experiments: 8 Science Experiments in One Hour or Less. (p. 1717)
—Tundra Experiments: 14 Science Experiments in One Hour or Less. (p. 1796)
—Water: Green Science Projects for a Sustainable Planet. (p. 1862)
—Weather Science Fair Projects, Revised & Expanded Using the Scientific Method. LaBaff, Tom, illus. (p. 1870)
—Weather Science Fair Projects Using Sunlight, Rainbows, Ice Cubes, & More. (p. 1870)
—Who Can Solve the Crime? Science Projects Using Detective Skills. (p. 1914)
—Who Forged This Document? Crime-Solving Science Projects. (p. 1915)
—Whose Bones Are These? Crime-Solving Science Projects. (p. 1921)
—Whose Fingerprints Are These? Crime-Solving Science Projects. (p. 1921)
—Wild Science Projects about Earth's Weather. LaBaff, Tom, illus. (p. 1930)
Gardner, Robert, jt. auth. see Anthony, Nathan.
Gardner, Robert & Conklin, Barbara Gardner. Ace Your Human Biology Science Project: Great Science Fair Ideas. (p. 8)
—Chemistry Science Fair Projects Using French Fries, Gumdrops, Soap, & Other Organic Stuff. (p. 297)
—Organic Chemistry Science Fair Projects, Revised & Expanded Using the Scientific Method. LaBaff, Tom & LaBaff, Stephanie, illus. (p. 1303)
Gardner, Robert & Goodstein, Madeline P. Ace Your Forces & Motion Science Project: Great Science Fair Ideas. (p. 8)
—Ace Your Space Science Project: Great Science Fair Ideas. (p. 8)
Gardner, Robert & Kemer, Eric. Easy Genius Science Projects with Temperature & Heat: Great Experiments & Ideas. (p. 500)
Gardner, Robert & Perry, Phyllis Jean. Ace Your Plant Science Project: Great Science Fair Ideas. (p. 8)
Gardner, Robert & Shortelle, Dennis. Slam Dunk! Science Projects with Basketball. (p. 1587)
Gardner, Robert & Tocci, Salvatore. Ace Your Weather Science Project: Great Science Fair Ideas. (p. 8)
Gardner, Robert, et al. Ace Your Animal Science Project: Great Science Fair Ideas. (p. 8)
—Ace Your Chemistry Science Project: Great Science Fair Ideas. (p. 8)
—Ace Your Ecology & Environmental Science Project: Great Science Fair Ideas. (p. 8)
—Ace Your Exercise & Nutrition Science Project: Great Science Fair Ideas. (p. 8)
—Ace Your Food Science Project: Great Science Fair Ideas. (p. 8)
—Ace Your Physical Science Project: Great Science Fair Ideas. (p. 8)
—Ace Your Science Project about the Senses: Great Science Fair Ideas. (p. 8)
—Ace Your Sports Science Project: Great Science Fair Ideas. (p. 8)
Gardner, Sally. Book of Princesses. (p. 211)
—I, Coriander. (p. 837)
—Maggot Moon. Crouch, Julian, illus. (p. 1071)
—Magical Kids: The Invisible Boy & the Strongest Girl in the World. Gardner, Sally, illus. (p. 1074)
—Niña Más Fuerte de Todos los Tiempos. Tapia, Sonia, tr. (p. 1256)
—Niño Invisible. Tapia, Sonia, tr. (p. 1257)
—Nino Que Podia Volar. Tapia, Sonia, tr. (p. 1257)
—Operation Bunny. Roberts, David, illus. (p. 1300)
—Red Necklace: A Story of the French Revolution. (p. 1454)
—Red Necklace. (p. 1454)
—Silver Blade. (p. 1576)
—Three Pickled Herrings: Book Two. Roberts, David, illus. (p. 1743)
—Vanishing of Billy Buckle. Roberts, David, illus. (p. 1833)
Gardner, Sally, illus. see Thomas, Frances.
Gardner, Sally, jt. auth. see Bach, Richard.
Gardner, Sally, tr. see Adams, Georgie & ADAMS, GEORGIE.
Gardner, Sally Faye, jt. auth. see Berry, Julie Gardner.
Gardner, Sara. Emma & the Dinosaur. (p. 519)
Gardner, Scot. Dead I Know. (p. 416)
Gardner, Sheldon. Converso Legacy. (p. 361)
Gardner, Stephen, illus. see Kulsa, Wha.
Gardner, Suzanne, jt. auth. see Balser, Erin.
Gardner, Timothy. Oil. (p. 1282)
Gardner, Yvonne. Scrawny the Tree. (p. 1532)
Gardos, Susan, illus. see Staunton, Ted.
Gardos, Susan, jt. auth. see Staunton, Ted.
Gardy, Jennifer. It's Catching: The Infectious World of Germs & Microbes. Holinaty, Josh, illus. (p. 896)
Gareis, Elisabeth. Novel Approach: The Color Purple. (p. 1268)
Gareth Stevens Editorial Staff. Dolphins. (p. 464)
—Elephants. (p. 511)
—Hippos. (p. 781)
—Oceans. (p. 1277)
—Pandas. (p. 1321)
—Parrots. (p. 1325)
—Wolves. (p. 1944)
Gareth Stevens Editorial Staff, jt. auth. see Gareth Stevens editorial staff.
Gareth Stevens Editorial Staff, jt. auth. see Howell, Laura.
Gareth Stevens editorial staff & Gareth Stevens Editorial Staff. Gareth Stevens Atlas of the World. (p. 656)
—Volcanoes. (p. 1849)
Gareth Stevens Editorial Staff, creator. Haunted. (p. 753)
Gareth Stevens Publishing, creator. Cursed Creatures. (p. 395)
—Doomed & the Dead. (p. 470)
—From the Grave. (p. 644)
—Grammar All-Stars Complete Set. (p. 706)
Gareth Stevens Publishing Staff & Porter, Malcolm. Children's Atlas of the World. (p. 303)
Gareth Stevens Publishing Staff, contrib. by. Camels. (p. 256)
—Chimpanzees. (p. 306)
—Crocodiles. (p. 384)
—Forensics. (p. 617)
—Frogs. (p. 641)
—Giraffes. (p. 677)
—Kangaroos. (p. 942)
—Lions. (p. 1021)
—Penguins. (p. 1337)
—Polar Bear. (p. 1378)
—Protists & Fungi. (p. 1412)
—Sharks. (p. 1562)
—Space Exploration. (p. 1619)
—Spiders. (p. 1626)
—Tigers. (p. 1749)
—Turtles. (p. 1798)
—Universe. (p. 1820)
—Zebras. (p. 1985)
Garett, K. J. Carrie's Christmas Wish. (p. 271)
Garey, Barbara J. Adventures of Princess Naomia (p. 22)
Garey, Marita & National Geographic Learning Staff. Kids Are Consumers. (p. 952)
Garfat, Thomas, ed. Child & Youth Care Approach to Working with Families. (p. 301)
Garfein, Stanley Joe. Tales of the Temple Mice. (p. 1703)
Garfield, Cari. After All, I'm Just a Ball: Children's Poetry Guessing Book. (p. 28)
Garfield, Henry. Lost Voyage of John Cabot. (p. 1057)
Garfield, Ken. Dale Earnhardt, Jr: Born to Race. (p. 401)
—Jeff Gordon: Rewriting the Record Book. (p. 911)
Garfield, Leon. Complete Bostock & Harris. (p. 352)
—Drummer Boy. (p. 487)
—John Diamond. (p. 921)
—Smith - The Story of a Pickpocket. (p. 1594)
Garfield, Leon & Blishen, Edward. God Beneath the Sea. Keeping, Charles, illus. (p. 688)
Garfield, Sol, jt. auth. see Garfield, Sol L.
Garfield, Sol L. & Garfield, Sol. Clinical Psychology: The Study of Personality & Behavior. (p. 333)
Garfield, Tom. Modern US History 1865 - Present. (p. 1159)
Garfield, Yvette. Handstand Kids Italian Cookbook. (p. 741)
Garfield, Yvette & Azima, Cricket. Handstand Kids Mexican Cookbook. DeRose, Kim, illus. (p. 741)
Garfinkle, Adam M. Israel. (p. 893)
—Israel. (p. 893)
Garfinkle, D. L. Stuck in the 70's. (p. 1668)
Garing, Ken. Planetoid Volume 1 TP. (p. 1368)
Garinger, Alan. Jeremiah Stokely Naturalist. (p. 913)
Garinger, Alan K. Alone: The Journey of the Boy Sims. (p. 48)
Garis, Howard. Adventures of Uncle Wiggily. Wisa, Louis, illus. (p. 24)
Garis, Howard R. Bed Time Stories: Uncle Wiggily's Travels. Wisa, Louis, illus. (p. 156)
—Bed Time Stories: Uncle Wiggily in the Woods. Wisa, Louis, illus. (p. 156)
—Bed Time Stories: Uncle Wiggily's Adventures. Wisa, Louis, illus. (p. 156)
—Curly & Floppy Twistytail. (p. 394)
—Curlytops & Their Pets. (p. 394)
—Curlytops & Their Playmates. (p. 394)
—Curlytops at Silver Lake. (p. 394)
—Curlytops at Uncle Frank's Ranch. (p. 394)
—Curlytops at Uncle Frank's Ranch; or, Little Folks on Ponyback. (p. 394)
—Curlytops on Star Island. (p. 394)
—Curlytops on Star Island; or, Camping Out with Grandpa. (p. 394)
—Dick Hamilton's Airship. (p. 435)
—Sammie & Susie Littletail. Wisa, Louis, illus. (p. 1507)
—Umboo, the Elephant. (p. 1810)
—Uncle Wiggily & Old Mother Hubbard. (p. 1812)
—Uncle Wiggily in the Woods. (p. 1812)
—Uncle Wiggily's Adventures. (p. 1812)
—Uncle Wiggily's Travels. (p. 1812)
Garis, Howard Roger. Bed Time Stories. (p. 156)
—Buddy & Brighteyes Pigg. (p. 234)
—Bully & Bawly No-Tail: (the Jumping Frogs) (p. 241)
—Curly & Floppy Twistytail. (p. 394)
—Curlytops at Uncle Franks Ranch. (p. 394)
—Curlytops at Uncle Frank's Ranch. (p. 394)
—Curlytops on Star Island. (p. 394)
—Daddy Takes Us Skating. (p. 399)
—Daddy Takes Us to the Garden. (p. 399)
—Daddy takes us to the Garden. (p. 399)
—Dick Hamiltons Airship. (p. 435)
—Dick Hamilton's Airship or, A Young Millionaire in the Clouds. (p. 435)
—Favorite Uncle Wiggily Animal Bedtime Stories. Kliros, Thea, illus. (p. 578)
—Johnnie & Billie Bushytail. (p. 923)
—Larry Dexter's Great Search or, the Hunt for the Missing Millionaire. (p. 976)
—Lulu, Alice & Jammie Wibble Wobble. (p. 1064)
—Lulu, Alice & Jimmie Wibblewobble. (p. 1064)
—Sammie & Susie Littletail. (p. 1507)
—Tom Cardiff's Circus. King, W. B., illus. (p. 1763)
—Umboo the Elephant. (p. 1810)
—Umboo, the Elephant. (p. 1810)
—Uncle Wiggily & the Littletails. (p. 1812)
—Uncle Wiggily Bedtime Stories: In Easy-to-Read Type. Kliros, Thea, illus. (p. 1812)
—Uncle Wiggily in the Country. (p. 1812)
—Uncle Wiggily on the Farm. (p. 1812)
—Uncle Wiggily's Adventures. (p. 1812)
—Uncle Wiggily's Airship. (p. 1812)
—Uncle Wiggily's Automobile. (p. 1812)
—Uncle Wiggily's Fortune. (p. 1812)
—Uncle Wiggily's Happy Days. (p. 1812)
—Uncle Wiggily's Travels. (p. 1812)
Garis, Lilian C. Girl Scout Pioneers; or, Winning the First B.C. (p. 679)
—Let's Play Circus. (p. 1000)
Garisch, Dawn. Babyshoes. (p. 129)
Garland, Betsy. Golden Rule. (p. 695)
Garland, Hamlin. Long Trail. (p. 1047)
Garland, Lynn Rockwell, illus. see Coppage, Merry Ann.

Garland, Michael. Americana Adventure. (p. 64)
—Car Goes Far. Garland, Michael, illus. (p. 265)
—Fish Had a Wish. Garland, Michael, illus. (p. 598)
—Grandpa's Tractor. Garland, Michael, illus. (p. 710)
—Hooray José! Garland, Michael, illus. (p. 796)
—King Puck. Garland, Michael, illus. (p. 959)
—Last Night at the Zoo. (p. 978)
—Last Night at the Zoo. Garland, Michael, illus. (p. 978)
—Lost Dog. (p. 1055)
—Miss Smith & the Haunted Library. (p. 1152)
—Miss Smith & the Haunted Library. Garland, Michael, illus. (p. 1152)
—Miss Smith Reads Again! (p. 1152)
—Miss Smith Reads Again! Garland, Michael, illus. (p. 1152)
—Miss Smith under the Ocean. Garland, Michael, illus. (p. 1152)
—Miss Smith's Incredible Storybook. (p. 1152)
—Miss Smith's Incredible Storybook. Garland, Michael, illus. (p. 1152)
—Oh, What a Christmas! Garland, Michael, illus. (p. 1281)
—Super Snow Day Seek & Find. (p. 1682)
—Tugboat. Garland, Michael, illus. (p. 1796)
—Where's My Homework? Garland, Michael, illus. (p. 1910)
Garland, Michael, illus. see Bertram, Debbie & Bloom, Susan.
Garland, Michael, illus. see Bloom, Susan & Bertram, Debbie.
Garland, Michael, illus. see Cuyler, Margery.
Garland, Michael, illus. see Keane, Michael.
Garland, Michael, illus. see Kroll, Steven & Droll.
Garland, Michael, illus. see Kroll, Steven.
Garland, Michael, illus. see Lord, Michelle.
Garland, Michael, illus. see O'Brien, Kathryn.
Garland, Michael, illus. see Patterson, James.
Garland, Michael, illus. see Tompert, Ann.
Garland, Michael, illus. see York, J.
Garland, Michael, jt. auth. see Estefan, Gloria.
Garland, Nicholas, illus. see McHenry, Eric.
Garland, Nick, jt. auth. see Phillips, Shannon.
Garland, Peter, jt. auth. see Warner, Emilia.
Garland, Sally Anne. Share. Garland, Sally Anne, illus. (p. 1561)
Garland, Sarah. Azzi in Between. (p. 122)
—Doing Christmas. (p. 463)
—Eddie's Garden: And How to Make Things Grow. (p. 503)
—Eddie's Kitchen. (p. 503)
—Eddie's Toolbox: And How to Make & Mend Things. (p. 504)
—Splash! (p. 1629)
Garland, Sarah & Quarto Generic Staff. Doing the Washing. (p. 463)
—Going Swimming. (p. 693)
—Going to Playschool. (p. 693)
Garland, Sherry. Best Horse on the Force (p. 170)
—Buffalo Soldier Himler, Ronald, illus. (p. 236)
—Children of the Dragon: Selected Tales from Vietnam Hyman, Trina Schart, illus. (p. 302)
—Lotus Seed. Kiuchi, Tatsuro, illus. (p. 1057)
—Voices of Gettysburg Hierstein, Judith, illus. (p. 1848)
—Voices of Pearl Harbor Johnson, Layne, illus. (p. 1848)
—Voices of the Alamo Himler, Ronald, illus. (p. 1848)
—Voices of the Dust Bowl Hierstein, Judith, illus. (p. 1848)
Garlando, Luigi. Gran Equipo: Gol 1. (p. 706)
—Union Hace la Fuerza: ¡Gol! (p. 1818)
—¡Nos Vamos a Brasil! ¡Gol! (p. 1266)
Garlick, Kim. Thank You. (p. 1725)
Garlick, Mark A. Astronomy Garlick, Mark A., illus. (p. 109)
—Atlas of the Universe. (p. 113)
—Universo en Expansion. Barois, Valerian Stooper, tr. (p. 1821)
Garlick, Mark A., illus. see Goldsmith, Mike.
Garlid, Ann, tr. see Koch, Miriam.
Garlington, Shudonica. I'm the Princess & My Daddy's My King. (p. 860)
Garlington, William R. Great Divide: Coloring & Activity Book. (p. 715)
—Great Divide: The Adventures of Billy Bean & Bobby Nut. (p. 715)
Garlock, Dorothy. Mother Road. (p. 1178)
Garlock, H. B. & Garlock, Ruthanne. Before We Kill & Eat You: The Miracles & Adventures of a Pioneer Missionary Couple in Africa. (p. 159)
Garlock, Ruthanne, jt. auth. see Garlock, H. B.
Garlock, Ruthanne, jt. auth. see Sherrer, Quin, Sr.
Garman, E. Thomas & Forgue, Raymond E. Personal Finance Handbook: A Guide to Securing Your Financial Future. (p. 1344)
Garmon, Anita. Alexander Graham Bell Invents. (p. 36)
Garmon, Larry Mike. Calamari Code: an Agatha Pixie Mystery. (p. 252)
Garn, Laura Aimee. Bella Basset Ballerina. Sokolova, Valerie, illus. (p. 162)
Garneau, Jean-Yves. Bedtime Prayers. (p. 157)
Garner, Alan. Elidor. (p. 512)
—Moon of Gomrath: A Tale of Alderley. (p. 1172)
—Owl Service. (p. 1315)
—Red Shift. (p. 1455)
—Weirdstone of Brisingamen: A Tale of Alderley. (p. 1873)
Garner, Albert. Adventures of Dimi. (p. 17)
Garner, Alex, ed. see Oprisko, Kris.
Garner, Andrew, jt. auth. see Horst, Heather A.
Garner, Carolyn. Teaching Library Media Skills in Grades K-6: A How-to-Do-It Manual. (p. 1710)
Garner, Eleanor Ramrath & Ramrath Garner, Eleanor. Eleanor's Story: An American Girl in Hitler's Germany (p. 508)
Garner, Ellen. Santa's Elves & the Tickets. Street, James, illus. (p. 1513)
Garner, Essex, illus. see Garner, Lama.
Garner, Jazzy. Cotton Tales of Pippa the Bunny. (p. 369)
Garner, Lama. Children's Book of Barack Obama Our 44th President. Garner, Essex, illus. (p. 303)
Garner, Linda. Some Secrets Hurt: A Story of Healing. Speth, Brandilyn, illus. (p. 1609)
Garner, Lynne. African Crafts: Fun Things to Make & Do from West Africa. (p. 27)
Garner, Phillip. Biff Cardova from Rooster Poot Kansas. (p. 177)
Garner, Simon. Berlin. Hunt, Miguel, photos by. (p. 167)
Garnett, Emmeline. Florence Nightingale's Nuns. (p. 606)
Garnett, Jana. How the Caterpillar Got Its Wings: (How Acknowledging Your Feelings Can Give You Flight) (p. 813)
Garnett, Kaila, jt. auth. see Taylor, Derrick.
Garnett, Sammie & Pallotta, Jerry. U. S. Navy Alphabet Book. Bolster, Rob, illus. (p. 1807)
Garnett, Sandy, creator. Rainbow Riders. (p. 1435)
Garnett, Tarreka. Sleepover. Damon Danielson, illus. (p. 1589)
Garns, Allen, illus. see Clark, Georgia.
Garns, Allen, illus. see Gauch, Sarah.
Garns, Allen, illus. see Penner, Lucille Recht.
Garnsey, Wayne, ed. see Pickles, Jonathan & Van Ackooy, Maureen.
Garnsey, Wayne, illus. see Milanese, Celestine Marie & Peck, Carolyn.
Garnsworthy, Marlo, ed. see Hayes, Kate.
Garnvin, Rebecka, illus. see Liddle, Sharon.
Garofalo, Gianluca, illus. see Jeffrey, Gary.
Garofalo, Rob, Jr. Winner by Any Standard: A Personal Growth Journey for Every American Teen. (p. 1937)
Garofoli, Viviana. Halloween Hugs: A HUGS Book. (p. 737)
Garofoli, Viviana, illus. see Auerbach, Annie.
Garófoli, Viviana, illus. see Genhart, Michael.
Garofoli, Viviana, illus. see Hall, Kirsten.
Garofoli, Viviana, illus. see Hubbell, Patricia.
Garofoli, Viviana, illus. see Inches, Alison.
Garofoli, Viviana, illus. see Kleiner, Mariela.
Garófoli, Viviana, illus. see Kochan, Vera.
Garofoli, Viviana, illus. see Kohuth, Jane.
Garofoli, Viviana, illus. see London, Jonathan.
Garofoli, Viviana, illus. see Man-Kong, Mary.
Garófoli, Viviana, illus. see Newman, Tracy.
Garofoli, Viviana, illus. see Park, Barbara.
Garófoli, Viviana, illus. see Rostoker-Gruber, Karen.
Garofoli, Viviana, illus. see Salas, Laura Purdie.
Garofoli, Viviana, illus. see Wolf, Jackie.
Garofoli, Wendy. Dancing with a Crew Vol. 4 (p. 403)
—Hip-Hop Culture (p. 780)
—Hip-Hop Dancing (p. 780)
—Hip-Hop History (p. 780)
—Popping, Locking, & Everything in Between (p. 1384)
Garofoli, Wendy & Garofoli Zamora, Wendy. Irish Step Dancing (p. 888)
—Swing Dancing (p. 1691)
Garofoli Zamora, Wendy. Hip-Hop History [Scholastic]. (p. 780)
Garofoli Zamora, Wendy, jt. auth. see Garofoli, Wendy.
Garon, Pierre, tr. see Down, Heather.
Garr, Hillary. Dino the Dog & His Day in the Country. Kirton, Pamela T., illus. (p. 441)
Garr, Rebecca. Adventures of Baroness of the Arizona Desert. Davisson, Vanessa, illus. (p. 16)
Garralón, Ana, et al. Si Ves un Monte de Espuma y Otros Poemas. Novoa, Teresa, tr. (p. 1572)
Garratt, Irene Joyce. Andrew's Activities: Two in One Stories. (p. 72)
—Happy Birthday: Two in One Stories. (p. 744)
Garratt, Richard. France (p. 627)
—United Kingdom (p. 1819)
Garratt, Richard, illus. see Allaby, Michael.
Garratt, Richard, illus. see Day, Trevor.
Garratt, Richard, illus. see Moore, Peter D.
Garratt, Richard, jt. auth. see Moore, Peter D.
Garraway, Kym, illus. see Remson, Billie.
Garraway, Kym W., illus. see Remson, Billie.
Garrelts, Christopher. Squarey Head Tells a Lie. Mayabb, Darrell, ed. (p. 1636)
Garretson, Dee. Wildfire Run. (p. 1931)
—Wolf Storm. (p. 1944)
Garretson, Jerri. Johnny Kaw: The Pioneer Spirit of Kansas. Dollar, Diane, illus. (p. 923)
—Kansas Tall Tales: Tenth Anniversary Anthology. Garretson, Jerri & Dollar, Diane A., illus. (p. 943)
—Twister Twyla: The Kansas Cowgirl. Dollar, Diane, illus. (p. 1803)
Garrett, Ann & Higney, Gene-Michael. Fins & Flippers, Scales & Nippers. (p. 589)
Garrett, Bradley. Learn to Say Your ABC's: With Help from the Holy Bible. (p. 984)
Garrett, Brandon. Right to Privacy. (p. 1472)
Garrett, Byron. ABC's of Life. (p. 4)
Garrett, Caroline S., illus. see Hicks, Esther & Hicks, Jerry.
Garrett, Caroline S., illus. see Hicks, Esther, et al.
Garrett, Caroline S., illus. see Ledbetter, Penny S.
Garrett, Caroline S., illus. see Underhill, Marjorie Fay.
Garrett, Caroline S., tr. see Underhill, Marjorie Fay.
Garrett, Christine. Dream Bunny's Tales - Saving the Land of Dreams. (p. 483)
Garrett, Cindy Crawford. Life's Lessons with the Silly Animals Out on the Ranch: What Is Wrong with Bob the Rooster? (p. 1013)
Garrett, Corrie. Aspen Experiments. (p. 107)
Garrett, Dan, ed. Friends & Neighbors. (p. 638)
—Girls. (p. 679)
—Masks & Faces. (p. 1102)
—Scapegoats. (p. 1519)
—Upheavals. (p. 1824)
Garrett, Debbie. Black Dolls: A Comprehensive Guide to Celebrating, Collecting, & Experiencing the Passion. (p. 196)
Garrett, Desta, ed. see Frank, Arnold L.
Garrett, Diane Marie. Buger the Butterfly & the Lion Kitties' First Adventure. Gulley, Hardrick M., illus. (p. 236)
Garrett, Ginger. Scientists Ask Questions. (p. 1528)
—Solids, Liquids, & Gases. (p. 1608)
Garrett, Jacqueline, photos by see Kirst, Kathleen & Kirst, Kat.
Garrett, Keith, illus. see Williams, Mark.
Garrett, Kelsey. Lennie's Pennies. Kopler, Joe, illus. (p. 991)
Garrett, Kenneth, photos by see Clifford, Barry.
Garrett, Leslie, jt. auth. see Jenner, Caryn.
Garrett, Leslie & Dorling Kindersley Publishing Staff. Earth Smart, Level 2. (p. 497)
—Helen Keller. (p. 762)
—Helen Keller, Level 3. (p. 763)
Garrett, Lisa. Four Little Chicks. (p. 625)
Garrett, Lyn. Horatio & the Sea Tornado. (p. 797)
Garrett, Meredith. Penny & the Polka Dot Shoes. (p. 1338)
Garrett, Myers, illus. see Moore, Mykela.
Garrett, Nicole. Cupid Factor. (p. 392)
Garrett, Scott, illus. see Oliver, Lin & Winkler, Henry.
Garrett, Scott, illus. see Winkler, Henry & Oliver, Lin.
Garrett, Stephanie. Girl's Guide to Wisdom & Virtue: Being a Lady in a Modern World. (p. 680)
Garrett, Tiffany & Seaman, Jim. Miami University of Ohio College Prowler off the Record. (p. 1134)
Garrett, Toni, illus. see Alston, E. B.
Garrett, Troy. Kramer's World. (p. 967)
Garrett, Winston. Let's Ride the School Bus! (p. 1000)
—What Does a Library Media Specialist Do? (p. 1883)
—What Does a Library Media Specialist Do? (¿Qué Hace el Especialista de Medios de la Biblioteca Escolar?) de la Vega, Eida, ed. (p. 1883)
—What Does the School Nurse Do? (p. 1884)
—What Does the School Nurse Do? (¿Qué Hace la Enfermera de la Escuela?) de la Vega, Eida, ed. (p. 1884)
—¡Vamos a Tomar el Autobús Escolar! / Let's Ride the School Bus! de la Vega, Eida, ed. (p. 1831)
Garrick, Lainie. Losing Papou: One Child's Journey Towards Understanding & Accepting Death. Mandarino, Gene, illus. (p. 1054)
Garrick, Veda. Place: Jello. (p. 1365)
Garrido, Felipe. Coyote Tonto. Gonzalez, Francisco, illus. (p. 374)
Garrido, Maria Teresa. Bernardo el Ermitano. (p. 167)
Garrido, Pedro Gelabert. Libro del Abuelo: Un Mundo de Aventuras Entre la Realidad y la Fantasma. Velert, Miriam, illus. (p. 1006)
Garriel, Barbara. I Know a Shy Fellow Who Swallowed a Cello. O'Brien, John, illus. (p. 840)
Garriel, Barbara S. I Know a Shy Fellow Who Swallowed a Cello. O'Brien, John, illus. (p. 840)
Garrigue, Roland, illus. see Leblanc, Catherine.
Garrigus, J. Encyclopedia of the Caribbean (p. 525)
Garrington, Sally. Focus on the United States. (p. 611)
—New York. Fairclough, Chris, photos by. (p. 1247)
Garrington, Sally, jt. auth. see Brooks, Clare.
Garris, Norma. Story of Christmas. (p. 1657)
Garris, Rebekah. Whither Thou Goest, I Will Go. (p. 1914)
Garrison, Barbara, illus. see Scheffrin-Falk, Gladys.
Garrison, Carri, illus. see Morgan, Marlo.
Garrison, Chris. If I Were a Tree. (p. 853)
—Ten Pickle Pie. (p. 1719)
Garrison, Gene K. Javelina: Have-Uh-What? (p. 910)
Garrison, Ron, illus. see Pearce, Claudia & Worley, Karen E.
Garrison, Ron, photos by see Pearce, Claudia & Worley, Karen E.
Garrison, Sue, illus. see Estes, Don.
Garrison, Tommy. Imagination Celebration. (p. 860)
Garrity, Jane & Doan, Laura, eds. Sapphic Modernities: Sexuality, Women & National Culture. (p. 1514)
Garrity, Jennifer Johnson. Calendar Quest: A 5,000 Year Trek Through Western History with Father Time. (p. 252)
Garrity-Riley, Kelsey, illus. see Krasner, Barbara.
Garrott, Dawn E. How Riley Rescued the Huffy Woofer. Mazibuko, Luthando, illus. (p. 812)
—How Riley Tamed the Invisible Monster. (p. 812)
Garrow, Linda, illus. see Evert, Laura.
Garrow, Rhonda. Michaela & the Christmas Village. (p. 1135)
—Saber & the Onion. (p. 1499)
Garry, J. W. Storm's Maine Vacation. (p. 1656)
Garry-McCord, Kathleen & Sonsky, Kim. Stamp It! Brush-Free Art Prints & Paint Projects. Sonsky, Kim, illus. (p. 1639)
Garsee, Jeannine. Before, after, & Somebody in Between. (p. 158)
—Say the Word. (p. 1518)
—Unquiet. (p. 1822)
Garsee, Linmarie. Annabelle's Vacation with Grandma Hayley: A Mountain Quiltfest Adventure. (p. 85)
Garside, Jeff. Extreme Environments: Living on the Edge. (p. 556)
Garson, Cindy. Welcome to Kristy's Farm, Book 2 (Black & White Version) (p. 1873)
—Welcome to Kristy's Farm, Book 4. (p. 1873)
Garson, Sarah. Daydream Dan. (p. 415)
—One, Two, Cockatoo! Garson, Sarah, illus. (p. 1297)
Garson, Sarah, illus. see Bankow, Henriette.
Garson, Sarah, illus. see Barkow, Henriette.
Garson, Sol, et al. Espaanol Mundial. (p. 536)
—Espanol Mundial 2. (p. 536)
—Libro de Ejercicios. (p. 1006)
Garst, Shannon. Silver Spurs for Cowboy Boots. Hargens, Charles, illus. (p. 1577)
Garstang, Michael. Ntombazana: A Story of an African Elephant Family. (p. 1269)
Garstecki, Julia. Life During the Industrial Revolution. (p. 1010)
—Life in Colonial America. (p. 1010)
—Rev up Your Writing in Informational Texts. Gallagher-Cole, Mernie, illus. (p. 1465)
—Rev up Your Writing in Nonfiction Narratives. Gallagher-Cole, Mernie, illus. (p. 1465)
Garstecki, Julia & Benchmark Education Co. Staff. Childhood in Different Times & Places. (p. 302)
Garth, M. & Garth, Maureen. Jardin Interior. (p. 909)
Garth, Maureen, jt. auth. see Garth, M.
Garth, Richard & Duncan, Vicky. Rabbits & Snakes. (p. 1430)
Garthwaite, Lynn D. Dirkle Smat Inside Mount Flatbottom. Howarth, Craig, illus. (p. 445)
Gartlan, Daniel. Poor Hannah. (p. 1383)
Gartland, Robert A. Cowboys & Cattle. (p. 374)
Gartner, Hans & Poppel, Hans. Osito ILmpio y Osito Sucio. (p. 1305)
Gartner, Kathleen, illus. see Aboff, Marcie.
Garton, Carol. Isabella Barella. (p. 891)
—Land of Carin. (p. 973)
Garton, Keith & Cutler, Nelida Gonzalez, eds. Time for Kids World Atlas. (p. 1751)
Garton, Kevan. Cockleton Mystery. (p. 337)
Garton, Leora, jt. auth. see Rubin, Barry M.
Garton, Michael. Countdown by the Sea. (p. 370)
Garton, Michael, illus. see Askew, Amanda & Marleau, Eve.
Garton, Michael, illus. see Marleau, Eve.
Garton, Sam. I Am Otter. Garton, Sam, illus. (p. 833)
—Otter in Space. Garton, Sam, illus. (p. 1307)
—Otter Loves Halloween! Garton, Sam, illus. (p. 1307)
Garty, Judy. Jeff Bezos: Business Genius of Amazon.com. (p. 911)
—Marching Band Competition. (p. 1091)
Garver, Lorie. Alligators. (p. 47)
Garver, Marianne & Garver, Mary. October's Promise: A Turtle Cove Novel. (p. 1277)
Garver, Mary, jt. auth. see Garver, Marianne.
Garver, Sonya. Peanut Butter Jelly Gang & Grandpa's Gift. (p. 1332)
Garvey, Amy. Cold Kiss. (p. 338)
—Glass Heart. (p. 682)
Garvey, Brann, illus. see Cosson, M. J.
Garvey, Brann, illus. see Gallagher, Diana G.
Garvey, Brann, illus. see MacPhail, C. & Cosson, M. J.
Garvey, Brann, illus. see Peschke, Marci & Townson, H.
Garvey, Brann, illus. see Peschke, Marci.
Garvey, Brann, illus. see Tayleur, Karen.
Garvey, Brann, illus. see Welvaert, Scott R.
Garvey, Brann, illus. see Welvaert, Scott R. & Jungman, Ann.
Garvey, James W. St. Paul Cathedral Parish: The Early Years - 1834-1903. (p. 1638)
Garvin, Elaine, illus. see Allan-Meyer, Kathleen.
Garvin, Elaine, illus. see Cowan, Charlotte.
Garvin, Elaine, illus. see Gutman, Dan.
Garvin, Elaine, illus. see Pingry, Patricia A.
Garvin, Elaine, illus. see Ross, Kathy.
Garvin, Elaine, illus. see Youd, Pauline.
Garvin, Kelly, illus. see Preszler, June.
Garvin, Kelly, illus. see Richardson, Adele & Richardson, Adele D.
Garvin, Mal. Christmas Gift: At a Time Christmas Is Leaving Many People Jaded, These Warm Hearted, Humorous Christmas Stories That Lift the Spirit, Come from Radio Spots by Award Winning Australian Broadcaster Mal Garvin, Compiled by His Wife Jenny. (p. 314)
Garvin, Sheri, illus. see Franck, Charlotte.
Garwin, Elaine & Youd, Pauline. Wonder Bible Storybook: 12 Little Stories for Little People. Scandinavia Publishing House Staff, ed. (p. 1947)
Garwood, Gord, illus. see Friedman, Becky.
Garwood, Gord, jt. illus. see Style Guide Staff.
Garwood, Mary. Pawprints upon My Heart II: The Journey Continues. (p. 1331)
Gary Clanciarulo, Gary, illus. see Scott, Robbie.
Gary, Glenn, illus. see VanRiper, Justin & VanRiper, Gary.
Gary, Ken, tr. Fire Stealers: A Hopi Story. (p. 591)
Gary, Litvin, ed. see Howell, Mark & Montgomery, Martha.
Gary, Meredith. Sometimes You Get What You Want. Brown, Lisa, illus. (p. 1610)
Gary, Paulsen. Hatchet. (p. 752)
—Nightjohn. (p. 1255)
Gary R Kirby. Stories of Sunshine & Funtime of Wonder & Thunder of Mystery & Magic for the Young to Grow On. (p. 1655)
Gary, Richard. Double Dare. (p. 472)
—My Dream. (p. 1202)
—Safari. (p. 1501)
Gary Ripper, illus. see Brice, Ginny.
Gary, Romain. Vie Devant Soi (p. 1841)
Garza, Amy Ammons. Sterlen: And a Mosaic of Mountain Women. Ammons, David F. & Ammons, Sherilyn, eds. (p. 1648)
Garza, Amy Ammons, ed. see Pafford, Nancy McIntosh.
Garza, Armando N. Itty Bitty & the Hide & Seek Adventure. (p. 900)
—Itty Bitty Saves the Day. (p. 900)
Garza, Ben. Entre Suenos. Julieta, Iria, illus. (p. 531)
Garza, Carmen Lomas. Cuadros de Familia. (p. 388)
—In My Family. (p. 864)
—Magic Windows: Ventanas Magicas. (p. 1074)
—Making Magic Windows. (p. 1081)
—Vejigante-Masquerader. (p. 1835)
Garza, Fabiola. Story of Saint John Paul II: A Boy Who Became Pope. Garza, Fabiola, illus. (p. 1659)
Garza, Francisco Xavier Gonzalez. "El Espiritu de Dios en la Ciencia" (p. 507)
Garza, Jenny. Beautiful. (p. 153)
Garza, Lois Ann. Lellie the Different Elephant. Martinez-Neal, Juana, illus. (p. 991)
Garza, R. Baby Blue Egg's Big Adventure. (p. 125)
Garza, Ray. Captain Christian. (p. 263)
Garza, Sarah. Action! Making Movies. (p. 10)
Garza, Xavier. Charro Claus & the Tejas Kid. (p. 294)
—Creepy Creatures & Other Cucuys. (p. 381)
—Great & Mighty Nikko. (p. 713)
—Juan & the Chupacabras/Juan y el Chupacabras. Ward, April, illus. (p. 930)
—Kid Cyclone Fights Devil & Other Stories/Kid Ciclon Se Enfrenta a el Diablo y Otras Historias. Ventura, Gabriela Baeza, tr. from ENG. (p. 951)
—Lucha Libre: The Man in the Silver Mask - A Bilingual Cuento. Garza, Xavier, illus. (p. 1062)
—Lucha Libre: The Man in the Silver Mask - A Bilingual Cuento. Crosthwaite, Luis Humberto, tr. (p. 1062)
—Maximilian & the Bingo Rematch: A Lucha Libre Sequel. (p. 1112)
—Maximilian & the Mystery of the Guardian Angel. (p. 1112)

G

Garza, Xavier & Villarroel, Carolina. Zulema & the Witch Owl/Zulema y la Bruja Lechuza. Garza, Xavier, illus. (p. 1990)
Gasal, Ben, illus. see Daugherty, Doug.
Gasca, Theresa & Juarez, Amanda. Mere Words Can Only Say... (p. 1127)
Gascoigne, Ingrid. Papua New Guinea. (p. 1323)
Gascoigne, John. Captain Cook: Voyager Between Worlds. (p. 264)
Gascoigne, Martin, jt. auth. see London, Jack.
Gascot, John, jt. auth. see Stout, Mary Gallagher.
Gash, Amy. What the Dormouse Said: Lessons for Grown-Ups from Children's Books. Le-Tan, Pierre, illus. (p. 1893)
Gashler, Stephen. Bent Sword. (p. 165)
Gaslor, Julie. Samy the Star. (p. 1510)
Gaskill, Rachel. Agnes de Mille. (p. 29)
—Agnes Demille. (p. 29)
Gaskin, Terri. Me & My Brother: Coloring Book. (p. 1115)
—Me & My Brother. (p. 1115)
Gasking, Terry, ed. see Pritchard, Mary.
Gaskins, Matthew D., tr. see Farquharson, Alex, et al.
Gaskins, Melda. Anit: The Chef. Kauffin, Karlynn, illus. (p. 84)
Gaskins, Pearl Fuyo. I Believe In... Christian, Jewish, & Muslim Young People Speak about Their Faiths. (p. 834)
Gaskins, Renee Guerry. Kevin Blue Can't Moo: And He Doesn't Know What to Do! (p. 949)
Gaskins, Terry & Treigle, Jimmy. Very Big Storm: Created by Terry Gaskins Inspired by Jimmy Treigle. (p. 1837)
Gasmen, Imelda Fines. Tuttle Tagalog for Kids. (p. 1799)
Gasmen, Imelda Fines, ed. see Fancy, Robin Lyn & Welch, Vala Jeanne.
Gasnick, Roy M. & Grycan, Julien. Serra: American Founding Father. (p. 1552)
Gasol, Anna, tr. see Plessix, Michel.
Gaspar, Joe. Albert Pujols: Amazing Hitter. (p. 34)
—Albert Pujols. (p. 34)
—Alex Rodriguez. (p. 36)
—Bald Eagle. (p. 133)
—Bald Eagle / el Guila Calva. Alamn, Eduardo, ed. (p. 133)
—Dustin Pedroia: Rising Star. (p. 490)
—Dustin Pedroia. (p. 490)
—Flag. (p. 601)
—Flag / la Bandera. Alamn, Eduardo, ed. (p. 601)
—Jimmy Rollins. (p. 918)
—Justin Morneau. (p. 940)
—Liberty Bell. (p. 1005)
—Liberty Bell / la Campana de la Libertad. Alamn, Eduardo, ed. (p. 1005)
—National Anthem. (p. 1231)
—National Anthem / el Himno Nacional. Alamn, Eduardo, ed. (p. 1231)
—Ryan Howard. (p. 1499)
—Statue of Liberty. (p. 1645)
—Statue of Liberty / la Estatua de la Libertad. Alamn, Eduardo, ed. (p. 1645)
—White House. (p. 1913)
—White House / la Casa Blanca. Alamn, Eduardo, ed. (p. 1913)
Gaspar, Joe & Weaver, Jack. Hunting. (p. 829)
Gaspar, Julian, et al. Introduction to Business. (p. 882)
Gaspar, Tamas, illus. see Riordan, Rick & Venditti, Robert.
Gaspard, Helen. Doctor Dan the Bandage Man. (p. 459)
Gasparro, Marie, jt. auth. see Falletta, Bernadette.
Gasparro, Marie & Falletta, Bernadette. Magnificent Hole. (p. 1076)
Gaspas, Diane & Creative Haven Staff. Creative Haven Chinese Designs Coloring Book. (p. 379)
Gaspas, Dianne. Southwest Indian Designs Coloring Book. (p. 1618)
Gass, Britney. C a P S. (p. 249)
Gass, Justin T. Alcohol. (p. 35)
Gass, Kenneth. Trilobites! (p. 1786)
Gass, Marja, tr. see Parkkola, Seita.
Gassler, Stephen, III, illus. see Schreck, Karen Halvorsen.
Gassman, Julie. Crabby Pants Watson, Richard, illus. (p. 375)
Gassman, Julie A. Cheerleading Really Is a Sport Santillan, Jorge H., illus. (p. 296)
—Crabby Pants Watson, Richard, illus. (p. 375)
—Eleanore Won't Share Mikhail, Jessica, illus. (p. 508)
—I Am on Strike Against Softball Santillan, Jorge H., illus. (p. 833)
—Lucille Gets Jealous Cooke, Charlotte, illus. (p. 1062)
—Nobody Wants to Play with a Ball Hog Santillan, Jorge H., illus. (p. 1262)
—Skating Is Hard When You're Homesick Santillan, Jorge H., illus. (p. 1584)
—You Can't Spike Your Serves Santillan, Jorge H., illus. (p. 1975)
—You Get What You Get Home, Sarah, illus. (p. 1975)
Gassman, Nathan, des. Math Fun Carabelli, Francesca, illus. (p. 1106)
Gassman, Nelson, jt. auth. see Parenzini, Charity.
Gassmann, Janice. Mimi's Happy Box. (p. 1145)
Gassós, Dolors, jt. auth. see Parramon Staff.
Gast, Christy & Krug, Jane. Caring for Myself: A Social Skills Storybook. (p. 269)
Gast, Linda, photos by see Frank, Rochelle.
Gastaldo, Walter, illus. see Barsy, Kalman.
Gastel, Tiffany & Benchmark Education Co. Staff. Red-Tail Angels. (p. 1455)
Gaster, Lucy & Squires, Amanda. Providing Quality in the Public Sector: A Practical Approach to Improving Public Services. (p. 1413)
Gaster, Valerie Land. Jesus Loves the Easter Bunny. (p. 916)
Gasteva, Julia, ed. see AZ Books Staff.
Gastineau, John. Nuclear Radiation with Vernier. (p. 1270)
gaston, carter j. How Do You Know When It's Time to Go to Bed? (p. 808)
Gaston, Carter J., illus. see Gaston, P. J.
Gaston County Museum of Art & History, ed. Secret Adventures of Hamster Sam: Attack of the Evil Boll Weevils! (p. 1540)
Gaston, Keith A., illus. see Pyatt, Sue.
Gaston, P. J. How Do You Know When It's Time to Go to Bed? Gaston, Carter J., illus. (p. 808)
Gaston, Sharon D. Clean Your Own House & Misery Loves Company. (p. 330)
—Who's Laughing Now? & Don't Burn Your Bridge. (p. 1920)
Gaston, Sierra, illus. see Wiedeman, Connie.
Gasztold, Carmen B. De, see De Gasztold, Carmen B.
Gatacre, Sophie. Please Don't Call Me Mad! (p. 1373)
Gatagan, T., illus. see Byars, Betsy.
Gatagán, Tino, tr. Poesía Española para Niños. (p. 1376)
Gatchell, Christine. Elementary Greek: Koine for Beginners: Year Three Textbook. (p. 510)
—Elementary Greek: Year Three Workbook: Koine for Beginners. Bogost, Abbey, ed. (p. 510)
Gatehouse, John. Demons & Elementals Windett, Dave, illus. (p. 426)
—Flying Fiends & Gruesome Creatures Windett, Dave, illus. (p. 610)
—Man-Monsters & Animal Horrors. Windett, Dave, illus. (p. 1085)
—Undead & Water Beasts Windett, Dave, illus. (p. 1813)
Gateley, Edwina. God Goes on Vacation. Gateley, Edwina, illus. (p. 688)
—God Goes to School. (p. 689)
Gatell, Angelina. Mis Primeras Lecturas Poeticas. (p. 1150)
Gateman, Ryan, creator. Spelling the Number Words: From a Child's View. (p. 1625)
Gates, Alexander E. & Ritchie, David. Encyclopedia of Earthquakes & Volcanoes. (p. 525)
Gates, Donald, illus. see Shelton, Rick.
Gates Ed D., James Terry. Georgie's Saturday Quest. (p. 665)
Gates Galvin, Laura. Alphabet of Art. Tabbutt, Steven, illus. (p. 49)
—de Adorable: Un Abecedario Fabuloso. Schwaeber, Barbie Heit, ed. (p. 416)
—First Look at Insects. Oh, Charlotte, illus. (p. 596)
Gates, Henry Louis, Jr., ed. see Crafts, Hannah.
Gates, Henry Louis, Jr., ed. see Gates, J.
Gates, J. Norton Anthology of African American Literature: Course Guide. Gates, Henry Louis, Jr. & McKay, Nellie Y., eds. (p. 1266)
Gates, J. F. Children of the White Tree: Brady Barrett & the Firstlings Assignment. (p. 302)
Gates, J. Gabriel & Keel, Charlene. Dark Territory. (p. 408)
—Ghost Crown. (p. 670)
Gates, Jeremy S., jt. auth. see Thorsen, Jody.
Gates, Josephine Scribner. April fool Doll. Keep, Virginia, illus. (p. 93)
—Captain Billie: Leads the way to the land of I don't want To. Sichel, Harold, illus. (p. 263)
—dolls in Fairyland. Keep, Virginia, illus. (p. 464)
—land of Delight: Child life on a Pony Farm. (p. 973)
—Little girl Blue: Lives in the woods till she learns to say Please. Keep, Virginia, illus. (p. 1028)
—Little Girl Blue plays I Spy. (p. 1028)
—Little red white & Blue. Keep, Virginia, illus. (p. 1035)
—Live Doll Series (p. 1039)
—live dolls' busy Days. Keep, Virginia, illus. (p. 1039)
—live dolls' house Party. Keep, Virginia, illus. (p. 1039)
—live dolls in Wonderland. Keep, Virginia, illus. (p. 1039)
—live dolls' play Days. Keep, Virginia, illus. (p. 1039)
—More about live Dolls. Keep, Virginia, illus. (p. 1173)
—Nannette & the baby Monkey. (p. 1229)
—Nannette goes to visit her Grandmother. (p. 1229)
—One day in Betty,s Life. Stuart, B. S., illus. (p. 1294)
—secret of the live Dolls. Archibald, A. L., illus. (p. 1542)
—Story of Live Dolls: Being an Account of How, on a Certain June Morning. (p. 1659)
—Story of Live Dolls: Being an account by Josephine Scribner Gates of how, on a certian June morning, all of the dolls in the Cloverdale came Alive. Keep, Virginia, illus. (p. 1659)
—story of the lost Doll. Keep, Virginia, illus. (p. 1661)
—Story of the three Dolls. Keep, Virginia, illus. (p. 1662)
—Sunshine Annie. Cory, Fanny Y., illus. (p. 1678)
—Tommy Sweet-Tooth & Little girl Blue. Churbuck, Esther V., illus. (p. 1765)
—Turkey Doll. Flass, E. C., illus. (p. 1797)
Gates, Laura. Very Good Smell. (p. 1838)
Gates, Margo. Antelopes. (p. 89)
—Centipedes. (p. 287)
—Honey Badgers. (p. 794)
—Jaguars. (p. 905)
—Sea Otters. (p. 1535)
—Snails. (p. 1596)
—Wombats. (p. 1945)
Gates, Mariam. Good Night Yoga: A Pose-By-Pose Bedtime Story Hinder, Sara Jane, illus. (p. 700)
Gates, Mysti. Noises in the Night. (p. 1262)
Gates, Pat. Apple Tree's Secret Hosselkus, Devin, illus. (p. 92)
Gates, Phyllis, illus. see Woodruff, Joe.
Gates, S. P. Monster in the Mudball (p. 1167)
Gates, Susan. Mole Who was Scared of the Dark. Breakespeare, Andrew, illus. (p. 1160)
—Pirate! Band 15. McClellan, Maddy, illus. (p. 1362)
Gates, Susan & Ceredigion, Cymdeithas Lyfrau. Babi Bag Siwgwr. Williams, Dylan, tr. from ENG. (p. 123)
Gates, Valerie. Other Colors: An ABC Book. Cutting, Ann, photos by. (p. 1306)
Gatewood, June S. Mandy Miller & the Brownie Troop. Connors, Mary, illus. (p. 1087)
Gatewood, Michael A. Ziploc War. (p. 1987)
Gatheing Place Publishers. Stones' Quest Redemption of the Curse: Redemption of the Curse. (p. 1653)
Gathering Place Publisher. Stones' Quest the Battles Begin (p. 1653)
Gathering Place Publishers. Stones' Quest in Search of Its Master: In Search of Its Master. (p. 1653)
—Stones' Quest in Search of Its Master. (p. 1653)
Gathigo, Cyrus Ngatia, illus. see Resman, Michael.
Gathorne-Hardy, Jonathan. Jane's Adventures: Jane's Adventures in & Out of the Book; Jane's Adventures on the Island of Peeg; Jane's Adventures in a Balloon. Hill, Nicolas, illus. (p. 908)
Gatker, Anna & Varacalli, Lauren. Babson College College Prowler off the Record. (p. 124)
Gatlin, Shawana. Now I Lay Me down to Sleep. (p. 1269)
Gatou, Shouji. Full Metal Panic - Overload! Nagai, Tomohiro, illus. (p. 646)
Gatt, Elizabeth, illus. see Miles, Victoria.
Gatta, Frank, jt. auth. see Furgang, Kathy.
Gattegno, Caleb, jt. auth. see Educational Solutions Staff.
Gatto, Horacio, illus. see Celcer, Irene.
Gatto, Kim, illus. see Wargin, Kathy-jo.
Gatto, Kimberly. Derek Jeter: A Baseball Star Who Cares. (p. 427)
—Kevin Garnett: A Basketball Star Who Cares. (p. 950)
—LeBron James: A Basketball Star Who Cares. (p. 987)
—Lionel Messi: A Soccer Star Who Cares. (p. 1021)
—Tom Brady: Never-Quit Quarterback. (p. 1762)
Gatto, Steve. Da Curse of the Billy Goat: The Chicago Cubs, Pennant Races, & Curses. (p. 398)
Gattuso, Joan. Lotus Still Blooms: Sacred Buddhist Teachings for the Western Mind. (p. 1057)
Gatty. Parables from Nature. (p. 1323)
Gatty, Alfred. Aunt Judy's Tales. (p. 115)
—Fairy Godmothers & Other Tales. (p. 563)
—Parables from Nature. (p. 1323)
—Parables from Nature (Classic Edition) (p. 1323)
—Parables from Nature (Yesterday's Classics) (p. 1323)
Gatz, Krissandra. Secret Inside. Elliott, Jeff, illus. (p. 1541)
Gau Family Studio, illus. see Cary, Amy.
Gauch, Patricia Lee. Christina Katerina & the Box. (p. 312)
—Impossible Major Rogers. Parker, Robert Andrew, illus. (p. 862)
—Thunder at Gettysburg. Gammell, Stephen, illus. (p. 1746)
Gauch, Patricia Lee, ed. see Eric Carle Museum of Picture Book Art Staff.
GAUCH, PATRICIA LEE, jt. auth. see Gauch, Patricia Lee.
Gauch, Patricia Lee & GAUCH, PATRICIA LEE. Tanya entre Bastidores. Ichikawa, Satomi, illus. (p. 1705)
Gauch, Sarah. Tomb Robber & King Tut. Gams, Allen, illus. (p. 1764)
Gauches, Claudia, jt. auth. see Rancourt, Heather.
Gaudasinska, Elzbieta, illus. see Prokofiev, Sergei.
Gaudenzi, Giacinto, illus. see Brocklehurst, Ruth.
Gaudenzi, Giacinto, illus. see Firth, Rachel.
Gaudenzi, Giacinto, illus. see Milbourne, Anna.
Gaudet, Christine, illus. see Rath, Tom H.
Gaudet, M. K. Marley & Me: Marley to the Rescue! (p. 1095)
—Marley to the Rescue! (p. 1095)
Gaudet, Mary Kate. Peppa Pig: Coloring & Activity Book & Crayons. (p. 1340)
Gaudiamo, Adi Darda, illus. see Avery, Ben & Rogers, Bud.
Gaudiamo, Adi Darda, illus. see Avery, Ben G.
Gaudiamo, Adi Darda, illus. see Avery, Ben.
Gaudin, Thierry. Planet of Gehom. Smith, Anne & Smith, Owen, trs. from FRE. (p. 1367)
Gaudioso, John. Smoky to the Rescue. (p. 1595)
Gaudissart, Martine. My Blue Lamb. (p. 1198)
Gauger, Kathleen. If You Want to Be Happy, Give Something Away. (p. 854)
Gaughen, A. C. Lady Thief. (p. 971)
—Lion Heart. (p. 1020)
—Scarlet. (p. 1520)
Gaughen, Shasta, ed. Coping with Death. (p. 365)
Gaugler, Gil. Samantha's Coloring Box (p. 1507)
Gauld, Tom, illus. see Dumas, Alexandre.
Gaulkin, Marianne Quigley. Playdance Studio. Baker, David, illus. (p. 1372)
Gault, Linda Fufford. Chosen Tree. (p. 311)
—Help Is on the Way: The Adventures of Madame Flutterby Book Iii. (p. 765)
Gaumont Cinémathèque Muse Staff & Chronicle Books Staff. Dogs. (p. 462)
Gaumont Cinémathèque Muse Staff & Museum of Modern Art Staff. Petit Cinema - Bridge. (p. 1348)
Gausa, Manuel, et al, contrib. by. Metapolis Dictionary of Advanced Architecture. (p. 1130)
Gausden, Vicki, illus. see Dale, Elizabeth.
Gausnell, Patricia. Oklahoma Tomboy: Childhood Memoirs of Agnes Gausnell Martin. (p. 1283)
Gauss, Rose, illus. see Meyers, Susan A.
Gausselin, Richard J. How the Grandmas & Grandpas Saved Christmas. (p. 813)
Gaustad, Edwin S. Benjamin Franklin: Inventing America. (p. 165)
Gauthier, Bertrand. Abracadabra, les Jumeaux Sont La! (p. 6)
—Jumeaux Bulle Series. Dumont, Daniel, illus. (p. 933)
—Revanche d'Ani Croche. (p. 1465)
—Tenebres Piegees Jorisch, Stéphane, illus. (p. 1720)
—Zunik dans le Grand Magicien. (p. 1990)
Gauthier, Corbert, illus. see Oke, Janette.
Gauthier, Elizabeth. Bald Chimpanzee: An Adventure in ABCs. Gauthier, Elizabeth & Bonney, Joan, illus. (p. 133)
—Bald Chimpanzee, an Adventure in ABC's. Gauthier, Elizabeth, illus. (p. 133)
—Out of the Nursery. Gauthier, Elizabeth, illus. (p. 1311)
Gauthier, Gail. Happy Kid! (p. 746)
Gauthier, Gilles. Beau Valentino Sort Ses Crocs. Derome, Pierre-Andre, tr. (p. 153)
—Gros Cadeau du Petit Marcus. (p. 725)
—Petite Lili Est un Genie. Derome, Pierre-André, illus. (p. 1348)
Gauthier, Gilles & Derome, Pierre-Andre. Pas de Prison pour Chausson. (p. 1326)
—Petit Chausson, Grande Babouche. (p. 1348)
Gauthier, Glenn G. A to Z Book. Gauthier, Glenn G., illus. (p. 1)
Gauthier, James & Martin, Ed. Last Chance. (p. 977)
Gauthier, Lance C., text. One-Eared Mouse of Pasture Hill. (p. 1294)
Gauthier, Manon, illus. see Heidbreder, Robert.
Gauthier, Manon, illus. see Slodovnick, Avi.
Gauthier, Manon, illus. see Spielman, Gloria.
Gauthier, Pamela. Adventures of Bernie the Moose: Bernie Meets Maria. (p. 16)
Gauvin, Edward, tr. see Guibert, Emmanuel & Sfar, Joann.
Gauvin, Edward, tr. see Joffo, Joseph.
Gauvin, Edward, tr. see Luciani, Brigitte.
Gauvin, Edward, tr. see Richard, Laurent.
Gauvin, Edward, tr. see Trondheim, Lewis.
Gauvin, Edward, tr. I Remember Beirut. (p. 844)
Gauvin, Matthew, illus. see Da Puzzo, Allegra & Da Puzzo, Jackson.
Gavagan, Cinda J. Old Haunted House. (p. 1284)
Gavalda, Anna. 95 Libras de Esperanza. (p. 1998)
Gave, Marc. American History Adds up & la historia de los Estados Unidos en Suma: 6 English, 6 Spanish Adaptations (p. 61)
—Come y Cuenta. (p. 347)
—historia de los Estados Unidos en Suma. (p. 782)
—Human Body & el cuerpo Humano: 6 English, 6 Spanish Adaptations (p. 825)
—Juegos de números alrededor del Mundo. (p. 931)
—Math to Munch on & Come y Cuenta: 6 English, 6 Spanish Adaptations (p. 1107)
—Number Games Around the World & Juegos de números alrededor del Mundo: 6 English, 6 Spanish Adaptations (p. 1271)
Gave, Marc, jt. auth. see Brunelle, Lynn.
Gave, Marc, told to. cuerpo Humano: Set Of 6. (p. 390)
Gaven, Jim. Friends Find Fun for Food: All about Alliterations. (p. 638)
Gavet, Nathalie, illus. see Robe, Adam D.
Gavet, Nathalie, illus. see Robe, Kim.
Gavidia, Derick. Most Painful Thing in Life. (p. 1177)
Gavigan, Karen W., jt. ed. see Albright, Kendra S.
Gavila, Robert. Nisha: Montana. (p. 1257)
Gavilanes, Enrique & Inniss, Michelle. Global Language Detective. (p. 684)
Gavin, Clara. Room for Bear. (p. 1488)
Gavin, Fred. Bedtime Stories. Klemek, Ryan, illus. (p. 157)
Gavin, Jamila. Blackberry Blue & Other Fairy Tales. Collingridge, Richard, illus. (p. 197)
—Tales from India. Hall, Amanda, illus. (p. 1701)
—Three Indian Princesses: The Stories of Savitri, Damayanti & Sita. (p. 1742)
Gavin, Jamila & Quarto Generic Staff. School for Princes: Stories from the Panchatantra. Willey, Bee, illus. (p. 1523)
Gavin, Rebecca Thompson. Adventures of Oakey Dokey Acorn: Oakey & Ivy. Gavin, Rebecca Thompson, illus. (p. 21)
Gavin, Rohan. Knightley & Son - K-9. (p. 964)
Gavin, Sherrie. Baptism & Boomerangs. (p. 137)
Gavioli, Gino & Gavioli, G. Candido, el Limpiador de Chimeneas. Brignole, Giancarla, tr. (p. 261)
Gaviraghi, Giuditta, illus. see Murray, Tamsyn.
Gavlak, Lawrence. Heavenly Visitors: True Stories of Angelic Intervention & Other Heavenly Encounters. (p. 761)
Gavlak, Lawrence J. Ghosts of Pennsylvania: From Across the State & from the Gettysburg Battlefield. (p. 672)
Gavlik, Sherry, jt. auth. see Rosle, Maura.
Gavoili, G., jt. auth. see Gavioli, Gino.
Gavril, David, illus. see Van Leeuwen, Jean.
Gavrilovskiy, Olga, illus. see Hunter, T. H.
Gavrilovskiy, Olga, illus. see Hunter, Todd H.
Gawade, Akansha A. This Is Who I Am. (p. 1737)
Gawne, Jeffrey. Hermie: And the Animals' Mixed-Up Ears. (p. 771)
Gawron, Gay. New Hampshire Coloring Book. (p. 1245)
Gawronski, J. D., et al. Mathematics Assessment Sampler, Grades 3-5: Items Aligned with NCTM's Principles & Standards. (p. 1108)
Gawthrop, Shaughn, illus. see D'Arcy, Megan.
Gay, Delmas Levi. Ears at the Top of the Stairs. (p. 494)
Gay, Francis. Friendship Book. (p. 639)
—Friendship Book 2004. D C Thomson Staff, ed. (p. 639)
Gay, Homel D. On the Road Again! More Travels with My Family. Gay, Marie-Louise, illus. (p. 1291)
Gay, John. Beggar's Opera. (p. 159)
Gay, Kathlyn. Abortion: Understanding the Debate. (p. 5)
—Aftermath of the Chinese Nationalist Revolution. (p. 28)
—Aftermath of the Russian Revolution. (p. 28)
—Am I Fat? The Obesity Issue for Teens. (p. 51)
—Are You Fat? The Obesity Issue for Teens. (p. 97)
—Bigotry & Intolerance: The Ultimate Teen Guide. (p. 185)
—Body Image & Appearance: The Ultimate Teen Guide. (p. 207)
—Cultural Diversity: Conflicts & Challenges. (p. 391)
—Death & Dying A-Z: By Kathlyn Gay. (p. 420)
—Divorce: The Ultimate Teen Guide. (p. 455)
—Do You Know What to Eat? (p. 458)
—Eating Disorders: Anorexia, Bulimia & Binge Eating. (p. 501)
—Food: The New Gold. (p. 612)
—Mao Zedong's China. (p. 1089)
—Religion & Spirituality in America: The Ultimate Teen Guide. (p. 1458)
—Scoop on What to Eat: What You Should Know about Diet & Nutrition. (p. 1529)
—Volunteering: The Ultimate Teen Guide. (p. 1850)
Gay, Kathlyn & McGarrahan, Sean. Epilepsy: The Ultimate Teen Guide. (p. 532)
Gay, Maria T., illus. see Hankey, Sandy.
Gay, Marie-Louise. Buenas Noches Samuel. (p. 235)
—Buenos Dias Samuel. (p. 235)
—Caramba (p. 265)
—Estela, la Estrella del Mar. (p. 538)
—Estela, Princesa de la Noche. (p. 538)
—Fat Charlie's Circus Gay, Marie-Louise, illus. (p. 577)
—Good Morning Sam. (p. 698)
—Good Night, Sam (p. 700)
—Mademoiselle Moon Gay, Marie-Louise, illus. (p. 1070)
—Rabbit Blue (p. 1429)
—Rainy Day Magic Gay, Marie-Louise, illus. (p. 1436)
—Roslyn Rutabaga & the Biggest Hole on Earth! (p. 1490)
—Rumpelstiltskin. (p. 1495)
—Rumplestinskin. (p. 1495)
—Stella - Fairy of the Forest. (p. 1646)
—Stella, Fee des Forets. (p. 1647)
—Stella, l'Etoile de Mer. (p. 1647)
—Stella, Princess of the Sky (p. 1647)
—Stella, Queen of the Snow. (p. 1647)

—Stella, Reine des Neiges. (p. 1647)
—Stella, Star of the Sea (p. 1647)
—Summer in the City. (p. 1674)
—Sur Mon Ile. (p. 1685)
—Three Little Pigs (p. 1743)
—What Are You Doing Sam? (p. 1880)
—When Stella Was Very, Very Small (p. 1904)
Gay, Marie-Louise, illus. see Gay, Homel D.
Gay, Marie-Louise, illus. see Gillmor, Don, et al.
Gay, Marie-Louise, illus. see Gillmor, Don.
Gay, Marie-Louise, illus. see Gilmore, Don.
Gay, Marie-Louise, illus. see Howe, James.
Gay, Marie-Louise, illus. see Leblanc, Louise.
Gay, Marie-Louise, illus. see Wishinsky, Frieda.
Gay, Marie-Louise, jt. auth. see Homel, David.
Gay, Marie-Louise, tr. see Leblanc, Louise.
Gay, Michel. Bibunde. (p. 177)
—Cochecito. (p. 337)
—Croninon. (p. 384)
—Doctor Bibunde. (p. 459)
—Vez Mas. (p. 1839)
Gay, Michel, illus. see Devernois, Elsa.
Gay, Michel & Michel, Gay. provision de besos de Zea/ Zea Temporary Kisses. (p. 1413)
Gay, Michele. Leoncio's Adventures. (p. 992)
Gay, Michelle. Brain Breaks for the Classroom: Quick & Easy Breathing & Movement Activities That Help Students Reenergize, Refocus, & Boost Brain Power-Anytime of the Day! (p. 221)
Gay, Oonagh & Leopold, Patricia, eds. Conduct Unbecoming? The Regulation of Parliamentary Behaviour. Gay, Oonagh & Leopold, Patricia, trs. (p. 356)
Gay, Romney. Bonny's Wish. (p. 209)
—Conny & Uncle Dick. (p. 358)
Gayatri Stein, Mari. Puddle Moon. (p. 1414)
Gaydon, S. Activators Riding. (p. 10)
Gaydos, Nora. All about the ABC's. Sams, B. B., illus. (p. 43)
—Clever Critters. Sullivan, Mary & Gray, Steve, illus. (p. 331)
—I'M a New Big Brother: Little Steps for Big Kids. (p. 858)
—I'M a New Big Sister. Gutierrez, Akemi, illus. (p. 858)
—Look Around! Sams, B. B., illus. (p. 1048)
—Math Madness (p. 1106)
—Now I'm Growing! - A Visit to the Doctor. Gutierrez, Akemi, illus. (p. 1269)
—Now I'm Growing! - First Day of School. Gutierrez, Akemi, illus. (p. 1269)
—Now I'm Growing! Hands Are Not for Hurting. Gutierrez, Akemi, illus. (p. 1269)
—Now I'm Growing! Prince of the Potty - Little Steps for Big Kids! Gutierrez, Akemi, illus. (p. 1269)
—Now I'm Reading! Slide, See & Say Flashcards - 50 Short Vowel Words! (p. 1269)
—Now I'm Reading! - My World. Sams, B. B., illus. (p. 1269)
—Phonics Comics: Pony Tales - Level 1. Hamilton, Pamela, illus. (p. 1352)
—Playful Pals Sams, B. B., illus. (p. 1372)
—Playful Pals. Sams, B. B., illus. (p. 1372)
—Princess of the Potty - Little Steps for Big Kids! Gutierrez, Akemi, illus. (p. 1405)
—Simply Science Independent Volume 1. (p. 1578)
—Snack Attack, Level 2. Sams, B. B., illus. (p. 1595)
—Word Play: Sight Words. Sullivan, Mary, illus. (p. 1951)
Gaydos, Stellisa. Lulu the Lucky Ladybug. (p. 1065)
Gaydosik, Victoria, jt. auth. see Brackett, Mary Virginia.
Gayesky, Fernando, tr. see Brown, Monica.
Gay-Kassel, Doreen, illus. see Jones, Melanie Davis.
Gayken, D. Rae. Grandma's Baseball Card: A Braynard Family Story. (p. 708)
Gayle, Amber. On the Naive but Honorable Self-Determination of Teenage Girls: My Evil Twin Sister No. 5. (p. 1291)
Gayle, Christine. Dottie the Sock: How I Found My Pair! (p. 472)
Gayle, Emi. Night & Day. (p. 1252)
Gayle, Juliet V. Emily & Beautiful & the Great Strawberry Whipped Cream Pie Mystery. (p. 518)
Gayle, Sharon. Harriet Tubman & the Freedom Train. Marshall, Felicia, illus. (p. 750)
Gayle, Sharon, jt. auth. see Gayle, Sharon Shavers.
Gayle, Sharon Shavers. Emma's Escape: A Story of America's Underground Railroad. Velasquez, Eric, illus. (p. 520)
Gayle, Sharon Shavers & Gayle, Sharon. Teddy Roosevelt: The People's President. Dacey, Bob & Bandelin, Debra, trs. (p. 1712)
Gayle, Sherri. Bubbles of Faith. (p. 233)
Gayle, Vandercook, illus. see Robert, Lytle.
Gayle-Evans, Guda. Annotated Bibliography of Multi-Cultural Literature for Children Three to Ten Years. (p. 87)
Gaylord, Glance. Culm Rock, the Story of a Year: What it Brought & What it Taught. (p. 390)
Gaylord, Laurel Porter. Quiero a Mi Mama Porque. Wolff, Ashley, illus. (p. 1428)
Gaylord, Susan Kapuscinski & Jabbour, Joyce. Make, Draw, & Design Your Own Book. Labat, Yancey C., illus. (p. 1079)
Gaynor, Kate. Bravest Girl in School. Murphy, Aileen, illus. (p. 223)
Gayzagian, Doris K. One White Wishing Stone: A Beach Day Counting Book. Swamer, Kristina, illus. (p. 1297)
Gazarik, Rebecca Renee. Caribbean Caribou's Ancient Discovery. Patterson, Aaron James, ed. (p. 268)
Gazdag, Adam. Non Born Heir. (p. 1263)
Gazlay, Suzy. David Suzuki: Doing Battle with Climate Change. (p. 411)
—Managing Green Spaces: Careers in Wilderness & Wildlife Management. (p. 1086)
—Re-Greening the Environment: Careers in Cleanup, Remediation, & Restoration. (p. 1441)
Gazlay, Suzy, jt. auth. see Owen, Ruth.
Gazlay, Suzy & Owen, Ruth. Growing & Eating Green: Careers in Farming, Producing, & Marketing Food. (p. 726)
Gazquez, Juan Pablo Hernandez, et al. Zurdo el Que lo Lea! Ugalde, Felipe, illus. (p. 1990)
Gazsi, Benjamin, illus. see Neer, P. J.
Gaztambide-Fernandez, Ruben A. Cultural Studies & Education: Perspectives on Theory, Methodology, & Practice. (p. 391)
Gazzal, Joanne. Candle Carrie the Birthday Fairy. (p. 261)
Gazzaneo, Lucia, illus. see Brignole, Giancarla, tr.
Gbala, Deswin R. Rock University: A Collection of Short Stories & Poems. Gbala, Deswin R., illus. (p. 1482)
Ge, Tang. Dragon Emperor: A Chinese Folktale. (p. 477)
Gear, Kathleen O'Neal. It Wakes in Me. (p. 894)
Gear, Kathleen O'Neal & Gear, W. Michael. Children of the Dawnland. (p. 302)
Gear, W. Michael, jt. auth. see Gear, Kathleen O'Neal.
Geary, Cailean McCarrick. Kelsey Shining Bright. (p. 948)
Geary, Judith. Getorix: The Eagle & the Bull. (p. 668)
Geary, Leslie. Ambulances. (p. 57)
Geary, Rick, illus. see Dickens, Charles.
Geary, Rick, jt. auth. see Wells, H. G.
Geary, Steve, illus. see Everson, Chance.
Geary, William L. Scandinavian Glass: Creative Energies (p. 1519)
Geason, Susan. Flight of the Falcon. (p. 604)
Geatches, Hazel. Cities, Level 2. (p. 322)
Geatches, Hazel, ed. see Northcott, Richard.
Geatches, Hazel, ed. Oxford Read & Discover - Electricity. (p. 1315)
Gebert, Helga, illus. see Amman, Jurg.
Gebert, Shirley M. Mighty Molly. (p. 1140)
—Silly Simon: Sound Series. (p. 1576)
GEbhard, Andy, illus. see BAtey, Kathey.
Gebhard, Wilfried. Lo Que Eduardo Sabe Hacer. Gebhard, Wilfried, illus. (p. 1044)
Gebhardt-Gayler, Winnie, illus. see Preussler, Otfried.
Gebhart, Ryan. There Will Be Bears. (p. 1730)
Gebolys, Danja. Little Ricky. (p. 1035)
Gebr, Jaroslav, illus. see Frees, Jessie Lynch.
Gecko, Gabriel, et al. Iron Man/War Machine: Hands of the Mandarin. (p. 888)
Gedacht, Daniel C. Art & Religion in Ancient Rome. (p. 101)
—Economy & Industry in Ancient Rome. (p. 503)
—George Washington: Leader of a New Nation. (p. 664)
—Home Life in Ancient Rome. (p. 792)
—Land & Resources in Ancient Rome. (p. 973)
—Land & Resources of Ancient Rome. (p. 973)
—Politics & Government in Ancient Rome. (p. 1381)
—Technology of Ancient Rome. (p. 1711)
Gedatus, Gustav Mark. Minnesota. (p. 1147)
Geddes, Anne. 10 en la Cama. (p. 1993)
—Lullaby & Good Night. (p. 1064)
—This Little Baby. (p. 1737)
Geddes, Anne, jt. auth. see Handford, Martin.
Geddes, Anne, photos by. Opposites. (p. 1300)
Geddes, Diana E. Baseball Fun. Kaeden Corp. Staff, ed. (p. 141)
—Hockey Practice. Palmer, Kate S., illus. (p. 786)
—Let's Play Basketball. Kaeden Corp. Staff, ed. (p. 1000)
Geddes, Melanie D. Learning to Dream with Your Eyes Open: A Survival Guide for Inner City Youth. (p. 985)
Geddes, Serena, illus. see Collum, Karen.
Geddes, Serena, illus. see Earhart, Kristin.
Geddes, Serena, illus. see Murrell, Belinda.
Geddes, Serena, illus. see Reynolds, Alison.
Gedeon, Gloria, illus. see Hoenecke, Karen.
Gedeon, Gloria, illus. see Oppenlander, Meredith.
Gedeon, Gloria, illus. see Spinelle, Nancy Louise.
Gedeon, Gloria, illus. see Urmston, Kathleen & Urmston, Grant.
Gedeon, Gloria, illus. see Urmston, Kathleen.
Gedeon, Gloria, illus. see Williams, Deborah.
Gedney, Mona K. Life & Times of Buddha. (p. 1008)
—Story of the Great Depression. (p. 1661)
Gedovius, Juan. From the Vine. Gedovius, Juan, illus. (p. 644)
—Purple Cubed. Gedovius, Juan, illus. (p. 1419)
—Tintodonte: Un Domingo Sin Desayuno. (p. 1756)
Gedovius, Juan, illus. see Hinojosa, Francisco.
Gedovius, Juan, illus. see Macias, Elva.
Gedrich, Colleen, illus. see Evans, Leah Beth.
Gedrich, Colleen, illus. see Mazur, Cathy.
Gedzyk, Emily. Paleo Cooking for Cavekids. (p. 1319)
Gee, Allison. Animal Dreams: Coloring Book. (p. 77)
Gee & Rey. Dinosaurios Guia de Campo. (p. 443)
Gee, Bonnie, illus. see Pallotta, Jerry.
Gee, Craighton Earl. Notes on the State of America: A Compilation of Less Commonly Discussed Facts & Historical Events. (p. 1268)
Gee, Denise. Southern Cocktails: Dixie Drinks, Party Potions, & Classic Libations. Peacock, Robert M., photos by. (p. 1617)
Gee, Evelyn. Daughter of Egypt (p. 409)
Gee, Isybilla, illus. see Caffee, Pat.
Gee, Lulu. Dolly's Wonderful New Life. (p. 464)
Gee, Maurice. Fire Raiser. (p. 590)
—Gool (p. 702)
—Limping Man (p. 1018)
—Priests of Ferris (p. 1399)
—Salt (p. 1505)
Gee, R., jt. auth. see Tyler, Jenny.
Gee, Randi. Everybody Has a Cat Named Molly. (p. 543)
—Goldfish & Poodle. (p. 695)
—Smart Cookie. (p. 1592)
Gee, T. S. Dress up for When I Grow Up. (p. 485)
Geehan, Wayne, illus. see Calvert, Pam.
Geehan, Wayne, illus. see Neuschwander, Cindy.
Geehan, Wayne, jt. auth. see Neuschwander, Cindy.
Geenberg, Michael, jt. auth. see Greenberg, Doreen.
Geer, Charles, illus. see Brinley, Bertrand R.
Geer, Charles, illus. see Elam Jr., Richard M.
Geer, Charles, illus. see Foster, Martha S.
Geer, Charles, illus. see Furman, A. L., ed.
Geer, Charles, illus. see Hicks, Clifford B.
Geer, Charles, illus. see Sorensen, Virginia.
Geer, Charles H., illus. see Coombs, Charles Ira.
Geer, Charles H., illus. see Coombs, Charles.
Geer, Charles H., illus. see Kroll, Francis Lynde.
Geer, William J., illus. see Grambling, Lois G.
Geer-Drummond, Vanessa T. Olivia's Trip to the Zoo. (p. 1287)
Geerling, Marjetta. Fancy White Trash. (p. 570)
Geesey, Kathleen. Black Fog. (p. 196)
Geeslin, Campbell. Elena's Serenade. Juan, Ana, illus. (p. 511)
Geeson, Andrew, illus. see Eason, Sarah.
Geffert, Karen L. Falling Star Is the Beginning of a Wish. (p. 567)
Gegner, Rose G. Detective Rooster Rue. (p. 431)
Gehl, Laura. And Then Another Sheep Turned Up. Adele, Amy, illus. (p. 71)
Gehl, Laura & Aesop. Hare & the Tortoise Race Across Israel. Goodreau, Sarah, illus. (p. 748)
—Hare & Tortoise Race Across Israel. Goodreau, Sarah, illus. (p. 748)
Gehr, Mary, illus. see Aldis, Dorothy Keeley.
Gehr, Mary, illus. see Warner, Gertrude Chandler.
Gehret, Jeanne. Don't-Give-Up Kid: And Learning Disabilities. LaDuca, Michael, illus. (p. 467)
—Don't-Give-Up Kid: And Learning Differences. DePauw, Sandra A., illus. (p. 467)
—Eagle Eyes: A Child's Guide to Paying Attention. LaDuca, Michael, illus. (p. 492)
—Susan B. Anthony: And Justice for All. (p. 1688)
Gehrke, Dolores, jt. auth. see Gehrke, William.
Gehrke, William & Gehrke, Dolores. Sonia's Choice. (p. 1612)
Gehrman, Jody. Confessions of a Triple Shot Betty. (p. 356)
Gehrmann, Katja. Goose the Bear. (p. 702)
Gehrt, Linda. My Trip, My Spaceship. (p. 1220)
Gehry, Frank O., jt. auth. see Bodden, Valerie.
Geier, Marguerita. San Buenaventura, Serra's Last Mission. (p. 1510)
Geiger, Beth. Clean Water. (p. 330)
—Geography of Canada: Set Of 6. (p. 662)
—Geography of Canada: Text Pairs. (p. 662)
—Inside Story of Jupiter. (p. 877)
—Inside Story of Saturn. (p. 877)
Geiger, Beth & Fuerst, Jeffrey B. Return to Earth. Wolk-Stanley, Jessica, illus. (p. 1465)
Geiger, Beth & National Geographic Learning (Firm) Staff. Earth's Changing Land. (p. 498)
Geiger, Eileen. Adventures of Christina Crankypants. (p. 17)
Geiger, Kay. Treasure. (p. 1781)
Geiger, Lorraine Lynch. Wild & Woolly Night. Vargo, Sharon, illus. (p. 1928)
Geiger, Nina Friant. Froblits of Round Pond. (p. 639)
Geiger Stephens, Pamela. Dropping in on Renaissance Artists. McNeill, Jim, illus. (p. 486)
Geiger-Pritchard, Jean. Cross Waddle. (p. 385)
Geiken, Brenda, illus. see Amundson, Susan.
Geiken, Brenda Joy, illus. see Amundson, Susan D.
Geimer, Allan F. I Can Read, You Can Read: Basic Reading Teaching Guide. (p. 836)
Geis, Alissa Imre, illus. see Moss, Peggy, et al.
Geis Conti, Patricia, jt. auth. see Geis, Patricia.
Geis, Jessica, illus. see Alano, Benny.
Geis, Patricia. Alexander Calder. (p. 36)
—Good-bye Diaper! Folch, Sergio, illus. (p. 697)
—Good-bye Pacifier! Folch, Sergio, illus. (p. 697)
—Henri Matisse: Meet the Artist! (p. 767)
—Let's Eat! Folch, Sergio, illus. (p. 996)
—Let's Get Dressed! Folch, Sergio, illus. (p. 997)
—Let's Get Well! Folch, Sergio, illus. (p. 997)
—Let's Go to Sleep! Folch, Sergio, illus. (p. 997)
—Let's Help! Folch, Sergio, illus. (p. 998)
—Let's Wash Up! Folch, Sergio, illus. (p. 1001)
—Néstor Tellini. Geis, Patricia, illus. (p. 1242)
—Pablo Picasso. (p. 1316)
—Paca Lamar. Geis, Patricia, illus. (p. 1317)
—Pascual Midón. Geis, Patricia, illus. (p. 1326)
Geis, Patricia & Geis Conti, Patricia. Alexander Calder. (p. 36)
—Andy Warhol. (p. 73)
—Meninas. (p. 1126)
Geise, Brenda & Merkle, Blair Geise. Love Spot. (p. 1060)
Geisen, Cynthia. We Are Different & Alike: A Book about Diversity. Fitzgerald, Anne, illus. (p. 1865)
—What Is God Like? Just for Me Book. Fitzgerald, Anne, illus. (p. 1889)
Geiser, Christina, jt. auth. see Reiff, Lauren.
Geiser, Traci Ferguson. Name Games: Using Children's Names to Link Oral Language & Print. Dobelmann, Collene L., ed. (p. 1228)
—Sequencing, Grade K. (p. 1552)
Geiser, Traci Ferguson & Boylan, Maureen McCourt. Leap into Literacy Fall. Cernek, Kim, ed. (p. 982)
—Leap into Literacy Spring. Cernek, Kim, ed. (p. 982)
—Leap into Literacy Winter. Cernek, Kim, ed. (p. 982)
Geisert, Arthur. Country Road ABC: An Illustrated Journey Through America's Farmland. (p. 372)
Geisert, Arthur, creator. Giant Seed. (p. 674)
—Thunderstorm. (p. 1746)
Geisler, Dagmar, illus. see International Center for Assault Prevention Staff & Pro Familia, Deutsche Gesellschaft für Sexualberatung und Familienplanung Staff.
Geisler, Dagmar, jt. auth. see Geisler, Dagmar.
Geisler, Ruth. It's a Great, Awful, In-Between Day: Devotions for Young Readers. (p. 895)
—Shine, Smiling Pumpkin. (p. 1566)
Geissler, Darry, ed. see Reynolds, Ralph V.
Geissler, Kimberly, ed. see Reynolds, Ralph V.
Geisst, Charles R. Encyclopedia of American Business History (p. 524)
Geist, Hans, illus. see Billiot, Christopher.
Geist, Ken. Three Little Fish & the Big Bad Shark. Gorton, Julia, illus. (p. 1742)
—Who's Who? Cole, Henry, illus. (p. 1921)
Geist, Ken, ed. see Grace, Will.
Geist, Ken, ed. see Warhola, James & Scholastic, Inc. Staff.
Geister, David, illus. see Bauer, Patricia.
Geister, David, illus. see Carlson, Nancy & McCool, Barry.
Geister, David, illus. see Swain, Gwenyth.
Geister, David, illus. see Verstraete, Larry.
Geister, David, illus. see Wargin, Kathy-jo.
Geithner, Carole. If Only. (p. 853)
Gekko, Alexander. Arena Warriors. (p. 97)
—Jewel Fighters: The Game. (p. 917)
Gelb, John. Power Nap Kit. (p. 1389)
Gelber, Dan, et al, des. Marvel Universe Roleplaying Game: Guide to Hulk & Avengers. (p. 1099)
Gelber, Lisa & Roberts, Jody. P Is for Peanut: A Photographic A-B-C. (p. 1316)
Gelber, Peter Frost. Dragon Who Lived Next Door. Tucker, Lewis R. & Mosher, Scott, illus. (p. 478)
Gelbwasser, Margie. Pieces of Us. (p. 1356)
Geldart, Thomas. Emilie the Peacemaker. (p. 518)
Geldart, William, illus. see Westall, Robert.
Geldart, William, jt. auth. see Doney, Meryl.
Gelder, Darren & Woodcock, Paul. Marketing & Promotional Strategy. (p. 1095)
Gelderman, Robert G. Yellow Dog with One Bad Eye. Students, Shelton Intermediate School Art & Weir, Susan, illus. (p. 1970)
Gelenius, Deb. My Mom, My Teacher. (p. 1214)
Gelev, Penko, illus. see Homer.
Gelfand, Dale Evva. Charlemagne. (p. 291)
—Coretta Scott King: Civil Rights Activist. (p. 367)
—Jimi Hendrix: Musician. (p. 918)
—Sean Combs. (p. 1536)
—Syria. (p. 1693)
Gelfand, Dale Evva, jt. auth. see Hull, Mary.
Gelfand, I. M. & Shen, Alexander. Algebra (p. 38)
Gelfand, Shoshana Boyd. Jewish Tales. Hall, Amanda, illus. (p. 917)
Gelfer, Regina. Kiss Box. (p. 961)
Gelford, Inga. Sophie Ma's Magical Glasses. (p. 1613)
Gelin, Antoinette. Captain Underfish: Superhero for the Underworld. (p. 264)
Gelinas, Ben, et al. World of Thedas Marshall, Dave, ed. (p. 1957)
Geller, Amy. My First Words OUTSIDE (p. 1208)
Geller, Barbara & DelBello, Melissa P., eds. Treatment of Bipolar Disorder in Children & Adolescents. (p. 1783)
Geller, Beverly. Ellies Shabbat Surprise. (p. 514)
Geller, Beverly Mach. My Family & Me. (p. 1202)
Geller, Kristin. Follow-the-Directions Draw & Write Activities: Step-by-Step Directions & Writing Prompts That Guide Children to Draw Pictures & Write Stories about Them. (p. 612)
Geller, Mark. Raymond. (p. 1441)
Gelletly, LeeAnne. AIDS & Health Issues. (p. 30)
—AIDS & Health Issues. Ojakorotu, Victor, ed. (p. 30)
—Bolivia Henderson, James D., ed. (p. 208)
—Bolivia. (p. 208)
—Colombia Henderson, James D., ed. (p. 341)
—Colombia. (p. 341)
—Ecological Issues. Ojakorotu, Victor & Rotberg, Robert I., eds. (p. 502)
—Equal Rights Amendment. (p. 533)
—Equal Rights Amendment. Harrington, A. Page, ed. (p. 533)
—Gift of Imagination: The Story of Roald Dahl. (p. 675)
—Kurds. (p. 968)
—Mexican Immigration. (p. 1131)
—Mid-Atlantic States: Delaware, Maryland, & Washington, D. C. (p. 1137)
—Modern-Day Pirates. (p. 1158)
—Monarchy. Colton, Timothy J., ed. (p. 1163)
—Oligarchy. Colton, Timothy J., ed. (p. 1285)
—Origins of the Women's Rights Movement. (p. 1304)
—Origins of the Women's Rights Movement. Harrington, A. Page, ed. (p. 1304)
—Seeking Th Right to Vote. (p. 1548)
—Seeking Th Right to Vote. Harrington, A. Page, ed. (p. 1548)
—Somalia. (p. 1608)
—Woman's Place in Early America. (p. 1945)
—Woman's Place in Early America. Harrington, A. Page, ed. (p. 1945)
Gellineau, Lloyd. Allen in the Flashlight. (p. 40)
Gellman, Ellie. Jeremy's Dreidel. Mola, Maria, illus. (p. 913)
Gellman, Ellie B. Netta & Her Plant. Ugliano, Natascia, illus. (p. 1242)
—Shai's Shabbat Walk. Conger, Holli, illus. (p. 1558)
—Tamar's Sukkah. Kahn, Katherine Janus, illus. (p. 1704)
Gellock, Ed. Top Dog Lives Indoors & My Neighbors Live Outside. (p. 1769)
Gelman, Amy, jt. auth. see Owens, Michael.
Gelman, Judy & Krupp, Vicki Levy. Kids' Book Club Book: Reading Ideas, Recipes, Activities, & Smart Tips for Organizing Terrific Kids' Book Clubs. (p. 952)
Gelsey, James. Baseball Boogeyman. (p. 141)
—Caper Gets Even. (p. 262)
—Mean Green Mystery Machine: Junior Chapter Book. Duendes Del Sur Staff, illus. (p. 1116)
—Scooby-Doo! & the Carnival Creeper. (p. 1529)
—Scooby-Doo! & the Frankenstein Monster. (p. 1529)
—Scooby-Doo! & the Groovy Ghost. (p. 1529)
—Scooby-Doo! & the Gruesome Goblin. (p. 1529)
—Scooby-Doo! & the Howling Wolfman. (p. 1529)
—Scooby-Doo! & the Spooky Strikeout. (p. 1529)
Gelsey, James, adapted by. Opposing Force. (p. 1300)
Gelsey, James & Duendes Del Sur Staff. Scooby-Doo & the Karate Caper. (p. 1529)
—Scooby-Doo & the Runaway Robot. (p. 1529)
—Scooby-Doo & the Sunken Ship. (p. 1529)
—Scooby-Doo & the Vampire's Revenge. (p. 1529)
—Scooby-Doo & the Witch Doctor. (p. 1529)
—Scooby-Doo & the Zombie's Treasure. (p. 1529)
Gelsinger, Dona. All Things Bright & Beautiful. (p. 46)
Gelsthorpe, Loraine, ed. see Geste, Mal, et al.
Geltrich, Brigitta, ed. In the Love of Animals. Baldwin, Christopher, illus. (p. 866)
Gemeinhart, Dan. Honest Truth. (p. 794)
Gemignani, Tony, jt. auth. see Morgan, Diane.
Geminario, Jo Ann, jt. auth. see Jamie, Schaefer-Wilson.
Gemmell, Kathy, ed. see Leigh, Susannah.

G

Gemmen, Heather. But It's True. Lagares, Luciano, illus. (p. 246)
—Learn-to-Read Bible. Wilber, Peggy M., ed. (p. 984)
Gempko, Gloria, jt. auth. see Weston, Alan.
Gemstone Publishing, creator. Donald Duck Adventures. (p. 465)
Gemstone, Rose. Boy Who Wouldn't Hug. Nahabedian, Dallas, illus. (p. 219)
Gemwitch, Ruby. Family of Silly Words: Mamma Words, Baby Words, & Other Words... (p. 568)
—Tayanna's Ballet Tutorial for Tiny Tots. (p. 1708)
Gendell, Megan. Rocking & Roving: Everything You Wanted to Know about Rockets, Rovers, & Robots. (p. 1483)
—Spanish Missions of California. (p. 1621)
—Spanish Missions of Texas. (p. 1621)
Gendell, Megan & Connolly, Rachel. Lost in Space: Everything You Wanted to Know about Planets, Stars, Galaxies, & Beyond. (p. 1055)
—Your Home in Space: Everything You Wanted to Know about Earth, the Sun, & the Moon. (p. 1980)
Gendell, Megan & O'Dea, Tierney. Shoot for the Stars: Everything You Wanted to Know about Astronomy, Stars, & Constellations. (p. 1568)
Gendell, Megan & Sweitzer, James. Spinning 'round the Sun: Everything You Wanted to Know about the Solar System & Everything in It. (p. 1628)
Gendler, Joel, jt. auth. see Sohn, Emily.
Gendler, Robert, photos by see Grice, Noreen.
Gendreau, Paula. Adventures of Lilly Lou: The First Day at Camp Who Who. (p. 19)
—Adventures of Lilly Lou: A Friday Night Sleepover & a Big Boo. (p. 19)
Gendron, Cathy, illus. see Barton, Chris.
Gendron, Elizabeth. In God's Playpen: For the Child in all of Us. (p. 863)
Gene, Barbara. Lamar Montgomery & the Freaky Faces Club. (p. 972)
Genechten, Guido van. Alex & the Tart. (p. 35)
—Because I Love You So Much. (p. 155)
—Big Potty Book. (p. 183)
—Floppy. (p. 606)
—Floppy in the Dark. (p. 606)
—Kangaroo Christine. Genechten, Guido van, illus. (p. 942)
—Porque Te Quiero Tanto. (p. 1386)
—Ricky. (p. 1470)
—Snowy's Special Secret. Genechten, Guido van, illus. (p. 1601)
Genechten, Guido van & Frippiat, Stéphanie. Ricky & Mia the Chicken. (p. 1470)
Genechten, Guido van, et al. Con los Abuelos. (p. 355)
Genechten, Guido van, tr. from DUT. Floppy in the Dark: Floppy Dans le Noir. (p. 606)
—Floppy in the Dark: Veshlapushi Ne Erresire. (p. 606)
Genell, Jacqueline. Books of the Bible: Memory Book. (p. 212)
Genereux, Andy. Yamnuska Rock: The Crown Jewel of Canadian Rockies Traditional Climbing (p. 1968)
Genet, John, jt. ed. see Kole, Ted.
Geneviève Douyon Flambert. Grace: The Mystical Caribbean Mission. (p. 704)
Genhart, Michael. Ouch Moments: When Words Hurt. Garófoli, Viviana, illus. (p. 1307)
Gennari, Jennifer. My Mixed-Up Berry Blue Summer. (p. 1214)
Gennifer, Choldenko. Al Capone Does My Shirts. (p. 32)
Genovés, Graciela, jt. auth. see Lázaro León, Georgina.
Genovese, Janell, illus. see Parker, Toni Trent.
Genovese, Michael A. & Han, Lori Cox. Encyclopedia of American Government & Civics (p. 524)
Gensler, Sonia. Dark Between. (p. 407)
—Ghostlight. (p. 672)
—Revenant. (p. 1465)
Gensmer, Laura. Score One for Math! (p. 1530)
—Where We Live. (p. 1910)
Gent, Mike, jt. auth. see Heatley, Michael.
Gent, Ron. Tale of Two Hamsters. (p. 1700)
Genth, Christina, illus. see Deich, Cheri Bivin.
Gentieu, Penny. Baby! Talk! Gentieu, Penny, illus. (p. 128)
Gentieu, Penny, illus. see Acredolo, Linda & Goodwyn, Susan.
Gentieu, Penny, photos by see Reiser, Lynn.
Gentieu, Penny, photos by see Spinelli, Jerry.
Gentile, Christopher, illus. see Bole, Kristen.
Gentilin, Isabella. Whispers of an Angel. (p. 1912)
Gentner, Norma L. & Young, Steve. Save a Tree for Me. (p. 1516)
Gentry, April, et al. Critical Companion to Herman Melville: A Literary Reference to His Life & Work. (p. 383)
Gentry, Brad. Hollywood Princess. (p. 789)
Gentry, Debra, illus. see Elwell, Sharon.
Gentry, J. B. Lily the Worm. (p. 1018)
Gentry, J. Richard & Craddock, Richard S. Nursery Rhyme Time. (p. 1273)
Gentry, Jennifer Mills. Maria Loves to Dance. (p. 1093)
—Maria the Cat (p. 1093)
—Maria's 4th of July. (p. 1093)
—Maria's Bedtime. (p. 1093)
Gentry, Kyle, illus. see Becker, Brooke.
Gentry, Marita, illus. see Casas, Dianne de Las.
Gentry, Marita, illus. see de Las Casas, Dianne.
Gentry, Marita, illus. see De Las Casas, Dianne.
Gentry, Marita, illus. see de Las Casas, Dianne.
Gentry, Marley. Chase Learns to Ride. (p. 294)
Gentry, Nancy. Little Blue, Little Gray. Keaggy, Sarah, illus. (p. 1024)
Gentry, Stephen. Journey to the Stars & Back. (p. 929)
Gentry, Susana, photos by see Sly, Stacey.
Gentry, T. Kyle, illus. see Earl, David G.
Gentry, T. Kyle, illus. see Enderle, Dotti & Sansum, Vicki.
Gentry, T. Kyle, illus. see Enderle, Dotti.
Gentry, Tony. Jesse Owens: Champion Athlete. (p. 914)
Gentry, Victory. Grandpa's Fairy Tales: Horatio the Hawk. (p. 709)
Gentzler, Yvonne S., jt. auth. see Liddell, Louise A.
Genzo, John Paul, illus. see Hollenbeck, Kathleen M.
Geo, illus. see Shin, Ji-Sang.
Geoff Hewitt, ed. see Adams, Keith.
Geoffroi, Remie, illus. see chickaDEE Magazine Staff.
Geoffroi, Remie, illus. see Mototsune, Kat.
Geoffroi, Remie, illus. see Pitt, Steve.
Geoffroi, Remie, illus. see Slavens, Elaine & Pitt, Steve.
Geoffroi, Remie, illus. see Staunton, Ted.
Geoghegan, G. P. Crosses Across America. (p. 385)
Geography Collective Staff. Mission: Explore Camping. Morgan-Jones, Tom, illus. (p. 1153)
—Mission: Explore on the Road. Morgan-Jones, Tom, illus. (p. 1153)
—Mission Explore Food. Morgan-Jones, Tom, illus. (p. 1153)
Georgalis, Frank Elias. Evangelist: At the Left Had of God. (p. 541)
Georgano, G. N. Cars of the Seventies & Eighties: Hatchbacks for the Sportsman. (p. 272)
—Vintage Years, 1920-1930: Mass Production & the Great Boom of Wheels. (p. 1843)
George, jt. auth. see Sharky.
George, Abigail. Freaky Bug Facts! Understand Place Value (p. 632)
George, Andrew. Epic of Gilgamesh. (p. 532)
George, Audra. Vagabonding. George, Audra, illus. (p. 1830)
George, Ben W. Wanda the Witch's Broom: How an Old School Witch Learns New Tricks. (p. 1856)
George, Bobby & George, June. Montessori: Letter Work. Nassner, Alyssa, illus. (p. 1170)
—Montessori: Number Work. Nassner, Alyssa, illus. (p. 1170)
—Montessori - Shape Work. Nassner, Alyssa, illus. (p. 1170)
George, Bobby, et al. Montessori: Map Work. (p. 1170)
George, Boy. I Hear... (p. 839)
George Cary Eggleston. Captain Sam: The Boy Scouts of 1814. (p. 264)
George, Charles. Black Nationalism. (p. 196)
george, charles. pyramids of Giza. (p. 1421)
George, Charles. Racism. Haugen, Hayley Mitchell, ed. (p. 1432)
George, Charles, jt. auth. see George, Linda.
George, Charles & Currie-McGhee, Leanne. Protecting Ecosystems. (p. 1412)
George, Charles & George, Linda. Beagle. (p. 149)
george, charles & george, linda. Biotech Research. (p. 190)
George, Charles & George, Linda. Boxer. (p. 217)
—Climate Change Research. (p. 332)
—Dachshund. (p. 398)
—Holocaust. (p. 789)
—Labrador Retriever. (p. 970)
—Mayan Civilization. (p. 1113)
—Miniature Schnauzer. (p. 1146)
—Shih Tzu. (p. 1566)
George, Charles, et al. Dalai Lama. (p. 401)
George, Christian Timothy. Charles Spurgeon: The Prince of Preachers. (p. 292)
George E. Keely, Jr. Happy Day Fable. (p. 745)
George, Elizabeth. Edge of Nowhere. (p. 504)
—Edge of the Shadows. (p. 504)
—Edge of the Water. (p. 504)
—Girl's Guide to Discovering Her Bible. (p. 680)
—Joven Conforme al Corazon de Dios. (p. 929)
—Little Girl after God's Own Heart: Learning God's Ways in My Early Days. Luenebrink, Judy, illus. (p. 1028)
George, Enzo. America in the Fifties. (p. 59)
—American Revolution. (p. 63)
—Civil Rights Movement. (p. 325)
—Civil War. (p. 325)
—Cold War. (p. 339)
—Colonial America. (p. 341)
—Expanding Frontier. (p. 548)
—Jazz Age & the Great Depression. (p. 910)
—Korean War: Showdown with China. (p. 967)
—Persian Gulf War: War Against Iraqi Aggression. (p. 1344)
—World War I. (p. 1958)
—World War II. (p. 1959)
George, Enzo, jt. auth. see Benjamin, Andrew.
George, Enzo, jt. auth. see Hatton, Thomas.
George, Enzo, jt. auth. see Peyton, Katherine.
George, Enzo, jt. auth. see Samuels, Charlie.
George, Erin. Cupid Cow: The Story of a Baby Bull Born on Valentines Day. (p. 392)
—Doggie Doodles: A Picture & Coloring Book of Dog Breeds. Wright, Richard, illus. (p. 462)
George, Francis. Mr G Clef & Friends. Wasvary, Marcia, illus. (p. 1185)
George, Gale. Life Cycle of a Maple Tree. (p. 1009)
—Seminole. (p. 1550)
—We're in the Band: Develop Understanding of Fractions & Numbers. (p. 1875)
George, Harold. Men of the 9th Ohio. (p. 1126)
George Hunter, Bonnie. Jimmy's First Christmas in Heaven. (p. 918)
George, Imelda, illus. see Major, Kevin.
George, Isabel & Jones, Rob Lloyd. Animals at War. (p. 82)
George, J. A. Camp Aconyte. (p. 257)
George, Jean Craighead. Autumn Moon. (p. 118)
—Charlie's Raven. George, Jean Craighead, illus. (p. 293)
—Crowbar. (p. 386)
—Dear Katie, the Volcano Is a Girl. (p. 419)
—Eagles Are Back. Minor, Wendell, illus. (p. 492)
—Frightful's Mountain. (p. 639)
—Galápagos George. Minor, Wendell, illus. (p. 653)
—Galapagos Picture Book. Minor, Wendell, illus. (p. 653)
—Goose & Duck. Lamont, Priscilla, illus. (p. 702)
—How to Talk to Your Cat. Truesdell, Sue & Meisel, Paul, illus. (p. 822)
—Ice Whale. Hendrix, John, illus. (p. 851)
—Julie of the Wolves. (p. 932)
—Julie of the Wolves. Schoenherr, John, illus. (p. 932)
—Julie y los Lobos. (p. 932)
—Last Polar Bear. Minor, Wendell, illus. (p. 978)
—Luck: The Story of a Sandhill Crane. Minor, Wendell, illus. (p. 1062)
—My Side of the Mountain. (p. 1218)
—Ratas de Rio, S. A. (p. 1440)
—Shark Beneath the Reef. (p. 1562)
—Snowboard Twist. Minor, Wendell, illus. (p. 1600)
—Special Gift for Grammy. Johnson, Steve & Fancher, Lou, illus. (p. 1623)
—Spring Moon. (p. 1635)
—Summer Moon. (p. 1674)
—Tierra Que Habla. (p. 1748)
—Winter Moon. (p. 1938)
—Wolves Are Back. (p. 1945)
—Wolves Are Back. Minor, Wendell, illus. (p. 1945)
George, Jean Craighead, jt. auth. see Cimarusti, Marie Torres.
George, Jean Craighead, et al. Pocket Guide to the Outdoors: Based on My Side of the Mountain. (p. 1375)
George, Jessica Day. Dragon Flight. (p. 477)
—Dragon Slippers. (p. 478)
—Dragon Spear. (p. 478)
—Princess of Glass. (p. 1404)
—Princess of the Midnight Ball. (p. 1404)
—Princess of the Silver Woods. (p. 1405)
—Silver in the Blood. (p. 1576)
—Sun & Moon, Ice & Snow. (p. 1676)
—Thursdays with the Crown. (p. 1746)
—Tuesdays at the Castle. (p. 1796)
—Wednesdays in the Tower. (p. 1871)
George, Jim. Boy's Guide to Discovering His Bible. (p. 220)
George, John, 3rd, illus. see Pope, Amy.
George, June, jt. auth. see George, Bobby.
George, Kallie. Flare. Cote, Genevieve, illus. (p. 602)
—Magical Animal Adoption Agency, Book 1 Clover's Luck. Boiger, Alexandra, illus. (p. 1074)
—Melancholic Mermaid. Halpin, Abigail, illus. (p. 1125)
—Spark. Côté, Geneviève, illus. (p. 1622)
—Splash. Cote, Genevieve, illus. (p. 1629)
George, Kallie, ed. see Lloyd, Jennifer.
George, Kallie, ed. see Winters, Kari-Lynn & Van Turennout, Paola.
George, Kallie, jt. auth. see Meister, Soizick.
George, Karen, illus. see Donaldson, Julia.
George, Kristine O'Connell. Emma Dilemma: Big Sister Poems. Carpenter, Nancy, illus. (p. 519)
—Fold Me a Poem. Stringer, Lauren, illus. (p. 611)
—Great Frog Race: And Other Poems. Kiesler, Kate, illus. (p. 716)
—Old Elm Speaks. Kiesler, Kate, illus. (p. 1283)
—¡Libro! Smith, Maggie, illus. (p. 1006)
George, Laura. Truth: About the Five Primary Religions & the Seven Rules of Any Good Religion. (p. 1793)
George, Leonard, Jr., illus. see Olson, Karen W.
George, Linda, jt. auth. see George, Charles.
george, linda, jt. auth. see george, charles.
George, Linda, jt. auth. see George, Charles.
George, Linda & George, Charles. Great Depression. (p. 715)
George, Lindsay B., jt. auth. see George, Lindsay Barrett.
George, Lindsay Barrett. Alfred Digs. George, Lindsay Barrett, illus. (p. 37)
—Inside Mouse, Outside Mouse. George, Lindsay Barrett, illus. (p. 876)
—Maggie's Ball. George, Lindsay Barrett, illus. (p. 1071)
—Secret. George, Lindsay Barrett, illus. (p. 1540)
—That Pup! George, Lindsay Barrett, illus. (p. 1726)
George, Lindsay Barrett, illus. see Schaefer, Lola M.
George, Lindsay Barrett & George, Lindsay B. Alfred Digs. George, Lindsay Barrett, illus. (p. 37)
—In the Garden: Who's Been Here? George, Lindsay Barrett, illus. (p. 866)
—Inside Mouse, Outside Mouse. George, Lindsay Barrett, illus. (p. 876)
George, Liz. Conflict Resolution: When Friends Fight. (p. 357)
—Empathy: I Know How You Feel! (p. 520)
—Thankfulness: A Gratitude Attitude! (p. 1725)
George, Lucy M. Holidays: Then & Now. (p. 788)
George, Lynn. 20 Questions: History (p. 1995)
—Beavers: Dam Builders. (p. 155)
—Calendars of Native Americans: Timekeeping Methods of Ancient North America. (p. 252)
—Civil War Recipes: Adding & Subtracting Simple Fractions. (p. 325)
—Coral: Reef Builders. (p. 366)
—Leaf Pile. (p. 982)
—Prairie Dogs: Tunnel Diggers. (p. 1392)
—Sammy's Sunglasses. (p. 1508)
—Super Sandwich. (p. 1680)
—Teotihuacan: Designing an Ancient Mexican City: Calculating Perimeters & Areas of Squares & Rectangles. (p. 1721)
—Termites: Mound Builders. (p. 1721)
—Wasps: Nest Builders. (p. 1860)
—What Do You Know about Colonial America? (p. 1883)
—What Do You Know about the Age of Exploration? (p. 1883)
—What Do You Know about the American Revolution? (p. 1883)
—What Do You Know about the Civil War? (p. 1883)
—What Do You Know about Westward Expansion? (p. 1883)
—Wombats: Burrow Builders. (p. 1945)
George, Lynn, jt. auth. see Schimel, Kate.
George, Lynn & Schimel, Kate. New York's Early Explorers. (p. 1248)
George, Madeleine. Looks. (p. 1051)
George, Marian M. Little Journey to Puerto Rico. (p. 1029)
George, Michael. Stars: Beacons in the Sky. (p. 1643)
—Volcanoes: The Fiery Mountains. (p. 1849)
George, Michele. Rainbow of Love. (p. 1435)
George, Mike. 1,001 Ways to Relax: An Illustrated Guide to Reducing Stress. (p. 2002)
George, Mindy Lee. Sugar Bugs. (p. 1672)
—These Hands. Hagan, Donell, illus. (p. 1731)
George, Olivia. Bravest Girls in the World. DuBurke, Randy, illus. (p. 223)
—Copy Cat. Hudson, Brett, illus. (p. 366)
—Weather. Fletcher, Rusty, illus. (p. 1869)
George, Olivia, jt. auth. see Scholastic, Inc. Staff.
George, Pamela & Brown, Walter M. North Carolina Alphabet. (p. 1265)
George, Patrick. I Smell... (p. 845)
—I Taste... George, Patrick, illus. (p. 846)
—I Touch .. George, Patrick, illus. (p. 847)
—Magic Colors. (p. 1072)
—Magic Opposites. (p. 1073)
George, Patrick & PatrickGeorge. Contrarios. (p. 361)
—Numeros. (p. 1273)
George, Paul S., ed. see Rudy, Carol-Ann.
George, Peter, illus. see Meister, Carl.
George R. Cathcart Jr. Ernie's Clever Plan. (p. 534)
George, Rebecca. Super Smart Math: 180 Warm-Ups & Challenging Activities. (p. 1682)
George, Sandy. Anika's Travel Diaries: The Lava Island Trip. (p. 76)
George, Susie. Let's Go on a Treasure Hunt. (p. 997)
George, Thomas. Diplodocus. (p. 445)
George Trad. Symph - In Search of Harmony. Beniamino Brady, illus. (p. 1693)
George-Lafazanis, Venetia. Tilly Tales. (p. 1750)
Georger, Lucie, illus. see Lammertink, Ilona.
Georges, Theodore K. Forever in My Arms. (p. 619)
George-Warren, Holly. Cowgirl Way: Hats off to America's Women of the West. (p. 374)
Georgi, Tamela & Wojna, Lisa. Canadian Women Adventurers: Stories of Daring & Courage. (p. 260)
Georgiady, Nicholas P., et al. Ohio Men Collins, Julia B., illus. (p. 1281)
Georgiana, Vanessa. Lulu: And the Garden of Life. (p. 1064)
Georgieva, Zoia. Herman the Earth Worm: Illustrated by Emma C. Van Dyke. (p. 771)
Georgiou, Tyrone. Formula 1. (p. 620)
—Funny Car Dragsters. (p. 649)
—Indy Cars. (p. 873)
—Pro Stock Dragsters. (p. 1408)
—Pro Stock Motorcycle Dragsters. (p. 1408)
—Top Fuel Dragsters. (p. 1769)
Gephart, Donna. As If Being 12 3/4 Isn't Bad Enough, My Mother Is Running for President! Kocsis, J. C., illus. (p. 105)
—Death by Toilet Paper. (p. 420)
—How to Survive Middle School. (p. 822)
—Olivia Bean, Trivia Queen. (p. 1286)
Gerace, Frank E. & Leslie, Clare Walker. Ancient Celtic Festivals: And How We Celebrate Them Today. (p. 68)
Geraci, Drew, illus. see Waid, Mark, et al.
Geraci, Maria. Boyfriend of the Month Club. (p. 220)
Geradts, Evert, et al. Uncle Scrooge #372. Clark, John, ed. (p. 1812)
Geraghty, Paul. Dinosaur in Danger. (p. 442)
—Dinosaur in Danger. Geraghty, Paul, illus. (p. 442)
—Help Me! Geraghty, Paul, illus. (p. 765)
—Hoppameleon. Geraghty, Paul, illus. (p. 797)
—Hunter. Geraghty, Paul, illus. (p. 828)
—Rotten & Rascal: The Two Terrible Pterosaur Twins. (p. 1490)
—Solo. Geraghty, Paul, illus. (p. 1608)
—Tortuga. (p. 1771)
Geraghty, Paul, jt. auth. see Bush, John.
Geragotelis, Brittany. Life's a Witch. (p. 1013)
—What the Spell. (p. 1893)
—Witch Is Back: A Life's a Witch Book. (p. 1941)
—Witch Is Back. (p. 1941)
Gerald, A. I. Hathlin Behind the Gates of Hell. (p. 752)
Gerald, Jay. Adventures of Geo, the Pebble. (p. 18)
Gerald, Tom. Traveling by Train: Read Well Level K Unit 19 Storybook. Weber, Philip A., Jr., illus. (p. 1780)
Geraldi, Michele J. Pennies at Piper Park. (p. 1337)
—Shell Story. (p. 1564)
—Way to Papou Lake. (p. 1864)
Geraldine Anderson. Bev's Amazing Adventures: The Kitten. (p. 173)
Geran, Chad. Oh, Baby! (p. 1280)
Geran, Chad, illus. see Norman, Kim.
Gerani, Gary. Dinosaurs Attack. (p. 444)
Gerard, Caleb, jt. auth. see Casey, Joe.
Gerard Clark. Crickley Meadow. (p. 382)
Gerard, Franck J. Time Waits for No One! Prioritize to Change Your Life! (p. 1753)
Gerard, James H. Blue Marble: How a Photograph Revealed Earth's Fragile Beauty (p. 203)
Gerard, Joe. Flight from Tokura. (p. 604)
Gerard, Joseph L. Out of Focus. (p. 1311)
Gerard, Justin. Beowulf: Grendel the Ghastly. Bk. 1 (p. 166)
—Lightlings. (p. 1015)
Gerard, Justin, illus. see Baucom, Ian.
Gerard, Justin, illus. see Hapka, Catherine, pseud.
Gerard, Justin, illus. see Heyman, Alissa.
Gerard, Justin, illus. see Hornby, Steven.
Gerard, Justin, illus. see Meade, Starr, et al.
Gerard, Justin, illus. see Sproul, R. C.
Gerard, Justin, jt. illus. see Grosvenor, Charles.
Gerard, Kevin. Diego's Dragon, Book Three: Battle at Tenochtitlan. Dreadfuls, Penny, ed. (p. 437)
Gerard, Maureen. Reader's Theater: Tall Tales. (p. 1444)
Gerard, Timothy. City Brigade & Remember the Music. (p. 323)
Gerardi, Jan. Eco People on the Go! (p. 502)
—Little Gardener. (p. 1028)
—Little Recycler. (p. 1034)
Gerardi, Jan, illus. see Golden Books Staff.
Gerardi, Jan, illus. see Greenburg, J. C.
Gerardi, Jan, illus. see Seuss, Dr.
Geras, Adèle. Apricots at Midnight: And Other Stories from a Patchwork Quilt. (p. 93)
—Cecily's Portrait. (p. 283)
—Ithaka. (p. 895)
—Lizzie's Wish. (p. 1043)
—My Ballet Dream. McNicholas, Shelagh, illus. (p. 1196)
—Pictures of the Night. (p. 1356)
—Tower Room. (p. 1773)
—Troy. (p. 1790)
—Voyage. (p. 1850)
—Watching the Roses: The Egerton Hall Novels, Volume Two (p. 1861)
Geras, Adèle & McNicholas, Shelagh. Tilly Tutu. McNicholas, Shelagh, illus. (p. 1750)

Gerber, Carole. 10 Busy Brooms. Fleming, Michael, illus. (p. 1993)
—Annie Jump Cannon, Astronomer Wald, Christina, illus. (p. 87)
—Jessica McBean, Tap Dance Queen. Barton, Patrice, illus. (p. 914)
—Jessica Mcbean, Tap Dance Queen. Barton, Patrice, illus. (p. 914)
—Leaf Jumpers. Evans, Leslie, illus. (p. 982)
—Little Red Bat Wald, Christina, illus. (p. 1034)
—Seeds, Bees, Butterflies, & More! Poems for Two Voices. Yelchin, Eugene, illus. (p. 1547)
—Spring Blossoms. Evans, Leslie, illus. (p. 1635)
—Stingrays! Underwater Fliers. Mones, Isidre, illus. (p. 1651)
—Tuck-in Time. Pearson, Tracey Campbell, illus. (p. 1795)
—Tundra Food Chains. (p. 1796)
—Twelve Days of Christmas in Ohio. Ebbeler, Jeffrey, illus. (p. 1800)
Gerber, Kathryn, illus. see Roraback, Amanda.
Gerber, Larry. Careers in Landscaping & Gardening. (p. 268)
—Cited! Identifying Credible Information Online. (p. 322)
—Cloud-Based Computing. (p. 334)
—Distortion of Facts in the Digital Age. (p. 454)
—Dream Jobs in Sports Refereeing. (p. 483)
—Second Amendment: The Right to Bear Arms. (p. 1539)
—Step-By-Step Guide to Problem Solving at School & Work. (p. 1647)
—Taliban in Afghanistan. (p. 1703)
—Top 10 Tips for Developing Money Management Skills. (p. 1768)
—Torture. (p. 1771)
—Truth about Steroids. (p. 1794)
Gerber, Linda. Death by Bikini. (p. 420)
—Death by Bikini Mysteries (p. 420)
—Death by Denim. (p. 420)
—Finnish Line. (p. 589)
—Lights, Camera, Cassidy - Celebrity, Episode One. (p. 1016)
—Lights, Camera, Cassidy: Drama. (p. 1016)
—Lights, Camera, Cassidy - Hacked. (p. 1016)
—Now & Zen. (p. 1269)
Gerber, Lisa Ann. Elaina's Sleuthing Days (p. 508)
Gerber, Mary Jane, illus. see Boehm, Rachel.
Gerber, Mary Jane, illus. see Downie, Mary Alice.
Gerber, Mary Jane, illus. see Porter, Pamela.
Gerber, Mary Jane, illus. see Rivera, Raquel.
Gerber, Patric, illus. see Lasater, Amy.
Gerber, Paul. Is It Alive? (p. 889)
Gerber, Pesach, illus. see Shollar, Leah Pearl.
Gerberding, Richard & Moran Cruz, Jo Ann Hoeppner. Medieval Worlds: An Introduction to European History, 300-1492. (p. 1119)
Gerbracht, Edie. Especially Me! Stoner, Alexis, illus. (p. 536)
Gerdes, Louise. Biodiversity. (p. 188)
—Cyberbullying. Greenhaven Press Editors, ed. (p. 396)
—Gun Violence. (p. 732)
—Guns & Crime. (p. 732)
—Homless. (p. 794)
—Latin America. (p. 979)
—National Service. (p. 1233)
—Teen Driving. (p. 1713)
—Urban America. (p. 1825)
Gerdes, Louise, ed. see Grover, Jan.
Gerdes, Louise, jt. auth. see Grover, Jan.
Gerdes, Louise, ed. Are Government Bailouts Effective? (p. 96)
—Cybercrime. (p. 396)
—Domestic Violence. (p. 465)
—How Safe Is America's Infrastructure? (p. 812)
—Hybrid & Electric Cars. (p. 831)
—Latin America. (p. 979)
—Nuclear Weapons. (p. 1270)
—Teen Dating. (p. 1713)
—Violence. (p. 1843)
—What Are the Causes of Prostitution? (p. 1880)
Gerdes, Louise I. 1992 Los Angeles Riots. Greenhaven Press Editors, ed. (p. 2003)
—9/11. (p. 1993)
—Drones. Greenhaven Press Editors & Gale Editors, eds. (p. 485)
—Drones. Greenhaven Press Editors & Gale, Anthony, eds. (p. 485)
—How Safe Is America's Infrastructure? (p. 812)
—Human Genetics. (p. 826)
—Medicine. (p. 1119)
—National Service. (p. 1234)
—Political Campaigns. (p. 1380)
—Robotic Technology. Greenhaven Press Editors, ed. (p. 1480)
—Should the US Close Its Borders? Greenhaven Press Editors & Gale, A. G., eds. (p. 1570)
—Should the US Close Its Borders? Greenhaven Press Editors & Gale Editors, eds. (p. 1570)
—Super Pacs. Greenhaven Press Editors, ed. (p. 1680)
—Super Pacs. Greenhaven Press Editors & Gale Editors, eds. (p. 1680)
—Vietnam War. (p. 1841)
—Wave & Tidal Power. Kiesbye, Stefan, ed. (p. 1864)
—World War II. (p. 1959)
Gerdes, Louise I., ed. Globalization. (p. 685)
—Medicine. (p. 1119)
—Patriot Act. (p. 1329)
—War. (p. 1857)
—What Are the Causes of Prostitution? (p. 1880)
Gerdes, Sarah. Catacombs & the Lava Bed Forest. (p. 278)
Gerdner, Linda & Langford, Sarah. Grandfather's Story Cloth. Loughridge, Stuart, illus. (p. 707)
Gerecke, Bretta, illus. see Christenson, Jonathan.
Geremia, Daniela, illus. see Stride, Lottie & Oliver, Martin.
Geremia, Denise. Pouty Puppy. (p. 1389)
Gerencher, Jane. Santa's Sugar. Patch, Michael, illus. (p. 1513)
Gerety, Ed. Combinations: Opening the Door to Student Leadership. (p. 347)
Gergely, Tibor. Tootle. Golden Books Staff, photos by. (p. 1768)
Gergely, Tibor, illus. see Crampton, Gertrude, et al.
Gergely, Tibor, illus. see Crampton, Gertrude.
Gergely, Tibor, illus. see Duplaix, Georges & Golden Books Staff.
Gergely, Tibor, illus. see Frank, Janet & Golden Books Staff.
Gergely, Tibor, illus. see Golden Books Staff & Miryam.
Gergely, Tibor, illus. see Golden Books Staff.
Gergely, Tibor, illus. see Golden Books.
Gergely, Tibor, illus. see Hoffman, Beth Greiner.
Gergely, Tibor, illus. see McGinley, Phyllis, et al.
Gergely, Tibor, illus. see Miryam.
Gergely, Tibor, illus. see North Bedford, Annie.
Gergen, Joe, et al. Football Book: All-Time Greats, Legendary Teams, & Today's Favorite Players-With Tips on Playing Like a Pro. (p. 615)
Gergley, Tibor. Occupaciones de Gente Ocupada. (p. 1275)
Gerhard, Ana. Listen to the Birds: An Introduction to Classical Music. Varela, Cecilia, illus. (p. 1022)
Gerhardt, Barbara. I Am of Scram. (p. 833)
Gerhardt, Michael J., jt. auth. see Wittekind, Erika.
Gerhardt, Paul L. Diversity King. (p. 454)
Gerheim, Su. Bayocor Adventures, the Secret Cave. (p. 147)
Gerhmann, Katja, jt. auth. see Langen, Annette.
Geringer, Laura, jt. auth. see Bass, L. G.
Geringer, Laura, jt. auth. see Joyce, William.
Geringswald, Rita T. Adventures of Ali Alligator. (p. 16)
—Benny: The bird who was too lazy to Fly. (p. 165)
Gerlach, Carolyn. Robert Lee. (p. 1479)
Gerlach, Elizabeth K. Apples for Cheyenne: A Story about Autism, Horses & Friendship. (p. 93)
Gerlach, Steve. Lake Mountain. (p. 972)
Gerlach, Susan, jt. auth. see Gerlach-Babb nee Maines, Mary.
Gerlach-Babb nee Maines, Mary & Gerlach, Susan. Best Christmas Gift. (p. 168)
Gerlings, Charlotte. Great Artists. (p. 713)
Gerlings, Rebecca. Enormouse! Gerlings, Rebecca, illus. (p. 531)
Gerlings, Rebecca, ed. Hey, Diddle, Diddle & Other Best-loved Rhymes. Ulkutay & Co Ltd, illus. (p. 774)
—Hey, Diddle, Diddle & Other Best-Loved Rhymes. Ulkutay Design Group Staff, illus. (p. 774)
—Itsy Bitsy Spider & Other Best-loved Rhymes. Ulkutay & Co Ltd, illus. (p. 900)
—Itsy Bitsy Spider & Other Best-Loved Rhymes. Ulkutay Design Group Staff, illus. (p. 900)
—Little Miss Muffet & Other Best-loved Rhymes. Ulkutay & Co Ltd, illus. (p. 1032)
—Little Miss Muffet & Other Best-Loved Rhymes. Ulkutay Design Group Staff, illus. (p. 1032)
—Mary Had a Little Lamb & Other Best-loved Rhymes. Ulkutay & Co Ltd, illus. (p. 1100)
—Mary Had a Little Lamb & Other Best-Loved Rhymes. Ulkutay Design Group Staff, illus. (p. 1100)
—Wee Willie Winkie & Other Best-Loved Rhymes. Ulkutay Design Group Staff, illus. (p. 1871)
—Wee Willie Winkie & Other Best-loved Rhymes. Ulkutay & Co Ltd & Ulkutay & Co Ltd, illus. (p. 1871)
—Yankee Doodle & Other Best-loved Rhymes. Ulkutay & Co Ltd, illus. (p. 1968)
—Yankee Doodle & Other Best-Loved Rhymes. Ulkutay Design Group Staff, illus. (p. 1968)
Gerlitz, Menachem. Return to the Heavenly City. (p. 1465)
Germadnik, Mary. How Do We Know the Age of the Universe? (p. 807)
Germain, Daniella, illus. see Holmes, Janet A.
Germain, Kerry. Kimo's Summer Vacation. Montes, Keoni, illus. (p. 957)
—Kimo's Surfing Lesson. Moore, Nicolette, illus. (p. 957)
Germain, Philippe, illus. see Hébert, Marie-Francine.
Germaine, Elizabeth & Burckhardt, Ann. Cooking the Australian Way. (p. 362)
German, Lana. Jake the Sadder Ladder. Miller, Mark, illus. (p. 906)
German, Roger. Porches & Sunrooms: Planning & Remodeling Ideas. (p. 1386)
Germano, Nicholas, illus. see Pepper, Sly.
Germano, Yveta. Bring Me Back. (p. 228)
Germein, Katrina. My Dad Thinks He's Funny. Jellett, Tom, illus. (p. 1201)
Gerner, Jochen. ARTastic! 200+ Art Smart Activities. (p. 103)
Gerner, Katy. Buddhism. (p. 234)
—Catholicism. (p. 280)
—Hinduism. (p. 780)
—Islam. (p. 891)
—Judaism. (p. 930)
—Protestantism. (p. 1412)
—Religions Around the World (p. 1458)
Gerner, Penny. Amoora Trilogy. (p. 65)
Gerngross, Günter, jt. auth. see Kaleta, Magda.
Gerngross, Günter, jt. auth. see Puchta, Herbert.
Gerngross, Günter & Puchta, Herbert. Join Us for English 1 Flashcards Polish Edition. (p. 924)
—Join Us for English 1 Portfolio Polish Edition. (p. 924)
—Join Us for English 1 Pupil's Book Polish Edition. (p. 924)
Gernhart, Carlie, illus. see Gernhart, Cyndi.
Gernhart, Cyndi. Adventures of Gertrude Mccluck, Chicken in Charge: The Missing Eggs Vol. 1 Gernhart, Carlie, illus. (p. 18)
—Adventures of Gertrude Mccluck, Chicken in Charge: The Great Crate Mystery Vol. 2 Gernhart, Carlie, illus. (p. 18)
—Adventures of Gertrude Mccluck, Chicken in Charge: A Midwinter Light's Dream Vol. 4 Gernhart, Carlie, illus. (p. 18)
—Adventures of Gertrude Mccluck, Chicken in Charge: The Yellow-Eyed Pond Monster Vol. 3 Gernhart, Carlie, illus. (p. 18)
—Gertrude Sees... On the Farm. Gernhart, Cyndi et al, illus. (p. 667)
Gero, Bernard F. Hike on a Bike. (p. 779)
Gerovasiliou, Oreanthy. Yuri the Lion: Three Stories. (p. 1983)
Gerowin, Sean. Catte au Lait & the Big Hurricane. (p. 281)
Gerra, Laurent. Man from Washington. (p. 1085)
Gerrell, Spike, illus. see Bennett, Howard J.
Gerrish, Howard H., et al. Electricity: Teaching Package. (p. 509)
—Electricity. (p. 509)
—Electricity & Electronics: Teaching Package. (p. 509)
—Electricity & Electronics: Interactive Software Site License. (p. 509)
—Electricity & Electronics: Interactive Software Individual License. (p. 509)
—Electricity & Electronics. (p. 509)
Gerrits, Julie & Newton, Sydney. Child Abuse. (p. 301)
Gerritsen, Paula, illus. see Van Lieshout, Elle & Van Os, Erik.
Gerrity, Arlene. Tale of Chicken Noodle & Rabbit Stew Number Two. (p. 1699)
Gerrold, David, et al. Diary of a Stinky Dead Kid Hack, Robert et al, illus. (p. 435)
—Wickeder. Parker, Rick et al, illus. (p. 1927)
Gerry, Bella Bashan. Sweetest Dreams. (p. 1690)
Gerry, Lisa, jt. auth. see National Geographic Kids Staff.
Gerry, Lisa M. Puppy Love: True Stories of Doggie Devotion. (p. 1418)
Gerry's 4. World of Round. (p. 1957)
Gersh, Camilla, jt. auth. see Dorling Kindersley Publishing Staff.
Gershator, David & Gershator, Phillis. Bread Is for Eating. Shaw-Smith, Emma, illus. (p. 224)
Gershator, Phillis. Listen, Listen. Jay, Alison, illus. (p. 1022)
—Little Lenty. (p. 1030)
—Moo, Moo, Brown Cow! Have You Any Milk? Potter, Giselle, illus. (p. 1171)
—Old House, New House Potter, Katherine, illus. (p. 1284)
—Rata-Pata-Scata-Fata: A Caribbean Story Meade, Holly, illus. (p. 1440)
—Sambalena Show-Off. (p. 1507)
—When It Starts to Snow. Matje, Martin, illus. (p. 1903)
—Who's in the Farmyard? McDonald, Jill, illus. (p. 1920)
—Who's in the Garden? McDonald, Jill, illus. (p. 1920)
Gershator, Phillis, jt. auth. see Gershator, David.
Gershator, Phillis, jt. auth. see Jay, Alison.
Gershator, Phillis & Green, Mim. Time for a Hug. Walker, David, illus. (p. 1751)
Gershator, Phillis & Walker, David. Time for a Bath. (p. 1751)
Gershator, Phyllis. Who's in the Forest? McDonald, Jill, illus. (p. 1920)
Gershel, Yolande. Alice. (p. 39)
—Clarabelle's Christmas. (p. 326)
Gershenfeld, Matti K., jt. auth. see Napier, Rodney W.
Gershenson, Harold P. America the Musical 1776-1899: A Nation's History Through Music. Chesworth, Michael, illus. (p. 59)
—Freddy Flamingo & the Kindertown Five. Mills, Christopher, illus. (p. 633)
—Kindertown Fire Brigade. Mills, Christopher, illus. (p. 957)
—Noodles from Scratch. Mills, Christopher, illus. (p. 1264)
Gershman, Jenifer. Where Did Mommy's Superpowers Go? Helping Kids Understand a Parent's Serious Illness. (p. 1906)
Gershman, Jo, illus. see Conlon, Mara.
Gershman, Jo, illus. see Miller, Sibley & Lenhard, Elizabeth.
Gershman, Jo, illus. see Miller, Sibley.
Gershman, Jo, illus. see Pieper, Martha Heineman.
Gershman, Regina. Animals from My Window. (p. 82)
Gershon, Neil. Other Side of the Frame. (p. 1306)
Gershtein, V. M. Two Stories about Nothing Significant. (p. 1804)
Gersing, James, illus. see Magellan, Marta.
Gersing, James, photos by see Magellan, Marta.
Gerson, Mary-Joan. Fiesta Femenina. Gonzalez, Maya Christina, illus. (p. 584)
Gerstein, David. Mickey & the Gang: Classic Stories In Verse. Clark, John, ed. (p. 1136)
Gerstein, David, ed. see Gottfredson, Floyd.
Gerstein, Francine, jt. auth. see Fromer, Liza.
Gerstein, Mordecai, illus. see Rosenstock, Barb.
Gerstein, Mordicai. Book. Gerstein, Mordicai, illus. (p. 210)
—Dear Hot Dog. (p. 419)
—First Drawing. (p. 594)
—How to Bicycle to the Moon to Plant Sunflowers: A Simple but Brilliant Plan in 24 Easy Steps. Gerstein, Mordicai, illus. (p. 815)
—Man Who Walked Between the Towers. (p. 1086)
—Man Who Walked Between the Towers. Gerstein, Mordicai, illus. (p. 1086)
—Minifred Goes to School. Gerstein, Mordicai, illus. (p. 1146)
—Mountains of Tibet. Gerstein, Mordicai, illus. (p. 1181)
—Night World. (p. 1254)
—Three Samurai Cats: A Story from Japan. (p. 1743)
—What Charlie Heard. Gerstein, Mordicai, illus. (p. 1881)
—White Ram: A Story of Abraham & Isaac. Gerstein, Mordicai, illus. (p. 1913)
—You Can't Have Too Many Friends! Gerstein, Mordicai, illus. (p. 1974)
Gerstein, Mordicai, illus. see Levy, Elizabeth & Coville, Bruce.
Gerstein, Mordicai, illus. see Levy, Elizabeth.
Gerstein, Mordicai, illus. see Lipson, Eden Ross.
Gerstein, Mordicai, illus. see Spires, Elizabeth.
Gerstein, Sherry. Great Cake. Bennett, Andy, illus. (p. 714)
—Hide & Peek: A Lift-A-Flap Letters Book. Bennett, Andy, illus. (p. 776)
—Imagination Vacation: A Color-Foil Shapes Book. Bennett, Andy, illus. (p. 860)
—Moo, Moo Who Are You? Bennett, Andy, illus. (p. 1171)
Gerstein, Yoni, illus. see Kugel, Bruriah.
Gersten, Dan, creator. Ask Curtis: Dog-Sense Advice from Curtis the Dog (p. 106)
Gerstenblit, Rivke. Baruch & His Disappearing Yarmulke. Judowitz, Chani, illus. (p. 140)
Gerstler, J. C. My Elephant Likes to Read. Alley, Ashleigh & Norona, Bill, illus. (p. 1202)
Gerstmyer, David. You or Me: Who Should I Be? (p. 1976)
Gerstner, Joanne. Detroit Tigers. (p. 431)
—Toronto Blue Jays. (p. 1770)
Gerstner, Joanne C. Detroit Pistons. (p. 431)
—Toronto Raptors. (p. 1770)
Gerszak, Rafal. Beyond Bullets: A Photo Journal of Afganistan. (p. 173)
Gerszak, Rafal, photos by see McKay, Sharon E.
Gerth, Melanie. Diez Pequeñas Mariquitas. Huliska-Beith, Laura, illus. (p. 437)
—Five Little Ladybugs. Huliska-Beith, Laura, illus. (p. 600)
—Five Little Ladybugs with Hand Puppet. Beith, Laura Huliska, illus. (p. 600)
—Ten Little Ladybugs. Huliska-Beith, Laura, illus. (p. 1719)
Gerth, Melanie, jt. illus. see Diaz, James.
Gertner, Sheina Sachar. Tree Stood Still. (p. 1783)
Gertz, Mercedes, jt. concept see Suarez, Nora.
Gervais, Bernadette, jt. auth. see Pittau, Francesco.
Gervais, Bernadette & Pittau, Francesco. Birds of a Feather. (p. 191)
Gervais, Josephine. Mommies Are Protecting Their Children. (p. 1162)
—Mommies Are Special People. (p. 1162)
Gervais, Ricky. Flanimals Pop-up. Steen, Rob, illus. (p. 602)
Gervais, Tiffany. Im Different & Im Happy. (p. 858)
Gervais, Tiffany Lee. There's a Mouse in the House! (p. 1731)
—This Is Me! (p. 1736)
Gervasi, Christine, illus. see McKenzie, Richard.
Gervasio, illus. see Collins, Terry, et al.
Gervasio, illus. see Jensen Shaffer, Jody, et al.
Gervasio, illus. see Jensen Shaffer, Jody.
Gervasio, illus. see Shaffer, Jody Jensen, et al.
Gervasio, illus. see Shaffer, Jody Jensen.
Gervasio, illus. see Weakland, Mark & Jensen Shaffer, Jody.
Gervasio, illus. see Weakland, Mark, et al.
Gervasio, illus. see Weakland, Mark.
Gervasio, Christine. Pandas Live to Eat. (p. 1321)
Gervay, Susanne. Always Jack. Wilcox, Cathy, illus. (p. 51)
—Butterflies. (p. 247)
—Daisy Sunshine. Culkin-Lawrence, Teresa, illus. (p. 400)
—I Am Jack. Cathy, Wilcox, illus. (p. 833)
—Super Jack. Wilcox, Cathy, illus. (p. 1680)
—SuperJack. Wilcox, Cathy, illus. (p. 1683)
—That's Why I Wrote This Song. (p. 1727)
Gervay, Susanne & Wilcox, Cathy. Always Jack. (p. 51)
Gerver, Jane E. Bath Time. Ovresat, Laura, illus. (p. 144)
—Christmas Shapes. Davis, Nancy & Davis, Kathryn Lynn, illus. (p. 315)
—Little Sister, Big Mess! Dieterichs, Shelley, illus. (p. 1036)
—Santa Snatcher. Spaziante, Patrick, illus. (p. 1513)
—Wait for Me! Reid, Mick, illus. (p. 1852)
—Who's at Home? Davis, Nancy & Davis, Kathryn Lynn, illus. (p. 1920)
Gerver, Jane E., et al. Let's Build with Barney Backhoe. (p. 994)
—Let's Grow with Allie Gator. (p. 998)
Gerver, Jane, et al. Biggest Pumpkin Ever! (p. 185)
—Tallest Building of All! (p. 1704)
Gerwitz, Christina, jt. auth. see Gerwitz, Felice.
Gerwitz, Felice. Literature: Keys to the Past: Unlocked. No. 3 (p. 1023)
—Literature: Dinosaur Quest at Diamond Peak. No. 2 (p. 1023)
Gerwitz, Felice & Gerwitz, Christina. Dinosaur Quest at Diamond Peak (p. 442)
—Keys to the Past: Unlocked (p. 951)
—Missing Link: Found (p. 1152)
Gerwitz, Felice & Whitlock, Jill. Creation Geology: A Study Guide to Fossils, Formations & the Flood. (p. 379)
Géser, Gretchen. One Bright Ring. Géser, Gretchen, illus. (p. 1294)
Geshell, Carmen. Mele da Mynah's Noisy 'Ohana. Pagay, Jeff, illus. (p. 1125)
—Surf Rats of Waikiki Beach. Pagay, Jeff, illus. (p. 1685)
—Waltah Melon: Local-Kine Hero. Pagay, Jeff, illus. (p. 1856)
Gesme, Carole & Pearson, Douglas. Time Together Learning about Family Values. (p. 1753)
Gesser, Bernadette. Adventures of Rocky, Croaker & Spot. Mavronis, Michelle, illus. (p. 22)
Gessner, Kati. What Do You See When You Look at Me. (p. 1883)
Geste, Mal, et al. Zoo Room. Gelsthorpe, Loraine & Rex, Sue, eds. (p. 1989)
Gesvalli, Domanick. Jason's Journeys: Swim to Me. (p. 910)
Geszel, Michael. Tribes: The Dog Years. (p. 1785)
Get Smart Skills Staff. HSPT Mathematics: New Jersey High School Proficiency Test. (p. 824)
—HSPT Reading: New Jersey High School Proficiency Test. (p. 824)
—HSPT Writing: New Jersey High School Proficiency Test. (p. 824)
—PSSA Reading: Pennsylvania System of School Assessment. (p. 1413)
—PSSA Writing: Pennsylvania System of School Assessment. (p. 1413)
Getha, Patricia & Maltseff, Michele. Drawing Horses: A Complete Kit for Beginners. (p. 482)
Getha, Patricia, et al. Art of Drawing & Painting Horses: Capture the Majesty of Horses & Ponies in Pencil, Oil, Acrylic, Watercolor & Pastel. (p. 102)
—Art of Drawing Animals: Discover all the techniques you need to know to draw amazingly lifelike Animals. (p. 102)
Getsinger, Mary. Dream Come True. (p. 483)
Getson, Denise. Dry Souls. (p. 487)
Gettelman, Elizabeth. Competitive Basketball for Girls. (p. 352)
Gettelman, Elizabeth, jt. auth. see Mableton, Barry.
Getti, C. Bear's Prayer. (p. 152)
Gettman, Cheryl. Molly Magee & the Jelly Bean Tree. (p. 1160)
Getty Images, Inc. Staff, contrib. by. Stars of the All Blacks Poster Book. (p. 1643)
Gettys, Katherine, illus. see Ferrier, Paul Eugene.
Getz, Jeanine Behr. Think Green! Nightingale, Jenny, illus. (p. 1734)
Getzinger, Donna. Special. (p. 1623)
—Triangle Shirtwaist Factory Fire. (p. 1785)

Getzinger, Donna & Felsenfeld, Daniel. Antonio Vivaldi & the Baroque Tradition. (p. 90)
—George Frideric Handel & Music for Voices. (p. 663)
—Johann Sebastian Bach & the Art of Baroque Music. (p. 920)
—Johannes Brahms & the Twilight of Romanticism. (p. 920)
—Richard Wagner & German Opera. (p. 1470)
Geuk-jin, Jeon & Jeon, Keuk-jin. Fighting!! Guidance. (p. 585)
Geurds, Patricia. Bedtime for Percy. (p. 157)
Gevertz, Rob, jt. auth. see Burnett, Betty.
Gevinson, Tavi. Rookie Yearbook Three. (p. 1487)
Gevirtz, Gila. Count Me In: Jewish Wisdom in Action. (p. 369)
Gevry, C. C. Christmas Kindness. Mabey, Coline, illus. (p. 314)
Gevry, Christine, illus. see Deprisco Wang, Dorothea.
Gevry, Claudine. One Little Penguin & His Friends: A Pushing, Turning, Counting Book. (p. 1295)
—Penguins in Paradise: A Colors Flap Book. (p. 1337)
Gévry, Claudine, illus. see Bowman, Crystal.
Gévry, Claudine, illus. see Cooper, Alexandra.
Gévry, Claudine, illus. see Depken, Kristen & Depken, Kristen L.
Gévry, Claudine, illus. see DePrisco, Dorothea.
Gévry, Claudine, illus. see Finbarr, Desmond.
Gévry, Claudine, illus. see Hood, Susan.
Gévry, Claudine, illus. see Lloyd-Jones, Sally.
Gevry, Claudine, illus. see Mitter, Matt.
Gévry, Claudine, illus. see Perez, Jessica.
Gévry, Claudine, illus. see Ranson, Erin.
Gévry, Claudine, illus. see Rovetch, L. Bob.
Gévry, Claudine, illus. see Top That Publishing Staff, ed.
Gévry, Claudine, illus. see Wang, Margaret C.
Gewirtz, Adina Rishe. Zebra Forest. (p. 1985)
Gewirtz, Elaine Waldorf. Fetch This Book: Train Your Dog to Do Almost Anything. (p. 582)
Geye, Susan & Reynolds, Janice. Orca Soundings Resource Guide (p. 1302)
Geyer, Clyde. Awesome Adventures of Chuckie Chopper & Friends. (p. 120)
Geyer, Donna M., jt. auth. see Bell, Marion R.
Geyer, Flora. Mao Zedong: The Rebel Who Led a Revolution. (p. 1089)
—Saladin: The Muslim Warrior Who Defended His People. (p. 1504)
Geyer, Flora, jt. auth. see MacDonald, Fiona.
Geyer, Kim. Go to Sleep, Monty! Geyer, Kim, illus. (p. 687)
Geyer, Mark Edward, illus. see Hicks, Deron R.
Geyer, Mark Edward, illus. see Moriarty, Chris.
Geyer, Mark Edward, illus. see Pollack, Pamela D. & Belviso, Meg.
Geyer, Mark Edward, illus. see Stine, Megan.
Ghahremani, Susie, illus. see Ward, Jennifer.
Ghani, Aisha. I Can Pray Anywhere! Zulkifli, Azhari, illus. (p. 836)
Ghani, Samna. Shoe, the Necklace, & the Giant. Williams, Nancy E., ed. (p. 1568)
—Tooth Fairy Goes to School. Williams, Nancy E., ed. (p. 1768)
Ghazi, Suhaib Hamid. Ramadan. Rayyan, Omar, illus. (p. 1437)
Ghent, Natale. Millhouse. (p. 1143)
Ghent, Rena. Adventures of Billy the Whale. (p. 16)
Gherasim, Gabriel & Gherasim, Louise. Story of the Queen Bee & Children's Corner (p. 1662)
Gherasim, Louise, jt. auth. see Gherasim, Gabriel.
Gherman, Beverly. Anne Morrow Lindbergh: Between the Sea & the Stars. (p. 86)
—First Mothers. Downing, Julie, illus. (p. 596)
—First Son & President: A Story about John Quincy Adams. Bird, Matthew, illus. (p. 597)
—Jimmy Carter. (p. 918)
Gherman, Beverly & Chronicle Books Staff. Sparky: The Life & Art of Charles Schulz. (p. 1622)
Gheysens, Francois, jt. auth. see Cadic, Olivier.
Ghez, Andrea Mia & Cohen, Judith Love. You Can Be A Woman Astronomer. Katz, David Arthur, illus. (p. 1973)
Ghiglieri, Carol. Easy Reader Biographies: Helen Keller: An Inspiring Life. (p. 500)
—Easy Reader Biographies: Squanto: A Friend to the Pilgrims. (p. 500)
—Easy Reader Biographies: Susan B. Anthony: Fighter for Women's Rights. (p. 500)
—Tree Homes. (p. 1783)
Ghiglione, Marco. Ultraheroes: Save the World. Vol. 1 Secchi, Riccardo, illus. (p. 1810)
Ghiglione, Marco & Randolph, Grace. Ultraheroes: Save the World. Secchi, Riccardo & Randoplh, Grace, illus. (p. 1810)
Ghigna, Charles. Adeline Porcupine. East, Jacqueline, illus. (p. 12)
—Alphabet Parade. Jatkowska, Ag, illus. (p. 50)
—Animal Tracks: Wild Poems to Read Aloud. Speirs, John, tr. (p. 80)
—Bobby Bear. East, Jacqueline, illus. (p. 206)
—Cuddle Bunny. East, Jacqueline, illus. (p. 389)
—Fury of Motion: Poems for Boys. (p. 650)
—Hail to Spring! Watson, Laura, illus. (p. 735)
—I See Fall Jatkowska, Ag, illus. (p. 845)
—I See Spring Jatkowska, Ag, illus. (p. 845)
—I See Summer Jatkowska, Ag, illus. (p. 845)
—I See Winter Jatkowska, Ag, illus. (p. 845)
—Learning Parade. Jatkowska, Ag, illus. (p. 985)
—Learning Parade [10 X 10]. Jatkowska, Ag, illus. (p. 985)
—Little Seeds Jatkowska, Ag, illus. (p. 1036)
—Little Seeds [Scholastic]. AG Jatkowska, illus. (p. 1036)
—Lucy Goose. East, Jacqueline, illus. (p. 1063)
—My Little School House. Jatkowska, Ag, illus. (p. 1213)
—Numbers at the Park: 1-10 Jatkowska, Ag, illus. (p. 1272)
—Numbers at the Park: 1 2 3 4 5 6 7 8 9 10. Jatkowska, Ag, illus. (p. 1272)
—Oh My, Pumpkin Pie! Spengler, Kenneth, illus. (p. 1281)
—Pick up the Park Jatkowska, Ag, illus. (p. 1354)
—Raindrops Fall All Around. Watson, Laura, illus. (p. 1436)
—Recycling Is Fun Jatkowska, Ag, illus. (p. 1453)
—Score! 50 Poems to Motivate & Inspire. Gorton, Julia, illus. (p. 1530)
—Shapes Are Everywhere! Jatkowska, Ag, illus. (p. 1560)
—Snow Wonder. Woolf, Julia, illus. (p. 1600)
—Springtime Weather Wonders. Watson, Laura, illus. (p. 1635)
—Sunshine Brightens Springtime. Watson, Laura, illus. (p. 1678)
—Veo el Invierno. Jatkowska, Ag, illus. (p. 1836)
—Veo el Otoño. Jatkowska, Ag, illus. (p. 1836)
—Veo el Verano. Jatkowska, Ag, illus. (p. 1836)
—Veo la Primavera. Jatkowska, Ag, illus. (p. 1836)
—We Need Water Jatkowska, Ag, illus. (p. 1867)
—Windy Day in Spring. Watson, Laura, illus. (p. 1936)
—Wonders of the Color Wheel. Jatkowska, Ag, illus. (p. 1949)
Ghigna, Charles & Ghigna, Debra. Barn Storm. Greenseid, Diane, illus. (p. 139)
Ghigna, Debra, jt. auth. see Ghigna, Charles.
Ghim, John Y. Ghim's Critical Exercises of High School Math. (p. 670)
—Ghim's Critical Exercises of High School Math Answers & Explanations. (p. 670)
Ghione, Yvette. Canada in Colours. Gurth, Per-Henrik, illus. (p. 260)
—Hockey Opposites. Gürth, Per-Henrik, illus. (p. 786)
Ghione, Yvette, jt. auth. see Dubuc, Marianne.
Ghione, Yvette, jt. auth. see McIntyre, Sasha.
Ghione, Yvette, tr. see Dubuc, Marianne.
Ghione, Yvette & Gagnon, Celeste, creators. This Is Daniel Cook at the Construction Site. (p. 1735)
—This Is Daniel Cook Making Honey. (p. 1735)
Ghione, Yvette & Gurth, Per-Henrik. Oh, Canada! Gurth, Per-Henrik, illus. (p. 1280)
Ghislain, Gary. How I Stole Johnny Depp's Alien Girlfriend. (p. 810)
Ghiuselev, Iassen, illus. see Carroll, Lewis, pseud.
Ghiuselev, Iassen, illus. see Grimm, Jacob, et al.
Ghiuselev, Iassen, illus. see Ruskin, John.
Ghlinn, Aine Ni. Lamhainni Glasa. Fagan, Martin, illus. (p. 972)
Gholar, Cheryl, ed. see Bonnice, Sherry.
Gholar, Cheryl, ed. see Brinkerhoff, Shirley.
Gholar, Cheryl, ed. see Intosh, Kenneth Mc & McIntosh, Kenneth.
Gholar, Cheryl, ed. see Libal, Joyce & Simons, Rae.
Gholar, Cheryl, ed. see Libal, Joyce.
Gholar, Cheryl, ed. see Riddle, John & Simons, Rae.
Gholar, Cheryl, ed. see Sanna, Ellyn.
Gholar, Cheryl, ed. see Simons, Rae & Gommer, Viola Ruelke.
Gholar, Cheryl, ed. see Vitale, Ann.
Ghorashi, Bahman. How to Become an Exceptionally Successful Young Person: A Guide to Early Planning & A Roadmap to Success PLUS How to Face Worry, Defeat, & Uncertainty & Rise above Them All. (p. 815)
Ghose, Sudhin N. Folk Tales & Fairy Stories from India. (p. 611)
Ghose, Sudhindra Nath. Flame of the Forest. (p. 602)
Ghosh, Nemai, photos by see Robinson, Andrew.
Ghosh, Premola. Ten Timeless Tales. (p. 1719)
Ghoshal, Sumantra & Westney, D. Eleanor, eds. Organization Theory & the Multinational Corporation. (p. 1303)
Ghoulstone, Rotterly. Undead Ed. Baines, Nigel, illus. (p. 1813)
Ghounem, Mohamed. 101 Ways Islam Gives Love to the Bible: The Quranic Teachings on Christianity. (p. 2000)
—Who Is Our Savior? Allah or Jesus (p. 1916)
Ghounem, Mohamed & Meskar, Sara. Corano e la Bibbia: Testimonianza di Verità (p. 366)
Ghun, Oh Rhe Bar, jt. auth. see Yoon, Je Ho.
Gi Gi. Adventures of Trueword the Bear. (p. 24)
Giacabello, John. Careers in the Fashion Industry. (p. 268)
—You & Violence in Your Family. (p. 1973)
Giachetti, Julia. Don't Give up! Lap Book. Evans, Antony, illus. (p. 467)
—I Was So Mad. Poole, Helen, illus. (p. 848)
—I Was So Mad Lap Book. Poole, Helen, illus. (p. 848)
—My Happy Day. Poole, Helen, illus. (p. 1210)
—My Happy Day Lap Book. Poole, Helen, illus. (p. 1210)
—Thanks for Sharing, Tommy. Mones, Marc, illus. (p. 1725)
—Thanks for Sharing, Tommy Lap Book. Mones, Marc, illus. (p. 1725)
Giachetti, Julia & Benchmark Education Co. Staff. Tail for a Tail - Cherokee Trickster Tales. (p. 1695)
Giacobbe, Beppe, illus. see Bartoletti, Susan Campbell.
Giacobbe, Beppe, illus. see Burleigh, Robert.
Giacobello, John. Bodyguards: Life Protecting Others. (p. 207)
—Choosing a Career in the Fashion Industry. (p. 310)
—Choosing a Career in the Toy Industry. (p. 310)
—Everything You Need to Know about Anxiety & Panic Attacks. (p. 545)
—Everything You Need to Know about the Dangers of Overachieving: A Guide for Relieving Pressure & Anxiety. (p. 546)
—You & Violence in Your Family. (p. 1973)
Giacobello, John, jt. auth. see Banks, Delilah.
Giacomini, Amanda, illus. see Hyde, Margaret.
Giacomo, Michael San. Phantom Jack. (p. 1349)
Giacomo, Renee San. Lily's Rainbow. Fernandez, Carina, illus. (p. 1018)
Giacomoni, Carol A. I can ski despite these Ducky feet on Me. (p. 836)
Giacomucci, Carol. New Home. (p. 1245)
Giallongo, Zach. Star Wars Doodles. Giallongo, Zach, illus. (p. 1641)
Giallongo, Zack. Broxo. Giallongo, Zack, illus. (p. 232)
Giallongo, Zack, illus. see Lendler, Ian.
Giallongo, Zack, illus. see Schweizer, Chris.
Giamanco, Candice (Bucky). Sweet Circus. (p. 1689)
Giambroni, Shannon. Tugger in the Country. (p. 1796)
Giambruno, Mark, jt. auth. see Hata, Kenjiro.
Giampa, Linda. Journey Through the Bible. (p. 928)
Gianakoulis, Theodore & MacPherson, Georgia. Fairy Tales of Modern Greece. (p. 564)
Gianatti, Silvia, et al. Tinker Bell & Her Magical Arrival. Melaranci, Elisabetta & Urbano, Emilio, illus. (p. 1755)
Giancamilli, Vanessa. Gecko Gathering. Kest, Kristin, illus. (p. 659)
—Patches Finds a Home. Hatala, Dan, illus. (p. 1328)
—Platypus Creek. Thivierge, Claude, illus. (p. 1370)
Giancanelli, Candace, illus. see Gard, Don.
Gianferrari, Maria. Penny & Jelly: Slumber under the Stars. Heder, Thyra, illus. (p. 1338)
—School Show. Heder, Thyra, illus. (p. 1523)
Giangrande, Cathy. Saint Petersburg: Museums, Palaces & Historic Collections. (p. 1504)
Giangregorio, Anthony. Only the Young Survive: An Apocalyptic Tale. (p. 1298)
—Zombies Are Cool. Collins, Andrew Dawe, illus. (p. 1988)
—Zombies Are People Too! (p. 1988)
Giangregorio, Kimberly A. Smelly Shoe. O'Toole, Julianne, illus. (p. 1593)
Giannakeff, Dianne D., adapted by. Young Actor's Bible: Stories from the Bible. (p. 1978)
Giannasi, Maddalena. Bianca & Her Alphabet Soup. (p. 175)
Gianni, Gary, jt. auth. see Henry, O.
Giannini, Claudia, tr. see Gonzalez, Ray.
Gianniny, Gary, jt. auth. see Fourment, Tiffany.
Giannotta, Andres Bernardo. Manga Stained Glass Coloring Book. (p. 1087)
Giannotta, Andres Bernardo & Drawing Staff. How to Draw Manga. (p. 818)
Gianopoulos, Andrea. Attractive Story of Magnetism with Max Axiom, Super Scientist. Martin, Cynthia & Schulz, Barbara, illus. (p. 114)
—Historia Atractiva del Magnetismo con Max Axiom, Supercientífico. Strictly Spanish, LLC., tr. from ENG. (p. 782)
Gianopoulos, Andrea & Barnett, Charles, III. Isaac Newton & the Laws of Motion Miller, Phil, illus. (p. 890)
Gianopoulos, Andrea & Barnett III, Charles. Isaac Newton & the Laws of Motion [Scholastic]. Miller, Phil, illus. (p. 890)
Gianopoulos, Andrea & Capstone Press Editors. Isaac Newton & the Laws of Motion Miller, Phil & Barnett, Charles, III, illus. (p. 890)
GIANTmicrobes(r). GIANTmicrobes — Cells Coloring Book. Cutting, David, illus. (p. 674)
—GIANTmicrobes — Germs & Microbes Coloring Book. Cutting, David, illus. (p. 674)
Giaquinta, Maria, illus. see Fabbella, Teresa.
Giardi, Sandy, jt. auth. see Clark, Seneca.
Giardino, Vittorio. Jew in Communist Prague: Rebellion Johnson, Joe, tr. from FRE. (p. 916)
—Jonas Fink: La Infancia. Vol. 1 (p. 925)
Giarrusso, Chris. G-Man Coming Home. (p. 651)
—G-Man Learning to Fly (p. 651)
—G-Man Super Journal: Awesome Origins. (p. 651)
—G-Man Volume 2: Cape Crisis: Cape Crisis. (p. 651)
—Mini Marvels: The Complete Collection. (p. 1146)
Giarrusso, Chris, illus. see Bell, Jake.
Gibala-Broxholm, Scott. Maddie's Monster Dad Gibala-Broxholm, Scott, illus. (p. 1069)
Gibala-Broxholm, Scott, illus. see Wax, Wendy.
Gibaldi, Lauren. Night We Said Yes. (p. 1254)
Gibb, Sarah. Rapunzel: Based on the Original Story by the Brothers Grimm. Gibb, Sarah, illus. (p. 1439)
Gibb, Sarah, illus. see French, Vivian.
Gibb, Sarah, illus. see Jones, Ursula.
Gibb, Sarah, illus. see Kessler, Liz.
Gibbins, Desiree. Book Keeper's Oracle. (p. 210)
Gibbon, Monk. Pupil: A Memory of Love. (p. 1417)
Gibbon, Rebecca. Bee Who Spoke: The Wonderful World of Belle & the Bee. (p. 157)
Gibbon, Rebecca, illus. see Bober, Natalie S.
Gibbon, Rebecca, illus. see Corey, Shana.
Gibbon, Rebecca, illus. see Preus, Margi.
Gibbon, Rebecca, illus. see Stone, Tanya Lee.
Gibbons, Alan. Blood Pressure. (p. 200)
—Charles Darwin. (p. 292)
—Demon Assassin. (p. 426)
—Dying Photo. (p. 491)
—Edge. (p. 504)
—Lost Boys' Appreciation Society. (p. 1055)
—Night Hunger. (p. 1253)
—Raining Fire. (p. 1436)
—Scared to Death. (p. 1519)
—Witch Breed. (p. 1941)
Gibbons, Alan, ed. see Donbavand, Tommy.
Gibbons, Alan, ed. see Rai, Bali.
Gibbons, Casey Hartley. Girl's Life with God. (p. 680)
Gibbons, Cassandra, illus. see Selig, Josh.
Gibbons, Charlie, et al. Graph Links Activity Package for Health: Macintosh. (p. 710)
—Graph Links Activity Package for Health. (p. 710)
—Teacher's Editions. (p. 1709)
Gibbons, Dave. Originals. (p. 1304)
Gibbons, Dave, illus. see Thomas, Roy, et al.
Gibbons, Dave, jt. auth. see Johns, Geoff.
Gibbons, David, ed. Timechart History of the World: 6000 Years of World History Unfolded. (p. 1753)
Gibbons, Deanna, illus. see Whitmore, Hugh.
Gibbons, Denis, ed. see Stewart, Mark.
Gibbons, Erin, ed. Whirl Story Bible: Lively Bible Stories to Inspire Faith. Keller, Matthew M., illus. (p. 1912)
Gibbons, Faye. Day the Picture Man Came. Meidell, Sherry, illus. (p. 414)
—Full Steam Ahead. Meidell, Sherry, illus. (p. 646)
—Mountain Wedding. Rand, Ted, illus. (p. 1181)
Gibbons, Gail. Alligators & Crocodiles. Gibbons, Gail, illus. (p. 47)
—Beavers. (p. 155)
—Beavers. Gibbons, Gail, illus. (p. 155)
—Chicks & Chickens. (p. 301)
—Clean Energy. (p. 330)
—Coral Reefs. Gibbons, Gail, illus. (p. 366)
—Corn. Gibbons, Gail, illus. (p. 367)
—Cowboys & Cowgirls. Gibbons, Gail, illus. (p. 374)
—De Sol a Sol. (p. 416)
—Dinosaur Discoveries. (p. 442)
—Dinosaurs. (p. 443)
—Dinosaurs! Gibbons, Gail, illus. (p. 443)
—Elephants of Africa. Gibbons, Gail, illus. (p. 512)
—From Seed to Plant. Gibbons, Gail, illus. (p. 643)
—From Sheep to Sweater. (p. 643)
—Fruits We Eat. (p. 646)
—Galaxies, Galaxies! Gibbons, Gail, illus. (p. 653)
—Galaxies, Galaxies. Gibbons, Gail, illus. (p. 653)
—Gorillas. Gibbons, Gail, illus. (p. 703)
—Grizzly Bears. Gibbons, Gail, illus. (p. 724)
—Groundhog Day! (p. 725)
—Groundhog Day. Gibbons, Gail, illus. (p. 725)
—Halloween Is... . (p. 738)
—Honey Makers. (p. 794)
—Horses! (p. 800)
—Horses! Gibbons, Gail, illus. (p. 800)
—Hurricanes! Gibbons, Gail, illus. (p. 830)
—Ice Cream: The Full Scoop. (p. 850)
—It's Raining! Gibbons, Gail, illus. (p. 898)
—It's Snowing! Gibbons, Gail, illus. (p. 898)
—Ladybugs. Gibbons, Gail, illus. (p. 971)
—Owls. (p. 1315)
—Owls. Gibbons, Gail, illus. (p. 1315)
—Planets. (p. 1368)
—Planets. Gibbons, Gail, illus. (p. 1368)
—Polar Bears. Gibbons, Gail, illus. (p. 1379)
—Quilting Bee. Gibbons, Gail, illus. (p. 1428)
—Say Woof! (p. 1519)
—Snakes. (p. 1596)
—Snakes. Gibbons, Gail, illus. (p. 1596)
—Surrounded by Sea: Life on a New England Fishing Island. Gibbons, Gail, illus. (p. 1686)
—Thanksgiving Is... (p. 1726)
—Tornadoes! (p. 1770)
—Tornadoes! Gibbons, Gail, illus. (p. 1770)
—Valentine's Day Is. Gibbons, Gail, illus. (p. 1830)
—Valentine's Day Is... Gibbons, Gail, illus. (p. 1830)
—Vegetables We Eat. (p. 1834)
Gibbons, Jim, ed. see Randall, Ron.
Gibbons, Jim, ed. see Reger, Rob & Huehner, Mariah.
Gibbons, Jolian A. Giggly Gaggle of Friends. (p. 676)
Gibbons, Joyce. What God Has Made! Johnson, Donna T., illus. (p. 1884)
Gibbons, Lynn. Sharks. (p. 1562)
Gibbons, Lynn, jt. auth. see Coode, Chris.
Gibbons, Lynn & Coode, Chris. Sharks. (p. 1562)
Gibbons, Rachelle. Big Buckaroo & Moose the Cow Dog. (p. 180)
Gibbons, Robert. Beyond Time New & Selected Work 1977-2007. (p. 174)
Gibbons, Susan. Love Grows: El Amor Crece. (p. 1059)
Gibbons, Ted & Wilcox, S. Michael. Modern Fables. McCune, Mark, illus. (p. 1158)
Gibbons, Teresa Dominguez. Greatest Gift. (p. 719)
—Pancakes Every Morning. (p. 1320)
Gibbons, Timothy M., illus. see Sutherland, Paul H.
Gibbons, Tony, illus. see Green, Tamara.
Gibbons, Tony & Snedden, Robert. Dinosaur Atlas. (p. 441)
Gibbs, Andrew, illus. see Pantone.
Gibbs, Anna. Mystery of the Healing Waters. (p. 1225)
Gibbs, D. L., jt. auth. see Fisher, Doris.
Gibbs, D. Renee. Special Little Christmas Tree. (p. 1623)
Gibbs, Dreene. Am I Pretty, Momma? (p. 51)
Gibbs, Edward. I Spy in the Sky. Gibbs, Edward, illus. (p. 846)
—I Spy on the Farm. Gibbs, Edward, illus. (p. 846)
—I Spy Pets. Gibbs, Edward, illus. (p. 846)
—I Spy under the Sea. Gibbs, Edward, illus. (p. 846)
—I Spy with My Little Eye. Gibbs, Edward, illus. (p. 846)
—Little Acorn Grows Up. (p. 1023)
—Little Bee. (p. 1024)
Gibbs, Gail L. What about Those Pants? (p. 1879)
Gibbs, Gretchen. Book of Maggie Bradstreet. (p. 211)
Gibbs, Jeanne. Collector's Book of Novelty Pans (p. 340)
Gibbs, Jon. Barnum's Revenge. (p. 139)
Gibbs, Lisa & Hellard, Bernadette. Netball Diary. (p. 1242)
Gibbs, Lynne. Mega Book of Motorcycles. (p. 1124)
—Mega Book of Trucks: Discover the Most Amazing Trucks on Earth! (p. 1124)
—Molly Mouse Is Shy: A Story of Shyness. Mitchell, Melanie, illus. (p. 1161)
—Time to Share: A Story of Sharing. Mitchell, Melanie, illus. (p. 1753)
Gibbs, Lynne & Morris, Neil. Mega Book of Cars. (p. 1124)
Gibbs, Maddie. Aardvarks: Cerdos Hormigueros. (p. 2)
—Aardvarks. (p. 2)
—African Buffalo. (p. 27)
—Amigos de la Granja / Farmyard Friends (p. 65)
—Antelope. (p. 89)
—Antelope / Antílopes. (p. 89)
—Chickens (p. 300)
—Clownfish. (p. 335)
—Clownfish / Los Peces Payaso. De La Vega, Eida, ed. (p. 335)
—Cows (p. 374)
—Crocodiles: Cocodrilos. (p. 384)
—Crocodiles. (p. 384)
—Ducks (p. 488)
—Farmyard Friends (p. 575)
—Flamingos: Flamencos. (p. 602)
—Flamingos. (p. 602)
—Goats (p. 687)
—Goldfish. (p. 695)
—Horses (p. 800)
—Hyenas: Hienas. (p. 831)
—Hyenas. (p. 831)
—Jackals: Chacales. (p. 903)
—Jackals. (p. 903)
—Jellyfish. (p. 912)
—Las Cabras / Goats (p. 976)
—Las Vacas / Cows (p. 977)
—Los Caballos / Horses (p. 1053)
—Los Patos / Ducks (p. 1054)
—Ostriches: Avestruces. (p. 1306)
—Ostriches. (p. 1306)
—Pigs (p. 1358)
—Rays. (p. 1441)
—Rays / Las Rayas. De La Vega, Eida, ed. (p. 1441)

—Sea Horses. (p. 1534)
—Sea Horses / Los Caballos de Mar. De La Vega, Eida, ed. (p. 1534)
—Sea Stars. (p. 1535)
—Sea Stars / Las Estrellas de Mar. De La Vega, Eida, ed. (p. 1535)
Gibbs, Maddie & Alamán, Eduardo. Goldfish: Los Carpines. (p. 695)
—Jellyfish: Las Medusas. (p. 912)
Gibbs, May. Complete Adventures of Snugglepot & Cuddlepie. (p. 352)
Gibbs, Megan, illus. see Crouch, Adele.
Gibbs, Noni & Kahrs, Christina. Rahab's Promise. Vieira, Andrei, illus. (p. 1433)
Gibbs Smith & Adams, Jennifer. Button-Lit Wearable Classic Literature Button Box Oliver, Alison, illus. (p. 248)
Gibbs Smith & Williams, Nate. Hank & Snoliver in Put down the Phone! Williams, Nate, illus. (p. 742)
Gibbs Smith Publisher Staff, jt. auth. see Lederer, Richard.
Gibbs, Stuart. Belly Up. (p. 163)
—Double Cross. (p. 472)
—Evil Spy School. (p. 546)
—Last Musketeer. (p. 978)
—Poached. (p. 1374)
—Spaced Out. (p. 1620)
—Spy Camp. (p. 1636)
—Spy School. (p. 1636)
—Traitor's Chase. (p. 1777)
Gibbs, Susie. Scary Poems to Make You Shiver. Chatterton, Martin, illus. (p. 1520)
Gibbs, Tracey, illus. see Banyard, Jen.
Gibbs, Tracy, illus. see Morgan, Sally.
Gibby, Bayne. You Mean the World to Me. Walker, David, illus. (p. 1976)
Gibeau, Claire Janvier. Active Alphabet. (p. 10)
—Circus in Grandpa's Day. (p. 322)
—Homonyms. (p. 794)
Gibelin, Christophe, jt. auth. see N'Guessan, Marc.
Giberson, Angela Bradford. Electric Voices. (p. 508)
Gibert, Jean Claude, illus. see Weiss, Ellen.
Gibler, Douglas M. & University of Alabama Staff. International Military Alliances, 1648-2000 (p. 880)
Giblett, Rod. Living with the Earth: Mastery to Mutuality. (p. 1042)
Giblin. Curl It, Braid It, Shave It. (p. 394)
Giblin, Brian E., ed. see Galvin, Laura Gates & Studio Mouse Staff.
Giblin, Brian E., ed. see Nussbaum, Ben.
Giblin, Erinn, ed. see Reed, Nicole.
Giblin, James Cross. Amazing Life of Benjamin Franklin. Dooling, Michael, illus. (p. 55)
—Good Brother, Bad Brother: The Story of Edwin Booth & John Wilkes Booth. (p. 697)
—Life & Death of Adolf Hitler. (p. 1007)
—Rise & Fall of Senator Joe McCarthy. (p. 1474)
Giblin, James Cross, ed. see Hansen, Joyce.
Giblin, James Cross, jt. auth. see Bunting, Eve.
Giblin, James Cross, jt. auth. see Peek, Merle.
Giblin, Sheri, photos by see Grunes, Barbara.
Giblin, Sheri, photos by see Spieler, Marlena.
Gibney, Shannon. See No Color. (p. 1546)
Gibons, Gail. Vegetables We Eat. (p. 1834)
Gibran, Khalil. Profeta; El Loco; Paginas Escogidas. Sfair, Antonio Chalita, tr. (p. 1409)
Gibs, Leighanne. Emo Poetry & Prose. (p. 520)
Gibsen, Cole. Katana. (p. 944)
—Life Unaware. (p. 1013)
—Senshi. (p. 1551)
—Shinobi. (p. 1567)
Gibson. Sail Yel Nf Colorful Animals. (p. 1503)
—Sail Yel Nf Out of the Egg. (p. 1503)
Gibson, Amy. By Day, by Night. So, Meilo, illus. (p. 249)
—Catching Kisses. van Lieshout, Maria, illus. (p. 279)
—Split! Splat! Björkman, Steve, illus. (p. 1630)
Gibson, Angela S. Colors of God. (p. 345)
Gibson, B. J. Grannie's World Record Collard Greens. (p. 710)
Gibson, B. W. Extra Innings: The Diamond Thieves. (p. 555)
Gibson, Barbara, illus. see Dodge, Andrew.
Gibson, Barbara, illus. see Penn, Audrey.
Gibson, Barbara L., illus. see Penn, Audrey.
Gibson, Barbara L., jt. auth. see Penn, Audrey.
Gibson, Barbara Leonard. Dragonfly Door. (p. 478)
Gibson, Barbara Leonard, illus. see Penn, Audrey.
Gibson, Barbara Leonard, illus. see Smith, Marie, et al.
Gibson, Beatrice. Legend of the Sandals. (p. 989)
Gibson, Betty & Denton, Kady MacDonald. Couac, la Petite Cane (Little Quack) (p. 369)
Gibson, Bonnie R. May I Keep You in My Pocket? (p. 1112)
Gibson, Brylee. Dinosaur Discoveries. (p. 442)
—Disease Detectives. (p. 450)
—Extreme Scientists. (p. 556)
—Keeping in Touch. (p. 947)
—Looking after Our World. (p. 1050)
—Megacities. (p. 1124)
—Scams. (p. 1519)
—Tails, Tails, Tails. (p. 1695)
—Unseen by the Eye. (p. 1822)
—Wildlife Detectives. (p. 1931)
—Wonders of the World Megastructures. (p. 1949)
—World Beyond Earth. (p. 1954)
Gibson, C. R., Company Staff. Ballet Slippers Diary. (p. 134)
—Story of Easter. (p. 1658)
Gibson, Carol Ann. Loopy. (p. 1052)
Gibson, Catherine. Through Sophie's Eyes. (p. 1745)
Gibson, Cay. Cajun 'Ti Beau & the Cocodries. D'Antoni, Colleen, illus. (p. 252)
—Catholic Mosaic: Living the Liturgical Year with Literature, an Illustrated Book Study for Children. Decaen, Rose, ed. (p. 280)
Gibson, Charles, illus. see Tullgren, Terrence.
Gibson, Chris. Acne Free in 3 Days: How I Cured My Acne Condition in 3 Days. (p. 9)
—No More Moles, Warts, or Skin Tags: How I Safely Removed Moles, Warts, & Skin Tags for Life. Universal Marketing Media, ed. (p. 1259)
Gibson, Clare. Secret Life of Dreams: Decoding the Messages from Your Subconscious. (p. 1541)
Gibson, Dave, illus. see Eggleton, Jill.
Gibson, Donovan. Ticker That Needed a Fixer. Rottinger, Amy, illus. (p. 1747)
Gibson, Douglas. Tales of a Fifth-Grade Knight. Tuya, Jez, illus. (p. 1702)
Gibson, Gary A. Tronix 2 Basic Digital Concepts: Basic Digital Concepts. (p. 1788)
Gibson, Ginger Foglesong. Tiptoe Joe. Rankin, Laura, illus. (p. 1757)
Gibson, Gregory V., illus. see Gibson, James E. & Gibson, Sylvia Scott.
Gibson, Gregory V., illus. see Gibson, Sylvia Scott & Gibson, James E.
Gibson, Gregory V., illus. see Gibson, Sylvia Scott.
Gibson, J. Phil & Gibson, Terri R. Natural Selection. (p. 1236)
—Plant Ecology. (p. 1369)
Gibson, James C., illus. see Gibson, Roxie C.
Gibson, James C., illus. see Gibson, Roxie Cawood.
Gibson, James E. Rico, the Mysterious Worm (p. 1470)
Gibson, James E., jt. auth. see Gibson, Sylvia Scott.
Gibson, James E. & Gibson, Sylvia Scott. Treetoe the Space Monster Gibson, Gregory V., illus. (p. 1784)
Gibson, Jennifer & Roth, Ashley. Gracie & Grandma & the Rock Star Birthday Party. (p. 705)
Gibson, Jim, illus. see Gibson, Roxie.
Gibson, Jo. Afraid. (p. 26)
—Obsessed. (p. 1275)
—Twisted. (p. 1802)
Gibson, Josephine. Is There a Mouse in the House? (p. 890)
Gibson, Julia Mary. Copper Magic. (p. 365)
Gibson, Karen. Adrian Peterson. (p. 13)
—Amazon River. (p. 56)
—Ancient Babylon. (p. 68)
—Railroad Comes to America (1820-1830) (p. 1434)
—San Antonio. (p. 1510)
—We Visit Nigeria. (p. 1868)
—What It's Like to Be George Lopez. de la Vega, Eida, tr. from ENG. (p. 1891)
—What It's Like to Be Jennifer Lopez. de la Vega, Eida, tr. from ENG. (p. 1891)
—What It's Like to Be Vladimir Guerrero. de la Vega, Eida, tr. (p. 1891)
Gibson, Karen B., jt. auth. see Gibson, Karen Bush.
Gibson, Karen Bush. Eli Whitney. (p. 512)
—Fury of Hurricane Andrew 1992. (p. 650)
—Herman Melville. (p. 771)
—Historic Fight for the 2008 Democratic Presidential Nomination: The Obama View. (p. 782)
—John Peter Zenger. (p. 922)
—Langston Hughes. (p. 974)
—Life & Times of Catherine the Great. (p. 1008)
—Mudslide in la Conchita, California 2005. (p. 1189)
—Native American History for Kids: With 21 Activities. (p. 1234)
—New Netherland: The Dutch Settle the Hudson Valley. (p. 1246)
—Samuel Adams. (p. 1509)
—Spotlight on Europe (p. 1634)
—Spotlight on North America (p. 1634)
—Spotlight on South America (p. 1634)
—Venezuela. (p. 1835)
—Vietnam War. (p. 1841)
—Ways to Help Children with Disabilities: A Guide to Giving Back. (p. 1865)
—Women Aviators: 26 Stories of Pioneer Flights, Daring Missions, & Record-Setting Journeys. (p. 1945)
—Women in Space: 23 Stories of First Flights, Scientific Missions, & Gravity-Breaking Adventures. (p. 1946)
Gibson, Karen Bush & Gibson, Karen B. Blackfeet: People of the Dark Moccasins (p. 197)
—Great Basin Indians: Daily Life in The 1700s (p. 714)
—Oklahoma Facts & Symbols. (p. 1283)
—Pawnee: Farmers & Hunters of the Central Plains. (p. 1331)
—Venezuela: A Question & Answer Book (p. 1835)
Gibson, Marley. Awakening. (p. 120)
—Counseling. (p. 369)
—Discovery. (p. 450)
—Guidance. (p. 730)
—Radiate. (p. 1432)
—Reason (p. 1450)
Gibson, Mary. Buried Treasure. (p. 243)
Gibson, Melissa A. Clarice the Charming Clarinet. (p. 327)
Gibson, Narie. Judah the Barracuda. (p. 930)
Gibson, Nichoel, illus. see Vogl, Nancy & Strange, David.
Gibson, R. Contar y Estampar. (p. 360)
—Juggling. (p. 932)
—Recortar y Pegar. (p. 1452)
—What Shall I Draw? (p. 1893)
—What Shall I Grow? (p. 1893)
—What Shall I Make? (p. 1893)
Gibson, R. & Watt, F. Summer Activities. (p. 1673)
—Things to Make & Do for Christmas. (p. 1733)
Gibson, Ray. Big Book of Things to Do: Combined Volume. Stitt, Sue, illus. (p. 179)
—Crayon Activities Pack. (p. 377)
—Drawing Animals Pack. (p. 481)
—I Can Cut & Stick, I Can Crayon, I Can Finger Paint, I Can Draw Animals, I Can Count, I Can Add up & Fun with Numbers. (p. 835)
—I Can Draw Animals Kid Kit. (p. 835)
—I Can Draw People. Watt, Fiona, ed. (p. 835)
—Ideas para Navidad. (p. 852)
—Little book of vacation Activities. (p. 1025)
—Things That Move Kid Kit. (p. 1733)
—What Shall I Grow? Watt, Fiona, ed. (p. 1893)
—What Shall I Paint? Everett, Felicity, ed. (p. 1893)
Gibson, Rex, ed. see Bevington, David & Shakespeare, William.
Gibson, Rex, ed. see Clamp, Mike.
Gibson, Rex, ed. see Innes, Sheila.
Gibson, Rex, ed. see Shakespeare, William.
Gibson, Rex & Shakespeare, William. As You Like It. Andrews, Richard, ed. (p. 105)
Gibson, Roxie. Talking with God. Gibson, Jim, illus. (p. 1704)
Gibson, Roxie C. Hey, God! Listen! Gibson, James C., illus. (p. 774)
—Hey God! What Is Christmas? Gibson, James C., illus. (p. 774)
—Hey, God! What Makes You Happy? Gibson, James C., illus. (p. 774)
Gibson, Roxie Cawood. Hey God, Where Are You? Gibson, James C., illus. (p. 774)
Gibson, Sabina, illus. see Hall, Kirsten.
Gibson, Sherri L. In the Mind of a Child: Children's Stories. (p. 866)
Gibson, Sonya. My Dog, Trinity. (p. 1202)
Gibson, Steve. Sparky the Firehouse Dog Weishampel, Winifred Ann, illus. (p. 1622)
Gibson, Sylvia Scott. Ricky the Skating Worm & Friends Gibson, Gregory V., illus. (p. 1470)
Gibson, Sylvia Scott, jt. auth. see Gibson, James E.
Gibson, Sylvia Scott & Gibson, James E. Latawnya the Naughty Horse Two Gibson, Gregory V., illus. (p. 979)
Gibson, Taylor, illus. see Clark, Steven & Clark, Justin.
Gibson, Terri R., jt. auth. see Gibson, J. Phil.
Gibson, Tonya. Hiking with Dad. (p. 779)
Gibson, William. All Tomorrow's Parties. (p. 46)
Gidali, Orit. Nora the Mind Reader. Gordon-Noy, Aya, illus. (p. 1264)
Gidaro, Ellen Glassman, jt. auth. see Vernick, Audrey Glassman.
Giddens, Jake, illus. see Leipold, Judith.
Giddens, Martha Anne. Unluckiest Kid in the Universe. (p. 1821)
Giddens, Owen, jt. auth. see Giddens, Sandra.
Giddens, Sandra. Chris Daughtry. (p. 311)
—Coping with Chemotherapy. (p. 365)
—Coping with Grieving & Loss. (p. 365)
—Everything You Need to Know about Crohn's Disease & Ulcerative Colitis. (p. 545)
—Frequently Asked Questions about Suicide. (p. 636)
—Future Techniques in Surgery. (p. 651)
—Making Smart Choices about Food, Nutrition, & Lifestyle. (p. 1082)
—Obsessive-Compulsive Disorder. (p. 1275)
—Suicide. (p. 1673)
—Timeline of the Constitutional Convention. (p. 1754)
—Timeline of the War of 1812. (p. 1754)
Giddens, Sandra, jt. auth. see McIntyre, Abigael.
Giddens, Sandra & Giddens, Owen. Coping with Chemotherapy. (p. 365)
—Coping with Grieving & Loss. (p. 365)
—Everything You Need to Know about Crohn's Disease & Colitis. (p. 545)
—Future Techniques in Surgery. (p. 651)
—Making Smart Choices about Food, Nutrition, & Lifestyle. (p. 1082)
Giddens, Sandra & Owen. Chinese Mythology. (p. 307)
Giddens-White, Bryon. Supreme Court & the Judicial Branch (p. 1684)
Giddings, Joshua. Exiles of Florida - or, the Crimes Committed by Our Government Against the Maroons Who Fled from South Carolina & Other Slave States Seeking Protection under Spanish Laws. (p. 548)
Giddings, Sharon, et al. Cystic Fibrosis. (p. 397)
Giddy Up Staff. Backyardigans Color Blast. (p. 131)
—Go Diego Go Water Wow! Book. (p. 686)
—Littlest Pet Shop Color N Carry II. (p. 1039)
—Littlest Pet Shop ColorBlast. (p. 1039)
—SpongeBob Abraca Dazzle. (p. 1630)
—Transformers Color N Carry II. (p. 1778)
—Transformers Gears & Games. (p. 1778)
Giddy Up Staff, contrib. by. Barbie Color Blast Mini. (p. 138)
—Barbie Color N Carry II. (p. 138)
—Barbie ColorBlast. (p. 138)
—Barbie Surprize Ink Book 2. (p. 138)
—Barbie Water Wow Book. (p. 138)
—Blendy Pen Small Blister Kit. (p. 199)
—Camp Rock Surprize Ink Book. (p. 257)
—Diego Color Blast. (p. 437)
—Diego Surprize Ink Book. (p. 437)
—Dora Color Blast Mini. (p. 470)
—Dora Rub N Color Mini. (p. 470)
—Dora Surprize Ink Book 3. (p. 471)
—Dora the Explorer Color N Carry II. (p. 471)
—Dora the Explorer ColorBlast. (p. 471)
—Dora Water Wow! Book. (p. 471)
—Hannah Montana Surprize Ink Book. (p. 742)
—Hello Kitty ColorBlast. (p. 764)
—High School Musical Surprize Ink Book. (p. 778)
—Littlest Pet Shop Rub N Color Mini Book. (p. 1039)
—Littlest Pet Shop Surprize Ink Book. (p. 1039)
—Littlest Pet Shop Surprize Ink Book 2. (p. 1039)
—Littlest Pet Shop Water Wow Book. (p. 1039)
—Littlests Pet Shop Color Blast Mini. (p. 1039)
—Mickey Color Blast Mini. (p. 1136)
—Mickey Surprize Ink Book. (p. 1136)
—Mickey Water Wow Book. (p. 1136)
—My Little Pony Color Blast Mini. (p. 1213)
—My Little Pony Surprize Ink Book 3. (p. 1213)
—My Little Pony Water Wow! Book. (p. 1213)
—Princess Pop Beads How to Book. (p. 1405)
—Princess Water Wow Book. (p. 1406)
—Rub N Color Large Kit. (p. 1493)
—Rub N Color Small Kit. (p. 1493)
—Sesame Street Licensed Color n Carry Ll. (p. 1553)
—Sesame Street Surprize Ink Book 2. (p. 1553)
—Sesame Street Water Wow! Book. (p. 1553)
—Spiderman Blendy Pen Poster Book. (p. 1626)
—Spiderman Color Blast Mini. (p. 1626)
—Spiderman Surprize Ink Book. (p. 1626)
—Spiderman Surprize Ink Book2. (p. 1626)
—Spiderman Water Wow Book. (p. 1626)
—Sponge Bob Rub N Color Mini. (p. 1630)
—Spongebob Color N Carry II. (p. 1630)
—SpongeBob ColorBlast. (p. 1630)
—SpongeBob Surprize Ink Book 4. (p. 1630)
—Spongebob Water Wow! Book. (p. 1630)
—Thomas Tank Rub N Color Mini Book. (p. 1739)
—Thomas Tank Surprize Ink Book. (p. 1739)
—Thomas Tank Water Wow Book. (p. 1739)
—Tigger & Pooh Surprize Ink Book. (p. 1749)
—Transformers Animated Water Wow Book. (p. 1778)
Gideon, Amos, jt. auth. see Zenko, Darren.
Gideon, Brook, jt. auth. see Kleinman, Liza.
Gideon, John. Little Soup Spoon. (p. 1036)
Gidney, Craig Laurance. Bereft. (p. 166)
Gidre, Linda, et al. Take Your Mark on Vacation. (p. 1697)
Gidwitz, Adam. Grimm Conclusion. (p. 724)
—Grimm Conclusion. D'Andrade, Hugh, illus. (p. 724)
—In a Glass Grimmly. (p. 863)
—In a Glass Grimmly. D'Andrade, Hugh, illus. (p. 863)
—Tale Dark & Grimm (p. 1699)
—Tale Dark & Grimm. (p. 1699)
—Tale Dark & Grimm. D'Andrade, Hugh, illus. (p. 1699)
Gidwitz, Adam, et al. Tale Dark & Grimm. D'Andrade, Hugh, illus. (p. 1699)
Giebfried, Rosemary, illus. see Markowsky, Judy Kellogg.
Giebfried, Rosemary, illus. see Stevens, Betsy T.
Giebink, Bruce. Minnesota Bug Hunt. Johnson, Bill, photos by. (p. 1147)
Giegreen, Alan, illus. see Cleary, Beverly.
Giella, Joe, illus. see Fox, Gardner & Broome, John.
Giella, Joe, illus. see Kanigher, Robert & Broome, John.
Gier, Kerstin. Dream a Little Dream. Bell, Anthea, tr. from GER. (p. 483)
—Emerald Green. (p. 517)
—Emerald Green. Bell, Anthea, tr. (p. 517)
—Ruby Red. Bell, Anthea, tr. (p. 1493)
—Ruby Red. Bell, Anthea, tr. from GER. (p. 1493)
—Sapphire Blue. Bell, Anthea, tr. (p. 1514)
—Sapphire Blue. Bell, Anthea, tr. from GER. (p. 1514)
Gierhart, Steve, ed. see Wines, Michael P.
Giersbach-Rascon, Susan, tr. see Bencastro, Mario.
Giese, Stephanie. Cookie Jar Parable. (p. 361)
Giesecke, Ernestine. Be Your Own Boss: Small Businesses. (p. 149)
—Governments Around the World (p. 704)
—Local Government (p. 1044)
—National Government (p. 1233)
—State Government (p. 1644)
Giesecke, Ernestine & Heinemann Library Staff. Governments Around the World (p. 704)
—Local Government (p. 1044)
—National Government (p. 1233)
—State Government (p. 1644)
Gieselmann, Reinhard. Happy Prince & Other Tales. (p. 746)
Gieser, Sherry. Opening Gifts: Marriage & Holy Orders. (p. 1300)
Giesler, Dagmar & Geisler, Dagmar. Max juega en la Arena. (p. 1111)
Gifaldi, David. Toby Scudder, King of the School. (p. 1760)
Giff, Patricia Reilly. All about Stacy. (p. 43)
—All the Way Home. (p. 46)
—Bears Beware. Bright, Alasdair, illus. (p. 151)
—B-E-S-T Friends. (p. 122)
—Big Something. Palmisciano, Diane, illus. (p. 184)
—Big Whopper. Bright, Alasdair, illus. (p. 184)
—Dias Sombrios. (p. 435)
—Don't Tell the Girls: A Family Memoir. (p. 468)
—Eleven. (p. 512)
—Fancy Feet. (p. 570)
—Fiercely & Friends: the Big Something. Palmisciano, Diane, illus. (p. 584)
—Fiercely & Friends: the Sneaky Snow Fox. Palmisciano, Diane, illus. (p. 584)
—Flying Feet. Bright, Alasdair, illus. (p. 610)
—Garden Monster. Palmisciano, Diane, illus. (p. 656)
—Gingersnap. (p. 677)
—Horas de Sol. (p. 797)
—House of Tailors. (p. 803)
—Hunter Moran Digs Deep. (p. 828)
—Hunter Moran Hangs Out. (p. 828)
—Hunter Moran Saves the Universe. (p. 828)
—Laura Ingalls Wilder. (p. 980)
—Maggie's Door. (p. 1071)
—Mystery of the Blue Ring. (p. 1225)
—Nory Ryan's Song. (p. 1266)
—Number One Kid. Bright, Alasdair, illus. (p. 1271)
—Patti Cake & Her New Doll. Bryant, Laura J., illus. (p. 1329)
—Pictures of Hollis Woods. (p. 1356)
—Powder Puff Puzzle. (p. 1389)
—R My Name Is Rachel. (p. 1429)
—Relato de un Verano. (p. 1458)
—Riddle of the Red Purse. (p. 1470)
—Secret at the Polk Street School. (p. 1540)
—Sky High. (p. 1586)
—Sneaky Snow Fox. Palmisciano, Diane, illus. (p. 1597)
—Soccer Song. Sims, Blanche, illus. (p. 1603)
—Stacy Says Good-Bye. (p. 1638)
—Star Time. Bright, Alasdair, illus. (p. 1641)
—Storyteller. (p. 1663)
—Super Surprise. Bright, Alasdair, illus. (p. 1682)
—Until I Find Julian. (p. 1823)
—Watch Out! Man-Eating Snake. (p. 1861)
—Water Street. (p. 1863)
—Wild Girl. (p. 1929)
—Willow Run. (p. 1934)
—Winter Sky. (p. 1938)
—Zigzag Zoom. Bright, Alasdair, illus. (p. 1986)
Giffen, Keith. What Were They Thinking?! Leib, Michael S., illus. (p. 1895)
Giffen, Keith & DeMatteis, J. M. Planetary Brigade. Abraham, Joe et al, illus. (p. 1368)
Giffen, Keith, et al. Jeremiah Harm. Lyra, Rael & Albuquerque, Rafael, illus. (p. 913)
—Rocket Raccoon: Guardian of the Keystone Quadrant. (p. 1483)
Giffin, Noelle, illus. see Chand, Emlyn.
Giffin, Noelle, illus. see Verstraete, Majanka.

Gifford, Carrie, illus. see Daneshvari, Gitty.
Gifford, Clare. Dick Whittington. Cerisier, Emmanuel, illus. (p. 436)
Gifford, Clive. 100 Grossest Facts. (p. 1998)
—100 Weirdest Facts. (p. 1999)
—Activator's Cycling. (p. 10)
—Activators Football. (p. 10)
—Amazing Applications & Perfect Programs. (p. 53)
—Arms Trade. (p. 100)
—Astronomy, Astronauts, & Space Exploration. (p. 109)
—Awesome Algorithms & Creative Coding. (p. 120)
—Ball Sports. (p. 134)
—Baseball. (p. 140)
—Basketball. (p. 143)
—Business of Soccer. (p. 245)
—Cars. (p. 271)
—Chasing the World's Most Dangerous Storms (p. 294)
—Child Labor. (p. 301)
—Computer Networks. (p. 355)
—Dead or Alive? Horne, Sarah, illus. (p. 417)
—Diggers & Cranes. (p. 439)
—Discover Science: Robots. (p. 448)
—Ducati. (p. 487)
—Empire Windrush. (p. 521)
—Explorers: Things That Go. Bull, Peter, illus. (p. 551)
—Extreme Motorcycle Racing (p. 556)
—Eye Benders: The Science of Seeing & Believing. (p. 557)
—Food & Cooking in Ancient Egypt. (p. 613)
—Food & Cooking in Ancient Greece. (p. 613)
—Food & Cooking in Ancient Rome. (p. 613)
—Food & Cooking in Viking Times. (p. 613)
—Food Technology. (p. 614)
—Football. (p. 614)
—Gangs. (p. 655)
—Golf: From Tee to Green-The Essential Guide for Young Golfers. (p. 696)
—Great Global Puzzle Challenge with Google Earth. Ings, William, illus. (p. 716)
—His Dark Materials? The Unofficial Quiz Book. (p. 781)
—How the World Works: Know It All, from How the Sun Shines to How the Pyramids Were Built. (p. 813)
—Inside Story of Motorsports. (p. 877)
—Inside Story of Soccer. (p. 877)
—Inside Story of Track & Field. (p. 877)
—Inside Story of World Cup Soccer. (p. 877)
—Karate. (p. 943)
—Kickboxing. (p. 951)
—Killer History: A Gruesome & Grisly Trip Through the Past. (p. 956)
—Kingfisher Book of Soccer Skills. (p. 960)
—Kingfisher Soccer Encyclopedia. (p. 960)
—Martial Arts. (p. 1097)
—Martial Arts Legends. (p. 1097)
—Motorbikes. (p. 1179)
—My First Soccer Book: A Brilliant Introduction to the Beautiful Game. (p. 1208)
—North Korea. (p. 1265)
—Official IRB Rugby World Cup 2015 Fact File. (p. 1280)
—Out of This World: All the Cool Stuff about Space You Want to Knkow. (p. 1311)
—Out of This World: All the Cool Stuff about Space You Want to Know. Pinder, Andrew, illus. (p. 1311)
—Planes & Helicopters. (p. 1367)
—Poverty. (p. 1389)
—Racism. (p. 1432)
—Racism. (p. 1432)
—Robots. (p. 1481)
—Robots. Picini, Frank, illus. (p. 1481)
—Running. (p. 1497)
—Science of Computers. (p. 1527)
—Skiing. (p. 1584)
—So You Think You Know David Beckham? (p. 1602)
—So You Think You Know Harry Potter: Over 1000 Wizard Quiz Questions. (p. 1602)
—So You Think You Know London? Over 100 Brilliant Quiz Questions. (p. 1602)
—So You Think You Know Narnia? Over 1,000 Quiz Questions about the Magical Narnia Books. (p. 1602)
—So You Think You Know Shakespeare? With over 1000 Questions about the Bard, His Life & His Works. (p. 1602)
—So You Think You Know the Olympics. (p. 1602)
—Soccer: The Ultimate Guide to the Beautiful Game. (p. 1603)
—Soccer. (p. 1603)
—Soccer Legends. (p. 1603)
—Soccer Players & Skills. (p. 1603)
—Soccer Rules & Regulations. (p. 1603)
—Solar System, Meteors, & Comets. (p. 1607)
—Sports. (p. 1632)
—Stars, Galaxies, & the Milky Way. (p. 1643)
—Super Trucks. (p. 1682)
—Swimming. (p. 1691)
—Swimming & Diving. (p. 1691)
—Teamwork in Soccer. (p. 1711)
—Technology. (p. 1711)
—Teenage Kicks: 101 Things to Do Before You're 16. (p. 1714)
—Tell Me about Sports. (p. 1716)
—Tennis. (p. 1720)
—Think Again! False Facts Attacked & Myths Busted. (p. 1734)
—Track & Field. (p. 1775)
—Tractors. (p. 1775)
—Trucks. (p. 1791)
—Universe, Black Holes, & the Big Bang. (p. 1820)
—Vietnam War. (p. 1841)
—Violence on the Screen. (p. 1843)
—Why Did the Vietnam War Happen? (p. 1923)
—World War II: True Stories. (p. 1959)
—Wrestling. (p. 1962)
Gifford, Clive, jt. auth. see Platt, Richard.
Gifford, Clive, jt. auth. see Tick Tock Staff.
Gifford, Clive, jt. auth. see Woods, Mark.
Gifford, Clive & Dorling Kindersley Publishing Staff. Skateboarding. (p. 1583)
Gifford, Clive & Phillips, Dee. Soccer World Cup. (p. 1604)
Gifford, Dorinda. Harriet the Ferret Luevano, Raul, illus. (p. 749)
Gifford, George E., Jr., ed. Dear Jeffie: Being the Letters from Jeffries Wyman to His Son Jeffries Wyman, Jr. (p. 419)
Gifford, Griselda. Second Sight. (p. 1539)
Gifford, Jerry. Squirrel Highway. (p. 1637)
Gifford, Myrna. Meet the Lit Kids: A Read-and-Sing Book. Cooper, Frances, illus. (p. 1123)
—Name Those Vowels: A Read-and-Sing Book. Cooper, Frances, illus. (p. 1228)
—Oh, Do You Know? A Read-and-Sing Book. Cooper, France, illus. (p. 1280)
—Spelling Families: A Read-and-Sing Book. Cooper, Frances, illus. (p. 1625)
—Talking & Walking: A Read-and-Sing Book. Cooper, Frances, illus. (p. 1703)
—Two Little Letters: A Read-and-Sing Book. Cooper, Frances, illus. (p. 1804)
—What's That Sound? A Read-and-Sing Book. Cooper, Frances, illus. (p. 1899)
Gifford, Myrna Ross. Outlaws: A Read-and-Sing Book. Cooper, Frances, illus. (p. 1312)
—Silent E: A Read-and-Sing Book. Cooper, Frances, illus. (p. 1575)
Gifford, P. S. Dr. Offig's Lessons from the Dark Side, Volume 1. (p. 475)
Gifford, Peggy. Great Big Green. Desimini, Lisa, illus. (p. 714)
—Moxy Maxwell Does Not Love Stuart Little. Fisher, Valorie, photos by. (p. 1184)
—Moxy Maxwell Does Not Love Writing Thank-You Notes. Fisher, Valorie, illus. (p. 1184)
Gifford, Scott. Piece = Part = Portion: Fractions = Decimals = Percents. Thaler, Shmuel, photos by. (p. 1356)
—Piece = Part = Portion. Thaler, Shmuel, photos by. (p. 1356)
Gifune, Greg F. Night Work. Kirkpatrick, Katrina, illus. (p. 1254)
Gigante, Carol. First Family: And Their Struggle to Survive. (p. 595)
Giganti, Paul. How Many Blue Birds Flew Away? A Counting Book with a Difference. Crews, Donald, illus. (p. 811)
—Numeros Importantes. Grbich, Aaron, illus. (p. 1273)
Gigarjian, Ani & Avedikian, Linda. My Second Book of Armenian Words. (p. 1218)
Giggenbach, Ellen. My Town. (p. 1220)
—My Zoo. (p. 1222)
Gigi. Adventures of Simsim: Based on a True Story. Alvarado, Eladia, illus. (p. 23)
Gigi, Jessy. Sky Ride of Jimmy & Friends. (p. 1587)
Giglio, James N. Stan Musial: Baseball Hero. (p. 1639)
Giglio, Judy. Communication Then & Now (p. 349)
—Dreaming of Great Ideas (p. 484)
—Sounds & How We Hear Them (p. 1615)
—Tapping Tale. (p. 1706)
—Tapping Tale. Cepeda, Joe, illus. (p. 1706)
—Third Grade Scholar. Boyer, Robin, illus. (p. 1734)
Giglio, Judy & Capstone Press Editors. Dreaming of Great Ideas (p. 484)
Giglio, Judy & Capstone Press Staff. Communication Then & Now (p. 349)
—Sounds & How We Hear Them (p. 1615)
Giglio, Louie. Wired: For a Life of Worship. (p. 1939)
Gigliotti, Jim. AFC North. (p. 26)
—Amazing NASCAR Races. (p. 55)
—Animal Sports (p. 79)
—Dale Earnhardt Jr. (p. 401)
—Defensive Backs. (p. 424)
—Famous NASCAR Tracks. (p. 569)
—Fantastic Finishes. (p. 571)
—Football. (p. 614)
—Football Superstars. (p. 615)
—Great Girl Golfers. (p. 716)
—Great NASCAR Teams. (p. 717)
—Hottest Dragsters & Funny Cars. (p. 802)
—Hurricanes. (p. 830)
—I Am #8: Roberto Clemente. (p. 831)
—Knight Life. (p. 964)
—Linebackers. (p. 1019)
—Linemen. (p. 1019)
—Monster Trucks. (p. 1168)
—Off-Road Racing. (p. 1279)
—Personal Watercraft. (p. 1344)
—Power Pitchers. (p. 1390)
—Powerboat Racing. (p. 1390)
—Receivers. (p. 1451)
—Skydiving. (p. 1587)
—Smoke Jumpers. (p. 1594)
—Smokin' Dragsters & Funny Cars. (p. 1594)
—Sports Arena & Event Management Ferrer, Al, ed. (p. 1632)
—STEM in Sports. (p. 1647)
—Teamwork at the Track. (p. 1711)
—Water Sports (p. 1863)
—Who Was Bruce Lee? (p. 1918)
—Who Was Bruce Lee? Hinderliter, John et al, illus. (p. 1918)
—Who Was Mother Teresa? Harrison, Nancy, illus. (p. 1919)
—Who Was Queen Victoria? (p. 1919)
—Who Was Queen Victoria? Harrison, Nancy & Hergenrother, Max, illus. (p. 1919)
Gigliotti, Jim & Walters, John. Sports in America, 2000-2009. (p. 1632)
Gigliotti, Sallie B. I'm Sorry, Said Denny. (p. 860)
Gijswijt-Hofstra, Marijke & Marland, Hilary. Cultures of Child Health in Britain & the Netherlands in the Twentieth Century. (p. 391)
Gikow, Louise. Day with Daddy. Mazali, Gustavo, illus. (p. 415)
—I Can Read. Patience, John, illus. (p. 836)
—Science. (p. 1524)
—What Do You See? Ulrich, George, illus. (p. 1883)
Gikow, Louise, jt. auth. see Lippman, Peter.
Gikow, Louise A. I Can Read. Patience, John, illus. (p. 836)
Gil, Carmen. Fantasma con Asma. Webster, Sarah, illus. (p. 571)
—Story of a Cockroach. (p. 1657)
Gil, Carmen & Gali, Merce. Ana Frank. (p. 66)
Gil, Carmen & Gil Martinez, Carmen. It's a Pain to Be a Princess! Montero Galan, Daniel, illus. (p. 896)
Gil, Lydia. Letters from Heaven. (p. 1002)
Gil, Lydia M. Mimi's Parranda/la Parranda de Mimi. Sosa, Hernan, illus. (p. 1145)
Gil Martinez, Carmen, jt. auth. see Gil, Carmen.
Gil, Rodolpho, illus. see Goza, Shelly.
Gil, Sabina, illus. see Jimenez, Angeles.
Gilani, Fawzia. Cinderella: An Islamic Tale. (p. 320)
—Snow White: An Islamic Tale. Adams, Shireen, illus. (p. 1599)
Gilani-Williams, Fawzia. Lost Ring: An Eid Story. Burgess, Kulthum, illus. (p. 1056)
Gilberstadt, Debra Pack. Unmarked Grave: Remembering an American Patriot. (p. 1821)
Gilbert, Adrian. Codes & Ciphers. (p. 338)
—Spy Files: Secret Agents. (p. 1636)
—Spy School. (p. 1636)
—Top Technology. (p. 1769)
Gilbert, Adrian D. Voices of the Foreign Legion: The History of the World's Most Famous Fighting Corps. (p. 1848)
Gilbert, Alma. Maxfield Parrish: Master of Make-Believe. (p. 1112)
Gilbert, Anne Yvonne, illus. see Pirotta, Saviour.
Gilbert, Anne Yvonne, illus. see Stoker, Bram.
Gilbert, Ariadne. More Than Conquerors. (p. 1175)
Gilbert, Barbara Snow. Paper Trail. (p. 1323)
Gilbert, Barbara Snow & Boyds Mills Press Staff. Stone Water. (p. 1653)
Gilbert, Betty. Buffy the Burrowing Owl. (p. 236)
Gilbert, Cecilia, illus. see Bey, Angelique.
Gilbert, Celia. Mama's Lullaby. (p. 1084)
Gilbert, D. Hide & Seek: A Mystery Novel for Children. (p. 776)
Gilbert, David D. Feodor Fitz: Journey to Harmony Ville. (p. 581)
Gilbert, Dawn, jt. auth. see Blunt, Julia.
Gilbert, Diana. Guided by the Light. (p. 730)
Gilbert, Douglas R., photos by see Rojas Cardona, Javier, ed.
Gilbert, Drexel. H Is for Heaven: The Bible Alphabet Book. Spradlin, Leslie, illus. (p. 734)
Gilbert, Elizabeth. Pilgrims. (p. 1358)
Gilbert, Elizabeth T. Watch Me Draw Tiggerific Tales. (p. 1861)
Gilbert, Elizabeth T., jt. illus. see Tucker, Marianne.
Gilbert, Frances. Today the Teacher Changed Our Seats. (p. 1761)
Gilbert, Geoffrey. Rich & Poor in America: A Reference Handbook (p. 1469)
Gilbert, George. George, Candy, & the Raccoon. Perez-Torres, Juliana, illus. (p. 663)
Gilbert, Grant. Tour de France. (p. 1773)
Gilbert, H. K. Reporting for Duty: A Day at the White House. (p. 1461)
Gilbert, Harry. Year of Sharing, Level 1. Oxford University Press Staff & Bassett, Jennifer, eds. (p. 1969)
Gilbert, Heather. Skyler the Pirate (p. 1587)
Gilbert, Heather & Nash, Kevin. Virginia Tech College Prowler off the Record: Inside Virginia Polytechnic Institute. (p. 1844)
Gilbert, Henry. King Arthur's Knights: The Tales Retold for Boys & Girls. (p. 958)
Gilbert, James. Big Jims Ten Years & Still Cartooning. (p. 182)
Gilbert, Janet, jt. auth. see Van Horn, William.
Gilbert, Janet, et al. Uncle Scrooge Clark, John, ed. (p. 1812)
Gilbert, Jeff. Trick or Shriek. (p. 1786)
Gilbert, Jim. Host of Ghosts. (p. 801)
Gilbert, Joan. More Missouri Ghosts: Fact, Fiction & Folklore. Graham, Adele, illus. (p. 1174)
—Mule Boy. Burke, Kathryn Schaar, illus. (p. 1189)
Gilbert, Joan Sewell. Missouri Horses: Gift to a Nation. Vol. 1 Graham, Adele, illus. (p. 1154)
Gilbert, Keith & Schuh, Leesa. TEENAGERS: Your Essential Guide to the Weird World of... Adults 2nd Edition. (p. 1714)
Gilbert, Kelly Loy. Conviction. (p. 361)
Gilbert, Kristen Stalvey. Sam & Ally. (p. 1506)
Gilbert, LaBritta. Do Touch: Instant, Easy, Hands-on Learning Experiences for Young Children. Charner, Kathleen, ed. (p. 457)
Gilbert, Laura. Everything You Need to Know about Compulsive Sexual Behavior. (p. 545)
—Skeletal System. (p. 1584)
Gilbert, Louise. Classworks Literacy Year 1. (p. 329)
Gilbert, Marcie. Zee: Adventure One: Borrowing China. Krebs, Patricia, illus. (p. 1985)
Gilbert, Matthew. Casey Chronicles (Teenage Mutant Ninja Turtles) Random House Editors & Spaziante, Patrick, illus. (p. 275)
—Friend or Foe? (Teenage Mutant Ninja Turtles) Random House, illus. (p. 637)
—Mutant Mayhem! (Teenage Mutant Ninja Turtles) Random House, illus. (p. 1194)
—Showdown with Shredder (Teenage Mutant Ninja Turtles) Random House Staff, illus. (p. 1571)
Gilbert, Melissa. Daisy & Josephine. Kuo, Julia, illus. (p. 400)
Gilbert, Michael T., et al. Mickey Mouse Adventures Clark, John, ed. (p. 1136)
—Walt Disney's Comics & Stories #693. Clark, John, ed. (p. 1855)
Gilbert, Nikki Murphy. Gilbert Green. (p. 676)
Gilbert, Pat, jt. auth. see Guzzetta, Torrie.
Gilbert, Rean. Capitan's Tale: A Colour Story Book. (p. 263)
Gilbert, Rob, illus. see Eagle, Kin.
Gilbert, Sara. American Food. (p. 60)
—Annie Oakley. (p. 87)
—Apatosaurus. (p. 91)
—Atlanta Braves. (p. 112)
—Baltimore Orioles. (p. 135)
—Boston Red Sox. (p. 215)
—Built for Success: The\Story of Starbucks. (p. 240)
—Built for Success: the Story of CNN. (p. 240)
—Built for Success: the Story of Facebook. (p. 240)
—Built for Success: the Story of FedEx. (p. 240)
—Built for Success: the Story of Target. (p. 240)
—Built for Success: the Story of Twitter. (p. 240)
—Bulldozers. (p. 240)
—Calamity Jane. (p. 252)
—Chicago Cubs. (p. 299)
—Chicago White Sox. (p. 299)
—Chinese Food. (p. 307)
—Cincinnati Reds. (p. 319)
—Concrete Mixers: Machines That Build. (p. 355)
—Concrete Mixers. (p. 355)
—Cranes. (p. 376)
—Death Valley. (p. 420)
—Diggers. (p. 439)
—Drilling Machines. (p. 485)
—Dump Trucks: Machines That Build. (p. 489)
—Dump Trucks. (p. 489)
—Everglades. (p. 542)
—French Food. (p. 635)
—Grand Canyon. (p. 707)
—Great Smoky Mountains. (p. 718)
—History of the Arizona Cardinals. (p. 784)
—History of the Cleveland Browns. (p. 785)
—History of the Seattle Seahawks. (p. 785)
—Italian Food. (p. 894)
—Los Angeles Angels of Anaheim. (p. 1053)
—Los Angeles Dodgers. (p. 1053)
—Mexican Food. (p. 1131)
—Miami Marlins. (p. 1134)
—Middle Eastern Food. (p. 1137)
—Minnesota Twins. (p. 1147)
—New York Mets. (p. 1248)
—New York Yankees. (p. 1248)
—NFL Today: Baltimore Ravens. (p. 1249)
—NFL Today: Buffalo Bills. (p. 1249)
—NFL Today: Cincinnati Bengals. (p. 1250)
—NFL Today: Cleveland Browns. (p. 1250)
—NFL Today: Dallas Cowboys. (p. 1250)
—NFL Today: Green Bay Packers. (p. 1250)
—NFL Today: Indianapolis Colts. (p. 1250)
—NFL Today: Minnesota Vikings. (p. 1250)
—NFL Today: Tennessee Titans. (p. 1250)
—NFL Today: Washington Redskins. (p. 1250)
—Philadelphia Phillies. (p. 1350)
—Play It Loud! The Rebellious History of Music (p. 1371)
—San Francisco Giants. (p. 1510)
—South Carolina. (p. 1616)
—St. Louis Cardinals. (p. 1638)
—Story of Amazon. Com. (p. 1657)
—Story of Amazon.com. (p. 1657)
—Story of Apple. (p. 1657)
—Story of Apple - Built for Success. (p. 1657)
—Story of CNN. (p. 1657)
—Story of EBay. (p. 1658)
—Story of eBay. (p. 1658)
—Story of Facebook. (p. 1658)
—Story of FedEx. (p. 1658)
—Story of Google. (p. 1658)
—Story of McDonald's. (p. 1659)
—Story of McDonald's - Built for Success. (p. 1659)
—Story of MTV. (p. 1659)
—Story of Pixar. (p. 1659)
—Story of Starbucks. (p. 1660)
—Story of Target. (p. 1660)
—Story of the Arizona Cardinals. (p. 1660)
—Story of the Arizona Diamondbacks. (p. 1660)
—Story of the Baltimore Orioles. (p. 1660)
—Story of the Baltimore Ravens. (p. 1660)
—Story of the Chicago Cubs. (p. 1660)
—Story of the Cincinnati Bengals. (p. 1660)
—Story of the Cleveland Browns. (p. 1660)
—Story of the Dallas Cowboys. (p. 1660)
—Story of the Detroit Tigers. (p. 1660)
—Story of the Florida Marlins. (p. 1661)
—Story of the Green Bay Packers. (p. 1661)
—Story of the Houston Astros. (p. 1661)
—Story of the Indianapolis Colts. (p. 1661)
—Story of the Kansas City Royals. (p. 1661)
—Story of the Los Angeles Angels of Anaheim. (p. 1661)
—Story of the Los Angeles Lakers. (p. 1661)
—Story of the Memphis Grizzlies. (p. 1661)
—Story of the Miami Heat. (p. 1661)
—Story of the Milwaukee Brewers. (p. 1661)
—Story of the Milwaukee Bucks. (p. 1661)
—Story of the Minnesota Timberwolves. (p. 1661)
—Story of the Minnesota Vikings. (p. 1661)
—Story of the New Orleans Hornets. (p. 1661)
—Story of the New Orleans Saints. (p. 1661)
—Story of the NFL. (p. 1661)
—Story of the Oakland Athletics. (p. 1661)
—Story of the Orlando Magic. (p. 1661)
—Story of the Philadelphia 76ers. (p. 1662)
—Story of the Seattle Seahawks. (p. 1662)
—Story of the St. Louis Cardinals. (p. 1662)
—Story of the Tampa Bay Buccanneers. (p. 1662)
—Story of the Tennessee Titans. (p. 1662)
—Story of the Texas Rangers. (p. 1662)
—Story of the Toronto Raptors. (p. 1662)
—Story of the Washington Redskins. (p. 1662)
—Story of Twitter. (p. 1662)
—Story of Wal-Mart. (p. 1663)
—Toronto Blue Jays. (p. 1770)
—Triceratops. (p. 1785)
—Tyrannosaurus Rex. (p. 1805)
—Vermont. (p. 1837)
—World Series Champs: Atlanta Braves. (p. 1958)
—World Series Champs: Baltimore Orioles. (p. 1958)
—World Series Champs: Chicago Cubs. (p. 1958)
—World Series Champs: Cincinnati Reds. (p. 1958)
—World Series Champs: la Angels of Anaheim. (p. 1958)
—World Series Champs: Los Angeles Dodgers. (p. 1958)
—World Series Champs: Miami Marlins. (p. 1958)
—World Series Champs: New York Yankees. (p. 1958)
—World Series Champs: Philadelphia Phillies. (p. 1958)
—Write Your Own Article: Newspaper, Magazine, Online. (p. 1964)
—Yellowstone. (p. 1970)
—Yosemite. (p. 1972)
Gilbert, Sara, jt. auth. see Cooperman, Sheila.

Gilbert, Sara, jt. auth. see Frisch, Aaron.
Gilbert, Sara & Clark, Tracey. Bulldozers. (p. 240)
Gilbert, Sara Dulaney, jt. auth. see Cooperman, Sheila.
Gilbert, Scott W. Adventures of Willie the Worm: Willie's Big Adventure. (p. 24)
Gilbert, Sharon K. Winds of Evil: The Laodicea Chronicles (p. 1936)
Gilbert Square Books. Fun of Rhyme Square Pears. (p. 648)
Gilbert, Steve, jt. ed. see Harrison, Maureen.
Gilbert, Wendy June. Our Beds Are Cars. (p. 1307)
Gilbert, William. Last Lords of Gardonal. (p. 978)
Gilbert, William S. Iolanthe: or The Prince & the Peri. Landes, William-Alan, ed. (p. 886)
—Mikado: or The Town of Titipu. Landes, William-Alan, ed. (p. 1141)
—Pirates of Penzance: or A Slave to Duty. Landes, William-Alan, ed. (p. 1363)
Gilbert, Yvonne, illus. see Andersen, Hans Christian.
Gilbert, Yvonne, illus. see Hickox, Rebecca.
Gilbert, Yvonne, illus. see Joel, Billy.
Gilbert, Yvonne, illus. see Picoult, Jodi & van Leer, Samantha.
Gilbert, Yvonne, illus. see Zahler, Diane.
Gilbert-Dumas, Mylène. Mystique. (p. 1226)
Gilbery, Barbara. Abby Helps Make It Happen. (p. 2)
Gilboa, Rinat, illus. see Thomas, Doni Zasloff & Lindberg, Eric.
Gilbreth, Frank B., Jr. & Carey, Ernestine Gilbreth. Cheaper by the Dozen. (p. 295)
Gilcher, William Harry, jt. auth. see Cohen, Hilda Stern.
Gilchrest-Unrau, Sally. Sam's Weird Afternoon. (p. 1509)
Gilchrist, Cherry. Calendar of Festivals. Cann, Helen, illus. (p. 252)
—Stories from the Silk Road. Mistry, Nilesh, illus. (p. 1654)
Gilchrist, Cherry & Cann, Helen. Calendar of Festivals: Celebrations from Around the World. Mistry, Nilesh, illus. (p. 252)
Gilchrist, Cherry & Pearson Education Staff. Princess Diana. (p. 1403)
Gilchrist, Ellen. Adventures of TinTin. (p. 24)
Gilchrist, J. Into the Land of Nede. (p. 881)
Gilchrist, Jan Spivey. Obama: The Day the World Danced. (p. 1275)
Gilchrist, Jan Spivey, illus. see Greenfield, Eloise & Greenfield.
Gilchrist, Jan Spivey, illus. see Greenfield, Eloise.
Gilchrist, Jan Spivey, illus. see Pettitt, Linda & Darrow, Sharon.
Gilchrist, Reona. Maile. Guy, Robert, illus. (p. 1077)
Gildea, Kathy. Adventures of Baylee Beagle—Annabelle Beagle. Larson, Amanda, illus. (p. 16)
—Adventures of Baylee Beagle—Greenville. (p. 16)
—Adventures of Baylee Beagle—Hurricane Hound. Larson, Amanda, illus. (p. 16)
Gildea, Ray Y. Letters Home: Children Learn Geography Through Communication with Parents Traveling/Working Abroad. (p. 1002)
Gildea, Shir. Loving All the Colors. Gildea, Shir, illus. (p. 1061)
Gilden, Mel. Secret of Spider Motel. Roe, David, illus. (p. 1542)
—Secret of the Spider Motel. Roe, David, illus. (p. 1543)
Gildenstein, Melanie & O'Donnell, Kerri. Primary Source Investigation of the Gold Rush. (p. 1400)
Gilder Lehrman Institute of American History. Abraham Lincoln & the Emancipation Proclamation. (p. 6)
Gilderdale, Alan, illus. see Gilderdale, Betty.
Gilderdale, Betty. Little Yellow Digger Goes to School. Gilderdale, Alan, illus. (p. 1038)
Gilders, Michelle. Why Am I Rare? Gilders, Michelle, photos by. (p. 1922)
Gilders, Michelle A. Kids' Guide to Zoo Animals (p. 954)
Gildersleeve, Amanda. Three Brothers Gruff: The Fairytale Everyone Thought They Knew. (p. 1741)
Gildersleeve, Mary C. Great Yarns for the Close-Knit Family: Over Two Dozen Original Hand-Knit Designs Inspired by One Dozen Family Read-alouds. (p. 719)
GIL-DOLZ, MAITE CARANZA, et al. Mauro Ojos Brillantes. (p. 1110)
Gile, John. Primer Bosque. Kohen-Klieman, Clarita, tr. (p. 1400)
Gilead, Jack, jt. auth. see Polsky, Milton.
Giles, Angela & Picthall, Chez. 123. Calver, Paul, illus. (p. 2000)
—Colours & Shapes. Calver, Paul, illus. (p. 346)
Giles, Bridget. Kenya. (p. 949)
—Nigeria. (p. 1252)
—West African Myths. (p. 1876)
Giles, Chauncey. Magic Spectacles: A Fairy Story. (p. 1073)
Giles, Christina M. Aidan & His Magic Wand. (p. 30)
Giles, Doris. Foursome. (p. 625)
Giles, Gail. Dark Song. (p. 408)
—Girls Like Us. (p. 680)
—Right Behind You. (p. 1472)
—Shattering Glass. (p. 1563)
—What Happened to Cass McBride? (p. 1885)
—What Happened to Cass McBride? A Novel. (p. 1885)
Giles, Geoff. Match the Views: Cut & Fold Puzzles to Imagine & Solve. (p. 1104)
Giles, Inga, jt. auth. see Heacock, David.
Giles, Katharine. Princess of Skye, an Archer Adventure. (p. 1404)
Giles, Lamar. Endangered. (p. 526)
—Fake ID. (p. 565)
Giles, Lisa. Adventures of Sunny the Bunny: The Easter Egg Hunt. (p. 23)
Giles, M. J. Young Adult's Guide to a Business Career. (p. 1978)
Giles, Mike. Baby Teeth Fall Out, Big Teeth Grow! (p. 128)
—Halloween Is Fun! (p. 738)
—Sleep & Dream of Happy Things. (p. 1588)
—Spring Showers Bring Flowers. (p. 1635)
Giles, Mike, illus. see Brooke, Samantha.
Giles, Mike, illus. see Kilpatrick, Irene.
Giles, Mike, illus. see Mattern, Joanne.
Giles, Mike, illus. see McMahon, Kara.
Giles, Mike, illus. see Rao, Lisa & Gallo, Tina.
Giles, Mike, illus. see Shaw, Natalie.
Giles, Mike, illus. see Thomas, Jim.
Giles, Polly. Have You Ever Been Afraid of Animals? (p. 754)
Giles, S. A. Home for All: How a Little Puppy Finds a Home. (p. 792)
—Home for All: How a Little Puppy Gets a Name. (p. 792)
Giles, Sophie. Children's Book of Green Habits. Davies, Kate, illus. (p. 303)
—Children's Book of Healthy Habits. Davies, Kate, illus. (p. 303)
—Children's Book of Success at School. (p. 303)
Giles, Sophie, jt. auth. see Fiona Fox Staff.
Giles, Sophie & Davies, Kate. Children's Book of Keeping Safe. (p. 303)
—Children's Book of Money Sense. (p. 303)
Giles, Sophie & Davis, Kate. My First 1000 Words. Peters, Andy & Hewett, Angela, illus. (p. 1203)
Giles, Sophie, et al. Children's Book of Manners. East, Jacqueline, illus. (p. 303)
—My First Picture Dictionary. Burton, Terry & Hicks, Angela, illus. (p. 1207)
Giles, Susan. Caribbean Cats. Giles, Susan, illus. (p. 268)
—Lola & Luigi. (p. 1045)
Giles, W. Marie. Open Your Mind, Open Your Heart: A Collection of Words of Wisdom, Heartfelt Thoughts, & Original Poetry. (p. 1300)
Gilfert, Shirley Tankersley. Other Side of Jordan: A Story of the Underground Railroad. (p. 1306)
Gilfillan, Ross. Losing It: The Growing Pains of a Teenage Vampire. (p. 1054)
Gilgal, Flora. Am Christ's Grades 1 And 2. (p. 51)
Gilgannon, Denise, illus. see Newhouse, Mark.
Gilgannon-Collins, Denise, illus. see Nass, Marcia Shoshana.
Gilgen, Paula L. C a T. (p. 249)
Gilhooly, Jack. Three Cat Tales. (p. 1741)
Gili Gaya, Samuel. Diccionario Obreviado de la Lengua Espanol: Vox. (p. 435)
Gili, Phillida. Cinderella: A Pop-up Book. Gili, Phillida, illus. (p. 320)
—Lost Ears. (p. 1055)
Giliewe, Unada, illus. see Bader, Joanne.
Gilkerson, Patricia. My Adventure in a Castle. (p. 1195)
—My Adventure in a Meadow. (p. 1195)
—My Adventure in an Enchanted Forest. (p. 1195)
—My Adventure in the Desert. (p. 1195)
—My Adventure Inside a Volcano. (p. 1195)
—My Adventure on a Ranch. (p. 1195)
—My Adventure Scuba Diving. (p. 1195)
—My Adventure with Dogs. (p. 1195)
—My Adventure with Eagles. (p. 1195)
—My Adventure with Owls. (p. 1195)
—My Adventure with Sea Horses. (p. 1195)
—My Adventure with Sea Turtles. (p. 1195)
—My Adventure with Sharks. (p. 1195)
—My Adventure with Squirrels. (p. 1195)
—My Adventure with Whales. (p. 1195)
—My Adventure with Wild Horses. (p. 1195)
—My Adventure with Wolves. (p. 1195)
Gilkerson, William. Pirate's Passage. (p. 1364)
—Pirate's Passage. Gilkerson, William, illus. (p. 1364)
—Thousand Years of Pirates. (p. 1740)
Gilkey, Gail. Freckles & the Circus. (p. 632)
—No More Garbage. Gilkey, Gail, ed. (p. 1259)
—Seashell Garden. (p. 1538)
Gilks, Tina M. My Dog Mo. (p. 1202)
Gill, Amber. Joseph's Summer. (p. 926)
Gill, Bill Pojo. Duel Masters. (p. 489)
—Pojo's Unofficial Guide to Neopets. (p. 1377)
Gill, Bob. Green-Eyed Mouse & the Blue-Eyed Mouse. (p. 721)
—What Colour Is Your World? (p. 1881)
Gill, Bob, illus. see Reid, Alastair.
Gill, Cheryl, jt. auth. see Gill, Mickey.
Gill, Damian. Robots: Endless Creative Possibilities. (p. 1481)
Gill, David Macinnis. Black Hole Sun. (p. 196)
—Graham Salisbury: Island Boy. (p. 705)
—Invisible Sun. (p. 886)
—Shadow on the Sun. (p. 1557)
—Soul Enchilada. (p. 1614)
Gill, Deirdre, jt. auth. see Rosenbaum, Andria Warmflash.
Gill, Heidi. 2 Kurious Kids: China. Carter, Kris, illus. (p. 1991)
—2 Kurious Kids: India. Carter, Kris, illus. (p. 1991)
—2 Kurious Kids: France. Carter, Kris, illus. (p. 1991)
—Egypt. Carter, Kris, illus. (p. 506)
Gill, Heidi & Carter, Kris. 2 Kurious Kids: Mexico. (p. 1991)
Gill, J. Duddy. Secret of Ferrell Savage. Chaghatzbanian, Sonia, illus. (p. 1542)
Gill, Jacqueline Paske. Monster in the Basement. Gill, Jacqueline Paske, illus. (p. 1167)
Gill, Janet. Basket Weaver & Catches Many Mice. Choi, Yangsook, illus. (p. 143)
Gill, Janie S. Just Like You. Lambson, Elizabeth, illus. (p. 939)
—When Grandma Comes to Visit. (p. 1902)
Gill, Jean. On the Other Hand. (p. 1291)
Gill, Jim. Soup Opera. Moose, David, illus. (p. 1615)
Gill, Joe. Unauthorized Tarzan. Wright, Brendan, ed. (p. 1811)
Gill, Joel Christian. Strange Fruit: Uncelebrated Narratives from Black History. Vol. 1 (p. 1665)
Gill, Judy A. Wish U Well. (p. 1940)
Gill, Kim, jt. auth. see DeNinno, Joanne.
Gill, Margaret. Brain Changers. (p. 221)
—Return of the Quetzal. (p. 1464)
Gill, Margery, illus. see Burnett, Frances Hodgson.
Gill, Margery, illus. see Cooper, Susan.
Gill, Mehmaz S. Yellow Butterfly. Ward, Lindsay, illus. (p. 1970)
Gill, Michael. Mitsuki. (p. 1156)
Gill, Mickey. Glam Slam! (p. 682)
Gill, Mickey & Gill, Cheryl. Dude Diary 2. (p. 489)
—Dude Diary 4: Write Stuff, Draw Randomly, Destroy If Needed! (p. 489)
—New! Girl Diary: Your Days, Your Way! (p. 1244)
Gill, Monica & Viegas, Jennifer. Lower Limbs in 3D. (p. 1061)
Gill, Monica K. Biopharmaceuticals. (p. 190)
Gill, Nancy & Pratt, Brendan. Parents' Guide to School Selection in San Mateo & Santa Clara Counties—Sixth Edition. (p. 1324)
Gill, Nav K. Under the Moonlit Sky. (p. 1813)
Gill, Patricia. Pabi, Beega & the Mongoose Monster. (p. 1316)
Gill, Paul. Centaurs: An Adventure Fantasy. (p. 287)
Gill, Pittar, jt. auth. see Pittar, Gill.
Gill, Raj. Monkey Ate My Pancakes. (p. 1165)
Gill, Roma, ed. see Shakespeare, William.
Gill, Roma, jt. auth. see Shakespeare, William.
Gill, Roma & Shakespeare, William. Measure for Measure. (p. 1117)
Gill, Shelley. Alaska. Endres, Patrick J., photos by. (p. 33)
—Alaska's Dog Heroes: True Stories of Remarkable Canines. James, Robin, illus. (p. 34)
—Big Blue. Barrow, Ann, illus. (p. 178)
—Hawai'i. Goto, Scott, illus. (p. 755)
—Prickly Rose. Cartwright, Shannon & Love, Judy, illus. (p. 1398)
—Sitka Rose. Cartwright, Shannon, illus. (p. 1582)
—Up on Denali: Alaska's Wild Mountain. Cartwright, Shannon, illus. (p. 1824)
Gill, Shelley & Cartwright, Shannon. Kiana's Iditarod. (p. 951)
Gill, Tim, illus. see Williams, Sam.
Gill, Timothy. Flip & Fin: We Rule the School! Numberman, Neil, illus. (p. 604)
—Flip & Fin: Super Sharks to the Rescue! Numberman, Neil, illus. (p. 604)
Gill, Vince. Emperor's New Clothes: A Country Storybook. Newsom, Carol, illus. (p. 521)
Gillam, David. Gingertown. Gilliam, David, illus. (p. 677)
Gillam, Scott. Andrew Carnegie: Industrial Giant & Philanthropist. (p. 72)
—Civil Liberties. (p. 324)
—Rachel Carson: Pioneer of Environmentalism. (p. 1431)
—Sigmund Freud: Famous Neurologist. (p. 1574)
—Steve Jobs: Apple ICon. (p. 1649)
—Steve Jobs: Apple & iPod Wizard. (p. 1649)
Gilland, Gary P. Turtle Train Troop. (p. 1798)
Gillanders, Ann. Fairy Fleur & Doug the Dragonfly's Adventures in London: Ann Gillanders. (p. 563)
Gillard, Arthur. Dieting. Greenhaven Press Editors, ed. (p. 437)
—Drug Abuse. (p. 486)
—Food Allergies. Greenhaven Press Editors, ed. (p. 613)
—Learning Disabilities. (p. 985)
—Marijuana (p. 1094)
—Marijuana. (p. 1094)
—Medical Marijuana. Greenhaven Press Editors, ed. (p. 1118)
—Sexual Harassment. Greenhaven Press Editors & Gale Editors, eds. (p. 1556)
—Stroke. (p. 1668)
—Vegetarianism. Gale Editors, ed. (p. 1834)
Gillard, Arthur, jt. ed. see Greenhaven Press Editors.
Gillard, Arthur, ed. Nuclear Power. (p. 1270)
—Traumatic Brain Injury. (p. 1780)
Gillard, Jason, illus. see Macht, Heather.
Gillard, Keith. Basic Map Reading. (p. 142)
Gille, Chaudron. College Vocabulary (p. 340)
Gilleard, Maria. Biff, the Lonely Great White Shark. (p. 177)
Gilleland, Linda. I Love You, Baby Deer. Irish, Leigh Ann, illus. (p. 843)
Gilleland, Rebecca. Swiss Family Robinson Study Guide. (p. 1691)
Gillen, Jim & Gillen, Lynea. Yoga Calm for Children: Educating Heart, Mind, & Body. (p. 1972)
Gillen, Kristin M. Raspberries on Tummies. (p. 1439)
Gillen, Lisa P. Spring Time. Gillen, Lisa P., illus. (p. 1635)
Gillen, Lisa P., illus. see Black, Jessica L.
Gillen, Lisa P., illus. see Hensley, Sarah M.
Gillen, Lisa P., illus. see Howard-Parham, Pam.
Gillen, Lisa P., illus. see Mullican, Judy & Crowell, Knox.
Gillen, Lisa P., illus. see Mullican, Judy.
Gillen, Lisa P., illus. see Parham, Pam H.
Gillen, Lisa P., illus. see Williams, Heather L.
Gillen, Lynea. Good People Everywhere. Swamer, Kristina, illus. (p. 700)
Gillen, Lynea, jt. auth. see Gillen, Jim.
Gillen, Rosemarie, illus. see Bucklaschuk, Angela.
Gillen, Rosemarie, illus. see Carroll, Jacquie Lund.
Gillen, Rosemarie, illus. see Dall, Ernestine.
Gillen, Rosemarie, illus. see Doti Chavez, Caryn.
Gillen, Rosemarie, illus. see Gainey, Gary.
Gillen, Rosemarie, illus. see Gober, Thomas.
Gillen, Rosemarie, illus. see Jolivert, Immaculine.
Gillen, Rosemarie, illus. see Lagneau, Mary.
Gillen, Rosemarie, illus. see Lancaster, Melinda.
Gillen, Rosemarie, illus. see Lee, Vanessa Rose.
Gillen, Rosemarie, illus. see O'Donnell, Candy.
Gillen, Rosemarie, illus. see Powell, Angela.
Gillen, Rosemarie, illus. see Thyroff, Brad.
Gillen, Rosemarie, illus. see Vance, Mimi Brian.
Gillen, Rosemarie, jt. auth. see Buford, Stanley G.
Gillen-Connell, Linda. Dumb Bunny. (p. 489)
—Laura the Loser. (p. 980)
Gillenwater, Chadwick. Anacondas (p. 66)
—Giant Anteaters (p. 673)
—Groundhogs (p. 725)
—Howler Monkeys (p. 823)
Gillenwater, Chadwick & Dunn, Mary R. South American Animals. (p. 1616)
Gilles, Almira Astudillo. Willie Wins Angel, Carl, illus. (p. 1934)
Gilles, Carol J., jt. auth. see Moore, Rita A.
Gilles-Gray, Carolyn, illus. see Taylor, Helen.
Gillespie, Andrew. As Business Studies. (p. 105)
—Business Studies. (p. 245)
Gillespie, Carol Ann. New Zealand. Gritzner, Charles F., ed. (p. 1249)
Gillespie, Elizabeth. Robbie's Beach Adventure. (p. 1478)
Gillespie, Eloyce. Framed. (p. 627)
Gillespie, Esther A. & Clark, Thomas Curtis, eds. Child's Thought of God: Religious Poems for Children. (p. 305)
Gillespie, Frances. Al Haya Al Bahriya Fee Qatar (Sea & Shore Life of Qatar) Shughry, Salam, tr. (p. 32)
—Birds of Qatar. (p. 192)
—Hasharat Qatar (Insects & Arachnids of Qatar) (p. 752)
—Insects & Arachnids of Qatar. (p. 876)
—Mammals of Qatar. (p. 1085)
—Plants of Qatar. (p. 1370)
—Reptiles & Amphibians of Qatar. (p. 1461)
—Sea & Shore Life of Qatar. (p. 1534)
—Thadiyat Qatar (Mammals of Qatar) (p. 1724)
—Toyoor Qatar (Birds of Qatar) (p. 1774)
—Zawahef Qatar (Reptiles & Amphibians of Qatar) (p. 1985)
Gillespie, Frances & Al-Naimi, Faisal. Hidden in the Sands - Arabic: Uncovering Qatar's Past. (p. 775)
—Hidden in the Sands - English: Uncovering Qatar's Past. (p. 775)
Gillespie, Gary Franklin. Storytime with Grandp. (p. 1664)
Gillespie, Greg G., illus. see Shelton, C. H. & Shelton, C. H.
Gillespie, Haven & Coots, J. Fred. Santa Claus Is Comin' to Town. Kellogg, Steven, tr. (p. 1511)
Gillespie, Hollis. Unaccompanied Minor. (p. 1811)
—We Will Be Crashing Shortly. (p. 1868)
Gillespie, Jane. Diving for Shapes in Hawaii: An Identification Book for Keiki. Bosgra, Johann, illus. (p. 455)
—Emma's Rainy Day. Aardema, John, illus. (p. 520)
—G Is for Gecko: An Alphabet Adventure in Hawai'i. Robinson, Don, illus. (p. 651)
—Happy Honu Takes a Bath. Cabanting, Ruth, illus. (p. 746)
—S Went Surfing: An ABC Book for Keiki. Cabanting, Ruth, illus. (p. 1499)
—S Went Surfing in Hawai'i. Moen, Ruth, illus. (p. 1499)
—There Was an Old Auntie. Aardema, John, illus. (p. 1730)
Gillespie, John T. Historical Fiction for Young Readers (Grades 4-8) An Introduction (p. 783)
Gillespie, John T. & Naden, Corinne J. Teenplots: A Booktalk Guide to Use with Readers Ages 12-18 (p. 1714)
Gillespie, Katie, jt. auth. see Craats, Rennay.
Gillespie, Katie, jt. auth. see Foran, Jill.
Gillespie, Katie, jt. auth. see Hamilton, Lynn.
Gillespie, Katie, jt. auth. see Lomberg, Michelle.
Gillespie, L. Sticker Dressing Warriors. Ordas, Emi, illus. (p. 1650)
Gillespie, Leslie. Motorcyles. (p. 1180)
Gillespie, Lisa. Trees. (p. 1784)
Gillespie, Lisa Jane. Sticker Dressing Extreme Sports. Ordas, Emi, illus. (p. 1650)
Gillespie, Natalie. Believing in Narnia: A Kid's Guide to Unlocking the Secret Symbols of Faith in C. S. Lewis' the Chronicles of Narnia (p. 162)
Gillespie, Natalie, jt. auth. see Feinberg, Margaret.
Gillespie, Peggy, jt. ed. see Beard, Jean J.
Gillespie, Sarah. Diary of Sarah Gillespie: A Pioneer Farm Girl (p. 435)
Gillespie, Tonnika. Queen's 3 Jewels. Anderson, Susan, illus. (p. 1425)
Gillet, Jean Wallace, jt. auth. see Roser, Nancy.
Gillet, Meg. Ecosystems. (p. 503)
Gillett, Chrissy, jt. auth. see Hewitt, Hazel.
Gillett, Hallie, illus. see Dacey, Richard.
Gillett, Jack. Access to Geography: Population. (p. 8)
Gillett, Jack & Gillett, Meg. Conservation-Area Maps. (p. 358)
—Energy-Resource Maps. (p. 528)
—Natural Resource Maps. (p. 1235)
—Natural-Resource Maps. (p. 1235)
—Physical Geography. (p. 1353)
—Transportation-Network Maps. (p. 1779)
Gillett, Meg, jt. auth. see Gillett, Jack.
Gillette, Henry S., illus. see Eberle, Irmengarde.
Gillette, Lesli. Coco's Identity Crisis. (p. 337)
Gillette, Tim, illus. see Bolme, Edward Sarah.
Gillette-Simms, Verdina. My Champion's Eyes: Blind but Not Defeated. (p. 1200)
Gilley, Jane. Adventures of Solly Polly & Georgie Porgy. (p. 23)
—Christmas on Troglodyte Hill - Book Three of the Troglodyte Trilogy. (p. 315)
—Phantom Pum. (p. 1349)
—Roodery's Birthday - Book One of the Troglodyte Trilogy. (p. 1487)
—Thibault Goes Missing - Book Two of the Troglodyte Trilogy. (p. 1732)
Gilley, Jeremy. Peace One Day. Blessen, Karen, illus. (p. 1331)
Gilley, Mel. Sam & the Sad Dinosaur. (p. 1506)
Gillezeau, Marcus. Hands On: A Practical Guide to Production & Technology in Film, TV & New Media. (p. 741)
Gillham, Bill, et al. Essential Skills (p. 537)
Gilliam, David, illus. see Gillam, David.
Gilliam, Jessie. Geno (p. 661)
Gilliam, Nancy, creator. LeBron James: King of the Court Companion Study Guide. (p. 987)
Gilliam, Thomas & Neill, Jane. Move It. Lose It. Live Healthy: Achieve a Healthier Workplace One Employee at a Time! (p. 1183)
Gillian, Chelsea, et al. Princess ABCs And 123s. (p. 1402)
Gillie, Brian. Guide to the Best Vocal Harmonies of Rock 'n' Roll: 1955 - 1985. (p. 730)
Gillies, Chuck, illus. see Lucado, Max.
Gillies, Isabel. Starry Night. (p. 1642)
Gillies, Mark. Imvula, Child of the Rain. (p. 862)
Gilligan, Alison. Pirate Treasure of the Onyx Dragon. (p. 1363)
—Search for the Black Rhino. (p. 1537)
Gilligan, Jeff, jt. auth. see Burrows, Roger.
Gilligan, Paul, jt. auth. see Madaras, Lynda.
Gilligan, Shannon. Case of the Silk King. (p. 275)
—Case of the Silk King. Pornkerd, Vorrarit et al, illus. (p. 275)
—Choose Your Own Adventure: The Case of the Silk King. (p. 310)
—Cup of Death. Nugent, Suzanne, illus. (p. 392)
—Ghost Island. Newton, Keith, illus. (p. 671)
—Lake Monster Mystery. Newton, Keith, illus. (p. 972)
—Mystery of Ura Senke. (p. 1226)
—Princess Island. (p. 1404)
—Struggle down Under. Burphon, S. et al, illus. (p. 1668)

Gilliland, C., compiled by. Great Flood. (p. 716)
Gilliland, Hap. Alone in the Wilderness. (p. 48)
Gilliland, Jillian Hulme, illus. see Downie, Mary Alice & Zola, Mequido.
Gilliland, Mary Ellen. Summit: A Gold Rush History of Summit County, Colorado. (p. 1675)
Gilliland, Tom. Adventures of Archie Aardvark. (p. 16)
Gillingham, Sara. How to Grow a Friend. (p. 820)
—In My Barn. Siminovich, Lorena, illus. (p. 864)
—In My Den. Siminovich, Lorena, illus. (p. 864)
—In My Forest. Siminovich, Lorena, illus. (p. 864)
—In My Jungle. Siminovich, Lorena, illus. (p. 864)
—In My Nest. Siminovich, Lorena, illus. (p. 864)
—In My Ocean. Siminovich, Lorena, illus. (p. 864)
—In My Pond. Siminovich, Lorena, illus. (p. 864)
—My Little Easter Egg. (p. 1212)
—My Little Stocking. (p. 1213)
—My Little Sweetheart. (p. 1213)
—On My Beach. Siminovich, Lorena, illus. (p. 1289)
—On My Leaf. Siminovich, Lorena, illus. (p. 1289)
—Snuggle the Baby. (p. 1601)
Gillingham, Sara, illus. see Krensky, Stephen.
Gillingham, Sara, jt. auth. see Paul Frank Industries.
Gillingham, Sara, jt. auth. see Simi, Gillingham.
Gillingham, Sara & Chronicle Books Staff. In My Flower. Siminovich, Lorena, illus. (p. 864)
—In My Meadow. Siminovich, Lorena, illus. (p. 864)
—T Is for Tugboat: Navigating the Seas from A to Z. (p. 1694)
Gillingham, Sara & Siminovich, Lorena. In My Tree. (p. 864)
Gillis, Bonnie, illus. see Elayne.
Gillis, Bonnie, illus. see Melania, Mother.
Gillis, Candie. Adventures of Divianna & Finn. (p. 17)
Gillis, Jane, illus. see Frenette, Liza.
Gillis, Jennifer B. Jobs on Wheels. (p. 919)
—Neighborhood Shopping. (p. 1240)
—You Are Here. (p. 1973)
Gillis, Jennifer Blizin. Benjamin Franklin (p. 164)
—Can It Live Here? (p. 258)
—Confederate Soldier. (p. 356)
—Dan the Ant. Brooks, Karen Stormer, illus. (p. 402)
—Estas Aqui/You Are Here. Duque, Olga, tr. (p. 538)
—Halloween (p. 737)
—Hogares para Todos/Homes for Everyone. Alemián, Manuel, tr. (p. 787)
—Life on the Lower East Side. (p. 1012)
—Milton Hershey: The Founder of Hershey's Chocolate. (p. 1144)
—Neighborhood Shopping. (p. 1240)
—Puedes Ayudar/You Can Help. Alemián, Manuel, tr. (p. 1414)
—Restored Villages. (p. 1464)
—Southeast (p. 1617)
—Time to Open! (p. 1753)
—Two Nice Mice. Krejca, Gary, illus. (p. 1804)
—What Do You Say? Losa, Ann, illus. (p. 1883)
—You Are Here. (p. 1973)
Gillis, Keith Alexander. My Quest to Ghana. (p. 1217)
Gillis, Peter & Alexander, Larry. Dr. Strange: Strange Tales. Shoemaker, Terry et al, illus. (p. 475)
Gillman, Kathy, photos by see Philipp, Cathy.
Gillmor, Don. Christmas Orange. (p. 315)
—Fabulous Song. Gay, Marie-Louise, illus. (p. 560)
—Yuck, a Love Story Gay, Marie-Louise, illus. (p. 1983)
—Yuck, a Love Story. Gay, Marie-Louise, illus. (p. 1983)
Gillmor, Don, et al. Fabulous Song. Gay, Marie-Louise, illus. (p. 560)
Gillmore, Inez Haynes. Maida's Little Shop. (p. 1076)
—Maida's Little Shop. (p. 1077)
Gillmore, Jean, illus. see Wenger, Brahm & Green, Alan.
Gillon, Gail T. Phonological Awareness: From Research to Practice. (p. 1352)
Gillooly, Eileen, ed. Poetry for Young People: Rudyard Kipling. Spector, Joel & Sharpe, Jim, illus. (p. 1376)
Gillooly, Jessica B. Before She Gets Her Period: Talking with Your Daughter about Menstruation. Orellana, Nery, illus. (p. 158)
Gillot, Laurence & Sebaoun, Elisabeth. Half & Half-Swimming with Dolphins. Rocco & Dorémus, Gaëtan, illus. (p. 736)
Gillott, C. M. Nelson 'n' Deck & Friends: How the Adventures Began. (p. 1241)
Gillrie Fraser, Marg. Dolphin Way. (p. 464)
Gillrie-Fraser, Margaret. Dolphin Way: Learn about the amazing underwater sea world of Mattie the Dolphin as he soars through one exciting adventure after Another! (p. 464)
—Dolphin Way. (p. 464)
Gilman, Charles. Professor Gargoyle. (p. 1409)
—Slither Sisters. (p. 1591)
—Tales from Lovecraft Middle School #4: Substitute Creature. (p. 1701)
—Teacher's Pest. (p. 1709)
Gilman, Christopher, illus. see Keller, Jeff, Jr.
Gilman, David. Blood Sun. (p. 200)
—Devil's Breath Bk. 1. (p. 432)
Gilman, Dorothy, see Butters, Dorothy Gilman, pseud.
Gilman, Dorothy Foster. Ted Gilman. Caley, Isabel W., illus. (p. 1712)
Gilman, Grace. Dixie. McConnell, Sarah, illus. (p. 455)
—Dixie & the Best Day Ever. Rogers, Jacqueline, illus. (p. 455)
—Dixie & the Big Bully. (p. 455)
—Dixie & the Big Bully. McConnell, Sarah, illus. (p. 455)
—Dixie & the Class Treat. (p. 455)
—Dixie & the Class Treat. Rogers, Jacqueline, illus. (p. 455)
—Dixie & the Good Deeds. (p. 455)
—Dixie & the Good Deeds. McConnell, Sarah, illus. (p. 455)
—Dixie & the School Trip. (p. 455)
—Dixie & the School Trip. McConnell, Sarah, illus. (p. 455)
—Dixie Loves School Pet Day. McConnell, Sarah, illus. (p. 455)
—Dixie Wins the Race. (p. 455)
—Dixie Wins the Race. Rogers, Jacqueline, illus. (p. 455)
Gilman, Jan Levinson. Murphy's Three Homes: A Story for Children in Foster Care. O'Malley, Kathy, illus. (p. 1192)
Gilman, Laura Anne. Camelot Spell. (p. 256)
—Coping with Cerebral Palsy. (p. 365)
Gilman, Laura Anne, jt. auth. see Truet, Turin.
Gilman, Phoebe. Balloon Tree. (p. 135)
—Jillian Jiggs & the Great Big Snow. (p. 917)
—Jillian Jiggs & the Secret Surprise. (p. 917)
—Pirate Pearl. (p. 1362)
—Something from Nothing. (p. 1610)
Gilman, Sara, illus. see Mayfield, Holly.
Gilmartin, Charles. Storybook Sign Language. (p. 1663)
Gilmartin, Erin. Stretched into Shadow with No End: A Collection of Poems (p. 1667)
Gilmartin, Mary. Adventures with Easton: The Magical Journey. (p. 25)
Gilmer, Evelyn. Maggie: The Beagle with a Broken Tail. (p. 1071)
—Maggie the Beagle & the Dude Ranch. (p. 1071)
—Maggie the Beagle & the Oil Spill. (p. 1071)
—Maggie the Beagle Goes to Summer Camp. (p. 1071)
Gilmore, Cathy. Bubbles & Fun. (p. 233)
—Fun at the Park with Ransom & Ripley. (p. 647)
Gilmore, Cathy, jt. auth. see Benoist, Cathy.
Gilmore, Cathy & Benoist, Carol. Easter Bunny's AMAZING Day. Sundy, Jonathan, illus. (p. 499)
Gilmore, David. Xavier University College Prowler off the Record. (p. 1967)
Gilmore, Don. Christmas Orange Gay, Marie-Louise, illus. (p. 315)
Gilmore, Dorina Lazo. Stone in the Soup. Hires, Josh, illus. (p. 1652)
Gilmore, Frederic. Lincoln Memorial. (p. 1018)
—Washington Monument. (p. 1860)
Gilmore, Grace. Big City. Brown, Petra, illus. (p. 180)
—Ghost of Juniper Creek. Brown, Petra, illus. (p. 671)
—Logan Pryce Makes a Mess. Brown, Petra, illus. (p. 1045)
—Lucky Wheel. Brown, Petra, illus. (p. 1063)
Gilmore, Jason & Peterson, Paul. Next Day. Jansen, Alex & Poplak, Richard, eds. (p. 1249)
Gilmore, Rachna. Catching Time Wakelin, Kirsti Anne, illus. (p. 279)
—Flute Biswas, Pulak, illus. (p. 608)
—Gift for Gita. Priestley, Alice, illus. (p. 675)
—Grandpa's Clock Meissner, Amy, illus. (p. 709)
—Making Grizzle Grow Watts, Leslie Elizabeth, illus. (p. 1081)
—Roses for Gita. Priestley, Alice, illus. (p. 1490)
—Screaming Kind of Day. (p. 1533)
—Sower of Tales (p. 1618)
—When-I-Was-a-Little-Girl Benoit, Renne, illus. (p. 1903)
Gilmour, Barbara, et al. Cool Kind Kid Camp Kit 4-6: Social Skills Shaping Futures. (p. 363)
Gilmour, H. B., jt. auth. see Reisfeld, Randi.
Gilmour, Karen, illus. see McNulty John.
Gilmour, Richard. Bible History. (p. 175)
Gilpatrick, Gil. Allagash Guide: What You Need to Know to Canoe This Famous Waterway. (p. 46)
Gilpen, Rebecca. Boy's Activity Book. (p. 220)
—Christmas Activity Book. (p. 312)
Gilpin, Caroline. National Geographic Readers: Amelia Earhart. (p. 1233)
Gilpin, Caroline Crosson. National Geographic Readers: Abraham Lincoln. (p. 1233)
Gilpin, Caroline Crosson, jt. auth. see National Geographic Kids Staff.
Gilpin, Dan, jt. auth. see Basher, Simon.
Gilpin, Dan & Brush, Jim. Police Units. (p. 1380)
Gilpin, Dan & Bull, Peter. Explorers: Planet Earth. (p. 551)
Gilpin, Daniel. Centipedes, Millipedes, Scorpions, & Spiders (p. 287)
—Dwarf Geckos, Rattlesnakes, & Other Reptiles (p. 491)
—Life-Size Sharks & Other Underwater Creatures. Knowelden, Martin, illus. (p. 1013)
—Lobsters, Crabs, & Other Crustaceans (p. 1044)
—Record-Breaking Animals. (p. 1452)
—Record-Breaking Buildings. (p. 1452)
—Record-Breaking Cars. (p. 1452)
—Record-Breaking People. (p. 1452)
—Snails, Shellfish, & Other Mollusks (p. 1596)
—Starfish, Urchins, & Other Echinoderms (p. 1642)
—Start Your Own Band. (p. 1643)
—Tree Frogs, Mud Puppies, & Other Amphibians. (p. 1783)
Gilpin, Daniel, jt. auth. see Parker, Steve.
Gilpin, Daniel & Basher, Simon. Planet Earth: What Planet Are You On? Basher, Simon, illus. (p. 1367)
Gilpin, Daniel & Pang, Alex. Machines Close-Up (p. 1068)
—Military Fighting Machines. (p. 1143)
—Modern Military Aircraft. (p. 1158)
—Modern Warships & Submarines. (p. 1159)
—Record Breakers. (p. 1452)
—Rescue Vehicles. (p. 1462)
—Spacecraft. (p. 1620)
Gilpin, Esther. How the Bear Got Its Hair. (p. 812)
Gilpin, R. Fairy Things to Make & Do. (p. 564)
Gilpin, R. & Atkinson, C. Christmas Cooking. (p. 313)
Gilpin, Rebecca. 30 Healthy Things to Cook & Eat. (p. 1996)
—Amazing Activity Book (formerly Boys' Activity Book) (p. 52)
—Animal Things to Make & Do. (p. 80)
—Christmas fairy things to make & Do. Fearn, Katrina, illus. (p. 313)
—Cosas de Hadas. (p. 368)
—Dangerous Animals (Level 1) - Internet Referenced. (p. 404)
—Fairy Things to Make & Do. (p. 564)
—Fairy Things to Make & Do Kid Kit. McCafferty, Jan, illus. (p. 564)
—Introduction to Word Processing: Using Microsoft Word 2000 or Microsoft Office 2000. (p. 882)
—Little Children's Cookbook. Sage, Molly & Larkum, Adam, illus. (p. 1026)
—Monster Things to Make & Do. Harrison, Erica et al, illus. (p. 1168)
—Pirate Things to make & Do. (p. 1363)
—Spiders. Kushii, Tetsuo et al, illus. (p. 1626)
—Spiders. Kushii, Tetsuo & Wright, David, illus. (p. 1626)
—Things to Make for Mother's Day. Figg, Non, illus. (p. 1733)
—Travel Activity Book. (p. 1780)
—Trucks & Tractors. (p. 1791)
—Valentine Things to Make & Do. (p. 1830)
Gilpin, Rebecca, ed. see Wilkes, Angela & Cartwright, Stephen.
Gilpin, Rebecca, jt. auth. see Lacey, Minna.
Gilpin, Rebecca, jt. auth. see Watt, Fiona.
Gilpin, Rebecca & Atkinson, Catherine. Easter Cooking. (p. 499)
—Fairy Cooking. (p. 563)
—Yummy Little Cookbook. (p. 1983)
—Yummy Little Cookbook. Taylor, Non et al, illus. (p. 1983)
Gilpin, Rebecca & Brocklehurst, Ruth. Wizard, Pirate & Princess Things to Make & Do. Harrison, Erica, illus. (p. 1943)
Gilpin, Rebecca & Pratt, Leonie. Big Book of Science Things to Make & Do. Thompson, Josephine, illus. (p. 179)
Gilpin, Stephen, illus. see Arena, Jennifer.
Gilpin, Stephen, illus. see Bolger, Kevin.
Gilpin, Stephen, illus. see Boniface, William.
Gilpin, Stephen, illus. see Braun, Eric.
Gilpin, Stephen, illus. see Fjelland Davis, Rebecca.
Gilpin, Stephen, illus. see Hall, John.
Gilpin, Stephen, illus. see Kimmel, Eric A.
Gilpin, Stephen, illus. see King, M. G.
Gilpin, Stephen, illus. see Lasky, Kathryn.
Gilpin, Stephen, illus. see Loewen, Nancy, et al.
Gilpin, Stephen, illus. see Loewen, Nancy.
Gilpin, Stephen, illus. see McMullan, Kate.
Gilpin, Stephen, illus. see Mellom, Robin.
Gilpin, Stephen, illus. see Oliver, Lin.
Gilpin, Stephen, illus. see Pilger, Seamus.
Gilpin, Stephen, illus. see Robertson, Si & Nelson, Ashley Howard.
Gilpin, Stephen, illus. see Rothstein, Nancy H. & Rothstein, Nancy.
Gilpin, Stephen, illus. see Stafford, Jean & Van Draanen, Wendelin.
Gilpin, Stephen, illus. see Stott, Ann.
Gilpin, Stephen, illus. see Thomson, Sarah L.
Gilpin, Stephen, illus. see Troupe, Thomas Kingsley.
Gilpin, Stephen, illus. see Underwood, Deborah.
Gilpin, Stephen, illus. see Van Draanen, Wendelin.
Gilpin, Stephen, illus. see Wax, Wendy & Wax, Naomi.
Gilpin, Stephen, jt. auth. see Hall, John.
Gilpin, Stephen, jt. auth. see Rothstein, Nancy H.
Gilroy, Caroline. Redolf. (p. 1456)
Gilson. Love Potions. Saincantin, Jerome, tr. from FRE. (p. 1060)
—Melusine: The Vampires' Ball. Vol. 3 (p. 1125)
—Melusine - Hocus Pocus. Clarke & Clarke, illus. (p. 1125)
Gilson, Estelle, tr. see Bontempelli, Massimo.
Gilson, Heather, photos by see Chronicle Books Staff.
Gilson, Jamie. Bug in a Rug. deGroat, Diane, illus. (p. 236)
—My Teacher Is an Idiom. Tilley, Debbie, illus. (p. 1220)
—Thirteen Ways to Sink a Sub. (p. 1735)
Gilson, Judith. That's Just Jesus. (p. 1727)
Gilsvik, Bob. Complete Book of Trapping. Gilsvik, David, illus. (p. 352)
Gilsvik, David, illus. see Gilsvik, Bob.
Gilvan-Cartwright, Chris. Who's in the Ocean? (p. 1920)
Gilvan-Cartwright, Chris, illus. see DePrisco, Dorothea.
Gilvan-Cartwright, Chris, illus. see Gondek, Heather J.
Gilvan-Cartwright, Chris, illus. see Gondek, Heather.
Gilvan-Cartwright, Chris, illus. see Hewitt, Sally.
Gilvan-Cartwright, Christopher, illus. see Boroson, Martin & Quarto Generic Staff.
Gilven, Edwin. Blubaugh, Spiritually Speaking. (p. 202)
Gimbel, Steven. René Descartes. (p. 1460)
Gimbergsson, Sara, illus. see Edvall, Lilian.
Giménez Llort, Lydia. man who wore a Panama Hat. (p. 1086)
Giménez, Paco, illus. see Cano, Carles & Cano Peiró, Carles.
Giménez, Paco, tr. see Cano, Carles & Cano Peiró, Carles.
Gimlin, Mihaela, illus. see Creanga, Ion.
Gimmell, K., jt. auth. see Elliot, K.
Gimpel, Diane. Monarchies. (p. 1163)
—Transcontinental Railroad. (p. 1778)
Gimpel, Diane Marczely. Columbine Shootings. (p. 346)
—Pompeii. (p. 1382)
—Terrell Owens. (p. 1721)
—Violence in Video Games. (p. 1843)
Gimpel, Lee. Fighting Wars, Planning for Peace: The Story of George C. Marshall. (p. 586)
Ginebra, Fidel. Guardian de la Sangre. (p. 728)
Ginesin, Lucia. Prince Jack, the Little Artist. Ginesin, Zack, illus. (p. 1401)
Ginesin, Zack, illus. see Ginesin, Lucia.
Ginevra, Dante, illus. see Bolte, Marissa.
Ginevra, Dante, illus. see Collins, Terry.
Ginevra, Dante, illus. see Hoffman, Mary.
Ginevra, Dante, illus. see Yomtov, Nel, et al.
Ginevra, Dante, illus. see Yomtov, Nel.
Ginevra, Dante, contrib. by. Peril in Pompeii! Nickolas Flux & the Eruption of Mount Vesuvius (p. 1343)
Gingeleski, Randolph J. War of Lord Capani. (p. 1857)
Ginger Illustration, illus. see Gould, Judith S. & Burke, Mary F.
Ginger Illustrations Staff, illus. see Enderle, Dotti.
Ginger Illustrations Staff, illus. see Tuszynski, Kathy & Yarber, Angela.
Ginger, Richard, jt. auth. see Kings, Gary.
Gingeras, Alison M. Guy Bourdin. Bourdin, Samuel, photos by. (p. 733)
Gingerich, Neeltje. Mini-Musicals for Christmas. (p. 1146)
Gingold, Janet. Danger, Long Division. (p. 404)
—Finch Goes Wild. (p. 587)
—My Adventure as a Birder: Advanced My Adventure. (p. 1195)
—My Adventure as a Camper: Advanced My Adventure. (p. 1195)
—My Adventure as a Scientist: Advanced My Adventure. (p. 1195)
—My Adventure on a Lake: Advanced My Adventure. (p. 1195)
—My Adventure with Arthropods: Advanced My Adventure. (p. 1195)
—My Adventure with Reptiles: Advanced My Adventure. (p. 1195)
Gingras, Charlotte. Boite a Bonheur. Jorisch, Stéphane, illus. (p. 208)
—Ecuyere. Dubois, Gérard, illus. (p. 503)
—Pieces of Me. Ouriou, Susan, tr. from FRE. (p. 1356)
Gingras, Gaston, jt. auth. see Brouwer, Sigmund.
Gingras, Marie Claude. Let's Spend Summer with Fred. (p. 1000)
Gingrich, Callista. From Sea to Shining Sea. Arciero, Susan, illus. (p. 643)
—Land of the Pilgrims Pride. Arciero, Susan, illus. (p. 973)
—Sweet Land of Liberty. Arciero, Susan, illus. (p. 1690)
—Yankee Doodle Dandy. Arciero, Susan, illus. (p. 1968)
Gingrich, Newt & Forstchen, William R. Grant Comes East. (p. 710)
Ginkel, Anne. I've Got an Elephant Bynum, Janie, illus. (p. 900)
Ginn, David. Clown Magic. (p. 335)
Ginn, Don. Principle: It Carries the Power to Change Our Destiny. (p. 1406)
Ginn, Janel D. Bilingual Education. (p. 186)
—Biological & Chemical Weapons. (p. 189)
Ginn, Jennifer. Lobsters on the Loose Krackow, Eric T., illus. (p. 1044)
—My Father Flies Kramer, David, illus. (p. 1203)
Ginnings, Miriam, jt. auth. see Latimer, Miriam.
Ginolfi, Art. Tiny Snowflake. (p. 1756)
—Tiny Star. (p. 1756)
Ginoschio De Osceola, Ibrahim. Enter the Corn Bunny (p. 531)
Ginsberg, Dvora, illus. see Yerushalmi, Miriam.
Ginsberg, Mort. Ukey & His Magical Ukulele. (p. 1808)
Ginsburg, Binyamin, ed. Parsha Page: Sefer Bereishis. (p. 1325)
Ginsburg, Herbert P., et al. Acorn Hunt. (p. 9)
—Big Math for Little Kids: Classroom Manipulative Kit. (p. 182)
—Dobee Doubler. (p. 458)
—Favorite Shapes. (p. 578)
—Jenny Saves the Day. (p. 913)
—Leftover Muffins. (p. 987)
—Rafael's Messy Room. (p. 1433)
—So Many Fives! (p. 1602)
—Table of Phinneas Fable. (p. 1694)
—Tick-Tock! (p. 1747)
—Trees of Mrs. Mcgee. (p. 1784)
—Two-Two the Tooth Fairy. (p. 1804)
Ginsburg, Lynn & Taylor, Mary. What Are You Hungry For? Women, Food, & Spirituality. (p. 1880)
Ginsburg, Richard D., et al. Whose Game Is It, Anyway? A Guide to Helping Your Child Get the Most from Sports, Organized by Age & Stage. (p. 1921)
Ginsburg, Sara. Look What My Parents Give Me. David, Racheli, illus. (p. 1050)
Ginsburgh, Judy. Complete Jewish Songbook for Children (p. 353)
Gintrac, Brigitte. Let's Play with Lou. (p. 1000)
Ginukov, Valentin, illus. see Shurin, Masha.
Ginyard, John. What Is the Job of a Corrections Officer? (p. 1890)
Gioffre, Rosalba. Fun with French Cooking. (p. 648)
—Fun with Italian Cooking. (p. 648)
Gioffre, Rosalba, et al. Kids' Cookbook: Recipes from Around the World. Wilson, Alison & Farrell, Helen, eds. (p. 953)
Giogas, Valarie. In My Backyard Zecca, Katherine, illus. (p. 864)
Giombi, Gary. Finding God in Prayer: A Backpack Journal for Teens. (p. 588)
Giono, Aline, jt. auth. see Giono, Jean.
Giono, Jean. Hombre Que Plantaba Arboles. (p. 791)
Giono, Jean & Giono, Aline. Man Who Planted Trees. Bray, Barbara, tr. from FRE. (p. 1086)
Giordana, D., illus. see Gaiman, Neil.
Giordano, illus. see Bellenson, Evelyn.
Giordano, Anne. Spencer, the Magic Rabbit. (p. 1625)
Giordano, Anthony. Another Boring Summer... Again! (p. 87)
Giordano, Dick. Dracula. (p. 476)
Giordano, Dick, illus. see Maggin, Elliot, et al.
Giordano, Dick, illus. see Perez, George, et al.
Giordano, Geraldine. Everything You Need to Know about Wicca: Ancient Beliefs for a Modern World. (p. 546)
—Oklahoma City Bombing. (p. 1283)
—Sandy Koufax. (p. 1511)
Giordano, Jean. Alphabet for Young Eckists. Epps, SArah, illus. (p. 49)
Giordano, Margaret A. Bowditchers. (p. 216)
Giordano, Paula J. Honey Bees Going to a New School. (p. 794)
Giordano, Pearl. Glasses for George. (p. 682)
Giordano, Virginia E. Duffy T. Mcgraw Makes New Friends: The Little Pug with the Big Heart. (p. 489)
Giorgio, Marg. Maxi's Magical Dream. (p. 1112)
Gioscia, Bob. Cutter Lives: The Principal Assassin Returns. (p. 396)
Gioseffi, Anthony P. Mainframe. (p. 1077)
Gioulis, Sue, illus. see Yeh, Kat.
Giovanni, Nikki. Lincoln & Douglass: An American Friendship. (p. 1018)
—Lincoln & Douglass: An American Friendship. Collier, Bryan, illus. (p. 1018)
—On My Journey Now: Looking at African-American History Through the Spirituals. (p. 1289)
—Rosa. Collier, Bryan, illus. (p. 1488)
—Rosa Storytime Set Collier, Bryan, illus. (p. 1489)
—Sun Is So Quiet. Bryan, Ashley, illus. (p. 1676)
Giovanni, Nikki, jt. auth. see Scholastic, Inc. Staff.
Giovannini, Jody, illus. see Jones, Carroll.
Giovannini, Vivia. Glass Ball. (p. 682)
Giovannoli, Renato. Misterio en Villa Jamaica. (p. 1155)
Giovanucci, Sharon, illus. see Voland, Wanda.
Giovine, Sergio, illus. see Buckey, Sarah Masters.
Giovine, Sergio, illus. see Reiss, Kathryn.
Gipp, Jennifer. Spotlight on Introduction to Computers. (p. 1634)
Gipson, Crash. Sheldon's Favorite Game. (p. 1564)
Gipson, Fred. Old Yeller. (p. 1285)
Gipson, Fred & Polson, Steven. Old Yeller. (p. 1285)

Gipson, Mary Willene. Tattered Feather. (p. 1707)
Gipson, Morrell. Surprise Doll. Lerch, Steffie, illus. (p. 1685)
Gipson, Morrell, ed. Stories of Mystery, Adventure & Fun from Calling All Girls. Dawson, Isabel, illus. (p. 1655)
Giraffe, Red, illus. see Hayler, Kate.
Giraffe, Red, illus. see Hofer, Charles.
Giraldo, Maria Cristina, tr. see Llewellyn, Claire.
Giraldo, Maria Loretta. Saints & Their Stories. Moran, Margaret Edward, tr. (p. 1504)
Giraldo, Paola. Gamal Abdel Nasser -el faraón Rojo. (p. 654)
Girard, Alexander. Alexander Girard Color. (p. 36)
—Alexander Girard Coloring Book. (p. 36)
—Alexander Girard Memory Game. (p. 36)
Girard, Franck. Baúl de Palabras. de Monfreid, Dorothée, illus. (p. 147)
—Mi Primer Baul de Palabras. Jonniaux, Isabelle, illus. (p. 1133)
Girard, Geoffrey. Project Cain. (p. 1410)
Girard, Philippe. Gustave et le Capitaine Planète. Girard, Philippe, illus. (p. 733)
—Gustave et les Sosies du Capitaine Planète. Girard, Philippe, illus. (p. 733)
Girard, Robert. American Flag: Learning to Identify Two-Digit Numbers up To 50. (p. 60)
Girard, Roger, illus. see Krensky, Stephen.
Girard, Thomas. Nameless Treasure. Girard, Thomas, illus. (p. 1228)
Girard, Vanessa, DM. Diversity Is U & Me (high school survival Guide) (p. 454)
Girard, Vanessa P. High School Survival Guide: United in Diversity. (p. 778)
Girasole, Alessia, illus. see Metzger, Steve.
Girasole, Alessia, illus. see Weiss, Ellen & Friedman, Mel.
Giraud, Jean & Charlier, Jean-Michel. Blueberry: El Raid Infernal. Martín, Andreu, tr. from FRE. (p. 204)
—Blueberry: Geronimo el Apache. Martín, Andreu, tr. from FRE. (p. 204)
—Blueberry: El Fantasma Balas de Oro. Martín, Andreu, tr. from FRE. (p. 204)
—Blueberry: La Mina del Alemán Perdido. Martín, Andreu, tr. from FRE. (p. 204)
—Blueberry: Último Tren Hacia Washington. Martín, Andreu, tr. from FRE. (p. 204)
Giraud, Teresa, illus. see Jordan, Lana.
Giraudon, David. Our Living Earth: A Story of People, Ecology, & Preservation. Arthus-Bertrand, Yann, photos by. (p. 1309)
Girdner, Randall P. Mr. Ping's Almanac of the Twisted & Weird presents Boyd Mccloyd & the Perpetual Motion Machine. (p. 1186)
Gire, Anna Marie Petrarca. Sal: A Tale of Many Feathers. (p. 1504)
Girel, Stephane. Bird in Winter: A Children's Book Inspired by Pieter Breugel. (p. 190)
Girel, Stephane, illus. see Elschner, Geraldine.
Girginov, Vassil, et al. Olympic Games Explained: A Student Guide to the Evolution of the Modern Olympic Games. (p. 1287)
Giricz, Irma Cantu. Goody, Goody Gumdrops. (p. 702)
Girls, B. J. Kahmal's Big Day! (p. 941)
Girl Scouts of the USA, creator. Ambassador Girl's Guide to Girl Scouting. (p. 56)
—Senior Girl's Guide to Girl Scouting. (p. 1550)
Girmay, Aracelis. Changing, Changing: Story & Collages. Girmay, Aracelis, illus. (p. 290)
Girner, Sebastian. Monsuno Combat Chaos. Vol. 3: Rise of the Ocean God. Height, Ray-Anthony, illus. (p. 1170)
Girod, Christina M. Indian Americans. (p. 871)
Giroir, Constance H. Mommy Did You Know... An Adoption Story. Longo, Jason, illus. (p. 1162)
Girolami, Lisa. Run to Me. (p. 1496)
Giron, Elizabeth, illus. see Olesen, Demetria Vassiliou.
Girouard, Patricia L., illus. see Stockstill, Gloria McQueen.
Girouard, Patrick, illus. see Bailer, Darice.
Girouard, Patrick, illus. see Browne, Yolanda.
Girouard, Patrick, illus. see Caffey, Don.
Girouard, Patrick, illus. see Crow, Melinda Melton.
Girouard, Patrick, illus. see Gagliardi, Tina.
Girouard, Patrick, illus. see Hall, Pamela.
Girouard, Patrick, illus. see Mahoney, Judy.
Girouard, Patrick, illus. see Millhouse, Jackie.
Girouard, Patrick, illus. see Moncure, Jane Belk.
Girouard, Patrick, illus. see StJohn, Amanda.
Girouard, Patrick, illus. see Stockstill, Gloria McQueen.
Girouard, Patrick, illus. see Thompson, Kim Mitzo.
Girourard, Patrick, illus. see Bullard, Lisa.
Giroux, Chris, jt. auth. see Noah, Jennifer.
Giroux, Henry A. America on the Edge: Henry Giroux on Politics, Culture, & Education. (p. 59)
Giroux, Henry A. & Giroux, Susan Searls. Take Back Higher Education: Race, Youth, & the Crisis of Democracy in the Post-Civil Rights Era. (p. 1696)
Giroux, Robert, ed. see Bishop, Elizabeth.
Giroux, Susan Searls, jt. auth. see Giroux, Henry A.
Girtz, Angie. Oliver's Amazing Imagination. (p. 1286)
Girvan, Gregor. Trial for Iris. (p. 1785)
Gisbert, Joan Manuel. Mirada Oscura. (p. 1149)
—Palacio de los Tres Ojos. Lucini, Chata, illus. (p. 1319)
Gisbert, Joan Manuel & Gisbert Ponsolé, Joan Manuel. Orion y Los Animales Magos. (p. 1304)
Gisbert, Montse & Gisbert, Montserrat. Salvador Dalí, Píntame un Sueño. (p. 1506)
Gisbert, Montserrat, jt. auth. see Gisbert, Montse.
Gisbert Ponsolé, Joan Manuel, jt. auth. see Gisbert, Joan Manuel.
Gischler, Victor. X-Men: With Great Power. Bachalo, Chris, illus. (p. 1967)
—X-Men - Curse of the Mutants. Medina, Paco, illus. (p. 1967)
Gish, Melissa. Airport. (p. 32)
—Alligators. (p. 47)
—Antelopes. (p. 89)
—Bats. (p. 144)
—Beavers. (p. 155)
—Bighorn Sheep. (p. 185)
—Bison. (p. 193)
—Bison - Living Wild. (p. 193)
—Brown Bears. (p. 231)
—Camels. (p. 256)
—Chameleons. (p. 289)
—Chimpanzees. (p. 306)
—Construction Site. (p. 360)
—Cougars. (p. 369)
—Crabs. (p. 375)
—Crocodiles. (p. 384)
—Dairy Farm. (p. 400)
—Eagles. (p. 492)
—Elephants. (p. 511)
—Energy. (p. 528)
—Falcons. (p. 566)
—Flamingos. (p. 602)
—Frogs. (p. 641)
—Geckos. (p. 659)
—Gorillas. (p. 703)
—Hawks. (p. 755)
—Hippopotamuses. (p. 781)
—Hummingbirds. (p. 826)
—Iguanas. (p. 856)
—Jaguars. (p. 905)
—Jellyfish. (p. 912)
—Kangaroos. (p. 942)
—Killer Whales. (p. 956)
—Komodo Dragons. (p. 966)
—Leopards. (p. 993)
—Light. (p. 1014)
—Living Wild - Alligators. (p. 1042)
—Living Wild: Antelopes. (p. 1042)
—Living Wild - Bats. (p. 1042)
—Living Wild: Beavers. (p. 1042)
—Living Wild: Brown Bears. (p. 1042)
—Living Wild: Camels. (p. 1042)
—Living Wild: Chameleons. (p. 1042)
—Living Wild: Chimpanzees. (p. 1042)
—Living Wild: Cougars. (p. 1042)
—Living Wild: Flamingos. (p. 1042)
—Living Wild: Frogs. (p. 1042)
—Living Wild: Geckos. (p. 1042)
—Living Wild: Hawks. (p. 1042)
—Living Wild: Hippos. (p. 1042)
—Living Wild - Kangaroos. (p. 1042)
—Living Wild - Leopards. (p. 1042)
—Living Wild - Moose. (p. 1042)
—Living Wild: Octopuses. (p. 1042)
—Living Wild: Piranhas. (p. 1042)
—Living Wild: Sea Lions. (p. 1042)
—Living Wild: Sea Turtles. (p. 1042)
—Living Wild: Skunks. (p. 1042)
—Living Wild: Tortoises. (p. 1042)
—Living Wild: Vultures. (p. 1042)
—Living Wild: Walruses. (p. 1042)
—Living Wild: Wild Horses. (p. 1042)
—Living Wild: Wolverines. (p. 1042)
—Living Wild: Woodpeckers. (p. 1042)
—Living Wild: Zebras. (p. 1042)
—Meerkats. (p. 1120)
—Monkeys. (p. 1165)
—Newspaper Publisher. (p. 1249)
—Octopuses. (p. 1278)
—Oklahoma. (p. 1282)
—Owls. (p. 1315)
—Pandas. (p. 1321)
—Piranhas. (p. 1362)
—Raccoons. (p. 1430)
—Rhinoceroses. (p. 1467)
—Sea Lions. (p. 1534)
—Sea Turtles. (p. 1535)
—Sharks. (p. 1562)
—Skunks. (p. 1586)
—Sound. (p. 1615)
—Storks. (p. 1655)
—Temperature. (p. 1717)
—Tennessee. (p. 1720)
—Tortoises. (p. 1771)
—Utah. (p. 1829)
—Vultures. (p. 1851)
—Walruses. (p. 1855)
—Washington. (p. 1859)
—Whales. (p. 1877)
—Wild Horses. (p. 1929)
—Wolverines. (p. 1944)
—Woodpeckers. (p. 1949)
—Zebras. (p. 1985)
Gish, Melissa & Shaw, Nancy J. Fossils. (p. 623)
Gish, Sarah. Summer Book 2006: A Guide to Houston Day Camps & Classes for Kids & Teens. (p. 1674)
Gish, Steven, et al. Ethiopia. (p. 539)
Gisnash, Sahara. Salt-N-Pepa. (p. 1505)
Gisnash, Sahara, jt. auth. see Spaulding, Jeffrey.
Gisser, George H. Happy Kappy-The Flying Kangaroo(Who couldn't hop!): "Without Our Tails" Bk. 1 Gisser, George H. et al, illus. (p. 746)
Gisser, Marshall C., illus. see Gisser, George H.
Gissing, Kathleen. Buddy & the Poi Puppy. Swiatoviak, Jeri, illus. (p. 234)
Gist, E. M., illus. see Olson, Arielle North & Schwartz, Howard.
Gist, Richard. Ayshus on the Inside. (p. 121)
Gitau, Terri. Annie & Kindness the Frog. (p. 86)
Gitchel, Sam & Foster, Lorri. Hablemos Acerca del S-E-X-O. Kaplan, Dori, tr. from ENG. (p. 735)
—Let's Talk about S-E-X: A Guide for Kids 9 to 12 & Their Parents. (p. 1001)
Gitelson. Study Guide: Used with ... Gitelson-American Government. (p. 1670)
Gitenstein, Judy. Alvin Alley. (p. 51)
Gitlin, Martin. 1980 U. S. Olympic Boycott: A History Perspectives Book. (p. 2002)
—Adrian Peterson: Record-Setting Running Back. (p. 13)
—Battle of Bull Run: A History Perspectives Book. (p. 146)
—Battle of the Little Bighorn. (p. 146)
—Billie Jean King: Tennis Star & Social Activist. (p. 187)
—Boston Celtics. (p. 215)
—Chris Rock: A Biography of a Comic Genius. (p. 311)
—Cincinnati Bengals. (p. 319)
—Cincinnati Reds. (p. 319)
—Cleveland Browns. (p. 331)
—Cleveland Cavaliers. (p. 331)
—Cleveland Indians. (p. 331)
—Connecticut Huskies. (p. 358)
—Cyber Attack. (p. 396)
—Darrell Waltrip: Racing Legend. (p. 409)
—David Wright: Gifted & Giving Baseball Star. (p. 411)
—Dirk Nowitzki: NBA Champion. (p. 445)
—Dream Jobs in Sports Finance & Administration. (p. 483)
—Dream Jobs in Sports Scouting. (p. 483)
—Drew Brees: Super Bowl Champ. (p. 485)
—EBay: The Company & Its Founder. (p. 501)
—Ed Reed. (p. 503)
—Extreme Sports & Their Greatest Competitors (p. 557)
—Florida Gators. (p. 607)
—Football Skills: How to Play Like a Pro. (p. 615)
—George S. Patton: World War II General & Military Innovator. (p. 663)
—Girls Play to Win Cheerleading. (p. 680)
—Girls Play to Win Softball. (p. 680)
—Great Depression & World War II: 1929-1945. (p. 715)
—Green Berets. (p. 721)
—Hills. (p. 780)
—Hockey. (p. 786)
—Holocaust. (p. 789)
—Jeff Gordon: Racing's Brightest Star. (p. 911)
—Jeremy Lin: Basketball Phenom. (p. 913)
—Jimmie Johnson: Racing Champ. (p. 918)
—Joe Flacco: Super Bowl MVP. (p. 920)
—Joseph Pulitzer: Historic Newspaper Publisher. (p. 926)
—Kevin Durant: NBA Superstar. (p. 950)
—Kobe Bryant: NBA Champion. (p. 966)
—Los Angeles Dodgers. (p. 1053)
—Los Angeles Lakers. (p. 1053)
—Louisville Cardinals. (p. 1059)
—Martial Arts & Its Greatest Fighters (p. 1097)
—Memphis Grizzlies. (p. 1126)
—Miami Heat. (p. 1134)
—Michigan Football. (p. 1135)
—Montgomery Bus Boycott: A History Perspectives Book. (p. 1170)
—My Super Sweet 16. (p. 1219)
—Ohio State Buckeyes. (p. 1281)
—Ole Miss Rebels. (p. 1285)
—Operation Desert Storm. (p. 1300)
—Peyton Manning: Superstar Quarterback. (p. 1349)
—Playing Pro Basketball. (p. 1372)
—Post-War United States: 1945-Early 1970s. (p. 1387)
—Randy Orton: A Living Legacy (p. 1438)
—Referee. (p. 1456)
—San Francisco Giants. (p. 1510)
—Shaun White: Snow & Skateboard Champion. (p. 1563)
—Soccer Star Robinho. (p. 1603)
—Sonia Sotomayor: Supreme Court Justice. (p. 1612)
—St. Louis Cardinals. (p. 1638)
—Stan Lee: Comic Book Superhero. (p. 1639)
—Stanley Cup: All about Pro Hockey's Biggest Event (p. 1640)
—Tennis. (p. 1720)
—Tom Brady: Super Bowl Quarterback. (p. 1762)
—Tyler Perry: A Biography of a Movie Mogul. (p. 1805)
—U. S. Involvement in Vietnam. (p. 1806)
—U. S. Sanctions on Cuba. (p. 1807)
—Vietnam War. (p. 1841)
—Vikings. (p. 1842)
—Walt Disney: Entertainment Visionary. (p. 1855)
—Weirdest Moments in Sports. (p. 1873)
—Wimbledon. (p. 1935)
—Wisconsin Badgers. (p. 1939)
—World War II on the Home Front: An Interactive History Adventure (p. 1959)
—World War II U. S. Homefront: A History Perspectives Book. (p. 1959)
—Wounded Knee Massacre (p. 1962)
Gitlin, Martin, jt. auth. see Heath, Steve.
Gitlin, Martin, jt. auth. see Lobby, Mackenzie.
Gitlin, Martin, jt. auth. see Swain, Gwenyth.
Gitlin, Martin & Goldstein, Margaret J. Cyber Attack. (p. 396)
Gitlin, Martin, et al. Winner Takes All. (p. 1937)
Gitlin, Marty. Baseball Legends in the Making (p. 141)
—Best Tennis Players of All Time. (p. 171)
—Brutal Games: History's Most Dangerous Sports. (p. 233)
—Carmelo Anthony. (p. 270)
—Chris Paul. (p. 311)
—Cincinnati Reds. (p. 319)
—Cleveland Indians. (p. 331)
—Kevin Love. (p. 950)
—Los Angeles Dodgers. (p. 1053)
—San Francisco Giants. (p. 1510)
—St. Louis Cardinals. (p. 1638)
—Totally Gross History of Medieval Europe. (p. 1771)
Gitlin, Marty, et al. Legends in the Making (p. 990)
Gittemeier, Tausha. Hmmm, I was Thinking... What If? (p. 786)
Gittens, Sandra L. Hooray! We're Making Memories Today! PA Illustrator, illus. (p. 796)
Gittens, Tessa, jt. auth. see Aarons, Maureen.
Gittings, Clare. What Are You Looking At? Band 14. (p. 1880)
Gittins, Sheri. Christmas Journey. (p. 314)
Gittoes-Singh, Xennia. One Drop: To Be the Color Black. (p. 1294)
Giuffre, Mary & Clark, Paul L. Scribble & Grin: 53 Rhymes for Inspiring Times. Sullivan, Troy, illus. (p. 1533)
Giuliani, Al. New Nanny. (p. 1246)
Giuliani, George A., jt. auth. see Pierangelo, Roger.
Giuliano, Kevin. When I Was Young. (p. 1903)
Giulieri, Anne. Aquarium (p. 93)
—Banana Spider (p. 136)
—Bugs Vanzet, Gaston, illus. (p. 237)
—Castle Kreinberg, Sylvia, photos by. (p. 276)
—Chocolate Banana Pops Kreinberg, Sylvia, photos by. (p. 309)
—Circus Tricks Meldrum, Ned, photos by. (p. 322)
—Cooking Pancakes Meldrum, Ned, photos by. (p. 362)
—Grandpa's Farm Bailey, Martin, illus. (p. 709)
—Here Is a Robot Kreinberg, Sylvia, photos by. (p. 770)
—In the Playhouse Aranda, Omar, illus. (p. 867)
—In the Water Hancock, Anna, illus. (p. 867)
—Little Sea Horse & the Big Crab Aranda, Omar, illus. (p. 1036)
—Little Sea Horse & the Big Storm Aranda, Omar, illus. (p. 1036)
—Look at Me Boyer, Susy, illus. (p. 1048)
—Look at the Picture Kreinberg, Sylvia, photos by. (p. 1049)
—Lost Sock Bailey, Martin, illus. (p. 1056)
—Make a Secret Playhouse Meldrum, Ned, photos by. (p. 1078)
—Make Two Crocodiles Kreinberg, Sylvia, photos by. (p. 1079)
—Max & the Balloons Bailey, Martin, illus. (p. 1110)
—My Big Sandcastle Boyer, Susy, illus. (p. 1197)
—My Birthday Kreinberg, Sylvia, photos by. (p. 1198)
—My Dinosaurs Meldrum, Ned, photos by. (p. 1202)
—My Rock Pool Meldrum, Ned, photos by. (p. 1217)
—My Shopping (p. 1218)
—Oral Language-Book A: Speaking & Listening in the Classroom. (p. 1301)
—Oral Language-Book B: Speaking & Listening in the Classroom. (p. 1301)
—School Garden Fleming, Garry, illus. (p. 1523)
—Secret Tree House Boyer, Susy, illus. (p. 1544)
—Sleepy Little Caterpillar Florian, Mélanie, illus. (p. 1590)
—Surprise Pancakes for Mom Boyer, Susy, illus. (p. 1686)
—To the Shops Florian, Mélanie, illus. (p. 1759)
—Volcano Bubbles Kreinberg, Sylvia, illus. (p. 1848)
—Volcano Sand Hill Boyer, Susy, illus. (p. 1848)
Giunta, Brian. Seven Presidents. Chapin, Patrick O., illus. (p. 1554)
Giurco, Diane. Adventures of Willy & Nilly. (p. 24)
Giusti, Katiuscia. Clean-Up Contest. (p. 330)
Given, Cate. Cartwheeling. Hill-Peterson, Jodi, illus. (p. 273)
—Great Pogo Stick. Hill-Peterson, Jodi, illus. (p. 718)
Givens, David. Love Signals: A Practical Field Guide to the Body Language of Courtship. (p. 1060)
Givens, David, ed. For the Kids! A Family-Friendly Guide to Outings & Activities. (p. 616)
Givens, Ed. Molly Maple: The Wishing Star. (p. 1160)
Givens, Florence Rosie. Little More Cream Please Poem Collection by Florence Rosie Givens. (p. 1032)
Givens, R. Eight Ball Bible: A Guide to Bar Table Play. Givens, R, illus. (p. 507)
Givens, Terryl L. Escamas de Dragon y Hojas de Sauce. Portwood, Andrew, illus. (p. 534)
Givnan, Tanner. Runaway Ornaments. (p. 1496)
Givner, Joan. Hills Are Shadows. (p. 780)
Gizicki, Carlie, jt. auth. see Gizicki-Lipson, Coryn.
Gizicki-Lipson, Coryn & Gizicki, Carlie. Angel in the Sky. Gizicki-Lipson, Coryn, illus. (p. 73)
Gizzi, Peter. Periplum & Other Poems, 1987—1992. (p. 1343)
Glabe, Scott & Rahimi, Joey. Dartmouth College College Prowler off the Record. (p. 409)
Glacel, Jenn, ed. see Oster, Kalab J.
Glad, Molly. I'm the Boy Who. (p. 860)
Gladden, DelSheree. Escaping Fate. (p. 535)
—Shaxoa's Gift: Book Two in the Twin Souls Saga. (p. 1563)
Gladden, Stephanie, illus. see Ottaviani, Jim.
Glade, Debbie. Travel Advenures of Lilly P Badilly: Costa Rica. (p. 1780)
Gladen, Jennifer. Angel Donor. Bell, Samantha, illus. (p. 73)
Gladfelter, Allen, illus. see Porter, Alan J.
Gladfelter, Scott, et al. Be the One! The Todd Beamer Story an Adaptation of Let's Roll! by Lisa Beamer & Todd Anderson. (p. 149)
Gladir, George, jt. auth. see Salicrup, Jim.
Gladir, George, et al. Ebenezer Stooge. Goldberg, Stan, illus. (p. 501)
—Three Stooges. Goldberg, Stan, illus. (p. 1744)
Gladstone, James, jt. auth. see Edwards, Ron.
Gladwell, Deborah L. Adventures of Shy Spy Time Traveler: The Ten Plagues of Egypt & the Parting of the Red Sea. (p. 23)
Gladwell, Michael. Slappers Maui Vacation. (p. 1588)
Gladwin, Harold Sterling. Men Out of Asia. (p. 1126)
Glaeser, David M. Trip to the Cottage with Bobo. (p. 1787)
Glaeser, Patricia Heinz. New Day for Foal. (p. 1244)
Glaessner, Gert-Joachim. German Democracy: From Post-World War II to the Present Day. (p. 666)
Glancey, Jonathan. Story of Architecture. (p. 1657)
Glancy, Diane. Rooms: New & Selected Poems. (p. 1488)
Glanville, Caroline, illus. see Johnson, Gail & Grell, Jane.
Glanville, K. L. 2108: Eyes Open. (p. 2003)
—Realm: The Awakening Begins (p. 1450)
Glanville, Toby, photos by see Carrarini, Rose & Carrarini, Jean Charles.
Glanzman, Louis, illus. see Rockwell, Carey & Ley, Willy.
Glanzman, Louis S., illus. see Ciardi, John.
Glanzman, Louis S., illus. see Lindgren, Astrid.
Glasbergen, Randy, illus. see Bradley, Michael J.
Glascodine, Carolyn, ed. Access Asia: Primary Teaching & Learning Units. Mo, Xiangyi, illus. (p. 8)
Glaser, Byron & Higashi, Sandra. Zolocolor! Doodling Between Black & White. Glaser, Byron & Higashi, Sandra, illus. (p. 1987)
—Zolocolor! Christmas Doodling. Glaser, Byron & Higashi, Sandra, illus. (p. 1987)
—Zolocolor! Doodle Canoodle. (p. 1987)
—Zolocolor! Toodle-Oo Doodle-Oo. (p. 1987)
Glaser, Chaya. Jupiter: The Biggest Planet. (p. 937)
—JUPiter: El Mayor de Los Planetas. (p. 937)
—Mercurio: El MÁS PequeÑo de Todos. (p. 1127)
—Mercury: The Smallest of All. (p. 1127)
—Saturn: Amazing Rings. (p. 1515)
—Saturno: Anillos Asombrosos. (p. 1516)
—Sol: Una Superestrella. (p. 1606)
—Sun: A Super Star. (p. 1675)
—Urano: Frío y Azul. (p. 1825)
—Uranus: Cold & Blue. (p. 1825)

Glaser, Chaya & Sawyer, J. Clark. Icy Comets: Sometimes Have Tails. (p. 851)
—Pluto: Not a Planet. (p. 1374)
Glaser, David, et al. Living with a Star: From Sunscreen to Space Weather. Hoyt, Richard, photos by. (p. 1042)
Glaser, Jason. Achilles (p. 9)
—Batter. (p. 145)
—Batters. (p. 145)
—Bearded Dragons Collins, Tami, illus. (p. 151)
—Buffalo Soldiers & the American West. Smith, Tod G. et al, illus. (p. 236)
—Career Building Through Using Digital Story Tools. (p. 266)
—Careers in Online Retailing. (p. 268)
—Catcher. (p. 279)
—Colds (p. 339)
—Colorado: The Centennial State. (p. 343)
—Danica Patrick. (p. 404)
—David Beckham. (p. 410)
—Flu (p. 608)
—Green Berets Martin, Cynthia, illus. (p. 721)
—Horned Lizards Collins, Tami, illus. (p. 798)
—Infielders. (p. 873)
—Jackie Robinson: Gran Pionero del Béisbol. Lentz, Bob, illus. (p. 904)
—Jackie Robinson: Baseball's Great Pioneer Lentz, Bob et al, illus. (p. 904)
—John Brown's Raid on Harpers Ferry. Milgrom, Al et al, illus. (p. 921)
—Kansas: The Sunflower State. (p. 943)
—Kentucky: The Bluegrass State. (p. 949)
—Komodo Dragons Collins, Tami, illus. (p. 966)
—Leif Eriksson (p. 991)
—Lewis & Clark (p. 1004)
—Louisiana. (p. 1058)
—Maria Sharapova. (p. 1093)
—Meet the Senate. (p. 1123)
—Minerals up Close. (p. 1146)
—Molly Pitcher: Young American Patriot Smith, Tod G. et al, illus. (p. 1161)
—Nevada. (p. 1242)
—Outfielders. (p. 1312)
—Patrick Henry: Liberty or Death. McDonnell, Peter, illus. (p. 1329)
—Pennsylvania. (p. 1337)
—Peyton Manning. (p. 1349)
—Pitcher. (p. 1364)
—Point Guard. (p. 1377)
—Power Forward. (p. 1389)
—Prospect. (p. 1412)
—Roger Federer. (p. 1484)
—Sea Turtles Collins, Tami, illus. (p. 1535)
—South Dakota: The Mount Rushmore State. (p. 1617)
—Sports Idols (p. 1632)
—Tiger Woods. (p. 1749)
—Tim Duncan. (p. 1750)
—Tim Lincecum. (p. 1750)
—Tom Brady. (p. 1762)
Glaser, Jason, jt. auth. see Olson, Nathan.
Glaser, Jason & Bowman, Laurel. Mars (p. 1096)
Glaser, Jason & Roley, Don. Ninja Martin, Cynthia, illus. (p. 1256)
Glaser, Linda. Alask. (p. 33)
—Dazzling Dragonflies: A Life Cycle Story. Posada, Mia, illus. (p. 415)
—Emma's Poem: The Voice of the Statue of Liberty. Nivola, Claire A., illus. (p. 520)
—Garbage Helps Our Garden Grow: A Compost Story. Rotner, Shelley, photos by. (p. 655)
—Hannah's Way. Gustavson, Adam, illus. (p. 743)
—Hello, Squirrels! Scampering Through the Seasons. Holland, Gay W., illus. (p. 765)
—Hoppy Hanukkah! Howarth, Daniel, illus. (p. 797)
—It's Fall! Swan, Susan, illus. (p. 896)
—It's Spring! Swan, Susan, illus. (p. 899)
—It's Summer! (p. 899)
—Mrs. Greenberg's Messy Hanukkah. Cote, Nancy, illus. (p. 1187)
—Not a Buzz to Be Found: Insects in Winter. Zollars, Jaime, illus. (p. 1266)
—On One Foot. Balaguer, Nuria, illus. (p. 1289)
—Singing Crickets. Feltes, Tess, illus. (p. 1579)
—Stone Soup with Matzoh Balls: A Passover Tale in Chelm. Tabatabaei, Maryam, illus. (p. 1653)
Glaser, Milton, illus. see Glaser, Shirley.
Glaser, P. H. Chrystallia & the Source of Light. (p. 317)
Glaser, Rebecca. Baby Moses & Other Bible Stories. Ferenic, Bill, illus. (p. 127)
—Dump Truck. (p. 489)
—Fall. (p. 566)
—Flowers. (p. 608)
—Good Samaritan & Other Bible Stories. Ferenc, Bill, illus. (p. 700)
—Holy Moly Christmas Story. Ferenc, Bill, illus. (p. 791)
—Holy Moly Story Bible: Exploring God's Awesome Word. Ferenic, Bill, illus. (p. 791)
—Jesus at the Temple & Other Bible Stories. Ferenc, Bill, illus. (p. 915)
—Jesus Feeds 5,000 & Other Bible Stories. Ferenc, Bill, illus. (p. 915)
—Jonah & the Big Fish & Other Bible Stories. Ferenic, Bill, illus. (p. 925)
—Joseph & His Brothers & Other Bible Stories. Ferenic, Bill, illus. (p. 926)
—Leaves. (p. 986)
—Maple Tree. (p. 1090)
—Mary & Martha & Other Bible Stories. Ferenc, Bill, illus. (p. 1100)
—Noah's Ark & Other Bible Stories. Ferenic, Bill, illus. (p. 1261)
—Oak Trees. (p. 1274)
—Red in Nature. (p. 1454)
—Rocks. (p. 1483)
—Seeds. (p. 1547)
—Spring. (p. 1634)
—Summer. (p. 1673)
—Winter. (p. 1937)
Glaser, Rebecca Stromstad. Border Collies Saunders-Smith, Gail, ed. (p. 213)
—Elephants Spray. (p. 512)
—Minnesota. (p. 1147)
—North Dakota. (p. 1265)
—Penguins Waddle. (p. 1337)
Glaser, Shirley. Alphazeds. Glaser, Milton, illus. (p. 50)
Glasgow, Yvonne M. Frankie the Firefly Belongs. (p. 630)
Glaspey, Terry & Kerr, Kathleen. Bible Basics for Kids: An Awesome Adventure Through God's Word. (p. 175)
Glass, Alberta. My Seeing Eye Glasses. Buehrle, Jacquelyn, illus. (p. 1218)
Glass, Alden C. Blue Moon over Fenway. (p. 203)
Glass, Andrew. Flying Cars: The True Story. (p. 609)
—Wondrous Whirligig: The Wright Brothers¿ First Flying Machine. Glass, Andrew, illus. (p. 1949)
Glass, Andrew, illus. see Bernstein, Dan.
Glass, Andrew, illus. see Hesse, Karen.
Glass, Andrew, illus. see Kimmel, Eric A.
Glass, Andrew, illus. see Smith, Susan Mathias.
Glass, Andrew, photos by see Wooldridge, Connie N. & Wooldridge, Connie Nordhielm.
Glass, Bryan J. L., jt. auth. see Oeming, Michael Avon.
Glass, Calliope. Around-The-World Safari. (p. 101)
—Disney Tails Figaro's Halloween Surprise. Disney Storybook Art Team, illus. (p. 453)
—Muppets Most Wanted Read-Along Storybook & CD. (p. 1191)
—Tiana: The Stolen Jewel. (p. 1746)
—Walking with Dinosaurs Handbook. (p. 1854)
Glass, Calliope, jt. auth. see Disney Book Group Staff.
Glass, Calliope, jt. auth. see Scholastic, Inc. Staff.
Glass, Calliope & Disney Book Group Staff. Around-the-World Safari. Disney Storybook Artists Staff et al, illus. (p. 101)
—I Love School! Ho, Winnie & Egan, Caroline LaVelle, illus. (p. 843)
—Monsters University Read-Along Storybook & CD. Disney Storybook Art Team, illus. (p. 1169)
—Tiana - The Stolen Jewel: A Jewel Story. Disney Storybook Artists Staff, illus. (p. 1746)
Glass, Doyle D. Lions of Medina: The Marines of Charlie Company & the Battle for Barrier Island. (p. 1021)
Glass, Eleri. Red Shoes. Spires, Ashley, illus. (p. 1455)
Glass, Eric, illus. see Estes, Don.
Glass, George. Narcotics: Dangerous Painkiller. (p. 1229)
Glass, Graeme. Bee's Kiss. Trone, Jo, illus. (p. 158)
Glass, Hilary Ann Love, illus. see Hipp, Helen C.
Glass House Graphics Staff, illus. see Dahl, Michael.
Glass House Graphics Staff, illus. see Lemke, Donald.
Glass, Ira. New Kings of Nonfiction. Glass, Ira, ed. (p. 1245)
Glass, June. Poker Fat: Takes a Vacation. (p. 1378)
Glass, Maya. Abigail Adams: Famous First Lady. (p. 5)
—Abigail Adams: Destacada Primera Dama. (p. 5)
—Abigail Adams: Famous First Lady / Destacada Primera Dama. (p. 5)
—Abigail Adams: Destacada Primera Dama (Abigail Adams: Famous First Lady) (p. 5)
—Benjamin Franklin: Early American Genius. (p. 164)
—Benjamin Franklin: Político e inventor Estadounidense. (p. 165)
—Benjamin Franklin: Early American Genius / Político e inventor Estadounidense. (p. 165)
—Benjamin Franklin: Político e inventor estadounidense (Benjamin Franklin: Early American Genius) (p. 165)
—Jumping Book. (p. 934)
—Jumping Book / Saltar. (p. 934)
—Jumping Book/Saltar. Brusca, Maria Cristina, tr. from ENG. (p. 934)
—Marching Book: Marchar. (p. 1092)
—Marching Book. (p. 1092)
—Running Book / Correr. (p. 1497)
Glass, Paula Kay. My Big, Blue Tractor. (p. 1197)
Glass, Roger, illus. see McGrath, Barbara Barbieri.
Glass, Shelby. Something Is Everything. (p. 1610)
Glass, Sherri & Wentzel, Jim. Cool Careers Without College for People Who Love Manga, Comics, & Animation. (p. 363)
Glass, Stephen. Sara Sparrow. (p. 1514)
Glass, Sue. Helping Hop. (p. 766)
Glass, Susan. Forensic Investigator: Measurement (p. 617)
—Great Eggscape Van Wright, Cornelius, illus. (p. 715)
Glass, Timothy. Sleepytown Beagles Penny's 4th of July. Mikle, Toby, illus. (p. 1590)
Glassbourg, Michael. Learn to Speak Film: A Guide to Creating, Promoting & Screening Your Movies. Kulak, Jeff & Owlkids Books Inc. Staff, illus. (p. 984)
Glassby, Cathie, illus. see Ractliffe, Justin.
Glasscock, Sarah. Skill-Building Mini-Lessons, Activities, & Games. (p. 1585)
—Southwest: Set Of 6. (p. 1617)
—Southwest: Text Pairs. (p. 1617)
—Western States: Set Of 6. (p. 1876)
—Western States: Text Pairs. (p. 1876)
Glasscock, Sarah, jt. auth. see Miller, Carol Rawlings.
Glasscock, Sarah, jt. auth. see Nickelsen, LeAnn.
Glasscock, Sarah, jt. auth. see Nickelsen, Leann.
Glasscock, Sarah, jt. auth. see Rawlings Miller, Carol.
Glasscock, Sarah, et al. How Nurses Use Math. (p. 811)
Glasser, Debbie & Schenck, Emily. New Kid, New Scene: A Guide to Moving & Switching Schools. (p. 1245)
Glasser, Judith M. Learning to Feel Good & Stay Cool: Emotional Regulation Tools for Kids with ADHD. (p. 985)
—Learning to Feel Good & Stay Cool: Emotional Regulation Tools for Kids with Ad/Hd. (p. 985)
Glasser, Judith M. & Kushner, Jill Menkes. Learning to Be Kind & Understand Differences: Empathy Skills for Kids with Ad/Hd. (p. 985)
Glasser, Robin Preiss, illus. see Cheney, Lynne.
Glasser, Robin Preiss, illus. see Feiffer, Kate.
Glasser, Robin Preiss, illus. see Ferguson, Sarah.
Glasser, Robin Preiss, illus. see Ferguson, The Duchess of York, Sarah, The Duchess of York.
Glasser, Robin Preiss, illus. see O'Connor, Jane & Harper Collins / LeapFrog.
Glasser, Robin Preiss, illus. see O'Connor, Jane.
Glasser, Robin Preiss, illus. see Scanlon, Elizabeth Garton & Scanlon, Elizabeth G.
Glasser, Robin Preiss, illus. see Viorst, Judith.
Glasser, Sophie. I've Known since I Was Eight. (p. 901)
Glassman, Bruce. Caring. (p. 269)
—Citizenship. (p. 323)
—Fairness. (p. 563)
—Respect. (p. 1463)
—Responsibility. (p. 1463)
—Six Pillars of Character (p. 1582)
—Trustworthiness. (p. 1793)
—Zoolidays. Kiaulevicius, Rolandas, illus. (p. 1989)
Glassman, Bruce S. Caring. (p. 269)
—Citizenship. (p. 323)
—Fairness. (p. 563)
—Respect. (p. 1463)
—Responsibility. (p. 1463)
—Trustworthiness. (p. 1793)
Glassman, Jackie. Berry Best Friends' Picnic. (p. 167)
—Conquering Everest & la conquista del Monte Everest: 6 English, 6 Spanish Adaptations (p. 358)
—conquista del Monte Everest. (p. 358)
—Grandes inventos y cómo Surgieron. Hanner, Albert, illus. (p. 707)
—Great Inventions & Where They Came from & Grandes inventos y cómo Surgieron: 6 English, 6 Spanish Adaptations Hanner, Albert, illus. (p. 716)
—Los Cumpleaños Alrededor Del Mundo: Set Of 6. (p. 1053)
Glassman, Michael, jt. auth. see Ely, Lisa.
Glassman, Michael & Ely, Lisa. Kinder Gardens: Games & Adventures (p. 957)
Glassman, Miriam. Call Me Oklahoma! (p. 254)
Glassman, Shira. Second Mango. (p. 1539)
Glassner, Andrew. Interactive Storytelling: Techniques for 21st Century Fiction. (p. 879)
Glastetter, KC & Hollman, Jeremie. Glacier National Park: An ABC Adventure. (p. 682)
Glastetter, KC & Hollman, Jeremie, photos by. Yellowstone Natl Park Abc Adv. (p. 1970)
Glasthal, Jacqueline B. Liberty on 23rd Street. Reingold, Alan, illus. (p. 1005)
Glatshteyn, Yankev. Emil & Karl. Shandler, Jeffrey, tr. (p. 518)
Glatt, Lisa & Greenberg, Suzanne. Abigail Iris: The One & Only. Allen, Joy, illus. (p. 5)
—Pet Project. Allen, Joy, illus. (p. 1345)
Glatt, Lisa, et al. Abigail Iris: The One & Only. (p. 5)
Glatthaar, Joseph T., jt. auth. see O'Neill, Robert John.
Glatzer, Jenna. Exploration of the Moon. (p. 550)
—George Ferris' Grand Idea: The Ferris Wheel. Dominguez, Stephanie, illus. (p. 663)
—Hattie, Get a Haircut! Kendall, Monica, illus. (p. 752)
—Native American Festivals & Ceremonies. Johnson, Troy, ed. (p. 1234)
—Story Behind the Name. (p. 1656)
Glatzmayer, Thomas, jt. auth. see Wendling, Nathalie.
Glave, Tom. Baltimore Ravens. (p. 135)
—Cincinnati Bengals. (p. 319)
—Cleveland Browns. (p. 331)
—Houston Texans. (p. 804)
—Indianapolis Colts. (p. 871)
—Jacksonville Jaguars. (p. 904)
—Pittsburgh Steelers. (p. 1365)
—Sprint Car Racing. (p. 1635)
—Tennessee Titans. (p. 1720)
Glavich, Mary Kathleen. Blessed Teresa of Calcutta: Missionary of Charity. Kiwak, Barbara, tr. (p. 199)
—Child's Book of Miracles. (p. 304)
—Child's Book of Parables. (p. 304)
—God's Angels, Our Friends: Stories & Activities about Angels. (p. 690)
—Gospel Theater for the Whole Community: 92 Plays for Education & Worship. (p. 703)
—Rosary: Gospel on Beads. (p. 1489)
—Saint Therese of Lisieux: The Way of Love. Esquinaldo, Virginia, tr. (p. 1504)
—Student Pack of Bible Stories. (p. 1669)
Glavin, Kevin. All the Things You'll Do! Grepo, Sarah, illus. (p. 46)
Glaze, Dave. Danger in Dead Man's Mine (p. 403)
—Last Flight of the Birdman (p. 977)
—Light-Fingered Gang (p. 1015)
Glaze, Dave & Coteau Books Staff. Waiting for Pelly (p. 1853)
Glazer, Devorah. Touch of the High Holidays: A Touch & Feel Book. Seva, illus. (p. 1772)
Glazer, Maryann. Adventures of Teddy Bark-Lee: Teddy Comes Home. (p. 23)
—Adventures of Teddy Bark-Lee: Teddy Goes to the Doctor. (p. 23)
Glazer, Tom. On Top of Spaghetti. (p. 1292)
—Tom Glazer's Treasury of Songs for Children. Seiden, Art, illus. (p. 1763)
Glazier, Garth, illus. see Friden, Chris.
Glazier, Loss Pequeño. Anatman, Pumpkin Seed, Algorithm. (p. 67)
Glazner, Allen F., jt. auth. see Sharp, Robert P.
Glazov, Sheila N. Princess Shayna's Invisible Visible Gift. (p. 1405)
Glazunova, Nadezda, illus. see Currier, Alvin Alexsi.
Gleadhill, Christa J. Here Comes Lucky! (p. 770)
Gleasner, Diana C. Popoki, the Hawaiian Cat: An Amazing Adventure with the Whale. Winton, Andrea Evans, illus. (p. 1384)
Gleason, Anita, illus. see Barry, Maureen.
Gleason, Barbara. My Hometown: Mashpee. (p. 1211)
—My Hometown: Barnstable. (p. 1211)
Gleason, Carrie. Biography of Cotton. (p. 189)
—Biography of Rubber. (p. 189)
—Biography of Silk. (p. 189)
—Biography of Tea. (p. 189)
—Biography of Tobacco. (p. 189)
—Biography of Wool. (p. 189)
—Chinese New Year. (p. 307)
—Day of the Dead. (p. 414)
—Environmental Activist. (p. 532)
—Feasting Bedbugs, Mites, & Ticks. (p. 579)
—Geothermal Energy: Using Earth's Furnace. (p. 665)
—Henry Hudson: Seeking the Northwest Passage. (p. 768)
—Ocean Storm Alert! (p. 1276)
Gleason, Carrie, jt. auth. see National Geographic Kids Staff.
Gleason, Carrie, jt. auth. see Rodger, Ellen.
Gleason, Carrie & Rodger, Ellen. Animal Rights Activist. (p. 79)
Gleason, Colleen. Clockwork Scarab. (p. 333)
—Spiritglass Charade. (p. 1629)
Gleason, John, ed. see Bolger, Janie, et al.
Gleason, Katherine. Awesome Science: A Chapter Book. (p. 121)
—Social Lives of Animals: A Chapter Book. (p. 1604)
Gleason, Katherine & Nichols, Catherine. Ripley's Believe it or Not! Virtual Odditorium. (p. 1474)
Gleason, Norma. Fun with Word Puzzles. (p. 649)
Gleed, Paul. Bloom's How to Write about William Shakespeare. (p. 201)
Gleeson, Bill. Weekends for Two in Southern California 2003: 50 Romantic Getaways. Longwood, Marc, photos by. (p. 1872)
—Weekends for Two in the Southwest: 50 Romantic Getaways. Hazlegrove, Cary, photos by. (p. 1872)
Gleeson, Brian. Anansi. Guarnaccia, Steven, illus. (p. 67)
—Finn McCoul. de Sève, Peter, illus. (p. 589)
—Koi & the Kola Nuts. Ruffins, Reynold, illus. (p. 966)
—Paul Bunyan. Meyerowitz, Rick, illus. (p. 1330)
—Pecos Bill. Raglin, Tim, illus. (p. 1334)
—Tiger & the Brahmin. Vargo, Kurt, illus. (p. 1748)
Gleeson, J. M., illus. see Kipling, Rudyard.
Gleeson, Joseph M. Just So Stories. (p. 939)
Gleeson, Libby. Banjo & Ruby Red. Blackwood, Freya, illus. (p. 136)
—Clancy & Millie & the Very Fine House. Blackwood, Freya, illus. (p. 326)
—Great Bear. Greder, Armin, illus. (p. 714)
—Half a World Away. Blackwood, Freya, illus. (p. 736)
—I Am Thomas. Greder, Armin, illus. (p. 834)
—Mahtab's Story. (p. 1076)
—Ray's Olympics. Cox, David, illus. (p. 1441)
Gleeson, Libby & Blackwood, Freya. Look, a Book! (p. 1048)
Gleich, Jacky, illus. see Fried, Amelie.
Gleich, Jacky, illus. see Orlev, Uri.
Gleich, Jacky, illus. see Pez, Alberto.
Gleick, Beth. Time Is When. Jocelyn, Marthe, illus. (p. 1752)
Gleim, Jc. Leprechaun Kate. (p. 993)
Gleisner, Jenna Lee. Bug Exterminator. (p. 236)
—How's the Weather in Spring? (p. 824)
—My Body Needs Food. (p. 1198)
—My Body Needs Rest. (p. 1198)
—My Body Needs to Be Clean. (p. 1198)
—Pig Farmer. (p. 1357)
—Planting a Garden in Spring. (p. 1369)
—We Celebrate Arbor Day in Spring. (p. 1866)
—We Celebrate Cinco de Mayo in Spring. (p. 1866)
—We Celebrate Earth Day in Spring. (p. 1866)
—What Blossoms in Spring? (p. 1880)
—What Do Animals Do in Spring? (p. 1882)
—What Do People Do in Spring? (p. 1882)
Gleisner, Tom, et al. Phaic Tan: Sunstroke on a Shoestring. (p. 1349)
Gleitzman, Morris. Now. (p. 1268)
—Once. (p. 1292)
—Then. (p. 1729)
—Toad Rage. (p. 1760)
Glencoe. Discovering Life Skills: Reteaching Activities. (p. 449)
Glencoe McGraw-Hill Staff. American Journey: Modern Times. (p. 62)
—American Journey. (p. 62)
—American Vision: Modern Times. (p. 63)
—American Vision: Modern Times, Spanish Reading Essentials & Note-Taking Guide. (p. 63)
—American Vision. (p. 63)
—Astronomy. (p. 109)
—Bon Voyage!, Level 3. (p. 208)
—¡Buen Viaje! (p. 235)
—Civics Today: Citizenship, Economics & You. (p. 324)
—Civics Today: Citizenship, Economics, & You. (p. 324)
—Earth Materials & Processes. (p. 496)
—Earth Science: Geology, the Environment, & the Universe. (p. 496)
—Earth Science. (p. 496)
—Exploring Our World: People, Places & Cultures. (p. 553)
—Exploring Our World - People, Places, & Cultures: Western Hemisphere, Europe, & Russia. (p. 553)
—Glencoe Accounting: First Year Course, School-to-Work Handbook. (p. 683)
—Glencoe Accounting: First Year Course, Chapter Reviews & Working Papers Chapters 14-29 with Peachtree Guides (p. 683)
—Glencoe Life Science, Reinforcement. (p. 683)
—Glencoe Middle School Spanish: ¿Cómo Te Va? B Nivel Azul. (p. 683)
—Glencoe Physical Science. (p. 683)
—Human Body Systems. (p. 826)
—¡Buen Viaje!, Level 1. (p. 850)
—Interactive Student Edition CD-ROM. (p. 879)
—Introduction to Physical Science. (p. 882)
—Journey Across Time. (p. 927)
—Journey Across Time, Early Ages, Reading Essentials & Study Guide, Workbook. (p. 927)
—Journey Across Time, Interactive Tutor Self Assessment CD-ROM. (p. 927)
—Microsoft Word 2007: Real World Applications. (p. 1137)
—Motion, Forces, & Energy. (p. 1179)
—Nature of Matter. (p. 1236)
—Physical Science. (p. 1353)
—Sociology & You. (p. 1605)
—Street Law, StudentWorks CD-ROM. (p. 1666)
—United States Government: Democracy in Action, StudentWorks with Audio Summaries. (p. 1819)

—Water Planet. (p. 1863)
—Waves, Sound, & Light. (p. 1864)
—World Geography & Cultures, Interactive Tutor Self-Assessment. (p. 1955)
—World Geography & Cultures, Standardized Test Practice Workbook. (p. 1955)
—World History. (p. 1955)
—¡Buen Viaje!, Level 3. (p. 235)
Glencoe McGraw-Hill Staff, jt. auth. see Booth, Kathryn A.
Glencoe McGraw-Hill Staff, jt. auth. see Fisher, Douglas.
Glencoe McGraw-Hill Staff, jt. auth. see McGraw-Hill Staff.
Glencoe McGraw-Hill Staff, jt. auth. see Merki, Mary Bronson.
Glencoe McGraw-Hill Staff, jt. auth. see Schmitt, Conrad J.
Glencoe McGraw-Hill Staff & Glencoe Staff. Microsoft PowerPoint 2007: Real World Applications. (p. 1136)
Glencoe McGraw-Hill Staff & McGraw-Hill Education Staff. American Vision, Spanish Reading Essentials & Note-Taking Guide Workbook. (p. 64)
—Economics: Today & Tomorrow. (p. 502)
Glencoe McGraw-Hill Staff & McGraw-Hill Education (Firm) Staff. Economics: Today & Tomorrow, Spanish Reading Essentials. (p. 502)
Glencoe McGraw-Hill Staff & McGraw-Hill Education Staff. Exploring Our World: People, Places, & Culture. (p. 553)
Glencoe McGraw-Hill Staff & McGraw-Hill Education (Firm) Staff. Exploring Our World, Student Edition. (p. 553)
Glencoe McGraw-Hill Staff & McGraw-Hill Education Staff. Glencoe Science: From Bacteria to Plants. (p. 683)
—Journey Across Time, Early Ages, Active Reading & Note-Taking Guide. (p. 927)
—Journey Across Time, Reading Essentials & Study Guide. (p. 927)
—Physical Science. (p. 1353)
—Street Law: A Course in Practical Law. (p. 1666)
Glencoe McGraw-Hill Staff, creator. Algebra 1: Volume Two: Integration Applications Connections (p. 38)
—Algebra 2: Integration, Applications, Connections. (p. 38)
—American Journey - Modern Times: Reading Essentials & Note-Taking Guide. (p. 62)
—American Journey: Modern Times, Spanish Reading Essentials & Note-Taking Guide. (p. 62)
—American Republic since 1877 Spanish Reading Essentials & Study Guide. (p. 63)
—American Republic to 1877 Reading Essentials & Study Guide Student Workbook. (p. 63)
—American Vision Reading Essentials & Study Guide Student Workbook. (p. 64)
—Changing Surface of Earth. (p. 290)
—Developing Child. (p. 431)
—Economics, Principles & Practices. (p. 503)
—Economics Today & Tomorrow: Spanish Reading Essentials & Study Guide: Student Workbook. (p. 503)
—Economics Today & Tomorrow StudentWorks. (p. 503)
—Exploring Our World - Eastern Hemisphere: People, Places, & Cultures. (p. 553)
—Geometry. (p. 662)
—Glencoe Health. (p. 683)
—Glencoe Science: Level Green. (p. 683)
—Glencoe Science: Level Blue - Reinforcement. (p. 683)
—Glencoe Science Level Blue (p. 683)
—Glencoe world history StudentWorks Plus. (p. 683)
—Glencoe Writer's Choice: Grammar & Composition, Grade 6. (p. 683)
—Impact Mathematics Course 3: Algebra & More. (p. 862)
—Journey Across Time - The Early Ages. (p. 927)
—Life Structure & Function. (p. 1013)
—Matematicas Curso 1: Aplicaciones y Conceptos. (p. 1104)
—Matematicas Curso 2: Aplicaciones y Conceptos. (p. 1104)
—Mathematics: Applications & Concepts. (p. 1107)
—Mathematics: Applications & Concepts, Course 3, Practice Skills Worbook. (p. 1108)
—Mathematics - Applications & Concepts. (p. 1108)
—Mathematics with Business Applications, School-to-Home Activity Workbook. (p. 1108)
—Quick Review Math Handbook: Hot Words, Hot Topics. Bk. 2 (p. 1427)
—Quick Review Math Handbook - Hot Words, Hot Topics (p. 1427)
—Repaso: A Review Workbook for Grammar, Communication, & Culture. (p. 1460)
—Repaso Breve Manual de Matematicas Libro 1: Palabras Importantes Temas de Actualidad. (p. 1460)
—Technology Student Workbook: Today & Tomorrow. (p. 1712)
—Timed Readings Plus in Social Studies (p. 1754)
—Timed Readings Plus in Social Studies Book 10 (p. 1754)
—Timed Readings Plus in Social Studies Book 4 (p. 1754)
—Today's Teen. (p. 1761)
—United States Government: Democracy in Action. (p. 1819)
—United States in the 20th Century. (p. 1819)
Glencoe McGraw-Hill Staff, et al. Glencoe Health (p. 683)
Glencoe Staff. Math '87. (p. 1105)
Glencoe Staff, jt. auth. see Glencoe McGraw-Hill Staff.
Glendenning, Debra Morgan. Little Lost Baxter. (p. 1031)
Glendinning, Eric. Oxford English for Careers - Technology. (p. 1315)
Glendinning, Richard, jt. auth. see Blassingame, Wyatt.
Glenn, Avery, et al. Women's Rights Movement. Javier, Emmanuel Xerx & Burton, Daniel, illus. (p. 1947)
Glenn, John. Civil Engineers! (p. 324)
—Civil Engineers. (p. 324)
Glenn, Joshua, jt. auth. see Larsen, Elizabeth Foy.
Glenn, Joshua & Larsen, Elizabeth Foy. Unbored Games: Serious Fun for Everyone. Kasunick, Heather & Reusch, Mister, illus. (p. 1811)
Glenn, Judith. Manassas, Please Slow Down. Colson, A. W. & Renda, Joseph, illus. (p. 1086)
Glenn, Kenny. First Race for Luvable Me. (p. 596)
Glenn, Lauren J. Where Is God. (p. 1908)
Glenn, Lexi & Nia. My Invention: How Lexi Glenn, a fourth grader, came up with an idea & got it in toy stores all over the world. A story of how you must first believe in Yourself. (p. 1211)
Glenn, Lon Bennet. Texas Prisons: Largest Hotel Chain in Texas. (p. 1724)
Glenn, Melissa, illus. see Ezpeleta, Laurie.
Glenn, Patricia Brown. Under Every Roof: A Kid's Style & Field Guide to the Architecture of American Houses. (p. 1813)
Glenn, Richard A. Right to Privacy: Rights & Liberties under the Law Stephenson, Donald Grier, ed. (p. 1472)
Glenn, Shelley. Gracie's Fall. (p. 705)
Glenn, Suki & Carpenter, Susan. Patterns in Arithmetic: Student Workbook. Bk. 2 (p. 1329)
—Patterns in Arithmetic: Student Workbook: Book 1 (p. 1329)
—Patterns in Arithmetic: Parent/Teacher Guide: Book 2. 2 Minns, Karen M. C., illus. (p. 1329)
—Patterns in Arithmetic: Student Workbook: Book 2. 2 Minns, Karen Marie Christa, illus. (p. 1329)
—Patterns in Arithmetic: Parent/Teacher Guide & Student Workbook: Book 1. Minns, Karen M. C., illus. (p. 1329)
Glenn, Walter, et al. Microsoft(r) Exchange Server 2007. (p. 1136)
Glenn, Wendy J. & Campbell. Sarah Dessen: From Burritos to Box Office. (p. 1514)
Glennon, Michelle. Duncan the Circus Dinosaur. Glennon, Michelle, illus. (p. 490)
—My Big Green Teacher: Taking the Green Road. Glennon, Michelle, illus. (p. 1197)
—My Big Green Teacher: Please Turn off the Lights. Glennon, Michelle, illus. (p. 1197)
—My Big Green Teacher: Seven Generations from Now. Glennon, Michelle, illus. (p. 1197)
—My Big Green Teacher: Don't Rock the Boat: Saving Our Oceans. Glennon, Michelle, illus. (p. 1197)
—My Big Green Teacher: Take a Deep Breath: Saving Our Rainforests. Glennon, Michelle, illus. (p. 1197)
—My Big Green Teacher: Recycling: It's Easy Being Green. Glennon, Michelle, illus. (p. 1197)
Glennon, William. Trial of the Arkansas Bear. (p. 1785)
Glesener, Loretta. Bringing Back Dinner Time. (p. 229)
Glessner, Gordon. Water Wars, Secrets Revealed. (p. 1863)
Glewwe, Eleanor. Sparkers. (p. 1622)
Glick, Dvorah. Red Is My Rimon: A Jewish Child's Book of Colors. Ackerman, Dena, illus. (p. 1454)
Glick, Nathan, illus. see Brown, Virginia Pounds & Owens, Laurella, eds.
Glick, Nathan H., illus. see Brown, Virginia Pounds & Owens, Laurella.
Glick, Sharon, illus. see Guy, Ginger Foglesong & Guy, Ginger F.
Glick, Shifra. Shikufitsky Glick, Shifra, illus. (p. 1566)
—Shikufitzky 5. (p. 1566)
Glick, Susan. Jemma's Got the Travel Bug Nash, Kelli, illus. (p. 912)
Glickman, Claudia. Skin Sense. (p. 1585)
Glickman, Susan. Bernadette & the Lunch Bunch Allard, Melanie, illus. (p. 167)
—Bernadette in the Doghouse (p. 167)
Glickman, Sylvia & Schleifer, Martha Furman, eds. From Convent to Concert Hall: A Guide to Women Composers (p. 642)
Glicksman, Caroline, illus. see Hutton, Simon.
Glickstein, Jennifer, ed. see Darling, Helen.
Glidewell, Steve. Inline Skating. (p. 874)
Glienke, Amelie, illus. see Sommer-Bodenburg, Angela.
Glimm, Adele. Gene Hunter: The Story of Neuropsychologist Nancy Wexler. (p. 660)
Glimmerveen, Ulco. Leaper: The Amazing Life of the Salmon. (p. 982)
Glines, Abbi. Because of Low. (p. 155)
—Breathe. (p. 226)
—Existence. (p. 548)
—Hold on Tight. (p. 788)
—Just for Now. (p. 938)
—Misbehaving. (p. 1150)
—Sea Breeze Collection: Breathe; Because of Low; While It Lasts; Just for Now. (p. 1534)
—Until Friday Night. (p. 1823)
—Vincent Boys. (p. 1842)
—Vincent Boys Collection: The Vincent Boys & the Vincent Brothers. Set (p. 1842)
—Vincent Brothers. Frost, Michael, photos by. (p. 1842)
—While It Lasts. (p. 1911)
Gliori, Debi. Alfie in the Bath. (p. 37)
—Dragon's Extraordinary Egg. (p. 479)
—Little Bear & the Wish Fish. (p. 1024)
—Mr. Arth Yn Gwarchod. (p. 1184)
—No Matter What. (p. 1259)
—Scariest Thing of All. Bloom, Clive, illus. (p. 1520)
—Scariest Thing of All. Gliori, Debi & Bloom, Clive, illus. (p. 1520)
—Stormy Weather. Gliori, Debi, illus. (p. 1656)
—Tobermory Cat. (p. 1760)
—Trouble with Dragons. Gliori, Debi, illus. (p. 1790)
—What's the Time, Mr Wolf? (p. 1900)
—Witch Baby & Me. (p. 1941)
—Witch Baby & Me after Dark (p. 1941)
Gliori, Debi, illus. see Bright, Rachel.
Gliori, Debi, illus. see Bruce, Lisa.
Gliori, Debi, illus. see Dunbar, Joyce.
Gliori, Debi, jt. auth. see Dunbar, Joyce.
Gliori, Debi, jt. auth. see Lively, Penelope.
Gliori, Debi & Bloom, Clive. What's the Time, Mr Wolf? (p. 1900)
Gliori, Debi & Hurst, Kelly. Witch Baby & Me on Stage. Gliori, Debi, illus. (p. 1941)
Glitschka, Von, illus. see Young, Rebecca.
Glitterpony, Jessica Noelle. Warkak & Snoozle. (p. 1858)
Global Fund for Children Staff. American Babies. (p. 59)
—Global Babies. Su, Keren et al, photos by. (p. 684)
—Global Babies (Bebes del Mundo) Su, Keren et al, photos by. (p. 684)
Global Fund for Children Staff, contrib. by. Global Baby Girls. (p. 684)
Globe-Fearon Staff. Changes. (p. 290)
—Contamination. (p. 360)
—Native American Biographies. (p. 1234)
—Sea-Wolf. (p. 1536)
—Spartacus. (p. 1622)
—Teenage Refugees from Bosnia-Herzegovina Speak Out. (p. 1714)
—Teenage Refugees from Russia Speak Out. (p. 1714)
—Working Together Against Destruction of the Environment. (p. 1953)
—Working Together Against Gun Violence. (p. 1953)
—Working Together Against Hate Groups. (p. 1953)
—Working Together Against Racism. (p. 1953)
Globe-Fearon Staff, ed. Jane Eyre, Grades 5-12. (p. 908)
Glock-Cooper, Allison, jt. auth. see Cooper, T.
Glocke, Robin. Tiny Fish. (p. 1756)
Glon, Nancy, illus. see Magness, Robert.
Gloor, Elizabeth. Cultural Institutions of New York City. (p. 391)
—New York City: An Urban Community. (p. 1248)
Gloria North. Dragon Dreams: Tales of Fun & Fantasy. (p. 477)
Gloria, Truitt. Baby Jesus Is Born. (p. 126)
Glossop, Jennifer. Kids Book of World Religions. Mantha, John, illus. (p. 952)
—Tattoo You! Color & Make Your Own Temporary Tattoo Designs. Klund, Barbara, illus. (p. 1707)
Glover, A. Libro de Pegatinas Perros. (p. 1006)
Glover, Clair. Fairy Penguin - the Penguin Who Loves to Play. (p. 563)
Glover, Daniel, ed. see Liszt, Franz.
Glover, Darryl. Pirate Kitty. Austin, Britta, ed. (p. 1362)
Glover, David. Cavern of Clues. (p. 282)
—Mansion of Mazes. (p. 1088)
—Museum of Mysteries. (p. 1193)
—Planet of Puzzles. (p. 1367)
Glover, David & Barnes, Jon. Machines. (p. 1068)
Glover, David & Glover, Penny. Cars in Action. (p. 272)
—Cranes. (p. 376)
—Digging Machines in Action. (p. 439)
—Growing. (p. 726)
—Motorcycles in Action. (p. 1180)
—Moving. (p. 1183)
—Owning a Pet Rabbit. (p. 1315)
—Planes in Action. (p. 1367)
—Senses. (p. 1551)
—Staying Healthy. (p. 1645)
—Tractors in Action. (p. 1776)
—Trucks in Action. (p. 1791)
Glover, Dennis W. Cat in the Woods. (p. 278)
—Goat Farm. (p. 687)
—Talking Flower. (p. 1703)
Glover, Emma M. Benjamin Jay Was a Bully. Snider, K. C., illus. (p. 165)
Glover, Harry. Dogs. (p. 462)
—Dogs Sticker Book. Francis, John & Testar, Sue, illus. (p. 463)
Glover, Maria Robinson. Who Do I Want to Be? Contemporary Black Women from A to Z. Glover, Maria Robinson, illus. (p. 1915)
Glover, Matt. But It's True. (p. 246)
Glover, Melissa. Mikey's Mr. Monster. (p. 1141)
Glover, Mildred C. Buddy Heads for Home: A Hurricane Katrina Pet Survivor Story. (p. 235)
Glover, Penny, jt. auth. see Glover, David.
Glover, Robert, illus. see Nuttbucket, Oliver S., III.
Glover, Rosanne Harper. Chloe, the Very Special Goat. Sites, Jennifer, illus. (p. 308)
Glover, Ruth E. Lost Labyrinth. (p. 1056)
Glover, Sandra. Dangerously Close. (p. 404)
—Identity. (p. 852)
Glover, Sophie, illus. see Bristow, Sophie.
Glowacki, Helen. God's Plan of Salvation. (p. 691)
Glowatsky, Phyllis. Light of Stars. Stringer, Karen, illus. (p. 1015)
Gluck, Larry. Art of Drawing: Creating Accurate Lines & Shapes. Pt. 1 (p. 102)
—Basic Painting Course. (p. 142)
Gluck, Leanne, jt. auth. see Shaw, Holly.
Glucksman, Jodi, jt. compiled by see Dawson, Kate.
Glueck, Michael Wells, ed. see Craig, Deborah Anne.
Glum, Felicity, jt. auth. see RH Disney Staff.
Glupker, Dianne. Great Tastes of Michigan. Delsi, Dawna, illus. (p. 718)
Glupker, Dianne & Delsi, Dawna. Great Lights of Michigan. Delsi, Dawna, illus. (p. 717)
Glur, D. Empire Contre Attaque. (p. 521)
Glut, Donald F., tr. Discover Dinosaurs. (p. 447)
Glyman, Caroline A. Forest House Firsts: Supplemental Selected Early Childhood Stories Biser, Dee, illus. (p. 618)
Glymph, Rikimah. Are You My Friend? (p. 97)
Glyn, Chris, illus. see Morgan, Ruth.
Glyn, Chris, tr. see Morgan, Ruth.
Glyn, Pamela. green light in the Mountains. (p. 722)
Glynn, Carol. Carol Out of the Box (p. 270)
Glynn, Chris, illus. see Hopwood, Mererid, et al.
Glynn, Chris, illus. see Kay, Francesca.
Glynn, Chris, illus. see Lewis, Siân.
Glynn, Eoin. Mischief at Se. (p. 1150)
Glynn, Gower. Stories Told in the Wigwam. (p. 1655)
Glynn, W. Celebrando a Diario con el Rey. (p. 283)
Gmeyner, Elizabeth. Key of the Kingdom: A Book of Stories & Poems for Children. Russell, Joyce, illus. (p. 950)
G-Mo. Shmu Songs. (p. 1568)
Gnanadesikan, Mrudulla. Art & Technique of Simulation. (p. 101)
Gnojewski, Carol. African-American Crafts Kids Can Do! (p. 26)
—American Indian Crafts Kids Can Do! (p. 62)
—Celebrating Cinco de Mayo. (p. 284)
—Cinco de Mayo: Se Celebra el Orgullo. Jusid, Carolina, tr. from ENG. (p. 319)
—Cinco de Mayo Crafts. (p. 319)
—Day of the Dead: A Latino Celebration of Family & Life. (p. 414)
—Dia de los Muertos - Una Celebracion de la Familia y la Vida. Cinquemani, Romina C., tr. from ENG. (p. 433)
—Dia de Martin Luther King, JR: Honramos a un Hombre de Paz. Jusid, Carolina, tr. from ENG. (p. 433)
—Earth Day Crafts. (p. 495)
—Fun St. Patrick's Day Crafts. (p. 648)
—Kwanzaa: Seven Days of African-American Pride. (p. 969)
—Kwanzaa Crafts. (p. 969)
—Madonna: Express Yourself. (p. 1070)
—Ramadan: A Muslim Time of Fasting, Prayer, & Celebration. (p. 1437)
—St. Patrick's Day Crafts. (p. 1638)
Gnoli, Domenico, illus. see Juster, Norton.
Gnoske, Alexandra. Loui Saves the Earth. (p. 1058)
Gnuse, Allison. My African Home. (p. 1195)
Go Office. Touch of Dynamism. (p. 1772)
Go Office Staff & Hayashi, Hikaru. Drawing Sensational Characters (p. 482)
Go, Ping-gam. Understanding Chinese Characters by their Ancestral Forms. (p. 1815)
Goad, Rachel. Joshua Jenkins & the Cookie Jar Conundrum. (p. 927)
Goad, Stephanie Davis. Day the Elephant Sat on Our Car. (p. 414)
Goba, Busisiwe, et al. Mathematics for Zambia Basic Education Grade 7 Pupil's Book. (p. 1108)
—Mathematics Matters Grade 7 Learner's Book. (p. 1108)
—Mathematics Matters Grade 7 Learner's Book Afrikaans Translation. (p. 1108)
—Study & Master Mathematical Literacy Grade 10 Learner's Book. (p. 1670)
—Study & Master Mathematical Literacy Grade 10 Learner's Book Afikaans Translation. (p. 1670)
Gobble, DeAnna Akers, illus. see Warmuth, Donna Akers.
Gober, Robert. Vija Celmins. (p. 1842)
Gober, Thomas. Dandylion the Duck. Gillen, Rosemarie, illus. (p. 403)
Gobert, R. Darren. Theatre of Caryl Churchill. (p. 1728)
Goble, Brant & Goble, Faith, eds. Gander Press Review: Fall/Winter 2008. Goble, Faith, illus. (p. 655)
Goble, Faith, jt. ed. see Goble, Brant.
Goble, Patrick. Symphony No. 2. (p. 1693)
Goble, Paul. All Our Relatives: Traditional Native American Thoughts about Nature. (p. 45)
—Boy & His Mud Horses: And Other Stories from the Tipi. (p. 217)
—Custer's Last Battle: Red Hawk's Account of the Battle of the Little Bighorn. (p. 395)
—Earth Made New: Plains Indian Stories of Creation. (p. 496)
—Girl Who Loved Wild Horses. (p. 679)
—Horse Raid: The Making of a Warrior. (p. 800)
—Mystic Horse. Goble, Paul, illus. (p. 1226)
—Red Cloud's War: Brave Eagle's Account of the Fetterman Fight. (p. 1453)
—Song of Creation. Goble, Paul, illus. (p. 1611)
—Walking Along: Plains Indian Trickster Stories. Goble, Paul, illus. (p. 1854)
Goble, Warwick, illus. see Kingsley, Charles.
Gobo. Animal Songs. (p. 79)
GoBo. Santa Baby: Boxed Set. (p. 1511)
Gobo Books, creator. My Magnetic Shapes & Colors: Flo & Zip's Busy Day. (p. 1214)
Gobo Books Staff. Ready for Numbers: Little Learners. (p. 1447)
—Sleepytime Songs. (p. 1590)
Gobo, creator. Baby Faces. (p. 126)
—Baby Farm Animals. (p. 126)
—Little Learners Ready to Read & Write. (p. 1030)
—My Baby. (p. 1196)
—My Magnetic First Words Runaway Cat. (p. 1214)
—My Magnetic Spelling Book Let's Pretend! (p. 1214)
—Santa Baby. (p. 1511)
—Up! Goes the Bunny! (p. 1824)
Göçmen, Dogan. Adam Smith Problem: Reconciling Human Nature & Society in the Theory of Moral Sentiments & Wealth of Nations. (p. 11)
Godbersen, Anna. Beautiful Days. (p. 153)
—Envy. (p. 532)
—Lucky Ones. (p. 1063)
—Luxe. (p. 1066)
—Luxe, Rumors, & Envy (p. 1066)
—Rumors. (p. 1495)
—Splendor. (p. 1630)
Godbey, Corey, illus. see Hunt, Susan.
Godbey, Cory, illus. see Anthony, Michelle.
Godbey, Cory, illus. see Candau, Brittany.
Godbey, Cory, illus. see Ebbers, Susan M.
Godbey, Cory, illus. see Morrow, Daniel & Strobel Morrow, Alison.
Godbout, Geneviève, illus. see Borden, Louise.
Godbout, Geneviève, illus. see Robert, Nadine.
Godbout, Neil. Disintegrate (p. 451)
—Dissolve (p. 453)
Godbout, Real, jt. auth. see Lavigne, Guy.
Godby, Giovanna. Quaddles, Dwaddles, & Elizabeth: The Tale of a Very Confused Chicken. (p. 1422)
Godby, Michele. Mommy... Would You Still Love Me If I Was a Squirrel. (p. 1162)
Godby, Ron. King of Imperial Hill. (p. 959)
Goddard, Angela. Writing for Assessment. (p. 1964)
Goddard, Brenda, illus. see Golden Books Staff & Carbone, Courtney.
Goddard, Brenda, illus. see Golden Books.
Goddard, Brenda, illus. see Tillworth, Mary.
Goddard, Carole. China. (p. 306)
Goddard, D. L. Agondray: The Guardian of the Clouds. (p. 30)
Goddard, Drew, et al. Wolves at the Gate Jeanty, Georges et al, illus. (p. 1945)
Goddard, Jennifer S. On the Road: The Savvy Girl's Guide to Cars. (p. 1291)
Goddard, Jerome. You Gonna Touch That? Student Edition. (p. 1975)
Goddard, Jolyon. Beavers. (p. 155)
—Hummingbirds. (p. 826)
—Inside the Human Body. (p. 877)
—Monarch Butterfly. (p. 1163)
Goddard, Mary Beth. How Would It Feel? Mycek-Wodecki, Anna, illus. (p. 823)
Goddard, Michael. Adventure of Mike & Matt. (p. 14)

Goddard, Phyllis M. Spratling Silver: Recognizing a Spratling Silver Treasure: a Field Guide. (p. 1634)
Godden, Rumer. Cockcrow to Starlight: A Day Full of Poetry. Kneen, Maggie, illus. (p. 337)
—Dolls' House. (p. 464)
—Episode of Sparrows. (p. 532)
—Mousewife. du Bois, William Pène, illus. (p. 1182)
—Story of Holly & Ivy. Cooney, Barbara, illus. (p. 1658)
Godden, Rumer, jt. auth. see De Gasztold, Carmen B.
Goddu, Krystyna Poray. George Washington's Presidency. (p. 665)
—Primary Source History of U. S. Independence. (p. 1400)
—What's Your Story, Paul Revere? (p. 1900)
—What's Your Story, Susan B. Anthony? (p. 1900)
—What's Your Story, Wilma Rudolph? (p. 1900)
Godeassi, Anna, illus. see Oh, DaYun.
Godell, Rick. My Grandpa Tom & Me Neighbor, Douglas, illus. (p. 1210)
Godfrey. Murder in the Shadows. (p. 1192)
Godfrey, Arthur Dwayne, illus. see McCarroll, Barbara.
Godfrey, Jan. God's Wonderful World. Adderley, Peter, illus. (p. 692)
—Mira! (p. 1148)
—My Baptism Bible Catholic Edition. Grudina, Paola Bertolina, illus. (p. 1196)
—My Sleepytime Bible. Doherty, Paula, illus. (p. 1219)
—Road to Christmas Day. Piwowarski, Marcin, illus. (p. 1477)
—Road to Easter Day. Piwowarski, Marcin, illus. (p. 1477)
—Ten Christmas Sheep. Ayres, Honor, illus. (p. 1718)
—Who Made the Morning? Ayres, Honor, illus. (p. 1916)
Godfrey, Jan & Grudina, Paola Bertolini. My Story Bible: 66 Favorite Stories. (p. 1219)
Godfrey, Jan, et al. Mi Biblia para la Hora de Dormir. Doherty, Paula, illus. (p. 1132)
Godfrey, Jessica E. Night Hamster. (p. 1253)
Godfrey, John. Green Enamel Kid. (p. 721)
Godfrey, Ken & Godfrey, Sandra. Practicing the Presence of God: The Story of Brother Lawrence. (p. 1392)
Godfrey, Linda S. Lake & Sea Monsters. (p. 972)
—Mythical Creatures. (p. 1227)
Godfrey, Mark, et al. Anri Sala. (p. 88)
Godfrey, Martyn. Mystery in the Frozen Lands (p. 1224)
Godfrey, Neale S. Check It Out: The Book about Banking: Classroom Set. (p. 295)
—Money Adventure: Earning, Saving, Spending, Sharing: Primary Home-School Kit. (p. 1163)
Godfrey, Sandra, jt. auth. see Godfrey, Ken.
Godi, illus. see Zidrou.
Godin, Thelma Lynne. Hula-Hoopin' Queen. Brantley-Newton, Vanessa, illus. (p. 825)
Godinez, Flory. Adventures of Max & Millie: The Notable Orchard. (p. 20)
Godinez, Mary, jt. auth. see Griffiths, Allen.
Godkin, Celia. Fire! The Renewal of a Forest (p. 590)
—Hurricane! (p. 829)
—Skydiver: Saving the Fastest Bird in the World. Godkin, Celia, illus. (p. 1587)
—When the Giant Stirred: Legend of a Volcanic Island Godkin, Celia, illus. (p. 1904)
—Wolf Island Godkin, Celia, illus. (p. 1944)
Godkin, Celia, illus. see Woods, Shirley E.
Godkin, Celia, tr. see Woods, Shirley E.
Godley, Christina. Lion at the Gateway. (p. 1020)
Godley, Marie. Special Christmas Bear. (p. 1623)
Godley-Sugrue, Mary, jt. auth. see Carden, Kathleen A.
Godolphin, Mary. Swiss Family Robinson Told in Words. (p. 1691)
—Swiss Family Robinson Told in Words of One Syllable. (p. 1691)
Godon, Ingrid, illus. see Cowell, Cressida.
Godon, Ingrid, illus. see Neeman, Sylvie.
Godon, Ingrid, illus. see Norac, Carl.
Godsey, J. P. "Gus". How Scooter Gets His Tail Back. Del Russo, John William, Sr., illus. (p. 812)
Godula, Brian, jt. see Godula, Ellen Kjelgaard.
Godula, Ellen Kjelgaard & Godula, Brian. Queen Mab, Musical Verses Volume 3. (p. 1425)
Godwin, Brian. Adventures of Kate: The Big Move & the Birthday Gift. (p. 19)
—Love - the Greatest Fruit of All. (p. 1059)
Godwin, Edward. Logic Puzzles (p. 1045)
Godwin, Jane. Falling from Grace. (p. 567)
Godwin, Laura. One Moon, Two Cats. Tanaka, Yoko, illus. (p. 1296)
—This Is the Firefighter [Board Book]. Hector, Julian, illus. (p. 1736)
Godwin, Laura, jt. auth. see Martin, Ann M.
Godwin, Laura & Buck, Nola. Christmas Goodnight. Wright, Sarah Jane, illus. (p. 314)
Godwin, Sam. Case of the Missing Caterpillar: A First Look at the Life Cycle of a Butterfly Abel, Simone, illus. (p. 274)
—Drop Goes Plop: A First Look at the Water Cycle Abel, Simone, illus. (p. 485)
—Hen Can't Help It: A First Look at the Life Cycle of a Chicken. Abel, Simone, illus. (p. 767)
—Seed in Need: A First Look at the Plant Cycle. Abel, Simone, illus. (p. 1547)
—Trouble with Tadpoles: A First Look at the Life Cycle of a Frog. Abel, Simone, illus. (p. 1790)
Goebel, Jenny. Firefighter. Psacharopulo, Alessandra, illus. (p. 591)
—Foreman Farley Has a Backhoe. Van Doninck, Sebastiaan, illus. (p. 617)
—Foreman Frankie Is Handy. Mack, Steve, illus. (p. 617)
—Grave Images. (p. 712)
Goebel, Kelly. Adventures in the Weeping Willow Tree. Murfield, Anna, illus. (p. 16)
Goebig, Ed. Jake & Julia Save the Butterfly. (p. 905)
Goecke, Michael P. American Mastodon. (p. 62)
—Baryonyx. (p. 140)
—Camarasaurus. (p. 255)
—Compsognathus. (p. 354)
—Dire Wolf. (p. 445)
—Giant Ape. (p. 673)
—Giant Armadillo. (p. 673)
—Giant Ground Sloth. (p. 673)
—Giant Rhino. (p. 674)
—Giganotosaurus. (p. 676)
—Irish Elk. (p. 887)
—Oviraptor. (p. 1314)
—Pachycephalosaurus. (p. 1317)
—Prehistoric Animals Set 1. (p. 1395)
—Saber-Toothed Cat. (p. 1499)
—Scimitar Cat. (p. 1529)
—Short-Faced Bear. (p. 1569)
—Woolly Mammoth. (p. 1950)
—Woolly Rhinoceros. (p. 1950)
Goedde, Kathy. Blogged Down. (p. 200)
Goedde, Steve Diet, photos by. Steve Diet Goedde - Kumi Postcard Collection. (p. 1649)
—Steve Diet Goedde - Masuimi Max Postcard Collection. (p. 1649)
Goede, Irene, illus. see Post, Hans & Heij, Kees.
Goede, Irene, illus. see Post, Hans.
Goedeken, Kathy, illus. see Cohen, Sasha & Maciel, Amanda.
Goedeken, Kathy, illus. see Cohen, Sasha.
Goeglein, T. M. Cold Fury. (p. 338)
—Embers & Ash. (p. 517)
—Flicker & Burn. (p. 603)
Goehner, Amy Lennard, ed. see Newman, Elizabeth.
Goeke, Mark, photos by see Urbigkit, Cat.
Goeken, Brook. My Mom's an Engineer. (p. 1214)
Goeken, Samir. My Favorite Children's Poems. (p. 1203)
Goeller, Dorothy. 4th of July. (p. 1992)
—Christmas. (p. 312)
—Halloween. (p. 737)
—St. Patrick's Day. (p. 1638)
—Thanksgiving Day. (p. 1726)
—Valentine's Day. (p. 1830)
Goelman, Ari. Path of Names. (p. 1328)
Goembel, Ponder. Animal Fair Goembel, Ponder, illus. (p. 77)
Goembel, Ponder, illus. see DiPucchio, Kelly.
Goembel, Ponder, illus. see Hopkins, Lee Bennett.
Goembel, Ponder, illus. see Ketteman, Helen.
Goembel, Ponder, illus. see Morrow, Barbara Olenyik.
Goembel, Ponder, illus. see Wheeler, Lisa.
Goepel, Meg. Farting Is Fun. (p. 575)
Goering, Laura. Whistling Wings Jacques, Laura, illus. (p. 1912)
Goertzen, Angelina. Tinsel the Christmas Tree. (p. 1756)
Goertzen, Glenda. City Dogs Hudecki, Peter, illus. (p. 323)
—Prairie Dogs Béha, Philippe, illus. (p. 1392)
Goerzen, Christy. Big Apple Effect (p. 177)
—Explore (p. 550)
—Farmed Out (p. 574)
Goessling, Ben. Minnesota Timberwolves. (p. 1147)
—Washington Nationals. (p. 1860)
Goetchius, Alex. Career Building Through Social Networking. (p. 266)
Goethals, Angela. Sisterhood of the Traveling Pants. (p. 1581)
Goethes Fairy Tale Staff. Green Snake & the Beautiful Lily. Allen, Joan deRis, ed. (p. 722)
Goetting, Waltraud, tr. see Davis, Jim.
Goetting, Waltraud, tr. see Watterson, Bill.
Goettling, Nickalas, illus. see Gaffney, Linda.
Goetz, Bracha. Because of a Smile. (p. 155)
—My Own Thank You Story in Rainbow Colored Land. (p. 1216)
—What Do You See at Home? (p. 1883)
Goetze, Jutta. Howl. (p. 823)
—Luna-C. (p. 1065)
—Snow Wings. (p. 1600)
Goetzl, Robert F., illus. see Bruchac, Joseph.
Goetzmann, William H., ed. see Brown, Janet Hubbard.
Goetzmann, William H., ed. see Crompton, Samuel Willard.
Goetzmann, William H., ed. see Davenport, John.
Goetzmann, William H., ed. see Koestler-Grack, Rachel A.
Goetzmann, William H., ed. see McNeese, Tim.
Goetzmann, William H., ed. see Mountjoy, Shane.
Gofen, Ethel. France. (p. 627)
Gofen, Ethel, jt. auth. see Otfinoski, Steven.
Gofen, Ethel, et al. Sweden. (p. 1689)
Goff, Brian, illus. see Staunton, Ted.
Goff, Elizabeth Hudson, jt. auth. see Anderson, Dale.
Goff, Elizabeth Hudson, jt. auth. see Brown, Jonatha A.
Goff, Elizabeth Hudson, jt. auth. see Uschan, Michael V.
Goff, Elizabeth Hudson & Anderson, Dale. First Moon Landing. (p. 596)
Goff, Elizabeth Hudson & Brown, Jonatha A. Anne Frank. (p. 85)
Goff, Elizabeth Hudson & Uschan, Michael V. Bombing of Pearl Harbor. (p. 208)
—California Gold Rush. (p. 253)
Goff, Elizabeth Hudson, et al. California Gold Rush. Floor, Guus, illus. (p. 253)
—Fiebre Del Oro en California. (p. 583)
—Primer Alunizaje. (p. 1400)
Goff, John. Take Over. Evans, Patricia, ed. (p. 1697)
Goff, Sissy & Trevathan, Melissa. Mirrors & Maps: A Girl's Guide to Becoming a Teen (p. 1149)
Goff, Terry. 44 Fast & Fun Microsoft Word Activities. (p. 1997)
Goffard, Christopher. Snitch Jacket. (p. 1598)
Goffe, Toni, illus. see Hindley, Judy.
Goffe, Toni, illus. see Kid, Penelope.
Goffe, Toni, illus. see Neff, LaVonne.
Goffe, Toni, illus. see Shepard, Aaron.
Goffe, Toni, illus. see Stinson, Kathy.
Goffe, Toni, illus. see Unwin, Mike.
Goff-Tuttle, Marie Jaume. Colors of Christmas: A Christmas Poem for Young & Old. Reschofsky, Jean, illus. (p. 345)
Gogarty, Brian. Shamrock Sean & the Bird's Nest. Burchartz, Roxanne, illus. (p. 1559)
—Shamrock Sean & the Wishing Well. Burchartz, Roxanne, illus. (p. 1559)
—Shamrock Sean Goes Fishing. (p. 1559)
Gogerly, Liz. Ancient Egypt (p. 68)
—Autumn. (p. 118)
—Cool Brands. (p. 362)
—Eating Well. Gordon, Mike, illus. (p. 501)
—Exercise. Gordon, Mike, illus. (p. 548)
—Film Stars. (p. 586)
—Fossil Fuels. (p. 623)
—Graffiti Culture. (p. 705)
—Greeks. (p. 721)
—Justin Bieber. (p. 940)
—Keeping Clean. Gordon, Mike, illus. (p. 947)
—Safety. Gordon, Mike, illus. (p. 1502)
—Street Dance. (p. 1666)
—Taking Medicine. Gordon, Mike, illus. (p. 1698)
—Taylor Momsen. (p. 1708)
—Teeth. Gordon, Mike, illus. (p. 1715)
—United States. (p. 1819)
Goggans, Janice W., ed. see Di Franco, Aaron.
Goggerly, Liz. Capoeira: Fusing Dance & Martial Arts. (p. 263)
Goggins, Jean. Adventures of Boo & Koty: Snow. (p. 16)
Gogh, Vincent van, see Bassil, Andrea & van Gogh, Vincent.
Gogh, Vincent van, see Bassil, Andrea & van Gogh, Vincent.
Gogh, Vincent van, see Lossani, Chiara & van Gogh, Vincent.
Gogh, Vincent van, see van Gogh, Vincent.
Gogna, Ruth M. Hollywood Nineteen Eighty Crossword Puzzle. (p. 789)
Gogol, Nikolai. Nose. (p. 1266)
Gogol, Nikolai & Sylvan Learning Staff. First Grade Reading Skill Builders (Sylvan Workbooks) (p. 595)
Gogolewski, Kathe. Tato. (p. 1707)
Gogolski, A. Wealding Word. (p. 1869)
Gogonya, Carol. Adventure of Red Robin in the African Forest. (p. 14)
—African Mermaid & Other Stories. (p. 27)
—Magical Crystal Island of Morzzagal Where the King & His Three Sons Lived. (p. 1074)
Goguen, Martha. Sissy Goes to Washington. Fowler, Faith, illus. (p. 1581)
Goguen, Martha M. Andromed: Dream Believe Achieve Series. Walker, Patricia M., illus. (p. 72)
Gogwilt, Christopher. Invention of the West: Joseph Conrad & the Double-Mapping of Europe & Empire. (p. 884)
Goh, Colin & Woo, Yen Yen. Enter the Dumpling Lee, Soo, illus. (p. 531)
Goh, Michelle. 10 Best Cinderella Stories in Sports. (p. 1993)
Goh, Sui Noi & Lim, Bee Ling. China. (p. 306)
Goh, Tai Hwa, illus. see Aryal, Aimee.
Gohari, Omid, jt. auth. see Benson, Elisa.
Gohari, Omid, jt. auth. see Campbell, Margaret.
Gohari, Omid, jt. auth. see Doctorick, Jonathan.
Gohari, Omid, jt. auth. see Friedman, Sarah.
Gohari, Omid, jt. auth. see Hasslebeck, Kellie.
Gohari, Omid, jt. auth. see Katz, Andrew.
Gohari, Omid, jt. auth. see Mahon, Amy.
Gohari, Omid, jt. auth. see Ross, Jordan.
Gohari, Omid, jt. auth. see Rudolph, Allyson.
Gohari, Omid, jt. auth. see Sendrowski, Brian, Jr.
Gohari, Omid, jt. auth. see Thompson, Camille.
Gohari, Omid, jt. auth. see Vance, Ashley.
Gohda, Hiroaki, illus. see Zappa, Go.
Gohman, Amy. I Have Just the Gift for You. (p. 839)
Goikeda, Shin-Ya & Capcom Japan Staff. Devil May Cry (p. 432)
Goin, Kenn. Football for Fun! (p. 615)
Goin, Miriam. National Geographic Readers - Storms! (p. 1233)
—Storms! (p. 1656)
Going, K. L. Dog in Charge. Santat, Dan, illus. (p. 461)
—Fat Kid Rules the World. (p. 577)
—Garden of Eve. (p. 656)
—King of the Screwups. (p. 959)
—Liberation of Gabriel King. (p. 1005)
—Saint Iggy. (p. 1503)
Goins, Debra Lynn. One Day I Tried to Catch the Sun. (p. 1294)
Goins, Heather Lea, illus. see Goodnight, Lora.
Gokhale, Ruby. Emma & Kelly. (p. 519)
Gokool, R. G. Miss Crumcake's Amazing Divining Rod. (p. 1151)
Gokurakuin, Sakurako. Category Freaks (p. 279)
—FLCL Clear Poster: Haruhara Haruko. (p. 603)
Gola, Mark. Winning Softball for Girls, Second Edition. (p. 1937)
Golabek, Mona & Cohen, Lee. Children of Willesden Lane: Beyond the Kindertransport - A Memoir of Music, Love & Survival. (p. 303)
Golan, Hanna. Bless the Children: A Mother's Journal. (p. 199)
Golan, Martin. Where Things Are When You Lose Them. (p. 1910)
Golan, Miriam, jt. auth. see Jackson, Paul.
Golant, Evgenia, illus. see Golant, Galina & Grant, Lisa.
Golant, Galina & Grant, Lisa. Play Checkers with Me. Golant, Evgenia, illus. (p. 1371)
Golay, Michael. Civil War. (p. 325)
—Spanish-American War. (p. 1620)
Gold, Annabelle. Tadpole Grows Up. (p. 1695)
Gold, August. Does God Forgive Me? Waller, Diane Hardy, photos by. (p. 460)
—Does God Hear My Prayer? Waller, Diane Hardy, photos by. (p. 460)
Gold, Avie. Pirkei Avos Horen, Michael & Halasz, Andras, illus. (p. 1364)
Gold, Carolyn J. Dragonfly Secret. (p. 478)
Gold, Claudia, jt. auth. see Gordon, Rachel.
Gold, Ethel. Outdoor Things. (p. 1312)
—Things That Go. (p. 1733)
Gold, Gina. Disney Mickey Mouse Clubhouse: Hugs from Mickey: A Hugs Book. Guell, Fernanado, illus. (p. 451)
—Disney Minnie Mouse Hugs for Friends: A Hugs Book. (p. 452)
—Disney Palace Pets Guess Who Castle Cuties. (p. 452)
—Minnie: Hocus Bow-Cus! (p. 1147)
—Minnie: A Walk in the Park. (p. 1147)
Gold, Gina, jt. auth. see Disney Book Group Staff.
Gold, Gina, jt. auth. see Reader's Digest Staff.
Gold, Jeffrey. Brianna & the Search for the Cloudmaker. (p. 227)
Gold, John C. Circulatory & Lymphatic Systems. (p. 321)
Gold, John Coopersmith. Learning about the Circulatory & Lymphatic Systems. (p. 984)
Gold, Kimberley. Four Seasons. (p. 625)
—Outer Space. (p. 1312)
Gold, M., ed. see Siegel, Jerry.
Gold, Martha V. Learning about the Nervous System. (p. 985)
—Nervous System. (p. 1241)
Gold, Maya. Spellbinding. (p. 1625)
—Swan Fake. (p. 1688)
Gold, Maya & Dorling Kindersley Publishing Staff. Mother Teresa. (p. 1178)
Gold, Maya & Fitzhugh, Louise. Harriet the Spy, Double Agent. (p. 749)
Gold, Michael, photos by see Cobb, Vicki.
Gold, Paul Daniel, jt. auth. see Jennings, Terri.
Gold, Rachel. Being Emily. (p. 161)
—Just Girls. (p. 938)
Gold, Rainbow. Dolphin Dreams. (p. 464)
Gold, Robin. Mr. Da Vinci's Time Machine. Zarb, Mike, illus. (p. 1184)
Gold, Rozanne. Eat Fresh Food: Awesome Recipes for Teen Chefs. Mansfield, Phil, illus. (p. 501)
—Kids Cook 1-2-3: Recipes for Young Chefs Using Only 3 Ingredients. Pinto, Sara, illus. (p. 953)
Gold, Susan Dudley. Americans with Disabilities ACT. (p. 64)
—Brown V. Board of Education: Separate but Equal? (p. 232)
—Civil Rights ACT of 1964. (p. 324)
—Clean Air & Clean Water Acts. (p. 330)
—Clear & Present Danger: Schenck V. United States. (p. 330)
—Digestive & Excretory Systems. (p. 438)
—Engel V. Vitale: Prayer in the Schools. (p. 529)
—Freedom of Information ACT. (p. 634)
—Harriet Tubman & the Underground Railroad. (p. 750)
—In Re Gault: Do Minors Have the Same Rights as Adults? (p. 864)
—Kathryn Bigelow. (p. 944)
—Korematsu V. United States: Japanese-American Internment. (p. 967)
—Learning about the Digestive & Excretory Systems. (p. 985)
—Learning about the Musculoskeletal System & the Skin. (p. 985)
—Learning about the Respiratory System. (p. 985)
—Loving V. Virginia: Lifting the Ban Against Interracial Marriage. (p. 1061)
—Lyndon B. Johnson. (p. 1066)
—McCulloch V. Maryland: State V. Federal Power. (p. 1114)
—Missouri Compromise. (p. 1154)
—Musculoskeletal System & the Skin. (p. 1192)
—New York Times Co. V. Sullivan: Freedom of the Press or Libel? (p. 1248)
—Parody of Public Figures: Hustler Magazine V. Falwell. (p. 1325)
—Parody of Public Figures: Hustler Magazine Inc. V. Falwell. (p. 1325)
—Protecting Hate Speech: R.A.V. V. St. Paul. (p. 1412)
—Respiratory System. (p. 1463)
—Roberts v. Jaycees: Women's Rights. (p. 1479)
—Saluting the Flag: West Virginia State Board of Education V. Barnette. (p. 1506)
—Sofia Coppola. (p. 1605)
—Son of Sam Case: Simon & Schuster V. Members of United States Crime Victims Board. (p. 1611)
—Taft-Hartley Act. (p. 1695)
—Tinker V. des Moines: Free Speech for Students. (p. 1756)
—United States V. Amistad: Slave Ship Mutiny. (p. 1820)
—Vernonia School District V. Action: Drug Testing in the Schools. (p. 1837)
—Worcester v. Georgia: Native American Rights. (p. 1950)
Gold, Susan Dudley, see Dudley Gold, Susan.
Gold, Tracie. Adventures of Bonnie the Bunny: With Freddy the Fox. (p. 16)
—Bonnie the Bunny. (p. 209)
Gold, Willa. Stella & Tulip: A Home for Us. (p. 1646)
Golda, Kata. Stories for Bedtime: A Keepsake Pocket & Tales to Cherish. (p. 1654)
Goldbaum, Myrna Lou. Diary of a Palm Reader. (p. 434)
Goldbeck, David, jt. auth. see Charney, Steve.
Goldberg, Barbara. Mindy's Passover Parsley. (p. 1145)
Goldberg, Barry. Bubble Blowers, Beware! (p. 233)
—Watch Me Draw SpongeBob's Underwater Escapades. (p. 1861)
Goldberg, Barry, illus. see Collins, Terry.
Goldberg, Barry, illus. see Fisch, Sarah & Bridwell, Norman.
Goldberg, Barry, illus. see Herman, Gail & Bridwell, Norman.
Goldberg, Becklan Fritz. Lie Awake Lake. (p. 1007)
Goldberg, Dana, jt. auth. see Gonzalez, Maya Christina.
Goldberg, Dana, ed. On My Block: Stories & Paintings by Fifteen Artists. (p. 1289)
Goldberg Eds, Gail C. Animals A-Z: Poems for Early Readers. (p. 82)
Goldberg, Ella, ed. Farm Life. (p. 574)
—Simple Shapes. (p. 1578)
Goldberg, Enid & Itzkowitz, Norman. Grigory Rasputin: Holy Man or Mad Monk? (p. 724)
—Valad the Impaler: The Real Count Dracula. (p. 1830)
Goldberg, Jake & Hart, Joyce. Hawai'i. (p. 755)
Goldberg, Jan. C-130 Hercules. (p. 249)
—Department of Commerce. (p. 427)
—Earth Imaging Satellites. (p. 496)
—Hernando de Soto: Trailblazer of the American Southeast. (p. 772)
—James Lovell: The Rescue of Apollo 13. (p. 907)
—Julius Caesar. (p. 932)
—Napoleon Bonaparte. (p. 1229)
Goldberg, Judy. Samantha's World: A Girl's-Eye View of the Turn of the 20th Century. Andreasen, Dan, illus. (p. 1507)
Goldberg, Lee. Mr. Monk & the Two Assistants (p. 1185)
Goldberg, Lynn, jt. auth. see Rasmussen, Donald.
Goldberg, Malky. What Else Do I Say? A Lift the Flap Book. Argoff, Patti, illus. (p. 1884)

Goldberg, Mara J. Issavich's Unruly Nest. (p. 893)
Goldberg, Marshall. Mirthful Medecine. (p. 1149)
—Natural Cancer Killers. (p. 1235)
Goldberg, Matthew J. So So Wisdom: The Misplaced Teachings of So So Gai. (p. 1602)
Goldberg, Moses. Sleeping Beauty (Dornroschen) (Play Script) (p. 1589)
Goldberg, Nancy Solomon. I Am Moxxy Dog! (p. 833)
Goldberg, Olly, jt. auth. see Llardon, Roberts.
Goldberg, Stan, illus. see Gladir, George, et al.
Goldberg, Stan, illus. see Kinney, Sarah & Petrucha, Stefan.
Goldberg, Stan, illus. see Kinney, Sarah.
Goldberg, Stan, illus. see Petrucha, Stefan & Kinney, Sarah.
Goldberg, Stan, illus. see Petrucha, Stefan, et al.
Goldberg, Stan, illus. see Salicrup, Jim & Gladir, George.
Goldberg, Tod. Fix. (p. 601)
Goldberg, Whoopi. Dancing Diva. Roos, Maryn, illus. (p. 402)
—Perfectly Prima Roos, Maryn, illus. (p. 1342)
—Sugar Plum to the Rescue! Roos, Maryn, illus. (p. 1673)
—Terrible Terrel. Roos, Maryn, illus. (p. 1721)
—Toeshoe Trouble. Roos, Maryn, illus. (p. 1761)
Goldberg, Whoopi & Underwood, Deborah. Plum Fantastic Bk. 1. Cato, Nancy & Roos, Maryn, illus. (p. 1374)
Goldblas, Amy, jt. auth. see Rotner, Shelley.
Goldblatt, David. Ball Is Round: A Global History of Soccer. (p. 134)
Goldblatt, Mark. Finding the Worm. (p. 588)
—Twerp. (p. 1801)
Goldblatt, Rob. Boy Who Didn't Want to Be Sad. (p. 219)
Goldblatt, Robert. Boy Who Didn't Want to Be Sad. (p. 219)
Golde, Evie. Freshwater & Saltwater Habitats. (p. 636)
Golde, Justin F. Yes, My Dear, Alligators Do Belong on the Moon. (p. 1970)
Goldeen, Bill, jt. auth. see Goldeen, Ruth.
Goldeen, Ruth & Goldeen, Bill. Alef-Bet Yoga for Kids. Goldeen, Bill, photos by. (p. 35)
Goldemberg, Silvana. Victoria (p. 1840)
Golden Books. ABC Animals (Dora the Explorer) Mcgee, Warner, illus. (p. 3)
—Art of the Ninja (Teenage Mutant Ninja Turtles) Golden Books, illus. (p. 102)
—Barbie 9 Favorite Fairy Tales (Barbie) (p. 138)
—Barbie & Ken Vintage Paper Dolls. Golden Books, illus. (p. 138)
—Barbie in Princess Power. (p. 138)
—Barbie Loves Parties (Barbie) Duarte, Pamela & Musselman, Christian, illus. (p. 138)
—Barbie's Beauty Salon (Barbie) (p. 138)
—Big Ballet Show (Dora the Explorer) Loter, Inc., illus. (p. 178)
—Big Boat Race! (Team Umizoomi) Riley, Kellee, illus. (p. 178)
—Big Book of Blaze & the Monster Machines. Golden Books, illus. (p. 179)
—Big Book of Ninja Turtles (Teenage Mutant Ninja Turtles) Golden Books, illus. (p. 179)
—Big Book of Paw Patrol (Paw Patrol) Golden Books, illus. (p. 179)
—Big City Friends! (Dora & Friends) Golden Books, illus. (p. 180)
—Blue Book of Fairy Tales. (p. 202)
—Boo Goes There? (SpongeBob SquarePants) Golden Books, illus. (p. 209)
—Bubble Bonanza! (Bubble Guppies) Golden Books, illus. (p. 233)
—Bubble Buddies! (Bubble Guppies) Golden Books, illus. (p. 233)
—Bubble Guppies Little Golden Book Favorites (Bubble Guppies) Golden Books, illus. (p. 233)
—Bubble Guppies Magnet Book (Bubble Guppies) Golden Books, illus. (p. 233)
—Bubble Party! (Bubble Guppies) Huxtable, John, illus. (p. 233)
—Bubble Pirates! (Bubble Guppies) Unten, Eren, illus. (p. 233)
—Buddy's Teeth (Dinosaur Train) Aikins, Dave, illus. (p. 235)
—Bunnies' ABC. Williams, Garth, illus. (p. 242)
—Christmas Countdown (Team Umizoomi) Fruchter, Jason, illus. (p. 313)
—Clash with the Kraang! (Teenage Mutant Ninja Turtles) Golden Books, illus. (p. 327)
—Class Pictures! (Bubble Guppies) Golden Books, illus. (p. 327)
—Creature Creations! (Teenage Mutant Ninja Turtles) Golden Books, illus. (p. 380)
—DC Super Friends Little Golden Book Favorites (DC Super Friends) (p. 415)
—DC Super Friends Little Golden Book Library (DC Super Friends) (p. 415)
—Dinosaur Dig! (Bubble Guppies) Jackson, Mike, illus. (p. 442)
—Disney Classics Little Golden Book Library (p. 451)
—Disney Junior Little Golden Book Library (Disney Junior) (p. 451)
—Doctor Is In! Unten, Eren, illus. (p. 459)
—Dora's Christmas Carol (Dora the Explorer) Goddard, Brenda & Haskett, Dan, illus. (p. 471)
—Dora's Sticker Adventure! (Dora the Explorer) Golden Books, illus. (p. 471)
—Eureka! Valeri, Jim, illus. (p. 540)
—Extreme Team! (SpongeBob SquarePants) Golden Books, illus. (p. 557)
—Fantastic Fairy Fan Book. Golden Books, illus. (p. 571)
—Fearless Firemoose! (Rocky & Bullwinkle) Golden Books, illus. (p. 579)
—Field Trip Time! (Bubble Guppies) Golden Books, illus. (p. 584)
—Fire Engine Book. Gergely, Tibor, illus. (p. 590)
—From Army Ants to Zebrafish: Animals That Hop, Fly & Swish! (Dr. Seuss/Cat in the Hat) Ruiz, Aristides, illus. (p. 642)
—Fry Cook Freak-Out! (SpongeBob SquarePants) Petrossi, Fabrizio, illus. (p. 646)
—Full Speed Ahead! (Blaze & the Monster Machines) Golden Books, illus. (p. 646)
—Giant Adventures. Golden Books, illus. (p. 673)
—Go for the Gold! (Dora the Explorer) Mcgee, Warner, illus. (p. 686)
—Good Knight SpongeBob (SpongeBob SquarePants) Golden Books & Aikins, Dave, illus. (p. 698)
—Good Morning, Bunny/Good Night, Bunny. (p. 698)
—Guppy Tales (Bubble Guppies) Golden Books, illus. (p. 732)
—Happy Holi-Doodles! Moroney, Christopher, illus. (p. 746)
—Here Comes Peter Cottontail. Golden Books, illus. (p. 770)
—Ho-Ho Holidays! (Bubble Guppies) Huxtable, John, illus. (p. 786)
—Hooray for Dora! (Dora the Explorer) Golden Books, illus. (p. 796)
—I See Seeds! Ruiz, Aristides, illus. (p. 845)
—Inventing Time! Golden Books, illus. (p. 883)
—It's Time for Christmas! (Bubble Guppies) Golden Books, illus. (p. 899)
—Join the Team! (Team Umizoomi) Golden Books, illus. (p. 924)
—Jumbo Coloring Adventures! (Nickelodeon) Golden Books, illus. (p. 933)
—Jurassic Fun (Dinosaur Train) Golden Books, illus. (p. 937)
—Just Yelp for Help! (PAW Patrol) Golden Books, illus. (p. 940)
—Let's Get Epic! (Teenage Mutant Ninja Turtles) Golden Books, illus. (p. 997)
—Let's Go, Guppies! (Bubble Guppies) Golden Books, illus. (p. 997)
—Let's Make a Splash! (Bubble Guppies) Golden Books, illus. (p. 999)
—Little Red Hen. Miller, J. P., illus. (p. 1034)
—Living the Dream Life (Barbie: Life in the Dream House) (p. 1041)
—Make It Count! (Big Time Rush) Golden Books, illus. (p. 1079)
—Mega-Mutations! (Teenage Mutant Ninja Turtles) Golden Books, illus. (p. 1124)
—Mighty Adventures (Team Umizoomi) Fruchter, Jason, illus. (p. 1139)
—Nickelodeon Fairy Tales (Nickelodeon) Aikins, David, illus. (p. 1251)
—Nickelodeon Little Golden Book Library (Nickelodeon) (p. 1251)
—Night of the Ghost Pirate (Paw Patrol) Lovett, Nate, illus. (p. 1254)
—Nine Classic Tales. (p. 1256)
—No Job Is Too Big! (Paw Patrol) Golden Books, illus. (p. 1258)
—Official Ninja Turtle Handbook (Teenage Mutant Ninja Turtles) Golden Books, illus. (p. 1280)
—On the Farm (Bubble Guppies) Jackson, Mike, illus. (p. 1290)
—Once upon a Princess (Dora the Explorer) Golden Books, illus. (p. 1293)
—One Spooky Night (Dora & Friends) Aikins, David, illus. (p. 1297)
—Out of This World! (Dr. Seuss/Cat in the Hat) Ruiz, Aristides, illus. (p. 1311)
—Paint the Town! (Dora & Friends) Sciarrone, Claudio, illus. (p. 1318)
—Paint with Pocoyo! (Pocoyo) (p. 1318)
—Painting Pals (Nickelodeon) Golden Books, illus. (p. 1318)
—Pat the Bunny: at the Apple Orchard. Vilela, Luiz, illus. (p. 1327)
—Pat the Pet (Pat the Bunny) Vilela, Luiz, illus. (p. 1327)
—Pat the Zoo (Pat the Bunny) LV Studio, illus. (p. 1327)
—Picture This (Pocoyo) Golden Books, illus. (p. 1356)
—Plank-Ton's Big Plan! Golden Books, illus. (p. 1368)
—Princess & the Pea. Christy, Jana, illus. (p. 1402)
—Princesses, Mermaids, Fairies & More! Golden Books, illus. (p. 1406)
—Puppy Birthday to You! (Paw Patrol) Petrossi, Fabrizio, illus. (p. 1418)
—Puppy Love! (Bubble Guppies) Golden Books, illus. (p. 1418)
—Purple Monkey Rescue! (Team Umizoomi) DiCicco, Sue, illus. (p. 1419)
—Race Against Time (Mr. Peabody & Sherman) Fransisco, Tina, illus. (p. 1430)
—Rainbow Rescue! (Dora the Explorer) Miller, Victoria, illus. (p. 1435)
—Ready for Battle! (Teenage Mutant Ninja Turtles) Golden Books, illus. (p. 1447)
—Ready, Set, Explore! (Dora the Explorer) Golden Books, illus. (p. 1447)
—Ready to Roll! (Paw Patrol) Golden Books, illus. (p. 1448)
—Ride the Tide (SpongeBob SquarePants) Golden Books, illus. (p. 1471)
—Rock on! (Julius Jr.) Golden Books, illus. (p. 1482)
—Royal Ball! (Dora & Friends) Miller, Victoria, illus. (p. 1492)
—Ruff-Ruff Rescues! (Paw Patrol) Golden Books, illus. (p. 1494)
—Saved by the Shell! (Teenage Mutant Ninja Turtles) Golden Books, illus. (p. 1517)
—Seafaring Friends (SpongeBob SquarePants) Golden Books, illus. (p. 1536)
—Sewer Squad. Chabot, Jacob, illus. (p. 1555)
—Silly Costume Contest (Team Umizoomi) Fruchter, Jason, illus. (p. 1575)
—Snow Wonder! (Frosty the Snowman) Golden Books, illus. (p. 1600)
—Sparkle, Skate, & Spin! (Dora the Explorer) Golden Books, illus. (p. 1622)
—SpongeBob Squarepants Movie Tie-In. Golden Books & Meurer, Caleb, illus. (p. 1630)
—Star Wars: Attack of the Clones (Star Wars) Beavers, Ethen, illus. (p. 1641)
—Start Your Engines! (Bubble Guppies) Golden Books, illus. (p. 1643)
—Sticker Celebration! (Nickelodeon) Golden Books, illus. (p. 1650)
—Sticker Swim-Sation! (Bubble Guppies) Golden Books, illus. (p. 1650)
—Sticky Situations! (SpongeBob SquarePants) Golden Books, illus. (p. 1650)
—Stroke of Genius (Mr. Peabody & Sherman) Golden Books, illus. (p. 1668)
—Super Skates! (Dora the Explorer) Aikins, David, illus. (p. 1681)
—T Is for Troll! Fruchter, Jason, illus. (p. 1694)
—Teenage Mutant Ninja Turtles. Golden Books, illus. (p. 1714)
—Thomas & Friends: Nine Favorite Tales (Thomas & Friends) A Little Golden Book Collection. (p. 1738)
—Thomas & the Dinosaur (Thomas & Friends) Lapadula, Thomas, illus. (p. 1738)
—Thomas Takes a Vacation (Thomas & Friends) Durk, Jim, illus. (p. 1739)
—Time Wave! (Mr. Peabody & Sherman) Golden Books, illus. (p. 1753)
—Trainloads of Color (Thomas & Friends) (p. 1777)
—Trains, Cranes & Troublesome Trucks (Thomas & Friends) (p. 1777)
—Troll Time! Golden Books, illus. (p. 1788)
—Turtle Power! (Teenage Mutant Ninja Turtles) Golden Books, illus. (p. 1798)
—Turtles to the Rescue! (Teenage Mutant Ninja Turtles) Johnson, Shane L., illus. (p. 1799)
—Ultimate Turtles Fan Book (Teenage Mutant Ninja Turtles) Golden Books, illus. (p. 1810)
—Umi Egg Hunt (Team Umizoomi) Golden Books & Aikins, David, illus. (p. 1810)
—Walkin' in a Sticker Wonderland! (Seuss/Cat in the Hat) Moroney, Christopher, illus. (p. 1854)
—Wally's Magical Adventures. Burch, Benjamin, illus. (p. 1855)
—We Can Do It! (Dora & Friends) Golden Books, illus. (p. 1866)
—We Totally Rock! (Bubble Guppies) Jackson, Mike, illus. (p. 1868)
—Welcome to the City! (Dora & Friends) Sciarrone, Claudio, illus. (p. 1874)
—Welcome to Wonderland! (Dora the Explorer) Miller, Victoria, illus. (p. 1874)
—Who's Hatching? (Dinosaur Train) Fruchter, Jason, illus. (p. 1920)
—Wonderful Winx (Winx Club) Golden Books, illus. (p. 1948)
—World of Barbie. Golden Books, illus. (p. 1956)
—You Can Count on Us! (Team Umizoomi) Golden Books, illus. (p. 1974)
—Zoom to the Rescue! (Team Umizoomi) Fruchter, Jason, illus. (p. 1989)
Golden Books, illus. see Awdry, W.
Golden Books, illus. see Awdry, Wilbert V.
Golden Books, illus. see Berrios, Frank.
Golden Books, illus. see Carbone, Courtney.
Golden Books, illus. see Cardona, Jose.
Golden Books, illus. see Depken, Kristen L.
Golden Books, illus. see Man-Kong, Mary.
Golden Books, illus. see Miller, Mona.
Golden Books, illus. see Muldrow, Diane.
Golden Books, illus. see Posner-Sanchez, Andrea.
Golden Books, illus. see Reisner, Molly, et al.
Golden Books, illus. see Tillworth, Mary.
Golden Books, illus. see Wrecks, Billy.
Golden Books & Berrios, Frank. Mutants Rule! (Teenage Mutant Ninja Turtles) Golden Books, illus. (p. 1194)
Golden Books Staff. All Paws on Deck! (Paw Patrol) Golden Books Staff & Lovett, Nate, illus. (p. 45)
—Animal Sounds. Battaglia, Aurelius, illus. (p. 79)
—Animal Tales. (p. 80)
—Baby Farm Animals. Williams, Garth, illus. (p. 126)
—Barbie & the Three Musketeers. (p. 138)
—Barbie & the Three Musketeers. Golden Books Staff, illus. (p. 138)
—Barbie in a Christmas Carol. (p. 138)
—Barbie Loves Ballet/Fashion Show Fun! Golden Books Staff, illus. (p. 138)
—Be a Ballerina! Mcgee, Warner, illus. (p. 147)
—Beautiful Barbie. Golden Books Staff, illus. (p. 153)
—Bee Mine. Golden Books Staff & Riley, Kellee, illus. (p. 157)
—Bengal Tiger Boo-Boo. Golden Books Staff, illus. (p. 164)
—Beyond the Clouds. Duarte, Pamela, illus. (p. 174)
—Big Book of Words (Nickelodeon) Golden Books Staff & Spaziante, Patrick, illus. (p. 179)
—Big Coloring Adventures! (Nickelodeon) Golden Books Staff, illus. (p. 180)
—Big Easter Adventure (Peter Cottontail) (p. 181)
—Brave Knight Dora (Dora the Explorer) Golden Books Staff & Fruchter, Jason, illus. (p. 223)
—Bunny Business. Aikins, Dave, illus. (p. 242)
—Bunny's Fuzzy Christmas. Golden Books Staff, illus. (p. 242)
—Bunny's Garden. Golden Books Staff, illus. (p. 242)
—Cars. Golden Books Staff, illus. (p. 271)
—Catch a Wave! Golden Books Staff, illus. (p. 279)
—Champions of the Sea! (SpongeBob SquarePants) Artifact Group Staff, illus. (p. 289)
—Christmas Fiesta. Fruchter, Jason, illus. (p. 314)
—Christmas Is Coming! (Dora the Explorer) Mcgee, Warner, illus. (p. 314)
—Christmas Magic. McGee, Warner, illus. (p. 314)
—Crystal Magic. Mcgee, Warner, illus. (p. 387)
—Danger from the Deep. (p. 403)
—Doodle Do It! (Nickelodeon) (p. 469)
—Dora the Explorer Fun Kit! Golden Books Staff, illus. (p. 471)
—Dora the Explorer Make Your Own Little Golden Book. (p. 471)
—Dora's Big Valentine! Golden Books Staff, illus. (p. 471)
—Dora's Super Silly Coloring Book (Dora the Explorer) Golden Books Staff, illus. (p. 471)
—Drawing Fiesta! (Dora the Explorer) Golden Books Staff, illus. (p. 481)
—Dreamy Dreamhouse (Barbie: Life in the Dream House) Duarte, Pamela, illus. (p. 484)
—Easter Deliveries. Golden Books Staff, illus. (p. 499)
—Easter Eggspress! Durk, Jim & Stubbs, Tommy, illus. (p. 499)
—Egg Surprise. Roper, Bob, illus. (p. 506)
—Eloise Wilkin Stories. Wilkin, Eloise, illus. (p. 516)
—Explore with Me! Golden Books Staff, illus. (p. 551)
—Fabulous Fashion. (p. 560)
—Fairy Magic (Dora the Explorer) Fruchter, Jason, illus. (p. 563)
—Farm Tales. (p. 574)
—Favorites: The Poky Little Puppy/Scuffy the Tugboat/The Saggy Baggy Elephant. (p. 578)
—Favorites: Thomas Breaks a Promise/Thomas & the Big, Big Bridge/May the Best Engine Win! (p. 578)
—Feel the Love (SpongeBob SquarePants) Schigiel, Gregg, illus. (p. 580)
—Find the Dinosaurs! (Team Umizoomi) Riley, Kellee et al, illus. (p. 587)
—Fire Engine Book. Gergely, Tibor, illus. (p. 590)
—Fly Like a Fish. Meurer, Caleb, illus. (p. 609)
—Follow the Ninja! Golden Books Staff & Lambe, Steve, illus. (p. 612)
—Forever Fairytopia. Harchy, Atelier Philippe, illus. (p. 619)
—Friends & Flowers (Dora the Explorer) Golden Books Staff, illus. (p. 638)
—Friends from Sodor. Hit Entertainment Staff, illus. (p. 638)
—Get Hooked! (p. 667)
—Giant Steps! (p. 674)
—Glamour Girl. Harchy, Atelier Philippe, illus. (p. 682)
—Going Buggy! Insects & Spiders to Paint. Ruiz, Aristides, illus. (p. 692)
—Golden Children's Bible. Miralles, Jose, illus. (p. 694)
—Great Crayon Race. (p. 715)
—Halloween Coloring Book. (p. 737)
—Here Comes Bubble Bunny! (Bubble Guppies) MJ Illustrations Staff, illus. (p. 770)
—Hooray for Best Friends! Zalme, Ron, illus. (p. 795)
—House That Jack Built. Miller, J. P., illus. (p. 803)
—Hugs & Fishes (SpongeBob SquarePants) (p. 825)
—In Action! Golden Books Staff, illus. (p. 863)
—It's Time for Bubble Puppy! Unten, Eren Blanquet, illus. (p. 899)
—Itty-Bitty Kitty Rescue (Paw Patrol) Golden Books Staff & Petrossi, Fabrizio, illus. (p. 900)
—Jumbo Coloring Party. Golden Books Staff, illus. (p. 933)
—King of Karate (SpongeBob SquarePants) Golden Books Staff & Aikins, Dave, illus. (p. 959)
—Kite Riders! (Team Umizoomi) Fruchter, Jason, illus. (p. 962)
—Let's Dance! Fruchter, Jason, illus. (p. 995)
—Little Bunny Bedtime. Riley, Kellee, illus. (p. 1025)
—Little Golden Book Favorites. Scarry, Richard & Golden Books Staff, illus. (p. 1028)
—Little Mermaid - Songs from the Heart. Marrucchi, Elisa, illus. (p. 1031)
—Lorax Deluxe Doodle Book. Gerardi, Jan, illus. (p. 1052)
—Lorax Doodle Book. Gerardi, Jan, illus. (p. 1052)
—Magical Mermaid Crown. Savitsky, Steven, illus. (p. 1075)
—May I Help You? (Pat the Bunny) Golden Books Staff & LV Studio Staff, illus. (p. 1112)
—May the Best Engine Win! Stubbs, Tommy, illus. (p. 1112)
—Mermaid Princess. Golden Books Staff, illus. (p. 1128)
—Mighty Monster Machines (Blaze & the Monster Machines) Golden Books Staff & Lambe, Steve, illus. (p. 1140)
—My Easter Basket. Karl, Linda, illus. (p. 1202)
—My Heart Is Happy! Fruchter, Jason, illus. (p. 1211)
—Nickelodeon Little Golden Book Favorites (Nickelodeon) Golden Books Staff, illus. (p. 1251)
—Nickelodeon Nursery Rhymes (Nickelodeon) Aikins, Dave, illus. (p. 1251)
—Oh, the Things Spring Brings! Ruiz, Aristides, illus. (p. 1281)
—P Is for Paint! Cartobaleno Staff, illus. (p. 1316)
—Paint the Town Pink! Golden Books Staff, illus. (p. 1318)
—Painting Power! (Team Umizoomi) Fruchter, Jason, illus. (p. 1318)
—Pets Are the Best! (Dora the Explorer) Fruchter, Jason, illus. (p. 1348)
—Plank-Ton to the Rescue! Golden Books Staff & Aikins, Dave, illus. (p. 1368)
—Prayers for Children. Wilkin, Eloise, illus. (p. 1393)
—Princess Dreams. Golden Books Staff, illus. (p. 1403)
—Princess Party. (p. 1405)
—Princess Stories: A Collection to Color. (p. 1405)
—Private Eyes (SpongeBob SquarePants) (p. 1407)
—Puppy Power! (Paw Patrol) Golden Books Staff & Lovett, Nate, illus. (p. 1418)
—Puzzle Party! (Dora the Explorer) Mcgee, Warner, illus. (p. 1421)
—Rainbow Adventure. Miller, Victoria, illus. (p. 1435)
—Ready, Set, Race! Fruchter, Jason & Golden Books Staff, illus. (p. 1447)
—Rescue Team! Durk, Jim, illus. (p. 1462)
—Ride along the Countryside. Santanach, Tino, illus. (p. 1471)
—Saddle Up! Mcgee, Warner, illus. (p. 1501)
—Santa's Big Big Book to Color. (p. 1513)
—Save the Unicorn King! Miller, Victoria, illus. (p. 1517)
—Scribblebob Doodlepants! (p. 1533)
—Share a Hug. Golden Books Staff & Fruchter, Jason, illus. (p. 1561)
—Shiver Me Timbers! Martinez, Heather, illus. (p. 1567)
—Sleepy Bunny. (p. 1589)
—Sleepytime Tales. (p. 1590)
—Snow Princess Spell. (p. 1599)
—Splash of Color! Golden Books Staff, illus. (p. 1629)
—Sponge in Space! (SpongeBob SquarePants) Martinez, Heather, illus. (p. 1630)
—SpongeBob for President! (SpongeBob SquarePants) Golden Books Staff & Aikins, Dave, illus. (p. 1630)
—SpongeBob SportyPants! (SpongeBob SquarePants) Golden Books Staff, illus. (p. 1630)
—SpongeBob's Best Days! Golden Books Staff, illus. (p. 1631)
—Standing Tall! Golden Books Staff, illus. (p. 1639)
—Stick Together! Meurer, Caleb, illus. (p. 1650)
—Sticker-Tastic! (Julius Jr.) Golden Books Staff & Valeri, Jim, illus. (p. 1650)
—Super Coloring Adventures! (Nick Jr.) Golden Books Staff, illus. (p. 1679)
—Super Coloring Fiesta! Golden Books Staff, illus. (p. 1679)
—Super Sponge-Tastic! (p. 1682)
—Take-Along Treasures. (p. 1696)
—Thomas & the Christmas Tree. Courtney, Richard, illus. (p. 1738)
—Thomas' Giant Coloring Book. (p. 1738)
—Three Little Pigs. Walt Disney Company Staff, illus. (p. 1742)
—Trainloads of Fun. Golden Books Staff, illus. (p. 1777)
—Travel with Thomas. Santanach, Tino, illus. (p. 1780)

G

—Tree for Me! Gerardi, Jan, illus. (p. 1783)
—Tree's Company. Mathieu, Joe & Ruiz, Aristides, illus. (p. 1784)
—Triceratops for Lunch. Meurer, Caleb, illus. (p. 1785)
—Twelve Days of Christmas: A Christmas Carol. Beckett, Sheilah, illus. (p. 1800)
—Twirly Whirly Flowers. Walston, Dave, illus. (p. 1802)
—Very Busy Sticker Book. Golden Books Staff, illus. (p. 1837)
—Very Krabby Christmas (SpongeBob SquarePants) Aikins, Dave, illus. (p. 1838)
—Vintage Valentines. (p. 1843)
—We Love Halloween! Fruchter, Jason, illus. (p. 1867)
—Wedding Bells. Sarl Aky-Aka Creations & Golden Books Staff, illus. (p. 1870)
—Welcome to Wally's World! VanTuyle, David, illus. (p. 1874)
—Wipe Out! (SpongeBob SquarePants) Golden Books Staff, illus. (p. 1939)
—World of Colors. Golden Books Staff, illus. (p. 1956)
Golden Books Staff, illus. see Awdry, W.
Golden Books Staff, illus. see Awdry, Wilbert V.
Golden Books Staff, illus. see Awdry, Wilbert V. & Awdry, Rev. W.
Golden Books Staff, illus. see Berrios, Frank & Mangual, Ines.
Golden Books Staff, illus. see Berrios, Frank & RH Disney Staff.
Golden Books Staff, illus. see Carbone, Courtney.
Golden Books Staff, illus. see Depken, Kristen L.
Golden Books Staff, illus. see Fontes, Justine & Korman, Justine.
Golden Books Staff, illus. see Kunhardt, Dorothy.
Golden Books Staff, illus. see Man-Kong, Mary & Hashimoto, Meika.
Golden Books Staff, illus. see Man-Kong, Mary & Tillworth, Mary.
Golden Books Staff, illus. see Man-Kong, Mary.
Golden Books Staff, illus. see McGuire, Molly.
Golden Books Staff, illus. see Miller, Mona.
Golden Books Staff, illus. see Posner-Sanchez, Andrea.
Golden Books Staff, illus. see Random House Editors.
Golden Books Staff, illus. see Reisner, Molly.
Golden Books Staff, illus. see RH Disney Staff & Hall, Klay.
Golden Books Staff, illus. see RH Disney Staff.
Golden Books Staff, illus. see Saxon, Victoria & Smiley, Ben.
Golden Books Staff, illus. see Scarry, Richard.
Golden Books Staff, illus. see Wrecks, Billy.
Golden Books Staff, jt. auth. see Bedford, Annie North.
Golden Books Staff, jt. auth. see Brown, Margaret Wise.
Golden Books Staff, jt. auth. see Duplaix, Georges.
Golden Books Staff, jt. auth. see Frank, Janet.
Golden Books Staff, jt. auth. see Henderson, Patti.
Golden Books Staff, jt. auth. see Muldrow, Diane.
Golden Books Staff, jt. auth. see Random House.
Golden Books Staff, jt. auth. see Ricci, Christine.
Golden Books Staff, jt. auth. see Scarry, Richard.
Golden Books Staff, jt. auth. see Simeon, S.
Golden Books Staff, jt. auth. see Teitelbaum, Michael.
Golden Books Staff, jt. auth. see Weiner, Eric.
Golden Books Staff, jt. auth. see Werner, Janet.
Golden Books Staff, photos by see Gergely, Tibor, illus.
Golden Books Staff & Artful Doodlers Limited Staff. Blue's Quilt. (p. 204)
Golden Books Staff & Benedict, Elizabeth. Classic Characters of Little Golden Books (p. 327)
Golden Books Staff & Carbone, Courtney. Grandma's House (Dora the Explorer) Goddard, Brenda & Haskett, Dan, illus. (p. 708)
Golden Books Staff & Cartobaleno Staff. Winx Forever! (Winx Club) Golden Books Staff, illus. (p. 1939)
Golden Books Staff & Jackson, Mike. Ready, Set, Paint! (p. 1447)
Golden Books Staff & Lewman, David. Junior Novelization. Golden Books Staff & Random House Value Publishing Staff, illus. (p. 936)
—Mutants in Space! Golden Books Staff, illus. (p. 1194)
Golden Books Staff & Man-Kong, Mary. Barbie Bedtime Story Collection (Barbie) (p. 138)
Golden Books Staff & Miryam. Happy Man & His Dump Truck. Gergely, Tibor, illus. (p. 746)
Golden Books Staff & Random House Staff. Enter the Lair (Teenage Mutant Ninja Turtles) Golden Books Staff & Random House Staff, illus. (p. 531)
Golden Books Staff & RH Disney Staff. Cars Little Golden Book Favorites. (p. 272)
—Wonderful Princess World. RH Disney Staff, illus. (p. 1948)
Golden Books Staff & Smith, Geof. Green vs. Mean (Teenage Mutant Ninja Turtles) Lambe, Steve, illus. (p. 722)
—Green vs. Mean (Teenage Mutant Ninja Turtles) Golden Books Staff & Lambe, Steve, illus. (p. 722)
—Mr. FancyPants! Meurer, Caleb, illus. (p. 1185)
Golden Books Staff, creator. Perfect Fit. (p. 1341)
Golden Books Staff, et al. Christmas Favorites. Catusanu, Mircea & Wilkin, Eloise, illus. (p. 313)
Golden, Brenda. Celebrity. (p. 285)
Golden, Brian M. Farmington: A Pictorial History Photograph Collection. (p. 574)
Golden, Christopher. Buffy the Vampire Slayer (p. 236)
—Buffy - The Vampire Slayer (p. 236)
—Ejercito Perdido. Mignola, Mike, illus. (p. 507)
—Lost Slayer. (p. 1056)
—When Rose Wakes. (p. 1904)
Golden, Christopher, jt. auth. see Randall, Thomas.
Golden, Christopher, jt. auth. see Sniegoski, Thomas E.
Golden, Christopher & Lebbon, Tim. Sea Wolves Bk. 2. Ruth, Greg, illus. (p. 1536)
—Wild. Ruth, Greg, illus. (p. 1928)
Golden, Christopher & Sniegoski, Thomas E. Un-Magician. (p. 1811)
Golden, Christopher, et al. Buffy the Vampire Slayer: Carnival of Souls; One Thing or Your Mother; Blooded. (p. 236)
—Halloween Rain - Bad Bargain - Afterimage. (p. 738)
—Talent Azaceta, Paul & Chee, illus. (p. 1701)
Golden Cosmos Staff, contrib. by. High Times: A History of Aviation. (p. 778)
Golden Eagle Productions Staff. Grandmother Moon & Sammy the Loon (p. 709)
Golden, Emily, jt. auth. see Webster, Grace.
Golden, Erin Lee. Halloween Scratchers. Nassner, Alyssa, illus. (p. 738)
Golden, Harriet, illus. see Andersen, Hans Christian.
Golden, Jess, illus. see Singleton, Linda Joy.
Golden, John. Kiley & the Love Struck Frog. (p. 956)
Golden, John Ashton, illus. see McIntosh, Kenneth.
Golden, Joseph. Johnny Moonbeam & the Silver Arrow: An Adventure for Young People in Narration & Mime. (p. 923)
Golden, Kathleen M. Cleopatra's Big Birthday BBQ. Golden, Kathleen M., illus. (p. 331)
Golden, Laura. Every Day After. (p. 542)
Golden, Lilly, illus. see Thom, Kara Douglass.
Golden, Mark, jt. auth. see Baker, Steve.
Golden, Michael, et al. 'Nam (p. 1228)
Golden, Mike & Vansant, Wayne. 'Nam (p. 1228)
Golden, Nancy. British Are Coming! The Midnight Ride of Paul Revere. (p. 229)
—Exploring Canada with the Five Themes of Geography. (p. 551)
—Exploring Mexico with the Five Themes of Geography. (p. 552)
—Exploring the United States with the Five Themes of Geography. (p. 554)
—Life with the Comanches: The Kidnapping of Cynthia Ann Parker. (p. 1013)
Golden, Pam. Lulu Learns about Reporting: Ending the Tattle Battle. Outohak, Diana, illus. (p. 1065)
Golden, R. M. Wings of Wonder: The Chronicles of Willie Wisdom. (p. 1936)
Golden, Rayna, illus. see Edwards, Wayne.
Golden, Robert Charles. Eve. Happel, Sally, illus. (p. 541)
—Pee Wee: The Blackcapped Chickadee. (p. 1334)
Golden, Robert N., et al. Rape. (p. 1439)
—Smoking. (p. 1595)
—Truth about Stress Management. (p. 1794)
Golden, Ryan. Shummys: Cooking Joy with Every Girl & Boy. Reda, Jaime, illus. (p. 1571)
Golden, Stacie. Cozette's Great Adventure. (p. 375)
Golden Twomey, Emily. Amazing Copycat Coloring Book: Cool Pictures to Copy & Complete. (p. 54)
Golden, William Lee. Noah, Didn't It Rain. Looney, Bill, illus. (p. 1261)
Goldenberg, Alisse Lee. Strings of the Violin. (p. 1667)
Goldenberg, Linda. Little People & a Lost World: An Anthropological Mystery. (p. 1033)
Goldenberg, Olly, jt. auth. see Liardon, Roberts.
Goldenburg, Dorothea & Killian, Bette. Treasury of Fairy Tales. LoFaro, Jerry et al, illus. (p. 1782)
Goldenstern, Joyce. Albert Einstein: Physicist & Genius. (p. 34)
—Albert Einstein: Genius of the Theory of Relativity. (p. 34)
Goldenthal, Jolene. Beautiful Truth: A One-Act Comedy Play. (p. 154)
Goldfarb, Ian M. & Silverstein, Janna. Searching for Close Encounters with Aliens. (p. 1537)
Goldfarb, James L. Her Husband's Heart. (p. 769)
Goldfield, Rebecca & Short, Mike. Captive of Friendly Cove: Based on the Secret Journals of John Jewitt. (p. 264)
Goldfinger, Jennifer P., illus. see Thomas, Charlie.
Goldfrank, David, et al. History of Russia: Peoples, Legends, Events, Forces. (p. 784)
Goldfrap, John Henry. Boy Aviators' Polar Dash: Or Facing Death in the Antarctic. (p. 217)
Goldgrab, Eli. Sidros Toldos, Vayeitsei, Vayishlach (p. 1573)
Goldhammer, Richard. Gotta Do Homework! Elephant Notes - Study Tips You'll Never Forget. (p. 704)
Goldhawk, Emma. Cuddly Koala. Lambert, Jonathan, illus. (p. 389)
—Little Lamb. Lambert, Jonathan, illus. (p. 1030)
—Snuggle Bunny. Lambert, Jonathan, illus. (p. 1601)
Goldie, Sonia. Ghosts. Boutavant, Marc, illus. (p. 672)
Goldie, Sophie, et al. Formula One Maths Gold. (p. 620)
Goldin, Barbara Diamond. Best Hanukkah Ever (p. 170)
—Cakes & Miracles: A Purim Tale Zollars, Jaime, illus. (p. 252)
—Family Book of Midrash: 52 Jewish Stories from the Sages. (p. 568)
—Mountain of Blintzes McGrory, Anik, illus. (p. 1181)
—Night Lights: A Sukkot Story. Carmi, Giora, illus. (p. 1253)
Goldin, Barbara Diamond, jt. auth. see Peretz, I. L.
Goldin, Barbara Diamond, et al. 40 Greatest Jewish Stories Ever Told Allon, Jeffrey, illus. (p. 1997)
Goldin, David. Meet Me at the Art Museum: A Whimsical Look Behind the Scenes. (p. 1121)
Goldin, David, illus. see Snyder, Laurel.
Goldin, David, illus. see Young, Karen Romano.
Goldin, Nan, et al. Devil's Playground. (p. 432)
Goldin, Sandy. Vanity Murders. (p. 1833)
Goldin, Stan, ed. see Beahm, George.
Golding, Claire Mowbray, jt. auth. see Choiniere, Joseph.
Golding, Elizabeth. Forty-Eight Funny Faces: Use the Cling-On Stickers to Make Funny Faces! Mallett, Lisa, illus. (p. 623)
—Make 24 Paper Planes: Includes Awesome Launcher Kit! Moerbeek, Kees, illus. (p. 1078)
—Moonlight Animals. Lodge, Ali, illus. (p. 1172)
—Moonlight Ocean. Lodge, Ali, illus. (p. 1172)
Golding, Elizabeth, jt. auth. see Butterfield, Moira.
Golding, J. C., illus. see Monroe, Guy.
Golding, Jacqueline. Healing Stories: Picture Books for the Big & Small Changes in a Child's Life. (p. 757)
Golding, Julia. Cat among the Pigeons. (p. 277)
—Cat's Cradle. (p. 281)
—Chimera's Curse (p. 306)
—Diamond of Drury Lane. (p. 434)
—Glass Swallow (p. 682)
—Gorgon's Gaze (p. 702)
—Mines of the Minotaur (p. 1146)
—Secret of the Sirens (p. 1543)
—Silver Sea (p. 1576)
Golding Moore, Michelle. Normal Is Me. (p. 1264)
Golding, Theresa Martin. Abby's Asthma & the Big Race. Lucas, Margeaux, illus. (p. 2)
—Niner. (p. 1256)
Golding, William. Senor de las Moscas. (p. 1550)
Goldish. Lights, Camera, Action: Small Books X6 (Discovery Phonics) (p. 1016)
Goldish, Meish. Accidental Inventions: (Or Made by Mistake) (p. 8)
—Air Force: Civilian to Airman. (p. 31)
—Amazing Amusement Park Rides. (p. 52)
—Amazing Water Frogs. (p. 56)
—Animal Control Officers to the Rescue. (p. 77)
—Army: Civilian to Soldier. (p. 100)
—Baby Bug Dishes. (p. 125)
—Baghdad Pups. (p. 132)
—Bald Eagles: A Chemical Nightmare. (p. 134)
—Bark Scorpion. (p. 139)
—Beautiful Butterflies. (p. 153)
—Bloodthirsty Mosquitoes. (p. 201)
—Bobcat. (p. 206)
—Bomb-Sniffing Dogs. (p. 208)
—Brave Hearts. (p. 223)
—Brown Bear: The Biggest Meat-Eater on Land. (p. 231)
—Bug-a-Licious. (p. 236)
—California Condors: Saved by Captive Breeding. (p. 253)
—Camel. (p. 256)
—City Firefighters. (p. 323)
—Coast Guard: Civilian to Guardian. (p. 336)
—Deadly Praying Mantises. (p. 418)
—Disabled Dogs. (p. 446)
—Disgusting Hagfish. (p. 450)
—Doctors to the Rescue. (p. 459)
—Dogs. (p. 462)
—Emperor Penguin: The World's Biggest Penguin. (p. 520)
—Empty Pot: A Chinese Legend. Treatner, Meryle, illus. (p. 521)
—Everything You Need to Know about Dyslexia. (p. 545)
—Firefighters to the Rescue. (p. 591)
—Florida Manatees: Warm Water Miracles. (p. 607)
—Fossa: A Fearsome Predator. (p. 623)
—Fossil Feud: Marsh & Cope's Bone Wars. (p. 623)
—Freaky-Big Airplanes. (p. 632)
—Giraffe: The World's Tallest Mammal. (p. 677)
—Gorillas. (p. 703)
—Ground Zero Dogs. (p. 725)
—Heart-Stopping Roller Coasters. (p. 760)
—Hidden Walkingsticks. (p. 776)
—Hollywood Dogs. (p. 789)
—Hollywood Horses. (p. 789)
—Hotshots. (p. 802)
—How Many Are Here? Meyerhoff, Jill, illus. (p. 811)
—Huge Earthmovers. (p. 824)
—Hungry Cockroaches. (p. 828)
—Inside the Worm's Hole. (p. 878)
—Jumping Spiders. (p. 934)
—Killer Bees. (p. 956)
—Leaping Grasshoppers. (p. 982)
—Lights! Camera! Action! (p. 1016)
—Little Newts. (p. 1032)
—Lost in a Desert. (p. 1055)
—Lost in the Woods. (p. 1056)
—Lost on a Mountain. (p. 1056)
—Mammal Menu. (p. 1085)
—Marine Corps: Civilian to Marine. (p. 1094)
—Marine Firefighters. (p. 1094)
—Michael Phelps: Anything Is Possible! (p. 1134)
—Moray Eel: Dangerous Teeth. (p. 1173)
—Navy: Civilian to Sailor. (p. 1238)
—Nice Vine, Quite Fine Sargent, Claudia Karabaic, illus. (p. 1250)
—Orangutans. (p. 1302)
—Pest-Sniffing Dogs. (p. 1345)
—Prison Puppies. (p. 1407)
—R. E. A. D. Dogs. (p. 1429)
—Red Imported Fire Ants: Attacking Everything. (p. 1454)
—Red Wolves: And Then There Were (Almost) None. (p. 1455)
—Reticulated Python: The World's Longest Snake. (p. 1464)
—Rottweiler: Super Courageous. (p. 1491)
—Science Dogs. (p. 1525)
—Sea Lions in the Navy. (p. 1535)
—Shark: The Shredder. (p. 1562)
—Shelter Dogs. (p. 1565)
—Siberian Tiger: The World's Biggest Cat. (p. 1572)
—Skydiving Dogs. (p. 1587)
—Slimy Salamanders. (p. 1590)
—Smelly Stink Bugs. (p. 1593)
—Smokejumpers. (p. 1594)
—Southern Elephant Seal: The Biggest Seal in the World. (p. 1617)
—Spectacular Skyscrapers. (p. 1624)
—Spider-Tizers & Other Creepy Treats. (p. 1626)
—Spooky Wolf Spiders. (p. 1631)
—Stonefish: Needles of Pain. (p. 1653)
—Surf Dog Miracles. (p. 1685)
—Tiger Sharks: Blue Blenders. (p. 1748)
—Titanic Trucks. (p. 1758)
—Toy Fox Terrier: America's Dog. (p. 1774)
—Toy Poodle: Oodles of Fun. (p. 1774)
—Tricky Trapdoor Spiders. (p. 1786)
—Warty Toads. (p. 1859)
—Whale Shark: The World's Biggest Fish. (p. 1877)
—Wildlife Rehabilitators to the Rescue. (p. 1931)
—Zack Can Fix It! Scruton, Clive, illus. (p. 1984)
Goldish, Meish & Aiello, Ron. War Dogs. (p. 1857)
Goldish, Meish & Parkhurst, Anthony. Horses, Donkeys, & Mules in the Marines. (p. 800)
Goldish, Meish & Ridgway, Sam H. Bottlenose Dolphins in the Navy. (p. 215)
Goldman, Arnold J. Study Guide: Used with ... Goldman-Business Law: Principles & Practices. (p. 1670)
Goldman, Chava. How to Succeed on Any Diet: A Jewish & Friendly Guide to Dieting & Exercise. (p. 821)
Goldman, Dan, jt. auth. see Goldman, Steven.
Goldman, Dara. Boris & Stella & the Perfect Gift. (p. 214)
Goldman, David J. Jewish Sports Stars: Athletic Heroes Past & Present. (p. 917)
—Presidential Losers. (p. 1397)
Goldman, Garnet, illus. see Underwood, Kim.
Goldman, Garnet, illus. see Underwood, Ralph Kim.
Goldman, Judy. Uncle Monarch & the Day of the Dead. Moreno, Rene King, illus. (p. 1812)
Goldman, Judy, tr. see Price, Mathew.
Goldman, Karen. Jordan & the Dreadful Golem. Moseley, Rachel, illus. (p. 925)
Goldman, Ken. Beginner's Guide- Acrylic: Learn the Basics of Acrylic Painting (p. 159)
Goldman, Ken, des. Charcoal Drawing. (p. 291)
Goldman, Laurie. Clean Energy. (p. 330)
Goldman, Laurie, jt. auth. see Laber-Warren, Emily.
Goldman, Laurie, jt. auth. see Warren, Emily Laber.
Goldman, Lena. Walking through the Maze: A Children's Guide for Loss & Grief. (p. 1854)
Goldman, Leslie. On the Job. (p. 1290)
Goldman, Leslie, jt. auth. see Sullivan, Kevin.
Goldman, Leslie & Trenc, Milan. Night at the Museum. (p. 1252)
Goldman, Linda Sarah, illus. see Herman, Debbie.
Goldman, Lisa Bear. Amadito & Spider Woman. Pena, Amado M., Jr., illus. (p. 51)
Goldman, Marcia, photos by. Lola & Tattletale Zeke. (p. 1045)
—Lola Goes to the Doctor. (p. 1045)
Goldman Marshall, Lauren. My Beautiful Bow: An Adoption Story. Marschell, Hannah, illus. (p. 1196)
Goldman, Phyllis B., ed. Monkeyshines on Rocks & Minerals. (p. 1166)
Goldman, Phyllis, ed. Monkeyshines on Mysteries in History. (p. 1166)
—Monkeyshines on the Library: For Your Information. (p. 1166)
—Monkeyshines on What's up down There: Exploring the World Underground. (p. 1166)
Goldman, Stan. CPCS Mental Health Proceedings in Massachusetts. (p. 375)
Goldman, Stanley M. Doorway to Forever: September 2nd, 1666, the First Day of Forever. (p. 470)
Goldman, Steven & Goldman, Dan. Everyman: Be the People. Bucco, Joe, illus. (p. 544)
Goldman, Todd. Bear in Long Underwear. Doodler, Todd H., illus. (p. 151)
—Bear's Underwear Mystery: A Count-and-Find-It Adventure. Doodler, Todd H., illus. (p. 152)
—What Color Is Bear's Underwear? Doodler, Todd H., illus. (p. 1881)
Goldman, Todd, et al. Bear in Underwear. (p. 151)
Goldman, Todd Harris. Boys Are Stupid, Throw Rocks at Them! Goldman, Todd Harris, illus. (p. 220)
Goldner, Harriet. Please, Don't Pass over the Seder Plate: A Haggadah for the Young & Young-at-Heart. (p. 1373)
Goldner, Joan. BusyBodyBook Personal & Family Organizer Jan-Dec 2009 Funky Floral: Funky Floral. (p. 246)
Goldner, John. Hockey Talk: The Language of Hockey from A-Z Heeley, Ted, illus. (p. 787)
Goldner, Rahel. Coloring Book Art Nouveau. (p. 344)
Goldner, Rahel, jt. auth. see Kutschbach, Doris.
Goldolphin, Mary. Sandford & Merton. (p. 1511)
Goldring, Jamie. I Believe. (p. 834)
Goldrush, Jds. Adventures of Chris & Tom's Grandp: Great Grand Pappy's Treasure Map & the Bat Gold Cave. (p. 17)
—Christmas Caf. (p. 313)
Golds, Alexandra Kimla, illus. see Kimla, Lenka J.
Goldsack, Gaby. Fairies Die Cut. (p. 563)
—Fire Engine. Lawson, Peter, illus. (p. 590)
—Fishing Boat. Lawson, Peter, illus. (p. 599)
—Little Lion & Daniel: A Finger Puppet Play & Read Story. (p. 1030)
—Ocean Animals. Bampton, Bob, illus. (p. 1276)
—Ultimate Sleepover Pack. Reeves, Sue, illus. (p. 1810)
Goldsack, Gaby & Dawson, Peter. Noah's Ark: My Little Bible Book. Lawson, Peter, illus. (p. 1261)
Goldsack, Gaby, et al. Little Fir Tree. (p. 1027)
Goldsberry, Booty. Scaredy-Cat, I'm Not. (p. 1519)
Goldsberry, Michelle. Life Series: First Day. (p. 1013)
Goldsberry, U'i. Shark Man of Hana. Chang, Roy, illus. (p. 1562)
Goldsberry, U'ilani. Is for Aloha: A Hawaii Alphabet. Yee, Tammy, illus. (p. 889)
Goldsborough, June, illus. see Lowery, Lawrence F.
Goldsby, Gabrielle. Paybacks. (p. 1331)
Goldschmidt, Gregory Walter, Jr., creator. Greg's Egyptian Adventure. (p. 723)
Goldsmann, Henri. Secret Agent Spanky Sheep in the mystery of: the Pooperous Pizza Plunderer. (p. 1540)
Goldsmith, Abby, illus. see Shelley, Rebecca.
Goldsmith, Bonnie. William Randolph Hearst: Newspaper Magnate. (p. 1933)
Goldsmith, Bonnie Zucker. Dr. Mary Edwards Walker: Civil War Surgeon & Medal of Honor Recipient. (p. 475)
Goldsmith, Carol. Book of Carols: Songs of Discovery on the Path to Enlightenment. (p. 211)
Goldsmith, Connie. Battling Malaria: On the Front Lines against a Global Killer. (p. 147)
—Cutting-Edge Medicine. (p. 396)
—Dietary Supplements. (p. 437)
—Hepatitis. (p. 769)
—Influenza: The Next Pandemic? (p. 873)
—Influenza. (p. 873)
—Invisible Invaders: Dangerous Infectious Diseases. (p. 885)
—Leukemia. (p. 1003)
—Meningitis. (p. 1126)
—Skin Cancer. (p. 1585)
—Superbugs Strike Back: When Antibiotics Fail. (p. 1682)
—Traumatic Brain Injury: From Concussion to Coma. (p. 1780)
Goldsmith, Emily & Nash, Kevin. Vassar College College Prowler off the Record. (p. 1833)
Goldsmith, Evelyn, et al. Collins Junior Illustrated Dictionary. (p. 340)
Goldsmith, Howard. John F. Kennedy & the Stormy Sea. Benoit, Renne, illus. (p. 921)

—John F. Kennedy & the Stormy Sea. Benoit, Renné, illus. (p. 921)
—Mark Twain at Work! Habbas, Frank, illus. (p. 1095)
—Thomas Edison to the Rescue! DiVito, Anna, illus. (p. 1738)
—Thomas Jefferson & the Ghostriders. Rose, Drew, illus. (p. 1739)
Goldsmith, Joel S. Class Lessons with Joel Goldsmith. (p. 327)
Goldsmith, Lynn. Angel Warriors. (p. 74)
Goldsmith, Marcia. Important Years: The 1980s. (p. 862)
Goldsmith, Marshall & Reiter, Mark. What Got You Here Won't Get You There: How Successful People Become Even More Successful! (p. 1885)
Goldsmith, Michael, jt. auth. see Reader's Digest Editors.
Goldsmith, Mike. Airport. Daubney, Kate, illus. (p. 32)
—Digging for Dinosaurs. Daubney, Kate, illus. (p. 439)
—Dinosaurs. Abbott, Simon, illus. (p. 443)
—Discover Science: Light & Sound. (p. 448)
—Discover Science: Materials. (p. 448)
—Eureka! The Most Amazing Scientific Discoveries of All Time. (p. 540)
—Everything You Need to Know about Science. (p. 546)
—Flip the Flaps: Planet Earth. Palin, Nicki, illus. (p. 605)
—Flip the Flaps: Weather. Butler, John, illus. (p. 605)
—I Wish I Knew That. (p. 848)
—In One End & Out the Other: What Happens to Poo When It Leaves You? Watson, Richard, illus. (p. 864)
—In One End & Out the Other. Watson, Richard, illus. (p. 864)
—Kingfisher Space Encyclopedia. (p. 960)
—Navigators: Stars & Planets (TP) (p. 1238)
—Recycling. (p. 1453)
—Solar System. (p. 1607)
—Space. (p. 1618)
—Space Adventure. Abbott, Simon, illus. (p. 1618)
—Under the Sea. Daubney, Kate, illus. (p. 1814)
—Universe: Journey into Deep Space. Garlick, Mark A., illus. (p. 1820)
Goldsmith, Mike, jt. auth. see Chancellor, Deborah.
Goldsmith, Mike, jt. auth. see Dorling Kindersley Publishing Staff.
Goldsmith, Mike, jt. auth. see Steele, Philip.
Goldsmith, Mike & Chancellor, Deborah. Caring for Our Bodies. (p. 269)
Goldsmith, Mike & Johnson, Jinny. Being Safe. (p. 161)
Goldsmith, Mike, et al. Space: Fun, Facts, & Star Gazing... (p. 1618)
Goldsmith, Oliver. Elegy on the Death of A Mad Dog. (p. 510)
—Elegy on the Glory of Her Sex Mrs Mary B. (p. 510)
—She Stoops to Conquer. Landes, William-Alan, ed. (p. 1564)
Goldsmith, Ros. Who Lives near the North Pole? (p. 1916)
Goldsmith, Rose. How Did the Vikings Come to Canada? (p. 806)
—Over & Under. (p. 1313)
Goldsmith, Tom, illus. see Eugster, Rachel.
Goldsmith, Tom, illus. see Linden, Joanne.
Goldson, Ashea S. Jayden & the Magic Pants. (p. 910)
Goldstein, A. Nancy, illus. see Williams, Laura E.
Goldstein, Alrica, ed. Polly Pocket Jumbo Color & Activity Book. (p. 1381)
—Polly Pocket Stylin' Color & Activity Book. (p. 1381)
Goldstein, Ann, tr. see Lakhous, Amara.
Goldstein, Bobby. Story of the Pink Gorilla Monster. (p. 1662)
Goldstein, Donald M., ed. see Ugaki, Matome.
Goldstein, Jessica & Inker, Inna, eds. Let My People Go! Carol, Racklin-Siegel, illus. (p. 994)
Goldstein, Joyce Esersky. Solo Suppers: Simple Delicious Meals to Cook for Yourself. Swinks, Judi, photos by. (p. 1608)
Goldstein, Lori A. Becoming Jinn. (p. 156)
Goldstein, Margaret, jt. auth. see Lindop, Edmund.
Goldstein, Margaret J. British in America. (p. 229)
—Bulgaria in Pictures. (p. 240)
—Earth. (p. 495)
—Everything You Need to Know about Multiple Sclerosis. (p. 545)
—Fuel under Fire: Petroleum & Its Perils. (p. 646)
—Haiti in Pictures. (p. 736)
—Irish in America. (p. 887)
—Israel in Pictures. (p. 893)
—Japanese in America. (p. 909)
—Lebanon in Pictures. (p. 986)
—Legalizing Drugs: Crime Stopper or Social Risk? (p. 988)
—Pluto. (p. 1374)
—Saturn. (p. 1515)
—Solar System. (p. 1607)
—Stars. (p. 1643)
—Sun. (p. 1675)
—Venus. (p. 1836)
—You Are Now on Indian Land: The American Indian Occupation of Alcatraz Island, California, 1969. (p. 1973)
Goldstein, Margaret J., jt. auth. see Gitlin, Martin.
Goldstein, Margaret J., jt. auth. see Taus-Bolstad, Stacy.
Goldstein, Mona Pastroff. Friends Forever: The Good Fight. (p. 638)
Goldstein, Monica. Children Go Green: Bus trip to Little Stars Elementary. (p. 302)
Goldstein, Natalie. Animal Hunting & Feeding. (p. 78)
—Arthropods at Sea: Crustaceans. (p. 103)
—Drought & Heat Waves: A Practical Survival Guide. (p. 486)
—Droughts & Heat Waves: A Practical Survival Guide. (p. 486)
—Germ Theory. (p. 666)
—Global Warming. (p. 684)
—How Do We Know the Nature of the Ocean? (p. 808)
—John Muir. (p. 922)
—Parkinson's Disease. (p. 1325)
—Photosynthesis & Other Plant Life Processes. (p. 1353)
—Vaccines. (p. 1830)
—Viruses. (p. 1844)
Goldstein, Natalie, jt. auth. see Campbell, Margaret Christine.
Goldstein, Natalie & Lockwood, Julie L. Biodiversity. (p. 188)
Goldstein, Phyllis. Uniquely Connecticut (p. 1818)
Goldstein, Rose B. Songs to Share. Schloss, E., illus. (p. 1612)
Goldstein, Sam, jt. auth. see Zentall, Sydney.
Goldstein, Sam & Desisto, Allie. Some Kids Just Can't Sit Still! Desisto, Allie, illus. (p. 1609)
Goldstein, Sam, et al. Angry Children, Worried Parents: Seven Steps to Help Families Manage Anger. (p. 75)
—Seven Steps to Help Your Child Worry Less: A Family Guide. (p. 1555)
Goldstein, Sidney. Wine Lover Cooks with Wine: Great Recipes for the Essential Ingredient. Moore, Paul, photos by. (p. 1936)
Goldstein, Sol. Baby Crane's Tale. (p. 125)
Goldstein, William. My Blood Feet. (p. 1198)
Goldston, Juli-Ette Robin. Bowtie Brownlee Goes to School. (p. 216)
Goldstone, Bruce. 100 Ways to Celebrate 100 Days. Goldstone, Bruce, illus. (p. 1999)
—Awesome Autumn. Goldstone, Bruce, photos by. (p. 121)
—Great Estimations. Goldstone, Bruce, illus. (p. 715)
—Greater Estimations. Goldstone, Bruce, illus. (p. 719)
—I See a Pattern Here. Goldstone, Bruce, illus. (p. 845)
—That's a Possibility! A Book about What Might Happen. (p. 1726)
Goldstone, Bruce & Poortvliet, Rien. Gnome's Christmas. (p. 685)
Goldstrom, Robert, illus. see Durango, Julia & Trupiano, Katie Belle.
Goldsworthy, Kaite. Aguila de Cabeza Blanca. (p. 30)
—Bald Eagle with Code. (p. 133)
—Burj Khalifa. (p. 243)
—Canada. (p. 260)
—Chichen Itza. (p. 299)
—Electricity. (p. 509)
—France. (p. 627)
—Gabrielle Giffords. (p. 652)
—Grey Cup. (p. 723)
—Halloween. (p. 737)
—Magnetism. (p. 1075)
—Monte Rushmore. (p. 1170)
—Mount Rushmore. (p. 1180)
—Mount Rushmore with Code. (p. 1180)
—Otters. (p. 1307)
—Producers. (p. 1409)
—St. Paul's Cathedral. (p. 1638)
Goldsworthy, Kaite, jt. auth. see Yasuda, Anita.
Goldsworthy, Katie, jt. auth. see Yasuda, Anita.
Goldsworthy, Steve. Alamo. (p. 33)
—Alamo with Code. (p. 33)
—Aleuts. (p. 35)
—Antarctica. (p. 88)
—Baseball. (p. 140)
—Brazil. (p. 224)
—Cheetahs. (p. 296)
—China. (p. 306)
—Constellations. (p. 359)
—Daredevil's Guide to Stunts (p. 406)
—Edward Kennedy. (p. 505)
—Estatua de la Libertad. (p. 538)
—Famous Explorers. (p. 569)
—Golf. (p. 696)
—Kremlin. (p. 967)
—Leopards. (p. 993)
—Mark Zuckerberg. (p. 1095)
—Municipal Government. (p. 1191)
—Pentagon. (p. 1338)
—Philippines. (p. 1350)
—Politics: African American History. (p. 1381)
—Puerto Rico. (p. 1415)
—Richard Branson. (p. 1469)
—Sarah Palin. (p. 1514)
—Scorching Supercars. (p. 1530)
—Soccer. (p. 1603)
—Statue of Liberty with Code. (p. 1645)
—Steve Jobs. (p. 1649)
—Tennis. (p. 1720)
—Travel Green. (p. 1780)
—World War I: 1914-1918. (p. 1958)
—Zombies: The Truth Behind History's Terrifying Flesh-Eaters. (p. 1988)
Goldsworthy, Steve, jt. auth. see Morrison, J. A.
Goldthorpe, Jake. Mommy! Daddy! Help! There's a Monster in My Room! (p. 1162)
Gold-Vukson, Marji. Grandpa & Me on Tu B'Shevat. Evans, Leslie, illus. (p. 709)
—Shapes of My Jewish Year. Springer, Sally, illus. (p. 1561)
—Sounds of My Jewish Year. Urban, Suzanne, illus. (p. 1615)
Gold-Vukson, Marji E. Numbers of My Jewish Year. Oeltjenbruns, Joni, illus. (p. 1272)
Goldwater, Mitchell. Molly Goes to the Farmer's Market: Use Place Value & Properties of Operations to Add. (p. 1160)
Golembe, Carla. Story of Hula. (p. 1658)
Golembe, Carla, illus. see Heiligman, Deborah.
Golembe, Carla, illus. see Tomecek, Steve.
Golen, Jessica, illus. see Plourde, Paulette.
Golenbock, Peter. ABCs of Baseball. Andreasen, Dan, illus. (p. 4)
—Hank Aaron: Brave in Every Way. Lee, Paul, illus. (p. 742)
—Miracle: Bobby Allison & the Saga of the Alabama Gang. (p. 1148)
Golert, Amanda, illus. see van der Zande, Irene.
Golf, Cali. Umkhuba: The Journal. (p. 1810)
Goliger, Janet. I Need to Be SAFE I'm Worth It! How to Protect Your Child from Danger. Bond, Amy, ed. (p. 844)
Golightly, Anne. Amelia Earhart: Female Aviator. (p. 58)
Golightly, Anne, jt. auth. see Mills, Nathan.
Golightly, Holly. School Bites: Blood Drinking 101 (p. 1522)
—Witches n Whatnot. (p. 1941)
Golightly, Holly, creator. School Bites. (p. 1522)
Golino, Mirto, illus. see Curtiss, A. B.
Golio, Gary. Bird & Diz. Young, Ed, illus. (p. 190)
—Jimi: Sounds Like a Rainbow - A Story of the Young Jimi Hendrix. Steptoe, Javaka, illus. (p. 918)
—Spirit Seeker: John Coltrane's Musical Journey. Gutierrez, Rudy, illus. (p. 1628)
—When Bob Met Woody: The Story of the Young Bob Dylan. Burckhardt, Marc, illus. (p. 1901)
Golio, Janet & Golio, Mike. Present from the Past. (p. 1396)
—Puzzle from the Past. (p. 1421)
Golio, Mike, jt. auth. see Golio, Janet.
Golke, Kristi Stenberg. Grape Meets Billy: The Bubblegum Gang. (p. 710)
Gollahon, Carleen Anderson. Sophie & the Mysterious Ring. (p. 1613)
Gollan, Stewart, illus. see Carbon, Sally & Langer, Justin.
Golliher, Bill. Best of Sabrina the Teenage Witch. G!, Holly, illus. (p. 170)
Golliher, Bill, illus. see Holland, Beth.
Golliher, Bill & Vaughan, Jack. Webber Interactive WH Questions Level 2: Whcd22. (p. 1870)
Gollogly, Gene, jt. auth. see Cordova, Amy.
Gollub, Matthew. Cool Melons - Turn to Frogs! The Life & Poems of Issa. (p. 364)
—Cool Melons-Turn to Frogs! The Life & Poems of Issa Stone, Kazuko G., illus. (p. 364)
—Jazz Fly 2: The Jungle Pachanga. Hanke, Karen, illus. (p. 911)
—Ten Oni Drummers. Stone, Kazuko G., illus. (p. 1719)
—Twenty-Five Mixtec Cats. Martinez, Leovigildo, illus. (p. 1801)
—Uncle Snake. Martinez, Leovigildo, illus. (p. 1812)
Gollub, Matthew W. Twenty-five Mixtec Cats. Martinez, Leovigildo, illus. (p. 1801)
Golly, Annemieke, jt. auth. see Sprague, Jeff.
Gologan, Trena. Alexandru's Gift. (p. 37)
—Butterflies to Remember. (p. 247)
—Esther's Younique Crown. (p. 538)
—Grandparents are Special. (p. 709)
Golosi, Rosanne. Best Friends Forever! Martini, Angela, illus. (p. 169)
Golson Books, Ltd. Staff. Handbooks to Life in America (p. 740)
Golson Books, Ltd. Staff & Carlisle, Rodney P. Day by Day: The Twenties (p. 412)
—Thirties (p. 1735)
Golson, J. Geoffrey, jt. ed. see Carlisle, Rodney P.
Golston, Sydele E. Death Penalty. (p. 420)
Golub, Osu. Penguins Go for the Gold. (p. 1337)
Golubeva, Evgeniia, illus. see Marshall, Linda Elovitz.
Golus, Carrie. Biography Russell Simmons. (p. 189)
—Josh Gibson. (p. 926)
—Muhammad Ali. (p. 1189)
—Russell Simmons: From Def Jam to Super Rich. (p. 1498)
—Take A Stand! What You Can Do about Bullying. (p. 1696)
—Tupac Shakur. (p. 1797)
Goly, Rozz. WOB: Where Does Bubblegum Come From? (p. 1943)
Goman, Carol Kinsey, jt. auth. see Jackson, Donna M.
Gomberg, David, ed. see Balestier, Courtney.
Gomberg, David, jt. auth. see Heimberg, Justin.
Gomberg, David, jt. ed. see Heimberg, Justin.
Gombert, Bobby, illus. see Hutchens, David.
Gombinski, Rita, illus. see Winitz, Harris, et al.
Gomboli, Mario. Abajo el Miedo! (p. 2)
—Comer Bien, Saber Comer. (p. 348)
—Ecoeducacion. (p. 502)
—Educacion Vial. (p. 505)
—Lavarse Es Divertido. (p. 980)
—Nadie Es Perfecto. (p. 1227)
Gombrich, E. H. Little History of the World: Illustrated Edition. (p. 1029)
—Little History of the World. (p. 1029)
—Little History of the World. Mustill, Caroline, tr. from GER. (p. 1029)
—Preference for the Primitive: Episodes in the History of Western Taste & Art. (p. 1395)
—Story of Art. (p. 1657)
Gomdori Co. Staff & Han, Hyun-dong. Survive! Inside the Human Body, Vol. 1: The Digestive System. (p. 1687)
—Survive! Inside the Human Body, Vol. 2: The Circulatory System. (p. 1687)
—Survive! Inside the Human Body, Vol. 3: The Nervous System. (p. 1687)
Gomel, Luc. Face-to-Face with the Ant: Energetic Worker. Amann, Remy & Stoffel, Dominique, photos by. (p. 560)
Gomer, Gwasg, jt. auth. see Huws, Emily.
Gomer, William, illus. see Bronson, Cary.
Gomes, Angus, illus. see Pulford, Elizabeth.
Gomes, Barbara K. Esau at the Big House. (p. 534)
Gomes, Filomena. My Mom Loves Me More Than Sushi Spires, Ashley, illus. (p. 1214)
—My Mom Loves Me More Than Sushi. Spires, Ashley, illus. (p. 1214)
Gomes, John, illus. see Curtis, Jennifer Keats.
Gomes, John, illus. see Keats Curtis, Jennifer.
Gomes, John, photos by see Curtis, Jennifer Keats.
Gomes, Julie. ABC Exercise with Me. Dungan, Julia, illus. (p. 3)
Gomes, Linda Nunes. Special Words: A Story about Multicultural Families & Their Pets. Levine, Lenora D., illus. (p. 1623)
Gomez, Alonso Restrepo. Antiguos Insectos: Los Sobrevivientes A los Dinosaurios. (p. 89)
Gomez, Blanca, illus. see Shannon, George.
Gomez Buendia, Blanca Ines & Henao De Brigard, Luis Carlos, compiled by. Artesanías de la Palabra. (p. 103)
Gomez Campo, Fernando. Al Final de la Noche. (p. 32)
Gómez, Carlos Humberto. Nos Comunicamos 1. (p. 1266)
—Nos Comunicamos 2. (p. 1266)
—Nos Comunicamos 4. (p. 1266)
—Nos Comunicamos 6. (p. 1266)
—Nos Comunicamos Kindergarten. (p. 1266)
—Workbook 1. (p. 1952)
—Workbook 2. (p. 1952)
—Workbook 3. (p. 1952)
—Workbook 4. (p. 1952)
—Workbook 6. (p. 1952)
—Workbook Kindergarten. (p. 1952)
Gómez Cerda, Alfredo. Barro de Medellín/ Mud of Medellin. Lopez, Xan, illus. (p. 140)
Gómez Cerdá, Alfredo. Botín de Atolondrado. (p. 215)
—Monstruo y la Bibliotecaria. (p. 1170)
Gómez Cerdá, Alfredo, jt. auth. see Equipo Staff.
Gómez Cerdá, Alfredo, et al. Dos Plumas de Aguila. Puebla, Teo, illus. (p. 472)
Gomez, Eddie Martinez, illus. see Anza, Ana Luisa.
Gomez, Elena. World of Prayers. (p. 1957)
Gomez, Elena, illus. see Emmett, Jonathan.
Gomez, Elena, illus. see Morgan, Michaela.
Gomez, Elena, illus. see Scott-Brown, Anna.
Gomez, Elisa, tr. see Paddock, Susan Star.
Gomez, Elizabeth, illus. see Argueta, Jorge & Alvarez, Cecilia Concepcion.
Gómez, Elizabeth, illus. see Argueta, Jorge.
Gómez, Elizabeth, illus. see Herrera, Juan Felipe.
Gomez, Georgina M. Argentina's Parallel Currency: The Economy of the Poor (p. 98)
Gomez, Jose Angel. Five Plus Two Equals Twelve: A Story about a Great Sowing & Reaping Miracle. (p. 601)
Gomez, Leticia & Rozario, Paul A. Bolivia. (p. 208)
Gomez, Luis Marcelino. Memorias de Angola: Cuentos Africanos. Vallejo, Esperanza, illus. (p. 1126)
Gomez, Marcela, illus. see Flor Ada, Alma.
Gomez, Mercedes. Komok, Nokek y los Flamencos. Castillo, Guillermo Graco, illus. (p. 966)
Gomez, Nancy McKell. Gracie Grey. (p. 705)
—Little Sylvia Seagull. (p. 1037)
Gomez, Nicole. Missing Piece. (p. 1152)
Gomez, Obed, illus. see Caraballo, Samuel.
Gomez, Patricia, jt. auth. see Jordan, Sara.
Gomez, Patricio, illus. see Santirso, Liliana.
Gomez, Patricio, illus. see Sarduy, Severo.
Gomez, Rebecca. Albert Einstein. (p. 34)
—George Washington Carver. (p. 664)
—Graduation Day at Elf School. (p. 705)
—Happy Easter, Hello Kitty! (p. 745)
—Jackie Robinson. (p. 903)
—Sally Ride. (p. 1505)
—Thomas Edison. (p. 1738)
—Thomas Jefferson. (p. 1739)
Gomez, Rebecca & ABDO Publishing Company Staff. First Biographies (p. 593)
Gomez, Rebecca J., jt. auth. see Schwartz, Corey Rosen.
Gomez, Rocio, ed. see Liberto, Lorenzo.
Gomez, Rocio, tr. see Liberto, Lorenzo.
Gomez, Sally. Too Many Freckles! Mitchell, Hazel, illus. (p. 1766)
Gomez Seitz, M. Stella. Master Cookie-Maker: A True Life Story for Children. (p. 1103)
Gomez, Selena. Selena Gomez Style Guide. (p. 1549)
Gomez, Sergio, illus. see Torres, Jotam D.
Gomez, Sonia & Benchmark Education Co., LLC Staff. It Can Fit! (p. 893)
Gomez, Yuliana. Bedtime Explorers!/¡Exploradores a la Hora de Dormir! (Dora the Explorer) Random House, illus. (p. 156)
—UmiCar's Big Race/la Gran Carrera de UmiCar (Team Umizoomi) Random House, illus. (p. 1810)
Gomez, Yuliana, jt. auth. see Lewman, David.
Gomez, Yuliana, tr. see Lewman, David.
Gomez, Yuliana, tr. see Tillworth, Mary.
Gomez-Centurion, Carlos. Armada Invencible. (p. 99)
Gomi, Taro. Bus Stops. (p. 244)
—Cheer up Doodle Book. (p. 296)
—Doodles: A Really Giant Coloring & Doodling Book. (p. 469)
—Everyone Poops. (p. 544)
—Great Day. (p. 715)
—Grumpy Doodle Book. (p. 727)
—Happy Doodle Book. (p. 745)
—Hide & Seek. (p. 776)
—Mommy! Mommy! (p. 1162)
—My Friends. (p. 1209)
—My Friends/Mis Amigos. (p. 1209)
—Peekaboo! (p. 1335)
—Play All Day: More Than 100 Punch-Out Pieces! (p. 1371)
—Scribbles: A Really Giant Drawing & Coloring Book. (p. 1533)
—Story Doodles Place Mats. (p. 1657)
—Taro Gomi's Playful Puzzles for Little Hands: 60+ Guessing Games, Twisty Mazes, Logic Puzzles, & More! (p. 1706)
—Wake up Doodle Book. (p. 1853)
—Wiggle! (p. 1927)
—Yummy Doodles Place Mats. (p. 1983)
Gomi, Taro & Chronicle Books Staff. Doodle 123! A Really Giant Doodling & Drawing Book. (p. 469)
Gomi, Taro & Cosmic Debris Etc., Inc. Staff. Squiggles: A Really Giant Drawing & Painting Book. (p. 1637)
Gommer, Viola Ruelke, jt. auth. see Simons, Rae.
Gomolski, Mark F. Ginny's Adventures: Little Ginny. (p. 677)
Gompertz, Haley. Pluto's Planet Problems. (p. 1374)
Gompper, Gail. Every Day by the Bay. Gompper, Gail, illus. (p. 542)
Gon, Adriano, illus. see Dunn, Opal.
Gon, Adriano, illus. see Jarman, Julia.
Gon, Zang Sung, jt. auth. see O'Donnell, Kevin.
Gonçalves da Silva, Fabio, illus. see Janesh, Ron.
Goncalves, Regina. Mathematics - what beast Is This? (p. 1108)
Goncharik, Irina, ed. see AZ Books Staff.
Gondek, Heather. Who's in the Jungle? Lift-the-Flap 'n' Learn. Gilvan-Cartwright, Chris, illus. (p. 1920)
Gondek, Heather J. Who's on the Farm? Lift-the-Flap 'n' Learn Book. Gilvan-Cartwright, Chris, illus. (p. 1921)
Gonder, Glen W. Poudre Canyon. Gonder, Sharon J., ed. (p. 1389)
Gonder, Sharon J., ed. see Gonder, Glen W.
Gondosch, Linda. How Did Tea & Taxes Spark a Revolution? And Other Questions about the Boston Tea Party. (p. 806)
—Where Did Sacagawea Join the Corps of Discovery? And Other Questions about the Lewis & Clark Expedition. (p. 1906)
Goneau, Martin, illus. see Cleary, Brian P.
Goneau, Martin, illus. see Cleary, Brian P. & Nelson, Jennifer K.
Goneau, Martin, jt. auth. see Cleary, Brian P.
Gongora, Oscar, tr. see Beylon, Cathy.
Gongora, Oscar, tr. see Petruccio, Steven.
Gonick, Larry. Cartoon History of the Modern World: From Columbus to the U. S. Constitution. Pt. 1, Vol. 6 (p. 273)

—Kokopelli & Company in Attack of the Smart Pies. (p. 966)
Gonina, Luba, illus. see Harary, Keith.
Goniwicha, William. Spike a Relli: The Mini Doberman. (p. 1627)
—Spike a Relli: A Week at the Lake. (p. 1627)
Gonnard, Christel. Planet of the Night Globes. (p. 1368)
Gonnard, Christel, et al. Planet of Okidians. (p. 1367)
Gonne, Maud, illus. see Young, Ella.
Gonsalves, Gloria D. Diamonds Forever: Never Let Your Inner Child Stop from Glittering. (p. 434)
Gonsalves, Rob, illus. see Thomson, Sarah L.
Gonsalves, Robert, illus. see Thomson, Sarah L.
Gonsalves, Samantha. Magic Archive. (p. 1071)
Gonsalves, Theresa J. Man in the Woods: Based on a True Story. (p. 1085)
Gonyea, Maria. Princess Maria. (p. 1404)
Gonyea, Mark. Book about Color: A Clear & Simple Guide for Young Artists. Gonyea, Mark, illus. (p. 210)
—Counting on Letters: From A to Z & 1 to 26. (p. 371)
—Spooky Box. Gonyea, Mark, illus. (p. 1631)
Gonzales, Adele J. Deepening Our Prayer: Participant's Guide. (p. 423)
Gonzales Bertrand, Diane. Sofia & the Purple Dress / Sofia y el Vestido Morado. Baeza Ventura, Gabriela, tr. (p. 1605)
—There's a Name for This Feeling / Hay un Nombre para lo Que Siento. Baeza Ventura, Gabriela, tr. (p. 1731)
Gonzales, Brittany, jt. auth. see Hillstead, McKensy.
Gonzales, Chuck, illus. see Barbo, Maria S.
Gonzales, Chuck, illus. see Borgenicht, David & Epstein, Robin.
Gonzales, Chuck, illus. see Borgenicht, David, et al.
GONZALES, Chuck, illus. see Mayer, Kirsten.
Gonzales, Chuck, illus. see Van King, L.
Gonzales, Chuck, illus. see Williams, Suzanne.
Gonzales, Diana, ed. see Fitzgibbon, Diana.
Gonzales, Doreen. Arctic Ocean: A MyReportLinks. com Book. (p. 96)
—Are We There Yet? Using Map Scales (p. 96)
—Atlantic Ocean: A MyReportLinks. com Book. (p. 112)
—Bats in the Dark. (p. 145)
—Corn/Maíz. (p. 367)
—Crickets in the Dark. (p. 382)
—Earthquakes. (p. 497)
—Floods & Tsunamis. (p. 605)
—Frigid Arctic Ocean. (p. 639)
—Grand Canyon National Park: Adventure, Explore, Discover. (p. 707)
—Huge Pacific Ocean. (p. 825)
—Hurricanes. (p. 830)
—Indian Ocean: A MyReportLinks. com Book. (p. 871)
—Look at the Second Amendment: To Keep & Bear Arms. (p. 1049)
—Mighty Atlantic Ocean. (p. 1139)
—Owls in the Dark. (p. 1315)
—Pacific Ocean: A MyReportLinks. com Book. (p. 1317)
—Raccoons in the Dark. (p. 1430)
—Rocky Mountain National Park: Adventure, Explore, Discover. (p. 1484)
—Scorpions in the Dark. (p. 1530)
—Secret of the Manhattan Project: Stories in American History. (p. 1542)
—Secret of the Manhattan Project. (p. 1542)
—Seven Wonders of the Modern World: A MyReportLinks. com Book. (p. 1555)
—Silly Cat Jokes to Tickle Your Funny Bone. (p. 1575)
—Skunks in the Dark. (p. 1586)
—Southern Ocean: A MyReportLinks. com Book. (p. 1617)
—Stormy Southern Ocean. (p. 1656)
—Thunderstorms. (p. 1746)
—Tornadoes. (p. 1770)
—Tropical Indian Ocean. (p. 1789)
—Up North & down South: Using Map Directions (p. 1824)
—Volcanoes. (p. 1849)
—What Are the 7 Wonders of the Modern World? (p. 1879)
Gonzales, Doreen & Graham, Amy. What Are the 7 Wonders of the Natural World? (p. 1879)
Gonzales, Doreen & Sanz, Ma Pilar. Corn: Maíz. (p. 367)
Gonzales, Felipe C. Little Folk Stories & Tales by Don Pablo: Bilingual Stories in Spanish & English = Chistes y Cuentos de Don Pablo: Cuentos Bilingües en Español e Inglés. (p. 1027)
Gonzales, Linda, ed. see Kiraithe, Jackie.
Gonzales, Lisa. Arroyo. (p. 101)
Gonzales, Nana, illus. see Crespo, Ana.
Gonzales, Rave And Linda. Saved: A Short Story. (p. 1517)
Gonzales, Rebecca. Beauty & the Basketcase. (p. 154)
Gonzales, Sharon. Airport Explorers: 2008 Activity Book. (p. 32)
Gonzales, Todd. Palestine in the News: Past, Present, & Future. (p. 1319)
Gonzalez, Ada Acosta. Mayte & the Bogeyman/Mayte y el Cuco. Rodriguez, Christina, illus. (p. 1113)
González, Althea, jt. auth. see Fogle, Llynda.
Gonzalez, Ana Carlota. Cucarachita Martina. Chaves, Guido, illus. (p. 389)
González, Angel Luis, illus. see Luna, Sagrario & Alcott, Louisa May.
González, Angel Luis, tr. see Luna, Sagrario & Alcott, Louisa May.
Gonzalez, Ashley, illus. see Kagna, Barbara.
Gonzalez, Aurora Adriana. Mystery of Leo: El misterio de Leo. Ballester Kniska, Lorena Ivonne, ed. (p. 1224)
Gonzalez Bertrand, Diane. Ruiz Street Kids (Los Muchachos de la Calle Ruiz) Ventura, Gabriela Baeza, tr. (p. 1495)
Gonzalez, Blanca Maciel. Cathy Meets Sofi. (p. 280)
Gonzalez, Bruno. Savior of the Rain Forest: An Adventure of Zalvator the Black Panther. (p. 1518)
Gonzalez, Carlos Mario, tr. see Hoffmann, E. T. A.
Gonzalez, Carolina Reoyo, jt. ed. see Gonzalez, Marisa Javierre.
Gonzalez, Christina Diaz. Red Umbrella. (p. 1455)
—Thunderous Whisper. (p. 1746)
Gonzalez, Crysol, illus. see Blumenthal, Bliss & Alarcon, Claudia.
Gonzalez, David J. There Are No Space Aliens! 12 Biblical Points Disproving Space Aliens. (p. 1729)
Gonzalez, Diana, jt. auth. see Weyn, Suzanne.
Gonzalez, Ed. DinoSk8ers a Counting Coloring Book. (p. 445)
Gonzalez, Emerald. Emmy. (p. 520)
Gonzalez, Francisco, illus. see Garrido, Felipe.
Gonzalez, Gabriela & Triana, Gaby. Backstage Pass. (p. 130)
Gonzalez, Genaro. So-Called Vacation. (p. 1601)
Gonzalez, Henry, illus. see Buitrago, Fanny.
Gonzalez, Henry, illus. see Kipling, Rudyard.
Gonzalez, Henry, illus. see Nino, Jairo Anibal.
Gonzalez, Henry, illus. see Niño, Hugo.
Gonzalez, Henry, illus. see Roman, Celso.
Gonzalez, Javier A., illus. see Lindeen, Mary.
Gonzalez Jensen, Margarita. Botas Negras. Sanchez, Enrique O., illus. (p. 215)
Gonzalez, Jorge, jt. auth. see Gunderson, Jessica.
Gonzalez, Jorge, jt. auth. see Hoena, Blake A.
Gonzalez, Jorge & Collodi, Carlo. Pinocchio Ruiz, Alfonso, illus. (p. 1360)
Gonzalez, Jorge & Shakespeare, William. Romeo & Juliet Cabrera, Eva, illus. (p. 1486)
Gonzalez, Jorge H., photos by see Neira, Maria Lia.
Gonzalez, Jose Antonio, illus. see Laban, Terry.
Gonzalez, Jose Cruz, see Cruz Gonzalez, Jose.
Gonzalez., Jose L., illus. see Adams, Marlene.
González, Juan Carlos. Francois Truffaut -una vida hecha Cine. (p. 628)
Gonzalez, L. M. R. Gifts Lucy. Terrible Monster. (p. 1721)
Gonzalez, Liana R., creator. Where These Feet Lead. (p. 1910)
Gonzalez, Libia. Geografia e Historia de los Estados Unidos. (p. 662)
Gonzalez, Lissette. Astronauts in Action. (p. 109)
—Bomb Squads in Action. (p. 208)
—Frequently Asked Questions about Human Papillomavirus. (p. 636)
—Police in Action. (p. 1380)
—Search & Rescue Specialists. (p. 1537)
—Stunt Performers & Stunt Doubles. (p. 1670)
—U. S. Military: Defending the Nation. (p. 1806)
González, Lola, et al. Rafael Alberti y los Niños. Ruiz Navarro, Jose, illus. (p. 1433)
Gonzalez, Lucia. Bossy Gallito. (p. 215)
Gonzalez, Lucia M. & Delacre, Lulu. Storyteller's Candle. (p. 1664)
Gonzalez, Luis Daniel. Guia de Clasicos de la Literatura Infantil y Juvenil 3. (p. 729)
Gonzalez, Maité. Magic Blue Coral. (p. 1071)
—Mrs Turtle & the Magic Pearl. (p. 1188)
Gonzalez, Maite. Tanya & Magicfly. (p. 1705)
Gonzalez, Margarita E., ed. see Rosa-Mendoza, Gladys.
Gonzalez, Marisa Javierre & Gonzalez, Carolina Reoyo, eds. Nuevo Espasa Ilustrado 2003: Diccionario Enciclopedico. (p. 1270)
Gonzalez, Maya Christina. My Colors, My World. (p. 1200)
—Yo Se Que el Rio Me Ama. (p. 1971)
Gonzalez, Maya Christina, illus. see Alarcón, Francisco X.
Gonzalez, Maya Christina, illus. see Alarcón, Francisco X. & Alarcon, Francisco.
Gonzalez, Maya Christina, illus. see Anzaldúa, Gloria.
Gonzalez, Maya Christina, illus. see Gerson, Mary-Joan.
Gonzalez, Maya Christina, illus. see Perez, Amada Irma & Children's Book Press Staff.
Gonzalez, Maya Christina, illus. see Pérez, Amada Irma.
Gonzalez, Maya Christina & Goldberg, Dana. Llámeme Árbol. (p. 1043)
Gonzalez, Maya Christina & Perez, Amada Irma. My Very Own Room: Mi Propio Cuartito. (p. 1221)
Gonzalez, Maytee Aspuro Y. Hesed. (p. 774)
Gonzalez, Militza. Dear Bully, I Send Blessings Your Way! (p. 418)
Gonzalez Montes, Fidencio & Beltran, Leonardo Arenas. Ultima Vida de un Gato. (p. 1809)
Gonzalez, Noni. Dream of Wings. Gonzalez, Tom, illus. (p. 483)
—Kubla, a Koi Story. Gonzalez, Tom, illus. (p. 968)
Gonzalez, Owner Lucy. Puppy Trapped in Cyberspace! (p. 1418)
Gonzalez, Pedro Julio, illus. see Huelin, Jodi.
Gonzalez, Rafael. Cookie Boy! (p. 361)
Gonzalez, Ralfka & Ruiz, Ana. Mi Primer Libro de Dichos. (p. 1133)
Gonzalez, Ray. conejito Claudio. (p. 356)
—Conejito Claudio (G) Para Bebés de 1 a 3 Años. Giannini, Claudia, tr. (p. 356)
Gonzalez Reyes, Amaury. De Mis Poemas Vividos. Hernández, René Mario, ed. (p. 416)
Gonzalez, Ricky, illus. see Blumenthal, Bliss & Alarcon, Claudia.
González, Rigoberto, jt. auth. see Gonzalez, Rigoberto.
González, Rigoberto & Alvarez, Cecilia Concepcion. Antonio's Card/la Tarjeta de Antonio. (p. 90)
Gonzalez, Rigoberto & González, Rigoberto. Soledad Sigh-Sighs. Ibarra, Rosa, illus. (p. 1607)
Gonzalez, Santiago, illus. see Delgado, Francisco.
Gonzalez, Santiago, illus. see Iturralde, Edna.
Gonzalez, Tesa, illus. see Ballesteros, Jose Manuel & Manuel, Ballesteros Pastor José.
Gonzalez, Tesa, illus. see Javaloyes, Inigo & Iñigo, Javaloyes.
Gonzalez, Thomas, illus. see Bernier-Grand, Carmen T.
Gonzalez, Thomas, illus. see Deedy, Carmen Agra.
Gonzalez, Thomas, illus. see Kittinger, Jo S.
Gonzalez, Thomas, illus. see Markle, Sandra.
Gonzalez, Thomas, illus. see McGinty, Alice B.
Gonzalez, Thomas, tr. see Hipp, Andrew.
Gonzalez, Tom, illus. see Gonzalez, Noni.
Gonzalez, Tomas, tr. see Egan, Tracie.
Gonzalez, Tomas, tr. see Harte, May.
Gonzalez, Tomas, tr. see Heller, Daryl.
Gonzalez, Tomas, tr. see Hipp, Andrew.
Gonzalez, Tomas, tr. see Houghton, Gillian.
Gonzalez, Tony & Brown, Greg. Tony Gonzalez: Catch & Connect. (p. 1766)
Gonzalez-Gallarza, Isabel, tr. see McCaughrean, Geraldine.
Gonzalez-Jensen, Margarita. Bird Who Ate Too Much. Wolff, Jason, illus. (p. 190)
Gonzalez-Villariny, Natali. Mirando y Mirando: La Gran Aventura. Cancio, Damian, illus. (p. 1149)
Gonzalo, Angela. Pig, Bear, & the Pear: The Pear Meets the Pig & Bear. (p. 1357)
Gonzßlez Valdts, Alberto Domingo. Sueños de Obama/Obama's Dreams. (p. 1672)
Goo, Maurene. Since You Asked... (p. 1578)
Goobie, Beth. Before Wings. (p. 159)
—Dream Where the Losers Go (p. 484)
—Fixed (p. 601)
—Hello, Groin (p. 764)
—Jason's Why (p. 910)
—Kicked Out. (p. 951)
—Lottery (p. 1057)
—Something Girl (p. 1610)
—Sticks & Stones (p. 1650)
—Throne (p. 1744)
—Who Owns Kelly Paddik? (p. 1917)
Goobie, Beth & Fernández, Queta. Ni un Día Más (p. 1250)
—Que Dirán (p. 1423)
Gooch, T. It Was My Star. (p. 894)
Gooch, Thelma, illus. see Malot, Hector & Crewe-Jones, Florence.
Gooch-Anderson, Stacy. Legend of the Star. (p. 989)
Good, Andi, jt. auth. see Asquith, Ros.
Good Books. Celebrating Cat. (p. 284)
—Happy Lemonade. (p. 746)
—Joyful Sunflower. (p. 930)
Good, Cynthia, jt. auth. see Humiston, Sharon.
Good, Dinah. Stay Away from Mean Jean! (p. 1645)
Good, Jackie. Houdini the Hamster's Great Escape. (p. 802)
Good, Jason. Must. Push. Buttons! Krosoczka, Jarrett J., illus. (p. 1194)
Good, Karen, illus. see Moulton, Mark Kimball & Chalmers, Josh.
Good, Karen, illus. see Moulton, Mark.
Good, Karen H., illus. see Moulton, Mark K.
Good, Karen H., illus. see Moulton, Mark Kimball.
Good, Karen Hillard, illus. see Moulton, Mark Kimball.
Good, Karen Hillard, illus. see Moulton, Mark.
Good, Karen Hillard, jt. auth. see Moulton, Mark Kimball.
Good, Keith. Shape It! Magnificent Projects for Molding Materials. (p. 1560)
Good, Linnea, et al. Adventures of the God Detectives. (p. 23)
Good, Merle. Reuben & the Fire. (p. 1465)
Good, Phyllis Pellman. Fix-It & Forget-It Kids' Cookbook: 50 Favorite Recipes to Make in a Slow Cooker. (p. 601)
Good, Sr., jt. auth. see Good, Yvonne.
Good, Yvonne & Good, Sr. Bubble Gum & Polka Dot. (p. 233)
Goodacre, Sonia, et al. Cambridge VCE Health & Human Development Units 3 & 4 Bundle. (p. 256)
Goodale, Krystahl, illus. see Riley, Brad.
Goodall, Barry, Jr. Glory Gone Forgotten: The Untold Story of the 12th Kentucky Cavalry. Embry, Eugene, ed. (p. 685)
Goodall, Jane, et al. Harvest for Hope: A Guide to Mindful Eating. (p. 751)
Goodall, John S., illus. see Read, Miss.
Goodall, Lian. Photographing Greatness: The Story of Karsh. Thompson, Samantha, illus. (p. 1353)
—Singing Towards the Future: The Story of Portia White. (p. 1579)
Goodan, Till. Gene Autry & Raiders of the Range. (p. 660)
Goodberry, Jo, illus. see Page, Nick & Page, Claire.
Goodbody, Slim. Avoiding Injuries. McGinnis, Ben, illus. (p. 120)
—Eating Right. McGinnis, Ben, illus. (p. 501)
—Exercising. McGinnis, Ben, illus. (p. 548)
—Keeping Clean. McGinnis, Ben, illus. (p. 947)
—Keeping Safe. McGinnis, Ben, illus. (p. 947)
—Staying Well. McGinnis, Ben, illus. (p. 1645)
Goodbody, Slim & Burstein, John. Big Fat Lies: Advertising Tricks. (p. 181)
—Birds. McGinnis, Ben, illus. (p. 191)
—Cats. McGinnis, Ben, illus. (p. 280)
—Dogs. McGinnis, Ben, illus. (p. 462)
—Energy In, Energy Out: Food As Fuel. (p. 528)
—Fast Food: Slowing Us All Down. (p. 576)
—Goldfish. McGinnis, Ben, illus. (p. 695)
—Grocery Shopping: It's in the Bag. (p. 725)
—Guinea Pigs. McGinnis, Ben, illus. (p. 731)
—Looking at Labels: The Inside Story. (p. 1050)
—Million Moves: Keeping Fit. (p. 1144)
—Rabbits. McGinnis, Ben, illus. (p. 1429)
—Shape of Good Nutrition: The Food Pyramid. (p. 1560)
—Snack Attack: Unhealthy Treats. (p. 1595)
Goodboy, Mary, et al. Pump Energy Food: A Revolutionary Cookbook & Eating Plan to Create the Body of Your Dreams. (p. 1416)
Goode, Ben. Fine Art of Worrying: The Official Guide Book for Worry Warts. (p. 589)
Goode, Caroline, jt. auth. see Reber, Deborah.
Goode, Diane. Most Perfect Spot. Goode, Diane, illus. (p. 1177)
—Thanksgiving Is Here! Goode, Diane, illus. (p. 1726)
Goode, Diane, illus. see Barden, Stephanie.
Goode, Diane, illus. see Brown, Margaret Wise.
Goode, Diane, illus. see Duchess of York Staff & Ferguson, Sarah.
Goode, Diane, illus. see Feiffer, Kate.
Goode, Diane, illus. see Harper, Charise Mericle.
Goode, Diane, illus. see Primavera, Elise.
Goode, Diane, illus. see Roberts, Cokie.
Goode, Diane, illus. see Rylant, Cynthia.
Goode, Diane, jt. auth. see Hautzig, Deborah.
Goode, Jeff. PRINCESS GRAY & the BLACK & WHITE KNIGHT. (p. 1404)
—Rumpelstiltskin. (p. 1495)
Goode, John. 151 Days. (p. 2000)
—Going the Distance. (p. 693)
Goode, Laura. Sister Mischief. (p. 1581)
Goode, Suzi. Lost Wizard Series Bk 1. (p. 1057)
Goode, Teresa. Jayhawk Adventures, a Day at the Zoo. Kotrous, Chad, illus. (p. 910)
—Jayhawk Adventures, Jed's Birthday Surprise. Kotrous, Chad, illus. (p. 910)
—Wildcat Adventures: A Vacation in the Big Apple. Kotrous, Chad, illus. (p. 1931)
Goodell, Jon, illus. see Andersen, Hans Christian.
Goodell, Jon, illus. see Andrews McMeel Publishing Staff & Moore, Clement C.
Goodell, Jon, illus. see Hopkins, Jackie Mims.
Goodell, Jon, illus. see Horning, Sandra.
Goodell, Jon, illus. see Moore, Clement C.
Goodell, Jon, illus. see Publications International Ltd. Staff, ed.
Goodell, Jon, illus. see Robbins, Maria Polushkin & Polushkin Robbins, Maria.
Goodell, Mary. Chicken Pox Puppy: Kate & Jen's Daily Adventures. Goodell, Mary, illus. (p. 300)
Gooden, Sean Lawrence. Mother of the Green Bear (p. 1178)
Goodenough, Arthur. Clergy of Litchfield County. (p. 331)
Goodenough, Jerry & Read, Rupert, eds. Film As Philosophy: Essays on Cinema after Wittgenstein & Cavell. (p. 586)
Goodenow, Ellen A. My Weather Journal. (p. 1221)
Gooderham, Andrew, illus. see Walters, Eric & Walters, Christina.
Gooderham, Andrew, jt. auth. see Ruurs, Margriet.
Gooderham, Chris. Even More Wicked Rhymes. (p. 541)
—More Wicked Rhymes. (p. 1175)
—Wicked Rhymes. (p. 1927)
Goodey, Diana & Goodey, Noel. Messages (p. 1129)
Goodey, Diana, et al. Messages 3 Student's Book (p. 1129)
Goodey, Madeline. Fred & Finn. Gordon, Mike, illus. (p. 632)
Goodey, Noel, jt. auth. see Goodey, Diana.
Goodfellow, Dan, illus. see Kats, Jewel.
Goodfellow, Greg. Epilepsy. (p. 532)
Goodhart, Pippa. Big Cat. (p. 180)
—Cake Test. McCafferty, Jan, illus. (p. 252)
—Dragon Boy. Ursell, Martin, illus. (p. 476)
—Fire Cat. (p. 590)
—Fun Race. Mason, Sue, illus. (p. 648)
—Ginny's Egg. Brouwer, Aafke, illus. (p. 677)
—Hoppy Birthday, Jo-Jo! Birkett, Georgie, illus. (p. 797)
—House that Jack Built. Parker, Andy, illus. (p. 804)
—Just Imagine. Sharratt, Nick, illus. (p. 938)
—Little Nelly's Big Book. Rowland, Andy, illus. (p. 1032)
—Milly. (p. 1144)
—Nature Detectives Mason, Sue, illus. (p. 1236)
—One Windy Day: Green Banana. Cassidy, Amber, illus. (p. 1297)
—Rescued by a Dog Called Flow. Lewis, Anthony, illus. (p. 1462)
—Slow Magic. Kelly, John, illus. (p. 1591)
—What's in Store? Dreidemy, Joëlle, illus. (p. 1898)
Goodhart, Pippa & Birkett, Georgie. Hoppy Birthday, Jo-Jo! (p. 797)
Goodhart, Pippa & Goodheart, Pippa. Dragon Magic. Danson, Lesley, illus. (p. 477)
—Slow Magic. Kelly, John, illus. (p. 1591)
Goodhart, Pippa & Sharratt, Nick. You Choose! (p. 1975)
Goodheart, Pippa, jt. auth. see Goodhart, Pippa.
Goodheart-Wilcox, creator. Architecture: Residential Drafting & Design. (p. 95)
Goodhue, Thomas W. Curious Bones: Mary Anning & the Birth of Paleontology. (p. 392)
Goodier, Eleanor, et al. Vermin Family Adventures (Book 1) (p. 1837)
Goodin, Carolyn M. Candy Land. Goodin, Carolyn M., illus. (p. 261)
Goodin, Robert. Kurdles. (p. 968)
Gooding, Mel, ed. see Shrigley, David.
Gooding-Alber, Karry. Red Shoelace (p. 1455)
Goodings, Christina. Bible & Prayers for Teddy & Me. Samuel, Janet, illus. (p. 175)
—Bible Stories for Girls. Bursi, Simona, illus. (p. 176)
—Christmas Story. Maddocks, Maria, illus. (p. 315)
—Growing Green: A Young Person's Guide to Taking Care of the Planet. Furukawa, Masumi, illus. (p. 726)
—Growing Strong: A Book about Taking Care of Yourself. Furukawa, Masumi, illus. (p. 726)
—Guess Who? Noah's Ark: A Flip-The-Flap Book. Muss, Angela, illus. (p. 729)
—In the Beginning. Carletti, Emanuela, illus. (p. 865)
—Lift-the-Flap. Hudson, Annabel, illus. (p. 1014)
—Lift-the-Flap Christmas Stories. Hudson, Annabel, illus. (p. 1014)
—Looking High & Low for One Lost Sheep. Ayliffe, Alex, illus. (p. 1051)
—Lost Sheep Story. Carletti, Emanuela, illus. (p. 1056)
—My Big Bright Bible Board Book. Barker, Stephen, illus. (p. 1197)
—My Little Bible Board Book Mitchell, Melanie, illus. (p. 1212)
—My Little Bible Board Book. Mitchell, Melanie, illus. (p. 1212)
—My Look & Point Bible. Hudson, Annabel, illus. (p. 1213)
—My Look & Point First Easter. Hudson, Annabel, illus. (p. 1213)
—My Look & Point in the Beginning Stick-A-Story Book. Hudson, Annabel, illus. (p. 1213)
—My Look & Point Jonah & the Whale Stick-a-Story Book. Hudson, Annabel, illus. (p. 1213)
—My Look & Point Story of Jesus Stick-A-Story Book. Hudson, Annabel, illus. (p. 1213)
—My Noah's Ark Jigsaw Book. Elliott, Rebecca, illus. (p. 1216)
—Noah's Ark. Carletti, Emanuela, illus. (p. 1261)
—Whizzy Bizzy Christmas Fun Book. (p. 1914)
Goodings, Christina & Hudson, Annabel. My Look & Point First Christmas Stick-a-Story Book. (p. 1213)
—My Look & Point Noah. (p. 1213)
Goodisman, Leonard David. Princess Bea. (p. 1403)
Goodkind, Terry. Naked Empire. (p. 1228)
Goodlett, Liza. Getting Ready for the Show. (p. 669)
Goodman, Alison. Eon: Dragoneye Reborn. (p. 532)
—Eon. (p. 532)

G

—Last Dragoneye. (p. 977)
—Singing the Dogstar Blues. (p. 1579)
Goodman, Allegra. Other Side of the Island. (p. 1306)
Goodman, Amy & Goodman, David. Static: Government Liars, Media Cheerleaders, & the People Who Fight Back. (p. 1644)
Goodman, Carol. Blythewood. (p. 204)
—Ravencliffe. (p. 1441)
Goodman, David, jt. auth. see Goodman, Amy.
Goodman, David & Miller, Zoe. Faces. (p. 561)
—Shape. (p. 1560)
Goodman, Dena & Wellman, Kathleen. Enlightenment. (p. 530)
Goodman, Emily. Plant Secrets. Tildes, Phyllis Limbacher, illus. (p. 1369)
Goodman, Errol. I Am Helpful. (p. 833)
—I Am Helpful / Soy Acomedida. (p. 833)
Goodman, Gabriel. Alliance. (p. 47)
—Confessional. (p. 356)
—Lightning's Run. (p. 1016)
—Plague Riders. (p. 1366)
Goodman, George. Boy They Thought Never Wanted to Work. (p. 219)
Goodman, George, et al. Adventures of Wally the Wheelbarrow: Book One. (p. 24)
Goodman, Hannah R. Fear of Falling. (p. 579)
Goodman, Heidi, jt. auth. see Chen, Shan-Shan.
Goodman, James A. Two Weeks Under: The Sheppton Mine Disaster Miracle. (p. 1804)
Goodman, Jill. Mustang, the Little Dog Who Was Afraid to Go to School. (p. 1194)
Goodman, Joan. Bernard Wants a Baby. Catalano, Dominic, illus. (p. 167)
Goodman, Joan Elizabeth. Ballet Bunnies (p. 134)
—Paradise: Inspired by a True Story of Survival. (p. 1323)
Goodman, John. Percy's Magical Adventures. (p. 1341)
Goodman, John, tr. see Langlois, Florence.
Goodman, Judith. Fairy's Tale about Honesty. (p. 565)
Goodman Koz, Paula, illus. see Huggins, Peter.
Goodman Koz, Paula, illus. see Olswanger, Anna.
Goodman, Larry. Clean up the Glup! (p. 330)
—Cowboy & Other Stories. (p. 373)
Goodman, Larry, illus. see Collier, Wayne Evans.
Goodman, Leandria D. Firecracker, Firecracker, Boom, Boom, Boom! (p. 591)
Goodman, Marlene. Let's Learn English Picture Dictionary. (p. 998)
—Let's Learn German Picture Dictionary. (p. 998)
—Let's Learn Hebrew Picture Dictionary. (p. 998)
—Let's Learn Italian Picture Dictionary. (p. 998)
—Let's Learn Japanese Picture Dictionary. (p. 998)
—Let's Learn Spanish Picture Dictionary. (p. 998)
Goodman, Marlene, illus. see Passport Books Staff, ed.
Goodman, Marlene K., illus. see Stein, Larry.
Goodman, Michael. World War I Spies. (p. 1959)
Goodman, Michael E. Buffalo Bill. (p. 235)
—CIA & Other American Spies. (p. 318)
—Civil War Spies. (p. 325)
—Cold War Spies. (p. 339)
—Dark Labyrinths. (p. 407)
—Detroit - Red Wings. (p. 431)
—History of the Atlanta Falcons. (p. 784)
—History of the Carolina Panthers. (p. 784)
—History of the New York Giants. (p. 785)
—History of the New York Jets. (p. 785)
—History of the Tampa Bay Buccaneers. (p. 785)
—History of the Washington Redskins. (p. 785)
—KGB & Other Russian Spies. (p. 951)
—Modern Spies. (p. 1159)
—Philadelphia - Flyers. (p. 1350)
—Revolutionary War Spies. (p. 1467)
—SIS & Other British Spies. (p. 1581)
—Spies Around the World: The Mossad & Other Israeli Spies. (p. 1627)
—Spies Around the World: the CIA & Other American Spies. (p. 1627)
—Spies Around the World: the KGB & Other Russian Spies. (p. 1627)
—Spies Around the World: the Mossad & Other Israeli Spies. (p. 1627)
—Story of the Atlanta Braves. (p. 1660)
—Story of the Atlanta Falcons. (p. 1660)
—Story of the Boston Red Sox. (p. 1660)
—Story of the Carolina Panthers. (p. 1660)
—Story of the Cincinnati Reds. (p. 1660)
—Story of the Colorado Rockies. (p. 1660)
—Story of the Montreal Canadiens. (p. 1661)
—Story of the New Jersey Nets. (p. 1661)
—Story of the New York Giants. (p. 1661)
—Story of the New York Jets. (p. 1661)
—Story of the New York Rangers. (p. 1661)
—Story of the Philadelphia Phillies. (p. 1662)
—Story of the Pittsburgh Pirates. (p. 1662)
—Story of the San Diego Padres. (p. 1662)
—Story of the San Francisco Giants. (p. 1662)
—Story of the Washington Nationals. (p. 1662)
—Story of the Washington Redskins. (p. 1662)
—Tiger Woods. (p. 1749)
—World War II Spies. (p. 1959)
—Wyatt Earp. (p. 1966)
Goodman, Nancy. Camping Kids Adventures. (p. 257)
Goodman, Peggy. Ritzi's Bath. Bunker, Thomas, illus. (p. 1475)
Goodman, Polly. Communities Today & Tomorrow. (p. 349)
—Energy Today & Tomorrow. (p. 528)
—Food, Farming, & the Future. (p. 613)
—Food in China. (p. 613)
—Food in India. (p. 613)
—Food in Italy. (p. 613)
—Food in the Carribbean. (p. 613)
—Transportation for the Future. (p. 1779)
—Understanding Fossil Fuels. (p. 1815)
—Understanding Water Power. (p. 1816)
—Understanding Wind Power. (p. 1816)
Goodman, Polly, jt. auth. see Lawson, Julia.
Goodman, Ruth Fisher, tr. see Mark, Yudel.
Goodman, Sarah, jt. auth. see Russell, Wendy Thomas.
Goodman, Sarah & Sorkin, Louis N. Bugs - Fandex Family Field Guides. (p. 237)
Goodman, Shawn. Kindness for Weakness. (p. 957)
—Something Like Hope. (p. 1610)
Goodman, Steve. Train They Call New Orleans. McCurdy, Michael, illus. (p. 1777)
—Train They Call the City of New Orleans. McCurdy, Michael, illus. (p. 1777)
Goodman, Sue. Beginning Topology. (p. 159)
Goodman, Susan, jt. auth. see Goodman, Susan E.
Goodman, Susan E. All in Just One Cookie. Bush, Timothy, illus. (p. 44)
—Choppers! Doolittle, Michael, photos by. (p. 310)
—First Step: How One Girl Put Segregation on Trial. Lewis, Earl B., illus. (p. 597)
—Hazelle Boxberg. Ettlinger, Doris, illus. (p. 756)
—How Do You Burp in Space? And Other Tips Every Space Tourist Needs to Know. Slack, Michael, illus. (p. 808)
—How Do You Burp in Space? And Other Tips Every Space Tourist Needs to Know. Slack, Michael H., illus. (p. 808)
—It's a Dog's Life: How Man's Best Friend Sees, Hears, & Smells the World. Slonim, David, illus. (p. 895)
—Monster Trucks! Doolittle, Michael, illus. (p. 1168)
—Motorcycles! Doolittle, Michael, illus. (p. 1179)
—Robert Henry Hendershot. Ettlinger, Doris, illus. (p. 1479)
—Saber-Toothed Cats. Maguire, Kerry, illus. (p. 1499)
—Saving the Whooping Crane. Saroff, Phyllis, illus. (p. 1517)
—Saving the Whooping Crane. Saroff, Phyllis V., illus. (p. 1517)
—See How They Run: Campaign Dreams, Election Schemes, & the Race to the White House. Smith, Elwood, illus. (p. 1546)
—See How They Run. (p. 1546)
—Trains! (p. 1777)
—Trains! Doolittle, Michael, illus. (p. 1777)
—Truth about Poop & Pee: All the Facts on the Ins & Outs of Bodily Functions. Smith, Elwood H., illus. (p. 1794)
—Ultimate Field Trip #5: Blasting off to Space Academy. Doolittle, Michael J., illus. (p. 1809)
—Unseen Rainbows, Silent Songs: The World of Animal Senses. Duncan, Beverly, illus. (p. 1822)
Goodman, Susan E. & Goodman, Susan. On This Spot: An Expedition Back Through Time. Christiansen, Lee, illus. (p. 1292)
Goodman, Susan E. & National Geographic Learning Staff. India in the Past & Present. (p. 871)
Goodman, Susan E. & Smith, Michael W., Jr. Women Work for Change. (p. 1946)
Goodman, Tama, illus. see Biers-Ariel, Matt.
Goodman Wright, Shelly. Twisted Roots: The Lost Scrolls. (p. 1802)
Goodman, Yetta M. Valuing Language Study: Inquiry into Language for Elementary & Middle Schools. (p. 1831)
Goodman-Schneps, Oriana. Seventh Chime. (p. 1555)
Goodney, Diane, jt. auth. see Silas, Elizabeth.
Goodnight, Craig. Condor the Police K-9 In: Never Talk to Strangers. (p. 356)
Goodnight, Lora. Ivy Tales: The First Irish Fairy. Goins, Heather Lea, illus. (p. 901)
Goodnight, Macy. Toad & the Dragonfly. (p. 1759)
Goodnight, Rosemary. Dear Old Granny's Nursery Rymes for the 21st Century. (p. 419)
—Dear Old Granny's Nursery Rymes for the 21st Century. Turner, Michael W., illus. (p. 419)
Goodnough, David. Debate over Human Cloning. (p. 421)
Goodnow, Patti, illus. see Parker, David.
Goodpaster, Nancy, illus. see Payne, Sandy.
Goodreau, Sarah, illus. see Gehl, Laura & Aesop.
Goodrich, C. C. Barnabee: Goes to Work. (p. 139)
—Barnabee: At the Picnic. (p. 139)
—Barnabee: Goes Shopping. (p. 139)
—Barnabee: In the Meadow. (p. 139)
—Barnabee: In the Beehive. (p. 139)
—Barnabee: Meets New Friends. (p. 139)
Goodrich, Carter. Hermit Crab. Goodrich, Carter, illus. (p. 771)
—Mister Bud Wears the Cone. Goodrich, Carter, illus. (p. 1155)
—Say Hello to Zorro! Goodrich, Carter, illus. (p. 1518)
—We Forgot Brock! Goodrich, Carter, illus. (p. 1867)
—Zorro Gets an Outfit. Goodrich, Carter, illus. (p. 1990)
Goodrich, Carter & Moore, Clement C. Creature Was Stirring: One Boy's Night Before Christmas. Goodrich, Carter, illus. (p. 380)
Goodrich, Charles Augustus. Child's History of the United States. (p. 305)
Goodrich, Juliette. Little Light Shines Bright: A True Story about the World's Longest Burning Lightbulb. (p. 1030)
Goodrich, Murleen. Think! Pete. (p. 1734)
Goodrich, Olivia. Timetraveler's Guide to Roman London. (p. 1754)
Goodrich, Peter, jt. auth. see Coveleskie, Sally.
Goodrich, Samuel G. Child's History of the United States. (p. 305)
—History of All Nations, from the Earliest Periods to the Present Time. (p. 783)
Goodrich, Samuel G., see Parley, Peter, pseud.
Goodrich, Samuel G. (Samuel Griswold). Famous Men of Ancient Times: By the Author of Peter Parley's Tales. (p. 569)
Goodrich, Samuel Griswol. Peter Parleys Tales about America & Au. (p. 1347)
Goodridge, Catherine. Jane Goodall & Jane Goodall (Spanish) 6 English, 6 Spanish Adaptations. (p. 908)
—Jane Goodall (Spanish) (p. 908)
—Michelle Kwan. (p. 1135)
—Michelle Kwan & Michelle Kwan (Spanish) 6 English, 6 Spanish Adaptations. (p. 1135)
—Michelle Kwan (Spanish) (p. 1135)
—Tiger Woods. (p. 1749)
—Tiger Woods & Tiger Woods (Spanish) 6 English, 6 Spanish Adaptations. (p. 1749)
Goodridge, Teresa. Happy Hedgehogs Stickers. (p. 746)
Goodridge, Walt F. J. Life Rhymes: For the Passion-Centered Life. (p. 1013)
—Lyrics for Living: Just Because I Am. Vol. 2 Owens-Waters, Zelda, ed. (p. 1067)
Goodrow, Carol. Happy Feet, Healthy Food: Your Child's First Journal of Exercise & Healthy Eating. Goodrow, Carol, illus. (p. 745)
—Kids Running: Have Fun, Get Faster, & Go Farther. (p. 955)
—Treasure of Health & Happiness. Goodrow, Carol, illus. (p. 1782)
Goodrum, L. E. Counting with G & Me. (p. 372)
Goodrum, Smith. Marble War: The game of chess as told to Steven. (p. 1091)
Goodspeed, Betsy. Reluctant Mountaineer. (p. 1458)
Goodspeed, Horace. Will's Neighborhood. (p. 1934)
Goodspeed, Jjdy. Perky Turkey's 4th of July Adventure. (p. 1343)
Goodspeed, Judy. Perky Turkey Finds a Friend. (p. 1343)
—Perky Turkey Finds a Friend. Taylor, Chet, illus. (p. 1343)
—Perky Turkey's Perfect Plan. (p. 1343)
—Perky Turkey's Perfect Plan. Taylor, Chet, illus. (p. 1343)
—Saddle Up. (p. 1501)
Goodstat, Alan, jt. auth. see Specialty Press.
Goodstein, Madeline. Sports Science Fair Projects. (p. 1633)
Goodstein, Madeline P. Goal! Science Projects with Soccer. (p. 687)
—Plastics & Polymers Science Fair Projects. LaBaff, Tom & LaBaff, Stephanie, illus. (p. 1370)
—Plastics & Polymers Science Fair Projects Using Hair Gel, Soda Bottles, & Slimy Stuff. (p. 1370)
—Water Science Fair Projects, Revised & Expanded Using the Scientific Method. LaBaff, Tom & LaBaff, Stephanie, illus. (p. 1863)
—Water Science Fair Projects Using Ice Cubes, Super Soakers, & Other Wet Stuff. (p. 1863)
—Wheels! Science Projects with Bicycles, Skateboards, & Skates. (p. 1901)
Goodstein, Madeline P., jt. auth. see Gardner, Robert.
Goodway, Simon, illus. see Montreuil, Gaetane.
Goodwin, Adrienne Annette, illus. see Bridges, Eunice.
Goodwin, Aimee. Fish Named Luke. (p. 598)
Goodwin, Ann. How to Dazzle at Information Technology. (p. 816)
Goodwin, Anne. No Business Like Ghost Business. (p. 1258)
Goodwin, Archie. Secret Agent Corrigan, 1977-1980 (p. 1540)
Goodwin, Brenda L., concept. Mangoes & the Kids: Teach A Child, Change the World. (p. 1087)
Goodwin, Brian. Pineapple Soap. (p. 1359)
Goodwin, Carol. Does This Belong Here? A Twiggyleaf Adventure. McDaniel, Thomas, illus. (p. 460)
—Great Acorn: A Twiggyleaf Adventure. McDaniel, Thomas, illus. (p. 713)
—Tippy Needs A Home: A Twiggyleaf Adventure. McDaniel, Thomas, illus. (p. 1757)
—What's the Hurry, Furry? A Twiggyleaf Adventure. McDaniel, Thomas, illus. (p. 1899)
Goodwin, Catherine. Seeking Shelter. (p. 1548)
Goodwin, Debbie Salter. Quick Start Drama for Kids: No Rehearsal Bible Skits for Classroom or Performance. (p. 1427)
—Quick Start Drama for Kids: Christmas: No Rehearsal Bible Skits for Classroom or Performance. (p. 1427)
Goodwin, Evelyn. Meet the Children from the Fifty States in Poetry. (p. 1122)
Goodwin, Harold Leland, jt. auth. see Blaine, John.
Goodwin, John. Arkful of Animal Stories. Macnaughton, Tina, illus. (p. 99)
—Lion Book of Five-Minute Animal Stories. Bendall-Brunello, John, illus. (p. 1020)
—Lion Book of Five-Minute Bedtime Stories. Waterhouse, Stephen, illus. (p. 1020)
—Lion Book of Five-Minute Christmas Stories. Johnson, Richard, illus. (p. 1020)
—Lion Book of Five-Minute Christmas Stories. Johnson, Richard A., illus. (p. 1020)
—Robin Hood. (p. 1479)
Goodwin, Josh, jt. auth. see Mills, Nathan.
Goodwin, Kathleen P. Point Reyes Visions Guidebook: Where to go, What to Do. Blair, Richard P., photos by. (p. 1377)
Goodwin, Leah, ed. see Bentow, Brian.
Goodwin, Susan Williams, jt. auth. see Whitley, Peggy J.
Goodwin, Vincent. Adventure of Abbey Grange. Dunn, Ben, illus. (p. 14)
—Adventure of the Blue Carbuncle. Dunn, Ben, illus. (p. 14)
—Adventure of the Cardboard Box. Dunn, Ben, illus. (p. 14)
—Adventure of the Copper Beeches. Dunn, Ben, illus. (p. 14)
—Adventure of the Dancing Men. Dunn, Ben, illus. (p. 14)
—Adventure of the Dying Detective. Dunn, Ben, illus. (p. 14)
—Adventure of the Empty House. Dunn, Ben, illus. (p. 14)
—Adventure of the Engineer's Thumb. Dunn, Ben, illus. (p. 14)
—Adventure of the Norwood Builder. Dunn, Ben, illus. (p. 14)
—Adventure of the Priory School. Dunn, Ben, illus. (p. 14)
—Adventure of the Red Circle. Dunn, Ben, illus. (p. 14)
—Adventure of the Red-Headed League. Dunn, Ben, illus. (p. 14)
—Adventure of the Second Stain. Dunn, Ben, illus. (p. 14)
—Adventure of the Six Napoleons. Dunn, Ben, illus. (p. 14)
—Adventure of the Solitary Cyclist. Dunn, Ben, illus. (p. 14)
—Adventure of the Speckled Band. Dunn, Ben, illus. (p. 14)
—Adventure of the Three Students. Dunn, Ben, illus. (p. 14)
—Adventure of Wisteria Lodge. Dunn, Ben, illus. (p. 14)
—Body-Snatcher. (p. 207)
—Call of Cthulhu. (p. 254)
—Moonlit Road. (p. 1173)
—Othello. Allen, Chris, illus. (p. 1306)
—Wendigo. (p. 1875)
Goodwin, Vincent & Shakespeare, William. Twelfth Night. Martin, Cynthia, illus. (p. 1800)
Goodwin, Wendy, illus. see Stalick, Garyanna.
Goodwine, Lashayla. My Mind Has Many Colors. (p. 1214)
Goodwyn, Susan. My First Spoken Words: Animals. (p. 1208)
Goodwyn, Susan, jt. auth. see Acredolo, Linda.
Goody, C. A. Charlie & the Rodent Queen Laaker, Terry, illus. (p. 292)
—Charlie Goes Camping: Charlie's Great Adventure #4. (p. 293)
Goody, Wendy, jt. auth. see Kelly, Veronica.
Goodyear-Brown, Paris. Gabby the Gecko. (p. 652)
Goodyer, Clive. Underwater Doodles: Amazing Scenes to Complete & Create. (p. 1817)
Gookin, Dan. Word 2003 for Dummies(r). (p. 1950)
Goomas, John, illus. see Holaves, Chris.
Goon, Geraldine. Grandma Tells Dozens of Stories. (p. 708)
Goonack, Cathy. Scaly-Tailed Possum & Echidna. Goonack, Katrina et al, illus. (p. 1519)
Goonack, Katrina, illus. see Goonack, Cathy.
Goopar, Rocio Arvea. Ro & Otilo: The Magic Train. (p. 1476)
Goopymart, illus. see Tausig, Ben.
Goose, Mother. Lets Move & Lets Sing 2 BK Pack. (p. 999)
—Lets Play & Sing 2 BK Pack. (p. 1000)
—Let's Sing, Lets Move & Let's Play. (p. 1000)
Gooseberry Staff. Kids in the Kitchen Cookbook: Recipes for Fun! (p. 954)
Goosen, Stephanie. Caleb's World. (p. 252)
Goosens, Philippe, illus. see Robberecht, Thierry.
Goosens, Philippe, jt. auth. see Friester, Paul.
Goosley, Stephen M. Fishing with Steve. (p. 599)
Goossens, Jesse. Right to Play. (p. 1472)
Goossens, Philippe. Knock! Knock! Knock! Who's There? (p. 965)
Goossens, Philippe, illus. see Friester, Paul.
Goossens, Philippe, illus. see Robberecht, Thierry.
Goossens, Philippe, jt. auth. see Friester, Paul.
Goossens, Philippe, jt. auth. see Robberecht, Thierry.
Gootel, Rifka. My First Learn & Do Jewish Holiday Book. Rosenberg, Amye, illus. (p. 1207)
Gootman, Marilyn E. When a Friend Dies: A Book for Teens about Grieving & Healing. (p. 1901)
—When a Friend Dies: A Book for Teens about Grieving & Healing. Espeland, Pamela, ed. (p. 1901)
Gootman, Marilyn E., jt. auth. see Karwoski, Gail.
Gopigian, Susan Kadian. Gadoo the Cat: An Armenian Folktale. Bolt, Susan Collier, illus. (p. 652)
Gopinath, Karin Ursula. Friends in the Garden. Sutanto, Tommy, illus. (p. 638)
Gopinath, Sujata, jt. auth. see Aronovsky, Ilona.
Goranson, Christopher. Careers as a Webmaster: Maintaining the Site. (p. 267)
Goranson, Christopher D. Careers as a Webmaster: Maintaining the Site. (p. 267)
—Danny Harf: Wakeboarding Superstar. (p. 405)
Göransson, Johannes, tr. see Berg, Aase.
Gorbachenok, Ekaterina, ed. see AZ Books Staff.
Gorbachev, Kostya, illus. see Gorbachev, Valeri.
Gorbachev, Mikhail, illus. see Roth, Carol.
Gorbachev, Mikhail, jt. auth. see Ikeda, Daisaku.
Gorbachev, Valeri. Best Cat. Gorbachev, Valeri, illus. (p. 168)
—Big Trip. Gorbachev, Valeri, illus. (p. 184)
—Cats Are Cats. Gorbachev, Valeri, illus. (p. 281)
—Catty Jane Who Hated the Rain. Gorbachev, Valeri, illus. (p. 281)
—Christopher Counting. Gorbachev, Valeri, illus. (p. 317)
—Dia de lluvia. Gorbachev, Valeri, illus. (p. 433)
—Doctor Nice. (p. 459)
—Goldilocks & the Three Bears. (p. 696)
—How to Be Friends with a Dragon. Gorbachev, Valeri, illus. (p. 815)
—Me Too! (p. 1116)
—Me Too! Gorbachev, Valeri, illus. (p. 1116)
—Ms. Turtle the Babysitter. Gorbachev, Valeri, illus. (p. 1188)
—That's What Friends Are For. Gorbachev, Valeri, illus. (p. 1727)
—Turtle's Penguin Day. (p. 1799)
—Two Little Chicks Go to School. (p. 1804)
—When Someone Is Afraid Gorbachev, Kostya, illus. (p. 1904)
—Whose Hat Is It? (p. 1921)
—Whose Hat Is It? Gorbachev, Valeri, illus. (p. 1921)
Gorbachev, Valeri, illus. see Ackerman, Tova.
Gorbachev, Valeri, illus. see Blanchard, Patricia & Suhr, Joanne.
Gorbachev, Valeri, illus. see Griswell, Kim T.
Gorbachev, Valeri, illus. see Horning, Sandra.
Gorbachev, Valeri, illus. see Martin, David Lozell.
Gorbachev, Valeri, illus. see Moser, Lisa.
Gorbachev, Valeri, illus. see Newman, Lesléa.
Gorbachev, Valeri, illus. see Roth, Carol.
Gorbachev, Valeri, illus. see Roth, Jurgen Philip Philip Philip Kevin Kevin P Geneen Philip Philip Philip Marie, Carol.
Gorbachev, Valeri, illus. see Stiegemeyer, Julie.
Gorbatov, Vadim, illus. see Patterson, Stacey.
Gorbaty, Norman, illus. see Ziefert, Harriet.
Gorbett, Danea. Adopted Teens Only: A Survival Guide to Adolescence. (p. 13)
Gorbounov, Stephanie. Little Happy Bird. (p. 1029)
Gordan, Gus, illus. see Dickens, Rosie & Courtauld, Sarah.
Gordeev, Denis, illus. see Peters, Stephanie True.
Gordenker, Leon, jt. auth. see Baehr, Peter R.
Gorder, Cheryl, jt. auth. see Harris, Samuel.
Gordh, Bill. Building a Children's Chapel: One Story at a Time. (p. 238)
Gordh, Bill & Pugliano-Martin, Carol. Barbie. Wolcott, Karen, illus. (p. 138)
Gordo, Aleix, illus. see Rodríguez-Nora, Tere.
Gordo, Françs, jt. ed. see Gordo, Lydia.
Gordo, Lydia & Gordo, Françs, eds. Celestina: Análisis y Estudio Sobre la Obra, el Autor y Su Época. (p. 286)
—Cien Años de Soledad. (p. 319)
—Lazarillode de Tormes: Análisis y Estudio Sobre la Obra, el Autor y Su Epoca. (p. 981)
—Poema de Mio Cid: Análisis y Estudio Sobre la Obra, el Autor y Su Epoca. (p. 1376)
Gordon, Amy. Gorillas of Gill Park. (p. 703)
—Painting the Rainbow. Tuschman, Richard, illus. (p. 1318)
—Return to Gill Park. (p. 1465)
—Shadow Collector's Apprentice. (p. 1557)
—Twenty Gold Falcons. (p. 1801)
Gordon, Andrew. Andy's Book. (p. 73)
Gordon, Andrew, illus. see Armitage, Ronda.

G

Gordon, Anne. Animals of the Ice & Snow. (p. 83)
Gordon, Ayala, illus. see Simon, Norma.
Gordon, B. & Parker, H. Wipe Clean ABC. (p. 1939)
Gordon, Barry & Johnson, Adam. Parasites Like Us. (p. 1324)
Gordon, Betsy, ed. see Headings, Peggy A.
Gordon, Bob. Carry-Me ABC. (p. 271)
—Giant See a Shape My Giant 123 Book. (p. 674)
—Lift & Learn Colors. Snaith, Andy, photos by. (p. 1014)
—Santa's Christmas. (p. 1513)
—Touch & Feel Noisy Puppy. (p. 1772)
—Touch & Sparkle Emergency. (p. 1772)
Gordon, Bob, et al. Wipe Clean 123. (p. 1939)
Gordon, Bonnie J. Escape from Goshen. (p. 535)
Gordon Brown, Doris. Jesus Brought Lazarus Back to Life. (p. 915)
—Lazarus; the Talk of the Town. (p. 981)
Gordon, Carl, illus. see Coyle, Carmela Lavigna.
Gordon, Carl, illus. see Davidson, Susanna.
Gordon, Carl, illus. see Lansky, Bruce, ed.
Gordon, Carl, illus. see Nesbitt, Kenn.
Gordon, Carl, illus. see Pottle, Robert.
Gordon, Carl, illus. see Walton, Rick.
Gordon, Carl, jt. illus. see Gordon, Mike.
Gordon, Carol. Super Smart Information Strategies: Make the Grade. (p. 1682)
Gordon, Danielle. Garage Cat. (p. 655)
Gordon, Danny, illus. see Smith-Leckie, Nina.
Gordon, David. Extremely Cute Animals Operating Heavy Machinery. (p. 557)
—Sink Your Teeth Into... Sharks! (p. 1579)
—Smitten. Gordon, David, illus. (p. 1594)
—Three Little Rigs. Gordon, David, illus. (p. 1743)
—Ugly Truckling. Gordon, David, illus. (p. 1808)
Gordon, David, illus. see Ciminera, Siobhan & Testa, Maggie.
Gordon, David, illus. see Downs, Mike.
Gordon, David, illus. see Holub, Joan.
Gordon, David, illus. see Jon Scieszkas Trucktown, et al.
Gordon, David, illus. see Olson, K. C.
Gordon, David, illus. see Scieszka, Jon.
Gordon, David George. Creepy Critters of the Southwest. (p. 381)
—Tarantula. (p. 1706)
—Uncover a Shark. Pringle, Betsy Henry, ed. (p. 1812)
Gordon, David George, illus. see Cyrus, Kurt.
Gordon, Dean, illus. see Richards, Kitty & Disney Book Group Staff.
Gordon, Domenica More. Archie. (p. 95)
—Archie's Vacation. (p. 95)
Gordon, Edwin, jt. auth. see Lowe, Marilyn.
Gordon, Edwin E. Am I Musical? Discover Your Musical Potential (Adults & Children Ages 7 & Up) (p. 51)
Gordon, Elaine R. Mommy, Did I Grow in Your Tummy? Where Some Babies Come From. Clo, Kathy, illus. (p. 1162)
Gordon, Elizabeth. Bird Children: The Little Playmates of the Flower Children. Ross, M. T., illus. (p. 190)
—Bird Children. Ross, M. T., illus. (p. 190)
—Flower Children: The Little Cousins of the Field & Garden. Ross, M. T., illus. (p. 607)
Gordon, Ellen. Verseful of Jewish Holidays. Katz, Avi, illus. (p. 1837)
Gordon, Emily. Kitty Book. Cagle, Terry R., illus. (p. 963)
Gordon, Eric A., illus. see Aptekar, Devan.
Gordon, Eric A., illus. see Bright, J. E.
Gordon, Eric A., illus. see Lemke, Donald.
Gordon, Eric A., illus. see Rosen, Lucy.
Gordon, Eric A., illus. see Santos, Ray.
Gordon, Eric A., illus. see Sazaklis, John.
Gordon, Eric A., illus. see Sutton, Laurie S.
Gordon, Eric A., illus. see Turner, Katharine.
Gordon, F. C., illus. see Pierson, Clara Dillingham.
Gordon, Fran & Tischler, Faye. Dutch Double. (p. 490)
Gordon, Freddie, jt. auth. see Levin, Freddie.
Gordon, Gaelyn. Tripswitch. (p. 1787)
Gordon, George W. & Walker, David. Police Encounters: The Black Man's Guide to Handling Encounters with the Police & Protecting Your Constitutional Rights. (p. 1380)
Gordon, Glenn. Bubble Heads. (p. 233)
Gordon, Gus. Herman & Rosie. Gordon, Gus, illus. (p. 771)
Gordon, Gus, illus. see Arena, Felice & Kettle, Phil.
Gordon, Gus, illus. see Arena, Felice, et al.
Gordon, Gus, illus. see Bancks, Tristan.
Gordon, Gus, illus. see Esbaum, Jill.
Gordon, Gus, illus. see Mawter, J. A.
Gordon, Gus, illus. see Sullivan, Bryan & French, Jackie.
Gordon, Ingrid, jt. auth. see Norac, Carl.
Gordon, Irene Ternier. Tecumseh: Diplomat & Warrior in the War of 1812. (p. 1712)
Gordon, Jacqueline. Hider's Story. (p. 777)
—Hider's Story Companion Journal. (p. 777)
Gordon, Janice Knuth. Eager Bunny. (p. 492)
Gordon, Jennifer. Broken Girl. (p. 230)
—Terrible Tales 2: The Bloodcurdling Truth about the Frog Prince, Jack & the Beanstalk, A Very Fowl Duckling, the Ghoulishly Ghoulish Snow White, A Really Crabby Princess, & A Very Squashed Pea. (p. 1721)
Gordon, Jo. Reciclar (Recycling) (p. 1451)
Gordon, Jo Ann. Articulation Tales: Stories for Articulation Remediation. (p. 104)
Gordon, John, illus. see Williams, Bonnie.
Gordon, John Stuart. Hitlers Head. (p. 786)
Gordon, Jon. Energy Bus for Kids: A Story about Staying Positive & Overcoming Challenges. Scott, Korey, illus. (p. 528)
Gordon, Josh & Pecsenye, Jessica. Pitzer College College Prowler off the Record. (p. 1365)
Gordon, Judy Ann. Grammie's Magical Garden: Beyond the Gate. (p. 706)
Gordon, Julie & Skindzier, Jon. George Washington University College Prowler off the Record. (p. 665)
Gordon, Kate. Thyla. (p. 1746)
—Vulpi. (p. 1851)
Gordon, Kathy L. I'm not sick, I have a Handicap. (p. 859)
Gordon, Keith & Kaye, Jacqueline. New Maths Frameworking - Year 9. (p. 1246)
Gordon, Leneé, photos by see Grimes-Herbert, Taryn.
Gordon, Leslie M. Homeless Christmas Tree. Bailey, Court, illus. (p. 793)
Gordon, Lily & Nash, Kevin. Union College College Prowler off the Record. (p. 1818)
Gordon, Lindsay. Bond. (p. 208)
—Domination Dolls. (p. 465)
—In Her Service. (p. 863)
—Rites of Obedience. (p. 1475)
Gordon, Lorell Cynthia. Tilly's Birthday: A Young Girl's Introduction to Menstruation. (p. 1750)
Gordon, Lynn. 52 Activities for Jewish Holidays. Johnson, Karen, illus. (p. 1997)
—52 Activities for You & Your Baby. Johnson, Karen, illus. (p. 1997)
—52 Adventures in San Francisco. Johnson, Karen, illus. (p. 1997)
—52 Boredom Busters for Kids! Johnson, Karen, illus. (p. 1997)
—52 Christmas Activities. Johnson, Karen, illus. (p. 1997)
—52 Fun Things to Do in the Car. Johnson, Karen & Synarski, Susan, illus. (p. 1997)
—52 Fun Things to Do on the Plane. Johnson, Karen & Synarski, Susan, illus. (p. 1997)
—52 Great Family Films. Johnson, Karen, illus. (p. 1997)
—Activities to Share with Your Grandchild. Johnson, Karen, illus. (p. 10)
—Big Collection of Phonics Flipbooks: 200 Reproducible Flipbooks That Target the Phonics & Word Study Skills Every Primary Student Needs to Know. (p. 180)
Gordon, Lynn & Chronicle Books Staff. Cool Tricks for Kids. Synarski, Susan & Johnson, Karen, illus. (p. 364)
—Rainy Day Activities. (p. 1436)
Gordon, Lynn, et al. Circus Fantastico. (p. 322)
Gordon, Marie Elaina. My Grand-Mom Told Me... Book 1. (p. 1210)
—My Grand-Mom Told Me-down by the Sea. (p. 1210)
Gordon, Matthew. Islam. (p. 891)
Gordon, Michele Lynne. Springing Singing Sprout: Little Tales of a Little Sprout. (p. 1635)
Gordon, Mick. Ride of Your Life. (p. 1471)
Gordon, Mike. Emperor's New Clothes. (p. 521)
—Frog Prince. (p. 640)
—Goldilocks & the Three Bears. (p. 696)
—Little Red Riding Hood. (p. 1035)
—Princess & the Pea. (p. 1402)
—Stories of Princesses. (p. 1655)
—Wish Fish. (p. 1940)
Gordon, Mike, illus. see Anderson, Judith.
Gordon, Mike, illus. see Callahan, Thera S.
Gordon, Mike, illus. see Coyle, Carmela Lavigna.
Gordon, Mike, illus. see Davidson, Susanna.
Gordon, Mike, illus. see Esham, Barbara.
Gordon, Mike, illus. see Esham, Barbaraa.
Gordon, Mike, illus. see Gogerly, Liz.
Gordon, Mike, illus. see Goodey, Madeline.
Gordon, Mike, illus. see Green, Jen.
Gordon, Mike, illus. see Imbody, Amy E. & Imbody, Amy.
Gordon, Mike, illus. see Lansky, Bruce, ed.
Gordon, Mike, illus. see Llewellyn, Claire.
Gordon, Mike, illus. see McNamara, Margaret.
Gordon, Mike, illus. see Namm, Diane.
Gordon, Mike, illus. see Nesbitt, Ken.
Gordon, Mike, illus. see Nesbitt, Kenn.
Gordon, Mike, illus. see Pottle, Robert.
Gordon, Mike, illus. see Rau, Dana Meachen.
Gordon, Mike, illus. see Robinson, Hilary.
Gordon, Mike, illus. see Sims, Lesley.
Gordon, Mike, illus. see Walton, Rick.
Gordon, Mike, jt. auth. see McNamara, Margaret.
Gordon, Mike, tr. see Namm, Diane.
Gordon, Mike & Gordon, Carl. Magic Porridge Pot. (p. 1073)
Gordon, Minette, et al. Understanding Women's Rights. (p. 1816)
Gordon, Murphy. Emy Moon. (p. 522)
Gordon, Nick. Air Force Air Commandos. (p. 31)
—Alberto Del Rio. (p. 35)
—Army Delta Force. (p. 100)
—Army Green Berets. (p. 100)
—Army Night Stalkers. (p. 100)
—Army Rangers. (p. 100)
—Bomb Squad Technician. (p. 208)
—Bone Chapel. (p. 208)
—Coal Miner. (p. 336)
—Coast Guard Rescue Swimmer. (p. 336)
—Deep Sea Fisherman. (p. 423)
—Dolph Ziggler. (p. 464)
—Edinburgh Castle. (p. 504)
—Fighter Pilot. (p. 585)
—Kofi Kingston. (p. 966)
—Lumberjack. (p. 1065)
—Marine Corps Force Recon. (p. 1094)
—Marine Expeditionary Units. (p. 1094)
—Mark Henry. (p. 1095)
—Monster Cars. (p. 1166)
—Monster Cranes. (p. 1167)
—Monster Diggers. (p. 1167)
—Monster Trains. (p. 1168)
—Monster Trucks. (p. 1168)
—Navy SEALs. (p. 1238)
—Rodeo Clown. (p. 1484)
—Smoke Jumper. (p. 1594)
—U. S. Air Force. (p. 1806)
—U. S. Army. (p. 1806)
—U. S. Coast Guard. (p. 1806)
—U. S. Marine Corps. (p. 1806)
—U. S. Navy. (p. 1807)
Gordon, Pauline C. Adventures of the Droplet Twins. (p. 23)
—Animals in My Backyard! Joey, the Flying Squirrel. (p. 83)
Gordon, Peggy T. Santa's Secret. (p. 1513)
Gordon, Rachel & Gold, Claudia. Potty Palooza: A Step-by-Step Guide to Using a Potty. Bergmann, Sarah, illus. (p. 1388)
Gordon, Ray. Depths of Depravation. (p. 427)
Gordon, Ray, jt. auth. see Rainey, Anne.
Gordon, Richard. Your Healing Hands: The Polarity Experience. (p. 1980)
Gordon, Robert. Can't Be Satisfied: The Life & Times of Muddy Waters. (p. 261)
Gordon, Roderick. Closer (p. 334)
—Deeper (p. 423)
—Spiral (p. 1628)
Gordon, Roderick & Williams, Brian. Caida Libre. Munoz, Adolfo, tr. (p. 251)
—Closer (p. 334)
—Closer. (p. 334)
—Deeper. (p. 423)
—Freefall. (p. 635)
—Spiral. (p. 1628)
—Tunnels Williams, Brian, illus. (p. 1797)
—Tunnels. (p. 1797)
—Tunnels #6: Terminal. (p. 1797)
Gordon, Roderick & Williams, Brian James. Terminal. (p. 1721)
Gordon, Ronni L., jt. auth. see Stillman, David M.
Gordon, Ronni L. & Stillman, David M. Cuaderno 1: A Beginning Workbook for Grammar & Communication: Answer Key & Progress Checks. (p. 387)
—Cuaderno 2: An Intermediate Workbook for Grammar & Communication: Answer Key & Progress Checks (p. 387)
Gordon, Sam, tr. see Alemagne, Beatrice.
Gordon, Samantha, jt. auth. see Bruening, Ari.
Gordon, Sandra, jt. auth. see Gordon, Sandra J.
Gordon, Sandra J. & Gordon, Sandra. Best Baby Products: The A to Z Guide to Everything You Need for Your Baby. Consumer Reports Staff, ed. (p. 168)
Gordon, Sharon. Adivina Quién. (p. 12)
—Adivina Quien Atrapa. (p. 12)
—Adivina Quien Baja en Picada. (p. 12)
—Adivina Quien Cambia. (p. 12)
—Adivina Quien Ruge. (p. 12)
—Adivina Quien Se Esconde. (p. 12)
—Adivina Quien Se Zambulle. (p. 12)
—Allergies. (p. 46)
—Amarillo. (p. 52)
—Anaranjado. (p. 67)
—Animales de la Montaña. Victory Productions, Inc. Staff, tr. from ENG. (p. 80)
—Animales de la Selva Tropical. Victory Productions, Inc. Staff, tr. from ENG. (p. 80)
—Animales de las Planicies. Victory Productions, Inc. Staff, tr. from ENG. (p. 81)
—Animales de los Humedales. (p. 81)
—Animales del Desierto. Victory Productions, Inc. Staff, tr. from ENG. (p. 81)
—Animales del Mar. Victory Productions, Inc. Staff, tr. from ENG. (p. 81)
—Animales Salvajes (p. 81)
—Animals in the Wild (p. 83)
—Arriba Abajo: Exactamente lo Opuesto. (p. 101)
—Asthma. (p. 108)
—At Home by the Ocean. (p. 110)
—At Home by the Ocean/Mi Casa Junto Al Mar. (p. 110)
—At Home in the City. (p. 110)
—At Home in the City/Mi Casa en la Ciudad. (p. 110)
—At Home in the Desert. (p. 110)
—At Home in the Desert/Mi Casa en el Desierto. (p. 110)
—At Home (Mi Casa) (p. 110)
—At Home on the Farm. (p. 110)
—At Home on the Farm/Mi Casa en la Granja. (p. 110)
—At Home on the Mountain. (p. 110)
—At Home on the Mountain/Mi Casa en la Montana. (p. 110)
—At Home on the Ranch. (p. 110)
—At Home on the Ranch/Mi Casa en el Rancho. (p. 110)
—Azul. (p. 122)
—Big/Small/Grande/Pequeno. (p. 185)
—Blue/El Azul. (p. 204)
—Bookworms: At Home (p. 213)
—Bookworms: Ready for School (p. 213)
—Canada. (p. 260)
—Colores (p. 344)
—Colors/Los Colores (p. 346)
—Compartimos: Listos para Ir a la Escuela. (p. 352)
—Decimos la Verdad. (p. 421)
—Desert Animals. (p. 428)
—Dirty Clean/Sucio Limpio. (p. 446)
—Dirty/Clean. (p. 446)
—Dives. (p. 454)
—Duro Blando. (p. 490)
—Earaches. (p. 492)
—Escuchamos. (p. 535)
—Exercise. (p. 548)
—Fast/Slow. (p. 576)
—Fast/Slow/Rapido/Lento. (p. 576)
—Grande, Pequeno. (p. 707)
—Green. (p. 721)
—Green/El Verde. (p. 722)
—Guess Who (Adivina Quién) (p. 729)
—Guess Who Bites: Adivina Quién Muerde. (p. 729)
—Guess Who Changes. (p. 729)
—Guess Who Changes/Adivina Quien Cambia. (p. 729)
—Guess Who Dives/Adivina Quien Se Zambulle. (p. 729)
—Guess Who Grabs. (p. 729)
—Guess Who Grabs/Adivina Quien Atrapa. (p. 729)
—Guess Who Hides/Adivina Quien Se Esconde. (p. 729)
—Guess Who Hisses: Adivina Quién Silba. (p. 729)
—Guess Who Hops: Adivina Quién Salta. (p. 729)
—Guess Who Roars. (p. 729)
—Guess Who Roars/Adivina Quien Ruge. (p. 729)
—Guess Who Runs: Adivina Quién Corre. (p. 729)
—Guess Who Runs. (p. 729)
—Guess Who Snaps: Adivina Quién Tritura. (p. 729)
—Guess Who Snaps. (p. 729)
—Guess Who Spins: Adivina Quién Teje. (p. 729)
—Guess Who Spins. (p. 729)
—Guess Who Swoops. (p. 729)
—Guess Who Swoops/Adivina Quien Baja en Picada. (p. 729)
—Hard/Soft. (p. 748)
—Hard/Soft/Duro/Blando. (p. 748)
—Hides. (p. 777)
—Just the Opposite (Exactamente lo Opuesto) (p. 940)
—Listos para ir a la Escuela (p. 1022)
—Mi Casa (p. 1132)
—Mi Casa en el Desierto. (p. 1132)
—Mi Casa en el Rancho. (p. 1132)
—Mi Casa en la Ciudad. (p. 1132)
—Mi Casa en la Granja. (p. 1132)
—Mi Casa en la Montana. (p. 1132)
—Mi Casa Junto al Mar. (p. 1132)
—Mojado Seco. (p. 1160)
—Morado. (p. 1173)
—Mountain Animals. (p. 1180)
—My Brain. (p. 1199)
—My Heart & Blood. (p. 1210)
—My Lungs. (p. 1213)
—My Skin. (p. 1219)
—My Stomach. (p. 1219)
—Ocean Animals. (p. 1276)
—Orange/El Anaranjado. (p. 1302)
—Pinkeye. (p. 1360)
—Plains Animals. (p. 1366)
—Purple/El Morado. (p. 1419)
—Que Hay Dentro de un Camion de Bomberos? (p. 1423)
—Que Hay Dentro de un Carro de Policia? (p. 1423)
—Que Hay Dentro de un Hospital? (p. 1423)
—Que Hay Dentro de una Ambulancia? (p. 1423)
—Que Hay Dentro de una Estacion de Policia? (p. 1423)
—Que Hay Dentro de una Estacion de Policia? / What's Inside a Police Station? (p. 1423)
—Rainforest Animals. (p. 1436)
—Rapido Lento. (p. 1439)
—Ready for School (Listos para Ir a la Escuela) (p. 1447)
—Red/El Rojo. (p. 1455)
—Respetamos las Reglas. (p. 1463)
—Roars. (p. 1478)
—Rojo. (p. 1485)
—Somos Amables. (p. 1611)
—Somos un Equipo. (p. 1611)
—Sucio Limpio. (p. 1672)
—United States. (p. 1819)
—Up Down (Arriba Abajo) (p. 1824)
—Up/down. (p. 1824)
—Verde. (p. 1836)
—We Are a Team. (p. 1865)
—We Are a Team/Somos un Equipo. (p. 1865)
—We Are Kind. (p. 1865)
—We Are Kind/Somos Amables. (p. 1865)
—We Follow the Rules. (p. 1867)
—We Follow the Rules/Respetamos Las Reglas. (p. 1867)
—We Listen. (p. 1867)
—We Listen/Escuchamos. (p. 1867)
—We Share. (p. 1868)
—We Share/Compartimos. (p. 1868)
—We Tell the Truth. (p. 1868)
—We Tell the Truth/Decimos la Verdad. (p. 1868)
—Wet/Dry. (p. 1877)
—Wet/Dry/Seco/Mojado. (p. 1877)
—Wetland Animals. (p. 1877)
—Whats Inside a Fire Truck? (¿Qué Hay Dentro de un Camión de Bomberos?) (p. 1898)
—What's Inside a Firehouse/Que Hay Dentro de un Cuartel de Bomberos? (p. 1898)
—What's Inside a Hospital? (p. 1898)
—What's Inside a Hospital?/Que Hay Dentro de un Hospital? (p. 1898)
—What's Inside a Police Car? (p. 1898)
—What's Inside a Police Car/Que Hay Dentro de un Carro de Policia? (p. 1898)
—What's Inside a Police Station? (p. 1898)
—What's Inside an Ambulance? (p. 1898)
—What's Inside an Ambulance?/Que Hay Dentro de una Ambulancia? (p. 1898)
—What's Inside? (¿Qué Hay Dentro?) (p. 1898)
—Yellow. (p. 1969)
—Yellow/El Amarillo. (p. 1970)
—You Are What You Eat. (p. 1973)
Gordon, Sharon, jt. auth. see Gordon, Sharon.
Gordon, Sharon & Gordon, Sharon. Exactamente lo Opuesto (p. 547)
Gordon, Sharon, ed. Que Hay Dentro de un Cuartel de Bomberos? (p. 1423)
Gordon, Sherri Mabry. Are You at Risk for Food Allergies? Peanut Butter, Milk, & Other Deadly Threats. (p. 97)
—Be Smart about Money: Money Management & Budgeting. (p. 149)
—Beyond Bruises: The Truth about Teens & Abuse. (p. 173)
—Downloading Copyrighted Stuff from the Internet: Stealing or Fair Use? (p. 474)
—Evolution Debate: Darwinism vs. Intelligent Design. (p. 546)
—Josh! Leading Man Josh Hutcherson. (p. 926)
—Peanut Butter, Milk, & Other Deadly Threats: What You Should Know about Food Allergies. (p. 1332)
—Using Technology. (p. 1828)
Gordon, Sherri Mabry, jt. auth. see Roy, Jennifer Rozines.
Gordon, Sherri Mabry & Library. Green & Clean Energy: What You Can Do. (p. 721)
Gordon, Sherri Mabry & Mabry-Gordon, Sherri. Are You Being Abused? (p. 97)
Gordon, Sol. When Living Hurts: For Teenagers, Young Adults, Their Parents, Leaders, & Counselors. (p. 1903)
Gordon Staff, jt. auth. see Mordecai.
Gordon, Stephanie Jacob, jt. auth. see Enderle, Judith Ross.
Gordon, Stephen G. Expressing the Inner Wild: Tattoos, Piercings, Jewelry, & Other Body Art. (p. 555)
—Jay-Z: CEO of Hip-Hop. (p. 910)
—Tim Tebow: Quarterback with Conviction. (p. 1750)
Gordon, Steven E., illus. see Aptekar, Devan.
Gordon, Steven E., illus. see Bright, J. E.
Gordon, Steven E., illus. see Huelin, Jodi.
Gordon, Steven E., illus. see Lemke, Donald.
Gordon, Steven E., illus. see Lime, Harry.
Gordon, Steven E., illus. see Rau, Zachary.

Gordon, Steven E., illus. see Rosen, Lucy.
Gordon, Steven E., illus. see Santos, Ray.
Gordon, Steven E., illus. see Sazaklis, John.
Gordon, Steven E., illus. see Sutton, Laurie S.
Gordon, Steven E., illus. see Teitelbaum, Michael.
Gordon, Steven E., illus. see Turner, Katharine.
Gordon, Stewart. Planning Your Piano Success: A Blueprint for Aspiring Musicians. (p. 1368)
Gordon, Susan. Meet the Mummy. (p. 1123)
—Montesquieu: The French Philosopher Who Shaped Modern Government. (p. 1170)
Gordon, Susie, illus. see Lyons, Jane & Bailey, Karen.
Gordon, Sylvia. Further Adventures of the Potty Wizard & His Cat, Muddles. (p. 650)
Gordon-Harris, Tory, jt. auth. see Arlon, Penelope.
Gordon-Harris, Tory, jt. auth. see Pinnington, Andrea.
Gordon-Lucas, Bonnie, illus. see Petersell, Shlomo, ed.
Gordon-Lucas, Bonnie, illus. see Petersell, Shlomo.
Gordon-Noy, Aya, illus. see Gidali, Orit.
Gordon-Noy, Aya, illus. see Keller, Elinoar & Peleg-Segal, Naama.
Gore, Al. Inconvenient Truth: The Crisis of Global Warming. (p. 869)
—Inconvenient Truth: The Planetary Emergency of Global Warming & What We Can Do about It. (p. 869)
Gore, Ariel, ed. Essential Hip Mama: Writing from the Cutting Edge of Parenting. (p. 537)
Gore, E. J. Taya Bayliss: Treasure Hunter. (p. 1707)
Gore, Emily. And Nick. Gore, Leonid, illus. (p. 71)
Gore, Jim. Witch Snatchit & Mr Grabbit. (p. 1941)
Gore, Kristin. Sammy's Hill. (p. 1508)
Gore, Leonid. Danny's First Snow. Gore, Leonid, illus. (p. 406)
—Mommy, Where Are You? Gore, Leonid, illus. (p. 1162)
—Worms for Lunch? Gore, Leonid, illus. (p. 1961)
Gore, Leonid, illus. see Frost, Helen.
Gore, Leonid, illus. see Gore, Emily.
Gore, Leonid, illus. see Hovey, Kate.
Gore, Leonid, illus. see Packard, Mary.
Gore, Leonid, illus. see Shepard, Aaron.
Gore, Leonid, illus. see Zarin, Cynthia.
Gore, Teresa. Christmas on Cherrybrook Lane. (p. 315)
Goreja, W. G. Shea Butter: The Nourishing Properties of Africa's Best-Kept Natural Beauty Secret. (p. 1564)
Gorelick, Victor, illus. see Ribeiro, Nelson & Spotlight Editors.
Gorelick, Victor, illus. see Ribeiro, Nelson.
Gorelick, Victor, illus. see Ribiero, Nelson & Spotlight Editors.
Gorelick, Victor, illus. see Spotlight Editors.
Goren, Ada. Collaborative Class Books from a to Z: Easy, Letter-By-Letter Books Children Create Together to Learn the Alphabet. (p. 339)
—Math Story Mats: 16 Ready-to-Use Story Mats That Boost Essential Listening & Math Skills. (p. 1107)
—Shoe Box Learning Centers - Sight Words: 30 Instant Centers with Reproducible Templates & Activities That Help Kids Learn 200+ Sight Words-Independently! (p. 1568)
Gorenburg, Steve, ed. see McCarthy, John.
Gorenman, Marcelo, illus. see Rudnick, Arnold.
Gorey, E., jt. auth. see Neumeyer, P.
Gorey, Edward. Osbick Bird. (p. 1305)
—Thoughtful Alphabets: The Just Dessert / The Deadly Blotter. (p. 1740)
—West Wing. (p. 1876)
—Wuggly Ump. Gorey, Edward, illus. (p. 1966)
Gorey, Edward, illus. see Bellairs, John.
Gorey, Edward, illus. see Ciardi, John.
Gorey, Edward, illus. see Jones, DuPre.
Gorey, Edward, illus. see Levine, Rhoda.
Gorey, Edward, illus. see Warner, Rex.
Gorey, Edward, illus. see Wells, H. G.
Gorey, Edward, jt. auth. see Neumeyer, Peter F.
Gorey, Edward & Donnelly, James. Three Classic Children's Stories. (p. 1741)
Gorey, Edward & Lear, Edward. Dong with the Luminous Nose. (p. 466)
—Jumblies. (p. 933)
Gorey, Haller, jt. auth. see Zondervan Publishing Staff.
Gorey, Jill & Haller, Nancy. Pups of the Spirit Melmon, Deborah, illus. (p. 1418)
Gorg, Gwyn. I Am the Blues. Alfandolo, Koffi, illus. (p. 834)
Görg, Holger, ed. see Greenaway, David.
Gorgas, Paula Blais. Little Lost Leprechaun. (p. 1031)
—Little Lost Leprechaun. Taylor, Chet, illus. (p. 1031)
—Perfect Purple Present. (p. 1342)
Gorges, Julie A. Just Call Me Goody-Two-Shoes. (p. 938)
Goril, Cindy. Lacey's Legacy: Stretch's Story. Jamison, Sharon, illus. (p. 970)
Goring, Ruth. Dias Festivos y Celebraciones. Palacios, Argentina, tr. (p. 435)
Gorini, Catherine A. Geometry. (p. 662)
Goris, Laura, illus. see Smith, Kimberly.
Gorissen, Dean, illus. see Bancks, Tristan.
Gorissen, Dean, illus. see Henson, Laura J. & Grooms, Duffy.
Gorissen, Dean, illus. see Roy, James.
Gorjanc, Adele A. Italian Conversation: A Practical Guide for Students & Travelers. (p. 894)
Gorky, Maksim, see Gorky, Maxim.
Gorky, Maxim. Lower Depths. Landes, William-Alan, ed. (p. 1061)
Gorla, Stefano. Donkey's Tale. Marchetti, Angela, illus. (p. 466)
Gorler, Rosemarie & Piscitelli, Donna. Just Like Mary. Sternhagen, Mimi, illus. (p. 939)
Gorlinski, Gini. 100 Most Influential Musicians of All Time. (p. 1998)
Gormally, Eleanor. Little Flower Bulb: Helping Children Bereaved by Suicide. Loki & Splink, illus. (p. 1027)
—Little One Asks. (p. 1032)
—St Paul: The Man with the Letters. (p. 1638)
Gorman, Carol. Games. (p. 654)
—Midsummer Night's Dork. (p. 1139)
Gorman, Carol & Findley, Ron J. Stumptown Kid (p. 1670)
Gorman, Carolyn Portier, ed. see Schmitt, Nannette Toups.
Gorman, Chris. Indi Surfs. (p. 870)
Gorman, Dl. Pudgy Wudgy: Pudgy Wudgy Meets a Friend. (p. 1414)
Gorman, Grey. Abridged but Out There: Six Months of Simon. (p. 7)
Gorman, Jacqueline & Guy, John. British Kings & Queens: 1,000 Years of Intrigue, Struggle, Passion & Power. (p. 229)
Gorman, Jacqueline Laks. Alcalde (Mayor) (p. 35)
—Aquarium. (p. 93)
—Aquarium (El Acuario) Acosta, Tatiana & Gutiérrez, Guillermo, trs. (p. 94)
—Aquarium/el Acuario. (p. 94)
—Biblioteca. (p. 177)
—Bus Drivers. Andersen, Gregg, photos by. (p. 244)
—Chris Rock. (p. 311)
—Cuáles Son Tus Derechos Básicos? (p. 388)
—Dentists. (p. 427)
—Doctors. (p. 459)
—Firefighters. Andersen, Gregg, photos by. (p. 591)
—Fossil Fuels. (p. 623)
—Gobernador (Governor) (p. 688)
—Governor. (p. 704)
—Judge. (p. 930)
—Juez (Judge) (p. 931)
—Library. (p. 1005)
—Library/La Biblioteca. Acosta, Tatiana & Gutiérrez, Guillermo, trs. (p. 1006)
—Mayor. (p. 1113)
—Miembro del Congreso (Member of Congress) (p. 1139)
—Museum. (p. 1192)
—Museum (El Museo) Acosta, Tatiana & Gutiérrez, Guillermo, trs. (p. 1192)
—Museum/El Museo. (p. 1193)
—Olsen Twins. (p. 1287)
—Playground: El Parque. (p. 1372)
—Playground. (p. 1372)
—Playground. Acosta, Tatiana & Gutiérrez, Guillermo, trs. (p. 1372)
—Police Officers. Andersen, Gregg, photos by. (p. 1380)
—Por Que Son Importantes las Elecciones? (p. 1386)
—Por Qué Son Importantes Las Elecciones? (p. 1386)
—President. (p. 1396)
—Presidente. (p. 1397)
—Quienes Gobiernan Nuestro Pais? (p. 1427)
—Quiénes Gobiernan Nuestro País? (p. 1427)
—Shopping Mall. (p. 1569)
—Shopping Mall (El Centro Comercial) (p. 1569)
—Vice President. (p. 1840)
—What Are Your Basic Rights? (p. 1880)
—Who Leads Our Country? (p. 1916)
—Why Are Elections Important? (p. 1922)
—Why Do We Have Laws? (p. 1924)
—Zoo. (p. 1988)
—Zoo (El Zoologico) (p. 1989)
—¿Por Qué Tenemos leyes? (p. 1386)
Gorman, Jacqueline Laks, jt. auth. see Bailey Association Staff.
Gorman, Jacqueline Laks, jt. auth. see Hart, Joyce.
Gorman, Jacqueline Laks, jt. auth. see Sanders, Doug.
Gorman, Jacqueline Laks & Laks Gorman, Jacqueline. Bus Drivers. Andersen, Gregg, photos by. (p. 244)
—Firefighters. Andersen, Gregg, photos by. (p. 591)
—Librarians. Andersen, Gregg, photos by. (p. 1005)
—Playground/El Parque. (p. 1372)
—Police Officers. Andersen, Gregg, photos by. (p. 1380)
—Shopping Mall/El Centro Comercial. (p. 1569)
—Zoo/El Zoológico. Acosta, Tatiana & Gutiérrez, Guillermo, trs. (p. 1989)
Gorman, Jacqueline Laks & Nations, Susan. Member of Congress. (p. 1125)
Gorman, Jacqueline Laks, et al. Apor Qu Tenemos Leyes? (p. 92)
—Cuáles Son Tus Derechos Básicos? (p. 388)
Gorman, Joe & Trammell, Jack. Conversations in History: 9 Important Historical Events & the People Who Starred in Them. (p. 361)
Gorman, John. Light: An Investigation. (p. 1014)
Gorman, Karyn. Rapunzel & the Prince of Pop. Anderson, Laura Ellen, illus. (p. 1439)
Gorman, Katie. Wondrous Adventures. (p. 1949)
Gorman, Ken. Atkinsen Ticket. (p. 112)
Gorman, Kyrsten, illus. see Gorman, Patrick.
Gorman, Lovenia. A Is for Algonquin: An Ontario Alphabet. Rose, Melanie, illus. (p. 1)
Gorman, Marsi. Night of the Plunger Knight. (p. 1254)
Gorman, Mike, illus. see Kerns, Ann.
Gorman, Mike, illus. see Service, Pamela F.
Gorman, Patrick. Alicia & Policia Gorman, Kyrsten, illus. (p. 40)
Gorman, Stan, illus. see Balfanz, Mary.
Gorman, Suzy, photos by see Session, Garry.
Gorman, Thomas. Old Neighborhood. (p. 1284)
Gormley, Beatrice. Adara. (p. 11)
—C. S. Lewis: The Man Behind Narnia. (p. 250)
—Diana, Princess of Wales: Young Royalty. (p. 434)
—Julius Caesar: Young Statesman. (p. 933)
—Laura Bush: America's First Lady. (p. 980)
—Malcolm X: A Revolutionary Voice. (p. 1083)
—Maria Mitchell: The Soul of an Astronomer. (p. 1093)
—Marie Curie: Young Scientist. (p. 1093)
—Nelson Mandela: South African Revolutionary. (p. 1241)
Gormley, Beatrice, jt. auth. see Weiss, Ellen.
Gormley, Greg. Daddy's Day at Work. (p. 399)
—Dog in Boots. Angaramo, Roberta, illus. (p. 461)
—Grandad's Busy Day. (p. 707)
—Grandma Goes to Tea. (p. 708)
—Mummy's Big Day Out. (p. 1191)
Gormley, Greg, jt. auth. see Hudson, Charlotte.
Gormley, Julia Ann, illus. see Neuhaus, Richard A.
Gorojan, Elena, ed. see AZ Books Staff.
Gorospe, Myriam, tr. see Cunningham, Steven C.
Gorrasi, Krista, ed. see Haring, Kevin A.
Gorrell, Gena K. Heart & Soul: The Story of Florence Nightingale. (p. 759)
—In the Land of the Jaguar: South America & Its People. Krystoforski, Andrej, illus. (p. 866)
—Say What? The Weird & Mysterious Journey of the English Language. (p. 1518)
—Working Like a Dog: The Story of Working Dogs Through History. (p. 1953)
Gorrell, Nancy. Anna Banana. (p. 85)
—Corey's Story. (p. 367)
Görrissen, Janina, illus. see Kerns, Ann.
Görrissen, Janina, illus. see Tsang, Evonne.
Gors, Steven E. Secret Files of Professor L. Otto Funn: Or, Stop Being a Slug, Open This Book, & Make Your Brain Happy. Carrington, Matt, illus. (p. 1540)
Gorski, Grzegorz. Bajka o Rybaku i Prawie Zŏotej Rybce. (p. 133)
Gorski-Sterner, Gail. Adventures of Isabelle the Lost Pot Belly Pig: Based on a True Story. (p. 19)
Gorsline, Douglas, illus. see Molloy, Anne Stearns Baker.
Gorsline, Douglas, illus. see Moore, Clement C., ed.
Gorsline, Douglas W., illus. see Malkus, Alida Sims.
Gorstein, Mordicai, illus. see Levy, Elizabeth.
Gorstko, Aleksandr. Daddy! Mom! at Last I Know Fractions! (p. 398)
Gortler, Rosemarie, jt. auth. see Piscitelli, Donna.
Gortler, Rosemarie & Piscitelli, Donna. Beatitudes for Children. Sternhagen, Mimi, illus. (p. 153)
—Mass Book for Children. Sternhagen, Mimi, illus. (p. 1102)
Gorton, Julia, illus. see Cobb, Vicki.
Gorton, Julia, illus. see Geist, Ken.
Gorton, Julia, illus. see Ghigna, Charles.
Gorton, Julia, illus. see Newman, Lesléa.
Gorton, Steve, illus. see Platt, Richard.
Gos & Peyo. Astrosmurf. Peyo, illus. (p. 109)
Gosalia, Kirit, tr. see Pundit Baraiya, Gopaldasji.
Goscinny, jt. auth. see Sempe.
Goscinny, R. Asterix & the Roman Agent. Uderzo, A., illus. (p. 108)
—Asterix Omnibus: Asterix & the Big Fight - Asterix in Britain - Asterix & the Normans. Vol. 3 Uderzo, A., illus. (p. 108)
—Asterix Omnibus 5: Asterix & the Cauldron - Asterix in Spain - Asterix & the Roman Agent. Uderzo, Albert, illus. (p. 108)
—Asterix Omnibus 7: Asterix & the Soothsayer - Asterix in Corsica - And Asterix & Caesar's Gift. Uderzo, A., illus. (p. 108)
—Asterix Omnibus 8: Includes Asterix & the Great Crossing #22, Obelix & Co. #23, & Asterix in Belgium #24. Uderzo, A., illus. (p. 108)
—Asterix Omnibus 9. Uderzo, A., illus. (p. 108)
—Seven Stories Morris Publishing Company Staff, illus. (p. 1555)
—Where's Asterix? Uderzo, A., illus. (p. 1910)
—Where's Dogmatix? Uderzo, A., illus. (p. 1910)
Goscinny, R., jt. auth. see Uderzo, A.
Goscinny, R. & Morris Publishing Company Staff. Oklahoma Land Rush. (p. 1283)
Goscinny, R. & Uderzo, A. Asterix & Cleopatra. Uderzo, A., illus. (p. 107)
—Asterix & the Golden Sickle. (p. 107)
—Asterix & the Great Crossing. (p. 107)
—Asterix Omnibus: Asterix & the Big Fight, Asterix in Britain, Asterix & the Normans. (p. 108)
—Asterix Omnibus: Asterix in Switzerland - The Mansion of the Gods - Asterix & the Laurel Wreath. No. 6 (p. 108)
—Asterix Omnibus: Asterix & the Magic Carpet - Asterix & the Secret Weapon - Asterix & Obelix All at Sea. (p. 108)
—Asterix Omnibus 11: Asterix & the Actress, Asterix & the Class Act, Asterix & the Falling Sky. (p. 108)
—Asterix Omnibus 2: Asterix the Gladiator, Asterix & the Banquet, Asterix & Cleopatra. (p. 108)
—Obelix et Compagnie. (p. 1275)
—Tour de Gaule d'Asterix. (p. 1773)
—Where's Asterix? (p. 1910)
Goscinny, R. & Uderzo, Albert. Asterix & the Big Fight. Uderzo, Albert, illus. (p. 107)
—Asterix & the Cauldron. Uderzo, Albert, illus. (p. 107)
—Asterix & the Chieftain's Shield. Uderzo, Albert, illus. (p. 107)
—Asterix & the Laurel Wreath. Uderzo, Albert, illus. (p. 108)
—Asterix & the Normans. Uderzo, Albert, illus. (p. 108)
—Asterix & the Roman Agent. Uderzo, Albert, illus. (p. 108)
—Asterix in Belgium. (p. 108)
—Asterix in Britain. (p. 108)
—Asterix Omnibus. (p. 108)
—Asterix Omnibus 1: Asterix the Gaul, Asterix & the Golden Sickle, Asterix & the Goths. (p. 108)
—Asterix Omnibus 5: Includes Asterix & the Cauldron, Asterix in Spain, & Asterix & the Roman Agent. (p. 108)
—Asterix Omnibus 6: Asterix in Switzerland - The Mansion of the Gods - Asterix & the Laurel Wreath. (p. 108)
—Asterix Omnibus 7: Includes Asterix & the Soothsayer #19, Asterix in Corsica #20, & Asterix & Caesar's Gift #21. (p. 108)
—Mansions of the Gods. Uderzo, Albert, illus. (p. 1088)
—Obelix & Co. (p. 1275)
Goscinny, Ren&eacute. Nicholas. Bell, Anthea, tr. from FRE. (p. 1250)
Goscinny, Rene. Apache Canyon (p. 91)
Goscinny, René. Asterix & the Normans. (p. 108)
—Asterix aux Jeux Olympiques. (p. 108)
—Asterix aux jeux Olympiques. (p. 108)
—Asterix Chez les Belges. (p. 108)
—Asterix en Hispanie. (p. 108)
—Asterix et Cleopatre. (p. 108)
—Asterix et les Goths. (p. 108)
—Asterix et les Normaands. (p. 108)
—Asterix le Gaulois. (p. 108)
—Bounty Hunter Morris Publishing Company Staff, illus. (p. 216)
—Caliph's Vacation. (p. 253)
—Cure for the Daltons Morris, Alfred, illus. (p. 392)
—Daltons Always on the Run. Morris, illus. (p. 401)
—Daltons in the Blizzard. (p. 401)
—Dashing White Cowboy. Morris, illus. (p. 409)
—Escort Morris Publishing Company Staff, illus. (p. 535)
—Grand Vizier Iznogoud Tabary, illus. (p. 707)
—Grande Traversee. (p. 707)
Goscinny, Rene. In the Shadow of the Derricks. (p. 867)
Goscinny, René. Iznogoud & the Day of Misrule. (p. 901)
—Iznogoud & the Magic Carpet. Tabary, illus. (p. 901)
—Iznogoud - Iznogoud & the Magic Computer (p. 901)
—Iznogoud - The Infamous Tabary, illus. (p. 901)
—Iznogoud Vol. 10: Iznogoud the Relentless. Tabary, Jean, illus. (p. 901)
Goscinny, Rene. Jesse James. Morris, Alfred, illus. (p. 914)
—Lucky Luke Versus Joss Jamon. Morris, illus. (p. 1062)
Goscinny, René. Ma Dalton. (p. 1067)
—Nicholas Again. Bell, Anthea, tr. from FRE. (p. 1250)
—Nicholas & the Gang. Bell, Anthea, tr. from FRE. (p. 1250)
—Nicholas on Vacation. Bell, Anthea, tr. (p. 1251)
—Nicholas on Vacation. Bell, Anthea, tr. from FRE. (p. 1251)
Goscinny, Rene. On the Daltons' Trail. (p. 1290)
Goscinny, René. Petit Nicolas. (p. 1348)
—Rivals of Painful Gulch. Morris Publishing Company Staff, illus. (p. 1475)
—Rockets to Stardom - Iznogoud Tabary, illus. (p. 1483)
—Stagecoach. Morris Publishing Company Staff, illus. (p. 1638)
—Tenderfoot. Morris, Alfred, illus. (p. 1719)
—Tortillas for the Daltons. Spear, Luke, tr. from FRE. (p. 1770)
—Wagon Train. Morris, Jean, illus. (p. 1852)
—Western Circus. Morris, Alfred, illus. (p. 1876)
—Wicked Wiles of Iznogoud Tabary, Armelle, illus. (p. 1927)
Goscinny, René, jt. auth. see Morris Publishing Company Staff.
Goscinny, Rene, jt. auth. see Morris.
Goscinny, Rene, jt. auth. see Uderzo, Albert.
Goscinny, René & Bell, Anthea. Nicholas. Sempé, Jean-Jacques, illus. (p. 1250)
Goscinny, René & Livre, Hachette. Asterix 600 Stickers. Uderzo, A., illus. (p. 107)
Goscinny, René & Morris Publishing Company Staff. Billy the Kid. (p. 187)
—Dalton Cousins. (p. 401)
—Daltons Redeem Themselves. (p. 401)
—Emperor Smith. (p. 521)
—Grand Duke. (p. 707)
—Rails on the Prairie. (p. 1434)
—Singing Wire. (p. 1579)
Goscinny, René & Sempé, Jean-Jacques. Nicholas in Trouble. Bell, Anthea, tr. from FRE. (p. 1251)
—Nicholas on Holiday. Bell, Anthea, tr. from FRE. (p. 1251)
Goscinny, Rene & Spear, Luke. Barbed Wire on the Prairie. Spear, Luke, tr. from FRE. (p. 137)
Goscinny, René & Tabary, Jean. Carrot for Iznogoud (p. 271)
Goscinny, René & Uderzo. Asterix French. (p. 108)
—Tour de Gaule d'Asterix. (p. 1773)
Goscinny, René & Uderzo, A. Asterix & Obelix's Birthday. (p. 107)
—Asterix in Switzerland. (p. 108)
Goscinny, René & Uderzo, Albert. Adivino. Uderzo, Albert, illus. (p. 13)
—Asterix & Caesar's Gift. (p. 107)
—Asterix & Cleopatra. (p. 107)
—Asterix & Obelix's Birthday: The Golden Book. (p. 107)
—Asterix & the Banquet. (p. 107)
—Asterix & the Banquet. Uderzo, Albert, illus. (p. 107)
—Asterix & the Big Fight. (p. 107)
—Asterix & the Cauldron. (p. 107)
—Asterix & the Class Act. (p. 107)
—Asterix & the Golden Sickle. (p. 107)
—Asterix & the Goths. (p. 107)
—Asterix & the Goths. Uderzo, Albert, illus. (p. 107)
—Asterix & the Great Crossing. (p. 108)
—Asterix & the Laurel Wreath. Uderzo, Albert, illus. (p. 108)
—Asterix & the Normans. Uderzo, Albert, illus. (p. 108)
—Asterix & the Soothsayer. Uderzo, Albert, illus. (p. 108)
—Asterix at the Olympic Games. Uderzo, Albert, illus. (p. 108)
—Asterix Chez les Helvetes. (p. 108)
—Asterix el Galo. Uderzo, Albert, illus. (p. 108)
—Astérix en Bélgica. Uderzo, Albert, illus. (p. 108)
—Astérix en Bretaña. Uderzo, Albert, illus. (p. 108)
—Asterix en Corse. (p. 108)
—Astérix en Helvecia. Uderzo, Albert, illus. (p. 108)
—Astérix en Hispania. Uderzo, Albert, illus. (p. 108)
—Asterix en Hispanie. (p. 108)
—Asterix en la India. Uderzo, Albert, illus. (p. 108)
—Asterix et le Bombe. (p. 108)
—Asterix French. (p. 108)
—Astérix Gladiador. Uderzo, Albert, illus. (p. 108)
—Asterix in Belgium. (p. 108)
—Asterix in Britain. Uderzo, Albert, illus. (p. 108)
—Asterix in Corsica. (p. 108)
—Asterix in Corsica. Uderzo, Albert, illus. (p. 108)
—Asterix in Spain. (p. 108)
—Asterix in Spain. Uderzo, Albert, illus. (p. 108)
—Asterix in Switzerland. Uderzo, Albert, illus. (p. 108)
—Astérix Legionario. Uderzo, Albert, illus. (p. 108)
Goscinny, Rene & Uderzo, Albert. Asterix Omnibus: Asterix the Legionary - Asterix & the Chieftain's Shield - Asterix at the Olympic Games. Vol. 4 (p. 108)
Goscinny, René & Uderzo, Albert. Asterix Omnibus 9. (p. 108)
—Asterix the Gaul. (p. 108)
—Asterix the Gaul. Uderzo, Albert, illus. (p. 108)
—Asterix the Gladiator. Uderzo, Albert, illus. (p. 108)
—Asterix the Legionary. (p. 108)
—Asterix the Legionary. Uderzo, Albert, illus. (p. 108)
—Asterix y Cleopatra. Uderzo, Albert, illus. (p. 108)
—Asterix y el Caldero. Uderzo, Albert, illus. (p. 108)
—Asterix y los Godos. Uderzo, Albert, illus. (p. 108)
—Bouclier Arverne. (p. 215)
—Cizaña. Uderzo, Albert, illus. (p. 326)
—Combate de los Jefes. Uderzo, Albert, illus. (p. 346)
—Escudo Arverno. Uderzo, Albert, illus. (p. 535)
—Hijo de Astérix. Uderzo, Albert, illus. (p. 779)
—How Obelix Fell into the Magic Potion: When He Was a Little Boy. (p. 811)
—Hoz de Oro. Uderzo, Albert, illus. (p. 824)

—Laureles del Cesar. (p. 980)
—Laureles Del Cesar. Uderzo, Albert, illus. (p. 980)
—Mansions of the Gods. Uderzo, Albert, illus. (p. 1088)
—Obelix & Co. (p. 1275)
—Obélix y Compañía. Uderzo, Albert, illus. (p. 1275)
—Regalo Del César. Uderzo, Albert, illus. (p. 1457)
—Vuelta a la Galia. (p. 1851)
—Vuelta a la Galia. Uderzo, Albert, illus. (p. 1851)
Goscinny, René & Uderzo, M. Adivino. (p. 13)
—Arvernerschild. (p. 105)
—Asterix el Galo. (p. 108)
—Cizana. (p. 326)
—Combate de los Jefes. (p. 346)
—Escudo Arverno. (p. 535)
—Falx Aurea. (p. 567)
—Geschenk Casars. (p. 667)
—Goldene Sichel. (p. 695)
—Gran Travesia. (p. 707)
—Grosse Uberfahrt. (p. 725)
—Hoz de Oro. (p. 824)
—Kampf der Hauptlinge. (p. 942)
—Kupferkessel. (p. 968)
—Laureles del Cesar. (p. 980)
—Lorbeeren des Casar. (p. 1052)
—Normannen. (p. 1264)
—Regalo del Cesar. (p. 1457)
—Residencia de los Dioses. (p. 1463)
—Seher. (p. 1548)
—Streit um Asterix. (p. 1667)
—Tour de Gaulle. (p. 1773)
—Trabantenstadt. (p. 1774)
—Vuelta a la Galia. (p. 1851)
Goscinny, René, et al. Asterix & the Chieftan's Shield. (p. 107)
—Asterix & the Class Act. Bell, Anthea & Hockridge, Derek, trs. from FRE. (p. 107)
—Lucky Luke: The Dashing White Cowboy. (p. 1062)
—Lucky Luke - Jesse James. (p. 1062)
—Lucky Luke - Ma Dalton. (p. 1062)
—Lucky Luke - the Tender Foot. (p. 1062)
—Nicholas Again. Bell, Anthea, tr. from FRE. (p. 1250)
Goscinny, René, text. Asterix Chez les Belges. (p. 108)
—Asterix le Gaulois. (p. 108)
Gose, Elijah Jude. Ryan Howard: Power Hitter. (p. 1499)
Gose, Senora. Flip Flop Spanish: Ages 3-5: Level 1. (p. 605)
Gose, Senora, jt. auth. see Batot, Yvonne.
Goshorn, Shan, illus. see Duncan, Barbara, ed.
Gosine, Aarti. Magic Cave: A Cascade Children's Book. (p. 1072)
Goskowski Kubus, Patricia. Amanda Finds Kristy Alone: The Amanda the Angel Series. (p. 52)
—Amanda Surprises Sarah: The Amanda the Angel Series. (p. 52)
Goslin, Angela. True Colours. (p. 1792)
Gosline, Andrea Alban. Happiness Tree: Celebrating the Gifts of Trees We Treasure. Bossi, Lisa Burnett, illus. (p. 744)
—Ten Little Wishes: A Baby Animal Counting Book. Bossi, Lisa Burnett, illus. (p. 1719)
Gosline, Andrea & Alban, Andrea. Anya's War. (p. 90)
Gosline, Sheldon, ed. see Mueller, Richard.
Gosling, Maureen, et al. You Can Be a Woman Movie Maker. (p. 1974)
Gosling, Sharon. Diamond Thief. (p. 434)
—Remy Brunel & the Circus Horse. (p. 1460)
—Ruby Airship. (p. 1493)
Gosman, Gillian. Abraham Lincoln. (p. 6)
—Baboons. (p. 124)
—Benjamin Franklin. (p. 164)
—Benjamín Franklin. (p. 164)
—Chris Colfer. (p. 311)
—Earth-Friendly Energy. (p. 496)
—Earth-Friendly Food. (p. 496)
—Earth-Friendly Shopping. (p. 496)
—Express It: Sharing Your Media Online (p. 554)
—Franklin D. Roosevelt. (p. 630)
—George Washington. (p. 664)
—Harriet Tubman. (p. 749)
—Howler Monkeys. (p. 823)
—I Have a Cold. (p. 839)
—I Have an Ear Infection. (p. 839)
—I Have Chicken Pox. (p. 839)
—I Have Pinkeye. (p. 839)
—I Have Strep Throat. (p. 839)
—I Have the Flu. (p. 839)
—Inclined Planes in Action. (p. 869)
—Jaden Smith. (p. 905)
—Jennifer Lawrence. (p. 912)
—Justin Bieber. (p. 940)
—Levers in Action. (p. 1004)
—Life Stories (p. 1013)
—Martin Luther King, Jr. (p. 1097)
—Meaghan Jette Martin. (p. 1116)
—Proboscis Monkeys. (p. 1408)
—Publish It: Sharing Your Writing Online (p. 1414)
—Pulleys in Action. (p. 1416)
—Rhesus Monkeys. (p. 1467)
—Rosa Parks. (p. 1488)
—Screws in Action. (p. 1533)
—Simple Machines & Holidays. (p. 1578)
—Simple Machines at School. (p. 1578)
—Simple Machines in Sports. (p. 1578)
—Simple Machines in the Great Outdoors. (p. 1578)
—Simple Machines in the Military. (p. 1578)
—Simple Machines in Your Home. (p. 1578)
—Spider Monkeys. (p. 1626)
—Tamarins. (p. 1704)
—Taylor Lautner. (p. 1708)
—Thomas Jefferson. (p. 1739)
—Wedges in Action. (p. 1871)
—What Do You Know about Earth's Atmosphere? (p. 1883)
—What Do You Know about Earth's Oceans? (p. 1883)
—What Do You Know about Plate Tectonics? (p. 1883)
—What Do You Know about Rocks? (p. 1883)
—What Do You Know about Weather & Climate? (p. 1883)
—Wheels & Axles in Action. (p. 1900)
Gosman, Gillian & Houghton Gosman, Gillian. What Do You Know about Plate Tectonics? (p. 1883)
Gosney, John W. Blogging for Teens. (p. 200)
Gospel Light. Bible Story Art Activities. (p. 176)
—Children's Ministry Smart Pages. (p. 303)
—Passport to Adventure: 13 Choices That Shape a Kid's Life. (p. 1327)
—Really Big Book of Kids' Sermons & Object Talks. (p. 1449)
Gospel Light Publications Staff. Baby Beginnings: I Love to Look! Bible Story Picture Cards. (p. 125)
—Big Book of Bible Story Activity Pages #1: Help Kids Play, Listen & Talk Through the Bible. No. 1 (p. 178)
—God's Story for Me: 104 Favorite Bible Stories for Children. (p. 692)
Gospel Light Publications Staff, creator. Best Gift: Forgiveness: A Read-to-Me Bible Story Coloring Book about Jesus & the Paralyzed Man. (p. 170)
Gospel Light Publications Staff, et al. Genesis. (p. 660)
Gospodinov, George, illus. see Wilson, Barbara E.
Goss, Anthony & Blair, Janet. Golden Dog Bone. (p. 694)
Goss, Gary. Blue Moon Soup: A Family Cookbook. Dyer, Jane, illus. (p. 203)
Goss, Jamie. Snake Without a Hiss (p. 1596)
Goss, John, illus. see Johnston, Annie Fellows.
Goss, John, illus. see Stein, Evaleen.
Goss, Leon. By the Light of the Moon. Luo, Shiyin Sean, illus. (p. 249)
—I'm Good, I'm Beautiful, I'm Smart. Mailey, Maria C. & Neuburger, Jenny, illus. (p. 859)
—In Your Seat, Mr. Pete! Velez, Jill Ondercin, illus. (p. 868)
—King for a Day. Nichols, Chris, illus. (p. 958)
—Selfus Esteemus Personalitus Low. Tunell, Ken, illus. (p. 1549)
Goss, Leon, 3rd. Selfus Esteemus Personalitus Low. Tunell, Ken, illus. (p. 1549)
Goss, Matt. Bear Crimbo. (p. 150)
Goss, Michael Anthony. Bat Who Wore Glasses. Longabough, Kristen, illus. (p. 143)
Goss, Mini, illus. see Edwards, Hazel & Anketell, Christine.
Goss, Mini, illus. see Wignell, Edel.
Goss, Nicole, et al. University of Georgia College Prowler off the Record. (p. 1820)
Goss, Shelia M. & Hughes, Vi. Once upon a Bathtime Shefrin, Sima Elizabeth, illus. (p. 1292)
Goss, Tim. Jupiter (p. 937)
—Mars (p. 1096)
—Mercury (p. 1127)
—Saturn (p. 1515)
—Venus (p. 1836)
Goss, Tim & Gyuk, Geza. Outer Planets (p. 1312)
Gosse, Jim. Jimmy Jaguar: Collection of Stories. (p. 918)
Gosse, Jonathan F., jt. auth. see Green, Denis.
Gosse, Jonathan F., jt. auth. see Proctor, Thomas E.
Gosse, Jonathan F. & Green, Denis. Industrial Maintenance. (p. 872)
Gosselin, Katie, tr. see Coming, Soon.
Gosselin, Kim. Smoking Stinks!! Buttner, Thom, illus. (p. 1595)
—Sportsercise: A School Story about Exercise-Induced Asthma. Ravanelli, Terry, illus. (p. 1633)
Gosselin, Suzanne Hadley, jt. auth. see Nappa, Jon.
Gosselink, John. Defense of Thaddeus A. Ledbetter. (p. 423)
—Free Thaddeus! (p. 634)
Gossett, Christian & Kayl, Bradley. Battle of Kar Dathra's Gate. (p. 146)
Gossett, Kelley & Nash, Kevin. Boston College College Prowler off the Record. (p. 215)
Gossett, Parthy. Jody, Quack, & Me. (p. 919)
Gossett, Robert A. Legend of Jake, the Salty Dog. Yarbrough, Mark, illus. (p. 988)
Gossett, Susan. True Superhero. (p. 1793)
Gossler, Renate Von. Little Weed. (p. 1037)
Gosule, Bette & Longmire, Lynda. Sneakers Hangs Out. Dewitt, Kenny, illus. (p. 1597)
Goswami, Danavir, compiled by. America Is Ready: Vaisnava Society 7. Vol. 7 (p. 59)
Got, Yves. Chambre de Didou. (p. 289)
—Mi Gran Libro de Las Palabras: Las Vacaciones de Dodo. (p. 1132)
—Sam's Pop-up Schoolhouse. Got, Yves, illus. (p. 1509)
Got, Yves & Zero to Ten Publication Staff. Greek Myths & Legends. (p. 721)
Gotch, Jaclyn. Linked by Love. (p. 1019)
Gothard, David, illus. see Saab, Julie.
Gotlieb, Jules, illus. see Olds, Helen Diehl.
Goto, Liu & Yatate, Hajime. Mobile Suit Gundam Seed Ogasawara, Tomofumi, illus. (p. 1157)
Goto, Scott. Perfect Sword. Goto, Scott, illus. (p. 1342)
Goto, Scott, illus. see Gill, Shelley.
Goto, Scott, illus. see Kakugawa, Francis.
Goto, Scott, illus. see Tolstoy, Alexei.
Gotoh, Keiji. Gatekeepers (p. 658)
Gotsch, Connie. Belle's Star. Cogan, John, illus. (p. 163)
—Belle's Trial. Cogan, John, illus. (p. 163)
Gotsch, Patrice. Cesar Chavez: Changing Lives. Arreola, Gil, illus. (p. 288)
—Martin Luther King, Jr: Changing Lives. Arreola, Gil, illus. (p. 1098)
Gotsubo, Masaru, jt. auth. see Manglobe.
Gotsubo, Masaru & Manglobe. Samurai Champloo Gotsubo, Masaru, illus. (p. 1509)
Gotsubo, Ryuji, creator. Sasameke (p. 1515)
Gott, Barry. Class Pets. (p. 327)
—Head, Shoulders, Knees, & Toes. (p. 756)
Gott, Barry, illus. see Bair, Sheila.
Gott, Barry, illus. see Barker, Henry.
Gott, Barry, illus. see Bowen, Anne.
Gott, Barry, illus. see Churchill, Ginger.
Gott, Barry, illus. see Danko, Dan & Mason, Tom.
Gott, Barry, illus. see David, Lawrence.
Gott, Barry, illus. see Driscoll, Laura.
Gott, Barry, illus. see Dussling, Jennifer.
Gott, Barry, illus. see Fishman, Cathy Goldberg.
Gott, Barry, illus. see French, Lisa S.
Gott, Barry, illus. see Hall, Kirsten.
Gott, Barry, illus. see Hopkins, Lee Bennett.
Gott, Barry, illus. see Knudsen, Michelle.
Gott, Barry, illus. see Kroll, Steven.
Gott, Barry, illus. see Larsen, Kirsten.
Gott, Barry, illus. see May, Eleanor.
Gott, Barry, illus. see Spinner, Stephanie.
Gott, Barry, illus. see Walker, Nan.
Gott, Barry, illus. see Wheeler, Lisa.
Gott, Barry, jt. auth. see Ziefert, Harriet.
Gott Dondey, Laura. Civil War Love Story: Spencer & Mary Lemira Lincoln. (p. 325)
Gott, Ricky. Horner. (p. 793)
—I Wish, I Wish... I Wish to Fish / IT. (p. 849)
—I Wish to Fish. (p. 849)
—It. (p. 893)
Gott, Robert. How to Be in the Wrong Place at the Wrong Time. (p. 815)
—Jinxed. (p. 919)
Gottardo, Alessandro, illus. see Lewis, Gill.
Gottesfeld, Jeff. Bank of Badness. (p. 136)
—Bank of Badness. (p. 136)
—Choices. (p. 309)
—Chopped! (p. 310)
—Code. (p. 338)
—Crush. (p. 386)
—Fight School (p. 585)
—Frenemies. (p. 636)
—Independence Day. (p. 870)
—Killer Flood (p. 956)
—Little Miss Miss (p. 1031)
—Love Mints (p. 1060)
—Meet Alana/Meet Kaylee. (p. 1120)
—Robinson's Hood (p. 1480)
—Robinson's Hood. (p. 1480)
—Showdown on the Strip. (p. 1571)
—Standing by Emma. (p. 1639)
—Starstruck (p. 1643)
—Too Many Dogs (p. 1766)
—Wedding Bell Blues. (p. 1870)
—Xo Ronette (p. 1967)
—Xo Ronette. (p. 1967)
Gottesman, Eric. Color Your Own Patriotic Posters. (p. 343)
—Fun with Wizards Stencils. (p. 649)
—Glow-in-the-Dark Tattoos Fantasy. (p. 685)
—Hooray for the USA! (p. 796)
—I Love America Stained Glass Coloring Book. (p. 841)
—Magical Dragons Tattoos. (p. 1074)
—Wizards & Dragons Stained Glass Coloring Book. (p. 1943)
—Wizards & Sorcerers Tattoos. (p. 1943)
Gottesman, Eric & Coloring Books for Adults. Classic Tattoo Designs Coloring Book. (p. 328)
Gottesman, Val, illus. see Poffenberger, Nancy.
Gottfred, B. T. Forever for a Year. (p. 619)
Gottfredson, Floyd. Race to Death Valley Gerstein, David & Groth, Gary, eds. (p. 1431)
Gottfredson, Floyd, et al. Walt Disney's Comics & Stories #700. (p. 1855)
Gottfried Hollander, Barbara. Conduct Disorder. (p. 356)
—Participating in Plays, Skits, & Debates with Cool New Digital Tools. (p. 1325)
Gottfried Hollander, Barbara, jt. auth. see Hollander, Barbara.
Gottfried, Maya. Our Farm: By the Animals of Farm Sanctuary. Zakanitch, Robert Rahway, illus. (p. 1308)
Gottfried, Ted. Censorship. (p. 287)
—Cold War. Reim, Melanie, illus. (p. 339)
—Fight for Peace: A History of Antiwar Movements in America. (p. 585)
—Millard Fillmore. (p. 1143)
Gottfried, Ted & Follett, Katherine. Facts about Alcohol. (p. 561)
Gottfried, Ted & Harkrader, Lisa. Marijuana. (p. 1094)
Gotthardt, Katherine. Furbily-Furld: Takes on the World. Williams, Shane, ed. (p. 650)
Gottheimer, Josh, ed. Ripples of Hope: Great American Civil Rights Speeches. (p. 1474)
Götting, Jean-Claude, illus. see Delval, Marie-Hélène.
Gottlieb, Dale. Are We There Yet? (p. 96)
Gottlieb. Earth & Beyond. (p. 495)
—Human Body. (p. 825)
—Land Animals. (p. 973)
—Matter, Motion & Machines. (p. 1109)
—Plant Life. (p. 1369)
—Water Life. (p. 1863)
Gottlieb, Jack, ed. see Bernstein, Leonard.
Gottlieb, Karen, jt. auth. see Ali, Anila.
Gottlieb, Wendy Ruth. Purr-Im Cat. (p. 1419)
Gottman, John. What Am I Feeling? Talaris Research Institute Staff, ed. (p. 1879)
Gottschalk, Bre. Lucky Necklace. (p. 1063)
Gottschalk, Deana, illus. see Wise, D. Rudd & Wise, Rachel.
Gottschalk, S. Life According to Max: Max's Friends Won't Get Lost. (p. 1007)
Gottschild, Brenda Dixon. Black Dancing Body: A Geography from Coon to Cool. (p. 195)
Gottwald, Siegfried, et al. Meyers Kleine Enzyklopädie Mathematik. (p. 1131)
Gotwald, Julie M. Maddy's Journey. (p. 1070)
Gotzen-Beek, Betina, illus. see Zoller, Elisabeth & Kolloch, Brigitte.
Gotzen-Beek, Betina, illus. see Zöller, Elisabeth & Kolloch, Brigitte.
Goudge, Elisabeth, jt. auth. see Goudge, Elizabeth.
Goudge, Elizabeth. I Saw Three Ships. Tomes, Margot, illus. (p. 845)
—Little White Horse. (p. 1037)
Goudge, Elizabeth & Goudge, Elisabeth. Pequeño Caballo Blanco. (p. 1341)
Gouge, Angela, illus. see Hasler, Brian.
Gouge, Angela, tr. see Hasler, Brian.
Gough, Bill. Adventures of Stumpman. (p. 23)
Gough, Bryan, illus. see Woloson, Eliza.
Gough, Bryan, tr. see Woloson, Eliza.
Gough, Simon. I Can'T Fly & I Can'T Swim. (p. 837)
Gough, Sue. Here Comes the Night. (p. 770)
Goulchoux, René. I Am Ivan Crocodile! Neuhaus, Julia, illus. (p. 833)
Goulart, Ron. Cheap Thrills. (p. 295)
—Comic Book Culture: An Illustrated History. Bennett, Ann Granning, ed. (p. 348)
Goulbourne, Nathaniel. Aliens Zoo. (p. 41)
Gould, Alan. Convection: A Current Event. Klofkorn, Lisa, illus. (p. 361)
—Hot Water & Warm Homes from Sunlight. Gould, Alan et al, illus. (p. 802)
Gould, Carol. My Native American School. Drzewiecki, Paul, illus. (p. 1215)
Gould, Cecily. Island of the White Toothed Shrew. (p. 892)
Gould, Ellen. Blue Number Counting Book. Kelly, Cathy, illus. (p. 203)
Gould, Evan Jay, jt. auth. see Gould, Judith S.
Gould, F. J. Children's Plutarch: Tales of the Romans. Crane, Walter, illus. (p. 304)
Gould, Francesca. Why Fish Fart: Gross but True Things You'll Wish You Didn't Know. Coovert, J. P., illus. (p. 1925)
Gould, Francesca & Haviland, David. Why Dogs Eat Poop: Gross but True Things You Never Knew about Animals. Coovert, J. P., illus. (p. 1924)
Gould, Jacqueline. Guessing Book: For 3 to 7 Year Olds. (p. 729)
Gould, Jane. At the Pond. (p. 111)
—In the Garden. (p. 866)
—World War I: 1914-1916 — a Terrible New Warfare Begins. (p. 1958)
Gould, Jane H. Alexander Hamilton. (p. 36)
—Benjamin Franklin. (p. 164)
—Ferdinand Magellan. (p. 581)
—Flying Dutchman. (p. 609)
—George Washington Carver. (p. 664)
—Henry Hudson. (p. 768)
—John Adams. (p. 921)
—John Henry. (p. 922)
—Steve Jobs. (p. 1649)
Gould, Jane H., jt. auth. see Miller, Reagan.
Gould, Jane H., jt. auth. see Roberts, Steven.
Gould, Jason, photos by see Wild, Margaret.
Gould, Joyce A. Beyond Location, Location, Location: A Systematic, Promotional Approach to Marketing Commercial Real Estate. (p. 174)
Gould, Judith S. & Burke, Mary F. Four Square: The Personal Writing Coach, Grades 7-9. Wheeler, Ron, illus. (p. 625)
—Four Square: The Personal Writing Coach, Grades 4-6. Ginger Illustration, illus. (p. 625)
—Write Now! Mitchell, Judith, ed. (p. 1963)
Gould, Judith S. & Gould, Evan Jay. Four Square: A Companion to the Four Square Writing Method: Writing in the Content Areas for Grades 1-4. Mitchell, Judy, ed. (p. 625)
Gould, Lorraine. Warren the Watchdog. (p. 1858)
Gould, M. & Gould, R. About Gossip: What Would Jesus Do Hurst, Debbie, illus. (p. 5)
Gould, M&R. Bleeks: The Bleek Family's First Christmas Hurst, Debbie, illus. (p. 199)
—What Would Jesus Do? Purity of Intention. (p. 1895)
Gould, Margee. Giant Plants. (p. 674)
—Meat-Eating Plants. (p. 1118)
—Poisonous Plants. (p. 1377)
—Prickly Plants. (p. 1398)
Gould, Mike, ed. see Kemp, Beth.
Gould, R., jt. auth. see Gould, M.
Gould, Robert. Big Rigs. (p. 183)
—Bugs Epstein, Eugene, illus. (p. 237)
—Dinosaurs. (p. 443)
—Father & Son Read-Aloud Old Testament Stories. Gurin, Lara, illus. (p. 577)
—Father & Son Read-Aloud Stories. Gurin, Lara, illus. (p. 577)
—Giant Earth Movers. (p. 673)
—Monster Trucks. (p. 1168)
—Racers. Gould, Robert, photos by. (p. 1431)
—Rescue Vehicles. Gould, Robert, photos by. (p. 1462)
—Sea Creatures. (p. 1534)
—Tractors. (p. 1775)
Gould, Robert, jt. auth. see Duey, Kathleen.
Gould, Robert, photos by see Big Guy Books Staff & Duey, Kathleen.
Gould, Robert, photos by see Duey, Kathleen.
Gould, Robert & Duey, Kathleen. Time Soldiers. (p. 1752)
—Time Soldiers - Rex. Epstein, Eugene, illus. (p. 1752)
Gould, Roberta. Kid's Book of Incredibly Fun Crafts. Martin Jourdenais, Norma Jean, illus. (p. 952)
—Kids' Multicultural Craft Book: 35 Crafts from Around the World. Jourdenais, Norma Jean, illus. (p. 954)
Gould, Sasha. Cross My Heart. (p. 385)
—Heart of Glass. (p. 759)
Gould, Shawn, illus. see Raff, Courtney Granet.
Gould, Susan Lynn. Gift from Grandma. Verkruysse, Toni, illus. (p. 675)
Gould, Terry. Adventures of Sir Sniffsalot & His Friends. (p. 23)
—Adventures of Sir Sniffsalot & His Friends. Proulx, Denis, illus. (p. 23)
Gould, Vera Dobson & Hughes, Patricia J. Dominie Thesaurus for Young Writers. (p. 465)
Gould, William, jt. auth. see Ward-Johnson, Chris.
Goulding, Celeste, illus. see Arengo, Sue.
Goulding, Dorothy J. Three Christmas Plays. (p. 1741)
Goulding, June, illus. see Baxter, Nicola.
Goulding, June, illus. see Blumberg, Margie.
Goulding, June, illus. see Ratnett, Michael.
Gouldthorpe, Peter, illus. see King, Corinne & Fenton, Corinne.
Goulet, Willette. Gizmo's Day Out. (p. 681)
Goulis, Julie. Something Shiny, Something Round. Ferguson, John, illus. (p. 1610)
—Things a String Can Be. Ferguson, John, illus. (p. 1733)
—Topsy-Turvy Towel. Ferguson, John H., illus. (p. 1769)
Goulston, Mark. Los 6 Secretos para Tener una Relacion Duradera. (p. 1053)
Gourbault, Martine, illus. see Pendziwol, Jean E.

G

Gourbault, Martine, illus. see Pendziwol, Jean E. & Pendziwol, Jean.
Gourbault, Martine, jt. auth. see Pendziwol, Jean E.
Gourlay, Candy. Tall Story. (p. 1704)
Gourlay, Catherine. Family Matters: Plays about Family Changes. (p. 568)
—Flashpoints! Plays about Controlling Anger. (p. 602)
—Friend or Foe? Plays about Bullying. (p. 637)
—Invisible Me: Plays about Self-Image. (p. 885)
—What's the Difference? Plays about Tolerance. (p. 1899)
—Where Do I Belong? Plays about Fitting In. (p. 1907)
Gourley, Barbara. Legacy of Tip: The Catahoula. (p. 987)
—True Adventures of Tip the Catahoula-Leopard Cowdog. (p. 1791)
Gourley, Catherine. Flappers & the New American Woman: Perceptions of Women from 1918 Through the 1920s. (p. 602)
—Gibson Girls & Suffragists: Perceptions of Women from 1900 to 1918. (p. 674)
—Gidgets & Women Warriors: Perceptions of Women in the 1950s & 1960s. (p. 674)
—Horrors of Andersonville: Life & Death Inside a Civil War Prison. (p. 799)
—Images & Issues of Women in the Twentieth Century. (p. 860)
—Ms. & the Material Girls: Perceptions of Women from the 1970s Through the 1990s. (p. 1188)
—Rosie & Mrs. America: Perceptions of Women in the 1930s & 1940s. (p. 1490)
—Who Is Maria Tallchief? Taylor, Val Paul, illus. (p. 1916)
Gourley, Robbin. Bring Me Some Apples & I'll Make You a Pie: A Story about Edna Lewis. (p. 228)
—First Garden: The White House Garden & How It Grew. (p. 595)
—Talkin' Guitar: A Story of Young Doc Watson. (p. 1703)
Gourse, Leslie. Sophisticated Ladies: The Great Women of Jazz. French, Martin, illus. (p. 1613)
Gous, M. M., jt. auth. see Barnard, Marietjie.
Gous, M.M., jt. auth. see Barnard, Marietjie.
Gousseff, Catherine. Perfect Knight. Negrin, Fabian, tr. from FRE. (p. 1342)
Gout, Leopoldo, jt. auth. see Patterson, James.
Gouveia, Keith. Children of the Dragon. (p. 302)
—Goblin Princess. (p. 688)
Gouveia, Keith & Peck, Garrett, eds. Small Bites. (p. 1591)
Govan, Christine Noble. Pink Maple House. Sari, illus. (p. 1360)
—Surprising Summer. Sari, illus. (p. 1686)
—Tilly's Strange Secret. (p. 1750)
Govan, Nina & Olive and Moss Staff. Louis the Lion. (p. 1058)
—Margot & Mo. (p. 1092)
—Michael the Monkey. (p. 1135)
Gove, Bill. Sky Route to the Quarries: History of the Barre Railroad. (p. 1587)
Gove, Doris. My Mother Talks to Trees Mallory, Marilynn H., illus. (p. 1214)
Gove, Frank Stanley, illus. see Ferris, Margaret Ann.
Gove, Susan E. Kids Get It: Shrinking Our Carbon Footprint. (p. 953)
Govenar, Alan. Life As a Sideshow Tattoo Artist: Stoney Knows How (p. 1008)
Govenar, Alan B. Extraordinary Ordinary People: Five American Masters of Traditional Arts. Govenar, Alan B., photos by. (p. 555)
Govoni, Dennis, photos by see Walls, Suzanne L.
Gow, Kailin. Activities Guide for 365 Days of the Year! Fun Things to Do for Kids & Grown-Ups That'll Help Develop Creativity, Social Skills, & Self-confidence! (p. 10)
—Audrey Club: A Fashion Fables Novel. (p. 115)
—Devil Wore Denim: A Fashion Fables Novel. (p. 432)
—Diary of a Discount Donna: A Fashion Fables Book: A Novel. (p. 434)
—Diary of A Discount Donna: A Fashion Fables Novel: A Novel. (p. 434)
—Loving Summer. (p. 1061)
—Reborn #1: Queen B Superheroine Series. (p. 1451)
—Stoker Sisters. (p. 1651)
—Tiffany at Tea Time: (A Tiffany T. Book) Dillman, Jennifer, illus. (p. 1748)
—Tiffany at the Top of the World: (A Tiffany T. Book) Dillman, Jennifer, illus. (p. 1748)
Gow, Kailin, creator. Queen B Superheroine: Book 1 - Reborn & Book 2 - Buzz Off. (p. 1424)
Gow, Mary. Archimedes: Genius Mathematician. (p. 95)
—Archimedes: Mathematical Genius of the Ancient World. (p. 95)
—Great Philosopher: Plato & His Pursuit of Knowledge. (p. 717)
—Great Thinker: Aristotle & the Foundations of Science. (p. 718)
—Greatest Doctor of Ancient Times: Hippocrates & His Oath. (p. 719)
—Johannes Kepler: Discovering the Laws of Planetary Motion. (p. 921)
—Johnstown Flood: The Day the Dam Burst. (p. 924)
—Measuring the Earth: Eratosthenes & His Celestial Geometry. (p. 1117)
—Rachel Carson: Ecologist & Activist. (p. 1431)
—Robert Boyle: Pioneer of Experimental Chemistry. (p. 1478)
—Robert Hooke: Creative Genius, Scientist, Inventor. (p. 1479)
—Stock Market Crash Of 1929: Dawn of the Great Depression. (p. 1651)
Gow, Nancy. Ten Big Toes & a Prince's Nose. Costanza, Stephen, illus. (p. 1718)
Gowack, Paul, jt. auth. see Torphy, William.
Gowan, Barbara. D Is for Desert: A World Deserts Alphabet. (p. 397)
—Desert Digits: An Arizona Number Book. Toddy, Irving, illus. (p. 429)
—Little Arizona. (p. 1023)
Gowans, Floyd W. Covenant Verses: The Book of Mormon. (p. 373)
Gowans, Jacob. Psion Beta. (p. 1413)
—Psion Gamma. (p. 1413)
Gowar, Mick. Baa Baa, Black Sheep & Baa Baa, Pink Sheep. (p. 123)
—Dad's Van. (p. 399)
—Leo's New Pet. Morgan, Richard, illus. (p. 993)
—Pie-Eating Contest. Hall, Francois, illus. (p. 1356)
—Rodeo Rider Hall, Francois, illus. (p. 1484)
Gowen, Fiona. How to Draw Amazing Animals & Incredible Insects. (p. 816)
—How to Draw Awesome Vehicles: Land, Sea, & Air. (p. 816)
—How to Draw Incredible Aliens & Cool Space Stuff. (p. 817)
Gowen, L. Kris & McKenna, Molly. Image & Identity: Becoming the Person You Are. (p. 860)
Gowen, Molly. Dragons of Jelly Mountain. (p. 479)
Gowens, Kyle, illus. see Kennis, Don.
Gower, Catherine & Zhihong, He. Long-Long's New Year. (p. 1047)
Gower, Jeremy, illus. see Meredith, Susan.
Gower, Jeremy, illus. see Watt, Fiona.
Gower, Jim, illus. see Eschberger, Beverly.
Gower, Jim, illus. see Habiger, Geoff.
Gower, Teri, illus. see Brocklehurst, Ruth.
Gower, Teri, illus. see Daynes, Katie.
Gower, Teri, illus. see Dickins, Rosie.
Gower, Teri, illus. see Doherty, Gillian, et al.
Gower, Teri, illus. see Doherty, Gillian.
Gower, Teri, illus. see Helbrough, Emma.
Gower, Teri, illus. see Johnson, Sue & Evans, Cheryl.
Gower, Teri, illus. see Jones, Rob Lloyd.
Gower, Teri, illus. see Lester, Anna.
Gower, Teri, illus. see Sims, Lesley.
Gower, Teri, illus. see Young, Caroline.
Gower, Teri, jt. auth. see Jones, Rob Lloyd.
Gowey, Christine Ann. Zip & Zap Take a Nap. Kleinman, Andi, illus. (p. 1987)
Gowing, Lawrence, ed. Facts on File Biographical Encyclopedia of Artists. (p. 561)
—Facts on File Encyclopedia of Art. (p. 561)
—Facts on File Encyclopedia of Art & Artists Set. (p. 561)
Gowing, Pattie. Mrs. Gowing's Kindergarten. vonderLuft, Lydia, illus. (p. 1187)
Gownley, Jimmy. Amelia & Her Three Kisses. (p. 57)
—Amelia in Fireflies & Time. (p. 58)
—Amelia in Heroes & Villains. (p. 58)
—Amelia in into Graceland. (p. 58)
—Amelia in Joy & Wonder. (p. 58)
—Amelia's Life During Wartime. (p. 58)
—Dumbest Idea Ever! (p. 489)
—Her Permanent Record. (p. 769)
—Her Permanent Record. Gownley, Jimmy, illus. (p. 769)
—Meaning of Life ... & Other Stuff. Gownley, Jimmy, illus. (p. 1117)
—Superheroes. (p. 1683)
—Superheroes. Gownley, Jimmy, illus. (p. 1683)
—True Things: Adults Don't Want Kids to Know. Gownley, Jimmy, illus. (p. 1793)
—Tweenage Guide to Not Being Unpopular. Gownley, Jimmy, illus. (p. 1799)
—Very Ninja Christmas. Gownley, Jimmy, illus. (p. 1838)
—What Makes You Happy. Gownley, Jimmy, illus. (p. 1892)
—When the Past Is a Present. Gownley, Jimmy, illus. (p. 1905)
—Whole World's Crazy. (p. 1920)
—Whole World's Crazy. Gownley, Jimmy, illus. (p. 1920)
Gowsell, Rosie, jt. auth. see Rodger, Ellen.
Goyal, Anuj, ed. Higher Ground. (p. 778)
Goyer, David S., jt. auth. see Johns, Geoff.
Goyer, David S. & Johns, Geoff. Darkness Falls Tomasi, Peter, ed. (p. 408)
—Jsa: Prince of Darkness. (p. 930)
Goyer, David S., et al. Stealing Thunder. (p. 1646)
Goyer, Deb. Billy's Fantasies. (p. 187)
—Raggedy Beggar. Johnson, Lauren, illus. (p. 1433)
Goyer, Katell. Princesses of the World. Misstigri, illus. (p. 1406)
Goyer, Tricia. Prayers That Changed History: From Christopher Columbus to Helen Keller, How God Used 25 People to Change the World (p. 1393)
Goyette, Linda. Northern Kids. (p. 1265)
—Rocky Mountain Kids (p. 1484)
Goza, Shelly. Mr. Meme. Gil, Rodolpho, illus. (p. 1185)
GPV. Guinea Pig Nativity. (p. 731)
Graaf, Anne De, see De Graaf, Anne.
Graaf, Anne De, see Dickens, Charles & De Graaf, Anne.
Grab, Daphne. Alive & Well in Prague, New York. (p. 41)
—Halftime. (p. 737)
Grabas, Peter, illus. see Nosek, Jude.
Grabell, Jeff, jt. auth. see Krech, Bob.
Grabenstein, Chris. Black Heart Crypt. (p. 196)
—Crossroads. (p. 385)
—Escape from Mr. Lemoncello's Library. (p. 535)
—Hanging Hill. (p. 742)
—I Funny: A Middle School Story. Patterson, James, ed. (p. 838)
—Riley Mack & the Other Known Troublemakers. (p. 1472)
—Riley Mack Stirs up More Trouble. (p. 1472)
—Smoky Corridor. (p. 1595)
Grabenstein, Chris, jt. auth. see Patterson, James.
Grabenstein, Chris & Patterson, James. I Funny: A Middle School Story. Park, Laura, illus. (p. 838)
Graber, Janet. Resistance. (p. 1463)
Graber, Jesse, illus. see Byrne, Marlene F.
Graber, Jesse, illus. see Byrne, Marlene.
Graber, Jesse, jt. auth. see Byrne, Marlene F.
Graber, Lois. Song in the Storm. (p. 1611)
Graber, Vickie, illus. see Bayne, Nancy.
Grabham, Tim, et al. Movie Maker: The Ultimate Guide to Making Films. Parsons, Garry, illus. (p. 1183)
Grabis, Bettina, et al. Nail Decorating. (p. 1227)
Grablewski, Alexandra, photos by see Hart, Jenny.
Grabo, Carl. Cat in Grandfather's House. (p. 278)
Grabowski, Angela. Encyclopedia of Tunisian Crochet. (p. 525)
Grabowski, Daniel, illus. see D'Amico, Christy.
Grabowski, John F. Alton Brown. (p. 50)
—Americans of Central American Heritage. (p. 64)
—Atlanta Braves. (p. 112)
—Bobby Flay. (p. 206)
—Detroit Redwings. (p. 431)
—Larry Fitzgerald. (p. 976)
—Minnesota Vikings. (p. 1147)
—New York Rangers. (p. 1248)
—Vietnamese Americans. (p. 1841)
Grabowski, Leo. Nathan's Thread. Hale, Pattie, illus. (p. 1231)
Grace, Amanda. But I Love Him. (p. 246)
—In Too Deep. (p. 868)
—No One Needs to Know. (p. 1259)
—Truth about You & Me. (p. 1794)
Grace, Ann Marie. Secret Gift. (p. 1541)
Grace, Aunt. Woodchuck OntOnt FairHolly WyattHiser Mcgallion & His Friends. (p. 1949)
Grace, Bill, illus. see Rogers Yaeger, Nancy.
Grace, Catherine O'Neill. How & Why: A Kids' Book about the Body. Barr, Loel, illus. (p. 804)
Grace, Catherine O'Neill, jt. auth. see Bruchac, Margaret M.
Grace, Catherine O'Neill & Bruchac, Margaret M. 1621: A New Look at Thanksgiving. Brimberg, Sisse & Coulson, Cotton, photos by. (p. 2002)
Grace, Elizabeth. Hollywood Tail. (p. 789)
Grace, Elora. Umbrellas Everywhere! (p. 1810)
Grace, Gloria. World Without Rules. (p. 1960)
Grace, Hannah. Popcorn MacHine. (p. 1384)
Grace, Jaylen. Porridge the Two Faced Parrot. (p. 1386)
Grace, Kathleen. Perfect Pug. (p. 1342)
Grace, L. E. Joey G. Can't Fall Asleep. (p. 920)
Grace, N. B. Battle of the Bands. (p. 146)
—Lights, Camera, Action! (p. 1016)
—Mummies Unwrapped! The Science of Mummy-Making. (p. 1191)
—Rev It Up! (p. 1465)
—UFO Lands in USA! Was a Spacecraft Crash Covered Up? (p. 1807)
—UFOs: What Scientists Say May Shock You! (p. 1808)
—UFO's: What Scientists Say May Shock You! (p. 1808)
Grace, Patricia. Mutuwhenua: The Moon Sleeps. (p. 1195)
Grace, Phillip. Lizard of Cupcake Lake. (p. 1042)
Grace, Samantha & Michael. My Little Boy. (p. 1212)
Grace, Sherrill E., et al, eds. Vision of the Orient: Texts, Intertexts, & Contexts of Madame Butterfly. (p. 1845)
Grace, Sina, illus. see Benson, Amber.
Grace, Susan, jt. auth. see Shields, Mary.
Grace, Will. Thank You Prayer. Geist, Ken, ed. (p. 1725)
—Who Do You See? (p. 1915)
Graceland Book Publishers, as told by. Little Girl by Chinyere Nwakanma. (p. 1028)
Grace-Smith, Briar. When Sun & Moon Collide. (p. 1904)
Gracey, Michael. Invisible Ideas. (p. 885)
Gracia, Amy A. Arby the Singing Cockatoo: Arby Finds His Voice. (p. 95)
Gracie, Anne. Stolen Princess. (p. 1652)
Grack, David. Birds of the Northwoods. (p. 192)
Grack, Rachel. American Paint Horse. (p. 62)
—American Saddlebred Horse. (p. 63)
Grade Class, Goslee's Fifth and Sixth. Amazing Body Book. (p. 54)
Gradisher, Martha, illus. see Linn, Margot.
Gradstein, Donna, jt. auth. see Jeffers, Susan.
Gradwell, John B., et al. Technology Shaping Our World: Wraparound Edition. (p. 1712)
—Technology Shaping Our World. (p. 1712)
Grady, Cynthia. I Lay My Stitches Down. Wood, Michele, illus. (p. 840)
Grady, Daniel John. Diego Forlan. (p. 437)
—Mario Yepes. (p. 1094)
Grady, Joi. Daddy Lets Me. (p. 398)
—I Like You & I Love You. (p. 841)
Grady, Karen. It's Not My Fault, She Started It. (p. 898)
Grady, Kit, illus. see Calvani, Mayra.
Grady, Kit, illus. see Harris, Sally M.
Grady, Kit, illus. see McIntyre, Mel & McIntyre, Mel.
Grady, Kit, illus. see McIntyre, Mel.
Grady, Kit, illus. see Reeg, Cynthia.
Grady, Kit, illus. see Shepherd, Donna J.
Grady, Kit, jt. auth. see Arnold, Connie.
Grady, Monica, et al. Stardust from Space. De Leiris, Lucia, illus. (p. 1642)
Grady, Sean M. Optics. (p. 1301)
Grady, Sean M. & Tabak, John. Biohazards. (p. 189)
Grady, Wayne, tr. Technology (p. 1711)
Graeber, Mark. Collin Conway: The First Adventure with. (p. 340)
Graef, Renee, illus. see Anderson, William T.
Graef, Renee, illus. see Arno, Iris Hiskey.
Graef, Renee, illus. see Bastianich, Lidia Matticchio.
Graef, Renee, illus. see Hinrichs, Alexandra S. D.
Graef, Renee, illus. see Hodgson, Mona Gansberg.
Graef, Renee, illus. see Lord, Jill Roman.
Graef, Renee, illus. see Mackall, Dandi Daley.
Graef, Renee, illus. see Patrick, Jean L. S.
Graef, Renee, illus. see Prieto, Anita C.
Graef, Renee, illus. see Rodgers, Richard & Hammerstein, Oscar, II.
Graef, Renee, illus. see Schulman, Janet.
Graef, Renee, illus. see Shaw, Janet.
Graef, Renée, illus. see Smith, Marie & Smith, Roland.
Graef, Renee, illus. see Wargin, Kathy-jo.
Graef, Renee, illus. see Wiley, Melissa.
Graegin, Stephanie, illus. see Hoffman, Judy.
Graegin, Stephanie, illus. see Jenkins, Emily.
Graegin, Stephanie, illus. see Latham, Irene.
Graegin, Stephanie, illus. see LeBox, Annette.
Graegin, Stephanie, illus. see McFadden, Deanna, et al.
Graegin, Stephanie, illus. see McFadden, Deanna.
Graegin, Stephanie, illus. see Namm, Diane.
Graegin, Stephanie, illus. see Scanlon, Liz Garton.
Graegin, Stephanie, illus. see Van Laan, Nancy.
Graf, Hilber H. Evil Never Dies. (p. 546)
Graf, Mike. Acadia National Park: Eye of the Whale. (p. 7)
—Arches & Canyonlands National Parks - In the Land of Standing Rocks. Leggitt, Marjorie, illus. (p. 95)
—Bryce Canyon & Zion National Parks: Danger in the Narrows. Leggitt, Marjorie, illus. (p. 233)
—Glacier National Park: Going to the Sun. Leggitt, Marjorie, illus. (p. 682)
—Grand Canyon National Park: Tail of the Scorpion. Leggitt, Marjorie, illus. (p. 707)
—Grand Teton National Park: to the Top of the Grand. (p. 707)
—Great Smokies National Park: Ridge Runner Rescue. Leggitt, Marjorie, illus. (p. 718)
—Mount Rushmore, Badlands, Wind Cave: Going Underground. Leggitt, Marjorie, illus. (p. 1180)
—Mudslide (p. 1189)
—My Yosemite: A Guide for Young Adventurers. Filice, Annette, illus. (p. 1222)
—Olympic National Park: Touch of the Tide Pool, Crack of the Glacier. Marjorie, Leggitt, illus. (p. 1288)
—Rock Climbing. (p. 1482)
—Rocky Mountain National Park: Peril on Long's Peak. Marjorie, Leggitt, illus. (p. 1484)
—Yellowstone National Park: Eye of the Grizzly. Leggitt, Marjorie, illus. (p. 1970)
—Yosemite National Park: Harrowing Ascent of Half Dome. Leggitt, Marjorie, illus. (p. 1972)
Graf, Mike, jt. auth. see McFarren, Kathleen.
Graf, Mike & Follett, Dave. Mudslide. (p. 1189)
Graf, Mike & Kaske, Anne. Dinosaur Canyon. Weston, Steve, illus. (p. 441)
Graf, Mike & Morden, Richard. Dirt on My Shoe. (p. 446)
Graf, Mike & Snedden, Robert. Everglades National Park. McMullen, Anne, illus. (p. 542)
—How Does a Cloud Become a Thunderstorm? (p. 808)
—How Does a Waterfall Become Electricity? (p. 808)
—Mapping Earth from Space (p. 1090)
—Mapping Earth from Space KJA Artists Staff, illus. (p. 1090)
—Montana. (p. 1170)
—Oregon. (p. 1302)
Graf, Mike, et al. How Does a Waterfall Become Electricity? (p. 808)
Graf, William, illus. see Sparks, Candi.
Grafe, Max, illus. see Elliott, David.
Grafe, Max, illus. see Schlitz, Laura Amy.
Graff, Lisa. Absolutely Almost. (p. 7)
—Double Dog Dare. (p. 472)
—Life & Crimes of Bernetta Wallflower: The Pros & Cons. (p. 1007)
—Lost in the Sun. (p. 1056)
—Sophie Simon Solves Them All. Beene, Jason, illus. (p. 1613)
—Tangle of Knots. (p. 1705)
—Thing about Georgie. (p. 1732)
—Umbrella Summer. (p. 1810)
Graff, Marie Louise, jt. auth. see Kohen, Elizabeth.
Graff, Rhonda. Instant Nonfiction Writing Frames: Reproducible Templates & Easy How-To's That Guide Children to Research & Write Successful Reports on the Topics You Teach. (p. 878)
Graffam, Merle, illus. see Walker, E. G.
Graffito Books Staff & Helm, Zebedee. Dogs of the World: Ultimate Guide Books to Everything! Helm, Zebedee, illus. (p. 463)
Grafflus, Richard. Great Groundhog Caper. (p. 716)
Graftinvine, D. J. Hobbledehoy: Salvation. (p. 786)
Grafton, Carol Belanger, ed. Cats in Art. (p. 281)
Gragg, Karla. Memphis Learns the Hard Way. Unger, Erin, illus. (p. 1126)
Gragg, Rod. George Washington: An Interactive Biography (p. 664)
Graham, Adele, illus. see Gilbert, Joan Sewell.
Graham, Adele, illus. see Gilbert, Joan.
Graham, Alastair. Full Moon Soup. (p. 646)
Graham, Alistair. Full Moon Soup. Graham, Alistair, illus. (p. 646)
Graham, Amy. Acadia National Park: Adventure, Explore, Discover. (p. 7)
—Astonishing Ancient World Scientists: Eight Great Brains. (p. 108)
—Be Smart about Your Career: College, Income, & Careers. (p. 149)
—Be Smart about Your Future: Risk Management & Insurance. (p. 149)
—Celebrated African-American Novelists. (p. 284)
—Choosing a Community Service Career: A How-to Guide. (p. 310)
—Discovering Antarctica's Land, People, & Wildlife: A MyReportLinks. com Book. (p. 448)
—Great Smoky Mountains National Park: Adventure, Explore, Discover. (p. 718)
—Iran in the News: Past, Present, & Future. (p. 886)
—Look at the Bill of Rights: Protecting the Rights of Americans. (p. 1049)
—Look at the Eighteenth & Twenty-First Amendments: The Prohibition & Sale of Intoxicating Liquors. (p. 1049)
—New Hampshire: A MyReportLinks.com Book. (p. 1245)
—Oregon Trail & the Daring Journey West by Wagon. (p. 1303)
—Seven Wonders of the Natural World: A MyReportLinks. com Book. (p. 1555)
—Thomas Edison: Wizard of Light & Sound. (p. 1738)
—What Are the 7 Wonders of the Natural World? (p. 1879)
Graham, Amy, jt. auth. see Gonzales, Doreen.
Graham, Amy & Haslam, William. Woodland Caribou: A MyReportLinks.com Book. (p. 1949)
Graham, Andrew S., illus. see Graham, Janice Barrett.
Graham, Audry. Boa Constrictor. (p. 205)
—Boa Constrictor / Boa Constrictora. (p. 205)
—King Cobra. (p. 958)
Graham, Baxter. Old King Stinky Toes. Martin, James R., illus. (p. 1284)
Graham, Bettina, jt. auth. see Boase, Petra.
Graham, Billy. God's Good News Bible Storybook (p. 691)
—Just As I Am: The Autobiography of Billy Graham. (p. 938)
Graham, Bob. April & Esme Tooth Fairies. Graham, Bob, illus. (p. 93)
—Benny: An Adventure Story. (p. 165)
—Bus Called Heaven. Graham, Bob, illus. (p. 244)
—How the Sun Got to Coco's House. Graham, Bob, illus. (p. 813)

G

—How to Heal a Broken Wing. Graham, Bob, illus. (p. 820)
—"Let's Get a Pup!" Said Kate. Graham, Bob, illus. (p. 996)
—Silver Button. Graham, Bob, illus. (p. 1576)
—Tales from the Waterhole. (p. 1702)
—Tales from the Waterhole. Graham, Bob, illus. (p. 1702)
—Trouble with Dogs... Said Dad. Graham, Bob, illus. (p. 1790)
—Vanilla Ice Cream. Graham, Bob, illus. (p. 1833)
Graham, Bob, illus. see Gray, Nigel.
Graham, Bob, illus. see Rosen, Michael.
Graham, Bob, illus. see Smith, Peter.
Graham, Bobby G. Jake the Snake. (p. 906)
Graham, Brandon. Perverts of the Unknown. Graham, Brandon, illus. (p. 1345)
—Prophet Volume 1: Remission TP: Remission TP. (p. 1411)
Graham, Brandon & Roy, Simon. Prophet Volume 2: Brothers TP: Brothers TP. (p. 1411)
—Prophet Volume 3: Empire TP: Empire TP. (p. 1411)
Graham, Buck. My First Big Book of Questions & Answers: Things That Go. (p. 1204)
Graham, C. E., illus. see Dukoff, K. D.
Graham, C. Toni. Gabby Giggles. (p. 652)
Graham, Carl, illus. see Williams, Paula.
Graham, Caroline. Character Cats: Tyler & the Tree of Courage. (p. 291)
Graham, Carolyn. Clifford's Big Ideas. (p. 332)
—Let's Chant, Let's Sing, Level 1 (p. 995)
—Young Children's Picture Dictionary. (p. 1978)
Graham, Cenesha. I Want to Help. (p. 848)
Graham, Cheryl. Special Project. (p. 1623)
—Stephanie's Shoes. (p. 1648)
Graham, Chris. So Many Snakes. (p. 1602)
—Spiders! (p. 1626)
Graham, Crystal L. My Little Teddy Bear: Has Anybody Seen.... (p. 1213)
Graham, David. Adventures of Inky - Escape from London. (p. 19)
Graham, Deborah. Magic Comes Back: A Max & Sam Adventure. (p. 1072)
Graham, Denise R. Curse of the Lost Grove. (p. 395)
Graham, Dennis, illus. see Ramos, Peregrina.
Graham, Dora, jt. auth. see Behn, Rosa.
Graham, Earnest, illus. see Graham, Shirley Smith.
Graham, Elspeth. Sandwich that Jack Made. Mould, Chris, illus. (p. 1511)
Graham, Elspeth, jt. auth. see Peet, Mal.
Graham, Evelyne. Think-a-Grams A1. (p. 1734)
—Think-a-Grams A2. (p. 1734)
—Think-a-Grams B1. (p. 1734)
—Think-a-Grams C1. (p. 1734)
Graham, Frank. Adventures of Lil' Bull. (p. 19)
Graham, Frederick. Why Me? (p. 1925)
Graham, Georgia. Cub's Journey Home. (p. 389)
—Nana's Getting Married. (p. 1228)
—Team Like No Other Graham, Georgia, illus. (p. 1710)
—Where Wild Horses Run (p. 1910)
Graham, Georgia, illus. see Azore, Barbara.
Graham, Georgia, illus. see Hartt-Sussman, Heather.
Graham, Georgia, illus. see Morck, Irene.
Graham, Georgia, illus. see Vaage, Carol.
Graham, Gillian. Rainbow Cookbook for Kids. (p. 1435)
Graham, Greg, jt. auth. see King, J. Eric.
Graham, H. P. & De Bats, M. On the Heels of the Hunted. (p. 1290)
Graham, H. Rachelle. Cursed. (p. 395)
Graham, Heather, illus. see Foggo, Cheryl.
Graham, Hilary Weisman. Reunited. (p. 1465)
Graham, Ian. Aircraft. (p. 31)
—Amazing Stadiums. (p. 56)
—Amazing Vehicles: Foldout Book. (p. 56)
—Asteroids & Comets. (p. 108)
—Be in the First Submarine! An Undersea Expedition You'D Rather Avoid. Antram, David, illus. (p. 148)
—Be on the Hindenburg! A Transatlantic Trip You'd Rather Skip. (p. 149)
—Build the Rocket. (p. 238)
—Build Your Own Cool Cars. (p. 238)
—Cars (p. 271)
—Cars. (p. 271)
—Cars & Bikes. (p. 272)
—Darkest Depths: And Other Underground Megastructures. (p. 408)
—Dump Trucks & Other Big Machines. (p. 489)
—Earth & the Universe. (p. 495)
—Earthquakes. (p. 497)
—Electricity! Walker, Rory, illus. (p. 509)
—Emergency! (p. 518)
—Emergency Vehicles. (p. 518)
—Fabulous Bridges. (p. 560)
—Farming & the Future. (p. 574)
—Fast Cars. (p. 576)
—Food Technology. (p. 614)
—Forces & Motion: Investigating a Car Crash Stayte, James, illus. (p. 617)
—Forensic Technology. (p. 617)
—From Crude Oil to Fast Food Snacks: An Energy Journey Through the World of Heat. (p. 642)
—From Falling Water to Electric Car: An Energy Journey Through the World of Electricity. (p. 642)
—Galaxies & Stars. (p. 653)
—Gigantic Lengths. (p. 676)
—Great Building Designs 1900-Today. (p. 714)
—Great Electronic Gadget Designs 1900-Today. (p. 715)
—In Space. (p. 865)
—In the Air. (p. 865)
—Judaism (p. 930)
—Judaism. (p. 930)
—Kenya. (p. 949)
—Machines & Inventions. Antram, David et al, illus. (p. 1068)
—Massive Monsters & Other Huge Megastructures. (p. 1103)
—Megastructures: Tallest, Longest, Biggest, Deepest. (p. 1124)
—Microscopic Scary Creatures. (p. 1136)
—Mighty Machines. (p. 1140)
—Mighty Machines, CARS, Scholastic BF Edition. (p. 1140)
—Military & Government Technology (p. 1142)
—Military Planes: Model Maker. (p. 1143)
—Military Technology. (p. 1143)
—Monster Trucks. (p. 1168)
—Motorcycles. (p. 1179)
—Nigeria. (p. 1252)
—On the Farm. (p. 1290)
—On the Rails. (p. 1291)
—On the Water. (p. 1291)
—Our Moon. (p. 1309)
—Our Sun. (p. 1310)
—Pakistan. (p. 1319)
—Planets Far from Earth. (p. 1368)
—Planets near Earth. (p. 1368)
—Robot Technology. (p. 1480)
—Science of a Bicycle: The Science of Forces. (p. 1527)
—Ships. (p. 1567)
—Slide & Discover: Space. (p. 1590)
—Spain. (p. 1620)
—Sun. (p. 1675)
—Towering Giants & Other Tall Megastructures. (p. 1773)
—Tremendous Tunnels. (p. 1784)
—Trucks. (p. 1791)
—Tsunami: Perspectives on Tsunami Disasters (p. 1795)
—What Do We Know about the Solar System? (p. 1882)
—You Wouldn't Want to Be a World War II Pilot! Air Battles You Might Not Survive. Antram, David, illus. (p. 1977)
—You Wouldn't Want to Be in the First Submarine! An Undersea Expedition You'd Rather Avoid. Antram, David, illus. (p. 1977)
—You Wouldn't Want to Be on Apollo 13! A Mission You'd Rather Not Go On. Antram, David, illus. (p. 1977)
—You Wouldn't Want to Be on the First Flying Machine! A High-Soaring Ride You'd Rather Not Take. Antram, David, illus. (p. 1977)
—You Wouldn't Want to Be on the First Flying Machine! - A High-Soaring Ride You'd Rather Not Take. (p. 1977)
—You Wouldn't Want to Be on the Hindenburg! (p. 1977)
—You Wouldn't Want to Be on the Hindenburg! A Transatlantic Trip You'd Rather Skip. (p. 1977)
—You Wouldn't Want to Be Sir Isaac Newton! A Lonely Life You'd Rather Not Lead. (p. 1977)
—You Wouldn't Want to Be Sir Isaac Newton! A Lonely Life You'd Rather Not Lead. Antram, David, illus. (p. 1977)
—You Wouldn't Want to Climb Mount Everest! A Deadly Journey to the Top of the World. (p. 1977)
—You Wouldn't Want to Work on the Hoover Dam! An Explosive Job You'd Rather Not Do. Antram, David, illus. (p. 1977)
—You Wouldn't Want to Work on the Railroad! (Revised Edition) (p. 1977)
Graham, Ian, jt. auth. see Coppendale, Jean.
Graham, Ian, jt. auth. see Farndon, John.
Graham, Ian, jt. auth. see Solway, Andrew.
Graham, Ian, jt. auth. see Spilsbury, Richard.
Graham, Ian & Jones, Geriant H. Exploring Science: Space an Amazing Fact File & Hands-On Project Book. (p. 553)
Graham, Ian & Morris, Neil. Handheld Gadgets (p. 740)
Graham, Ian, et al. Mighty Machines: Fun, Facts, & Crazy Machines. (p. 1140)
Graham, J. Time of His Life. Hornbeck, Ken, illus. (p. 1752)
Graham, J. Lee. In the Nick of Time. (p. 867)
Graham, Jack, illus. see Otfinoski, Steve.
Graham, Janice Barrett. Me Tarzan, You Jane. Graham, Andrew S. & Ribeira, Lili, illus. (p. 1116)
Graham, Janice C. Little Country Girl & Frisky the Squirrel. Allen, S. Joan & Graham, Jerry L., illus. (p. 1026)
Graham, Jerry L., illus. see Graham, Janice C.
Graham, Joan Bransfield. Flicker Flash. Davis, Nancy, illus. (p. 603)
Graham, Joan Claire. Minnesota Memories 3. (p. 1147)
Graham, Joan Claire, compiled by. Minnesota Memories 5. (p. 1147)
Graham, JoanClaire, compiled by. Minnesota Memories 4. (p. 1147)
Graham, Joanne, jt. auth. see Hairston, Lisa Lee.
Graham, Joseph. Who's Gonna Save Me? It's Time to Tell Your Secrets. (p. 1920)
Graham, Judith A. Didley-Doo's (p. 437)
—Didley-Doo's Go on an Adventure (p. 437)
Graham, Karen. Chloe's Pet. (p. 309)
Graham, Kevin, jt. auth. see Chandler, Gary.
Graham, L. B. All My Holy Mountain. (p. 45)
—Beyond the Summerland. (p. 174)
—Bringer of Storms. (p. 229)
Graham, Lauren N. I Wanna Be a Chef! (p. 847)
Graham, Leland, jt. auth. see Dankberg, Tracy.
Graham, Leland, jt. auth. see Ledbetter, Darril.
Graham, Leland & McCoy, Isabelle. World Geography, Grades 4-6: Where in the World Are You? (p. 1955)
Graham, Lindsay, illus. see Workman Publishing Company Staff.
Graham, Lloyd A. Ingenious Mathematical Problems & Methods. (p. 874)
Graham, Lorenz. North Town. Graham, Lorenz, illus. (p. 1265)
—Return to South Town. Graham, Lorenz, illus. (p. 1465)
—South Town. Graham, Lorenz, illus. (p. 1617)
—Whose Town? Graham, Lorenz, illus. (p. 1922)
Graham Lotz, Anne, jt. auth. see Lotz, Anne Graham.
Graham, Margaret Bloy, illus. see Zion, Gene & Zion.
Graham, Margaret Bloy, illus. see Zion, Gene.
Graham, Mark. Hello, I Am Fiona from Scotland. Sofilas, Mark, illus. (p. 764)
Graham, Mark, illus. see Dixon, Ann.
Graham, Mark, illus. see Howard, Ellen.
Graham, Mark, illus. see Oates, Joyce Carol.
Graham, Mark, illus. see Ryder, Joanne.
Graham, Michael. Great Inhibinator. (p. 716)
—I am Nate. (p. 833)
Graham, Michael, illus. see Greene, Reggie.
Graham, Michael, illus. see Ramos, Odalys Q.
Graham, Michele, illus. see Ring, Susan.
Graham, Monty Dr. My First Big Book of Questions & Answers: Under the Sea. (p. 1204)
Graham, Noel, jt. auth. see Blundell, Gillian.
Graham, Noel & Blundell, Graham. Graph Pack. (p. 710)
Graham, Oakley. 123 Dreams. Orkrania, Alexia, illus. (p. 2000)
—Animals on the Farm. Byrne, Mike, illus. (p. 83)
—I'm Just a Little Sheep. Green, Barry, illus. (p. 859)
—When I Dream of 123. (p. 1902)
Graham, Oakley, jt. auth. see Hopgood, Sally.
Graham, Othello Leneer. Animal Sisters. (p. 79)
Graham, Pamela, et al. Frog Has a Sticky Tongue. (p. 640)
Graham Parry Jones, Terence, see Fairgray, Richard & Jones, Terry.
Graham Parry Jones, Terence, see Jones, Terry.
Graham, Pat, et al. Children's Songbook Companion. Grover, Nina, illus. (p. 304)
Graham, Patti. And That Is Why We Teach: A Celebration of Teachers. Wellman, Megan D., illus. (p. 71)
Graham, Richard. Jack y el Monstruo. Varley, Susan, illus. (p. 903)
Graham, Rita Z. Big Brother Little Brother. Vadalia, Hemali, illus. (p. 179)
Graham, Roland. How We Make Music. (p. 823)
—Let's Vote! Learning to Use Simple Bar Graphs. (p. 1001)
—Let's Vote! Learning to Use Simple Bar Graphs. (p. 1001)
—Making Money. (p. 1081)
Graham, Rosemary. Thou Shalt Not Dump the Skater Dude: And Other Commandments I Have Broken. (p. 1740)
Graham, Ruth Bell. Prodigals & Those Who Love Them. (p. 1409)
Graham, S. Jewels for the Journey. (p. 917)
Graham, Sabrina Depina. Breanna. (p. 225)
—Breanna & Amber: Help Each Other Achieve Their Dreams (Christian Version) (p. 225)
Graham, Sadie, jt. auth. see Stevens, Emily.
Graham, Shirley Smith. Unlikely Chosen: A Graphic Novel Translation of the Biblical Books of Jonah, Esther, & Amos. Graham, Earnest, illus. (p. 1821)
Graham, Stacey. Girls' Ghost Hunting Guide. (p. 680)
Graham, Stedman. Move Without the Ball: Put Your Skills & Your Magic to Work for You. (p. 1183)
Graham, Stella. Forces & Motion at the Playground. (p. 617)
Graham, Tamara. Little Miss Litterbug. (p. 1031)
Graham, Tatiana. Vét. (p. 1839)
Graham, Wendy. High Jinx: Sloanes Beach, Skateboard Hero, Rock on, Bearded Toad. (p. 777)
Graham-Barber, Lynda. Animals' Winter Sleep. Willis, Nancy Carol, illus. (p. 84)
—KokoCat, Inside & Out. Lane, Nancy, illus. (p. 966)
—Say Boo! Lehman, Barbara, illus. (p. 1518)
Graham-Dixon, Andrew, jt. auth. see Dorling Kindersley Publishing Staff.
Grahame, Abby. Wentworth Hall. (p. 1875)
Grahame, Deborah A. Austria. (p. 116)
—Sweden. (p. 1689)
Grahame, Howard. Wishing Book. (p. 1940)
—Wishing Book 2 - Return to Mars. (p. 1940)
Grahame, Kenneth. Dream Days. Shepard, Ernest H., illus. (p. 483)
—Gates of Dawn. Johnson, Joe, tr. (p. 658)
—Golden Age. (p. 694)
—Mr. Toad Johnson, Joe, tr. from FRE. (p. 1186)
—Open Road. Iosa, Ann, illus. (p. 1299)
—Reluctant Dragon. Shepard, Ernest H., illus. (p. 1458)
—Royal Raven Counter. (p. 1492)
—Viento en los Sauces. (p. 1841)
—Wind in the Willows. (p. 1935)
—Wind in the Willows. Iosa, Ann, illus. (p. 1935)
—Wind in the Willows. Daily, Don, illus. (p. 1935)
—Wind in the Willows. Hanft, Joshua, ed. (p. 1935)
—Wind in the Willows. Taso, Alex, illus. (p. 1935)
—Wind in the Willows. Akib, Jamel, illus. (p. 1935)
—Wind in the Willows. Moore, Inga, illus. (p. 1935)
—Wind in the Willows. Kliros, Thea, illus. (p. 1935)
—Wind in the Willows. Leplar, Anna, illus. (p. 1935)
—Wind in the Willows. Bransom, Paul, illus. (p. 1935)
—Wind in the Willows. Roberts, David, illus. (p. 1935)
—Wind in the Willows. Barnhart, Nancy, illus. (p. 1935)
—Wind in the Willows. Rackham, Arthur, illus. (p. 1935)
—Wind in the Willows. Ingpen, Robert R., illus. (p. 1935)
—Wind in the Willows. Shepard, Ernest H., illus. (p. 1935)
—Wind in the Willows. Grahame, Kenneth & McKowen, Scott, illus. (p. 1935)
Grahame, Kenneth, jt. auth. see Baum, L. Frank.
Grahame, Kenneth, jt. auth. see Grahame, Kenneth.
Grahame, Kenneth, jt. auth. see Kelly, Jacqueline.
Grahame, Kenneth, jt. auth. see Woodside, Martin.
Grahame, Kenneth & Grahame, Kenneth. Wind in the Willows. Oxford University Press Staff & Bassett, Jennifer, eds. (p. 1935)
Grahame, Kenneth & Hill, Susan. Wind in the Willows: A Fine Welcome. (p. 1935)
Grahame, Kenneth & Lerer, Seth. Wind in the Willows. Lerer, Seth, ed. (p. 1935)
Grahame, Kenneth & Plessix, Michel. Panic at Toad Hall. Johnson, Joe, tr. from FRE. (p. 1321)
Grahame, Kenneth & Todd, Justin. Wind in the Willows. (p. 1935)
Grahame, Kenneth & Williams, Nicholas. Gwyns I'n Helyk. Shepard, Ernest H., illus. (p. 733)
Grahame-Smith, Deborah. Dr. Seuss. (p. 475)
—Lois Lowry. (p. 1045)
Grahame-Smith, Deborah, contrib. by. Countdown to Catastrophe. (p. 370)
—First Bloody Battles. (p. 593)
—Horrific Invasions. (p. 799)
Graham-Kennedy, Elaine. Dinosaurs: Where Did They Come from & Where Did They Go? (p. 444)
Graham-Larkin, Debbie. Magic in the Air. (p. 1072)
Graham-Morgan, Ivet. Grandma's Garden. (p. 708)
—Peter the Parrot Misses Home: Misses Home. (p. 1347)
Grahn, Barbara, jt. auth. see Maltz, Susan.
Grailey, Trevor. Cree. (p. 380)
Graimes, Nicola. Kids' Fun & Healthy Cookbook. Shooter, Howard, photos by. (p. 953)
Grainger, A. J. Captive. (p. 264)
Grainger, D. Night Santa Got Lost. (p. 1254)
Grainger, Ragnil, jt. auth. see Sanders, Jane.
Grainger-Valvano, Claire Lcsw. My Daddy Sits upon a Star: A Book to Help Console a Child Whose Father Has Died. (p. 1201)
Grajczyk, Shane, illus. see Roth, Rhonda.
Gralla, Howard, jt. auth. see Young, Timothy.
Gralley, Jean. Sweetie. (p. 1690)
Gram, Golden. Gail the Snail: Night Owl. (p. 652)
—Gail the Snail: A Holiday Tale. (p. 652)
—Gail the Snail: How I Met Gail. (p. 652)
—Gail the Snail: Snailing Around. (p. 652)
—Gail the Snail: Goes on Vacation. (p. 652)
Gram, Patrick, illus. see Nicholas, Melissa.
Grama, Batsheva. HaSifronim Sheli Series Four (p. 752)
—HaSifronim Sheli Series One (p. 752)
—HaSifronim Sheli Series Three (p. 752)
Grama, Getta. Swirling Designs. (p. 1691)
Gramatky, Hardie. Little Toot. Burgess, Mark, illus. (p. 1037)
—Little Toot. Gramatky, Hardie, illus. (p. 1037)
Grambling, jt. auth. see Grambling, Lois G.
Grambling, Lois G. Can I Bring My Pterodactyl to School, Ms. Johnson? Love, Judy, illus. (p. 258)
—Can I Bring Saber to New York, Ms. Mayor? Love, Judy, illus. (p. 258)
—Can I Bring Woolly to the Library, Ms. Reeder? Love, Judy, illus. (p. 258)
—Here Comes T. Rex Cottontail. Davis, Jack E., illus. (p. 770)
—Nicky Jones & the Roaring Rhinos. Geer, William J., illus. (p. 1251)
—T. Rex & the Mother's Day Hug. Davis, Jack E., illus. (p. 1694)
—T. Rex Trick-or-Treats. Davis, Jack E., illus. (p. 1694)
—Witch Who Wanted to Be a Princess. Love, Judy, illus. (p. 1941)
Grambling, Lois G. & Grambling. Shoo! Scat! Newman, Barbara Johansen, illus. (p. 1568)
Grambo, Ashleigh Deese. C Is for Chicago. (p. 249)
Grambo, Rebecca L. Borealis: A Polar Bear Cub's First Year Cox, Daniel J., illus. (p. 214)
—Digging Canadian Dinosaurs Bonder, Dianna, illus. (p. 439)
—Digging Canadian History (p. 439)
Grambs, David L. & Levine, Ellen S. So You Think You Can Spell? Killer Quizzes for the Incurably Competitive & Overly Confident. (p. 1602)
Gramby, Shirley. Boxing Championship: A Tee Am Sam Story. (p. 217)
Grami, B. Help! I Have Rats in My Hair! (p. 765)
Gramma Debbie. Poop Book. (p. 1383)
Grammer, Maurine. Navajo Brothers & the Stolen Herd. Cleveland, Fred, illus. (p. 1237)
Grammy Pammy. Biggest Catch. (p. 185)
—Day the Elephant Escaped from the Zoo. (p. 414)
Grammy Sunshine. Adventures of Mouse: The Mouse Who Wanted to Be A Pig. (p. 20)
Gramont, Nina de. Meet Me at the River. (p. 1121)
Grampa Ralph. Santa's New Boots (p. 1513)
Grams, Kimberly. Smedley & the Sprinkle Machine. (p. 1593)
Gran, Mary Alice. Child Is Born. (p. 301)
Gran, Meredith. Marceline & the Scream Queens. Gran, Meredith, illus. (p. 1091)
Granada, Nancy, illus. see Kipling, Rudyard.
Granados, Antonio. Insomniopteros. (p. 878)
—Poemas de Juguete 1. (p. 1376)
—Versos de Dulce y de Sal. (p. 1837)
Granados, Lucia. Bemba's Secret Garden. (p. 163)
Granahan, Shirley. John Newbery: Father of Children's Literature. (p. 922)
Granata, Charles L., jt. auth. see Ramone, Phil.
Granata, Diana. Come & Meet Baci (p. 347)
Granata, Nancy. Perfect Porch for Witch Watching. (p. 1342)
Granberry, Debra & Skindzier, Jon. Furman University College Prowler off the Record. (p. 650)
Grand, Dee Ann. Child's First Prayers. (p. 305)
Grand Pre, Mary, illus. see Rowling, J. K.
Grandbear the Storyteller. Tales of Tails from the Blue Heron Ranch Crawford, Dale, illus. (p. 1702)
Grandchildren, jt. auth. see Brooks, G. Alan.
Grande, Gabrielle. Fluffy's Book. (p. 608)
Grandelis, Leiah, illus. see Dickson, Vivian.
Granderson, Curtis. All You Can Be: Dream It, Draw It, Become It! (p. 46)
Grandfeather Press. Roly Poly Napoleon Discovers Colors. (p. 1485)
Grandfield, Meg & DeMakas, Meg. Captain Jeb, Pirate Cat. Grandfield, Meg & DeMakas, Meg, illus. (p. 264)
Grandfield, Meg Ellen. How the Wellswood Cat Came to Be. (p. 813)
Grandin, Temple, jt. auth. see Montgomery, Sy.
Grandison, Alice & Chambers Harrap Publishers Staff. Mini School Dictionary. (p. 1146)
Grandits, John. Blue Lipstick: Concrete Poems. Grandits, John, illus. (p. 203)
—Technically, It's Not My Fault: Concrete Poems. (p. 1711)
—Ten Rules You Absolutely Must Not Break If You Want to Survive the School Bus. Austin, Michael Allen, illus. (p. 1719)
Grandlic, Miha. Tasmanian Devil. (p. 1707)
Grandma. Harry's Adventure (p. 751)
—There Is a Vampire in Our Cellar: Adventures of Butterfly Nectar Meadows. (p. 1730)
Grandma Bette. Excellent Adventures of Max & Madison: Bedtime Stories for Youngsters. (p. 547)
Grandma Fudgie. Day at the Beach. (p. 412)
—Walk to the Park. (p. 1854)
Grandma Geny Heywood, jt. auth. see Grandma Geny Heywood, Geny Heywood.
Grandma Geny Heywood, Geny Heywood & Grandma Geny Heywood. Proto: What do you do when a dinosaur is born in your Garden? (p. 1412)
Grandma Janet Mary. Grandma's Treasure Chest. Pennington, Craig, illus. (p. 709)
—Grandpa's Fishin' Friend. Pennington, Craig, illus. (p. 709)
Grandma, Little. Tiny. (p. 1756)
Grandma Poo Poo. Tessie the Toad. Olen, Jennifer, illus. (p. 1723)
Grandma Sue. Bubba the Bear. (p. 233)

Grandma, Sue. Rocky the Rocking Horse. (p. 1484)
Grandmother Littlewolf. Littlestar Macpherson, Carol, illus. (p. 1039)
Grandolt, Jean. In the Quest for Inshalla: Simbies of the Caribbean at the World Under. (p. 867)
Grandpa. Beginning of Meet the Müsh-Mice: (a Visit to the North Pole) (p. 159)
Grandpa Bob. Dirty Nose Series. (p. 446)
—Dirty Nose Series - Olander. (p. 446)
Grandpa Casey. Another Müsh-Mice Adventure: Florida Vacation Brennan, Lisa, illus. (p. 88)
—Another Müsh-Mice Adventure. Brennan, Lisa, illus. (p. 88)
—Going Green: Another Mush-Mice Adventure Brennan, Lisa, illus. (p. 692)
—Meet the Müsh-Mice. Brennan, Lisa, illus. (p. 1123)
—Trilogy: Three Adventures of the Müsh-Mice. Brenn, Lisa, illus. (p. 1786)
Grandpa Dennis, as told by. George Washington's Smallest Army: The Miracle Before Trenton. (p. 665)
Grandpa Peeps. Squire & the White Dragon. (p. 1637)
Grandpré, Karen Haus, illus. see Henry, Marguerite.
GrandPré, Mary, illus. see Achebe, Chinua & Iroaganachi, John.
GrandPré, Mary, illus. see Blumenthal, Deborah.
GrandPré, Mary, illus. see Brown, Jason Robert.
GrandPré, Mary, illus. see MacDonald, Betty Bard.
GrandPré, Mary, illus. see MacDonald, Betty.
GrandPré, Mary, illus. see Mitton, Tony.
GrandPré, Mary, illus. see Prelutsky, Jack.
GrandPré, Mary, illus. see Rosenstock, Barb.
GrandPré, Mary, illus. see Rowling, J. K.
GrandPré, Mary, illus. see Williams, Rozanne Lanczak.
GrandPré, Mary, illus. see Yep, Laurence & Ryder, Joanne.
Grandreams Staff. Deborah the Dozy Duckling: A Squeaky Storybook. (p. 421)
Grandt, Eve, illus. see Thielbar, Melinda.
Granfield, Linda. Amazing Grace: The Story of the Hymn. (p. 54)
—Circus. (p. 322)
—Legend of the Panda. (p. 989)
—Out of Slavery: The Journey to Amazing Grace. Wilson, Janet, illus. (p. 1311)
—What Am I? Herbert, Jennifer, illus. (p. 1879)
—Where Poppies Grow: A World War I Companion (p. 1909)
Grange, Emma. Empire Strikes Back. (p. 521)
—Lego Star Wars: A New Hope. (p. 990)
—Lego Star Wars: The Return of the Jedi. (p. 990)
—Lego Star Wars: The Empire Strikes Back. (p. 990)
—New Hope. (p. 1245)
—Return of the Jedi. (p. 1464)
Grange, James. 1990s Coloring Book: All That & a Box of Crayons (Psych! Crayons Not Included.) (p. 2002)
Granger, Barbara. Down to Earth with a Bump. (p. 474)
Granger, Persis R. Adirondack Gold. (p. 12)
Granger, Ronald. Day at the Zoo: Compare Numbers. (p. 412)
—Exploring Earth's Surface. (p. 552)
—Know Your Leaves. (p. 965)
Granger, Ronald, jt. auth. see Mills, Nathan.
Granger, Shane, illus. see Henderson, Jason.
Granger, Trudi. Always There Bear. Llewhellin, Gareth, illus. (p. 51)
Granhold, Adriana. Mattie Knowsmath & the Great Shape Hunt. (p. 1110)
G'rani, Elizebeth. Learning with Kailey & Anthony: Kailey Meets Anthony (p. 986)
Grannij, Joan, jt. auth. see Gannij, Joan.
Grannis, Greg. Lottie Bright & the Starmaker's Universe. Vargas, Robert, illus. (p. 1057)
Granny J. Pinky Makes a New Friend: Pinky Frink's Adventures. (p. 1360)
—Pinky Visits Outer Space: Pinky Frink's Adventures. (p. 1360)
Granny, Smith. Granny Smith's Sudoku Solver: For Beginners & Other Wise People. (p. 710)
Granowsky, Alvin. More Consonants: Set of 6. (p. 1174)
—Readiness Skills (Auditory, Visual, & Motor) Set of 6. (p. 1444)
—SRA Phonics: Grade 1 (p. 1637)
—SRA Phonics: Grade 2 (p. 1637)
—SRA Phonics: Grade 3 (p. 1637)
Granson, Steven. Zando. (p. 1984)
Granström, Brita, illus. see Davies, Nicola.
Granström, Brita, illus. see Dunbar, Joyce.
Granström, Brita, illus. see Henderson, Kathy.
Granström, Brita, illus. see Hindley, Judy.
Granström, Brita, illus. see Manning, Mick & Brita, Granström.
Granström, Brita, illus. see Manning, Mick.
Granström, Brita, illus. see Quarto Generic Staff.
Granstrom, Brita, jt. auth. see Manning, Mick.
Granström, Brita, jt. illus. see Manning, Mick.
Grant, Alaric. Alaric Time Traveling. (p. 33)
Grant, Alice. Dear Mr President, Please Send My Daddy Home. (p. 419)
Grant, Amanda. Grow It, Cook It with Kids. (p. 726)
Grant, Amanda, ed. see Phaidon Press Editors.
Grant, Amanda & Yorke, Francesca. Kids' Kitchen: Good Food Made Easy. (p. 954)
Grant, Arenett. Christmas Tag. (p. 316)
Grant, Callie. Mud Puddle Hunting Day. Magee, Melanie, illus. (p. 1188)
Grant, Carolyn E. Christmas in Maggie's Neighborhood. (p. 314)
—Maggie's Neighborhood. (p. 1071)
Grant, Carrie and David. Elephant's Birthday Bells: Jump up & Join In. Busby, Ailie, illus. (p. 512)
—Lion's Speedy Sauce: Jump up & Join In. Busby, Ailie, illus. (p. 1021)
Grant, Catherine Miles. Lenses on Learning Series: Readings Book. (p. 991)
—Lenses on Learning Series: Facilitator's Book. (p. 991)
Grant, Cheryl, illus. see Byers, Marcella.
Grant, Christopher. Teenie. (p. 1714)
Grant, Cindy M. Itty-Bitty Jesus Is Born Christmas Storybook. (p. 900)
Grant, Cj. Princess & the Swan. (p. 1403)
Grant, Crystal. Warrior Boy. (p. 1858)
Grant, Damian. Salman Rushdie. (p. 1505)
Grant, David N. Christmas Present. (p. 315)
Grant, Debbie. American Bison. (p. 60)
Grant, Donald. Atlas of Space. (p. 113)
—Avion. (p. 120)
—Desert. Grant, Donald, illus. (p. 428)
—Deserts. (p. 429)
—Flying. Grant, Donald, illus. (p. 609)
—Homes. Grant, Donald, illus. (p. 793)
—In the Sky. Grant, Donald, illus. (p. 867)
—Let's Look at the Sky. Grant, Donald, illus. (p. 999)
Grant, Donald, illus. see Prunier, James.
Grant, Donald & Chabot, Jean-Philippe. Cavernicolas. (p. 282)
Grant, Donald & Delafosse, Claude. Dinosaurs at Large. Grant, Donald, illus. (p. 444)
—Let's Look at Dinosaurs. Grant, Donald, illus. (p. 998)
Grant, Donald & Vallon, Jacqueline. Halloween. Valat, Pierre-Marie, illus. (p. 737)
Grant, Donald, et al. Casa. (p. 273)
Grant, Donna. Hungrige Begierde. (p. 828)
Grant, Donna, jt. auth. see DeBerry, Virginia.
Grant, Douglas, illus. see Burroughs, Edgar Rice.
Grant, Edward. Science & Religion, 400 B. C. to A. D. 1550: From Aristotle to Copernicus (p. 1525)
Grant, Elaine Y. & Elliott, Sharon M. Little Book of Baseball. (p. 1025)
Grant, Eleanor. Ministering Angels. (p. 1147)
Grant, Gavin J., jt. ed. see Link, Kelly.
Grant, Gavin J. & Link, Kelly, eds. Steampunk! an Anthology of Fantastically Rich & Strange Stories. (p. 1646)
Grant, Holly. League of Beastly Dreadfuls (p. 982)
Grant, Jacob. Little Bird's Bad Word. (p. 1024)
—Scaredy Kate. (p. 1519)
Grant, Jacqueline. My Name Is Noel. (p. 1215)
Grant, James. Children of Venus: An Experiment in Three Parts. (p. 303)
Grant, Jim, see Child, Lee, pseud.
Grant, Joan. Cat & Fish. Curtis, Neil, illus. (p. 277)
—Cat & Fish Go to See. Curtis, Neil, illus. (p. 277)
—Monster That Grew Small. Xoul, illus. (p. 1168)
—Winged Pharaoh. (p. 1936)
Grant, Joan Marshall. Redskin Morning & Other Stories. Lavers, Ralph, illus. (p. 1456)
—Scarlet Fish & Other Stories. Lavers, Ralph, illus. (p. 1520)
Grant, John. Debunk It! How to Stay Sane in a World of Misinformation. (p. 421)
—Littlenose Collection: The Explorer. Collins, Ross, illus. (p. 1038)
—Littlenose Collection - The Magician. Collins, Ross, illus. (p. 1038)
—Littlenose the Magician. Collins, Ross, illus. (p. 1038)
Grant, John & Stocks, Mike. Classic Horror. (p. 328)
Grant, Joyce. Gabby Dolby, Jan, illus. (p. 652)
—Gabby Drama Queen Dolby, Jan, illus. (p. 652)
Grant, Judyann. Chicken Said, "Cluck!" Truesdell, Sue, illus. (p. 300)
Grant, Judyann Ackerman. Chicken Said, "Cluck!" Truesdell, Sue, illus. (p. 300)
Grant, K. M. Blaze of Silver. (p. 198)
—Blood Red Horse. (p. 200)
—How the Hangman Lost His Heart. (p. 813)
—Paradise Red. (p. 1323)
—White Heat. (p. 1913)
Grant, Karima. Nelson Mandela. (p. 1240)
—Sofie & the City. Montecalvo, Janet, illus. (p. 1605)
Grant, Katy. Acting Out. (p. 10)
—Fearless. (p. 579)
—Friends Forever. (p. 638)
—Hide & Seek (p. 776)
—Pranked. (p. 1393)
—Rumors. (p. 1495)
—Tug-of-War. (p. 1796)
Grant, Kevin Patrick. Exploration in the Age of Empire, 1750-1953, Revised Edition. (p. 550)
Grant, L. Trevor. Carnivalitis: The Conflicting Discourse of Carnival (p. 270)
Grant, Leigh, illus. see Bulla, Clyde Robert & Bulla.
Grant, Lisa, ed. see Darby, Joel, et al.
Grant, Lisa, jt. auth. see Golant, Galina.
Grant, Mackensey. Roman's Road Trip: Understand Place Value. (p. 1486)
Grant, Margriet, illus. see Mahany, Patricia Shely.
Grant, Mark J. Lila: The Sign of the Elven Queen. (p. 1017)
Grant, Melvyn, illus. see Kingsley, Kaza.
Grant, Michael. Call. (p. 253)
—Fear. (p. 579)
—Gone. (p. 697)
—Hunger. (p. 827)
—Key. (p. 950)
—Lies. (p. 1007)
—Light. (p. 1014)
—Messenger of Fear. (p. 1129)
—Plague. (p. 1366)
—Power. (p. 1389)
—Tattooed Heart. (p. 1707)
—Trap. (p. 1779)
Grant, Michael, jt. auth. see Applegate, Katherine.
Grant, Michael & Applegate, Katherine. Eve & Adam. (p. 541)
Grant, Moyra. Government & Politics. (p. 704)
Grant, Myrna. Gladys Aylward - No Mountain Too High. (p. 682)
—Ivan & the American Journey. (p. 900)
—Ivan & the Daring Escape. (p. 900)
—Ivan & the Hidden Bible. (p. 900)
—Ivan & the Informer. (p. 900)
—Ivan & the Moscow Circus. (p. 900)
—Ivan & the Secret in the Suitcase. (p. 900)
Grant, Nancy. Maggie & the Backyard Helpers. (p. 1071)
Grant, Neil. Eric the Red. (p. 533)
—Every Day Life in Ancient Rome. Cappon, Manuela, tr. (p. 542)
—Everyday Life of the Aztecs, Incas & Mayans. Cappon, Manuela et al, illus. (p. 544)
—Everyday Life of the Celts. Cappon, Manuela, illus. (p. 544)
—Everyday Life of the Vikings. (p. 544)
—Indo Dreaming. (p. 872)
—Medieval Europe. (p. 1119)
—Rhino Chasers. (p. 1467)
Grant, Nicola. Don't Be So Nosy, Posy! Warnes, Tim, illus. (p. 467)
Grant, R. G. Communism. (p. 349)
—Great Depression. (p. 715)
—Hiroshima. (p. 781)
—Moments in History - Why Did World War I Happen? (p. 1162)
—Vietnam War. (p. 1841)
—Why Did Hiroshima Happen? (p. 1923)
—Why Did the Great Depression Happen? (p. 1923)
—World War I. (p. 1958)
Grant, R. J., jt. auth. see Field, Jacob.
Grant, Reg. Cold War. (p. 339)
—Korean War. (p. 967)
—World War II: Europe. (p. 1959)
Grant, Richard E. & Bently, Peter. Wah-Wah Diaries: The Making of a Film. 3 CDs. Cort, Ben, illus. (p. 1852)
Grant, Robert. American Ethics & the Virtuous Citizen: The Blessings of Liberty. (p. 60)
—Jack in the Bush or A Summer on a Salmon River. (p. 903)
Grant, Robert, jt. auth. see Grant, Robert D.
Grant, Robert D. & Grant, Robert. Representations of British Emigration, Colonisation & Settlement: Imagining Empire, 1800-1860. (p. 1461)
Grant, Ron & Ovadia, Ron. First Dog of 1600 Pooch'Lvania Avenue: My First Year in Arf, Arf Office!! Garbot, Dave, illus. (p. 594)
Grant, Rose. Right Where You Need Me. Bryant, Julie, illus. (p. 1472)
Grant, Ruthie. Oh, No! Fancy-Free Amy Gets Bad News. (p. 1281)
Grant, Sara. Half Lives. (p. 736)
Grant, Sarah, illus. see Lewis, Anne Margaret.
Grant, Sharon. Mr. Special Visits Mrs. Precious' Class. (p. 1186)
Grant, Shauntay. Apples & Butterflies: A Poem for Prince Edward Island Thiebaux-Heikalo, Tamara, illus. (p. 92)
—City Speaks in Drums Tooke, Susan, illus. (p. 324)
—Up Home Tooke, Susan, illus. (p. 1824)
Grant, Sheryl. Gumnut Gully Gang: Billy's Bright Idea. (p. 731)
Grant, Sophia, illus. see Donald, Margaret.
Grant Sr, Hector J. Sybil: The Trials & Triumphs of a Jamaican Girl. (p. 1692)
Grant, Stephen, jt. auth. see Gruenwald, Mark.
Grant, Steven, jt. auth. see Brooks, Yvonne.
Grant, Susan. Cambridge IGCSE Economics Student's Book. (p. 255)
—Cambridge IGCSE Economics Workbook. (p. 255)
—Cambridge o Level Economics Student's Book. (p. 255)
—Tell Me a Story. Dall, Christopher M., illus. (p. 1716)
Grant, Susan McKenna. Piano, Piano, Pieno: Authentic Food from a Tuscan Farm. (p. 1354)
Grant, Tess. Flying in the Dark. (p. 610)
Grant, Tim, jt. ed. see diMauro, Laurie.
Grant, Tina, jt. ed. see diMauro, Laurie.
Grant, V. F. Stories from Grimley Forest. (p. 1654)
Grant, Vicki. B Negative (p. 123)
—Cochonnet: (Pigboy) (p. 337)
—Comeback (p. 347)
—Dead-End Job (p. 416)
—Halifax Citadel. Pilsworth, Graham, illus. (p. 737)
—Hold the Pickles (p. 788)
—I. D. (p. 837)
—Identification (p. 852)
—Nine Doors (p. 1256)
—No te Vayas (p. 1260)
—Pigboy (p. 1357)
—Pigboy. (p. 1357)
—Puppet Wrangler (p. 1417)
—Quid Pro Quo (p. 1427)
—Res Judicata (p. 1462)
—Trabajo Sin Futuro (p. 1774)
—Triggered (p. 1786)
Grant, Virginia. Australia's Greatest Landmarks & Locations. (p. 116)
Grant-Adamson, Andrew. Cyber Crime. (p. 396)
Grantham, Jared James. Ashley & the Dollmaker. (p. 106)
Grant-McRae, Denise B. Mr. Apple's Penny Candy Bus. (p. 1184)
Grantner, Anne M. & Haggart, Gary. Without a Home. Hannon, Kenneth, photos by. (p. 1942)
Granville, Bryan. Goldie's Gold & the Monkey Girl. (p. 696)
Grapes, Bryan J. Events That Changed the World - 1980-2000. (p. 541)
Graphic Manufacture, illus. see Martinez, Roland.
Graphics Factory, illus. see Irving, Harry.
Graphics, Nataly, illus. see Taher, Amr.
Graphman, W. M. . Matthew. Chel & Riley Adventures: The Great Mountain Adventure. (p. 297)
Graphman, Wm. Matthew. Chel & Riley Adventures: The K9 Kidnapping Adventure. (p. 297)
Grashkina, Alexandra. Williams College College Prowler off the Record. (p. 1933)
Grass, Jeff, photos by see Henry, Patti.
Grass, Michael. Impolite Village. (p. 862)
Grassby, Donna. Seaside Alphabet. Tooke, Susan, illus. (p. 1538)
Grassi, Anna, jt. auth. see Branciforte, Suzanne.
Grassi, Jennifer. Sally's Favorite Color. (p. 1505)
Grasskamp, Walter, et al. Hans Haacke. (p. 743)
Grasso, Craig A., illus. see Dike, Diane.
Grasso, Julie A. Return to Cardamom. Blackwell, David, illus. (p. 1465)
Grasso, Julie Anne. Escape from the Forbidden Planet. Blackwell, David, illus. (p. 535)
—Stellarcadia. Mann, Lawrence, illus. (p. 1647)
Grasso, Lorraine. Short Stories, Tall Tales. (p. 1569)
Grasso, Mary Ann. Tale of a Tooth or Two or Three. (p. 1699)
Grasso, Samantha A., illus. see Dike, Diane.
Graston, Arlene, illus. see Mathes, Charles.
Grate, Gina. Project Noah. (p. 1410)
Grateful Steps Publishing & Tipton, Angela. Butterflies Don't Crawl. Irvine, Wil, illus. (p. 247)
Grater, Lindsay, illus. see Lunn, Janet.
Grater, Michael. Papercraft Projects with One Piece of Paper. (p. 1323)
—Puppets, Jumping Jacks & Other Paper People. (p. 1417)
Gratiot, Jim. Cootie Kisser Convention on Canterbury Court. (p. 365)
Grattan, Charmae. Becky Bear Goes to Town. (p. 156)
Grattan-Dominguez, Alejandro. Stuff of Dreams. (p. 1670)
Gratton, Tessa. Apple Throne. (p. 92)
—Blood Magic. (p. 200)
—Lost Sun. (p. 1056)
Gratton, Tessa, et al. Storybook: A Collection of Stories. (p. 1663)
Grattopp, Matthew, jt. auth. see Carlile-Grattopp, Kari.
Gratz, Alan. Brooklyn Nine. (p. 231)
—Dragon Lantern: A League of Seven Novel. (p. 477)
—Fantasy Baseball. (p. 572)
—League of Seven. Helquist, Brett, illus. (p. 982)
—Samurai Shortstop. (p. 1510)
—Something Rotten. (p. 1610)
—Something Wicked. (p. 1610)
Gratz, Alan, jt. auth. see Barba, Rick.
Gratz, Ali. Rudy Gets A Transplant. (p. 1494)
Gratz, Jo, jt. auth. see Gratz, Wendi.
Gratz, Wendi & Gratz, Jo. Creature Camp: Make Your Own 18 Softies to Draw, Sew & Stuff. (p. 380)
Gratzer, Walter. Giant Molecules: From Nylon to Nanotubes. (p. 673)
Grau, Andre, jt. auth. see Dorling Kindersley Publishing Staff.
Grau, Maritta, ed. ABCs of Frederick Maryland: A Historic Coloring Book. Grau, Ryon, illus. (p. 4)
Grau, Ryon, illus. see Grau, Maritta, ed.
Grau, Sheila. Dr. Critchlore's School for Minions: Book 1. Sutphin, Joe, illus. (p. 475)
Graubart, Norman D. Ambulances (p. 57)
—Beavers in American History. (p. 155)
—Bison in American History. (p. 193)
—Cattle in American History. (p. 281)
—Cement Mixers (p. 286)
—Fire Trucks (p. 591)
—Horses in American History. (p. 800)
—How to Track a Deer (p. 822)
—How to Track a Rabbit (p. 822)
—How to Track a Turkey (p. 822)
—Laila Ali: Champion Boxer. (p. 972)
—Laila Ali. (p. 972)
—Mules in American History. (p. 1189)
—Neil DeGrasse Tyson: Spokesperson for Science. (p. 1240)
—Science of Baseball. (p. 1527)
—Science of Basketball. (p. 1527)
—Tractor-Trailers (p. 1775)
Graubart, Norman D. & Tyson, Neil deGrasse. Neil DeGrasse Tyson: Spokesperson for Science. (p. 1240)
Graudin, Ryan. All That Burns. (p. 45)
—All That Glows. (p. 45)
Graullera, Fabiola, illus. see Alberto, Eliseo.
Graullera, Fabiola, illus. see Alvarez, Leticia Herrera.
Graullera, Fabiola, illus. see Cordova, Soledad.
Graullera, Fabiola, illus. see Marti, Jose.
Graullera, Fabiola, illus. see Zepeda, Monique.
Graullera, Fabiolla, illus. see Laínez, René Colato.
Graullera Ramírez, Fabiola, illus. see Laínez, René Colato.
Graun, Ken. Our Constellations & Their Stars. (p. 1308)
Graunke, Susan M., illus. see Hill, Meggan.
Graux, Amélie. I Love to Eat. Graux, Amélie, illus. (p. 843)
Graux, Amélie, et al. I Love to Sleep. Graux, Amélie, illus. (p. 843)
Gravatt, Andrea R. Lavender Ribbon. (p. 981)
Gravdahl, John. Curious Catwalk. (p. 392)
Gravel, Elise. Adopt a Glurb! (p. 13)
—Blast off with Doodle Tom: A Space Doodle-Odyssey. (p. 198)
—Cranky Ballerina. (p. 376)
Gravel, Élise. Day in the Office of Doctor Bugspit. (p. 413)
Gravel, Élise. Fly. (p. 609)
—Head Lice. (p. 756)
Gravel, Elise. How Do You Doodle? (p. 808)
Gravel, Élise. Jessie Elliot Is a Big Chicken. Gravel, Élise, illus. (p. 914)
—Let's Draw & Doodle Together! (p. 996)
Gravel, Elise. Rat. (p. 1440)
—Slug. (p. 1591)
—Spider. (p. 1626)
Gravel, Élise. Worm. (p. 1961)
Gravel, Élise, illus. see Mass, Wendy & Brawer, Michael.
Gravel, Élise, illus. see Phillips, Karen.
Gravelle, Jennifer, jt. auth. see Gravelle, Karen.
Gravelle, Karen. Eight Little Legs. Davis, Nelle, illus. (p. 507)
Gravelle, Karen & Gravelle, Jennifer. Period Book: Everything You Don't Want to Ask (But Need to Know) Palen, Debbie, illus. (p. 1343)
Gravenhorst, Edna Campos. Ay, Mijo! Why Do You Want to Be an Engineer? (p. 121)
Gravenkamp, Kim. C Is for Cameron but also for Cecil. (p. 249)
Graver, Jane. How You Are Changing: For Boys Ages 10-12 & Parents. Ebert, Len, illus. (p. 823)
Graver, Jane, jt. auth. see Ameiss, Bill.
Graves, Alfred Perceval. Irish Fairy Book. (p. 887)
Graves, Andy Jane. Zeezee Goes to the Duck Park. (p. 1985)
Graves, Anna Louise. How Can You Lose Something as Big as a Farm? (p. 805)
Graves, Annie. Demon Babysitter. McElhinney, Glenn, illus. (p. 426)
—Dog's Breakfast. McElhinney, Glenn, illus. (p. 462)
—Frankenkids. (p. 629)
—Frankenkids. McElhinney, Glenn, illus. (p. 629)
—Guinea Pig Killer. McElhinney, Glenn, illus. (p. 731)
—Hatching. McElhinney, Glenn, illus. (p. 752)

G

—Help! My Brother's a Zombie. McElhinney, Glenn, illus. (p. 766)
—Mirrored. (p. 1149)
—Mirrored. McElhinney, Glenn, illus. (p. 1149)
—Wolfling's Bite. McElhinney, Glenn, illus. (p. 1944)
Graves, Brandon Beebe. In Beaner's Backyard. (p. 863)
Graves, Charles P. Annie Oakley: The Shooting Star. Cary, illus. (p. 87)
Graves, Damien. Cat Lady. (p. 278)
—Deadly Catch. (p. 417)
—I Can See You. (p. 836)
—Shut Your Mouth. (p. 1572)
Graves, Dan. Pparcel's Notebook Presents: The Search for the Giant Stone Monkey Head, Truth, Friends & Strange Food. Graves, Dan, illus. (p. 1391)
Graves, Dennis, illus. see Elfrig, Kate.
Graves, Dennis, illus. see Evans, Karen & Urmston, Kathleen.
Graves, Dennis, illus. see Hoenecke, Karen.
Graves, Dennis, illus. see Urmston, Kathleen & Evans, Karen.
Graves, Dennis, illus. see Williams, Deborah.
Graves, Dennis, illus. see Yannone, Deborah.
Graves, Emily, illus. see Turner, Mark.
Graves, Gayle. It Was All Done in Six Days. (p. 894)
Graves, Gayle, jt. auth. see Graves, Tyler.
Graves, Gayle & Graves, Tyler. True Meaning of Christmas. (p. 1792)
Graves, Harmon. I'm Only Three¿ & Look at All the Things That I Can Do! Ritchie, Scot, illus. (p. 859)
Graves, Jennifer. Ava's Awful Fright! (p. 118)
Graves, Jeseca. Bessie Coleman: The Story of an Aviation Pioneer. (p. 168)
Graves, Jonathan. Isabella Propeller & the Magic Beanie. Haley, Gail E., illus. (p. 891)
Graves, Judith. Under My Skin. Cox, Val, illus. (p. 1813)
Graves, Justin. Sorceress: The Pixy Dust Diaries. (p. 1614)
Graves, K. Mars Moon Colony One - Carmen's Revenge: Dream Casters II. (p. 1096)
Graves, Karen D. But That's Not Fair! (p. 246)
Graves, Karen M., jt. auth. see Graves, Karen Marie.
Graves, Karen Marie & Graves, Karen M. Ballet Dance (p. 134)
—Tap Dancing (p. 1705)
Graves, Kassie. Brave Little Sailboat. Graves, Kassie, illus. (p. 223)
Graves, Keith. Chicken Big. (p. 300)
—Frank Was a Monster Who Wanted to Dance. (p. 629)
—Monsterator. (p. 1168)
—Orphan of Awkward Falls. (p. 1304)
—Second Banana. (p. 1539)
Graves, Keith, illus. see Asher, Sandy.
Graves, Keith, illus. see Fontenot, Mary Alice.
Graves, Keith, illus. see Jackson, Alison.
Graves, Keith, illus. see Lewis, J. Patrick.
Graves, Keith, illus. see Palatini, Margie.
Graves, Kerry A. Constitution: The Story Behind America's Governing Document. (p. 359)
—Declaration of Independence: The Story Behind America's Founding Document. (p. 422)
—I Have a Dream: The Story Behind Martin Luther King JR.'s Most Famous Speech. (p. 839)
—Irish Americans. (p. 887)
Graves, Linda, illus. see Anderson, William.
Graves, Linda, illus. see Gruber, Michael.
Graves, Linda, illus. see Yolen, Jane.
Graves, Linda Dockey, illus. see Weyn, Suzanne.
Graves, Lisa. History's Witches. Graves, Lisa, illus. (p. 785)
Graves, Mab. Little Lost Girls Paper Dolls. (p. 1031)
Graves, Mary. Adventures of Peanut George. (p. 21)
Graves, Michael A. R. Henry VIII. (p. 768)
Graves, Michael F., jt. auth. see Philippot, Raymond.
Graves, Michelle, illus. see Williams, Hap.
Graves, Peter, pref. Cats (Domestic) Calendar (p. 281)
—Cows Calendar (p. 374)
Graves, Renee. Malcolm X. (p. 1083)
—Scopes Trial. (p. 1530)
Graves, Robert. Two Wise Children. Dean, Venitia, illus. (p. 1804)
Graves, Robert, tr. see Suetonius.
Graves, Robin. Space Diaries: The Saga of Robby, Boy Astronaut. (p. 1619)
Graves, Rose M. Mudwalker. (p. 1189)
Graves, Samantha. Sight Unseen. (p. 1574)
Graves, Sue. Bad Luck, Lucy! Williams, Lisa, illus. (p. 132)
—Ben & the Big Balloon. Jackson, Helen, illus. (p. 163)
—Ben & the Big Balloon. Jackson, Helen, illus. (p. 163)
—Blackbeard's Treasure. Chapman, Neil A., illus. (p. 197)
—But What If? Guicciardini, Desideria, illus. (p. 246)
—Cake for Dinner. (p. 252)
—Crabby Gabby. Guicciardini, Desideria, illus. (p. 375)
—Fizz Whiz. (p. 601)
—Georgie & the Dragon. Hall, Francois, illus. (p. 665)
—Harry & the Horse. (p. 750)
—Harry's Hat. Worsley, Belinda, illus. (p. 751)
—I Hate Everything! Guicciardini, Desideria, illus. (p. 839)
—Meet Erdene. (p. 1121)
—Mop Top. McClelland, Maddy, illus. (p. 1173)
—Night, Night. (p. 1253)
—Oh, George! Collins, Ross, illus. (p. 1280)
—Take a Deep Breath. Guicciardini, Desideria, illus. (p. 1696)
—The Messy Cake. (p. 1728)
—Tom's Big Nap. Holmes, Stephen, illus. (p. 1765)
—Tubby Tabby. Cope, Jane, illus. (p. 1795)
—What Is the Bible? (p. 1890)
Graves, Sue & Guicciardini, Desideria. I Didn't Do It! (p. 837)
Graves, Sue & Kavanagh, Peter. Too Sleepy! (p. 1767)
Graves, Susan Elaine. Lily the Lucky Ducky (p. 1018)
—Rescued & Making New Friends. (p. 1462)
Graves, Tyler, jt. auth. see Graves, Gayle.
Graves, Tyler & Graves, Gayle. Don't Let It Bug You. (p. 468)
—Where Are They Now. (p. 1906)
Graves, Will. Best Hockey Players of All Time. (p. 170)
—Best NBA Guards of All Time. (p. 170)
—Best NBA Teams of All Time. (p. 170)
—Best NFL Defenses of All Time. (p. 170)
—Best NFL Offenses of All Time. (p. 170)
—Robert Griffin III: NFL Sensation: RGIII. (p. 1479)
Gravett, Christopher. Castle. (p. 276)
—DK Eyewitness Books: Knight: Knight. (p. 456)
—Knight. (p. 964)
—Real Knights: Over 20 True Stories of Chivalrous Deeds. James, John, illus. (p. 1448)
Gravett, Emily. Again! Gravett, Emily, illus. (p. 29)
—Bear & Hare Go Fishing. Gravett, Emily, illus. (p. 150)
—Blue Chameleon. Gravett, Emily, illus. (p. 202)
—Dogs. (p. 462)
—Dogs. Gravett, Emily, illus. (p. 462)
—Little Mouse's Big Book of Beasts. (p. 1032)
—Little Mouse's Big Book of Fears. Gravett, Emily, illus. (p. 1032)
—Matilda's Cat. Gravett, Emily, illus. (p. 1109)
—Meerkat Mail. Gravett, Emily, illus. (p. 1120)
—Monkey & Me. Gravett, Emily, illus. (p. 1165)
—Odd Egg. Gravett, Emily, illus. (p. 1278)
—Orange Pear Apple Bear. Gravett, Emily, illus. (p. 1302)
—Rabbit Problem. Gravett, Emily, illus. (p. 1429)
—Spells. Gravett, Emily, illus. (p. 1625)
—Wolf Won't Bite! Gravett, Emily, illus. (p. 1944)
—Wolves. Gravett, Emily, illus. (p. 1944)
Gravett, Emily, illus. see Harrold, A. F.
Gravier, Anne, illus. see Levivier, Juliette.
Gravier, Anne, jt. auth. see Avril, Adeline.
Gravitt, Bill, illus. see Madore, Michele.
Gravley, Debbie Bybee. Golden Lace & the Magical Mossy Woods. (p. 695)
Gravois, Michael. 25 Totally Terrific Science Projects: Easy How-To's & Templates for Projects That Motivate Students to Show What They Know about Key Science Topics. (p. 1996)
—Fill-In Flip Books for Grammar, Vocabulary, & More, Grades 3-5: 25 Interactive Study AIDS That Kids Fill Out & Use Again & Again to Reinforce Essential Language Arts Content. (p. 586)
—Hands-On History: Colonial America. (p. 741)
—Reading Response Scrapbooking Activities: Reproducible Fonts, Clip Art, & Templates with Easy Step-by-Step Directions & Presentation Tips to Help All Students Showcase Their Learning. (p. 1446)
Graw, Christine Werts. Day I Gave My Stuff Away: The Story of Ashley Mae. (p. 413)
Graw, Victoria. Rounded Notes: From Years Long & Short. (p. 1491)
Gray, Alice, compiled by. Stories for the Extreme Teen's Heart: Over One Hundred Treasures to Touch Your Soul. (p. 1654)
Gray, Amy. How to Be a Vampire: A Fangs-On Guide for the Newly Undead. Erwert, Scott, illus. (p. 815)
—It's Good to Give. (p. 897)
Gray, Amy & Valentina, Serena. How to Be a Zombie. (p. 815)
Gray, Angela M., illus. see Smith, Jennifer Lynne.
Gray, Anne. Healer's Touch (p. 757)
—Rites of the Healer (p. 1475)
Gray, Anthony. Confederate Adventure of Jed Bodine & Ruefus: The Old Tulip Train Raid. (p. 356)
Gray, Betty. Legend of CaseyRock. (p. 988)
Gray, Bianca. Back to School: Adventures of Alex & Joey. (p. 130)
Gray, Bronwen, tr. see Futterer, Kurt.
Gray, Carolyn. Aboriginal Treaties. (p. 5)
—All about M. E. Manners & Etiquette for TWEENS & TEENS. (p. 42)
Gray, Charlotte. Bible Folks Shape Books. Henderson, Liz, illus. (p. 175)
—My Bible Box in Color. Henderson, Liz, illus. (p. 1197)
—Traveling Through the Bible with Bible Folks. Henderson, Liz, illus. (p. 1780)
Gray, Christopher. Moondene Prince. (p. 1172)
—There Be Goblins in the Wood!™ (p. 1729)
Gray, Cissy, illus. see Coste, Marion.
Gray, Claudia. Afterlife: An Evernight Novel. (p. 28)
—Afterlife. (p. 28)
—Balthazar: An Evernight Novel. (p. 135)
—Evernight. (p. 542)
—Fateful. (p. 577)
—Hourglass. (p. 802)
—Sorceress. (p. 1614)
—Spellcaster. (p. 1625)
—Stargazer. (p. 1642)
—Steadfast. (p. 1645)
—Ten Thousand Skies above You. (p. 1719)
Gray, Claudia, et al. Grim. Johnson, Christine, ed. (p. 724)
Gray, Clio. Peder & the Skincatcher. (p. 1334)
Gray, Coral, jt. auth. see Gray, Rick.
Gray, Dan, jt. ed. see Bustamante, Frank.
Gray, Dawn. S.P.I.R.I.T. Fire Storm. (p. 1628)
Gray, Dean, illus. see Butterfield, Moira & Golding, Elizabeth.
Gray, Deanne. Ante: Strangers. (p. 89)
Gray, Deborah, jt. auth. see Starwoman, Athena.
Gray, Dee. Po Cats (9 Lives) Cultural Adventure Series: 2 Low-Income Felines Share Their Musings on Travel, Colonialism, & Geopolitics (p. 1374)
Gray, Diane. Bears with Unruly Hairs. (p. 152)
Gray, Dianne & Gray, Dianne E. Holding up the Earth. (p. 788)
Gray, Dianne E., jt. auth. see Gray, Dianne.
Gray, E. Travis. Ridalin Phymes: Poetry for the ADHD Generation. (p. 1470)
Gray, Elizabeth. Giraffe for a Pet Valente, Christa, illus. (p. 677)
Gray, Elizabeth Janet. Adam of the Road. Lawson, Robert, illus. (p. 11)
Gray, Eric & Gray, Wendy. Kay-T & the Star-Maker. (p. 946)
Gray, Erick S. Booty Call *69. Whitney, Leah, ed. (p. 213)
—It's Like Candy: An Urban Novel. (p. 897)
—Nasty Girls: An Urban Novel. (p. 1230)
Gray, Frederick Ransom. Unrequited Love Club: Episode 2. (p. 1822)
—Unrequited Love Club: Three girls against the World. (p. 1822)
Gray, Grandpa. Land of the Three Elves: Beginnings. Vol. 1 (p. 973)
—Land of the Three Elves: Inside the Curve of the River. (p. 973)
Gray, H. Peter. Exhaustion of the Dollar: Its Implications for Global Prosperity. (p. 548)
Gray, Heather M. & Phillips, Samantha. Real Girl Real World: A Guide to Finding Your True Self. (p. 1448)
Gray, Hetty. Bee on Your Face! (p. 157)
Gray, J. M. L., illus. see Weiss, Ellen.
Gray, J. Sadie. My Appalachian Story & Coloring Book Volume 1: Second Edition. (p. 1196)
Gray, Jacky. Rory. (p. 1488)
Gray, Jane. Princess Backwards Milkau, Liz, illus. (p. 1403)
Gray, Jane, illus. see Clarke, Jane.
Gray, Jennifer & Swift, Amanda. Guinea Pigs Online: Furry Towers. Horne, Sarah, illus. (p. 731)
Gray, Jennifer, et al. Guinea Pigs Online: Viking Victory. (p. 731)
Gray, Joanna. Little Raindrop. Kolanovic, Dubravka, illus. (p. 1034)
Gray, Judith, jt. auth. see Ellison, Sheila.
Gray, Judy Silverstein. U. S. Coast Guard & Military Careers. (p. 1806)
Gray, Judy Silverstein & Kiland, Taylor Baldwin. Careers in the US Coast Guard. (p. 268)
Gray, Justin & Palmiotti, Jimmy. Uncle Sam & the Freedom Fighters. (p. 1812)
Gray, Karen, illus. see Mitchell, Lindy.
Gray, Karlin. Nadia: The Girl Who Couldn't Sit Still. Davenier, Christine, illus. (p. 1227)
Gray, Keith. Chain. (p. 288)
—Creepers. (p. 381)
—Dead Trouble. Scruton, Clive, illus. (p. 417)
—Ghosting. (p. 672)
—Ostrich Boys. (p. 1306)
Gray, Keith, ed. see Burgess, Melvin, et al.
Gray, Kes. Cluck O'Clock. McQuillan, Mary, tr. (p. 335)
—Daisy & the Trouble with Burglars. Sharratt, Nick & Parsons, Garry, illus. (p. 400)
—Daisy & the Trouble with Giants. Sharratt, Nick & Parsons, Garry, illus. (p. 400)
—Daisy & the Trouble with Kittens. Sharratt, Nick & Parsons, Garry, illus. (p. 400)
—Daisy & the Trouble with Life. Sharratt, Nick & Parsons, Garry, illus. (p. 400)
—Daisy & the Trouble with Sports Day. Sharratt, Nick, illus. (p. 400)
—First Day. Paul, Korky, illus. (p. 594)
—Leave Me Alone: A Tale of What Happens When You Stand up to a Bully. Wildish, Lee, illus. (p. 986)
—Mummy Goes to Work. (p. 1191)
—Nelly, the Monster Sitter. Hanson, Stephen, illus. (p. 1240)
—Nuddy Ned. Parsons, Garry, illus. (p. 1270)
—You Do! (p. 1975)
—Zoe Gets the Jitters! McQuillan, Mary, illus. (p. 1987)
Gray, Kes & Parsons, Garry. Billy's Bucket. (p. 187)
Gray, Kes, et al. Bebé a Bordo. Nayler, Sarah, illus. (p. 155)
Gray, Kevan. Spelman College College Prowler off the Record. (p. 1625)
Gray, Kevan, jt. auth. see Ballow, Jonah.
Gray, Kevan, jt. auth. see Bohler, Victoria.
Gray, Kevan, jt. auth. see C. Ridley, Jol.
Gray, Kevan, jt. auth. see Chasan, Emily.
Gray, Kevan, jt. auth. see Klein, Jennifer.
Gray, Kevan, jt. auth. see Nicole, Bridget.
Gray, Kim. I'm from India. (p. 859)
Gray, Larry. Canada's World War II Aces: Heroic Pilots & Gunners of the Wartime Skies. (p. 260)
—Canadians in the Battle of the Atlantic. (p. 260)
Gray, Laurel. Selfish Shellfish. (p. 1549)
Gray, Laurie. Maybe I Will. (p. 1113)
—Summer Sanctuary. (p. 1675)
Gray, Leon. Amazing Animal Communicators. (p. 53)
—Amazing Animal Engineers. (p. 53)
—Amazing Animal Shape-Shifters. (p. 53)
—Amazing Animal Super-Sleuths. (p. 53)
—Amazing Animal Tool-Users & Tool-Makers. (p. 53)
—Animal Scientists. (p. 79)
—Basics of the Periodic Table. (p. 142)
—Cane Toad: The World's Biggest Toad. (p. 261)
—Cybercrime. (p. 396)
—Deserts. (p. 429)
—Electricity. (p. 509)
—Flemish Giant Rabbit: The World's Biggest Bunny. (p. 603)
—Food Webs. (p. 614)
—Forces & Motion. (p. 617)
—Genetic Modification: Should Humans Control Nature? (p. 660)
—Giant Pacific Octopus: The World's Largest Octopus. (p. 673)
—Global Positioning System: Who's Tracking You? (p. 684)
—King Cobra: The World's Longest Venomous Snake. (p. 958)
—Life in Extreme Places. (p. 1010)
—Light. (p. 1014)
—Magnetism. (p. 1075)
—Missouri River. (p. 1154)
—Plant Classification. (p. 1369)
—Puberty. (p. 1414)
—Rivers. (p. 1476)
—Solving the Mysteries of Stonehenge. (p. 1608)
—Trumpeter Swan: The World's Largest Waterbird. (p. 1793)
—Virtual Crime! Solving Cybercrime. (p. 1844)
—Walking Sticks: The World's Longest Insects. (p. 1854)
—What Is a Blog & How Do I Use It? (p. 1888)
—What Is a Search Engine & How Do I Use It? (p. 1888)
—What Is a Social Network & How Do I Use It? (p. 1888)
—What Is a Wiki & How Do I Use It? (p. 1888)
—Zinc. (p. 1987)
Gray, Leon, jt. auth. see Woodward, John.
Gray, Leon & U. S. National Geographic Society Staff. Iran. (p. 886)
Gray, Leslie, illus. see Bowdish, Lynea.
Gray, Libba Moore. Is There Room on the Feather Bed? (p. 890)
—Miss Tizzy. Rowland, Jada, illus. (p. 1152)
Gray, Luli. Ant & Grasshopper. Ferri, Giuliano, illus. (p. 88)
Gray, M., illus. see Moore, Alan.
Gray, Margaret, jt. auth. see Tuchman, Gail.
Gray, Mary. Dollhouse Asylum. (p. 464)
Gray, Mary T. Watchable Birds of the Southwest. (p. 1861)
Gray, Maureen, illus. see Hooper, M.
Gray Mayo, Jo Ann, illus. see Hawkins Harris, Jennifer.
Gray, Michael Loyd. King Biscuit. (p. 958)
Gray, Mick, jt. auth. see Moore, Alan.
Gray, Millie. All for Mairi's Wedding. (p. 44)
—Filabeg International. (p. 586)
Gray, Miranda, illus. see Smith, Lucy.
Gray, Mitchel, jt. auth. see Asai, Carrie.
Gray, Nick & Scandifflo, Laura. Escape from Tibet: A True Story. (p. 535)
Gray, Nigel. Country Far Away. Philippe, Dupasquier, illus. (p. 372)
—Time to Play! Graham, Bob, illus. (p. 1753)
Gray, P. J. Accident. (p. 8)
—Accident Book 2 (p. 8)
—Lab (p. 969)
—Lab Book 3 (p. 969)
—Searching for Answers. (p. 1537)
—Trippin' (p. 1787)
—Trippin' Book 1 (p. 1787)
—Truth. (p. 1793)
Gray, Paula, illus. see Warner, Penny.
Gray, Peter. Animals. (p. 81)
—Female Action Figures. (p. 581)
—Heroes & Villains. (p. 772)
—How to Draw Butterflies & Other Insects. (p. 817)
—How to Draw Cats & Dogs & Other Pets. (p. 817)
—How to Draw Dolphins & Other Sea Creatures. (p. 817)
—How to Draw Tigers & Other Big Cats. (p. 819)
—Let's Draw: Animals, People, Cars, Cartoons. (p. 995)
—Male Action Figures. (p. 1083)
—Monsters. (p. 1168)
—Robots. (p. 1481)
Gray, Peter C. Female Action Figures. (p. 581)
—Male Action Figures. (p. 1083)
—Robots. (p. 1481)
Gray, Peter Winslow. Who Was Who in America: Their Childhood Years (p. 1919)
—Who Was Who in America Volume II: Their Childhood Years. (p. 1919)
Gray, R. Haiku. (p. 735)
Gray, Rev. Maxine A. Children's Lessons on Morality: Don't Use Your Friends. (p. 303)
Gray, Richard, jt. auth. see Harrison, Jordan.
Gray, Rick & Gray, Coral. Evangel Meets Orsen Whale. Headley, Aaron, illus. (p. 541)
Gray, Rita. Flowers Are Calling. Pak, Kenard, illus. (p. 608)
—Have You Heard the Nesting Bird? Pak, Kenard, illus. (p. 754)
Gray, Sara, illus. see Aboff, Marcie.
Gray, Sara, illus. see Blaisdell, Molly & Lyons, Shelly.
Gray, Sara, illus. see Blaisdell, Molly.
Gray, Sara, illus. see Dahl, Michael & Loewen, Nancy.
Gray, Sara, illus. see Dahl, Michael & Picture Window Books Staff.
Gray, Sara, illus. see Dahl, Michael.
Gray, Sara, illus. see Healy, Nicholas M.
Gray, Sara, illus. see Healy, Nick & Healy, Nicholas M.
Gray, Sara, illus. see Loewen, Nancy & Dahl, Michael.
Gray, Sara, illus. see Loewen, Nancy.
Gray, Sara, illus. see Lyons, Shelly & Blaisdell, Molly.
Gray, Sara, illus. see Lyons, Shelly.
Gray, Sara, illus. see Shaskan, Trisha Speed.
Gray, Shannon. Growing up Cranberry. Murfield, Anna, illus. (p. 726)
Gray, Shelly. Cat Called Spot. (p. 277)
Gray, Shirley W. Philippines. (p. 1350)
Gray, Shirley W. & Gray, Shirley Wimbish. Vietnam. (p. 1841)
Gray, Shirley Wimbish. Philippines. (p. 1350)
Gray, Shirley Wimbish, jt. auth. see Gray, Shirley W.
Gray, Sondra. According to Phoenix. (p. 8)
—According to Punkin. (p. 8)
—According to Taffy. (p. 8)
Gray, Stacy A., illus. see Hensley, Sarah M.
Gray, Stacy A., illus. see Mullican, Jody.
Gray, Stacy A., illus. see Mullican, Judy.
Gray, Stephen J. For the Love of a Cloud Maker. (p. 616)
Gray, Steve, illus. see Baker, Ken.
Gray, Steve, illus. see Duffield, Katy.
Gray, Steve, illus. see Gaydos, Nora.
Gray, Steve, illus. see Stephenson, Midji.
Gray, Steve, illus. see Trumbauer, Lisa.
Gray, Steve, illus. see Ward, Jennifer.
Gray, Steve, jt. auth. see Trumbauer, Lisa.
Gray, Susan. All Across Ohio: A Bird's Eye View with Worthington Cardinal Messer, Celia, illus. (p. 43)
—Colorful Ohio! A Bird's Eye View with Worthington Cardinal Gray, Susan & Messer, Celia, illus. (p. 344)
—Plain & Simple: A Bird's Eye View with Worthington Cardinal Messer, Celia, illus. (p. 1366)
—River Ride: A Bird's Eye View with Worthington Cardinal Messer, Celia, illus. (p. 1476)
—Wagon-O! A Bird's Eye View with Worthington Cardinal Messer, Celia, illus. (p. 1852)
—We Can Fly! A Bird's Eye View with Worthington Cardinal Messer, Celia, illus. (p. 1866)
Gray, Susan H. Allosaurus. (p. 47)
—American Alligator. (p. 59)
—American Mink. (p. 62)
—Animals Helping to Detect Diseases. (p. 82)
—Ankylosaurus. (p. 84)
—Apatosaurus. (p. 91)
—Artificial Limbs. (p. 104)
—Australian Spotted Jellyfish. (p. 116)
—Beagles. (p. 150)
—Bioengineer. (p. 188)

—Bulldogs. (p. 240)
—Bullfrog. (p. 240)
—Camels Have Humps. (p. 256)
—Circulatory System. (p. 321)
—Compsognathus. (p. 354)
—Dachshunds. (p. 398)
—Digestive System. (p. 438)
—Dinosaur Armor. (p. 441)
—Dinosaur Dig! (p. 442)
—Dinosaur Eggs. (p. 442)
—Dinosaur Teeth. (p. 443)
—Dinosaur Tracks. (p. 443)
—Disease Control. (p. 450)
—Ecology: The Study of Ecosystems. (p. 502)
—Elephant Seal. (p. 511)
—Emerald Ash Borer. (p. 517)
—Emergency Care. (p. 518)
—Experiment with Bugs. (p. 549)
—Experiment with Plants. (p. 549)
—Experiment with Seeds. (p. 549)
—Experiments with Electricity. (p. 549)
—Experiments with Motion. (p. 549)
—Food Webs: Interconnecting Food Chains Schultz, Ashlee, illus. (p. 614)
—Geology: The Study of Rocks. (p. 662)
—German Shepherds. (p. 666)
—Giant African Snail. (p. 673)
—Gray Whale. (p. 713)
—Hearing. (p. 759)
—Horse Shows. (p. 800)
—Iguanodon. (p. 856)
—Jellyfish. (p. 912)
—Key Deer. (p. 950)
—Life Cycle of Birds (p. 1009)
—Life Cycle of Insects (p. 1009)
—Life Cycle of Mammals (p. 1009)
—Lionfish. (p. 1021)
—Maiasaura. (p. 1076)
—Mongolian Wild Horse. (p. 1164)
—Muscular System. (p. 1192)
—Nervous System. (p. 1241)
—Nudibranch. (p. 1270)
—Oviraptor. (p. 1314)
—Paleontology: The Study of Prehistoric Life. (p. 1319)
—Penguins Can't Fly. (p. 1337)
—Pomeranians. (p. 1382)
—Rays. (p. 1441)
—Respiratory System. (p. 1463)
—Scholastic News Nonfiction Readers: Prehistoric World (p. 1522)
—Scottish Terriers. (p. 1532)
—Sea Star. (p. 1535)
—Skeletal System. (p. 1584)
—Spinosaurus. (p. 1628)
—Spinosaurus. Squier, Robert, illus. (p. 1628)
—Starling. (p. 1642)
—Stegosaurus. (p. 1646)
—Super Cool Science Experiments: Bugs. (p. 1679)
—Super Cool Science Experiments: Seeds. (p. 1679)
—Super Cool Science Experiments: Plants. (p. 1679)
—Transplants. (p. 1779)
—Triceratops. (p. 1785)
—Triceratops. Squier, Robert, illus. (p. 1785)
—Tyrannosaurus Rex. (p. 1805)
—Velociraptor. (p. 1835)
—Vision. (p. 1844)
—Walking Catfish. (p. 1854)
—Whooping Crane. (p. 1920)
—Zebra Mussel. (p. 1985)
Gray, Susan H., jt. auth. see Gray, Susan Heinrichs.
Gray, Susan H., jt. auth. see Somervill, Barbara.
Gray, Susan H. & Somervill, Barbara A. Bald Eagle. (p. 133)
—California Condor. (p. 253)
—Termite. (p. 1721)
Gray, Susan Heinrichs. Ecology: The Study of Ecosystems. (p. 502)
—Geology: The Study of Rocks. (p. 662)
—Germany. (p. 666)
—Mako Sharks. (p. 1083)
—Oceanography: The Study of Oceans. (p. 1277)
Gray, Susan Heinrichs & Gray, Susan H. Basset Hounds. (p. 143)
—Border Collies. (p. 213)
—Cocker Spaniels. (p. 337)
—Pugs. (p. 1415)
—Rottweilers. (p. 1491)
—Yorkshire Terriers. (p. 1972)
Gray, Susannah. Alligators Coming! Jones, Zach, illus. (p. 47)
—Gotta See Nathan! Jones, Nathan, illus. (p. 704)
Gray, T. L. Keezy's 10 Awesome Rules for Teenaged Dating! (p. 948)
Gray, Tricia. Wondrous Adventures of St. Francis of Assisi. (p. 1949)
Gray, Virginia Butler. My Magic Glasses. (p. 1213)
Gray, Virginia, illus. see Lee, Cora & O'Reilly, Gillian.
Gray, Wendy, jt. auth. see Gray, Eric.
Graybar, Shmuel, illus. see Mindel, Nissan.
Graybill, Guy, Jr. Dogs of Saint George: The Dogs of St George (p. 463)
Graybill, Joni, illus. see Aryal, Aimee.
Graydon, Shari. Made You Look: How Advertising Works & Why You Should Know. Lamoreaux, Michelle, illus. (p. 1070)
Graydon, William Murray. Canoe Boys & Campfires: Adventures on Winding Waters. (p. 261)
—Jungle Boy; or, Sexton Blake's Adventures in India. (p. 935)
Grayer, Dianna. Deonna's Unveiling: a Girl, a Teacher, a Turtle, & an Eagle. (p. 427)
Grayer, Luther. If You Play, You Must Pay. (p. 854)
Gray-Martin, Rita. Erick. (p. 533)
Graymont, Barbara. Iroquois. (p. 888)
Grayson, Augustus. What Is the Weather Today? (p. 1890)
Grayson, Barry/Scott. Twisted Yarns: Bedtime Stories for Hip Kids. (p. 1802)
Grayson, Cary, ed. see Farnette, Cherrie, et al.
Grayson, Cary, ed. see Frank, Marjorie & Norris, Jill.
Grayson, Devin, jt. auth. see Westerfeld, Scott.
Grayson, Devin, et al. Black Widow: The Itsy-Bitsy Spider. Hampton, Scott, illus. (p. 197)
—War Crimes. Woods, Pete & Camuncoli, Giuseppe, illus. (p. 1857)
Grayson, Devin K., jt. auth. see Gale, Bob.
Grayson, Rick, illus. see Allen, Margaret.
Grayson, Rick, illus. see Cernek, Kim.
Grayson, Rick, illus. see Flores, Debra, et al.
Grayson, Rick, illus. see Heidrich, Delana.
Grayson, Rick, illus. see Hex, Kathleen.
Grayson, Rick, illus. see Jennett, Pamela & Marchant, Sherry.
Grayson, Rick, illus. see Jones, Carmen S.
Grayson, Rick, illus. see Jordano, Kimberly & Adsit, Kim.
Grayson, Rick, illus. see Klawitter, Pamela Amick.
Grayson, Rick, illus. see Lewis, Sue & Stern, Amy.
Grayson, Rick, illus. see Morton, Debra & Stover, Elizabeth.
Grayson, Rick, illus. see Schwartz, Linda.
Grayson, Rick, illus. see Williams, Rozanne Lanczak.
Grayson, Robert. Amistad. (p. 65)
—Biggest Loser. (p. 185)
—California's Gold Rush. (p. 253)
—Careers in Network Engineering. (p. 268)
—Dancing with the Stars. (p. 403)
—Ed Begley, Jr. Living Green. (p. 503)
—Estée Lauder: Businesswoman & Cosmetics Pioneer. (p. 538)
—FBI & Cyber Crimes. (p. 578)
—FBI & National Security. (p. 578)
—FBI & Public Corruption. (p. 578)
—John Cena. (p. 921)
—Managing Your Digital Footprint. (p. 1086)
—Military. (p. 1142)
—Plaxico Burress. (p. 1370)
—Revolutionary War. (p. 1466)
—Sony: The Company & Its Founders. (p. 1613)
—SWAT Teams: The Missions (p. 1689)
—Transportation. (p. 1779)
—U. S. Civil War: Why They Fought. (p. 1806)
—U. S. Industrial Revolution. (p. 1806)
—United States. (p. 1819)
—US Air Force. (p. 1826)
—Voters: From Primaries to Decision Night. (p. 1850)
Grayson, Robert, jt. auth. see Delmar, Pete.
Grayson, Robert, jt. auth. see Ellis, Carol.
Grayson, Robert & Delmar, Pete. American Special Ops. (p. 63)
Grayson-Jones, Timothy. Cholera. (p. 309)
—Polio. (p. 1380)
Gray-Wilburn, Renée. Earthquakes! Sotirovski, Aleksandar, illus. (p. 497)
—Volcanoes! Sotirovski, Aleksandar, illus. (p. 1849)
—What You Need to Know about Meningitis. (p. 1896)
Gray-Wilburn, Renée, jt. auth. see Aboff, Marcie.
Gray-Wilburn, Renée & Beehive Illustrations Staff. Volcanoes! Sotirovski, Aleksandar, illus. (p. 1849)
Gray-Wilburn, Renée & Katz, Jill. Floods: Be Aware & Prepare (p. 605)
—Hurricanes: Be Aware & Prepare (p. 830)
Gray-Wilburn, Renée & Rustad, Martha E. H. Weather Aware (p. 1870)
Graziani, E. War in My Town (p. 1857)
Graziani, Maria. Adventures of Valeria Veterinarian: Las Aventuras de Valeria Veterinaria Elejalde, Eliana, illus. (p. 24)
—Black Cat on Halloween: Un Gato Negro en Dia de Brujas. Elejalde, Eliana, illus. (p. 195)
Graziani, Mary. Fat Pigs Fly! (p. 577)
Graziano, Alexandra Marie. Colors of Rayne. (p. 345)
Graziano, Carlo. Dialoghi Simpatici. (p. 434)
Graziano, Claudia. Meerkat's Safari. Barbera, Michelle, illus. (p. 1120)
Graziano, Jim. Johnny Depp. (p. 923)
Graziano, John. Woof! Funny Pet Stories. (p. 1950)
Graziano, John, illus. see Ripley's Inc. Staff.
Graziano-Straus, Laura. Happy Crabby Crying Happy Family's Blessing (p. 745)
Grbich, Aaron, illus. see Giganti, Paul.
Greager, Clay, jt. auth. see Burnett, Iris.
Great, Alex. Balkan Tales. (p. 134)
Great Books Foundation (U.S.) Staff, contrib. by. Junior Great Books. (p. 936)
Great Source Education Group Staff. Math on Call: A Mathematics Handbook. (p. 1106)
—Math on Call. (p. 1106)
Great Source Education Group Staff, creator. Math to Know Book A: Problem Solving. (p. 1107)
Greater Truth Publishers, ed. see Murray, Andrew.
Greathead, Helen. Clothes & Shoes. (p. 334)
Greathouse, Cindy. Robin the Abused Child. (p. 1480)
—Sophie the Missing Bunny. (p. 1613)
—Wilbur Learns to Forgive (p. 1928)
Greathouse, Justin, illus. see Loewen, Nancy.
Greathouse, Lisa. Backstage Pass: Fashion (p. 130)
—Backstage Pass: Fashion. (p. 130)
—Bakery. (p. 133)
—Bicicletas y Tablas. (p. 177)
—Big Digs: Construction Site (p. 181)
—Big Digs - Construction Site. (p. 181)
—Cómo Funcionan los Juguetes. (p. 351)
—Cómo Funcionan los Parques de Diversiones. (p. 351)
—Count Me In! School Carnival. (p. 369)
—Count Me In! - School Carnival. (p. 369)
—Count Me In! Soccer Tournament. (p. 369)
—Count Me In! What's for Lunch? (p. 369)
—Eat Healthy. (p. 501)
—Emergency! Be Prepared. (p. 518)
—Escalar y Saltar. (p. 534)
—Farm Animals: Classifying & Sorting. (p. 573)
—Find Your Sport. (p. 587)
—Fun in the Sun. (p. 648)
—Games Are Fun. (p. 654)
—Get Moving. (p. 667)
—Healthy Habits, Healthy You. (p. 758)
—Johnny Appleseed. (p. 923)
—Make It Healthy. (p. 1079)
—Pet Store. (p. 1345)
—Recess Time: Patterns. (p. 1451)
—Snack Shop. (p. 1595)
—Sweet: Inside a Bakery. (p. 1689)
—Toy Store. (p. 1774)
—What's for Lunch? (p. 1897)
—Wild Animals, Level K. (p. 1928)
Greathouse, Lisa, jt. auth. see Herwick Rice, Dona.
Greathouse, Lisa & Kuligowski, Stephanie. Unsolved! Mysterious Events. (p. 1822)
Greathouse, Lisa E. Astronomers Through Time. (p. 109)
—Food Webs. (p. 614)
—Nutrient Cycle. (p. 1274)
—Skygazers: From Hypatia to Faber (p. 1587)
Greathouse, Rebecca. Katie & Riley's Magical Adventures: Journey to the Amazon. (p. 944)
Greaux, Romea, illus. see Quetel, Linda.
Greaves, Bettina Bien, ed. see von Mises, Ludwig.
Greaves, Helen & Greaves, Simon. Doodle Yourself Smart ... Math. (p. 469)
Greaves, Margaret. Mice of Nibbling Village. Pinkney, Jane, illus. (p. 1134)
—Mouse Mischief. Pinkney, Jane, illus. (p. 1182)
—Stories from the Ballet. Kopper, Lisa, tr. (p. 1654)
—Tattercoats. Chamberlain, Margaret, illus. (p. 1707)
Greaves, Nick & du Plessis, David. When Bat Was a Bird: And Other Animal Tales from Africa. (p. 1901)
Greaves, Simon. Time Tables (p. 1752)
—Times Tables (p. 1754)
—Times Tables Practice Age 7-11. (p. 1754)
Greaves, Simon, jt. auth. see Greaves, Helen.
Greban, Quentin. Mommy, I Love You. (p. 1162)
—Mommy, I Love You. Greban, Quentin, illus. (p. 1162)
Greban, Quentin, illus. see Andersen, Hans Christian.
Greban, Quentin, illus. see Collodi, Carlo.
Greban, Quentin, illus. see Greban, Tanguy.
Greban, Quentin, illus. see Grimm, Jacob & Grimm, Wilhelm.
Greban, Tanguy. Sarah So Small. Greban, Quentin, illus. (p. 1514)
Greber, Barbara. Curvey's Christmas Wish. Medeiros, Jennifer, illus. (p. 395)
Grebin, Margaret. Baseball Forever! A Boy's Book on Grief, Loss, & Healing. (p. 141)
Grebing, Diane J. & Haas, Jane Elling. Bible Craft Potpourri: 50 Clever Bible Craft Projects. (p. 175)
Grecian, Alex. Rocketbots. (p. 1483)
Grecian, Alexander. Rocketbots: Trouble in Time: Trouble in Time. (p. 1483)
Greck-Ismair, Michaela, jt. auth. see Leleu, Sinead.
Greco, E. D., illus. see Reinstedt, Randall A.
Greco, Francesca. Cyril the Mandrill (p. 397)
Greco, Theresa. ABC Town. (p. 3)
Greder, Armin. City. Greder, Armin, illus. (p. 323)
—Island. Greder, Armin, illus. (p. 892)
Greder, Armin, illus. see Gleeson, Libby.
Greeff, Annie. Resilience (p. 1463)
—Resilience: Personal Skills for Effective Learning Vol. 1 (p. 1463)
Greek Baby and Kids Staff. Greek Alphabet Phonics Book. (p. 720)
Greek, Joe. Career in Computer Graphics & Design (p. 267)
—Incredible Projects Using 3D Printing (p. 869)
—Parkour. (p. 1325)
—Righteous Gentiles: Non-Jews Who Fought Against Genocide. (p. 1472)
—What Is Soil? (p. 1890)
—What Is the Atmosphere & How Does It Circulate? (p. 1890)
Greek, Joseph. Writing Term Papers with Cool New Digital Tools. (p. 1965)
Greeley, August. Fading Forests: The Destruction of Our Rainforests. (p. 562)
—Fallout: Nuclear Disasters in Our World. (p. 567)
—Mayan Writing in Mesoamerica. (p. 1113)
—Pistols & Politics: Alexander Hamilton's Great Duel. (p. 1364)
—Pistols & Politics: Alexander Hamilton Duels Aaron Burr. (p. 1364)
—Poisoned Planet: Pollution in our World. (p. 1377)
—Sludge & Slime: Oil Spills in Our World. (p. 1591)
—Toxic Waste: Chemical Spills in Our World. (p. 1774)
—Writing in Ancient Egypt. (p. 1965)
—Writing in Ancient India. (p. 1965)
—Writing in Ancient Mesopotamia. (p. 1965)
—Writing in Ancient Phoenicia. (p. 1965)
Greeley, David. Seven Friends Marquis, KariAnn, illus. (p. 1554)
Green, Adolph, jt. auth. see Comden, Betty.
Green, Alan, jt. auth. see Wenger, Brahm.
Green, Alice. Celebrating Id-Ul-Adha: A Muslim Festival. (p. 285)
Green, Alison. Fox in the Dark. Allwright, Deborah, illus. (p. 626)
—Mother Goose's Nursery Rhymes: And How She Came to Tell Them. Scheffler, Axel, illus. (p. 1178)
Green, Alison, jt. auth. see Scheffler, Axel.
Green, Amy. Escape from Riddler's Pass (p. 535)
Green, Andi. Lonely Little Monster. (p. 1046)
—Monster in the Bubble. (p. 1167)
—Monster Who Couldn't Decide. (p. 1168)
Green, Andrew. Jazz Guitar Structures: Boosting Your Solo Power. (p. 911)
Green, Ann L. Sgt. Dusty's New Home. (p. 1556)
Green, Babs Brumer. Take Her Back: An Andy-Bear Tale. (p. 1696)
Green, Barry. How to Draw 101 Animals. Green, Dan, illus. (p. 816)
—How to Draw 101 Baby Animals. Green, Dan, illus. (p. 816)
—How to Draw 101 Dinosaurs. Green, Dan, illus. (p. 816)
—How to Draw 101 Funny People. Green, Dan, illus. (p. 816)
—How to Draw 101 Monsters. Green, Dan, illus. (p. 816)
—How to Draw 101 Spooky Things. Green, Dan, illus. (p. 816)
Green, Barry, illus. see Graham, Oakley.
Green, Barry, illus. see Kings, Gary & Ginger, Richard.
Green, Barry, illus. see Lambert, Nat.
Green, Barry, illus. see Thompson, Kate.
Green, Bea, et al. Five-Minute Warm-Ups for Elementary Grades. Bosarge, Charlotte, ed. (p. 601)
—Five-Minute Warm-Ups for Middle Grades. Bosarge, Charlotte, ed. (p. 601)
Green, Ben K. Color of Horses: A Scientific & Authoritive Identification of the Color of the Horse. (p. 343)
Green, Burt, illus. see Wiley, Jean.
Green, Carl R. Alcohol: A MyReportLinks.com Book. (p. 35)
—Apollo 11 Rockets to First Moon Landing: A MyReportLinks. com Book. (p. 91)
—Cortés: Conquering the Powerful Aztec Empire. (p. 368)
—Custer's Stunning Defeat by American Indians at the Little Bighorn. (p. 395)
—Gemini 4 Spacewalk Mission: A MyReportLinks. com Book. (p. 659)
—Giant Panda: A MyReportLinks. com Book. (p. 673)
—Gorilla: A MyReportLinks. com Book. (p. 703)
—Koala: A MyReportLinks. Com Book. (p. 966)
—Nicotine & Tobacco: A Myreportlinks. com Book. (p. 1251)
—Spacewalk: The Astounding Gemini 4 Mission. (p. 1620)
—Tiger: A MyReportLinks.com Book. (p. 1748)
—Vietnam War: A MyReportLinks. Com Book. (p. 1841)
—Walking on the Moon: The Amazing Apollo 11 Mission. (p. 1854)
Green, Carl R., jt. auth. see Katirgis, Jane.
Green, Carl R., jt. auth. see Sanford, William R.
Green, Carl R. & Sanford, William R. Amazing Out-of-Body Experiences. Kelley, Gerald, illus. (p. 55)
—Astonishing Mind Powers. Kelley, Gerald, illus. (p. 108)
—Belle Starr. (p. 163)
—Billy the Kid. (p. 187)
—Butch Cassidy. (p. 246)
—Discovering Past Lives. Kelley, Gerald, illus. (p. 449)
—Jesse James. (p. 914)
—Mysterious Secrets of Dreams. Kelley, Gerald, illus. (p. 1223)
—Mystery of Fortune-Telling. Kelley, Gerald, illus. (p. 1224)
—Sensing the Unknown. Kelley, Gerald, illus. (p. 1551)
—Wild Bill Hickok. (p. 1929)
—Wyatt Earp. (p. 1966)
Green, Caroline. Drug Resistance. (p. 486)
—Stem Cells. (p. 1647)
Green, Cathy, et al. Great Ships on the Great Lakes: A Maritime History. (p. 718)
—Great Ships on the Great Lakes Teacher's Guide: A Maritime History. (p. 718)
Green, Chris Marie. Drop of Red (p. 486)
Green, Connie Jordan. Emmy. (p. 520)
—War at Home. (p. 1857)
Green, Connie R. & Oldendorf, Sandra Brenneman. Religious Diversity & Children's Literature: Strategies & Resources. (p. 1458)
Green, Corey. Brainstorm: Buckley School Books #2. (p. 222)
—Managing Stan: Buckley School Books #1. (p. 1086)
Green, D. L. Zeke Meeks Alves, Josh, illus. (p. 1985)
—Zeke Meeks vs His Big Phony Cousin Alves, Josh, illus. (p. 1985)
—Zeke Meeks vs the Annoying Princess Sing-Along Alves, Josh, illus. (p. 1985)
—Zeke Meeks vs the Big Blah-Rific Birthday Alves, Josh, illus. (p. 1985)
—Zeke Meeks vs the Crummy Class Play Alves, Josh, illus. (p. 1985)
—Zeke Meeks vs the Gruesome Girls Alves, Josh, illus. (p. 1986)
—Zeke Meeks vs the Horrendous Halloween Alves, Josh, illus. (p. 1986)
—Zeke Meeks vs the Horrifying TV-Turnoff Week Alves, Josh, illus. (p. 1986)
—Zeke Meeks vs the Mother's Day Meltdown. Alves, Josh, illus. (p. 1986)
—Zeke Meeks vs the No-Fun Fund-Raiser Alves, Josh, illus. (p. 1986)
—Zeke Meeks vs the Pain-In-the-Neck Pets Alves, Josh, illus. (p. 1986)
—Zeke Meeks vs the Putrid Puppet Pals Alves, Josh, illus. (p. 1986)
—Zeke Meeks vs the Stinkin' Science Fair Alves, Josh, illus. (p. 1986)
—Zeke Meeks vs the Stinky Soccer Team. Alves, Josh, illus. (p. 1986)
—Zeke Meeks vs the Super Stressful Talent Show Alves, Josh, illus. (p. 1986)
Green, Dan. Elements. (p. 510)
—Essentially English. (p. 537)
—Rocks & Minerals. (p. 1483)
—Technology: A Byte-Sized World! (p. 1711)
Green, Dan, illus. see Green, Barry.
Green, Dan, jt. auth. see Basher, Simon.
Green, Dan, jt. auth. see Harras, Bob.
Green, Dan & Basher, Simon. Biology: Life as We Know It! Basher, Simon, illus. (p. 189)
Green, Dan & Clark, Tom. How to Improve at Playing Guitar. (p. 820)
Green, Dan & Harrod, Elisa. How to Improve at Playing Piano. (p. 820)
Green, Dan & McMillan, Sue. How to Improve at Drawing. (p. 820)
—How to Improve at Making Jewelry. (p. 820)
Green, Dawn A. Marianne Wellman's School for Girls. (p. 1093)
Green, Denis, jt. auth. see Gosse, Jonathan F.
Green, Denis & Gosse, Jonathan F. Industrial Maintenance: Answer Key. (p. 872)
—Industrial Maintenance: Resource Guide. (p. 872)
Green, Donna, illus. see Urmy, Deanne, ed.
Green, Edna. My Special Thoughts: Designed for African-American Children. (p. 1219)
—My Special Thoughts. (p. 1219)
Green, Elaine. Adventures of Abigale Green in Spain, Alston, Brad, illus. (p. 16)
Green, Elizabeth Crick. Of Butterflies & Elephants! (p. 1279)

Green, Emily. Bears. (p. 151)
—Beavers. (p. 155)
—Circulatory System. (p. 321)
—Coyotes. (p. 374)
—Digestive System. (p. 438)
—Foxes. (p. 626)
—Frogs. (p. 641)
—Muscular System. (p. 1192)
—Nervous System. (p. 1241)
—Opossums. (p. 1300)
—Porcupines. (p. 1386)
—Raccoons. (p. 1430)
—Respiratory System. (p. 1463)
—Skeletal System. (p. 1584)
—Skunks. (p. 1586)
—Snakes. (p. 1596)
—Turtles. (p. 1798)
—Wolves. (p. 1944)
Green, Emily K. Ants. (p. 90)
—Beavers. (p. 155)
—Bumblebees. (p. 241)
—Caves. (p. 282)
—Chickens. (p. 300)
—Cockroaches. (p. 337)
—Cows. (p. 374)
—Crickets. (p. 382)
—Deserts. (p. 429)
—Dragonflies. (p. 478)
—Fall. (p. 566)
—Fireflies. (p. 592)
—Forests. (p. 618)
—Fruits. (p. 645)
—Goats. (p. 687)
—Grains. (p. 705)
—Grains. (p. 706)
—Grasshoppers. (p. 711)
—Healthy Eating. (p. 758)
—Horses. (p. 800)
—Keeping Fit. (p. 947)
—Lakes. (p. 972)
—Meat & Beans. (p. 1118)
—Milk, Yogurt, & Cheese. (p. 1143)
—Mountains. (p. 1181)
—Oceans. (p. 1277)
—Oils. (p. 1282)
—Pigs. (p. 1358)
—Rivers. (p. 1476)
—Sheep. (p. 1564)
—Vegetables. (p. 1834)
—Volcanoes. (p. 1849)
—Walkingsticks. (p. 1854)
Green, Francis. Neighbors in Need. (p. 1240)
Green, Gail. Animals & Teens: The Ultimate Teen Guide. (p. 82)
—Kids' Guide to Projects for Your Pet (p. 953)
Green, Gail D. Pretty Presents: Paper Creations to Share (p. 1398)
Green, Gail D. & Price, Sean Stewart. Kids' Guides. (p. 954)
Green, Gail, et al. Paper Artist: Creations Kids Can Fold, Tear, Wear, or Share. (p. 1322)
Green, George & Brooke, Amy/ J. George Green's, the Lion Who Couldn't Roar. (p. 663)
Green, Gladys, jt. auth. see Green, Michael.
Green, Gladys & Green, Michael. Night Attack Gunships: The AC-130H Spectres. (p. 1252)
—Stealth Attack Fighters: The F-117A Nighthawks. (p. 1646)
Green, Holly G. Don't Slam the Door. Scott, Sarah Chamberlin, illus. (p. 468)
Green, Ivah E. Animals under Your Feet. Reece, Maynard, illus. (p. 84)
Green, Jack. Dusty the Dust Devil. (p. 490)
—Microchip Kid. (p. 1136)
Green, Jackie Fourcade, illus. see McMahon, Bea Prior.
Green, Jackie Fourcade, jt. auth. see McMahon, Bea Prior.
Green, Jacqueline. Kiss & Tell. (p. 961)
—Secrets & Lies. (p. 1544)
—Truth or Dare. (p. 1794)
Green, Jane. Second Chance. (p. 1539)
Green, Janessa. Perimeters of the Ancient World: Recognize Perimeter (p. 1343)
Green, Janice D. Creation. (p. 379)
Green, Jared F., ed. DJ, Dance, & Rave Culture. (p. 455)
Green, Jay P., Sr., ed. Interlinear Greek-English New Testament. (p. 880)
Green, Jedda Ngwarai, illus. see Kunoth, Mark & Turner, Margaret.
Green, Jen. 1993 Mississippi River Floods. (p. 2003)
—3-D Explorer: Bugs. Veres, Laszlo, illus. (p. 1991)
—Advertising. (p. 25)
—Africans: We Came to North America. (p. 28)
—Air We Breathe. (p. 31)
—Ancient Celts: Archaeology Unlocks the Secrets of the Celts' Past. (p. 68)
—Ancient Greek Myths. (p. 69)
—Arctic Ocean. (p. 96)
—Atlantic Ocean. (p. 112)
—Audacious Aviators: True Stories of Adventurers' Thrilling Flights (p. 114)
—Aztecs. (p. 122)
—Barron's Amazing Fact-Packed, Fold-Out Atlas of the World: With Awesome Pop-Up Map! Engel, Christiane, illus. (p. 140)
—Barron's Totally Wild Fact-Packed, Fold-Out Animal Atlas. Engel, Christiane, illus. (p. 140)
—Bears. (p. 151)
—Big Cats & Wild Dogs: Explore the Incredible World & Lions, Tigers, Cheetahs, Leopards, Wolves, Hyenas, Dingos & Other Hunting Dogs. (p. 180)
—California Sea Lion. (p. 253)
—Caribbean. (p. 268)
—Caribbean Sea & Gulf of Mexico. (p. 268)
—Caring for Habitats. (p. 269)
—Changing Climates. (p. 290)
—China. (p. 306)
—Chinese & Japanese Myths. (p. 307)
—Coastlines Around the World. (p. 336)
—Coasts. (p. 336)
—Collins Big Cat Progress - Non-Fiction: Lime Band 11/Copper Band 12. (p. 340)
—Crocodiles. (p. 384)
—Cuba. (p. 388)
—Day & Night. (p. 412)
—Deserts & Polar Regions Around the World. (p. 429)
—Earthquake. (p. 497)
—Egyptians. (p. 507)
—Elephants. (p. 511)
—Energy for the Future. (p. 528)
—Evolution: Investigating the Origin & Development of the Species. (p. 546)
—Evolution. (p. 546)
—Exploring Nature: Beetles & Bugs. (p. 552)
—Exploring Nature: Incredible Insects. (p. 552)
—Exploring Nature: Examine the Wonderful World of Wolves, Jackals, Coyotes, Foxes & Other Wild Dogs, Shown in 190 Exciting Images: Wolves - Life in the Wild. (p. 552)
—Extreme Survival. (p. 557)
—Find Out about Birds: With 16 Projects & More Than 250 Pictures. (p. 587)
—Find Out about Insects. (p. 587)
—Find Out about Rainforests: With 20 Projects & More Than 250 Pictures. (p. 587)
—Focus on Egypt. (p. 610)
—Focus on Italy. (p. 610)
—Focus on South Africa. (p. 611)
—Food & Farming (p. 613)
—Frozen Extremes. (p. 645)
—Gandhi & the Quit India Movement: Days of Decision (p. 655)
—Garbage & Litter. (p. 655)
—Geology: Investigating the Science of the Earth. (p. 662)
—Great White Shark. (p. 719)
—Greece. (p. 720)
—Hail! Ancient Egyptians. (p. 735)
—Hail! Ancient Greeks. (p. 735)
—Hail! Aztecs. (p. 735)
—Hippopotamus. (p. 781)
—How the Water Cycle Works. (p. 813)
—Hurricane Andrew. (p. 829)
—Indian Ocean. (p. 871)
—Inheritance & Reproduction (p. 874)
—Inheritance of Traits: Why Is My Dog Bigger Than Your Dog? (p. 874)
—Inside Animals. (p. 876)
—Islands Around the World. (p. 892)
—Japón. (p. 909)
—Koalas. (p. 966)
—Leopards. (p. 993)
—Life in a Backyard. (p. 1010)
—Life in a Coral Reef. (p. 1010)
—Life in the Desert. (p. 1011)
—Life on the Tundra. (p. 1012)
—Making Air Cleaner. (p. 1080)
—Medicine. (p. 1119)
—Mediterranean Sea. (p. 1120)
—México. (p. 1131)
—Mighty Rivers. (p. 1140)
—Mississippi River. (p. 1154)
—Moray Eel. (p. 1173)
—Mount St. Helens. (p. 1180)
—Mountains. (p. 1181)
—Mountains Around the World. (p. 1181)
—Mumbai. Fairclough, Chris, photos by. (p. 1190)
—National Geographic Countries of the World - Vietnam. (p. 1231)
—Oil Disaster. (p. 1282)
—Pacific Ocean. (p. 1317)
—Porcupines. (p. 1386)
—Projects with Plants. (p. 1411)
—Projects with the Seaside. (p. 1411)
—Rabbits. (p. 1429)
—Raccoons. (p. 1430)
—Rain Forest Extremes. (p. 1434)
—Rainforests at Risk. (p. 1436)
—Red Fox. (p. 1454)
—Reducing Air Pollution. (p. 1456)
—Reducing & Recycling Waste. (p. 1456)
—Reducing Pollution & Waste (p. 1456)
—Reducing Pollution & Waste Ward, Geoff, illus. (p. 1456)
—Rhinoceros. (p. 1467)
—River Otters. (p. 1476)
—Rocks & Soil. (p. 1483)
—Saving Energy. (p. 1517)
—Saving Water. (p. 1518)
—Sea Lions. (p. 1534)
—Sea Otter. (p. 1535)
—Sharks. (p. 1562)
—Slide & Discover: Dinosaur Atlas. (p. 1590)
—Slide & Discover: World Atlas. (p. 1590)
—Snakes. (p. 1596)
—Surviving Natural Disasters. (p. 1687)
—Sustaining Our Natural Resources (p. 1688)
—Understanding Volcanoes & Earthquakes. (p. 1816)
—Using Energy Wisely. (p. 1828)
—Volcanoes Around the World. (p. 1849)
—Wasps. (p. 1860)
—Water. (p. 1862)
—Weather & Seasons. (p. 1870)
—Whales. (p. 1877)
—Why Should I Protect Nature? Gordon, Mike, illus. (p. 1926)
—Why Should I Recycle? Gordon, Mike, illus. (p. 1926)
—Why Should I Save Energy? Gordon, Mike, illus. (p. 1926)
—Why Should I Save Water? Gordon, Mike, illus. (p. 1926)
—Wildlife in Danger. (p. 1931)
—Wolves. (p. 1944)
—World's Oceans. (p. 1960)
Green, Jen, jt. auth. see Taylor, Barbara.
Green, Jen & Martineau, Susan. Wolves. (p. 1944)
Green, Jen & Molnar, Michael. Bears. (p. 151)
—Sharks. (p. 1562)
—Snakes. (p. 1596)
Green, Jen, et al. Show Me Science (p. 1570)
Green, Jessica. Diary of a Would-Be Princess: The Journal of Jillian Jones, 5b. (p. 435)
—Scratch Kitten & the Ghost Ship. Vane, Mitch, illus. (p. 1532)
—Scratch Kitten & the Terrible Beasties. Vane, Mitch, illus. (p. 1532)
Green, Jim. Ghost Dancer. (p. 670)
—Shadows of the Moon... Dancing. (p. 1558)
Green, Joanne. American Hero. (p. 61)
—Hootah's Baby. (p. 796)
—Story of Thumper the Cleft-Affected Bunny. (p. 1662)
Green, Joey. Jolly President: Or Letters George W. Bush Never Read. Green, Joey, illus. (p. 924)
Green, John. Abundance of Katherines. (p. 7)
—Arabian Nights Coloring Book. (p. 94)
—Beowulf. (p. 166)
—Big Book of Horses to Color. (p. 179)
—Buscando a Alaska. (p. 244)
—Cathedrals of the World Coloring Book. (p. 280)
—Charles Darwin. (p. 292)
—Creative Haven Wildflowers Stained Glass Coloring Book. (p. 379)
—Dogs to Paint or Color. (p. 463)
—Fairy World Stained Glass Coloring Book. (p. 564)
—Fault in Our Stars. (p. 577)
—Favorite Horses. (p. 578)
—Fun with Horseback Riding Stencils. (p. 648)
—Great Racehorses. (p. 718)
—Great Scenes from Horror Stories. (p. 718)
—Heavenly Snowflakes Stained Glass Coloring Book. (p. 761)
—Horse Anatomy. (p. 799)
—Horse Scenes to Paint or Color. (p. 800)
—Horses in Battle. (p. 800)
—Horses of the Old West. (p. 800)
—Horses Stained Glass Coloring Book. (p. 800)
—Horses Tattoos. (p. 800)
—Indian Life in Pre-Columbian North America Coloring Book. (p. 871)
—Kings & Queens of England. (p. 960)
—Language of Flowers Coloring Book. (p. 975)
—Looking for Alaska. (p. 1051)
—Midsummer Night's Dream Stained Glass Coloring Book. (p. 1139)
—Monkeys & Apes Coloring Book. (p. 1166)
—Musical Instruments Stained Glass Coloring Book. (p. 1194)
—Old Testament Scenes Stained Glass Coloring Book. (p. 1285)
—Paper Towns. (p. 1323)
—Pirate Queens: Notorious Women of the Sea. (p. 1363)
—Pirates Stained Glass Coloring Book. (p. 1364)
—Ponies Stickers. (p. 1382)
—Popes Coloring Book. (p. 1384)
—Saints Stained Glass Coloring Book. (p. 1504)
—Samurai Stained Glass Coloring Book. (p. 1510)
—Samurai Warriors. (p. 1510)
—Shiny Horses Stickers. (p. 1567)
—Sparta! Warriors of the Ancient World. (p. 1622)
—Teorema Katherine. (p. 1721)
—Terdellaline: A Free-Spirited, Energeti. (p. 1721)
—War of the Worlds. (p. 1857)
—Who Lives on the Farm? (p. 1916)
—Wildflowers GemGlow Stained Glass Coloring Book. (p. 1931)
—Will Grayson, Will Grayson. (p. 1932)
—Women of the Bible. (p. 1946)
—Wonderful World of Horses Coloring Book. (p. 1948)
—World of Cats to Paint or Color. (p. 1956)
Green, John, illus. see Dumas, Alexandre.
Green, John, illus. see London, Jack.
Green, John, illus. see MacKenzie, Donald A.
Green, John, illus. see Roman, Dave.
Green, John, jt. auth. see Blaisdell, Bob.
Green, John & Appelbaum, Stanley. Life in Old Japan Coloring Book. (p. 1010)
Green, John & Blaisdell, Bob. Great Scenes from Dickens' Novels. (p. 718)
Green, John & Coloring Books Staff. Amazing Angels Stained Glass Coloring Book. (p. 52)
—Glorious Angels Coloring Book. (p. 685)
Green, John & Drawing Staff. How to Draw Horses. (p. 817)
Green, John & Levithan, David. Will Grayson, Will Grayson. (p. 1932)
Green, John & Negri, Paul. Great Composers. (p. 715)
Green, John, et al. Let It Snow: Three Holiday Romances. (p. 994)
—Merry Christmas! Stained Glass Coloring Book. (p. 1129)
Green, Jon, jt. creator see DeShazer, Dennis.
Green, Jonathan. Amadeus, the Leghorn Rooster. (p. 51)
Green, Jonathan, illus. see Lauture, Denize.
Green, Jonathan, et al. Christmas Unwrapped: A Kid's Winter Wonderland of Holiday Trivia. (p. 316)
Green, Jonathon & Karolides, Nicholas J. Encyclopedia of Censorship. (p. 525)
Green, Jose. Castro's Diary. (p. 277)
Green, Joyce. Adventures of Chuck the Duck. (p. 17)
Green, Judith. Family Secret. Hammah, Aisha, illus. (p. 568)
Green, Judy. Little Blue Octopus. (p. 1024)
Green, Julia. Tilly's Moonlight Garden. (p. 1750)
Green, Julie. Super Smart Information Strategies: Write It Down. (p. 1682)
—Super Smart Information Strategies: Shooting Video to Make Learning Fun. (p. 1682)
Green, Julie, ed. see Berwick, Gwen & Thorne, Sydney.
Green, K. C. Regular Show Vol. 1. (p. 1457)
Green, Kate. Number of Animals. Wormell, Christopher, illus. (p. 1271)
—Number of Animals Nesting Blocks. Wormell, Christopher, illus. (p. 1271)
Green, Katie May. Seen & Not Heard. Green, Katie May, illus. (p. 1548)
Green, Katie May, illus. see Yolen, Jane.
Green, Ken. Love in a Dustbin. (p. 1059)
—Not a Chance. (p. 1266)
—Reptiles - Weird Wildlife (p. 1461)
Green, Kevin M. Livy Bug & Ally Gator in Best Friends. (p. 1042)
Green, Kim. Rinny Rhino Wants Pink Pearls & a Polka Dotted Penguin. (p. 1473)
Green, Leslie. Hi Mom, It's Me. (p. 775)
Green, Lila & Benchmark Education Co., LLC Staff. Mr. Dan Has a Plan. (p. 1184)
Green, Lucyna A. M. Love You Little Brother. (p. 1060)
Green, M. I. Primeros Auxilios para Ninos (First Aid for Children) (p. 1400)
Green, M. L. Underneath My Favorite Tree. (p. 1815)
Green, Marian. Book of Spells II. (p. 211)
Green, Marilyn. Fantasias en tu Cabello. (p. 571)
—My Anytime Anywhere Autograph Book. (p. 1196)
Green, Mary. Rivers in Action. (p. 1476)
Green, Mary, jt. auth. see Hiatt, Kay.
Green, Mary Alayne. Night Shadows: A Journal of Hominid Research (p. 1254)
Green, Matthew, illus. see Valenzuela, Kristine.
Green, Meg. Everything You Need to Know about Credit Cards & Fiscal Responsibility. (p. 545)
Green, Meg, jt. auth. see Berg, David W.
Green, Megan, illus. see Bilbrey, Heather.
Green, Megan, illus. see Paige, Nancy.
Green, Melissa J. & G., Melissa J. Mona Whine'ona: (the List) G., Ashley R., illus. (p. 1163)
Green, Michael. U. S. Military Forces. (p. 1806)
—United States Air Force (p. 1819)
—United States Army (p. 1819)
—United States Marines (p. 1819)
—United States Navy (p. 1819)
Green, Michael, jt. auth. see Green, Gladys.
Green, Michael & Green, Gladys. Carrier-Based Jet Fighters: The F-14 Tomcats. (p. 271)
—Long Range Bombers: The B-1B Lancers. (p. 1047)
Green, Michelle Y. Strong Right Arm: The Story of Mamie Peanut Johnson. Nelson, Kadir, illus. (p. 1668)
Green, Mim, jt. auth. see Gershator, Phillis.
Green, Mischa. Wounded Voices Unwise Choices: The Truth from Our Youth. (p. 1962)
Green, Mischa P. Sacred: 100 Affirmations for Girls. (p. 1500)
—What Tough Times Taught Me: ... that I just gotta teach You. (p. 1894)
Green, Naima. Meet Frankenstein. (p. 1121)
Green, Naima, jt. auth. see Merlin, Hope.
Green, Nehanda. Adventures of Jaja & Jamila Going to Africa: Going to Africa (p. 19)
Green, Noel, illus. see Robinson, Beth.
Green, Paige. Family over Everything. (p. 568)
Green, Paula. Flamingo Bendalingo: Poems from the Zoo. Hight, Michael, illus. (p. 602)
Green, Phillip. Littoral Combat Ships. (p. 1039)
Green, Poppy. Emerald Berries. Bell, Jennifer A., illus. (p. 517)
—Forget-Me-Not Lake. Bell, Jennifer A., illus. (p. 619)
—Looking for Winston. Bell, Jennifer A., illus. (p. 1051)
—New Friend. Bell, Jennifer A., illus. (p. 1244)
Green, Rayna & Fernandez, Melanie. Encyclopedia of the First Peoples of North America. (p. 525)
Green, Rich. Pearlsus. (p. 1333)
Green, Richard, jt. auth. see Green, Roger Lancelyn.
Green, Richard L. Salute to Historic African Kings & Queens. (p. 1506)
Green, Richard L., et al, eds. Salute to Black Civil Rights Leaders. Dobson, S. Gaston, illus. (p. 1506)
Green, Rico, jt. auth. see Disney Book Group Staff.
Green, Risa. Projection. (p. 1410)
Green, Robert. Bicycles. (p. 177)
—Cars. (p. 271)
—Cause & Effect the French Revolution: The French Revolution. (p. 282)
—Cause & Effect the September 11 Attacks: The September 11 Attacks. (p. 282)
—Coal. (p. 336)
—Expect the Most - Provide the Best: How High Expectations & Outstanding Instruction Help All Learners Succeed. (p. 548)
—From Waste to Energy. (p. 644)
—Global Warming. (p. 684)
—How Renewable Energy Is Changing Society. (p. 812)
—Immigration. (p. 861)
—Overpopulation. (p. 1314)
—Pandemics. (p. 1321)
—Pollution. (p. 1381)
—Poverty. (p. 1389)
—Skateboards. (p. 1583)
—Terrorism. (p. 1722)
—Woodrow Wilson. (p. 1949)
Green, Robert, jt. auth. see Flammang, James M.
Green, Robert, jt. auth. see Loeb, Jason.
Green, Robert James. Hawk of the Nile. Miller, Shane, illus. (p. 755)
Green, Rod. Emergency Vehicles. Biesty, Stephen, illus. (p. 518)
—Giant Vehicles. Biesty, Stephen, illus. (p. 674)
—Santa Claus: The Magical World of Father Christmas. (p. 1511)
Green, Roger Lancelyn. Adventures of Robin Hood. Hall, Arthur, illus. (p. 22)
—King Arthur & His Knights of the Round Table. Reiniger, Lotte, illus. (p. 958)
—Tale of Troy. Baynes, Pauline, illus. (p. 1700)
—Tales of Ancient Egypt. (p. 1702)
—Tales of the Greek Heroes. (p. 1702)
Green, Roger Lancelyn & Green, Richard. Adventures of Robin Hood. Hall, Arthur & Terrazzini, Daniela Jaglenka, illus. (p. 22)
Green, Roger Lancelyn & Langford, Alan. Myths of the Norsemen. (p. 1227)
Green, Roger Lancelyn, ed. Once upon a Time: Folk & Fairy Tales of the World. Kubasta, Vojtech, illus. (p. 1293)
Green, Ross Gordo & Healy, Kearney F. Tough on Kids: Rethinking Approaches to Youth Justice. (p. 1772)
Green, Ruth. Noisy Neighbors. (p. 1263)
Green, S. E. Killer Instinct. (p. 956)
—Killer Within. (p. 956)

Green, Sally. Half Bad. (p. 736)
—Half Wild. (p. 737)
Green, Sara. Apple. (p. 92)
—Arabian Horse. (p. 94)
—Basset Hounds. (p. 143)
—Beagles. (p. 150)
—Belgian Horse. (p. 161)
—Bill Gates. (p. 186)
—Blacktip Reef Shark. (p. 198)
—Blue Shark. (p. 203)
—Bomb-Sniffing Dogs. (p. 208)
—Border Collies. (p. 213)
—Boxers. (p. 217)
—Bulldogs. (p. 240)
—Camping. (p. 257)
—Canoeing. (p. 261)
—Cheerleading. (p. 296)
—Cheerleading Basics. (p. 296)
—Cheerleading Camp. (p. 296)
—Cheerleading Competitions. (p. 296)
—Cheerleading Professionals. (p. 296)
—Cheerleading Squads. (p. 296)
—Cheerleading Tryouts. (p. 296)
—Chihuahuas. (p. 301)
—Coca-Cola. (p. 337)
—Cocker Spaniels. (p. 337)
—Collies. (p. 340)
—Crayola. (p. 377)
—Dachshunds. (p. 398)
—Dalmatians. (p. 401)
—Disney. (p. 451)
—Doberman Pinschers. (p. 459)
—Elon Musk. (p. 516)
—Fire Dogs. (p. 590)
—Freshwater Fishing. (p. 637)
—Friesian Horse. (p. 639)
—Goblin Shark. (p. 688)
—Great White Shark. (p. 719)
—Guide Dogs. (p. 730)
—Hershey's. (p. 774)
—Hiking. (p. 779)
—Jeff Bezos. (p. 911)
—Kayaking. (p. 946)
—Kellogg's. (p. 948)
—Larry Page. (p. 976)
—Lego. (p. 990)
—Lipizzan Horse. (p. 1021)
—Mako Shark. (p. 1082)
—Marissa Mayer. (p. 1094)
—Mark Zuckerberg. (p. 1095)
—McDonald's. (p. 1114)
—Military Dogs. (p. 1142)
—Morgan Horse. (p. 1175)
—Mountain Climbing. (p. 1180)
—Nike. (p. 1255)
—Oceanic Whitetip Shark. (p. 1277)
—Police Dogs. (p. 1380)
—Pomeranians. (p. 1382)
—Relgian Horse. (p. 1458)
—Rottweilers. (p. 1491)
—Sergey Brin. (p. 1552)
—Service Dogs. (p. 1553)
—Shetland Pony. (p. 1566)
—Snow Search Dogs. (p. 1599)
—Steve Jobs. (p. 1649)
—Target. (p. 1706)
—Tennessee Walking Horse. (p. 1720)
—Therapy Dogs. (p. 1729)
—Thoroughbred Horse. (p. 1740)
—Water Rescue Dogs. (p. 1863)
—West Highland White Terriers. (p. 1876)
—Wilderness Search Dogs. (p. 1931)
—Yorkshire Terriers. (p. 1972)
Green, Scooter. Ituke's First Hunt. (p. 900)
Green, Shayla. What's in My House? (p. 1897)
—What's in My House? Number Names & Count Sequence. (p. 1898)
Green, Steve, illus. see Pernell, Pasha.
Green, Sue, illus. see Richter, Bernd & Richter, Susan.
Green, Susan Eikov. Don't Pick on Me: Help for Kids to Stand up to & Deal with Bullies. (p. 468)
Green, Sylvia. Soft-Hearted Sheepdog. Kavanagh, Peter, illus. (p. 1606)
Green, Tamara. Dodo: Extinct Species. Gibbons, Tony, illus. (p. 460)
Green, Tammy L., et al. Ruby Explores the World of Wellness. (p. 1493)
—Ruby Learns about the World of Wellness. (p. 1493)
—Sydney Travels Through the World of Wellness. (p. 1692)
—T. J.'s Adventures in the World of Wellness. (p. 1694)
Green, Teri & Taylor, Sue. Littlest Soldier (p. 1039)
Green, Terry. Moonstone. (p. 1173)
Green Thumb Theatre Staff, ed. see Gardiner, Meghan, et al.
Green, Tim. Baseball Great. (p. 141)
—Best of the Best: A Baseball Great Novel. (p. 170)
—Best of the Best. (p. 170)
—Big Time. (p. 184)
—Deep Zone. (p. 423)
—First Team. (p. 597)
—Football Champ. (p. 615)
—Football Genius. (p. 615)
—Football Hero. (p. 615)
—Force Out. (p. 617)
—Kid Owner. (p. 951)
—Lost Boy. (p. 1055)
—New Kid. (p. 1245)
—Perfect Season. (p. 1342)
—Pinch Hit. (p. 1359)
—Rivals: A Baseball Great Novel. (p. 1475)
—Trainer Tim's Camp Fitness. (p. 1777)
—Trainer Tim's down on the Farm. (p. 1777)
—Trainer Tim's Gym. (p. 1777)
—Trainer Tim's Troubled Friend. (p. 1777)
—Unstoppable. (p. 1822)
Green, Timothy. Mystery of Coyote Canyon. Green, Timothy, illus. (p. 1224)
—Powerpoint Made Very Easy! Easy Step-by-Step Lessons & Projects That Help Every Kid - & Every Teacher - Master the Essentials of PowerPoint, Grades 4-8. (p. 1391)
Green, Toby, ed. see Johnson, Gail & Grell, Jane.
Green, Victoria Peace. Give Me Five for Fangs, Feathers, & Faith! A Devotional for Tweenagers. (p. 681)
Green, Wendy. Helen & Nicky: A Story of a Special Great Dane & Her Wonderful Girl. (p. 762)
Green, Yuko. Camina from Brazil Sticker Paper Doll. (p. 256)
—Greek Girl & Boy Paper Dolls. (p. 720)
—Japanese Word Book. (p. 909)
—Let's Learn about JAPAN: Activity & Coloring Book. (p. 998)
—Let's Learn about MEXICO: Activity & Coloring Book. (p. 998)
—Naia & Kohola. (p. 1227)
—Nativity Activity & Coloring Book. (p. 1235)
Green, Yuko, illus. see Hearn, Lafcadio, et al.
Green, Yuko, illus. see Hirschi, Ron.
Greenacres, Levi. Ham in a Pram. (p. 739)
—Mommy's New Tattoo: A Bedtime Story for People (p. 1163)
Greenagel, Frank L., photos by. Think Like a Photographer! How to Take Better Pictures Than Anyone in Your Family. (p. 1734)
Greenaven Press, ed. see Mackay, Jennifer.
Greenaven Press Staff, ed. see Boyd, Christie Brewer.
Greenaven Press Staff, ed. see Henningfeld, Diane Andrews.
Greenaven Press Staff, ed. see Mackay, Jenny.
Greenaven Press Staff, ed. see Uschan, Michael V.
Greenaven Press Staff, ed. see Wilcox, Christine.
Greenaven Press Staff, ed. Adele. (p. 12)
Greenaway, David. Globalization & Productivity Growth: Theory & Evidence. Greenaway, David et al, eds. (p. 685)
Greenaway, Frank, photos by see Clarke, Barry & Dorling Kindersley Publishing Staff.
Greenaway, Frank, photos by see Rayner, Matthew & BVetMed MRCVS Staff.
Greenaway, Kate. Kate Greenaway's Birthday Book. (p. 944)
—Mother Goose Coloring Book. Perkins, Nancy, illus. (p. 1178)
Greenaway, Theresa. Animals: Foldout Book. (p. 81)
Greenaway, Theresa, jt. auth. see Dorling Kindersley Publishing Staff.
Greenaway, Theresa, ed. Ocean: A Foldout Book & Wall Chart. (p. 1276)
Greenbaum, Fay, tr. see Pinet, Michele.
Greenbaum, Harry. Brazil. Gritzner, Charles F., ed. (p. 224)
—Iceland. (p. 851)
Greenberg, Anne, ed. see Caletti, Deb.
Greenberg, Carmel. Who Stole Pop Pop's Underwear? Jennings, Randy, illus. (p. 1917)
Greenberg, Dan. Fractions & Decimals: 25 Tales with Computation & Word Problems to Reinforce Key Skills. (p. 626)
—Reading Skills Mysteries, Grades 3-6: 'Whodunits' with Comprehension Questions That Help Kids Identify the Main Idea, Draw Conclusions, Determine Cause & Effect, & More. (p. 1446)
Greenberg, Daniel A. Lizards. (p. 1042)
—Wilderness Search Dogs. (p. 1931)
Greenberg, Daniel A. & Hess, Nina. Whales. (p. 1877)
Greenberg, Daniel A. & Wilsdon, Christina. Chimpanzees. (p. 306)
Greenberg, David. Calvin Coolidge. Schlesinger, Arthur M., Jr., ed. (p. 255)
—Don't Forget Your Etiquette! The Essential Guide to Misbehavior. Westcott, Nadine Bernard, illus. (p. 467)
—Super Silly School Poems. Woodruff, Liza, illus. (p. 1681)
—Tugging String: A Novel about Growing up During the Civil Rights Era. (p. 1796)
Greenberg, David E. Ugly Brown Pear. (p. 1808)
Greenberg, Doreen & Geenberg, Michael. Drive to Win: The Story of Nancy Lieberman-Cline. (p. 485)
Greenberg, Doris & Shandley, Pandré. Legend of L'Esprit: Dance Legacy Series. (p. 988)
Greenberg, James, jt. auth. see Universal Dreamworks Pictures Staff.
Greenberg, Jan, jt. auth. see Jordan, Sandra.
Greenberg, Jan & Jordan, Sandra. Action Jackson. Parker, Robert Andrew, illus. (p. 10)
—Andy Warhol, Prince of Pop. (p. 73)
—Ballet for Martha: Making Appalachian Spring. Floca, Brian, illus. (p. 134)
—Mad Potter: George E. Ohr, Eccentric Genius. (p. 1069)
—Vincent Van Gogh: Portrait of an Artist. (p. 1843)
Greenberg, Jan, ed. Side by Side: New Poems Inspired by Art from Around the World. (p. 1573)
Greenberg, Joanne. I Never Promised You a Rose Garden. (p. 844)
Greenberg, Keith. Bill & Hillary: Working Together in the White House. (p. 186)
Greenberg, Keith Elliot. Derek Jeter: Spectacular Shortstop. (p. 427)
—Forensics. (p. 617)
Greenberg, Martin. Dinosaur Fantastic. (p. 442)
Greenberg, Martin, et al, eds. Civil War Ghosts. (p. 325)
Greenberg, Melanie Hope, illus. see Cohen, Miriam.
Greenberg, Michael. Sword of a Champion: The Sharon Monplaisir Story. (p. 1692)
Greenberg, Nicki. Naughtiest Reindeer. Greenberg, Nicki, illus. (p. 1237)
Greenberg, Penny. Adventures of Toby the Turtle & Mighty Magoo. (p. 24)
Greenberg, Scott. Sandbags & the Fire: How Leaders Cut Loose Their Hang-Ups & Soar to Success. (p. 1511)
Greenberg, Sidney & Silverman, Morris. Siddurenu. (p. 1573)
Greenberg, Sidney & Sugarman, Allan S. Junior Contemporary Prayer Book for the High Holidays. (p. 936)
Greenberg, Suzanne, jt. auth. see Glatt, Lisa.
Greenberger, Robert. Careers in Artificial Intelligence. (p. 267)
—Christina Aguilera. (p. 312)
—Cool Careers Without College for People Who Love to Organize, Manage, & Plan. (p. 363)
—Deserts: The Living Landscape. (p. 429)
—Gus Grissom: The Tragedy of Apollo 1. (p. 732)
—Gus Grissom. (p. 732)
—Historical Atlas of Pakistan. (p. 783)
—How Do We Know the Nature of Energy. (p. 808)
—Juan Ponce de Leon: The Exploration of Florida & the Search for the Fountain of Youth. (p. 930)
—Lou Gehrig. (p. 1057)
—Meet Godzilla. (p. 1121)
—Suicide Bombers. (p. 1673)
—Technology of Ancient China. (p. 1711)
—Will Eisner. (p. 1932)
—Wilt Chamberlain. (p. 1935)
Greenberger, Robert, jt. auth. see Clemens, Nora.
Greenberger, Robert, jt. auth. see Vincent, Beverly.
Greenberger, Robert & Loughridge, Lee. Arctic Attack. Kruse, Jason T., illus. (p. 96)
Greenberger, Robert, et al. Robin's First Flight. Schigiel, Gregg, illus. (p. 1480)
Greenberger, Tehilla. Gifts to Treasure. Toron, Eli, illus. (p. 676)
Greenblatt, C. H., illus. see Banks, Steven & Hillenburg, Stephen.
Greenblatt, C. H., illus. see Banks, Steven.
Greenblatt, Kim Isaac. Practical Money Making: Surviving Recession, Layoffs, Credit Problems, Generating Passive Income Streams, Working Full Time or Part Time & Retirement. (p. 1392)
Greenblatt, Miriam. Han Wu Di & Ancient China. (p. 740)
—Julius Caesar & the Roman Republic. (p. 933)
—Napoleon Bonaparte & Imperial France. (p. 1229)
—War of 1812. (p. 1857)
Greenblatt, Miriam, jt. auth. see Orr, Tamra.
Greenblatt, Miriam & Lemmo, Peter S. Human Heritage: A World History. (p. 826)
Greenblatt, Miriam, et al. Glencoe Human Heritage: A World History. (p. 683)
Greenburg, Dan. Don't Count on Dracula. Davis, Jack E., illus. (p. 467)
—Dude, Where's My Spaceship? Pamintuan, Macky, illus. (p. 489)
—How I Went from Bad to Verse. Davis, Jack E., illus. (p. 810)
—It's Itchcraft! Davis, Jack E., illus. (p. 897)
—Just Add Water... & Scream! Davis, Jack E., illus. (p. 937)
—Just Add Water... And Scream! Davis, Jack E., illus. (p. 937)
—Secrets of Dripping Fang: The Onts. Fischer, Scott M., illus. (p. 1545)
—Secrets of Dripping Fang: Attack of the Giant Octopus. Fischer, Scott M., illus. (p. 1545)
—Secrets of Dripping Fang: Fall of the House of Mandible. Fischer, Scott M., illus. (p. 1545)
—Secrets of Dripping Fang: The Shluffmuffin Boy Is History. Fischer, Scott M., illus. (p. 1545)
—Secrets of Dripping Fang: Treachery & Betrayal at Jolly Days. Fischer, Scott M., illus. (p. 1545)
—Secrets of Dripping Fang: The Vampire's Curse: Book 3: Book 3. Fischer, Scott M., illus. (p. 1545)
—Secrets of Dripping Fang: When Bad Snakes Attack Good Children. Fischer, Scott M., illus. (p. 1545)
—Secrets of Dripping Fang: Please Don't Eat the Children: Book 7: Book 7. Fischer, Scott M., illus. (p. 1545)
—Secrets of Dripping Fang, Book Eight: When Bad Snakes Attack Good Children. Fischer, Scott M., illus. (p. 1545)
—Secrets of Dripping Fang, Book Four: Fall of the House of Mandible. Fischer, Scott M., illus. (p. 1545)
—Secrets of Dripping Fang, Book One: The Onts. Fischer, Scott M., illus. (p. 1545)
—Secrets of Dripping Fang, Book Seven: Please Don't Eat the Children. Fischer, Scott M., illus. (p. 1545)
—Secrets of Dripping Fang, Book Six: Attack of the Giant Octopus. Fischer, Scott M., illus. (p. 1545)
—Secrets of Dripping Fang, Book Two: Treachery & Betrayal at Jolly Days. Fischer, Scott M., illus. (p. 1545)
—Shluffmuffin Boy Is History Fischer, Scott M., illus. (p. 1568)
Greenburg, Dan & DiTerlizzi, Angela. Vampire's Curse Fischer, Scott M., illus. (p. 1832)
Greenburg, J. C. In the Deep. Gerardi, Jan, illus. (p. 865)
—In the Desert. Gerardi, Jan, illus. (p. 865)
—In the Garbage. Gerardi, Jan, illus. (p. 866)
—In the Garden. Palen, Debbie, illus. (p. 866)
—In the Ice Age. Gerardi, Jan, illus. (p. 866)
—In the Jungle. (p. 866)
—In the Whale. Reed, Mike, illus. (p. 868)
—In Time. Gerardi, Jan, illus. (p. 868)
—In Uncle Al Gerardi, Jan, illus. (p. 868)
—On Earth. Gerardi, Jan, illus. (p. 1288)
—On the Reef. Reed, Mike, tr. (p. 1291)
—Under Water. Reed, Mike, illus. (p. 1814)
—With the Bats. Gerardi, Jan, illus. (p. 1942)
—With the Dinosaurs. Gerardi, Jan, illus. (p. 1942)
—With the Frogs. Gerardi, Jan, illus. (p. 1942)
Greenburg, Nicki. Octopus Has Deadly Spit. Greenburg, Nicki & Greenburg, Nicki, illus. (p. 1278)
Greenburger, Sanford Jerome, tr. see Salten, Felix.
Greendyk, William, tr. see Bunyan, John.
Greendyk, William, tr. see Friendly, Aunt.
Greendyk, William, tr. DOS Osos. (p. 472)
—Hierba Mala. (p. 777)
—Niños de la Biblia. (p. 1257)
—Primeras Impresiones de Dios. (p. 1400)
Greendyk, William, tr. from ENG. Doce Historias de la Tia Margarita. (p. 459)
—Hijo de la Viuda. (p. 779)
Greene, Bette. Drowning of Stephan Jones. (p. 486)
—I've Already Forgotten Your Name, Philip Hall! Jenkins, Leonard, illus. (p. 900)
—Morning Is a Long Time Coming. (p. 1175)
—Philip Hall Likes Me, I Reckon Maybe. (p. 1350)
—Summer of My German Soldier. (p. 1674)
Greene, Brenda. Dog Gone: Boomer's Story. Cheryl H. Hahn, illus. (p. 461)
Greene, Buddy, jt. auth. see Lowry, Mark.
Greene, Carol. 13 Days of Halloween. Raglin, Tim, illus. (p. 1995)
—Cat & the Bear. (p. 277)
—I Love Our Air. (p. 842)
—I Love Our Animals. (p. 842)
—I Love Our Forests. (p. 842)
—I Love Our Land. (p. 842)
—I Love Our People. (p. 842)
—I Love Our Water. (p. 842)
—Please, Wind? Sharp, Gene, illus. (p. 1373)
—Snow Joe. Sharp, Paul, illus. (p. 1599)
—Story of Halloween. Bronson, Linda, illus. (p. 1658)
—Why Boys & Girls Are Different. (p. 1923)
—Why Boys & Girls Are Different. Dorankamp, Michelle, illus. (p. 1923)
Greene, Chad. Ronni, the Little Jewish Girl Who Loved Israel. (p. 1487)
Greene, Chad Felix. What's That Thing on Your Head? Greene, Chad Felix, illus. (p. 1899)
Greene, Constance C. Beat the Turtle Drum. (p. 152)
—Girl Called Al. (p. 678)
Greene, Daryl C. Benjamin's Dog Joseph: A Three Legged Hero. Akers-Bell, Mary, illus. (p. 165)
Greene, Edgar. Tony Hawk. (p. 1766)
Greene, Graham. Brighton Rock. (p. 228)
Greene, Graham, jt. auth. see Greene, Graham.
Greene, Graham & Greene, Graham. Gun for Sale. (p. 732)
Greene, Hamilton, illus. see Hill, Monica.
Greene, Ida. Anger Management for Children, Elementary. (p. 75)
—Looking for Love in All the Wrong Places. (p. 1051)
Greene, Inez. Adonde Esta Me Topito? Flor Ada, Alma, tr. (p. 13)
—Mi Perrito Flor Ada, Alma, tr. (p. 1133)
Greene, Jacqueline. Nathan's Hanukkah Bargain Hierstein, Judith, illus. (p. 1231)
—Rebecca Story Collection. Hirsch, Jennifer, ed. (p. 1450)
—Secrets at Camp Nokomis: A Rebecca Mystery. Hirsch, Jennifer, ed. (p. 1544)
Greene, Jacqueline Dembar. 2001 World Trade Center Attack. (p. 2003)
—Grizzly Bears: Saving the Silvertip. (p. 724)
—Secret Shofar of Barcelona. Chayka, Doug, illus. (p. 1543)
—Secret Shofar of Barcelona. Chayka, Douglas, illus. (p. 1543)
—Speak up, Tommy! Melmon, Deborah, illus. (p. 1623)
—Triangle Shirtwaist Factory Fire. (p. 1785)
Greene, Janice. 75-Cent Son (p. 1998)
—Blood & Basketball. (p. 200)
—Breaking Point (p. 225)
—Dark Lady. (p. 407)
—Escape from Earth (p. 534)
—Eye of the Hurricane (p. 557)
—Fat Boy (p. 577)
—Girl Who Had Everything (p. 679)
—Hamlet's Trap (p. 739)
—House on the Hill (p. 803)
—I Spy E-Spy (p. 846)
—No Exit (p. 1258)
—No Way to Run (p. 1261)
—Plot (p. 1374)
—Read My Lips. (p. 1443)
—Read Reflect Respond (p. 1443)
—Read, Reflect, Respond (p. 1443)
—Ritual (p. 1475)
—Strange but True (p. 1664)
—Strange but True Book 1 (p. 1665)
—Strange but True Stories Book 1: The Presidential Ghost, Mystery Spots on Earth, UFO or Weather Balloon? ... & More. (p. 1665)
—Strange but True Stories Book 5. (p. 1665)
—Tough Girl. (p. 1772)
—Under Siege (p. 1813)
—White Fang. (p. 1912)
—White Room (p. 1913)
Greene, Janice, jt. auth. see Quinley, Elliot.
Greene, Janice, jt. auth. see Suter, Joanne.
Greene, Janice, jt. auth. see Thomas, Terri.
Greene, Janice & Thomas, Terri. Read My Lips (p. 1443)
Greene, Joanne. Lippy the Lion. (p. 1021)
Greene, John McBride. Encounter at Ogre Island. Julich, Jenniffer, illus. (p. 524)
Greene, John Robert. George H. W. Bush Years. (p. 663)
—Nixon-Ford Years. (p. 1257)
Greene, Joshua M. Kaliya, Serpent King. Wire, Patrick, illus. (p. 942)
—Krishna & the Mystery of the Stolen Calves. Amendola, Dominique, illus. (p. 967)
—Littlest Giant: The Story of Vamana. Moore, Emma V., illus. (p. 1039)
Greene, Judybeth. Mommy, Open up the Secrets of the World. (p. 1162)
Greene, Karen. Adventures of Jack. (p. 19)
Greene, Kathi. Betty Gets Ready for the Doctor. (p. 172)
Greene, Kathy B. How I Love You! (p. 810)
Greene, Kelly Evelyn, illus. see Evans, Barbara Greene.
Greene, Kimberly. Fame Game & Me. (p. 567)
—My Life on TV. (p. 1212)
—My Sister's a Pop Star. (p. 1218)
Greene, Kristy. How Penguins Lost Their Flight. (p. 812)
Greene, Leslie. Papa & Breannah Bear on a Treasure Hunt. (p. 1321)
Greene, Lila. Henry Ford's Fantastic Factory: Identify & Explain Patterns in Arithmetic. (p. 768)
Greene, Linda Lee, jt. auth. see Welch, Debra Shiveley.
Greene, Marjorie. Cassie's Big Day. (p. 276)
Greene, Mary. Lizzy Gets Another Brother. (p. 1043)
Greene, Meg. B-52 Stratofortress. (p. 122)
—Careers in the National Guards' Search & Rescue Units. (p. 268)
—Hunt for Osama Bin Laden. (p. 828)
—Hunt for Osama bin Laden. (p. 828)
—Japan: A Primary Source Cultural Guide. (p. 909)
—Obesity. (p. 1275)
—Polish Americans. (p. 1380)
—Rest in Peace: A History of American Cemeteries. (p. 1464)
—Technology of Ancient Japan. (p. 1711)

—Transcontinental Treaty 1819: A Primary Source Examination of the Treaty Between the United States & Spain over the American West. (p. 1778)
Greene, Meg & Malvasi, Meg Greene. Into the Land of Freedom: African Americans in Reconstruction. (p. 881)
Greene, Melanie W., et al. Goodnight, Boone. Marlowe, Susan B., illus. (p. 701)
Greene, Michele Dominguez. Keep Sweet. (p. 947)
Greene, Montrell. Magic in Me Series #1: Magical Me. (p. 1072)
—Magic in Me Series #3: Believing in Me. (p. 1072)
Greene, Montrell & Greene, Robie. Magic in Me Series #2: Imagine Me. (p. 1072)
Greene, Narcissa. Adventures of Veree Knowland. (p. 24)
—Wandering Jack & Other Stories. (p. 1856)
Greene, Reggie. Adventures of Swami Somewhere- the Supermarket. Graham, Michael, illus. (p. 23)
Greene, Rhonda Gowler. Daddy Is a Cozy Hug. Smith, Maggie, illus. (p. 398)
—Firebears, the Rescue Team. Andreasen, Dan, illus. (p. 591)
—Mail Monkeys. Bender, Robert, illus. (p. 1077)
—Mommy Is a Soft, Warm Kiss. Smith, Maggie, illus. (p. 1162)
—No Pirates Allowed! Said Library Lou. Ajhar, Brian, illus. (p. 1259)
—Noah & the Mighty Ark Spengler, Margaret L., illus. (p. 1261)
—Only God Can Make a Kitten (p. 1298)
—Santa's Stuck. Cole, Henry, illus. (p. 1513)
—Very First Thanksgiving Day. Gaber, Susan, illus. (p. 1838)
Greene, Richard. Lawrence the Locomotive. (p. 981)
Greene, Robert. World War I. (p. 1958)
Greene, Roberta, jt. auth. see Greene, Roberta R.
Greene, Roberta R. & Greene, Roberta. Human Behavior Theory & Social Work Practice. (p. 825)
—Social Work with the Aged & Their Families. (p. 1605)
Greene, Roble, jt. auth. see Greene, Montrell.
Greene, Sanford, illus. see Pryce, Trevor & Naftali, Joel.
Greene, Sanford, illus. see Pryce, Trevor.
Greene, Sanford, illus. see Torres, J., et al.
Greene, Sefton. Space Painters. (p. 1619)
Greene, Sheppard M., jt. auth. see Miller, J. Philip.
Greene, Stephanie. Christmas at Stony Creek. Sheban, Chris, illus. (p. 312)
—Falling into Place. (p. 567)
—Happy Birthday, Sophie Hartley. (p. 745)
—Moose Crossing Mathieu, Joe, illus. (p. 1173)
—Moose's Big Idea Mathieu, Joe, illus. (p. 1173)
—Owen Foote, Money Man. Weston, Martha, illus. (p. 1314)
—Owen Foote, Super Spy. Weston, Martha, illus. (p. 1314)
—Pig Pickin' Mathieu, Joe, illus. (p. 1357)
—Pocketful of Princess Posey: First Grade Parade-Perfect Present-Next-Door Dog. Roth Sisson, Stephanie, illus. (p. 1375)
—Princess Posey & the Christmas Magic. (p. 1405)
—Princess Posey & the Christmas Magic. Sisson, Stephanie Roth, illus. (p. 1405)
—Princess Posey & the First Grade Ballet. Roth Sisson, Stephanie, illus. (p. 1405)
—Princess Posey & the First Grade Parade Roth Sisson, Stephanie, illus. (p. 1405)
—Princess Posey & the First Grade Parade Sisson, Stephanie Roth, illus. (p. 1405)
—Princess Posey & the First-Grade Boys. Sisson, Stephanie Roth, illus. (p. 1405)
—Princess Posey & the Monster Stew. Sisson, Stephanie Roth, illus. (p. 1405)
—Princess Posey & the Perfect Present Sisson, Stephanie Roth, illus. (p. 1405)
—Princess Posey & the Tiny Treasure. Sisson, Stephanie Roth, illus. (p. 1405)
—Queen Sophie Hartley. (p. 1425)
—Show-Off Mathieu, Joe, illus. (p. 1571)
—Sophie Hartley & the Facts of Life. (p. 1613)
—Sophie Hartley, on Strike. (p. 1613)
Greene, Stephen M. T. Tales of the Unknown. (p. 1703)
Greene, Steven & Elder, Laurel. Politics of Parenthood: Causes & Consequences of the Politicization & Polarization of the American Family. (p. 1381)
Greene, Thomas. Whacked Out Wrestling: Memorial - A tale of Headlocks, Hurricanrana, & High School. (p. 1877)
Greene, Tracy, illus. see Ross, Eric.
Greene, Victor. Life of Benjamin Franklin. (p. 1011)
Greeneish, Susan, illus. see Cusick, Dawn & O'Sullivan, Joanne.
Greeneish, Susan, illus. see Fielding, Beth.
Greene's 29 after school art students, K., illus. see Marino, Angie.
Greenes, Carol. Hot Math Topics: Estimation & Computation with Large Numbers. (p. 801)
—Tops Beginning Problem Solving: Big Book. (p. 1769)
Greenes, Carol, et al. Addition & Subtraction. (p. 12)
—Estimations & Logical Reasoning. (p. 538)
—Fractions & Decimals. (p. 626)
—Geometry & Measurements. (p. 662)
—Multiplication & Division. (p. 1190)
—Number Sense. (p. 1271)
—Number Sense & Computation. (p. 1271)
—Patterns & Reasoning. (p. 1329)
—Spatial Sense. (p. 1622)
—Time & Money. (p. 1751)
Greenes, Carole E., et al. Navigating through Problem Solving & Reasoning in Grade 2. House, Peggy A. & Greenes, Carole E., eds. (p. 1238)
Greenes, Carole, et al. Hot Math Topics: Algebraic Reasoning. (p. 801)
—Money & Time. (p. 1164)
Greenes, Shimra, illus. see Kleiman, Deanna M.
Greenfeld, Barbara & Weinstein, Robert A. Kids' College Almanac Fourth Edition: A First Look at College. (p. 953)
Greenfeld, Howard. Promise Fulfilled: Theodor Herzl, Chaim Weizmann, David Ben-Gurion, & the Creation of the State of Israel. (p. 1411)
Greenfelder, Jill, illus. see Bogel, Rachel Anne.
Greenfield, jt. auth. see Greenfield, Eloise.
Greenfield, Amy Butler. Chantress Alchemy. (p. 291)
—Chantress Fury. (p. 291)
Greenfield, Anne. Songs of Life: Psalm Meditations from the Catholic Community at Stanford Soos, Eva, photos by. (p. 1612)
Greenfield Educational Center Staff. Words Through Poetry (p. 1952)
Greenfield, Eloise. Brothers & Sisters: Family Poems. Gilchrist, Jan Spivey, illus. (p. 231)
—Brothers & Sisters. (p. 231)
—Friendly Four. Gilchrist, Jan Spivey, illus. (p. 638)
—Great Migration: Journey to the North. Gilchrist, Jan Spivey, illus. (p. 717)
—How They Got Over: African Americans & the Call of the Sea. (p. 814)
—Me & Neesie. Gilchrist, Jan Spivey, illus. (p. 1115)
—Paul Robeson. Ford, George, illus. (p. 1330)
—Poetry Anthology. Gilchrist, Jan Spivey, illus. (p. 1376)
—She Come Bringing Me That Little Baby Girl. Steptoe, John, illus. (p. 1564)
—When the Horses Ride By: Children in the Times of War. Gilchrist, Jan Spivey, illus. (p. 1904)
—William & the Good Old Days. (p. 1933)
Greenfield, Eloise & Ford, George. Paul Robeson. (p. 1330)
Greenfield, Eloise & Greenfield. In the Land of Words: New & Selected Poems. Gilchrist, Jan Spivey, illus. (p. 866)
Greenfield, Nancy Reuben. When Mommy Had a Mastectomy. Butler, Ralph M., illus. (p. 1903)
Greenfield, Tonya. Nonnie's Kitchen: Fun & Food in the Kitchen with Kids. (p. 1263)
Greenfield, Tonya G. Nonnies Kitchen Fun & Food in the Kitchen with Kids. (p. 1263)
Greengaard, Alex, illus. see Lister, Tresina.
Greenhalgh, Miranda. Rapid Duck. (p. 1439)
Greenhalgh, Rachel, illus. see Cook, Bob.
Greenham, Caz. Adventures of Eric Seagull. Homfray, Nick, illus. (p. 18)
—Adventures of Eric Seagull 'Story-Teller' Book 2 a Fairy's Wish. Homfray, Nick, illus. (p. 18)
Greenhaven Press Editors. Adoption. (p. 13)
—Are Books Becoming Extinct? (p. 96)
—Birth Control. (p. 192)
—Celiac Disease. (p. 286)
—Columbine School Shootings. (p. 346)
—Education. (p. 505)
—Egyptian Mythology. Mckerley, Jennifer Guess, ed. (p. 507)
—Genocide. (p. 661)
—History of Jazz. (p. 784)
—History of Rap & Hip-Hop. (p. 784)
—Lindsey Vonn. (p. 1019)
—Mrsa. Williams, Mary E., ed. (p. 1188)
—Native Americans. (p. 1234)
—Online Social Games. (p. 1298)
—Taylor Lautner. (p. 1708)
Greenhaven Press Editors, ed. see Abramovitz, Melissa.
Greenhaven Press Editors, ed. see Berlatsky, Noah.
Greenhaven Press Editors, ed. see Bily, Cynthia A.
Greenhaven Press Editors, ed. see Bryfonski, Dedria.
Greenhaven Press Editors, ed. see Busby, Barbara Sheen.
Greenhaven Press Editors, ed. see Cartlidge, Cherese.
Greenhaven Press Editors, ed. see Chalk, Frank.
Greenhaven Press Editors, ed. see Currie, Stephen.
Greenhaven Press Editors, ed. see Dunn, John M.
Greenhaven Press Editors, ed. see Emert, Phyllis Raybin.
Greenhaven Press Editors, ed. see Engdahl, Sylvia.
Greenhaven Press Editors, ed. see Espejo, Roman.
Greenhaven Press Editors, ed. see Fisanick, Christina.
Greenhaven Press Editors, ed. see Francis, Amy.
Greenhaven Press Editors, ed. see Friedman, Lauri S.
Greenhaven Press Editors, ed. see Gerdes, Louise I.
Greenhaven Press Editors, ed. see Gerdes, Louise.
Greenhaven Press Editors, ed. see Gillard, Arthur.
Greenhaven Press Editors, ed. see Haerens, Margaret.
Greenhaven Press Editors, ed. see Haugen, David M.
Greenhaven Press Editors, ed. see Haugen, David.
Greenhaven Press Editors, ed. see Hay, Jeff.
Greenhaven Press Editors, ed. see Henningfeld, Diane Andrews.
Greenhaven Press Editors, ed. see Hiber, Amanda.
Greenhaven Press Editors, ed. see Hillstrom, Kevin.
Greenhaven Press Editors, ed. see Johnson, Claudia Durst.
Greenhaven Press Editors, ed. see Kallen, Stuart A.
Greenhaven Press Editors, ed. see Langwith, Jacqueline.
Greenhaven Press Editors, ed. see Lankford, Ronald D.
Greenhaven Press Editors, ed. see Loonin, Meryl.
Greenhaven Press Editors, ed. see Mackay, Jennifer & Mackay, Jennifer.
Greenhaven Press Editors, ed. see MacKay, Jennifer.
Greenhaven Press Editors, ed. see Merino, Noel.
Greenhaven Press Editors, ed. see Merino, Noel.
Greenhaven Press Editors, ed. see Merino, Noel.
Greenhaven Press Editors, ed. see Merino, Noel.
Greenhaven Press Editors, ed. see Merino, Noël.
Greenhaven Press Editors, ed. see Merino, Noël.
Greenhaven Press Editors, ed. see Merino, Noël.
Greenhaven Press Editors, ed. see Merino, Noël.
Greenhaven Press Editors, ed. see Miller, Debra A.
Greenhaven Press Editors, ed. see Naff, Clay Farris.
Greenhaven Press Editors, ed. see Nardo, Don.
Greenhaven Press Editors, ed. see Nelson, David E.
Greenhaven Press Editors, ed. see Riggs, Thomas.
Greenhaven Press Editors, ed. see Roleff, Tamara L.
Greenhaven Press Editors, ed. see Rosenthal, Beth.
Greenhaven Press Editors, ed. see Scherer, Lauri S.
Greenhaven Press Editors, ed. see Tardiff, Joe.
Greenhaven Press Editors, ed. see Thompson, Tamara.
Greenhaven Press Editors, ed. see Ullmann, Carol.
Greenhaven Press Editors, ed. see Uschan, Michael V.
Greenhaven Press Editors, ed. see Watkins, Christine.
Greenhaven Press Editors, ed. see Watson, Stephanie.
Greenhaven Press Editors, ed. see Wilcox, Christine.
Greenhaven Press Editors, ed. see Williams, Mary E.
Greenhaven Press Editors, ed. see Woog, Adam.
Greenhaven Press Editors, ed. see Wukovits, John F.
Greenhaven Press Editors, jt. ed. see Gale Editor.
Greenhaven Press Editors & Bryfonski, Dedria. Standardized Testing. (p. 1639)
Greenhaven Press Editors & Busby, Barbara Sheen. Foods of Indonesia. (p. 614)
Greenhaven Press Editors & Craig, Lizabeth. History of Nursing. Hardman, Lizabeth, ed. (p. 784)
Greenhaven Press Editors & Fisanick, Christina, eds. Ovarian Cancer. (p. 1313)
Greenhaven Press Editors & Gale Editors, eds. Privacy. (p. 1407)
Greenhaven Press Editors & Gillard, Arthur, eds. War in Afghanistan. (p. 1857)
Greenhaven Press Editors & Haerens, Margaret. Genocide. (p. 661)
Greenhaven Press Editors & Haugen, David. Are Books Becoming Extinct? (p. 96)
—Health Care Legislation. (p. 758)
Greenhaven Press Editors & Haugen, David M. Alternative Medicine. Zott, Lynn, ed. (p. 50)
Greenhaven Press Editors & Kallen, Stuart A. History of Country Music. (p. 783)
Greenhaven Press Editors & MacKay, Jennifer, eds. Gun Control. (p. 731)
Greenhaven Press Editors & Schwartz, Heather E. Cheerleading. (p. 296)
Greenhaven Press Editors & Szumski, Bonnie. Stephen Colbert. (p. 1648)
Greenhaven Press Editors & Zott, Lynn, eds. Congressional Ethics. (p. 357)
Greenhaven Press Editors, ed. Cyberbullying. (p. 396)
—Education. (p. 505)
—Fibromyaligia. (p. 583)
—Garbage & Recycling. (p. 655)
—Population. (p. 1385)
—Welfare. (p. 1874)
Greenhaven Press Staff, ed. see Berlatsky, Noah.
Greenhaven Press Staff, ed. see Boyd, Christie Brewer.
Greenhaven Press Staff, ed. see Cartlidge, Cherese.
Greenhaven Press Staff, ed. see Engdahl, Sylvia.
Greenhaven Press Staff, ed. see Espejo, Roman.
Greenhaven Press Staff, ed. see Garbus, Julia.
Greenhaven Press Staff, ed. see Garbus, Julie.
Greenhaven Press Staff, ed. see Haugen, David.
Greenhaven Press Staff, ed. see Hoover, Elizabeth.
Greenhaven Press Staff, ed. see Lansford, Tom.
Greenhaven Press Staff, ed. see Merino, Noel.
Greenhaven Press Staff, ed. see Merino, Noel.
Greenhaven Press Staff, ed. see Merino, Noël.
Greenhaven Press Staff, ed. see Merino, Noël.
Greenhaven Press Staff, ed. see Reid, Scott.
Greenhaven Press Staff, ed. see Scherer, Lauri S.
Greenhaven Press Staff, ed. see Scherer, Randy.
Greenhaven Press Staff, ed. see Szumski, Bonnie.
Greenhaven Press Staff, ed. see Thompson, Tamara.
Greenhaven Press Staff, ed. see Williams, Mary E.
Greenhaven Press Staff, ed. Mitt Romney. (p. 1156)
—Muammar El-Qaddafi. (p. 1188)
—Multiracial America. (p. 1190)
—Nuclear Power. (p. 1270)
—Prince Harry. (p. 1401)
—Teen Drug Abuse. (p. 1713)
—Wyclef Jean. (p. 1966)
Greenhead, Bill, illus. see Adams, Alison.
Greenhead, Bill, illus. see Fuerst, Jeffrey B.
Greenhead, Bill, illus. see Smith, Carrie.
Greenhill, Ms Jane. Jolly Olde Teenage Alien. (p. 924)
Greenhut, Josh & Brown, Jeff. Flying Chinese Wonders. Pamintuan, Macky, illus. (p. 609)
Greenidge, Kirsten. Familiar. (p. 567)
Greenland, Katharine Hayward, jt. auth. see Alden, Raymond MacDonald.
Greenland, Paul R., et al. Career Opportunities in Conservation & the Environment. (p. 267)
Greenland, Shannon. Down to the Wire. (p. 474)
—Summer My Life Began. (p. 1674)
—Winning Element (p. 1937)
Greenlaw, Linda. All Fishermen Are Liars: True Tales from the Dry Dock Bar. (p. 44)
Greenlaw, M. Jean. Flood. (p. 605)
—Inundacion. (p. 883)
Greenlaw, Steven A. Doing Economics: A Guide to Understanding & Carrying Out Economic Research. (p. 463)
Greenleaf, E. Who Wants to Nap? (p. 1918)
Greenleaf, Lisa, illus. see Brennan, Linda Crotta.
Greenleaf, Lisa, illus. see Buell, Janet & Sisters, Write.
Greenleaf, Lisa, illus. see Darragh, Marty & Pitkin, Jo.
Greenleaf, Lisa, illus. see Lyman Schremmer, Patty.
Greenleaf, Lisa, illus. see Mayr, Diane & Sisters, Write.
Greenleaf, Lisa, illus. see Murphy, Andrea & Ray, Joyce.
Greenlee, Carolyn Wing, illus. see BlueWolf, James Don.
Greenlee, Don. This Countryboy Guardian Was Heaven Sent. (p. 1735)
Greenley, Amanda & Evans, Linda. Birthday Party - Ali & Sam Help Out - Well Spotted! (p. 193)
—Gang: Learning about the Victorians; Ali & Sam's School Trip. (p. 655)
—Sledmere Stories: The Gameboy; Thanks Sophie!, Stop Thief! Bk. 2 (p. 1588)
Greenley, Victoria. I Don't Like My Grumpy Face! (p. 837)
Greens, Olivia. My Dream. (p. 1202)
Greensall, Maxine. Keith the Kite. (p. 948)
Greenseid, Diane, illus. see Dragonwagon, Crescent.
Greenseid, Diane, illus. see Ghigna, Charles & Ghigna, Debra.
Greenseid, Diane, illus. see Ketteman, Helen.
Greensfelder, Saundra. Adventures of Top Hat Crow. (p. 24)
Greensill, Rowina Anne. James Goes to Play School. (p. 907)
Greenslade, David & Rushton, Rhian Wyn. Gloria Ar Berlian Bupur. (p. 685)
Greensmith, Wayne. Everybody's Magic. (p. 543)
Greenspan, Alice. Thanking God for You. (p. 1725)
Greenspan, Deborah. Kids' Day. (p. 953)
Greenspan, Paul. Crystal of Dreams. (p. 387)
Greenspan, Shari Dash. Shemot Muzarim. Katz, Avi, illus. (p. 1565)
Greenspon, Thomas S. What to Do When Good Enough Isn't Good Enough: The Real Deal on Perfectionism: A Guide for Kids. (p. 1894)
Greenstein, Elaine, illus. see Christiansen, Candace.
Greenstein, Susan, illus. see Forest, Heather.
Greenstein, Susan, illus. see Prager, Ellen J.
Greenstone, Brian. Pangea Software's Ultimate Game Programming Guide for Mac OS X. (p. 1321)
Greenwald, Lisa. Dog Beach Unleashed: The Seagate Summers Book Two. (p. 461)
—My Life in Pink & Green. (p. 1212)
—My Summer of Pink & Green: Pink & Green Book Two. (p. 1219)
—My Summer of Pink & Green. (p. 1219)
—Pink & Green Is the New Black: Pink & Green Book Three. (p. 1359)
—Reel Life Starring Us. (p. 1456)
—Sweet Treats & Secret Crushes. (p. 1690)
—Welcome to Dog Beach: The Seagate Summers Book One. (p. 1873)
Greenwald, Lisa, jt. auth. see Paley, Sasha.
Greenwald, Marni Leigh. What Kind of Bagel Am I? (p. 1891)
Greenwald, Susan. Five Times Five Is Not Ten: Make Multiplication Easy. (p. 601)
Greenwald, Todd J., jt. creator see Disney Modern Publishing.
Greenwald, Todd J., contrib. by. Wizards of Waverly Place Party Planner. (p. 1943)
—Wizards of Waverly Place Sticker Activity Book. (p. 1943)
—Wizards of Waverly Place Ultimate Puzzle Book. (p. 1943)
Greenwald, Tommy. Charlie Joe Jackson's Guide to Extra Credit. (p. 293)
—Charlie Joe Jackson's Guide to Extra Credit. Coovert, J. P., illus. (p. 293)
—Charlie Joe Jackson's Guide to Not Reading. (p. 293)
—Charlie Joe Jackson's Guide to Not Reading. Coovert, J. P., illus. (p. 293)
—Charlie Joe Jackson's Guide to Summer Vacation. Coovert, J. P., illus. (p. 293)
—Jack Strong Takes a Stand. (p. 903)
—Jack Strong Takes a Stand. Mendes, Melissa, illus. (p. 903)
—Katie Friedman Gives up Texting! And Lives to Tell about It. Coovert, J. P., illus. (p. 945)
Greenwald, Zee. Loving Kindness: Stories of Chessed from Our Sages. (p. 1061)
Greenwall, Jessica. First Sticker Book Circus. (p. 597)
—First Sticker Book Fairies. (p. 597)
—First Sticker Book Princesses. Finn, Rebecca, illus. (p. 597)
Greenwall, Jessica & Brooks, Felicity. First Sticker Book Monkeys. (p. 597)
Greenwalt, Mary, illus. see Wheeler, Opal & Deucher, Sybil.
Greenwalt, Mary, illus. see Wheeler, Opal.
Green-Warren, Loretta M. Chyna 's Secret Place Adventure. (p. 318)
—Counting, Rhyming & Body Parts. (p. 371)
Greenway, Bethany. Waikiki Lullaby. America, illus. (p. 1852)
Greenway, Betty. Aidan Chambers: Master Literary Choreographer. (p. 30)
Greenway, Betty, ed. Twice-Told Children's Tales: The Influence of Childhood Reading on Writers for Adults. Vol. 35 (p. 1801)
Greenway, Glen. Ant Cook & the Giant Sangom. (p. 88)
Greenway, Shirley. Exploration of North America. (p. 550)
Greenway, Shirley, et al. Great Explorers. (p. 715)
Greenwell, Ivo. Ancestor. (p. 67)
Greenwell, Jessica. Animal Coloring Book with Stickers. (p. 77)
—Dinosaurs. Scott, Peter, illus. (p. 443)
—Fairies Sticker Coloring Book. (p. 563)
—Farm Coloring Sticker Book. (p. 573)
—First Colors Sticker Book. (p. 593)
—First Sticker Book Christmas. (p. 597)
—First Sticker Book Easter. (p. 597)
—My First Coloring Book. (p. 1206)
—Noisy Body Book. (p. 1263)
—Noisy Monsters. Wildish, Lee, illus. (p. 1263)
—Pets Sticker Book. (p. 1348)
—This Is My Car. (p. 1736)
—This Is My Digger. (p. 1736)
—Wipe-Clean Telling the Time. Scott, Kimberley, illus. (p. 1939)
Greenwell, Jessica & Taplin, Sam. Big Sticker Book of Animals. (p. 184)
Greenwell, Jessical. Farm Animals Lift & Look. (p. 573)
Greenwood, Anna. Beyond the Grey Wall. (p. 174)
—Children at St Bartholomew's Hospital. (p. 302)
Greenwood, Arin. Save the Enemy. (p. 1516)
Greenwood, Barbara. Factory Girl. (p. 561)
—Kids Book of Canada. MacRae, Jock, illus. (p. 952)
Greenwood Brown, Anne. Deep Betrayal. (p. 422)
—Lies Beneath. (p. 1007)
—Promise Bound. (p. 1411)
Greenwood, Carmel & Taylor, Chris. Wake up Mum: A Mother & Son's True Crisis Story of Overcoming Drug Addiction with Love, Laughter & Miraculous Insights. (p. 1853)
Greenwood, Cathleen, jt. auth. see Hambleton, Vicki.
Greenwood, Charles R., et al, eds. Schoolwide Prevention Models: Lessons Learned in Elementary Schools. (p. 1524)
Greenwood, Chris. Tanya Talia Plants A Tree. (p. 1705)
—Tanya Talia Plats a Tree. (p. 1705)
Greenwood, Diana. Insight (p. 878)
Greenwood, Dwayne. Tales of Wally the Whale & Sammy the Salmon. (p. 1703)
Greenwood Elementary School. Twigs Tells a Story. (p. 1801)
Greenwood, Elinor & Dorling Kindersley Publishing Staff. Get Talking Chinese: Mandarin Chinese for Beginners. (p. 668)
Greenwood, Grace. History of My Pets by Grace Greenwood [Pseud], with Engravings from Designs by Billings. (p. 784)
—Stories from Famous Ballads for Children by Grace Greenwood [Pseud] with Illustrations by Billings. (p. 1654)

Greenwood, Janette Thomas. Gilded Age: A History in Documents. (p. 676)
Greenwood, Janice. Lucy Ladybug's Hugs. (p. 1063)
Greenwood, Kerry. Alien Invasions. (p. 41)
—Evan's Gallipoli. (p. 541)
Greenwood, Lori. Vision Link: 60 Keys to Fulfilling Your Future. (p. 1844)
Greenwood, Marion, illus. see Sherer, Mary (Huston).
Greenwood, Mark. Donkey of Gallipoli: A True Story of Courage in World War I. Lessac, Frané, illus. (p. 466)
—Greatest Liar on Earth. Lessac, Frané, illus. (p. 720)
—Mayflower. Lessac, Frané, illus. (p. 1113)
—Midnight. Lessac, Frané, illus. (p. 1138)
Greenwood, Mark & Lessac, Frané. Drummer Boy of John John. (p. 487)
Greenwood, R. L. Visit to the Kingdom of Camelot. (p. 1845)
Greenwood, Rosie. I Wonder Why Columbus Crossed the Ocean: And Other Questions about Explorers. (p. 849)
—I Wonder Why Volcanoes Blow Their Tops: And Other Questions about Natural Disasters. (p. 849)
Greenwood, Susan, jt. auth. see Dowswell, Paul.
Greer, Ana, illus. see Custard, P. T.
Greer, Dan, ed. see Moeller, Bill & Moeller, Jan.
Greer, Dan, ed. see Moulton, Candy.
Greer, Dan, ed. see Pittman, Ruth.
Greer, Daniel, ed. see Ewing, Sherm.
Greer, Daniel, ed. see Metz, Leon C.
Greer, Gregg & Greer, Karen. Broken Toys: China's Song. (p. 230)
Greer, Hannah. Castle Ivengless: The Velvet Bag Memoirs (p. 277)
—Gift of Re, the Adventures of the Whiz Kids. (p. 675)
—Lighthouse Summer Greer, Tica, illus. (p. 1015)
—Pharos Legacy Book: The Whiz Kids Adventures. (p. 1350)
—Velvet Bag Memoirs (p. 1835)
Greer, Karen, jt. auth. see Greer, Gregg.
Greer, Rob, photos by see Friedericy Dolls, illus.
Greer, Terri Gregory & Judy. Amazing Adventures of Peanut & PeeWee at Church. (p. 52)
Greer, Tica, illus. see Greer, Hannah.
Greer, Tom. Honey Visits Grandpa Smith. (p. 794)
Greer, Tom C. Honey's Peanut Butter Adventure. Faust, Laurie A., illus. (p. 795)
Greetham, Bryan. Philosophy. (p. 1351)
Greg. When I'm Bigger. (p. 1903)
Greg, Neri. Yummy: The Last Days of a Southside Shorty. (p. 1983)
Greg, Tang, jt. auth. see Tang, Greg.
Gregar, Steve. Al the Alien. (p. 33)
—Buzz the Fly. (p. 248)
—Littlest Elephant. (p. 1039)
Gregory, Vicki, illus. see Stratton, Erin.
Gregersen, Erik. Astronomical Observations: Astronomy & the Study of Deep Space. (p. 109)
—Inner Solar System: The Sun, Mercury, Venus, Earth, & Mars. (p. 875)
—Manned Spaceflight. (p. 1087)
—Milky Way & Beyond: Stars, Nebulae, & Other Galaxies. (p. 1143)
—Outer Solar System: Jupiter, Saturn, Uranus, Neptune, & the Dwarf Planets. (p. 1312)
—Universe: A Historical Survey of Beliefs, Theories, & Laws. (p. 1820)
—Unmanned Space Missions. (p. 1821)
Gregersen, Erik, ed. Britannica Guide to Analysis & Calculus. (p. 229)
—Britannica Guide to Statistics & Probability. (p. 229)
—Britannica Guide to the History of Mathematics. (p. 229)
Gregerson, Judy. Bad Girls Club. (p. 131)
Gregerson, Lajuan. Child's Tour of the Holy Land. (p. 305)
Gregg, Anna, photos by see Williams, Carol Lynch & Gregg, L. B.
Gregg, Emma, et al. Rough Guide to East Coast Australia. (p. 1491)
Gregg, John Hunter. Where Dogs Run. (p. 1907)
Gregg, L. B., jt. auth. see Williams, Carol Lynch.
Gregg, Paula, jt. auth. see Norvell, Candyce.
Gregg, Randy. Advanced Drills & Goalie Drills for Hockey. (p. 13)
—Puck Control Drills for Hockey. (p. 1414)
—Skating Drills for Hockey. (p. 1584)
—Team Drills for Hockey. (p. 1710)
Gregg, Stacy. Angel & the Flying Stallions. (p. 73)
—Auditions. (p. 115)
—Blaze & the Dark Rider. (p. 198)
—Comet & the Champion's Cup. (p. 348)
—Destiny & the Wild Horses. (p. 431)
—Flame & the Rebel Riders. (p. 602)
—Fortune & the Golden Trophy. (p. 623)
—Island of Lost Horses. (p. 892)
—Liberty & the Dream Ride (p. 1005)
—Mystic & the Midnight Ride. (p. 1226)
—Nightstorm & the Grand Slam. (p. 1255)
—Princess & the Foal. (p. 1402)
—Riding Star. (p. 1471)
—Showjumpers (p. 1571)
—Stardust & the Daredevil Ponies. (p. 1642)
—Storm & the Silver Bridle. (p. 1655)
—Victory & the All-Stars Academy. (p. 1840)
Gregg, Stephen. S. P. A. R. a play / (p. 1499)
Gregoire, Fabian. Ninos de la Mina. Malagarriga, Carlos Fanlo, tr. (p. 1257)
Gregoire, Maia. Grammaire Progressive du Francais: Debutant. (p. 706)
Gregoire, Maryellen. All Kinds of Sounds (p. 45)
—Animales en el Bosque (Animals in the Forest) (p. 81)
—Animals in the Forest (p. 83)
—Apple Trees. (p. 92)
—At the Beach. (p. 110)
—Bandera (the Flag) (p. 136)
—Cachorro de Tigre (a Tiger Cub) (p. 250)
—Computers (p. 355)
—Contar Crayones (Counting Crayons) (p. 360)
—Counting Crayons (p. 371)
—En la Playa (at the Beach) (p. 522)
—Escuelas Viejas y Nuevas (p. 535)
—Escuelas Viejas y Nuevas (Old & New Schools) (p. 535)
—Flag. (p. 601)
—Fun Days! (p. 647)
—Ganar Dinero (Making Money) (p. 655)
—Help (p. 765)
—Insects. (p. 875)
—Life in a Desert (p. 1010)
—Making Money (p. 1081)
—Morning Meals Around the World Yesh, Jeff, illus. (p. 1175)
—Moving Fast (p. 1183)
—My Family. (p. 1202)
—Old & New Schools (p. 1283)
—Our Sun (p. 1310)
—Staying Warm. (p. 1645)
—Storytime. (p. 1664)
—Structures (p. 1668)
—Things in Space (p. 1733)
—Tiger Cub (p. 1748)
—Trees. (p. 1784)
—Vida en el Desierto (Life in a Desert) (p. 1840)
—We All Have Shadows (p. 1865)
—We All Need Plants. (p. 1865)
—What Is Water? (p. 1891)
—Yo Puedo Ayudar (I Can Help) (p. 1971)
—Your Five Senses. (p. 1980)
Gregor, Karri. Something Special. (p. 1610)
Gregor, Karri J. What's the Matter Bob. (p. 1899)
—Who Is E? (p. 1915)
Gregor, Terril, illus. see Dodson, Merilee.
Gregori, Anthony. Meet the Itslts. (p. 1122)
Gregorich, Barbara. Beginning Sounds. (p. 159)
—Brain Quest, Grade 4: A Whole Year of Curriculum-Based Exercises & Activities in One Fun Book! McGee, Patty, ed. (p. 222)
—Same or Different. (p. 1507)
—Shapes & Colors. (p. 1560)
Gregorich, Barbara & Hoffman, Joan. Counting 1-10. (p. 370)
Gregorich, Barbara & Jennison, Christopher. Racing Math: Cherckered Flag Activities & Projects for Grades 4-8. (p. 1432)
Gregorich, Barbara, et al. Lowercase Alphabet. (p. 1061)
—Uppercase Alphabet. (p. 1825)
Gregories, Rachel. Connor Goes to Camp: Subtract Within 20. (p. 358)
Gregorio, Giuliana, illus. see Brooks, Felicity.
Gregorio, I. W. None of the Above. (p. 1263)
Gregorovius, Ferdinand. History of the City of Rome in the Middle Ages: 1200-1304 A. D. Vol. 5 Hamilton, Annie, tr. (p. 784)
Gregorovna, Anna. Inside Earth: Rocks & Minerals. (p. 876)
Gregorowski, Christopher. Fly, Eagle, Fly: An African Tale. Daly, Niki, illus. (p. 609)
Gregory, Byron. Little Gray & the Wockelbog Woods. (p. 1028)
Gregory, C. Matt. Golf Secrets 4 U & Me. (p. 696)
Gregory, Cam. When Do I Go to School? (p. 1902)
—Where Can I Find A Good Friend? (p. 1906)
—Where Do Tall Trees Grow? (p. 1907)
—Who Lives Here? (p. 1916)
—Who Should Follow Signs? (p. 1917)
—Why Are Polar Bears in Danger? (p. 1922)
Gregory, Caroline. Puppy Stew. Suorsa, Michael, illus. (p. 1418)
Gregory, Charles, II. Edison Diamond Disc Record Labels & Discography Leggitt, Linda, ed. (p. 504)
Gregory, Charles Matthew. Mika's Musik Coloring Book. (p. 1141)
Gregory, Daniel. Solid State Lasers for the Laser Enthusiast - Pulse Edition American LaserTechnic, ed. (p. 1607)
Gregory, David. Visions of Reality. (p. 1845)
Gregory, Dee. Accidental Daughter: A Children's Story about Hope. (p. 8)
Gregory, Dorothy Lake, illus. see Judson, Clara Ingram.
Gregory, Fran, illus. see Armistead, John.
Gregory, Fran, jt. auth. see Armistead, John.
Gregory, Heather. Ben & the Geocache Treasure. (p. 163)
Gregory, Helen. All about Homes (p. 42)
—All about Mammals (p. 42)
—All about Snakes & Lizards (p. 43)
—Bread Around the World. (p. 224)
—Celebrations Around the World (p. 285)
—Changing the Land. (p. 290)
—Find Out about Farming (p. 587)
—Firefighter's Day (p. 591)
—Firefighter's Day. (p. 591)
—Getting There. (p. 669)
—Harvest Season (p. 752)
—Healthy Eating (p. 758)
—How Things Move (p. 814)
—Lugares Donde Trabajamos (p. 1064)
—Park. (p. 1324)
—Places to Work (p. 1366)
—Pushes & Pulls (p. 1420)
—Team Work (p. 1710)
—Teamwork (p. 1710)
—We Need Money (p. 1867)
—Wings (p. 1936)
Gregory, Helen, jt. auth. see Moore, Elizabeth.
Gregory, Helen & Moore, Elizabeth. Wonder Readers Next Steps: Science. (p. 1947)
Gregory, Isabella Augusta. Rising of the Moon. (p. 1475)
Gregory, Jeannette. Honor Your Father & Mother. (p. 795)
—Once upon A Time. (p. 1293)
Gregory, Jeannette T. Speaking Our Language. (p. 1623)
—Who Am I? Removing the Mask with the Word of God. (p. 1914)
Gregory, Jenny, illus. see Baglio, Ben M.
Gregory, Jenny, illus. see Baglio, Ben M. & Daniels, Lucy.
Gregory, Jillian. Breaking Secret Codes (p. 225)
—Making Secret Codes (p. 1082)
Gregory, Josh. Aardvarks. (p. 2)
—Abraham Lincoln: The 16th President. (p. 6)
—Adjectives. Petelinsek, Kathleen, illus. (p. 13)
—Adverbs. Petelinsek, Kathleen, illus. (p. 25)
—Aircraft Pilot. (p. 31)
—Anacondas. (p. 66)
—Andrew Jackson: The 7th President. (p. 72)
—Andrew Luck. (p. 72)
—Animal Predators. (p. 79)
—Animation. (p. 84)
—Apps: From Concept to Consumer. (p. 93)
—Avionics Technician. (p. 120)
—Bill & Melinda Gates. (p. 186)
—Bill Clinton. (p. 186)
—Blake Griffin. (p. 198)
—Cesar Chavez. (p. 288)
—Chef. (p. 297)
—Climate Scientist. (p. 332)
—Diplodocus. (p. 445)
—Dolphins. (p. 464)
—Drills. (p. 485)
—Elephants. (p. 511)
—Experiment with Solids. (p. 549)
—Franklin D. Roosevelt: The 32nd President. (p. 630)
—Frederick Douglass. (p. 633)
—French Revolution. (p. 636)
—From Bats to... Radar. (p. 642)
—From Birds to... Aircraft. (p. 642)
—From Butterfly Wings to Display Technology. (p. 642)
—From Thistle Burrs to... Velcro. (p. 644)
—From Woodpeckers to... Helmets. (p. 644)
—George Washington: The 1st President. (p. 664)
—Gettysburg. (p. 670)
—Gettysburg Address. (p. 670)
—Giraffes. (p. 677)
—Great White Sharks. (p. 719)
—Hammers. (p. 739)
—Hedgehogs. (p. 762)
—Henry Ford: Father of the Auto Industry. (p. 768)
—Hunt for Bin Laden: Operation Neptune Spear. (p. 828)
—Hydrologist. (p. 831)
—Ichthyosaur. (p. 851)
—Information Systems Technician. (p. 874)
—Jackie Robinson. (p. 903)
—Koalas. (p. 966)
—Lebron James. (p. 986)
—Martin Luther King Jr. (p. 1097)
—Meerkats. (p. 1120)
—Monarch Butterflies. (p. 1163)
—Monkeys. (p. 1165)
—Moose. (p. 1173)
—Nouns. Petelinsek, Kathleen, illus. (p. 1268)
—Owls. (p. 1315)
—Persian Gulf War. (p. 1344)
—Plumber. (p. 1374)
—Polar Bears. (p. 1379)
—Rats. (p. 1440)
—Rattlesnakes. (p. 1440)
—Red Wolves. (p. 1455)
—Revolutionary War. (p. 1466)
—Screwdrivers. (p. 1533)
—Sloths. (p. 1591)
—Special Ops. (p. 1623)
—Spinosaurus. (p. 1628)
—Steve Jobs. (p. 1649)
—Superstorm Hurricane Sandy. (p. 1684)
—Theodore Roosevelt: The 26th President. (p. 1729)
—Thomas Jefferson: The 3rd President. (p. 1739)
—Verbs. Petelinsek, Kathleen, illus. (p. 1836)
—Vultures. (p. 1851)
—What Do They Do? Doctors. (p. 1882)
—What Do They Do? Veterinarians. (p. 1882)
—What Does It Do? Ambulance. (p. 1884)
—What Does It Do? Crane. (p. 1884)
—What Does It Do? Fire Truck. (p. 1884)
—What Does It Do? Tractor. (p. 1884)
—Wolf Spiders. (p. 1944)
—Working Dogs. (p. 1952)
—World War I. (p. 1958)
—Wrenches. (p. 1962)
Gregory, Josh & Bose, Meenekshi. James Madison: The 4th President. (p. 907)
—John Adams: The 2nd President. (p. 921)
Gregory, Josh & Wilner, Barry. Peyton Manning. (p. 1349)
Gregory, Joy. Buckingham Palace. (p. 234)
—Field Museum of Natural History. (p. 584)
—Israel. (p. 893)
—Metropolitan Museum of Art. (p. 1130)
—St. Patrick's Cathedral. (p. 1638)
Gregory, Kristiana. Bronte's Book Club. (p. 230)
—Cannons at Dawn: The Second Diary of Abigail Jane Stewart, Valley Forge, Pennsylvania, 1779. (p. 261)
—Clue at the Bottom of the Lake. Farcy, Patrick, illus. (p. 335)
—My Darlin' Clementine. (p. 1201)
—Winter of Red Snow. (p. 1938)
Gregory, Kristiana & Campbell, Mary Exa Atkins. Earthquake at Dawn. (p. 497)
Gregory, Larry. Christmas Surprise. Woolmer, Nancy, illus. (p. 315)
Gregory, Lorraine NAR NEEDED. One, Two, Tie Your Shoes! Carlson, Nancy Gayle, illus. (p. 1297)
Gregory, Manju. Ali Baba & the Forty Thieves. Jago, illus. (p. 39)
—Dragon's Tears: Lotet e Kucedres. Le, Guo, illus. (p. 479)
—Dragon's Tears: Les Larmes du Dragon. Le, Guo, illus. (p. 479)
—Dragon's Tears. Le, Guo, illus. (p. 479)
—Jill & the Beanstalk. Anstey, David, illus. (p. 917)
Gregory, Matt. Ski Tales. (p. 1584)
Gregory, Nan. How Smudge Came Lightburn, Ron, illus. (p. 812)
—Wild Girl & Gran. (p. 1929)
Gregory, Nicky. Georgie Jones ... & You Thought Your Family Was Weird! (p. 665)
Gregory, Paul R. & Stuart, Robert C. Comparing Economic Systems in the Twenty-First Century. (p. 352)
Gregory, Peter. Allman Brothers. (p. 47)
—Allman Brothers Band. (p. 47)
—Queen. (p. 1424)
Gregory, Philippa. Changeling. (p. 290)
—Changeling. Taylor, Sally & van Deelen, Fred, illus. (p. 290)
—Changeling. van Deelen, Fred & Taylor, Sally, illus. (p. 290)
—Fools' Gold. van Deelen, Fred, illus. (p. 614)
—Stormbringers. van Deelen, Fred, illus. (p. 1656)
Gregory, Raven. Waking. (p. 1853)
Gregory, Raven, ed. see Kalvoda, Mike.
Gregory, Raven & Ruditis, Paul. Charmed Season 9 Volume 2 (p. 294)
Gregory, Regina. Mollie & Ike Find Jesus in a Hotair Balloon? (p. 1160)
Gregory, Sally, illus. see Blyton, Enid.
Gregory, Stefan. Life along the Nile. (p. 1007)
Gregory, Steven. Lion's Drum: A Retelling of an African Folk Tale. Obata, Claudia, illus. (p. 1021)
Gregson, Agatha. Fast & Formidable Animals. (p. 576)
—Grossest Animal Tricks. (p. 725)
—Tooth & Nail: Deadly Jaws & Claws. (p. 1768)
Gregson, Bob. Incredible Indoor Games, Grades 1 - 5. (p. 869)
Gregson, Margaret M. Story of Our Trees: In Twenty-Four Lessons. (p. 1659)
Gregson, Susan R. Cyber Literacy: Evaluating the Reliability of Data. (p. 396)
—Investigating Demons, Possessions, & Exorcisms (p. 884)
Greif, Barbara Lynn. Born from the Heart. (p. 214)
Greig, Allison. Stacey's Adventures. (p. 1638)
Greig, Charlotte. Oceania. (p. 1277)
Greig, Elna. Bye-Bye! (p. 249)
—Hello! (p. 763)
Greig, Noel, adapted by. Tin Soldier: And Other Plays for Children. (p. 1755)
Greil, Marlene, jt. auth. see Crabtree Publishing Company Staff.
Greimann, Dorothy Burgess. Treehouse Orphans. (p. 1784)
Grein, Josh. Petunia Bobbin & the Baby Robin: A Christmas Adventure. (p. 1349)
Greiner, Gail. Patchwork Helps a Friend. Schmidt, Jacqueline, illus. (p. 1328)
Greiner, Ruth. Satan, the Enemy of God: New Testament Volume 2: Life of Christ Part 2. Vol. 2 Neal, Sharon et al, eds. (p. 1515)
Greiner, Ruth B. Christ & the Church: New Testament Volume 42 Revelation Part 1. Vol. 42 Olson, Ed, illus. (p. 311)
—Crucifixion Part 1 ... the Road to the Cross: New Testament Volume 11 Life of Christ Part 11. Pt. I, Vol. 11 Mayer, Melody & Olson, Ed, illus. (p. 386)
—Crucifixion Part 2 Christ Sacrifice Our Salvation: New Testament Volume 12 Life of Christ Part 12. Pt. 2, Vol. 12 Mayer, Melody & Olson, Ed, illus. (p. 386)
—Faith: New Testament. Volume 5 Hertzler, Frances H.. et al, illus. (p. 565)
—Judgment the Wrath of God: New Testament Volume 44 Revelation Part 3. Vol. 44 Mayer, Melody & Olson, Ed, illus. (p. 930)
—Repentance: New Testament Volume 6, Life of Christ, Part 6. Vol. 6 (p. 1461)
—Saviour: New Testament Volume 3: the Life of Christ Part 3: Everybody Needs Jesus. Vol. 3 Hertzler, Frances H.. et al, illus. (p. 1518)
Greiner, Ruth B., et al. Eternity: New Testament , Revelation Part 4: the Lord Reigns Forever. Vol. 45 Henkel, Vernon et al, illus. (p. 539)
—GOD His Son, His Book, His Home: New Testament Introductory Volume. Hertzler, Frances H.. & Olson, Ed, illus. (p. 689)
—Sin: New Testament Volume 4, Life of Christ, Part 4. Vol. 4 Hertzler, Frances H.. et al, illus. (p. 1578)
Greisen, Steve, ed. see Soleim, Heather.
Greisman, Joan, jt. auth. see Wittels, Harriet.
Greitens, Eric. Warrior's Heart: Becoming a Man of Compassion & Courage. (p. 1859)
Greive, Bradley Trevor. Blue Day Book for Kids: A Lesson in Cheering Yourself Up. (p. 202)
—Every Day Is Christmas: Living the Holiday Spirit Throughout the Year Without Damaging Your Health or Driving Everyone Crazy. (p. 542)
—Teaspoon of Courage for Kids: A Little Book of Encouragement for Whenever You Need It. (p. 1711)
Greive, Bradley Trevor & Easton, Samantha. Querida Mama: Gracias por Todo. (p. 1425)
Grejniec, Michael. Buenos Dias, Buenas Noches/Good Morning, Good Night. Alejandro, Alis, tr. from ENG. (p. 235)
—What Do You Like? Grejniec, Michael, illus. (p. 1883)
Grejniec, Michael & Bright Connections Media. Taste of the Moon. Grejniec, Michael, illus. (p. 1707)
Grekul, Lisa. Kalyna's Song (p. 942)
Grell, Jane, jt. auth. see Johnson, Gail.
Grelsamer, Ronald P. What Your Doctor May Not Tell You about Hip & Knee Replacement Surgery: Everything You Need to Know to Make the Right Decisions. (p. 1896)
Gremila, Elaine Demetri. Seasons of the Heart. (p. 1538)
Gremillion, Barry, illus. see Aliberti, Frances C.
Grena, G. M. LMLK—A Mystery Belonging to the King (p. 1044)
Grenevitch, Betsy Coffman. Paths of Light. (p. 1328)
Grenfell, Susan. Religious Studies for Common Entrance. (p. 1458)
Grenier, Christian, jt. auth. see Kemoun, Hubert Ben.
Grenier, Daniel, illus. see Daigle, Evelyne.
Grennan, Michael F. Adventures of E-Lane: Maple Syrul Heaven. (p. 17)
Grenz, Suzanna M., jt. auth. see Stone, Ilene.
Grepo, Sarah, illus. see Glavin, Kevin.
Gresh, Dannah. Danika's Totally Terrible Toss. (p. 405)
—It's Great to Be a Girl! A Guide to Your Changing Body. (p. 897)
—My Secret Keeper Girl(r) Diary. (p. 1218)
—Secret Keeper Girl Pajama Party. (p. 1541)
Gresh, Dannah & Anderson, Chizuruoke. Yuzi's False Alarm. (p. 1983)
Gresh, Dannah & Mylin, Janet. Just Call Me Kate. (p. 938)

Full bibliographic information is available on the Title Index page number referenced in parentheses at the end of each entry

G

Gresh, Dannah K. & Weibel, Suzy. T Is for AnTONIa. (p. 1693)
Gresh, Lois H. Divergent Companion: The Unauthorized Guide to the Series. (p. 454)
—Divergent Companion. (p. 454)
—Mortal Instruments Companion: City of Bones, Shadowhunters, & the Sight: the Unauthorized Guide. (p. 1176)
—Ultimate Unauthorized Eragon Guide: The Hidden Facts Behind the World of Alagaesia. (p. 1810)
Gresham, Delia, illus. see Lael, Anita.
Gresham, Eddie. Footfalls. (p. 615)
—Man Who Murdered Love. (p. 1086)
Gresham, Evelyn. Sweet Sweet Carabee. Sponaugle, Kim, illus. (p. 1690)
Gresham, Joel. Bible Bears: Featuring the Imagination Bears. (p. 175)
—Our Bearable World: Featuring the Imagination Bears. (p. 1307)
Gresham, Nakae (Nikki). Nephew with a Thousand Ms Questions. (p. 1241)
Gresham, P. A. Anything Could Be Any Thing. (p. 91)
Gresham, Xanthe. Princess & the Pea. Clara, Miss, illus. (p. 1402)
Gresko, Marcia S. Israel. (p. 893)
—Medieval Castle. (p. 1119)
Gressel, Tina. Baby Haley's World: Exploring Heaven. (p. 126)
Gressett, William H., Jr. Nor all your Piety nor Wit... . (p. 1264)
Gressler, Jeanne, ed. Offerings of the Spirit: Tributes to Brother Thomas. Israel, David et al, photos by. (p. 1280)
Gressman, Carylee Anne. Draw & Write Through History: Creation Through Jonah. Wolf, Aaron D., ed. (p. 480)
Greste, Peter, illus. see Hatkoff, Craig, et al.
Greste, Peter, photos by see Hatkoff, Craig, et al.
Grethe, James. Weird & Wondrous Tales of Woodland Wyre. (p. 1872)
Gretta, J. Clemens, illus. see Burtis, Thomson.
Grettenberg, Joel. Saeeb & the Chocolate Ant. (p. 1501)
Gretter, J. Clemens, illus. see Dixon, Franklin W.
Gretzer, John, illus. see Cavanna, Betty.
Greubel, Joseph E., ed. see Wissolik, Richard David.
Greulich, Deborah Ripoll. I Choose You. (p. 837)
Greve, Hannah K., illus. see McCusker, Tammy.
Greve, Meg. Birdhouse That Jack Built. Poole, Helen, illus. (p. 190)
—Chili Challenge. Myer, Ed, illus. (p. 305)
—Friends. (p. 638)
—From Empty Lot to Building. (p. 642)
—Go North! Mones, Marc, illus. (p. 687)
—Humpty Dumpty. Poole, Helen, illus. (p. 827)
—Integrity. (p. 879)
—Internet. (p. 880)
—Keys & Symbols on Maps. (p. 950)
—Let's Get Pizza. Poole, Helen, illus. (p. 997)
—Maps Are Flat, Globes Are Round. (p. 1090)
—Mountain Thrill. Myer, Ed, illus. (p. 1181)
—Mud Pie Queen. Poole, Helen, illus. (p. 1188)
—Museum Mystery. Mones, Marc, illus. (p. 1193)
—North, South, East, & West. (p. 1265)
—Painting Party. Anglicas, Louise, illus. (p. 1318)
—River Rafting. Anglicas, Louise, illus. (p. 1476)
—Science Projects. (p. 1527)
—Ship & Shells. Myer, Ed, illus. (p. 1567)
—Speakers. (p. 1623)
—Swim for It! Dufalla, Anita, illus. (p. 1690)
—Taking Notes & Close Reading. (p. 1698)
—Watch for Whales! Myer, Ed, illus. (p. 1861)
—Wet & Wild Waterpark. Mones, Marc, illus. (p. 1877)
—Writing an Opinion Paper. (p. 1964)
Greve, Meg & Robertson, J. Jean. Camiones: Trucks. (p. 256)
Greve, Meg & Sturm, Jeanne. Mi Mascota: Pet Tricks. (p. 1132)
Greve, Tom. Angel Island. (p. 73)
—Buzzing Bugs. (p. 249)
—Buzzing Bugs. Rourke Publishing Staff, ed. (p. 249)
—Creeping Crawlers. Rourke Publishing Staff, ed. (p. 381)
—Emt: Crisis Care for Injuries & Illness. (p. 521)
—Firefighters: Battling Smoke & Flames. (p. 591)
—Fossils, Uncovering the Past. (p. 624)
—Freshwater Fish. (p. 636)
—Giant Pandas. (p. 674)
—Hockey Goalies. (p. 786)
—Linebackers. (p. 1019)
—Plate Tectonics & Disasters. (p. 1370)
—Police: Protect & Serve. (p. 1379)
Greve Tom. Reptiles. (p. 1461)
Greve, Tom. Reptiles. (p. 1461)
—Running Backs. (p. 1497)
—Snakes. (p. 1596)
—Swat: Special Weapons & Tactics. (p. 1689)
—Thanks, NASA! (p. 1725)
—Thanks, Nasa! (p. 1725)
—Whales. (p. 1877)
—World Trade Center. (p. 1958)
Greven, Alec. How to Talk to Dads. Acedera, Kei, illus. (p. 822)
—How to Talk to Girls. Acedera, Kei, illus. (p. 822)
—How to Talk to Moms. Acedera, Kei, illus. (p. 822)
—How to Talk to Santa. Acedera, Kei, illus. (p. 822)
—Rules for School. Acedera, Kei, illus. (p. 1495)
Greven, Doris, illus. see Sijercic, Hedina.
Greves, Julie, et al. Upside down & Backwards: A Sibling's Journey Through Childhood Cancer. (p. 1825)
Grew, David. Wild Dog of Edmonton. Segner, Ellen, illus. (p. 1929)
Grey, Ada, illus. see Salzano, Tammi.
Grey, Allan. Alienology. Steer, Dugald A., ed. (p. 41)
Grey, Amelia. Gentleman Says "I Do" (p. 661)
Grey, Andrew, illus. see Canfield, Nancy Lee.
Grey, C. R. Legacy of the Claw. Madsen, Jim, illus. (p. 987)
Grey, Chelsea Gilian. Erna the Rhinoceros. (p. 517)
—Jeshi the Gorilla. (p. 914)
—Jeshi the Gorilla. Leeper, Christopher, ed. (p. 914)
—Jeshi the Gorilla. Leeper, Christopher J., illus. (p. 914)
—Jeshi the Gorilla. Leeper, Chris & Leeper, Chris, illus. (p. 914)
—Leperit the Zebra: African Wildlife Foundation. Denman, Michael L. & Huiett, William J., illus. (p. 993)
—Leperit the Zebra. (p. 993)
—Leperit the Zebra. Denman, Michael & Huiett, William, illus. (p. 993)
—Princess Colors. (p. 1403)
Grey, Chelsea Gillian, jt. auth. see Shriver, Chelsea.
Grey, Christopher, jt. auth. see Grey, Christopher Peter.
Grey, Christopher Peter & Grey, Christopher. Leonardo's Shadow: Or, My Astonishing Life As Leonardo Da Vinci's Servant. (p. 992)
Grey, Cristina. My Messy Room: Count to Tell the Number of Objects. (p. 1214)
Grey, Erika. Alphabet Bears: Spook-Tales Collection. Grey, Erika, illus. (p. 49)
Grey, Jacob. Ferals. (p. 581)
Grey, Kevan. Geneva College College Prowler off the Record. (p. 661)
Grey Larsen, jt. auth. see Larsen, Grey.
Grey, Melissa. Girl at Midnight. (p. 678)
Grey, Mini. Adventures of the Dish & the Spoon. (p. 23)
—Biscuit Bear. (p. 193)
—Egg Drop. (p. 506)
—Hermelin the Detective Mouse. (p. 771)
—Three by the Sea. (p. 1741)
—Toys in Space. (p. 1774)
—Traction Man & the Beach Odyssey. (p. 1775)
—Traction Man Is Here! (p. 1775)
—Very Smart Pea & the Princess-To-Be. (p. 1838)
Grey, Mini, illus. see King-Smith, Dick.
Grey, Mini & Gardner, Lyn. Into the Woods. Grey, Mini, illus. (p. 881)
Grey, Rochelle, text. My RiverPlace on the Schuylkill Coloring Book. (p. 1217)
Grey, Zane. Cabin Gulch: A Western Story. (p. 250)
—Redheaded Outfield. (p. 1455)
Greyling, Emma. Mystical Life of the Dog with Three Legs. (p. 1226)
Gribben, Valerie. Fairytale Trilogy: Fairytale, the Emperor's Realm, & the Three Crowns. (p. 565)
Gribbin, John, jt. auth. see Charlesworth, Kate.
Gribbin, John, jt. auth. see Gribbin, Mary.
Gribbin, Mary & Gribbin, John. Misterios de la Materia Oscura: Conoce las Claves del Universo de Philip Pullman. Sanchez Abuli, Enrique, tr. (p. 1155)
—Science of Philip Pullman's His Dark Materials. (p. 1527)
Gribbin-Lindemon, Sharon. Do Martians Recycle? (p. 457)
Gribble, John. Grandpas' Book: For the Grandpa Who's Best at Everything. Woodroffe, David, illus. (p. 709)
Gribble, Julie. Bubblegum Princess. Hanson, Lori, illus. (p. 233)
Gribbon, Sean, illus. see Burnett, Frances Hodgson.
Gribbon, Sean, tr. see Burnett, Frances Hodgson.
Gribel, Christiane & Orlando. No Voy a Dormir/I Am Not Going to Sleep. Gribel, Christiane & Orlando, illus. (p. 1261)
Gribnau, Joe. Kick the Cowboy Tans, Adrian, illus. (p. 951)
—Rocky Mountain Night Before Christmas Alikhan, Salima, illus. (p. 1484)
Grice Lynch, Linda, illus. see Grice Neely, Edwina.
Grice Neely, Edwina. Thank You God for My Body. Grice Lynch, Linda, illus. (p. 1725)
Grice, Noreen. Little Moon Phase Book. Gendler, Robert, photos by. (p. 1032)
Gricol, Sharon. Life's Captivity. (p. 1013)
Gridina, Anna, ed. see AZ Books Staff.
Gridley, J. Tales of Ryan Foster: The Land of Eternal Rain. Chamberlain, Calum, illus. (p. 1702)
Gridley, Steven. Lovers in the Park: A Ten-Minute Comedy Duet. (p. 1061)
Grieb, Wendy, illus. see Czajak, Paul.
Griebel, Roberta L. Joyful Noise! (p. 930)
Griechen, Jane M. Theodore B a Turkey. (p. 1729)
Griegg, Linda, illus. see Gilbert, LaBritta.
Griego, Margarita. Monkeys Like Bananas! a Los Monos les Gustan Los Platanos! (p. 1166)
griego, Mito. Rey Midas. Ruiz, Margarita, illus. (p. 1467)
Griego, Tony, illus. see Tuchman, Gail & Gray, Margaret.
Griehl, Manfred. Jet Planes of the Third Reich: The Secret Projects Vol. 2 (p. 916)
Griek, Susan Vande. Loon. Reczuch, Karen, illus. (p. 1052)
Grier, Gary, illus. see Scholastic, Inc. Staff, et al.
Grier, Gene & Everson, Lowell. Midnight Miracle: Singer's Edition. (p. 1139)
—Midnight Miracle: A Musical Christmas Story. (p. 1139)
—Midnight Miracle: Accompanist Edition, Singer's Edition. (p. 1139)
—Midnight Miracle: A Musical Christmas Story: Singer's Edition. Singer's Edition (p. 1139)
Grier, Geoffrey, illus. see Stefansson, Vilhjalmur & Irwin, Violet.
Grier, Kerry. Jabari Makes a Splash. Nettis, Donna, illus. (p. 902)
Grier, Laura, illus. see Bottner, Barbara.
Grier, Laura, photos by see Bottner, Barbara.
Grier, Paul. Recycling Paper. (p. 1453)
Grierson, Ruth. Is for Acadia: Mount Desert Island from A to Z. Johnson, Richard, illus. (p. 889)
Gries, Frederica, tr. Little Rabbit Talks on the Phone & Other Children's Poems from the Chinese. (p. 1034)
Gries, John P. & Griesemer, James. Roadside Geology of South Dakota. (p. 1477)
Griesemer, James, jt. auth. see Gries, John P.
Griesemer, James, jt. auth. see Hasselstrom, Linda M.
Grieser, Jeanne K. Touch & Feel Petting Zoo. Pedler, Caroline, illus. (p. 1772)
Griesmer, Russell. My Hometown. Wong, Priscilla, illus. (p. 1211)
Griessman, Annette, jt. auth. see Czerneda, Julie E.
Grieve, Walter G., illus. see Talbot, Ethel.
Grifalconi, Ann. Village That Vanished. Nelson, Kadir, illus. (p. 1842)
Grifalconi, Ann, illus. see Dorros, Arthur.
Grifalconi, Ann, illus. see Myers, Walter Dean.
Grifalconi, Ann, illus. see Williams, Karen Lynn.
Griff, illus. see Dalton, Annie.
Griffen, C. W. Crucified by Pontius Pilate. (p. 386)
Griffeth, Bunny, illus. see Latimer, Kiki.
Griffey, Harriet. Earthquakes & Other Natural Disasters, Level 4. (p. 497)
—Secrets of the Mummies. (p. 1545)
Griffey, Harriet & Dorling Kindersley Publishing Staff. Secrets of the Mummies, Level 4. (p. 1545)
Griffie, Sandra. Snow Dancer. (p. 1598)
Griffie, Sandra Kay. How Elmer Lost His Hop. (p. 809)
Griffin, A. C. America's Child. (p. 64)
Griffin, Adele. All You Never Wanted. (p. 46)
—Amandine. (p. 52)
—Julian Game. (p. 932)
—Knaveheart's Curse. (p. 964)
—Loud Awake & Lost. (p. 1057)
—Sons of Liberty. (p. 1613)
—Tighter. (p. 1749)
—Unfinished Life of Addison Stone: a Novel. (p. 1817)
—Where I Want to Be. (p. 1908)
Griffin, Adele & Brown, Lisa. Picture the Dead. (p. 1356)
Griffin, Bethany. Dance of the Red Death. (p. 402)
—Fall. (p. 566)
—Masque of the Red Death. (p. 1102)
Griffin, C. R. Runt & the Two Roses. (p. 1497)
Griffin, Carolee G. Santa's New Suit. (p. 1513)
Griffin, Cheri, illus. see Batton, Doris.
Griffin, Claire J. Nowhere to Run. (p. 1269)
Griffin, Curtis. We Real People: A Documentary in Poetry (p. 1868)
Griffin, D. J. Rose of Silence. (p. 1489)
Griffin, Daniel. Adventures of Merlin the Mouse (p. 20)
Griffin, Dawnell. Osenpiots! (p. 1305)
Griffin, Dexter, jt. auth. see Wright, Sabrina L.
Griffin, Don, illus. see Gall, Ginnie.
Griffin, Donna. Dani & the Bananas. (p. 404)
—Twelve Days of Christmas in Indiana. Cummings, Troy, illus. (p. 1800)
Griffin, Dorothy J. What Goes Around Comes Around. (p. 1885)
Griffin, Esther M. Alex, the Lonely, Black-Footed Penguin. (p. 36)
Griffin, Geoff. How Can the Poor Be Helped? (p. 805)
Griffin, Geoff, ed. Are Athletes Good Role Models? (p. 96)
Griffin, Georgene. Dinosaurs, Meat-Eaters. (p. 445)
—Endangered Mammals. (p. 526)
Griffin, Georgene, jt. illus. see McKee, Karen.
Griffin, Georgene & Jael. Cool Wheels. (p. 364)
Griffin, Grace, ed. see Canaday, Matt & Canaday, Cindi.
Griffin, Grant, jt. auth. see Griffin, Martha.
Griffin, Hedley, illus. see Top That!, ed.
Griffin, Ingrid. Story of Cassiopeia. (p. 1657)
—Story of Hercules. (p. 1658)
—Story of the Great Bear. (p. 1661)
Griffin, Jason, jt. auth. see Reynolds, Jason.
Griffin, Jennifer. Feeling Bag. (p. 580)
Griffin, Jim, illus. see Osborne, Rick.
Griffin, Julia Andrew. Bonny Bunny & the Golden Rule. (p. 209)
Griffin, Kasana, ed. see Taylor, Vincent.
Griffin, Keith. Carry-Me 123. (p. 271)
Griffin, Kitty. Ride: The Legend of Betsy Dowdy. Priceman, Marjorie, illus. (p. 1471)
Griffin, Kitty & Combs, Kathy. Stinker & the Onion Princess. Manders, John, illus. (p. 1651)
Griffin, L. D. Cold Mountain Hunter. (p. 338)
Griffin, Lisa M., illus. see McCumbee, Stephie.
Griffin, Lydia. BeBa & the Curious Creature Catchers. Lostimolo, Stephanie, illus. (p. 155)
—Prunes & Rupe. Hunt, Judith, illus. (p. 1413)
—Susan Anderson: Colorado's Doc Susie. (p. 1687)
Griffin, Maave. Constitution Day. (p. 359)
Griffin, Maeve. Ciara. (p. 318)
—Plant Parts: Roots, Stems, & Leaves. (p. 1369)
Griffin, Marcia. Debbie's Letter to God. Davies, Michelle, illus. (p. 421)
Griffin, Margaret. Today's U. S. Army (p. 1761)
Griffin, Margot. Dance of Life (p. 402)
—Pioneers: Challenges from the Past. (p. 1361)
Griffin, Mark. Just in Time. (p. 938)
Griffin, Marlin, illus. see Cox Gray, Marjorie.
Griffin, Martha & Griffin, Grant. Sam's Birthmark. Smiley, Mary Anne, illus. (p. 1509)
Griffin, Mary. Our Needs & Wants. (p. 1309)
Griffin, Michele. It's Haircut Time! How one little boy overcame his fear of haircut Day. (p. 897)
—Picky, Picky Pete. (p. 1355)
Griffin Mims, Nancy. Christmas Geese. (p. 314)
Griffin, Molly Beth. Rhoda's Rock Hunt. Bell, Jennifer A., illus. (p. 1468)
—Silhouette of a Sparrow. (p. 1575)
Griffin, N. Smashie Mcperter & the Mystery of Room 11. Hindley, Kate, illus. (p. 1593)
—Whole Stupid Way We Are. (p. 1920)
Griffin, Patsy. Luigi Pirandello. Bloom, Harold, ed. (p. 1064)
Griffin, Paul. Adrift. (p. 13)
—Orange Houses. (p. 1301)
—Stay with Me. (p. 1645)
—Ten Mile River. (p. 1719)
Griffin, Paul, illus. see Swift, Gayle H. & Swift, Casey Anne.
Griffin, Philip. Ursula's Maiden Army. (p. 1826)
Griffin, Rachel. Celebration Gift Wrap. (p. 285)
Griffin, Rachel, illus. see Batt, Tanya Robyn.
Griffin, Rachel, illus. see Mhlophe, Gcina.
Griffin, Ralph G., ed. see Church, J. R.
Griffin, Ramona Rorie. Gift That Grandma Gave: Including Bloom's Leveled Questions Study Guide. Tunstel Jr., Robert L., illus. (p. 675)
—My Mind Looks Back & Wonders ... Tunstel Jr., Robert L., illus. (p. 1214)
Griffin, Randall C. Winslow Homer: An American Vision. Ace, Jane, ed. (p. 1937)
Griffin, Ricky W. Fundamentals of Management. (p. 649)
Griffin, Ricky W. & Morable, Linda. Management. (p. 1086)
Griffin, Sandi Z. Yea Us Series (Tails with a Moral) Griffin, Sandi Z., illus. (p. 1969)
Griffin, Sandra. Big & Little ABC. (p. 177)
Griffin, Saundra J. Which Should I Be? (p. 1911)
Griffin, Starla. Girl, 13: A Global Snapshot of Generation E. (p. 678)
Griffin, Stella. Little Girl Who Loved Joy. (p. 1028)
Griffin, W. E. B. Hunters (p. 828)
Griffin, Wiley Chase. Chase the Shark: Flies Like a Bird. (p. 294)
Griffin, William D., jt. auth. see Ortiz-Griffin, Julia.
Griffin-Scott, Janet, illus. see Hapka, Catherine, pseud & Hapka, Cathy.
Griffis, Albert R. Ancient American Anthropography. (p. 67)
Griffis, Molly. Buffalo in the Mall. Doner, Kim, illus. (p. 235)
Griffis, Molly Levite. Great American Bunion Derby. (p. 713)
—Rachel Resistance. (p. 1432)
—Simon Says. (p. 1577)
Griffis, William. Dutch Fairy Tales for Young Folks. (p. 490)
Griffis, William Elliot. Dutch Fairy Tales for Young Folks. (p. 490)
—Young People's History of the Pilgrims. (p. 1979)
Griffith, A. J. America's Child. (p. 64)
Griffith, Andrew. Transformers: Movie Prequel: Foundation: Vol 2. (p. 1778)
—Transformers: Movie Prequel: Foundation: Vol 1: Dark of the Moon. (p. 1778)
Griffith, Bev. Cougar Times. (p. 369)
Griffith, Christina. Jubilee & Ashanti Find Insects. (p. 930)
—Why Jubilee & Ashanti go to the Doctor? (p. 1925)
Griffith, Dawn. That Makes Me So Mad! Second Edition. (p. 1726)
Griffith, Diane. Granny's Magic Garden. (p. 710)
Griffith, George. Tsar Wars Episode One: Angel of the Revolution. Rowland, Marcus L., ed. (p. 1795)
—Tsar Wars Episode Two: Syren of the Skies. Rowland, Marcus L., ed. (p. 1795)
Griffith, Gershom, illus. see Brandt, Keith & Mattern, Joanne.
Griffith, Gershom, illus. see deRubertis, Barbara.
Griffith, Gershom, illus. see DeRubertis, Barbara.
Griffith, Gershom, illus. see Mortensen, Lori.
Griffith, Gretchen. When Christmas Feels Like Home. Farias, Carolina, illus. (p. 1901)
Griffith, Helen V. Moonlight. Dronzek, Laura, illus. (p. 1172)
Griffith, Indigo, jt. photos by see Bilik-Franklin, MidiAna.
Griffith, Jeana R. Tale of Two Athletes: The Story of Jumper & the Thumper: Workbook: Steps to Tackle Childhood Obesity. (p. 1700)
Griffith, Jeana R., jt. auth. see Griffith, M. Christopher.
Griffith, John Anthony. Scientific Golfer: Improving Your Golf Game Through Baselining Griffith, John Anthony, illus. (p. 1528)
Griffith, Linda Hill. Best Ever Ring Bearer. (p. 169)
—Most Special Flower Girl. (p. 1177)
Griffith, M. Christopher & Griffith, Jeana R. Tale of Two Athletes: The Story of Jumper & the Thumper a True Story on Understanding & Combating Childhood Obesity. (p. 1700)
Griffith, Mari, jt. auth. see Dickins, Rosie.
Griffith, Michelle & Conder, Jen. Rosie's Quilt. (p. 1490)
Griffith, Samuel B., tr. see Sun-Tzu.
Griffith, Timothy. Orbis Naturalis. (p. 1302)
Griffith, Travis. Your Father Forever. Abreu, Raquel, illus. (p. 1980)
Griffith, Victoria. Fabulous Flying Machines of Alberto Santos-Dumont. Montanari, Eva, illus. (p. 560)
Griffiths, Allen & Godinez, Mary. Rusty Finds a Home: A Christmas Miracle. Ulrich, Kelly, illus. (p. 1498)
Griffiths, Andy. 13-Story Treehouse. Denton, Terry, illus. (p. 1995)
—26-Story Treehouse. Denton, Terry, illus. (p. 1996)
—39-Story Treehouse. Denton, Terry, illus. (p. 1996)
—Big Fat Cow That Goes Kapow. Denton, Terry, illus. (p. 181)
—Cat on the Mat Is Flat. Denton, Terry, illus. (p. 278)
—Cat, the Rat, & the Baseball Bat. (p. 278)
—Cat, the Rat, & the Baseball Bat. Denton, Terry, illus. (p. 278)
—Day My Butt Went Psycho! (p. 413)
—Ed & Ted & Ted's Dog Fred. (p. 503)
—Ed & Ted & Ted's Dog Fred. Denton, Terry, illus. (p. 503)
—Killer Koalas from Outer Space: And Lots of Other Very Bad Stuff That Will Make Your Brain Explode! Denton, Terry, illus. (p. 956)
—Killer Koalas from Outer Space & Lots of Other Very Bad Stuff That Will Make Your Brain Explode! Denton, Terry, illus. (p. 956)
—Treasure Fever! (p. 1781)
—What Body Part Is That? A Wacky Guide to the Funniest, Weirdest, & Most Disgustingest Parts of Your Body. Denton, Terry, illus. (p. 1880)
Griffiths, Annie, jt. auth. see Honovich, Nancy.
Griffiths, Bill. Mud Fort. (p. 1188)
Griffiths, Corinne Escobar. Corky Eckelsbriar. (p. 367)
Griffiths, Dean, illus. see Bogart, Jo Ellen & Bogart, Jill.
Griffiths, Dean, illus. see Bogart, Jo Ellen.
Griffiths, Dean, illus. see Bogart, Jo Ellen.
Griffiths, Dean, illus. see Bouchard, David.
Griffiths, Dean, illus. see Brouwer, Sigmund & Gingras, Gaston.
Griffiths, Dean, illus. see Brouwer, Sigmund.
Griffiths, Dean, illus. see Hamilton, Arlene.
Griffiths, Dean, illus. see Kulling, Monica.
Griffiths, Dean, illus. see Wilson, Troy.
Griffiths, Dean, illus. see Wishinsky, Frieda.
Griffiths, Dean, jt. auth. see Wishinsky, Frieda.
Griffiths, Deborah. Heather's Amazing Discovery: A True Story of Paleontology. Lundquist, Robert, illus. (p. 760)
Griffiths, Gary Wayne. Hawaiian Ponies: A Mystery in Paradise (p. 755)
Griffiths, Georgina. Granny Carstairs: The Wrinkled Fairy. (p. 710)
Griffiths, Katie. Rihanna. (p. 1472)
—Vampires. (p. 1832)
Griffiths, Mark. Hanging on Every Word: 48 of the World's Greatest Stories, Retold for Reading Aloud (p. 742)

—Impossible Boy. (p. 862)
—Technoslime Terror! Chatterton, Martin, illus. (p. 1712)
Griffiths, Marlene. Crafty Crane of Potpourri Pond. (p. 376)
Griffiths, Neil & Nash, Doug. Florence Was No Ordinary Fairy. (p. 606)
Griffiths, Philip Jones & Chomsky, Noam. Vietnam Inc. (p. 1841)
Griffiths, Rachel. What's the Address? (p. 1899)
—Why Do Bridges Arch? Level 3 Factbook. (p. 1923)
—Why Do Leaves Change Colour? Level 3 Factbook. (p. 1923)
Griffiths, Rachel, jt. auth. see Clyne, Margaret.
Griffiths, Rebecca, illus. see Hodgson, Karen J.
Griffiths, Richard A., jt. auth. see Taylor, Barbara.
Griffiths, Robert. Adventures of Clive. (p. 17)
Griffiths, Sara. Thrown a Curve. (p. 1745)
Griffiths-Jones, Sam & Moog, Bob. Sudoku for Kids. (p. 1672)
Griffo, Daniel, illus. see Clay, Kathryn.
Griffo, Daniel, illus. see Lynn, Sarah.
Griffo, Michael. Starfall. (p. 1642)
—Unwelcome. (p. 1823)
Griffor, Edward. Encyclopedia of Science & Technology (p. 525)
Griffune, Donna L. I Love You with My Heart. (p. 844)
Griftner, Rebecca, illus. see Pruitt, Kat.
Griggs, Charles, ed. see Taylor, Vincent.
Griggs, Howard. Native American Mound Builders. (p. 1234)
Griggs, John R. Learning to Play Guitar. (p. 986)
Griggs, Joyce. Imanis Good Deed. (p. 861)
Griggs, Rosemarie. Adventures of Donkey Tom Volume 2: Crystal Forest. (p. 17)
Griggs, Terry. Nieve. L'Hirondelle, Cheryl, illus. (p. 1252)
—Silver Door Teacher Guide. (p. 1576)
Grigg-Saito, Katrina. Sound of Silence. Kuo, Julia, illus. (p. 1615)
Griggs-Burr, Alexander, illus. see Hickey, David.
Grignon, R. Querida. (p. 1425)
Grigorov, Yassen. Ángeles de la Guarda. (p. 74)
Grigorovich, Yuri, et al. Authorized Bolshoi Ballet Book of Romeo & Juliet. (p. 117)
Grigsby, Ann, jt. creator see Thompson, Kristin.
Grigsby, Cynthia. Hollow Creek: A Haunted Beginning (p. 789)
Grigsby, Susan. First Peas to the Table: How Thomas Jefferson Inspired a School Garden. Tadgell, Nicole, illus. (p. 596)
—In the Garden with Doctor Carver. Tadgell, Nicole, illus. (p. 866)
—In the Garden with Dr. Carver. Tadgell, Nicole, illus. (p. 866)
—Wisteria's Show & Tell Spectacular: Older Than the Dinosaurs. Miller, Alexandra, illus. (p. 1941)
Grill, Gerald, illus. see Merrill, Karen Grill.
Grill, William. Shackleton's Journey. (p. 1556)
Grill-Merrill, Karen. Muk & Tuk Tales. (p. 1189)
Grillo, Trine. I'm Not Afraid of That. (p. 859)
Grillo, Tyran, tr. see Sena, Hideaki.
Grillo-Marxuach, Javier. Middle Man: Volume 1. McClaine, Les, illus. (p. 1137)
Grim, Katie. Gingerbread Land. Johnson, Jake, illus. (p. 677)
Grimaldi. My Amazing Dinosaur. Burrell, Carol Klio, tr. from FRE. (p. 1196)
—Welcome to the Tribe! Bannister, illus. (p. 1874)
Grimaldi, Catherine. It's Raining! A Pop-Up Book with Patterns. Grimaldi, Catherine, illus. (p. 898)
Grimaldi, Flora. My Amazing Dinosaur. Burrell, Carol Klio, tr. (p. 1196)
Grimard, Gabrielle, illus. see Chartrand, Lili.
Grimard, Gabrielle, illus. see Demers, Dominique.
Grimard, Gabrielle, illus. see Dumont, Claire & Lacoursiere, Suzanne.
Grimard, Gabrielle, illus. see Jordan-Fenton, Christy & Pokiak-Fenton, Margaret.
Grimard, Gabrielle, illus. see Kingsbury, Karen.
Grimard, Gabrielle, illus. see Lee, Ingrid.
Grimard, Gabrielle, illus. see Pelletier, Maryse.
Grimball, Meta, illus. see Welsh, Charles, ed.
Grimberg, Tina. Out of Line: Growing up Soviet. (p. 1311)
Grimbol, William R. Jesus in Your Backpack: A Teen's Guide to Spiritual Wisdom. Halberstadt, Bridget, illus. (p. 915)
Grime, L. L. Do You Love Me? (p. 458)
—Little Tree. (p. 1037)
—Make up Story. (p. 1079)
Grimes, Charles J. Boys! (p. 220)
Grimes, Cookie. New Year's Family. Grimes, Cookie, illus. (p. 1247)
Grimes, Craig & Washington, Aimee. Yabut the Rabbit. MikeMotz.com, illus. (p. 1968)
Grimes, Janice D. Before You Were Born - Our Wish for A Baby - Egg Donation: Version 3: Egg Donation. (p. 159)
Grimes, Kristopher, illus. see Jones, Brittany.
Grimes, Linda. Jiggery-Jee's Eden Valley Stories. (p. 917)
Grimes, Liz, ed. see Robins, Jeannie.
Grimes, Nikki. Almost Zero: A Dyamonde Daniel Book. Christie, R. Gregory, illus. (p. 48)
—At Break of Day. Collier, John & Morin, Paul, illus. (p. 110)
—At Jerusalem's Gate: Poems of Easter. Frampton, David, illus. (p. 110)
—Barack Obama: Son of Promise, Child of Hope. (p. 137)
—Barack Obama: Son of Promise, Child of Hope. Collier, Bryan, illus. (p. 137)
—Bronx Masquerade. (p. 230)
—Chasing Freedom: The Life Journeys of Harriet Tubman & Susan B. Anthony, Inspired by Historical Facts. Wood, Michele, illus. (p. 294)
—Danitra Brown, Class Clown. Lewis, E. B., illus. (p. 405)
—Dark Sons (p. 408)
—Girl Named Mister (p. 678)
—Halfway to Perfect: A Dyamonde Daniel Book Christie, R. Gregory, illus. (p. 737)
—It's Raining Laughter. Pinkney, Myles C., photos by. (p. 898)
—Make Way for Dyamonde Daniel. Christie, R. Gregory, illus. (p. 1079)
—My Man Blue. Lagarrigue, Jerome, illus. (p. 1214)
—Oh, Brother! Benny, Mike, illus. (p. 1280)
—On the Road to Paris. (p. 1291)
—Planet Middle School. (p. 1367)
—Poems in the Attic. Zunon, Elizabeth, illus. (p. 1376)
—Rich. Christie, R. Gregory, illus. (p. 1469)
—Road to Paris. (p. 1477)
—Tai Chi Morning: Snapshots of China. Young, Ed, illus. (p. 1695)
—Thanks a Million. Cabrera, Cozbi A., illus. (p. 1725)
—Voices of Christmas Velasquez, Eric, illus. (p. 1848)
—Welcome, Precious. Collier, Bryan, illus. (p. 1873)
—What Is Goodbye? (p. 1889)
—When Daddy Prays. Ladwig, Tim, illus. (p. 1901)
—Words with Wings. (p. 1952)
Grimes, Nikki, jt. auth. see Scholastic, Inc. Staff.
Grimes, Terri & Timmons, Jasmine. Pony Named Penny. (p. 1382)
Grimes, Valerie. Tails of Castle Hill Acres. (p. 1695)
Grimes-Herbert, Taryn. I've Got Feelings: An Activity Book for Grinning, Grimacing, & Shouting Out Loud! Gordon, Leneé, photos by. (p. 900)
Grimly, Gris. Gris Grimly's Wicked Nursery Rhymes. Grimly, Gris, illus. (p. 724)
—Gris Grimly's Wicked Nursery Rhymes II. (p. 724)
—Little Jordan Ray's Muddy Spud. Grimly, Gris, illus. (p. 1029)
Grimly, Gris, illus. see Crimi, Carolyn.
Grimly, Gris, illus. see Gaiman, Neil.
Grimly, Gris, illus. see Grimm, Jacob, et al.
Grimly, Gris, illus. see Leuck, Laura.
Grimly, Gris, illus. see Messer, Stephen.
Grimly, Gris, illus. see Pearson, Susan.
Grimly, Gris, illus. see Poe, Edgar Allen.
Grimly, Gris, illus. see Scieszka, Jon, et al.
Grimly, Gris, illus. see Shelley, Mary.
Grimm. Bola de cristal. (p. 208)
—Hija del molinero. (p. 779)
—Repunzel. (p. 1462)
—Schoensten Kinder und Hausmaerchen. (p. 1521)
—Tres pelos diablo. (p. 1784)
Grimm, jt. auth. see Grimm, Jacob.
Grimm, Dave, illus. see Grimm, Kristi.
Grimm, Debi, illus. see Siefker, Eunice.
Grimm, Hannelore. Kittens: Keeping & Caring for Your Pet. (p. 963)
Grimm, Hermanos. Caperucita Roja. (p. 262)
Grimm, J., jt. auth. see Grimm, J. & W.
Grimm, J. & W. Sleeping Beauty. Dusikova, Maja, illus. (p. 1589)
—Three Little Pigs. Watts, Edith M B. B., Bernadette, illus. (p. 1742)
Grimm, J. & W. & Brothers Grimm. Six Swans. Raidt, Gerda, illus. (p. 1582)
Grimm, J. & W. & Grimm, J. Frog Prince: Or Iron Henry. Hager, Christian & Schroeder, Binette, illus. (p. 640)
Grimm, J. L. C., jt. auth. see Grimm, W. C.
Grimm, Jacob. Cinderella/Cenicienta. (p. 320)
—Cinderella/Cenicienta Take Home Version. (p. 320)
—Elves & the Shoemaker. (p. 517)
—Grimm's Fairy Stories. (p. 724)
—Tom Thumb/Pulgarcito. (p. 1764)
Grimm, Jacob, jt. auth. see Grimm, Wilhelm K.
Grimm, Jacob, jt. auth. see Sendak, Maurice.
Grimm, Jacob & Grimm. Cuentos de Grimm. Rackham, Arthur, illus. (p. 390)
Grimm, Jacob & Grimm, Wilhelm. Classic Collection of Fairy Tales. Shuttleworth, Cathy, illus. (p. 328)
—Grimm's Fairy Tales. McKowen, Scott, illus. (p. 724)
—Grimm's Fairy Tales. Taylor, Edgar & Edwardes, Marian, trs. (p. 724)
—Grimm's Household Tales. Peake, Mervyn, illus. (p. 724)
—Hansel & Gretel. Archipova, Anastasiya, illus. (p. 743)
—Little Red Riding Hood. Sourdais, Clémentine, illus. (p. 1035)
—Rapunzel. Bell, Anthea, tr. from GER. (p. 1439)
—Sleeping Beauty & Other Fairy Tales. (p. 1589)
—Snow White: A Tale from the Brothers Grimm. Santore, Charles, illus. (p. 1599)
—Snow White. Greban, Quentin, illus. (p. 1599)
—Story of Little Red Riding Hood. Bing, Christopher H., illus. (p. 1659)
Grimm, Jacob & Grimm, Wilhelm K. Brave Little Tailor. (p. 223)
—Bremen Town Musicians: A Tale about Working Together. Catalano, Dominic, illus. (p. 226)
—Cinderella & Other Tales. (p. 320)
—Complete Fairy Tales of the Brothers Grimm. Zipes, Jack D., tr. from GER. (p. 352)
—Cuentos de Grimm. (p. 390)
—Doctor All-Knowing: A Folk Tale from the Brothers Grimm. Boiger, Alexandra, illus. (p. 459)
—Fairy Tales (p. 564)
—Fisherman & His Wife: A Tale about Being Happy & Satisfied. Ebert, Len, illus. (p. 599)
—Fisherman & His Wife. Bryan, Diana, illus. (p. 599)
—Fisherman & His Wife/ El Pescador y Su Esposa. (p. 599)
—Frog Prince/ El Principe Sapo. (p. 640)
—Golden Goose / La Oca de Oro. (p. 694)
—Grandpa Mouse & Little Mouse: A Tale about Respect for Elders. Lonaytis, Olga, illus. (p. 709)
—Grimm's Fairy Stories. (p. 724)
—Grimms Fairy Tales. (p. 724)
—Grimm's Fairy Tales. (p. 724)
—Grimm's Fairy Tales. Hunt, Margaret, tr. from GER. (p. 724)
—Hans My Hedgehog: A Tale from the Brothers Grimm. Nickle, John, illus. (p. 743)
—Hansel & Gretel. Duntze, Dorothee, illus. (p. 743)
—Hansel & Gretel. Price, Margaret Evans, illus. (p. 743)
—Hansel & Gretel/Hansel y Gretel. (p. 743)
—Hut in the Forest Lawson, Polly, tr. from GER. (p. 830)
—Little Red Riding Hood: Caperucita Roja. Surges, James, tr. (p. 1035)
—Little Red Riding Hood/Caperucita Roja. (p. 1035)
—Rapunzel/Raponchigo. (p. 1439)
—Rumpelstiltskin. (p. 1495)
—Rumpelstiltskin. Watts, Bernadette, illus. (p. 1495)
—Sleeping Beauty. (p. 1589)
—Sleeping Beauty / La Bella Durmiente. (p. 1589)
—Snow White. (p. 1599)
—Snow White & Other Fairy Tales. (p. 1599)
—Snow White/Blancanieves. (p. 1600)
—Star Child. Watts, Edith & Watts, Bernadette, illus. (p. 1640)
—Tom Thumb/Pulgarcito. (p. 1764)
—Water of Life/ El Aqua de Vida. (p. 1863)
Grimm, Jacob, et al. Animal Fables Roederer, Charlotte, illus. (p. 77)
—Bremen Town Musicians: A Grimm Graphic Novel Weber, Lisa K., illus. (p. 226)
—Caperucita Roja. Rovira, Francesc, illus. (p. 262)
—Caperucita Roja. Watts, Bernadette, illus. (p. 262)
—Cinderella. Lavreys, Debbie, illus. (p. 320)
—Cuentos de los Hermanos Grimm. Archipowa, A. & Martinez B. de Quirós, Eladio, trs. (p. 390)
—Elves & the Shoemaker: A Grimm Graphic Novel Rodriquez, Pedro, illus. (p. 517)
—Family Favorites Thibault, Dominique & Durual, Christophe, illus. (p. 568)
—Garbancito. Serra, Sebastia, illus. (p. 656)
—Golden Goose: A Grimm Graphic Novel Ferraz, Thiago, illus. (p. 694)
—Goose Girl. (p. 702)
—Gris Grimly's Tales from the Brothers Grimm: Being a Selection from the Household Stories Collected by Jacob & Wilhelm Grimm. Hunt, Alfred William & Grimly, Gris, illus. (p. 724)
—Hansel & Gretel. (p. 743)
—Hansel & Gretel. Rowe, Louise, illus. (p. 743)
—Princess Tales Deru, Myriam et al, illus. (p. 1405)
—Queen Bee. Ghiuselev, Iassen & James, Elizabeth, illus. (p. 1424)
—Snow White & the Seven Dwarfs. (p. 1600)
Grimm, Jacob i Wilhelm (Germans Grimm), jt. auth. see Boada i Moret, Francesc.
Grimm, Jakob & Grimm, Wilhelm K. Grimm's Fairy Tales. Freeberg, Eric, illus. (p. 724)
Grimm, Jeanette. Living with Grandma & Grandpa. (p. 1042)
Grimm, Kristi. Mommy, Tell Me a Story about a Car, 2nd Edition. Grimm, Dave, illus. (p. 1162)
—Mommy, Tell Me a Story about a Fish. (p. 1162)
—Mommy, Tell Me a Story about a Plane, 2nd Edition. Grimm, Dave, illus. (p. 1162)
Grimm, Sandra. Baby Farm Animals. Sodré, Julie, illus. (p. 126)
Grimm, The Brothers, et al. Complete Grimm's Fairy Tales. (p. 353)
Grimm, W. C. & Grimm, J. L. C. Grimm's Fairy Tales. (p. 724)
Grimm, Wilhelm, jt. auth. see Grimm, Jacob.
Grimm, Wilhelm K. Dear Mili. Manheim, Ralph, tr. (p. 419)
Grimm, Wilhelm K., jt. auth. see Grimm, Jacob.
Grimm, Wilhelm K., jt. auth. see Grimm, Jakob.
Grimm, Wilhelm K. & Grimm, Jacob. Grimm's Fairy Tales Volume 2. (p. 724)
—Little Red Cap. Zwerger, Lisbeth, illus. (p. 1034)
—Little Red Riding-Hood: A Grimm's Fairy Tale. Lawson, Polly, tr. from GER. (p. 1035)
—Tales from Grimm. Gág, Wanda, tr. (p. 1701)
Grimm, Wilhelm K., et al. Elves & Shoemaker. (p. 517)
—Grimm's Fairy Tales. (p. 724)
—Rapunzel. (p. 1439)
—Twelve Dancing Princesses. Barrager, Brigette, illus. (p. 1800)
Grimme, Don & Grimme, Sheryl. New Manager's Tool Kit: 21 Things You Need to Know to Hit the Ground Running. (p. 1246)
Grimme, Jeannette, ed. see Morgan, Mario.
Grimme, Sheryl, jt. auth. see Grimme, Don.
Grimmer, Constance Marie. Santa's Christmas Dogs: A Legend Begins... (p. 1513)
Grimsdell, Jeremy. Bushbaby Night. (p. 244)
Grimshaw, Luke. Sniffle, Sneeze, Cough Back Off! Brzozowski, Christina, illus. (p. 1597)
—Sniffle, Sneeze, Cough... Back Off! Brzozowski, Christina, illus. (p. 1597)
Grimshaw, Melanie, et al. Make It! (p. 1079)
Grimsley, Barbara J. to Z of Animal Poetry for Children. (p. 1759)
Grimsley, Patsy. Miracle of the Purple Martin Gourds. (p. 1148)
Grimwood, Tracie, illus. see Lock, Kath.
Grimwood, Tracie, illus. see Trussell-Cullen, Alan.
Grinapal, Corinne. Racial Profiling & Discrimination: Your Legal Rights. (p. 1432)
Grinapol, Corinne. Harvey Milk: Pioneering Gay Politician (p. 752)
—Racial Profiling & Discrimination: Your Legal Rights. (p. 1432)
—Reed Hastings & Netflix. (p. 1456)
Grindele, Jenny. Josh, the Jock of High School. (p. 926)
Grindell, Joan, illus. see Langeler, Gerard.
Grindell, Mark, illus. see Langeler, Gerard.
Grindley, Sally. Archie's Amazing Adventure. Bendall-Brunello, John, tr. (p. 95)
—Bravo, Max! Ross, Tony, illus. (p. 224)
—Captain Pepper's Pets. Parkins, David, illus. (p. 264)
—Danger in the Dust. (p. 404)
—Feather Wars. (p. 579)
—Feathers in the Wind. (p. 579)
—Goat in a Boat. Phillips, Mike, illus. (p. 687)
—Home for Christmas. Littlewood, Karin, illus. (p. 792)
—Hurricane Wills. (p. 830)
—Keep Out! Bears About! (p. 947)
—Little Ballerina. (p. 1023)
—Paw Prints in the Snow. Frost, Adam, illus. (p. 1331)
—Poppy & Max & the Noisy Night. Gardiner, Lindsey, illus. (p. 1385)
—Poppy & Max & the River Picnic. Gardiner, Lindsey, illus. (p. 1385)
—Puff Flies. Fuller, Jeremy, illus. (p. 1415)
—Queen Ella's Feet. Aguilar, Sandra, illus. (p. 1424)
—Shadows under the Sea. (p. 1558)
—Shhh! (p. 1566)
—Shhh! Utton, Peter, illus. (p. 1566)
—Snail Trail. Phillips, Mike, illus. (p. 1596)
Grindley, Sally, jt. auth. see Varley, Susan.
Grindley, Sally & Dorling Kindersley Publishing Staff. Little Ballerina, Level 2. (p. 1023)
Grindley, Sally & Foreman, Michael. Playa de Pedro. (p. 1372)
Grindley, Sally & Lucas, D J. Dear Max. Ross, Tony, illus. (p. 419)
Grindley, Sally & Max, Querido. Querido Max. Ross, Tony, illus. (p. 1426)
Grindley, Sally, compiled by. Classic Animal Stories. (p. 327)
Grindley, Sally, et al. Pam Mae'r Awyr Yn Las? Stori Gan Sally Grindley. (p. 1320)
Grindstaff, Kit. Flame in the Mist. (p. 602)
Grine, Chris. Chickenhare. (p. 300)
Grine, Frederick, jt. ed. see Grine, Frederick E.
Grine, Frederick E. & Grine, Frederick, eds. Evolutionary History of the "Robust" Australopithecines. (p. 547)
Griner, Jack. Archibald My Pet Pig. Knudson, Dana, illus. (p. 95)
—Best Paw Forward. (p. 171)
—Creature or Critter? Chase, Linda, illus. (p. 380)
Griner, Sophia Maria. Hooray for Saturday! (p. 796)
Gringhuis, Dirk, illus. see Warner, Gertrude Chandler.
Grinnell, George Bird. Blackfeet Indian Stories. (p. 197)
—Jack among the Indians. (p. 902)
—Jack in the Rockies or A Boys Adventures. (p. 903)
Grinnell, Suzanne. Where Is Beau? Peter, Joshua, illus. (p. 1908)
Grinstead, Billy. Volunteer. (p. 1850)
Grinstead, Krista. Frenchie & Friends: The Walk. (p. 636)
Grinti, Mike & Grinti, Rachel. Claws. (p. 330)
Grinti, Rachel, jt. auth. see Grinti, Mike.
Grinvald, Zeev & Zryl, Laya. Watching My Words: An Illustrated Children's Guide to the Laws of Shemiras Halashon. Baifus, Rut, illus. (p. 1861)
Grinvalsky, Peggy, illus. see Burns, Mary E.
Griotto, Sophie, jt. auth. see Vendittelli, Marie.
Gripari, Pierre. Gentil Petit Diable: Et Autres Contes de la Rue Broca. Rosado, Puig, illus. (p. 661)
—Good Little Devil & Other Tales. Lewis, Sophie, tr. (p. 698)
Gripe, Harold, illus. see Gripe, Maria.
Gripe, Maria. Elvis Karlsson. Gripe, Harold, illus. (p. 517)
Gripe, Maria, jt. auth. see Gripe, Maria.
Gripe, Maria & Gripe, Maria. Hijos del Vidriero. (p. 779)
Grippando, James. Leapholes. (p. 982)
Grippo, Daniel. Playing Fair, Having Fun: A Kid's Guide to Sports & Games. Alley, R. W., illus. (p. 1372)
—When Mom or Dad Dies: A Book of Comfort for Kids. Alley, R. W., illus. (p. 1903)
Griscom, Laura. Boy Named 27091: A Teenager's Struggle for Survival during the Holocaust. (p. 218)
Griser, Carol. Breona's New Life. (p. 226)
Grisewood, Therese U., ed. see Peralas, Jorge.
Grisham, Betty, illus. see Newell, Carol Donsky.
Grisham, Jason, illus. see Nivens, Karen.
Grisham, John. Abduction. (p. 4)
—Abduction. (p. 4)
—Accused. (p. 8)
—Activist. (p. 10)
—Casa Dipinta. (p. 273)
—Fugitive. (p. 646)
—Kid Lawyer. (p. 951)
—Theodore Boone Box Set (p. 1729)
Grisham, Jonathan. Death of the Universe. (p. 420)
Grisham, Sharon Casey. God's Child: A Fellow Scholar Choice. (p. 691)
Grishaver, Joel Lurie. I Can Celebrate the Jewish Holidays. Bleicher, David, illus. (p. 835)
Grishaver, Joel Lurie, jt. auth. see Berman, Melanie.
Grisinger Reilly, Teresa Kathryn. Etiquette Lessons: Modern Manners. Vol. 2 (p. 539)
—Etiquette Lessons: Girls & Boys at the Table, Teens at the Table, Table Manners, American Cotillion. Part I,Part II (p. 539)
Griskey, Michele. Beverly Cleary. (p. 173)
—Emily Dickinson. (p. 518)
—Harriet Beecher Stowe. (p. 749)
—Ray Bradbury. (p. 1441)
Grissom, Michael Andrew. You Might Be Southern If ... (p. 1976)
Grissom, Michael Andrew, jt. auth. see McBroom, Christopher Erik.
Grist, Julie. Flying: Just Plane Fun. Grist, Julie, illus. (p. 609)
Grist, Paul. 39th Precinct. (p. 1996)
—Rabbit Hunt. (p. 1429)
—Untouchable Rico Costas & Other Stories. (p. 1823)
Grist, Paul, jt. auth. see Cooke, Darwyn.
Griswell, Kim T. Rufus Goes to School. Gorbachev, Valeri, illus. (p. 1494)
—Rufus Goes to Sea. Gorbachev, Valeri, illus. (p. 1494)
Griswold, Cliff. Fall Leaves. (p. 566)
—Let's Go Apple Picking! (p. 997)
—Let's Go on a Hayride! (p. 997)
—Pumpkin Patch. (p. 1416)
Griswold del Castillo, Richard. Cesar Chavez: The Struggle for Justice/la Lucha Por la Justicia. Colin, Jose Juan, tr. (p. 288)
—Cesar Chavez: The Struggle for Justice (La Lucha por la Justicia) Colin, Jose Juan, tr. (p. 288)
Griswold, Earleen, illus. see Picayo, Mario.
Griswold, Elaine. Fairy Walk: A True Story of Imagination. (p. 564)
Griswold, Grampa. Grampa's Bedtime Rhymes. (p. 706)
Griswold, Melissa. Friends, Like You: Educator's Guide. (p. 638)
—Friends, Like You: Children's Activity Book. Fisher, Cynthia, illus. (p. 638)
—Friends, Like You. Fisher, Cynthia, illus. (p. 638)
Griswold, Phillip, illus. see Miller, Lindsey Michael.
Griswold-Ford, Valerie. Last Rites. (p. 978)
Griswood, John, ed. Biblia Juvenil Ilustrada. Sanz Falcon, Maria Teresa, tr. from ENG. (p. 176)
Gritton, Steve. ... & Then I... (p. 71)
—Kandy Witch. (p. 942)
—Plain Fish. (p. 1366)
—Super Dupers. Gritton, Steve, illus. (p. 1680)

—Trouble with Sisters & Robots. (p. 1790)
Gritzner, Charles & Gritzner, Yvonne. Peru. (p. 1345)
Gritzner, Charles F. Changing Climates. (p. 290)
—Deserts. (p. 429)
—Environment & Natural Resources. (p. 532)
—Feeding a Hungry World. (p. 580)
—Haiti. (p. 736)
—Latin America. (p. 979)
—Mexico. (p. 1131)
—Nicaragua. (p. 1250)
—Polar Regions. (p. 1379)
—Tropics. (p. 1789)
—United States. (p. 1819)
Gritzner, Charles F., ed. see Benhart, John & Pomeroy, George.
Gritzner, Charles F., ed. see Crooker, Richard A.
Gritzner, Charles F., ed. see Desaulniers, Kristi.
Gritzner, Charles F., ed. see Gillespie, Carol Ann.
Gritzner, Charles F., ed. see Greenbaum, Harry.
Gritzner, Charles F., ed. see Lopez, Jose Javier.
Gritzner, Charles F., ed. see Pavlovic, Zoran.
Gritzner, Charles F., ed. see Phillips, Douglas A.
Gritzner, Charles F., ed. see Whitefield, Gary T.
Gritzner, Charles F., jt. auth. see Crooker, Richard A.
Gritzner, Charles F., jt. auth. see Dendinger, Roger E.
Gritzner, Charles F., jt. auth. see Kheirabadi, Masoud.
Gritzner, Charles F., jt. auth. see Wingfield, George.
Gritzner, Charles F. & Phillips, Douglas. Japan. (p. 909)
Gritzner, Charles F. & Phillips, Douglas A. Dominican Republic. (p. 465)
Gritzner, Charles F. & Swanson, Linnea C. Panama. (p. 1320)
Gritzner, Charles F., contrib. by. Global Connections (p. 684)
Gritzner, Charles F., ed. Modern World Nations, (p. 1159)
Gritzner, Janet H. Jamaica. (p. 906)
Gritzner, Jason, jt. auth. see Lineback, Mandy.
Gritzner, Yvonne, jt. auth. see Gritzner, Charles.
Grivas, Vasilis. Zaf the Persian Cat. (p. 1984)
Grivas, Vasilis, illus. see McRae, J. R.
Griver, Jeanette A. CURIO a Shetland Sheepdog & Friends: A Story of Change for Children of All Ages. (p. 392)
—CURIO a Shetland Sheepdog & her Pals: All ages Will enjoy the Tales of Friendship. (p. 392)
—Curio, a Shetland Sheepdog Meets the Crow: A Story of Friendship For Children of All Ages (p. 392)
Grizinski, Yolande, jt. auth. see Holzhauser-Peters, Leslie.
Grizzard, Sue H. Princess Caylee: An Incredible Birthday Wish Come True. (p. 1403)
Grizzell, Kenneth. Father's Gift. (p. 577)
Grizzell, Larry. Star: A Christmas Song. (p. 1640)
—What Would You Like to Do Today? Fun in the Snow. (p. 1895)
Grizzell, Larry, creator. What Would You Like to Do Today? (p. 1895)
Grizzell, Whitney. HaleyBeth & Pink Rose Meet for the First Time. (p. 736)
Gro, Wright. Matchword/Prog Set. (p. 1104)
Grob, John-Marc. FriendFish. (p. 637)
Grobbelaar, Pieter W. & Verster, Sean. Famous South African Folk Tales. (p. 569)
Grobet, Veronique, illus. see Zidrou.
Grobler, Piet. All the Wild Wonders: Poems of Our Earth. (p. 46)
—Little Bird's ABC. Grobler, Piet, illus. (p. 1024)
Grobler, Piet, illus. see Cooling, Wendy & Quarto Generic Staff.
Grobler, Piet, illus. see Cooling, Wendy.
Grobler, Piet, illus. see De Vos, Philip.
Grobler, Piet, illus. see Dijkstra, Lida.
Grobler, Piet, illus. see Luján, Jorge.
Grobler, Piet, illus. see Naidoo, Beverley.
Grobler, Piet, illus. see Quarmby, Katharine.
Grobler, Piet, illus. see Ravishankar, Anushka.
Grobler, Piet, jt. auth. see Hofmeyr, Dianne.
GROBLER, Piet, jt. auth. see QUARMBY, Katharine.
Grobler, Piet, et al. Rights of a Child. (p. 1472)
Groce, Mandy. What Is the Gospel? (p. 1890)
Groce, Michelle. Jasper. Duis, Laura, illus. (p. 910)
Grochowski, Brad. Secret Weakness of Dragons: And Other Tales a Fairy Whispered in My Ear. (p. 1544)
Grocki, Jennifer. From A to Zamboni, the Alphabet Hockey Style! Flyers Edition. Lendway, Andy, illus. (p. 641)
Grodin, Elissa. D Is for Democracy: A Citizen's Alphabet. Juhasz, Victor, illus. (p. 397)
Grodin, Elissa, jt. auth. see Wilde, Oscar.
Grodin, Elissa D. Yankee Doodle Numbers: A Connecticut Number Book. Brookfield, Maureen K., illus. (p. 1968)
Grodin, Elissa D., et al. C Is for Ciao: An Italy Alphabet. Ventura, Marco, illus. (p. 249)
Grody, Laura. Grace & Dignity. (p. 704)
Groebner, Dominic, illus. see Khanduri, Kamini, et al.
Groebner, Dominic, illus. see Pearcey, Alice.
Groebner, Dominic, illus. see Sims, Lesley.
Groenboom, Roger, et al. King Jesus. (p. 958)
—Light of the World Is Jesus. (p. 1015)
—Rough Waves? Jesus Saves! (p. 1491)
—Sharable Parables. (p. 1561)
Groenendyk, Doretta. Bully 101 (p. 241)
—Hockey Morning Noon & Night (p. 786)
—Step Outside (p. 1648)
Groenendyk, Doretta, jt. auth. see Hope-Simpson, Lila.
Groenendyk, Doretta, jt. auth. see Murray, Shannon.
Groenewald, Catherine. I Could Be Anywhere. (p. 837)
—Jingle-Jingle in My Pocket. (p. 918)
—Little Girl Who Didn't Want to Grow Up. (p. 1028)
Groenewald, Catherine, jt. auth. see Oosthuizen, Sarah.
Groenewald, Frans, illus. see Scotford, Groenewald & Scotford, Tina.
Groenewald, Frans, illus. see Scotford, Tina.
Groeneweg, Nicole. Interactive Projects & Displays: Ideas for a Student-Created Learning Environment. F, Stacey, ed. (p. 879)
—One Word Pearl. Mitchell, Hazel, illus. (p. 1297)
Groenewegen, Peter, jt. auth. see Vaggi, Gianni.
Groening, Matt. Bart Simpson - Out to Lunch. (p. 140)
—Big Bad Book of Bart Simpson. (p. 177)
—Simpsons Comics Colossal Compendium Volume 2. (p. 1578)
—Simpsons Comics Get Some Fancy Book Learnin' (p. 1578)
—Simpsons Ultra-Jumbo Rain-or-Shine Fun Book. (p. 1578)
Groening, Matt, creator. Beach Blanket Bongo. (p. 149)
Groenink, Chuck, illus. see Stein, Mathilde.
Groenink, Chuck, illus. see Bram, Elizabeth.
Groenink, Chuck, illus. see Chapin, Tom & Forster, John.
Groenink, Chuck, illus. see Heide, Florence Parry.
Groenink, Chuck, illus. see Palatini, Margie.
Groenink, Chuck, illus. see Yeh, Kat.
Groethe, Kd. Boy Who Would Walk on Air. (p. 219)
—Virtual Adventures of Megan & Timmy. (p. 1844)
Grof, Stanislav, illus. see Sullivan, Melody.
Groff, David, illus. see Bader, Bonnie.
Groff, David, illus. see Belviso, Meg & Pollack, Pam.
Groff, David, illus. see Demuth, Patricia Brennan.
Groff, David, illus. see Kelley, True.
Groff, David, illus. see Medina, Nico.
Groff, David, illus. see O'Connor, Jim.
Groff, David, illus. see Pascal, Janet.
Groff, David, illus. see Spinner, Stephanie.
Groff, David, illus. see Stine, Megan.
Groffman, Simcha. Awesome Days. (p. 121)
—Simcha's Kinder Torah: Torah Stories & Thoughts on the Weekly Parasha. (p. 1577)
—Simcha's Kinder Torah Presents Awesome Days: Torah Stories & Thoughts for the Yomim Noraim & Succos to Enhance Your Yom Tov Table. (p. 1577)
Grogan, Jerry, jt. auth. see Fitzpatrick, Tom.
Grogan, John. Bad Dog, Marley! Cowdrey, Richard, illus. (p. 131)
—Bad Dog, Marley! Beloved Book & Plush Puppy. Cowdrey, Richard, illus. (p. 131)
—Christmas Is Coming. Cowdrey, Richard & Koelsch, Michael, illus. (p. 314)
—Dog Who Ate My Homework. (p. 462)
—Dog Who Cried Woof. Cowdrey, Richard, illus. (p. 462)
—Farm Dog. Cowdrey, Richard, illus. (p. 573)
—Firehouse Dog. (p. 592)
—Marley: Not a Peep! (p. 1095)
—Marley: A Dog Like No Other. (p. 1095)
—Marley: Firehouse Dog. Cowdrey, Richard & Halverson, Lydia, illus. (p. 1095)
—Marley: The Dog Who Ate My Homework. Cowdrey, Richard & Whipple, Rick, illus. (p. 1095)
—Marley & the Kittens. Cowdrey, Richard, illus. (p. 1095)
—Marley Goes to School. Cowdrey, Richard, illus. (p. 1095)
—Marley Learns a Lesson. (p. 1095)
—Marley Learns a Lesson. Cowdrey, Richard, illus. (p. 1095)
—Marley Looks for Love. Cowdrey, Richard, illus. (p. 1095)
—Marley - Not a Peep! Cowdrey, Richard & Whipple, Rick, illus. (p. 1095)
—Marley - Springs Ahead. Cowdrey, Richard, illus. (p. 1095)
—Marley Steals the Show. Cowdrey, Richard & Lyon, Tammie, illus. (p. 1095)
—Marley Storybook Treasury. Cowdrey, Richard, illus. (p. 1095)
—Marley's Big Adventure. (p. 1095)
—Marley's Christmas Pageant. Cowdrey, Richard, illus. (p. 1095)
—Marley's World Reusable Sticker Book. Cowdrey, Richard, illus. (p. 1095)
—Messy Dog. Cowdrey, Richard, illus. (p. 1130)
—Not a Peep! Cowdrey, Richard & Whipple, Rick, illus. (p. 1266)
—Sit, Marley, Sit! Cowdrey, Richard & Lyon, Tammie, illus. (p. 1581)
—Snow Dog Marley. Cowdrey, Richard, illus. (p. 1599)
—Thanks, Mom & Dad! Cowdrey, Richard, illus. (p. 1725)
—Thanksgiving to Remember. Cowdrey, Richard & Whipple, Rick, illus. (p. 1726)
—Trick or Treat, Marley! Cowdrey, Richard, illus. (p. 1786)
—Very Marley Christmas. Cowdrey, Richard, illus. (p. 1838)
Grogan, John & Hill, Susan. Marley & the Runaway Pumpkin. Cowdrey, Richard & Halverson, Lydia, illus. (p. 1095)
—Marley's Big Adventure. Cowdrey, Richard & Halverson, Lydia, illus. (p. 1095)
—Strike Three, Marley! Beier, Ellen & Cowdrey, Richard, illus. (p. 1667)
—Strike Three, Marley! Cowdrey, Richard & Beier, Ellen, illus. (p. 1667)
Grogan, Joy. Into the Fold. (p. 881)
Grogan, Patrick. Birding for Children. (p. 191)
Grogan, Shannon. From Where I Watch You. (p. 644)
Groggins, Anita. Adventures of Little Cappedo: Cobwebs in the Sky. (p. 19)
Grolier Educational (Firm) Staff, contrib. by. Nature's Children. (p. 1237)
Grolier Educational Staff, contrib. by. Amazing Animals of the the World 2 (p. 53)
—Argentina. (p. 97)
—Biology Matters! (p. 189)
—Civil War (p. 325)
—Flash Focus (p. 602)
—Grolier Student Encyclopedia (p. 725)
—Insects & Other Invertebrates (p. 876)
—Reformation, Exploration, & Empire (p. 1456)
—Space Science (p. 1619)
—USA 1950s (p. 1826)
Grolier (Firm) Staff, contrib. by. Amazing Animals of the the World 3. (p. 53)
—World War II (p. 1959)
Grolier Incorporated Staff, contrib. by. Amazing Animals of the World (p. 53)
—Amazing Animals of the World. (p. 53)
Grolier Publishing Company Staff, contrib. by. Hispanic American Biographies (p. 781)
Grollman, Earl A. Talking about Death: A Dialogue Between Parent & Child. (p. 1703)
—Talking about Divorce & Separation: A Dialogue Between Parent & Child. Pitzer, Suzanne, illus. (p. 1703)
Grollman, Earl A. & Johnson, Joy. Complete Book about Death for Kids. Donner, Brad, photos by. (p. 352)
Gromosiak, Paul. Owahonton: Maid of the Mist. (p. 1314)
Grondel, April, illus. see McNeill, Audrey.
Grondin, Peter. Lifetime of Deception. (p. 1014)
Groneman, William, III, et al. David Crockett: Hero of the Common Man. (p. 411)
Groner, Judye & Wikler, Madeline. Let's Visit Israel. Nathan, Cheryl, illus. (p. 1001)
Groner, Judyth. My First Hebrew Word Book. Marzel, Pépi, illus. (p. 1206)
Groner, Judyth & Wikler, Madeline. Thank You, God! A Jewish Child's Book of Prayers. Haas, Shelly, illus. (p. 1725)
Groner, Judyth Saypol & Wikler, Madeline. Maccabee Meals: Food & Fun for Hanukkah. Roma, Ursula, illus. (p. 1068)
Gronquist, D. E. Time Trap. (p. 1753)
Groome, Harry. Wing Walking. (p. 1936)
Groome, W. H. C., illus. see Whistler, Charles W.
Grooms, Duffy, jt. auth. see Henson, Laura J.
Grooms, Molly. We Are Dolphins. Oda, Takashi, illus. (p. 1865)
—We Are Horses. (p. 1865)
—We Are Puppies. (p. 1865)
Groot, Bob de. Jade Vol. 5. Rodrigue, illus. (p. 905)
Groot, De. Black Moon. Spear, Luke, tr. from FRE. (p. 196)
Groot, Nicole, illus. see O'Connor, Frankie.
Groover, Shaunessi T. He Leadeth Me Beside the Still Water. (p. 756)
Grose, Carl. Hansel & Gretel. (p. 743)
Grose, Crystal. Eat & Drink Your ABCs. (p. 501)
Grose, Michael. Why First Borns Rule the World & Last Borns Want to Change It. (p. 1924)
Grosgebauer, Clare Ham. My Snickerdoodle Doodle Book: Creative Writing & Drawing Adventures. (p. 1219)
—Snickerdoodle! a Tall Tale about a Powerful Pee-Wee! Rissing, Karen, illus. (p. 1597)
—Snickerdoodle & the Roller-Skating Horse! Rissing, Karen, illus. (p. 1597)
—Snickerdoodle's Star-Spangled Fourth of July! Rissing, Karen, illus. (p. 1597)
Groshek, Jodie. Brush, Brush, Brush. (p. 232)
Groshelle, Dave, illus. see Saunders, Helen.
Grosinger, Paula, ed. see Schweitzer, Arlette.
Grosjean, Didier. Yo, Barbarroja. (p. 1971)
Gross, Andrew, jt. auth. see Patterson, James.
Gross, Arthur. Child's Garden of Bible Stories. Barr, Marilyn, illus. (p. 305)
Gross, Arthur William. Child's Garden of Bible Stories: The Classic Edition. (p. 305)
Gross, Carmen. Ryan Elias Finds: The Truth Behind Lying. Dixon, Nehemiah F., illus. (p. 1499)
Gross, Craig & Foster, Mike. Questions You Can't Ask Your Mama: 68 1/2 Questions for Craig & Mike. (p. 1426)
Gross, Edward. Spider-Man Confidential: From Comic Icon to Hollywood Hero. (p. 1626)
Gross, Fannie. Shakespeare Two Thousand: Two Thousand Questions & Answers on All of Shakespeare's Plays. (p. 1559)
Gross, Frederick C. & Chace, Reeve. Truth about Marijuana. (p. 1794)
Gross, Inge E. Memories of Opportunities, Family & Adventures. (p. 1126)
Gross, Jen & Hoch, Jen. Visit up & down Wall Street. Gross, Margaret, illus. (p. 1845)
Gross, John. After Shakespeare: Writing Inspired by the World's Greatest Author. (p. 28)
Gross, Judith, et al. Celebrate: A Book of Jewish Holidays. Weissman, Bari, illus. (p. 283)
Gross, Kaiya, jt. auth. see Gross, Kimberley.
Gross, Kimberley & Gross, Kaiya. Multiplication Monster. Gross, Sanai, illus. (p. 1190)
Gross, M. J. How to Draw the Life & Times of William Jefferson Clinton. (p. 819)
Gross, Maia, illus. see Sutherland, Rowan.
Gross, Margaret, illus. see Gross, Jen & Hoch, Jen.
Gross, Miriam. All about Astronauts. (p. 42)
—All about Rockets. (p. 43)
—All about Satellites. (p. 43)
—All about Space Missions. (p. 43)
—All about Space Shuttles. (p. 43)
—All about Space Stations. (p. 43)
—How to Draw the Life & Times of James Monroe. (p. 819)
—John Adams: Patriot, Diplomat, & Statesman. (p. 921)
Gross, Miriam J. All about Astronauts. (p. 42)
—All about Satellites. (p. 43)
—All about Space Missions. (p. 43)
—All about Space Shuttles. (p. 43)
—All about Space Stations. (p. 43)
—How to Draw the Life & Times of William Jefferson Clinton. (p. 819)
—Jellyfish. (p. 912)
—Moray Eel. (p. 1173)
—Octopus. (p. 1278)
—Sea Dragon. (p. 1534)
—Sea Slug: Nudibranchs. (p. 1535)
—Stingray. (p. 1651)
Gross, Richard D. & Rolls, Geoff. Essential A2 Psychology for AQA. (p. 536)
—Essential AS Psychology for AQA Specification A. (p. 536)
Gross, Rod. Church Mouse Named Joy. (p. 318)
Gross, Roxanna. Pit Monster. (p. 1364)
Gross, Ruth Belov & Björkman, Steve. Book about Your Skeleton. (p. 210)
Gross, S. D. Blue Frog. (p. 202)
—Freddie. (p. 632)
—Freddie, Fireman Mike. (p. 632)
—Mugallumps. (p. 1189)
Gross, Sanai, illus. see Gross, Kimberley & Gross, Kaiya.
Gross, Sandra & Busch, Leah. Toast to Counting: Toast to Baby. Hutton, John, ed. (p. 1760)
Gross, Scott. Scooby-Doo & the Aliens of Area 49. (p. 1529)
Gross, Scott, illus. see Weakland, Mark.
Gross, Sherie, tr. see Rosenberg, Tziporah.
Gross, Sue, illus. see Bercun, Brenda.
Gross, Susan, illus. see Stillman, Sarah.
Gross-Andrew, Susannah, illus. see Coon, Nora E., ed.
Grossbard, H. A. Driving in Florida: The Politically Incorrect Guide to Surviving the Roadways of the Sunshine State. (p. 485)
Grossberg, Blythe. Applying to College for Students with ADD or LD: A Guide to Keep You (and Your Parents) Sane, Satisfied, & Organized Through the Admission Process. (p. 93)
—Test Success: Test-Taking & Study Strategies for All Students, Including Those with ADD & LD. (p. 1723)
Grossberg, Blythe, jt. auth. see Grossberg, Blythe N.
Grossberg, Blythe N. & Grossberg, Blythe. Making ADD Work: On-the-Job Strategies for Coping with Attention Deficit Disorder. (p. 1080)
Grossblatt, Ben. Extreme Animals: Sharks. (p. 556)
—Keep Out! Door Alarm: Build Your Own Key-Card Security System! (p. 947)
—Slapshot Science: SmartLab. (p. 1588)
Grossblatt, Ben & Klutz Editors. Gotcha Gadgets. (p. 704)
Grossblatt, Ben & Rippley, P. U. Jurassic Farts: A Spotter's Guide. Palmer, Evan, illus. (p. 937)
Grosschmid, Pablo - Ecjegoyen, jt. auth. see Juventud Staff.
Grossel, David, et al. Tudor Years. Lotherington, John, ed. (p. 1796)
Grosset & Dunlap. Angelina & the Easter Bonnet. (p. 74)
—Baby's First Words. Aikins, Dave, illus. (p. 129)
—Bedtime for Baby. Aikins, Dave, illus. (p. 156)
—Buzzbee the Magician. (p. 249)
—Celebrate Thanksgiving with Max & Ruby! (Sticker Stories) (p. 284)
—Chipping Cheddar Christmas. Artful Doodlers Ltd., illus. (p. 308)
—Learn to Draw. (p. 983)
—Max Goes Fishing. (p. 1111)
—Octonauts & the Decorator Crab. (p. 1277)
—Octonauts & the Whale Shark. (p. 1278)
—Octonauts Creature Report. (p. 1278)
—Scaredy Bee. (p. 1519)
—Underwater Adventures. (p. 1817)
—Zoom! Things That Go. Aikins, Dave, illus. (p. 1989)
Grosset & Dunlap & Beakman, Onk. Mask of Power: Cynder Confronts the Weather Wizard. No. 2 (p. 1102)
—Mask of Power - Terrafin Battles the Boom Brothers. (p. 1102)
Grosset & Dunlap & Campbell, Hannah S. Take Flight & Fight! (p. 1696)
Grosset and Dunlap Editors, jt. auth. see Holabird, Katharine.
Grosset and Dunlap Editors & Hutchison, Barry. Book of Elements - Life & Undead. (p. 211)
Grosset & Dunlap Inc. Staff. Away We Go. (p. 120)
—Fun with Dick & Jane. (p. 648)
Grosset and Dunlap Staff. Angelina's Best Friend Dance. Artful Doodlers Ltd., illus. (p. 74)
—Angelina's Spring Fling. (p. 74)
—Baby's ABC. Aikins, Dave, illus. (p. 128)
—Baby's First Easter. Aikins, Dave, illus. (p. 129)
—Costume Fun! (p. 368)
—Day to Play! (p. 414)
—Funny Bunny Tales. (p. 649)
—Hungry Bunny Tales. (p. 828)
—I Would Like to Actually Keep It. (p. 849)
—Max & Ruby Celebrate Easter. (p. 1110)
—Max & Ruby's Four Seasons. (p. 1110)
—Max & Ruby's Storybook Treasury. (p. 1110)
—Max Makes a Friend. (p. 1111)
—Max to the Rescue. (p. 1111)
—Merry Bunny Christmas. (p. 1128)
—My ABC Book. Seiden, Art, illus. (p. 1195)
—Octonauts & the Colossal Squid. (p. 1277)
—Octonauts & the Undersea Eruption. (p. 1278)
—Our First Snow. (p. 1308)
—Ruby Gets Crafty. (p. 1493)
—Ruby's Cupcakes. (p. 1493)
—Ruby's Falling Leaves. (p. 1493)
—Ruby's Rainbow. (p. 1493)
—Silly Bunny Tales. (p. 1575)
—Spooky Bunny Tales. (p. 1631)
—Sporty Bunny Tales. (p. 1633)
—Super Bunny Tales. (p. 1679)
—Surprise for Mom! (p. 1685)
Grosset and Dunlap Staff, jt. auth. see Duey, Kathleen.
Grosset and Dunlap Staff, jt. auth. see Penguin Group (USA) Staff.
Grosset and Dunlap Staff, jt. auth. see Wells, Rosemary.
Grosset and Dunlap Staff & Activision Publishing, Inc., Staff. Skylanders Giants: Master Eon's Official Guide. (p. 1587)
—Skylanders Swap Force - Master Eon's Official Guide. (p. 1587)
Grosset and Dunlap Staff & Child, Lauren. I Slightly Want to Go Home. (p. 845)
Grosset and Dunlap Staff & Hutchison, Barry. Book of Elements - Air & Earth. (p. 211)
Grosset and Dunlap Staff & Penguin Young Readers Group Staff. Away We Go. (p. 120)
—Beach Day! (p. 149)
—Go Away, Spot (p. 686)
—Ruby Scores a Goal. (p. 1493)
—We Play. (p. 1868)
—We See. (p. 1868)
—We Work. (p. 1869)
—Who Can Help? (p. 1914)
Grosset and Dunlap Staff, contrib. by. We Play Outside. (p. 1868)
—World of Dick & Jane Anderson. (p. 1956)
Grosset and Dunlap Staff, et al. Max's Checkup. (p. 1112)
—Skylanders Trap Team: Master Eon's Official Guide. (p. 1587)
Grosset, et al. Max Goes Fishing. (p. 1111)
Grosshandler, Janet. Drugs & Driving. (p. 487)
Grosshandler, Janet, jt. auth. see Mendralla, Valerie.

Grosshauser, Peter. My Week. (p. 1221)
Grosshauser, Peter, illus. see Hetherington, Debra Thorpe, ed.
Grosshauser, Peter, illus. see Rosa-Mendoza, Gladys.
Grosshauser, Peter, illus. see Smith, E. K.
Grosshauser, Peter, illus. see Smith, Martina.
Grosshauser, Peter, illus. see Wesley, Milliana, ed.
Grossinger, Tania. Jackie & Me: A Very Special Friendship. Esperanza, Charles George, illus. (p. 903)
Grossman, Andrea, jt. auth. see Carola, Leslie Conron.
Grossman, Bill. Cowboy Ed. Wint, Florence, illus. (p. 374)
—My Little Sister Ate One Hare. Hawkes, Kevin, illus. (p. 1213)
—My Little Sister Hugged an Ape. Hawkes, Kevin, illus. (p. 1213)
Grossman, Chaya. Cherry on Top: A Kosher Junior Cookbook. (p. 298)
Grossman, David. Be My Knife: A Novel. Gurantz, Maya & Almog, Vered, trs. (p. 148)
—Her Body Knows: Two Novellas. Cohen, Jessica, tr. (p. 769)
—Hug. Schoffman, Stuart, tr. (p. 824)
—Someone to Run With: A Novel. Almog, Vered & Gurantz, Maya, trs. (p. 1609)
—Zig Zag Kid. Rosenberg, Betsy, tr. (p. 1986)
Grossman, Gene. ...Until Proven Innocent. (p. 1823)
Grossman, Leonard S. In the Name of Greed. (p. 866)
Grossman, Linda Sky & Toronto Child Abuse Centre Staff. I'M a Great Little Kid (p. 858)
—I'm a Great Little Kid (p. 858)
Grossman, Lynne, jt. auth. see Herman, Alison.
Grossman, Mahesh. Silly Rubber Band Handbook: The Ultimate Guide to Collecting & Trading Shaped Bandz. (p. 1576)
Grossman, Mark. World Military Leaders: A Biographical Dictionary. (p. 1956)
Grossman, Max & Benchmark Education Co., LLC. Idea Machine: My Inventor's Journal. (p. 852)
Grossman, Mendel, photos by see Smith, Frank Dabba & Quarto Generic Staff.
Grossman, Nancy, illus. see Caudill, Rebecca.
Grossman, Rena. Carry Me (p. 271)
—Carry Me (Spanish/English) Fiol, Maria A., tr. (p. 271)
—Eating the Rainbow (p. 501)
—Families (p. 567)
Grossmann, Dan, illus. see Standard Publishing Staff.
Grossmann-Hensel, Katharina. How Mommy Met Daddy. Ward, Rachel, tr. from GER. (p. 811)
—Papa is a Pirate. Grossmann-Hensel, Katharina, illus. (p. 1322)
Grosso, Alissa. Ferocity Summer. (p. 582)
Grosso, Salvatore. Butterfly & the Dinosaur: A true story of fiction Inspired by a Beautiful Butterfly. (p. 247)
Grosvenor, Charles, illus. see Auerbach, Annie & PopCap Games Staff.
Grosvenor, Charles, illus. see Hapka, Catherine, pseud.
Grosvenor, Charles & Gerard, Justin. Dragon Mountain Adventure. (p. 477)
Grosvenor, Charles, et al. Tale of Dragons. (p. 1699)
Grosvenor, Mary B., jt. auth. see Smolin, Lori A.
Groth, Gary, ed. see Gottfredson, Floyd.
Groth, Jeanette L. Prayer: Learning How to Talk to God. (p. 1393)
Groth, Lynn. Buttons' Bouquet of Flowers. (p. 248)
—Buttons in the Dark. (p. 248)
—Buttons' Picnic. (p. 248)
—Buttons Visits Grandma. (p. 248)
Groth-fleming. Professor Fergus Fahrenheit & His Wonderful Weat. (p. 1409)
Grotholt, Yannick. Chi Quest! (p. 299)
—High Risk! (p. 778)
—Power of Fire Chi. (p. 1389)
—Right Decision. (p. 1472)
Grotius, Hugo. Truth of the Christian Religion, with Jean le Clerc's Additions. (p. 1794)
Grotke, Christopher A., illus. see Salisbury, Linda G.
Groucutt, Jonathan. Foundations of Marketing. (p. 624)
Group, Brown Reference. Festive Foods: China. (p. 582)
—Festive Foods: India. (p. 582)
—Festive Foods: Italy. (p. 582)
—Festive Foods: Japan. (p. 582)
—Festive Foods: France. (p. 582)
—Festive Foods: Mexico. (p. 582)
—Festive Foods: Germany. (p. 582)
—Festive Foods: United States. (p. 582)
Group Publishing Staff. Christmas Extras! Faith-Filled Ideas for Celebrating Christmas. (p. 313)
—Gigantic Book of Games for Youth Ministry (p. 676)
—Pray & Play Bible 2: For Young Children (p. 1393)
Group Publishing Staff & Tyndale House Publishers Staff, contrib. by. Live: Holy Bible: New Living Translation. (p. 1039)
Group Publishing Staff, contrib. by. All-Star Bloopers from All-Star Youth Leaders. (p. 45)
—Kids' Travel Guide to the 23rd Psalm. (p. 955)
Group Publishing Staff, creator. Baby Beakers: Infants, Toddlers & Twos. (p. 125)
—Bible Memory Buddy Care Cards. (p. 175)
—Flip Flops, Pre-K - K: Group's Buzz: the Instant Sunday School Three-Lesson Mini-Kit. (p. 605)
—Gator Guidebook: A Kid-Sized Bit of the Bible. (p. 658)
—Grapple - Spring: Preteens' Toughest Questions, the Bible's Smartest Answers (p. 711)
—Moose Mountain: Where Kids Build Friendships That Last Forever. (p. 1173)
—Name Badges: Junior Funologist. (p. 1228)
—On the Spot: No-Prep Games for Children's Ministry. (p. 1291)
—Preteen Launchables: All the Stuff You Need to Launch Your Preteen Ministry: Upper Elementary. (p. 1398)
Group Publishing Staff, ed. Quick Children's Sermons: Did Adam & Eve Have Bellybuttons? (p. 1427)
Group, The Monotheist. Message: A Translation of the Glorious Qur'an. (p. 1129)
Group/McGraw-Hill, Wright. 13th Floor: Level O (p. 1995)
—Abraham Lincoln: The Civil War President (p. 6)
—Africa: Rich in Land & History (p. 26)
—African Art: Level E (p. 27)
—Against the Odds: Magazine Anthology - Level 3 (p. 29)
—Al Ataque! (p. 32)
—All's Well that End Well: Level N (p. 48)
—Amazing Asia (p. 53)
—Ancient Egypt: The Realm of Pharaohs (p. 68)
—And the Winner Is: Level N (p. 71)
—Animal Advocates (p. 76)
—Animal Mysteries (p. 79)
—Animales Domesticos (p. 81)
—Animals Go Mad: Level 2 (p. 82)
—Aranas (p. 94)
—Around the World: Level 7 (p. 100)
—Art Show (p. 103)
—Aunt Jewel's Ghost (p. 115)
—Aunt Victoria's Monster: Level P (p. 115)
—Australia: Urban & Outback (p. 116)
—Autumn Leaves: Complete Set. (p. 118)
—Autumn Leaves: Classroom Library Set. (p. 118)
—Aztec, Maya, & Inca (p. 122)
—Aztec People: Level I (p. 122)
—Babies: Collection 1. (p. 123)
—Bad News Good News: Level N (p. 132)
—Bats about Bats! Level M (p. 145)
—Bazaar (p. 147)
—Benjamin Franklin: Man of Words & Wisdom (p. 165)
—Black Tooth the Pirate: Level G (p. 197)
—Blow your Top: Magazine Anthology: Level 6 (p. 202)
—Bobcat Level: Lesson Plan Set. (p. 206)
—Bobcat Level: Adventure Journal Set. (p. 206)
—Bobcat Level: Wildcats Bobcat Complete Kit. (p. 206)
—Book2web Sets: History Each of 12 Titles, Teacher Guide, Storage Unit. (p. 212)
—Book2web Sets: Geography Each of 12 Titles, Teacher Guide, Storage Unit. (p. 212)
—Book2web Sets: Famous People Each of 12 Titles, Teacher Guide, Storage Unit. (p. 212)
—Book2web Sets: Complete Set - 6 Each of 72 Titles, 6 Teacher Guides, 6 Storage Units. (p. 212)
—Book2web Sets: Earth & Physical Science Each of 12 Titles, Teacher Guide, Storage Unit. (p. 212)
—Bugs don't Bug Me: Level K (p. 237)
—Building the Railroads (p. 239)
—Burned: Magazine Anthology: Level 7 (p. 244)
—Butterfly: Collection 2. (p. 247)
—Buttons: Collection 1. (p. 248)
—Buzz the Beekeeper: Level 6 (p. 248)
—C & P Pies: Level H (p. 249)
—Calendar: Level G (p. 252)
—Canada Coast to Coast (p. 260)
—Caretakers of the Earth (p. 268)
—Castle Life in the Middle Ages (p. 277)
—Cat Culture: Level O (p. 277)
—Cats: Collection 4. (p. 281)
—Celebrating the New Year: Level I (p. 285)
—Cheetah Conservation: Level P (p. 296)
—Chinampa: Level I (p. 307)
—Cold Facts about Ice Ages (p. 338)
—Como nos Transportamos (p. 351)
—Complete Level Sets: Level 3 Complete Set. (p. 353)
—Complete Level Sets: Level 4 Complete Set. (p. 353)
—Complete Level Sets: Level 5 Complete Set. (p. 353)
—Complete Level Sets: Level 6 Complete Set. (p. 353)
—Complete Level Sets: Level 7 Complete Set. (p. 353)
—Complete Level Sets: Levels 1-2 Complete Set. (p. 353)
—Complete Program Set: Fluency Strand. (p. 353)
—Complete Program Set: Word Work Strand. (p. 353)
—Complete Program Set: Comprehension Strand. (p. 353)
—Complete Program Set. (p. 353)
—Comprehension: Level 1. (p. 354)
—Comprehension: Level 2. (p. 354)
—Comprehension: Level 3. (p. 354)
—Comprehension: Level 5. (p. 354)
—Comprehension: Level 6. (p. 354)
—Comprehension: Level 7. (p. 354)
—Comprehension Evaluation: Evaluation Guides: Level 2. (p. 354)
—Comprehension Placement Assessment. (p. 354)
—Comprehension Teacher Guide: Teacher Guides: Level 4. (p. 354)
—Cougar Level: Lesson Plan. Set (p. 369)
—Cougar Level: Adventure Journal. Set (p. 369)
—Cougar Level: Wildcats Cougar Complete Kit. (p. 369)
—Crazy Adventurers: Magazine Anthology: Level 6 (p. 377)
—Creature Talk (p. 380)
—Crias de Los Animales (p. 382)
—Day to Remember: Level I (p. 414)
—D-Man & Beans: Complete Set. (p. 398)
—D-Man & Beans: Classroom Library Set. (p. 398)
—D-Man's Escape (p. 398)
—Dog-Sled Racer: Level 5 (p. 461)
—Dom's Dragon: Level E (p. 465)
—Donde Vive la Gente (p. 466)
—Donde Viven Algunos Animales (p. 466)
—Don't Go Out: Level F (p. 467)
—Double Dare. (p. 472)
—Dreams of Flight (p. 484)
—Early Emergent Guided Reading Kit 1: Complete Kit. (p. 493)
—Early Emergent Guided Reading Kit 1: Lesson Plans. (p. 493)
—Early Emergent Guided Reading Kit 1: Student Books. (p. 493)
—Early Emergent Guided Reading Kit 4: Student Books (p. 493)
—Early Emergent Guided Reading Kit 4: Lesson Plans. Vol. 4 (p. 493)
—Early Fluency Guided Reading Kit 1: Lesson Plans. (p. 493)
—Early Fluency Guided Reading Kit 1: Student Books. (p. 493)
—Early Fluency Guided Reading Kit 5: Lesson Plans (p. 493)
—Early Fluency Guided Reading Kit 5: Student Books (p. 493)
—Early Fluency Kit 1: Complete Kit. (p. 493)
—Early Fluency Kit 1: Lesson Plans. (p. 493)
—Early Fluency Kit 1: Student Books. (p. 493)
—Early Fluency-Fluency Writing Kit. (p. 493)
—Earth & Physical Science: Color & Light (p. 495)
—Earth & Physical Science: Our Solar System (p. 495)
—Earth & Physical Science: Exploring Electricity (p. 495)
—Earthquakes: The Earth-Shaking Facts (p. 497)
—Earthworms: Level E (p. 498)
—Emergent Writing Kit. (p. 518)
—Erosion de la Tierra (p. 534)
—E-search: Level O (p. 492)
—Europe's Many Cultures (p. 540)
—Explorers: Fluency - Complete Kit. (p. 551)
—Explorers Fluency Complete Kit 2 (p. 551)
—Famous Shipwrecks (p. 569)
—FDR & Eleanor: Triumphs & Tragedies (p. 578)
—Fibonacci's Cows: Level O (p. 583)
—Fire at the Museum: Decodable Books (p. 590)
—Fire at the Museum Play 11: Decodable Plays (p. 590)
—First Explorers: Upper Emergent - Complete Kit. (p. 594)
—First Explorers: Student Book Set - 1 Each of 12 Titles. (p. 594)
—First Explorers: Upper Emergent-Early Fluency - Complete Kit. (p. 594)
—First Explorers: Upper Emergent - Lesson Plan Set - 1 Each of 12 Lesson Plans. (p. 594)
—First Explorers: Upper Emergent-Early Fluency - Student Book Set - 1 Each of 12 Titles. (p. 594)
—First Explorers: Upper Emergent-Early Fluency - Lesson Plan Set - 1 Each of 12 Lesson Plans. (p. 594)
—Five Little Frogs: Collection 1. (p. 600)
—Fluency Guided Reading Kit 3: Lesson Plans Vol. 3 (p. 608)
—Fluency Guided Reading Kit 3: Student Books Vol. 3 (p. 608)
—Fluency Teacher Guide: Level 2 (p. 608)
—Fluency Teacher Guide: Level 3 (p. 608)
—Fluency Teacher Guide: Level 4 (p. 608)
—Fluency Teacher Guide: Level 5 (p. 608)
—Fluency Teacher Guide: Level 6 (p. 608)
—Fluency Teacher Guide: Level 7 (p. 608)
—Forces of Nature: Level K (p. 617)
—Formas de Moverse (p. 620)
—Fossils Reveal Clues about Ancient Life (p. 624)
—Found & Lost (p. 624)
—Frederick Douglass: A Voice for Civil Rights (p. 633)
—Friend in the Wild: Level Q (p. 637)
—From Plan to House: Level H (p. 643)
—Fuerzas de la Naturaleza (p. 646)
—Fun with Fizz & Frost: Level O (p. 648)
—Gear Up! Early Fluency - Complete Kit (p. 659)
—Gear Up! Early Emergent - Complete Kit (p. 659)
—Gear Up!: Upper Emergent - Complete Kit. Vol. 3 (p. 659)
—Gear Up! Upper Emergent- Student Book Each of 16 Titles. (p. 659)
—Gear Up! Early Emergent - 1 Each of 8 Student Books: Level A. (p. 659)
—Gear Up!: Early Emergent - Gear up! for Guided Reading. Vol. 2 (p. 659)
—Gear Up! Early Emergent - Student Book Set - 1 Each of 16 Titles (p. 659)
—Gear Up!: Early Emergent - Gear up! Guided Reading Overview. Vol. 2 (p. 659)
—Gear Up! Early Emergent - Lesson Plan Set - 1 Each of 16 Lesson Plans (p. 659)
—Gear Up!: Early Fluency - Student Book Set - 1 Each of 16 Titles. Vol. 2 (p. 659)
—Gear Up!: Upper Emergent - Student Book Set - 1 Each of 16 Titles. Vol. 3 (p. 659)
—Gear Up! Upper Emergent-Early Fluency - 1 Each of 8 Student Books: Level J. (p. 659)
—Gear Up!: Early Fluency - Lesson Plan Set - 1 Each of 16 Lesson Plans. Vol. 2 (p. 659)
—Gear Up!: Upper Emergent - Lesson Plan Set - 1 Each of 16 Lesson Plans. Vol. 3 (p. 659)
—Geography: Central & South America (p. 662)
—George Washington: A Quiet Leader (p. 664)
—Ger Up! Upper Emergent - 1 Each of 8 Student Books: Level E. (p. 666)
—Going Places: Level I (p. 693)
—Gourmet Delights (p. 704)
—Great Aviators Take Flight (p. 713)
—Groovy Gran & the Karaoke Kid: Level S (p. 725)
—Guided Reading Kits: Early Emergent Kit 1 (Lesson Plans) (p. 730)
—Guided Reading Kits: Upper Emergent Kit 1 (Lesson Plans) (p. 730)
—Guided Reading Kits: Upper Emergent Kit 1 (Student Books) (p. 730)
—Guided Reading Kits: Upper Emergent Kit 2 (Lesson Plans) Vol. 2 (p. 730)
—Guided Reading Kits: Upper Emergent Kit 3 (Lesson Plans) Vol. 3 (p. 730)
—Guided Reading Kits: Upper Emergent Kit 4 (Lesson Plans) Vol. 4 (p. 730)
—Guided Reading Kits: Early Emergent Kit 2: Student Books. Vol. 2 (p. 730)
—Guided Reading Kits: Early Emergent Kit 4: Student Books. Vol. 4 (p. 730)
—Guided Reading Kits: Upper Emergent Kit 1: Student Books. (p. 730)
—Guided Reading Kits: Upper Emergent Kit 3: Student Books. Vol. 3 (p. 730)
—Heat: Level F (p. 760)
—Helen Keller: Level 3 (p. 763)
—History: World War I (p. 783)
—History: World War II (p. 783)
—History: The Civil War (p. 783)
—History: The Oregon Trail (p. 783)
—History: Revolutionary War (p. 783)
—History: Space Exploration (p. 783)
—Holly's Birthday Cake: Collection 2. (p. 789)
—How not to Catch the Moon: Level L (p. 811)
—Humpback Tedy: Level E (p. 827)
—I am the Walrus: Level N (p. 834)
—I Dig Dinosaurs: Level K (p. 837)
—I Want Some Honey: Level E (p. 847)
—In the Rain Forest (p. 867)
—Inventors Create Tomorrow (p. 884)
—Klutzy Cat: Level N (p. 964)
—Lagunas y Rios (p. 971)
—Lazy Moon: Level G (p. 981)
—Legends of the Wild West: Level O (p. 990)
—Leopard Level: Lesson Plan Set. (p. 993)
—Leopard Level: Adventure Journal Set. (p. 993)
—Leopard Level: Wildcats Leopard Complete Kit. (p. 993)
—Let's make a Pinata: Collection 4. (p. 999)
—Lewis & Clark: Mapping the West (p. 1004)
—Life in the Deserts (p. 1011)
—Lights Out! 6 Each of 1 Anthology (p. 1016)
—Lion Level: Lesson Plan Set. (p. 1020)
—Lion Level: Adventure Journal Set. (p. 1020)
—Lion Level: Wildcats Lion Complete Kit. (p. 1020)
—Magic Shoes: Level N (p. 1073)
—Magnificent Masks: 6 Each of 1 Anthology (p. 1076)
—Make a Raft: Level E (p. 1078)
—Make, Bake, Take: Collection 2. (p. 1079)
—Make me Laugh! 6 Each of 1 Anthology (p. 1079)
—Making Sense of Sound & Music (p. 1082)
—Maps: Level I (p. 1090)
—Materials Que Hay en la Tierra (p. 1104)
—Measuring: Collection 2. (p. 1117)
—Mexico: Land of Old & New (p. 1131)
—Mira Hacia el Cielo (p. 1148)
—Mischief & Mayhem: Level O (p. 1150)
—Mosquito Attack: Level 4 (p. 1176)
—Mountain Majesty (p. 1181)
—Mountain Peaks: Complete Set. (p. 1181)
—Mountain Peaks: Classroom Library Set. (p. 1181)
—Mouse Mapper: Level I (p. 1182)
—Move it & Shake It! 6 Each of 1 Anthology (p. 1183)
—Movie Magic (p. 1183)
—Mundo de Las Plantas (p. 1191)
—Music Scene (p. 1193)
—My School, Your School: Level E (p. 1218)
—My Word! what a Bird! Collection 4. (p. 1221)
—New House: Level H (p. 1245)
—No Hay Nadie Como Tu (p. 1258)
—No Room, New Rules (p. 1260)
—Nuestros Cinco Sentidos (p. 1270)
—On the Move: Level H (p. 1291)
—On the Prowl: 6 Each of 1 Anthology (p. 1291)
—On-the-Mark Assessment Kits: Early & Upper Emergent - Nonfiction Set. (p. 1291)
—On-the-Mark Assessment Kits: Early Fluency & Fluency - Nonfiction Set. (p. 1291)
—Opposites: Collection 4. (p. 1300)
—Our World's Oceans (p. 1310)
—Outback School: Level E (p. 1312)
—Panther Level: Lesson Plan Set. (p. 1321)
—Panther Level: Adventure Journal Set. (p. 1321)
—Panther Level: Wildcats Panther Complete Kit. (p. 1321)
—Paper Capers: Level N (p. 1322)
—Para Que Construye el Hombre (p. 1323)
—Party: Collection 1. (p. 1325)
—Pat's Picture: Level E (p. 1329)
—People on the Path Toward Human Rights (p. 1339)
—Pet Show: Collection 4. (p. 1345)
—Phonics & Word Study Complete Kits: Phonics & Word Study: Level A. (p. 1352)
—Picture This! 6 Each of 1 Anthology (p. 1356)
—Pigeon Princess: Level O (p. 1357)
—Pixels & Paint (p. 1365)
—Plagues: Magazine Anthology: Level 7 (p. 1366)
—Planet Race: Level F (p. 1368)
—Planets: Level F (p. 1368)
—Playground Chant: Collection 1. (p. 1372)
—Por Que se Mueven Las Cosas (p. 1385)
—Possibilities (p. 1387)
—Puppets: 6 Each of 1 Anthology (p. 1417)
—Queen of the Trail Play 8: Decodable Plays (p. 1425)
—Raging Rivers: Complete Set. (p. 1433)
—Raging Rivers: Classroom Library Set. (p. 1433)
—Reading Recovery Kits: Reading Recovery Complete Set. (p. 1446)
—Ready, Set, Pop! Collection 3. (p. 1447)
—River Wild: 6 Each of 1 Anthology (p. 1476)
—Riverboat Bill: Level H (p. 1476)
—Rivers: Level H (p. 1476)
—Rivers: From Beginning to End (p. 1476)
—Rocks & Minerals Tell Earth's Story (p. 1483)
—Rollers & Blades: Level H (p. 1485)
—Roma Roller Skater: Level H (p. 1485)
—Samantha's Sea: Level Q (p. 1507)
—Sand: Collection 3. (p. 1510)
—Savage Storms: Tornadoes & Hurricanes (p. 1516)
—Saws Don't Pounce Play 9: Decodable Plays (p. 1518)
—Secret Socer Ball Maker: Level G (p. 1544)
—Secrets & Strays (p. 1544)
—Seiko the Watchdog: Level N (p. 1548)
—Set 1: Los Alimentos (p. 1553)
—Set 2: La Luz (p. 1553)
—Set 2: Los Dinosaurios (p. 1553)
—Sign Language Alphabet Cards. (p. 1574)
—Sky Colors: Collection 3. (p. 1586)
—Slimed! 6 Each of 1 Anthology (p. 1590)
—So You Want this Job, do You? Magazine Anthology: Level 6 (p. 1602)
—SoCer: Level I (p. 1604)
—Song Box Social Studies Songs: 1 Each of 4 Big Books. (p. 1611)
—Song Box Social Studies Songs: 1 Each of 4 Cassettes. (p. 1611)
—Song Box Social Studies Songs: 1 Each of 4 Student Books. (p. 1611)
—Song Box Social Studies Songs: 6 Each of 4 Student Books. (p. 1611)
—Sonido (p. 1612)
—Speed: Magazine Anthology: Level 6 (p. 1624)
—Spider & Buffalo: Level N (p. 1626)
—Stories on Stage (p. 1655)
—Story Box: Early Fluency - Student Book Set - 1 Each of 16 Titles. (p. 1657)
—Story Box: Upper Emergent - Lesson Plan Set - 1 Each of 16 Lesson Plans (p. 1657)

G

—Story Box: Early Emergent Kit 3- Lesson Plan Set - 1 Each of 16 Lesson Plans. Vol. 3 (p. 1657)
—Story Box, Leveled Books. (p. 1657)
—Storyteller: Upper Emergent - Complete Kit (p. 1663)
—Storyteller: Early Emergent - Complete Kit. Vol. 2 (p. 1663)
—Storyteller: Upper Emergent - Upper Emergent - Complete Kit (p. 1663)
—Storyteller: Early Emergent - 1 Each of 3 Student Books: Level A. (p. 1663)
—Storyteller: Early Emergent - 1 Each of 16 Student Books: Level D. (p. 1663)
—Storyteller: Upper Emergent - 1 Each of 14 Student Books: Level G. (p. 1663)
—Storyteller: Upper Emergent - Lesson Plan Set - 1 Each of 16 Lesson Plans. (p. 1663)
—Storyteller: Upper Emergent-Early Fluency - 1 Each of 4 Student Books: Level K. (p. 1663)
—Storyteller: Upper Emergent-Early Fluency - 1 Each of 14 Student Books: Level I. (p. 1663)
—Storyteller: Early Emergent - Lesson Plan Set - 1 Each of 16 Lesson Plans. Vol. 2 (p. 1663)
—Storyteller: Upper Emergent - Student Book Set - 1 Each of 16 Fiction & Nonfiction Titles. (p. 1663)
—Storyteller: Early Emergent - Student Book Set - 1 Each of 16 Fiction & Nonfiction Titles. (p. 1663)
—Storyteller: Early Emergent - Student Book Set - 1 Each of 16 Fiction & Nonfiction Titles. (p. 1663)
—Storyteller: Early Emergent - Student Book Set - 1 Each of Fiction & Nonfiction Titles. Vol. 2 (p. 1663)
—Storyteller Chapter Books: Fluency - 1 Each of 2 Title: Level U. (p. 1663)
—Storyteller Chapter Books: Fluency - 1 Each of 2 Titles: Level R. (p. 1663)
—Storyteller Chapter Books: Early Fluency-Fluency - 1 Each of 4 Titles: Level P. (p. 1663)
—Storyteller Chapter Books: Early Fluency-Fluency - 1 Each of 10 Titles: Level O. (p. 1663)
—Storyteller Chapter Books: Upper Emergent-Early Fluency - 1 Each of 4 Titles: Level J. (p. 1663)
—Storyteller Chapter Books: Upper Emergent-Early Fluency - 1 Each of 18 Titles: Level M. (p. 1663)
—Storyteller Early Emergent Guided Reading Complete Kit 1. (p. 1663)
—Storyteller Early Emergent Guided Reading Kit 1 Lesson Plans. (p. 1663)
—Storyteller Upper Emergent Guided Reading Complete Kit 2 (p. 1664)
—Storyteller Upper Emergent Guided Reading Complete Kit 1. (p. 1664)
—Storyteller Upper Emergent Guided Reading Kit (p. 1664)
—Storyteller Upper Emergent Guided Reading Kit: 4 Lesson Plans (p. 1664)
—Storyteller Upper Emergent Guided Reading Kit 1 Lesson Plans. (p. 1664)
—Storyteller Upper Emergent Guided Reading Kit 2 (p. 1664)
—Storyteller Upper Emergent Guided Reading Kit 2 Lesson Plans (p. 1664)
—Stranger Than Fiction: 6 Each of 1 Anthology (p. 1665)
—Summer Skies: Complete Set. (p. 1675)
—Summer Skies: Classroom Library Set. (p. 1675)
—Sunshine: Early Emergent - Complete Kit. (p. 1677)
—Sunshine: Early Emergent - Group 3:1 Each of 4 Student Books: Level B. (p. 1677)
—Sunshine: Early Emergent - Group 3: 1 Each of 4 Student Books: Level A. (p. 1677)
—Sunshine: Early Fluency - Enrichment Library: 1 each of 5 titles: Level N. (p. 1677)
—Sunshine: Early Fluency - Enrichment Library: 1 each of 12 titles: Level L. (p. 1677)
—Sunshine: Early Emergent-Upper Emergent - Group 2: 1 Each of 8 Student Books: Level E. (p. 1677)
—Sunshine: Early Emergent-Upper Emergent - Groups 1-2: 1 Each of 16 Student Books: Level E. (p. 1677)
—Sunshine: Fluency-Group 3: 1 each of 6 Titles: Level P. (p. 1678)
—Sunshine: Fluency - Group 3: 1 Each of 4 Titles: Level S. (p. 1678)
—Sunshine: Early Fluency-Group 3: 1 each of 8 Titles: Level L. (p. 1678)
—Sunshine: Early Fluency-Group 1; 1 each of 11 titles: Level N. (p. 1678)
—Sunshine: Early Fluency - Group 3: 1 each of 8 Titles: Level K. (p. 1678)
—Sunshine: Early Fluency - Group 1: 1 each of 11 titles: Level K. (p. 1678)
—Sunshine: Early Fluency-Groups 1-2; 1 each of 17 titles: Level N. (p. 1678)
—Sunshine: Early Fluency - Groups 1-2: 1 each of 17 titles: Level K. (p. 1678)
—Sunshine: Upper Emergent-Group 2: 1 each of 5 student books: Level J. (p. 1678)
—Sunshine: Upper Emergent - Group 3:1 Each of 6 Student Books: Level G. (p. 1678)
—Sunshine: Upper Emergent-Group 3: 1 each of 10 student books: Level I. (p. 1678)
—Sunshine: Upper Emergent-Group 3: 1 each of 12 Student Books: Level N. (p. 1678)
—Sunshine: Early Fluency-Enrichment Library; 1 each of 7 titles: Level M. (p. 1678)
—Sunshine: Upper Emergent-Nonfiction: 1 each of 3 student books: Level H. (p. 1678)
—Sunshine: Upper Emergent - Nonfiction:1 Each of 3 Student Books: Level G. (p. 1678)
—Sunshine: Upper Emergent-Groups 1-2: 1 each of 16 student books: Level I. (p. 1678)
—Sunshine: Upper Emergent - Groups 1-2:1 Each of 15 Student Books: Level F. (p. 1678)
—Sunshine: Upper Emergent - Group 1:1 Each of 8 Student Books: Level G. Group 1. (p. 1678)
—Sunshine: Upper Emergent - Group 2: 1 Each of 8 Student Books: Level G. Group 1. (p. 1678)
—Sunshine: Upper Emergent-Enrichment Library: 1 each of 5 student books: Level J. (p. 1678)

—Sunshine: Early Fluency - Enrichment Library, Groups 1-2: 1 each of 11 titles: Level K. (p. 1678)
—SUNSHINE Early Emergent Guided Reading Kit 4 (p. 1678)
—SUNSHINE Early Fluency Guided Reading Kit 5 (p. 1678)
—SUNSHINE Fluency Guided Reading Kit 3 (p. 1678)
—Sunshine Upper Emergent Guided Reading Kit 5 (p. 1679)
—Survival in Cyberspace: Level T (p. 1686)
—Take Twos: Fluency - 1 Each of 4 Titles: Level S. (p. 1697)
—Take Twos: Upper Emergent - 1 Each of 8 Titles: Level E. (p. 1697)
—Take Twos: Fluency - Group 1: 1 each of 12 Titles: Level R. (p. 1697)
—Take Twos: Fluency - Group 1: 1 each of 6 Lesson Plans: Level R. (p. 1697)
—Take Twos: Upper Emergent - Level H: 1 Each of 4 Lesson Plans: Level H. (p. 1697)
—Take-Twos: Fluency - 1 each of 12 Titles: Level O. (p. 1697)
—Take-Twos: Upper Emergent - 1 Each of 10 Titles: Level J. (p. 1697)
—Take-Twos: Fluency - Group 1; 1 each of 12 Titles: Level P. (p. 1697)
—Take-Twos: Fluency - Group 2; 1 Each of 4 (New) Titles: Level P. (p. 1697)
—Take-Twos: Fluency - Groups 1 & 2; 1 Each of 16 Titles: Level P. (p. 1697)
—Take-Twos Adventure: Fluency - Complete Kit. Vol. 3 (p. 1697)
—Take-Twos Adventure: Fluency - Student Book Set - 1 Each of 12 Titles. Vol. 3 (p. 1697)
—Take-Twos Adventure: Fluency - Lesson Plan Set - 1 Each of 6 Lesson Plans. Vol. 3 (p. 1697)
—Take-Twos Animals: Early Fluency - Complete Kit (p. 1697)
—Take-Twos Animals: Early Fluency - Student Book Set - 1 Each of 12 Titles. Vol. 4 (p. 1697)
—Take-Twos Animals: Early Fluency - Lesson Plan Set - 1 Each of 6 Lesson Plans. Vol. 4 (p. 1697)
—Take-Twos Circles & Cycles: Upper Emergent - Upper Emergent - Complete Kit. Vol. 2 (p. 1697)
—Take-Twos Circles & Cycles: Upper Emergent - Student Book Set 1 Each of 12 Titles. Vol. 2 (p. 1697)
—Take-Twos Circles & Cycles: Upper Emergent - Lesson Plan Set - 1 Each of 16 Lesson Plans. Vol. 2 (p. 1697)
—Take-Twos Cultures: Upper Emergent - Complete Kit. (p. 1697)
—Take-Twos Cultures: Upper Emergent - Student Book Set - 1 Each of 12 Titles. (p. 1697)
—Take-Twos Cultures: Upper Emergent - Lesson Plan Set - 1 Each of 16 Lesson Plans. (p. 1697)
—Take-Twos Earth Links: Upper Emergent - Complete Kit. Vol. 3 (p. 1697)
—Take-Twos Earth Links: Upper Emergent - Student Book Set - 1 Each of 12 Titles. Vol. 3 (p. 1697)
—Take-Twos Earth Links: Upper Emergent - Lesson Plan Set - 1 Each of 16 Lesson Plans. Vol. 3 (p. 1697)
—Take-Twos Finding Out: Fluency - Complete Kit. Vol. 6 (p. 1697)
—Take-Twos Finding Out: Fluency - Student Book Set - 1 Each of 12 Titles. Vol. 6 (p. 1697)
—Take-Twos Finding Out: Fluency - Lesson Plan Set - 1 Each of 6 Lesson Plans. Vol. 6 (p. 1697)
—Take-Twos Land & Air: Early Fluency - Complete Kit (p. 1697)
—Take-Twos Land & Air: Early Fluency - Student Book Set - 1 Each of 12 Titles. (p. 1697)
—Take-Twos Land & Air: Early Fluency - Lesson Plan Set - 1 Each of 6 Lesson Plans. (p. 1697)
—Take-Twos Making Things: Early Fluency - Complete Kit. Vol. 3 (p. 1697)
—Take-Twos Making Things: Early Fluency - Student Book Set - 1 Each of 12 Titles. Vol. 3 (p. 1697)
—Take-Twos Making Things: Early Fluency - Lesson Plan Set - 1 Each of 6 Lesson Plans. Vol. 3 (p. 1697)
—Take-Twos Old to New: Fluency - Complete Kit. Vol. 4 (p. 1697)
—Take-Twos Old to New: Fluency - Student Book Set - 1 Each of 12 Titles. Vol. 4 (p. 1697)
—Take-Twos Old to New: Fluency - Lesson Plan Set - 1 Each of 6 Lesson Plans. Vol. 4 (p. 1697)
—Take-Twos Play Time: Upper Emergent - Upper Emergent - Complete Kit. Vol. 4 (p. 1697)
—Take-Twos Play Time: Upper Emergent - Student Book Set - 1 Each of 12 Titles. Vol. 4 (p. 1697)
—Take-Twos Play Time: Upper Emergent - Lesson Plan Set - 1 Each of 16 Lesson Plans. Vol. 4 (p. 1697)
—Take-Twos Slither, Swim, & Soar: Fluency - Complete Kit. (p. 1697)
—Take-Twos Slither, Swim, & Soar: Fluency - Student Book Set - 1 Each of 12 Titles. (p. 1697)
—Take-Twos Slither, Swim, & Soar: Fluency - Lesson Plan Set - 1 Each of 6 Lesson Plans. (p. 1697)
—Take-Twos Social Studies: Fluency - Complete Kit. Vol. 2 (p. 1697)
—Take-Twos Social Studies: Fluency - Student Book Set - 1 Each of 12 Titles. Vol. 2 (p. 1697)
—Take-Twos Social Studies: Fluency - Lesson Plan Set - 1 Each of 6 Lesson Plans. Vol. 2 (p. 1697)
—Take-Twos Sports: Early Fluency - Complete Kit. Vol. 2 (p. 1697)
—Take-Twos Sports: Early Fluency - Student Book Set - 1 Each of 12 Titles. Vol. 2 (p. 1697)
—Take-Twos Sports: Early Fluency - Lesson Plan Set - 1 Each of 6 Lesson Plans. Vol. 2 (p. 1697)
—Take-Twos Stories & Legends: Fluency - Complete Kit. Vol. 5 (p. 1697)
—Take-Twos Stories & Legends: Fluency - Student Book Set - 1 Each of 12 Titles. Vol. 5 (p. 1697)
—Take-Twos Stories & Legends: Fluency - Lesson Plan Set - 1 Each of 6 Lesson Plans. Vol. 5 (p. 1697)
—Teacher Guide: History (p. 1709)
—Teacher Guide: Famous People (p. 1709)
—Teeth: Level G (p. 1715)
—Tiger Level: Lesson Plan Set. (p. 1748)
—Tiger Level: Adventure Journal Set. (p. 1748)
—Tiger Level: Wildcats Tiger Complete Kit. (p. 1748)
—Toys, Then & Now: Level E (p. 1774)

—Tropical Treasure: The Rain Forest (p. 1789)
—Turtle: Collection 2. (p. 1798)
—Turtles, Tortoises & Terrapins: Level M (p. 1799)
—Tv Times: 6 Each of 1 Anthology (p. 1799)
—Twentieth-Century Explorers (p. 1801)
—Twig Books: Student Book Set - 1 Each of 16 Titles. (p. 1801)
—Twig Books: Early Emergent - 1 each of 16 student books: Level A. (p. 1801)
—Twig Books: Upper Emergent - 1 each of 16 student books: Level F. (p. 1801)
—Twig Books: Upper Emergent - Student Book Set -1 Each of 16 Titles. Vol. 4 (p. 1801)
—Twig Books: Upper Emergent - Student Book Set - 1 Each of 16 Titles. Vol. 3 (p. 1801)
—Twig Books: Upper Emergent - Upper Emergent - 1 each of 16 student books: Level D. (p. 1801)
—Under the Sea (p. 1814)
—United States Coast to Coast (p. 1819)
—Upper Emergent Guided Reading Complete Kit 1. (p. 1825)
—Upper Emergent Guided Reading Kit 1: Lesson Plans. (p. 1825)
—Upper Emergent Guided Reading Kit 1: Student Books. (p. 1825)
—Upper Emergent Guided Reading Kit 2: Lesson Plans Vol. 2 (p. 1825)
—Upper Emergent Guided Reading Kit 2: Student Books Vol. 2 (p. 1825)
—Upper Emergent Guided Reading Kit 5: Lesson Plans Vol. 5 (p. 1825)
—Upper Emergent Guided Reading Kit 5: Student Books Vol. 5 (p. 1825)
—Upper Emergent Guided Reading Kit 6: Lesson Plans Vol. 6 (p. 1825)
—Upper Emergent Guided Reading Kit 6: Student Books Vol. 6 (p. 1825)
—Upper Emergent Kit 1: Complete Kit. (p. 1825)
—Upper Emergent Kit 1: Lesson Plans. (p. 1825)
—Upper Emergent Kit 2: Complete Kit Vol. 2 (p. 1825)
—Upper Emergent Kit 2: Lesson Plans Vol. 2 (p. 1825)
—Upper Emergent Kit 2: Student Books Vol. 2 (p. 1825)
—Vegetarians: Level H (p. 1834)
—Vida de Los Insectos (p. 1840)
—Vida en el Oceano (p. 1840)
—Vida en la Selva Tropical (p. 1840)
—Volcanoes: The Hottest Spots on Earth (p. 1849)
—Washington D. C. Heartbeat of a Nation (p. 1860)
—Waves: Collection 3. (p. 1864)
—Wear your Art: 6 Each of 1 Anthology (p. 1869)
—Welcome to the Big Top: 6 Each of 1 Anthology (p. 1873)
—What If? Collection 4. (p. 1887)
—What Sport Is It? Collection 3. (p. 1893)
—Where in the World? Collection 3. (p. 1908)
—Whispering Pines: Complete Set. (p. 1912)
—Whispering Pines: Classroom Library Set. (p. 1912)
—Who Is Tuffy 2000? (p. 1916)
—Why Things Change? (p. 1926)
—Wildcats Strand Kits: People & Places Strand. (p. 1931)
—Wildcats Strand Kits: Sports & Action Strand. (p. 1931)
—Wildcats Strand Kits: Animals & Nature Strand. (p. 1931)
—Wildcats Strand Kits: Arts & Entertainment Strand. (p. 1931)
—Wildcats Strand Kits: Science & Technology Strand. (p. 1931)
—Wildcats Strand Kits: Myths & Misconceptions Strand. (p. 1931)
—Winter Weather: Collection 2. (p. 1938)
—Wolf Master: Level R (p. 1944)
—Wonder World: Early Fluency - Student Book Set - 1 Each of 16 Titles. (p. 1947)
—Wonder World: Upper Emergent - Student Book Set - 1 Each of 16 Titles. (p. 1947)
—Wonder World: Early Emergent - Student Book Set - 1 Each of 16 Titles. (p. 1947)
—Wonder World Complete Sets: Math Set - 1 Each of 30 Titles. (p. 1947)
—Wonder World Complete Sets: Science Set - 1 Each of 97 Titles. (p. 1947)
—Wonder World Complete Sets: Social Studies Set - 1 Each of 73 Titles. (p. 1947)
—Wonder World Early & Upper Emergent Sets: Math Set - 1 Each of 20 Titles. (p. 1947)
—Wonder World Early & Upper Emergent Sets: Science Set - 1 Each of 49 Titles. (p. 1947)
—Wonder World Early & Upper Emergent Sets: Social Studies Set - 1 Each of 43 Titles. (p. 1947)
—Wonder World Early Fluency & Fluency: Math Set - 1 Each of 10 Titles. (p. 1947)
—Wonder World Early Fluency & Fluency: Science Set - 1 Each of 48 Titles. (p. 1947)
—Wonder World Early Fluency & Fluency: Social Studies Set - 1 Each of 30 Titles. (p. 1947)
—Word Word Word Study. (p. 1951)
—Working Like a Dog: 6 Each of 1 Anthology (p. 1953)
—World Leaders through the Ages (p. 1956)
—Worm Farm: Level E (p. 1961)
—Wright Skills: Level A Sets - Short Vowels only: 1 Each of 19 Titles. (p. 1963)
—Wright Skills: Level B Sets - 1 Each of 40 Titles (includes long Vowels) (p. 1963)
—Wright Skills: Level B Sets - 6 Each of 40 Titles (includes long Vowels) (p. 1963)
—Wright Skills: Level A Sets - 1 Each of 40 Titles (includes Short Vowels) (p. 1963)
—Wright Skills: Level A Sets - 6 Each of 40 Titles (includes Short Vowels) (p. 1963)
—Young & Wild: 6 Each of 1 Anthology (p. 1978)
—Zoo Tales: 6 Each of 1 Anthology (p. 1989)
Grout, Claire. Emil & Ordi: Friends for All Time. (p. 518)
Grout, Paul A., illus. see Windeatt, Mary F.
Grout, Phil. Harvest of Hope. (p. 751)
Grove, Christine, illus. see Bardaus, Anna W.
Grove, Christine, illus. see Snead, Kathi.
Grove, Craig J. Frog Water. (p. 640)
Grove, Ella. Surprise for Tommy. (p. 1686)
Grove, Gladys, illus. see Gonder, Glen W.

Grove, Linda, ed. see Hamashita, Takeshi.
Grove, Malachai. Malachai Grove Plunt Solinairy: The Song of Malachai. (p. 1083)
—Return of Malachai. (p. 1464)
Grove, Philip D., et al. World War II: The War at Sea. (p. 1959)
Grove, S. E. Glass Sentence. (p. 682)
—Golden Specific. (p. 695)
Grove, Tim. First Flight Around the World: The Adventures of the American Fliers Who Won the Race. (p. 595)
—Transportation. Gerdes, Louise, ed. (p. 1779)
Grover, Jan. Free Speech. (p. 634)
Grover, Jan & Gerdes, Louise. Transportation. (p. 1779)
Grover, Jan Zita. Home for Dakota. (p. 792)
Grover, Kuloa A. Charlie the Snake. (p. 293)
Grover, Lorie Ann. Big Hug for Little Cub. Kightley, Rosalinda, illus. (p. 181)
—Hold Me Tight. (p. 787)
—Loose Threads. (p. 1052)
—On Pointe. (p. 1289)
Grover, Neha Lamba. Shaurya's Adventures. (p. 1563)
Grover, Nina, illus. see Graham, Pat, et al.
Groves. Ant Eggs. (p. 88)
—Back to School (p. 130)
—Bee & the Sea (p. 157)
—Best Duster Bk. 5. (p. 169)
—C. P. O. (p. 250)
—Duck in the Box (p. 488)
—Hatching Is Catching. (p. 752)
—Jumpers. (p. 934)
—Knots & Knocks (p. 965)
—Mud Cake (p. 1188)
—Pond Monster (p. 1382)
—Scoop of Plays. (p. 1529)
—Six Silly Plays. (p. 1582)
—Snatch & Grab. (p. 1597)
—Sticky Trousers. (p. 1650)
—Tea Break. (p. 1708)
Groves, Marcia, et al. Science & Technology in the Middle Ages. (p. 1525)
Groves, Marsha. Inventing the Computer. (p. 883)
—Manners & Customs in the Middle Ages. (p. 1088)
—Medieval Projects. (p. 1119)
—Medieval Projects You Can Do! (p. 1119)
Groves, Odessa M. Playful Teeth: Login. (p. 1372)
Grovet, Heather. Beanie, the Horse That Wasn't a Horse. (p. 150)
—Blondie's Big Ride. (p. 200)
—Friend for Zipper. (p. 637)
—Sarah Lee & a Mule Named Maybe. (p. 1514)
—Super Star Problems. (p. 1682)
—What's Wrong with Rusty. (p. 1900)
Grovet, Heather Marie. Marvelous Mark & His No-Good Dog. (p. 1099)
Grozdanovic, Sava, et al. Volleyball for Boys & Girls. (p. 1849)
Grubb, W. B., illus. see Heyliger, William.
Grubbs, Angela. Chosen to Believe. (p. 311)
Grubbs, Darlene. Children of the Ember: World War III (p. 302)
Grube, Edward C. Martin Luther. White, Deborah J., illus. (p. 1097)
—Teens Pray: Conversations with God. (p. 1715)
Grube, George. Church Fathers for Young People Thomas, Michael, illus. (p. 318)
Gruber, Ben. Next Generation (p. 1249)
Gruber, Beth. Ancient Iraq: Archaeology Unlocks the Secrets of Iraq's Past. (p. 69)
—Cheerleading for Fun! (p. 296)
—Gymnastics for Fun! (p. 734)
—Mexico. (p. 1131)
—Snowboarding for Fun! (p. 1600)
Gruber, Beth, et al. Ancient Inca: Archaeology Unlocks the Secrets of the Inca's Past. (p. 69)
Gruber, Daveda. Castle of Ice. (p. 277)
—More Tales of a Tiny Dog. (p. 1175)
—Red Barn & other Short Stories. (p. 1453)
—Tales of a Tiny Dog. (p. 1702)
Gruber Jr., Fernan M. Santa's Reindeer Hay. (p. 1513)
Gruber, Lorin. Journey to Mars. (p. 929)
Gruber, Michael. Legend of the Brog. Gruber, Michael & Graves, Linda, illus. (p. 989)
Gruber, Yehudit. Power of Giving. (p. 1389)
Grubish, Donald. Scenario Paintball: Tips, Tools, & Tactics from the Trenches. (p. 1521)
Grubman, Bonnie. How Do You Get a Mouse to Smile? Van Wright, Cornelius, illus. (p. 808)
Grubnedor Press. Tuppy the Turtle Puppy. (p. 1797)
Grucella, A. J. Prairie Dogs in Danger. (p. 1392)
Grucella, Ann. Bobcats. (p. 206)
Grucella, Cali. Look at Landforms. (p. 1048)
Grucella, Ethan. Cheetahs. (p. 296)
—Hyenas. (p. 831)
—Kanye West. (p. 943)
—Rhinoceroses. (p. 1467)
Grudem, Wayne A., jt. auth. see Poythress, Vern.
Grudina, Paola Bertolina, illus. see Godfrey, Jan.
Grudina, Paola Bertolini, illus. see Howie, Vicki.
Grudina, Paola Bertolini, illus. see Wright, Sally Ann.
Grudina, Paola Bertolini, jt. auth. see Godfrey, Jan.
Grudzina, Douglas, ed. see Hawthorne, Nathaniel.
Grudzina, Douglas, ed. see London, Jack.
Grudzina, Joanne, Rebecca and Tangorra & Benchmark Education Co. Staff. Opinions about the Trail of Tears. (p. 1300)
Grudzina, Rebecca. Baby Bumblebee. Boyer, Lyn, illus. (p. 125)
—Baby Bumblebee for Mommy. Boyer, Lyn, illus. (p. 125)
—Mary, Mary, Quite Contrary. Harrington, David, illus. (p. 1100)
—Pease Porridge, Please! Harrington, David, illus. (p. 1333)
—Red Roses, Blue Violets, And... ? Ledger, Bill, illus. (p. 1455)
Gruebele, Michelle, illus. see Waibel, Stacy Raye.
Gruelle, Johnny. Raggedy Andy Stories. (p. 1433)
—Raggedy Ann & Andy: A Read-Aloud Treasury. (p. 1433)
—Raggedy Ann & Andy & the Camel with the Wrinkled Knees. Moerbeek, Kees, illus. (p. 1433)

For book reviews, descriptive annotations, tables of contents, cover images, author biographies & additional information, updated daily, subscribe to www.booksinprint2.com

2301

—Raggedy Ann & Rags. Palmer, Jan, illus. (p. 1433)
—Raggedy Ann in Cookie Land: (Classic) Gruelle, Johnny, illus. (p. 1433)
—Raggedy Ann Stories. (p. 1433)
Gruelle, Johnny, illus. see Grimm, Jacob & Grimm, Wilhelm K.
Gruelle, Johnny, illus. see Malot, Hector & Crewe-Jones, Florence.
Gruelle, Justin C., illus. see Titchenell, Elsa-Brita.
Gruen, Chuck, illus. see Salter-Mathieson, Nigel C. S.
Gruen, John, photos by see Ronci, Kelli.
Gruen, K. W. Teaching the Message of the Lord's Prayer. (p. 1710)
Gruenbaum, Michael. Somewhere There Is Still a Sun: A Memoir of the Holocaust. (p. 1610)
Gruenbaum, Michael & Hasak-Lowy, Todd. Somewhere There Is Still a Sun: A Memoir of the Holocaust. (p. 1610)
Gruenberg, Leif A. Korean War. (p. 967)
Gruener, Jack, et al. Prisoner B-3087. (p. 1407)
Gruenfelder, Robin, illus. see Olek, Lisa B.
Gruenwald, Mark. Captain America: The Captain. Dwyer, Kieron, illus. (p. 263)
Gruenwald, Mark & Grant, Stephen. Essential Defenders Perlin, Don et al, illus. (p. 536)
Gruffudd, Elena. Gelert. (p. 659)
Gruffudd, Elena & Owen, Carys Eurwen. Clustiau March. (p. 336)
Gruffudd, Garmon, jt. auth. see Ioan, Elwyn.
Gruffudd, Heini. It's Welsh! A Welsh Course for the Young. (p. 899)
Gruffudd, Lefi, jt. auth. see Ioan, Elwyn.
Gruffudd, Robat, tr. see Rogers, Alan.
Gruffydd, Stella. Haws Dweud: Gweithgareddau Lleferedd, Darllen Ac Ysgrifennu I Blant Cyfnod Allweddol 2. (p. 755)
Grumet, Bridget Hall & Baker, Lawrence W. Primary Sources - Reconstruction Era. (p. 1400)
Grummett, Danny. Duffy: The Adventures of a Superdog. (p. 489)
—Duffy Dog's Christmas: A Duffy the Superdog Book. (p. 489)
Grummett, Tom, illus. see Thomas, Rich, Jr.
Grummett, Tom, illus. see Wyatt, Chris.
Grummett, Tom, jt. auth. see Gage, Christos.
Grumpy Cat, Grumpy. Grumpy Cat Coloring Book. (p. 727)
—Grumpy Cat Paper Dolls. (p. 727)
—Grumpy Cat Stickers. (p. 727)
—Grumpy Cat Tattoos. (p. 727)
Grün, Anselm, et al. Legend of Saint Nicholas. Ferri, Giuliano, illus. (p. 988)
Grund, Carol A. Anna Mei, Blessing in Disguise. (p. 85)
—Anna Mei, Cartoon Girl. (p. 85)
—Anna Mei, Escape Artist. (p. 85)
Grunden, Kimberly, illus. see Lockhart, Barbara M.
Grunden, Kimberly, illus. see Morris, Cathy.
Grundon, Holly, jt. auth. see Novelli, Joan.
Grundy, Jessica, illus. see Brooks, Charlie.
Grundy, Peter, illus. see Rogers, Simon.
Gruner, Jessica, jt. auth. see Reger, Rob.
Grunes, Barbara. Wok Every Day: From Fish & Chips to Chocolate Cake, Recipes & Techniques for Steaming, Poaching, Grilling, Deep Frying, Smoking, Braising, & Stir-frying in the World's Most Versatile Pan. Van Vynckt, Virginia & Giblin, Sheri, photos by. (p. 1943)
grunion. Adventures of Poppy the Golf Ball. (p. 21)
Grunke, Julie. You & Me & the King. (p. 1973)
Grunwell, Jeanne Marie. Mind Games. (p. 1145)
Grupo Editorial Norma Staff. Dia Cualquiera. (p. 433)
Grupo Editorial Norma Staff, ed. Chicken Littel - Cuento Clasico. (p. 300)
—Chicken Littel - Gran Coleccion. (p. 300)
—Chicken Little - Libro Con Autoadhesivos. (p. 300)
—Chicken Little - Ultimate Stickers Book. (p. 300)
Gruskin, Edward I. Roy Rogers: Robin Hood of the Range. Hess, Erwin L., illus. (p. 1492)
Gruszka, Chris A., illus. see Christian, Betsy & Christian, George.
Grutzik, Becky, illus. see Barriman, Lydia.
Gruver, Sara. Reading Skills Mini-Lessons. (p. 1446)
Grycan, Julien, jt. auth. see Gasnick, Roy M.
Grylls, Pinny. Very Hopeless Sheepdog. Wellesley, Rosie, illus. (p. 1838)
Gryski, Camilla. Camilla Gryski's Favorite String Games. Sankey, Tom, illus. (p. 256)
Grzelak, Kyle, illus. see Dooley, Larry.
Grzelak, Kyle, illus. see Siebler, Stephanie.
Grzimek, Bernhard & McDade, Melissa C. Birds (p. 191)
—Grzimek's Student Animal Life Resource. (p. 728)
—Mammals (p. 1085)
Gs Troop 1358. Thanksgiving Poem. (p. 1726)
Gschwandtner, L. B. Page Truly & the Journey to Nearandfar. (p. 1318)
GSUSA Staff. Del Suelo Al Cielo: La guia para principiantes de como explorar la naturaleza en su Vecindario. (p. 424)
Gu, George Zhibin. China's Global Reach. (p. 307)
Gu, Licheng & Hambleton, Laura. Chinese with Lulu & Maomao. (p. 308)
Guadalupe, Jezabel, tr. see Vermillion, Patricia.
Guanci, Anne Marie. David & the Worry Beast: Helping Children Cope with Anxiety. Attia, Caroline, illus. (p. 410)
Guanzhong, Luo. Three Kingdoms. Chiang, Shirley, illus. (p. 1742)
Guara, Ig. Avengers vs. Pet Avengers. (p. 119)
Guara, Ig, illus. see Baltazar, Art & Franco.
Guard, Anara. What If a Stranger Approaches You? Madden, Colleen M., illus. (p. 1887)
—What If There Is a Fire? Pfleegor, Gina, illus. (p. 1887)
—What If You Get Lost? Jones, Dani, illus. (p. 1887)
—What If You Need to Call 911? Laughead, Mike, illus. (p. 1887)
Guard, Candy. Turning to Jelly Guard, Candy, illus. (p. 1798)
Guardado, Maria. Frog That Went to the Moon. Valentin, Jeannette, illus. (p. 640)
Guardino, Dawn M. Nightmare Echoes: Short Scary Stories for Young Teens. (p. 1255)
Guardino, Dot. Otto Meets Huba, Honey, Hunchy, Herbey, Tuba & Wuba at the Zoo. (p. 1307)
Guardo, Attilio. Halloween at Clear Creek. (p. 737)
—Special Time in Clear Creek. (p. 1623)
Guare, Richard, jt. auth. see Dawson, Peg.
Guare, Sarah, ed. see Storey Publishing Staff.
Guarente, Gabe. Satan's Prep: A Graphic Novel. Fox, Dave, illus. (p. 1515)
Guarino, Deborah. If the Shoe Fits. (p. 854)
—Is Your Mama a Llama? Kellogg, Steven, illus. (p. 890)
Guarino, Deborah & Kellogg, Steven. Ta Maman Est-Elle un Lama? (p. 1694)
Guarino, Deborah & Scholastic Book Editors. Is Your Mama a Llama? (p. 890)
Guarino, Robert. Me & My Feelings: What Emotions Are & How We Can Manage Them. Jackson, Jeff, illus. (p. 1115)
Guarnaccia, Steven. Cinderella: A Fashionable Tale. (p. 320)
—Goldilocks & the Three Bears: A Tale Moderne. (p. 696)
—Three Little Pigs: An Architectural Tale. (p. 1743)
Guarnaccia, Steven, illus. see Gleeson, Brian.
Guarnaccia, Steven, illus. see Hopkinson, Deborah.
Guarnaccia, Steven, illus. see Shugaar, Antony & International Spy Museum Staff.
Guarneri, Carl J. America Compared: American History in International Perspective to 1877 Vol. 1 (p. 59)
—America Compared: American History in International Perspective - Since 1865 Vol. 2 (p. 59)
Guarneri, Cristina. Invincible (p. 885)
—Magic Tree. (p. 1074)
—Wiley's Adventure. (p. 1932)
Guarneri, Lauren. Do You Know Who I Am Now? (p. 458)
Guarnieri, Rossana. Fiabe della Buonanotte. (p. 583)
Guarnotta, Lucia. We Are Tigers. (p. 1866)
Guatemala, Anne. Story of Señor Pico. Frazao, Catia, illus. (p. 1660)
Guay, Rebecca, illus. see Casey, Dawn, et al.
Guay, Rebecca, illus. see Koller, Jackie French.
Guay, Rebecca, illus. see Krensky, Stephen.
Guay, Rebecca, illus. see Muten, Burleigh.
Guay, Rebecca, illus. see Yolen, Jane & Stemple, Heidi E. Y.
Guay, Rebecca, illus. see Yolen, Jane, et al.
Gubernatis, Loretto. Dimitrius & the Gladiolas. (p. 440)
—Dragons N Things. (p. 479)
Gubianas, Valenti. Saint-Exupery Asi Imagine el Planeta de un Pequeño Principe. (p. 1503)
Gubitosi, Lillian, illus. see Blackman, S. A.
Gubitosi, Lillian, illus. see D'Aurio, Ariana.
Gubitosi-D'Aurio, Gina, illus. see D'Aurio, Ariana.
Guckian, Mara Ellen & Teacher Created Resources Staff. Alphabet Mystery Pictures, PreK-1. (p. 49)
—Number Mystery Pictures, Prek-1. (p. 1271)
Gude, Paul. Surprise for Giraffe & Elephant. Gude, Paul, illus. (p. 1685)
—When Elephant Met Giraffe. Gude, Paul, illus. (p. 1902)
Gudelunas, David. Confidential to America: Newspaper Advice Columns & Sexual Education. (p. 356)
Gudeon, Adam. Me & Meow. Gudeon, Adam, illus. (p. 1115)
—Ping Wants to Play. Gudeon, Adam, illus. (p. 1359)
Gudeon, Adam, illus. see Sternberg, Julie.
Gudeon, Adam, jt. auth. see Gudeon, Adam.
Gudeon, Adam & Gudeon, Adam. Ping Wants to Play. (p. 1359)
Gudeon, Karla, illus. see Michelson, Richard.
Gudeon, Karla, illus. see Ziefert, Harriet.
Guderjahn, Ernie L. Children's Trilogy: Ali's Flying Rug, the Shadow Workers, & the Magic Cricket (Playscript) (p. 304)
Gudgeon, Chris. Ghost Trackers: The Unreal World of Ghosts, Ghost-Hunting, & the Paranormal. (p. 672)
Gudino Kieffer, E. Giraluna (Moonflower) (p. 678)
Gudmundson, C. J. When I Take the Sacrament, I Remember Jesus. Tenney, Shawna J. C., illus. (p. 1903)
Gudule. Nouille Vivante. (p. 1268)
Guek Cheng, P. & Pang, Guek Cheng. Grenada. (p. 723)
Gueldenpfennig, Sonia. Spectacular Women in Space (p. 1624)
—Women in Space Who Changed the World. (p. 1946)
Guell, Fernanado, illus. see Gold, Gina.
Guene, Faiza, jt. auth. see Ahlberg, Allan.
Guénette, Geneviève, illus. see Rosseau, Paul.
Guenette, Genevieve, illus. see Rousseau, Paul.
Guenther, Kim, illus. see Schiffner, Frederick A.
Guera, R. M., illus. see Aaron, Jason.
Guerard, Mathieu, jt. auth. see Vincent, Annick.
Guerard, Paula. MaryLou Found a Really Big Shoe. (p. 1101)
Guerber, H. A. Story of the Romans (Yesterday's Classics) (p. 1662)
Guerber, Hélène Adeline. Yourself & Your House Wonderful. (p. 1982)
Guerin, F. A. Witch at NO46: Verbrola. (p. 1941)
Guerlais, Gérald. Story of Orion: A Roman Constellation Myth (p. 1659)
—Story of Ursa Major & Ursa Minor: A Roman Constellation Myth (p. 1662)
Guerlais, Gérald, illus. see Capstone Press Editors.
Guerlais, Gérald, illus. see Capstone Press Staff.
Guerlais, Gérald, illus. see Loewen, Nancy & Braun, Eric.
Guerlais, Gérald, illus. see Loewen, Nancy & Gunderson, Jessica.
Guerlais, Gérald, illus. see Loewen, Nancy, et al.
Guerlais, Gérald, illus. see Loewen, Nancy.
Guerlais, Gérald, illus. see Shaskan, Trisha Speed.
Guerlais, Gérald, illus. see Stewart, Whitney.
Guernsey, Joann Bren. Hillary Rodham Clinton: Secretary of State. (p. 780)
Guerra, Elisa Puricelli. City of Lizards. Zeni, Marco, tr. from ITA. (p. 324)
—Forest of Talking Trees. Zeni, Marco, tr. (p. 618)
—Legend of Black Bart Pernigotti, Chiara, tr. from ITA. (p. 988)
—Merlin's Island Pernigotti, Chiara, tr. from ITA. (p. 1128)
—Minerva Mint (p. 1146)
—Night of the Blue Turtles. Zeni, Marco, tr. from ITA. (p. 1253)
—Order of the Owls Bernstein, Gabo León, illus. (p. 1302)
Guerra, Elisa Speckman. Quien Es Criminal? un Recorrido Por el Delito, la Ley, la Justicia y el Castigo en Mexico: Desde el Virreinato Hasta el Siglo XX. Magallanes, Alejandro, illus. (p. 1427)
Guerra Frontera, Ernesto. Tú, ellos y los Otros. (p. 1795)
Guerra, Miguel & Dias, Suzy. Samurai Elf: Set Apart. Vol. 1 (p. 1509)
Guerra, Pia, illus. see Vaughan, Brian K.
Guerra, Pia, illus. see Vaughan, Brian K. & Marzon, Jose.
Guerra, Pia, illus. see Vaughan, Brian K. & Sudzuka, Goran.
Guerra, R. R. Gabirochi y la Isla de la Vid. (p. 652)
Guerra, S. F. Billy the Kid Is Not Crazy (p. 187)
Guerra, Stephanie. Torn (p. 1770)
Guerras Safia. Lou Lou. Kemble, Mai S., illus. (p. 1057)
Guerras, Safia. Lou Lou. (p. 1057)
Guerrera, Debra. Adventures of Baby Caterpillar & His Traveling Butterfly Family. (p. 16)
Guerrera, Jeannette D. Christmas Witch. (p. 316)
—Dumb-Dumb Angel. (p. 489)
—Pot of Gold. (p. 1388)
Guerrero, Andrés. Noche. Guerrero, Andrés, illus. (p. 1262)
Guerrero, Andrés, illus. see Vallejo-Nagera, Alejandra.
Guerrero, Andrés, jt. auth. see Guerrero, Andres.
Guerrero, Andres & Guerrero, Andrés. Gigante Pequeño. (p. 676)
Guerrero, Ernesto, tr. see Markel, Michelle.
Guerrero, Ernesto, tr. from ENG. Family Stories (Cuentos Familiares) Castro, Maria Elena et al, illus. (p. 568)
Guerrero, Pablo. Mi Laberinto. Urberuaga, Emilio, illus. (p. 1132)
Guerrero, Rhonda. It's Me, Penny! The Hot Air Balloon Adventure. Leech, Jacob, illus. (p. 897)
Guerrieri, Donald J., et al. Glencoe Accounting: Real-World Applications & Connections (p. 683)
—Glencoe Accounting: Real-World Applications & Connections, Advanced Course. (p. 683)
Guertin, Chantel. Rule of Thirds. (p. 1495)
Guéry, Anne & Dussutour, Olivier. Alphab'art: Find the Letters Hidden in the Paintings. Parkin, Antonia, tr. from FRE. (p. 48)
Guess, Alison. No Bones about It, Skeleton Jokes. White, David, illus. (p. 1257)
Guess, Bob. Hey Mister, How's Your Sister? (p. 774)
Guess, Catherine Ritch. Friendly Beasts. (p. 637)
—Kipper Finds a Home: A White Squirrel Parable Volume 1. Pace, Christine, illus. (p. 961)
—Rudy & the Magic Sleigh. (p. 1494)
—Rudy el Puerco Rojo. (p. 1494)
—Rudy the Red Pig. Haynes, Jason & Oke, Rachel, illus. (p. 1494)
Guess McKerley, Jennifer, ed. Football. (p. 614)
Guess, R. J. Frog That Would Not Jump. (p. 640)
Guess, Roberta J. Two Wings (p. 1804)
Guest, Charlotte. Peredur the Son of Evrawc. (p. 1341)
Guest, Elissa Haden. Bella's Rules. Halpin, Abigail, illus. (p. 162)
—Harriet's Had Enough! Meisel, Paul, illus. (p. 750)
—Iris & Walter: True Friends. (p. 887)
—Iris & Walter: The Sleepover. (p. 887)
—Iris & Walter: The School Play. (p. 887)
—Iris & Walter: Lost & Found. Davenier, Christine, illus. (p. 887)
—Iris & Walter. (p. 887)
—Iris & Walter. Davenier, Christine, illus. (p. 887)
—Iris & Walter & Baby Rose. Davenier, Christine, illus. (p. 887)
—Iris & Walter & Cousin Howie. Davenier, Christine, illus. (p. 887)
—Iris & Walter & the Birthday Party. Davenier, Christine, illus. (p. 887)
—Iris & Walter & the Field Trip. (p. 887)
—Iris & Walter & the Field Trip. Davenier, Christine, illus. (p. 887)
—Iris & Walter & the Substitute Teacher. Davenier, Christine, illus. (p. 887)
—Iris & Walter Book & CD. Davenier, Christine, illus. (p. 887)
—Iris & Walter: Substitute Teacher. Davenier, Christine, illus. (p. 887)
—Iris & Walter: the School Play. Davenier, Christine, illus. (p. 887)
—Iris & Walter - The School Play. Davenier, Christine, illus. (p. 887)
—Iris & Walter, the Sleepover. Davenier, Christine, illus. (p. 887)
—Iris & Walter: the Sleepover. Davenier, Christine, illus. (p. 887)
—Iris & Walter: True Friends. Davenier, Christine, illus. (p. 887)
—Who's My Cupcake? Fedotova, Marina, illus. (p. 1920)
Guest, Elissa Haden & Blackstone, Margaret. Girl Stuff: A Survival Guide to Growing Up. Pollak, Barbara, illus. (p. 679)
Guest, Jacqueline. At Risk (p. 110)
—Belle of Batoche (p. 163)
—Dream Racer (p. 483)
—Fire Fight. (p. 590)
—Ghost Messages (p. 671)
—Outcasts of River Falls Peetoom, Laura, ed. (p. 1312)
—Racing Fear (p. 1432)
—Secret Signs (p. 1543)
—Soccer Star! (p. 1603)
—War Games (p. 1857)
—Wild Ride (p. 1930)
Guest, Jacqueline & Bossley, Michele Martin. Goal in Sight (p. 687)
Guest, Jacqueline & Leavey, Peggy Dymond. Growing up Ivy. (p. 726)
Guest, John. Amazing True Facts. (p. 56)
—Collective Worship Unwrapped: 33 Tried & Tested Story-Based Assemblies for Primary Schools. (p. 340)
Guest, Peggy, illus. see Barile, Mary Collins.
Guetov, Dimitar, ed. see Nalbantsky, Danail.
Guetov, Dimitar D., ed. see Bulychev, Kirill.
Guetov, Dimitar D., des. Bulgarian Orthodox Bible: (Pravoslavna Biblia) (p. 240)
Guettier, Bénédicte. At the Circus. (p. 111)
—Dinosaur Dinners. (p. 442)
—Dinosaurs. Guettier, Bénédicte, illus. (p. 443)
—In the Jungle. (p. 866)
—Me Visto... Y Te Como! (p. 1116)
—On the Farm. (p. 1290)
Guettier, Nancy. Circus in the Sky. (p. 322)
—Jude's Moon. Walsh, Tina, illus. (p. 930)
—Mermaids on Mars. (p. 1128)
—Roy G. Biv Is Mad at Me Because I Love Pink! (p. 1492)
—Roy G. Biv Is Mad at Me Because I Love Pink! Vera, Andrew, illus. (p. 1492)
Guevara, Dennis Villanueva, illus. see Iturrondo, Angeles Molina.
Guevara, Linda L., ed. see Mueller, Doris.
Guevara, Linda L., ed. see Waters, Tony.
Guevara, Melva Vizcarrondo. My Grandma, My Hero. (p. 1210)
Guevara, Susan, illus. see Elya, Susan Middleton.
Guevara, Susan, illus. see Johnston, Tony.
Guevara, Susan, illus. see Kimmel, Eric A.
Guevara, Susan, illus. see Soto, Gary.
Guevara, Susan, illus. see Winter, Jonah.
Gueyfier, Judith, illus. see Heine, Theresa & Barefoot Books Staff.
Guffey, Greg & Guffey, Greg L. Golden Age of Indiana High School Basketball. (p. 694)
Guffey, Greg L., jt. auth. see Guffey, Greg.
Guffey, Laurel R. Littlest Penguins. (p. 1039)
Guffrey, Lindsey. Psalm for the Solar System. (p. 1413)
Guggenheim, Jaenet. Next Week When I'm Big. Verelst, Suana, illus. (p. 1249)
Guggenheim, Jaenet, illus. see Riley, Barbara.
Guggenheim, Jaenet & Lucas, Spencer G. Triassic Hall: Building the Triassic Exhibit from the Ground Up. Lucas, Spencer G., ed. (p. 1785)
Guggenheim, Marc. Resurrection Volume 2. Jones, James Lucas, ed. (p. 1464)
Gugle, Marie, jt. auth. see Hilkene, Ruth Miller.
Gugler, Laurel Dee. Catching Forever (p. 279)
—Piece of Forever (p. 1356)
—There's a Billy Goat in the Garden. Beaton, Clare, illus. (p. 1730)
Guglielmo, Amy, jt. auth. see Appel, Julie.
Gugliuzza, Susan M. Growing a Healthy Baby: One Spoonful at a Time. Lamberth, Christine, ed. (p. 726)
Gugu, Abdul M., illus. see Burgess, Lisa Maria.
Guhe, Irmtraud, illus. see von Kessel, Carola.
Guia, Elizabeth. Veces Riendo, A Veces Llorando. (p. 1834)
Guiberson, Brenda Z. Disasters: Natural & Man-Made Catastrophes Through the Centuries. Guiberson, Brenda Z., illus. (p. 447)
—Earth: Feeling the Heat. Wallace, Chad, illus. (p. 495)
—Emperor Lays an Egg. Schonhorst, Elizabeth, ed. (p. 520)
—Frog Song. Spirin, Gennady, illus. (p. 640)
—Greatest Dinosaur Ever. Spirin, Gennady, illus. (p. 719)
—Ice Bears. Spirin, Ilya, illus. (p. 850)
—Into the Sea. Berenzy, Alix, illus. (p. 881)
—Life in the Boreal Forest. Spirin, Gennady, illus. (p. 1011)
—Moon Bear. Young, Ed, illus. (p. 1171)
—Most Amazing Creature in the Sea. Spirin, Gennady, illus. (p. 1177)
—Mummy Mysteries: Tales from North America. (p. 1191)
—Mummy Mysteries: Tales from North America. Guiberson, Brenda Z., illus. (p. 1191)
Guibert, Emmanuel. Alan's War: The Memories of G. I. Alan Cope. Guibert, Emmanuel, illus. (p. 33)
—Beautiful Cow. (p. 153)
—Bizbilla Hits the Bullseye. (p. 194)
—Happy as a Pig... (p. 744)
—Just a Donkey Like You & Me. (p. 937)
—Just a Donkey Like You & Me. Boutavant, Marc, illus. (p. 937)
—Nasty Cat. (p. 1230)
—Sardine in Outer Space 5. Pezzali, Walter & Sfar, Joann, illus. (p. 1515)
—Sardine in Outer Space 6. Sfar, Joann, illus. (p. 1515)
—Space Pirate Sardine vs. the Brainwashing Machine. Sfar, Joann, illus. (p. 1619)
—Thunder Horse. (p. 1746)
—Thunder Horse. Boutavant, Marc, illus. (p. 1746)
—Where's Petula? (p. 1910)
Guibert, Emmanuel & Boutavant, Marc. Happy as a Pig... Boutavant, Marc, illus. (p. 744)
Guibert, Emmanuel & Sfar, Joann. Sardine in Outer Space. Watson, Sasha, tr. from FRE. (p. 1514)
—Sardine in Outer Space Gauvin, Edward, tr. from FRE. (p. 1515)
—Sardine in Outer Space Brizzi, Elisabeth & Siegel, Alexis, trs. from FRE. (p. 1515)
Guibert, Susan Mullen & O'Shaughnessy, Brendan. Clashmore Mike Comes Home. Pynaert, Andrea, illus. (p. 327)
—Clashmore Mike_Dublin to Dome. Pynaert, Andrea, illus. (p. 327)
Guibord, Charity, illus. see Liebenow, Todd, et al.
Guibord, Maurissa. Warped. (p. 1858)
Guicciardini, Desideria. Rumpelstiltskin. (p. 1495)
Guicciardini, Desideria, illus. see Brooks, Felicity.
Guicciardini, Desideria, illus. see Graves, Sue.
Guicciardini, Desideria, jt. auth. see Graves, Sue.
Guicciardini, Desideria & McNicholas, Shelagh. Hop, Skip & Jump. (p. 796)
Guice, Butch, illus. see Beatty, Scott.
Guice, Butch, illus. see Brubaker, Ed & Breitweiser, Mitch.
Guice, Butch, illus. see Waid, Mark & Beatty, Scott.
Guice, Butch, illus. see Waid, Mark.
Guice, Butch, et al. What If?: Classic. Vol. 7 (p. 1887)
Guice, Jackson, illus. see Brubaker, Ed.
Guice, Jackson, illus. see Busiek, Kurt, et al.
Guice, Jackson, jt. auth. see Ellis, Warren.
Guida, Liisa, illus. see Beall, Pamela Conn & Nipp, Susan Hagen.
Guida, Liisa C., illus. see Tomecek, Steve.
Guida, Liisa Chauncy, illus. see Beall, Pamela Conn & Nipp, Susan Hagen.
Guida, Liisa Chauncy, illus. see Tomecek, Steve.

Guideposts Associates Staff, contrib. by. Power of Kindness for Teens: True Stories Written by Teens for Teens from the Pages of Guideposts. (p. 1389)
Guideposts Editors, ed. Daily Guideposts 2005. (p. 399)
—Daily Guideposts Journal 2005. (p. 399)
—Guideposts for the Spirit: Stories of Courage. (p. 730)
Guideposts, From the Pages of. Power of Love for Teens: True Stories Written by Teens: From the Pages of Guideposts. (p. 1389)
Guidera, Daniel, illus. see Einhorn, Kama.
Guidera, Daniel, illus. see Krensky, Stephen.
Guidi, Guido, illus. see Rao, Lisa.
Guidi, Victoria. Who on Earth Is Jane Goodall? Champion for the Chimpanzees. (p. 1917)
Guidici, Cynthia. Mario Molina (p. 1094)
Guidobaldi, Serena, jt. auth. see Totaro, Roberto.
Guidone, Julie. Frogs. (p. 641)
—Frogs (Ranas) (p. 641)
—Jaguars. (p. 905)
—Jaguars (Jaguares) (p. 905)
—Monkeys. (p. 1165)
—Monkeys; Monos. (p. 1166)
—Sloths. (p. 1591)
—Sloths; Perezosos. (p. 1591)
—Snakes. (p. 1596)
—Snakes (Serpientes) (p. 1597)
—Snakes/Serpientes. (p. 1597)
—Toucans & Other Birds. (p. 1772)
—Toucans & Other Birds; Tucanes y otras Aves. (p. 1772)
Guidone, Lisa M. What Happens at a Crayon Factory? (p. 1885)
—What Happens at a Crayon Factory? ¿Qué Pasa en una Fábrica de Crayones? (p. 1885)
—What Happens at a Crayon Factory?/¿Qué Pasa en una Fábrica de Crayones? (p. 1885)
—What Happens at a Magazine? (p. 1885)
—What Happens at a Magazine?/¿Qué Pasa en la Editorial de una Revista? (p. 1885)
—What Happens at a Museum? (p. 1885)
—What Happens at a Museum? (¿Qué pasa en un Museo?) (p. 1885)
—What Happens at a Museum?/¿Qué Pasa en un Museo? (p. 1885)
—What Happens at a Zoo? (p. 1885)
—What Happens at a Zoo?/¿Qué pasa en un Zoológico? (p. 1885)
Guidone, Lisa M. & Nations, Susan. What Happens at a Magazine?/¿Qué Pasa en la Editorial de una Revista? (p. 1885)
—What Happens at a Zoo?;¿Qué pasa en un Zoológico? (p. 1885)
Guidoux, Valerie. Little Bears. (p. 1024)
—Little Dolphins. (p. 1027)
—Little Polar Bears. (p. 1033)
—Little Zebras. (p. 1038)
—Ositos. (p. 1305)
Guidoux, Valerie, jt. auth. see Texier, Ophélie.
Guldry, C. Adventures of Moochie the Moosh Mouse & Mr. Waddles the Duck: Welcome to Sugarbush Swamp. (p. 20)
Guiffre, William. Angelita's Song. Baron, Cheri Ann, illus. (p. 74)
—First Gift of Christmas. Baron, Cheri Ann, illus. (p. 595)
—Gramma's Glasses. Pippin, Barbara, illus. (p. 706)
—Wrong Side of the Bed. Baron, Cheri Ann, illus. (p. 1965)
Guiffre, William A. Angelita's Song. Baron, Cheri Ann, illus. (p. 74)
—Eddie, the Elf Who Would Be Elvis. Fannon, Chris, illus. (p. 503)
—First Gift of Christmas. Baron, Cheri Ann, illus. (p. 595)
—Gramma's Glasses. Pippin, Barbara, illus. (p. 706)
—Wrong Side of the Bed. Baron, Cheri Ann, illus. (p. 1965)
Guignard, Lars. Yogi's Curse. (p. 1972)
Guih, Line Carol. Momo the Historian: The Powerful Ivorian Boy. (p. 1163)
Guild, Shena, ed. see Barber, Antonia & Quarto Generic Staff.
Guile, Gill. Bobby the Bulldozer. (p. 206)
—Danny the Digger. (p. 406)
—In My Garden. (p. 864)
—My Nursery Rhyme Pop-up Book. (p. 1216)
—Tiny the Train. (p. 1757)
—Tommy the Tractor. (p. 1765)
Guile, Gill, illus. see B&H Editorial Staff, ed.
Guile, Gill, illus. see Davies, Gill.
Guile, Gill, illus. see Hubbard, Ben.
Guile, Gill, illus. see Jordan, Jennifer.
Guile, Gill, illus. see Powell-Tuck, Maudie.
Guile, Gill, illus. see Rabe, Tish.
Guiley, Rosemary. Fairies. (p. 562)
—Ghosts & Haunted Places. (p. 672)
Guiley, Rosemary Ellen. Dreams & Astral Travel. (p. 484)
—Encyclopedia of Angels. (p. 524)
—Fairies. (p. 562)
—Ghosts & Haunted Places. (p. 672)
—Spirit Communications. (p. 1628)
—Vampires. (p. 1832)
—Witches & Wiccans. (p. 1941)
Guiley, Rosemary Ellen & Dennett, Preston E. Bigfoot, Yeti, & Other Ape-Men. (p. 185)
Guilfoile, Patrick. Chicken Pox. (p. 300)
Guilfoile, Patrick G. Human Papillomavirus. (p. 826)
Guilfoyle, Kim. Why Do You Love Me? (p. 1924)
Guilhaumond, Gregory, illus. see Riordan, Rick & Venditti, Robert.
Guilhaumond, Gregory, illus. see Venditti, Robert & Riordan, Rick.
Guili, Z., jt. ed. see Ping, Chen.
Guillain, Adam. Bella Balistica & the African Safari. (p. 162)
—Bella Balistica & the Forgotten Kingdom. (p. 162)
—Bella Balistica & the Indian Summer. (p. 162)
—Bella Balistica & the Temple of Tikal. (p. 162)
—Marshmallows for Martians. Guillain, Charlotte & Wildish, Lee, illus. (p. 1096)
Guillain, Adam, jt. auth. see Guillain, Charlotte.
Guillain, Adam & Guillain, Charlotte. Pirate Pie Ship. Van Wyk, Rupert, illus. (p. 1363)
Guillain, Adam & Guillain, Charlotte. Doughnuts for a Dragon. Wildish, Lee, illus. (p. 473)
—Three Frilly Goats Fluff. Littler, Phil, illus. (p. 1742)
Guillain, Adam & Steiner, Elke. Bella's Brazilian Football. Steiner, Elke, illus. (p. 162)
Guillain, Charlotte. 101 Ways to Be a Great Role Model (p. 2000)
—A. A. Milne (p. 1)
—Ahorrar Agua (p. 30)
—Ahorrar Energía (p. 30)
—Alimentos de los Insectos. (p. 41)
—Amazing Elephants (p. 54)
—Animal Fairy Tales Beacon, Dawn, illus. (p. 77)
—Animal Fairy Tales Big Book Collection. Beacon, Dawn, illus. (p. 77)
—Animal Fairy Tales Bind Up 1. (p. 77)
—Animal Life Stories (p. 78)
—Animals (p. 81)
—Art (p. 101)
—Astronauts (p. 109)
—Aztec Warriors (p. 122)
—Bats (p. 144)
—Beatrix Potter (p. 153)
—Brave Nurses. (p. 223)
—Brillante U Opaco (p. 228)
—Bug Babies (p. 236)
—Bug Food (p. 236)
—Bug Homes (p. 236)
—Bug Parts (p. 236)
—Bug Senses (p. 236)
—Bugs on the Move (p. 237)
—Building Things (p. 239)
—Caliente o Frío (p. 253)
—Caring for Nature (p. 269)
—Casas de los Insectos. (p. 273)
—Cat & the Beanstalk Beacon, Dawn, illus. (p. 277)
—Cats. Elsom, Clare, illus. (p. 280)
—Cheetahs (p. 296)
—Ciclismo (p. 318)
—Cleaning up Litter (p. 330)
—Comparing Bugs (p. 351)
—Comparing Properties. (p. 352)
—Comparing Shapes. (p. 352)
—Computers (p. 355)
—Coping with Bullying (p. 365)
—Coping with Moving Away (p. 365)
—Crías de los Insectos. (p. 382)
—Cuidar de la Naturaleza (p. 390)
—Czech Republic (p. 397)
—Different Sounds (p. 438)
—Dogs (p. 462)
—Dr. Seuss (p. 475)
—Duro o Blando (p. 490)
—Earth (p. 495)
—Earth (Space Series - Arabic) (p. 497)
—Elephants (p. 511)
—Emperor Penguin's New Clothes Beacon, Dawn, illus. (p. 521)
—Empty Pot: A Chinese Folk Tale Dorado, Steve, illus. (p. 521)
—Es Rigido o Se Dobla (p. 534)
—Estrellas. (p. 538)
—Exploring Space. (p. 553)
—Extreme Animals. (p. 556)
—Extreme Athletes: True Stories of Amazing Sporting Adventurers (p. 556)
—Fairies (p. 562)
—Fierce Fighters (p. 584)
—Finn MacCool & the Giant's Causeway: An Irish Folk Tale Dorado, Steve, illus. (p. 589)
—Floating or Sinking (p. 605)
—Flores (p. 606)
—Flota o Se Hunde (p. 607)
—Flowers (p. 608)
—Folk Tales from Around the World Dorado, Steve, illus. (p. 611)
—Foolish, Timid Rabbit: An Indian Folk Tale Dorado, Steve, illus. (p. 614)
—Fruits (p. 645)
—Frutas (p. 646)
—Fútbol (p. 650)
—Get Drawing! (p. 667)
—Get Writing! (p. 668)
—Gladiators & Roman Soldiers (p. 682)
—Goldiclucks & the Three Bears Beacon, Dawn, illus. (p. 695)
—Great Art Thefts (p. 713)
—Great Escapes (p. 715)
—Great Explorers. (p. 715)
—Greek Warriors (p. 721)
—Hard or Soft (p. 748)
—Heavy or Light (p. 761)
—History (p. 783)
—Hojas (p. 787)
—Hot or Cold (p. 802)
—How Do We Hear? (p. 807)
—How Does My Body Work? (p. 809)
—Hungary (p. 827)
—Insectos en Movimiento. (p. 875)
—Islamic Culture (p. 891)
—Jaguars (p. 905)
—Kitten Who Cried Dog Beacon, Dawn, illus. (p. 962)
—Las Casas de Los Insectos (p. 976)
—Leaves (p. 986)
—Life Cycles (p. 1009)
—Life Story of a Butterfly (p. 1013)
—Life Story of a Frog (p. 1013)
—Life Story of a Ladybug (p. 1013)
—Life Story of a Salamander (p. 1013)
—Liso O Áspero. (p. 1022)
—Little Red Riding Duck Beacon, Dawn, illus. (p. 1035)
—Looking at Literature. (p. 1051)
—Luna (p. 1065)
—Magnets. (p. 1076)
—Making Sounds (p. 1082)
—Math (p. 1104)
—Maurice Sendak (p. 1110)
—Medieval Knights (p. 1119)
—Mermaids (p. 1128)
—Mighty Lions (p. 1140)
—Moon (p. 1171)
—Moon (Space Series - Arabic) (p. 1172)
—Music (p. 1193)
—Music: From the Voice to Electronica. (p. 1193)
—My First Day at a New School (p. 1206)
—My First Sleepover (p. 1208)
—Natación (p. 1230)
—Neil Gaiman: Rock Star Writer. (p. 1240)
—New Brother or Sister (p. 1243)
—Ninja (p. 1256)
—Nuestra Piel (p. 1270)
—Nuestra Sangre (p. 1270)
—Nuestros Cerebros (p. 1270)
—Nuestros Corazones (p. 1270)
—Nuestros Estómagos (p. 1270)
—Nuestros Huesos (p. 1270)
—Nuestros Músculos (p. 1270)
—Nuestros Pulmones (p. 1270)
—Our Blood (p. 1307)
—Our Bodies (p. 1307)
—Our Bones (p. 1308)
—Our Brains (p. 1308)
—Our Hearts (p. 1309)
—Our Lungs (p. 1309)
—Our Muscles (p. 1309)
—Our Skin (p. 1310)
—Our Stomachs (p. 1310)
—Pandarella Beacon, Dawn, illus. (p. 1320)
—Partes de los Insectos. (p. 1325)
—Pesado o Liviano (p. 1345)
—Planetas. (p. 1368)
—Planets (p. 1368)
—Planets. (p. 1368)
—Poland (p. 1378)
—Polar Regions. (p. 1379)
—Poodle & the Pea Beacon, Dawn, illus. (p. 1383)
—Portugal (p. 1387)
—Powerful Polar Bears (p. 1390)
—Producir Sonidos (p. 1409)
—Properties of Materials (p. 1411)
—Pumas (p. 1416)
—Punk: Music, Fashion, Attitude! (p. 1417)
—Rabbits. Elsom, Clare, illus. (p. 1429)
—Rabbits - Animal Family Albums. Elsom, Clare, illus. (p. 1430)
—Raíces (p. 1433)
—Ratpunzel Beacon, Dawn, illus. (p. 1440)
—Reading & Writing (p. 1445)
—Recoger la Basura (p. 1452)
—Reusing & Recycling (p. 1465)
—Rigido O Se Dobla. (p. 1472)
—Roald Dahl (p. 1477)
—Rocks & Soil (p. 1483)
—Roots (p. 1488)
—Rumplesnakeskin Beacon, Dawn, illus. (p. 1495)
—Samurai (p. 1509)
—Saving Energy (p. 1517)
—Saving Water (p. 1518)
—Science (p. 1524)
—Seeds (p. 1547)
—Semillas (p. 1550)
—Sentidos de los Insectos. (p. 1551)
—Shiny or Dull (p. 1567)
—Shocking Sharks (p. 1568)
—Sleeping Badger Beacon, Dawn, illus. (p. 1588)
—Smooth or Rough (p. 1595)
—Sneaky Spies (p. 1597)
—Soaring Eagles (p. 1603)
—Soccer (p. 1603)
—Sol (p. 1606)
—Sonidos Diferentes (p. 1612)
—Sonidos Que Nos Rodean. (p. 1612)
—Spain (p. 1620)
—Sports (p. 1632)
—Spot the Difference: Plants (p. 1633)
—Spreading the Word. (p. 1634)
—Stars (p. 1643)
—Stars. (p. 1643)
—Stems (p. 1647)
—Stiff or Bendable (p. 1650)
—Stories of Women's Suffrage: Votes for Women! (p. 1655)
—Sun (p. 1675)
—Sun (Space Series - Arabic) (p. 1676)
—Super Spiders (p. 1682)
—Tallos (p. 1704)
—Tierra (p. 1748)
—Tree of Life: An Amazonian Folk Tale Dorado, Steve, illus. (p. 1783)
—Unhappy Stonecutter: A Japanese Folk Tale Dorado, Steve, illus. (p. 1817)
—Usar de Nuevo y Reciclar (p. 1826)
—Vampires (p. 1832)
—Vietnam (p. 1841)
—Vikings (p. 1842)
—Visiting the Dentist (p. 1845)
—Walk on the Wild Side. (p. 1854)
—What Is a Graphic Novel? (p. 1888)
—What Is a Novel? (p. 1888)
—What Is a Poem? (p. 1888)
—What Is a Short Story? (p. 1888)
—What Is Creative Nonfiction? (p. 1889)
—What Is Informational Writing? (p. 1889)
—What Is Instructional Writing? (p. 1889)
—What Is Persuasive Writing? (p. 1890)
—Why the Spider Has Long Legs: An African Folk Tale Dorado, Steve, illus. (p. 1926)
—World of Bugs (p. 1956)
—¿Cómo Oímos? (p. 351)
—¿Qué es el Sonido? (p. 1423)
Guillain, Charlotte, illus. see Guillain, Adam.
Guillain, Charlotte, jt. auth. see Guillain, Adam.
Guillain, Charlotte, jt. auth. see Guillain, Adam.
Guillain, Charlotte, jt. auth. see Smith, Sian.
Guillain, Charlotte, jt. auth. see Weil, Ann.
Guillain, Charlotte & Aesop. Kitten Who Cried Dog. Beacon, Dawn, illus. (p. 962)
Guillain, Charlotte & Andersen, Hans Christian. Poodle & the Pea. Beacon, Dawn, illus. (p. 1383)
Guillain, Charlotte & Baraclough, Sue. Life Cycles (p. 1009)
—Push & Pull (p. 1420)
—Rocks & Soil (p. 1483)
—Teeth (p. 1715)
—Water (p. 1862)
Guillain, Charlotte & Claybourne, Anna. Animal Abilities. (p. 76)
Guillain, Charlotte & Colson, Mary. Dream It, Do It! (p. 483)
Guillain, Charlotte & Guillain, Adam. Spaghetti with the Yeti. Wildish, Lee, illus. (p. 1620)
Guillain, Charlotte & Heinemann Library Staff. Astronautas (p. 109)
—Different Sounds (p. 438)
—Floating or Sinking (p. 605)
—Hard or Soft (p. 748)
—Heavy or Light (p. 761)
—Hot or Cold (p. 802)
—How Do We Hear? (p. 807)
—Las Estrellas (p. 976)
—Los Planetas (p. 1054)
—Luna (p. 1065)
—Making Sounds (p. 1082)
—Shiny or Dull (p. 1567)
—Smooth or Rough (p. 1595)
—Sol (p. 1606)
—Stiff or Bendable (p. 1650)
—Tierra (p. 1748)
—What Is Sound? (p. 1890)
Guillain, Charlotte & Mason, Paul. Animal Family Albums. Elsom, Clare, illus. (p. 77)
Guillain, Charlotte & Perrault, Charles. Pandarella. Beacon, Dawn, illus. (p. 1321)
Guillain, Charlotte, et al. Living in the Wild: Big Cats (p. 1041)
Guillaume, Andrea M. Classroom Mathematics Inventory for Grades K-6: An Informal Assessment. (p. 329)
Guille, Rosanne, illus. see Turnbull, Stephanie.
Guillén, Nicolás. Por el Mar de las Antillas Anda un Barco de Papel. (p. 1385)
Guillerey, Aurélie, illus. see Badreddine, Delphine.
Guillermo-Newton, Judith. Competitive Tennis for Girls. (p. 352)
Guillermo-Newton, Judy. Competitive Tennis for Girls. (p. 352)
Guillet, Francois, illus. see Guillet, Jean-Pierre.
Guillet, Jean-Pierre. Puce Cosmique et le Rayon Bleuge. Guillet, Francois, illus. (p. 1414)
Guillian, Adam & Guillain, Charlotte. Emma Peror & the Tutu That Wasn't There. (p. 520)
Guillon, Eric, illus. see Paul, Cinco & Daurio, Ken.
Guillope, Antoine, illus. see London, Jack.
Guillope, Antoine. One Scary Night. (p. 1296)
Guilloppé, Antoine. One Scary Night. (p. 1296)
Guilloppé, Antoine, illus. see Heard, Georgia.
Guillory, Mike, jt. auth. see Yanez, Anthony.
Guillory, Sarah. Reclaimed. (p. 1452)
Guillot, Angela K. Day Frasier the Frog Jumped High. Ashley Comeaux-Foret, illus. (p. 413)
Guillou, Philippe Le, see Le Guillou, Philippe.
Guilmette, Patty. Finding Kyle Some Style Whitman, Diana McManus, illus. (p. 588)
Guimaraes, Santi Román i, illus. see Rodriguez-Nora, Tere.
Guimond, Rick, jt. auth. see Berton, Judy.
Guin, Anatoly. Smart Tales from Brainy the Cat. (p. 1593)
Guin, Ursula K. Le, see Le Guin, Ursula K.
Guin, Valerie. In the City. (p. 865)
—In the Country. (p. 865)
—On the Move. (p. 1291)
—Where We Live. (p. 1910)
Guinan, Paul, illus. see Willingham, Bill.
Guinard, Geraldine, illus. see Smith, Helene.
Guinn, Dolores Hollyfield. Frederick Frog & His Family: Being a Bully. (p. 633)
—Stubborn & Disobedient Box, Paul, illus. (p. 1668)
Guinn, Jeff. Christmas Chronicles. (p. 313)
Guinnard, Auguste. Tres años de esclavitud entre los Patagones. Duviols, Jean-Paul, ed. (p. 1784)
Guinness, Louise, ed. Everyman Book of Nonsense Verse. (p. 544)
Guinness, Paul. Globalisation. (p. 685)
Guinness, Paul & Nagle, Garrett. Data Response Questions for AS Geography. (p. 409)
Guinta, Peter & Cribbs, Randy. Illumination Rounds. (p. 857)
Guinzburg, Michael. Evergreen Review on CD Issues 21 To 30. (p. 542)
Guion, Melissa. Baby Penguins Everywhere! Guion, Melissa, illus. (p. 127)
—Baby Penguins Love Their Mama. Guion, Melissa, illus. (p. 127)
Guion, Tamara, illus. see Steinmann, Donna.
Guion, Wilma F. Blue Blue Elephant: (I Am Somebody) (p. 202)
Guipre, Jewel. Nightmare Trolls. (p. 1255)
Guipre, Jewel Moreland. Dance with Me. (p. 402)
Guirao, David, illus. see Maestro, Pepe.
Guitard, Agnes, tr. see Ward, John.
Guix, Joan Carles, tr. see Carlson, Dale.
Guix, Joan Carles, tr. see Warner, Penny.
Guix, Juan Gabriel Lopez, tr. see Saki.
Guiza, Vic. Bat in the Bunk: Summer Camp Stories Seires. (p. 143)
Guiza, Victor, illus. see Barret, Marie.
Guiza, Victor, illus. see Burgess, Starr.
Guiza, Victor, illus. see Purtle, Louise.
Guiza, Victor, illus. see Robertson, Karen.
Guiza, Victor, illus. see Shammas, Anna.
Guiza, Victor, illus. see Sloyer, Elliot.
Gul, Hasibe & Balci, Erkan. My Wonderful Body. (p. 1221)

—Nutritious Vegetables. (p. 1274)
Gulack, Robin. Root Beer Cats. (p. 1488)
Gulacy, Paul, illus. see Moench, Doug.
Gulbis, Stephen. Old MacDonald Had a Barn. (p. 1284)
—Wheels on the Bus. (p. 1901)
Gulbis, Stephen, illus. see Lewis, Jill.
Guler, Greg, illus. see Peterson, Scott.
Gulick, Bill. Roadside History of Oregon. (p. 1477)
Gulick, Luther & Luther Gulick. Camp Fire Girls. (p. 257)
Gulino, ViTina Corso. Peter Rabbit & My Tulips. Murariu, Lorraine, illus. (p. 1347)
Gulkin, Sidney & Notkin, Jerome J. How & Why Wonder Book of MacHines. Zaffo, George J., illus. (p. 804)
Gulko, Candace S. Accounting, Business, & Finance. (p. 8)
—Film. (p. 586)
Gulla, Rosemarie. On the Wings of the Swan. Undercuffler, Gary, illus. (p. 1292)
Gullard, Pamela & Lund, Nancy. Life on the San Andreas Fault: A History of Portola Valley. (p. 1012)
Gulledge, Laura Lee. Page by Paige. (p. 1318)
—Will & Whit. (p. 1932)
Gullens, Lee M., illus. see Cochran, Jean M.
Gulley, Hardrick M., illus. see Garrett, Diane Marie.
Gulley, Martha, illus. see Blackman, Dorothy L.
Gulley, Martha, illus. see Messner, Kate.
Gulley, Robin, ed. see Gulley Sr, Wayne A.
Gulley, Robin R., ed. see Prevedel, Brenda.
Gulley Sr, Wayne A. Michelangelo Tangelo - a Bully No More. Gulley, Robin, ed. (p. 1135)
Gulley SR, Wayne A., illus. see Gulley Sr, Wayne A.
Gulley Sr, Wayne A., illus. see Prevedel, Brenda.
Gullible, Ru. Phantom. (p. 1349)
Gulliksen, Anne. Boy from Nøtterøy. (p. 218)
—Smartest Dog on the Planet. (p. 1593)
Gulliksen, Eivind, illus. see Lennard, Kate.
Gulliver, A. & Cartwright, S. Snap. (p. 1597)
Gulliver, Amanda. Colors. (p. 344)
—Pets. (p. 1348)
—Underwater. (p. 1817)
—Zoo. (p. 1988)
Gulliver, Amanda, illus. see Dale, Jay.
Gulliver, Amanda, illus. see Powell, Jillian.
Gulliver, Amanda, illus. see Traditional.
Gulliver, Amanda & Turnbull, Stephanie. Things to Make & Do with Paper. Sage, Molly, illus. (p. 1733)
Gullo, Arthur. Tornadoes. (p. 1770)
—Tsunamis. (p. 1795)
—Volcanoes. (p. 1849)
Gullo, Jim. Travel Guide to the Plantation South. (p. 1780)
Gullotti, Pat, illus. see LaSala, Paige.
Gully, Mario, jt. auth. see Hammond, Marc.
Gulotta, Charles. Learn This! Stuff You Need to Know, & Mistakes You Need to Stop Making, Before You Step Foot into High School. (p. 983)
Gulzeth, Ray, illus. see Becklund, Annette L.
Gumboli, Mario. Buenos Modales. (p. 235)
—Peligro! (p. 1336)
Gumbs, Al-Tariq. Turtle Who Bullied. (p. 1798)
Gumede, William. Kite's Flight. Sereda, Maja, illus. (p. 962)
Gumm, Amy L. Let It Grow, Let It Grow, Let It Grow: Hands-on Activities to Explore the Plant Kingdom. (p. 994)
Gumm, Merry L. Help! I'm in Middle School... How Will I Survive? (p. 765)
Gumm, Susan Kathleen, illus. see Lewin, Terry.
Gumm, Susan Kathleen, illus. see Papazoglu, Paula.
Gumm, Susan Kathleen, illus. see Piccirillo, Renee.
Gummelt, Donna & Melchiorre, Dondino. Cow Puppies. Wall, Randy Hugh, ed. (p. 373)
—Do Fish Kiss? Wall, Randy Hugh, ed. (p. 456)
—Don't Get My Honey... . HONEY. Wall, Randy Hugh, ed. (p. 467)
—I'm All Blown Up. Wall, Randy Hugh, ed. (p. 858)
—Michelina the Magical Musical Good Witch of the Forest. Wall, Randy Hugh, ed. (p. 1135)
—My Sunshine Friend. Wall, Randy Hugh, ed. (p. 1219)
—Your Name Is Mud. Wall, Randy Hugh, ed. (p. 1981)
Gummer, Chiele. Family of Geese. (p. 568)
Gumnut, I. B. Daniel's Pushbike. (p. 405)
—Mad Dogs. (p. 1069)
Gump, Granny. Giraffe Who Went to School. (p. 677)
Gunby, Shirley & Laman, Judi-Lynn. Extinct & Endangered: Big Animals Small World - Painting for Peanuts. (p. 555)
Gunby, Stephanie. Clever Clouds. (p. 331)
Gundel, Jean. Mystery Key at Camp Green Meadow. Robertson, R. H., illus. (p. 1224)
Gunderman, Shelby & Burns, Adam. UC San Diego College Prowler off the Record: Inside University of California San Diego. (p. 1807)
Gundersen, Bev. Grow Through the Bible: 52 Bible Lessons from Genesis to Revelation for Ages 8-12. (p. 726)
Gundersen, Ralph, jt. auth. see Tinerella, Paul P.
Gunderson, Cory. Boston Tea Party. (p. 215)
—Great Depression. (p. 715)
Gunderson, Cory Gideon. 2000 Presidential Election. (p. 2003)
—Afghanistan's Struggles. (p. 26)
—Battle in Baghdad. (p. 146)
—Battle of the Alamo. (p. 146)
—Dred Scott Decision. (p. 484)
—Islamic Fundamentalism. (p. 891)
—Israeli-Palestinian Conflict. (p. 893)
—Need for Oil. (p. 1239)
—Religions of the Middle East. (p. 1458)
—Swedish Americans. (p. 1689)
—Terrorist Groups. (p. 1722)
—U. N. Weapons Inspectors. (p. 1805)
—When Diplomacy Fails. (p. 1902)
Gunderson, J. Fire & Snow: A Tale of the Alaskan Gold Rush. Townsend, Shannon, illus. (p. 590)
—Last Rider: The Final Days of the Pony Express. Ruiz, Jose Alfonso Ocampo & Woodman, Ned, illus. (p. 978)
—Ropes of Revolution: The Boston Tea Party Schoonover, Brent, illus. (p. 1488)
Gunderson, Jessica. Alamo: Myths, Legends, & Facts (p. 33)
—Benedict Arnold: Battlefield Hero or Selfish Traitor? (p. 164)
—Biography of Malcolm X. Hayden, Seitu, illus. (p. 189)
—Christopher Columbus: New World Explorer or Fortune Hunter? (p. 316)
—Conquistadors. (p. 358)
—Don't Break the Balance Beam! Santillan, Jorge H., illus. (p. 467)
—Elephant Dancer: A Story of Ancient India Hu, Caroline, illus. (p. 511)
—Emma's New Beginning. Foti, Anthony J., illus. (p. 520)
—Energy Dilemma. (p. 528)
—Global Warming. (p. 684)
—Gothic Art: Movements in Art. (p. 704)
—Gothic Art. (p. 704)
—Horse on the Hill: A Story of Ancient India Hu, Caroline, illus. (p. 800)
—How Big? Wacky Ways to Compare Size Keino, illus. (p. 805)
—How Long? Wacky Ways to Compare Length Sinkovec, Igor, illus. (p. 810)
—I Broke into Gymnastics Camp Santillan, Jorge H., illus. (p. 834)
—I Just Have to Ride the Halfpipe! Santillan, Jorge H., illus. (p. 840)
—Impressionism: Movements in Art. (p. 862)
—Impressionism. (p. 862)
—Jay-Z: Hip-Hop Icon Kinsella, Pat, illus. (p. 910)
—King's Warrior: A Story of Ancient India Hu, Caroline, illus. (p. 961)
—Life on the Mayflower Dumm, Brian Caleb, illus. (p. 1012)
—Little Red Riding Hood Stories Around the World: 3 Beloved Tales Madden, Colleen et al, illus. (p. 1035)
—Methods of Warfare. (p. 1130)
—Mount Rushmore: Myths, Legends, & Facts (p. 1180)
—Ninjas: A Guide to the Ancient Assassins (p. 1256)
—Ohio. (p. 1281)
—Pennsylvania. (p. 1337)
—Pilgrims' First Thanksgiving Lucke, Deb, illus. (p. 1358)
—Pivotal Moments. (p. 1365)
—Realism: Movements in Art. (p. 1449)
—Realism. (p. 1449)
—Really, Rapunzel Needed a Haircut! The Story of Rapunzel As Told by Dame Gothel. Alonso, Denis, illus. (p. 1450)
—Really, Rapunzel Needed a Haircut! The Story of Rapunzel, as Told by Dame Gothel. Alonso, Denis, illus. (p. 1450)
—Rebel among Redcoats: A Revolutionary War Novel. (p. 1450)
—Romanticism: Movements in Art. (p. 1486)
—Romanticism. (p. 1486)
—Second Continental Congress (p. 1539)
—Secret Weapons: A Tale of the Revolutionary War Aburto, Jesus, illus. (p. 1544)
—Servant & the Water Princess: A Story of Ancient India Hu, Caroline, illus. (p. 1552)
—Snorkeling for Fun! (p. 1598)
—Snow White Stories Around the World: 4 Beloved Tales Belloni, Valentina et al, illus. (p. 1600)
—Songs of Stones River: A Civil War Novel. (p. 1612)
—Stranger on the Silk Road: A Story of Ancient China Hu, Caroline, illus. (p. 1665)
—Thanksgiving Then & Now Shin, Hayoung, illus. (p. 1726)
—There's a Hurricane in the Pool! Santillan, Jorge H., illus. (p. 1731)
—U. S. Navy True Stories: Tales of Bravery. (p. 1807)
—Vikings. (p. 1842)
—Wound Is Mortal: The Story of the Assassination of Abraham Lincoln. (p. 1962)
—X: A Biography of Malcolm X. Hayden, Seitu, illus. (p. 1966)
—Your Life as a Cabin Attendant on the Titanic. Dougherty, Rachel, illus. (p. 1981)
—Your Life as a Cabin Boy on a Pirate Ship. Burns, Mike, illus. (p. 1981)
—Your Life As a Pharaoh in Ancient Egypt Ebbeler, Jeff, illus. (p. 1981)
—Your Life As a Pioneer on the Oregon Trail. Dougherty, Rachel, illus. (p. 1981)
—Your Life As a Private on the Lewis & Clark Expedition Madden, Colleen, illus. (p. 1981)
Gunderson, Jessica, jt. auth. see Braun, Eric.
Gunderson, Jessica, jt. auth. see Gunderson, Jessica Sarah.
Gunderson, Jessica, jt. auth. see Loewen, Nancy.
Gunderson, Jessica, jt. auth. see Yomtov, Nel.
Gunderson, Jessica A. How to Keep a Secret for Detectives. (p. 820)
Gunderson, Jessica & Collins, Terry. American Graphic. Kinsella, Pat & Byers, Michael, illus. (p. 61)
Gunderson, Jessica & Gonzalez, Jorge. Full Court Pressure Ruiz, Alfonso, illus. (p. 646)
Gunderson, Jessica & Loewen, Nancy. Really, Rapunzel Needed a Haircut! The Story of Rapunzel As Told by Dame Gothel. Alonso, Denis & Tayal, Amit, illus. (p. 1450)
Gunderson, Jessica & Meister, Cari. Multicultural Fairy Tales Madden, Colleen et al, illus. (p. 1190)
Gunderson, Jessica & Weakland, Mark. Wacky Comparisons. (p. 1852)
—Wacky Comparisons. Bolton, Bill & Sinkovec, Igor, illus. (p. 1852)
Gunderson, Jessica, et al. Monumental History (p. 1170)
—You Choose: Fractured Fairy Tales. (p. 1975)
Gunderson, Jessica Sarah. Sacagawea: Journey into the West Martin, Cynthia & Schulz, Barbara, illus. (p. 1500)
—Sacagawea: Journey into the West Martin, Cynthia & Schultz, Barbara, illus. (p. 1500)
—Your Life As a Pharaoh in Ancient Egypt Ebbeler, Jeff, illus. (p. 1981)
—Your Life As a Private on the Lewis & Clark Expedition Madden, Colleen, illus. (p. 1981)
Gunderson, Jessica Sarah & Gunderson, Jessica. Lewis & Clark Expedition Erwin, Steve et al, illus. (p. 1004)
—Triangle Shirtwaist Factory Fire Miller, Phil et al, illus. (p. 1785)
Gunderson, Jessica Sarah, et al. Eli Whitney & the Cotton Gin Acerno, Gerry, illus. (p. 512)
—Eli Whitney & the Cotton Gin Acerno, Gerry et al, illus. (p. 512)
Gunderson, Megan M. Andrew Jackson. (p. 72)
—Andrew Johnson. (p. 72)
—Australian Shepherds. (p. 116)
—Banks & Banking. (p. 136)
—Bears: Level 1. Keimig, Candice, illus. (p. 151)
—Bears Eat & Grow: Level 2. Keimig, Candice, illus. (p. 151)
—Bears in the Mountains: Level 3. Keimig, Candice, illus. (p. 152)
—Benjamin Harrison. (p. 165)
—Franklin D. Roosevelt. (p. 630)
—Gerald Ford. (p. 666)
—James A. Garfield. (p. 906)
—James Buchanan. (p. 907)
—James Madison. (p. 907)
—James Monroe. (p. 907)
—John F. Kennedy. (p. 921)
—John Tyler. (p. 923)
—Labor & Management. (p. 969)
—Lyndon B. Johnson. (p. 1066)
—Scottish Deerhounds. (p. 1531)
—Whippets. (p. 1912)
—William McKinley. (p. 1933)
Gunderson, Vivian D. Bible Is the Best Book. Why? Mowery, Linda Williams & Murphy, Emmy Lou, illus. (p. 175)
Gundert, Margaret. D. Q. & the SOOYOO Gundert, Marjorie, illus. (p. 398)
Gundert, Marjorie, illus. see Gundert, Margaret.
Gunes, Aysenur. Makkah & Madinah Activity Book. Polat, Ercan, illus. (p. 1082)
—Mosques of the World Activity Book. Polat, Ercan, illus. (p. 1176)
Gunetsreiner, Nina, jt. auth. see Schoene, Kerstin.
Gunhus, Jeff. Jack Templar & the Monster Hunter Academy. (p. 903)
—Jack Templar Monster Hunter. (p. 903)
Gunlock, Sheila. Groovy Granny & the Character Bees. (p. 725)
Gunn, Barbara. Inuit Tales: Read Well Level K Unit 10 Storybook. Jerde, Susan, illus. (p. 883)
—Old MacDonald's Farm: Read Well Level K Unit 7 Storybook. Marier, Chuck, illus. (p. 1284)
Gunn, Barbara, jt. auth. see Jones, Shelley V.
Gunn, Barbara & Dunn, Richard. Flowers: Read Well Level K Unit 9 Storybook. Nolte, Larry, illus. (p. 608)
Gunn, Barbara, et al. Mark & Dan Go West: Read Well Level K Unit 17 Storybook. Weber, Philip A., Jr., illus. (p. 1095)
Gunn, Dusty M. Paul & Peter Possum. (p. 1330)
Gunn, Joni & Owenby, Ina. Santa's Wedding. (p. 1513)
Gunn, Linda, illus. see Poulter, J. R.
Gunn, Murray. Dragon Bones: Two Years Beneath the Skin of a Himalayan Kingdom. (p. 476)
Gunn, Richard. Monster Movers. (p. 1168)
—Racing Cars. (p. 1432)
Gunn, Robin Jones. Christy Miller Collection (p. 317)
—Christy Miller Collection Vol. 3. (p. 317)
—Christy Miller Collection, Vol 1 (p. 317)
—Close Your Eyes (p. 334)
—Mrs. Rosey Posey & the Fine China Plate Schofield, Christina Diane, illus. (p. 1187)
—Open Your Heart Vol. 3 (p. 1300)
—Sierra Jensen Collection (p. 1573)
—Sierra Jensen Collection, Vol 1 (p. 1573)
—Whispers. (p. 1912)
Gunnell, Beth, jt. illus. see Davies, Hannah.
Gunnell, Beth, et al. Summer Fun Doodles: Sunny Full-Color Pictures to Complete & Create. (p. 1674)
Gunnella, illus. see McMillan, Bruce.
Gunnery, Sylvia. Out of Bounds. (p. 1311)
—Personal Best (p. 1344)
Gunney, Lynn Tuttle. Meet Jesus: The Life & Lessons of a Beloved Teacher. Conteh-Morgan, Jane, illus. (p. 1121)
Gunning, Monica. Shelter in Our Car. Pedlar, Elaine, illus. (p. 1565)
—Under the Breadfruit Tree: Island Poems. Broeck, Fabricio Vanden, illus. (p. 1813)
Gunning, P. M. Adventures of Corrie & Trix. (p. 17)
Gunnufson, Charlotte. Halloween Hustle Atteberry, Kevan, illus. (p. 738)
Gunson, Dave, illus. see Martin, Justin McCory.
Gunson, Jonathan. Divine Calling. (p. 454)
Gunston, Bill, et al. World of Flight. (p. 1956)
Gunston, Bill Tudor & Guy, John. Battle Machines. (p. 146)
Gunston, Bill Tudor & Parker, Steve. Fasten Your Seatbelt! Mind-Boggling Machines. (p. 576)
Gunter, Frances. Golden Horseshoe (p. 695)
—Golden Horseshoe 2 (p. 695)
Gunter, Jacob Ben, et al. Daily Bugle Stories. (p. 399)
Gunter, Jill H. Three Dinosaur Friends. (p. 1742)
Gunter, Miles & Shannon, Kelsey. Yeti vs. Vampire. (p. 1971)
Gunter, Tina. Monday. (p. 1163)
Gunther, Chat, photos by see Dunn, Anthony, illus.
Gunther, Joseph. Bluff Sabiston, Susan, illus. (p. 204)
Gunther, Richard, illus. see Suter, Janine.
Gunther, Vanessa. Chief Joseph: A Biography (p. 301)
Gunthridge, Jack. Life. (p. 1007)
Gunton, Mark, jt. auth. see Russell, Willy.
Gunton, Sharon. Date & Acquaintance Rape. (p. 409)
Gunton, Sharon, ed. Learning Disabilities. (p. 985)
Gunzenhauser, Kelly, jt. auth. see Reeves, Diane Lindsey.
Gunzi, jt. auth. see Picthall, Chez.
Gunzi, Christane. 1 2 3. (p. 1990)
—ABC. (p. 2)
—Colours. (p. 346)
—Farm. (p. 573)
—My Body. Murrell, Deborah, ed. (p. 1198)
—My Favourite Things. (p. 1203)
—My Lovely Day. (p. 1213)
—Opposites. Murrell, Deborah, ed. (p. 1300)
—Pets. (p. 1348)
—Words. (p. 1951)
—Zoo. Zwemmer, Dominic, ed. (p. 1988)
Gunzi, Christiane. Big Noisy Tractors. (p. 183)
—Big Noisy Trucks. (p. 183)
—Clothes. (p. 334)
—Colores. (p. 344)
—Colours. (p. 346)
—Fluffy Babies. (p. 608)
—Formas. (p. 620)
—Friendly Pets. (p. 638)
—Furry Kittens. (p. 650)
—In the House. (p. 866)
—Let's Count Noisy Kittens. (p. 995)
—Let's Count Noisy Puppies. (p. 995)
—Little Ponies: A Feels Real Book to Touch & Share. (p. 1033)
—Little Ponies. (p. 1033)
—My Home. (p. 1211)
—Numbers. (p. 1271)
—Numeros. (p. 1273)
—On the Farm. (p. 1290)
—Pigs in Pink. (p. 1358)
—Tamanos. (p. 1704)
—Under the Sea. (p. 1814)
—Who's Hiding? at the Zoo. (p. 1920)
—Words. (p. 1951)
Gunzi, Christiane, ed. see Picthall, Chez.
Gunzi, Christiane, jt. auth. see Calver, Paul.
Gunzi, Christiane, contrib. by. Colores. (p. 344)
Gunzi, Christiane. Shapes. (p. 1560)
Gunzi, Christiane, jt. auth. see Gunzi, Christiane.
Gunzi, Christiane, jt. auth. see Picthall, Chez.
Gunzi, Christiane & Gunzi, Christiane. Colours. (p. 346)
Guo, Amy. Vhonk. (p. 1839)
Guo, Jinsong. Touching Stories by Dr. Guo. (p. 1772)
Gupta, Garima, illus. see Ramanathan, Priya.
Gupta, Jennifer. Love Shapes. (p. 1060)
—May I? (p. 1112)
—Silly Turtle! That's Not on the Menu! (p. 1576)
Gupta, Ranu. Campfires & Creepy Calls. (p. 257)
Guptara, Jyoti, jt. auth. see Guptara, Suresh.
Guptara, Suresh & Guptara, Jyoti. Conspiracy of Calaspia. (p. 359)
Gura, Timothy & Lee, Charlotte. Oral Interpretation. (p. 1301)
Guralnick, Peter. Nighthawk Blues: A Novel. (p. 1255)
Gurantz, Maya, tr. see Grossman, David.
Gurden, Gloria. Adventures of Wersel Driftwood. (p. 24)
—Wersel Goes to Hong Kong. (p. 1875)
Gurevich, David A., tr. see Schneersohn, Yosef Yitzchak.
Gurevich, Leonid M. Russian-English Lexicon of Chess Praxis (p. 1498)
Gurevich, Margaret. Balancing ACT. Hagel, Brooke, illus. (p. 133)
—Chloe by Design Hagel, Brooke, illus. (p. 308)
—Chloe by Design: Making the Cut Hagel, Brooke, illus. (p. 308)
—Design Destiny Hagel, Brooke, illus. (p. 429)
—Design Disaster. Hagel, Brooke, illus. (p. 429)
—Design Diva Hagel, Brooke, illus. (p. 429)
—Fashion Week Finale. Hagel, Brooke, illus. (p. 576)
—First Cut Hagel, Brooke, illus. (p. 594)
—Intern Ambition. Hagel, Brooke, illus. (p. 880)
—Runway Rundown. Hagel, Brooke, illus. (p. 1497)
—Unraveling Hagel, Brooke, illus. (p. 1822)
Gurewitz, Samantha & Polay, Ellyn. Marvin Mcgunk & All of His Junk. (p. 1099)
Gurihiru Staff, illus. see Sumerak, Marc.
Gurihiru Staff, illus. see Yang, Gene Luen & DiMartino, Michael Dante.
Gurihiru Staff, jt. illus. see Di Vito, Andrea.
Gurin, Lara, illus. see Duey, Kathleen.
Gurin, Lara, illus. see Gould, Robert.
Gurin, Lara, illus. see Duey, Kathleen.
Guritz, Linda F., illus. see Button, Kevin.
Gurkow, Malkie. Building a Better Me: Student's Workbook. (p. 238)
Gurley, James. Oracle of Delphi. (p. 1301)
Gurley, Russ, ed. see Hamper, Robbie.
Gurley, Russ, ed. see Moran, Theresa & Malone, Dan.
Gurman, Sarah, jt. text see Kavanaugh, Missy.
Gurney, Beth. Sand & Soil. (p. 1510)
Gurney, James. Dinotopia: The World Beneath. (p. 445)
—Dinotopia: The World Beneath. Gurney, James, illus. (p. 445)
—Dinotopia: Journey to Chandara. Gurney, James, illus. (p. 445)
—Dinotopia - First Flight. (p. 445)
Gurney, James, jt. auth. see Gurney, James.
Gurney, James & Gurney, James. Land Apart from Time. Gurney, James & Gurney, James, illus. (p. 973)
Gurney, John Steven. Dinosaur Train. (p. 443)
Gurney, John Steven, illus. see Dower, Laura.
Gurney, John Steven, illus. see Earhart, Kristin.
Gurney, John Steven, illus. see Finch, Kate.
Gurney, John Steven, illus. see Moore, Clement C.
Gurney, John Steven, illus. see Moore, Clement C. & Linz, Peter.
Gurney, John Steven, illus. see Roy, Ron.
Gurney, John Steven, illus. see Roy, Ronald.
Gurney, John Steven, illus. see Usian, Michael E.
Gurney, John Steven, illus. see Wallace, Carol & Wallace, Bill.
Gurney, John Steven, tr. see Roy, Ron.
Gurney, Stella. Aventuras de Pinocho. Basic, Zdenko, illus. (p. 119)
—Mr. Bickle & the Ghost. Raga, Silvia, illus. (p. 1184)
—Not so Silly Sausage. Million, Liz, illus. (p. 1267)
—Sally Sets Sail. Worsley, Belinda, illus. (p. 1505)
Gurney, Stella, jt. auth. see Sparklington, Madame.
Gurney, Stella & Tailfeather, Speck Lee. Architecture According to Pigeons. (p. 95)
Gurnick, Isabella Grace & Beals, Stephen Naayvek. Girls Have Eyelashes. (p. 680)
Gurock, Jeffrey S. Judaism's Encounter with American Sports. (p. 930)
Gurovich, Natalia, illus. see Robleda, Margarita.
Gurqui, Montserrat, tr. see Donelly, Joe & Donnelly, Joe.
Gurr, Simon, illus. see Byrne, Eugene.
Gurrentz, Sheryl, jt. auth. see Singer, Cindy.
Gurstelle, William. Art of the Catapult: Build Greek Ballistae, Roman Onagers, English Trebuchets, & More Ancient Artillery. (p. 102)
Gurstien, Shari, jt. auth. see Erichson, Carey.

Full bibliographic information is available on the Title Index page number referenced in parentheses at the end of each entry

Gürth, Per-Henrik. ABC of Toronto. (p. 3)
—Canada All Year. (p. 260)
—Canada in Colours. (p. 260)
—Canada in Colours. Gürth, Per-Henrik, illus. (p. 260)
—Canada in Words. Gürth, Per-Henrik, illus. (p. 260)
—First Hockey Words. Gürth, Per-Henrik, illus. (p. 595)
Gurth, Per-Henrik. Snowy Sports: Ready, Set, Play! (p. 1601)
GüRth, Per-Henrik. When Wishes Come True. (p. 1905)
Gurth, Per-Henrik, illus. see Bellefontaine, Kim.
Gurth, Per-Henrik, illus. see Ghione, Yvette.
Gurth, Per-Henrik, jt. auth. see Ghione, Yvette.
Gurtler, Janet. 16 Things I Thought Were True. (p. 1995)
—Beaver. (p. 154)
—Cora's Decision. Wood, Katie, illus. (p. 366)
—How I Lost You. (p. 810)
—If I Tell. (p. 853)
—I'm Not Her. (p. 859)
—Maple Leaf. (p. 1090)
—Rachel's Secret. Wood, Katie, illus. (p. 1432)
—Secrets Beneath the Sea. Wood, Katie, illus. (p. 1544)
—Shyanna's Song. Wood, Katie, illus. (p. 1572)
—Shyanna's Wish. Wood, Katie, illus. (p. 1572)
—Small Game. (p. 1592)
—Truth about Us. (p. 1794)
—Who I Kissed. (p. 1915)
Guruge, Anura. Pup Is Not a Toy. (p. 1417)
Gurule, Jennifer. Look at Aunt Clare's Hair. Gurule, Jennifer, illus. (p. 1048)
Gurule, Teri. Izzy the Dizzy Dragonfly. (p. 901)
Gurvis, Laura K. Learn & Do Bible Book. Ben-Moshe, Jana, illus. (p. 982)
Guscott, Maggie. On the Job, Book 3. (p. 1290)
Guscott, Maggie, jt. auth. see McKay, Lucia.
Gushue, Brenda. Through the Storm (p. 1745)
Gussoni, Clizia. Awesome Book of Bugs! (p. 121)
Gustafon, Karen. Mongolia Cries Out for Prayer: Will You Be the One to Answer the Cry? (p. 1164)
Gustafson, Angela. Imagine a House: A Journey to Fascinating Houses Around the World. (p. 860)
Gustafson, Chris. Acting Cool! Using Reader's Theater to Teach Math & Science in Your Classroom (p. 9)
—Acting Cool! Using Reader's Theater to Teach Language Arts & Social Studies in Your Classroom (p. 9)
Gustafson, Jenna. Saving Fort Smoky. (p. 1517)
Gustafson, Monica. Quick Make Artic Activities. (p. 1427)
Gustafson, Sandra A. Great Sleeps Italy: Florence, Rome, Venice. (p. 718)
Gustafson, Sarah. Whales, Dolphins, & More Marine Mammals. (p. 1878)
Gustafson, Scott. Cuentos y Cantos de Navidad. (p. 390)
—Eddie: The Lost Youth of Edgar Allan Poe. Gustafson, Scott, illus. (p. 503)
—Favorite Nursery Rhymes from Mother Goose. (p. 578)
Gustafson, Scott W. Biblical Amnesia: A Forgotten Story of Redemption. (p. 176)
Gustafson, Troy, illus. see Brooks, John R.
Gustaitis, Joseph. Figure Skating. (p. 586)
—Snowboard. (p. 1600)
—Speed Skating. (p. 1624)
Gustaitis, Joseph Alan. Arctic Trucker. (p. 96)
—Chinese Americans. (p. 307)
—Storm Chasers. (p. 1655)
Gustavson, Adam, illus. see Blumenthal, Deborah.
Gustavson, Adam, illus. see Borden, Louise.
Gustavson, Adam, illus. see Edwards, Michelle.
Gustavson, Adam, illus. see Einhorn, Edward.
Gustavson, Adam, illus. see Glaser, Linda.
Gustavson, Adam, illus. see Harley, Bill.
Gustavson, Adam, illus. see Harris, John.
Gustavson, Adam, illus. see Holm, Jennifer L.
Gustavson, Adam, illus. see Kimmelman, Leslie.
Gustavson, Adam, illus. see Laminack, Lester L.
Gustavson, Adam, illus. see Lendroth, Susan.
Gustavson, Adam, illus. see Lucas, Eileen.
Gustavson, Adam, illus. see Ludwig, Trudy.
Gustavson, Adam, illus. see Lunde, Darrin.
Gustavson, Adam, illus. see Robertson, Sebastian.
Gustavson, Adam, illus. see Weber, Elka.
Gustavson, Adam, jt. auth. see Borden, Louise.
Gustavson, Adam, tr. see Borden, Louise.
Gusterson, Leigh, illus. see de Rham, Mickey.
Gusti. Half of an Elephant. Gusti, illus. (p. 736)
Gusti, illus. see Alcantara, Ricardo.
Gusti, illus. see Alcántara, Ricardo.
Gusti, illus. see Alcántara, Ricardo.
Gusti, illus. see Bucay, Jorge.
Gusti, illus. see Farre, Lluis.
Gusti, illus. see Montes, Graciela & Montes, Graciela.
Gustke, Carol Davis. Angel's First Job. (p. 75)
Gustlin, Zoe. Samantha, Abby & Jake: A Surprise Discovery. (p. 1507)
—Samantha, Abby & Jake Finding Gold. (p. 1507)
—Samantha, Abby & Jake Lost in the War. (p. 1507)
—Samantha, Abby & Jake Moving West. (p. 1507)
Gustovich, Michael, illus. see Siembieda, Kevin.
Gutch, Michael. Sticky, Sticky, Stuck! Björkman, Steve, illus. (p. 1650)
Gutelle, jt. auth. see Puckett.
Gutenberg, S. R. Abby Longbotham & the Quilt. (p. 2)
Guthman, Deborah, tr. see Tepper, Yona.
Guthridge, Bettina, illus. see Ende, Debra.
Guthridge, Bettina, illus. see Shanahan, Lisa.
Guthridge, Bettina, illus. see Walker, Lois.
Guthrie, Janelle. Rachel & the Pink & Green Dragon. (p. 1431)
Guthrie, Lewis, illus. see Satterfield, April.
Guthrie, Randy. Rain-the Civil War Years. (p. 1435)
Guthrie, Woody. Enviarme a Ti Flor Ada, Alma, tr. (p. 531)
—Riding in My Car. (p. 1471)
Gutierez, Francisco, illus. see Dupont, Matthew.
Gutierrez, Akemi, illus. see Balsley, Tilda.
Gutierrez, Akemi, illus. see Gaydos, Nora.
Gutierrez, Akemi, illus. see Martin, David.
Gutierrez, Akemi, illus. see Ramos, Jorge.
Gutierrez, Akemia, illus. see Newman, Vivian.
Gutiérrez Bello, Marta, jt. auth. see Bennet, Archie.
Gutierrez, Chris, illus. see Sanchez, Elizabeth.
Gutierrez, Dave, jt. auth. see Irving, Washington.
Gutierrez, Dave & Irving, Washington. Legend of Sleepy Hollow Smith, Tod & Smith, Tod G., illus. (p. 988)
Gutierrez, Debbi Miller. Cactus Factory. (p. 250)
Gutierrez, Elisa. Picturescape. (p. 1356)
Gutiérrez, Elisa, jt. auth. see Acheson, Alison.
Gutiérrez, Elisa & Owlkids Books Inc. Staff. Letter Lunch (p. 1002)
Gutierrez, Gloria, tr. see Repko, Marya.
Gutierrez, Guillermo, tr. see Barnham, Kay.
Gutierrez, Guillermo, tr. see Brown, Jonatha A.
Gutiérrez, Guillermo, tr. see Gorman, Jacqueline Laks & Laks Gorman, Jacqueline.
Gutiérrez, Guillermo, tr. see Gorman, Jacqueline Laks.
Gutierrez, Guillermo, tr. see Mezzanotte, Jim.
Gutierrez, Jose Angel. Making of a Civil Rights Leader: Jose Angel Gutierrez. (p. 1082)
Gutierrez, Michaela Mahsetky. Jummy the Turtle. (p. 933)
Gutierrez, Rochelle. Dear Monster. (p. 419)
—Melvin Munch Wants My Lunch. (p. 1125)
Gutierrez, Rudy, illus. see Brown, Monica.
Gutierrez, Rudy, illus. see Dorros, Arthur.
Gutierrez, Rudy, illus. see Golio, Gary.
Gutierrez, Rudy, illus. see Sol & K'naan.
Gutierrez-Green, Sandra. Colors in My Garden. (p. 345)
Gutierrez-Haley, Lisa. New Pet: Adventures of Hayden & Jace. (p. 1246)
—Wiggly Tooth: Adventures of Hayden & Jace. (p. 1928)
Gutknecht, Allison. Cast Is the Perfect Accessory: And Other Lessons I've Learned. Lewis, Stevie, illus. (p. 276)
—Don't Wear Polka-Dot Underwear with White Pants: And Other Lessons I've Learned. Lewis, Stevie, illus. (p. 469)
—Never Wear Red Lipstick on Picture Day: And Other Lessons I've Learned. Lewis, Stevie, illus. (p. 1243)
—Pizza Is the Best Breakfast: And Other Lessons I've Learned. Lewis, Stevie, illus. (p. 1365)
Gutman, Anne. Cadeau de Noel. (p. 250)
—Gaspard & Lisa's Christmas Surprise. Hallensleben, Georg, illus. (p. 657)
—Gaspard et Lisa au Musee. (p. 657)
—Lisa a New York. (p. 1021)
—Lisa's Baby Sister. Hallensleben, Georg, illus. (p. 1022)
Gutman, Anne, jt. auth. see Hallensleben, Georg.
Gutman, Anne & Hallensleben, Georg. Daddy Cuddles. (p. 398)
—Daddy Kisses. (p. 398)
—Mommy Hugs. (p. 1162)
—Mommy Loves. (p. 1162)
Gutman, Anne, et al. Baños. Hallensleben, Georg, illus. (p. 136)
—Besitos. (p. 168)
—Colores. (p. 344)
—Numeros. (p. 1273)
—Ruidos. (p. 1494)
—Sueños. (p. 1672)
Gutman, Bill. Lance Armstrong: A Biography. (p. 973)
Gutman, Colas & Seegmuller, Stephanie. Pointless Leopard: What Good Are Kids Anyway? Perret, Delphine, illus. (p. 1377)
Gutman, Dan. Abner & Me. (p. 5)
—Babe Ruth & the Ice Cream Mess. Garvin, Elaine, illus. (p. 123)
—Back in Time with Benjamin Franklin. (p. 130)
—Back to School, Weird Kids Rule! (p. 130)
—Back to School, Weird Kids Rule! Paillot, Jim, illus. (p. 130)
—Bunny Double, We're in Trouble! Paillot, Jim et al, illus. (p. 242)
—Casey Back at Bat. Johnson, Steve et al, illus. (p. 275)
—Christmas Genie. Santat, Dan, illus. (p. 314)
—Coach Hyatt Is a Riot! Paillot, Jim, illus. (p. 336)
—Day Roy Riegels Ran the Wrong Way. Talbott, Kerry, illus. (p. 414)
—Deck the Halls, We're off the Walls! (p. 421)
—Deck the Halls, We're off the Walls! Paillot, Jim, illus. (p. 421)
—Dr. Brad Has Gone Mad! (p. 475)
—Dr. Brad Has Gone Mad! Paillot, Jim, illus. (p. 475)
—Dr. Carbles Is Losing His Marbles! Paillot, Jim, illus. (p. 475)
—Dr. Nicholas Is Ridiculous! (p. 475)
—Dr. Nicholas Is Ridiculous! Paillot, Jim, illus. (p. 475)
—Election! A Kid's Guide to Picking Our President 2012. (p. 508)
—From Texas with Love. (p. 644)
—Funny Boy Meets the Airsick Alien from Andromeda. Dykes, John S., illus. (p. 649)
—Funny Boy Meets the Dumbbell Dentist from Deimos (with Dangerous Dental Decay) Dietz, Mike, illus. (p. 649)
—Funny Boy Takes on the Chit-Chatting Cheeses from Chattanooga. Dietz, Mike, illus. (p. 649)
—Funny Boy Versus the Bubble-Brained Barbers from the Big Bang. Dietz, Mike, illus. (p. 649)
—Genius Files #4: from Texas with Love. (p. 661)
—Get Rich Quick Club. (p. 668)
—Getting Air. (p. 669)
—Homework Machine. (p. 794)
—Honus & Me. (p. 795)
—It's Halloween, I'm Turning Green! (p. 897)
—It's Halloween, I'm Turning Green! Paillot, Jim, illus. (p. 897)
—Jackie & Me. (p. 903)
—Jackie Robinson & the Big Game. Garvin, Elaine, illus. (p. 904)
—Jim & Me. (p. 917)
—Johnny Hangtime. (p. 923)
—Kid Who Ran for President. (p. 952)
—License to Thrill. (p. 1007)
—Mayor Hubble Is in Trouble! (p. 1113)
—Mayor Hubble Is in Trouble! Paillot, Jim, illus. (p. 1113)
—Mickey & Me. (p. 1136)
—Million Dollar Putt. (p. 1144)
—Million Dollar Shot. (p. 1144)
—Million Dollar Strike. (p. 1144)
—Miss Brown Is Upside Down! Paillot, Jim, illus. (p. 1151)
—Miss Child Has Gone Wild! Paillot, Jim, illus. (p. 1151)
—Miss Daisy Is Crazy! Paillot, Jim, illus. (p. 1151)
—Miss Holly Is Too Jolly! Paillot, Jim, illus. (p. 1151)
—Miss Klute Is a Hoot! (p. 1151)
—Miss Klute Is a Hoot! Paillot, Jim, illus. (p. 1151)
—Miss Kraft Is Daft! Paillot, Jim, illus. (p. 1151)
—Miss Laney Is Zany! (p. 1151)
—Miss Laney Is Zany! Paillot, Jim, illus. (p. 1151)
—Miss Lazar Is Bizarre! Paillot, Jim, illus. (p. 1151)
—Miss Mary Is Scary! Paillot, Jim, illus. (p. 1151)
—Miss Small Is off the Wall! Paillot, Jim, illus. (p. 1152)
—Miss Suki Is Kooky! Paillot, Jim, illus. (p. 1152)
—Mission Unstoppable. (p. 1153)
—Mr. Burke Is Berserk! (p. 1184)
—Mr. Burke Is Berserk! Paillot, Jim, illus. (p. 1184)
—Mr. Cooper Is Super! Paillot, Jim, illus. (p. 1184)
—Mr. Docker Is off His Rocker! Paillot, Jim, illus. (p. 1184)
—Mr. Granite Is from Another Planet! Paillot, Jim, illus. (p. 1185)
—Mr. Harrison Is Embarrassin'! Paillot, Jim, illus. (p. 1185)
—Mr. Hynde Is Out of His Mind! Paillot, Jim, illus. (p. 1185)
—Mr. Jack Is a Maniac! (p. 1185)
—Mr. Jack Is a Maniac! Paillot, Jim, illus. (p. 1185)
—Mr. Klutz Is Nuts! Paillot, Jim, illus. (p. 1185)
—Mr. Louie Is Screwy! Paillot, Jim, illus. (p. 1185)
—Mr. Macky Is Wacky! Paillot, Jim, illus. (p. 1185)
—Mr. Sunny Is Funny! Paillot, Jim, illus. (p. 1186)
—Mr. Tony Is Full of Baloney! Paillot, Jim, illus. (p. 1186)
—Mrs. Cooney Is Loony! Paillot, Jim, illus. (p. 1187)
—Mrs. Dole Is Out of Control! Paillot, Jim, illus. (p. 1187)
—Mrs. Jafee Is Daffy! (p. 1187)
—Mrs. Jafee Is Daffy! Paillot, Jim, illus. (p. 1187)
—Mrs. Kormel Is Not Normal! Paillot, Jim, illus. (p. 1187)
—Mrs. Lane Is a Pain! (p. 1187)
—Mrs. Lilly Is Silly! Paillot, Jim, illus. (p. 1187)
—Mrs. Lizzy Is Dizzy! (p. 1187)
—Mrs. Lizzy Is Dizzy! Paillot, Jim, illus. (p. 1187)
—Mrs. Patty Is Batty! Paillot, Jim, illus. (p. 1187)
—Mrs. Roopy Is Loopy! Paillot, Jim, illus. (p. 1187)
—Mrs. Yonkers Is Bonkers! Paillot, Jim, illus. (p. 1188)
—Ms. Beard Is Weird! (p. 1188)
—Ms. Beard Is Weird! Paillot, Jim, illus. (p. 1188)
—Ms. Coco Is Loco! Paillot, Jim, illus. (p. 1188)
—Ms. Cuddy Is Nutty! Paillot, Jim, illus. (p. 1188)
—Ms. Hannah Is Bananas! Paillot, Jim, illus. (p. 1188)
—Ms. Krup Cracks Me Up! Paillot, Jim, illus. (p. 1188)
—Ms. Lagrange Is Strange! Paillot, Jim, illus. (p. 1188)
—Ms. Leakey Is Freaky! Paillot, Jim, illus. (p. 1188)
—Ms. Leakey Is Freaky! No. 12. Paillot, Jim, illus. (p. 1188)
—Ms. Sue Has No Clue! (p. 1188)
—Ms. Sue Has No Clue! Paillot, Jim, illus. (p. 1188)
—Ms. Todd Is Odd! Paillot, Jim, illus. (p. 1188)
—My Weird School Collection Paillot, Jim, illus. (p. 1221)
—My Weird School Daze! Paillot, Jim, illus. (p. 1221)
—My Weird School Daze 12-Book Box Set Paillot, Jim, illus. (p. 1221)
—My Weird School Special: Bunny Double, We're in Trouble. (p. 1221)
—My Weird School Special: Back to School, Weird Kids Rule! Paillot, Jim, illus. (p. 1221)
—My Weird School Special: Bunny Double, We're in Trouble! Paillot, Jim, illus. (p. 1221)
—My Weird School Special: Deck the Halls, We're off the Walls! Paillot, Jim, illus. (p. 1221)
—My Weird School Special - Oh, Valentine, We've Lost Our Minds! Paillot, Jim, illus. (p. 1221)
—My Weird Writing Tips. Paillot, Jim, illus. (p. 1221)
—My Weirder School #10: Mr. Jack Is a Maniac! Paillot, Jim, illus. (p. 1221)
—My Weirder School #9: Ms. Sue Has No Clue! Paillot, Jim, illus. (p. 1221)
—My Weirdest School #2: Ms. Cuddy Is Nutty! Paillot, Jim, illus. (p. 1221)
—Never Say Genius. (p. 1243)
—Nightmare at the Book Fair. (p. 1255)
—Officer Spence Makes No Sense! Paillot, Jim, illus. (p. 1280)
—Oh, Valentine, We've Lost Our Minds! (p. 1281)
—Race for the Sky: The Kitty Hawk Diaries of Johnny Moore. (p. 1431)
—Rappy the Raptor. Bowers, Tim, illus. (p. 1439)
—Ray & Me. (p. 1441)
—Recycle This Book: 100 Top Children's Book Authors Tell You How to Go Green. (p. 1453)
—Return of the Homework Machine. (p. 1464)
—Roberto & Me. (p. 1479)
—Satch & Me. (p. 1515)
—Shoeless Joe & Me. (p. 1568)
—Talent Show. (p. 1701)
—Ted & Me. (p. 1712)
—Willie & Me. (p. 1934)
—You Only Die Twice. (p. 1976)
Gutman, Dan, ed. Recycle This Book: 100 Top Children's Book Authors Tell You How to Go Green. (p. 1453)
Gutner, Howard. America's Secret Weapon: The Navajo Code Talkers of World War II. (p. 64)
—Drums: The World's Heartbeat. (p. 487)
—Egypt. (p. 506)
—Puerto Rico. (p. 1415)
—Speaker of the House. (p. 1623)
Gutsche, Brigitte. Intruder. (p. 883)
Gutsche, Henry. Hitler's Willing Warrior. (p. 786)
Guttentag, Devora. Saving Soraya. (p. 1517)
Guttier, Benedicte. At the Circus - Welsh Edition. (p. 111)
—Dinosaur Dinners - Welsh Edition. (p. 442)
Guttiere, Benedicte. When Christmas Comes. (p. 1901)
—When Christmas Comes - Welsh Edition. Guttiere, Benedicte, illus. (p. 1901)
Guttilla, Peter. Your Personal Guide to Psychic Development. (p. 1981)
Guttmacher, Joyce. Harvesting Medicine on the Hill. (p. 752)
Guttman, Burton S. Genetics: The Code of Life. (p. 661)
Guttman, S. Daniel. Passover Zoo Seder Ratner, Phillip, illus. (p. 1327)
Guttormsen, Trygve Lund, illus. see Vars, Elle Márjá.
Gutwein, Austin & Hillard, Todd. Take Your Best Shot: Do Something Bigger Than Yourself (p. 1697)
Gutwein, Gwendolyn, illus. see Molnar, Cheri Eplin.
Gutwein, Gwendolyn, illus. see Mustaine Hettinger, Cynthia.
Gutwein, Mary Lee. Invitation to Lunch. (p. 886)
Gutzschhahn, Uwe-Michael. Lighthouse under the Clouds. Docherty, Thomas, illus. (p. 1015)
Guy, Belinda. First Aid Manual for Children: In the Form of Three Short Stories. (p. 592)
Guy, Big, jt. auth. see Nemec, Gale.
Guy, Ginger F., jt. auth. see Guy, Ginger Foglesong.
Guy, Ginger Foglesong. Bravo! Moreno, Rene King, illus. (p. 224)
—Dias y Dias: Days & Days. Moreno, Rene King, illus. (p. 435)
—Fiesta! Moreno, Rene King, illus. (p. 584)
—Go Back to Bed! Bernardin, James, illus. (p. 686)
—Mi Abuelita. Escrivá, Vivi, illus. (p. 1132)
Guy, Ginger Foglesong & Guy, Ginger F. Fiesta! Board Book. Moreno, Rene King, illus. (p. 584)
—Siesta. Moreno, Rene King, illus. (p. 1573)
—Siesta Board Book. Moreno, Rene King, illus. (p. 1573)
—¡Perros! ¡Perros! Glick, Sharon, illus. (p. 1344)
Guy, Glen. Adventure Fire: Adventures of Dusty Sourdough. (p. 14)
Guy, John. Drake & the Elizabethan Explorers. (p. 479)
—Egyptian Life. (p. 506)
—Elizabeth I & the Armada. (p. 513)
—Ghosts. (p. 672)
—Henry VIII & His Six Wives. (p. 768)
—Kings & Queens (p. 960)
—Medieval Life. (p. 1119)
—Roman Life. (p. 1486)
—Tudor & Stuart Life. (p. 1796)
—Victoria. (p. 1840)
—Victorian Life. (p. 1840)
Guy, John, jt. auth. see Gorman, Jacqueline.
Guy, John, jt. auth. see Gunston, Bill Tudor.
Guy, Joseph. One Childs Cry for Hope. (p. 1294)
Guy, K. T., jt. auth. see Cayce, Jw.
Guy, Only A. Hard Questions about Christianity. (p. 748)
—Hard Questions about the End Times. (p. 748)
Guy, Pauline. Let's Count. (p. 995)
Guy, Pauline & Pierre-Louis, Jerry. Alphabet Rocks: Happy Kids Rock. (p. 50)
Guy, Robert, illus. see Gilchrist, Reona.
Guy, Sue, illus. see Gagliano, Eugene M.
Guy, Sue, illus. see Whitney, Gleaves & Whitney, Louise.
Guy, Susan, illus. see Gagliano, Eugene.
Guy, Susan, illus. see Whitney, Gleaves & Whitney, Louise Doak.
Guy, Susan, illus. see Whitney, Gleaves & Whitney, Louise.
Guy, Will, illus. see Ulick, Michael Ackerman.
Guyatt, Ben. Billy Green Saves the Day. (p. 187)
Guymon, Jennette King, illus. see Midgley, Elizabeth Cole.
Guymon-King, jt. auth. see Ross, Melanie H.
Guymon-King, Jennette, illus. see Ross, Mary H.
Guymon-King, Jennette, jt. auth. see Ross, Melanie H.
Guyot, Céline, illus. see Amblard, Odile.
Guyot, Rebecca. Flyin' Ryan the Rescue Ranger: In: the Puzzleton Storm (p. 609)
Guyton, M. Little Remembrance. (p. 1035)
Guzaldo, Jessica. Murder & Betrayal DeFalco, Julie & Cowhey, Dennis R., eds. (p. 1192)
Guze, Tessa, illus. see Tetlow, Karin.
Guzek, Greta, illus. see Clark, Catherine Anthony.
Guzek, Greta, illus. see Perry, Robert.
Guzek, Greta, illus. see White, Howard.
Guzman, Carlos Jose, illus. see Petrucha, Stefan & Kinney, Sarah.
Guzman Ferrer, Martin Luis, tr. see Adamson, Thomas K.
Guzman Ferrer, Martin Luis, tr. see Hall, Margaret C. & Hall, Margaret.
Guzman Ferrer, Martin Luis, tr. see Schuh, Mari C.
Guzman Ferrer, Martin Luis, tr. see Schuh, Mari C. & Schuh, Mari.
Guzman, Jacob, illus. see Guzman, Raquel.
Guzman, Jaime. I've Got 10! Understanding Addition. (p. 900)
Guzman, Lila. Kichi in Jungle Jeopardy. Johnson, Regan, illus. (p. 951)
Guzman, Lila & Guzman, Rick. Cesar Chavez: Fighting for Fairness. (p. 288)
—Cesar Chavez: La Lucha Por lo Justo. (p. 288)
Guzmán, Lila & Guzmán, Rick. César Chávez: La Lucha Por lo Justo. (p. 288)
—Diego Rivera: Artist of Mexico. (p. 437)
—Diego Rivera: Artista de Mexico. (p. 437)
—Ellen Ochoa: First Latina Astronaut. (p. 514)
—Ellen Ochoa: La Primera Astronauta Latina. (p. 514)
—Frida Kahlo: Pinto su Vida. (p. 637)
Guzman, Lila & Guzman, Rick. Frida Kahlo: Painting Her Life. (p. 637)
Guzmán, Lila & Guzmán, Rick. George Lopez: Comedian & TV Star. (p. 663)
—George Lopez: Latino King of Comedy. (p. 663)
—George Lopez: Comediante y Estrella de TV. (p. 663)
Guzman, Lila & Guzman, Rick. Lorenzo & the Turncoat. (p. 1053)
—Lorenzo's Revolutionary Quest. (p. 1053)
—Lorenzo's Secret Mission. (p. 1053)
Guzmán, Lila & Guzmán, Rick. Roberto Clemente: Baseball Hero. (p. 1479)
—Roberto Clemente: Heroe del Beisbol. (p. 1479)
Guzman, Lula, illus. see Bradley, Debby.
Guzman, Maria Del C. Sheep of Many Colors: Coloring Book. Lovell, Edith, illus. (p. 1564)
Guzman, Martin Luis, tr. see Schwartz, David M.
Guzman, Minerva, illus. see Olker, Constance.
Guzman, Raquel. Adventures of Eliseo & Stefano: My Daddy Can Fly! Guzman, Jacob, illus. (p. 17)
Guzman, Rick, jt. auth. see Guzman, Lila.
Guzman, Rick, jt. auth. see Guzman, Lila.
Guzman, Rick, jt. auth. see Guzman, Lila.
Guzman, Rick, jt. auth. see Guzman, Lila.
Guzmán, Rick, jt. auth. see Guzmán, Lila.
Guzmán, Rick, jt. auth. see Guzmán, Lila.

G

Guzmán, Rick, jt. auth. see Guzmán, Lila.
Guzmán, Rick, jt. auth. see Guzmán, Lila.
Guzmán, Rick, jt. auth. see Guzmán, Lila.
Guzman, Sienna. Visiting Death Valley: Represent & Interpret Data. (p. 1845)
Guzman, Stephanie. Adventures of Oliver the Clownfish: Acting Cool. (p. 21)
—Oliver the Clownfish: The Invitation Slip-up. (p. 1285)
Guzy, Adam, jt. auth. see Hawksworth, Lorraine.
Guzzardi, Mary. Magical Ice Skates. (p. 1074)
Guzzetta, Torrie & Gilbert, Pat. Glyphs* & Math: How to Use Picture Writing to Collect, Interpret, & Analyze Data. (p. 685)
Guzzio, Tracie Church, ed. see Samuels, Wilfred D.
Gwalch, Gwasg Carreg, jt. auth. see Dafydd, Myrddin ap.
Gwaltney, Doris. Homefront. (p. 793)
Gwanas, Bethan. Ramboy. (p. 1437)
Gwangjo, illus. see Subramaniam, Manasi.
Gwartney, Becky, et al. Lead On: Destination Reality. (p. 981)
Gwent (Wales), Staff Development Unit Staff & Acen Staff, contrib. by. Croeso I Gartref Llew. (p. 384)
—Nos Da, Arthur. (p. 1266)
Gwilym, Mari & Thomas, Dylan. Am Ddolig! (p. 51)
Gwinn, Saskia, ed. see Claybourne, Anna.
Gwinnell, Esther & Adamec, Christine. Encyclopedia of Addictions & Addictive Behaviors. (p. 524)
Gwinner, Patricia, illus. see Hooker, Adele.
Gwyer, Gillian K. Podnockery Forest - Owl & the Trickster. (p. 1375)
Gwyn, Brian M. Not Another Overdraft! How to Get Your Money Back... Responsibly! (p. 1267)
Gwyn, Richard. Pierre Elliott Trudeau (p. 1357)
Gwynne, Alexander, jt. auth. see Capstone Press Staff.
Gwynne, Fred, illus. see Martin, George W.
Gwynne, Phillip. Queen with the Wobbly Bottom. Whatley, Bruce, illus. (p. 1425)
—What's Wrong with the Wobbegong? Rogers, Gregory, illus. (p. 1900)
—Yobbos Do Yoga. Joyner, Andrew & Joyner, Louise, illus. (p. 1972)
Gwynne, Phillip & McCann, Eliza. Little Piggy's Got No Moves. Jellett, Tom, illus. (p. 1033)
Gyatso, Geshe Kelsang. Story of Angulimala: Buddhism for Children Level 1. (p. 1657)
—Story of Buddha: Buddhism for Children Level 2. (p. 1657)
—What Is Buddhism? Buddhism for Children Level 3. (p. 1889)
—What Is Meditation? Buddhism for Children Level 4. (p. 1889)
Gyekye, Sami. North: Reunion. (p. 1265)
Gygax, Gary & Mona, Erik. Infernal Sorceress. (p. 873)
Gynux, illus. see Dotlich, Rebecca Kai.
Gynux, illus. see Viau, Nancy & Bolinao, Mela.
Gynux, illus. see Viau, Nancy.
Gyuk, Geza, jt. auth. see Goss, Tim.

H

H & T Imaginations Unlimited, Inc. Home Run Derby with Professor Woodpecker. (p. 792)
—Kid's Sand Box Fun with Professor Woodpecker: Good Old Fashion Wholesome Fun Children's Story. (p. 955)
—Professor Woodpecker's Strawberry Patch! Wholesome, Fun children's story with Professor Woodpecker. (p. 1409)
—Sand Castles with Professor Woodpecker. (p. 1510)
—Toy Trains with Professor Woodpecker. (p. 1774)
—Vegetable Gardening with Professor Woodpecker. (p. 1834)
H. Gray, Susan. Experiments with Electricity. (p. 549)
H. J. Ford, illus. see Andrew Lang, ed.
H M Bricker & Bricker, Howard Michael. Christmas Santa Had No Beard. Dall, John, illus. (p. 315)
H. P. Lawrence. Adventures of Wilfred & Henri: The Staff of Knowledge. (p. 24)
H., Yves & Hermann. Manhattan Beach 1957. (p. 1087)
Ha, Thu Huong. Hail Caesar. (p. 735)
Ha, Ying-Hwa, illus. see Shahan, Sherry.
Ha, Ying-Hwa, tr. see Shahan, Sherry.
Haab, Rachel. Hadas. Esteve, Laura, tr. (p. 735)
Haab, Sherri. Clay So Cute! 21 Polymer Clay Projects for Cool Charms, Itty-Bitty Animals, & Tiny Treasures. (p. 330)
—Divertidas. (p. 454)
—Mis pulseras Favoritas. (p. 1150)
—Nail Art. (p. 1227)
Haab, Sherri & Klutz Editors. Holiday Picture Bracelets: Everything You Need to Make Your Own Personal Picture Bracelets. (p. 788)
Haack, Kelly J. Iowa: A MyReportLinks. Com Book. (p. 886)
—Nebraska: A MyReportLinks. Com Book. (p. 1239)
Haag, Bob, illus. see Haag, Ruth.
Haag, Ruth. Guide to Cottage Architecture As Seen in Lakeside, Ohio. Haag, Bob, illus. (p. 730)
Haagen, Debra. Amazing Animals by Design. (p. 53)
Haaglund, Lois F. Tough, Willing & Able: Tales of a Montana Family. McKenna, Gwen, ed. (p. 1773)
Haaji. Black Moon. (p. 196)
Haak, Harold H. Mubox Bugs. (p. 1188)
Haak, René & Pudelko, Markus, eds. Japanese Management: In Search of a New Balance Between Contuity & Change. (p. 909)
Haak, Rieneke. Kari, Meraai en Die Rollende, Tollende Lemoene. (p. 943)
Haake, Martin, illus. see Donovan, Sandy.
Haake, Susana, tr. see Winner, Ramana Moreno.
Haan, Linda de & Nijland, Stern. King & King. Haan, Linda de & Nijland, Stern, illus. (p. 958)
Haan, Wanda. Macaroon Moon: A Book of Poems & Rhymes for Children. Christensen, Donald, illus. (p. 1067)
Haar, Jaap Ter & Mearns, Martha. Boris. Poortvliet, Rien, illus. (p. 214)
Haaren, John. Famous Men of Greece. (p. 569)
—Famous Men of Modern Times. (p. 569)
—Famous Men of Rome. (p. 569)
Haaren, John H. John H Haaren's Complete Famous Men Series. (p. 922)
Haaren, John H. & Poland, A. Famous Men of Greece (Yesterday's Classics) (p. 569)
Haaren, John H. & Poland, A. B. Famous Men of Ancient Rome: Lives of Julius Caesar, Nero, Marcus Aurelius & Others. (p. 569)
—Famous Men of Rome (Yesterday's Classics) (p. 569)
Haarsma, P. J. Awakening on Orbis 4. (p. 120)
—Betrayal on Orbis. (p. 171)
—Softwire: Betrayal on Orbis 2. (p. 1606)
—Softwire: Wormhole Pirates on Orbis 3. (p. 1606)
—Wormhole Pirates on Orbis (p. 1961)
Haas, Abigail. Dangerous Girls. (p. 404)
Haas, Carolyn B. Big Book of Fun: Creative Learning Activities for Home & School. Phillips, Jane B., illus. (p. 179)
Haas, Deborah, illus. see Rhodes, Sam.
Haas, Esti, illus. see Fuks, Menuhah & Tager, Gavriella.
Haas, Franklin C. & Burrows, Roger. Birds of Pennsylvania. (p. 191)
Haas, Irene. Bess & Bella. Haas, Irene, illus. (p. 168)
Haas, Jane Elling, jt. auth. see Grebing, Diane J.
Haas, Jessie. Birthday Pony. Apple, Margot, illus. (p. 193)
—Bramble & Maggie: Give & Take. Friend, Alison, illus. (p. 222)
—Bramble & Maggie: Horse Meets Girl. Friend, Alison, illus. (p. 222)
—Bramble & Maggie Give & Take. Friend, Alison, illus. (p. 222)
—Chase. (p. 294)
—Horse Crazy! 1,001 Fun Facts, Craft Projects, Games, Activities, & Know-How for Horse-Loving Kids. (p. 799)
—Horse Meets Girl. Friend, Alison, illus. (p. 799)
—Saige. Davis, Sarah, illus. (p. 1503)
—Saige Paints the Sky. Davis, Sarah, illus. (p. 1503)
—Spooky Season. Friend, Alison, illus. (p. 1631)
Haas, Jessie, jt. auth. see Wedekind, Annie.
Haas, Jessie & Wedekind, Annie. Mercury's Flight: The Story of a Lipizzaner Stallion. (p. 1127)
Haas, Kristin. Shape Family Babies Bersani, Shennen, illus. (p. 1560)
Haas, Kristin, et al. Los Bebés de la Familia Geométrica Bersani, Shennen, illus. (p. 1053)
Haas, Nicole. Freedom Bee. (p. 634)
Haas, Peter Michael. Geschichten Für Akkordeon - 25 Lustige und Wehmütige Kinderstücke. (p. 667)
Haas, Rick De, see De Haas, Rick.
Haas, Robert. I Dreamed of Flying Like a Bird: My Adventures Photographing Wild Animals from a Helicopter. Haas, Robert, illus. (p. 838)
Haas, Robert B. African Critters. (p. 27)
Haas, Shelly, illus. see Groner, Judyth & Wikler, Madeline.
Haas, Shelly O., illus. see Figley, Marty Rhodes.
Haas, Shelly O., illus. see Portnoy, Mindy Avra.
Haase, Claudia. My First Bilingual Book of Symbols. (p. 1204)
Haase Wittler, Penny S. Emma, the Big Red Cow. (p. 520)
Haave, Meghan. Christopher's Bedtime Story. Rittmueller, Jeanne, illus. (p. 317)
—Christopher's Night at Grandma & Grandpa's. (p. 317)
Habashi, Azza, jt. auth. see Browne, Eileen.
Habashi, Azza, jt. auth. see McDonnell, Flora.
Habbas, Frank, illus. see Goldsmith, Howard.
Habbley, Kathleen, illus. see Singer, Marilyn.
Habeeb, William Mark. Africa: Facts & Figures. (p. 26)
—Africa: Facts & Figures. Rotberg, Robert I., ed. (p. 26)
—Arab Americans. (p. 94)
—Civil Wars in Africa. Ojakorotu, Victor & Rotberg, Robert I., eds. (p. 326)
—Egypt. (p. 506)
—Egypt. Rotberg, Robert I., ed. (p. 506)
—Iran (p. 886)
—Iran. (p. 886)
—Islamic Fundamentalism. (p. 891)
—Ivory Coast. (p. 901)
—Ivory Coast. Rotberg, Robert I., ed. (p. 901)
—Turkmenistan. (p. 1797)
Habek, Wendy. Good Boy, Troy! (p. 697)
Habel, Helen, illus. see Kaleta, Don.
Habel, Lia. Dearly, Departed. (p. 419)
Haber, Jan, illus. see Haber, Shel.
Haber, Karen. Crossing Infinity. (p. 385)
Haber, Melissa Glenn. Dear Anjali. (p. 418)
—Your Best Friend, Meredith. (p. 1980)
Haber, Shel. Animals' Vacation. Haber, Jan, illus. (p. 84)
Haber, Tiffany Strelitz. Monster Who Lost His Mean. Edmunds, Kirstie, illus. (p. 1168)
—Ollie & Claire. Cordell, Matthew, illus. (p. 1287)
Haberdasher, Violet. Knightley Academy. (p. 964)
—Secret Prince: A Knightley Academy Book. (p. 1543)
—Secret Prince. (p. 1543)
Haberkern, E., jt. auth. see Kaserman.
Haberle, Susan E. North Carolina Colony. (p. 1265)
—South Carolina Colony. (p. 1616)
Haberler, Julia. Carnival Pony. (p. 270)
Haberlin, Brian. Manhunter Project Vol 1 (p. 1087)
Haberman, Lia. About Face: Beauty Tricks & Tips. (p. 5)
Haber-Schaim, Uri. Introductory Physical Science. (p. 883)
Haber-Schaim, Uri, et al. Force, Motion, & Energy Assessment Package. (p. 616)
Haberstroh, Anne, illus. see Dahl, Michael & Moore, Mark.
Haberstroh, Anne, illus. see Doudna, Kelly.
Haberstroh, Anne, illus. see Hanson, Anders.
Haberstroh, Anne, illus. see Kompelien, Tracy.
Haberstroh, Anne, illus. see Salzmann, Mary Elizabeth.
Haberstroh, Anne, illus. see Scheunemann, Pam.
Haberstroh, Anne, illus. see Ziegler, Mark & Dahl, Michael.
Haberstroh, Marilyn & Panik, Sharon. Quetzalcóatl Tale of Corn. Castle, Lynn, illus. (p. 1426)
Haberstroh, Marilyn, et al. Tale of Chocolate. (p. 1699)
Habib, Linda, ed. see Jamiol, Paul.
Habiger, Geoff. Dinosaur Learning Activity Book. Habiger, Geoff & Gower, Jim, illus. (p. 442)
Habinger, Renate, illus. see Härtling, Peter.
Habitat For Humanity Of The Chesapeake, ed. Peace by Piece: Illustrations by Christian, Jewish & Muslim Children Ages 5-17. (p. 1331)
Habjan, Peter, illus. see Diamond, Jeremy.
Habnit, Eleonora. Permanent Makeup & Reconstructive Tattooing (p. 1343)
Habro Transformers Staff. Transformers Rescue Bots Roll to the Rescue! A Lift-The-Flap Book. (p. 1778)
Hach, Heather, jt. auth. see Rodgers, Mary.
Hachette Children's Books Staff, jt. auth. see Barker, Geoff.
Hachette Children's Books Staff, jt. auth. see Barraclough, Sue.
Hachette Children's Books Staff, jt. auth. see Brush, Jim.
Hachette Children's Books Staff, jt. auth. see Butterfield, Moira.
Hachette Children's Books Staff, jt. auth. see Dowswell, Paul.
Hachette Children's Books Staff, jt. auth. see Hibbert, Clare.
Hachette Children's Books Staff, jt. auth. see Lestrade, Ursula.
Hachette Children's Books Staff, jt. auth. see Mason, Paul.
Hachette Children's Books Staff, jt. auth. see Tonkin, Rachael.
Hachler, Bruno. I Am Who I Am. Wolferman, Iris, illus. (p. 834)
Hachler, Bruno & Muller, Birte. Farley Farts. (p. 573)
Hacht, Anne Marie. Literary Themes for Students (p. 1022)
Hacikyan, Talleen, illus. see Rosen, Michael.
Hack, Brittany. American Sign Language, Counting with Sea Creatures. (p. 63)
—Glitter Princess. (p. 684)
Hack, Richard. Hughes: The Private Diaries, Memos & Letters. (p. 825)
Hack, Robert, illus. see Gerrold, David, et al.
Hackbarth, Judith A. Plays, Players & Playing: How to Start Your Own Children's Theatre Company. Fife, Bruce, ed. (p. 1373)
Hackenberg, Rachel G. Writing to God. (p. 1965)
Hackenberg, Richard. Moose Hunting in Alaska: The Secrets to Success. Russ, Tony & O'Loughlin, Diane, eds. (p. 1173)
Hacker, Carlotta. 1950: Canadian Decades. (p. 2002)
—Kids Book of Canadian History. Mantha, John, illus. (p. 952)
Hacker, Carlotta, jt. auth. see Lemieux, Carlotta.
Hacker, Caryn Sabes. Bully Grows Up: Erik Meets the Wizard: Adult Guide Edition Boureau, Silvere, illus. (p. 241)
Hacker, Erin. Baker of Sweet City (p. 133)
—Harley's Tale. (p. 749)
Hacker, John. Getting Older Is Not for Wimps. (p. 669)
Hacker, Randy, illus. see Dean, Sara.
Hackett, J. J. Even Cows Wear Moo Moos. Pearn, Kayley, illus. (p. 541)
Hackett, Jane & Dorling Kindersley Publishing Staff. Ballerina: A Step-by-Step Guide to Ballet. Handley, David, photos by. (p. 134)
Hackett, Michael, illus. see Baden, Robert.
HacklFander, F. W. (Friedrich Wilhelm). Enchanting & Enchanted; from the German of Hackfander by Mrs a L Wister. (p. 523)
Hackman, Evelyn, illus. see Martin, Elaine S. Bowman.
Hackman, Sue. Hodder Reading Project 5-6 Reader: Highlights of English Literature. (p. 787)
Hackmann, Bethany, illus. see Baliko, Janelle.
Hackney Blackwell, Amy & Manar, Elizabeth P. UXL Encyclopedia of Science. (p. 1829)
Hackney Blackwell, Amy & Matters, Print. Ramadan. (p. 1437)
Hackworth, Debbie. Catch Your Wave. (p. 279)
Hacohen, Dean. Tuck Me In! Scharschmidt, Sherry, illus. (p. 1795)
—Who's Hungry? Scharschmidt, Sherry, illus. (p. 1920)
Hacohen, Dean & Scharschmidt, Sherry. Tuck Me In! (p. 1795)
Hadadi, Hoda, illus. see Cunnane, Kelly.
Hadcroft, Will. Anne Droyd & Century Lodge. (p. 85)
—Anne Droyd & the Ghosts of Winter Hill. (p. 85)
Haddad Ikonomopoulos, Marcia, jt. auth. see Dostis, Isaac.
Haddad, Yousif & Ingle, Jack. Simple Arabic: A Comprehensive Course. (p. 1577)
Haddad-Hamwi, Louise, illus. see Craig, Joni.
Haddi, Javon, jt. auth. see Smith, Darshiel.
Haddis, Seyoum. Kuku. (p. 968)
Haddix, Margaret Peterson. 39 Clues # 10: El Desafío Final. (p. 1996)
—Always War. (p. 51)
—Among the Barons. (p. 65)
—Among the Betrayed. (p. 65)
—Among the Brave. (p. 65)
—Among the Enemy. (p. 65)
—Among the Free. (p. 65)
—Among the Hidden. (p. 65)
—Because of Anya. (p. 155)
—Caught. (p. 281)
—Claim to Fame. (p. 326)
—Dexter the Tough. Elliott, Mark, illus. (p. 433)
—Don't You Dare Read This, Mrs. Dunphrey. (p. 469)
—Double Identity. (p. 473)
—Escape from Memory. (p. 535)
—Found. (p. 624)
—Full Ride. (p. 646)
—Game Changer. (p. 654)
—House on the Gulf. (p. 803)
—Into the Gauntlet. (p. 881)
—Just Ella. (p. 938)
—Leaving Fishers. (p. 986)
—Palace of Lies. (p. 1319)
—Palace of Mirrors. (p. 1319)
—Redeemed. (p. 1455)
—Risked. (p. 1475)
—Running Out of Time. (p. 1497)
—Sabotaged. (p. 1500)
—Say What? (p. 1518)
—Say What? Bernardin, James, illus. (p. 1518)
—Sent. (p. 1551)
—Shadow Children (p. 1557)
—Shadow Children: Among the Hidden; Among the Impostors; Among the Betrayed; Among the Barons; Among the Brave; Among the Enemy; Among the Free. (p. 1557)
—Shadow Children Books: Among the Hidden; Among the Impostors Vols. 1 & 2 (p. 1557)
—Takeoffs & Landings. (p. 1697)
—Torn. (p. 1770)
—Turnabout. (p. 1798)
—Uprising: Three Young Women Caught in the Fire That Changed America. (p. 1825)
Haddix, Margaret Peterson & Heath, Mike. Missing Collection: Found; Sent; Sabotaged; Torn; Caught. (p. 1152)
Haddock, Patricia. Careers in Banking & Finance. (p. 267)
Haddon, Dawn. Paddy Stories. (p. 1317)
Haddon, Jean. It's a Beautiful Day! Enright, Vicky, tr. (p. 895)
—It's a Beautiful Day! Enright, Vicky, illus. (p. 895)
—Make Sense! DiRocco, Carl, illus. (p. 1079)
Haddon, Mark. Boom! (p. 213)
—Curious Incident of the Dog in the Night-Time. (p. 394)
—Footprints on the Moon. Birmingham, John & Birmingham, Christian, illus. (p. 615)
Haden, Robbie. Run Girl Run. (p. 1496)
Hader, Berta and Elmer. Big Snow & Other Stories: A Treasury of Caldecott Award Winning Tales. (p. 184)
—Mother Goose Picture Book. (p. 1178)
Hader, Berta & Hader, Elmer. Reindeer Trail: A Long Journey from Lapland to Alaska. (p. 1457)
Hader, Elmer, jt. auth. see Hader, Berta.
Hadi, Aryo. Fall, Learn, Rise. (p. 566)
Hadithi, Mwenye. Cross Crocodile. Kennaway, Adrienne, illus. (p. 385)
—Running Rhino. Kennaway, Adrienne, illus. (p. 1497)
Hadithi, Mwenye, jt. auth. see Kennaway, Mwalimu.
Hadithi, Mwenye & Kennaway, Adrienne. Crafty Chameleon. (p. 376)
—Handsome Hog. (p. 741)
—Laughing Giraffe. (p. 980)
Hadithi, Mweyne. Bumping Buffalo. Kennaway, Adrienne, illus. (p. 241)
Hadkins, Helen & Lewis, Samantha. Interactive, Level 2. (p. 879)
Hadkins, Helen, et al. Interactive (p. 879)
Hadland, W. Into the Night. (p. 881)
Hadley, Caroline. Woodside; or, Look, Listen & Learn. (p. 1950)
Hadley Clark, Harriett. Cheep-Cheep! The Little Bird Who Said His Name. (p. 295)
Hadley, Joyce M. Dorothy Arnold: Joe Dimaggio's First Wife. (p. 471)
Hadley, Margie. Looking Back in the Mirror. (p. 1051)
Hadley, Sally C. Little Sally Girl's Greatest Adventure Series. (p. 1036)
Hadley, Suzanne. Faithgirlz Handbook: How to Let Your Faith Shine Through. (p. 565)
Hadnot, Victor. Wheels of God. (p. 1901)
Haefele, Steve, illus. see Aboff, Marcie.
Haefele, Steve, illus. see Field, Ellen.
Haefele, Steve, illus. see Lee, Quinlan B.
Haefele, Steve, illus. see Lee, Quinlan B. & Bridwell, Norman.
Haefele, Steve, illus. see Marsoli, Lisa Ann & Bridwell, Norman.
Haefele, Steve, illus. see Pugiano-Martin, Carol & Bridwell, Norman.
Haefele, Steve, illus. see Shepherd, Jodie.
Haefele, Steve, illus. see Stamper, Judith B.
Haefele, Steve, illus. see Stamper, Judith Bauer, et al.
Haefele, Steve, illus. see Stamper, Judith.
Haegele, Katie. Cool Careers Without College for Nature Lovers. (p. 362)
—E-Advertising & E-Marketing: Online Opportunities. (p. 491)
—E-Advertising & E-Marketing Online Opportunities. (p. 491)
—Monte Irvin. (p. 1170)
Haehnel, Alan. Blender: A One-Act Dark Comedy Play. (p. 199)
—Hank Morgan: A One-Act Comedy Play. (p. 742)
—Heubner the Reluctant. (p. 774)
—Remotely Related: Comedy Monologue. (p. 1460)
—Twisting-Turning Death Machine: Ten-Minute Comedy Duet. (p. 1803)
—What the Doctor Ordered: Ten-Minute Comedy Duet. (p. 1893)
—WWBF: Dramatic Play. (p. 1966)
Haehnel, Alan, jt. auth. see Sacco, Christopher.
Haeick, Noah. Welcome to My Class! Count to Tell the Number of Objects. (p. 1873)
Haeick, Reese. Marlon's Trip to the Marina: Multiply Within 100 (p. 1096)
Haen, Teri R. Treasure to Love. (p. 1782)
Haerens, Margaret. Aging Population. Greenhaven Press Editors & Gale Editors, eds. (p. 29)
—Aging Population. Greenhaven Press Editors & Gale Research Staff, eds. (p. 29)
—Birth Control. Greenhaven Press Editors & Gale Editors, eds. (p. 192)
—Eating Disorders. (p. 501)
—Government Gridlock. (p. 704)
—Illegal Immigration. (p. 856)
—International Adoptions. (p. 880)
—Malnutrition. (p. 1084)
—Mandatory Minimum Sentencing. (p. 1087)
—Mass Media. Greenhaven Press Editors, ed. (p. 1102)
—Mass Media. Greenhaven Press Editors & Gale Editors, eds. (p. 1102)
—Mexico's Drug War. Greenhaven Press Editors, ed. (p. 1131)
—Mixed Marriage. Gale, ed. (p. 1156)
—Obesity. (p. 1275)
—Offshore Drilling. (p. 1280)
—Oil. (p. 1282)
—Organ Donation. (p. 1303)
—Professional Athletes. Greenhaven Press Editors, ed. (p. 1409)
—Social Justice. (p. 1604)
—Television. (p. 1716)

H

—Tibet. (p. 1747)
—US Airport Security. Zott, Lynn, ed. (p. 1826)
—Veterans. (p. 1839)
—War Crimes. (p. 1857)
—World Peace. (p. 1958)
—World Trade Organization. (p. 1958)
Haerens, Margaret, jt. auth. see Greenhaven Press Editors.
Haerens, Margaret, ed. Eating Disorders. (p. 501)
—Human Trafficking. (p. 826)
—Juvenile Crime. (p. 941)
—Obesity. (p. 1275)
—Organ Donation. (p. 1303)
Haeringen, Annemarie Van, see Van Haeringen, Annemarie.
Haes, Jennifer Louise. Changes in Crystal Springs. (p. 290)
Haesche, Richard Paul, Sr. Magic of the Leprechaun. (p. 1073)
—My Pet Dinosaur. (p. 1217)
—Mystery of Dismal Swamp. (p. 1224)
—Stories & Poems for Juveniles. (p. 1654)
—Treasure of Pirates Cave. (p. 1782)
Haesche, Richard, Sr. Big Race. (p. 183)
—Bull of Death. (p. 240)
—Dog Named Wishbone. (p. 461)
—Ghost Wolf. (p. 672)
—Legend of the Unicorn. (p. 989)
—Mystery of Monster Manor. (p. 1224)
—Werewolf Syndrome. (p. 1875)
Haezer, Jane, illus. see Kropik, Linda Kristine.
Haf, Eurgain & Wen, Dref. Fferm Ffion. (p. 583)
Hafer, Jedd, jt. auth. see Hafer, Todd.
Hafer, Todd, jt. auth. see Meyer, Joyce.
Hafer, Todd & Hafer, Jedd. Stranger in the Chat Room: How Far Would You Go to Prove Your Faith? (p. 1665)
Hafer, Tom. Lemonade Crash. Terry, Brian, illus. (p. 991)
Haffmann, Janet & Richardson, Adele D. Bugbooks (p. 236)
Haffner, Kirstin. Born to Be Free. (p. 214)
Hafiz, Caroline Owen. Return of the Fossil. (p. 1464)
Hafiz, Dilara, et al. American Muslim Teenager's Handbook. (p. 62)
Hafiz, Imran, et al. American Muslim Teenager's Handbook. (p. 62)
Hafner, Marylin. Adventures of Molly & Emmett. (p. 20)
Hafner, Marylin, illus. see Berger, Melvin.
Hafner, Marylin, illus. see Dodds, Dayle Ann.
Hafner, Marylin, illus. see Horvath, Polly.
Hafner, Marylin, illus. see Katz, Bobbi.
Hafner, Marylin, illus. see Lasky, Kathryn.
Hafner, Marylin, illus. see Prelutsky, Jack.
Hafner, Marylin, illus. see Schotter, Roni.
Haft, Sheryl. I Love You, Blankie. Massey, Jane, illus. (p. 843)
Hagan, Donell, illus. see George, Mindy Lee.
Hagan, Jack. Always & in All Ways. (p. 51)
Hagan, Jeannine Marie. Bethany. (p. 171)
Hagan, Scott. Big Bad Bible Bullies. Horne, Doug, illus. (p. 177)
—Buscapleitos de la Biblia. Horne, Doug, illus. (p. 244)
Hagan, Stacy, illus. see Toh, Irene.
Hagan, Theda. Contemporary Zone. (p. 360)
Hage, Mike. Back Pain Book: A Self-Help Guide for the Daily Relief of Back & Neck Pain Dirr, Karen, illus. (p. 130)
Hagee, Alison. Educating the Heart: Standards-Based Activities to Foster Character, Community, & Self-Reflection. (p. 505)
Hagee, Brooks. Paloma: The Dove Who Was Afraid to Fly. (p. 1320)
Hagel, Brooke, illus. see Bolte, Mari.
Hagel, Brooke, illus. see Bolte, Marissa.
Hagel, Brooke, illus. see Gurevich, Margaret.
Hagel, Brooke, illus. see Klein, Marissa.
Hagelberg, Michael, illus. see Davidson, Elizabeth W.
Hagelberg, Michael, illus. see Storad, Conrad J.
Hageman, Erik, illus. see Sterns, Michael.
Hagemann, Anneliese. Radiestesia/Adivinanza: La Llave Dorada Para Aprovechar las Energias. (p. 1432)
Hagemann, Anneliese & Hagemann, Doris. Divine Principles of Truth. (p. 454)
—Healing Our Energy Fields. (p. 757)
—Nature Communication: A Further Application of the Inner Art of Dowsing. (p. 1236)
Hagemann, Bernhard. Charlie Gallina Ciega. (p. 293)
Hagemann, Doris, jt. auth. see Hagemann, Anneliese.
Hagen, Bethany. Jubilee Manor. (p. 930)
—Landry Park. (p. 974)
—Landry Park. Conescu, Nancy, ed. (p. 974)
Hagen, Carol L. Night Henry Ford Met Santa. Faulkner, Matt, illus. (p. 1253)
Hagen, Charles. Mary Ellen Mark. (p. 1100)
Hagen, Debra. Harvest on the Farm - Lapbook: Kinney, Cyndi, ed. (p. 751)
—Harvest on the Farm - Lapbook: Assembled. Kinney, Cyndi, ed. (p. 752)
Hagen, E. Happiness. (p. 744)
Hagen, George. Gabriel Finley & the Raven's Riddle. Bakal, Scott, illus. (p. 652)
Hagen, Kelly. Jake & Jesus. (p. 905)
Hagen, Oddmund. Campo Abierto (Open Field) Santos, Nuria G., tr. from NOR. (p. 258)
Hagen, Stefan, illus. see Tanen, Sloane.
Hagen, Stefan, photos by see Tanen, Sloane.
Hager, Alan. Encyclopedia of 16th, 17th, & 18th Century British Writers (p. 524)
Hager, Alan, et al. Encyclopedia of British Writers, 16th to 20th Centuries. (p. 525)
Hager, Christian, illus. see Grimm, J. & W. & Grimm, J.
Hager, Holly J. Heroin = Busted! (p. 773)
Hager, Janet. Truly Julie. (p. 1793)
Hager, Jenna Bush. Historia de Ana: Un Camino Lleno de Esperanza. de La Concha, Bertha Ruiz, tr. (p. 782)
Hager, Jenna Bush, jt. auth. see Bush, Laura.
Hager, Kendra M. Alexander. Potty Praise for Boys & Girls. (p. 1388)
Hager, Mandy. Into the Wilderness. (p. 881)
—Resurrection. (p. 1464)
Hager, Mickey. Clarence Duntz & the Monkey Spell. (p. 327)
Hager, Robert. Saurcana: Terror from the Sea. (p. 1516)
Hagerman, Andrew. Digital Music Making for Teens. (p. 439)
Hagerman, Carr & Lundin, Stephen C. Top Performer: A Bold Approach to Sales & Service. (p. 1769)
Hagerman, Jessica, illus. see Burt, Steve.
Hagerup, Klaus. Markus & Diana. Chace, Tara, tr. from NOR. (p. 1095)
—Markus & the Girls. Chace, Tara, tr. from NOR. (p. 1095)
Haggard, H. Rider. Allan Quatermain #3: Allan+s Wife. (p. 46)
—King Solomon's Mines. Marcos, Pablo, illus. (p. 959)
—Lysbeth: A Tale of the Dutch. (p. 1067)
—Minas del Rey Salomon. (p. 1145)
—Minas del Rey Salomon. Eric, F. Rowe, illus. (p. 1145)
—Pearl-Maiden. Kou, Christopher D. & McHugh, Michael J., eds. (p. 1333)
—Red Eve. (p. 1453)
Haggart, Gary, jt. auth. see Grantner, Anne M.
Haggarty, Holly. Summer Dragons. (p. 1674)
Haggarty, S. Little Muddy Bear. (p. 1032)
Haggerty, Andrew. Harper Lee: To Kill a Mockingbird. (p. 749)
—Jane Austen: Pride & Prejudice & Emma. (p. 908)
Haggerty, Robert. Bailey's Day. (p. 133)
Haggerty, Tim, illus. see Beckett-Bowman, Lucy.
Haggerty, Tim, illus. see Bone, Emily.
Haggerty, Tim, illus. see Kreisman, Rachelle.
Haggerty, Tim, illus. see Milbourne, Anna.
Haggerty, Tim, illus. see Pratt, Leonie.
Haggerty, Tim, illus. see Sweeny, Sheila.
Haggerty, Tim, illus. see Turnbull, Stephanie.
Haggis-On-Whey, Benny, jt. auth. see Haggis-On-Whey, Doris.
Haggis-On-Whey, Doris & Haggis-On-Whey, Benny. Cold Fusion. (p. 338)
—Giraffes? Giraffes! (p. 677)
Hagihara, Rie, tr. see Shigeno, Shuichi.
Hagin, Karen. If I Could Reach the Sky. (p. 853)
—Jeremy, the Giraffe Who Was Afraid of Heights. (p. 913)
Hagin, Randall S. Awesome ABC. (p. 120)
Hagin, Sally, illus. see Duder, Tessa, ed.
Hagin, Sally, illus. see Turhan, Sedat.
Hagin, Sally, jt. auth. see Turhan, Sedat.
Hagler, Barbara. Henrietta's Hope: A Hope Farm Series Book. (p. 767)
—Julia's Joy. (p. 932)
—Luca Loves. (p. 1062)
—Pack of Alpaca. (p. 1317)
—Speedy Steve the Rocket Rabbit: Hope Farm Adventures. (p. 1625)
Hagler, Chris E. Big Jim & the Squirrel. (p. 182)
Hagler, Gina. ADA Lovelace. (p. 10)
—Careers As a First Responder. (p. 267)
—Careers for Tech Girls in Math. (p. 267)
—Creating Book Reports with Cool New Digital Tools. (p. 378)
—Discovering Quantum Mechanics (p. 449)
—Money-Making Opportunities for Teens Who Are Artistic. (p. 1164)
—Sarah Dessen. (p. 1514)
—Step-by-Step Experiments with Electricity. Ostrom, Bob, illus. (p. 1647)
—Step-by-Step Experiments with Magnets. Ostrom, Bob, illus. (p. 1647)
—Step-by-Step Experiments with Soils. Ostrom, Bob, illus. (p. 1647)
—Top STEM Careers in Engineering. (p. 1769)
—Understanding Freedom of the Press. (p. 1815)
Hagler, Jack, jt. auth. see Hagler, Liz.
Hagler, Liz & Hagler, Jack. Hooked on the Book: Patrick's Adventures Through the Books of the Bible. (p. 795)
Hagman, Harvey Dixon. Majesty from Assateague Aiken, David, illus. (p. 1078)
Hague, Devon, jt. auth. see Hague, Michael.
Hague, Jane. Very Busy Week: Stories from Tilly's Number Town. (p. 1837)
Hague, Kathleen, jt. auth. see Hague, Michael.
Hague, Mel. Twisted River. (p. 1802)
Hague, Michael. Book of Fairies. Hague, Michael, illus. (p. 211)
—Michael Hague's Magical World of Unicorns. Hague, Michael, illus. (p. 1134)
—Michael Hague's Read-To-Me Book of Fairy Tales. Hague, Michael, illus. (p. 1134)
—Treasured Classics. (p. 1782)
Hague, Michael, illus. see Aylesworth, Jim.
Hague, Michael, illus. see Barbo, Maria S.
Hague, Michael, illus. see Barrie, J. M.
Hague, Michael, illus. see Berlin, Irving.
Hague, Michael, illus. see Hill, Susan & Barrie, J. M.
Hague, Michael, illus. see Potter, Beatrix.
Hague, Michael, illus. see Williams, Margery.
Hague, Michael & Hague, Devon. Book of Ghosts. Hague, Michael & Hague, Devon, illus. (p. 211)
Hague, Michael & Hague, Kathleen. Michael Hague's Treasury of Christmas Carols. (p. 1134)
Hague, Michael, ed. Child's Book of Prayers (p. 304)
—Child's Book of Prayers. (p. 304)
Hahm, Jennifer, tr. see Woo.
Hahn, Betty Brandt. Grandma's House. (p. 708)
Hahn, Beverly. Twenty Acres of Love: Irrigation Time. Hahn, Beverly, illus. (p. 1801)
—Twenty Acres of Love: Little Bit Hahn, Beverly & Silva, Tom, illus. (p. 1801)
Hahn, Blair. My Purple Kisses. Nation, Tate, illus. (p. 1217)
—My Purple Toes. Nation, Tate, illus. (p. 1217)
Hahn, Brian. It's Not the Yellow Fever. (p. 898)
Hahn, Cathe. Step Up! Artley, Bob, illus. (p. 1648)
Hahn, Chanda. Steele Wolf. (p. 1646)
Hahn, Daniel. Happiness Is a Watermelon on Your Head. Dreis, Stella, illus. (p. 744)
Hahn, Daniel, illus. see McCann, Michelle Roehm & Welden, Amelie.
Hahn, David, illus. see McCann, Michelle Roehm & Welden, Amelie.
Hahn, David, illus. see McCann, Michelle Roehm.
Hahn, Don. Alchemy of Animation: Making an Animated Film in the Modern Age. (p. 35)
—Animation Magic. (p. 84)
Hahn, Donna M. Staying Safe When I Go Out. (p. 1645)
Hahn, Fredrick. Strong Kids, Healthy Kids: The Revolutionary Program for Increasing Your Child's Fitness in 30 Minutes a Week (p. 1668)
Hahn, Jan. Albert & the Milk Pail. (p. 34)
Hahn, Jill. to Z Idioms. (p. 1759)
Hahn, Kathy. Racial Profiling. (p. 1432)
Hahn, Kelly. No Good Rain. (p. 1258)
Hahn, Laura. Mount Rushmore: Memorial to Our Greatest Presidents. Moreno, Barry, ed. (p. 1180)
Hahn, Marika. Things to Wear. (p. 1733)
Hahn, Mary Downing. All the Lovely Bad Ones. (p. 46)
—As Ever, Gordy. (p. 105)
—Closed for the Season. (p. 334)
—Daphne's Book. (p. 406)
—Dead Man in Indian Creek. (p. 417)
—Deep & Dark & Dangerous: A Ghost Story. (p. 422)
—Deep & Dark & Dangerous. (p. 422)
—Doll in the Garden: A Ghost Story. (p. 463)
—Doll in the Garden; The Old Willis Place. (p. 463)
—Gentleman Outlaw & Me: In the Old West, It's Easier to Be an Outlaw Than a Girl. (p. 661)
—Ghost of Crutchfield Hall. (p. 671)
—Hear the Wind Blow. (p. 759)
—Look for Me by Moonlight. (p. 1049)
—Mister Death's Blue-Eyed Girls. (p. 1155)
—Old Willis Place. (p. 1285)
—Promises to the Dead. (p. 1411)
—Stepping on the Cracks. (p. 1648)
—Tallahassee Higgins. (p. 1704)
—Time for Andrew: A Ghost Story. (p. 1751)
—Took: A Ghost Story. (p. 1767)
—Wait till Helen Comes: A Ghost Story. (p. 1852)
—Where I Belong. (p. 1908)
—Witch Catcher. (p. 1941)
Hahn, Michael T. Dad's Deer Tactics: Tom Hahn's Hunting Secrets Revealed by His Son. 1000 Hahn, Michael T., photos by. (p. 399)
Hahn, Molly. Under the Sneep Tree: The Wamboozling of a Village. (p. 1814)
Hahn, Nancy. One Lost Boy. Ayoub, Hamid, illus. (p. 1296)
Hahn, Pamela. Star Who Almost Wasn't There. (p. 1642)
Hahn, Phil. Henrietta: The Homely Duckling. Coker, Paul, Jr., illus. (p. 767)
Hahn, Rebecca. Creature of Moonlight. (p. 380)
—Shadow Behind the Stars. (p. 1557)
Hahn, Samuel J. Stories Told under the Sycamore Tree: Bible Plant Object Lessons. Patton, Scott, tr. (p. 1655)
Hahn, Sierra, ed. see Allie, Scott, et al.
Hahn, Sierra, ed. see Duarte, Gustavo.
Hahn, Sierra, ed. see Espenson, Jane & Bell, Brad.
Hahn, Sierra, ed. see Gage, Christos.
Hahn, Sierra, ed. see Jackson, Dan.
Hahn, Sierra, ed. see Jeanty, Georges, et al.
Hahn, Sierra, ed. see Ryan, Sara.
Hahn, Sierra, ed. see Taylor, Corey.
Hahn, Sierra, ed. see Whedon, Joss, et al.
Hahne, Michelle. Song School Greek. (p. 1611)
Hahner, Aaron. Magic of Midnight. (p. 1073)
Hahner, Chris, illus. see Cheshire, Marc.
Hahnke. Through the Eyes of a Raptor. (p. 1745)
Hahnl, John. Pocket & Toast Hahnl, Olivia, illus. (p. 1375)
Hahnl, Olivia, illus. see Hahnl, John.
Haibara, Yak. Sengoku Basara: Samurai Legends Volume 2: Samurai Legends Volume 2 (p. 1550)
Haidar, Hanna. Earl's Big Adventure in Costa Rica. Hutcheson, Meredith, ed. (p. 493)
—Earl's Big Adventure in Costa Rica. Newton, Kimberly, illus. (p. 493)
—Earl's Big Adventure in Japan. Newton, Kimberly, illus. (p. 493)
Haidle, David, illus. see Haidle, Helen.
Haidle, David, jt. auth. see Haidle, Helen.
Haidle, Elizabeth, illus. see Fisher, Donna R.
Haidle, Helen. Journey to the Cross & Victory: The Complete Easter Story of Jesus' Death & Resurrection. Haidle, David, illus. (p. 929)
—Lord Is My Shepherd. (p. 1052)
Haidle, Helen & Haidle, David. Creation Story for Children. Haidle, Helen & Haidle, David, illus. (p. 379)
Haig, Brian. Mortal Allies. (p. 1176)
Haig, Matt. Samuel Blink & the Forbidden Forest. (p. 1509)
—Shadow Forest. (p. 1557)
—To Be a Cat. Curtis, Stacy, illus. (p. 1758)
Haig-Brown, Roderick. Panther. (p. 1321)
Haig-Brown, Roderick, jt. auth. see Haig-Brown, Roderick L.
Haig-Brown, Roderick L. & Haig-Brown, Roderick. Starbuck Valley Winter. (p. 1642)
—Whale People. (p. 1877)
Haigentz, Misak. Bridges of Dream River. (p. 227)
Haigh, Alan, et al. Oxford International Primary Science, Stage 1. (p. 1315)
Haigh, Jane G., jt. auth. see Murphy, Claire Rudolf.
Haigh, Jean, jt. auth. see Webber, Beryl.
Haigh, Joanne. What a Silly Pottimus. (p. 1878)
Haight, Angela. Crow Said No. Spurll, Barbara, illus. (p. 386)
Haight, Joelle, illus. see Albright, David Edward.
Haight, Travis. 2:30 AM: Wired on Coffee; Six Premium Blended (Not So) Shorts. (p. 1991)
Haiku, Apache. Bambino Royale: A Jimmy Bee Secret Agent Adventure. (p. 135)
—Diapers Are Forever: A Jimmy Bee Secret Agent Adventure. (p. 434)
Hail, Nathan. Complaint. (p. 352)
Haile, Carol J. Christmas Cows. Haile, Carol J., illus. (p. 313)
—Dream Vacation. Miller, Robert, illus. (p. 484)
—Elephant Overboard! Haile, Carol J., illus. (p. 511)
—Princess Tree: A Tale of Fairies, Elves & Magic. (p. 1406)
Haile, Matthew. Worms Is Fool. (p. 1961)
Hailes, Ronald. Pink Rabbit. (p. 1360)
Hailstone, Ruth. White Ox. Burr, Dan, illus. (p. 1913)
Haimura, Kiyotaka, illus. see Kamachi, Kazuma.
Haines, Doris. 1 Goat, 2 Goat, 3 Goat, 4. (p. 1991)
Haines, Genny, illus. see Wang, Margaret.
Haines, Geri Berger. Little Lost Lamb. Haines, Geri Berger, illus. (p. 1031)
Haines, J. D. Put the Boys In: The Story of the Virginia Military Institute Cadets at the Battle of New Market. (p. 1420)
Haines, Jayne. Cry for the Moon. (p. 387)
Haines, Kathryn Miller. Girl Is Trouble. (p. 678)
Haines, Lise. Girl in the Arena. (p. 678)
Haines, Marie. Lion-Hearted Quakers. Putman, Stanley, illus. (p. 1020)
Haining, Peter. Magician's Circle: More Spellbinding Stories of Wizards & Wizardry. (p. 1075)
—Magicians' Circle. (p. 1075)
Hain-Jun, Yue & Soldevilla, Juan Manuel. Marco Polo: La Ruta de las Maravillas. (p. 1092)
Hainnu, Rebecca & Ziegler, Anna. Walk on the Tundra Leng, Qin, illus. (p. 1854)
Hains, Harriet, jt. auth. see Boyee, Claire.
Hainsworth, B. R. Boris the Lost Badger. Perkins, Mair, illus. (p. 214)
Hainsworth, Emily. Through to You. (p. 1745)
Hairs, Joya, photos by see Amado, Elisa.
Hairsine, Trevor, illus. see Bendis, Brian Michael & Quesada, Joe.
Hairston, Angelica. Did Noah Have Whales on the Ark? Ferguson, Tamara, illus. (p. 436)
Hairston, K. C. Past Prayers That Worked - & the Forgotten Rules: The 28 Forgotten Rules of Prayer. (p. 1327)
Hairston, Kennard. World's Best Recreational Activity Bears. (p. 1960)
Hairston, Kennard Lee. Rosie Bear Plays Baseball. (p. 1490)
Hairston, Lisa Lee. Victoria Has A Secret. (p. 1840)
Hairston, Lisa Lee & Graham, Joanne. Luckiest Girl in Luckyville. (p. 1062)
Hairston, Maxine & Keene, Michael. Successful Writing. (p. 1672)
Hairston-Piggee, Tameko. My Daddy Lives with God. (p. 1201)
Haisch, Joshua, illus. see Soske, Becky.
Haisha, Lisa. Whispers from Children's Hearts. (p. 1912)
Haislip, Phyllis Hall. Anybody's Hero: The Battle of Old Men & Young Boys. (p. 91)
—Between the Lines: A Revolutionary War Slave's Journey to Freedom. (p. 173)
—Divided Loyalties: A Revolutionary War Fifer's Story. (p. 454)
—Lili's Gift: A Civil War Healer's Story. (p. 1017)
—Lottie's Courage: A Contraband Slave's Story. (p. 1057)
Haisten, Tiffany. Red Is the Color Of... (p. 1454)
Haitani, Kenjiro. Rabbit's Eyes. Sminkey, Paul, tr. from JPN. (p. 1430)
Haith, Sera, illus. see Surratt, Denise.
Haitz, Rochelle. Aesop's Angel. Ewanits, Tara, photos by. (p. 25)
—House on the Hill in Stinkyville. Motz, Mike, illus. (p. 803)
Hajde, Jeremy, illus. see Peterson, S. L.
Hajdinjak-Krec, Marsela, illus. see Redmond, Shirley Raye.
Hajdusiewicz, Babs Bell. Bridge Is Up! Hefferan, Rob, illus. (p. 227)
Hajdyla, Ken, illus. see Arrathoon, Leigh A.
Hajeski, Nancy J. Beatles: Here, There & Everywhere. (p. 153)
—Big Book of Presidents: From George Washington to Barack Obama. (p. 179)
Hajime, Yatate & Koruda, Yousuke. Infinite Ryvius (p. 873)
Hajime, Yatate & Kuroda, Yosuke. Infinite Ryvius (p. 873)
Hajj, Sharon. Zula Blackburn & the Rising Sun Festival. (p. 1990)
Hakala, Joann. Baby Brother! Oh No! Shaw-Peterson, Kimberly, illus. (p. 125)
Hakamada, Mera. Fairy Idol Kanon Volume 4 (p. 563)
—Fairy Idon Kanon (p. 563)
Hakamada, Mera, jt. auth. see Udon Kids Staff.
Hakase, Mizuki. Demon Ororon (p. 426)
Hake, Mary A. Creation Homeschool Curriculum: 12 Lesson CD. (p. 379)
Hake, Stephen, jt. auth. see Saxon Publishers Staff.
Hake, Stephen & Saxon, John. Math 76: An Incremental Development: Test Forms. (p. 1105)
—Saxon Math 5/4: An Incremental Development. (p. 1518)
—Saxon Math 6/5. (p. 1518)
—Saxon Math 7/6. (p. 1518)
—Saxon Math 8/7. (p. 1518)
Hakes, Matthew. What Catholic Teens Should Know about Ecstacy. Larkin, Jean, ed. (p. 1881)
—What Catholic Teens Should Know about Going to War. Larkin, Jean, ed. (p. 1881)
—What Catholic Teens Should Know about What Muslims Believe. Larkin, Jean K., ed. (p. 1881)
—What Catholic Teens Should Know When Scandal Hits the Church. Larkin, Jean, ed. (p. 1881)
Hakim, Joy. Age of Extremes, 1880-1917. (p. 29)
—All the People: Since 1945. (p. 46)
—All the People. (p. 46)
—All the People since 1945. (p. 46)
—An Age of Extremes, 1880-1917. (p. 66)
—First Americans: Prehistory-1600. (p. 593)
—First Americans Prehistory 1600. (p. 593)
—From Colonies to Country, 1735-1791. (p. 642)
—History of Us (p. 785)
—History of US: Ten-volume Set (p. 785)
—History of US: Sourcebook & Index. (p. 785)
—History of US: All the People since 1945. Bk. 10 (p. 785)
—Liberty for All, 1789-1850 (p. 1005)
—Liberty for All, 1820-1860. (p. 1005)
—Making Thirteen Colonies, 1600-1740. (p. 1082)
—New Nation, 1789-1850. (p. 1246)
—Reconstructing America, 1865-1890. (p. 1452)
—Story of Science: Newton at the Center. (p. 1660)
—War, Peace, & All That Jazz, 1918-1945. (p. 1858)
—War, Terrible War, 1855-1865 Bk. 6. (p. 1858)
—War, Terrible War, 1855-1865. (p. 1858)
Hakit, Ruben. Keith Urban. (p. 948)
Hakizimana, Laurence. Quadrature: Pi, at Last, a Rational Number Equal to 3.125. (p. 1422)
Hakkarainen, Anna-Liisa, illus. see Bucchino, John.

Hakohen, Israel Meir, et al. Parabolas de Sabiduria. (p. 1323)
Hakowski, Maryann. Vine & Branches Price, Carolyn, illus. (p. 1843)
—Vine & Branches Stamschror, Robert P., ed. (p. 1843)
—Vine & Branches. St. George, Carolyn, illus. (p. 1843)
Hal Leonard Corp. Staff. Children's Songs (p. 304)
—Children's Songs: Budget Books (p. 304)
—Children's Songs for Ukulele Strummers. (p. 304)
Hal Leonard Corp. Staff, jt. creator see AMSCO Publications Staff.
Hal Leonard Corp. Staff, contrib. by. Experiencing Choral Music, Advanced Mixed: Grades 9-12. (p. 548)
Hal Leonard Corp. Staff, creator. 15 Recital Songs in English. (p. 1995)
—211. the Big Book of Nursery Rhymes & Children's Songs. (p. 2001)
—Christmas Classics for Harmonica: 25 Timeless Melodies for Easy Harmonica. (p. 313)
—Christmas Favorites for Harmonica. (p. 314)
—Classical Favorites: Hal Leonard Recorder Songbook. (p. 328)
—Disney Movie Hits: Cello. (p. 452)
—Disney Movie Hits: Flute. (p. 452)
—Disney Movie Hits: Viola. (p. 452)
—Disney Movie Hits: F Horn. (p. 452)
—Disney Movie Hits: Violin. (p. 452)
—Disney Movie Hits: Trumpet. (p. 452)
—Disney Movie Hits: Alto Sax. (p. 452)
—Disney Movie Hits: Clarinet. (p. 452)
—Disney Movie Hits: Tenor Sax. (p. 452)
—Disney Movie Hits: Trombone/Baritone. (p. 452)
—Disney's My First Songbook: A Treasury of Favorite Songs to Sing & Play. (p. 453)
—Disney's My First Songbook - Volume 4. (p. 453)
—Easy Disney Fake Book. (p. 500)
—Fantastic Big Book of Children's Songs. (p. 571)
—First Nursery Rhymes: Fun Repertoire for Beginner Pianists Complementing Any Piano Course. (p. 596)
—Great Songs for Children. (p. 718)
—Jazzy Opera Classix: For Violin. (p. 911)
—Jazzy Opera Classix: For Clarinet. (p. 911)
—Kids' Collection: Recorder Fun! 3-Book Bonus Pack. (p. 953)
—Kids' Fun Songs: Learn & Play Recorder Pack. (p. 953)
—Musical Theatre Anthology for Teens. (p. 1194)
—Songs Children Can Sing! Pro Vocal Boys' & Girls' Edition Volume 1. (p. 1611)
—Songs for Kids - Audition Songs: Piano/Vocal/Guitar Arrangements with CD Backing Tracks. (p. 1612)
—Teaching Little Fingers to Play Broadway Songs. (p. 1710)
—Teaching Little Fingers to Play More Broadway Songs: Mid to Later Elementary Level. (p. 1710)
—Violin Classics - Advanced Level. (p. 1843)
—Worship Together Favorites for Kids. (p. 1961)
Hal Leonard Music Books Staff. Still More Disney Solos for Kids: Voice & Piano with Online Recorded Performances & Accompaniments. (p. 1650)
hal, marcovitz. Is Offshore Oil Drilling Worth the Risks? (p. 889)
Haladay, Max. Max Gets Mad. (p. 1111)
Halam, Ann. Dr. Franklin's Island. (p. 475)
—Shadow on the Stairs. (p. 1557)
—Snakehead. (p. 1596)
Halasz, Andras, illus. see Gold, Avie.
Halberstadt, Bridget, illus. see Grimbol, William R.
Halberstam, David. Firehouse. (p. 592)
Halbert, Patricia, ed. see Randol, Susan, et al.
Halbower, Susan J., illus. see Birkelbach, Alan.
Halbower, Susan J., illus. see Rubin, Donna.
Halbrook, Kristin. Every Last Promise. (p. 542)
Halbur, Donna. Puppy & the Guppy. (p. 1418)
Halcarz, Jim. Tales Before Time. (p. 1701)
Halcomb, Suzanne. Mcfee Family Harvest. (p. 1114)
Halcoop, Ursula Lily. Journey. (p. 927)
Haldane, Carol. Dannie's Dilemma - Book Two. (p. 405)
Haldane, Rachael. Nymphas' World. (p. 1274)
Haldeman, Dakley, jt. auth. see Autry, Gene.
Haldeman, Myrtle L. Cassie after Antietam. (p. 276)
Haldy, Emma E. Abraham Lincoln. Bane, Jeff, illus. (p. 6)
—Eleanor Roosevelt. Bane, Jeff, illus. (p. 508)
—Frederick Douglass/By Emma E. Haldy ; Illustrated by Jeff Bane. Bane, Jeff, illus. (p. 633)
—Martin Luther King, Jr. Bane, Jeff, illus. (p. 1097)
—Rosa Parks. Bane, Jeff, illus. (p. 1488)
Hale, Aaron. Addy Gets Made. (p. 12)
Hale, Bruce. Adventures of Space Gecko. (p. 23)
—Afraid of the Dark. Francis, Guy, illus. (p. 26)
—Big Bad Baby. Breen, Steve, illus. (p. 177)
—Big Bad Detective Agency. (p. 178)
—Big Nap. (p. 182)
—Big Nap. Hale, Bruce, illus. (p. 182)
—Chameleon Wore Chartreuse. (p. 289)
—Clark the Shark. Francis, Guy, illus. (p. 327)
—Clark the Shark Dares to Share. Francis, Guy, illus. (p. 327)
—Clark the Shark Takes Heart. Francis, Guy, illus. (p. 327)
—Clark the Shark - Tooth Trouble. Francis, Guy, illus. (p. 327)
—Curse of the Were-Hyena: A Monstertown Mystery. (p. 395)
—Dial M for Mongoose: A Chet Gecko Mystery. (p. 433)
—Ends of the Earth. Dorman, Brandon, illus. (p. 527)
—Farewell, My Lunchbag. (p. 573)
—Farewell, My Lunchbag. Hale, Bruce, illus. (p. 573)
—Fat Cat of Underwhere. Hillman, Shane, illus. (p. 577)
—From Russia with Lunch: A Chet Gecko Mystery. (p. 643)
—Give My Regrets to Broadway. (p. 681)
—Hamster of the Baskervilles. (p. 740)
—Hiss Me Deadly. Hale, Bruce, illus. (p. 781)
—Key Lardo: A Chet Gecko Mystery. Hale, Bruce, illus. (p. 950)
—Malted Falcon. (p. 1084)
—Malted Falcon. Hale, Bruce, illus. (p. 1084)
—Mole Men of Underwhere. Hillman, Shane, illus. (p. 1160)
—Monsters on the Loose! A Seek & Solve Mystery! Garbot, Dave, illus. (p. 1169)
—Murder, My Tweet. (p. 1192)
—Murder, My Tweet. Hale, Bruce, illus. (p. 1192)
—Mystery of Mr. Nice. (p. 1224)
—Mystery of Mr. Nice. Hale, Bruce, illus. (p. 1224)
—Mystery of Mr. Nice. Hale, Bruce, illus. (p. 1225)
—Pirates of Underwhere. Hillman, Shane, illus. (p. 1364)
—Possum Always Rings Twice. Hale, Bruce, illus. (p. 1387)
—Prince of Underwhere. Hillman, Shane, illus. (p. 1401)
—Santa on the Loose! Garbot, Dave, illus. (p. 1513)
—School for SPIES Book 2 Thicker Than Water. Dorman, Brandon, illus. (p. 1523)
—School for SPIES Book One Playing with Fire. Dorman, Brandon, illus. (p. 1523)
—School for SPIES Thicker Than Water. Dorman, Brandon, illus. (p. 1523)
—Snoring Beauty. Fine, Howard, illus. (p. 1598)
—This Gum for Hire. (p. 1735)
—This Gum for Hire. Hale, Bruce, illus. (p. 1735)
—Tooth Trouble. (p. 1768)
—Trouble Is My Beeswax: A Chet Gecko Mystery. (p. 1790)
—Trouble Is My Beeswax. (p. 1790)
—Trouble Is My Beeswax. Hale, Bruce, illus. (p. 1790)
Hale, Christy. East-West House: Noguchi's Childhood in Japan. Hale, Christy, illus. (p. 498)
Hale, Christy, illus. see Kirk, Connie Ann.
Hale, Christy, illus. see Morrison, Lillian.
Hale, Christy, illus. see Stuve-Bodeen, Stephanie.
Hale, Christy, illus. see Thompson, Lauren.
Hale, Christy, jt. auth. see Stuve-Bodeen, Stephanie.
Hale, Christy, tr. It Rained All Day That Night: Autograph Album Verses & Inscriptions. (p. 894)
Hale, Cole, illus. see Lynch, Jason.
Hale, Connie. Elementary Guitar. Holl, Brent, ed. (p. 510)
Hale, Daniel J. & LaBrot, Matthew. Red Card. (p. 1453)
Hale, Dean. Scapegoat: The Story of a Goat Named Oat & a Chewed-Up Coat. Slack, Michael, illus. (p. 1519)
Hale, Dean, jt. auth. see Hale, Shannon.
Hale, Dean & Hale, Shannon. Scapegoat: The Story of a Goat Named Oat & a Chewed-Up Coat. Slack, Michael, illus. (p. 1519)
Hale, Derek. Brain Freeze Ain't for Sissies: Dinwiddie Dunn & His Bowlegged Sons. (p. 221)
Hale, Edward E. Man Without a Country. (p. 1086)
Hale, Edward Everett. Margaret Percival in America; a Tale Ed by a New England Minister, a B Being a Sequel to Margaret Percival a Tale Ed by Rev William Sewell, B. (p. 1092)
Hale, Gloria, jt. auth. see Hale, James.
Hale, Glorya, ed. Read-Aloud Poems: 50 of the World's Best-Loved Poems for Parent & Child to Share. (p. 1442)
Hale, Helen. Dale Evans & Danger in Crooked Canyon. Luhrs, Henry, illus. (p. 401)
Hale, J. P., illus. see Hall, Eve D.
Hale, James & Hale, Gloria. Faithfulnes of God - Our Testimony. (p. 565)
Hale, James Graham, illus. see Pfeffer, Wendy.
Hale, James Graham, illus. see Zoehfeld, Kathleen Weidner.
Hale, Jason, illus. see Lynn, Richard & Nova Blue.
Hale, Jenny, illus. see Munro, Maisie.
Hale, Jenny, illus. see Novick, Mary.
Hale, Jenny, illus. see Reed, Jonathan.
Hale, Jenny, jt. auth. see Novick, Mary.
Hale, Jenny, jt. auth. see Reed, Jonathan.
Hale, Joseph. Nory the 3rd Grade: Case of the Missing Toys. (p. 1266)
Hale, Kathleen. No One Else Can Have You. (p. 1259)
—Nothing Bad Is Going to Happen. (p. 1268)
Hale, Linda. Activity Story Book: Sunshine & Her Big Blarney Smile. Liao, Yivian, illus. (p. 10)
—Sunshine & Her Big Blarney Smile. Liao, Yivian, illus. (p. 1678)
Hale, Lucretia. Peterkin Papers. Brett, Harold M., illus. (p. 1347)
Hale, Lucretia P. Peterkin Papers. (p. 1347)
Hale, Lucretia Peabody. Last of the Peterkins: With Others of Their Kin. (p. 978)
Hale, Marian. Dark Water Rising. (p. 408)
—Goodbye Season. (p. 701)
—Truth about Sparrows. (p. 1794)
Hale, Mary. Karly & Sheila's Walk. (p. 944)
Hale, Natalie. Oh, Brother! Growing up with a Special Needs Sibling. Sternberg, Kate, tr. (p. 1280)
—So Many Colors. (p. 1602)
—So Many Feelings. (p. 1602)
—Spaghetti! (p. 1620)
Hale, Nathan. Devil You Know. Hale, Nathan, illus. (p. 432)
—Nathan Hale's Hazardous Tales: One Dead Spy. (p. 1231)
—Nathan Hale's Hazardous Tales: Big Bad Ironclad! (p. 1231)
—Nathan Hale's Hazardous Tales: Donner Dinner Party. (p. 1231)
—Nathan Hale's Hazardous Tales: The Underground Abductor. (p. 1231)
—Nathan Hale's Hazardous Tales: Treaties, Trenches, Mud, & Blood (a World War I Tale) (p. 1231)
—Twelve Bots of Christmas. Hale, Nathan, illus. (p. 1800)
Hale, Nathan, illus. see Hale, Shannon & Hale, Dean.
Hale, Nathan, illus. see Kipling, Rudyard.
Hale, Nathan, illus. see Muecke, Anne & Moore, Clement C.
Hale, Nathan, illus. see Peacock, L. A.
Hale, Nathan, illus. see Ryan, Candace.
Hale, Nathan, illus. see Walton, Rick.
Hale, Nathan, illus. see Zoehfeld, Kathleen Weidner.
Hale, Nick. Edge. (p. 504)
Hale, Ohara. Who Did It? Who Farted? Who Burped? Who Pooped? Who Peed? Who Sneezed? (p. 1915)
Hale, Pattie, illus. see Grabowski, Leo.
Hale, Phil, illus. see King, Stephen.
Hale, R. A. Best Friends. (p. 169)
Hale, Rachael. 101 Cataclysms: For the Love of Cats. (p. 1999)
—Baby Colors. (p. 125)
—Baby Giggles. (p. 126)
—Baby's Best Friend. (p. 128)
—Furry Friends. (p. 650)
—Hugs & Kisses. (p. 825)
—Love Tails. (p. 1060)
—Santa Paws. (p. 1513)
—Somebunny Loves You. (p. 1609)
Hale, Rachael, photos by. Baby Animals. (p. 124)
—Bedtime Buddies. (p. 156)
Hale, Randy, illus. see Ritz, Lee F.
Hale, Rhonda. Workplace Devotions. (p. 1953)
Hale, Sally, illus. see McGougan, Kathy.
Hale, Samantha. Everything Changes. (p. 544)
Hale, Sarah Elder, ed. see Waryncia, Lou.
Hale, Sarah Elder, jt. ed. see Chorlian, Meg.
Hale, Sarah Elder, ed. Jefferson Davis & the Confederacy. (p. 912)
—Rebuilding a Nation: Picking up the Pieces. (p. 1451)
—Robert E. Lee: Duty & Honor. (p. 1479)
—Stonewall Jackson: Spirit of the South. (p. 1653)
Hale, Sarah Josepha. Mary Had a Little Lamb Huliska-Beith, Laura, illus. (p. 1100)
—Mary Had a Little Lamb. dePaola, Tomie, illus. (p. 1100)
Hale, Shannon. Austenland. Hale, Shannon, ed. (p. 116)
—Book of a Thousand Days. Smith, James Noel, illus. (p. 210)
—Dangerous. (p. 404)
—Enna Burning. (p. 530)
—Ever after High: Once upon a Time: A Story Collection. (p. 541)
—Ever after High: the Storybox of Legends Boxed Set. (p. 541)
—Fire & Ice. (p. 590)
—Forest Born. (p. 618)
—Forgotten Sisters. (p. 620)
—Goose Girl. (p. 702)
—Palace of Stone. (p. 1319)
—Princess Academy. (p. 1402)
—Princess in Black. (p. 1404)
—River Secrets. (p. 1476)
—Storybook of Legends. (p. 1663)
—Unfairest of Them All. (p. 1817)
—Wonderlandiful World. (p. 1948)
Hale, Shannon, jt. auth. see Hale, Dean.
Hale, Shannon & Hale, Dean. Calamity Jack. Hale, Nathan, illus. (p. 252)
—Princess in Black. Pham, LeUyen, illus. (p. 1404)
—Rapunzel's Revenge. Hale, Nathan, illus. (p. 1439)
Hale, Sheila. I Am Me. (p. 833)
Hale, Wendy A., jt. auth. see Lantz, Peggy Sias.
Hale, Wendy & Lantz, Peggy. Young Naturalist's Guide to Florida. (p. 1979)
Hales, J. Rulon, illus. see Driggs, Howard R.
Halevy, Hanita H. Dragonlions & the Spacemen. Heler, Shraga, illus. (p. 478)
Haley, A. Santa's Big Night. (p. 1513)
Haley, Alex. Autobiography of Malcolm X. Bloom, Harold, ed. (p. 117)
Haley, Alex, jt. auth. see Weisberg, Barbara.
Haley, Amanda. 3-2-1 School Is Fun! (p. 1991)
—Easter Has Eggs. (p. 499)
—Mundo de Peques. (p. 1191)
—Music Class. (p. 1193)
—Ready, Alice? (p. 1447)
Haley, Amanda, illus. see Byars, Betsy.
Haley, Amanda, illus. see Cox, Judy.
Haley, Amanda, illus. see Lawler, Janet.
Haley, Amanda, illus. see Linn, Margot.
Haley, Amanda, illus. see Metzger, Steve.
Haley, Amanda, illus. see Packard, Mary.
Haley, Amanda, illus. see Schubert, Leda.
Haley, Amanda, illus. see Winthrop, Elizabeth.
Haley, Amanda, illus. see Ziefert, Harriet & Ehrlich, Fred.
Haley, Amanda, illus. see Ziefert, Harriet.
Haley, Amanda, illus. see Zondervan Publishing Staff.
Haley, Annie. Rumpus & Bumpus: If we could do Anything... ... ... (p. 1495)
Haley, Barbara. Boot Camp. (p. 213)
—Purple Heart. (p. 1419)
—Singing Soldiers: And Other Bible Stories You've Gotta Hear. Apps, Fred, illus. (p. 1579)
Haley, Carrie. Three Little Female Pigs. (p. 1742)
Haley, Dennis, jt. auth. see Brown, Marcy.
Haley, Dennis & Brown, Marci. We Both Read-When I Grow Up. (p. 1866)
Haley, Gail E., illus. see Graves, Jonathan.
Haley, Gail E., jt. auth. see Konigsburg, E. L.
Haley, Gail E., tr. Kokopelli, Drum in Belly. (p. 966)
Haley, James. Stephen Austin & the Founding of Texas. (p. 1648)
—Women in the Military. (p. 1946)
Haley, James L. Stephen F. Austin & the Founding of Texas. (p. 1648)
Haley, Jeannette. Adventures of Zack & Mira. (p. 24)
Haley, John, et al. Abuse. (p. 7)
Haley, Olivia. Jellybeans. (p. 912)
Haley, Patricia, jt. auth. see Burkhart, Jessica.
Haley-Christian, Diana. Broken Rules. (p. 230)
Halfman, Janet. Polar Bear Horizon. Chesterman, Adrian, illus. (p. 1378)
Halfman, Patti. 100% Language Intermediate. (p. 1998)
Halfman, Patti, jt. auth. see Johnson, Paul F.
Halfmann, Janet. Alligator at Saw Grass Road. Anzalone, Lori, illus. (p. 47)
—Animal Teachers. O'Byrne, Nicola & Hudson, Katy, illus. (p. 80)
—Canada Goose at Cat Tail Lane. Stegos, Daniel, illus. (p. 260)
—Canada Goose at Cattail Lane. Stegos, Daniel J., illus. (p. 260)
—Dolphin's Rescue: The Story of a Pacific White-Sided Dolphin. (p. 465)
—Dolphin's Rescue: The Story of a Pacific White-Sided Dolphin. Petruccio, Steven James, illus. (p. 465)
—Dolphin's Rescue. Petruccio, Stephen & Petruccio, Stephen, illus. (p. 465)
—Eggs 1 2 3: Who Will the Babies Be? Johnson, Betsy & Thompson, Betsy, illus. (p. 506)
—Fur & Feathers Klein, Laurie Allen, illus. (p. 650)
—Garter Snake at Willow Creek Lane. Wertheim, Anne, illus. (p. 657)
—Good Night, Little Sea Otter Williams, Wish, illus. (p. 699)
—Good Night, Little Sea Otter (Burmese Karen/English) Williams, Wish, illus. (p. 699)
—Good Night, Little Sea Otter (Burmese/English) Williams, Wish, illus. (p. 699)
—Good Night, Little Sea Otter (Hmong/English) Williams, Wish, illus. (p. 699)
—Good Night, Little Sea Otter (Portuguese/English) Williams, Wish, illus. (p. 699)
—Hermit Crab's Home: Safe in a Shell. Dacey, Bob, illus. (p. 771)
—Hermit Crab's Home: Safe in a Shell. Dacey, Bob & Bandelin, Debra, illus. (p. 771)
—Home in the Cave Bersani, Shennen, illus. (p. 792)
—Little Black Ant on Park Street. Rietz, Kathleen, illus. (p. 1024)
—Little Skink's Tail Klein, Laurie Allen, illus. (p. 1036)
—Mongoose. (p. 1164)
—Narwhal: Unicorn of the Sea. Petruccio, Steven James, illus. (p. 1230)
—Narwhal: The Unicorn of the Sea. Petruccio, Steven James, illus. (p. 1230)
—Pelican's Catch. Dacey, Bob & Bandelin, Debra, illus. (p. 1335)
—Plant Tricksters. (p. 1369)
—Polar Bear Horizon. Chesterman, Adrian, illus. (p. 1378)
—Red Bat at Sleep Hollow Lane. Buchs, Thomas, illus. (p. 1453)
—Red Bat at Sleep Hollow Lane. Stegos, Daniel, illus. (p. 1453)
—Red Bat at Sleepy Hollow Lane. Stegos, Daniel, illus. (p. 1453)
—Seven Miles to Freedom: The Robert Smalls Story. Smith, Duane, illus. (p. 1554)
—Star of the Sea: A Day in the Life of a Starfish. Paley, Joan, illus. (p. 1640)
Halfmann, Janet & Smith, Duane. Seven Miles to Freedom: The Robert Smalls Story (p. 1554)
Halfmann, Janet & Smithsonian Institution Staff. horizonte del Oso Polar: Polar Bear Horizon. (p. 798)
Halfmann, Janet & Stegos, Daniel. Canada Goose at Cattail Lane. (p. 260)
Halfpenny, James C. Yellowstone Wolves in the Wild. (p. 1970)
Halilbegovich, Nadja. My Childhood under Fire: A Sarajevo Diary. (p. 1200)
Haling, Elizabeth. Look at Life. (p. 1048)
Halka, Monica & Nordstrom, Brian. Halogens & Noble Gases. (p. 739)
—Periodic Table of the Elements (p. 1343)
Halkin, Hillel, tr. see Orlev, Uri.
Halkyard, Harriet & Halkyard, John. 99 Days to Panama: An Exploration of Central America by Motorhome. How a Couple & their Dog Discovered this New World in their RV. (p. 1998)
Halkyard, John, jt. auth. see Halkyard, Harriet.
Hall / Waltz. Mortimer Jones: The Bubble Gum Nerd (p. 1176)
Hall, Adam Z. Little Purple Puppy. (p. 1034)
Hall, Alice Eby. Echoes of Eden: Life at Hallcienda Farms. (p. 502)
Hall, Alvin D., jt. auth. see Dorling Kindersley Publishing Staff.
Hall, Amanda. Barefoot Book of Animal Tales. (p. 139)
—Giant Tales from Around the World. Waters, Fiona, illus. (p. 674)
—In Andal's House. (p. 863)
—Stolen Sun. Hall, Amanda, illus. (p. 1652)
Hall, Amanda, illus. see Aesop.
Hall, Amanda, illus. see Gavin, Jamila.
Hall, Amanda, illus. see Gelfand, Shoshana Boyd.
Hall, Amanda, illus. see Joslin, Mary.
Hall, Amanda, illus. see Markel, Michelle & Rousseau, Henri.
Hall, Amanda, illus. see Self, David.
Hall, Amanda, illus. see Smucker, Anna Egan.
Hall, Amanda, tr. Giant Tales. (p. 674)
Hall, Andrew, jt. auth. see Feinman, Anthony.
Hall, Angela Marie. Priscilla Pennybrook: Hello World, I Have Arrived! (p. 1407)
Hall, Annalisa. Blanket of Comfort. (p. 198)
—Holy Ghost Is Like a Blanket. Egbert, Corey, illus. (p. 791)
—I Want to Be Baptized. Egbert, Corey, illus. (p. 847)
—Momma, i hold You. (p. 1162)
—Tak & Lolly: Santa Clause at Church. (p. 1696)
Hall, Arthur, illus. see Green, Roger Lancelyn & Green, Richard.
Hall, Arthur, illus. see Green, Roger Lancelyn.
Hall, August, illus. see Appelt, Kathi.
Hall, August, illus. see Barron, T. A.
Hall, Barbara. Dixie Storms. (p. 455)
—Noah Confessions. (p. 1261)
—That Is Choice! (p. 1726)
Hall Beadore, Sondra. God Knew You Before You Were Born. (p. 689)
Hall, Becky. Morris & Buddy: The Story of the First Seeing Eye Dog Ettlinger, Doris, illus. (p. 1176)
Hall, Betty L. & Jones, Helen. West Virginia Survival. (p. 1876)
Hall, Beverly H., illus. see Fisher, Nancy.
Hall, Bob, illus. see Simonson, Louise.
Hall, Bob, jt. illus. see Buscema, John.
Hall, Bradley H. Legal Issues in Career & Technical Education. (p. 987)
Hall, Brianna. Freedom from Slavery: Causes & Effects of the Emancipation Proclamation (p. 634)
—Great Women of the American Revolution. (p. 719)
—Hair-Raising Monster Stories (p. 736)
—Mummies of Ancient Egypt (p. 1191)
—Strike It Rich! The Story of the California Gold Rush (p. 1667)
Hall, Brianna & Levine, Becky. Cause & Effect (p. 282)
Hall, Brianna, et al. Adventures on the American Frontier (p. 24)
—Scared! (p. 1519)
—Story of the American Revolution. (p. 1660)
Hall, Bruce, jt. auth. see Hall, Bruce Edward.
Hall, Bruce Edward & Hall, Bruce. Henry & the Kite Dragon. Low, William, tr. (p. 767)

Hall, Bureda Ann Greathouse. Stories of My Little Blue Monkey. (p. 1655)
Hall, C. Aubrey. Call of Eirian (p. 254)
Hall, C. Aubrey & Zuckerman, Al. Mage Fire (p. 1071)
Hall, Carol S. & Hansen, T. J. This Is Arizona. (p. 1735)
—This Is Idaho. (p. 1736)
—This Is Utah. (p. 1736)
Hall, Caroline V. Rhett & Abby: Abby's New Home. (p. 1467)
Hall, Christina. Can Checkers Come Too? Hall, Lowell, illus. (p. 258)
Hall, David, jt. auth. see Rhodes, Mary Jo.
Hall, Deborah. Keepers of the Garden. (p. 947)
Hall, Dee. Can You Imagine? Hall, Dee & Hesselbein, Kent, illus. (p. 259)
Hall, Derek. Africa. (p. 26)
—Asia. (p. 106)
—Chemistry, Earth, & Space Sciences. (p. 297)
—Europe. (p. 540)
—Life Sciences. (p. 1013)
—North America. (p. 1264)
—Physical Sciences. (p. 1353)
Hall, Derek, jt. auth. see Ryles, Briony.
Hall, Derek, ed. Philosophy, Invention, & Engineering. (p. 1351)
Hall, Desis. Christmas in Jamaica & Other Stories. (p. 314)
Hall, Donald. Lucy's Christmas. McCurdy, Michael, illus. (p. 1063)
—Lucy's Summer. McCurdy, Michael, illus. (p. 1063)
Hall, Dorothy. Story of Little Granny Munklestump. (p. 1659)
Hall, Dorothy & Daniel, Marie. Guess the Covered Word for Seasons & Holidays. (p. 729)
Hall, Dorothy, et al. Big Words for Big Kids: Systematic Sequential Phonics & Spelling. (p. 184)
Hall, Dorothy Louise, illus. see Cohen, Barbara S.
Hall, Dorothy P. Guess the Covered Word for Character Development, Grades 1 - 5. (p. 729)
Hall, Dorothy P. & Cunningham, Patricia M. Administrator's Guide to the Four Blocks(r), Grades 1 - 3. (p. 13)
Hall, Dorothy P. & Tillman, CeCe. Book Club Groups: A Multilevel Four-Blocks Reading Strategy. Bland, Joey, ed. (p. 210)
Hall, Duncan. Brambleholme Summer. (p. 222)
Hall, Erin & Skindzier, Jon. University of Texas College Prowler off the Record. (p. 1821)
Hall, Eve D. Dontay's Alphabet Book of Color. Hale, J. P., illus. (p. 469)
Hall, Evelyn, told to. Dante's Poetic Playground. (p. 406)
Hall, Francie. Appalachian Christmas ABCs. Oehm, Kent, illus. (p. 92)
Hall, Francois. Emperor's New Clothes. (p. 521)
Hall, Francois, illus. see Gowar, Mick.
Hall, Francois, illus. see Graves, Sue.
Hall, Frank. Prince Who Did Not Want to be King. (p. 1401)
Hall, Frostie. Dread Champions for the King, Book 2: For the King! (p. 482)
—Dread Champions of the King: The Humble Beginning. (p. 482)
Hall, Geoff. Literature in Language Education. (p. 1023)
Hall, Gladys. Red Riding Hood. (p. 1454)
Hall, Godfrey. Games: Traditions Around the World. (p. 654)
Hall, Greg, illus. see Thomas, Keltie.
Hall, H. Tom. Golden Tombo. (p. 695)
Hall, Hannah, jt. auth. see Thomas Nelson Publishing Staff.
Hall, Hannah C. God Bless My Boo Boo Whitlow, Steve, illus. (p. 688)
—God Bless Our Fall Whitlow, Steve, illus. (p. 688)
Hall, Homer L. High School Journalism. (p. 778)
—High School Journalism Teacher's Workbook & Guide. (p. 778)
—Junior High Journalism. (p. 936)
—Student's Workbook for Junior High Journalism. (p. 1669)
Hall, Homer L. & Aimone, Logan. Student's Workbook for Junior High Journalism. (p. 1669)
Hall, Homer L. & Aimone, Logan H. High School Journalism. (p. 778)
Hall, Howard. Charm of Dolphins: The Threatened Life of a Flippered Friend. León, Vicki, ed. (p. 294)
—Frenzy of Sharks: The Surprising Life of a Perfect Predator. Leon, Vicki, ed. (p. 636)
—Secrets of Kelp Forests: Life's Ebb & Flow in the Sea's Richest Habitat. Leon, Vicki, ed. (p. 1545)
Hall, J. Darroll. Lollipop Club. (p. 1046)
Hall, Jacque. Tommy Turns Dtective. (p. 1765)
Hall, James Norman, jt. auth. see Nordhoff, Charles.
Hall, James W. & Zumdahl, Steven S. Introductory Chemistry: A Foundation. (p. 883)
Hall, Jamie. One Gemini's Poetic Ideology. (p. 1295)
Hall, Jason. Pistolwhip - Yellow Menace. (p. 1364)
Hall, Jean-Blaise, photos by see Spieler, Marlena & Oxmoor House Staff.
Hall, Jennie. Viking Tales. (p. 1842)
—Viking Tales (Yesterday's Classics) Lambdin, Victor R., illus. (p. 1842)
Hall, Jennifer. Reginald's Broken Arm. (p. 1457)
—Winston Rabbit & other Poems. (p. 1937)
Hall, Joan Upton. RX for Your Writing Ills. (p. 1499)
Hall, John. Is He or Isn't He? (p. 889)
—Jeffrey Takes on the World. (p. 912)
—What If I Pulled This Thread. Gilpin, Stephen, illus. (p. 1887)
Hall, John & Gilpin, Stephen. If the Earth Had a Zipper. (p. 854)
Hall, John R. Angels Working Overtime. (p. 75)
Hall, Julie. Hot Planet Needs Cool Kids: Understanding Climate Change & What You can do About it. (p. 802)
—Reptiles & Amphibians: Grades 2 & 3. (p. 1461)
—Weather: Grades 2 & 3. (p. 1869)
Hall, Kate W. Richmond Rocks! (p. 1470)
Hall, Katharine. Amphibians & Reptiles. (p. 66)
—Amphibians & Reptiles: A Compare & Contrast Book. (p. 66)
—Árboles: Un Libro de Comparación y Contraste (p. 95)
—Nubes: Un Libro de Comparación y Contraste (p. 1269)
—Polar Bears & Penguins: a Compare & Contrast Book (p. 1379)
Hall, Katherine. Polar Bears & Penguins: A Compare & Contrast Book (p. 1379)
Hall, Kathleen. Billy & Bobby's Adventures. (p. 187)
Hall, Katy, pseud & Eisenberg, Lisa. Dino Riddles. Rubel, Nicole, illus. (p. 441)
Hall, Kelly. Legend of the Light Keeper. (p. 989)
Hall, Kenneth. Johnny & the Heaters. (p. 923)
Hall, Kirk. Carina & Her Care Partner Gramma. Paolini, Alison, illus. (p. 269)
—Carson & His Shaky Paws Grampa. Paolini, Alison, illus. (p. 272)
Hall, Kirsten. African Elephant: The World's Biggest Land Mammal. (p. 27)
—Animal Hearing. (p. 78)
—Animal Hearing/El Oido en los Animales. (p. 78)
—Animal Sight: La Vista de los Animales. (p. 79)
—Animal Sight. (p. 79)
—Animal Sight/La Vista de los Animales. (p. 79)
—Animal Smell. (p. 79)
—Animal Smell (El Olfato en los Animales) (p. 79)
—Animal Taste. (p. 80)
—Animal Taste (El Gusto en los Animales) (p. 80)
—Animal Taste (el Gusto en los Animales) (p. 80)
—Animal Touch. (p. 80)
—Animal Touch (El Tacto en los Animales) (p. 80)
—Ballerina Girl. (p. 134)
—Big Sled Race. Burnett, Lindy, illus. (p. 183)
—Birthday Beastie: All about Counting. Luedecke, Bev, illus. (p. 192)
—Bunny, Bunny. Wilburn, Kathy, illus. (p. 242)
—Buried Treasure: All about Using a Map. Luedecke, Bev, illus. (p. 243)
—Deep Sea Adventures: A Chapter Book. (p. 423)
—Double Trouble: All about Colors. Luedecke, Bev, illus. (p. 473)
—Duck, Duck, Goose! (p. 488)
—First Day of School: All about Shapes & Sizes. Luedecke, Bev, illus. (p. 594)
—Glow-In-The-Dark Zombie Science. Myers, Lawrence E., illus. (p. 685)
—Good Times: All about the Seasons. Luedecke, Bev, illus. (p. 700)
—Grandma's House. Calderas, Gloria, illus. (p. 708)
—Great Bustard: The World's Heaviest Flying Bird. (p. 714)
—Help! All about Telling Time. Luedecke, Bev, illus. (p. 765)
—Hide-And-Seek: All about Location. Luedecke, Bev, illus. (p. 776)
—Hide-and-Seek: All about Location. Luedecke, Bev, illus. (p. 776)
—I'm a Princess. DeRosa, Dee, illus. (p. 858)
—I'm Not Scared. Holub, Joan, illus. (p. 859)
—Jacket. Tolstikova, Dasha, illus. (p. 903)
—Kids in Sports. (p. 954)
—Leatherback Turtle: The World's Heaviest Reptile. (p. 986)
—Let's Trade: All about Trading. Luedecke, Bev, illus. (p. 1001)
—Little Bird, Be Quiet! Gibson, Sabina, illus. (p. 1024)
—Little Lies: All about Math. Luedecke, Bev, illus. (p. 1030)
—My New School. Gott, Barry, illus. (p. 1216)
—My New Town. Suzan, Gerardo, illus. (p. 1216)
—Perfect Day: All about the Five Senses. Luedecke, Bev, illus. (p. 1341)
—Revamp Your Room. (p. 1465)
—Slider's Pet: All about Nature. Luedecke, Bev, illus. (p. 1590)
—Toot! Alder, Charlie, illus. (p. 1767)
—Tooth Fairy. Apperley, Dawn, illus. (p. 1768)
—Top Secret. Simard, Remy, illus. (p. 1769)
—Tug-of-War: All about Balance. Luedecke, Bev, illus. (p. 1796)
—Up Close & Gross. Jankowski, Dan, illus. (p. 1824)
—Vote for Me: All about Civics. Luedecke, Bev, illus. (p. 1850)
—What a Mess! All about Numbers. Luedecke, Bev, illus. (p. 1878)
—Zoom, Zoom, Zoom. Garofoli, Viviana, illus. (p. 1989)
Hall, Kirsten, jt. auth. see Flaxman, Jessica.
Hall, Kirsten, jt. auth. see Seltzer, Eric.
Hall, Kirsten & Flaxma, Jessica. Who Says? (p. 1917)
Hall, Klay, jt. auth. see RH Disney Staff.
Hall, KrisAnne. Bedtime Stories for Budding Patriots. (p. 157)
Hall, LaMarcus J. I Refuse to Let You Give Up: To My Teens Who Feel All Hope Is Gone... (p. 844)
Hall, Leanne. This Is Shyness. (p. 1736)
Hall, Linley Erin. Careers in Biotechnology. (p. 267)
—DNA & RNA. (p. 456)
—Doomsday Scenarios: Separating Fact from Fiction: Killer Viruses. (p. 470)
—Killer Viruses. (p. 956)
—Reducing Your Carbon Footprint in the Kitchen. (p. 1456)
—Starvation in Africa. (p. 1644)
—Transactinides: Rutherfordium, Dubnium, Seaborgium, Bohrium, Hassium, Meitnerium, Darmstadtium, & Roentgenium. (p. 1778)
Hall, Linley Erin, ed. Critical Perspectives on Energy & Power. (p. 383)
—Laws of Motion: An Anthology of Current Thought. (p. 981)
Hall, Lisa. Burton the Sneezing Cow. Keaton, Pam, illus. (p. 244)
Hall, Lowell, illus. see Hall, Christina.
Hall, Lucy. From England to Jamestowne: A Journey to Find My Father. (p. 642)
Hall, Lynn Bradford. Shaka, Warrior King of the Zulu. Hermans, Rene, illus. (p. 1558)
Hall, M. C. First Grade Scholar. Boyer, Robin, illus. (p. 595)
—Leonardo Da Vinci. (p. 992)
—Madam C. J. Walker. (p. 1069)
—Martin Luther King, Jr. Civil Rights Leader. Soud, illus. (p. 1098)
—National Anthem. Ouren, Todd, illus. (p. 1231)
—Second Grade Scholar. Boyer, Robin, illus. (p. 1539)
—Skin Deep: Functions of Skin (p. 1585)
—Welcome to Denali National Park. (p. 1873)
Hall, M. C. & Hall, Margaret. Christmas. (p. 312)
Hall, Maggie. Conspiracy of Us. (p. 359)
Hall, Marcella Runell & Cameron, Andrea. 10 Most Influential Hip Hop Artists. (p. 1994)
Hall, Marcellus, illus. see Hopkins, Lee Bennett.
Hall, Marcellus, illus. see Krull, Kathleen.
Hall, Marcellus, illus. see North, Sherry.
Hall, Marcellus, illus. see Wilson, Karma.
Hall, Margaret. Abraham Lincoln: 16th U. S. President. Soud, illus. (p. 6)
—Ants (p. 90)
—Ants [Scholastic]. (p. 90)
—Bancos (p. 136)
—Banks (p. 136)
—Beavers Saunders-Smith, Gail, ed. (p. 155)
—Cows & Their Calves (p. 374)
—Cows & Their Calves [Scholastic]. (p. 374)
—Dinero (p. 440)
—Ducks & Their Ducklings (p. 488)
—Ducks & Their Ducklings [Scholastic]. (p. 488)
—Elephants & Their Calves (p. 511)
—Estaciones del Año. (p. 538)
—Grasshoppers (p. 711)
—Grasshoppers [Scholastic]. (p. 711)
—Hanukkah. (p. 743)
—Herons Saunders-Smith, Gail, ed. (p. 773)
—Hibernar. (p. 775)
—Homes. (p. 793)
—Ladybugs [Scholastic]. (p. 971)
—Little World Holidays & Celebrations (p. 1038)
—Martin Luther King, Jr. Day. (p. 1098)
—Muskrats Saunders-Smith, Gail, ed. (p. 1194)
—Penguins & Their Chicks (p. 1337)
—Schools. (p. 1524)
—Spiders (p. 1626)
—Tarjetas de Crédito y Cheques (p. 1706)
—Thanksgiving. (p. 1725)
—Tigers & Their Cubs. (p. 1749)
—Tu Dinero (p. 1795)
—Wetland Animals Saunders-Smith, Gail, ed. (p. 1877)
Hall, Margaret, jt. auth. see Hall, M. C.
Hall, Margaret, jt. auth. see Hall, Margaret C.
Hall, Margaret C. Ants. (p. 90)
—Centipedes (p. 287)
—Cicadas (p. 318)
—Clothing. (p. 334)
—Crickets. Saunders-Smith, Gail, ed. (p. 382)
—Day & Night Saunders-Smith, Gail, ed. (p. 412)
—Festivals. (p. 582)
—Food. (p. 612)
—Grasshoppers. (p. 711)
—Hibernation Saunders-Smith, Gail, ed. (p. 775)
—Irish Americans. (p. 887)
—Ladybugs. (p. 971)
—Praying Mantises. (p. 1393)
—Seasons of the Year Saunders-Smith, Gail, ed. (p. 1538)
—Transportation. (p. 1779)
—Vietnamese Americans. (p. 1841)
Hall, Margaret C. & Hall, Margaret. Arañas. Guzman Ferrer, Martin Luis, tr. from ENG. (p. 94)
—Beetles (p. 158)
—Credit Cards & Checks (p. 380)
—Day & Night Miller, Jo, illus. (p. 412)
—Dragonflies (p. 478)
—Fireflies (p. 592)
—Hormigas. Guzman Ferrer, Martin Luis, tr. from ENG. (p. 798)
—Mantis Religiosas. Guzman Ferrer, Martin Luis, tr. from ENG. (p. 1088)
—Mariquitas. Guzman Ferrer, Martin Luis, tr. from ENG. (p. 1094)
—Money (p. 1163)
—Mosquitoes Saunders-Smith, Gail, ed. (p. 1176)
—Saltamontes. Guzman Ferrer, Martin Luis, tr. from ENG. (p. 1505)
—Seasons of the Year Miller, Jo, illus. (p. 1538)
—Venom & Visions: Art of the Southwest. (p. 1836)
—Your Allowance (p. 1979)
Hall, Marjorie. Talisman Tales: Wiggleton's Courageous Adventure. No. 1 (p. 1703)
Hall, Marjory. Gold-Lined Box. (p. 693)
Hall, Mark & West, Matthew. City on the Hill. Vania, Tatio, illus. (p. 324)
Hall, Mark, et al. Thrive Student Edition: Digging Deep, Reaching Out (p. 1744)
Hall, Martha Gamble. Note from Sant. (p. 1267)
Hall, Mary, illus. see Castle, Amber.
Hall, Mary, illus. see Oakes, Loretta.
Hall, Mary Kathleen. Marland's Mysterious Mazes: Past the Mailbox. (p. 1095)
Hall, Matthew Henry. Phoebe & Chub. Aldridge, Sheila, illus. (p. 1351)
Hall, Megan Kelley & Jones, Carrie. Dear Bully: 70 Authors Tell Their Stories. (p. 418)
Hall, Melanie, illus. see Busch, Melinda Kay.
Hall, Melanie, illus. see Cohen, Deborah.
Hall, Melanie, illus. see Fishman, Cathy Goldberg.
Hall, Melanie, illus. see Hopkins, Lee Bennett.
Hall, Melanie, illus. see Rosenstock, Barb.
Hall, Melanie, illus. see Schram, Peninnah.
Hall, Melanie, illus. see Swartz, Nancy Sohn.
Hall, Melanie W., illus. see Berger, Barry W.
Hall, Melanie W., illus. see Fishman, Cathy Goldberg.
Hall, Melanie W., illus. see Hopkins, Lee Bennett.
Hall, Melanie W., illus. see Johnson, William.
Hall, Melanie W., illus. see Jules, Jacqueline & Hechtkopf, Jacqueline.
Hall, Melanie W., jt. auth. see Fishman, Cathy Goldberg.
Hall, Melissa. Legend of Athlon. Ryan, Ashley, illus. (p. 988)
Hall, Michael. Cat Tale. Hall, Michael, illus. (p. 278)
—Frankencrayon. Hall, Michael, illus. (p. 629)
—It's an Orange Aardvark! Hall, Michael, illus. (p. 896)
—My Heart Is Like a Zoo. Hall, Michael, illus. (p. 1211)
—Perfect Square. Hall, Michael, illus. (p. 1342)
—Red: A Crayon's Story. Hall, Michael, illus. (p. 1453)
Hall, Mike. Chirpi. (p. 308)
Hall, Milton, illus. see Carothers, Sue & Henke, Elizabeth.
Hall, Nancy. Get Set for the Code Book B. (p. 668)
—Go for the Code Book C. (p. 686)
—Spellwell B: Grade 3. (p. 1625)
Hall, Nancy R. My Grandparents Live in an RV Hall, Nancy R., illus. (p. 1210)
Hall, Natalie Susan. Andy Anole's Adventure (p. 73)
Hall, Noelle. Emily & the Captain. D'Souza, Mel, illus. (p. 518)
Hall, Noelle Chason & Joanne Beeker Clurman. Sweetpea County's Secret Quilt. Caprara, Collette, illus. (p. 1690)
Hall, Norris, illus. see Booth-Alberstadt, Sheila.
Hall, Norris, illus. see Hensley, Terri Anne.
Hall, Norris, illus. see Jaques, Jon.
Hall, Norris, illus. see Moore, Jim.
Hall, Pam. Odds Get Even. Chapman, Lynne, illus. (p. 1278)
Hall, Pamela. 5 Steps to Drawing Dinosaurs. Girouard, Patrick, illus. (p. 1992)
—5 Steps to Drawing Farm Animals. Lane Holm, Sharon, illus. (p. 1992)
—Bully-Free Bus. Ostrom, Bob, illus. (p. 241)
—Bully-Free Party. Ostrom, Bob, illus. (p. 241)
—Bully-Free Playground. Ostrom, Bob, illus. (p. 241)
—Bully-Free School. Ostrom, Bob, illus. (p. 241)
—Code Blue Calling All Capitals! Currant, Gary, illus. (p. 338)
—Discover Dirt. Yamada, Jane, illus. (p. 447)
—Discover Shadows. Yamada, Jane, illus. (p. 448)
—Discover Sound. Yamada, Jane, illus. (p. 448)
—ELEMENOPEE, the Day I, M, N, O & P Left the Abc's. Williamson, James, illus. (p. 510)
—Find Your Function at Conjunction Junction. Currant, Gary, illus. (p. 587)
—Making a Bully-Free World. Ostrom, Bob, illus. (p. 1080)
—Miss You Like Crazy. Bell, Jennifer A., illus. (p. 1152)
—Muscle-Bound Compounds. Currant, Gary, illus. (p. 1192)
—Punk-Tuation Celebration. Currant, Gary, illus. (p. 1417)
—Rectangles. Holm, Sharon, illus. (p. 1452)
—Rena & Rio Build a Rhyme. Pilo, Cary, illus. (p. 1460)
—Squares. Holm, Sharon, illus. (p. 1636)
—Stand-in Pronouns Save the Scene! Currant, Gary, illus. (p. 1639)
—Staying Bully-Free Online. Ostrom, Bob, illus. (p. 1645)
—Wheel of Subject-Verb Agreement. Currant, Gary, illus. (p. 1900)
Hall, Pat, illus. see Takayama, Sandi.
Hall, Patricia. Honest-to-Goodness Story of Raggedy Andy Wannamaker, Joni Gruelle, illus. (p. 794)
—Old Friends, New Friends. Winfield, Alison, illus. (p. 1283)
Hall, Petisamaria G. Why Grandmas Go to Heaven. (p. 1925)
HALL, Prentice. Young Children's Picture Dictionary: Teacher's Resource Book with CD-ROM. (p. 1978)
Hall, Raelene. New Puppy. Collier, Kevin Scott & LeBlanc, Giselle, illus. (p. 1247)
Hall, Randal C. Lamborghini. (p. 972)
Hall, Rebecca. A Is for Arches: A Utah Alphabet. Larson, Katherine & Langton, Bruce, illus. (p. 1)
Hall, Rich. Things Snowball. (p. 1733)
Hall, Richard E. Strategic Planninhg for a Small Business. (p. 1666)
Hall, Rocky Lane. Fan (p. 570)
Hall, Roger, illus. see Perry, Phyllis.
Hall, Rohan. Little Boy. (p. 1025)
Hall, Ron, illus. see Armstrong, Jeannette C.
Hall, Rose. After the Storm. Jazvic, Beryl, illus. (p. 28)
Hall, Rosemary. Kids Knee Garden from the Adventures with Lamb E. Boy Series. (p. 954)
Hall, S. M. & Quarto Generic Staff. Breaking the Circle. (p. 225)
Hall, Sandy. Gibson Speaks: The World's Tallest Dog Talks about His Life. (p. 674)
—Little Something Different. (p. 1036)
Hall, S.C. Turns of Fortune & Other Tales. (p. 1798)
Hall, Sharon J. Ridgeway Middle School: Choosing to Embrace Diversity 360 Degrees. (p. 1471)
Hall, Shirley. Adventure of Molly the Mouse. (p. 14)
—Buggy Buggy. Ledger, Faye, illus. (p. 236)
—Fairy Tale. (p. 564)
—Monkey Monkey. (p. 1165)
Hall, Shyima. Hidden Girl: The True Story of a Modern-Day Child Slave. (p. 775)
Hall, Stan And Carol. Carl Barconey & Friends. (p. 269)
Hall, Stephen. Exploring the Oceans. (p. 554)
Hall, Stephen M. Shepherd's Son. (p. 1565)
Hall, Stuart, jt. auth. see Stanley, Andy.
Hall, Susan. Dolphin Named Tag. (p. 464)
—Dora's Cousin Diego. (p. 471)
—Finding Home: The Story of Two Penguins. (p. 588)
—Mr. Fixit's Lucky Day. (p. 1185)
—Robot Repairman to the Rescue! (p. 1480)
Hall, Susan, illus. see Beinstein, Phoebe.
Hall, Susan, illus. see Koeppel, Ruth.
Hall, Susan, illus. see Lindner, Brooke.
Hall, Susan, illus. see Ottersley, Martha T.
Hall, Susan, illus. see Random House Staff.
Hall, Susan, illus. see Ricci, Christine.
Hall, Susan, illus. see Valdes, Leslie.
Hall, Susan, jt. illus. see Hall, Susan.
Hall, Susan & Hall, Susan. Diego Saves the Tree Frogs. (p. 437)
—Surf That Wave! (p. 1685)
Hall, Susan Liberty. Scented Adventures of the Bouquet Sisters in Fairyland. Josephine, Wall, illus. (p. 1521)
Hall, Susan T. ABC Sign & Color: A Beginner's Book of American Sign Language. (p. 3)
—Happy Halloween Coloring Book. (p. 745)
—Presentamos a Diego! (p. 1396)
—Watch Me Draw Diego's Animal Adventures. (p. 1861)
Hall, Tamika. Nita, la Mariquita the Ladybug: A Spanglish Kids Book. (p. 1257)
Hall, Tara. Good Girls Do. Raluca, Cristina Cirti, illus. (p. 698)
Hall, Teri. Away. (p. 120)
—Line. (p. 1019)
Hall, Terri L. Denny & Denise: A Story of Two Ducks: Introducing Pretty Boy & Fella Hall, Terri L. & Babeaux, Dennis, photos by. (p. 426)
Hall, Terri L. & Babeaux, Denise L. Story of Chester the Chow Chow. (p. 1657)
Hall, Tessa Emily. Purple Moon. (p. 1419)
Hall, Tim K. Shadow of the Wolf. (p. 1557)
Hall, Timothy L. Religion in America. (p. 1458)
Hall, Traci. Diary of a Bad Boy. (p. 434)
—Her Wiccan, Wiccan Ways. (p. 769)

H

—Wiccan Cool. (p. 1927)
Hall, Tracy, illus. see Irving, Washington.
Hall, Wendell E., illus. see Brown, Roberta Simpson.
Hall, Wendell E., illus. see Jameson, W. C.
Hall, Wendell E., illus. see Jones, Loyal & Wheeler, Billy Edd.
Hall, Wendell E., illus. see Taylor, Shirley A.
Hall, William. Just Like Me: My Diggety Dog - Paws4Learning. (p. 939)
Hall, William H., jt. auth. see Baker, Paul R.
Hallagen Ink, ed. see Johnson, Kevin Wayne.
Hallagin, Janet. Way of Courage. (p. 1864)
Hallam, Chrystal. Treasure of the Soul. (p. 1782)
Hallam, Colleen and Peggy, illus. see Ross, Marlene.
Hallam, Gwion. Creadyn: Neu, Huw Dafis A'r Draenog Wnaeth Gnoi at y Gwaed, A'r Corryn Sy'n Crwydro'i Hunllefau. (p. 378)
—Disgwyl a Disgwyl. (p. 451)
Hallam, Gwion & Thomas, Rhianedd. Breuddwyd Roc a Rôl. (p. 226)
Hallam, Serena Sax, illus. see Kettles, Nick.
Hallaway, Tate. Almost to Die For. (p. 48)
Hallawell, Francis. Introducing Great Britain. (p. 882)
—London. (p. 1046)
Hallberg, Garth Risk. Penny: A Little History of Luck. (p. 1338)
Halle. Brunnert und Partners, Flughafen Leipzig/Halle: Opus 52. (p. 232)
Hallenleben, Georg, jt. auth. see Magnier, Thierry.
Hallensleben, Georg, illus. see Banks, Kate.
Hallensleben, Georg, illus. see Gutman, Anne, et al.
Hallensleben, Georg, illus. see Gutman, Anne.
Hallensleben, Georg, jt. auth. see Gutman, Anne.
Hallensleben, Georg & Gutman, Anne. Mommy & Daddy Boxed Set (p. 1162)
Haller, Christine A. Chippy: The sea lion that lost its Way. Lund, Nancy M., illus. (p. 308)
Haller, Heather, ed. see Kemeny, Esther.
Haller, Nancy, jt. auth. see Gorey, Jill.
Haller, Reese. Adventures Begin. Lynn, Galsterer, illus. (p. 15)
—Giving & Receiving. Haller, Reese, illus. (p. 681)
—Making Friends Galsterer, Lynne, illus. (p. 1081)
—Rescuing Freedom. Haller, Thomas, illus. (p. 1462)
Haller, Thomas, illus. see Haller, Reese.
Hallett, Cynthia J. & Huey, Peggy J., eds. New Casebooks - J. K. Rowling: Harry Potter. (p. 1244)
Hallett, Joy Davies, illus. see Davies, Leah.
Hallett, Mark, illus. see Becker, John.
Hallett, R. B. 10 Most Decisive Battles on American Soil. (p. 1993)
Halley, Jane E. Unidentified Flight-Less Object. (p. 1818)
Halley, Marilyn. Apple-Green Eyes. (p. 92)
Halley, Wendy Stofan. Inside Out. Collier-Morales, Roberta, illus. (p. 877)
Halliday, Ayun. Peanut. Hoppe, Paul, illus. (p. 1332)
Halliday, Gemma. Deadly Cool. (p. 417)
—Social Suicide. (p. 1605)
Halliday, John. Shooting Monarchs. (p. 1568)
Halliday, Keith. Aurore of the Yukon: A Girl's Adventure in the Klondike Gold Rush. (p. 116)
Halliday, M. Ladder, a BBQ & a Pillar of Salt. (p. 970)
Halliday, M. A. K. Instructor Solutions Guide for Fundamentals of Physics. (p. 878)
—Instructor's Manual for Fundamentals of Physics. (p. 878)
—Test Bank for Fundamentals of Physics. (p. 1723)
Halliday, Marc & Potter, Ian. Red Sea, a Burning Bush & a Plague of Frogs. (p. 1455)
—Tent Peg, a Jawbone & a Sheepskin Rug. (p. 1720)
Halliday, Susan. Quiz Champs. Jellett, Tom, illus. (p. 1429)
Halliday-King, Michaela. Pennine Mouse. (p. 1337)
Halligan, Chris, jt. auth. see Aryal, Aimee.
Halligan, Jim & Newman, John. Seeing Red. (p. 1548)
Halligan, Kelly C., illus. see Carey, Keelin, et al.
Halligan, Terry. Funny Skits & Sketches. Behr, Joyce, illus. (p. 650)
Hallinan, James D. Poem Power: A Miracle for You. (p. 1376)
Hallinan, P. K. ABC I Love You. (p. 3)
—Brothers Forever. Hallinan, P. K., illus. (p. 231)
—Christmas at Grandma's House. (p. 312)
—Easter at Our House. (p. 499)
—Forever Friends! (p. 619)
—Grandma Loves You. (p. 708)
—Grandma Loves You! Kirkland, Katherine, illus. (p. 708)
—Grandpa Loves You! Kirkland, Katherine, illus. (p. 709)
—Happy Birthday! (p. 744)
—Heartprints. (p. 760)
—Holidays & Special Feelings (p. 788)
—How Do I Love You? (p. 807)
—How Do I Love You? Hallinan, P. K., illus. (p. 807)
—How Do I Love You/Como Te Amo. (p. 807)
—I Know Jesus Loves Me. (p. 840)
—I Know Jesus Loves Me. Hallinan, P. K., illus. (p. 840)
—I'm Thankful Each Day. (p. 860)
—I'm Thankful Each Day!/Doy Gracias Cada Dia! (p. 860)
—Just Open a Book. (p. 939)
—Let's Be Fit. (p. 994)
—Let's Be Friends. (p. 994)
—Let's Be Happy. Hallinan, P. K., illus. (p. 994)
—Let's Be Helpful. (p. 994)
—Let's Be Helpful. Hallinan, P. K., illus. (p. 994)
—Let's Be Honest. (p. 994)
—Let's Be Kind. (p. 994)
—Let's Be Kind. Hallinan, P. K., illus. (p. 994)
—Let's Be Patient. (p. 994)
—Let's Be Polite. (p. 994)
—Let's Be Safe. (p. 994)
—Let's Be Thankful. (p. 994)
—Let's Be Thankful. Hallinan, P. K., illus. (p. 994)
—Let's Learn All We Can! (p. 998)
—Let's Play As a Team. (p. 1000)
—Let's Share. (p. 1000)
—Let's Share. Hallinan, P. K., illus. (p. 1000)
—Looking Book. Barton, Patrice, illus. (p. 1051)
—Love Letter from God. Watson, Laura, illus. (p. 1060)
—My Brother & I. (p. 1199)
—My Daddy & I. (p. 1201)
—My Mommy & I. (p. 1214)
—My Sister & I. (p. 1218)
—My Teacher's My Friend. (p. 1220)
—Rainbow of Friends. (p. 1435)
—Sisters Forever. Hallinan, P. K., illus. (p. 1581)
—Thank You, God. (p. 1725)
—Thanksgiving at Our House. (p. 1725)
—That's What a Friend Is! (p. 1727)
—Today Is Christmas! Hallinan, P. K., illus. (p. 1760)
—Today Is Easter! (p. 1760)
—Today Is Halloween! (p. 1760)
—Today Is Halloween! Hallinan, P. K., illus. (p. 1760)
—Today Is Thanksgiving! Hallinan, P. K., illus. (p. 1760)
—We're Very Good Friends, My Father & I. (p. 1875)
—We're Very Good Friends, My Grandma & I. (p. 1875)
—When I Grow Up. (p. 1902)
Hallinan, Susan, illus. see Canfield, Andrea.
Hallinan, Val. Rhode Island. (p. 1468)
Halling, Jonathan, illus. see National Geographic Kids Staff.
Halling, Jonathan, illus. see U. S. National Geographic Society Staff & National Geographic Kids Staff.
Hallman, Patsy Johnson. Creating Positive Images: A Guide for Young People. (p. 378)
Hallmark, Danna G. How Do I Feel Happy? How Do I Feel Sad? (p. 807)
Hallmark, Darla. More Dragons: Coloring Book by Darla Hallmark. (p. 1174)
Hallock, Charles. Origin of the American Indigenes. (p. 1304)
Hallock, Marilyn R. Central Glass Company: The First Thirty Years, 1863-1893 (p. 287)
Halloran, Corey. Our Neighborhood Food Drive: Extend the Counting Sequence. (p. 1309)
—Our Neighborhood Food Drive. (p. 1309)
Halloran, Craig. Chronicles of Dragon: Terror at the Temple (Book 3) (p. 317)
—Chronicles of Dragon: Dragon Bones & Tombstones (Book 2) (p. 317)
—Chronicles of Dragon: The Hero, the Sword & the Dragons (Book 1) (p. 317)
Hallowell, Edward M. & Mayer, Bill. Walk in the Rain with a Brain. (p. 1853)
Hallowell, George & Holub, Joan. Wagons Ho! Avril, Lynne, illus. (p. 1852)
Hallowell, Scot. Spellbound: Essie's Garden. (p. 1625)
Halls, Kelly Milner. Alien Investigation: Searching for the Truth about UFOs & Aliens. Spears, Rick, illus. (p. 41)
—Animals. Cosgrove, Lee, illus. (p. 81)
—Astronaut. (p. 109)
—Blazing Courage. Parks, Phil, illus. (p. 199)
—Dinosaur Parade: A Spectacle of Prehistoric Proportions. Spears, Rick, illus. (p. 442)
—Dinosaurs. Cosgrove, Lee, illus. (p. 443)
—In Search of Sasquatch. (p. 864)
—Life During the Civil War. (p. 1010)
—Look What You Can Make with Craft Sticks. Halls, Kelly, Milner, ed. (p. 1050)
—Story of the Hoover Dam: A History Perspectives Book. (p. 1661)
—Tiger in Trouble! And More True Stories of Amazing Animal Rescues. (p. 1748)
—Virtual Reality Specialist. (p. 1844)
—Wild Dogs: Past & Present. (p. 1929)
Halls, Kelly Milner & Holland, Simon. Lie Detector. Cosgrove, Lee, illus. (p. 1007)
Halls, Kelly Milner & Sumner, William. Saving the Baghdad Zoo: A True Story of Hope & Heroes. Sumner, William, illus. (p. 1517)
Halls, Kelly Milner, ed. Girl Meets Boy: Because There Are Two Sides to Every Story. (p. 678)
Halls, Kelly Milner, et al. Tales of the Cryptids: Mysterious Creatures That May or May Not Exist. (p. 1702)
Hall-Smith, Rachel. Tlk2me: God's Answer for Today. (p. 1758)
Hallstrand, John & Sarah & Hawley, Karen. Zoey Helps the Mystery Dog Find a Home. (p. 1987)
Hallwood, Cheri L. Curious Polka-Dot Present. Rose, Patricia M., illus. (p. 394)
—Winter's First Snowflake. Rose, Patricia M., illus. (p. 1938)
Hallworth, Grace. Dancing to the River ELT Edition. (p. 403)
—Sleep Tight. Kopper, Lisa, illus. (p. 1588)
Hally, Ashleigh. Abraham Lincoln. (p. 6)
—Coretta Scott King. (p. 367)
—Jackie Cochran. (p. 903)
—Juliette Gordon Low. (p. 932)
—Lugenia Burns Hope. (p. 1064)
—Martha Berry. (p. 1097)
—Rosalynn Carter. (p. 1489)
Halpenny, Karen, ed. see Galvin, Laura Gates.
Halper, Sharon. To Learn Is to Do: A Tikkun Olam Road Map. Koffsky, Ann D., illus. (p. 1759)
Halper, Sharon D. Holy Days, Holy Ways. Rauchwerger, Lisa, illus. (p. 791)
—Teacher's Guide for to Learn Is to Do: A Tikkun Olam Roadmap. Koffsky, Ann D., illus. (p. 1709)
Halperin, Wendy, illus. see Galbraith, Kathryn O.
Halperin, Wendy Anderson, illus. see Bruchac, Joseph.
Halperin, Wendy Anderson, illus. see Burnett, Frances Hodgson.
Halperin, Wendy Anderson, illus. see King James Bible Staff.
Halperin, Wendy Anderson, illus. see Rylant, Cynthia.
Halperin, Wendy Anderson, illus. see Wood, Douglas.
Halperin, Wendy Anderson, jt. auth. see Rylant, Cynthia.
Halperin, Wendy Anderson, et al. Peace. Halperin, Wendy Anderson, illus. (p. 1331)
Halpern, Chalky. Hamentash That Ran Away. (p. 739)
Halpern, Gina. Where Is Tibet? Halpern, Gina, illus. (p. 1909)
Halpern, Jake & Kujawinski, Peter. Dormia. (p. 471)
—Nightfall. (p. 1255)
Halpern, Julie. F - It List. (p. 559)
—Get Well Soon. (p. 668)
—Have a Nice Day. (p. 754)
—Into the Wild Nerd Yonder. (p. 881)
Halpern, Monica. All about Light. (p. 42)
—All about Tide Pools. (p. 43)
—Building the Transcontinental Railroad. (p. 239)
—Moving North: African Americans & the Great Migration 1915-1930. (p. 1183)
—Railroad Fever: Building the Transcontinental Railroad 1830-1870. (p. 1434)
—Railroad Fever: Building the Transcontinental Railroad, 1830-1870. (p. 1434)
—Rivers of Fire: The Story of Volcanoes. (p. 1476)
—Three Immigrant Communities New York City In 1900: Set Of 6. (p. 1742)
—Three Immigrant Communities: New York City In 1900: Text Pairs. (p. 1742)
—Underground Towns, Treetops, & Other Animal Hiding Places. (p. 1815)
—Venus Flytraps, Bladderworts & Other Wild & Amazing Plants. (p. 1836)
Halpern, Monica & National Geographic Learning Staff. Great Migration: African Americans Move to the North, 1915-1930. (p. 717)
—Home Front During World War II. (p. 792)
—Progressives. (p. 1410)
Halpern, Paul. Faraway Worlds: Planets Beyond Our Solar System. Cook, Lynette R., illus. (p. 573)
Halpern, Shari. Dinosaur Parade. Halpern, Shari, illus. (p. 442)
Halpern, Shari, illus. see Masurel, Claire.
Halpern, Shari, illus. see Sturges, Judy Sue Goodwin.
Halpern, Shari, illus. see Sturges, Philemon.
Halpernl, Wendy Anderson, illus. see Galbraith, Kathryn O.
Halpert, Ben. Savvy Cyber Kids at Home: The Defeat of the Cyber Bully. Southerland, Taylor, illus. (p. 1518)
Halpin, Abigail, illus. see Brauner, Barbara & Mattson, James Iver.
Halpin, Abigail, illus. see Cheng, Andrea.
Halpin, Abigail, illus. see George, Kallie.
Halpin, Abigail, illus. see Guest, Elissa Haden.
Halpin, Abigail, illus. see Krishnaswami, Uma.
Halpin, Abigail, illus. see Lloyd, Megan Wagner.
Halpin, Abigail, illus. see Patron, Susan.
Halpin, Abigail, illus. see Simon, Coco.
Halpin, Abigail, illus. see Snyder, Laurel.
Halpin, Angela Demos, jt. auth. see Fine, Edith Hope.
Halpin, Brendan & Franklin, Emily. Jenna & Jonah's Fauxmance. (p. 912)
—Tessa Masterson Will Go to Prom. (p. 1722)
Halpin, D. I Learn about Jesus Col/Act Bk. (p. 840)
—My Guardian Angel Col/Act Bk. (p. 1210)
Halpin, D. Thomas. Beatitudes Coloring & Activity Book. Richards, Virginia Helen, illus. (p. 153)
—Holy Eucharist. Richards, Virginia Helen, illus. (p. 791)
Halpin, D. Thomas, illus. see Richards, Virginia Helen.
Halpin, D. Thomas, jt. auth. see Richards, Virginia Helen.
Halpin, D. Thomas & Richards, Virginia Helen. Saint Paul. Halpin, D. Thomas & Richards, Virginia Helen, illus. (p. 1504)
Halpin, Mikki. It's Your World—If You Don't Like It, Change It: Activism for Teenagers. (p. 899)
—It's Your World—If You Don't Like It, Change It. (p. 899)
Halsema, Thea B. van, see Van Halsema, Thea B.
Halsey, Alan. Not Everything Remotely. (p. 1267)
Halsey, Jacqueline. Bluenose Adventure. Orchard, Eric, illus. (p. 204)
—Peggy's Letters (p. 1335)
Halsey, Jacqueline, jt. auth. see Muller, Carrie.
Halsey, Megan. 3 Pandas Planting Halsey, Megan, illus. (p. 1991)
Halsey, Megan, illus. see Chin-Lee, Cynthia.
Halsey, Megan, illus. see Farmer, Jacqueline.
Halsey, Megan, illus. see Hubbell, Patricia.
Halsey, Megan, illus. see Rockwell, Anne F.
Halsey, Megan, illus. see Zimmer, Tracie Vaughn.
Halsey-Cody, J. E. Story Time. (p. 1663)
Halstead, J. Oliver. Last Letter. (p. 978)
Halstead, Jayce N. True Legend of White Crow: Adventures of the Fudge Sisters. Twomey-Lange, Marianna, photos by. (p. 1792)
Halstead, Rachel, jt. auth. see Reid, Struan.
Halstead, Rachel & Reid, Struan. Everyday Life in the Ancient World: Learn about Houses, Homes & What the Romans, Celts, Egyptians & Other Peoples of the Past Used to Eat. (p. 543)
Halstead, Stefanie Merle. Night of the Festival. (p. 1254)
Halsted, John D., ed. Peachy Princesses & Impetuous Princes - for Girls Only! (p. 1332)
Halsted, John David, ed. Dragon's Tales for Boys Only! (p. 479)
—East of the Sun & West of the Moon & Other Moon Stories. (p. 498)
Halteman, Laverne K. Mommy Goes to Heaven. (p. 1162)
Halter, Loretta. Lacy's Journey: The Life of a Decorator Crab. (p. 970)
—Voice for the Redwoods. du Houx, Emily, illus. (p. 1847)
—Voice for the Redwoods. Bartczak, Peter, illus. (p. 1847)
Halter, Reese & Turner, Nancy J. Native Trees of British Columbia. Pearse, Stephen, tr. (p. 1235)
Halterman, Randy. Randall's Rhymes & Toddler Treats: Bedtime Love Stories. (p. 1438)
—Randall's Rhymes & Toddlers Treats: The Animal ABCs. (p. 1438)
—Randall's Rhymes & Toddlers Treats: Children Are Precious, Lovable, & Sweet: Fun to Read & Learning Made Easy. (p. 1438)
Haltermon, Becky, illus. see Clare, Caitlen.
Haltigan, Susanne. Seymour the Sea Turtle Saves His Sea Friends. (p. 1556)
Haltom, Cris. Stranger of the Table. (p. 1665)
Haltom, Gerald. Santa Shares His Mitten. (p. 1513)
Haluska, David. Jesus Loves Trucks. Ford, Emily, illus. (p. 916)
Halverson, Barbara. Farm Friends Forever: Everyone Needs Friends. (p. 574)
Halverson, Delia Touchton. My Cup Runneth Over. (p. 1200)
—Oak Street Chronicles & the Good News: Everyday Life & Christian Faith. Dotts, M. Franklin, ed. (p. 1274)
—Teaching Prayer in the Classroom: Experiences for Children & Youth. (p. 1710)
Halverson, Jim. Spelling Works. (p. 1625)
Halverson, Lydia. Nursery Rhymes. (p. 1273)
Halverson, Lydia, illus. see Grogan, John & Hill, Susan.
Halverson, Lydia, illus. see Grogan, John.
Halverson, Lydia, illus. see Riehecky, Janet.
Halverson, Lydia, illus. see Ritchie, Joseph R.
Halverson, Lydia, illus. see Ritchie, Joseph.
Halverson, Lydia, illus. see Rollins, Jack & Nelson, Steve.
Halverson, Lydia, illus. see Schaefer, Peggy.
Halverson, Lydia, illus. see Spinelli, Eileen.
Halverson, Mathew. Concord Cunningham Pursues the Clues: The Scripture Sleuth 5. (p. 355)
Halverson, Tom, illus. see Dunlop, Ed.
Halvorson, Adeline, illus. see Tyson, Ian.
Halvorson, Karin. Inside the Blood. (p. 877)
—Inside the Bones. (p. 877)
—Inside the Brain. (p. 877)
—Inside the Ears. (p. 877)
—Inside the Eyes. (p. 877)
—Inside the Heart. (p. 877)
—Inside the Kidneys. (p. 877)
—Inside the Lungs. (p. 877)
—Inside the Muscles. (p. 877)
—Inside the Skin, Hair, & Nails. (p. 877)
—Inside the Stomach. (p. 877)
—Inside Your Germs. (p. 878)
Halvorson, Marilyn. Blood Brothers (p. 200)
—Blue Moon (p. 203)
—Blue Moon. (p. 203)
—Bull Rider (p. 240)
—Dare (p. 406)
—Let It Go (p. 994)
—Monteur de Taureau: (Bull Rider) (p. 1170)
Halvorson, Michelle. All My Wishes for You. (p. 45)
Ham, Becky. Periodic Table. (p. 1343)
Ham, Catherine. Step Inside! A Look Inside Animal Homes. (p. 1648)
—Step Inside! A Look inside Animal Homes. (p. 1648)
Ham, Ken. Answer Book for Kids: 25 Questions on Creation & the Fall. (p. 88)
—Answers Book for Kids, Volume 3: 22 Questions from Kids on God & the Bible. (p. 88)
—Answers Book for Kids, Volume 4: 22 Questions from Kids on Sin, Salvation, & the Christian Life. (p. 88)
—Dinosaurs for Kids. (p. 444)
—My Creation Bible: Teaching Kids to Trust the Bible from the Very First Verse. Taylor, Jonathan, illus. (p. 1200)
—Six Days or Millions of Years? (p. 1582)
—What Really Happened to the Dinosaurs? (p. 1893)
Ham, Ken, jt. auth. see Hansel, Karen.
Ham, Ken & Davis, Buddy. It's Designed to Do What It Does Do. (p. 896)
Ham, Ken & Ham, Mally. Is for Adam: The Gospel from Genesis. (p. 889)
Ham, Mally, jt. auth. see Ham, Ken.
Hama, Larry. Battle of Antietam: The Bloodiest Day of Battle. (p. 146)
—Battle of Antietam: The Bloodiest Day of Battle. Moore, Scott, illus. (p. 146)
—Battle of First Bull Run: The War Begins! (p. 146)
—Battle of First Bull Run: The Civil War Begins. (p. 146)
—Battle of First Bull Run: The Civil War Begins. Moore, Scott, illus. (p. 146)
—Battle of Guadalcanal: Land & Sea Warfare in the South Pacific. (p. 146)
—Battle of Iwo Jima: Guerilla Warfare in the Pacific. (p. 146)
—Battle of Iwo Jima: Guerilla Warfare in the Pacific. (p. 146)
—Battle of Iwo Jima: Guerilla Warfare in the Pacific. Williams, Anthony, illus. (p. 146)
—Battle of Shiloh: Surprise Attack! (p. 146)
—Battle of Shiloh: Surprise Attack! Moore, Scott, illus. (p. 146)
—Classic G. I. Joe Volume 8 (p. 328)
—Island of Terror: Battle of Iwo Jima. Erskine, Gary & Williams, Anthony, illus. (p. 892)
—Omega Team. (p. 1288)
—Real American Hero (p. 1448)
Hama, Larry, jt. auth. see Cain, Bill.
Hama, Larry & Cain, Bill. Tank of Tomorrow: Stryker. (p. 1705)
—Unmanned Aerial Vehicles. (p. 1821)
Hama, Larry & Dixon, Chuck. G. I. JOE: the IDW Collection Volume 1: The IDW Collection Volume 1. (p. 651)
Hama, Larry, et al. Age of Apocalypse. Erskine, Steve et al, illus. (p. 29)
—G. I. Joe: A Real American Hero. Vol. 6 (p. 651)
Hama, Larry, text. Captain America: The Death of Captain America Prose Novel. (p. 263)
Hamad, Elnour, illus. see Harris, Kate W., ed.
Hamad, Munir. AutoCAD 2009 Essentials. (p. 117)
Hamaguchi, Carla. Letters, Numbers, Color & Shape Learning Centers. (p. 1002)
Hamaguchi, Carla, ed. see Barr, Linda.
Hamaguchi, Carla, ed. see Burch, Regina G.
Hamaguchi, Carla, ed. see Callella, Trisha.
Hamaguchi, Carla, ed. see Cernek, Kim, et al.
Hamaguchi, Carla, ed. see Hatch, Thomas & Purney, Dawn.
Hamaguchi, Carla, ed. see Hatch, Tom & Purney, Dawn.
Hamaguchi, Carla, ed. see Hults, Alaska.
Hamaguchi, Carla, ed. see Johnson, Virginia.
Hamaguchi, Carla, ed. see Lewis, Sue & Stern, Amy.
Hamaguchi, Carla, ed. see Morss, Martha.
Hamaguchi, Carla, ed. see Purney, Dawn & Hatch, Thomas.
Hamaguchi, Carla, ed. see Putnam, Jeff.
Hamaguchi, Carla, ed. see Schorr, Andrew.
Hamaguchi, Carla, ed. see Williams, Rozanne Lanczak.
Hamaguchi, Karyn M. Journey to Salvation: The Inspiring Story of a Young Rape Survivor's Recovery. (p. 929)
Hamaker, Steve, illus. see Smith, Jeff.
Hamanaka, Sheila. Grandparents Song. Hamanaka, Sheila, illus. (p. 709)
—Space. (p. 1618)
Hamann, Hilary, jt. auth. see Sefusatti, Emiliano.

Hamann, Hilary Thayer. Anthropology of an American Girl. (p. 89)
Hamashita, Takeshi. China, East Asia & the Global Economy: Regional & Historical Perspectives. Grove, Linda & Selden, Mark, eds. (p. 306)
—China, East Asia & the Global Economy: Regional & Historical Perspectives. Selden, Mark & Grove, Linda, eds. (p. 306)
Hamazaki, Tatsuya. .Hack: //Legend of the Twilight Kokubo, Naomi, tr. from JPN. (p. 735)
—. hack //Legend of the Twilight, Volume 1: Kaplan SAT/ACT Vocabulary-Building Manga. Izumi, Rei, illus. (p. 735)
—.hack//Legend of the Twilight: The Complete Collection. (p. 735)
—Legend of the Twilight Bracelet Izumi, Rei, illus. (p. 989)
Hamazaki, Tatsuya & Tatsuya, Hamazaki. Hack//Ai Buster Idumi, Rei, illus. (p. 735)
Hambleton, Anne. Raja: Story of a Racehorse. Peggykauffman.com Staff & Kauffman, Margaret, illus. (p. 1437)
Hambleton, Laura. Bugs. (p. 237)
—Chameleon Races (p. 289)
—Chameleon Races Erdogan, Faith, tr. from ENG. (p. 289)
—Chameleon Races Choudhury, Dorbesh, tr. from ENG. (p. 289)
—Chameleon Swims (p. 289)
—Chameleon Swims Choudhury, Dorbesh, tr. from ENG. (p. 289)
—Safari Animals. (p. 1501)
Hambleton, Laura, illus. see Erdogan, Fatih.
Hambleton, Laura, illus. see Traynor, Tracy & Pérez, Maria.
Hambleton, Laura, illus. see Traynor, Tracy.
Hambleton, Laura, jt. auth. see Collins Educational Staff.
Hambleton, Laura, jt. auth. see Gu, Licheng.
Hambleton, Laura & Turhan, Sedat. Telling Tails: Fun with Homonyms. Hambleton, Laura, illus. (p. 1717)
Hambleton, Vicki & Greenwood, Cathleen. So, You Want to Be a Writer? How to Write, Get Published, & Maybe Even Make It Big! (p. 1602)
Hamblin, George, illus. see Fort, Holli, et al.
Hamblin, George, illus. see Malaspina, Ann.
Hamblin, Hope. Kyl. (p. 969)
Hambly, Barbara. Circle of the Moon. (p. 321)
Hamblyn, Richard, ed. see Defoe, Daniel.
Hambrick, Sharon. Brain Games. (p. 221)
—Tommy's Clubhouse. Manning, Maurie J., tr. (p. 1765)
—Tommy's Race. Manning, Maurie J., illus. (p. 1765)
—Tommy's Rocket. Manning, Maurie J., illus. (p. 1765)
Hamburg, Jennifer. Monkey & Duck Quack Up! Fotheringham, Edwin, illus. (p. 1164)
—Moose That Says Moo. Truesdell, Sue, illus. (p. 1173)
Hamburger, Carole. Zippity-Do-Dot: The Dot Who Dared to Pick Her Knows. Hamburger, Carole, illus. (p. 1987)
Hamburger, Maria. Story of Aum. (p. 1657)
Hamby, Joe & Kluever, Karen Trogdon. Synago Gear for the Road Leader. (p. 1693)
—Synago Gear for the Road Student. (p. 1693)
Hamdan, Noah, illus. see Dean, Ramsey.
Hamdani, Ibrahim. American Muslims & Jihad. (p. 62)
—Baba Jee: A Tribute & Brief Biography of Hazrat Syed Ghulam Abbas Shah Hamdani (RA) (p. 123)
—Salah: The Prescribed Daily Prayers. (p. 1504)
Hamed, Maissa. Last Night of Ramadan. El Wakil, Mohamed, illus. (p. 978)
Hameister, Ann, illus. see Welles, Lee.
Hameister, Elaine. Ladybug: Her Travels with Jesus. (p. 971)
Hamel, Caroline, illus. see Dube, Pierrette.
Hamel, Christopher de, see de Hamel, Christopher.
Hamel, Jonathan, jt. auth. see Holm, Jennifer L.
Hamel, Mike. Sword & the Flute. (p. 1692)
Hamel, Raymond & Britannica Encyclopaedia, Inc. Staff. Encyclopedia Britannica General KnowledgeTrivia. (p. 524)
Hamelin, Marie-Micheline, illus. see Kruger, Leanne Flett.
Hamelin, Marie-Micheline, illus. see Lecoy, Denise.
Hamelin, Marie-Micheline, illus. see Olson, Karen W.
Hamelin, Marie-Micheline, illus. see Olson, Karen.
Hamelin, Marie-Micheline, illus. see Wagner, Elaine J. & Wagner, Elaine.
Hamel-Mcevoy, Kristen & Chin, Jonathan L. My Little Leo. (p. 1212)
Hamen, Susan E. Ancient Rome. (p. 70)
—Australia. (p. 116)
—Clara Barton: Civil War Hero & American Red Cross Founder. (p. 326)
—Germany. (p. 666)
—Google: The Company & Its Founders. (p. 702)
—How to Analyze the Films of James Cameron. (p. 814)
—How to Analyze the Films of the Coen Brothers. (p. 814)
—John D. Rockefeller: Entrepreneur & Philanthropist. (p. 921)
—Lewis & Clark Expedition. (p. 1004)
—New Deal. (p. 1244)
—Pearl Harbor. (p. 1333)
—Thirteen Colonies. (p. 1734)
—US Navy. (p. 1826)
—World War II. (p. 1959)
—Wright Brothers. (p. 1963)
Hamernik, Cathy. What Do You See? (p. 1883)
Hames, Annette & McCaffrey, Monica, eds. Special Brothers & Sisters: Stories & Tips for Siblings of Children with a Disability or Serious Illness. McCaffrey, Brendan, illus. (p. 1623)
Hamil, Nicole. Magic of Ellie. (p. 1072)
Hamil, Sara. My Feeling Better Workbook: Help for Kids Who Are Sad & Depressed. (p. 1203)
Hamill, Dion. Amazeing Ruins: Journey Through Lost Civilisations. Hamill, Dion, illus. (p. 52)
—Twelve Tasks of Hercules. (p. 1800)
Hamill, Jeff, et al. Uncle Scrooge Clark, John, ed. (p. 1812)
Hamill, Pete. Forever. (p. 619)
Hamill, Pete, ed. see Liebling, A. J.
Hamilton, A., jt. auth. see Roos, Am.
Hamilton, Alice. Loving Hands of Grandma: A True Story. (p. 1061)
Hamilton, Allen, illus. see Wilson-Max, Ken.
Hamilton, Amy. Indigo Dreaming: Meditations for Children. (p. 872)
Hamilton, Andrew, illus. see Punter, Russell.
Hamilton, Anna Housel. Poor Little Slave Girl. (p. 1383)
Hamilton, Annie. Unforgettable Night. (p. 1817)
Hamilton, Annie, tr. see Gregorovius, Ferdinand.
Hamilton, Arlene. Only a Cow Griffiths, Dean, illus. (p. 1298)
Hamilton, Benny. Goat in the Coat. (p. 687)
Hamilton, Bernard. Religion in the Medieval West. (p. 1458)
Hamilton, Bethany. Ask Bethany. (p. 106)
—Ask Bethany: FAQs - Surfing, Faith & Friends (p. 106)
—Body & Soul: A Girl's Guide to a Fit, Fun & Fabulous Life (p. 207)
—Rise Above: A 90-Day Devotional (p. 1474)
Hamilton, Bethany & Bundschuh, Rick. Soul Surfer: A True Story of Faith, Family, & Fighting to Get Back on the Board. (p. 1614)
Hamilton, C. After Ever Happily. (p. 28)
Hamilton, Carol. I'm Not from Neptune. (p. 859)
Hamilton, Christopher. Understanding Philosophy for AS Level. (p. 1816)
Hamilton, Clarice. Special Delivery. (p. 1623)
Hamilton, Clem, et al. Trees of Illinois. (p. 1784)
Hamilton, Covette J. Begethie Wenferd Meets King Tut. (p. 159)
Hamilton, Craig, illus. see Croall, Marie P.
Hamilton, David E., jt. auth. see Hamilton, Elizabeth L.
Hamilton, Dawn. Passing Exams: A Guide for Maximum Success & Minimum Stress. (p. 1326)
Hamilton, Deborah E. Why are You my Mother? A Mother's Response to Her Adopted Daughter. Andrules, Jamie L., illus. (p. 1922)
Hamilton, Dennis Stephen. Higher Ground. (p. 778)
Hamilton, Dianne, ed. see Smith, Annie Laura.
Hamilton, Dianne, ed. see Vaught, Susan.
Hamilton, Dorothy, illus. see Blyton, Enid.
Hamilton, Edmond, et al. Martian Manhunter. (p. 1097)
—Superman - Batman: The Greatest Stories Ever Told. Vol. 1 (p. 1683)
Hamilton, Elizabeth L. Charley Chimp's Jungle Fairness. (p. 292)
—Christopher Cat's Character Club. (p. 316)
—Cubby Bear's Big Responsibility. (p. 388)
—Date with Responsibility. (p. 409)
—Dorrie Donkey's Cooperation Camp. (p. 472)
—Georgey Giraffe's Giant Respect: Character Critter Series #6. (p. 665)
—Jeremy Rabbit's Honesty Pie. (p. 913)
—Katie Kangaroo's Leap of Courage. (p. 945)
—Little Zoh's Submissive Trunk. (p. 1038)
—Lost on Superstition Mountain. (p. 1056)
—Mystery at Lake Cachuma. (p. 1223)
—Pandora Puppy's Caring Circle. (p. 1321)
—Pansy Pig's Patience Pit. (p. 1321)
—Ricky Raccoon's Trustworthiness Tree. (p. 1470)
—Stinky Skunk's Self-Control. (p. 1651)
—Surprise at Pearl Harbor. (p. 1685)
Hamilton, Elizabeth L. & Hamilton, David E. Courage. (p. 372)
Hamilton, Emma Walton, ed. see Olbrys, Brooks.
Hamilton, Emma Walton, jt. auth. see Andrews, Julie.
Hamilton, Emma Walton, jt. auth. see Edwards, Julie Andrews.
Hamilton, Eric E. Buddy the Bassett Hound Follows His Nose. (p. 235)
Hamilton, Erika. Spirit of Danley Manor. (p. 1628)
Hamilton, Fran Santoro. Hands-on English. Hamilton, Michael, illus. (p. 741)
Hamilton, Garry. Frog Rescue: Changing the Future for Endangered Wildlife. (p. 640)
—Rhino Rescue: Changing the Future for Endangered Wildlife. (p. 1467)
Hamilton, Garry, jt. auth. see Crepeau, Pierre.
Hamilton, George. Seeing Red: Story Seeds Vol 1. Hazel, Andrew, illus. (p. 1548)
Hamilton, Gina L. Light. (p. 1014)
—Light Q & A. (p. 1015)
Hamilton, Harriet. Ribbons of the Sun. (p. 1469)
Hamilton, Harriet, tr. see Evento, Susan.
Hamilton, Harriet, tr. see Ribke, Simone T.
Hamilton, Harriet, tr. see Walker, Cynthia.
Hamilton, Helen, illus. see West, Jerry.
Hamilton, Iona, et al. Science Pathways Year 9. (p. 1527)
Hamilton, James, illus. see Hamilton, Kersten.
Hamilton, Janet. James Watson: Solving the Mystery of DNA. (p. 907)
Hamilton, Janice. Canada. (p. 260)
—Canadians in America. (p. 260)
—Jamaica in Pictures. (p. 906)
—Nigeria in Pictures. (p. 1252)
—Norman Conquest of England. (p. 1264)
—Somalia in Pictures. (p. 1608)
—South Africa in Pictures. (p. 1616)
Hamilton, Jean. Secrets of Tropical Rainforests: Hot & Humid & Teeming with Life. Leon, Vicki, ed. (p. 1546)
Hamilton, Jen, ed. Canadian Poems for Canadian Kids. Fearon, Merrill, illus. (p. 260)
Hamilton, Jill. Activism. (p. 10)
—Bankruptcy. (p. 136)
—Bullying & Hazing. (p. 241)
—Foster Care. (p. 624)
—Juvenile Crime. (p. 941)
—Music Industry. (p. 1193)
—U. S. Economy. (p. 1806)
—Video Games. (p. 1841)
Hamilton, John. A-10 Thunderbolt Ii. (p. 1)
—Abrams Tanks. (p. 7)
—Ac-130H/U Gunship. (p. 7)
—AH-64D Apache Longbow. (p. 30)
—Aircraft Carriers. (p. 31)
—Aircraft of World War I. (p. 31)
—Aliens. (p. 41)
—Allied Forces. (p. 47)
—American Revolution: Road to War. (p. 63)
—America's Military. (p. 64)
—Amphibious Assault Ships. (p. 66)
—Anderson Silva. (p. 72)
—Avalanches. (p. 118)
—B. J. Penn. (p. 123)
—B-2 Spirit Stealth Bomber. (p. 122)
—B-52 Stratofortress. (p. 122)
—Bareback Riding. (p. 139)
—Barrel Racing. (p. 140)
—Battles of World War I. (p. 147)
—Bmx. (p. 204)
—Bradley Fighting Vehicles. (p. 221)
—Bull Riding. (p. 240)
—Castles & Dungeons. (p. 277)
—Cougars. (p. 369)
—Cruisers. (p. 386)
—Death Valley National Park. (p. 420)
—Destroyers. (p. 431)
—Dog Friday. (p. 461)
—Drag Racers. (p. 476)
—Dragons. (p. 478)
—Droughts. (p. 486)
—Early Battles of the American Revolution. (p. 493)
—Elves & Fairies. (p. 517)
—Events Leading to World War I. (p. 541)
—F/A-18 Super Hornet. (p. 559)
—F-16 Fighting Falcon. (p. 559)
—F-22 Raptor. (p. 559)
—F-35 Lightning II. (p. 559)
—Fantasy & Folklore. (p. 572)
—Fantasy & Folklore Set II. (p. 572)
—Final Frontier. (p. 586)
—Final Years of the American Revolution. (p. 587)
—Final Years of World War I. (p. 587)
—Formula One Cars. (p. 620)
—Forrest Griffin. (p. 623)
—Frigates. (p. 639)
—Future Societies. (p. 651)
—Georges St-Pierre. (p. 665)
—Goblins & Trolls. (p. 688)
—Go-Kart Racing. (p. 686)
—Golden Age & Beyond. (p. 694)
—Grand Teton National Park. (p. 707)
—Great Smoky Mountains National Park. (p. 718)
—Greatest Hits. (p. 720)
—Green Berets. (p. 721)
—Haunted Places. (p. 753)
—History of Pirates. (p. 784)
—Humvees. (p. 827)
—Hydroplanes. (p. 831)
—Inline Skating. (p. 875)
—Inside the Octagon. (p. 877)
—Knights & Heroes. (p. 964)
—Landslides. (p. 974)
—Leaders & Generals of the American Revolution. (p. 981)
—Lightning. (p. 1015)
—Magic Rings & Other Magical Things. (p. 1073)
—Man-Made Horrors. (p. 1085)
—Mission to Mars (p. 1153)
—Modern Masters of Science Fiction. (p. 1158)
—Motocross. (p. 1179)
—Muscle Cars. (p. 1192)
—National Parks Set 2 (p. 1233)
—Nature's Fury Set 2. (p. 1237)
—Navy SEALs. (p. 1238)
—New Worlds. (p. 1247)
—Ogres And Giants. (p. 1280)
—Olympic National Park. (p. 1288)
—Paladins. (p. 1319)
—Pioneers of Science Fiction. (p. 1361)
—Pirate Ships & Weapons. (p. 1363)
—Pirate's Life. (p. 1363)
—Princesses & Heroines. (p. 1406)
—Real-Time Reporting. (p. 1449)
—Robots & Androids. (p. 1481)
—Rocky Mountain National Park. (p. 1484)
—Roping. (p. 1488)
—Saddle Bronc Riding. (p. 1501)
—Skateboarding. (p. 1583)
—Snowboarding. (p. 1600)
—Spaceships. (p. 1620)
—Sports Cars. (p. 1632)
—Steer Wrestling. (p. 1646)
—Stock Cars. (p. 1651)
—Strykers. (p. 1668)
—Submarines. (p. 1671)
—Theodore Roosevelt National Park. (p. 1729)
—Time Travel. (p. 1753)
—Trench Fighting of World War I. (p. 1784)
—Tsunamis. (p. 1795)
—Turning Points of the American Revolution. (p. 1798)
—UAVs: Unmanned Aerial Vehicles. (p. 1807)
—Uh-60 Black Hawk. (p. 1808)
—Unicorns & Other Magical Creatures. (p. 1818)
—United States Air Force. (p. 1819)
—United States Armed Forces (p. 1819)
—United States Army. (p. 1819)
—United States Marine Corps. (p. 1819)
—United States Navy. (p. 1819)
—V-22 Osprey. (p. 1829)
—Vampires. (p. 1832)
—Weapons of Fantasy & Folkore. (p. 1869)
—Weapons of Science Fiction. (p. 1869)
—Weapons of the American Revolution. (p. 1869)
—Weapons of the Twenty-First Century. (p. 1869)
—Weapons of World War I. (p. 1869)
—Wildfires. (p. 1931)
—Witches. (p. 1941)
—Wizards & Witches. (p. 1943)
—World War II: Weapons. (p. 1959)
—World War II: Early Battles. (p. 1959)
—World War II: Turning Points. (p. 1959)
—World War II: War in the Air. (p. 1959)
—World War II: The Final Years. (p. 1959)
—World War II: Leaders & Generals. (p. 1959)
—Xtreme UFC (p. 1967)
—You Write It! Horror. (p. 1977)
—You Write It! Fantasy. (p. 1977)
—You Write It! Mystery. (p. 1977)
—You Write It! Screenplay. (p. 1977)
—You Write It! Graphic Novel. (p. 1977)
—You Write It! Science Fiction. (p. 1977)
—Zion National Park. (p. 1987)
Hamilton, John, jt. auth. see Wade, Linda R.
Hamilton, John C. Lewis & Clark: An Illustrated Journey. Hamilton, John C., photos by. (p. 1004)
Hamilton, Katharine E. Susie at Your Service. (p. 1688)
Hamilton, Kersten. In the Forests of the Night. (p. 866)
—Ire of Iron Claw: Gadgets & Gears, Book 2. Hamilton, James, illus. (p. 887)
—Mesmer Menace. Hamilton, James, illus. (p. 1129)
—Police Officers on Patrol. Alley, R. W., illus. (p. 1380)
—Red Truck. Petrone, Valeria, illus. (p. 1455)
—Tyger Tyger: A Goblin Wars Book. (p. 1805)
—When the Stars Threw down Their Spears: The Goblin Wars, Bk. 3 (p. 1905)
—When the Stars Threw down Their Spears. (p. 1905)
—Yellow Copter. Petrone, Valeria, illus. (p. 1970)
Hamilton, L. Ninos y la Naturaleza. (p. 1257)
Hamilton, Laura. Cones. Mitter, Kathryn, illus. (p. 356)
—Cubes. Mitter, Kathryn, illus. (p. 389)
—Cylinders. Mitter, Kathryn, illus. (p. 397)
—Prisms. Mitter, Kathryn, illus. (p. 1407)
—Pyramids. Mitter, Kathryn, illus. (p. 1421)
—Spheres. Mitter, Kathryn, illus. (p. 1626)
Hamilton, Laura, reader. Sheila Rae, the Brave. (p. 1564)
—Vera's First Day of School. (p. 1836)
Hamilton, Laurell K. Bloody Bones. (p. 201)
—Cerulean Sins (p. 288)
Hamilton, Laurell K., et al. Bite: All-New Stories of Dark Seduction. (p. 194)
Hamilton, Laurie, illus. see Hillert, Margaret.
Hamilton, Leslie. Story of Peter Little Bear: A Lamprey River Adventure. (p. 1659)
Hamilton, Libby. Fairy Tale Handbook. Tomic, Tomislav, illus. (p. 564)
—Ultimate Pirate Handbook. Leyssenne, Mathieu & Kraft, Jason, illus. (p. 1809)
Hamilton, Libby, ed. see Stoddard, Rosie & Marshall, Phillip.
Hamilton, Lily & Myers, Barbara. Lily & Nana. Sellaro, Brendan, illus. (p. 1017)
—Lily Goes to School. Sellaro, Brendan, illus. (p. 1018)
Hamilton, Linda. Big-Hearted Monkey & the Crocodile. (p. 181)
—Meet the Meerkats. (p. 1123)
—Smile & Say Cheetah! Brown, Kevin, illus. (p. 1594)
—Wise Old Turtle. (p. 1940)
Hamilton, Lynn. Bird. (p. 190)
—Caring for Your Bird. (p. 269)
—Caring for Your Ferret. (p. 269)
—Caring for Your Fish. (p. 269)
—Caring for Your Turtle. (p. 269)
—Ferret. (p. 582)
—Fish. (p. 598)
—Labor Day. (p. 969)
—Memorial Day. (p. 1125)
—Presidents' Day. (p. 1397)
—Turtle: My Pet. (p. 1798)
—Turtle. (p. 1798)
Hamilton, Lynn A. Caring for Your Bird. Marshall, Diana & Nault, Jennifer, eds. (p. 269)
—Caring for Your Fish. Kissock, Heather & Marshall, Diana, eds. (p. 269)
—Caring for Your Turtle. (p. 269)
Hamilton, Lynn & Gillespie, Katie. Ferret. (p. 582)
—Turtle. (p. 1798)
Hamilton, Martha, jt. auth. see Weiss, Mitch.
Hamilton, Martha & Weise, Mutch. Scared Witless: Thirteen Eerie Tales to Tell. Pope, Kevin, illus. (p. 1519)
Hamilton, Martha & Weiss, Mitch. Ghost Catcher: A Bengali Folktale. Balouch, Kristen, illus. (p. 670)
—Hidden Feast: A Folktale from the American South. Tate, Don, illus. (p. 775)
—How & Why Stories: World Tales Kids Can Read & Tell. Lyon, Carol, illus. (p. 804)
—How Fox Became Red. O'Malley, Kathy, illus. (p. 809)
—Noodlehead Stories: World Tales Kids Can Read & Tell. Elsammak, Ariane, illus. (p. 1264)
—Priceless Gifts: A Tale from Italy. Kanzler, John, illus. (p. 1398)
—Stolen Smell. Wrenn, Tom, illus. (p. 1652)
—Tale of Two Frogs. Wrenn, Tom, illus. (p. 1700)
—Through the Grapevine: World Tales Kids Can Read & Tell. Lyon, Carol, illus. (p. 1745)
—Two Fables of Aesop. MacDonald, Bruce, illus. (p. 1803)
—Well of Truth: A Folktale from Egypt. Wrenn, Tom, illus. (p. 1874)
—Why Animals Never Got Fire: A Story of the Couer d'Alene Indians. MacDonald, Bruce, illus. (p. 1922)
—Why Koala Has a Stumpy Tail. Wrenn, Tom, illus. (p. 1925)
Hamilton, Martha & Weiss, Mitch, retold by. Forty Fun Fables: Tales That Trick, Tickle & Teach. (p. 623)
Hamilton, Martha, et al. Noodlehead Stories: World Tales Kids Can Read & Tell. (p. 1264)
Hamilton, Mary. Sensory Training Simplified: A Guide to Despook Your Horse. (p. 1551)
Hamilton, Matthew. Bobby's Dove. Sosebee, Cheryl, illus. (p. 206)
Hamilton, Meredith. They're Poets & They Know It! A Collection of 30 Timeless Poems. (p. 1732)
Hamilton, Meredith, illus. see Driscoll, Michael.
Hamilton, Meredith, jt. auth. see Alexander, Heather.
Hamilton, Michael, illus. see Hamilton, Fran Santoro.
Hamilton, Mimi. Kevin & Tak. (p. 949)
Hamilton, Neil A. 1970s. (p. 2002)
Hamilton, Pamela, illus. see Gaydos, Nora.
Hamilton, Pamela Greenhalgh. Snow Day. (p. 1598)
Hamilton, Pat. Peaches the Private Eye Poodle: The Missing Muffin Caper. (p. 1332)

H

Hamilton, Patricia Birdsong. Why do you Walk Funny? (p. 1924)
Hamilton, Patricia Birdsong & Scripts Publishing Staff. What's Up: William Explains Ataxia to His New Friends. (p. 1900)
Hamilton, Patricia D. Peaches the Private Eye Poodle: Finding Dipsey Doodle. (p. 1332)
—Peaches the Private Eye Poodle: Finding Foster a Home. (p. 1332)
—Peaches the Private Eye Poodle: Where Is Loosey Goosey? (p. 1332)
Hamilton, Penny, ed. see Mathias, Adeline.
Hamilton, Peter, ed. Max Weber (p. 1111)
Hamilton, Phelesha. Promised King: There Is a King in You. (p. 1411)
Hamilton, Phyllis McAllister, jt. auth. see Burke, Arlene Avery.
Hamilton, Prissy. Rainbow Within: An Introduction to the Emotional Energies for Children. Hamilton, Prissy, ed. (p. 1436)
Hamilton, Robert. Encyclopedia of Amazing Places: Discover Famous Wonders of the World. (p. 524)
Hamilton, Robert M. Amazing Hummingbird. (p. 54)
—Dimes! (p. 440)
—Dolares - Dollar Bills. (p. 463)
—Dollar Bills! (p. 463)
—Going Places: On a Boat. (p. 693)
—In a Car. (p. 862)
—Mia's Five Senses. (p. 1134)
—On a Bike. (p. 1288)
—On a Bus. (p. 1288)
—On a Plane. (p. 1288)
—On a Train. (p. 1288)
—Ticks. (p. 1747)
Hamilton, Ruth. Billy London's Girls. (p. 187)
—Nest of Sorrows. (p. 1242)
Hamilton, S. J. Cat's Eye View. (p. 281)
Hamilton, S. L. America's Cup. (p. 64)
—Ants. (p. 90)
—Astronaut Firsts. (p. 109)
—Barracuda. (p. 140)
—Base Jumping. (p. 140)
—Bears. (p. 151)
—Beasts. (p. 152)
—Beetles. (p. 158)
—Big Cats. (p. 180)
—Big Game Fishing. (p. 181)
—Biking. (p. 186)
—Bugs. (p. 237)
—Catfish. (p. 280)
—Cats. (p. 280)
—Dogs. (p. 462)
—Earthquakes. (p. 497)
—Eels. (p. 505)
—Exploration. (p. 550)
—Flies. (p. 604)
—Floods. (p. 605)
—Fly Fishing. (p. 609)
—Freshwater Fishing. (p. 637)
—Ghosts. (p. 672)
—Hurricanes. (p. 830)
—Ice Fishing. (p. 850)
—Iditarod. (p. 852)
—Indianapolis 500. (p. 871)
—Kentucky Derby. (p. 949)
—Lizards. (p. 1042)
—Mantis. (p. 1088)
—Marlin. (p. 1096)
—Mummies. (p. 1190)
—Piranha. (p. 1362)
—Reno Air Races. (p. 1460)
—Reptiles. (p. 1461)
—Roaches. (p. 1476)
—Robots & Rovers. (p. 1481)
—Rodeo. (p. 1484)
—Saltwater Fishing. (p. 1506)
—Sharks. (p. 1562)
—Sky Watch. (p. 1587)
—Snakes. (p. 1596)
—Solar System. (p. 1607)
—Spearfishing. (p. 1623)
—Spiders. (p. 1626)
—Stars. (p. 1643)
—Sturgeon. (p. 1670)
—Surfing. (p. 1685)
—Tornadoes. (p. 1770)
—Tour de France. (p. 1773)
—Volcanoes. (p. 1849)
—Werewolves. (p. 1875)
—White Water. (p. 1913)
—Wolves. (p. 1944)
—Xtreme Fishing. (p. 1967)
—Xtreme Insects. (p. 1967)
—Xtreme Monsters (p. 1967)
—Xtreme Predators (p. 1967)
—Xtreme Space (p. 1967)
—Xtreme Sports (p. 1967)
—Zombies. (p. 1988)
Hamilton, Sable. Free Spirit. (p. 634)
—Star Is Born. (p. 1640)
—Stardust Stables. (p. 1642)
—Wildfire. (p. 1931)
Hamilton, Sam. Discovering Mission San Buenaventura. (p. 449)
—Discovering Mission San Diego de Alcalá. (p. 449)
Hamilton, Seymour. Laughing Princess. (p. 980)
Hamilton, Sharon. Shine On. (p. 1566)
Hamilton, Sue. Air & Sea Mysteries. (p. 31)
—Ambushed by a Cougar. (p. 57)
—Attacked by a Crocodile. (p. 114)
—Bartholomew Roberts. (p. 140)
—Bermuda Triangle. (p. 167)
—Bitten by a Rattlesnake. (p. 194)
—Close Encounters of the Wild Kind (p. 333)
—Creatures of the Abyss. (p. 380)
—Eaten by a Shark. (p. 501)
—Ghosts & Goblins. (p. 672)
—Jack Kirby. (p. 903)
—Joe Simon. (p. 920)
—Joe Sinnott. (p. 920)
—John Buscema. (p. 921)
—John Romita, Sr. (p. 922)
—Lost Cities. (p. 1055)
—Mauled by a Bear. (p. 1110)
—Monsters. (p. 1168)
—Monsters of Mystery. (p. 1169)
—Swarmed by Bees. (p. 1689)
—Unsolved Mysteries (p. 1822)
Hamilton, Sue L. Ballroom. (p. 135)
—Blackbeard. (p. 197)
—Captain Kidd. (p. 264)
—Country & Western. (p. 372)
—Crime Scene Investigation (p. 382)
—DNA Analysis: Forensic Fluids & Follicles. (p. 456)
—Fingerprint Analysis: Hints from Prints. (p. 589)
—Forensic Artist: Solving the Case with a Face. (p. 617)
—Forensic Ballistics: Styles of Projectiles. (p. 617)
—Forensic Entomology: Bugs & Bodies. (p. 617)
—Henry Morgan. (p. 768)
—Hip-Hop. (p. 780)
—Incredible Hulk. (p. 869)
—Latin. (p. 979)
—Masters of Horror. (p. 1103)
—Nature on the Rampage. (p. 1236)
—Pirates! (p. 1363)
—Rock. (p. 1481)
—Stan Lee. (p. 1639)
—Swing. (p. 1691)
—Xtreme Dance (p. 1967)
—Zombies. (p. 1988)
Hamilton, Susan & Peters, Laura. Best Garden Plants for Tennessee. (p. 169)
Hamilton, Tim. Big Fib. Hamilton, Tim, illus. (p. 181)
—But! Hamilton, Tim, illus. (p. 246)
—Is That a Cat? (p. 890)
Hamilton, Tisha. Animals of Asia: Set Of 6. (p. 83)
—Animals of Asia: Text Pairs. (p. 83)
—Mickey Mouse Clubhouse. Disney Storybook Artists Staff, illus. (p. 1136)
—Piratas del Caribe. el viaje al fin del Mundo: Pirates of the Caribbean: at the World's End. (p. 1362)
Hamilton, Tisha, jt. auth. see Reader's Digest Editors.
Hamilton, Tisha, adapted by. Barbie Fairytopia: A Junior Novelization. (p. 138)
Hamilton, Toby G. Busta Rhymes. (p. 245)
—Dmx. (p. 456)
—Fat Joe. (p. 577)
—Ice Cube. (p. 850)
Hamilton, Trenton. History of Western Dance. (p. 785)
Hamilton, Virginia. House of Dies Drear. (p. 803)
—M. C. Higgins, the Great (p. 1067)
—M. C. Higgins, the Great. (p. 1067)
—People Could Fly: The Picture Book. (p. 1339)
—People Could Fly: The Picture Book. Dillon, Leo & Dillon, Diane, illus. (p. 1339)
—People Could Fly: American Black Folktales. Dillon, Leo & Dillon, Diane, illus. (p. 1339)
—Planet of Junior Brown. (p. 1367)
—Primos. (p. 1401)
—Zeely. (p. 1985)
—Zeely. Shimin, Symeon, illus. (p. 1985)
Hamilton, Virginia, et al. Plain City. (p. 1366)
Hamilton Waxman, Laura & Waxman, Laura. Fabulous Fashion Inventions. (p. 560)
Hamilton, Wendy. Feeding Tree. (p. 580)
Hamilton, Williams. Sly the Fly Goes on an Adventure. (p. 1591)
Hamilton Wright Mabie. Heroes Every Child Should Know. (p. 772)
Hamilton-Emery, Chris. 101 Ways to Make Poems Sell: The Salt Guide to Getting & Staying Published. (p. 2000)
Hamilton-Fairley, Fiona. Little Cooks: 30 Delicious Recipes to Make & Enjoy. (p. 1026)
Hamilton-Sturdy, K. Tree of Dreams. (p. 1783)
Hamilton-Wilkes, Viola, jt. auth. see Wilkes, Donald.
Hamlett, Martha. Bats in the Air, Bats in My Hair. (p. 145)
Hamley, Dennis. Badger's Fate. (p. 132)
—Beautiful Games. Fenoughty, Charles, illus. (p. 153)
—Divided Loyalties. (p. 454)
—Ghosts Who Waited. (p. 673)
—Haunted United. Fenoughty, Charles, illus. (p. 754)
—Hawk's Vision. (p. 755)
—Oxford Anthology of Mystery Stories. (p. 1315)
—Pageants of Despair. (p. 1318)
—Very Far from Here. (p. 1838)
—Without Warning: Ellen's Story, 1914-1918. (p. 1942)
—Yule Logs. (p. 1983)
Hamley, Harold, ed. How to Write & Sell. (p. 823)
Hamlin, Janet, illus. see Allman, Barbara.
Hamlin, Janet, illus. see Humphrey, Mary.
Hamlin, Janet, illus. see Stewart, Melissa.
Hamlin, John. Tales of an Old Lumber Camp: A Story of Early Days in A Great Industry. Bernard, C. E. B., illus. (p. 1702)
Hamlin, Robyn Maria. Polly Dactyl's Magic Castle Missions. (p. 1381)
Hamlin, Willie. Great First where it All Began. (p. 716)
Hamlisch, Marvin. Marvin Makes Music. Madsen, Jim, illus. (p. 1099)
Hamlyn. Princess Cupcakes (p. 1403)
Hamlyn, Jean. Clumsy Daisy: Meet Clumsy Daisy & her Family. (p. 336)
—Clumsy Daisy Goes on Holiday: Book 3. (p. 336)
—Clumsy Daisy Goes to School. (p. 336)
Hamm, Barbara R. Media Center Discovery: 180 Ready-to-Use Activities for Language Arts, Grades 5-8. (p. 1118)
Hamm, Diane Johnston. Rock-a-Bye Farm. Natchev, Alexi, illus. (p. 1481)
Hamm, Lisa. Buddy the Duck. (p. 235)
Hamm, Mia. Winners Never Quit! Thompson, Carol, illus. (p. 1937)
Hammack, Debi, illus. see Olson, Kevin Noel.
Hammack, Sandra, illus. see Zemanick, Patty.
Hammack, Sayamwong E., jt. auth. see Toufexis, Donna.
Hammah, Aisha. Image Game. Stubblefield, Linda, ed. (p. 860)
Hammah, Aisha, illus. see Green, Judith.
Hammari, Kimiko. Teeny Tiny Talks IV: My Eternal Family. Miller, Rebecca, illus. (p. 1715)
Hamme, Jean Van, see Rosinski & Van Hamme, Jean.
Hamme, Jean Van, see Van Hamme, Jean.
Hamme, Van. Thorgal Vol. 14: Giants. Rosinski, illus. (p. 1740)
Hammel, Bob, jt. auth. see Knight, Bob.
Hammelef, Danielle S. Awesome Special Effects. (p. 121)
—Building a Car (p. 238)
—Building an Airplane (p. 238)
—Case of the Ad That Subtracts & Other True Math Mysteries for You to Solve (p. 273)
—Explosive Scenes: Fireballs, Furious Storms, & More Live Special Effects. (p. 554)
—Eye-Popping CGI: Computer-Generated Special Effects. (p. 558)
—Fun with Fives. (p. 648)
—Mind-Blowing Makeup in Special Effects. (p. 1145)
—Mystery of the Missing Cookies. (p. 1225)
—Numbers Big & Small. (p. 1272)
—Shopping with the Nicholas Family. (p. 1569)
—That Figures! A Crash Course in Math (p. 1726)
—This Book Beats the Odds: A Collection of Amazing & Startling Odds (p. 1735)
Hammelef, Danielle S. & Omoth, Tyler. See How It's Made (p. 1546)
Hammelef, Danielle S., et al. Seriously True Mysteries. (p. 1552)
—Super Trivia Collection. (p. 1682)
Hammer. Willy's Wild Weekend: Friday. (p. 1934)
Hammer, Cully, et al. Shellshocked. Martin, Cynthia, illus. (p. 1565)
Hammer, David, jt. auth. see Levin, Daniel T.
Hammer, Larry. Eagles of Lincoln. Nutt, Don, illus. (p. 492)
Hammer, Max. Superstars of the Atlanta Braves. (p. 1684)
—Superstars of the Boston Red Sox. (p. 1684)
—Superstars of the Chicago Cubs. (p. 1684)
—Superstars of the Los Angeles Dodgers. (p. 1684)
—Superstars of the Miami Heat. (p. 1684)
—Superstars of the Oklahoma City Thunder. (p. 1684)
Hammer, Maxwell. Boston Red Sox: World Series Champions. (p. 215)
—LeBron James: NBA MVP & Champion. (p. 987)
—Oklahoma City Thunder. (p. 1283)
—Peyton Manning: NFL MVP & Champion. (p. 1349)
—Sidney Crosby: NHL MVP & Champion. (p. 1573)
Hammer, Randy, jt. auth. see Blokland, Suzanne.
Hammer, Rusty, compiled by. Guide to Inner Tubing. (p. 730)
Hammer, Sheila. Chorkie: A Cross Between a Chihuahua & a Yorkshire Terrier (p. 310)
—Tyrannosaurus Rex: Mighty Meat-Eater Dove, Jason, illus. (p. 1805)
Hammerquist, Theresa, illus. see Davidson, Jean.
Hammersley, Karen, illus. see Wellings, Chris R.
Hammerslough, J. Fandex Family Guide: Dinosaurs. (p. 570)
Hammerslough, Jane. Dinosaurs. (p. 443)
—Everything You Need to Know about Teen Motherhood. (p. 546)
—Langur Monkey's Day. Buelt, Laura, tr. (p. 975)
—Langur Monkey's Day. Buelt, Laura, illus. (p. 975)
Hammerslough, Jane & Smithsonian Institution Staff. Langur Monkey's Day. Buelt, Laura, illus. (p. 975)
Hammerslough, Nancy. Almost Lost, Nearly Found: A Novel of Sisters & Secrets. (p. 48)
Hammersmith, Craig. Life in the Pond (p. 1011)
—Water Cycle (p. 1862)
Hammersmith, Craig, et al. Habitats Around the World. (p. 735)
Hammerstein, Oscar, II, jt. auth. see Rodgers, Richard.
Hammerstrom, Kent, illus. see Neimark, Susie.
Hammett, Dashiell. Maltese Falcon (p. 1084)
Hammill, Elizabeth, ed. Over the Hills & Far Away: A Treasury of Nursery Rhymes. (p. 1314)
Hammill, Faye, et al, eds. Encyclopedia of British Women's Writing, 1900-1950. (p. 525)
Hammill, Matt. Sir Reginald's Logbook. Hammill, Matt, illus. (p. 1580)
Hammill, Matt, illus. see Hyde, Natalie.
Hammock, Lee & Jacobson, Justin. Dawning Star: Operation Quick Launch. Moretti, Danilo, illus. (p. 412)
Hammock, Mary B. Msn Cpnp. Princess Reagan & the Paci Fairy. (p. 1405)
Hammock, Sarah Owens. You Can't Get into More Trouble Than Gator Pervis!! Cocciolone, Kathy Roberts, illus. (p. 1974)
Hammon, Darrel L. Christmas Beneath the Lake: From the Adventures of Bob the Bullfrog. (p. 312)
Hammon, Inc. Staff, ed. Historical Atlas of the World. (p. 783)
Hammond, Andrew. Blood Eagle Tortures. (p. 200)
—Gallows Curse. (p. 653)
—Guardians' Reckoning. (p. 728)
—Mask of Death. (p. 1102)
—Traitor's Revenge. (p. 1777)
Hammond, Andy, illus. see Blane, Francisco.
Hammond, Andy, illus. see Hurwitz, Johanna.
Hammond, Andy, illus. see Owen, Anna.
Hammond, Andy, illus. see Peet, Mal.
Hammond, Ashlie. Captain Dan Takes a Day Off. Ault, Dane, illus. (p. 264)
Hammond, Barbara. Duffy Chronicles. (p. 489)
Hammond, Brean & Regan, Shaun. Making the Novel: Fiction & Society in Britain, 1660-1789. (p. 1082)
Hammond, Brean S. Pope Amongst the Satirists. (p. 1384)
Hammond, Charmaine. Toby, the Pet Therapy Dog, & His Hospital Friends. Prevac, Rose Anne, illus. (p. 1760)
—Toby, the Pet Therapy Dog, Says Be a Buddy, Not a Bully. (p. 1760)
—Toby, the Pet Therapy Dog, Says Be a Buddy Not a Bully. Prevec, Rose Anne, illus. (p. 1760)
Hammond Editors, ed. Trains. (p. 1777)
Hammond, Edward. Jesus the Way: The Child's Guide to Heav. (p. 916)
Hammond, Elaine Breault. Sky Pony (p. 1587)
Hammond, Gaye, illus. see Smedley, Gord.
Hammond, Gaye, illus. see Wolczuk, Alice.
Hammond Inc, ed. World Almanac Notebk Atlas 2010. (p. 1953)
Hammond Inc Staff, ed. Scholastic New Headline World Atlas. (p. 1522)
Hammond, James F. Ski Challenge. (p. 1584)
Hammond, Jo. Home Before Dark (p. 792)
Hammond, John. Benedictine Legacy of Peace: The Life of Abbot Leo A. Rudloff. (p. 164)
Hammond, John & Hutchison, Gary. Bewildering Bond: A Novel for Teenagers. (p. 173)
Hammond, John, as told by. Lucky in Life. (p. 1062)
Hammond, Julie, illus. see Jones, Lori M.
Hammond, Julie, illus. see Kelso, Mary Jean.
Hammond, Julie, illus. see McDine, Donna M.
Hammond, Julie, jt. auth. see Kelso, Mary Jean.
Hammond, Marc & Gully, Mario. Reality Bites. (p. 1449)
Hammond, Meredith. World According to Tiffany: The Airplane Trip. (p. 1953)
Hammond, Michelle McKinney. How to Make Love Work. (p. 820)
Hammond, Nancy Robinson, illus. see Mara, Sarah Robinson.
Hammond, Paula. Atlas of Endangered Animals: Wildlife under Threat Around the World. (p. 112)
—Atlas of the World's Most Dangerous Animals: Mapping Nature's Born Killers. (p. 113)
—Atlas of the World's Strangest Animals. (p. 113)
—Italy & Switzerland. (p. 895)
Hammond, Rebecca. Winds Cove. (p. 1936)
Hammond, Richard & Dorling Kindersley Publishing Staff. Car Science. (p. 265)
Hammond, Roger. Pelican Files: The Case of the Missing Fish! (p. 1335)
Hammond, Roger, photos by see Cussen, Sarah R.
Hammond, Roger, photos by see Cussen, Sarah.
Hammond, Ron J. Dig: Journey of a Lost Tribe. (p. 438)
Hammond, Sandra. Day with Duke. (p. 415)
Hammond, Susan. Susan Hammond's Classical Kids: A New Music-Based Curriculum: Grades K-8. (p. 1688)
Hammond, Tasha. Boogey Monster. (p. 210)
Hammond, Ted, illus. see Amstel, Marsha.
Hammond, Ted, illus. see Brennan, Patricia & Demuth, Patricia Brennan.
Hammond, Ted, illus. see Brill, Marlene Targ.
Hammond, Ted, illus. see Buckley, James, Jr.
Hammond, Ted, illus. see Burgan, Michael.
Hammond, Ted, illus. see Demuth, Patricia Brennan.
Hammond, Ted, illus. see Figley, Marthy Rhodes & Figley, Marty Rhodes.
Hammond, Ted, illus. see Figley, Marty Rhodes.
Hammond, Ted, illus. see Herman, Gail & Harrison, Nancy.
Hammond, Ted, illus. see Holub, Joan.
Hammond, Ted, illus. see Littlefield, Holly.
Hammond, Ted, illus. see Patrick, Jean L. S.
Hammond, Ted, illus. see Pollack, Pamela D. & Belviso, Meg.
Hammond, Ted, illus. see Ransom, Candice.
Hammond, Ted, illus. see Stine, Megan.
Hammond, Tim & Dorling Kindersley Publishing Staff. Sports. (p. 1632)
Hammond, Veronica. Wash Those Hands. (p. 1859)
Hammond World Atlas Corporation Staff. American History Through Maps. (p. 61)
—Asia. (p. 106)
—Children's World Atlas. (p. 304)
—Christmas. (p. 312)
—Explorer Atlas. (p. 551)
—Presidents: An Illustrated History of America's Leaders. (p. 1397)
—World Almanac Notebook Atlas 2008. (p. 1953)
Hammond World Atlas Corporation Staff, creator. Discovering Maps: A Children's World Atlas. (p. 449)
—Student World Atlas. (p. 1669)
—Student's Notebook Atlas. (p. 1669)
Hammond World Atlas Corporation Staff, ed. Globes in a Box. (p. 685)
—Planet Earth: Our Planet as You've Never Seen It Before. (p. 1367)
—World. (p. 1953)
—World Almanac Notebk Atlas 2009. (p. 1953)
—World Passport: Atlas & Travelmate. (p. 1958)
Hammonds, Claudia Muttart. Dreaming in Color. (p. 484)
Hammonds, Heather. Modellieren MIT Knete. (p. 1158)
Hammonds, Theresa D. God's Invisible Fruit of Love. (p. 691)
Hammonds-Smith, Maxine, jt. auth. see Stephens, Karen.
Hammons, Barbara, illus. see McAtee, Rick.
Hammons, Mark, illus. see Hartman, Colleen Kelley.
Hammontree, Marie. Walt Disney. Irvin, Frank, illus. (p. 1855)
Hammserstein. In My Own Little Corner. (p. 864)
Hamod, Rania. I Am Good. (p. 833)
—I Am Lovable. (p. 833)
Hamon, Susan E. Engineering. (p. 529)
Hamper, Robbie. Crested Gecko in Captivity. (p. 381)
—Leopard Gecko in Captivity. Gurley, Russ, ed. (p. 992)
Hampl, Dori. Talara-Ninja Hy & Her Band of Feathered Samurai. (p. 1699)
Hample, Stoo, jt. auth. see Hample, Stuart E.
Hample, Stuart E. & Hample, Stoo. Silly Book. Hample, Stoo, illus. (p. 1575)
—Silly Book. Hample, Stuart E. & Hample, Stoo, illus. (p. 1575)
Hampshire, Anthony. Fast Track (p. 576)
—Fast Track. (p. 576)
—Full Throttle (p. 646)
—Full Throttle. (p. 646)
—G-Force (p. 651)
—On the Limit (p. 1290)
—On the Limit. (p. 1290)

—Title Run (p. 1758)
—Title Run. (p. 1758)
Hampstead, Tom. Kingdom of the Two Great Houses. (p. 960)
Hampton, Brooke. Enchanted Cedar: The Journey Home. (p. 523)
Hampton, David. Living in Australia. Hampton, David, photos by. (p. 1041)
Hampton, David, illus. see Thomson, Ruth.
Hampton, David, photos by see Kent, Su.
Hampton, David, photos by see Thomson, Ruth.
Hampton, DeAnne. My Look-Like-Me Mommy. (p. 1213)
Hampton, Francesca. Children's Voyage the Long Journey Home. (p. 304)
Hampton, Jeff. Snowman Uprising on Hickory Lane. (p. 1601)
Hampton, John, illus. see Fannin, Cole.
Hampton, John W., illus. see Patten, Lewis B.
Hampton, Julian Vaughan. Limbus (p. 1018)
Hampton, Lin, illus. see Simmons, Lynn Sheffield.
Hampton, Patrick. Down by the Mulberry Tree (p. 474)
Hampton, Randall. Christmas Kiss. (p. 314)
Hampton, Scott, illus. see Brin, David.
Hampton, Scott, illus. see Carey, Mike.
Hampton, Scott, illus. see Grayson, Devin, et al.
Hampton, Sue. Aliens & Angels: Three Stories for Christmas. (p. 41)
—Gorilla Dreams. (p. 703)
—Pomp & Circumstances. (p. 1382)
Hampton, Wilborn. Elvis Presley: A Twentieth Century Life. (p. 517)
—September 11, 2001: Attack on New York City. (p. 1551)
—War in the Middle East: A Reporter's Story: Black September & the Yom Kippur War. (p. 1857)
Hampton-Johnson, Rasheeda. Mommy Where Is Daddy? (p. 1162)
Hamrick, Frank, et al. Clay to Conquest: The Faith of Eight. Wright, Ben, ed. (p. 330)
—Clay to Conquest. Wright, Benjamin, ed. (p. 330)
Hamrick, Karla. From Captive to Captain. (p. 642)
Hamsa, Bobbie. Animal Babies. Dunnington, Tom, illus. (p. 76)
—Dirty Larry. Catanese, Donna, illus. (p. 446)
Han, Carolyn. Koa's Seed. Peterson, Kathleen, illus. (p. 966)
Han, Heung-gi, illus. see Han, Suzanne C.
Han, Hyun-dong, jt. auth. see Gomdori Co. Staff.
Han, Jenny. Clara Lee & the Apple Pie Dream. (p. 326)
—Complete Summer I Turned Pretty Trilogy: The Summer I Turned Pretty; It's Not Summer Without You; We'll Always Have Summer. (p. 353)
—It's Not Summer Without You (p. 898)
—It's Not Summer Without You. (p. 898)
—P. S. I Still Love You. (p. 1316)
—Shug. (p. 1571)
—Summer I Turned Pretty. (p. 1674)
—To All the Boys I've Loved Before. (p. 1758)
—We'll Always Have Summer. (p. 1874)
Han, Jenny & Vivian, Siobhan. Burn for Burn. (p. 243)
—Fire with Fire. (p. 591)
Han, John J. Little Guy Haiku: Life with Bailey, a Maltese. Han, Joy, illus. (p. 1028)
Han, Joon-ho, illus. see Collodi, Carlo.
Han, Joy, illus. see Han, John J.
Han, Kakao. Journey into the Human Body Yoon, Seok, illus. (p. 928)
Han, Lori Cox, jt. auth. see Genovese, Michael A.
Han, Lori Cox, jt. auth. see Han, Tomislav.
Han, Mylene, illus. see Settel, Jim.
Han, Oki, illus. see Myers, Tim J.
Han, Oki S., illus. see Myers, Tim.
Han, Oki S., illus. see Whelan, Gloria & Nolan, Jenny.
Han, Seung Won. Princess 3 (p. 1402)
Han, Soma, illus. see Stickler, John.
Han, Soma, jt. auth. see Stickler, John C.
Han, SooJin, illus. see Kim, Cecil.
Han, Suzanne C. Let's Color Korea-Traditional Lifestyles. (p. 995)
—Let's Visit Korea. Han, Heung-gi, illus. (p. 1001)
Han, Than T., illus. see Hendtlass, Jane & Nichols, Alan.
Han, Tomislav & Han, Lori Cox. Handbook to American Democracy (p. 740)
Han, Xuemei. Brave Little Mongolian Sisters. Han, Xuemei, illus. (p. 223)
—Radish & the Girl with Long Hair. Han, Xuemei, illus. (p. 1433)
Han, Yu-Mei. Brave Servant: A Tale from China. (p. 223)
—Glitter Halloween Stickers. (p. 684)
—Glitter Santas Stickers. (p. 684)
Han, Yu-Mei, illus. see Pelleschi, Andrea.
HaNa, Lee & Park, KangHo. Heavenly Executioner Chiwoo (p. 761)
Hanak, Elizabeth. Princess of Cliffwood. (p. 1404)
Hanamaki, Anna. Nephilim (p. 1241)
Hanasaki, Akira, illus. see Kariya, Tetsu.
Hanauer, Jodi. Child of the 80's Looks Back. (p. 301)
Hanawalt, Barbara. European World, 400-1450. (p. 540)
Hanawalt, Barbara A. European World, 400-1450. (p. 540)
Hanawalt, Josh, illus. see Dierenfeldt, Jane.
Hanawalt, Lisa, illus. see Bradford, Arthur.
Hanbidge, Patricia, jt. auth. see Peters, Laura.
Hanbidge, Patricia & Peters, Laura. Annuals for Saskatchewan & Manitoba (p. 87)
Hanbury-Murphy, Trudy. Solving the Mysteries of Ancient Rome. (p. 1608)
Hanby, Benjamin Russell. Up on the Housetop. Snyder, Robert, illus. (p. 1824)
Hancock, Anna, illus. see Dale, Jay.
Hancock, Anna, illus. see Giulieri, Anne.
Hancock, Chris. Starting Playschool- Mini-Pals Go, Too. (p. 1644)
Hancock, Claire & Hanrahan, Gareth. Titanic Notebook: The Story of the World's Most Famous Ship. (p. 1758)
Hancock, David, illus. see Chandler, Fiona, et al.
Hancock, David, illus. see Chandler, Fiona.
Hancock, David, illus. see Daynes, Katie.
Hancock, David, illus. see Dowswell, Paul.
Hancock, David, illus. see Firth, Rachel.
Hancock, David, illus. see Khanduri, Kamini.
Hancock, David, illus. see Lloyd Jones, Rob.
Hancock, David, illus. see Taplin, Sam.
Hancock, Dennis. Goodnight on the Farm. Hancock, Uyen, illus. (p. 701)
Hancock, Dennis & Hancock, Shawn. What If There Are No Colors. Hancock, Uyen, illus. (p. 1887)
Hancock, Dennis & Uyen. Tree House on the Bluff. Hancock, Uyen, illus. (p. 1783)
Hancock, H. Irving. Dave Darrin at Vera Cruz. (p. 410)
—Dave Darrin's First Year at Annapolis. (p. 410)
—Dave Darrin's Fourth Year at Annapolis. (p. 410)
—Dave Darrin's Second Year at Annapolis. (p. 410)
—Dave Darrin's Second Year at Annapolis, or Two Midshipmen As Naval Academy Youngsters. (p. 410)
—Dave Darrin's Third Year at Annapolis. (p. 410)
—Dick Prescott's First Year at West Point. (p. 436)
—Dick Prescott's Fourth Year at West Point. (p. 436)
—Dick Prescott's Second Year at West Point. (p. 436)
—Dick Prescott's Third Year at West Point. (p. 436)
—Grammar School Boys in Summer Athletics. (p. 706)
—High School Boys' Canoe Club. (p. 778)
—High School Boys' Fishing Trip. (p. 778)
—High School Boys in Summer Camp. (p. 778)
—High School Boys' Training Hike. (p. 778)
—High School Captain of the Team. (p. 778)
—High School Freshmen. (p. 778)
—High School Left End. (p. 778)
—High School Left End, or Dick & Co. Grilling on the Football Gridiron. (p. 778)
—High School Pitcher. (p. 778)
—Uncle Sam's Boys with Pershing's Troops. (p. 1812)
—Uncle Sam's Boys with Pershing's Troops, or Dick Prescott at Grips with the Boche. (p. 1812)
—Young Engineers in Arizona. (p. 1978)
—Young Engineers in Arizona, or Laying Tracks on the Man-Killer Quicksand. (p. 1978)
—Young Engineers in Colorado. (p. 1978)
—Young Engineers in Mexico. (p. 1978)
—Young Engineers in Nevada. (p. 1978)
—Young Engineers on the Gulf. (p. 1978)
Hancock, James Gulliver, illus. see Price, Jane.
Hancock, Joey. Golden Retriever Christmas. (p. 695)
Hancock, Lee. Lorenzo de' Medici: Florence's Great Leader & Patron of the Arts. (p. 1053)
Hancock, Lyn. Tabasco the Saucy Raccoon Kemp, Loraine, illus. (p. 1694)
Hancock, Maryann & Hempstead, Anne. águila Calva. (p. 30)
—Bandera (p. 136)
—Casa Blanca (p. 273)
—Corte Suprema (p. 368)
—Estatua de la Libertad (p. 538)
Hancock Ms Lsc, Dionna. Where Did My Half-Brother Come From: Book 1 of the Half-Brother/Step-Brother Children's Series. (p. 1906)
Hancock, Nicky, jt. auth. see Sunderland, Margot.
Hancock, Nicky & Sunderland, Margot. Helping Children Who Are Anxious or Obsessional: A Guidebook. Nunes, Terezinha & Bryant, P., eds. (p. 766)
Hancock, Pat. Kids Book of Canadian Prime Ministers. Mantha, John, illus. (p. 952)
Hancock, R. C. Uncommon Blue. (p. 1812)
Hancock, Robert, tr. see Dixon, Tom, et al.
Hancock, Rusty. Dedicated Dads: Stepfathers of Famous People. Van Kampen, Megan, illus. (p. 422)
Hancock, Shawn, jt. auth. see Hancock, Dennis.
Hancock, Stefanie, illus. see Traylor, Waverley.
Hancock, Susan G. Wind & Little Cloud. Simmons, Robert, illus. (p. 1935)
Hancock, Uyen, illus. see Hancock, Dennis & Hancock, Shawn.
Hancock, Uyen, illus. see Hancock, Dennis & Uyen.
Hancock, Uyen, illus. see Hancock, Dennis.
Hancock, Vicki, jt. auth. see Tidwell, Mae B.
Hancock, W. Allan, illus. see Ruurs, Margriet.
Hancock, William. Bo Bunny. (p. 205)
Hancocks, Helen. Penguin in Peril. Hancocks, Helen, illus. (p. 1337)
Hancox, Lucy, jt. auth. see Renfrew, C. E.
Hand. Westlife. (p. 1876)
Hand, Carol. Abortion: Interpreting the Constitution. (p. 5)
—Amazing Feats of Environmental Engineering. (p. 54)
—Biomass Energy. (p. 189)
—Careers for Tech Girls in Technology. (p. 267)
—Climate Change: Our Warming Earth. (p. 332)
—Colombia. (p. 341)
—Community, Urban, & Home Gardens. (p. 350)
—Cool Careers Without College for People Who Love Animals. (p. 362)
—Creation of Glaciers. (p. 379)
—Dead Zones. (p. 417)
—Epidemiology: The Fight Against Ebola & Other Diseases. (p. 532)
—Existence of Sasquatch & Yeti. (p. 548)
—Experiments with Rocks & Minerals. (p. 549)
—Great Hope for an Energy Alternative: Laser-Powered Fusion Energy. (p. 716)
—Introduction to Genetics. (p. 882)
—Is There Life Out There? The Likelihood of Alien Life & What It Would Look Like. (p. 890)
—Jane Goodall. (p. 908)
—Living with Food Allergies. (p. 1042)
—Norway. (p. 1266)
—Science Lab: Weather Patterns. (p. 1526)
—Special Ops: Search & Rescue Operations (p. 1623)
—Vaccines. (p. 1830)
Hand, Cynthia. Boundless. (p. 216)
—Hallowed: An Unearthly Novel. (p. 737)
—Hallowed. (p. 737)
—Last Time We Say Goodbye. (p. 979)
—Unearthly. (p. 1817)
Hand, Elizabeth. Illyria. (p. 858)
—New Threat. (p. 1247)
Hand, Jason, illus. see RH Disney Staff & Hall, Klay.
Hand, Jenny. P.S. I Still Love You. (p. 1413)
Hand, Jimmie. Long Way Around. (p. 1047)
Hand, Jimmie, told to. Jimmy Spencer: Don't Ever Quit! (p. 918)
Hand, Lewis. Dwellers of the Dark. (p. 491)
Hand, Renne. What Would You Do If You Were Left at the Zoo? Mathieu, Middy, illus. (p. 1895)
Hand, Reuben. Jumping Jack: Drill Sergeant Bear Volume 1. (p. 934)
—Knee Bender: Drill Sergeant Bear Volume 3 Fiebiger, John, illus. (p. 964)
—Push Up: Drill Sergeant Bear Volume 2. Fiebiger, John, illus. (p. 1420)
—Turn & Bounce Fiebiger, John, illus. (p. 1797)
Hand, Reuben W. Thirst for Life (p. 1734)
Hand, Terry, illus. see McRae, J. R.
Hand, Terry, illus. see Poulter, J. R.
Handa, Nimret. Good Night Stories. (p. 700)
Handberg, Irene. Body & Senses PAK: Learning Center (p. 207)
Handelman, Dorothy, photos by see Eaton, Deborah.
Handelman, Dorothy, photos by see Leonard, Marcia.
Handelman, Dorothy, photos by see Simon, Charnan.
Handelman, Dorothy, photos by see Tidd, Louise Vitellaro.
Handelsman, Valerie. Birdies' Seaside Gym. Jasmin, Lynn, illus. (p. 191)
—Coral Reef Neighborhood. Handelsman, Valerie, illus. (p. 366)
—Sleepy Pelican Police. Miller, Erin L., illus. (p. 1590)
Handelsman, Valerie J. Lobster Monica: Dream, Dream, Dream - Monica Was Always Dreaming. Handelsman, Valerie J., illus. (p. 1044)
Handford, Martin. Donde Esta Wally? En Hollywood. (p. 466)
—Incredible Paper Chase. Handford, Martin, illus. (p. 869)
—Nuevo - ¿Donde Esta Wally Ahora? Sánchez Abulí, Enrique, tr. (p. 1270)
—Spectacular Poster Book. Handford, Martin, illus. (p. 1624)
—Where's Waldo? (p. 1911)
—Where's Waldo? Handford, Martin, illus. (p. 1911)
—Where's Waldo? in Hollywood. (p. 1911)
—Where's Waldo? in Hollywood. Handford, Martin, illus. (p. 1911)
—Where's Waldo Now? (p. 1911)
—Where's Waldo Now? Handford, Martin, illus. (p. 1911)
—Where's Waldo? Spaer Adventure: The Great Space Adventure. (p. 1911)
—Where's Waldo? The Fantastic Journey. Handford, Martin, illus. (p. 1911)
—Where's Waldo? the Fantastic Journey. Handford, Martin, illus. (p. 1911)
—Where's Waldo? the Great Picture Hunt. (p. 1911)
—Where's Waldo? the Great Picture Hunt. Handford, Martin, illus. (p. 1911)
—Where's Waldo? the Incredible Paper Chase. (p. 1911)
—Where's Waldo? the Magnificent Mini Boxed Set. Handford, Martin, illus. (p. 1911)
—Where's Waldo? the Search for the Lost Things. Handford, Martin, illus. (p. 1911)
—Where's Waldo? the Sticker Book! Handford, Martin, illus. (p. 1911)
—Where's Waldo? the Totally Essential Travel Collection. Handford, Martin, illus. (p. 1911)
—Where's Waldo? the Ultimate Travel Collection. Handford, Martin, illus. (p. 1911)
—Where's Waldo? the Wonder Book. Handford, Martin, illus. (p. 1911)
—Wow Collection: Six Amazing Books & a Puzzle. Handford, Martin, illus. (p. 1962)
Handford, Martin & Geddes, Anne. Diario del Bebe. Sánchez Abulí, Enrique, tr. (p. 434)
Handford, S. A. Aesop's Fables. Salter, Safaya, illus. (p. 25)
—Aesop's Fables. Winter, Nilo, illus. (p. 26)
Handford, S. A. & Lawrence, Jacob. Aesop's Fables. (p. 25)
Handford, Tom. Chinchillas (p. 307)
Handleman, Philip. Dream of Pilots Kodera, Craig, illus. (p. 483)
Handler, Daniel. Girls Standing on Lawns. Kalman, Maira, illus. (p. 681)
—Why We Broke Up. (p. 1926)
—Why We Broke Up. Kalman, Maira, illus. (p. 1926)
Handler, Daniel, see Snicket, Lemony, pseud.
Handley, Bill. Speed Math for Kids: The Fast, Fun Way to Do Basic Calculations. (p. 1624)
Handley, David, photos by see Hackett, Jane & Dorling Kindersley Publishing Staff.
Handley, Rod, et al. Team Studies on Character: Inspiration for Life & Sports. (p. 1710)
Handloser, Rick. Sneezy Neezy. Byous, Shawn, illus. (p. 1597)
Handprint Staff. Traffic Town. (p. 1776)
Handron, Kerry, jt. auth. see Sumners, Carolyn T.
Hands, Cynthia. In Flight! Disney Storybook Artists Staff, illus. (p. 863)
—Takeoff! Disney Storybook Artists Staff, illus. (p. 1697)
Hands, Cynthia, jt. auth. see Carbone, Courtney.
Hands, Cynthia, jt. auth. see RH Disney Staff.
Hands, Gill, jt. auth. see Equipo Staff.
Hands, Nikki. Lilly Bunny Goes to the Doctor. (p. 1017)
Handwerk, Marina. Hey Cool, I've Never Seen a Teacher with His Head Cut off Before! (p. 774)
Handy, Femida & Carpenter, Carole H. Sandy's Incredible Shrinking Footprint Steele-Card, Adrianna & Second Story Press Staff, illus. (p. 1511)
Handy, Libby & Newnham, Jack. Boss for a Week. (p. 215)
Handyside, Chris. History of Blues. (p. 783)
—History of Country. (p. 783)
—History of Folk. (p. 784)
—History of Jazz. (p. 784)
—History of Rock & Roll. (p. 784)
—History of Soul & R&B. (p. 784)
Haneberg, Janet. Alamander, the Orange Salamander. (p. 33)
—Eggie Rabbit. (p. 506)
—Mighty Mitt. (p. 1140)
Hanegar, Renee. Activités de Noël. Bauer, Larry, illus. (p. 10)
Hanel, Rachael. Ancient Rome: An Interactive History Adventure (p. 70)
—Can You Survive an Earthquake? An Interactive Survival Adventure (p. 259)
—Can You Survive Antarctica? An Interactive Survival Adventure (p. 259)
—Cheetahs. (p. 296)
—Climate Fever: Stopping Global Warming (p. 332)
—Identity Theft. (p. 852)
—Koalas. (p. 966)
—Life as a Knight: An Interactive History Adventure. (p. 1008)
—Lions. (p. 1021)
—Mexican Immigrants in America: An Interactive History Adventure. (p. 1131)
—Nebraska. (p. 1239)
—Nevada. (p. 1242)
—Parrots. (p. 1325)
—Penguins. (p. 1337)
—Polar Bears. (p. 1379)
—Smell. (p. 1593)
—Tigers. (p. 1749)
—West Virginia. (p. 1876)
—Wyoming. (p. 1966)
Hanel, Rachael, jt. auth. see Schaefer, Lola M.
Hanel, Rachael & Lassieur, Allison. You Choose: Survival. (p. 1975)
Hanel, Rachael, et al. You Choose: Survival. (p. 1975)
Hanel, Rachel. Gladiators. (p. 682)
—Israeli-Palestine Conflict. (p. 893)
—Knights. (p. 964)
—Pirates. (p. 1363)
—Samurai. (p. 1509)
Hanel, Wolfram. Merry Christmas, Mr. Snowman! Rossell, Judith, illus. (p. 1129)
Hänel, Wolfram, jt. auth. see Hanel, Wolfram.
Hanel, Wolfram & Hänel, Wolfram. Christmas for the Snowmen. Waas, Uli, illus. (p. 314)
Hanes, Don, illus. see Wilcox, Jean K. & Cameron, E. Jane.
Hanes, Marina C. Ling Ling: The Kitten Who Changed Her Ways. Bowman, Ethan T., illus. (p. 1019)
Hanes, Richard C., ed. see Thomson Gale Staff & Hermsen, Sarah.
Hanes, Richard C., ed. see Thomson Gale Staff.
Hanes, Richard Clay, jt. auth. see McNeill, Allison.
Hanes, Richard Clay, et al. American Home Front in World War II: Almanac. (p. 61)
—American Homefront in World War II: Biographies. (p. 61)
—Prejudice in the Modern World. (p. 1395)
—Shaping America Cumulative Index (p. 1561)
—Shaping of America, 1783-1815, Reference Library (p. 1561)
Hanes, Rosann. Diamond H Ranch: Told by: Val - Loyal Ranch Dog. (p. 434)
Hanes, Sharon M., ed. see Thomson Gale Staff.
Hanes, Sharon M. & McNeill, Allison. American Homefront in World War II: Primary Sources. (p. 61)
Hanes, Sharon M., et al. Cold War: Almanac (p. 339)
—Cold War: Biographies (p. 339)
—Cold War - Primary Sources. (p. 339)
—Cold War Reference Library: Includes Cumulative Index (p. 339)
Hanes, Tracey. Adventures of Kung Foo Poo. (p. 19)
Haney, Bob & Kanigher, Robert. Brave & the Bold Team-Up - Archives. (p. 223)
Haney, Bob & Sekowsky, Mike. Brave & the Bold Presents: Batman Team-Ups. (p. 223)
Haney, Donald W. My Name Is Snappy! (p. 1215)
Haney, Johannah. Abortion Debate: Understanding the Issues. (p. 5)
—Alcohol: Rules, Regulations, & Responsibilities. (p. 35)
—Capoeira. (p. 263)
—Dolphins. (p. 464)
—Ferrets. (p. 582)
—Frogs. (p. 641)
—Michigan. (p. 1135)
—Nuclear Energy. (p. 1269)
—Parrots. (p. 1325)
—Shel Silverstein. (p. 1564)
—Small Birds. (p. 1591)
—Turtles. (p. 1798)
—Whales. (p. 1877)
Haney, Johannah, jt. auth. see Roy, Jennifer Rozines.
Haney, Johannah & Haney-Withrow, Anna. Seals. (p. 1536)
Haney, Johannah & Hantula, Richard. Michigan. (p. 1135)
Haney Perez, Jessica. My First 100 Words Book: A Lift-the-Flap, Pull-Tab Learning Book. March, Chloe, illus. (p. 1203)
Haney-Withrow, Anna. Tae Kwon Do. (p. 1695)
Haney-Withrow, Anna, jt. auth. see Haney, Johannah.
Hanford, Juliana. Werewolf Moon. Pillo, Cary, illus. (p. 1875)
Hanft, Joshua, ed. see Grahame, Kenneth.
Hanft, Joshua E. Jackie Robinson. Marcos, Pablo, illus. (p. 903)
Hanh, Thich Nhat. Coconut Monk. Mai, Vo-Dinh, illus. (p. 337)
—Is Nothing Something? Kids' Questions & Zen Answers about Life, Death, Family, Friendship, & Everything in Between. McClure, Jessica, illus. (p. 889)
—Pebble for Your Pocket. Ames, Philippe & Hop, Nguyen Thi, illus. (p. 1333)
Hanh, Thich Nhat & Parallax Press Staff. Hermit & the Well. Mai, Vo-Dinh, illus. (p. 771)
Hanifin, Laura, photos by see Capucilli, Alyssa Satin.
Hanington, John G. Adventures of Quick Fox. (p. 21)
Hank, Thomas. No Time for Kings. (p. 1260)
Hanke, Karen, illus. see Gollub, Matthew.
Hanke, Karen, illus. see Scelsa, Greg.
Hanke, Karen, illus. see Williams, Rozanne Lanczak.
Hanke, Maureen & Leedham, Jacalyn. Alligator Raggedy-Mouth: Making Music with Poems & Rhymes. (p. 47)
Hankes, Judith E. & Fast, Gerald R. Lost & Found & Found Again: A Math Adventure. (p. 1054)
Hankey, Sandy. Sweet Little Girl. Gay, Maria T., illus. (p. 1690)
Hankey, Wilbur. Skinny the Bull: As Told to Me by Grandpa. (p. 1585)
Hankin, Don. Cat Island. (p. 278)

H

Hankin, Rosemary. Chinese Cookbook for Kids. (p. 307)
—French Cookbook for Kids. (p. 635)
—Indian Cookbook for Kids. (p. 871)
—Italian Cookbook for Kids. (p. 894)
Hankin, Rosie. Chinese Cookbook for Kids. (p. 307)
—Cut & Paste Farm Animals. (p. 395)
—Cut & Paste Sea Creatures. (p. 396)
—Cut & Paste Trucks, Trains, & Big Machines. (p. 396)
—French Cookbook for Kids. (p. 635)
—Italian Cookbook for Kids. (p. 894)
—Mediterranean Cookbook for Kids. (p. 1120)
—Mexican Cookbook for Kids. (p. 1131)
Hankins, Chelsey, jt. auth. see RJF Publishing Staff.
Hankins, Jim. Teddy Scares: Rasputin's Revenge GN: Rasputin's Revenge GN. (p. 1712)
—Teddy Scares: Toastie TP: Toastie TP. (p. 1712)
—Teddy Scares Volume 1. (p. 1712)
Hankins, Larry. Stickboy at the Fair. (p. 1650)
Hankins, M. Lil' Mikie Tells It Like It Is. (p. 1017)
Hankinson, Kim, et al. Paper Pets: 10 Pets to Pop Out & Play With! (p. 1322)
Hankison, McP. Surfing the Internet Safely: A Guide for Teens & Adults. (p. 1685)
Hankison, Whitney. Surfing the Internet Safely: A Workbook for Children. (p. 1685)
Hanks, Carol, illus. see Slaughter, Kristi.
Hanks, Karoline. Exploring Our Biomes (Boxed Set) South Africa (p. 553)
Hanks, Larry R. Stickboy (p. 1650)
Hanks, Scott. Take Heed to Thyself for Teens. (p. 1696)
Hanley, Elizabeth A., ed. World of Dance. (p. 1956)
Hanley, John, illus. see Herzog, Brad.
Hanley, Shirley. Horse Memories of Luck Ahead. (p. 799)
Hanley, Sinéad, illus. see Whiten, Jan.
Hanley, Victoria. Seize the Story: A Handbook for Teens Who Like to Write. (p. 1548)
Hanley, Zachary, illus. see Tata, Cb.
Hanlin, Beverly Austin. Little Lamb: A Christmas Story. (p. 1030)
Hanlon, jt. auth. see Eisele.
Hanlon, Abby. Dory & the Real True Friend. (p. 472)
—Dory Fantasmagory. (p. 472)
—Ralph Tells a Story (p. 1437)
Hanlon, Jennifer. Shadow's Tale. (p. 1558)
Hanlon, Leslie, illus. see Brundige, Patricia.
Hanlon, Michael. Science of the Hitchhiker's Guide to the Galaxy. (p. 1527)
Hanmer, Clayton, illus. see Kelsey, Elin.
Hanmer, Clayton, illus. see Kyi, Tanya Lloyd.
Hann, Harry Henry & Johnson, Nancy. Down in the Tropics. Langille, Elaine, illus. (p. 474)
Hanna, D. M. Man in the Cowboy Hat. (p. 1085)
Hanna, Dan, illus. see Diesen, Deborah.
Hanna, Dawn. Best Hikes & Walks of Southwestern British Columbia (p. 170)
Hanna, Ellen, ed. see Diggs, Linda.
Hanna, Gary, illus. see Spilsbury, Louise.
Hanna, Gary, illus. see Spilsbury, Richard.
Hanna, H. Y. Curse of the Scarab (Big Honey Dog Mysteries #1) Curse of the Scarab. (p. 395)
Hanna, Heather. Daniel Asks about Baptism & Communion. (p. 404)
Hanna, James Milton, Sr. Once upon a Time in the South. (p. 1293)
Hanna, Janice & Thompson, Janice. 3-Minute Devotions for Girls: 180 Inspirational Readings for Young Hearts. (p. 1991)
Hanna, Janice, et al. Operation: Excitement! 3 Stories In 1. (p. 1300)
Hanna, John Fairbanks. Vincent J Muggs: What If? (p. 1842)
Hanna, Kevin & Fagan, Dave. Creature Academy GN. (p. 380)
Hanna, Margaret Leis. Canneh, the Reluctant Christmas Camel. Weltner, Dave, illus. (p. 261)
Hanna, Michelle. Awakening the Other Side: Poems & Art Illustrations. (p. 120)
Hanna, Tim. One Good Run: The Legend of Burt Munro. (p. 1295)
Hanna, Virginie. Rosy Posey Is Not Dirty! Desmoineaux, Christel, illus. (p. 1490)
—Secret Life of Princesses. Delanssay, Cathy, illus. (p. 1541)
—Shelby the Flying Snail Piu, Amandine, illus. (p. 1564)
Hannaford, Linda S. Petie the Parrot's Amazing Adventures: P. D. Q. Lee, George T., illus. (p. 1348)
Hannah, Eileen. Learning about the Library. (p. 985)
Hannah, Helen Elizabeth. Let's Help Little Polka Dot Find His Way Home. (p. 998)
Hannah Lane. Frog Named Dude. (p. 640)
Hannah, Martha. Ghost of Hampton Court. Dowell, Larry, illus. (p. 671)
Hannah, Sophie. Monogram Murders: The New Hercule Poirot Mystery. (p. 1166)
Hannah, Sophie, tr. see Jansson, Tove.
Hannah, Sue. Crafty Concoctions: 101 Craft Supply Recipes. (p. 376)
Hannah, Tess, jt. auth. see Hannah, Tom.
Hannah, Tom & Hannah, Tess. Endless String: Poems for Children (and the people who read to Them) (p. 527)
Hannah, Vickie. There's A Schnoozle in My Closet. (p. 1731)
Hannah, Wood, illus. see Tiger Tales Staff, ed.
Hannam, John-Pierre M., Sr. Uncle Jake's Hat. (p. 1811)
Hannan, Peter. Freddy! Deep-Space Food Fighter. Hannan, Peter, illus. (p. 633)
—Freddy! King of Flurb. Hannan, Peter, illus. (p. 633)
—Freddy! Locked in Space. Hannan, Peter, illus. (p. 633)
—Greatest Snowman in the World! Hannan, Peter, illus. (p. 720)
—My Big Mouth: 10 Songs I Wrote That Almost Got Me Killed. Hannan, Peter, illus. (p. 1197)
—Petlandia. Hannan, Peter, illus. (p. 1348)
Hannel, Gerardo Ivan. Highly Effective Questioning. (p. 779)
Hanneman, Monika, et al. Gardening with Children. Tomasello, Sam, illus. (p. 656)
Hanner, Albert, illus. see Brewster, Joy.
Hanner, Albert, illus. see Cameron, Ken.
Hanner, Albert, illus. see Glassman, Jackie.
Hanner, Albert, illus. see Lunis, Natalie.
Hanner, Albert, illus. see McCay, William.
Hanner, Albert, illus. see Prigioniero, Lily.
Hanner, Albert, illus. see Smith, Carrie.
Hanner, Albert, illus. see Sullivan, Erin.
Hanner, Albert, illus. see Sullivan, Erin.
Hannigan, Kate. Cupcake Cousins. Hughes, Brooke Boynton, illus. (p. 392)
—Detective's Assistant. (p. 431)
—Summer Showers Hughes, Brooke Boynton, illus. (p. 1675)
Hannigan, Katherine. Emmaline & the Bunny. Hannigan, Katherine, illus. (p. 520)
—Gwendolyn Grace. Hannigan, Katherine, illus. (p. 733)
—Ida B: And Her Plans to Maximize Fun Avoid Disaster, & (Possibly) Save the World. (p. 851)
—Ida B: ... And Her Plans to Maximize Fun, Avoid Disaster, & (Possibly) Save the World. (p. 851)
—True (... Sort Of) (p. 1791)
Hannigan, Lynne. Sam's Passover. (p. 1509)
Hannigan, Paula. Hugs for You. Brown, Heather, illus. (p. 825)
—New York City. Chandler, Shannon, illus. (p. 1248)
—Stencil Art. Klutz Editors, ed. (p. 1647)
—Under Construction. Brown, Heather, illus. (p. 1813)
Hannigan, Paula, jt. auth. see Accord Publishing Staff.
Hannigan, Paula, jt. auth. see Kirkova, Milena.
Hannigan, Paula & Accord Publishing Staff. Music Star. Slade, Christian, illus. (p. 1193)
—Under Construction. Brown, Heather, illus. (p. 1813)
Hannigan, Paula & Croyle, Paula. Washington, D. C. Chandler, Shannon, illus. (p. 1860)
Hanning, Jacob. Mommy's Little Helper: That's Me. (p. 1163)
—There Is a Bird at My Window. (p. 1729)
Hannon, Holly, illus. see Meachen Rau, Dana.
Hannon, Holly, illus. see Rouss, Sylvia A.
Hannon, Holly, illus. see Rouss, Sylvia.
Hannon, Kenneth, photos by see Grantner, Anne M. & Haggart, Gary.
Hannon, Patrice. Dear Jane Austen: A Heroine's Guide to Life & Love. (p. 419)
Hannon, Robert A. J. L. Cowen's Postwar Lionel Trains: O-Gauge Reference Manual II, Motorized Units, Rolling Stock & Accessories. (p. 901)
Hannon, Rose. Finding Agate: An Epic Story of a Poodle's Heart & His Will to Survive. (p. 587)
Hannon, Sharon M. Punks: A Guide to an American Subculture (p. 1417)
Hannula, Kate. Forever, Jewel. (p. 619)
Hanny, Diane. Wispy Willy. Baskey, Kim, illus. (p. 1941)
Hano, Patricia. Tyler Meets the Moon. (p. 1805)
Hanrahan, Abigail & McSweeny, Catherine. 50 Quick Play Reading Games. (p. 1997)
Hanrahan, Brendan. Great Day Trips in the Connecticut Valley of the Dinosaurs. (p. 715)
Hanrahan, Christina K. That Evelyn Margaret! (p. 1726)
—What Would Evelyn Margaret Think, Say, & Do? (p. 1895)
Hanrahan, Clare. Legal System. (p. 988)
Hanrahan, Clare, ed. see Hanrahan, Clare M.
Hanrahan, Clare, ed. see Haugen, David M.
Hanrahan, Clare, ed. Global Resources. (p. 684)
Hanrahan, Clare M. Legal System. Hanrahan, Clare, ed. (p. 988)
Hanrahan, Gareth, jt. auth. see Hancock, Claire.
Hanrahan, Val. Additional Mathematics for Ocr. Porkess, R., ed. (p. 12)
Hanrion, Patricia. Jingle Bell Bum. (p. 918)
Hanrott, Robert & Horsley, Martha. Telling Tales. (p. 1717)
Hans, Stephanie, illus. see Lockwood, Vicki.
Hans, Stephanie, illus. see Seven, John.
Hansard, Peter. Field Full of Horses. Lilly, Kenneth, illus. (p. 583)
Hansel, Karen & Ham, Ken. Charlie & Trike Grand Canyon Adventure. (p. 292)
Hansell, Donna. Adventures of Kirbey the Kidney. (p. 19)
Hansell, Robin. Mason & Monkey's Big Adventure. (p. 1102)
Hansen, jt. auth. see Johnson, Steve.
Hansen, Ace. Julius Caesar Brown & the Green Gas Mystery. (p. 933)
Hansen, Alli. Huevos Rancheros. (p. 824)
Hansen, Amelia. It's Raining Pups & Dogs! (p. 898)
Hansen, Amelia, illus. see Bix, Daisy.
Hansen, Amelia, illus. see Buchwald, Claire.
Hansen, Amelia, illus. see Prevost, Jeanne.
Hansen, Amy. Floating & Sinking. (p. 605)
—Fossil Fuels: Buried in the Earth. (p. 623)
—Geothermal Energy: Hot Stuff! (p. 665)
—Hydropower: Making a Splash! (p. 831)
—Matter Comes in All Shapes. (p. 1109)
—Nuclear Energy: Amazing Atoms. (p. 1269)
—Solar Energy: Running on Sunshine. (p. 1606)
—Solid or Liquid? (p. 1607)
—What Is It Made Of? (p. 1889)
—Where Did the Water Go? (p. 1906)
—Wind Energy: Blown Away! (p. 1935)
Hansen, Amy S. Bugs & Bugsicles: Insects in the Winter. Kray, Robert C., illus. (p. 237)
—Fossil Fuels: Buried in the Earth. (p. 623)
—Geothermal Energy: Hot Stuff! (p. 665)
—How Do We Stay on Earth? A Gravity Mystery Scott, Korey, illus. (p. 808)
—Hydropower: Making a Splash! (p. 831)
—Matter Comes in All Shapes. (p. 1109)
—Nuclear Energy: Amazing Atoms. (p. 1269)
—Solar Energy: Running on Sunshine. (p. 1606)
—Where Does the Sun Go at Night? An Earth Science Mystery Scott, Korey, illus. (p. 1907)
—Wind Energy: Blown Away! (p. 1935)
Hansen, Amy S. & Ollen, Rebecca. First Graphics: Science Mysteries: A Science Mystery. Scott, Korey & McDee, Katie, illus. (p. 595)
—First Graphics: Science Mysteries. Scott, Korey & McDee, Katie, illus. (p. 595)
Hansen, Andra. Quest: A Story of a Stow Away, Who Eventually Ends up Owning the Ship. For the Barton Reading & Spelling System. (p. 1426)
—Tax Man: A Tax Preparer Can't Get His First Computer to work, in One Syllable Words, Written for the Barton Reading & Spelling System. (p. 1707)
Hansen, Angela, illus. see Holzer, Angela.
Hansen, Anya, jt. auth. see Sohn, Emily.
Hansen, Bjarne, illus. see Tomasi, Peter J.
Hansen, Brandy A. Madd Maddox: Sister for Sale. (p. 1069)
Hansen, Caroline, jt. auth. see Hansen, Francis.
Hansen, Chance. Green Pea Makes a Flourless Cookie. (p. 722)
Hansen, Christine, illus. see Holden, Pam, et al.
Hansen, Christine, illus. see Holden, Pam.
Hansen, Clint, illus. see Burton, Martin Nelson.
Hansen, Clint, illus. see Ellis, Gwen.
Hansen, Diane. Those are MY Private Parts. Charlotte Hansen, illus. (p. 1740)
Hansen, Doug. Mother Goose in California. (p. 1178)
—Sierra Adventure Coloring Book: Featuring Yosemite National Park. (p. 1573)
Hansen, Doug, illus. see Brumage, Katherine.
Hansen, Doug & Aesop. Aesop in California. (p. 25)
Hansen, Eric. Great White Judgment. Moody, Julie, illus. (p. 719)
—Ian, Ceo, North Pole. (p. 849)
—Isle of Nam. Meier, Paul, illus. (p. 893)
Hansen, Ernest, illus. see Rasmussen, Knud.
Hansen, Francis & Hansen, Caroline. Finally a Friend. (p. 587)
Hansen, Gaby, illus. see Bedford, David.
Hansen, Gaby, illus. see Doney, Meryl.
Hansen, Gaby, illus. see Freedman, Claire.
Hansen, Gaby, illus. see Johnson, Jane.
Hansen, Gaby, illus. see Leeson, Christine.
Hansen, Gaby, illus. see Lobel, Gill.
Hansen, Grace. Abraham Lincoln. (p. 6)
—Alligators. (p. 47)
—Animal Facts to Make You Smile! (p. 77)
—Ants. (p. 90)
—Barack Obama. (p. 137)
—Bees. (p. 157)
—Beetles. (p. 158)
—Bill Clinton. (p. 186)
—Butterflies. (p. 247)
—Chameleons. (p. 289)
—Dolphins. (p. 464)
—Dragonflies. (p. 478)
—Franklin D. Roosevelt. (p. 630)
—Franklin Delano Roosevelt. (p. 630)
—George Washington. (p. 664)
—History Maker Biographies. (p. 783)
—Iguanas. (p. 856)
—Jackie Robinson: Baseball Legend. (p. 904)
—Jane Goodall: Chimpanzee Expert & Activist. (p. 908)
—Jellyfish. (p. 912)
—John F. Kennedy. (p. 921)
—Komodo Dragons. (p. 966)
—Machines to Thrill You! (p. 1068)
—Malala Yousafzai: Education Activist. (p. 1083)
—Mariposas. (p. 1094)
—Martin Luther King, Jr. Civil Rights Leader. (p. 1098)
—Mosquitoes. (p. 1176)
—Ocean Life. (p. 1276)
—Octopuses. (p. 1278)
—Places to Amaze You! (p. 1366)
—Pope Francis: Religious Leader. (p. 1384)
—Science Facts to Surprise You! (p. 1526)
—Seahorses. (p. 1536)
—Seeing Is Believing. (p. 1548)
—Snakes. (p. 1596)
—Tropical Fish. (p. 1789)
—Turtles. (p. 1798)
—Walt Disney: Animator & Founder. (p. 1855)
—Weird Animals to Shock You! (p. 1872)
—Whales. (p. 1877)
—World Records to Wow You! (p. 1958)
Hansen, Grace, jt. auth. see ABDO Publishing Company Staff.
Hansen, Grace, et al. Abejas. (p. 4)
—Caimanes. (p. 252)
—Camaleones. (p. 255)
—Dragones de Komodo. (p. 478)
—Escarabajos. (p. 535)
—Hormigas. (p. 798)
—Iguanas. (p. 856)
—Libélulas. (p. 1005)
—Mosquitos. (p. 1177)
—Serpientes. (p. 1552)
—Tortugas. (p. 1771)
Hansen, Henry. Mayor Teddy. (p. 1113)
Hansen, Holly T., jt. auth. see Johnson, Jennifer Hunt.
Hansen, Holly T. & Johnson, Jennifer Hunt. Life in Your Town (p. 1011)
—Memories of the Railroad (p. 1126)
—Remembering Mother (p. 1459)
Hansen, Jane, et al. Prek-2 Writing Classroom: Growing Confident Writers. (p. 1395)
Hansen, Janis. Creation: God's Wonderful Gift Fransisco, Wendy, illus. (p. 379)
—David & His Giant Battle Francisco, Wendy, illus. (p. 410)
—Jesus: The Birthday of the King Francisco, Wendy, illus. (p. 914)
—Jonah & His Amazing Voyage Francisco, Wendy, illus. (p. 924)
Hansen, Jeanne. Wow! an Upside down Cake Birthday Party! (p. 1962)
Hansen, Jeff. Alibriana Visits the Branch Office. (p. 39)
Hansen, Jeffry Scott. Warpath. (p. 1858)
Hansen, Jennifer. Lucy's Grade School Adventure. Marsden, Ken, illus. (p. 1063)
Hansen, Jim. How to Draw Superheroes. (p. 818)
Hansen, Jim & Burns, John. How to Draw Dragons. (p. 817)
—How to Draw Superheroes. (p. 818)
Hansen, Jimmy, illus. see Abnett, Dan.
Hansen, Jimmy, illus. see Rimmer, Ian.
Hansen, Joyce. Gift-Giver. (p. 675)
—I Thought My Soul Would Rise & Fly: The Diary of Patsy, a Freed Girl, Mars Bluff, South Carolina 1865. (p. 846)
—One True Friend. Giblin, James Cross, ed. (p. 1297)
—Yellow Bird & Me. (p. 1970)
Hansen, Joyce & McGowan, Gary. Freedom Roads: Searching for the Underground Railroad. Ransome, James E., illus. (p. 635)
Hansen, Judith. Seashells in My Pocket: AMC's Family Guide to Exploring the Coast from Maine to Florida. Sabaka, Donna, illus. (p. 1538)
Hansen, Justin LaRocca. Brothers Unite. (p. 231)
—Monster Hunter. (p. 1167)
Hansen, Kate. Spike the Sewer Cat. Illustrations byVoigt, Karen S., illus. (p. 1627)
Hansen, Katharine, jt. auth. see Hansen, Randall S.
Hansen, Keli. Nala's Story. (p. 1228)
Hansen, Laurie, illus. see Smith, Kathleen.
Hansen Literary Agency Staff, jt. auth. see Deutsch, Barry.
Hansen, Lorie, illus. see Prindle, Twyla D.
Hansen, Lorie Miller, illus. see Prindle, Twyla.
Hansen, Lynne. Change: Heritage of Horror Series. (p. 289)
—Reckless Revolution. (p. 1451)
—Shades of Blue & Gray. (p. 1557)
—Time for Witches. (p. 1752)
Hansen, Lynne & Bosco, Sally. AltDeath.com. (p. 50)
Hansen, Marc. Ralph Snart Adventures: Comic Collection #1. (p. 1437)
Hansen, Mark & Ferber, Kevin S. Success 101 for Teens: Dollars & Sense for a Winning Financial Life. (p. 1671)
Hansen, Mark Victor. Richest Kids in America: How They Earn It, How They Spend It, How You Can Too. (p. 1470)
Hansen, Mark Victor, jt. auth. see Canfield, Jack.
Hansen, Mary Heetderks. Breaking Free. (p. 225)
Hansen, MaryAnn Shelley. Sam the Second. (p. 1507)
Hansen, Melissa, illus. see Henderson, Tim.
Hansen, Merrily P. Close-Up Look at Plants: A Content Area Reader-Science. (p. 334)
—Homes Around the World: A Content Area Reader-Social Studies. (p. 793)
Hansen Moench, Megan. Know Your State Activity Book Utah Padavick, Nate, illus. (p. 965)
—Know Your State Activity Book Washington Padavick, Nate, illus. (p. 965)
Hansen, Ole Steen. A-10 Thunderbolt. Pang, Alex, illus. (p. 1)
—AH-64 Apache Helicopter Pang, Alex, illus. (p. 30)
—Air Combat. (p. 31)
—B-2 Spirit Stealth Bomber Pang, Alex, illus. (p. 122)
—Commercial Aviation: Military Aircraft of World War One. (p. 349)
—F/A-22 Raptor. Pang, Alex, illus. (p. 559)
—Flying for Fun. (p. 610)
—Helicopters. (p. 763)
—Seaplanes & Naval Aviation. (p. 1537)
—Space Flight. (p. 1619)
—Story of Flight (p. 1658)
—Story of Flight. (p. 1658)
—Weird & Wonderful Aircraft. (p. 1872)
Hansen, Paisley, illus. see French, Joyce.
Hansen, Paul. Adventures of Gray Tail. (p. 18)
—When Snakes Attack! (p. 1904)
Hansen, Peter & Skindzier, Jon. University of Richmond College Prowler off the Record. (p. 1821)
Hansen, Randall S. & Hansen, Katharine. Complete Idiot's Guide to Study Skills. (p. 353)
Hansen, Red, illus. see Gamble, Adam & Jasper, Mark.
Hansen, Red, illus. see Gamble, Adam.
Hansen, Red, illus. see Hodgson, Mona Gansberg.
Hansen, Red, illus. see Lears, Laurie.
Hansen, Red, illus. see Redmond, Shirley Raye.
Hansen, Robin. Ice Harbor Mittens. Hogan, Jamie, illus. (p. 850)
Hansen, Roland. Jingle Jangles Smith. (p. 918)
—Story of a Butterfly Called Bee. (p. 1657)
—Tim the Cat. (p. 1750)
—Tim the Cat. Jackson, Brittany Janay, illus. (p. 1750)
Hansen, Rosanna. Caring Animals. (p. 269)
—Caring for Cheetahs: My African Adventure. (p. 269)
—Jupiter. (p. 937)
—Mysteries in Space: Exploration & Discovery. (p. 1222)
—Seven Wonders of the Sun & Other Stars. (p. 1555)
Hansen, Sarah. Abraham Lincoln. (p. 6)
—Dwight D. Eisenhower. (p. 491)
—When Mountain Lions Attack! (p. 1904)
Hansen, Sharon A. Executive Functioning Workbook for Teens: Help for Unprepared, Late, & Scattered Teens. (p. 548)
Hansen, Sophia, jt. auth. see Sophia Hansen, Hansen.
Hansen, Sue. 50 Reproducible, Leveled Game Sheets That Kids Can Use Independently or in Small Groups to Practice Important Math Skills. (p. 1997)
—Little Bitty Bella in a Big, Big World. (p. 1024)
Hansen, Susan. Flying Quilt. (p. 610)
Hansen, T. J., jt. auth. see Hall, Carol S.
Hansen, Tammy A., ed. see Berggren, Jeff.
Hansen, Taylor. Little Boy & the Christmas Tale. (p. 1025)
Hansen, Thomas S., jt. auth. see Dollenmayer, David B.
Hansen, Thore, illus. see Bringsvaerd, Tor Age.
Hansen, Thore, illus. see Rorvik, Bjorn F.
Hansen-Krening, Nancy, et al, eds. Kaleidoscope: A Multicultural Booklist for Grades K-8. (p. 941)
Hansen-Smith, Bradford. Folding Circle Tetrahedra: Truth in the Geometry of Wholemovement. (p. 611)
Hanson, Anders. Adell & the Secret Well. (p. 12)
—Ant King. Haberstroh, Anne, illus. (p. 88)
—Archaeologist's Tools. (p. 95)
—Awesome Abyssinians. Doucet, Bob, illus. (p. 120)
—Beetle Mania. (p. 158)
—Bold Boxers. Doucet, Bob, illus. (p. 208)
—Can You See Me? (p. 259)
—Career for Mr. Lear. (p. 266)
—Chuck Has a Big Truck. (p. 318)
—Claire's Bear Scare. (p. 326)
—Come in & Swim! (p. 347)
—Cow with a Plow. (p. 373)
—Cuddly Cats. (p. 389)

—Deer on Mount Ranier. (p. 423)
—Do Something for Others: The Kids' Book of Citizenship. (p. 457)
—Don't Hop with Pop! (p. 467)
—Drills. (p. 485)
—Dunk-Tank Frank. (p. 490)
—Elaine's Rain Cane. (p. 508)
—Elephant. (p. 511)
—Elephants Are Not Little! (p. 511)
—Elephants Are Not Little. (p. 512)
—Eli & the High Pie. (p. 512)
—Everyone Is Equal: The Kids' Book of Tolerance. (p. 544)
—Giant Animals. (p. 673)
—Go for It! (p. 686)
—Hammers. (p. 739)
—Handsome Horses. (p. 741)
—Here Comes the Sun. (p. 770)
—Hun Plays One-On-One. (p. 827)
—Hun Plays One-on—One. (p. 827)
—I Like My Family! (p. 841)
—Iguana Mama. (p. 856)
—Jill & John. (p. 917)
—Jill & the Giant Spill. (p. 917)
—Joe Grows Tomatoes. (p. 920)
—Kangaroo Boxers. Nobens, C. A., illus. (p. 942)
—Kangaroo Boxers. Nobens, Cheryl A., illus. (p. 942)
—Kay's Maze Phase. (p. 946)
—Keeping the Peace: The Kids' Book of Peacemaking. (p. 948)
—Kim & Ken. (p. 956)
—Land of the Free: The Kids' Book of Freedom. (p. 973)
—Let's Go by Airplane. (p. 997)
—Let's Go by Boat. (p. 997)
—Let's Go by Bus. (p. 997)
—Let's Go by Cable Car. Craig, Diane, ed. (p. 997)
—Let's Go by Car. (p. 997)
—Let's Go by Helicopter. (p. 997)
—Let's Go by Hot Air Balloon. (p. 997)
—Let's Go by Hovercraft. (p. 997)
—Let's Go by Motorcycle. (p. 997)
—Let's Go by RV. (p. 997)
—Let's Go by Train. (p. 997)
—Let's Go by Truck. (p. 997)
—Let's Sled Instead. (p. 1000)
—Little Like Me. (p. 1030)
—Lively Lizards. (p. 1040)
—Liz & Len. (p. 1042)
—Lone Shark. Haberstroh, Anne, illus. (p. 1046)
—May by the Bay. (p. 1112)
—Meg & Mark. (p. 1124)
—Meteorologist's Tools. (p. 1130)
—Monkey Business. Chawla, Neena, illus. (p. 1165)
—Nan & Nick. (p. 1228)
—Nate Is Great. (p. 1230)
—Neil & His Meal Mobile. (p. 1240)
—Night Owl. Haberstroh, Anne, illus. (p. 1254)
—No Bullies Allowed! The Kids' Book of Dealing with Bullies. (p. 1258)
—Olga & Olaf. (p. 1285)
—Olive & Oscar. (p. 1285)
—Owl Swings a Dowel. (p. 1315)
—Pam & Pete. (p. 1320)
—Pantaloncillos del Canguro. Nobens, C. A., illus. (p. 1321)
—Pest with a Vest. (p. 1345)
—Pig with a Wig. (p. 1357)
—Pig with the Wig. (p. 1357)
—Pink Mink. (p. 1360)
—Pliers. (p. 1374)
—Quinn & Quenton. (p. 1428)
—Rhino Horns. Nobens, C. A., illus. (p. 1467)
—Rhino Horns. Nobens, Cheryl A., illus. (p. 1467)
—Rob the Blob. (p. 1478)
—Ruth & Rob. (p. 1498)
—Sara & Sam. (p. 1514)
—Saws. (p. 1518)
—Scientist's Tools. (p. 1529)
—Seasons Come & Go. (p. 1538)
—Shaggy Shih Tzus. Doucet, Bob, illus. (p. 1558)
—Sharon & Shawn. (p. 1563)
—Simone on the Throne. (p. 1577)
—Sleek Siamese. Doucet, Bob, illus. (p. 1588)
—Snowman's Clothes. (p. 1601)
—Stand up for Yourself: The Kids' Book of Courage. (p. 1639)
—Terrific Turtles. (p. 1721)
—Tools of the Trade. (p. 1767)
—Tuba Del Rinoceronte. Nobens, C. A., illus. (p. 1795)
—Tuba del Rinoceronte. Nobens, C. A., illus. (p. 1795)
—Waste Is Traced. (p. 1860)
—We Say Hooray! (p. 1868)
—Whale Tale. (p. 1877)
—What Do I Look Like? (p. 1882)
—What in the World Is a Cone? (p. 1887)
—What in the World Is a Cylinder? (p. 1887)
—What in the World Is a Prism? (p. 1887)
—What in the World Is a Pyramid? (p. 1888)
—What in the World Is a Sphere? (p. 1888)
—Wrenches. (p. 1962)
—You & I Can Read! (p. 1973)
—You & I Can Read! Craig, Diane, ed. (p. 1973)
Hanson, Anders, jt. auth. see ABDO Publishing Company Staff.
Hanson, Anders, jt. auth. see Nakata, Ritsuko.
Hanson, Anders & Craig, Diane. Sea Turtle. (p. 1535)
Hanson, Anders & Hengel, Katherine. Biggest, Baddest Book of Pirates. (p. 185)
Hanson, Anders & Mann, Elissa. Biggest, Baddest Book of Beasts. (p. 185)
—Biggest, Baddest Book of Bugs. (p. 185)
—Biggest, Baddest Book of Dinosaurs. (p. 185)
—Biggest, Baddest Book of Monsters. (p. 185)
—Cool Flexagon Art: Creative Activities That Make Math & Science Fun for Kids! (p. 363)
—Cool Optical Illusions: Creative Activities That Make Math & Science Fun for Kids! (p. 364)
—Cool Paper Folding: Creative Activities That Make Math & Science Fun for Kids! (p. 364)
—Cool String Art: Creative Activities That Make Math & Science Fun for Kids! (p. 364)
—Cool Structures: Creative Activities That Make Math & Science Fun for Kids! (p. 364)
—Cool Tessellations: Creative Activities That Make Math & Science Fun for Kids! (p. 364)
Hanson, Anders, et al. First Rhymes (set of 47 Titles) (p. 596)
Hanson, Ann. Flicker's Round Trip. (p. 603)
Hanson, Anne E. Ambulances in Action (p. 57)
—Fire Trucks in Action (p. 591)
Hanson, Bonnie Compton. Escape from Camp Porcupine. (p. 534)
—Impossible Christmas Present. (p. 862)
—Lost on Monster Mountain. (p. 1056)
—Meet the Ponytail Girls. (p. 1123)
—Stormy Spring. (p. 1656)
Hanson, Cindy L. Be Loved Eagle: A Beloved Bird: Book 2. (p. 148)
—Mighty Eagle: A Beloved Bird: the Search for True Love. (p. 1140)
—Soar Higher Eagle: A Beloved Bird: the Search for True Love Series. (p. 1603)
Hanson, Dana, illus. see Ahlman, Larry.
Hanson, Ed. African Safari. (p. 28)
—Amazon Adventure. (p. 56)
—Danger at 20 Fathoms. (p. 403)
—Desert Ordeal. (p. 429)
—Disaster in Oceania. (p. 446)
—Falsely Accused. (p. 567)
—Floodgates. (p. 605)
—Forest Fire. (p. 618)
—Free Fall. (p. 634)
—Hostages. (p. 801)
—Hurricane. (p. 829)
—Iron Mountain. (p. 888)
—Lost at Sea. (p. 1055)
—Mountain Blizzard. (p. 1180)
—Mystery at Bear Lake. (p. 1223)
—Pass. (p. 1326)
—Ransom. (p. 1438)
—Sunken Treasure. (p. 1677)
—Swamp. (p. 1688)
Hanson, Faye. Cinderella's Secret Diary. Hanson, Faye, illus. (p. 320)
—Wonder. Hanson, Faye, illus. (p. 1947)
Hanson III, Andrew C., ed. Ice Age Trail Atlas 2005. (p. 850)
Hanson, Jackie, jt. auth. see Hanson, Ted.
Hanson, Jacquelyn. Parker House & Other Stories. (p. 1324)
Hanson, Janell. I Will Help You. (p. 848)
Hanson, Jean V. Pudding Town. (p. 1414)
Hanson, Jeanne K. Caves. (p. 282)
Hanson, Jennifer L. Mongolia. (p. 1164)
Hanson, John, et al. GCSE Humanities for AQA. (p. 659)
Hanson, Jon, jt. auth. see Hanson, Paige.
Hanson, Jon, jt. auth. see Hanson, Sue.
Hanson, Jonathan. Victor el Zopilote Renuente! Duffek, Kim Kanoa, illus. (p. 1840)
—Victor, the Reluctant Vulture. Duufek, Kim Kanoa, illus. (p. 1840)
Hanson, Joyce A. Mary McLeod Bethune & Black Women's Political Activism. (p. 1101)
Hanson, Krista Finstad. Great Barrier Reef. (p. 713)
Hanson, Lori, illus. see Gribble, Julie.
Hanson, Lynne. Worm World: Clue Books. (p. 1961)
Hanson, Maria. Dog Heaven: Somewhere over the Rainbow Bridge. D'Amico, Dee Densmore, illus. (p. 461)
Hanson, Martina D. & Benchmark Education Co. Staff. Analytical Arguments about Courage. (p. 67)
Hanson, Mary. How to Save Your Tail: If You Are a Rat Nabbed by Cats Who Really Like Stories about Magic Spoons, Wolves with Snout-Warts, Big, Hairy Chimney Trolls ... & Cookies, Too. (p. 821)
Hanson, P. H. My Granny's Purse. (p. 1210)
—My Mommy's Tote. (p. 1214)
Hanson, Paige & Hanson, Jon. Harry Spotter: The Incontinent Puppy Sellers, Amy, illus. (p. 751)
Hanson, Paul & Nagourney, Eric. My Silly Body: A User's Manual for Boys & Girls. (p. 1218)
Hanson, Peter E., illus. see Roop, Peter & Roop, Connie.
Hanson, Robert. Bluey & the Great Spirit Moon. (p. 204)
Hanson, Robert Karl. Bluey & the Great Spirit Moon. (p. 204)
Hanson, Sandy. Camel's Story: A Search for the Messiah. Hanson, Sandy & Delage, Kristi, illus. (p. 256)
—Camel's Story, I Met the Lamb. (p. 256)
Hanson, Sharon. 10 Best Love Poems. (p. 1993)
Hanson, Shelley. K9 Crew Beginnings. (p. 941)
Hanson, Stephen, illus. see Gray, Kes.
Hanson, Sue & Hanson, Jon. All about Mancala: Its History & How to Play. (p. 42)
Hanson, Susan Jo, illus. see Jacobsen, Annie.
Hanson, Sydney, illus. see Davies, Jacqueline.
Hanson, Ted & Hanson, Jackie. Dakota's First Roundup. (p. 401)
Hanson, Tippi, jt. auth. see Russell, Lyndsay.
Hanson, Tracie. New World Baby - the Collection. (p. 1247)
Hanson, Tracie, des. New World Baby - French. (p. 1247)
—New World Baby - German. (p. 1247)
—New World Baby - Italian. (p. 1247)
—New World Baby - Spanish. (p. 1247)
Hanson, Vic Jan Fegley. Healing Child's Friend. (p. 757)
Hanson, Warren. Bugtown Boogie. Johnson, Steve & Fancher, Lou, illus. (p. 237)
—Grandpa Has a Great Big Face. Elliott, Mark, illus. (p. 709)
—It's Monday, Mrs. Jolly Bones! Tusa, Tricia, illus. (p. 897)
—Kiki's Hats: Our Gifts Live on & On. Hanson, Warren, illus. (p. 955)
—Sea of Sleep. LaMarche, Jim, illus. (p. 1535)
Hanson, Warren, illus. see Kupchella, Rick.
Hanson, Warren, jt. auth. see Hegg, Tom.
Hanson-Harding, Alexandra. Activism: Taking on Women's Issues. (p. 10)
—Albert Einstein. (p. 34)
—Beekeeping. (p. 157)
—How to Beat Physical Bullying. (p. 815)
—Step-By-Step Guide to Win-Win Negotiating Every Day. (p. 1647)
—Texas. (p. 1723)
—What Is Matter? (p. 1889)
—Wyoming. (p. 1966)
Hanson-Harding, Alexandra & Benchmark Education Co. Staff. Science of Flight. (p. 1527)
Hanson-Harding, Alexandra L. Wyoming. (p. 1966)
Hanson-Harding, Brian. Dairy: From the Farm to Your Table. (p. 400)
Hanson-Roberts, Mary. Cinderella: A Tale of Kindness. (p. 320)
Hansson, Martina & Benchmark Education Co. Staff. Great Native American Leaders. (p. 717)
Hanstick, Kevin, illus. see Polley, JoAnn.
Hanstick, Kevin R., illus. see Polley, J. Patrick & Polley, JoAnn.
Hantel, Johanna, illus. see Bacon, Arthur & Bacon, Henry.
Hantel, Johanna, illus. see Jensen, Patricia & Demar, Regier.
Hantel, Johanna, illus. see Jensen, Patricia.
Hantel, Johanna, illus. see Neasi, Barbara J.
Hanton, Sophie. Colors by the Sea. (p. 345)
—First Words in the Garden. (p. 597)
—Hugs: Tuck Each Baby into a Loving Hug. (p. 825)
—Numbers in the Jungle. (p. 1272)
—Shapes on the Farm. (p. 1561)
Hanton, Sophie, illus. see Williamson, Karen.
Hantula, Richard. Electricity & Forces. (p. 509)
—Jonas Salk. (p. 925)
—Plants & Animals. (p. 1369)
—Rocks & Fossils. (p. 1483)
—Science at Work in Auto Racing. (p. 1525)
—Science at Work in Baseball. (p. 1525)
—Science at Work in Basketball. (p. 1525)
—Science at Work in Football. (p. 1525)
—Science at Work in Snowboarding. (p. 1525)
—Science at Work in Soccer. (p. 1525)
—Thomas Edison. (p. 1738)
Hantula, Richard, jt. auth. see Asimov, Isaac.
Hantula, Richard, jt. auth. see Bjorklund, Ruth.
Hantula, Richard, jt. auth. see Derzipilski, Kathleen.
Hantula, Richard, jt. auth. see Dornfeld, Margaret.
Hantula, Richard, jt. auth. see Haney, Johannah.
Hantula, Richard, jt. auth. see Hart, Joyce.
Hantula, Richard & Bjorklund, Ruth. Puerto Rico. (p. 1415)
Hantula, Richard, et al. How Do Cell Phones Work? (p. 806)
—How Do Solar Panels Work? (p. 807)
—Nuclear Power. (p. 1270)
—Solar Power. (p. 1606)
Hantula, Timothy James, illus. see Sharp, N. L.
Hantz, Sara. Will the Real Abi Saunders Please Stand Up? (p. 1932)
Hanzie, Christopher. Punch: All about Boxing Intermediate Book with Online Access. (p. 1416)
Hanzik, Sharon. Raccoons Don't Use Spoons. (p. 1430)
Hao, K. T. Best Friends. Kung, Annie, tr. (p. 169)
—Magic Book. Ferri, Giuliano, illus. (p. 1071)
—Where's My Mommy? Toni, Alessandra, illus. (p. 1910)
—Who Did This? Bernatene, Poly, illus. (p. 1915)
Hao, K. T., jt. auth. see Kim, Byung-Gyu.
Hao, K. T. & Fulla, Monserrat. Scott y Amundsen: La Conquista del Polo Sur. Ingpen, Robert R., illus. (p. 1531)
Haoa Cardinali, Viki, tr. see Orliac, Catherine.
Hapipi, Rafiz, jt. auth. see Foley, Erin.
Hapka, C. A. Leyenda de los Toa. (p. 1004)
Hapka, Catherine, adapted by see Hapka, Cathy, pseud.
Hapka, Catherine, jt. auth. see Bloomberg, Georgina.
Hapka, Catherine, jt. auth. see Destiny, A.
Hapka, Catherine, jt. auth. see Disney Book Group Staff.
Hapka, Catherine, see Hapka, Cathy, pseud.
Hapka, Catherine, pseud. Always Dreamin' (p. 51)
—ASPCA Pet Rescue Club: the Lonely Pony. (p. 107)
—At the Show. Kennedy, Anne, illus. (p. 111)
—Back in the Saddle. Kennedy, Anne, illus. (p. 130)
—Blast from the Past. (p. 198)
—Blue Ribbon Day. (p. 203)
—Blue Ribbon Day. Kennedy, Anne, illus. (p. 203)
—Blue Ribbon Summer. (p. 203)
—Chasing Gold. (p. 294)
—Disney Sofia the First: Sweet Dreams, Sofia! Cardona, Jose, illus. (p. 453)
—Don't Meddle with Miss Nettle. (p. 468)
—Enchanted Science Fair. (p. 523)
—Forever Free. (p. 619)
—Friends 4 Ever? (p. 638)
—Holiday in Enchancia. (p. 788)
—Horse Diaries #12: Luna. Sanderson, Ruth, illus. (p. 799)
—How to Train Your Dragon: Meet the Dragons. Grosvenor, Charles & Gerard, Justin, illus. (p. 822)
—Jingle Bells. (p. 918)
—Jingle Bells (Horse Diaries Special Edition) Sanderson, Ruth, illus. (p. 918)
—Love on Cue. (p. 1060)
—Meet the Buddies! Lyon, Tammie, illus. (p. 1122)
—Mermaids in the Backyard. Madrid, Erwin & Castelao, Patricia, illus. (p. 1128)
—Moonlight Mile. (p. 1172)
—New Home for Truman. Regan, Dana, illus. (p. 1245)
—New Pony. (p. 1246)
—New Pony. Kennedy, Anne, illus. (p. 1246)
—No Time for Hallie. Regan, Dana, illus. (p. 1260)
—One Big Blue Family. (p. 1294)
—Over the Top. (p. 1314)
—Plants vs. Zombies: Save Your Brains! (p. 1370)
—Plants vs. Zombies. (p. 1370)
—Pony Crazy. Kennedy, Anne, illus. (p. 1382)
—Pony Party. (p. 1382)
—Pony Scouts: The Camping Trip. (p. 1383)
—Pony Scouts - Pony Party. Kennedy, Anne, illus. (p. 1383)
—Pony Scouts: the Camping Trip. Kennedy, Anne, illus. (p. 1383)
—Pony Scouts - The Camping Trip. Kennedy, Anne, illus. (p. 1383)
—Really Riding! Kennedy, Anne, illus. (p. 1450)
—Rio: Blu & Friends. (p. 1473)
—Rio 2: Vacation in the Wild. (p. 1473)
—Rio - Learning to Fly. (p. 1473)
—Roaring In. (p. 1478)
—Runaway Ponies! (p. 1496)
—Runaway Ponies! Kennedy, Anne, illus. (p. 1496)
—Sofia the First: Our Mother's Day Surprise. (p. 1605)
—Something Borrowed. (p. 1609)
—Together We Can Do It. (p. 1762)
—Trail Ride. Kennedy, Anne, illus. (p. 1776)
—Twelve Dates of Christmas. (p. 1800)
—Vacation in the Wild. (p. 1830)
—Walking with Dinosaurs: The Winter Ground. (p. 1854)
—Walking with Dinosaurs: the Winter Ground. (p. 1854)
—Winning Gift. (p. 1937)
—Yatimah. Sanderson, Ruth, illus. (p. 1968)
Hapka, Catherine, pseud & Bloomberg, Georgina. A Circuit. (p. 1)
—My Favorite Mistake: An a Circuit Novel. (p. 1203)
—Off Course. (p. 1279)
Hapka, Catherine, pseud & Disney Book Group Staff. Amulet & the Anthem. Disney Storybook Art Team, illus. (p. 66)
—Holiday in Enchancia. Disney Storybook Art Team, illus. (p. 788)
—Pooh's Secret Garden. Disney Storybook Art Team, illus. (p. 1383)
—Sofia the First Princesses to the Rescue! Purchase Includes a Digital Song! Disney Storybook Artists Staff & Lee, Grace, illus. (p. 1605)
—Sofia the First the Floating Palace. Lee, Grace, illus. (p. 1605)
—Sweet Dreams, Roo. Disney Storybook Art Team, illus. (p. 1689)
Hapka, Catherine, pseud & Echols, Jennifer. Winter's Kiss: The Ex Games - The Twelve Dates of Christmas. (p. 1938)
Hapka, Catherine, pseud & Hapka, Cathy. Elska. Griffin-Scott, Janet & Sanderson, Ruth, illus. (p. 516)
Hapka, Catherine, pseud & Rey, H. A. Curious George's Dinosaur Discovery. Hines, Anna Grossnickle, illus. (p. 394)
Hapka, Catherine, pseud, et al. Dinosaur Discovery Hines, Anna Grossnickle, illus. (p. 442)
Hapka, Cathy, jt. auth. see Disney Book Group Staff.
Hapka, Cathy, jt. auth. see Hapka, Catherine, pseud.
Hapka, Cathy, jt. auth. see Scholastic, Inc. Staff.
Hapka, Cathy, see Hapka, Catherine, pseud.
Hapka, Cathy, pseud. Dancing. (p. 402)
—Dawn of the Dead. (p. 411)
—Echo's Lucky Charm. Hibbert, Hollie, illus. (p. 502)
—Giving Thanks. Byrne, Mike, illus. (p. 681)
—Halloween Visitor. (p. 739)
—Jungle Adventure. (p. 935)
—LEGO Friends: Mystery in the Whispering Woods (Chapter Book #3) (p. 990)
—Lights, Camera, Girl Power! (p. 1016)
—My Little Doctor Bag Book. Sharp, Paul, illus. (p. 1212)
—My Sparkle Purse. (p. 1219)
—Mystery in the Whispering Woods. (p. 1224)
—Pardon My French. (p. 1324)
—Picture Me Christmas Princess. Hill, Heather C. & Roush, April, illus. (p. 1355)
—Picture Me to the Rescue. Roush, April, illus. (p. 1355)
—Pretend & Play Kitty: With Real Crown You Can Wear! Borlasca, Hector, illus. (p. 1398)
—Royal Games. (p. 1492)
—Sparkle Purse. Schwaner, Lynne, illus. (p. 1622)
Hapka, Cathy, pseud, adapted by. Fantastic 4: The Movie Storybook. (p. 571)
Hapka, Cathy, pseud & Disney Book Group Staff. Pooh's Easter Basket. Disney Storybook Art Team, illus. (p. 1383)
—Sofia Makes a Friend. Disney Storybook Artists Staff, illus. (p. 1605)
Hapka, Cathy, pseud & Titlebaum, Ellen. How Not to Babysit Your Brother. Palen, Debbie, illus. (p. 811)
—How Not to Start Third Grade. Palen, Debbie, illus. (p. 811)
Hapka, Cathy, pseud, et al. Pooh's Halloween Pumpkin. Disney Storybook Artists Staff, illus. (p. 1383)
—Royal Slumber Party. Disney Storybook Art Team, illus. (p. 1492)
Happel, Kathleen. Smartest Kid I Ever Met. Behles, Liza, illus. (p. 1593)
Happel, Roberta L. Lynd. (p. 1066)
Happel, Sally, illus. see Golden, Robert Charles.
Happel-Holtz, Ruby H. Kool Kat Charlie of Cocoa Beach. (p. 967)
Happpy Books. Day at the Farm. (p. 412)
Happy Books. Day at the Circus. (p. 412)
—Little Butterfly. (p. 1025)
—Little Frog. (p. 1028)
—Little Ladybug. (p. 1030)
Happy Books, creator. Bunny's Egg Hunt. (p. 242)
Happy, I. M. Thoughts & Feelings. (p. 1740)
Haptie, Charlotte. Daring Rescue. (p. 407)
—Otto & the Bird Charmers: The Second Book of the Karmidee. (p. 1307)
—Otto & the Flying Twins. (p. 1307)
Haqq, Shahada Sharelle Abdul. Noble Women of Faith: Asiya, Mary, Khadija, Fatima. (p. 1262)
Haque, Jameel, jt. auth. see Kwek, Karen.
Haque, Mary Baca. Madalynn the Monarch Butterfly & Her Quest to Michoacan. Jones, Francisco Lancaster, tr. from ENG. (p. 1069)
Hara, Masahiro. Toco & the Rabbit Jack. Yanai, Tetsuo, tr. (p. 1760)
Harada, Shotaro. Na Na Na Na (p. 1227)
Harary, Keith. Owls of the Enchanted Forest. Gonina, Luba, illus. (p. 1315)
—Owls of the Enchanted Forest - 2007 Special Collector's Edition. Gonina, Luba, illus. (p. 1315)
Harasimowicz, Ellen, illus. see Burns, Loree Griffin.
Harasimowicz, Ellen, photos by see Burns, Loree Griffin.
Harasymiw, M. Alexander. British Colonies. (p. 229)

H

—Pararescuemen. (p. 1324)
Harasymiw, Malcolm J. Dwight Howard: Emerging Basketball Superstar. (p. 491)
Harasymiw, Mark. Alligators Are Not Pets! (p. 47)
—Army. (p. 100)
—Bird Watcher's Guide to Chickadees. (p. 190)
—Bizarre Life Cycle of A Salmon. (p. 194)
—Chasing a Tornado. (p. 294)
—Extreme Jobs in Extreme Places: Life on a Submarine. (p. 556)
—Heroes of the US Navy. (p. 773)
—Mapping South America. (p. 1090)
—Military Helicopters. (p. 1143)
—Rangers. (p. 1438)
Harasymiw, Mark & Harasymiw, Mark J. Alligators Are Not Pets! (p. 47)
—Mapping South America. (p. 1090)
Harasymiw, Mark & Harasymiw, Therese. Native Americans in Early America. (p. 1234)
Harasymiw, Mark J. Be an Archaeologist. (p. 148)
—Legend of Rip Van Winkle. (p. 988)
—Termites. (p. 1721)
Harasymiw, Mark J., jt. auth. see Harasymiw, Mark.
Harasymiw, N. D. Condors in Danger. (p. 356)
Harasymiw, R. Mann. Problem Solving with Pigs. (p. 1408)
Harasymiw, R. P. Cheetahs. (p. 296)
Harasymiw, R. P., jt. auth. see Harasymiw, Raymond.
Harasymiw, Raymond & Harasymiw, R. P. Problem Solving with Pigs. (p. 1408)
Harasymiw, Roman. Devils Tower. (p. 432)
Harasymiw, Teppo. Customs & Celebrations Across America. (p. 395)
Harasymiw, Therese. Causes & Effects of the Texas Revolution. (p. 282)
—Graph It! (p. 710)
—Hedgehogs in the Dark. (p. 762)
—How Do I Use a Library? (p. 807)
—Life in a Colonial City. (p. 1010)
—Louisiana Purchase. (p. 1058)
—Making Venn Diagrams. (p. 1082)
—Meerkats. (p. 1120)
—Ostriches. (p. 1306)
—World Holidays. (p. 1955)
Harasymiw, Therese, jt. auth. see Harasymiw, Mark.
Harat, Christopher. Draw Manga. (p. 481)
Harazin, S. A. Painless. (p. 1318)
Harbeke, Dan. Get In! How to Market Yourself & Become Successful at a Young Age. (p. 667)
Harber, Chris. Simon the Policeman on Safari - Claude the Camel. Harber, Hulya, illus. (p. 1577)
—Simon the Policeman on the Number Planet. Harber, Hulya, illus. (p. 1577)
Harber Freeman, Anna. Love You More Than Anything. Henry, Jed, illus. (p. 1060)
Harber, Hulya, illus. see Harber, Chris.
Harberts, Bernie. Woody & Maggie Walk Across America. (p. 1950)
Harbison, Lawrence, ed. 2007: The Best Ten-Minute Plays for Two Actors. (p. 2003)
—2007: The Best Ten-Minute Plays for Three or More Actors. (p. 2003)
Harbison, Paige. New Girl. (p. 1244)
Harbo, Christopher. Flip-Side Nursery Rhymes. Jack, Colin & Chatzikonstantinou, Danny, illus. (p. 605)
—Origami Paperpalooza. (p. 1304)
Harbo, Christopher L. Bill Gates (p. 186)
—Co-Pilot, Level 2. (p. 336)
—Easy Animal Origami. (p. 500)
—Easy Holiday Origami (p. 500)
—Easy Magician Origami (p. 500)
—Easy Ocean Origami (p. 500)
—Easy Origami. (p. 500)
—Easy Origami. (p. 500)
—Easy Origami Toys (p. 500)
—Easy Space Origami (p. 500)
—Explosive World of Volcanoes with Max Axiom, Super Scientist Smith, Tod, illus. (p. 554)
—Frankenstein's Monster & Scientific Methods Aón, Carlos, illus. (p. 629)
—Frankenstein's Monster & Scientific Methods. An, Carlos, illus. (p. 629)
—Humpty Dumpty Flip-Side Rhymes. Chatzikonstantinou, Danny, illus. (p. 827)
—Jack & Jill Flip-Side Rhymes. Jack, Colin, illus. (p. 902)
—Kids' Guide to Paper Airplanes. (p. 953)
—Little Bo Peep Flip-Side Rhymes. Chatzikonstantinou, Danny, illus. (p. 1025)
—Little Miss Muffet Flip-Side Rhymes. Jack, Colin, illus. (p. 1032)
—Monster Science. An, Carlos, illus. (p. 1168)
—Monster Science. Aón, Carlos, illus. (p. 1168)
—Mundo Explosivo de los Volcanes con Max Axiom, Supercientífico. Strictly Spanish, LLC., tr. (p. 1191)
—My First Guide to Paper Airplanes. (p. 1206)
—Origami Explosion: Scorpions, Whales, Boxes, & More! (p. 1304)
—Origami Folding Frenzy: Boats, Fish, Cranes, & More! (p. 1304)
—Origami Palooza: Dragons, Turtles, Birds, & More! (p. 1304)
—Origami Paperpalooza! (p. 1304)
—Origami Papertainment: Samurai, Owls, Ninja Stars, & More! (p. 1304)
—Paper Airplanes, Captain Level 4 (p. 1322)
—Paper Airplanes, Flight School Level 1 (p. 1322)
—Pilot, Level 3. (p. 1359)
—Shapes. Banks, Timothy, illus. (p. 1560)
—Ultimate Guide to Paper Airplanes: 35 Amazing Step-by-Step Designs! (p. 1809)
Harbo, Christopher L., jt. auth. see Barnhill, Kelly Regan.
Harbo, Christopher L., et al. Business Leaders (p. 245)
—Secrets of Martial Arts: An Isabel Soto History Adventure. (p. 1545)
Harbo, Gary. Northern Woods Adventure: Early Reader. Harbo, Gary, illus. (p. 1266)
—Northern Woods Adventure: Advanced Reader Harbo, Gary, illus. (p. 1266)
—Where Is My Sister? (p. 1909)
Harbor, Missy. Susan of Bluebonnet Hill (p. 1688)
Harbou, Thea Von, see von Harbou, Thea & Von Harbou, Thea.
Harbour, Elizabeth, illus. see Shields, Gillian.
Harbour, Jonathan, jt. auth. see Sethi, Maneesh.
Harbourt, Kathi. Adventures of Kat VanDrat. (p. 19)
Harbridge, Paul. Helena's Voyage: A Mystic Adventure. (p. 763)
Harburg, E. Y. Over the Rainbow. Noonan, Julia, illus. (p. 1314)
Harburg, E. Y. & Arlen, Harold. Over the Rainbow. Noonan, Julia, illus. (p. 1314)
Harby, Melanie. All Aboard for Dreamland! Valerio, Geraldo, illus. (p. 42)
Harchy, Atelier Philippe. Chicken Little: A Tale about Common Sense. (p. 300)
Harchy, Atelier Philippe, illus. see Arps, Melissa & Lagonegro, Melissa.
Harchy, Atelier Philippe, illus. see Golden Books Staff.
Harchy, Atelier Philippe, illus. see Lagonegro, Melissa & RH Disney Staff.
Harchy, Atelier Philippe, illus. see Marsoli, Lisa Ann.
Harchy, Atelier Philippe, illus. see Parent, Nancy.
Harchy, Atelier Philippe, illus. see Weinberg, Jennifer Liberts & RH Disney Staff.
Harcourt Achieve, creator. Avenues. (p. 119)
—Images. (p. 860)
—People. (p. 1339)
—Top Line Math: Data, Tables & Graphs. (p. 1769)
—Windows. (p. 1936)
Harcourt Brace Staff. Astro Algebra: Grades 6-8 Net Version Software Package. (p. 109)
Harcourt, creator. Achieve Arizona Mathematics 5. (p. 8)
—I Know Big & Small: Math Concept Reader. (p. 840)
—I Know Numbers: Math Concept Reader. (p. 840)
—I Know Shapes: Math Concept Reader. (p. 840)
—Summertime Math: Math Concept Reader. (p. 1675)
Harcourt, Inc Staff, jt. auth. see Clark, Diane C.
Harcourt, Lalie & Wortzman, Rickie. Red Riding Hood's Math Adventure. Mazille, Capucine, illus. (p. 1455)
Harcourt, Mike, jt. auth. see Warren, Steph.
Harcourt School Publishers, creator. Earth's Changing Crust: Lessons 3-5. (p. 498)
—Ecosystems: Lessons 3-4. (p. 503)
—Energy Transfer & Weather: Lessons 2-3. (p. 528)
—Human Body. (p. 825)
—Invisible Pull: Electricity & Magnets. (p. 886)
—Matter Matters! (p. 1109)
—Professional Development for Math: Fraction Operations, Grades 3-6. (p. 1409)
Harcourt School Publishers Staff. 1st Place Reading: Title 1 Program Kit. (p. 1991)
—All about People (p. 43)
—All the People (p. 46)
—Alphabet Construction. (p. 49)
—Art. (p. 101)
—Art Big Book. (p. 101)
—Art Everywhere: Artist's Workshop Activities. (p. 102)
—Art, Grade 1: Teacher Resource Book. (p. 102)
—Art, Grade 1. (p. 102)
—Art, Grade 2. (p. 102)
—Art, Grade 3. (p. 102)
—Art, Grade 4: Teacher Resource Book. (p. 102)
—Art, Grade 4. (p. 102)
—Art, Grade 5. (p. 102)
—Assessment & Information Instruction, Grades K-6: Professional Development in Reading - Participant's Guide. (p. 107)
—Assessment & Information Instructions, Grades K-6: Professional Development for Reading: Guide to Video. (p. 107)
—Assessment Guide Harcourt. (p. 107)
—At Home with the Family (p. 110)
—Banner Days Level 2-2. (p. 136)
—Be Active! Movement Flipchart. (p. 148)
—Be Active! Strength Flipchart. (p. 148)
—Be Active! Flexibility Flipchart. (p. 148)
—Be Active! Cardiovascular Flipchart. (p. 148)
—Be Active! Instant Activity Cards Collection. (p. 148)
—Be Active!, Grade 3-6: Resource Binder Tabs. (p. 148)
—Be Active!, Grade K-2: Resource Binder Tabs. (p. 148)
—Be Active! Program: Health & Fitness. (p. 148)
—Beginnings 1877. (p. 160)
—Beginnings 2005. (p. 160)
—Being a Citizen (p. 160)
—Big Book Art 2006 - Grade 1. (p. 178)
—Big Book of Rhymes. (p. 179)
—Catch a Dream Level 1-2. (p. 279)
—Changing Patterns Level 3-1. (p. 290)
—Collections: Phonics Activity Book. (p. 340)
—Decodable Book (p. 422)
—Decoding & Word Recognition Assessment. (p. 422)
—Distant Voyages. (p. 453)
—Esl Support Book Horizons. (p. 536)
—Family Involvement. (p. 568)
—Flower Garden Lap Book. (p. 607)
—Going Outside to Play. (p. 692)
—Going to School (p. 693)
—Going to School Big Book No. 1. (p. 693)
—Good Citizen (p. 697)
—Harcourt Ciencias: CA & National Big Book. (p. 747)
—Harcourt Ciencias, Grade 1: Grade Level Set: Texas/National Edition. (p. 747)
—Harcourt Ciencias, Grade 3: Life Science, Unit A&B (p. 747)
—Harcourt Ciencias, Grade 3: Earth Science. Unit C&D (p. 747)
—Harcourt Ciencias, Grade 3: Physical Science. Unit E&F (p. 747)
—Harcourt Language: Vocabulary Power. (p. 747)
—Harcourt Language Arts: Standardized Test Preparation. (p. 747)
—Harcourt Matematicas: Resource Package. (p. 747)
—Harcourt Matematicas: Practice Workbook. (p. 747)
—Harcourt Matematicas: Challenge Workbook. (p. 747)
—Harcourt Matematicas: Reteaching Workbook. (p. 747)
—Harcourt Matematicas: Answer Key/Enrichment Book. (p. 747)
—Harcourt Matematicas: Checklist for Knowledge Enrichment. (p. 747)
—Harcourt Matematicas: Checklist for Knowledge Enrichment. (p. 747)
—Harcourt Matematicas: CA & National Family Involvement Activities. (p. 747)
—Harcourt Matematicas: Problem Solving & Reading Strategies Workbook. (p. 747)
—Harcourt Matematicas, Grade 1: Assessment Guide. (p. 747)
—Harcourt Matematicas, Grade 1: Challenge Workbook. (p. 747)
—Harcourt Matematicas, Grade 1: Reteaching Workbook. (p. 747)
—Harcourt Matematicas, Grade 1: Teacher's Resource Book. (p. 747)
—Harcourt Matematicas, Grade 1. (p. 747)
—Harcourt Matematicas, Grade 3: Practice Workbook. (p. 747)
—Harcourt Matematicas, Grade 3: Problem Solving & Reading Strategies Workbook. (p. 747)
—Harcourt Matematicas, Grade K: Assessmetn Guide. (p. 747)
—Harcourt Matemáticas Práctica. (p. 747)
—Harcourt Math: Practice Workbook. (p. 747)
—Harcourt Math: MEAP Resource Book. (p. 747)
—Harcourt Math: Eresource 1 Year Access. (p. 747)
—Harcourt Math. (p. 747)
—Harcourt Math Collection, Grade 1 (p. 747)
—Harcourt Math Collection, Grade 6 (p. 748)
—Harcourt Math, Grade 1. (p. 748)
—Harcourt Math, Grade K Vol. 2. (p. 748)
—Harcourt Physical Education Posters, Grades 3-6. (p. 748)
—Harcourt School Publishers Art Everywhere. (p. 748)
—Harcourt School Publishers Horizons: Us History 2003. Vol. 1 (p. 748)
—Harcourt School Publishers Matematicas. (p. 748)
—Harcourt School Publishers Science California: Lab Manual Student Edition Science 08 Grade 4. (p. 748)
—Harcourt Science: Standard Test Preparation. (p. 748)
—Harcourt Science: Earth Instant Reader CD-ROM Teacher's Guide. (p. 748)
—Harcourt Science: Physical Science Instant Reader CD-ROM Teacher's Guide. (p. 748)
—Harcourt Science. (p. 748)
—Harcourt Trophies. (p. 748)
—Health & Fitness: Activity Book. (p. 757)
—Health & Fitness: Resources for Spanish Speakers. (p. 757)
—Health & Fitness 5-Pack: Activity Book. (p. 757)
—Health & Fitness, Grade 3-6. (p. 757)
—Here & There 2003 Level 1-3. (p. 770)
—Herman the Helper Lap Book. (p. 771)
—Horizons: US History. (p. 797)
—Horizons: Texas Edition. (p. 797)
—Horizons: Indiana Edition. (p. 797)
—Horizons: States & Regions. (p. 797)
—Horizons: Assessment Program. (p. 797)
—Horizons: "All About Me" Unit. (p. 797)
—Horizons: World Regions. Bk. 2 (p. 797)
—Horizons: North Carolina Edition. (p. 797)
—Horizons: Time for Kids Readers: US History. (p. 797)
—Horizons. (p. 797)
—Horizons 2003: States & Regions. Vol. 1 (p. 797)
—Horizons Big Book. (p. 797)
—Horizons Big Book Collection Unit 1. (p. 797)
—Horizons Big Book Collection Unit 2. (p. 797)
—Horizons Big Book Collection Unit 3. (p. 797)
—Horizons Big Book Collection Unit 4. (p. 797)
—Horizons Big Book Collection Unit 5. (p. 797)
—Horizons Big Book Collection Unit 6. (p. 797)
—Horizons Big Book Collection. (p. 797)
—Horizons ESL Summary. (p. 797)
—Horizons ESL Summary with Ancient Civilizations. (p. 798)
—Horizons, Grade 1: Time for Kids Readers. (p. 798)
—Horizons, Grade 1. (p. 798)
—Horizons, Grade 2: Time for Kids Readers. (p. 798)
—Horizons, Grade 3. (p. 798)
—Horizons, Grade K: Time for Kids Readers. (p. 798)
—Horizons, Grade K. (p. 798)
—Horizons with Ancient Civilizations. (p. 798)
—Horizons with Ancient Civilizations, Grade 3. (p. 798)
—Horizontes: Big Book. (p. 798)
—Horizontes: US History. (p. 798)
—Horizontes: World Regions. (p. 798)
—Horizontes: States & Regions. (p. 798)
—Horizontes: Unit Big Book Collection. (p. 798)
—Horizontes. (p. 798)
—Horizontes, Grade 1. (p. 798)
—Horizontes, Grade 2. (p. 798)
—Horizontes, Grade 3. (p. 798)
—Horizontes, Grade 4: States & Regions. (p. 798)
—How the Sky Got Its Starr. (p. 813)
—In & Around the Land (p. 863)
—Jobs People Do. (p. 919)
—Just for You Level 2-1. (p. 938)
—Land Around (p. 973)
—Leaders for Peace. (p. 981)
—Learn about People (p. 982)
—Learn about the People No. 4. (p. 982)
—Lets Visit Museum, Above Level Reader Grade K: Harcourt School Publishers Social Studies. (p. 1001)
—Library Package. (p. 1006)
—Little Quack Lap Book. (p. 1034)
—Little Red Hen Lap Book. (p. 1035)
—Little Red Hen Library Book Grade K: Harcourt School Publishers Storytown. (p. 1035)
—Living in a Community (p. 1041)
—Living in the Community (p. 1041)
—Looking at the Earth (p. 1051)
—Looking at the Earth Big Book No. 3. (p. 1051)
—Looking Back (p. 1051)
—Looking Back Big Book No. 5. (p. 1051)
—Matemáticas. (p. 1104)
—Matematicas 2005 (p. 1104)
—Math 2004: National Teachers Edition. Vol. 3 (p. 1105)
—Math Program Development, Grades 3-6: Fraction Concepts Binder Package. (p. 1107)
—Math Program Development, Grades K-2: Number Sense Binder Package. (p. 1107)
—Mathematicas. (p. 1107)
—Months of School. (p. 1170)
—Moving into English. (p. 1183)
—Moving into English Big Books: Leveled Library Collection. (p. 1183)
—Moving into English, Grade 2. (p. 1183)
—Moving into English Teacher's Kit, Grade 1. (p. 1183)
—My Heros (p. 1211)
—My World (p. 1221)
—On Your Mark Level 3-2. (p. 1292)
—Oral Reading Fluency Assessment. (p. 1301)
—Our Government. (p. 1309)
—Past & Present (p. 1327)
—Past & Present Big Book No. 5. (p. 1327)
—People & Work Big Book No. 6. (p. 1339)
—People at Work (p. 1339)
—People in History (p. 1339)
—People in Time (p. 1339)
—Problem Solving. (p. 1408)
—School Days (p. 1522)
—Social Studies: Stories in Time: Library Book Collection. (p. 1604)
—Social Studies: States & Regions: Library Book Collection. (p. 1604)
—Social Studies, Grade 5: United States. (p. 1604)
—Social Studies Library. (p. 1604)
—Standardized Test Preparation Grade1 2002. (p. 1639)
—Teacher's Edition Package: Texas Edition. (p. 1709)
—Test Best MCT Reading (p. 1723)
—TIME for Kids: World Regions. (p. 1751)
—TIME for Kids: World Region Bk. 11 (p. 1751)
—TIME for Kids. (p. 1751)
—TIME for Kids 5 Pack. (p. 1751)
—Time/Kids (p. 1754)
—Timefor Kids (p. 1754)
—Timeless Treasure. (p. 1754)
—Trophies Theme 1 (p. 1788)
—Trophies Theme 2 (p. 1788)
—Trophies Theme 3 (p. 1788)
—Trophies Theme 4 (p. 1788)
—Trophies Theme 5 (p. 1788)
—Trophies Theme 6 (p. 1788)
—Trophies: Lead the Way. (p. 1788)
—Trophies: Stories & More. (p. 1788)
—Trophies: Distant Voyages. (p. 1788)
—Trophies: Mr. Putter & Tabby (p. 1788)
—Trophies Theme 1, Level 2-1. (p. 1788)
—Trophies Theme 1, Level 2-2. (p. 1788)
—Trophies Theme 2, Level 3-1. (p. 1788)
—Trophies Theme 2, Level 3-2. (p. 1788)
—Trophies Theme 3, Level 3-1. (p. 1788)
—Trophies: Timeless Treasures. (p. 1788)
—Trophies: Guess Who. Level 1-1 (p. 1788)
—Trophies: Banner Days. Level 2-2 (p. 1788)
—Trophies: Here & There. Level 1-3 (p. 1788)
—Trophies: Just for You. Level 2-1 (p. 1788)
—Trophies: On Your Mark. Level 3-2 (p. 1788)
—Trophies: Time Together. Level 1-4 (p. 1788)
—Trophies: Gather Around. Level 1-5 (p. 1788)
—Trophies: Catch the Dream. Level 1-2 (p. 1788)
—Trophies: Changing Patterns. Level 3-1 (p. 1788)
—Trophies. (p. 1788)
—Trophies Collection. (p. 1788)
—Trophies, Grade 1: Teacher Bag. (p. 1788)
—Trophies, Grade 1: Here & There. Level 1-3 (p. 1788)
—Trophies, Grade 1: Time Together. Level 1-4 (p. 1788)
—Trophies, Grade 1: Gather Around. Level 1-5 (p. 1788)
—Trophies, Grade 1-5: Dry-Erase Board. (p. 1788)
—Trophies, Grade 2: Teacher Bag. (p. 1788)
—Trophies, Grade 2 Theme 2, Level 2-1. (p. 1789)
—Trophies, Grade 2 Theme 2, Level 2-2. (p. 1789)
—Trophies, Grade 2 Theme 3, Level 2-1. (p. 1789)
—Trophies, Grade 2 Theme 3, Level 2-2. (p. 1789)
—Trophies, Grade 3: Teacher Bag. (p. 1789)
—Trophies, Grade 3 Theme 1, Level 3-1. (p. 1789)
—Trophies, Grade 3 Theme 1, Level 3-2. (p. 1789)
—Trophies, Grade 3 Theme 3, Level 3-2. (p. 1789)
—Trophies, Grade 4 Theme 2. (p. 1789)
—Trophies, Grade 4 Theme 3. (p. 1789)
—Trophies, Grade 4 Theme 4. (p. 1789)
—Trophies, Grade 4 Theme 5. (p. 1789)
—Trophies, Grade 4 Theme 6. (p. 1789)
—Trophies, Grade 4: Teacher Bag. (p. 1789)
—Trophies, Grade 5 Theme 1. (p. 1789)
—Trophies, Grade 5 Theme 2. (p. 1789)
—Trophies, Grade 5 Theme 3. (p. 1789)
—Trophies, Grade 5 Theme 4. (p. 1789)
—Trophies, Grade 5 Theme 5. (p. 1789)
—Trophies, Grade 5 Theme 6. (p. 1789)
—Trophies, Grade 5: Teacher Bag. (p. 1789)
—Trophies, Grade 6 Theme 1. (p. 1789)
—Trophies, Grade 6 Theme 2. (p. 1789)
—Trophies, Grade 6 Theme 3. (p. 1789)
—Trophies, Grade 6 Theme 4. (p. 1789)
—Trophies, Grade 6 Theme 5. (p. 1789)
—Trophies, Grade 6 Theme 6. (p. 1789)
—Trophies, Grade 6: Teacher Bag. (p. 1789)
—Trophies, Grade K Theme 1-4. (p. 1789)
—Trophies, Grade K Theme 5-8. (p. 1789)
—Trophies, Grade K Theme 9-12. (p. 1789)
—Trophies, Grade K: Teacher Bag. (p. 1789)
—Trophies Reading Program: Nursery Rhymes Anthology. (p. 1789)
—Trophies Reading Program, Grade K. (p. 1789)
—U. S. History. (p. 1806)
—United States History 2003 (p. 1819)
—United States History Beginnings (p. 1819)
—United States History Civil War to Present. (p. 1819)

Full bibliographic information is available on the Title Index page number referenced in parentheses at the end of each entry

—US History: The Civil War to the Present (p. 1826)
—US History. (p. 1826)
—US History - Beginning to the Civil War. (p. 1826)
—US History - Civil War to the Present. (p. 1826)
—US History, Grade 5: Beginnings. Vol. 2 (p. 1826)
—Watch This! Level 1-5 Grade 1: Harcourt School Publishers Storytown Florida. (p. 1861)
—We Belong in Groups (p. 1866)
—We Work Together (p. 1869)
—When Storm Library Book Grade K: Harcourt School Publishers Storytown. (p. 1904)
—Where We Live (p. 1910)
—World History (p. 1955)
—World History: States & Regions. (p. 1955)
—World History: Time for Kids Reader 5-Pack (p. 1955)
—World History: The Civil War to the Present. (p. 1955)
—World History, Grade 4: States & Regions. Vol. 2 (p. 1955)
—World Regions. (p. 1958)
—World Regions Horizon. (p. 1958)
—Writing Express Espanol, Grade 1. (p. 1964)
—Writing Express, Grade 6. (p. 1964)
—Your Health. (p. 1980)
—Your Health Reader: The Doctor. (p. 1980)
—Your Health Reader: The Dentist. (p. 1980)
—Your Health Reader: The Morning. (p. 1980)
—Zoo Zillions: User's Guide. (p. 1989)
Harcrow, Melissa. Where're Your Manners, William? (p. 1910)
Hardaway, Francine. Foster Mom: A Journey of Self-Discovery. (p. 624)
Hardcastle, Henry. Explorer: A Daring Guide for Young Adventurers. Steer, Dugald A., ed. (p. 551)
Hardcastle, Michael. Hit It! Moulder, Bob, illus. (p. 785)
—My Brother's a Keeper Moulder, Bob, illus. (p. 1199)
Hardcastle, Nick, illus. see Calhoun, Marmaduke Randolph.
Hardcastle, Nick, illus. see O'Brien, Johnny.
Hardegree, Maureen. Haint Misbehavin' (p. 735)
—Haint She Sweet. (p. 735)
—Hainted Love. (p. 735)
Harden, Mark E. Bug in the Big White Forest. (p. 236)
Harden, Pamela. Abc's from the Whippety Wood: The Magic in Nature. (p. 4)
Harden, Perry Lee. Percy Hargrove Stories: It's All Elementary. (p. 1341)
Harder, Christopher. It's Tough to Nap on a Turtle. Harder, Rolf, illus. (p. 899)
Harder, Eleanor. What'd Ya Do Today, Billy Joe? (p. 1896)
Harder, Linda Janet. Kittens in the Classroom. (p. 963)
Harder, Rolf, illus. see Harder, Christopher.
Harder Tangvald, Christine. Someone I Love Died. (p. 1609)
—Thank You, God, for My Two Hands. (p. 1725)
Hardesty, Ann A. Lucy's Trials in the Black Hills. (p. 1063)
Hardesty, Constance. Teen-Centered Writing Club: Bringing Teens & Words Together (p. 1713)
Hardesty, Michael. Who Made the Sun, Mommy? (p. 1916)
Hardesty, Von. Flight. (p. 604)
Hardge, A. Terrence. Bobby's Big Birthday Bash. (p. 206)
Hardgrave, Gayle. Daniel Goes to Pre-K. (p. 405)
Hardgraves, Dalon. Little Boy Named U. (p. 1025)
Hardie, Chris, illus. see Kahn, doc, Robert.
Hardie Grant Books. Kooky 3D Kids' Cookbook. (p. 967)
Hardie Grant Books Staff. I Heart One Direction Journal - 100% Unofficial. (p. 839)
Hardie Grant Books Staff & Sticker Family Staff. For You, Dad: The Sticker Family. (p. 616)
Hardie, Jill. Sparkle Box: The Story of a Very Special Christmas Gift. Kornacki, Christine, illus. (p. 1622)
—Sparkle Egg. Kornacki, Christine, illus. (p. 1622)
Hardie, Kerry. Bird Woman. (p. 190)
—Winter Marriage: A Novel. (p. 1938)
Hardie, Richard. Leap of Faith. (p. 982)
Hardie, Samantha. Samantha's Oracle: A Fortune Teller for Teenage Witches. (p. 1507)
Hardiman, Richard & Speelman, Helen. In the Footsteps of Abraham: The Holy Land in Hand-Painted Photographs. (p. 866)
Hardin, Allen. Drive Like a Champ: A Safe Start to Driving Smart. (p. 485)
Hardin, Becky. Shug E Bear. (p. 1571)
Hardin, Holly. Aurora of the Northern Lights. (p. 116)
Hardin, J. R. Kalvin the Kudzu Monster. (p. 942)
Hardin, Lori. Squiggly & the Bully. (p. 1637)
Hardin, Melinda. Hero Dad Langdo, Bryan, illus. (p. 772)
—Hero Mom Langdo, Bryan, illus. (p. 772)
Hardin, Teresa, illus. see Medders, James.
Hardin, Travis. Called to Serve. (p. 254)
Harding, David. Race to the Finish. Whitby, Charlotte, illus. (p. 1431)
Harding, David & Kelly, Helen. Four Paws Collection (p. 625)
Harding, Davilla. Math Graphic Organizers 1-2: Simple & Effective Strategies for Solving Math Word Problems. Hults, Alaska, ed. (p. 1106)
Harding, James. From Wibbleton to Wobbleton: Adventures with the Elements of Music & Movement. Noyes, Eli, illus. (p. 644)
Harding, Jennie. Ellie Bean the Drama Queen: A Children's Book about Sensory Processing Disorder. Padgett, Dave, illus. (p. 514)
Harding, Kat. Lesbian Kama Sutra. (p. 993)
Harding, Keith, jt. auth. see Walker, Robin.
Harding, Lauri. Do Veterans Receive Adequate Health Care? (p. 457)
Harding, Lauri R., ed. DNA Databases. (p. 456)
Harding, Les. McCurdy & the Silver Dart (p. 1114)
Harding, Niall, illus. see Arps, Melissa & Lagonegro, Melissa.
Harding, Niall, illus. see Bak, Jenny.
Harding, Niall, illus. see Lagonegro, Melissa & RH Disney Staff.
Harding, Robert, jt. auth. see Symes, R. F.
Harding, Robyn. My Parents Are Sex Maniacs: A High School Horror Story. (p. 1216)
Harding, Samuel. Story of the Middle Ages. (p. 1661)
Harding, Samuel Bannister. Story of the Middle Ages (Yesterday's Classics) (p. 1661)
Harding, Sandra & Figueroa, Robert, eds. Science & Other Cultures. (p. 1525)
Harding, Susan. Here I Am! (p. 770)
Hardinge, Frances. Cuckoo Song. (p. 389)
—Fly by Night. (p. 609)
—Fly Trap. (p. 609)
—Lost Conspiracy. (p. 1055)
Hardison, Brian, illus. see Mitchell-Tulloss, Delores.
Hardison, Buist, illus. see Coffee, Karen Lynn.
Hardison, Buist E. 5 Little Shorties. Hardison, Buist E., illus. (p. 1992)
Hardiyono, illus. see Bunanta, Murti.
Hardman, Christy. Against the Giant. (p. 29)
Hardman, Jessica, jt. auth. see Hardman, Ron.
Hardman, John. Bush Adventure. (p. 244)
—Little Miss Daredevil. Beach, Bryan, illus. (p. 1031)
—Mr. Bump in: Lights, Camera, Bump! Britton, Matthew, illus. (p. 1184)
Hardman, Lizabeth. Baseball. (p. 140)
—History of Medicine. (p. 784)
—Plague. (p. 1366)
Hardman, Lizabeth, ed. see Greenhaven Press Editors & Craig, Lizabeth.
Hardman, Lizabeth, ed. see Mattern, Joanne.
Hardman, Lizabeth, jt. auth. see Peak, Lizabeth.
Hardman, Lizabeth, jt. auth. see Silverthorne, Elizabeth.
Hardman, Ron & Hardman, Jessica. Shadow Fox: Sons of Liberty. Barnecut, Suzanne, ed. (p. 1557)
—Shadow Fox: Sons of Liberty Teacher's Edition. Barnecutt, Suzanne, ed. (p. 1557)
Hardrick, Jackie. Imani in Never Say Goodbye. (p. 861)
Hardtke, Karen J. Honesty & Sincerity: An American Possibility. (p. 794)
Hardwell, Gary D. Boo Bears' Story: Stormy Night. (p. 209)
Hardwick, Holly, illus. see Pottle, Robert.
Hardwick, Susan. Brazil: World-Wise Kids Guides. (p. 224)
—China: World-Wise Kids Guides. (p. 306)
—Greece: World-Wise Kids Guides. (p. 720)
—Iraq: World-Wise Kids Guides. (p. 887)
Hardwick, Susan, ed. Egypt. (p. 506)
—Ireland. (p. 887)
—Mexico. (p. 1131)
Hardy, A. S. Sea Stories for Wonder Eyes. (p. 1535)
Hardy, Candace J., illus. see Wiesner, Karen Sue.
Hardy, Chris, illus. see Thompson, Yvonne.
Hardy, Cindy & Masterman, Lorrine A. Egg Island Reader (p. 506)
Hardy, Daniel J. Israeli Heat. (p. 893)
—Last Angel. (p. 977)
—Rapture 101. (p. 1439)
—Wrath of God. (p. 1962)
Hardy, Donna, jt. auth. see Coe, Jara.
Hardy, E. Stuart, illus. see Bennett, Virginia.
Hardy, Ed & Young, Jim. Pollywogs & Other Friends. Motley, Chris and Jim Young, illus. (p. 1381)
Hardy, Edward. Where Is Fred? Pye, Ali, illus. (p. 1908)
Hardy, Emelia J. Adventures of Maureen & Maury: For Children of All Ages! (p. 20)
Hardy, Emma. My First Craft Book. Akass, Susan, ed. (p. 1206)
Hardy, Emma-Rose. Vampuric Slayer Blood. (p. 1832)
Hardy, Frank, illus. see Windham, Kathryn Tucker.
Hardy, Gary D. Pj the Water Breathing Dragon: In Being Different Is a Good Thing. (p. 1365)
Hardy, Janet Norris. Four in One: The Four Gospels from the King James Version Merged into a Single Narrative. (p. 625)
Hardy, Janice. Blue Fire (p. 202)
—Darkfall. (p. 408)
—Healing Wars: Book II: Blue Fire. (p. 757)
—Shifter. (p. 1566)
Hardy, Joshua O. A B C Book on Protecting Yourself from Strangers: A-z. (p. 1)
Hardy, LeAnne. Between Two Worlds: A Novel. (p. 173)
Hardy, Lorién Trover. Firefly Summer Yilmaz, Necdet, illus. (p. 592)
Hardy, Mary Smith. Uncle Hubbard & the Burlap Sack. (p. 1811)
Hardy, Melissa. Geomancer's Compass. (p. 662)
Hardy, P. Stephen & Hardy, Sheila. Extraordinary People of the Civil Rights Movement. (p. 555)
Hardy, Pris, illus. see Jeanne Taylor Thomas Illustrator: Pr.
Hardy, Rachael. Cézanne (p. 288)
Hardy, S. F. Empress' New Hair. (p. 521)
Hardy, Sarah, jt. ed. see Wiedmer, Caroline.
Hardy, Sarah C. Silver Winged Dragon. (p. 1577)
Hardy, Sarah Frances. Paint Me! Hardy, Sarah Frances, illus. (p. 1318)
—Puzzled by Pink. (p. 1421)
Hardy, Sheila, jt. auth. see Hardy, P. Stephen.
Hardy, Sherrie. Just Say No. (p. 939)
Hardy, Thomas. Mayor of Casterbridge. (p. 1113)
—Mayor of Casterbridge Level 5 Upper-Intermediate. (p. 1113)
—Plpr4: Far from the Madding Crowd RLA. (p. 1374)
Hardy, Vincent, illus. see Petrovic, Svetlana.
Hardy, Zoey. Brockway High. (p. 230)
—Everything Changes. (p. 544)
Hardyman, Robyn. Apes & Monkeys. (p. 91)
—Bugs. (p. 237)
—Camping. (p. 257)
—Celebrate: China. (p. 283)
—Celebrate: India. (p. 283)
—Celebrate: Italy. (p. 283)
—Celebrate: Japan. (p. 283)
—Celebrate: France. (p. 283)
—Celebrate: Mexico. (p. 283)
—Celebrate: Germany. (p. 283)
—Celebrate: United States. (p. 283)
—Celebrate! Set, 8-Volumes. (p. 284)
—Dolphins. (p. 464)
—Eating Well. (p. 501)
—Fighting Malaria. (p. 585)
—Fighting the Flu. (p. 586)
—Fishing. (p. 599)
—Healthy Bodies. (p. 758)
—How a Solar-Powered Home Works. (p. 804)
—Hunting. (p. 829)
—Kayaking & Canoeing. (p. 946)
—Nikola Tesla & Thomas Edison. (p. 1255)
—Pierre & Marie Curie. (p. 1357)
—Race to Control the Population. (p. 1431)
—Race to End Epidemics. (p. 1431)
—Relationships. (p. 1457)
—Safe & Healthy. (p. 1502)
—Snow & Blizzards. (p. 1598)
—Whales. (p. 1877)
—Wind & Storms. (p. 1935)
Hardyment, Christina. Arthur Ransome & Captain Flint's Trunk. (p. 104)
Hare, Christopher. Bayard the Good Knight Without Fear & Without Reproach. (p. 147)
Hare, Eric B. Clever Queen. (p. 331)
—Curse Proof. (p. 395)
—Dr. Rabbit. Bohlmann, Siegfried, illus. (p. 475)
—Jungle Heroes & Other Stories. (p. 935)
—Skyscrapers: 365 Stories That Build You up: Daily Devotions for Juniors. (p. 1587)
Hare, John, illus. see McVicker, Maryellen.
Hare, John, illus. see Offutt, Jason.
Hare, John, illus. see Olson, Greg.
Hare, John, illus. see Russell, Greta.
Hare, Mary Alyce, illus. see Crosby, Sarah.
Hare, Mimi & Naylor, Clare. First Assistant: A Continuing Tale from Behind the Hollywood Curtain. (p. 593)
Hare, Ralph. Geography in the School Grounds. Lye, Michael, illus. (p. 662)
Hare, Tony. Capa de Ozono. (p. 262)
—Polucion de los Mares. (p. 1381)
—Residuos Toxicos (Toxic Residues) (p. 1463)
Harea, Maria. Who Does That? Jobs in Your Community. (p. 1915)
Hareas, John. NBA Slam Dunk 3-D. (p. 1238)
Hareas, John & Smallwood, John. Steve Nash. (p. 1649)
Harel, Moshe. Elf Prince. (p. 512)
Harel, Nirah. Lev Katan Gadol: Sipuro Shel Hertsl. (p. 1003)
Harelkin, Mary. Tunnels of Treachery (p. 1797)
Harewood, Sean C. It's Only the First Day. (p. 898)
Harfey, Alfred D., Jr. How to Develop Your Heavenly Prayer Language: Five Steps to a Better Understanding of Praying in the Spirit. (p. 816)
Harff, David. Mouse Mayhem (p. 1182)
Hargens, Charles, illus. see Garst, Shannon.
Harger, Teresa. Nicky & the Princess. (p. 1251)
Hargett, Paul R. Me & My Bass Guitar: The Life & Music of Victor Lemonte Wooten. (p. 1115)
Hargis, Alvin. Kingdom of Mystique Series: Book 1. (p. 959)
Hargis, Wes, illus. see Koehler-Pentacoff, Elizabeth.
Hargis, Wes, illus. see Walton, Rick & Kraus, Franz.
Hargis, Wes, illus. see Walton, Rick.
Hargis, Wes, illus. see Yankovic, Al, pseud.
Hargrave, John. Mischief Maker's Manual. (p. 1150)
—Sir John Hargrave's Mischief Maker's Manual. (p. 1580)
Hargraves, Orin. Big Book of Spelling Tests. (p. 179)
—Slang Rules! A Practical Guide for English Learners. (p. 1587)
Hargraves, Orin, jt. auth. see Seward, Pat.
Hargreaves, Adam. Little Miss Hug. Hargreaves, Adam, illus. (p. 1031)
—Little Miss Princess. (p. 1032)
—Mr. Moustache. Hargreaves, Adam, illus. (p. 1185)
Hargreaves, Adam, illus. see Hargreaves, Roger.
Hargreaves, Adam, jt. auth. see Hargreaves, Roger.
Hargreaves, Adam & Hargreaves, Roger. Little Miss Birthday. Hargreaves, Adam, illus. (p. 1031)
—Little Miss Naughty & the Good Fairy. Hargreaves, Adam, illus. (p. 1032)
—Mr. Birthday. Hargreaves, Adam, illus. (p. 1184)
—Mr. Tickle & the Scary Halloween. (p. 1186)
Hargreaves, G. N. Douglas. (p. 473)
Hargreaves, Greg, illus. see Gardiner, John Reynolds.
Hargreaves, Roger. Little Miss Bad. (p. 1031)
—Little Miss Giggles. (p. 1031)
—Little Miss Greedy. (p. 1031)
—Little Miss Late. (p. 1031)
—Little Miss Princess & the Very Special Wedding. (p. 1032)
—Little Miss Quick. (p. 1032)
—Little Miss Scary. (p. 1032)
—Little Miss Splendid & the Princess. Hargreaves, Adam, illus. (p. 1032)
—Little Miss Tidy. (p. 1032)
—Little Miss Whoops. (p. 1032)
—Mr. Christmas Sticker Activity Book. Hargreaves, Adam, illus. (p. 1184)
—Mr. Cool. (p. 1184)
—Mr. Fussy. (p. 1185)
—Mr. Good. (p. 1185)
—Mr. Happy. (p. 1185)
—Mr. Men 40th Anniversary Box Set. (p. 1185)
—Mr. Messy. (p. 1185)
—Mr. Muddle. (p. 1185)
—Mr. Nervous. (p. 1185)
—Mr. Nobody. Hargreaves, Adam, illus. (p. 1186)
—Mr. Rude. (p. 1186)
—Mr. Silly. (p. 1186)
—Mr. Stingy. (p. 1186)
—Mr. Tickle. (p. 1186)
—Mr. Uppity. (p. 1187)
—Mr. Worry. (p. 1187)
—Mr. Wrong. (p. 1187)
—Night Before Christmas. Hargreaves, Adam, illus. (p. 1252)
Hargreaves, Roger, jt. auth. see Deutsch, Stacia.
Hargreaves, Roger, jt. auth. see Downes, Alice.
Hargreaves, Roger, jt. auth. see Hargreaves, Adam.
Hargreaves, Roger, jt. auth. see Ryals, Lexi.
Hargreaves, Roger & Hargreaves, Adam. Little Miss Sunshine & the Wicked Witch. Hargreaves, Adam, illus. (p. 1032)
—Little Miss Trouble & the Mermaid. Hargreaves, Adam, illus. (p. 1032)
—Mr. Tickle & the Dragon. Hargreaves, Adam, illus. (p. 1186)
Hargrove, Jason. Looking Good, Cody Greer. (p. 1051)
Hargrove, Julia. Bostons Trail to Freedom. (p. 215)
—Tomb of the Unknowns. (p. 1764)
Harimann, Sierra. All in the Family. (p. 44)
—Ballet School. Workman, Lisa, illus. (p. 134)
—Diploma Day. (p. 445)
—Easter Egg Hunt. (p. 499)
—Ice Age: Dawn of the Dinosaurs - Momma Mix-Up. (p. 850)
—Puppies on Parade. (p. 1418)
—Puppy Love. (p. 1418)
—Puppy Tale. (p. 1418)
—Water Pups. (p. 1863)
—We Love You, Strawberry Shortcake! Beighley, Marci, illus. (p. 1867)
Haring, Keith. Nina's Book of Little Things. Haring, Keith, illus. (p. 1256)
Haring, Keith, et al. Art for Baby: High-Contrast Images by Eleven Contemporary Artists to Explore with Your Child. (p. 102)
Haring, Kevin A. Where Do I Hide My Hippopotamus? There Is an Adventurer in All of Us. Gorrasi, Krista, ed. (p. 1907)
Haring, Mary, illus. see Krohn, Gretchen & Johnson, John Norton.
Haris, Kimberli, jt. auth. see Haris, Martha.
Haris, Martha & Haris, Kimberli. Adventures of Fairyella the Tooth Fairy & Dragonfly Floyd. (p. 18)
Harisiades, Jamie, jt. auth. see Rebello, Gleeson.
Hariton, Anca, illus. see Richards, Jean.
Harjo, Joy. For a Girl Becoming. McDonald, Mercedes, illus. (p. 615)
Harker, George A., illus. see Shaw, Charles D.
Harker, Jillian. I Love You, Grandma. (p. 843)
—I Wish... McLean, Gill, illus. (p. 848)
Harker, John B. Betsy Ross's Five Pointed Star: Elizabeth Claypoole, Quaker Flag Maker: A Historical Perspective. (p. 172)
—Betsy Ross's Five Pointed Star: Elizabeth Claypoole, Quaker Flag Maker - A Historical Perspective. (p. 172)
Harker, Lesley. Baby's Book of Rhymes. (p. 128)
Harker, Lesley, illus. see Hooper, Mary.
Harker, Lesley, illus. see Thomas, Pat.
Harkes, Willy. Little Dutch Girl in World War II. Blair, Jocelyn, illus. (p. 1027)
Harkey, Faith. Genuine Sweet. (p. 661)
Harkham, Rachel & Thomas, Doni Zasloff. Get Cooking: A Jewish American Family Cookbook & Rockin' Mmama Doni Celebration. (p. 667)
harkins, charles. Naptime Adventures of Luksi the Turtle. (p. 1229)
Harkins, Nathan, illus. see Rossman, Alicia.
Harkins, Philip. Knockout. (p. 965)
Harkins, Susan. Carolinas: Sir George Carteret & Sir Anthony Ashley Cooper. (p. 270)
Harkins, Susan, jt. auth. see Harkins, William.
Harkins, Susan & Harkins, William H. Life & Times of King Arthur: The Evolution of the Legend. (p. 1008)
—Life & Times of Patrick Henry. (p. 1008)
Harkins, Susan and William. Walter Dean Myers. (p. 1856)
Harkins, Susan Sales. Breaking the Sound Barrier: The Story of Chuck Yeager. (p. 225)
Harkins, Susan Sales, jt. auth. see Harkins, William H.
Harkins, Susan Sales & Harkins, William H. Assassination of John F. Kennedy 1963. (p. 107)
—Betsy Ross. (p. 172)
—Care for a Pet Bunny. (p. 266)
—Colonial Virginia. (p. 341)
—Design Your Own Butterfly Garden. (p. 430)
—Design Your Own Pond & Water Garden. (p. 430)
—Donner Party. (p. 466)
—Fall of the Soviet Union 1991. (p. 566)
—Georgia: The Debtors Colony. (p. 665)
—King Tut. (p. 959)
—Life & Times of Clara Barton. (p. 1008)
—Life & Times of Father Jacques Marquette. (p. 1008)
—Life & Times of John Paul Jones. (p. 1008)
—Life & Times of Pythagoras. (p. 1008)
—Life & Times of Richard the Lionheart. (p. 1008)
—Life & Times of William the Conqueror. (p. 1008)
—Perseus. (p. 1344)
—Pochantas. (p. 1375)
—Sam Houston. (p. 1506)
—Threat to the Whooping Crane. (p. 1741)
Harkins, William & Harkins, Susan. Earthquake in Loma Prieta, California 1989. (p. 497)
Harkins, William H., jt. auth. see Harkins, Susan Sales.
Harkins, William H., jt. auth. see Harkins, Susan.
Harkins, William H. & Harkins, Susan Sales. Jamestown: The First Colony. (p. 907)
Harkness, Karen. Coralee's Best Run Yet. (p. 366)
—Obama, Our Hero. (p. 1275)
Harkness, Peter T. Andy the Acrobat: Out with the Greatest Show on Earth. (p. 73)
—Andy the Acrobat. (p. 73)
—Andy the Acrobat or Out with the Greatest Show on Earth. (p. 73)
Harkness, Susan. Little Graham Cracker House. (p. 1028)
Harko, Lubov, ed. see AZ Books Staff.
Harkrader, L. D. Airball: My Life in Briefs. (p. 31)
Harkrader, Lisa. Adventures of Beanboy. (p. 16)
—Cheetah: A MyReportLinks. com Book. (p. 296)
—Cool Beans: The Further Adventures of Beanboy. (p. 362)
—Cuba: A MyReportLinks.com Book. (p. 388)
—Daisy Diaz Shakes up Camp. Nez, John A., illus. (p. 400)
—Grizzly Bear. A MyReportLinks.com Book. (p. 724)
—India: A MyReportLinks. com Book. (p. 870)
—Orangutan: A Myreportlinks. com Book. (p. 1302)
—Reconstruction & Aftermath of the Civil War: A MyReportLinks. com Book. (p. 1452)
—Ruby Makes It Even! Odd/Even Numbers. Wummer, Amy, illus. (p. 1493)
—South Korea: A MyReportLinks. com Book. (p. 1617)
Harkrader, Lisa, jt. auth. see Gottfried, Ted.
Harkrader, Lisa, jt. auth. see Katirgis, Jane.
Harl, Joelean. Wintertime Fun: Snow. (p. 1939)
Harlan. My Best Friend. (p. 1196)

Harlan, Noah, jt. auth. see Ostow, Micol.
Harlan Rowe Junior High. Everyday Heroes; Biographies & Memoirs from the Athens Area School District Eighth Grade Oral History Project. (p. 543)
Harlan, Thomas. Storm of Heaven: Book Three of the oath of empire: A Historical Novel. (p. 1656)
Harland, Jackie, illus. see Fairley, Melissa.
Harland, Jackie, illus. see Wallace, Karen.
Harland, Joan & Timmons, Nick. As Film Studies. (p. 105)
Harland, Richard. Liberator. (p. 1005)
—Worldshaker. (p. 1961)
Harlen, Jonathan. Circus Berzerkus. (p. 322)
—Cockroach War. (p. 337)
Harley, Alexis, jt. ed. see Bloom, Harold.
Harley, Avis. African Acrostics: A Word in Edgeways. Noyes, Deborah, illus. (p. 26)
—African Acrostics: A Word in Edgeways. Noyes, Deborah, photos by. (p. 26)
—Monarch's Progress: Poems with Wings. Harley, Avis, illus. (p. 1163)
—Sea Stars: Saltwater Poems. Butschler, Margaret, photos by. (p. 1535)
Harley, Bill. Amazing Flight of Darius Frobisher (p. 54)
—Bear's All-Night Party. Ferreira, Melissa, illus. (p. 151)
—Charlie Bumpers vs. the Really Nice Gnome Gustavson, Adam, illus. (p. 292)
—Charlie Bumpers vs. the Teacher of the Year Gustavson, Adam, illus. (p. 292)
—Dear Santa: The Letters of James B. Dobbins. Alley, R. W., illus. (p. 419)
—Dirty Joe the Pirate: A True Story. Davis, Jack E., illus. (p. 446)
—Lost & Found Gustavson, Adam, illus. (p. 1054)
—Night of the Spadefoot Toads (p. 1254)
—Sitting down to Eat. (p. 1582)
Harley, E. K. But Where Was Louise? And Other Literary Adventures. (p. 246)
Harley, Jason. Journey to the Light. (p. 929)
Harley, Rex. Baby, Now That I've Found You. (p. 127)
Harley, Stephen. Christmastime Dog Rescue. (p. 316)
Harlin, Greg, illus. see Cheney, Lynne.
Harlin, Greg, illus. see Krensky, Stephen.
Harlin, Greg, tr. see Krensky, Stephen.
Harlin, Sybel, illus. see Novick, Mary & Hale, Jenny.
Harlin, Sybel, illus. see Novick, Mary.
Harline, Leigh & Washington, Ned. When You Wish upon a Star. Puybaret, Eric, illus. (p. 1905)
Harling, Birgit, jt. auth. see Uriz, Francisco J.
Harlow, Brent W. Peetie the Awesome Possum. (p. 1335)
Harlow, Honey. Honey's Shoes. (p. 795)
Harlow, Janet, illus. see Gallery, Philip D.
Harlow, Janet L., illus. see Gallery, Philip D.
Harlow, Janet L., jt. auth. see Gallery, Philip D.
Harlow, Janet L., tr. see Gallery, Philip D.
Harlow, Joan Hiatt. Blown Away! (p. 202)
—Firestorm! (p. 592)
—Joshua's Song. (p. 927)
—Midnight Rider. (p. 1139)
—Secret of the Night Ponies. (p. 1542)
—Shadows on the Sea. (p. 1558)
—Thunder from the Sea. (p. 1746)
Harlow, Patty Fayerweather. Rock with Rodney and, Party with Perky to Preserve Wildlife. (p. 1482)
Harman, Debbie. Book of Mormon Says. (p. 211)
Harman, Debbie G. Jesus Said- (p. 916)
—My Baptism: The Best Day Ever. (p. 1196)
Harman, Fred. Bronc Peeler: The Lone Cowboy. (p. 230)
Harman, Graham. Guerrilla Metaphysics: Phenomenology & the Carpentry of Things. (p. 728)
Harman, Hollis Page. Money Sense for Kids. (p. 1164)
Harman, Ian. Adventures of Terry Tool Bench: Book 1 Terry Is Born. (p. 23)
Harman, Micah, illus. see Dwyer, Kevin & Dwyer, Shawnae.
Harman, Michael. Loro y la Higuera. (p. 1053)
—Parrot & the Fig Tree. (p. 1325)
Harman, Paul, ed. Guide to UK Theatre for Young Audiences. (p. 730)
Harman, Rebecca. Carbon-Oxygen & Nitrogen Cycles: Respiration, Photosynthesis, & Decomposition (p. 265)
—Earth's Changing Crust: Plate Tectonics & Extreme Events (p. 498)
—Earth's Resources: Renewable & Non-Renewable (p. 498)
—Earth's Weather: Changing Patterns & Systems (p. 498)
—Rock Cycles: Formation, Properties, & Erosion. (p. 1482)
—Water Cycle: Evaporation, Condensation & Erosion (p. 1862)
Harman, Teri. Black Moon: The Moonlight Trilogy. (p. 196)
—Blood Moon: The Moonlight Trilogy. (p. 200)
—Blood Moon: The Blood Inheritance Trilogy. (p. 200)
—Storm Moon. (p. 1656)
Harmel, Kristin. Blonde Theory. (p. 200)
Harmening, Gail. How Did Clancey Get His Color? (p. 806)
Harmer, David. There's a Monster in the Garden: The Best of David Harmer. Archbold, Tim, illus. (p. 1731)
Harmer, David, jt. auth. see Cookson, Paul.
Harmer, Sharon, illus. see Braun, Eric.
Harmer, Wendy. I Lost My Mobile at the Mall. (p. 841)
—I Made Lattes for a Love God. (p. 844)
—Pearlie & Great Aunt Garnet. Taylor, Gypsy, illus. (p. 1333)
—Pearlie & Her Pink Shell. Taylor, Gypsy, illus. (p. 1333)
—Pearlie & Jasper. Zarb, Mike & Taylor, Gypsy, illus. (p. 1333)
—Pearlie & Opal. Zarb, Mike, illus. (p. 1333)
—Pearlie & Sapphire. Taylor, Gypsy, illus. (p. 1333)
—Pearlie & the Big Doll. Zarb, Mike, illus. (p. 1333)
—Pearlie & the Cherry Blossom Fairy. Taylor, Gypsy, illus. (p. 1333)
—Pearlie & the Christmas Angel. Taylor, Gypsy & Zarb, Mike, illus. (p. 1333)
—Pearlie & the Fairy Queen. Taylor, Gypsy, illus. (p. 1333)
—Pearlie & the Flamenco Fairy. Taylor, Gypsy, illus. (p. 1333)
—Pearlie & the Lost Handbag. Zarb, Mike, illus. (p. 1333)
—Pearlie & the Silver Fern Fairy. Taylor, Gypsy, illus. (p. 1333)
—Pearlie Goes to Rio. Taylor, Gypsy, illus. (p. 1333)
—Pearlie in Central Park. Taylor, Gypsy, illus. (p. 1333)
—Pearlie in Paris. Taylor, Gypsy, illus. (p. 1333)
—Pearlie in the Park. Zarb, Mike, illus. (p. 1333)
Harmin, Karen Leigh. J. K. Rowling: Author of Harry Potter—An Unauthorized Biography. (p. 901)
Harmon, Alison L. Adventures of Feeda Fox; Everybody's Different. (p. 18)
Harmon, Casey Sean. Everafter Chronicles: Reign of the Night Creatures. (p. 542)
Harmon, Dan, et al. Monster House - La Casa de los Sustos. (p. 1167)
Harmon, Daniel. Super Pop! Pop Culture Top Ten Lists to Help You Win at Trivia, Survive in the Wild, & Make It Through the Holidays. (p. 1680)
Harmon, Daniel E. Al Gore & Global Warming. (p. 32)
—Algeria. (p. 38)
—Algeria. Rotberg, Robert I., ed. (p. 38)
—Andrew Jackson. (p. 72)
—Ayatollah Ruhollah Khomeini. (p. 121)
—Career As an Electrician. (p. 266)
—Careers As a Marketing & Public Relations Specialist. (p. 267)
—Careers in Explosives & Arson Investigation. (p. 267)
—Careers in Internet Security. (p. 268)
—Careers in Roofing & Flooring. (p. 268)
—Cassandra Clare (p. 276)
—Chemical & Biological Weapons: Agents of War & Terror. (p. 297)
—Dream Jobs in Sports Media. (p. 483)
—Explorers of the South Pacific. (p. 551)
—First Job Smarts. (p. 595)
—Fish, Meat, & Poultry: Dangers in the Food Supply. (p. 598)
—Frequently Asked Questions about Overscheduling & Stress. (p. 636)
—Haunted Places & Ghostly Encounters. (p. 753)
—How to Start Your Own Band. (p. 821)
—Hudson River. (p. 824)
—Jobs in Environmental Cleanup & Emergency Hazmat Response. (p. 919)
—Kyrgyzstan. (p. 969)
—Leukemia. (p. 1003)
—Libya. (p. 1007)
—Lower Atlantic: Florida, Georgia, South Carolina (p. 1061)
—Managing Your Band. (p. 1086)
—Minnesota: Past & Present. (p. 1147)
—New Medicines: Issues of Approval, Access, & Product Safety. (p. 1246)
—Notre Dame Football. (p. 1268)
—Obesity. (p. 1275)
HARMON, Daniel E. Pervez Musharraf: President of Pakistan. (p. 1345)
Harmon, Daniel E. Pervez Musharraf: President of Pakistan. (p. 1345)
—Poultry: From the Farm to Your Table. (p. 1389)
—Powering up a Career in Software Development & Programming. (p. 1391)
—Publishing Your E-Book. (p. 1414)
—Smart Strategies for Buying a Car. (p. 1593)
—South Carolina: Past & Present. (p. 1616)
—Special Ops: Military Intelligence (p. 1623)
—Turkey. (p. 1797)
—Washington: Past & Present. (p. 1859)
—Werewolves. (p. 1875)
—Woodrow Wilson. (p. 1949)
—Working As a Law Enforcement Officer in Your Community. (p. 1952)
Harmon, Daniel E., jt. auth. see Lily, Henrietta M.
Harmon, Deborah A. & Jones, Toni Stokes. Elementary Education: A Reference Handbook (p. 510)
Harmon, Douglas. Momma Whats a Stranger. (p. 1162)
Harmon, Gedge, illus. see Windeatt, Mary F.
Harmon, Glenn, illus. see Jensen, Kimberly.
Harmon, Glenn, illus. see Potter, George.
Harmon, Glenn, illus. see Rowley, Deborah Pace.
Harmon, Glenn, illus. see Setzer, Lee Ann.
Harmon, Glenn, illus. see Setzer, LeeAnn.
Harmon, Heather, photos by see Chronicle Books Staff.
Harmon, Jeannie. Joshua's New Job. (p. 927)
—Let's Pretend. (p. 1000)
—Prayer. (p. 1393)
Harmon, Jeannie, jt. auth. see Cook, David C. Publishing Staff.
Harmon, Julian. My Dad Pays Taxes. (p. 1201)
Harmon, Kitty, ed. see Chronicle Books Staff.
Harmon, Leesa, et al. Bullets & Bayonets: A Battle of Frankin Primer. (p. 240)
Harmon, Michael. Brutal. (p. 233)
—Chamber of Five. (p. 289)
—Last Exit to Normal. (p. 977)
—Skate. (p. 1583)
—Stick. (p. 1649)
Harmon, Michael B. Under the Bridge. (p. 1813)
Harmon, Michael B., jt. auth. see Shea, John.
Harmon, Minnie. Golden's Routine. (p. 695)
Harmon, Minnie P. Golden's Animal Friends. (p. 695)
—Golden's Shapes & Colors. (p. 695)
Harmon, Paul. Mora: All Beasts Will Show Their Teeth. Vol. 1 (p. 1173)
Harmon, Ruth. Christmas Story. (p. 315)
Harmon, Steve, illus. see Curtis, Jessica Lynn.
Harmon, Victoria Marie. Say Hello to My Little Green Friend Tiki. (p. 1518)
Harms, Carol. What If? (p. 1887)
Harms, Cathy, ed. see McCray, Ed.
Harms, Jeanine. Boss Mouse Coloring Book & Theme Song. (p. 215)
Harms, Julia. Recipe & Craft Guide to Italy. (p. 1451)
Harnadek, Anita. Algebra Word Problems (p. 38)
—Critical Thinking: Problem Solving, Reasoning, Logic, & Arguments. Bk. 1 (p. 383)
—Critical Thinking Book One - Instruction/Answer Guide: Problem Solving, Reasoning, Logic, & Arguments. (p. 383)
—Math Word Problems Level C: Mixed Concepts: Whole Numbers to Percents. (p. 1107)
—Mind Benders A1: Deductive Thinking Skills. (p. 1145)
—Mind Benders A2: Deductive Thinking Skills. (p. 1145)
—Mind Benders A4: Deductive Thinking Skills. (p. 1145)
—Mind Benders B1: Deductive Thinking Skills. (p. 1145)
—Mind Benders B2: Deductive Thinking Skills. (p. 1145)
—Mind Benders B3: Deductive Thinking Skills. (p. 1145)
—Mind Benders B4: Deductive Thinking Skills. (p. 1145)
—Mind Benders C1: Deductive Thinking Skills. (p. 1145)
—Mind Benders C2: Deductive Thinking Skills. (p. 1145)
—Mind Benders C3: Deductive Thinking Skills. (p. 1145)
Harnden, Chris. Pickidilly O. & the Storm. (p. 1354)
Harned, Bert. Any Ole Bush: Christ Living in You. Skinner, Kerry L., ed. (p. 90)
Harner, Jennifer L. Reading & Learning from Informational Text. Petelinsek, Kathleen, illus. (p. 1445)
Harner, Ron. Cool It Frida! Surrey, Michael, illus. (p. 363)
—Move It Milton! Surrey, Michael, illus. (p. 1183)
—Suck It up Tate! Surrey, Michael, illus. (p. 1672)
Harness, Cheryl. Abe Lincoln Goes to Washington: 1837-1865. (p. 4)
—Adventurous Life of Myles Standish & the Amazing-but-True Survival Story of Plymouth Colony: Barbary Pirates, the Mayflower, the First Thanksgiving, & Much, Much More. (p. 25)
—Adventurous Life of Myles Standish & the Amazing-but-True Survival Story of Plymouth Colony. Harness, Cheryl, illus. (p. 25)
—Flags over America: A Star-Spangled Story. Harness, Cheryl, illus. (p. 602)
—George Washington. (p. 664)
—Ghosts of the Civil War. Harness, Cheryl, illus. (p. 672)
—Ghosts of the Nile. Harness, Cheryl, illus. (p. 672)
—Groundbreaking, Chance-Taking Life of George Washington Carver & Science & Invention in America. Harness, Cheryl, illus. (p. 725)
—Literary Adventures of Washington Irving: American Storyteller. (p. 1022)
—Mary Walker Wears the Pants: The True Story of the Doctor, Reformer, & Civil War Hero. Molinari, Carlo, illus. (p. 1101)
—Our Colonial Year. Harness, Cheryl, illus. (p. 1308)
—Remarkable Benjamin Franklin. (p. 1458)
—Remarkable Benjamin Franklin. Harness, Cheryl, illus. (p. 1458)
—Remarkable Rough-Riding Life of Theodore Roosevelt & the Rise of Empire America. (p. 1459)
—Remember the Ladies: 100 Great American Women. (p. 1459)
—Remember the Ladies: 100 Great American Women. Harness, Cheryl, illus. (p. 1459)
—Revolutionary John Adams. (p. 1466)
—Thomas Jefferson. (p. 1739)
—Tragic Tale of Narcissa Whitman & a Faithful History of the Oregon Trail. Harness, Cheryl, illus. (p. 1776)
—Trailblazing Life of Daniel Boone & How Early Americans Took to the Road. (p. 1776)
—Young Abe Lincoln: The Frontier Days: 1809-1837. (p. 1978)
Harness, Cheryl, illus. see Allen, Thomas B.
Harness, Cheryl, illus. see Anderson, William.
Harness, Cheryl, illus. see Cummins, Julie & Cummins, Julia.
Harness, Cheryl, illus. see Cummins, Julie.
Harness, Cheryl, illus. see Hutton, Stacie Vaughn.
Harness, Cheryl, jt. auth. see U. S. National Geographic Society Staff.
Harness, Peter, et al. Singular Voices. (p. 1579)
Harnest, Faye. Girl Fight (p. 678)
Harnett, Lynn, jt. auth. see Philbrick, Rodman.
Harney, D. G. Meet Mr. Ugly (p. 1121)
Harney Jr., Robert. Clumsiest Spider. Scott, Jennifer, illus. (p. 336)
Harnick, Sheldon. Sunrise, Sunset. Schoenherr, Ian, illus. (p. 1677)
Harnish, Alexander, illus. see Harnish, Jeannette.
Harnish, Coach Dave, jt. auth. see Schaller, Bob.
Harnish, Jeannette. Duck Who Drove a Boat. Harnish, Alexander, illus. (p. 488)
Harnsberger, L. C. Christmas Favorites for Recorder: Book & Recorder. (p. 314)
Harnsberger, L. C., jt. auth. see Manus, Ron.
Harnsberger, L. C. & Manus, Ron. Alfred's Kid's Guitar Course Complete: The Easiest Guitar Method Ever! (p. 38)
Harnum, Robert. Exile in the Kingdom: A Novel. (p. 548)
Harold, Elsie Louise. Stop Bullying: An ABC Guide for Children & the Adults Who Interact with Them. Harold, Elsie Louise, illus. (p. 1653)
Harold, Gwyneth. Bad Girls in School. (p. 131)
Harow, Penny. Festival of Lights: A Delightful Collection of Handmade Chanukiot. (p. 582)
Harp, Georgieanna. This Is Your Earthday. (p. 1737)
Harp, Jerry. Creature. (p. 380)
Harp, Kim, jt. auth. see Bird, Roy.
Harp, Susan. Evie Goes Clean & Green. Siau, Jon, illus. (p. 546)
—Retrieving with Evie. Siau, John, illus. (p. 1464)
Harpan, Gaile. Ballad of Calvin the Cat. Reddy, Sneha, illus. (p. 134)
—Ballad of Omar the Cat. Reddy, Sneha, illus. (p. 134)
—Ballad of Snowball the Cat. Reddy, Sneha, illus. (p. 134)
—Ballad of Victor the Cat. Reddy, Sneha, illus. (p. 134)
—True Puppy Tails. (p. 1792)
Harpan, Gaile, ed. see Dimarcello, Pete.
Harpan, Gaile, jt. auth. see Panks, Kristin.
Harpan, Gaile & DiMarcello, Pete. Another Dolphin's Tale, a Love Story. Baker, Edmund, illus. (p. 87)
HarPaz, Natan. Kiki Kangaroo. (p. 955)
Harper, Aimee. Crystal. (p. 387)
—Dream Dogs - Nugget. (p. 483)
Harper, Amelia. Literary Lessons from The Lord of the Rings. Howe, John, illus. (p. 1022)
Harper, Anita. It's Not Fair. McQuillan, Mary, illus. (p. 898)
Harper, Ben. Super Friends: Going Bananas. Random House Staff, illus. (p. 1680)
—Superdog & Bat Hound to the Rescue. (p. 1683)
Harper, Benjamin. Greetings from Rio! (p. 723)
—Hot Wheels: To the Extreme. Wisinski, Ed & White, Dave, illus. (p. 802)
—Star Wars Rebels: the Secret Jedi: The Adventures of Kanan Jarrus: Rebel Leader & Jedi Master. (p. 1642)
Harper, Benjamin, jt. auth. see Dorling Kindersley Publishing Staff.
Harper, Benjamin, jt. auth. see Poe, Edgar Allen.
Harper, Benjamin & Poe, Edgar Allen. Tell-Tale Heart Calero, Dennis, illus. (p. 1717)
Harper, Benjamin & Scieszka, Jon. All Around Trucktown. Shannon, David et al, illus. (p. 44)
Harper, Betty. Color My World: Early Elvis (Coloring Book) Vol. 1 Harper, Betty, illus. (p. 343)
Harper, C. J. Wilderness. (p. 1931)
Harper, Candy. Keep the Faith. (p. 947)
Harper, Charise Mericle. Alien Encounter. Harper, Charise Mericle, illus. (p. 40)
—Ball. (p. 134)
—Bean Dog & Nugget: the Ball. (p. 150)
—Bean Dog & Nugget: the Cookie. (p. 150)
—Cookie. (p. 361)
—Cupcake. Harper, Charise Mericle, illus. (p. 392)
—Dreamer, Wisher, Liar. (p. 484)
—Go! Go! Go! Stop! (p. 686)
—Go, Go, Go, Stop! (p. 686)
—Henry's Heart: A Boy, His Heart, & a New Best Friend. Harper, Charise Mericle, illus. (p. 769)
—If Waffles Were Like Boys. Magoon, Scott, illus. (p. 854)
—Just Grace. Harper, Charise Mericle, illus. (p. 938)
—Just Grace & the Double Surprise. (p. 938)
—Just Grace & the Snack Attack. (p. 938)
—Just Grace & the Snack Attack. Harper, Charise Mericle, illus. (p. 938)
—Just Grace & the Super Sleepover. (p. 938)
—Just Grace & the Trouble with Cupcakes. (p. 938)
—Just Grace Gets Crafty. Harper, Charise Mericle, illus. (p. 938)
—Just Grace Goes Green. (p. 938)
—Just Grace, Star on Stage. (p. 938)
—Just Grace Walks the Dog. (p. 938)
—Pink Me Up. (p. 1360)
—Power of Cute. (p. 1389)
—Star on Stage. (p. 1641)
—Still Just Grace. (p. 1650)
—Still Just Grace. Harper, Charise Mericle, illus. (p. 1650)
—Super Sasquatch Showdown. Harper, Charise Mericle, illus. (p. 1680)
—Superlove. Goode, Diane & Chambers, Mark, illus. (p. 1683)
—Wedgieman: A Hero Is Born. Shea, Bob, illus. (p. 1871)
—Wedgieman & the Big Bunny Trouble. Shea, Bob, illus. (p. 1871)
Harper, Charise Mericle, illus. see Markle, Sandra.
Harper, Charise Mericle & Malk, Steven. Just Grace & the Flower Girl Power. Harper, Charise Mericle, illus. (p. 938)
Harper, Charise Mericle & Mericle Harper, Charise. Princess Patty Finds Her Prince. (p. 1405)
Harper, Charles. Alphabet Children Puzzle Book. (p. 49)
Harper, Charley. Charley Harper Tree of Life. (p. 292)
—Charley Harper's a Partridge in a Pear Tree. (p. 292)
—Charley Harper's Birds. (p. 292)
—Charley Harper's Sticky Birds: An Animal Sticker Kit. (p. 292)
Harper, Charley, illus. see Burke, Zoe.
Harper, Chris. Dogges of Barkshire - the Charge of the Light Brigade. (p. 462)
—Dogges of Barkshire - the Grand Kennel. Harper, Chris, illus. (p. 462)
Harper, Clay & Ingram, Jas. Are You Sure That Was A Rabbit? (p. 97)
Harper, Clifford, illus. see Gombrich, E. H.
Harper Collins. Paddington. (p. 1317)
Harper Collins / LeapFrog, jt. auth. see Collins, Harper.
Harper Collins / LeapFrog, jt. auth. see O'Connor, Jane.
Harper, Dan. Sit, Truman! Moser, Barry & Moser, Cara, illus. (p. 1582)
Harper, David R. & Harper, Meg. Animal Crazy. (p. 77)
Harper, Demetria R. God, Help Me, I Keep Failing! The Cries of a Young Teenager's Heart. (p. 689)
Harper, Donna. Hello God: Are You Here? (p. 764)
Harper, E. T. & Taylor, Dan. Dylan's Amazing Dinosaur: the Stegosaurus: With Pull-Out, Pop-Up Dinosaur Inside! (p. 491)
—Dylan's Amazing Dinosaur: the Tyrannosaurus Rex: With Pull-Out, Pop-Up Dinosaur Inside! (p. 491)
Harper, Eleanor. Honey & Harebell. (p. 794)
Harper, Ellen. Fun with Egyptian Symbols Stencils. (p. 648)
Harper, Fred, illus. see O'Connor, Jim.
Harper, Fred, illus. see Pascal, Janet B.
Harper, Fred, illus. see Tomecek, Steve.
Harper, Fred, illus. see Washington, George.
Harper, Glyn & Richardson, Colin. Bravest & Best: Kiwis Awarded the Victoria Cross. (p. 223)
Harper, Helena. Pep, Polish & Paint. McKinney, Malachy, illus. (p. 1340)
Harper, Hill. Letters to a Young Sister: DeFINE Your Destiny. (p. 1002)
Harper, Jamie. Miles to Go. Harper, Jamie, illus. (p. 1142)
—Miss Mingo & the Fire Drill. Harper, Jamie, illus. (p. 1151)
—Miss Mingo & the First Day of School. (p. 1151)
—Miss Mingo & the First Day of School. Harper, Jamie, illus. (p. 1151)
—Miss Mingo Weathers the Storm. Harper, Jamie, illus. (p. 1151)
—Splish Splash, Baby Bundt: A Recipe for Bath Time. Harper, Jamie, illus. (p. 1630)
Harper, Jamie, illus. see Wallace, Rich & Warner, Sally.
Harper, Jamie, illus. see Warner, Sally.
Harper, Jamie, jt. auth. see Warner, Sally.
Harper, Jessica. Lizzy's Ups & Downs: NOT an Ordinary School Day. Dupont, Lindsay Harper, illus. (p. 1043)
—Place Called Kindergarten. Karas, G. Brian, illus. (p. 1365)
—Uh-Oh, Cleo. Berkeley, Jon, illus. (p. 1808)
Harper, Jo. I Could Eat You Up! Chorao, Kay, illus. (p. 837)
—Mayor Jalapeno Hal from Presidio, Texas. (p. 1113)
—Whistling Willie. (p. 1912)
—Wilma Rudolph: Olympic Runner. Henderson, Meryl, illus. (p. 1934)

Harper, Jo & Harper, Josephine. Finding Daddy: A Story of the Great Depression. Mazellan, Ron, illus. (p. 588)
Harper, Joel. All the Way to the Ocean. Spusta, Marq, illus. (p. 46)
Harper, John. Denny Hamlin. (p. 426)
—Time Lapse: Collapse. (p. 1752)
Harper, Josephine, jt. auth. see Harper, Jo.
Harper, Judith. Unique Places. (p. 1818)
Harper, Judith E. Andrew Johnson. (p. 72)
—Unique Places. (p. 1818)
Harper, Julie-Ann. Pick-a-WooWoo -Frolicking with the Fairies: Two Enchanting Fairytales Rose, Carolyn Maree, illus. (p. 1354)
—Pick-a-WooWoo - My Angels Advice: A Story about Love Rose, Carolyn Maree, illus. (p. 1354)
—Pick-a-WooWoo -the Happy Little Spirit: Each of us has a Spirit but what Is it & where did it come From? Forrest, Genevieve, illus. (p. 1354)
—Pick-a-WooWoo - Wizards Words of Wisdom Bellinger, Marie, illus. (p. 1354)
—Pick-a-WooWoo - Yep I See Spirit: The Gift of Sight Bellinger, Marie, illus. (p. 1354)
—Pick-a-WooWoo- Grandma's Great Advice: The Art of Listening Lee, Roslyn, illus. (p. 1354)
Harper, Ken. Mystery in Mansfield. (p. 1224)
Harper, Kristine. Hurricane Andrew. (p. 829)
—Mount St. Helens Volcanic Eruption. (p. 1180)
Harper, Lee. Emperor's Cool Clothes (p. 521)
—Snow! Snow! Snow! Harper, Lee, illus. (p. 1599)
Harper, Lee, illus. see Helakoski, Leslie.
Harper, Lee, illus. see Myers, Walter Dean.
Harper, Lee, illus. see Silvano, Wendi J.
Harper, Leslie. Cómo Dar un Discurso. (p. 350)
—Cómo Escribir un Artículo de Opinion. (p. 350)
—Cómo Escribir un Artículo Editorial. (p. 350)
—Cómo Mantenerse Informado. (p. 351)
—Cómo Mantenerse Informados. (p. 351)
—Cómo Recaudar Fondos para una Causa. (p. 351)
—How Do Elections Work? (p. 807)
—How Do Laws Get Passed? (p. 807)
—How to Give a Speech. (p. 820)
—How to Raise Money for a Cause. (p. 821)
—How to Stay Informed. (p. 821)
—How to Write an Op-Ed Piece. (p. 823)
—What Are Checks & Balances? (p. 1879)
—What Are Rights & Responsibilities? (p. 1879)
—What Is Citizenship? (p. 1889)
Harper, Lisa. You Belong to Me Little One. (p. 1973)
Harper, Marrisa and Normita. ABC Book. (p. 3)
Harper, Marvin. Our War Stories. (p. 1310)
Harper, Meg. My Mum & the Green-Eyed Monster. (p. 1215)
—My Mum & the Gruesome Twosome. (p. 1215)
—No More School. (p. 1259)
Harper, Meg, jt. auth. see Harper, David R.
Harper, Michael J. & Arrington, Jay. Baby Do It. (p. 125)
—Little Entrepreneur: Takes Flight. (p. 1027)
—Teenage Entrepreneur. (p. 1714)
Harper, P. Thandi Hicks. Hip-Hop Development. (p. 780)
Harper, Piers. Christmas Doodles: Over 100 Pictures to Complete & Create. (p. 313)
Harper, Piers, illus. see Simon, Mary Manz.
Harper, Richard. Richie Gets a Dog: A Father & Son Book about Adopting Animals Shelter Dogs & Cats. (p. 1470)
Harper, Robert Alexander & Subanthore, Aswin. Saudi Arabia. (p. 1516)
Harper, Ruth E., illus. see Penn, Audrey & Cosgrove, Stephen.
Harper, Ruth E., illus. see Penn, Audrey.
Harper, Sandy. Educational Toys for Kids of All Ages. (p. 505)
Harper, Scott. Clouds! (p. 335)
—Morgan's Birthday Surprise: Understanding Subtraction. (p. 1175)
Harper, Stephan J. Black Sheep Beach, Mary FitzGerald, illus. (p. 196)
—One Christmas Story. Steuerwald, Joy, illus. (p. 1294)
Harper, Steven, jt. auth. see Flaherty, Patrick F.
Harper, Suzanne. 10 Most Tragic Romances. (p. 1994)
—Gaggle of Goblins. (p. 652)
—Gust of Ghosts. (p. 732)
—Juliet Club. (p. 932)
—Mischief of Mermaids. (p. 1150)
—Secret Life of Sparrow Delaney. (p. 1541)
—Unseen World of Poppy Malone: A Gaggle of Goblins. No. 1 (p. 1822)
Harper, Suzanne, illus. see Earnest, Peter.
Harper, Suzanne & Sheppard, Bonnie. 10 Most Extreme Vacations. (p. 1994)
Harper, Valentina. Creative Coloring Animals: Art Activity Pages to Relax & Enjoy! (p. 379)
Harper, Valerie, jt. auth. see Allen, Connie.
Harper, Vicky. Selah (p. 1549)
Harpercollins. Writing (p. 1964)
HarperCollins Children's Books, creator. England the Facts Sticker Book: All the Facts, All the Stats, All the Stickers! (p. 529)
HarperCollins Publishers Ltd. Staff. Birthday Cake Book. (p. 192)
—Charming Classics Box Set No. 3: Charming Horse Library. (p. 294)
—Collins Illustrated Dictionary. (p. 340)
—My Little Pony. (p. 1213)
HarperCollins Publishers Ltd. Staff, jt. auth. see Collins Maps Staff.
HarperCollins Publishers Ltd. Staff, jt. auth. see Finn, Perdita.
HarperCollins Publishers Ltd. Staff, jt. auth. see Oliver, Alison.
HarperCollins Publishers Ltd. Staff & Auerbach, Annie. Paddington: Paddington's Adventures. (p. 1317)
—Paddington - Meet Paddington. (p. 1317)
HarperCollins Publishers Ltd. Staff & Frantz, Jennifer. Voyage of the Dawn Treader: Aboard the Dawn Treader. (p. 1850)
—Voyage of the Dawn Treader: Quest for the Lost Lords. (p. 1850)
HarperCollins Publishers Ltd. Staff, ed. Home on the Range. (p. 792)
HarperCollins Publishers Ltd. Staff, et al. I Can Read Halloween Treat Zimmer, Dirk, illus. (p. 836)
—James Cameron's Avatar. (p. 907)
—Origins No. 5. (p. 1304)
—Paddington: Paddington's World. (p. 1317)
—Paddington: Paddington in London. (p. 1317)
Harpercollins Staff. Collins First Atlas. (p. 340)
—Collins - First Atlas: Learn with Maps. (p. 340)
—Collins First Dictionary. (p. 340)
—Collins Student Atlas. (p. 341)
—Collins Very First Spanish Dictionary. (p. 341)
Harpercollins Staff, jt. auth. see Collins Dictionaries.
Harpercollins Staff, jt. auth. see Donbavand, Tommy.
HarperCollins UK. Phonics & Spelling. (p. 1351)
HarperCollins UK Staff. Cobuild Essential English Dictionary. (p. 337)
—Counting (p. 370)
—England World Cup Dream Team: Live Your Own World Cup Dream! (p. 529)
—England World Cup Junior Companion: Everything you Need to Know about the 2006 World Cup. (p. 529)
—Grammar & Punctuation Practice. (p. 706)
—Junior Atlas. (p. 936)
—New Maths Frameworking - Matches the Revised Ks3 Framework - Year 7. (p. 1246)
—Real Heroes: Courage under Fire. Vol. 2 (p. 1448)
—Skills for the Tofel iBT Test. (p. 1585)
—Times Tables Practice. (p. 1754)
HarperCollins UK Staff, jt. auth. see Catling, Simon.
HarperCollins UK Staff, jt. auth. see Collins Easy Learning Staff.
HarperCollins UK Staff, jt. auth. see Collins Easy Learning.
HarperCollins UK Staff & Collins Staff. My First Book of World Flags. (p. 1205)
Harpine, Elaine C. Christment Tree Pattern: 21 Christian Ornaments on the Meaning of Christmas. (p. 316)
Harpine, Elaine Clanton. Come, Follow Me!: Sessions 1-26 Vol. 1 (p. 347)
—Come, Follow Me!: Sessions 27-59 Vol. 2 (p. 347)
Harpster, Steve. 1-100 Dot-to-Dots. (p. 1990)
—Arnold Gets Angry: An Emotional Literacy Book. (p. 100)
—Baby Animals. (p. 124)
—Betty Stops the Bully: An Emotional Literacy Book. (p. 172)
—Catherine Finds Her Courage: An Emotional Literacy Book. (p. 280)
—Debra Doesn't Take the Dare: An Emotional Literacy Book. (p. 421)
—First Word Search: Easy First Words. (p. 597)
—First Word Search: Fun First Phonics. (p. 597)
—First Word Search: Fun First Words. (p. 597)
—First Word Search: Reading Made Easy. (p. 597)
—Growing up Happy: Arnold Gets Angry, Betty Stops the Bully & Catherine Finds Her Courage: the Emotional Literacy Series (p. 726)
—Pencil, Paper, Draw! - Animals. (p. 1336)
—Pencil, Paper, Draw! - Cars & Trucks. (p. 1336)
—Pencil, Paper, Draw! - Dogs. (p. 1336)
—Pencil, Paper, Draw! - Fantasy Creatures. (p. 1336)
—Pencil, Paper, Draw!(r) - Dinosaurs. (p. 1336)
—Pencil, Paper, Draw!(r) - Horses. (p. 1336)
Harpster, Steve, illus. see Adams, Alison.
Harpster, Steve, illus. see Hoena, Blake A.
Harpster, Steve, illus. see Houts, Amy.
Harpster, Steve, illus. see Lemke, Amy J.
Harpster, Steve, illus. see Lord, Michelle.
Harpster, Steve, illus. see Meister, Cari.
Harpster, Steve, illus. see Mooney, Carla.
Harpster, Steve, illus. see Nickel, Scott.
Harpster, Steve, illus. see Pattison, Darcy.
Harpster, Steve, illus. see Shapiro, Lawrence E.
Harpster, Steve, illus. see Shapiro, Lawrence.
Harpster, Steve, illus. see Smith, Carrie.
Harpster, Steve, illus. see Temple, Bob.
Harpster, Steve, illus. see Torres, J.
Harpster, Steve, illus. see Yasuda, Anita.
Harpster, Steve, jt. auth. see Yasuda, Anita.
Harpur, James. Celtic Myth: A Treasury of Legends, Art, & History. (p. 286)
—Crusades: The Two Hundred Years War: The Clash Between the Cross & the Crescent in the Middle East 1096-1291. (p. 386)
Harr, Alexandra. Make a Stand: When Life Gives You Lemons, Change the World! (p. 1079)
Harr, Lynn, illus. see Spoon, Cynthia.
Harrad, Matthew, illus. see Koontz, Robin Michal.
Harrah, Judith. Come Inside the Ark. Foster, Jack, illus. (p. 347)
—Jesus, I Believe. Kukreja, Julie, illus. (p. 915)
Harrald-Pilz, Marilee. Hide-and-Seek Puzzles: Animal Friends. (p. 777)
Harrald-Pilz, Marilee, illus. see Berry, Eileen M.
Harrald-Pilz, Marilee, illus. see Metzger, Steve.
Harrald-Pilz, Marilee, illus. see Schmauss, Judy Kentor.
Harrald-Pilz, Marilee, jt. auth. see Ashour, Monica.
Harrald-Pilz, Marilee, jt. auth. see Slater, Teddy.
Harrap. French Student's Dictionary. (p. 636)
Harrar, Frank W. Wee Dragonslayers. Galan-Robles, Francisco, illus. (p. 1871)
Harrar, George. Not As Crazy As I Seem. (p. 1267)
—Trouble with Jeremy Chance. Thayer, Elizabeth, illus. (p. 1790)
Harras, Bob & Green, Dan. World Without a Justice League. (p. 1959)
Harrast, Tracy. Miracles of Jesus Corke, Estelle, illus. (p. 1149)
—My Giant Fold-Out Book: Christmas. Doherty, Paula, illus. (p. 1209)
—Oh Holy Night. Corke, Estelle, illus. (p. 1280)
—Picture That! Bible Storybook over 65 Stories Colby, Garry, illus. (p. 1356)
—Story of the Nativity Corke, Estelle, illus. (p. 1661)
—¿Adivina Que? Historias de la Biblia Sharp, Alice & Sharp, Paul, illus. (p. 12)
Harrast, Tracy & Readers Digest Childrens Publishing Inc. Staff. Long Ago in Bethlehem. Corke, Estelle, illus. (p. 1046)
Harrast, Tracy L. My Learn to Read Bible: Stories in Words & Pictures Schneider, Christine M., illus. (p. 1211)
Harrel, Tina, illus. see Picone, Emma Lee.
Harrell, Angel R., jt. auth. see Sebastian, Teresa L.
Harrell, Antoinette. Nurturing My Family Tree: Genealogy for Children. (p. 1273)
Harrell, Bill. Gabriel & the Secret of the Rainbow: A Story to Inspire Hope. (p. 652)
Harrell, Deborah A. Pintos Hope. (p. 1361)
Harrell, Kim, illus. see Bachmann, Elaine Rice.
Harrell, Kim, illus. see Dans, Peter E.
Harrell, Maurice, illus. see Yolanda And Reese.
Harrell, Michael, illus. see Moore, Carol Hair.
Harrell, Micheael, illus. see Moore, Carol H.
Harrell, Nancy. Ninos de el Mundo/ Children of the World. (p. 1257)
Harrell, Rob. Trouble with Weasels. (p. 1790)
Harrell, Symear, illus. see Londa And Pop-Pop.
Harries, Brigitte. Puppies: Keeping & Caring for Your Pet. (p. 1418)
Harries, Tony. Zeegpaw & the Cat Cult. (p. 1985)
Harriet Kasak Portfolio Staff, illus. see Wheeler, Lisa.
Harriet, Ziefert, jt. auth. see Ziefert, Harriet.
Harrigan, Matt. Zoo's Annual Piggyback Race. Beavers, Melinda, illus. (p. 1990)
Harrigan, Mike, illus. see Hardman, Ron & Hardman, Jessica.
Harrill, Cory, illus. see Pecora, Bet Shoshannah.
Harriman, Marinell & Harriman, Robert. Myriad of Minstrels. Harriman, Marinell & Harriman, Robert, illus. (p. 1222)
Harriman, Robert, jt. auth. see Harriman, Marinell.
Harrington, A. Page, ed. see DeAngelis, Therese.
Harrington, A. Page, ed. see Gelletly, LeeAnne.
Harrington, A. Page, ed. see Humphrey, Elizabeth King.
Harrington, A. Page, ed. see Jennings, Terry Catasús.
Harrington, A. Page, ed. see Roppelt, Donna.
Harrington, Claudia. My Grandparents. Persico, Zoe, illus. (p. 1210)
—My Military Mom. Persico, Zoe, illus. (p. 1214)
—My Mom & Dad. Persico, Zoe, illus. (p. 1214)
—My Two Dads. Persico, Zoe, illus. (p. 1220)
—My Two Homes. Persico, Zoe, illus. (p. 1220)
—My Two Moms. Persico, Zoe, illus. (p. 1220)
Harrington, Daniel. What Am I. (p. 1879)
—What Am I? A Hawai'i Animal Guessing Game. Brandt, Susan, illus. (p. 1879)
Harrington, David, illus. see Alfaro, Manuel.
Harrington, David, illus. see Balsley, Tilda.
Harrington, David, illus. see Brolsma, Jody.
Harrington, David, illus. see Chrismer, Melanie.
Harrington, David, illus. see Duckworth, Liz.
Harrington, David, illus. see Grudzina, Rebecca.
Harrington, David, illus. see Harris, Brooke.
Harrington, David, illus. see McGuire, Andy.
Harrington, David, illus. see McManis, Margaret.
Harrington, David, illus. see Nappa, Mike.
Harrington, David, illus. see Rosenberg, Aaron.
Harrington, David, illus. see Shally, Celeste.
Harrington, David, illus. see Sorenson, Margo.
Harrington, David, illus. see Strauss, Kevin.
Harrington, David, illus. see Thomasian, Sara.
Harrington, David, illus. see Wesemann, Tim.
Harrington, David, jt. auth. see McConduit, Denise.
Harrington, Dylan, et al. Harrington Five & the Case of the School Sandals Err Vandals. (p. 750)
Harrington, Fred H. Ethiopian Wolf. (p. 539)
—Gray Wolf. (p. 713)
—Red Wolf. (p. 1455)
Harrington, Geri. Gray Squirrel at Pacific Avenue. Roosevelt, Michele Chopin, illus. (p. 713)
Harrington, Glenn, illus. see Kasten, David Scott & Kastan, Marina, eds.
Harrington, Hannah. Speechless. (p. 1624)
Harrington, James. Last Laugh. (p. 978)
Harrington, Jane. Extreme Pets. (p. 556)
—Four Things My Geeky-Jock-of-a-Best-Friend Must Do in Europe. (p. 625)
Harrington, Janice N. Busy-Busy Little Chick. Pinkney, Brian, illus. (p. 246)
—Chicken-Chasing Queen of Lamar County. Jackson, Shelley, illus. (p. 300)
—Going North. Lagarrigue, Jerome, illus. (p. 692)
Harrington, Janine. Soul Sister. (p. 1614)
Harrington, John. Meet Mindy: A Native Girl from the Southwest. Secakuku, Susan, photos by. (p. 1121)
Harrington, John, photos by see Belarde-Lewis, Miranda.
Harrington, John, photos by see Secakuku, Susan.
Harrington, John, photos by see Tayac, Gabrielle.
Harrington, John P., jt. auth. see Clark, Ann Nolan.
Harrington, K. A. Forget Me. (p. 619)
Harrington, Karen. Sure Signs of Crazy. (p. 1685)
Harrington, Kim. Clarity. (p. 327)
—Dead & Buried. (p. 416)
—Framed & Dangerous. (p. 627)
—Partners in Crime. (p. 1325)
—Perception. (p. 1341)
—Sleepover Stakeout. (p. 1589)
—Sleuth or Dare #2: Sleepover Stakeout. (p. 1590)
Harrington, Leslie, illus. see Allen, Susan.
Harrington, Leslie, illus. see Winans, Carvin.
Harrington, Linda. Holly's Backyard Adventures (p. 789)
Harrington, Linda, illus. see Arrington, R. Region.
Harrington, Lisa. Rattled (p. 1440)
Harrington, Paul. Secret to Teen Power. (p. 1544)
Harrington, Rich, illus. see Alfonsi, Alice.
Harrington, Rich, illus. see West, Tracey.
Harrington, Sean. Jack-in-the-Box Madness. (p. 903)
Harrington, Shelley. Eyes of Rain. (p. 558)
—Gugly Ugly Gaboo. (p. 729)
Harrington, Tim. Nose to Toes, You Are Yummy! Harrington, Tim, illus. (p. 1266)
—This Little Piggy. Harrington, Tim, illus. (p. 1737)
Harrinsson, Nelson. Mario, Donkey Cuco & the Mango Tree. (p. 1094)
Harris, Abaghoul. Monster High Drop Dead Diary. (p. 1167)
Harris, Amber. Black, White & Beautiful. Mamata, Sue, illus. (p. 197)
Harris, Andrew, illus. see Cobb, Vicki.
Harris, Andrew, illus. see Harris, Trudy.
Harris, Andrew J. R., jt. ed. see Taylor, Helen.
Harris, Andy. Tick-Tock Grandad's Sweetshop Skills for Life. (p. 1747)
Harris, Angela. Night Light. (p. 1253)
Harris, Angela Brent -. Sweet Jamaican Summertime at Grandma's. (p. 1690)
Harris, Angela L. Mommy What Is a Ceo? Chapman, Debbie, illus. (p. 1162)
Harris, Annabel. Look Out, it's the First of October! (p. 1050)
Harris, Annaka. I Wonder. Rowe, John, illus. (p. 849)
Harris, Annmarie. Nutcracker. Jay, Alison, illus. (p. 1273)
Harris, Ashley Rae. Arms Trade. (p. 100)
—Cliques, Crushes, & True Friends: Developing Healthy Relationships. (p. 333)
—Do You Love Me? Making Healthy Dating Decisions. (p. 458)
—Facebook: The Company & Its Founders. (p. 560)
—Girl in the Mirror: Understanding Physical Changes. (p. 678)
—Graphic Novels. (p. 711)
—Microsoft: The Company & Its Founders. (p. 1136)
—Nicki Minaj: Rapper & Fashion Star. (p. 1251)
—Prank. (p. 1393)
—Tupac Shakur: Multi-Platinum Rapper. (p. 1797)
—Txt Me L8r: Using Technology Responsibly. (p. 1804)
Harris, Bill. Phantom (p. 1349)
Harris, Bonnie. When Your Kids Push Your Buttons: And What You Can Do about It. (p. 1906)
Harris, Brandy, illus. see Harris, Mary.
Harris, Brenda. Ride Like the Wind. (p. 1471)
Harris, Brian. Joe's Bedtime Stories for Boys & Girls. (p. 920)
Harris, Brian, illus. see Hodge, Deborah.
Harris, Brian, photos by see Hodge, Deborah.
Harris, Brian J. Snare Drum Plays the Zoo: Beginning Snare Drum Method (p. 1597)
Harris, Brooke. Are You Sleeping? Oliver, Mark, illus. (p. 97)
—Baby Gets a Cake. Beckstrand, Jared, illus. (p. 126)
—Brother John, Wake Up! (p. 231)
—Fun with Our Friends: Lap Book. (p. 649)
—Healthy Snacks: Lap Book. (p. 759)
—Jack & Jill Play on the Hill. (p. 902)
—Little Boy Blue, Where are You? (p. 1025)
—London Bridge. Boyer, Lyn, illus. (p. 1046)
—London Bridge Has Fallen Down. Boyer, Lyn, illus. (p. 1046)
—Mary's Garden: How Does it Grow? Xin, Xiao, illus. (p. 1101)
—Playing at My House: Lap Book. (p. 1372)
—Purple Cow. Hohnstadt, Cedric, illus. (p. 1419)
—This Little Pig, That Little Pig. (p. 1737)
—This Little Piggy. Ledger, Bill, illus. (p. 1737)
—Twinkle, Twinkle, Little Star. Harrington, David, illus. (p. 1802)
—Twinkling Stars. Harrington, David, illus. (p. 1802)
—Where Has My Dog Gone? Harrington, David, illus. (p. 1907)
—Where Has My Little Dog Gone? (p. 1907)
—Working on the Railroad. (p. 1953)
Harris, Calvin & Rustad, Martha E. Apple Harvest Saunders-Smith, Gail, ed. (p. 92)
—Scarecrows (p. 1519)
Harris, Carol & Brown, Mike. Accessories. (p. 8)
—Ceremonial Costumes. (p. 287)
—Children's Costumes. (p. 303)
—Men's Costumes. (p. 1126)
—Military Uniforms. (p. 1143)
—Women's Costumes. (p. 1946)
Harris, Carol Flynn. Place for Joey. (p. 1365)
Harris, Carol Gahara. My Name is Leona. Fujiwara, Kim, illus. (p. 1215)
Harris, Caroline. Discover Science: Whales & Dolphins. (p. 448)
—Discover Science: Weather. (p. 448)
—Whales & Dolphins. (p. 1878)
Harris, Carolyn. RV in NZ: How to Spend Your Winters Freedom Camping South—Way South—in New Zealand. (p. 1499)
Harris, Carrie. Bad Hair Day. (p. 131)
—Demon Derby. (p. 426)
—Sally Slick & the Steel Syndicate. Valentine, Amanda, ed. (p. 1505)
Harris, Charisse N. Mama Please. (p. 1084)
Harris, Charlaine. Bone to Pick (p. 209)
—Fool & His Honey. (p. 614)
—Real Murders. (p. 1448)
—Shakespeare's Christmas. (p. 1559)
—Shakespeare's Trollop. (p. 1559)
Harris, Charlaine & Kelner, Toni L. P., eds. Many Bloody Returns. (p. 1089)
Harris, Charles Edward. Ice Angels. (p. 850)
Harris, Christine. Audrey Goes to Town. James, Ann, illus. (p. 115)
—Audrey of the Outback. James, Ann, illus. (p. 115)
—Audrey of the Outback Collection. James, Ann, illus. (p. 115)
—Audrey's Big Secret. James, Ann, illus. (p. 115)
—Four Tails: An Anthology of Four Tales for Children. (p. 625)
—It's a Miroocool! James, Ann, illus. (p. 895)
—Silver Path. (p. 1576)
—Undercover Girl #5: Twisted. (p. 1814)
Harris, Christy D. Froggie Fiasco. (p. 640)
Harris, Cindy C. Raoke & the Camp Raid. (p. 1438)
Harris, Coy F., ed. see McCook, William.
Harris, - Crystal, illus. see Saleem-Muhammad, Rasheedah.
Harris, Daniel C., photos by see Harris, Donna L.
Harris, Danielle. Big Move to the Little House. (p. 182)
—Second Chance Sant. (p. 1539)
Harris, Dave. Daredevils & Show-offs. (p. 406)
—Great Escapes. (p. 715)
—Survival! (p. 1686)
—Weird & Wacky Festivals. (p. 1872)
Harris, Dave & Thomson, Russell. Who Invented That? (p. 1915)
Harris, Dave & Van Til, Meaghan. Eye See. (p. 558)

H

Harris, David. Pussy Footin' (p. 1420)
Harris, Deanna Lynn. Taters Go to School: The Feud. (p. 1707)
—Taters Go to Washington: The Feud. (p. 1707)
—Taters of the Ozarks: The Feud. (p. 1707)
Harris, Dede. Sammy: Child Survivor of the Holocaust Teachers Guide & Workbook. (p. 1508)
Harris, Dee. Croaker Sack Bunny. Bohart, Lisa, illus. (p. 384)
—I Am Not a Hippopotamus, I Am a Little Girl , Book. Bohart, Lisa, illus. (p. 833)
Harris, Denise. Are You Sleeping? Easy Easter Dramas, Speeches, & Recitations for Children. (p. 97)
Harris, Destiny. Beauty Secrets for Girls. (p. 154)
Harris, Devon & Cortés, Ricardo. Yes, I Can! The Story of the Jamaican Bobsled Team. (p. 1970)
Harris, Devon D. Yes I Can. (p. 1970)
Harris, Diane Banks. Eagle & the Chickens. (p. 492)
Harris, Don. Bluebird Story. (p. 204)
Harris, Donna. Dust Bunnies Do Love Donuts. (p. 490)
—Lucie & the Garden Fairies. (p. 1062)
—Ruff Life. (p. 1494)
Harris, Donna L. Lost Kitten & How He Was Found. AnnDrewArt, illus. (p. 1056)
Harris, Dorothy Joan. Cameron & Me. (p. 256)
—Perro Muy Diferente. Rioja, Alberto Jimenez, tr. from ENG. (p. 1344)
Harris, Dorthy. Taylor's Dream Ends Summer School Nightm. (p. 1708)
Harris, E. Lynn. Diaries of a Light-Skinned Colored Boy (p. 434)
Harris, Elle. Lullaby World. (p. 1064)
Harris, Erin. Elephant on My Roof. Harris, Erin, illus. (p. 511)
Harris, Errol E. Twenty-First Century Democratic Renaissance PBK: From Plato to Neoliberalism to Planetary Democracy. (p. 1801)
Harris, Evelyn. Two Harrises & One Day Go Camping. (p. 1803)
Harris, Frankco. David Saves the Day: An African American Depiction of David & Goliath. (p. 411)
Harris, Geraldine. Ancient Egypt. (p. 68)
—From My Spirit to Yours in Prose & Poetry. (p. 643)
Harris, Gina. I Kiss Girls. (p. 840)
Harris, Godfrey, jt. auth. see Leonardo.
Harris, Godfrey, et al. Life & Contributions of Leonardo Da Vinci. (p. 1007)
Harris, Grace L. Lord, Those Church Folks. (p. 1052)
Harris, Harris. Union Cross: New Seasons. (p. 1818)
Harris, Heather. Changing Tree. (p. 290)
Harris, Irene. African American Migrations in North America. (p. 27)
Harris, Isobel. Little Boy Brown. François, André, illus. (p. 1025)
Harris, J. Henry & Everson, Michael. Phyllis in Piskie-Land: A Tale of Cornwall, Inspired by Lewis Carroll's Wonderland. (p. 1353)
Harris, Jack, illus. see Souza, D. M.
Harris, Jane Ellen. Room for One More. Cole, Al, illus. (p. 1488)
Harris, Janelle. Bree's Building Blocks: Work with 11-19 to Gain Foundations for Place Value. (p. 226)
Harris, Janice. Journey: Subtle Lessons in Spiritual Awakening. (p. 927)
Harris, Janice L. & Lisech, Howard. Discovering Christlike Habits (Book 3) CHRISTIAN SCHOOL Edition: Student Workbook. Snyder, Barb, ed. (p. 449)
Harris, Janice L., et al. Discovering Christlike Habits (Book 3) HOME SCHOOL Edition: Student Workbook. Snyder, Barb, ed. (p. 449)
Harris, Jeffrey. Color Book Bible: Parted Waters for Kids. (p. 342)
Harris, Jennifer Beck, illus. see Landolf, Diane Wright.
Harris, Jennifer Beck, illus. see Williams, Rozanne Lanczak.
Harris, Jenny B., illus. see Williams, Rozanne Lanczak.
Harris, Jessica. Ella the Elephant Visits Granny & Pa. (p. 514)
Harris, Jim. Dinosaur's Night Before Christmas Harris, Jim, illus. (p. 445)
Harris, Jim, illus. see Artell, Mike.
Harris, Jim, illus. see Davis, David.
Harris, Jim, illus. see Harris, Marian.
Harris, Jim, illus. see Lowell, Susan.
Harris, Jim, illus. see Ode, Eric.
Harris, Jim, illus. see Schnetzler, Pattie.
Harris, Jim, jt. auth. see Harris, Marian.
Harris, Joanne. Blackberry Wine. (p. 197)
Harris, Joe. Belly Book. Harris, Joe, illus. (p. 163)
—Narda. (p. 1229)
—Wars in Toyland. (p. 1859)
Harris, Joe, jt. auth. see Connolly, Sean.
Harris, Joel, illus. see Vecchione, Glen.
Harris, Joel Chandle. Told by Uncle Remus: New Stories of the. (p. 1762)
Harris, Joel Chandler. Mingo. (p. 1146)
—Nights with Uncle Remus. (p. 1255)
—Story of Brer Rabbit & the Wonderful Tar Baby. Drescher, Henrik, illus. (p. 1657)
—Uncle Remus: His Songs & His Sayings. (p. 1812)
—Uncle Remus & Brer Rabbit the Complete Tales. (p. 1812)
—Uncle Remus His Songs & His Sayings. (p. 1812)
Harris, Joel Chandler, jt. auth. see Kessler, Brad.
Harris, Joel Chandler, jt. auth. see Schomp, Virginia.
Harris, Joel Chandler, et al. Classic Tales of Brer Rabbit. (p. 328)
—Classic Tales of Brer Rabbit. Daily, Don, illus. (p. 328)
—Tar Baby & Other Rhymes of Uncle Remus. (p. 1706)
Harris, John. Jingle Bells: How the Holiday Classic Came to Be Gustavson, Adam, illus. (p. 918)
—My Monster Notebook. Todd, Mark, illus. (p. 1214)
—Pop-Up Aesop. Brown, Calef, illus. (p. 1384)
—Strong Stuff: Herakles & His Labors. Baseman, Gary, illus. (p. 1668)
Harris, John, jt. auth. see Holmes, Mary Tavener.
Harris, John & Lorenz, Catherine. Cats. (p. 280)
—Discovering Art Dogs. (p. 448)
—Discovering Art Kids. (p. 448)
Harris, Jonathan, jt. auth. see Venning, Timothy.
Harris, Jonathan M. Environmental & Natural Resource Economics: A Contemporary Approach. (p. 532)
Harris, Joseph. 1980s. (p. 2002)
—Space Exploration: The Impact of Science & Technology. (p. 1619)
—Tibet. (p. 1747)
—Transportation: The Impact of Science & Technology. (p. 1779)
—What Are Human Rights? (p. 1879)
Harris, Joseph, jt. auth. see Kavanagh, Terry.
Harris, Joseph R., jt. auth. see Turkington, Carol A.
Harris, Joshua. I Kissed Dating Goodbye: A New Attitude Toward Relationships & Romance. (p. 840)
—I Kissed Dating Goodbye Study Guide. (p. 840)
Harris, Julie, reader. Puss in Boots. (p. 1420)
Harris, Kandi. Prince, the Future King: A Father's Example Wyman, M. C. & Anderson, Bill, illus. (p. 1401)
—Princess, the Future Queen: A Mother's Guidance. Rippon, Jor-El, illus. (p. 1406)
Harris, Kate W., ed. Clever Sheikh of the Butana: Sudanese Folk Tales. Hamad, Elnour, illus. (p. 331)
Harris, Keith. On the Street: Thoughts of a Born Again Biker. (p. 1291)
Harris, Kimberly Anne. Only in a Dream Series: Caught in a Web ~ the Trees Are My Friends~What Is All the Buzz About? (p. 1298)
Harris, L. Little Girl in Paris. (p. 1028)
Harris, La Verne Abe, illus. see Carr, Sheryl.
Harris, Lauren, jt. auth. see Crawford, Sheryl Ann.
Harris, Laurie Lanzen. Biography for Beginners: Inventors. (p. 189)
—Biography for Beginners: All Authors. (p. 189)
—Biography for Beginners: African-American Leaders. (p. 189)
—Biography for Beginners: Women Who Made a Difference. (p. 189)
—Colonial America & the Revolutionary War: The Story of the People of the Colonies, from Early Settlers to Revolutionary Leaders. (p. 341)
—How to Analyze the Works of Abraham Lincoln. (p. 814)
—Presidents of the United States. (p. 1397)
Harris, Laurie Lanzen, ed. Biography for Beginners: World Explorers. (p. 189)
—Biography for Beginners: African-American Leaders. Vol. 2 (p. 189)
Harris, Lee. Carla & the Great Talent Show. (p. 270)
Harris, Lewis. Taste for Red. (p. 1707)
Harris, Linda. What Is a Me-Ma? (p. 1888)
Harris, Lisa Delmedico. Official Princess Handbook: A Little Girl's Guide to Beauty, Poise, & Righteousness. (p. 1280)
—Princess Charm School: A Godly Approach to Beauty, Poise, & Righteousness. (p. 1403)
Harris, Lois V. Charlie Russell: Tale-Telling Cowboy Artist (p. 293)
—Mary Cassatt: Impressionist Painter Cassatt, Mary, illus. (p. 1100)
—Maxfield Parrish: Painter of Magical Make-Believe (p. 1112)
Harris, Loretta. Gangsta's Life. (p. 655)
—Hard Life. (p. 748)
—Inside Struggle. (p. 877)
—Who Did It & Why? (p. 1915)
Harris, Lorrayne R., illus. see Lewis, L. W.
Harris, M. G. Ice Shock. (p. 850)
—Invisible City. (p. 885)
—Zero Moment. (p. 1986)
Harris, M. S. Ed, jt. auth. see Harris, M. S. Ed Rebecca a.
Harris, M. S. Ed Rebecca a. & Harris, M. S. Ed. Megan's Monster. Lee, Joe, illus. (p. 1124)
Harris, Madeline S., ed. see Allen, Catherine Judge.
Harris, Madeline S., ed. see Evans, Arthur V.
Harris, Marian. Ten Little Kittens. Harris, Jim, illus. (p. 1719)
—Ten Little Puppies. Harris, Jim, illus. (p. 1719)
Harris, Marian & Harris, Jim. Ten Little Kittens. (p. 1719)
Harris, Marie. Girl Who Heard Colors. Newton, Vanessa Brantley, illus. (p. 679)
—Primary Numbers: A New Hampshire Numbers Book. Holman, Karen, illus. (p. 1399)
Harris, Mark Jonathan. Come the Morning. Rosa, Marrisa, photos by. (p. 347)
Harris, Mary. Freckles from Heaven. Harris, Brandy, illus. (p. 632)
Harris, Mary Beth. Susie Sunflower. Pederson, Gunda, illus. (p. 1688)
Harris, Michael. Deviant. (p. 432)
—Heaven's War. (p. 761)
—Teenagers. (p. 1714)
—TEENAGERS II: High School Blowout!!! (p. 1714)
—Young Marques Becomes a Quiet Storm. (p. 1979)
Harris, Michael C. Artificial Intelligence. (p. 104)
—Spare Parts for People. (p. 1622)
—Unusual Diseases. (p. 1823)
Harris, Michele Zink. Plain Little Yellow Pencil: Leading by Placing Yourself Below. (p. 1366)
Harris, Miki, illus. see Jones, Teresa Chin.
Harris, Milt. Foxy Roxy: The Adventures of a Smooth Fox Terrier. (p. 626)
Harris, Missy. I'm Allergic: Imma Lurgic's Story. (p. 858)
—I'm Allergic. (p. 858)
Harris, Monica. Black Widow Spider. (p. 197)
—My First Book of Animals. (p. 1205)
—Paper Wasp. (p. 1323)
—Tarantula. (p. 1706)
—Tick. (p. 1747)
—Walking Stick. (p. 1854)
Harris, Nancy. águila Calva. (p. 30)
—Amarillo (p. 52)
—American Flag (p. 60)
—Amphetamines. (p. 65)
—Azul (p. 122)
—Bald Eagle (p. 133)
—Bandera Estadounidense (p. 136)
—Black (p. 194)
—Blanco (p. 198)
—Blue (p. 202)
—Brown (p. 231)
—Campana de la Libertad (p. 257)
—Capitol Building (p. 263)
—Capitolio (p. 263)
—Casa Blanca (p. 273)
—Colors (p. 345)
—Comparing Colors. (p. 351)
—Estatua de la Libertad (p. 538)
—Green (p. 721)
—Himno Nacional (p. 780)
—In These Walls & Floors (p. 868)
—In This Bathroom (p. 868)
—In This Bedroom (p. 868)
—In This Kitchen (p. 868)
—In This Living Room (p. 868)
—Is an Inchworm an Inch? Measuring with Fractions. (p. 889)
—Juramento de Lealtad (p. 937)
—Liberty Bell (p. 1005)
—Lincoln Memorial (p. 1018)
—Marrón. (p. 1096)
—Mashed Potatoes: Collecting & Reporting Data. (p. 1102)
—Monte Rushmore (p. 1170)
—Monumento a Lincoln (p. 1171)
—Monumento a Washington (p. 1171)
—Mount Rushmore (p. 1180)
—Naranja (p. 1229)
—National Anthem (p. 1231)
—Negro (p. 1240)
—Orange (p. 1301)
—Pledge of Allegiance (p. 1373)
—Red (p. 1453)
—Right to Die. (p. 1472)
—Rojo (p. 1485)
—Shapes & Patterns We Know. (p. 1560)
—Statue of Liberty (p. 1645)
—Sticky Fingers: Exploring the Number 5. (p. 1650)
—Sticky Fingers Exploring the Number 5. (p. 1650)
—Verde (p. 1836)
—Violet (p. 1843)
—Violeta (p. 1843)
—Washington Monument (p. 1860)
—What Are Elections? (p. 1879)
—What Are the Amendments? (p. 1879)
—What's a City Council? (p. 1896)
—What's a Governor? (p. 1896)
—What's a Mayor? (p. 1896)
—What's a President & Vice President? (p. 1896)
—What's Congress? (p. 1896)
—What's Government? (p. 1897)
—What's Lurking in This House? (p. 1898)
—What's the Bill of Rights? (p. 1899)
—What's the Declaration of Independence? (p. 1899)
—What's the State Judicial Branch? (p. 1899)
—What's the State Legislative Branch? (p. 1899)
—What's the Supreme Court? (p. 1899)
—What's the U. S. Constitution? (p. 1900)
—White (p. 1912)
—White House (p. 1913)
—Yellow (p. 1969)
—¿Qué es la Carta de Derechos? (p. 1423)
—¿Qué es la Constitución? (p. 1423)
—¿Qué es la Corte Suprema? (p. 1423)
—¿Qué Es la Declaracion de Independencia? (p. 1423)
—¿Qué es la Declaracion de Independencia? (p. 1423)
—¿Qué es la Rama Judicial Estatal? (p. 1423)
—¿Qué es la Rama Legislativa Estatal? (p. 1423)
—¿Qué es un Alcalde? (p. 1423)
—¿Qué es un Congreso? (p. 1423)
—¿Qué es un Consejo Municipal? (p. 1423)
—¿Qué es un Gobernador? (p. 1423)
—¿Qué es un Gobierno? (p. 1423)
—¿Qué es un Presidente y un Vicepresidente? (p. 1423)
—¿Qué Son Elecciones? (p. 1424)
—¿Qué Son las Enmiendas? (p. 1424)
Harris, Nancy & Armstrong, Lynn, eds. Volcanoes. (p. 1849)
Harris, Nancy & Rissman, Rebecca. Be the Best at Math (p. 149)
—Be the Best at Reading (p. 149)
—Be the Best at Science (p. 149)
Harris, Nancy, ed. Tornadoes. (p. 1770)
Harris, Nathaniel. 1960s. (p. 2002)
—1970s. (p. 2002)
—Ancient Maya: Archaeology Unlocks the Secrets of the Maya's Past. (p. 70)
—Atlas of the World's Deserts. (p. 113)
—Burma (Myanmar) (p. 243)
—Crime Fighting: The Impact of Science & Technology. (p. 382)
—Debate about Globalization. (p. 421)
—Drug Trafficking. (p. 487)
—Monarchy. (p. 1163)
—Mosaics. (p. 1176)
—National Geographic Investigates: Ancient Maya: Archaeology Unlocks the Secrets of the Maya's Past. (p. 1231)
—Paul Cézanne. (p. 1330)
—Terrorism. (p. 1722)
—Wall Paintings. (p. 1854)
—World War II. (p. 1959)
Harris, Nathaniel, jt. auth. see Heinemann Library Staff.
Harris, Nelson. Andrew of the Antimites. (p. 72)
Harris, Nic. Alaska. (p. 33)
—How Cool Is Cold! Low Intermediate Book with Online Access. (p. 806)
—Science of Heat. (p. 1527)
—Wonders of the World High Beginning Book with Online Access. (p. 1949)
Harris, Nic & Naughton, Diane. Growing up: from Baby to Adult High Beginning Book with Online Access. (p. 726)
Harris, Nicholas. Day in a City. (p. 413)
—Empire: Rise & Fall. (p. 521)
—First Humans. Dennis, Peter, illus. (p. 595)
—Glow in the Dark Book of Space: The Book You Can Read in the Dark! Sebastian Quigley, Sebastian, illus. (p. 685)
—Greatest Invention of All Time. (p. 720)
—Let's Explore a Castle. Lee, Brian, illus. (p. 996)
—Let's Explore a Pirate Ship. Lee, Brian, illus. (p. 996)
—Medicine: Old & New. (p. 1119)
—Pyramid. Dennis, Peter, illus. (p. 1421)
—Rainforest. (p. 1436)
—Viaje Increíble al Centro de la Tierra. (p. 1839)
—Year at a Construction Site. (p. 1969)
—Year at a Farm. (p. 1969)
Harris, Nicholas, jt. auth. see Harris, Nicholas.
Harris, Nicholas & Dennis, Peter. Volcano. (p. 1848)
Harris, Nicholas & Harris, Nicholas. Viaje Increíble a los Planetas. (p. 1839)
—Viaje Increíble al Fondo del Mar. (p. 1839)
—Viaje Increíble por el Cuerpo Humano. (p. 1839)
Harris, Nicholas & Joanna, Turner. Porque de las Cosas: Naturaleza y Ciencia. (p. 1386)
Harris, Nicholas, text. Dinosaurs. (p. 443)
—Panoramas: Ocean Life. (p. 1321)
Harris, Nick. Wooden Horse of Troy (p. 1949)
Harris, Nick, illus. see Dixon, Andy.
Harris, Nick, illus. see Evans, Hestia.
Harris, Nicolas. Castles Through Time. (p. 277)
—Dinosaurs Through Time. Dennis, Peter, illus. (p. 445)
—Earthquakes Through Time. (p. 498)
—Libro de Saber: Civilizaciones y Conocimiento. (p. 1006)
—Pyramids Through Time. (p. 1421)
—Volcanoes Through Time. (p. 1849)
Harris, Nikki. Adventures in Friendship for Benji Butterfly & Tom Turkey. (p. 15)
Harris, Odis Clinton. Wee Willie & the Lonely Pine. (p. 1871)
Harris, P & Brewe. Improve Sight-Singing: High & Medium Voice. (p. 862)
Harris, P. M. G. History of Human Populations: Migration, Urbanization, & Structural Change Vol. II (p. 784)
Harris, Patrice. Grandma Asks: Were You Good at School Today? Harrison, Nicholas, illus. (p. 708)
Harris, Patricia. Garden of My Heart. (p. 656)
Harris, Patricia Taylor. I Believe I'll Testify: A True Story about the Power of Prayer. Taylor Harris Photography, photos by. (p. 834)
Harris, Patrick. Waterman Chronicles: Rise of the Elementals. (p. 1863)
—Where the Day Takes You volume One. (p. 1909)
Harris, Patrick O'Neil, illus. see Welch, Michelle Rose.
Harris, Paul & Brewer, Mike. Improve Sight-Singing! Low/Medium Voice - Elementary level. (p. 862)
Harris, Peter. Night Pirates. Allwright, Deborah, illus. (p. 1254)
Harris, Philip. Inky Pinky. (p. 874)
—Trever & the Phoenix. (p. 1785)
Harris, Philip R. Launch Out. (p. 980)
Harris, Phyllis, illus. see Brown, Margaret.
Harris, Phyllis, illus. see Derico, Laura Ring.
Harris, Phyllis, illus. see Marsaw, Roy.
Harris, Phyllis, illus. see Novack, Danielle.
Harris, Phyllis, illus. see Simon, Mary Manz.
Harris, Pj. Fat, Fat, What's Wrong with That? The Importance of Diet & Exercise. (p. 577)
Harris, Polly. Peep Peep, You're a Duck, Not a People! (p. 1335)
Harris, R. Craig, illus. see Harris, Richard.
Harris, R. P. Tua & the Elephant. (p. 1795)
—Tua & the Elephant. Yoo, Taeeun, illus. (p. 1795)
Harris, Rachel. Tale of Two Centuries. (p. 1700)
Harris, Rae Ann & Weintraub, David. Sereena's Secret. Craft, Danna, illus. (p. 1552)
Harris, Richard. I'm Walking, I'm Running, I'm Jumping, I'm Hopping. Harris, R. Craig, illus. (p. 860)
Harris, Rita & Long, Paul. 19 Cats of Alabama. (p. 1995)
Harris, Robert & Yolen, Jane. Girl in a Cage. (p. 678)
Harris, Robert E. Rose That Grew Out the Concrete (p. 1489)
Harris, Robert J., jt. auth. see Yolen, Jane.
Harris, Robie H. Adios, Ratoncito. Rioja, Alberto Jiménez, tr. (p. 12)
—David Dinosaur-Rrr! What It's Like to Be 3. Emberley, Michael, illus. (p. 411)
—Day Leo Said I Hate You! Bang, Molly, illus. (p. 413)
—Goodbye Mousie. Ormerod, Jan, illus. (p. 701)
—Harris Untitled Book of First. (p. 750)
—I Am Not Going to School Today! Ormerod, Jan, illus. (p. 833)
—It's Not the Stork! A Book about Girls, Boys, Babies, Bodies, Families & Friends. Emberley, Michael, illus. (p. 898)
—It's Perfectly Normal. (p. 898)
—It's So Amazing! A Book about Eggs, Sperm, Birth, Babies, & Families. Emberley, Michael, illus. (p. 899)
—Mail Harry to the Moon! Emberley, Michael, illus. (p. 1077)
—Maybe a Bear Ate It! Emberley, Michael, illus. (p. 1113)
—Sexo... Que Es? (p. 1556)
—Untitled Harris Book of First. (p. 1823)
—What's in There? All about Before You Were Born. Emberley, Michael & Westcott, Nadine Bernard, illus. (p. 1898)
—What's So Yummy? All about Eating Well & Feeling Good. Westcott, Nadine Bernard, illus. (p. 1899)
—When Lions Roar. Raschka, Chris, illus. (p. 1903)
—Who Has What? All about Girls' Bodies & Boys' Bodies. Westcott, Nadine Bernard, illus. (p. 1915)
—Who's in My Family? All about Our Families. Westcott, Nadine Bernard, illus. (p. 1920)
Harris, Robie H. & Cousins, Lucy. Sexo: Que es? Desarrollo, Cambios Corporales, Sexo y Salud Sexual. Saslavsky, Irene, tr. (p. 1556)
Harris, Roy. Recipes & Reminiscence: A Celebration of My Friends in the Theatre. (p. 1451)
Harris, Sally M. Color Me Happy. Paplinksie, Cecilia, illus. (p. 343)
—Rainbow Nights. Grady, Kit, illus. (p. 1435)
Harris, Samuel & Gorder, Cheryl. Sammy: Child Survivor of the Holocaust. (p. 1507)
Harris, Samuel R. Sammy Child Survivor of the Holocaust. (p. 1508)
Harris, Sharon, illus. see Vecchione, Glen.
Harris, Shelly J. Snowman's Love (p. 1601)
Harris, Shelly Jones. Little Elephant Is a Lifesaver. (p. 1027)
Harris, Stanley. First Shot: A Tale of a Boy's Trip Through Time to the Battle of Lexington. (p. 596)
Harris, Stephanie C. Wonders of Monkey Mac! (p. 1948)

Harris, Stephen. Ballroom Bonanza: A Hidden Pictures ABC Book. Rycroft, Nina, illus. (p. 135)
Harris, Stephen L. Fire Mountains of the West: The Cascade & Mono Lake Volcanoes. (p. 590)
Harris, Steve J., illus. see Hixon, Mara Uman.
Harris, Steven, illus. see Kelly, Joe.
Harris, Sue. ABC: A Busy Fingers Book. Chrystall, Claire, illus. (p. 3)
—Little Seal Finds a Friend. Boey, Stephanie, illus. (p. 1036)
Harris, Tammy. Fairy Flower Alphabet. (p. 563)
Harris, Ted. Catney Reid Who Needs Money? (p. 280)
Harris, Teresa E. Perfect Place. (p. 1342)
—Summer Jackson: Grown Up. Ford, A. G., illus. (p. 1674)
Harris, Terrell. Volcanoes Change the Land. (p. 1849)
Harris, Tiffany, illus. see Burch, Sharon.
Harris, Tim. Alligators. (p. 47)
—Amphibians. (p. 65)
—Animal Kingdom. (p. 78)
—Australia & South East Asia. (p. 116)
—Crocodiles & Alligators. (p. 384)
—Eagles. (p. 492)
—Earth Science. (p. 496)
—Europe. (p. 540)
—Frogs. (p. 641)
—Grouse. (p. 725)
—Hawks. (p. 755)
—Life Science. (p. 1013)
—Lizards. (p. 1042)
—Mackenzie River. (p. 1068)
—Mountains & Highlands (p. 1181)
—Nonvenomous Snakes. (p. 1263)
—North & South America. (p. 1264)
—Pelicans. (p. 1335)
—Physical Science. (p. 1353)
—Snakes. (p. 1596)
—South & Central Asia. (p. 1616)
—Space Science. (p. 1619)
—Sport: Almost Everything You Ever Wanted to Know. (p. 1631)
—Transportation Technology. (p. 1779)
—Turtles. (p. 1799)
—Venomous Snakes. (p. 1836)
Harris, Tim, ed. Birds. (p. 191)
—Elephants. (p. 511)
—Fish. (p. 598)
—Invertebrates. (p. 884)
—Lions. (p. 1021)
—Mammals of the Southern Hemisphere. (p. 1085)
—Penguins. (p. 1337)
—Reptiles & Amphibians. (p. 1461)
—Wolves. (p. 1944)
Harris, Todd, illus. see Healy, Christopher.
Harris, Todd V. Heroes & Haters. (p. 772)
Harris, Tony. Invincible Iron Man(r): Disassembled. (p. 885)
—There's a Wombat in My Bed. (p. 1731)
Harris, Tricia. Fairy Tales for Fashionistas. (p. 564)
Harris, Trudy. Clock Struck One: A Time-Telling Tale. Hartman, Carrie, illus. (p. 333)
—Jenny Found a Penny. Hovell, John, illus. (p. 913)
—Over, under, in, & Ouch! Haskamp, Steve, illus. (p. 1314)
—Royal Treasure Measure. Stevanovic, Ivica, illus. (p. 1492)
—Say Something, Perico. RéBora, Cecilia, illus. (p. 1518)
—Splitting the Herd: A Corral of Odds & Evens. Julian, Russell, illus. (p. 1630)
—Tally Cat Keeps Track. Harris, Andrew, illus. (p. 1704)
Harris, Tumeka. Broken Law. Sea Breeze Productions & Phelps, Janice, eds. (p. 230)
—Goody Bag. Sea Breeze Productions, ed. (p. 701)
—Home Sweet Home. Sea Breeze Productions, ed. (p. 793)
—Trouble in Paradise. Sea Breeze Productions & Phelps, Janice, eds. (p. 1789)
Harris, V. Perception Rules! Personal Success: The Story of Brandin the Misunderstood Bull. (p. 1341)
Harris, Valerie. Saga of Henry Box Brown: A Play for Black History Month. (p. 1502)
Harris, Valerie F. & Jones, Eula V. Mariah's Diary. (p. 1093)
—My Teacher Doesn't Like Me. (p. 1219)
—Shaping up for Sight Word Success. (p. 1561)
—We Are One. (p. 1865)
Harris, Virginia. Charlie's Cage. (p. 293)
Harris, Walter, jt. auth. see Antell, Gerson.
Harris, Wayne, illus. see Baillie, Allan.
Harris, Wayne, illus. see Morgan, Anne.
Harris, Wayne, jt. auth. see Morgan, Anne.
Harris, Wendell. Elton's Shoes. (p. 516)
Harris, Wendy. Technology. (p. 1711)
Harris, William. Water Makes Hydropower. (p. 1863)
Harris, William C. & Harris, William C., Jr. Wassaw Sound. (p. 1860)
Harris, William C., Jr., jt. auth. see Harris, William C.
Harris Wilson, P., jt. auth. see Leatherman, Greg.
Harris, Yvonne. Oahu Hikes: The Best Hikes & Walks on the Island. (p. 1274)
Harris-Davies, Dafydd, et al. Caleb a Tyg. (p. 252)
Harrison, illus. see Eding, June.
Harrison Adams, Troon & Adams, Troon Harrison. Nuclear Energy: Power from the Atom. (p. 1270)
Harrison Adams, Troon & Harrison, Troon. Marijuana. (p. 1094)
Harrison, Andy. Vital Skills: How to Related to Authority. (p. 1846)
Harrison, Anna, ed. see Yorke, Jane & Dorling Kindersley Publishing Staff.
Harrison, Anne-Marie. Babies Are Noisy: A Book for Big Brothers & Sisters Including Those on the Autism Spectrum. Byrne, Beth, illus. (p. 123)
Harrison, Benjamin. Aliens, Sasquatches, Flowers, & Plants: Volume I. (p. 41)
—Aliens, Sasquatches, Flowers, & Plants. (p. 41)
Harrison, Brenda Sue. Frances Faye Freeman's Almost Perfect Pig. (p. 627)
Harrison, Brian, jt. auth. see Gabolinscy, Jack.
Harrison, Casey. I'm an Ostrich. (p. 858)
Harrison, Charles. Generals Die in Bed: 100th Anniversary of World War I Special Edition. (p. 660)
Harrison, Charles C. Dick Turpin. (p. 436)
Harrison, Christy Gremore. Once upon A Monday. (p. 1293)
Harrison, Colin. Using Technology to Improve Reading & Learning. (p. 1828)
Harrison, Cora. Debutantes: In Love. (p. 421)
—Secret Spy from Drumshee. Wolfhound Publishing Editors, ed. (p. 1544)
—Titanic Voyage from Drumshee. (p. 1758)
—Two Mad Dogs. Myler, Terry, illus. (p. 1804)
—Wolf in the Midnight Forest. (p. 1944)
Harrison, David L. Alligator in the Closet: And Other Poems Around the House. Kendall, Jane, illus. (p. 47)
—Connecting Dots: Poems of My Journey. Cousineau, Kelley & Cunningham, Kelley, illus. (p. 358)
—Cowboys: Voices in the Western Wind. Burr, Dan, illus. (p. 374)
—Earthquakes: Earth's Mightiest Moments. Nathan, Cheryl, illus. (p. 497)
—Farmer's Dog Goes to the Forest: Rhymes for Two Voices. Johnson-Petrov, Arden, illus. (p. 574)
—Farmer's Garden: Rhymes for Two Voices. Johnson-Petrov, Arden, illus. (p. 574)
—Glaciers: Nature's Icy Caps. Nathan, Cheryl, illus. (p. 682)
—Mammoth Bones & Broken Stones: The Mystery of North America's First People. Hilliard, Richard, illus. (p. 1085)
—Monster Is Coming! Wilhelm, Hans, illus. (p. 1167)
—Mountains: The Tops of the World. Nathan, Cheryl, illus. (p. 1181)
—Oceans: The Vast, Mysterious Deep. Nathan, Cheryl, illus. (p. 1277)
—Paul Bunyan: My Story. Kanzler, John, illus. (p. 1330)
—Perfect Home for a Family. Angaramo, Roberta, illus. (p. 1342)
—Pirates. Burr, Dan, illus. (p. 1363)
—Rivers: Nature's Wondrous Waterways. Nathan, Cheryl, illus. (p. 1476)
—Vacation: We're Going to the Ocean. Shepperson, Rob, illus. (p. 1829)
Harrison, Dorothy. Better Tomorrow? (p. 172)
Harrison, Emma. Best Girl. (p. 170)
—From Head to Toe: The Girls' Life Guide to Taking Care of You. Montagna, Frank, illus. (p. 642)
—Love under Wraps. (p. 1060)
—Phoebe Who? (p. 1351)
—Sacked: A Rival High Novel. (p. 1500)
—That's a Wrap: A Rival High Novel. (p. 1726)
—Toe the Line: A Rival High Novel. (p. 1761)
Harrison, Erica. Box of Fairies. (p. 216)
—Monster Snap. Harrison, Erica, illus. (p. 1168)
Harrison, Erica, illus. see Bone, Emily.
Harrison, Erica, illus. see Bowman, Lucy & MacLaine, James.
Harrison, Erica, illus. see Gilpin, Rebecca & Brocklehurst, Ruth.
Harrison, Erica, illus. see Gilpin, Rebecca.
Harrison, Erica, illus. see MacLaine, James & Bowman, Lucy.
Harrison, Erica, illus. see MacLaine, James.
Harrison, Erica, illus. see Watt, Fiona.
Harrison, F. Bayford. Battlefield Treasure. (p. 147)
Harrison, Francesca. Obus the Eucalyptus Tree Fairy. (p. 1275)
Harrison, Freya, illus. see Deak, JoAnn & Deak, Terrence.
Harrison, Geoffrey C. & Scott, Thomas F. Church & State. Stewart, Mark & Kennedy, Mike, eds. (p. 318)
—Fight for Freedom. Stewart, Mark & Kennedy, Mike, eds. (p. 585)
Harrison, Hannah E. Bernice Gets Carried Away. (p. 167)
—Extraordinary Jane. (p. 555)
Harrison, Hannah E., illus. see Hawkes, Kevin.
Harrison, Harry. Stainless Steel Trio. (p. 1638)
—Toy Shop. (p. 1774)
Harrison, Harry, illus. see Brennan, Sarah.
Harrison, Harry, illus. see Fletcher, Chris.
Harrison, Hazel. Watercolours Made Easy: Learn How to Use Watercolours with Step-by-Step Techniques & Projects to Follow, in 150 Colour Photographs. (p. 1863)
Harrison, Jack. Bozo the Criminal Dog. (p. 220)
Harrison, James. Rainforests. (p. 1436)
Harrison, James, ed. see Ballingall, Peter & Spieler, Marlena.
Harrison, Jean. Home. (p. 791)
—Safety. (p. 1502)
Harrison, Jean & Cristnogol, Cymorth. Shompa o India. (p. 1568)
Harrison, Jo. Jewellery Box Fairies. (p. 917)
Harrison, Joanna, illus. see Wells, Kitty.
Harrison, Joanna & Briggs, Raymond. Snowman & the Snowdog. (p. 1601)
Harrison, John. Fergal Onions. (p. 582)
—Fergal Onions. Harrison, John, illus. (p. 582)
Harrison, Jordan & Gray, Richard. Hans Christian Anderson's the Flea & the Professor. (p. 743)
Harrison, Kenny. Hide & Seek Harry at the Playground. Harrison, Kenny, illus. (p. 776)
—Hide & Seek Harry on the Farm. Harrison, Kenny, illus. (p. 776)
Harrison, Kevin. I Know a Rhino. Blue, Buster, illus. (p. 840)
Harrison, Kim, pseud. Early to Death, Early to Rise. (p. 494)
—Once Dead, Twice Shy. (p. 1292)
—Something Deadly This Way Comes. (p. 1609)
Harrison, Laura, illus. see Mortensen, Erik.
Harrison, Lisi. Alphas. (p. 50)
—Back & Deader Than Ever. (p. 130)
—Belle of the Brawl. (p. 163)
—Best Friends for Never. (p. 169)
—Boys R Us. (p. 220)
—Bratfest at Tiffany's (p. 222)
—Bratfest at Tiffany's. (p. 223)
—Charmed & Dangerous: The Clique Prequel. (p. 294)
—Clique. (p. 333)
—Clique. (p. 333)
—Clique - Charmed & Dangerous. (p. 333)
—Clique Collection. (p. 333)
—Dial L for Loser. (p. 433)
—Ghoul Next Door. (p. 673)
—Invasion de las Robachicos. Porras-Ballard, Patricia, tr. (p. 883)
—Invasion of the Boy Snatchers. (p. 883)
—It's Not Easy Being Mean (p. 898)
—It's Not Easy Being Mean. (p. 898)
—Monster High. (p. 1167)
—Monster High: the Scary Cute Collection. (p. 1167)
—Monster High: Where There's a Wolf, There's a Way. (p. 1167)
—Movers & Fakers. (p. 1183)
—My Little Phony. (p. 1212)
—P. S. I Loathe You. (p. 1316)
—Pretenders. (p. 1398)
—Pretty Committee Strikes Back (p. 1398)
—Revenge of the Wannabes. (p. 1466)
—Sealed with a Diss. (p. 1536)
—Tale of Two Pretties. (p. 1700)
—These Boots Are Made for Stalking. (p. 1731)
—Top of the Feud Chain. (p. 1769)
—Where There's a Wolf, There's a Way. (p. 1909)
Harrison, Lisi, creator. Dylan. (p. 491)
Harrison, Logan. What Was It Like in Ancient China? (p. 1894)
Harrison, Logan, jt. auth. see Harrison, Lorraine.
Harrison, Lorraine. All Kinds of Rocks. (p. 45)
—Flat Shapes, Solid Shapes: Identify & Describe Shapes. (p. 603)
—Mites. (p. 1156)
—My Fourth of July. (p. 1209)
—Pisces. (p. 1364)
—Sioux. (p. 1580)
Harrison, Lorraine & Harrison, Logan. What Was It Like in Ancient China? (p. 1894)
Harrison, Marie P. Sir Jack Cat & Friends. (p. 1580)
Harrison, Marybeth. Left Out Lucie. (p. 987)
Harrison, Maureen & Gilbert, Steve, eds. Speeches of Abraham Lincoln. (p. 1624)
Harrison, Megan Bernadette. Adventures of Kitty Tom & Blossom: Book One. (p. 19)
—Fears, Tears, & Laughter: The Adventures of Kitty Tom & Blossom Book Two (p. 579)
Harrison, Mette Ivie. Princess & the Bear. (p. 1402)
—Princess & the Hound. (p. 1402)
Harrison, Micah. Perimeters of Ancient Buildings: Recognize Perimeter. (p. 1343)
Harrison, Michael. Cop's Night Before Christmas Miles, David, illus. (p. 366)
Harrison, Michael & Stuart-Clark, Christopher. One Hundred Years of Poetry for Children. (p. 1295)
—Oxford Book of Christmas Poems. (p. 1315)
—Oxford Book of Story Poems. (p. 1315)
Harrison, Michelle. 13 Curses. (p. 1995)
—13 Secrets. (p. 1995)
—13 Treasures. (p. 1995)
—Thirteen Curses. (p. 1735)
—Thirteen Secrets. (p. 1735)
—Thirteen Treasures. (p. 1735)
Harrison, Nancy. Who's on Mount Rushmore? Box Set (p. 1921)
Harrison, Nancy, illus. see Abramson, Ann.
Harrison, Nancy, illus. see Anderson, Kirsten.
Harrison, Nancy, illus. see Bader, Bonnie.
Harrison, Nancy, illus. see Berendes, Mary & Aesop.
Harrison, Nancy, illus. see Brennan, Patricia & Demuth, Patricia Brennan.
Harrison, Nancy, illus. see Buckley, James, Jr.
Harrison, Nancy, illus. see Burgan, Michael.
Harrison, Nancy, illus. see Demuth, Patricia Brennan.
Harrison, Nancy, illus. see Dubowski, Cathy East & Pascal, Janet.
Harrison, Nancy, illus. see Edgers, Geoff.
Harrison, Nancy, illus. see Eding, June.
Harrison, Nancy, illus. see Edwards, Roberta.
Harrison, Nancy, illus. see Fabiny, Sarah.
Harrison, Nancy, illus. see Fradin, Dennis Brindell.
Harrison, Nancy, illus. see Frith, Margaret.
Harrison, Nancy, illus. see Gigliotti, Jim.
Harrison, Nancy, illus. see Herman, Gail.
Harrison, Nancy, illus. see Holub, Joan.
Harrison, Nancy, illus. see Hopkinson, Deborah.
Harrison, Nancy, illus. see Joachim, Jean C.
Harrison, Nancy, illus. see Kelley, True.
Harrison, Nancy, illus. see Kramer, Sydelle.
Harrison, Nancy, illus. see Labrecque, Ellen.
Harrison, Nancy, illus. see Manzanero, Paula K.
Harrison, Nancy, illus. see McDonough, Yona Zeldis.
Harrison, Nancy, illus. see Medina, Nico & Putra, Dede.
Harrison, Nancy, illus. see Medina, Nico.
Harrison, Nancy, illus. see Milton, Joyce.
Harrison, Nancy, illus. see Morgan, Ellen.
Harrison, Nancy, illus. see O'Brien, John A.
Harrison, Nancy, illus. see O'Brien, John A. & Thompson, Gare.
Harrison, Nancy, illus. see O'Connor, Jim.
Harrison, Nancy, illus. see Pascal, Janet.
Harrison, Nancy, illus. see Pollack, Pam & Belviso, Meg.
Harrison, Nancy, illus. see Pollack, Pam, et al.
Harrison, Nancy, illus. see Pollack, Pamela D. & Belviso, Meg.
Harrison, Nancy, illus. see Prince, April Jones.
Harrison, Nancy, illus. see Rau, Dana Meachen.
Harrison, Nancy, illus. see Spinner, Stephanie.
Harrison, Nancy, illus. see Stevenson, Robert Louis.
Harrison, Nancy, illus. see Stewart, Whitney.
Harrison, Nancy, illus. see Stine, Megan.
Harrison, Nancy, illus. see Thompson, Gare.
Harrison, Nancy, illus. see Waldron, Ann.
Harrison, Nancy, jt. auth. see Herman, Gail.
Harrison, Nicholas. Day in a City. (p. 413)
—Year at a Construction Site. (p. 1969)
—Year at a Farm. (p. 1969)
Harrison, Nicholas, illus. see Harris, Patrice.
Harrison, Patrick Gb. Who says Kist Can't Fight Global Warming. (p. 1917)
Harrison, Paul. 1950s. (p. 2002)
—Amazing Book of 3D Thrillers: Fantastic Eye-Popping Experiences. (p. 54)
—Ancient Roman Clothes. (p. 70)
—Ancient Roman Homes. (p. 70)
—Animal Fun. (p. 78)
—Billy on the Ball. Raga, Silvia, illus. (p. 187)
—Brilliant Book of 3D Thrillers: Get Ready for the Ultimate 3d Adventure! (p. 228)
—Cold War. (p. 339)
—Elephant Rides Again. Million, Liz, illus. (p. 511)
—Extreme Supercars. (p. 557)
—Gravity-Defying Stunt Spectaculars. (p. 712)
—Let's Work Together. (p. 1001)
—Mega Machines: Roar into Action with These Super-Charged Racers! (p. 1124)
—Micro Bugs. (p. 1136)
—Monster Trucks. (p. 1168)
—My Pet. (p. 1217)
—Noisy Books. Fiorin, Fabiano, illus. (p. 1263)
—On the Move. (p. 1291)
—Perfect Prince. Mason, Sue, illus. (p. 1342)
—Pirates. (p. 1363)
—Racing Supercars. (p. 1432)
—Reptiles. (p. 1461)
—Sea Monsters. (p. 1535)
—Snakes. (p. 1596)
—Space. (p. 1618)
—Speed Machines. (p. 1624)
—Superbikes. (p. 1682)
—Superboats. (p. 1682)
—Supercars. (p. 1682)
—Supercopters. (p. 1682)
—Superplanes. (p. 1684)
—Supertrucks. (p. 1684)
—T. Rex. (p. 1694)
—Uncovering Mummies & Other Mysteries of the Ancient World (p. 1812)
—Undersea Adventure. Nascimbeni, Barbara, illus. (p. 1815)
—Why Did the Cold War Happen? (p. 1923)
—Yummy in My Tummy! Worsley, Belinda, illus. (p. 1983)
Harrison, Paul, jt. auth. see Amery, Heather.
Harrison, Paul, jt. auth. see Montague-Smith, Ann.
Harrison, Paul, jt. auth. see Robinson, Nick.
Harrison, Paul & Arcturus Publishing Staff. Bugs & the World's Creepiest Microbugs. (p. 237)
Harrison, Paul & Montague-Smith, Ann. Extension for All Through Problem Solving. (p. 555)
Harrison, Paul & Robbins, Amanda. Gravity-Defying Stunt Spectaculars (p. 712)
Harrison, Paul & Robinson, Nick. Origami X (p. 1304)
Harrison, Paula. Golden Shell. (p. 695)
—Ice Diamond. (p. 850)
—Lost Gold. (p. 1055)
—Magic Rings. (p. 1073)
—Moonlight Mystery. (p. 1172)
—Rainbow Opal. (p. 1435)
—Rescue Princesses #11: the Rainbow Opal. (p. 1462)
—Secret Promise. (p. 1543)
—Shimmering Stone. (p. 1566)
—Silver Locket. (p. 1576)
—Snow Jewel. (p. 1599)
—Stolen Crystals. (p. 1652)
—Wishing Pearl. (p. 1940)
Harrison, Peter & Hunt, Norman Bancroft. Amazing World of the Wild West: Discover the Trailblazing History of Cowboys, Outlaws & Native Americans. (p. 56)
Harrison, Robert. Oriel's Travels. (p. 1303)
Harrison, Sam. Zing! Five Steps & 101 Tips for Creativity on Command. (p. 1987)
Harrison, Sarah. Day at a Zoo. (p. 412)
—Day at an Airport. (p. 412)
Harrison, Scott. Choosing a Career in Carpentry. (p. 310)
Harrison, Scott, jt. auth. see Ross, Allison J.
Harrison, Scott & Ross, Allison J. Choosing a Career in Waste Management. (p. 310)
Harrison, Sharon, et al. Mathemateg Newydd Caergrawnt. (p. 1107)
Harrison, Steve, illus. see Maddox, Mike & Anderson, Jeff.
Harrison, T., illus. see Seigel, Mike.
Harrison, Ted. Northern Alphabet. (p. 1265)
—O Canada. (p. 1274)
Harrison, Troon. Dream Collector. (p. 483)
—Eye of the Wolf (p. 558)
—Poetry & Potatoes. Hellard, Susan, illus. (p. 1376)
—Twilight Box. (p. 1801)
Harrison, Troon, jt. auth. see Harrison Adams, Troon.
Harrison, Vanessa. Activities: 101 Ideas for Children & Adults. (p. 10)
Harrison, Winston E. Rockmaster System: Relating Ongoing Chords to the Keyboard - Rock. Harrison, Winston E. & Montgomery, Robert, eds. (p. 1483)
Harrison, Zac. Crash Landing (p. 376)
—Frozen Enemies (p. 645)
—Galactic Battle (p. 652)
—Hyperspace High (p. 831)
—Robot Warriors (p. 1480)
—Space Plague (p. 1619)
—Warlord's Revenge (p. 1858)
Harrison-Lever, Brian, illus. see Jorgensen, Norman.
Harrison-Lever, Brian, illus. see Jorgensen, Norman.
Harrison-Lever, Brian, jt. auth. see Jorgensen, Norman.
Harrison-Lever, Brian, jt. auth. see Wolfer, Dianne.
Harris-Wyrick, Wayne. Kimmy Finds Her Key. Liz Warren, illus. (p. 957)
—Why Am I Me? Macquignon, Stephen, illus. (p. 1922)
Harriton, Maxine. School Trip to the Fruit Planet (p. 1523)
Harr-Loudin, Cindy. Danny the Backward Duck. (p. 406)
—Not So Odd Friends. (p. 1267)
Harrod, Elisa, jt. auth. see Green, Dan.
Harrod-Eagles, Cynthia. Biggest Pumpkin Ever! Woodruff, Liza, illus. (p. 185)
—Cave Homes. (p. 282)
—Changeling. (p. 290)
—Church Anniversary. (p. 318)

H

—Fantastic Ants. (p. 571)
—I Love You to the Moon. Poh, Jennie, illus. (p. 844)
—It's Holiday Time! Baccala, Gladys, illus. (p. 897)
—It's Spring Time! Baccala, Gladys, illus. (p. 899)
—Stars & Constellations. (p. 1643)
Harrod-Eagles, Cynthia & Bennett, Elizabeth. Curious about Fishes. (p. 392)
Harrold, A. F. Fizzlebert Stump: The Boy Who Cried Fish. (p. 601)
—Fizzlebert Stump: The Boy Who Ran Away from the Circus (And Joined the Library) (p. 601)
—Fizzlebert Stump & the Bearded Boy. (p. 601)
—Fizzlebert Stump & the Girl Who Lifted Quite Heavy Things. (p. 601)
—Imaginary. Gravett, Emily, illus. (p. 860)
Harrold, Brian, illus. see Thompson, Tolya L.
Harrold, Kimberly. Sometimes, MS Is Yucky. Whitfield, Eric, illus. (p. 1610)
Harrold, Stephanie Marie. Pirate's Eye. (p. 1363)
Harrold, Yvette. With Butterfly Eyes. Henriksen, Rebecca, illus. (p. 1942)
Harron, Nancy. Harron's Nest Floor Decor & More. (p. 750)
Harrop, Isobel. Isobel Journal (p. 893)
Harrow, Jeremy. Basketball in the Pac-10 Conference. (p. 143)
—Crystal Meth. (p. 387)
Harrow, Jeremy, jt. auth. see Michaels, Vanessa Lynn.
Harrub, Brad. God Made Dinosaurs. (p. 689)
—God Made Fish. (p. 689)
Harry How Books. Just Luke. (p. 939)
Harry, Pamela. My Body & Me (p. 1198)
Harry, Rebecca. Little Lion. (p. 1030)
—Snow Bunny's Christmas Wish. Harry, Rebecca, illus. (p. 1598)
Harry, Rebecca, illus. see Emmett, Jonathan.
Harry-Jennings, Pamela. This Is Who I Am. (p. 1737)
Harshbarger, D. Treasures of Dawn. (p. 1782)
Harshman, Marc. All the Way to Morning. Dávalos, Felipe, illus. (p. 46)
Harshman, Marc & Ryan, Cheryl. Red Are the Apples. Zahares, Wade, illus. (p. 1453)
Harsley, Tricia. Sandy Rella. (p. 1511)
Harstad, Johan. 172 Hours on the Moon. (p. 2000)
Harstad, Johan & Chace, Tara. 172 Hours on the Moon. (p. 2000)
Harston, David. Michigan Coloring Book. (p. 1135)
Harston, David, illus. see Mindes, Erin.
Harston, Jerry. More of My First Book of Mormon Stories. (p. 1174)
Harston, Jerry, illus. see Buck, Deanna Draper.
Harston, Jerry, illus. see Hiris, Monica.
Harston, Jerry, illus. see Johnson, Alice W. & Warner, Allison H.
Harston, Jerry, illus. see Oppenlander, Meredith.
Harston, Jerry, illus. see Passey, Marion.
Harston, Jerry, illus. see Wach, Randy-Lynne.
Harston, Jerry, illus. see Worthington, Lisa & Moon, Susan.
Hart, Alison. Anna's Blizzard Bachem, Paul, illus. (p. 85)
—Bell's Star. Sanderson, Ruth, illus. (p. 163)
—Darling, Mercy Dog of World War I Montgomery, Michael G., illus. (p. 409)
—Dive Right In. Studios, Arcana, illus. (p. 454)
—Emma's River Bachem, Paul, illus. (p. 520)
—Fires of Jubilee. (p. 592)
—Gabriel's Horse (p. 652)
—Gabriel's Horses (p. 652)
—Gabriel's Journey (p. 652)
—Gabriel's Triumph (p. 652)
—Risky Chance. Sanderson, Ruth, illus. (p. 1475)
—Spy on the Home Front: A Molly Mystery. Tibbles, JeanPaul, illus. (p. 1636)
—Taking the Reins. Studios, Arcana, illus. (p. 1698)
—Whirlwind. (p. 1912)
—Wolfgang Puck. (p. 1944)
Hart, Alison, jt. auth. see Leonhardt, Alice.
Hart, Amber. After Us. (p. 28)
—Before You. (p. 159)
Hart, Anne. Dogs with Careers: Ten Happy-Ending Stories of Purpose & Passion. (p. 463)
—Roman Justice: Too Roman to Handle. (p. 1485)
Hart, Arianna. Take Your Medicine. (p. 1697)
Hart, Beth Ellen. Just Be Big about It: Clean up Your Room. (p. 938)
Hart, Carla. Kid Named Cancer: A Story about a Bully & How He Got Treated. (p. 951)
Hart, Caryl. Catch That Rat. McLaughlin, Tom, illus. (p. 279)
—Don't Put Your Pants on Your Head, Fred! Hodgkinson, Leigh, illus. (p. 468)
—How to Catch a Dragon. Eaves, Ed, illus. (p. 815)
—Princess & the Peas. Warburton, Sarah, illus. (p. 1403)
—Princess & the Presents. Warburton, Sarah, illus. (p. 1403)
—Rhino? What Rhino? Horne, Sarah, illus. (p. 1467)
—Whiffy Wilson: The Wolf Who Wouldn't Wash. Lord, Leonie, illus. (p. 1911)
Hart, Caryl & Lord, Leonie. Whiffy Wilson: The Wolf Who Wouldn't Go to School. (p. 1911)
Hart, Chris. Drawing the New Adventure Cartoons: Cool Spies, Evil Guys & Action Heroes. (p. 482)
—Manga Mania Romance: Drawing Shojo Girls & Bishie Boys. (p. 1087)
Hart, Chris, jt. auth. see Hart, Christopher.
Hart, Chrissi. Hermit, the Icon, & the Emperor: The Holy Virgin Comes to Cyprus. Chocheli, Niko, illus. (p. 771)
—Under the Grapevine: A Miracle by Saint Kendeas of Cyprus. Brandenburg, Claire, illus. (p. 1813)
Hart, Christine. Best Laid Plans (p. 170)
—Stalked (p. 1638)
—Watching July (p. 1861)
Hart, Christopher. Cartoon Faces: How to Draw Faces, Features & Expressions. (p. 273)
—Cartoonist's Big Book of Drawing Animals. (p. 273)
—Draw Manga! (p. 481)
—Draw Manga Monsters! (p. 481)
—Draw Manga Super Cute Characters Drawing Kit. (p. 481)
—Draw Manga Villains! (p. 481)
—Drawing Animals Shape by Shape: Create Cartoon Animals with Circles, Squares, Rectangles & Triangles. (p. 481)
—Drawing Vampires: Gothic Creatures of the Night. (p. 482)
—Drawing Wizards, Witches & Warlocks. (p. 482)
—Fashion Design Studio: Learn to Draw Figures, Fashion, Hairstyles & More. (p. 575)
—Figure It Out! The Beginner's Guide to Drawing People. (p. 586)
—Girl Power! Drawing Fabulous Females for Japanese Comics. (p. 678)
—How to Draw Amazing Comic Book Characters Drawing Kit. (p. 816)
—How to Draw Cartoon Animals Drawing Kit. (p. 817)
—How to Draw Chic Fashions Drawing Kit. (p. 817)
—Kids Draw Animals. (p. 953)
—Kids Draw Big Book of Everything Manga. (p. 953)
—Kids Draw Manga. (p. 953)
—Kids Draw Manga Monsters. (p. 953)
—Kids Draw Manga Shoujo. (p. 953)
—Magna Martial Arts Masters Drawing Kit. (p. 1075)
—Magna Teen Characters Drawing Kit. (p. 1075)
—Xtreme Art: Ultimate Book of Trace-and-Draw Manga. (p. 1967)
—You Can Draw Cartoon Animals: A Simple Step-by-Step Drawing Guide! (p. 1974)
—Young Artists Draw Animals. (p. 1978)
—Young Artists Draw Manga. (p. 1978)
—¡Dibuja Manga! Nivel Básico. Miralles, Charles, tr. (p. 435)
Hart, Christopher & Hart, Chris. Shonen: Drawing Action-Style Japanese Comics. (p. 1568)
Hart, Dave, jt. auth. see Calu, John.
Hart, Derek. Secret of the Dragon's Eye. (p. 1542)
Hart, Diane H., ed. see Hill, Z. B.
Hart, Diane H., ed. see James, Sara.
Hart, Diane H., ed. see Scott, Celicia.
Hart, George. Ancient Egypt. (p. 68)
Hart, Greg & Arundale, Jackie. Investigating Geography. (p. 884)
Hart, Haley. I (Heart) Zac Efron. (p. 839)
Hart, Harold. Organische Chemie. (p. 1303)
Hart, J. Tristan. Adventures of Friendly & Barnackel: Book 2. (p. 18)
—Adventures of Friendly & Barnackel: Book 3 Ollie the Octopus. (p. 18)
—Adventures of Friendly & Barnackel: Book 4 Jaybird the BlueJay. (p. 18)
—Adventures of Friendly & Barnackel: Book 1 Friendly & Barnackel. (p. 18)
Hart, James, illus. see Loughlin, Patrick.
Hart, Janice. Henry & the Oranges: Henry's Wild Adventures. McDonald, Suzi, illus. (p. 767)
Hart, Jason, illus. see Gamble, Adam & Jasper, Mark.
Hart, Jeff. Eat, Brains, Love. (p. 501)
—Undead with Benefits. (p. 1813)
Hart, Jenny. Sublime Stitching: Hundreds of Hip Embroidery Patterns & How-To. Grablewski, Alexandra, photos by. (p. 1671)
Hart, John. Mammoth Boy: A Lad's Epic Journey to Find Mammoths in the Ice Age. (p. 1085)
Hart, Joy F. New Family for Semoj. (p. 1244)
Hart, Joyce. Alabama. (p. 33)
—Big Dogs. (p. 181)
—Cats. (p. 280)
—Frequently Asked Questions about Being Part of a Military Family. (p. 636)
—How Inflation Works. (p. 810)
—How Inflation Works (Real World Economics) (p. 810)
—Kim Jong Il: Leader of North Korea. (p. 956)
—Native Son: The Story of Richard Wright. (p. 1235)
—Ohio. (p. 1281)
—Oregon. (p. 1302)
—Small Dogs. (p. 1592)
—Snakes. (p. 1596)
Hart, Joyce, jt. auth. see Baldwin, Guy.
Hart, Joyce, jt. auth. see Bennett, Michelle.
Hart, Joyce, jt. auth. see Dornfeld, Margaret.
Hart, Joyce, jt. auth. see Goldberg, Jake.
Hart, Joyce, jt. auth. see Hoffman, Nancy.
Hart, Joyce, jt. auth. see Morrice, Polly Alison.
Hart, Joyce, jt. auth. see Peters, Stephen.
Hart, Joyce, jt. auth. see Shirley, David.
Hart, Joyce & Bass, Elissa. Alabama. (p. 33)
Hart, Joyce & Chang, Perry. Florida. (p. 606)
Hart, Joyce & Gorman, Jacqueline Laks. Oregon. (p. 1302)
Hart, Joyce & Hantula, Richard. Pennsylvania. (p. 1338)
Hart, Joyce & Herrington, Lisa M. Ohio. (p. 1281)
Hart, Joyce & Zeinert, Karen. Wisconsin. (p. 1939)
Hart, Julie Anne. Miss Molly Mare. (p. 1151)
Hart, Karen. Butterflies in May. (p. 247)
Hart, Katherine & Barker, Elsa. Letters from the Afterlife: A Guide to the Other Side. (p. 1002)
Hart, Kim. Beatrice & Raymond: A Universal MessagesTM Book. (p. 153)
Hart, Kingsley, tr. see Jansson, Tove.
Hart, Lauri J. Day in the Life of Nicholas B. (p. 413)
Hart, Linda. When Mummy Says. (p. 1904)
Hart, Liz. Un-Written Rules or Single Sex. (p. 1811)
Hart, Louise. Rosie's Rule. (p. 1490)
Hart, Melissa. Guide for Using the Tale of Despereaux in the Classroom. (p. 730)
—Guide for Using Walk Two Moons in the Classroom. (p. 730)
—Mind Twisters, Grade 3. (p. 1145)
Hart, Melissa, jt. auth. see Housel, Debra J.
Hart, Melissa, jt. auth. see Housel, Debra.
Hart, Micah K. Tinseland: Christopher's Christmas Adventure. (p. 1756)
Hart, Penny. Our Forever Home Tails of the Cozy Red Barn. (p. 1308)
Hart, Phillip S. Bessie Coleman. (p. 168)
Hart, Rebecca, tr. see Reiser, Lynn.
Hart, Rhiannon. Blood Song. (p. 200)
—Blood Storm. (p. 200)
Hart, Roger, illus. see Reed, A. W.
Hart, Sam, illus. see Lee, Tony.
Hart, Sue. Tales of the Full Moon. Harvey, Chris, illus. (p. 1702)
Hart, Sura & Kindle Hodson, Victoria. Compassionate Classroom: Relationship Based Teaching & Learning. (p. 352)
Hart, Susan. Teacher's Guide to Motor Development: Essential For. (p. 1709)
Hart, Teresa. Ant & the Alligator. (p. 88)
—Ant & the Lost Spider (p. 88)
Hart, William E., ed. see Synge, John M.
Hartas, Leo, illus. see Morris, Dave.
Harte, Harlee. I (Heart) Taylor Lautner. (p. 839)
—I (Heart) Taylor Swift. (p. 839)
—I Justin Bieber. (p. 840)
—Jonas Brothers. (p. 925)
—Robert Pattinson. (p. 1479)
—Selena Gomez. (p. 1549)
Harte, Lawrence. Home Media Networks Quick Course; Systems, Technology & Operation: Audio, Video & Data Distribution in the Home. (p. 792)
—Introduction to CDMA: IS-95 & CDMA2000 Radio Channels, Logical Channels, & Operation. (p. 882)
—Introduction to CHTML. (p. 882)
—Introduction to Email Marketing. (p. 882)
—Introduction to EVDO: Physical Channels, Logical Channels, Network, & Operation. (p. 882)
—Introduction to GPRS & EDGE: Physical Channels, Logical Channels, Network, & Operation. (p. 882)
—Introduction to GSM: Physical Channels, Logical Channels, Network, & Operation. (p. 882)
—Introduction to Internet Marketing. (p. 882)
—Introduction to Internet Web Keyword Advertising. (p. 882)
—Introduction to IP Television: Why & How Companies are Providing Television Through Data Networks. (p. 882)
—Introduction to IP Video: Digitization, Compression & Transmission. (p. 882)
—Introduction to Mobile Data, Circuit Switched, Packet Switched, Mobitex, CDPD, GPRS, EVDO & Cellular Packet Data, 2nd Edition. (p. 882)
—Introduction to MPEG; MPEG-1, MPEG-2 & MPEG-4. (p. 882)
—Introduction to Online Stores. (p. 882)
—Introduction to Paging Systems: One-Way, Two-Way, Pocsag, Ermes, Flex, Reflex, & Inflexion. (p. 882)
—Introduction to Private Land Mobile Radio: Dispatch, LTR, APCO, MPT1327, IDEN & TETRA. (p. 882)
—Introduction to SS7; SSP; SCP; STP, & SS7 Protocol Layers Operation. (p. 882)
—Introduction to Wideband Code Division Multiple Access (WCDMA) Physical Channels, Logical Channels, Network, & Operation. (p. 882)
—Mobile Systems. (p. 1157)
—Web Marketing Dictionary. (p. 1870)
Harte, Lawrence, jt. auth. see Ofrane, Avi.
Harte, Lawrence, jt. auth. see Robert, Belt.
Harte, Lawrence & Bowler, David. Introduction to SIP IP Telephony Systems: Technology Basics, Services, Economics, & Installation. (p. 882)
—Introduction to SS7 & IP, Call Signaling Using SIGTRAN, MGCP, SCTP, SIP, & H. 323. (p. 882)
Harte, Lawrence & Clee, Stephen. Introduction to Mobile Video, How to Send Live TV & Streaming Video to 2G & 3G Multimedia Telephones. (p. 882)
Harte, Lawrence & Sutton, Kyle. Introduction to Search Engine Optimization, SEO: How to Manage SEO Projects & Increase Search Engine Ranking. Luck, Carolyn, ed. (p. 882)
Harte, Lawrence, et al. Introduction to CDMA: Physical Channels, Logical Channels, Network Functions, & Operation. (p. 882)
—Signaling System 7 (SS7) Basics. (p. 1574)
Harte, May. 1, 2, 3 in My House. (p. 1990)
—ABCs in My House. (p. 4)
—ABC's in My House. (p. 4)
—Halloween. (p. 737)
—Halloween. Gonzalez, Tomas, tr. from ENG. (p. 737)
—Hide & Seek Kids. (p. 776)
—Hide & Seek Pets. (p. 777)
—Hide-and-Seek Kids. (p. 776)
—Hide-and-Seek Pets. (p. 777)
—Thanksgiving. (p. 1725)
Harte, Will, tr. see Nurk, Enn & Telgmaa, Aksel.
Hartel, Traudel & Traudel, Hartel. Acontecimientos Felices: Invitaciones y Felicitaciones. (p. 9)
Hartelius, Margaret A. Zoom! (reissue) The Complete Paper Airplane Kit. Hartelius, Margaret A. & Eagle, Cameron, illus. (p. 1989)
Hartell, Jason G. Organic Chemistry. (p. 1303)
Hartenaus, P. J. Belden Boy: - the adventures of Peter Mcdugal. (p. 161)
Harter, Adam, jt. auth. see Sohn, Emily.
Harter, Debbie. Animal Boggie. (p. 76)
—Animal Boogie. (p. 76)
—Animal Boogie. Harter, Debbie, illus. (p. 76)
—Animal Boogie. Blackstone, Stella, illus. (p. 76)
—Animal Boogie. (p. 77)
—Animal Boogie. Penner, Fred, illus. (p. 77)
—Bear about Town Gift Wrap. (p. 150)
—Bear's Busy Year. (p. 151)
—Cha-Cha-Cha en la Selva. Canetti, Yanitzia, tr. (p. 288)
—Cha-Cha-Cha en la Selva. Harter, Debbie, illus. (p. 288)
—De Paseo Por la Selva. Ugalde, Raquel, tr. (p. 416)
—"Find the stars in the dark" (Bear in a Square) (p. 587)
—"Find the triangles on the wave" (Bear in a Square) (p. 587)
—Herb's Vegetable Patch. (p. 769)
—Herb's Vegetable Patch Gift Wrap. (p. 769)
—Snow Bear Gift Wrap. (p. 1598)
—Walking Through the Jungle. (p. 1854)
—Walking Through the Jungle. Harter, Debbie, illus. (p. 1854)
Harter, Debbie, illus. see Bass, Jules.
Harter, Debbie, illus. see Blackstone, Stella & Barefoot Books Staff.
Harter, Debbie, illus. see Blackstone, Stella & Barefoot Books.
Harter, Debbie, illus. see Blackstone, Stella & Champion, Servane.
Harter, Debbie, illus. see Blackstone, Stella & Meza-Riedewald, Leticia.
Harter, Debbie, illus. see Blackstone, Stella & Parker, Elizabeth.
Harter, Debbie, illus. see Blackstone, Stella.
Harter, Debbie, illus. see Langham, Tony.
Harter, Debbie, illus. see Seaworthy, Oscar & Collins, Mark.
Harter, Debbie, illus. see Steinberg, Laya.
Harter, Debbie, jt. auth. see Bass, Jules.
Harter, Debbie, jt. auth. see Blackstone, Stella.
Harter, Debbie, jt. auth. see Langham, Tony.
Harter, Debbie & Barefoot College Staff. Animal Boogie Fun Activities. Harter, Debbie, illus. (p. 77)
Harter, Debbie & Beaton, Clare. 1 To 20. (p. 1991)
—to Z. (p. 1759)
Harter, Debbie, tr. Walking Through the Jungle: Duke Ecur Neper Xhungel. (p. 1854)
—Walking Through the Jungle: Marchant a Travers la Jungle. (p. 1854)
Harter, Gage. Sly the Fly: The Doctor's Office. Teich, Melle, illus. (p. 1591)
Harter, Marjorie B., jt. auth. see Ryder, Verdene.
Harter, Penny. Beastie Book: An Alphabestiary. Miller, Alexandra, illus. (p. 152)
Hartgers, Katarina, tr. see Aizpuriete, Amanda.
Hartgraves, Richard. Little Cedar. (p. 1026)
Harthan, Jan. B-I-B-L-E: Paraphrase of Proverbs & Romans for Children. Vol. 3 (p. 122)
Harthorne, Clydell. Adventures of Libbi Rae. (p. 19)
Harthorne, Clydell, jt. auth. see Harthorne, Clydell.
Harthorne, Clydell & Harthorne, Clydell. Adventures of Libbi Rae. (p. 19)
Hartigan, Meg, illus. see Lite, Lori.
Hartigan, Sue. Essential GCSE Pe for Edexcel. (p. 537)
Hartin. Very Important Christmas Pageant the Story of the Birth of Christ Told with Humor, Mystery & Awe! (p. 1838)
Hartinger, Brent. Geography Club. (p. 662)
—Project Sweet Life. (p. 1410)
—Split Screen: Attack of the Soul-Sucking Brain Zombies; Bride of the Soul-Sucking Brain Zombies. (p. 1630)
Hartland, Jessie. Bon Appétit! The Delicious Life of Julia Child. Hartland, Jessie, illus. (p. 208)
—How the Dinosaur Got to the Museum. (p. 813)
—How the Meteorite Got to the Museum. (p. 813)
—Steve Jobs: Insanely Great. (p. 1649)
Hartland, Jessie, illus. see Franco, Betsy.
Hartle, James B. How to Succede in Prison. (p. 821)
Hartley, Alicia Byrd. I Like Being Me. (p. 841)
Hartley, Audrey. Colors for Michaela. (p. 345)
Hartley Bellows, Carol. Icabog Bear. (p. 850)
—Icey. (p. 851)
Hartley, Bob. Childrens Adoration Prayer Book. Clonts, E. M. M., illus. (p. 303)
Hartley, Debra. My Sticker Album: Boys Sticker Collection. (p. 1219)
—My Sticker Album. (p. 1219)
Hartley, Grandpa. Further Jolly Bedtime Tales for Big & Little People. (p. 650)
Hartley, James. Berlina's Quest. Legge, Barbara, ed. (p. 167)
Hartley, Jill, photos by. Fruits of India. (p. 646)
—Vegetables of India. (p. 1834)
Hartley, John. Holt American Civics. (p. 789)
Hartley, Joshua, illus. see The Guide Dog, Thelma.
Hartley, Karen & Macro, Chris. Ant (p. 88)
—Bee (p. 157)
—Ladybug (p. 971)
—Snail (p. 1595)
Hartley, Karen, et al. Caterpillar (p. 279)
—Centipede. (p. 287)
—Flea (p. 603)
—Grasshopper (p. 711)
—Head Louse (p. 756)
—Spider (p. 1626)
—Stick Insect (p. 1649)
Hartley Steiner. This Is Gabriel Making Sense of School: A Book about Sensory Processing Disorder. (p. 1735)
Hartley, Stephanie Olga. Between Hither & Yon Where Good Things Go On! Hartley, Stephanie Olga, illus. (p. 172)
Hartley, Steve. Attack of the Alien Brain. Lum, Bernice, illus. (p. 113)
—Oliver Fibbs: The Clash of the Mega Robots. Vol. 4 Lum, Bernice, illus. (p. 1285)
—Oliver Fibbs & the Abominable Snow Penguin. Lum, Bernice, illus. (p. 1285)
—Oliver Fibbs & the Giant Boy-Munching Bugs. Lum, Bernice, illus. (p. 1285)
—World's Biggest Bogey. (p. 1960)
Hartley, Susan. Abby's Adventures: Abby the Pirate. Kane, Brenden, illus. (p. 2)
—Bienvenido a nuestra Escuela: Fiction-to-Fact Big Book. (p. 177)
—Family Celebration: Set Of 6. (p. 568)
—Family Celebration. (p. 568)
—I Am in - Version 2: Set Of 6. (p. 833)
—Jake's Sleepover: Set Of 6. (p. 906)
—Jake's Sleepover. (p. 906)
—Stephanie Investigates: Small Book. (p. 1648)
—Stephanie Investigates. (p. 1648)
—Welcome to Our School. (p. 1873)
Hartley, Susan, jt. auth. see Campbell, Jane.
Hartley, Susan & Schieber, Jennifer. Red Riding Hood. (p. 1454)
Härtling, Peter. Abuela. Mizsenko, Ingrid, illus. (p. 7)
—Ben Liebt Anna. (p. 163)
—Viejo John. Habinger, Renate, illus. (p. 1841)
—viejo John. Habinger, Renate, illus. (p. 1841)
Hartlove, Chris, photos by see Falick, Melanie.
Hartman, Adrienne, illus. see Banks, Ann.
Hartman, Bob. Big Pig Stampede: And a Bunch More Amazing Miracles. (p. 183)
—Easter Angels. Williams, Sophy, illus. (p. 499)
—Lion Storyteller Bedtime Book. Nagy, Krisztina Kállai, illus. (p. 1020)
—Lion Storyteller Bible Kallai Nagy, Krisztina, illus. (p. 1020)

—Lion Storyteller Christmas Book. Nagy, Krisztina Kallai, illus. (p. 1020)
—Lion Storyteller Easter Book. (p. 1020)
—More Bible Tales. (p. 1174)
—Mr Aesop's Story Shop. Jago, illus. (p. 1184)
—Noah's Big Boat. Samuel, Janet, illus. (p. 1261)
—Noisy Stable & Other Christmas Stories. Hudson, Brett, illus. (p. 1263)
—Sheep in Wolf's Clothing. Raglin, Tim, illus. (p. 1564)
—Stories from the Stable. Hudson, Brett, illus. (p. 1654)
—Wolf Who Cried Boy. Rayla, Tim, illus. (p. 1944)
—Wolf Who Cried Boy. Raglin, Tim, illus. (p. 1944)
Hartman, Bob & Abel, Simone. Who Frightened the Fishermen? (p. 1915)
Hartman, Bob & Hudson, Brett. Polly & the Frog: And Other Folk Tales. (p. 1381)
Hartman, Bob & Nagy, Krisztina Kallai. Lion Storyteller Bedtime Book. (p. 1020)
Hartman, Bob & Poole, Susie. Lion Storyteller Book of Animal Tales. (p. 1020)
Hartman, Brett. Cadillac Chronicles. (p. 250)
Hartman, Carrie. Child of Mine. (p. 301)
Hartman, Carrie, illus. see Cook, Julia.
Hartman, Carrie, illus. see Harris, Trudy.
Hartman, Carrie, illus. see Mermelstein, Yael.
Hartman, Carrie, illus. see Snow, Todd & Snow, Peggy.
Hartman, Carrie, illus. see Snow, Todd.
Hartman, Cassie, photos by see Patent, Dorothy Hinshaw.
Hartman, Colleen Kelley. My Grandma Calls Me Lovey. Hammons, Mark, illus. (p. 1210)
Hartman, Dan, illus. see Patent, Dorothy Hinshaw.
Hartman, Eve & Meshbesher, Wendy. Animal Classification: Do Cats Have Family Trees? (p. 77)
—Changing Life on Earth De Angelis, Maurizio et al, illus. (p. 290)
—Climate Change (p. 332)
—Digestion & Nutrition: What Happens to the Food We Eat? (p. 438)
—Do Scientists Care about Animal Welfare? (p. 457)
—Fossil Fuels (p. 623)
—Health & Wellness (p. 757)
—Light & Sound (p. 1014)
—Magnetism & Electromagnets (p. 1076)
—Mission to Mars (p. 1153)
—Scientists Behind Medical Advances (p. 1529)
—Scientists Behind Space (p. 1529)
—Searching for Arctic Oil (p. 1537)
—What Are the Issues with Genetic Technology? (p. 1880)
—What Is the Threat of Invasive Species? (p. 1890)
Hartman, Eve, et al. Changing Life on Earth De Angelis, Maurizio et al, illus. (p. 290)
—Climate Change (p. 332)
—Fossil Fuels (p. 623)
—Health & Wellness (p. 757)
—Light & Sound (p. 1014)
—Role of Genes (p. 1485)
—Science Ethics & Controversies Escott, Ian, illus. (p. 1525)
Hartman, Holly, ed. see McLoone, Margo.
Hartman, Holly, ed. see Siegel, Alice.
Hartman, Jack & Hartman, Judy. Exchange Your Worries for God's Perfect Peace. (p. 547)
Hartman, John, illus. see Zimmerman, Kathleen.
Hartman, Judith Allen. Upside down Harry. (p. 1825)
Hartman, Judy, jt. auth. see Hartman, Jack.
Hartman, Kurt, illus. see Fein, Eric.
Hartman, Kurt, illus. see Rifkin, L.
Hartman, Kurt, illus. see Rifkin, L. (Lauren).
Hartman, Mike. Take Your Dreams to the ICE. (p. 1697)
Hartman, Moreta. Adventures of the Rocky Mountain Tea Twerps. Mantzke, Jurgen, illus. (p. 23)
Hartman, Ms. Joan. Mischiefs & Misadventures of the Hooligans. (p. 1150)
Hartman, Nancy Lee, illus. see Hayward, Mark Brauner.
Hartman, Rachel. Seraphina. (p. 1552)
—Shadow Scale. (p. 1558)
Hartman, Randall J. Cakewalk Crosswords. (p. 252)
Hartman, Sara. Mary Magdalene's Easter Story. Koehler, Ed, illus. (p. 1100)
—Ten Plagues. Murphy, Terri, illus. (p. 1719)
—When Jesus Was Born. Mitter, Kathy, illus. (p. 1903)
Hartman, Sarah. Asian-American Crafts Kids Can Do! (p. 106)
—Middle Eastern Crafts Kids Can Do! Ponte, June, illus. (p. 1137)
Hartman, Scott, illus. see American Museum of Natural History Staff.
Hartman, Tony & Fafalios, Chris. Whistle Pig. (p. 1912)
Hartman, Wayne. Beyond Imagination: 2003 Musings (p. 174)
—Beyond Imagination: Best of Notes. (p. 174)
—Beyond Imagination: 2003 Musings. Vol. 1 (p. 174)
—Beyond Imagination: 2003 Musings. Vol. II (p. 174)
—Beyond Imagination: The Search for Center. (p. 174)
—Beyond Imagination: Best Passages from 2002 Musings. (p. 174)
—Beyond Imagination Quotes. (p. 174)
Hartmann, Andrea. 3, 2, 1... Blastoff! (p. 1991)
Hartmann, Annabelle. As Big As a Mountain. (p. 105)
Hartmann, April, illus. see Leman, Nora.
Hartmann, Dario. Gallery Girls Collection: Mermaid. (p. 653)
Hartmann, Diana. What Was That Bug That Flew By. (p. 1895)
Hartmann, Jennifer. Kristofur Kitty: Crossing the Street. (p. 967)
Hartmetz, Richard, ed. see Nesbit, E.
Hartnell, Andy. Army of Darkness: Ashes 2 Ashes. (p. 100)
Hartness, Jim & Eskelin, Neil. 24 Hour Turn-Around: Use 24 One-Hour time Periods To Turn Your Life Around. (p. 1996)
Hartnett, Edith E. Breath on the Water. (p. 225)
—Once upon a Time. (p. 1293)
Hartnett, Edmond. Dreams. (p. 484)
Hartnett, Sonya. Butterfly. (p. 247)
—Children of the King. (p. 302)
—Midnight Zoo. McNaughtt, Jonathan & Offermann, Andrea, illus. (p. 1139)
—Sadie & Ratz. James, Ann, illus. (p. 1501)
—Silver Donkey. Powers, Don, illus. (p. 1576)
—Silver Donkey. Spudvilas, Anne, illus. (p. 1576)
—Stripes of the Sidestep Wolf. (p. 1667)
—What the Birds See. (p. 1893)
Hartog, Arnold, jt. auth. see Streltski, Mies.
Hartov, Steven, jt. auth. see Durant, Michael J.
Hartpence, Craig. SHOTS Project (SuperHero's Operating Through Syringes) (p. 1569)
Hart-Plaugher, Teresa. Little Bird & the Wind. Swope, Brenda, illus. (p. 1024)
Hartry, Nancy. Jocelyn & the Ballerina Hendry, Linda, illus. (p. 919)
—Smokescreen. (p. 1594)
—Watching Jimmy. (p. 1861)
Hartsell, Sandra. Let's Go Feed the Animals. (p. 997)
Hartsfield, Mariella G., jt. auth. see Wheeler, Jacque.
Hartshorne, Holly L. School Time for the Three Little Fish (p. 1523)
Hartsock, Conner, jt. auth. see Schreiber, Hannah.
Hartson. Willa's New World: The Novel Study. (p. 1933)
Hartt, Autumn. Believe in A Dream: Overcoming Adversity to Make Childhood Dreams Come True. Hartt, Judy, illus. (p. 161)
Hartt, Judy, illus. see Hartt, Autumn.
Hartter, Sean, illus. see Shannon, Jason.
Hartt-Snowbell, Sarah. Vivian Untangled. (p. 1846)
Hartt-Sussman, Heather. Here Comes Hortense! Graham, Georgia, illus. (p. 770)
—Nana's Summer Surprise. Graham, Georgia, illus. (p. 1228)
—Noni Is Nervous. Côté, Geneviève, illus. (p. 1263)
—Noni Says No. Côté, Geneviève, illus. (p. 1263)
Hartung, Susan Kathleen, illus. see Akin, Sara Laux.
Hartung, Susan Kathleen, illus. see Bergstein, Rita M.
Hartung, Susan Kathleen, illus. see Bowman, Crystal.
Hartung, Susan Kathleen, illus. see Faulconer, Maria Fasal.
Hartung, Susan Kathleen, illus. see Mannis, Celeste Davidson.
Hartung, Susan Kathleen, illus. see Markes, Julie.
Hartung, Susan Kathleen, illus. see Schaefer, Lola M.
Hartwell, Dana S. Angry Tree. (p. 75)
Hartwiger, Heidi. Tricorn Trivia: Colonial Facts & Fun for Kids. (p. 1786)
Hartwright, Gianna. Befana Drama. (p. 158)
Hartzell, Andy. Fox Bunny Funny. (p. 626)
Hartzler, Aaron. Rapture Practice: A True Story about Growing up Gay in an Evangelical Family. (p. 1439)
—Rapture Practice. (p. 1439)
—What We Saw. (p. 1895)
Hartzler, Maria, illus. see Zimmerman, Mary Joyce.
Haruch, Tony. Kurtal Explores Australian Aboriginal Art. (p. 968)
Harukaze, Santa, jt. auth. see Kusaka, Hidenori.
Haruta, Nana. Cactus's Secret. Haruta, Nana, illus. (p. 250)
Harvancik, Monica, illus. see Revere, John J.
Harvell, Richard Brian. Adventures of the Book Battling Kids: The Carson Corners Chronicles. (p. 23)
Harven, Emile de, see de Harven, Emile.
Harvest House Publishers. Easter Story Sticker Book. (p. 499)
—Jesus the Miracle Worker. (p. 916)
—Jesus the Miracle Worker Sticker Book. (p. 916)
—Joseph the Dreamer. (p. 926)
—Joseph the Dreamer Sticker Book. (p. 926)
—Very Special Baby. (p. 1838)
—Very Special Baby Sticker Book. (p. 1838)
Harvest House Publishers & Emmerson-Hicks, J. Complete Illustrated Children's Bible. (p. 353)
Harvest House Publishers Staff, jt. auth. see Fletcher, Betty.
Harvey, A. W. Llewellyn. Christmas Stories: For the Young & Young at Heart. (p. 315)
Harvey, Alex. Dancing with the Star. (p. 403)
—OLIVIA & the Kite Party. Spaziante, Patrick, illus. (p. 1286)
Harvey, Alyxandra. Bleeding Hearts. (p. 199)
—Blood Feud. (p. 200)
—Blood Moon. (p. 200)
—Blood Prophecy. (p. 200)
—Breath of Frost. (p. 225)
—Haunting Violet. (p. 754)
—Hearts at Stake. (p. 760)
—Stolen Away. (p. 1652)
—Whisper the Dead. (p. 1912)
Harvey, Amanda, illus. see Fenner, Carol.
Harvey, Anne, jt. auth. see Farjeon, Eleanor.
Harvey, Autumn. Putty. (p. 1420)
Harvey, Barbara. Inner City Nursery Rhymes. (p. 875)
Harvey, Bev. Animal Families (p. 77)
—Animal Kingdom (p. 78)
—Birds: Set of 6 (p. 191)
—Fish. (p. 598)
—Reptiles. (p. 1461)
Harvey, Bev, et al. Birds: Set of 6 Mettler, René, illus. (p. 191)
Harvey, Bob, illus. see Brontë, Charlotte.
Harvey, Bob, illus. see Doyle, Arthur.
Harvey, Bob, illus. see Stevenson, Robert Louis.
Harvey, Bonnie C. Jane Addams: Social Worker & Nobel Peace Prize Winner. (p. 908)
Harvey, Bonnie Carman. Jane Addams: Social Worker & Nobel Peace Prize Winner. (p. 908)
Harvey, Brian K. Roman Lives: Ancient Roman Life as Illustrated by Latin Inscriptions. (p. 1486)
Harvey, Carol. Lulu, the Friendly Giraffe. (p. 1065)
Harvey, Charlene A. Adventures of the Tiger Club. (p. 23)
Harvey, Chris, illus. see Hart, Sue.
Harvey, Damian. Aquanauts. Oliver, Mark, illus. (p. 93)
—Gift for the King. Remphry, Martin, illus. (p. 675)
—Mr. Fox's Socks. Rescek, Sanja, illus. (p. 1185)
—Snail's Legs. Paul, Korky, illus. (p. 1596)
—Tunnel Racers. Oliver, Mark, illus. (p. 1797)
—Whizzy Witch. Dumortier, Marjorie, illus. (p. 1914)
Harvey, Damian, jt. auth. see Collins Educational Staff.
Harvey, Damian & Remphry, Martin. Robin & the Friar. (p. 1479)
—Robin & the Monk. (p. 1479)
Harvey, Damien. Dinosaur Rock. Ward, Matt, illus. (p. 442)
Harvey, Dan. Rocky Mountain: Colorado, Utah, Wyoming (p. 1484)
Harvey, G. & Dickens, R. Little Book of Riding & Pony Care. (p. 1025)
—Riding & Pony Care. (p. 1471)
Harvey, Gayle, illus. see Forte, Imogene.
Harvey, Gil, illus. see Punter, Russell.
Harvey, Gill. Crime & Detection. (p. 382)
—Orphan of the Sun. (p. 1304)
—Starting Cooking - Internet Linked. (p. 1644)
—Starting Cooking Kid Kit. (p. 1644)
—True Desert Adventures. (p. 1792)
—True Desert Adventures. Woodcock, John, illus. (p. 1792)
—True Stories of Crime & Detection. (p. 1792)
—True Stories of Crime & Detection. Chisholm, Jane, ed. (p. 1792)
—Tutankhamun. McNee, Ian, illus. (p. 1799)
Harvey, Gill, jt. auth. see Dowswell, Paul.
Harvey, Gill & Reid, Struan. Encyclopedia of Ancient Egypt. (p. 524)
—Encyclopedia of Ancient Egypt - Internet Linked. (p. 524)
Harvey, Gwen. Esperanza Means Hope. Porfirio, Guy, illus. (p. 536)
Harvey, Gwendolyn Fowlkes. Backyard Plum Tree. (p. 131)
Harvey, Ian & Chasemore, Richard. Tanks. (p. 1705)
Harvey II, Alvin, illus. see Weber, Erec-Michael Ollier.
Harvey, Irene J. William the Fairground Car. (p. 1933)
Harvey, Jacqueline. Alice-Miranda at Camp. (p. 39)
—Alice-Miranda at School. (p. 39)
—Alice-Miranda at the Palace. (p. 39)
—Alice-Miranda in New York. (p. 39)
—Alice-Miranda in Paris. (p. 39)
—Alice-Miranda on Vacation. (p. 39)
—Alice-Miranda Shines Bright. (p. 39)
—Alice-Miranda Shows the Way. (p. 39)
—Alice-Miranda Takes the Stage. (p. 39)
—Clementine Rose & the Ballet Break-In. (p. 330)
—Clementine Rose & the Famous Friend. Yi, J., illus. (p. 330)
—Clementine Rose & the Farm Fiasco. Yi, J., illus. (p. 330)
—Clementine Rose & the Movie Magic. (p. 330)
—Clementine Rose & the Pet Day Disaster. Yi, J., illus. (p. 330)
—Clementine Rose & the Seaside Escape. (p. 331)
—Clementine Rose & the Surprise Visitor. Yi, J., illus. (p. 331)
—Clementine Rose & the Treasure Box. (p. 331)
—Clementine Rose Busy Day Book. Yi, J., illus. (p. 331)
—Sound of the Sea. Crossett, Warren, illus. (p. 1615)
Harvey, Jayne. Busy Bugs: A Book about Patterns. Adnet, Bernard, illus. (p. 246)
—Cat Show. Petrosino, Tamara, illus. (p. 278)
Harvey, Jeanne Walker. Astro: The Steller Sea Lion Bersani, Shennen, illus. (p. 109)
—My Hands Sing the Blues: Romare Bearden's Childhood Journey Zunon, Elizabeth, illus. (p. 1210)
Harvey, Joanna & Crabtree, Marc. Meet My Neighbor, the Dentist. (p. 1121)
—Meet My Neighbor, the Hair Stylist. (p. 1121)
—Meet My Neighbor, the Paramedic. (p. 1121)
—Meet My Neighbor, the Restaurant Owner. (p. 1121)
Harvey, John. My New Skates. (p. 1216)
Harvey, Karen, jt. auth. see Wolford, Merle.
Harvey, Kathleen, illus. see Dannenbring-Eichstadt, Lana.
Harvey, Keith. Oscar & the Magic Table: A Story about a Little Boy Who For got His Table Manners. (p. 1305)
—Tiberius & the Chocolate Cake. Kirk, Heather, illus. (p. 1747)
—Tiberius & the Friendly Dragon. Kirk, Heather, illus. (p. 1747)
—Tiberius Goes to School. Brown, Kait, illus. (p. 1747)
—Tiberius Goes to School. Brown, Kate & Hickman, Paula, illus. (p. 1747)
—Tiberius Meets Sneaky Cat. Hickman, Paula, illus. (p. 1747)
Harvey, Keith & Beard, Lauren. Say Please, Louise! A Story of a Little Girl With Monstrous Manners. (p. 1518)
Harvey, Keith & Hickman, Paula. Tiberius & the Rainy Day. (p. 1747)
Harvey, Keith & Kirk, Heather. Tiberius & the Friendly Dragon. (p. 1747)
Harvey, Ken. 'Fridge Games. Hermes, Mary Sue, illus. (p. 637)
—Leftovers. Hermes, Mary Sue, illus. (p. 987)
—Quest: Brothers of the Storm: A Tale of Boys Born to Fight. (p. 1426)
Harvey, Kim. Bully Book: An Interactive Educational Workbook for Ages 6-13. (p. 241)
Harvey, Lisa, illus. see Swain, Gwenyth.
Harvey, M. A. Attack of the Jaguar: Dare to Take the Test. (p. 113)
—Riddle of Bear Cave: Dare to Take the Test. (p. 1470)
—Scorpion Secret: Dare to Take the Test. (p. 1530)
—Shark Island Mystery: Dare to Take the Test. (p. 1562)
—Wannabes Pop Diva: For Girls Who Know What They Want to Be. (p. 1856)
Harvey, Martin, photos by see Schindel, John.
Harvey, Matt. Shopping with Dad. Latimer, Miriam, illus. (p. 1569)
Harvey, Matt & Latimer, Miriam. Shopping with Dad. Latimer, Miriam, illus. (p. 1569)
Harvey, Matthea. Cecil the Pet Glacier. Potter, Giselle, illus. (p. 283)
Harvey, Matthew, jt. auth. see Aikman, Louise.
Harvey, Michael C., illus. see Ketchum, Sally.
Harvey, Miles. Look What Came from Africa. (p. 1050)
Harvey, Missy. Epaminondas: Where Is Your Common Sense? (p. 532)
Harvey Mph, Janera P. What Mommy Does. Utley, J. Stacy, illus. (p. 1892)
Harvey, Natalie. Peppermint Pixie. Winfield, Amy, illus. (p. 1340)
Harvey, Pam & Panckridge, Michael. Faster Than Lightning. (p. 576)
—Ghost of a Chance. (p. 671)
—In the Deep End. (p. 865)
—Into the Fire. (p. 881)
—Taking the Chequered Flag. (p. 1698)
Harvey, Paul & Pearson Education Staff. Surfer! (p. 1685)
Harvey, Paul E., Jr. Adventures of Shamus the Leprechaun. (p. 22)
Harvey, Paul, Jr. E: A Tale For Everybody. Butler, Bryan C., illus. (p. 491)
Harvey, Rich, ed. see Anderson, Lars.
Harvey, Robert. Fall of Apartheid: The Inside Story from Smuts to Mbeki. (p. 566)
Harvey, Robin, illus. see Taylor, Gwen.
Harvey, Roger & Sévigny, Eric. Caillou Goes Camping. (p. 251)
Harvey, Roland. At the Beach: Postcards from Crabby Spit. Harvey, Roland, illus. (p. 110)
—In the Bush: Our Holiday at Wombat Flat. Harvey, Roland, illus. (p. 865)
—In the City: Our Scrapbook of Souvenirs. (p. 865)
—In the City: Our Scrapbook of Souvenirs. Harvey, Roland, illus. (p. 865)
—On the Farm: Our Holiday with Uncle Kev. Harvey, Roland, illus. (p. 1290)
—To the Top End: Our Trip Across Australia. Harvey, Roland, illus. (p. 1759)
Harvey, Roland, illus. see Lester, Alison.
Harvey, Roland, jt. auth. see Lester, Alison.
Harvey, Ronald. Wombats Go on Camp. Harvey, Ronald, illus. (p. 1945)
Harvey, Ruth S. Farm of Barney B. Brown. (p. 574)
Harvey, Sarah N. Blanco (p. 198)
—Bull's Eye (p. 240)
—Deadly (p. 417)
—Death Benefits (p. 420)
—Lit Report (p. 1022)
—Plastic (p. 1370)
—Puppies on Board Cowles, Rose, illus. (p. 1418)
—Shattered (p. 1563)
—Three Little Words (p. 1743)
Harvey, Sarah N. & Buffam, Leslie. Great Lakes & Rugged Ground: Imagining Ontario Charko, Kasia, illus. (p. 717)
—West Is Calling: Imagining British Columbia Bonder, Dianna, illus. (p. 1876)
Harvey, Sharon M. Legend of the Pumpkin Carver. (p. 989)
—One Egg-stra-Ordinary Invention. (p. 1294)
—Virginia's Travel Basket. (p. 1844)
Harvey, Stephanie, et al. Ladders Social Studies 4: the Pacific Coast (on-Level) (p. 970)
—Ladders Social Studies 5: the Maya (on-Level) (p. 970)
—Living on the Coast. (p. 1041)
Harvey, Tom. Creature Teachers. (p. 380)
—Gnome Home. (p. 685)
—Guido, the Swan with an Attitude. (p. 730)
—Rat in the Red Truck. (p. 1440)
—Top Dog. (p. 1769)
Harvey, Tom, et al. Tiger Pups. Philpott, Keith, illus. (p. 1748)
Harvey, William C. Ingles para Ninos: English for Children. (p. 874)
—Spanish Every Day: A Learning Adventure for Young Readers. (p. 1621)
Harvey-Fitzhenry, Alyxandra. Broken (p. 230)
—Waking (p. 1853)
Harvie, Ronald Anthony. Adventures of Peter Potato & Friends. (p. 21)
Harvill, Kitty, illus. see Shapiro, Jody Fickes.
Harward, Barnaby, ed. Romeo & Juliet: Interfact Shakespeare. (p. 1486)
Harwell, Andrew. Spider Ring. (p. 1626)
Harwell, Wiley D. Knowing Truth by Name: The Stories of White Bear. (p. 965)
Harwich, Mary Belle, jt. auth. see Hay, John.
Harwood, Beth. Amazing Baby Go Baby Go. (p. 53)
—One Snowy Night. Ronchi, Susanna, illus. (p. 1297)
Harwood, John, jt. auth. see Nixon, Joan Lowery.
Harwood, Kelsey. Still Alive. (p. 1650)
Hasak-Lowy, Todd. 33 Minutes. Barton, Bethany, illus. (p. 1996)
—Me Being Me Is Exactly As Insane As You Being You. (p. 1115)
Hasak-Lowy, Todd, jt. auth. see Gruenbaum, Michael.
Hasan, Heather. Aluminum. (p. 50)
—Archimedes: The Father of Mathematics. (p. 95)
—Bone Cancer. (p. 208)
—Caffeine & Nicotine: A Dependent Society. (p. 251)
—Caffeine & Nicotine. (p. 251)
—Cervical Cancer: Current & Emerging Trends in Detection & Treatment. (p. 288)
—Fluorine. (p. 608)
—Frequently Asked Questions about Everyday First Aid. (p. 636)
—How to Produce, Release, & Market Your Music. (p. 821)
—Iron. (p. 888)
—Kepler & the Laws of Planetary Motion. (p. 949)
—Meat: From the Farm to Your Table. (p. 1117)
—Nitrogen. (p. 1257)
—Pennsylvania: Past & Present. (p. 1338)
—Primary Source History of the Colony of South Carolina. (p. 1400)
—Skateboarding Today & Tomorrow. (p. 1583)
—Wikipedia, 3.5 Million Articles & Counting: Using & Assessing the People's Encyclopedia. (p. 1928)
Hasan, Heather, jt. auth. see Jones, Viola.
Hasan, Heather, ed. How Mathematical Models, Computer Simulations, & Exploration Can Be Used to Study the Universe: An Anthology of Current Thought. (p. 811)
Hasan, Jamal I. Journey to Remember. (p. 929)
Hasan, K. A. Rufus' Big Scare. Primmasone, Bruce, illus. (p. 1494)
Hasan, Rashad, compiled by. Early African American Women Writers & Social Activists. (p. 493)
—Florida Federal Writers Project - American Life Histories & Slave Narratives 1936-1940. (p. 607)
Hasan, Tahara. Anthrax Attacks Around the World. (p. 89)
Hasany, Syed M. Stop the Train, Monkey! (p. 1654)
—Where Is My Stethoscope? (p. 1909)
Hasbro. Dancing in the Clouds. Stein, Erin, ed. (p. 403)
—Friends Are Never Far Away Hurchalla, Elizabeth, ed. (p. 638)
—G. I. Joe Valor vs. Venom (p. 651)

—My Little Pony: Ponyville Reading Adventures. (p. 1213)
HASBRO. My little pony V5. (p. 1213)
Hasbro. Runaway Rainbow. (p. 1496)
—Transformers: Roll Out & Read Adventures. (p. 1778)
—Transformers Rescue Bots: Reading Adventures: Passport to Reading Level 1. (p. 1778)
—Transformers: Roll Out & Read Adventures. (p. 1778)
—Transformers: Ultimate Storybook Collection. (p. 1778)
—Ultimate Betrayal (p. 1809)
—Very Minty Christmas. (p. 1838)
Hasbro & King, Trey. Transformers Rescue Bots. (p. 1778)
Hasbro & Shea, Lisa. Transformers: Rescue Bots: Meet Chase the Police-Bot. (p. 1778)
Hasbro Industries Incorporated Staff. My Little Pony Winning Style: Stories, Activites, & Tattoos. (p. 1213)
Hasbro My Little Pony, Hasbro My. My Little Pony New Episode 2014. (p. 1213)
—My Little Pony Pony Friends Are Forever/la Amistad de Los Ponis Es para Siempre: An English/Spanish Lift-The-Flap Book. (p. 1213)
Hasbro, prod. Ultimate Betrayal (p. 1809)
Hasbro Staff. Elements of Harmony: Friendship Is Magic. (p. 510)
—My Little Pony Pony Friends Are Forever. (p. 1213)
Hasbro, told to. Transformers More Than Meets the Eye: 3D Book with Glasses. (p. 1778)
Hasbrouck, Jan & Denton, Carolyn. Reading Coach: A How-to Manual for Success. (p. 1445)
Hasbrouck, Ph.D., Jan, contrib. by. Quick Phonics Assessment. (p. 1427)
Hascall, Glenn. Power Prayers for Boys. (p. 1390)
Hascall, Glenn, jt. auth. see Baker, Tim.
Hascall, Glenn & Barbour Publishing Staff. 3-Minute Devotions for Guys: 180 Encouraging Readings for Teens. (p. 1991)
Hascamp, Steve. Eight Silly Monkeys. (p. 507)
Hasday, Judy. So You Think You Can Dance. (p. 1602)
—Tiger Woods. (p. 1749)
Hasday, Judy & Hasday, Judy L. Americans of Eastern European Heritage. (p. 64)
Hasday, Judy L. Agnes de Mille. (p. 29)
—Albert Einstein: The Giant of 20th Century Science. (p. 34)
—Americans of Eastern European Heritage. (p. 64)
—Apollo 13 Mission: Overcoming Adversity. (p. 91)
—Civil Rights Act Of 1964: An End to Racial Segregation. (p. 324)
—Davy Crockett. (p. 411)
—Extraordinary People in the Movies. (p. 555)
—Facebook & Mark Zuckerberg. (p. 560)
—Forty-Nine Minutes of Madness: The Columbine High School Shooting. (p. 623)
—Japanese Americans. (p. 909)
—Libya. (p. 1007)
—Libya. Rotberg, Robert I., ed. (p. 1007)
—Marie Curie: Pioneer on the Frontier of Radioactivity. (p. 1093)
—Michael Jordan. (p. 1134)
—Oprah Winfrey. (p. 1301)
—Sierra Leone. (p. 1573)
—Sierra Leone. Rotberg, Robert I., ed. (p. 1573)
—Tiger Woods. (p. 1749)
—Women in the Civil Rights Movement. (p. 1946)
Hasday, Judy L., jt. auth. see Hasday, Judy.
Hasday, Judy L. & Crompton, Samuel Willard. Barry Sanders. (p. 140)
Hasday, Judy L. & Worth, Richard. Donovan Mcnabb. (p. 466)
Hasekura, Isuna. Spice & Wolf. (p. 1626)
Haseley, Dennis. Invisible Moose. Kellogg, Steven, illus. (p. 886)
—My Father Doesn't Know about the Woods & Me. (p. 1203)
—Old Banjo. Gammell, Stephen, illus. (p. 1283)
Haseley, et al. Oso Que Amaba Los Libros. (p. 1305)
Haselhurst, Maureen. Emperor's New Uniform. Kennedy, Kelly, illus. (p. 521)
Hasenecz Calvert, Ellen. Nine Goldfish in David's Pond. (p. 1256)
Hash, Bill W. Jahmon's Adventure Home. (p. 905)
Hash, John A. Best of Bible Pathway 2004. (p. 170)
Hash, Stella. Christmas Caravan. (p. 313)
Hashanah, Rosh & Kippur, Yom. Rosh Hashanah & Yom Kippur Coloring Book. (p. 1490)
Hashey, Heather. I'm A Big Sister. Hashey, Kim, photos by. (p. 858)
Hashey, Kim, photos by see Hashey, Heather.
Hashimoto, Daniel & Richardville, Mandy. Action Movie Kid: All New Adventures Part 1. Fabbretti, Valerio, illus. (p. 10)
Hashimoto, Meika, jt. auth. see Man-Kong, Mary.
Hashimoto, Meika & Tillworth, Mary. I Am Buzz Lightyear (Disney/Pixar Toy Story) RH Disney Staff, illus. (p. 832)
Hashmi-Alikhan, Saira. Snuggly Baby. (p. 1601)
Hashway, Kelly. Stalked by Death. (p. 1638)
Hasibe, Gul & Balci. Delicious Fruits. (p. 425)
Hasiuk, Brenda. Where the Rocks Say Your Name. (p. 1909)
—Your Constant Star (p. 1980)
Haskamp, Steve. Este Cerdito. (p. 538)
—Five Silly Monkeys. (p. 601)
—Ocho Monitos. (p. 1277)
Haskamp, Steve, illus. see Harris, Trudy.
Haskamp, Steve, illus. see Imperato, Teresa.
Haskamp, Steven. Eight Silly Monkeys. (p. 507)
—Five Silly Monkeys. (p. 601)
Haskell, J. P. Earth's Many Landforms. (p. 498)
Haskell, L. Sweet Story of Old: A Life of Christ for Children. (p. 1690)
Haskell, Merrie. Castle Behind Thorns. (p. 276)
—Handbook for Dragon Slayers. (p. 740)
—Princess Curse. (p. 1403)
Haskell, Rachael. Biggest Little Hero. (p. 185)
Haskett, Dan, illus. see Golden Books Staff & Carbone, Courtney.
Haskett, Dan, illus. see Golden Books.
Haskett, Dan, illus. see Tillworth, Mary.
Haskett, J. A. Morgan & Friends. (p. 1175)
Haskett, Wendy. Wendy Haskett's Backward Glances (p. 1875)
Haskew, Michael E. Tanks: Inside & Out. (p. 1705)
Haski, Pierre, ed. see Yan, Ma.
Haski, Pierre, jt. auth. see Yan, Ma.
Haskins, Amanda. God Is My Daddy. (p. 689)
Haskins, James. Black Stars of the Civil War Times. (p. 197)
—Black Stars of the Civil Rights Movement. (p. 197)
—Delivering Justice: W. W. Law & the Fight for Civil Rights. Andrews, Benny, illus. (p. 425)
—Freedom Rides: Journey for Justice. (p. 635)
—Harlem Renaissance. (p. 749)
—March on Washington. (p. 1091)
Haskins, James & Benson, Kathleen. Africa: A Look Back. (p. 26)
—African American Religious Leaders. (p. 27)
Haskins, James, et al. Rise of Jim Crow. (p. 1474)
Haskins, Jim. African American Entrepreneurs. (p. 27)
Haskins, Jim, ed. see Sullivan, Otha Richard.
Haskins, Jim, jt. auth. see Benson, Kathleen.
Haskins, Jim & Benson, Kathleen. Count Your Way Through South Africa. Neibert, Alissa, illus. (p. 370)
—Count Your Way Through Zimbabwe. Park, Janie Jaehyun, illus. (p. 370)
Haskins, Jim, et al. John Lewis in the Lead: A Story of the Civil Rights Movement (p. 922)
Haskins, Lori. Butterfly Fever. Smath, Jerry, illus. (p. 247)
—Locura Por Las Mariposas (Butterfly Fever) Smath, Jerry, illus. (p. 1045)
—No Money? No Problem! Nez, John A., illus. (p. 1259)
—Sled Dogs. (p. 1588)
Haskins, Lori & Ramirez, Alma. Locura por las Mariposas. Smath, Jerry, illus. (p. 1045)
Haslam, Andrew. Arctic Peoples. (p. 96)
—Earth. (p. 495)
—Insects. (p. 875)
Haslam, Andrew, jt. auth. see Baker, Wendy.
Haslam, Andrew, et al. Body. (p. 206)
—Building. (p. 238)
—Earth. (p. 495)
—Flight. (p. 604)
—Sound. (p. 1615)
—Space. (p. 1618)
—Time. (p. 1750)
Haslam, John, illus. see Marsico, Katie.
Haslam, John, illus. see Rosselson, Leon.
Haslam, William, jt. auth. see Graham, Amy.
Hasler, Ben, illus. see Turner, Tracey.
Hasler, Brian. Casper & Catherine Move to America: An Immigrant Family's Adventures, 1849-1850. Gouge, Angela, tr. (p. 276)
Hasler, Doris, et al. Nutrition & Wellness (p. 1274)
Hasler, Eveline. En Suenos Puedo Volar. (p. 523)
—In My Dreams I Can Fly. Bhend, Kathi, illus. (p. 864)
Haslett, Katherine A. Day Amy Met the Prime Minister & Mrs. Blair. (p. 412)
Hasley, Jessica Williams. Could We? A Book of Wishes. (p. 369)
Hasling, Jack. Little Rock & Other Stories: And Other Stories. Rogers, Denny, illus. (p. 1036)
—Salamander the Great! (p. 1504)
Haspiel, Dean, illus. see Keenan, Sheila & Stine, R. L.
Haspiel, Dean, illus. see Lynch, Jay.
Haspiel, Dean, jt. auth. see Lynch, Jay.
Haspiel, Dean, jt. auth. see Pekar, Harvey.
Haspiel, Dean, jt. auth. see Wald, Mark.
Haspiel, Dean & Doe, Juan. X-Men: First Class: Class Portraits. (p. 1967)
Haspiel, Dean & Lynch, Jay. Mo & Jo Fighting Together Forever. (p. 1157)
Hass, Estie, illus. see Fuchs, Menucha.
Hassall, Angela. Ella Moves House. Ewen, Caroline, illus. (p. 514)
Hassan, Marian A. Bright Star, Blue Sky. (p. 228)
Hassan, Masood. Madeline & Friends: Fruits & Veggies vs Candy. Lady Josephine, illus. (p. 1070)
Hassan, Michael. Crash & Burn. (p. 376)
Hassan, Miriam & Benchmark Education Co., LLC Staff. Gabe, Kate, Dave. (p. 652)
—Go up, up, Up. (p. 687)
—Win, Win, Win! (p. 1935)
Hassard, Jack. Science As Inquiry. (p. 1525)
Hassed, Craig. Essence of Health: The Seven Pillars of Wellbeing. (p. 536)
Hassel, Bryan C., jt. auth. see Hassel, Emily A.
Hassel, Emily A. & Hassel, Bryan C. Picky Parent Guide: Choose Your Child's School with Confidence, the Elementary Years (K-6) (p. 1355)
Hasselbring, Janet. Ossie the Brave Fish Hawk: Tales from Pelican Cove: Book 3. (p. 1306)
—What Do You See, Mrs Night Heron? De Vries, Bruce, illus. (p. 1883)
Hasselfeldt, Lori. under the Ocean Alphabet Book. Hasselfeldt, Lori, illus. (p. 1813)
Hasselius, Michelle M. Lyndon B. Johnson (p. 1066)
—Richard M. Nixon (p. 1469)
Hasselius, Michelle M. & Tucker, Rosalyn. Presidential Biographies (p. 1397)
Hasselstrom, Linda M. & Griesemer, James. Roadside History of South Dakota. (p. 1477)
Hassett, Ann. Finest Christmas Tree. Hassett, John, illus. (p. 589)
Hassett, Ann, jt. auth. see Hassett, John.
Hassett, Ann & Hassett, John. Come Back, Ben. Hassett, Ann & Hassett, John, illus. (p. 347)
Hassett, John, illus. see Hassett, Ann.
Hassett, John, jt. auth. see Hassett, Ann.
Hassett, John & Hassett, Ann. Come Back, Ben. (p. 347)
Hassig, Susan M. & Al Adely, Laith Muhmood. Iraq. (p. 887)
Hassig, Susan M. & Latif, Zawiah Abdul. Somalia. (p. 1608)
Hassig, Susan M. & Muhmood, Laith. Iraq. (p. 887)
Hassig, Susan M. & Quek, Lynette. Panama. (p. 1320)
Hassinger, Peter W. Shakespeare's Daughter. (p. 1559)
Hassinger, Peter W., jt. auth. see Haussinger, D.
Hasslebeck, Kellie & Gohari, Omid. Depauw University College Prowler off the Record. (p. 427)
Hassler, Jill K. Beyond the Mirrors: The Study of the Mental & Spiritual Aspects of Horsemanship. Bartholomew, Jane, ed. (p. 174)
—In Search of Your Image: A Practical Guide to the Mental & Spiritual Aspects of Horsemanship. Jahiel, Jessica, ed. (p. 865)
Hassler, Jon. Staggerford Flood. (p. 1638)
—Staggerford Murders. (p. 1638)
Hassler, Kurt. Diva V Poe. (p. 454)
Hassler-Scoop, Jill K., et al. Equestrian Instruction: The Integrated Approach to Teaching & Learning. Covington, Emily, illus. (p. 533)
—Riding Experience & Beyond: Personal Development for Riders. Kolb, Robin, ed. (p. 1471)
Haste, Dianne. C C Cookie Bear's Cookbook. (p. 249)
Hastedt, Glenn. Espionage: A Reference Handbook Vasan, Mildred, ed. (p. 536)
Hasting, Lori A. Green with N. V. (p. 722)
Hastings, Avery. Feuds. (p. 583)
—Torn. (p. 1770)
Hastings, Derek. Penguins - Pb: A Portrait of the Animal World. (p. 1337)
Hastings, Eileen. Rufus & Christopher Series (p. 1494)
Hastings, Howard L., illus. see Heyliger, William.
Hastings, Howard L., illus. see White, Ramy Allison.
Hastings, Jacqueline. Jay's Tales. (p. 910)
Hastings, John. Drawing Breakthrough Kit: Taking the Mystery Out of Learning to Draw. (p. 481)
Hastings, Jon. Terrabella Smoot & the Unsung Monsters. (p. 1721)
Hastings, Juliet. White Rose Ensnared. (p. 1913)
Hastings, Ken, illus. see Creed, Julie.
Hastings, Leon. Trixie - the Christmas Cow. McLeod, David, illus. (p. 1788)
Hastings, Robert. Blue Kangaroo: It's Nice to Be Different. (p. 203)
Hastings, Rook. Nearly Departed. (p. 1239)
Hastings, Selina. Children's Illustrated Bible. Thomas, Eric, illus. (p. 303)
Hastings, Selina, jt. auth. see Dorling Kindersley Publishing Staff.
Hastings, Suanne. Many Moods of Maddie: Bossy Boots. Crabtree, Andy, illus. (p. 1089)
Haston, Meg. How to Rock Best Friends & Frenemies. (p. 821)
—How to Rock Braces & Glasses. (p. 821)
—How to Rock Break-Ups & Make-Ups. (p. 821)
—Paperweight. (p. 1323)
Hasty, Shaudalon. My Body. (p. 1198)
Hasty, Vicki Sterling. Eliza & the Analogies of Burnshire. (p. 513)
Hasu, Sarah Toshiko. Megume & the Trees. (p. 1124)
Hasumi, Toui. Othello. (p. 1306)
Haswell, Peter. Whales. (p. 1877)
Hata, Donald T. & Hata, Nadine. Japanese Americans & World War II: Exclusion, Internment & Redress. (p. 909)
Hata, Kenjiro. Hayate the Combat Butler. Hata, Kenjiro, illus. (p. 755)
Hata, Kenjiro & Giambruno, Mark. Hayate the Combat Butler Hata, Kenjiro, illus. (p. 755)
Hata, Kenjiro, et al. Hayate the Combat Butler. Hata, Kenjiro, illus. (p. 755)
Hata, Kowshiro, illus. see Kimura, Yuichi.
Hata, Nadine, jt. auth. see Hata, Donald T.
Hatakeyama, Hiroshi, illus. see Hood, Karen Jean Matsko.
Hatakeyama, Hiroshi, tr. see Hood, Karen Jean Matsko.
Hatala, Dan, illus. see Giancamilli, Vanessa.
Hatala, Dan, illus. see O'Donnell, Liam.
Hatala, Dan, jt. auth. see Boyer, Allen B.
Hatam, Samer, illus. see Holden, Pam & Aesop.
Hatam, Samer, illus. see Holden, Pam.
Hatanaka, Kellen. Drive (p. 485)
—Work: An Occupational ABC (p. 1952)
Hatch, Alden. General George Patton: Old Blood & Guts. (p. 660)
Hatch, Andrew. Examining Airplane Crashes. (p. 547)
Hatch, Bee. Grandma Talks to Me. (p. 708)
Hatch, Ines Arnsberger. Marsha's Song: A Celebration of Life. (p. 1096)
Hatch Jr., B. J. Butch. Professor Rock Ltd. Chatham, Dennis J., illus. (p. 1409)
Hatch, Justina. Charlie the Caterpillar (p. 293)
Hatch, Laurence. Cultivars of Woody Plants (A-C) (p. 390)
Hatch, Morgan John. Where Dreams Are Made. (p. 1907)
Hatch, Richard & Linaweaver, Brad. Battlestar Galactica: Paradis. (p. 147)
Hatch, Thomas. History of Hip-Hop: The Roots of Rap. (p. 784)
—Larry the Moose. (p. 976)
Hatch, Thomas, jt. auth. see Purney, Dawn.
Hatch, Thomas & Purney, Dawn. Advantage Grammar Grade 6: High Interest Skill Building for Home & School. Vol. 8142 Hamaguchi, Carla, ed. (p. 14)
—Advantage Grammar Grade 7: High Interest Skill Building for Home & School Hamaguchi, Carla, ed. (p. 14)
Hatch, Tom & Purney, Dawn. Advantage Grammar Grade 3: High Interest Skill Building for Home & School. Vol. 8139 Hamaguchi, Carla, ed. (p. 13)
Hatcher, Bill. National Geographic Photography Field Guide: Action & Adventure. Hatcher, Bill, photos by. (p. 1233)
Hatcher, John. Ali's Dream. (p. 41)
Hatfield, Cynthia, illus. see Lewis-Brown, Alscess.
Hatfield, Justin, jt. auth. see Hatfield, Tyrel.
Hatfield, Justin R., jt. auth. see Hatfield, Tyrel S.
Hatfield, Kara. Real Story of Sant. (p. 1449)
Hatfield, Kari, ed. see Hatfield, Tyrel & Hatfield, Justin.
Hatfield, Lisa, ed. see Hatfield, Tyrel & Hatfield, Justin.
Hatfield, Ron. Love Notes from God. Boehm, Annette, ed. (p. 1060)
Hatfield, Ruth. Book of Storms. Call, Greg, illus. (p. 212)
Hatfield, Tommy, illus. see Carrier, Therese & Carrier, Stephen.
Hatfield, Tyrel & Hatfield, Justin. Fix Your Eyes on Jesus. Hatfield, Lisa & Hatfield, Kari, eds. (p. 601)
—Mystery of Christ. Hatfield, Lisa & Hatfield, Kari, eds. (p. 1224)
—Righteous Roundup: Wanted: Righteous children of God. Hatfield, Tyrel, illus. (p. 1472)
Hatfield, Tyrel S. & Hatfield, Justin R. Fix your eyes on Jesus. Hatfield, Tyrel S., illus. (p. 601)
Hathaway, Barbara. Missy Violet & Me. (p. 1155)
Hathaway, Jaime L. Necklace. (p. 1239)
Hathaway, Jeff. Masterpiece. (p. 1103)
Hathaway, Jill. Impostor. (p. 862)
—Slide. (p. 1590)
Hathaway, Karen, illus. see Salton, Liz.
Hathaway, Lucinda Churchman. 'Round the World: Takashi Sails Home. (p. 1491)
Hathorn, Libby. Baby for Loving. Ainslie, Tamsin, illus. (p. 126)
—Caravan Kids. Connor, Julie, illus. (p. 265)
—Eu Amo Você, Livro. Dalla, Juliana, tr. from ENG. (p. 540)
—Outside. Voutila, Ritva, illus. (p. 1313)
—River. Wong, Stanley, illus. (p. 1475)
Hathorn, Libby & Magerl, Caroline. Over the Moon. (p. 1314)
Hathorn, Sarah Alexandra. Teenagents: World Challenge. (p. 1714)
Hatke, Ben. Julia's House for Lost Creatures. Hatke, Ben, illus. (p. 932)
—Legends of Zita the Spacegirl. (p. 990)
—Legends of Zita the Spacegirl. Hatke, Ben, illus. (p. 990)
—Zita the Spacegirl. (p. 1987)
—Zita the Spacegirl. Hatke, Ben, illus. (p. 1987)
Hatke, Ben, illus. see DeDomenico, Elizabeth Marie.
Hatke, Ben, illus. see Doman, Regina.
Hatke, Ben, illus. see Hicks, Betty.
Hatke, Ben, illus. see Lozano, Neal.
Hatke, Ben, illus. see Pochocki, Ethel.
Hatkoff, Craig. Knut: How One Little Polar Bear Captivated the World. (p. 966)
—Panda Patrol. (p. 1320)
Hatkoff, Craig, jt. auth. see Yates, David.
Hatkoff, Craig & Hatkoff, Juliana Lee. Good-Bye Tonsils! Mets, Marilyn, illus. (p. 697)
Hatkoff, Craig & Yates, David. Hope for Winter: The True Story of a Remarkable Dolphin Friendship. (p. 796)
Hatkoff, Craig, et al. Knut: How One Little Polar Bear Captivated the World. (p. 966)
—Owen & Mzee: The Language of Friendship. Greste, Peter, photos by. (p. 1314)
—Owen & Mzee: The True Story of a Remarkable Friendship. Greste, Peter, illus. (p. 1314)
Hatkoff, Juliana, et al. Knut: La Historia del Osito Polar Que Cautivo Al Mundo Entero. (p. 966)
—Winter's Tail: How One Little Dolphin Learned to Swim Again. (p. 1938)
Hatkoff, Juliana Lee, jt. auth. see Hatkoff, Craig.
Hatley, A. L. Little Pinky's Day. (p. 1033)
Hatley, Shannon. Young Princess & the Brave Knight. (p. 1979)
Hatori, Bisco. Host Club (p. 801)
—Host Club. Hatori, Bisco, illus. (p. 801)
—Ouran High School Host Club (p. 1310)
Hatori, Koshiro, tr. see Maekawa, Jun & Origami.
Hatrick, Gloria. Masks. (p. 1102)
Hatt, Christine. African-American Slave Trade. (p. 27)
—American West. (p. 64)
—Ancient Greece (p. 69)
Hattan, Ann. Jake & Bobby's Magical Christmas. (p. 905)
Hattaway, Carol. Dinky Duck's Adventure. Cotton, Sue Lynn, illus. (p. 440)
Hattemer, Kate. Vigilante Poets of Selwyn Academy. (p. 1842)
Hattenhauer, Ina. Dollhouse Sticker Book. (p. 464)
Hatter, Hilda E. Bananas & Balloons: Inspirational Stories of Motorcycling Adventures. (p. 136)
Hattle, Jay. Boy Who Didn't Try. (p. 219)
Hatton, Caroline. Night Olympic Team: Fighting to Keep Drugs Out of the Games. (p. 1254)
Hatton, Fran. Learning about Earning. (p. 984)
Hatton, Fredrick D. Dusty & a Gift for a King (p. 490)
Hatton, Jenny. Finding Aunt Joan. Rankin, Joan, illus. (p. 588)
—Moving House. Rankin, Joan, illus. (p. 1183)
—Swimming in the Sun. Rankin, Joan, illus. (p. 1691)
Hatton, Laura. Fairy's Garden. (p. 565)
Hatton, Libby. Pete Puffin's Wild Ride Cruising Alaska's Currents. Hatton, Libby, illus. (p. 1346)
Hatton, Thomas & George, Enzo. Afghanistan & Iraq Wars: War Against Extremism. (p. 26)
Hattori, Chihiro. Kanji de Manga Special Edition: Yoji-Jukugo: Yoji-Jukugo. (p. 942)
Hattrup, Cheryl. Little Woman Handbook. (p. 1038)
Hattstein, Markus. Prehistory, First Empires, & the Ancient World: From the Stone Age to 900 CE. (p. 1395)
Hattstein, Markus, jt. auth. see Berndl, Klaus.
Hattstein, Markus & Udelhoven, Hermann-Josef. Middle Ages & the Early Modern Period: From the 5th Century to the 18th Century. (p. 1137)
Hatzfeld, Jean. Antelope's Strategy: Living in Rwanda after the Genocide. Coverdale, Linda, tr. (p. 89)
Hau, Joseph, illus. see Hau, Stephanie.
Hau, Stephanie. I Can Live To 100! Secrets Just for Kids. Hau, Joseph, illus. (p. 836)
Hauber, Jennifer. Just Like Om. (p. 939)
Hauck, Christie, illus. see Culver, Kathy.
Hauck, Max M. Science versus Crime. (p. 1528)
Hauck, Melissa, illus. see Jensen, Elizabeth.
Hauenstein, Michael. Speedboat Racers. (p. 1624)
Hauenstein, Sandra. Little Flowers. (p. 1027)
Hauf, Kyle. Annabelle Discovers the Missing Lunch Money. PA Illustrator, illus. (p. 85)
Hauff, Wilhelm & Pak, Boris. Little Mook & Dwarf Longnose. (p. 1032)
Haugaard, Erik. Prince Boghole. (p. 1401)
Haugaard, Erik C., jt. auth. see Haugaard, Erik Christian.
Haugaard, Erik Christian. Hakon of Rogen's Saga. Dillon, Leo & Dillon, Diane, illus. (p. 736)
—Little Fishes. Johnson, Milton, illus. (p. 1027)

Haugaard, Erik Christian & Haugaard, Erik C. Boy & the Samurai. (p. 217)
—Revenge of the Forty-Seven Samurai. (p. 1466)
—Samurai's Tale. (p. 1510)
Haugaard, Kay. Day the Dragon Danced. Barritt, Carolyn Reed, illus. (p. 414)
—No Place. (p. 1259)
Hauge, Carl, illus. see Burgess, Thornton W.
Hauge, Mary, illus. see Burgess, Thornton W.
Haugen, Brenda. Abraham Lincoln: Great American President. (p. 6)
—Adolf Hitler: Dictator of Nazi Germany (p. 13)
—African Elephants (p. 27)
—Birthdays. Ouren, Todd, illus. (p. 193)
—Black Dahlia: Shattered Dreams (p. 195)
—Christmas. Ouren, Todd, illus. (p. 312)
—Crazy Horse: Sioux Warrior (p. 377)
—Douglas MacArthur: America's General (p. 473)
—Easter. Boyd, Sheree, illus. (p. 499)
—Giant Pandas (p. 674)
—Holidays & Celebrations (p. 788)
—Johnathan Toews. (p. 923)
—Langston Hughes: The Voice of Harlem (p. 974)
—Martha Washington: First Lady of the United States. (p. 1097)
—Sheamus: Pro Wrestling Superstar (p. 1564)
—Thanksgiving. Ouren, Todd, illus. (p. 1725)
—Valentine's Day. Ouren, Todd, illus. (p. 1830)
—Zodiac Killer: Terror & Mystery (p. 1987)
Haugen, Brenda, jt. auth. see Moreno, Barry.
Haugen, Brenda & Compass Point Books Staff. Teens in Australia (p. 1715)
—Thurgood Marshall: Civil Rights Lawyer & Supreme Court Justice (p. 1746)
Haugen, David. Children of Undocumented Immigrants. Greenhaven Press Editors, ed. (p. 303)
—Russia. Greenhaven Press Editors, ed. (p. 1498)
—Technology & the Cloud. Greenhaven Press Staff, ed. (p. 1711)
—War. Greenhaven Press Editors, ed. (p. 1857)
Haugen, David, jt. auth. see Greenhaven Press Editors.
Haugen, David, jt. auth. see Henningfeld, Diane Andrews.
Haugen, David, jt. auth. see Watkins, Christine.
Haugen, David M. Attack on Pearl Harbor. Gale Editors, ed. (p. 114)
—BP Oil Spill. (p. 221)
—Bullying. Greenhaven Press Editors, ed. (p. 241)
—Can the War on Terrorism Be Won? (p. 258)
—China. (p. 306)
—Coal. (p. 336)
—Criminal Justice. (p. 382)
—Democracy. (p. 425)
—Disabilities. Greenhaven Press Editors & Gale Editors, eds. (p. 446)
—Discipline & Punishment. (p. 447)
—Discrimination. Greenhaven Press Editors, ed. (p. 450)
—Drilling in the Gulf of Mexico. (p. 485)
—Ethics of Cloning. (p. 539)
—Food/the Food Industry in Eric Schlosser's Fast Food Nation. (p. 614)
—Genetic Engineering (p. 660)
—Global Resources. Hanrahan, Clare, ed. (p. 684)
—Globalization. (p. 685)
—Health Care. (p. 757)
—Human Rights. (p. 826)
—Interracial Relationships. (p. 881)
—Iran. (p. 886)
—Is Global Warming a Threat? (p. 889)
—Islam (p. 891)
—Islam. (p. 891)
—Legalized Gambling. (p. 988)
—Media Violence. (p. 1118)
—Middle Class. (p. 1137)
—National Security. (p. 1233)
—Nuclear & Toxic Waste. (p. 1269)
—Nutrition. (p. 1274)
—Outsourcing. (p. 1313)
—Parenting. Greenhaven Press Editors, ed. (p. 1324)
—Popular Culture. (p. 1385)
—Sexality in the Comedies of Shakesprear. Gale, ed. (p. 1556)
—Sexually Transmitted Diseases. Gale, ed. (p. 1556)
—Should the Federal Government Bail Out Private Industry? (p. 1570)
—Should the U. S. Reduce Its Consumption? (p. 1570)
—Terrorism. (p. 1722)
—Unemployment. (p. 1817)
—Vietnam War. Gale Editors, ed. (p. 1841)
—War in Hemingway's a Farewell to Arms. Gale, ed. (p. 1857)
—Welfare. (p. 1874)
Haugen, David M., ed. see Friedman, Lauri S.
Haugen, David M., ed. see Musser, Susan.
Haugen, David M., jt. auth. see Greenhaven Press Editors.
Haugen, David M., jt. auth. see Watkins, Christine.
Haugen, David M. & Bauder, Julia. Is the Political Divide Harming America? (p. 890)
Haugen, David M. & Egendorf, Laura K. Islam in America. (p. 891)
Haugen, David M. & Musser, Susan. Can the War on Terrorism Be Won? (p. 258)
—Holocaust. (p. 789)
—Pandemics. (p. 1321)
—Religion in America. (p. 1458)
Haugen, David M. & Musser, Susan, eds. Pandemics. (p. 1321)
Haugen, David M., ed. Alternative Medicine. (p. 50)
—Democracy. (p. 425)
—Food/the Food Industry in Eric Schlosser's Fast Food Nation. (p. 614)
—Is Foreign Aid Necessary? (p. 889)
—Millennial Generation. (p. 1143)
—Renewable Energy. (p. 1460)
—Sex. (p. 1556)
—Space Exploration. (p. 1619)
Haugen, David M., et al. American Values. (p. 63)
—Energy Alternatives. (p. 528)
—Great Depression. (p. 715)
—Iraq (p. 887)
—Iraq. (p. 887)
—Middle East. (p. 1137)
Haugen, Hayley Mitchell. Disaster Relief. (p. 446)
—Internet Safety. (p. 880)
—Life in a Coral Reef. (p. 1010)
—Lupus. (p. 1066)
—People with Disabilities. (p. 1340)
Haugen, Hayley Mitchell, ed. see George, Charles.
Haugen, Hayley Mitchell, jt. auth. see Ferguson, Olivia.
Haugen, Hayley Mitchell, ed. Race in Ralph Ellison's Invisible Man. (p. 1431)
Haugen, Peter. Biology: Decade by Decade. Cannon, William J., ed. (p. 189)
Haugen, Ryan, illus. see Blackaby, Susan & Jones, Christianne C.
Haugen, Ryan, illus. see Blackaby, Susan.
Haugen, Ryan, illus. see Dahl, Michael & Ziegler, Mark.
Haugen, Ryan, illus. see Dahl, Michael, et al.
Haugen, Ryan, illus. see Dahl, Michael.
Haugen, Ryan, illus. see Donahue, Jill L., et al.
Haugen, Ryan, illus. see Jones, Christianne C.
Haugen, Ryan, illus. see Seuling, Barbara.
Haugen, Ryan, illus. see Stockland, Patricia M.
Haugen, Ryan, jt. auth. see Blackaby, Susan.
Haugen, Timothy A. Castle of Gloom (p. 277)
Haugen, Victoria J. Big Blue's Wish. (p. 178)
Haugen-McLane, Janie. Real-World Picture Words Software - Household Words. (p. 1449)
—Real-World Picture Words Software - Kitchen/Bathroom Words. (p. 1449)
Haughey, Jennifer. NOT a Stupid Baby Book: Top Secret: Boys Only! (p. 1266)
Haughom, Lisa. People, Places & Things. (p. 1340)
—Things That Go! (p. 1733)
Haughton, Chris. Little Owl Lost. Haughton, Chris, illus. (p. 1032)
—Oh No, George! Haughton, Chris, illus. (p. 1281)
—Shh! We Have a Plan. Haughton, Chris, illus. (p. 1566)
Haughton, Emma. Drug Abuse? (p. 486)
—Equality of the Sexes? (p. 533)
Haughton, Hugh, ed. see Carroll, Lewis, pseud.
Haughwout, Pixie & Folsom, Ralph. Canal Cruising in the South of France: The Romantic Canal Du Midi. (p. 260)
Haulley, Fletcher. Critical Perspectives on 9/11. (p. 383)
—Deparment of Homeland Security. (p. 427)
—Department of Homeland Security. (p. 427)
—Primary Source History of the Colony of New Hampshire. (p. 1400)
Haulley, Fletcher, ed. Critical Perspectives On 9/11. (p. 383)
Hauman, Carrie. Zoe the Magic Love Dog. (p. 1987)
Hauman, Doris, illus. see Piper, Watty.
Hauman, George, illus. see Piper, Watty.
Hauman, George and Doris, illus. see Piper, Watty.
Haun, Janine. Three Steps to Heaven. (p. 1744)
Haun, Wayne, et al. Island Christmas: A Kids' Musical about Giving. (p. 892)
Haupt, Wolfgang & Bland, Janice. Tales of the Little Hedgehogs: Fairy Plays. Mouraviova, Yulia, illus. (p. 1702)
Haus, Carl. Father of Many Nations. (p. 577)
Haus, Carl Hoyt. Brand-New World. (p. 222)
—God Makes a Promise. (p. 690)
Haus, Estudio. Ancient Myths. (p. 70)
Haus, Estudio, illus. see Atwood, Megan.
Haus, Estudio, illus. see Enz, Tammy.
Haus, Estudio, illus. see Wheeler-Toppen, Jodi.
Haus, Jean. With the Band (p. 1942)
Haus, Robyn. Create a Year-Round Wildlife Habitat: For Urban & Suburban Small Spaces. (p. 378)
Hauser, Bill, illus. see Schmatz, Pat.
Hauser, Bill, illus. see Tabs, Judy & Steinberg, Barbara.
Hauser, Bill, illus. see Willey, Margaret.
Hauser, Dana. Imagination's Amazing Planet (p. 860)
Hauser, Jill Frankel. Kid's Guide to Becoming the Best You Can Be! Developing 5 Traits You Need to Achieve Your Personal Best. Kline, Michael, illus. (p. 953)
—Kindergarten Success: Helping Children Excel Right from the Start. Hauser, Savlan, illus. (p. 957)
—Kindergarten Success. Hauser, Salvan, illus. (p. 957)
—Little Hands Celebrate America: Learning about the U. S. A. through Crafts & Activities. Kline, Michael, illus. (p. 1029)
—Little Hands Celebrate America! Learning about the U.S.A Through Crafts & Activities. (p. 1029)
—Science Play: Beginning Discoveries for 2 to 6 Year Olds. Kline, Michael, illus. (p. 1527)
—Science Play. Kline, Michael, illus. (p. 1527)
—Super Science Concoctions. Kline, Michael, illus. (p. 1680)
Hauser, Judy. Legend of Punzel's Pond. (p. 988)
Hauser, Lisa Kay. 1-2-3, & God Made Me! (p. 1990)
—1-2-3, Special Like Me! (p. 1990)
Hauser, Michele. Crystal Palace: Rescue of the Baby Fairy Prince. (p. 387)
—Crystal Palace Ii: Rebellion in Fairyland. (p. 387)
—The, Crystal Palace Iii: The Fairy War. (p. 1728)
Hauser, Mindy Moser. Vo-Tech Track to Success in Hospitality & Tourism. (p. 1847)
Hauser, Salvan, illus. see Hauser, Jill Frankel.
Hauser, Savlan, illus. see Hauser, Jill Frankel.
Hauser, Sheri. Abrea Ansus. Peck, Karna, illus. (p. 7)
—Corianta: Heart Song. (p. 367)
—Corianta Love Notes I. (p. 367)
—Corianta Love Notes II. (p. 367)
—Frog Frey Fun. (p. 640)
—Glory Bound Bindings. (p. 685)
—Holy Hum. Brown, Ron, illus. (p. 791)
—Me Mesa. (p. 1116)
—Sharing Ole Lumpy. (p. 1561)
—Tomasena: Moving from Doubt to Faith. Peck, Karna, illus. (p. 1764)
Hauser, Sheri, photos by see Tolpen, Stanley.
Hausfater, Rachel. Little Boy Star: An Allegory of the Holocaust. Zimmerman, Joelle, tr. from FRE. (p. 1025)
Hausfater-Douïeb, Rachel. Nino Estrella. Latyk, Olivier, illus. (p. 1257)
Häusler, Thomas. Viruses vs. Superbugs: A Solution to the Antibiotics Crisis? Leube, Karen, tr. from GER. (p. 1844)
Hausman, Gerald. Otter, the Spotted Frog & the Great Flood: A Creek Indian Story. Shiloh, Ramon, illus. (p. 1307)
—Timeswimmer. (p. 1754)
Hausman, Gerald & Hausman, Loretta. Farewell, Josephine: The Romance of Josephine & Napoleon. (p. 573)
—Mind with Wings: The Story of Henry David Thoreau. (p. 1145)
Hausman, Loretta, jt. auth. see Hausman, Gerald.
Hausman, Michelle. Amelia's Eyes. (p. 58)
Hausman, Sid. Cactus Critter Bash. Hausman, Sid, illus. (p. 250)
Hausmann, Gisela. Hands on Mathemagical Dice. (p. 741)
—Obvious Letters: The Alphabet Every Child Will Remember. (p. 1275)
Hausmann, Rex, illus. see Senneff, John A.
Hausner, Xenia. Xenia Hausner: Heart Matters (p. 1967)
Haussinger, D. & Hassinger, Peter W. Susanna the Snake. (p. 1688)
Haussler, Stuart. Skin Tight: A Red Tail Hawk Production. (p. 1585)
Hautala, Beth. Waiting for Unicorns. (p. 1853)
Hauth, Katherine B. What's for Dinner? Quirky, Squirmy Poems from the Animal World. Clark, David, illus. (p. 1897)
Hautman, Pete. All-In. (p. 44)
—Big Crunch. (p. 180)
—Blank Confession. (p. 198)
—Cydonian Pyramid. (p. 397)
—Eden West. (p. 504)
—Flinkwater Factor: A Novel in Five Thrilling Episodes. (p. 604)
—Godless. (p. 690)
—Hole in the Sky. (p. 788)
—How to Steal a Car. (p. 821)
—Invisible. Hautman, Pete, illus. (p. 885)
—Klaatu Terminus. (p. 963)
—Mr. Was. (p. 1187)
—No Limit. (p. 1258)
—Obsidian Blade. (p. 1275)
—Rash. (p. 1439)
—Sweetblood. (p. 1690)
—What Boys Really Want. (p. 1880)
Hautman, Pete & Logue, Mary. Doppelganger. (p. 470)
—Skullduggery. (p. 1586)
—Snatched. (p. 1597)
Hautzig, Deborah. Hey, Dollface (p. 774)
—L. Frank Baum's Wizard of Oz. (p. 969)
—Lewis Carroll's Alice in Wonderland. Rathke, Kathryn, illus. (p. 1004)
—Little Witch Learns to Read. Wickstrom, Sylvie K., illus. (p. 1038)
Hautzig, Deborah & Goode, Diane. Story of the Nutcracker Ballet. Goode, Diane, illus. (p. 1661)
Hautzig, Esther, tr. see Peretz, I. L.
Hauvette, Marion, illus. see Knight, Deborah Janet.
Havard, Amanda. Survivors: Point of Origin. (p. 1687)
—Survivors. (p. 1687)
Havard, Christian. Face-to-Face with the Chicken. (p. 560)
—Wolf: Night Howler. Jacana Agency, photos by. (p. 1943)
Havel, Geoff. Babies Bite. (p. 123)
—Graves of the Roti Men. (p. 712)
Havel, K. Gravitation: Master Key to the Universe. (p. 712)
Havelin, Kate. Hoopskirts, Union Blues, & Confederate Grays: Civil War Fashions from 1861 to 1865. (p. 795)
—Victoria Woodhull: Fearless Feminist. (p. 1840)
Havemeyer, Janie. Catherine de' Medici: "The Black Queen" Malone, Peter, illus. (p. 280)
—Njinga the Warrior Queen. Malone, Peter, illus. (p. 1257)
Haven, Gayle Jeanine. Love from Both Houses, My Parents Love. (p. 1059)
Haven, Kendall. 100 Greatest Science Discoveries of All Time (p. 1998)
—New Year's to Kwanzaa: Original Stories of Celebration. (p. 1247)
Haven, Kendall F. Alexander Graham Bell: Inventor & Visionary. (p. 36)
—Women at the Edge of Discovery: 40 True Science Adventures (p. 1945)
Haven, Paul. Two Hot Dogs with Everything. Jessell, Tim, illus. (p. 1803)
Havener, Katherine. Nursies When the Sun Shines: A Little Book on Night Weaning. Burrier, Sara, illus. (p. 1273)
Havens, Diane, jt. auth. see Bernardi, Philip.
Havens, J. C. In My World: The Beginning. (p. 864)
Havens, Sarita. My Grandma Is an Angel Now. Perunko, Linda, illus. (p. 1210)
Havercroft, Elizabeth. Year in the World of Dinosaurs. (p. 1969)
—Year on a Pirate Ship. (p. 1969)
Haverfield, Mary, illus. see Byrne, Gayle.
Haverfield, Mary, illus. see Kurtz, Jane.
Havergal, Frances Ridley. Children's Devotions. (p. 303)
—Little Pillows & Morning Bells: Good-Night Thoughts & Waking Thoughts for the Little Ones. (p. 1033)
Haverich, Beatrice. Instant Expert. (p. 878)
—Photography: How to Take Awesome Photos (p. 1353)
Havers, R. P. W. & O'Neill, Robert John. World War II: Europe, 1944-1945. (p. 1959)
Haverty, Doug, adapted by. Flavia & the Dream Maker: The Musical. (p. 603)
Havice, L. K. Peanut the Tiny Horse. Bessey, Brandan, illus. (p. 1332)
Havice, Susan, illus. see Taylor-Butler, Christine.
Haviland, C. S. Faith & Fairies. (p. 565)
Haviland, David, jt. auth. see Gould, Francesca.
Havill, Juanita. Call the Horse Lucky. Lane, Nancy, illus. (p. 254)
—Flower Garden. O'Brien, Anne Sibley, illus. (p. 607)
—Grow Kodman, Stanislawa, illus. (p. 725)
—Grow Kodman, Stanislawa, illus. (p. 725)
—Jamaica Tag-Along O'Brien, Anne Sibley, illus. (p. 906)
—Jamaica's Blue Marker. O'Brien, Anne Sibley, illus. (p. 906)
—Jamaica's Find O'Brien, Anne Sibley, illus. (p. 906)
Havlan, J. R., jt. auth. see Levy, Elizabeth.
Havran, Melissa. George Washington. (p. 664)
Haw, Brenda, illus. see Dolby, Karen.
Haw, Brenda, illus. see Heywood, Rosie, ed.
Haw, Brenda, illus. see Heywood, Rosie.
Haw, Brenda, illus. see Leigh, Susannah.
Haw, Jennie. Score! The Story of Soccer. (p. 1530)
Haw, Mark. Middle World: The Restless Heart of Matter & Life. (p. 1138)
Hawa, Christine Elias. Joy the Girl How Never Smiled. (p. 929)
Hawaii Winter Baseball. Major Mynah & Da Menehune Crew. (p. 1078)
Hawass, Zahi. Curse of the Pharaohs: My Adventures with Mummies. (p. 395)
Hawass, Zahi A. Tutankhamun: The Mystery of the Boy King. (p. 1799)
—Tutankhamun: The Mysteries of the Boy King. (p. 1799)
Hawcock, David. Ant. Montgomery, Lee, illus. (p. 88)
—Bee. Montgomery, Lee, illus. (p. 157)
—Dinosaurs! Pop-Up Paper Designs. Hawcock, David, illus. (p. 444)
—Fantastic Press-Out Flying Airplanes: Includes 18 Flying Models. Montgomery, Lee & Pastor, Terry, illus. (p. 572)
—Stegosaurus. Hawcock, David, illus. (p. 1646)
—Triceratops. Hawcock, David, illus. (p. 1785)
Hawcock, David, illus. see Elzbieta.
Hawcock, David & Kentley, Eric. Pop-Up Book of Ships. (p. 1384)
Hawcock, David & Montgomery, Lee. Fly. (p. 609)
—Wasp. (p. 1860)
Hawcock, David, tr. Tyrannosaurus. (p. 1805)
Hawes, Adrienne Hill. Moving Danielle. (p. 1183)
Hawes, Alison. Extreme Places: Could You Live Here? (p. 556)
—Go Greek! (p. 686)
—Landscape Detective: Tracking Changes in Your Surroundings. (p. 974)
—My Exercise Diary: Band 02B/Red B. (p. 1202)
—Roman Soldier's Handbook. (p. 1486)
—School Trip. Mould, Chris, illus. (p. 1523)
—Water Wise! (p. 1863)
—Weather Report: Band 02a/Red A. Stojic, Manya, illus. (p. 1870)
—What Are You Making? Band 02b/Red B. Elworthy, Antony, illus. (p. 1880)
—What the Romans Did for the World. (p. 1893)
—Who's Who in WWII. (p. 1921)
Hawes, Alison, jt. auth. see Collins Educational Staff.
Hawes, Carlin. Abigail's Bunny. (p. 5)
Hawes, Charles Boardman. Dark Frigate. (p. 407)
Hawes, Dorothy. Invisible Julian. Reaves, Daniel, illus. (p. 885)
Hawes, Jason & Wilson, Grant. Ghost Hunt: Chilling Tales of the Unknown. (p. 670)
Hawes, Louise & Sharratt, Mary. Vanishing Point. (p. 1833)
Hawes, Rachelle. Dan the Rescue Man: Fire at Farmer Dave's. (p. 402)
Hawk, Benjamin. Meadow Mystery. (p. 1116)
Hawk, Delores. Edge of Finall. (p. 504)
Hawk, Fran. Count down to Fall Neidigh, Sherry, illus. (p. 369)
Hawk, Frank. Story of the H. L. Hunley & Queenie's Coin. Nance, Dan, illus. (p. 1661)
Hawk, J. L. If I Were a Creature under the Seaa. (p. 853)
Hawk Planners. Easy Guide to Soccer Rules 2008-2009. (p. 500)
Hawk, Steve. Waves. (p. 1864)
Hawke, Jay Jordan. Pukawiss the Outcast. (p. 1415)
Hawke, Rosanne. Keeper. (p. 947)
—Sailmaker. (p. 1503)
—Spirit of a Mountain Wolf. (p. 1628)
Hawker, Frances & Alicavusoglu, Leyla. Islam in Turkey. Campbell, Bruce, photos by. (p. 891)
Hawker, Frances & Bhatia, Mohini. Sikhism in India. Campbell, Bruce, photos by. (p. 1575)
Hawker, Frances & Paz, Noemi. Christianity in Mexico. Campbell, Bruce, photos by. (p. 312)
Hawker, Frances & Resi, Putu. Hinduism in Bali. Campbell, Bruce, photos by. (p. 780)
Hawker, Frances & Sunantha Phusomsai. Buddhism in Thailand. Campbell, Bruce, photos by. (p. 234)
Hawker, Frances & Taub, Daniel. Judaism in Israel. Campbell, Bruce, photos by. (p. 930)
Hawker, Kate "Ayasta". Faces of Our Children. (p. 561)
Hawker, Louise. Colonialism in Chinua Achebe's Things Fall Apart. (p. 342)
—Genocide in Elie Wiesel's Night. (p. 661)
—Womens Rights. (p. 1946)
Hawker, Louise & Bryfonski, Dedria. Industrialism in John Steinbeck's: The Grapes of Wrath. (p. 873)
—Industrialism in John Steinbeck's the Grapes of Wrath. (p. 873)
Hawker, Louise, ed. Womens Rights. (p. 1946)
Hawkes, Andrea Constantine. Same Great Struggle: The History of the Vickery Family of Unity, Maine, 1634-1997. (p. 1507)
Hawkes, Brian. History of the Dallas Cowboys. (p. 785)
—History of the Indianapolis Colts. (p. 785)
—History of the Jacksonville Jaguars. (p. 785)
—History of the Kansas City Chiefs. (p. 785)
—Story of the San Diego Padres. (p. 1662)
—Story of the Washington Nationals. (p. 1662)
Hawkes, Chris. Human Body: Uncovering Science. (p. 825)
Hawkes, Kevin. Remy & Lulu. Hawkes, Kevin & Harrison, Hannah E., illus. (p. 1460)
—Wicked Big Toddlah. (p. 1927)
—Wicked Big Toddlah Goes to New York. (p. 1927)
Hawkes, Kevin, illus. see Aiken, Joan.
Hawkes, Kevin, illus. see Anderson, M. T.
Hawkes, Kevin, illus. see Barrett, Judi.
Hawkes, Kevin, illus. see Beaty, Andrea.
Hawkes, Kevin, illus. see Bertrand, Lynne.
Hawkes, Kevin, illus. see Black, Michael Ian.
Hawkes, Kevin, illus. see Fleischman, Paul.

H

Hawkes, Kevin, illus. see Grossman, Bill.
Hawkes, Kevin, illus. see Hoberman, Mary Ann.
Hawkes, Kevin, illus. see Ibbotson, Eva.
Hawkes, Kevin, illus. see Isaacs, Anne.
Hawkes, Kevin, illus. see Knudsen, Michelle.
Hawkes, Kevin, illus. see Krull, Kathleen.
Hawkes, Kevin, illus. see Kuskin, Karla.
Hawkes, Kevin, illus. see Lindbergh, Anne M.
Hawkes, Kevin, illus. see Madison, Alan.
Hawkes, Kevin, illus. see Rasmussen, Halfdan Wedel, et al.
Hawkes, Kevin, illus. see Stutson, Caroline.
Hawkes, Kevin, illus. see Trumbauer, Lisa.
Hawkes, Kevin, illus. see Willard, Nancy.
Hawkes, Kevin, illus. see Winter, Jonah.
Hawkes, Nigel, jt. auth. see Hawkes, Nigel.
Hawkes, Nigel & Hawkes, Nigel. Misterios del Universo. (p. 1155)
Hawkes, Spencer. Beagles in My Bed Coloring Book. (p. 150)
Hawkes, Steve. Tennessee River. (p. 1720)
Hawkesworth, Asha. Grandma's Roses. Kathie, Gabriel, illus. (p. 709)
Hawking, Lucy, jt. auth. see Hawking, Stephen W.
Hawking, Lucy & Hawking, Stephen W. George & the Big Bang. Parsons, Garry, illus. (p. 663)
—George's Cosmic Treasure Hunt. Parsons, Garry, illus. (p. 665)
Hawking, Stephen W., jt. auth. see Hawking, Lucy.
Hawking, Stephen W. & Hawking, Lucy. George & the Big Bang. Parsons, Garry, illus. (p. 663)
—George's Cosmic Treasure Hunt. Parsons, Garry, illus. (p. 665)
—George's Secret Key to the Universe. Parsons, Garry, illus. (p. 665)
Hawkins, A. D. Time Princess. (p. 1752)
Hawkins, Aaron. Year Money Grew on Trees. (p. 1969)
Hawkins, Al. April Is Born: Adventures of a New Quarter Horse Filly. Erickson, Terri, illus. (p. 93)
Hawkins, Anastacia. Larkspur. (p. 975)
Hawkins, Andy, jt. ed. see Nuttall, Neil.
Hawkins, Bret R. ButtieBear. (p. 248)
Hawkins, Brett. Triune Tale of Diminutive Swine. (p. 1788)
Hawkins, Clyde. Harley Davidson (p. 749)
Hawkins, Colin. Foxy Doesn't Feel Well. (p. 626)
—Mr Wolf's Week. (p. 1187)
—Mr. Wolf's Week. (p. 1187)
—Pirate Ship: A Pop-up Adventure. Hawkins, Colin et al, illus. (p. 1363)
—What's the Time,Mr. Wolf? Mini Pop-Up. (p. 1900)
Hawkins, Colin, illus. see Brandreth, Gyles.
Hawkins, Colin & Hawkins, Jacqui. Foxy & Friends Go Racing. (p. 626)
—Here's a Happy Elephant (p. 771)
—Here's a Happy Kitten (p. 771)
—Here's a Happy Pig (p. 771)
—Here's a Happy Puppy (p. 771)
—Pirate Treasure Map: A Fairytale Adventure. Hawkins, Colin & Hawkins, Jacqui, illus. (p. 1363)
—Snap! Snap! (p. 1597)
—Witch Pigs. (p. 1941)
Hawkins, Dave, photos by see Trahan, Kendra.
Hawkins, David R. Reality, Spirituality & Modern Man. (p. 1449)
Hawkins, Delta Michelle. Cassandra's Journey. (p. 276)
Hawkins, Denise. Plight of Sanna, the Polar Bear (p. 1374)
Hawkins, Desiree. Book of Power. (p. 211)
Hawkins, Dorothy. Mouse in My House. (p. 1182)
Hawkins, Elizabeth. Ben's Birthdays. Cemmick, Paul, illus. (p. 165)
Hawkins, Emily. Good Night, Little Bunny: A Changing-Picture Book. Butler, John, illus. (p. 699)
Hawkins, Emily, ed. see Aronnax, Pierre.
Hawkins, Emily, ed. see De Lesseps, Ferdinand Zoticus.
Hawkins, Frank C. & Laube, Greta L. B. Book of Bad Habits for Young (and Not So Young!) Men & Women: How to Chuck the Worst & Turn the Rest to Your Advantage. Hong, Richard, illus. (p. 210)
Hawkins, Grace, jt. auth. see Johnson, Earl L.
Hawkins, Grace M., ed. see Johnson, Earl L.
Hawkins Harris, Jennifer. Love: The Book of Love for Kids. Gray Mayo, Jo Ann, illus. (p. 1059)
Hawkins, Jacqui, jt. auth. see Hawkins, Colin.
Hawkins, Jay. Bright Ideas: The Science of Light. (p. 228)
—Hot Stuff: The Science of Heat & Cold. (p. 802)
—It's Alive! The Science of Plants & Living Things. (p. 896)
—Material World: The Science of Matter. (p. 1104)
—Push & Pull: The Science of Forces. (p. 1420)
—Really Horrible Animal Facts. (p. 1450)
—Really Horrible Body Facts. (p. 1450)
—Really Horrible History Facts. (p. 1450)
—Really Horrible Science Facts. (p. 1450)
—Super Sonic: The Science of Sound. (p. 1682)
Hawkins, Jeff. Biggest Chokes in Sports. (p. 185)
—Playing Pro Hockey. (p. 1372)
—World Series. (p. 1958)
Hawkins, Jeri. Dandelion Tea. (p. 403)
Hawkins, Jim. Daddy, Tell Me a Story about the First Day of School. (p. 399)
Hawkins, John. Air Disasters. (p. 31)
—Aliens & UFOs. (p. 41)
—Atlantis & Other Lost Worlds. (p. 112)
—Bigfoot & Other Monsters. (p. 185)
—Earthquake Disasters. (p. 497)
—Hauntings. (p. 754)
—Hurricane Disasters. (p. 829)
—Shipwreck Disasters. (p. 1567)
—Tsunami Disasters. (p. 1795)
—Volcano Disasters. (p. 1848)
—World's Strangest Unexplained Mysteries. (p. 1961)
Hawkins, Jonny, illus. see Elliott, Rob.
Hawkins, Jonny, jt. auth. see Phillips, Bob.
Hawkins, June Morris. When Tony Caught a Fish. (p. 1905)
Hawkins, Jyren. Shot to Victory. (p. 1569)
Hawkins, Karen. Seduction of Sara. (p. 1546)
Hawkins, Kirk A. Political Culture of Democracy in Venezuela 2007: 2007. (p. 1380)
Hawkins, Kristen, illus. see Holley, Kim.
Hawkins, Linda, illus. see Heyde, Christiane.
Hawkins, Linda J. Alexander & the Great Vegetable Feud. Bowles, Jennifer, illus. (p. 36)
—Catering to Children: With Recipes for Memorable Tea Parties. Yonts, Barbara, photos by. (p. 279)
—Who Gives a Hoot? Hunter Hoot,the Great Horned Owl. (p. 1915)
Hawkins, Loreatha V. Prince & the Musical Castle. (p. 1401)
Hawkins, Matt. Think Tank. (p. 1734)
—Think Tank Volume 2 TP. (p. 1734)
Hawkins, Matt, jt. auth. see Silvestri, Marc.
Hawkins, Mia K. Broken Guild of Twelve Pirates (p. 230)
Hawkins, Nicole. Blue. (p. 202)
Hawkins, Phycillia Maria. What's up Chuck? The Little Boy with ADHD. (p. 1900)
Hawkins, Rachel. Demonglass. (p. 426)
—Hex Hall (p. 774)
—Miss Mayhem. (p. 1151)
—Rebel Belle. (p. 1450)
—School Spirits. (p. 1523)
—Spell Bound (a Hex Hall Novel) (p. 1625)
Hawkins, Tim. Awesome on the Inside. (p. 121)
Hawkins, Trisha. Everything You Need to Know about Measles & Rubella. (p. 545)
Hawkins, Vickie Vernon. Stranger Danger: Children Beware. (p. 1665)
Hawkins, Wanda. Geronimo Discovers Faith. (p. 667)
Hawkins, Wendy. Binky Goes to School. (p. 188)
Hawkins-Rodgers, Donzella. No Bulley Destroys Chloe's Hairdo. (p. 1257)
—No Bulley Destroy's Chloe's Hairdo. Hewins, Shirley, illus. (p. 1257)
Hawkins-Walsh, Elizabeth & Pierson-Solis, Lennard. Katie's Premature Brother = el Hermano Prematuro de Katie. Blake, Anne Catharine, illus. (p. 945)
Hawks, K. J. Lu-Don & the Kingdoms of Trent. (p. 1061)
Hawks, Robb. Legend of Billy Adams: A Cowboy Story with a Message for Every Child. Davenport, Andy, illus. (p. 988)
Hawksley, Gerald. Amazing Journey of Noah & His Incredible Ark. (p. 54)
—Danny Dog's Car: Press Out Parts Make a Car Carrying Danny Dog! (p. 405)
—Good Puppy. Stanley, Mandy, illus. (p. 700)
—Mommies & Babies on the Farm. Calitri, Susan, illus. (p. 1162)
—Patty Cow's Tractor: Press Out Parts Make a Tractor Carrying Patty Cow. (p. 1329)
—Quacky Duck's Plane: Press Out Parts Make an Airplane Carrying Quacky Duck! (p. 1422)
—See Through Safari. Spengler, Margaret, illus. (p. 1547)
—Splashy Dolphin's Boat: Press Out Parts Make a Boat Carrying Splashy Dolphin. (p. 1629)
Hawksley, L. Dickens, jt. auth. see Dickens, Charles.
Hawksworth, Lorraine. Masked Intruder. (p. 1102)
Hawksworth, Lorraine & Guzy, Adam. Fables from the Largetooth Animal Refuge. (p. 559)
Hawley, Bill. Diente Suelto de Carlitos (p. 437)
Hawley, Bobby. By Golly, Molly, You're Right. (p. 249)
—Matt & the Wonder of Wishes (p. 1109)
Hawley, Ella. Exploring Ecosystems. (p. 552)
—Exploring Food & Nutrition. (p. 552)
—Exploring Food Chains & Food Webs. (p. 552)
—Exploring Heredity. (p. 552)
—Exploring Our Impact on the Environment. (p. 553)
—Exploring the Classification of Living Things. (p. 553)
—Number 1. (p. 1270)
—Number 2. (p. 1271)
—Number 3. (p. 1271)
—Number 4. (p. 1271)
—Number 5. (p. 1271)
—Numbers 1, 2, 3, 4, 5. (p. 1272)
Hawley, Greg. Don't Let the Bedbugs Bite. Regan, Dana, illus. (p. 468)
Hawley, Jim. Homer & Friends. (p. 793)
Hawley, Karen, jt. auth. see Hallstrand, John & Sarah.
Hawley, Kelvin. My Things (p. 1220)
—Vacation: Individual Title Six-Packs. (p. 1829)
Hawley, Kelvin, illus. see Eggleton, Jill.
Hawley, Kelvin, illus. see Holden, Pam.
Hawley, Mabel C. Four Little Blossoms & Their Winter Fun. (p. 625)
—Four Little Blossoms on Apple Tree Island. (p. 625)
Hawley, Mary, jt. auth. see Moran, Lisa.
Hawley, Michael. Bhutan: An Odyssey in Shangri-la with Choki & Gyelsey. Lhamo, Choki & Loday, Gyelsey, photos by. (p. 174)
Hawley, Michael, Jr. Bhutan: A Visual Odyssey Across the Last Himalayan Kingdom (p. 174)
Hawley, R. Spencer, illus. see Hawley, Richard And Elizabeth.
Hawley, Rebecca. Corvette. (p. 368)
—Ferrari. (p. 582)
—Lamborghini. (p. 972)
—Mustang. (p. 1194)
—Porsche. (p. 1386)
—Superfast Cars (p. 1683)
—Viper. (p. 1843)
Hawley, Richard. Paul & Juliana: A Novel. (p. 1330)
Hawley, Richard And Elizabeth. There's a Monster in My Nose. Hawley, R. Spencer, illus. (p. 1731)
Hawley, Samuel. I Just Ran: Percy Williams, World's Fastest Human. (p. 840)
Hawley, Sandra, et al. Enduring Vision: A History of the American People. Vol. 2 (p. 527)
Hawn Foundation Staff, contrib. by. Brain-Focused Strategies for Learning-And Living. (p. 221)
—Mindup Curriculum, Grades 6-8: Brain-Focused Strategies for Learning-And Living. (p. 1145)
—Mindup Curriculum - Grades Prek-2: Brain-Focused Strategies for Learning-And Living. (p. 1145)
Haworth, Danette. Me & Jack. (p. 1115)
—Summer of Moonlight Secrets. (p. 1674)
—Violet Raines Almost Got Struck by Lightning. (p. 1843)
—Whole Lot of Lucky. (p. 1920)
Haworth, Dianne. Paddy the Wanderer. (p. 1317)
Haworth, Hennie, illus. see Broom, Jenny.
Haworth, Margaret. It's My Birthday. Edwards, Paul, illus. (p. 897)
—Jarry, Garry Palas: Cat Tail Stories. Haworth, Margaret, photos by. (p. 909)
—New Kid: Rusty Book. Edwards, Paul, illus. (p. 1245)
—Oh Holly Dallig: Cat Tail Stories. Haworth, Margaret, photos by. (p. 1280)
—When Daddy Goes Away: Rusty Books. Edwards, Paul, illus. (p. 1901)
Haworth-Attard, Barbara. My Life from Air-Bras to Zits. (p. 1212)
Hawran, Mary. How to Be A Recycling Hero. (p. 814)
Haws, Dallin, jt. auth. see Breeze, Johnny.
Haws, Ileen. Feet are Neat. (p. 580)
—Nothin' 2 Do. (p. 1268)
Haws, Jacob. Telarthia: The Taln Crystal. (p. 1716)
Hawthorn, P. Little Book of Bedtime Stories. (p. 1025)
—Little Book of Fairy Stories. (p. 1025)
Hawthorn, P., jt. auth. see Tyler, Jenny.
Hawthorn, Paul, illus. see Helliwell, Sheila.
Hawthorn, Philip & Tyler, Jenny. Who's Making That Mess? Cartwright, Stephen, illus. (p. 1920)
Hawthorn, Phillip. Usborne Stories for Bedtime. Tyler, Jenny, ed. (p. 1827)
Hawthorn, Phillip, jt. auth. see Tyler, Jenny.
Hawthorn, Phillip & Tyler, Jenny. There's A Monster in My House. (p. 1731)
Hawthorne, Grace. Healthy Air: Book C of Healthy Me Blyth, Eileen, illus. (p. 758)
—Healthy Bodies: Book A of Healthy Me Blyth, Eileen, illus. (p. 758)
—Healthy Food: Book B of Healthy Me Blyth, Eileen, illus. (p. 758)
—Healthy Me. Blyth, Eileen C., illus. (p. 758)
Hawthorne, Jonathan. Scarlet Letter - Literary Touchstone Edition. (p. 1520)
Hawthorne, Kate & Sheppard, Daniela. Young Person's Guide to the Internet: The Essential Website Reference Book for Young People, Parents & Teachers. (p. 1979)
Hawthorne, Mike. Machine Teen: History 101001. (p. 1068)
Hawthorne, Nathaniel. Classics Illustrated #6: the Scarlet Letter. Thompson, Jill, illus. (p. 328)
—Grandfather's Chair: A History for Youth. (p. 707)
—Nathaniel Hawthorne. McConnell, James, illus. (p. 1231)
—Scarlet Letter. (p. 1520)
—Scarlet Letter. Moliken, Paul, ed. (p. 1520)
—Scarlet Letter - Spotlight Edition. Grudzina, Douglas, ed. (p. 1520)
—Tanglewood Tales. Pogány, Willy, illus. (p. 1705)
—Tanglewood Tales. Sterrett, Virginia, illus. (p. 1705)
—Tanglewood Tales for Girls & Boys. (p. 1705)
—Timeless Classics Low Level: Scarlet Letter (p. 1754)
—Wonder Book: Heroes & Monsters of Greek Mythology. (p. 1947)
—Wonder Book & Tanglewood Tales. (p. 1947)
—Wonder Book for Girls & Boys. (p. 1947)
Hawthorne, Philip & Tyler, Jenny. Who's Making That Noise? Cartwright, Stephen, illus. (p. 1920)
Hawthorne, Rachel. Boyfriend League. (p. 220)
—Boyfriend Project. (p. 220)
—Caribbean Cruising. (p. 268)
—Crocodile Who Was Afraid of the Water. (p. 384)
—Dark of the Moon. (p. 408)
—Full Moon. (p. 646)
—Island Girls & Boys. (p. 892)
—Labor of Love. (p. 969)
—Love on the Lifts. (p. 1060)
—Moonlight. (p. 1172)
—One Perfect Summer: Labor of Love & Thrill Ride. (p. 1296)
—Shadow of the Moon. (p. 1557)
—Snowed In. (p. 1600)
—Suite Dreams. (p. 1673)
—Thrill Ride. (p. 1744)
—Trouble from the Start: A Companion to the Boyfriend Project. (p. 1789)
—Year in Europe. (p. 1969)
Hawthorne, Reita Rea. Finding Christmas. (p. 588)
Hawvermale, Lance. Discretionist. (p. 450)
Hawxhurst, Joan C. Bubbe & Gram: My Two Grandmothers. Bynum-Nwulu, Jane, illus. (p. 233)
Hawyard, Charlie O., illus. see Caldwell, Bruce.
Haxhia, Miranda. Andy's Cherry Tree. Deisadze, Zaur, illus. (p. 73)
—Dolls Nose. Kohler, Ursula, illus. (p. 464)
Haxton, Charles. Grandpa Goes to College. Haxton-Johns, Rebecca, illus. (p. 709)
Haxton-Johns, Rebecca, illus. see Haxton, Charles.
Hay, Angela. Grace S Incredible! Unforgettable! Summer! (p. 705)
Hay, Barbara. Lesson of the White Eagle. Hay, Peter, illus. (p. 993)
Hay Bright, Jean. Meanwhile, Next Door to the Good Life. (p. 1117)
Hay DeSimone, Corkey. Air & Space Activity & Coloring Book: An Early Introduction to the History of Flight. Hay DeSimone, Corkey, illus. (p. 31)
—Dinosaur Explore Activity & Coloring Book: Dinosaurs designed for their littlest Fans. Hay DeSimone, Corkey, illus. (p. 442)
—Future Sports Legend Board Book: An Early Introduction to Sports in Maryland. Hay DeSimone, Corkey, illus. (p. 651)
—Mammal Animal Board Book 2nd Edition. Hay DeSimone, Corkey, illus. (p. 1084)
—Mammal Animal Coloring & Activity Book: What Is a mammal? You are a mammal Too! (p. 1084)
—Panda Promise Activity & Coloring Book. Hay DeSimone, Corkey, illus. (p. 1320)
Hay, Jeff. Amendment XIV: Citizenship for All. (p. 58)
—Amendment XV: Race & the Right to Vote. (p. 58)
—Arab-Israeli Six-Day War. (p. 94)
—Crisis in Darfur. Gale Editors, ed. (p. 383)
—Holocaust. Greenhaven Press Editors, ed. (p. 789)
—Japanese American Internment. Wukovits, John, ed. (p. 909)
—Pollution. (p. 1381)
—Tibet. Greenhaven Press Editors & Gale Editors, eds. (p. 1747)
Hay, Jeff, ed. Hinduism. (p. 780)
Hay, Jerry M. & Pollema-Cahill, Phyllis. Goose Named Gilligan. (p. 702)
Hay, John & Harwich, Mary Belle. Dancing Hands: Signs of Learning. Wapahi, Robert, illus. (p. 403)
Hay, Kathleen. Quest of Happy Hearts. (p. 1426)
Hay, Louise L. Adventures of Lulu. Smith-Moore, J. J., illus. (p. 20)
Hay, Louise L. & Tracy, Kristina. I Think, I Am! Teaching Kids the Power of Affirmations. Schwarz, Manuela, illus. (p. 846)
Hay, Peter. Canned Laughter: The Best Stories from Radio & Television. (p. 261)
Hay, Peter, illus. see Hay, Barbara.
Hay, Sam. Beth & the Bugs. Johns, Ann, illus. (p. 171)
—Chuck & Duck. Johns, Ann, illus. (p. 318)
—Goldfish from Beyond the Grave. (p. 695)
—Goldfish from Beyond the Grave #4. Cooper, Simon, illus. (p. 695)
—Night of the Howling Hound Cooper, Simon, illus. (p. 1254)
—Night of the Howling Hound. (p. 1254)
—Return of the Hungry Hamster. Cooper, Simon, illus. (p. 1464)
—Revenge of the Phantom Furball Cooper, Simon, illus. (p. 1466)
—Revenge of the Phantom Furball. (p. 1466)
—Rise of the Zombie Rabbit. (p. 1475)
—Rise of the Zombie Rabbit #5. Cooper, Simon, illus. (p. 1475)
—That Dog! Oelofsen, Vian, illus. (p. 1726)
—Wish Fish. May, Kate, illus. (p. 1940)
Haya, Erwin, illus. see Chatzky, Jean.
Haya, Erwin, illus. see Fogarty, Mignon.
Haya, Erwin, illus. see Strauss, Ed.
Haya, Erwin, illus. see Wacholtz, Anthony.
Hayashi, Fumino. Neon Genesis Evangelion (p. 1241)
Hayashi, Hikaru. Personajes Femeninos. (p. 1344)
Hayashi, Hikaru, jt. auth. see Go Office Staff.
Hayashi, Hikaru & Office, Go. Basics of Characters & Materials. (p. 142)
Hayashi, Leslie Ann. Celebrating Holidays in Hawaii. Bishop, Kathleen Wong, illus. (p. 285)
—Fables Beneath the Rainbow. Bishop, Kathleen Wong, illus. (p. 559)
—Fishy Alphabet in Hawaii. Bishop, Kathleen Wong, illus. (p. 599)
Hayashi, Nancy, illus. see Adams, Diane.
Hayashi, Nancy, illus. see Bottner, Barbara.
Hayashi, Nancy, illus. see Rodman, Mary Ann.
Hayashi, Nancy, illus. see Spinelli, Eileen & Spinelli.
Hayashi, Nancy, illus. see Spinelli, Eileen.
Hayashi, Nancy, tr. see Spinelli, Eileen & Spinelli.
Hayashi, Nancy, tr. see Spinelli, Eileen.
Hayashi, Yoshio, illus. see Sakade, Florence.
Hayashi, Yoshio, jt. auth. see Sakade, Florence.
Hayashida, Q., jt. auth. see Hayashida, Q.
Hayashida, Q. & Hayashida, Q. Dorohedoro. Hayashida, Q., illus. (p. 471)
Hayashiya, Shizuru. Sister Red #1 (p. 1581)
Hayashiya, Shizuru, jt. auth. see Kuroda, Yosuke.
Hayatian, MaryAnn. Cookie, a cat's Tale. (p. 361)
—Flower Child. (p. 607)
Haycraft, Howard, ed. see Doyle, Arthur.
Haycraft, Marilynn J., illus. see Edgell, Ernest.
Haycraft, Melissa Story. Alex the Alligator. (p. 36)
Haydel, Catherine. the Cat & Hurricane Katrina. (p. 1728)
Haydel-Vicidomina, Lisa. Run Ru Run: A Story of the Thin, Pink-Chested Dog. (p. 1496)
Hayden, jt. auth. see Hayden.
Hayden & Hayden. Matter of Attitude. (p. 1109)
Hayden, Erika. Carli & the Magic Tea Party. (p. 270)
Hayden, Gwendolen Lampshire. Mary Martha's Really Truly Stories: Book 1. (p. 1100)
—Mary Martha's Really Truly Stories: Book 2. (p. 1100)
—Mary Martha's Really Truly Stories: Book 3. (p. 1100)
—Mary Martha's Really Truly Stories: Book 4. (p. 1100)
—Mary Martha's Really Truly Stories: Book 5. (p. 1100)
—Mary Martha's Really Truly Stories: Book 6. (p. 1100)
—Mary Martha's Really Truly Stories: Book 7. (p. 1100)
—Mary Martha's Really Truly Stories: Book 8. (p. 1100)
Hayden, Jeanne. Last Minute Wilma & Her Toad Soup. (p. 978)
Hayden, Jennifer, illus. see Trimble, Marcia.
Hayden, Jennifer H., illus. see Trimble, Marcia J.
Hayden, Kate. Amazing Buildings. (p. 54)
Hayden, Kate, jt. auth. see Lock, Deborah.
Hayden, Kate & Lock, Deborah. Amazing Buildings (p. 54)
Hayden, Kate, et al. Starry Sky. (p. 1642)
Hayden, Patrick Nielsen, jt. auth. see Yolen, Jane.
Hayden, Paul. Byron the Lonely Christmas Tree. (p. 249)
Hayden, Seito, illus. see Banks, Calvin J.
Hayden, Seitu, illus. see Biskup, Agnieszka.
Hayden, Seitu, illus. see Chandler, Alton.
Hayden, Seitu, illus. see Collins, Terry, et al.
Hayden, Seitu, illus. see Fogerty, Ramona.
Hayden, Seitu, illus. see Gunderson, Jessica.
Hayden, Sonserra V. Reflections of Sonserra. (p. 1456)
Haydon, David J. Spuds - the Circus Comes to Town. (p. 1635)
—Spuds - the Fancy Dress Party. Ferns, Kevin, illus. (p. 1635)
—Spuds - the Windy Day. Ferns, Kevin, illus. (p. 1635)
Haydon, Elizabeth. Thief Queen's Daughter Chan, Jason, illus. (p. 1732)
—Tree of Water. Dorman, Brandon, illus. (p. 1783)
Haydon, Julie. Farm: Lift-A-Flap. (p. 573)
—First 1000 Words. (p. 592)
—Locust Plague (p. 1045)
Haydu, Corey Ann. Life by Committee. (p. 1008)
—Making Pretty. (p. 1082)
—OCD Love Story. (p. 1275)
—Rules for Stealing Stars. (p. 1495)

Haye, Lucy. ABCD & an Ant's Story. (p. 3)
Hayek, F. A. Fortunes of Liberalism: Essays on Austrian Economics & the Ideal of Freedom. Kresge, S., ed. (p. 623)
Hayes, Amy. ADA Lovelace. (p. 10)
—Big Bulldozers. (p. 180)
—Big Cranes. (p. 180)
—Big Diggers. (p. 181)
—Big Loaders. (p. 182)
—Big Tractors. (p. 184)
—Celebrate Earth Day. (p. 283)
—Celebrate Independence Day. (p. 283)
—Celebrate Martin Luther King Jr. Day. (p. 284)
—Celebrate Memorial Day. (p. 284)
—Celebrate Passover. (p. 284)
—Celebrate Valentine's Day. (p. 284)
—Discovering STEM at the Museum. (p. 449)
—Dump Trucks Are Big Trucks. (p. 489)
—Garnets. (p. 657)
—Hornets. (p. 798)
—Medusa & Pegasus. (p. 1120)
—Seed Becomes a Dandelion. (p. 1547)
—Turning Cotton into Clothes. (p. 1798)
—Turning Sand into Glass. (p. 1798)
—Turning Sap into Maple Syrup. (p. 1798)
—Turning Wheat into Bread. (p. 1798)
—Turning Wool into Sweaters. (p. 1798)
—Valentine's Day. (p. 1830)
—We Need Worms. (p. 1867)
Hayes, Amy, jt. auth. see Reynolds, Wendy A.
Hayes, Angela. Just an Existence. (p. 937)
—Mop Heads Polly Jr., Jimmy Wayne, illus. (p. 1173)
Hayes, Arvid. Little Bird Saves a Little Boy's Life. (p. 1024)
Hayes, Betsy, illus. see Alford, Douglas.
Hayes, Beverly. Charlie Chicken Hawk Ashcraft Jr, D. C., illus. (p. 293)
Hayes, Bill. Landmarks: Historical U. S. Supreme Court Decisions. Hayes, Bill, ed. (p. 974)
Hayes, Carolyn. School Starts Today: The Mccool School Series. (p. 1523)
Hayes, Celeste. Cacao & the Jaded Orb: A Sphinx & Trevi Adventure. (p. 250)
—Enchanted Fairyland: A Sphinx & Trevi Adventure. (p. 523)
—Puzzle Box of Nefertiti: A Sphinx & Trevi Adventure. Bishop, Christina, illus. (p. 1420)
Hayes, Christine. Mothman's Curse. Hindle, James K., illus. (p. 1179)
Hayes, Clair W. Boy Allies at Verdun. (p. 217)
—Boy Allies at Verdun or Saving France from the Enemy. (p. 217)
—Boy Allies in Great Peril. (p. 217)
—Boy Allies in the Balkan Campaign. (p. 217)
—Boy Allies in the Balkan Campaign or the Struggle to Save a Nation. (p. 217)
—Boy Allies in the Trenches: Midst Shot & Shell along the Aisne. (p. 217)
—Boy Allies in the Trenches. (p. 217)
—Boy Allies on the Firing Line. (p. 217)
—Boy Allies on the Firing Line or Twelve Days Battle along the Marne. (p. 217)
—Boy Allies with Haig in Flanders. (p. 217)
Hayes, Clair Wallace. Boy Allies at Verdun: Saving France from the Enemy. (p. 217)
Hayes, Clyde & Jacobson, Pat. Tunnels of Tecsuna. (p. 1797)
Hayes, Dale. Kc the Good Little Diggy Dog Who Does Naughty Things... Is Going Home. (p. 946)
Hayes, Dan. Thanksgiving. (p. 1725)
Hayes, Daniel. Flyers. (p. 609)
Hayes, David, illus. see Shubin, Masha.
Hayes, Denis. Silly Animal Stories for Kids. (p. 1575)
—Silly Fishy Stories for Kids. (p. 1575)
—Silly Ghost Stories for Kids. (p. 1576)
Hayes, Don. Easter. (p. 499)
Hayes, Doris. Tony the Trailer's Travels. (p. 1766)
Hayes, Drew, jt. auth. see Davidsen, Keith.
Hayes, Elvin. Lesson for Lexi: From a Bully's Prospective. (p. 993)
Hayes, Felix. Doctor Monkey. Broadway, Hannah, illus. (p. 459)
—In the Garden. Broadway, Hannah, illus. (p. 866)
—In the Snow. Broadway, Hannah, illus. (p. 867)
—Monkey & Robot: In the Snow. (p. 1165)
Hayes, Fiona, illus. see Rivers, Moore Debbie & Henning, Heather.
Hayes, Geoffrey. Benny & Penny in Just Pretend. (p. 165)
—Benny & Penny in Just Pretend. Hayes, Geoffrey, illus. (p. 165)
—Benny & Penny in Just Pretend, Level 2. Hayes, Geoffrey, illus. (p. 165)
—Benny & Penny in Lights Out! (p. 165)
—Benny & Penny in Lost & Found! (p. 165)
—Benny & Penny in the Big No-No! (p. 165)
—Benny & Penny in the Big No-No! Mouly, Francoise, ed. (p. 165)
—Benny & Penny in the Toy Breaker. (p. 165)
—Benny & Penny in the Toy Breaker. Mouly, Francoise, ed. (p. 165)
—Benny & Penny in the Toy Breaker, Level 2. (p. 165)
—Bunny's Night-Light: A Glow-in-the-Dark Search. (p. 243)
—Night-Light for Bunny. (p. 1253)
—Night-Light for Bunny. Hayes, Geoffrey, illus. (p. 1253)
—Otto & Uncle Tooth Adventures. (p. 1307)
—Patrick Eats His Peas & Other Stories. Hayes, Geoffrey, illus. (p. 1329)
—Poor Excuse for a Dragon. (p. 1383)
—Poor Excuse for a Dragon. Hayes, Geoffrey, illus. (p. 1383)
Hayes, Geoffrey, illus. see Spiegelman, Art.
Hayes, Geoffrey, jt. auth. see Hayes, Geoffrey.
Hayes, Geoffrey & Hayes, Geoffrey. Patrick in a Teddy Bear's Picnic & Other Stories. (p. 1329)
Hayes, Geoffrey & Rosenstiehl, Agnes. Toon Books. (p. 1767)
Hayes, Gwen. Dreaming Awake. (p. 484)
—Falling Under. (p. 567)
Hayes, J. B. Freddy the Frog's First Christmas. (p. 633)
Hayes, J. D. & Younce, Eldon, compiled by. Anthony, Kansas: Celebrating 125 Years. (p. 89)
Hayes, James. Tuggy the Little Tug Boat. (p. 1796)
Hayes, Jennifer & Doubilet, David. Face to Face with Sharks. (p. 560)
Hayes, Joe. Baila, Nana, Baila: Cuban Folktales in English & Spanish. Trenard Sayago, Mauricio, illus. (p. 132)
—Coyote Debajo de la Mesa. Castro L., Antonio, illus. (p. 374)
—Coyote under the Table (El Coyote Debajo de la Mesa) Castro L., Antonio, illus. (p. 374)
—Cucuy! A Bogeyman Cuento in English & Spanish. Robledo, Honorio, illus. (p. 389)
—Dance, Nana, Dance (Baila, Nana, Baila) Trenard Sayago, Mauricio, illus. (p. 402)
—Día que Nevaron Tortillas. Hayes, Joe, tr. (p. 433)
—Don't Say a Word, Mama / No Digas Nada, Mama. (p. 468)
—Ghost Fever (Mal de Fantasma) (p. 670)
—Ghost Fever (Mal de Fantasma) Pennypacker, Mona, illus. (p. 670)
—Gum-Chewing Rattler. (p. 731)
—Gum-Chewing Rattler. Castro L., Antonio, illus. (p. 731)
—Juan Verdades - El Hombre Que No Sabía Mentir. Fiedler, Joseph Daniel, illus. (p. 930)
—Llorona - The Weeping Woman: An Hispanic Legend Told in Spanish & English. Hill, Vicki Trego & Pennypacker, Mona, illus. (p. 1043)
—Lovesick Skunk. Castro L., Antonio, illus. (p. 1061)
—My Pet Rattlesnake. (p. 1217)
—Pajaro Verde. Castro L., Antonio, illus. (p. 1319)
—Spoon for Every Bite. Leer, Rebecca, illus. (p. 1631)
Hayes, Joe, tr. see Argueta, Jorge.
Hayes, Joe, tr. see Flor Ada, Alma & Campoy, F. Isabel.
Hayes, Joe, tr. see Flor Ada, Alma.
Hayes, John C. Splurge & the Theatre of Magic. (p. 1630)
Hayes, Juliana. Ari Sylph Valley. (p. 98)
Hayes, K. M. My Little Brony: An Unofficial Novel about Finding the Magic of Friendship. (p. 1212)
Hayes, Karel. Amazing Journey of Lucky the Lobster Buoy. (p. 54)
—Christmas Visitors. (p. 316)
—Snowflake Comes to Stay. (p. 1600)
—Summer Visitors Hayes, Karel, illus. (p. 1675)
—Winter Visitors. (p. 1938)
Hayes, Karel, illus. see Hodgkins, Fran.
Hayes, Karel, illus. see Train, Mary.
Hayes, Kate. All about Poop. Gamsworthy, Mario, ed. (p. 43)
Hayes, Kathryn. Balloon Fairy. (p. 135)
Hayes, Kathy, illus. see Shubin, Masha.
Hayes, Kevin J., jt. ed. see Bloom, Harold.
Hayes, Kimberly Wasserman. Princesses & Dinosaurs. (p. 1406)
Hayes, Ladene M. Continuing Saga of Rikki Tikki Tavi. (p. 361)
—Continuing Saga of Rikki Tikki Tavi - Book Two. (p. 361)
Hayes, Larry. My Name Starts with K. Anderson, Airlie, illus. (p. 1215)
Hayes, Larry E. My Name Starts with A (Library Version) (p. 1215)
—My Name Starts with J. Anderson, Airlie, illus. (p. 1215)
—My Name Starts with S (Library Version) Anderson, Airlie, illus. (p. 1215)
Hayes, Linda. Grandma's First Computer. (p. 708)
Hayes, Mabel Ditch. Would Grandma Still Love Me? (p. 1962)
Hayes, Malcolm. Dreamcatchers. (p. 484)
Hayes, Marilyn. Jumbo Health Yearbook: Grade 3. (p. 933)
—Jumbo Health Yearbook: Grade 4. (p. 933)
—Jumbo Nutrition Yearbook: Grade 4. (p. 933)
—Jumbo Nutrition Yearbook: Grade 5. (p. 933)
—Jumbo Social Studies Yearbook: Grade 5. (p. 933)
Hayes, Matt & Nash, Kevin. College of the Holy Cross College Prowler off the Record. (p. 340)
Hayes, Michael. James Little Elk: Meeting His Family. (p. 907)
Hayes, Mj. Emma's House of Sound. Robinson-Chavez, Kathryn A. & Madzel, D. E., illus. (p. 520)
Hayes, Nicky, jt. auth. see Wagner, Wolfgang.
Hayes, Nicole. Whole of My World. (p. 1920)
Hayes, Paul A. Harem of Books. (p. 748)
Hayes, Rebecca, ed. see Brown, Valcine.
Hayes, Rosemary. Loose Connections. (p. 1052)
—Magic Sword. (p. 1073)
—Mixing It. (p. 1156)
—Payback. (p. 1331)
Hayes, Sabrina. Saturday Morning & Sneaky. (p. 1515)
Hayes, Sadie. Next Big Thing. (p. 1249)
—Social Code. (p. 1604)
Hayes, Sarah. Nine Ducks Nine. (p. 1256)
Hayes, Sarah M. Cowboy Wyatt. (p. 374)
Hayes, Sonia. Eye Candy. (p. 557)
—Ms. Thang. (p. 1188)
—Urban Goddess. (p. 1825)
Hayes, Stephen. Seventh Sorcerer: The Magic Crystals. (p. 1555)
Hayes, Steve, illus. see Norton, J. Renae.
Hayes, Susan. Read It Build It Space. Abbott, Simon, illus. (p. 1443)
Hayes, Susan, jt. auth. see Arlon, Penelope.
Hayes, Terri. Day the Blue Puff Trees Bloomed. (p. 414)
Hayes, Tracey J. Bartina in Trouble Again. (p. 140)
Hayes, Trudie L. & Perkins, Kenneth B. Of All the People in the World to Be I Am Glad That I Am Me! (p. 1279)
Hayes, Vicki C. Garden Troll (p. 656)
—Out of Gas (p. 1311)
—Sky Watchers. (p. 1587)
—Zuze & the Star (p. 1990)
Hayes-Knoll, Carolyn. Ista Cante. (p. 893)
Hayford, Jack W. Acts Bible Story Book: What Kids Want to Know about the Holy Spirit. (p. 10)
—Fatal Attractions: Why Sex Sins Are Worse Than Others. (p. 577)
—Jack Hayford Presenta Hechos una Historia de la Biblia. Foote, Dan, illus. (p. 903)
Hayford, James. Knee-Deep in Blazing Snow: Growing up in Vermont. McCurdy, Michael, illus. (p. 964)
Hayhurst, Chris. Bill Russell. (p. 186)
—Careers in E-Commerce Security & Encryption. (p. 267)
—Cholera. (p. 309)
—Cool Careers Without College for Animal Lovers. (p. 362)
—Euclid: The Great Geometer. (p. 540)
—Everything You Need to Know about Food Additives. (p. 545)
—Israel's War of Independence: Al-Nakba. (p. 893)
—Israel's War of Independence. (p. 893)
—Jobs in Environmental Law. (p. 919)
—John Sutter: California Pioneer. (p. 922)
—John Sutter: California Pioneer / Pionero de California. (p. 922)
—John Sutter: Pionero de California (John Sutter: California Pioneer) (p. 922)
—Lungs: Learning How We Breathe. (p. 1066)
—Neptune. (p. 1241)
—Pluto. (p. 1374)
—Pluto & Other Dwarf Planets. (p. 1374)
—Sitting Bull: Sioux War Chief. (p. 1582)
—Sitting Bull / Toro Sentado: Sioux War Chief / Jefe Sioux. (p. 1582)
—Stay Cool: A Guy's Guide to Handling Conflict. (p. 1645)
—Toro Sentado: Jefe Sioux. (p. 1770)
—Toro Sentado: Jefe sioux (Sitting Bull: Sioux War Chief) (p. 1770)
—Ultra Marathon Running. (p. 1810)
Hayhurst, Chris, jt. auth. see Becker, Jack.
Hayhurst, Chris, jt. auth. see Campbell, Josette.
Hayhurst, Chris, jt. auth. see Concord, Parker.
Hayhurst, Chris, jt. auth. see Wayne, Melody.
Hayhurst, James L. Adventures of Mercury Lane: Bad Commandments (p. 20)
Hayhurst/Parascension Press, James/Lyle. Adventures of Mercury Lane: Bad Commandments (p. 20)
Haylamaz, Resit. Abu Bakr: The Pinnacle of Truthfulness. (p. 7)
—Ali: Hero of Chivalry. (p. 38)
—Luminous Life of Our Prophet. (p. 1065)
—Zayd: The Rose That Bloomed in Captivity. (p. 1985)
Hayler, Kate. Volcano Alert! Team Mission: A Pop-up Book. Giraffe, Red & Doughty, Clare, illus. (p. 1848)
Hayles, Brian. Doctor Who & the Ice Warriors. (p. 459)
Hayles, Marsha. Breathing Room. (p. 226)
—Bunion Burt. Davis, Jack E., illus. (p. 242)
Haymond, Mary & Lee, Linda. Building Independent Readers - A Systematic Approach: 30 Mini-Lessons That Teach Students the Strategies They Need for Successful Sustained Independent Reading-All Year Long! (p. 239)
Hayn, Carter. Bo's Seed Pot. (p. 214)
—Drawing Dragons. (p. 481)
—Drawing Ghosts. (p. 481)
—Drawing Vampires. (p. 482)
—Drawing Werewolves. (p. 482)
—Drawing Witches & Wizards. (p. 482)
—Drawing Zombies. (p. 482)
—New York City: Old & New. (p. 1248)
—New York City's Historical Heritage. (p. 1248)
Hayn, Walter, illus. see Hoffmann, Heinrich.
Haynali, Carolyn A. (Nesto). Goldie: The little horse that didn't Listen. (p. 695)
Hayne, Mark, illus. see Jones, Erasmus W.
Hayner, Linda K. Ellanor's Exchange. (p. 514)
Haynes, Anne S. Little Tree Makes a New Year's Resolution. (p. 1037)
Haynes, Betsy. Cowslip. (p. 374)
—Creepazoid's Nostrils. (p. 381)
—My Adventure Panning for Gold. (p. 1195)
Haynes, Cate. Groovy Granny. Tholen, Shane, illus. (p. 725)
Haynes, Charles C., et al. First Freedoms: A Documentary History of First Amendment Rights in America. (p. 595)
Haynes, David & Landsman, Julie, eds. Welcome to Your Life: Writings for the Heart of Young America. (p. 1874)
Haynes, Debra. Surprise for Chico. (p. 1685)
Haynes, Diane & Swanson, Diane. Flight or Fight (p. 604)
—Gaia Wild (p. 652)
Haynes, Emily, jt. auth. see Patel, Sanjay J.
Haynes, Emily, jt. auth. see Patel, Sanjay.
Haynes, Gaile F. Winning Team: A Guidbook for Junior Showmanship. (p. 1937)
Haynes, Georgia. Trixie, the Treat Fairy: A Halloween Fable. (p. 1788)
Haynes, India K. Sweet Shana. (p. 1690)
Haynes, Jason, illus. see Guess, Catherine Ritch.
Haynes, Joyce, illus. see Allbritton, Stacy.
Haynes, Joyce, illus. see Osseo-Asare, Fran.
Haynes, Joyce, illus. see Petrick, Neila Skinner.
Haynes, Joyce, illus. see Toner, Gerald R.
Haynes, Lori. Wallenda Witches Flying School. (p. 1855)
Haynes, M. Gator & Moose. Connaught, illus. (p. 658)
—Mrs. Alligator's First Movie: Gator at Indy. (p. 1187)
Haynes, Marilee. A. K. A. Genius. (p. 1)
—Genius under Construction. (p. 661)
Haynes, Martha Sue. Ladies of Color. (p. 970)
Haynes, Natalie. Great Escape. (p. 715)
Haynes, Penny, illus. see Littlefield, Eireann.
Haynes, Sara. Gauguin (p. 658)
Haynes, Simon. Hal Spacejock: Second Course. (p. 736)
Haynes, Tammi. Boy on the Side of the Road. (p. 218)
Haynes-Mayes, Ingrid. Recipe of Ideas for Phonemic Awareness & Phonics: Hands-on Activities for Primary Grades. (p. 1451)
Haynie, Cindie. Cuz: Tuning in with Tuny. (p. 396)
Haynie, Rachel. First, You Explore: The Story of Young Charles Townes. Cook, Trahern, illus. (p. 598)
Hays, Anna. Portia's Exclusive & Confidential Rules on True Friendship. (p. 1386)
—Portia's Ultra Mysterious Double Life. (p. 1386)
Hays, Anna Jane. Here Comes Silent E! Adinolfi, JoAnn, illus. (p. 770)
—Kindergarten Countdown. Davick, Linda, illus. (p. 957)
—Pup Speaks Up. Petrone, Valeria, illus. (p. 1417)
—Secret of the Circle-K Cave. Smath, Jerry, illus. (p. 1542)
—Smarty Sara. Kantorovitz, Sylvie & Wickstrom, Sylvie, illus. (p. 1593)
—So Big! Moroney, Christopher, illus. (p. 1601)
—Spring Surprises. Wittwer, Hala Swearingen, illus. (p. 1635)
Hays, Barrett K. Mars, Jimmy & Me. (p. 1096)
—Odelette. (p. 1278)
Hays, Ethel. One, Two, Buckle My Shoe: an Alphabet & Counting Book. (p. 1297)
—Town Mouse & the Country Mouse. (p. 1773)
Hays, Helen Ashe. Adventures of Prince Lazybones: And Other Stories. (p. 22)
Hays, K. D. & Weidman, Meg. Toto's Tale. Martinez, April, illus. (p. 1772)
Hays, Michael, illus. see Layne, Steven, et al.
Hays, Michael, illus. see Seeger, Pete & Jacobs, Paul DuBois.
Hays, Patricia Quinn. First Dog. (p. 594)
Hays, Phillip. Porka-Bella-Snu & the Mystery of the Letters. Spencer, Chip, illus. (p. 1386)
Hays, Samuel P. Wars in the Woods: The Rise of Ecological Forestry in America. (p. 1859)
Hays, Sharon. Tumbleweed Family. (p. 1796)
Hays, Steve. Beauty & the Boy: An Old Man's Story for a Dying Boy. (p. 154)
Hays, Summer. Mrs. Gambel the Quirky Quail. (p. 1187)
Hays, Susan. Nature Friends Creativity Book. (p. 1236)
Hays, Tommy. Pleasure Was Mine. (p. 1373)
Hayskar, Bonnie, ed. see Silva Lee, Alfonso.
Hayskar, Bonnie J., ed. see Silva Lee, Alfonso.
Haysom, John, illus. see Doyle, Christopher.
Haysom, John, illus. see Jeffs, Stephanie.
Hayton, Althea. Two Little Birds. Schlitt, RaRa, illus. (p. 1804)
Hayward, Allan J. Lost Little Fish. (p. 1056)
Hayward, Annie, illus. see Muir, Nicola.
Hayward, Dave. Teaching & Assessing Practical Skills in Science. (p. 1709)
Hayward, Ian Benfold, jt. auth. see Huggins-Cooper, Lynn.
Hayward, Jason. Teddy Bear Adventures. (p. 1712)
Hayward, Katherine. Fire Extinguisher Training. (p. 590)
Hayward, Laura. Why? (p. 1922)
Hayward, Linda. Monster Bug. Palmisciano, Diane, illus. (p. 1166)
—Sesame Street Dictionary. Mathieu, Joe, illus. (p. 1553)
Hayward, Linda, et al. I Spy: A Game to Read & Play. Cooke, Tom, illus. (p. 846)
Hayward, Mark Brauner. I See Without My Eyes. Hartman, Nancy Lee, illus. (p. 845)
—I'm a Magician's Helper. (p. 858)
Hayward, Roy, illus. see Scott, D. P.
Haywood, Carolyn. B Is for Betsy. (p. 122)
—Back to School with Betsy. (p. 130)
—Betsy & Billy. (p. 172)
—Betsy & the Boys. (p. 172)
—Here's a Penny. (p. 771)
—Penny & Peter. (p. 1338)
—Primrose Day. (p. 1401)
—Two & Two Are Four. (p. 1803)
Haywood, Chris & Mac an Ghaill, Mairtin. Men & Masculinities: Theory, Research & Social Practice. (p. 1126)
Haywood, David & Adamson, Peter. Hidden Talent of Albert Otter. (p. 776)
Haywood, Ebony. There Was Once a Potato. (p. 1730)
Haywood, Ian Benfold, illus. see Coates, Paul.
Haywood, Ian Benfold, illus. see Kerner, Susan.
Haywood, Jennifer Johnson, jt. auth. see Bozzuti-Jones, Mark Francisco.
Haywood, John. Home, Family & Everyday Life Through the Ages: Compare the Food, Homes & Daily Lives of Ancient People from All the Major Civilizations. (p. 792)
—Through the Ages: Gods, Beliefs & Ceremonies. (p. 1745)
—West African Kingdoms. (p. 1876)
Haywood, John, ed. Illustrated History Encyclopedia Everyday Life in the Ancient World: How People Lived & Worked Through the Ages. (p. 857)
Haywood, John, et al, eds. Children's Encyclopedia of the Ancient World. (p. 303)
Haywood, Karen. Eagles. (p. 492)
—Hawks & Falcons. (p. 755)
—Skeletal System. (p. 1584)
Haywood, Karen Diane. Bears. (p. 151)
—Georgia. (p. 665)
Haywood, R. Dinosaurios. (p. 443)
Hazan, Maurice. Animaux et les verbes flash card Set. (p. 84)
—Chiffres, couleurs, verbes et phrases flash card Set. (p. 301)
—French (p. 635)
—French. (p. 635)
—Saber, Deber, Querer, Poder: Symtalk Verb + Verb Infinitive Game for Spanish. (p. 1499)
Hazan, Maurice, illus. see Figueras, Ligaya, ed.
Hazan, Maurice, illus. see Travis, Joelle & Figueras, Ligaya, eds.
Hazan, Maurice, illus. see Travis, Joelle, ed.
Hazan, Maurice, creator. Camino: Practicing Everyday Vocabulary. (p. 256)
—Chemin: Practicing Everyday Vocabulary for French. (p. 297)
—Chinese Dialogue Game: Level 1. (p. 307)
—Chinese Objects, Colors & Numbers Bingo. (p. 307)
—Conversation Game for French. (p. 361)
—Conversation Game for Spanish. (p. 361)
—Dime quien Es: Spanish Dialogues Level 1. (p. 440)
—Dis moi qui c Est: French Dialogues Level 1. (p. 446)
—Escrivons: Introduction to Writing in French. (p. 535)
—ESL Dialogue Game: Level 1. (p. 536)
—ESL Dialogues Game: Level 2. (p. 536)
—ESL Objects, Colors & Numbers Bingo. (p. 536)
—ESL Practicing Vocabulary Game. (p. 536)
—ESL Verb Bingo. (p. 536)
—Frases y Fotos: Long Sentence Bingo. (p. 631)
—French Conjugating Cards. (p. 635)
—French Question Game. (p. 636)
—German Dialogue Game: Level 1. (p. 666)
—German Dialogue Game: Level 2. (p. 666)
—German Practicing Vocabulary Game. (p. 666)
—German Resto Presto Game. (p. 666)
—Guiseppe e i suoi Amici: Italian Big Book. (p. 731)
—Hebrew Dialogues Game Level 1. (p. 761)
—Italian Dialogues Game: Level 1. (p. 894)
—Italian Dialogues Game: Level 2. (p. 894)
—Italian Practicing Vocabulary Game. (p. 894)

H

—Italian Resto Presto Game. (p. 894)
—Japanese Dialogue Game: Level 1. (p. 909)
—Japanese Objects, Colors & Numbers Bingo. (p. 909)
—Object, Color & Number Bingo. (p. 1275)
—Objects, Colors & Numbers Bingo for French. (p. 1275)
—Perdidos: Directions in the City. (p. 1341)
—Phrases et Photos: Long sentence Bingo. (p. 1353)
—Prom Game for Spanish. (p. 1411)
—Resto Presto. (p. 1464)
—Resto Presto French. (p. 1464)
—Savoir, devoir, vouloir, Pouvoir: Symtalk Verb + Verb Infinitive Game for French. (p. 1518)
—Spanish Conjugating Cards. (p. 1621)
—Symtalk French Book 1 Package. (p. 1693)
—Symtalk French Book 4 Package: Plein la Vue. (p. 1693)
—Symtalk French Junior Book Package. (p. 1693)
—Symtalk Italian Book 1 Package. (p. 1693)
—Symtalk Spanish Book 1 Package. (p. 1693)
—Symtalk Spanish Book 4 Package: En Plena Vista. (p. 1693)
—Symtalk Spanish Junior Book Package. (p. 1693)
—Verbes: Symtalk Verb Bingo. (p. 1836)
—Verbos: Symtalk Verb Bingo. (p. 1836)
Hazard, Andrea, illus. see Perez, Angela J.
Hazard, John, illus. see Alimonti, Frederick & Tedesco, Ann.
Hazard, John, illus. see Pilon, Cindy Jett.
Hazard, Mary Jo. Peacocks of Palos Verdes. (p. 1332)
Hazareesingh, Sudhir. Saint-Napoleon: Celebrations of Sovereignty in Nineteenth-Century France. (p. 1503)
Haze, Armand. Beautiful Blossom. (p. 153)
Hazekamp, Michelle R. Rainbow in My Pocket. Buehrle, Jacquelyn, illus. (p. 1435)
Hazel, Andrew, illus. see Hamilton, George.
Hazel Bell. When Fred the Rooster Crowed. (p. 1902)
Hazel, Jan. Marshall Meets the Little Dragons. (p. 1096)
Hazelaar, Cor, illus. see Shelby, Anne.
Hazelett, Robert. Grandpa's Fairy Tales. (p. 709)
Hazell, Carolyn. Pav the Plumber Saves the Day. (p. 1331)
Hazell, Mark. Flight of the Cloud Sailor. (p. 604)
—Gift of the Wind Dancers. (p. 675)
—Miners of the Rainbow Stone (the Forest Children Series) (p. 1146)
Hazeltine, Alice I., jt. auth. see Smith, Elva S.
Hazelton, Jack W. Charlie Duck. Hazelton, Jack W., illus. (p. 293)
Hazelton, Tanya & Bonanni, Constance. Ian's Golden Passage. (p. 849)
Hazelwood, C. Jessie's Window. (p. 914)
Hazelwood, K. D. Coyotebat. Mathis, Leslie, illus. (p. 374)
Hazen, Barbara Shook. Noah's Ark. Catusanu, Mircea, illus. (p. 1261)
—Please & Thank You Book. Chollat, Emilie, illus. (p. 1373)
Hazen, Les. South Wind: A Story of Best Friends. (p. 1617)
Hazen, Lynn E. Amazing Trail of Seymour Snail. Cushman, Doug, illus. (p. 56)
Hazen, Robert M., jt. auth. see Trefil, James.
Hazen, Walter. Ancient Times. (p. 70)
—Middle Ages. (p. 1137)
—Reform Movement. (p. 1456)
Hazen, Walter A. Civil War. (p. 325)
—Colonial Times: With Cross-Curricular Activities in Each Chapter: Colonial Times. (p. 341)
—Communication. (p. 349)
—Everyday Life: Reform in America. (p. 543)
—Everyday Life: Revolutionary War. (p. 543)
—Frontier: With Cross-Curricular Activities in Each Chapter: the Frontier. (p. 644)
—Immigration. (p. 861)
Hazlegrove, Cary, photos by see Gleeson, Bill.
Hazlehurst, Pam. Santa's Dilemm. (p. 1513)
Hazleton, Kim. Officer Kaboodle Goes to School. (p. 1280)
Hazlett, Richard W. & Hyndman, Donald W. Roadside Geology of Hawaii. (p. 1477)
Hazlett, V. Jake's Junction: Henry's Listening Ears. Tucker, E., illus. (p. 906)
Hazlewood, Leyland. Chester Goes to Afric. (p. 298)
Hazuka, Tom. Last Chance for First. (p. 977)
Hazuki, Kanae. Say I Love You (p. 1518)
HB Staff. Alien Vacation. (p. 41)
—All Fall Down. (p. 44)
—Baby. (p. 124)
—Bird's Bad Day. (p. 191)
—Davy Crockett & the Wild Cat. (p. 411)
—Every Cat. (p. 542)
—Fantastic Phonics Practice! (p. 572)
—Four Very Big Beans. (p. 625)
—Frog's Day. (p. 641)
—Good-bye, Fox. (p. 697)
—Help! Said Jed. (p. 766)
—Henry. (p. 767)
—How the Sky Got It's Stars. (p. 813)
—I Was Just about to Go to Bed. (p. 848)
—Just Like You. (p. 939)
—King Who Loved to Dance. (p. 959)
—Let's Visit the Moon. (p. 1001)
—Little Chicks Sing. (p. 1026)
—Lunch in Space. (p. 1065)
—My Family Band. (p. 1202)
—My Sister Is My Friend. (p. 1218)
—My Wild Woolly. (p. 1221)
—One Little Slip. (p. 1295)
—Perfect Pet. (p. 1342)
—Play Ball! (p. 1371)
—Silly Aunt Tilly. (p. 1575)
—Today Is Monday. (p. 1760)
—What a Shower! (p. 1878)
—Where Babies Play. (p. 1906)
He, Xu. Happy Flight. (p. 745)
—Happy Taichichuan. (p. 746)
He, Zihong, jt. auth. see Olive, Guillaume.
Heacock, David & Giles, Inga. Child of Oz. (p. 301)
Head, Alison, jt. auth. see Huggins-Cooper, Lynn.
Head, Carol Carwile & Tom Head. Turbulent 60s - 1966. (p. 1797)
Head, David L. Granville T. Woods: African American Communication & Transportation Pioneer. (p. 710)
Head, Debby & Pollett, Libby. BBY Practice Pages: Making Ten. (p. 147)
—BBY Practice Pages: Choosing Coins. (p. 147)
—BBY Practice Pages: Addition Facts 0-10. (p. 147)
—BBY Practice Pages: Addition Facts 11-20. (p. 147)
—BBY Practice Pages: Numbers & Words 0-10. (p. 147)
—BBY Practice Pages: Numbers & Words 11-20. (p. 147)
—BBY Practice Pages: Modeling Numbers 0-100. (p. 147)
—BBY Practice Pages: Subtraction Facts 0-10. (p. 147)
—BBY Practice Pages: Beginning Addition 0-10. (p. 147)
—BBY Practice Pages: Subtraction Facts 11-20. (p. 147)
—BBY Practice Pages: Making Change Through $1. 00. (p. 147)
Head, Diane. Grammy Dee Solves the Case of the Red-Hot Screamies. (p. 706)
Head, Edwina, et al. Amazing Animal Families. (p. 53)
Head, Heno. God Made Dinosaurs. Fletcher, Rusty, illus. (p. 689)
Head, Honor. Amazing Fish. (p. 54)
—Amazing Mammals. (p. 55)
—Amazing Plants. (p. 55)
—Beans & Nuts: On Your Plate. (p. 150)
—Cats. (p. 280)
—Cats & Kittens. (p. 281)
—Celebrating Harvest Festivals Around the World. (p. 284)
—Celebrating Yom Kippur: The Jewish New Year. (p. 285)
—Dairy. (p. 400)
—Family & Friends. (p. 568)
—Famous Spies. (p. 569)
—Fish. (p. 598)
—Healthy Eating. (p. 758)
—Horses & Ponies. (p. 800)
—How to Handle Cyberbullying. (p. 820)
—Keeping Clean. (p. 947)
—Keeping Fit. (p. 947)
—Mammals. (p. 1085)
—Milk, Cheese, & Eggs. (p. 1143)
—Plants. (p. 1369)
—Rain. Taylor, Lauren, ed. (p. 1434)
—Salad. (p. 1504)
—Snow. Taylor, Lauren, ed. (p. 1598)
—Wind. Taylor, Lauren, ed. (p. 1935)
Head, Jason. Sui Companion Set. (p. 1673)
Head, Jean. Andrew's Christmas Dream. (p. 72)
Head, Jeff. Dragon's Fury - World War against America & the West. Durkin, Chris & Fischer, Joanie, eds. (p. 479)
Head, Mat. Warduff & the Corn Cob Caper. Head, Mat, illus. (p. 1858)
—Warduff & the Pelican Pirates. (p. 1858)
Head, Murray, illus. see White, Alexina B.
Head, Murray, photos by see Lurie, Susan.
Head, Murray, photos by see White, Alexina B.
Head, Pat, illus. see Marlow, Herb.
Head, Tom. Ancient Mesopotamia. (p. 70)
—Freedom of Religion. (p. 634)
Head, Vivian. Pull-The-Tab Times Tables Book. (p. 1415)
Head, Vivien. Pull the Tab - Times Tables Book. (p. 1415)
Headcase Design, illus. see Aronson, Marc & Newquist, H. P.
Headford, Cheryl. Face in the Window. (p. 560)
Headings, Joseph E., illus. see Headings, Peggy A.
Headings, Peggy A. Friends for Keeps. Gordon, Betsy, ed. (p. 638)
Headlam, Catharine & Catherine, Headlam. Enciclopedia de las Ciencias (p. 523)
Headley, Aaron, illus. see Gray, Rick & Gray, Coral.
Headley, James. Rigging. (p. 1472)
Headley, Julia. Yanina Ballerina. (p. 1968)
Headley, Justina Chen. Patch. Vane, Mitch, illus. (p. 1328)
Headley, Justina Chen & Chen, Justina. North of Beautiful. (p. 1265)
Headley, Maria Dahvana. Magonia. (p. 1076)
Headley, Shannon. Writing Organizers. (p. 1965)
Headlund, Peggy L. Consequence: Importance of the Spirit. (p. 358)
Headrick, Gordon T. Chronicles of Em-Haborn. (p. 317)
Headrick, Julianna. Our New Addition. Baker, David, illus. (p. 1309)
Headrick, Tammy Hill. That Famous Bird, Sir Thornton the Third. (p. 1726)
Headstream, John H. Bright Stories & Little Literature for Children. (p. 228)
Headstrom, Richard. Adventures with a Hand Lens. (p. 25)
Head-Weston, Alex, illus. see Matthews, Rupert.
Heady, Heather. What's at the Beach? Storch, Ellen N., illus. (p. 1896)
Heal, Edith. How the World Began. Nelson, Don, illus. (p. 813)
Healan, Tammy. Ladybug's Defense: Part One of the Fascinating Bug's Series. Hill, Malissa, illus. (p. 971)
Heald, Glenn. Santa Talks! The Life Story of Saint Nicholas. (p. 1513)
Heale, Jay. African Animal Tales. (p. 27)
Heale, Jay, jt. auth. see Stewart, Dianne.
Heale, Jay & Koh, Angeline. Portugal. (p. 1387)
Heale, Jay & Latif, Zawiah Abdul. Madagascar. (p. 1069)
Heale, Jay & Wong, Winnie. Tanzania. (p. 1705)
Heale, Jay & Yong, Jui Lin. Democratic Republic of the Congo. (p. 426)
Heale, Jonathan, illus. see McAllister, Angela.
Healer, Stephanie A. My Angel Michael. (p. 1196)
Healey, Bruce. Delightfully Dreadful Tale of King Drod (p. 425)
Healey, Karen. Shattering. (p. 1563)
—When We Wake. (p. 1905)
—While We Run. (p. 1911)
Healey, Richard (Dick). Holly the Christmas Dove. (p. 789)
Healey, Tim. 1960s. (p. 2002)
Healey, Tim & Carter, Alex. Insider's Guide for High School Students: A Handbook for the Ninth Grade Year. (p. 878)
Health New England, creator. Sammie Sportz My Summer of Sports Safety. (p. 1507)
HealthTeacher. HealthTeacher: K-1. (p. 758)
Healy, A. J. Tommy Storm & the Galactic Knights. (p. 1765)
Healy, Aaron. Making the Trade: Stocks, Bonds, & Other Investments. (p. 1082)
Healy, Christopher. Hero's Guide to Being an Outlaw. Harris, Todd, illus. (p. 773)
—Hero's Guide to Saving Your Kingdom. Harris, Todd, illus. (p. 773)
—Hero's Guide to Storming the Castle. Harris, Todd, illus. (p. 773)
Healy, Jeane, illus. see Wilmes, Liz & Wilmes, Dick.
Healy, Kearney F., jt. auth. see Green, Ross Gordo.
Healy, Maggie, illus. see Heinz, Brian J.
Healy, Nicholas M. If You Were a Period Gray, Sara, illus. (p. 855)
—If You Were a Period [LTD Commodities]. Gray, Sara, illus. (p. 855)
Healy, Nicholas M., jt. auth. see Healy, Nick.
Healy, Nick. American Flag. (p. 60)
—Billy the Kid. (p. 187)
—Christopher Columbus. (p. 316)
—Giovanni Da Verrazano. (p. 677)
—Liberty Bell. (p. 1005)
—Marie Curie. (p. 1093)
—Muhammad Ali. (p. 1189)
—Piano. (p. 1354)
—Star-Spangled Banner. (p. 1641)
—Statue of Liberty. (p. 1645)
—White House. (p. 1913)
Healy, Nick & Healy, Nicholas M. If You Were a Period Gray, Sara, illus. (p. 855)
—Roberto Clemente: Baseball Legend (p. 1479)
—Sammy Sosa: Baseball Superstar (p. 1508)
—World's Deadliest Sharks (p. 1960)
—World's Most Dangerous Bugs (p. 1960)
Healy, Reneé. You Are Safe in the Universe. (p. 1973)
Healy, Shay. Beastly Jokes. (p. 152)
—More Beastly Jokes. (p. 1174)
Healy, Tim. Birthday Chronicles: Volume I. (p. 192)
Heaney Dunn, John. Little Red House with No Doors & No Windows & A Star Inside. (p. 1035)
Heaney, Shane. Food from Around the World: Represent & Solve Problems Involving Division. (p. 613)
—Scotch-Irish Immigration to America: Economic Hardship in Ireland (1603-1775) (p. 1530)
Heap, Bridgette. Pursuit of Pizan Chodagiri, Shanthi, illus. (p. 1419)
Heap, Jonathon, illus. see Mulherin, Jennifer & Frost, Abigail.
Heap, Sue. Danny's Drawing Book. Heap, Sue, illus. (p. 406)
—Espera y Veras. (p. 536)
—Fabulous Fairy Feast. Heap, Sue, illus. (p. 560)
—Four Friends Together. Heap, Sue, illus. (p. 625)
—Mine! Heap, Sue, illus. (p. 1145)
Heap, Sue, illus. see French, Vivian.
Heap, Sue, illus. see Heapy, Teresa.
Heap, Sue, illus. see Lloyd-Jones, Sally.
Heap, Sue, illus. see Wilson, Jacqueline.
Heap, Will, photos by see Knowlden, Martin.
Heape, David R. That's What Friends Do. (p. 1727)
Heaphy, Paula, illus. see Frankel, Erin.
Heapy, Teresa. Japanese Culture (p. 909)
—Very Little Red Riding Hood. Heap, Sue, illus. (p. 1838)
Heard, Foreman. Tales of Pinkie Posie. (p. 1702)
Heard, Georgia. Arrow Finds Its Mark: A Book of Found Poems. Guilloppé, Antoine, illus. (p. 101)
Heard, Georgia, ed. Falling down the Page: A Book of List Poems. (p. 566)
—Falling down the Page. (p. 566)
Heard, Margaret. It's Water Time. (p. 899)
Hearld, Mark, illus. see Davies, Nicola.
Hearn, Diane Dawson. Anna in the Garden. (p. 85)
Hearn, Diane Dawson, illus. see Bauer, Marion Dane.
Hearn, Diane Dawson, illus. see Krensky, Stephen.
Hearn, Diane Dawson, illus. see Levinson, Nancy Smiler.
Hearn, Emily. Batchawana Silly Stuff. Valleau, Gailon, illus. (p. 143)
—Franny & the Music Girl Thurman, Mark & Second Story Press Staff, illus. (p. 631)
Hearn, Emily & Milne, Marywinn, eds. Our New Home: Immigrant Children Speak (p. 1309)
Hearn, Jeff. Cutting Yards on Mars: Writer's Block. (p. 396)
Hearn, Julie. Hazel: A Novel. (p. 756)
—Hazel. (p. 756)
—Ivy. (p. 901)
—Minister's Daughter. (p. 1147)
Hearn, Julie & Yankus, Marc. Sign of the Raven. (p. 1574)
Hearn, Lafcadio. In Ghostly Japan. (p. 863)
—Interpretations of Literature. (p. 880)
Hearn, Lafcadio, et al. Boy Who Drew Cats & Other Japanese Fairy Tales. Green, Yuko, illus. (p. 219)
Hearn, Lian. Heaven's Net Is Wide. (p. 761)
—Leyendas de los Otori I. (p. 1004)
Hearn, Marilyn, illus. see Carson, Shonette.
Hearn, Michael Patrick. Porcelain Cat. Dillon, Leo & Dillon, Diane, illus. (p. 1386)
Hearn, Sam, illus. see Adkins, Laura.
Hearn, Sam, illus. see Smith, J. L.
Hearn, Samuel, illus. see Rees, Gwyneth.
Hearne, Betsy. Canine Connection: Stories about Dogs & People. (p. 261)
—Seven Brave Women. Andersen, Bethanne, illus. (p. 1554)
—Wishes, Kisses, & Pigs. (p. 1940)
Hearse, Rai Jayne. Life & Loves of Cherry Bakewell: Year One. (p. 1007)
Hearson, Ruth, illus. see McQuinn, Anna, et al.
Hearson, Ruth, illus. see McQuinn, Anna.
Hearst, Allyson. White Pajamas: A Karate Story. (p. 1913)
Hearst, Michael. Extraordinary People. Scamihorn, Aaron, illus. (p. 555)
—Unusual Creatures: A Mostly Accurate Account of Earth's Strangest Animals. (p. 1823)
—Unusual Creatures: A Mostly Accurate Account of Some of the Earth's Strangest Animals. Noordeman, Jelmer et al, illus. (p. 1823)
Heart, Angelina. Teaching of Little Crow: The Journey of the Soul. (p. 1710)
Heart Of Dakota. Little Hands to Heaven. (p. 1029)
Heart, Sandra. Pemanna & Yerbo, the Toe-Tamals Family & Friends. (p. 1343)
Hearth, Amy Hill. Delany Sisters Reach High. Ladwig, Tim, illus. (p. 424)
Hearth, Liese. My Dog Burps. (p. 1202)
Heartney, Eleanor. Art & Today. (p. 101)
Heary, E. A., tr. see Sophocles.
Heasley, Gwendolyn. Don't Call Me Baby. (p. 467)
—Long Way from You. (p. 1047)
—Where I Belong. (p. 1908)
Heaston, Rebecca J., illus. see Nixon, Joan Lowery.
Heater, Derek. Citizenship: The Civic Ideal in World History, Politics & Education. (p. 323)
Heath, Alan & Bainbridge, Nicki. Baby Massage: The Calming Power of Touch. Fisher, Julie, photos by. (p. 127)
Heath, Beverly C. Bedtime Lullaby. Floyd, John, Jr., illus. (p. 157)
—Counting with Colors. Floyd, John, Jr., illus. (p. 372)
—My Parts Equal Me! Floyd, John, Jr., illus. (p. 1216)
—Opposites. Floyd, John, Jr., illus. (p. 1300)
Heath, Christopher. Against the Drimlith. (p. 29)
Heath, Clyde. Kids Have Ups & Downs Too! (p. 954)
Heath, Erin. Doctors in Our Community. (p. 459)
Heath, Jack. Lab. (p. 969)
—Money Run. (p. 1164)
Heath, Kathy. Camp Crazy Kids. (p. 257)
Heath, Kathy & Martin, Karla. Logan's Journey. Omoff, Theresa, illus. (p. 1045)
Heath, Kay S. Books Are NOT My Favorite Things. (p. 212)
Heath, Michael. Garlic Bread for Eugene. (p. 657)
Heath, Mike, jt. auth. see Haddix, Margaret Peterson.
Heath, Paul Reaves, illus. see DeStout, Carole.
Heath, Paulette Powell. Break Through Reflections. (p. 224)
—In the Mist. (p. 866)
Heath, Sarah. Why Is My Cat Doing That? (p. 1925)
Heath, Shanon. Boy Named George: The True Story of George Washington. (p. 218)
Heath, Steve & Gitlin, Martin. Arizona Cardinals. (p. 98)
Heathcote, Peter. Lizards (p. 1043)
Heather, jt. auth. see Adamson, Thomas K.
Heather C Hudak. Ants. (p. 90)
Heather C Hudak & Hudak, Heather C. Ants. (p. 90)
Heather, Cherry. Surviving High School: The Journey of an Angst Filled Teen (p. 1687)
Heather Heath Pruett. Happy House. (p. 746)
Heather, Miss. Creepy Crypt of ABC. Heather, Miss, illus. (p. 381)
Heather Rose Brabant. Moon Princess. (p. 1172)
Heather Zschock. Solar System Scratch & Sketch. (p. 1607)
Heatherly, C. L. Chuck. My Piece of the Sky. (p. 1217)
Heathfield, Lisa. Seed. (p. 1547)
Heatley, David, illus. see Potter, Ellen.
Heatley, Michael. Katy Perry. (p. 946)
Heatley, Michael & Gent, Mike. Taylor Swift. (p. 1708)
Heaton, J. Barrett. Careers in Teaching. (p. 268)
Heaton, Jr., illus. see Hulslander, Dyan.
Heaton, Layce, illus. see Page, Lawana.
Heaton, Layce D. Many Tracks of Lap'n Tap Heaton, Layce D., illus. (p. 1089)
Heaton, Maria. Kangaroos Say Sorry, Too. (p. 942)
Heaton, Mark. Ruth Tells the Truth. (p. 1498)
Heaviside, Oliver. Electromagnetic Theory: Including an Account of Heaviside's Unpublished Notes Set (p. 509)
Heavner, Jodi, illus. see Randall, Marilyn Mae.
Hebert, Catherine, ed. see Donnell, Frances.
Hebert, Charles G. Christmas for Friends: With the Bush Buddies. (p. 314)
Hebert, David L., ed. Freedom of the Press. (p. 634)
Hebert, J. J. Weepy the Dragon. (p. 1872)
Hébert, Marie-Francine. Maison dans la Baleine. Germain, Philippe, illus. (p. 1077)
—Petite Fille Qui Detestait l'Heure du Dodo. (p. 1348)
—This Side of the Sky Ouriou, Susan, tr. from FRE. (p. 1737)
Hebert, Pamela. Elliot Finley's Jus' Plain Ole Daisy. (p. 514)
Hébert-Collins, Sheila. Jacques et la Canne à Sucre: A Cajun Jack & the Beanstalk Lyne, Alison Davis, illus. (p. 905)
—Jean-Paul Hébert Was There/Jean-Paul Hébert Etait Là Bergeron, John W., illus. (p. 911)
—Petite Rouge: A Cajun Twist to an Old Tale Lyne, Alison, illus. (p. 1348)
Hebert-Ford, Linda. Tough Choices: Beyond Anger Management. (p. 1772)
Hebler, Michael. Night after Christmas. Driessen, Anita, illus. (p. 1252)
Hebron, Yvette C. Ross. Cherry Blossom Kids & the Three-legged Dog. (p. 298)
Hecht, Alan. Antidepressants & Antianxiety Drugs. (p. 89)
—Cancer Treatment Drugs. (p. 261)
—Mumps. (p. 1191)
—Polio. (p. 1380)
Hecht, Alan & Yannielli, Len. Lyme Disease. (p. 1066)
Hecht, Jeff. Vanishing Life: The Mystery of Mass Extinctions. (p. 1833)
Hecht, Kristina. 1, 2, 3, My Daddy & Me. (p. 1990)
—Bird & a Bee (p. 190)
Hecht, Randi, ed. see FHM Magazine Staff.
Hechter, Janice, illus. see Simhaee, Rebeka.
Hechter, Janice, illus. see Townsend, Una Belle.
Hechtkopf, H., illus. see Fuchs, Menucha.
Hechtkopf, Jacqueline, jt. auth. see Jules, Jacqueline.
Hechtman, Betty Jacobson. Blue Schwartz & Nefertiti's Necklace: A Mystery with Recipes. (p. 203)
Heck, C. S. Memory-Kisses. (p. 1126)
Heck, Claudia, tr. see Maddox, Jake.
Heck, Claudia M., jt. auth. see Suen, Anastasia.
Heck, Claudia M., tr. see Crow, Melinda Melton.
Heck, Claudia M., tr. see Maddox, Jake.
Heck, Claudia M., tr. see Meister, Cari.
Heck, Claudia M., tr. see Suen, Anastasia.
Heck, Don. Marvel Masterworks: The Avengers - Volume 4. (p. 1099)
Heck, Don, illus. see Friedrich, Mike.
Heck, Don, jt. illus. see Colan, Gene.
Heck, Don, jt. illus. see Lieber, Larry.

Heck, Don, et al. Invaders Classic: The Complete Collection. Vol. 1 (p. 883)
Heck, Ed. Monkey Lost. (p. 1165)
Heck, Tom. Toobeez Teambuilding Activity Workbook: The Toobeez Teambuilding Activity workbook helps teams to exercise their creative problem-solving, communication & collaboration Skills. Anderson, Victoria, ed. (p. 1767)
Hecke, Stephanie. Fishy Dreams. (p. 599)
Hecker, Cindy. Legend of Patrick Tierney. Chambliss, Marilyn, illus. (p. 988)
Hecker, Vera. Home for Rainbow. (p. 792)
—Mystic World Coloring Book. Hecker, Vera, illus. (p. 1226)
Hecker, Vera, illus. see Banta, Sandra F.
Hecket, Jessica. Gideon's Dragons. (p. 674)
—Lamb That Got Away. (p. 972)
Heckler, Naomi & Kyelberg, Hope. Adventures of Little Caesar ... Little Caesar's Christmas Adventure. (p. 19)
Heckman, Ashley. Last Three Words. (p. 979)
Heckman, Dennise. Mountain Doggies. (p. 1180)
Heckman, Mark, illus. see Newman, Mark.
Heckman, Philip. Saving Money. (p. 1517)
Heckscher, Melissa & Shulman, Mark. Explorer's Gazette: Amazing Stories of 30 Real-Life Journeys. (p. 551)
Heckt, Jackie. Colony of Virginia. (p. 342)
—Immigration to Colonial America. (p. 861)
—What the Clouds Are Telling You. (p. 1893)
Hector, Julian. Gentleman Bug. Hector, Julian, illus. (p. 661)
Hector, Julian, illus. see Godwin, Laura.
Hector, Julian, illus. see Levine, Arthur A.
Hector, Julian, illus. see Muir, Leslie.
Hector, Nancy. Juniper. (p. 936)
Hector, Rachel. Re-Ride. (p. 1442)
Hedde, Rebecca. Science with Magnets. (p. 1528)
Hedderich, Tom, illus. see Field, Matthew S.
Hedderwick, Mairi. Island Stories. Hedderwick, Mairi, illus. (p. 892)
—Katie Morag & the Big Boy Cousins. Hedderwick, Mairi, illus. (p. 945)
—Katie Morag & the Birthdays. Hedderwick, Mairi, illus. (p. 945)
—Katie Morag & the Grand Concert. Hedderwick, Mairi, illus. (p. 945)
—Katie Morag & the Riddles. Hedderwick, Mairi, illus. (p. 945)
—Katie Morag & the Two Grandmothers. Hedderwick, Mairi, illus. (p. 945)
—Katie Morag Delivers the Mail. Hedderwick, Mairi, illus. (p. 945)
—Katie Morag of Course! (p. 945)
—Utterly Otterleys. (p. 1829)
—Walk with Grannie. (p. 1854)
Heddle, Jennifer, jt. auth. see Disney Book Group Staff.
Heddle, Rebecca. Puzzle Journey through Time. Spenceley, Annabel, illus. (p. 1421)
—Science in the Kitchen. Edom, Helen, ed. (p. 1526)
Hédelin, Pascale. Animal Babies: Lift the Flap & Learn. Herrbach, Stéphanie & Owlkids Books Inc. Staff, illus. (p. 76)
—Earth & Sky: A Lift-the-Flap Guide to Our World & Solar System. Richard, Laurent & Owlkids Books Inc. Staff, illus. (p. 495)
—Face-to-Face with the Duck. (p. 560)
—Human Body: Lift the Flap & Learn. Barborini, Robert, illus. (p. 825)
Heder, Thyra. Fraidyzoo. (p. 627)
Heder, Thyra, illus. see Gianferrari, Maria.
Hedgecock, Lucie, illus. see DePrisco, Dorothea.
Hedgecock, Sean, illus. see Soleim, Heather.
Hedger, Ralph. Limits & Degrees. (p. 1018)
Hedges, A. A. C. Bottles & Bottle Collecting. (p. 215)
Hedges, David. Step into Shadows: Learning to Trust Beyond the Visible. (p. 1648)
Hedges, Rachael, illus. see Colby, J. Z.
Hedgman, Janis. Party in the Garden. (p. 1326)
Hedicker, Lisa, illus. see Kenney, Karen Latchana.
Hedji, Charles. Fields of Discovery. (p. 584)
Hedley, Alistair, selected by. Read to Me Daddy. (p. 1443)
Hedlund, Daniel Levine. Trouble with Tomatoes. (p. 1790)
Hedlund, Jody. Uncertain Choice (p. 1811)
Hedlund, Stephanie. Autumn. Bauer, Stephanie, illus. (p. 118)
—Bedtime with Mother Goose. Tugeau, Jeremy, illus. (p. 157)
—Seasons. Bauer, Stephanie, illus. (p. 1538)
—Spring. Bauer, Stephanie, illus. (p. 1634)
—Summer. Bauer, Stephanie, illus. (p. 1673)
—Winter. Bauer, Stephanie, illus. (p. 1937)
Hedman, Jack. Gift of Gab: A Collection of Recollections. (p. 675)
Hedrick, David, photos by see Murray, Libby.
Hedrick, Helen Groves. Tails, Trails & Pies: An Appalachian Cattle Drive. Spiker, Sue Ann Maxwell, illus. (p. 1695)
Hedrick, Larry, ed. see Xenophon.
Hedrick, Mandy, illus. see Porter, Harry.
Hedstrom, Leigh, illus. see Watson, Rhonda.
Hedstrom-Page, Deborah. From Colonies to Country with George Washington. Martinez, Sergio, illus. (p. 642)
—From Log Cabin to White House with Abraham Lincoln. Martinez, Sergio, illus. (p. 643)
—From Settlement to City with Benjamin Franklin. Martinez, Sergio, illus. (p. 643)
—From Slavery to Freedom with Harriet Tubman. Martinez, Sergio, illus. (p. 643)
Hee, Lee Yun. Demon Diary Na, Lauren, tr. from KOR. (p. 426)
Heebner, Mary D., illus. see Craig, Sienna R.
Heeg, Berg Heeg. Voyage to Victory: The Voice of a Sailor in the Pacific 1943-1945. (p. 1850)
Heegaard, Marge Eaton. Adopted & Wondering: Drawing Out Feelings. (p. 13)
—Drawing Together to Accept & Respect Differences. (p. 482)
—Drawing Together to Learn about Feelings. (p. 482)
—Living Well with My Serious Illness. (p. 1042)
Hee-Joon, Son. Dorothy of Oz (p. 472)
—Phantasy Degree (p. 1349)
—PhD: Phantasy Degree. (p. 1350)
—PhD: Phantasy Degree. Vol. 1 (p. 1350)
—PhD: Phantasy Degree. Vol. 1 Hee-Joon, Son, illus. (p. 1350)
Heeley, Ted, illus. see Goldner, John.
Heembrock, Roberta. Why Kids Can't Spell: A Practical Guide to the Missing Component in Language Proficiency. (p. 1925)
Heeney, Bronwyn. Dragon Called Wilbur: How a Fire-Breathing Dragon Made Friends. Fekete, Lucy, illus. (p. 476)
—Nibbles. Sayers, Rachel, illus. (p. 1250)
Heer, Andrew De. Story of Kwesi Appiah: The GHANAIAN AMERICAN BOY, for young Readers. (p. 1658)
—Three African Short Stories for Young Readers: For Young Readers. (p. 1741)
Heer, Andy. Fundamental Wesleyan Catechism. Reasoner, Vic, ed. (p. 649)
Heer, Dusty Rhoades. Forest That Rains Frogs. (p. 618)
Heermann, Barry. Noble Purpose: Igniting Extraordinary Passion for Life & Work. (p. 1262)
Heers, Alli, jt. auth. see Susedik, Tina.
Heers, Matt, illus. see Turnipseed, Susan.
Heers, Nate, illus. see Turnipseed, Susan.
Heerschap, Bonnie. I Love You Oodles & Boodles & Chicken & Noodles. (p. 844)
Hees, Bradford. Light of Nor. (p. 1015)
Hees, Miriam. Adventures of Jilly & Brad: Noises in the Attic. Kinneman, D. Michael, illus. (p. 19)
Heese, Susan & Paquet, Cathy. Social Science Matters Grade 6 Learner's Book. (p. 1604)
—Social Science Matters Grade 6 Learner's Book Afrikaans Edition. (p. 1604)
Hefferan, Rob. My Pop-up Nursery Rhymes. (p. 1217)
—My Sparkling Nursery Rhymes. (p. 1219)
Hefferan, Rob, illus. see Fontes, Justine.
Hefferan, Rob, illus. see Hajdusiewicz, Babs Bell.
Hefferan, Rob, illus. see Williams, Rozanne Lanczak.
Heffernan, Danielle. Puppy Dog Tales. (p. 1418)
Heffernan, Margaret McKay. Crystal Grove. (p. 387)
Heffernan, Anne Eileen. 57 Stories of Saints. Rizzo, Jerry, illus. (p. 1997)
Heffernan, Colleen. Kind of Courage (p. 957)
Heffernan, Eileen. Fifty-Seven Stories of Saints. Rizzo, Jerry, illus. (p. 585)
Heffernan, John. Horse Called Elvis. (p. 799)
Heffernan, Mary A., jt. text see Gangwer, Rosalie M.
Hefflin, Toby, illus. see Winn, Don M.
Heffick, LaMonte. Story of Big Dog. (p. 1657)
—Story of Boney & Clyde. (p. 1657)
—Story of Ninja Cat. (p. 1659)
Heflin, Jenifer. Puertas Abiertas Kit: Open Doors to Spanish Level 1 (p. 1414)
Heflin, Jenifer, jt. illus. see Thrall, Gordon.
Heflin, Ronald. Caddo Lake. (p. 250)
Hefner, Bobby E. Trial of Billy the Kid. (p. 1785)
Hefner, Elizabeth. Great Laundry Rebellion. (p. 717)
Hefner, Shayna. Delicate Balance. (p. 425)
Hegamin, Tonya Cherie. Willow. (p. 1934)
Hegan, Robin, illus. see Oelschlager, Vanita.
Hegarty, Carol, ed. Teacher's Resource Guide. (p. 1709)
Hegarty, Pat. If I Were a... Ballerina. Pope, Liz & Pope, Kate, illus. (p. 853)
—If I Were a... Firefighter. Pope, Liz & Pope, Kate, illus. (p. 853)
—If I Were a... Princess. Pope, Liz & Pope, Kate, illus. (p. 853)
—If I Were a... Soccer Star. Pope, Liz & Pope, Kate, illus. (p. 853)
Hegarty, Patricia. Five Black Cats. Woolf, Julia, illus. (p. 600)
—Five Busy Elves. Woolf, Julia, illus. (p. 600)
—Five Little Ghosts. Woolf, Julia, illus. (p. 600)
Hegarty, Shane. Legends Begin. (p. 989)
Hege, Evelyn. Letter for Titus. (p. 1002)
Hege, Lynnita. Little Black Hen. Keyes, Tina Misrasi, illus. (p. 1024)
Hegedus, Bethany. Between Us Baxters. (p. 173)
Hegedus, Bethany, jt. auth. see Gandhi, Arun.
Hegel, Claudette. African-American Musicians. (p. 27)
—African-American Musicians. Hill, Marc Lamont, ed. (p. 27)
—Randolph Caldecott: An Illustrated Life. (p. 1438)
—Tigers (p. 1749)
Heger, Bryan. Valor & Virtues from the Mind of a Child (p. 1831)
Heger, Laurel. Professor Lightfoot's Mushroom Expedition: In Search of Woodland Treasures. (p. 1409)
Heger, Siegfried. Gina's Poems: Adventures in Love. (p. 676)
Hegerhorst, Bethany. Baseball Princess: Samantha's Summer & the Unicorn Flu. Abbott, Kristin, illus. (p. 141)
—Soccer Princess: Josephina & the Gown Fashion Runway Show Abbott, Kristin, illus. (p. 1603)
Hegerhorst, Bethany Brady, illus. see Brady, S. Lamar.
Hegg, Tom & Hanson, Warren. Peef & the Baby Sister. Hegg, Tom & Hanson, Warren, illus. (p. 1334)
Heggerty, Michael. Phonemic Awareness: The Skills That They Need to Help Them Succeed! (Kindergarten Version) (p. 1351)
Heggum, Lisa. All Sleek & Skimming Stories (p. 45)
Hegley, John. Stanley's Stick. Layton, Neal, illus. (p. 1640)
Hehenberger, Shelly, illus. see Barchers, Suzanne.
Hehenberger, Shelly, illus. see Beinhard, B. J.
Hehenberger, Shelly, illus. see Lane, Sandra & Miles, Brenda.
Hehenberger, Shelly, illus. see Rubenstein, Lauren.
Hehenberger, Shelly, illus. see Rubenstein, Laurence Z.
Hehir, Tim. Julius & the Watchmaker. (p. 932)
Hehner, Barbara, jt. auth. see Suzuki, David T.
Hei, Pamela Bray Vande. Teacher's Lounge. (p. 1709)
Heibel, Dorothy. Message for a Spy. (p. 1129)
Heiberg, Anette. I Can Count One Two Three. (p. 835)
—I Can See Colors. (p. 836)
—I Can Spot Shapes. (p. 836)
—I Know My Alphabet. (p. 840)
Heible, Bev. Collection of Short Tails. (p. 340)
Heible, Beverly. Christmas Party on River Row. (p. 315)
—River Row: Andrew & Luke Fishing with Grandpa. (p. 1476)
Heichberger, Robert L. Tell Me A Story Grandpa. (p. 1716)
Heid, Karen, illus. see Stagliano, Katie.
Heidari, Mahdi. Little Red Fire. Taylor, Adam, illus. (p. 1034)
Heidbreder, Robert. Black & Bittern Was Night. Gauthier, Manon & Martz, John, illus. (p. 194)
—Crocodiles Play! Mate, Rae, illus. (p. 384)
—Crocodiles Say... Mate, Rae, illus. (p. 384)
—Drumheller Dinosaur Dance. Slavin, Bill et al, illus. (p. 487)
—Lickety-Split. Petricic, Dusan, illus. (p. 1007)
—Sea-Wishing Day. Denton, Kady MacDonald, illus. (p. 1536)
—See Saw Saskatchewan. Ritchie, Scot, illus. (p. 1547)
—Shake Awakes Mongeau, Marc, illus. (p. 1558)
Heide, Florence Parry. How to Be a Hero. Groenink, Chuck, illus. (p. 814)
—Princess Hyacinth. Smith, Lane, illus. (p. 1404)
—Promise Is a Promise. Auth, Tony, illus. (p. 1411)
—Shrinking of Treehorn. (p. 1571)
—Some Things Are Scary. Feiffer, Jules, illus. (p. 1609)
—That's What Friends Are For. Meade, Holly, illus. (p. 1727)
Heide, Florence Parry & Clief, Sylvia Van. That's What Friends Are For. Meade, Holly, illus. (p. 1727)
Heide, Iris van der. Intercambio Magico. De Sterck, Goedele, tr. (p. 879)
Heide, William van der, see van der Heide, William.
Heidecker, Rosemary. Emmie. (p. 520)
Heidecker, Samie. Who's Looking at Whom? Christmas (p. 1920)
Heidell, Valerie. Mirika's Story. (p. 1149)
Heiden, Gina. Zippy, Lolly & Surfer Dude. (p. 1987)
Heiden, Pete. I Luv U 2: Understanding Relationships & Dating. (p. 844)
—Pakistan. (p. 1319)
—Penelope & Pip Build a Prose Poem. Huntington, Amy, illus. (p. 1336)
Heidenreich, Franziska. Crochet for Kids: Basic Techniques & Great Projects That Kids Can Make Themselves (p. 384)
Heiderer, Conrad. Alpha-Blocke: Alpha-Blocke.com Learning Forum Animals, Art & the Alphabet Series with Case & Talking CD. (p. 48)
Heiderstadt, Dorothy. Indian Friends & Foes: A Baker's Dozen Portraits from Pocahontas to Geronimo. Miller, David Humphreys, illus. (p. 871)
Heidhausen, Bud. Sinking Castle. Skinner, Michael, illus. (p. 1579)
Heidrich, Delana. Figuratively Speaking: Using Classic Literature to teach 40 Literary Terms Clark, Kim, ed. (p. 586)
Heidtke, John. Family Golf Adventures on Michigan Links. (p. 568)
—Family Outdoor Journal. (p. 568)
—Hey! Take Me Fishing, Again. (p. 774)
—Summer's Passage on Sutter's Bay. (p. 1675)
Heierbacher, Michael. Yo Ho Ho Merry Christmas. (p. 1971)
Heigh, Stephen. Mr. George & the Red Hat. Burton, Kevin, ed. (p. 1185)
—Snowman in the Moon. Burton, Kevin, ed. (p. 1601)
Height, Ray. Shadowland: Power Man. (p. 1558)
Height, Ray-Anthony, illus. see Girner, Sebastian.
Heighton, Mary Beth & Laskey, Andrew. What I Do When You're Not Home (p. 1886)
Heighway-Bury, Robin, illus. see Hooper, Meredith.
Heij, Kees, jt. auth. see Post, Hans.
Heike, Mark, illus. see Miller, Connie Colwell.
Heikes, Callie. Postcards from Boston with Sela. (p. 1388)
Heiks, James, ed. Alice Parker's Hand Me Down Songs. (p. 39)
Heil, Christopher. Wish Rings: A Second Beginning. (p. 1940)
Heilbron, J. L. Ernest Rutherford: And the Explosion of Atoms. (p. 533)
Heilbroner, Joan. Pet Named Sneaker. Lemaitre, Pascal, illus. (p. 1345)
Heiligman, Deborah. Boy Who Loved Math: The Improbable Life of Paul Erdős. Pham, LeUyen, illus. (p. 219)
—Celebrate Christmas: With Carols, Presents, & Peace. (p. 283)
—Celebrate Diwali: With Sweets, Lights, & Fireworks. (p. 283)
—Celebrate Easter: With Colored Eggs, Flowers, & Prayer. (p. 283)
—Celebrate Halloween: With Pumpkins, Costumes, & Candy. (p. 283)
—Celebrate Hanukkah: With Light, Latkes, & Dreidels. (p. 283)
—Celebrate Independence Day: With Parades, Picnics, & Fireworks. (p. 283)
—Celebrate Passover: With Matzah, Maror, & Memories. (p. 284)
—Celebrate Ramadan & Eid Al-Fitr: With Praying, Fasting, & Charity. (p. 284)
—Celebrate Rosh Hashanah & Yom Kippur: With Honey, Prayers, & the Shofar. (p. 284)
—Celebrate Thanksgiving: With Turkey, Family, & Counting Blessings. (p. 284)
—Celebremos la Navidad: Con Villancicos, Regalos y Paz. (p. 285)
—Charles & Emma: The Darwins' Leap of Faith. (p. 291)
—Cool Dog, School Dog (p. 363)
—From Caterpillar to Butterfly. Weissman, Bari, illus. (p. 642)
—From Caterpillar to Butterfly Big Book. Weissman, Bari, illus. (p. 642)
—Fun Dog, Sun Dog Bowers, Tim, illus. (p. 647)
—High Hopes: A Photobiography of John F. Kennedy. Feresten, Nancy, ed. (p. 777)
—Honeybees. Golembe, Carla, illus. (p. 794)
—Intentions. (p. 879)
—Snow Dog, Go Dog Bowers, Tim, illus. (p. 1599)
Heiligman, Deborah & Dennis, Matthew. Celebrate Independence Day: With Parades, Picnics, & Fireworks. (p. 283)
Heiligman, Deborah & U. S. National Geographic Society Staff. Celebrate Halloween. (p. 283)
Heiligman, Deborah & Yavari, Neguin. Celebrate Ramadan & Eid Al-Fitr. (p. 284)
Heilman, Carl, II, illus. see Weber, Sandra.
Heim, Barbara. Hudson Beavers & the New Neighbourhood. (p. 824)
—Hudson Beavers Build a Lodge. (p. 824)
Heim, Josephine. Through the Eyes of a Child. (p. 1745)
Heim, Julia & Dami, Elisabetta. Little Book of Happiness. Bluecheese, Wally, illus. (p. 1025)
Heim, Robert. Squeaking Earl. (p. 1636)
Heiman, Diane, jt. auth. see Suneby, Liz.
Heiman, Diane & Suneby, Elizabeth. Origami Fortune Tellers. Archer, Christine, illus. (p. 1304)
Heiman, Diane & Suneby, Liz. See What You Can Be: Explore Careers That Could Be for You! Wood, Tracey, illus. (p. 1547)
—That's a Mitzvah. Molk, Laurel, illus. (p. 1726)
Heiman, Herb. Running on Dreams. (p. 1497)
Heiman, Laura. My Favorite Michael. Keen, Sophie, illus. (p. 1203)
Heimann, Rolf. Brain Busting Bonanza. Heimann, Rolf, illus. (p. 221)
—Dinomazia. (p. 441)
—Dragonmazia. (p. 478)
—Life's Like a Crocodile. Heimann, Rolf, illus. (p. 1013)
—Puzzle Mazia. Heimann, Rolf, illus. (p. 1421)
Heimberg, Justin. Spirit Glass: A Book of Magically Hidden Images. (p. 1628)
Heimberg, Justin, ed. see Balestier, Courtney.
Heimberg, Justin, jt. auth. see Borgenicht, David.
Heimberg, Justin & Gomberg, David. Doubly Disgusting: Over 300 All New Crazy Questions Plus Extra Pages to Make up Your Own! (p. 473)
—Extra Extremely Extreme: Over 1,200 Positively Preposterous Dilemmas to Ponder. (p. 555)
—Gross Out: Over 300 Crazy Questions Plus Extra Pages to Make up Your Own! (p. 725)
—Radically Repulsive: Over 400 Crazy Questions! (p. 1432)
—Would You Rather... ? for Kids! (p. 1962)
—Would You Rather... ? Terrifically Twisted: Over 300 Crazy Questions! (p. 1962)
—Would You Rather... ? Wonderfully Weird: Over 400 Crazy Questions! (p. 1962)
Heimberg, Justin & Gomberg, David, eds. Would You Rather... ? BFF: Over 300 Fiercely Fascinating Questions to Ask Your Friends. (p. 1962)
—Would You Rather... ? LOL: Over 300 Intensely Intriguing Questions to Ask Your Friends. (p. 1962)
Heimbuch, Carol. Shadow Stallion. (p. 1558)
Heimbuch, Carol Jo. Condor Caper. Martin, Fred, illus. (p. 356)
—Twilight Tracks. (p. 1801)
Heimdallson, Freydis, et al. Kindertales: Stories Old & New for the Children of the Folk. (p. 957)
Heimerdinger, Chris. Drums of Desolation: A Novel. (p. 487)
—Escape from Zarahemla. (p. 535)
—Kingdoms & Conquerors: A Novel. (p. 960)
—Tower of Thunder: A Novel. Vol. 9 (p. 1773)
—Warriors of Cumorah (p. 1859)
Heimerl, Caitlin, illus. see Danneberg, Julie & Monet, Claude.
Heimerl, Caitlin, illus. see Danneberg, Julie.
Heimlich, C. Thomas the Autonomous Hippopotamus. (p. 1739)
Heims, Freya, ed. see Keene, Michael.
Heims, Neil. Allen Ginsburg. (p. 46)
—J. R. R. Tolkien. (p. 902)
—Reading Johnny Tremain. (p. 1446)
—Reading the Adventures of Tom Sawyer. (p. 1446)
—Reading the Diary of Anne Frank. (p. 1446)
—Tortured Noble: The Story of Leo Tolstoy. (p. 1771)
Heims, Neil, ed. see Shakespeare, William.
Heims, Neil, jt. ed. see Bloom, Harold.
Hein. Instructor's Manual & Test Bank to Accompany Foundations of College Chemistry 11e & Alternate 11editions. (p. 878)
Hein, Connie L. Toliver in Time: For a Fourth of July Celebration. Theobald, Denise, illus. (p. 1762)
—Toliver in Time; for a Journey West: History in a Nutshell. Theobald, Denise, illus. (p. 1762)
Hein, Eckhard, et al. Wages, Employment, Distribution & Growth: International Perspectives. (p. 1852)
Hein, Jessica, et al, eds. GirlSpoken: From Pen, Brush & Tongue (p. 681)
Hein, Joy Fisher, illus. see Appelt, Kathi.
Hein, Joy Fisher, illus. see Colburn, Cherie Foster.
Hein, Joy Fisher, illus. see Wade, Mary Dodson.
Hein, Marilyn B. Math Phonics Pre-Algebra. Wheeler, Ron, illus. (p. 1107)
—Math Phonics(tm) Pre-Geometry. (p. 1107)
Hein, Michelle & Skindzier, Jon. Muhlenberg College College Prowler off the Record. (p. 1189)
Hein, Simeon. Planetary Intelligence: 101 Easy Steps to Energy, Well-Being, & Natural Light. Liss, Ira & Sorensen, Peter, illus. (p. 1368)
Heinberg, Allan. Who Is Wonder Woman? (p. 1916)
Heinberg, Allan, jt. auth. see Johns, Geoff.
Heine, Florian. 13 Architects Children Should Know. (p. 1994)
—13 Art Inventions Children Should Know. (p. 1994)
—13 Painters Children Should Know. (p. 1995)
—Impressionism: 13 Artists Children Should Know. (p. 862)
Heine, Helme. Abenteurer. (p. 4)
—Cuentas de Elefante. (p. 389)
—Maravilloso Viaje a Traves de la Noche. (p. 1091)
—Ricardo. Heine, Helme, illus. (p. 1469)
—Trois Amis. (p. 1788)
—Wunderbare Reise Durch Die Na. (p. 1966)
Heine, Laura & Tomko, Karen. Rodney the Repo Reindeer: A Cautionary Tale to Be Shared after Christmas. (p. 1484)
Heine, Patricke, jt. auth. see Heine, Patricke Johns.
Heine, Patricke Johns & Heine, Patricke. Personality in Social Theory. (p. 1344)
Heine, Teresa & Heine, Theresa. Elephant Dance: Memories of India. Moxley, Sheila, illus. (p. 511)
Heine, Theresa. Baile del Elefante: Recuerdos de la India. Moxley, Sheila, illus. (p. 132)
—Elephant Dance: A Journey to India. Moxley, Sheila, illus. (p. 511)
Heine, Theresa, jt. auth. see Heine, Teresa.
Heine, Theresa & Barefoot Books Staff. Chandra's Magic Light: A Story in Nepal. Gueyfier, Judith, illus. (p. 289)
—Chandra's Magic Light. Gueyfier, Judith, illus. (p. 289)

H

Heine, Theresa & Tavares, Victor. Star Seeker: A Journey to Outer Space. Tavares, Victor, illus. (p. 1641)
Heinecke, Liz Lee. Kitchen Science Lab for Kids: 52 Family Friendly Experiments from the Pantry. (p. 962)
Heinemann Educational Ltd. Publishing Staff. Minibeasts Up Close Package. (p. 1145)
—True Crime Package 6-Pack. (p. 1792)
—Wild Side of Pets Package. (p. 1930)
Heinemann Library, jt. auth. see Fitzgerald, Stephanie.
Heinemann Library Staff. Culture in Action (p. 391)
—Sci-Hi: Earth & Space Science Set (p. 1524)
Heinemann Library Staff, jt. auth. see Ansary, Mir Tamim.
Heinemann Library Staff, jt. auth. see Ballard, Carol.
Heinemann Library Staff, jt. auth. see Barraclough, Sue.
Heinemann Library Staff, jt. auth. see Claybourne, Anna.
Heinemann Library Staff, jt. auth. see Cregan, Elizabeth R.
Heinemann Library Staff, jt. auth. see Cribben, Patrick.
Heinemann Library Staff, jt. auth. see Davis, Barbara J.
Heinemann Library Staff, jt. auth. see Feinstein, Stephen.
Heinemann Library Staff, jt. auth. see Galko, Francine.
Heinemann Library Staff, jt. auth. see Ganeri, Anita.
Heinemann Library Staff, jt. auth. see Giesecke, Ernestine.
Heinemann Library Staff, jt. auth. see Guillain, Charlotte.
Heinemann Library Staff, jt. auth. see Hermann, Spring.
Heinemann Library Staff, jt. auth. see Herr, Melody.
Heinemann Library Staff, jt. auth. see Hurley, Michael.
Heinemann Library Staff, jt. auth. see Latham, Donna.
Heinemann Library Staff, jt. auth. see Mason, Paul.
Heinemann Library Staff, jt. auth. see Miles, Liz.
Heinemann Library Staff, jt. auth. see Morris, Neil.
Heinemann Library Staff, jt. auth. see Oxlade, Chris.
Heinemann Library Staff, jt. auth. see Parker, Steve.
Heinemann Library Staff, jt. auth. see Parker, Vic.
Heinemann Library Staff, jt. auth. see Penrose, Jane.
Heinemann Library Staff, jt. auth. see Rand, Casey.
Heinemann Library Staff, jt. auth. see Raum, Elizabeth.
Heinemann Library Staff, jt. auth. see Royston, Angela.
Heinemann Library Staff, jt. auth. see Schonberg, Marcia.
Heinemann Library Staff, jt. auth. see Shannon, Sarah.
Heinemann Library Staff, jt. auth. see Smith, Sian.
Heinemann Library Staff, jt. auth. see Snedden, Robert.
Heinemann Library Staff, jt. auth. see Solway, Andrew.
Heinemann Library Staff, jt. auth. see Spilsbury, Louise.
Heinemann Library Staff, jt. auth. see Stewart, Mark.
Heinemann Library Staff, jt. auth. see Stewart, Melissa.
Heinemann Library Staff, jt. auth. see Tagliaferro, Linda.
Heinemann Library Staff, jt. auth. see Whitehouse, Patricia.
Heinemann Library Staff, jt. auth. see Williams, Brian.
Heinemann Library Staff & Harris, Nathaniel. Great Depression. (p. 715)
Heinemann Library Staff & Schaefer, A. R. Exercise (p. 548)
—Healthy Food (p. 758)
—Staying Healthy (p. 1645)
Heinemann Staff. Ethiopia. (p. 539)
Heinen, Sandy, illus. see Sanford, Agnes.
Heinerke, Kristina, jt. auth. see Telles, Cecilia R.
Heiney, Sue P. Zig the Pig Goes to School. Charles, Akins, illus. (p. 1986)
Heinlein, Robert A. Sixth Column. (p. 1583)
—Time for the Stars. (p. 1752)
Heinlein, Stuart. Century Dragon: The Beginning. (p. 287)
—Century Dragon: The Second Battle. (p. 287)
Heinlen, Marieka, illus. see Agassi, Martine & Verdick, Elizabeth.
Heinlen, Marieka, illus. see Agassi, Martine, et al.
Heinlen, Marieka, illus. see Agassi, Martine.
Heinlen, Marieka, illus. see Verdick, Elizabeth & Agassi, Martine.
Heinlen, Marieka, illus. see Verdick, Elizabeth.
Heinlen, Marieka, jt. auth. see Verdick, Elizabeth.
Heinrich, Christian, illus. see Le Normand, Bruno.
Heinrich, Erik. Survival Debate: A Rip-Roaring Game of Either-Or Questions. (p. 1686)
—This or That Survival Debate: A Rip-Roaring Game of Either/or Questions. (p. 1737)
—This or That Survival Debate: A Rip-Roaring Game of Either - Or Questions. (p. 1737)
Heinrich, Erik, et al. This or That? (p. 1737)
Heinrich, Julie. Bob White & Whippoorwill. (p. 205)
Heinrich, Tyson. Where Is My Honey? (p. 1908)
Heinrichs, Ann. Amazon Rain Forest. (p. 56)
—Aztecs. (p. 122)
—Barber. (p. 137)
—Brazil. (p. 224)
—Chinese New Year. Huang, Benrei, illus. (p. 307)
—Cinco de Mayo. Petelinsek, Kathleen, illus. (p. 319)
—Conjunctions. McGeehan, Dan & Moore, David, illus. (p. 357)
—Continents. (p. 360)
—Delaware (Revised Edition) (p. 424)
—Dust Bowl (p. 490)
—Egypt. (p. 506)
—Father's Day. Alley, illus. (p. 577)
—Fire Investigator. (p. 590)
—Forensic Psychologist. (p. 617)
—Great Recession. (p. 718)
—Greece. (p. 720)
—Halloween. Weidner, Teri, illus. (p. 737)
—Independence Day. Squier, Robert, illus. (p. 870)
—Interjections. McGeehan, Dan & Moore, David, illus. (p. 880)
—Islands. (p. 892)
—Jamaica. (p. 906)
—Japanese-American Internment: Innocence, Guilt, & Wartime Justice. (p. 909)
—Luxembourg. (p. 1066)
—Maine. (p. 1077)
—Minnesota (Revised Edition) (p. 1147)
—Mother's Day. Alley, illus. (p. 1178)
—Mount Everest. (p. 1180)
—Nanotechnologist. (p. 1229)
—Nebraska. (p. 1239)
—Netherlands. (p. 1242)
—Nevada. (p. 1242)
—Nigeria. (p. 1252)
—Nile River. (p. 1255)
—North Carolina. (p. 1264)
—Nouns. McGeehan, Dan & Moore, David, Jr., illus. (p. 1268)
—Oceans. (p. 1277)
—Patrick Henry: Orator & Patriot. (p. 1329)
—Prefixes & Suffixes. McGeehan, Dan & Moore, David, Jr., illus. (p. 1395)
—Printing Press. (p. 1407)
—Pronouns. McGeehan, Dan & Moore, David, illus. (p. 1411)
—Sahara Desert. (p. 1503)
—Samuel Adams: Father of the Revolution. (p. 1509)
—Shipbuilder. (p. 1567)
—Shoemaker. (p. 1568)
—St. Patrick's Day. Snyder, Joel, illus. (p. 1638)
—Storm Chaser. (p. 1655)
—Sustaining Earth's Energy Resources. (p. 1688)
—Sweden. (p. 1689)
—Thanksgiving. Jordan, Charles, illus. (p. 1725)
—Verbs. McGeehan, Dan & Moore, David, illus. (p. 1836)
—Vermont (Revised Edition) (p. 1837)
—Voices of World War I: Stories from the Trenches (p. 1848)
—Wales. (p. 1853)
—We the People - Civil War Era (p. 1868)
—West Virginia (Revised Edition) (p. 1876)
Heinrichs, Ann & Burgan, Michael. Henry Clay: The Great Compromiser. (p. 767)
—John Paul Jones. (p. 922)
Heinrichs, Ann & Compass Point Books Staff. Surrender of Cornwallis (p. 1686)
Heinrichs, Ann & Heinrichs, Anne. Ethiopia. (p. 539)
Heinrichs, Anne, jt. auth. see Heinrichs, Ann.
Heinrichs, Cynthia. Mermaids. Lee, Jumin, illus. (p. 1128)
Heinrichs, Jane, illus. see Miles, Brenda & Patterson, Colleen A.
Heins, Tanya, illus. see Dharkar, Anuja & Tapley, Scott.
Heinst, Marie. My First Number Book. (p. 1207)
—My First Number Book. Scholastic, Inc. Staff, ed. (p. 1207)
Heintzelman, Greta & Smith Howard, Alycia. Tennessee Williams A to Z: The Essential Reference to His Life & Work. (p. 1720)
Heinz, Brian. Butternut Hollow Pond. Marstall, Bob, illus. (p. 248)
—Mocha Dick: The Legend & the Fury. Enos, Randall, illus. (p. 1157)
—Wolves. Fuchs, Bernie, illus. (p. 1944)
Heinz, Brian J. Barnyard Cat. (p. 139)
—Cheyenne Medicine Hat. Manchess, Gregory, illus. (p. 299)
—Coming of Winter in the Adirondacks. Healy, Maggie, illus. (p. 348)
—Kayuktuk: An Arctic Quest. Van Zyle, Jon, illus. (p. 946)
—Nanuk, Lord of the Ice. Manchess, Gregory, illus. (p. 1229)
—Nathan of Yesteryear & Michael of Today. Friar, Joanne, illus. (p. 1231)
—Red Fox at McCloskey's Farm. Sheban, Chris, illus. (p. 1454)
Heinz, R. M. Bunny Is Born. (p. 242)
Heinz, Renata Perpetua. Nail's Life. (p. 1228)
Heinze, Monica Bacon. Day with Shapes. Dow, S. B., illus. (p. 415)
Heinzen, Kory S., illus. see Lorbiecki, Marybeth.
Heiser, Aline, illus. see Brewer, Michael.
Heiser, Aline, illus. see Cory, Diane.
Heiser, Aline, illus. see Klammer, Lynn.
Heiser, Aline, illus. see Totilo, Rebecca Park.
Heiser, Aline L., illus. see Patrick, Patsy S.
Heiser, Jorg, jt. contrib. by see Siegel, Katy.
Heishman, Rebecca. Misadventures of Millie. (p. 1150)
Heisinger, Denise. Adventures on the Farm. Schleich, Mary B., illus. (p. 25)
Heisler, H. T. A. Innkeeper's Daughter: A Christmas Story & Music Score. (p. 875)
Heiss, Renee. Ducklings in a Row. (p. 488)
Heiss, Renée. Feng Shui for the Classroom: 101 Easy-to-Use Ideas. (p. 581)
—Helping Kids Help: Organizing Successful Charitable Projects. (p. 766)
Heiss, Renee. Somebody Cares! (p. 1609)
Heiss, Rolland L. Tapestries: A Play in One ACT. (p. 1705)
Heit Schwaeber, Barbie. Alphabet of Dogs. (p. 49)
—Bailey & the Beagle Brigade. Neidigh, Sherry, illus. (p. 133)
Heiter, Celeste. Costumes of Asia: A Connoisseur's Coloring Book. Pulido, Rene, illus. (p. 368)
—Fashion Asia: Patterns & Designs of Traditional Cultures. Pulido, Rene, illus. (p. 575)
Heitritter, Laura. I Love You Just Because. Villim, Jim, illus. (p. 843)
Heits, Rudolph T. Ben Roethlisberger. (p. 163)
—Ben Rothlisberger. (p. 163)
—Communism. Colton, Timothy J., ed. (p. 349)
—DeMarcus Ware. (p. 425)
—Jason Witten. (p. 910)
—Mass Murderers. (p. 1102)
Heitz, Bruce. Historia Fantastica. (p. 782)
Heitz, Tim, illus. see Oliver, Lin & Winkler, Henry.
Heitz, Tim, illus. see Wallace, Rich.
Heitz, Tim, illus. see Winkler, Henry & Oliver, Lin.
Heitzmann, Connie & Koch, Janie. Gulf Coast Memory Scrapbook: A Pictorial Journey of Hope & Healing. (p. 731)
Heitzmann, William Ray. Opportunities in Sports & Fitness Careers. (p. 1300)
Helakoski, Leslie. Big Chickens. Cole, Henry, illus. (p. 180)
—Big Chickens Fly the Coop. Cole, Henry, illus. (p. 180)
—Big Chickens Go to Town. Cole, Henry, illus. (p. 180)
—Big Pigs. Helakoski, Leslie, illus. (p. 183)
—Doggone Feet! Helakoski, Leslie, illus. (p. 462)
—Fair Cow (p. 562)
—Woolbur. (p. 1950)
—Woolbur. Harper, Lee, illus. (p. 1950)
Helbig-Miller, Theresa. Benny the Raccoon (p. 165)
—Nana & the Jabbywalker Evans, Sherri, illus. (p. 1228)
Helbrough, Emma. 1001 Bugs to Spot. (p. 2001)
—1001 Bugs to Spot. Gower, Teri, illus. (p. 2002)
—Bears. Kushii, Tetsuo & Larkum, Adam, illus. (p. 151)
—Book of Knowledge. (p. 211)
—Day in the Life of a Native American. (p. 413)
—Day in the Life of a Native American. Firenze, Inklink, illus. (p. 413)
—Day in the Life of a Pharaoh. (p. 413)
—Day in the Life of a Pirate. (p. 413)
—Day in the Life of a Pirate. Firenze, Inklink, illus. (p. 413)
—Dogs. Donaera, Patrizia & Mayer, Uwe, illus. (p. 462)
—Great Planet Earth Search. Jackson, Ian, illus. (p. 717)
—Great Planet Earth Search. Milbourne, Anna, ed. (p. 717)
—How Flowers Grow. (p. 809)
—How Flowers Grow. Silver, Maggie & Mayer, Uwe, illus. (p. 809)
—Usborne Internet-Linked Book of Knowledge. (p. 1827)
Helbrough, Emma, jt. auth. see Turnbull, Stephanie.
Helbrough, Emma & Brooks, Felicity. First Picture Trucks. Van Wyk, Hanri & Newell, Keith, illus. (p. 596)
Helbrough, Emma, retold by. Nutcracker. (p. 1273)
Held, George. Neighbors: The Yard Critters Too. Kim, Joung Un, illus. (p. 1240)
—Phased: Poems, Etc. Held, Jean, photos by. (p. 1350)
Held, Jean, photos by see Held, George.
Heldring, Thatcher. Roy Morelli Steps up to the Plate. (p. 1492)
—Toby Wheeler: Eighth Grade Benchwarmer. (p. 1760)
Hele, Bonita Jewel. Adventures That Lead to Home. Butler, Lisa, illus. (p. 25)
Helean, April K. Love Can Build a Bridge. (p. 1059)
Helemano, Butch. Sleeping Giant of Waimea. (p. 1589)
Helen, Grace. Ms. Marpol Always Says: (Small Experiences) (p. 1188)
—Santa's Way. (p. 1513)
—Vicky Sticky Lips: Putting Others to the Test. (p. 1840)
Helenek, Sophie. My First Book FRUITS: GOLD Mom's Choice Awards. (p. 1205)
—My First Book MUSICAL INSTRUMENTS: GOLD Mom's Choice Awards Recipient. (p. 1205)
—My First Book SHAPES: GOLD Mom's Choice Awards Recipient. (p. 1206)
—My First Book SKY WONDERS: BOOK of the YEAR 2014 for Babies & Toddlers Category by Creative Child Magazine. (p. 1206)
Helenthal, Janet. Helen Keller. (p. 762)
Heler, Shraga, illus. see Halevy, Hanita H.
Helfand, Lewis. 400 BC: The Story of the Ten Thousand. Singh, Lalit Kumar, illus. (p. 2001)
—Abraham Lincoln: From the Log Cabin to the White House - Campfire Heroes Line. Jones, K. L. & Manikandan, illus. (p. 6)
—Conquering Everest: The Lives of Edmund Hillary & Tenzing Norgay. Tayal, Amit, illus. (p. 358)
—Mother Teresa: Saint of the Slums. Banerjee, Sankha & Nagar, Sachin, illus. (p. 1178)
—Muhammad Ali: The King of the Ring. Sharma, Lalit Kumar, illus. (p. 1189)
—Photo Booth. Nagar, Sachin, illus. (p. 1352)
—They Changed the World: Bell, Edison & Tesla. Kumar, Naresh, illus. (p. 1732)
—Wright Brothers. Banerjee, Sankha, illus. (p. 1963)
Helfand, Lewis & Teitelbaum, Michael. Martin Luther King. Banerjee, Sankha, illus. (p. 1097)
Helfenbein, DeWayne. Treasure Hunt. (p. 1781)
Helfer, Ralph. World's Greatest Elephant. Lewin, Ted, illus. (p. 1960)
Helfinstine, Robert F. & Roth, Jerry D. Texas Tracks & Artifacts: Do Texas Fossils Indicate Coexistence of Man & Dinosaurs? (p. 1724)
Helft, Claude. Dulces Suenos, Teddy! (p. 489)
Helgerson, Joseph. Crows & Cards. (p. 386)
—Horns & Wrinkles. Ceccoli, Nicoletta, illus. (p. 798)
Helgesen, Marian C. Claudia's Magic Cupboard. (p. 329)
—Oscar Owl's Cottage. (p. 1305)
Helget, Nicole. Beetles. (p. 158)
—Cochroaches. (p. 337)
—Dragonflies. (p. 478)
—Fireflies. (p. 592)
—Moths. (p. 1179)
—Snow. (p. 1598)
—Wonder at the Edge of the World. (p. 1947)
Helget, Nicole Lea. Barbarians. (p. 137)
—Giraffes. (p. 677)
—Mongols. (p. 1164)
—Swans. (p. 1689)
Helgren. People, Places & Change: The Western World. (p. 1339)
—People, Places & Change: The Eastern Hemisphere. (p. 1339)
—People, Places & Change: Online Edition Plus. (p. 1339)
Helgren, David M. People, Places & Change: Enhanced Online Edition. (p. 1339)
—World Geography Today: Online Edition. (p. 1955)
Helguera, Luis Ignacio. Gracias a Johannes. Morales, Judith, illus. (p. 705)
Heliadore. Animals at Night. Heliadore, illus. (p. 82)
—Butterfly. Heliadore, illus. (p. 247)
Heliadore, illus. see Jeunesse, Gallimard & Delafosse, Claude.
Héliadore & Joly, Dominique. Mountains. (p. 1181)
Héliadore, et al. Butterfly. (p. 247)
—Let's Look at Animals by Night. (p. 998)
Helidoniotis, Kathy. Horse Mad Academy (p. 799)
—Horse Mad Academy. (p. 799)
—Horse Mad Heights (p. 799)
—Horse Mad Heroes (p. 799)
—Horse Mad Heroes. (p. 799)
—Horse Mad Summer (p. 799)
—Horse Mad Summer. (p. 799)
—Horse Mad Western (p. 799)
—Horse Mad Western. (p. 799)
—Horse Mad Whispers (p. 799)
—Totally Horse Mad. (p. 1771)
Heling, Kathryn. Clothesline Clues to Jobs People Do. (p. 334)
Heling, Kathryn & Hembrook, Deborah. Clothesline Clues to Jobs People Do. Davies, Andy Robert, illus. (p. 334)
—Clothesline Clues to Sports People Play. Davies, Andy Robert, illus. (p. 334)
—I Wish I Had Freckles Like Abby. Adamson, Bonnie, illus. (p. 848)
—I Wish I Had Freckles Like Abby/Quisiera Tener Pecas Como Abby. Adamson, Bonnie, illus. (p. 848)
—I Wish I Had Glasses Like Rosa. Adamson, Bonnie, illus. (p. 848)
—I Wish I Had Glasses Like Rosa/Quisiera Tener Lentes Como Rosa. de La Vega, Eida, tr. (p. 848)
—I Wish I Was Strong Like Manuel. Adamson, Bonnie, illus. (p. 849)
—I Wish I Was Strong Like Manuel/Quisiera Ser Fuerte Como Manuel. Adamson, Bonnie, illus. (p. 849)
—I Wish I Was Tall Like Willie. Adamson, Bonnie, illus. (p. 849)
—I Wish I Was Tall Like Willie/Quisiera Ser Tan Alto Como Willie. Adamson, Bonnie, illus. (p. 849)
—Mouse's Hide-and-Seek Words. Joseph, Patrick, illus. (p. 1182)
—Ten Grouchy Groundhogs. Johnson, Jay, illus. (p. 1718)
—Ten Lucky Leprechauns. (p. 1719)
—Ten Lucky Leprechauns. Johnson, Jay, illus. (p. 1719)
Heling, Kathryn, et al. I Wish I Had Freckles Like Abby/Quisiera Tener Pecas Como Abby. de La Vega, Eida, tr. (p. 848)
Heliot, Éric, illus. see Cali, Davide.
Helixon, Tracy Schuldt. Little Isaac's Big Adventure. Foster, Jack, illus. (p. 1029)
Helland, L. HellandBack Kids: Be Careful What You Wish For. (p. 763)
Hellard, Bernadette, jt. auth. see Gibbs, Lisa.
Hellard, Sue, illus. see Bradman, Tony.
Hellard, Sue, illus. see Kingfisher, Rupert.
Hellard, Sue, illus. see Lum, Kate.
Hellard, Sue, illus. see McAllister, Angela & Hooper, Mary.
Hellard, Susan, illus. see Bradman, Tony.
Hellard, Susan, illus. see Crebbin, June.
Hellard, Susan, illus. see Dale, Jenny.
Hellard, Susan, illus. see Harrison, Troon.
Hellard, Susan, illus. see Mooney, Bel.
Hellberg, Joanne S. Alv. Hellberg, Kristian & Hellberg, Madalyn, illus. (p. 51)
—Soltee's Indian. (p. 1608)
—Thomas S Tucker & the Silver Buckle. (p. 1739)
Hellberg, Kristian, illus. see Hellberg, Joanne S.
Hellberg, Madalyn, illus. see Hellberg, Joanne S.
Helldorfer, M. C. Anne of Green Gables. Beier, Ellen, illus. (p. 86)
—Cabbage Rose. Downing, Julie, illus. (p. 250)
—Daniel's Gift. (p. 405)
Helle, Lucy, illus. see Williams, Rozanne Lanczak.
Hellen, N. Touch & Peek with Teddy & Me. (p. 1772)
Hellen, Nancy. My Magic House. (p. 1213)
—Visit to the Farm: Pop-up. Hellen, Nancy, illus. (p. 1845)
Heller, Alyson. Let's Go Skating! Björkman, Steve, illus. (p. 997)
—Raggedy Ann's Beach Bag. Thomas, Laura, illus. (p. 1433)
—Soccer Day. Björkman, Steve, illus. (p. 1603)
—Time for T-Ball. Björkman, Steve, illus. (p. 1751)
—Touchdown! Björkman, Steve, illus. (p. 1772)
Heller, Andrew. Fine Mess. (p. 589)
—No Bones about It. Rene, Perez, illus. (p. 1257)
Heller Budnick, Stacy, illus. see Dyer, Wayne W.
Heller, D. M. Let's Make a Bike with Everyday Materials. (p. 999)
—Let's Make a Dump Truck with Everyday Materials. (p. 999)
—Let's Make a Fish with Everyday Materials. (p. 999)
—Let's Make a Lion with Everyday Materials. (p. 999)
—Let's Make a Monkey with Everyday Materials. (p. 999)
—Let's Make an Owl with Everyday Materials. (p. 999)
Heller, Dana, ed. Selling Of 9/11: How a National Tragedy Became a Commodity. (p. 1550)
Heller, Daryl. Hannukah. (p. 743)
—Hanukkah / Jánuca. (p. 744)
—Hanukkah/Januca. (p. 744)
—Kwanzaa. (p. 968)
—Kwanzaa. Gonzalez, Tomas, tr. from ENG. (p. 968)
—Kwanzaa / Kwanzaa. (p. 969)
Heller, Donna & Payne, James. Enchanted Tree. Zamboni, David, illus. (p. 523)
Heller, Elaine. Half 'n Half Animals A1: Think, Draw, & Color. (p. 736)
Heller, Esther Susan. Menorah under the Sea. (p. 1126)
Heller, Janet Ruth. How the Moon Regained Her Shape Hodson, Ben, illus. (p. 813)
Heller, Joseph & Henkin, William A. Bodywise: An Introduction to Hellerwork for Regaining Flexibility & Well-Being. (p. 207)
Heller, Julek, illus. see Delaney, Joseph.
Heller Korin, Ellen S. Asperger Syndrome an Owner's Manual: What You, Your Parents & Your Teachers Need to Know. (p. 107)
Heller, Linda. Castle on Hester Street. Kulikov, Boris, illus. (p. 277)
—How Dalia Put a Big Yellow Comforter Inside a Tiny Blue Box: And Other Wonders of Tzedakah. McQueen, Stacey Dressen, illus. (p. 806)
Heller, Lora. Sign Language ABC. (p. 1574)
—Sign Language for Kids: A Fun & Easy Guide to American Sign Language. (p. 1574)
Heller, Marcy. Loco Dog & the Dust Devil in the Railyard. Poes, Nancy, illus. (p. 1045)
—Loco Dog in the Santa Fe Rail Yard (p. 1045)
Heller, Maryellen. My Big Sister's First Day of School. Soman, David, illus. (p. 1197)
—My Favorite Place. Friar, Joanne, illus. (p. 1203)
Heller, Michael. Exigent Futures: New & Selected Poems. (p. 548)
—Uncertain Poetries: Selected Essays on Poets, Poetry & Poetics. (p. 1811)
Heller, Pete. Peppy Learns to Play Baseball. Kinsey, Thomas D., ed. (p. 1340)
Heller, Ruth. Animals Born Alive & Well. (p. 82)
—Chickens Aren't the Only Ones. (p. 300)
—Feathers. (p. 579)
—Galapagos Means Tortoises. Heller, Ruth, illus. (p. 653)
—Motivo de una Flor (Reason for a Flower) (p. 1179)

—Nous Ne Sommes Pas Nes/Oeuf! (p. 1268)
—Reason for a Flower. (p. 1450)
—Sea Life. Heller, Ruth, illus. (p. 1534)
—Sea within a Sea: Secrets of the Sargasso. Heller, Ruth, illus. (p. 1536)
—Spring Has Sprung. (p. 1635)
—Wildflowers. (p. 1931)
Heller, Ruth, illus. see Merriam-Webster, Inc. Staff.
Heller, Ruth, illus. see Renberg, Dalia Hardof.
Heller, Sarah. Tinker Bell My Music MP3 Player: Storybook & Personal Music Player. (p. 1755)
Heller, Sarah & Reader's Digest Staff. Disney Fairies Music Player. (p. 451)
Heller, Silvia. Woodman's Rose. (p. 1949)
Heller, Steven. Merz to Emigre & Beyond: Progressive Magazine Design of the Twentieth Century. (p. 1129)
Heller, Tania. Eating Disorders: A Handbook for Teens, Families & Teachers. (p. 501)
Hell-Höflinger, Philippa. My First Coloring Dictionary from a to Z. (p. 1206)
Hellier, Catherine. Baby's Friends. Ferri, Francesca, illus. (p. 129)
—Baby's World of Colors. Ferri, Francesca, illus. (p. 129)
Hellier, Lorraine. Wayward Wagon. (p. 1865)
Hellier, Scott, illus. see Lambert, Kate.
Helling, Paxton L. Head over Blue Heal: The Story of Rita Rumble. (p. 756)
Hellings, Collete & Jacobs, Nadine. Bebe Caido del Cielo. Jacobs, Nadine, illus. (p. 155)
Hellisen, Cat. Beastkeeper. (p. 152)
Helliwell, Sheila. Gammy. Hawthorn, Paul & Hopkins, Simon, illus. (p. 655)
—Hoonraki Moon: The Murphy Stories. (p. 795)
Hellman, Charles. Adventures in Sportsand - the Baseball Bully (with accompanying CD) The Baseball Bully. Tiritilli, Robert, illus. (p. 15)
—Adventures in SportsLand - the Basketball Bully (with accompanying CD) Tiritilli, Robert, illus. (p. 15)
—Adventures in SportsLand - the Football Bully (with accompanying CD) Tiritilli, Robert, illus. (p. 15)
—Adventures in SportsLand - the Soccer Bully (with accompanying CD) Tiritilli, Robert, illus. (p. 15)
—Fun Is... (p. 648)
Hellman, Charles & Tiritilli, Robert. Beisbol Humor. (p. 161)
—Futbol Humor. (p. 651)
—Golf Humor. (p. 696)
—Tennis Humor. (p. 1720)
Hellman, Charles S. Baseball Bully. Tiritilli, Robert A., illus. (p. 141)
—Baseball Challenge: Defenders of Sportsland. Tiritilli, Robert A., illus. (p. 141)
—Bogie: Golf... As It Was. (p. 207)
—Discovering Sportsland. Tiritilli, Robert A., illus. (p. 449)
—Football Bully. Tiritilli, Robert A., illus. (p. 615)
—Hockey Bully. Tiritilli, Robert A., illus. (p. 786)
—Luckysports Abc's Coloring Book. Tiritilli, Robert A., illus. (p. 1063)
—Volleyball Bully. Tiritilli, Robert A., illus. (p. 1849)
Hellman, Charles S. & Tiritilli, Robert A. Tennis Bully. (p. 1720)
Hellman, Sue. Little Red Crab. (p. 1034)
Hellmann-Hurpol, Odile. Devuelvanme Mi Perro. (p. 432)
Hellmich, Mittie. Mini Bar - Rum: Little Book of Big Drinks. Stojanovic, Laura & Frankeny, Frankie, photos by. (p. 1146)
—Sangria: Fun & Festive Recipes. Pearson, Victoria, photos by. (p. 1511)
—Ultimate Bar Book: The Comprehensive Guide to over 1,000 Cocktails. Mount, Arthur, illus. (p. 1809)
Hellweg, Paul. American Heritage Children's Thesaurus. (p. 61)
Hellweg, Paul, jt. auth. see American Heritage Dictionary Editors.
Helm, Charles & Owlkids Books Inc. Staff. Daniel's Dinosaurs: A True Story of Discovery. Zimmer, Joan, illus. (p. 405)
Helm, Joanna, jt. auth. see Bernstein, Laurie.
Helm, Julie G. Lost Monster Tales. Cary, Debbi, illus. (p. 1056)
—Merlin for Sherman. Cary, Debbi G., photos by. (p. 1128)
Helm, Zebedee, jt. auth. see Graffito Books Staff.
Helman, Andrea. Hide & Seek: Nature's Best Vanishing Acts. Jecan, Gavriel, illus. (p. 776)
—Northwest Animal Babies. Wolfe, Art, photos by. (p. 1266)
—O Is for Orca: An Alphabet Book. Wolfe, Art, photos by. (p. 1274)
—Southwest Colors. Jecan, Gavriel, photos by. (p. 1617)
Helmer, Barbara, jt. auth. see Suzuki, David T.
Helmer, Der-Shing, illus. see Beauregard, Lynda.
Helmer, Der-Shing, illus. see Thielbar, Melinda.
Helmer, Jay & Skindzier, Jon. Kenyon College College Prowler off the Record. (p. 949)
Helmer, Marilyn. Adventures at Camp Lots-O-Fun Deas, Mike, illus. (p. 15)
—Fog Cat. (p. 611)
—Fossil Hunters Walshe, Dermot, illus. (p. 623)
—Funtime Riddles. Kurisu, Jane, illus. (p. 650)
—Great Garage Sale Deas, Mike, illus. (p. 716)
—One Splendid Tree. Eastman, Dianne, illus. (p. 1297)
—Pirate Island Treasure Parkins, David, illus. (p. 1362)
—Sharing Snowy Charko, Kasia, illus. (p. 1561)
Helmes, Amy, jt. auth. see Askew, Kim.
Helmetag Murdock, Kita. Future Flash. (p. 651)
Helmetag, Patricia, jt. auth. see Murdock, Kita Helmetag.
Helming, Troy. Clean Power Revolution (p. 330)
Helmintoller, Matt & Baiz, Mark. One December Night. (p. 1294)
Helmore, Jim. Letterbox Lil: A Cautionary Tale. (p. 1002)
—My Little Library Wall, Karen, illus. (p. 1212)
—Oh No, Monster Tomato! Wall, Karen, illus. (p. 1281)
Helmore, Jim, jt. auth. see Helmore Wall Staff.
Helmore, Jim & Wall, Karen. Letterbox Lil. (p. 1002)
Helmore Wall Staff & Helmore, Jim. Oh No, Monster Tomato! Wall, Karen, illus. (p. 1281)
Helmrath, M. O. & Bartlett, J. L. Bobby Bear Series (p. 206)
Helms, Andrea, et al. Introduction to Geospatial Technology: 2nd Edition. (p. 882)
Helms, Antje, jt. auth. see von Holleben, Jan.
Helms, Buddy. Alienated. (p. 41)
Helms, Dana, illus. see Bowlby, Linda S.
Helms, Hal M., jt. auth. see Pochocki, Ethel.
Helms, Jo. Grizz's Story-A Greater Courage: A Dog's Journey. (p. 724)
—In the Paw Prints of an Angel: Sarge & Kodi's Story. (p. 867)
Helms, Rhonda. Promposal. (p. 1411)
Helms, Rhonda, jt. auth. see Destiny, A.
Helms, Selah & Thompson, Susan. Small Talks on Big Questions: A Historical Companion to the Children's Catechism Vol. 2 Whitney, Caffy, illus. (p. 1592)
Helms, Selah, et al. Small Talks on Big Questions: A Historical Companion to the Children's Catechism Vol. 1 Whitney, Caffy, illus. (p. 1592)
Helms, Tina, photos by see Korty, Carol.
Helmso, Candy Grant. Cakewalk. Taylor, Stephen, illus. (p. 252)
—Freedom Quilt. Friar, Joanne, illus. (p. 634)
Helou, Sandra & Chown, Xanna Eve. Grover on the Case: Follow the Reader Level 1. (p. 725)
Helowicz, Cathy. On Grandpop's Lap (p. 1288)
Helquist, jt. auth. see Helquist, Brett.
Helquist, Brett. Bedtime for Bear. Helquist, Brett, illus. (p. 156)
—Grumpy Goat. Helquist, Brett, illus. (p. 727)
—Roger, the Jolly Pirate. (p. 1484)
—Roger, the Jolly Pirate. Helquist, Brett, illus. (p. 1484)
—Scary Stories 3: More Tales to Chill Your Bones. (p. 1520)
Helquist, Brett, illus. see Ashburn, Boni.
Helquist, Brett, illus. see Balliett, Blue.
Helquist, Brett, illus. see Corey, Shana.
Helquist, Brett, illus. see Dickens, Charles.
Helquist, Brett, illus. see Dumas, Alexandre.
Helquist, Brett, illus. see Farrey, Brian.
Helquist, Brett, illus. see Gaiman, Neil.
Helquist, Brett, illus. see Gratz, Alan.
Helquist, Brett, illus. see Howe, James.
Helquist, Brett, illus. see Martin, Ann M. & Godwin, Laura.
Helquist, Brett, illus. see Schwartz, Alvin.
Helquist, Brett, illus. see Scieszka, Jon.
Helquist, Brett, illus. see Smith, Jennifer E.
Helquist, Brett, illus. see Snicket, Lemony, pseud.
Helquist, Brett, illus. see Trafton, Jennifer.
Helquist, Brett & Helquist. Roger: The Jolly Pirate. Helquist, Brett, illus. (p. 1484)
—Roger, the Jolly Pirate. Helquist, Brett, illus. (p. 1484)
Helsby, Genevieve. Those Amazing Musical Instruments! Your Guide to the Orchestra Through Sounds & Stories. (p. 1740)
Helsel, Larry D. & Liu, Peter. Industrial Materials. (p. 872)
Helsel, Sandra. Pokey & the Rooster. Snyder, Joe, illus. (p. 1378)
Helsley, Donalisa. I Love You Better Than Chocolate Chip Cookies. (p. 843)
Helsom, Geoff, illus. see Dykema, Marjorie.
Helson, Jan & Helson, Rachel Annette. Philanthropy: A Big Word for Big Hearted People. Helson, Rachel Annette, illus. (p. 1350)
Helson, Rachel Annette, jt. auth. see Helson, Jan.
Helstrom, Kraig. Crop Circles. (p. 385)
—Knights. (p. 964)
Helton, David, illus. see Hillert, Margaret.
Helton, Dianne. I Like Pumpkins! Me Gustan Las Calabazas! (p. 841)
Heltzel, Anne. Charlie, Presumed Dead. (p. 293)
—Circle Nine. (p. 321)
Helvey, Rebecca. Greta's Purpose. Helvey, Rebecca, illus. (p. 723)
Helwani, Najiyah Diana. Sophia's Journal: Time Warp 1857. (p. 1613)
Helweg, Hans, illus. see Bedford, Annie North.
Helweg, Laura. Eastern Great Lakes: Indiana, Michigan, Ohio (p. 500)
Helwig, Teresa L., ed. see Pritchard, Herman S.
Hembree, G. Wil. Willisby Orphans: In the Keys to the Bottomless Pit. (p. 1934)
Hembrook, Deborah, jt. auth. see Heling, Kathryn.
Hemby, Margaret, illus. see Shaw, Wendy M.
Hemdal, Jay F. Mini-Aquariums: Basic Aquarium Setup & Maintenance. (p. 1146)
Hemenway, Priya. Little Book of Jesus. (p. 1025)
Hemenway, Scott. Anthracite Collieries & Railroads of the Western Middle Field. (p. 89)
Hemery, Kathleen Maresh. Sunflower Promise. Bordelois, Augusto, illus. (p. 1676)
Heming, Leah-Ellen, illus. see Durant, Alan.
Hemingway, Al. Chuck Norris. (p. 318)
Hemingway, Albert. American Naval Forces in the Vietnam War. (p. 62)
—Barack Obama. (p. 137)
—Chuck Norris. (p. 318)
Hemingway, Amanda. Poisoned Crown. (p. 1377)
Hemingway, Edith M. Road to Tater Hill. (p. 1477)
Hemingway, Edward. Bad Apple: A Tale of Friendship. Hemingway, Edward, illus. (p. 131)
—Bad Apple's Perfect Day. Hemingway, Edward, illus. (p. 131)
Hemingway, Edward, illus. see Bailey, Mark & Oatman, Michael.
Hemingway, Mike. Legend of Vysallimore. (p. 989)
Hemmel, David. Living in the Key West Style Anywhere: A Complete Guide to Planning a Home in the Charming Key West Style. (p. 1041)
Hemmel, David Lee & Knutson, Janette C. Alexis' Island: Growing up in the Tropical Paradise of Key West. (p. 37)
Hemmer, Kurt, ed. Encyclopedia of Beat Literature: The Essential Guide to the Lives & Works of the Beat Writers. (p. 525)
Hemmerle, Jamie. Lost & Found Summer. (p. 1054)
Hemming, Denny, ed. see Dahlberg, Laurie.
Hemming, Heidi & Savage, Julie Hemming. Women Making America. (p. 1946)
Hemminger, Marcia. Comprehension Crosswords Grade 4 McAskin, Denice, illus. (p. 354)
—Comprehension Crosswords Grade 6 Adams Marks, Elizabeth, illus. (p. 354)
Hemmings, Kaui Hart. Juniors. (p. 936)
Hemmings, Lisa & O'Keefe, Allan. Imagine Me with the Three Owls: Feeling Great. (p. 861)
Hemmingson, Nancy S., illus. see Crow, Stanford.
Hempel, Marc. Gregory Treasury. (p. 723)
Hemperly, Ilona K. & Nanni, Lyn. Koa'e Kea. (p. 966)
Hemphill, Helen. Adventurous Deeds of Deadwood Jones. (p. 25)
—Long Gone Daddy. (p. 1047)
—Runaround. (p. 1496)
Hemphill, Kris. Ambush in the Wilderness. (p. 57)
Hemphill, Michael & Angleberger, Tom. Stonewall Hinkleman & the Battle of Bull Run. (p. 1653)
Hemphill, Rick. Adventures of Kirra & Rincon: Li'l Kids, Big Waves. (p. 19)
Hemphill, Stephanie. Hideous Love: The Story of the Girl Who Wrote Frankenstein. (p. 777)
—Sisters of Glass. (p. 1581)
—Wicked Girls: A Novel of the Salem Witch Trials. (p. 1927)
—Your Own, Sylvia: A Verse Portrait of Sylvia. (p. 1981)
—Your Own, Sylvia: A Verse Portrait of Sylvia Plath. (p. 1981)
Hempstead, Anne. Capitolio (p. 263)
—Statue of Liberty (p. 1645)
Hempstead, Anne, jt. auth. see Hancock, Maryann.
Hempstead, Jim. Come, Journey to Bethlehem. (p. 347)
Hempstock, Becky, jt. auth. see Medcalf, Carol.
Hemrich-Skomer, Denise, jt. auth. see Tyrtania, Joachim.
Hemry, Melanie & Lynnes, Gina. Anointing for Children w/ anointing oil Vial. (p. 87)
Hemstock, Annie. Moose (p. 1173)
Hemstock, Annie Wendt. Bow Hunting. (p. 216)
—Horseshoe Crabs (p. 800)
—Hunting Gear. (p. 829)
—Hunting Laws & Safety. (p. 829)
—Hunting with Rifles. (p. 829)
—Hunting with Shotguns. (p. 829)
—Know Your Quarry. (p. 965)
—Living Fossils (p. 1041)
Hemstock, Whitney M. ABC's of Traffic Safety. (p. 4)
Hemstreet, Keith, jt. auth. see Wheeler, Patti.
Hemyng, Bracebridge. Jack Harkaway & His Son's Escape from the Brigands of Greece. (p. 903)
—Jack Harkaway & His Son's Escape from the Brigand's of Greece. (p. 903)
Hen, Horseradish. You Have Permission. (p. 1975)
Hen, Ms. Lucky Lottie. (p. 1062)
Hen, Yitzhak. Roman Barbarians: The Royal Court & Culture in the Early Medieval West. (p. 1485)
Henaff, Carole, illus. see Lupton, Hugh, et al.
Hénaff, Carole, illus. see Lupton, Hugh.
Henaff, Carole, illus. see Tarnowska, Wafa'.
Henao De Brigard, Luis Carlos, jt. compiled by see Gomez Buendia, Blanca Ines.
Hench, Larry. Boing-Boing the Bionic Cat & the Jewel Thief. Steed, Tobias, ed. (p. 208)
—Boing-Boing the Bionic Cat & the Space Station. Morgan-Jones, Tom, illus. (p. 208)
Henchey, Agnes Braceland. This 'N' That. (p. 1737)
Hendee, Barb & Hendee, J. C. Dhampir. (p. 433)
—Rebel Fay (p. 1450)
Hendee, J. C., jt. auth. see Hendee, Barb.
Hendershot, Eric. At Season's End. (p. 110)
—Horse for Christmas. (p. 799)
Henderson, Aileen Kilgore. Hard Times for Jake Smith: A Story of the Depression Era. (p. 748)
Henderson, Aimee M. Just Like My Dad. (p. 939)
Henderson, Ann, ed. see Huancal, Yang, et al.
Henderson, Ashlee. Adventures of the Ruler Twins: The Twins Earn Their Ruler Names. (p. 23)
—Adventures of the Ruler Twins. (p. 23)
Henderson, Barbara. Down in Mr Brown's Garden. (p. 474)
Henderson, Bonnie. UFOS: Out of the Black. (p. 1808)
Henderson, Brandon. Legend of the Kukui Nut. (p. 989)
Henderson, C. J. Baby's First Mythos. (p. 129)
Henderson, Cecil, illus. see Alexander, Carmen.
Henderson, Charles. Goodnight Saigon: The True Story of the U. S. Marines' Last Days In. (p. 701)
Henderson, Charles, Jr., et al. Latin for Americans (p. 979)
Henderson, Christine Dunn, ed. see Addison, Joseph, et al.
Henderson, Clifford. Middle of Somewhere. (p. 1137)
Henderson, Dana, illus. see Arenella, Betsy Bottino.
Henderson, Dave. Story of Three Trees: And the miracle of Prayer. (p. 1662)
Henderson, Dianne. Frightening Old Mansion. (p. 639)
Henderson, Elisabeth & Armstrong, Nancy. 100 Questions You'd Never Ask Your Parents. (p. 1998)
Henderson, Harry. Communications & Broadcasting: From Wired Words to Wireless Web. (p. 349)
—Computer Viruses. (p. 355)
—Curie Family. (p. 392)
—Digital Age. (p. 439)
—Encyclopedia of Computer Science & Technology. (p. 525)
—Gun Control. (p. 732)
—How Mobile Devices Are Changing Society. (p. 811)
—Online Privacy & Government. (p. 1298)
—Power of the News Media. (p. 1389)
—Privacy in the Information Age. (p. 1407)
Henderson, Harry, rev. Capital Punishment. (p. 262)
Henderson, Helene. Patriotic Holidays of the United States: An Introduction to the History, Symbols, & Traditions Behind the Major Holidays & Days of Observance. (p. 1329)
Henderson, Hugh. VanDland. (p. 1833)
Henderson, Jack. Jack - Draws Anything. (p. 902)
Henderson, Jackie S. Growing up Underexposed: Lessons Learned from My Daddy. (p. 727)
Henderson, James D., ed. see Colleen Madonna Flood Williams.
Henderson, James D., ed. see Gelletly, LeeAnne.
Henderson, James D., ed. see Hernandez, Roger E.
Henderson, James D., ed. see Hernandez, Roger.
Henderson, James D., ed. see Hernandez, Romel.
Henderson, James D., ed. see Kozleski, Lisa.
Henderson, James D., ed. see Orr, Tamra.
Henderson, James D., ed. see Shields, Charles J.
Henderson, James D., ed. see Temple, Bob.
Henderson, James D., ed. Discovering South America (p. 449)
—Discovering the Caribbean (p. 449)
Henderson, Jason. Psy-Comm. Granger, Shane, illus. (p. 1413)
—Triumph of Death. (p. 1788)
—Vampire Rising. (p. 1832)
—Voice of the Undead. (p. 1848)
Henderson, Jason & Salvaggio, Tony. Psy-Comm Karmaga, Ramanda, illus. (p. 1413)
Henderson, Jeanine. Ever after High - A Wonderlandiful Doodle Book. (p. 541)
Henderson, Kathy. And the Good Brown Earth. Henderson, Kathy, illus. (p. 71)
—Dog Story. Granström, Brita, illus. (p. 461)
—Look at You! A Baby Body Book. Howard, Paul, illus. (p. 1049)
—Pets, Pets, Pets! Fisher, Chris, illus. (p. 1348)
—Tabby Cat's Secret. (p. 1694)
Henderson, Kathy & Quarto Generic Staff. Hush, Baby, Hush! Lullabies from Around the World. Smy, Pam, illus. (p. 830)
Henderson, Kathy, et al. Cars, Cars, Cars! (p. 272)
Henderson, Ken, illus. see Adams, Pamela L.
Henderson, Kris. Animalimericks! Burt, Kelly, illus. (p. 81)
Henderson, Lauren. Kiss in the Dark. (p. 961)
—Kiss Me Kill Me. (p. 961)
—Kiss of Death. (p. 961)
—Kissing in Italian. (p. 962)
Henderson, Liz, illus. see Gray, Charlotte.
Henderson, Mary Anne. Adventures of Linda's Little Frog. (p. 19)
Henderson, McDavid, illus. see Clements, Andrew.
Henderson, Melva. Maizie & the Sorcerer's Spell. (p. 1078)
—Mischief Reigns. (p. 1150)
Henderson, Meryl. Indoor Things. (p. 872)
—Things to Play With. (p. 1733)
Henderson, Meryl, illus. see Dunn, Herb.
Henderson, Meryl, illus. see Eboch, M. M.
Henderson, Meryl, illus. see Harper, Jo.
Henderson, Meryl, illus. see Jackson, Max.
Henderson, Meryl, illus. see Kudlinski, Kathleen.
Henderson, Meryl, illus. see Mantell, Paul.
Henderson, Meryl, illus. see Pringle, Laurence.
Henderson, Meryl, illus. see Sloate, Susan.
Henderson, Meryl, illus. see Stanley, George E.
Henderson, Meryl, illus. see Stanley, George Edward.
Henderson, Meryle, illus. see Pringle, Laurence.
Henderson, Milagros. Lulu the Bouncing Kangaroo. (p. 1065)
Henderson, Myrna. Twin Lands. (p. 1802)
Henderson, Patti & Golden Books Staff. Blessing from Above. Edge, Elizabeth, illus. (p. 199)
Henderson, Richard. One Christmas Night. Shackelford, David, illus. (p. 1294)
Henderson, Robin. Bella, the Green Puppy: An Eco-Friendly Tale (Second Edition) (p. 162)
Henderson, Sam. Scene but Not Heard. (p. 1521)
Henderson, Sara. Howie Finds a Hug Zenz, Aaron, illus. (p. 823)
—Howie's Tea Party Zenz, Aaron, illus. (p. 823)
Henderson, Sara & Zenz, Aaron. Howie Goes Shopping(Fido Va de Compras) Henderson, Sara & Zenz, Aaron, illus. (p. 823)
—Howie Wants to Play Henderson, Sara & Zenz, Aaron, illus. (p. 823)
Henderson, Scott. I Want to Be a Pig. (p. 847)
Henderson, Scott B., illus. see Robertson, David Alexander.
Henderson, Scott B., illus. see Robertson, David.
Henderson, Stewart. All Things Weird & Wonderful. (p. 46)
—All Things Weird & Wonderful. Baines, Nigel, illus. (p. 46)
Henderson, Susan & White, Emily. Raising the Roof: Destination Reality. (p. 1437)
Henderson, Susan Sinclair. Penelope's Journey Home. (p. 1336)
Henderson, Tim. Butterflies & Magic Dreams. Hansen, Melissa, illus. (p. 247)
Henderson, Virginia. Zippy the Dreamer. (p. 1987)
Hendesi, Roya. Ancient Queendom. (p. 70)
Hendin, Josephine Gattuso. Heartbreakers: Women & Violence in Contemporary Culture & Literature. (p. 760)
Hendler, Muncie. Dover Masterworks: Color Your Own Modern Art Paintings. (p. 473)
—Infinite Designs Coloring Book. (p. 873)
Hendley, Jeff. Stump. Hendley, Tess, illus. (p. 1670)
Hendley, Tess, illus. see Hendley, Jeff.
Hendra, Sue. Barry the Fish with Fingers. (p. 140)
—Barry the Fish with Fingers & the Hairy Scary Monster. (p. 140)
—Busy Day, Busy Night: Rainforest. (p. 246)
—Busy Day, Busy Night: Rain Forest. (p. 246)
—Dave. Pichon, Liz, illus. (p. 410)
—Dave's Breakfast Blast-Off! Wildish, Lee, illus. (p. 410)
—My Mermaid Counting Book. (p. 1214)
Hendra, Sue, illus. see Freedman, Claire.
Hendra, Sue, illus. see Hicks, Barbara Jean.
Hendra, Sue, illus. see Kertell, Lynn Maslen.
Hendra, Sue, illus. see Maslen, Bobby Lynn & Kertell, Lynn Maslen.
Hendra, Sue, illus. see Mayfield, Sue.
Hendra, Sue, illus. see Powell, Richard.
Hendrick, Betty Acey, illus. see Furcron, Bertha Phillips.
Hendrick-Lockyer, Veronica. Moon Boy. (p. 1172)
Hendricks, Brenda K. Much More to Christmas. Hendricks, Brenda K., illus. (p. 1188)
—What's Better Than That, Seren Dippity? Hendricks, Brenda K., illus. (p. 1896)
—What's the Buzz, Bumbly Bee? Hendricks, Brenda K., illus. (p. 1899)
Hendricks, Brenda K., illus. see Lickel, Lisa J.

H

Hendricks, D. J., et al. Essential Statistics for the Behavioral Sciences. (p. 537)
Hendricks, Damion, jt. auth. see Simonson, Louise.
Hendricks, Elizabeth. Nzinga's Tribe. (p. 1274)
Hendricks, Hansie. NSSC Accounting Answer Book. (p. 1269)
—NSSC Accounting Module 1. (p. 1269)
Hendricks, Jeff, jt. auth. see LeVert, Suzanne.
Hendricks, Linda K. Rainbow Egg. (p. 1435)
Hendricks, Sandy, illus. see Mason, Bonita.
Hendricks, Tim. Mentor: The True Story of an Hourly Factory Employee who Became Financially Independent. (p. 1127)
Hendricks, Tracey, illus. see Robbins-Turner, Darlene.
Hendrickson, Alyce. Healing Words. (p. 757)
Hendrickson, Clyde. Altos: A Clyde Hendrickson Joint. (p. 50)
—Special Places. (p. 1623)
—Squirrel. (p. 1637)
Hendrickson, David H. Cracking the Ice. (p. 375)
Hendrickson, Kenneth E. & Hendrickson, Kenneth E., Jr. Primary Source Accounts of the Spanish-American War. (p. 1399)
Hendrickson, Kenneth E., Jr., jt. auth. see Hendrickson, Kenneth E.
Hendrickson, Kevis. Legend of Witch Bane. (p. 989)
Hendrickson, Mary K., jt. auth. see Peacock, Kathy Wilson.
Hendrickson, Peggy, jt. auth. see Popkin, Michael H.
Hendrickson Publishers, creator. Economy Bible-NRSV-Apocrypha. (p. 503)
—Explorer Bible. (p. 551)
Hendrickson, Terry D. What Is Choo-Choo? Choo Choo Is A Cat. (p. 1889)
Hendrickx, Melissa. From My Window. (p. 643)
Hendrix, Amanda, ed. see Moran, Raphael.
Hendrix, Bryan, illus. see Bader, Bonnie.
Hendrix, E. B. Angel & Evie: Catching a Unicorn. (p. 73)
Hendrix, Emilia. Seals & Pups. (p. 1536)
Hendrix, Heather. What Should I Be for Halloween? (p. 1893)
Hendrix, Jennifer & Schmitt, Laura. Oscar. (p. 1305)
Hendrix, John. Drawing Is Magic: Discovering Yourself in a Sketchbook. (p. 482)
—Shooting at the Stars: The Christmas Truce of 1914. (p. 1568)
Hendrix, John, illus. see Angleberger, Tom.
Hendrix, John, illus. see Fleischman, Sid.
Hendrix, John, illus. see George, Jean Craighead.
Hendrix, John, illus. see Hopkinson, Deborah.
Hendrix, John, illus. see Moss, Marissa.
Hendrix, John, illus. see Schulz, Heidi.
Hendrix, John, illus. see Singer, Marilyn.
Hendrix, Lisa. Immortal Warrior. (p. 861)
Hendrix, Mary E. What Makes a Boy Strong? What Makes a Girl Pretty? (p. 1892)
Hendry, Diana. Harvey Angel y la Nina Fantasma. Alban, Rafael Segovia, tr. (p. 752)
—Oodles of Noodles. Massini, Sarah, illus. (p. 1298)
—Que Noche Mas Ruidosa! Chapman, Jane, illus. (p. 1424)
—Very Snowy Christmas. Chapman, Jane, illus. (p. 1838)
Hendry, Frances. Atlantis. (p. 112)
—Quest for a Kelpie. (p. 1426)
—Quest for a Queen: The Lark. (p. 1426)
—Quest for a Queen: The Falcon. (p. 1426)
—Quest for a Queen: The Jackdaw. (p. 1426)
—Quest for Atlantis. (p. 1426)
—Seer's Stone. (p. 1548)
—Wee Malkie. (p. 1871)
Hendry, Joy. Reclaiming Culture: Indigenous People & Self-Representation. (p. 1452)
Hendry, Linda. Horse Crafts. Hendry, Linda, illus. (p. 799)
Hendry, Linda, illus. see Borsky, Mary.
Hendry, Linda, illus. see Hartry, Nancy.
Hendry, Linda, illus. see Hood, Susan.
Hendry, Linda, illus. see Irvine, Joan.
Hendry, Linda, illus. see Kenny, Chantal Lacourcière.
Hendry, Linda, illus. see Tokio, Marnelle.
Hendry, Linda, illus. see Wishinsky, Frieda.
Hendry, Linda, jt. auth. see Hood, Susan.
Hendry, Linda, jt. auth. see Irvine, Joan.
Hendry, Linda & Farris, Katherine. Mon Plus Bel Album de Mots Illustres. (p. 1163)
Hendtlass, Jane & Nichols, Alan. Media Ethics: Ethics, Law & Accountability in the Australian Media. Han, Than T., illus. (p. 1118)
Hendy, Jenny. Best-Ever Step-By-Step Kid's First Gardening: Fantastic Gardening Ideas for 5-12 Year Olds, from Growing Fruit & Vegetables & Fun with Flowers to Wildlife Gardening & Craft Projects. (p. 169)
—Fun Gardening for Kids - 30 Creative Outdoor Projects: Imaginative Ideas for Great Activities for 5-12 Year Olds, Shown in 500 Fantastic Step-By-Step Pictures. (p. 648)
—Gardening Projects for Kids: Fantastic Ideas for Making Things, Growing Plants & Flowers & Attracting Wildlife, with 60 Practical Projects & 175 Photographs. (p. 656)
—Kids' First Gardening Book: Fantastic Gardening Ideas for 5-12 Year Olds, from Growing Fruit & Vegetables & Fun with Flowers to Wildlife Gardening & Craft Projects. (p. 953)
Hendy, Jenny, jt. auth. see McDougall, Nancy.
Heneghan, James. Grave (p. 712)
—Hit Squad (p. 785)
—Hit Squad. (p. 785)
—Payback (p. 1331)
—Safe House (p. 1502)
Heneghan, James, jt. auth. see McBay, Bruce.
Heneghan, James & Charles, Norma M. Bank Job (p. 136)
Heneghan, James & McBay, Bruce. Nannycatch Chronicles Valério, Geraldo, illus. (p. 1229)
Heneghan, James B. Torn Away (p. 1770)
Heneghan, Judith. Love Your Cat. (p. 1061)
—Love Your Dog. (p. 1061)
—Love Your Hamster. (p. 1061)
—Love Your Rabbit. (p. 1061)
—Magician's Apprentice. (p. 1075)
Heneghan, Lou. Turnarounders & the Arbuckle Rescue. Maguire, Jake, illus. (p. 1798)
Heney, Clare, illus. see Boyce, Frank Cottrell.
Heney, Clare, photos by see Boyce, Frank Cottrell.
Hengel, Katherine. Amazing American Curls. Doucet, Bob, illus. (p. 52)
—Apple State Treasure Hunt: A Story about Washington. Doucet, Bob, illus. (p. 92)
—Before the Snap (p. 158)
—Brainy Brittanys. Doucet, Bob, illus. (p. 222)
—Burly Bulldogs. Doucet, Bob, illus. (p. 243)
—Chipper Chihuahuas. Doucet, Bob, illus. (p. 308)
—Cool Birds & Bugs: Great Things to Do in the Great Outdoors. (p. 362)
—Cool Parks & Trails: Great Things to Do in the Great Outdoors. (p. 364)
—Delightful Devon Rexes. Doucet, Bob, illus. (p. 425)
—Ears Are for Earrings: The Sense of Hearing. (p. 494)
—Eyes Are for Winking: The Sense of Sight. (p. 558)
—Garden to Table: A Kid's Guide to Planting, Growing, & Preparing Food. (p. 656)
—Handoff (p. 741)
—Hands Are for Holding: The Sense of Touch. (p. 741)
—Hip Himalayans. Doucet, Bob, illus. (p. 780)
—Hit Just Right (p. 785)
—It's a Baby Australian Fur Seal! (p. 895)
—It's a Baby Flying Fox! (p. 895)
—It's a Baby Koala! (p. 895)
—It's a Baby Spiny Anteater! (p. 895)
—It's a Baby Tasmanian Devil! (p. 895)
—It's B! (p. 896)
—It's G! (p. 897)
—It's H! (p. 897)
—It's M! (p. 897)
—It's Q! (p. 898)
—It's R! (p. 898)
—It's V! (p. 899)
—It's X! (p. 899)
—Monty's Ice Pick: A Story about Alaska. Doucet, Bob, illus. (p. 1170)
—Mouths Are for Smiling: The Sense of Taste. (p. 1183)
—No Easy Race (p. 1258)
—Noses Are for Picking: The Sense of Smell. (p. 1266)
—Outgoing Oriental Shorthairs. Doucet, Bob, illus. (p. 1312)
—Proud Portuguese Water Dogs. Doucet, Bob, illus. (p. 1412)
—Rupert & the Liberty Bell: A Story about Pennsylvania. Doucet, Bob, illus. (p. 1497)
—Senses Are for Everything: The Five Senses. (p. 1551)
—Sherice: Blind Trust. (p. 1565)
—Smooth Sphynx. Doucet, Bob, illus. (p. 1595)
—Strong Siberian Huskies. Doucet, Bob, illus. (p. 1668)
—Sweet Scottish Folds. Doucet, Bob, illus. (p. 1690)
—Taking Control (p. 1698)
—Terrific Tabbies. Doucet, Bob, illus. (p. 1721)
—Wings (p. 1936)
Hengel, Katherine, jt. auth. see Hanson, Anders.
Henggeler, Mary F. Where's Wendy? The Curious Cat. (p. 1911)
Henham, R. D. Black Dragon Codex. (p. 196)
—Brass Dragon Codex. (p. 222)
—Bronze Dragon Codex. (p. 230)
—Red Dragon Codex. (p. 1453)
Henig, Sherry. Goodbye to Bedtime Fears: A Children's Book. (p. 701)
—Group Rules! The Social Skills & Ground Rules for Children's Groups. (p. 725)
—Sara Makes Her Mother Proud & Learns Good Behavior: A Children's Book. (p. 1514)
Henighan, Tom. Boy from Left Field. (p. 218)
—Demon in My View. (p. 426)
—Doom Lake Holiday. (p. 470)
—Mercury Man. (p. 1127)
—Viking Terror. (p. 1842)
Henisz, Jerzy E. SOPHIE in PARIS & other Stories. (p. 1613)
Henisz, Jerzy E. & Henisz, Sophie, illustrator. TEDDY BEAR who went on a Trip around the World & other Stories. (p. 1712)
Henisz, Sophie, illustrator, jt. auth. see Henisz, Jerzy E.
Henity, Kristi. Kimi's Grand Adventures (p. 957)
Henk, Roy. Unlock Rocks: Explore Clues in Crystals with Kitchen Science. (p. 1821)
Henke, Elizabeth, jt. auth. see Carothers, Sue.
Henkel, D. B., VIII, illus. see Henkel, Donald G.
Henkel, Donald G. Painted Treasures or the Original 288 Tree Gnomes. Henkel, D. B., VIII, illus. (p. 1318)
Henkel, Julie Anne. Jungle Seek in the Rainforest: An Enchanted Fairy Tale. (p. 935)
Henkel, Pat. Jeffrey's Great Day. Elliott, Luke, illus. (p. 912)
Henkel, Vernon, illus. see Greiner, Ruth B., et al.
Henkel, Vernon, illus. see Kiefer, Velma, et al.
Henkel, Vernon & Tweed, Sean. Esther: Old Testament Volume 28: Esther. Vol. 28 (p. 538)
Henkes, Kevin. All Alone. Henkes, Kevin, illus. (p. 43)
—Bird Lake Moon. (p. 190)
—Birds. Dronzek, Laura, illus. (p. 191)
—Birthday Room. (p. 193)
—Box Full of Lilly: Lilly's Big Day. Henkes, Kevin, illus. (p. 216)
—Box of Treats: Five Little Picture Books about Lilly & Her Friends. Henkes, Kevin, illus. (p. 216)
—Chester's Way. (p. 298)
—Chrysanthemum. (p. 317)
—Chrysanthemum. Henkes, Kevin, illus. (p. 317)
—Crisantemo. Mlawer, Teresa, tr. from ENG. (p. 383)
—Good Day. Henkes, Kevin, illus. (p. 697)
—Good Day Board Book. Henkes, Kevin, illus. (p. 697)
—Gran Dia de Lily. Posada, Maria Candelaria, tr. from ENG. (p. 706)
—Julius, the Baby of the World. (p. 933)
—Julius, the Baby of the World. Henkes, Kevin, illus. (p. 933)
—Julius's Candy Corn. Henkes, Kevin, illus. (p. 933)
—Junonia. (p. 936)
—Junonia. Henkes, Kevin, illus. (p. 936)
—Kitten's First Full Moon. Henkes, Kevin, illus. (p. 963)
—Kitten's First Full Moon Board Book. Henkes, Kevin, illus. (p. 963)
—Lilly Adore l'École! (p. 1017)
—Lilly's Big Day. (p. 1017)
—Lilly's Big Day. Henkes, Kevin, illus. (p. 1017)
—Lilly's Big Day Standee. (p. 1017)
—Lilly's Chocolate Heart. Henkes, Kevin, illus. (p. 1017)
—Lilly's Purple Plastic Purse. (p. 1017)
—Lilly's Purple Plastic Purse. Henkes, Kevin, illus. (p. 1017)
—Lily y Su Bolso de Plastico Morado. (p. 1018)
—Little White Rabbit. Henkes, Kevin, illus. (p. 1037)
—Little White Rabbit Board Book. Henkes, Kevin, illus. (p. 1037)
—My Garden. Henkes, Kevin, illus. (p. 1209)
—Old Bear. Henkes, Kevin, illus. (p. 1283)
—Old Bear Board Book. Henkes, Kevin, illus. (p. 1283)
—Olive's Ocean. (p. 1286)
—Penny & Her Doll. (p. 1338)
—Penny & Her Doll. Henkes, Kevin, illus. (p. 1338)
—Penny & Her Marble. (p. 1338)
—Penny & Her Marble. Henkes, Kevin, illus. (p. 1338)
—Penny & Her Song. (p. 1338)
—Penny & Her Song. Henkes, Kevin, illus. (p. 1338)
—Primera Luna Llena de Gatita. Henkes, Kevin, illus. (p. 1400)
—Protecting Marie. (p. 1412)
—Sheila Rae, the Brave. Henkes, Kevin, illus. (p. 1564)
—So Happy! Lobel, Anita, illus. (p. 1602)
—Sun & Spoon. (p. 1676)
—Two under Par. Henkes, Kevin, illus. (p. 1804)
—Waiting. Henkes, Kevin, illus. (p. 1852)
—Wemberly Worried. (p. 1875)
—Wemberly Worried. Henkes, Kevin, illus. (p. 1875)
—Wemberly's Ice-Cream Star. Henkes, Kevin, illus. (p. 1875)
—When Spring Comes. Dronzek, Laura, illus. (p. 1904)
—Words of Stone. (p. 1952)
—Year of Billy Miller. (p. 1969)
—Year of Billy Miller. Henkes, Kevin, illus. (p. 1969)
—Zebra Wall. (p. 1985)
Henkes, Kevin & Kevin, Henkes. Owen. (p. 1314)
Henkin, Bill, jt. auth. see Wallace, Amy.
Henkin, Roxanne. Confronting Bullying: Literacy as a Tool for Character Education. (p. 357)
Henkin, William A., jt. auth. see Heller, Joseph.
Henkoski, Alexander. Adventures of Rathdrum Willie & His Motor Car. (p. 22)
Henley, Christian A. Adventures with Norky: Teamwork. (p. 25)
Henley, Claire. Jonah & the Big Fish. (p. 925)
—Noah & the Flood. (p. 1261)
Henley, Claire, illus. see Top That Publishing Staff, ed.
Henley, Ivan. Kitty Milo Says the Alphabet (A Read-Aloud Book for Children) (p. 963)
Henley, K. P. Historia de Dios (God's Story) (p. 782)
Henley, Karyn. Arts & Crafts, Volume 1: Bible Story Activities for ages 2 To 5 (p. 105)
—Day by Day Begin-to-Read Bible. Sapulich, Joseph, illus. (p. 412)
—Day by Day Devotions: A Year of Character Building Devotions for Kids. (p. 412)
—Exploring God's World Through Simple Science: Bible Story Activities for Ages 2 To 5. (p. 552)
—God Gave Me a Place to Live. (p. 688)
—God Is with Me All the Time. (p. 689)
—God Is with Me Everywhere. (p. 689)
—God Made All Kinds of Friends. (p. 689)
—God Made Animals. (p. 689)
—God Made Food. (p. 689)
—God Made Land, Sea, & Sky. (p. 689)
—God Made My Family. (p. 690)
—God Made Plants. (p. 690)
—Hablame de Dios. Erickson, David L., illus. (p. 735)
—I am Kind to My Friends. (p. 833)
—I Give. (p. 838)
—I Grow. (p. 838)
—I Help. (p. 839)
—I Listen. (p. 841)
—I Obey My Parents. (p. 844)
—I Praise God. (p. 844)
—I Pray. (p. 844)
—I Say Thank-You. (p. 845)
—I Share. (p. 845)
—I Take Care of My Body. (p. 846)
—I Take Care of My Pets. (p. 846)
—I Take Care of My Room. (p. 846)
—I Take Care of the Earth. (p. 846)
—I Trust God at Night. (p. 847)
—I Trust God When It Rains. (p. 847)
—Jesus Is Alive! Easter. (p. 915)
—Jesus Is God's Son: Christmas. (p. 915)
—Jesus Is My Friend. (p. 915)
—Jesus Made People Well. (p. 916)
—Marvy Gets the Thumps. (p. 1100)
—Monday, Tuesday, Oopsday! (p. 1163)
—Pot Luck Supper. (p. 1388)
—Story Telling: Bible Class Activities for Ages 2 To5. (p. 1663)
—Tell Me about God. Erickson, David, illus. (p. 1716)
Henley, Karyn F. Love Trumps Karma: Uncovering the Truth You Know You Know. (p. 1060)
—Sword Fighting. (p. 1692)
Henley, Ralph. Action Rhymes & Active Games: Over 200 Bible Story Activities for Ages 2 to 5. (p. 10)
Henley, Tracy, jt. auth. see Thorne, B. Michael.
Henn, Astrid, illus. see Weigelt, Udo.
Henn, Pamela. Nick & Slim: The Legend of the Falcon Mine. (p. 1251)
Henn, Sophy. Where Bear? Henn, Sophy, illus. (p. 1906)
Henne, R. J. Talking Rabbit & the Farmer. (p. 1703)
Henne, R. J. & Wilson, Marlys. Harley Boogle & His Bulldog Buster (p. 749)
Henneberg, Susan. Creating Science Fair Projects with Cool New Digital Tools. (p. 379)
—Defeating Addiction & Alcoholism. (p. 423)
—I Have Been Raped, Now What? (p. 839)
—Investigating Ghosts & the Spirit World (p. 884)
—James Baldwin (p. 907)
—Money-Making Opportunities for Teens Who Like Working with Kids. (p. 1164)
—Step-By-Step Guide to Effective Job Hunting & Career Preparedness. (p. 1647)
—Twitter Safety & Privacy: A Guide to Microblogging. (p. 1803)
—Vo-Tech Track to Success in Health Care. (p. 1847)
—What Is a Song? (p. 1888)
Henneberger, Robert, illus. see Christopher, Matt.
Henneberry, Dottie. I Still Believe in Butterflies. Scherer, Viki, ed. (p. 846)
Hennessey, David G. Cricket's Christmas: the Bethlehem Story. (p. 382)
Hennessey, Dick. Me Tarzan - You Jane. (p. 1116)
—Survival. (p. 1686)
Hennessey, Jimmy. TAE KWON DO Just for You. (p. 1695)
Hennessey, Thomas. Origins of the Troubles. (p. 1304)
Hennessy, B. G. Boy Who Cried Wolf. Kulikov, Boris, illus. (p. 219)
—Claire & the Unicorn Happy Ever After. Mitchell, Susan, illus. (p. 326)
—Corduroy Goes to the Beach. McCue, Lisa, illus. (p. 367)
—Mr. Ouchy's First Day. Meisel, Paul, illus. (p. 1186)
—Once upon a Time Map Book: Take a Tour of Six Enchanted Lands. Joyce, Peter, illus. (p. 1293)
—Scary Places Map Book: Seven Terrifying Tours. Madrid, Erwin, illus. (p. 1520)
Hennessy, B. G., jt. auth. see Freeman, Don.
Hennessy, Barbara G. Once upon a Time Map Book: Take a Tour of Six Enchanted Lands. Joyce, Peter, illus. (p. 1293)
Hennessy, Brendan. Essay to Write? (p. 536)
Hennessy, Claire. Afterwards. (p. 29)
Hennessy, James. Shane's Game. (p. 1559)
Hennessy, Mary L. Spring Breezes & Sneezes. (p. 1635)
Hennessy, Mary-Christine. My Hidden Friend. (p. 1211)
Hennessy-Howell, Heather. Dangles: The Adventures of Dangles. (p. 404)
Hennesy, Carolyn. Pandora Gets Angry. (p. 1321)
—Pandora Gets Frightened. (p. 1321)
—Pandora Gets Greedy. (p. 1321)
—Pandora Gets Heart (p. 1321)
—Pandora Gets Jealous. (p. 1321)
—Pandora Gets Lazy. (p. 1321)
—Pandora Gets Vain. (p. 1321)
Henning, Ann. Cow Patty Patti. (p. 373)
Henning, Heather. Christmas. Bull, Nicola, ed. (p. 312)
—Creation. Bull, Nicola, ed. (p. 379)
—God Sent a Baby King. Atkins, Alison, illus. (p. 690)
—When God Created the World. (p. 1902)
Henning, Heather, jt. auth. see Rivers, Moore Debbie.
Henninger, Michelle, illus. see Nolen, Jerdine, et al.
Henninger, Michelle, illus. see Nolen, Jerdine.
Henninger, Michelle, illus. see Wallace, Nancy K.
Henningfeld, Diane Andrews. Adoption. (p. 13)
—Charter Schools. (p. 294)
—Death Penalty. (p. 420)
—Disasters. Greenaven Press Staff & Gale Editors, eds. (p. 447)
—Disasters. Greenhaven Press Editors & Gale Editors, eds. (p. 447)
—Family Violence. (p. 569)
—Famine. (p. 569)
—Health & Disease. (p. 757)
—North & South Poles. (p. 1264)
—Should Women Be Allowed to Serve in Combat in the U. S. Armed Forces? (p. 1570)
—Women in Islam. (p. 1945)
Henningfeld, Diane Andrews & Haugen, David. Hurricane Katrina. (p. 830)
Henningfeld, Diane Andrews, ed. Adoption. (p. 13)
—Family Violence. (p. 569)
—Haiti Earthquake. (p. 736)
Henningfield, Diane Andrews. Disposal of the Dead. (p. 453)
Henningfield, Jack E., ed. see Chastain, Zachary.
Henningfield, Jack E., ed. see Etingoff, Kim.
Henningfield, Jack E., ed. see Miller, Malinda.
Henningfield, Jack E., ed. see Nelson, Sheila.
Henningfield, Jack E., ed. see Sanna, E. J.
Henningfield, Jack E., ed. see Walker, Ida.
Henny, Rose. Teddy Finds His Way: A Teddy Tale. Henny, Rose, illus. (p. 1712)
Heno, Christy C. Christmas Pageant. Scott, Maren J., illus. (p. 315)
Henretta, James A. America's History: High School Edition. (p. 64)
Henrichs, Wendy. I Am Tama, Lucky Cat: A Japanese Legend Jaeggi, Yoshiko, illus. (p. 834)
—When Anju Loved Being an Elephant. Butler, John, illus. (p. 1901)
Henricks, Dana. George Clooney. (p. 663)
Henrickson, Beth. Marquis de Lafayette & Other International Champions of the American Revolution. (p. 1096)
Henriksen, Rebecca, illus. see Harrold, Yvette.
Henrikson, Jerilynn. Teddy, the Ghost Dog of Red Rocks. (p. 1713)
Henrikson, Peggy & Moore, Lorraine O. Creating Balance in Children: Activities to Optimize Learning & Behavior - A Guide for Teachers & Parents of Children Ages 5 to 14. (p. 378)
Henrique, Paulo, illus. see Conway, Gerry.
Henrique, Paulo, illus. see Farshtey, Greg.
Henrique, Paulo, illus. see Lobdell, Scott.
Henrique, Paulo, illus. see Petrucha, Stefan.
Henrique, Paulo, jt. auth. see Petrucha, Stefan.
Henriques, Ben. Max & the Memory Machine. (p. 1110)
Henriques, S. M. My Little Book of Prayer. (p. 1212)
Henriquez, Cesar. Jonathan's Colorful Campus Tour - University of Connecticut A-Z. (p. 925)
—Sebastian's Colorful Campus Tour - University of Miami A-Z. (p. 1539)
Henriquez, Emile, illus. see Pushker, Gloria Teles & Tarman, Mel.
Henriquez, Emile, illus. see Townsend, Una Belle.
Henriquez, Emile, illus. see Williams Evans, Freddi & Evans, Freddi Williams.
Henriquez, Emile F., illus. see McConduit, Denise Walter.
Henry, A. Underwood. Kitching, Laura, illus. (p. 1817)
Henry, April. Blood Will Tell. (p. 200)
—Body in the Woods. (p. 207)
—Girl, Stolen. (p. 679)

—Girl Who Was Supposed to Die. (p. 679)
—Night She Disappeared. (p. 1254)
—Shock Point. (p. 1568)
Henry, Blake, illus. see Smith, Greg Leitich.
Henry, Brian. American Incident. (p. 61)
Henry, Chaz. St. Mulligan & the History of Golf. (p. 1638)
Henry, Daphne. Victory over the Silent Consequences of Divorce. (p. 1840)
Henry, Deborah. Not Too Young to Pray. (p. 1267)
Henry, Deborah, ed. My Devotions: Fifty Years. (p. 1201)
Henry, Debra. Best Behavior: A Celebration of Good Manners for Our African-American Children. Deal, David, photos by. (p. 168)
Henry, Dick O. Everyday Happenings. (p. 543)
Henry, Freeman G. Geo/Graphies: Mapping the Imagination in French & Francophone Literature & Film. (p. 662)
Henry, Gordon, jt. auth. see Cornell, George.
Henry, Heather French. Claire's Magic Sades. Henry, Heather French, illus. (p. 326)
—Claire's Magic Shoes. Henry, Heather French, illus. (p. 326)
—Cornbread Kitchen: A Thanksgiving Day Story. (p. 367)
—Flying Away. Henry, Heather French, illus. (p. 609)
—Pepper's Purple Heart: A Veteran's Day Story. (p. 1340)
—Pepper's Purple Heart: A Veteran's Day Story. Henry, Heather French, illus. (p. 1340)
—Volando. (p. 1848)
—What Freedom Means to Me: A Flag Day Story. Henry, Heather French, illus. (p. 1884)
—Zapatas Magicas de Claire. (p. 1985)
Henry, Henther French. Life, Liberty & the Pursuit of Jellybeans: A Fourth of July Story. Henry, Henther French, illus. (p. 1011)
—Life, Liberty & the Pursuit of Jellybeans: An Independence Day Story. Henry, Henther French, illus. (p. 1011)
Henry, Isabelle. Hundred-Penny Rub. (p. 827)
Henry, J. Big Gray House II: More Adventures of Franklin Meyers. (p. 181)
Henry, J., illus. see Altsheler, Joseph A.
Henry, James. Cabinet of Curiosities. (p. 250)
—Real Thing & Other Tales. (p. 1449)
Henry, Jed. Cheer up, Mouse! Henry, Jed, illus. (p. 296)
—Good Night, Mouse! Henry, Jed, illus. (p. 699)
—I Speak Dinosaur! (p. 846)
Henry, Jed, illus. see Becker, Kate M.
Henry, Jed, illus. see Chall, Marsha Wilson.
Henry, Jed, illus. see Detlefsen, Lisl H.
Henry, Jed, illus. see Harber Freeman, Anna.
Henry, Jed, illus. see Hood, Susan.
Henry, Jed, illus. see Myracle, Lauren.
Henry, Jed, illus. see Parker, Marjorie Blain.
Henry, Jed, illus. see Taylor Kent, Derek.
Henry, Jonathan. Astronomy Book. (p. 109)
Henry, Judy. Uniquely Alaska (p. 1818)
—Woodland Stories for Our Grandchildren. (p. 1949)
Henry, Juliann. Little Shepherd Girl: A Christmas Story. Madsen, Jim, illus. (p. 1036)
Henry, Kristina. Rat Tank Ambler, Laura & Brown, Amanda, illus. (p. 1440)
—Turtle Tank Ambler, Laura & Brown, Amanda, illus. (p. 1798)
Henry, Kristina, et al. Fish Tank (p. 598)
Henry, LaTosha. Dino Treasure Hunt Friesen, Wayne, illus. (p. 441)
Henry, Laura & Phillips-Green, Jeanette. Senses. (p. 1551)
Henry, Lenworth. Gilbert the Mighty Hurricane: A Jamaican Experience. (p. 676)
Henry, Lewis. Gaulin & the Dove. (p. 658)
Henry, Lucia Kemp, jt. auth. see Moore, Suzanne.
Henry, Lynn. Think Like a Pony: Foundation Book. (p. 1734)
—Think Like a Pony on the Ground (p. 1734)
Henry, Maggie, illus. see Mahoney, Liana.
Henry, Mandy. Elephants in Our House. (p. 512)
Henry, Marcia. Madeline Island ABC Coloring Book. Parsons, Sally, illus. (p. 1070)
Henry, Marguerite. Benjamin West & His Cat Grimalkin. Dennis, Wesley, illus. (p. 165)
—Brighty of the Grand Canyon. (p. 228)
—Cinnabar, the One o'Clock Fox. Dennis, Wesley, illus. (p. 321)
—Gaudenzia, Pride of the Palio. Ward, Lynd, illus. (p. 658)
—Justin Morgan Had a Horse. (p. 940)
—Justin Morgan Had a Horse. Dennis, Wesley, illus. (p. 940)
—King of the Wind: The Story of the Godolphin Arabian. (p. 959)
—King of the Wind: The Story of the Godolphin Arabian. Dennis, Wesley, illus. (p. 959)
—Marguerite Henry Complete Collection (p. 1093)
—Misty of Chincoteague. Dennis, Wesley, illus. (p. 1155)
—Misty's Twilight. Grandpré, Karen Haus, illus. (p. 1155)
—Sea Star: Orphan of Chincoteague. Dennis, Wesley, illus. (p. 1535)
—Stormy, Misty's Foal. Dennis, Wesley, illus. (p. 1656)
—White Stallion of Lipizza. (p. 1913)
—White Stallion of Lipizza. Dennis, Wesley, illus. (p. 1913)
Henry, Marilyn. Marilyn Monroe Paper Dolls. Henry, Marilyn, illus. (p. 1094)
Henry, Martha J. & Pollack, Daniel. Adoption in the United States: A Reference for Families, Professionals, & Students. (p. 13)
Henry, Matthew. Comentario Matthew Henry: Poeticos: Matthew Henry's Commentary: Matthew Henry. Vol. II (p. 348)
Henry, Michèle. Cleveland Drive Mysteries: The Hunt. (p. 331)
Henry, Mike. Tell Me about the Presidents: Lessons for Today's Kids from America's Leaders. (p. 1716)
Henry, Mike, illus. see Kapai, Tommy.
Henry, Nancy. Where's Papa? (p. 1910)
Henry, Natasha L. Talking about Freedom: Celebrating Emancipation Day in Canada. (p. 1703)
Henry, Nathan L. Good Behavior. (p. 697)
Henry, O. Gift of the Magi: A Story about Giving. Jaekel, Susan M., illus. (p. 675)
—Gift of the Magi. Lynch, P. J., illus. (p. 675)
—Gift of the Magi. Zwerger, Lisbeth, illus. (p. 675)
—Ransom of Red Chief. Delessert, Etienne, illus. (p. 1438)
Henry, O., jt. auth. see Escott, John.
Henry, O., jt. auth. see Shipton, Paul.
Henry, O. & Gianni, Gary. Gift of the Magi. (p. 675)
Henry, O., et al. Graphic Classics - O. Henry Pomplun, Tom, ed. (p. 710)
Henry, Pam. Cold Call. (p. 338)
Henry, Patrick. Spectacular Adventures of John Cross. (p. 1624)
Henry, Patsy M. My Hare Line & the Dead Pine Tree. (p. 1210)
—My Hare Line & the Hat. (p. 1210)
—My Hare Line Meets the Brown Rabbit. (p. 1210)
Henry, Patti. Emotionally Unavailable Man: A Blueprint for Healing. Grass, Jeff, photos by. (p. 520)
Henry, Regene. Barefoot Boys of Fayette. Stich, Carolyn R., illus. (p. 139)
Henry, Rohan. Gift Box. (p. 675)
Henry, Sally. Card Making. (p. 265)
—Clay Modeling. (p. 330)
—Collage. (p. 339)
—Drawing. (p. 481)
—Make Your Own Art (p. 1079)
—Painting. (p. 1318)
—Paper Folding. (p. 1322)
Henry, Sally, jt. auth. see Cook, Trevor.
Henry, Sally & Cook, Trevor. Brilliant Book of Experiments. (p. 228)
—Cool Stuff to Do: Jam-Packed with Brilliant Things to Make & Do! (p. 364)
—Eco Crafts. (p. 502)
—Make Your Own Art (p. 1079)
—Making Masks. (p. 1081)
—Making Mosaics. (p. 1081)
—Making Puppets. (p. 1082)
—Origami. (p. 1303)
—Papier-Mâché. (p. 1323)
Henry, Sandi. Making Amazing Art! 40 Activities Using the 7 Elements of Art Design. Cole, Sarah, illus. (p. 1080)
—Using Color in Your Art! Choosing Colors for Impact & Pizzazz. Rakitin, Sarah, illus. (p. 1828)
—Using Color in Your Art! Chossing Colors for Impact & Pizzazz. Rakitin, Sarah, illus. (p. 1828)
Henry, Sandy. Child's Bedtime Companion. Pavlova, Vera, illus. (p. 304)
Henry, Shanta. When Thugs Cry. (p. 1905)
Henry, Sherrie. Last of the Summer Tomatoes. (p. 978)
—Last of the Summer Tomatoes [Library Edition]. (p. 978)
Henry, Steve. Cat Got a Lot. (p. 278)
—Happy Cat. (p. 745)
—Happy Cat. Henry, Steve, illus. (p. 745)
—Here Is Big Bunny. (p. 770)
Henry, Steven, illus. see Colby, Rebecca.
Henry, Sue. Refuge (p. 1456)
Henry, T. K. Rickey & Rachel, the Cats without Tails & Their Awesome Adventure. (p. 1470)
Henry, Thomas, illus. see Crompton, Richmal.
Henry, Tom. Paul Bunyan on the West Coast. La Fave, Kim, illus. (p. 1330)
Henry, W., ed. see Bloom, Harold.
Henry, W., et al. Bloom's BioCritiques. (p. 201)
Henry, William. Growing up Country: Life on the Farm. (p. 726)
—Tir na NOg: A New Adventure. Arnault, Delphine, illus. (p. 1757)
Hensdill, Norma Mae. Friends Are Forever. (p. 638)
—I'm Granny's Little Mess, Just Look at the Rest. (p. 859)
Hense, Mary, et al. How Astronauts Use Math. (p. 805)
—How Fighter Pilots Use Math. (p. 809)
Hensel, Boots. Zoopendous Surprise! Gabriel, Andrea, illus. (p. 1990)
Hensel, Gege. a B C Animal Adventures. (p. 1)
Hensel, Rita. Humble Stew in Going Country. (p. 826)
—Whooo's the Chicken Thief, a Humble Stew Book (p. 1920)
Hensel, Sylvia. a B C Animal Adventures. (p. 1)
Henshall, Kenneth G., et al. Guide to Reading & Writing Japanese: A Comprehensive Guide to the Japanese Writing System. (p. 730)
Henshon, Suzanna. Mildew on the Wall. (p. 1142)
Henshon, Suzanna E. Spiders on the Ceiling. (p. 1627)
Hensie, Terry W., jt. ed. see Chmiel, David.
Hensler, K. Why Worry? The Adventures of Bay/Bob/A/Loo/Bop Everything in Moderation. (p. 1927)
Hensler, Sue. Cage Fight. (p. 251)
Hensley, Annemarie. Freeman Out of Water. (p. 635)
Hensley, Janice. Sparkie & Barney Discover the Power of Prayer. (p. 1622)
Hensley, Joy N. Rites of Passage. (p. 1475)
Hensley, Judith Victoria. Sir Thomas the Eggslayer. (p. 1580)
—Terrible Tin. (p. 1721)
Hensley, Laura. Advertising Attack (p. 25)
—Art for All: What Is Public Art? (p. 102)
—How to Read a Work of Art (p. 821)
Hensley, Nathaniel. Strange Tale of Hector & Hannah Crowe. (p. 1665)
Hensley, Sarah M. I Can Be. Teeple, Jackie, illus. (p. 834)
Hensley, Sarah M. At the Park. Crowell, Knox, illus. (p. 111)
—Caillou Goes to the Fair. Coray, Stacy A., illus. (p. 251)
—Caillou's Trip to the Harbor. Gillen, Lisa P., illus. (p. 252)
—Caillov Visits the Circus. Storch, Ellen N., illus. (p. 252)
—Helping Farmer Joe. Crowell, Knox, illus. (p. 766)
—Helping in My Town. Middleton, Mikell, illus. (p. 766)
—I Want to Ride. Gray, Stacy A., illus. (p. 848)
—Katie's Snacks. Coray, Stacy A., illus. (p. 945)
—Water Fun. Crowell, Knox, illus. (p. 1862)
Hensley, Terri Anne. Henry visits the Veterinarian. (p. 768)
—Henry's new Home. (p. 769)
—Silliest Bug & Insect Book Ever. Hall, Norris, illus. (p. 1575)
—Tobias Andrew Bartholomew. Hall, Norris, illus. (p. 1760)
Hensley, Wendie & Licata, Annette. Science. (p. 1524)
Henson, Andora. Shelby's 'Doption Story. Moody, Julie, illus. (p. 1564)
Henson, Brooke, illus. see Burnette, Margarette.
Henson, Gaby, illus. see Baxter, Nicola.
Henson, Heather. Angel Coming. Gaber, Susan, illus. (p. 73)
—Dream of Night. (p. 483)
—Grumpy Grandpa. MacDonald, Ross, illus. (p. 727)
—Here's How I See It - Here's How It Is. (p. 771)
—Here's How I See It—Here's How It Is. (p. 771)
—Making the Run. (p. 1082)
—That Book Woman. Small, David, illus. (p. 1726)
Henson, Heather, et al. Vampire Bunny. Mack, Jeff, tr. (p. 1832)
Henson, Jim & Juhl, Jerry. Tale of Sand. Christy, Stephen & Robinson, Chris, eds. (p. 1700)
Henson, Laura J. & Grooms, Duffy. Ten Little Elvi. Gorissen, Dean, illus. (p. 1719)
Henson, Susan, jt. auth. see Bishop, Jennie.
Henson, Tara. Littlest Blue Jay. (p. 1038)
Hensperger, Beth. Bread Bible: Beth Hensperger's 300 Favorite Recipes. Bates, Harry, illus. (p. 224)
Henterly, Jamichael, illus. see Ward, Jennifer.
Hentges, Katie. Your First Boyfriend. (p. 1980)
Hentley, Sheila Rose. Nursery Rhymes & Nursery Riddles for All Ages. (p. 1273)
Henty, A. G. With Frederick the Great. (p. 1942)
Henty, G. A. At Aboukir & Acre: A Story of Napoleon's Invasion of Egypt (Henty Homeschool History Series) (p. 110)
—At Agincourt: A Tale of the White Hoods of Paris. (p. 110)
—At Agincourt: A Story of the White Hoods of Paris. (p. 110)
—At Agincourt (Deluxe Heirloom Edition) A Story of the White Hoods of Paris (Deluxe Heirloom Edition) (p. 110)
—Beric the Briton: A Story of the Roman Invasion. (p. 167)
—Bonnie Prince Charlie: A Tale of Fontenoy & Culloden. (p. 209)
—Boy Knight: A Tale of the Crusades. (p. 218)
—Bravest of the Brave. (p. 223)
—By Conduct & Courage: A Story of the Days of Nelson. (p. 249)
—By Sheer Pluck: A Tale of the Ashanti War. (p. 249)
—Captain Bayley's Heir: A Tale of the California Gold Fields. (p. 263)
—Cat of Bubastes: A Tale of Ancient Egypt. (p. 278)
—Cat of Bubastes. (p. 278)
—Dragon & the Raven: The Days of King Alfred. (p. 476)
—Dragon & the Raven. (p. 476)
—Dragon & the Raven: or the Days of King Alfred. (p. 476)
—For Name & Fame: Or Through Afghan Passes. (p. 616)
—For Name & Fame: Or, Through Afghan Passes. (p. 616)
—For Name & Fame (Deluxe Heirloom Edition) Or, Through Afghan Passes (Deluxe Heirloom Edition) (p. 616)
—Friends Though Divided: A Tale of the Civil War. (p. 639)
—G. A. Henty Short Story Collection: Featuring: Sole Survivors, the Frontier Girl, the Ranch in the Valley, & on the Track (p. 651)
—G. A. Henty Short Story Collecton (Deluxe Heirloom Edition) Featuring: Sole Survivors, the Frontier Girl, the Ranch in the Valley, & on the Track (Deluxe Heirloom Edition) (p. 651)
—In Freedom's Cause: A Tale of Wallace & Bruce. (p. 863)
—In Freedom's Cause: A Story of Wallace & Bruce. (p. 863)
—In the Heart of the Rockies: An Adventure on the Colorado River. (p. 866)
—In the Heart of the Rockies. (p. 866)
—In the Reign of Terror: The Adventures of a Westminster Boy. (p. 867)
—Lion of Saint Mark: A Story of Venice in the Fourteenth Century. (p. 1020)
—March on London: A Story of Wat Tyler's Insurrection. (p. 1091)
—March on London: Being a Story of Wat Tyler's Insurrection. (p. 1091)
—March on London (Deluxe Heirloom Edition) A Story of Wat Tyler's Insurrection (Deluxe Heirloom Edition) (p. 1091)
—No Surrender! A Tale of the Rising in la Vendee. (p. 1260)
—No Surrender! (Deluxe Heirloom Edition) A Tale of the Rising in la Vendee (Deluxe Heirloom Edition) (p. 1260)
—On the Pampas: Or the Young Settlers. (p. 1291)
—Orange & Green: A Tale of the Boyne & Limerick. (p. 1301)
—Orange & Green (Deluxe Heirloom Edition) A Tale of the Boyne & Limerick (Deluxe Heirloom Edition) (p. 1301)
—St. George for England: A Tale of Cressy & Poitiers. (p. 1638)
—St. George for England. (p. 1638)
—Stone Chest or the Secret of Cedar Island. (p. 1652)
—Tale of the Western Plains. Pearse, Alfred, illus. (p. 1700)
—Through Russian Snows: A Story of Napoleon's Retreat from Moscow. (p. 1745)
—Through Three Campaigns: A Story of Chitral Tirah & Ashanti. (p. 1745)
—Tiger of Mysore: A Story of the War with Tippoo Saib. (p. 1748)
—Tiger of Mysore (Deluxe Heirloom Edition) A Story of the War with Tippoo Saib (Deluxe Heirloom Edition) (p. 1748)
—To Herat & Cabul: A Story of the First Afghan War. (p. 1759)
—To Herat & Cabul (Deluxe Heirloom Edition) A Story of the First Afghan War (Deluxe Heirloom Edition) (p. 1759)
—Treasure of the Incas: The Treasure of the Incas. (p. 1782)
—True to the Old Flag: A Tale of the American War of Independence. (p. 1793)
—True to the Old Flag: A Novel of the Loyalists in the American War of Independence. (p. 1793)
—True to the Old Flag. (p. 1793)
—Under Drake's Flag: A Tale of the Spanish Main. (p. 1813)
—Under Wellington's Command: A Tale of the Peninsular War. (p. 1814)
—Under Wellington's Command (Deluxe Heirloom Edition) A Tale of the Peninsular War (Deluxe Heirloom Edition) (p. 1814)
—When London Burned: A Story of Restoration Times & the Great Fire. (p. 1903)
—Winning His Spurs: A Tale of the Crusades. (p. 1937)
—With Buller in Natal: Or a Born Leader. (p. 1942)
—With Clive in India: Or the Beginnings of an Empire. (p. 1942)
—With Clive in India. (p. 1942)
—With Frederick the Great: A Tale of the Seven Years' War. (p. 1942)
—With Lee in Virgini: A Story of the American Civil War. (p. 1942)
—With Lee in Virgini. (p. 1942)
—With Lee in Virginia: A Story of the American Civil War. (p. 1942)
—With Lee in Virginia. (p. 1942)
—With Moore at Corunna: A Tale of the Peninsular War. (p. 1942)
—With the Allies to Pekin: A Tale of the Relief of the Legations. (p. 1942)
—With the Allies to Pekin (Deluxe Heirloom Edition) A Tale of the Relief of the Legations (Deluxe Heirloom Edition) (p. 1942)
—With Wolfe in Canad: The Winning of a Continent. (p. 1942)
—With Wolfe in Canada: The Winning of a Continent. (p. 1942)
—Wulf the Saxon: A Story of the Norman Conquest. Peacock, Ralph, illus. (p. 1966)
—Wulf the Saxon. (p. 1966)
—Young Buglers: A Tale of the Peninsular War. (p. 1978)
—Young Carthaginian: A Tale of the Times of Hannibal. (p. 1978)
—Young Carthaginian: A Story of the Times of Hannibal. (p. 1978)
Hentzell, Brittany. Annie & Amie's Arduous Afternoon. (p. 86)
Henwood, Doug. After the New Economy. (p. 28)
Henzel, Cynthia Kennedy. Great Barrier Reef. (p. 713)
—Great Wall of China. (p. 719)
—Pyramids of Egypt. (p. 1421)
—Stonehenge. (p. 1653)
—Taj Mahal. (p. 1696)
Henzel, Richard, ed. Chapters from My Autobiography. Narrated by Richard Henzel. (p. 291)
Heo, Min, jt. auth. see Fowler, Gloria.
Heo, Yumi. Green Frogs: A Korean Folktale. (p. 721)
—Red Light, Green Light. Heo, Yumi, illus. (p. 1454)
—Sun & Moon Have a Tea Party. (p. 1676)
—Ten Days & Nine Nights: An Adoption Story. Heo, Yumi, illus. (p. 1718)
Heo, Yumi, illus. see Look, Lenore.
Heo, Yumi, illus. see Lupton, Hugh.
Heo, Yumi, illus. see Vail, Rachel.
Heo, Yumi, jt. auth. see MacDonald, George.
Heos, Bridget. Alabama: Past & Present. (p. 33)
—Alabama Football. (p. 33)
—At the Eleventh Hour: And Other Expressions about Money & Numbers. (p. 111)
—Be Safe Around Fire. Baroncelli, Silvia, illus. (p. 149)
—Be Safe Around Water. Baroncelli, Silvia, illus. (p. 149)
—Be Safe on the Internet. Baroncelli, Silvia, illus. (p. 149)
—Be Safe on the Playground. Baroncelli, Silvia, illus. (p. 149)
—Be Safe on Your Bike. Baroncelli, Silvia, illus. (p. 149)
—Brain in Your Body (p. 221)
—Brain Quest Workbook: Grade 5. Rockefeller, Matt, illus. (p. 222)
—Career as a Hairstylist. (p. 266)
—Colorado: Past & Present. (p. 343)
—Cool As a Cucumber: And Other Expressions about Food. (p. 362)
—Counting Change. Longhi, Katya, illus. (p. 371)
—Creation of Peninsulas. (p. 379)
—Do You Really Want a Cat? Longhi, Katya, illus. (p. 458)
—Do You Really Want a Guinea Pig? Longhi, Katya, illus. (p. 458)
—Do You Really Want a Hamster? Longhi, Katya, illus. (p. 458)
—Do You Really Want a Horse? Longhi, Katya, illus. (p. 458)
—Do You Really Want a Lizard? Longhi, Katya, illus. (p. 458)
—Do You Really Want to Visit a Coral Reef? Fabbri, Daniele, illus. (p. 458)
—Do You Really Want to Visit a Prairie? Fabbri, Daniele, illus. (p. 458)
—Do You Really Want to Visit a Temperate Forest? Fabbri, Daniele, illus. (p. 458)
—Do You Really Want to Visit Neptune? Fabbri, Daniele, illus. (p. 458)
—Do You Really Want to Visit Saturn? Fabbri, Daniele, illus. (p. 458)
—Getting a Job in Hair Care & Makeup. (p. 668)
—Human Genome. (p. 826)
—I, Fly. Plecas, Jennifer, illus. (p. 838)
—Ice Fishing. (p. 850)
—Jay-Z. (p. 910)
—Just Like Us!, Ants. (p. 939)
—Just Like Us!, Birds. (p. 939)
—Kofi Kingston: Champ of Smackdown. (p. 966)
—Lady Gaga. (p. 970)
—Let's Meet a Construction Worker. Moran, Mike, illus. (p. 999)
—Let's Meet a Dentist. Poling, Kyle, illus. (p. 999)
—Let's Meet a Doctor. Moran, Mike, illus. (p. 999)
—Let's Meet a Teacher. Poling, Kyle, illus. (p. 999)
—Making Graphs. Longhi, Katya, illus. (p. 1081)
—Manners at a Friend's House. Longhi, Katya, illus. (p. 1088)
—Manners at a Restaurant. Longhi, Katya, illus. (p. 1088)
—Manners at School. Longhi, Katya, illus. (p. 1088)
—Manners at the Store. Longhi, Katya, illus. (p. 1088)
—Manners on Vacation. Longhi, Katya, illus. (p. 1088)
—Manners with Technology. Longhi, Katya, illus. (p. 1088)
—Measure It. Longhi, Katya, illus. (p. 1117)
—Mustache Baby. Ang, Joy, illus. (p. 1194)
—Mustache Baby Meets His Match. Ang, Joy, illus. (p. 1194)
—Polluted Water & Your Vital Organs. (p. 1381)
—Rey Mysterio: Giant Killer. (p. 1467)
—Rihanna. (p. 1472)
—Ronde & Tiki Barber: Football Stars. (p. 1487)
—Ronde & Tiki Barber: Football Stars (Sports Families) (p. 1487)
—So You Want to Grow a Pie? Fabbri, Daniele, illus. (p. 1602)
—So You Want to Grow a Pizza? Fabbri, Daniele, illus. (p. 1602)
—So You Want to Grow a Taco? Fabbri, Daniele, illus. (p. 1602)
—Stronger Than Steel: Spider Silk DNA & the Quest for Better Bulletproof Vests, Sutures, & Parachute Rope. Comins, Andy, illus. (p. 1668)
—Telling Time. Longhi, Katya, illus. (p. 1717)
—Triple H: No Mercy. (p. 1787)
—What Are Measurements? (p. 1879)
—What to Expect When You're Expecting Hatchlings: A Guide for Crocodilian Parents (and Curious Kids) Jorisch, Stéphane, illus. (p. 1894)

—What to Expect When You're Expecting Joeys: A Guide for Marsupial Parents (And Curious Kids) Jorisch, Stéphane, illus. (p. 1894)
—What to Expect When You're Expecting Larvae: A Guide for Insect Parents (And Curious Kids) Jorisch, Stéphane, illus. (p. 1894)
—Wisconsin: Past & Present. (p. 1939)
—Your First Girlfriend. (p. 1980)
Heos, Bridget & Powell, Marie. Do You Really Want a Bird? Longhi, Katya, illus. (p. 458)
Hepburn, C J. Reading & Language Arts: Level J. (p. 1445)
Hepburn, Debby, ed. see Hepburn, Richard D.
Hepburn, Greg. Liam Goes to Independence Hall. (p. 1004)
Hepburn, Richard D. History of American Naval Dry Docks. Hepburn, Debby et al, eds. (p. 783)
Hepfler, Caroline Ann. Huckleberrys Hiccups. (p. 824)
Hepker, Sue. This Is the Challah. Wummer, Amy, illus. (p. 1736)
Hepler, Chris, jt. auth. see Hepler, Jennifer Brandes.
Hepler, Heather. Cupcake Queen. (p. 392)
—Love? Maybe. (p. 1059)
Hepler, Heather, jt. auth. see Barkley, Brad.
Hepler, Jennifer Brandes & Hepler, Chris. M. I. T. H. Operation Smoking Jaguar. (p. 1067)
Hepler, Linda McGhee. How to Survive Seventh Grade (If You're Lucky) (p. 822)
Hepola, Catherine R. Great Toadie. (p. 718)
Hepperman, Christina. Samurai. (p. 1509)
Heppermann, Christine. City Chickens. (p. 323)
—Poisoned Apples: Poems for You, My Pretty. (p. 1377)
—Samurai. (p. 1509)
—Twitter: The Company & Its Founders. (p. 1803)
—Whitney Houston: Recording Artist & Actress. (p. 1914)
Heppermann, Christine & Friedman, Richard D. Bush v. Gore: The Florida Recounts of the 2000 Presidential Election. (p. 244)
Heppermann, Christine & Koertge, Ronald. Sadie's Story. Marcero, Deborah, illus. (p. 1501)
Hepplewhite, Peter. Knights. (p. 964)
—Loos, Poos, & Number Twos: A Disgusting Journey Through the Bowels of History! (p. 1052)
—Roman Soldiers. (p. 1486)
—Royals, Rebels, & Horrible Headchoppers: A Bloodthirsty History of the Terrifying Tudors! (p. 1492)
—Thomas Crapper, Corsets, & Cruel Britannia: A Grim History of the Vexing Victorians! (p. 1738)
—True Stories from World War I. (p. 1792)
Hepworth, Emily. Stray Dog. (p. 1666)
Herald, Jacqueline. Fashions of a Decade: The 1920s. (p. 576)
—Fashions of a Decade: The 1970s. (p. 576)
Heran, Michelle, illus. see Waters, Galadriel, ed.
Heras, Theo. What Will We Do with the Baby-O? Herbert, Jennifer, illus. (p. 1895)
Herbach, Geoff. Fat Boy vs. the Cheerleaders. (p. 577)
—Gabe Johnson Takes Over. (p. 652)
—I'm with Stupid. (p. 860)
—Nothing Special. (p. 1268)
—Stupid Fast. (p. 1670)
Herbauts, Anne. Monday. (p. 1163)
—Prince Silencio. Bedrick, Claudia Z., tr. from FRE. (p. 1401)
Herbert, Bethany Zohner. Perfect Fool. (p. 1341)
Herbert, Brian, et al. Road to Dune. (p. 1477)
Herbert Carter. Boy Scouts' First Camp Fire. (p. 218)
Herbert, David. Charles Darwin's Religious Journey. (p. 292)
Herbert, Denis. Mon Enfance Lilloise Racontee a ma Fille: Recits d'Antan (1950 A 1955) Silver, Joanne S., ed. (p. 1163)
Herbert, Denis & Silver, Joanne. Complément éducatif: Mon Enfance Lilloise Racontée à Ma Fille: Récits D'antan (1950 à 1955) (p. 352)
Herbert, Frances. Fran's Van & the Magic Box. Herbert, Frances, illus. (p. 631)
—Fran's Van & the Naughty Terrier. Herbert, Frances, illus. (p. 631)
Herbert, Frank. Hellstrom's Hive. (p. 765)
Herbert, Gail, jt. auth. see Hutchins, Hazel.
Herbert, George. Complete English Poems. Tobin, John, ed. (p. 352)
Herbert Hoover National Historic Site (U.S), ed. see Romero, Kyle & Padron, Maria Lorena.
Herbert, James. Rats. (p. 1440)
Herbert, Janis. Abraham Lincoln for Kids: His Life & Times with 21 Activities. (p. 7)
Herbert, Jennifer, illus. see Granfield, Linda.
Herbert, Jennifer, illus. see Heras, Theo.
Herbert, Marcus P. Bertie at Bedtime. (p. 168)
Herbert, Patricia M. Life of the Buddha. (p. 1012)
Herbertson, Lisa. Swimming Along. Kennedy, Catherine, illus. (p. 1691)
Herbold, Marvin. Marvin Teaches Fingerspelling. (p. 1100)
Herbold, Marvin, jt. compiled by see Neal, Vonda.
Herbsman, Cheryl Renée. Breathing. (p. 226)
Herbst, Benjamin. What Happens When I Cough? (p. 1886)
Herbst, Gabriele, tr. see Schulz, Charles M.
Herbst, Judith. Aliens. (p. 41)
—Beyond the Grave. (p. 174)
—Germ Theory. (p. 666)
—History of Transportation. (p. 785)
—History of Weapons. (p. 785)
—Hoaxes. (p. 786)
—Lands of Mystery. (p. 974)
—Monsters. (p. 1168)
—UFOs. (p. 1807)
—Vanished. (p. 1833)
Herbst, Kailee. Lots of Clocks: Learning about Tools That Measure Time. (p. 1057)
—Who's Short? Who's Tall? Learning to Compare Heights. (p. 1921)
Herbstritt, Rj. God Loves You More Than Rainbows & Butterflies! Herbstritt, T. J., illus. (p. 689)
Herbstritt, T. J., illus. see Herbstritt, Rj.
Herda, D. J. Dred Scott Case: Slavery & Citizenship. (p. 484)
—Furman V. Georgia: The Death Penalty Case. (p. 650)
—New York Times V. United States: National Security & Censorship. (p. 1248)
Herda, Frank A. Cup of Death: Cronicles of the Dragons of the Magi. (p. 392)
Herdegen, Lance J. Men Stood Like Iron: How the Iron Brigade Won Its Name. (p. 1126)
Herder, Ronald. Great Works for Piano Four Hands. Herder, Ronald, ed. (p. 719)
Herdling, Glenn. African Mythology: Anansi. (p. 27)
—Greek Mythology: Jason & the Golden Fleece. (p. 720)
—Jason & the Golden Fleece: A Greek Myth. (p. 910)
—Mitología Africana: Anansi. Obregon, Jose Maria, illus. (p. 1156)
Herdling, Glenn & Obregón, José María. Mitología Griega: Jasón y el Vellocino de Oro. (p. 1156)
Heredia, Maria Fernanda. Donde Esta Mama? (p. 466)
—Oso, el Mejor Amigo del Hombre. (p. 1305)
—Por Si No Te Lo He Dicho. (p. 1386)
—Premio Con el Que Siempre Sone. (p. 1395)
—Quieres Saber la Verdad? (p. 1428)
Hereford, L. F. Gerry the Grape. Skardarasy, Doreen L., illus. (p. 667)
Herfurtner, Ralph. Niki y el Perrito. (p. 1255)
Hergé. Adventures of Tintin (p. 24)
—America. (p. 58)
—Arumbaya-Fetisch. (p. 105)
—Asunto Tornasol. (p. 109)
—Aterrizaje en la Luna. (p. 111)
—Aventures de Tintin au Pays des Soviets. (p. 119)
—Black Island. (p. 196)
—Blaue Lotos. (p. 198)
—Blue Lotus. (p. 203)
—Broken Ear. (p. 230)
—Calculus Affair. (p. 252)
—Cangrejo Pinzas Oro. (p. 261)
—Castafiore Emerald. (p. 276)
—Cetro de Ottokar. (p. 288)
—Cigares du Pharaon. (p. 319)
—Cigarros del Faraon. (p. 319)
—Cigars of the Pharaoh. (p. 319)
—Crab with the Golden Claws. (p. 375)
—Crabe aux Pinces d'Or. (p. 375)
—Destination Moon. (p. 430)
—Drago Blu. (p. 476)
—Estrella Misteriosa. (p. 538)
—Explorers of the Moon. (p. 551)
—Fall Bienlein. (p. 566)
—Flight 714. (p. 604)
—Flug 714 nach Sydney. (p. 608)
—Geheimnis der "Einhorn" (p. 659)
—Geheimnisvolle Stern. (p. 659)
—Granchio d'Oro. (p. 707)
—Ile Noire. (p. 856)
—Im Reiche des Schwarzen Goldes. (p. 860)
—Isla Negra. (p. 891)
—Joyas de la Castafiore. (p. 930)
—Juwelen der Sangerin. (p. 941)
—King Ottokar's Sceptre. (p. 959)
—Kohle an Bord. (p. 966)
—Konig Ottokar's Zepter. (p. 967)
—Krabbe mit den Goldenen Scheren. (p. 967)
—Land of Black Gold. (p. 973)
—Lo Scettro di Ottokar. (p. 1044)
—Loto Azul. (p. 1057)
—Lotus Bleu. (p. 1057)
—Objectif Lune. (p. 1275)
—Objetivo la Luna. (p. 1275)
—On a Marche sur la Lune. (p. 1288)
—Oreille Cassee. (p. 1303)
—Oreja Rota. (p. 1303)
—Peppy & Virginny in Lapinoland. (p. 1340)
—Prisoners of the Sun. (p. 1407)
—Red Rackham's Treasure. (p. 1454)
—Red Sea Sharks. (p. 1455)
—Reiseziel Mond. (p. 1457)
—Sceptre d' Ottokar. (p. 1521)
—Schatz Rackhams des Roten. (p. 1521)
—Schritte auf dem Mond. (p. 1524)
—Schwarze Insel. (p. 1524)
—Secret de la Licorne. (p. 1540)
—Secret of the Unicorn. (p. 1543)
—Secreto del Unicornio. (p. 1544)
—Segreto del Liocorno. (p. 1548)
—Sept Boules de Cristal. (p. 1551)
—Sette Sfere di Cristallo. (p. 1554)
—Seven Crystal Balls. (p. 1554)
—Shooting Star. (p. 1568)
—Sieben Kristallkugeln. (p. 1573)
—Siete Bolas de Cristal. (p. 1573)
—Sigari del Faraone. (p. 1573)
—Sonnentempel. (p. 1612)
—Stock de Coque. (p. 1651)
—Temple du Soleil. (p. 1718)
—Templo del Sol. (p. 1718)
—Tesoro de Rackham el Rojo. (p. 1722)
—Tesoro di Rakam. (p. 1722)
—Tim und der Haifischsee. (p. 1750)
—Tim und die Picaros. (p. 1750)
—Tim und Struppi 19. Tim in Tibet. (p. 1750)
—Tintín: Descubro Las Letras. (p. 1756)
—Tintín: Descubro Los Números. (p. 1756)
—Tintín: Descubro Los Animales. (p. 1756)
—Tintín: Descubro Los Transportes. (p. 1756)
—Tintín: El cangrejo de las pinzas de Oro. (p. 1756)
—Tintin & Alph-Art. (p. 1756)
—Tintin & the Golden Fleece. (p. 1756)
—Tintin & the Lake of Sharks. (p. 1756)
—Tintin & the Picaros. (p. 1756)
—Tintin au Congo. (p. 1756)
—Tintin au Pays de l'Or Noir. (p. 1756)
—Tintin au Tibet. (p. 1756)
—Tintin en Amerique. (p. 1756)
—Tintin en el Congo. (p. 1756)
—Tintin en el Pais del Oro Negro. (p. 1756)
—Tintin en Tibet. (p. 1756)
—Tintin et le Lac aux Requins. (p. 1756)
—Tintin et les Picaros. (p. 1756)
—Tintin im Amerika. (p. 1756)
—Tintin im Kongo. (p. 1756)
—Tintin in America. (p. 1756)
—Tintin in the Land of the Soviets. (p. 1756)
—Tintin in Tibet. (p. 1756)
—Tintin y los Picaros. (p. 1756)
—Tresor de Rackham le Rouge. (p. 1785)
—Vol 714 Pour Sydney: Flight 714 for Sydney. Vol. 714 (p. 1848)
—Vuelo 714 para Sidney. (p. 1851)
—Y las Naranjas Azules. (p. 1968)
—Zigarren des Pharaos. (p. 1986)
Hergé & Egmont Books Staff. Tintin & the Picaros. (p. 1756)
—Tintin in Tibet. (p. 1756)
Hergé & I, Herge-tintin Rustica. Cigarros del Faraon. (p. 319)
—Isla Negra. (p. 891)
—Oreja Rota. (p. 1303)
—Tintin en Amerique. (p. 1756)
—Tintin en el Congo. (p. 1756)
Hergé & Ii, Herge-tintin Cartone. Tesoro de Rackham el Rojo. (p. 1722)
Hergé & Ii, Herge-tintin Rustica. Estrella Misteriosa. (p. 538)
—Secreto del Unicornio. (p. 1544)
Hergé & Iii, Herge-tintin Rustica. Tintin el Pais del Oro Negro. (p. 1756)
Hergé & Iv, Herge-tintin Rustica. Tintin y los Picaros. (p. 1756)
—Vuelo 714 para Sidney. (p. 1851)
Hergé, et al. Aterrizaje en la Lune. (p. 112)
—Cetro de Ottokar. (p. 288)
—Objetivo la Luna. (p. 1275)
—Secret of the Unicorn. (p. 1543)
—Siete Bolas de Cristal. (p. 1573)
—Stock de Coque. (p. 1651)
—Tesoro de Rackham el Rojo. (p. 1722)
Hergenroeder, Ernie. Little Drop of Water. (p. 1027)
Hergenroeder, Ernie, illus. see Mitchell, Kathy.
Hergenroeder, Ernie, illus. see Pacheco, Maria & Garcia-Martinez, Julia.
Hergenrother, Max, illus. see Buckley, James, Jr.
Hergenrother, Max, illus. see Fabiny, Sarah.
Hergenrother, Max, illus. see Gigliotti, Jim.
Hergenrother, Max, illus. see MacDowell, Maureen.
Herges, Connie, illus. see Simonson, Lona Marie.
Herges, Connie, illus. see Simonson, Lona.
Herglotz, Pam Herglotz. Ichabod & the Chipmunks. (p. 851)
Herigstad, Sally. Help! I Can't Pay My Bills: Surviving a Financial Crisis. (p. 765)
Hering, Marianne, jt. auth. see McCusker, Paul.
Hering, Marianne & Sanders, Nancy I. Captured on the High Seas. (p. 265)
Hering, Marianne & Younger, Marshal. Escape to the Hiding Place. (p. 535)
Hering, Marianne, et al. Doomsday in Pompeii. (p. 470)
Heritage & Almeida, Artie. Music Proficiency: Doggone Dynamics. (p. 1193)
Heritage, Anne, tr. see Neumann, Dietrich.
Herkenhoff, Paulo, et al. Louise Bourgeois. (p. 1058)
Herkert, Barbara. Birds in Your Backyard. (p. 191)
Herkimer, Barbara. Our New Neighbors. (p. 1309)
Herlihy, Matt & Clarke, Nzingha, selected by. Sweet Fancy Moses: Book 2. (p. 1689)
Herlong, M. H. Buddy. (p. 234)
—Great Wide Sea. (p. 719)
Herman, Alison & Grossman, Lynne. Dolly Goes on Vacation. Eve, Lealand, illus. (p. 464)
—Dolly Goes to the Beach. Eve, Lealand, illus. (p. 464)
—Dolly Goes to the Supermarket. Eve, Lealand, illus. (p. 464)
Herman, Alley, jt. auth. see Mills, Nathan.
Herman, Carli. Good Graffiti Teen Talk on Tough Issues. (p. 698)
Herman, Charlotte. My Chocolate Year: A Novel with 12 Recipes. Pham, LeUyen, illus. (p. 1200)
Herman, Daniel, ed. see Collins, Katherine.
Herman, Daniel, ed. see Lawrence, James.
Herman, Debbie. Carla's Sandwich. Bailey, Sheila, illus. (p. 270)
—From Pie Town to Yum Yum: Weird & Wacky Place Names Across the United States. Goldman, Linda Sarah, illus. (p. 643)
Herman, Eleanor. Legacy of Kings. (p. 987)
Herman, Emmi S. We All Fall for Apples. Kennedy, Annie, illus. (p. 1865)
Herman, Gail. Ariel: The Shimmering Star Necklace. (p. 98)
—Boo on the Loose. (p. 210)
—Boo on the Loose (Disney/Pixar Monsters, Inc.) Tilley, Scott, illus. (p. 210)
—Buried in the Backyard. Smath, Jerry, illus. (p. 243)
—Christmas Wishes. Marderosian, Mark, illus. (p. 316)
—Creeping Tide. (p. 381)
—Creeping Tide. Nez, John, illus. (p. 381)
—Enterrado en el Jardin. Smath, Jerry, illus. (p. 531)
—Enterrado en el Jardin; Buried in the Backyard. (p. 531)
—Fall Fright. Duendes Del Sur Staff, illus. (p. 566)
—Flower Girl. Billin-Frye, Paige, illus. (p. 607)
—Haunted Halloween Party. Duendes Del Sur Staff, illus. (p. 753)
—Make-a-Splash Writing Rules. (p. 1079)
—New Dog in Town. Nez, John, illus. (p. 1244)
—Peppa Pig & Her Best Friend. (p. 1340)
—Scooby-Doo: A Scooby-Rific Reader. (p. 1529)
—Scooby-Rific Reader. Duendes Del Sur Staff, illus. (p. 1529)
—Snowboarding Similes & Metaphors. (p. 1600)
—What Is the World Series? Anderson, Scott, illus. (p. 1890)
—Who Is Derek Jeter? Thomson, Andrew, illus. (p. 1915)
—Who Was Davy Crockett? (p. 1918)
—Who Was Davy Crockett? Squier, Robert & Harrison, Nancy, illus. (p. 1918)
—Who Was Jackie Robinson? Harrison, Nancy & O'Brien, John, illus. (p. 1918)
Herman, Gail & Amatrula, Michele. Climbing Everest (Totally True Adventures) (p. 333)
Herman, Gail & Bridwell, Norman. Halloween Howl. Goldberg, Barry, illus. (p. 737)
Herman, Gail & Harrison, Nancy. Who Is Wayne Gretzky? (p. 1916)
—Who Is Wayne Gretzky? Hammond, Ted, illus. (p. 1916)
Herman, Gail & Voege, Debra. Catch-a-Wave Compounds. (p. 279)
—Karate Contractions. (p. 943)
—Pedaling to Perfect Punctuation. (p. 1334)
Herman, George & Seaton, Kristen. Nine Dragons: A Contemporary Fable. (p. 1256)
Herman, Mark & Apter, Ronnie, trs. from RUS. Moscow Ballet Great Russian Nutcracker. Fedorov, Valentin, illus. (p. 1176)
Herman, R. A. Littlest Christmas Tree. Rogers, Jacqueline, illus. (p. 1039)
—Littlest Pumpkin. Ogden, Betina, illus. (p. 1039)
—Pal & Sal's New Friend. (p. 1319)
—Pal Saves the Day. Ogden, Betina, illus. (p. 1319)
Herman, Scott, illus. see Delea, Pattie.
Herman, Stephanie. Cost Benefit Jr: Self-Contained: How Free Markets Work. Bk. 1 (p. 368)
—Cost Benefit Jr: Bound Text with Looseleaf Q & A - Answer Key: How Free Markets Work. Bk. 1 (p. 368)
Herman, Susan. Bad, Sophie, Bad! (p. 132)
Hermann, jt. auth. see H., Yves.
Hermann, Spring. Anne Frank: Hope in the Shadows of the Holocaust. (p. 85)
—Making Their Mark (p. 1082)
—Struggle for Equality: Women & Minorities in America. (p. 1668)
—Struggle for Freedom (p. 1668)
—Student's Guide to Eugene O'Neill. (p. 1669)
—Student's Guide to Tennessee Williams. (p. 1669)
Hermann, Spring & Heinemann Library Staff. Making Their Mark (p. 1082)
—Struggle for Freedom (p. 1668)
Herman-O'Neal, Jackie. Moctezuma's Zoo: A Tale from an Enchanted City. (p. 1157)
Hermans, Rene, illus. see Hall, Lynn Bradford.
Hermanski, Carol. Ordinary Cat. (p. 1302)
Hermanson, Kyle, illus. see Jones, Christianne C.
Hermanson, Tammy. Did You Ever Wonder? (p. 437)
Hermansson, Casie. How to Analyze the Films of Clint Eastwood. (p. 814)
—Parental Guidance Ratings. (p. 1324)
Hermes, Mary Sue, illus. see Harvey, Ken.
Hermes, Patricia. Black Cloud. (p. 195)
—Black Cloud. Sheckels, Astrid, illus. (p. 195)
—Emma Dilemma & the Camping Nanny Carter, Abby, illus. (p. 519)
—Emma Dilemma & the New Nanny Carter, Abby, illus. (p. 519)
—Emma Dilemma & the Two Nannies Carter, Abby, illus. (p. 519)
—Emma Dilemma, the Nanny, & the Best Horse Ever Carter, Abby, illus. (p. 519)
—Emma Dilemma, the Nanny, & the Secret Ferret Carter, Abby, illus. (p. 519)
—Emma Dilemma, the Nanny, & the Wedding (p. 519)
—Fly Away Home. (p. 609)
—Horse Diaries - Koda. Sanderson, Ruth, illus. (p. 799)
—Wild Year: Joshua's Oregon Trail Diary. Bk. 3 (p. 1931)
—You Shouldn't Have to Say GoodBye: It's Hard Losing the Person You Love The Most. (p. 1976)
Hermes, Patricia, et al. Fly Away Home. (p. 609)
Hermes, Trismegistus. Divine Pymander of Hermes Mercuris Trismegistus, in XVII Books. Everard, John, tr. (p. 454)
Hermit, Acrid. Misty Forest Fables. (p. 1155)
Hermoso, A. S., et al. Curso Practico de la Gramatica de Espanol Lengua Extranjera: Curso Practico I. (p. 395)
—Curso Practico de la Gramatica de Espanol Lengua Extranjera: Curso Practico II. (p. 395)
—Curso Practico de la Gramatica de Espanol Lengua Extranjera: Curso Practico III. (p. 395)
Hermsen, Ronald. Story of Giraffe. Pigni, Guido, illus. (p. 1658)
Hermsen, Sarah. Space Exploration Library Cumulative Index. (p. 1619)
Hermsen, Sarah, jt. auth. see Thomson Gale Staff.
Hermsen, Sarah, et al. American Reference Library. (p. 63)
Hermstad, Melanie. Bird, I Love You. (p. 190)
Hern & Ez, Daniel. Endangered Lions. (p. 526)
Hernandez, Alejandro. Tres Cabezas y un Volcan. BEFEC Mulguin and Associates Staff, illus. (p. 1784)
Hernandez, Anna Marie Eloise. O Holy Night. (p. 1274)
Hernandez, Annette. Captain Holo's Journey through the Alphabet: An ABC Book. (p. 264)
Hernandez, Aurora, tr. see Ludwig, Trudy.
Hernandez, Bibi, illus. see Shaw, Sandra Anne.
Hernandez, Carlos. It's the Law! (p. 899)
Hernandez, Christopher. Animal Superpowers. (p. 80)
—Animals on the Farm. Scholastic, Inc. Staff, illus. (p. 83)
—Scaredycrow. (p. 1520)
Hernandez, Claudia. Redondo: O Cuando los Circulos Se Convierten en Esferas. Pombo, Luis G. & Pombo, Luis, illus. (p. 1456)
Hernandez, Claudia, et al. Con Cuatro Alcanza. Magallanes, Alejandro, illus. (p. 355)
Hernandez, Dan. Come to the Tree. (p. 347)
Hernandez, Daniel. They Call Me a Hero: A Memoir of My Youth. (p. 1732)
Hernandez, David. Land of the Pharaohs (p. 973)
—Mighty Armor (p. 1139)
—No More Us for You. (p. 1259)
—Suckerpunch. (p. 1672)
Hernandez, Elaine. Welcome to Humming Meadow Ranch. Hernandez, Stacy, illus. (p. 1873)
Hernandez, Eufemia. Palabrerias: Retahilas, trabalenguas, Colmos y otros juegos de palabras. Maa'Dhoor, Lilian, illus. (p. 1319)
Hernández, Evan. Little Tiger Sisters. (p. 1037)
Hernández, Gabriel, illus. see Andruetto, María Teresa.
Hernandez, Gabriel, illus. see Stine, R. L.

Hernandez, Georgina. Tinta de Las Moras. Cardenas, Patricia Karla Marquez & Cardenas, Patricia Karla, illus. (p. 1756)
Hernandez, Gilbert. Adventures of Venus. (p. 24)
Hernandez, Gilbert, illus. see Various Authors.
Hernández, Guillermo. Ortografía Norma y Estilo: Actividades de Autoaprendizaje. (p. 1305)
Hernández, Guillermo & Rellan, Clara. Aprendo a Escribir 2: Narrar y Describir. (p. 93)
Hernandez, Jaime. Locas Volumen 1. (p. 1044)
Hernandez, Janice. Lisa & the Light Dancer. (p. 1022)
Hernandez, Jewel. Being Born: The Doula's Role. Mithuna, R. Michael, illus. (p. 161)
Hernandez, Jewel & Mithuna, R. Michael. Nacimiento: El Papel de una Doula = Being Born: The Doula's Role. Mithuna, R. Michael, illus. (p. 1227)
Hernandez, Jo Ann Yolanda. Throwaway Piece. (p. 1745)
Hernandez, Jose. Martin Fierro. (p. 1097)
Hernandez, Jose Francisco. Ingles para Ninos-Un Metodo Facil y Efectivo para Sus Hijos. (p. 874)
Hernández, Juan A., jt. auth. see Andreu Iglesias, Cesar.
Hernandez, Karina, tr. see Bertrand, Diane Gonzales.
Hernández, Karina, tr. see De Anda, Diane.
Hernandez, Keith. First-Base Hero: A Lift-the-Flap Pop-up Book. Manders, John, illus. (p. 593)
Hernandez, Lea. Clockwork Angels: Texas Steampunk II. (p. 333)
Hernandez, Lea, illus. see Fisch, Sholly.
Hernandez, Leeza. Cat Napped. Hernandez, Leeza, illus. (p. 278)
—Dog Gone! Hernandez, Leeza, illus. (p. 461)
Hernandez, Leeza, illus. see Donovan, Sandy.
Hernandez, Leeza, illus. see Lithgow, John.
Hernandez, Leeza, illus. see McCallum, Ann.
Hernandez, Mario. Ninas de la Tierra: Sowbugs (p. 1256)
Hernandez, Mary L. Como el Viento Paso a Ser Tormenta. Maval Publishing Inc. Staff, illus. (p. 350)
Hernández, Miguel, jt. auth. see Hernández, Miguel.
Hernández, Miguel & Hernández, Miguel. Miguel Hernandez para Ninos. Alonso, Juan Ramon, illus. (p. 1141)
Hernandez Mora, Victor. From the Winds of Manguito Desde los vientos de Manguito: Cuban Folktales in English & Spanish, Cuentos Folklóricos de Cuba, en Inglés y Español Perez, Elvia et al, eds. (p. 644)
Hernandez, Natalie. Stowaway to California: Adventures with Father Junipero Serra (p. 1664)
Hernandez, Natalie Nelson. Aventuras Con Padre Serra. (p. 119)
—Captain Sutter's Fort: Adventures with John A. Sutter. (p. 264)
—Mapmakers of the Western Trails: Adventures with John Chries Fremont (p. 1090)
Hernández, Oscar, jt. auth. see Gamblin, Rose Tooley.
Hernàndez, Pau Joan, tr. see Husson, Severin & Veyret, Yvette.
Hernandez, Peter. New Day with Rhyming Robin. (p. 1244)
Hernández, Rafael, jt. auth. see Cluster, Dick.
Hernandez, Regina. Jail Break Spells Double the Trouble: Jake the Beagle's Crazy Adventures. Woods, Carol, ed. (p. 905)
—Texas Roundup: Jake the Beagle's Crazy Adventures. Woods, Carol, ed. (p. 1724)
Hernández, René Mario, ed. see González Reyes, Amaury.
Hernández, René Mario, ed. see San Jorge, José.
Hernández, René Mario, illus. see Mederos, Miriam.
Hernandez, Roger. Cuba Henderson, James D., ed. (p. 388)
Hernández, Roger E. 1898 to World War II. (p. 2002)
—Civil War, 1840s-1890s. (p. 325)
—Cuba. (p. 388)
—Cuban Immigration. (p. 388)
—Early Explorations: The 1500s. (p. 493)
Hernandez, Roger E. Immigration. (p. 861)
Hernandez, Roger E. New Spain: 1600-1760s. (p. 1247)
Hernandez, Roger E. Paraguay Henderson, James D., ed. (p. 1323)
Hernandez, Roger E. Paraguay. (p. 1323)
—South America: Facts & Figures. (p. 1616)
Hernandez, Roger E. South America: Facts & Figures Henderson, James D., ed. (p. 1616)
Hernández, Roger E. Spanish-American War. (p. 1620)
Hernandez, Roger E. Teens & Relationships. (p. 1715)
—Teens & Relationships. Developed in Association with the Gallup Organization Staff, ed. (p. 1715)
Hernández, Roger E. Teens & the Media. (p. 1715)
Hernandez, Roger E. Teens & the Media. Developed in Association with the Gallup Organization Staff, ed. (p. 1715)
Hernandez, Romel. Caribbean Islands: Facts & Figures. (p. 268)
—Caribbean Islands: Facts & Figures Henderson, James D., ed. (p. 268)
—Immigration from Central America. (p. 861)
—Puerto Rico Henderson, James D., ed. (p. 1415)
—Puerto Rico. (p. 1415)
—Trinidad & Tobago Henderson, James D., ed. (p. 1786)
—Trinidad & Tobago. (p. 1786)
Hernandez, Ruben. Elisa Escuchaba el Canto de Las Ballenas. Corichi, Yadhira, illus. (p. 513)
Hernandez, Stacy, illus. see Hernandez, Elaine.
Hernandez, Stephanie, illus. see Whitt, Stephen.
Hernandez, Steven, illus. see Berton, Judy.
Hernandez, Tino Santanach, illus. see Korhonen, Kari, et al.
Hernandez Vera, Rene & Panamericana Staff, eds. Breviario de Colombia: Una Guia para Todos. (p. 226)
Hernandez, Vince. Soulfire: Shadow Magic Volume 1 TP: Shadow Magic Volume 1 TP. (p. 1614)
Hernandez Walta, Gabriel, illus. see Kim, Chuck, et al.
Hernandez-Divers, Sonia. Geckos (p. 659)
—Snakes (p. 1596)
Herndon, Christopher, illus. see Shapiro, David R.
Herndon, Lee G. Land of Always & Forever: The Trilogy (p. 973)
Herndon, Roblyn, jt. auth. see Phillips, Betty Lou.
Herndon, Ryan, jt. auth. see Calkhoven, Laurie.
Herndon, Ryan, jt. auth. see Hirschmann, Kris.
Herndon, Ryan, jt. compiled by see Hirschmann, Kris.
Herndon, Ryan, jt. compiled by see Lee, Celeste.
Herndon, Ryan, jt. compiled by see Mattern, Joanne.
Herndon, Ryan, compiled by. 3-D Deep-Sea Creatures! (p. 1991)
—3-D Extreme! (p. 1991)
Herndon, S. N. Uncle Deek's Boating Adventure. (p. 1811)
Herndon, Susan A. Janie's World: Under the Rock. (p. 908)
—Janie's World: Walk with Me Through Nature's Door. (p. 908)
Herning, Kathy, ed. see Belczyk, David.
Herodotus. Wright Brothers Adventure. (p. 1963)
Herold, Dallas J. Bear Who Was Washed Too Much: A Nicholas & Bunky Book. (p. 151)
Herold, Marlette. Luvable Lucind: Jacob & the Bullies. (p. 1066)
Herold, Vickey. Breaking the Sound Barrier. (p. 225)
—Cattle Town: Forth Worth. (p. 281)
—Discover a Cattle Town: Forth Worth. (p. 447)
—Discover A Gold Rush Community: San Francisco. (p. 447)
—Discover A Whaling Community: Nantucket. (p. 447)
—Discover Light. (p. 447)
—Discover Science During the Renaissance. (p. 448)
—Discover Sound. (p. 448)
—Discover the Renaissance in England. (p. 448)
—Discover the Renaissance in Italy. (p. 448)
—Discover the Sound Barrier. (p. 448)
—Gold Rush Community: San Francisco. (p. 694)
—Light & Color. (p. 1014)
—Renaissance in England. (p. 1460)
—Renaissance in Italy. (p. 1460)
—Science During the Renaissance. (p. 1525)
—Sound Is Energy. (p. 1615)
—Whaling Community: Nantucket. (p. 1878)
Heroldt, Richard, illus. see Bader, Joanne.
Heron, Andrew. Kids' Sudoku for Dummies. (p. 955)
Heron, Jackie. Get Moving in the City. Avakyan, Tatevik, illus. (p. 667)
—Let's Move in the Outdoors. Avakyan, Tatevik, illus. (p. 999)
Heron, Jeanette, tr. see Bold, Emily.
Herpin, K. K., illus. see Riebel, Jessica Mire.
Herr, Brandy. Adventures of Freddie Spaghetti & Meat Ball. (p. 18)
Herr, Charlotte. How Freckle Frog Made Herself Pretty. (p. 809)
Herr, Ethel. Dr. Oma: The Healing Wisdom of Countess Juliana Von Stolberg. (p. 475)
Herr, Judy. Mastering CDA Competencies. (p. 1103)
—Working with Young Children: Resource Portfolio. (p. 1953)
—Working with Young Children: Teaching Package Exam View(r) Test Generator Software. (p. 1953)
—Working with Young Children: Teaching Package Answer key, Mastering CDA Competencies. (p. 1953)
—Working with Young Children. (p. 1953)
Herr, Judy & Libby-Larson, Yvonne. Creative Resources for Bulletin Boards in the Early Childhood Classroom. (p. 380)
Herr, Margaret J. Fritz, the Donut-Tailed Dog. (p. 639)
Herr, Melody. Exploring the New World: An Interactive History Adventure (p. 554)
—Sitting for Equal Service: Lunch Counter Sit-Ins, United States, 1960s. (p. 1582)
—Slave Trade (p. 1588)
Herr, Melody & Darnell, Regna. Edward Sapir: Linguist, Anthropologist, Humanist. (p. 505)
Herr, Melody & Heinemann Library Staff. African Roots (p. 28)
Herr, Tad, illus. see Oetting, Judy.
Herran, Joe, jt. auth. see Thomas, Ron.
Herranz Brooks, Jacqueline, tr. see Perez, Annette.
Herrbach, Stéphanie, illus. see Hédelin, Pascale.
Herren, Greg. Dark Tide. (p. 408)
—Lake Thirteen. (p. 972)
—Sleeping Angel. (p. 1588)
—Sorceress. (p. 1614)
Herren, Ray V. Exploring Agriscience. (p. 551)
Herrera, Aaron Jeremiah, illus. see McGhee, Katie Mariah.
Herrera, Alberto. Músik: A Delightfully Harmonic Tale of the Origin of Music. (p. 1194)
Herrera, Debbi. Clara's Choice. (p. 326)
Herrera, Erik, et al. Acquire the Fire: 40 Teen Devotionals Mauss, Doug, ed. (p. 9)
Herrera, Francisco, illus. see Way, Daniel & Medina, Paco.
Herrera, Hanna, jt. auth. see Walker-Jones, Alexandra.
Herrera, J. Ignacio. 125 Refranes Infantiles. Torcida, Maria Luisa, illus. (p. 2000)
Herrera, Joaquin. Horris, Little Eli & the Lens of Truth. (p. 799)
Herrera, Joaquin Ramon. Scary: A Book of Horrible Things for Kids. (p. 1520)
Herrera, Juan, jt. auth. see Herrera, Juan Felipe.
Herrera, Juan Felipe. Canto de las Palomas/Calling the Doves. (p. 262)
—Cinnamon Girl: Letters Found Inside a Cereal Box. (p. 321)
—Featherless: Desplumado. Cuevas, Ernesto & Cuevas, Ernesto, Jr., illus. (p. 579)
—Grandma & Me at the Flea: Los Meros Meros Remateros. De Lucio-Brock, Anita, illus. (p. 708)
—Portraits of Hispanic American Heroes. Colón, Raúl, illus. (p. 1387)
—SkateFate. (p. 1583)
—Upside down Boy. Gómez, Elizabeth, illus. (p. 1825)
Herrera, Juan Felipe & Cuevas, Ernesto. Featherless. (p. 579)
Herrera, Juan Felipe & Herrera, Juan. Supermina del Cilantro. Robledo Tapia, Honorio, illus. (p. 1684)
Herrera, Juan Ignacio. Haced Sitio a Mi Hermano. (p. 735)
Herrera, Mario, jt. auth. see Hojel, Barbara.
Herrera, Mario & Hojel, Barbara. Balloons: Picture Cards. (p. 135)
—Balloons: Storybooks Package. (p. 135)
—Balloons: Mascot Puppet Lucky Ducky. (p. 135)
—Balloons: Mascot Puppet Sunny Bunny. (p. 135)
—Balloons: Mascot Puppet Funny Froggy. (p. 135)
—Balloons. (p. 135)
Herrera, Matthew D. History Guide to Old Mission San Luis Obispo de Tolosa. (p. 783)
Herrera, Nicholas. High Riders, Saints & Death Cars: A Life Saved by Art Denne, John, photos by. (p. 778)
Herrera, Raquel, tr. see Barry, Dave & Pearson, Ridley.
Herrera, Robin. Hope Is a Ferris Wheel. (p. 796)
Herrera, Velino, illus. see Clark, Ann Nolan.
Herrera-Sobek, María & Salem Press Staff. House on Mango Street, by Sandra Cisneros. (p. 803)
Herrero, M. N. Mi Libro de Seguridad Infantil. (p. 1132)
Herrero, Teresa, jt. auth. see Martin, Carme.
Herrick, Amy. Time Fetch. (p. 1751)
Herrick, Ann. Perfect Guy. (p. 1342)
—Summer Replacement. (p. 1675)
—Walk Softly & Watch Out for Bigfoot. (p. 1854)
Herrick, Mark, illus. see Smith, Tim.
Herrick, Mark J., illus. see Sams, Carl R., II & Stoick, Jean.
Herrick, Mark J., illus. see Stephens, Edna Cucksey.
Herrick, Robert. Delight in Disorder: Selected Poems. (p. 425)
Herrick, Steven. Black Painted Fingernails. (p. 196)
—Cold Skin. (p. 338)
—Do-Wrong Ron. Magerl, Caroline, illus. (p. 457)
—Kissing Annabel: Love, Ghosts, & Facial Hair & a Place Like This. (p. 962)
—Love, Ghosts, & Facial Hair. (p. 1059)
—Naked Bunyip Dancing. Norling, Beth, illus. (p. 1228)
—Simple Gift. (p. 1577)
—Slice: Juicy Moments from My Impossible Life. (p. 1590)
—Wolf. (p. 1943)
Herridge, Debbie, illus. see Wakem, Samantha.
Herridon, Lynne. Peter & the Wolf. (p. 1346)
Herriges, Ann. Clouds. (p. 335)
—Corals. (p. 366)
—Crabs. (p. 375)
—Dolphins. (p. 464)
—Fall. (p. 566)
—Jellyfish. (p. 912)
—Lightning. (p. 1015)
—Manatees. (p. 1086)
—Octopuses. (p. 1278)
—Rain. (p. 1434)
—Sea Horses. (p. 1534)
—Sea Stars. (p. 1535)
—Sea Turtles. (p. 1535)
—Snow. (p. 1598)
—Spring. (p. 1634)
—Summer. (p. 1673)
—Sunshine. (p. 1677)
—Whales. (p. 1878)
—Wind. (p. 1935)
—Winter. (p. 1937)
Herriman, George & Yoe, Craig. Krazy & Ignatz in Tiger Tea. Yoe, Craig, ed. (p. 967)
Herrin, Roberta Teague. Appalachian Children's Literature: An Annotated Bibliography. (p. 92)
Herring, Aimée, photos by see Strand, Jessica.
Herring, Bruce D. Wizard of Wonderland (p. 1943)
Herring, James E. Internet & Information Skills: A Guide for Teachers & School Librarians. (p. 880)
Herring, John, tr. see Martins, Isabel Minhós.
Herring, Kip, illus. see Stone, Jodi.
Herring, M. L., illus. see Li, Judith L.
Herring, Trudy, jt. auth. see Tucker, S. J.
Herringshaw, DeAnn. Dorothy Dandridge: Singer & Actress. (p. 471)
—Harlem Renaissance. (p. 749)
—Lucille Ball: Actress & Comedienne. (p. 1062)
—United States Enters the 20th Century. (p. 1819)
Herrington, Chris. Harry & Hannah: The American Adventure. Pacheco, Jorge M., illus. (p. 750)
Herrington, Lisa M. Acorn to Oak Tree. (p. 9)
—Amazing Mammals. (p. 55)
—American Flag. (p. 60)
—Back-to-School Safety. (p. 130)
—Bald Eagle. (p. 133)
—Beans to Chocolate. (p. 150)
—Bicycle Safety. (p. 177)
—Butterflies & Moths. (p. 247)
—Car Safety. (p. 265)
—Caterpillar to Butterfly. (p. 279)
—Cheetahs & Leopards. (p. 296)
—Crocodiles & Alligators. (p. 384)
—Fire Safety. (p. 590)
—Freaky Fish. (p. 632)
—Frogs & Toads. (p. 641)
—Groundhog Day. (p. 725)
—Hanukkah. (p. 743)
—How Do You Know It's Fall? (p. 808)
—How Do You Know It's Spring? (p. 808)
—I Broke My Arm. (p. 834)
—I Have a Cavity. (p. 839)
—I Have a Cold. (p. 839)
—I Like to Exercise. (p. 841)
—I Lost a Tooth. (p. 841)
—I Need Stitches. (p. 844)
—Incredible Insects. (p. 869)
—Internet Safety. (p. 880)
—It's a Good Thing There Are Bees. (p. 895)
—It's a Good Thing There Are Butterflies. (p. 895)
—It's a Good Thing There Are Snakes. (p. 895)
—It's a Good Thing There Are Spiders. (p. 895)
—Kwanzaa. (p. 968)
—Martin Luther King Jr. Day. (p. 1098)
—Milk to Ice Cream. (p. 1143)
—Monkeys & Apes. (p. 1166)
—Remarkable Reptiles. (p. 1459)
—Seed to Plant. (p. 1547)
—Statue of Liberty. (p. 1645)
—Stranger Safety. (p. 1665)
—Tadpole to Frog. (p. 1695)
—Thanksgiving. (p. 1725)
—Tomatoes to Ketchup. (p. 1764)
—Trees to Paper. (p. 1784)
—Turtles & Tortoises. (p. 1799)
—White House. (p. 1913)
Herrington, Lisa M., jt. auth. see Hart, Joyce.
Herrington, Lisa M., jt. auth. see Petreycik, Rick.
Herrington, Russel M. & Shoemacher, Paul. USAF Flight Test Engineering Manual. (p. 1826)
Herriot, James. Every Living Thing (p. 543)
—It Shouldn't Happen to a Vet (p. 894)
—James Herriot's Treasury for Children: Warm & Joyful Tales by the Author of All Creatures Great & Small. Brown, Ruth & Barrett, Peter, illus. (p. 907)
—James Herriot's Treasury of Inspirational Stories for Children: Warm & Joyful Tales by the Author of All Creatures Great & Small. Brown, Ruth & Barrett, Peter, illus. (p. 907)
—Lord God Made Them All (p. 1052)
—Vet in a Harness (p. 1839)
—Vet in a Spin (p. 1839)
—Vets Might Fly (p. 1839)
Herriott, Charlotte. Boa Constrictor vs. Grizzly Bear. (p. 205)
—Cheetah vs. Ostrich. (p. 296)
—Rat vs. Cockroach. (p. 1440)
Herrmann, Angela, jt. auth. see McKinney, Donna.
Herrndorf, Wolfgang. Why We Took the Car. Mohr, Tim, tr. from GER. (p. 1926)
—You, Me, & a Russian Jeep. (p. 1976)
Herrnson, Paul S., et al. Guide to Political Campaigns in America Medvic, Stephen K., ed. (p. 730)
Herrod, Mike. Comics to Go! 19 Stories for You to Finish! And More... (p. 348)
—Doggie Dreams. (p. 462)
—Hiccup! (p. 775)
Herrod, Robin & Kerrod, Robin. Space Pioneers. (p. 1619)
—Space Shuttles. (p. 1619)
Herrold. City & Village Planning & Zon. (p. 323)
Herrold, Karen L. Ice Cream Truck. (p. 850)
Herron, Carolivia. Always an Olivia: A Remarkable Family History. Tugeau, Jeremy, illus. (p. 51)
Herron, Carolivia, photos by. Little Georgia & the Apples: A Retelling of Aunt Georgia's First Catalpa Tale (p. 1028)
Herron, Dorothy, illus. see Lorraine, Nancy.
Herron, Edward A. Return of the Alaskan: Mailboat in the Outpost. Langley, Gene, illus. (p. 1464)
Herron, Edwin, illus. see Schneider, Herman & Schneider, Nina.
Herron, Mark, illus. see Lombardo, Michelle.
Herron, Paul, ed. Cafe in Space: The Anais Nin Literary Journal (p. 251)
Herschap, Heather, MDiv. My Friends & I. (p. 1209)
Herschbach, Elisabeth. Lower Plains: Kansas, Nebraska (p. 1061)
Herscovitch, Arthur. Everything You Need to Know about Drug Abuse. (p. 545)
Hersey, Bob. Norman Rockwell: A Pop-Up Art Experience. (p. 1264)
Hersey, Bob, illus. see Clarke, Penny.
Hersey, Bob, illus. see Legg, Gerald.
Hersey, Bob, illus. see Skevington, Andrea.
Hersey, Jodi. Achy Ali. Peabody, Rob, illus. (p. 9)
Hersey, Suzanne Buzby. My Maine. Fazio, Nicole, illus. (p. 1214)
Hersh, Iffy. Mommy Is an Histologist. (p. 1162)
Hersh, Richard H. & Merrow, John. Declining by Degrees: Higher Education at Risk. Hersh, Richard H. & Merrow, John, eds. (p. 422)
Hershberger, Carol, jt. auth. see Kelley, Gail.
Hershberger, Fannie. Kinder Kookin' Amish Children Share Their Own Recipes. (p. 957)
Hershenhorn, Esther. Chicken Soup by Heart. Litzinger, Rosanne, illus. (p. 300)
—Fancy That. Lloyd, Megan, illus. (p. 570)
—Little Illinois. Monroe, Michael Glenn, illus. (p. 1029)
—S Is for Story: A Writer's Alphabet. Pullen, Zachary, illus. (p. 1499)
—Txtng Mama Txtng Baby. (p. 1804)
Hershenson, Ken, jt. auth. see Shepherd, Wendy.
Hershey, Katherine. Tabernacle, Part 2 A Picture of the Lord Jesus: Old Testament Volume 10 Exodus Part 5. Vol. 10, Pt. 2 Willoughby, Yuko, illus. (p. 1694)
Hershey, Katherine, jt. auth. see Piepgrass, Arlene.
Hershey, Mary. 10 Lucky Things That Have Happened to Me since I Nearly Got Hit by Lightning. (p. 1993)
—My Big Sister Is So Bossy She Says You Can't Read This Book. (p. 1197)
Hersholt, Jean, tr. see Andersen, Hans Christian.
Hersholt, Jean P., tr. see Andersen, Hans Christian.
Hershon, Robert, et al. When We Were Countries. (p. 1905)
Hersko, Ralph E. Braddock's Road Across Northern & Western Virginia: A 250th Anniversary Retrospective. (p. 221)
Herskowitz, Benjie. David & Goliath with a Twist. (p. 410)
Herskowitz, Sol. Horrible Happening. (p. 798)
Hersom, P. Dinosaurs Funny & Weird Extinct Animals: Learn with Amazing Dinosaur Pictures & Fun Facts about Dinosaur Fossils, Names & More, a Kids Book about Dinosaurs. (p. 444)
—Sea Life Funny & Weird Marine Animals: Learn with Amazing Photos & Facts about Ocean Marine Sea Animals. (p. 1534)
Hersov, Kate, jt. auth. see Chilman-Blair, Kim.
Herstek, Amy Paulson. Emily Dickinson: Solitary & Celebrated Poet. (p. 518)
Hertan, Charles. Power Chess for Kids: More Ways to Think Ahead & Become One of the Best Players in Your School (p. 1389)
—Power Chess for Kids: Learn How to Think Ahead & Become One of the Best Players in Your School. (p. 1389)
Hertel, Kerry. Tidy Tess. (p. 1747)
Hertkorn, Michaela C. Little Cloud Upset. Ayala, Joseph, illus. (p. 1026)
Hertling, Heiner, illus. see Sams, Laura & Sams, Robert.
Hertsgaard, Mark. Eagle's Shadow: Why America Fascinates & Infuriates the World. (p. 492)
Hertzler, Frances, illus. see Lyster, R. Iona, et al.
Hertzler, Frances, illus. see St. John, Patricia, et al.
Hertzler, Frances B. & Ober, Jonathan. Eternal God: New Testament. Vol. 1 (p. 539)
Hertzler, Frances H.., illus. see Carvin, Rose-Mae.
Hertzler, Frances H.., illus. see Greiner, Ruth B.

H

Hertzler, Frances H., illus. see Greiner, Ruth B., et al.
Hertzog, Nancy, et al. Around My House! (p. 100)
—Let's Go to the Market! (p. 997)
—Let's Play! (p. 999)
Herumin, Wendy. Censorship on the Internet: From Filters to Freedom of Speech. (p. 287)
—Child Labor Today: A Human Rights Issue. (p. 301)
Herweck, Diana. All in a Day's Work: ER Doctor. (p. 44)
—All in a Day's Work: Police Officer. (p. 44)
—All in a Day's Work - Police Officer. (p. 44)
—Davy Crockett. (p. 411)
—ER Doctor. (p. 533)
—In the Game: An Athlete's Life (p. 866)
—In the Game - An Athlete's Life (p. 866)
—On the Scene: A CSI's Life (p. 1291)
—On the Scene: A CSI's Life. (p. 1291)
Herweck, Don. Albert Einstein: Gentle Genius. (p. 34)
—Albert Einstein: And His Theory of Relativity (p. 34)
—All about Energy. (p. 42)
—All about Mechanical Engineering. (p. 43)
—Energy. (p. 528)
—Gravity. (p. 712)
—Making It Go: The Life & Work of Robert Fulton. (p. 1081)
—Mechanical Engineering (p. 1118)
—Robert Fulton: Engineer of the Steamboat (p. 1479)
Herweck, Dona. Day in the Life of a Ballet Dancer. (p. 413)
—Day in the Life of a Cowhand. (p. 413)
—Day in the Life of a Firefighter. (p. 413)
—George Washington. (p. 664)
—Martin Luther King Jr. (p. 1098)
—Susan B. Anthony. (p. 1688)
Herwick Rice, Dona & Bradley, Kathleen. Reconstruction: After the Civil War. (p. 1452)
Herwick Rice, Dona & Conklin, Wendy. Causes of the Civil War. (p. 282)
Herwick Rice, Dona & Greathouse, Lisa. Annie Oakley. (p. 87)
Herwick Rice, Dona & Isecke, Harriet. Cold War: Communism on Trial. (p. 339)
—Sojourner Truth Story. (p. 1606)
Herwick Rice, Dona & Paris, Stephanie. Sal Fink. (p. 1504)
Herwick Rice, Dona & Sugarman, Dorothy. World War I: In Flanders Fields. (p. 1958)
Herxheimer, Sophie, illus. see Clayton, Sally.
Herz, Henry, et al. Monster Goose Nursery Rhymes Larson, Abigail, illus. (p. 1167)
Herz, Irene. Paul Harris, Grow Up! A Book for Children about the Founder of Rotary. Herz, Irene & Herz, Irene L., illus. (p. 1330)
Herz, Irene L., illus. see Herz, Irene.
Herzberg, Max J. Myths & Their Meaning. (p. 1227)
Herzberger, Magda. Tales of the Magic Forest. (p. 1702)
Herzig, Alison Cragin. Gran Dilema. (p. 706)
Herzing, Nancy. Night the Angels Came. (p. 1254)
Herzog, Alex, tr. see Schnurr, J., ed.
Herzog, Arthur. Earthsound. (p. 498)
Herzog, Arthur, Jr., jt. auth. see Holiday, Billie.
Herzog, Brad. Awesome Stories of Generosity in Sports. (p. 121)
—E Is for Extreme: An Extreme Sports Alphabet. Rose, Melanie, illus. (p. 492)
—Francis & Eddie: The True Story of America's Underdogs. Pullen, Zachary, illus. (p. 627)
—Full Count: A Baseball Number Book. Langton, Bruce, illus. (p. 646)
—H Is for Home Run: A Baseball Alphabet. Rose, Melanie, illus. (p. 734)
—I Spy with My Little Eye: Baseball. Milne, David, illus. (p. 846)
—Incredible Stories of Courage in Sports. (p. 869)
—Inspiring Stories of Sportsmanship. (p. 878)
—Is for Amazing Moments: A Sports Alphabet. Rose, Melanie, illus. (p. 889)
—K Is for Kick: A Soccer Alphabet. Rose, Melanie, illus. (p. 941)
—Little Baseball. Bowles, Doug, illus. (p. 1023)
—Little Basketball. Bowles, Doug, illus. (p. 1023)
—Little Football. Bowles, Doug, illus. (p. 1028)
—Little Soccer. Bowles, Doug, illus. (p. 1036)
—P Is for Putt: A Golf Alphabet. Langton, Bruce, illus. (p. 1316)
—Powerful Stories of Perseverance in Sports. (p. 1391)
—R Is for Race: A Stock Car Alphabet. Bready, Jane Gilltrap, illus. (p. 1429)
—Remarkable Stories of Teamwork in Sports. (p. 1459)
—S Is for Save the Planet: A How-to-Be Green Alphabet. Ayriss, Linda Holt, illus. (p. 1499)
—T Is for Touchdown: A Football Alphabet. Braught, Mark, illus. (p. 1694)
—T Is for Touchdown: A Football Alphabet. Stacy, Alan & Braught, Mark, illus. (p. 1694)
—W Is for Wrigley: A Friendly Confines Alphabet. Hanley, John, illus. (p. 1851)
Herzog, Brad & Bowles, Doug. G Is for Gold Medal: An Olympics Alphabet. Bowles, Doug, illus. (p. 651)
Herzog, Dagmar. Intimacy & Exclusion: Religious Politics in Pre-Revolutionary Baden. (p. 881)
Herzog, George, jt. auth. see Courlander, Harold.
Herzog, Inge, illus. see Shue, Jenna.
Herzog, Joyce. Budding Authors: Then & Now. (p. 234)
—Budding Authors: Zooming Ahead. (p. 234)
—Budding Authors: Step into Writing. (p. 234)
—Budding Authors: Adventures in Writing. (p. 234)
—Budding Authors: Writing U. S. History. (p. 234)
—Budding Authors: Twirling Around. Sinclair, Angie et al, eds. (p. 234)
—Draw & Write 2. (p. 480)
—Draw & Write I. (p. 480)
—Excursion into Reading Reader: Part of the Little Beginner's Book Series. (p. 547)
—Excursion into Words: Student Activity Book. Sinclair, Angie & Sinclair, Dan, eds. (p. 547)
—Expedition with Vowels: Student Activity Book. Sinclair, Angie & Sinclair, Dan, eds. (p. 548)
—Expedition with Vowels Reader: Part of the Little Beginner's Book Series. (p. 548)
—Exploring the Alphabet: Student Activity Book. Sinclair, Angie & Sinclair, Dan, eds. (p. 553)
—History in His Hands, Volume 1: Study Guide. (p. 783)
—LetterMaster: Comic Book. (p. 1002)
—School in a Box: Mini-Book. (p. 1523)
—Todder School in a Box: Mini Book. (p. 1761)
Herzog, Kimberly. All That We Could Give. (p. 45)
Herzog, Mary Ann. Buddy Tails. (p. 235)
Herzog, Michael & Pickering, Kenneth. Troilus & Criseyde. (p. 1788)
Herzog, Pearl. Amazing Fishing Rod. Bodel, Itai, photos by. (p. 54)
—Pink Dollhouse. (p. 1359)
Heschke, Elena, illus. see Berne, Emma Carlson.
Heschke, Elena, illus. see Hunt, Sara R. & Kenney, Karen Latchana.
Heschke, Elena, illus. see Kenney, Karen Latchana.
Heshka, Ryan. Ryan Heshka's ABC Spookshow. (p. 1499)
—Welcome to Robot Town. Heshka, Ryan, illus. (p. 1873)
Hesik, Annameekee. Driving Lessons: A You Know Who Girls Novel. (p. 485)
Heskett, Tracie. Informational Reading, Grades 1-2. (p. 874)
—Math Strategies to Use with English Language Learners, Grade 1-2. (p. 1107)
—Math Strategies to Use with English Language Learners, Grades 5-6. (p. 1107)
—Strategies to Use with Your English Language Learners, Grade 1-3. (p. 1666)
—Strategies to Use with Your English Language Learners, Grades 4-6. (p. 1666)
—Traits of Good Writing, Grades 1-2. (p. 1777)
—Traits of Good Writing, Grades 5-6. Fields, Kim et al, eds. (p. 1777)
Hesleden, Michael. Benjamin Franklin: American Diplomat. (p. 164)
Heslep, William. Tower of London. (p. 1773)
Hespe, Robert. Jingle Bear on Ice. Booker, Carly-Jean, illus. (p. 918)
Hesper, Sam. Animal Cannibals (p. 77)
—Black Widow Spiders (p. 197)
—Praying Mantises (p. 1393)
Hess, Amy, jt. auth. see Carson, Penny.
Hess, Anna, jt. auth. see Dannenbring, Cheryl.
Hess, Brian F. Lynquest & the Search for Greatness. (p. 1066)
Hess, Deborah. American Flag. (p. 60)
—Liberty Bell. (p. 1005)
—Star-Spangled Banner. (p. 1641)
—White House. (p. 1913)
Hess, Debra. On Trial in Rome: Cicero Versus Caesr. (p. 1292)
Hess, Debra, jt. auth. see Apte, Sunita.
Hess, Debra, jt. auth. see Carangelo, Audrey.
Hess, Debra, jt. auth. see Robbins, Trina.
Hess, Debra, jt. auth. see Sandler, Michael.
Hess, Debra & McGeveran, William. South Carolina. (p. 1616)
Hess, Debra & Olson, Tod. Modern Olympics: Battling for Peace. (p. 1158)
Hess, Debra & Wiesenfeld, Lori P. Florida. (p. 606)
Hess, Debra, et al. South Carolina. (p. 1616)
Hess, Erwin L., illus. see Gruskin, Edward I.
Hess, Erwin L., illus. see Winterbotham, R. R.
Hess, Frederick M. Common Sense School Reform. (p. 349)
Hess, Harvalee, illus. see Hess, Kathryn.
Hess, Ingrid. Amish Alphabet. (p. 65)
—Sleep in Peace. (p. 1588)
—Walk in Peace. (p. 1853)
Hess, Ingrid, illus. see Peifer, Jane Hoober.
Hess, Ingrid, illus. see Weaver, Lisa D.
Hess, Joan Tauke-. Cowboy Execution - Justified? (p. 374)
Hess, Karl. Capitalism for Kids: Growing up to Be Your Own Boss. Williams, Jane A. & Daniels, Kathryn, eds. (p. 262)
Hess, Kathryn. Whitepaws Fabio Giorgio Don Gato Hess. Hess, Harvalee, illus. (p. 1914)
Hess, Mark, illus. see Turner, Ann Warren.
Hess, Nina. Practical Guide to Monsters. Whitman, Stacy, ed. (p. 1392)
—Whose Feet? Kanzler, John, tr. (p. 1921)
Hess, Nina, jt. auth. see Greenberg, Daniel A.
Hess, Paul. Animal Worlds. (p. 80)
—Farmyard Animals. Hess, Paul, illus. (p. 575)
—Polar Animals. Hess, Paul, illus. (p. 1378)
—Rainforest Animals. (p. 1436)
—Rainforest Animals. Hess, Paul, illus. (p. 1436)
—Safari Animals. Hess, Paul, illus. (p. 1501)
Hess, Paul, illus. see Barber, Antonia & Quarto Generic Staff.
Hess, Paul, illus. see Cave, Kathryn & Quarto Generic Staff.
Hess, Paul, illus. see Lisle, Rebecca.
Hess, Paul, illus. see MacDonald, Alan.
Hess, Paul, illus. see Maddern, Eric & Williamson, Duncan.
Hess, Paul, illus. see Maddern, Eric.
Hess, Paul, illus. see Tavaci, Elspeth & Quarto Generic Staff.
Hess, Paul, jt. auth. see Poole, Josephine.
Hess, Ron. Hard Case. (p. 748)
Hesse, Diane. Charlie Catfish & the Big Mistake. (p. 293)
Hesse, George. Malcolm & the Magic Shoe... a Peek into Heaven. (p. 1083)
Hesse, Hermann. Bajo la Rueda. (p. 133)
—Demian: Die Geschichte von Emil Sinclairs Jugend. (p. 425)
Hesse, Hermann & SparkNotes Staff. Siddhartha. Kestler, Justin & Florman, Ben, eds. (p. 1573)
Hesse, Joseph M. Régions de France. (p. 1457)
Hesse, Karen. Aleutian Sparrow. Zerbetz, Evon, illus. (p. 35)
—Aleutian Sparrow. McGillivray, Kim & Zerbetz, Evon, illus. (p. 35)
—Brooklyn Bridge. Sheban, Chris, illus. (p. 231)
—Cats in Krasinski Square. Watson, Wendy, illus. (p. 281)
—Come on, Rain! (p. 347)
—Lavender. Kimmel, Eric A. & Glass, Andrew, illus. (p. 981)
—Light in the Storm: The Diary of Amelia Martin, Fenwick Island, Delaware 1861. (p. 1015)
—Music of Dolphins. (p. 1193)
—Out of the Dust. (p. 1311)
—Phoenix Rising. (p. 1351)
—Sable. Sewall, Marcia, illus. (p. 1500)
—Safekeeping. (p. 1502)
—Spuds. Watson, Wendy, illus. (p. 1635)
—Stowaway. (p. 1664)
—Wish on a Unicorn. (p. 1940)
—Witness. (p. 1942)
—Young Hans Christian Andersen. Blegvad, Erik, illus. (p. 1978)
Hesse, Laura. Great Pumpkin Ride. (p. 718)
Hesse, Laura L. One Frosty Christmas. (p. 1295)
Hesse, Leah. Colin Counts To 50. (p. 339)
—How Do Dams Work? (p. 806)
—Let's Count Down: Understanding Subtraction. (p. 995)
Hesselbein, Deborah A. Tail Talks. Claycomb, Norma L., illus. (p. 1695)
Hesselbein, Kent, illus. see Hall, Dee.
Hessman, Amy. Understanding Special Needs Kids: Seizures. (p. 1816)
Hest, Amy. Beso de Buenas Noches. Rubio, Esther, tr. (p. 168)
—Charley's First Night. Oxenbury, Helen, illus. (p. 292)
—Dog Who Belonged to No One. Bates, Amy, illus. (p. 462)
—Don't You Feel Well, Sam? Jeram, Anita, illus. (p. 469)
—Guess Who, Baby Duck! Barton, Jill, illus. (p. 729)
—Kiss Good Night: Book & Toy Gift Set. Jeram, Anita, illus. (p. 961)
—Kiss Good Night. Jeram, Anita, illus. (p. 961)
—Kiss Good Night Lap-Size Board Book. Jeram, Anita, illus. (p. 961)
—Letters to Leo. Denos, Julia, illus. (p. 1002)
—Little Chick: Three Little Stories. (p. 1026)
—Little Chick. Jeram, Anita, illus. (p. 1026)
—Mr. George Baker. (p. 1185)
—Mr. George Baker. Muth, Jon J., illus. (p. 1185)
—Reader Castillo, Lauren, illus. (p. 1444)
—Remembering Mrs. Rossi. Maione, Heather, illus. (p. 1459)
—Tu Puedes Hacerlo, Sam. Jeram, Anita, illus. (p. 1795)
—When Charley Met Grampa. Oxenbury, Helen, illus. (p. 1901)
—When Jessie Came Across the Sea. (p. 1903)
—When Jessie Came Across the Sea. Lynch, P. J., illus. (p. 1903)
—You Can Do It, Sam. Jeram, Anita, illus. (p. 1974)
Hester, Beth Landis. Lego Ninjago: Secret World of the Ninja. (p. 990)
Hester, Beth Landis & Dorling Kindersley Publishing Staff. Secret World of the Ninja. (p. 1544)
Hester, Carla. Sunday School Sarah: A Book of Children's Bible Stories. (p. 1676)
Hester, Denia Lewis. Grandma Lena's Big Ol' Turnip. Urbanovic, Jackie, illus. (p. 708)
—Grandma Lena's Big Ol'Turnip. Urbanovic, Jackie, illus. (p. 708)
Hester, Elizabeth, ed. see Yorke, Jane & Dorling Kindersley Publishing Staff.
Hester, Elizabeth & Dorling Kindersley Publishing Staff. North American Birds. (p. 1264)
Hester, Elliott Neal. Plane Insanity: A Flight Attendant's Tales of Sex, Rage, & Queasiness at 30,000 Feet. (p. 1367)
Hester, Jimmy. Tlw: Introduction to True Love Waits. (p. 1758)
Hester, John C. Three Days in Hell. (p. 1742)
Hester, Lyn. Mary Lou Likes Blue. (p. 1100)
—Stop Drop & Roll. (p. 1653)
Hester, Phil. Firebreather (p. 591)
—Kestus. Morrissey, Paul, ed. (p. 949)
—T. H. U. N. D. E. R. Agents Volume 1. (p. 1693)
Hester, Sallie. Diary of Sallie Hester: A Covered Wagon Girl (p. 435)
Hestermann, Bethanie, jt. auth. see Hestermann, Josh.
Hestermann, Josh & Hestermann, Bethanie. Zoology for Kids: Understanding & Working with Animals, with 21 Activities. (p. 1989)
Hestler, Anna & Spilling, Jo-Ann. Wales. (p. 1853)
—Yemen. (p. 1970)
Heston, Charles, illus. see Martini, Teri.
Heston, L. L. Story of Pan Doo: A Panda's Progress. (p. 1659)
Hetherington, Debra Thorpe, ed. Spark Story Bible: Spark a Journey Through God's Word. Grosshauser, Peter, illus. (p. 1622)
Hetherington, Ian, et al. Realizing Change: Vipassana Meditation in Action. (p. 1449)
Hetherington, Jan, illus. see Hetherington, Sally.
Hetherington, Lisa. Oscar & Willie: Silly Oscar's Days of the Week. Lawrey, Derek, illus. (p. 1305)
Hetherington, Sally. Where's Pa? Hetherington, Jan, illus. (p. 1910)
Heti, Sheila. We Need a Horse. Rojas, Clare, illus. (p. 1867)
Hetland, Beth, illus. see Brown, Cynthia Light & McGinty, Patrick.
Hetland, Beth, illus. see Kavin, Kim.
Hetland, Beth, illus. see Latham, Donna.
Hetrick, Hans. Hydroplanes (p. 831)
—NBA - A History of Hoops: The Story of the San Antonio Spurs. (p. 1238)
—Outrageous Hockey Rivalries. (p. 1313)
—Play Baseball Like a Pro: Key Skills & Tips (p. 1371)
—Rolling Stones: Pushing Rock's Boundaries. (p. 1485)
—Six Degrees of Peyton Manning: Connecting Football Stars. (p. 1582)
—Sport Bikes (p. 1631)
—Story of the Miami Heat. (p. 1661)
—Story of the San Antonio Spurs. (p. 1662)
—Super Bowl: All about Pro Football's Biggest Event (p. 1679)
—This Book's Got Game: A Collection of Awesome Sports Trivia (p. 1735)
—World Series: All about Pro Baseball's Biggest Event (p. 1958)
Hetrick, Hans, et al. Winner Takes All. (p. 1937)
Hetticher, Patricia. Forty Weeks from Monday. (p. 623)
Hetzel, D. June & Lee, Michelle, eds. Beauty Is Soul Deep: 180 Devotions for Growing a Meaningful Inner Life. (p. 154)
Hetzer, Michael. Footprints on the Ceiling: Your Child's Footprint Completes the Story. Clayton, Kim, illus. (p. 615)
—Footprints on the Ceiling (Collector's Edition) Your Child's Footprint Completes the Story. Clayton, Kim, illus. (p. 615)
—Get Well Picture. Clayton, Kim, illus. (p. 668)
—Hug for Percy Porcupine. Clayton, Kim, illus. (p. 824)
—No More Handprints: Your Child's Handprint Completes the Story. Clayton, Kim, illus. (p. 1259)
Heuchert, Richard, jt. auth. see Barth, Katrin.
Heuer, Christoph. Lola & Fred & Tom. (p. 1045)
Heuer, Steve. Spectacular Experiments & Mad Science Kids Love: Science That Dazzles @ Home, School or on the Go! (p. 1624)
Heuninck, Ronald. Rain or Shine. Heuninck, Ronald, illus. (p. 1435)
Heurtelou, Maude. Makso. Louissaint, Louis, illus. (p. 1083)
—Makso's Farm. Vilsaint, Fequiere, ed. (p. 1083)
—Sandra: Cinderalla in Haiti. (p. 1511)
Heuscher, Julius E., tr. see Goethes Fairy Tale Staff.
Heuston, Kimberley. Book of Jude. (p. 211)
—Mao Zedong. (p. 1089)
—Napoleon I: Emperor & Conqueror. (p. 1229)
—Otto von Bismarck: Iron Chancellor of Germany. (p. 1307)
—Shakeress. (p. 1559)
Heuston, Kimberley & Heuston, Kimberley Burton. Napoleon I: Emperor & Conqueror. (p. 1229)
Heuston, Kimberley B. Dante's Daughter. (p. 406)
Heuston, Kimberley Burton. Mao Zedong. (p. 1089)
Heuston, Kimberley Burton, jt. auth. see Heuston, Kimberley.
Heuston, Kimberley Burton, jt. auth. see Kenoyer, Jonathan M.
Heuston, Kimberley Burton, jt. auth. see Kenoyer, Jonathan Mark.
Heuston, Kimberly. Shakeress. (p. 1559)
Heuvel, Elizabeth Vanden. From Seedlings That Sprouted: The Boon Family History 1575-2014. (p. 643)
Heuvel, Eric & Miller, Lorraine T. Family Secret. Miller, Lorraine T., tr. from DUT. (p. 568)
Heuvel, Eric, et al. Search. Miller, Lorraine T., tr. from DUT. (p. 1537)
Hevesi, Gabriel. 100% Leadership: Guidelines to be an Effective Leader. (p. 1998)
Hevesi, Rachel. I Am a Monkey. Tyson, Liz, illus. (p. 832)
—Peppy - a Long Way from Home. Parathian, Hannah, illus. (p. 1340)
Heward, L. Richard. Personal Finance Simplified. Jarvis, Sharon Downing, ed. (p. 1344)
Hewat, Jo-Anne. Where's Grandma Daddy? (p. 1910)
Hewes, Agnes Danforth. Spice & the Devil's Cave. Ward, Lynd, illus. (p. 1626)
Hewetson, Nicholas, illus. see MacDonald, Fiona.
Hewetson, Nicholas J., illus. see MacDonald, Fiona.
Hewetson, Nicholas J., illus. see Meredith, Susan.
Hewetson, Nicholas J., illus. see Morley, Jacqueline.
Hewetson, Nick, illus. see Stewart, David.
Hewett, Angela. Bumper Junior Art: Colour by Numbers. (p. 241)
—Colours & Shapes: Touch & Trace Early Learning Fun! Duck Egg Blue (Firm) Staff et al, illus. (p. 346)
Hewett, Angela, illus. see Award, Anna.
Hewett, Angela, illus. see Giles, Sophie & Davis, Kate.
Hewett, Angela, illus. see Picthall, Chez.
Hewett, Edgar L. Circular Relating to Historic & Prehistoric Ruins of the Southwest & Their Preservation. (p. 321)
—Government Supervision of Historic & Prehistoric Ruins. (p. 704)
—Groundwork of American Archaeology. (p. 725)
Hewett, Katherine. Magic Bubble Bath. (p. 1072)
—Smile Doodle Bug! (p. 1594)
Hewins, Shirley. Rainy Brown & the Seven Midgets. (p. 1436)
Hewins, Shirley, illus. see Hawkins-Rodgers, Donzella.
Hewitson, Mark. Germany & the Causes of the First World War. (p. 666)
Hewitt, Beth Edington. Sermones Que Cautivan A los Ninos: Como Preparar y Presentar Sermones Infantiles Poderosos. Ballesta, Alfredo, tr. (p. 1552)
Hewitt, Christine. Mystical Journey. (p. 1226)
Hewitt, David. Uncle Sam's America. Hewitt, Kathryn, illus. (p. 1812)
Hewitt, Elizabeth, illus. see Jacobs, Karen & Miller, Leah.
Hewitt, Franz. Monster Doctor, M. D. (p. 1167)
Hewitt, Geoff, ed. see Adams, Keith.
Hewitt, Hazel & Gillett, Chrissy. Locust Ate My Daddy's Underwears. (p. 1045)
Hewitt, Ibrahim, ed. see Kayani, M. S.
Hewitt, Kathryn, illus. see Bunting, Eve.
Hewitt, Kathryn, illus. see Hewitt, David.
Hewitt, Kathryn, illus. see Krull, Kathleen.
Hewitt, Megan. Eagle Rises. (p. 492)
Hewitt, Monica. Hewidoos-The First Day of School. (p. 774)
Hewitt, Nick & Jackson, Andrea V., eds. Handbook of Atmospheric Science: Principles & Applications. (p. 740)
Hewitt, Paul G., et al. Conceptual Physical Science. (p. 355)
Hewitt, Sally. Amazing Electricity. (p. 54)
—Amazing Forces & Movement. (p. 54)
—Amazing Light. (p. 55)
—Amazing Materials. (p. 55)
—Amazing Plants. (p. 55)
—Amazing Sound. (p. 55)
—By the Sea. (p. 249)
—Caring for Our Earth. (p. 269)
—Caring for the Earth. (p. 269)
—Cars. (p. 271)
—Dark & Light. (p. 407)
—Earth & Space. (p. 495)
—Egyptians. (p. 507)
—Energy. (p. 528)
—Face to Face Safari. Gilvan-Cartwright, Chris, illus. (p. 560)
—First Experiences: Going to the Dentist. (p. 594)
—Forces & Motion. (p. 617)
—Fruit. (p. 645)
—Going to the Dentist. (p. 693)
—Grains & Cereals. (p. 706)
—Greeks. (p. 721)
—Happy Birthday. Cameron, Craig, illus. (p. 744)
—Happy Doctor. Cameron, Craig, illus. (p. 745)

—Happy Dresser. Cameron, Craig, illus. (p. 745)
—Hear This! (p. 759)
—Hogares de Animales: Animal Homes. (p. 787)
—Homes. (p. 793)
—Keeping Healthy. (p. 947)
—Life Cycles: From Caterpillar to Butterfly. (p. 1010)
—Life Cycles from Tadpole to Frog (p. 1010)
—Listen Up! (p. 1022)
—Look Here! (p. 1049)
—Maps. (p. 1090)
—Meat & Fish. (p. 1118)
—Milk & Cheese. (p. 1143)
—Minibeasts. (p. 1146)
—Mountains. (p. 1181)
—My Bones. (p. 1198)
—My Brain. (p. 1199)
—My Digestive System. (p. 1202)
—My Heart & Lungs. (p. 1210)
—My Stepfamily. (p. 1219)
—Our New Baby. (p. 1309)
—Planes. (p. 1367)
—Plants. (p. 1369)
—Project Geography - Rivers. (p. 1410)
—Pull & Push. (p. 1415)
—Racism. (p. 1432)
—Reduce & Reuse. (p. 1456)
—Romans. (p. 1486)
—Smell It! (p. 1593)
—Smell That! (p. 1593)
—Sound. (p. 1615)
—Spick-and-Span Fairy (p. 1626)
—Tastes Good! (p. 1707)
—Touch That! (p. 1772)
—Transportation. (p. 1779)
—Using Energy. (p. 1828)
—Using Machines. (p. 1828)
—Using Water. (p. 1829)
—Vegetables. (p. 1834)
—Vikings. (p. 1842)
—Waste & Recycling. (p. 1860)
—Water. (p. 1862)
—Weather. (p. 1869)
—When People Die. (p. 1904)
—Where's My Shirt? (p. 1910)
—Your Food. (p. 1980)
—Your Local Enviornment. (p. 1981)
—Your Local Environment. (p. 1981)
Hewitt, Sally & Royston, Angela. My Body: A Fun Way to Find Out All the Facts about Your Body. (p. 1198)
Hewitt, Sally, et al. Teimlo'n Genfigennus. (p. 1715)
Hewitt, William. Across the Wide River. (p. 9)
Hewitt-Barker, Marsha E. Dachshund Who Sprouted Wings. (p. 398)
Hewlett, Gill. Entry Level Mathematics (p. 531)
Hewling, Amy Megan. Wishes. (p. 1940)
Hewson, Maggie, jt. auth. see Angliss, Sarah.
Hex, Kathleen. Grammar Minutes: 100 Minutes to Better Basic Skills. Kim, Regina Hurh & Snoddy, Gillian, eds. (p. 706)
—Using the Standards, Grade 3: Building Grammar & Writing Skills. (p. 1828)
Heyde, Christiane. Happy Girl. Hawkins, Linda, illus. (p. 745)
Heydlauff, Lisa. Going to School in India. Upadhye, Nitin, photos by. (p. 693)
Heydt, Scott. Mice Don't Taste Like Chicken. Aaron, Rich, illus. (p. 1134)
Heyen, William. Poetics of Hiroshima. (p. 1376)
Heyens, Gudrun & Engel, Gerhard. Fun & Games with the Alto Recorder: Tune. Bk. 1 (p. 647)
—Fun & Games with the Alto Recorder: Tuto. Bk. 1 (p. 647)
—Fun & Games with the Alto Recorder: Tune. Bk. 2 (p. 647)
Heyer, Carol. Christmas Story. (p. 315)
—Easter Story. (p. 499)
—Excalibur. (p. 547)
—First Christmas. (p. 593)
—First Christmas. Heyer, Carol, illus. (p. 593)
—First Easter. (p. 594)
—First Easter. Heyer, Carol, illus. (p. 594)
—Humphrey's First Christmas. Heyer, Carol, illus. (p. 827)
—Humphrey's First Palm Sunday. Heyer, Carol, illus. (p. 827)
Heyer, Carol, illus. see Aesop.
Heyer, Carol, illus. see Fry, Sonali.
Heyer, Carol, illus. see O'Malley, Kevin.
Heyer, Carol, illus. see Smith, Maggie Caldwell.
Heyer, Carol, illus. see Winkler, Henry & Oliver, Lin.
Heyer, Sandra. True Stories Behind the Songs. (p. 1792)
Heyes, Eileen. O'Dwyer & Grady Starring in Tough Act to Follow. (p. 1278)
Heyes, Jane, illus. see David, Juliet.
Heyge, Lorna Lutz. Music Garden for Babies from Birth to 18 Months: Songbook 1. (p. 1193)
Heying, Teresa. Fishing with Grandpa. (p. 599)
—No Matter What You Do. (p. 1259)
Heyliger, William. Bill Darrow's Victory. Salg, Bert, illus. (p. 186)
—Hot Dog Partners. Hastings, Howard L., illus. (p. 801)
—Jerry Hicks, Explorer. Salg, Bert, illus. (p. 913)
—Jerry Hicks, Ghost Hunter. Salg, Bert, illus. (p. 913)
—Quarterback Hothead. Grubb, W. B., illus. (p. 1422)
Heyman, Alissa. Twelve Dancing Unicorns. Gerard, Justin, illus. (p. 1800)
Heyman, Carly. My Extra Special Brother: How to Love, Understand, & Celebrate Your Sibling with Special Needs. Conley, Stephanie, illus. (p. 1202)
Heyman, Frank J., ed. see Heymann, Irene Rommel.
Heyman, Ken, photos by see Morris, Ann.
Heyman, Richard, jt. auth. see Heyman, Richard.
Heyman, Richard & Heyman, Richard. Jack the Surfer Dude ..... Hit the Road Jack Book 3: Hit the Road Jack. (p. 903)
Heymann, Irene Rommel. Fanciful Tales & Poems: For Grandchildren of Any Age. Heyman, Frank J., ed. (p. 570)
Heymelaux, Jasmin. Caco the Little Orphan Cat: O Gatinho Órfão. Canuto, Louise, tr. from ENG. (p. 250)
Heymelaux, Jasmin & Biggs, Harry. Coco: The Little Orphan Cat. Perroud, Benoît, illus. (p. 337)
Heyne, Kara. Locket's Secret. (p. 1045)
Heyward, DuBose. Country Bunny & the Little Gold Shoes 75th Anniversary Edition. Flack, Marjorie, illus. (p. 372)
—Country Bunny & the Little Gold Shoes Gift Edition with Charm. Flack, Marjorie, illus. (p. 372)
Heywood, Grandma Geny. Stegot: ... the Great. (p. 1646)
—Tirano: Another Dinosaur Is Born! (p. 1757)
Heywood, Grand-Mere Geny. Proto: Que faire quand un dinosaure nait dans votre Jardin? Connors, Mary, illus. (p. 1412)
Heywood, La Abuelita Geny. Proto: ¿Qué hacer cuando un dinosaurio nace en tu Jardín? (p. 1412)
Heywood, Rosie. Great Balloon Race. (p. 713)
—Great City Search. (p. 714)
—Great Dinosaur Search. Wingate, Philippa, ed. (p. 715)
—Puzzle Car Race. Haw, Brenda, illus. (p. 1420)
Heywood, Rosie, ed. Travel Puzzles Sticker Book. Haw, Brenda, illus. (p. 1780)
Heyworth, Heather, illus. see Carlson, Amie.
Heyworth, Heather, illus. see Dale, Jay.
Heyworth, Heather, illus. see Matthew, Anna.
Heyworth, Heather, illus. see Rische, Stephanie.
Heyworth, Heather, illus. see Troupe, Thomas Kingsley.
Hezlep, Amber, illus. see Higbee, Heidi.
Hezlep, William. Bigfoot! (p. 184)
—Bog Bodies. (p. 207)
—Cayman Duppy: Playscript. (p. 282)
—Curse of the Tomb Raiders. (p. 395)
—How Come Christmas? (p. 806)
—Kokopelli's Cave. (p. 966)
—Merlin's Cave. (p. 1128)
—Nessie: Playscript. (p. 1242)
—Pharaoh's Dagger: Playscript. (p. 1349)
—Plays of the Past: Three American One-Acts. (p. 1373)
—Plays of the Present: Three American One-Acts. (p. 1373)
—Red Cloud's Revenge. (p. 1453)
—Shipwrecked. Landes, William Alan, ed. (p. 1567)
—Time Travelers (p. 1753)
—Treasure of the Mayans. (p. 1782)
Hezlep, William, ed. Trouble in the Mountains. (p. 1790)
Hiaasen, Carl. Basket Case. (p. 142)
—Chomp. (p. 309)
—Double Whammy. (p. 473)
—Flush. (p. 608)
—Hoot. (p. 796)
—Lucky You. (p. 1063)
—Nature Girl. (p. 1236)
—Scat. (p. 1521)
—Skink - No Surrender. (p. 1585)
—Strip Tease. (p. 1667)
Hiamey, Godfred Kwaku. Dovito & the Little Ant. (p. 474)
Hiatt, Fred. Nine Days. (p. 1256)
Hiatt, Kay & Green, Mary. Collins Primary Literacy. (p. 341)
Hibbard, Derrick. College Fast Track: Essential Habits for Less Stress & More Success. (p. 340)
Hibbeler, Stephen Paul. Wonderful, Magical World. (p. 1948)
Hibben, Frank Cummings. Lost Americans. (p. 1054)
Hibbert, Adam. Life in a Pond. (p. 1010)
—Terrorism. (p. 1722)
—World Wonders. (p. 1960)
Hibbert, Adam, jt. auth. see Hibbert, Clare.
Hibbert, Claire. Birds. (p. 191)
—Butterflies & Moths. (p. 247)
—Fish. (p. 598)
—Snakes & Lizards. (p. 1596)
—Spiders. (p. 1626)
Hibbert, Clare. Beetles. (p. 158)
—China. (p. 306)
—Dakota Fanning. (p. 401)
—Day That Changed History: The Assassination of John F Kennedy. (p. 414)
—Elephant Orphans (p. 511)
—Hamster. (p. 739)
—If You Were a Cat. (p. 854)
—If You Were a Dog. (p. 854)
—If You Were a Dolphin. (p. 855)
—If You Were a Horse. (p. 855)
—If You Were a Shark. (p. 855)
—If You Were a Snake. (p. 855)
—Jaden Smith. (p. 905)
—My Busy Week. (p. 1200)
—Real Pirates. James, John, illus. (p. 1448)
—Rich & Poor in Ancient Egypt. (p. 1469)
—Salamanders. (p. 1504)
—Save the Animals (p. 1516)
Hibbert, Clare, jt. auth. see Dorling Kindersley Publishing Staff.
Hibbert, Clare & Hachette Children's Books Staff. Fashion Model: Find Out How the Top Fashion Models Made It! (p. 575)
—Movie Star - Celeb: Find Out How Your Favorite Movie Stars Made It! (p. 1183)
—Pop Star - Celeb: Find Out How Your Favorite Pop Stars Made It! (p. 1384)
Hibbert, Clare & Hibbert, Adam. Twentieth Century. Woolf, Alex, ed. (p. 1801)
Hibbert, Dee. Share Day Hibbert, Rhonda, illus. (p. 1561)
Hibbert, Hollie, illus. see Hapka, Cathy, pseud.
Hibbert, Hollie, illus. see Maccarone, Grace.
Hibbert, Rhonda, illus. see Hibbert, Dee.
Hibbett, Myles. Zephyr Spheres & the Lost Spell. (p. 1986)
Hibbitts, Mark. Alfie Potts: Alfie & the Mind Virus. Purchase, Brendan, illus. (p. 37)
—Alfie Potts: Alfie & the Seminar. Purchase, Brendan, illus. (p. 37)
Hibbs, Carmen Arlene. Captivity in the Contemporary Zone My True Story. (p. 265)
Hibbs, Gillian. Tilly's at Home Holiday. Hibbs, Gillian, illus. (p. 1750)
Hibbs, Linda. All about Indonesia: Stories, Songs & Crafts for Kids. (p. 42)
Hibbs, Lisa. Allie Doogledorf & the Mighty Mess. (p. 47)
Hibbs, Sasha. Black Amaranth. (p. 194)
Hiber, Amanda. Alternative Lending. (p. 50)
—Are Adoption Policies Fair? (p. 96)
—Do Tax Breaks Benefit the Economy? (p. 457)
—Gangs. (p. 655)
—Is the U. S. Ready for a Minority President? (p. 890)
—Is the United States Ready for a Minority President? (p. 890)
—Islamic Militancy. (p. 892)
—Sexual Violence. Greenhaven Press Editors, ed. (p. 1556)
—Sexual Violence. Greenhaven Press Editors & Gale Editors, eds. (p. 1556)
—Should Cameras Be Allowed in Courtrooms? (p. 1569)
—Should Governments Negotiate with Terrorists? (p. 1569)
—What Is the Future of the U. S. Economy? (p. 1890)
Hibschman, Barbara. 52 Ways to Teach Children to Share the Gospel. (p. 1997)
Hicer, Nancy. Maps & New York City. (p. 1090)
—New York City's Five Boroughs. (p. 1248)
Hichens, Joanne. Stained. (p. 1638)
Hichs, Donald E. & Demers, Aimee. Proactive Discipline. Maximilian Press Publishers staff, ed. (p. 1408)
Hickerson, Brandy. My Brother & Me. (p. 1199)
Hickerson, Joel. ImagineLand's Bubble Gum Trouble (p. 861)
Hickey, Barbara. Ms Sincerely Kind Goes Out & About: (Where Good Manners Matter) (p. 1188)
Hickey, Brenda, illus. see Curnow, Bobby.
Hickey, Caroline. Isabelle's Boyfriend. (p. 891)
Hickey, David. Very Small Something. Griggs-Burr, Alexander & Griggs-Burr, Alexander, illus. (p. 1838)
Hickey, Josh, illus. see Elmore, Amber.
Hickey, Joshalyn M. Good Morning Lovey! Chaveevah, Banks Ferguson, illus. (p. 698)
—Travis, It's NOT Your Birthday! Ferguson, Chaveevah Banks, illus. (p. 1781)
Hickey, Laura L. What's in the Woods. (p. 1898)
Hickey, Marilyn & Bowling, Sarah. Blessing the Next Generation: Creating a Lasting Family Legacy with the Help of a Loving God. (p. 199)
Hickey, Matt. Ebby Meets Felicity. Corr, Christopher, illus. (p. 501)
Hickey, Michael, jt. auth. see Brownworth, Thom.
Hickey, Sally. Empty Shoes. (p. 521)
Hickey, Tony. Where's Jacko? Myler, Terry, illus. (p. 1910)
Hickman, B. Jo. Old Cat, Fat Rat, & Boo. (p. 1283)
Hickman, Claire, jt. auth. see Meredith, Susan.
Hickman, Clare, jt. auth. see Rogers, Kirsteen.
Hickman, Clare & Meredith, Sue. Usborne Encyclopedia of World Religions: Internet-Linked. Rogers, Kirsteen, ed. (p. 1827)
Hickman, Debbie. Exasperated Clock. Taylor, Adam, illus. (p. 547)
Hickman, Gregory. Jack of All Trades. (p. 903)
Hickman, Jonathan. Avengers - Rogue Planet (p. 118)
—Everything Dies. (p. 544)
—Fantastic Four by Jonathan Hickman - Volume 3. (p. 571)
—Fantastic Four by Jonathan Hickman - Volume 6. Choi, Mike & Camuncoli, Giuseppe, illus. (p. 571)
—Ultimate Comics Ultimates Ribic, Esad & Peterson, Brandon, illus. (p. 1809)
Hickman, Jonathan, jt. auth. see Colak, Mirko.
Hickman, Jonathan, jt. auth. see Dragotta, Nick.
Hickman, Jonathan, jt. auth. see Spencer, Nick.
Hickman, Jonathan & Dragotta, Nick. Fantastic Four Epting, Steve & Brooks, Mark, illus. (p. 571)
Hickman, Jonathan, text. Ultimate Comics Thor. (p. 1809)
Hickman, Kirt. Purple. Olson, Julie, illus. (p. 1419)
Hickman, Pamela. Animals & Their Mates: How Animals Attract, Fight for & Protect Each Other. Stephens, Pat, illus. (p. 82)
—Animals & Their Young: How Animals Produce & Care for Their Babies. Stephens, Pat, illus. (p. 82)
—Animals Hibernating: How Animals Survive Extreme Conditions. Stephens, Pat, illus. (p. 82)
—Birds of Prey Rescue: Changing the Future for Endangered Wildlife. (p. 192)
—How Animals Eat. Stephens, Pat, illus. (p. 804)
—How Animals Move. Stephens, Pat, illus. (p. 804)
—How Animals Use Their Senses. Stephens, Pat, illus. (p. 805)
—It's Moving Day! Valerio, Geraldo, illus. (p. 897)
—Turtle Rescue: Changing the Future for Endangered Wildlife. (p. 1798)
Hickman, Pamela & Cavalluzzo, Jean Smith. Righting Canada's Wrongs: Italian Canadian Internment in the Second World War. (p. 1472)
Hickman, Pamela & Federation of Ontario Naturalists. Naturaleza Divertida. Shore, Judie, illus. (p. 1236)
—Naturaleza y Tú. Shore, Judie, illus. (p. 1236)
Hickman, Pamela & Taraschi-Carr, Gola. Righting Canada's Wrongs: the Komagata Maru & Canada's Anti-Indian Immigration Policies in the Twentieth Century. (p. 1472)
Hickman, Paula, illus. see Harvey, Keith.
Hickman, Paula, jt. auth. see Harvey, Keith.
Hickman, Ruth. Going Through Puberty: A Boy's Manual for Body, Mind, & Health. (p. 693)
—Going Through Puberty: A Girl's Manual for Body, Mind, & Health. (p. 693)
Hickman, Sondra, Jr. Snowman to Dixxebell. (p. 1601)
Hickner, Hayden. Bear & the Bees. (p. 150)
Hickox, Rebecca. Per & the Dala Horse. Gilbert, Yvonne, illus. (p. 1341)
Hicks, Alan and Aaron, illus. see Richardson, Robert.
Hicks, Angela, illus. see Giles, Sophie, et al.
Hicks, Angie. Alien. (p. 40)
—Butterfly. (p. 247)
—Colour by Numbers. (p. 346)
—Colour by Numbers - Pirate. (p. 346)
—Fairy Horse. (p. 563)
—Fish. (p. 598)
—Mermaid. (p. 1128)
—Moonlight & the Mermaid. (p. 1172)
—Pirate. (p. 1362)
—Shark. (p. 1561)
Hicks, Angie, illus. see King, Karen.
Hicks, Aniya & Hicks, Michelle. Fun Back in Ruskin Town. (p. 647)
Hicks, Aubrey. Advertising: Does Advertising Tell the Truth? (p. 25)
Hicks, Barbara Jean. I Like Black & White. Prap, Lila, illus. (p. 841)
—I Like Colors. Prap, Lila, illus. (p. 841)
—Monsters Don't Eat Broccoli. Hendra, Sue, illus. (p. 1169)
Hicks, Barbara Jean, jt. auth. see Disney Book Group Staff.
Hicks, Barbara Jean & Disney Book Group Staff. Sister More Like Me. Disney Storybook Artists Staff et al, illus. (p. 1581)
Hicks, Benjamin. Arithmecation. (p. 98)
—Byron's Tie. Hicks, Benjamin & Hicks, Rosetta, eds. (p. 249)
Hicks, Betty. Basketball Bats / Goof-Off Goalie. McCauley, Adam, illus. (p. 143)
—Out of Order. (p. 1311)
—Swimming with Sharks / Track Attack. McCauley, Adam, illus. (p. 1691)
—Worm Whisperer. Hatke, Ben, illus. (p. 1961)
Hicks, Betty & McCauley, Adam. Scaredy-Cat Catcher. (p. 1519)
Hicks, Bob. Cornelius, the Little Dragon Book. Hicks, Bob, illus. (p. 367)
—Narvick the Whark (or a Shwale) (p. 1230)
Hicks, Charlotte, jt. auth. see Patenaude, Jeremy.
Hicks, Clifford B. Alvin Fernald, Foreign Trader. Schluenderfritz, Theodore, illus. (p. 51)
—Alvin Fernald, Mayor for a Day. Sokol, Bill, illus. (p. 51)
—Alvin Fernald, Mayor for a Day. Schluenderfritz, Theodore, illus. (p. 51)
—Alvin Fernald's Incredible Buried Treasure. Bradfield, Roger, illus. (p. 51)
—Alvin's Secret Code. Sokol, Bill, illus. (p. 51)
—Marvelous Inventions of Alvin Fernald. Geer, Charles, illus. (p. 1099)
Hicks, Constance. Florabelle Bunny & the Sparrow. (p. 606)
Hicks, Deron R. Secrets of Shakespeare's Grave. Geyer, Mark Edward, illus. (p. 1545)
—Tower of the Five Orders: The Shakespeare Mysteries, Book 2. Geyer, Mark Edward, illus. (p. 1773)
—Tower of the Five Orders. Geyer, Mark Edward, illus. (p. 1773)
Hicks, Diana, jt. auth. see Littlejohn, Andrew.
Hicks, Diana & Littlejohn, Andrew. American English Primary Colors 1. (p. 60)
—American English Primary Colors 2 Vocabulary Cards. (p. 60)
—Primary Colours (p. 1399)
—Primary Colours Level 2. (p. 1399)
—Primary Colours, Level 4. (p. 1399)
—Primary Colours Level 5 Activity Book. (p. 1399)
—Primary Colours Level 5 Pupil's Book. (p. 1399)
Hicks, Donn, jt. auth. see Hynes, Mary Ellen.
Hicks, Dwayne. Composting. (p. 354)
—Paul Revere: American Patriot. (p. 1330)
Hicks, Dwayne, jt. auth. see Mills, Nathan.
Hicks, Esther & Hicks, Jerry. Sara: A Talking Owl Is Worth a Thousand Words! Bk. 3 Garrett, Caroline S., illus. (p. 1514)
—Solomon's Fine Featherless Friends. (p. 1608)
Hicks, Esther, et al. Sara Learns the Secret about the Law of Attraction. Garrett, Caroline S., illus. (p. 1514)
Hicks, et al. ¡Ñec-Ñec, Ris-Ras! (p. 1239)
Hicks, Faith, illus. see Kelly, Claire.
Hicks, Faith Erin. Adventures of Superhero Girl. Edidin, Rachel, ed. (p. 23)
—Friends with Boys. Hicks, Faith Erin, illus. (p. 639)
Hicks, Faith Erin, illus. see Kim, Susan & Klavan, Laurence.
Hicks, Faith Erin, illus. see Shen, Prudence.
Hicks, Faith Erin, illus. see Torres, J.
Hicks, Faith Erin & Druckmann, Neil. Last of Us: American Dreams. Wright, Brendan, ed. (p. 978)
Hicks, Greg & Foster, Rick. Martha Is Mine: An Almost True Story. Sheldon, Kristin, illus. (p. 1097)
Hicks, Hannah. Jessica's Fairies: The Lost Wand. (p. 914)
Hicks, Holly Floyd. Ella's Birthday Wish. (p. 514)
Hicks, Holly Floyd, ed. Ella's Birthday Wish. (p. 514)
Hicks, Jamara. Calvin Gets a Family. (p. 255)
Hicks, Jerry, jt. auth. see Hicks, Esther.
Hicks, John. Divided World. (p. 454)
—My Buddypack. (p. 1199)
Hicks, John B. Ghost of Fire Company 18. (p. 671)
Hicks, John Bryant. Day Charlie Lost His Weirdiness. (p. 412)
Hicks, Kay. Dukes the Ginger Dog. (p. 489)
Hicks, Kaylee, illus. see Bruton, Seth.
Hicks, Keli L. I Use a Mouse. (p. 847)
Hicks, Kelli. Airplanes. (p. 32)
—Analyze This: Testing Ingredients. (p. 67)
—Animal Sanctuaries. (p. 79)
—Companion & Therapy Animals. (p. 351)
—Escalators. (p. 534)
—I Can Prove It! Investigating Science. (p. 836)
—I Can Prove It! Investigating Science. (p. 836)
—Let's Classify Organisms. (p. 995)
—Using Tools to Understand Our World. (p. 1828)
—What Happens When You Flush? (p. 1886)
—Zip Lines. (p. 1987)
Hicks, Kelli L. Dav Pilkey Byers, Michael, illus. (p. 410)
—Honesty. (p. 794)
—I Use a Mouse. (p. 847)
—I Use Science Tools. (p. 847)
—Jeff Kinney Byers, Michael, illus. (p. 912)
—Let's Classify Animals! (p. 995)
—Living or Nonliving? (p. 1041)
—Natural or Man-Made? (p. 1235)
—Nocturnal Animals (p. 1262)
—Responsibility. (p. 1463)
—Science Safety Rules. (p. 1528)
Hicks, Kelli L. & Weber, Michael. Rourke's Complete History of Our Presidents Encyclopedia (p. 1491)
Hicks, Kelli L., ed. Complete History of Our Presidents Encyclopedia (p. 353)
Hicks, Kelli L., et al. Learn about Animal Behavior. (p. 982)
Hicks, Kelli Shay. Hot Air Ballooning. (p. 801)

Hicks, Kim, jt. auth. see Hicks, Rob.
Hicks, Kyra E. Martha Ann's Quilt for Queen Victoria. Fodi, Lee Edward, illus. (p. 1097)
—Martha Ann's Quilt for Queen Victoria. Födi, Lee Edward, illus. (p. 1097)
Hicks, Linda Ashman. Just Another Amazing Morning. (p. 937)
Hicks, Mack R. Unfit for Murder. (p. 1817)
Hicks, Michael Christopher. Tales of Drake: The Tale of the Lost Dog. (p. 1702)
Hicks, Michelle. Vbs 2004 Youth Leader: Rickshaw Rally from Virtual to Spir. (p. 1834)
—Vital Skills: How to Develop Unity. (p. 1846)
Hicks, Michelle, jt. auth. see Hicks, Aniya.
Hicks, Mindy, ed. see Bucki, Jo Dee & O'Malley, John.
Hicks, Peter. Barack Obama: President for Change. (p. 137)
—Documenting the Industrial Revolution. (p. 460)
—Documenting Women's Suffrage. (p. 460)
—How Castles Were Built. (p. 805)
—Lance Armstrong - Racing Hero. (p. 973)
—You Wouldn't Want to Live in a Wild West Town! Dust You'd Rather Not Settle. Antram, David, illus. (p. 1977)
Hicks, R. Animals in Art. (p. 83)
Hicks, Rebecca. Little Vampires. Hicks, Rebecca, illus. (p. 1037)
Hicks, Rob & Hicks, Kim. Amelia, A to Z. Bolton-Eells, Sharon, illus. (p. 57)
Hicks, Robert. Widow of the South. (p. 1927)
Hicks, Robert Z. Tommie Turtle's Secret. Rolseth, Ruthie, illus. (p. 1764)
Hicks, Rosetta, ed. see Hicks, Benjamin.
Hicks, Terry Allan. Allergies. (p. 46)
—Bald Eagle. (p. 133)
—Capitol. (p. 263)
—Chumash. (p. 318)
—Common Cold. (p. 349)
—Declaration of Independence. (p. 422)
—Earth & the Moon. (p. 495)
—Ellis Island. (p. 515)
—How Do Mountains Form? (p. 807)
—Karate. (p. 943)
—Maine. (p. 1077)
—Mandan. (p. 1087)
—Nevada. (p. 1242)
—New Hampshire. (p. 1244)
—Obesity. (p. 1275)
—Pledge of Allegiance. (p. 1373)
—Pros & Cons of Biofuel. (p. 1412)
—Pros & Cons of Oil. (p. 1412)
—Saturn. (p. 1515)
—Symbols of America Group 2 (p. 1693)
—Uncle Sam. (p. 1812)
—Washington, D. C. (p. 1860)
—Washington D.C. (p. 1860)
—Why Do Leaves Change Color? (p. 1923)
—Why Does the Sun Set? (p. 1924)
—Zuni. (p. 1990)
Hicks, Terry Allan, jt. auth. see Hudson, Amanda.
Hicks, Terry Allan, et al. Maine. (p. 1077)
—Nevada. (p. 1242)
Hicks, Wendi N., jt. auth. see Arline-Hicks, Patience.
Hicks-Alessi, Nicole. Raccoon Hollow: Marky's Troubles. (p. 1430)
Hidaka, Banri. V. B. Rose Volume 10. (p. 1829)
—V. B. Rose Volume 9. (p. 1829)
Hidaka, Banri & Banri, Hidaka. V. B. Rose (p. 1829)
Hidalgo, Ethel. Mona's not Afraid. (p. 1163)
Hidalgo, Manolo. Renato. (p. 1460)
Hidalgo, Maria. Hearing. (p. 759)
—Heat. (p. 760)
—Lightning. (p. 1015)
—Sight. (p. 1574)
—Taste. (p. 1707)
—Touch. (p. 1772)
Hidalgo, Pablo. Head-to-Head Tag Teams. (p. 756)
—Phantom Menace. (p. 1349)
—Star Wars Rebels: Head to Head. (p. 1641)
—Star Wars Rebels: Head to Head. (p. 1641)
Hidalgo, Pablo, jt. auth. see Disney Book Group Staff.
Hidalgo, Pablo, jt. auth. see Sansweet, Stephen J.
Hidalgo-Robert, Alberto. Fat No More: A Teenager's Victory over Obesity. (p. 577)
Hiday, Thomas A. Remove the Mystery from Digital Photography: A Remove the Mystery Guidebook. (p. 1460)
Hidier, Tanuja DeSai. Bombay Blues. (p. 208)
Hidier, Tanuja Desai. Born Confused. (p. 214)
Hie, Vanessa, jt. auth. see Massenot, Véronique.
Hieber, Leanna Renee. Darker Still. (p. 408)
Hiebert. Ready Readers Study Guide to the Big Book Collection. (p. 1447)
Hiebert, Elfrieda H. Eyes Are Everywhere. (p. 558)
—Five Little Dinosaurs. (p. 600)
—Humpback Whales. (p. 827)
—Mr. Wink. (p. 1187)
—Quickreads: Level E Complete Program. (p. 1427)
—Quickreads: Windows Classroom Program. (p. 1427)
—Quickreads: Macintosh Classroom Program. (p. 1427)
—Quickreads: Level B Windows Classroom Package. (p. 1427)
—Quickreads: Level C Windows Classroom Package. (p. 1427)
—Quickreads: Level D Windows Classroom Package. (p. 1427)
—Quickreads: Level B Macintosh Classroom Package. (p. 1427)
—Quickreads: Level C Macintosh Classroom Package. (p. 1427)
—Quickreads: Level D Macintosh Classroom Package. (p. 1427)
—Quickreads. (p. 1427)
—Ready Read. (p. 1447)
—Ready Read, Stage 1 Take Home Books. (p. 1447)
—Ready Read, Stage 2 Take Home Books. (p. 1447)
Hiebert, Elfrieda H. & Juel, Connie. At the Track. (p. 111)
—Ben's New Trick. (p. 165)
—Best Birthday Mole Ever Had. (p. 168)
—Bike That Spike Likes. (p. 185)
—Blastoff! (p. 198)
—Blue Sue. (p. 203)
—Can a Cow Hop? (p. 258)
—Cat That Broke the Rules. (p. 278)
—Dee & Me. (p. 422)
—Doctor Has the Flu. (p. 459)
—Dragon's Lunch. (p. 479)
—Eight Friends in All. (p. 507)
—Eric & the Three Goats. (p. 533)
—Fourth of July. (p. 625)
—Fun Place to Eat. (p. 648)
—Good-Bye Summer, Hello Fall. (p. 697)
—Good-Bye Zoo. (p. 697)
—Goose Chase. (p. 702)
—Haddie's Caps. (p. 735)
—Hiccups Would Not Stop. (p. 775)
—Hunt for Clues. (p. 828)
—Jump Right In. (p. 934)
—Kangaroo in the Kitchen. (p. 942)
—Let's Go Marching. (p. 997)
—Let's Move! (p. 999)
—Lion Roars. (p. 1020)
—Little Frog's Monster Story. (p. 1028)
—Lobster Fishing at Dawn. (p. 1044)
—Looking for Angus. (p. 1051)
—Lucky Duck. (p. 1062)
—Merry Go Round. (p. 1129)
—Mess. (p. 1129)
—Molly's Broccoli. (p. 1161)
—Mr. Fin's Trip. (p. 1185)
—Mrs. Tuck's Little Tune. (p. 1187)
—My Clock Is Sick. (p. 1200)
—My Hamster, Van. (p. 1210)
—My Lost Top. (p. 1213)
—My Monster & Me. (p. 1214)
—My Shadow. (p. 1218)
—Nanny Goat's Nap. (p. 1229)
—Night & Day. (p. 1252)
—Night Animals. (p. 1252)
—Night Sky. (p. 1254)
—Nut Pie for Jud. (p. 1273)
—Once upon a Time. (p. 1293)
—Pat's Perfect Pizza. (p. 1329)
—Polly's Shop. (p. 1381)
—Pop Pops the Popcorn. (p. 1384)
—Princess Who Couldn't Cry. (p. 1406)
—Quack. (p. 1422)
—River Grows. (p. 1476)
—Roll Out the Red Rug. (p. 1485)
—Rush, Rush, Rush. (p. 1498)
—Sally's Spaceship. (p. 1505)
—Sandy. (p. 1511)
—Save That Trash. (p. 1516)
—Six Fine Fish. (p. 1582)
—Six Go By. (p. 1582)
—Something to Munch. (p. 1610)
—Sparky's Bone. (p. 1622)
—Steve's Room. (p. 1649)
—Stop That! (p. 1653)
—Terrific Shoes. (p. 1721)
—That Cat. (p. 1726)
—That Fly. (p. 1726)
—Three Silly Cowboys. (p. 1743)
—Too High. (p. 1766)
—Too Much Ketchup. (p. 1767)
—Trip. (p. 1787)
—True Or False? (p. 1792)
—Very Big (p. 1837)
—Vultures on Vacation. (p. 1851)
—We Are Singing. (p. 1865)
—What Rhymes with Cat? (p. 1893)
—When Bob Woke Up Late. (p. 1901)
—When I Go See Gram. (p. 1902)
—When We Are Big. (p. 1905)
—Where Do They Live? (p. 1907)
—Where Does the Rabbit Hop? (p. 1907)
—Where Is the Queen? (p. 1909)
—Who Came Out? (p. 1914)
—Who Has a Tail? (p. 1915)
—Who Is Ready? (p. 1916)
—Who's in the Jungle? (p. 1920)
—Wilma's Wagon. (p. 1934)
Hiebert, Elfrieda H. & Sailors, Misty, eds. Finding the Right Texts: What Works for Beginning & Struggling Readers. (p. 588)
Hief, Gina, illus. see Rothchild, Erik.
Hierl, Christine Gormican. Wyatt Walker Turbo Talker. Thompson, Michelle Gormican & Thompson, Janet M., illus. (p. 1966)
Hierlmaier, Joy, illus. see Hierlmaier Nelson, Christine M.
Hierlmaier Nelson, Christine M. Green Yellow Go! Nat Knows Bananas. Hierlmaier, Joy, illus. (p. 722)
Hieronymus, Carol Fegley. Blackie & Her Kittens: A True Story. (p. 197)
Hiers, Christopher, illus. see Limbaugh, Rush H., III & Limbaugh, Kathryn Adams.
Hierstein, Judith, illus. see Crawford, Laura.
Hierstein, Judith, illus. see Garland, Sherry.
Hierstein, Judith, illus. see Greene, Jacqueline.
Hierstein, Judith, illus. see Lipson, Greta Barclay.
Hierstein, Judith, illus. see Pittman, Rickey.
Hierstein, Judith, illus. see Pushker, Gloria Teles.
Hierstein, Judy, illus. see Fetty, Margaret, ed.
Hiesberger, Jean Marie, jt. auth. see Gallagher, Maureen.
Hietpas, Polly. Hello Rosie Cat. (p. 765)
—Rosie Cat's Bad Fur Day. (p. 1490)
Higashi, Sandra, jt. auth. see Glaser, Byron.
Higashi, Sandra, jt. illus. see Glaser, Byron.
Higashino, Keigo. Naoko. Yasar, Kerim, tr. from JPN. (p. 1229)
Higbee, Heidi. It Could Happen... on the Bus. Hezlep, Amber, illus. (p. 894)
Higdon, Hal. Run, Dogs, Run! Summers, Dana, illus. (p. 1496)
Higdon, Keathley B. Big Mouth Herman. (p. 182)
Higdon, Patrick A. Grandpa & My Report (p. 709)
Higesanbon. Mo Mo Mo Mo Monster: Mon Monster. (p. 1157)
Higgie, Will K., illus. see Fox, Frances Margaret.
Higginbotham, Anastasia. Divorce Is the Worst. (p. 455)
Higginbotham, Liz. Drake the Dragon. (p. 480)
Higginbotham, Mary. Only Feature. (p. 1298)
Higginbotham Nichols, Vivian. Henny & Penny: A Story of Sharing & Caring. (p. 767)
Higgins. Elementary Grammar (p. 510)
Higgins, Ann Elizabeth. Baxter the Bully. (p. 147)
Higgins, Anne Keenan. I Love It When... Higgins, Anne Keenan, illus. (p. 842)
Higgins, Anne Keenan, illus. see Ain, Beth.
Higgins, Anne Keenan, illus. see Morris, Taylor.
Higgins, Anne Keenan, illus. see Phillips, Karen.
Higgins, B. T. Master of Disaster. (p. 1103)
Higgins, Chris. Secrets Club - Alice in the Spotlight. (p. 1544)
Higgins, Clark L., illus. see Higgins, Tiffany A.
Higgins, Dalton. Hip Hop World (p. 780)
—Hip-Hop World. (p. 780)
Higgins, Derek. Fred the Tiki: Misunderstandings. (p. 632)
Higgins, Dusty, illus. see Venditti, Robert.
Higgins, F. E. Black Book of Secrets. (p. 195)
—Bone Magician. (p. 209)
—Eyeball Collector. (p. 558)
—Game of Ghouls. (p. 654)
—Lunatic's Curse. (p. 1065)
—Tangle of Traitors. (p. 1705)
Higgins, F. E., et al. Mago de los Huesos. Perez, Nuria Marti, tr. (p. 1076)
Higgins, Frank. Slave Dancer's Choice. (p. 1588)
Higgins, Gladys. Goodnight, Charlie. (p. 701)
Higgins, Heather. Foal That Doesn't Have a Family. (p. 610)
Higgins, Helen Boyd. Alexander Hamilton: Young Statesman. Underdown, Harold D., ed. (p. 36)
Higgins, Iain, tr. see Czerniawski, Adam.
Higgins, Jack. Brought in Dead. (p. 231)
Higgins, Jack & Richards, Justin. Death Run. (p. 420)
—First Strike. (p. 597)
—Sharp Shot. (p. 1563)
—Sure Fire. (p. 1685)
Higgins, Jane. Bridge. (p. 227)
Higgins, Jim. Enchanted Nursery: Nessie's Friends. (p. 523)
—Enchanted Nursery: Heather & Hamish, Fun in Florida, Reggie Rabbit at the Seaside, Percy Penguin's Friends. (p. 523)
Higgins, Joanna. Waiting for the Queen: A Novel of Early America. (p. 1853)
Higgins, Kathy, jt. auth. see Cosgrove, Stephen.
Higgins, Kitty. As the Crow Flies. Leon, Karen, illus. (p. 105)
—Mushing in Alaska. (p. 1193)
—Three Sisters. Corcoran, Mark, illus. (p. 1744)
—Wild Bill Hiccups. (p. 1929)
Higgins, Kitty, jt. auth. see Cosgrove, Stephen.
Higgins, Kitty, jt. told to see Cosgrove, Stephen.
Higgins, Krystal, illus. see Aryal, Aimee.
Higgins, Lawrence. Demons & Dragons: Time, Space & Magic. (p. 426)
Higgins, M. G. Bi-Normal (p. 174)
—Blow Out. (p. 202)
—Body Switch (p. 207)
—Falling Out of Place (p. 567)
—Falling Out of Place. (p. 567)
—Fish Boy (p. 598)
—Flyer (p. 609)
—I'm Just Me. (p. 859)
—Lost House. (p. 1055)
—Offside. (p. 1280)
—Power Hitter. (p. 1389)
—Racer. (p. 1431)
—Soldier. (p. 1607)
Higgins, M. G., jt. auth. see Higgins, M. g.
Higgins, M. g. & Higgins, M. G. Power Hitter. (p. 1389)
Higgins, Marguerite & Berg, Rea. Jessie Benton Fremont: California Pioneer. (p. 914)
Higgins, Maria Mihalik. Benjamin Franklin: Revolutionary Inventor. (p. 165)
Higgins, Matt. Air Out There: How Clean Is Clean? (p. 31)
—Clear Choices: The Water You Drink. (p. 330)
Higgins, Melissa. Anacondas (p. 66)
—Boa Constrictors (p. 205)
—Celebrating Differences. (p. 284)
—Cobras (p. 337)
—Dodos. (p. 460)
—I Am a Good Citizen (p. 832)
—I Am Caring (p. 832)
—I Am Fair (p. 832)
—I Am Respectful (p. 833)
—I Am Responsible (p. 833)
—I Am Trustworthy (p. 834)
—I Don't Bully (p. 837)
—Jamestown Colony. (p. 907)
—Jennifer Lawrence: Breakout Actress. (p. 912)
—Julian Assange: WikiLeaks Founder. (p. 932)
—Let's Play! Awesome Activities Every Babysitter Needs to Know (p. 999)
—Living with Substance Addiction. (p. 1042)
—Mitt Romney. (p. 1156)
—Night Dad Went to Jail: What to Expect When Someone You Love Goes to Jail Kirwan, Wednesday, illus. (p. 1253)
—Night Dad Went to Jail: What to Expect When Someone You Love Goes to Jail. Kirwan, Wednesday, illus. (p. 1253)
—Pushing Isn't Funny: What to Do about Physical Bullying. Shin, Simone, illus. (p. 1420)
—Sabertooth Cats. (p. 1499)
—Sgt. Reckless - The War Horse: Korean War Hero. Iglesias, Alvaro, illus. (p. 1556)
—Teasing Isn't Funny: What to Do about Emotional Bullying. Shin, Simone, illus. (p. 1711)
—Teen Self-Injury. (p. 1714)
—We All Come from Different Cultures (p. 1865)
—We All Have Different Abilities (p. 1865)
—We All Have Different Families (p. 1865)
—We All Look Different (p. 1865)
—Weekends with Dad: What to Expect When Your Parents Divorce Kirwan, Wednesday, illus. (p. 1872)
—Wind Energy. (p. 1935)
—Woolly Mammoths. (p. 1950)
—You're in Charge: Basic Rules Every Babysitter Needs to Know (p. 1982)
Higgins, Melissa, jt. auth. see Doering, Amanda F.
Higgins, Melissa, jt. auth. see Frisch-Schmoll, Joy.
Higgins, Melissa & Dellapenna, Joseph W. Roe v. Wade: Abortion & a Woman's Right to Privacy. (p. 1484)
Higgins, Melissa & Dunn, Mary R. Snakes. (p. 1596)
Higgins, Melissa & Houser, Aimee. Taylor Swift: Country & Pop Superstar. (p. 1708)
Higgins, Melissa & Rissman, Rebecca. Babysitter's Backpack (p. 129)
—Babysitter's Backpack: Everything You Need to Be a Safe, Smart, & Skilled Babysitter (p. 129)
Higgins, Myrta. Little Gardens for Boys & Girls. (p. 1028)
Higgins, Nadia. Area 51. (p. 97)
—Avast, Ye Dog Thief! Holder, Jimmy, illus. (p. 118)
—Aye, My Eye! Holder, Jimmy, illus. (p. 121)
—Beauty & the Beast. Petelinsek, Kathleen, illus. (p. 154)
—Bella Thorne: Shaking up the Small Screen. (p. 162)
—Blimey, That's Slimy! Holder, Jimmy, illus. (p. 199)
—Break a Sea Leg, Shrimp-Breath! Holder, Jimmy, illus. (p. 224)
—Brilliant Beauty Inventions. (p. 228)
—Bruno Mars: Pop Singer & Producer. (p. 232)
—Carly Rae Jepsen: Call Her Amazing. (p. 270)
—Cinderella. Petelinsek, Kathleen, illus. (p. 320)
—Deadliest Adorable Animals. (p. 417)
—Deadly Adorable Animals. (p. 417)
—Defending the Land: Causes & Effects of Red Cloud's War. (p. 423)
—Discover Water. Yamada, Jane, illus. (p. 448)
—Down, Zombie, Down! Zombie Zappers Book 4. (p. 474)
—Dwarf Planets: Pluto & the Lesser Planets. (p. 491)
—Electricity Is Everywhere. Ricci, Andres Martinez, illus. (p. 509)
—Electricity Is Everywhere CD+Book. Martinez Ricci, Andres, illus. (p. 509)
—Electricity Is Everywhere Site CD+Book. Martinez Ricci, Andres, illus. (p. 509)
—Emma Watson: From Wizards to Wallflowers. (p. 520)
—Excited about Energy CD+Book. Martinez Ricci, Andres, illus. (p. 547)
—Excited about Energy Site CD+Book. Martinez Ricci, Andres, illus. (p. 547)
—Experiment with a Plant's Living Environment. (p. 549)
—Experiment with a Plant's Roots. (p. 549)
—Experiment with Parts of a Plant. (p. 549)
—Experiment with Photosynthesis. (p. 549)
—Experiment with Pollination. (p. 549)
—Experiment with What a Plant Needs to Grow. (p. 549)
—Fun Food Inventions. (p. 647)
—Get Moving with Friends & Family. Avakyan, Tatevik, illus. (p. 667)
—Ghosts. (p. 672)
—Hansel & Gretel. Petelinsek, Kathleen, illus. (p. 743)
—Haunted Houses. (p. 753)
—Henry & Hala Build a Haiku. Dumm, Brian, illus. (p. 767)
—Issun Boshi (One-Inch Boy) A Japanese Folktale. Morrow, J. T., illus. (p. 893)
—It's a Thunderstorm! Ward, Damian, illus. (p. 896)
—It's a Tornado! Ward, Damian, illus. (p. 896)
—It's a Tsunami! Ward, Damian, illus. (p. 896)
—It's Hailing! Ward, Damian, illus. (p. 897)
—It's Raining! Ward, Damian, illus. (p. 898)
—It's Snowing! Ward, Damian, illus. (p. 899)
—Jennifer Lawrence: The Hunger Games' Girl on Fire. (p. 913)
—Justin Bieber: Pop & R & B Idol. (p. 940)
—Katy Perry: From Gospel Singer to Pop Star. (p. 946)
—Last Stand: Causes & Effects of the Battle of the Little Bighorn. (p. 978)
—Life Science Through Infographics. Waananen, Lisa, illus. (p. 1013)
—Little Red Riding Hood. Petelinsek, Kathleen, illus. (p. 1035)
—Logan Lerman: The Perks of Being of an Action Star. (p. 1045)
—Marvelous Motion. Ricci, Andres Martinez, illus. (p. 1099)
—Marvelous Motion CD+Book. Martinez Ricci, Andres, illus. (p. 1099)
—Marvelous Motion Site CD+Book. Martinez Ricci, Andres, illus. (p. 1099)
—Mighty Magnet CD+Book. Martinez Ricci, Andres, illus. (p. 1140)
—Mighty Magnet Site CD+Book. Martinez Ricci, Andres, illus. (p. 1140)
—Mighty Magnets. Ricci, Andres Martinez, illus. (p. 1140)
—Moon Landing. (p. 1172)
—National Geographic Kids Everything Vikings: All the Incredible Facts & Fierce Fun You Can Plunder. (p. 1232)
—Natural Disasters Through Infographics. Sciuto, Alex, illus. (p. 1235)
—Nicholas Hoult: Beast of the Silver Screen. (p. 1251)
—Pegleg Gets Stumped. Holder, Jimmy, illus. (p. 1335)
—Perspective Flip Books (p. 1344)
—Science Rocks! Set 2 - 6 Titles (p. 1527)
—Solar System Through Infographics. Waananen, Lisa, illus. (p. 1607)
—Solar Systems: Planets, Stars, & Orbits. (p. 1607)
—Spanish Missions of the Old West. (p. 1621)
—Split History of the Civil Rights Movement: A Perspectives Flip Book. (p. 1630)
—Stupendous Sound. Ricci, Andres Martinez, illus. (p. 1670)
—Stupendous Sound CD+Book. Martinez Ricci, Andres, illus. (p. 1670)
—Stupendous Sound Site CD+Book. Martinez Ricci, Andres, illus. (p. 1670)
—Super Apostrophe Saves the Day! Gallagher-Cole, Mernie, illus. (p. 1679)
—Super Comma Saves the Day! Gallagher-Cole, Mernie, illus. (p. 1679)

—Super Exclamation Point Saves the Day! Gallagher-Cole, Mernie, illus. (p. 1680)
—Super Period Saves the Day! Gallagher-Cole, Mernie, illus. (p. 1680)
—Super Question Mark Saves the Day! Gallagher-Cole, Mernie, illus. (p. 1680)
—Super Quotation Marks Saves the Day! Gallagher-Cole, Mernie, illus. (p. 1680)
—Super Shadows. Ricci, Andres Martinez, illus. (p. 1681)
—Super Shadows CD+Book. Martinez Ricci, Andres, illus. (p. 1681)
—Super Shadows Site CD+Book. Martinez Ricci, Andres, illus. (p. 1681)
—UFOs. (p. 1807)
—US Culture Through Infographics. Kulihin, Vic, illus. (p. 1826)
—US Culture Through Infographics. Thompson, Bryon & Kulihin, Vic, illus. (p. 1826)
—US Government Through Infographics. Sciuto, Alex, illus. (p. 1826)
—Walk the Plank, Plankton. Holder, Jimmy, illus. (p. 1854)
—Weather Watchers Ward, Damian, illus. (p. 1870)
—Welcome to Everglades National Park. (p. 1873)
—What's Great about Minnesota? (p. 1897)
—Whole Truth: Writing Fearless Nonfiction. (p. 1920)
—World's Oddest Inventions. (p. 1960)
—Your Mission to Jupiter. (p. 1981)
—Zombie Camp: Zombie Zappers Book 1. (p. 1988)
—Zombie Field Day: Zombie Zappers Book 2. (p. 1988)
—Zombie Next Door: Zombie Zappers Book 3. (p. 1988)
Higgins, Nadia Abushanab. Feminism 3.0: Reinventing the F Word. (p. 581)
Higgins, Nadia & Ricci, Andres Martinez. Excited about Energy. (p. 547)
Higgins, Nadia & Schwartz, Heather E. Cause & Effect: American Indian History. (p. 282)
Higgins, Paul, ed. see Kemp, Beth.
Higgins, Quentin R. Hippity Has a Hot Idea. Higgins, Quentin R., illus. (p. 780)
Higgins, Rada/Ruth & Blackwell, Maxine. Revelations: Disaster: the Inner Life of Jasmine. (p. 1465)
Higgins, Richard Stockton. Trace of the True Cross. (p. 1774)
Higgins, Ryan. Wilfred. Higgins, Ryan, illus. (p. 1932)
Higgins, Sean, tr. see Delano, Poli.
Higgins, Simon. Moonshadow #2: the Nightmare Ninja. (p. 1173)
—Moonshadow: Rise of the Ninja. (p. 1173)
Higgins, Tiffany A. We've Seen Sant. Higgins, Clark L., illus. (p. 1877)
Higgins, Wendy. Sweet Evil. (p. 1689)
—Sweet Peril. (p. 1690)
—Sweet Reckoning. (p. 1690)
—Sweet Temptation. (p. 1690)
Higginson, Hadley. Keeker & the Crazy, Upside-Down Birthday. Perrett, Lisa, illus. (p. 946)
—Keeker & the Pony Camp Catastrophe Perrett, Lisa, illus. (p. 946)
—Keeker & the Springtime Surprise. Perrett, Lisa, illus. (p. 946)
Higginson, Mel. Beaks & Bills. (p. 150)
—Hibernation. (p. 775)
—Picos/Beaks & Bills. Sarfatti, Esther, tr. (p. 1355)
Higginson, Sheila Sweeny. Chilly Catches a Cold. (p. 306)
—Diego rescata al bebé manatí (Diego's Manatee Rescue) McGee, Warner, illus. (p. 437)
—Disasters of Technology: Set Of 6. (p. 447)
—Doc Mcstuffins: A Very Mcstuffins Christmas. (p. 459)
—Drip, Drop! the Rain Won't Stop! Your Turn, My Turn Reader. Yee, Josie, illus. (p. 485)
—Henry Loves Beckett. (p. 768)
—Jake & the Never Land Pirates: Cubby's Mixed-Up Map. (p. 905)
—Jingle Bell Doc. Disney Book Group Staff et al, illus. (p. 918)
—Leilani's Luau. Disney Storybook Artists Staff, illus. (p. 991)
—Minnie Wishing on a Bow. (p. 1148)
—Pulling Back the Curtain on Magic! McClurkan, Rob, illus. (p. 1416)
—Welcome to Roarsville. (p. 1873)
—You're Getting a Baby Brother! Williams, Sam, illus. (p. 1982)
—You're Getting a Baby Sister! Williams, Sam, illus. (p. 1982)
Higginson, Sheila Sweeny, jt. auth. see Disney Book Group Staff.
Higginson, Sheila Sweeny & Disney Book Group Staff. Brontosaurus Breath. Disney Storybook Art Team, illus. (p. 230)
—Bubble Trouble. Disney Storybook Artists Staff & Disney Storybook Art Team, illus. (p. 233)
—Caught Blue-Handed. Disney Storybook Art Team, illus. (p. 281)
—Chilly Catches a Cold. Disney Storybook Art Team, illus. (p. 306)
—Jake & the Never Land Pirates Cubby's Mixed-Up Map. Disney Storybook Art Team, illus. (p. 905)
—Loud Louie. Disney Storybook Artists Staff, illus. (p. 1057)
—Mermaid Dives In. Disney Storybook Art Team, illus. (p. 1128)
—Minnie's Rainbow. Loter Inc. Staff & Disney Storybook Art Team, illus. (p. 1148)
—Minnie's Valentine. Loter Inc. Staff & Disney Storybook Art Team, illus. (p. 1148)
—Run-Down Racecar. Disney Storybook Art Team, illus. (p. 1496)
—Up, up, & Away! Disney Storybook Artists Staff & Disney Storybook Art Team, illus. (p. 1824)
—Whose Birthday Is It? Disney Storybook Artists Staff, illus. (p. 1921)
Higginson, Sheila Sweeny, et al. All Stuffed Up. Disney Storybook Artists Staff, illus. (p. 45)
—Chilly Catches a Cold. (p. 306)
Higginson, Sheryl. Dilbert's Pets (p. 440)
Higginson, Thomas W. Young Folks' History of the United States. (p. 1978)
Higgs, Carolyn. Little Knight (p. 1030)
—One Village Boy Loses His Friends. (p. 1297)
Higgs, Liz Curtis. Parable of the Lily Munger, Nancy, illus. (p. 1323)
—Parabola del Lirio. Munger, Nancy, illus. (p. 1323)
—Pine Tree Parable. (p. 1359)
—Pumpkin Patch Parable. (p. 1416)
—Sunflower Parable Munger, Nancy, illus. (p. 1676)
Higgs, Matthew, et al. Uta Barth. (p. 1829)
Higgy, M. J. Creator's Dream. (p. 380)
High, Amy, tr. see Falconer, Ian.
High, Gracia. I am not going to sleep Now. (p. 833)
High, Linda. Lap Talks with Granny at Easter. (p. 975)
High, Linda Oatman. Cemetery Keepers of Gettysburg. Filippucci, Laura Francesca, illus. (p. 286)
—Heart Like Ringo Starr (p. 759)
—Tenth Avenue Cowboy. Farnsworth, Bill, illus. (p. 1720)
High School, West Scranton & Mazzino, Christopher. Four Years to Life. (p. 625)
Higham, Amanda, illus. see Phinn, Gervase.
Higham, Charles. Howard Hughes: The Secret Life. (p. 823)
Higham, Cindy. Snowflakes for All Seasons: 72 Fold & Cut Paper Snowflakes. (p. 1600)
Highet, Alistair. Lucas. Delessert, Etienne, illus. (p. 1062)
Highley, Rainey Marie. Long Lost Tale of the Dragon & the Whale. (p. 1047)
Highlights for Children, compiled by. Fun at School. (p. 647)
—Good Sports. (p. 700)
—Highlights Hidden Picture Playground: on Vacation. (p. 779)
—Playful Pets. (p. 1372)
Highlights for Children Editorial Staff. Amazing Mazes - Follow Your Nose! (p. 55)
—Doodlerama: Oldies of Doodling, Coloring, & Puzzling Fun! (p. 469)
—Farm Puzzles. (p. 574)
—Hit the Trail. (p. 786)
—Laugh It Up! 501 Super-Silly Jokes, Riddles, & Cartoons from Highlights. Coulson, David, illus. (p. 980)
—Look What You Can Make with Plastic Containers. Schneider, Hank & Filipski, J. W., photos by. (p. 1050)
—Puzzlemania School Puzzles. (p. 1421)
—Puzzlemania(r) Halloween Puzzles. (p. 1421)
—Puzzlemania(r) Winter Puzzles. (p. 1421)
—Ticklish Tales. (p. 1747)
—Travel Puzzles. (p. 1780)
Highlights for Children Editorial Staff, ed. see Boyds Mills Press Staff.
Highlights for Children Editorial Staff, jt. auth. see Boyds Mills Press Staff.
Highlights for Children Editorial Staff & Boyds Mills Press Staff. Hidden Pictures Sticker Fun. (p. 776)
—Highlights Hidden Pictures Sticker Fun (p. 779)
—Look What You Can Make with Paper Plates: Creative Crafts from Everyday Objects. Richmond, Margie Hayes, ed. (p. 1050)
Highlights for Children Editorial Staff, compiled by. Amazing Mazes - Off We Go! (p. 55)
Highlights for Children Editorial Staff, creator. Amazing Mazes: Lost & Found. (p. 55)
Highlights for Children Staff. Say It Again! 501 Wacky Word Puzzles from Highlights. Dammer, Mike, illus. (p. 1518)
Highlights USA for Children Staff. Puzzlemania. (p. 1421)
Highstreet, Harry. Melanie Ann. (p. 1125)
Hight, Lloyd R., illus. see Johnson, Nancy Pelander.
Hight, Michael, illus. see Green, Paula.
Hightman, J. P. Spirit. (p. 1628)
Hightman, Jason. Saint of Dragons. (p. 1504)
Hightower, Paul. Father of Geometry: Euclid & His 3-D World. (p. 577)
—Galileo: Astronomer & Physicist. (p. 653)
—Greatest Mathematician: Archimedes & His Eureka! Moment. (p. 720)
Hightower, Paul W. Galileo: Genius Astronomer. (p. 653)
Hight-Sullins, Paula, jt. auth. see Hight-Sullins, Paula.
Hight-Sullins, Paula & Hight-Sullins, Paula. Promised Land of Texas. (p. 1411)
Highway, Tomson. Caribou Song Rombough, John, illus. (p. 269)
—Dragonfly Kites: Kiweeginapiseek. (p. 478)
—Fox on the Ice Deines, Brian, illus. (p. 626)
Highway, Tomson, et al. Living Stories: Godi Weghàà Ets' Eèda Macintosh, Tessa, photos by. (p. 1041)
Higi, Laf. Sock Thing. (p. 1605)
Higman, Anita. Living Darkness: Texas Caves. (p. 1040)
Higman, B. W. Plantation Jamaica, 1750-1850: Capital & Control in a Colonial Economy. (p. 1369)
Higney, Gene-Michael, jt. auth. see Garrett, Ann.
Higson, Charlie. Dead (new Cover) (an Enemy Novel) (p. 417)
—Double or Die (p. 473)
—Enemy (new Cover) (an Enemy Novel) (p. 527)
—Fallen (an Enemy Novel) (p. 566)
—Fear (new Cover) (an Enemy Novel) (p. 579)
—Hunted (an Enemy Novel) (p. 828)
—Hurricane Gold (p. 829)
—Sacrifice. (p. 1500)
—Sacrifice (an Enemy Novel) (p. 1501)
—SilverFin (p. 1577)
Higuchi, Daisuke. Re-Start Higuchi, Daisuke, illus. (p. 1442)
—Whistle! (p. 1912)
—Whistle! Higuchi, Daisuke, illus. (p. 1912)
—Whistle! Kokubo, Naomi, tr. from JPN. (p. 1912)
Higuchi, Daisuke, jt. auth. see Moyoco, Anno.
Higuchi, Daisuke & Daisuke, Higuchi. Whistle! Higuchi, Daisuke, illus. (p. 1912)
Hiiasen, Carl. Hoot. (p. 796)
Hiiepuu, Ene, jt. auth. see Hiisjärv, Piret.
Hiiragi, Aoi. Baron: The Cat Returns. Hiiragi, Aoi, illus. (p. 140)
Hiiragi, Aoi, illus. see Morita, Hiroyuki.
Hiisjärv, Piret & Hiiepuu, Ene. Estonia. Bultje, Jan Willem, photos by. (p. 538)
Hijioka, Makoto. Giratina & the Sky Warrior! Hijioka, Makoto, illus. (p. 678)
—Giratina & the Sky Warrior! Ani-Manga. (p. 678)
Hijuelos, Oscar. Dark Dude. (p. 407)
Hijuelos, Oscar & Oscar, Hijuelos. Dark Dude. Roja, Alberto Jimenenz, tr. (p. 407)
Hikadova, Katerina, illus. see Dusek, Jiri, et al.
Hikawa, Kyoko. From Far Away (p. 642)
—From Far Away Hikawa, Kyoko, illus. (p. 642)
—From Far Away. Hikawa, Kyoko, illus. (p. 642)
Hilaire, Jean Vilmond, tr. see Silva Lee, Alfonso.
Hilary, Jay. Quotient Club. (p. 1429)
Hilb, Nora. Itsy Bitsy Spider. (p. 900)
Hilb, Nora, illus. see Maine, Margarita.
Hilb, Nora, illus. see Pearson, Debora.
Hilb, Nora, illus. see Spinelli, Eileen.
Hilbert, David. Foundations of Geometry. Townsend, E. J., tr. (p. 624)
Hilbrandt, Sarah Perrin. Jacob & the Taloon. (p. 904)
Hilburn, Dora. Between. (p. 172)
Hilburn, L. M. Little Princesses to the Rescue. (p. 1034)
Hilda, Perera, jt. auth. see Perera, Hilda.
Hildahl, Esther J. Meadow Pnd. (p. 1116)
Hildahl, Melita K. Life Is an Adventure with Ernie. (p. 1011)
Hildahl, Violetta R. Peacock of Taj Mahal. (p. 1332)
HildaRose, illus. see Barber, Jill.
HildaRose, illus. see Fitch, Sheree.
Hildebrand, Cody. How the Skunk Earned His Stripes: A Pet Parent's Guide to Having a Skunk in the Family. (p. 813)
Hildebrand, Jens. Team 002: The Abduction of the Queen. Garcia, Juan F., illus. (p. 1710)
—Team 002 und das Utopia-Element. Garcia, Juan F., illus. (p. 1710)
—Team 002 und Die Entführung der Queen. Garcia, Juan F., illus. (p. 1710)
Hildebrand, Jens & Ridge, Sally. Cyberstalker. (p. 396)
Hildebrand, Jens, et al. Art of Team 002. (p. 102)
Hildebrandt, Laurel & Chell, Jenny. Shadow People. (p. 1557)
Hildebrandt, Lowell, illus. see Kaneko, Amanda Bullard.
Hildebrandt, Lowell, illus. see Torres, Christopher S.
Hilder, Rowland, illus. see Masefield, John.
Hilderbrand, Barbara. Birthday of the Church. (p. 193)
—David Becomes King. (p. 410)
Hilderbrand, Karen Mitzo, jt. adapted by see Thompson, Kim Mitzo.
Hilderbrand, Karen Mitzo, jt. adapted by see Twin Sisters(r) Staff.
Hilderbrand, Karen Mitzo, jt. auth. see Thompson, Kim Mitzo.
Hilderbrand, Karen Mitzo & Thompson, Kim Mitzo. Essential Preschool Skills. (p. 537)
Hilderbrandt, Sandra June. Wilbur's Great Adventure. Merrell, Vernon R., illus. (p. 1928)
—Wilbur's Great Adventure. Whispering Pine Press International, Inc. Staff, ed. (p. 1928)
Hilding, Norma. Muffet & the Dust Storm. (p. 1189)
Hilditch, Kevin M. Kevin & the Smiling Dog. (p. 949)
Hildreth, Joann R. Nicholas James & Missy. Aughe, Roger, illus. (p. 1251)
Hildreth, Ruth Erixon. Fun Lovin' Delanie Jo. Aughe, Roger, illus. (p. 648)
Hile, Doretta. Place for All of Us. Barnes, William, illus. (p. 1365)
Hile, Kevin. Animal Rights. (p. 79)
—Centaur. (p. 287)
—Cesar Chavez. (p. 288)
—Ghost Ships. (p. 671)
—Video Games. (p. 1841)
—Weather. (p. 1869)
Hile, Kevin, jt. auth. see Lynette, Rachel.
Hile, Lori. Aliens & UFOs. (p. 41)
—Aliens & UFOs. King, Chris, illus. (p. 41)
—Animal Survival. (p. 80)
—Bullying (p. 241)
—Daily Life in Shang Dynasty China. (p. 400)
—Gangs (p. 655)
—Getting Ahead: Drugs, Technology, & Competitive Advantage (p. 669)
—Getting Ahead: Drugs, Technology, & Competitive Advantage Lingard, Darren, illus. (p. 669)
—Loch Ness Monster (p. 1044)
—Loch Ness Monster. (p. 1044)
—Mermaids (p. 1128)
—Rachel Carson: Environmental Pioneer (p. 1431)
—Science of Snowboarding (p. 1527)
—Social Networks & Blogs. (p. 1604)
—Surviving Extreme Sports (p. 1687)
Hile, Lori, jt. auth. see Bingham, Jane.
Hile, Lori, et al. Daily Life In... (p. 399)
—Science of Speed (p. 1527)
—Solving Mysteries with Science. (p. 1608)
Hileman, Jane. Will You Go? Bianchi, John, illus. (p. 1932)
Hileman, Jane, jt. auth. see Pitt, Marilyn.
Hileman, Jane & Pitt, Marilyn. Come with Me. Bianchi, John, illus. (p. 347)
—Home Alone. Bianchi, John, illus. (p. 791)
—I Love to Sleep. Bianchi, John, illus. (p. 843)
—I Want a Dog. Bianchi, John, illus. (p. 847)
—Let Me In. Bianchi, John, illus. (p. 994)
—Snow Dog. Bianchi, John, illus. (p. 1598)
—Storm. Bianchi, John, illus. (p. 1655)
—Time for a Bath. Bianchi, John, illus. (p. 1751)
—You Can't Have It! Bianchi, John, illus. (p. 1974)
Hileman, Linda L. Dawn's Secret. (p. 412)
Hiley, Lisa & Langrish, Bob. Horse Breeds Poster Book. (p. 799)
Hilgartner, Carol. Elizabeth Cady Stanton. (p. 513)
Hilgemann, Werner, jt. auth. see Kinder, Hermann.
Hilgenberg, Bob & Muir, Roberto. Tinker Bell & the Great Fairy Rescue. Storino, Sara & Zanotta, Roberta, illus. (p. 1755)
Hilgendorf, L. B. Orville Oak & Friends. Dow, S. B., illus. (p. 1305)
Hilgendorf, Sarah. Thesaurus of Synonmys & Antonyms: Canadian Edition. (p. 1731)
Hili, Marvin. Playland. (p. 1373)
Hilinski, Clint, illus. see Croall, Marie P.
Hilinski, Clint, illus. see Croall, Marie.
Hilinski, Clint, illus. see Limke, Jeff.
Hilkene, Ruth Miller & Gugle, Marie. Willie Fox's Diary. (p. 1934)
Hill, Alan J. Tremain, Book One: The Seven Faiths. (p. 1784)
—Tremain Book Two: Underworld & Overland. (p. 1784)
Hill, Amanda. Brush with the Super Dentists. (p. 232)
Hill, Amye Rose. Amazing Mr. Buddy. (p. 55)
Hill, Andrew G. Song of the Seraphim. (p. 1611)
Hill, Anita R., jt. auth. see Hill, David W.
Hill, Anne E. Kirsten Dunst. (p. 961)
—Lebron James: King of Shots. (p. 987)
—Michelle Kwan. (p. 1135)
—Sasha Cohen. (p. 1515)
—Ten American Movie Directors: The Men Behind the Camera. (p. 1718)
—Tyra Banks: From Supermodel to Role Model. (p. 1805)
Hill, Annemarie. Meaty Treats. (p. 1118)
Hill, Barbara, jt. auth. see Landman, Yael.
Hill, Bartha. Kiwi Adventures. (p. 963)
Hill, Becky. Duck That Stayed Behind. (p. 488)
Hill, Bert & Watterson, Steve. Conditioning: How to Get in Football Shape. (p. 356)
Hill, Beth, illus. see Kantner, Seth.
Hill, Bethanne, illus. see Downing, Johnette.
Hill, Bodhi, illus. see Dunn, Jill.
Hill, Bonnie Hearn. Aries Rising. (p. 98)
—Taurus Eyes. (p. 1707)
Hill, Brenda. Messages of God Written in Rhyme. (p. 1129)
Hill, C. J. Echo in Time. (p. 502)
—Erasing Time. (p. 533)
—Slayers. (p. 1588)
—Slayers: Friends & Traitors. (p. 1588)
Hill, Carol A. Rodgers, see Rodgers Hill, Carol A.
Hill, Carolyn L. Journey Through Eclipses (p. 928)
Hill, Carolyn Swan. Summer to Remember. (p. 1675)
Hill, Chelsie & Love, Jessica. Push Girl: A Novel. (p. 1420)
Hill, Cheryl E. R Is for Reading Books. Pierce, Dave G., illus. (p. 1429)
Hill, Chris, illus. see Little Pickle Press & DiOrio, Rana.
Hill, Christina. Community Leaders Then & Now. (p. 350)
—Earth's Moon. (p. 498)
—Inside a Plant. (p. 876)
—What Makes a Plant? (p. 1892)
Hill, Christine M. Gwendolyn Brooks: Poetry Is Life Distilled. (p. 733)
—Lance Armstrong: Cycling, Surviving, Inspiring Hope. (p. 973)
Hill, Clare. Granddad's Circus & Other Stories. (p. 707)
Hill, Clarissa. God Deserves Your Best. Hill, Stephanie, illus. (p. 688)
Hill, Constance. Most Important Question. (p. 1177)
Hill, Dave. Scotland. (p. 1530)
Hill, Dave, illus. see Baker, Robert C.
Hill, Dave, illus. see Davidson, Susanna.
Hill, Dave, illus. see Jaeger, Elizabeth.
Hill, Dave, illus. see Mackall, Dandi Daley.
Hill, Dave, illus. see Sanna, Charles A.
Hill, Dave, jt. auth. see Deere, John.
Hill, Dave, jt. auth. see John, Deere.
Hill, David. Coming Back. (p. 348)
—Ghosts & Ghoulies. (p. 672)
Hill, David, illus. see Hoyt, Megan.
Hill, David, illus. see McKnight, Scot & McKnight Barringer, Laura.
Hill, David W., ed. see Pember, G. H.
Hill, David W. & Hill, Anita R. Case Of: Is Santa Claus Real? (p. 273)
Hill, Donna. In My Bedroom. (p. 864)
Hill, Douglas. Brujas y Magos. Wilson, Alex, illus. (p. 232)
—Dragon Charmer. (p. 476)
—Dragon Charmer. Melnyczuk, Peter, illus. (p. 476)
—Galactic Warlord. (p. 652)
—Warriors Wasteland: The Huntsmen. (p. 1859)
Hill, E. C. Earth the Water Planet: Set Of 6. (p. 497)
—Earth: the Water Planet: Text Pairs. (p. 497)
Hill, Emma. My First Book of Animals: A Pull-Out Toddler Book. (p. 1205)
—My First Book of Colors: A Pull-Out Toddler Book. (p. 1205)
—My First Book of Numbers: A Pull-Out Toddler Book. (p. 1205)
Hill, Eric. Buenas Noches Spot. (p. 235)
—Cumpleaños de Spot. (p. 392)
—Donde Esta Spot? (p. 466)
—Drawing Fun with Spot. (p. 481)
—First Christmas. Hill, Eric, illus. (p. 593)
—Good Night, Spot. Hill, Eric, illus. (p. 700)
—Hide & Seek. Hill, Eric, illus. (p. 776)
—Jugar Con Spot. (p. 931)
—Juguetes de Spot. (p. 932)
—Night-Night, Spot. (p. 1253)
—Night-Night, Spot. Hill, Eric, illus. (p. 1253)
—Primera Navidad de Spot. (p. 1400)
—S. S. Happiness Crew: Book of Numbers. (p. 1499)
—Spot Aprende los Colores. (p. 1633)
—Spot Ayuda en la Casa. (p. 1633)
—Spot Bakes a Cake. Hill, Eric, illus. (p. 1633)
—Spot Can Count. (p. 1633)
—Spot Can Count. Hill, Eric, illus. (p. 1633)
—Spot en Casa. (p. 1633)
—Spot en el Jardin. (p. 1633)
—Spot en la Granja. (p. 1633)
—Spot Goes Shopping. Hill, Eric, illus. (p. 1633)
—Spot Goes to School. Hill, Eric, illus. (p. 1633)
—Spot Goes to the Farm. (p. 1633)
—Spot Goes to the Farm. Hill, Eric, illus. (p. 1633)
—Spot Goes to the Park. Hill, Eric, illus. (p. 1633)
—Spot Loves His Daddy. Hill, Eric, illus. (p. 1633)
—Spot Loves His Friends. Hill, Eric, illus. (p. 1633)
—Spot Loves His Grandma. Hill, Eric, illus. (p. 1633)
—Spot Loves His Mommy. Hill, Eric, illus. (p. 1633)
—Spot Loves School. Hill, Eric, illus. (p. 1633)
—Spot Loves Sports. Hill, Eric, illus. (p. 1633)
—Spot on the Move. Hill, Eric, illus. (p. 1633)
—Spot Says Please. Hill, Eric, illus. (p. 1633)
—Spot's Baby Sister. Hill, Eric, illus. (p. 1634)
—Spot's Balloon. Hill, Eric, illus. (p. 1634)
—Spot's Birthday Party. Hill, Eric, illus. (p. 1634)
—Spot's Christmas. Hill, Eric, illus. (p. 1634)
—Spot's Christmas Plush Doll. Hill, Eric, illus. (p. 1634)

—Spot's Easter Surprise. Hill, Eric, illus. (p. 1634)
—Spot's Favorite Shapes. Hill, Eric, illus. (p. 1634)
—Spot's Favorite Things. Hill, Eric, illus. (p. 1634)
—Spot's First Colors. Hill, Eric, illus. (p. 1634)
—Spot's First Numbers. Hill, Eric, illus. (p. 1634)
—Spot's First Shapes. Hill, Eric, illus. (p. 1634)
—Spot's First Walk. (p. 1634)
—Spot's First Walk. Hill, Eric, illus. (p. 1634)
—Spot's First Words. Hill, Eric, illus. (p. 1634)
—Spot's Fun First Words. Hill, Eric, illus. (p. 1634)
—Spot's Halloween. Hill, Eric, illus. (p. 1634)
—Spot's Opposites. (p. 1634)
—Spot's Toys. Hill, Eric, illus. (p. 1634)
—What Do You See, Spot? Hill, Eric, illus. (p. 1883)
—Where's Spot? (p. 1910)
—Where's Spot? Hill, Eric, illus. (p. 1910)
—Who's There, Spot? (p. 1921)
Hill, Eric M. Deliverance from Demons & Diseases: Freedom from Incurable Diseases & Persistent Problems (p. 425)
Hill, Eveline. Hugo & Oscar Go Travelling: Continuing the Adventures of Hugo & Oscar. (p. 825)
Hill, Ezra M. Black Red Tail Angels: The Story of a Tuskegee Airman & the Aviators. (p. 196)
Hill, Genita. My Very Special Brother. McCall, William L., illus. (p. 1221)
Hill, Genita S. President Obama's Ghost. (p. 1397)
Hill, George. Conquest of Ireland, an Historical & Genealogical Account of the Plantation of Ulster: An Archival Record of the old Irish & of new families that settled in Ireland (p. 358)
—Fall of Irish Chiefs & Clans & the Plantation of Ulster: Including the Names of Irish Catholics, & Protestant Settlers. (p. 566)
—Special Census of Northern Ireland, Pynnars Survey of Land Holders: Including Names & Locations of Protestants & Catholics Affected. (p. 1623)
Hill, George & Pope, Franklin. Names in the Land Grants in Northern Ireland: From the Plantation of Ulster. (p. 1228)
Hill, George, et al. County Londonderry Lands & Families in Northern Ireland: Names & Locations from the Plantation of Ulster. (p. 372)
Hill, Gordon. Fun Pack More Magic Tricks. (p. 648)
Hill, Grace Brooks. Corner House Girls in a Play. (p. 367)
Hill, Grace Livingston. Best Birthday: A Christmas Entertainment for Children. (p. 168)
—Cloudy Jewel. (p. 335)
Hill, Graham. Chemistry Counts. (p. 297)
Hill, Harriet. Star That Could Not Twinkle. (p. 1641)
Hill, Heather C., illus. see Hapka, Cathy, pseud.
Hill, Ingrid. Ursula, Under. (p. 1826)
Hill, Isabel. Building Stories (p. 239)
Hill, Isabel T. Urban Animals Hill, Isabel T., photos by. (p. 1825)
Hill, James. Larry the Lunker. (p. 976)
Hill, Jane, et al. Integrating English Language Learners in the Science Classroom (p. 879)
Hill, Janet Muirhead. Horse & the Crow: A Miranda & Starlight Story. (p. 799)
—Kendall & Kyleah. Leonhard, Herb, illus. (p. 948)
—Kendall's Storm. Leonhard, Herb, illus. (p. 948)
—Kyleah's Tree. Leonhard, Herb, illus. (p. 969)
—Many Adventures of Miranda & Starlight: Six Books in One Package. (p. 1089)
—Miranda & Starlight. (p. 1149)
—Miranda & Starlight: (the Starlight Books, 1) Revised Edition Lehmkuhl, Pat, illus. (p. 1149)
Hill, Jeff. Prohibition. (p. 1410)
—WPA—Putting America to Work. (p. 1962)
Hill, Jen. Percy & TumTum: A Tale of Two Dogs. (p. 1341)
Hill, Jenn, illus. see Hilton, Perez.
Hill, Jessie, illus. see Johnson, Rachel N.
Hill, JoAnn. Missy's Babies. (p. 1155)
Hill, Jonathan David, illus. see Reed, M. K.
Hill, Joy. Berry the Bird Learns How to Fly. (p. 168)
Hill, Joyce. Penny in My Pocket. (p. 1338)
Hill, Judith J. Champion for Grace. (p. 289)
Hill, Julia G. Cyril the Serious Cirrus Cloud. (p. 397)
Hill, Justin. Zodaccia: Realms of Chaos. (p. 1987)
Hill, Karen. All God's Creatures. Fancher, Lou & Johnson, Steve, illus. (p. 44)
—Cat Tails. (p. 278)
—Something Wonderful: A Christmas Story. Reagan, Susan, illus. (p. 1610)
Hill, Karen, ed. see Byrd-Hill, Ida.
Hill, Kathi Harper. Christmas Closet & Other Works. (p. 313)
Hill, Kathleen Thompson. Career Opportunities in the Food & Beverage Industry. (p. 267)
Hill, Kathy, jt. auth. see Sandusky, Thomas.
Hill, Katie Rain. Rethinking Normal: A Memoir in Transition. (p. 1464)
Hill, Kevin. Lady Bug's Can't Be Tall. (p. 970)
— Z Animal Coloring & Activity Book: English & Spanish. (p. 1984)
Hill, Kevin, illus. see Byrd-Hill, Ida.
Hill, Kevin Kelvin. Red Baron, the Knight of Many Talents. (p. 1453)
—Supreme Sorcerer Ollie Tooth Pick & His Two Henchmen versus the Magical Dragons. (p. 1685)
Hill, Kirkpatrick. Bo at Ballard Creek. Pham, LeUyen, illus. (p. 205)
—Bo at Iditarod Creek. Pham, LeUyen, illus. (p. 205)
—Dancing at the Odinochka. (p. 402)
—Do Not Pass Go. (p. 457)
—Miss Agnes & the Ginger Tom. (p. 1151)
—Winter Camp. (p. 1938)
—Year of Miss Agnes. (p. 1969)
Hill, Laban Carrick. Dave the Potter: Artist, Poet, Slave. (p. 410)
—Dave the Potter: Artist, Poet, Slave. Collier, Bryan, illus. (p. 410)
—Harlem Stomp! A Cultural History of the Harlem Renaissance. (p. 749)
—When the Beat Was Born: DJ Kool Herc & the Creation of Hip Hop. Taylor, Theodore, III, illus. (p. 1904)
Hill, Laban Carrik. Dave the Potter: Artist, Poet, Slave. (p. 410)
Hill, Laura, jt. auth. see Mills, Nathan.
Hill, Leah. Adventures of Prince Phillip & the Fairytale Creatures: The Giant Problem. (p. 22)
Hill, Lee Sullivan, jt. auth. see Hill, Lee Sullivan.
Hill, Lee Sullivan. Earthmovers on the Move. (p. 497)
Hill, Lee Sullivan. Earthmovers on the Move. (p. 497)
—Jets. (p. 916)
—Motorcycles. (p. 1179)
—Motorcycles on the Move. (p. 1180)
—Palas Mecánicas. Translations.com Staff, tr. from ENG. (p. 1319)
—Trains on the Move. (p. 1777)
Hill, Lee Sullivan & Hill, Lee Sulivan. Motorcycles on the Move. (p. 1180)
—Trains on the Move. (p. 1777)
Hill, Leonard. Punxsutawney Phyllis. Ebbeler, Jeffrey, illus. (p. 1417)
Hill, Lexie. Kissing Booth. (p. 962)
Hill, Lisa. Gravity (p. 712)
Hill, Lyn. Enduring Spirit. (p. 527)
—Thr Politics of Plunder: A Viking Tale. (p. 1740)
Hill, Lynn, illus. see Pyatt, A. K.
Hill, M., ed. see Siegel, Jerry.
Hill, Malissa, illus. see Healan, Tammy.
Hill, Marc Lamont, ed. see Armstrong, Linda J.
Hill, Marc Lamont, ed. see Davidson, Tish.
Hill, Marc Lamont, ed. see Ellis, Carol.
Hill, Marc Lamont, ed. see Hegel, Claudette.
Hill, Marc Lamont, ed. see Lusted, Marcia Amidon.
Hill, Marc Lamont, ed. see Main, Mary & Thomason, Cathy.
Hill, Marc Lamont, ed. see Massie, Elizabeth.
Hill, Marc Lamont, ed. see Nasium, James.
Hill, Marc Lamont, ed. see Perry, M. LaVora.
Hill, Marc Lamont, ed. see Scarbrough, Mary Hertz.
Hill, Maree. Nurse Nerid. (p. 1273)
Hill, Margaret Bateson, see Bateson Hill, Margaret.
Hill, Marjorie B. Xeno Oaks. (p. 1967)
Hill, Mary. Let's Go to a Movie. (p. 997)
—Let's Go to a Park. (p. 997)
—Let's Go to a Science Center. (p. 997)
—Pennies. (p. 1337)
—Serena & Venus Williams. (p. 1552)
—Signs at the Airport. (p. 1574)
—Signs at the Park. (p. 1574)
—Signs at the Store. (p. 1574)
—Spending & Saving. (p. 1625)
Hill, Mary Lea. Saint Paul: The Thirteenth Apostle. Archambault, Matthew, illus. (p. 1504)
Hill, Meggan. Nico & Lola: Kindness shared between a boy & a dog. (p. 1251)
—Nico & Lola: Kindness Shared Between a Boy & a Dog. Graunke, Susan M., illus. (p. 1251)
Hill, Melissa. Barn Owls. (p. 139)
—Burrowing Owls. (p. 244)
—Golden Eagles. (p. 694)
—Great Horned Owls. (p. 716)
—Owls. (p. 1315)
—Peregrine Falcons. (p. 1341)
—Red-Tailed Hawks. (p. 1455)
—Snowy Owls. (p. 1601)
Hill, Melissa, jt. auth. see Dunn, Mary R.
Hill, Merle Roddy. Kitty Goes Splash. Diez-Luckie, Cathy, illus. (p. 963)
—Let's Count Again! (p. 995)
Hill, Michael. Access to Geography: Urban Settlement & Land Use. (p. 8)
—Coasts & Coastal Management. (p. 336)
—Rural Settlement & the Urban Impact on the Countryside. (p. 1497)
Hill, Michael, ed. see Morrison, Grant.
Hill, Michelle M. Stanley. (p. 1639)
Hill, Monica. Dale Evans & the Lost Gold Mine. Crawford, Mel, illus. (p. 401)
—Rin Tin Tin & the Lost Indian. Greene, Hamilton, illus. (p. 1473)
Hill, Nancy. If Body Parts Could Grow on Trees. (p. 852)
Hill, Nancy S. One Year Did You Know Devotions. (p. 1298)
—One Year Did You Know Devotions 2. (p. 1298)
Hill, Napoleon. Piense y Hagase Rico - Think & Grow Rich. (p. 1357)
Hill, Nick. Carlton Casey: Alien Incident. (p. 270)
Hill, Nicolas, illus. see Gathorne-Hardy, Jonathan.
Hill, Orlah. My Day at the Library. (p. 1201)
Hill, Pamela Smith. Laura Ingalls Wilder: A Writer's Life. (p. 980)
Hill, Pascoe. Fifty Days on Board of a Slave Vessel. (p. 585)
Hill, Prescott, illus. see Cecil, Lauren & Scholastic, Inc. Staff.
Hill, Prescott, illus. see Cecil, Lauren.
Hill, Prescott, illus. see Simon, Jenne.
Hill, Raine. Growing up Pagan: A Workbook for Wiccan Families Pearce, Gillian M., illus. (p. 727)
Hill, Randal C. Aston Martin. (p. 108)
—Lamborghini (p. 972)
Hill, Robert E. Day of the Monarch. (p. 414)
Hill, Ros. Shamoo: A Whale of a Cow. (p. 1559)
—Shamoo, a Whale of a Cow. (p. 1559)
—Shamooo: A Whale of a Cow. Hill, Ros, illus. (p. 1559)
—Unexpected Tails. (p. 1817)
Hill, Rowland, tr. see Curtiss, Dominique.
Hill, Ryan. J P Trouble. (p. 901)
Hill, Sandra. Down & Dirty (p. 474)
—Pearl Jinx. (p. 1333)
—Pink Jinx. (p. 1360)
Hill, Sandy. Heaven, Just Believe. (p. 761)
Hill, Sarah. Posie Pixie & the Copper Kettle. O'Gorman, Sarah, ed. (p. 1387)
—Posie Pixie & the Lost Matchbox. O'Gorman, Sarah, ed. (p. 1387)
Hill, Shannon, illus. see Owens, Wanda.
Hill, Stephanie, illus. see Hill, Clarissa.
Hill, Steve, illus. see Scott, Keith.
Hill, Stuart. Blade of Fire. (p. 198)
—Last Battle of the Icemark. (p. 977)
Hill, Susan. Pure in Heart. (p. 1419)
—Rolling Stones. (p. 1485)
—Ruby Bakes a Cake Moore, Margie, illus. (p. 1493)
—Ruby Bakes a Cake. Moore, Margie, illus. (p. 1493)
—Ruby Paints a Picture Moore, Margie, illus. (p. 1493)
—Ruby's Perfect Day Moore, Margie, illus. (p. 1493)
—Ruby's Perfect Day. Moore, Margie, illus. (p. 1493)
Hill, Susan, jt. auth. see Grahame, Kenneth.
Hill, Susan, jt. auth. see Grogan, John.
Hill, Susan & Barrie, J. M. Peter Pan: Lost & Found. (p. 1347)
—Peter Pan: Lost & Found. Hague, Michael, illus. (p. 1347)
Hill, Susan & Sewell, Anna. Black Beauty & the Thunderstorm. Farnsworth, Bill, illus. (p. 195)
Hill, Susanna Leonard. Airplane Flight! Larrañaga, Ana Martín, illus. (p. 32)
—April Fools, Phyllis! Ebbeler, Jeffrey, illus. (p. 93)
—Can't Sleep Without Sheep. Wohnoutka, Mike, illus. (p. 262)
—Freight Train Trip! A Lift-the-Flap Adventure. Larrañaga, Ana Martín, illus. (p. 635)
—No Sword Fighting in the House. Kelley, True, illus. (p. 1260)
—Not yet, Rose. Rutten, Nicole, illus. (p. 1267)
—Punxsutawney Phyllis. Ebbeler, Jeffrey, illus. (p. 1417)
Hill, T. J., illus. see Hipp, Diane.
Hill, Tara Theresa. What Can You Do with Two Mommies? (p. 1881)
Hill, Taven. My Travel Book. (p. 1220)
Hill, Terri-Sue. I'm Healthy & Colorful from the Bottom Up. (p. 859)
—I'm Thankful. (p. 860)
Hill, Tim & Clayton, Marie, compiled by. Beatles. (p. 153)
Hill, Tony. Curse of the Crooked Spire & Other Fairy Tales. (p. 395)
Hill, Tracy, illus. see McKy, Katie.
Hill, Tracy, illus. see Mcky, Katie.
Hill, Trish, illus. see Zail, Suzy.
Hill, Valerie. Australia. (p. 116)
—Korea. (p. 967)
—New Zealand. (p. 1249)
—Thailand. (p. 1724)
Hill, Vicki Trego, illus. see Hayes, Joe.
Hill, Will. Battle Lines: A Department 19 Novel. (p. 146)
—Rising: A Department 19 Novel. (p. 1475)
—Zero Hour. (p. 1986)
Hill, William. Department 19. (p. 427)
—Department Nineteen. (p. 427)
Hill, Z. B. 50 Cent. (p. 1997)
—Art Festivals & Galleries: The Art of Selling Art. (p. 102)
—Beyoncé. (p. 173)
—Ciara. (p. 318)
—Core Workouts. Hart, Diane H., ed. (p. 367)
—Eating Right & Additional Supplements for Fitness. Hart, Diane H., ed. (p. 501)
—Eminem. (p. 519)
—Endurance & Cardio Training. Hart, Diane H., ed. (p. 527)
—Envy & Jealousy. Croft, Cindy, ed. (p. 532)
—Gallup Guides for Youth Facing Persistent Prejudice. (p. 653)
—Happiness. Croft, Cindy, ed. (p. 744)
—LL Cool J. (p. 1043)
—Loneliness. Croft, Cindy, ed. (p. 1046)
—Mary J. Blige. (p. 1100)
—Music & Musicians. (p. 1193)
—Notorious B.I.G. (p. 1268)
—Optimism & Self-Confidence. Croft, Cindy, ed. (p. 1301)
—Painting. (p. 1318)
—Performing Arts. (p. 1343)
—Players & the Game Around the World. (p. 1372)
—Romantic Attraction. Croft, Cindy, ed. (p. 1486)
—Sadness. Croft, Cindy, ed. (p. 1501)
—Sean "Diddy" Combs. (p. 1536)
—Snoop Dogg. (p. 1598)
—Tupac. (p. 1797)
—Usher. (p. 1828)
Hill, Z. B., jt. auth. see Earl, C. F.
Hill, Z. B. & Earl, C. F. Mary J. Blige. (p. 1100)
Hillam, Corbin, illus. see Allen, Margaret.
Hillam, Corbin, illus. see Callella, Trisha.
Hillam, Corbin, illus. see Connolly, Debbie & Danley, Laurie.
Hillam, Corbin, illus. see Ellermeyer, Deborah & Rowell, Judy.
Hillam, Corbin, illus. see Hults, Alaska, ed.
Hillam, Corbin, illus. see Jennett, Pamela & Marchant, Sherry.
Hillam, Corbin, illus. see Kim, Hy.
Hillam, Corbin, illus. see Sylvester, Diane.
Hillan, Pam & Dyan, Penelope. Dem Bones, Dem Bones! (p. 425)
Hillan, Pamela & Dyan, Penelope. Discovery in the Old Mine. Weigand, John, photos by. (p. 450)
—Hidden Treasure at Dragon Lake. (p. 776)
—Jewels of the Crown. Weigand, John, photos by. (p. 917)
—Mummy's Secret. Weigand, John, photos by. (p. 1191)
—Mystery on Burgundy Street. (p. 1226)
—Ring of Evil. Weigand, John D., photos by. (p. 1473)
—Secret at Fort Huachuca. (p. 1540)
Hillard Good, Karen, illus. see Moulton, Mark Kimball.
Hillard, Shirley. One Big Hug. (p. 1294)
—Who's Not Asleep? (p. 1921)
Hillard, Todd, jt. auth. see Gutwein, Austin.
Hillary, Marlana. Zoo's News: Just Be You. (p. 1990)
Hillenbrand, Jane. What a Treasure! Hillenbrand, Will, illus. (p. 1878)
Hillenbrand, Laura. Unbroken: An Olympian's Journey from Airman to Castaway to Captive. (p. 1811)
Hillenbrand, Will. All for a Dime! A Bear & Mole Story. (p. 44)
—Asleep in the Stable. (p. 106)
—Cock-a-Doodle Christmas! (p. 337)
—Down by the Barn (p. 474)
—Kite Day: A Bear & Mole Story. Hillenbrand, Will, illus. (p. 962)
—Look Out, Jack! the Giant Is Back! (p. 1050)
—Mother Goose Picture Puzzles Hillenbrand, Will, illus. (p. 1178)
—Off We Go! A Bear & Mole Story. (p. 1279)
—Off We Go! A Bear & Mole Story. Hillenbrand, Will, illus. (p. 1279)
—Spring Is Here! Hillenbrand, Will, illus. (p. 1635)
—Spring Is Here. Hillenbrand, Will, illus. (p. 1635)
Hillenbrand, Will, illus. see Adler, David A.
Hillenbrand, Will, illus. see Cuyler, Margery.
Hillenbrand, Will, illus. see Hillenbrand, Jane.
Hillenbrand, Will, illus. see Kutner, Merrily.
Hillenbrand, Will, illus. see Livingston, Myra Cohn.
Hillenbrand, Will, illus. see Miller, Bobbi.
Hillenbrand, Will, illus. see Odanaka, Barbara.
Hillenbrand, Will, illus. see Pinkwater, Daniel M.
Hillenbrand, Will, illus. see Root, Phyllis.
Hillenbrand, Will, illus. see St. George, Judith.
Hillenbrand, Will, illus. see Wilson, Karma.
Hillenbrand, Will, illus. see Wright, Maureen.
Hillenburg, Stephen. Spongebob Squarepants Bikini Bottom's Most Wanted. (p. 1630)
Hillenburg, Stephen, jt. auth. see Banks, Steven.
Hillenburg, Steven. Meow... Like a Snail?! (p. 1127)
—SpongeBob SquarePants. (p. 1630)
—SpongeBob SquarePants: Another Day Another Dollar (p. 1630)
—Spy Kids 3-D Game Over. (p. 1636)
Hillenburg, Steven, creator. Crime & Funishment Vol. 4 (p. 382)
—Saves the Day (p. 1517)
—SpongeBob SquarePants: Krusty Krab Adventures Vol. 1 (p. 1630)
—Spongebob Squarepants the Movie. (p. 1630)
—SpongeBob SquarePantsTM: Friends Forever. (p. 1630)
Hiller, Sandi J., jt. auth. see Miller, Reagan.
Hiller, Sandra J. Annie Oakley. (p. 87)
—Life of a Colonial Blacksmith. (p. 1011)
—Life of a Colonial Printer. (p. 1011)
Hillerman, Tony. Buster Mesquite's Cowboy Band. (p. 245)
Hillert, Margaret. Away Go the Boats. Masheris, Robert, illus. (p. 120)
—Baby Bunny. (p. 125)
—Baby Bunny. Masheris, Robert, illus. (p. 125)
—Ball Book. Brooks, Nan, illus. (p. 134)
—Birthday Car. Oechsli, Kelly, illus. (p. 192)
—Boy & the Goats. Miyake, Yoshi, illus. (p. 217)
—Cinderella at the Ball. Lasalle, Janet, illus. (p. 320)
—Circus Fun. Raphael, Elaine, illus. (p. 322)
—City Fun. Corey, Barbara, illus. (p. 323)
—Come Play with Me. (p. 347)
—Come Play with Me. Craft, Kinuko, illus. (p. 347)
—Come to School, Dear Dragon. Helton, David, illus. (p. 347)
—Cookie House. Craft, Kinuko, illus. (p. 361)
—Cow That Got Her Wish. (p. 373)
—Dear Dragon Eats Out. Schimmell, David, illus. (p. 418)
—Dear Dragon Flies a Kite. Pullan, Jack, illus. (p. 418)
—Dear Dragon Gets a Hole-In-One. Pullan, Jack, illus. (p. 418)
—Dear Dragon Gets a Pet. Pullan, Jack, illus. (p. 418)
—Dear Dragon Goes Camping. Schimmell, David, illus. (p. 418)
—Dear Dragon Goes to Grandpa's Farm. Pullan, Jack, illus. (p. 418)
—Dear Dragon Goes to the Aquarium. Pullan, Jack, illus. (p. 419)
—Dear Dragon Goes to the Bank. Schimmell, David, illus. (p. 419)
—Dear Dragon Goes to the Beach. Pullan, Jack, illus. (p. 419)
—Dear Dragon Goes to the Carnival. Schimmell, David, illus. (p. 419)
—Dear Dragon Goes to the Dentist. Schimmell, David, illus. (p. 419)
—Dear Dragon Goes to the Firehouse. Schimmell, David, illus. (p. 419)
—Dear Dragon Goes to the Library. Schimmel, David, illus. (p. 419)
—Dear Dragon Goes to the Market. Schimmell, David, illus. (p. 419)
—Dear Dragon Goes to the Police Station. Pullan, Jack, illus. (p. 419)
—Dear Dragon Goes to the Zoo. Schimmell, David, illus. (p. 419)
—Dear Dragon Grows a Garden. Schimmell, David, illus. (p. 419)
—Dear Dragon Learns to Read. Pullan, Jack, illus. (p. 419)
—Dear Dragon's A Is for Apple. Schimmell, David, illus. (p. 419)
—Dear Dragon's Colors 1,2,3. Schimmell, David, illus. (p. 419)
—Dear Dragon's Colors 123. Schimmell, David, illus. (p. 419)
—Dear Dragon's Day with Father. Schimmell, David, illus. (p. 419)
—Dear Dragon's Fun with Shapes. del Risco, Eida, tr. (p. 419)
—Dear Dragon's Fun with Shapes. Schimmell, David, illus. (p. 419)
—Dragon Goes to the Farm. (p. 477)
—Es Hora de Ir a la Cama, Querido Dragón: It's Bedtime, Dear Dragon. Fernandez, Queta, tr. (p. 534)
—Es Primavera, Querido Dragón/It's Spring, Dear Dragon. Schimmell, David, illus. (p. 534)
—Es primavera, querido dragón/It's Spring, Dear Dragon. del Risco, Eida, tr. from ENG. (p. 534)
—Es un Buen Juego, Querido Dragón/It's a Good Game, Dear Dragon. Schimmell, David, illus. (p. 534)
—Es un Buen Juego, Querido Dragón/It's a Good Game, Dear Dragon. Del Risco, Eida, tr. from ENG. (p. 534)
—Four Good Friends. Stasiak, Krystyna, illus. (p. 625)
—Friend for Dear Dragon. Helton, David, illus. (p. 637)
—Fun Days. (p. 647)
—Fun Days. Rogers, Joe, illus. (p. 647)
—Funny Baby. Depper, Hertha, illus. (p. 649)
—Funny Ride. Sumichrast, Jozef, illus. (p. 650)
—Go to Sleep, Dear Dragon. Helton, David, illus. (p. 687)
—Happy Birthday, Dear Dragon. Kock, Carl, illus. (p. 744)
—Happy Easter, Dear Dragon. Kock, Carl, illus. (p. 745)
—Happy Hanukkah, Dear Dragon. Schimmell, David, illus. (p. 745)
—Happy Mother's Day, Dear Dragon (p. 746)
—Help for Dear Dragon. Helton, David, illus. (p. 765)
—House for Little Red. Oechsli, Kelly, illus. (p. 803)
—I Can Do It: For the Earliest Reader. (p. 835)

—I Did It, Dear Dragon. Schimmell, David, illus. (p. 837)
—I Like Things. (p. 841)
—I Like Things. Axeman, Lois, illus. (p. 841)
—I Love You, Dear Dragon. Kock, Carl, illus. (p. 843)
—I Need You, Dear Dragon. Helton, David, illus. (p. 844)
—It's a Good Game, Dear Dragon. Schimmell, David, illus. (p. 895)
—It's Bedtime Dear Dragon. Schimmell, David, illus. (p. 896)
—It's Circus Time, Dear Dragon. Helton, David, illus. (p. 896)
—It's Earth Day, Dear Dragon: For the Earliest Reader. (p. 896)
—It's Fall, Dear Dragon. Schimmell, David, illus. (p. 896)
—It's Ground Hog Day Dear Dragon. Schimmell, David, illus. (p. 897)
—It's Halloween, Dear Dragon. Kock, Carl, illus. (p. 897)
—It's Spring, Dear Dragon. Schimmell, David, illus. (p. 899)
—It's St. Patrick's Day, Dear Dragon. del Risco, Eida, tr. (p. 899)
—It's St. Patrick's Day, Dear Dragon. Schimmell, David, illus. (p. 899)
—It's Summer, Dear Dragon. Schimmell, David, illus. (p. 899)
—It's Winter, Dear Dragon. Schimmell, David, illus. (p. 899)
—Juega, Juega, Juega, Querido Dragón/Play, Play, Play, Dear Dragon. del Risco, Eida, tr. (p. 931)
—Juega, Juega, Juega, Querido Dragon/Play, Play, Play, Dear Dragon. Del Risco, Eida, tr. from ENG. (p. 931)
—Let's Go, Dear Dragon. Kock, Carl, illus. (p. 997)
—Let's Have a Play. Elzaurdia, Sharon, illus. (p. 998)
—Little Cookie. Charles, Donald, illus. (p. 1026)
—Little Cowboy & the Big Cowboy. Siculan, Dan, illus. (p. 1026)
—Little Puff. Jordan, Sid, illus. (p. 1034)
—Little Red Riding Hood. (p. 1035)
—Little Red Riding Hood. Connelly, Gwen, illus. (p. 1035)
—Little Runaway. Anderson, Irv, illus. (p. 1036)
—Magic Beans. Pekarsky, Mel, illus. (p. 1071)
—Magic Nutcracker. (p. 1072)
—Magic Nutcracker. Iversen, Portia, illus. (p. 1072)
—Merry Christmas, Dear Dragon. Kock, Carl, illus. (p. 1128)
—Not I, Not I. Magnuson, Diana, illus. (p. 1267)
—Not Too Little to Help (p. 1267)
—No-Tail Cat or, I Like What I Am (p. 1260)
—No-Tail Cat or, I Like What I Am: Or, I Like What I Am. (p. 1260)
—Penguin, Penguin: For the Earliest Reader (p. 1337)
—Pinocchio. Hamilton, Laurie, illus. (p. 1360)
—Play Ball. Martin, Dick, illus. (p. 1371)
—Play, Play, Play Dear Dragon. Schimmell, David, illus. (p. 1371)
—Pumpkin, Pumpkin: For the Earliest Reader. Starfall Education, photos by. (p. 1416)
—Purple Pussycat. Stasiak, Krystyna, illus. (p. 1419)
—Querido Dragón, Los Colores y 1, 2, 3 /Dear Dragon's Colors 1, 2, 3. del Risco, Eida, tr. (p. 1425)
—Querido dragón, los colores y 1, 2, 3 /Dear Dragon's Colors 1, 2, 3. del Risco, Eida, tr. from ENG. (p. 1425)
—Querido Dragon Pasa el Dia con Papa/Dear Dragon's Day with Father. Del Risco, Eida, tr. from ENG. (p. 1425)
—Querido Dragón Quiere Ayudar: Dear Dragon Helps Out. Fernandez, Queta, tr. (p. 1426)
—Querido Dragón Va a la Biblioteca/Dear Dragon Goes to the Library. del Risco, Eida, tr. (p. 1426)
—Querido Dragón Va a la Biblioteca/Dear Dragon Goes to the Library. Del Risco, Eida, tr. from ENG. (p. 1426)
—Querido Dragón Va a la Estación de Bomberos/Dear Dragon Goes to the Firehouse. de', Eida, tr. (p. 1426)
—Querido Dragón Va Al Banco: Dear Dragon Goes to the Bank. Fernandez, Queta, tr. (p. 1426)
—Querido dragón va al cuartel de bomberos/Dear Dragon Goes to the Firehouse. del Risco, Eida, tr. from ENG. (p. 1426)
—Querido Dragón Va Al Mercado/Dear Dragon Goes to the Market. Schimmell, David, illus. (p. 1426)
—Querido dragón va al mercado/Dear Dragon Goes to the Market. del Risco, Eida, tr. from ENG. (p. 1426)
—Snow Baby. Dauber, Liz, illus. (p. 1598)
—Take a Walk, Johnny. Miyake, Yoshi, illus. (p. 1696)
—Three Bears. Wilde, Irma, illus. (p. 1741)
—Three Goats . Pekarsky, Mel, illus. (p. 1742)
—Three Little Pigs. Wilde, Irma, illus. (p. 1743)
—Three Little Plays (p. 1743)
—Tom Thumb. Hockerman, Dennis, illus. (p. 1764)
—Touchdown! Dear Dragon. Schimmell, David, illus. (p. 1772)
—Up, up, & Away. Masheris, Robert, illus. (p. 1824)
—Up, up, up, Dear Dragon. Schimmell, David, illus. (p. 1824)
—We Can Help, Dear Dragon. Schimmell, David, illus. (p. 1866)
—What Am I? Elzaurdia, Sharon, illus. (p. 1879)
—What's in My Pocket, Dear Dragon? Schimmell, David, illus. (p. 1898)
—What's in the Pond, Dear Dragon? Schimmell, David, illus. (p. 1898)
—What's in the Sky, Dear Dragon? Schimmel, David, illus. (p. 1898)
—What's in the Sky, Dear Dragon? Schimmell, David, illus. (p. 1898)
—What's in the Woods, Dear Dragon? Schimmell, David, illus. (p. 1898)
—Where Is Dear Dragon? Schimmell, David, illus. (p. 1908)
—Who Goes to School? Brooks, Nan, illus. (p. 1915)
—Why We Have Thanksgiving. Siculan, Dan, illus. (p. 1926)
—Witch Who Went for a Walk. Stasiak, Krystyna, illus. (p. 1941)
—Wolves: For the Earliest Reader. Starfall Education, ed. (p. 1945)
—Yellow Boat. Young, Ed, illus. (p. 1970)
—¿Dónde Está Querido Dragón? Where Is Dear Dragon? Fernandez, Queta, tr. from ENG. (p. 466)
—¿Qué Hay en el Cielo, Querido Dragón? What's in the Sky, Dear Dragon? Fernandez, Queta, tr. from ENG. (p. 1423)
—¿Qué Hay en el Estanque, Querido Dragón? What's in the Pond, Dear Dragon? Fernandez, Queta, tr. (p. 1423)
—¿Qué Tengo en el Bolsillo, Querido Dragón? What's in My Pocket, Dear Dragon? Fernandez, Queta, tr. (p. 1424)

Hillert, Margaret & Fernández, Queta. ¿Que Hay en el Bosque, Querido Dragon? What's in the Woods, Dear Dragon? Schimmell, David, illus. (p. 1423)
Hillery, Susie Moore. Count Your Blessings. (p. 370)
Hilley, Thomas, illus. see Danley, Jerry J.
Hilliam, Corbin, illus. see Harding, Davilla.
Hilliam, Corbin, illus. see Jennett, Pamela.
Hilliam, David. Castles & Cathedrals: The Great Buildings of Medieval Times. (p. 277)
—Castles & Cathedrals. (p. 277)
—Eleanor of Aquitaine: The Richest Queen in Medieval Europe. (p. 508)
—Joan of Arc: Heroine of France. (p. 919)
—Philip II: King of Spain & Leader of the Counter-Reformation. (p. 1350)
—Philip II: Kong of Spain & Leader of the Counter-reformation. (p. 1350)
—Richard the Lionheart & the Third Crusade: The English King Confronts Saladin in AD 1191. (p. 1470)
—Richard the Lionhearted & the Third Crusade: The English King Confronts Saladin, AD 1191. (p. 1470)
—Thomas Becket: English Saint & Martyr. (p. 1738)
—William Shakespeare: England's Greatest Playwright & Poet. (p. 1933)
Hilliam, Paul. Elizabeth I: Queen of England's Golden Age. (p. 513)
—William the Conqueror: First Norman King of England. (p. 1933)
Hilliam, Rachel. Galileo Galilei: Father of Modern Science. (p. 653)
Hilliard, Carol, illus. see Cheehy, Debra/Ilene.
Hilliard, Michael. Butter Bee Grows up Too Fast! (p. 247)
Hilliard, Regina Foster. Tim & Tom: Frog Friends. (p. 1750)
Hilliard, Richard. Godspeed, John Glenn. (p. 692)
—Lucky 13: Survival in Space. (p. 1062)
—Neil, Buzz, & Mike Go to the Moon. (p. 1240)
Hilliard, Richard, illus. see Harrison, David L.
Hilliker, Phillip, illus. see Brezenoff, Steve.
Hilliker, Phillip, illus. see Muldoon, Kathleen M.
Hillings, Pamela, jt. auth. see Hillings, Phyllis.
Hillings, Phyllis & Hillings, Pamela. Web of Good Manners - Grown-up Manners for Young People. Mumper-Drumm, Heidrun, illus. (p. 1870)
Hillman, Iris H. Back Yard Critters: Things That Go Bump in the Night. (p. 130)
Hillman, John E. Ancient Stories of the Hodj. (p. 70)
Hillman, Laura. I Will Plant You a Lilac Tree: A Memoir of a Schindler's List Survivor. (p. 848)
Hillman, Shane, illus. see Hale, Bruce.
Hillmann, Joe, illus. see Reich, J. J.
Hillmerle Roddy. All under the Bright Yellow Sun. (p. 46)
Hillner, Brenda. Invisible Girl. (p. 885)
Hill-Peterson, Jodi, illus. see Given, Cate.
Hills, Aaron Merritt, jt. auth. see Mahan, Asa.
Hills, Alan, photos by see Cotterell, Arthur, et al.
Hills, Curt. Hannah's Legalized Kidnapping: A Rush to React Took Her Away for 207 Days. (p. 743)
Hills, Frederic F. & Hills, Tad. Rocket's 100th Day of School. (p. 1483)
Hills, Jodi. Believe. Hills, Jodi, illus. (p. 161)
—Hope-So. Bjornson, Barbara, illus. (p. 796)
Hills, Ken. 1940s. (p. 2002)
Hills, Laila. Elephant. (p. 511)
—Squirty Bath Books - Duck. (p. 1637)
Hills, Laila, illus. see Su, Tami.
Hills, Louis Edward. New Light on American Archaeology. (p. 1246)
—Short Work on the Popol & the Traditional History of the Ancient Americans, by Lxt-lil-Xochitl. (p. 1569)
Hills, Melanie. Gingerbread Kids. (p. 677)
Hills, Tad. Drop It, Rocket! (p. 485)
—Duck & Goose: How Are You Feeling? Hills, Tad, illus. (p. 488)
—Duck & Goose. Hills, Tad, illus. (p. 488)
—Duck & Goose, 1, 2, 3. Hills, Tad, illus. (p. 488)
—Duck & Goose Colors. Hills, Tad, illus. (p. 488)
—Duck & Goose Go to the Beach. (p. 488)
—Duck & Goose, Goose Needs a Hug. Hills, Tad, illus. (p. 488)
—Duck & Goose, Here Comes the Easter Bunny! Hills, Tad, illus. (p. 488)
—Duck, Duck, Goose. Hills, Tad, illus. (p. 488)
—Find a Pumpkin. Hills, Tad, illus. (p. 587)
—How Rocket Learned to Read. Hills, Tad, illus. (p. 812)
—It's Time for Christmas! Hills, Tad, illus. (p. 899)
—R Is for Rocket: an ABC Book. (p. 1429)
—Rocket Writes a Story. Hills, Tad, illus. (p. 1483)
—Rocket's Learning Box Hills, Tad, illus. (p. 1483)
—Rocket's Mighty Words. (p. 1483)
—What's up, Duck? A Book of Opposites. Hills, Tad, illus. (p. 1900)
Hills, Tad, jt. auth. see Hills, Frederic F.
Hillson, Ted. Tae Kwon Do Classic Forms: 21 Hyung—Novice White Belt Through Advanced Black Belt. Kligge, Elizabeth, illus. (p. 1695)
Hillstead, McKensy & Gonzales, Brittany. One Day. (p. 1294)
Hillstrom & Hillstrom, Laurie C. Jackie Robinson & the Integration of Baseball. (p. 904)
Hillstrom, Kevin. Gay Marriage. Greenhaven Press Editors, ed. (p. 659)
—Great Depression & the New Deal. (p. 715)
—Harlem Renaissance. (p. 749)
—Internet Revolution. (p. 880)
—McCarthyism & the Communist Threat. (p. 1114)
—Medical Marijuana. Gale, G., ed. (p. 1118)
—Natural Disaster Response. Lucent Books Staff, ed. (p. 1235)
—Nuclear Energy. Greenhaven Press Editors, ed. (p. 1269)
—Progressive Era. (p. 1410)
—Watergate. (p. 1863)
Hillstrom, Kevin, jt. auth. see Dougherty, Terri.
Hillstrom, Kevin, jt. auth. see Hillstrom, Laurie.
Hillstrom, Kevin, jt. auth. see Ruffner, Peter.
Hillstrom, Kevin, jt. ed. see Abbey, Cherie D.
Hillstrom, Kevin & Hillstrom, Laurie Collier. Al Gore. (p. 32)
—Dale Earnhardt, Jr. (p. 401)
—War in the Persian Gulf: Biographies. (p. 1857)
—War in the Persian Gulf - Primary Sources: From Operation Desert Storm to Operation Iraqi Freedom. (p. 1857)
Hillstrom, Kevin & Hillstrom, Laurie Collier, eds. Automobiles, Mining & Petroleum, Textiles (p. 117)
—Industrial Revolution in America - Overview/Comparison (p. 872)
Hillstrom, Kevin, ed. Eating Disorders. (p. 501)
Hillstrom, Laurie. Frida Kahlo, Painter. (p. 637)
—Gabriel Garcia Marquez. (p. 652)
—Online Social Networks. (p. 1298)
Hillstrom, Laurie, ed. see Boyd, Christie Brewer.
Hillstrom, Laurie & Hillstrom, Kevin. Diego Rivera, Muralist. (p. 437)
Hillstrom, Laurie C., jt. auth. see Hillstrom.
Hillstrom, Laurie Collier. Jay-Z. (p. 910)
—Kelly Clarkson. (p. 948)
—Pele: Soccer Superstar. (p. 1335)
—Underground Railroad. (p. 1814)
—Voting Rights Act of 1965. (p. 1850)
—War in the Persian Gulf: From Operation Desert Storm to Operation Iraqi Freedom Reference Library (p. 1857)
—War in the Persian Gulf Almanac: From Operation Desert Storm to Operation Iraqi Freedom. Carnagie, Julie, ed. (p. 1857)
Hillstrom, Laurie Collier, jt. auth. see Hillstrom, Kevin.
Hillstrom, Laurie Collier, jt. ed. see Hillstrom, Kevin.
Hillstrom, Laurie, ed. Food Regulation & Safety. (p. 614)
—Vaccinations. (p. 1830)
Hill-Sullivan, Shunice. Son, Do You Know How Truly Blessed You Are? (p. 1611)
Hilltree, Angela. ABC Coloring Book: Creation Science & Geology. (p. 3)
Hillyard, Samantha. Sociology of Rural Life. (p. 1605)
Hillyer, Brenda L. Mystery in the Marsh. (p. 1224)
Hillyer, Lexa. Proof of Forever. (p. 1411)
—Rio. (p. 1473)
Hillyer, Rhonda. Butterfly Magic. Wood, Steve, illus. (p. 248)
Hillyer, V. M. Child's History of the World. (p. 305)
Hilmer, Evelyn, illus. see Counter, Marlow & Counter, Marlow.
Hilmo, Tess. Skies Like These. (p. 1584)
—With a Name Like Love. (p. 1942)
Hilsenrad, Michael. Theatre of Innocence. (p. 1728)
Hilson, R. Phantoms of the Fort. (p. 1349)
Hilton, Bing. Greentown Glass Company Price Advisor 2003 (p. 723)
Hilton, Charlotte. Adventure of the Pen Pot Pals. (p. 14)
Hilton, Fern A. Jesse & Henry Save the Day. (p. 914)
—Jesse & Wee. (p. 914)
Hilton, George Woodman. Great Lakes Car Ferries. (p. 717)
Hilton, John & Sweat, Anthony. How? Essential Skills for Living the Gospel. (p. 804)
Hilton, K. Magic of Finkleton. (p. 1073)
Hilton, Marcel. Magical Web. (p. 1075)
Hilton, Marilyn. Found Things. (p. 624)
—Full Cicada Moon. (p. 646)
Hilton, Marilyn Copley. Christian Girl's Guide to Your Mom. (p. 311)
Hilton, N. E. Spell. (p. 1625)
Hilton, Nette. Grave Catastrophe. (p. 712)
—Living Next to Lulah. (p. 1041)
—Sprite Downberry. (p. 1635)
—Web. Millard, Kerry, illus. (p. 1870)
—Woolly Jumpers. (p. 1950)
Hilton, Perez. Boy with Pink Hair. Hill, Jenn, illus. (p. 219)
Hilton, Samantha. 3-D Baby Animals. (p. 1991)
—Big Cats & Amazing Jungle Animals. (p. 180)
—Nature's Neighborhoods. Holmes, Steve, illus. (p. 1237)
—World of Insects. Holmes, Steve, illus. (p. 1956)
Hilts, Ben, illus. see Czajak, Paul & Brothers Hilts Staff.
Hilts, Brothers, jt. auth. see Wolf, Karina.
Hilty, Bertha, illus. see Brown, W. C.
Hime, Stanley E. Stanley's Quilt Book / Sue Stays Busy. (p. 1640)
Himekawa, Akira. Four Swords Himekawa, Akira, illus. (p. 625)
—Four Swords Pt. 2 Himekawa, Akira, illus. (p. 625)
—Legend of Zelda (p. 989)
—Legend of Zelda: Phantom Hourglass. Himekawa, Akira, illus. (p. 989)
—Link to the Past. Himekawa, Akira, illus. (p. 1019)
—Majora's Mask. Himekawa, Akira, illus. (p. 1078)
—Minish Cap. Himekawa, Akira, illus. (p. 1147)
—Ocarina of Time. Himekawa, Akira, illus. (p. 1275)
—Oracle of Ages Himekawa, Akira, illus. (p. 1301)
Himekawa, Akira, et al. Legend of Zelda: Hyrule Historia. Thorpe, Patrick, ed. (p. 989)
Himes, John. Adventures of an Alligator Named Ally. (p. 16)
—Beauty. (p. 154)
—Everyone Is Special. (p. 544)
Himes, Kathy. Major Prairie Tramp - the Many ADV of a Hunting Dog. (p. 1078)
Himle, Lisa. Hands as Warm as Toast. Langton, Bruce, illus. (p. 741)
Himler, Ronald. Dancing Boy Himler, Ronald, illus. (p. 402)
—Girl on the Yellow Giraffe Himler, Ronald, illus. (p. 678)
Himler, Ronald, illus. see Adler, David A.
Himler, Ronald, illus. see Adler, David A. & Adler, Michael S.
Himler, Ronald, illus. see Bunting, Eve.
Himler, Ronald, illus. see Coerr, Eleanor.
Himler, Ronald, illus. see Cohen, Miriam.
Himler, Ronald, illus. see Cole, Barbara H.
Himler, Ronald, illus. see Cole, Barbara.
Himler, Ronald, illus. see DeLaCroix, Alice.
Himler, Ronald, illus. see Garland, Sherry.
Himler, Ronald, illus. see Howard, Ellen.
Himler, Ronald, illus. see Khan, Rukhsana.
Himler, Ronald, illus. see Newman, Lesléa.
Himler, Ronald, illus. see Swain, Gwenyth.
Himler, Ronald, illus. see Van Steenwyk, Elizabeth.
Himler, Ronald, illus. see Vander Zee, Ruth.
Himler, Ronald, illus. see Wright, Betty Ren.
Himler, Ronald, illus. see Zolotow, Charlotte.
Himler, Ronald, jt. auth. see Cohen, Miriam.
Himmelman, Jeff, illus. see Rubin, Susan Goldman.
Himmelman, John. Basic Illustrated Guide to Frogs, Snakes, Bugs, & Slugs. (p. 142)
—Chickens to the Rescue. Himmelman, John, illus. (p. 300)
—Cows to the Rescue. Himmelman, John, illus. (p. 374)
—Duck to the Rescue. Himmelman, John, illus. (p. 488)
—Frog in a Bog. Himmelman, John, illus. (p. 640)
—Katie & the Puppy Next Door. Himmelman, John, illus. (p. 944)
—Katie Loves the Kittens. Himmelman, John, illus. (p. 945)
—Noisy Bird Sing-Along. Himmelman, John, illus. (p. 1263)
—Noisy Bug Sing-Along. Himmelman, John, illus. (p. 1263)
—Noisy Frog Sing-Along. Himmelman, John, illus. (p. 1263)
—Pigs to the Rescue. Himmelman, John, illus. (p. 1358)
—Tales of Bunjitsu Bunny. Himmelman, John, illus. (p. 1702)
—Tudley Didn't Know Himmelman, John, illus. (p. 1796)
Himmelman, John, illus. see Stewart, Melissa.
Himmelreich, Cheri. Does It Hurt? (p. 460)
Himmler, Ronald, illus. see Cohen, Miriam.
Himonas, Alex & Howard, Alan. Calculus, Student Solutions Manual: Ideas & Applications. (p. 252)
Himsl, Sharon M. Events That Changed the World - 1940-1960. (p. 541)
Hina. Di Gi Charat Theater - Leave it to Piyoko (p. 433)
Hina, Paul & Hina, Sarah. Anxiety Disorders. Gale Editors, ed. (p. 90)
Hina, Sarah, jt. auth. see Hina, Paul.
Hinako, Ashihara. Forbidden Dance (p. 616)
Hinbest, Wendy. Frizzy Tizzy Camps In. (p. 639)
—Frizzy Tizzy Cleans Up. (p. 639)
—Frizzy Tizzy Dances. (p. 639)
—Frizzy Tizzy Gets New Shoes. (p. 639)
—Frizzy Tizzy Goes to the Park. (p. 639)
Hinchcliffe, L. T. For the Love of Prudence Possum. (p. 616)
Hincher, Theresa B. Baldy the Balloon. (p. 134)
Hinchliffe, Stuart Jarod. Princess Tiffany Arabella & the Time of Dreams. (p. 1406)
Hinckley, Betts. Adventure's of Charlie Girl. (p. 17)
—Mr Bumble. (p. 1184)
Hinckley, Greg, illus. see Cahn, Yehudah.
Hincks, Gary, jt. auth. see Malam, John.
Hind, Devon & Bergstresser, Kate, trs. Jesse Owens: World's Fastest Human. (p. 914)
Hind, Rebecca. Sacred Places. (p. 1500)
Hinder, Sara Jane, illus. see Gates, Mariam.
Hinder, Sarah Jane, illus. see Brown, Gina Bates.
Hinderliter, John, illus. see Gigliotti, Jim.
Hinderliter, John, illus. see Kelley, True.
Hinderliter, John, illus. see Kinney, Patrick.
Hinderliter, John, illus. see Koontz, Robin.
Hinderliter, John, illus. see Medina, Nico.
Hinderliter, John, illus. see O'Connor, Jim.
Hindle, James K., illus. see Hayes, Christine.
Hindley, J. Knights & Castles. (p. 964)
Hindley, Judy. Do Like A Duck Does! (p. 457)
—Do Like a Duck Does! Bates, Ivan, illus. (p. 457)
—Eyes, Nose, Fingers, & Toes: A First Book All about You. Granström, Brita, illus. (p. 558)
—Knights & Castles. Wheatley, Abigail, ed. (p. 964)
Hindley, Judy, et al. Time Traveler: Visit Medieval Times, the Viking Age, the Roman World & Ancient Egypt. (p. 1753)
Hindley, Kate, illus. see Bee, William.
Hindley, Kate, illus. see Griffin, N.
Hindley, Kate, illus. see Robinson, Michelle.
Hindman, Susan. Carpenter. (p. 271)
—Think Like a Scientist in the Classroom. (p. 1734)
—Working at a Movie Theater. (p. 1952)
Hindmarch, Will & Kobar, Christopher. Ordo Dracul. (p. 1302)
Hindmarsh, Ted C. Elf & the Magic Windows: A Christmas Fairy Tale. (p. 512)
Hinds, Gareth. Beowulf. (p. 166)
—Macbeth. Hinds, Gareth, illus. (p. 1067)
—Merchant of Venice. Hinds, Gareth, illus. (p. 1127)
—Odyssey. Hinds, Gareth, illus. (p. 1278)
—Romeo & Juliet. Hinds, Gareth, illus. (p. 1486)
—Romeo & Juliet (Graphic Adaptation) (p. 1486)
Hinds, Gareth, illus. see Lunge-Larsen, Lise.
Hinds, Gareth & Shakespeare, William. Merchant of Venice. Hinds, Gareth, illus. (p. 1127)
Hinds, Kathryn. Ancient Celts: Europe's Tribal Ancestors. (p. 68)
—Church. (p. 318)
—City. (p. 323)
—Countryside. (p. 372)
—Daily Living. (p. 400)
—Early Germans: Peoples of the North. (p. 493)
—Elizabeth & Her Court. (p. 513)
—Everyday Life in Medieval Europe. (p. 543)
—Everyday Life in the Renaissance. (p. 543)
—Everyday Life in the Roman Empire. (p. 544)
—Faith. (p. 565)
—Goths. (p. 704)
—Huns. (p. 828)
—Life in Ancient Egypt (p. 1010)
—Life in Elizabethan England (p. 1010)
—Life in the Medieval Muslim World (p. 1011)
—Lin In The Roman Empire Series (p. 1018)
—Mermaids. (p. 1128)
—Palace. (p. 1319)
—Patricians. (p. 1329)
—Pharaoh's Court. (p. 1349)
—Religion. (p. 1458)
—Scythians & Sarmatians. (p. 1534)
—Sphinxes & Centaurs. (p. 1626)
—Unicorns. (p. 1818)
—Vikings: Masters of the Sea. (p. 1842)
Hinds, Kathryn, jt. auth. see Schomp, Virginia.
Hinds, Maurene. Emily Dickinson. (p. 518)
Hinds, Maurene J. Antarctica. (p. 88)
—Ferguson Guide to Resumes & Job Hunting Skills: A Step-by-Step Guide to Preparing for Your Job Search. (p. 582)

H

—Ferguson Guide to Resumes & Job Hunting Skills: A Handbook for Recent Graduates & Those Entering the Workplace for the First Time. (p. 582)
—Fighting the AIDS & HIV Epidemic: A Global Battle. (p. 586)
—Furman V. Georgia & the Death Penalty Debate: Debating Supreme Court Decisions. (p. 650)
—Halle Berry. (p. 737)
—How to Analyze the Works of Toni Morrison. (p. 814)
—John Steinbeck: Banned, Challenged, & Censored. (p. 922)
—Reader's Guide to Richard Wright's Black Boy. (p. 1444)
—Witchcraft on Trial: From the Salem Witch Hunts to the Crucible. (p. 1941)
—You Have the Right to Know Your Rights: What Teens Should Know. (p. 1975)
Hinds, Ruth McNaughton. Puppy & I. (p. 1418)
Hinds, Sandra A. I Love You Every. (p. 843)
Hinduja, Sameer, jt. auth. see Patchin, Justin W.
Hine, Christine, ed. Virtual Methods: Issues in Social Research on the Internet. (p. 1844)
Hine, Darlene Clark, et al. African-American Odyssey since 1865 Ball, Alan, ed. (p. 27)
Hine, David. Redemption. (p. 1455)
Hine, Eileen. Desert Opposites. (p. 429)
Hine, Lewis, photos by see Mann, Elizabeth.
Hine, Robert. Facts on File Dictionary of Biology. (p. 561)
Hineman, Jonathan. Goodbye, Santa. Cruz, Cheryl, illus. (p. 701)
Hiner, Danielle E. Mommy Can I Play with Tommy? Based on Joseph Hiner, a boy with Cerebral Palsy. (p. 1162)
Hines, Amanda Conley. Grandma, Why Didn't God Make me a Bird? (p. 708)
Hines, Amber. Maggie & the Moo Bully. (p. 1071)
Hines, Anna Grossnickle. 1, 2, Buckle My Shoe. (p. 1990)
—I Am a Tyrannosaurus. Hines, Anna Grossnickle, illus. (p. 832)
—Peaceful Pieces: Poems & Quilts about Peace. Hines, Anna Grossnickle, illus. (p. 1332)
—Pieces: A Year in Poems & Quilts. Hines, Anna Grossnickle, illus. (p. 1356)
—Whistling. (p. 1912)
—Winter Lights: A Season in Poems & Quilts. Hines, Anna Grossnickle, illus. (p. 1938)
Hines, Anna Grossnickle, illus. see Driscoll, Laura & Rey, H. A.
Hines, Anna Grossnickle, illus. see Driscoll, Laura, et al.
Hines, Anna Grossnickle, illus. see Hapka, Catherine, pseud & Rey, H. A.
Hines, Anna Grossnickle, illus. see Hapka, Catherine, pseud, et al.
Hines, Anna Grossnickle, illus. see Perez, Monica & Houghton Mifflin Company Editors.
Hines, Anna Grossnickle, illus. see Rey, H. A.
Hines, Anna Grossnickle, illus. see Rey, H. A. & Rey, Margret.
Hines, Anna Grossnickle, illus. see Rey, Margret & Rey, H. A.
Hines, Chrissie & Ferreras, Alberto. Perro y el Gato. Winslow, Justin, illus. (p. 1344)
Hines, Connie. Ballerinas Don't Get Pickles. (p. 134)
—Whisper the Baby Butterfly. (p. 1912)
Hines, D. H. L. College Mouse. (p. 340)
Hines, Danise. Ziona Learns to Be a Good Samaritan. (p. 1987)
Hines, Erin & Faulconer-Lippert, Gwin. Number Fun with Ally Dog. (p. 1271)
Hines, Irene, illus. see Arnold, Shauna.
hines, j. Finding Raven. (p. 588)
Hines, Janet. Inside America's CIA: The Central Intelligence Agency. (p. 876)
Hines, Jerry E. Silly & Stinky Stories My Grandpa Tells. (p. 1575)
Hines, Jim C. Goblin Quest. (p. 688)
Hines, Laura Freeman, illus. see Lewison, Wendy Cheyette.
Hines, Marcel, illus. see Dunagan, Jennifer.
Hines, Thomas. Bubble Machine. (p. 233)
Hines-Stephens, Sarah, jt. auth. see Mason, Jane B.
Hines-Stephens, Sarah, jt. auth. see Stephens, Sarah Hines.
Hines-Stephens, Sarah, et al. Do It Now! Crafts: Cool Art Projects & Tasty Snacks. (p. 457)
Hingoro, Samira, creator. Marriage Proposal. (p. 1096)
Hinkel, Patricia. Frog in My Bucket. (p. 640)
Hinkelman, Carole & Rebik, Nan. Herman Chronicles: *Herman the Horrible Trailer Mouse *Herman & the Donkeys * Herman's Midnight Trek * Herman's Vacation. (p. 771)
Hinkes, Enid. Police Cat. (p. 1380)
—Police Cat. Rasmussen, Wendy, illus. (p. 1380)
Hinkle, Cynthia. Star of Wonder. van der Sterre, Johanna, illus. (p. 1641)
Hinkle, Cynthia A. Thankful Leper: The Story of the Ten Lepers: Luke 17:11-19 & 2 Kings 5:1-15 for Children. Collier-Morales, Roberta, illus. (p. 1725)
Hinkle, Donald. Ronald Reagan: A MyReportLinks.com Book. (p. 1486)
Hinkle, Donald Henry. Oklahoma: A MyReportLinks. Com Book. (p. 1283)
Hinkle, Marcus. CNC Milling Machine & Router DIY For $300: Everything you need to know to build an inexpensive CNC machine, write G code & locate free Software. (p. 336)
Hinkler Books, creator. 101 First Words: Animals. (p. 1999)
—101 First Words: At Home. (p. 1999)
—101 First Words: Things That Go. (p. 1999)
—101 First Words. (p. 1999)
—Pop Diva Make-Up Kit. (p. 1384)
—Princess Make-Up Kit. (p. 1404)
Hinkler Books, ed. Baby Animals. (p. 124)
—Baby's First Birthday. (p. 129)
—Baby's First Numbers. (p. 129)
—Baby's First Thanksgiving. (p. 129)
—Funky Things to Draw. (p. 649)
—Ghostly Glow in the Haunted House. (p. 672)
—Little Princess Tea Party. (p. 1034)
—Littlest Pet Shop Cat & Mouse. (p. 1039)
—Littlest Pet Shop Hamster & Dalmation. (p. 1039)
—Littlest Pet Shop Spaniel & Monkey. (p. 1039)
—Mighty Movers. (p. 1140)
—My Amazing Sticker Activity Book. (p. 1196)
—My Designer Doll's House to Make & Decorate. (p. 1201)
—My Pretty Pink Tea Party. (p. 1217)
—My Treasury of Princess Tales. (p. 1220)
—Scooby Doo! & the Gang's Spooky Snacks. (p. 1529)
—You Can Draw. (p. 1974)
Hinkler Books Staff. 1 2 3. (p. 1990)
—ABC. (p. 3)
—Balloon Animals. (p. 135)
—CD Storybook: Beauty & the Beast; The Little Mermaid; Cinderella; Snow White. (p. 283)
—Dinosaurs. (p. 443)
—Dinosaurs. Kiely, Rob, illus. (p. 444)
—Farm Lift the Flap. Penton Overseas, Inc. Staff, ed. (p. 574)
—My Cool Box of Dress-up Dolls. (p. 1200)
—My Treasury of Bedtime Tales. (p. 1220)
—My Treasury of Fairytales. (p. 1220)
Hinkler Books Staff, ed. see Cuthbert, Kate.
Hinkler Books Staff, ed. see Tovey, Peter.
Hinkler Books Staff, ed. Baby's First Animals. (p. 129)
—Baby's First Colors. (p. 129)
—Casper the Caterpillar. (p. 276)
—Dress-up Fashion Dolls: Designer Collection. (p. 485)
—Early Math. (p. 493)
—Funny Fish. (p. 649)
—Hungry Frog. (p. 828)
—Phonics. (p. 1351)
—Spelling. (p. 1625)
Hinkler Books Staff, reader. Barney Says "Play Safely" (p. 139)
—Barney's Big Balloon. (p. 139)
—Barney's Outer Space Adventure. (p. 139)
—Come on over Barneys House. (p. 347)
Hinkler Editors, ed. On the Farm. (p. 1290)
Hinkler Studios Staff., ed. Baby's First Christmas. (p. 129)
—Baby's First Halloween. (p. 129)
—Big Bumper Book of Paper Models. (p. 180)
—Cars: Numbers & Early Math. (p. 272)
—Disney Princess: Counting & Spelling. (p. 452)
—Dora the Explorer Story Vision. (p. 471)
—Jack & the Beanstalk. (p. 902)
—Little Red Riding Hood. (p. 1035)
—Mickey Mouse Clubhouse: Preschool Skills. (p. 1136)
Hinkler Studios Staff, ed. Snow White. (p. 1599)
Hinkler Studios Staff., ed. Sponge Bob Story Vision. (p. 1630)
—Three Little Pigs. (p. 1742)
—Winnie the Pooh: ABC & First Words. (p. 1937)
Hinks, Roy H. Cybo Soccer & Heavens Above. (p. 396)
Hinlicky, Gregg, illus. see Sportelli-Rehak, Angela.
Hinman, Bobbie. Belly Button Fairy. Adams, Mark Wayne, illus. (p. 163)
—Fart Fairy. Adams, Mark Wayne, illus. (p. 575)
—Knot Fairy. Bridgeman, Kristi, illus. (p. 965)
—Sock Fairy. Bridgeman, Kristi, illus. (p. 1605)
Hinman, Bonnie. Basic Genealogy for Kids. (p. 141)
—Eternal Vigilance: The Story of Ida B. Wells-Barnett. (p. 539)
—Executive Branch. (p. 548)
—Extreme Cycling with Dale Holmes. (p. 556)
—Florence Nightingale & the Advancement of Nursing. (p. 606)
—John Legend. (p. 922)
—Life & Times of William Penn. (p. 1008)
—Life During the Revolutionary War. (p. 1010)
—Massachusetts Bay Colony: The Puritans Arrive from England. (p. 1102)
—Mount Everest. (p. 1180)
—Paula Deen. (p. 1330)
—Pennsylvania: William Penn & the City of Brotherly Love. (p. 1338)
—Scoop on School & Work in Colonial America (p. 1529)
—Stranger in My Own House: The Story of W. E. B. du Bois. (p. 1665)
—Thanksgiving/Accion de Gracias. de la Vega, Eida, tr. from ENG. (p. 1726)
—Threat to the Leatherback Turtle. (p. 1741)
—Tony Blair. (p. 1766)
—We Visit Pakistan. (p. 1868)
—We Visit Panama. (p. 1868)
—We Visit Peru. (p. 1868)
Hinman, Bonnie, jt. auth. see Asselin, Kristine Carlson.
Hinman, Bonnie & Benchmark Education Co. Staff. Opinions about Presidential Speeches. (p. 1300)
Hinman, Christmas. Christmas/Navidad. de la Vega, Eida, tr. from ENG. (p. 316)
Hinman, John. Reminiscences of a Doctor. (p. 1460)
Hinn, Benny. Buenos Dias, Espiritu Santo (p. 235)
Hinnant, Henry. Showdown at Dry Gulch: Singer's Edition. (p. 1571)
—Showdown at Dry Gulch: Leader Accompanist Edition. (p. 1571)
—Showdown at Dry Gulch: Value Pak: Leader'S/Accompanist Editions, Singer's Edition & Listening Cassette. (p. 1571)
Hinnant, Skip, jt. auth. see Morgan, Michaela.
Hino, Hideshi. Bug Boy: Hino Horror: A Graphic Novel. No. 2 Hino, Hideshi, illus. (p. 236)
Hino, Matsuri. Captive Hearts. Hino, Matsuri, illus. (p. 264)
—MeruPuri. Hino, Matsuri, illus. (p. 1129)
—Vampire Knight Hino, Matsuri, illus. (p. 1832)
—Vampire Knight. Bates, Megan, ed. (p. 1832)
—Vampire Knight. Hino, Matsuri, illus. (p. 1832)
Hino, Matsuri & Kimura, Tomo. Vampire Knight. Hino, Matsuri, illus. (p. 1832)
Hinojosa, Francisco. Ana, Verdad? Gedovius, Juan, illus. (p. 66)
—Aníbal y Melquiades. (p. 76)
—Peor Señora del Mundo. (p. 1340)
—Yanka, Yanka. Hinojosa, Francisco, illus. (p. 1968)
Hinrichs, Alexandra S. D. Therese Makes a Tapestry. Graef, Renee, illus. (p. 1731)
Hinrichs, Tambra. Ryley's World (p. 1499)
Hinrichsen, Natalie, illus. see Magona, Sindiwe.
Hinrichsen, Natalie, illus. see Walton, Ann.
Hinrichsen, Tamsin, illus. see Walton, Ann.
Hinsberger, Paul. Beyond the Shadows. (p. 174)
Hinson, E. Glenn. Feeding on the Word: Participant's Book. (p. 580)
Hinson, Paw Paw. Country Days: Duck Pond. (p. 372)
Hinton, Amber. Mister Ego & the Bubble of Love. Zintoll, Gabreyhl, illus. (p. 1155)
Hinton, Cheryl. Kayla's Magic Eyes. Ellis, Althia Melody, ed. (p. 946)
Hinton, John. Ancient China. (p. 68)
—Hot or Cold? Describe & Compare Measurable Attributes. (p. 802)
Hinton, Kaa Vonia. Jacqueline Woodson. (p. 905)
Hinton, KaaVonia. Brown V. Board of Education, Topeka, KS, 1954. (p. 232)
—Desegregating America's Schools. (p. 428)
—Martin Luther King, Jr. (p. 1097)
—Story of the Underground Railroad. (p. 1662)
—To Preserve the Union: Causes & Effects of the Missouri Compromise (p. 1759)
Hinton, Kerry. Career As an Operating & Stationary Engineer. (p. 266)
—Cool Careers Without College for Music Lovers. (p. 362)
—Cool Careers Without College for People Who Love Food. (p. 363)
—Pythons. (p. 1422)
—Terrorist Attack: A Practical Survival Guide. (p. 1722)
—Terrorist Attacks: A Practical Survival Guide. (p. 1722)
—Trial of Sacco & Vanzetti: A Primary Source Account. (p. 1785)
Hinton, Maureen. William's Troublesome Tongue. (p. 1934)
Hinton, Nigel. 2 Die 4. (p. 1991)
—Collision Course. (p. 341)
—Walk the Wild Road. (p. 1854)
Hinton, Paul Richard. Rammy (p. 1438)
Hinton, S. E. Esto Ya Es Otra Historia. (p. 538)
—Outsiders. (p. 1313)
—Rebeldes. (p. 1451)
—Rumble Fish. (p. 1495)
—Some of Tim's Stories. (p. 1609)
—Taming the Star Runner. (p. 1704)
—Tex. (p. 1723)
Hinton, S. E., jt. auth. see Romer, Marcus.
Hinton, S. E. & Ashe, Jade. Batman & Friends. (p. 144)
Hinton, S. E. & Hinton, Susan E. Ley de la Calle. Lacruz, Javier, tr. (p. 1004)
Hinton, Sophie. Peekaboo! Sea. Hinton, Sophie, illus. (p. 1335)
—Peekaboo! Snow. Hinton, Sophie, illus. (p. 1335)
Hinton, Steph. Let's Learn First Words with Stickers. (p. 998)
Hinton, Stephanie. Busy Book for Boys: 550 Things to Find. (p. 246)
Hinton, Stephanie, illus. see Hopgood, Sally.
Hinton, Susan E., jt. auth. see Hinton, S. E.
Hinton, Susan E. & E Hinton, Susan. Ley de la Calle. (p. 1004)
Hintz, Allison, jt. auth. see Kazemi, Elham.
Hintz, Amy, illus. see Bigler, Ashley Hansen.
Hintz, Martin. Bahamas. (p. 132)
—Croatia. (p. 384)
—Israel. (p. 893)
—Monaco. (p. 1163)
—Netherlands. (p. 1242)
—New York Colony. (p. 1248)
—Pennsylvania Colony. (p. 1338)
Hintze, Amy. I'm So Glad When Daddy Comes Home. (p. 860)
Hinwood, Christine. Returning. (p. 1465)
Hipp, Andrew. Árbol del Olivo: Por Dentro y Por fuera. (p. 94)
—Assassin Bugs. (p. 107)
—Corn: Inside & Out. (p. 367)
—Corn. (p. 367)
—Dung Beetles. (p. 490)
—Gardening Ants. (p. 656)
—Girasol: Por dentro y por fuera (Sunflower:Inside & Out) (p. 678)
—Girasol: Por Dentro y Por Fuera. Brusca, Maria Cristina, tr. (p. 678)
—Leafhoppers. (p. 982)
—Life Cycle of a Duck. (p. 1009)
—Life Cycle of a Mouse. (p. 1009)
—Life Cycle of a Painted Turtle. (p. 1009)
—Life Cycle of a Praying Mantis. (p. 1009)
—Life Cycle of an Earthworm. (p. 1009)
—Maiz: Por dentro y por fuera (Corn: Inside & Out) (p. 1078)
—Maiz: Por Dentro y Por Fuera. González, Thomas, tr. (p. 1078)
—Oak. (p. 1274)
—Oak Trees: Inside & Out. (p. 1274)
—Olive Tree. (p. 1285)
—Olive Trees: Inside & Out. (p. 1285)
—Orchid Mantises. (p. 1302)
—Peanut-Head Bugs. (p. 1332)
—Really Wild Life of Insects (p. 1450)
—Roble: Por dentro y por fuera (Oak Tree: Inside & Out) (p. 1480)
—Roble: Por Dentro y Por Fuera. Gonzalez, Tomas, tr. from ENG. (p. 1480)
—Sunflower. (p. 1676)
—Sunflowers: Inside & Out. (p. 1676)
Hipp, Diane. Stuart the Donkey: A Tale of His Tail. Hill, T. J., illus. (p. 1668)
Hipp, Earl. Disfrutas Tu Vida? Aprende a Manejar las Tensiones y Preocupaciones para Ser Feliz. (p. 450)
—Fighting Invisible Tigers: Stress Management for Teens. (p. 585)
Hipp, Helen C. Different Kind of Safari. Diaco, Paula Tedford, ed. (p. 438)
Hipp, Ryan, illus. see Kammeraad, Kevin & Kammeraad, Stephanie.
Hippely, Hilary Horder. Song for Lena. Baker, Leslie, illus. (p. 1611)
Hippie Bob. God's Cook Book What a Creation! A Hippie Bob Tale. (p. 691)
—Jesus Believes in Santa Claus: A Christmas Dream... (p. 915)
—Robbie & the Magic Mirror: Who Do You See? (p. 1478)
—Tab-Boo & the Witches of Candy Land. (p. 1694)
Hippler, Arthur M. Citizens of the Heavenly City: A Catechism of Catholic Social Teaching. (p. 323)
Hippocrene Books Staff. Children's Illustrated Czech Dictionary: English-Czech/Czech-English. (p. 303)
—Children's Illustrated German Dictionary: English-German, German-English. (p. 303)
—Hippocrene Hindi Children's Picture Dictionary. Martin, Robert Stanly, ed. (p. 781)
Hippocrene Books Staff, creator. Children's Picture Dictionary. (p. 304)
—Hippocrene Polish Children's Dictionary: English-Polish/Polish-English. (p. 781)
Hippocrene Books Staff, ed. Bengali Children's Picture Dictionary: English-Bengali/Bengali-English. (p. 164)
—Children's Illustrated Korean Dictionary: English-Korean/Korean-English. (p. 303)
—Chinese Children's Picture Dictionary: English-Chinese/Chinese-English. (p. 307)
—Hebrew Children's Picture Dictionary: English-Hebrew/Hebrew-English. (p. 761)
—Norwegian Children's Picture Dictionary: English-Norwegian/Norwegian-English. (p. 1266)
Hipps, Amelia. Islam, Christianity, Judaism. (p. 891)
Hipscher, Jerome. White Slavery. (p. 1913)
Hira, Susan. Werwolf on Eagle's Nest Mountain: A Snowboarding Adventure Turned Deadly When Kids Discover Plundered World War II Nazi Treasure Hidden in a Secret Mountain Lair. (p. 1875)
Hirabayashi, Suzanne. Open & Loving Heart: Gentle Words of Self-Endearment. Van Hoorn, Aurea, illus. (p. 1299)
Hirahara, Naomi. 1001 Cranes. (p. 2002)
Hirakawa, Diane M. Math 101 for Busy Families: K-6 Monthly Activities. (p. 1105)
Hiranandani, Veera. Cooking Club Chaos! #4. Dreidemy, Joëlle, illus. (p. 361)
—Lunch Will Never Be the Same! Dreidemy, Joelle, illus. (p. 1065)
—Lunch Will Never Be the Same! Dreidemy, Joëlle, illus. (p. 1065)
—Olivia & Her Ducklings. (p. 1286)
—Olivia & Her Ducklings. Johnson, Shane L., illus. (p. 1286)
—Passport to Pastries #3. Dreidemy, Joëlle, illus. (p. 1327)
—Phoebe G. Green Farm Fresh Fun. Dreidemy, Joelle, illus. (p. 1351)
—Phoebe G. Green - Farm Fresh Fun Dreidemy, Joëlle, illus. (p. 1351)
—Whole Story of Half a Girl. (p. 1920)
Hirano, Cathy, jt. auth. see Uehashi, Nahoko.
Hirano, Cathy, tr. see Uehashi, Nahoko.
Hirano, Cathy, tr. see Yumoto, Kazumi.
Hirano, Kohta. Hellsing (p. 765)
—Hellsing Johnson, Duane, tr. from JPN. (p. 765)
Hirao, Amiko, illus. see Norworth, Jack & Simon, Carly.
Hirao, Amiko, illus. see Sunami, Kitoba & Sunami, Christopher.
Hirashima, Jean, illus. see Ferrier, Charlotte.
Hirashima, Jean, illus. see Sanrio Company, Ltd Staff.
Hirashima, Jean, illus. see Sanrio Company, LTD.
Hirashima, Jean, jt. auth. see Sanrio Company, Ltd Staff.
Hirashima, Jean & Sanrio Company, Ltd Staff. Hello Kitty, Hello Spring! (p. 764)
Hires, Josh, illus. see Gilmore, Dorina Lazo.
Hires, Josh, photos by see Lazo, Dorina.
Hiriart, Sherry. It Came Out of Nowhere: The Woody Chronicles. (p. 893)
Hiriart, Sherry, ed. see Zwaniga, Jennifer.
Hiris, Monica. Just Like Dad. Drzewiecki, Paul, illus. (p. 939)
—Just Like Mom. Sierra, Holly, illus. (p. 939)
—Sleepy Polar Bear. Harston, Jerry, illus. (p. 1590)
Hiro, Mashima. Rave Master (p. 1441)
Hiro, Mashima, jt. auth. see Mashima, Hiro.
Hiroe, Ikoi, tr. see Ikumi, Mia & Yoshida, Reiko.
Hiroe, Ikoi, tr. see Judal.
Hiroe, Ikoi, tr. see Taniguchi, Tomoko.
Hiroe, Ikoi, tr. see Yoshida, Reiko.
Hiroe, Ikoi, tr. Comic Party: Another Round (p. 348)
Hiron. Rhombo Continuo. (p. 1468)
Hironaka, Heisuke & Sugiyama, Yoshishige, eds. Tokyo Shoseki's Mathematics 4 for Elementary School (Grade 4A & 4B, 2 vol. Set) (p. 1762)
—Tokyo Shoseki's Mathematics 5 for Elementary School (Grades 5A & 5B, 2 vol. Set) (p. 1762)
Hirose, George, photos by see Lewis, Richard.
Hirose, George, photos by. I Catch My Moment: Art & Writing by Children on the Life of Play. (p. 837)
Hirota, Denise. Circus Poster. (p. 322)
—Little Zippy Duffelbag Goes to France. (p. 1038)
Hirsch, Ancilla. Holy Mass Col & Act Bk. (p. 791)
Hirsch, Bette & Thompson, Chantal. Moments Littéraires: An Anthology for Intermediate French. (p. 1162)
Hirsch, Charmaine, illus. see Magers, Ramona Hirsch.
Hirsch, Davida, jt. auth. see Nelson, Esther.
Hirsch, E. D., Jr., ed. Age of Exploration (p. 29)
—American Revolution (p. 63)
—Americans Move West. (p. 64)
—Ancient China. (p. 68)
—Ancient Egypt. (p. 68)
—Ancient Greece. (p. 69)
—Ancient India. (p. 69)
—Ancient Rome: Level 3. (p. 70)
—Civil Rights Leaders. (p. 324)
—Civil War (p. 325)
—Early Explorers & Settlers. (p. 493)
—Europe in the Middle Ages (p. 540)
—From Colonies to Independence. (p. 642)
—Geography of the Americas. (p. 662)
—Geography of the United States (p. 662)
—History & Geography: Level 4. (p. 783)
—History & Geography: Level 5. (p. 783)

—Immigration (p. 861)
—Independence for Latin America (p. 870)
—Industrialization & Urbanization in America (p. 873)
—Making the Constitution. (p. 1082)
—Native Americans: Cultures & Conflicts (p. 1234)
—Renaissance (p. 1460)
—United States Constitution (p. 1819)
—Westward Expansion after the Civil War (p. 1876)
—Westward Expansion Before the Civil War (p. 1876)
Hirsch, E. D., Jr., et al. New First Dictionary of Cultural Literacy: What Your Child Needs to Know. (p. 1244)
Hirsch, Edward & Darhansoff, Liz. Demon & the Angel: Searching for the Source of Artistic Inspiration. (p. 426)
Hirsch, Esther. Counting on Friends. (p. 371)
Hirsch, James. Great White Shark. (p. 719)
Hirsch, Jeff. Breakaway. (p. 224)
—Darkest Path. (p. 408)
—Eleventh Plague. (p. 512)
—Magisterium. (p. 1075)
Hirsch, Jennifer. Bitty Twins on the Go. Lohmann, Renate, illus. (p. 194)
—Minute Mysteries: Brainteasers, Puzzlers, & Stories to Solve. (p. 1148)
Hirsch, Jennifer, ed. see Greene, Jacqueline.
Hirsch, Jennifer, ed. see Kurtz, Jane.
Hirsch, Jennifer, ed. see Reiss, Kathryn.
Hirsch, Jennifer & Jones, Michelle. Kit's Cooking Studio. Witkowski, Teri, ed. (p. 962)
Hirsch, Jennifer & Sisson, Stéphanie Roth. Bitty Twins' Bedtime Story. (p. 194)
—Bitty Twins' Halloween. (p. 194)
Hirsch, Judd, reader. Fireboat: The Heroic Adventures of the John J. Harvey. (p. 591)
Hirsch, Kerry, illus. see Silk, Max V.
Hirsch, Mary. April Fool's Fun. (p. 93)
Hirsch, Odo. Darius Bell & the Glitter Pool. (p. 407)
Hirsch, Rebecca. Arctic Tern Migration. (p. 96)
—Buffalo Migration. (p. 235)
—Caribou Migration. (p. 269)
—Crystals. (p. 387)
—Dall Sheep Migration. (p. 401)
—Green Sea Turtle Migration. (p. 722)
—Life Cycles of Plants. (p. 1010)
—Monarch Butterfly Migration. (p. 1163)
—New Zealand. (p. 1249)
—Platypuses: Web-Footed Billed Mammals. (p. 1370)
—Rock Cycle. (p. 1482)
—Save the Planet: Growing Your Own Garden. (p. 1516)
—Save the Planet: Helping Endangered Animals. (p. 1516)
—Save the Planet: Protecting Our Natural Resources. (p. 1516)
—Science Lab: Motion & Forces. (p. 1526)
—Science Lab: Properties of Matter. (p. 1526)
—Science Lab: The Life Cycles of Plants. (p. 1526)
—Sedimentary Rocks. (p. 1546)
—Soil. (p. 1606)
Hirsch, Rebecca E. Africa. (p. 26)
—African Elephants: Massive Tusked Mammals. (p. 27)
—American Alligators: Armored Roaring Reptiles. (p. 59)
—Australia. (p. 116)
—Boa Constrictors: Prey-Crushing Reptiles. (p. 205)
—Europe. (p. 540)
—Galápagos Tortoises: Long-Lived Giant Reptiles. (p. 653)
—Gray Wolves: Howling Pack Mammals. (p. 713)
—Grizzly Bears: Huge Hibernating Mammals. (p. 724)
—How the Executive Branch Works. (p. 813)
—Humpback Whales: Musical Migrating Mammals. (p. 827)
—Hydrogen & Fuel Cells. (p. 831)
—King Cobras: Hooded Venomous Reptiles. (p. 958)
—Komodo Dragons: Deadly Hunting Reptiles. (p. 966)
—Leatherback Sea Turtles: Ancient Swimming Reptiles. (p. 986)
—Microbiomes. (p. 1136)
—Mountain Gorillas: Powerful Forest Mammals. (p. 1180)
—North America. (p. 1264)
—Panther Chameleons: Color-Changing Reptiles. (p. 1321)
—Platypuses: Web-Footed Billed Mammals. (p. 1370)
—Ruby-Throated Hummingbirds: Tiny Hovering Birds. (p. 1493)
—Siberian Tigers: Camouflaged Hunting Mammals. (p. 1572)
—Snowy Owls. (p. 1601)
—South America. (p. 1616)
—Top 50 Reasons to Care about Polar Bears: Animals in Peril. (p. 1769)
—Tuataras: Dinosaur-Era Reptiles. (p. 1795)
—Vampire Bats: Nighttime Flying Mammals. (p. 1831)
—What's Great about Arizona? (p. 1897)
—What's Great about Washington, DC? (p. 1897)
Hirsch, Rebecca E. & Cottle, John. Antarctica. (p. 88)
Hirsch, Rebecca E. & Cybriwsky, Roman A. Asia. (p. 106)
Hirschfeld, Leila & Hirschfeld, Tom. You Decide, Ben Franklin! Weber, Lisa K., illus. (p. 1975)
Hirschfeld, Robert. Martians Are People, Too. (p. 1097)
Hirschfeld, Tom, jt. auth. see Hirschfeld, Leila.
Hirschfelder, Arlene, ed. see Paquette, Penny Hutchins & Tuttle, Cheryl Gerson.
Hirschfelder, Arlene, jt. auth. see Ajmera, Maya.
Hirschfelder, Arlene, jt. auth. see Dennis, Yvonne Wakim.
Hirschfield, Beth. What's Eating You, Girls 'n Boysenberries? Veno, Joe, illus. (p. 1897)
Hirschfield, Lisa. A. E. Housman. (p. 1)
Hirschi, Ron. Ocean Seasons Carlson, Kirsten, illus. (p. 1276)
—Searching for Grizzlies. Cooper, Deborah, illus. (p. 1537)
—Searching for Grizzlies. Mangelsen, Thomas D. & Cooper, Deborah, illus. (p. 1537)
—Swimming with Humuhumu: A Young Snorkeler's First Guide to Hawaiian Sea Life. Yee, Tammy, illus. (p. 1691)
—When Morning Comes. Mangelsen, Thomas, photos by. (p. 1903)
—When Night Comes. Mangelsen, Thomas, photos by. (p. 1904)
—Winter Is for Whales: A Book of Hawaiian Seasons. Green, Yuko, illus. (p. 1938)
Hirschmann, Kris. Are You Related to a Rock Star? A Guide to Unlocking Your Secret Family History. (p. 97)
—Blast Off. (p. 198)
—Burt Rutan: Aircraft Designer. (p. 244)
—Coral. (p. 366)
—Demons. (p. 426)
—Ebola Virus. (p. 501)
hirschmann, kris. Frankenstein. (p. 629)
Hirschmann, Kris. Going Green. (p. 692)
—HDTV: High Definition Television. (p. 756)
—Hello, Bunny! Hutto, Victoria, illus. (p. 763)
—Is a Paw a Foot? All about Measurement. (p. 889)
—Jonathan Ive: Designer of the IPod. (p. 925)
—Kuwaiti Oil Fires. (p. 968)
—LEGO Toys. (p. 990)
—Lobsters. (p. 1044)
—Montana: The Treasure State. (p. 1170)
—Owls, Bats, Wolves & Other Nocturnal Animals. (p. 1315)
—Reflections of Me: Girls & Body Image (p. 1456)
—Rocks & Minerals. (p. 1483)
—Sea Turtles. (p. 1535)
—Serious Case of the Sillies. Jennings, C. S., illus. (p. 1552)
—South Dakota: The Mount Rushmore State. (p. 1617)
—South Dakota. (p. 1617)
—Space & the Planets. Bollinger, Peter, illus. (p. 1618)
—Tickety Toc: Triple Trouble Time. (p. 1747)
—Triple Trouble Time. (p. 1787)
—Utah. (p. 1829)
—Vampires in Literature. (p. 1832)
—Walrus. (p. 1855)
hirschmann, kris. Werewolf. (p. 1875)
Hirschmann, Kris. Your Sexuality. (p. 1981)
Hirschmann, Kris, jt. auth. see Woog, Adam.
Hirschmann, Kris & Herndon, Ryan. Test Your Smarts! (p. 1723)
—Test Your Smarts! Science. (p. 1723)
Hirschmann, Kris & Herndon, Ryan, compiled by. Guinness World Records: Records of Overwhelming Size. (p. 731)
—Guinness World Records. (p. 731)
—Guinness World Records, up Close. (p. 731)
Hirschmann, Kris & Langdo, Bryan. We're Going on a Ghost Hunt. (p. 1875)
Hirschmann, Kristine. Geography of South America: Set Of 6. (p. 662)
—Geography of South America: Text Pairs. (p. 662)
Hirsh, Alice, illus. see Ruchlis, Hyman.
Hirsh, Marilyn, illus. see Adler, David A.
Hirsh, Mia & Benchmark Education Co., LLC Staff. Cat in a Cap. (p. 278)
—Val Is a Vet. (p. 1830)
Hirsheimer, Christopher, photos by see Johnson, Margaret M.
Hirsheimer, Christopher & Knickerbocker, Peggy. San Francisco Ferry Plaza Farmers' Market Cookbook: A Comprehensive Guide to Impeccable Produce Plus 130 Seasonal Recipes. Hirsheimer, Christopher, photos by. (p. 1510)
Hirshmann, Kris. Impressionism. (p. 862)
Hirsinger, Julien, jt. auth. see Surget, Alain.
Hirst, Alexandra. RSPCA Bumper Book of Pets & Other Animals. (p. 1493)
Hirst, Carla, jt. auth. see Johnson, Julia.
Hirst, Damien, illus. see Fryer, Paul.
Hirst, Mike. Freedom of Belief. (p. 634)
His Feast Publishing. Pursuing His Presence: A Place in Him. (p. 1419)
Hische, Jessica, illus. see Nesbit, E.
Hiscock, Bruce. Big Caribou Herd: Life in the Arctic National Wildlife Refuge. Hiscock, Bruce, illus. (p. 180)
—Big Storm. (p. 184)
—Big Tree. Hiscock, Bruce, illus. (p. 184)
—Coyote & Badger: Desert Hunters of the Southwest. (p. 374)
—Ookpik: The Travels of a Snowy Owl. (p. 1298)
Hiscock, Bruce, illus. see Swinburne, Stephen R.
Hiscock, Bruce, jt. auth. see Swinburne, Stephen R.
Hiscocks, Dan, ed. see Bristow, Sophie.
Hiscocks, Dan, ed. see Burden, Peter.
Hiscox, Don. Sled. (p. 1588)
Hiskey, Iris. Hannah & the Hippo's No Mud Day. (p. 742)
Hiss, Jill. Peppeto's Magic Jelly Bean. (p. 1340)
Hissey, Jane. Cuellolargo. (p. 389)
—Old Bear. (p. 1283)
Hissom, Jennie. Wheels on the Move: Driving with Andy. Catusanu, Mircea, illus. (p. 1901)
Historical Pages Company, compiled by. Historical Pages First Edition: Story of Vermont. (p. 783)
—Roxies: The story the fries the fifty Years. (p. 1492)
History Channel, History & Steinberg, Don. Ancient Aliens. (p. 67)
—Young Investigator's Guide to Ancient Aliens. (p. 1979)
Hit Entertainment. Lost at Sea! Stubbs, Tommy, illus. (p. 1055)
—Mike & the Invisible Monster. (p. 1141)
—Mike & the Mighty Shield. (p. 1141)
HIT Entertainment, H. I. T. Evie the Knight. (p. 546)
—Fireless Dragon. (p. 592)
—Mike & the Invisible Monster. (p. 1141)
—Mike's Daring Book of Doodles. (p. 1141)
HIT Entertainment Staff. Adventures in Glendragon. (p. 15)
—Amazing Egg. (p. 54)
—Great Mom Rescue. (p. 717)
—Journey to Dragon Mountain. (p. 928)
—Meet Mike! (p. 1121)
—Mike & Friends Mini Library. (p. 1141)
—Mike & the Mighty Shield. (p. 1141)
—Mike the Knight & Sir Trollee. (p. 1141)
—Quest for the King's Crown. (p. 1426)
—Tricky Trail. (p. 1786)
—Welcome to Mike's World. (p. 1873)
HIT Entertainment Staff, illus. see Evans, Cordelia.
HIT Entertainment Staff, illus. see Gallo, Tina.
Hit Entertainment Staff, illus. see Golden Books Staff.
HIT Entertainment Staff, illus. see Pendergrass, Daphne.
HIT Entertainment Staff, illus. see Reader's Digest Staff.
Hitch, Brian. Ultimates - Super-Human. (p. 1810)
Hitch, Bryan. Gods & Monsters (p. 690)
—Homeland Security Vol. 2. (p. 793)
Hitch, David, illus. see Winter, Ariel S.
Hitchcock, Alfred. Misterio de la Arana de Plata. (p. 1155)
—Misterio de la Calavera Parlante. (p. 1155)
—Misterio de la Cueva de los Lamentos. (p. 1155)
—Misterio de la Montana del Monstruo. (p. 1155)
—Misterio de la Serpiente Susurrante. (p. 1155)
—Misterio de Leon Mervioso. (p. 1155)
—Misterio del Dragon. (p. 1155)
—Misterio del Gato de Trapo. (p. 1155)
—Misterio del Lago Fantasma. (p. 1155)
—Misterio del Testamento Sorprendiente. (p. 1155)
Hitchcock, Jan Hoag. Rosie's Flight. (p. 1490)
Hitchcock, Jane Stanton. One Dangerous Lady. (p. 1294)
Hitchcock, S. C. & Flynn, Tom. Disbelief 101: A Young Person's Guide to Atheism. White, Leslie, illus. (p. 447)
Hitchcock, Susan Tyler. Karen Horney: Pioneer of Feminine Psychology. (p. 943)
—Rita Levi-Montalcini. (p. 1475)
—Roe V. Wade: Protecting a Woman's Right to Choose. (p. 1484)
Hitchens, Christopher. Thomas Jefferson: Author of America. (p. 1739)
Hitchins, Pat. Rosie's Walk. (p. 1490)
Hite, Kenneth. Where the Deep Ones Are. (p. 1909)
Hites, Kati. Winnie & Waldorf. Hites, Kati, illus. (p. 1937)
Hiti, Sam, illus. see Doeden, Matt.
Hiti, Samuel. Waga's Big Scare. Hiti, Samuel, illus. (p. 1852)
Hiti, Samuel, illus. see Doeden, Matt.
Hiti, Samuel, illus. see Levine, Michelle.
Hiti, Samuel, illus. see Midthun, Joseph.
Hiti, Samuel, illus. see Sonneborn, Liz.
Hiti, Samuel, jt. auth. see Midthun, Joseph.
Hiti, Samuel, creator. End Times - Tiempos Finales: English / Spanish. Vol. 1 (p. 526)
Hitschler, Cynthia. Gleb... the Terrible! (p. 682)
—Perils of Pink Cat. (p. 1343)
—World of Jacky Blue & Other Cats. (p. 1957)
Hitz, Dustin, illus. see Rex, Judith.
Hitzges, Norm. Princess Bible St. Angelo, Ron, photos by. (p. 1403)
Hiwatari, Saki. Please Save My Earth (p. 1373)
—Please Save My Earth Hiwatari, Saki, illus. (p. 1373)
—Please Save My Earth. Hiwatari, Saki, illus. (p. 1373)
Hix, H. L. Legible Heavens. (p. 990)
Hix, Jax, jt. auth. see Porras, Nikki Jo.
Hix, John. Glasshouse. (p. 682)
Hix, Melvin. Magic Speech Flower: Or Little Luke & His Animal Friends. (p. 1073)
Hix, Zack. Bully Bad. (p. 241)
Hixon, Mara Uman. Turtle's Way: Loggy, Greeny & Leather. Harris, Steve J., illus. (p. 1799)
Hixson, Bryce. Anatomy Academy. Hixson, Bryce, illus. (p. 67)
—Digits, Midgets, & Degrees Kelvin. Hixson, Bryce, illus. (p. 440)
—Galactic Cookie Dough. Hixson, Bryce, illus. (p. 652)
—Get Your Poop in a Group. Hixson, Bryce, illus. (p. 668)
—Great Graphs in Ten Days. Hixson, Bryce, illus. (p. 716)
—Newton Take 3. Hixson, Bryce, illus. (p. 1249)
—Original World Wide Web. Hixson, Bryce, illus. (p. 1304)
—Plant Stigmas & Other Botanical Concerns. Hixson, Bryce, illus. (p. 1369)
—What's Up? Hixson, Bryce, illus. (p. 1900)
Hixson, Bryce, illus. see DeWitt, Lockwood.
Hizer, David V., jt. auth. see Rosenberg, Arthur D.
Hjertaas, Trevor. Elephant, Elephant (p. 511)
HL Studios, H. L., illus. see Spilsbury, Louise & Spilsbury, Richard.
HL Studios Staff, illus. see Barber, Nicola.
HL Studios Staff, illus. see Burgan, Michael.
HL Studios Staff, illus. see Claybourne, Anna.
HL Studios Staff, illus. see Hunter, Nick.
HL Studios Staff, illus. see Shuckburgh, Emily & Chambers, Catherine.
HL Studios Staff, illus. see Spilsbury, Louise & Spilsbury, Richard.
HL Studios Staff, illus. see Spilsbury, Richard.
HL Studios Staff, illus. see Tuffen, Hugh & Waldron, Melanie.
Hlad, Carole. Daisy's Dance Party: (from the Amanda's Cats Series) (p. 401)
Hladik, Terry L. Timid Timmy the Brave. Bouthyette, Valerie, illus. (p. 1754)
Hlinka, Michael, jt. auth. see Sylvester, Kevin.
Hliva, Diana. My Pet Lunecat. (p. 1217)
Hlobil, Karel. Forest Friends & the Three-Headed Dragon. (p. 618)
Hnatiuk, Charlie, illus. see Ouellet, Debbie.
Hnatov, Catherine. Hip, Hop (p. 780)
—Hip, Hop (Arabic/English) (p. 780)
—Hip, Hop (Hmong/English) (p. 780)
—Hip, Hop (Portuguese/English) Icibaci, Neusa, tr. from ENG. (p. 780)
—Hip, Hop (Spanish/English) Del Risco, Eida, tr. (p. 780)
—Yum, Yum (p. 1983)
—Yum, Yum (Spanish/English) (p. 1983)
Hnatov, Catherine, illus. see Whiteside, Andy.
Ho, Betty Yulin. How to Live a Long Life. (p. 820)
Ho, David, illus. see Catanese, P. W.
Ho, Jane. ABC Alphabet Book (p. 3)
Ho, Jannie. Great Matzoh Hunt. Ho, Jannie, illus. (p. 717)
—Guess Who? Ho, Jannie, illus. (p. 729)
—Light the Menorah. (p. 1015)
—Muddle Zoo. (p. 1188)
Ho, Jannie, illus. see Capstone Press Staff, et al.
Ho, Jannie, illus. see Crow, Nosy.
Ho, Jannie, illus. see Dahl, Michael.
Ho, Jannie, illus. see Dinardo, Jeff.
Ho, Jannie, illus. see Meister, Cari.
Ho, Jannie, illus. see Metzger, Steve.
Ho, Jannie, illus. see Nosy Crow.
Ho, Jannie, illus. see Teitelbaum, Michael.
Ho, Jannie, illus. see Trumbauer, Lisa.
Ho, Jannie, jt. auth. see Bruning, Matt.
Ho, Jannie, jt. auth. see Cerato, Mattia.
Ho, Jannie, jt. auth. see Sexton, Brenda.
Ho, Jannie, et al. Easy to Draw Animals Ho, Jannie & Sexton, Brenda, illus. (p. 500)
Ho, Jason, illus. see Shelley, Mary.
Ho, Louise, illus. see Freeman, Claire.
Ho, Louise, illus. see Steven, Kenneth.
Ho, Minfong. Hush! A Thai Lullaby. (p. 830)
Ho, Mingfong. Hush! A Thai Lullaby. Meade, Holly, illus. (p. 830)
Ho, Nicola C. Farting Bunny. (p. 575)
Ho, Oliver. Ultimate Book of Family Card Games. (p. 1809)
Ho, Winnie, illus. see Glass, Calliope & Disney Book Group Staff.
Hoadley, Jo. Miss Creant: The Adventures of a little Red Hen. (p. 1151)
Hoagland, Victor. Illustrated Rosary for Children. (p. 858)
Hoak, Benjamin T. Jacob. (p. 904)
—Joseph. (p. 926)
Hoang, Melanie Rowland. Gift. (p. 674)
Hoar, Gail, illus. see Schoen, Robin.
Hoard, Angela, illus. see Coburn, Claudia.
Hoard, Carolyn, jt. auth. see Bonnice, Sherry.
Hoard, Julia. God, What Is the Gift of Tongues? (p. 690)
Hoare, Ben. Cat. (p. 277)
—Endangered Animals. (p. 526)
—Eyewitness - Endangered Animals. (p. 558)
—Temperate Grasslands (p. 1717)
Hoare, Ben, et al. Incredible Journeys: Amazing Animal Migrations. (p. 869)
Hoare, Jerry, illus. see Burgan, Michael.
Hoare, Jerry, illus. see Demuth, Patricia Brennan.
Hoare, Jerry, illus. see Fabiny, Sarah.
Hoare, Jerry, illus. see Hoobler, Dorothy & Hoobler, Thomas.
Hoare, Jerry, illus. see Labrecque, Ellen.
Hoare, Jerry, illus. see Lowell, Barbara.
Hoare, Jerry, illus. see Rau, Dana Meachen.
Hoare, Pauline M. My Naughty Brother, David: And Other Stories. (p. 1215)
Hoare, Stephen. Computer World. (p. 355)
Hoare, William. Musical Director in Amateur Theatre. (p. 1194)
Hoban, Julia. Willow. (p. 1934)
Hoban, Lillian. Arthur's Honey Bear. (p. 104)
Hoban, Lillian, illus. see Hoban, Russell.
Hoban, Malcolm. Yolanda's Yard Sale: Add & Subtract Within 20. (p. 1972)
—Yolanda's Yard Sale. (p. 1972)
Hoban, Russell. Baby Sister for Frances. Hoban, Lillian, illus. (p. 128)
—Bargain for Frances. Hoban, Lillian, illus. (p. 139)
—Best Friends for Frances. (p. 169)
—Best Friends for Frances. Hoban, Lillian, illus. (p. 169)
—Birthday for Frances. (p. 192)
—Birthday for Frances. Hoban, Lillian, illus. (p. 192)
—Bread & Jam for Frances. Hoban, Lillian, illus. (p. 224)
—How Tom Beat Captain Najork & His Hired Sportsmen. Blake, Quentin, illus. (p. 823)
—Jim's Lion. Deacon, Alexis, illus. (p. 918)
—Little Brute Family. Hoban, Lillian, illus. (p. 1025)
—Little Brute Family. Peck, Lillian Hoban, illus. (p. 1025)
—Near Thing for Captain Najork. Blake, Quentin, illus. (p. 1239)
—Rosie's Magic Horse. Blake, Quentin, illus. (p. 1490)
—Soonchild. Deacon, Alexis, illus. (p. 1613)
—Sorely Trying Day. Hoban, Lillian, illus. (p. 1614)
Hoban, Tana. Black & White. Hoban, Tana, illus. (p. 195)
—I Wonder. (p. 849)
—Over, under & Through. Hoban, Tana, illus. (p. 1314)
Hobar, Linda Lacour. Mystery of History, Volume 1: Creation to the Resurrection. (p. 1224)
Hobbes, Elena. How Do Eggs Hatch? (p. 807)
Hobbie, Holly. Charming Opal. (p. 294)
—Charming Opal. Hobbie, Holly, illus. (p. 294)
—Everything but the Horse. (p. 544)
—Fanny & Annabelle. (p. 571)
—Gem. (p. 659)
—I'll Be Home for Christmas. (p. 856)
—Let It Snow. (p. 994)
—One & Only. (p. 1293)
—Present for Toot. (p. 1396)
—Toot & Puddle. (p. 1767)
—Toot & Puddle. Hobbie, Holly, illus. (p. 1767)
—Top of the World. (p. 1769)
—Wish You Were Here. (p. 1940)
—You Are My Sunshine. (p. 1973)
Hobbie, Jocelyn, illus. see Hobbie, Nathaniel.
Hobbie, K. R., et al. Weird & Wacky Facts. (p. 1872)
Hobbie, Nathaniel. Priscilla & the Great Santa Search. Hobbie, Jocelyn, illus. (p. 1407)
—Priscilla & the Pink Planet. Hobbie, Jocelyn, illus. (p. 1407)
—Priscilla & the Pixie Princess. Hobbie, Jocelyn, illus. (p. 1407)
Hobbs, Anne Stevenson, jt. auth. see Cotsen, Margit Sperling.
Hobbs, Brice Edward. Beth's Woodpecker. (p. 171)
Hobbs, Chris & Perryman, Richard. Largest Number Smaller Than Five. (p. 975)
Hobbs, Constance. Bugsy's Special Event. (p. 237)
—Dreamers. (p. 484)
Hobbs, Craig, jt. auth. see Hobbs, Traci.
Hobbs, Ellen Youngs. Oh ! Hannah. (p. 1280)
Hobbs, Joseph J. Egypt. (p. 506)
Hobbs, Julia Ann, jt. auth. see Fisher, Carla Dawn.
Hobbs, Leigh. Hooray for Horrible Harriet. Hobbs, Leigh, illus. (p. 796)
—Horrible Harriet. Hobbs, Leigh, illus. (p. 798)
—Horrible Harriet's Inheritance. (p. 798)
—Mr Badger & the Big Surprise. (p. 1184)
—Mr Badger & the Magic Mirror. Hobbs, Leigh, illus. (p. 1184)
—Mr Badger & the Missing Ape. (p. 1184)
—Old Tom, Man of Mystery Hobbs, Leigh, illus. (p. 1285)
—Old Tom's Holiday. Hobbs, Leigh, illus. (p. 1285)
Hobbs, Leigh, illus. see Lawrenson, Diana.
Hobbs, Leigh, illus. see May, Ruthie.
Hobbs, Mike. Communications. (p. 349)
—Entertainment. (p. 531)

—Fashion. (p. 575)
—Food & Drink. (p. 613)
—Superbikes (p. 1682)
Hobbs, Olivia. Summer of Violet. (p. 1674)
Hobbs, Pamela. Secret Elf. (p. 1540)
—Where Is Chic. (p. 1908)
Hobbs, Richard R. Naval Science 2: Maritime History, Leadership, & Nautical Sciences for the NJROTC Student. 2 (p. 1237)
—Naval Science 3: Naval Knowledge & Skills for the NJROTC Student. (p. 1237)
Hobbs, Ruth & Miller, Lester, contrib. by. Time to Plant. (p. 1753)
Hobbs, Traci & Hobbs, Craig. God Thank You for My Pockets. (p. 690)
Hobbs, Valerie. Carolina Crow Girl. (p. 270)
—Defiance. (p. 424)
—Maggie & Oliver or a Bone of One's Own. Thermes, Jennifer, illus. (p. 1071)
—Minnie McClary Speaks Her Mind. (p. 1147)
—Sheep. (p. 1564)
—Sweetie McGinnis Solves Them All. (p. 1690)
—Wolf. (p. 1943)
Hobbs, Will. Beardance. (p. 151)
—Beardream. Kastner, Jill, illus. (p. 151)
—Big Wander. (p. 184)
—Changes in Latitudes. (p. 290)
—Crossing the Wire. (p. 385)
—Downriver. (p. 474)
—Go Big or Go Home. (p. 686)
—Jackie's Wild Seattle. (p. 904)
—Kokopelli's Flute. (p. 966)
—Leaving Protection. (p. 986)
—Never Say Die. (p. 1243)
—Take Me to the River. (p. 1696)
Hobbs, Will, jt. auth. see Hobbs, William.
Hobbs, Will & Hobbs, William. Far North. (p. 572)
—Wild Man Island. (p. 1929)
Hobbs, William. Down the Yukon. (p. 474)
—Ghost Canoe. (p. 670)
—Jason's Gold. (p. 910)
—Leaving Protection. (p. 986)
Hobbs, William, jt. auth. see Hobbs, Will.
Hobbs, William & Hobbs, Will. Bearstone. (p. 152)
Hobbs-Wyatt, Debz, ed. Wild N Free. (p. 1929)
—Wild N Free Too. (p. 1929)
Hobby, Blake. Student's Encyclopedia of Great American Writers (p. 1669)
Hobby, Blake, ed. see Bloom, Harold.
Hobby, Blake, jt. auth. see Bloom, Harold.
Hobby, Blake, ed. Bloom's Literary Themes: Rebirth & Renewal. (p. 201)
Hobby, Nathan. Fur. (p. 650)
Hobden, Helen. Be in the Place. (p. 148)
Hoberman, Mary Ann. And to Think That We Thought That We'd Never Be Friends. Hawkes, Kevin, illus. (p. 71)
—Eensy-Weensy Spider. Westcott, Nadine Bernard, illus. (p. 505)
—Forget-Me-Nots: Poems to Learn by Heart. Emberley, Michael, illus. (p. 619)
—House Is a House for Me. Fraser, Betty, illus. (p. 803)
—I Like Old Clothes. Barton, Patrice, illus. (p. 841)
—It's Simple, Said Simon. So, Meilo, illus. (p. 898)
—Llama Who Had No Pajama: 100 Favorite Poems. Fraser, Betty, illus. (p. 1043)
—Miss Mary Mack. Bernard Westcott, Nadine & Westcott, Nadine Bernard, illus. (p. 1151)
—My Song Is Beautiful: Poems & Pictures in Many Voices. (p. 1219)
—Seven Silly Eaters. Frazee, Marla, illus. (p. 1554)
—Strawberry Hill. (p. 1666)
—Very Short Tall Tales to Read Together. Emberley, Michael, illus. (p. 1838)
—You Read to Me, I'll Read to You: Very Short Fairy Tales to Read Together. (p. 1976)
—You Read to Me, I'll Read to You: Very Short Mother Goose Tales to Read Together. (p. 1976)
—You Read to Me, I'll Read to You: Very Short Fables to Read Together. Emberley, Michael, illus. (p. 1976)
—You Read to Me, I'll Read to You: Very Short Stories to Read Together. Emberley, Michael, illus. (p. 1976)
—You Read to Me, I'll Read to You: Very Short Fairy Tales to Read Together. Emberley, Michael, illus. (p. 1976)
—You Read to Me, I'll Read to You: Very Short Scary Tales to Read Together. Emberley, Michael, illus. (p. 1976)
—You Read to Me, I'll Read to You: Very Short Mother Goose Tales to Read Together. Emberley, Michael, illus. (p. 1976)
—You Read to Me, I'll Read to You: Very Short Fables to Read Together. Emberley, Michael, illus. (p. 1976)
—You Read to Me, I'll Read to You - Very Short Mother Goose Tales to Read Together. Emberley, Michael, illus. (p. 1976)
Hoberman, Mary Ann & Emberley, Michael. You Read to Me, I'll Read to You: Very Short Scary Tales to Read Together. No. 2 Emberley, Michael, illus. (p. 1976)
Hobkirk, Lori. James Earl Carter. (p. 907)
—Madam C. J. Walker. (p. 1069)
Hoblin, Paul. Aaron Rodgers: Super Bowl MVP. (p. 2)
—Amazing Basketball Records. (p. 54)
—Amazing Football Records. (p. 54)
—Andrew Luck: Rising NFL Star. (p. 72)
—Biggest Blunders in Sports. (p. 185)
—Boston Strangler. (p. 215)
—Carmelo Anthony: Superstar Scorer. (p. 270)
—Colin Kaepernick: NFL Phenom. (p. 339)
—Derrick Rose: NBA's Youngest MVP. (p. 427)
—Girls Play to Win Swimming & Diving. (p. 680)
—Gladiators. (p. 682)
—Great Hitters of the Negro Leagues. (p. 716)
—Great Pitchers of the Negro Leagues. (p. 717)
—Rock Crawling: Tearing It Up. (p. 1482)
—Superstars of the New York Knicks. (p. 1684)
—Superstars of the San Antonio Spurs. (p. 1684)
Hoblin, Paul & Hueller, Patrick. Archenemy. (p. 95)
—Beast. (p. 152)
—Foul. (p. 624)
—Tractor Pulling: Tearing It Up. (p. 1775)
Hobson, Charles, illus. see Hobson, Mary Daniel & Rauh, Anna Isabel.
Hobson, Joseph. Snake River Adventures: Floating the Snake. (p. 1596)
Hobson, Mark. Raindrop. (p. 1436)
Hobson, Mark, jt. auth. see Pirz, Therese S.
Hobson, Mark, tr. Language Helper German: Helpin you speak more German. (p. 975)
Hobson, Mary Daniel & Rauh, Anna Isabel. Wolf Who Ate the Sky. Hobson, Charles, illus. (p. 1944)
Hobson, Meg. True Story of Sam Who Became a Fish. (p. 1793)
Hobson, Richard, et al. General Studies for AQA B. (p. 660)
Hobson, Ryan, illus. see Honovich, Nancy.
Hobson, Ryan, illus. see Perry, Phyllis.
Hoce, Charley. Beyond Old McDonald: Funny Poems from down on the Farm. Fernandes, Eugenie, illus. (p. 174)
Hoch, Doug, illus. see Derrick Patricia.
Hoch, Jeff. Guess Who Saves the Rain Forest? Hoch, Jeff, ed. (p. 729)
Hoch, Jen, jt. auth. see Gross, Jen.
Hoch, Kevin, illus. see Simpson, Richard.
Hochain, Serge. Building Liberty: A Statue Is Born. (p. 239)
—Building Liberty: A Statue Is Born. Hochain, Serge, illus. (p. 239)
Hochenauer, Mary & Hochenauer-Fox, Lois. Sunny & Wondrous, Cat Cousins. (p. 1677)
Hochenauer-Fox, Lois, jt. auth. see Hochenauer, Mary.
Hochman, David & Kennison, Ruth. Potty Train. Anderson, Derek, illus. (p. 1389)
Hochman, Eleanor, tr. see Dumas, Alexandre.
Hochman, Marisa. Walk in Pirate's Cove. Woodland, Bette, illus. (p. 1853)
Hochstadt, Steve. Sources of the Holocaust. (p. 1616)
Hochstatter, Daniel J. Italian. (p. 894)
—Just Look 'n Learn English Picture Dictionary. (p. 939)
—Just Look 'n Learn Spanish Picture Dictionary. (p. 939)
Hochstatter, Daniel J., contrib. by. Just Look 'n Learn English Picture Dictionary. (p. 939)
Hochstetler, Kathryn, et al, eds. Palgrave Advances in International Environmental Politics. (p. 1320)
Hocing, Justin. Skateboard Design & Construction: How Your Board Gets Built. (p. 1583)
Hock, Dan. Afternoon Auction: An Iggy & Igor Mystery. (p. 29)
—Birthday Bash An Iggy & Igor Mystery (#2) 2 vols. Hock, Dan, illus. (p. 192)
Hock, Peggy. Clean Energy. (p. 330)
—Helping Out. (p. 766)
—Making Less Trash. (p. 1081)
—Saving Energy. (p. 1517)
—Saving Water. (p. 1518)
Hockbridge, Derek, tr. see Uderzo, Albert & Goscinny, René.
Hockenberry, Dee. Collecting Golliwogs: Teddy Bear's Best Friend (p. 339)
Hockensmith, Steve. Holmes on the Range. (p. 789)
Hockensmith, Steve, jt. auth. see Pflugfelder, Bob.
Hocker, Katherine M. Frozen in Motion: Alaska's Glaciers. Brubaker, Jill, ed. (p. 645)
Hockerman, Dennis. Country Mouse & the City Mouse: A Tale of Tolerance. (p. 372)
—Lion & the Mouse: A Tale about Being Helpful. (p. 1020)
—Little Seed: A Tale about Integrity. (p. 1036)
Hockerman, Dennis, illus. see Aesop.
Hockerman, Dennis, illus. see Barbe, Walter B.
Hockerman, Dennis, illus. see Christensen-Hall, Nancy.
Hockerman, Dennis, illus. see Hillert, Margaret.
Hockerman, Dennis, illus. see Williams, Rozanne Lanczak.
Hockerman, Dennis, illus. see Wilsdon, Christina.
Hockerman, Dennis, et al. Folktales from Ecosystems Around the World. (p. 611)
Hockett, M. A. & Hockett, Margaret. Language Mechanic: Tuning up English with Logic. (p. 975)
Hockett, Margaret. Punctuation Puzzler - Commas & More B1. (p. 1417)
—Punctuation Puzzler - Run-ons A1. (p. 1417)
Hockett, Margaret, jt. auth. see Hockett, M. A.
Hockett, Rosemary Lou. Mom's on the Job. (p. 1163)
Hocking, Amanda. Ascend. (p. 105)
—Crystal Kingdom. (p. 387)
—Elegy. (p. 510)
—Frostfire. (p. 645)
—Ice Kissed. (p. 850)
—Lullaby. (p. 1064)
—Switched. (p. 1691)
—Switched. (p. 1692)
—Tidal. (p. 1747)
—Torn. (p. 1770)
—Wake. (p. 1853)
Hocking, Amanda, ed. see Letts, Jason.
Hocking, Deborah, illus. see Markle, Sandra.
Hocking, Geoff, illus. see Marwood, Lorraine.
Hocking, Justin. Dream Builders: The World's Best Skatepark Creators. (p. 483)
—Dream Builders: The World's Best Skate Park Creators. (p. 483)
—Off the Wall: A Skateboarder's Guide to Riding Bowls & Pools. (p. 1279)
—Rippin' Ramps: A Skateboarder's Guide to Riding Halfpipes. (p. 1474)
—Rippin' Ramps: A Skateboarder's Guide to Riding Half-Pipes. (p. 1474)
—Skate Parks. (p. 1583)
—Skateboarder's Guide to Skate Parks, Halp-Pipes, Bowls, & Obstacles (p. 1583)
—Skateboarding Competitions. (p. 1583)
—Skateboarding Design & Construction: How Your Board Gets Built. (p. 1583)
—Skateboarding Half-Pipes, Ramps, & Obstacles. (p. 1583)
—Skateboarding Half-pipes, Ramps, & Obstacles. (p. 1583)
—Taking Action: How to Get Your City to Build a Public Skatepark. (p. 1698)
—Taking Action: How to Get Your City to Build a Public Skate Park. (p. 1698)
—World's Greatest Skate Parks. (p. 1960)
Hockinson, Liz. Marcello: The Movie Mouse. Otoshi, Kathryn, illus. (p. 1091)
—Marie Antoinette "Madame Deficit" Malone, Peter, illus. (p. 1093)
Hocknell, Barbara. Gifts for God. (p. 675)
—Mouse Who Attended the Last Supper: And Other Stories. (p. 1182)
—Robins & the Bell. (p. 1480)
Hockney, Deborah. Jocasta's Gift. (p. 919)
Hockridge, Derek, tr. see Goscinny, René, et al.
Hockridge, Derek, tr. see Uderzo, Albert & Goscinny, René.
Hockridge, Derek, tr. see Uderzo, Albert, et al.
Hocutt, Rose (Webber). Spoon Family. (p. 1631)
Hoda, Rubina, illus. see Sood, Sana Hoda.
Hodakov, Levi. I Go to the Ohel. Rosenfeld, D. L. & Leverton, Yossi, eds. (p. 838)
Hodder, Beth. Ghost of Schafer Meadows. (p. 671)
—Stealing the Wild. (p. 1646)
Hodder Children's Books Staff, jt. auth. see Whiteford, Rhona.
Hodes, Loren. Thirty-One Cakes: A Hashvas Aveida Adventure. Rosenfeld, Devorah Leah, ed. (p. 1735)
—Who Would Have Guessed? It's All for the Best! Hodes, Loren, illus. (p. 1919)
Hodge, A. D. Bubbles & Boundaries. (p. 233)
—Saucy Bossy Princess. (p. 1516)
Hodge, Anthony. Collage. (p. 339)
Hodge, Bill. Cyril: Tales of a Teenage Cyrano. (p. 397)
Hodge, Bonnie. Rocky Mountain Horses (p. 1484)
Hodge, Darlene F. Jubilee Principle: The Long Way Back to Eternity (p. 930)
Hodge, Darren, jt. auth. see Rowe, Eva McKenzie.
Hodge, Deborah. Bees. Mulock, Julian, illus. (p. 157)
—Desert Animals. Stephens, Pat, illus. (p. 428)
—Emma's Story. Zhang, Song Nan, illus. (p. 520)
—Forest Animals. Stephens, Pat, illus. (p. 618)
—Kids Book of Canada's Railway: And How the CPR Was Built. Mantha, John, illus. (p. 952)
—Kids Book of Canadian Immigration. Mantha, John, illus. (p. 952)
—Lily & the Mixed-Up Letters. Brassard, France, illus. (p. 1018)
—Looking at Bears. Stephens, Pat, illus. (p. 1050)
—Looking at Wild Cats. Ogle, Nancy Gray, illus. (p. 1051)
—Polar Animals. Stephens, Pat, illus. (p. 1378)
—Rain Forest Animals. Stephens, Pat, illus. (p. 1434)
—Rescuing the Children: The Story of the Kindertransport. (p. 1462)
—Savanna Animals. Stephens, Pat, illus. (p. 1516)
—Up We Grow! A Year in the Life of a Small, Local Farm. Harris, Brian, photos by. (p. 1824)
—Watch Me Grow! A Down-to-Earth Guide to Growing Food in the City. Harris, Brian, illus. (p. 1861)
—West Coast Wild: A Nature Alphabet Reczuch, Karen, illus. (p. 1876)
—Wetland Animals. Stephens, Pat, illus. (p. 1877)
—Wild Dogs: Wolves, Coyotes & Foxes. Stephens, Pat, illus. (p. 1929)
Hodge, Judith. Plants We Use: Set Of 6. (p. 1370)
—Plants We Use & Las plantas que Usamos: 6 English, 6 Spanish Adaptations. (p. 1370)
—Riches from Earth: Set Of 6. (p. 1470)
—Riches from Earth & Las riquezas de la Tierra: 6 English, 6 Spanish Adaptations. (p. 1470)
Hodge, Marie, jt. auth. see Berne, Emma Carlson.
Hodge, Merle. For the Life of Laetitia. (p. 616)
Hodge, Rosamund. Crimson Bound. (p. 382)
—Cruel Beauty. (p. 386)
Hodge, Russ. Genetics & Evolution (p. 661)
Hodge, Susie. Ancient Egyptian Art (p. 68)
—Ancient Greek Art (p. 69)
—Ancient Roman Art (p. 70)
—Animals. Roberts, Steve, illus. (p. 81)
—Celebrity Snapper: Taking the Ultimate Celebrity Photo (p. 285)
—Dinosaurs. (p. 443)
—Dinosaurs. Roberts, Steve, illus. (p. 443)
—Forbidden City. (p. 616)
—Global Warming. (p. 684)
—How to Draw Animals. Roberts, Steve, illus. (p. 816)
—How to Draw Dinosaurs. Roberts, Steve, illus. (p. 817)
—How to Survive Modern Art. (p. 822)
—Masks. (p. 1102)
—Prehistoric Art. (p. 1395)
—Puppets. (p. 1417)
—Toxic! Killer Cures & Other Poisonings (p. 1774)
—Toxic! [Scholastic]: Killer Cures & Other Poisonings. (p. 1774)
Hodge, Susie, jt. auth. see Mason, Paul.
Hodge, Susie & Mason, Paul. Investigating UFOs & Aliens. (p. 885)
Hodge, Susie & Picasso, P. Pablo Picasso. (p. 1316)
Hodgekiss, Jo. Libro de los Numeros (Book of Numbers) (p. 1006)
Hodges, Annell. Angel's Tattoo. (p. 75)
Hodges, Benjamin, illus. see Wymarra, Elizabeth & Wymarra, Wandihnu.
Hodges, Betty. Jamie & the Haunted Lighthouse. (p. 907)
Hodges, Diane & Warner, Penny. 501 TV-Free Activities for Kids. (p. 2001)
Hodges, Gary, jt. auth. see Chapman, Garry.
Hodges, George. Castle of Zion. (p. 277)
—Garden of Eden: Stories from the Fir. (p. 656)
—Saints & Heroes to the End of the Middle Ages (Yesterday's Classics) (p. 1504)
Hodges, Henry & Engel, Margaret. How to Act Like a Kid: Backstage Secrets of a Young Performer. (p. 814)
Hodges, Jared. Peach Fuzz. (p. 1332)
Hodges, Jared, jt. auth. see Cibos, Lindsay.
Hodges, Jared & Cibos, Lindsay. Peach Fuzz—Scholastic Exclusive. (p. 1332)
Hodges, Jean A. Drinking Dragon Sam Learns Drinking Doesn't Pay. (p. 485)
Hodges, Jim. Electronic Lollipops. (p. 509)
Hodges, Lynn & Buchanan, Sue. I Love You This Much Bendall-Brunello, John, illus. (p. 844)
Hodges, Lynn, et al. I Love You This Much Bendall-Brunello, John, illus. (p. 844)
Hodges, Margaret. Legend of Saint Christopher. Watson, Richard J., illus. (p. 988)
—Legend of Saint Christopher. Watson, Richard Jesse, illus. (p. 988)
—Saint George & the Dragon. (p. 1503)
Hodges, Margaret & Malory, Thomas. Merlin & the Making of the King. Hyman, Trina Schart, tr. (p. 1128)
Hodges, Meredith. Jasper: A Christmas Caper. Shields, Bonnie, illus. (p. 910)
—Jasper: A Fabulous Fourth. Shields, Bonnie, illus. (p. 910)
—Jasper: The Story of a Mule. Shields, Bonnie, illus. (p. 910)
Hodges, Quae, jt. auth. see Johnson, Linda.
Hodges, Rick. What Muslims Think, & How They Live. (p. 1892)
Hodges, Ronald. Buff Bears. (p. 235)
Hodges, Tammy. Breakfast with the Blues. (p. 225)
Hodgin, Duane, compiled by. Best of Character II. (p. 170)
Hodgin, Molly, jt. auth. see Brooks, Riley.
Hodgkins, jt. auth. see Hodgkins, Fran.
Hodgkins, Craig. Friends Church: One-Hundred Years of Following Christ Together. (p. 638)
Hodgkins, Dorothy. Darlington's Margaret. (p. 409)
Hodgkins, Fran. Andre the Famous Harbor Seal. Frenkel, Yetti, illus. (p. 72)
—Champions of the Ocean. Arbo, Cris, illus. (p. 289)
—Half & Half-Earthquake! Hunt, Judith, illus. (p. 736)
—Horses. (p. 800)
—How People Learned to Fly. (p. 812)
—How People Learned to Fly. Kelley, True, illus. (p. 812)
—Idaho. (p. 851)
—If You Were My Baby: A Wildlife Lullaby. Bryant, Laura J., illus. (p. 855)
—Little Loon. Hayes, Karel, illus. (p. 1030)
—Massachusetts. (p. 1102)
—Mexico: A Question & Answer Book (p. 1131)
—Missouri. (p. 1154)
—Secret Galaxy Taylor, Mike, photos by. (p. 1540)
—West Virginia. (p. 1876)
—Who's Been Here? A Tale in Tracks. Hayes, Karel, illus. (p. 1920)
Hodgkins, Fran & Hodgkins. How People Learned to Fly. Kelley, True, illus. (p. 812)
Hodgkinson, Jo. Big Day for Migs. Hodgkinson, Jo, illus. (p. 180)
—Talent Show. Hodgkinson, Jo, illus. (p. 1701)
Hodgkinson, Leigh. Boris & the Snoozebox. Hodgkinson, Leigh, illus. (p. 214)
—Boris & the Wrong Shadow. (p. 214)
—Boris & the Wrong Shadow. Hodgkinson, Leigh, illus. (p. 214)
—Goldilocks & Just One Bear. Hodgkinson, Leigh, illus. (p. 696)
—Limelight Larry. Hodgkinson, Leigh, illus. (p. 1018)
—Smile! Hodgkinson, Leigh, illus. (p. 1593)
—Troll Swap. Hodgkinson, Leigh, illus. (p. 1788)
Hodgkinson, Leigh, illus. see Edwards, Marnie.
Hodgkinson, Leigh, illus. see Hart, Caryl.
Hodgman, Ann. Do Touch! Don't Touch! Barnard, Lucy, illus. (p. 457)
—How to Die of Embarrassment Every Day. Hodgman, Ann, photos by. (p. 816)
—Monsters Dance. Wood, Hannah, illus. (p. 1169)
—That's My Mommy! Logan, Laura, illus. (p. 1727)
—Uh-Oh! Oh No! Barnard, Lucy, illus. (p. 1808)
Hodgman, Joan, jt. auth. see Hoppenbrouwers, Toke.
Hodgson, Christy. Debra's First Day of School. (p. 421)
Hodgson, Jesse. Pongo. (p. 1382)
Hodgson, Joan. Hullo Sun. Ripper, Peter, illus. (p. 825)
—Our Father. Ripper, Peter, illus. (p. 1308)
Hodgson, Julie. Earth Child. (p. 495)
—Fun with Number Rhymes for the Early Years. (p. 648)
—Juno & the Half -Man. (p. 936)
—Juno & the Windwalker. (p. 936)
—Magic of Christmas. (p. 1072)
—Miniature Horse Tales. (p. 1146)
—Mothaich. (p. 1177)
—Polly Mae. (p. 1381)
Hodgson, Julie, jt. ed. see Rhodes, Judith.
Hodgson, Karen J. Bella's Bubble. Griffiths, Rebecca, illus. (p. 162)
—Boris the Boastful Frog. Cox, Steve, illus. (p. 214)
—Hugh's Blue Day. Collins, Ross, illus. (p. 825)
—I Don't Care! Said Claire. Rowe, Harriet, illus. (p. 837)
—King Who Wanted More. Dina, Madalina, illus. (p. 959)
—Robot Who Couldn't Cry. Dina, Madalina, illus. (p. 1480)
Hodgson, Karen J., jt. auth. see Lambert, Sally Anne.
Hodgson, Louise & Jones, Eric. Delyth y Ddraig. (p. 425)
Hodgson, Miriam. Love from Dad: Stories about Fathers & Daughters. (p. 1059)
Hodgson, Mona. Thank You God for Rain Jahier, Milena, illus. (p. 1725)
Hodgson, Mona Gansberg. Bedtime in the Southwest. Graef, Renee, illus. (p. 157)
—Desert Critter Friends Set (p. 429)
—Princess Twins & the Birthday Party Hansen, Red, illus. (p. 1406)
—Princess Twins & the Puppy Hansen, Red, illus. (p. 1406)
—Princess Twins & the Tea Party Hansen, Red, illus. (p. 1406)
—Princess Twins Play in the Garden Hansen, Red, illus. (p. 1406)
Hodgson, Sandra. Toof Fairies. (p. 1767)
Hodgson, William Hope. Sea Horses. (p. 1534)
Hodkin, Faith. What Was My Mother Thinking? Militello, Joy, illus. (p. 1894)
Hodkin, Michelle. Evolution of Mara Dyer. (p. 547)
—Retribution of Mara Dyer. (p. 1464)
—Unbecoming of Mara Dyer. (p. 1811)
Hodnefjeld, Hilde, illus. see Di Fiore, Mariangela.
Hodnett, Valerie. Three for the Birds (asi) A Collection of New Fairy Tales in the Old Style. (p. 1742)
Hodsdon-Carr, Sandra, ed. see Messick, Maxine.
Hodson, Ann. Ben the Deer. (p. 163)

Hodson, Ann & Mason, David. Adventures of Kef, Dael & Emma. (p. 19)
Hodson, Ben, illus. see Beck, Carolyn.
Hodson, Ben, illus. see Bolger, Kevin.
Hodson, Ben, illus. see Boutilier, Joanna.
Hodson, Ben, illus. see Crawford, Laura.
Hodson, Ben, illus. see Heller, Janet Ruth.
Hodson, Ben, illus. see Ipcizade, Catherine.
Hodson, Ben, illus. see Schwartz, Ellen.
Hodson, Ben, illus. see Stewart, Shannon.
Hodson, Ben, illus. see Watts, Gillian.
Hodson, Ben, illus. see Winters, Kari-Lynn.
Hodson, Christopher. Little Library Literacy: Lizo's Song Ndebele. Pulles, Elizabeth, illus. (p. 1030)
—Little Library Literacy: Lizo's Song Xhosa. Pulles, Elizabeth, illus. (p. 1030)
Hodson, Debbie. Mountain Rainbow. (p. 1181)
Hodson, Jewel, illus. see Rowley, Deborah Pace.
Hodson, Sally. Granny's Clan: A Tale of Wild Orcas. Jones, Ann, illus. (p. 710)
Hodson, Sarah E. Early Social Skills Stories: Going Potty. Platt, Jason, illus. (p. 494)
—Wh- Questions. (p. 1877)
Hodus, Brett, jt. auth. see Blumenthal, Scott.
Hoe, Susan. Rosa Parks. (p. 1488)
Hoe, Susan C. Environments. (p. 532)
—Habitats. (p. 734)
—Resources. (p. 1463)
—Rosa Parks. (p. 1488)
—Where We Live. (p. 1910)
Hoe, Susan C., jt. auth. see Hoe, Susan C.
Hoe, Susan C. & Hoe, Susan C. Environments. (p. 532)
—Where We Live. (p. 1910)
Hoeben, Peter, jt. auth. see Owen, Steve.
Hoedl, Lee. Jesse the Wait of the Wood. Hoedl, Lee, photos by. (p. 914)
Hoefer, Jacqueline, ed. More Abundant Life: New Deal Artists & Public Art in New Mexico. Berrett, Pat, photos by. (p. 1174)
Hoeffner, Betty. Stop Bullying Handbook: A Guide for Students & Their Friends. (p. 1653)
Hoeffner, Deb, illus. see Messer, Celeste M.
Hoeffner, Deb, illus. see Whitman, Lynn.
Hoeffner, Karol Ann. Surf Ed. (p. 1685)
Hoefler, Kate & Bean, Jonathan. Real Cowboys. Hoefler, Kate & Bean, Jonathan, illus. (p. 1448)
Hoeft, Jen. FUNdamental Fitness: Playground Exercises for Grownups (p. 649)
Hoehn, Ron. Windy Night: It happened one Night. (p. 1936)
Hoehn, Roxy. God's Adventurers. (p. 690)
Hoehne, Marcia. Anne Bradstreet: America's Puritan Poet. (p. 85)
Hoeksema, Gertrude. Come, Ye Children: A Bible Storybook for Young Children. Steenholdt, Jeff, illus. (p. 347)
Hoel, Charlotte. Magical Mischief Maker. (p. 1075)
Hoelscher, Wolfgang, ed. see McGee, Brenda Holt & Keiser, Debbie Triska.
Hoena, B. A. Can You Survive an Alien Invasion? An Interactive Doomsday Adventure. Fisher-Johnson, Paul, illus. (p. 259)
—Cyclopes (p. 397)
—Jack & the Beanstalk: An Interactive Fairy Tale Adventure. Tayal, Amit, illus. (p. 902)
—Jason & the Argonauts: A Graphic Retelling. (p. 910)
—Livewire! Schoening, Dan, illus. (p. 1040)
—Odysseus (p. 1278)
—Poseidon (p. 1387)
—Science of Hockey with Max Axiom, Super Scientist. (p. 1527)
—Theseus & the Minotaur: A Graphic Retelling. (p. 1732)
—Washington, D.C: The U.S. Capital. (p. 1860)
Hoena, B. A., jt. auth. see Hoena, Blake A.
Hoena, B. A. & Barrie, J. M. Peter Pan. Cano, Fernando, illus. (p. 1347)
Hoena, Blake. Baseball. (p. 140)
—Basketball. (p. 143)
—Brains vs. Brawn. Regan, Dana, illus. (p. 222)
—Building the Golden Gate Bridge: An Interactive Engineering Adventure (p. 239)
—Coming Clean. Regan, Dana, illus. (p. 348)
—Daring Cano, Fernando, illus. (p. 406)
—Football. (p. 614)
—Gymnastics. (p. 733)
—Halloween Scream. Regan, Dana, illus. (p. 738)
—Hockey. (p. 786)
—Hurricane Katrina: An Interactive Modern History Adventure (p. 830)
—Mississippi. (p. 1154)
—Museum Mystery. Regan, Dana, illus. (p. 1193)
—National Geographic Kids Everything Dinosaurs: Chomp on Tons of Earthshaking Facts & Fun. (p. 1232)
—National Geographic Kids Everything Soccer: Score Tons of Photos, Facts, & Fun. (p. 1232)
—North Dakota. (p. 1265)
—Oklahoma. (p. 1282)
—Riddler's Ransom. Beavers, Ethen, illus. (p. 1471)
—Robert Louis Stevenson's Treasure Island (p. 1479)
—School Bus Bully. Regan, Dana, illus. (p. 1522)
—Science of Hockey with Max Axiom, Super Scientist. Cacau, Caio, illus. (p. 1527)
—Skateboard Scare. Regan, Dana, illus. (p. 1583)
—Soccer. (p. 1603)
—Stubby the Dog Soldier: World War I Hero Hurst, Oliver, illus. (p. 1668)
—Swimming. (p. 1691)
—Tennis. (p. 1720)
—Trouble with Cheating. Regan, Dana, illus. (p. 1790)
—Video Game Zombie. Regan, Dana, illus. (p. 1841)
—Washington, D. C. (p. 1860)
Hoena, Blake, jt. auth. see Doeden, Matt.
Hoena, Blake, jt. auth. see Dreier, David L.
Hoena, Blake, jt. auth. see Field, Jon Eben.
Hoena, Blake, jt. auth. see National Geographic Kids Staff.
Hoena, Blake, jt. auth. see Perritano, John.
Hoena, Blake A. Ack's New Pet Harpster, Steve, illus. (p. 9)
—Athena (p. 112)
—Beyond the Black Hole. Harpster, Steve, illus. (p. 174)
—Big Mistake Harpster, Steve, illus. (p. 182)
—Black Hole Report Harpster, Steve, illus. (p. 196)
—Eek & Ack Early Chapter Books (p. 505)
—Eek & Ack vs the Wolfman Harpster, Steve, illus. (p. 505)
—Eek Discovers Earth Harpster, Steve, illus. (p. 505)
—Estacion de Bomberos. (p. 538)
—Estación de Bomberos. (p. 538)
—Harley Quinn's Shocking Surprise Schoening, Dan, illus. (p. 749)
—If an Egg Hatches... & Other Animal Predictions. (p. 852)
—If Books. (p. 852)
—If It's Really Cold... & Other Weather Predictions. (p. 853)
—If You Have a Magnet... And Other Science Predictions. (p. 854)
—If You Have a Magnet... & Other Science Predictions. (p. 854)
—If You Plant a Seed... & Other Nature Predictions (p. 854)
—If You Plant a Seed... & Other Nature Predictions. (p. 854)
—Invaders from the Great Goo Galaxy. Harpster, Steve, illus. (p. 883)
—Livewire! Schoening, Dan, illus. (p. 1040)
—Ooze Slingers from Outer Space. Harpster, Steve, illus. (p. 1299)
—Puzzling Pluto Plot: Eek & Ack Harpster, Steve, illus. (p. 1421)
—Raw Cano, Fernando, illus. (p. 1441)
—Raw. Cano, Fernando, illus. (p. 1441)
—Rival Cano, Fernando, illus. (p. 1475)
—Swamp Sting! Facio, Sebastian, illus. (p. 1688)
—Under the Red Sun Schoening, Dan, illus. (p. 1814)
—Weather ABC: An Alphabet Book (p. 1869)
—Zeus (p. 1986)
—Zombified: Volume Nine Majado, Caio, illus. (p. 1988)
Hoena, Blake A., jt. auth. see Burgan, Michael.
Hoena, Blake A., jt. auth. see Fuentes, Benny.
Hoena, Blake A., jt. auth. see Loughridge, Lee.
Hoena, Blake A., jt. auth. see Saunders-Smith, Gail.
Hoena, Blake A. & Coughlan Publishing Staff. Visit to the Farm (Una Visita a la Granja) (p. 1845)
Hoena, Blake A. & Fuentes, Benny. Spotlight Striker Sandoval, Gerardo, illus. (p. 1634)
Hoena, Blake A. & Gonzalez, Jorge. Kickoff Blitz. Ruiz, Alfonso, illus. (p. 951)
Hoena, Blake A. & Hoena, B. A. Athena (p. 112)
—Cyclopes (p. 397)
—Langston Hughes: Great American Writer. (p. 974)
—Livewire! Schoening, Dan, illus. (p. 1040)
—Matthew Henson: Arctic Adventurer Miller, Phil et al, illus. (p. 1109)
—Odysseus (p. 1278)
—Poseidon (p. 1387)
—Shackleton & the Lost Antarctic Expedition Hoover, Dave et al, illus. (p. 1556)
—Venus (p. 1836)
—Zeus (p. 1986)
Hoena, Blake A. & Loughridge, Lee. Cosmic Bounty Hunter Burchett, Rick, illus. (p. 368)
Hoena, Blake A. & Terrell, Brandon. Tony Hawk's 900 Revolution. (p. 1766)
Hoena, Blake A. & Tortosa, Wilson. Amplified Ito, Leonardo, illus. (p. 66)
—Zombified Majado, Caio, illus. (p. 1988)
Hoena, Blake A., et al. Poison Ivy's Deadly Garden (p. 1377)
—You Choose: Modern History (p. 1975)
Hoena, Blake & Doeden, Matt. You Choose: Doomsday. Nathan, James, illus. (p. 1975)
Hoena, Blake, et al. You Choose: Engineering Marvels (p. 1975)
Hoena, Blake, retold by. 12 Labors of Hercules: A Graphic Retelling. (p. 1994)
—Voyages of Odysseus: A Graphic Retelling. (p. 1851)
Hoenecke, Karen. At the Park. (p. 111)
—Little Mouse. Gedeon, Gloria, illus. (p. 1032)
—Snake Hunts for Lunch. Drzewiecki, Paul, illus. (p. 1596)
—Tree House. Graves, Dennis, illus. (p. 1783)
—What's for Dinner? (p. 1897)
—What's Inside? Biddle, Bruce, illus. (p. 1898)
Hoepfner, John P. Tale of Magic Pixie Dust. (p. 1699)
Hoercher, Donald F. Duckie Walk. Zaharias, Terrilynn, illus. (p. 488)
Hoerner, L. Cat & Dog Dress up Sticker Paper Dolls. (p. 277)
—Fanciful Fairies & Dazzling Dragons Coloring Book. (p. 570)
Hoes, Holly. When Aliens Took over the World. (p. 1901)
Hoese, Ray. My Dad Is an Ironman. Steinbach, Coreen, illus. (p. 1201)
Hoessle, Maureen. Under Three Flags: Exploring Early St. Louis History. Mulkey Young, Kim, illus. (p. 1814)
Hoestlandt, Jo. Emile bille de Clown. (p. 518)
—Robin del Bosque. (p. 1479)
Hoey, Joseph. St. Michaels. (p. 1638)
Hoeye, Michael. Cuestion de Tiempo. (p. 390)
—Sands of Time: A Hermux Tantamoq AdventureTM. (p. 1511)
—Sands of Time. (p. 1511)
—Time Stops for No Mouse: A Hermux Tantamoq AdventureTM. (p. 1752)
—Time Stops for No Mouse. (p. 1752)
Hof, Marjolijn. Against the Odds Prins, Johanna, tr. (p. 29)
—Mother Number Zero Prins, Johanna, tr. from DUT. (p. 1178)
Hofer, Charles. Airplanes. (p. 32)
—Bullet Trains. (p. 240)
—Meet Dracula. (p. 1121)
—Motorcycles. (p. 1179)
—Race Cars. (p. 1430)
—Saturn. (p. 1515)
—Spacecraft. (p. 1620)
—Speedboats. (p. 1624)
—Tonka Construction Zone. Giraffe, Red, illus. (p. 1765)
Hofer, Debra. Kido the Dragon. (p. 952)
Hofer, Ernst & Hofer, Nelly. Wild Swans. (p. 1930)
Hofer, Joan. Sherbert. (p. 1565)
—Sherbert's Waterlogged Tail. (p. 1565)
Hofer, Klaus C., tr. see Pohlmann-Eden, Bernd.
Hofer, Nelly, jt. illus. see Hofer, Ernst.
Hoff, Mary. Crocodiles. (p. 384)
—Fighting Back. (p. 585)
—Life at Night. (p. 1008)
—Metamorphosis. (p. 1130)
—Penguins. (p. 1337)
—Pollination. (p. 1381)
—Snakes. (p. 1596)
Hoff, Mary King. Koalas. (p. 966)
—Monkeys. (p. 1165)
—Polar Bears. (p. 1379)
—Swans. (p. 1689)
—Tigers. (p. 1749)
Hoff, Syd. DANIELITO Y EL DINOSAURIO. (p. 405)
—Danny & the Dinosaur. Hoff, Syd, illus. (p. 405)
—Littlest Leaguer. Hoff, Syd, illus. (p. 1039)
—Syd Hoff's Dinosaur Stories & More. (p. 1692)
Hoffa, Darlene. Bible Stories about Jesus. (p. 176)
—Through the Year with Jesus. (p. 1745)
Hoffbauer, Wyng, illus. see Eakins, Bonny Mae.
Hoffecker, Carol E. Delaware: The First State. (p. 424)
Hoffelt, Jane. We Share One World. Husted, Marty, illus. (p. 1868)
Hoffer, Rod. Strange Christmas Dream. (p. 1665)
Hoffert, John. Time of Reckoning. (p. 1752)
—Zero Factor. (p. 1986)
Hoffert, John & Hoffert, John F. Aphrodite's Redemption: The Lion Roars. (p. 91)
Hoffert, John F., jt. auth. see Hoffert, John.
Hoffert, Kara & Fribley, Kara. Find the Right Words with Thesauruses. (p. 587)
Hoffman, Aaron M. Building Trust: Overcoming Suspicion in International Conflict. Rosenau, James N. & Stone, Russell, eds. (p. 239)
Hoffman, Alice. Foretelling. (p. 618)
—Green Angel. (p. 721)
—Green Heart. (p. 722)
—Green Witch. (p. 722)
—Incantation. (p. 868)
—Indigo. (p. 872)
—Nightbird. (p. 1255)
—Seventh Heaven. (p. 1555)
—Skylight Confessions. (p. 1587)
Hoffman, Amalia. Klezmer Bunch. (p. 963)
Hoffman, Beth Greiner. Animal Gym. Gergely, Tibor, illus. (p. 78)
Hoffman, Betty N. Liberation: Stories of Survival from the Holocaust. (p. 1005)
Hoffman, Bridget Kilroy. Full-Color Math Games. (p. 646)
Hoffman, C. J. Hiss: A Story about Love, Trust & Growing Up. (p. 781)
Hoffman, Cj. Dragons & the Simmies: A Friendly Story. (p. 479)
Hoffman, Diana / Lynne. Lighting the Earth. Brough, Karen, illus. (p. 1015)
Hoffman, Don. Sparky the Fire Dog. Dakins, Todd, illus. (p. 1622)
—Wanderer: The Monarch Butterfly. (p. 1856)
Hoffman, Emily, jt. auth. see Huang, Linda.
Hoffman, Emily Allen. Friend of the Enemy. (p. 637)
Hoffman, Gretchen. Osteoporosis. (p. 1306)
Hoffman, Isobel, illus. see Dabritz, Evelyn.
Hoffman, J. Ann. Special Purpose. (p. 1623)
Hoffman, Jane. Backyard Scientist A Science Wonderland for the Very Young: Simple, fun-to-do Science Experiments Ages 2 To 7. (p. 131)
Hoffman, Joan. 1-25 Dot-to-Dot. (p. 1990)
—ABC Dot-to-Dot. (p. 3)
—Alphabet Fun. Boyer, Robin, illus. (p. 49)
—Crosswords. (p. 385)
—First Grade Basics. (p. 595)
—Hide & Seek Number Skills. (p. 777)
—Kindergarten Basics. (p. 957)
—Kindergarten Basics. Boyer, Robin, illus. (p. 957)
—Preschool Basics. (p. 1396)
—Preschool Practice. (p. 1396)
—Reading Readiness. (p. 1446)
—Second Grade Basics. (p. 1539)
—Tracing Trails Pre-Writing Skills. (p. 1775)
Hoffman, Joan, jt. auth. see Gregorich, Barbara.
Hoffman, Joey. Greedy Courier. (p. 720)
Hoffman, Judy. Art of Flying: A Novel. Graegin, Stephanie, illus. (p. 102)
Hoffman, Juliet. 24 Hours: From Day to Night. (p. 1996)
Hoffman, Kamri Alexis. Buddy Saves the Day: Will Shawn stay safe on Vacation? (p. 235)
Hoffman, Karen Burkinshaw. Story about Tee Low: A Mouse with a Knot in His Tail. (p. 1656)
Hoffman, Kathelin, ed. see Burroughs, William S.
Hoffman, Kathryn A. & Teraoka, Masami. Ascending Chaos: The Art of Masami Teraoka, 1966-2006. (p. 105)
Hoffman, Kimberly, illus. see Hoppey, Tim.
Hoffman, Kolby John. Racing Days. (p. 1432)
Hoffman, Kurt. How Cars Changed the World. (p. 805)
—Young Heroes, a Learner's Guide to Changing the World: Abolish Slavery Edition. (p. 1978)
Hoffman, Lawrence A. & Wolfson, Ron. What You Will See Inside a Synagogue. Aron, Bill, photos by. (p. 1896)
Hoffman, Mary. Amazing Grace. (p. 54)
—Bravo, Grace! (p. 224)
—City of Secrets. (p. 324)
—City of Ships. (p. 324)
—Clever Katya: A Fairy Tale from Old Russia. Cameron, Marie, illus. (p. 331)
—Colores de Casa. Littlewood, Karin, illus. (p. 344)
—David. (p. 410)
—Dracula's Daughter. (p. 476)
—Encore, Grace! (p. 524)
—Falconer's Knot: A Story of Friars, Flirtation & Foul Play. (p. 565)
—First Book of Fairy Tales. Downing, Julie, illus. (p. 593)
—Great Big Book of Families. Asquith, Ros, illus. (p. 714)
—Great Big Book of Feelings. Asquith, Ros, illus. (p. 714)
—Lines in the Sand: New Writing on War & Peace. Lassiter, Rhiannon, ed. (p. 1019)
—Princess Grace. Van Wright, Cornelius & Hu, Ying-Hwa, illus. (p. 1404)
—Special Powers. (p. 1623)
—Stravaganza: City of Ships. (p. 1666)
—Stravaganza: City of Swords. (p. 1666)
—Sword in the Stone. Ginevra, Dante, illus. (p. 1692)
—Trace in Space. (p. 1774)
—Twelve Dancing Princesses. Clara, Miss, illus. (p. 1800)
—Welcome to the Family. Asquith, Ros, illus. (p. 1874)
—Women of Camelot: Queens & Enchantresses at the Court of King Arthur. Balit, Christina, illus. (p. 1946)
Hoffman, Mary & Martins, Pam. How to Be a Cat. (p. 814)
Hoffman, Mary Ann. Alamo. (p. 33)
—Alex Rodriguez: Baseball Star. (p. 36)
—Alex Rodriguez: Baseball Star/Estrella del Beisbol. (p. 36)
—Alex Rodriguez: Baseball Star/Estrella del Beisbol. Alaman, Eduardo, tr. (p. 36)
—Animal Features. (p. 77)
—Bananas for Breakfast! (p. 136)
—Caleb's Car Wash. (p. 252)
—David Ortiz: Baseball Star. (p. 411)
—David Ortiz: Baseball Star/Estrella del Beisbol. (p. 411)
—David Ortiz: Baseball Star/Estrella del Beisbol. Alaman, Eduardo, tr. (p. 411)
—Dwayne Wade: Basketball Star. (p. 491)
—Dwayne Wade: Basketball Star/Estrella del Baloncesto. (p. 491)
—Dwayne Wade: Basketball Star/Estrella del Baloncesto. Alaman, Eduardo, tr. (p. 491)
—Elbert Takes a Trip. (p. 508)
—Guard Dogs. (p. 728)
—Happy Birthday, Rita Raccoon! (p. 745)
—Helping Dogs. (p. 766)
—Herding Dogs. (p. 769)
—History of the Maya: Using Computational Skills in Problem Solving. (p. 785)
—How Do Penguins Survive the Cold? (p. 807)
—Hurricane Katrina. (p. 830)
—I Am a Good Citizen. (p. 832)
—I Am a Good Citizen / Soy un buen Ciudadano. (p. 832)
—Jeff Gordon. (p. 911)
—Kyle Busch. (p. 969)
—LeBron James: Basketball Star. (p. 987)
—Lebron James: Basketball Star. (p. 987)
—LeBron James: Basketball Star/Estrella del Baloncesto. (p. 987)
—Lebron James: Basketball Star/Estrella del Baloncesto. Alaman, Eduardo, tr. from ENG. (p. 987)
—Loch Ness Monster. (p. 1044)
—Maple Tree Mystery. (p. 1090)
—Missing Wheel. (p. 1153)
—misterio en el árbol (the Maple Tree Mystery) (p. 1155)
—Molly Makes a Milkshake. (p. 1160)
—Panama Canal: Global Gateway. (p. 1320)
—Parrot for Pam. (p. 1325)
—Peyton Manning: Football Star. (p. 1349)
—Peyton Manning: Football Star/Estrella del Futbol Americano. Alaman, Eduardo, tr. (p. 1349)
—Piñata Party. (p. 1359)
—Plant Experiments: What Affects Plant Growth? (p. 1369)
—Police Dogs. (p. 1380)
—Scientific Inquiry in Action: Chemical Reaction! (p. 1528)
—Scott Joplin: King of Ragtime. (p. 1531)
—Shaun Alexander: Football Star. (p. 1563)
—Shaun Alexander: Football Star/Estrella del futbol Americano. (p. 1563)
—Shaun Alexander: Football Star/Estrella del Futbol Americano. Alaman, Eduardo, tr. (p. 1563)
—Watch Apple Trees Grow. (p. 1860)
—Watch Apple Trees Grow / ¡Mira cómo crece el Manzano! (p. 1860)
Hoffman, Mary Hramiec. Elizabeth Whitney Williams & the Little Traverse Light. (p. 513)
—Lolek the Boy Who Became Pope John Paul II. Hoffman, Mary Hramiec, illus. (p. 1046)
Hoffman, Mary Y. Great Big Green Book. Asquith, Ros, illus. (p. 714)
Hoffman, Michael. I'm Only Three. (p. 859)
Hoffman, Nancy, ed. see Smith, Robert W.
Hoffman, Nancy & Hart, Joyce. South Carolina. (p. 1616)
—West Virginia. (p. 1876)
Hoffman, Nina. Meeting. (p. 1123)
Hoffman, Nina Kiriki. Spirits That Walk in Shadow. (p. 1629)
—Stir of Bones. (p. 1651)
—Thresholds. (p. 1744)
Hoffman, Onalee Lytle. Mattie Goes Home. (p. 1110)
Hoffman, Pam. Sadie Dog. (p. 1501)
Hoffman, Pat. Antics: Perspective on an Ant's World. (p. 89)
Hoffman, Patricia. Bethlehem Town: Where Jesus Was Born. Munger, Nancy, illus. (p. 171)
Hoffman, Paul. King's Gambit: A Son, a Father, & the World's Most Dangerous Game. (p. 960)
—Wings of Madness: Alberto Santos-Dumont & the Invention of Flight. (p. 1936)
Hoffman, Paul G., illus. see Ingham, Donna.
Hoffman, Paul G., illus. see Schlosser, S. E.
Hoffman, Peter. ferret in a Garret. Olson, Cindy, illus. (p. 582)
Hoffman, Richard L., jt. auth. see Baker, Nancy.
Hoffman, Robert M. Adventures of Mia & Squeaky: Tails of Imagination. (p. 20)
Hoffman, Ronald. Mr. Lucky. (p. 1185)
—Neighborhood. (p. 1240)
Hoffman, Rosekrans, illus. see Miranda, Anne.
Hoffman, Sanford. Too Much Tooting. (p. 1767)
Hoffman, Sanford, illus. see Keller, Charles.
Hoffman, Sanford, illus. see Linn, Margot.
Hoffman, Sanford, illus. see Pellowski, Michael J.
Hoffman, Sanford, illus. see Rosenbloom, Joseph.
Hoffman, Sara E. Gases. (p. 657)
Hoffman, Stephanie. Sharp Teeth, Flat Teeth. (p. 1563)
Hoffman, Steve, illus. see Roberts, Tom.
Hoffman, Steven M. Fossils: History in the Rocks. (p. 624)
—Gems, Crystals, & Precious Rocks. (p. 660)
—Rock Study: A Guide to Looking at Rocks. (p. 1482)
—Rocks & Soil. (p. 1483)

—Volcanoes & Earthquakes: Making & Moving Rock. (p. 1849)
—Weathering & Erosion: Wearing down Rocks. (p. 1870)
Hoffman, Terri. Sly Fly & the Gray Mare. BURNS, Theresa, illus. (p. 1591)
Hoffman, Yair. Misguiding the Perplexed: The Laws of Lifnei Iver. (p. 1150)
Hoffmann, Arthur W. Blue King. (p. 203)
Hoffmann, Burton R. Millicent the Magnificent. du Houx, Emily C., illus. (p. 1144)
Hoffmann, Catherine E. & Hoffmann, Dana Marie. Here Little Teacup! up! Up! O'Leary Brown, Erin, illus. (p. 770)
Hoffmann, Dana. Golden Tale: A Goldentail Adventure Story Book. O'Leary Brown, Erin, illus. (p. 695)
Hoffmann, Dana Marie. Cuento Dorado, un Libro de Aventura, la Historia de Goldentail. O'Leary Brown, Erin, illus. (p. 389)
—Golden Tale, A Goldentail Adventure Story Book. O'Leary Brown, Erin, illus. (p. 695)
Hoffmann, Dana Marie, jt. auth. see Hoffmann, Catherine E.
Hoffmann, E. T. A. Hombre de la Arena. Toro, Jorge & Gonzalez, Carlos Mario, trs. (p. 791)
—Nutcracker. (p. 1273)
—Nutcracker. Kliros, Thea, illus. (p. 1273)
—Nutcracker. Julian, Alison, illus. (p. 1273)
—Nutcracker. Manheim, Ralph, tr. from GER. (p. 1273)
—Nutcracker & the Golden Pot. (p. 1274)
—Nutcracker & the Mouse King. Scheiner, A. & Wenckebach, L. W. R., illus. (p. 1274)
Hoffmann, E. T. A., jt. auth. see McCaughrean, Geraldine.
Hoffmann, E. T. A. & Neugroschel, Joachim. Nutcracker. (p. 1273)
Hoffmann, E. T. A. & Ventura, Paola Fratalocchi. Nutcracker. (p. 1273)
Hoffmann, Eric, illus. see Cooper, Sharon Katz & Compass Point Books Staff.
Hoffmann, Eric, illus. see Stille, Darlene R.
Hoffmann, Erich, illus. see Stille, Darlene R.
Hoffmann, Frank. Rhythm & Blues, Rap, & Hip-Hop. (p. 1468)
Hoffmann, Gretchen. Chickenpox. (p. 300)
—Digestive System. (p. 438)
—Flu. (p. 608)
—Mononucleosis. (p. 1166)
Hoffmann, Heinrich. Slovenly Betsy: the American Struwwelpeter: From the Struwwelpeter Library. Hayn, Walter, illus. (p. 1591)
—Slovenly Kate & Other Stories: From the Struwwelpeter Library. Hosemann, Theodor, illus. (p. 1591)
—Struwwelpeter: Or Pretty Stories & Funny Pictures. Hoffmann, Heinrich, illus. (p. 1668)
Hoffmann, Kerry Cohen. Easy. (p. 500)
—It's Not You, It's Me. (p. 898)
Hoffmann, Laurence D. & Bradley, Gerald L. Calculus: For Business, Economics, & the Social & Life Sciences. (p. 252)
Hoffmann, Omer, illus. see Landau, Orna.
Hoffmann, Peggy. Miss B's First Cookbook: Twenty Family-Sized Recipes for for the Youngest Cook. Hunter, Gerald, illus. (p. 1151)
Hoffmann, Sara. Going from Here to There. (p. 692)
—Kinds of Flowers. (p. 957)
—Kinds of Fruits. (p. 957)
—Kinds of Grains. (p. 957)
—Kinds of Vegetables. (p. 957)
—Liquids. (p. 1021)
—Little Book of Space. (p. 1025)
—Made of Cloth. (p. 1070)
—Made of Paper. (p. 1070)
—Made of Wood. (p. 1070)
—Rolling. (p. 1485)
—Solids. (p. 1607)
—Spinning. (p. 1628)
—Sri Lanka in Pictures. (p. 1637)
—Staying Still. (p. 1645)
Hoffmann, Sara E. Ana & the Pet Show. Strange, Katie, illus. (p. 66)
—Ana & the Rainy Day. Strange, Katie, illus. (p. 66)
—Ben Gives a Gift. Dieterichs, Shelley, illus. (p. 163)
—Fall Fun for Kit. Roraback, Robin, illus. (p. 566)
—Holidays with Joe. Bueno, Lisa, illus. (p. 788)
—Nan Swims. Roraback, Robin, illus. (p. 1228)
—Nia Bakes Cookies. Strange, Katie, illus. (p. 1250)
—Party with Joe. Bueno, Lisa, illus. (p. 1326)
—Picnic with Kit. Roraback, Robin, illus. (p. 1355)
—Sam Is Six. Dieterichs, Shelley, illus. (p. 1506)
—Sam Sees Snow. Dieterichs, Shelley, illus. (p. 1507)
—School for Ken. Bueno, Lisa, illus. (p. 1522)
Hoffmann, Stefan-Ludwig. Civil Society: 1750-1914. (p. 325)
Hoffmire, A. B. Ogre Bully. (p. 1280)
Hoffmire, Baird. Anansi & the Tug O' War. (p. 67)
—Big Wide-Mouth Frog. (p. 184)
—How Tiger Got His Stripes: A Folktale from Vietnam. (p. 814)
Hoffmire, Baird, illus. see Cleveland, Rob.
Hoffmire, Baird, illus. see Norfolk, Bobby & Norfolk, Sherry.
Hoffmire, Baird, illus. see Weiss, Mitch & Hamilton, Martha.
Hoffpauir, J. R. Wibeau Flies! (p. 1927)
Hofher, Cathy, illus. see Parker, Sandy.
Hofher, Cathy, illus. see Stoutland, Allison.
Hoflus, Sarah & Skindzier, Jon. Ithaca College College Prowler off the Record. (p. 895)
Hofkin, Sabrina. Magnolia (p. 1076)
Hofland. Barbadoes Girl: A Tale for Young People. (p. 137)
—Little Manuel, the Captive Boy. (p. 1031)
Hofmann, Ginnie. Bear Next Door. (p. 151)
—One Teddy Bear Is Enough! (p. 1297)
—Runaway Teddy Bear. (p. 1496)
—Who Wants an Old Teddy Bear? Hofmann, Ginnie, illus. (p. 1918)
Hofmann, Ginnie, illus. see Dracker, Pune.
Hofmann, Michael, tr. see Keun, Irmgard.
Hofmann-Maniyar, Ariane. Ice in the Jungle. (p. 850)
Hofmeister, Alan, et al. Ann & Nan. (p. 84)
—Ann & the Hat. (p. 84)
—Ant & the Bee. (p. 88)
—Bad Men. (p. 132)
—Balloons & Bandits. (p. 135)
—Banks & Boats. (p. 136)
—Barrels & Blimps. (p. 140)
—Bat. (p. 143)
—Bat Rat. (p. 143)
—Beaches & Boulders. (p. 149)
—Bee. (p. 157)
—Ben the Ant. (p. 163)
—Birds & Bikes. (p. 191)
—Birds & Bowls. (p. 191)
—Books & Bears. (p. 212)
—Bottles & Bats. (p. 215)
—Bracelet Mystery. (p. 221)
—Bracelets & Barbers. (p. 221)
—Bud & the Tree. (p. 234)
—Bulls & Bulldogs. (p. 240)
—Bus. (p. 244)
—Cages & Jars. (p. 251)
—Camels & Colors. (p. 256)
—Cans & Drums. (p. 261)
—Canyons & Creatures. (p. 262)
—Captains & Canoes. (p. 264)
—Carnivals & Closets. (p. 270)
—Cartons & Clocks. (p. 272)
—Carts & Cars. (p. 273)
—Caves & Camps. (p. 282)
—Clowns & Crowns. (p. 335)
—Creatures of Loon. (p. 380)
—Dash Has Fun. (p. 409)
—Diets & Diamonds. (p. 437)
—Dogs & Dust. (p. 462)
—Ducks & Ponds. (p. 488)
—Faces & Storms. (p. 561)
—Feathers & Fudge. (p. 579)
—Fish & Fires. (p. 598)
—Fog & Fisherman. (p. 611)
—Foxes & Farms. (p. 626)
—Freckles & Forests. (p. 632)
—From Out of the Past. (p. 643)
—Fun Fish. (p. 647)
—Fun with the Sheet. (p. 649)
—Goats & Gold. (p. 687)
—Gold of Eagle Island. (p. 693)
—Great Covered Wagon Race. (p. 715)
—Hat. (p. 752)
—I See Sam. (p. 845)
—In a Tub. (p. 863)
—In the Mud. (p. 866)
—In the Tent. (p. 867)
—It Is Ann. (p. 894)
—Laughs & Landings. (p. 980)
—Legend of Rudolfo. (p. 988)
—Lids & Logs. (p. 1007)
—Loggers & Lunches. (p. 1045)
—Mask. (p. 1102)
—Mat. (p. 1104)
—Mat & the Nut. (p. 1104)
—Mat at Bat. (p. 1104)
—Mat Did It. (p. 1104)
—Mat in the Hat. (p. 1104)
—Mat in the Sun. (p. 1104)
—Mat Is Wet. (p. 1104)
—Mat the Rat. (p. 1104)
—Meet Mit. (p. 1121)
—Men. (p. 1126)
—Mice & Ice. (p. 1134)
—Mit & the Weed. (p. 1155)
—Mit Is Wet. (p. 1155)
—Nan & the Man. (p. 1228)
—Nan Sits. (p. 1228)
—Nat. (p. 1230)
—Nell & Ed. (p. 1240)
—Not Yet, Tip. (p. 1267)
—Paths & Places. (p. 1328)
—Pears & Planes. (p. 1333)
—Pets & Plums. (p. 1348)
—Pianos & Police. (p. 1354)
—Pipes & Mules. (p. 1362)
—Pits & Wells. (p. 1364)
—Plum. (p. 1374)
—Pond. (p. 1382)
—Popsicles & Poems. (p. 1385)
—Potions & Pictures. (p. 1388)
—Puzzles & Purses. (p. 1421)
—Riders & Rocks. (p. 1471)
—Rivers & Races. (p. 1476)
—Rocks. (p. 1483)
—Ruff. (p. 1494)
—Run, Feet, Run. (p. 1496)
—Sam. (p. 1506)
—Sam Is Mad. (p. 1506)
—Sam Sat. (p. 1507)
—Scars & Screams. (p. 1520)
—See It. (p. 1546)
—See Mat. (p. 1546)
—See Me. (p. 1546)
—See Sam. (p. 1547)
—See Them. (p. 1547)
—Seed. (p. 1547)
—Sell the Shell. (p. 1550)
—Shell. (p. 1564)
—Shells & Rocks. (p. 1565)
—Sherrifs & Showers. (p. 1566)
—Ship. (p. 1567)
—Shirts & Sandwiches. (p. 1567)
—Sid. (p. 1572)
—Sid & the Mess. (p. 1572)
—Sis. (p. 1581)
—Sis in a Mess. (p. 1581)
—Sis in the Well. (p. 1581)
—Sit on It. (p. 1581)
—Smash It. (p. 1593)
—Smiles & Surprises. (p. 1594)
—Snap Plays a Song. (p. 1597)
—Songs & Sticks. (p. 1611)
—Spaceships & Saddles. (p. 1620)
—Spells & Space. (p. 1625)
—Storms & Stardust. (p. 1656)
—Swim with Us. (p. 1691)
—Tip Plays a Trick. (p. 1757)
—To Camp. (p. 1758)
—To the Den. (p. 1759)
—Tracks & Trails. (p. 1775)
—Trick on Ruff. (p. 1786)
—Trip. (p. 1787)
—Trip in a Ship. (p. 1787)
—Trunks & Things. (p. 1793)
—Up the Path. (p. 1824)
—Up We Go. (p. 1824)
—Was It Wet? (p. 1859)
—Watch Dogs & Waves. (p. 1860)
—Watches & Rings. (p. 1861)
—We Will Run. (p. 1868)
—We Will See. (p. 1868)
—Wells & Wishes. (p. 1874)
—Who Am I? (p. 1914)
—Will We Win? (p. 1932)
Hofmeister, Nick. Adventures of Eli Deuce - SPECIAL EDITION - Fourth & Final Part Added. (p. 17)
Hofmeyr, David. Stone Rider. (p. 1652)
Hofmeyr, Dianne. Eye of the Moon. (p. 557)
—Eye of the Sun. (p. 558)
Hofmeyr, Dianne & Grobler, Piet. Magic Bojabi Tree. Grobler, Piet, illus. (p. 1071)
Hofmeyr, Dianne & Quarto Generic Staff. Zeraffa Giraffa. Ray, Jane, illus. (p. 1986)
Hofner, Cathy, illus. see Stoutland, Allison.
Hofsess, William. My Very First Dinosaur. (p. 1221)
Hofstad, Maryanne. Hi, Mommy & Daddy! I'm Here! (p. 775)
Hofstetter, Adam. Olympic Basketball. (p. 1287)
Hofstetter, Adam, jt. auth. see Baker, Jayne.
Hofstetter, Adam B. Olympic Basketball. (p. 1287)
—Olympic Gymnastics. (p. 1287)
—Softball: Rules, Tips, Strategy, & Safety. (p. 1606)
Hofstrand, Skip. Tears for Nanertak: Text & Watercolors by Skip Hofstrand. (p. 1711)
Hogan & Wiggers. Ultimate Geography & Timeline. (p. 1809)
Hogan, Anne Harmon. Three Amigos. (p. 1741)
Hogan, Barbora. How Ryan & Aiden Saved the Ocean. (p. 812)
Hogan, Edward. Daylight Saving. (p. 415)
—Messengers. (p. 1129)
Hogan, Edward Patrick, jt. auth. see Fouberg, Erin Hogan.
Hogan, Edward Patrick, jt. tr. see Fouberg, Erin Hogan.
Hogan, Edward Patrick, et al. Sweden. (p. 1689)
Hogan, Ellis. Tyrannosaurus Rex In: I've Got to Start Changing My Ways. (p. 1805)
Hogan, Eric, illus. see McNair, Barbara.
Hogan II, Haywood. Horse, the Dog, & the Bird. (p. 800)
Hogan, Jamie. Seven Days of Daisy Hogan, Jamie, illus. (p. 1554)
Hogan, Jamie, illus. see Arnold, Caroline.
Hogan, Jamie, illus. see Blackaby, Susan.
Hogan, Jamie, illus. see Danneberg, Julie.
Hogan, Jamie, illus. see Hansen, Robin.
Hogan, Jamie, illus. see Perkins, Mitali.
Hogan, Jamie, illus. see Sayre, April Pulley.
Hogan, Janice M. As Big as the Sky. (p. 105)
Hogan, Jayne. Callie Cow. Reiter, Cheryl, ed. (p. 254)
Hogan, Joyce W., jt. auth. see Lollis, Sylvia.
Hogan, Joyce W., jt. auth. see Peterson, Tara.
Hogan, Julie. Ideals Treasury of Best-Loved Christmas Stories. (p. 852)
Hogan, Maggie S. Student History Notebook of America. (p. 1669)
Hogan, Mary. Perfect Girl. (p. 1342)
—Pretty Face. (p. 1398)
—Serious Kiss. (p. 1552)
Hogan, Micki. Midnight's Lullaby: Volume One. Brown, Bobby, illus. (p. 1139)
Hogan, Peter. Welcome to Earth! Simon, Philip, ed. (p. 1873)
Hogan, Robb Dragon. There Was a Time: A Journey into Black & White with Taz. (p. 1730)
Hogan, Robb Dragon Taz. Moonlight's Spell: Rhymes for Younger Readers by TAZ. (p. 1173)
Hogan, Sean O., ed. Judicial Branch of State Government: People, Process, & Politics (p. 931)
Hogan, Sophie, photos by see Watters, Debbie, et al.
Hogan, Stephen. Johnny Lynch: Road to Camden. (p. 923)
—Johnny Lynch: Patriot Drummerboy. (p. 923)
Hogan, Tamara Anne. Mary Bea Says Why Is for Yog. Tortop, Anil, illus. (p. 1100)
Hogan, Tom, illus. see Hogan, Wes.
Hogan, Wes. Balloons. Hogan, Wes & Hogan, Tom, illus. (p. 135)
Hogarth, Ainslie. Boy Meets Girl Massacre (Annotated) (p. 218)
Hoge, Patricia, jt. ed. see Fontana, Lynn.
Hogen, Hildegard, jt. auth. see Ohlig, Rudolf.
Hogenkamp, S. All Sorts of Sports: Learning the or Sound. (p. 45)
—My Birthday: Learning the IR Sound. (p. 1198)
—They Crawl! Learning the CR Sound. (p. 1732)
Hogg, Gary. Beautiful Buehla & the Zany Zoo Makeover. Chess, Victoria, illus. (p. 153)
Hogg, Glenda, jt. auth. see Martin, Lynn.
Hogg, James. Magical Mermaids. Atkins, Alison, illus. (p. 1075)
Hoggard, Brian. Crusader Castles: Christian Fortresses in the Middle East. (p. 386)
Hoggatt, Jack, jt. auth. see Trabel, Diana.
Hoggatt, Jack P. & Shank, Jon A. Computer Applications & Keyboarding. (p. 354)
Hoggatt, Pamla. Day the Oil Took My Beach Away. (p. 414)
—You Did It All for Me. Hoggatt, Pamla, illus. (p. 1975)
Hoggins, Matthew. Nora's Pink Boots. (p. 1264)
—Speedy Story. (p. 1625)
Hoglen, Jeffrey & Hoglen, Tonya. Obeying the Call: A 14 Day Pre-Mission Devotional & Trip Journal. (p. 1275)
Hoglen, Tonya, jt. auth. see Hoglen, Jeffrey.
Hoglund, Anna, illus. see Stark, Ulf.
Hogner, Dorothy Childs. Our American Horse. Hogner, Nils, illus. (p. 1307)
Hogner, Nils, illus. see Hogner, Dorothy Childs.
Hogrogian, Nonny. One Fine Day. Hogrogian, Nonny, illus. (p. 1295)
Hogrogian, Nonny, illus. see Kherdian, David.
Hogue, Cheryl Porter. Nicodemus & Pedro: Their First Christmas. (p. 1251)
Hogue, Richard, Sr. We Were the Third Herd. (p. 1868)
Hoguet, Susan Ramsay. Maine ABC. (p. 1077)
Hoh, Molly. Creating the Purrfect Tale. (p. 379)
Hohenthal, K. D. Herman Goes Home: A Duffy Family Adventure. (p. 771)
Hohenthal, K. D., creator. Reading & Writing Connection Journal with Herman the Crab: What Is the Story About? No. 1 (p. 1445)
—Reading & Writing Connection with Herman the Crab: Story Problem & Solution. No. 2 (p. 1445)
—Reading & Writing Connection with Herman the Crab: Story Beginning, Middle, End. No. 3 (p. 1445)
—Reading & Writing Connection with Herman the Crab: Story Problem, Solution, Beginning, Middle, End. No. 4 (p. 1445)
Hohl, Nikki. Changing Planets: The Prince Is Found. (p. 290)
Hohl, Richard. Prairie: A Novelette. (p. 1392)
Hohl, Valicity. When I Grow Up. (p. 1902)
Hohlbein, Wolfgang. Avalon Projekt. (p. 118)
Hohlt, Janie. Basic Writing 2. (p. 142)
—Basic Writing Binder 2. (p. 142)
Hohmeier, Maria. Amazingly Wonderful Things. Weber, Penny, illus. (p. 56)
Hohn, David, illus. see Howell, Trisha Adelena.
Hohn, David, illus. see Mackall, Dandi Daley.
Hohn, David, illus. see Reisberg, Joanne.
Höhn, Jessica. Please Don't Pick the Flowers I Am Watching You. (p. 1373)
Hohn, Tracy, illus. see Durden, Angela K.
Hohn, Tracy, illus. see McClarnon, Marciann.
Hohnstadt, Cedric, illus. see Comfort, Ray.
Hohnstadt, Cedric, illus. see Harris, Brooke.
Hohnstadt, Cedric, illus. see Metzger, Steve.
Hohnstadt, Cedric, illus. see Nickel, Scott.
Hohnstadt, Cedric, jt. auth. see Metzger, Steve.
Hoien, Ruth S. Ruthie's Four Hearts. (p. 1499)
Hoit, Richard, illus. see Holden, Pam.
Hoit, Richard, illus. see McDaniel, Becky Bring.
Hoit, Richard, illus. see Smith, Annette.
Hojel, Barbara, jt. auth. see Herrera, Mario.
Hojel, Barbara & Herrera, Mario. Pockets 3. (p. 1375)
Hokanson, Lars, illus. see Finkelstein, Norman H.
Hokanson, Lois, illus. see Finkelstein, Norman H.
Hoke, Jason, illus. see Dara Cicciarelli.
Hoke, Jeehyun. Boy & the Little Violet Flower. (p. 217)
Hoke, Jeenhyun, illus. see Thomas, Mark Lawton.
Hoke, Laurence. @Large (p. 975)
Hoke, Nick. Great Character Development Workbook: An Educational Workbook of Values & Virtues for Children of All Ages. (p. 714)
Hokenson, Linda, jt. auth. see Modéré, Armelle.
Hokenson, Terry. Winter Road. (p. 1938)
Hokie, illus. see Houghton, Amelia C.
Hoku, Nani. Unstoppable, Unbreakable Hearts. (p. 1823)
Hol, Coby. Punch & His Friends. (p. 1416)
Holabird, Katharine. Angelina & Alice. Craig, Helen, illus. (p. 74)
—Angelina & Henry. Craig, Helen, illus. (p. 74)
—Angelina & the Princess. Craig, Helen, illus. (p. 74)
—Angelina & the Royal Wedding. Craig, Helen, illus. (p. 74)
—Angelina & the Tummy Butterflies. (p. 74)
—Angelina at the Fair. Craig, Helen, illus. (p. 74)
—Angelina at the Palace. (p. 74)
—Angelina Ballerina. Craig, Helen, illus. (p. 74)
—Angelina Has the Hiccups! Craig, Helen, illus. (p. 74)
—Angelina Ice Skates. Craig, Helen, illus. (p. 74)
—Angelina Takes a Bow. (p. 74)
—Angelina Takes a Bow. Craig, Helen, illus. (p. 74)
—Angelina's Baby Sister. Craig, Helen, illus. (p. 74)
—Angelina's Big City Ballet. Craig, Helen, illus. (p. 74)
—Angelina's Birthday. Craig, Helen, illus. (p. 74)
—Angelina's Christmas. Craig, Helen, illus. (p. 74)
—Angelina's Halloween. Craig, Helen, illus. (p. 74)
—Angelina's Perfect Party. Craig, Helen, illus. (p. 74)
—Angelina's Silly Little Sister. Craig, Helen, illus. (p. 74)
—Angelina's Spring Fling. (p. 74)
—Angelina's Surprise Show. Craig, Helen, illus. (p. 74)
—Chipping Cheddar Christmas. (p. 308)
—Dance of Friendship. Craig, Helen, illus. (p. 402)
—Day at Miss Lilly's. Craig, Helen, illus. (p. 412)
—Nutcracker. Craig, Helen, illus. (p. 1273)
—Rose Fairy Princess. Craig, Helen, illus. (p. 1489)
—Shining Star Trophy. Craig, Helen, illus. (p. 1566)
—Very Special Tea Party. Craig, Helen, illus. (p. 1838)
Holabird, Katharine, jt. auth. see Craig, Helen.
Holabird, Katharine & Craig, Helen. Angelina's New School. (p. 74)
Holabird, Katharine & Grosset and Dunlap Editors. Angelina Loves... Craig, Helen, illus. (p. 74)
Holabird, Katherine. Twinkle. Warburton, Sarah, illus. (p. 1802)
Holaves, Chris. Even the Dead Get up for Milk. Goomas, John, illus. (p. 541)
—Running with the Bats: Corriendo con los Murcielagos. Medina, Candace, tr. (p. 1497)
Holba, Annette. Handbook for the Humanities Doctoral Student. (p. 740)
Holben, Jennifer Mellus. Brothers of Liberty. (p. 231)
Holbert, Raymond, illus. see Battle-Lavert, Gwendolyn.
Holbrook, Denise. Doors. (p. 470)
Holbrook, Flannery B. Great Day in Portsmouth. (p. 715)
Holbrook, Florence. Why the Crocodile Has a Wide Mouth: And Other Nature Myths. (p. 1926)
Holbrook, James. Emily I Think I Saw Heaven. Brittingham, Jennifer, illus. (p. 519)

Holbrook, John Robert. Gingerbread Jimmi: Magical Storybook. Scott, Catherine, ed. (p. 677)
Holbrook, L. E. Victoria & the Door to Travarnis. (p. 1840)
Holbrook, Ramona Webb. Baby Buck Arrives at the Big Red Barn. (p. 125)
Holbrook, Sara. By Definition: Poems of Feelings. Mattern, Scott, illus. (p. 249)
—Zombies! Evacuate the School! Sandstrom, Karen, illus. (p. 1988)
Holbrook, Sara & Wolf, Allan. More Than Friends: Poems from Him & Her. (p. 1175)
Holbrook, Sara E. Weird? (Me, Too!) Let's Be Friends. Sandstrom, Karen, illus. (p. 1872)
—Zombies! Evacuate the School. Sandstrom, Karen, illus. (p. 1988)
Holbrook, Stewart H. Swamp Fox of the Revolution. (p. 1688)
Holcomb, Carrie E. Dragons: A Fantasy Made Real. Holcomb, Carrie E., ed. (p. 478)
Holcomb, Carrie E., ed. Buggin' with Ruud. (p. 236)
—Monster Nation JR. (p. 1168)
Holcomb, J. Paul, jt. auth. see Holcomb, Sue A.
Holcomb, Mark. Beach Boys. (p. 149)
Holcomb, Michele, illus. see MacMillan, Lesley.
Holcomb, Nicholas, illus. see Sisler, Stephanie.
Holcomb, Sue A. & Holcomb, J. Paul. Tex R Masaur: Down in the Dump. Holcomb, Sue A., illus. (p. 1723)
Holcomb, T. Toot-Toot & Her Troubles: Name Calling. (p. 1767)
Holcomb, William R. Teleport. (p. 1716)
Holcroft, John, illus. see Candlewick Press, Candlewick.
Holcroft, John & Candlewick Press Staff. Space Exploration: Panorama Pops. Holcroft, John, illus. (p. 1619)
Holcroft, Trevor. Adventures with Astro the Alien. Bourgonje, Chantal, illus. (p. 25)
—Amazing Adventures of Abigail & Her Magnificent Magic Bed. (p. 52)
—MORE Adventures with ASTRO the ALIEN. (p. 1174)
Holczer, Tracy. Secret Hum of a Daisy. (p. 1541)
Holdcroft, Tina. Hidden Depths: Amazing Underwater Discoveries. Holdcroft, Tina, illus. (p. 775)
—Hidden Treasures: Amazing Stories of Discovery. Holdcroft, Tina, illus. (p. 776)
—Spy, Spy Again: True Tales of Failed Espionage. (p. 1636)
Holdcroft, Tina, illus. see Hutchins, Hazel.
Holdcroft, Tina, illus. see Scandiffio, Laura.
Holdeen, Bonnie, illus. see Boynton, Jeannette.
Holden, Anthony. Massie. (p. 1103)
Holden, Anthony, illus. see Bondor-Stone, Annabeth & White, Connor.
Holden, Arianne, jt. auth. see Llewellyn, Claire.
Holden, Chanler, illus. see Mese, John R. & Kelsey, Dawn M.
Holden, Courtney. Cloud Factories & Wind Chargers. (p. 334)
Holden, Edward S. Sciences. (p. 1528)
Holden, H. Plutarch's Life of Pericles. (p. 1374)
Holden, Henry M. American Alligator: A MyReportLinks. Com Book. (p. 59)
—American Women of Flight: Pilots & Pioneers. (p. 64)
—Coolest Job in the Universe: Working Aboard the International Space Station. (p. 364)
—Danger in Space: Surviving the Apollo 13 Disaster. (p. 403)
—Living & Working Aboard the International Space Station: A MyReportLinks.com Book. (p. 1040)
—New Jersey: A MyReportLinks. Com Book. (p. 1245)
—Persian Gulf War: A MyReportLinks.com Book. (p. 1344)
—Pioneering Astronaut Sally Ride: A MyReportLinks.com Book. (p. 1361)
—Space Shuttle Disaster: The Tragic Mission of the Challenger. (p. 1619)
—Tragedy of the Space Shuttle Challenger: A MyReportLinks.com Book. (p. 1776)
—Trailblazing Astronaut John Glenn: A MyReportLinks.com Book. (p. 1776)
—Triumph over Disaster Aboard Apollo 13: A MyReportLinks.com Book. (p. 1788)
—Wisconsin: A MyReportLinks. Com Book. (p. 1939)
—Woodrow Wilson: A MyReportLinks.com Book. (p. 1949)
Holden, J. T. Alice in Verse the Lost Rhymes of Wonderland: The Lost Rhymes of Wonderland. Johnson, Andrew, illus. (p. 39)
Holden, Pam. About Lighthouses. (p. 6)
—Animal Art Storey. Jim, illus. (p. 76)
—Are You Hungry? Hawley, Kelvin, illus. (p. 97)
—Baby Whale's Mistake Aziz, Lamia, illus. (p. 128)
—Big Bad Wolf Hawley, Kelvin, illus. (p. 178)
—Caterpillar to Butterfly. (p. 279)
—Dance, Dance, Dance! (p. 402)
—Dinosaur Hunters Storey, Jim & Hawley, Kelvin, illus. (p. 442)
—Farm Friends Hawley, Kelvin, illus. (p. 574)
—Fire in the Jungle Hatam, Samer, illus. (p. 590)
—Flying Monkey East, Jacqueline, illus. (p. 610)
—Fruit for You Cooper, Jenny, illus. (p. 645)
—Gentle Giant Hatam, Samer, illus. (p. 661)
—Going Up Hawley, Kelvin, illus. (p. 693)
—Good Things from Trees. (p. 700)
—Greedy Gus the Pirate Whimp, Pauline, illus. (p. 720)
—Happy Birthday Hawley, Kelvin, illus. (p. 744)
—Hoppity Hop Morris, Sandra, illus. (p. 797)
—Huff & Puff! Storey, Jim, illus. (p. 824)
—Hungry Boy. (p. 828)
—Hunting for Treasure Whimp, Pauline, illus. (p. 829)
—I Like to Paint (p. 841)
—King of the Zoo Cammell, Sandra, illus. (p. 959)
—Knock, Knock! Hoit, Richard, illus. (p. 965)
—Learn about Birds. (p. 982)
—Learning to Swim. (p. 986)
—Let's Play Ball Webb, Philip, illus. (p. 1000)
—Long, Long Ride Storey, Jim, illus. (p. 1047)
—Look at My Home East, Jacqueline, illus. (p. 1048)
—Look in the Mirror. (p. 1049)
—Magic Stone Soup. (p. 1073)
—Mailbox Man. (p. 1077)
—Masks. (p. 1102)
—Max Monkey East, Jacqueline, illus. (p. 1111)

—Message from Camp Webb, Philip, illus. (p. 1129)
—My Hands Hawley, Kelvin, illus. (p. 1210)
—Naughty Goldilocks Hoit, Richard, illus. (p. 1237)
—Our Puppet Show. (p. 1309)
—Paper Chains (p. 1322)
—Paper Trail Hawley, Kelvin, illus. (p. 1323)
—Pass It On Hawley, Kelvin, illus. (p. 1326)
—Paulo the Pilot Whimp, Pauline, illus. (p. 1331)
—Pin the Tail on the Donkey Hawley, Kelvin, illus. (p. 1359)
—Presents for Grace Hawley, Kelvin, illus. (p. 1396)
—Quick Picnic Ross, Christine, illus. (p. 1427)
—Rainbow Party Whimp, Pauline, illus. (p. 1435)
—Red Riding Hood Hawley, Kelvin, illus. (p. 1454)
—Ringing Bells. (p. 1473)
—Sally Snip Snap's Party Storey, Jim, illus. (p. 1505)
—See Me Ride East, Jacqueline, illus. (p. 1546)
—Show Me a Shape Cooper, Jenny, illus. (p. 1570)
—Sneaky Spider Storey, Jim, illus. (p. 1597)
—So Fast Webb, Philip, illus. (p. 1602)
—Stickybeak the Parrot East, Jacqueline, illus. (p. 1650)
—Stone Soup Hawley, Kelvin, illus. (p. 1652)
—Surprise from the Sky Whimp, Pauline, illus. (p. 1686)
—Surprise Visitor Hoit, Richard, illus. (p. 1686)
—Thirsty Baby Elephant. (p. 1734)
—Three Billy Goats Gruff Hawley, Kelvin, illus. (p. 1741)
—Three Little Pigs Storey, Jim, illus. (p. 1742)
—Tin Lizzy Hawley, Kelvin, illus. (p. 1755)
—Too Big & Heavy Hatam, Samer, illus. (p. 1766)
—Toys That Can Go (p. 1774)
—Trip, Trap! Hawley, Kelvin, illus. (p. 1787)
—Turtle Is Lost. (p. 1798)
—Two Pirates Whimp, Pauline, illus. (p. 1804)
—Umbrellas Go Up. (p. 1810)
—Watch Me Swim Hansen, Christine, illus. (p. 1861)
—Watch Out for Whales Aziz, Lamia, illus. (p. 1861)
—Watch the Ball Whimp, Pauline, illus. (p. 1861)
—Water from Rain. (p. 1862)
—Whale Rescue Aziz, Lamia, illus. (p. 1877)
—When I Grow Up. East, Jacqueline, illus. (p. 1902)
—Who Wins the Race? (p. 1919)
Holden, Pam, jt. auth. see Lockyer, John.
Holden, Pam & Aesop. Clever Crow. Hatam, Samer, illus. (p. 331)
Holden, Pam, et al. Mira Como Nado. Hansen, Christine, illus. (p. 1148)
Holden, Robert. Pied Piper of Hamelin. Zak, Drahos, illus. (p. 1356)
Holden, Susan. Sparky Dog: the Pensive Pup. Aspen, Lydia, illus. (p. 1622)
—Sparky Dog: the Trash Hound Beagle. Aspen, Lydia, illus. (p. 1622)
Holden-Rowley, Tim & Blewitt, John. AS Citizenship. Mitchell, Mike, ed. (p. 105)
Holder, Amy. Lipstick Laws. (p. 1021)
Holder, Jennifer. Brave & Beautiful Queen Esther. Julien, Terry, illus. (p. 223)
—Daniel & His Faithful Friends. Julien, Terry, illus. (p. 404)
—Go, Jonah, Go! (p. 686)
—God Made You Special. Nobens, C. A., illus. (p. 690)
—God Said & Moses Led. (p. 690)
—God Was with Joseph. (p. 690)
—My Story of Jesus. Munger, Nancy, illus. (p. 1219)
—Old Testament Faith Heroes. (p. 1284)
—Peter Said Yes! (p. 1347)
Holder, Jennifer, jt. auth. see Stortz, Diane.
Holder, Jimmy, illus. see Beech, Sandy.
Holder, Jimmy, illus. see Higgins, Nadia.
Holder, Jimmy, illus. see Wallace, Rich.
Holder, Jimmy, illus. see Walton, Rick.
Holder, John, illus. see Ganeri, Anita.
Holder, Larry & Howell, Brian. New Orleans Saints. (p. 1246)
Holder, Mig, et al. Papa Panov's Special Day. (p. 1322)
Holder, Nancy. Evil Within. (p. 546)
—On Fire. (p. 1288)
—Pretty Little Devils. (p. 1398)
—Rose Bride: A Retelling of "The White Bride & the Black Bride" (p. 1489)
—Screaming Season. (p. 1533)
—Spirited. (p. 1629)
Holder, Nancy, jt. auth. see Viguie, Debbie.
Holder, Nancy & Viguié, Debbie. Crusade. (p. 386)
—Damned. (p. 401)
—Legacy & Spellbound. (p. 987)
—Resurrection. (p. 1464)
—Vanquished. (p. 1833)
Holder, Nancy & Viguie, Debbie. Wicked: Witch & Curse. (p. 1927)
Holder, Nancy & Viguié, Debbie. Wicked: Witch & Curse. (p. 1941)
Holder, Ramona V. Paco & Lexus Are Good Friends: Paco y Lexus son Buen Amigos. (p. 1317)
Holder, Sherie. More Amazing Sports Photos: More Funny, Famous, & Fantastic Photographs from the World of Sports. (p. 1174)
Holderness, Grizelda, illus. see Koralek, Jenny.
Holdiman, Kim S. Hurt in My Heart. (p. 830)
Holding, James Malcolm, 3rd, et al. Mullet Masters (p. 1189)
Holding, Sarah. SeaBEAN: Book 1 of the SeaBEAN Trilogy. (p. 1536)
Holdman, Shirley Terrill. Adventures of Giggles & Owen: A True Story. Riecks Goss, Carol, illus. (p. 18)
Holdredge, Jon, illus. see Winick, Judd.
Holdren, Maria K., illus. see Weaver, Kimberly & Murphy, Allyson.
Holdren, Mark W. Spirit Wolf. (p. 1629)
Holdstein, Deborah. Challenging Perspectives: Reading Critically about Ethics & Values. (p. 289)
Holdsworth, Henry, photos by see Krauskopf, Sharma.
Holdsworth, John. Old Testament. (p. 1284)
Hole, Jim. Bulbs: Practical Advice & the Science Behind It (p. 240)
—Locations: Favorite Plants for Better Yards. (p. 1044)
—Problems: Favorite Plants for Better Yards Vol. 2 (p. 1408)
—What Grows Here? Favorite Plants for Better Yards. (p. 1885)

—What Grows Here? Indoors: Favorite Houseplants for Every Situation. Matsubuchi, Akemi, photos by. (p. 1885)
Hole, Jim, jt. auth. see Hole, Lois.
Hole, Jim, ed. Hole's Dictionary of Hardy Perennials: The Buyer's Guide for Professionals, Collectors & Gardeners. (p. 788)
Hole, Lois. Lois Hole's Perennial Favorites: 100 Best for Beauty & Hardiness. Keane-Dawes, Jennifer M., ed. (p. 1045)
—Trees & Shrubs: Practical Advice & the Science Behind It Vol. 5 (p. 1834)
—Vegetables: Practical Advice & the Science Behind It (p. 1834)
Hole, Lois & Hole, Jim. Lois Hole's Bulbs: Better Choices, Better Gardens. (p. 1045)
Hole, Stian. Anna's Heaven. (p. 85)
—Garmann's Secret. Hole, Stian, illus. (p. 657)
—Garmann's Summer. Bartlett, Don, tr. from NOR. (p. 657)
Hole, Stian & Bartlett, Don. Garmann's Street. (p. 657)
Holechek, Max. Edsel Mcfarlan's New Car. Toland, Darrell, illus. (p. 505)
Holeman, Linda. Search of the Moon King's Daughter. (p. 1537)
—Toxic Love. (p. 1774)
Holford, Karen. I Miss Grandpa: A Story to Help Your Child Understand Death— & Eternal Life. (p. 844)
Holgate, Doug, illus. see Carvell, Tim.
Holgate, Doug, illus. see Kroll, Steven.
Holgate, Doug, illus. see Savage, J. Scott.
Holgate, Douglas, illus. see Anderson, Brian.
Holgate, Douglas, illus. see Cotler, Steve.
Holgate, Douglas, illus. see Dahl, Michael & Collins, Daryll.
Holgate, Douglas, illus. see Dahl, Michael.
Holgate, Douglas, illus. see Kalz, Jill.
Holgate, Douglas, illus. see Lemke, Donald B.
Holgate, Douglas, illus. see Lemke, Donald.
Holgate, Douglas, illus. see Taor, Adam.
Holgren, Anna C., illus. see Collins, C. B.
Holguin, Elvira Rodriguez. Camina, Camino. (p. 256)
Holguin, Magdalena, tr. see Horvath, Polly.
Holguin, Magdalena, tr. see Spinner, Stephanie.
Holguin, Magdalena, tr. see Wang, Gabrielle.
Holics, Laszlo. 300 Creative Physics Problems with Solutions. (p. 2001)
Holiday, Billie. God Bless the Child. Pinkney, Jerry, illus. (p. 688)
Holiday, Billie & Herzog, Arthur, Jr. God Bless the Child. Pinkney, Jerry, illus. (p. 688)
—God Bless the Child. Pinckney, Jerry, illus. (p. 688)
Holiday, J. D. Janoose the Goose. Holiday, J. D., illus. (p. 908)
Holiday, Jane. Exploring Argentina with the Five Themes of Geography. (p. 551)
—Exploring Brazil with the Five Themes of Geography. (p. 551)
—Exploring Chile with the Five Themes of Geography. (p. 551)
Holiday, Michael. Clam Land: Lessons in Life. (p. 326)
Holiday, Moody. No Ordinary Love, Selena's Revenge (p. 1259)
Holifield, Vicky, illus. see Homan, Tim.
Holinaty, Josh, illus. see Gardy, Jennifer.
Holinaty, Josh, illus. see Szpirglas, Jeff.
Holjes, Kerry, ed. see Willard, Hugh.
Holkins, Jerry. Attack of the Bacon Robots! Krahulik, Mike, illus. (p. 113)
Holko, Suzanne L. Grampy & Me. (p. 706)
Holl, jt. auth. see Holl, Kristi D.
Holl, Brent, ed. see Amchin, Robert.
Holl, Brent, ed. see Hale, Connie.
Holl, Brent, ed. see Kennedy, Steven.
Holl, Kristi. Chat Freak. (p. 294)
—Discovering the Nature of Gravity (p. 450)
—Girlz Rock: Devotions for Girls (p. 681)
—Shazam & Chris Barton, Philip Inghelbrecht, Dhiraj Mukherjee, & Avery Wang (p. 1563)
—Shine on Girl: Devotions to Keep You Sparkling (p. 1566)
—What's a Girl to Do? Finding Faith in Everyday Life (p. 1896)
Holl, Kristi & Adams, Michelle Medlock. No Boys Allowed: Devotions for Girls (p. 1257)
Holl, Kristi D. Invisible Alex. (p. 885)
Holl, Kristi D. & Holl. Chick Chat: 90-Day Devotional (p. 299)
Holl, Robert. Apúrate, Teddy: Fiction-to-Fact Big Book. Forss, Ian, illus. (p. 93)
—Teddy on the Move. (p. 1712)
Holladay, Drew. Stories by Drew Holladay: With Grandma Shirley Holladay. (p. 1654)
Holladay, Reggie, illus. see Ottolenghi, Carol.
Holladay, Riley. Jake, the Clumsy Astronaut: With a Bonus Story, Bob, the Scorpion (p. 906)
Holladay, Shirley. Gail the Snail. (p. 652)
—Little H 2 O: A Story about the Rain Cycle. Smith, Mindy, illus. (p. 1028)
—Oh Gary, Dr. Berry Isn't Scary: Visiting the Doctor Can Be a Comfortable, Pleasant Experience. (p. 1280)
Holland, jt. auth. see Berg.
Holland, Amy L. Adventures of Bubba & Sis: Book One. (p. 17)
Holland, Beth. Webber HearBuilder Following Directions Fun Sheets: Hbbk55. Ink, Bruce & Golliher, Bill, illus. (p. 1870)
Holland, Cheron. Bully: Carmen & Artela. (p. 241)
Holland, Diane. Sally Butterfield Goes Fishing! (p. 1505)
Holland, Dwayne K. Princess Laura & the Magic Waterfall. (p. 1404)
Holland, Eva, jt. auth. see Minnick, Chris.
Holland, Frances. Ryan's Praying Mantis (p. 1499)
Holland, Francis. KoKo's New Home. (p. 966)
Holland, Gay W., illus. see Glaser, Linda.
Holland, Gay W., illus. see Kavasch, E. Barrie.
Holland, Gill. Louisvle Counts! A Children's Counting & Art Book. Brothers, Stephanie, ed. (p. 1059)
Holland, Gini. Alive & Not Alive. (p. 41)
—Alive & Not Alive/Vivo y no Vivo (p. 41)
—Alive & Not Alive/Vivo y No Vivo. (p. 41)
—American Shorthairs. (p. 1259)
—Empire State Building: How It Was Built & How It Is Used. (p. 521)
—Holiday Crafts. (p. 788)

—Hot & Cold. (p. 801)
—Hot & Cold/Caliente y Frio. (p. 801)
—I Live in a Town. (p. 841)
—I Live in a Town/Vivo en un Pueblo. Coffey, Colleen & Carrillo, Consuelo, trs. (p. 841)
—I Live in the City. (p. 841)
—I Live in the City/Vivo en la Ciudad. Coffey, Colleen & Carrillo, Consuelo, trs. (p. 841)
—I Live in the Country. (p. 841)
—I Live in the Country/Vivo en el Campo. Coffey, Colleen & Carrillo, Consuelo, trs. (p. 841)
—I Live in the Desert. (p. 841)
—I Live in the Desert/Vivo en el Desierto. Coffey, Colleen & Carrillo, Consuelo, trs. (p. 841)
—I Live in the Mountains. (p. 841)
—I Live in the Mountains/Vivo en las Montañas. Coffey, Colleen & Carrillo, Consuelo, trs. (p. 841)
—I Live near the Ocean. (p. 841)
—I Live near the Ocean/Vivo cerca del Mar. Coffey, Colleen & Carrillo, Consuelo, trs. (p. 841)
—Light & Heavy. (p. 1014)
—Light & Heavy/ Ligero y Pesado. (p. 1014)
—Light & Heavy/Ligero y Pesado. (p. 1014)
—Paper Crafts. (p. 1322)
—Ragdolls. (p. 1433)
—Soft & Hard. (p. 1605)
—Soft & Hard/Blando Y Duro. (p. 1606)
—Where I Live. (p. 1908)
Holland, Gini, jt. auth. see O'Hern, Kerri.
Holland, Gini & O'Hern, Kerri. Louis Armstrong. Spay, Anthony & Campbell, Alex, illus. (p. 1058)
—Nelson Mandela. (p. 1240)
—Nelson Mandela. McHargue, D., illus. (p. 1240)
Holland, Gretchen. Because He Loves Me. (p. 155)
Holland, James. Duty Calls - Dunkirk. (p. 491)
Holland, James R. Diamonds Are Waiting for You: Crater of Diamonds, Where Dreams Can & Do Come True. (p. 434)
Holland, Jennifer S. Dog & the Piglet. (p. 461)
—Leopard & the Cow. (p. 992)
—Unlikely Friendships for Kids: The Monkey & the Dove - And 4 Other Stories of Animal Friendships. (p. 1821)
—Unlikely Friendships for Kids: The Dog & the Piglet - And Four Other Stories of Animal Friendships. (p. 1821)
—Unlikely Friendships for Kids: the Leopard & the Cow. And Four Other Stories of Animal Friendships. (p. 1821)
Holland, Joe, illus. see McIntosh, Kenneth.
Holland, John Flint. Please Take Me to a Christmas Play Today. (p. 1373)
Holland, Karen. Garden Gang. (p. 656)
Holland, Kathy, illus. see Dunlap, Jim.
Holland, L. Tam. Counterfeit Family Tree of Vee Crawford-Wong. (p. 370)
Holland, Lee. Chair in Time: A Playdate with History. (p. 288)
—Welcome to My Chair: Tales of Adventure from Grumpy's Living Room. (p. 1873)
Holland, Leslie J. Dr. Martin Luther King Jr.'s - I Have a Dream Speech: What It Really Means. (p. 475)
—Dr. Martin Luther King Jr.'s I Have a Dream Speech: In Translation What It Really Means. (p. 475)
Holland, Lisa Tomms, illus. see Engram, Teta.
Holland, Loretta. Fall Leaves. MacKay, Elly, illus. (p. 566)
Holland, Marci. Birth Day Letter: An Alzheimer's Story. (p. 192)
—Birth Day Letter. (p. 192)
Holland, Mary. Animal Mouths (p. 78)
—Beavers' Busy Year (p. 155)
—Beavers' Busy Year Holland, Mary, photos by. (p. 155)
—Ferdinand Fox's First Summer (p. 581)
—Milkweed Visitors. Holland, Mary, photos by. (p. 1143)
—Primer Verano Del Zorro Fernando (p. 1400)
Holland, Maryjo. Broken Shadow. (p. 230)
Holland, NiColle & Holland, Savage Steve. I Have a Hero. (p. 839)
Holland, Nikki Richardson. Meet Lancearnus Jones: A Special Kid with Special Needs. (p. 1121)
Holland, Richard, illus. see Attard, Enebor.
Holland, Richard, illus. see Clynes, Kate, et al.
Holland, Richard, illus. see Landman, Tanya.
Holland, Richard, illus. see Mark, Jan.
Holland, Richard, illus. see Rosen, Michael.
Holland, Rick, illus. see Willis, McKenzie.
Holland, Robert. Black Queen. (p. 196)
—Crossing the River. (p. 385)
—Ghost Who Came to Tea: A Novel of Sports & Mystery. (p. 672)
—Spooks: A Charles Oliver Jones, P.I. (p. 1631)
Holland, Ruth, illus. see Wrench, Peter.
Holland, Savage Steve, jt. auth. see Holland, NiColle.
Holland, Simon. Human Body. Cosgrove, Lee, illus. (p. 825)
—Oceans: Can You Tell the Facts from the Fibs? Cosgrove, Lee, illus. (p. 1277)
Holland, Simon, jt. auth. see Halls, Kelly Milner.
Holland, Stephanie. Personal Safety. (p. 1344)
—Social Behaviour. Friedl, Peter, illus. (p. 1604)
Holland, Trish. Build It from A to Z. (p. 238)
—I Can Do It! Newton, Vanessa Brantley, illus. (p. 835)
—Lasso the Moon. Petrone, Valeria, illus. (p. 977)
—Neighborhood Song. (p. 1240)
—Trees: Count. (p. 1784)
—Wash & Dry. Kumar, Vinay, illus. (p. 1859)
—Who Lives in Trees? (p. 1916)
—Who's Got the Button? (p. 1920)
—World of Families. (p. 1956)
Holland, Trish & Ford, Christine. Soldiers' Night Before Christmas. Manders, John, illus. (p. 1607)
Holland, Wayne. George: A Pitch Dark Comedy. (p. 663)
Holland, Zoraida. A Somewhat Odd Tale of Love. (p. 971)
—Lagoon: A Somewhat Odd Tale of Love. (p. 971)
Holland-Boatwright, Terry. God's Animals, My Friends. (p. 690)
Holland-Davis, Tami. Purple Tulip. (p. 1419)
Hollander, Barbara. Booms, Bubbles, & Busts (p. 213)
—Booms, Bubbles, & Busts: The Economic Cycle. (p. 213)
—How Credit Crises Happen. (p. 806)
—How Currency Devaluation Works. (p. 806)

For book reviews, descriptive annotations, tables of contents, cover images, author biographies & additional information, updated daily, subscribe to www.booksinprint2.com

2347

—How the World Bank & International Monetary Fund Work. (p. 813)
—Money Matters: An Introduction to Economics. (p. 1164)
—Paying for College: Practical, Creative Strategies. (p. 1331)
—Top 10 Secrets for Investing Successfully. (p. 1768)
—Top 10 Secrets for Spending Your Money Wisely. (p. 1768)
Hollander, Barbara & Gottfried Hollander, Barbara. Top 10 Secrets for Investing Successfully. (p. 1768)
—Top 10 Secrets for Spending Your Money Wisely. (p. 1768)
Hollander, Barbara Gottfried. Bitcoins: Navigating Open Source Currency (p. 194)
—Ellen DeGeneres: Television's Funniest Host (p. 514)
—Marriage Rights & Gay Rights: Interpreting the Constitution. (p. 1096)
Hollander, Benjamin. Rituals of Truce & the Other Israeli. (p. 1475)
Hollander, Cass. Keeping Fit (p. 947)
Hollander, Cass & Capstone Press Editors. Keeping Fit (p. 947)
Hollander, Michael, jt. auth. see Hollander, Michael R.
Hollander, Michael & Hollander, Michael R. Helping Teens Who Cut: Understanding & Ending Self-Injury. (p. 766)
Hollander, Michael R., jt. auth. see Hollander, Michael.
Hollander, Michael R. & Hollander, Michael. Helping Teens Who Cut: Understanding & Ending Self-Injury. (p. 766)
Hollander, Sarah, illus. see Archambault, John & Plummer, David.
Hollander, Sarah, illus. see Plummer, David & Archambault, John.
Hollander, Sarah, illus. see Ransom, Candice.
Hollands, Judith. Mrs. Mudgie & Mr. James. (p. 1187)
Hollar, Cheryl Faye. Billy the Bunny Goes to the State Fair. (p. 187)
Hollar, Sherman. Ancient Egypt. (p. 68)
—Astronomy: Understanding the Universe. (p. 109)
—Basketball & Its Greatest Players. (p. 143)
—Biographies of Colonial America: From Sir Walter Raleigh to Phillis Wheatley. (p. 188)
—Biographies of Colonial America: Sir Walter Raleigh, Powhatan, Phillis Wheatley, & More. (p. 188)
—Biographies of the New American Nation: From George Washington to Frederick Douglass. (p. 188)
—Biographies of the New American Nation: George Washington, Thomas Jefferson, Frederick Douglass, & More. (p. 188)
—Closer Look at Bacteria, Algae, & Protozoa. (p. 334)
—Closer Look at Biology, Microbiology, & the Cell. (p. 334)
—Closer Look at Plant Classifications, Parts, & Uses. (p. 334)
—Closer Look at the Animal Kingdom. (p. 334)
—Inner Planets: Mercury, Venus, & Mars. (p. 875)
—Investigating Earth's Desert, Grassland, & Rainforest Biomes. (p. 884)
—Investigating Earth's Polar Biomes. (p. 884)
—Mesopotamia. (p. 1129)
—Outer Planets: Jupiter, Saturn, Uranus, & Neptune. (p. 1312)
—Pioneers in Medicine: From the Classical World to Today. (p. 1361)
—Pioneers in the World of Weather & Climatology. (p. 1361)
—Pioneers of the Industrial Age: Breakthroughs in Technology. (p. 1361)
—Protecting the Environment. (p. 1412)
—Soccer & Its Greatest Players. (p. 1603)
—Sound. (p. 1615)
Hollar, Sherman, contrib. by. Andrew Jackson. (p. 72)
—Barack Obama. (p. 137)
—George Washington. (p. 664)
—John F. Kennedy. (p. 921)
Hollar, Sherman, ed. Electronics. (p. 509)
Hollaway, David. Quigley Mccormick: And the Curse of the Polka Dotted Pig (p. 1428)
Hollein, Max, jt. auth. see Hollein, Nina.
Hollein, Nina & Hollein, Max. Cut-Out Fun with Matisse. (p. 396)
Hollen, Kathryn H. Reproductive System (p. 1461)
Hollenbeck, Kathleen. Penguins Family: The Story of a Humboldt Penguin. Stegos, Daniel, illus. (p. 1337)
—Penguins Family: Story of a Humboldt Penguin Hardcover. Stegos, Daniel, illus. (p. 1337)
—Penguin's Family: The Story of a Humboldt Penguin. Stegos, Daniel, illus. (p. 1337)
Hollenbeck, Kathleen & Smithsonian Institution Staff. Penguin's Family (la familia del Pinguino) (p. 1337)
Hollenbeck, Kathleen M. Dancing on the Sand: A Story of an Atlantic Blue Crab. (p. 403)
—Dancing on the Sand: A Story of an Atlantic Blue Crab. Popeo, Joanie, illus. (p. 403)
—Fluency Practice Mini-Books: 15 Short, Leveled Fiction & Nonfiction Mini-Books with Research-Based Strategies to Help Students Build Word Recognition, Fluency, & Comprehension. (p. 608)
—Islands of Ice: The Story of a Harp Seal. Genzo, John Paul, illus. (p. 892)
—Lobster's Secret. Weiman, Jon, illus. (p. 1044)
—Penguin's Family: The Story of the a Humboldt Penguin. Stegos, Daniel J., illus. (p. 1337)
—Red Fox at Hickory Lane. Smith, Wendy, tr. (p. 1454)
—Red Fox at Hickory Lane. Smith, Wendy, illus. (p. 1454)
Hollenbeck, Patricia. Eat Your Colors. (p. 501)
Holler, Sue Farrell. Lacey & the African Grandmothers (p. 970)
Holley, Kim. Rollie Pollie Review. Hawkins, Kristen, illus. (p. 1485)
Holley, Linda A. Tipis, Tepees, Teepees: History & Design of the Cloth Tipi (p. 1757)
Holley, M. E. Jonah & the Last Great Dragon: Legend of the Heart Eaters. (p. 925)
—Menace of the Night Creatures. (p. 1126)
Holley, Marietta. Samantha at the St. Louis Exposition. (p. 1507)
—Samantha at the World's Fair. (p. 1507)
Holley, Pam Spencer. Quick & Popular Reads for Teens. (p. 1427)
Holley, Rebecca L. Cow-racter A Lesson in Kindness: Barnyard Blessings. (p. 373)
Holley, Vanessa, illus. see Scholastic, Inc. Staff & Roberson, Karla.
Holliday, Andrea. Squissy, the Little Grey Squirrel That Got a Second Chance. (p. 1637)
Holliday, Anne. No More Puppet Shows. (p. 1259)
Holliday, Berchie, et al. Algebra 1. (p. 38)
—Algebra 2. (p. 38)
Holliday, Bobby. Hamor: The Road to Jerusalem. (p. 739)
—Lump of Clay. Price, Rebecca, illus. (p. 1065)
Holliday, D. L. Adventures of Tommy. (p. 24)
Holliday, Diane & Malone, Bobbie. Digging & Discovery, Teachers Guide & Student Materials, 2nd Edition, on CD: Wisconsin Archaeology. (p. 439)
Holliday, Diane Young. Mountain Wolf Woman: A Ho-Chunk Girlhood. (p. 1181)
Holliday, Diane Young & Malone, Bobbie. Digging & Discovery: Wisconsin Archaeology. (p. 439)
Holliday, Holly, illus. see Keithley, Laura Lee.
Holliday, Laurel. Dreaming in Color Living in Black & White: Our Own Stories of Growing up Black in America. (p. 484)
Holliday, Mary Martin, tr. see Ponti, Claude.
Holliday, Patricia. I Look in the Mirror. (p. 841)
—Is for Anjelina. (p. 889)
—Is for Anjelina: an Introduction to ABC's And 123's. (p. 889)
—You & me makes Two. (p. 1973)
Holliday, Reggie, illus. see Jacks, Cyndie & Lewis, Dawn.
Holliday, S. L. My Identity Christ-Is: Stay in the Game. (p. 1211)
Holliday, Susan. Dream Cave. (p. 483)
—Riding the Storm. (p. 1471)
—Time Street Gang & the Rag & Bone Boy. (p. 1752)
Holliday, Taliba, jt. auth. see North, Tiana.
Hollier, Jo. Roary O'Rourke Challenge of the Trolls (p. 1478)
—Roary O'Rourke, Quest for the Secret of Bramble Castle. (p. 1478)
—Roary O'Rourke the Princess & Dooley Do (p. 1478)
—Roary O'Rourke Victorious Duo (p. 1478)
Holligan, Susan. Grandma Smells Like Love. (p. 708)
Hollihan, Kerrie Logan. Carnival in Latin America: Carnaval en Latinoamérica. Sanz, Ma Pilar, tr. (p. 270)
—Christmas Traditions in Latin America: Tradiciones Navidenas en Latinoamérica. Sanz, Ma Pilar, tr. (p. 316)
—Day of the Dead: Día de Los Muertos. (p. 414)
—Elizabeth I, the People's Queen: Her Life & Times, 21 Activities. (p. 513)
—Hispanic Heritage Month: Mes de la Herencia Hispana. Sanz, Ma Pilar, tr. (p. 781)
—Isaac Newton & Physics for Kids: His Life & Ideas with 21 Activities. (p. 890)
—Reporting under Fire: 16 Daring Women War Correspondents & Photojournalists. (p. 1461)
—Rightfully Ours: How Women Won the Vote, 21 Activities. (p. 1472)
—Theodore Roosevelt for Kids: His Life & Times, 21 Activities. (p. 1729)
Hollihan, Tony. Crazy Horse: Warrior Spirit of the Sioux. (p. 377)
—Disasters of Western Canada: Courage Amidst the Chaos. Vol. 1 (p. 447)
—Mountain Men: Frontier Adventurers Alone Against the Wilderness (p. 1181)
—Mounties March West: The Epic Trek & Early Adventures of the Mounted Police. (p. 1181)
Hollihan-Elliot, Sheila. Ancient History of China. (p. 69)
—Ancient History of China. Wang, Jianwei, ed. (p. 69)
—Art & Architecture of China. Wang, Jianwei, ed. (p. 101)
—Chinese Art & Architecture. (p. 307)
—Muslims in China. (p. 1194)
Holliman, Lynn. Best Day Ever! (p. 168)
Hollindale, Peter & Barrie, J. M. Peter Pan & Other Plays: The Admirable Crichton; Peter Pan; When Wendy Grew up; What Every Woman Knows; Mary Rose. (p. 1347)
Holling, Holling Clancy. Holling Clancy Holling's Stories from Many Lands. (p. 789)
Holling, Prudence. Grace Has a Secret. (p. 704)
Hollinger, Deanne, illus. see Johnston, Johanna.
Hollinger, Elizabeth M. Star Ocean(r) Till the End of Time: Official Strategy Guide. (p. 1640)
Hollinger, Lisa. Academic Word Power 1. (p. 7)
Hollinger, Valerie Bunch, illus. see O'Connor, Crystal Ball.
Hollingsworth, Kenneth D. Planting the Seeds That Reap the Harvest: A Guide to Understanding the Basics of Christian Witnessing & Evangelism. (p. 1369)
Hollingsworth, Mary. My Bible Journey Supersaver. (p. 1197)
Hollingsworth, Mary, jt. auth. see Wilde, Oscar.
Hollingsworth, Suzi. Birding with Bobbie. (p. 191)
Hollingsworth, Tamara. Anne Frank: A Light in the Dark (p. 85)
—Anne Frank: A Light in the Dark. (p. 85)
—Helen Keller: A New Vision (p. 762)
—Helen Keller: A New Vision. (p. 762)
—Martin Luther: A Reforming Spirit. (p. 1097)
—Nelson Mandela: Leading the Way (p. 1241)
—Nelson Mandela: Leading the Way. (p. 1241)
—Reformation: A Religious Revolution. (p. 1456)
—Unforgettable Catastrophes. (p. 1817)
—Unforgettable Natural Disasters. (p. 1817)
—Unforgettable News Reports. (p. 1817)
Hollingsworth, Toni, jt. auth. see Pitches, Neale.
Hollingum, Ben. Maps & Measurement. (p. 1090)
—Travel Maps. (p. 1780)
—Understanding Maps of Our World: Maps & Mapping the World. (p. 1815)
Hollingworth, Denise & Searle, Carole. Jammin' in the Jungle! (p. 907)
Hollinrake, Chriss, illus. see Apted, Violet.
Hollins, Jack. Charlie's Christmas Adventure. (p. 293)
Hollins, Paula. Christmas Makes Words! A Selection of Words That Can Be Made from the Letters in the Word Christmas, with Humorous Poems & Colorful Illustr. (p. 314)
—Christopher Makes Words! A Personalized World of Words Based on the Letters in the Name Christopher, with Humorous Poems & Colorful Illustrations. (p. 317)
—Isabella Makes Words! A Personalized World of Words Based on the Letters in the Name Isabella, with Humorous Poems & Colorful Illustrations. (p. 891)
—Isabelle Makes Words! A Personalized World of Words Based on the Letters in the Name Isabelle, with Humorous Poems & Colorful Illustrations. (p. 891)
—Katherine Makes Words! A Personalized World of Words Based on the Letters in the Name Katherine, with Humorous Poems & Colorful Illustrations. (p. 944)
—Michael Makes Words! A Personalized World of Words Based on the Letters in the Name Michael, with Humorous Poems & Colorful Illustrations. (p. 1134)
—Sophie Makes Words! A Personalized World of Words Based on the Letters in the Name Sophie, with Humorous Poems & Colorful Illustrations. (p. 1613)
Hollis, Charles, jt. auth. see Rushforth, Keith.
Hollis, Ginger. Pumpkin Gift. Scarborough, Casey, illus. (p. 1416)
Hollis Iv, John H., jt. see Natera, Jasmin A.
Hollis, John H., 4th. Art & graffiti Iraq: Soldier's Art, Graffiti, Flags, & Flashes in Iraq (p. 101)
—Psd/set teams of Iraq: A Pictorial of DOD Contractor Teams in Iraq (p. 1413)
—Saf weapons of Iraq: A Pictorial of Small Arms Fire Weapons in OIF I, II, III, & IV (p. 1501)
Hollis, Matthew. Jada Makes Jewelry: Use Place Value Understanding & Properties of Operations to Add & Subtract. (p. 905)
Hollis, Michael, illus. see Trembley, Skip & Ochs, Susan A.
Hollis, Mignonne, jt. auth. see Dalkin, Monika.
Hollis, Nicole Phillips. My Neighborhood Super Kids. (p. 1216)
Hollis, Randy. Meet Sneazle Rahn, Jess, illus. (p. 1122)
Hollis, Trish. Light Bulb Buddies. (p. 1015)
Hollis, Tyler, illus. see Gaddy, Kathi.
Hollis, Tyler, illus. see Tuttle, Brad.
Hollister, Milan. Adventures of Meg: Wiggles Learns about Telling the Truth. (p. 20)
—Adventures of Meg: Meg Sniffs Out the Endangered Pink River Dolphin. (p. 20)
Hollman, Jeremie, jt. auth. see Glastetter, KC.
Hollman, Jeremie, jt. photos by see Glastetter, KC.
Hollmann, Clide Anne & Plummer, Myrtes Marie. Jim Bridger: King of Scouts. (p. 917)
Hollmann, Robert E. Davy Crockett. (p. 411)
—William Barret Travis. (p. 1933)
Hollo, Anselm. Braided River: New & Selected Poems, 1965-2005. (p. 221)
Hollon, Frank Turner, et al. Glitter Girl & the Crazy Cheese. Dulemba, Elizabeth O., illus. (p. 684)
Hollow, Michele C. Animal Jokes to Tickle Your Funny Bone. (p. 78)
—Grateful Dead: What a Long, Strange Trip It's Been. (p. 712)
—Nifty Thrifty Math Crafts. Ponte, June, illus. (p. 1252)
—Nifty Thrifty Sports Crafts. Ponte, June, illus. (p. 1252)
Holloway, Christina. Irish Selkie. (p. 888)
Holloway, Christopher. Gloumain Chronicles Book 1. the Aznadac Heir. (p. 685)
Holloway, Ethan. Numbers at the Market: Number Names & Count Sequence. (p. 1272)
Holloway, Jamie. Jimmy Is Not a Fish. (p. 918)
Holloway, Jimmie Frances. Little Bit Finds His Kin or Does He? Hum! (p. 1024)
Holloway, John N. History of Kansas: The conflict of free & slave labor in the settlement of Kansas, & the overthrow of the latter, with all other items of general Interest ... : American slavery, & its onward March. (p. 784)
Holloway, Julie M., jt. auth. see Brown, Brett T.
Holloway, Karl. I Can Show the Way: Monte's Rocket Launch. Vagreti, Eva, illus. (p. 836)
Hollowell, Lorraine L. Oatmeal Bath: And Other Poems That Make Kids Laugh. (p. 1275)
—Outside Is Where I'd Rather Be: And Other Poems for Kids Like Me. (p. 1313)
Hollows, Joanne & Moseley, Rachel, eds. Feminism in Popular Culture. (p. 581)
Holly, Davison, illus. see Sylvia, Davison.
Holly, Emma. Catching Midnight. (p. 279)
—Fairyville. (p. 565)
Holly, Julia. Mrs Winkler's Cure. Holly, Julia, illus. (p. 1188)
Hollyer, Beatrice. Let's Eat: What Children Eat Around the World. (p. 996)
—Our World of Water: Children & Water Around the World. (p. 1310)
—Todos a la Mesa Que Comen Los Niños y Niñas Del Mundo. (p. 1761)
Hollyer, Belinda. River Song. (p. 1476)
—Secrets, Lies & My Sister Kate. (p. 1545)
Hollyer, Belinda & Brontë, Charlotte. Jane Eyre. (p. 908)
Holm, Amy E., jt. auth. see Crawford, Leslie.
Holm, Anne. I Am David. Kingsland, L. W., tr. from DAN. (p. 832)
Holm, Barbara. Visit to Hawaii. Ingram, Anne, illus. (p. 1845)
Holm, Bill. Windows of Brimnes: An American in Iceland. (p. 1936)
Holm, H. R. Against an Amber Sky. (p. 29)
—Forever Santa. (p. 619)
Holm, Jennifer L. Adventure. (p. 14)
—Claim. (p. 326)
—Creek. (p. 380)
—Eighth Grade Is Making Me Sick: Ginny Davis's Year in Stuff. Castaldi, Elicia, illus. (p. 507)
—Fourteenth Goldfish. (p. 625)
—Middle School Is Worse Than Meatloaf: A Year Told Through Stuff. Castaldi, Elicia, illus. (p. 1137)
—Our Only May Amelia. (p. 1309)
—Penny, Caída del Cielo: Retrato de una Familia Italoamericana. Diez, Lola, tr. (p. 1338)
—Penny from Heaven. (p. 1338)
—Trouble with May Amelia. Gustavson, Adam, illus. (p. 1790)
—Turtle in Paradise. (p. 1798)
—Wilderness Days. (p. 1931)
Holm, Jennifer L., jt. auth. see Holm, Matthew.
Holm, Jennifer L., jt. auth. see Meigs, Cornelia.
Holm, Jennifer L. & Hamel, Jonathan. Postman Always Brings Mice. Weinman, Brad, illus. (p. 1388)
—To Scratch a Thief. Weinman, Brad, illus. (p. 1759)
Holm, Jennifer L. & Holm, Matt. Babymouse for President. (p. 128)
—Bad Babysitter. Holm, Jennifer L. & Holm, Matt, illus. (p. 131)
—Captain Disaster. (p. 264)
—Captain Disaster. Holm, Jennifer L. & Holm, Matt, illus. (p. 264)
—Extreme Babymouse. (p. 556)
—Extreme Babymouse. Holm, Jennifer L. & Holm, Matt, illus. (p. 556)
—Fear the Amoeba. (p. 579)
—Game On! (p. 654)
—Happy Birthday, Babymouse. (p. 744)
—Power of the Parasite. (p. 1389)
—Power of the Parasite. Holm, Jennifer L. & Holm, Matt, illus. (p. 1389)
Holm, Jennifer L. & Holm, Matthew. Babymouse for President. Holm, Jennifer L. & Holm, Matthew, illus. (p. 128)
—Beach Babe. (p. 149)
—Brave New Pond. Holm, Jennifer L. & Holm, Matthew, illus. (p. 223)
—Burns Rubber. (p. 244)
—Burns Rubber. Holm, Jennifer L. & Holm, Matthew, illus. (p. 244)
—Camp Babymouse. (p. 257)
—Cupcake Tycoon. Holm, Jennifer L. & Holm, Matthew, illus. (p. 392)
—Deadly Disease of Doom. Holm, Jennifer L. & Holm, Matthew, illus. (p. 417)
—Dragonslayer. Holm, Jennifer L. & Holm, Matthew, illus. (p. 479)
—Fear the Amoeba Holm, Jennifer L. & Holm, Matthew, illus. (p. 579)
—Fear the Amoeba. Holm, Jennifer L. & Holm, Matthew, illus. (p. 579)
—Game On! Holm, Jennifer L. & Holm, Matthew, illus. (p. 654)
—Happy Birthday, Babymouse! Holm, Jennifer L. & Holm, Matthew, illus. (p. 744)
—Heartbreaker. (p. 760)
—Mad Scientist. Holm, Jennifer L. & Holm, Matthew, illus. (p. 1069)
—Monster Mash. (p. 1167)
—Monster Mash. Holm, Jennifer L. & Holm, Matthew, illus. (p. 1167)
—Musical. Holm, Jennifer L. & Holm, Matthew, illus. (p. 1194)
—Our Hero. (p. 1309)
—Puppy Love. (p. 1418)
—Queen of the World! (p. 1425)
—Rock Star. (p. 1482)
—Skater Girl. (p. 1584)
—Super Amoeba. Holm, Jennifer L. & Holm, Matthew, illus. (p. 1679)
—Very Babymouse Christmas. Holm, Jennifer L. & Holm, Matthew, illus. (p. 1837)
Holm, Jennifer L., et al. Comics Squad: Recess! (p. 348)
Holm, Kirsten C. Everyday Life in Ancient China. (p. 543)
—Everyday Life in Ancient Greece. (p. 543)
—Everyday Life in Ancient Rome. (p. 543)
—Everyday Life in the Maya Civilization. (p. 543)
Holm, M. S. Arborist. (p. 95)
—How Mohammed Saved Miss Liberty. (p. 811)
Holm, Matt, jt. auth. see Holm, Jennifer L.
Holm, Matthew, jt. auth. see Holm, Jennifer L.
Holm, Matthew & Holm, Jennifer L. Skater Girl. (p. 1584)
Holm, Sharon, illus. see Atwood, Megan.
Holm, Sharon, illus. see Brynie, Faith Hickman.
Holm, Sharon, illus. see Hall, Pamela.
Holm, Sharon, illus. see Lorbiecki, Marybeth.
Holm, Sharon, illus. see Ross, Kathy.
Holm, Sharon, illus. see Vogel, Julia.
Holm, Sharon, illus. see Williams, Rozanne Lanczak.
Holm, Sharon Lane. Zoe's Hats: A Book of Colors & Patterns. Holm, Sharon Lane, illus. (p. 1987)
Holm, Sharon Lane, illus. see Blackaby, Susan.
Holm, Sharon Lane, illus. see Brynie, Faith Hickman.
Holm, Sharon Lane, illus. see Ross, Kathy.
Holm, Sharon Lane, illus. see Taylor, Jane.
Holm, Sharon Lane, illus. see Thompson, Kim Mitzo.
Holm, Sharon Lane, illus. see Tourville, Amanda Doering.
Holm, Sharon Lane, tr. see Ross, Kathy.
Holman. Science Spectacular: Physics: Online Edition Upgrade. (p. 1528)
—Science Spectacular: Physics: Enhanced Online Edition. (p. 1528)
Holman Bible Staff, jt. auth. see Broadman and Holman Publishers Staff.
Holman, Bobby Joe. Diatonic Harmonica. (p. 435)
Holman, Donna Buckman. Little Angel Friends. (p. 1023)
Holman, Doris Anne. Come with Me to the Pond. (p. 347)
—Oscar, the River Otter. (p. 1305)
Holman, Felice. Cricket Winter. Thomas, Robyn, illus. (p. 382)
—Slake's Limbo. (p. 1587)
Holman, Karen, illus. see Harris, Marie.
Holman, Karen Busch, illus. see Arenstam, Peter.
Holman, Karen Busch, illus. see Wargin, Kathy-jo.
Holman, Nedra. Beautiful Queen. Velitchenko, Olga, illus. (p. 154)
Holman, T. A. Stop It, Tyrone! (p. 1653)
Holmberg, Ansgar, illus. see Fischer, Carl.
Holmberg, Bo R. Day with Dad. Eriksson, Eva, illus. (p. 415)
Holmberg, James J. Into the Wilderness: The Lewis & Clark Expedition. (p. 881)
Holmberg, John. Mooring Madness. (p. 1173)
Holme, Sharon, illus. see Blackaby, Susan.
Holmen, Lene. Kittens. (p. 963)
—Lift & Learn Opposites. Snaith, Andy, photos by. (p. 1014)
Holmes. Gateway Science (p. 658)
Holmes, A. M. X., jt. auth. see Brush Creations.
Holmes & Thom. Dawn of the Dinosaur Age: The Triassic Period. (p. 412)
—Early Life: The Cambrian Period. (p. 493)
—First Vertebrates. (p. 597)

—Time of the Giants: The Mid-Late Jurassic Periods. (p. 1752)
—Time of the Giants. (p. 1752)
Holmes, Andy. Bible for Me: 12 Favorite Stories Voltz, Ralph, illus. (p. 175)
—Building God's Kingdom - Diggit Saves the Day de Giorgi, Sergio, illus. (p. 239)
—If You Give a Boy a Bible. (p. 854)
—Mi Biblia Pijama. O'Connor, Tim, illus. (p. 1132)
—My Princess Bible. Eliseev, Sergey, illus. (p. 1217)
—Tipper Tells a Lie de Giorgi, Sergio, illus. (p. 1757)
Holmes, Andy & Voltz, Ralph. Biblia para Mi (p. 176)
Holmes, Anna. Emmet's Awesome Day. (p. 520)
—Emmet's Awesome Day. Scholastic, Inc. Staff, illus. (p. 520)
—Scorpion Strike! Ameet Studio Staff, illus. (p. 1530)
—Tickety Toc: Pirate Time. (p. 1747)
—Welcome to Tickety Town. (p. 1874)
—Wyldstyle: The Search for the Special. (p. 1966)
—Wyldstyle - The Search for the Special. (p. 1966)
Holmes, Anna & Scholastic, Inc. Staff. Tickety Toc: Welcome to Tickety Town. (p. 1747)
Holmes, Ardy. 4 Seasons of Color. (p. 1992)
Holmes, Bill. Mark Martin. (p. 1095)
Holmes, Christopher P. Slugs: On G.I. Gurdjieff's Beelzebub's Tales to His Grandson. (p. 1591)
Holmes, David, jt. auth. see Warn, Sue.
Holmes, Denise, illus. see Aulenback, Stephany.
Holmes, Denise, illus. see Beliveau, Kathy.
Holmes, Donna M. Jacob & Isabell (p. 904)
Holmes, Ekua, illus. see Weatherford, Carole Boston.
Holmes, Elizabeth. Normal Kid. (p. 1264)
Holmes, Ellen & White, Ellen. Complete Record Book. (p. 353)
Holmes, Ellen White, jt. auth. see Carson-Dellosa Publishing Staff.
Holmes, F., jt. auth. see Davies, H.
Holmes, Fay. Happy Little Ghost: A Halloween Tale. Holmes, Fay, illus. (p. 746)
Holmes, Geni. Adventures of Papa & Jaycee: With Duckey. (p. 21)
Holmes, Gerald L., illus. see Erickson, John R.
Holmes, Gerald L., jt. illus. see Erickson, John R.
Holmes, Guy D. Chicken Froze His Little Toes. (p. 300)
Holmes, Harold H. Tale of the Purple Chicken & Orange Frog. (p. 1700)
Holmes, Heidi L. Best Man. (p. 170)
—Costs & Expenses. (p. 368)
—Maid of Honor. (p. 1076)
—Speeches & Toasts. (p. 1624)
Holmes, Helen, illus. see Ifans, Rhiannon.
Holmes, J. Leigh. That Darn Tooth Fairy! (p. 1726)
Holmes, Janet A. Have You Seen Duck? Bentley, Jonathan, illus. (p. 754)
—Me & You. Rossell, Judith, illus. (p. 1115)
—My Little Library - Me & You. Rossell, Judith, illus. (p. 1212)
—Pink. Bentley, Jonathan, illus. (p. 1359)
—Snap! Germain, Daniella, illus. (p. 1597)
Holmes, Jeremy. There Was an Old Lady. (p. 1730)
Holmes, Jeremy, illus. see Kuhlman, Evan.
Holmes, Jeremy, illus. see Lewis, J. Patrick & Florian, Douglas.
Holmes, Jeremy, illus. see Weiner, Ellis.
Holmes, Jon, ed. see Jaffe, Gail Lois.
Holmes, Joshua D., illus. see Firely, G. M.
Holmes, Julia, jt. auth. see Shapiro, Lawrence.
Holmes, Julienne R. Girl Who Wore Her Shoes on the Wrong Feet. (p. 679)
Holmes, Karen. Slow Motion: Taking Your Time High Beginning Book with Online Access. (p. 1591)
Holmes, Katherine L. Wide Awake Loons. (p. 1927)
Holmes, Kathryn. Distance Between Lost & Found. (p. 453)
Holmes, Kimberly. Digibots Classroom Adventures. Lawson, Devin, illus. (p. 439)
Holmes, Laurie, jt. auth. see Holmes, Thom.
Holmes, Lynda. Spring Cleaning. (p. 1635)
Holmes, Mary Tavener. My Travels with Clara. Cannell, Jon, illus. (p. 1220)
Holmes, Mary Tavener & Harris, John. Elephant from Baghdad Cannell, Jon, illus. (p. 511)
—Giraffe Goes to Paris Cannell, Jon, illus. (p. 677)
Holmes, Matthew, illus. see Dobson, Christina.
Holmes, Melisa & Hutchison, M.D., Patricia. Girlology: A Girl's Guide to Stuff That Matters. (p. 679)
Holmes, Melisa & Hutchison, Patricia. Girlology's There's Something New about You: A Girl's Guide to Growing Up. (p. 679)
Holmes, Melisa & Hutchison, Trish. Hang-Ups, Hook-Ups, & Holding Out: Stuff You Need to Know about Your Body, Sex, & Dating. (p. 742)
Holmes, Mike, illus. see Yang, Gene Luen.
Holmes, Mike, jt. auth. see Comeau, Joey.
Holmes, Oliver Wendell, Sr. Grandmother's Story of Bunker Hill Battle. (p. 709)
—Path of the Law: Learning, Understanding, & Mastering the Law. Kunz, Joseph C., Jr., ed. (p. 1328)
Holmes, Parker. Alabama Crimson Tide. (p. 33)
—Alabama vs. Auburn. (p. 33)
—Amazing Snakes of the Northeast. (p. 55)
—Amazing Snakes of the Southwest & West Coast. (p. 55)
—Auburn Tigers. (p. 114)
—Lakers vs. Celtics. (p. 972)
—Packers vs. Bears. (p. 1317)
—Texas vs. Oklahoma. (p. 1724)
—Tim Tebow. (p. 1750)
Holmes, Quentin. Real Street Kidz: Chasing Action. (p. 1449)
—Real Street Kidz: Art of Authenticity. (p. 1449)
Holmes, Rebecca. Allie's Art Class: Analyze, Compare, Create, & Compose Shapes. (p. 47)
Holmes, Rebecca, illus. see Sithole, Thelma.
Holmes, Richard. Battle. (p. 145)
Holmes, Richard Walker. Ratters of Lightning Ridge. (p. 1440)
Holmes, Robert, photos by see Luebbermann, Mimi.
Holmes, S. D. Adventures of Mister. (p. 20)
Holmes, Sara. Operation Yes. (p. 1300)
Holmes, Sara Lewis. Letters from Rapunzel. (p. 1002)
—Operation Yes. (p. 1300)
Holmes, Stephanie. Grady Goes to Puppy School. (p. 705)
Holmes, Stephen. Alphabet Zoo. (p. 50)
—Number Farm. (p. 1271)
Holmes, Stephen, illus. see Graves, Sue.
Holmes, Stephen, jt. auth. see Faulkner, Keith.
Holmes, Steve. Animales Marinos: Mezcla y Diviertete. (p. 81)
Holmes, Steve, illus. see Hilton, Samantha.
Holmes, Steve, illus. see Wilkes, Angela, et al.
Holmes, Thom. Age of Mammals: The Oligocene & Miocene Periods. (p. 29)
—Dinosaur Scientist: Careers Digging up the Past. (p. 442)
—Early Humans: The Pleistocene & Holocene Epochs. (p. 493)
—Evolution. (p. 546)
—Jazz. (p. 910)
—Last of the Dinosaurs: The Late Cretaceous Period. (p. 978)
—Paleontologists: Searching for Dinosaur Bones. (p. 1319)
—Prehistoric Earth Set, 10-Volumes. (p. 1395)
—Primates & Human Ancestors: The Pliocene Epoch. (p. 1400)
—Rise of the Mammals: The Paleocene & Eocene Periods. (p. 1475)
Holmes, Thom, jt. auth. see Chin, Karen.
Holmes, Thom & Holmes, Laurie. Baby Dinosaurs: Eggs, Nests, & Recent Discoveries. Skrepnick, Michael William, illus. (p. 125)
—Great Dinosaur Expeditions & Discoveries: Adventures with the Fossil Hunters. Skrepnick, Michael William, illus. (p. 715)
—Prehistoric Flying Reptiles: The Pterosaurs. Skrepnick, Michael William, illus. (p. 1395)
Holmes, Timothy & Wong, Winnie. Zambia. (p. 1984)
Holmes, Victoria. Horse from the Sea: An Epic Horse Story. (p. 799)
—Horse from the Sea. (p. 799)
—Rider in the Dark: An Epic Horse Story. (p. 1471)
Holmes, Wayne & Pelletier, Christine. Lost & Found Teaching Unit. Kalvoda, LeAnn, illus. (p. 1054)
Holmes, Will, Jr., jt. auth. see Farrell, Eric L.
Holmes, William H. Handbook of Aboriginal American Antiquities. (p. 740)
—On the Race History & Facial Characteristics of the Aboriginal Americans. (p. 1291)
—Study of the Textile Art in Its Relation to the Development of Form & Ornament. (p. 1670)
Holmes-Denson, Carol. Fun of the World. (p. 648)
Holmes-Merritt, Angela. LINK Fairflies & Fairies. (p. 1019)
Holmlund, Heather D., illus. see Loyie, Larry & Brissenden, Constance.
Holmlund, Mona. Inspiring Women: A Celebration of Herstory. Youngberg, Gail, ed. (p. 878)
Holmqvist, Carin. African Tales. (p. 28)
Holmstadt, Pearl L. Shane's Demise. (p. 1559)
Holmwood, Anna, tr. see Blackcrane, Gerelchimeg.
Holness, Allison. Bath Time. (p. 144)
Holob, Victoria. Arco Iris Del Sr. Paloma: The Spanish Edition. Holob, Victoria, tr. (p. 95)
—Indiana Birdman: Grandpa Bud Aviation Stories, the Complete Collection. Holob, Victoria, illus. (p. 871)
—Miss Stella, the Child Care Magician. Holob, Victoria, illus. (p. 1152)
—Mr. Dove's Rainbow. Holob, Victoria, tr. (p. 1184)
—Trilogy: Three Airplane Stories for Children. Holob, Victoria, photos by. (p. 1786)
Holocaust Human Rights Center of Maine, jt. auth. see Stillman, Lorry.
Holofcener, Mark. Evan's Earthly Adventure. (p. 541)
Holokai, Ben W., Jr. Myths & Legends of Hawai'i Coloring Book. (p. 1227)
Holoska, Jiri, photos by see Krcmár, Karol.
Holquist, Diana. Make Me a Match. (p. 1079)
Holroyd, Geraldine, illus. see Pavese, Candace.
Holroyd, Irene. Slam Dunk State Side. (p. 1587)
Holsather, Bill, illus. see Holsather, Kent.
Holsather, Kent. Henry of York: The Secret of Juan de Vega. Holsather, Bill, illus. (p. 768)
Holsather, Kent /Wilson. Sara's Moon. (p. 1514)
Holsey, Alvin I. Dinosaur Haunt. (p. 442)
Holsey, Chanda Nicole. Precious Pete, Will You Remember Me, When I Am Out to Sea? A Salute to All Navy Dads. (p. 1394)
Holsey, Chanda Nicole, jt. auth. see Holsey, Dr Chanda Nicole.
Holsey, Dr Chanda Nicole & Holsey, Chanda Nicole. Savvie Sunshine, Will You Remember Daddy When I Am Out to Sea? A Salute to All Navy Dads. (p. 1518)
Holsinger, Carol, illus. see Moore, Sheila.
Holsinger, Rosemary. Shasta Indian Tales. Piemme, P. I., illus. (p. 1563)
Holst, Jerome Alphonse. Gretchen & the Gremlins. Krajenbrink Hulin, Yvonne, illus. (p. 723)
Holstad, Kathy, jt. auth. see Tillamook County Creamery Association.
Holstein, Ima. Dragons Daydream. (p. 479)
Holston-Holloway, Angela M. Apple Pie Kids. (p. 92)
Holt, Alex. Kung-Fu Frogs: From the Planet Intellectica. (p. 968)
Holt, Anne. What Never Happens. Dickson, Kari, tr. from NOR. (p. 1892)
Holt Ayriss, Linda, illus. see Smith, Roland & Smith, Marie.
Holt, Carmen & Jim. Betun: The Story of a Rascalero As Told by His Companeros. (p. 172)
Holt, Christopher. Dark Waters. (p. 408)
—Journey's End. (p. 929)
—Last Dogs: The Vanishing. Call, Greg, illus. (p. 977)
—Last Dogs: Dark Waters. Douglas, Allen, illus. (p. 977)
—Last Dogs: Journey's End. Douglas, Allen, illus. (p. 977)
—Last Dogs: the Long Road. Douglas, Allen, illus. (p. 977)
—Last Dogs - The Vanishing. (p. 977)
—Long Road. (p. 1047)
—Vanishing. Call, Greg, illus. (p. 1833)
Holt, Cija. Zwarkowski & the Show & Tell Collection. (p. 1990)
Holt, David & Mooney, Bill. Spiders in the Hairdo: Modern Urban Legends. (p. 1627)
Holt, David & Mooney, Bill, eds. More Ready-to-Tell Tales from Around the World. (p. 1174)
—Ready-to-Tell Tales: Sure-Fire Stories from America's Favorite Storytellers. (p. 1448)
Holt, Deloris L. Black History Playing Card Deck: With 52 Portraits of Distinguished Black Americans. Newman, Langley, illus. (p. 196)
Holt, Denver W., jt. auth. see Ford, Ansley Watson.
Holt, E. J. This Little Corner of Nowhere. (p. 1737)
Holt, Edwin B., tr. see Münsterberg, Hugo.
Holt, Gretta Scott. Reindeer Who Was Afraid to Fly. (p. 1457)
Holt, Jane E. In Madera Canyon. (p. 864)
Holt, Jeri. Little Sugar Cube. (p. 1037)
Holt, Jessica. Night in the Life of a Tooth Fairy. (p. 1253)
Holt, Julia. Beyonce. (p. 173)
—Jackie Chan (p. 903)
—Osbournes. (p. 1305)
—Victoria Beckham. (p. 1840)
—Will Smith. (p. 1932)
Holt, Julia & Woodcock, Sandra. Keanu Reeves. (p. 946)
Holt, Julia, et al. Robbie Williams. (p. 1478)
Holt, Julie. Conner's Giant Secret. (p. 358)
Holt, K. A. Mike Stellar: Nerves of Steel. (p. 1141)
—Rhyme Schemer. (p. 1468)
Holt, K. A., jt. auth. see Roy, Keri Anne.
Holt, Kimberly Willis. Adventures of Granny Clearwater & Little Critter. Hulska-Beith, Laura, illus. (p. 18)
—Dancing in Cadillac Light. (p. 403)
—Dear Hank Williams. (p. 419)
—Dinner with the Highbrows. Brooker, Kyrsten, illus. (p. 441)
—Keeper of the Night. (p. 947)
—My Louisiana Sky. (p. 1213)
—Navy Brat. Davenier, Christine, illus. (p. 1238)
—Part of Me: Stories of a Louisiana Family. (p. 1325)
—Piggy's Sweet Potato Pie Lesson. (p. 1358)
—Piper Reed, Campfire Girl. Davenier, Christine, illus. (p. 1361)
—Piper Reed, Clubhouse Queen. Davenier, Christine, illus. (p. 1361)
—Piper Reed, Forever Friend. Davenier, Christine, illus. (p. 1361)
—Piper Reed Gets a Job. Davenier, Christine, illus. (p. 1361)
—Piper Reed - Navy Brat. Davenier, Christine, illus. (p. 1361)
—Piper Reed, Party Planner. Davenier, Christine, illus. (p. 1362)
—Piper Reed, Rodeo Star. Davenier, Christine, illus. (p. 1362)
—Waiting for Gregory. Swiatkowska, Gabi, illus. (p. 1852)
—Water Seeker. (p. 1863)
—When Zachary Beaver Came to Town. (p. 1906)
Holt, Laurence. Stikky Night Skies. (p. 1650)
Holt, Lindsey, illus. see Love, Makada H.
Holt, Lindsey Leann. Green Jellybean: A Book of Children's Poems (p. 722)
Holt, Madeline. My Angel Next Door. Kovalevich, Denise, ed. (p. 1196)
Holt, Mark & Muir, Hamish. 8vo: On the Outside (p. 1993)
Holt, Martha. Adventures of Jillian & Sam: Tiger in Our Town. (p. 19)
Holt, Martin. Alfie George & the Chocolate Thieves. (p. 37)
HOLT MCDOUGAL. Go Math! Student Interactive Worktext Accelerated 7 2014. (p. 686)
—Holt Mcdougal Algebra 1: Student Interactive Worktext 2014. (p. 790)
Holt, Nick, ed. see Brookes, Archer.
Holt, Norah, jt. auth. see Berten, Jinny Powers.
Holt, Rebecca. Have You Ever Seen a Rooster Ride a Bicycle? (p. 754)
HOLT, RINEHART AND WINSTON. World History: People & Nations. (p. 1955)
Holt, Rinehart and Winston Staff. Algebra 2: Everyday Resources: Kentucky Edition. (p. 38)
—Allez Viens! Online Edition (p. 47)
—Allez Viens!: Reading Strategies Guide. Level 1 (p. 47)
—American Civics: Online Edition Plus. (p. 60)
—American Civics: Guided Reading Strategies. (p. 60)
—American Civics: Chapter Tutorials for Students. (p. 60)
—American Civics: Answer Key for Guided Reading Strategies. (p. 60)
—American Nation: Guide to Reading Strategies. (p. 62)
—Are You Ready? Intervention Middle School Math. (p. 97)
—Are You Ready? Intervention. (p. 97)
—Astronomy (p. 109)
—Biology: Assessments. (p. 189)
—Biology: Quick Data & Math. (p. 189)
—Biology: Chapter Resource Package. (p. 189)
—Biology: Practice & Experimental Labs. (p. 189)
—Biology: Special Needs Activities & Answer Key. (p. 189)
—Biology. (p. 189)
—Call to Freedom: Beginning 1877 - Texas Online Edition. (p. 254)
—Chemistry: Chapter Resource File. (p. 297)
—Decision Making: Math Context. (p. 421)
—Decisions for Health Blue. (p. 421)
—Decisions for Health Green. (p. 421)
—Decisions for Health: Blue Edition. (p. 421)
—Decisions for Health: Decision-Making. Red (p. 421)
—Decisions for Health: Decision-Making. Blue (p. 421)
—Decisions for Health: Safety. Blue, Chptr. 19 (p. 421)
—Decisions for Health: Tobacco. Blue, Chptr. 14 (p. 421)
—Decisions for Health: Alcohol. Blue, Chptr. 15 (p. 421)
—Decisions for Health: Decision-Making Workbook. Green (p. 421)
—Decisions for Health: Preventing Abuse. Blue, Chptr. 13 (p. 421)
—Decisions for Health: Conflict Management. Blue, Chptr. 12 (p. 421)
—Decisions for Health: Infectious Diseases. Blue, Chptr. 17 (p. 421)
—Decisions for Health: Health & Environment. Blue, Chptr. 21 (p. 421)
—Decisions for Health: Noninfectious Diseases. Blue, Chptr. 18 (p. 421)
—Decisions for Health: Medicine & Illegal Drugs. Blue, Chptr. 16 (p. 421)
—Decisions for Health: Chapter Resource Introduction Booklet. Red (p. 421)
—Decisions for Health: Chapter Resource Introduction Booklet. Blue (p. 421)
—Decisions for Health: Chapter Resource Introduction Booklet. Green (p. 421)
—Decisions for Health Green: Health & Safety. Chptr. 15 (p. 421)
—Decisions for Health Green: Tobacco & Alcohol. Chptr. 14 (p. 421)
—Decisions for Health Green: Understanding Drugs. Chptr. 13 (p. 421)
—Decisions for Health Red: Teens & Drugs. Chptr. 13 (p. 421)
—Decisions for Health Red: Teens & Alcohol. Chptr. 12 (p. 421)
—Decisions for Health Red: Personal Safety. Chptr. 17 (p. 421)
—Decisions for Health Red: Your Changing Body. Chptr. 16 (p. 421)
—Decisions for Health Red: Infectious Diseases. Chptr. 14 (p. 421)
—Decisions for Health Red: Noninfectious Diseases. Chptr. 15 (p. 421)
—Digging Numbers: Math/Context. (p. 439)
—Earth Science: Study Guide. (p. 496)
—Earth Science: Models of Earth. No. 3 (p. 496)
—Earth Science: Earth Chemistry. No. 4 (p. 496)
—Earth Science: The Rock Record. No. 8 (p. 496)
—Earth Science: Resources & Energy. No. 7 (p. 496)
—Earth Science: Earth & It's Systems. No. 2 (p. 496)
—Earth Science: Minerals & Earth's Crust. No. 5 (p. 496)
—Earth Science: Directed Reading & Vocabulary Workbook. (p. 496)
—Earth Science. (p. 496)
—Economics: Reteaching. (p. 502)
—Elemental Literature - Elements of Literature. (p. 510)
—Elements of Language: Literacy Handbook. (p. 510)
—Elements of Language: Spelling - Grade 6. (p. 510)
—Elements of Language: Developing Language Skills. (p. 510)
—Elements of Language: Developing Language Skills Answer Key. (p. 510)
—Elements of Language: Vocational Workshop Answer Key - Grade 6. (p. 510)
—Elements of Literature: Spelling. (p. 510)
—Elements of Literature: Holt Reader. (p. 510)
—Elements of Literature: Adapted Reader. (p. 510)
—Elements of Literature: Holt Adapted Reader. (p. 510)
—Elements of Literature: Mississippi Edition. (p. 510)
—Elements of Literature: Holt Reading Solutions. (p. 510)
—Elements of Literature: Vocabulary Development. (p. 510)
—Elements of Literature: Supporting Instructions. (p. 510)
—Elements of Literature: Language Handbook Worksheets. (p. 510)
—Elements of Literature: Family Involvement Activities. (p. 510)
—Elements of Literature: Holt Adapted Reader Answer Key. (p. 510)
—Elements of Literature: Language Handbook Worksheets Answer Key. (p. 510)
—Elements of Literature: Mississippi with Enhanced Online Edition. (p. 510)
—Elements of Literature: Writing, Listening, Speaking: Assessment. (p. 510)
—Elements of Literature: Language Handbook, Worksheets & Answer Key. (p. 510)
—Elements of Literature: Terra Nova Test Preparation with Answer Key. (p. 510)
—Elements of Literature: Assessment: Literature, Reading & Vocabulary. (p. 510)
—Elements of Literature: Holt Reader: Interactive Worktext - Georgia Edition. (p. 510)
—Elements of Literature: Holt Reader: Interactive Worktext - Mississippi Edition. (p. 510)
—Elements of Literature 2005 - The Holt Reader. (p. 510)
—Elements of Literature - Adapted Reader. (p. 510)
—Elements of Literature, Grade 6: Holt Reader. (p. 510)
—Elements of Literature, Grade 6: Holt Reader: Interdisciplinary Worktext - Georgia Edition. (p. 510)
—Elements of Literature, Grade 7: Holt Reader. (p. 511)
—Elements of Literature, Grade 7: Holt Reader: Interactive Worktext - Florida Edition. (p. 511)
—Elements of Literature, Grade 7: Holt Reader: Interdisciplinary Worktext - Georgia Edition. (p. 511)
—Elements of Literature, Grade 9: Holt Reader: Interactive Worktext. (p. 511)
—Elements of Literature - Holt Adapted Reader. (p. 510)
—En Avant: Online Edition. (p. 522)
—En Avant/En Route. (p. 522)
—En Route: Online Edition. (p. 522)
—Environmental Science: Assessments. (p. 532)
—Environmental Science: Air. Chptr. 12 (p. 532)
—Environmental Science: Land. Chptr. 14 (p. 532)
—Environmental Science: Waste. Chptr. 19 (p. 532)
—Environmental Science: Biodiversity. Chptr. 10 (p. 532)
—Environmental Science: Renewable Energy. Chptr. 18 (p. 532)
—Environmental Science: Food & Agriculture. Chptr. 15 (p. 532)
—Environmental Science: Nonrenewable Energy. Chptr. 17 (p. 532)
—Environmental Science: The Human Population. Chptr. 9 (p. 532)
—Environmental Science: Atmosphere & Climate. Chptr. 13 (p. 532)
—Environmental Science: Population & Communities. Chptr. 8 (p. 532)
—Environmental Science: Mining & Mineral Resources. Chptr. 16 (p. 532)
—Environmental Science: Environment & Human Health. Chptr. 20 (p. 532)
—Environmental Science: Economics, Policy & the Future. Chptr. 21 (p. 532)
—Environmental Science. (p. 532)
—Environmental Science 2004. (p. 532)
—Expresate: Premier Online Edition. (p. 554)
—Florida Preparation & Response in English/Language Arts/FCAT. (p. 607)

H

—Harcourt Science & Technology: Strategies & Practice Answer Key. (p. 748)
—Healthcare: Consumer Health. Blue, Chptr. 20 (p. 758)
—Holt Adapted Reader. (p. 789)
—Holt Adapted Reader 2003 - Elemental Literature. (p. 789)
—Holt American Civics. (p. 789)
—Holt Biology 2004: Texas Edition. (p. 789)
—Holt Biology 2004. (p. 789)
—Holt Chemistry: Enhanced Online Edition. (p. 789)
—Holt Chemistry: Covalent Bonds. Chptr. 6 (p. 789)
—Holt Chemistry: Ionic Compounds. Chptr. 5 (p. 789)
—Holt Chemistry: Chemical Equations/Reactions. Chptr. 8 (p. 789)
—Holt Chemistry: Molecules/Chemical Compositions. Chptr. 7 (p. 789)
—Holt Chemistry: Strategies & Practice for Reading: New York Edition. (p. 789)
—Holt Chemistry: Gases. Chptr. 12 (p. 790)
—Holt Chemistry: Solutions. Chptr. 13 (p. 790)
—Holt Chemistry: Reaction Rates. Chptr. 16 (p. 790)
—Holt Chemistry: Causes of Change. Chptr. 10 (p. 790)
—Holt Chemistry: Nuclear Chemistry. Chptr. 18 (p. 790)
—Holt Chemistry: Carbon & Organics. Chptr. 19 (p. 790)
—Holt Chemistry: Oxidation/Reduction. Chptr. 17 (p. 790)
—Holt Chemistry: Biological Chemistry. Chptr.20 (p. 790)
—Holt Chemistry: Chemical Equilibrium. Chptr. 14 (p. 790)
—Holt Chemistry: States of Matter & Forces. Chptr. 11 (p. 790)
—Holt Chemistry 2: Stoichiometry. Chptr. 9 (p. 790)
—Holt Chemistry 2: Atoms & Molecules. Chptr. 3 (p. 790)
—Holt Chemistry 2: The Periodic Table. Chptr. 4 (p. 790)
—Holt - Decisions. (p. 789)
—Holt Geometry 2003: South Carolina Practice Workbook. (p. 790)
—Holt Handbook: Activities & Tests. (p. 790)
—Holt Handbook: Activities & Tests Online. (p. 790)
—Holt Handbook: Language Practice - Grade 9. (p. 790)
—Holt Handbook: Language Practice - Grade 10. (p. 790)
—Holt Handbook: Chapter Tests with Answer Key. (p. 790)
—Holt Handbook: Language Practice with Answer Key - Grade 9. (p. 790)
—Holt Handbook, Grade 10: Developing Language Skills/Practice Answer Key. (p. 790)
—Holt Handbook, Grade 11: Developing Language Skills/Practice. (p. 790)
—Holt Handbook, Grade 6: Developing Language Skills/Practice. (p. 790)
—Holt Handbook, Grade 8: Developing Language Skills/Practice Answer Key. (p. 790)
—Holt Literature & Language Arts: Universal Access: Support in Spanish. (p. 790)
—Holt Literature & Language Arts: Vocabulary Development - California Edition. (p. 790)
—Holt Literature & Language Arts: Unlimited Access Introduction to Reading - California Edition. (p. 790)
—Holt Literature & Language Arts: Unlimited Access Introduction to Reading - California Edition - Grade 8. (p. 790)
—Holt Literature & Language Arts: Unlimited Access Introduction to Reaading - California Edition - Grade 10. (p. 790)
—Holt Literature & Language Arts, Grade 10: Language Skills - California Edition. (p. 790)
—Holt Literature & Language Arts, Grade 12: At Home, a Guide to Standards Mastery: Instructional Support. (p. 790)
—Holt Mathematics: Homework & Practice Workbook. Course 3 (p. 790)
—Holt Physics: Premier Online Edition. (p. 790)
—Holt Reader. (p. 790)
—Holt Science & Technology: Inquiry Labs. (p. 790)
—Holt Science & Technology: Life Science. (p. 790)
—Holt Science & Technology: Earth Science. (p. 790)
—Holt Science & Technology: Labs You Can Eat. (p. 790)
—Holt Science & Technology: Physical Science. (p. 790)
—Holt Science & Technology: Chapter Resources. (p. 790)
—Holt Science & Technology: Science Fair Guide. (p. 790)
—Holt Science & Technology: Math Skills Worksheets. (p. 790)
—Holt Science & Technology: Online Edition Upgrade. (p. 790)
—Holt Science & Technology: Life Science Study Guide. (p. 790)
—Holt Science & Technology: Whiz-Bang Demonstrations. (p. 790)
—Holt Science & Technology: Earth Science Study Guide. (p. 790)
—Holt Science & Technology: Science Skills Worksheets. (p. 790)
—Holt Science & Technology: Ecolabs & Field Activities. (p. 790)
—Holt Science & Technology: Directed Reading Answer Key. (p. 790)
—Holt Science & Technology: Program Introduction Booklet. (p. 790)
—Holt Science & Technology: Assessment Checklist & Rubrics. (p. 790)
—Holt Science & Technology: Life Science: Teaching Resources. (p. 790)
—Holt Science & Technology: Life Science: Heredity. Chapter 5 (p. 790)
—Holt Science & Technology: Earth Science: Teaching Resources. (p. 790)
—Holt Science & Technology: Earth Science: Volcanoes. Chapter 9 (p. 790)
—Holt Science & Technology: Long-Term Projects & Research Ideas. (p. 790)
—Holt Science & Technology: Life Science: Genes & DNA. Chapter 6 (p. 790)
—Holt Science & Technology: Life Science: Special Needs Workbook. (p. 790)
—Holt Science & Technology: Earth Science: Earthquakes. Chapter 8 (p. 790)
—Holt Science & Technology: Earth Science: Special Needs Workbook. (p. 790)
—Holt Science & Technology: Life Science: Enhanced Online Edition. (p. 790)
—Holt Science & Technology: Calculator for Biological Science Labs. (p. 790)
—Holt Science & Technology: Earth Science: Enhanced Online Edition. (p. 790)
—Holt Science & Technology: Enhanced Online Edition - Short Course. (p. 790)
—Holt Science & Technology: Life Science: Invertebrates. Chapter 15 (p. 790)
—Holt Science & Technology: Life Science: Classification. Chapter 9 (p. 790)
—Holt Science & Technology: Physical Science: Special Needs Workbook. (p. 790)
—Holt Science & Technology: Life Science: Plant Processes. Chapter 13 (p. 790)
—Holt Science & Technology: Earth Science: The Atmosphere. Chapter 15 (p. 790)
—Holt Science & Technology: Earth Science: Rocks & Fossils. Chapter 6 (p. 790)
—Holt Science & Technology: Earth Science: Plate Tectonics. Chapter 7 (p. 790)
—Holt Science & Technology: Physical Science: Enhanced Online Edition. (p. 790)
—Holt Science & Technology: Life Science: Protists & Fungi. Chapter 11 (p. 790)
—Holt Science & Technology: Earth Science: Energy Resources. Chapter 5 (p. 790)
—Holt Science & Technology: Life Science: The Cell in Action. Chapter 4 (p. 790)
—Holt Science & Technology: Life Science: Evolution & Living. Chapter 7 (p. 790)
—Holt Science & Technology: Life Science: Reading & Comprehension Guide. (p. 790)
—Holt Science & Technology: Life Science: Bacteria & Viruses. Chapter 10 (p. 790)
—Holt Science & Technology: Physical Science: Periodic Table. Chapter 12 (p. 790)
—Holt Science & Technology: Life Science: Animals & Behavior. Chapter 14 (p. 790)
—Holt Science & Technology: Life Science: Cells - Basic Units. Chapter 3 (p. 790)
—Holt Science & Technology: Physical Science: Work & Machines. Chapter 8 (p. 790)
—Holt Science & Technology: Earth Science: Reading & Comprehension Guide. (p. 790)
—Holt Science & Technology: Earth Science: Weathering of Soil. Chapter 10 (p. 790)
—Holt Science & Technology: Physical Science: States of Matter. Chapter 3 (p. 790)
—Holt Science & Technology: Physical Science: Matter in Motion. Chapter 5 (p. 790)
—Holt Science & Technology: Physical Science: Forces in Motion. Chapter 6 (p. 790)
—Holt Science & Technology: Physical Science: Forces in Fluids. Chapter 7 (p. 790)
—Holt Science & Technology: Physical Science: Chemical Bonding. Chapter 13 (p. 790)
—Holt Science & Technology: Life Science: It's Alive!! or Is It? Chapter 2 (p. 790)
—Holt Science & Technology: Earth Science: Exploring the Oceans. Chapter 13 (p. 790)
—Holt Science & Technology: Physical Science: Reading & Comprehension Guide. (p. 790)
—Holt Science & Technology: Life Science: Introduction to Plants. Chapter 12 (p. 790)
—Holt Science & Technology: Earth Science: Movement of the Ocean. Chapter 14 (p. 790)
—Holt Science & Technology: Physical Science: Chemical Reactions. Chapter 14 (p. 790)
—Holt Science & Technology: Physical Science: Chemical Compounds. Chapter 15 (p. 790)
—Holt Science & Technology: Physical Science: Properties of Matter. Chapter 2 (p. 790)
—Holt Science & Technology: Life Science: History of Life on Earth. Chapter 8 (p. 790)
—Holt Science & Technology: Life Science: The World of Life Science. Chapter 1 (p. 790)
—Holt Science & Technology: Earth Science: The Flow of Fresh Water. Chapter 11 (p. 790)
—Holt Science & Technology: Earth Science: Minerals & Earth's Crust. Chapter 3 (p. 790)
—Holt Science & Technology: Earth Science: Rocks - Mineral Mixtures. Chapter 4 (p. 790)
—Holt Science & Technology: Physical Science: Introduction to Atoms. Chapter 11 (p. 790)
—Holt Science & Technology: Earth Science: The World of Earth Science. Chapter 1 (p. 790)
—Holt Science & Technology: Physical Science: Heat & Heat Technology. Chapter 10 (p. 790)
—Holt Science & Technology: Earth Science: Maps & Models of the Earth. Chapter 2 (p. 790)
—Holt Science & Technology: Strategies & Practice for Reading - Tennessee Edition. (p. 790)
—Holt Science & Technology: Physical Science: Energy & Energy Resources. Chapter 9 (p. 790)
—Holt Science & Technology: Physical Science: The World of Physical Science. Chapter 1 (p. 790)
—Holt Science & Technology: Physical Science: Elements, Compounds, & Mixtures. Chapter 4 (p. 790)
—Holt Science & Technology. (p. 790)
—Holt Science & Technology: Electricity & Magnetism. Pt. N (p. 791)
—Holt Science & Technology: Earth Science: Climate. Chapter 17 (p. 791)
—Holt Science & Technology: Inside the Restless Earth. Level F (p. 791)
—Holt Science & Technology: Life Science: Body Defenses. Chapter 27 (p. 791)
—Holt Science & Technology: Life Science: Birds & Mammals. Chapter 17 (p. 791)
—Holt Science & Technology: Earth Science: Studying Space. Chapter 18 (p. 791)
—Holt Science & Technology: Life Science: Staying Healthy. Chapter 28 (p. 791)
—Holt Science & Technology: Life Science: Cycles in Nature. Chapter 19 (p. 791)
—Holt Science & Technology: Earth Science: Exploring Space. Chapter 22 (p. 791)
—Holt Science & Technology: Physical Science: Atomic Energy. Chapter 16 (p. 791)
—Holt Science & Technology: Life Science: Body Organization. Chapter 22 (p. 791)
—Holt Science & Technology: Life Science: Earth's Ecosystems. Chapter 20 (p. 791)
—Holt Science & Technology: Physical Science: Electromagnetism. Chapter 18 (p. 791)
—Holt Science & Technology: Physical Science: Light & Our World. Chapter 23 (p. 791)
—Holt Science & Technology: Earth Science: The Family of Planets. Chapter 21 (p. 791)
—Holt Science & Technology: Physical Science: The Energy of Waves. Chapter 20 (p. 791)
—Holt Science & Technology: Physical Science: The Nature of Sound. Chapter 21 (p. 791)
—Holt Science & Technology: Physical Science: The Nature of Light. Chapter 22 (p. 791)
—Holt Science & Technology: Life Science: Communication & Control. Chapter 25 (p. 791)
—Holt Science & Technology: Physical Science: Electronic Technology. Chapter 19 (p. 791)
—Holt Science & Technology: Life Science: Circulation & Respiration. Chapter 23 (p. 791)
—Holt Science & Technology: Earth Science: Understanding the Weather. Chapter 16 (p. 791)
—Holt Science & Technology: Life Science: Reproduction & Development. Chapter 26 (p. 791)
—Holt Science & Technology: Life Science: Digestive & Urinary Systems. Chapter 24 (p. 791)
—Holt Science & Technology: Life Science: Fishes, Amphibians, & Reptiles. Chapter 16 (p. 791)
—Holt Science & Technology: Earth Science: Formation of the Solar System. Chapter 20 (p. 791)
—Holt Science & Technology: Physical Science: Introduction to Electricity. Chapter 17 (p. 791)
—Holt Science & Technology: Life Science: Interactions with Living Things. Chapter 18 (p. 791)
—Holt Science & Technology: Earth Science: Stars, the Galaxy, & the Universe. Chapter 19 (p. 791)
—Holt Science & Technology: Life Science: Environmental Problems & Solutions. Chapter 21 (p. 791)
—Holt Science & Technology Online Edition. (p. 791)
—Holt Science Spectrum: Forces. Chptr. 11 (p. 791)
—Holt Science Spectrum: Solutions. Chptr. 7 (p. 791)
—Holt Science Spectrum: Planet Earth. Chptr. 21 (p. 791)
—Holt Science Spectrum: The Atmosphere. Chptr. 22 (p. 791)
—Holt Science Spectrum: States of Matter. Chptr. 3 (p. 791)
—Holt Science Spectrum: The Solar System. Chptr. 19 (p. 791)
—Holt Science Spectrum: Using Natural Resources. Chptr. 23 (p. 791)
—Holt Science Spectrum: A Physical Approach - Spanish Study Guide. (p. 791)
—Holt Texas! (p. 791)
—Horizons: Time for Kids Collection (p. 797)
—Human Journey: Online Edition. (p. 826)
—Human Journey: The Modern World: Online Edition. (p. 826)
—Human Journey: The Ancient World: Online Edition. (p. 826)
—Insights & Data: Math/Context. (p. 878)
—Internet Access 2003: Enrollment 750. (p. 880)
—Komm Mit!: Ubungsheft. Level 1 (p. 966)
—Komm Mit!: Grammatikheft. Level 1 (p. 966)
—Komm Mit!: Storytelling Book. Level 1 (p. 966)
—Life Science: Study Guide. (p. 1013)
—Life Science: Directed Reading & Vocabulary Workbook. (p. 1013)
—Life Science. (p. 1013)
—Life Science 2005. (p. 1013)
—Lifetime of Health: Life Skills. (p. 1014)
—Lifetime of Health: Tobacco. Chptr. 11 (p. 1014)
—Lifetime of Health: HIV & AIDS. Chptr. 21 (p. 1014)
—Lifetime of Health: Illegal Drugs. Chptr. 12 (p. 1014)
—Lifetime of Health: Other Diseases. Chptr. 15 (p. 1014)
—Lifetime of Health: Lifestyle Diseases. Chptr. 14 (p. 1014)
—Lifetime of Health: Marriage & Parenthood. Chptr. 17 (p. 1014)
—Lifetime of Health: Prevention of Diseases. Chptr. 13 (p. 1014)
—Lifetime of Health: Adolescence & Adulthood. Chptr. 16 (p. 1014)
—Lifetime of Health: Building Relationships. Chptr. 19 (p. 1014)
—Lifetime of Health: Reproduction & Pregnancy. Chptr. 18 (p. 1014)
—Lifetime of Health: Risks of Sexual Activity. Chptr. 20 (p. 1014)
—Lifetime of Health: Chapter Resource File Introduction Booklet. (p. 1014)
—Math: Middle School: Chapter Resources. Course 1 (p. 1105)
—Math: Middle School: Chapter Resources. Course 2 (p. 1105)
—Math: Middle School: Chapter Resources. Course 3 (p. 1105)
—Math: Middle School: Standard Test Practice. Course 2 (p. 1105)
—Math: Middle School: Standard Test Practice. Course 3 (p. 1105)
—Math: Middle School: Interactive Posters & Worksheets. (p. 1105)
—Math: CIM Test Preparation Book: Oregon High School Edition. (p. 1105)
—Math: Middle School: Interactive Posters & Worksheets. Course 1 (p. 1105)
—Math: Middle School: Interactive Posters & Worksheets. Course 3 (p. 1105)
—Math: Middle School: Standard Test Practice with Answer Key. Course 2 (p. 1105)
—Math Chapter Resources: Maine Edition. (p. 1105)
—Math Chapter Resources: Arizona Edition. (p. 1105)
—Math Chapter Resources: New Jersey Edition. (p. 1105)
—Math Chapter Resources: Pennsylvania Edition. (p. 1105)
—Math in Context Summer School Program. (p. 1106)
—Math Know-It Notebook: Middle School. (p. 1106)
—Microorganisms, Fungi, & Plants. (p. 1136)
—Middle School Math: Resource Book. Chapter 4 (p. 1137)
—Middle School Math: Resource Book. Chapter 5 (p. 1137)
—Middle School Math: Resource Book. Chapter 6 (p. 1137)
—Middle School Math: Resource Book. Chapter 7 (p. 1137)
—Middle School Math: Resource Book. Chapter 8 (p. 1137)
—Middle School Math: Resource Book. Chapter 9 (p. 1137)
—Middle School Math: Resource Book. Chapter 10 (p. 1137)
—Middle School Math: Resource Book. Chapter 11 (p. 1137)
—Middle School Math: Resource Book. Chapter 12 (p. 1137)
—Middle School Math: Maryland Edition. Course 2 (p. 1137)
—Middle School Math: Maryland Edition. Course 3 (p. 1137)
—Middle School Math: Family Involvement. Course 3 (p. 1137)
—Middle School Math: Tech Lab Activities. Course 3 (p. 1137)
—Middle School Math: Hands-on Lab Activities. Course 3 (p. 1137)
—Middle School Math: Consumer/Career Mathematics. Course 3 (p. 1137)
—Middle School Math: Chapter Resources: Oregon Edition. Course 1 (p. 1137)
—Middle School Math: Chapter Resources: Oregon Edition. Course 2 (p. 1137)
—Middle School Math: Chapter Resources: Oregon Edition. Course 3 (p. 1137)
—Middle School Math: New York Review & Test Preparation Workbook. (p. 1137)
—Middle School Math: Chapter Resources: New YorkEdition. Course 2 (p. 1137)
—Middle School Math: Chapter Resources: New York Edition. Course 3 (p. 1137)
—Middle School Math: Success for English Language Students. Course 3 (p. 1137)
—Middle School Math: Homework/Practice Workbook with Answers. Course 3 (p. 1137)
—Middle School Math: Homework/Practice Workbook with Answer Key - Spanish Edition. Course 3 (p. 1137)
—Middle School Math 2: Spanish Homework & Practice Workbook. (p. 1137)
—Middle School Math Test Preparation Workbook: Pennsylvania Edition. (p. 1138)
—Middle School Practice for Middle School English Subject Area. (p. 1138)
—Modern Biology. (p. 1158)
—New in Numbers. (p. 1245)
—Number Tools: Math Context. (p. 1271)
—Number Tools: Math/Context. Vol. 2 (p. 1271)
—Number Tools Workbook Math/Contt. (p. 1271)
—NY Strategy & Practice for Reading 2004: Science Spectrum. (p. 1274)
—OH Strategy & Practice for Reading 2004: Science Spectrum. (p. 1281)
—People, Places & Change: Texas Online Edition. (p. 1339)
—People, Places & Change: The East: Map Activities. (p. 1339)
—People, Places & Change: The East: Chapter Tutorials. (p. 1339)
—People, Places & Change: The West: Chapter Tutorials. (p. 1339)
—People, Places & Change: The East: Main Idea Activities. (p. 1339)
—People, Places & Change: An Introduction to World Studies. (p. 1339)
—People, Places & Change: The East: Guided Reading Strategies. (p. 1339)
—People, Places & Change: The West: Guided Reading Strategies. (p. 1339)
—People, Places & Change: The East: Geography & Life Activities. (p. 1339)
—People, Places & Change: The West: Geography & Life Activities. (p. 1339)
—People, Places & Change: The East: Critical Thinking Activities. (p. 1339)
—People, Places & Change: The East: Graphic Organizer Activities. (p. 1339)
—People, Places & Change: The West: Critical Thinking Activities. (p. 1339)
—People, Places & Change: The West: Graphic Organizer Activities. (p. 1339)
—People, Places & Change: Western Hemisphere: Main Idea Activities. (p. 1339)
—Physical Science: Chapter Resources. (p. 1353)
—Physical Science: Directed Reading & Vocabulary Workbook. (p. 1353)
—Physical Science. (p. 1353)
—Physical Science 2005. (p. 1353)
—Physics: Premier Online Edition. (p. 1353)
—Physics: Science Special - Assessments. (p. 1353)
—Pre-Algebra: Chapter Resources. (p. 1393)
—Pre-Algebra: Are You Ready: Intervention. (p. 1393)
—Pre-Algebra. (p. 1393)
—Pre-Algebra: Solution Key. (p. 1394)
—Pre-Algebra: Multilingual Glossary. (p. 1394)
—Pre-Algebra: Standard Test Preparation. (p. 1394)
—Pre-Algebra: Test Preparation Tool Kit. (p. 1394)
—Pre-Algebra: Tech Lab Activities with Answer Key. (p. 1394)
—Pre-Algebra: Readiness Activities with Answer Key. (p. 1394)
—Pre-Algebra: Success for English Language Learners. (p. 1394)
—Pre-Algebra: Math: Reading, Writing & Content Areas. (p. 1394)
—Pre-Algebra: Resource Book with Answer Key. Chptr. 2 (p. 1394)
—Pre-Algebra: Resource Book with Answer Key. Chptr. 4 (p. 1394)
—Pre-Algebra: Resource Book with Answer Key. Chptr. 5 (p. 1394)
—Pre-Algebra: Resource Book with Answer Key. Chptr. 9 (p. 1394)
—Pre-Algebra: Hands-on Lab Activities with Answer Key. (p. 1394)
—Pre-Algebra: Homework & Practice Workbook Answer Key. (p. 1394)
—Pre-Algebra: Interactive Study Guide with Answer Key. (p. 1394)

H

—Pre-Algebra: Resource Book with Answer Key. Chptr. 10 (p. 1394)
—Pre-Algebra: Resource Book with Answer Key. Chptr. 11 (p. 1394)
—Pre-Algebra: Resource Book with Answer Key. Chptr. 12 (p. 1394)
—Pre-Algebra: Resource Book with Answer Key. Chptr. 13 (p. 1394)
—Pre-Algebra: Resource Book with Answer Key. Chptr. 14 (p. 1394)
—Pre-Algebra: Standard Test Preparation with Answer Key. (p. 1394)
—Pre-Algebra: Interactive Problem Solving with Answer Key. (p. 1394)
—Pre-Algebra Know-It Notebook. (p. 1394)
—Precalculus: A Graphing Approach. (p. 1394)
—Preparation & Construct Response: Elemental Literature. (p. 1395)
—Preparation & Construction Response: Elemental Literature. (p. 1395)
—Reader Fourth Course. (p. 1444)
—Reading Guide Program Lifehealth Sexual Resource. (p. 1446)
—Reflections & Numbers: Math/Context. (p. 1456)
—Science Puzzlers, Twisters & Teasers. (p. 1527)
—Science Skills Workshop. (p. 1528)
—Science Spectrum: Physics Math Skills. (p. 1528)
—Standard Test Practice Workbook: South Carolina Edition - Algebra. (p. 1639)
—Standart Test Practice Workbook: South Carolina Edition - Geometry. (p. 1639)
—Taks Practice Exams Biology. (p. 1699)
—Teaching Math to All Students Package. (p. 1710)
—Ven Conmigo!: Cuaderno/Act. Level 1 (p. 1835)
—Ven Conmigo!: Cuaderno de Act. Level 2 (p. 1835)
—Ven Conmigo!: Cuadero/Hispanic. Level 1 (p. 1835)
—Ven Conmigo!: Cuadero/Hispanic. Level 2 (p. 1835)
—Ven Conmigo!: Storytelling Book. Level 1 (p. 1835)
—Ven Conmigo!: Cuaderno de Grammar. Level 1 (p. 1835)
—Ven Conmigo!: Cuaderno de Grammar. Level 2 (p. 1835)
—Vocabulary Workshop: Tests. (p. 1847)
—Vocabulary Workshop. (p. 1847)
—World Geography Today: Guided Reading Strategies. (p. 1955)
—World History: The Human Journey: Online Edition. (p. 1955)
—World History: The Human Journey: Online Edition Plus. (p. 1955)
—World History & Doc-B's Questions: New York Edition. (p. 1955)
Holt, Rinehart and Winston Staff & Thomas, W. Laverne. Sociology: The Study of Human Relationships Set (p. 1605)
Holt, Sharon. Did My Mother Do That? Lovelock, Brian, illus. (p. 436)
—Make Your Own Joke Book. Kinnaird, Ross, illus. (p. 1080)
Holt, Sharon & Mitchell, Julie. Metal Mouth (p. 1130)
Holt, Sharon & Proudfoot, Dean. Don't Embarrass Me, Dad! (p. 467)
Holt, Simon. Devouring #2: Soulstice. (p. 432)
Holt, Stephen. Whistling Stallion. Crowell, Pers, illus. (p. 1912)
Holt, Stephen & Lewis, Oscar. We Were There with the California Forty-Niners. Lufkin, Raymond, illus. (p. 1868)
Holt, Steven, illus. see Schindel, John.
Holt, Steven, jt. auth. see Schindel, John.
Holt, Steven, photos by see Schindel, John.
Holt, Tabby. Henhouse Gang. (p. 767)
Holt, Tami. Friends Forever. (p. 638)
Holt, Theresa. What If I Wet My Pants. (p. 1887)
Holt, William T. Brand New Shoes Coloring & Activity Book. (p. 222)
Holtam, Elizabeth T. Possum in My Pocket. (p. 1387)
Holtei, Christa. Nanuk Flies Home. Vohwinkel, Astrid, illus. (p. 1229)
Holtei, Christa & Woofter, Susi. In the New World: A Family in Two Centuries. Raidt, Gerda, illus. (p. 867)
Holter, Bjarden. Man on My Back: Jesus & His Four-Legged Helpers. (p. 1085)
Holter, James. Dirt Bike Racers. (p. 446)
Holt-Giménez, Eric & Patel, Raj, eds. Food Rebellions: Crisis & the Hunger for Justice. (p. 614)
Holthaus, Abbey. Treasures of Christmas. Downs, Braden, illus. (p. 1782)
Holtje, Bert & Collins, Christine. Amnesia & Related Disorders. (p. 65)
Holton Crawford, Joyce. Killer B's Plan Revenge. (p. 956)
Holton, Jim. Chinook Jargon: The Hidden Language of the Pacific Northwest. (p. 308)
Holton, Robert J. Making Globalization. (p. 1081)
Holtsclaw, Josh, illus. see Depken, Kristen L.
Holtwijk, Ineke & Boyds Mills Press Staff. Asphalt Angels. Boeke, Wanda, tr. (p. 107)
Holtz, Eric Siegfried. Nueva Jersey. Porras, Carlos & D'Andrea, Patricia, trs. from ENG. (p. 1270)
Holtz, Lara Tankel, jt. ed. see Whittington, Melanie.
Holtz, Mary Elizabeth, jt. auth. see Mills, Nathan.
Holtz, Monica Stauber. Behind the Zoo: Find Out What the Animals Eat & Do at Irvine Park Zoo, Chippewa Falls, Wisconsin. Opatz, Shane, illus. (p. 160)
Holtz, Thomas R. Dinosaurs: The Most Complete, Up-to-Date Encyclopedia for Dinosaur Lovers of All Ages. Rey, Luis V., illus. (p. 444)
Holtz, Thomas R., jt. auth. see Brett-Surman, Michael K.
Holtz, Thomas R., jt. auth. see Random House Staff.
Holtz, Thomas R. & Random House Staff. T. Rex: Hunter or Scavenger? Skrepnick, Michael, illus. (p. 1694)
Holtz, Thomas R., Jr. Digging for Brachiosaurus: A Discovery Timeline. (p. 439)
—Digging for Stegosaurus: A Discovery Timeline. (p. 439)
—Digging for Triceratops: A Discovery Timeline. (p. 439)
—Digging for Tyrannosaurus Rex: A Discovery Timeline. (p. 439)
—Dinosaur Discovery Timelines. (p. 442)
Holtz-Bacha, Christina. Second Chance. (p. 1539)
Holtzman, Caren, jt. auth. see Bresser, Rusty.
Holtzman, Claudia Ann. Why Are They Called... Grandparents! (p. 1922)
Holub, Joan. Apple Countdown. Smith, Jan, illus. (p. 92)
—Ballet Stars. (p. 134)
—Ballet Stars. McNicholas, Shelagh, illus. (p. 134)
—Be Careful, Icarus! Patricelli, Leslie, illus. (p. 148)
—Be Patient, Pandora! Patricelli, Leslie, illus. (p. 149)
—Bed, Bats, & Beyond. Gallagher-Cole, Memie, illus. (p. 156)
—Big Heart! A Valentine's Day Tale. Terry, Will, illus. (p. 181)
—Brush Your Hair, Medusa! Patricelli, Leslie, illus. (p. 232)
—Cleopatra & the King's Enemies: Based on a True Story of Cleopatra in Egypt. Aleshina, Nonna, illus. (p. 331)
—Danielle's Dollhouse Wish. (p. 405)
—Dig, Scoop, Ka-Boom! Gordon, David, illus. (p. 438)
—Do Not Open! The Story of Pandora's Box. (p. 457)
—Dragon Dance: A Chinese New Year. Huang, Benrei, illus. (p. 477)
—Elizabeth & the Royal Pony: Based on a True Story of Elizabeth I of England. Aleshina, Nonna, illus. (p. 513)
—Good Luck! A St. Patrick's Day Story. Terry, Will, illus. (p. 698)
—Groundhog Weather School: Fun Facts about Weather & Groundhogs. Sorra, Kristin, illus. (p. 725)
—Groundhog Weather School. Sorra, Kristin, illus. (p. 725)
—Isabel Saves the Prince: Based on a True Story of Isabel I of Spain. Aleshina, Nonna, illus. (p. 890)
—Itty Bitty Kitty. Burks, James, illus. (p. 900)
—Itty Bitty Kitty & the Rainy Play Day. Burks, James, illus. (p. 900)
—Kiss for You. Church, Caroline Jayne, illus. (p. 961)
—Knights Before Christmas. Magoon, Scott, illus. (p. 964)
—Little Red Writing. Sweet, Melissa, illus. (p. 1035)
—Lydia & the Island Kingdom: A Story Based on the Real Life of Princess Liliuokalani of Hawaii. Aleshina, Nonna, illus. (p. 1066)
—Make a Wish, Midas! Patricelli, Leslie, illus. (p. 1079)
—Mighty Dads. Dean, James, illus. (p. 1140)
—More Snacks! A Thanksgiving Play. Terry, Will, illus. (p. 1175)
—One-Eyed People Eater: The Story of Cyclops. (p. 1294)
—One-Eyed People Eater: The Story of Cyclops. Jones, Dani, illus. (p. 1294)
—Picnic! A Day in the Park. Terry, Will, illus. (p. 1355)
—Play Nice, Hercules! Patricelli, Leslie, illus. (p. 1371)
—Please Share, Aphrodite! Patricelli, Leslie, illus. (p. 1373)
—Pumpkin Countdown. Smith, Jan, illus. (p. 1416)
—Quién Fue Marco Polo? O'Brien, John & Harrison, Nancy, illus. (p. 1427)
—Scaredy-Pants! A Halloween Story. Terry, Will, illus. (p. 1519)
—Shampoodle. Bowers, Tim, illus. (p. 1559)
—Snow Day! A Winter Tale. Terry, Will, illus. (p. 1598)
—Spring Is Here! A Story about Seeds. Terry, Will, illus. (p. 1635)
—Surprise, Trojans! The Story of the Trojan Horse. Jones, Dani, illus. (p. 1686)
—Twinkle, Star of the Week. Nicholls, Paul, illus. (p. 1802)
—What Is the Statue of Liberty? (p. 1890)
—What Is the Statue of Liberty? Mantha, John et al, illus. (p. 1890)
—What Was the First Thanksgiving? (p. 1895)
—What Was the Gold Rush? (p. 1895)
—What Was the Gold Rush? Tomkinson, Tim, illus. (p. 1895)
—What Were the Salem Witch Trials? Putra, Dede & McVeigh, Kevin, illus. (p. 1895)
—Who Was Babe Ruth? (p. 1918)
—Who Was Babe Ruth? Hammond, Ted & Harrison, Nancy, illus. (p. 1918)
—Who Was Jim Henson? Harrison, Nancy, illus. (p. 1918)
—Who Was Johnny Appleseed? DiVito, Anna, illus. (p. 1918)
—Who Was Marco Polo? O'Brien, John, illus. (p. 1918)
—Who Was Marco Polo? O'Brien, John et al, illus. (p. 1918)
—Why Do Birds Sing? DiVito, Anna, illus. (p. 1923)
—Why Do Horses Neigh? DiVito, Anna, illus. (p. 1923)
—Why Do Rabbits Hop? And Other Questions about Rabbits, Guinea Pigs, Hamsters, & Gerbils. DiVito, Anna, illus. (p. 1924)
—Why Do Snakes Hiss? And Other Questions about Snakes, Lizards, & Turtles. DiVito, Anna, illus. (p. 1924)
—Zero the Hero. Lichtenheld, Tom, illus. (p. 1986)
Holub, Joan, illus. see deRubertis, Barbara.
Holub, Joan, illus. see Hall, Kirsten.
Holub, Joan, illus. see Mullins, Patty Rutland.
Holub, Joan, illus. see Nobisso, Josephine.
Holub, Joan, illus. see Scholastic, Inc. Staff.
Holub, Joan, jt. auth. see Hallowell, George.
Holub, Joan & Williams, Suzanne. Amphitrite the Bubbly. (p. 66)
—Aphrodite the Beauty. (p. 91)
—Aphrodite the Diva. (p. 91)
—Aphrodite the Fair. (p. 91)
—Apollo & the Battle of the Birds. (p. 91)
—Apollo & the Battle of the Birds. Phillips, Craig, illus. (p. 91)
—Ares & the Spear of Fear. Phillips, Craig, illus. (p. 97)
—Artemis the Brave. (p. 103)
—Artemis the Loyal. (p. 103)
—Athena the Brain. (p. 112)
—Athena the Proud. (p. 112)
—Athena the Wise. (p. 112)
—Cassandra the Lucky. (p. 276)
—Cinderella Stays Late. (p. 320)
—Crius & the Fright of Night. Phillips, Craig, illus. (p. 384)
—Crius & the Night of Fright. (p. 384)
—Cronus & the Threads of Dread. (p. 384)
—Girl Games: Super Special. (p. 678)
—Girl Games. (p. 678)
—Girls' Games - Super Special. (p. 680)
—Goddess Girls: Athena the Brave - Persephone the Phony; Aphrodite the Beauty; Artemis the Brave. Set, Bks. 1-4 (p. 690)
—Goddess Girls the Glittering Collection: Athena the Wise - Aphrodite the Diva - Artemis the Loyal - Medusa the Mean. (p. 690)
—Goldilocks Breaks In. (p. 696)
—Hades & the Helm of Darkness. (p. 735)
—Hades & the Helm of Darkness. Phillips, Craig, illus. (p. 735)
—Hephaestus & the Island of Terror. (p. 769)
—Hyperion & the Great Balls of Fire. Phillips, Craig, illus. (p. 831)
—Iris the Colorful. (p. 887)
—Medusa the Mean. (p. 1120)
—Medusa the Rich. (p. 1120)
—Pandora the Curious. (p. 1321)
—Persephone the Daring. (p. 1344)
—Persephone the Phony. (p. 1344)
—Pheme the Gossip. (p. 1350)
—Poseidon & the Sea of Fury. (p. 1387)
—Poseidon & the Sea of Fury. Phillips, Craig, illus. (p. 1387)
—Rapunzel Cuts Loose. (p. 1439)
—Red Riding Hood Gets Lost. (p. 1455)
—Sleeping Beauty Dreams Big. (p. 1589)
—Snow White Lucks Out. (p. 1600)
—Typhon & the Winds of Destruction. (p. 1805)
—Typhon & the Winds of Destruction. Phillips, Craig, illus. (p. 1805)
—Zeus & the Thunderbolt of Doom. Phillips, Craig, illus. (p. 1986)
Holub, Joan, et al. Aphrodite the Diva. (p. 91)
Holub, Sharon R. Adventures of the Big Green Van. (p. 23)
—Callie Cakes Finds Her Treasures. (p. 254)
Holubitsky, Katherine. Big Snapper (p. 184)
—Hippie House (p. 780)
—Mountain That Walked (p. 1181)
—Tweaked (p. 1799)
Holybee, Christine Monday. Big Arrival of Spot the Cow Pig. (p. 177)
Holyfield, John, illus. see Bildner, Phil.
Holyfield, John, illus. see Nolan, Nina.
Holyfield, John, illus. see Smothers, Ethel Footman & Smothers, Ethel F.
Holyfield, John, illus. see Stauffacher, Sue.
Holyfield, John, illus. see Stroud, Bettye & Ramsey, Calvin Alexander.
Holyoak, Kathleen & Summers, Sherry. Flowers in Heaven. (p. 608)
Holyoke, Nancy. Smart Girl's Guide: Manners. (p. 1592)
—Smart Girl's Guide to Manners: The Secrets to Grace, Confidence, & Being Your Best. Watkins, Michelle, ed. (p. 1592)
Holyoke, Polly. Neptune Challenge. (p. 1241)
—Neptune Project. (p. 1241)
Holzach, Cornelie. Schatzsuche MIT Schmucki der Perlsau: Im Schmuckmuseum Pforzheim Für Groß und Klein. (p. 1521)
Holzbauer, David, jt. auth. see Trudeau, Scott.
Holzer, Angela. Fat Freddy. Tucker, Barclay, illus. (p. 577)
—Gooey Gummy Geese. Smith, Ashley, illus. (p. 702)
—Lovely Lily. Hansen, Angela, illus. (p. 1061)
—My Dog, Eddie. Funk, Debbie, illus. (p. 1202)
Holzer, David. Make & Play Airplanes. Galvani, Maureen, illus. (p. 1079)
—Prime Suspect: Suspect Identification System. (p. 1400)
Holzer, Harold. Father Abraham: Lincoln & His Sons. (p. 577)
—Lincoln: How Abraham Lincoln Ended Slavery in America - A Companion Book for Young Readers to the Steven Spielberg Film. (p. 1018)
—Lincoln: How Abraham Lincoln Ended Slavery in America: A Companion Book for Young Readers to the Steven Spielberg Film. (p. 1018)
—President Is Shot! The Assassination of Abraham Lincoln. (p. 1397)
Holzer, Julie. Maggie's Forever Home. (p. 1071)
Holzhauser-Peters, Leslie & Grizinski, Yolande. Thinking Through Problems at School: Social Problem Solving Scenarios to Enhance Communication, Thinking, & Decision Making Skills. (p. 1734)
Holzhey, Magdalena. Frida Kahlo: The Artist in the Blue House. (p. 637)
Holzmann, Angela, illus. see Steinkühler, Martina.
Holzschuher, Cythnia. Our Country Thematic Unit. (p. 1308)
Holzwarth, Werner. I Wish I Were A... Jeschke, Stefanie, illus. (p. 849)
—Story of the Little Mole Who Knew It Was None of His Business. Erlbruch, Wolf, illus. (p. 1661)
Holzwarth, Werner, jt. auth. see Erlbruch, Wolf.
Holzwarth, Werner & Erlbruch, Wolf. Story of the Little Mole Who Knew It Was None of His Business. (p. 1661)
—Story of the Little Mole Who Went in Search of Whodunit. (p. 1661)
Hom, John, illus. see Wax, Wendy.
Hom, Nancy, illus. see Spagnoli, Cathy.
Hom, Susan & Richardson, Phillip. Message in a Bottle. Björkman, Steve, illus. (p. 1129)
Homan, Lynn M. & Reilly, Thomas. Girls Fly! Shepherd, Rosalie M., tr. (p. 680)
—Women Who Fly Shepherd, Rosalie M., illus. (p. 1946)
Homan, Michael. Grendel Gander the Sinister Goose. Duggins, Peat, illus. (p. 723)
Homan, Tim. Hiking the Benton MacKaye Trail Holifield, Vicky, illus. (p. 779)
Homberg, Ansgar, illus. see Fischer, Carl.
Homberg, Ruth. Jewels for a Princess. (p. 917)
—Jewels for a Princess (Disney Princess) RH Disney Staff, illus. (p. 917)
—Little Mermaid. (p. 1031)
—Little Mermaid Step into Reading (Disney Princess) RH Disney Staff, illus. (p. 1031)
—Princess Charm School. Random House Staff, illus. (p. 1403)
—Racing for Good. (p. 1432)
—Racing for Good (Disney/Pixar Cars) RH Disney Staff, illus. (p. 1432)
—Sticker Hunt! (Julius Jr.) Random House, illus. (p. 1650)
Home, Henry & Kames, Lord. Principles of Equity. (p. 1406)
Homel, David, tr. see Stinson, Kathy.
Homel, David & Gay, Marie-Louise. Travels with My Family (p. 1780)
Homemaker, Nellie. Journey with a Woman of the Gullah Cultu. (p. 929)
Homer. Classic Starts - The Iliad. Freeberg, Eric, illus. (p. 328)
—Iliad. Tsilis, Thanos, illus. (p. 856)
—Iliad. Fagles, Robert & Bloom, Harold, eds. (p. 856)
—Iliada. (p. 856)
—Iliada y la Odisea. (p. 856)
—Odisea. (p. 1278)
—Odyssey. Freeberg, Eric, illus. (p. 1278)
—Odyssey. Fagles, Robert, tr. from GRE. (p. 1278)
—Odyssey. (p. 1279)
—Odyssey. Gelev, Penko, illus. (p. 1279)
—Odyssey. Tsilis, Thanos, illus. (p. 1279)
Homer, jt. auth. see Bowman, Patrick.
Homer, jt. auth. see Fagles, Robert.
Homer & Martín, Jean. Cuentos y Leyendas de la Iliada. Campos, Paz, tr. (p. 390)
Homer & Rouse, W. H. D. Odyssey. Rouse, W. H. D., tr. from GEC. (p. 1279)
Homer, Elizabeth. Peter Wolfe & the Scepter of Myleah. (p. 1347)
Homer, Katie. Brainstorming Creative Guide to Help Parents & Children Through Severe Weather. (p. 222)
Homer, Larona. Shore Ghosts & Other Stories of New Jersey. Bock, William Sauts, illus. (p. 1569)
Homewood, Terry Stewart. From Then until Now. (p. 644)
Homeyer, Henry. Wobar & the Quest for the Magic Calumet. Yunger, Joshua, illus. (p. 1943)
Homfray, Jenny. Adventures of Parker the Parrot. (p. 21)
Homfray, Nick, illus. see Greenham, Caz.
Homzie, Hillary. Hot List. (p. 801)
—Things Are Gonna Get Ugly. (p. 1733)
Honda, Liana. Kou Lima. Kukahiko, Puni, illus. (p. 967)
—Kou Wawae. Kukahiko, Puni, illus. (p. 967)
Hondel, Gary. Pudgee Woodchuck. Hondel, Gary, illus. (p. 1414)
Honderich, Lou. Ricki. (p. 1470)
Honders, Christine. Bloodsucking Birds. (p. 201)
—Buffalo Soldiers. (p. 236)
—How Cats & Other Animals See at Night. (p. 805)
—How Sharks & Other Animals Sense Electricity. (p. 812)
—Steve Jobs: Father of the Digital Revolution. (p. 1649)
—Steve Jobs: Visionary of the Digital Revolution. (p. 1649)
—Trip Inside a Tornado. (p. 1787)
—What Is Gravity? (p. 1889)
—When Hail Hits. (p. 1902)
Honders, Jamie. Coral Snake. (p. 366)
—Flying Foxes Are Not Foxes! (p. 610)
—Our Community Helpers. (p. 1308)
Honders, Jamie, jt. auth. see Mills, Nathan.
Hondo. Dream World Tales. (p. 484)
Hondorp, Michael & Nash, Kevin. University of Michigan College Prowler off the Record. (p. 1820)
Hondru, Ovi, illus. see Fuerst, Jeffrey B. & Benchmark Education Co., LLC.
Hone, Blaine. Intergalactic Commandos: Defense of the Squid Heads. (p. 880)
Hone, Brettell. My African Bedtime Rhymes. (p. 1195)
Hone, Sallie. Phoenix. (p. 1351)
Honea, Helen. Shedding the Light: Stories from the Bible. (p. 1564)
Honegger, Mark. English Grammar for Writing. (p. 530)
Honey, Alison. My Ashmolean Discovery Book. (p. 1196)
Honey, Elizabeth. Ballad of Cauldron Bay. (p. 134)
—I'm Still Awake, Still! Honey, Elizabeth & Johnson, Sue, illus. (p. 860)
—That's Not a Daffodil! Honey, Elizabeth, illus. (p. 1727)
Honey, Elizabeth, illus. see Mattingley, Christobel.
Honey, Elizabeth & Brandt, Heike. To the Boy in Berlin. Honey, Elizabeth, illus. (p. 1759)
Honeybourne, John. BTEC National Sport Textbook: Development, Coaching & Fitness. Bk. 1 (p. 233)
Honeybourne, John, et al. Advanced Physical Education & Sport for A-Level. (p. 13)
Honeycutt, Brad. Exceptional Eye Tricks. (p. 547)
Honeycutt, Brad & Stickels, Terry. Art of the Illusion: Deceptions to Challenge the Eye & the Mind. (p. 102)
Honeycutt, Gene. Alexander's Long Trip Home. (p. 37)
Honeycutt, Natalie. Best-Laid Plans of Jonah Twist. (p. 170)
Honeycutt, Scarlet. Turkeys in Disguise. Aarvig, Cindy, illus. (p. 1797)
Honeyman, Kay. Fire Horse Girl. (p. 590)
Honeyman-Lowe, Gina & Lowe, John C. Your Guide to Metabolic Health. (p. 1980)
Honeywill, Chris, jt. auth. see Ellse, Mark.
Hong, Andrew, jt. auth. see Hong, Denise.
Hong, Catherine Thao. Adventures of Miss Turtle. Pipe, Jasper, illus. (p. 20)
Hong, Chen Jian. Leyenda De la Cometa. (p. 1004)
Hong, Chen Jiang. Little Eagle. (p. 1027)
—Magic Horse of Han Gan. Bedrick, Claudia Z., tr. from FRE. (p. 1072)
—Mao & Me. Bedrick, Claudia Z., tr. from FRE. (p. 1089)
Hong, Chia Swee, et al. Sensory Motor Activities for Early Development. (p. 1551)
Hong, Denise & Hong, Andrew. Why I Love My Mom: The Ultimate Gift of the Heart. Lopez, Paul & Hong, Denise, illus. (p. 1925)
Hong, J. Gabriela Gil. Chaos & Mother Earth / Caos y Madre Tierr. (p. 291)
Hong, Jihae, tr. Threads of Time Young Noh, Mi, illus. (p. 1741)
Hong, K. L. Life Freaks Me Out: And Then I Deal with It. (p. 1010)
Hong, Kathryn L., ed. see Fisher, Deborah.
Hong, Lily T., illus. see Butler, Andrea.
Hong, Lily Toy. Two of Everything. (p. 1804)
Hong, Lily Toy, jt. auth. see Tucker, Kathy.
Hong, Richard, illus. see Hawkins, Frank C. & Laube, Greta L. B.
Hong, Seonna. Animus. (p. 84)
Hongo, Akiyoshi. Digimon (p. 439)
—Digimon Sheh, Stephanie, tr. (p. 439)
—Digimon Yuen Wong Yu, illus. (p. 439)
—Digimon Tamers (p. 439)
—Digimon Tamers Sheh, Stephanie, tr. from JPN. (p. 439)
—Digimon Zero Two (p. 439)
Hongo, Akiyoshi, creator. Digimon Tamers (p. 439)
Honig, Bruce. In Pursuit of the Aha! & Ha! Ha! Ha!: Games & Activities for Kids & Their Parents. (p. 864)

—Pursuit of the Aha & Ha! Ha! Ha!: Games & Activities That Support, Challenge & Use Creative Thinking (Divergent) in the Classroom. (p. 1419)
Honig, Dave, et al. LL Cool J's Platinum Workout: Sculpt Your Best Body Ever with Hollywood's Fittest Star. (p. 1043)
Honig, Debbie, jt. auth. see Karlitz, Gail.
Honigsberg, Peter Jan. Armful of Memories. Morse, Tony, illus. (p. 99)
—Pillow of Dreams. Morse, Tony, illus. (p. 1359)
Honigsberg, Peter John. Too Much Picnic. Jones, Ryan, illus. (p. 1767)
Honigsheim, Paul. Outline for the Study of Primitive Peoples in North, Central, & South America. (p. 1313)
Honnor, Sylvia & Mascie-Taylor, Heather. Encore Tricolore (p. 524)
Honolulu Theatre for Youth Staff. Christmas Talk Story. (p. 316)
Honor Books Publishing Staff, contrib. by. God's Little Devotional Book for Boys. (p. 691)
—Pocket Guide for Teens. (p. 1375)
Honovich, Nancy. Color & Play: Jungle Animals. (p. 342)
—Field Guide to Dinosaurs. Dando, Marc & Hobson, Ryan, illus. (p. 583)
—Field Guide to Rainforest Animals: Explore the Amazon Jungle. (p. 583)
—Immigration from the Former Yugoslavia. (p. 861)
Honovich, Nancy, jt. auth. see Murawski, Darlyne.
Honovich, Nancy & Beer, Julie. National Geographic Kids Get Outside Guide: All Things Adventure, Exploration, & Fun! (p. 1232)
Honovich, Nancy & Griffiths, Annie. National Geographic Kids Guide to Photography: Tips & Tricks on How to Be a Great Photographer from the Pros & Your Pals at My Shot. (p. 1232)
Honowitz, Stacey. Genius with a Penis, Don't Touch! (p. 661)
—My Privates Are Private. (p. 1217)
Honowitz, Stacey & Brenner, Jordyn. My Privates Are Private. (p. 1217)
Honsaker, Arthur J. Heart of a Dove: Believe. (p. 759)
Honsinger, Alise, illus. see Honsinger, Linda.
Honsinger, Laura. Mike's New Friends. (p. 1141)
Honsinger, Linda. Leonard Lou: Beautiful, Brave, Strong, & True. Honsinger, Alise, illus. (p. 992)
Hoobler, David. Zonk & the Secret Lagoon: The Further Adventures of Zonk the Dreaming Tortoise. Hoobler, David, illus. (p. 1988)
Hoobler, Dorothy, jt. auth. see Hoobler, Thomas.
Hoobler, Dorothy & Hoobler, Thomas. Demon in the Teahouse. (p. 426)
—Ghost in the Tokaido Inn. (p. 671)
—In Darkness, Death. (p. 863)
—Monsters: Mary Shelley & the Curse of Frankenstein. (p. 1168)
—Seven Paths to Death. (p. 1554)
—Sword That Cut the Burning Grass. (p. 1692)
—Where Are the Great Pyramids? Hoare, Jerry, illus. (p. 1906)
Hoobler, Dorothy, et al. Captain John Smith: Jamestown & the Birth of the American Dream. (p. 264)
Hoobler, Thomas, jt. auth. see Hoobler, Dorothy.
Hoobler, Thomas & Hoobler, Dorothy. Real American Girls Tell Their Own Stories: Messages from the Heart & Heartland. (p. 1448)
Hood, Alaine. Hard Blue Midnight. (p. 748)
Hood, Alaine & Bond, Primula. Switching Hands. (p. 1692)
Hood, Ann. Alexander Graham Bell Master of Sound. Zilber, Denis, illus. (p. 36)
—Amelia Earhart - Lady Lindy Zilber, Denis, illus. (p. 58)
—Anastasia Romanov - The Last Grand Duchess Zilber, Denis, illus. (p. 67)
—Anastasia Romanovs - The Last Grand Duchess Zilber, Denis, illus. (p. 67)
—Clara Barton - Angel of the Battlefield. Kwasney, Karl et al, illus. (p. 326)
—Crazy Horse - Brave Warrior. Altmann, Scott, illus. (p. 377)
—Crazy Horse - Brave Warrior. Altmann, Scott & Zilber, Denis, illus. (p. 377)
—Harry Houdini - Prince of Air. Altmann, Scott & Zilber, Denis, illus. (p. 750)
—Jewel of the East. Kwasny, Karl et al, illus. (p. 917)
—Leonardo Da Vinci: Renaissance Master. No. 9 Zilber, Denis, illus. (p. 992)
—Little Lion Kwasney, Karl et al, illus. (p. 1030)
—Prince of Air Altmann, Scott & Zilber, Denis, illus. (p. 1401)
—Queen Liliuokalani - Royal Prisoner. Altmann, Scott & Zilber, Denis, illus. (p. 1425)
Hood, Ann & Altmann, Scott. Alexander Hamilton - Little Lion Kwasney, Karl & Zilber, Denis, illus. (p. 36)
—Angel of the Battlefield. Kwasney, Karl & Zilber, Denis, illus. (p. 74)
Hood, Ann & Zilber, Denis. Alexander Graham Bell: Master of Sound. No. 7 (p. 36)
Hood, Ann Howle. Put It Back. (p. 1420)
Hood, Brandyn. My Favorite Foods in the Grocery Store. (p. 1203)
Hood, Christine & Muschla, Judith. Practice, Practice, Practice! Multiplication & Division: 50 Independent Practice Pages That Help Kids Master Essential Math Skills - And Meet the NCTM Standards. (p. 1392)
Hood, Cortney Thomas. Miss Sippi Sass: Seriously Southern. Seriously Sassy. (p. 1152)
Hood, Dana, jt. auth. see Bryant, Sharon.
Hood, Dominic & Skindzier, Jon. Harvard University College Prowler off the Record. (p. 751)
Hood, Douglas. Stone Hat. Simonton, Tom, illus. (p. 1652)
Hood, Evelyn. Wake for Donald. (p. 1853)
Hood, George W., illus. see Wilhelm, Richard, ed.
Hood, Jack B. Legend of Holly Boy. (p. 988)
Hood, James G. Dr. James G. Hood, Author: Book, Freelance Service & Gift Catalog. Whispering Pine Press International, ed. (p. 475)
Hood, Joyce, illus. see Ketch, Ann.
Hood, Kared Jean Matsko. My Special Care Scrapbook for Foster Children: A Special Scrapbook for Foster Children Whispering Pine Press International, ed. (p. 1219)
Hood, Karen Jean Matsko. Adventure Travel: A Daily Journal Whispering Pine Press International, Inc. Staff, ed. (p. 15)
—Adventure Travel Activity & Coloring Book: Activity & Coloring Book Series. (p. 15)
—Adventure Travel Activity & Coloring Book. Whispering Pine Press International, ed. (p. 15)
—Adventures of My Dentist & the Tooth Fairy: Activity & Coloring Book Whispering Pine Press International, Inc. Staff, ed. (p. 21)
—Adventures of My Dentist & the Tooth Fairy Activity & Coloring Book Second Edition. (p. 21)
—Adventures of My Dentist & Tooth Fairy Activity & Coloring Book: Activity & Coloring Book. Whispering Pine Press International, Inc. Staff, ed. (p. 21)
—Angels, Angels Way up High Whispering Pine Press International, ed. (p. 75)
—Apple Delights Cookbook, Translated Italian: A Collection of Apple Recipes Whispering Pine Press International, ed. (p. 92)
—Apples: Apple Board Book Whispering Pine Press International, ed. (p. 92)
—Arizona Saguaro: A Collection of Poetry Whispering Pine Press International, ed. (p. 99)
—Arizona Saguaro: A Collection of Poetry Whispering Pine Press International Staff, ed. (p. 99)
—Gaited Horse Activity & Coloring Book. Whispering Pine Press International, ed. (p. 652)
—Gaited Horse Activity & Coloring Book-English/German/Spanish Edition. Whispering Pine Press International, Inc. Staff, ed. (p. 652)
—Gaited Horse Journal: A Daily Journal Whispering Pine Press International, Inc. Staff, ed. (p. 652)
—Getaway Country Kitchen Catalog: Gourmet & Country Grocery, Take-Out Food & Catering Service Products Whispering Pine Press International, ed. (p. 668)
—Girls Can Do Activity & Coloring Book. Whispering Pine Press International, Inc. Staff, ed. (p. 679)
—Girls Can Do Activity & Coloring Book Whispering Pine Press International, ed. (p. 680)
—Girls Can Do Journal: A Daily Journal Whispering Pine Press International, ed. (p. 680)
—Goodnight, I Wish You Goodnight Whispering Pine Press International, Inc. Staff, ed. (p. 701)
—Goodnight, I Wish You Goodnight, Bilingual English & Icelandic Whispering Pine Press International, ed. (p. 701)
—Grandma Bert's Favorite Christmas Sweets Recipes: A Collection of Recipes from Grandma Bert Whispering Pine Press International, ed. (p. 708)
—Icelandic Horse: A Daily Journal Whispering Pine Press International, ed. (p. 851)
—Icelandic Horse Activity & Coloring Book Whispering Pine Press International, ed. (p. 851)
—Icelandic Horse Activity & Coloring Book: Activity & Coloring Book Whispering Pine Press International, ed. (p. 851)
—Jesus Loves the Little Children: Activity & Coloring Book Whispering Pine Press International, ed. (p. 916)
—Karen Jean Matsko Hood, Inc. Parenting Book & Gift Catalog. Whispering Pine Press International, ed. (p. 943)
—Kids' Kindness: Adventures in Learning Whispering Pine Press International, ed. (p. 954)
—Kids' Kindness Activity & Coloring Book Whispering Pine Press International, ed. (p. 954)
—Kids' Kindness Journal: A Daily Journal Whispering Pine Press International, ed. (p. 954)
—Lost Medal Whispering Pine Press International, Inc. Staff, ed. (p. 1056)
—Lost Medal, Christian Edition: With Bible Verses & Christian Themes. Whispering Pine Press International, ed. (p. 1056)
—My Adoption Celebration Scrapbook: A Special Celebration of My Adoption Whispering Pine Press International, ed. (p. 1195)
—My Birth Celebration Journal: A Daily Journal Whispering Pine Press International, Inc. Staff, ed. (p. 1198)
—My Birth Celebration Scrapbook: A Celebration of My Birth Scrapbook for Children (p. 1198)
—My Birth Celebration Scrapbook: A Celebration of My Birth Scrapbook for Children Whispering Pine Press International, Inc. Staff, ed. (p. 1198)
—My Dentist & the Tooth Fairy: Activity & Coloring Book Whispering Pine Press International, Inc. Staff, ed. (p. 1201)
—My Holiday Memories Journal: A Daily Journal Whispering Pine Press International, ed. (p. 1211)
—My Holiday Memories Scrapbook for Adopted Kids: A Holiday Memories Scrapbook for Kids Whispering Pine Press International, ed. (p. 1211)
—My Holiday Memories Scrapbook for Foster Kids: A Holiday Memories Scrapbook for Kids Whispering Pine Press International, ed. (p. 1211)
—My Holiday Memories Scrapbook for Kids Whispering Pine Press International, ed. (p. 1211)
—My Holiday Memories Scrapbook for Kids Whispering Pine Press International, Inc. Staff, ed. (p. 1211)
—My Special Care Journal for Adopted Children: A Daily Journal Whispering Pine Press International, ed. (p. 1219)
—My Special Care Journal for Foster Children: A Daily Journal Whispering Pine Press International, ed. (p. 1219)
—My Special Care Scrapbook for Adopted Children: A Special Scrapbook for Adopted Children Whispering Pine Press International, ed. (p. 1219)
—My Special Care Scrapbook for Adopted Children: A Special Care Scrapbook for Adopted Children Whispering Pine Press International, ed. (p. 1219)
—My Special Care Scrapbook for Children: A Special Scrapbook for Children Whispering Pine Press International, Inc. Staff, ed. (p. 1219)
—Opening Day. Whispering Pine Press International, ed. (p. 1300)
—Petting Farm Fun: Hood Picture Book Series (p. 1348)
—Petting Farm Fun Whispering Pine Press International, ed. (p. 1348)
—Petting Farm Fun: Hood Picture Book Series - Book 3 Whispering Pine Press International Staff, ed. (p. 1348)
—Petting Farm Fun, Bilingual English & Hindi. Whispering Pine Press International, ed. (p. 1348)
—Petting Farm Fun, Bilingual English & Marathi Edition: Hood Picture Book Series- Book 3. (p. 1348)
—Petting Farm Fun, Bilingual English & Portuguese. Whispering Pine Press International, ed. (p. 1348)
—Petting Farm Fun, Bilingual English & Spanish Whispering Pine Press International, ed. (p. 1348)
—Petting Farm Fun, Translated Hindi Whispering Pine Press International, ed. (p. 1349)
—Petting Farm Fun, Translated Marathi Edition: Hood Picture Book Series- Book 3. (p. 1349)
—Petting Farm Fun, Translated Portuguese Whispering Pine Press International, ed. (p. 1349)
—Spokane Falls. Whispering Pine Press International, ed. (p. 1630)
—Stinky Feet & Other Unpleasant Items: A Collection of Children's Poetry. (p. 1651)
—Tanka Thoughts: A Collection of Poetry Whispering Pine Press International, ed. (p. 1705)
—There's a Toad in the Hole: A Big Fat Toad in the Hole Whispering Pine Press International, ed. (p. 1731)
—Under the Lilacs: A Collection of Children's Poetry Whispering Pine Press International, ed. (p. 1813)
—Washington State: Activity & Coloring Book. (p. 1860)
Hood, Karen Jean Matsko & Hood, Kyler. My Holiday Memories Scrapbook for Kids, Translated Hindi Edition (p. 1211)
Hood, Korey K. Type 1 Teens: A Guide to Managing Your Diabetes. Ishe, Bryan, illus. (p. 1805)
Hood, Kyler, jt. auth. see Hood, Karen Jean Matsko.
Hood, Philip, illus. see Brown, Harriet & Witowski, Teri.
Hood, Robert. Gadgets & Gizmos. (p. 652)
Hood, Sue. Monkey Business. Chapman, Susan, illus. (p. 1165)
Hood, Susan. Ada's Violin: The Story of the Recycled Orchestra. Comport, Sally Wern, illus. (p. 11)
—Brainiac's Road Trip. (p. 222)
—Caterpillar Spring, Butterfly Summer: 10th Anniversary Edition. Gevry, Claudine, illus. (p. 279)
—Caterpillar Spring, Butterfly Summer. Gévry, Claudine, illus. (p. 279)
—Just Say Boo! Henry, Jed, illus. (p. 939)
—Mission: Back to School: Top Secret Info for Rookie Students. Lundquist, Mary, illus. (p. 1153)
—Mission: New Baby. Lundquist, Mary, illus. (p. 1153)
—Pup & Hound. Hendry, Linda, illus. (p. 1417)
—Pup & Hound at Sea. Hendry, Linda, illus. (p. 1417)
—Pup & Hound Catch a Thief. Hendry, Linda, illus. (p. 1417)
—Pup & Hound Hatch an Egg. Hendry, Linda, illus. (p. 1417)
—Pup & Hound in Trouble. Hendry, Linda, illus. (p. 1417)
—Pup & Hound Lost & Found. Hendry, Linda, illus. (p. 1417)
—Pup & Hound Move In. Hendry, Linda, illus. (p. 1417)
—Pup & Hound Play Copycats. Hendry, Linda, illus. (p. 1417)
—Pup & Hound Scare a Ghost. Hendry, Linda, illus. (p. 1417)
—Pup & Hound Stay up Late. Hendry, Linda, illus. (p. 1417)
—Rooting for You. Cordell, Matthew, illus. (p. 1488)
—Spike: The Mixed-Up Monster. Sweet, Melissa, illus. (p. 1627)
—Tooth Mouse. Nadeau, Janice, illus. (p. 1768)
Hood, Susan, jt. auth. see Albee, Sarah.
Hood, Susan & Hendry, Linda. Pup & Hound. Hendry, Linda, illus. (p. 1417)
Hood, Thomas & Pearson Education Staff. Man Two Shadow & Other Ghost Stories. (p. 1086)
Hood, Tyline M. I Love You So Much, Goodnight. (p. 844)
Hood-Caddy, Karen. Howl. (p. 823)
—Saving Crazy. (p. 1517)
—Truth about Brave. (p. 1794)
Hooff Andreozzi, Maremi, illus. see Hooff, Gudren.
Hooff, Gudren. I. M. Green. Hooff Andreozzi, Maremi, illus. (p. 844)
Hoofnagle, Therese, illus. see Dawson, J. M.
Hoog, Mark. Your Song: A Growing Field Adventure. Aukerman, Robert J., illus. (p. 1981)
Hoog, Mark E. Dream Machine: A Growing Field Adventure. Aukerman, Robert J., illus. (p. 483)
Hoogenboom, Lynn. Amerigo Vespucci. (p. 64)
—Amerigo Vespucci: A Primary Source Biography. (p. 65)
—Christopher Columbus: A Primary Source Biography. (p. 316)
—Christopher Columbus. (p. 316)
—Ferdinand Magellan: A Primary Source Biography. (p. 581)
—Ferdinand Magellan. (p. 581)
—Francisco Pizarro: A Primary Source Biography. (p. 628)
—Francisco Pizarro. (p. 628)
—Juan Ponce de Leon: A Primary Source Biography. (p. 930)
—Juan Ponce de Leon. (p. 930)
—Sir Francis Drake: A Primary Source Biography. (p. 1580)
—Sir Francis Drake. (p. 1580)
—William Tecumseh Sherman: The Fight to Preserve the Union. (p. 1933)
Hooghe, Marc & Stolle, Dietlind. Generating Social Capital: Civil Society & Institutions in Comparative Perspective. (p. 660)
Hoogstad, Alice. BOLDER & BOAT. (p. 208)
Hoogstad, Alice, illus. see Van Os, Erik & Van Lieshout, Elle.
Hook. Shipwrecks - Mysteries of the Past. (p. 1567)
—Wrinkled Crinkled Grapes: A Purple Monster. (p. 1963)
Hook, Adam, illus. see Dargie, Richard & Compass Point Books Staff.
Hook, Carol A. Before There Were Stars: An Orange Dragon. (p. 158)
Hook, Christa, illus. see Castle, Ian.
Hook, Dena, jt. auth. see Pino, Santo.
Hook, Derek. He Walked & He Walked & He Walked. (p. 756)
Hook, Dianne J. DJ Inkers Plan Book. (p. 455)
—DJ Inkers Record Book. (p. 455)
Hook, Dianne J., creator. All about Me: Creative Scrapbooking Templates & Clip Art for Classroom & Home. (p. 43)
—Schooltime Borders: Creative Borders for Classroom & Home. (p. 1524)
Hook, Frances, jt. illus. see Hook, Richard.
Hook, Francis. Finding the Djinn. (p. 588)
Hook, J. E. Magic Square. (p. 1073)
Hook, Jacqueline A. You're Going to Be a Flower Girl. (p. 1982)
Hook, Jason. Where's the Dragon? Hook, Richard, illus. (p. 1911)
Hook, Melissa. Ethics in Victim Services. (p. 539)
Hook, Richard, illus. see Hook, Jason.
Hook, Richard, illus. see Nohl, Frederick.
Hook, Richard & Hook, Frances. Jesus the Friend of Children. (p. 916)
Hook, Sue & Jackson, Carolyn, eds. All about People: How We Grow, How Our Bodies Work, & How We Feel. (p. 43)
Hook, Sue Vander. Writing Intriguing Informational Pieces. (p. 1965)
—Writing Notable Narrative Nonfiction. (p. 1965)
Hook, Sue Vander, see Englar, Mary & Vander Hook, Sue.
Hook, Sue Vander, see Vander Hook, Sue.
Hook, Sue Vander & Kamisar, Yale. Miranda v. Arizona: An Individual's Rights When under Arrest. (p. 1149)
Hooke, R. Schuyler. Thomas & the Great Discovery. Stubbs, Tommy, illus. (p. 1738)
—Thomas & the Jet Engine. (p. 1738)
—Thomas & the Treasure. Palone, Terry & Permane, Terry, photos by. (p. 1738)
—Thomas' Night Before Christmas. Courtney, Richard, illus. (p. 1739)
Hooke, R. Schuyler, jt. auth. see Awdry, Wilbert V.
Hooker, Adele. Sailor the Cat. Gwinner, Patricia, illus. (p. 1503)
Hooker, Forrestine Cooper. Child of the Fighting Tenth: On the Frontier with the Buffalo Soldiers. Wilson, Steve, ed. (p. 301)
Hooker, Jennifer, jt. auth. see Robertson, Kathy.
Hooker, Karen. Camping. Biddle, Bruce, illus. (p. 257)
Hooker, Lou. Puppies & Pet Crows. (p. 1418)
—Year of the Fire. (p. 1969)
Hooker, Ronessa Blair. What Color Am I? (p. 1881)
Hooker, Worthington. Child's Book of Nature. (p. 304)
Hooks, Bell. Be Love, Baby Love. Freeman, Laura, illus. (p. 148)
Hooks, Earnest. Let's go see Mother Wilkerson's Farm. (p. 997)
Hooks, Gwendolyn. Best Trick: A Pet Club Story Byrne, Mike, illus. (p. 171)
—Cat Food Mystery: A Pet Club Story Byrne, Mike, illus. (p. 278)
—Find the Cat! A Pet Club Story Byrne, Mike, illus. (p. 587)
—Freshwater Feeders: Studying Food Webs in Freshwater. (p. 636)
—Lucky Charm: A Pet Club Story Byrne, Mike, illus. (p. 1062)
—Noisy Night: A Pet Club Story Byrne, Mike, illus. (p. 1263)
—Pet Club. Byrne, Mike, illus. (p. 1345)
—Pet Costume Party: A Pet Club Story Byrne, Mike, illus. (p. 1345)
—Pet Wash: A Pet Club Story Byrne, Mike, illus. (p. 1346)
—Pets at the Party: A Pet Club Story Byrne, Mike, illus. (p. 1348)
—Three's a Crowd. Walker, Sylvia, illus. (p. 1744)
Hooks, Gwendolyn, jt. auth. see Scholastic, Inc. Staff.
Hooks, Margaret. Tina Modotti. Modotti, Tina, photos by. (p. 1755)
Hoole, Elissa Janine. Kiss the Morning Star (p. 961)
—Sometimes Never, Sometimes Always. (p. 1610)
Hooley, Rachelle B. & Butler, Mackay M. Halloween Chase. Jarman, Brandy S., illus. (p. 737)
Hoomes, Eleanor W. Laughing Matters: Creative Writing Book. (p. 980)
Hoop, Cathy C. PowerXpress Easter: Peter's Story Unit. (p. 1391)
Hooper, jt. auth. see Fry.
Hooper, Caroline. Learn Songwriting. (p. 983)
Hooper, Caroline, ed. see O'Brien, Eileen.
Hooper, Caroline & Danes, Emma. Little Book of Nursery Rhymes. (p. 1025)
Hooper, Carrie Lynn. Harley & the Hummingbird. (p. 749)
Hooper, Hadley, illus. see Corey, Shana.
Hooper, Hadley, illus. see MacLachlan, Patricia.
Hooper, Hadley, illus. see Nelson, Marilyn.
Hooper, Hadley, illus. see Person, Naomi, et al.
Hooper, Jaci. Gary: #Exodus 20. (p. 657)
Hooper, James. Nelly. (p. 1240)
Hooper, Kaye D., et al. Encyclopedia of Multiple Sclerosis. (p. 525)
Hooper, Leta. Dream That Saved Grizzly Forest. (p. 484)
Hooper, M. Haunting of Julia Gray, Maureen & Lynch, Josh, illus. (p. 754)
Hooper, Mary. Down to Earth. Harker, Lesley, illus. (p. 474)
—Fallen Grace. (p. 566)
—Ghoul at School. Harker, Lesley, illus. (p. 673)
—Katie: The Revolting Bridesmaid. Vayssiere, Frederique, illus. (p. 944)
—Newes from the Dead. (p. 1249)
—Revolting Baby. Vayssiere, Frederique, illus. (p. 1466)
—Revolting Holiday. Vayssiere, Frederique, illus. (p. 1466)
—Revolting Wedding. Vayssiere, Frederique, illus. (p. 1466)
—Round the Rainbow. Harker, Lesley, illus. (p. 1491)
—Velvet. (p. 1835)
Hooper, Mary, jt. auth. see McAllister, Angela.
Hooper, Meredith. Egyptian Tomb: The Tomb of Nebamun. (p. 507)
—River Story. Willey, Bee, illus. (p. 1476)
—Tom Crean's Rabbit: A True Story from Scott's Last Voyage. Kitchen, Bert, illus. (p. 1763)
—Who Built the Pyramid? Heighway-Bury, Robin, illus. (p. 1914)
Hooper, Meredith & Quarto Generic Staff. Ponko & the South Pole. Ormerod, Jan, illus. (p. 1382)
Hooper, Nancy. Everywhere Coquis. Quinones, Jacqueline, tr. (p. 546)
Hooper, R. M. J. Secret of Crescent Grey. (p. 1542)
Hooper, Ruth. Santa's Factory. Charbonnel, Olivier & Mostyn, David, illus. (p. 1513)
Hoopes, Sandra. Original Cin. (p. 1304)
Hoople, Barrie, ed. see Armstrong, Linda.
Hoople, Barrie, ed. see Mullarkey, Lisa.

Hoopmann, Kathy. All Cats Have Asperger Syndrome. (p. 44)
—All Dogs Have ADHD. (p. 44)
Hoops, Kevin, photos by see Vendera, Jaime & McGee, Anne Loader.
Hoorn, Aurea Van, see Hirabayashi, Suzanne.
Hoose, Hannah, jt. auth. see Hoose, Phillip.
Hoose, Philip M. It's Our World, Too. (p. 898)
Hoose, Phillip. Boys Who Challenged Hitler: Knud Pedersen & the Churchill Club. (p. 220)
—Claudette Colvin: Twice Toward Justice. (p. 329)
—Moonbird: A Year on the Wind with the Great Survivor B95 (p. 1172)
—Race to Save the Lord God Bird. (p. 1431)
Hoose, Phillip & Hoose, Hannah. Oye, Hormiguita. Tilley, Debbie, illus. (p. 1316)
Hooser, Betty. Flying House for Entertainment. (p. 610)
Hooser, Betty J. Kids with Large Insects & Flowers & Unusual Things. (p. 955)
Hooten, Emily & Student Life Staff. 31 Verses - Here & Now: Every Teenager Should Know. (p. 1996)
Hooten, K. J. Egg Nanny Tales. (p. 506)
—Stories to Amuse the Kids (p. 1655)
Hooton, David James. Carrots in Candy Land. (p. 271)
—It Circled Twice. (p. 893)
Hooton, Margaret. Laughing Pot & Other Stories: More Tales for All the Children of the World. (p. 980)
Hoover, Charity, illus. see Martin, Mary.
Hoover, Dave. Fighting Chance - Denial (p. 585)
Hoover, Dave, illus. see Doeden, Matt.
Hoover, Dave, illus. see Hoena, Blake A. & Hoena, B. A.
Hoover, Dave, illus. see Martin, Michael & Martin, Michael J.
Hoover, Dave, illus. see Martin, Michael J.
Hoover, Dave, illus. see Olson, Nathan.
Hoover, Elizabeth. Suzanne Collins. (p. 1688)
—Walter Dean Myers. Greenhaven Press Staff, ed. (p. 1856)
Hoover, Helen. Great Wolf & the Good Woodsman. Bowen, Betsy, illus. (p. 719)
Hoover, John J., photos by see Toki, Wilfred.
Hoover, Krystal Dawn. Tabby Town. (p. 1694)
Hoover, Laney Laube. Tale of the Tailless Cat. (p. 1700)
Hoover, Leighnne W. Festus & his Fest Favorites. (p. 582)
Hoover, Melanie. Name the Missing Shape: Analyze, Compare, Create, & Compose Shapes. (p. 1228)
Hoover, Nadine. A, B, C Awal. Bardo, Yuyun, illus. (p. 1)
Hoover, Nicolas. Red Merit Badge of Courage. (p. 1454)
Hoover, P. J. Emerald Tablet. (p. 517)
—Navel of the World. (p. 1237)
—Solstice. (p. 1608)
—Tut: The Story of My Immortal Life. (p. 1799)
Hoover, Paul. Rehearsal in Black. (p. 1457)
Hoover, Paulette. What's That Lump in Your Bed? (p. 1899)
Hoover, Sarah. If My Dirty Shoes Could Fly. (p. 853)
Hoover, Steve. Hannah Chronicles: The Door in the Floor: the Adventures of Hannah Hadley, Girl Spy. Bk. 1 (p. 742)
Hoover, T. A. Last Eagle. Kaths, Kathy, illus. (p. 977)
Hooymans, Robert. Mildly Adventurous Doings of Piedlow Twerne. (p. 1142)
HOP, LLC. Hooked on ABCs Super Activity Kit. (p. 795)
—Hooked on Animals in the Wild Super Activity Kit. (p. 795)
—Hooked on Animals on the Farm Super Activity Kit. (p. 795)
—Hooked on Animals Pets Super Activity Kit. (p. 795)
—Hooked on Bible Stories. (p. 795)
—Hooked on Bible Stories NT Stories. (p. 795)
—Hooked on Bible Stories Old Testament Stories. (p. 795)
—Hooked on Bible Stories Premium Edition. (p. 795)
—Hooked on Boats Super Activity Kit. (p. 795)
—Hooked on Chinese. (p. 795)
—Hooked on French. (p. 795)
—Hooked on Handwriting Learn to Print. (p. 795)
—Hooked on Kindergarten. (p. 795)
—Hooked on Learning Coloring. (p. 795)
—Hooked on Learning Handwriting. (p. 795)
—Hooked on Learning Puzzles & Mazes. (p. 795)
—Hooked on Numbers. (p. 795)
—Hooked on Phonics Beginning Reading with Bible Stories. (p. 795)
—Hooked on Phonics Learn to Read (Kindergarten & First Grade) (p. 795)
—Hooked on Phonics Reading Comprehension. (p. 795)
—Hooked on Phonics Word Games. (p. 795)
—Hooked on Pre-K. (p. 795)
—Hooked on Spanish. (p. 795)
—Hooked on Spanish Beginning Spanish. (p. 795)
—Hooked on Spelling. (p. 795)
—Hooked on Trains, Planes, & Cars Super Activity Kit. (p. 795)
—Hooked on Trucks Super Activity Kit. (p. 795)
—Super Activity 3-pack - Hooked on Animals. (p. 1679)
—Super Activity 3-pack - Hooked on Things That Go. (p. 1679)
—Sylvan School Success. (p. 1692)
HOP LLC Staff. Hooked on Math - Addition & Subtraction. (p. 795)
—Hooked on Math - Division. (p. 795)
—Hooked on Math - Multiplication. (p. 795)
—Hooked on Phonics - Learn to Read Kindergarten. (p. 795)
HOP LLC Staff, ed. Hooked on Phonics - Learn to Read First Grade. (p. 795)
Hop, Nguyen Thi, illus. see Hanh, Thich Nhat.
Hopcus, Sharron. Kanka the Kankapotamus. (p. 942)
—Ollie the Collie Takes a Ride on the Trolley. (p. 1287)
—Poppie Takes a Ride on a Hot Air Balloon. (p. 1384)
—Poppie the One-Eyed Pug. (p. 1384)
—Poppie the One-Eyed Pug & His New Friend. (p. 1384)
—Poppie the One-Eyed Pug Visits the North Pole. (p. 1384)
—Poppie's Pot of Gold. (p. 1384)
Hope, Anthony. Prisionero de Zenda. (p. 1407)
Hope, B. T. Curse of the Bone Pirates: Nui Island Eco-Logical Adventures. (p. 394)
Hope, Bill, illus. see Matheson, Jason.
Hope, Charles. Solar System. (p. 1607)
Hope, David. Fireside Book 2004. D C Thomson Staff, ed. (p. 592)
Hope, Gloria. Harry's Club. (p. 751)
Hope, Harry S. Elements of Lore - Volume 1 of the Books of Lore. (p. 511)
Hope, J., et al. Mental Math in Junior High. (p. 1126)
Hope, Kathleen. Isiah Thomas & the Mysterious Castle Mcscary. (p. 891)
—Jack Eagle the Pirate & Other Mysterious Tales. (p. 903)
Hope, Laura. Bobbsey Twins. (p. 206)
—Bobbsey Twins at the County Fair. (p. 206)
—Bobbsey Twins on Blueberry Island. (p. 206)
—Bobbsey Twins or Merry Days Indoors and. (p. 206)
—Bunny Brown & His Sister Sue Giving A. (p. 242)
—Story of a Plush Bear. (p. 1657)
Hope, Laura Lee. Bobbsey Twins: The First Fifteen Stories, Including Merry Days Indoors & Out, in the Country, at the Seashore, at School, at Snow Lodge, on A. (p. 206)
—Bobbsey Twins. (p. 206)
—Bobbsey Twins at Home. (p. 206)
—Bobbsey Twins at Meadow Brook. (p. 206)
—Bobbsey Twins at School. (p. 206)
—Bobbsey Twins at Snow Lodge. (p. 206)
—Bobbsey Twins at the County Fair. (p. 206)
—Bobbsey Twins at the Seashore. (p. 206)
—Bobbsey Twins in a Great City. (p. 206)
—Bobbsey Twins in the Country. (p. 206)
—Bobbsey Twins in the Great West. (p. 206)
—Bobbsey Twins in Volcano Land. (p. 206)
—Bobbsey Twins in Washington. (p. 206)
—Bobbsey Twins on A House Boat. (p. 206)
—Bobbsey Twins on a House Boat. (p. 206)
—Bobbsey Twins on Blueberry Island. (p. 206)
—Bunny Brown & His Sister Sue. (p. 242)
—Bunny Brown & his Sister Sue. (p. 242)
—Bunny Brown & His Sister Sue & Their Shetland Pony. (p. 242)
—Bunny Brown & His Sister Sue at Aunt Lu's City Home. (p. 242)
—Bunny Brown & His Sister Sue at Camp R. (p. 242)
—Bunny Brown & His Sister Sue Giving A. (p. 242)
—Bunny Brown & His Sister Sue Giving a Show. (p. 242)
—Bunny Brown & His Sister Sue in the Sunny South. (p. 242)
—Bunny Brown & His Sister Sue Keeping Store. (p. 242)
—Bunny Brown & His Sister Sue on an Auto Tour. (p. 242)
—Bunny Brown & His Sister Sue on Grandpa's Farm. (p. 242)
—Freddie & Flossie. Pyle, Chuck, illus. (p. 632)
—Freddie & Flossie & Snap. Pyle, Chuck, illus. (p. 632)
—Freddie & Flossie & the Leaf Monster. Ruppert, Larry, illus. (p. 632)
—Freddie & Flossie & the Train Ride. Pyle, Chuck, illus. (p. 632)
—Freddie & Flossie at the Beach. Pyle, Chuck, illus. (p. 632)
—Moving Picture Girls at Oak Farm: Or, Queer Happenings While Taking Rural Plays. (p. 1184)
—Moving Picture Girls at Oak Farm. (p. 1184)
—Moving Picture Girls at Sea: Or A Pictured Shipwreck That Became Real. (p. 1184)
—Moving Picture Girls at Sea. (p. 1184)
—Moving Picture Girls under the Palms: Or Lost in the Wilds of Florida. (p. 1184)
—Moving Picture Girls under the Palms. (p. 1184)
—Mystery at School. (p. 1224)
—Outdoor Girls at Ocean View: Or the Box That Was Found in the Sand. (p. 1312)
—Outdoor Girls at Ocean View. (p. 1312)
—Outdoor Girls at Rainbow Lake. (p. 1312)
—Outdoor Girls at the Hostess House: Or, doing their best for the Soldiers. (p. 1312)
—Outdoor Girls at the Hostess House. (p. 1312)
—Outdoor Girls at Wild Rose Lodge: The Outdoor Girls at Wild Rose Lodge. (p. 1312)
—Outdoor Girls at Wild Rose Lodge. (p. 1312)
—Outdoor Girls in a Motor Car. (p. 1312)
—Outdoor Girls in Army Service: Or Doing Their Bit for the Soldier Boys. (p. 1312)
—Outdoor Girls in Army Service. (p. 1312)
—Outdoor Girls in Florida: Or Wintering in the Sunny South. (p. 1312)
—Outdoor Girls in Florida. (p. 1312)
—Outdoor Girls in the Saddle: Or the Girl Miner of Gold Run. (p. 1312)
—Outdoor Girls in the Saddle. (p. 1312)
—Outdoor Girls of Deepdale: Or Camping & Tramping for Fun & Health. (p. 1312)
—Outdoor Girls of Deepdale. (p. 1312)
—Outdoor Girls on Pine Island: Or A Cave & What It Contained. (p. 1312)
—Short Works of Laura Lee Hope. (p. 1569)
—Six Little Bunkers at Cousin Tom's. (p. 1582)
—Six Little Bunkers at Cowboy Jack's. (p. 1582)
—Six Little Bunkers at Grandma Bell's. (p. 1582)
—Six Little Bunkers at Mammy Junes. (p. 1582)
—Story of a Nodding Donkey. (p. 1657)
Hope, Lauryne. Little Kitty. (p. 1030)
Hope, Lee Laura. Bunny Brown & His Sister Sue & Their Shetland Pony. (p. 242)
—Outdoor Girls in a Motor Car: The Haunted Mansion of Shadow Valley. (p. 1312)
—Outdoor Girls in a Motor Car or the Haunted Mansion of Shadow Valley. (p. 1312)
—Outdoor Girls in a Winter Camp: Glorious Days on Skates & Ice Boats. (p. 1312)
—Outdoor Girls in a Winter Camp or Glorious Days on Skates & Ice Boats. (p. 1312)
—Six Little Bunkers at Aunt Jo's. (p. 1582)
—Six Little Bunkers at Cowboy Jack's. (p. 1582)
Hope, Michelle, illus. see Galjanic, Lisa.
Hope, Rinnah Y. Gossip Queen. Joyart, B., illus. (p. 703)
Hopeless, Dennis, jt. auth. see Norton, Mike.
Hope-Simpson, Lila & Groenendyk, Doretta. Fiddles & Spoons: Journey of an Acadian Mouse (p. 583)
Hopgood, Andrew, illus. see Condon, Bill.
Hopgood, Andrew, illus. see Reynolds, Alison.
Hopgood, Kevin, illus. see Claybourne, Anna.
Hopgood, Sally. Trip to Busy Town: A Pull-The-Tab Book. Hinton, Stephanie, illus. (p. 1787)
Hopgood, Sally & Graham, Oakley. Arctic Wonders. Wood, Hannah, illus. (p. 96)
—Safari Wonders. Wood, Hannah, illus. (p. 1502)
Hopgood, Tim. Here Comes Frankie! (p. 770)
—Hooray for Hoppy! (p. 796)
—Little Answer. (p. 1023)
—Ping & Pong Are Best Friends (Mostly) (p. 1359)
—Unpoppable. (p. 1822)
—Wow! Said the Owl. Hopgood, Tim, illus. (p. 1962)
Hopgood, Tim, illus. see Thiele, Bob & Weiss, George David.
Hopkins, Adrianna & Lyon, Abby. University of North Carolina College Prowler off the Record. (p. 1821)
Hopkins, Albert A., ed. Magic: Stage Illusions, Special Effects & Trick Photography. (p. 1071)
Hopkins, Amy. Girlfriends Make the Best Friends. (p. 679)
Hopkins, Andrea. Damsels Not in Distress: The Lives of Medieval Women. (p. 401)
—Damsels Not in Distress: The True Story of Women in Medieval Times. (p. 401)
—Day in the Life of a Knight. (p. 413)
—Day in the Life of a Knight. Firenze, Inklink, illus. (p. 413)
—Viking Explorers & Settlers. (p. 1842)
—Viking Families & Farms. (p. 1842)
—Viking Gods & Legends. (p. 1842)
—Viking Longships. (p. 1842)
—Viking Raiders & Traders. (p. 1842)
—Vikings: The Norse Discovery of America. (p. 1842)
Hopkins, Andy & Potter, Joc. Animals in Danger, Level 1. Lindop, Christine, ed. (p. 83)
Hopkins, Audrey. Vinny Drake Is One. Flook, Helen, illus. (p. 1843)
Hopkins, Cathy. Besties: Mates, Dates, & Sleepover Secrets; Mates, Dates, & Sole Survivors; Mates, Dates, & Mad Mistakes. (p. 171)
—Friend Me: Mates, Dates, & Inflatable Bras; Mates, Dates, & Cosmic Kisses; Mates, Dates, & Designer Divas. (p. 637)
—Love Lottery. (p. 1060)
—Mates, Dates, & Chocolate Cheats. (p. 1104)
—Mates, Dates, & Diamond Destiny. (p. 1104)
—Mates, Dates, & Great Escapes. (p. 1104)
—Mates, Dates, & Inflatable Bras. (p. 1104)
—Mates, Dates, & Mad Mistakes. (p. 1104)
—Mates, Dates, & Sleepover Secrets. (p. 1104)
—Mates, Dates, & Tempting Trouble. (p. 1104)
—Mates, Dates Guide to Life, Love, & Looking Luscious. (p. 1104)
—Princess of Pop. (p. 1404)
—Teen Queens & Has-Beens. (p. 1713)
—White Lies & Barefaced Truths. (p. 1913)
Hopkins, Cathy, jt. auth. see Hopkins, Cathy.
Hopkins, Cathy & Hopkins, Cathy. White Lies & Barefaced Truths. (p. 1913)
Hopkins, Charles. Santa's Frost Covered Sleigh Lay Broken in the Snow. (p. 1513)
Hopkins, Cynthia. Vital Skills: How to Pray Using Scripture. (p. 1846)
Hopkins, Dave, jt. auth. see Boyle, Bill.
Hopkins, David. John Dryden. (p. 921)
Hopkins, Douglas. Princess June & the Shadow Pirates (p. 1404)
Hopkins, Ellen. Burned. (p. 243)
—Crank. (p. 376)
—Crank Trilogy: Crank; Glass; Fallout. (p. 376)
—Fallout. (p. 567)
—Fly Fishing. (p. 609)
—Freshwater Fishing: The Great Outdoors. (p. 637)
—Glass. (p. 682)
—Identical. (p. 852)
—Impulse. (p. 862)
—Perfect. (p. 1341)
—Smoke. (p. 1594)
—Tilt. (p. 1750)
—Tricks. (p. 1786)
Hopkins, Ellen, ed. Flirtin' with the Monster: Your Favorite Authors on Ellen Hopkins' Crank & Glass. (p. 605)
—New Dawn: Your Favorite Authors on Stephenie Meyer's Twilight Series. (p. 1244)
Hopkins, Ellen H. Storming the Skies: The Story of Katherine & Marjorie Stinson: Pioneer Women Aviators. (p. 1656)
Hopkins, Emily, illus. see Willeford, Tammy Jean.
Hopkins, Eva, jt. auth. see Linser, Joseph Michael.
Hopkins, H. Joseph. Tree Lady: The True Story of How One Tree-Loving Woman Changed a City Forever. McElmurry, Jill, illus. (p. 1783)
Hopkins, Howard. Nightmare Club #2: the Deadly Dragon. (p. 1255)
—Nightmare Club #3: the Willow Witch. (p. 1255)
Hopkins, Jackie Mims. Gallinita de la Pradera Cole, Henry, illus. (p. 653)
—Gold Miner's Daughter: A Melodramatic Fairy Tale Goodell, Jon, illus. (p. 693)
—Goldie Socks & the Three Libearians. Manders, John, illus. (p. 695)
—Joe Bright & the Seven Genre Dudes. Manders, John, illus. (p. 920)
—Our Texas. Spearing, Craig J., illus. (p. 1310)
—Picture Book & Library Lessons. Thornburgh, Rebecca, illus. (p. 1355)
—Prairie Chicken Little Cole, Henry, illus. (p. 1392)
—Shelf Elf. Thornburgh, Rebecca McKillip, illus. (p. 1564)
—Shelf Elf Helps Out. Thornburgh, Rebecca McKillip, illus. (p. 1564)
—Three Armadillies Tuff Brooks, S. G., illus. (p. 1741)
Hopkins, Jane. Diving for Colors in Hawaii: A Color Identification Book for Keiki. Bosgra, Johann, illus. (p. 454)
—Diving for Numbers in Hawaii. Bosgra, Johann, illus. (p. 455)
Hopkins, Jeanette. Juggler. (p. 932)
Hopkins, Jeff, illus. see Nallboff, Jane.
Hopkins, Jerry. In the Name of the Boss Upstairs: The Father Ray Brennan Story. (p. 866)
Hopkins, K. C. Night the Spirits Danced. (p. 1254)
Hopkins, Karen Ann. Belonging. (p. 163)
—Forever. (p. 619)
—Temptation. (p. 1718)
Hopkins, Lee Bennett. All the World's a Stage. Billout, Guy, illus. (p. 46)
—Alphathoughts. Baggetta, Marla, illus. (p. 50)
—Amazing Faces. Soentpiet, Chris K., illus. (p. 54)
—Been to Yesterdays: Poems of a Life. Rendeiro, Charlene, illus. (p. 157)
—Behind the Museum Door: Poems to Celebrate the Wonders of Museums. Dressen-McQueen, Stacey, illus. (p. 160)
—Christmas Presents: Holiday Poetry. Hall, Melanie W., illus. (p. 315)
—City I Love. Hall, Marcellus, illus. (p. 323)
—Days to Celebrate: A Full Year of Poetry, People, Holidays, History, Fascinating Facts, & More. Alcorn, Stephen, illus. (p. 415)
—Dizzy Dinosaurs: Silly Dino Poems. Gott, Barry, illus. (p. 455)
—Full Moon & Star. Hall, Marcellus, illus. (p. 646)
—Give Me Wings. Goembel, Ponder, illus. (p. 681)
—Got Geography! Stanton, Philip, illus. (p. 703)
—Halloween Howls: Holiday Poetry. Schuett, Stacey, illus. (p. 737)
—Hamsters, Shells, & Spelling Bees: School Poems. Yoshikawa, Sachiko, illus. (p. 740)
—Hanukkah Lights: Holiday Poetry. Hall, Melanie, illus. (p. 744)
—I Am the Book. Yayo, illus. (p. 834)
—Incredible Inventions. Sarcone-Roach, Julia, illus. (p. 869)
—Lee Bennett Hopkins Mother Goose. (p. 987)
—Manger. Cann, Helen, illus. (p. 1087)
—Mary's Song. Alcorn, Stephen, illus. (p. 1101)
—Mother Goose & Her Animal Friends. Fehlau, Dagmar et al, illus. (p. 1177)
—Mother Goose & Her Children. Fehlau, Dagmar et al, illus. (p. 1177)
—Mother Goose Around the World. Fehlau, Dagmar et al, illus. (p. 1178)
—Mother Goose Through the Seasons. Fehlau, Dagmar et al, illus. (p. 1178)
—Nasty Bugs. Terry, Will, illus. (p. 1230)
—Pet for Me. Manning, Jane, illus. (p. 1345)
—Valentine Hearts: Holiday Poetry. Adinolfi, JoAnn, illus. (p. 1830)
—Worlds of Poetry (p. 1960)
Hopkins, Lee Bennett & Alcorn, Stephen. Little Bill: Extra Thankful Thanksgiving. (p. 1024)
Hopkins, Lee Bennett & Boyds Mills Press Staff. Alphathoughts: Alphabet Poems. Baggetta, Marla, illus. (p. 50)
Hopkins, Lee Bennett & Moore, Gigi. Hear My Prayer (p. 759)
Hopkins, Lee Bennett, ed. America at War. Alcorn, Stephen, illus. (p. 59)
Hopkins, Leslie. World Apart. (p. 1954)
Hopkins, Louisa Parsons, jt. auth. see Andrews, Jane.
Hopkins, Mary Rice. Animal Alphabet: On the Land, in the Sky or Sea, Meet God's Creatures from a to Z. Francisco, Wendy, illus. (p. 76)
Hopkins, Mildred Elaine. Friends to the Rescue. (p. 639)
Hopkins, Nicolla. What was Grandma Doing? Wiggins, Margaret W., illus. (p. 1894)
Hopkins, Simon, illus. see Farrelly, Linda.
Hopkins, Simon, illus. see Helliwell, Sheila.
Hopkins, Susan R. Madison's Retreat. (p. 1070)
Hopkins, Suzette. Little Wolf's Christmas. Taylor, Jill, illus. (p. 1038)
Hopkins, Therese. Animal Dens. (p. 77)
—Bird Nests. (p. 190)
—Burrows. (p. 244)
—Insect Homes. (p. 875)
—Shells. (p. 1565)
—Underwater Homes. (p. 1817)
Hopkins, Virginia, jt. auth. see Lee, John R.
Hopkins, William G. Photosynthesis & Respiration. (p. 1353)
—Plant Biotechnology. (p. 1368)
Hopkins, William G., ed. see Stephens, Nicholas.
Hopkins, William G., ed. see Tornqvist, Carl-Erik.
Hopkins, William G., ed. see Wiedenhoeft, Alex C.
Hopkins, William G., ed. Plant Development. (p. 1369)
Hopkins, William J. Sandman: His Farm Stories (Yesterday's Classics) (p. 1511)
—Sandman: His House Stories (Yesterday's Classics) (p. 1511)
—Sandman: His Sea Stories (Yesterday's Classics) Home, Diantha W., illus. (p. 1511)
—Sandman: His Ship Stories (Yesterday's Classics) Home, Diantha W., illus. (p. 1511)
—Sandman: More Farm Stories (Yesterday's Classics) Williamson, Ada Clendenin, illus. (p. 1511)
Hopkinson, Courtney, jt. auth. see Reilly, Carmel.
Hopkinson, Deborah. Abe Lincoln Crosses a Creek: A Tall, Thin Tale (Introducing His Forgotten Frontier Friend) Hendrix, John, illus. (p. 4)
—Annie & Helen. Colón, Raúl, illus. (p. 86)
—Apples to Oregon: Being the (Slightly) True Narrative of How a Brave Pioneer Father Brought Apples, Peaches, Pears, Plums, Grapes, & Cherries (and Children) Across the Plains. Carpenter, Nancy, illus. (p. 93)
—Apples to Oregon. (p. 93)
—Billy & the Rebel: Based on a True Civil War Story. Floca, Brian, illus. (p. 187)
—Billy & the Rebel: Based on a True Civil War Story. Anderson, Bethanne & Floca, Brian, illus. (p. 187)
—Boy Called Dickens. Hendrix, John, illus. (p. 217)
—Cabin in the Snow. Farcy, Patrick, illus. (p. 250)
—Fannie in the Kitchen: The Whole Story from Soup to Nuts of How Fannie Farmer Invented Recipes with Precise Measurements. Carpenter, Nancy, illus. (p. 571)
—First Family. Ford, A. G., illus. (p. 594)
—From Slave to Soldier: Based on a True Civil War Story. Floca, Brian, illus. (p. 643)
—Girl Wonder: A Baseball Story in Nine Innings. Widener, Terry, illus. (p. 679)
—Girl Wonder. Widener, Terry, illus. (p. 679)
—Great Trouble: A Mystery of London, the Blue Death, & a Boy Called Eel. (p. 719)
—Independence Cake: A Revolutionary Confection Inspired by Amelia Simmons, Whose True History Is Unfortunately Unknown, Embellished with Scrumptious Illustrations. (p. 870)

H

—Into the Firestorm: A Novel of San Francisco 1906. (p. 881)
—John Adams Speaks for Freedom. Orback, Craig, illus. (p. 921)
—Keep On! The Story of Matthew Henson, Co-Discoverer of the North Pole Alcorn, Stephen, illus. (p. 947)
—Knit Your Bit: A World War I Story. Guarnaccia, Steven, illus. (p. 964)
—Long Trail. Farnsworth, Bill, illus. (p. 1047)
—Maria's Comet. Lanino, Deborah, illus. (p. 1093)
—Michelle. Ford, A. G., illus. (p. 1135)
—Our Kansas Home. Faricy, Patrick, illus. (p. 1309)
—Pioneer Summer. Faricy, Patrick, illus. (p. 1361)
—Sailing for Gold. Farnsworth, Bill, illus. (p. 1503)
—Shutting Out the Sky: Life in the Tenements of New York, 1880-1924. (p. 1572)
—Sky Boys: How They Built the Empire State Building. Ransome, James E., illus. (p. 1586)
—Steamboat School. Husband, Ron, illus. (p. 1646)
—Susan B. Anthony: Fighter for Women's Rights. Bates, Amy, illus. (p. 1688)
—Susan B. Anthony: Fighter for Women's Rights. Bates, Amy June, illus. (p. 1688)
—Sweet Land of Liberty Jenkins, Leonard, illus. (p. 1690)
—Titanic: Voices from the Disaster. (p. 1757)
—Under the Quilt of Night. Ransome, James E., illus. (p. 1814)
—Up Before Daybreak: Cotton & People in America. (p. 1824)
—Who Was Charles Darwin? Harrison, Nancy, illus. (p. 1918)
Hopkinson, Deborah & Carpenter, Nancy. Apples to Oregon: Being the (Slightly) True Narrative of How a Brave Pioneer Father Brought Apples, Peaches, Pears, Plums, Grapes, & Cherries (and Children) Across the Plains. (p. 93)
Hopkinson, Nalo. Chaos. (p. 291)
Hopkinson, Nalo, ed. see Dunnion, Kristyn.
Hopkinson, Simon. Roast Chicken & Other Stories. Bayley, Flo, illus. (p. 1478)
Hopman, Philip. Valentine & His Violin. (p. 1830)
Hopman, Philip, illus. see Dickins, Rosie.
Hopman, Philip, illus. see Durant, Alan.
Hopman, Philip, illus. see Tak, Bibi Dumon & Dumon Tak, Bibi.
Hopman, Philip, illus. see Tak, Bibi Dumon.
Hopman, Philip, illus. see van Lieshout, Ted.
Hopman, Philip, illus. see Veldkamp, Tjibbe.
Hoppa, Jocelyn. Isaac Asimov: Science Fiction Trailblazer. (p. 890)
Hoppe, Bethany A. Molly B. Golly's Wonderful Dancing Debut. Ayotte, Andie C., illus. (p. 1160)
Hoppe, Gail, ed. see schneider, Sandra.
Hoppe, Jessica, jt. auth. see Fonte, Mary Roessler.
Hoppe, Ludwig Augustin. Die Epiklesis Der Griechischen Und Orientalischen Liturgieen Und Der Römische Consekrationskanon (German Edition) (p. 437)
Hoppe, Paul. Hat. Hoppe, Paul, illus. (p. 752)
—Woods. (p. 1949)
Hoppe, Paul, illus. see Barton, Chris.
Hoppe, Paul, illus. see Halliday, Ayun.
Hoppe, Paul, illus. see Pakkala, Christine.
Hoppe, Paul, illus. see Reynolds, Aaron.
Hoppen, Kelly. Kelly Hoppen Home: From Concept to Reality. Knapp, Vincent, photos by. (p. 948)
Hoppenbrouwers, Toke & Hodgman, Joan. Sids. (p. 1573)
Hoppenstedt, Elbert M. President Harrison's Horse Race. (p. 1397)
Hopper, Andy Lee, illus. see Hopper, Bobby E.
Hopper, Billy, illus. see Bertch, David P. & Bertch, Barbara A.
Hopper, Bobby E. Bleep the Purple Bear. Hopper, Andy Lee, illus. (p. 199)
Hopper, Celia. Blade & the Story of the Little Spotted Dog. (p. 198)
—Merry Adventures of Blade & Friends. (p. 1128)
—Violets. (p. 1843)
Hopper, Celia Brashear. Blade & the Story of the Pearl Princess. (p. 198)
Hopper, Christopher, jt. auth. see Batson, Wayne Thomas.
Hopper, Jessica. Girls' Guide to Rocking: How to Start a Band, Book Gigs, & Get Rolling to Rock Stardom. (p. 680)
Hopper, Karyn. There's a Monster in My Opu. (p. 1731)
Hopper, Linda. Counselling & Psychotherapy with Children & Adolescents. (p. 369)
Hopper, Missy. Peggy Sue & the Pepper Patch. Bowden, Cecelia, illus. (p. 1335)
Hopper, Paul. Living with Globalization. (p. 1042)
Hopper, Pegge, illus. see Finney, Jefferson.
Hopper, Shay E., et al. Arkansas History for Young People. (p. 99)
Hopper, Whitney. Life Cycle of a Frog. (p. 1009)
—Time to Go to the Science Museum! Work with Time. (p. 1753)
Hoppey, Tim. Good Fire Helmet. McElrath-Eslick, Lori, illus. (p. 698)
—Jungle Scout: A Vietnam War Story Espinoza, Ramon, illus. (p. 935)
—Pedro, the Pirate. Bonder, Dianna, illus. (p. 1334)
—Tito, the Firefighter/Tito, el Bombero. de la Vega, Eida, tr. (p. 1758)
Hoppey, Tim, illus. see Rivera, Rafael, et al.
Hopping, Lorraine Jean. Bone Detective: The Story of Forensic Anthropologist Diane France. (p. 208)
—Chief Joseph: The Voice for Peace. (p. 301)
—Crossing the Atlantic: One Family's Story. (p. 385)
—Space Rocks: The Story of Planetary Geologist Adriana Ocampo. (p. 1619)
Hopping, Lorran Egan. Solar System. (p. 1607)
Hoppner, Gabi. Backyard Fun. (p. 131)
—Beach Fun. (p. 149)
—Fun on Wheels. (p. 648)
—Fun with Animals. (p. 648)
Hopson, Hal H. Shepherd's Story. (p. 1565)
—World Sings Noel: The Christmas Story in Global Song. (p. 1958)
Hopton, Stan. To Dance Beneath a Diamond Sky. (p. 1758)
Hopwood, James. Cool Distance Assistants: Fun Science Projects to Propel Things. (p. 363)
—Cool Gravity Activities: Fun Science Projects about Balance. (p. 363)
Hopwood, Mererid, et al. Byd Llawn Hud. Glynn, Chris, illus. (p. 249)
Horacek, Judy. Story of Growl. Horacek, Judy, illus. (p. 1658)
—Yellow Is My Color Star. Horacek, Judy, illus. (p. 1970)
Horacek, Judy, illus. see Fox, Mem.
Horacek, Judy, jt. auth. see Fox, Mem.
Horacek, Judy & Fox, Mem. Where Is the Green Sheep? (p. 1909)
Horácek, Petr. Animal Opposites. Horácek, Petr, illus. (p. 79)
—Beep Beep. Horácek, Petr, illus. (p. 157)
—Butterfly Butterfly: A Book of Colors. Horácek, Petr, illus. (p. 247)
—Choo Choo. Horácek, Petr, illus. (p. 310)
—Fly. Horácek, Petr, illus. (p. 609)
—Honk, Honk! Baa, Baa! Horácek, Petr, illus. (p. 795)
—Jonathan & Martha. (p. 925)
—Las Fresas Son Rojas. Horácek, Petr, illus. (p. 976)
—Look Out, Suzy Goose. Horácek, Petr, illus. (p. 1050)
—Mouse Who Ate the Moon. Horácek, Petr, illus. (p. 1182)
—My Elephant. Horácek, Petr, illus. (p. 1202)
—Puffin Peter. Horácek, Petr, illus. (p. 1415)
—Silly Suzy Goose. Horácek, Petr, illus. (p. 1576)
—Surprise for Tiny Mouse. Horácek, Petr, illus. (p. 1686)
—Suzy Goose & the Christmas Star: Midi Edition. Horácek, Petr, illus. (p. 1688)
—Suzy Goose & the Christmas Star. Horácek, Petr, illus. (p. 1688)
—Time for Bed. Horácek, Petr, illus. (p. 1751)
Horácek, Petr, illus. see Kim, Cecil.
Horak, Mila, illus. see Rauzi, Kelly Emerling.
Horan, David M., jt. ed. see Horan, Rodney S.
Horan, Mark, et al. Disabilities & Disorders in Literature for Youth: A Selective Annotated Bibliography for K-12. (p. 446)
Horan, Pamela. Newman the Gnome. (p. 1249)
Horan, Rodney S. & Horan, David M., eds. Spelling English: A Concise Guide to Spelling, Punctuation & Style. (p. 1625)
Horas, Elena, tr. see Newton, Robyn & Barber, Nicola, eds.
Horatio Alger Jr. Cash Boy. (p. 276)
—Cast upon the Breakers. (p. 276)
Horcasitas, Barbara. My Pet Alphabet. (p. 1217)
Hord, Colleen. Clean & Green Energy. (p. 330)
—Everyone Visits Family. (p. 544)
—From Farm to Restaurant. (p. 642)
—From Power Plant to House. (p. 643)
—Itsy Bitsy Spider. Poole, Helen, illus. (p. 900)
—Joe Acaba. (p. 920)
—Keep Your Chin Up. Dufalla, Anita, illus. (p. 947)
—Little Miss Midge. Poole, Helen, illus. (p. 1031)
—Michael J. Fox: Little World Biographies. (p. 1134)
—Muhammad Ali. (p. 1189)
—My Green Lunch. (p. 1210)
—My Safe Community. (p. 1218)
—Need It or Want It? (p. 1239)
—What's My Role? (p. 1898)
—Who's Mr. Goldfluss? Poole, Helen, illus. (p. 1920)
—Writing a Research Paper. (p. 1964)
Hord, Janice. Walking Stick Adventure. (p. 1854)
Hordern, Bob, et al. Managing Issues in Geography. (p. 1086)
Hordos, Sandra. Marissa Plans a Princess Tea Party. Allen, Joshua, illus. (p. 1094)
Hore, Rosie. Sticker Dolly Dressing Wartime Fashion IR. (p. 1650)
Horen, Michael. My Blessings for Food. (p. 1198)
Horen, Michael, illus. see Gold, Avie.
Horender, Philip M. Brave New Mouse: Ellis Island Approved Immigrant. Wolek, Guy, illus. (p. 223)
—Head West, Young Mouse: Transcontinental Railroad Traveler. Wolek, Guy, illus. (p. 756)
—Homeward Bound: Civil Rights Mouse Leader. Wolek, Guy, illus. (p. 794)
—Mighty Maximilian: Samuel Clemens's Traveling Companion. Wolek, Guy, illus. (p. 1140)
—Patriotic Mouse: Boston Tea Party Participant. Wolek, Guy, illus. (p. 1329)
—Yankee Mouse: Gettysburg Address Observer. Wolek, Guy, illus. (p. 1968)
Horenstein, Henry. Black & White Photography: A Basic Manual. (p. 195)
Hori, Hatsuki, illus. see Whipple, Laura.
Horlacher, Bill, jt. auth. see Horlacher, Kathy.
Horlacher, Bill & Horlacher, Kathy. I'm Glad I'm Your Mother. Johnson, Meredith, illus. (p. 859)
Horlacher, Kathy, jt. auth. see Horlacher, Bill.
Horlacher, Kathy & Horlacher, Bill. I'm Glad I'm Your Grandma. Johnson, Meredith, illus. (p. 859)
Horman, John. Angel Band: A Christmas Musical Based on Luke 2:1-20. (p. 73)
—Angel Band: A Christmas Musical Based on Luke 2:1-20. Value Pak (p. 73)
—Angel Band: A Christmas Musical Based on Luke 2:1-20. Singer's Edition (p. 73)
—Angel Band. (p. 73)
—Angel Band: a Christmas Musical Based on Luke 2:1-20: Bulletins. (p. 73)
Horman, John D. Something Old, Something New: Hymns to Explore Things to Do. (p. 1610)
Horman, John D., et al. Something Old, Something New: Hymns to Explore, Things to Do. Vol. 2 Keithahn, Mary Nelson, ed. (p. 1610)
Horman, Marnie. Carrie's Silver Christmas Tree. (p. 271)
Hormeo, Marielo Gil, illus. see Perez Saez, Lucrecia, et al.
Horn, Andrea Jean. In Search of the Sunbeam: A Wylie & Grayson Adventure. (p. 865)
Horn, Bernd. Battle Cries in the Wilderness: The Struggle for North America in the Seven Years' War. (p. 145)
—Men of Steel: Canadian Paratroopers in Normandy 1944. (p. 1126)
Horn, Carl Gustav, ed. see Clamp Staff.
Horn, Carl Gustav, ed. see Fujishima, Kosuke.
Horn, Carl Gustav, ed. see Yoshimura, Takumi.
Horn, Carl Gustav, tr. see Yamada, Masaki.
Horn, Carl Gustav, ed. Tokyo Babylon (p. 1762)
Horn, Dennis, et al. Wildflowers of Tennessee & the East Central States (p. 1931)
Horn, Elizabeth L. Coastal Wildflowers of the Pacific Northwest: Wildflowers & Flowering Shrubs from British Columbia to Northern California. Ort, Kathleen, ed. (p. 336)
—Sierra Nevada Wildflowers. Ort, Kathleen, ed. (p. 1573)
Horn, Emily. Excuse Me... Are You a Witch? Pawlak, Pawel, illus. (p. 548)
Horn, Geoffrey M. Adam Sandler. (p. 11)
—Albert Pujols. (p. 34)
—Alicia Keys. (p. 40)
—Barack Obama. (p. 137)
—Beyonce. (p. 173)
—Cabinet & Federal Agencies. (p. 250)
—Camera Operator. (p. 256)
—Cameron Diaz. (p. 256)
—Construction Worker. (p. 360)
—Crime Scene Investigator. (p. 382)
—Dale Earnhardt, Jr. (p. 401)
—Environmental Engineer. (p. 532)
—FBI Agent. (p. 578)
—Jamie Foxx. (p. 907)
—John McCain. (p. 922)
—John Mccain. (p. 922)
—Laila Ali. (p. 972)
—Margaret Mead. (p. 1092)
—Meteorologist. (p. 1130)
—Michelle Wie. (p. 1135)
—Movie Acting. (p. 1183)
—Movie Animation. (p. 1183)
—Movie Makeup, Costumes, & Sets. (p. 1183)
—Movie Soundtracks & Sound Effects. (p. 1183)
—Movie Stunts & Special Effects. (p. 1183)
—Nancy Pelosi. (p. 1229)
—Oil Rig Roughneck. (p. 1282)
—Peyton Manning. (p. 1349)
—Pit Crew Worker. (p. 1364)
—Political Parties, Interest Groups & the Media. (p. 1380)
—Presidency. (p. 1396)
—Sewer Inspector. (p. 1555)
—Sports Therapist. (p. 1633)
—Supreme Court. (p. 1684)
—Test Pilot. (p. 1723)
—Thurgood Marshall. (p. 1746)
—Usher. (p. 1828)
—Washington, D. C. (p. 1860)
—Writing, Producing, & Directing Movies. (p. 1965)
Horn, Geoffrey M., jt. auth. see Sanders, Doug.
Horn, Geoffrey M. & Bjorklund, Ruth. South Dakota. (p. 1617)
Horn, Geoffrey M., et al. Biofuels. (p. 188)
—Coal, Oil, & Natural Gas. (p. 336)
Horn, Geoffrey Michael. John Brown: Putting Actions above Words. (p. 921)
Horn, Greg. Art of Greg Horn (p. 102)
Horn, Mildred D. Teeny the Squirrel Meets the Outside World. (p. 1715)
Horn, Neithard. Evi, My Little Monkey: A Good Night Book for You & for Grown-ups, Too (p. 546)
Horn, Pam, ed. Read-Aloud Classics: 24 Ten-Minute Selections from the World's Best-Loved Children's Books. (p. 1442)
Horn, Peter. Best Father of All. James, J. Alison, tr. from GER. (p. 169)
—When I Grow Up... Kadmon, Cristina, illus. (p. 1902)
Horn, Randy. You Gotta Be Kidding! The Crazy Book of Would You Rather... ? Questions. (p. 1975)
Horn, Robert, jt. auth. see Elish, Dan.
Horn, Sandra. I Can't Hear You! I Can't See You! (p. 837)
—Silkie. (p. 1575)
Horn, Sandra & Ulasowski, Muza. Suvi & the Sky Folk. (p. 1688)
Horn, Sandra Ann, jt. auth. see Roberts, Sheena.
Horn, Shannon. Pirates of the Mississippian: The Adventures of Jerry & Draco. (p. 1364)
Horn, William Van, see Cole, Joanna & Van Horn, William.
Horn, William Van, see Rawson, Dave & Van Horn, William.
Horn, William Van, see Van Horn, William.
Hornback, Christine. Jenny Lynn's Secret Mission. (p. 913)
Hornback, Christine Gilliam. Caleb's Cereal. (p. 252)
Hornbeck, Ken, illus. see Graham, J.
Hornbeck, P. J. Chance & Charlie Go Flying. (p. 289)
Hornby, Hugh. Soccer. (p. 1603)
Hornby, Hugh & Dorling Kindersley Publishing Staff. Soccer. (p. 1603)
Hornby, Nick. Slam. (p. 1587)
Hornby, Simonetta Agnello. Almond Picker. McEwen, Alastair, tr. (p. 48)
Hornby, Steven. Secrets of a Christmas Box. Gerard, Justin, illus. (p. 1545)
Horne, Arthur M., et al, eds. Best Practices in Prevention. (p. 171)
Horne, Constance. Emily Carr's Woo. Calvert, Lissa, illus. (p. 518)
—Tenth Pupil. (p. 1720)
Horne, Diantha W., illus. see Hopkins, William J.
Horne, Diantha W., illus. see Johnston, Annie Fellows.
Horne, Doug, illus. see Hagan, Scott.
Horne, Douglas V., ed. Christian Leaders Home Discipleship Hymnbook. (p. 312)
Horne, Fiona. Witchin' A Handbook for Teen Witches. (p. 1941)
Horne, Glenda Burton & Burton, Beth Windsor. My Daydreams (p. 1201)
Horne, Grace, illus. see Rossitter, Derek.
Horne, J., illus. see Bugbird, T.
Horne, Jane. 101 First Things That Go. (p. 1999)
—Baby First Concepts: Colors. (p. 126)
—Busy Baby Noisy Book. (p. 245)
—Busy Baby Sparklies 4 Volume Boxed Set: Baby's First Box of Books. (p. 245)
—Flip & Find 123. (p. 604)
—Flip & Find Abc. (p. 604)
—Rough & Tough: Tractors & Trucks/Cars/Diggers & Dumpers/Emergency. (p. 1491)
—Rough & Tough Emergency. (p. 1491)
—Sparklies Colors. (p. 1622)
Horne, Jane & Page, Claire. I Really Like Puppies. (p. 844)
—Magnetics Fashion Show. (p. 1075)
Horne, Jay. Published Youth Volume Two. (p. 1414)
Horne, Nathan, illus. see Booth, Sara.
Horne, Philip, ed. see James, Henry.
Horne, Philip, illus. see Mackerel, Seymour & RH Disney Staff.
Horne, Richard, illus. see Turner, Tracey.
Horne, Richard & Szirtes, Helen. 101 Things to Do Before You're Old & Boring. Horne, Richard, illus. (p. 2000)
—101 Ways to Become a Superhero... or an Evil Genius. (p. 2000)
Horne, Ronald Wil. Forgotten Faces: A Window into Our Immigrant Past (5x8-BW) (p. 619)
Horne, Ronald William. Forgotten Faces: A Window into Our Immigrant Past (5x8-Clr-BW) (p. 619)
Horne, Sarah, illus. see Andersen, Hans Christian & Sandoval, Gerardo.
Horne, Sarah, illus. see Beauvais, Clémentine.
Horne, Sarah, illus. see Coburn, Ann.
Horne, Sarah, illus. see Davies, Kate, ed.
Horne, Sarah, illus. see Gassman, Julie A.
Horne, Sarah, illus. see Gifford, Clive.
Horne, Sarah, illus. see Gray, Jennifer & Swift, Amanda.
Horne, Sarah, illus. see Hart, Caryl.
Horne, Sarah, illus. see Lane, Kathleen, et al.
Horne, Sarah, illus. see Lane, Kathleen.
Horne, Sarah, illus. see MacKinnon, Mairi.
Horne, Sarah, illus. see Robinson, Mark.
Horne, Sarah, illus. see Saddlewick, A. B.
Horne, Sarah, illus. see Scholastic, Inc. Staff & Stevens, Chris.
Horne, Sarah, illus. see Stanley, Malaika Rose.
Horne, Sarah, illus. see Wines, Jacquie.
Horne, William Reginald. Germany. (p. 666)
Horne-Ingram, Gloria. Yonna Bonna & the Big Book. (p. 1972)
—Yonna Bonna the Purple Ballerin. (p. 1972)
Horner, D. M. & O'Neill, Robert John. World War II: The Pacific. (p. 1959)
Horner, Doogie, illus. see Stabler, David.
Horner, Emily. Love Story: Starring My Dead Best Friend. (p. 1060)
Horner, Jack. Digging up Dinosaurs. Rath, Robert & Wilson, Phil, illus. (p. 439)
Horner, John Arthur. Prayer of Matthias: And other plays for Worship. (p. 1393)
Horner, Randall. Navigating the Awkward Years: Useful Ideas & Concepts for Dealing with Life in High School & for Life after Graduation. (p. 1238)
Horner, Susan. Mission: An Angel's Most Important Assignment. Allen, Joe, illus. (p. 1153)
—What Is God's Design for My Body? (p. 1889)
Hornidge, Marilis. That Yankee Cat: The Maine Coon Cat. (p. 1726)
Horniman, Joanne. About a Girl. (p. 5)
—Little Wing. (p. 1037)
—My Candlelight Novel. (p. 1200)
—Secret Scribbled Notebooks. (p. 1543)
Horning, Jonathan. Simple Shelters: Tents, Tipis, Yurts, Domes & Other Ancient Homes. (p. 1578)
Horning, Katherine. World of Shadows. (p. 1957)
Horning, Lauren. Poppy. (p. 1385)
Horning, Mandy Cha'rae. Defenders: Rise of the Perfected. (p. 423)
Horning, Sandra. Biggest Pumpkin Stone-Barker, Holly, illus. (p. 185)
—Chicks! Goodell, Jon, illus. (p. 301)
—Giant Hug. Gorbachev, Valeri, illus. (p. 673)
Hornsby, Ashley. Pretty Little Lilly & the Magical Light. Couch, Greg, illus. (p. 1398)
Hornsby, Ashley Brooke. Pretty Little Lilly & the Land of Sweet Dreams (Paperback) Hranilovich, Barbara, illus. (p. 1398)
—Pretty Little Lilly & the Land of Sweet Dreams (Hard Bound) Hranilovich, Barbara, illus. (p. 1398)
—Pretty Little Lilly & the Magical Night (paperback) (p. 1398)
Hornsey, Chris & Perkins, Gwyn. Why Do I Have to Eat off the Floor? (p. 1923)
Hornstein, Lucy. Medical Haiku: A Bunch of Silly Poems. (p. 1118)
Hornung, E. W. Return Match. (p. 1464)
Hornung, Phyllis, illus. see Ellis, Julie.
Hornung, Phyllis, illus. see LoPresti, Angeline Sparagna.
Hornung, Phyllis, illus. see Taylor, Bonnie Highsmith.
Hornung, Phyllis, tr. see Taylor, Bonnie Highsmith.
Hornyak, Eva. Fishing Rainbows. (p. 599)
Horowitz, Alena Netia. Tlytiettlym Tree. Horowitz, Alena Netia & De La Fuente, Mary, illus. (p. 1758)
Horowitz, Alexandra. Inside of a Dog: What Dogs See, Smell, & Know (Young Reader's Edition) (p. 877)
Horowitz, Anthony. Ark Angel. (p. 99)
—Bloody Horowitz. (p. 201)
—Cayo Esqueleto. (p. 283)
—Complete Horowitz Horror. (p. 353)
—Crocodile Tears (p. 384)
—Crocodile Tears. (p. 384)
—Devil & His Boy. (p. 432)
—Eagle Strike. (p. 492)
—Evil Star. (p. 546)
—Falcon's Malteser. (p. 566)
—Golpe del Aguila. (p. 697)
—Greek Who Stole Christmas. (p. 721)
—Groosham Grange. (p. 725)
—Horowitz Horror. (p. 798)
—Necropolis (p. 1239)
—Necropolis. (p. 1239)
—Nightrise. (p. 1255)
—Oblivion. (p. 1275)

—Point Blanc. (p. 1377)
—Point Blank. (p. 1377)
—Public Enemy Number Two. (p. 1414)
—Raven's Gate. (p. 1441)
—Return to Groosham Grange: The Unholy Grail. (p. 1465)
—Russian Roulette: The Story of an Assassin. (p. 1498)
—Russian Roulette. (p. 1498)
—Scorpia. (p. 1530)
—Scorpia Rising. (p. 1530)
—Skeleton Key. (p. 1584)
—Skeleton Key. Kanako & Yuzuru, illus. (p. 1584)
—Snakehead. (p. 1596)
—South by Southeast. (p. 1616)
—Stormbreaker. (p. 1656)
—Stormbreaker. Damerum, Kanako et al, illus. (p. 1656)
—Switch. (p. 1691)
—Three of Diamonds. (p. 1743)
Horowitz, Anthony & Johnston, Antony. Point Blank. Yuzuru & Kanako, illus. (p. 1377)
Horowitz, Dave. Duck Duck Moose. Horowitz, Dave, illus. (p. 488)
—Five Little Gefiltes. Horowitz, Dave, illus. (p. 600)
—Humpty Dumpty Climbs Again. Horowitz, Dave, illus. (p. 827)
—Little Big Horse. (p. 1024)
—Monkey among Us. Horowitz, Dave, illus. (p. 1164)
—Scholastic Reader Level 1: Little Big Horse. (p. 1522)
—Twenty-Six Pirates: An Alphabet Book. Horowitz, Dave, illus. (p. 1801)
—Twenty-Six Princesses: An Alphabet Story. Horowitz, Dave, illus. (p. 1801)
—Twenty-Six Princesses. Horowitz, Dave, illus. (p. 1801)
—Ugly Pumpkin. Horowitz, Dave, illus. (p. 1808)
Horowitz, Eli, ed. see McSweeney's Books Staff.
Horowitz, Jeanine. Latch Key Kid. (p. 979)
—My First Playing Lesson. (p. 1207)
—Toady Toad's Move. (p. 1760)
Horowitz, Joseph. Dvoerak in America. (p. 491)
—Dvorak in America: In Search of the New World. (p. 491)
Horowitz, Lena. Dancing with Molly. (p. 403)
Horowitz, Marilyn. How to Write a Screenplay in 10 Weeks: A Fast & Easy Toolbox for All Writers. (p. 822)
Horowitz, Nancy Ellis. Nicely Dunn & the Lost Little Sister. (p. 1250)
Horowitz, Ruth. Crab Moon. Kiesler, Kate, illus. (p. 375)
Horrell, Charles, illus. see Vaizey, George de Horne.
Horrigan, David J. Spark in the Sea: Adventures in Marine Science (p. 1622)
Horrobin, Peter. Complete Junior Praise Words. (p. 353)
Horrobin, Peter J. Most Powerful Prayer on Earth. (p. 1177)
Horrocks, Anita. Almost Eden. (p. 48)
—Silas' Seven Grandparents Flook, Helen, illus. (p. 1575)
—What They Don't Know (p. 1894)
—What They Don't Know. (p. 1894)
Horrocks, Savannah, illus. see Temple, Bob.
Horrocks, Steve, illus. see Matthews, Andrew.
Horse, Harry. Last Castaways. Horse, Harry, illus. (p. 977)
—Last Cowboys. Horse, Harry, illus. (p. 977)
—Last Gold Diggers: Being as It Were, an Account of a Small Dog's Adventures, down Under. Horse, Harry, illus. (p. 977)
—Last Polar Bears. Horse, Harry, illus. (p. 978)
—Little Rabbit Goes to School. Horse, Harry, illus. (p. 1034)
—Little Rabbit Lost. Horse, Harry, illus. (p. 1034)
—Little Rabbit Runaway. Horse, Harry, illus. (p. 1034)
—Little Rabbit's Christmas. Horse, Harry, illus. (p. 1034)
—Little Rabbit's New Baby. Horse, Harry, illus. (p. 1034)
—Little Rabbit's New Baby / Book & Doll Package. (p. 1034)
Horsfall, Jacqueline. For the Love of Strangers. Kelly, Mary B., illus. (p. 616)
—Kids' Silliest Jokes. Jones, Buck, illus. (p. 955)
—Silly Riddles to Make You Giggle. Snider, Jackie, illus. (p. 1576)
—Super Goofy Jokes. Collinet, Rob, illus. (p. 1680)
Horsfall, Jacqueline, ed. see delMazo, Deborah.
Horsfall, Jacqueline, jt. auth. see Tait, Chris.
Horsfall, Jacqueline & Pierce, Terry. Laughin' Jammin' Slammin' Jokefest. (p. 980)
Horsfall, Kyla May & May, Kyla. As an International Super Spy. Horsfall, Kyla May & Horsfall, Kyla May, illus. (p. 105)
Horsfall, S. J. Jodie & Lilly... & the Fake Mansion. (p. 919)
—Jodie & Lilly & the Joy of Christmas. (p. 919)
Horsfield, Alan & Horsfield, Elaine. Talking about Food & the Environment. (p. 1703)
—Talking about the Dangers of Alcohol, Tobacco, & Caffeine. (p. 1703)
Horsfield, Elaine, jt. auth. see Horsfield, Alan.
Horsley, Andrew. How to Improve at Skateboarding. (p. 820)
Horsley, Andy. Skateboarding. (p. 1583)
Horsley, Martha, jt. auth. see Hanrott, Robert.
Horsman, Paul. Out of the Blue: A Journey Through the World's Oceans. Seapics.com Staff, photos by. (p. 1311)
Horst, Heather A. & Garner, Andrew. Jamaican Americans. (p. 906)
Horst, Melisa, illus. see Bowman, Silas.
Horsted, Paul. Custer State Park: From the Mountains to the Plains. Horsted, Paul, photos by. (p. 395)
Horstman, Lisa. Smoky Mountain Wee Ones. Kemp, Steve, ed. (p. 1595)
—Squawking Matilda (p. 1636)
Horstman, Lisa, illus. see Ketel, Debbie M.
Horstmann. Big Java & Ap Study Guide Set. (p. 182)
—Computing Concepts with Java Essentials. (p. 355)
Horstmann, Deborah McFillin. Sylvester the One-Legged Seagull. Buehrle, Jacquelyn, illus. (p. 1692)
Horstschäfer, Felicitas. Flowers: Make Your Own Mobile Inspired by Emil Nolde. (p. 608)
Hort, John, ed. see Shakespeare, William.
Hort, John & Hort, Leela. Hamlet: The Inessential Shakespeare. (p. 739)
Hort, Leela, ed. see Shakespeare, William.
Hort, Leela, jt. auth. see Hort, John.
Hort, Lenny. George Washington: A Photographic Story of a Life. (p. 664)
—Seals on the Bus. Karas, G. Brian, illus. (p. 1536)
—Seals on the Bus. Karas, G. Brian & Karas, G., illus. (p. 1536)
Hort, Lenny, et al. Nelson Mandela. (p. 1240)
Hortens, Mike, illus. see Cameron, Ken.
Horton, Anthony, jt. see Landowne, Youme.
Horton, Babs. Dandelion Soup. (p. 403)
Horton, Carter, jt. auth. see Horton, Nancy Jane.
Horton, Casey. French: From New France to Louisiana. (p. 635)
—Jews: We Came to North America. (p. 917)
Horton, Cynthia. Wiggle Tales: A Collection of Hopson's Haywood from the Brownsville States-Graphic. (p. 1927)
Horton, David, 2nd. Negro Intellect: A Guide for Young Black Males. (p. 1240)
Horton, Eleanor. Blue Birds at Willow Bridge. (p. 202)
Horton, Elizabeth. Pick Me, Pick Me. Kinsley, Sean, illus. (p. 1354)
Horton, Jeanette. God's Alphabet. (p. 690)
Horton, Jim. Foot Log Incident. (p. 614)
Horton, Joan. I Brought My Rat for Show-and-Tell. Siegel, Melanie, tr. (p. 834)
Horton, Loren O., jt. auth. see Hutt, Sarah.
Horton, Lori, illus. see Opheim, Sandra.
Horton, Michael. Original Animals. (p. 1304)
Horton, Nancy Jane & Horton, Carter. Big, Fat, Bald Head! (p. 181)
Horton, Rich, ed. see Beagle, Peter S. & Link, Kelly.
Horton, Ronald Arthur. British Literature for Christian Schools. (p. 229)
Horton, Steve. Amala's Blade: Spirits of Naamaron: Spirits of Naamaron. Warner, Chris, ed. (p. 52)
Horton, Susan. Inside Lily's World. (p. 876)
Hortten, Jacqueline Faye. Pu Beach. (p. 1414)
Horvath, David, jt. auth. see Nichols, Travis.
Horvath, Ferdinand H., illus. see Slaughter, Charles E.
Horvath, James. Build, Dogs, Build: A Tall Tail. Horvath, James, illus. (p. 238)
—Dig, Dogs, Dig: A Construction Tail. Horvath, James, illus. (p. 438)
—Work, Dogs, Work: A Highway Tail. Horvath, James, illus. (p. 1952)
Horvath, Janet. Playing (less) Hurt - an Injury Prevention Guide for Musicians. (p. 1372)
Horvath, Joan. What Scientists Actually Do. (p. 1893)
Horvath, Joshua W. Slinky My Alien Friend. (p. 1590)
Horvath, Polly. Canning Season. (p. 261)
—Everything on a Waffle (p. 545)
—Everything on a Waffle. (p. 545)
—Lord & Lady Bunny - Almost Royalty! Blackall, Sophie, illus. (p. 1052)
—Mr. & Mrs. Bunny: Detectives Extraordinaire! Blackall, Sophie, illus. (p. 1184)
—Mr. & Mrs. Bunny. (p. 1184)
—Mr. & Mrs. Bunny—Detectives Extraordinaire! Blackall, Sophie, illus. (p. 1184)
—My One Hundred Adventures. (p. 1216)
—Northward to the Moon. (p. 1266)
—One Year in Coal Harbor. (p. 1298)
—Pepins & Their Problems. Hafner, Marylin, illus. (p. 1340)
—Pepins & Their Problems. Hafner, Marylin, illus. (p. 1340)
—Todo Sobre una Waffle. Holguin, Magdalena, tr. (p. 1761)
—Trolls. (p. 1788)
—Vacation (p. 1829)
Horwitz, ElinorLander. When the Sky Is Like Lace Cooney, Barbara, illus. (p. 1905)
Hosack, Karen. Drawings & Cartoons (p. 482)
—What Is Art? (p. 1889)
Hosack, Leona. Kamal's Day. (p. 942)
Hosaka, Toshi, tr. see Zappa, Go.
Hosch, Jenifer. 50 Bible Activities for Creative Minds. (p. 1997)
Hosch, William L. Korean War & the Vietnam War: People, Politics, & Power. (p. 967)
—World War I: People, Politics, & Power. (p. 1958)
—World War II: People, Politics, & Power. (p. 1959)
Hosch, William L., ed. see Curley, Robert.
Hosch, William L., ed. Britannica Guide to Algebra & Trigonometry. (p. 229)
—Britannica Guide to Numbers & Measurement. (p. 229)
—World War I: People, Politics, & Power. (p. 1958)
Hose, Ryan, illus. see Edward, J. P.
Hosegood, Lynn, illus. see Pittman, Rickey E.
Hosein, Ann. History of Theatre. (p. 785)
—Key Figures of World War I. (p. 950)
—Political Science: The Study of Nations, Government, & Governing. (p. 1380)
—Technology of the Ancient World. (p. 1712)
Hosein, Ann, ed. Key Figures of World War I. (p. 950)
Hoseley, Rantz, illus. see Kiyosaki, Robert T. & Lechter, Sharon L.
Hosemann, Theodor, illus. see Hoffmann, Heinrich.
Hosford, Eric, illus. see Clark, Marc.
Hosford, Kate. Big Birthday. Clifton-Brown, Holly, illus. (p. 178)
—Big Bouffant. Clifton-Brown, Holly, illus. (p. 179)
—Feeding the Flying Fanellis: And Other Poems from a Circus Chef. Kawa, Cosei, illus. (p. 580)
—Infinity & Me. Swiatkowska, Gabi, illus. (p. 873)
—Perfect Cup of Tea. Swiatkowska, Gabi, illus. (p. 1341)
Hosford, William. ABalloonC. Hosford, William, illus. (p. 2)
Hosford, William G. Geo the Geode. Hosford, William G., illus. (p. 661)
Hoshine, Ken, illus. see SparkNotes Staff.
Hoshino, Felicia. Sora & the Cloud. (p. 1614)
Hoshino, Felicia, illus. see Bahk, Jane.
Hoshino, Felicia, illus. see Lee-Tai, Amy.
Hoshino, Felicia, jt. auth. see Lord, Michelle.
Hoshino, Katsura. D. Gray-Man. (p. 397)
—D. Gray-Man. Hoshino, Katsura, illus. (p. 397)
Hoshino, Katsura & Katsura, Hoshino. D. Gray-Man Hoshino, Katsura, illus. (p. 397)
—D. Gray-Man. Hoshino, Katsura, illus. (p. 397)
Hosie, Donna. Devil's Dreamcatcher. (p. 432)
—Devil's Intern. (p. 432)
Hosken, John. Sophie Storme. (p. 1613)
Hosking, Wayne. Asian Kites. (p. 106)
Hoskins, Ruth. No Time for down Time. (p. 1260)
Hoskinson, Susan, jt. auth. see Sundberg, Wayne C.
Hosler, Danamarie, illus. see Bryan, Jennifer Liu.
Hosler, Danamarie, illus. see Bryan, Jennifer.
Hosler, Jay. Last of the Sandwalkers. (p. 978)
—Sandwalk Adventures. (p. 1511)
Hosley, Maria. Airplanes. (p. 32)
—Cars. (p. 272)
—Cats. (p. 280)
—Dinosaurs. (p. 443)
—Dogs. (p. 462)
—People. (p. 1339)
Hosmer-Dillard, Mollie, tr. see Michaelis, Antonia.
Hosoe, Eikoh, photos by see Lifton, Betty Jean.
Hossain, Farhana, illus. see Cooper, Sharon Katz & Compass Point Books Staff.
Hossain, Farhana, illus. see Nardo, Don.
Hossain, Farhana, illus. see Stille, Darlene R.
Hossain, Farhana, illus. see Stille, Darlene R. & Compass Point Books Staff.
Hosselkus, Devin, illus. see Gates, Pat.
Hossell, Karen & U. S. National Geographic Society Staff. Delaware, 1638-1776. (p. 424)
Hossell, Karen Price. Bill of Rights. (p. 186)
—Declaration of Independence. (p. 422)
—Irish Americans. (p. 887)
—United States Constitution. (p. 1819)
Hossfeld, Harald. Rapacious Kings Sagacious Kids. (p. 1439)
Hossler, Margaret. Spenser Rose Is Born. (p. 1625)
Höst, Andrea K. Hunting. (p. 829)
Hosta, Dar. I Love the Alphabet. (p. 843)
—I Love the Night. Hosta, Dar, illus. (p. 843)
—Mavis & Her Marvelous Mooncakes. (p. 1110)
Hostetler, Bob, jt. auth. see McDowell, Josh.
Hostetler, Robert P., jt. auth. see Larson, Ron.
Hostetler, Robert P. & Larson, Ron. Precalculus. (p. 1394)
—Trigonometry. (p. 1786)
Hostetter, Joyce Moyer. Blue. (p. 202)
—Comfort. (p. 348)
Hoston, Jim, illus. see Ford, Juwanda G.
Hoston, Jim, illus. see Scholastic, Inc. Staff & Ford, Juwanda G.
Hoston, William T. No Bullies in the Huddle - Redskins - Casebound. (p. 1258)
—No Bullies in the Huddle - Redskins - Perfect Bound. (p. 1258)
Hot Off the Press Staff. Alphabet Tiles. (p. 50)
—Alphabet Tiles #2. (p. 50)
Hotaling, Gwenn. Child's Book of Seasons. (p. 304)
Hotchkiss, Andrea. Adventures of Napkin Boy & the Beads of Condensation. (p. 21)
Hotchkiss, Conrad, illus. see Foggo, Cheryl.
Hotchkiss, Gerald G. Emily in Kara Koto: A Young Girl's Adventure in Mongolia. (p. 519)
Hotchkiss, Gerry. Emily & the Lost City of Urgup: An Adventure in Arabia. (p. 518)
Hotchkiss, Ron. Matchless Six: The Story of Canada's First Women's Olympic Team. (p. 1104)
Hotchner, Tracie. Dog Bible: Everything Your Dog Wants You to Know. (p. 461)
Hoth, Iva. Biblia Ilustrada. LeBlanc, Andre, illus. (p. 176)
—New Testament Picture Bible. (p. 1247)
—Picture Bible. (p. 1355)
Hotta, Yumi. Hikaru No Go Vol. 4. Obata, Takeshi, illus. (p. 779)
—Hikaru No Go Hotta, Yumi & Obata, Takeshi, illus. (p. 779)
—Hikaru No Go. Obata, Takeshi, illus. (p. 779)
Hotta, Yumi & Shindo, Hikaru. Hikaru No Go. Shindo, Hikaru & Obata, Takeshi, illus. (p. 779)
Hotte, Sylvain. Power Forward. Roberts, Casey, tr. (p. 1389)
Hotter, Ashley. Filly for Laura. (p. 586)
Hotton, Rick. Holy Mole: Life Is What You Make It: Subtle Wisdom from an Unconventional Comic Strip. (p. 791)
Hotz, Donna. Aaron's Surprise! (p. 2)
—Christmas Star. (p. 315)
Houblon, Marie. World of Colors: Seeing Colors in a New Way. (p. 1956)
Houbre, Gilbert. Light. Houbre, Gilbert, illus. (p. 1014)
—Vegetables. Houbre, Gilbert, illus. (p. 1834)
Houbre, Gilbert, illus. see De Bourgoing, Pascale, et al.
Houbre, Gilbert, jt. auth. see Valat, Pierre-Marie.
Houbre, Gilbert & Jeunesse, Gallimard. Tortuga. Houbre, Gilbert & Barroso, Paz, trs. (p. 1771)
Houck, Colleen. Reawakened. (p. 1450)
—Tiger's Curse (p. 1749)
—Tiger's Curse. (p. 1749)
—Tiger's Destiny. (p. 1749)
—Tiger's Destiny (Book 4 in the Tiger's Curse Series) (p. 1749)
—Tiger's Quest. (p. 1749)
—Tiger's Voyage (p. 1749)
—Tiger's Voyage (Book 3 in the Tiger's Curse Series) (p. 1749)
Houck, Max M. Trace Evidence. (p. 1774)
Houde, Monique. Blinded by Love. (p. 199)
Houdek, Andi. J P S Halloween Parade. Collier, Kevin, illus. (p. 901)
—Mice in My Tummy. (p. 1134)
—Stop That Pudding! Collier, Kevin, illus. (p. 1653)
Houdek, Andrea. Mice in My Tummy. Collier, Kevin Scott, illus. (p. 1134)
Houdeshell, Jennifer T., illus. see Zajac, Kristen J.
Houdeshell, Jennifer Thomas, illus. see Reed, Jennifer Bond.
Houdeshell, Jennifer Thomas, illus. see Zajac, Kristen K.
Hougasian, Amy. Big Foot Sun. (p. 181)
Hough, Charlotte, illus. see Sewell, Anna.
Hough, Hannah Bliss, illus. see Lewis, Joan Lane.
Hough, Susan Elizabeth. Finding Fault in California: An Earthquake Tourist's Guide. (p. 588)
Houghton, Amelia C. Life & Adventures of Santa Claus (Yesterday's Classics) Hokie, illus. (p. 1007)
Houghton, Chris, illus. see Carney, Larry.
Houghton, Christopher, illus. see MacDangereuse, T. T.
Houghton, Diane R., illus. see Finnegan, Evelyn M.
Houghton, Diane R., illus. see Lonborg, Rosemary.
Houghton, Gillian. Abejas: Por dentro y por fuera (Bees: Inside & Out) (p. 4)
—Abejas: Por Dentro y Por Fuera. Velazquez De Leon, Mauricio, tr. (p. 4)
—Aranas: Por Dentro y Por Fuera. Gonzalez, Tomas, tr. (p. 94)
—Aranas: Por dentro y por fuera (Spiders: Inside & Out) (p. 94)
—Balancing a Checkbook. (p. 133)
—Bee. (p. 157)
—Bees: Inside & Out. (p. 158)
—Bones: The Skeletal System. (p. 209)
—Breath: The Respiratory System. (p. 225)
—Breath: the Respiratory System. (p. 225)
—Buhos: Por dentro y por fuera (Owls: Inside & Out) (p. 237)
—Buhos: Por Dentro y Por Fuera. Gonzalez, Tomas, tr. (p. 237)
—Careers in Urban Planning. (p. 268)
—Cash & ATMs. (p. 276)
—Christmas. (p. 312)
—Circulatory System. (p. 321)
—Creating a Budget. (p. 378)
—Digestive System. (p. 438)
—Easter. (p. 499)
—Ellis Island: A Primary Source History of an Immigrant's Arrival in America. (p. 515)
—Goods & Services. (p. 701)
—Guts: The Digestive System. (p. 733)
—How Banks Work. (p. 805)
—How Credit Cards Work. (p. 806)
—Mildred Taylor. (p. 1142)
—Muscles: The Muscular System. (p. 1192)
—Muscles: the Muscular System. (p. 1192)
—Muscular System. (p. 1192)
—Nervous System. (p. 1241)
—Oneida of Wisconsin. (p. 1298)
—Owl. (p. 1314)
—Owls: Inside & Out. (p. 1315)
—Respiratory System. (p. 1463)
—Skeletal System. (p. 1584)
—Spider. (p. 1626)
—Spiders: Inside & Out. (p. 1627)
—Tortugas: Por Dentro y Por Fuera. Gonzalez, Tomas, tr. (p. 1771)
—Tortugas: Por dentro y por fuera (Turtles: Inside & Out) (p. 1771)
—Turtle. (p. 1798)
—Turtles: Inside & Out. (p. 1799)
—Wreck of the Andrea Gail: Three Days of a Perfect Storm. (p. 1962)
Houghton, Gillian, jt. auth. see Merrick, Caitlin.
Houghton Gosman, Gillian. What Do You Know about Weather & Climate? (p. 1883)
Houghton Gosman, Gillian, jt. auth. see Gosman, Gillian.
Houghton, Jackolyn. Detective Billy Pears & the Missing Hat. (p. 431)
Houghton, Jill Ziereis. Let's Volunteer. Thompson, Chad, illus. (p. 1001)
Houghton Mifflin and Company Publishing Staff & Rey, H. A. Family Christmas Treasury with CD & Downloadable Audio. (p. 568)
Houghton Mifflin Company Editors, jt. auth. see Perez, Monica.
Houghton Mifflin Company Editors, jt. auth. see Rey, H. A.
Houghton Mifflin Company Staff. Birthday Fun with Curious George. (p. 192)
—Fire Truck Fun with Curious George. (p. 591)
—Hobbit: the Desolation of Smaug Sticker Book. (p. 786)
—Splish, Splash, Curious George. (p. 1630)
Houghton Mifflin Company Staff, jt. auth. see Rey, H. A.
Houghton Mifflin Company Staff, creator. EEdition: the Americans. (p. 505)
—Math Practice Workbook, Grade 3. (p. 1107)
—Math-Trips, Grades 4-6. (p. 1107)
Houghton Mifflin Harcourt Children's Group Staff & Rey, H. A. Family Storybook Treasury: Tales of Laughter, Curiosity, & Fun. (p. 568)
Houghton Mifflin Harcourt Children's Group Staff, jt. creator see Learning Company, Inc. Staff.
Houghton Mifflin Harcourt Publishing Company Staff. Girl Power 5-Minute Stories. (p. 679)
Houghton Mifflin Harcourt Publishing Company Staff & Kempshall, Paddy. Hobbit: The Battle of the Five Armies. (p. 786)
Houghton Mifflin Harcourt Publishing Company Staff & Hughes, Natasha. Hobbit: the Battle of the Five Armies — Movie Storybook. (p. 786)
Houghton Mifflin Harcourt Publishing Company Staff. Hobbit: the Desolation of Smaug Activity Book. (p. 786)
—Hobbit: the Desolation of Smaug — the Movie Storybook. (p. 786)
Houghton Mifflin Harcourt Publishing Company Staff & Rey, H. A. Start Your Engines 5-Minute Stories. (p. 1643)
Houghton, Peggy M., et al. APA: The Easy Way! (p. 91)
—Houghton & Houghton Manual of Style: A Guide to Writing Research Papers. (p. 802)
Houghton, Raymond C. Revolutionary War Road Trip on US Route 202: Spend a Revolutionary Day along One of America's Most Historic Routes. (p. 1466)
—Revolutionary War Road Trip on US Route 4: Spend a Revolutionary Day along One of America's Most Historic Routes (p. 1466)
—Revolutionary War Road Trip on US Route 7: Spend a Revolutionary Day along One of America's Most Historic Routes. (p. 1466)
—Revolutionary War Road Trip on US Route 9: Spend a Revolutionary Day along One of America's Most Historic Routes. (p. 1467)
—Revolutionary War Road Trip on US Route 9W: Spend a Revolutionary Day along One of America's Most Historic Routes. (p. 1467)
Houghton, Roswitha, illus. see Crispin, Barbara.
Houghton, Sarah. Bloodsuckers: Bats, Bugs, & Other Bloodthirsty Creatures (p. 201)
—Elie Wiesel: A Holocaust Survivor Cries Out for Peace. (p. 512)

H

—Elie Wiesel: A Holocaust Survivor Cries Out for Peace Set (p. 512)
Houghton, Shane. Reed Gunther Volume 2 TP. (p. 1456)
Houghton, Shane, jt. auth. see Schulz, Charles M.
Houghton, Steve, jt. auth. see Black, Dave.
Hougue, Heather, ed. Snowman Band. (p. 1601)
Houk, Amanda. Mommy's New Heart (p. 1163)
Houk, Katherine. Little Book of Sticky Isms. (p. 1025)
Houk Maley, Adrienne, jt. auth. see Chiger, Arielle.
Houlbrook, Matt & Cocks, Harry, eds. Palgrave Advances in the Modern History of Sexuality. (p. 1320)
Houlder, Dominic J., jt. auth. see Ananda, Kul.
Houle, Donna Lee. Eastern Bluebird: A Guide for Young Birdwatchers. Chambliss, Matthew et al, photos by. (p. 499)
Houle, Kelly. Gracie's Gallery: A Magic Mirror Book. (p. 705)
Houle, Michelle E. Lindsey Williams: Gardening for Impoverished Families. (p. 1019)
Houle, Michelle E., ed. Cesar Chavez. (p. 288)
Houle, Michelle M. AIDS in the 21st Century: What You Should Know. (p. 30)
—Gods & Goddesses in Greek Mythology Rock! Bock, William Sauts, illus. (p. 690)
—Mark Twain: Banned, Challenged, & Censored. (p. 1095)
—Modern British Poetry: "The World Is Never the Same" (p. 1158)
—Modern British Poetry- The World Is Never the Same. (p. 1158)
—Roald Dahl: Author of Charlie & the Chocolate Factory. (p. 1477)
Houng, Jane. Lantau Life. (p. 975)
Hounslow, Gaynor. Snoop & Sniffy Wiffy - the Tale of Two Hedgehogs: The Children's Book of Wildlife Stories. (p. 1598)
Houran, Lori Haskins. $25,000 Flight. Lowe, Wesley, illus. (p. 2003)
—Bloody Horned Lizards. (p. 201)
—Busy Tractors, Busy Days. (p. 246)
—Dig Those Dinosaurs. Marquez, Francisca, illus. (p. 438)
—Dozen Cousins. Usher, Sam, illus. (p. 474)
—Flarg Ate My Homework. Warrick, Jessica, illus. (p. 602)
—Flat Stanley & the Firehouse. Pamintuan, Macky, illus. (p. 603)
—How to Spy on a Shark. Marquez, Francisca, illus. (p. 821)
—I Will Keep You Safe & Sound. Brown, Petra, illus. (p. 848)
—Make a Wish, Albert: 3-D Shapes. Melmon, Deborah, illus. (p. 1079)
—Pug: What a Mug! (p. 1415)
—Spooky & Spookier: Four American Ghost Stories. Diaz, Viviana, illus. (p. 1631)
—Thousand Theos: Doubling. Pilz, M. H., illus. (p. 1740)
—Too Many Cats. Mathieu, Joe, illus. (p. 1766)
—Trip into Space: An Adventure to the International Space Station. Marquez, Francisca, illus. (p. 1787)
Hourglass Press, Hourglass, jt. auth. see Dover.
Hourglass Press, Hourglass & Sauza, Saul. Super-Deluxe, Epic Journal of Awesomeness. (p. 1679)
Hourihan, Kelly. 4 to 16 Characters. (p. 1992)
Hourlier, Sylvaine. Blacky & the Enchanted Mountain (p. 198)
House, B. J. What's Wrong with Pauly? Cash, Paul, illus. (p. 1900)
House, Brandy. Adam Ant (p. 11)
—Prince Eric & the Island of Despair. (p. 1401)
—Scorch the Dragon (p. 1530)
—Under a Toadstool (p. 1813)
House, Catherine. Hanan the Peanut Seller. (p. 740)
—Little Elephant. Whelan, Olwyn, illus. (p. 1027)
—Little Zebra. Whelan, Olwyn, illus. (p. 1038)
—Voices Against Injustice: Ten Christians Who Spoke Out for Justice. (p. 1848)
—Voices Against Slavery: Ten Christians Who Spoke Out for Freedom. (p. 1848)
—Where Did Grandad Go? Ayres, Honor, illus. (p. 1906)
House, Catherine & Quarto Generic Staff. Stork in a Baobab Tree: An African Twelve Days of Christmas. Alakija, Polly, illus. (p. 1655)
House, Darrell. Miller the Green Caterpillar. Argoff, Patti, illus. (p. 1143)
House, David James. Key to Space. (p. 950)
House, Edward Mandell. Intimate Papers of Colonel House: Arranged as a Narrative by Charles Seymour (p. 881)
House, Katherine L. Lighthouses for Kids: History, Science, & Lore with 21 Activities. (p. 1015)
—White House for Kids: A History of a Home, Office, & National Symbol, with 21 Activities. (p. 1913)
House, Matthew M. You've Got to Be Kidding Me! (p. 1982)
House, Megan. Big Black Bear. (p. 178)
House, Nancy, ed. see Kirst, Kathleen & Kirst, Kat.
House, Peggy. Prairie Anna. (p. 1392)
House, Peggy A., ed. see Greenes, Carole E., et al.
House, Peggy A., ed. see Yeatts, Karol, et al.
House, Peggy & Day, Roger P. Mission Mathematics II. (p. 1153)
House, Silas. Eli the Good. (p. 512)
House, Silas & Vaswani, Neela. Same Sun Here. Schenker, Hilary, illus. (p. 1507)
Houseal, Phil, et al. Sam Has Ants. (p. 1506)
Housel, Debra. Charlotte's Web: An Instructional Guide for Literature (p. 294)
Housel, Debra, jt. auth. see Rice, Dona Herwick.
Housel, Debra & Hart, Melissa. Main Idea, Grade 4. (p. 1077)
Housel, Debra J. Ecologists: From Woodward to Miranda (p. 502)
—Ecosystems (p. 503)
—Famous Immigrants. (p. 569)
—Forces. (p. 617)
—Immigration. (p. 861)
—Incredible Invertebrates. (p. 869)
—Industrial Giants. (p. 872)
—Industrial Revolution. (p. 872)
—Inside Ecosystems & Biomes. (p. 876)
—Inventions in Communications. (p. 884)
—Mammal Mania. (p. 1085)
—Motion. (p. 1179)
—Nature of Matter. (p. 1236)
—Pioneering Ecologists. (p. 1361)
—Slithering Reptiles & Amphibians. (p. 1591)
Housel, Debra J. & Doak, Robin S. Investigating Storms (p. 885)
—Weather Scientists (p. 1870)
Housel, Debra J. & Hart, Melissa. Main Idea, Grade 2. (p. 1077)
—Main Idea, Grade 3. (p. 1077)
Housel, Debra J. & Rice, Dona. Buy It! History of Money. (p. 248)
—Right Environment. (p. 1472)
Housel, Debra J. & Rice, Dona Herwick. Buy It! History of Money (p. 248)
Houselander, Caryll. Catholic Tales for Boys & Girls. (p. 280)
—More Catholic Tales for Boys & Girls. (p. 1174)
Houseman, D. L. Harvey & His Friends Great Fishing Adventure. (p. 752)
Housenick, Nicole. It's All about Sam-Or Is It? Sam's Terrible Day-Or Billy's? (p. 896)
Houser, Aimee. Tragedy in Tucson: The Arizona Shooting Rampage. (p. 1776)
—Venezuela. (p. 1835)
Houser, Aimee, jt. auth. see Higgins, Melissa.
Houser, Marlin. Secret of Squirrel Meadow. (p. 1542)
Houser, Marlin L. Adventures of Little Fox, Book Four, Escape. (p. 19)
—Adventures of Little Fox Book One, Generations: Teacher's Guide & Student Reproducibles. (p. 19)
—Adventures of Little Fox, Book Three, Unfamiliar Territory. (p. 19)
—Adventures of Little Fox, Generations (p. 19)
Houser, Tina. God's Campground. (p. 691)
Housley, Cathren, illus. see Wallace, Nancy.
Housley Dave. Ryan Seacrest Is Famous. (p. 1499)
Housman, Clemence, illus. see Housman, Laurence, ed.
Housman, Laurence. Field of Clover. (p. 584)
Housman, Laurence, ed. Moonshine & Clover. Housman, Clemence, illus. (p. 1173)
Houssais, Emmanuelle, illus. see Roy, Sandrine Dumas.
Houston, Alecia. Stories True of Gabby Cockatoo. Luna, Lauren, illus. (p. 1655)
Houston, Anna. Daisy's Bug. (p. 401)
Houston, Bronwyn, illus. see Dann, Lucy & Dann, Kiefer.
Houston, Debby. Mervous Tames Ocd. (p. 1129)
Houston, Dick. Bulu: African Wonder Dog. (p. 241)
Houston, Gloria M. Miss Dorothy & Her Bookmobile. Lamb, Susan Condie, illus. (p. 1151)
—Miss Dorothy's Bookmobile. (p. 1151)
Houston, Jack. Jumbo Health Yearbook: Grade 5. (p. 933)
—Jumbo Health Yearbook: Grade 6. (p. 933)
—Jumbo Health Yearbook: Grade 7. (p. 933)
—Jumbo Health Yearbook: Grade 8. (p. 933)
—Jumbo Science Yearbook: Grade 3. (p. 933)
—Jumbo Science Yearbook: Grade 5. (p. 933)
—Jumbo Science Yearbook: Grade 6. (p. 933)
—Jumbo Science Yearbook: Grade 7. (p. 933)
—Jumbo Science Yearbook: Grade 8. (p. 933)
Houston, Julian. New Boy. (p. 1243)
Houston, Larriesha. Princess Sarai. (p. 1405)
Houston, Lauren, illus. see Disney Book Group Staff.
Houston, Mark, et al. Hypertension: The Revolutionary Nutrition & Lifestyle Program to Help Fight High Blood Pressure. (p. 831)
Houston, Melissa, illus. see Jordan, Stephanie.
Houston, Meradeth. Colors Like Memories. (p. 345)
Houston, Nancy. Always the Hills. (p. 51)
Houston, Rebecca. Cat's Visitors. (p. 281)
—My Butterfly. (p. 1200)
Houston, Scott. Play Piano in a Flash Fake Book for Kids! A song book for kids in lead sheet Format (p. 1371)
—Play Piano in a Flash for Kids! A Fun & Easy Way for Kids to Start Playing the Piano. (p. 1371)
Houston, Scott & Sowash, Bradley. Play Piano in a Flash! the Next Step: The Next Step. (p. 1371)
Houtman, Jacqueline. Reinvention of Edison Thomas. (p. 1457)
Houtman, Jacqueline, et al. Bayard Rustin: The Invisible Activist. (p. 147)
Houts, Amy. Cooking Around the Country with Kids: USA Regional Recipes & Fun Activities. (p. 361)
—Down on the Farm Harpster, Steve, illus. (p. 474)
—God's People & Me: Boz's Big Book of Bible Fun. Davidson, Leigh, ed. (p. 691)
—Rachel Maddow (p. 1432)
Houts, Michelle. Beef Princess of Practical County. (p. 157)
—Winterfrost. (p. 1938)
Houts, Richard. Thief's Journey. (p. 1732)
Houx, Emily Marie Cornell du, illus. see Moss, Barbara E.
Hovaguimian, Vroni. Deep in the Woods. (p. 423)
Hovanec, Deb. Lots & Lots of Friends! (p. 1057)
Hovanec, Erin. Careers as a Content Provider for the Web. (p. 267)
Hovanec, Erin, jt. auth. see Chong, Elaine S.
Hovanec, Erin M. Careers as Content Provider for the Web. (p. 267)
—Everything You Need to Know about Phobias. (p. 545)
—Online Visit to Africa. (p. 1298)
—Online Visit to Antarctica. (p. 1298)
—Online Visit to Asia. (p. 1298)
—Online Visit to Australia. (p. 1298)
—Online Visit to Europe. (p. 1298)
—Online Visit to North America. (p. 1298)
—Online Visit to South America. (p. 1298)
Hovanec, Helene. Easy First Puzzles. Shems, Ed, illus. (p. 500)
—Letter Fun. Shems, Ed, illus. (p. 1002)
—Reading Games. Shems, Ed, illus. (p. 1446)
—Ultimate Puzzle Challenge: Head Twisters. LaCoste, Gary, illus. (p. 1809)
—Ultimate Puzzle Challenge: Mind Mashers. Luxich, Matt, illus. (p. 1809)
Hovanec, Helene, jt. auth. see Merrell, Patrick.
Hovanec, Helene & Merrell, Patrick. Barnyard Games & Puzzles: 100 Mazes, Word Games, Picture Puzzles, Jokes & Riddles, Brainteasers, & Fun Activities for Kids. (p. 140)
—Chicken Games & Puzzles: 100 Word Games, Picture Puzzles, Fun Mazes, Silly Jokes, Codes, & Activities for Kids. (p. 300)
—Great Outdoors Games & Puzzles: Bring the Outdoors Inside with 100 Mazes, Word Games, Picture Puzzles, Jokes & Riddles, Brainteasers, & Fun-Packed Activities. (p. 717)
Hovell, John, illus. see Harris, Trudy.
Hovemann, Anisa Claire, illus. see Malnor, Bruce & Malnor, Carol.
Hovemann, Anisa Claire, illus. see Malnor, Carol L. & Malnor, Bruce.
Hovemann, Anisa Claire, illus. see Myers, Tim.
Hovemann, Anisa Claire, illus. see Rinehart, Susie Caldwell.
Hovey, Kate. Ancient Voices. Kimber, Murray, illus. (p. 71)
—Arachne Speaks. Drawson, Blair, illus. (p. 94)
—Voices of the Trojan War. Gore, Leonid, illus. (p. 1848)
Hovey, Kendra A., et al. Banking on Self-Help Groups: Twenty Years On. (p. 136)
Hovhannisyan, Nune, illus. see Velikanje, Kathryn.
Hoving, Wilma, tr. see Bultje, Jan Willem.
Hovius, Christopher. Fitness & Nutrition. McDonnell, Mary Ann & Forman, Sara, eds. (p. 599)
Hovius, Christopher, jt. auth. see Libal, Autumn.
Hovland, Gary, illus. see Kesterson, Casie.
Hovland, Gary, illus. see O'Connor, Jane.
Hovland, Henrik & Bartlett, Don. John Jensen Feels Different. Kove, Torill, illus. (p. 922)
Hovland, Oivind, illus. see Orme, David.
Hovland, Stephenie. Isaac Blesses Jacob & Esau. (p. 890)
—Lydia Believes. Dorenkamp Repa, Michelle, illus. (p. 1066)
Hovland, Stephenie M. Heinrich Melchior Muhlenberg. Johnson, Larry, illus. (p. 762)
Hovsepian, Ann-Margret. One Year Designer Genes Devo. (p. 1297)
How, Barbara. My Friend: Beth. (p. 1209)
Howard, A. Louis the Furred - Volume One: The Days of Reckoning. (p. 1058)
Howard, A. G. Ensnared. (p. 531)
—Splintered. (p. 1630)
—Unhinged. (p. 1817)
Howard, Adeline, jt. auth. see Mohr, Janet.
Howard, Akime, jt. auth. see Howard, Jennie.
Howard, Alan, jt. auth. see Himonas, Alex.
Howard, Alison. Ocean Life. (p. 1276)
Howard, Amalie. Almost Girl. (p. 48)
—Alpha Goddess. (p. 48)
—Oceanborn. (p. 1277)
—Waterfell. (p. 1863)
Howard, Ann. Mystery of Dragon Bridge: A Peach Blossom Village Story. (p. 1224)
Howard, Annabelle. Alex in Numberland. DuFalla, Anita, illus. (p. 36)
—As the Mayan Calendars Turn. (p. 105)
—Battle for the Ballot. Leon, Karen, illus. (p. 145)
—Big Cheese. Leon, Karen, illus. (p. 180)
—Cry Out Liberty: Sarah Winnemucca, Indian Princess. (p. 387)
—Father, His Son, & Their Donkey: An Aesop's Fable. (p. 577)
—Hammurabi's Law & Order. (p. 739)
—Keelboat Annie: An American Tall Tale. (p. 946)
—King's New Crown. DuFalla, Anita, illus. (p. 960)
—Three Greek Myths: Pandora, Icarus & Midas. (p. 1742)
Howard, Annie Louise. Who's That Voice in the Woods (p. 1921)
Howard, Arthur. When I Was Five. (p. 1903)
Howard, Arthur, illus. see Appelt, Kathi.
Howard, Arthur, illus. see Cuyler, Margery.
Howard, Arthur, illus. see Lobel, Arnold & Rylant, Cynthia.
Howard, Arthur, illus. see Perl, Erica S.
Howard, Arthur, illus. see Pfeffer, Susan Beth.
Howard, Arthur, illus. see Rylant, Cynthia.
Howard, Arthur, illus. see Scanlon, Liz Garton.
Howard, Arthur, jt. auth. see Rylant, Cynthia.
Howard, Assuanta. Doggie Bets. Sandoz, Matt, illus. (p. 462)
Howard, Assuanta, jt. auth. see Mitchell, Derrick Lee.
Howard, Ayanna. On the Job with an Engineer. (p. 1290)
Howard, Barb. Dewpoint Show (p. 432)
Howard, Barnaby. Best Book of Pirates. (p. 168)
Howard, Becky L. Harrison Goes Camping. Pine, Margherita N., ed. (p. 750)
Howard, Brenda Lynette. Cadi's Weekend Adventure. (p. 250)
Howard, Britt, jt. auth. see Howard, Madeleine.
Howard, Catherine, tr. see Francia, Giada.
Howard, Cheryl L. Duster Dustbunny's Seven Days of the Week & Twelve Months in a Year. (p. 490)
—It's Turtle Time. Kapart, illus. (p. 899)
—Mikhael the Mighty: Be True to Who You Are & You Can Never Go Wrong. (p. 1141)
Howard, Cheryl Lee. Daisy Dustbunny Seven Days a Week: Learning to spell the days of the week is fun with Daisy Dustbunny. (p. 400)
Howard, Cheryl Lynne. Captured by Love: A Wild Horse Story Based on Psalm 139. (p. 265)
Howard, Chris. Rootless. (p. 1488)
Howard, Chrys, jt. auth. see Robertson, Korie.
Howard, Clark & Meltzer, Mark. Clark Smart Parents, Clark Smart Kids: Teaching Kids of Every Age the Value of Money. (p. 327)
Howard, Colin, illus. see Black, Robyn Hood.
Howard, Colin, illus. see Colich, Abby.
Howard, Dave. Lady's Day to Play. Howard, Dave, illus. (p. 971)
Howard Davis, Starla. Paul & the House Full of Donuts. (p. 1330)
Howard, Denise. Greentown Elementary: The Seafood Nightmare. (p. 723)
—Jameela's Big Adventure. (p. 906)
Howard, Devon, photos by see Smith, Ryan A.
Howard, E., ed. see Avi.
Howard Ed.D., Tequila E. All about Me! (p. 42)
—Earth Day. (p. 495)
Howard, Edgar B. Evidence of Early Man in North America, Based on Geological & Archaeological Work in New Mexico. (p. 546)
Howard, Elisabeth. ABCs of Vocal Harmony: Music Reading, Ear Training. (p. 4)
Howard, Elisabeth & Austin, Howard. Born to Sing. (p. 214)
Howard, Elizabeth Fitzgerald. Aunt Flossie's Hats (and Crab Cakes Later) Ransome, James, illus. (p. 115)
—Chita's Christmas Tree. (p. 308)
—Flower Girl Butterflies. Kromer, Christiane, illus. (p. 607)
—Train to Lulu's. Casilla, Robert, illus. (p. 1777)
—Virgie Goes to School with Us Boys. Lewis, E. B., illus. (p. 1844)
Howard, Ellen. Big Seed. (p. 183)
—Crimson Cap. (p. 382)
—Different Kind of Courage. (p. 438)
—Edith Herself. (p. 504)
—Gate in the Wall. (p. 658)
—Log Cabin Wedding. Himler, Ronald, illus. (p. 1045)
—Murphy & Kate. Graham, Mark, illus. (p. 1192)
Howard, Ellie Nothaus, illus. see Ball, S. N.
Howard, Fran. Asteroids, Comets, & Meteoroids. (p. 108)
—Badgers: Active at Night (p. 132)
—Bumble Bees. (p. 241)
—Bumble Bees [Scholastic]. (p. 241)
—Butterflies. (p. 247)
—Butterflies [Scholastic]. (p. 247)
—Deserts. (p. 429)
—Dwarf Planets. (p. 491)
—Earth. (p. 495)
—Forests. (p. 618)
—Grasslands. (p. 712)
—Jupiter. (p. 937)
—Kuiper Belt. (p. 968)
—Lakes & Ponds. (p. 972)
—Mars. (p. 1096)
—Mercury. (p. 1127)
—Milky Way. (p. 1143)
—Moon. (p. 1171)
—Moths. (p. 1179)
—Mountains. (p. 1181)
—Neptune. (p. 1241)
—Oceans. (p. 1277)
—Parrots (p. 1325)
—Parrots: Colorful Birds (p. 1325)
—Rivers & Streams. (p. 1476)
—Saturn. (p. 1515)
—Solar System. (p. 1607)
—Stars. (p. 1643)
—Sun. (p. 1675)
—Universe (p. 1820)
—Uranus. (p. 1825)
—Venus. (p. 1836)
—Walkingsticks. (p. 1854)
—Wetlands. (p. 1877)
Howard, Grahame. Wishing Book 3 - Extermination. (p. 1940)
Howard, Ian T. One Love, Two Worlds. Bishop, Tracey, illus. (p. 1296)
Howard, J. J. That Time I Joined the Circus. (p. 1726)
—Tracers. (p. 1775)
Howard, Jane R. Maria's Loom: An Original Fairy Tale with Music (play Script) (p. 1093)
Howard, Jennie & Howard, Akime. Creepy Colored Creatures. (p. 381)
Howard, Jennifer. Lucy & the Land of Lost Socks. (p. 1063)
Howard, Jenny. Bittersweet Voyage. (p. 194)
Howard, Jeremy. Countdown: The Adventures of Starforce. (p. 370)
Howard, Jim & Welsh-Howard, Paula. Tell Me Tell Me If You Can. (p. 1716)
—Tell Me, Tell Me, What You See. Knight, Vanessa, illus. (p. 1716)
Howard, Joan. Story of Mark Twain. Meadowcroft, Enid Lamonte, ed. (p. 1659)
Howard, Jonathan L. Katya's War. (p. 946)
—Katya's World. (p. 946)
Howard, Josh. Dead@17: Blood of Saints. Howard, Josh, illus. (p. 417)
—Dead@17: The Complete First Series. Howard, Josh, illus. (p. 417)
Howard, Judy. Heavenly Patchwork: Quilt Stories Stitched with Love. (p. 761)
Howard, Juliana. Catie the Copycat. (p. 280)
Howard, Julie. College Vocabulary (p. 340)
—Take Out Your Crayons. (p. 1697)
Howard, Juliet, illus. see Kollin, Dani.
Howard, Kate. Big-Top. Duendes Del Sur Staff, illus. (p. 184)
—Duck Vinci Code & Other Tales. (p. 488)
—Frozen Giant. (p. 645)
—Haunting of Pirate Cove. (p. 754)
—Hotel of Horrors. (p. 802)
—Hotel of Horrors. Duendes Del Sur Staff, illus. (p. 802)
—Lego Movie: Junior Novel. (p. 990)
—Lego Movie. (p. 990)
—Ninja vs. Ninja. (p. 1256)
—Rescue Mission. (p. 1462)
—Scooby-Doo! Mystery #3: the Haunting of Pirate Cove. Duendes Del Sur Staff, illus. (p. 1529)
—Search for Zane. (p. 1537)
—Stage Fright. Duendes Del Sur Staff, illus. (p. 1638)
—Techno Strike! (p. 1711)
Howard, Kate, jt. auth. see West, Tracey.
Howard, Kate & Duendes Del Sur Staff. Frozen Giant. (p. 645)
Howard, Ken. Young Chieftain. (p. 1978)
Howard, Kimberley, ed. see Rhodes, Sam.
Howard, Krystle, jt. auth. see Howard, Ryan.
Howard, Lee. Haunted Halloween. Scholastic, Inc. Staff & Alcadia SNC Staff, illus. (p. 753)
—Merry Scary Holiday. Alcadia SNC Staff, illus. (p. 1129)
Howard, Lee, jt. auth. see ABDO Publishing Company Staff.
Howard, Lee & Khan, Nahnatchka. Haunted Halloween. (p. 753)

—Merry Scary Holiday. (p. 1129)
Howard, Linda & Dockray, Tracy Arah. Mi Gran Libro de Palabras Play-Doh. (p. 1132)
Howard, Lisa Bob, jt. auth. see Bob, Steven M.
Howard, Madeleine & Howard, Britt. Little B's Safety Coaching. (p. 1025)
Howard, Marie. Punkin & the Peanut. (p. 1417)
Howard, Mark. Journey to Stone Village: Mark Howard. (p. 929)
Howard, Martin. Germs! Stimpson, Colin, illus. (p. 666)
—Germs! An Epic Tale on a Tiny Scale! Stimpson, Colin, illus. (p. 667)
—How to Cook Children: A Grisly Recipe Book for Gruesome Witches. Stimpson, Colin, illus. (p. 816)
—How to Slay a Werewolf: Advice, Tips & Fantastical Rules for the Budding Werewolf Slayer. (p. 821)
—Shaun the Sheep Movie - the Junior Novel. (p. 1563)
—Shaun the Sheep: the Beast of Soggy Moor. Janes, Andy, illus. (p. 1563)
—Shaun the Sheep: the Flock Factor. Janes, Andy, illus. (p. 1563)
—White Wand. Stimpson, Colin, illus. (p. 1913)
—Wild Winter. Stimpson, Colin, illus. (p. 1930)
Howard, Martin, jt. auth. see Cartaya, Pablo.
Howard, Megz, illus. see Bristol, P. L. & Branda, Barnabus.
Howard, Melanie A. Black Mambas (p. 196)
—Boa Constrictors (p. 205)
—Bowhunting for Kids (p. 216)
—Camping for Kids (p. 257)
—Civil Rights Marches. (p. 324)
—Copperheads. (p. 366)
—Corn Snakes (p. 367)
—Freshwater Fishing for Kids (p. 637)
—Stock Cars (p. 1651)
—Wild about Snakes. (p. 1928)
Howard, Melanie A., et al. Into the Great Outdoors. (p. 881)
—Wild about Snakes (p. 1928)
Howard, Monique. Moon Creeper. (p. 1172)
—Moon Creeper (Simplified Chinese & English) Li, Helen, tr. (p. 1172)
Howard, Nancy Shroyer. Mischief in Tuscany: Running Wild in a Famous Italian Painting. (p. 1150)
Howard, Norma, illus. see Tingle, Tim.
Howard, Pam, illus. see Scott, Liz, et al.
Howard, Patricia, illus. see Thurston, Cheryl Miller & Etzel, Laurie Hopkins.
Howard, Paul. Bugville - Home to the Bravest Bugs in the Universe! (p. 237)
Howard, Paul, illus. see Cooke, Trish.
Howard, Paul, illus. see Henderson, Kathy.
Howard, Paul, illus. see Rosen, Michael, ed.
Howard, Paul, illus. see Tomlinson, Jill.
Howard, Paul, illus. see Willis, Jeanne.
Howard, Pauline Rodriguez. Icy Watermelon/Sandia Fria: CD & Book Set. (p. 851)
Howard, Pauline Rodriguez, illus. see Galindo, Mary Sue.
Howard, Peggy Ann. Zorees: Land of Dreams. (p. 1990)
Howard, Philip, illus. see Penn, Audrey.
Howard, Pyle. Modern Aladdin or the Wonderful Adventures of Oliver Munier: an Extravaganza in Four Acts. (p. 1158)
Howard, Rebecca. Flagtastic Flags. (p. 602)
Howard, Reginald. Big, Big Wall. Aruego, Jose & Dewey, Ariane, illus. (p. 178)
—Big, Big Wall. Dewey, Ariane & Aruego, Jose, illus. (p. 178)
—Big, Big Wall/No Puedo Bajar. Ada, Alma Flora & Campoy, F. Isabel, trs. (p. 178)
Howard, Rex. Nobody's Somebody. (p. 1262)
Howard, Richard, tr. see de Saint-Exupéry, Antoine.
Howard, Richard, tr. see Saint-Exupéry, Antoine de.
Howard, Robert E., jt. auth. see Russell, P. Craig.
Howard, Robert E., jt. auth. see Thomas, Roy.
Howard, Roger. Oil Hunters: Exploration & Espionage in the Middle East. (p. 1282)
—Safety First. (p. 1502)
Howard, Rushton. Sebastian Reckless. Howard, Rushton, illus. (p. 1539)
Howard, Ryan & Howard, Krystle. Little Rhino #1: My New Team. Madrid, Erwin, illus. (p. 1035)
—Little Rhino #2: the Best Bat. Madrid, Erwin, illus. (p. 1035)
—Little Rhino #2: the Best Bat - Library Edition. Madrid, Erwin, illus. (p. 1035)
—Little Rhino #3: Dugout Hero. Madrid, Erwin, illus. (p. 1035)
—My New Team. Madrid, Erwin, illus. (p. 1216)
Howard, S. Paul. Hawehyo's Tale (p. 755)
Howard, Takesha. Where Are You Dad? (p. 1906)
Howard, Tim. Keeper: The Unguarded Story of Tim Howard. (p. 947)
—Keeper - The Unguarded Story of Tim Howard. (p. 947)
Howard, Vanetta, ed. see Johnson, Harvell.
Howard, Velma Swanston, tr. see Lagerlöf, Selma.
Howard, Velma Swanston, tr. Wonderful Adventures of Nils. (p. 1948)
Howard, Vera. My Gran: Country Stories for Young Children. (p. 1210)
Howard, Vernon. Monologues for Teens. Landes, William-Allan, ed. (p. 1166)
Howard, Victoria. Adventures of Max: The Bolognese Dog. (p. 20)
—Adventures of Max: Max & His Friends Save the World. (p. 20)
—Adventures of Max & Molly: A Love Story about a Dog & a Horse. (p. 20)
Howard, Victoria M. Adventures of Max: Max & His Friends Save the World. (p. 20)
—Adventures of Max & Molly: A Love Story about a Dog & a Horse. (p. 20)
—Max Goes to School. (p. 1111)
Howard, Virginia, illus. see Prieto, Anita C.
Howard, Zachariah, illus. see Sniegoski, Thomas E.
Howard-Barr, Elissa, et al. Sexual Behavior & Unplanned Pregnancy. (p. 1556)
Howard-Hess, Susan. Harriet Higby. Leamer, Vickie, illus. (p. 749)
Howard-Jones, Ruth. Whispers of Berg: Polo. (p. 1912)
Howard-Parham, Pam. Caillou Finds Colors. Gillen, Lisa P., illus. (p. 251)
—Caillou Gets in Shape. Gillen, Lisa P., illus. (p. 251)
—Caillou Waits for Dinner. Crowell, Knox, illus. (p. 251)
—Dinosaur Surprise. Neveu, Fred, illus. (p. 443)
—Loving Our Country. Teeple, Jackie, illus. (p. 1061)
—Playing on the Playground. Crowell, Knox, illus. (p. 1372)
—Spending Time Outdoors. Teeple, Jackie, illus. (p. 1625)
—This Is Farmer Greg. Coates, Jennifer, illus. (p. 1735)
Howard-Parnam, Pam. If You Go into the Forest. Meier, Kerry L., illus. (p. 854)
Howarth, Craig, illus. see Francis, JennaKay.
Howarth, Craig, illus. see Garthwaite, Lynn D.
Howarth, Craig, illus. see Kruse, Donald W.
Howarth, Craigh, illus. see Mair, J. Samia.
Howarth, Daniel. Goose That Laid the Golden Eggs. (p. 702)
Howarth, Daniel, illus. see Butler, M. Christina.
Howarth, Daniel, illus. see Cabral, Jeane.
Howarth, Daniel, illus. see Callahan, Sean.
Howarth, Daniel, illus. see Carr, Jan.
Howarth, Daniel, illus. see Castle, Caroline.
Howarth, Daniel, illus. see Conchie, Kathryn.
Howarth, Daniel, illus. see Fischel, Emma.
Howarth, Daniel, illus. see Glaser, Linda.
Howarth, Daniel, illus. see Howarth, Heidi.
Howarth, Daniel, illus. see Loughrey, Anita.
Howarth, Daniel, illus. see MacKinnon, Mairi, ed.
Howarth, Daniel, illus. see Mason, Conrad.
Howarth, Daniel, illus. see McAllister, Angela & Scholastic, Inc. Staff.
Howarth, Daniel, illus. see Smallman, Steve.
Howarth, Daniel, illus. see Spinner, Stephanie.
Howarth, Daniel, illus. see Williams, Becky.
Howarth, Heidi. How to Catch a Falling Star. Howarth, Daniel, illus. (p. 815)
—Otter Who Loved to Hold Hands. Howarth, Daniel, illus. (p. 1307)
Howarth, Lesley. Edge of the World. (p. 504)
Howat, Irene. 100 Fascinating Bible Facts. (p. 1998)
—Bobby Boast a Lot. De Boer, Michel, illus. (p. 206)
—George Müller: The Children's Champion. (p. 663)
—Granny Grump a Lot. De Boer, Michel, illus. (p. 710)
—Harry Help a Lot. De Boer, Michel, illus. (p. 750)
—Isobel Kuhn - Lights in Lisuland. (p. 893)
—James Chalmers: The Rainmaker's Friend. (p. 907)
—Jim Elliot: He Is No Fool... (p. 917)
—John Newton: A Slave Set Free. (p. 922)
—Life Is an Adventure. (p. 1011)
—Lorna Look a Lot. De Boer, Michel, illus. (p. 1053)
—Lucy Lie a Lot. De Boer, Michel, illus. (p. 1063)
—On His Majesty's Service. (p. 1289)
—Ten Boys Who Changed the World. (p. 1718)
—Ten Boys Who Didn't Give In. (p. 1718)
—Ten Boys Who Made a Difference. (p. 1718)
—Ten Boys Who Made History. (p. 1718)
—Ten Boys Who Used Their Talents. (p. 1718)
—Ten Girls Who Changed the World. (p. 1718)
—Ten Girls Who Didn't Give In. (p. 1718)
—Ten Girls Who Made a Difference. (p. 1718)
—Ten Girls Who Made History. (p. 1718)
—Ten Girls Who Used Their Talents. (p. 1718)
—William Work a Lot. De Boer, Michel, illus. (p. 1933)
Howat, Irene, et al. Gweni Gweld Bob Dim. (p. 733)
—Huw Helpu Pawb. (p. 830)
Howatt, Sandra J. Sleepyheads. Wan, Joyce, illus. (p. 1590)
Howden, Iris. Bright Future. (p. 228)
—Mother Teresa. (p. 1178)
—Nelson Mandela. (p. 1240)
Howe, Alan, et al. Core English Ks3 - Real Progress in Reading. (p. 367)
Howe, Cindy T., illus. see Nikolet, C. T.
Howe, Deborah & Howe, James. Bunnicula. Daniel, Alan, illus. (p. 242)
—Rabbit-Tale of Mystery. (p. 1429)
Howe, James. Addie on the Inside. (p. 11)
—Also Known As Elvis. (p. 50)
—Brontorina. (p. 230)
—Brontorina. Cecil, Randy, illus. (p. 230)
—Bud Barkin, Private Eye. Helquist, Brett, illus. (p. 234)
—Bunnicula in a Box: Bunnicula; Howliday Inn; the Celery Stalks at Midnight; Nighty-Nightmare; Return to Howliday Inn; Bunnicula Strikes Again; Bunnicula Meets Edgar Allan Crow. Payne, C. F., illus. (p. 242)
—Bunnicula Meets Edgar Allan Crow. Fortune, Eric, illus. (p. 242)
—Bunnicula Strikes Again! (p. 242)
—Bunnicula Strikes Again! Daniel, Alan, illus. (p. 242)
—Celery Stalks at Midnight. (p. 285)
—Celery Stalks at Midnight. Morrill, Leslie H., illus. (p. 285)
—Color of Absence: 12 Stories about Loss & Hope. (p. 343)
—Creepy-Crawly Birthday. Mack, Jeff, illus. (p. 381)
—Fright Before Christmas. Mack, Jeff, illus. (p. 639)
—Harold & Chester Stories. (p. 749)
—Horace & Morris but Mostly Dolores. Walrod, Amy, illus. (p. 797)
—Horace & Morris, but Mostly Dolores. Waldrod, Amy, illus. (p. 797)
—Horace & Morris Join the Chorus (but What about Dolores?) Walrod, Amy, illus. (p. 797)
—Horace & Morris Say Cheese (Which Makes Dolores Sneeze!) Walrod, Amy, illus. (p. 797)
—Hot Fudge. Mack, Jeff, tr. (p. 801)
—Hot Fudge. Mack, Jeff, illus. (p. 801)
—Houndsley & Catina. (p. 802)
—Houndsley & Catina. Gay, Marie-Louise, illus. (p. 802)
—Houndsley & Catina & the Birthday Surprise. Gay, Marie-Louise, illus. (p. 802)
—Houndsley & Catina & the Quiet Time. Gay, Marie-Louise, illus. (p. 802)
—Houndsley & Catina Plink & Plunk. Gay, Marie-Louise, illus. (p. 802)
—Howie Monroe & the Doghouse of Doom. (p. 823)
—Howie Monroe & the Doghouse of Doom. Helquist, Brett, illus. (p. 823)
—Howie Monroe & the Screaming Mummies of the Pharoah's Tomb II. (p. 823)
—Howliday Inn. (p. 824)
—Howliday Inn. Munsinger, Lynn, illus. (p. 824)
—Invasion of the Mind Swappers from Asteroid 6! (p. 883)
—Invasion of the Mind Swappers from Asteroid 6! Helquist, Brett, illus. (p. 883)
—It Came from Beneath the Bed! (p. 893)
—It Came from Beneath the Bed! Helquist, Brett, illus. (p. 893)
—Misfits. (p. 1150)
—Nighty-Nightmare. (p. 1255)
—Nighty-Nightmare. Morrill, Leslie, illus. (p. 1255)
—Odorous Adventures of Stinky Dog. Helquist, Brett, illus. (p. 1278)
—Otter & Odder: A Love Story. Raschka, Chris, illus. (p. 1307)
—Plink & Plunk. Gay, Marie-Louise, illus. (p. 1374)
—Rabbit-Cadabra! Mack, Jeff, illus. (p. 1429)
—Return to Howliday Inn. (p. 1465)
—Return to Howliday Inn. Daniel, Alan, illus. (p. 1465)
—Scared Silly. Mack, Jeff, illus. (p. 1519)
—Screaming Mummies of the Pharaoh's Tomb II. Helquist, Brett, illus. (p. 1533)
—Totally Joe. (p. 1771)
—Vampire Bunny. Mack, Jeff, illus. (p. 1832)
Howe, James, jt. auth. see Howe, Deborah.
Howe, James & Walrod, Amy. Horace & Morris but Mostly Dolores. Walrod, Amy, illus. (p. 797)
Howe, James, ed. 13: Thirteen Stories That Capture the Agony & Ecstasy of Being Thirteen. (p. 1994)
—Color of Absence: 12 Stories about Loss & Hope. (p. 343)
Howe, John, illus. see Harper, Amelia.
Howe, Katherine. Conversion. (p. 361)
Howe, Katherine, jt. auth. see Edelstein, Judy.
Howe, Kim. American Life Series: Family, Teacher, Friend (p. 62)
Howe, LeAnne. Evidence of Red: Poems & Prose. (p. 546)
Howe, Maggy G. & Bagby, Susan. Magical Future Song. (p. 1074)
Howe, Norma. Adventures of Blue Avenger. (p. 16)
—Angel in Vegas: The Chronicles of Noah Sark. (p. 73)
Howe, Norma, illus. see Tye, Peter.
Howe, Peter. Waggit Again. Rayyan, Omar, illus. (p. 1852)
—Waggit Forever. Rayyan, Omar, illus. (p. 1852)
—Waggit's Tale. Rayyan, Omar, illus. (p. 1852)
—Warriors of the Black Shroud. (p. 1859)
Howe, Philip, illus. see Koss, Amy Goldman.
Howe, Richard. FlameThrowin Fish: Flame Throwin Fish. (p. 602)
Howe, Tina Field. Alysa of the Fields: Book One in the Tellings of Xunar-kun. (p. 51)
—Snailsworth, a slow lttle Story. Howe, Tina Field, illus. (p. 1596)
Howe, Tom. Stonebringer: A Novel of Individuation. (p. 1653)
Howe, Zoë. Stevie Nicks: Visions, Dreams, & Rumors. (p. 1649)
Howell. Wesley-Hampton Academy - The Weatherman. (p. 1876)
Howell, Alice O. Lara's First Christmas. Mailer, Maggie, illus. (p. 975)
Howell, Ann C. & Chandler, Alton. Salute to Black Inventors: Coloring Learning Activities. Vol. 2 Chapman, L., ed. (p. 1506)
Howell, Brian. Amazing Auto Racing Records. (p. 53)
—Amazing Baseball Records. (p. 54)
—Amazing Hockey Records. (p. 54)
—Atlanta Braves. (p. 112)
—Auburn Tigers. (p. 114)
—Chicago Bears. (p. 299)
—Chicago Bulls. (p. 299)
—Colorado Rockies. (p. 343)
—Demolition Derby: Tearing It Up. (p. 426)
—Denver Broncos. (p. 427)
—Denver Nuggets. (p. 427)
—Derek Jeter: Yankee Great. (p. 427)
—Detroit Lions. (p. 431)
—Duke Blue Devils. (p. 489)
—Florida Gators. (p. 607)
—Football. (p. 615)
—Girls' Softball. (p. 680)
—Golf. (p. 696)
—Great Moments in Olympic Snowboarding. (p. 717)
—Green Bay Packers. (p. 721)
—Joe Mauer: All-Star Catcher. (p. 920)
—Kansas City Chiefs. (p. 943)
—Kentucky Wildcats. (p. 949)
—Kung Fu. (p. 968)
—LeBron James: Basketball Icon. (p. 987)
—Masters. (p. 1103)
—Miami Hurricanes. (p. 1134)
—Minnesota Vikings. (p. 1147)
—Monster Trucks: Tearing It Up. (p. 1168)
—Mud Truck Racing: Tearing It Up. (p. 1188)
—New York Yankees. (p. 1248)
—Notre Dame Fighting Irish. (p. 1268)
—Oakland Athletics. (p. 1274)
—Oakland Raiders. (p. 1275)
—Playing Pro Baseball. (p. 1372)
—Rally Car Racing: Tearing It Up. (p. 1437)
—San Diego Chargers. (p. 1510)
—Sports. (p. 1632)
—U. S. Growth & Change in the 19th Century, 1801 to 1861. (p. 1806)
—US Civil War & Reconstruction. (p. 1826)
—U.S. Civil War & Reconstruction. (p. 1826)
—U.S. Growth & Change in the 19th Century. (p. 1826)
—Utah Jazz. (p. 1829)
—You Have Been Invited! Collins Powell, Judy, illus. (p. 1975)
Howell, Brian, jt. auth. see Holder, Larry.
Howell, Catherine. My First Pocket Guide to Backyard Wilderness. Emmett, Jennifer, ed. (p. 1207)
Howell, Catherine H. Flora Mirabilis: How Plants Have Shaped World Knowledge, Health, Wealth, & Beauty. (p. 606)
Howell, Ches Lee. Old Lady's Story. (p. 1284)
Howell, Corin, illus. see Wyatt, Chris
Howell, David. Swan Songs-in Search of the Staffstone. (p. 1688)
Howell, Deanne, jt. auth. see Howell, Dusti.
Howell, Deanne, jt. prod. see Howell, Dusti.
Howell, Des. Abcs of Good Manners. (p. 4)
Howell, Dusti & Howell, Deanne. Vocabbusters SAT Vol. 1: Make vocabulary fun, meaningful & memorable using a multi-sensory Approach (p. 1847)
—Vocabusters SAT: Make Vocabulary Fun, Meaningful & Memorable Using a Multi-sensory Approach. Vol. 2 (p. 1847)
Howell, Dusti & Howell, Deanne, prods. Dr. Wiley Makes Sense. (p. 475)
Howell, Gail L. Sarah & the Blue Sled: Sarah's World (Series) (p. 1514)
—Sarah's World: Sarah Meets her Cousins by the Sea. (p. 1514)
Howell, Gill. Selkie Child. Keen, Sophie, illus. (p. 1550)
—Snow King. Cann, Helen, illus. (p. 1599)
—Tortoise & the Baboon. Woody, illus. (p. 1771)
Howell, Hayley L. Sammy's Two Left Feet: Groovin' with Mr. Smooth: Discovering How to Believe in Yourself. (p. 1508)
Howell, Heather. Emanuele Goes to the Zoo. (p. 517)
—Emily's Ballet Recital. (p. 519)
Howell, Jason W., illus. see Crain, Suzanne L.
Howell, Jennifer. Tracking down the Parts of Speech Game. (p. 1775)
Howell, Jessica. Lilly Lu & the Pink Tutu. (p. 1017)
Howell, John. Life & Adventures of Alexander Selkirk, the Real Robinson Crusoe: A Narrative Founded on Facts. (p. 1007)
Howell, Julie. Pepper Tree, How the Seeds Were Planted! LaGrange, Tiffany, illus. (p. 1340)
Howell, Julie Ann. Finnigan the Dragon. Zamboni, David, illus. (p. 589)
—Mrs Owl's Nest of Rhymes. LaGrange, Tiffany, illus. (p. 1187)
—Pepper Tree, How the Seeds Were Planted! LaGrange, Tiffany, illus. (p. 1340)
—Tooth Be Told. Cotton, Sue Lynn, illus. (p. 1768)
Howell, Kathy. Skoob: The Kingdom Awaits. (p. 1586)
—Skoob. Linton, Vera, illus. (p. 1586)
Howell, Keith, tr. see Dickens, Charles.
Howell, Keith, tr. see Shakespeare, William & McDonald, John.
Howell, Keith, tr. see Shakespeare, William.
Howell, Laura. Gerbils. Fox, Christyan, illus. (p. 666)
—Guinea Pigs. Fox, Christyan, illus. (p. 731)
—Hundreds of Silly Jokes. (p. 827)
—Introduction to Weather & Climate Change. (p. 882)
—Introduction to Weather & Climate Change. Furnival, Keith, illus. (p. 882)
—Monkeys Sticker Book. (p. 1166)
—Princess & the Pea. (p. 1402)
Howell, Laura, jt. auth. see Smith, Alastair.
Howell, Laura & Gareth Stevens Editorial Staff. Weather & Climate. (p. 1869)
Howell, Laura & Rogers, Kirsteen. Animal World. (p. 80)
—Earth & Space. (p. 495)
—World of Plants. (p. 1957)
Howell, Laura, ed. Animal Jokes. Rolland, Leonard Le, illus. (p. 78)
—Jokes. (p. 924)
—Usborne Book of Really Awful Jokes: About School & Other Stuff. Le Rolland, Leonard, illus. (p. 1827)
—Usborne Book of Silly Jokes. Le Rolland, Leonard, illus. (p. 1827)
Howell, Lauren. If I Was the Mayor. Dawson, Sheldon, illus. (p. 853)
Howell, Maria L. Catholicism. (p. 280)
—Divorce & Children. (p. 455)
Howell, Maria L., ed. Emancipation Proclamation. (p. 517)
Howell, Mark & Montgomery, Martha. Be Prepared for the AP Calculus Exam. Gary, Litvin, ed. (p. 149)
Howell, Richard, jt. illus. see Milgrom, Al.
Howell, Robert. Third Times the Charm. (p. 1734)
Howell, Ruth. Fairy Friends. Bachmann, B. L., illus. (p. 563)
Howell, Sara. American Revolution: Frontline Soldiers & Their Families. (p. 63)
—Camino a la Ciudadanía. (p. 256)
—Civil War: Frontline Soldiers & Their Families. (p. 325)
—Famous Immigrants & Their Stories. (p. 569)
—Fireflies (p. 592)
—First-Generation Americans. (p. 595)
—How Do Animals Communicate? (p. 806)
—Immigrants' Rights, Citizens' Rights. (p. 861)
—Inmigrantes Famosos y Sus Historias. (p. 875)
—Lantern Fish (p. 975)
—Los Derechos de Los Inmigrantes, Los Derechos de Los Ciudadanos. (p. 1053)
—Los Inmigrantes Indocumentados. (p. 1054)
—Los Refugiados. (p. 1054)
—Path to Citizenship. (p. 1328)
—Primera Generación de Estadounidenses. (p. 1400)
—Refugees. (p. 1456)
—Undocumented Immigrants. (p. 1817)
Howell, Theresa. A Is for Airplane. Brooks, David, illus. (p. 1)
Howell, Theresa, jt. auth. see Campoy, F. Isabel.
Howell, Theresa, ed. Baby Animals of the Southwest. (p. 124)
Howell, Trisha Adelena. Addie, the Playful Pekingese. Hohn, David, illus. (p. 11)
—Adventures of Melon & Turnip. Lopez, Paul, illus. (p. 20)
—Poopy Pekinese. Marshall, Jamie, illus. (p. 1383)
—Princess & the Pekinese. (p. 1403)
—Stinky Shepherd. Marshall, Jamie, illus. (p. 1651)
—Talia & the Great Sapphire of Knowledge. Hohn, David, illus. (p. 1703)
Howell, Troy. Dragon of Cripple Creek. (p. 477)
—First Prayers: A Celebration of Faith & Love. (p. 596)
Howell, Troy, illus. see Bates, Katharine Lee & Bates, Katharine.
Howell, Troy, illus. see Burnett, Frances Hodgson.
Howell, Troy, illus. see Cooper, James Fenimore.
Howell, Troy, illus. see Dumas, Alexandre.
Howell, Troy, illus. see Edwards, Pamela Duncan.
Howell, Troy, illus. see Friddell, Claudia.

H

Howell, Troy, illus. see Leroux, Gaston.
Howell, Troy, illus. see Rubin, Susan Goldman.
Howell, Troy, illus. see Wells, H. G.
Howell, Vickie. Finger Knitting Fun: 30 Cute, Clever, & Creative Projects for Kids. (p. 589)
Howells, Amanda. Summer of Skinny Dipping. (p. 1674)
Howells, Andrea. Finding Peace & the True Soul. (p. 588)
Howells, Angela. Tails of Victoria Way. (p. 1695)
Howells, Graham, illus. see Meek, Elin.
Howells, Graham, illus. see Randall, Daniel & Randall, Ronne.
Howells, Graham, illus. see Randall, Ronne.
Howells, Graham, illus. see West, Tracey.
Howells, Mike. Gettysburg College College Prowler off the Record. (p. 670)
Howells, Shelley. Making Sense of Your Senses: Set Of 6. (p. 1082)
—Making Sense of Your Senses & Tus sentidos tienen Sentido: 6 English, 6 Spanish Adaptations. (p. 1082)
Howells, Tania, illus. see Button, Lana.
Howells, Tania, illus. see Johnson, Tera.
Howells, William Dean. Christmas Every Day. (p. 313)
—Christmas Every Day & Other Stories. (p. 313)
Hower, Fred & Beck, Alison. Tree & Shrub Gardening for Ohio (p. 1783)
Howerton, James. Blue River Valley. (p. 203)
Howerton Moore, Donna. Billy the Bully's Big Awakening. (p. 187)
Howerton-Willis, Deborah. Amos the Aardvark. (p. 65)
Howes, Bryan Arthur, illus. see Coughlin, Jennie Rose.
Howes, Kelly King & Baker, Lawrence W. Almanac, Reconstruction Era. (p. 48)
Howes, Kelly King & Carnagie, Julie L. Roaring Twenties Almanac & Primary Sources. (p. 1478)
—Roaring Twenties Biographies. (p. 1478)
Howey, Bill. Actor's Menu: A Character Preparation Handbook. (p. 10)
Howey, Paul M. Freckles: The Mystery of the Little White Dog in the Desert. Zabriskie, Judy Mehn, illus. (p. 632)
Howie, Betsy. Unscripted by Lainey McBride. Lowery, Mike, illus. (p. 1822)
Howie, Vicki. Easter Swallows. Grudina, Paola Bertolini, illus. (p. 499)
—Have You Seen Christmas? Pedlar, Caroline, illus. (p. 754)
—Silent Night. Kallai, Kriszta Nagy, illus. (p. 1575)
—Story Plays for Christmas: Three Plays Complete with Stories & Interactive Activities. Doggett, Sue, ed. (p. 1663)
Howie, Vickie. Knock, Knock! Who's There at Christmas? MacLean, Moira, illus. (p. 965)
Howie, Vickie & MacLean, Moira. Easter Surprise: A Lift-the-Flap Board Book. (p. 499)
Howie, Vicky & MacLean, Moira. Cnoc, Cnoc! Pwy Sy 'Na? Llyfr Fflapiau Stori'r Nadolig. Wyn, Delyth, tr. from ENG. (p. 336)
Howington, C. D. Aunt Cindy's House. (p. 115)
Howitt, Carolyn. British Museum Quiz Book. (p. 230)
Howitt, Jeri. Tale of Two Loves. (p. 1700)
Howitt, Mary. Spider & the Fly: 10th Anniversary Edition. DiTerlizzi, Tony, illus. (p. 1626)
Howitt, Mary Botham. Strive & Thrive a Tale by Mary Howitt. (p. 1668)
Howker, Janni. Tejon de la Barca: Y Otras Historias. Tovar Cross, Juan Elias, tr. (p. 1716)
—Walk with a Wolf: Read, Listen & Wonder. Fox-Davies, Sarah, illus. (p. 1854)
Howland, Ashley. Ghostnapped. (p. 672)
—Homework Goblin. (p. 794)
—Obi the Super Puppy & the Mystery of the Red Mist. (p. 1275)
Howland, Leila. Forget-Me-Not Summer. Kim, Ji-Hyuk, illus. (p. 619)
—Nantucket Blue. (p. 1229)
—Nantucket Red. (p. 1229)
Howland, Michele. Flying Boy (p. 609)
Howland, Naomi. Better-Than-Best Purim (p. 172)
—Latkes, Latkes, Good to Eat: A Chanukah Story. (p. 980)
—Latkes, Latkes, Good to Eat Send-A-Story. (p. 980)
—Princess Says Goodnight. Small, David, illus. (p. 1405)
Howland, Naomi, illus. see Adelson, Leone.
Howland, Naomi, illus. see Dewhurst, Carin.
Howland, Naomi, tr. see Adelson, Leone.
Howlett, Bruce & Pitcher, Jeff, creators. Hop, Skip & Jump into Reading Software: For Six Students. (p. 796)
—Hop, Skip & Jump into Reading Software: For Two Students. (p. 796)
Howlett, Bruce, et al. Hop, Skip & Jump into Reading. Pitcher, Jeff, illus. (p. 796)
Howlett, Winston A., jt. auth. see Lorrah, Jean.
Howling, Adam, illus. see Swatman, Simon.
Howling, Eric. Drive (p. 485)
—Hoop Magic (p. 795)
—Kayak Combat (p. 946)
—Red Zone Rivals (p. 1455)
Howse, Emily. Zitface (p. 1987)
Howse, Jennifer. Boxing Day: Canadian Celebrations. (p. 217)
—British Museum. (p. 230)
—Civil War. (p. 325)
—Crabs. (p. 375)
—Great Synagogue of Budapest. (p. 718)
—Inclined Planes. (p. 869)
—Lendemain de Noël: Les Célébrations Canadiennes. Karvonen, Tanjah, tr. from ENG. (p. 991)
—Levers. (p. 1003)
—Louvre. (p. 1059)
—Manning Brothers. (p. 1088)
—Métis: Les Autochtones du Canada. Karvonen, Tanjah, tr. from ENG. (p. 1130)
—Miley Cyrus. (p. 1142)
—NASCAR Sprint Cup. (p. 1230)
—Neuschwanstein Castle. (p. 1242)
—Ours Esprit: Les Animaux du Canada. Karvonen, Tanjah, tr. from ENG. (p. 1310)
—Palace of Versailles. (p. 1319)
—Reconstruction. (p. 1452)
—Rihanna: Remarkable People. (p. 1472)
—Sandra Day O'Connor. (p. 1511)
—Spirit Bears. (p. 1628)
—Sports: African American History. (p. 1632)
—State Hermitage Museum. (p. 1644)
—Totem Poles: Canadian Icons. (p. 1771)
—Totems: Les Emblèmes Canadiens. McMann, Julie, tr. from ENG. (p. 1772)
—Trees. (p. 1784)
—Wedges. (p. 1871)
Howse, Jennifer & Kissock, Heather. Métis. (p. 1130)
Howson, Imogen. Linked. (p. 1019)
—Unravel. (p. 1822)
Howson, Imogen & Smith, Ali. Linked. (p. 1019)
Howver, Jen, et al. Wisdom on ... Getting along with Parents (p. 1939)
Hoyes, Amy & Reimann, A. J. Happy the Hippo: Eats Healthy Food. Stewart, K. L., illus. (p. 747)
Hoyes, Kerry, illus. see Yanisko, Thomas.
Hoyland, Christa. Beautiful Butterfly. (p. 153)
Hoyle, Geoffrey. 2011: Living in the Future. Anderson, Alasdair, illus. (p. 2003)
Hoyle, K. B. Scroll. (p. 1533)
—Six. (p. 1582)
Hoyle, R. L. Peru. (p. 1345)
Hoyle, Tom. Thirteen. (p. 1734)
Hoylie, Gerry. Byron Unleashed. (p. 249)
Hoyos, Hector. Siete Mejores Cuentos Chinos. Cuellar, Olga, illus. (p. 1573)
Hoyt, Ard, illus. see Anderson, Laurie Halse.
Hoyt, Ard, illus. see Brendler, Carol & Brendler, Carol H.
Hoyt, Ard, illus. see Casanova, Mary.
Hoyt, Ard, illus. see Demas, Corinne.
Hoyt, Ard, illus. see Kennedy Center Staff.
Hoyt, Ard, illus. see Kidd, Ronald, et al.
Hoyt, Ard, illus. see Layne, Steven L.
Hoyt, Ard, illus. see Lithgow, John.
Hoyt, Ard, illus. see Meadows, Michelle.
Hoyt, Ard, illus. see Sadler, Marilyn.
Hoyt, Ard, illus. see Shannon, Molly.
Hoyt, Ard, illus. see Skeers, Linda.
Hoyt, Ard, illus. see Spradlin, Michael P.
Hoyt, Ard, illus. see Weis, Carol.
Hoyt, Beth Caldwell & Ritter, Erica. Ultimate Girls' Guide to Science: From Backyard Experiments to Winning the Nobel Prize. Palen, Debbie, illus. (p. 1809)
Hoyt, Charlene. Where the Leprechauns Hide. Fischer, Sandi, illus. (p. 1909)
Hoyt, Elizabeth. Raven Prince. (p. 1441)
Hoyt, Erich. Weird Sea Creatures. (p. 1872)
—Whale Rescue: Changing the Future for Endangered Wildlife. (p. 1877)
Hoyt, Holly. Purple Widow. (p. 1419)
Hoyt, Kathleen. Kerloon & Cooley. (p. 949)
Hoyt, Linda & Therriault, Teresa. Mastering the Mechanics: Ready-to-Use Lessons for Modeled, Guided, & Independent Editing. (p. 1103)
Hoyt, Megan. Hildegard's Gift. Hill, David, illus. (p. 779)
Hoyt, Peggy R., jt. auth. see Farnsworth, Scott.
Hoyt, Richard, photos by see Ahouse, Jeremy John & Barber, Jacqueline.
Hoyt, Richard, photos by see Barber, Jacqueline.
Hoyt, Richard, photos by see Echols, Jean C.
Hoyt, Richard, photos by see Erickson, John & Willard, Carolyn.
Hoyt, Richard, photos by see Glaser, David, et al.
Hoyt, Richard, photos by see Gould, Alan.
Hoyt, Richard, photos by see Sutter, Debra, et al.
Hoyt, Sarah, et al, eds. Something Magic This Way Comes. (p. 1610)
Hoyte, Carol-Ann. And the Crowd Goes Wild! A Global Gathering of Sports Poems. Roemer, Heidi Bee, ed. (p. 71)
Hoyt-Goldsmith, Diane. Celebrating Chinese New Year. Migdale, Lawrence, photos by. (p. 284)
—Cinco de Mayo: Celebrating the Traditions of Mexico. Migdale, Lawrence, illus. (p. 319)
—Three Kings Day: A Celebration at Christmastime. Migdale, Lawrence, illus. (p. 1742)
Hozjan, Michael. Adventures of Tibo & Friends. (p. 24)
Hrachovec, Anna. Adventures in Mochimochi Land: Tall Tales from a Tiny, Knitted World. (p. 15)
Hranilovich, Barbara, illus. see Hornsby, Ashley Brooke.
Hranilovich, Barbara, illus. see Newell, Jeff.
Hrdlicka, Ales. Melanesians & Australians & the Peopling of America. (p. 1125)
—Recent Discoveries Attributed to Early Man in America. (p. 1451)
—Report on an Additional Collection of Skeletal Remains, from Arkansas & Louisiana: Made, & Presented to the Naional Museum in 1909, by Mr. Clarence B. Moore by Dr. Ales Hrdlicka. (p. 1461)
Hrdlitschka, Shelley. Allegra (p. 46)
—Gotcha! (p. 704)
—Kat's Fall (p. 945)
—Kat's Fall. (p. 945)
—Sister Wife (p. 1581)
—Sun Signs (p. 1676)
Hren, Andrea. Max's Special Birthday Gift. (p. 1112)
HRH Prince of Wales Staff, jt. auth. see Prince of Wales Publishing Co. Staff.
Hritzay, Tami. Hole in the Wall: J. B. & the Pirates. (p. 788)
Hronas, Georgia. Tell Us a Story, Grandma: More of Grandma's Orthodox Spiritual Stories. (p. 1717)
Hru, Dakari. Joshua's Masai Mask. Rich, Anna, illus. (p. 927)
Hruby, Emily. Counting in the Garden. Hruby, Patrick, illus. (p. 371)
Hruby, Emily, jt. auth. see Hruby, Patrick.
Hruby, Patrick. ABC Is for Circus. (p. 3)
—ABC Is for Circus (Chunky) (p. 3)
—Natural Wonders: A Patrick Hruby Coloring Book. (p. 1236)
Hruby, Patrick, illus. see Hruby, Emily.
Hruby, Patrick & Hruby, Emily. Counting in the Garden. (p. 371)
Hrutkay, Leigh Ann. Rise & Shine, Little Child. (p. 1474)
Hsia, Pei Chen. Little Dumpling. (p. 1027)
Hsiao, Christie. Journey to Rainbow Island. (p. 929)
HSP Staff. Band of Angels Challenge Trade Book Grade 2: Harcourt School Publishers Storytown. (p. 136)
—Eager Challenge Trade Book Grade 6: Harcourt School Publishers Storytown. (p. 492)
—Grandpa Stre Challenge Trade Book Grade 2: Harcourt School Publishers Storytown. (p. 709)
—Loser Challenge Trade Book Grade 6: Harcourt School Publishers Storytown. (p. 1054)
—My Rows & Cns Challenge Trade Book Grade 2: Harcourt School Publishers Storytown. (p. 1218)
Hsu, Florence, illus. see Keay, Ben.
Hsu, Jack, illus. see Yeh, Julie.
Hsu, Kim & Benchmark Education Co., LLC Staff. Read a USA Time Line. (p. 1442)
Hsu, Lewis. Hope & Destiny Jr: The Adolescent's Guide to Sickle Cell Diseases. (p. 796)
Hsu, Stacey W. Old Mo. Ritter, Adam, illus. (p. 1284)
Hsu, Yi Ling. Typhoon Holidays: Taiwan. Cowley, Joy, ed. (p. 1805)
Hsuan Hua. Buddha's Wisdom. Yeh, Alicia, illus. (p. 234)
—Dew Drops: Pearls of Wisdom by the Venerable Master Hua = [Zhao Lu: Xuanhuashangren Yi Li Ming Zhu]. (p. 432)
Hu, Bin, tr. see Crouch, Adele.
Hu, Caroline, illus. see Gunderson, Jessica.
Hu, Caroline, illus. see Pelleschi, Andrea.
Hu, Caroline, illus. see Robinson, Joanna Jarc.
Hu, Jennifer. Dodo's Story: Journey in America. (p. 460)
Hu, Lorna. Pili the 'Iwa Bird Shares the Letter B: Book #1 in the Gift of Reading Series. Omoto, Garrett, illus. (p. 1359)
Hu, Vicky. Muses: Greek Mythology (Mitologia Griega) (p. 1192)
—Titans & Cyclops/ Titanes y Ciclopes. (p. 1758)
Hu, Ying-Hwa, illus. see Black, Sonia W.
Hu, Ying-Hwa, illus. see Bridges, Ruby & Maccarone, Grace.
Hu, Ying-Hwa, illus. see Chinn, Karen.
Hu, Ying-Hwa, illus. see da Costa, Deborah.
Hu, Ying-Hwa, illus. see Hoffman, Mary.
Hu, Ying-Hwa, illus. see Medearis, Angela Shelf.
Hu, Ying-Hwa, illus. see Pringle, Laurence.
Hu, Ying-Hwa, illus. see Scholastic, Inc. Staff & Black, Sonia.
Hu, Ying-Hwa, illus. see Scholastic, Inc. Staff & Medearis, Angela Shelf.
Hu, Ying-Hwa, illus. see Schroeder, Alan.
Hu, Ying-Hwa, illus. see Starr, Meg.
Hu, Ying-Hwa, illus. see Wright, Rebecca Hu-Van & Asbjornsen, Peter Christen.
Hu, Ying-Hwa, jt. illus. see Van Wright, Cornelius.
Huadi, illus. see Bornemann, Elsa.
Huadi, illus. see Sugobono, Nahuel.
Hualde, Antonio C. Confirmacion: Sacramento Del Espiritu. (p. 356)
Huancai, Yang, et al. Drawing Fun: Animals. Liu, Xuemei & Henderson, Ann, eds. (p. 481)
Huang, Benrei, illus. see Bateman, Teresa.
Huang, Benrei, illus. see Heinrichs, Ann.
Huang, Benrei, illus. see Holub, Joan.
Huang, Benrei, illus. see Imperato, Teresa.
Huang, Benrei, illus. see Min, Laura.
Huang, Benrei, illus. see Packard, Mary.
Huang, Benrei, illus. see Simon, Charnan.
Huang, Benrei, illus. see Stohs, Anita Reith.
Huang, Benrei, illus. see Truelt, Trudi Strain.
Huang, Benrei, illus. see Wangerin, Walter, Jr.
Huang, Christine & Nash, Kevin. UC Berkeley College Prowler off the Record: Inside University of California Berkeley. (p. 1807)
Huang, Chungliang Al. Chinese Book of Animal Powers. (p. 307)
Huang, Fannie, ed. Quantum Physics: An Anthology of Current Thought. (p. 1422)
Huang, H Y, illus. see Yang-Huan & Yang-Huan.
Huang, Kathryn, illus. see Lasky, Kathryn.
Huang, Linda & Hoffman, Emily. Why Are You So Strong, Stanley? Stanley Shares with His Friend Walter His Secret to Being Healthy, Happy, & Strong. (p. 1922)
Huang, SuHua. Faithful Reading Partner: A Story from a Hakka Village. (p. 565)
Huang, Yu-Hsuan. Baby Bear: Finger Puppet Book. (p. 125)
—Baby Elephant: Finger Puppet Book. (p. 126)
—Baby Reindeer: Finger Puppet Book. (p. 127)
—Baby Tiger: Finger Puppet Book. (p. 128)
Huat, Tan Eng & Pearson, Jason. Punisher. (p. 1417)
Hub, Ulrich. Be at the Ark by Eight. Mühle, Jörg, illus. (p. 148)
Hub, Ulrich & Ragg-Kirkby, Helena. Becoming the Wolf. Mühle, Jörg, illus. (p. 156)
Hubbard, Ben. Hi Tech World: Cool Stuff. (p. 775)
—Hi Tech World: Code Breakers. (p. 775)
—Hi Tech World: High Level Security. (p. 775)
—History of Pop. (p. 784)
—My Very Own Kitten. Guile, Gill, illus. (p. 1221)
—My Very Own Puppy. Guile, Gill, illus. (p. 1221)
—Neil Armstrong & Getting to the Moon. (p. 1240)
—Top 10 Biggest. (p. 1768)
—Top 10 Longest. (p. 1768)
—Top 10 Smallest. (p. 1768)
—Tornado: Perspectives on Tornado Disasters (p. 1770)
—Yuri Gagarin & the Race to Space. (p. 1983)
Hubbard, Ben, jt. auth. see Cornish, Melanie J.
Hubbard, Ben & Langley, Andrew. Adventures in Space. (p. 15)
Hubbard, Ben, et al. Women's Stories from History. (p. 1947)
Hubbard, Bobbie, jt. auth. see Lindy J.
Hubbard, Crystal. Alive & Unharmed. (p. 41)
—Catching the Moon: The Story of a Young Girl's Baseball Dream Duburke, Randy, illus. (p. 279)
—Catching the Moon: The Story of a Young Girl's Baseball Dream. DuBurke, Randy, illus. (p. 279)
—Last Black King of the Kentucky Derby: The Story of Jimmy Winkfield. McGuire, Robert, illus. (p. 977)
Hubbard, Crystal & Belford, Kevin. Game, Set, Match, Champion Arthur Ashe. (p. 654)
Hubbard, Crystal & McGuire, Robert. Last Black King of the Kentucky Derby. (p. 977)
Hubbard, Diane. Remembering Rachel. (p. 1459)
Hubbard, Elaine. Student Solutions Manual: Used with ... Hubbard-Prealgebra. (p. 1669)
Hubbard, Frances K. & Spencer, Lauren. Writing to Inform. (p. 1965)
Hubbard, Gillian. Stray Puppy's Tale. (p. 1666)
Hubbard, Jennifer. Try Not to Breathe. (p. 1794)
Hubbard, Jenny. And We Stay. (p. 71)
—Paper Covers Rock. (p. 1322)
Hubbard, Jill & McCabe, Ginny. Secrets Young Women Keep (p. 1546)
Hubbard, Jim. Lives Turned Upside Down: Homeless Children in Their Own Words & Photographs. (p. 1040)
Hubbard, Joel D. Prealgebra Math Space. (p. 1394)
Hubbard, Julia, jt. auth. see Reynolds, John.
Hubbard, Kirsten. Like Mandarin. (p. 1017)
—Wanderlove. (p. 1856)
—Watch the Sky. (p. 1861)
Hubbard, L. Ron. All Frontiers Are Jealous. (p. 44)
—Cattle King for a Day. (p. 281)
—Crossroads. (p. 385)
—Destiny's Drum. (p. 431)
—Grammar & Communication for Children. (p. 706)
—Great Secret. (p. 718)
—If I Were You: Literature Guide for Teachers & Librarians, Based on Common Core ELA Standards for Classrooms 6-9 (p. 853)
—Matter of Matter. (p. 1109)
—Orders Is Orders. (p. 1302)
—Sea Fangs. (p. 1534)
—Trail of the Red Diamonds. (p. 1776)
Hubbard, L. Ron, contrib. by. Carnival of Death: Literature Guide for Teachers & Librarians Based on Common Core ELA Standards for Classrooms 6-9. (p. 270)
—Common Core Literature Guide: Dead Men Kill: Literature Guide for Teachers & Librarians Based on Common Core ELA Standards for Classrooms 6-9. (p. 349)
—Crossroads: Literature Guide for Teachers & Librarians, Based on Common Core ELA Standards for Classrooms 6-9. (p. 385)
—If I Were You: Literature Guide for Teachers & Librarians, Based on Common Core ELA Standards for Classrooms 6-9. (p. 853)
—On Blazing Wings: Literature Guide for Teachers & Librarians Based on Common Core ELA Standards for Classrooms 6-9. (p. 1288)
—Tomb of the Ten Thousand Dead: Literature Guide for Teachers & Librarians Based on Common Core ELA Standards for Classrooms 6-9. (p. 1764)
—Toughest Ranger: Literature Guide for Teachers & Librarians, Based on Common Core ELA Standards for Classrooms 6-9. (p. 1773)
Hubbard, Mandy. Fool Me Twice: An If Only Novel. (p. 614)
—Fool Me Twice. (p. 614)
—You Wish. (p. 1976)
Hubbard, Margaret Ann. Saint Louis & the Last Crusade. Barton, Harry, illus. (p. 1503)
Hubbard O.D., Kristopher T. Iggie's Telescope. (p. 855)
Hubbard, Rita & Hubbard, Rita Lorraine. Getting a Job in the Food Industry. (p. 669)
Hubbard, Rita L. Getting the Most Out of MOOC: Massive Open Online Courses (p. 669)
—What Degree Do I Need to Pursue a Career in Health Care? (p. 1881)
Hubbard, Rita Lorraine, jt. auth. see Hubbard, Rita.
Hubbard, SharronY. Link & Rosie Pick Berries. Schleihs, Krostin, illus. (p. 1019)
—Link & Rosie's Pets. Schleihs, Kristin, illus. (p. 1019)
—Rosie's New Bike. Schleihs, Kristin, illus. (p. 1490)
Hubbard, Sue. Ghost Station. (p. 671)
Hubbard, Suzanna. Lady Who Lived in a Car. (p. 971)
—Lady Who Lived in a Car. Hubbard, Suzanna, illus. (p. 971)
Hubbard-Brown, Janet. Abigail Adams: First Lady. (p. 5)
—Chaucer: Celebrated Poet & Author. (p. 295)
—Condoleezza Rice: Stateswoman. (p. 356)
—Eleanor Roosevelt: First Lady. (p. 508)
—How the Constitution Was Created. (p. 813)
—Joan of Arc. (p. 919)
—Labonte Brothers. (p. 969)
—Ray Charles. (p. 1441)
—Scott Joplin: Composer. (p. 1531)
—Shirin Ebadi: Champion for Human Rights in Iran. (p. 1567)
—Tina Fey. (p. 1755)
Hubbell, jt. auth. see Hubbell, Patricia.
Hubbell, Mary A. Miracle of Annie's Ring. (p. 1148)
Hubbell, Patricia. Black All Around! Tate, Don, illus. (p. 194)
—Boats: Speeding! Sailing! Cruising! Halsey, Megan & Addy, Sean, illus. (p. 205)
—Cars: Rushing! Honking! Zooming! Halsey, Megan & Addy, Sean, illus. (p. 272)
—Check It Out! Reading, Finding, Helping Speir, Nancy, illus. (p. 295)
—Every Orchard Tree. Broxon, Janet, illus. (p. 543)
—Firefighters! Speeing! Spraying! Saving! Garofoli, Viviana, illus. (p. 591)
—Firefighters! Speeding! Spraying! Saving! Garofoli, Viviana, illus. (p. 591)
—Horses: Trotting! Prancing! Racing! Mathieu, Joe, illus. (p. 800)
—Hurray for Spring. Morley, Taia, illus. (p. 829)
—My First Airplane Ride Speir, Nancy, illus. (p. 1204)
—Papa Fish's Lullaby. Eaddy, Susan, illus. (p. 1322)
—Shaggy Dogs, Waggy Dogs Wu, Donald, illus. (p. 1558)
—Snow Happy! Nakata, Hiroe, illus. (p. 1599)
—Teacher! Sharing, Helping, Caring Speir, Nancy, illus. (p. 1709)
—Trains: Steaming! Pulling! Huffing! (p. 1777)
—Trucks: Whizz! Zoom! Rumble! Halsey, Megan, illus. (p. 1791)
Hubbell, Patricia & Hubbell. Boo! Halloween Poems & Limericks Spackman, Jeff, illus. (p. 209)
Hubbell, Patricia & Tate, Don. Black All Around! (p. 194)
Hubbell, Will. Apples Here! (p. 93)

Hubble, Meagan R. Where Your Underwear Goes. (p. 1910)
Hubble, Miles & Bryant, Justin. Bob & the Fowl War: Book One in the Poultry Series. (p. 205)
Hubbs, Brian. Mountain Kings: A Collective Natural History of California, Sonoran, Durango & Queretaro Mountain Kingsnakes (p. 1181)
Hubbs, M. E. Secret of Wattensaw Bayou. Lyndon, Tracy S., illus. (p. 1543)
Hubenthal, Dayna, illus. see Fey, Jaki.
Huber, Becca, illus. see Sugg, Nan.
Huber, Jim, illus. see Chambers, Cindy & Demme, Tina.
Huber, Joe M., des. Ice Cream. (p. 850)
Huber, Joyce, illus. see Lofting, Hugh.
Huber, June, illus. see Cameron, Anne.
Huber, Mike. All in One Day. Cowman, Joseph, illus. (p. 44)
—Amazing Erik. Cowman, Joseph, illus. (p. 54)
—Bree Finds a Friend. Cowman, Joseph, illus. (p. 226)
—Evette's Invitation. Cowman, Joseph, illus. (p. 546)
—Mama's Gloves. Cowman, Joseph, illus. (p. 1084)
—Rita & the Firefighters. Cowman, Joseph, illus. (p. 1475)
Huber, Morgan. Nanite. (p. 1229)
Huber, Randolph. Monsters from the ID. (p. 1169)
Huber, Randy. Of Heroes & Heroines. (p. 1279)
Huber, Raymond. Flight of the Honey Bee. Lovelock, Brian, illus. (p. 604)
Huberman, Leo. Bienes Terrenales del Hombre. (p. 177)
—Man's Worldly Goods - the Story of the W. (p. 1088)
Hubert. Adrian & the Tree of Secrets. Caillou, Marie, illus. (p. 13)
Hubert, Jerry. They Were Not Gods: A Space-Age Fairytale. (p. 1732)
Hubert, Marie-Luce, illus. see Frattini, Stephane.
Hubert, Marie-Luce, photos by see Tracqui, Valérie.
Huberts, Al. Hockey Canada's Learn All about Hockey: Color & Activity. Bailey, Frank, illus. (p. 786)
—Learn All about Soccer: Color & Activity. Bailey, Frank, illus. (p. 982)
Hubery, Julia. My Daddy. Elliot, Rebecca, illus. (p. 1201)
—When Grandma Saved Christmas. Pedler, Caroline, illus. (p. 1902)
Hubler, Marsha. Blue Ribbon Champ (p. 203)
—Horse to Love (p. 800)
—Leading the Way (p. 982)
—Long Ride Home (p. 1047)
—On the Victory Trail (p. 1291)
—Southern Belle's Special Gift (p. 1617)
—Summer Camp Adventure (p. 1674)
—Whispering Hope (p. 1912)
Hubner, Carol Korb. Devora Doresh Mysteries. (p. 432)
—Devora Doresh Mysteries 2. (p. 432)
Hubner, Franz. Moaning Morris. Kessler, Mario, illus. (p. 1157)
Hubner, Franz & Franz, Hübner. Abuelita. (p. 7)
Hubner, Marie. Call Me Jacob! Wolfermann, Iris, illus. (p. 254)
Huchel, Gerald. She-Devil the Sassy Kitten. (p. 1564)
Huchel, Gerald D. She-Devil & the Pup. (p. 1564)
Huchthausen, Peter. America's Splendid Little Wars: A Short History of U. S. Engagements from the Fall of Saigon to Baghdad. (p. 64)
Huck, Jeremy. Charlie, the Christmas Caterpillar. (p. 293)
—Charlie, the Christmas Caterpillar, & Marvin Mouse. (p. 293)
Huckaby, Anna Sixkiller, tr. see Rumford, James.
Huckaby, Fred. Evolving Behind Water. (p. 547)
Huckeby, Ed. Judy Plays the Tuba, Johnny Plays the Flute. (p. 931)
Huckin, Amanda. Grandma's Garden. (p. 708)
Huckin, J. J. Inspire. Huckin, J. J., photos by. (p. 878)
Huckleberry, Alyssa. Rescuing Racei. (p. 1462)
Hucklesby, Jill. Samphire Song. (p. 1508)
Hucks, Doris. I Am a Shining Star. (p. 832)
—Quackie the Bunny. (p. 1422)
Hucks, Robin, ed. see Locke, Terry.
Hudak, Heather C. Air Pollution. (p. 31)
—Air Pollution with Code. (p. 31)
—Alligators. (p. 47)
—Australia. (p. 116)
—Banking. (p. 136)
—Bears. (p. 151)
—Bees. (p. 157)
—Birds. (p. 191)
—BMX. (p. 204)
—Butterflies. (p. 247)
—Caring for Your Chinchilla. (p. 269)
—Carnivores. (p. 270)
—Cattle. (p. 281)
—Chickens. (p. 300)
—Chinchilla. (p. 307)
—Dragonflies. (p. 478)
—Ducks. (p. 488)
—Eagles. (p. 492)
—Election Day. (p. 508)
—Election Day with Code. (p. 508)
—Fireflies. (p. 592)
—Fish. (p. 598)
—Goats. (p. 687)
—Grasshoppers. (p. 711)
—Hummingbirds. (p. 826)
—Insects. (p. 875)
—Land Mammals. (p. 973)
—Llamas. (p. 1043)
—Mapping. (p. 1090)
—Marine Mammals. (p. 1094)
—MotoX. (p. 1180)
—Oceans. (p. 1277)
—Omnivores. (p. 1288)
—Oprah Winfrey. (p. 1301)
—Pigs. (p. 1358)
—Ponies. (p. 1382)
—Praying Mantises. (p. 1393)
—Reptiles & Amphibians. (p. 1461)
—Robins: Watch Them Grow. (p. 1480)
—Roles & Responsibilities of Canadian Citizens: Government of Canada. (p. 1485)
—Sheep. (p. 1564)
—Spending. (p. 1625)
—Thumbelina. (p. 1745)

—Wolves. (p. 1944)
Hudak, Heather C., ed. see Bekkering, Annalise.
Hudak, Heather C., ed. see Diemer, Lauren.
Hudak, Heather C., ed. see Hurtig, Jennifer.
Hudak, Heather C., ed. see Webster, Christine.
Hudak, Heather C., jt. auth. see Heather C Hudak.
Hudak, Heather C., jt. auth. see Lupo, Tamar.
Hudak, Heather C., ed. Alligators. (p. 47)
—Bears. (p. 151)
—Bees. (p. 157)
—Eagles. (p. 492)
—Federal Government. (p. 580)
—Hummingbirds. (p. 826)
—Roles & Responsibilities of Canadian Citizens: Government of Canada. (p. 1485)
—Wolves. (p. 1944)
Hudak, Michal. Uproar at Bethlehem. (p. 1825)
Huddle, Lorena & Schleifer, Jay. Teen Suicide. (p. 1714)
Huddle, Rusty & Viegas, Jennifer. Eye in 3D. (p. 557)
Huddleston, Courtney, illus. see Ford, Adam B.
Huddleston, Courtney, illus. see Jolley, Dan.
Huddleston, Courtney, illus. see Scalera, Buddy.
Huddleston, Courtney, illus. see Schweizer, Chris.
Huddleston, Courtney, illus. see Williams, Eli & Jensen, Donald D.
Huddleston, Courtney, illus. see Young, J. E.
Huddleston, Courtney & Zirkel, Scott. Bit Haywire. Huddleston, Courtney, illus. (p. 194)
Hudec-Ignatescu, Donna. Time Out. (p. 1752)
Hudecki, Peter, illus. see Goertzen, Glenda.
Hudgens, Melica. Film Flam & Other Such Gobbledygook. (p. 604)
Hudgins, Andrew, ed. see Agee, James.
Hudgins, Ellis A. Good Man Who Came Out of Nazareth: A Biography of Jesus for Young Teen Readers. (p. 698)
Hudgins, Larry. My Dog Spike (p. 1202)
Hudgins, Mary Jane. Quacker Jack the Duck (p. 1422)
—Town of Nowhere Hudgins, Tim, illus. (p. 1773)
Hudgins, Tim, illus. see Hudgins, Mary Jane.
Hudicourt, Caroline. Mango for Grandpa. Sainsilus, Ismer, illus. (p. 1087)
Hudinger, Paul Edward. Controllers & Rollers: Do You Control or Roll. (p. 361)
Hudnall, Ken. Manhattan Conspiracy: Angel of Death. (p. 1087)
—Northwood Conspiracy. (p. 1266)
—Occult Connection: The Hidden Race. (p. 1275)
—Occult Connection: UFOs, Secret Societies & Ancient Gods (p. 1275)
—Spirits of the Border: History & Mystery of el Paso Del Norte. (p. 1629)
—Spirits of the Border: The History & Mystery of Fort Bliss Hudnall, Ken, photos by. (p. 1629)
—Spirits of the Border: The History & Mystery of New Mexico (p. 1629)
—Spirits of the Border: The History & Mystery of the Rio Grande (p. 1629)
Hudnall, Ken & Hudnall, Sharon. Spirits of the Border: The History & Mystery of New Mexico. (p. 1629)
Hudnall, Ken & Wang, Connie. Spirits of the Border: History & Mystery of el Paso Del Norte (p. 1629)
Hudnall, Ken, told to. Where No Car Has Gone Before. (p. 1909)
Hudnall, Sharon, jt. auth. see Hudnall, Ken.
Hudon-Verrelli, Jacqueline, illus. see Larsen, Andrew.
Hudrisier, Cecile, illus. see Ledu, Stephanie.
Hudrisier, Cecile, illus. see Ledu, Stéphanie.
Hudson. God Gave Me. (p. 688)
Hudson, Amanda. Michelle Obama. (p. 1135)
—This Is My Ball. (p. 1736)
—This Is My Bear. (p. 1736)
—This Is My Book. (p. 1736)
—This Is My Book/Este Es Mi Libro. (p. 1736)
—This Is My Truck. (p. 1736)
—This Is My Truck (Este es mi Camión) (p. 1736)
—This Is My Truck/Este Es Mi Camión. (p. 1736)
Hudson, Amanda, jt. auth. see Derzipliski, Kathleen.
Hudson, Amanda & Hicks, Terry Allan. Maine. (p. 1077)
Hudson, Amanda & Nations, Susan. This Is My Ball/Esta es mi Pelota. (p. 1736)
—This Is My Bear: Este Es Mi Oso. (p. 1736)
—This Is My Bear/Este Es Mi Oso. (p. 1736)
Hudson, Angus. Historias Favoritas de la Biblia (Favorite Bible Stories) (p. 782)
—Localiza la Diferencia (Find the Difference) Parabolas Que Jesus Relato. (p. 1044)
—Nacimiento Especial (Special Birthday) (p. 1227)
Hudson, Annabel, illus. see Goodings, Christina.
Hudson, Annabel, illus. see Goodings, Christina.
Hudson, Arthur K. Lonesome Gnome. Whittemore, Constance, illus. (p. 1046)
Hudson, B. Saint Tamika & Josh: Heaven & Christmas. (p. 1504)
—Saint Tamika & Josh: Jamaica & the African Safari. (p. 1504)
Hudson, Brett, illus. see George, Olivia.
Hudson, Brett, illus. see Hartman, Bob.
Hudson, Brett, jt. auth. see Hartman, Bob.
Hudson, Charlotte & Gormley, Greg. Monkey Words. (p. 1165)
Hudson, Cheryl. Songs I Love to Sing. (p. 1612)
Hudson, Cheryl & Hudson, Wade. My Holy Bible for African-American Children (p. 1211)
Hudson, Cheryl Willis. Book of Opposites. Simpson, Howard, illus. (p. 211)
—Book of Seasons. Simpson, Howard, illus. (p. 211)
—Clothes I Love to Wear: (p. 334)
—Come by Here Lord: Everyday Prayers for Children. (p. 347)
—Construction Zone. Sobol, Richard, photos by. (p. 360)
—Hands Can. (p. 741)
—Hands Can. Bourke, John-Francis, illus. (p. 741)
—Hands Can: Bourke, John-Francis, photos by. (p. 741)
—Las Manos. Bourke, John-Francis, illus. (p. 976)
—Many Colors of Mother Goose. (p. 1089)
—My Friend Maya Loves to Dance. Velasquez, Eric, illus. (p. 1209)
—What to Do When Bad Habits Take Hold: A Kid's Guide to Overcoming Nail Biting & More. Matthews, Bonnie, illus. (p. 1894)
Hudson, Cheryl Willis, jt. auth. see Hudson, Katura J.
Hudson, Cheryl Willis, jt. auth. see Scholastic, Inc. Staff.

Hudson, Christopher. Bible Tell Me - Who: Lessons from Amazing People of the Bible. (p. 176)
Hudson, Cullan. Strange State: Mysteries & legends of Oklahoma. Centennial edition, expanded & Revised Hudson, Cullan, illus. (p. 1665)
Hudson, David L. Gay Rights. (p. 659)
—Juvenile Justice. (p. 941)
—Rights of Students. (p. 1472)
—Smoking Bans. (p. 1595)
Hudson, David L., Jr. Educational Standards. (p. 505)
—Open Government. Marzilli, Alan, ed. (p. 1299)
—Prisoners' Rights. (p. 1407)
Hudson, David L., Jr. & Marzilli, Alan. Child Custody Issues. (p. 301)
Hudson, David W., photos by see Urne, Anne.
Hudson, Don, illus. see Hunter, Erin & Jolley, Dan.
Hudson, Don, illus. see Hunter, Erin.
Hudson, Ella. Hudson Hates School. (p. 824)
Hudson, Finn. Mowing for Money: Relate Area to Multiplication & to Addition. (p. 1184)
Hudson Goff, Elizabeth & Brown, Jonatha A. Ana Frank. (p. 66)
Hudson Goff, Elizabeth & Uschan, Michael V. Ataque a Pearl Harbor. (p. 111)
—ataque a Pearl Harbor (the Bombing of Pearl Harbor) (p. 111)
Hudson Goff, Elizabeth, et al. César Chávez. (p. 288)
Hudson, Iris. Mac & the Messmaker. Smath, Jerry, illus. (p. 1067)
Hudson, Jeffrey, pseud & Crichton, Michael. Case of Need. (p. 273)
Hudson, Judith. Bayo a Good African Boy. (p. 147)
Hudson, Kalyn B. Surfin' Sam Just Will Not Listen. (p. 1685)
Hudson, Karina. My Two Houses. (p. 1220)
Hudson, Katura J. Afro-Bets Quotes for Kids: Words for Kids to Live By. Simpson, Howard, illus. (p. 28)
—I'm a Big Sister Now. (p. 858)
Hudson, Katura J. & Hudson, Cheryl Willis. Langston's Legacy: 101 Ways to Celebrate the Life & Work of Langston Hughes. Hudson, Stephan, photos by. (p. 974)
Hudson, Katy. Bear & Duck. Hudson, Katy, illus. (p. 150)
Hudson, Katy, illus. see Halfmann, Janet.
Hudson, Lauriece. Prayers for the Smallest Hands. (p. 1393)
Hudson, Lisa. Meet Lisa Jo: First Day of School & Words Can Hurt. (p. 1121)
Hudson, Margaret Parker. Blue Umbrella. (p. 203)
Hudson, Marilyn A. Annie Oklahoma: Tales of the Plains. (p. 87)
—Elephant Hips Are Expensive! A Tale of the Sooner State. Fulco, Haley, illus. (p. 511)
—Night Voices: In the dead of Night. (p. 1254)
—Those Pesky Verses of Paul: Women & the New Testament. (p. 1740)
Hudson, Mary C. 13 stories of Povorina. (p. 1995)
—Chippy. (p. 308)
—Colors of Rainbow. (p. 345)
—Crossing the Chasm: The Sled. (p. 385)
—Horse That Can Fly. (p. 800)
—I like Xmas better when. (p. 841)
Hudson, Maryann. Girls' Golf. (p. 680)
Hudson, Phillip. Saying Goodbye, Sam's Love Story. Cook, Jennifer, ed. (p. 1519)
Hudson, Rachel. Objects in the Sky. (p. 1275)
Hudson, Rachel, jt. auth. see Mills, Nathan.
Hudson, Rho Titus. Cub & the Caterpillar. (p. 388)
Hudson, Ryan. Bible Puzzles on Bible People: 60 Word Searches & Fill in the Blank Puzzles on Favorite Bible Characters: For Kids, by Kids! (p. 176)
Hudson, Stephan, photos by see Hudson, Katura J. & Hudson, Cheryl Willis.
Hudson, Stephen J., illus. see Hudson, Wade.
Hudson, Sue. I Love You. Watanabe, Kaori, illus. (p. 843)
Hudson, Tara. Arise. (p. 98)
—Elegy. (p. 510)
—Hereafter. (p. 771)
Hudson, Ted, illus. see Uitti, Dan.
Hudson, Terry, et al. Oxford International Primary Science (p. 1315)
—Oxford International Primary Science: Primary 4-11 Oxford International Primary Science. Bk. 2 (p. 1315)
—Oxford International Primary Science 4. (p. 1315)
—Oxford International Primary Science, Stage 3. (p. 1315)
Hudson, Trevor. Mile in My Shoes: Cultivating Compassion. (p. 1142)
Hudson, Wade. Feelings I Love to Share. (p. 580)
—Friends I Love to Meet. (p. 638)
—God Gave Me: Wade Hudson. Pillo, Cary, illus. (p. 688)
—God Smiles When. (p. 690)
—It's Church Going Time. (p. 896)
—Pioneers. Hudson, Stephen J., illus. (p. 1361)
—Places I Love to Go. (p. 1366)
—Puddin' Jeffrey & Leah. (p. 1414)
—Puddin', Jeffrey Leah. (p. 1414)
—Puddin' Jeffrey & Leah: Happy Birthday Puddin'! Happy Birthday Puddin'! (p. 1414)
—Scientists Healers & Inventors (p. 1529)
—Two Tyrones. Page, Mark, illus. (p. 1804)
—Underground Railroad. (p. 1814)
Hudson, Wade, jt. auth. see Hudson, Cheryl.
Hudson, Wonderland D. Believer under Fire 40-Day Devotional & Journal: Daily Inspiration for People Who Love Jesus That Are Going Through the Times of Fiery Trial & Testing. (p. 162)
Hudson-Monger, Nadine. Brooke-Lynn's Trip to the Botanical Gardens with Grandm. (p. 230)
Hudspeth, Jodi. Unconditional Love. (p. 1812)
Hudspith, Will. Stairgate - Gordon's Adventures on Everest. (p. 1638)
Hue, Wendy. Topé Arrives. (p. 1769)
Hueber, Jolene Samanatha. Trunkels. (p. 1793)
Huebner, Dawn. Sometimes I Worry Too Much: A Book to Help Children Who Worry When They Don't Need To. Schader, Karen, ed. (p. 1610)
—What to Do When Bad Habits Take Hold: A Kid's Guide to Overcoming Nail Biting & More. Matthews, Bonnie, illus. (p. 1894)

—What to Do When You Dread Your Bed: A Kid's Guide to Overcoming Problems with Sleep. Matthews, Bonnie, illus. (p. 1894)
—What to Do When You Grumble Too Much: A Kid's Guide to Overcoming Negativity. Matthews, Bonnie, illus. (p. 1894)
—What to Do When You Worry Too Much: A Kid's Guide to Overcoming Anxiety. Candace, Bonnie & Ellen, illus. (p. 1894)
—What to Do When Your Brain Gets Stuck: A Kid's Guide to Overcoming Ocd. Matthews, Bonnie, illus. (p. 1894)
—What to Do When Your Temper Flares: A Kid's Guide to Overcoming Problems with Anger. Matthews, Bonnie, illus. (p. 1894)
Huebsch, Dave. Village Assignment: True Stories of Humor, Adventure, & Drama in Guatemala's Highland Villages. (p. 1842)
Huebsch, Rand, illus. see Clement-Davies, David.
Huegel, Kelly. GLBTQ: The Survival Guide for Gay, Lesbian, Bisexual, Transgender, & Questioning Teens. (p. 682)
Huehner, Mariah, jt. auth. see Reger, Rob.
Huelin, Jodi. Alvin & the Big Art Show. (p. 51)
—Alvin & the Chipmunks: Alvin & the Big Art Show. Artful Doodlers Limited Staff, illus. (p. 51)
—Alvin & the Chipmunks: Alvin & the Substitute Teacher. Artful Doodlers Limited Staff, illus. (p. 51)
—Alvin & the Chipmunks: Alvin's Easter Break. Artful Doodlers Limited Staff & Carzon, Walter, illus. (p. 51)
—Alvin & the Substitute Teacher. (p. 51)
—Batman & the Toxic Terror. Gordon, Steven E., illus. (p. 144)
—Batman Versus Bane. Tong, Andie, illus. (p. 144)
—Dark Knight Rises: Batman Versus Bane. (p. 407)
—Reason for the Season. Artful Doodlers Ltd Staff, illus. (p. 1450)
—Rio: The Movie Storybook. (p. 1473)
—Tools of the Trade. (p. 1767)
—Tools of the Trade. Gordon, Steven E., illus. (p. 1767)
—Turtles. Gonzalez, Pedro Julio, illus. (p. 1799)
Hueller, Andy. Dizzy Fantastic & Her Flying Bicycle. (p. 455)
—Skipping Stones at the Center of the Earth: A Middle Grade Novel. (p. 1586)
Hueller, Patrick, jt. auth. see Hoblin, Paul.
Huerta, Catherine, illus. see Bentley, Catherine & Bentley, Dawn.
Huerta, Catherine, illus. see Bentley, Dawn.
Huerta, Catherine, illus. see Dreyer, Ellen.
Huerta, Catherine, illus. see Emmer, E. R.
Huerta, Catherine, illus. see O'Donnel, Liam.
Huerta, Catherine, illus. see O'Donnell, Liam.
Huerta, Catherine, illus. see Schwaeber, Barbie H.
Huerta, Catherine, illus. see Schwaeber, Barbie Heit.
Huerta, Jorge A., ed. Necessary Theatre: Six Plays about the Chicano Experience. (p. 1239)
Hueske, Edward. Firearms & Fingerprints. (p. 591)
Hueston, M. P. Christmas Eve with Mrs. Claus. Weidner, Teri, illus. (p. 313)
Huether, Amy, jt. auth. see Huether, Michael.
Huether, Michael & Huether, Amy. Ju Ju & the Sunblock. (p. 930)
Huey, Debbie, illus. see Lee, Laura.
Huey, Lois Miner. American Archaeology Uncovers the Earliest English Colonies. (p. 59)
—American Archaeology Uncovers the Underground Railroad. (p. 59)
—American Archaeology Uncovers the Vikings. (p. 59)
—American Archaeology Uncovers the Westward Movement. (p. 59)
—American Archeology Uncovers the Dutch Colonies. (p. 59)
—Forgotten Bones: Uncovering a Slave Cemetery. (p. 619)
—Ick! Yuck! Eew! Our Gross American History. (p. 851)
—Voices of the American Revolution: Stories from the Battlefields (p. 1848)
—Voices of the American Revolution. (p. 1848)
—Voices of World War II: Stories from the Front Lines (p. 1848)
Huey, Peggy J., jt. auth. see Hallett, Cynthia J.
Huff, Ariella, illus. see Ferro, Ursula.
Huff, Bailey, jt. auth. see Furman, Necah Stewart.
Huff, Charlotte. Raising a Child with Arthritis: A Parent's Guide. Afshar, Bethany, ed. (p. 1437)
Huff, Jeane, illus. see Sargent, Dave & Sargent, Pat.
Huff, Jeane, illus. see Sargent, David M.
Huff, Jeane Lirley, illus. see Sargent, Dave M., Jr.
Huff, Jeane Lirley, illus. see Sargent, David M., Jr.
Huff, Mac, jt. auth. see Jacobson, John.
Huff, Mary Scott. Creative Kids Complete Photo Guide to Knitting. (p. 379)
Huff, Regan A. Eli Whitney: The Cotton Gin & American Manufacturing. (p. 512)
Huff, Richard. Jarretts. (p. 909)
Huff, Tim. Cardboard Shack Beneath the Bridge. (p. 265)
Huff, Tim, illus. see Fukumoto, Jan.
Huff, Toby E. Age of Science & Revolutions, 1600-1800. (p. 29)
Huffine, Erik, illus. see Sewell, James C.
Hufflines, Alan C. Texas War of Independence. (p. 1724)
Huffington, Arianna. On Becoming Fearless: In Love, Work, & Life. (p. 1288)
Huffman, Beth. Awesome Andrea. (p. 120)
Huffman, Cindy, ed. see Matheson, Dawn.
Huffman, Dolores M., et al. Health Problems in the Classroom 6-12: An A-Z Reference Guide for Educators. (p. 758)
Huffman, Ivy & Kwong, Julia. Dream of Gold Mountain. (p. 483)
Huffman, Jared. Lost Piece. Huffman, Jared & Rampley, Leigh, illus. (p. 1056)
Huffman, Karen. Psychology in Action: Instructor's Resource CD-ROM. (p. 1413)
Huffman, Nancy E. Misadventures of Taylor R. Bailey. (p. 1150)
Huffman, Nancy Salfrank. Old Dan Meets a Snake: A River Bluffs Adventure Book. (p. 1283)
Huffman, Tom, illus. see Terban, Marvin.
Huffman, Tonya. Spreading the Gospel. (p. 1634)
Huffmaster, Elizabeth, illus. see Schiavi, Sherry.
Huffmon, Betty, jt. auth. see Sloat, Teri.

For book reviews, descriptive annotations, tables of contents, cover images, author biographies & additional information, updated daily - subscribe to www.booksinprint2.com

2359

Hufford, Deborah. Greeting Card Making: Send Your Personal Message (p. 723)
—Room Decorating: Make Your Space Unique (p. 1488)
Hufford, Lottie. God's Talking Child Rocks. (p. 692)
Huffstead, C. V. Wielder of the Sengans: Including the Tomes of Ithren (p. 1927)
Hufnagel, Henry M. Buck's Loot. (p. 234)
Hufnal, Amy. Language of Color. (p. 975)
—Let's Explore Bugs: A Look at God's Smallest Creatures. (p. 996)
Hugel, Bob. I Did It Without Thinking: True Stories about Impulsive Decisions That Changed Lives. (p. 837)
—Secret-Code Math: Grades 3-5. (p. 1540)
Hugel, William K., ed. see Magnolia, B.
Hugelmeyer, Michele. Alex King, Famous Fourth Grader. (p. 36)
Huget, Jennifer LaRue. Beginner's Guide to Running Away from Home. (p. 159)
Huggens, Karin, illus. see Rainey.
Hugger, M. A. Danny Malloy & His Mississippi River Samurai. (p. 406)
Huggett, Christopher. Magic Man. (p. 1072)
Huggins, Carl, illus. see Baron, Lindamichelle.
Huggins, Michael J. 2005 ESPRIT Fundamentals. (p. 2003)
Huggins, Nathan I., ed. see Krauss, Peter.
Huggins, Nathan I., ed. see Lawler, Mary.
Huggins, Pat, jt. auth. see Shakarian, Lorraine.
Huggins, Pauline. Henry Wants to Be Different. (p. 769)
Huggins, Peter. In the Company of Owls. Goodman Koz, Paula, illus. (p. 865)
—Trosclair & the Alligator Gardiner. Lindsey, illus. (p. 1789)
Huggins-Cooper, Lynn. Alien Invaders/Invasores Extraterrestres. de la Vega, Eida, tr. from ENG. (p. 40)
—Beastly Bugs. (p. 152)
—Big Cats. (p. 180)
—Minibeasts. (p. 1146)
—Ravenous Reptiles. (p. 1441)
—Savage Sharks. (p. 1516)
—Scary Spiders. (p. 1520)
—Slithering Snakes. (p. 1591)
Huggins-Cooper, Lynn & Hayward, Ian Benfold. One Boy's War. (p. 1294)
Huggins-Cooper, Lynn & Head, Alison. Premier English. (p. 1395)
Huggins-Cooper, Lynne, et al. Extraordinary English. (p. 555)
—Mysterious Maths. (p. 1223)
Hughan, Judy. Make Better Story (p. 1079)
Hughartr, Ron. Place Beyond the Dust Bowl. (p. 1365)
Hughes, Alison. Lost in the Backyard (p. 1055)
—On a Scale of Idiot to Complete Jerk (p. 1288)
—Poser (p. 1387)
Hughes, Ann. Kaitlyn & the Moonman. (p. 941)
Hughes, Annie, jt. auth. see Thomas, Susan.
Hughes, Arthur, illus. see MacDonald, George, ed.
Hughes, Arthur, illus. see MacDonald, George.
Hughes, Avah W., ed. see Coffin, Rebecca J.
Hughes, Barbara. Then & Now. (p. 1729)
Hughes, Bettany. Crystal Drop. (p. 387)
Hughes, Bill. Soul Break: An Introduction to Souled Out. (p. 1614)
—Souled Out. (p. 1614)
—Texas History Coloring Book & Punch Out Playset. (p. 1724)
Hughes, Brooke Boynton, illus. see DiTerlizzi, Angela.
Hughes, Brooke Boynton, illus. see Hannigan, Kate.
Hughes, Carol. Princess & the Unicorn. (p. 1403)
Hughes, Catherine D. First Big Book of Animals. (p. 593)
—First Big Book of the Ocean. (p. 593)
—Little Kids Big Book of Animals. (p. 1029)
—National Geographic Little Kids First Big Book of Bugs. (p. 1232)
—National Geographic Little Kids First Big Book of Space. Aguilar, David A., illus. (p. 1232)
—National Geographic Little Kids First Big Book of Dinosaurs. Tempesta, Franco, illus. (p. 1232)
Hughes, Cathy, illus. see Alligator Books Staff & Fabiny, Sarah.
Hughes, Cathy, illus. see Miller, Jocelyn.
Hughes, Charlie & Jeanes, William. Branding Iron: Branding Lessons from the Meltdown of the US Auto Industry. (p. 222)
Hughes, Cheryl. Jackson, the Pigeon Who Was Afraid of Heights. (p. 904)
Hughes, Chris. Constitutional Convention. (p. 359)
Hughes, Christina Margaret Ann. Lucy & Her Unusual Pet. (p. 1063)
Hughes, Christopher. Civil War. (p. 325)
—Cuba. (p. 388)
—Rwanda. (p. 1499)
—Yugoslavia. (p. 1983)
Hughes, Clair. Dressed in Fiction. (p. 485)
Hughes, Colin & Wade, Winnie. How to Be a Wizard at Science Investigations. (p. 815)
—How to Be Brilliant at Living Things. (p. 815)
—How to Be Brilliant at Science Investigations. Ford, Kate, illus. (p. 815)
Hughes, D. Gift That Saved Christmas. (p. 675)
Hughes, David Pierce. One Sea. (p. 1296)
Hughes, David Pierce & Perot, Richard. One Tree. (p. 1297)
Hughes, Dawn Marie. Deadwood: Haunted Stories. (p. 418)
—Oakley Farm Friends. (p. 1275)
Hughes, Dean. As Wide As the River. (p. 105)
—Facing the Enemy. (p. 561)
—Missing in Action. (p. 1152)
—Search & Destroy. (p. 1537)
—Soldier Boys. (p. 1607)
—Under the Same Stars. (p. 1814)
Hughes, Devon. Unnaturals: The Battle Begins. Richardson, Owen, illus. (p. 1822)
Hughes, Diane. Wilbur Goes to School. (p. 1928)
—Wilbur Meets Aunt Lucy. (p. 1928)
Hughes, Diane Marie. Meet Wilbur the Squirrel. (p. 1123)
Hughes, Donna L. Charly's Adventure Johnson, Kenny Ray, illus. (p. 294)
Hughes, Emily. Little Gardener. (p. 1028)
—Wild. (p. 1928)
Hughes, Emily, illus. see Doyle, Roddy.
Hughes, Emily C. Boxtrolls: The Stinkiest Cheese in Cheesebridge. (p. 217)
—Marvel's Avengers - The Doodle Book. (p. 1099)
—My Little Pony: Ponies Love Pets! (p. 1213)
—My Little Pony: the Cutie Mark Crusaders Doodle Book. (p. 1213)
—Plants vs. Zombies - Brain Busters. (p. 1370)
—Ponies Love Pets! (p. 1382)
Hughes, Evan, illus. see Boekestein, William.
Hughes, Fox Carlton. Rainbow Rhino. Hughes, Fox Carlton, illus. (p. 1435)
Hughes, George, illus. see Clifford, Eth.
Hughes, Greg. Shapes & Colors Bible. Hughes, Greg, illus. (p. 1560)
Hughes, Gregory. Unhooking the Moon. (p. 1817)
Hughes, Haley. What's near & Far? Describe & Compare Measurable Attributes. (p. 1898)
Hughes, Helga. Cooking the Austrian Way. (p. 362)
Hughes, Holly. Hoofbeats of Danger. (p. 795)
—What's near & Far? Describe & Compare Measurable Attributes. (p. 1898)
Hughes, Huw John, et al. Bwystfilod Bychain. (p. 249)
Hughes, Huw John, tr. from ENG. Cadi Deud Celwydd. (p. 250)
Hughes, Jack. Dachy's Deaf. (p. 398)
—Emmy's Eczema. (p. 520)
—Rex's Specs. (p. 1467)
—Steggie's Stutter. (p. 1646)
Hughes, Janet, illus. see Sroda, George.
Hughes, Jennifer L. Nature of Numbers. (p. 1236)
Hughes, Jenny. Audrey's Tree House. Bentley, Jonathan, illus. (p. 115)
—Dark Horse. (p. 407)
—Fantasy Horse. (p. 572)
—Horse by Any Other Name. (p. 799)
—Horse in the Diary. (p. 799)
—Horse in the Mirror. (p. 799)
—Horse in the Portrait. (p. 799)
—Journeys of Jeff & Jessie, Book 3: Ranching. (p. 929)
—Legend of the Island Horse. (p. 989)
—Lilac Ladies. Bentley, Jonathan, illus. (p. 1017)
—Model Horse. (p. 1157)
—Mystery at Black Horse Farm. (p. 1223)
—Sea Horses. (p. 1534)
Hughes, Jenny, jt. auth. see Shepherd, Sandra.
Hughes, John. Surfer Prodigy. (p. 1685)
Hughes, John Ceiriog. All Through the Night. Boulton, Harold, tr. from WEL. (p. 46)
Hughes, John H. B. Jiminy Tish - the Animal's Christmas. (p. 918)
Hughes, John P. Wish for Little Tommy Turtle. White, Tara B., illus. (p. 1940)
Hughes, Jon. What Happened to Dinosaurs? Band 13. Hughes, Jon, illus. (p. 1885)
Hughes, Jon, illus. see Frost, Helen.
Hughes, Jon, illus. see Lindeen, Carol K.
Hughes, Jon, illus. see Lindeen, Carol K. & Capstone Press Staff.
Hughes, Jon, illus. see Lindeen, Carol K. & Lugtu, Carol J.
Hughes, Jon, illus. see Lindeen, Carol K., et al.
Hughes, Jon, illus. see Riehecky, Janet & Capstone Press Staff.
Hughes, Jon, jt. auth. see Bishop, Nic.
Hughes, Julie. Fantastic Christmas. Sharpley, Kate, illus. (p. 571)
Hughes, Karyn & Stone, Susan. Mango Tree: A delightful true story of simplicity & Fun! (p. 1087)
Hughes, L. Sara Chronicles: Book Three- the Return. (p. 1514)
—Sara Chronicles Book 5: The Great Unknown & all that Lies Beneath It. (p. 1514)
Hughes, Langston. I, Too, Am America. Collier, Bryan, illus. (p. 846)
—Lullaby (for a Black Mother) Qualls, Sean, illus. (p. 1064)
—My People. Smith, Charles R., Jr., illus. (p. 1216)
—Sail Away. Bryan, Ashley, illus. (p. 1503)
—Simple Speaks His Mind. (p. 1578)
—Thank You, M'am. Molinari, Carlo, illus. (p. 1725)
Hughes, Langston & Pinkney, Brian. Dream Keeper & Other Poems. Pinkney, Brian, illus. (p. 483)
Hughes, Laura. Don't Ask. (p. 466)
—Sara Chronicles: The Beginning, Book 1. (p. 1514)
Hughes, Laura, illus. see Wohl, Lauren L.
Hughes, Libby. George W. Bush: From Texas to the White House. (p. 664)
Hughes, Lisa. Activators Computers Unlimited. (p. 10)
—Internet. (p. 880)
Hughes, Lynn Gordon. To Live a Truer Life: A Story of the Hopedale Community. Lindro, illus. (p. 1759)
Hughes, Mair Wynn. Pwy All Famu? (p. 1421)
—Y Dewis. (p. 1968)
Hughes, Mair Wynn & Davidson, Nadine. Colli Pêl. (p. 340)
Hughes, Mair Wynn & Davies, Tracy. Brawd Newydd. (p. 224)
Hughes, Mair Wynn & Jones, Steven. Dwyn Afalau. (p. 491)
Hughes, Mair Wynn & Ward, Jonathan. Ffrindiau Pennaf. (p. 583)
Hughes, Mair Wynn & West, Alex. Ragsi Ragsan. (p. 1433)
Hughes, Marghanita. Toffee at Home on the Farm. (p. 1761)
—Toffee Goes Camping. (p. 1761)
Hughes, Marilynn. Former Angel - A Children's Tale. (p. 620)
Hughes, Mark Peter. Crack in the Sky. (p. 375)
—I Am the Wallpaper. (p. 834)
—Lemonade Mouth. (p. 991)
—Lemonade Mouth Puckers Up. (p. 991)
Hughes, Melissa. Myles & Otis: A Story of Friendship. (p. 1222)
Hughes, Melissa & Lenzo, Caroline. Colorful File Folder Games, Grade 3: Skill-Building Center Activities for Language Arts & Math. (p. 344)
Hughes, Mónica. Big Turnip. Moon, Cliff, ed. (p. 184)
Hughes, Monica. Blaine's Way (p. 198)
Hughes, Mónica. Carry Me. (p. 271)
—Cars. (p. 272)
—Fighting Dinosaurs. (p. 585)
—Flying Giants. (p. 610)
Hughes, Monica. Game. (p. 654)
—Golden Aquarians. (p. 694)
—Hunter in the Dark (p. 828)
—Keeper of the Isis Light. (p. 947)
—Ladybugs. (p. 971)
Hughes, Mónica. Little Mouse Deer & the Crocodile. Moricuchi, Mique, illus. (p. 1032)
—More Little Mouse Deer Tales. Clemenston, John, illus. (p. 1174)
—Pushing & Pulling. (p. 1420)
—Pushing & Pulling. Coote, Mark, illus. (p. 1420)
—Really Big Dinosaurs & Other Giants. (p. 1449)
—Shapes: Band 01A/Pink A. (p. 1560)
Hughes, Monica. Snails (p. 1596)
—Space Trap. (p. 1620)
—Spiders. (p. 1626)
Hughes, Mónica. Stripes. (p. 1667)
—Swimming Giants. (p. 1691)
Hughes, Monica. Weather Patterns. (p. 1870)
Hughes, Monica, jt. auth. see Collins Educational Staff.
Hughes, Mónica, jt. auth. see Hughes, William.
Hughes, Monica & Ganeri, Anita. Migration. (p. 1141)
—Water Cycle. (p. 1862)
Hughes, Mónica & Ripley, Frances. 350 Words. (p. 2001)
Hughes, Mónica & Zlatic, Tomislav. Lights. (p. 1016)
Hughes, Morgan. Baseball. (p. 140)
—Basketball. (p. 143)
—Cheerleading. (p. 296)
—Ice Skating. (p. 850)
—Soccer. (p. 1603)
Hughes, Natasha, jt. auth. see Houghton Mifflin Harcourt Publishing Company Staff.
Hughes, Patricia A. Tommy Learns a Great Secret. (p. 1765)
—Tommy Learns It's Not So Scary. (p. 1765)
Hughes, Patricia J., jt. auth. see Gould, Vera Dobson.
Hughes, Pennie Jean & Robinson, Keith. Vultures in the Cemetery. (p. 1851)
Hughes, Peter. Blueroads: Selected Poems. (p. 204)
Hughes, R. E. Stanley the Christmas Tree, A Wish Come True. (p. 1640)
Hughes, Richard E. Adventures into the Unknown! Simon, Philip, ed. (p. 16)
Hughes, Rick. Dream Dragon. (p. 483)
Hughes, Sananjaleen June. Joanna's World. (p. 919)
Hughes, Sarah Anne. Reptiles & Amphibians. Peterson, Roger Tory, ed. (p. 1461)
Hughes, Sarah Anne, illus. see Pyle, Robert Michael & Peterson, Roger Tory.
Hughes, Selwyn. Christ-Empowered Living: Reflecting God's Design. (p. 311)
Hughes, Serifati, illus. see Salardino, Nicholas.
Hughes, Shirley. Alfie & the Big Boys. Hughes, Shirley, illus. (p. 37)
—Alfie & the Birthday Surprise. Hughes, Shirley, illus. (p. 37)
—Alfie Gets in First. Hughes, Shirley, illus. (p. 37)
—Alfie Gives a Hand. Hughes, Shirley, illus. (p. 37)
—Alfie Weather. Hughes, Shirley, illus. (p. 37)
—Alfie Wins a Prize. Hughes, Shirley, illus. (p. 37)
—Alfie's Alphabet. (p. 37)
—Alfie's Christmas. (p. 37)
—Alfie's Feet. (p. 37)
—Alfie's Feet. Hughes, Shirley, illus. (p. 37)
—Alphie's Numbers. (p. 50)
—Big Alfie & Annie Rose. Hughes, Shirley, illus. (p. 177)
—Big Alfie Out of Doors Storybook. Hughes, Shirley, illus. (p. 177)
—Bobbo Goes to School. Hughes, Shirley, illus. (p. 206)
—Brush with the Past, 1900-1950: The Years That Changed Our Lives. (p. 232)
—Christmas Eve Ghost. Hughes, Shirley, illus. (p. 313)
—Daisy Saves the Day. Hughes, Shirley, illus. (p. 400)
—Digby o'Day & the Great Diamond Robbery. Vulliamy, Clara, illus. (p. 438)
—Digby o'Day in the Fast Lane. Vulliamy, Clara, illus. (p. 438)
—Dogger Hughes, Shirley, illus. (p. 462)
—Don't Want to Go! Hughes, Shirley, illus. (p. 469)
—Enchantment in the Garden. (p. 523)
—Evening at Alfie's. Hughes, Shirley, illus. (p. 541)
—Hero on a Bicycle. (p. 772)
—Jonadab & Rita. Hughes, Shirley, illus. (p. 924)
—Life Drawing: Recollections of an Illustrator. (p. 1010)
—Lucy & Tom's Christmas. (p. 1063)
—Out & About: A First Book of Poems. Hughes, Shirley, illus. (p. 1310)
—Sally's Secret. (p. 1505)
—Stories by Firelight. Hughes, Shirley, illus. (p. 1654)
Hughes, Shirley, illus. see Edwards, Dorothy.
Hughes, Shirley, illus. see Streatfeild, Noel.
Hughes, Stephen B. Adventures of Bruno a Dogg & Bowser T Houn' (p. 17)
Hughes, Steven, illus. see McClintock, Norah.
Hughes, Susan. Case Closed? Nine Mysteries Unlocked by Modern Science. Wandelmaier, Michael, illus. (p. 273)
—Does It Sink or Float? (p. 460)
—Earth to Audrey. Poulin, Stephane, illus. (p. 497)
—Is It Heavy or Light? (p. 889)
—Is It Hot or Cold? (p. 889)
—Is It Transparent or Opaque? (p. 889)
—Lester B. Pearson (p. 994)
—Let's Call It Canada: Amazing Stories of Canadian Place Names. Dobson, Clive et al, illus. (p. 995)
—No Girls Allowed: Tales of Daring Women Dressed as Men for Love, Freedom & Adventure. Dawson, Willow, illus. (p. 1258)
—Virginia. (p. 1844)
Hughes, Susan & Fast, April. Cuba: The People. (p. 388)
—Cuba: The Culture. (p. 388)
—Cuba - The Land. (p. 388)
Hughes, Susan & Owlkids Books Inc. Staff. Off to Class: Incredible & Unusual Schools Around the World. (p. 1279)
Hughes, Susan & Wandelmaier, Michael. Case Closed? Nine Mysteries Unlocked by Modern Science. Wandelmaier, Michael, illus. (p. 273)
Hughes, Ted. Iron Giant. (p. 888)
Hughes, Ted & Downer, Jim. Timmy the Tug. Hughes, Ted, illus. (p. 1755)
Hughes, Ted & Quarto Generic Staff. How the Whale Became: And Other Stories. Morris, Jackie, illus. (p. 813)
Hughes, Theodore E. & Klein, David. Executor's Handbook: A Step-by-Step Guide to Settling an Estate for Executors, Administrators, & Beneficiaries. (p. 548)
Hughes, Thomas. Tom Brown's School Days by an Old Boy. (p. 1763)
—Tom Browns Schooldays. (p. 1763)
Hughes, Tim. Here I Am to Worship: Never Lose the Wonder of Worshiping the Savior. (p. 770)
Hughes, Trevor. Oxenholme Hounds. (p. 1315)
Hughes, V. I. Aziz the Story Teller. Czernecki, Stefan, illus. (p. 122)
Hughes, Vi. Graveyard Hounds Liest, Christina, illus. (p. 712)
Hughes, Vi, jt. auth. see Goss, Sheila M.
Hughes, Vicki Million. Growing up with Buck (p. 727)
Hughes, Virginia. Peggy Finds the Theater. Leone, Sergio, illus. (p. 1335)
Hughes, William & Hughes, Monica. Creepy Creatures (p. 381)
Hughes, William & Hughes, Mónica. Pill Bugs. (p. 1359)
Hughes, William J. Chayce Jackson Bounty Hunter: Crisis in the Federation. (p. 295)
Hughes-Hallett, Deborah. Instructor's Resource to Accompany Applied Calculus. (p. 878)
—Instructor's Solutions Manual to Accompany Applied Calculus. (p. 878)
Hughes-Hallett, Deborah, et al. Calculus: Single & Multivariable. (p. 252)
—Calculus: Single Variable Update. (p. 252)
—Hughes-Hallett Calculus Update. (p. 825)
Hughes-Odgers, Kyle, illus. see McKinlay, Meg.
Hughey, Sue C. Herby's Secret Formula. Hughey, Sue C., illus. (p. 769)
Hughley-Edwards, Phyllis. Nana's Magical Closet: First Edition. (p. 1228)
Hugo, Pierre de. Seashore. (p. 1538)
Hugo, Pierre de, illus. see Allaire, Caroline & Krawczyk, Sabine.
Hugo, Victor. Hunchback of Notre Dame Rebis, Greg, illus. (p. 827)
—Hunchback of Notre Dame: With a Discussion of Compassion. Butterfield, Ned, tr. (p. 827)
—Hunchback of Notre Dame. (p. 827)
—Hunchback of Notre-Dame. Corvino, Lucy, illus. (p. 827)
—Miserables. (p. 1150)
—Misérables. Flores, Catty, illus. (p. 1150)
Hugo, Victor Marie. Hunchback of Notre Dame Laurel Associates Inc. Staff, ed. (p. 827)
Huguet, Andrea L. When God Turns off the Lights. (p. 1902)
Huidobro, Matías, intro. hijo Noveno. (p. 779)
Huidobro, Montes, prologue by. Lo que te cuente es Poco. (p. 1044)
Huiett, William, illus. see Galvin, Laura Gates.
Huiett, William, illus. see Grey, Chelsea Gillian.
Huiett, William J., illus. see Fraggalosch, Audrey.
Huiett, William J., illus. see Galvin, Laura Gates.
Huiett, William J., illus. see Grey, Chelsea Gillian.
Huiett, William J., illus. see Suen, Anastasia.
Huiett, William J., illus. see Tourville, Amanda Doering.
Huiett, William J., tr. see Galvin, Laura Gates.
Hui-Jin, Park. Chronicles of the Cursed Sword (p. 317)
—Chronicles of the Cursed Sword Beop-Ryong, Yuy, illus. (p. 317)
Hui-Jin, Park, illus. see Beop-Ryong, Yeo.
Hui-Jin, Park, illus. see Beop-Ryong, Yuy.
Hui-Jin, Park, illus. see Yeo, Beop-Ryong.
Huiner, Jacque. Anna Ate. (p. 85)
Huisingh, Rosemary. At the Library. (p. 111)
—Vocabulary Stories for Toddlers: Seasons. (p. 1847)
—Vocabulary Stories for Toddlers: Getting Ready for Bed. (p. 1847)
—Vocabulary Stories for Toddlers: My Body's Just Right for Me. (p. 1847)
Huismann, Duane, illus. see Fisher, Barbara.
Huizenga, Nathaniel. Justice in Winter: Justice the Dog Series. (p. 940)
Huizinga, Johan. Waning of the Middle Ages. (p. 1856)
Hujeer, Majeda, jt. auth. see Tommalieh, Fakhri.
Hukill, Lesa. Sweet Apple Cider & Cinnamon Sticks. (p. 1689)
Hulbert, Laura. Who Has These Feet? Brooks, Erik, illus. (p. 1915)
—Who Has This Tail? Brooks, Erik, illus. (p. 1915)
Hulbert, Mark. I'm Not Afraid. (p. 859)
Hulen, Laurie. Paw Prints. (p. 1331)
Hulet, Debra. Independence Rock. (p. 870)
Hulet, Paul. Bruce the Moose Is on the Loose. (p. 232)
Hulin, Pamela. Down under in Australia. Mendoza, Carlos, illus. (p. 474)
Hulin, Rachel. Flying Henry. (p. 610)
Huling, Jan. Ol Bloo's Boogie-Woogie Band & Blues Ensemble Sørensen, Henri, illus. (p. 1283)
—Puss in Cowboy Boots. Huling, Phil, illus. (p. 1420)
Huling, Phil, illus. see Huling, Jan.
Huling, Phil, illus. see Kimmel, Eric A.
Huliska-Beith, Laura. Cinco Pequenas Mariquitas. (p. 319)
Huliska-Beith, Laura, illus. see Dobbins, Jan & Bernal, Natalia.
Huliska-Beith, Laura, illus. see Dobbins, Jan.
Huliska-Beith, Laura, illus. see Feiffer, Kate.
Huliska-Beith, Laura, illus. see Gerth, Melanie.
Huliska-Beith, Laura, illus. see Hale, Sarah Josepha.
Huliska-Beith, Laura, illus. see Holt, Kimberly Willis.
Huliska-Beith, Laura, illus. see Johnson, Angela.
Huliska-Beith, Laura, illus. see Kimmel, Eric A.
Huliska-Beith, Laura, illus. see Mendelson, Edward, ed.
Huliska-Beith, Laura, illus. see Sobel, June.
Huliska-Beith, Laura, illus. see Wheeler, Lisa.
Hull, Biz, illus. see Chapman, Linda.
Hull, Bunny. Dream a World: A Child's Journey to Self-Discovery Dreamer's Activity Kit. Saint-James, Synthia, illus. (p. 483)

—Friendship Seed. Fleming, Kye, illus. (p. 639)
—Happy, Happy Kwanzaa: Kwanzaa for the World. Saint-James, Synthia, illus. (p. 745)
—Young Masters: The Magic Eye. Fleming, Kye, illus. (p. 1979)
Hull, Claire. Frozen in Time. (p. 645)
—Isn;T That Silly. (p. 893)
Hull, Claudia. Cock-a-Doodle-Not! (p. 337)
—Procrastimonsters! They're Everywhere. Mikle, Toby, illus. (p. 1409)
Hull, Deborah. Donut Butt: The Bighorn Sheep. (p. 469)
Hull, Dennis G. Passing Thoughts of Christmas. (p. 1326)
Hull, Iva Brown. Just Me: A Collection of Poems. (p. 939)
Hull, Jennifer Bingham. Beyond One: Growing a Family & Getting a Life. (p. 174)
Hull, Jim, illus. see Thayer, Ernest L. & Gardner, Martin.
Hull, Kathryn B. Pure Luck: A Novel. (p. 1419)
—Sarah's in-Line Skating Olympics. (p. 1514)
Hull, Mary. Mary Todd Lincoln: Civil War's First Lady. (p. 1101)
—Rosa Parks: Civil Rights Leader. (p. 1489)
—Witness the Boston Tea Party in United States History. (p. 1942)
Hull, Mary & Gelfand, Dale Evva. Rosa Parks. (p. 1489)
Hull, Mary E. Mary Todd Lincoln: Civil War's First Lady. (p. 1101)
—Witness the Boston Tea Party in United States History. (p. 1942)
Hull, Maureen. Lobster Fishing on the Sea Jones, Brenda, illus. (p. 1044)
—Rainy Days with Bear. (p. 1436)
—View from a Kite (p. 1841)
Hull, Norman. Joyce's Holiday in France. (p. 930)
—Robin's Big Brother. (p. 1480)
Hull, Robert. Ancient Greece. (p. 69)
—Aztec Empire. (p. 122)
—Entertainment & the Arts. (p. 531)
—Merchant. (p. 1127)
—Nun. (p. 1273)
—Peasant. (p. 1333)
—Stonemason. (p. 1653)
—Trade & Warfare. (p. 1776)
Hull, Teresa Travous. Love's Complete: A Russian Adoption Journey. (p. 1061)
Hullinger, C. D., illus. see Cifuentes, Carolina, ed.
Hullinger, C. D., illus. see Cifuentes, Carolina.
Hullinger, C. D., illus. see Rosa-Mendoza, Gladys.
Hullinger, C. D. & Brighter Child Publishing Staff. Mother Goose Rhymes (Las Rimas de Mama Oca), Grades PK - 3. (p. 1178)
Hulme, Janet A. Bladder & Bowel Issues for Kids: A Handy Guide for Kids Ages 4-12. (p. 198)
Hulme, John & Wexler, Michael. Glitch in Sleep. (p. 683)
—Seems: The Lost Train of Thought. (p. 1548)
—Seems: Un Segundo Perdido. Vidal, Jordi, tr. (p. 1548)
—Seems the Lost Train of Thought. (p. 1548)
Hulme, Joy N. Climbing the Rainbow. (p. 333)
—Easter Babies: A Springtime Counting Book. Andreasen, Dan, illus. (p. 499)
—Eerie Feary Feeling: A Hairy Scary Pop-up Book. Ely, Paul & Dudley, Dick, illus. (p. 505)
—Mary Clare Likes to Share: A Math Reader. Rockwell, Lizzy, illus. (p. 1100)
—Wild Fibonacci: Nature's Secret Code Revealed. Schwartz, Carol, illus. (p. 1929)
Hulme, Lucy V. Passages Redpath, Dale, illus. (p. 1326)
Hulme, Peter, ed. see Shakespeare, William.
Hulme-Cross, Benjamin. Gladiator's Victory. Rinaldi, Angelo, illus. (p. 682)
—House of Memories. Evergreen, Nelson, illus. (p. 803)
—Knight's Enemies. Rinaldi, Angelo, illus. (p. 964)
—Marsh Demon. Evergreen, Nelson, illus. (p. 1096)
—Red Thirst. Evergreen, Nelson, illus. (p. 1455)
—Samurai's Assassin. Rinaldi, Angelo, illus. (p. 1510)
—Ship of Death. Evergreen, Nelson, illus. (p. 1567)
—Stone Witch. Evergreen, Nelson, illus. (p. 1653)
—Viking's Revenge. Rinaldi, Angelo, illus. (p. 1842)
—Wolf Trap. Evergreen, Nelson, illus. (p. 1944)
Huls, Kathy. Sometimes Grandma Forgets. (p. 1610)
Hulse, Gillian, illus. see Morris, Ting & Morris, Neil.
Hulse, Kris. Cowhand Christmas. Hulse, Kris, illus. (p. 374)
Hulse, Terra, jt. auth. see Hyde, Jerry.
Hulslander, Dyan. God's Precious Gift. (p. 691)
—I Just Love You So Much. Heaton, Jr., illus. (p. 840)
Hulst, W. G. van de. Bible Stories for Our Little Ones. Isings, J. H., illus. (p. 176)
Hulst, W. G. van de & Hulst, Willem G. van de. Annie & the Goat. (p. 86)
—Basket. (p. 142)
—Black Kitten. (p. 196)
—Bruno the Bear. (p. 232)
—Footprints in the Snow. (p. 615)
—Herbie, the Runaway Duck. (p. 769)
—Kittens, Kittens Everywhere. (p. 963)
—Little Wooden Shoe. (p. 1038)
—Pig under the Pew. (p. 1357)
—Rockity Rowboat. (p. 1483)
—Search for Christmas. (p. 1537)
—Secret Hiding Place. (p. 1541)
—Secret in the Box. (p. 1541)
—Three Foolish Sisters. (p. 1742)
—Through the Thunderstorm. (p. 1745)
—Woods Beyond the Wall. (p. 1950)
Hulst, Willem G. van de, jt. illus. see Hulst, W. G. van de.
Hulstedt, Linda. My Brother's Secret: Opening Communication Lines for Families. (p. 1199)
Hult, Gene & Bright, J. E. Cat Commander. Vecchio, Luciano, illus. (p. 277)
Hult, Robert William. Time Dancer. (p. 1751)
Hults, Alaska. Reading First: Unlock the Secrets to Reading Success with Research-Based Strategies Hamaguchi, Carla, ed. (p. 1445)
—Writing Makeovers 1-2: Improving Skills - Adding Style. Rous, Sheri, ed. (p. 1965)
—Writing Makeovers 3-4: Improving Skills - Adding Style. Rous, Sheri, ed. (p. 1965)
Hults, Alaska, ed. see Allen, Margaret.
Hults, Alaska, ed. see Callella, Trisha.
Hults, Alaska, ed. see Ellermeyer, Deborah & Rowell, Judy.
Hults, Alaska, ed. see Harding, Davilla.
Hults, Alaska, ed. see Jennett, Pamela.
Hults, Alaska, ed. see Kupperstein, Joel.
Hults, Alaska, ed. American History Reader's Theater: Develop Reading Fluency & Text Comprehension Skills. Vol. 2244 Hillam, Corbin & Vangsgard, Amy, illus. (p. 61)
—Philosophers to Astronauts Reader's Theater: Develop Reading Fluency & Text Comprehension Skills. Vol. 2243 Hillam, Corbin & Vangsgard, Amy, illus. (p. 1351)
Human, Deborah. Pinky Promise. (p. 1360)
Human, Katy, ed. Biological Evolution: An Anthology of Current Thought. (p. 189)
Human Relations Media. Kidsdom: An Alcohol Prevention Curriculum. (p. 955)
Human Relations Media, prod. Clued in! on Saying No. (p. 336)
Human Sciences Research Council Staff. Every Step of the Way: The Journey to Freedom in South Africa. (p. 543)
Humann, Amanda. Out of Sync. (p. 1311)
Humann, Walter J. Little Crescent Moon & the Bright Evening Star. Bodeker, Brian, illus. (p. 1026)
Humbach. Expresate: Premier Online Edition. (p. 554)
—Ven Conmigo: Online Edition (p. 1835)
Humberstone, E. C. Usborne First Book of Knowledge. (p. 1827)
Humberstone, Eliot. Everyday Things. (p. 544)
Humbert, Ellen. Bible Crafts on a Shoestring Budget. (p. 175)
Humble, Darryl. India. (p. 870)
Humble, Mark. Elmo Raps. (p. 515)
Humble-Jackson, Sally. Miracle Maker: The Greatest Story Ever Told. (p. 1148)
Hume, David D. Beyond the Long-Eared Mountains. (p. 174)
Hume, Desmond. Earth's Water. (p. 498)
Hume, Desmond, jt. auth. see Mills, Nathan.
Hume, Gladys Gooch. Cloud Circus. (p. 334)
Hume, Jeff, illus. see Ballard, John.
Hume, John, illus. see Johnson, Annie P. & Johnson, Russell.
Hume, Lotta Carswell & Lo, Koon-Chiu. Favorite Children's Stories from China & Tibet. Koon-Chiu, Lo, illus. (p. 578)
Hume, Margaret Anne. Just May Reader: Mary Grannan Selected Stories. Evans, Joyce, illus. (p. 939)
Hume, Maureen. Pizza Gang: Facing the Witch. (p. 1365)
Hume, Stephen Eaton. Ben Franklin's War. (p. 163)
Humenick, Muriel & Peters, Laura. Roses for Northern California. (p. 1490)
Humes, Kristin Joy. My Dad Wears Polka-Dotted Socks! Barr, Loel, illus. (p. 1201)
Humes, Nancy. Papa & Nana Almost Always Say Yes. (p. 1321)
Humfrey, Peter. Titian. (p. 1758)
Humiston, Sharon & Good, Cynthia. Vaccinating Your Child: Questions & Answers for the Concerned Parent Atkinson, William, ed. (p. 1830)
Humm, Sharlene. Jack & Jill in the Special Wish. (p. 902)
Hummel, Jim. Bubble C. (p. 233)
—Hunters. (p. 828)
—Imagination: On Planet Hic-Cup. (p. 860)
Hummel, Jim, illus. see DeBrecht, Katharine.
Hummel, Patti M., compiled by. This Is Now: A Girl-to-Girl Devotional for Teens. (p. 1736)
Hummell, Victoria R. A. Friends of Jesus: Stories & Activities for Chrldren, Parents, & Teachers. (p. 638)
Hummingbird, Jesse T., illus. see Robinson, Gary.
Hummingbird, Jesse T., jt. auth. see Hummingbird, Sandy.
Hummingbird, Sandy & Hummingbird, Jesse T. Cherokee Clothing Activity Book. (p. 298)
Humphrey, Anna. Mission (un)Popular. (p. 1153)
—Rhymes with Cupid. (p. 1468)
—Ruby Goldberg's Bright Idea. Newton, Vanessa Brantley, illus. (p. 1493)
Humphrey, Art & Humphrey, Pat. Don't Sweat It: Ask Art & Pat. Butler, Tad, illus. (p. 468)
Humphrey, Bobby, photos by see Nixon, James.
Humphrey, Corinne. Tao of Rudy. (p. 1705)
Humphrey, Eleanor Cairns. Building Santa's Work Shop from Tales of the Crystal Cave. (p. 239)
Humphrey, Elizabeth King. Feminist Movement Today. (p. 581)
—Feminist Movement Today. Harrington, A. Page, ed. (p. 581)
Humphrey, Jeff & O'Donnell, Kerri. American Revolution in New York. (p. 63)
Humphrey, Joanne Fenton. Windmaster: A Mother's Dialogue with her Son. (p. 1936)
Humphrey, Lisa. Mother's Promise. Danioth, David, illus. (p. 1179)
Humphrey, Mary. Kids' Yoga Book of Feelings Hamlin, Janet, illus. (p. 955)
Humphrey, Matthew J. Coastal Magic. (p. 336)
Humphrey, Pat, jt. auth. see Humphrey, Art.
Humphrey, Paul. Building a Castle. (p. 238)
—How to Make a Card. Fairclough, Chris, photos by. (p. 820)
—How to Make a Mask. Fairclough, Chris, photos by. (p. 820)
—How to Make a Present. Fairclough, Chris, photos by. (p. 820)
Humphrey, Robert Lee, see Lee Humphrey, Robert, ed.
Humphrey, Sandra McLeod. Dare to Dream! 25 Extraordinary Lives. (p. 406)
—Hot Issues, Cool Choices: Facing Bullies, Peer Pressure, Popularity, & Put-Downs. (p. 801)
—Keepin' It Real: A Young Teen Talks with God. (p. 947)
—They Stood Alone! 25 Men & Women Who Made a Difference. (p. 1732)
Humphrey, Sandra McLeod & Barker, Dan. More-If You Had to Choose, What Would You Do? Strassburg, Brian, illus. (p. 1174)
Humphrey, T. Lewis. Price of Love. (p. 1398)
Humphrey Williams, Ann, illus. see Mayfield-Ingram, Karen.
Humphrey Williams, Ann, illus. see Ramirez, Alma.
Humphreys, Alastair. Boy Who Biked the World: Riding the Americas. Morgan-Jones, Tom, illus. (p. 219)
—Boy Who Biked the World: On the Road to Africa. Morgan-Jones, Tom, illus. (p. 219)
Humphreys, Audrey. Dragon Princess. (p. 477)
Humphreys, C. C. Hunt of the Unicorn. (p. 828)
Humphreys, Colin. Miracles of Exodus: A Scientist's Discovery of the Extraordinary Natural Causes of the Biblical Stories. (p. 1149)
Humphreys, David, photos by see Clegg, Holly.
Humphreys, Dolores. Adventures of J. G. & Echo: The Land of All Creatures & the Swamp Creature (p. 19)
Humphreys, Graham, illus. see Brooks, Felicity.
Humphreys, Jessica Dee & Chikwanine, Michel. Child Soldier: When Boys & Girls Are Used in War. Dávila, Claudia, illus. (p. 301)
Humphreys, Kevin S. First Kiss: The Way of a Man with a Maiden: the Way of a Man with a Maiden. (p. 595)
Humphreys, Neil. I Trapped a Dolphin but It Really Wasn't My Fault. Cheng, Puay Koon, illus. (p. 847)
—Picking up a Penguin's Egg Really Got Me into Trouble. Cheng, Puay Koon, illus. (p. 1354)
—Secrets of the Swamp. Koon, Cheng Puay, illus. (p. 1546)
Humphreys, Patrick B. 1-2-3 Kitties: A Cat Counting Book. (p. 1990)
—Love of Tin Robots. (p. 1060)
Humphreys, Pauline A. Romance of the Airman. (p. 1486)
Humphreys, Sandra Ann. Kittens Have the Smallest Chins. (p. 963)
Humphreys, Stephen. Harold Saves Christmas: A Harold & Charlie adventure Story. (p. 749)
Humphries, Jennifer & DiCampli, Nicki. Rebekah Grace the Practically Perfect Princess. (p. 1450)
Humphries, Jessie. Killing Ruby Rose (p. 956)
Humphries, Tudor, illus. see Allen, Judy.
Humphries, Tudor, illus. see Ganeri, Anita.
Humphries, Tudor, illus. see Lewis, C. S.
Humphries, Tudor, illus. see Lewis, C. S. & Orem, Hiawyn.
Humphries, Tudor, illus. see Oram, Hiawyn.
Humphries, Tudor, illus. see Wallace, Karen.
Humphries, Tudor, jt. auth. see Johnson, Jinny.
Humphries, Tudor & Allen, Judy. Are You a Ladybug? (p. 97)
Humphry, Christy. Fire & Water. (p. 590)
Humphrys-Bajaj, Holly, illus. see Humphrys-Dunne, Deanie.
Humphrys-Dunne, Deanie. Charlene the Star. (p. 291)
—Tails of Sweetbrier. Humphrys-Bajaj, Holly, illus. (p. 1695)
Huna Smith, Ryan, illus. see Yazzie, Seraphine G.
Hund, Marjolein, illus. see Boshouwers, Suzan.
Hund, Thomas. Toby T-Rex: Lightning Strikes. (p. 1760)
Hundal, Nancy. Camping Deines, Brian, illus. (p. 257)
—Kaleidoscopes & Butterfly Dreams. (p. 942)
—Number 21 Deines, Brian, illus. (p. 1271)
—Prairie Summer Deines, Brian, illus. (p. 1392)
—Twilight Fairies (p. 1801)
Hundley, Sam, illus. see Suhay, Lisa.
Huneck, Stephen. Sally at the Farm. (p. 1505)
—Sally Gets a Job. Huneck, Stephen, illus. (p. 1505)
—Sally Goes to Heaven. (p. 1505)
—Sally Goes to the Vet. Huneck, Stephen, illus. (p. 1505)
—Sally in the Forest. (p. 1505)
—Sally in the Sand. (p. 1505)
—Sally in the Snow. (p. 1505)
—Sally's Great Balloon Adventure. (p. 1505)
—Sally's Snow Adventure. Huneck, Stephen, illus. (p. 1505)
Hunefeldt, Christine. Peru. (p. 1345)
Huneke, Amanda. Monster at School. Wolek, Guy, illus. (p. 1166)
—Monster in the Park. Wolek, Guy, illus. (p. 1167)
—Monster on the Bus. Wolek, Guy, illus. (p. 1168)
—Monster on the Loose. Wolek, Guy, illus. (p. 1168)
Hünermann, Wilhelm. Crucified Heart: A Novel of St. Herman Joseph. Szanto, Hubert, tr. from GER. (p. 386)
Hung, Yating. Where Is Mama? A Pop-Up Story. (p. 1908)
Hunger, Bill. When Two Saints Meet. Ripley, Jill, ed. (p. 1905)
Hunger, Chrissy. Kuna Caught a Tun. (p. 968)
Hungerford, Thomas W. Contemporary College Algebra & Trigonometry: A Graphing Approach. (p. 360)
Hunkel, Cary, illus. see Field, Nancy & Karasov, Corliss.
Hunkins, Boehm Armstrong & McGraw-Hill Education Staff. Exploring Our World: People, Places, & Cultures. (p. 553)
Hunkins, Liz & Hunkins, P. J. Herbie the Erbie: What Are These Things Called Feelings? (p. 769)
Hunkins, P. J., jt. auth. see Hunkins, Liz.
Hunner, Trina L., illus. see Malnor, Carol L.
Hunner, Trina L., illus. see Thomas, Patricia.
Hunner, Trina L., jt. auth. see Malnor, Carol L.
Hunnicutt, M. E. Giants of Wonder. (p. 674)
—Wedding Wonderful. (p. 1871)
Hunnicutt, Susan. Organ Transplants. (p. 1303)
Hunnicutt, Susan C. Casualties of War. (p. 277)
—Federal Budget Deficit. (p. 580)
—Middle East Peace Process. (p. 1137)
—Tobacco & Smoking. (p. 1760)
—Universal Health Care. (p. 1820)
—World Hunger. (p. 1955)
Hunnicutt, Susan C., ed. Is the Western Diet Making the World Sick? (p. 890)
—World Hunger. (p. 1955)
Hunnisett, Jean. Period Costume for Stage & Screen: Dominos, Dolmans, Coats, Pelisses, Spencers, Callashes, Hoods & Bonnets. Vol. 5 Foulkes, Fiona et al, illus. (p. 1343)
Hunsaker, Debbie. Reading Rug. (p. 1446)
Hunsaker, Joan. Dagger in Time. (p. 399)
—Dagger in Time - the Web of Spies. (p. 399)
Hunsaker, Joyce Badgley. They Call Me Sacagawea. (p. 1732)
Hunsaker, L. K. Finishing Touches. (p. 589)
Hunsicker, Jennifer. Young Andrew Jackson in the Carolinas: A Revolutionary Boy. (p. 1978)
Hunsicker, Kelley. Chinese Immigrants in America: An Interactive History Adventure (p. 307)
Hunsicker, Ranelda Mack. Faerie Gold: A Guide for Teachers & Students. (p. 562)
—Heidi: A Guide for Teachers & Students. (p. 762)
—Little Women: A Guide for Teachers & Students. (p. 1038)
Hunsicker, Ranelda Mack, ed. see Spyri, Johanna.
Hunsicker, Ranelda Mack, jt. ed. see Lindskoog, Kathryn.
Hunsinger, J. A. Settlers. (p. 1554)
Hunt, Alfred William, illus. see Grimm, Jacob, et al.
Hunt, Amelia C. Little Blue Duck. (p. 1024)
Hunt, Angela. Calico Bear: A Story about Unchanging Love. Kiryakova, Niya, illus. (p. 253)
—True Princess. (p. 1792)
Hunt, Angela Elwell. Tres Árboles: Cento Tradicional. Jonke, Tim, illus. (p. 1784)
Hunt, B. B. Samantha Stone & the Mermaid's Quest. (p. 1507)
Hunt, Bonnie. Danger! Keep Out! The Grayson Twins Adventures. (p. 404)
—Missing Chimp: A Grayson Twins Adventures (p. 1152)
Hunt, Charles. Perfect Diet: The Ultimate Weight Solution for Every Body. (p. 1341)
Hunt, Chris. Stream Dreams: A Fly Fisher's Guide to Eastern Idaho's Small Water (p. 1666)
Hunt, Christopher. Victory after High School: Survive or Thrive—You Choose! (p. 1840)
Hunt, Connie. Hooray for Feet! Melmon, Deborah, illus. (p. 796)
—Hooray for Hands! Melmon, Deborah, illus. (p. 796)
—Planting Love: A Tale of Love & Growing. (p. 1369)
Hunt, Craig J. S., illus. see Hunt, Debbie Colleen.
Hunt, Darleen L. Baby's Fraction Lunch. Komarck, Michael, illus. (p. 129)
—Bob's Busy Year: Months of the Year. Komarck, Michael, illus. (p. 206)
—Dad's Pancakes: Number Reduction. Komarck, Michael, illus. (p. 399)
—Dog & Cat Compare: Comparing Amounts. Komarck, Michael, illus. (p. 461)
—Dog's Dollars: Patterns. Komarck, Michael, illus. (p. 462)
—Ellen Elizabeth's Peanut Butter Jar: Counting. Komarck, Michael, illus. (p. 514)
—Harvey T. Crow Puts It All Together: Addition. Komarck, Michael, illus. (p. 752)
—Lyle & Mildred Are a Pair: Counting by 2's. Komarck, Michael, illus. (p. 1066)
—Mr. Reed's Class Estimates: Estimating. Komarck, Michael, illus. (p. 1186)
—Samanta Uses Patterns: Patterns. Komarck, Michael, illus. (p. 1507)
—Samantha Visits Grandpa Geo: Shapes. Komarck, Michael, illus. (p. 1507)
—Spider Inventories: Count & Record. Komarck, Michael, illus. (p. 1626)
Hunt, Dawson J. Farmers Market Measurements (p. 574)
Hunt, Debbie Colleen. Dinosaur Who Loved to Bake & Eat Cakes. Hunt, Craig J. S., illus. (p. 443)
—Wollie the Wheelbarrow. Burket, Shelia, illus. (p. 1944)
Hunt, Des. Moa Cave. (p. 1157)
—Shadows in the Ice. (p. 1558)
—Tooth. (p. 1768)
Hunt, Desmond. Where Cuckoos Call. (p. 1906)
Hunt, E. Marlene. Every Apple. Hunt, E. Marlene, illus. (p. 542)
Hunt, Elizabeth Singer. Caper of the Crown Jewels (p. 262)
—Fight for the Frozen Land Williamson, Brian, illus. (p. 585)
—Mystery of the Mona Lisa Williamson, Brian, illus. (p. 1225)
—Peril at the Grand Prix - Italy (p. 1343)
—Pursuit of the Ivory Poachers - Kenya Williams, Brian, illus. (p. 1419)
—Puzzle of the Missing Panda Williamson, Brian, illus. (p. 1421)
—Quest for Aztec Gold - Mexico (p. 1426)
—Search for the Sunken Treasure: Australia. Bk. 2 (p. 1537)
—Search for the Sunken Treasure. Williamson, Brian, illus. (p. 1537)
—Secret Agent Jack Stalwart: The Deadly Race to Space: Russia. (p. 1540)
—Secret Agent Jack Stalwart: The Secret of the Sacred Temple - Cambodia. Williamson, Brian, illus. (p. 1540)
—Secret Agent Jack Stalwart: The Escape of the Deadly Dinosaur - USA. Bk. 1 Williamson, Brian, illus. (p. 1540)
—Secret Agent Jack Stalwart: Book 13: the Hunt for the Yeti Skull: Nepal. (p. 1540)
—Secret Agent Jack Stalwart: Book 14: the Mission to Find Max: Egypt. (p. 1540)
—Theft of the Samurai Sword: Japan #11. (p. 1728)
Hunt, Elizabeth Singer & Weinstein Books Staff. Theft of the Samurai Sword - Japan. Williamson, Brian, illus. (p. 1728)
Hunt, Emily M. & Pantoya, Michelle L. Engineering Elephants. (p. 529)
Hunt, Graham. Smillbow & the Land of Titch'wee. (p. 1594)
Hunt, Irene. Up a Road Slowly. (p. 1824)
Hunt, J. Timothy, jt. auth. see Jacob, P. L., pseud.
Hunt, James. I Have A New Puppy! Now What? (p. 839)
—I Have a New Puppy! Now What? A Puppy Survival Guide for Kids. Dickens, Christina, illus. (p. 839)
Hunt, James F. Pedro the Donkey: His Quest for Love & Acceptance. (p. 1334)
Hunt, James Milton. Don't condo my Lighthouse: HOW JAMES HUNT SAVED pONCE de lEON lIGHTHOUSE from aDJACENT DEVELOPMENT. (p. 467)
—Rye Grass Roots Activist Bible: Stop global Warming. (p. 1499)
—Rye Grass Roots Activist Bible: Save an Oak Tree, Stop Climate Change. (p. 1499)
Hunt, Jamie. Getting Stronger, Getting Fit: The Importance of Exercise. (p. 669)
—Homophobia: From Social Stigma to Hate Crimes. (p. 794)
—Tired of Being Teased: Obesity & Others. (p. 1757)
—Truth about Diets: What's Right for You? (p. 1794)
Hunt, Jane, illus. see Ayers, Linda.
Hunt, Janie. Shapes. Chrystall, Claire, illus. (p. 1560)
Hunt, Jeanne. Celebrating Saints & Seasons: Hundreds of Activities for Catholic Children. (p. 285)
Hunt, Jilly. Fair Trade (p. 562)
—Greece (p. 720)
—Greek Myths & Legends (p. 721)
—Leaders (p. 981)

H

—Popular Culture: 1900-1919 (p. 1385)
—Popular Culture: 1980-1999 (p. 1385)
—Roman Myths & Legends (p. 1486)
—Rookery of Penguins: And Other Bird Groups (p. 1487)
—Russia (p. 1498)
—Safety. (p. 1502)
Hunt, Jim, illus. see Clarke, Angelique.
Hunt, Jim, illus. see Lara, Sahai.
Hunt, Jim, illus. see Stroud, Scott.
Hunt, Jocelyn. Britian, 1846-1919. (p. 229)
Hunt, John, illus. see Hunter, Erin.
Hunt, Johnny. Bedtime Devotions with Jesus: My Daily Devotional for Kids (p. 156)
Hunt, Joni Phelps. Chorus of Frogs: The Risky Life of an Ancient Amphibian. Leon, Vicki, ed. (p. 310)
—Shimmer of Butterflies: The Brief, Brilliant Life of a Magical Insect. León, Vicki, ed. (p. 1566)
Hunt, Joni Phelps & London Town Press Staff. Band of Bears: The Rambling Life of a Lovable Loner. León, Vicki, ed. (p. 136)
Hunt, Joyce, jt. auth. see Selsam, Millicent E.
Hunt, Judith, illus. see Griffin, Lydia.
Hunt, Judith, illus. see Hodgkins, Fran.
Hunt, Judith, illus. see McKay, Sindy.
Hunt, Judith A., illus. see Kenney, Karen Latchana.
Hunt, Julie. Ghost Hunter. Norling, Beth, illus. (p. 670)
—On the Run. Norling, Beth, illus. (p. 1291)
—Song for a Scarlet Runner. (p. 1611)
—Trick Rider. Norling, Beth, illus. (p. 1786)
Hunt, Korey, jt. auth. see Freeman, Chris W.
Hunt, Leo. Thirteen Days of Midnight. (p. 1735)
Hunt, Lisa, illus. see Mortensen, Lori.
Hunt, Lynda Mullaly. Fish in a Tree. (p. 598)
—One for the Murphys. (p. 1295)
Hunt, Mabel Leigh. Peddler's Clock. Jones, Elizabeth Orton, illus. (p. 1334)
Hunt, Margaret, tr. see Grimm, Jacob & Grimm, Wilhelm K.
Hunt, Marigold. Book of Angels: Stories of Angels in the Bible. (p. 210)
—First Christians: The ACts of the Apostles for Children. (p. 593)
—Life of Our Lord for Children. (p. 1012)
—St. Patrick's Summer: A Children's Adventure Catechism. (p. 1638)
Hunt, Matt, illus. see Arena, Jen.
Hunt, Meg. Interstellar Cinderella. (p. 881)
Hunt, Miguel, photos by see Garner, Simon.
Hunt, Nancy Nye & Bradley, Nina Leopold. Aldo Leopold's Shack: Nina's Story. (p. 35)
Hunt, Norman Bancroft. Living in Ancient Egypt. (p. 1041)
—Living in Ancient Greece. (p. 1041)
—Living in Ancient Mesopotamia. (p. 1041)
—Living in Ancient Rome. (p. 1041)
—Living in the Ancient World. (p. 1041)
—Living in the Middle Ages. (p. 1041)
Hunt, Norman Bancroft, jt. auth. see Harrison, Peter.
Hunt, Paul, illus. see Oldfield, Jenny.
Hunt, Paul, jt. auth. see Dorling Kindersley Publishing Staff.
Hunt, Peter. Fairy Penguin's Lesson & Other Tales. (p. 563)
Hunt, Peter, ed. see Burnett, Frances Hodgson.
Hunt, Rameck, et al. We Beat the Street: How a Friendship Pact Led to Success. (p. 1866)
Hunt, Rhian G. Acrohelion Campaign Setting. (p. 9)
Hunt, Robert. Art & the Way. (p. 101)
Hunt, Robert, illus. see Ashby, Ruth.
Hunt, Robert, illus. see Carson, Mary Kay.
Hunt, Robert, illus. see Greene, Jacqueline.
Hunt, Robert, illus. see McDonald, Megan.
Hunt, Robert, illus. see Sandler, Martin W.
Hunt, Robert, illus. see Wyss, Johann David.
Hunt, Roderick. Camping Adventure. Brychta, Alex, illus. (p. 257)
Hunt, Santana. Bloodsucking Mosquitoes. (p. 201)
—Geronimo. (p. 667)
—Grand Canyon National Park. (p. 707)
—Osceola. (p. 1305)
Hunt, Sara. Stay Fit: Your Guide to Staying Active. (p. 1645)
Hunt, Sara, ed. see Calkhoven, Laurie & Laskey, Shannon.
Hunt, Sara, et al. Healthy Me. (p. 758)
Hunt, Sara R. You've Got Spirit! Cheers, Chants, Tips, & Tricks Every Cheerleader Needs to Know. Perrett, Lisa, illus. (p. 1982)
Hunt, Sara R. & Kenney, Karen Latchana. Hair Care Tips & Tricks. Heschke, Elena, illus. (p. 736)
Hunt, Scott, illus. see Testa, Maria.
Hunt, Susan. Sammy & His Shepherd. Godbey, Corey, illus. (p. 1507)
Hunt, Tiffani "Paradise". Glamorous 5: In the City of Garden Valley. (p. 682)
Hunt, Virginia D. Carter. Grandnanny, What Color Is God? (p. 709)
Hunt, Wayne. Zack & the Validators: Good As Gold. (p. 1984)
Hunt, Zoe. Azarels Christmas Wish. (p. 121)
Hunt, Zoe Paton. Azrael's Magical Moment. (p. 122)
Hunter, Adriana, tr. see Zenatti, Valerie.
Hunter, Alex. Game Over. Rew, Jen, illus. (p. 654)
—Game over - Book Three. (p. 654)
Hunter, Amy N. Ancient Land with a Fascinating Past: The History of Mexico. (p. 69)
—History of Mexico. (p. 784)
—Tony Gonzalez. (p. 1766)
Hunter, Anne. Cricket Song. (p. 382)
Hunter, Anne, illus. see Obed, Ellen Bryan.
Hunter, Archie. Power & Passion in Egypt: A Life of Sir Eldon Gorst, 1861-1911. (p. 1389)
Hunter, Barbara, see Cordoves, Barbara, pseud.
Hunter, Bernice Thurman. Girls They Left Behind (p. 681)
Hunter, C. C. Awake at Dawn. (p. 120)
—Born at Midnight. (p. 214)
—Chosen at Nightfall. (p. 310)
—Eternal: Shadow Falls: After Dark. (p. 539)
—Eternal. (p. 539)
—Reborn. (p. 1451)
—Shadow Falls - Next Chapter: Taken at Dusk - Whispers at Moonrise (p. 1557)
—Taken at Dusk: A Shadow Falls Novel. (p. 1697)
—Taken at Dusk. (p. 1697)
—Whispers at Moonrise. (p. 1912)
Hunter, Carl, illus. see Boyce, Frank Cottrell.
Hunter, Carl, photos by see Boyce, Frank Cottrell.
Hunter, Charlene, illus. see Stripling, Joe.
Hunter, Cheryl, jt. auth. see Ashcraft, Shelly.
Hunter, Dave. Along Florida's Expressways. (p. 48)
Hunter, David. Antidepressants & Advertising: Marketing Happiness. (p. 89)
—Antidepressants & the Pharmaceutical Companies: Corporate Responsibilities. (p. 89)
—Born to Smoke: Nicotine & Genetics. (p. 214)
—But Smoking Makes Me Happy: The Link Between Nicotine & Depression. (p. 246)
—Teen Life among the Amish & Other Alternative Communities: Choosing a Lifestyle. (p. 1713)
—Thousands of Deadly Chemicals: Smoking & Health. (p. 1740)
Hunter, David & Livingston, Phyllis. Youth with Bipolar Disorder: Achieving Stability. (p. 1982)
Hunter, Derek. Brainwash Escape Victims (p. 222)
—Pirate Club (p. 1362)
Hunter, Dette. 38 Ways to Entertain Your Babysitter. MacEachern, Stephen, illus. (p. 1996)
Hunter, Donna K. Hunterston Happenings: Kilts, Casts & Castles. (p. 829)
Hunter, Dorretta Day. Rainbows & Kisses. (p. 1436)
Hunter, Dru. How Do We Apply Science? (p. 807)
—How Does It Work? (p. 809)
—What Is Out There? (p. 1890)
—What Is the Reason? (p. 1890)
—Where Do We Look for Life? (p. 1907)
—Why Do We Behave Like That? (p. 1924)
Hunter, Elizabeth. Home Oasis. (p. 792)
Hunter, Emily. Bible-Time Nursery Rhyme Book. (p. 176)
Hunter, Erica C. D. Ancient Mesopotamia. (p. 70)
Hunter, Erin. After the Flood. (p. 28)
—After the Flood. Barry, James L. & Hunt, John, illus. (p. 28)
—Battles of the Clans. (p. 147)
—Beyond the Code. Barry, James L., illus. (p. 174)
—Blazing Star. (p. 199)
—Bluestar's Prophecy. McLoughlin, Wayne, illus. (p. 204)
—Broken Path. (p. 230)
—Burning Horizon. (p. 244)
—Cats of the Clans. McLoughlin, Wayne, illus. (p. 281)
—Clan in Need. Barry, James L., illus. (p. 326)
—Code of the Clans. McLoughlin, Wayne, illus. (p. 338)
—Crookedstar's Promise. (p. 384)
—Crookedstar's Promise. (p. 385)
—Dangerous Path. (p. 404)
—Dangerous Path. Stevenson, Dave, illus. (p. 404)
—Dangerous Path. Richardson, Owen & Stevenson, Dave, illus. (p. 404)
—Dark River. (p. 408)
—Darkest Hour. (p. 408)
—Darkest Hour. Stevenson, Dave, illus. (p. 408)
—Darkest Hour. Richardson, Owen & Stevenson, Dave, illus. (p. 408)
—Darkness Falls. (p. 408)
—Dawn. (p. 411)
—Dawn. Stevenson, Dave, illus. (p. 411)
—Dawn. Richardson, Owen & Stevenson, Dave, illus. (p. 411)
—Eclipse. (p. 502)
—Empty City. (p. 521)
—Empty City & a Hidden Enemy. (p. 521)
—Endless Lake. (p. 527)
—Enter the Clans. (p. 531)
—Fading Echoes. Richardson, Owen & Douglas, Allen, illus. (p. 562)
—Fire & Ice. (p. 590)
—Fire & Ice. Stevenson, Dave, illus. (p. 590)
—Fire & Ice. Richardson, Owen & Stevenson, Dave, illus. (p. 590)
—Fire in the Sky. (p. 590)
—Firestar's Quest. (p. 592)
—Firestar's Quest. Chalk, Gary, illus. (p. 592)
—First Battle. (p. 593)
—First Battle. McLoughlin, Wayne & Douglas, Allen, illus. (p. 593)
—Forest Divided. McLoughlin, Wayne & Douglas, Allen, illus. (p. 618)
—Forest of Secrets. (p. 618)
—Forest of Secrets. Stevenson, Dave, illus. (p. 618)
—Forest of Secrets. Richardson, Owen & Stevenson, Dave, illus. (p. 618)
—Forest of Secrets, In to the Wild, Fire & Ice. (p. 618)
—Forest of Wolves. (p. 618)
—Forgotten Warrior. (p. 620)
—Forgotten Warrior. Richardson, Owen & Douglas, Allen, illus. (p. 620)
—Fourth Apprentice. Richardson, Owen & Douglas, Allen, illus. (p. 625)
—Great Bear Lake. (p. 714)
—Heart of a Warrior. Barry, James L., illus. (p. 759)
—Hidden Enemy. (p. 775)
—Into the Wild. (p. 881)
—Into the Wild. Stevenson, Dave, illus. (p. 881)
—Into the Wild. Richardson, Owen & Stevenson, Dave, illus. (p. 881)
—Into the Woods. Hudson, Don, illus. (p. 881)
—Island of Shadows. (p. 892)
—Kallik's Adventure. Kurkoski, Bettina M., illus. (p. 942)
—Last Hope. (p. 978)
—Last Hope. Richardson, Owen & Douglas, Allen, illus. (p. 978)
—Last Wilderness. (p. 979)
—Long Shadows. (p. 1047)
—Lost Warrior (p. 1057)
—Melting Sea. (p. 1125)
—Midnight. (p. 1138)
—Midnight. Stevenson, Dave, illus. (p. 1138)
—Midnight. Richardson, Owen & Stevenson, Dave, illus. (p. 1138)
—Moonrise. (p. 1173)
—Moonrise. Stevenson, Dave, illus. (p. 1173)
—Moonrise. Richardson, Owen & Stevenson, Dave, illus. (p. 1173)
—New Prophecy (p. 1247)
—Night Whispers. Richardson, Owen & Douglas, Allen, illus. (p. 1254)
—Outcast. (p. 1312)
—Power of Three (p. 1390)
—Power of Three Set (p. 1390)
—Quest Begins. (p. 1426)
—Quest Begins. Chalk, Gary, illus. (p. 1426)
—Rescue. Barry, James L., illus. (p. 1462)
—Return to the Clans. Hudson, Don, illus. (p. 1465)
—Rise of Scourge. Kurkoski, Bettina M., illus. (p. 1474)
—Rising Storm. (p. 1475)
—Rising Storm. Stevenson, Dave, illus. (p. 1475)
—Rising Storm. Richardson, Owen & Stevenson, Dave, illus. (p. 1475)
—River of Lost Bears. (p. 1476)
—River of Lost Bearsrs No. 3. (p. 1476)
—Secrets of the Clans. McLoughlin, Wayne, illus. (p. 1545)
—Seekers: Return to the Wild #4: Forest of Wolves. (p. 1548)
—Shattered Peace. Barry, James L., illus. (p. 1563)
—Sight. (p. 1574)
—Sign of the Moon. (p. 1574)
—Sign of the Moon. Richardson, Owen & Douglas, Allen, illus. (p. 1574)
—Skyclan's Destiny. McLoughlin, Wayne, illus. (p. 1587)
—Smoke Mountain. (p. 1594)
—Spirits in the Stars. (p. 1629)
—Starlight. (p. 1642)
—Starlight. Stevenson, Dave, illus. (p. 1642)
—Starlight. Richardson, Owen & Stevenson, Dave, illus. (p. 1642)
—Storm of Dogs. (p. 1656)
—Sun Trail. (p. 1676)
—Sun Trail. McLoughlin, Wayne & Douglas, Allen, illus. (p. 1676)
—Sunrise. (p. 1677)
—Sunset. (p. 1677)
—Sunset. Stevenson, Dave, illus. (p. 1677)
—Sunset. Richardson, Owen & Stevenson, Dave, illus. (p. 1677)
—Survivors: the Gathering Darkness #1: a Pack Divided. Kubinyi, Laszlo, illus. (p. 1687)
—Tales from the Clans. (p. 1701)
—Tales from the Packs. (p. 1702)
—Tallstar's Revenge. (p. 1704)
—Tallstar's Revenge. Barry, James L., illus. (p. 1704)
—Thunder Rising. (p. 1746)
—Thunder Rising. McLoughlin, Wayne & Douglas, Allen, illus. (p. 1746)
—Toklo's Story. Kurkoski, Bettina M., illus. (p. 1762)
—Twilight. (p. 1801)
—Twilight. Stevenson, Dave, illus. (p. 1801)
—Twilight. Richardson, Owen & Stevenson, Dave, illus. (p. 1801)
—Untold Stories. McLoughlin, Wayne, illus. (p. 1823)
—Warriors (p. 1859)
—Warriors: The First Battle. (p. 1859)
—Warriors: Into the Wild, Fire & Ice, Forest of Secrets. (p. 1859)
—Warriors: The Ultimate Guide. McLoughlin, Wayne, illus. (p. 1859)
—Warriors: The First Battle. McLoughlin, Wayne & Douglas, Allen, illus. (p. 1859)
—Warriors. (p. 1859)
—Warriors Boxed Set: Rising Storm; A Dangerous Path; The Darkest Hour. (p. 1859)
—Warriors: Dawn of the Clans #6: Path of Stars. McLoughlin, Wayne, illus. (p. 1859)
—Warriors Manga - Graystripe's Adventure Barry, James, illus. (p. 1859)
—Warriors: Omen of the Stars Box Set: Volumes 1 To 6. (p. 1859)
—Warrior's Refuge. (p. 1859)
—Warrior's Return. (p. 1859)
—Warriors - Sunrise. (p. 1859)
—Warriors Super Edition: Bramblestar's Storm. (p. 1859)
—Warriors - The New Prophecy Richardson, Owen, illus. (p. 1859)
—Yellowfang's Secret. (p. 1970)
—Yellowfang's Secret. Barry, James L., illus. (p. 1970)
Hunter, Erin, jt. auth. see Jolley, Dan.
Hunter, Erin & Jolley, Dan. Escape from the Forest. Hudson, Don, illus. (p. 535)
—Warrior's Return Barry, James L., illus. (p. 1859)
Hunter, Erin E., illus. see Kurtz, Kevin.
Hunter, Erin E., illus. see Slade, Suzanne.
Hunter, Erin, et al. Moth Flight's Vision. Barry, James L. & Richardson, Owen, illus. (p. 1177)
Hunter, G. Scott, jt. auth. see Edwards, Gabrielle I.
Hunter, Georgia. Yubi & the Blue-Tailed Rat. (p. 1983)
Hunter, Gerald, illus. see Hoffmann, Peggy.
Hunter, Gerald S. Haunted Michigan, Volume 1: Recent Encounters with Active Spirits. (p. 753)
—More Haunted Michigan: New Encounters with Ghosts of the Great Lakes State. (p. 1174)
Hunter, GerlSpenser. Mother's House. (p. 1178)
Hunter, Gordon. How Are You, Mother Earth? We're Taking You to the Doctor! (p. 805)
Hunter, Ian. Scaredy Jack. (p. 1519)
Hunter, Jana. Trick or Treat. (p. 1786)
Hunter, Jana Novotny, et al. I Can Do It! Richards, Lucy, illus. (p. 835)
Hunter, John C., et al. Learning Basic Mathematics: Placement Tests. (p. 985)
—Learning Basic Mathematics. (p. 985)
—Mathematics: Placement Tests. (p. 1108)
Hunter, John Holmes. Treasured Moments. (p. 1782)
Hunter, John P. Red Thunder: Secrets, Spies, & Scoundrels at Yorktown. (p. 1455)
Hunter, Julius K. Absurd Alphabedtime Stories. Bauman, Todd, illus. (p. 7)
Hunter, K. N. Hollow: N2 the Hollow World. (p. 789)
Hunter, Kendall. Miff the Martian. (p. 1139)
Hunter, Kevin. Dude 101. (p. 489)
Hunter, Laura E., ed. see Lashley, Steven. E.
Hunter, Lee Hargus. Welby the Worm Who Lost His Wiggle. Thompson, Lydia, illus. (p. 1873)
Hunter, Llyn. Little Book of Magical Beings. Hunter, Llyn, illus. (p. 1025)
—Little Book of Monsters. Hunter, Llyn, illus. (p. 1025)
—Sea Life GemGlow Stained Glass Coloring Book. (p. 1534)
Hunter, M. S. Killing in Paradise. (p. 956)
Hunter, Mandy. Bug Crazy. (p. 236)
Hunter, Miranda. Latino Americans & Immigration Laws: Crossing the Border. (p. 979)
—Story of Latino Civil Rights: Fighting for Justice. (p. 1658)
Hunter, Miranda & Hunter, William. Sexually Transmitted Infections. Forman, Sara & McDonnell, Mary Ann, eds. (p. 1556)
—Sexually Transmitted Infections. McDonnell, Mary Ann & Forman, Sara, eds. (p. 1556)
—Women in the World of India. (p. 1946)
—Women's Issues: Global Trends (p. 1946)
Hunter, Mollie. Mermaid Summer. (p. 1128)
—Thirteenth Member. (p. 1735)
Hunter, Muata. Check Up. (p. 295)
Hunter, Myra, jt. ed. see Singer, Dani.
Hunter, Nick. 2000 & Beyond. (p. 2003)
—2012 London Olympics. (p. 2003)
—Alexander the Great (p. 36)
—Ancient Treasures (p. 71)
—Campaigns of World War I (p. 257)
—Catherine, Duchess of Cambridge (p. 280)
—Charles Darwin (p. 292)
—Christopher Columbus & Neil Armstrong. (p. 317)
—Comets (p. 348)
—Cyber Bullying (p. 396)
—Daily Life in Ancient Sumer. (p. 400)
—Daily Life in the Maya Civilization. (p. 400)
—Deserts: An Explorer Travel Guide HL Studios Staff, illus. (p. 429)
—Disaster Relief (p. 446)
—Earth (p. 495)
—Eclipses (p. 502)
—Energy for Everyone? the Business of Energy. (p. 528)
—Fighting Fires (p. 585)
—Finding Out about Your Family History (p. 588)
—Fun Magic Tricks (p. 648)
—High-Tech Olympics (p. 778)
—History Around You (p. 783)
—History at Home (p. 783)
—Home Fronts in World War I. (p. 792)
—Hoping for Peace in Afghanistan. (p. 797)
—Hoping for Peace in Libya. (p. 797)
—How Carbon Footprints Work. (p. 805)
—How Electric & Hybrid Cars Work. (p. 809)
—Internet Safety (p. 880)
—Julius Caesar Edwards, Mat, illus. (p. 932)
—Julius Caesar (p. 933)
—Libya (p. 1007)
—Life on the Western Front (p. 1012)
—Louis Pasteur (p. 1058)
—Military Survival (p. 1143)
—Morocco (p. 1175)
—New Worlds (p. 1247)
—Night Sky: & Other Amazing Sights. (p. 1254)
—Northern Lights (p. 1266)
—Offshore Oil Drilling (p. 1280)
—Pirate Treasure (p. 1363)
—Popular Culture: 1940-1959 (p. 1385)
—Rain Forests: An Explorer Travel Guide (p. 1434)
—Remembering World War I. (p. 1460)
—Science vs. Animal Extinction. (p. 1528)
—Science vs. Climate Change. (p. 1528)
—Science vs. the Energy Crisis. (p. 1528)
—Seas. (p. 1538)
—Shipwrecks (p. 1567)
—Silly Circus Tricks (p. 1575)
—Space (p. 1618)
—Stars & Constellations (p. 1643)
—Steve Jobs (p. 1649)
—Sun (p. 1675)
—Surviving Disasters (p. 1687)
—Suzanne Collins (p. 1688)
—Talking about the Past (p. 1703)
—Terrorism & Security (p. 1722)
—Winter Olympics. (p. 1938)
—Women in World War I (p. 1946)
—World of Olympics (p. 1957)
—World War I: Frontline Soldiers & Their Families. (p. 1958)
—World War I - Unclassified: Secrets Revealed! (p. 1959)
—World War II: Frontline Soldiers & Their Families. (p. 1959)
Hunter, Nick, jt. auth. see Bancroft, Tom.
Hunter, Nick, jt. auth. see Labrecque, Ellen.
Hunter, Nick & Faure, Florence. Alexander the Great (p. 36)
Hunter, Nick, et al. Hero Journals. (p. 772)
—Treasure Hunters. (p. 1781)
Hunter, Norman. Incredible Adventures of Professor Branestawm. (p. 869)
—Peculiar Triumph of Professor Branestawm. (p. 1334)
Hunter, R., illus. see Ruzycki, Dandan.
Hunter, R. C. Moon Kids. (p. 1172)
Hunter, R. Chase, illus. see Ruzycki, Dan Dan.
Hunter, Rebecca. Climate Change. (p. 332)
—Earth. (p. 495)
—Energy Supply. (p. 528)
—Facts about Electricity. (p. 561)
—Living Organisms. (p. 1041)
—Rain Forests. (p. 1434)
—Saving Wildlife. (p. 1518)
—Waste & Recycling. (p. 1860)
—Water Supply. (p. 1863)
Hunter, Rebecca & Walker, Kathryn. Growing up in the Forties. (p. 726)

—Growing up in the Thirties. (p. 726)
Hunter, Robbie Chase, illus. see Ruzycki, Dan Dan.
Hunter, Roy. Larry the Bookworm Saves the Day. (p. 976)
Hunter, Ryan Ann. In Disguise! Stories of Real Women Spies. (p. 863)
—In Disguise! Undercover with Real Women Spies. Little, Jeanette, illus. (p. 863)
Hunter, Ryan Ann, et al. Into the Air: An Illustrated Timeline of Flight. Nascimbene, Yan, illus. (p. 881)
Hunter, Sally. Humphrey's Playtime. (p. 827)
Hunter, Sara Hoagland. Every Turtle Counts. Spellman, Susan, illus. (p. 543)
—Lighthouse Santa. Miner, Julia, illus. (p. 1015)
—Unbreakable Code. Miner, Julia, illus. (p. 1811)
Hunter, Scott. Ley Lines of Lushbury. (p. 1004)
Hunter, Skillman "Kim". Becerrito en Valle Grande. Ritthaler, Sarah Pilcher, tr. (p. 155)
Hunter, T. H. Car Key Elves. Gavrilovskiy, Olga, illus. (p. 265)
Hunter, Tammy. Tede's Search for his Mom. (p. 1713)
Hunter, Thomas, Jr. I Can Be Anything I Want to Be. (p. 835)
Hunter, Todd H. Elf Night: A Christmas Story. Gavrilovskiy, Olga, illus. (p. 512)
Hunter, Travis. Two the Hard Way. (p. 1804)
Hunter, Valerie. Journey to Uranus (p. 929)
Hunter, Wade. Dark Glimmers. (p. 407)
Hunter, William. DNA Analysis. (p. 456)
—DNA Analysis. Noziglia, Carla Miller & Siegel, Jay A., eds. (p. 456)
—Mark & Trace Analysis. (p. 1095)
—Mark & Trace Analysis. Siegel, Jay A., ed. (p. 1095)
—Medications & Surgeries for Weight Loss: When Dieting Isn't Enough. (p. 1119)
—Nature & Nurture: The Causes of Obesity. (p. 1236)
—Nature & Nurture: The Causes of Obesity. Garcia, Victor, ed. (p. 1236)
—Solving Crimes with Physics. (p. 1608)
—Solving Crimes with Physics. Noziglia, Carla Miller & Siegel, Jay A., eds. (p. 1608)
—Surgery & Medicine for Weight Loss. Garcia, Victor, ed. (p. 1685)
Hunter, William, jt. auth. see Hunter, Miranda.
Hunter, Zach. Generation Change: Roll up Your Sleeves & Change the World (p. 660)
Hunter-Gault, Charlayne. To the Mountaintop: My Journey Through the Civil Rights Movement. (p. 1759)
Huntington, Amy, illus. see Anderson, Jill.
Huntington, Amy, illus. see Beckhorn, Susan Williams.
Huntington, Amy, illus. see Clark, Katherine.
Huntington, Amy, illus. see Clark, Katie.
Huntington, Amy, illus. see Heiden, Pete.
Huntington, Amy, illus. see Meyer, Susan.
Huntington, Amy, illus. see Norworth, Jack.
Huntington, Geoffrey. Blood Moon. (p. 200)
Huntington, Harriet E. Forest Giants: The Story of the California Redwoods. (p. 618)
Huntington, Hugh Mike, Jr. & Huntington, Thomas. Story of Your Life: A 'Fill in the Blanks' Autobiography. (p. 1663)
Huntington, Thomas, jt. auth. see Huntington, Hugh Mike, Jr.
Huntley, Amy. Everafter. (p. 541)
Huntley, Doris, illus. see Dowell, Vivian
Huntley, Helen. Essential Academic Vocabulary: Mastering the Complete Academic Word List. (p. 536)
Huntley, Theresa. Women in the Renaissance. (p. 1946)
Hunton, Carroll David. Son of the Eastern Plains (p. 1611)
Hunton, Robert L. Secrets of the Medicine Pouch. (p. 1545)
Huntrods, David. For the Love of Scuba. (p. 616)
—Jaguars. (p. 905)
—Scuba. (p. 1533)
Hunt-Ullock, Kathy, et al. Because You Teach: A Dynamic Musical Resource for Innovative Staff Development. Norris, Jill, ed. (p. 155)
—Middle School Matters: Innovative Classroom Activities. Norris, Jill, ed. (p. 1138)
Huntzinger, Erica. Cosmo Finds His Forever Home. (p. 368)
—How Much I Love You. (p. 811)
—When We Say Goodnight. (p. 1905)
Hunziker, Raymond E. Marine Aquariums: Basic Aquarium Setup & Maintenance. (p. 1094)
Hupf, Mitchell, jt. auth. see Hupf, Zetta.
Hupf, Mitchellx, jt. auth. see Hupf, Zetta.
Hupf, Zetta & Hupf, Mitchell. Henry Goes to the Park Hupf, Zetta, illus. (p. 768)
Hupf, Zetta & Hupf, Mitchellx. Detective Buddy & the Case of the Missing Football Hupf, Zetta, illus. (p. 431)
Hupp, Abby. Wizard in the Kitchen: Magical recipes for Kids of All Ages. (p. 1943)
Huppert, Beth L. Tale of the Scarlet Knight. (p. 1700)
Huppert, Susan. Perfect Gift. White, Rachel, illus. (p. 1342)
Huras, Lynne, illus. see Pavelka, Joe.
Hurchalla, Elizabeth, ed. see Hasbro.
Hurcomb, Fran. Going Places (p. 692)
Hurd. Physical Science. (p. 1353)
Hurd, jt. auth. see Hurd, Thacher.
Hurd, Clement, illus. see Brown, Margaret Wise & Brown, Wise M.
Hurd, Clement, illus. see Brown, Margaret Wise.
Hurd, Clement, illus. see Stein, Gertrude & Hurd, Thacher.
Hurd, Edith Thacher & Brown, Margaret Wise. Two Little Gardeners. Elliot, Gertrude, illus. (p. 1804)
Hurd, Owen. Chicago History for Kids: Triumphs & Tragedies of the Windy City Includes 21 Activities. (p. 299)
Hurd, Pamela. Switch Witch: An Old Fashioned Witch Learns a New Trick. (p. 1691)
Hurd, T. Mama Don't Allow. Hurd, Thacher, photos by. (p. 1084)
Hurd, Thacher. Bad Frogs. Hurd, Thacher, illus. (p. 131)
—Cat's Pajamas. (p. 281)
—Mama Don't Allow. (p. 1084)
—Pea Patch Jig. (p. 1331)
Hurd, Thacher, jt. auth. see Hurd, Thacher.
Hurd, Thacher, jt. auth. see Stein, Gertrude.
Hurd, Thacher, photos by see Hurd, T.
Hurd, Thacher & Hurd. Art Dog. Hurd, Thacher, illus. (p. 102)
—Mama Don't Allow. Hurd, Thacher, illus. (p. 1084)
Hurd, Thacher & Hurd, Thacher. Mystery on the Docks. Hurd, Thacher, illus. (p. 1226)
Hurd, Will. Changing States: Solids, Liquids, & Gases (p. 290)
Hurdman, Charlotte. Hands-on History! Stone Age. (p. 741)
—Stone Age. (p. 1652)
Hurdman, Charlotte, ed. World History Encyclopedia: 4 Million Years Ago to the Present Day. (p. 1955)
Hurdman, Charlotte, et al. Find Out about Ancient Egypt, Rome & Greece: Exploring the Great Classical Civilizations, with 60 Step-By-Step Projects & 1500 Exciting Images. (p. 587)
—Living History: What Life Was Like in Ancient Times. (p. 1041)
Hurley, Andrew, tr. see Borges, Jorge Luis.
Hurley, Andrew, tr. see Pérez-Reverte, Arturo.
Hurley, Ann Hollinshead. John Donne's Poetry & Early Modern Visual Culture. (p. 921)
Hurley, Crystal. Witch with an Itch. (p. 1941)
Hurley, J. M. Dance with Life (p. 402)
Hurley, Jeanette Clinger. Crystal Prince: Love Is the Only Way. (p. 387)
Hurley, Jo. Looking Good! How to Get Stylin' with Your Friends. Morley, Taia, illus. (p. 1051)
—Scooby-Doo! & the Phantom Prankster. (p. 1529)
—Scooby-Doo's Super Fun Book. (p. 1529)
—Slumber-Ific! Great Sleepover Ideas for You & Your Friends. Morley, Taia, illus. (p. 1591)
Hurley, Jorey. Fetch. Hurley, Jorey, illus. (p. 582)
—Nest. Hurley, Jorey, illus. (p. 1242)
Hurley, Meagan, jt. auth. see Reis, Jason.
Hurley, Michael. A-Z of the World Cup (p. 2)
—Baseball (p. 140)
—Basketball (p. 143)
—Canada (p. 260)
—Fantastic Sports Facts. (p. 572)
—Football (p. 615)
—Great Olympic Moments (p. 717)
—Ice Hockey (p. 850)
—Racing (p. 1432)
—Soccer (p. 1603)
—Surviving the Wilderness (p. 1687)
—United States of America (p. 1820)
—World Cup (p. 1954)
—World Cup 2010 (p. 1954)
—World Cup 2014 (p. 1954)
—World Cup Fever (p. 1954)
—World Cup Heroes (p. 1954)
—World Cup Nations (p. 1954)
—World of Soccer (p. 1957)
—World's Most Amazing Bridges (p. 1960)
—World's Most Amazing Lakes (p. 1960)
—World's Most Amazing Mountains (p. 1960)
—World's Most Amazing Skyscrapers (p. 1960)
—World's Most Amazing Stadiums (p. 1960)
Hurley, Michael & Heinemann Library Staff. World's Most Amazing Lakes (p. 1960)
—World's Most Amazing Mountains (p. 1960)
Hurley, Tonya. Blessed. Watkins, Abbey, illus. (p. 199)
—Ghostgirl. (p. 672)
—Ghostgirl. Frieyro, Alicia, tr. (p. 672)
—Homecoming. (p. 793)
—Lovesick. (p. 1061)
—Passionaries. (p. 1327)
—Precious Blood. Watkins, Abbey, illus. (p. 1394)
Hurley, Trish. 10 Most Enduring Fashion Trends. (p. 1993)
—10 Most Outrageous Outlaws. (p. 1994)
Hurley, Wes. How the Winter Frog Came to Was: Or, How to Get a Nice Surprise on Thanksgiving! Lee, Susan, illus. (p. 813)
Hurmence, Belinda. Girl Called Boy. (p. 678)
Hurrell, Dianne. Tom Burrows & Friends: Short Stories, Rhymes & Poems. (p. 1763)
Hurry, Helen. Peepo! Boo! Who Are You? (p. 1335)
Hursky, Kim. Ropald Needs a New Home. (p. 1488)
Hurst, Brandon Franklin. M-Trait. (p. 1067)
Hurst, Brooklynn. Fitness for Teens: Getting you Motivated for Life by Providing Principles for Healthy Living. (p. 599)
Hurst, Carol Otis. Picture Books in the Classroom: Addressing Concepts & Skills throughout the Curriculum Through Literature Kindergarten through Grade 2 (p. 1355)
—Terrible Storm. (p. 1721)
Hurst, Ceri, illus. see Virr, Paul.
Hurst, Christine. Symphony Smythe Wants a Pet. (p. 1693)
Hurst, Debbie, illus. see Gould, M&R.
Hurst, Debbie, illus. see Gould, M. & Gould, R.
Hurst, Donna L. & Taylor, Allison Wagner. Green Alphabet - a First Look at Ecology. (p. 721)
Hurst, Elise, illus. see Trussell-Cullen, Alan.
Hurst, Elva. Autumn Days: Based on a True Story. (p. 118)
—Pony Cart Adventure: A True Story. (p. 1382)
—Pony Cart Adventure. (p. 1382)
—Summer on the Farm: A True Story. (p. 1674)
—Summer on the Farm. (p. 1674)
—When School Bells Call: Based on a True Story. (p. 1904)
Hurst, Heidi. Jennifer Lopez. (p. 913)
Hurst, Joshua. One Day at the North Pole. Johnson, Jared, illus. (p. 1294)
Hurst, Kelly, jt. auth. see Gliori, Debi.
Hurst, Margaret, illus. see Gabriele, Joseph.
Hurst, Melissa E. Edge of Forever. (p. 504)
Hurst, Oliver, illus. see Hoena, Blake.
Hurst, Oliver, illus. see Knight, Richard, et al.
Hurst, Rich. Goodnight Thing. Sprague, Lois Rosio, illus. (p. 701)
Hurst-Archer, Lisa. How to Make a Wave (p. 820)
Hurston, Nancy S. Enchanted Pixie Gardens. (p. 523)
Hurston, Zora Neale. Six Fools. Tanksley, Ann, illus. (p. 1582)
—Three Witches. Ringgold, Faith, illus. (p. 1744)
—Zora Neale Hurston's Their Eyes Were Watching God. Bloom, Harold, ed. (p. 1990)
Hurston, Zora Neale & Thomas, Joyce Carol. Lies & Other Tall Tales. (p. 1007)
—Lies & Other Tall Tales. Myers, Christopher, illus. (p. 1007)
—Six Fools. Tanksley, Ann, illus. (p. 1582)
—Three Witches. Ringgold, Faith, illus. (p. 1744)
Hurt, Barbara. Dragons & Dragoons. Hurt, Barbara, illus. (p. 478)
—Great Tree of Milden Worf. (p. 719)
Hurt, John Washington, reader. Rabbit Ears World Tales. (p. 1429)
Hurt, Laurie. Jay & the Old Big Blue Truck. (p. 910)
Hurt, Laurie S. What I Think I Want to Be. (p. 1887)
Hurtado, Adrian M. Mary Had a Little Lamb. (p. 1100)
Hurtado, Bobadilla, jt. auth. see del Carmen, Maria.
Hurtado, Ernest R. Freddy the Unfixer. (p. 633)
Hurtado, Patricia. Magical Feline & the White Haven. (p. 1074)
Hurteau, Dave, jt. auth. see Bestful, Scott.
Hurth, Barbi. Butterfly & the Bee. Meyer, Chloe, illus. (p. 247)
Hurtig, Jennifer. Beatrix Potter. (p. 153)
—Butterflies. (p. 247)
—Butterflies. Hudak, Heather C., ed. (p. 247)
—Capitals. (p. 262)
—Deciduous Forests. (p. 421)
—Field Hockey. (p. 584)
—For the Love of Field Hockey. (p. 616)
—Maurice Sendak. (p. 1110)
—Natural Landmarks. (p. 1235)
—Raccoons. (p. 1430)
—Raccoons. Hudak, Heather C., ed. (p. 1430)
—Statue of Liberty. (p. 1645)
—Uluru: Sacred Rock of the Australian Desert. (p. 1810)
Hurtig, Jennifer & Kissock, Heather. Statue of Liberty. (p. 1645)
Hurt-Newton, Tania. Vamos de Paseo. (p. 1831)
—Yee-Ha Harvey. (p. 1969)
Hurvitz, Mitchell M., jt. auth. see Karesh, Sara E.
Hurwicz, Claude. Henry the Navigator. (p. 768)
Hurwin, Davida Wills. Freaks & Revelations. (p. 631)
—Time for Dancing. (p. 1751)
Hurwit, Jeffrey M. Acropolis in the Age of Pericles. (p. 9)
Hurwitz, Jane. Choosing a Career in Animal Care. (p. 310)
Hurwitz, Johanna. Amazing Monty. McGrory, Anik, illus. (p. 55)
—E is for Elisa. Tilley, Debbie, illus. (p. 492)
—Ethan Out & about Big Book: Brand New Readers. Floca, Brian, illus. (p. 539)
—Fourth-Grade Fuss. Hammond, Andy, illus. (p. 625)
—Magical Monty. McGrory, Anik, illus. (p. 1075)
—Mighty Monty: More First-Grade Adventures. McGrory, Anik, illus. (p. 1140)
—Mighty Monty. McGrory, Anek, illus. (p. 1140)
—Two & Only Kelly Twins. Mourning, Tuesday, illus. (p. 1803)
Hurwitz, Johanna & McCrory, Anik. Mostly Monty. McGrory, Anik, illus. (p. 1177)
Hurwitz, Johanna, ed. I Fooled You: Ten Stories of Tricks, Jokes & Switcheroos. Nihoff, Tim, illus. (p. 838)
Hurwitz, Kathleen A. Timothy's Tic. Mc Kelvey, Shawn, illus. (p. 1755)
Hurwitz, Laura. Disappear Home. (p. 446)
Hurwitz, Laura, jt. auth. see Lumry, Amanda.
Hurwitz, Michele Weber. Calli Be Gold. (p. 254)
—Summer I Saved the World ... in 65 Days. (p. 1674)
Hus, Jarred O., jt. auth. see Huseby, Adam J.
Husain, Aliya. Neither This nor That. (p. 1240)
Husain, Farzana, jt. auth. see Mortenson, Greg.
Husain, Shahrukh. Indian Myths. Willey, Bee, illus. (p. 871)
—Vikings. (p. 1842)
—Wise Fool. Archer, Micha, illus. (p. 1940)
Husain, Shahrukh & Mayhew, James. Barefoot Book of Stories from the Opera. (p. 139)
Husain, Zakir & Mishra, Samina. Sunshine for Amma. Pottenkulam, Pooja, illus. (p. 1678)
Husar, Jaco & Husar, Stephane. Hello, I Am Lily from New York City. Rigaudie, Mylene, illus. (p. 764)
Husar, Lisa, photos by see Schindel, John.
Husar, Lisa & Husar, Mike. Grand Canyon Babies. (p. 707)
Husar, Lisa & Husar, Mike, photos by. Bobcat Babies. (p. 206)
Husar, Mike, jt. auth. see Husar, Lisa.
Husar, Mike, jt. photos by see Husar, Lisa.
Husar, Mike, photos by see Schindel, John.
Husar, Stephane. Hello, I Am Charlie from London. Robert, Yannick, illus. (p. 764)
—Hello, I Am Max from Sydney. Sofilas, Mark, illus. (p. 764)
—Paolo from Rome. Le Grand, Claire, illus. (p. 1321)
Husar, Stephane, jt. auth. see Husar, Jaco.
Husband, Amy. Dear Teacher. (p. 419)
Husband, Amy, illus. see Barr, Catherine & Williams, Steve.
Husband Haddow, Barbara. One More Than Enough. (p. 1296)
Husband, Ron, illus. see Hopkinson, Deborah.
Husberg, Rob, illus. see Bernstein, Daryl.
Husby, Greg. Zoebirds. (p. 1987)
Husebo, Sara. Cinderella's Treasures. (p. 320)
Huseby, Adam J. & Hus, Jarred O. Adventures of Captain Kaleb: Pirate's Treasure. (p. 17)
Huseby, Victoria. Butterfly. (p. 247)
—Cat. (p. 277)
—Chicken. (p. 299)
—Daisy. (p. 400)
—Frog. (p. 639)
—Oak Tree. (p. 1274)
Huseman, Ryan, illus. see Oramas, Jennifer.
Huser, Glen. Runaway (p. 1496)
—Skinnybones & the Wrinkle Queen (p. 1585)
—Skinnybones & the Wrinkle Queen. (p. 1585)
—Stitches (p. 1651)
Huser, Glen & Rose, Martin. Jeremy's Christmas Wish. (p. 913)
Huskins, Suzanne Hallier. No Matter What! (p. 1259)
Huskins, Suzanne Hallier, illus. see Wyont, Wanda.
Huskins, T. A. I Am a Whosoever. (p. 832)
Huss, Sally, illus. see Lang, Rocky.
Hussain, Nelupa, illus. see Watt, Fiona.
Hussain, Saima S. Arab World Thought of It: Inventions, Innovations, & Amazing Facts. (p. 94)
Hussenot, Victor. Land of Lines. (p. 973)
Hussey, Charmian. Valley of Secrets. Crump, Christopher, illus. (p. 1831)
Hussey, Christopher, ed. see Davey, Peter.
Hussey, Don. Chesapeake Station: It Began with Serenity. (p. 298)
Hussey, Lorna. Little Lost Unicorn. (p. 1031)
Hussey, Lorna, illus. see Capucilli, Alyssa Satin.
Hussey, Lorna, illus. see Carroll, Lewis, pseud.
Hussey, Lorna, illus. see Courtauld, Sarah.
Hussey, Maria. Rise of the Jim Crow ERA. (p. 1475)
Hussey, Maria, ed. Rise of the Jim Crow Era. (p. 1475)
Hussl Krassnig, Gloria. What a Family. (p. 1878)
Husson, Severin & Veyret, Yvette. Nuestro Planeta, la Tierra. Hernández, Pau Joan, tr. (p. 1270)
Hust, Duke. Last Flight of the Gooney Bird. (p. 977)
Husted, Louella M. Elwood the Doubting Elf. (p. 517)
Husted, Marty, illus. see Hoffelt, Jane.
Husted, Terri. Math Detective B1: Higher-Order Thinking Reading Writing in Mathematics. (p. 1105)
Husted, Terri, jt. auth. see Critical Thinking Publishing Staff.
Husted, Ursula. Making Rain. (p. 1082)
Husting, Chad. Chemistry Student Lab Manual. (p. 297)
Hustins, Shelley, illus. see Riddle, Peter H.
Huston, Charlie. Sleepless: A Novel. (p. 1589)
Huston, Deirdre. Jake, Zee-Bee & the Crystal Quest. (p. 906)
Huston, Donna. Inch by Inch. (p. 868)
—Mr. O'Toole, the Diabetic Mule. (p. 1186)
—Vincent Rocks. (p. 1842)
—Woe down Clown. (p. 1943)
Huston, Harriette "Ree". Rescue of Buster Bus: A True Adventure Mystery with Sparkling Intrigue for All Ages. (p. 1462)
Huston, Jennifer L. U2: Changing the World Through Rock 'n' Roll. (p. 1807)
Huston, Kyle, illus. see Leon, Loni.
Huszar, Susan, photos by see Bailey, Debbie.
Hutchcraft, Steve. B Is for Bufflehead: Flying Through the ABC's with Fun Feathered Friends. Hutchcraft, Steve, photos by. (p. 123)
Hutchens, Calvin. Adventures of Otis Possum. (p. 21)
Hutchens, David. PageLand: A Story about Love & Sharing & Working Together. Gombert, Bobby, illus. (p. 1318)
Hutcherson, Darren, illus. see Norton, George.
Hutcheson, John C. Tom Finch's Monkey. (p. 1763)
Hutcheson, Meredith, ed. see Haidar, Hanna.
Hutchings, Amy. What Happens at a Horse Farm? (p. 1885)
—What Happens at a Horse Farm? ¿Qué Pasa en una Granja de Caballos? (p. 1885)
—What Happens at a Horse Farm? (¿Qué Pasa en una Granja de Caballos?) (p. 1885)
—What Happens at a Horse Farm?/¿Qué Pasa en una Granja de Caballos? (p. 1885)
—What Happens at a Supermarket? (p. 1885)
—What Happens at a Supermarket?/Qué Pasa en un Supermercado? (p. 1885)
—What Happens at a Vet's Office? (p. 1885)
—What Happens at a Vet's Office?/Que Pasa En Una Clinica Veterinaria? (p. 1885)
—What Happens at a Vet's Office?/¿Qué Pasa en Una Clínica Veterinaria? (p. 1885)
—What Happens at an Airport? (p. 1885)
—What Happens at an Airport? (¿Qué pasa en un Aeropuerto?) (p. 1885)
—What Happens at an Amusement Park? ¿Qué pasa en un parque de Diversiones? (p. 1885)
—What Happens at an Amusement Park?/¿Qué Pasa en un Parque de Diversiones? (p. 1886)
Hutchings, Amy & Nations, Susan. What Happens at a Party Store? (p. 1885)
—What Happens at a Party Store?/¿Qué Pasa en una Tienda de Cosas para Fiestas) (p. 1885)
—What Happens at a Supermarket?/Qué Pasa en un Supermercado? (p. 1885)
—What Happens at a TV Station? (p. 1885)
—What Happens at a TV Station? (¿Qué pasa en una emisora de Televisión?) (p. 1885)
—What Happens at a TV Station?/¿Qué Pasa en Una Emisora de Televisión? (p. 1885)
—What Happens at an Airport? (?:¿Qué pasa en un Aeropuerto?) (p. 1885)
—What Happens at an Airport?/¿Qué Pasa en un Aeropuerto? (p. 1885)
—What Happens at an Amusement Park? (p. 1885)
Hutchings, Harriet Anne. Amanda & the Angel. Cragg, Marcelyn Martin, illus. (p. 52)
Hutchings, Melinda. It Will Get Better: Finding Your Way Through Teen Issues. (p. 894)
Hutchings, Paul. Don't Eat That! Rhyming Words. (p. 467)
—Halloween Tails. (p. 739)
Hutchings, Tony. Week at the Seaside. (p. 1871)
Hutchings, Tony, illus. see Dorman, Clive & Dorman, Helen.
Hutchings, Tony, illus. see Dorman, Helen & Dorman, Clive.
Hutchins, Annie H., illus. see Brown, Pamela.
Hutchins, Elizabeth. Personal Best: Snowbored, All That Jazz, Thief! (p. 1344)
Hutchins, Eric, jt. auth. see Anderson, Matt.
Hutchins, Hazel. Robyn Makes the News. Cathcart, Yvonne, illus. (p. 1481)
—Robyn's Monster Play Cathcart, Yvonne, illus. (p. 1481)
—Robyn's Monster Play. Cathcart, Yvonne, illus. (p. 1481)
—Robyn's Party in the Park Cathcart, Yvonne, illus. (p. 1481)
—Robyn's Party-in-the-Park. Cathcart, Yvonne, illus. (p. 1481)
—Sarah & the Magic Science Project. Delezenne, Christine, illus. (p. 1514)
—Second Is a Hiccup: A Child's Book of Time. Denton, Kady MacDonald, illus. (p. 1539)
—Skate, Robyn, Skate Cathcart, Yvonne, illus. (p. 1583)
—Skate, Robyn, Skate. Cathcart, Yvonne, illus. (p. 1583)
—TJ & the Haunted House (p. 1758)
—TJ & the Quiz Kids (p. 1758)
—TJ & the Rockets (p. 1758)
—TJ & the Sports Fanatic (p. 1758)

H

—What the Snakes Wrote. Holdcroft, Tina, illus. (p. 1893)
Hutchins, Hazel, jt. auth. see Hutchins, Hazel J.
Hutchins, Hazel & Herbert, Gail. Mattland. Petricic, Dusan, illus. (p. 1110)
Hutchins, Hazel J. Ben's Snow Song: A Winter Picnic. (p. 165)
—I'd Know You Anywhere. (p. 851)
—It's Raining, Yancy & Bear. (p. 898)
—Second Is a Hiccup: A Child's Book of Time. Denton, Kady MacDonald, illus. (p. 1539)
Hutchins, Hazel J. & Hutchins, Hazel. Beneath the Bridge. Ohi, Ruth, illus. (p. 164)
—Robyn Makes the News Cathcart, Yvonne, illus. (p. 1481)
—Sidewalk Rescue. Ohi, Ruth, illus. (p. 1573)
—Skate, Robyn, Skate. Cathcart, Yvonne, illus. (p. 1583)
Hutchins, J. Spanish First Words (Primeras Palabras en Espanol) (p. 1621)
—Spanish First Words - Primeras Palabras en Español. (p. 1621)
Hutchins, Jennifer J. Just Plain Nora. (p. 939)
Hutchins, Laurence. I'm the King of the Castle! And Other Plays for Children. Hutchins, Laurence, illus. (p. 860)
Hutchins, Pat. Barn Dance! Hutchins, Pat, illus. (p. 139)
—Doorbell Rang. (p. 470)
—Rosie's Walk. (p. 1490)
—Titch. (p. 1758)
Hutchins, Paul. Secret Doorway: Beyond Imagination. (p. 1540)
Hutchinson, Alberta. Mystical Mandala Coloring Book. (p. 1226)
Hutchinson, Alberta, jt. auth. see Bartfeld, Martha.
Hutchinson, Alberta & Creative Haven Staff. Lotus Designs. (p. 1057)
—Square Mandalas. (p. 1636)
Hutchinson, Barry. Book of Elements: Fire & Water. (p. 211)
Hutchinson, Cheryl, ed. see Loesch, Joe.
Hutchinson, David, illus. see Dunn, Joeming.
Hutchinson, Emily. Car & Driver. (p. 265)
—Descriptive Writing Saddleback Educational Publishing Staff, ed. (p. 428)
—Everyday Household Tasks. (p. 543)
—Expository Writing Saddleback Educational Publishing Staff, ed. (p. 554)
—Man in the Iron Mask. (p. 1085)
—Moving Out on Your Own. (p. 1183)
—Narrative Writing Saddleback Educational Publishing Staff, ed. (p. 1229)
—Swiss Family Robinson. (p. 1691)
Hutchinson, Isabel, tr. see Rasmussen, Knud.
Hutchinson, John. Designing with Pro/DESKTOP: A Classroom Guide for Students Using Pro/DESKTOP V8. (p. 430)
Hutchinson, Joy, illus. see Aston, Al.
Hutchinson, Kerrian. Fish People. (p. 598)
Hutchinson, Mark. Reptiles. (p. 1461)
Hutchinson, Mark, tr. see Jonquet, Francois.
Hutchinson McMullen, Angela. I Like Me. (p. 841)
Hutchinson, M.D., Patricia, jt. auth. see Holmes, Melisa.
Hutchinson, Michelle, illus. see Ten Hagen, Evelyn.
Hutchinson, Shaun David. Deathday Letter. (p. 420)
—Fml. (p. 610)
—Violent Ends: A Novel in Seventeen Points of View. (p. 1843)
Hutchinson, Shaun David, et al. Violent Ends: A Novel in Seventeen Points of View. (p. 1843)
Hutchinson, Stefan. First Death of Laurie Strode (p. 594)
Hutchinson, Tim. Battle Scars. (p. 147)
Hutchinson, Tim, illus. see Cheshire, Gerard & Tango Books Staff.
Hutchinson, Tim, illus. see Crosbie, Duncan.
Hutchinson, Tim, illus. see Qing, Zheng.
Hutchinson, Tim, illus. see Regan, Lisa.
Hutchinson, Tim, illus. see Tango Books Staff.
Hutchinson, Tim, illus. see Taylor, Dereen.
Hutchinson, Wanda Phillips. Bee Man. (p. 157)
Hutchinson, William, illus. see Barr, Gladys H.
Hutchison, Barry. Mr Mumbles. (p. 1185)
Hutchison, Barry, jt. auth. see Grosset and Dunlap Editors.
Hutchison, Barry, jt. auth. see Grosset and Dunlap Staff.
Hutchison, D. C., illus. see Altsheler, Joseph A.
Hutchison, D. W. Storm Hags. (p. 1656)
Hutchison, David. Dragon Arms: Chaos Blade. Vol. 2 (p. 476)
—Dragon Arms: Blood & Steel Pocket Manga. Vol. 1 (p. 476)
—Junction 17 Color Pocket Manga. (p. 934)
Hutchison, David, jt. auth. see Baum, L. Frank.
Hutchison, Dot. Wounded Name. (p. 1962)
Hutchison, G. F. How to Handle Your Parents: A Guide for Teens. (p. 820)
Hutchison, Gary, jt. auth. see Hammond, John.
Hutchison, Patricia. Blue Whales. (p. 203)
—Sea Otters. (p. 1535)
—Snow Leopards. (p. 1599)
Hutchison, Patricia, jt. auth. see Holmes, Melisa.
Hutchison, Patricia & Peterson, Sheryl. Polar Bears. (p. 1379)
Hutchison, Trish, jt. auth. see Holmes, Melisa.
Hutchman, Laurence & D'Alimonte, Dan. Still Waters (p. 1650)
Huth, Michael, jt. auth. see Melville, Herman.
Huthmacher, J. Joseph. Nation of Newcomers. (p. 1231)
Huthmaker, Dixie. Trapped in Half Position. (p. 1779)
Hutmacher, Kimberly. Fossils & Rocks. (p. 624)
—Night Sky. (p. 1254)
—Paws, Claws, Hands, & Feet Rogers, Sherry, illus. (p. 1331)
—Studying Our Earth, Inside & Out. (p. 1670)
—Wonderful Water Cycle. (p. 1948)
Hutmacher, Kimberly M. Caves (p. 282)
—Deltas (p. 425)
—Hours (p. 802)
—Hours. (p. 802)
—I Want a Cat (p. 847)
—I Want a Dog (p. 847)
—I Want a Goldfish (p. 847)
—I Want a Hamster (p. 847)
—I Want a Pet. (p. 847)
—Islands (p. 892)
—It's about Time. (p. 896)
—Minutes. (p. 1148)
—Mountains (p. 1181)
—Perros de Terapia/Therapy Dogs (p. 1344)
—Perros de Trineo/Sled Dogs (p. 1344)
—Seconds (p. 1540)
—Sled Dogs (p. 1588)
—Television & Movie Star Dogs (p. 1716)
—Therapy Dogs (p. 1729)
—Your Senses at the Beach (p. 1981)
—Your Senses at the Dentist's Office. (p. 1981)
—Your Senses at the Fire Station (p. 1981)
—Your Senses at the Grocery Store (p. 1981)
—Your Senses at the Zoo (p. 1981)
Hutnick, Theresa & Phillips, Karen. Insectos Insolitos. Fox, Peter, photos by. (p. 875)
Hutsell-Manning, Linda. Jason & the Wonder Horn. (p. 910)
Hutson, Matt. Inside Story of the Moon. (p. 877)
—Inside Story of the Sun. (p. 877)
—Totally Amazing Careers in Aerospace. (p. 1771)
—Totally Amazing Careers in Engineering. (p. 1771)
—What Do You Want to Be? Explore Aerospace. (p. 1883)
Hutson-Nechkash, Peg. Help Me Write: Frames & Rubrics for Classroom Writing Success. (p. 765)
Hutson-Thompson, Holliday & Staggs, Kelley. Water Wonderful: An Activity Book for Grade K-3. (p. 1863)
Hutt, Aletha. Mama & Baba's First Chinese Words. (p. 1084)
Hutt, Sarah. Missing (p. 1152)
Hutt, Sarah & Horton, Loren O. Uniquely Iowa (p. 1818)
Hutto, Victoria, illus. see Hirschmann, Kris.
Hutto, Victoria, illus. see Sauer, Tammi.
Huttoe, Norma. Rusty - the Kissing Horse. (p. 1498)
Hutton, Clare. Zombie Dog. (p. 1988)
Hutton, Fiona. Adventures of Henrietta - the Camden Girl. (p. 18)
Hutton, Galia. Frank the Colorful Frog. Knox, Anna Mae, illus. (p. 629)
Hutton, Janice Turney. When My Shoes Aren't Cool. (p. 1904)
Hutton, Jason, illus. see Pettitt, Emily.
Hutton, John. Ball: Baby Unplugged. Hutton, John, ed. (p. 134)
—Beach: Baby Unplugged. Kang, Andrea, illus. (p. 149)
—Blanket: Baby Unplugged. Kang, Andrea, illus. (p. 198)
—Blocks: Baby Unplugged. Hutton, John, ed. (p. 200)
—Book: Baby Unplugged. Hutton, John, ed. (p. 210)
—Box: Baby Unplugged. Kang, Andrea, illus. (p. 216)
—Flowers for Mr. President. (p. 608)
—Pets: Baby Unplugged. Kang, Andrea, illus. (p. 1348)
—Sister Maus: A Small Tale of Sisters House in Salem. (p. 1581)
—Wet: Baby Unplugged. Hutton, John, ed. (p. 1877)
—Yard: Baby Unplugged. Kang, Andrea, illus. (p. 1968)
Hutton, John, ed. see Gross, Sandra & Busch, Leah.
Hutton, Kallie, et al. Mathematics for Zambia Basic Education Grade 5 Pupil's Book. (p. 1108)
—Stepping into Mathematics Grade 5 Learner's Book. (p. 1648)
—Stepping into Mathematics Grade 5 Learner's Book Afrikaans Translation. (p. 1648)
—Stepping into Mathematics Matters Grade 4 Learner's Book. (p. 1648)
—Stepping into Mathematics Matters Grade 4 Learner's Book Afrikaans Translation. (p. 1648)
Hutton, Linda. Every Monday Morning. Murley, Karen O., illus. (p. 543)
Hutton, Sam. Deep End. (p. 423)
—Final Shot. (p. 586)
—Kiss & Kill. (p. 961)
Hutton, Simon. Brilliant Billy's Big Book of Dinosaurs. Glicksman, Caroline, illus. (p. 228)
Hutton, Stacie. Jr. Social Studies Investigator. (p. 930)
Hutton, Stacie Vaughn. Shovelful of Sunshine. Harness, Cheryl, illus. (p. 1570)
Hutton Turner, Elisabeth, et al. Calder Miró. (p. 252)
Hutts Aston, Dianna, jt. auth. see Aston, Dianna Hutts.
Huusmann, Thomas-Bo & Fables, Aesops. Lion & the Mouse. (p. 1020)
Huven, Kim. Birthday Bears. Padron, Alicia, illus. (p. 192)
Huws, Emily. Anghenfil o Joc. (p. 75)
—Nid Fy Mai I. Lawrie, Robin, illus. (p. 1251)
Huws, Emily, jt. auth. see Impey, Rose.
Huws, Emily & Gomer, Gwasg. Nadolig Cae Berllan. (p. 1227)
Huxley, Aldous. Crows of Pearblossom. (p. 386)
—Crows of Pearblossom. Blackall, Sophie, illus. (p. 386)
Huxley, Dee, illus. see Norrington, Leonie.
Huxley, Sheila M. One Lovely Summer: The Stories of One Little Butterfly & His Friends. (p. 1296)
Huxman, K. D. Dragon Talk. (p. 478)
—Dragon Talk. Farrington, Teresa, illus. (p. 478)
—Grizzelda Gorilla. (p. 724)
Huxman, Karin (K. D.). Dragon Talk. (p. 478)
Huxtable, Ada Louise. Frank Lloyd Wright: A Life. (p. 628)
Huxtable, John, illus. see Bryant, Megan E.
Huxtable, John, illus. see Golden Books.
Huxtable, John, illus. see Nagaraj, Josephine.
Huxtable, Tonja, illus. see Bryant, Megan E.
Huy, Barbara. Llamas Need Pajamas. (p. 1043)
Huyck, David, illus. see Bar-el, Dan.
Huysmans, Joris-Karl. Against Nature. Baldick, Robert, tr. from FRE. (p. 29)
Hveem, Todd. Adventures of Celtic: Road Trip. (p. 17)
—Adventures of Celtic. (p. 17)
Hvezda, Chris, jt. auth. see Ballew, Vince.
Hvolboll, Eric P., jt. contrib. by see Chapman, Chris.
Hwa, Kim Dong. Color of Earth Na, Lauren, tr. from KOR. (p. 343)
Hwang, Frances. Transparency: Stories. (p. 1779)
Hwang, Jung Sun, illus. see Lee, Young Shin & Rogers, Buddy.
Hwang, Jung Sun, illus. see Rogers, Bud & Lee, Young Shin.
Hwang, Sun-Mi. Hen Who Dreamed She Could Fly. (p. 767)
Hwang, William Liang & Mian, Matthew K., eds. InnoWorks: Explorations, Student Edition. (p. 875)
Hwang, Yong-Su & Yang, Kyung-Il. Blade of Heaven. (p. 198)
Hwang, YoSeob, illus. see Kim, JiYu.
Hyams, Tor, et al. World of Happiness: Book & CD. (p. 1956)
Hyatt, Greg. Moises y la serpiente de bronce (Moses & the Bronze Snake) (p. 1160)
—Moses & the Bronze Snake. (p. 1176)
Hyatt, Joe, illus. see Bix, Daisy.
Hyatt, Patricia Rusch. Quite Contrary Man: A True American Tale. Brown, Kathryn, illus. (p. 1428)
Hyatt, Sean, illus. see White.
Hyatt, Sean, jt. auth. see White.
Hyde. Television & Radio Announcing. (p. 1716)
Hyde, Andrew. Experience the Point: Unofficial Guidebook to Cedar Point. (p. 548)
Hyde, Catherine, illus. see Morris, Jackie.
Hyde, Catherine, illus. see Pirotta, Saviour.
Hyde, Catherine Ryan. Becoming Chloe. (p. 156)
—Day I Killed James. (p. 413)
—Jumpstart the World. (p. 934)
—Year of My Miraculous Reappearance. (p. 1969)
Hyde, Catherine Ryan, illus. see Duffy, Carol Ann.
Hyde, E. A. Watson. Little Sisters to the Camp Fire Girls. (p. 1036)
Hyde, Heidi Smith. Elan, Son of Two Peoples. Prevost, Mikela, illus. (p. 508)
—Emanuel & the Hanukkah Rescue. Akib, Jamel, illus. (p. 517)
—Feivel's Flying Horses. van der Sterre, Johanna, illus. (p. 581)
—Mendel's Accordion. van der Sterre, Johanna, illus. (p. 1126)
—Shanghai Sukkah. Tsong, Jing Jing, illus. (p. 1559)
Hyde, Jerry & Hulse, Terra. Child Survival Skills: How to Detect & Avoid Dangerous People. (p. 301)
Hyde, Judith Jensen. Indiana. (p. 871)
—Louisiana. (p. 1058)
Hyde, Katherine. Lucia: Saint of Light. (p. 1062)
Hyde, Lara. Mosquito Bites. (p. 1176)
Hyde, Margaret. Mo Smells Blue: A Scentsational Journey. Giacomini, Amanda, illus. (p. 1157)
—Mo Smells Christmas: A Scentsational Journey. Giacomini, Amanda, illus. (p. 1157)
—Mo Smells Green: A Scentsational Journey. Giacomini, Amanda, illus. (p. 1157)
—Mo Smells Pink: A Scentsational Journey. Giacomini, Amanda, illus. (p. 1157)
—Mo Smells the Ballpark. Chaudhary, Aman, illus. (p. 1157)
—Mo Smells the Holidays: A Scentsational Journey. Giacomini, Amanda, illus. (p. 1157)
Hyde, Margaret E. DreddieLocks & the Three Slugs. Parker, Curtis, illus. (p. 484)
—Mo Smells Sweet Dreams: A Scentsational Journey. Chaudhary, Aman, illus. (p. 1157)
Hyde, Margaret E., ed. Cassatt for Kids (p. 276)
—Impressionists for Kids. (p. 862)
—Matisse for Kids (p. 1109)
—Picasso for Kids (p. 1354)
—Renoir for Kids (p. 1460)
Hyde, Margaret, ed. Dreddielocks & the Three Slugs Parker, Curtis, illus. (p. 484)
—Picasso for Kids (p. 1354)
—Van Gogh for Kids (p. 1833)
Hyde, Margaret O. Robert Cormier. (p. 1478)
Hyde, Margaret O. & Forsyth, Elizabeth. Safe Sex 101: An Overview for Teens. (p. 1502)
Hyde, Margaret O. & Forsyth, Elizabeth H. Stress 101: An Overview for Teens. (p. 1667)
Hyde, Margaret O. & Keene, Frances W. Hobby Fun Book: For Grade School Boys & Girls. (p. 786)
Hyde, Margaret O. & Setaro, John F. Drugs 101: An Overview for Teens. (p. 487)
—Smoking 101: An Overview for Teens. (p. 1595)
Hyde, Maureen, illus. see Nobisso, Josephine.
Hyde, Michelle Hazelwood. Night Night, Birmingham. (p. 1253)
Hyde, Natalie. Alcatraz. (p. 35)
—Animal Fossils. (p. 77)
—Black Tuesday & the Great Depression. (p. 197)
—Changing Direction. (p. 290)
—Classified: Spies at Work. (p. 328)
—Conquering Everest. (p. 358)
—Cryptic Canada: Unsolved Mysteries from Coast to Coast. Hammill, Matt & Owlkids Books Inc. Staff, illus. (p. 387)
—Cultural Traditions in Sweden. (p. 391)
—Deep Sea Extremes. (p. 423)
—Desert Extremes. (p. 429)
—Dinosaur Fossils. (p. 442)
—DNA. (p. 456)
—Expedition to the Arctic. (p. 548)
—Explore with Leif Eriksson. (p. 550)
—History Mysteries Revealed. (p. 783)
—Hockey Girl (p. 786)
—How to Be a Rock Collector. (p. 815)
—How to Write a Fantasy Story. (p. 822)
—How to Write an Adventure Story. (p. 822)
—Human Body Mysteries Revealed. (p. 825)
—Human Fossils. (p. 826)
—I Owe You One (p. 844)
—Immigration. (p. 861)
—King Tut. (p. 959)
—Life in a Mining Community. (p. 1010)
—Live It: Courage. (p. 1040)
—Live It: Fairness. (p. 1040)
—Micro Life in Soil. (p. 1136)
—Ninjas. (p. 1256)
—Plant Fossils. (p. 1369)
—Population Patterns: What Factors Determine the Location & Growth of Human Settlements? (p. 1385)
—Pushing & Pulling. (p. 1420)
—Significant People of World War II. (p. 1574)
—Soccer Science. (p. 1603)
—Soil Erosion & How to Prevent It. (p. 1606)
—Speeding up, Slowing Down. (p. 1624)
—Traits & Attributes. (p. 1777)
—Understanding Greek Myths. (p. 1815)
—Understanding Mesoamerican Myths. (p. 1816)
—What Are Fossils? (p. 1879)
—What Are Minerals? (p. 1879)
—What Are Sedimentary Rocks? (p. 1879)
—What Is Germ Theory? (p. 1889)
—What Is Motion? (p. 1890)
—What Is the Rock Cycle? (p. 1890)
—World War I: The Cause for War. (p. 1958)
Hyde, Natalie, jt. auth. see Crabtree Publishing Co. Staff.
Hyde, Natalie, jt. auth. see Crabtree Staff.
Hyde, Natalie, jt. auth. see Miller, Reagan.
Hyde, Noreen. Adventures of Miss Chief: Miss Chief Goes to School. Pushee, Marisa, illus. (p. 20)
Hyde, Shannon. Super Sam's Backyard Adventures. (p. 1680)
Hyde, Willie. Paddles the Amazing Rabbit. (p. 1317)
—Paddles the Amazing Rabbit - Color. (p. 1317)
Hydeck, Michelle A. R. Wings Up: All with a Little Help from Our Angels. (p. 1936)
Hyder, M. A. Donia: Stolen Raindrops or Honour among Thieves. (p. 466)
Hydrick, Stacey Wall. Unlikely Adventures of Stella Mickler. (p. 1821)
Hye-Kyung, Baek. Bring It On! (p. 228)
Hygh, Angela, ed. see Neiman, Tommy & Reynolds, Sue.
Hyland, Betty. Tressa & the Lost Circus of Ireland. (p. 1785)
Hyland, Greg, illus. see Landers, Ace & Doodle Pictures Studio Staff.
Hyland, Ken. Second Language Writing. (p. 1539)
Hyland, Tony. Emergency. (p. 518)
—Multiplying & Dividing at the Bake Sale (p. 1190)
Hyland, Tony & Brush, Jim. Border Defense. (p. 213)
Hyland, Tony & Scarborough, Kate. Killer Pets. (p. 956)
—Robot World. (p. 1480)
Hyland, Tony & Smart Apple Media Staff. Astronauts. (p. 109)
—Divers. (p. 454)
—Film & Fiction Robots. (p. 586)
—High-Rise Workers. (p. 778)
—High-Risk Robots. (p. 778)
—Miners & Drillers. (p. 1146)
—Robots at Work & Play. (p. 1481)
—Scientific & Medical Robots. (p. 1528)
—Space Robots. (p. 1619)
—Stunt Performers. (p. 1670)
—Zookeepers. (p. 1989)
Hyler, Nelson W. How & Why Wonder Book of Rocks & Minerals. Blackwood, Paul E., ed. (p. 804)
Hyles, Jack. Science of the Christian Life: Volume I (p. 1527)
Hylton, Adlyn. A-B-C Smarts: Book 1. (p. 1)
Hylton, Maxine. True Friend: A Story for All about Healing. (p. 1792)
Hyma, Albert, jt. auth. see Stanton, Mary.
Hyman, Adam. Managing the Digital Classroom: Dozens of Awesome Teacher-Tested Ideas That Help You Manage & Make the Most of Every Digital Tool in Your Classroom. (p. 1086)
Hyman, Bruce M. & Pedrick, Cherry. Anxiety Disorders. (p. 90)
—Obsessive-Compulsive Disorder. (p. 1275)
Hyman, Corine & Bryant, Julie. Why We Give Gifts at Christmas Time. (p. 1926)
Hyman, Frieda Clark. Victory on the Walls: A Story of Nehemiah. (p. 1840)
Hyman, Helen Kandel, jt. auth. see Falk, Barbara Bustetter.
Hyman, Jack G. Breakfast with the Birds. (p. 225)
Hyman, Miles, illus. see Craipeau, Jean-Lou & Dutrieux, Brigitte.
Hyman, Miles, illus. see Craipeau, Jean-Lou & Dutrieux, Julien.
Hyman, Teisha Lashe'. Uh Oh! a Human. (p. 1808)
Hyman, Teresa L. Coyotes. (p. 374)
—North Carolina. (p. 1264)
—Pyramids of Giza. (p. 1421)
Hyman, Trina Schart. Hershel & the Hanukkah Goblins. (p. 774)
—Self-Portrait: Trina Schart Hyman. (p. 1549)
Hyman, Trina Schart, illus. see Fritz, Jean.
Hyman, Trina Schart, illus. see Garland, Sherry.
Hyman, Trina Schart, illus. see Hodges, Margaret & Malory, Thomas.
Hyman, Trina Schart, illus. see Kimmel, Eric A.
Hyman, Trina Schart, illus. see Moeri, Louise.
Hyman, Trina Schart, illus. see Serwer-Berstein, Blanche.
Hyman, Trina Schart, illus. see Tchana, Katrin Hyman.
Hyman, Trina Schart, illus. see Updike, John.
Hyman, Trina Schart, tr. see Hodges, Margaret & Malory, Thomas.
Hyman, Zachary. Bambino & Me. Pullen, Zachary, illus. (p. 135)
Hymas, Anna, illus. see Mealer, Bryan & Kamkwamba, William.
Hymel, Gloria. Plays & Payasadas: Thinking Out of the Box. (p. 1373)
Hymper, W., illus. see Stretton, Hesba.
Hyndman, Donald W., ed. see Chronic, Halka.
Hyndman, Donald W., ed. see Frye, Keith.
Hyndman, Donald W., ed. see Van Diver, Bradford B.
Hyndman, Donald W., jt. auth. see Alt, David D.
Hyndman, Donald W., jt. auth. see Hazlett, Richard W.
Hynes, Margaret. Discover Science: Mountains. (p. 448)
—Discover Science: Polar Lands. (p. 448)
—Human Body: Amazing Information-Right Before Your Eyes! (p. 825)
—Navigators: Extreme Weather. (p. 1238)
—Picture This! Animals: Amazing Information-Right Before Your Eyes! (p. 1356)
—Polar Lands. (p. 1379)
Hynes, Margaret & White, Mike. Best Book of Early People. (p. 168)
Hynes, Mary Ellen & Hicks, Donn. Mission Mathematics II: Grades 3-5. (p. 1153)
Hynes, Mary Ellen, et al. Mission Mathematics II. (p. 1153)
Hynes, Michael C., et al. Mission Mathematics II: Grades 6-8. (p. 1153)
Hynes, Patricia. Electric Power Grid. (p. 508)

Hynes, Patricia Freeland. Cyber Cop. (p. 396)
—Electric Power Grid. (p. 508)
—Rights & Values. (p. 1472)
—Sound Engineer. (p. 1615)
Hynes, Robert, illus. see Dennard, Deborah.
Hynes, Robert, illus. see O'Donnell, Liam & O'Donnell, Laura.
Hynes, Robert, illus. see O'Donnell, Liam.
Hynes, Robert, illus. see Savageau, Cheryl.
Hynes, Robert, illus. see Smith, Stephanie & Smith, Stephanie A.
Hynes, Robert, illus. see Smith, Stephanie.
Hynes, Robert, illus. see Woelfle, Gretchen.
Hynson, Colin. Ancient Rome: The Complete Homework Solution. (p. 70)
—Be an Inca Mummy! A One-Way Journey You'D Rather Not Make. Antram, David, illus. (p. 148)
—Civil Rights Movement. (p. 325)
—Columbus & the Renaissance Explorers. (p. 346)
—Exploration of Africa. (p. 550)
—History of Railroads. (p. 784)
—How People Lived in Ancient Greece. (p. 812)
—How People Lived in Viking Times. (p. 812)
—In Ancient Greece. (p. 863)
—Magellan & the Americas. (p. 1071)
—Mesopotamia. (p. 1129)
—Plant-Eating Dinosaurs. Staunton, Joseph & Rey, Luis, illus. (p. 1369)
—Understanding Indian Myths. (p. 1815)
—What Can We Do about Obesity? (p. 1881)
—You Wouldn't Want to Be an Inca Mummy! A One-Way Journey You'd Rather Not Make. Antram, David, illus. (p. 1977)
Hynson, Colin, jt. auth. see Crabtree Staff.
Hynson, Colin, jt. auth. see Staunton, Joseph.
Hyong, Lee Chi. Demon Diary. Kara, György, illus. (p. 426)
Hyperion. Meridian Magic. (p. 1127)
Hyperion Staff. Enchanted Music. (p. 523)
—Finger Spelling Pack. (p. 589)
—First Signing ABC. Williams, Sam, illus. (p. 596)
—Walt Disney World: Where Magic Lives 2006. (p. 1855)
Hysen, Sylvia. Very Dairy Christmas. (p. 1837)
Hysom, Dennis Joe & Walker, Christine. Wooleycat's Musical Rhyme Time Theater. (p. 1950)
—Wooleycat's Musical Theater. Walker, Christine, illus. (p. 1950)
Hyun, Jinsun, illus. see Cordell, Greg.
Hyun, You. Faeries' Landing (p. 562)
—Faeries' Landing Hyun, You, illus. (p. 562)
—Faeries' Landing. (p. 562)
—Faeries' Landing. Hyun, You, illus. (p. 562)
Hyun, You, creator. Faeries' Landing (p. 562)
Hyun, You, ed. Faeries' Landing (p. 562)
Hyung Kim, Tae. Planet Blood (p. 1367)
Hyung, Min-Woo. Choir of Wolves Vol. 12 (p. 309)
—Dirge for the Unwanted. (p. 445)
—Justice N Mercy (p. 940)
—Priest (p. 1399)
—Priest: Stygian Mode (p. 1399)
—Priest Forbes, Jake T., ed. (p. 1399)
—Priest Hyung, Min-Woo, illus. (p. 1399)
—Priest Kim, Jessica, tr. from JPN. (p. 1399)
Hyung, Min-Woo, creator. Priest: Strain of the Dispossessed. Vol. 13 (p. 1399)
Hywel-Davis, Jack. Life of Smith Wigglesworth. (p. 1012)
Hyzy, Julie. State of the Onion (p. 1644)

I

I, Calvin, jt. auth. see Burnett, James.
I., D. Frost Bite. (p. 644)
I, Herge-tintin Rustica, jt. auth. see Hergé.
Iacobucci, Vincent. Little Book All about Fluguls. (p. 1025)
Iacopo, Bruno, illus. see Adler, Irene.
Iacovello, Dick, jt. auth. see Iacovello, Dick.
Iacovello, Dick & Iacovello, Dick. Grasshopper on the Moon. Iacovello, Dick, photos by. (p. 711)
Iacovone, Lauren Marie. Here Lies Thomas Crawford (p. 770)
Iakovos-Dalalakis, Helen. Nicholas Wins the Prize: Young Nicholas Experiences the Sacrament of Confession. 1 Gabrili, Alexandra, illus. (p. 1251)
Ian, Crowe, illus. see Nietzsche, Friedrich.
Ian, Johnston, tr. see Nietzsche, Friedrich.
Ian Pugh. Wolfstorm: The First Danny Piper Adventure. (p. 1944)
Ian, Shickle, illus. see Cameron, Kristy.
Ianieri, Tom. Polar Pals. (p. 1379)
Iannaco, G., jt. auth. see Davies, Helen.
Iannantuano, Theresa. Who Took My Lunch? (p. 1917)
Iantorno, Danlyn, illus. see Pearl, Sydelle.
Iasevoli, Brenda, jt. auth. see Time for Kids Editors.
Iasevoli, Brenda, told to. Plants! (p. 1369)
Ibaceta, Herminia D. Incertidumbre de Las Hojas. (p. 868)
Ibanez, Armando P., et al, eds. On the Wings of an Angel. (p. 1292)
Ibanez, Francisco Montana. Andres, Perro y Oso en el Pais de los Miedos. Acosta, Patricia, illus. (p. 72)
Ibañez, Vicente Blasco & Lorente, Mariano J. Last Lion & Other Stories. (p. 978)
Ibarra, Maria Teresa Ornelas. Penny & Me. (p. 1338)
Ibarra, Rosa, illus. see Gonzalez, Rigoberto & González, Rigoberto.
Ibarrola, Begonia. Adventures of a Water Drop. Tejado, Irene, illus. (p. 16)
—Chusco the Stray Dog. Souto, Jose, illus. (p. 318)
—Crisol & His Star. Pita, Lorena, illus. (p. 383)
—Story of a Can. Amado, Antonio, illus. (p. 1657)
Ibatoulline, Bagram, illus. see Andersen, Hans Christian.
Ibatoulline, Bagram, illus. see Bass, L. G. & Geringer, Laura.
Ibatoulline, Bagram, illus. see Booth, Philip.
Ibatoulline, Bagram, illus. see DiCamillo, Kate.
Ibatoulline, Bagram, illus. see Fleischman, Paul.
Ibatoulline, Bagram, illus. see Frederick, Heather Vogel.
Ibatoulline, Bagram, illus. see Lowry, Lois.
Ibatoulline, Bagram, illus. see Park, Linda Sue.
Ibatoulline, Bagram, illus. see Rabin, Staton.
Ibatoulline, Bagram, illus. see Rubin, Susan Goldman.
Ibatoulline, Bagram, illus. see Stanley, Diane.
Ibatoulline, Bagram, illus. see Wells, Rosemary.
Ibatoulline, Bagram, illus. see Wyeth, Sharon Dennis.
Ibatoulline, Bagram, illus. see Yolen, Jane.
Ibbetson, Paul. Oliver's Tale: A Squirrel's Story of Love, Courage, & Revolution. Wagle, Gina, ed. (p. 1286)
Ibbitson, John. Landing. (p. 974)
Ibbotson, Eva. Abominables. Robinson, Fiona, illus. (p. 5)
—Dial-a-Ghost. Hawkes, Kevin, illus. (p. 433)
—Dragonfly Pool. (p. 478)
—Great Ghost Rescue. Hawkes, Kevin, illus. (p. 716)
—Haunting of Granite Falls. Hawkes, Kevin, illus. (p. 754)
—Journey to the River Sea. (p. 929)
—Journey to the River Sea. Hawkes, Kevin, illus. (p. 929)
—Not Just a Witch. Hawkes, Kevin, illus. (p. 1267)
—Ogre of Oglefort. (p. 1280)
—One Dog & His Boy. (p. 1294)
—Star of Kazan. (p. 1640)
—Star of Kazan. Hawkes, Kevin, illus. (p. 1640)
Ibbotson, Eva, jt. auth. see Ibbotson, Eva.
Ibbotson, Eva & Ibbotson, Eva. Misión Mostruosa. (p. 1150)
—¡Menuda Bruja! (p. 1127)
Ibbott, Penny. Scarcode. (p. 1519)
Ibbs, Katharine, jt. auth. see Dorling Kindersley Publishing Staff.
Ibeas Delgado, Juan Manuel, tr. see Dupasquier, Philippe.
Ibeh, Chinwe. Moment That Sandra Won. (p. 1161)
—Tishan Worst Moment. (p. 1757)
Ibelings, Anne, illus. see Paxmann, Christine.
Ibitokun, Bernadette O. Kids, Know Your Vitamins. (p. 954)
Ibn Munqidh, Usama, jt. auth. see Ibn Munqidh, Usama.
Ibn Munqidh, Usama & Ibn Munqidh, Usama. Book of Contemplation: Islam & the Crusades. Cobb, Paul M., tr. from ARA. (p. 211)
Ibrahim, Idore, ed. see Ibrahim, Zafar Y.
Ibrahim, Nouran, tr. see Bone, Emily.
Ibrahim, Nouran, tr. see Carnavas, Peter.
Ibrahim, Nouran, tr. see Clarke, Catriona.
Ibrahim, Nouran, tr. see Patchett, Fiona.
Ibrahim, Nouran, tr. see Pratt, Leonie.
Ibrahim, Nouran, tr. see Turnbull, Stephanie.
Ibrahim, Yasmin. I Can Make Du'a Anywhere! Zulkifli, Azhari, illus. (p. 836)
—I Can Read the Qur'an Anywhere! Zulkifli, Azhari, illus. (p. 836)
—I Can Say Bismillah Anywhere! Zulkifli, Azhari, illus. (p. 836)
—I Can Wear Hijab Anywhere! Zulkifli, Azhari, illus. (p. 837)
Ibrahim, Zafar Y. Folie a Deux: Shared Psychosis. Ibrahim, Zafar Y. & Ibrahim, Idore, eds. (p. 611)
Ibsen, Henrik. Doll's House. Archer, William, tr. from NOR. (p. 464)
—Doll's House - Literary Touchstone Edition. (p. 464)
—Hedda Gabler. Downer, Alan S., ed. (p. 761)
—Ibsen's Selected Plays. Johnston, Brian, ed. (p. 850)
—John Gabriel Borkman. Landes, William-Alan, ed. (p. 921)
—Master Builder. Landes, William-Alan, ed. (p. 1103)
—Peer Gynt. Landes, William-Alan, ed. (p. 1335)
—Pillars of Society. (p. 1359)
—Rosmersholm. Landes, William-Alan, ed. (p. 1490)
Ibsen, Henrik, illus. see Landes, William-Alan, ed.
Ibsen, Henrik, tr. see Landes, William-Alan, ed.
Ibsen, Henrik & Landes, William-Alan, eds. Enemy of the People. (p. 527)
—Hedda Gabler. (p. 761)
Icanberry, Mark. LooLeDo. (p. 1051)
—Picnic on a Cloud. Mount, Arthur, illus. (p. 1355)
—Pirate's Feast. (p. 1363)
Icanberry, Mark & Mount, Arthur. Picnic on a Cloud. (p. 1355)
—Super Salads. (p. 1680)
Icanberry, Mark, creator. Electric Lunch. (p. 508)
Ice, D. C., illus. see Bolte, Mari.
Ice, D. C., illus. see Troupe, Thomas Kingsley.
Ice, Rod. Cat & the Strat. (p. 277)
Ice Water Press Staff. Secrets of the Deep. (p. 1545)
Icenoggle, Jodi. Schenck V. United States & the Freedom of Speech Debate: Debating Supreme Court Decisions. (p. 1521)
—'Til the Cows Come Home. Chartier, Normand, illus. (p. 1750)
Ichikawa, Santomi, illus. see Kadono, Eiko.
Ichikawa, Satomi. Come Fly with Me. Ichikawa, Satomi, illus. (p. 347)
—En Busca De Tesoros. (p. 522)
—En Busca de Tesoros. (p. 522)
—My Little Train. Ichikawa, Satomi, illus. (p. 1213)
Ichikawa, Satomi, illus. see Gauch, Patricia Lee & GAUCH, PATRICIA LEE.
Ichikawa, Satomi, illus. see Love, Maryann Cusimano.
Ichikawa, Satomi, illus. see Love, Maryann Cusimano.
Icibaci, Neusa, tr. see Hnatov, Catherine.
Icibaci, Neusa, tr. see Star Bright Books.
Icibaci, Neusa, tr. Eating the Rainbow (Portuguese/English) (p. 501)
Icilda. God Made Me Perfect & Wonderful: To Do What? (p. 689)
Icinori. Issun Boshi: The One-Inch Boy. (p. 893)
Idaho Writers League Coeur d'Alene Chapter. Kaleidoscope: A Collection of Tantalizing Tales. (p. 941)
Ide, Laurie S. & Langcaon, Jeff. Super Puffy. (p. 1680)
Ide, Laurie Shimizu. Okazu at the Zoo. Kanekuni, Daniel, illus. (p. 1282)
Idea Network LA Inc. Origami: 15 Easy & Fun Origami Designs. (p. 1303)
IDEA Staff, ed. Debatabase Book: A Must Have Guide for Successful Debate. (p. 420)
Ideals Children's Books Staff, creator. Hands-on Highlights Riddles: A Summer of Laughs. (p. 741)
—Hidden Pictures: Sun & Games. (p. 776)
—My Big Book of Wild Animals. (p. 1197)
—My First Words: Fun to Play Bilingual Learning Game! (p. 1208)
Ideals Publications Inc. Staff. Animals. (p. 81)
—Thomas & Friends Write, Slide & Learn: Numbers. (p. 1738)
Ideals Publications Inc. Staff, creator. Hands-on Highlights Rebus Fun: Animal Tales. (p. 741)
Ideals Publications Inc. Staff, ed. My Book of Wild Animals. (p. 1199)
Idee, Ari. Delicious Japan by Month. (p. 425)
—Great Peacemaker. (p. 717)
—What's Your Snack? (p. 1900)
IDEO Staff, jt. auth. see Suri, Jane Fulton.
Idiaghe, Efosa Francis. Day of a Monkey: Tricky the Monkey. (p. 414)
Idle, Molly. Brother, Can You Spare a Dime? (p. 231)
—Camp Rex. Idle, Molly, illus. (p. 257)
—Emma's Gift. (p. 520)
—Flora & the Flamingo. (p. 606)
—Flora & the Penguin. (p. 606)
—Heads Up: The Story of One Quarter. (p. 757)
—Nighty Night, Noah. (p. 1255)
—Sea Rex. Idle, Molly, illus. (p. 1535)
—Tea Rex. (p. 1708)
Idle, Molly, illus. see Accord Publishing Staff.
Idle, Molly, illus. see Crow, Kristyn.
Idle, Molly, illus. see Stevenson, Robert Louis.
Idle, Molly, illus. see Zondervan Publishing Staff.
Idowu, Cathy. Light for the Sacra Vellum: The Graceville Chronicles Book One. (p. 1015)
Idrac, Armand. My Normandy: A Teenager Lives Through World War II. Silver, Joanne S., tr. from FRE. (p. 1216)
Idumi, Rei, illus. see Hamazaki, Tatsuya & Tatsuya, Hamazaki.
Idzikowski, Lisa. What Is Friction? (p. 1889)
Ieda, Hitoshi, ed. Sustainable Urban Transport in an Asian Context (p. 1688)
IEEE Signal Processing Society, Machine Learning for Signal Processing Technical Committee Staff, jt. contrib. by see Institute of Electrical and Electronics Engineers, Inc. Staff.
Iegg, Gerard. Minibeasts. (p. 1146)
Ieronimo, Christine. Thirst for Home: A Story of Water Across the World. Velasquez, Eric, illus. (p. 1734)
If. 'Remaking' the World - The Nose on the Back of My Head. (p. 1458)
If, jt. auth. see Ralph, Gordon.
Ifans, Rhiannon. Magic of the Mabinogion. Holmes, Helen, illus. (p. 1073)
—Owain Glyndwr: Prince of Wales. Jones, Margaret, illus. (p. 1314)
—Tales from the Celtic Countries. Jones, Margaret, illus. (p. 1701)
—Tales from Wales. Holmes, Helen, illus. (p. 1702)
Ifkovic, Ed & Tang, Eric M. Dragon on a Ten-Speed. (p. 477)
Ifrim, Clelia. Cui Apartine Ziua de Ieri? (p. 390)
Iggulden, Conn & Duncan, Lizzy. Tollins 2: Dynamite Tales (p. 1762)
Iggulden, Fleur, jt. auth. see Allen, Julia.
Igl, Janeane. Winter, Spring, Summer, Fall: (A Sing-Song Book) (p. 1938)
Iglesias, Alvaro, illus. see Higgins, Melissa.
Iglesias, Cesar Andreu, see Andreu Iglesias, Cesar.
Iglesias González, Natalia. Nursery rhymes for the English Classroom. (p. 1273)
Ignatius, Adi, et al, eds. TIME: President Obama: The Path to the White House. Shell-Aurora, Callie, photos by. (p. 1752)
Ignato, Shirley. Wing ding my Chameleon. (p. 1936)
Ignatow, Amy. Awesomely Awful Melodies of Lydia Goldblatt & Julie Graham-Chang. (p. 121)
—Love & Other Fiascos with Lydia Goldblatt & Julie Graham-Chang (p. 1059)
—Popularity Papers: Book Four: the Rocky Road Trip of Lydia Goldblatt & Julie Graham-Chang. (p. 1385)
—Popularity Papers: The Long-Distance Dispatch Between Lydia Goldblatt & Julie Graham-Chang. (p. 1385)
—Popularity Papers: Book Six: Love & Other Fiascos with Lydia Goldblatt & Julie Graham-Chang. (p. 1385)
—Popularity Papers: The Less-Than-Hidden Secrets & Final Revelations of Lydia Goldblatt & Julie Graham-Chang. (p. 1385)
—Popularity Papers: Research for the Social Improvement & General Betterment of Lydia Goldblatt & Julie Graham-Chang. (p. 1385)
—Popularity Papers. (p. 1385)
—Popularity Papers - The Awesomely Awful Melodies. (p. 1385)
—Research for the Social Improvement & General Betterment of Lydia Goldblatt & Julie Graham-Chang. (p. 1462)
—Words of (Questionable) Wisdom. (p. 1951)
—Words of (Questionable) Wisdom from Lydia Goldblatt & Julie Graham-Chang. (p. 1951)
Ignatow, Amy & Allen, Rinne. Popularity Papers: The Long-Distance Dispatch Between Lydia Goldblatt & Julie Graham-Chang. Bk. 2 (p. 1385)
Ignatowicz, Nina, tr. see Taravant, Jacques.
Ignatz, Marie, jt. auth. see Windeatt, Mary Fabyan.
Igneri, David S. Boy & Girl Who Hated History. Wigley, Audrey Watson, illus. (p. 217)
Ignite! Learning, compiled by. Social Studies COW Subscription. (p. 1604)
—Social Studies Texas COW Subscription. (p. 1604)
—SuperCOW - Science & Social Studies Subscription: Science & Social Studies US. (p. 1682)
—SuperCOW - Science & Social Studies TX Subscription: Science & Social Studies TX. (p. 1683)
Iguchi, Bryan. Jovenes Aficionados al Snowboard (The Young Snowboarder) (p. 929)
Iguerabide, Juan Cruz, et al. Jonas y el Frigorifico Miedoso. (p. 925)
Iguina, Adriana, jt. auth. see Iturrondo, Angeles Molina.
Igus, Toyomi. Going Back Home: An Artist Returns to the South. Wood, Michele, illus. (p. 692)
—I See the Rhythm. Wood, Michele, illus. (p. 845)
—I See the Rhythm of Gospel Wood, Michele, illus. (p. 845)
—Two Mrs. Gibsons. Wells, Daryl, illus. (p. 1804)
Ihara, Shigekatsu. Diamond & Pearl Adventure! Ihara, Shigekatsu, illus. (p. 434)
—Pokeman - Diamond & Pearl Adventure! Ihara, Shigekatsu, illus. (p. 1377)
—Pokémon Diamond & Pearl Adventure! Ihara, Shigekatsu, illus. (p. 1378)
I-Haun. Real - Fake Princess. (p. 1448)
—Real/Fake Princess Zhao, Yun, tr. (p. 1449)
I-Haun, jt. auth. see I-Huan.
I-Haun, jt. auth. see Zhao, Yun.
Ihebereme, Chidozie . N. Dad Says Write. (p. 398)
Ihm, Dar-Young. Zero Park, Sung-Woo, illus. (p. 1986)
Iht. International Herald Tribune: On the Record. (p. 880)
I-Huan. Real - Fake Princess (p. 1448)
I-Huan & I-Haun. Real Fake Princess (p. 1448)
II, Herge-tintin Cartone, jt. auth. see Hergé.
II, Herge-tintin Rustica, jt. auth. see Hergé.
Iida, Haruko. Crescent Moon (p. 381)
—Crescent Moon Rymer, Nan, tr. from JPN. (p. 381)
Iida, Haruko, creator. Crescent Moon (p. 381)
Iida, Toshitsugu, illus. see Nobumoto, Keiko.
III, Herge-tintin Rustica, jt. auth. see Hergé.
Iinuma, Yuuki. Itsuwaribito , Vol. 14. (p. 900)
Ijiwola, Gregory. Just Before You Say, I Do: A RoadMap for Singles. (p. 938)
Ikala Aten, Dayle Marc, illus. see Talaro, Theresa.
Ikaris, Despoina. Little Red Jacket: A True Almost Christmas Almost Mystery Almost Ghost Story for Children And Certain Grown-Ups. (p. 1035)
Ikeda, Akihisa. Rosario+Vampire - Season II Vol. 1 Ikeda, Akihisa, illus. (p. 1489)
—Rosario+Vampire - Season II. Ikeda, Akihisa, illus. (p. 1489)
Ikeda, Daisaku. Cherry Tree. McCaughrean, Geraldine, tr. from JPN. (p. 298)
—Over the Deep Blue Sea. McCaughrean, Geraldine, tr. from JPN. (p. 1314)
—Princess & the Moon. McCaughrean, Geraldine, tr. from JPN. (p. 1402)
—Snow Country Prince. McCaughrean, Geraldine, tr. from JPN. (p. 1598)
Ikeda, Daisaku & Gorbachev, Mikhail. Moral Lessons of the Twentieth Century: Gorbachev & Ikeda on Buddhism & Communism. Gage, Richard L., tr. (p. 1173)
Ikegwuonu, Patricia Ryan. I Love My Hair, Too! (p. 842)
Ikeya, Sarah, tr. see Crouch, Adele.
Ikids. Fashion Girls Around the World. (p. 575)
—Soft Shapes: Ducks: (Baby's First Book + Puzzle) (p. 1606)
IKids, creator. Soft Shapes Chunky Puzzle Playset:outer space (Foam Puzzle & Playset) (p. 1606)
Ikids Staff. 10 Little Monkeys. King, Travis, illus. (p. 1993)
—Animals Everywhere. Phillips, Jillian, illus. (p. 82)
—Farm Faces: A Book of Masks. Larranaga, Ana Martin, illus. (p. 574)
—Fast Facts - Division. (p. 576)
—Fast Facts - Multiplication. (p. 576)
—Five Senses. (p. 601)
—Green Start - Little Helpers. Phillips, Jillian, illus. (p. 722)
—Ibaby - Goodnight, Baby: Tuck All the Babies into Their Beds. Larranaga, Ana Martin, illus. (p. 849)
—Junior Groovies: Things That Fly (Storybook, Fun Facts & Toys) (p. 936)
—Junior Groovies: Trains (Storybook, Fun Facts & Toys) (p. 936)
—Just Like My Mommy. Baruzzi, Agnese, illus. (p. 939)
—Little Turtles. Larranaga, Ana, illus. (p. 1037)
—Made with Love for Mom. Kalis, Jennifer, illus. (p. 1070)
—Math Gear: Fast Facts - Addition. (p. 1106)
—Math Gear: Fast Facts - Subtraction. (p. 1106)
—Old MacDonald's Farm. King, Travis, illus. (p. 1284)
—Pets. Francis, Guy, illus. (p. 1348)
—Race Cars. Randazzo, Tony, illus. (p. 1430)
—Shapes. Larranaga, Ana Martin, illus. (p. 1560)
—Soft Shapes: Dinosaurs (Baby's First Book + Puzzle) (p. 1606)
—Soft Shapes: Trucks (Baby's First Book + Puzzle) (p. 1606)
—Softs Shapes Ocean. (p. 1606)
—Tiny Tugboats. Larranaga, Ana, illus. (p. 1757)
—Trucks. Larranaga, Ana Martin, illus. (p. 1791)
—Why Do We Recycle? Science Made Simple! Pérez, Sara Rojo, illus. (p. 1924)
—Why Does the Wind Blow? Science Made Simple! Pérez, Sara Rojo, illus. (p. 1924)
Ikids Staff, jt. auth. see Bockol, Leslie.
Ikids Staff & Schimel, Lawrence. Is a Spider an Insect? Perez, Sara, illus. (p. 889)
—What's in the Egg? Perez, Sara, illus. (p. 1898)
Ikin, Susan. Alex & the Night-tide Dragon. (p. 35)
Ikomi, Tai. 70 Names of God. (p. 1998)
Ikonen, Jani, illus. see Parkkola, Seita.
Ikpe, Ernest & Madge. African Stories about the Tortoise. (p. 28)
Ikumi, Mia. Tokyo Mew Mew Yoshida, Reiko, illus. (p. 1762)
—Tokyo Mew Mew 6 (p. 1762)
—Tokyo Mew Mew a la Mode (p. 1762)
—Tokyo Mew Mew Volume 1 (p. 1762)
—Tokyo Mew Mew Volume 2 Yoshida, Reiko, illus. (p. 1762)
—Tokyo Mew-Mew: Volume 5 Yoshida, Reiko, illus. (p. 1762)
Ikumi, Mia, illus. see Kodansha.
Ikumi, Mia & Yoshida, Reiko. Tokyo Mew Mew (p. 1762)
—Tokyo Mew Mew Hiroe, Ikoi, tr. from JPN. (p. 1762)
Ikuwa, Robert Lono. Face of Her King. (p. 560)
Ilagan, Roland Mechael. Baba the Bear. (p. 123)
Ilaria, Harry. Automobile Ads Pre-War Classics: Auburn - Cord - Chrysler Airflow - Desoto Airflow - Duesenberg - Lasalle - Lincoln-Zephyr - Jordan - Pierce-Arrow. (p. 117)
—Automobile Ads the Other Guys: HenryJ - Hudson - Kaiser-Frazer - Nash/Rambler - Packard - Studebaker. (p. 117)
—British Sports Car Ads - the Assault on America: Austin-Healey - MGB - Triumph. (p. 230)

I

—Buick Ads of the 1950s And 1960s: Buick - Riviera - Special/Skylark. (p. 237)
—Cadillac Ads of the 1950s And 1960s. (p. 250)
—Chevrolet Ads of the 1950s And 1960s: Camaro - Chevelle - Chevrolet - Chevy II - Corvair - Corvette. (p. 299)
—Chevrolet Super Sports - the SS Muscle Cars: Camaro - Chevelle - Impala - Monte Carlo. (p. 299)
—Chrysler 300 Ads - from the Beginning. (p. 317)
—Classic American Cars of The 1950s. (p. 327)
—Corvair Ads 1960 - 1969. (p. 368)
—Corvair Anthology 1960 - 1969. (p. 368)
—Corvette Anthology 2008. (p. 368)
—Corvette Sales Brochures 1953 - 2009. (p. 368)
—Dodge & Desoto Ads of the 1950s And 1960s. (p. 460)
—Edsel Ads 1958 - 1959 - 1960. (p. 505)
—Firebird Anthology 1967 - 2002. (p. 591)
—General Motors Personal Luxury Car Ads: Grand Prix - Monte Carlo - Riviera - Toronado. (p. 660)
—GTO Ads 1964 - 2006. (p. 728)
—Lincoln Ads of the 1950s And 1960s. (p. 1018)
—Mercury Ads of the 1950s And 1960s: Mercury - Comet - Cougar. (p. 1127)
—Mercury Comet Ads 1960 - 1971. (p. 1127)
—Mustang Anthology 1964 - 2009. (p. 1194)
—Oldsmobile Ads of the 1950s And 1960s: Oldsmobile - Cutlass - Toronado. (p. 1285)
—Plymouth Ads of the 1950s And 1960s: Plymouth - Barracuda - Valiant. (p. 1374)
—Plymouth Barracuda Ads 1964 - 1974. (p. 1374)
—Plymouth Valiant & Duster Ads: 1960 - 1976. (p. 1374)
—Pontiac Ads of the 1950s And 1960s: Pontiac - Grand Prix - Tempest/GTO - Firebird. (p. 1382)
—Porsche 911 Anthology 1964 - 2009. (p. 1386)
—Thunderbird Anthology 2005. (p. 1746)
—Z Anthology 1970 - 2008. (p. 1984)
Ilasco, Meg Mateo. You Can Wear It Again: A Celebration of Bridesmaids' Dresses. (p. 1974)
Iles, Greg. Sleep No More. (p. 1588)
Ilg, Steve. Total Body Transformation: A 3-Month Personal Fitness Prescription for a Strong, Lean Body & a Calmer Mind. (p. 1771)
Iliand, Valentina. Gift of Joy & Laughter - Podarok Radosti I Smeha (in Russian Language) Po Sledam Detskogo Lepeta. Anoli, illus. (p. 675)
Iligan, Marlon, jt. auth. see Sherman, M. Zachary.
Ilin, Segal. Como el Hombre Llega A Ser Gigante. (p. 350)
Ilka, Benjamin Alexander. Boy & His Shadow. Ilka, Benjamin Alexander, illus. (p. 217)
Ilkumi, Mia & Yoshida, Reiko. Tokyo Mew Mew a la mode (en Español) (p. 1762)
Ill, Noel, illus. see Del Rio, Adam.
Illek, Nuala. Chinese Sausage Dog, the Panicky Porcupine & Mrs Shoo an Animal Tale of Friendship in Chin. (p. 307)
Illich, Maria. Morcant Twins & the Curse of the Griseum. (p. 1173)
Illidge, Joseph Phillip, ed. see Petersen, David.
Illingworth, Sasha, photos by see Patterson, James & Raymond, Emily.
IllusionWorks Staff. Amazing Optical Illusions. (p. 55)
Illustrated by: Charles Duke, illus. see Carr, Suzanna & Crutchfield, Tylicia.
Illustrations byVoigt, Karen S., illus. see Hansen, Kate.
Ilogienboh, Caroline. Nowhere to Hide. (p. 1269)
Ilya, illus. see Shakespeare, William.
Ilyas, Adnan. Tale of Five Whales. (p. 1699)
Im, Hye-Young, tr. see Seock Seo, Hong & Studio Redstone.
Im, Hye-Young, tr. see Studio Redstone & Studio Redstone.
Im, HyeYoung, tr. see Young-You, Lee.
Im, Hye-Young, tr. Dragon Hunter Seock Seo, Hong, illus. (p. 477)
Image Books Staff. Little Chick: Finger Puppet Book. Put, Klaartje van der, illus. (p. 1026)
—Little Chicken. Put, Klaartje van der, illus. (p. 1026)
—Little Dolphin. Put, Klaartje van der, illus. (p. 1027)
—Little Seal: Finger Puppet Book. Put, Klaartje van der, illus. (p. 1036)
Image Books Staff, jt. auth. see Chronicle Books Staff.
Image Books Staff & Chronicle Books Staff. Little Bunny. van der Put, Klaartje, illus. (p. 1025)
—Little Butterfly. van der Put, Klaartje, illus. (p. 1025)
—Little Pig. Put, Klaartje van der, illus. (p. 1033)
ImageBooks Staff. Little Cow. (p. 1026)
—Little Dog: Finger Puppet Book. (p. 1026)
—Little Horse: Finger Puppet Book. Put, Klaartje van der, illus. (p. 1029)
—Little Monkey. Put, Klaartje van der, illus. (p. 1032)
—Little Mouse. (p. 1032)
—Little Owl Finger Puppet Book. (p. 1032)
—Little Sea Turtle: Finger Puppet Book. (p. 1036)
—Little Shark: Finger Puppet Book. Put, Klaartje van der, illus. (p. 1036)
—Little Zebra. Put, Klaartje van der, illus. (p. 1038)
—Snow Baby Finger Puppet Book. (p. 1598)
ImageBooks Staff, jt. auth. see Chronicle Books Staff.
ImageBooks Staff & Chronicle Books Editors. Little Bat Finger Puppet Book. (p. 1023)
—Little Turkey. (p. 1037)
ImageBooks Staff & Chronicle Books Staff. Little Crab Finger Puppet Book. (p. 1026)
—Little Fish Finger Puppet Book. (p. 1027)
—Little Fox: Finger Puppet Book. Put, Klaartje van der, illus. (p. 1028)
—Little Kitten. van der Put, Klaartje, illus. (p. 1030)
—Little Puppy. Van Der Put, Klaatje, illus. (p. 1034)
—Little Spider Finger Puppet Book. van der Put, Klaartje, illus. (p. 1036)
ImageBooks Staff & Mulligan, Lenz. Little Panda Finger Puppet Book. (p. 1033)
—Little Polar Bear Finger Puppet Book. (p. 1033)
ImageBooks Staff, et al. Little Snowman. (p. 1036)
Imagination Movers Staff. Imagination Movers: Songs from Playhouse Disney. (p. 860)
Imagineers Staff & Wright, Alex. Imagineering Field Guide to Disneyland. (p. 861)
Imagineers Staff, et al. Imagineering Field Guide to Disney's Animal Kingdom at Walt Disney World. (p. 861)
Imai, Ayano. 108th Sheep. Imai, Ayano, illus. (p. 2000)
Imai, Hizuru, jt. auth. see Asano, Atsuko.
Imai, Yasue. B. B. Explosion. Imai, Yasue & Imai, Yasue, illus. (p. 122)
Imai, Yasue & Anzai, Nobuyuki. B. B. Explosion Imai, Yasue, illus. (p. 122)
Imam, Ibrahim, jt. auth. see Imam, Seema.
Imam, Seema & Imam, Ibrahim. I am Listening. (p. 833)
Imamori, Mitsuhiko. Everybody Kirigami! (p. 543)
Imamura, Keiko. Biographical Comics: the Wright Brothers: Challengers of the AIR. Oobayashi, Kaoru, illus. (p. 188)
Imamura, Keiko, jt. auth. see Imamura, Keiko.
Imamura, Keiko & Imamura, Keiko. Biographical Comics: the Wright Brothers: Challengers of the AIR. Oobayashi, Kaoru, illus. (p. 188)
Imbarrato, Susan Clair & Berkin, Carol. Encyclopedia of American Literature (p. 524)
Imbeau, Marcia B., jt. auth. see Tomlinson, Carol Ann.
Imbernón, Maite & Dickens, Charles. Oliver Twist. (p. 1286)
Imbernón, Teresa & Twain, Mark. Huckleberry Finn. Rodriguez, Lorenzo, tr. (p. 824)
Imbimbo, Anthony. Steve Jobs: The Brilliant Mind Behind Apple. (p. 1649)
Imbody, Amy, jt. auth. see Imbody, Amy E.
Imbody, Amy E. & Imbody, Amy. Snug as a Bug Gordon, Mike, illus. (p. 1601)
Imbriaco, Alison. California Condor: Help Save This Endangered Species! (p. 253)
—Causes of the Civil War: A MyReportLinks. com Book. (p. 282)
—Giant Panda: Help Save This Endangered Species! (p. 673)
—Incas: A MyReportLinks. com Book. (p. 868)
—Mountain Gorilla: Help Save This Endangered Species! (p. 1180)
—Otter: A MyReportLinks. com Book. (p. 1307)
—Red Wolf: Help Save This Endangered Species! (p. 1455)
—Sperm Whale: Help Save This Endangered Species! (p. 1625)
—Vietnam: A MyReportLinks. com Book. (p. 1841)
—Whooping Crane: Help Save This Endangered Species! (p. 1920)
Imes, Jarod. Age Ain't Nothing but a Number. (p. 29)
Imes, Jarold. Hold on Be Strong. (p. 787)
—Never Too Much - the Remix. (p. 1243)
—Rollin' Wit the Punches. (p. 1485)
Imes, Jarold, adapted by. U Can't Break Me. (p. 1805)
Imholtz, August & Tannenbaum, Alison. Alice Eats Wonderland. Carr, A. E. K., illus. (p. 39)
Imler, Kathryn. New Year's Day. (p. 1247)
—Valentine's Day (p. 1830)
Imler, Kathryn A. Año Nuevo (p. 87)
—Valentine's Day (p. 1830)
Imler, Kathryn A., jt. auth. see Imler, Kathryn.
Imler, Kathryn & Imler, Kathryn A. New Year's Day (p. 1247)
Immanuel, Anthony, jt. auth. see Stickels, Terry.
Immedium Staff. Space Cadet Topo: The Day the Sun Turned Off. (p. 1618)
Immel, Mary Blair. Captured! A Boy Trapped in the Civil War. (p. 265)
Immell, Myra. Creation of the State of Israel. (p. 379)
—Cuban Missle Crisis. Gale Editors, ed. (p. 388)
—Dissolution of the Soviet Union. (p. 453)
—Homeland Security. (p. 793)
—Israel. (p. 893)
—McCarthy Era. Gale Editors, ed. (p. 1114)
Immell, Myra, jt. auth. see Gale Editors.
Immell, Myra, ed. Cuban Revolution. (p. 388)
—Homeland Security. (p. 793)
—Uganda. (p. 1808)
Immelman, Sarita, illus. see Wyss, Tyan.
Immenschuh, Marilyn Y. Samantha & the Kids of Room 220. (p. 1507)
Immonen, Kathyrn. Wolverine & Jubilee: Curse of the Mutants. Noto, Phil, illus. (p. 1944)
Immonen, Laurel. Werepuppy. (p. 1875)
Immonen, Stuart. Magnetic North. (p. 1075)
Immonen, Stuart, et al. Ultimatum Companion. (p. 1810)
Imodraj. Brave Little Tailor. (p. 223)
Imodraj, illus. see Everett, Melissa.
Impact Books Editors. Enchanting Fantasy Dot to Dot. (p. 523)
—I Heart Manga Dot to Dot. (p. 839)
—Magical Creatures Dot to Dot. (p. 1074)
—Mean Machines Dot to Dot. (p. 1116)
Imperato, Teresa. Colors All Around: A Turn & Pop Book. Petrone, Valeria, illus. (p. 345)
—Fiona's Fairy Magic. Huang, Benrei, illus. (p. 589)
—Good Morning, Good Night! Mitchell, Melanie, illus. (p. 698)
—How Many Ducks in a Row? A Turn & Pop Book. Petrone, Valeria, illus. (p. 811)
—On the Farm: A Barnyard Book. Rayner, Olivia, illus. (p. 1290)
—On the Go! A Transportation Book. Rayner, Olivia, illus. (p. 1290)
—Speed Machines: A Pop-up Book with Moving Gears. Robinson, Keith, illus. (p. 1624)
—Ten Christmas Lights: Count the Lights from One to Ten! Parry, Jo, illus. (p. 1718)
—This Little Piggy. Haskamp, Steve, illus. (p. 1737)
—Trick or Treat! A Halloween Shapes Book. Winston, Jeannie, illus. (p. 1786)
Imperato, Teresa, jt. auth. see Wang, Dorothea DePrisco.
Impey, Allison, illus. see Hurley, Tonya.
Impey, Martin. Rapunzel. (p. 1439)
Impey, Martin, illus. see Dolan, Penny.
Impey, Martin, illus. see Nash, Margaret.
Impey, Rose. Best Friends! (p. 169)
—Introducing Scarlett Lee. (p. 882)
—Kerching! (p. 949)
—Spiders. (p. 1626)
Impey, Rose & Huws, Emily. Dymuniad Mewn Eiliad. (p. 491)
Imutan, Jordan. Axel Gabe's Adventure in Angeles City: Grown up Lessons for Our Children. (p. 121)
Imwalle, Candice, et al. Sir Morgan & the Kingdom of Horrible Food. (p. 1580)
In Den Bosch, Nicole, illus. see Ross, Kathy.
Inacio, Maria St. Katie's Big Move! (p. 945)
Inada, Koji. Beet the Vandel Buster Inada, Koji, illus. (p. 158)
Inada, Koji, illus. see Sanjo, Riku.
Inada, Koji, jt. auth. see Sanjo, Riku.
Inada, Koji & Sanjo, Riku. Beet the Vandel Buster Kawasaki, Beth, ed. (p. 158)
—Beet the Vandel Buster Sanjo, Riku, illus. (p. 158)
Inagaki, Riichird & Inagaki, Riichiro. Eyeshield 21 Murata, Yusuke, illus. (p. 558)
Inagaki, Riichiro. Eyeshield 21 (p. 558)
—Eyeshield 21. Murata, Yusuke, illus. (p. 558)
Inagaki, Riichiro, jt. auth. see Inagaki, Riichird.
Inagaki, Riichiro & Toriyama, Akira. Dragon Ball Z Inagaki, Riichiro & Toriyama, Akira, illus. (p. 476)
Inches, Alison. Adventures of a Plastic Bottle: A Story about Recycling. Whitehead, Pete, illus. (p. 16)
—Adventures of an Aluminum Can: A Story about Recycling. Whitehead, Pete & Chambers, Mark L., illus. (p. 16)
—Big Sister Dora! Aikins, Dave, illus. (p. 183)
—Diego's Buzzing Bee Adventure. Zalme, Ron, illus. (p. 437)
—Dora Loves Boots (Dora the Explorer) Random House Beginners Books Staff & MJ Illustrations Staff, illus. (p. 470)
—Dora Quiere Mucho a Boots. Saunders, Zina, illus. (p. 470)
—I Can Save the Earth! One Little Monster Learns to Reduce, Reuse, & Recycle. Garofoli, Viviana, illus. (p. 836)
—I Can Save the Ocean! The Little Green Monster Cleans up the Beach. Garofoli, Viviana, illus. (p. 836)
—I Love My Papi! (Dora the Explorer) Aikins, David, illus. (p. 842)
—Just Like Dora! Aikins, Dave, illus. (p. 939)
—My Visit with Periwinkle. Levy, David B., illus. (p. 1221)
—Quinceañera. Aikins, Dave, illus. (p. 1428)
—Santa Claus Is Green! How to Have an Eco-Friendly Christmas. Kirwan, Wednesday, illus. (p. 1511)
—School Gyrls POW Scrapbook. (p. 1523)
—Súper Bebés! Miller, Victoria, illus. (p. 1679)
Inches, Alison, jt. auth. see Man-Kong, Mary.
Inches, Alison & Weiner, Eric. Dora Loves Boots. Saunders, Zina, illus. (p. 470)
Incrocci, Rick. Psalms for Toddlers. (p. 1413)
Incrocci, Rick, illus. see Adams, Anne.
Incrocci, Rick, illus. see Larsen, Carolyn & Baker Publishing Group Staff.
Incrocci, Rick, illus. see Larsen, Carolyn.
Indante, Dan & Marks, Karl. Complete A**Hole's Guide to Handling Chicks. (p. 352)
Indenbaum, Dorothy, jt. auth. see Shichtman, Sandra H.
Indovino, Shaina. Women in Anthropology. Lee-Karlon, Ann, ed. (p. 1945)
—Women in Engineering. Lee-Karlon, Ann, ed. (p. 1945)
—Women in Information Technology. Lee-Karlon, Ann, ed. (p. 1945)
—Women in Physics. Lee-Karlon, Ann, ed. (p. 1946)
—Women in the Environmental Sciences. Lee-Karlon, Ann, ed. (p. 1946)
—Women Inventors. Lee-Karlon, Ann, ed. (p. 1946)
Indovino, Shaina C. Rachael Ray: From Candy Counter to Cooking Show. (p. 1431)
—Russell Simmons: From Drug Dealer to Music Mogul. (p. 1498)
—Simon Cowell: From the Mailroom to Idol Fame. (p. 1577)
Indovino, Shaina C., jt. auth. see Docalavich, Heather.
Indovino, Shaina C., jt. auth. see Etingoff, Kim.
Indovino, Shaina C., jt. auth. see Sadek, Ademola O.
Indovino, Shaina C., jt. auth. see Sanna, Jeanine.
Indovino, Shaina C., jt. auth. see Simons, Rae.
Indovino, Shaina C., jt. auth. see Walker, Ida.
Indovino, Shaina Carmel. Blake Griffin. (p. 198)
—Bulgaria. (p. 240)
—Dracula & Beyond: Famous Vampires & Werewolves in Literature & Film. (p. 476)
—Dwight Howard. (p. 491)
—European Union: Facts & Figures. (p. 540)
—Iceland. (p. 851)
—Kevin Durant. (p. 950)
—Kobe Bryant. (p. 966)
—Lebron James. (p. 986)
—Rachael Ray: From Candy Counter to Cooking Show. (p. 1431)
—Romania. (p. 1486)
—Russell Simmons: From Drug Dealer to Music Mogul. (p. 1498)
—Simon Cowell: From the Mailroom to Idol Fame. (p. 1577)
—Transylvania & Beyond: Vampires & Werewolves in Old Europe. (p. 1779)
—Women in Space. (p. 1946)
—Women in Space. Lee-Karlon, Ann, ed. (p. 1946)
Indovino, Shaina Carmel, jt. auth. see Docalavich, Heather.
Indovino, Shaina Carmel, jt. auth. see Etingoff, Kim.
Indovino, Shaina Carmel, jt. auth. see Libal, Autumn.
Indovino, Shaina Carmel, jt. auth. see Sadik, Ademola O.
Indovino, Shaina Carmel, jt. auth. see Sanna, Jeanine.
Indovino, Shaina Carmel, jt. auth. see Sia, Nicole.
Indovino, Shaina Carmel, jt. auth. see Simons, Rae.
Indovino, Shaina Carmel, jt. auth. see Stafford, James.
Indovino, Shaina Carmel, jt. auth. see Walker, Ida.
Inez, Peggy. Gully. (p. 731)
Infante, Begona. Bali, Yo Soy de la China (I'm from China) (p. 134)
—Fatima Yo Soy de El Salvador. (p. 577)
—Minu Yo Soy de India (I'm from India) (p. 1148)
—Takao Yo Soy de Japon (I'm from Japan) (p. 1696)
Infante, Francesc, illus. see Bailer, Darice, et al.
Infante, Francesc, illus. see Carrasco, Xavier.
Infante, Marisol. Adventures of the Smilees: Understanding Our Friends. (p. 23)
Infantil. Aprendo a Escribir 2. (p. 93)
Infantino, Carmine, illus. see Fox, Gardner & Broome, John.
Infantino, Carmine, illus. see Kanigher, Robert & Broome, John.
Infobase Publishing Staff, creator. Chemistry. (p. 297)
—Writing. (p. 1964)
Infurnari, Joe, illus. see Yakin, Boaz.
Ing, Dean. It's up to Charlie Hardin. (p. 899)
Ingalls, Ann. Basic Manners. Rooney, Ronnie, illus. (p. 142)
—Being a Good Guest. Rooney, Ronnie, illus. (p. 160)
—Christmas Traditions Around the World. Chavarri, Elisa, illus. (p. 316)
—Good Manners During Special Occasions. Rooney, Ronnie, illus. (p. 698)
—Good Manners in Public. Rooney, Ronnie, illus. (p. 698)
—Good Manners on the Phone. Rooney, Ronnie, illus. (p. 698)
—Good Manners with Family. Rooney, Ronnie, illus. (p. 698)
—Good Table Manners. Rooney, Ronnie, illus. (p. 700)
—Ice Cream Soup. (p. 850)
—Isabella & Ivan Build an Interview. Siegel, Melanie, illus. (p. 891)
—Piranha. (p. 1362)
—Piranha Paperback. (p. 1362)
—Scholastic Reader Level 1: Biggety Bat: Hot Diggety, It's Biggety! Zenz, Aaron, illus. (p. 1522)
—Seth & Savannah Build a Speech. Lee, Karen, illus. (p. 1554)
Ingalls, Ann, jt. auth. see MacDonald, Maryann.
Ingalls, Laura, jt. auth. see Wilder, Laura Ingalls.
Ingalls, Melodi J. Everyone Is Differphant. (p. 544)
Ingber Drohan, Michele, jt. auth. see Katirgis, Jane.
Ingebretsen, Karen, et al. Human Space Exploration. (p. 826)
Ingell, Jessica. Mommy Does God See Me? (p. 1162)
Ingelow, Jean. Mopsa the Fairy. (p. 1173)
Ingels, Diane, jt. auth. see Woebkenberg, Valerie.
Ingenieros, Jose. Hombre Mediocre. (p. 791)
Ingersol, Julie. Baptist & Methodist Faiths in America. (p. 137)
Ingersoll, Donna. Grandpa's Garden. (p. 710)
—Rock-A-Bye, Little Child of Mine. (p. 1481)
—Ten Tempting Tongue Twisters. (p. 1719)
Ingham, Anne. Ball Book. (p. 134)
Ingham, Dave, jt. auth. see Child, Lauren.
Ingham, Donna. Tales with a Texas Twist: Original Stories & Enduring Folklore from the Lone Star State. Hoffman, Paul G., illus. (p. 1703)
Ingham, Janis. Flip & Flop Celebrate Family. (p. 604)
Ingham, Julie, illus. see Eliot, Hannah.
Ingham, Julie, illus. see Magruder, Trula & American Girl Editors, eds.
Ingkavet, Andrew. Play Piano for Kids: Penguins Don't Play Piano, but You Can! (p. 1371)
Ingle, Annie & Klimo, Kate. Dog Diaries #2: Buddy. Jessell, Tim, illus. (p. 461)
Ingle, Jack, jt. auth. see Haddad, Yousif.
Ingle, L. G. Little Willy Wiggle & Johnny Amigo. (p. 1037)
Ingle, Michelle. LeLe's Passport. (p. 991)
Ingle, Rosalie Vandewater. Stage Is Coming! Hallie's Stage Stop Journey. (p. 1638)
Ingle, Sheila C. Courageous Kate: A Daughter of the American Revolution. (p. 373)
Inglee, K. B. Farmer's Daughter, Miller's Son. (p. 574)
Inglese, Judith. I Have a Friend. Inglese, Judith, illus. (p. 839)
Inglese, Judith, illus. see King, Dedie.
Inglis, Fiona. Garden Cook: Grow, Cook & Eat with Kids. (p. 656)
Inglis, Karen. Ferdinand Fox's Big Sleep Colouring Book. Kundalic, Damir, illus. (p. 581)
Inglis, Kate. Dread Crew: Pirates of the Backwoods Smith, Sydney, illus. (p. 482)
Inglis, Lillian. One That Caught Away. (p. 1297)
Ingman, Bruce. When Martha's Away. (p. 1903)
Ingman, Bruce, illus. see Ahlberg, Allan.
Ingman, Bruce, illus. see Feiffer, Kate.
Ingman, Bruce & Ahlberg, Allan. Runaway Dinner. Ingman, Bruce, illus. (p. 1496)
Ingoglia, Gina. Tree Book for Kids & Their Grown-Ups. (p. 1783)
Ingold, Jeanette. Big Burn. (p. 180)
—Hitch. (p. 786)
—Mountain Solo. (p. 1181)
—Paper Daughter. (p. 1322)
—Window. (p. 1936)
Ingold, Jeanette & Egan, Timothy. Big Burn: Teddy Roosevelt & the Fire That Saved America. (p. 180)
Ingpen, Robert R., illus. see Barrie, J. M.
Ingpen, Robert R., illus. see Burnett, Frances Hodgson.
Ingpen, Robert R., illus. see Carroll, Lewis, pseud.
Ingpen, Robert R., illus. see Grahame, Kenneth.
Ingpen, Robert R., illus. see Hao, K. T. & Fulla, Monserrat.
Ingpen, Robert R., illus. see Kipling, Rudyard.
Ingpen, Robert R., illus. see Lachenmeyer, Nathaniel.
Ingpen, Robert R., illus. see Rosen, Michael.
Ingpen, Robert R., illus. see Stevenson, Robert Louis.
Ingpen, Robert R., illus. see Thiele, Colin.
Ingpen, Robert R., illus. see Twain, Mark, pseud.
Ingpen, Robert R., illus. see Verne, Jules.
Ingraham, Corinne. Peacock & the Wishing-Fairy & Other Stories. (p. 1332)
Ingraham, Prentiss, ed. see Majors, Alexander.
Ingram, Anne, illus. see Holm, Barbara.
Ingram, Charles, illus. see Wicks, Valerie.
Ingram, Chris, illus. see Oldman, James.
Ingram, Christine, et al. Vegetarian & Vegetable Cooking: The Essential Encyclopedia of Healthy Eating. (p. 1834)
Ingram, Doreen. My Sanctuary: A Place I Call Home - Keepers of the Wild. Josh Green, illus. (p. 1218)
—My Sanctuary, a Place I Call Home. (p. 1218)
Ingram, Fiona. Secret of the Sacred Scarab. (p. 1543)
Ingram, Glenda Brown, illus. see Weaver, Jack.
Ingram, Jacquelyn. Dakota's Doggie Tale. (p. 401)
Ingram, Jan, illus. see Lovvorn, Ann R.
Ingram, Jas, jt. auth. see Harper, Clay.
Ingram, Joan. Your ABCs. (p. 1979)
Ingram, Rachel. Jackson & the Donut Shop. (p. 904)
Ingram, Richard. Land of the Giddiwonks. (p. 973)

Ingram, Roger. Clinical Notes on Trumpet Playing: (or, What I did During My Summer Vacation) Clarke, Victoria, ed. (p. 333)
Ingram, Scott. Battle of Valcour Bay. (p. 147)
—Chernobyl Nuclear Disaster. (p. 298)
—Dolphins. (p. 464)
—Greek Immigrants. (p. 720)
—Japanese Immigrants. (p. 909)
—Kansas: The Sunflower State. (p. 943)
—Korean Americans. (p. 967)
—Mexican Americans. (p. 1131)
—Nicolaus Copernicus: Father of Modern Astronomy. (p. 1251)
—Paul Revere. (p. 1330)
—South Asian Americans. (p. 1616)
—Stock Market Crash of 1929. (p. 1651)
—Tsunami! The 1946 Hilo Wave of Terror. (p. 1795)
—Writing of The Star-Spangled Banner. (p. 1965)
Ingram, Scott, jt. auth. see Crewe, Sabrina.
Ingram, Scott, jt. auth. see Martin, Michael.
Ingram, Scott & Asher, Robert. Polish Immigrants. (p. 1380)
Ingram, W. J. Evelyn. Saint Crispin & Other Quaint Conceits. (p. 1503)
Ingram, W. Scott. Kansas. (p. 942)
—Marijuana. (p. 1094)
Ingram-Jackson, Mandi. My Name Is Guenavere & I Talk Through My Eyes. (p. 1215)
Ingri, D'Aulaire & Parin, D'Aulaire Edgar. D'Aulaires Book of Greek Myths. (p. 410)
Ingrid. Peekaboo Book. (p. 1335)
Ings, William, illus. see Gifford, Clive.
Ingwersen, Faith, tr. see Bredsdorff, Bodil.
Iñigo, Javaloyes, jt. auth. see Javaloyes, Inigo.
Ink, Bruce, illus. see Foster, Beverly & Foster, Stacy Lynn.
Ink, Bruce, illus. see Holland, Beth.
Ink, Bruce, illus. see Webber, Sharon, et al.
Ink, Johnny. Inklings: Kids. (p. 874)
Ink, Lancman. Hotel Pioho's Palace. (p. 802)
Ink, Lancman, illus. see Walsh, Maria Elena.
Ink, Oliver. My Allowance. (p. 1195)
Inker, Inna, jt. ed. see Goldstein, Jessica.
Inklow, Dimiter. Yo, Clara y el Papagayo Pipo. (p. 1971)
—Yo, Clara y el Poni Miguelin. (p. 1971)
Inklow, Dimitier. Como Decidi Convertirme en Hermano Mayor (How I Decided to Become an Older Brother) (p. 350)
—Hurra, Susanita Ya Tiene Dientes! (Hurray, Little Susan Has Teeth Now!) (p. 829)
Inklow, Ditier. Orfeo, Sísifo y Cía. Castellanos, Diana, illus. (p. 1303)
Inklink Staff, illus. see Brookes, Olivia.
Inklink, Studio, illus. see Gallavotti, Barbara.
Inkpen, Chloe, jt. auth. see Inkpen, Mick.
Inkpen, Chloë & Inkpen, Mick. Hello Ladybird! (p. 764)
—Hello Oscar! (p. 764)
—Look at Me! - Zoe & Beans. (p. 1048)
—Magic Hoop! (p. 1072)
—Pirate Treasure! (p. 1363)
Inkpen, Chloe & Inkpen, Mick. We're Not Scared! (p. 1875)
—Where Is Binky Boo? (p. 1908)
Inkpen, Mick. Beachmoles & Bellvine. (p. 149)
—Beachmoles & Bellvine. MC, ed. (p. 149)
—Bear. (p. 150)
—Bokobikes. (p. 208)
—Don't Lose Pigley, Wibbly Pig! (p. 468)
—Everyone Hide from Wibbly Pig. (p. 544)
—Hide Me, Kipper! (p. 777)
—Is It Bedtime Wibbly Pig? (p. 889)
—Kipper. (p. 961)
—Kipper & Roly. (p. 961)
—Kipper's (p. 961)
—Kipper's A to Z: An Alphabet Adventure. (p. 961)
—Kipper's Christmas Eve. (p. 961)
—Kipper's Monster. (p. 961)
—Kipper's Snowy Day. (p. 961)
—Kipper's Toybox. (p. 961)
—Kipper's Toybox. Inkpen, Mick, illus. (p. 961)
—Lullabyhullaballoo! Inkpen, Mick, illus. (p. 1064)
—One Year with Kipper. (p. 1298)
—Ploo & the Terrible Gnobbler. (p. 1374)
—Rollo & Ruff & the Little Fluffy Bird. Inkpen, Mick, illus. (p. 1485)
—This Is My Book. Inkpen, Mick, illus. (p. 1736)
—Threadbear. (p. 1741)
—Wibbly Pig Has 10 Balloons. (p. 1927)
Inkpen, Mick, illus. see Butterworth, Nick.
Inkpen, Mick, jt. auth. see Butterworth, Nick.
Inkpen, Mick, jt. auth. see Inkpen, Chloe.
Inkpen, Mick, jt. auth. see Inkpen, Chloe.
Inkpen, Mick, jt. auth. see Inkpen, Chloë.
Inkpen, Mick, jt. auth. see Inkpen, Chloë.
Inkpen, Mick & Butterworth, Nick. Just Like Jasper! (p. 939)
Inkpen, Mick & Inkpen, Chloe. Zoe & Beans: Zoe's Christmas List. (p. 1987)
Inky. Dottie Goes to the Circus. (p. 472)
Inmaculada, Díaz, jt. auth. see Diaz, Inmaculada.
Inman, George, Jr., et al. Bumpy Pumpkin. Lyle, Avis, illus. (p. 241)
Inman, John. Tonk & the Battle of The 200. (p. 1765)
Inman, Robert. Christmas Bus. Baskin, Lyle, illus. (p. 313)
Inman, Roy. Judo Handbook. (p. 931)
Innerst, Stacy, illus. see Johnston, Tony.
Innerst, Stacy, illus. see Krull, Kathleen & Brewer, Paul.
Innerst, Stacy, illus. see Krull, Kathleen.
Innes, Brian. Ancient Roman Myths. (p. 70)
—Forensic Science. (p. 617)
—International Terrorism. (p. 880)
—Major Unsolved Crimes. (p. 1078)
Innes, Brian & Singer, Jane. DNA & Body Evidence. (p. 456)
—Fingerprints & Impressions. (p. 589)
Innes, Calvin, illus. see Nass, Marcia & Campisi, Stephanie.
Innes, Sheila. Measure for Measure. Gibson, Rex, ed. (p. 1117)
Innes, Shona & Agocs, Irisz. Friendship Is Like a Seesaw. (p. 639)
—Life Is Like the Wind. (p. 1011)
Innes, Stephanie & Endrulat, Harry. Bear in War Deines, Brian, illus. (p. 151)
—Bear on the Homefront Deines, Brian, illus. (p. 151)
Innes, Sue, illus. see Blazon, Nina.
Innis, Amy. Adventures of Princess Lilyan: The Shimmering Beauty Ball. (p. 22)
Innis, Roy. Energy Keepers Energy Killers: The New Civil Rights Battle. (p. 528)
Inniss, Michelle, jt. auth. see Gavilanes, Enrique.
Innis-Weisseneder, Emma May. Silky: The Dog That Saved the Day. Sherrard, Laura, illus. (p. 1575)
Innocenti, Jane. Aunt Jane's Summer Garden. (p. 115)
Innocenti, Roberto, illus. see Collodi, Carlo.
Innocenti, Roberto, illus. see Dickens, Charles.
Innocenti, Roberto, illus. see Gallaz, Christophe.
Innocenti, Roberto, illus. see Lewis, J. Patrick.
Innocenti, Roberto, illus. see Perrault, Charles.
Innocenti, Roberto, illus. see Vander Zee, Ruth.
Innocenti, Roberto, jt. auth. see Lewis, J. Patrick.
Innocenti, Roberto & Gallaz, Christophe. Rosa Blanca. (p. 1488)
Innovative Kids Staff. Baby Animals. (p. 124)
—Counting: E-Z Page Turners. Larrañaga, Ana Martin, illus. (p. 370)
—In the Garden. (p. 866)
—Shapes - Soft Shapes. (p. 1560)
—Sugar & Spice - Fashion Girls. Perrett, Lisa, illus. (p. 1672)
Innovative Kids Staff, jt. auth. see Larrañaga, Martin.
Innovative Kids Staff, jt. auth. see Page, Liza.
Innovative Kids Staff, creator. Playful Penguins. (p. 1372)
—Soft Shapes - Animals. (p. 1606)
—Soft Shapes - Colors. (p. 1606)
—Soft Shapes - Counting. (p. 1606)
—Soft Shapes Photo Books: Kittens. (p. 1606)
—Soft Shapes Photo Books: Tropical Fish. (p. 1606)
—Vehicles. (p. 1834)
Inns, Chris, jt. auth. see Woods, Dave.
Inns, Chris & Woods, Dave. Florence Nightingirl. (p. 606)
—Henry 1/8th. (p. 767)
Inny. Epiphany Rose-the Message. (p. 532)
Inokuma, Shinobu, jt. auth. see Murozumi, Hikaru.
Inoue, Junya, creator. Btoom! (p. 233)
Inoue, Kazurou. Midori Days. Inoue, Kazurou & Inoue, Kazurou, illus. (p. 1139)
Inoue, Momota. Genesect & the Legend Awakened. Inoue, Momota, illus. (p. 660)
—Kyurem vs. the Sword of Justice. (p. 969)
—Victini & Zekrom. (p. 1840)
Inoue, Santa. Tokyo Tribes (p. 1762)
Inoue, Santa, creator. Tokyo Tribes (p. 1762)
Inoue, Sora, jt. auth. see Saiga, Reiji.
Inoue, Takehiko. Slam Dunk. Inoue, Takehiko, illus. (p. 1587)
—Slam Dunk, Vol. 23. Inoue, Takehiko, illus. (p. 1587)
—Vagabond: The Letter. Vol. 14 Inoue, Takehiko, illus. (p. 1830)
Inoue, Takehiko, jt. auth. see Yoshikawa, Eiji.
Inouye, Carol, illus. see Fahy, Davene & Mueller, Dagmar H.
Inouye, Carol, illus. see Fahy, Davene.
Inouye, Carol, illus. see Paul, Alleen.
Insel, Eunice, jt. auth. see Edson, Ann.
InSeon, Chae. Handy Mr. Hippo. YouDae, Kim, illus. (p. 742)
Inserra, Rosa. Captain of the Toilet. (p. 264)
—Queen of the Toilet. (p. 1425)
Inserra, Rose. Birds. (p. 191)
—Mammals. (p. 1085)
—Worms. (p. 1961)
Inskipp, Carol. Healthy Seas. (p. 759)
—Reducing & Recycling Waste. (p. 1456)
—Travel & Tourism. (p. 1780)
Inslee, Francine. Charlie's Walk. (p. 293)
In-Soo, Na. King of Hell Jae-Hwan, Na, illus. (p. 958)
—King of Hell Jae-Hwan, Kim, illus. (p. 958)
In-Soo, Ra. King of Hell (p. 959)
—King of Hell Jae-Hwan, Kim, illus. (p. 959)
In-Soo, Ra, illus. see Jae-Hwan, Kim.
In-Soo, Ra & Jae-Hwan, Kim. King of Hell. (p. 958)
In-Soo, Ra & Ra, In-Soo. King of Hell Jae-Hwan, Kim, illus. (p. 958)
Inspirio Staff, jt. auth. see Zondervan Publishing Staff.
Institute for Creation Research Staff. Guide to Dinosaurs. (p. 730)
Institute of Electrical and Electronics Engineers, Inc. Staff & IEEE Signal Processing Society, Machine Learning for Signal Processing Technical Committee Staff, contrib. by. 2005 IEEE International Workshop on Machine Learning for Signal Processing. (p. 2003)
Instruc, Shurley. Shurley English 1 Kit H/S Ed. (p. 1572)
—Shurley English 1 Stu Workbook. (p. 1572)
—Shurley English 2 Kit H/S Ed. (p. 1572)
—Shurley English 2 Stu Workbook. (p. 1572)
—Shurley English 3 Kit H/S Ed. (p. 1572)
—Shurley English 3 Stu Workbook. (p. 1572)
—Shurley English 4 Kit H/S Ed. (p. 1572)
—Shurley English 4 Stu Workbook. (p. 1572)
—Shurley English 5 Kit H/S Ed. (p. 1572)
—Shurley English 5 Stu Workbook. (p. 1572)
—Shurley English 6 Stu Workbook. (p. 1572)
Interaction Publishers, Inc. Staff. Into Islam. (p. 881)
Interiano, Jeffrey. Critters of Forest City. (p. 384)
Interior Dept. (U.S.) & Land Management Bureau (U.S.), eds. Junior Explorer Geology & Fossils Activity Book. (p. 936)
Interlink Resources International. New Bridges - Book 3: Connecting People Through Language & Culture. (p. 1243)
Intermediate School, Parkview, compiled by. School Memories. (p. 1523)
International Center for Assault Prevention Staff & Pro Familia, Deutsche Gesellschaft für Sexualberatung und Familienplanung Staff. My Body Belongs to Me from My Head to My Toes. Geisler, Dagmar, illus. (p. 1198)
International Correspondence School, creator. 1902 Handbook of Steam Engineering: Elevators, Pumps & Steam Heating. (p. 2002)
—Mining: The Classic Mine Technology Book from 1907. (p. 1147)
—Mining: Hoisting the Classic Mine Technology Book From 1907. (p. 1147)
International Spy Museum Staff, jt. auth. see Shugaar, Antony.
International Thriller Writers Association Staff. Fear: 13 Stories of Suspense & Horror. Stine, R. L., ed. (p. 579)
Inthof, Marian. Aunt Marian's Abc Book (p. 115)
—Our Friends at Farmer John's Meadow. (p. 1308)
Intosh, Kenneth Mc & McIntosh, Kenneth. Clergy. Riggs, Ernestine G. & Gholar, Cheryl, eds. (p. 331)
Intrater, Roberta Grobel. Peek-a-Boo, You! Intrater, Roberta Grobel, photos by. (p. 1335)
Intravia, Emily & Swope, Gretchen. Fordham University College Prowler off the Record. (p. 617)
Intriago, Patricia. Dot. Intriago, Patricia, illus. (p. 472)
Inui, Sekihiko. Comic Party (p. 348)
—Comic Party Kiefl, Mike, tr. from JPN. (p. 348)
Inui, Sekihiko, creator. Comic Party (p. 348)
InVision Communications Staff, contrib. by. Inactive History Native Americans. (p. 868)
Invoke A Blessing Inc., Staff. Uncommon Boy. (p. 1812)
Inyard, April, jt. auth. see Inyard, Gordon.
Inyard, Gordon & Inyard, April. Adventures of Abe: An Autobiography of a Copper Penny. (p. 16)
Inzana, Ryan. Ichiro. (p. 851)
Ioan, Elwyn. Ici'r Ddôl A'r Cathod Nadolig. (p. 851)
—Ici'r Ddôl A'r Corrach Coch. (p. 851)
Ioan, Elwyn & Gruffudd, Garmon. Arthur A'r Cleddyf: Llyfr Lliwio. (p. 103)
—Llywelyn a Gelert: Llyfr Lliwio (p. 1044)
Ioan, Elwyn & Gruffudd, Lefi. Llyfr Lliwio Guto Nyth Brân. (p. 1044)
Ioannides, Mara W. Cohen. Shout in the Sunshine. (p. 1570)
Ioannou, Gregory Phillip, ed. see MacGregor, Kim.
Iola, Kate. Deadstock. (p. 418)
Ionesco, Eugène. Stories 1,2,3,4. Delessert, Etienne, illus. (p. 1654)
Ionescu, Angela C. Cuentos y Leyendas de Rumania. (p. 390)
Ionescu, Julian. Mango & His Friends Have a Party. Daranga, Ana-Maria, illus. (p. 1087)
—Tomato & Her Friends Have a Party. Daranga, Ana-Maria, illus. (p. 1764)
Iorillo, Kristin. Wacko Baby. (p. 1852)
Iorio, Nicole. Interactive Whiteboard Activities - Addition & Subtraction Facts Made Easy: Ready-to-Use Mini-Lessons & Activities That Help Students Master Math Facts. (p. 879)
—Joe Biden. (p. 920)
Iorio, Nicole, jt. auth. see Time for Kids Editors.
Iorio, Nicole & Time for Kids Editors. Spiders! (p. 1626)
Iorizzo, Carrie. Anxiety & Phobias. (p. 90)
—Schizophrenia & Other Psychotic Disorders. (p. 1521)
—Schizophrenia & Psychotic Disorders. (p. 1521)
Iorizzo, Carrie, jt. auth. see Crabtree Publishing Company Staff.
Iorizzo, Carrie, jt. auth. see Cross, Carrie L.
Iosa, Ann. Jobs in My Neighborhood. (p. 919)
Iosa, Ann, illus. see Callella, Trisha.
Iosa, Ann, illus. see Flores, Debra, et al.
Iosa, Ann, illus. see Grahame, Kenneth.
Iosa, Ann, illus. see Rosa-Mendoza, Gladys.
Iosa, Ann, illus. see Rouss, Sylvia A. & Rouss, Shannan.
Iosa, Ann, illus. see Schulz, Kathy.
Iosa, Ann W., illus. see Callella, Trisha.
Iosa, Ann W., illus. see Morton, Debra & Stover, Elizabeth.
Iosue, Marilyn. Santa's Busy Day. (p. 1513)
Ip, Ivy S. Clues at the Carnival. (p. 336)
Iparraguirre, Sylvia, et al. Terminemos el Cuento. (p. 1721)
Ipcar, Dahlov. Animal Hide & Seek (p. 78)
—Black & White. (p. 195)
—Bright Barnyard. (p. 228)
—Brown Cow Farm. (p. 232)
—Dahlov Ipcar's Farmyard Alphabet. (p. 399)
—Deep Sea Farm. (p. 423)
—Horses of Long Ago. (p. 800)
—I Like Animals. (p. 841)
—Ipcar's Maine Alphabet. (p. 886)
—One Horse Farm Ipcar, Dahlov, illus. (p. 1295)
—Stripes & Spots (p. 1667)
—Wonderful Egg. (p. 1948)
—World Full of Horses. (p. 1955)
Ipcizade, Catherine. BIG Boats. (p. 178)
—BIG Bugs. (p. 180)
—BIG Buildings. (p. 180)
—BIG Dinosaurs (p. 181)
—BIG Mouths (p. 182)
—BIG Pets. (p. 183)
—BIG Predators. (p. 183)
—BIG Roller Coasters (p. 183)
—BIG Trucks (p. 184)
—Dish on Mac & Cheese (p. 451)
—Fastest Animals (p. 576)
—Favorite Food Facts. (p. 578)
—Giraffes (p. 677)
—Giraffes Saunders-Smith, Gail, ed. (p. 677)
—Giraffes [Scholastic]. (p. 678)
—H Is for Honk! A Transportation Alphabet (p. 734)
—How to Make Frightening Halloween Decorations (p. 820)
—Lions (p. 1021)
—Lions Saunders-Smith, Gail, ed. (p. 1021)
—Lions [Scholastic]. (p. 1021)
—Russia in Colors (p. 1498)
—Scoop on Ice Cream (p. 1529)
—Skinny on Hot Dogs (p. 1585)
—Slowest Animals (p. 1591)
—Strongest Animals (p. 1668)
—T Is for Tiara: A Princess Alphabet (p. 1694)
—'Twas the Day Before Zoo Day Hodson, Ben, illus. (p. 1799)
—Zebras (p. 1985)
—Zebras Saunders-Smith, Gail, ed. (p. 1985)
—Zebras [Scholastic]. (p. 1985)
Ipcizade, Catherine, et al. Pucks, Clubs, & Baseball Gloves: Reading & Writing Sports Poems Loveridge, Matt et al, illus. (p. 1414)
Ipellie, Alootook & MacDonald, David. Inuit Thought of It: Amazing Arctic Innovations. (p. 883)
Ippisch, Hanneke. Spotted Bear: A Rocky Mountain Folktale. Ort, Kathleen, ed. (p. 1634)
Ippolito, Eva Marie. Donkey's Tale. Ippolito, Eva Marie, illus. (p. 466)
—Hear, O Lord. Ippolito, Eva Marie, ed. (p. 759)
Ippolito, Heidi. Bobo's New Home. (p. 206)
Iqbal, Michele. Jake: A Soul's Journey Through Time. (p. 905)
Irani, Dinaz. Indigo Fairy & the Frogs. (p. 872)
IraqiGirl. IraqiGirl: Diary of a Teenage Girl in Iraq. Wrigley-Field, Elizabeth & Ross, John, eds. (p. 887)
Irbinskas, Heather. Lost Kachina. Albert, Robert & Anthis, Brian, illus. (p. 1056)
—Pauly the Adventurous Pallid Bat. Anthis, Brian, illus. (p. 1331)
Irby, Rob, photos by see Stone, Sandra & Stone, James.
Ireland, Barb. Diaper Cake Know How. Suman, Michelle, ed. (p. 434)
Ireland, Bernard. Fall of Toulon: The Royal Navy & the Royalist Last Stand Against the French Revolution. (p. 566)
Ireland, Cameron Robert. Missing Left Shoe. (p. 1152)
—Say the 'K', Kay! (p. 1518)
Ireland, Charles E. Toolbox. Dlienno, Trish, illus. (p. 1767)
Ireland, Justina. Promise of Shadows. (p. 1411)
—Vengeance Bound. (p. 1835)
Ireland, Kenneth. Big Cats. (p. 180)
—Ghost Train. (p. 672)
—Noises in the Night. (p. 1262)
—Sleep Well. (p. 1588)
—Werewolf Mask. (p. 1875)
Ireland, Kevin. How to Catch a Fish. (p. 815)
Ireland, Mary E. & Brandstaedter, German H. Vacaciones de Eric,Las. Clingan, Darrell, tr. (p. 1829)
Iriarte, Tomas De & de, Iriarte Tomás. Fabulas de Iriarte. (p. 559)
Iribarren, Elena, tr. see Amado, Elisa.
Iribarren, Elena, tr. see Mora, Pat & Martinez, Libby.
Iribarren, Elena, ed. Mambru se fue a la Guerra. Calderon, Gloria, illus. (p. 1084)
Iribarren, Leopoldo, tr. see Amado, Elisa.
Irick, Angela. Ashley Wins the First Day of School. (p. 106)
Irish, Janice. Gift of Words: A Resource for Parents & Educators. (p. 675)
Irish, Leigh Ann, illus. see Gilleland, Linda.
Irish, Martin, illus. see Faulkner, Keith.
Irish, Rosario A. Lamy. (p. 972)
Irish, Terry. Tree Secrets. (p. 1783)
Iriyama, Satoshi. Good Night, Chirp. (p. 699)
—Happy Spring, Chirp! (p. 746)
Iriye, Akira, et al. World of Asia. (p. 1956)
Irly, I. R. Why Crocodile Does Not Smile. (p. 1923)
Iroaganachi, John, jt. auth. see Achebe, Chinua.
Irons, Cal and Rosie. Baker Bill. (p. 133)
Irons, Calvin. Fun Room. (p. 648)
—Long Long Ride. (p. 1047)
—Muffins at the Fair. (p. 1189)
—Shirts & Skirts. (p. 1567)
Irons, Calvin, jt. auth. see Burnett, Calvin.
Irons, Calvin, jt. auth. see Burnett, James.
Irons, Rosemary. Mix & Match Flip Chart. (p. 1156)
Irons Royalty, Cal. Five Minutes More. (p. 601)
—Shape Race in Outer Space. (p. 1560)
Ironside, Meredith. Spoon Creek Mystery. (p. 1631)
Ironside, Virgina & Ironside, Virginia. Huge Bag of Worries. Rodgers, Frank, illus. (p. 824)
Ironside, Virginia, jt. auth. see Ironside, Virgina.
Irvin, Barbara Band. Time, Money & Fractions. (p. 1752)
Irvin, Barbara Bando. Multiplication Facts. Boyer, Robin, illus. (p. 1190)
Irvin, Christine. Isaac the Frog. Less, Sally, illus. (p. 890)
Irvin, Christine M. Craft Stick Mania. (p. 375)
—Milk Carton Mania. (p. 1143)
—Paper Cup Mania. (p. 1322)
—Pie Pan Mania. (p. 1356)
—Pipe Cleaner Mania. (p. 1361)
Irvin, David. Rusty, the Rainbow Trout: Moving Day. Irvin, Sioux, illus. (p. 1498)
Irvin, Feliza, jt. auth. see Irvin, Feliza.
Irvin, Feliza & Irvin, Feliza. Idaly's Learning Chest, Series 1: Learning Body Parts. Vigil, Sabrina, ed. (p. 852)
Irvin, Frank, illus. see Hammontree, Marie.
Irvin, Juanita. Zack the Cool Cat. (p. 1984)
Irvin, Sioux, illus. see Irvin, David.
Irvin, Vanessa. Jack's Perfect World. (p. 904)
Irvin, William. Adventures of Winston & Hazel: Episode 1: the Silver Medallion. (p. 24)
Irvine, Alex. Captain America: The First Avenger. (p. 263)
—Phase One: Iron Man. (p. 1350)
—Phase One: Marvel's the Avengers. (p. 1350)
—Phase One: the Incredible Hulk. (p. 1350)
—Phase One: Thor. (p. 1350)
Irvine, Alex, adapted by. Adventures of Tintin. (p. 24)
Irvine, Alexander. Dungeons & Dragons: Dark Sun - Ianto's Tomb: Dark Sun - Ianto's Tomb. (p. 490)
—Rapture. (p. 1439)
Irvine, Alexander C. & Preiss, Byron. Have Robot, Will Travel. (p. 754)
Irvine, Chippy, jt. auth. see Douglas, Murray.
Irvine, Coco. Through No Fault of My Own: A Girl's Diary of Life on Summit Avenue in the Jazz Age. (p. 1745)
Irvine, Jenny. My Friend, Mi Amigo. (p. 1209)
Irvine, Joan. How to Make Super Pop-Ups. Hendry, Linda, illus. (p. 820)
Irvine, Joan & Hendry, Linda. Outside the Box! Creative Activities for Ecology-Minded Kids. Hendry, Linda, illus. (p. 1313)
Irvine, Mat, jt. auth. see Jefferis, David.

Irvine, Patricia McCune. Beyond the Greenest Hill: A Fairy Tale. (p. 174)
—Haunted Pavilion: And Other Short Stories. (p. 753)
Irvine, Ron S. ABC's of Your Body (p. 4)
Irvine, Wil, illus. see Grateful Steps Publishing & Tipton, Angela.
Irving, Barrington & Peppe, Holly. Touch the Sky. (p. 1772)
Irving, Dianne. Measuring Time at a Race (p. 1117)
—Perimeter & Area at the Amusement Park (p. 1343)
—Volume & Hot Air Balloons (p. 1850)
Irving, Dianne, jt. auth. see Lockyer, John.
Irving Ed.D., Harry R. Image-Word D'Enfants et Livre Simple de Phrase: Version Francaise Catégories Primaires. (p. 860)
Irving, Frazer, illus. see Reed, Gary & Shelley, Mary.
Irving, Frazer, illus. see Shelley, Mary.
Irving, Frazier, jt. illus. see Bachalo, Chris.
Irving, George S., illus. see Schwartz, Alvin & Alvin, Schwartz.
Irving, Harry. Picture-Word Quizzes Assessment Sheets & Solution Book: For the Children's Picture-Word & Simple Sentence Book. Graphics Factory, illus. (p. 1356)
Irving, Jan. Stories NeverEnding: A Program Guide for Schools & Libraries Vol. 1 (p. 1654)
Irving, N. Improve Your English. (p. 862)
Irving, N., jt. auth. see Daynes, Katie.
Irving, N., jt. auth. see Denne, B.
Irving, Nicole. Improve Your Punctuation. (p. 862)
Irving, Nicole, ed. see Amery, Heather.
Irving, Nicole, ed. see Davies, Helen.
Irving, Nicole, ed. see Leigh, Susannah.
Irving, Washington. Devil & Tom Walker. (p. 432)
—Legend of Sleepy Hollow. (p. 988)
—Legend of Sleepy Hollow. Van Nutt, Robert, illus. (p. 988)
—Legend of Sleepy Hollow & Other Stories. McKowen, Scott, illus. (p. 988)
—Legend of Sleepy Hollow & Other Stories from the Sketch Book. (p. 988)
—Rip Van Winkle. (p. 1473)
—Rip Van Winkle & Other Stories. (p. 1473)
—Washington Irving. Hall, Tracy, illus. (p. 1860)
Irving, Washington, jt. auth. see Foehner, Ashley.
Irving, Washington, jt. auth. see Gutierrez, Dave.
Irving, Washington & Busch, Jeffrey. Rip Van Winkle. (p. 1473)
Irving, Washington & Gutierrez, Dave. Leyenda Del Jinete Sin Cabeza Tobon, Sara, tr. from ENG. (p. 1004)
Irving, Washington, et al. Halloween Classics Pomplun, Tom, ed. (p. 737)
Irvin-Marston, Hope. My Little Book of Bald Eagles. (p. 1212)
—My Little Book of Burrowing Owls. Magdalena-Brown, Maria, illus. (p. 1212)
—My Little Book of Painted Turtles. Magdalena-Brown, Maria, illus. (p. 1212)
—My Little Book of River Otters. Magdalena-Brown, Maria, illus. (p. 1212)
—My Little Book of Timber Wolves. Magdalena-Brown, Maria, illus. (p. 1212)
—My Little Book of Whitetails. Magdalena-Brown, Maria, illus. (p. 1212)
—My Little Book of Wood Ducks. Magdalena-Brown, Maria, illus. (p. 1212)
Irwin, April, illus. see Clark, Danell.
Irwin, Bindi & Black, Jess. Bouncing off the Menu. (p. 216)
—Bushfire! (p. 244)
—Guest Appearance. (p. 729)
—Rescue! Bindi Wildlife Adventures. (p. 1462)
—Roar! (p. 1478)
—Totally Bindi: Access All Areas: Games & Quizzes, Facts & Photos. (p. 1771)
Irwin, Bindi & Costain, Meredith. Dive in Deeper. (p. 454)
—Ghostly Tale. (p. 672)
Irwin, Bindi & Kunz, Chris. Camouflage. (p. 257)
—Croc Capers: Bindi Wildlife Adventures. (p. 384)
—Trouble at the Zoo. (p. 1789)
—Whale of a Time. (p. 1877)
—Wildlife Games. (p. 1931)
Irwin, Bindi & Nathar, Marisa. Island Escape. (p. 892)
Irwin, Bindi, et al. Surfing with Turtles: Bindi Wildlife Adventures. (p. 1685)
Irwin, Chris. Nightmare of Shadows. (p. 1255)
Irwin, Dana, illus. see Mellor, Colleen Kelly.
Irwin, Dana M., illus. see Mellor, Colleen Kelly.
Irwin, Daniel. Adventures of Tylor Bear & Mana. (p. 24)
Irwin, Esther. Jesse & His New Friends. Puett, Gayle, ed. (p. 914)
—White Cloud: A Little Boy's Dream. Puett, Gayle, ed. (p. 1912)
Irwin, Gayle. Sage Learns to Share Araujo, Katie, illus. (p. 1502)
Irwin, Gerald. Harry the Spider & His Friend Charlie. (p. 751)
Irwin, Inez. Maida's Little Shop. (p. 1076)
Irwin, Inez Haynes. Maida's Little House. (p. 1076)
Irwin, James. Destination Moon. (p. 430)
Irwin, Jane, et al. Clockwork Faerie (p. 333)
Irwin, John B. Natural Way to a Trouble-Free Pregnancy: The Toxemia-Thiamine Connection. (p. 1236)
Irwin, John P. Cubby Files; Tales of a Pennsylvania Black Bear Growing Up. (p. 388)
Irwin, Judy. What's It to You? (p. 1898)
Irwin, Kate. Alfie's Great Escape. Elsom, Clare, illus. (p. 37)
Irwin, Kendra, illus. see Lyttle, Marcy.
Irwin, Ms. Judy. We're Done. (p. 1875)
—What Did You Say? (p. 1882)
Irwin, Robert, jt. auth. see Wells, Jack.
Irwin, Robert & Wells, Jack. Ambush at Cisco Swamp. Creagh, Lachlan, illus. (p. 57)
—Armoured Defence. Creagh, Lachlan, illus. (p. 100)
—Dinosaur Feather. Creagh, Lachlan, illus. (p. 442)
—Discovery. Creagh, Lachlan, illus. (p. 450)
—Robert Irwin, Dinosaur Hunter: The Wilderness Collection (p. 1479)
Irwin, Sue. Safety Stars: Players Who Fought to Make the Hard-Hitting Game of Professional Hockey Safer (p. 1502)
Irwin, Susan, jt. auth. see Bluestone, Carol.
Irwin, Violet, jt. auth. see Stefansson, Vilhjalmur.
Irwin-Ayotte, Tracy. Bilingual Songs: English-French. (p. 186)
—Bilingual Songs: English-French. Vol. 1 (p. 186)
Isaac, Andrew, jt. auth. see Rustad, Alan.
Isaac, Denise. Agape to You. (p. 29)
Isaac, Kendall. Lifeology... the Course We Needed but School Didn't Offer. (p. 1013)
Isaac, Lowell. Mr. Cat & the End of the World. (p. 1184)
Isaac, W. Smiley, illus. see Arceneaux, Kitty.
Isaacs, Anne. Dust Devil. Zelinsky, Paul O., illus. (p. 490)
—Ghosts of Luckless Gulch. Santat, Dan, illus. (p. 672)
—Meanwhile, Back at the Ranch. Hawkes, Kevin, illus. (p. 1117)
Isaacs, April. Tornadoes, Hurricanes, & Tsunamis: A Practical Survival Guide. (p. 1770)
Isaacs, April, ed. Critical Perspectives on Al Qaeda. (p. 383)
Isaacs, Christos, jt. auth. see Gage, Christos.
Isaacs Ferrer, Jorge, ed. Maria. (p. 1093)
Isaacs, John. Doggone Good Story. (p. 462)
Isaacs, Kathleen T. Bugs, Bogs, Bats, & Books: Sharing Nature with Children Through Reading. (p. 237)
Isaacs, Latricia. Mason & Baylee Learn to Count. (p. 1102)
—Mason & Hayden Visit Grandma. (p. 1102)
—Mason & Lilly Visit Grandpa. (p. 1102)
Isaacs, Michael. Fuzzy Escape Artists. Artigas, Alexandra, illus. (p. 651)
Isaacs, Rebekah, illus. see Mayo, Gretchen Will & O'Hern, Kerri.
Isaacs, Ronald H., jt. auth. see Rostoker-Gruber, Karen.
Isaacs, Sally. Bill & Melinda Gates. (p. 186)
—Understanding the Articles of Confederation. (p. 1816)
—Understanding the Bill of Rights. (p. 1816)
—Understanding the Declaration of Independence. (p. 1816)
—Understanding the US Constitution. (p. 1816)
Isaacs, Sally & Bedeksy, Baron. Understanding the Articles of Confederation. (p. 1816)
—Understanding the Bill of Rights. (p. 1816)
—Understanding the Declaration of Independence. (p. 1816)
—Understanding the US Constitution. (p. 1816)
Isaacs, Sally Senzell. Bill & Melinda Gates (p. 186)
—Gold Rush. (p. 693)
—Great Land Rush. (p. 717)
—Helen Thayer's Arctic Adventure: A Woman & a Dog Walk to the North Pole. Sasheva, Iva, illus. (p. 763)
—Lewis & Clark Expedition. (p. 1004)
—Stagecoaches & Railroads. (p. 1638)
—Trail of Tears. (p. 1776)
—West (p. 1876)
—What Caused the War of 1812? (p. 1881)
Isaacson, Philip M. Short Walk Around the Pyramids & Through the World of Art. (p. 1569)
Isaacson, Rick. Magic Museum. (p. 1072)
Isaak, Armond, jt. auth. see Carlson, Nancy.
Isabel, Delgado Maria. Chaves Memories los Recuerdos de Chave. Yvonne, Symank, illus. (p. 295)
Isabel, Isaias, tr. see Browne, Paula.
Isabel, Michelle. Murtle the Sea Turtle. Isabel, Michelle & Thomas, Franselica, illus. (p. 1192)
Isabella, Jude. Chitchat: Celebrating the World's Languages. Boake, Kathy, illus. (p. 308)
—Red Bicycle: The Extraordinary Story of One Ordinary Bicycle. Shin, Simone, illus. (p. 1453)
—Steve Jobs: Visionary Entrepreneur of the Digital Age. (p. 1649)
Isabelle, Decenciere, illus. see Drachman, Eric.
Isadora, Rachel. Bea at Ballet. Isadora, Rachel, illus. (p. 149)
—Hansel & Gretel. Isadora, Rachel, illus. (p. 743)
—Happy Belly, Happy Smile. Isadora, Rachel, illus. (p. 744)
—Jake at Gymnastics. Isadora, Rachel, illus. (p. 906)
—Mr. Moon. (p. 1185)
—Nick Plays Baseball. Isadora, Rachel, illus. (p. 1251)
—Night Before Christmas. (p. 1252)
—Night Before Christmas. Isadora, Rachel, illus. (p. 1252)
—Old Mikamba Had a Farm. Isadora, Rachel, illus. (p. 1284)
—On Your Toes: A Ballet ABC. (p. 1292)
—Peekaboo Morning. Isadora, Rachel, illus. (p. 1335)
—Princess & the Pea. (p. 1402)
—Say Hello! Isadora, Rachel, illus. (p. 1518)
—There Was a Tree. Isadora, Rachel, illus. (p. 1730)
—Twelve Dancing Princesses. Isadora, Rachel, illus. (p. 1800)
—What a Family! A Fresh Look at Family Trees. (p. 1878)
Isadora, Rachel, illus. see Kurtz, Jane.
Isadora, Rachel, illus. see Vaughan, Carolyn.
Isadora, Rachel, jt. auth. see Brothers Grimm, Becky.
Isaksen, Lisa A., illus. see Bozanich, Tony L. & Wight, Joe.
Isaksen, Patricia, ed. see Bozanich, Tony L. & Wight, Joe.
Isakson, Debra K. It's Nice to Be Nice: Tommy Learns a Lesson in Manners. (p. 897)
Isau, Ralf. Circulo del Crepusculo I: El Nino del Siglo. Bernet, Roberto, tr. (p. 322)
—Circulo del Crepusculo IV: El Fuego Ultraterreno. Bernet, Roberto, tr. (p. 322)
Isaza, Juanita, illus. see Nino, Jairo Anibal.
Isaza, Juanita, illus. see Quiroga, Horacio.
Isaza, Juanita, illus. see Vasco, Irene.
Isbell, R. & Raines, S. C. Arte de Contar: Cuentos a los Ninos. (p. 103)
Isbell, Rebecca & Buchanan, Marilyn. Everyone Has a Story to Tell. Bledsoe, William B., illus. (p. 544)
Isbell, Sarah. Book of Green Goo. (p. 211)
Isbell, Shaun. Mouse & the Witch (p. 1182)
Isbell, Susan & Jones, Robert. Noah's Very Big Boat. (p. 1262)
Isbell, Tessa J. Animal Adventures: Goosey & Beauty Take a Mystery Magic Carpet Ride to Jamaica. (p. 76)
Isbell, Toby, illus. see Campbell, Anna.
Isbell, Tom. Capture. (p. 265)
—Prey. (p. 1398)
Ische, Bryan, illus. see Quinn, Patricia O. & Maitland, Theresa E. Laurie.
Isdell, Wendy. Chemy Called Al by Wendy Isdell. (p. 297)
Isecke, Harriet. Finding Texas: Exploration in New Lands. (p. 588)
—Lyndon B. Johnson: A Texan in the White House. (p. 1066)
—Lyndon B. Johnson: Un Texano en la Casa Blanca / Lyndon B. Johnson - A Texan in the White House. (p. 1066)
—Stephen F. Austin: The Father of Texas. (p. 1648)
—Susan B. Anthony & Elizabeth Cady Stanton: Early Suffragists. (p. 1688)
—Texas en el Siglo XX (Texas in the 20th Century) (p. 1724)
—Texas Hoy: Guiando a los Estados Unidos Hacia el Futuro. (p. 1724)
—Texas in the 20th Century: Building Industry & Community. (p. 1724)
—Texas Today: Leading America into the Future. (p. 1724)
—Women's Suffrage: Fighting for Women's Rights. (p. 1947)
Isecke, Harriet, jt. auth. see Herwick Rice, Dona.
Isecke, Harriet, jt. auth. see Rice, Dona Herwick.
Isecke, Harriet & Kuligowski, Stephanie. Descubriendo Texas. (p. 428)
—Stephen F. Austin: El Padre de Texas / Stephen F. Austin - The Father of Texas. (p. 1648)
Iselin, Tom. Bread of Life: For the Table ... for Eternity (p. 224)
Isely, Chad, illus. see Jones, Kip.
Iseminger, Jonathan, illus. see Carey-Costa, Denise.
Iseminger, Jonathon, illus. see Carey-Costa, Denise.
Isenberg. High Five. (p. 777)
Isenberg, Barbara. Making It Big: The Diary of a Broadway Musical. (p. 1081)
Isenberg, Marty. Animated (p. 84)
—Renegades Vol. 1 (p. 1460)
Isenhoff, Michelle. Quill Pen. (p. 1428)
Iserles, Inbali. Tygrine Cat. (p. 1805)
Isern, Carol, tr. see Gaiman, Neil.
Isern, Carol, tr. see Kluver, Cayla.
Isern, Carol, tr. see Paolini, Christopher.
Isern, Carol, tr. see Small, Charlie.
Isern, Susanna. Magic Ball of Wool. (p. 1071)
Iserson, David. Firecracker. (p. 591)
Iserson, Kenneth V. Get into Medical School! A Guide for the Perplexed. (p. 667)
Ishe, Bryan, illus. see Hood, Korey K.
Isherwood, Christopher. Down There on a Visit: A Novel. (p. 474)
Isherwood, Matthew, illus. see Litton, Jonathan.
Ishibash, Toshiharu, illus. see Mizuno, Junko & Anzal, Yuko.
Ishida, Jui. Who Says Baa? A Touch & Feel Board Book. (p. 1917)
—Who Says Moo? A Touch & Feel Board Book. (p. 1917)
Ishida, Jui, illus. see Matsuda, Christine.
Ishida, Jui, illus. see Prelutsky, Jack.
Ishida, Jui, illus. see Yolen, Jane.
Ishida, Sanae. Little Kunoichi, the Ninja Girl. (p. 1030)
Ishihara, Satoru. Kimi Shiruya - Dost Thou Know? (p. 957)
Ishii, Minako. Girls' Day/Boys' Day. Ishii, Minako, photos by. (p. 680)
Ishii, Momoko. Gorrion de la Lengua Cortada. Akaba, Suekichi, illus. (p. 703)
Ishikawa, Elina, tr. see Ohta, Akiyoshi.
Ishikawa, Katsuhiko, jt. auth. see Yoshinaga, Masayuki.
Ishikawa, Shiho. AlphaPets. (p. 50)
Ishizuka, Kathy. John Grisham: Best-Selling Author. (p. 922)
Ishkanian, Charlotte. Best Ever Mission Stories: Kids in Action Around the World. (p. 169)
Ish-Kishor, Sulamith. Boy of Old Prague. Shahn, Ben, illus. (p. 218)
Ishtar Design. Mom's Authentic Assyrian Recipes. (p. 1163)
Ishwaran, Wobine. Journey into Space: Kary to the Moon. (p. 928)
—Shashi & Maya: A Life of Courage. (p. 1563)
Isik, Sernur, illus. see Ganeri, Anita.
Isik, Sernur, illus. see Newman, Tracy.
Isik, Sernur, illus. see Phillips, Ruby Ann.
Isings, J. H., illus. see Hulst, W. G. van de.
Isis, Watalia. Ronald's Adventures Throught Time & Imagination. (p. 1487)
Iskowitz, Joel, illus. see Burg, Ann.
Islam, Hina. Eid for Everyone. (p. 507)
Islam, M. N. Hamza's Journey of a Lifetime. (p. 740)
Islam, Sabirul. World at Your Feet: Three Strikes to a Successful Entrepreneurial Life. (p. 1954)
Islam, Shireen. Dinosaurs: The Final Chapter. (p. 444)
Island, Fiona. Wishbone's Magic Garden. (p. 1940)
Isle, Mick. Aristotle: Pioneering Philosopher & Founder of the Lyceum. (p. 98)
—Everything You Need to Know about Food Poisoning. (p. 545)
—Malaria. (p. 1083)
—Timeline of the Supreme Court. (p. 1754)
—Tom Hanks & Colin Hanks. (p. 1763)
Isle, Mick, jt. auth. see Roscoe, Kelly.
Isler, Claudia. Right to Vote. (p. 1472)
Isler, Claudia, jt. auth. see Ganchy, Sally.
Isler, Claudia, jt. auth. see Quinn, Barbara.
Isler, Linda Germano. It's Elementary, Funny Things Kids Say in School. Santitoro, Theresa & Tumminello, Giovanna, illus. (p. 896)
Isles, Deborah, jt. auth. see Stevens, Neil.
Ismail, Nafisah, jt. auth. see Morris, Kerry-Ann.
Ismail, Vehbi. Muhammad: The Last Prophet. (p. 1189)
Ismail, Yasmeen. Inside, Outside, Upside Down. (p. 877)
—Time for Bed, Fred! (p. 1751)
Ismail, Yasmeen, illus. see Averbeck, Jim.
Isner Studios, Will. Sheena: Queen of the Jungle. (p. 1564)
Isogawa, Yoshihito. LEGO Technic Idea Book: Wheeled Wonders (p. 990)
—Lego Technic Idea Book: Fantastic Contraptions (p. 990)
Isol. It's Useful to Have a Duck Amado, Elisa, tr. from SPA. (p. 899)
—Regalo Sorpresa. Isol, illus. (p. 1457)
—Secreto de Familia. (p. 1544)
—Tener un patito es util. (p. 1720)
—Vida de Perros. (p. 1840)
Isol, illus. see Luján, Jorge.
Isol, illus. see Montes, Graciela.
Isol Staff, illus. see Luján, Jorge.
Isom, Lori Boyd. Swoosh! Wise, Noreen, ed. (p. 1692)
Isom, Michelle. Human Dogs. (p. 826)
Isop, Laurie. How Do You Hug a Porcupine? Millward, Gwen, illus. (p. 808)
Isozaki, Arata & Oshima, Ken Tadashi. Arata Isozaki. (p. 94)
Israel, David, photos by see Gressler, Jeanne, ed.
Israel, Elaine. Hilary Duff. (p. 779)
Israel, Fred L., jt. ed. see Schlesinger, Arthur M., Jr.
Israel, Susan E. Be Just Me. (p. 148)
Israel-Clark, Anani. 7 Spiritual Laws of Money. (p. 1993)
Israeli, Raphael. Piracy in Qumran: The Battle over the Scrolls of the Pre-Christ Era. (p. 1362)
Israelievitch, Gabrielle. Where's Home? (p. 1910)
Issa, Joanna. I Can Make a Bunch of Flowers (p. 836)
—I Can Make a Mask (p. 836)
—I Can Make a Monster (p. 836)
—I Can Make a Truck (p. 836)
—These Are My Senses (p. 1731)
—What Can I Feel? (p. 1880)
—What Can I Hear? (p. 1880)
—What Can I Make Today? (p. 1880)
—What Can I See? (p. 1880)
—What Can I Smell? (p. 1880)
—What Can I Taste? (p. 1880)
Issa, Kate Hannigan, jt. auth. see Duncan, Karen.
Issa, Rose & Avedissian, Chant. Chant Avedissian: Cairo Stencils. (p. 290)
Issac, Michael. Historical Atlas of Oman. (p. 783)
Issaluk, Johnny. Games of Survival: Traditional Inuit Games for Elementary Students Maruyama, Ed, photos by. (p. 655)
Isserman, Maurice. Across America: The Lewis & Clark Expedition, Revised Edition. (p. 9)
—Exploring North America, 1800-1900, Revised Edition. (p. 553)
—Korean War. (p. 967)
—Vietnam War. (p. 1841)
—World War II. (p. 1959)
Issim, Beth. Empty Christmas Sack. (p. 521)
Istakhorov, Selma. Solving Real World Problems with Aerospace Engineering. (p. 1608)
Istvan & Schritter "Istvansch", Istvan. Federica Aburrida. (p. 580)
Ita, Sam. Odyssey: A Pop-Up Book. (p. 1279)
Italia, John. Birds of the Harbor. Caravela, Elena, illus. (p. 192)
Itani, Frances. Best Friend Trouble Després, Geneviève, illus. (p. 169)
Itchyka-Dana. Asian Nursery Rhymes. (p. 106)
Ithaca, Sciencenter, NY. How Small Is Nano? (p. 812)
—Is That Robot Real? (p. 890)
Ito, Akihiro. Geobreeders 1 Ito, Akihiro, illus. (p. 661)
Ito, Akira, jt. auth. see Takahashi, Kazuki.
Ito, Akira & Takahashi, Kazuki. Yu-Gi-Oh! R Ito, Akira, illus. (p. 1983)
Ito, Jerilyn. Double Rainbow Island: The Mauka Adventure. Wong, Melissa Oliaivar, illus. (p. 473)
Ito, Joel, illus. see Bruhn, Aron.
Ito, Kazunori. Hack//Another Birth - Infection (p. 735)
Ito, Leonardo, illus. see Hoena, Blake A. & Tortosa, Wilson.
Ito, Leonardo, illus. see Manning, Matthew K. & Majado, Caio.
Ito, Leonardo, illus. see Terrell, Brandon & Majado, Caio.
Ito, Leonardo, illus. see Terrell, Brandon & Tortosa, Wilson.
Ito, Willie, illus. see Bazaldua, Barbara.
Itoh, Shimei. Hyper Dolls (p. 831)
Itoh, Shimpei. Hyper Dolls. (p. 831)
Itoiz, Mayana. Search & Find: Fairy Tales as Children Have Never Seen Them Before! (p. 1537)
Itow, Rebecca Chiyoko, jt. auth. see Anderson II, Norman E.
Itow, Rebecca Chiyoko & Anderson II, Norman E. Boy, A Dog & Persnickety Log. (p. 217)
It's Good 2B Good Staff & Zerner, Sandra. It's Good 2B Good: Why It's Not Bad to Be Good. (p. 897)
Itterman, Bert. Growing up with Grandpa. (p. 727)
Iturralde, Edna. Caminantes del Sol. Gonzalez, Santiago et al, illus. (p. 256)
—Conoce a Miguel de Cervantes: Get to Know Miguel de Cervantes. (p. 358)
—Los pájaros no tienen fronteras: Leyendas y mitos de América Latina. (p. 1054)
—Martina, Las Estrellas y un Cachito de Luna. Chaves, Guido, illus. (p. 1098)
—Verde Fue Mi Selva. Arroba, Doris et al, eds. (p. 1836)
—Verde fue mi selva. Cornejo, Eulalia et al, illus. (p. 1836)
Iturralde, Edna & Chamorro, Marco. Torbellino. (p. 1769)
Iturrondo, Angeles Molina. Pepitina. Guevara, Dennis Villanueva, illus. (p. 1340)
—Sapo Sapito Sapote. Umpierre, Migdalia, illus. (p. 1514)
Iturrondo, Angeles Molina & Iguina, Adriana. Lost Sock. Ortiz Montanez, Nivea, illus. (p. 1056)
Itzkowitz, Norman, jt. auth. see Goldberg, Enid.
Ius, Dawn. Anne & Henry. Watcher, Jill, illus. (p. 85)
Iv, Herge-tintin Rustica, jt. auth. see Hergé.
Ivan & Moxo, illus. see Auerbach, Annie.
Ivan, Benson. Snow That Just Wouldn't Stop. Scott, Rosseau, illus. (p. 1599)
Ivancic, Linda. What Is a Wave? (p. 1888)
—What Is the Color Spectrum? (p. 1890)
Ivanke. Sparkling Easter Eggs: A Glittery Counting Book. (p. 1622)
Ivanke, illus. see Krensky, Stephen.
Ivanke & Lola, illus. see Bryant, Megan E. & O'Ryan, Ellie.
Ivanko, John D., jt. auth. see Ajmera, Maya.
Ivanoff, George. Gamers' Challenge. (p. 654)
—Gamers' Quest. (p. 654)
—How to Make a Fake Death Ray into a Real Laser. (p. 820)
—Life Death & Detention: Short Stories about School & Other Stuff. (p. 1010)
—Long-Lost Relatives. Rankin, Bruce H., illus. (p. 1047)
—Moon Bubble (p. 1172)
—My Best Friend's a Genius (p. 1197)
Ivanoff, George & Quarmby, Toby. My Best Friend Thinks I'm a Genius. (p. 1196)
Ivanov, A., illus. see Farley, Robin.
Ivanov, Aleksey, illus. see Broach, Elise.

Ivanov, Aleksey, illus. see Domain Public Staff.
Ivanov, Aleksey, illus. see Engle, Margarita.
Ivanov, Aleksey, illus. see Farley, Robin.
Ivanov, Aleksey, illus. see Feldman, Thea, et al.
Ivanov, Aleksey, illus. see Martin, Ann M., ed.
Ivanov, Aleksey, illus. see McCombs, Margi.
Ivanov, Aleksey, illus. see O'Connor, Jane.
Ivanov, Aleksey, illus. see Parente, Peter.
Ivanov, Aleksey, illus. see Yorinks, Arthur.
Ivanov, Alex, photos by see Reynolds, David West, et al.
Ivanov, Alexsey, illus. see Magnin, Joyce.
Ivanov, Evgueni, illus. see Tavadze, Olesya.
Ivanov, O., illus. see Farley, Robin.
Ivanov, Olga, illus. see Broach, Elise.
Ivanov, Olga, illus. see Domain Public Staff.
Ivanov, Olga, illus. see Engle, Margarita.
Ivanov, Olga, illus. see Farley, Robin.
Ivanov, Olga, illus. see Feldman, Thea, et al.
Ivanov, Olga, illus. see Magnin, Joyce.
Ivanov, Olga, illus. see Martin, Ann M., ed.
Ivanov, Olga, illus. see McCombs, Margi.
Ivanov, Olga, illus. see Yorinks, Arthur.
Ivanova, Kalina, tr. see Downie, David.
Ivanovich, Nikolai. Sources of Energy. (p. 1616)
Ivans, Marcia S. Over Easy. (p. 1313)
Ivers Casserly, Ricci. Kathy's Adventures. (p. 944)
Ivers, Gregg, jt. auth. see Segal Diascro, Jennifer.
Ivers, Steven. Family Menaces: The Beginning. (p. 568)
Ivers, Steven A. Family Menaces: Runaway Babies. (p. 568)
Ivers, Zoey & Uphoff, Pam. Barton Street Gym. (p. 140)
Iversen, Jeremy. 21. (p. 1996)
—Rush. (p. 1497)
Iversen, Portia, illus. see Hillert, Margaret.
Iversen, Sandra. Alphabet Book Aa. (p. 49)
—Alphabet Book Bb. (p. 49)
—Alphabet Book Cc. (p. 49)
—Alphabet Book Dd. (p. 49)
—Alphabet Book Ee. (p. 49)
—Alphabet Book Ff. (p. 49)
—Alphabet Book Gg. (p. 49)
—Alphabet Book Hh. (p. 49)
—Alphabet Book Ii. (p. 49)
—Alphabet Book Jj. (p. 49)
—Alphabet Book Kk. (p. 49)
—Alphabet Book Ll. (p. 49)
—Alphabet Book Mm. (p. 49)
—Alphabet Book Nn. (p. 49)
—Alphabet Book Oo. (p. 49)
—Alphabet Book Pp. (p. 49)
—Alphabet Book Zz. (p. 49)
—Day on the Mountain. (p. 414)
—What Is It? (p. 1889)
Iverson, Diane. My Favorite Tree: Terrific Trees of North America. (p. 1203)
—Rascal, the Tassel Eared Squirrel. (p. 1439)
Iverson, Diane, illus. see Allred, Sylvester.
Iverson, Diane, illus. see Allsop, Marcus.
Iverson, Diane, illus. see April, Elyse, et al.
Iverson, Diane, jt. auth. see Allred, Sylvester.
Iverson, Diane, jt. auth. see Allsop, Marcus.
Iverson, Gregory. Tyler's Big Blue Truck. Fritz, Siegfried, illus. (p. 1805)
Iverson, Gregory. Katie's Day. Fritz, Siegfried, illus. (p. 945)
Iverson, Jenna. Smile a Day: A Child's Daily Journal. (p. 1594)
Iverson, Mary. Horse Drawing Studio. (p. 799)
Iverson-Noel, Gayle. Brown Beary's Adventures with Jon-Paul. (p. 231)
Ivery, Rachel. Daniel, the Fastest Horse. (p. 405)
Ives, Bob. Three Ants & Mother Bird. Deskov, Vladimir, ed. (p. 1741)
—Three Ants & the Cat. Fairy, Meg, illus. (p. 1741)
Ives, Burl. Sailing on a Very Fine Day. Myers, Bernice & Myers, Lou, illus. (p. 1503)
Ives, David. Scrib. (p. 1533)
Ives, Pastor Carla. Healed from the Inside Out! (p. 757)
Ives, Penny. 5 Little Ducks W. (p. 1992)
—Celestine, Drama Queen. (p. 286)
—Five Little Ducks. (p. 600)
—Rabbit Pie. (p. 1429)
—Rabbit Pie. Ives, Penny, illus. (p. 1429)
Ives, Penny, illus. see Lewis, Paeony.
Ives, Rob. Make Your Own Movie Machine: Build a Paper Zoetrope & Learn to Make Animation Cells. (p. 1080)
Ives, Robert G. R. G. Ives Short Stories. (p. 1429)
Ives, Sarah Noble, illus. see Lindsay, Maud.
Ives, Suzanne Lintz. Bob, the Tree who Became a Star. (p. 205)
Ivey, Allen E., et al. Developmental Counseling & Therapy: Promoting Wellness over the Lifespan. (p. 432)
Ivey, Angela. My Butterfly Wings. (p. 1200)
Ivey, Casey Murray. Rojo the Prideful Little Rooster. (p. 1485)
Ivey, Catherine. Totally Amazing Careers in Health Sciences. (p. 1771)
—Totally Amazing Careers in Space Sciences. (p. 1771)
Ivey, Douglas G. Three Cows. (p. 1741)
Ivey, Lisa. Christmas Tree That Didn't Get Picked. (p. 316)
Ivey, Pamela. Mom! I'm Special I Am Fearfully & Wonderfully Made! (p. 1161)
Ivey, Randall. Jay & the Bounty of Books Galey, Chuck, illus. (p. 910)
Ivie, Emily, illus. see Reger, Rob & Huehner, Mariah.
Ivinskaya, Snezhana, ed. see AZ Books Staff.
Ivo. Charles & Amand: The Adventuresome Frogs. (p. 291)
Ivy, Cheryl. Little Miss D: What did you SEE? (p. 1031)
Ivy, Elena T., illus. see Lockwood, Mark W.
Ivy, Elena T., illus. see Zappler, Georg.
Iwai, Melissa. Soup Day. Iwai, Melissa, illus. (p. 1615)
Iwai, Melissa, illus. see Auerbach, Annie.
Iwai, Melissa, illus. see Cook, Julie Kidd.
Iwai, Melissa, illus. see Jules, Jacqueline.
Iwai, Melissa, illus. see Markell, Denis.
Iwai, Melissa, illus. see Payne, Lauren Murphy.
Iwai, Melissa, illus. see Rau, Dana Meachen.
Iwai, Melissa, illus. see Rosen, Michael J.
Iwai, Melissa, illus. see Sobel, June.
Iwai, Melissa, illus. see Swartz, Daniel J.
Iwai, Melissa, jt. auth. see Rockwell, Anne.
Iwai, Melissa, jt. auth. see Sobel, June.
Iwamura, Kazuo. Hooray for Fall! Iwamura, Kazuo, illus. (p. 796)
Iwamura, Kazuo. Bedtime in the Forest. (p. 157)
—Familia Raton Se Va A Dormir. (p. 567)
—Hooray for Snow! Iwamura, Kazuo, illus. (p. 796)
—Hooray for Spring! Iwamura, Kazuo, illus. (p. 796)
—Hooray for Summer! (p. 796)
—Seven Little Mice Have Fun on the Ice. (p. 1554)
Iwamura, Kazuo, jt. auth. see Carle, Eric.
Iwamura, Kazuo & Yamashita, Haruo. Seven Little Mice Go to School. (p. 1554)
—Seven Little Mice Go to the Beach. (p. 1554)
Iwanaga, Kent, illus. see Squadrito, Vanessa.
Iwasaki, Glen, illus. see Aihara, Chris.
Iwasaki, Masakazu. Popo Can Iwasaki, Masakazu, illus. (p. 1384)
Iwinski, Melissa. Wind at Work. (p. 1935)
Iwo, Tomoharu, tr. see Akino, Matsuri.
Iyengar, Godha. Stinkiest Day in May: The Story of a Stink. (p. 1651)
Iyengar, Malathi. Dance & Devotion: A Hand Book on 'Bharatanatyam' Dance & Traditional Prayers for Students Pursuing Indian Classical Dance. (p. 402)
Iyengar, Malathi Michelle. Romina's Rangoli. Wanardi, Jennifer, illus. (p. 1486)
—Tan to Tamarind: Poems about the Color Brown. Akib, Jamel, illus. (p. 1705)
Iyengar, Uma. Shoshan. Iyengar, Uma, illus. (p. 1569)
Iyer, Lisa H., jt. auth. see Antonian, Armen.
Iyer, Rani. Endangered Energy: Investigating the Scarcity of Fossil Fuels. (p. 526)
—Endangered Rain Forests: Investigating Rain Forests in Crisis. (p. 527)
—Endangered Rivers: Investigating Rivers in Crisis. (p. 527)
Iyer, Rani & Rake, Jody Sullivan. Endangered Earth. (p. 526)
Izenwata, Chinwendu, illus. see Ajiri, Ijeoma.
Izmaylov, Michelle. Galacteran Legacy: Galaxy Watch (p. 652)
Izquierdo, Ana, tr. Caritas Felices: Winnie-the-Pooh. (p. 269)
Izu, Kenro, photos by. Passage to Angkor. (p. 1326)
Izubuchi, Yutaka. Rahxephon Momose, Takeaki, illus. (p. 1433)
—Rahxephon. Momose, Takeaki, illus. (p. 1433)
Izubuchi, Yutaka & Ohnogi, Hiroshi. Rahxephon (p. 1433)
Izumi, Kaneyoshi. Doubt! Izumi, Kaneyoshi, illus. (p. 473)
—Doubt!! Izumi, Kaneyoshi, illus. (p. 473)
—Doubt!!TM. Kokubo, Naomi, tr. (p. 473)
—Seiho Boys' High School!, Vol. 3. Izumi, Kaneyoshi, illus. (p. 1548)
Izumi, Rei. Hack//Ai Buster. (p. 735)
Izumi, Rei, illus. see Hamazaki, Tatsuya.
Izuora, Ikechukwu. Dazzle-Kids Book of Nursery Rhymes & Poems: Book of Nursery Rhymes & Poems. (p. 415)
Izzo, David Garrett. Maximus in Catland/Purring Heights. (p. 1112)
Izzo, Donna. Frilly Lilly. (p. 639)
—Frilly Lilly's Candyland Express. (p. 639)
—Mischievous Michael's 1st Day of School. (p. 1150)
Izzo, Jean-Claude. Sun for the Dying. Curtis, Howard, tr. from FRE. (p. 1676)

J

J. G. Ferguson Publishing Company Staff. Exploring Health Care Careers. (p. 552)
J. G. Ferguson Publishing Company Staff, contrib. by. Discovering Careers for Your Future: English. (p. 449)
J, Granny. Pinky Gets a New Puppy: Pinky Frink's Adventures. (p. 1360)
J., Henry. Big Gray House: The Adventures of Franklin Meyers. (p. 181)
J., Jaylin. Go Dad Go. (p. 686)
J. Katyn. Boo & the Halloween Grin. (p. 209)
J. Long, William. Secrets of the Woods. (p. 1546)
J M Artworks, creator. Totally Horses: Jigsaw Book. (p. 1771)
J., Mary & Davis, Wayne R. Spur of the Moment Preschool. (p. 1635)
Jabaley, Jennifer. Crush Control. (p. 386)
—Lipstick Apology. (p. 1021)
Jabar, Cynthia, illus. see Kimmelman, Leslie.
Jabar, Cynthia, illus. see Murphy, Stuart J.
Jabar, Cynthia, illus. see O'Garden, Irene.
Jabar, Cynthia, illus. see Parenteau, Shirley.
Jabbour, Alan, ed. see Arkham, Thomas.
Jabbour, Alan, ed. see Palmer, Bill.
Jabbour, Alan, ed. see Snedeker, Gus.
Jabbour, Alan, ed. Folk Speech (p. 611)
Jabbour, Joyce, jt. auth. see Gaylord, Susan Kapuscinski.
Jablecki, Joseph S. & Marshall, Julia. Adventures of Mary Jo Beth: Book 1: the Beginning of Tiny Travels. (p. 20)
Jablon, Shmuel. Student's Pesach Haggadah. (p. 1669)
Jablonski, Carla. Defiance Purvis, Leland, illus. (p. 424)
—Resistance Purvis, Leland, illus. (p. 1463)
—Shadow of the Sphinx. (p. 1557)
—Thicker Than Water. (p. 1732)
—Travelers (p. 1780)
—Victory: Resistance Book 3. Purvis, Leland, illus. (p. 1840)
Jablonski, Carrie. Spot the Duck: A Real Story. (p. 1633)
—Spots New Friends. (p. 1634)
Jablonski, Patricia E., jt. auth. see Wallace, Susan Helen.
Jablonski, Patricia Edward. Saint Andre Bessette: Miracles in Montreal. Kiwak, Barbara, illus. (p. 1503)
Jablow, Renee. Hey, That's Not Trash! But Which Bin Does It Go In? Byrne, Mike, illus. (p. 774)
Jabour, Anya. Major Problems in the History of American Families & Children: Documents & Essays. (p. 1078)
Jacana Agency, photos by see Havard, Christian.
Jacen, Kris, ed. Lost & Found. (p. 1054)
Jachimczyk, Victoria. Max's Tale: Home Sweet Home. (p. 1112)
Jack, Alex, ed. see Shakespeare, William & Marlowe, Christopher.
Jack, Colin, illus. see Bailey, Linda.
Jack, Colin, illus. see Degman, Lori.
Jack, Colin, illus. see Harbo, Christopher L.
Jack, Colin, illus. see Harbo, Christopher.
Jack, Colin, illus. see Lachenmeyer, Nathaniel.
Jack, Colin, illus. see O'Ryan, Ray.
Jack, Colin, illus. see Vernick, Audrey.
Jack, Colin, jt. auth. see Brake, Mark.
Jack In The Box Staff. Favorite Children's Stories by Jack in T. (p. 578)
Jack, Keats Ezra. Peter's Chair. (p. 1347)
—Snowy Day. (p. 1601)
Jack, Lizzie. Little Loony Tales: Hatched. Bonnell, B. T., illus. (p. 1030)
Jack Myers Ministries, jt. auth. see Myers, Jack.
Jack R. Wilder. Devil with a Halo. (p. 432)
Jack Stanley. Coaster Cats Go to the Amusement Park. Breuer, Paul, illus. (p. 336)
Jack, Tickle, illus. see Steve, Smallman.
Jackaman, Philippa. ABC Kaleidoscope Book. Walsh, Mike, illus. (p. 3)
—Fun to Learn Opposites: Kaleidoscope Book. Daniel, Carol, illus. (p. 648)
Jackie, Glassman. Amazing Arctic Animals, Vol. 2. (p. 53)
Jacklin, Karl. It's Magic. (p. 897)
—Space in Time. (p. 1619)
Jackman, Joan. Jovenes Gimnastas. (p. 929)
Jackman, John. Collins Primary Focus - Comprehension (p. 341)
—Comprehension. (p. 354)
Jackman, John, ed. see Lindsay, Sarah.
Jackman, John, ed. see Wren, Wendy.
Jackman, Tammy. My Wondrous Words for Children. (p. 1221)
Jackowski, Amélie, illus. see Petz, Moritz.
Jackowski, Rosemarie. Busy Ants under Red Bricks. (p. 245)
—Super Duper Diaper-Poopin' Hero. (p. 1679)
JacKris Publishing, creator. Growing with Grammar Grade 3 Student Manual. (p. 727)
—Growing with Grammar Grade 3 Student Workbook & Answer Key. (p. 727)
Jacks, C. S. Adventures of Pisten Billy: Pisten Billy Makes the Grade! (p. 21)
Jacks, Cyndie, jt. auth. see Lewis, Dawn.
Jacks, Cyndie & Lewis, Dawn. Test Prep with a Twist Grade 2 Rous, Sheri, ed. (p. 1723)
Jackson, A. Isaiah J. Jiffy: You, You, You. Bully! (p. 891)
Jackson, Aariane R. Can You Hear Me Smiling? A Child Grieves a Sister. (p. 259)
Jackson, Aaron. Milton Da Rat: A Family Barbeque. (p. 1144)
Jackson, Abby. Fancy Feet. (p. 570)
—Homes (p. 793)
—Homes. (p. 793)
—Making Money. (p. 1081)
Jackson, Abby, jt. auth. see Cipriano, Jeri S.
Jackson, Aimee, jt. auth. see McCurry, Kristen.
Jackson, Al, Jr. Adventures of Middle School: The Handbook. (p. 20)
Jackson, Alisha. Noah's Fire Engine. (p. 1262)
Jackson, Alison. Desert Rose & Her Highfalutin Hog. Graves, Keith, illus. (p. 429)
—Rainmaker. (p. 1436)
—Thea's Tree. Pedersen, Janet, illus. (p. 1728)
—When the Wind Blew. Barrette, Doris, illus. (p. 1905)
Jackson, Amani D. I'm a Big Boy Now. (p. 858)
Jackson, Andrea V., jt. ed. see Hewitt, Nick.
Jackson, Anitha L. Gabby'may Digsby: When I grow up, I wanna Be.... (p. 652)
Jackson, Ann. Rags the Recycled Doll. O'Connor, Shannon, illus. (p. 1433)
Jackson, Anna. Catullus for Children. (p. 281)
Jackson, Anthony B., illus. see McBride, Maurice & Wallace, Jessica K.
Jackson, Antonia. Easter Story. Ferri, Giuliano, illus. (p. 499)
—My Advent Calendar Christmas Book. Kallai Nagy, Krisztina, illus. (p. 1195)
Jackson, April Eley, illus. see Jones, Alice Eley.
Jackson, Armitra L. Eating Safe with Ace & Mace! (p. 501)
Jackson, Aurelia. Amazon(r): How Jeff Bezos Built the World's Largest Online Store. (p. 56)
—Carmelo Anthony. (p. 270)
—Chris Paul. (p. 311)
—Disney's Pixar(r): How Steve Jobs Changed Hollywood. (p. 453)
—Dwyane Wade. (p. 491)
—Google(Tm) How Larry Page & Sergey Brin Changed the Way We Search the Web. (p. 702)
—Netflix: How Reed Hastings Changed the Way We Watch Movies & TV. (p. 1242)
—Rajon Rondo. (p. 1437)
—Tumblr(r): How David Karp Changed the Way We Blog. (p. 1796)
Jackson, B., jt. auth. see Jackson, Kathryn.
Jackson, Barbara. New Zealand. (p. 1249)
Jackson, Barry, illus. see Kessler, Brad.
Jackson, Barry E. Danny Diamondback. Jackson, Barry E., illus. (p. 405)
Jackson, Bernice, ed. see Boutin, Lesa.
Jackson Black, Amy Sue. Mercy Said No. (p. 1127)
Jackson, Bobby L. Boon the Raccoon & Easel the Weasel. Rodriguez, Christina, illus. (p. 213)
—Makimba's Animal World. Jones, Julienne, illus. (p. 1080)
Jackson, Bradley, jt. auth. see Fry, Michael.
Jackson Braun, Lilian, see Braun, Lilian Jackson.
Jackson, Brenda. Bachelor Undone. (p. 130)
—Henrietta & the Pot-Bellied Pig. (p. 767)
—No More Playas. (p. 1259)
—Savvy Sistahs. (p. 1518)
—Some Like It Hot. (p. 1609)
—What a Woman Wants. (p. 1878)
Jackson, Bridgett. Bobos Save the Day: Book One of Tales from the Creek. (p. 206)
—Monster on the Moon: Book Three of Tales from the Creek. (p. 1168)
—Princess & the Pink Palace: Book Two of Tales from the Creek. (p. 1403)
Jackson, Brittany Janay, illus. see Hansen, Roland.
Jackson, Byron & Jackson, Kathryn. Day at the Seashore. (p. 412)
Jackson, Carl. Alien Invasion: Invasive Species Become Major Menaces. (p. 40)
—Bugs That Build. (p. 237)
—Bugs That Destroy. (p. 237)
—Revolution in Computers. (p. 1466)
Jackson, Carol A., jt. auth. see Route 52 Staff.
Jackson, Carolyn, jt. ed. see Hook, Sue.
Jackson, Carolyn E. Tales from the Master. (p. 1702)
Jackson, Clandress. Chloe the Jumbo Jet: A Problem of Olympic Proportions. (p. 308)
—Chloe the Jumbo Jet: Fantastic Friends Around the World. (p. 308)
—Chloe the Jumbo Jet: First Class to Seoul! Let's Rock & Roll. (p. 308)
—Chloe the Jumbo Jet the Best Cancelled Christmas Ever. (p. 308)
Jackson, Cody. Pint-Sized Patriots. (p. 1361)
Jackson, Colin. Jovenes Atletas. (p. 929)
Jackson, Colter. Elephants Make Fine Friends. (p. 512)
Jackson, Constance L. Over the River: Life of Lydia Maria Child, Abolitionist for Freedom, 1802-1880. (p. 1314)
Jackson, Corrine. If I Lie. (p. 853)
—Ignited. (p. 856)
Jackson, Dan. Angel & Faith Volume 3: Family Reunion: Family Reunion. Allie, Scott & Hahn, Sierra, eds. (p. 73)
Jackson, Dave. Philadelphia 76ers. (p. 1350)
—Philadelphia Phillies. (p. 1350)
Jackson, Dave & Jackson, Neta. Exiled to the Red River: Chief Spokane Garry. (p. 548)
—Featuring David Livingstone & Other Christian Heroes. (p. 580)
—Hero Tales Vol. 2 (p. 772)
—Heroes in Black History: True Stories from the Lives of Christian Heroes. (p. 773)
Jackson, Dave, et al. Featuring Harriet Tubman & Other Christian Heroes. (p. 580)
—Hero Tales: A Family Treasury of True Stories from the Lives of Christian Heroes. Vol. 1 (p. 772)
—Trailblazers: Featuring Amy Carmichael & Other Christian Heroes. (p. 1776)
Jackson, Deb. Creamy Goes to Heaven. (p. 378)
Jackson, Debra. Canines on Patrol: Special Lessons. (p. 261)
Jackson, Debra Ann. Canines on Patrol. (p. 261)
Jackson, Demi. How Does a Light Bulb Work? (p. 808)
—How Is Paper Made? (p. 810)
—Paintball. (p. 1318)
—Parkour. (p. 1325)
—Roller Derby. (p. 1485)
Jackson, Demond, Sr. Turnaround Book of Poetry: Complete Series. (p. 1798)
Jackson, Denise. Mom Lovd Me A Blizzard: A Young Boy's Journey Through Grief. (p. 1161)
Jackson, Dennis, jt. auth. see Wheeler, Jordan.
Jackson, Derek. Brother Word. (p. 231)
Jackson, Dessi. Saint & His Bees. Brandenburg, Claire, illus. (p. 1503)
Jackson, Dominic, jt. auth. see Coronado, Mark.
Jackson, Dona. Let's Get Moving! Tell & Write Time. (p. 997)
Jackson, Donna M. Bug Scientists. (p. 236)
—ER Vets: Life in an Animal Emergency Room. (p. 533)
—Extreme Scientists: Exploring Nature's Mysteries from Perilous Places. (p. 556)
—Wildlife Detectives: How Forensic Scientists Fight Crimes Against Nature. Shattil, Wendy & Rozinski, Bob, photos by. (p. 1931)
Jackson, Donna M., jt. auth. see O'Connell, Caitlin.
Jackson, Donna M. & Goman, Carol Kinsey. Every Body's Talking: What We Say Without Words. (p. 542)
Jackson, Edwin L. & Stakes, Mary E. Georgia Studies Book: Our State & the Nation. (p. 665)
Jackson, Elaine. America. (p. 58)
—Discover Turkey. (p. 448)
—Egypt. (p. 506)
—India. (p. 870)
Jackson, Ellen. Abe Lincoln Loved Animals. Ettlinger, Doris, illus. (p. 4)
—Beastly Babies. Wenzel, Brendan, illus. (p. 152)
—Cinder Edna. (p. 320)
—Cupcake Thief. (p. 392)
—Cupcake Thief. Sims, Blanche, illus. (p. 392)
—Mysterious Universe: Supernovae, Dark Energy, & Black Holes. Bishop, Nic, illus. (p. 1223)
—Mysterious Universe: Supernovae, Dark Energy, & Black Holes. Bishop, Nic, photos by. (p. 1223)
—Tooling Around: Crafty Creatures & the Tools They Use. Benoit, Renne, illus. (p. 1767)
Jackson, Ellen B. Ballad of Booster Bogg. Carolan, Christine, illus. (p. 134)
—Cinnamon Brown & the Seven Dwarfs. Brown, Elbrite, illus. (p. 321)
—It's Back to School We Go! First Day Stories from Around the World. Ellis, Jan Davey, illus. (p. 896)
—Seven Seas. Slavin, Bill & Melo, Esperanca, illus. (p. 1554)
—Tree of Life: The Wonders of Evolution. Wiley, Judeanne Winter, illus. (p. 1783)
—Turn of the Century: Eleven Centuries of Children & Change. Ellis, Jan Davey, illus. (p. 1797)
—Winter Solstice. Ellis, Jan Davey, illus. (p. 1938)
Jackson, Emma. Home for Dixie: The True Story of a Rescued Puppy. Carey, Bob, illus. (p. 792)
Jackson, Everett E. Kimme Gets a Valentine. (p. 957)
—Kimme Meets Squirrelly D. (p. 957)
Jackson, G. A. Twelve Yellow Ducks. (p. 1800)
Jackson, Gabrielle E. Caps & Capers: A Story of Boarding-School Life. Relyea, C. M., illus. (p. 263)
—Caps & Capers. (p. 263)

J

—Peggy Stewart. (p. 1335)
Jackson, Gabrielle Emilie Snow. Caps & Capers: A Story of Boarding-school Life. (p. 263)
—Caps & Capers: A story of boarding-school Life. (p. 263)
—Caps & Capers: A Story of Boarding School Life (1901) Relyea, C. M., illus. (p. 263)
—Caps & Capers, a Story of Boarding-School Life. (p. 263)
Jackson, Gary. Sunny Side of the Apple. (p. 1677)
Jackson, Glenda K. Friends of the Hills. (p. 638)
Jackson, Gwendolyn. Adventures of Super T: The Missing Blanket Scott-Daniel, Toni, illus. (p. 23)
Jackson, Harry, Jr., jt. auth. see Barna, George.
Jackson, Heidi. Rat's Tale II: Escape from Rattovia. (p. 1440)
Jackson, Helen, illus. see Graves, Sue.
Jackson, Helen, jt. auth. see Webster, Helen.
Jackson, Helston, illus. see Jackson, Penny.
Jackson, Ian, illus. see Bingham, Jane.
Jackson, Ian, illus. see Bramwell, Martyn.
Jackson, Ian, illus. see Clarke, Phillip & Khan, Sarah.
Jackson, Ian, illus. see Davidson, Susanna & Unwin, Mike.
Jackson, Ian, illus. see Helbrough, Emma.
Jackson, Ian, illus. see Kahn, Sarah, ed.
Jackson, Ian, illus. see Marks, Anthony & Tingay, Graham.
Jackson, Ian, illus. see Mitchell, Andrew.
Jackson, Ian, illus. see Needham, Kate.
Jackson, Ian, illus. see Parker, Steve.
Jackson, Ian, illus. see Peach, Susan & Millard, Anne.
Jackson, Ian, illus. see Regan, Lisa.
Jackson, Ian, illus. see Young, Caroline & Needham, Kate.
Jackson, Ian, illus. see Young, Caroline.
Jackson, J. S. Bye-Bye, Bully: A Kid's Guide for Dealing with Bullies. Alley, R. W., tr. (p. 249)
—Keeping Family First: A Kid's Guide. Alley, R. W., illus. (p. 947)
Jackson, Jack. New Texas History Movies. (p. 1247)
Jackson, Jack & Magruder, Jana. New Texas History Movies. Jackson, Jack, illus. (p. 1247)
Jackson, James. Dancing with David. (p. 403)
Jackson, Jasmine. Robert's Really Restless. (p. 1479)
Jackson, Jason. Stronger Than Ever: Heavenly Advice for Earthly Life. (p. 1668)
Jackson, Jeannie, illus. see Stone, Chuck.
Jackson, Jeannie, tr. see Stone, Chuck.
Jackson, Jeff, illus. see Guarino, Robert.
Jackson, Jeff, illus. see Shah, Idries.
Jackson, Jeff, illus. see Sobel, David S.
Jackson, Jennifer. Punkydoos Take the Stage. Andreasen, Dan, illus. (p. 1417)
Jackson, Jill & Miller, Sy. Let There Be Peace on Earth: And Let It Begin with Me. Diaz, David, illus. (p. 994)
Jackson, Joann. Green Light, Red Light, Go! (p. 722)
Jackson, Jocelyn. Ariel's Adventures: the Series: Ariel's New Home. (p. 98)
Jackson, John. Tales for Great Grandchildren: Folk Tales from India & Nepal. Terrazzini, Daniela Jaglenka, illus. (p. 1701)
Jackson, John C. Piikani Blackfeet: A Culture under Siege. Bodmer, Karl, illus. (p. 1358)
Jackson, Johnny M. Survivors of the Alien Holocaust. (p. 1687)
Jackson, Katherine. Leaping from Public High to a Top University. (p. 982)
Jackson, Kathryn. Animals' Merry Christmas. Scarry, Richard, illus. (p. 83)
—Nurse Nancy. Malvern, Corinne, illus. (p. 1273)
—Puss in Boots. (p. 1420)
—Tawney Scrawny Lion. Tenggren, Gustaf, illus. (p. 1707)
—Tawny Scrawny Lion: Classic Edition. Tenggren, Gustaf, illus. (p. 1707)
Jackson, Kathryn, jt. auth. see Depken, Kristen L.
Jackson, Kathryn, jt. auth. see Jackson, Byron.
Jackson, Kathryn & Jackson, B. Saggy Baggy Elephant: Classic Edition. Tenggren, Gustaf, illus. (p. 1503)
—Saggy Baggy Elephant. Tenggren, Gustaf, illus. (p. 1503)
Jackson, Katy. Doodles Movie Star: Sensational, Show-Stopping Pictures to Create & Complete. (p. 469)
—Doodles Pop Star: Fabulous & Funky Pictures to Create & Complete. (p. 469)
—Draw Cute Pictures. (p. 480)
—Draw Magical Pictures. (p. 481)
—Draw Pretty Pictures. (p. 481)
—Pretty Fashions: Beautiful Fashions to Color! (p. 1398)
Jackson, Katy, illus. see Dale, Jay.
Jackson, Katy, jt. auth. see Ryan, Nelly.
Jackson, Kay. Armored Vehicles in Action. (p. 100)
—Explore the Desert (p. 550)
—Explore the Grasslands. (p. 550)
—Explore the Ocean. (p. 550)
—Military Helicopters in Action. (p. 1143)
—Military Planes in Action. (p. 1143)
—Military Tanks in Action. (p. 1143)
—Navy Ships in Action. (p. 1238)
—Navy Submarines in Action. (p. 1238)
—Oceans McMullen, Anne, illus. (p. 1277)
—Ways to Find Your Way: Types of Maps. (p. 1865)
Jackson, Kay, illus. see Whisler, Barbara.
Jackson, Kay Whytock, illus. see Scott, Elizabeth M.
Jackson, Keith. I Forgot My Lunch Money. (p. 838)
Jackson, Kendra. Bella's New Wings: An Adventure. (p. 162)
Jackson, Kimberly. Fate of America in the Ninth Hour. (p. 577)
—Volcano Adventures of Keikilani. Spachner, Karen D., illus. (p. 1848)
Jackson, Kristina. Plot Bunny. Winfield, Amy, illus. (p. 1374)
Jackson, Ladain. Rare Vision. (p. 1439)
Jackson, Lance, illus. see Pea, Uncle & Pomerantz, Joel.
Jackson, Laura, tr. see Morinaga, Ai.
Jackson, Laura, tr. see Tomizawa, Hitoshi.
Jackson, Laura Gower. Snowman & the Magic Eyeglasses. (p. 1601)
Jackson, Lee M. Careers in Focus: Family & Consumer Sciences. (p. 267)
—Careers in Focus: Family & Consumer Sciences: Education & Communication, Science & Technology, Human Services, Business, Art. (p. 267)
Jackson, Leona Novy. Littlest Christmas Kitten. Dupre, Kelly, illus. (p. 1039)
Jackson, Leslie L. Melodies from Heaven. (p. 1125)
—Treasures from Heaven. (p. 1782)
Jackson, Lisa, illus. see Bailey, Ellen.
Jackson, Lisa, illus. see Massey, Eithne.
Jackson, Livia, jt. auth. see Thompson, Lauren.
Jackson, Lora Z. Around the Clock: A Story about Telling Time. Martin, Miles J., illus. (p. 100)
Jackson, Loretta, jt. auth. see Britton, Vickie.
Jackson, Louise A. Exiled! From Tragedy to Triumph on the Missouri Frontier. (p. 548)
Jackson, Lyn D. Perilous Journey Home. (p. 1343)
Jackson, Lynda Jane. Maris Goes to Paris. (p. 1094)
Jackson, Marcus. Because My Teacher Said I Can. (p. 155)
Jackson, Marilee. Midnight Runner. (p. 1139)
Jackson, Marilyn Malloy, ed. Mother Goose on the Loose in Guam A Chamorro Adaptation of Traditional Nursery Rhymes. Tayama, Thomas, illus. (p. 1178)
Jackson, Marjorie. Beach Feet. Cohen, Lynda, illus. (p. 149)
Jackson, Mark, illus. see Cheng, Christopher.
Jackson, Mark, illus. see Wignell, Edel.
Jackson, Mary Helene. Weaver of Song: The Birth of Silent Night. Winstead, Leo, illus. (p. 1870)
Jackson, Maureen. You Count Too. (p. 1975)
Jackson, Max. Mickey Mantle: All-Star Athlete. Henderson, Meryl, illus. (p. 1136)
Jackson, Melanie. Big Dip (p. 181)
—Fast Slide (p. 576)
—High Wire (p. 778)
—Mask on the Cruise Ship (p. 1102)
—Queen of Disguises (p. 1425)
—Shadows on the Train (p. 1558)
—Summer of the Spotted Owl (p. 1674)
Jackson, Michael. Whiskey. (p. 1912)
Jackson, Michael C., jt. auth. see Maag, John W.
Jackson, Mike. Best Dog House Ever! (p. 168)
Jackson, Mike, illus. see Depken, Kristen L.
Jackson, Mike, illus. see Golden Books.
Jackson, Mike, illus. see Nagaraj, Josephine.
Jackson, Mike, illus. see Random House Staff.
Jackson, Mike, illus. see Random House.
Jackson, Mike, illus. see Tillworth, Mary.
Jackson, Mike, jt. auth. see Dixon-Engel, Tara.
Jackson, Mike, jt. illus. see Golden Books Staff.
Jackson, Monica. Teach Me about Jesus. (p. 1708)
Jackson, Monica Y. I Have a Book Idea! Now What? A Step-by-Step Guide to Self-Publishing. (p. 839)
Jackson, Neecie. Heeson's Arrival Brings Love & Excitement. (p. 762)
Jackson, Nellie O. Worst Day of My Life. (p. 1961)
Jackson, Neta, jt. auth. see Jackson, Dave.
Jackson, Nikki. Georgia & Reeds: The AL-PHA-BET Book. (p. 665)
—Georgia & Reed's: My Potty & Me. (p. 665)
Jackson, Ovetta. Beanie & Skooda & the Buddifly Gang. (p. 150)
Jackson, Patrick & Kimura, Rie. Potato Pals. (p. 1388)
Jackson, Paul. Best Ever Paper Planes That Really Fly! (p. 169)
—Origami Toys: That Fly, Tumble, & Spin (p. 1304)
—Surefire Paper Plane Kit. (p. 1685)
Jackson, Paul & Golan, Miriam. Origami Zoo: 25 Fun Paper Animal Creations! (p. 1304)
Jackson, Paul B. Luke & Mcnashty's Treasure. (p. 1064)
Jackson, Penny. Pepere's Little Girl. Jackson, Helston & Anderson, Betheny, illus. (p. 1340)
Jackson, Phil & Delehanty, Hugh. Sacred Hoops: Spiritual Lessons of a Hardwood Warrior. (p. 1500)
Jackson, Randy. Get Ready for Hazardous Weather: Learning Through Puzzles, Games & Exercises. (p. 668)
Jackson, Randy, et al. 2003 Tropical Weather Tracking Book. (p. 2003)
—Tropical Weather Tracking Book. (p. 1789)
Jackson, Richard. All Ears, All Eyes. Tillotson, Katherine, illus. (p. 44)
Jackson, Richelle. Running for Class President: Represent & Solve Problems Involving Division. (p. 1497)
Jackson, Rob. Animal Mischief. Jacobsen, Laura, illus. (p. 78)
Jackson, Robert. 101 Great Bombers. (p. 1999)
—101 Great Fighters. (p. 1999)
—101 Great Tanks. (p. 1999)
—101 Great Warships. (p. 1999)
—101 Greatest Weapons of All Times (p. 1999)
—Meet Me in St. Louis: A Trip to the 1904 World's Fair. (p. 1121)
—Warships: Inside & Out. (p. 1859)
Jackson, Robert B. Remarkable Ride of the Abernathy Boys. (p. 1459)
Jackson, Robert Bradley. Weekend Mischief. Beech, Mark, illus. (p. 1872)
Jackson, Robert, Jr. Amazing Liberteens. (p. 54)
Jackson, Ruth Montgomery. Bit of Magic with Wee Willie & Double Trouble. (p. 194)
Jackson, Sadara J. Cows Are Not Just for Milk: Las Vacas No Solamente Nos Dan Leche. (p. 374)
Jackson, Sarah. Preep II: More Tales of Early Texas. Jenkins, Delores, illus. (p. 1395)
—Preep of Old Washington Square: A Collection of East Texas Tales. Jenkins, Delores, illus. (p. 1395)
Jackson, Sarah, jt. auth. see Templeton, Robyn.
Jackson, Sharinese. Choices: Upper Elementary. Nyamor, Eric, illus. (p. 309)
—Choices. (p. 309)
Jackson, Shawn David. Holiness. com Dating Survival Guide. (p. 789)
Jackson, Shelley, illus. see Davis, David.
Jackson, Shelley, illus. see Harrington, Janice N.
Jackson, Shelley Ann, jt. auth. see Crosby, Jeff.
Jackson, Shelley Ann & Crosby, Jeff. Harness Horses, Bucking Broncos & Pit Ponies: A History of Horse Breeds. Jackson, Shelley Ann & Crosby, Jeff, illus. (p. 749)
Jackson, Sherard. You Can Draw Transforming Robots. (p. 1974)
Jackson, Shirley. Haunting of Hill House. (p. 754)
—We Have Always Lived in the Castle. Ott, Thomas, illus. (p. 1867)
Jackson, Spring. Little Faucet That Never Stopped Dripping. (p. 1027)
Jackson, Stephen. Mirrorworld: The World's Most Addictive Adventure Game Ever! (p. 1149)
—Mundoespejo. (p. 1191)
Jackson, Steve. Citadel of Chaos. (p. 322)
—House of Hell. (p. 803)
—How Is Paper Recycled? (p. 810)
—Sixty Bloodbones. (p. 1583)
Jackson, Steve & Livingstone, Ian. Worlock of Firetop Mountain. (p. 1961)
Jackson, Sue Ann. Gift of the Butterfly Box. (p. 675)
—Vessel for the King. (p. 1839)
Jackson, Susan. Secret of Mermaid Island. (p. 1542)
Jackson, Tom. Animal Card Box: 101 Amazing Fact Cards. (p. 77)
—Animal Trackers. (p. 80)
—Arkansas River. (p. 99)
—Basics of Atoms & Molecules. (p. 142)
—Beastly Bugs. (p. 152)
—Bighorn Sheep. (p. 185)
—Black Bears. (p. 195)
—Buildings & Structures. (p. 239)
—Caribou. (p. 269)
—Columbia River. (p. 346)
—Complete Book of Animals: A World Encyclopedia of Amphibians, Reptiles & Mammals with over 500 Detailed Illustrations. (p. 352)
—Cougars. (p. 369)
—Coyote. (p. 374)
—Dangerous Dinosaurs. (p. 404)
—Deadly Snakes. (p. 418)
—Destination Earth. (p. 430)
—Elk. (p. 513)
—Experiments with Light & Color. (p. 549)
—Exploring Nature: Macaws, Hummingbirds, Flamingos, Toucans & Other Exotic Species, All Shown in More Than 180 Pictures: Parrots & Rainforest Birds. (p. 552)
—Ferocious Sharks. (p. 582)
—Green Sea Turtle. (p. 722)
—Gulls. (p. 731)
—Illustrated Guide to the Animals of America: A Visual Encyclopedia of Amphibians, Reptiles & Mammals in the United States, Canada & South America, with over 350 Illustrations. (p. 857)
—Inside the Mind of a Clever Dolphin. (p. 877)
—Inside the Mind of a Deadly Cobra. (p. 877)
—Inside the Mind of a Fierce Lion. (p. 877)
—Land & Water Transportation. (p. 973)
—Lithium. (p. 1023)
—Mice. (p. 1134)
—Military & Security. (p. 1142)
—Monster Crocs. (p. 1167)
—Musk Ox. (p. 1194)
—Ohio River. (p. 1281)
—Piranhas & Other Small Deadly Creatures. (p. 1362)
—Power & Energy. (p. 1389)
—Prairie Dogs. (p. 1392)
—Pronghorns. (p. 1411)
—Radioactive Elements. (p. 1433)
—Saltwater Crocodile. (p. 1506)
—Saving Animal Species. (p. 1517)
—Scary Sea Monsters. (p. 1520)
—Seals. (p. 1536)
—Shark Attack. (p. 1562)
—Sharks. (p. 1562)
—Snake Bite. (p. 1596)
—South Korea. (p. 1617)
—Spiders. (p. 1627)
—Spooky Spiders. (p. 1631)
—Squirrels. (p. 1637)
—Tracking Animal Identity. (p. 1775)
—Tracking Animal Movement. (p. 1775)
—Tracking Animal Numbers. (p. 1775)
—Tropical Forests (p. 1789)
—Walrus. (p. 1855)
—Wild Horses. (p. 1929)
Jackson, Tom, jt. auth. see Cole, Joanna.
Jackson, Tom, jt. auth. see Crabtree Publishing Company Staff.
Jackson, Toneal M. Four Girls: A Lot of Choices. (p. 625)
Jackson, Tyrone. Save Our Home. (p. 1516)
Jackson, Vanessa Wyse. Recipes for Life: Fifty Ready-To-Use Spiritual Talks for Children. (p. 1451)
Jackson, Vicky. Poepal's Purpose. (p. 1376)
Jackson, Wayne P. Don't Let the Spoon Get Taken Out of Your Mouth (p. 468)
Jackson, Wayne T., frwd. In Search of a Father. (p. 864)
Jackson, Wendy. Charlie Mace & the Big Stink. (p. 293)
Jackson, William E. Flight from Babylon: The Legend & Quest of Draxie Dread. (p. 604)
Jackson-Beavers, Rose, et al. Hole in My Heart. (p. 788)
Jackson-Carter, Stuart, illus. see Ganeri, Anita.
Jackson-McCurdy, Patrecia K. Where 'Once upon a Time' Began. (p. 1909)
Jaco, Paul. Leopards of Sh'ong. (p. 993)
Jacob, Annie. When I Was a Kid. (p. 1903)
Jacob, Bill & Fosnot, Catherine Twomey. California Frog-Jumping Contest - Algebra. (p. 253)
Jacob, C. W. Tipperary Bird. (p. 1757)
Jacob, E. Como Leer un Codice. (p. 351)
Jacob, Ellen, et al. My Train Book. Vandenberg, Michael, photos by. (p. 1220)
Jacob, Murv, illus. see Bruchac, Joseph.
Jacob, Murv, illus. see Duvall, Deborah L.
Jacob, Murv, illus. see Ross, Gayle.
Jacob, P. L., pseud & Hunt, J. Timothy. Madame de Sévigné & Her Children at the Court of Versailles. (p. 1069)
Jacob, Sona &, illus. see Dekel, Amir.
Jacob, Violet. Golden Heart, & Other Fairy Stories. Sandheim, May, illus. (p. 694)
Jacobbe, Barbara A. Trusting in God... I Am More Than I Think I Am. (p. 1793)
Jacobelli, Frank, et al. ADD/ADHD Drug Free: Natural Alternatives & Practical Exercises to Help Your Child Focus. (p. 11)
Jacobellis, Michelle. Dachshund Tales: Adventures on the Great South Bay. (p. 398)
Jacober, Virginia. Trail Followers in India. (p. 1776)
Jacobi, Adam J. Student Congress Debate. (p. 1669)
Jacobo, Daysi, ed. see Triplett, Donald & Eiland, Marie.
Jacobs, Alan, et al. Beginning Algebra with Arithmetic Review. (p. 159)
Jacobs, Breena. Daddy's Girl. Austrew, Neva, illus. (p. 399)
Jacobs, Brian C. Case of the Old Man in the Mailbox. (p. 274)
Jacobs, Carmita. My Nana Has A Boyfriend. (p. 1215)
Jacobs, Caroline E. S. W. F. Club. (p. 1499)
Jacobs Cfp, Sheila. Jake's Big Bang. (p. 906)
Jacobs, Christian. Goon Holler: Goon Fishin' Jacobs, Parker, illus. (p. 702)
—Welcome to Goon Holler. Jacobs, Parker, illus. (p. 1873)
Jacobs, D. K., illus. see Thomas, Kerrie Annette.
Jacobs, Daniel. Big Babies. (p. 177)
—City Shapes (p. 324)
—City Shapes. (p. 324)
—Count Your Chickens. (p. 370)
—For Your Information. (p. 616)
—Patterns. (p. 1329)
Jacobs, Dean. Wondrous Journey: The World Is Waiting for You. (p. 1949)
Jacobs, Edgar P. Atlantis Mystery. (p. 112)
—Blake & Mortimer Vol. 15: The Secret of the Swordfish Part 1. (p. 198)
—Blake & Mortimer Vol. 17: the Secret of the Swordfish Part 3. (p. 198)
—Mystery of the Great Pyramid. (p. 1225)
—S. O. S. Meteors. (p. 1499)
—Secret of the Swordfish. (p. 1543)
—Yellow "M" (p. 1970)
Jacobs, Elaina & Benchmark Education Co. Staff. Dust Bowl. (p. 490)
Jacobs, Eli. Brothers Divided: A Novel of Intrigue. (p. 231)
Jacobs, Erin. Earth Angels. (p. 495)
Jacobs, Evan. Clan Castles (p. 326)
—Screaming Quietly (p. 1533)
—Screaming Quietly. (p. 1533)
—Varsity 170 (p. 1833)
—Zombies! (p. 1988)
Jacobs, Frank & Bursill, Henry. Hand Shadow Fun. (p. 740)
Jacobs, Frank, ed. Looney Limericks. Daste, Larry, illus. (p. 1052)
Jacobs, Ginger, ed. see Jacobs, Mike.
Jacobs, Greg. Everything Kids' Baseball Book: Today's Superstars, Great Teams, Legends—and Tips on Playing Like a Pro. (p. 545)
—Kids' Football Book: The All-Time Greats, Legendary Teams, Today's Superstars & Tips on Playing Like a Pro. (p. 953)
Jacobs, Greg, et al. Everything Kids' Baseball Book: From Baseball's History to Today's Favorite Players - With Lots of Home Run Fun in Between! (p. 545)
Jacobs, Heidi Hayes & LeVasseur, Michal L. World Studies: Medieval Times to Today: With Text Purchase, Add StudentEXPRESS. (p. 1958)
Jacobs, Holly. Too Little Hero. (p. 1766)
Jacobs, James. Legacy of Fire. (p. 987)
Jacobs, Jeanean, jt. auth. see Lorig, Steffanie.
Jacobs, Jerry L. Adventures on the Farm. Conyers, Courtney, illus. (p. 25)
—Koda. (p. 966)
Jacobs, Jessica, jt. auth. see Ureel, Jessica.
Jacobs, Joanne. Our School: The Inspiring Story of Two Teachers, One Big Idea, & the School That Beat the Odds. (p. 1310)
Jacobs, John. I Wanna Be. (p. 847)
Jacobs, John Hornor. Conformity. (p. 357)
—Shibboleth. (p. 1566)
—Twelve-Fingered Boy. (p. 1800)
Jacobs, John Hornor & Priest, A. Breakthrough. (p. 225)
Jacobs, Jonathan A. Ethics A-Z. (p. 539)
Jacobs, Jordan. Samantha Sutton & the Labyrinth of Lies. (p. 1507)
—Samantha Sutton & the Winter of the Warrior Queen. (p. 1507)
Jacobs, Joseph. Indian Fairy Tales. Batten, John D., illus. (p. 871)
—Jack & the Beanstalk. Crane, Walter, illus. (p. 902)
—Most Delectable History of Reynard the F. (p. 1177)
Jacobs, Joseph, ed. see Andersen, Hans Christian, et al.
Jacobs, Joseph, ed. English Fairy Tales. (p. 530)
—Europa's Fairy Book. Batten, John D., illus. (p. 540)
Jacobs, Joyce M., illus. see Connelly, Claire K.
Jacobs, Karen & Miller, Leah. How Full Is Sophia's Backpack? Hewitt, Elizabeth, illus. (p. 809)
Jacobs, Lana. Brand-New Look. (p. 222)
—Lost & Found. (p. 1054)
—Paint Book. Farley, Rick, illus. (p. 1318)
—Show-And-Tell. (p. 1570)
—Strawberry Shortcake's Spooky Night. MJ Illustrations Staff, illus. (p. 1666)
Jacobs, Laura. Landscape with Moving Figures: A Decade on Dance. (p. 974)
Jacobs, Laurie A. Box of Candles. Ephraim, Shelly Ephraim, illus. (p. 216)
Jacobs, Lee. Beaver. (p. 154)
—Crow. (p. 385)
—Turtle. (p. 1798)
Jacobs, Leslie. Adventure of the Tall giraffe & the Short Duck. (p. 14)
Jacobs, Lily. Littlest Bunny: An Easter Adventure. Dunn, Robert, illus. (p. 1038)
—Littlest Bunny in Alabama: An Easter Adventure. (p. 1038)
—Littlest Bunny in Alaska: An Easter Adventure. (p. 1038)
—Littlest Bunny in Albuquerque: An Easter Adventure. Dunn, Robert, illus. (p. 1038)
—Littlest Bunny in Arizona: An Easter Adventure. (p. 1038)
—Littlest Bunny in Arkansas: An Easter Adventure. (p. 1038)

—Littlest Bunny in Bentonville: An Easter Adventure. (p. 1038)
—Littlest Bunny in Boise: An Easter Adventure. (p. 1038)
—Littlest Bunny in Boston: An Easter Adventure. (p. 1038)
—Littlest Bunny in Calgary: An Easter Adventure. Dunn, Robert, illus. (p. 1038)
—Littlest Bunny in California: An Easter Adventure. Dunn, Robert, illus. (p. 1038)
—Littlest Bunny in Canada: An Easter Adventure. Dunn, Robert, illus. (p. 1038)
—Littlest Bunny in Charleston: An Easter Adventure. (p. 1038)
—Littlest Bunny in Chicago: An Easter Adventure. (p. 1038)
—Littlest Bunny in Cincinnati: An Easter Adventure. Dunn, Robert, illus. (p. 1038)
—Littlest Bunny in Colorado: An Easter Adventure. (p. 1038)
—Littlest Bunny in Connecticut: An Easter Adventure. (p. 1038)
—Littlest Bunny in Delaware: An Easter Adventure. Dunn, Robert, illus. (p. 1038)
—Littlest Bunny in Edmonton: An Easter Adventure. Dunn, Robert, illus. (p. 1038)
—Littlest Bunny in Florida: An Easter Adventure. Dunn, Robert, illus. (p. 1038)
—Littlest Bunny in Georgia: An Easter Adventure. (p. 1038)
—Littlest Bunny in Hawaii: An Easter Adventure. (p. 1038)
—Littlest Bunny in Idaho: An Easter Adventure. (p. 1038)
—Littlest Bunny in Illinois: An Easter Adventure. Dunn, Robert, illus. (p. 1038)
—Littlest Bunny in Indiana: An Easter Adventure. Dunn, Robert, illus. (p. 1038)
—Littlest Bunny in Iowa: An Easter Adventure. (p. 1038)
—Littlest Bunny in Kansas: An Easter Adventure. (p. 1038)
—Littlest Bunny in Kansas City: An Easter Adventure. Dunn, Robert, illus. (p. 1038)
—Littlest Bunny in Kentucky: An Easter Adventure. Dunn, Robert, illus. (p. 1038)
—Littlest Bunny in Las Vegas: An Easter Adventure. (p. 1038)
—Littlest Bunny in Los Angeles: An Easter Adventure. (p. 1038)
—Littlest Bunny in Louisiana: An Easter Adventure. Dunn, Robert, illus. (p. 1038)
—Littlest Bunny in Maine: An Easter Adventure. (p. 1039)
—Littlest Bunny in Maryland: An Easter Adventure. Dunn, Robert, illus. (p. 1039)
—Littlest Bunny in Massachusetts: An Easter Adventure. (p. 1039)
—Littlest Bunny in Minnesota: An Easter Adventure. Dunn, Robert, illus. (p. 1039)
—Littlest Bunny in Mississippi: An Easter Adventure. Dunn, Robert, illus. (p. 1039)
—Littlest Bunny in Missouri: An Easter Adventure. Dunn, Robert, illus. (p. 1039)
—Littlest Bunny in Montana: An Easter Adventure. Dunn, Robert, illus. (p. 1039)
—Littlest Bunny in Nebraska: An Easter Adventure. Dunn, Robert, illus. (p. 1039)
—Littlest Bunny in Nevada: An Easter Adventure. Dunn, Robert, illus. (p. 1039)
—Littlest Bunny in New England: An Easter Adventure. Dunn, Robert, illus. (p. 1039)
—Littlest Bunny in New Hampshire: An Easter Adventure. Dunn, Robert, illus. (p. 1039)
—Littlest Bunny in New Jersey: An Easter Adventure. Dunn, Robert, illus. (p. 1039)
—Littlest Bunny in North Carolina: An Easter Adventure. Dunn, Robert, illus. (p. 1039)
—Littlest Bunny in North Dakota: An Easter Adventure. Dunn, Robert, illus. (p. 1039)
—Littlest Bunny in Ohio: An Easter Adventure. Dunn, Robert, illus. (p. 1039)
—Littlest Bunny in Oklahoma: An Easter Adventure. Dunn, Robert, illus. (p. 1039)
—Littlest Bunny in Omaha: An Easter Adventure. Dunn, Robert, illus. (p. 1039)
—Littlest Bunny in Oregon: An Easter Adventure. Dunn, Robert, illus. (p. 1039)
—Littlest Bunny in Ottawa: An Easter Adventure. Dunn, Robert, illus. (p. 1039)
—Littlest Bunny in Pennsylvania: An Easter Adventure. Dunn, Robert, illus. (p. 1039)
—Littlest Bunny in Philadelphia: An Easter Adventure. Dunn, Robert, illus. (p. 1039)
—Littlest Bunny in Pittsburgh: An Easter Adventure. Dunn, Robert, illus. (p. 1039)
—Littlest Bunny in Portland: An Easter Adventure. Dunn, Robert, illus. (p. 1039)
—Littlest Bunny in San Francisco: An Easter Adventure. Dunn, Robert, illus. (p. 1039)
—Littlest Bunny in South Carolina: An Easter Adventure. Dunn, Robert, illus. (p. 1039)
—Littlest Bunny in South Dakota: An Easter Adventure. Dunn, Robert, illus. (p. 1039)
—Littlest Bunny in St. Louis: An Easter Adventure. Dunn, Robert, illus. (p. 1039)
—Littlest Bunny in Tampa Bay: An Easter Adventure. Dunn, Robert, illus. (p. 1039)
—Littlest Bunny in Tennessee: An Easter Adventure. Dunn, Robert, illus. (p. 1039)
—Littlest Bunny in Texas: An Easter Adventure. Dunn, Robert, illus. (p. 1039)
—Littlest Bunny in Toronto: An Easter Adventure. Dunn, Robert, illus. (p. 1039)
—Littlest Bunny in Tulsa: An Easter Adventure. Dunn, Robert, illus. (p. 1039)
—Littlest Bunny in Utah: An Easter Adventure. Dunn, Robert, illus. (p. 1039)
—Littlest Bunny in Vancouver: An Easter Adventure. Dunn, Robert, illus. (p. 1039)
—Littlest Bunny in Vermont: An Easter Adventure. Dunn, Robert, illus. (p. 1039)
—Littlest Bunny in Virginia: An Easter Adventure. Dunn, Robert, illus. (p. 1039)
—Littlest Bunny in Washington: An Easter Adventure. (p. 1039)
—Littlest Bunny in Washington, DC: An Easter Adventure. Dunn, Robert A., illus. (p. 1039)
—Littlest Bunny in West Virginia: An Easter Adventure. (p. 1039)
—Littlest Bunny in Wisconsin: An Easter Adventure. (p. 1039)
—Littlest Bunny in Wyoming: An Easter Adventure. (p. 1039)
Jacobs, Liza. Chimpanzees. (p. 306)
—Koalas. (p. 966)
—Ostriches. (p. 1306)
—Owls. (p. 1315)
—Snails. (p. 1596)
Jacobs, M. L. RestStop: Jeff & Jeanine. (p. 1464)
Jacobs, Marc, jt. auth. see Boone, Mary.
Jacobs, Marjorie, jt. auth. see Yung Dong, Venerable.
Jacobs, Mike. Holocaust Survivor: Mike Jacobs' Triumph over Tragedy. Jacobs, Ginger, ed. (p. 789)
Jacobs, Nadine. Zefir, la Cebrita en Peligro. Vicens, Paula, tr. (p. 1985)
Jacobs, Nadine, jt. auth. see Hellings, Collete.
Jacobs, Nathaniel, jt. auth. see Zabrosky, Joseph.
Jacobs, Parker. Super Gabba Friends! (p. 1680)
Jacobs, Parker, illus. see Jacobs, Christian.
Jacobs, Pat. I Wonder Why Penguins Can't Fly: And Other Questions about Polar Lands. (p. 849)
—I Wonder Why Penguins Can't Fly. (p. 849)
—I Wonder Why Pirates Wore Earrings: And Other Questions about Piracy. (p. 849)
Jacobs, Pat & MacDonald, Fiona. I Wonder Why Romans Wore Togas. (p. 849)
Jacobs, Pat & Steele, Philip. I Wonder Why Countries Fly Flags. (p. 849)
Jacobs, Paul DuBois, jt. auth. see Seeger, Pete.
Jacobs, Paul DuBois & Swender, Jennifer. Children's Songbag. (p. 304)
—Count on the Subway. Yaccarino, Dan, illus. (p. 369)
—Count on the Subway. Yaccarino, Dan, illus. (p. 370)
—Fire Drill. Lee, Huy Voun, illus. (p. 590)
—My Subway Ride. Alko, Selina, illus. (p. 1219)
—My Taxi Ride Alko, Selina, illus. (p. 1219)
Jacobs, Robbie. Kylie Cow Learns Colors. (p. 969)
Jacobs, Ruth Krehbiel, ed. Collected Notes on Children's Choirs: Compiled from the Choristers' Guild Letters of September, 1949 to June 1954. (p. 339)
Jacobs, Sheila. Aliens & Strangers. (p. 41)
—It's My Life. (p. 897)
—Jake Earns A Treat: A Life & Money Book. (p. 906)
—Jake Saves the Day: A Life & Money Book. (p. 906)
Jacobs, Sherry. "Bobby the Bully" (p. 206)
—Grampa's Teeth. (p. 706)
Jacobs, Thomas A. Teen Cyberbullying Investigated: Where Do Your Rights End & Consequences Begin? (p. 1713)
—Teens on Trial: Young People Who Challenged the Law - And Changed Your Life. (p. 1715)
—They Broke the Law - You Be the Judge: True Cases of Teen Crime. (p. 1732)
—What Are My Rights? Q&A about Teens & the Law. (p. 1879)
Jacobs, Timothy & Roberts, Russell. 100 Athletes Who Shaped Sports History. (p. 1998)
Jacobs, W. W. Monkey's Paw. (p. 1166)
Jacobs, Wm. Edwin. Answers to Unanswered Questions of Life & Religion. (p. 88)
Jacobs, Z. D. Ari & the Dybbuk. (p. 98)
Jacobsen, Amie, illus. see Brooks, Melanie & Spenser and Mom Staff.
Jacobsen, Amie, illus. see Spenser & Brooks, Melanie.
Jacobsen, Amie, illus. see Spenser & Mom.
Jacobsen, Annie. Ivar, the Short, but Brave Viking. Hanson, Susan Jo, illus. (p. 900)
—Ole Mackerel. Everson, Mya, illus. (p. 1285)
—Terrible Troll Cat. Hanson, Susan Jo, illus. (p. 1721)
Jacobsen, Barbara O. Love Leaps. (p. 1060)
Jacobsen, Laura. Boy & the North Wind: A Tale from Norway. (p. 217)
Jacobsen, Laura, illus. see Jackson, Rob.
Jacobsen, Laura, illus. see Kemmetmueller, Donna Jean.
Jacobsen, Laura, illus. see Mead, Maggie.
Jacobsen, Laura, illus. see Mobin-Uddin, Asma.
Jacobsen, Terry, illus. see Chandler, Michael.
Jacobsen, Wayne. He Loves Me! Learning to Live in the Father's Affection. (p. 756)
Jacobsen, Wayne & Coleman, Dave. So You Don't Want to Go to Church Anymore: An Unexpected Journey. (p. 1602)
Jacobson, Andrew, jt. auth. see Epstein, Adam Jay.
Jacobson, Bob. Ole Evinrude & His Outboard Motor. (p. 1285)
—Paul: Guitar Wizard. (p. 1330)
—Paul: Guitar Wizard. (p. 1331)
Jacobson, Bonny B. Whale Fables. (p. 1877)
Jacobson, Christopher. Chase Is on the Case: The Case of the Missing Truck. (p. 294)
Jacobson, Darlene Beck. Wheels of Change. (p. 1901)
Jacobson, David, illus. see Linn, Margot.
Jacobson, David M. & Kokkinos, Nikos. Herod & Augustus: Papers Presented at the IJS Conference, 21st-23rd June 2005. Jacobson, David M. & Kokkinos, Nikos, eds. (p. 772)
Jacobson, Fiona. Lindsey Helps at the Library: Subtract Within 20. (p. 1019)
—Nikola Tesla Lights the World. (p. 1255)
Jacobson, Harold Karan, et al, eds. Shaping of Foreign Policy. (p. 1561)
Jacobson, Jack. No Ordinary Boy. (p. 1259)
Jacobson, Jennifer Richard. Andy Shane & the Barn Sale Mystery. Carter, Abby, illus. (p. 73)
—Andy Shane & the Pumpkin Trick. Carter, Abby, illus. (p. 73)
—Andy Shane & the Queen of Egypt. (p. 73)
—Andy Shane & the Queen of Egypt. Carter, Abby, illus. (p. 73)
—Andy Shane & the Very Bossy Dolores Starbuckle. Carter, Abby, illus. (p. 73)
—Andy Shane, Hero at Last. Carter, Abby, illus. (p. 73)
—Andy Shane Is Not in Love. (p. 73)
—Andy Shane Is Not in Love. Carter, Abby, illus. (p. 73)
—Complete History of Why I Hate Her. (p. 353)
—Hero at Last. Carter, Abby, illus. (p. 772)
—Math: 12 Whole-Class, Super-Fun Games That Teach Addition & Subtraction, Place Value, Simple Fractions, & More. (p. 1104)
—Paper Things. (p. 1323)
—Reading: 12 Whole-Class, Super-Fun Games That Teach Phonics, Sight Words,, Reading Comprehension & More. (p. 1444)
—Small as an Elephant. (p. 1591)
—Stained. (p. 1638)
Jacobson, Jim, photos by see Bill, Tannis.
Jacobson, John. ImagiBOP: Creative Movement & Songs for Grades K-2. (p. 860)
—Quest: Adventure Story & Songs. Wilson, Roberta, illus. (p. 1426)
Jacobson, John & Day, Janet. Say Hello Wherever You Go: Music Strategies, Songs & Activities for Grades K-2. (p. 1518)
Jacobson, John & Huff, Mac. North Pole Musical: One Singular Sensational Holiday Revue. (p. 1265)
Jacobson, Judith, illus. see Flor Ada, Alma.
Jacobson, Justin, jt. auth. see Hammock, Lee.
Jacobson, Leonard. In Search of the Light. (p. 865)
Jacobson, Linda. Our Super Solar System. (p. 1310)
Jacobson, Pat, jt. auth. see Hayes, Clyde.
Jacobson, Rick. Mona Lisa Caper. Jacobson, Rick & Fernandez, Laura, illus. (p. 1163)
—Picasso: Soul on Fire. Jacobson, Rick & Fernandez, Laura, illus. (p. 1354)
Jacobson, Rick, illus. see Cowling, Douglas.
Jacobson, Rick, illus. see Trottier, Maxine.
Jacobson, Robert. Illegal Drugs America's Anguish. (p. 856)
Jacobson, Ryan. Case of the Florida Freeze. Belkholm, Erica, illus. (p. 274)
—Caught in a Pickle Garcia, Eduardo & Ferrara, Eduardo, illus. (p. 282)
—Constellations Activity Book Nitzsche, Shane, illus. (p. 359)
—Eleanor Roosevelt: First Lady of the World. Purcell, Gordon & Schulz, Barbara, illus. (p. 508)
—Exciting Entertainment Inventions. (p. 547)
—Get a Job at a Business. Cannell, Jon, illus. (p. 667)
—Get a Job Helping Others. Cannell, Jon, illus. (p. 667)
—Get a Job Making Stuff to Sell. Cannell, Jon, illus. (p. 667)
—Get a Summer Adventure Job. Cannell, Jon, illus. (p. 667)
—How MP3 Players Work. Mullaly, Glen, illus. (p. 811)
—How Telescopes, Binoculars, & Microscopes Work. Mullaly, Glen, illus. (p. 812)
—How Toilets Work. Mullaly, Glen, illus. (p. 823)
—How Wind Turbines Work. Mullaly, Glen, illus. (p. 823)
—Jack London's Call of the Wild - A Choose Your Path Book. (p. 903)
—Marvelous Medical Inventions. (p. 1099)
—Orange Juice Before the Store. McGeehan, Dan, illus. (p. 1301)
—Shoes Before the Store. McGeehan, Dan, illus. (p. 1568)
—Step-by-Step Experiments with Light & Vision. Ostrom, Bob, illus. (p. 1647)
—Story of the Star-Spangled Banner Martin, Cynthia & Beatty, Terry, illus. (p. 1662)
—William Penn: Founder of Pennsylvania. Stiles, Tim, illus. (p. 1933)
Jacobson, Tasha. Let's Meet a Marine Educator. (p. 999)
Jacobus, Tim, illus. see Kingsley, Kaza.
Jacoby, Nickolina Dye, illus. see Eberhard, Phyllis Lunde Brees.
Jacoby, Sue. Sneakies in Las Vegas: A Coby Jay Adventure. (p. 1597)
Jacome, Mauricio, illus. see Garcia, Edgar Allan.
Jacono, Mary Kaye. Lenny's Gift. (p. 991)
Jacq, Christian. Cuentos y Leyendas de la Epoca de Las Pirámides. Corral, Mercedes, tr. from FRE. (p. 390)
Jacque, David, jt. text see Branch, Elizabeth.
Jacqueline Juin Snow. Potato Tale. (p. 1388)
Jacqueline, Thomas. Birthday Picnic. (p. 193)
Jacqueline, Wilson, jt. auth. see Wilson, Jacqueline.
Jacqueline, Woodson. Locomotion. (p. 1045)
Jacquemain, Patti. Journey of the Great Bear: Through California's Golden Past. Jacquemain, Patti, illus. (p. 928)
Jacquemier, Sue, ed. see Kilpatrick, Cathy.
Jacquemier, Sue, ed. see Mitchell, Andrew.
Jacques. Sauver a Tete. (p. 1516)
Jacques, Brian. Angel's Command. (p. 75)
—Angel's Command. Elliot, David & Schoenherr, Ian, illus. (p. 75)
—Bellmaker. Curless, Allan, illus. (p. 163)
—Castaways of the Flying Dutchman. Schoenherr, Ian, illus. (p. 276)
—Doomwyte. (p. 470)
—Doomwyte. Elliot, David, illus. (p. 470)
—Eulalia! (p. 540)
—High Rhulain Elliott, David, illus. (p. 778)
—High Rhulain. (p. 778)
—High Rhulain. Elliot, David, illus. (p. 778)
—Legend of Luke. (p. 988)
—Loamhedge. (p. 1044)
—Loamhedge. Elliot, David, illus. (p. 1044)
—Long Patrol: A Tale from Redwall. Curless, Allan, illus. (p. 1047)
—Lord Brocktree. Fangorn, illus. (p. 1052)
—Mariel of Redwall. (p. 1093)
—Mariel of Redwall. Chalk, Gary, illus. (p. 1093)
—Marlfox: A Tale from Redwall. (p. 1096)
—Martin the Warrior: The Prisoner & the Tyrant; Actors & Searchers; The Battle of Marshank. (p. 1098)
—Martin the Warrior. Chalk, Gary, illus. (p. 1098)
—Mattimeo. (p. 1110)
—Mattimeo. Chalk, Gary, illus. (p. 1110)
—Mauer. (p. 1110)
—Outcast of Redwall: A Tale from Redwall. (p. 1312)
—Outcast of Redwall. (p. 1312)
—Pearls of Lutra. (p. 1333)
—Rakkety Tam (p. 1437)
—Rakkety Tam. (p. 1437)
—Rakkety Tam. Elliot, David, illus. (p. 1437)
—Redwall. Chalk, Gary, illus. (p. 1456)
—Redwall. Blevins, Bret, illus. (p. 1456)
—Redwall Cookbook. Denise, Christopher, illus. (p. 1456)
—Rogue Crew. (p. 1485)
—Rogue Crew. Rubin, Sean, illus. (p. 1485)
—Sable Quean (p. 1500)
—Sable Quean Elliot, David, illus. (p. 1500)
—Sable Quean. Elliot, David, illus. (p. 1500)
—Salamandastron. Chalk, Gary, illus. (p. 1504)
—Seven Strange & Ghostly Tales. (p. 1555)
—Taggerung. (p. 1695)
—Taggerung. Standley, Peter & Chalk, Gary, illus. (p. 1695)
—Triss. (p. 1787)
—Triss. Elliot, David & Curless, Allan, illus. (p. 1787)
—Voyage of Slaves: A Tale from the Castaways of the Flying Dutchman. (p. 1850)
Jacques, Faith, illus. see Dahl, Roald.
Jacques Hulswood, illus. see Mineulttie, Abike.
Jacques, Laura, illus. see Curtis, Jennifer Keats.
Jacques, Laura, illus. see Fields, Terri.
Jacques, Laura, illus. see Goering, Laura.
Jacques, Laura, illus. see Thomas, Peggy.
Jacques, Marcie. Booba-Lou. (p. 210)
Jacques, Michele Siuda. Teen Driving. (p. 1713)
Jacques, Philip M., jt. auth. see Caron, Lucille.
Jacques, Suzanne. Pee-Wee (p. 1334)
Jacques, Taryn Elise. What's Wrong with the New Girl? Reilly, Meghan M., illus. (p. 1900)
Jacquet, Luc. March of the Penguins: The Official Children's Book. Maison, Jerome, photos by. (p. 1091)
Jacquet-Acea, Russell LaMar. Sons & daughters of Jean Baptiste Jacquet: A History of the Black Jacquet Families in Louisiana. (p. 1613)
Jade, Torea, et al. Northwestern University College Prowler off the Record. (p. 1266)
Jaden, Denise. Losing Faith. (p. 1054)
—Never Enough. (p. 1242)
Jadestone, Justin. Mr Schemfumnickel: The Little Elf with the Real Bright Buttons! (p. 1186)
Jador, Monisha Annabel. Before You Were Born. (p. 159)
Jadoul, Emile. All by Myself! (p. 44)
—Good Night, Chicky. (p. 699)
—¡Todo el Mundo Va! (p. 1761)
Jae Hoo, Yoon, creator. In Dream World (p. 863)
Jae, Paloma. World's Most Unusual Machines (p. 1960)
Jaeger, Elizabeth. It's Easter, Little Bunny! Boyer, Robin, illus. (p. 896)
—It's Halloween, Little Pumpkin! Boyer, Robin, illus. (p. 897)
—Pentecost Story. Hill, Dave, illus. (p. 1338)
Jaeger, Pamela. Fiona No No. (p. 589)
Jaeger, Paul T., jt. ed. see Bowman, Cynthia Ann.
Jaeger, Peter. Eckhart Cars. (p. 502)
Jaeger, Winifred, jt. auth. see MacDonald, Margaret Read.
Jaegermann, Judith. My Childhood in the Holocaust. (p. 1200)
Jaeggi, Yoshiko, illus. see Henrichs, Wendy.
Jaeggi, Yoshiko, illus. see Nitz, Kristin Wolden.
Jaeggi, Yoshiko, illus. see Sheth, Kashmira.
Jaegly, Peggy. Sweetheart's Gift: A Healing Chincoteague Pony Story. (p. 1690)
Jaehne, Julie, et al. Glencoe Keyboarding Connections: Projects & Applications (p. 683)
Jae-Hwan, Kim. Dragon Hunt: World of Warcraft (p. 477)
—King of Hell (p. 959)
—King of Hell Na, Lauren, tr. from KOR. (p. 959)
Jae-Hwan, Kim, illus. see In-Soo, Na.
Jae-Hwan, Kim, illus. see In-Soo, Ra & Ra, In-Soo.
Jae-Hwan, Kim, illus. see In-Soo, Ra.
Jae-Hwan, Kim, illus. see Na, In-Soo.
Jae-Hwan, Kim, illus. see Ra, In-Soo.
Jae-Hwan, Kim, jt. auth. see In-Soo, Ra.
Jae-hwan, Kim, jt. auth. see Knaak, Richard A.
Jae-Hwan, Na, illus. see In-Soo, Na.
Jaekel, Susan. Tortoise & the Hare: A Tale about Determination. (p. 1771)
Jaekel, Susan, illus. see Mortensen, Lori.
Jaekel, Susan, illus. see Wilsdon, Christina.
Jaekel, Susan M. Stone Soup: A Tale about Sharing. (p. 1653)
—Tug of War: A Tale about Being Resourceful. (p. 1796)
Jaekel, Susan M., illus. see Henry, O.
Jael, illus. see Burnett, Frances Hodgson.
Jael, jt. illus. see Griffin, Georgene.
Jael, tr. see Burnett, Frances Hodgson.
Jafarzadeh, Alireza. Iran Threat: President Ahmadinejad & the Coming Nuclear Crisis. (p. 886)
Jaffa, Alisa, tr. see Steinhöfel, Andreas.
Jaffae, Olga. Cammie & Alex's Adventures in Gloryland. (p. 256)
—Cammie & Alex's Adventures in Skating History. (p. 256)
—Cammie & Alex's Adventures in the Icy Park. (p. 256)
—Cammie & Alex's Adventures in the Olympic Year. (p. 256)
Jaffe, Amy V. & Gardner, Luci. My Book Full of Feelings: How to Control & React to the Size of Your Emotions. (p. 1198)
Jaffe, Charlotte & Doherty, Barbara. Space Race. (p. 1619)
Jaffe, Charlotte & Roberts, Barbara. Across Five Aprils: L-I-T Guides. (p. 9)
—Anne Frank: The Diary of a Young Girl: L-I-T Guide. (p. 85)
—Cay: L-I-T Guide. (p. 282)
—Charlie & the Chocolate Factory: L-I-T Guide. (p. 292)
—Charlotte's Webb: L-I-T Guide. (p. 294)
—Day No Pigs Would Die: L-I-T Guide. (p. 414)
—Dear Mr. Henshaw: L-I-T Guide. (p. 419)
—From the Mixed-Up Files of Mrs. Basil E. Frankweiler: L-I-T Guide. (p. 644)
—Giver: L-I-T Guide. (p. 681)
—Hatchet: L-I-T Guide. (p. 752)
—House of Dies Drear: L-I-T Guide. (p. 803)
—Indian in the Cupboard: L-I-T Guide. (p. 871)
—Johnny Tremain: L-I-T Guide. (p. 923)
—Julie of the Wolves: L-I-T Guide. (p. 932)
—Maniac Magee: L-I-T Guide. (p. 1087)
—Midwife's Apprentice: L-I-T Guide. (p. 1139)
—Missing May: L-I-T Guide. (p. 1152)
—Number the Stars: L-I-T Guide. (p. 1271)
—Shiloh: L-I-T Guide. (p. 1566)
—Sign of the Beaver: L-I-T Guide. (p. 1574)
—Sing down the Moon: L-I-T Guide. (p. 1579)
—Summer of the Swans. (p. 1674)
—To Kill a Mockingbird: L-I-T Guide. (p. 1759)
—Tuck Everlasting: L-I-T Guide. (p. 1795)

J

—Walk Two Moons: L-I-T Guide. (p. 1854)
—Where the Red Fern Grows: L-I-T Guide. (p. 1909)
—Whipping Boy: L-I-T Guide. (p. 1912)
Jaffe, Deborah, jt. auth. see Frank, Vivien.
Jaffe, Elizabeth Dana. Ellen Ochoa. (p. 514)
Jaffe, Elizabeth Dana, jt. auth. see Evento, Susan.
Jaffe, Ellen. Feast of Lights (p. 579)
Jaffe, Gail Lois. Enchanted Mirror. Holmes, Jon, ed. (p. 523)
Jaffe, Ilene. Gobblie Goo from the Planet Goo. ColiaStudios, illus. (p. 688)
Jaffé, Laura. Book of When. Cointe, François, illus. (p. 212)
Jaffe, Marc & Gaido, Peter. Goo Goo Gaa Gaa: The Baby Talk Dictionary & Phrase Book. (p. 697)
Jaffe, Max. My Money, Myself: Lessons on Keeping More of What You Make. (p. 1214)
Jaffe, Michele. Bad Kitty. (p. 132)
—Kitty Kitty. (p. 963)
—Minders. (p. 1145)
Jaffe, Nina. Flor de Oro: Un Mito Taino de Puerto Rico. Ventura, Gabriela Baeza, tr. from ENG. (p. 606)
—Golden Flower: A Taino Myth from Puerto Rico. Sanchez, Enrique O., illus. (p. 694)
—Sing, Little Sack! I Canta, Saquito!: a Folktale from Puerto Rico. Cruz, Ray, illus. (p. 1579)
Jaffrey, Alizeh. Silly Ghost (p. 1576)
Jag, Shaani S. Little Small Book of Pictures & Poems. (p. 1036)
Jägel, Jason, jt. auth. see McMullen, Brian.
Jager, Hartmut. Secret of the Green Paint: Annette Vetter Adventure #2. (p. 1542)
Jäger, Jan, et al. My First Book of Knots. Jäger, Jan, illus. (p. 1205)
Jager, Korin Elizabeth, illus. see Jager, Phyllis.
Jager, Petrina. Gerald's Fast Food Foray. (p. 666)
Jager, Phyllis. Introducing Myself. Jager, Korin Elizabeth, illus. (p. 882)
Jaggi, Harleen. Mystery at the Book Store. (p. 1224)
Jago. Ali Baba & the Forty Thieves. (p. 39)
Jago, illus. see Cohen, Deborah Bodin.
Jago, illus. see Fry, Stella.
Jago, illus. see Gregory, Manju.
Jago, illus. see Hartman, Bob.
Jago, illus. see Johnson, Richard & Barkow, Henriette.
Jago, illus. see Lloyd-Jones, Sally.
Jago, illus. see Rosenthal, Betsy R.
Jago, illus. see Wigger, J. Bradley.
Jago, jt. auth. see Balsley, Tilda.
Jagodits, Carolyn Lee, illus. see Ernest, Brother.
Jagodits, Carolyn Lee, illus. see Flavius, Brother.
Jagodits, Carolyn Lee, illus. see Pelous, Donald.
Jagodits, Carolyn Lee, illus. see Roberto, Brother.
Jagucki, Marek, illus. see Meister, Cari & Loewen, Nancy.
Jagucki, Marek, illus. see Meister, Cari.
Jagucki, Marek, illus. see O'Hara, Mo.
Jahanforuz, Rita. Girl with a Brave Heart. Mintzi, Vali, illus. (p. 679)
Jahangiri, Holly. Trockle. (p. 1788)
Jahchan, Camila. Drama Queens. (p. 480)
Jahiel, Jessica, ed. see Hassler, Jill K.
Jahier, Milena, illus. see Hodgson, Mona.
Jahn, Benny. Ah-Choo - God Bless You. Scott, Chelsey, illus. (p. 30)
Jahn-Clough, Lisa. Country Girl, City Girl. (p. 372)
—Felicity & Cordelia: A Tale of Two Bunnies. Jahn-Clough, Lisa, illus. (p. 581)
—Me, Penelope. (p. 1116)
—My Friend & I. (p. 1209)
—Nothing but Blue. (p. 1268)
Jâho. What If Sheep Could Fly? JudyBee, tr. (p. 1887)
Jahsmann, Allan Hart & Simon, Martin P. Little Visits with God. White, Deborah, illus. (p. 1037)
Jaime, Catherine. Alphabet Fun Unit Study. (p. 49)
—Creatures, Creation, & Creator at the Galapagos Islands. Solid, Silas, photos by. (p. 380)
Jaime, Daniel, illus. see Caballero, Eduardo.
Jaime, Daniel, illus. see Calderon, Eduardo Caballero.
Jaimet, Kate. Break Point (p. 224)
—Dunces Anonymous (p. 490)
—Dunces Rock (p. 490)
—Edge of Flight (p. 504)
—Slam Dunk (p. 1587)
Jaimungal, Richard Neal. Hungry Bird & the Lonely Fish. (p. 828)
Jain, Devaki. Women, Development, & the Un: A Sixty-Year Quest for Equality & Justice. (p. 1945)
Jain, Manoj. Mahavira: The Hero of Nonviolence. Demi, illus. (p. 1076)
Jain, Priti, illus. see Marsh, Mike.
Jain, Shefalee, jt. auth. see Namjoshi, Suniti.
Jain, Varun. Understanding American Politics: A Book for Teenangers. (p. 1815)
Jainschigg, Nicholas, illus. see Bujold, Lois McMaster.
Jakab, Cheryl. Ecological Footprints. (p. 502)
—Food Supplies. (p. 614)
—Global Warming. (p. 684)
—Greenhouse Gases. (p. 723)
—Natural Wonders. (p. 1236)
—Pollution. (p. 1381)
—Protecting Natural Environments. (p. 1412)
—Renewable Energy. (p. 1460)
—Sustainable Cities. (p. 1688)
—Toxic Waste. (p. 1774)
—Waste Management. (p. 1860)
—Water Supply. (p. 1863)
Jakab, Cheryl & Keystone, David. Junior Science (p. 936)
Jakab, Cheryl & Smart Apple Media Staff. Artists at Work Wood. (p. 104)
—Circulatory System. (p. 321)
—Digestive System. (p. 438)
—Nervous System. (p. 1241)
—Our Body Skeletal System. (p. 1308)
Jakary, Lin. I Lost My Sock. Olson, Ryan, illus. (p. 841)
Jake D. Puppy Child Smiles Again. (p. 1418)
Jake, T. F., jt. auth. see Forbes, Jake T.
Jakesevic, Nenad, illus. see Fletcher, Susan.
Jaklich, Brian. Fireflies' Christmas. (p. 592)
Jako, Miklos. Truth about Religion: Book Three. (p. 1794)
—Truth about Religion. (p. 1794)
Jakobitz, Marilee. Martha Lu & the Whobegots. (p. 1097)
Jakobs, D. Anti-Villain League Handbook. (p. 89)
—Despicable Me 2: the Anti-Villain League Handbook. (p. 430)
—Holly, Jolly Harmony. (p. 789)
—Meet Blades the Copter-Bot. (p. 1120)
—My Little Pony: Tricks & Treats. (p. 1213)
—My Little Pony: Holly, Jolly Harmony. (p. 1213)
—My Little Pony: Tricks & Treats. (p. 1213)
—Transformers Rescue Bots: Meet Blades the Copter-Bot. (p. 1778)
Jakobsen, Kathy. My New York. Jakobsen, Kathy, illus. (p. 1216)
Jakobsen, Lars. Mysterious Manuscript. Jakobsen, Lars, illus. (p. 1223)
—Red Ruby. Jakobsen, Lars, illus. (p. 1455)
—Santa Fe Jail. Jakobsen, Lars, illus. (p. 1511)
—Secret Mummy. Jakobsen, Lars, illus. (p. 1542)
Jakobsen, Lars & Chapman, Robyn. Red Ruby. Jakobsen, Lars, illus. (p. 1455)
Jakopovich, Kathy. Paint on a Happy Face (p. 1318)
Jakoubek, Robert. Martin Luther King Jr. (p. 1097)
Jakoubek, Robert E. Martin Luther King, Jr. Civil Rights Leader. (p. 1098)
Jakovic, Chanakhya. Homeward Bound. (p. 794)
Jakson, Helen, illus. see Graves, Sue.
Jakubiak, David. Smart Kid's Guide to Online Bullying. (p. 1592)
Jakubiak, David J. How Our Government Works (p. 811)
—Kids Online (p. 954)
—Protecting Our Planet: What Can We Do about Toxins in the Environment? (p. 1412)
—Protecting Our Planet: What Can We Do about Oil Spills & Ocean Pollution? (p. 1412)
—Smart Kid's Guide to Avoiding Online Predators. (p. 1592)
—Smart Kid's Guide to Doing Internet Research. (p. 1592)
—Smart Kid's Guide to Internet Privacy. (p. 1592)
—Smart Kid's Guide to Online Bullying. (p. 1592)
—Smart Kid's Guide to Playing Online Games. (p. 1593)
—Smart Kid's Guide to Social Networking Online. (p. 1593)
—What Can We Do about Acid Rain? (p. 1880)
—What Can We Do about Deforestation? (p. 1880)
—What Can We Do about Ozone Loss? (p. 1881)
—What Does a Congressional Representative Do? (p. 1883)
—What Does a Governor Do? (p. 1883)
—What Does a Mayor Do? (p. 1883)
—What Does a Senator Do? (p. 1884)
—What Does a Supreme Court Justice Do? (p. 1884)
—What Does the President Do? (p. 1884)
Jakubowski, Kristan E. Paint the Town. (p. 1318)
Jakubowski, Michele. Beach Bummer. Waters, Erica-Jane, illus. (p. 149)
—Big Bike. Waters, Erica-Jane, illus. (p. 178)
—Big Dog Decisions Montalto, Luisa, illus. (p. 181)
—Dodgeball, Drama, & Other Dilemmas. Montalto, Luisa, illus. (p. 460)
—Outside Surprise. Waters, Erica-Jane, illus. (p. 1313)
—Party Pooper. Waters, Erica-Jane, illus. (p. 1326)
—Perfectly Poppy (p. 1342)
—Poppy's Puppy. Waters, Erica-Jane, illus. (p. 1385)
—Sidney & Sydney (p. 1573)
—Snowy Blast. Waters, Erica-Jane, illus. (p. 1601)
—Soccer Star. Waters, Erica-Jane, illus. (p. 1603)
—Talent Trouble. Waters, Erica-Jane, illus. (p. 1701)
—Third Grade Mix-Up. Montalto, Luisa, illus. (p. 1734)
Jakubowsky, Frank. God Looked down & Saw a Baby. (p. 689)
Jakubsen, Ryan. Portals III , Band of Rogues. (p. 1386)
Jal, David. David's Journey: The Story of David Jal, One of the Lost Boys of Sudan. Bezesky, Tracy, illus. (p. 411)
Jalali, Reza. Moon Watchers: Shirin's Ramadan Miracle O'Brien, Anne Sibley, illus. (p. 1172)
Jalali, Yassaman. Celebrating Norouz (Persian New Year) Zamanian, Marjan, illus. (p. 285)
Jalbert, Brad, jt. auth. see Peters, Laura.
Jalonen, Nicole. Baby's Magical Night. (p. 129)
—Magical Animal Army Adventures. (p. 1074)
Jalonen, Riitta. Tundra Mouse Mountain. Ledgard, J. M., tr. from FIN. (p. 1796)
Jalynn, Bailey. Dark Dust. (p. 407)
Jam, Teddy. Night Cars Beddows, Eric, illus. (p. 1253)
—This New Baby. Johnson, Virginia, illus. (p. 1737)
J.A.M.A.D., illus. see Washburn, Patrik.
Jamal L. Q'Ettelle. Jayden & the Return of the Jalon Warriors. (p. 910)
Jamaldinian, Joe. Bob Winging It. Jamaldinian, Joe, illus. (p. 205)
Jamana, Pharida, illus. see Savedoff, Barbara E. & Elissa, Barbara.
Jameel, Hiba. Pogo Entertained! (p. 1376)
Jamerson, Bettye J. For the Love of Beulah: Discovering Your Purpose in Life Begins with Love. (p. 616)
James, Adam, ed. see Chaline, Eric.
James, Adam, ed. see Chesterman, Barnaby.
James, Adam, ed. see Johnson, Nathan.
James, Adele. Adding with Apes. (p. 11)
James, Andrea. Adventures at Ja-Mar Farms: Pup-Pup, Padluck & PIG Take a Walk in the Wet Woods (p. 15)
James, Ann. Bird & Bear. James, Ann, illus. (p. 190)
James, Ann, illus. see Bedford, David.
James, Ann, illus. see Brian, Janeen.
James, Ann, illus. see Carthew, Mark & Rosen, Michael.
James, Ann, illus. see Fienberg, Anna.
James, Ann, illus. see Harris, Christine.
James, Ann, illus. see Hartnett, Sonya.
James, Ann, illus. see Kroll, Jeri.
James, Ann, illus. see Rippin, Sally.
James, Ann, illus. see Wild, Margaret.
James, Ann, jt. auth. see Bedford, David.
James, Ann, jt. auth. see Kroll, Jeri.
James, Annabelle. Abigail's Ballet Class. (p. 5)
—Abigail's Ballet Class. Beckes, Shirley, illus. (p. 5)
—Abigail's Bedtime. Beckes, Shirley, illus. (p. 5)
—Jack & the Beanstalk Story in a Box. Ackerman, Michele L., illus. (p. 902)
—Noah's Ark: Story in a Box. (p. 1261)
James, Anne. !Ataque de las Hormigas! Ramirez, Alma B., tr. from ENG. (p. 111)
James, Annie, illus. see Kubik, Dorothy.
James, Arthur. Jason & the Kodikats. (p. 910)
James Baldwin. Fifty Famous Stories Retold. (p. 585)
James Barter. Roman Gladiator. (p. 1485)
James, Ben. Tres Reyes Magos, the Three Wise Men. (p. 1784)
James, Bethan. First Christmas Sticker Book. (p. 593)
—My Toddler Bible. Sgouros, Yorgos, illus. (p. 1220)
James, Bethany & Shady, Leigh. Matilda Turnip's Endless Belly Button. (p. 1109)
James, Betsy. Listening at the Gate. James, Betsy, illus. (p. 1022)
—Word & Picture Books: For Year B/C Set 1 (p. 1950)
James, Betty R. Against All Odds: Artist Dean Mitchell's Story. (p. 29)
James, Brant. Formula One Racing. (p. 620)
James, Brian. Ahoy, Ghost Ship Ahead! Zivoin, Jennifer, illus. (p. 30)
—Attack on the High Seas! Zivoin, Jennifer, illus. (p. 114)
—Curse of Snake Island. Zivoin, Jennifer, illus. (p. 394)
—Dirty Liar. (p. 446)
—Easter Bunny's on His Way! (p. 499)
—Eight Spinning Planets. Benfanti, Russell, illus. (p. 507)
—Port of Spies. Zivoin, Jennifer, illus. (p. 1386)
—Treasure Trouble. Zivoin, Jennifer, illus. (p. 1782)
—Yo-Ho-Ho! Zivoin, Jennifer, illus. (p. 1971)
—Zombie Blondes. (p. 1988)
James, Brokenlily. Pine Needle Shoes. (p. 1359)
James, Caleb. Haffling. (p. 735)
James, Carol. Lady Who Loved Hats (p. 971)
James, Carol Ann. Baby's Sleepy Time Adventure. (p. 129)
James, Caroline Joy. Elee. (p. 510)
James, Cate, jt. auth. see Don, Lari.
James, Catherine. Bobby Cottontail's Gift. Collier, Kevin Scott, illus. (p. 206)
—Sad Little House. Collier, Kevin Scott, illus. (p. 1501)
James, Cheryl D. Leah's Treasure Book. (p. 982)
James, Cindy. Ten Easy Tips for Staying Safe. (p. 1718)
James, Clarence L., Sr. Lost Generation? or Left Generation! Confronting the Youth Crisis in Black America. (p. 1055)
James, Colin, ed. see Barrette, Melanie.
James, Colin, photos by see Barrette, Melanie.
James, Corinne M. Zoo Party. (p. 1989)
James, D. B. That Cat Is a Brat! (p. 1726)
James, Dalton. Heroes of Googley Woogley. (p. 773)
—Mudhogs. (p. 1189)
—Sneakiest Pirates. (p. 1597)
James, Danielle, jt. auth. see Danielle, Sara.
James, David. Sherlock Holmes & the Midnight Bell. Wilkes, Ian, ed. (p. 1565)
James, Dawn. Neighborhood Math. (p. 1240)
—Playground Math. (p. 1372)
—Store Math. (p. 1654)
James, Debra & James, Jessica. Social Pyramid. (p. 1604)
James, Diane. Baa, Baa, Black Sheep. (p. 123)
—En la Granja. (p. 522)
—Here We Go. (p. 770)
—Pat-a-Cake. (p. 1327)
—Three Blind Mice. (p. 1741)
James, Diane, illus. see Bulloch, Ivan.
James, Diane, jt. auth. see Bulloch, Ivan.
James, Elizabeth. Kids of Castle Grace. (p. 954)
James, Elizabeth, ed. see Petretti, Silvia I.
James, Elizabeth, illus. see Grimm, Jacob, et al.
James, Ellie. Shattered Dreams: A Midnight Dragonfly Novel. (p. 1563)
James, Emma J. Surprise for Santa. James, Emma J., illus. (p. 1686)
James, Eric. Halloween Scare at My House. Le Ray, Marina, illus. (p. 738)
—Halloween Scare in Alabama. La Ray, Marina, illus. (p. 738)
—Halloween Scare in Alaska. La Ray, Marina, illus. (p. 738)
—Halloween Scare in Albuquerque. La Ray, Marina, illus. (p. 738)
—Halloween Scare in Arkansas. La Ray, Marina, illus. (p. 738)
—Halloween Scare in Bentonville. La Ray, Marina, illus. (p. 738)
—Halloween Scare in Boise. La Ray, Marina, illus. (p. 738)
—Halloween Scare in Boston. La Ray, Marina, illus. (p. 738)
—Halloween Scare in Calgary. La Ray, Marina, illus. (p. 738)
—Halloween Scare in California. Le Ray, Marina, illus. (p. 738)
—Halloween Scare in Canada. Le Ray, Marina, illus. (p. 738)
—Halloween Scare in Charleston. La Ray, Marina, illus. (p. 738)
—Halloween Scare in Chicago. Le Ray, Marina, illus. (p. 738)
—Halloween Scare in Colorado. Le Ray, Marina, illus. (p. 738)
—Halloween Scare in Connecticut. La Ray, Marina, illus. (p. 738)
—Halloween Scare in Delaware. La Ray, Marina, illus. (p. 738)
—Halloween Scare in Edmonton. La Ray, Marina, illus. (p. 738)
—Halloween Scare in Florida. Le Ray, Marina, illus. (p. 738)
—Halloween Scare in Georgia. Le Ray, Marina, illus. (p. 738)
—Halloween Scare in Hawaii. La Ray, Marina, illus. (p. 738)
—Halloween Scare in Idaho. La Ray, Marina, illus. (p. 738)
—Halloween Scare in Illinois. La Ray, Marina, illus. (p. 738)
—Halloween Scare in Indiana. Le Ray, Marina, illus. (p. 738)
—Halloween Scare in Iowa. Le Ray, Marina, illus. (p. 738)
—Halloween Scare in Kansas. La Ray, Marina, illus. (p. 738)
—Halloween Scare in Kansas City. La Ray, Marina, illus. (p. 738)
—Halloween Scare in Kentucky. Le Ray, Marina, illus. (p. 738)
—Halloween Scare in Las Vegas. La Ray, Marina, illus. (p. 738)
—Halloween Scare in Los Angeles. La Ray, Marina, illus. (p. 738)
—Halloween Scare in Louisiana. Le Ray, Marina, illus. (p. 738)
—Halloween Scare in Maine. La Ray, Marina, illus. (p. 738)
—Halloween Scare in Maryland. Le Ray, Marina, illus. (p. 738)
—Halloween Scare in Massachusetts. La Ray, Marina, illus. (p. 738)
—Halloween Scare in Minnesota. Le Ray, Marina, illus. (p. 738)
—Halloween Scare in Mississippi. La Ray, Marina, illus. (p. 738)
—Halloween Scare in Missouri. Le Ray, Marina, illus. (p. 738)
—Halloween Scare in Montana. La Ray, Marina, illus. (p. 738)
—Halloween Scare in Nebraska. La Ray, Marina, illus. (p. 738)
—Halloween Scare in Nevada. La Ray, Marina, illus. (p. 738)
—Halloween Scare in New England. Le Ray, Marina, illus. (p. 738)
—Halloween Scare in New Hampshire. La Ray, Marina, illus. (p. 738)
—Halloween Scare in New Jersey. Le Ray, Marina, illus. (p. 738)
—Halloween Scare in New Mexico. La Ray, Marina, illus. (p. 738)
—Halloween Scare in New York. Le Ray, Marina, illus. (p. 738)
—Halloween Scare in North Carolina. La Ray, Marina, illus. (p. 738)
—Halloween Scare in North Dakota. La Ray, Marina, illus. (p. 738)
—Halloween Scare in Ohio. Le Ray, Marina, illus. (p. 738)
—Halloween Scare in Oklahoma. La Ray, Marina, illus. (p. 738)
—Halloween Scare in Omaha. La Ray, Marina, illus. (p. 738)
—Halloween Scare in Oregon. La Ray, Marina, illus. (p. 738)
—Halloween Scare in Pennsylvania. Le Ray, Marina, illus. (p. 738)
—Halloween Scare in Philadelphia. La Ray, Marina, illus. (p. 738)
—Halloween Scare in Pittsburgh. La Ray, Marina, illus. (p. 738)
—Halloween Scare in Portland. La Ray, Marina, illus. (p. 738)
—Halloween Scare in Rhode Island. La Ray, Marina, illus. (p. 738)
—Halloween Scare in San Francisco. La Ray, Marina, illus. (p. 738)
—Halloween Scare in South Carolina. La Ray, Marina, illus. (p. 738)
—Halloween Scare in South Dakota. La Ray, Marina, illus. (p. 738)
—Halloween Scare in St. Louis. La Ray, Marina, illus. (p. 738)
—Halloween Scare in Tampa Bay. La Ray, Marina, illus. (p. 738)
—Halloween Scare in Tennessee. Le Ray, Marina, illus. (p. 738)
—Halloween Scare in Texas. Le Ray, Marina, illus. (p. 738)
—Halloween Scare in the Carolinas. Le Ray, Marina, illus. (p. 738)
—Halloween Scare in Toronto. La Ray, Marina, illus. (p. 738)
—Halloween Scare in Tulsa. La Ray, Marina, illus. (p. 738)
—Halloween Scare in Utah. La Ray, Marina, illus. (p. 738)
—Halloween Scare in Vancouver. La Ray, Marina, illus. (p. 738)
—Halloween Scare in Vermont. La Ray, Marina, illus. (p. 738)
—Halloween Scare in Virginia. Le Ray, Marina, illus. (p. 738)
—Halloween Scare in Washington. Le Ray, Marina, illus. (p. 738)
—Halloween Scare in Washington, DC. La Ray, Marina, illus. (p. 738)
—Halloween Scare in West Virginia. La Ray, Marina, illus. (p. 738)
—Halloween Scare in Wisconsin. Le Ray, Marina, illus. (p. 738)
—Halloween Scare in Wyoming. La Ray, Marina, illus. (p. 738)
—Up & Down. (p. 1824)
James, Eric, illus. see Poleahla, Anita.
James, Estes, illus. see Rose, Williams.
James, Frank A. J. L., ed. Christmas at the Royal Institution: An Anthology of Lectures by M Faraday, J Tyndall, R S Ball, S P Thompson, E R Lankester, W H Bragg, W L Bragg, R L Gregory, & I Stewart. (p. 312)
James, Frank A. L., ed. Christmas at the Royal Institution: An Anthology of Lectures by M Faraday, J Tyndall, R S Ball, S P Thompson, E R Lankester, W H Bragg, W L Bragg, R L Gregory, & I Stewart. (p. 312)
James G. Normand. Santa's Secret Trick. (p. 1513)
James, Gilmory. Island of Ice: And the Snowmites. Dawson, Ken, illus. (p. 892)
James, Gordon, illus. see McKissack, Patricia C.
James, Gordon C., illus. see McKissack, Patricia C.
James, Gregory & Walkinshaw, Jean, eds. Model & Talent Directory - the International Directory of Model & Talent Agencies & Schools: The International Directory of Model & Talent Agencies & Schools (p. 1157)
James, Harry. Graphing with Pets (p. 711)
James, Hartwell. Enchanted Castle. (p. 523)
James, Hel, jt. auth. see Martineau, Susan.
James, Hel, jt. auth. see Martinneau, Susan.
James, Helen, illus. see Butterfield, Moira.
James, Helen, illus. see Butterworth Moira.
James, Helen Foster. E Is for Enchantment: A New Mexico Alphabet. Twinem, Neecy, illus. (p. 492)
—Grandma Loves You! Brown, Petra, illus. (p. 708)
—S Is for S'Mores: A Camping Alphabet. Judge, Lita, illus. (p. 1499)
James, Helen Foster & Loh, Virginia Shin-Mui. Paper Son: Lee's Journey to America. Ong, Wilson, illus. (p. 1323)
James, Helen Foster & Wilbur, Helen L. Little California. Urban, Helle, illus. (p. 1025)
James, Henry. Abasement of the Northmores. (p. 2)
—Album. (p. 35)
—Alexandra's Accident: A Little Girl Comes to Grief While Out with Her Pa. (p. 37)
—Altar of the Dead. (p. 50)
—Ambassadors. (p. 56)
—Ambassadors. Home, Philip, ed. (p. 56)
—Ambassadors. 1stWorld Library, ed. (p. 56)
—American Scene. (p. 63)
—Art of Fiction. (p. 102)
—Art of the Novel: Critical Prefaces. (p. 102)
—Beast in the Jungle. (p. 152)
—Beldonald Holbein. (p. 161)
—Better Sort. (p. 172)
—Birthplace. (p. 193)
—Breville Fane. (p. 226)
—Broken Wings. (p. 230)
—Chaperon. (p. 291)
—Coxon Fund. (p. 374)
—Daisy Miller. (p. 400)

—Daisy Miller. Lodge, David & Horne, Philip, eds. (p. 400)
—Death of the Lion. (p. 420)
—English Hours. (p. 530)
—Essays in London & Elsewhere. (p. 536)
—Europe. (p. 540)
—Europeans. (p. 540)
—Figure in the Carpet. (p. 586)
—Finer Grain. (p. 589)
—Flickerbridge. (p. 603)
—French Poets & Novelists. (p. 636)
—Friends of the Friends. (p. 638)
—Golden Bowl. (p. 694)
—Great Good Place. (p. 716)
—Guy Domville. (p. 733)
—Henry James - Novels 1901-1902: The Sacred Fount - The Wings of the Dove. (p. 768)
—High Bid. (p. 777)
—In the Cage. (p. 865)
—Italian Hours. (p. 894)
—Ivory Tower. (p. 901)
—Lesson of Balzac. (p. 993)
—Little Tour in France. (p. 1037)
—Middle Years. (p. 1138)
—Miss Gunton of Poughkeepsie. (p. 1151)
—Mrs. Medwin. (p. 1187)
—Next Time. (p. 1249)
—Notes of a Son & Brother. (p. 1268)
—Notes on Novelists: With Some Other Notes. (p. 1268)
—Outcry. (p. 1312)
—Owen Wingrave. (p. 1314)
—Partial Portraits. (p. 1325)
—Paste. (p. 1327)
—Picture & Text. (p. 1355)
—Portrait of a Lady. (p. 1386)
—Portraits of Places. (p. 1387)
—Private Life. (p. 1407)
—Pupil. (p. 1417)
—Real Right Thing. (p. 1448)
—Reprobate. (p. 1461)
—Sacred Fount. (p. 1500)
—Sense of the Past. (p. 1551)
—Small Boy & Others. (p. 1592)
—Soft Side. (p. 1606)
—Spoils of Poynton. (p. 1630)
—Story in It. (p. 1657)
—Terminations: The Death of the Lion, the Coxon Fund, the Middle Years, the Altar of the Dead. (p. 1721)
—Tree of Knowledge. (p. 1783)
—Turn of the Screw. (p. 1797)
—Turn of the Screw & Other Short Novels. (p. 1797)
—Two Faces. (p. 1803)
—Views & Reviews. (p. 1842)
—Washington Square. (p. 1860)
—Washington Square. Banta, Martha & Horne, Philip, eds. (p. 1860)
—William Wetmore Story & His Friends. (p. 1933)
—Wings of the Dove. (p. 1936)
—Wings of the Dove. Bell, Millicent & Horne, Philip, eds. (p. 1936)
James, Hilary. Emma Enslaved. (p. 519)
—Emma's Humiliation. (p. 520)
—Emma's Secret Diaries. (p. 520)
—Emma's Secret Domination. (p. 520)
—Emma's Secret World. (p. 520)
—Emma's Submission. (p. 520)
James, Hollis. Teenage Mutant Ninja Turtles Deluxe Step into Reading (Teenage Mutant Ninja Turtles) Random House, illus. (p. 1714)
James, Hollis, jt. auth. see Smith, James J.
James, Howe. Misfits. (p. 1150)
—Pinky & Rex & the Bully. (p. 1360)
James, Ian. Gingerbread Boy Uptown. (p. 677)
—Why Mosquitos Buzz in People's Ears: A Folktale from West Africa. (p. 1925)
—Why the Sky Is Far Away: A Tale from Nigeria. (p. 1926)
James, Ian, ed. Oceans. (p. 1277)
James, J. Alison. Eucalyptus Wings. Demi, illus. (p. 540)
—Runa. (p. 1496)
—Sing for a Gentle Rain. (p. 1579)
James, J. Alison, tr. see Horn, Peter.
James, J. Alison, tr. see Loupy, Christophe.
James, J. Alison, tr. see Pfister, Marcus.
James, J. Alison, tr. see Pin, Isabel.
James, J. Alison, tr. see Poppenhager, Nicole.
James, J. Alison, tr. from GER. Where Does Pepper Come From. Olten, Manuela, illus. (p. 1907)
James, Jack. How to Let Your Parents Raise a Millionaire: A Kid-to-Kid View on How to Make Money Make a Difference & Have Fun Doing Both. (p. 820)
James, Jake. Jake s Short Stories. (p. 906)
James, Jason. Johnny Repeat 1: The End of the Way That Was (p. 923)
James, Jeanie. Turkey! A Cook's How-to Survival Guide to the Holidays. (p. 1797)
James, Jenni. Pride & Popularity. (p. 1398)
James, "Jerry" John. Grandpa's Little White Truck. (p. 710)
James, Jessica, jt. auth. see James, Debra.
James, Jessica, creator. Shades of Gray: A Novel of the Civil War in Virginia. (p. 1557)
James, Jim. Paris, Wyoming. (p. 1324)
James, Joanne. Three Quest Plays: For Children (p. 1743)
—Three Quest Plays. (p. 1743)
James, John, illus. see Gravett, Christopher.
James, John, illus. see Hibbert, Clare.
James, John, illus. see MacDonald, Fiona & Donnelly, S. E.
James, John, illus. see MacDonald, Fiona.
James, John, illus. see Morley, Jacqueline.
James, John, illus. see Ratliff, Thomas.
James, John, illus. see Stewart, David.
James, Joyce. Bees. (p. 157)
James, Kari, adapted by. Barbie & the Magic of Pegasus: A Junior Novelization. (p. 138)
James, Karim. Kids Time to Rhyme: Read & Rhyme at the same Time. (p. 955)
James, Katy. My Favorite Summer Vacations. (p. 1203)
James, Keen. Stoopnagle's Tale Is Twisted: Spoonerisms Run Amok. (p. 1653)
James, Kelle. Smile for the Camera: A Memoir. (p. 1594)
James, Kennon, illus. see Benge, Janet.
James, Kennon, illus. see Sommer, Carl.
James, Kennon, illus. see Uglow, Loyd.
James, Kristopher. Lyrian. (p. 1067)
James, L. Dale Jarrett. (p. 401)
James L. Fuller. Lost Coal Mine to Oz. (p. 1055)
James, Larry W. Captain Petey: An Adventure at Sea. Ramos, Violet M., ed. (p. 264)
James, Laura, illus. see Senior, Olive.
James, Lincoln. Bugs up Close. (p. 237)
—Dale Jarrett. (p. 401)
—Deadly Poison Dart Frogs. (p. 418)
—Death Adder. (p. 420)
—Death Adder / Víboras de la Muerte. (p. 420)
—Hedgehogs Are Not Hogs! (p. 762)
—Making History: The Liberty Bell. (p. 1081)
—Mars: The Red Planet. (p. 1096)
—Mercury: The Iron Planet. (p. 1127)
—Native American Homes. (p. 1234)
—Prickle of Porcupines. (p. 1398)
—Prickle of Porcupines / una Manada de Puercoespines. (p. 1398)
—Sal Sleeps In. (p. 1504)
—Solar Eclipses. (p. 1606)
—Street Fair. (p. 1666)
—Sun: Star of the Solar System. (p. 1675)
—Venus: The Masked Planet. (p. 1836)
—What Happens When I Sweat? (p. 1886)
—Where Does the Garbage Go? (p. 1907)
James Lorimer & Company Ltd., Publishers. Fishing for Trouble. (p. 599)
James Lorimer and Company Ltd. Staff, jt. auth. see Laurence, Margaret.
James Lorimer and Company Ltd. Staff, jt. auth. see Slavens, Elaine.
James, M. R. Five Jars. (p. 600)
—Old Testament Legends: Being Stories Out of Some of the Less Known Apocryphal Books of the Old Testament 1913. (p. 1284)
James, M. R. & Pearson Education Staff. Crown. (p. 386)
James M.A., Deborah. Tangerine, Spark, & Rainbow's Story. (p. 1705)
James, Margaret Ray, illus. see Lundy, Charlotte.
James, Martha. Jack Tenfield's Star: A Story of Yankee. (p. 903)
James, Martin. William Is Going Green. (p. 1933)
James, Martin, illus. see Singh, Asavari.
James, Martin, illus. see Vigil, Angel.
James, Martin & Newman, Gary. Fishing. (p. 599)
James, Matt, illus. see Croza, Laurel.
James, Matt, illus. see Porter, Pamela.
James, Matt, illus. see Rogers, Stan.
James, McKelvy Walker, illus. see Folloni, Larry.
James, Melody. Signs of Love: Destiny Date. (p. 1574)
James, Melody, illus. see Ballard, George Anne.
James, Melody A., illus. see Ballard, George Anne.
James, Michael, jt. auth. see James, Shilah.
James, Midge, ed. see Reed, Rosemary.
James, Mike. Bootsie - & the Team. (p. 213)
—Bootsie - Just One More. (p. 213)
James, Muirden. Universo. (p. 1821)
James, Nick. Pearl Wars. (p. 1333)
—Skyship Academy: Crimson Rising. (p. 1587)
—Skyship Academy: Strikeforce. (p. 1587)
James, Oliver. China. (p. 306)
James, Otto. AIDS. (p. 30)
—Focus on Australia. (p. 610)
James, Rhian Nest, illus. see Fussell, Sandy.
James, Rhian Nest, illus. see Murphy, Sally.
James, Richard E., III. Adventures of the Elements: Dangerous Games. Vol. 3 Lyle, Maryann, ed. (p. 23)
James, Rob. As/A Level Physical Education: Skills Acquisition & Sports Psychology. (p. 105)
James, Robert. How the Camel Got His Hump. (p. 812)
—How the Elephant Got Its Trunk. (p. 813)
—People Who Care for Our Health Discovery Library (p. 1340)
James, Robert F., jt. auth. see Johnson, Rich.
James, Robert L., jt. auth. see Roland-James, Patricia.
James, Robin, illus. see Cosgrove, Stephen.
James, Robin, illus. see Gill, Shelley.
James, Robin, illus. see Penn, Audrey & Cosgrove, Stephen.
James, Rosalind. Bertie Rides Again. (p. 168)
James, Rosemary. What Do Scientists Do? Solve Problems Involving Measurement & Estimation (p. 1882)
James, Ryan M., jt. auth. see James, Syrie.
James, Sabrina. Spring Fling. (p. 1635)
James, Sabrina & Scognamiglio, John. Secret Santa. (p. 1543)
James, Sara. Flexibility & Agility. Hart, Diane H., ed. (p. 603)
—Photography. (p. 1353)
—Safety. (p. 1502)
—Sculpting. (p. 1533)
—Self-Defense. (p. 1549)
—Self-Discipline. (p. 1549)
—Self-Esteem. (p. 1549)
—Step Aerobics & Aerobic Dance. Hart, Diane H., ed. (p. 1647)
—Writing: Stories, Poetry, Song & Rap. (p. 1964)
—Yoga & Pilates. Hart, Diane H., ed. (p. 1972)
James, Sara, jt. auth. see Ruckdeschel, Liz.
James, Sarah-Louise. One Direction: The Ultimate Photo Collection: Follow the World's Greatest Boy Band. (p. 1294)
James, Scilla. Ponies at Owls' Wood. (p. 1382)
—Princess Phoebe - a Greyhound's Adventure. (p. 1405)
James, Setria. Doodles: Alphabet Coloring Fun. (p. 469)
James, Shilah & James, Michael. Little Land Adventures - Little Bird. Castles, Heather, illus. (p. 1030)
—Little Land Adventures - Little Iguan. Castles, Heather, illus. (p. 1030)
—Little Land Adventures - Little Pig. Castles, Heather, illus. (p. 1030)
—Little Land Adventures - Little Racoon. Castles, Heather, illus. (p. 1030)
James, Simon. Ancient Rome. (p. 70)
—Baby Brains: The Smartest Baby in the Whole World. James, Simon, illus. (p. 125)
—Days Like This: A Collection of Small Poems. (p. 415)
—DK Eyewitness Books: Ancient Rome: Ancient Rome. (p. 455)
—George Flies South. (p. 663)
—Leon y Beto. (p. 992)
—Little One Step. James, Simon, illus. (p. 1032)
—Nurse Clementine. (p. 1273)
—Querido Salvatierra. de la Vega, Eida, tr. from ENG. (p. 1426)
James, Soloman & Salt, Allan. Little Book of Animals. (p. 1025)
James, Steve, illus. see Carman, Patrick.
James, Steve, illus. see Myron, Vicki & Witter, Bret.
James, Steve, illus. see Riordan, Rick.
James, Steven. 24 Tandem Bible Hero Story Scripts for Children's Ministry. (p. 1996)
—24 Tandem Bible Story Scripts for Children's Ministry. (p. 1996)
—Believe It! Bible Basics That Won't Break Your Brain. Lee, Jared, illus. (p. 161)
—Blur (p. 204)
James, Steven, illus. see Malaspina, Ann.
James, Suzi. Matilda Bear & Father Bear: I Love You Father Bear. (p. 1109)
James, Syrie & James, Ryan M. Forbidden. (p. 616)
James, Tamara. World Is Your Oyster. SanCartier, Emma, illus. (p. 1956)
James, Thomas & Thomas, James. What Will I Play While You Are Away? (p. 1895)
James, Tina. Sarabeth Palmer: 1963-1964. (p. 1514)
James, Tom. Fun on the Move: With Pen & Wipe-Clean Fold-Out Pages. (p. 648)
—Play Day Colors: With Pen & Wipe-Clean Fold-Out Pages. (p. 1371)
James, Trisha. Cattle & Oil: The Growth of Texas Industries. (p. 281)
—Celebrating Texas: Patriotic Symbols & Landmarks. (p. 285)
James, Will. All in the Day's Riding. (p. 44)
—Big-Enough. McKenna, Gwen, ed. (p. 181)
—Cow Country. (p. 373)
—Cowboy in the Making. (p. 374)
—Cowboys North & South. DeRoo, John, ed. (p. 374)
—Dark Horse James, Will, illus. (p. 407)
—Dark Horse. (p. 407)
—Drifting Cowboy. (p. 485)
—Flint Spears: Cowboy Rodeo Contestant. (p. 604)
—Home Ranch. (p. 792)
—Horses I've Known. (p. 800)
—Lone Cowboy: My Life Story. (p. 1046)
—Look-See with Uncle Bill. (p. 1050)
—My First Horse (p. 1206)
—Sand. (p. 1510)
—Smokey: The Cowhorse. Vol. 1 (p. 1594)
—Smoky Cowhorse, the Cowhorse. (p. 1595)
—Smoky, the Cow Horse. (p. 1595)
—Smoky the Cowhorse. (p. 1595)
—Sun Up: Tales of the Cow Camps. (p. 1676)
—Three Mustangeers. (p. 1743)
—Uncle Bill: A Tale of Two Kids & a Cowboy. (p. 1811)
—Will James Cowboy Book (p. 1932)
—Young Cowboy. (p. 1978)
James, William. Energies of Men. (p. 528)
—Essays in Radical Empiricism. (p. 536)
—Letters (p. 1002)
—Meaning of Truth. (p. 1117)
—Pragmatism. (p. 1392)
—Principles of Psychology (p. 1406)
—Psychology: Briefer Course. (p. 1413)
—Some Problems of Philosophy. (p. 1609)
—Talks to Teachers on Psychology & to Students on Some of Life's Ideals. (p. 1704)
—Will to Believe & Other Essays in Popular Philosophy. (p. 1932)
James, William, ed. Varieties of Religious Experience. (p. 1833)
James, Wilson. SONS & BROTHERS in SEATTLE. (p. 1613)
James, Yolanda. In Spain. Brodie, Neale, illus. (p. 865)
James, Yolanda, et al. Bertie Wiggins' Amazing Ears. Brodie, Neale & McCarthy, Pat, illus. (p. 168)
James-Carde, Genice. Father for Me. Thomas, Michael Lee, illus. (p. 577)
—Go Away Bully! (p. 686)
Jameson, Bernadette. Boy Who Played His Way to Freedom. (p. 219)
Jameson, Catherine. Zoe & the Fawn. Flett, Julie, illus. (p. 1987)
Jameson, Louise. Christmas in Gabba Land. Style Guide Staff, illus. (p. 314)
Jameson, Pam. Betty Book! The Life & Times of Betty. (p. 172)
Jameson, Rosemary. Mortimer & Teasdale's Adventures. (p. 1176)
Jameson, Steven. Beyond: the Coloring Book Edition: Beyond, yet Still with You (There, of Course, Is God) Brown, Erin, illus. (p. 174)
—Byen Lwen, Poutan Toujou Avèk Ou: Se Sèten, Bondye La. Dugué, Georges, Jr., tr. (p. 249)
Jameson, W. C. Atlantic Coast: Legends of Sunken Pirate Treasures, Mysterious Caches, & Jinxed Ships, from Maine to Florida. (p. 112)
—Buried Treasures of California. Hall, Wendell E., illus. (p. 243)
—Buried Treasures of New England. (p. 243)
—Buried Treasures of Texas: Legends of Outlaw Loot, Pirate Hoards, Buried Mines, Ingots in Lakes, & Santa Anna's Pack-Train Gold. (p. 243)
—Buried Treasures of the American Southwest: Legends of Lost Mines, Hidden Payrolls & Spanish Gold. (p. 243)
—Buried Treasures of the Appalachians: Legends of Homestead Caches, Indian Mines & Loot from Civil War Raids. (p. 243)
—Buried Treasures of the Great Plains. (p. 243)
—Buried Treasures of the Mid-Atlantic States: Legends of Island Treasure, Jewelry Caches & Secret Tunnels. (p. 243)
—Buried Treasures of the Ozarks: Legends of Lost Gold, Hidden Silver & Forgotten Caches. (p. 243)
—Buried Treasures of the Pacific Northwest: Secret Indian Mines, Lost Outlaw Hoards, & Stolen Payroll Coins. (p. 243)
—Buried Treasures of the Rocky Mountain West: Legends of Lost Mines, Train Robbery Gold, Caves of Forgotten Riches, & Indians' Buried Silver. (p. 243)
—Buried Treasures of the South: Legends of Lost, Buried, & Forgotten Treasures, from Tidewater Virginia to Coastal Carolina to Cajun Louisiana. (p. 243)
Jamesson, Christine. Adventures of Samantha the Black Racer Snake. (p. 22)
Jamie, Humphries. Xtreme Electric Guitar. (p. 1967)
Jamie, Meckel. Noodles for Baby. (p. 1264)
Jamie, Schaefer-Wilson & Geminario, Jo Ann. Baby Rules: The Insider's Guide to Raising Your Parents. (p. 128)
Jamieson, Alison. Can the War on Terrorism Be Won? (p. 258)
Jamieson, B. Goldstrike. (p. 696)
Jamieson, Eden, illus. see Fiddick, Calay.
Jamieson, Marianne & Benchmark Education Co. Staff. Analytical Arguments about Four Pioneers of Flight. (p. 67)
Jamieson, Mark. Ico Island. (p. 851)
Jamieson, Patrick E. Mind Race: A Firsthand Account of One Teenager's Experience with Bipolar Disorder. (p. 1145)
Jamieson, Paul F. & Burdick, Neal S. Adirondack Reader. (p. 12)
Jamieson, Sandy, illus. see Benesch, Walter.
Jamieson, Victoria. Bea Rocks the Flock. (p. 149)
—Olympig! (p. 1288)
—Roller Girl. (p. 1485)
Jamieson, Victoria, illus. see Cameron, Anne.
Jamieson, Victoria, illus. see Feldman, Jody.
Jamieson, Victoria, illus. see Poploff, Michelle.
Jamieson, Victoria, illus. see Singlehurst, Naomi.
Jamiol, Paul. Bikers Are Animals: A Children's Book on Motorcycling. Habib, Linda, ed. (p. 185)
—Bikers Are Animals 4: Working & Riding. (p. 185)
Jamiolkowski, Raymond M. Baby Doesn't Make the Man: Alternative Sources of Power & Manhood for Young Men. (p. 125)
Jamison, Bob. Cambridge Checkpoints VCE Physical Education 2005. (p. 255)
Jamison, Heather & Meckenstock, Shay. Taste of Home. Marconette, Gennifer, ed. (p. 1707)
Jamison, Jo Lynn & Elliott, Lela Mae. Siren's Call of the Caves (p. 1580)
Jamison, Jocelyn. Baby Mood Swings. (p. 127)
Jamison, Kathy. Looking for the Alphabet. (p. 1051)
Jamison, Linc, jt. auth. see Mills, Nathan.
Jamison, Lori. Running for Dave. (p. 1497)
Jamison, Lori, jt. auth. see Kropp, Paul.
Jamison, Sharon, illus. see Goril, Cindy.
Jan, Emily. Monedas de Oro. (p. 1163)
—Pieces of Gold. (p. 1356)
Jan, Gamma. Something Really Important: All Around the World. (p. 1610)
Jan, R. R., illus. see Abraham, M. K.
Jan, Romero Stevens. Carlos Digs to China Carlos Excava Hasta la China. Jeanne, Arnold, illus. (p. 270)
Jan, Stephanie Liu, photos by see Yan, Martin.
Jan, Young. Orange Slipknot Curriculum Unit. (p. 1302)
—Starting the Colt. (p. 1644)
Jana, Laura, jt. auth. see Cook, Julia.
Janacone, Matt. Finny the Friendly Shark. Druschel, Bob, illus. (p. 589)
Janco, Tania, illus. see Howker, Janni.
Janczewski, Dariusz. One Day Everyone Was Late for School: A Bedtime Story Rhyme. (p. 1294)
Janda, David H. Awakening of a Surgeon: A Family Guide to Preventing Sports Injuries & Deaths. (p. 120)
Janda, Laura A., tr. see Vars, Elle Márjá.
Jander, Martha Streufert. Easter Gift. (p. 499)
Jane, Fred T., illus. see Griffith, George.
Jane, Hale. Boomland. (p. 213)
Jane, Johnson. Are You Ready for Bed. Gaby, Hansen, illus. (p. 97)
Jane, Kelsey. Autumn Adventure. (p. 118)
Jane, LaRue. Bulwinkle Who. (p. 241)
Jane, Mary, illus. see Auch, Mary Jane.
Jane, Musano Mary. Littlest Jingle Bell. (p. 1039)
Jane, Nance', illus. see Sullivan, Mary M.
Jane, Pamela. Little Elfie One. Manning, Jane, illus. (p. 1027)
—Little Goblins Ten. Jane, Pamela & Manning, Jane, illus. (p. 1028)
—Milo & the Flapjack Fiasco! Johnson, Meredith, ed. (p. 1144)
—Monster Mischief. Rosenberry, Vera, illus. (p. 1167)
—Noelle of the Nutcracker. Brett, Jan, illus. (p. 1262)
—Winky Blue Goes Wild! Tilley, Debbie, illus. (p. 1936)
Jane, Rebecca. Hamster Heroes to the Rescue: The Mystery of the Shadow in the Yard & Retirement. (p. 739)
Jane, Sarah. Hope's Garden. Ferrigno, Angela, illus. (p. 797)
Jane, Shasta. Standing Invisible. (p. 1639)
Jane, Yolen. Devil's Arithmetic. (p. 432)
Janeczko, Leah D., tr. see Baccalario, Pierdomenico.
Janeczko, Paul B. Dark Game: True Spy Stories from Invisible Ink to CIA Moles. (p. 407)
—Death of the Hat: A Brief History of Poetry in 50 Objects. Raschka, Chris, illus. (p. 420)
—Foot in the Mouth: Poems to Speak, Sing, & Shout. Raschka, Chris, illus. (p. 614)
—Foot in the Mouth. (p. 614)
—Hey, You! Poems to Skyscrapers, Mosquitoes, & Other Fun Things. Rayevsky, Robert, illus. (p. 774)
—Poetry from A to Z: A Guide for Young Writers. Bobak, Cathy, illus. (p. 1376)

—Requiem: Poems of the Terezin Ghetto. (p. 1462)
—Worlds Afire. (p. 1960)
Janeczko, Paul B., ed. Poke in the I: A Collection of Concrete Poems. Raschka, Chris, illus. (p. 1377)
—Top Secret: A Handbook of Codes, Ciphers & Secret Writing. LaReau, Jenna, illus. (p. 1769)
Janelle, Dick. Salmon Falls 1956. (p. 1505)
Janelle, Nicole & Cholette, Daniel. Naby Recycles. (p. 1227)
Janer, Montserrat. Rey Listo y el Rey Fuerte. (p. 1467)
Janes, Andy, illus. see Howard, Martin.
Janes, Lewis George. Health & a Day. (p. 757)
—Samuell Gorton: A Forgotten Founder of Our Liberties. (p. 1509)
—Study of Primitive Christianity. (p. 1670)
Janese, Julie. Little Booger Book. (p. 1025)
Janesh, Ron. Ariela Aparecida E O Vale Da Neblina Da Cachoeir. Gonçalves da Silva, Fabio, illus. (p. 98)
Janetzke, Adele K. Garden Home. (p. 656)
Janeway, Paul. Dragon Eye Connection. (p. 477)
Jang, EunJoo, illus. see Lee, WonKyeong.
Jang, Ki-hwa & Kim, In-sook. Good Friends: Symbiotic Relationships. Cowley, Joy, ed. (p. 698)
Jang, Yeong-seon, illus. see Barrie, J. M.
Jang, Yeong-seon, illus. see Barrie, James Matthew.
Janger, Kathleen, jt. auth. see Korenblit, Michael.
Jangjiravat, Somjai. Who Is Mr Piggy Pig? (p. 1916)
Jango-Cohen, Judith. American Flag. (p. 60)
—Aparato Respiratorio. Translations.com Staff, tr. (p. 91)
—Aparato Respiratorio (the Respiratory System) Translations.com Staff, tr. (p. 91)
—Armadillos. (p. 99)
—Bald Eagle. (p. 133)
—Bandera Estadounidense. Translations.com Staff, tr. from ENG. (p. 136)
—Bees. (p. 157)
—Bionics. (p. 190)
—Camels. (p. 256)
—Chinese New Year. Chin, Jason, illus. (p. 307)
—Dump Trucks on the Move. (p. 489)
—Fire Trucks on the Move. (p. 591)
—Flying Squirrels. (p. 610)
—Hippopotamuses. (p. 781)
—History of Food. (p. 784)
—Hovering Hummingbirds. (p. 804)
—Hungry Ladybugs. (p. 828)
—Kangaroos. (p. 942)
—Let's Look at Armadillos. (p. 998)
—Let's Look at Iguanas. (p. 999)
—Liberty Bell. (p. 1005)
—Librarians. (p. 1005)
—Mount Rushmore. (p. 1180)
—Octopuses. (p. 1278)
—Porcupines. (p. 1386)
—Respiratory System. (p. 1463)
—Volquetes. Translations.com Staff, tr. from ENG. (p. 1849)
—Volquetes (Dump Trucks) Translations.com Staff, tr. (p. 1849)
—Why Does It Rain? Feltes, Tess, illus. (p. 1924)
—Your Respiratory System. (p. 1981)
Janguay, Patricia, illus. see Stuefloten, Helen.
Jani, Mahendra & Jani, Vandana. What You Will See Inside a Hindu Temple. Bhargava, Neirah & Dave, Vijay, photos by. (p. 1896)
Jani, Vandana, jt. auth. see Jani, Mahendra.
Janic, Susan. Living the Dream: Hannah Montana & Miley Cyrus - The Unofficial Story. (p. 1041)
Janic, Susan & Thomas, Scott. Jonas Brothers Forever: The Unofficial Story of Kevin, Joe & Nick. (p. 925)
Janice Turner & Colleen Connelly. Colleen Goes to the Farmer's Market. Ron Frazier, photos by. (p. 340)
Janicke, Gregory. Conquerors Janicke, Gregory, illus. (p. 358)
—Dark Mystery of the Shadow Beasts. (p. 408)
—Lost & Found (p. 1054)
—Shadow Beasts Janicke, Gregory, illus. (p. 1557)
Janik, Dan. Sourdough Scott's Bedtime Fairy Tales from Alaska. (p. 1616)
Janin, Hunt & Besheer, Margaret. Saudi Arabia. (p. 1516)
Janis, Tim. Shine Like a Lighthouse. Steve, Lavigne, illus. (p. 1566)
Janisch, Heinz. En Casa. Rodriguez Aguilar, Christina, tr. (p. 522)
—Fantastic Adventures of Baron Munchausen. Cooper, Belinda, tr. from GER. (p. 571)
—King & the Sea. (p. 958)
Janisch, Heinz, jt. auth. see Leffler, Silke.
Janisch, Heinz & Bansch, Helga. Good Night Giants. (p. 699)
Janisch, Heinz & Leffler, Silke. Why Is the Snow White? (p. 1925)
Janjua, Sajid. Dusty the Kitten. (p. 490)
Jankéliowitch, Anne. 50 Ways to Save the Earth. Bourseiller, Philippe, photos by. (p. 1997)
Jankeliowitch, Anne. Kids Who Are Changing the World. Arthus-Bertrand, Yann, photos by. (p. 955)
Janko, Denise. Alexis-Mae. (p. 37)
—Buttercup. (p. 247)
Jankowki, Dan, jt. auth. see Fuqua, Nell.
Jankowski, Connie. All about Light & Sound (p. 42)
—All about Light & Sound. (p. 42)
—Astronomers: From Copernicus to Crisp. (p. 109)
—Hippocrates: Father of Medicine (p. 781)
—Hippocrates: Making the Way for Medicine. (p. 781)
—Human Body (p. 825)
—Investigating the Human Body. (p. 885)
—Jane Goodall: Animal Scientist & Friend. (p. 908)
—Jane Goodall: Primatologist & Animal Activist (p. 908)
—Pioneers of Light & Sound (p. 1361)
—Pioneers of Light & Sound. (p. 1361)
—Space Exploration (p. 1619)
Jankowski, Connie, jt. auth. see Science Readers Staff.
Jankowski, Dan, illus. see Hall, Kirsten.
Jankowski, Dan, illus. see Sauer, Cat.
Jankowski, Daniel, illus. see Salzano, Tammi J.
Jankowski, Daniel, illus. see Sauer, Cat.
Jankowski, Emily. History of the Great Lakes. (p. 785)
—Mapping North America. (p. 1090)
—Reaching Everest's Summit. (p. 1442)
—Soccer's Greatest Records (p. 1604)
Jankowski, Susan. Egypt in the News: Past, Present, & Future. (p. 506)
—Everglades National Park: Adventure, Explore, Discover. (p. 542)
—Jordan in the News: Past, Present, & Future. (p. 925)
—Olympic National Park: Adventure, Explore, Discover. (p. 1288)
—Say No to a Bully. (p. 1518)
Jankowski, Susan & Library. True Ocean Rescue Stories. (p. 1792)
—True Wilderness Rescue Stories. (p. 1793)
Jannazo, Michelle A. Isabella's Shoes. (p. 891)
Janner, Hans. Hans Janner, Sr. Playing Cards: Boxed, Custom Designed, Deluxe Poker-Size Playing Cards. (p. 743)
Janney, Connie. Most Extraordinary Farm. (p. 1177)
Janni, Rebecca. Every Cowgirl Goes to School. Avril, Lynne, illus. (p. 542)
—Every Cowgirl Loves a Rodeo. Avril, Lynne, illus. (p. 542)
—Every Cowgirl Needs a Horse. Avril, Lynne, illus. (p. 542)
—Every Cowgirl Needs Dancing Boots. Avril, Lynne, illus. (p. 542)
—Jammy Dance Dockray, Tracy, illus. (p. 907)
—Nellie Sue, Happy Camper. (p. 1240)
—Nellie Sue, Happy Camper. Avril, Lynne, illus. (p. 1240)
Janning, Scarlett. Therese's Terrarium. (p. 1731)
Janosch. Feliz Cumpleanos, Pequeno Tigre! (p. 581)
—Just One Apple. (p. 939)
—Pequeno Tigre y el Osito en la Ciudad. (p. 1341)
—Yo Te Curare, Dijo el Pequeno Oso. Janosch, illus. (p. 1971)
Janoski, Elizabeth. Mountain Song. (p. 1181)
Janover, Caroline D. Josh: A Boy with Dyslexia. (p. 926)
—Zipper: The Kid with ADHD. (p. 1987)
Janovich, Leah. Patty's Pictures. Billin-Frye, Paige, illus. (p. 1330)
Janovitz, Marilyn. Baby Baby Baby. (p. 125)
—Go Baby Go. (p. 686)
—I Will Try. Janovitz, Marilyn, illus. (p. 848)
—Look Out, Bird! (p. 1049)
—Play Baby Play! (p. 1371)
—Te Puedo Ayudar?/Can I Help? Fernandez, Queta, tr. (p. 1708)
—We Love Christmas! (p. 1867)
—We Love School! Janovitz, Marilyn, illus. (p. 1867)
—We Love School (¡Nos Encanta la Escuela!) Janovitz, Marilyn, illus. (p. 1867)
Janovitz, Marilyn, illus. see Burg, Ann E.
Janovitz, Marilyn, illus. see Meister, Cari & Stone Arch Books Staff.
Janovitz, Marilyn, illus. see Meister, Cari.
Janovitz, Marilyn, illus. see Rabe, Tish.
Janow, Jody. Eddie's Great Escape. (p. 503)
Janowski, Alice. Adventures of Inka the Feline. Smith, Jerry, illus. (p. 19)
Janowski, Alice & Boyer, Colleen McKinnon. Dakota & the Magical Gardens. (p. 401)
Janry. Spirou & Fantasio Vol. 4: Valley of the Exiles. (p. 1629)
Janry, illus. see Tome.
Jansdotter, Lotta. Simple Sewing: Patterns & How-To for 24 Fresh & Easy Projects. Jansdotter, Lotta, illus. (p. 1578)
Jansen, Adrienne, ed. Curioseum: Collected Stories of the Odd & Marvellous. Laing, Sarah, illus. (p. 392)
Jansen, Alex, ed. see Gilmore, Jason & Peterson, Paul.
Jansen, Curt, et al. Badger & Her Babies. (p. 132)
—Bobcat & Her Babies. (p. 206)
Jansen, Hanna. Over a Thousand Hills I Walk with You. Crawford, Elizabeth D., tr. from GER. (p. 1313)
Jansen, Karen. Coming of an Astronaut. (p. 348)
—Mardi Gras in New Orleans: An Alphabet Book. (p. 1092)
Jansen, Patty. Far Horizon. (p. 572)
Jansen Van Rensburg, Bianca. When Tomorrow Doesn't Come. (p. 1905)
Janski, Beverly. Little Birdie Told Me. (p. 1024)
Janson, Klaus, illus. see Mack, David.
Janson, Klaus, illus. see Mackie, Howard & Kavanagh, Terry.
Janson, Marilyn June. Tommy Jenkins: First Teleported Kid: A Fearless Series Book. (p. 1765)
Janssen, Ian. Perils of Pierre Book 1, Gold Fever. (p. 1343)
—Perils of Pierre Book 2, Hunger Rules. (p. 1343)
Janssen, Mark, illus. see Rieu, Jean-Philippe.
Janssen, Mark, jt. auth. see Rieu, Jean-Philippe.
Janssen, Patricia E., ed. see Benton, James.
Janssen, Patricia E., ed. see Lersch, Jean.
Janssen, Patricia E., ed. see Minges, Barbara.
Janssen, Patricia E., ed. see Wehrheim, Carol.
Janssen, Robert B. & Tessen, Daryl D. Birds of Minnesota & Wisconsin. (p. 191)
Janssen, Sarah. World Almanac for Kids 2014. (p. 1953)
Janssen, Sarah, ed. see World Almanac Editors.
Janssen, Sarah, ed. see World Almanac Staff.
Janssen-Mathes, Mieke M. E. Unlocking the Secret of Otherland: A Story & Activity Book for Children Living Abroad. Kwakkenbos, Frans, illus. (p. 1821)
Jansson, Alexander, illus. see Bachmann, Stefan, et al.
Jansson, Alexander, illus. see Wexler, Django.
Jansson, Kristin, jt. auth. see Freshman, Wendy.
Jansson, Lars, jt. auth. see Jansson, Tove.
Jansson, Tove. Book about Moomin, Mymble & Little My. Hannah, Sophie, tr. from SWE. (p. 210)
—Comet in Moominland. Portch, Elizabeth, tr. (p. 348)
—Finn Family Moomintroll. (p. 589)
—Finn Family Moomintroll. Portch, Elizabeth, tr. from SWE. (p. 589)
—Lift-the-Flap Hide & Seek. (p. 1014)
—Moomin & the Birthday Button. Jansson, Tove, illus. (p. 1171)
—Moomin & the Golden Tail. (p. 1171)
—Moomin & the Martians. (p. 1171)
—Moomin & the Sea. (p. 1171)
—Moomin Builds a House. (p. 1171)
—Moomin Falls in Love. (p. 1171)
—Moomin on the Riviera. (p. 1171)
—Moominland Midwinter. Warburton, Thomas, tr. (p. 1171)
—Moominpappa at Sea. Hart, Kingsley, tr. (p. 1171)
—Moominpappa's Memoirs. Warburton, Thomas, tr. (p. 1171)
—Moomin's Desert Island. (p. 1171)
—Moomin's Little Book of Numbers. (p. 1171)
—Moomin's Little Book of Words. (p. 1171)
—Moomin's Winter Follies. (p. 1171)
—Moominsummer Madness. Warburton, Thomas, tr. (p. 1171)
—Moominvalley in November. Hart, Kingsley, tr. (p. 1171)
—Moominvalley Turns Jungle. (p. 1171)
—Tales from Moominvalley. Warburton, Thomas, tr. (p. 1701)
Jansson, Tove & Jansson, Lars. Moomin & the Comet. (p. 1171)
Jantner, Janos. Drawing Fantasy Monsters. (p. 481)
—Drawing Horror-Movie Monsters. (p. 482)
—Drawing Monsters from Great Books. (p. 482)
—Drawing Mythological Monsters. (p. 482)
—Drawing Science-Fiction Monsters. (p. 482)
—Drawing Unexplained-Mystery Monsters. (p. 482)
Jantzen, Dot. 1 Little, 2 Little, 3 Little Orphans. (p. 1991)
Jantzen, Doug. Henry Hyena, Why Won't You Laugh? Claude, Jean, illus. (p. 768)
January, Brendan. Aftermath of the Wars Against the Barbary Pirates. (p. 29)
—Air Force One. (p. 31)
—Arab Conquests of the Middle East. (p. 94)
—Fidel Castro: Cuban Revolutionary. (p. 583)
—Genocide: Modern Crimes Against Humanity. (p. 661)
—Gettysburg: July 1-3 1863. (p. 670)
—Information Insecurity: Privacy under Siege. (p. 874)
—Iranian Revolution. (p. 886)
—Leonardo Da Vinci: Renaissance Painter. (p. 992)
—Leonardo Da Vinci. (p. 992)
—Little Bighorn: June 25, 1876. (p. 1024)
—Louis Armstrong. (p. 1058)
—Ludwig Van Beethoven: Musical Genius. (p. 1064)
January, Brendan & Seidman, David. Jimmy Carter: Peacemaker & President. (p. 918)
January, Rick. Come Out to the Garden. January, Stella, illus. (p. 347)
January, Rick & January, Stella. Come Out to the Garden. (p. 347)
January, Stella, illus. see January, Rick.
January, Stella, jt. auth. see January, Rick.
Janus, jt. auth. see Fearon Staff.
Janus Kahn, Katherine, illus. see Rouss, Sylvia.
Janus Kahn, Katherine, jt. auth. see Rouss, Sylvia A.
Janveau, Teri-Lynn & Thompson, Allister. Sailing for Glory: The Story of Captain Angus Walters & the Bluenose. Thompson, Samantha, illus. (p. 1503)
Janvier Gibeau, Claire. Discoveries. (p. 448)
—Here Comes Grandpa Now. (p. 770)
—My Favorite Animal. (p. 1203)
Jappa, Anthony W., creator. Anthony Jappa's Xigatu Warriors (p. 89)
Jaques, Jon. Two-Tone Frog. Hall, Norris, illus. (p. 1804)
Jaques, Laura, illus. see Fields, Terri.
Jaques-Plester, Carol. Grandma Goes to Heaven. (p. 708)
Jaquith, A., jt. auth. see Jaquith, A.
Jaquith, A. & Jaquith, A. Bee in the Yellow Jacket. Jaquith, A., illus. (p. 157)
Jara, Fatima de la, see de la Jara, Fatima.
Jara, Jose, illus. see Villasenor, Victor.
Jaraiz, David, illus. see Friden, Chris & Rodriguez Braojos, Alberto.
Jaramillo, Ann. Linea. (p. 1019)
Jaramillo, Gloria. Busy Kids' Colors, Shapes & Sizes. Poirier, Nadine, illus. (p. 246)
Jaramillo, J.C. Best Buggies (p. 168)
Jaramillo, Raquel, illus. see Barrie, J. M.
Jaramillo, Raquel, illus. see Clements, Andrew.
Jaramillo, Raquel, photos by see Barrie, J. M.
jarbeaux, tl. UpHill Skis. (p. 1825)
Jarboe, Tracy & Sadler, Stefani. Cut, Paste & Write ABC Activity Pages: 26 Lessons That Use Art & Alliterative Poetry to Build Phonemic Awareness, Teach Letter Sounds, & Help Children Really Learn the Alphabet. (p. 396)
Jardine, Alan. Sloop John B: A Pirate's Tale. Pickering, Jimmy, illus. (p. 1591)
Jardine, Ashley, jt. auth. see Jardine, Kathy.
Jardine, David, illus. see Sherrard, Valerie.
Jardine, Kathy & Jardine, Ashley. Durples: Go to School. (p. 490)
Jardy, Adam & Pecsenye, Jessica. Ohio State University College Prowler off the Record. (p. 1282)
Jareaux, Marlena. 26 Things to Teach Your Parents. (p. 1996)
Jared, Hodges. Peach Fuzz (p. 1332)
Jarek, Janice. Dominic & the Sandcastle. (p. 465)
—Emma & Her Angels. (p. 519)
—Mya & the Mermaid. (p. 1222)
Jarkins, Sheila. Adv Marco Flamingo Under Sea. Jarkins, Sheila, illus. (p. 13)
—Adventures of Marco Flamingo in the Jungle. Jarkins, Sheila, illus. (p. 20)
—Marco Flamenco. de la Vega, Eida, tr. (p. 1092)
—Marco Flamingo Under the Sea. (p. 1092)
—Marco Flamingo Under the Sea/ Las Aventuras Submarinas de Marco Flamenco. (p. 1092)
—Marco Flamingo under the Sea/Las Aventuras Submarinas de Marco Flamenco. (p. 1092)
—Marco Flamingo/Marco Flamenco. de la Vega, Eida, tr. (p. 1092)
Jarkins, Sheila, illus. see Gabbert, Rosalie M.
Jarman, Benjamin. Tony's Last Touchdown. (p. 1766)
Jarman, Brandy S., illus. see Hooley, Rachelle B. & Butler, Mackay M.
Jarman, Colin M. Science Museum Book of Sport. (p. 1526)
Jarman, Julia. Ants in Your Pants! Parker-Rees, Guy, illus. (p. 90)
—Best Kiss. Waters, Erica-Jane, illus. (p. 170)
—Big Blue Train. Reynolds, Adrian, illus. (p. 178)
—Class Three at Sea. Chapman, Lynne, illus. (p. 327)
—Class Two at the Zoo. Chapman, Lynne, illus. (p. 327)
—Friend in Need! Pankhurst, Kate, illus. (p. 637)
—Ghost Writer. (p. 672)
—Hangman. (p. 742)
—Harry the Clever Spider at School. Fowkes, Charlie, illus. (p. 751)
—Little Bad Riding Hood. (p. 1023)
—Lovely Old Lion. Varley, Susan, illus. (p. 1061)
—Magic Backpack. Gon, Adriano, illus. (p. 1071)
—Make Friends - Break Friends. Pankhurst, Kate, illus. (p. 1079)
—Molly & the Giant. Sholto, Walker, illus. (p. 1160)
—New Friend Old Friends. Pankhurst, Kate, illus. (p. 1244)
—Stowaway? Oldroyd, Mark, illus. (p. 1664)
—Time-Travelling Cat & the Aztec Sacrifice. (p. 1753)
—Time-Travelling Cat & the Egyptian Goddess. (p. 1753)
—Time-Travelling Cat & the Great Victorian Stink. (p. 1753)
—Time-Travelling Cat & the Roman Eagle. (p. 1753)
—Time-Travelling Cat & the Tudor Treasure. (p. 1753)
—Time-Travelling Cat & the Viking Terror. (p. 1753)
—Two Shy Pandas. Varley, Susan, illus. (p. 1804)
Jarmes, Jon Jeffery. Jason Post: Magic at the Downs. (p. 910)
Jarnicki, Harold. No Boring Practice, Please! Parts of Speech: Reproducible Practice Pages Plus Easy-to-Score Quizzes That Reinforce the Correct Use of Nouns, Verbs, Adjectives, Adverbs, & More. (p. 1257)
Jarnot, Lisa. Ring of Fire. (p. 1473)
Jarnow, Jesse. Adventures of Huckleberry Finn & Race in America. (p. 18)
—Davy Crockett: Frontier Hero / Defensor de la Frontera. (p. 411)
—Davy Crockett: Defensor de la frontera (Davy Crockett: Frontier Hero) (p. 411)
—Johnny Bench. (p. 923)
—Manifest Destiny: A Primary Source History of the Settlement of the American Heartland in the Late 19th Century. (p. 1087)
—Oil, Steel, & Railroads: America's Big Businesses in the Late 1800s. (p. 1282)
—Patrick Henry's Liberty or Death Speech: A Primary Source Investigation. (p. 1329)
—Phillis Wheatley. (p. 1350)
—Phillis Wheatley: African American Poet / Poeta Afroamericana. (p. 1351)
—Phillis Wheatley: Poeta afroamericana (Phillis Wheatley: African American Poet) (p. 1351)
—Socialism: A Primary Source Analysis. (p. 1605)
—Telegraph & Telephone Networks: Groundbreaking Developments in American Communications. (p. 1716)
—Telegraph & Telephone Networks: Ground Breaking Developments in American Communications. (p. 1716)
Jarnow, Jill. Writing to Instruct. (p. 1965)
Jarocki, Martin. Daily Zoo. (p. 400)
Jaroszko, Mike. Away in a Manger. (p. 120)
—Away in a Manger Devotional. (p. 120)
Jarratt, Laura. By Any Other Name. (p. 249)
—Skin Deep. (p. 1585)
Jarrell, Jane & Saathoff, Deborah. Address: Planet Earth. (p. 12)
—Number Wonder. (p. 1271)
—Off to Work We Go. (p. 1279)
Jarrell, Katherine. Shape Shakedown: The Case of the Missing Triangles. (p. 1560)
Jarrell, Pamela R. Caillou Finds a Caterpillar. Storch, Ellen N., illus. (p. 251)
—Caillou's Family & Friends. Meier, Kerry L., illus. (p. 251)
—Flitter, Flutter Butterfly. Middleton, Mikell, illus. (p. 605)
—Nice Cool Drink. Teeple, Jackie, illus. (p. 1250)
—Planting a Seed. Meier, Kerry L., illus. (p. 1369)
—Time for Bed. Coillen, Lisa P., illus. (p. 1751)
—Tod Squad Can Pretend. (p. 1760)
—Who Is in the Backyard? Crowell, Knox, illus. (p. 1916)
Jarrell, Pamela R., jt. auth. see Muench-Williams, Heather.
Jarrell, Randal C., ed. see Loux, Matthew.
Jarrell, Randall. Gingerbread Rabbit. Williams, Garth, illus. (p. 677)
Jarrell, Randall, tr. see Bechstein, Ludwig.
Jarrell, Randall, tr. see Segal, Lore, et al.
Jarrell, Robert. Sunday Afternoon Walk. (p. 1676)
Jarrett, Judy, illus. see Ramshaw, Gail.
Jarrett, Clare. Dancing Maddy. (p. 403)
Jarrett, Judy. Billy the Kid. (p. 187)
Jarrett, Judy, jt. auth. see Musleah, Rahel.
Jarrett, Mark. Mastering New York's Elementary Social Studies Standards: Grade 5. (p. 1103)
Jarrett, Michael, illus. see Williams, Rozanne Lanczak.
Jarrett, Michael, photos by see Burch, Regina G. & Donovan Guntly, Jenette.
Jarrett, Michael, photos by see Williams, Rozanne Lanczak.
Jarrett, Sandra, illus. see Neal, Sharon, ed.
Jarrow, Gail. Amazing Harry Kellar: Great American Magician. (p. 54)
—Fatal Fever: Tracking down Typhoid Mary. (p. 577)
—Lincoln's Flying Spies: Thaddeus Lowe & the Civil War Balloon Corps. (p. 1019)
—Red Madness: How a Medical Mystery Changed What We Eat. (p. 1454)
—Robert H. Jackson: New Deal Lawyer, Supreme Court Justice, Nuremberg Prosecutor. (p. 1479)
Jars, David La, see La Jars, David.
Jarski, Rosemarie. How to Be a Celebrity. (p. 814)
Jarvie, Gordon. Clans. (p. 326)
Jarvie, Gordon, ed. Irish Folk & Fairy Tales. (p. 887)
Jarvis. Lazy Dave. Jarvis, illus. (p. 981)
Jarvis, illus. see Marchesani, Laura & Medina, Zenaides A., Jr.
Jarvis, Alan, jt. auth. see Beavon, Rod.
Jarvis, Alan, jt. auth. see Chapman, Brian.
Jarvis, Ana. Aventuras Literarias. (p. 119)
Jarvis, Ana C. Basic Spanish. (p. 142)
—Como Se Dice... ? (p. 351)
—Spanish for Business & Finance. (p. 1621)
Jarvis, Ana C. & Lebredo, Raquel. Spanish for Medical Personnel. (p. 1621)
Jarvis, Cathy. Red Beard Santa's Biker Buddy. (p. 1453)
Jarvis, Daniel W. Revolution: A New Order Is Rising. (p. 1466)

Full bibliographic information is available on the Title Index page number referenced in parentheses at the end of each entry

Jarvis, James & Waterman, Russell. Vortigern's Machine: And the Great Sage of Wisdom. Jarvis, James, illus. (p. 1850)
Jarvis, Kay, jt. auth. see Burnett, Garry.
Jarvis, Kellah. Miss Kathy Sailon. (p. 1151)
Jarvis, Mary Rowles. Dick Lionheart. (p. 435)
Jarvis, Matt Russell, et al. Angles on Psychology. (p. 75)
Jarvis, Robin. Dancing Jax. (p. 403)
—Dark Waters of Hagwood. (p. 408)
—Fighting Pax. (p. 586)
—Freax & Rejex. (p. 632)
—Thorn Ogres of Hagwood. (p. 1740)
Jarvis, Rowles Mary. Dick Lionheart. (p. 435)
Jarvis, Sharon Downing, ed. see Heward, L. Richard.
Jarwin. Love in the Springtime. (p. 1059)
Jarzab, Anna. All Unquiet Things. (p. 46)
—Opposite of Hallelujah. (p. 1300)
—Tandem. (p. 1705)
Jarzabek, Ela, illus. see Mitter, Matt.
Jasheway, Leigh Anne. 101 Comedy Games for Children & Grown-Ups. (p. 1999)
Jasinski, Aaron, illus. see Curry, Don L.
Jasinski, Aaron, illus. see Kimmel, Eric A.
Jasinski, Diane, jt. auth. see Fetty, Margaret.
Jasinski, Diane, jt. ed. see Fetty, Margaret.
Jaske, Kat. For Honor: An Adventure of What Might Have Been: Book One of by Honor Bound. (p. 615)
Jaskiel, Stan, illus. see Capone, Deb.
Jaskiel, Stan, illus. see Lewis, Michael.
Jaskiewicz, A. E. Hickory & the Big Clock. (p. 775)
Jaskol, Julie & Lewis, Brian. City of Angels: In & Around Los Angeles. Kleven, Elisa, illus. (p. 323)
Jaskolka, Anna. Teen Dreams & What They Mean. (p. 1713)
Jaskulka, Marie. Lost Marble Notebook of Forgotten Girl & Random Boy. (p. 1056)
Jaskwhich, Cynthia Sheperd. Mema Says Good-Bye. Mazibuko, Luthando, illus. (p. 1125)
Jasmin, Lynn, illus. see Handelsman, Valerie.
Jasmine, Jean-Pierre. It's Raining Uber. (p. 898)
Jasner, Andy. Baltimore Ravens. (p. 135)
—Buffalo Bills. (p. 235)
Jasnoch, Dorothy. Adventure of Little Mouse Maggie. Kern, Kimberly, ed. (p. 14)
—Adventures of Oskar: Oskar's New School. Korzeniowski, Samson O., ed. (p. 21)
—Frankie the Bunny: Woodland Warning. Korzeniowski, Samson, ed. (p. 630)
—Frankie the Bunny: Newfound Friends. Korzeniowski, Samson O., ed. (p. 630)
—Frankie the Bunny: Woodland Warning. Korzeniowski, Samson O., ed. (p. 630)
—Frankie the Bunny: Helping the Birds. Korzeniowski, Samson O., ed. (p. 630)
—Frankie the Bunny: Wheels of Fortune. Korzeniowski, Samson O., ed. (p. 630)
—Frankie the Bunny: Mystery in the Forest. Korzeniowski, Samson O., ed. (p. 630)
—Frankie the Bunny: The Fall Scramble Begins. Korzeniowski, Samson O., ed. (p. 630)
—Frankie the Bunny Helping the Birds. Korzeniowski, Samson, ed. (p. 630)
—Frankie the Bunny the Fall Scramble Begins. Korzeniowski, Samson, ed. (p. 630)
Jasnoch, Dorothy, illus. see Saldivar, Jose A.
Jason. Jason & Edeia. (p. 910)
Jason Burkhardt, Sara Kendall and. Backdoor Trio: Which Way Did They Go. (p. 130)
Jason, Daniel, jt. auth. see Texas Golden Retriever, Casanova.
Jasper, Elizabeth. Golden Cuckoo. (p. 694)
Jasper, J. J. When I Grow Up. Bullock, Brad, illus. (p. 1902)
Jasper, Mark. Good Night Charleston. Kelly, Cooper, illus. (p. 699)
—Good Night Florida Keys. Rosen, Anne, illus. (p. 699)
—Good Night Israel. Rosen, Anne, illus. (p. 699)
Jasper, Mark, illus. see Gamble, Adam.
Jasper, Mark, illus. see Gamble, Jasper, et al.
Jasper, Mark, jt. auth. see Gamble, Adam.
Jasper, Mark & Gamble, Adam. Good Night Galaxy. Kelly, Cooper, illus. (p. 699)
Jasper, Mark & Kelly, Cooper. Good Night Ocean. Veno, Joe & Kelly, Cooper, illus. (p. 700)
Jasper, Rick & Reece, Richard. Catch. (p. 278)
—Late Bus. (p. 979)
—Out of Control. (p. 1311)
—Skin. (p. 1585)
—Thaw. (p. 1728)
Jasspon, Ethel Reed. Ritual & Dramatized Folkways. (p. 1475)
Jastrzebski, Brandy, illus. see Reimiller, Diane L.
Jastrzebski, Brandy, illus. see Reimiller, Diane.
Jastrzembski, Joseph C. Apache Wars: The Final Resistance. (p. 91)
Jastrzembski, Joseph C. & Rosier, Paul C. Apache. (p. 91)
Jasuna, Aija, illus. see Corwin, Katherine.
Jasuna, Aija, illus. see Lovascio, Jane.
Jasuna, Aija, illus. see Oltchick, Peter.
Jasuna, Aija, illus. see Sauers, Charlotte.
Jasuna, Aija, illus. see Sax, Anita.
Jatkowska, Ag. Christmas Treasure Hunt. (p. 316)
Jatkowska, Ag, illus. see Ghigna, Charles.
Jatkowska, Ag, illus. see Loewen, Nancy & Speed Shaskan, Trisha.
Jatkowska, Ag, illus. see Marley, Ziggy.
Jatkowska, Ag, illus. see Marshall, Linda Elovitz.
Jatkowska, Ag, illus. see Newman, Lesléa.
Jatkowska, Ag, illus. see Wiley, Melissa.
Jaunn, Adele, illus. see Morgan, Sally.
Jaunn, Adele, illus. see Walters, Celeste.
Jauregui, Diego. Libros de Arte para Ninos: Diego Rivera. (p. 1007)
Jauregui, Patricia. Sentimientos. Jauregui, Reginald, ed. (p. 1551)
Jauregui, Reginald, ed. see Jauregui, Patricia.
Jaurequi, Leticia, tr. see Paddock, Susan Star.
Jauss, Anne Marie, illus. see Frisch, Wilhelmine.
Jauss, Anne Marie, illus. see Myers, Byrona.
Javaherbin, Mina. Goal! Ford, A. G., illus. (p. 687)
—Soccer Star. Alarcao, Renato, illus. (p. 1603)
Javaloyes, Inigo & Iñigo, Javaloyes. Tortuga Numero Cien. Gonzalez, Tesa, illus. (p. 1771)
Javernick, Ellen. Birthday Pet O'Malley, Kevin, illus. (p. 193)
—What If Everybody Did That? Madden, Colleen M., illus. (p. 1887)
Javier, Emmanuel Xerx, illus. see Glenn, Avery, et al.
Javins, Marie. Marvel's Guardians of the Galaxy: The Art of the Movie Slipcase. (p. 1099)
Javins, Marie, jt. auth. see Chronicle Books Staff.
Javna, John, et al. New 50 Simple Things Kids Can Do to Save the Earth. Montez, Michele & Bodger, Lorraine, illus. (p. 1243)
Jawa, Sadhvi, illus. see Viswanath, Shobha.
Jaworowicz, Grace. Chelsea's Cheerleading Squad: Add Within 20. (p. 297)
Jaworski, Sabrina K. & Chehoski, Robert. Skin Care. (p. 1585)
Jaworski, Sarah. Gabe's Garden Food Chain. (p. 652)
Jax, T. L. Fraidy-Frieda's Light Show. Jax, T. L., illus. (p. 627)
Jaxartes, Alaric. Tattered Flags. (p. 1707)
Jaxland, Sheila. Mylo. (p. 1222)
Jay, Alison. 1 2 3: A Child's First Counting Book. (p. 1990)
—1 2 3 a Child's First Counting Book. (p. 1990)
—ABC: A Child's First Alphabet Book. Jay, Alison, illus. (p. 3)
—Alice's Adventures in Wonderland Board Book. (p. 40)
—Red, Green, Blue: A First Book of Colors. (p. 1454)
—Welcome to the Zoo! (p. 1874)
Jay, Alison, illus. see Barefoot Books Staff.
Jay, Alison, illus. see Catchpool, Michael.
Jay, Alison, illus. see Curtis, Carolyn, et al.
Jay, Alison, illus. see Curtis, Carolyn.
Jay, Alison, illus. see Gershator, Phillis.
Jay, Alison, illus. see Harris, Annmarie.
Jay, Alison, illus. see Lawler, Janet.
Jay, Alison, illus. see Lodding, Linda Ravin.
Jay, Alison, illus. see Rock, Lois.
Jay, Alison & Curtis, Carolyn. I Took the Moon for a Walk. (p. 847)
Jay, Alison & Gershator, Phillis. Listen, Listen. (p. 1022)
Jay, Asher. Thirteen Reasons Why. (p. 1735)
Jay, Aye. Punk Rock Fun Time Activity Book. (p. 1417)
Jay, Basil. Adventures of Twig. (p. 24)
Jay, Caroline. Seeds of Hope Bereavement & Loss Activity Book: Helping Children & Young People Cope with Change Through Nature. Dale, Unity-Joy, illus. (p. 1548)
Jay, Caroline & Thomas, Jenni. What Does Dead Mean? A Book for Young Children to Help Explain Death & Dying. Dale, Unity-Joy, illus. (p. 1884)
Jay, Eli. Poppy & the Fat Puppy. (p. 1385)
—Poppy & the Stranger. (p. 1385)
—Poppy, the Wandering Balloon. (p. 1385)
Jay, Em. Once. (p. 1292)
Jay, Eric. Jug-a-Ro-Mack-a-la-Lulu-e-Quack-a-la-Lulu-e-Zack-a-la-Lulu-O-Pippin & the Bullies of Badgersville. Kuang, Miao, illus. (p. 931)
Jay, Erwin. How to Take Back Control of the Seven Most Important Areas of Your Life. (p. 822)
Jay, Gina & Beattie, Julie. Hope the Hip Hippo. Turner, Cherie, illus. (p. 796)
Jay, Hilda L., jt. auth. see Jay, M. Ellen.
Jay, Joshua. Big Magic for Little Hands: 25 Astounding Tricks for Young Magicians. (p. 182)
Jay, Larsen. What If Cows Could...? (p. 1887)
Jay, Leisten, illus. see Marz, Ron.
Jay, Lorraine A. Sea Turtle Journey: The Story of a Loggerhead Turtle. Lee, Katie, illus. (p. 1535)
Jay, M. Ellen & Jay, Hilda L. Teaching with Computers: Strategies That Work in Grades K-6. (p. 1710)
Jay, Natasha. Avril Lavigne: She's Complicated (p. 120)
Jay, Pamela. Little Jaybird & the Prince of Light. (p. 1029)
Jay, Ruth Johnson. Mary Slessor: Missionary to Calabar. (p. 1101)
Jay, Samuel. Shadow of Guilt. (p. 1557)
Jay, Stacey. Juliet Immortal. (p. 932)
—Of Beast & Beauty. (p. 1279)
—Princess of Thorns. (p. 1405)
—Romeo Redeemed. (p. 1486)
—Valentine's Day of the Undead: Megan Berry, Book 2 And 1/3. (p. 1830)
Jayasuriya, Michael. Time MacHine. (p. 1752)
Jayne, Ann M. Kory's Jungle. (p. 967)
Jayne, Hannah. Dare. (p. 406)
—Escape. (p. 534)
—Truly, Madly, Deadly. (p. 1793)
Jayne, Mitch. Forest in the Wind. (p. 618)
Jayne, Waring -, jt. auth. see Waring, Richard.
Jaynie R. Wood, M. s. & Jo Berkus. Going to the Hospital What Will I See? And Who are Those People Wearing Funny Clothes? (p. 693)
Jaysree. Drama. (p. 480)
Jaz. Lost Lake: An Adventure for Kids of All Ages. (p. 1056)
Jazvic, Beryl, illus. see Hall, Rose.
Jazwierska, Jennifer & Popiel, Candice Bataille. Discovery of Glow. (p. 450)
Jazynka, Kitson. Mission: Wolf Rescue. (p. 1153)
—Nate's Story Orback, Craig, illus. (p. 1231)
—National Geographic Kids Mission: Tiger Rescue: All about Tigers & How to Save Them. (p. 1232)
—National Geographic Kids Mission: Wolf Rescue: All about Wolves & How to Save Them. Raven-Ellison, Daniel, ed. (p. 1232)
—National Geographic Readers: Martin Luther King, Jr. (p. 1233)
—National Geographic Readers: Rosa Parks. (p. 1233)
—Sacagawea. (p. 1500)
Jazynka, Kitson & Tripp, Valerie. Boys Camp: Zee's Story. Orback, Craig, illus. (p. 220)
Jazz. Gizmo & Scatz: A Tail of Friendship. (p. 681)
JBible Visuals International, compiled by. God's Discipline: Old Testament. Vol. 13 (p. 691)
Jean. Jean's Story. (p. 911)
Jean, April. Little Dachshund's Tale. Cross, Kevin, illus. (p. 1026)
Jean, David, illus. see Bouchard, David.
Jean, Emiko. We'll Never Be Apart. (p. 1874)
Jean Emily Myers, jt. auth. see Jean Emily Myers, Emily Myers.
Jean Emily Myers, Emily Myers & Jean Emily Myers. Mickey's Mini Farm. Tanner Voyles, illus. (p. 1136)
Jean, Grama. Timothy & Tabitha's Adventure down the Pathway, Thru the Forest: Grama Jean's Story Time Coloring Book. (p. 1755)
Jean, Heather. Secret of the Golden Pyramid. (p. 1542)
Jean, James, jt. auth. see Willingham, Bill.
Jean, Linda. Izzy's Summer: A Novel. (p. 901)
Jean Marie. Me, My Peeps & My Manners. (p. 1116)
Jean, Penny. Holding Grace. (p. 788)
Jean, S. L., illus. see Pierce, Darlene.
Jean, Texier, illus. see Joe, O'Brien.
Jeanba, Malahkee. Makeda Goes to the Beach. (p. 1080)
Jean-Baptiste, Marie V. Goodnight & Seeyoutomorrow. (p. 701)
Jeanes, William, jt. auth. see Hughes, Charlie.
Jeanette, Canyon, illus. see Marianne, Berkes.
Jeanfield. Twinkle, a Christmas Story. (p. 1802)
Jeanmarie, Michele. Curiosity, Curiosity: Lost in an Array. (p. 392)
Jeanne, Arnold, illus. see Jan, Romero Stevens.
Jeanne, Diana. Nathalie's Socks. Rose, Nathalie, illus. (p. 1231)
Jeanne, DuPrau. City of Ember. (p. 323)
Jeanne Grieser & Pearson, Mary Rose. Worship Bulletins for Kids: Fall & Winter. (p. 1961)
—Worship Bulletins for Kids: Spring & Summer. (p. 1961)
Jeanne, Miss, illus. see Weeks, Timothy.
Jeanne Taylor Thomas Illustrator: Pr. Austin & Harlow's First Adventure. Hardy, Pris, illus. (p. 116)
Jeannine & Egan, Jennifer. Jack the Brave Conquers the Snow. (p. 903)
Jeannotte, Lawrence, illus. see Utsler, Elaine.
Jean-P, Tibbles, illus. see Alison, Hart.
Jeans, Marcia. Creating Smart Board Lessons - Yes, You Can! Easy Step-by-Step Directions for Using Smart Notebook Software to Develop Powerful, Interactive Lessons That Motivate All Students. (p. 379)
Jeanty, Georges, illus. see Espenson, Jane, et al.
Jeanty, Georges, illus. see Goddard, Drew, et al.
Jeanty, Georges, illus. see Tieri, Frank.
Jeanty, Georges, et al. Core Allie, Scott & Hahn, Sierra, eds. (p. 367)
Jeanty, Richard. Meeting Ms. Right. (p. 1123)
Jeapes, Ben. His Majesty's Starship. (p. 781)
Jeb. Destinations in Time. (p. 430)
Jebb, R. C., tr. see Sophocles.
Jebiwool Art Museum Staff. Destination Blackbeard: Destinations in Time, Book 2 (p. 430)
Jecan, Gavriel, illus. see Helman, Andrea.
Jecan, Gavriel, photos by see Helman, Andrea.
Jecan, Gavriel, photos by see Vanasse, Deb.
Jedele, Christie, illus. see Klippenstein, Blaine.
Jedicke, Peter. Cosmology: Exploring the Universe. (p. 368)
—Exploring the Ocean Depths. (p. 554)
—Gravity, & How It Works. (p. 712)
—Great Inventions of the 20th Century. (p. 716)
—Great Moments in Space Exploration. (p. 717)
—Seti: The Search for Alien Intelligence. (p. 1554)
Jednik, Alice. What Does It Look Like? (p. 1884)
Jedson, Lee. Treaty of Paris 1783: A Primary Source Examination of the Treaty That Recognized American Independence. (p. 1783)
Jee-Hyung, Lee. Demon Diary Lim, Kara, illus. (p. 426)
Jeep, Elizabeth McMahon. Blessings & Prayers through the Year: A Resource for School & Parish. (p. 199)
—Children's Daily Prayer 2005 - 2006. (p. 303)
Jeetze, Hartmut von. Creative Steps in the Development of the Social Dimensions of Agriculture. (p. 380)
Jeeva Raghunath & Nayar, Deeya. Malli. Nancy Raj, illus. (p. 1083)
Jeevan, Dhamindra, illus. see Cutting, Robert.
Jeff Albrecht Studios Staff, illus. see Moberg, Julia.
Jeff, Brown. Flat Stanley - His Original Adventure! (p. 603)
Jeff, Marsh, illus. see O'Ryan, Ellie.
Jeff, Youngquist, ed. see Byrne, John A.
Jefferies, Cindy. Reach for the Stars. (p. 1442)
—Tara's Triumph. (p. 1706)
Jefferies, Marc John. Volcano. (p. 1848)
Jefferis. Racing Cars 6-Pack. (p. 1432)
Jefferis, David. Black Holes: And Other Bizarre Space Objects. (p. 196)
—Earth: Our Home Planet. (p. 495)
—Extreme Structures: Mega-Constructions of the 21st Century. (p. 557)
—Galaxies: Immense Star Islands. (p. 653)
—Gas Giants: Huge Far off Worlds. (p. 657)
—Green Power: Eco-Energy Without Pollution. (p. 722)
—Hot Planets: Mercury & Venus. (p. 802)
—Ice Dwarfs: Pluto & Beyond. (p. 850)
—Mars: Distant Red Planet. (p. 1096)
—Micro Machines: Ultra-Small World of Nanotechnology. (p. 1136)
—Mighty Megaplanets: Jupiter & Saturn. (p. 1140)
—Moon: Earth's Neighbor. (p. 1171)
—Planes. (p. 1367)
—Race Cars. (p. 1430)
—Robot Brains. (p. 1480)
—Robot Voyagers. (p. 1480)
—Robot Warriors. (p. 1480)
—Robot Workers. (p. 1480)
—Space Probes: Exploring Beyond Earth. (p. 1619)
—Star Spotters: Telescopes & Observatories. (p. 1641)
—Stars: Glowing Spheres in the Sky. (p. 1643)
—Sun: Our Local Star. (p. 1675)
Jefferis, David & Irvine, Mat. Exploring Planet Mars. (p. 553)
—Flight into Orbit. (p. 604)
—Race into Space. (p. 1431)
—Return to the Moon. (p. 1465)
Jeffers, Dawn. Beautiful Moon. Leick, Bonnie, illus. (p. 153)
—Beautiful Moon/Bella Luna. Del Risco, Eida, tr. (p. 153)
—Vegetable Dreams/Huerto Sonado. de La Vega, Eida, tr. (p. 1834)
Jeffers, Karen. Tosh. (p. 1771)
Jeffers, Oliver. Cómo Atrapar una Estrella. Lujan, Jorge, tr. (p. 350)
—Great Paper Caper. Jeffers, Oliver, illus. (p. 717)
—Heart & the Bottle. Jeffers, Oliver, illus. (p. 759)
—How to Catch a Star. Jeffers, Oliver, illus. (p. 815)
—Incredible Book Eating Boy. Jeffers, Oliver, illus. (p. 869)
—Increíble Niño Comelibros. (p. 870)
—It Wasn't Me. Jeffers, Oliver, illus. (p. 894)
—Lost & Found. Jeffers, Oliver, illus. (p. 1054)
—New Sweater: The Hueys, Book 1. Jeffers, Oliver, illus. (p. 1247)
—New Sweater. Jeffers, Oliver, illus. (p. 1247)
—None the Number: A Hueys Book. Jeffers, Oliver, illus. (p. 1263)
—None the Number. Jeffers, Oliver, illus. (p. 1263)
—Once upon an Alphabet: Short Stories for All the Letters. Jeffers, Oliver, illus. (p. 1293)
—Perdido y Encontrado. (p. 1341)
—Stuck. Jeffers, Oliver, illus. (p. 1668)
—This Moose Belongs to Me. Jeffers, Oliver, illus. (p. 1737)
—Up & Down. Jeffers, Oliver, illus. (p. 1824)
—Way Back Home. Jeffers, Oliver, illus. (p. 1864)
Jeffers, Oliver, illus. see Almond, David.
Jeffers, Oliver, illus. see Boyne, John.
Jeffers, Oliver, illus. see Colfer, Eoin.
Jeffers, Oliver, illus. see Daywalt, Drew.
Jeffers, Stewart. Collapse of the Crew. (p. 339)
Jeffers, Sunni. Eyes on the Prize. (p. 558)
Jeffers, Susan. Hansel & Gretel. (p. 743)
—My Pony. Jeffers, Susan, illus. (p. 1217)
—Nutcracker. Jeffers, Susan, illus. (p. 1274)
—Twelve Days of Christmas. (p. 1800)
—Twelve Days of Christmas. Jeffers, Susan, illus. (p. 1800)
Jeffers, Susan, illus. see Ehrlich, Amy.
Jeffers, Susan, illus. see Frost, Robert.
Jeffers, Susan, illus. see Lerner, Sharon & Sewell, Anna.
Jeffers, Susan, illus. see Wells, Rosemary.
Jeffers, Susan, jt. auth. see Wells, Rosemary.
Jeffers, Susan & Ehrlich, Amy. Cinderella. Battcock, Gregory, ed. (p. 320)
Jeffers, Susan & Gradstein, Donna. I Can Handle It! 50 Confidence-Building Stories to Empower Your Child. (p. 835)
Jefferson, A. C. Adventures of Lucy the Wiener Dog. (p. 20)
Jefferson, Anita. Climb Every Obstacle: Eliminate Your Limits! (p. 333)
Jefferson, Barbara. Luck of the Dragonfly. Jefferson, Daniel E., illus. (p. 1062)
Jefferson, Cassandra And Maya. King Martin. (p. 958)
Jefferson, Coretta Carte. Beautiful Lizzie. (p. 153)
—Cranky Christopher. (p. 376)
Jefferson, Courtney. Shoo Bobby Don't Bother Me. (p. 1568)
Jefferson, Daniel E., illus. see Jefferson, Barbara.
Jefferson, Dave, jt. auth. see Mills, Nathan.
Jefferson, E. Louis. Little Caterpillar-A Story of Kindness. (p. 1026)
—Little Caterpillar-A Story of Kindness-Companion Coloring Book. (p. 1026)
—Little Tadpole-A Story of Friendship: Companion Coloring Book. (p. 1037)
—Terry-The Little Tadpole-Making New Friends. (p. 1722)
Jefferson Elementary Art Club. Domino. (p. 465)
Jefferson, Iesha. Children of the Future. (p. 302)
Jefferson, Jemiah, ed. see Fushimi, Tsukasa.
Jefferson, Jemiah, ed. see Nocenti, Ann.
Jefferson, Jewell E. I'm Going to Be A Big Sister! (p. 859)
Jefferson, Joanne K. Lightning & Blackberries (p. 1016)
Jefferson, Leila. He's A Keeper. (p. 774)
Jefferson, Patti Brassard. How Long Will You Love Me? Jefferson, Patti Brassard, illus. (p. 810)
Jefferson, Robert Louis, illus. see Cretan, Gladys Yessayan.
Jefferson, Steve. Lil Super Snoopers Club: Kid's Forensic Science Detectives. (p. 1017)
Jefferson, Thomas. Quotations of Thomas Jefferson. U-Inspire Inc, ed. (p. 1429)
Jeffery, Gary & Petty, Kate. Abraham Lincoln: The Life of America's Sixteenth President. Lacey, Mike, illus. (p. 6)
Jeffery, Lisa. Isles of Langerhans, a Magical Kingdom, & Diabetes: A Story to Help Children Understand Diabetes & Develop the Courage to Live with It. (p. 893)
Jeffery, Marika. Carrie Underwood. (p. 271)
—Jennifer Garner. (p. 912)
Jeffery, Megan E., illus. see Lingo, Susan L.
Jeffery, P. Growing Up: Issues Ben Faces as a Christian Teenager. (p. 726)
Jeffirs, Matt, illus. see Kasso, Martin.
Jefford, Nikki. Aurora Sky: Vampire Hunter, Vol. 1. (p. 116)
Jeffords, Stephanie & Branum, Anita. Jumpy the Turtle. May, Ashley, illus. (p. 934)
Jeffrey, Dennis. It's Beautiful to Be Different & Being Different Is Beautiful! Campanelli, Mario, illus. (p. 896)
Jeffrey, Erica, jt. auth. see Dérib.
Jeffrey, Erica, tr. see Cinebook.
Jeffrey, Gary. Abraham Lincoln: The Life of America's Sixteenth President. (p. 6)
—Achilles & the Trojan War. (p. 9)
—African Myths. (p. 27)
—Autopsies: Pathologists at Work. (p. 117)
—Autopsies: Pathologists at Work. Riley, Terry, illus. (p. 117)
—Battle for the Atlantic. (p. 145)
—Battle of the Alamo. Spender, Nick, illus. (p. 146)
—Battle of the Little Bighorn. Spender, Nick, illus. (p. 146)
—Black Death. (p. 195)
—Bob Marley: The Life of a Musical Legend. Riley, Terry, illus. (p. 205)
—Castles. (p. 277)
—Centaurs. Poluzzi, Alessandro, illus. (p. 287)
—Cleopatra: The Life of an Egyptian Queen. (p. 331)

J

—Crusades. (p. 386)
—Dark Ages & the Vikings. (p. 407)
—Defying Death at Sea. Riley, Terry, illus. (p. 424)
—Defying Death in the Desert. (p. 424)
—Dragons. (p. 478)
—Eastern Front. (p. 500)
—Egyptian Myths. (p. 507)
—Egyptian Myths. Felmang, Romano, illus. (p. 507)
—Elasmosaurus: The Long-Necked Swimmer. Riley, Terry, illus. (p. 508)
—Explorations of Lewis & Clark. Riley, Terry, illus. (p. 550)
—Firebirds. Cappoli, Sara, illus. (p. 591)
—Gallipoli & the Southern Theaters. (p. 653)
—George Washington & the Winter at Valley Forge. (p. 664)
—Giants. (p. 674)
—Goblins. Verma, Dheeraj, illus. (p. 688)
—Gold Rush. Boccanfuso, Emanuele, illus. (p. 693)
—Hercules Fights the Nemean Lion. (p. 769)
—History of Flight. (p. 784)
—Hurricane Hunters & Tornado Chasers. (p. 829)
—Hurricane Hunters & Tornado Chasers. Garofalo, Gianluca, illus. (p. 829)
—Hurricanes. Lacey, Mike, illus. (p. 830)
—Incredible Space Missions: By Gary Jeffrey: Illustrated by Mike Lacey. Lacey, Mike, illus. (p. 869)
—Incredible Space Missions. (p. 869)
—Incredible Space Missions. Lacey, Mike, illus. (p. 869)
—Jason & the Argonauts. (p. 910)
—John Adams & the Boston Massacre. (p. 921)
—Julius Caesar: The Life of a Roman General. (p. 933)
—Knights. (p. 964)
—Lawrence of Arabia & the Middle East & Africa. (p. 981)
—Little Rock Nine & the Fight for Equal Education. (p. 1036)
—Loch Ness Monster & Other Lake Mysteries. (p. 1044)
—Loch Ness Monster & Other Lake Mysteries. Moulder, Bob, illus. (p. 1044)
—Loch Ness Monster & Other Lake Mysteries. Spender, Nik & Moulder, Bob, illus. (p. 1044)
—Malcolm X & the Fight for African American Unity. (p. 1083)
—Martin Luther King Jr: The Life of a Civil Rights Leader. (p. 1098)
—Martin Luther King Jr: The Life of a Civil Rights Leader. Forsey, Chris, illus. (p. 1098)
—Martin Luther King Jr: The Life of a Civil Rights Leader. Forsey, Christopher, illus. (p. 1098)
—Martin Luther King Jr. & the March on Washington. (p. 1098)
—Medgar Evers & the NAACP. (p. 1118)
—Medical Breakthroughs. (p. 1118)
—Medical Breakthroughs. Riley, Terry, illus. (p. 1118)
—Mermaids. Boccanfuso, Emanuele, illus. (p. 1128)
—North Africa & the Mediterranean. (p. 1264)
—Odysseus & the Odyssey. (p. 1278)
—Ogres. (p. 1280)
—On the Eastern Front. (p. 1290)
—On the Western Front. (p. 1292)
—Oprah Winfrey: The Life of a Media Superstar. (p. 1301)
—Oprah Winfrey: The Life of a Media Superstar. Riley, Terry, illus. (p. 1301)
—Oregon Trail. Poluzzi, Allesandro, illus. (p. 1303)
—Paul Revere & His Midnight Ride. (p. 1330)
—Perseus Slays the Gorgon Medusa. (p. 1344)
—Pony Express. Riley, Terry, illus. (p. 1382)
—Rebellion & Revolt. (p. 1451)
—Rosa Parks & the Montgomery Bus Boycott. (p. 1489)
—Samuel Adams & the Boston Tea Party. (p. 1509)
—Sea Monsters. (p. 1535)
—Secret Agents. (p. 1540)
—Secret Agents. Riley, Terry, illus. (p. 1540)
—Secret War. (p. 1544)
—Sitting Bull: The Life of a Lakota Chief. (p. 1582)
—Solving Crimes with Trace Evidence. (p. 1608)
—Solving Crimes with Trace Evidence. Richardson, Peter, illus. (p. 1608)
—Soviet War in Afghanistan. Spender, Nik, illus. (p. 1618)
—Spectacular Shipwrecks. (p. 1624)
—Spectacular Shipwrecks. Saraceni, Claudia, illus. (p. 1624)
—Stegosaurus: The Plated Dinosaur. Field, James, illus. (p. 1646)
—Theseus Battles the Minotaur. (p. 1732)
—Thomas Jefferson & the Declaration of Independence. (p. 1739)
—Thomas Paine Writes Common Sense. (p. 1739)
—Tornadoes & Superstorms. (p. 1770)
—Tornadoes & Superstorms. Riley, Terry, illus. (p. 1770)
—Tsunamis & Floods. (p. 1795)
—UFOs. (p. 1807)
—UFOs: Alien Abduction & Close Encounters. (p. 1808)
—Unicorns. Verma, Dheeraj, illus. (p. 1818)
—Vampires. Verma, Dheeraj, illus. (p. 1832)
—War at Sea. (p. 1857)
—War in the Air. (p. 1857)
—War in the Pacific. (p. 1857)
—Werewolves: Stories of Deadly Shapeshifters. (p. 1875)
—Werewolves. (p. 1875)
—Western Front. (p. 1876)
Jeffrey, Gary, jt. auth. see Kalman, Bobbie.
Jeffrey, Gary & Ganeri, Anita. Cleopatra: The Life of an Egyptian Queen. (p. 331)
Jeffrey, Gary & Newport, Kate. African Myths. Riley, Terry, illus. (p. 27)
Jeffrey, Gary & Petty, Kate. Julius Caesar: The Life of a Roman General. (p. 933)
—Sitting Bull: The Life of a Lakota Sioux Chief. (p. 1582)
Jeffrey, Gary & Riley, Terry. Cuban Missile Crisis. (p. 388)
—Korean War. (p. 967)
Jeffrey, Gary & Shone, Rob. Defying Death at the North & South Poles. Spender, Nik, illus. (p. 424)
Jeffrey, Gary & Spender, Nik. Vietnam War. (p. 1841)
Jeffrey, Ian. Magnum Landscape. (p. 1076)
Jeffrey, Ian & Phaidon Press Editors. Photography Book. (p. 1353)
Jeffrey, Laura S. All about Braille: Reading by Touch. (p. 42)
—Amazing American Inventors of the 20th Century. (p. 52)
—Birds: How to Choose & Care for a Bird. (p. 191)
—Cats: How to Choose & Care for a Cat. (p. 281)
—Celebrate Martin Luther King, Jr., Day. (p. 284)
—Celebrate Ramadan. (p. 284)
—Celebrate Tet. (p. 284)
—Choosing a Bird: How to Choose & Care for a Bird. (p. 310)
—Choosing a Cat: How to Choose & Care for a Cat. (p. 310)
—Choosing a Dog: How to Choose & Care for a Dog. (p. 310)
—Choosing a Fish: How to Choose & Care for a Fish. (p. 310)
—Choosing a Hamster, Gerbil, Guinea Pig, Rabbit, Ferret, Mouse, or Rat: How to Choose & Care for a Small Mammal. (p. 310)
—Choosing a Horse: How to Choose & Care for a Horse. (p. 310)
—Def Leppard: Arena Rock Band. (p. 423)
—Dogs: How to Choose & Care for a Dog. (p. 462)
—Fish: How to Choose & Care for a Fish. (p. 598)
—Hamsters, Gerbils, Guinea Pigs, Rabbits, Ferrets, Mice, & Rats: How to Choose & Care for a Small Mammal. (p. 740)
—Horses: How to Choose & Care for a Horse. (p. 800)
—Marijuana = Busted! (p. 1094)
—Pink Floyd: The Rock Band. (p. 1360)
Jeffrey, Leonard J. Journeys of the Mind-Book. (p. 929)
Jeffrey Manufacturing Co., creator. 1924 Jeffrey Coal & Ashes Handling Machinery Catalog. (p. 2002)
Jeffrey, Mark. Max Quick: The Pocket & the Pendant. (p. 1111)
Jeffrey, Megan, illus. see Reed, G L.
Jeffrey, Rosemary. Allio, Are you Free. (p. 47)
Jeffrey, Sarah. Me & My Invisible Guy. (p. 1115)
Jeffrey, Sean, illus. see Jennings, Sharon & Bourgeois, Paulette.
Jeffrey, Sean, illus. see Jennings, Sharon.
Jeffrie, Sally. Guide to Being a Goddess. (p. 730)
Jeffries, Alison. Sam & the Bag. Andreasen, Dan, illus. (p. 1506)
Jeffries, Joyce. Bedbugs. (p. 156)
—Big & Small. (p. 177)
—Caribou. (p. 269)
—Colony of North Carolina. (p. 342)
—Colony of South Carolina. (p. 342)
—Dinosaur Birthday Party. (p. 441)
—Dinosaur Holidays. (p. 442)
—Dinosaur School: Set 4. (p. 442)
—Dinosaur School: Sets 1-4. (p. 442)
—Dinosaurs in the Fall. (p. 445)
—Dinosaurs in the Spring. (p. 445)
—Dinosaurs in the Summer. (p. 445)
—Dinosaurs in the Winter. (p. 445)
—Freaky Freeloaders: Bugs That Feed on People Set. (p. 632)
—Heavy & Light. (p. 761)
—Hot & Cold. (p. 801)
—Long & Short. (p. 1047)
—Meet Amy's Family. (p. 1120)
—Meet the Baker. (p. 1122)
—Meet the Baker / Te Presento A Los Panaderos. (p. 1122)
—Meet the Bus Driver. (p. 1122)
—Meet the Bus Driver / Te Presento A Los Conductores de AutobúS. (p. 1122)
—Meet the Construction Worker. (p. 1122)
—Meet the Construction Worker / Conoce a Los Trabajadores de la Construccin. (p. 1122)
—Meet the Farmer. (p. 1122)
—Meet the Farmer / Conoce a Los Granjeros. (p. 1122)
—Meet the Fireman. (p. 1122)
—Meet the Fireman / Te Presento A Los Bomberos. (p. 1122)
—Meet the Librarian. (p. 1123)
—Meet the Librarian / Conoce a Los Bibliotecarios. (p. 1123)
—Meet the Mayor. (p. 1123)
—Meet the Mayor / Conoce a Los Alcaldes. (p. 1123)
—Meet the Nurse. (p. 1123)
—Meet the Nurse / Te Presento A Los Enfermeros. (p. 1123)
—Meet the Pilot. (p. 1123)
—Meet the Pilot / Conoce a Los Pilotos. (p. 1123)
—Meet the Policeman. (p. 1123)
—Meet the Policeman / Te Presento A Los PolicíAs. (p. 1123)
—Meet the Teacher. (p. 1123)
—Meet the Teacher / Te Presento A Los Maestros. (p. 1123)
—Meet the Vet. (p. 1123)
—Meet the Vet/Conoce a Los Veterinarios. (p. 1123)
—Mountains of the United States. (p. 1181)
—Near & Far. (p. 1238)
—Shapes at School: Identify & Describe Shapes. (p. 1560)
—Which Is Different? (p. 1911)
Jeffries, Katherine. Plants Grow: Lap Book. (p. 1370)
—Tim's Head, Shoulders, Knees, & Toes. Price, Nick, illus. (p. 1755)
Jeffs, Dixie. Baby to Love. (p. 128)
—Happy Lightning Bug. (p. 746)
—Little Pink Dress. (p. 1033)
—Molly's Promise. (p. 1161)
—Old Man. (p. 1284)
—Pokey's Chance. (p. 1378)
Jeffs, Sandy. Poems from the Madhouse. (p. 1376)
Jeffs, Stephanie. Baby Jesus. Tulip, Jenny, illus. (p. 126)
—Come into the Ark with Noah. Reynolds, Annette, ed. (p. 347)
—Feed a Crowd with Jesus. (p. 580)
—Follow the Star with the Wise Men. Reynolds, Annette, ed. (p. 612)
—Giant, a Crown & an Open Air Bus. (p. 673)
—If You'd Been There in Bible Times. Thomas, Jacqui, illus. (p. 855)
—Jacob: Wrestler with God. (p. 904)
—Jenny: Coming to Terms with the Death of a Sibling. Thomas, Jacqui, illus. (p. 913)
—Joshua: Warrior for God. (p. 926)
—March Round the Walls with Joshua. Reynolds, Annette, ed. (p. 1091)
—March 'Round the Walls with Joshua. (p. 1091)
—People Jesus Met. Tulip, Jenny, illus. (p. 1339)
—Peter: Fisherman for God. (p. 1346)
—Share Out the Food with Jesus. Reynolds, Annette, ed. (p. 1561)
—Stories Jesus Told. Tulip, Jenny, illus. (p. 1654)
—Story of Christmas. (p. 1657)
—Story of Christmas. Haysom, John, illus. (p. 1657)
—Things Jesus Did. Tulip, Jenny, illus. (p. 1733)
—Where's Jesus. Laver, Sarah, 8th, illus. (p. 1910)
Jeffs, Stephanie & Tulip, Jenny. My First Find Out about Series. (p. 1206)
Jeffs, Stephanie, et al. Bywyd Iesu. (p. 249)
—Llygoden y Nadolig. (p. 1044)
Jeffus, Sharon. Art Adventures in Namia. (p. 101)
Jeffus, Sharon, as told by. Artsy Animals: In the Ocean. (p. 105)
Jeffus, Sharon2006, as told by. Artsy Animals: Learn to Read. (p. 105)
Jefimenko, Oleg D., ed. see Francis, G. W.
Jehl, Douglas, jt. ed. see McDonald, Bernadette.
Jelenek, Frank X. Journey to the Heart: Centering Prayer for Children. Boyajian, Ann, illus. (p. 929)
Jellen, Michelle. Spain or Shine. (p. 1620)
Jellett, Tom, illus. see Bedford, David.
Jellett, Tom, illus. see Dumbleton, Mike.
Jellett, Tom, illus. see Germein, Katrina.
Jellett, Tom, illus. see Gwynne, Phillip & McCann, Eliza.
Jellett, Tom, illus. see Halliday, Susan.
Jellett, Tom, illus. see Knight, Linsay, ed.
Jellett, Tom, illus. see Saxby, Claire.
Jelliroll. Echo Booming Monologues. (p. 502)
Jelloun, Tahar. Racisme Explique a Ma Fille. (p. 1432)
Jelloun, Tahar Ben. Papa, Que Es el Racismo? (p. 1322)
Jelsma, Amber. Noah's Little Lamb Pease, Tristyn, illus. (p. 1262)
Jemaine, Bret. Sugarland. (p. 1673)
—Tim McGraw. (p. 1750)
Jemas, Bill & Watson, Andi. Namor: Sea & Sand. Larroca, Salvador, illus. (p. 1228)
Jemison, Mae, jt. auth. see Rau, Dana Meachen.
Jemison, Mae & Rau, Dana Meachen. 100 Year Starship. (p. 1999)
—Discovering New Planets. (p. 449)
—Exploring Our Sun. (p. 553)
—Journey Through Our Solar System. (p. 928)
Jempsa, Alice B. Why Does Everything Happen to Me? (p. 1924)
Jen, Kailin, photos by see Joanna, Harris.
Jēn, Ruth, jt. auth. see Jones, Marlis.
Jendresen, Erik & Villoldo, Alberto. First Story Ever Told. Yoshi, illus. (p. 597)
Jendrey, Julie. Loyola University New Orleans College Prowler off the Record. (p. 1061)
—San Diego State University College Prowler off the Record. (p. 1510)
Jendrey, Julie, jt. auth. see Spiro, Ian.
Jendrey, Julie, jt. auth. see Ugarte, Julia.
Jenisch, Betty. Rennie. (p. 1460)
Jenkins, A. M. Beating Heart. (p. 152)
—Night Road. (p. 1254)
—Out of Order. (p. 1311)
—Repossessed. (p. 1461)
Jenkins, Alan & N. Ray. Jokes for Kids 2. (p. 924)
Jenkins, Amanda. City Kids, Country Kids. (p. 323)
—Hodja's Fine Coat: A Tale from Turkey. (p. 787)
—How the Turtle Cracked its Shell: A Tale from Guatemala. (p. 813)
—Leaf Monster: A Spanish American Tale. (p. 982)
—Lion & the Mouse Shoot Hoops. (p. 1020)
—Mere Moments A Story of Pearl Harbor, the Day the Towers Fell. (p. 1127)
—Mutant Bugs. (p. 1194)
—Pecos Bill & Sluefoot Sue: An American Tall Tale. (p. 1334)
—Strong & the Weak Hammurabi's Code, Tomb Robbers! A Story of Ancient Egypt. (p. 1668)
—Tornado! (p. 1770)
—Why Mole Lives Underground: A Folktale from Peru. (p. 1925)
Jenkins, Amanda, jt. auth. see Anastasio, Dina.
Jenkins, Amanda & Benchmark Education Co., LLC. Secret Life of Wally Smithers. Fagan, Martin, illus. (p. 1541)
Jenkins, Antonio. Exposing Racism & Sexism in the American Arts: Jenkins Versus Metropolitan Opera. (p. 554)
Jenkins, Barbie. Legend of the Christmas Kiss. (p. 989)
Jenkins Bathe, Bettina. Violet the Pilot in Canada. (p. 1843)
Jenkins, Beverly. Belle. (p. 162)
—Josephine. (p. 926)
—Josephine & the Soldier. (p. 926)
Jenkins, C. S., illus. see McLean, P. J.
Jenkins, Carla LaVern. Disappearance of Mrs. Brown: A Jenkins Girl Mystery. (p. 446)
Jenkins, Celeste. Lost (and Found) Balloon. Bogade, Maria, illus. (p. 1054)
Jenkins, Debra Reid, illus. see Appelt, Kathi.
Jenkins, Debra Reid, illus. see Carlstrom, Nancy White.
Jenkins, Debra Reid, illus. see Kroll, Virginia.
Jenkins, Debra Reid, illus. see Park, Frances & Park, Ginger.
Jenkins, Delores, illus. see Jackson, Sarah.
Jenkins, Diana R. All Year Long! Funny Readers Theatre for Life's Special Times. (p. 46)
—Goodness Graces! Ten Short Stories about the Sacraments. (p. 701)
—Just Deal with It! Funny Readers Theatre for Life's Not-So-Funny Moments. (p. 938)
—Saints of Note: The Comic Collection. Storms, Patricia, illus. (p. 1504)
—Spotlight on Saints! A Year of Funny Readers Theater for Today's Catholic Kids. Richards, Virginia Helen, illus. (p. 1634)
—STALKER MOM & OTHER PLAYS. (p. 1639)
—Stepping Stones Journals. (p. 1648)
Jenkins, Donna. When I Grow up, I Want to Be a Builder. (p. 1903)
—When I Grow up, I Want to Be a Doctor. (p. 1903)
—When I Grow up, I Want to Be a Football Player. (p. 1903)
Jenkins, Elizabeth B. Journey to Q'ero: Golden Cradle of the Inka. (p. 929)
Jenkins, Emily. Cinco Criaturas. Cortes, Eunice, tr. (p. 319)
—Dangerous Pumpkins. Bliss, Harry, illus. (p. 404)
—Fine Dessert: Four Centuries, Four Families, One Delicious Treat. Blackall, Sophie, illus. (p. 589)
—Five Creatures. Bogacki, Tomek, illus. (p. 600)
—Fun Book of Scary Stuff. Yum, Hyewon, illus. (p. 647)
—Invisible Inkling. Bliss, Harry, illus. (p. 885)
—Lemonade in Winter: A Book about Two Kids Counting Money. Karas, G. Brian, illus. (p. 991)
—Little Bit Scary People. Boiger, Alexandra, illus. (p. 1024)
—Skunkdog. Pratt, Pierre, illus. (p. 1586)
—Small Medium Large Bogacki, Tomek, illus. (p. 1592)
—Small, Medium, Large Bogacki, Tomek, illus. (p. 1592)
—That New Animal. Jenkins, Emily, illus. (p. 1726)
—Toy Dance Party: Being the Further Adventures of a Bossyboots Stingray, a Courageous Buffalo, & a Hopeful Round Someone Called Plastic. Zelinsky, Paul O., illus. (p. 1774)
—Toy Dance Party. Zelinsky, Paul O., illus. (p. 1774)
—Toys Come Home: Being the Early Experiences of an Intelligent Stingray, a Brave Buffalo, & a Brand-New Someone Called Plastic. Zelinsky, Paul O., illus. (p. 1774)
—Toys Go Out: Being the Adventures of a Knowledgeable Stingray, a Toughy Little Buffalo, & Someone Called Plastic. Zelinsky, Paul O., illus. (p. 1774)
—Toys Meet Snow. Zelinsky, Paul O., illus. (p. 1774)
—Water in the Park: A Book about Water & the Times of the Day. Graegin, Stephanie, illus. (p. 1863)
—Whoopie Pie War. Bliss, Harry, illus. (p. 1920)
Jenkins, Emily & Jenkins, Emily P. That New Animal. Pratt, Pierre, illus. (p. 1726)
Jenkins, Emily P., jt. auth. see Jenkins, Emily.
Jenkins, Emily S. Quicketty Splits, Original Edition. (p. 1427)
Jenkins, Garry, jt. auth. see Bowen, James.
Jenkins, Gerald & Bear, Magdalen. Codes & Ciphers: Clever Devices for Coding & Decoding to Cut Out & Make. (p. 338)
—Tarquin Number Challenges: A Collection of 50 Puzzles to Test Your Mathematical Skills. (p. 1706)
Jenkins, Gloria. Storm: The Peace Maker. (p. 1655)
Jenkins, Henry A. Adventures of Monkey Squirrel & Frogman: Sand Trap. (p. 20)
Jenkins, J. J., jt. auth. see Petersen, George.
Jenkins, Jacqueline. Eve, Abigail, Sapphira. (p. 541)
Jenkins, Jacqueline, illus. see Kauffman, Christopher G.
Jenkins, Jean & Loewer, Peter. Inside-Out Stomach: An Introduction to Animals Without Backbones. (p. 877)
Jenkins, Jennifer Meghan. 10 Deadliest Predators. (p. 1993)
Jenkins, Jerry B. Crash at Cannibal Valley. (p. 376)
—Disaster in the Yukon. (p. 446)
—Terror: In Branco Grande. (p. 1722)
Jenkins, Jerry B., jt. auth. see Fabry, Chris.
Jenkins, Jerry B., jt. auth. see LaHaye, Tim.
Jenkins, Jerry B. & Fabry, Chris. Author's Blood. (p. 117)
—Book of the King. (p. 212)
—Canyon Echoes. (p. 262)
—Changeling. (p. 290)
—Dead End. (p. 416)
—Double Fault. (p. 472)
—Escaping Darkness. (p. 535)
—Grave Shadows. (p. 712)
—Hidden Riches. (p. 776)
—Hollywood Holdup. (p. 789)
—Instant Menace. (p. 878)
—Libro del Rey. (p. 1006)
—Minions of Time. (p. 1147)
—Missing Pieces. (p. 1152)
—Phantom Writer. (p. 1349)
—Stolen Secrets. (p. 1652)
—Sword of the Wormling. (p. 1692)
—Wild Rescue. (p. 1930)
—Wind Chill. (p. 1935)
—Windy City Danger. (p. 1936)
Jenkins, Jerry B. & LaHaye, Tim. Heat Wave: Surviving the Fourth Bowl Judgment. (p. 760)
—Mark of the Beast: Witness Behind Bars. (p. 1095)
—Mark of the Beast. (p. 1095)
—Perils of Love: Breaking Through the Darkness. (p. 1343)
—Pursued. (p. 1419)
—Rescued. (p. 1462)
—Rise of False Messiahs: Carpathia's Evil Tricks. (p. 1474)
—Shaken. (p. 1558)
—Taken. (p. 1697)
—Unmasked. (p. 1821)
Jenkins, Jerry B., et al. Deceived. (p. 421)
—Frantic. (p. 631)
—Ominous Choices - The Race for Life. (p. 1288)
—Protected. (p. 1412)
—Stung. (p. 1670)
Jenkins, June M. All about Me: Tales for Tiny Tots. (p. 43)
Jenkins, Leonard, illus. see Greene, Bette.
Jenkins, Leonard, illus. see Hopkinson, Deborah.
Jenkins, Leonard, illus. see Kessler, Cristina.
Jenkins, Leonard, illus. see Morrow, Barbara Olenyik.
Jenkins, Leonard, illus. see Myers, Walter Dean.
Jenkins, Leonard, illus. see Siebert, Diane.
Jenkins, Leonard, tr. see Myers, Walter Dean.
Jenkins, Lizzie L. P. R. Real Rosewood. (p. 1448)
Jenkins, Lyll Becerra De, see Becerra de Jenkins, Lyll.
Jenkins, Mark, ed. Worlds to Explore: Classic Tales of Travel & Adventure from National Geographic. (p. 1961)
Jenkins, Martin. Ape. White, Vicky, illus. (p. 91)
—Can We Save the Tiger? White, Vicky, illus. (p. 258)
—Chameleons Are Cool. Shields, Sue, illus. (p. 289)
—Emperor's Egg. Chapman, Jane, illus. (p. 521)
—Emperor's Egg Big Book: Read & Wonder Big Book. Chapman, Jane, illus. (p. 521)
—Grandma Elephant's in Charge. Bates, Ivan, illus. (p. 708)
—History of Money: From Bartering to Banking. Kitamura, Satoshi, illus. (p. 784)
—Titanic: Disaster at Sea. (p. 1757)
—Titanic. Sanders, Brian, illus. (p. 1757)
Jenkins, Meghan. 10 Most Amazing Birds. (p. 1993)
Jenkins, Merryann. Nehemiah the Postman: Journey Through the Alphabet. (p. 1240)
Jenkins, Mike. Child of Dust. (p. 301)

—Poems for Underage Thinkers. (p. 1376)
Jenkins, Missy & Croyle, Willliam. I Choose to Be Happy: A School Shooting Survivor's Triumph over Tragedy. (p. 837)
Jenkins, N. Ray. Jokes for Kids. (p. 924)
Jenkins, Noel, et al. This Is Geography Elearning Activities. (p. 1736)
Jenkins, Paul. Here There Be the Monsters Scott, Damion, illus. (p. 770)
—Prelude to Schism. De La Torre, Roberto et al, illus. (p. 1395)
Jenkins, Peter. When Father Christmas Resigned. Jenkins, Sandra, illus. (p. 1902)
Jenkins, Priscilla Belz. Nest Full of Eggs. Rockwell, Lizzy, illus. (p. 1242)
Jenkins, Reid Debra, illus. see Appelt, Kathi.
Jenkins, Saffy. Boy Who Cried Wolf Broadley, Leo, illus. (p. 219)
Jenkins, Sandra. My Play & Learn Book. (p. 1217)
Jenkins, Sandra, illus. see Jenkins, Peter.
Jenkins, Sara D. Prose Marmion a Tale of the Scottish. (p. 1412)
—Prose Marmion A Tale of the Scottish Border. (p. 1412)
Jenkins, Sharon I. Remember the Ten Commandments with Jam & Jean Jellybean. Jenkins, Sharon I., illus. (p. 1459)
Jenkins, Simon, illus. see Aiken, Nick.
Jenkins, Steve. Actual Size. (p. 10)
—Almost Gone: The World's Rarest Animals. Jenkins, Steve, illus. (p. 48)
—Animal Book: A Collection of the Fastest, Fiercest, Toughest, Cleverest, Shyest - And Most Surprising - Animals on Earth. Jenkins, Steve, illus. (p. 77)
—Beetle Book. Jenkins, Steve, illus. (p. 158)
—Bones: Skeletons & How They Work. Jenkins, Steve, illus. (p. 209)
—Dogs & Cats. (p. 462)
—Down, down, Down: A Journey to the Bottom of the Sea. Jenkins, Steve, illus. (p. 474)
—Hottest, Coldest, Highest, Deepest. (p. 802)
—Just a Second: A Different Way to Look at Time. (p. 937)
—Living Color. Jenkins, Steve, illus. (p. 1040)
—Looking Down. (p. 1051)
—Never Smile at a Monkey: And 17 Other Important Things to Remember. Jenkins, Steve, illus. (p. 1243)
—Prehistoric Actual Size. (p. 1395)
Jenkins, Steve, illus. see Crump, Marty.
Jenkins, Steve, illus. see Fox, Mem.
Jenkins, Steve, illus. see Franco, Betsy & Franco-Feeney, Betsy.
Jenkins, Steve, illus. see Franco, Betsy.
Jenkins, Steve, illus. see Page, Robin.
Jenkins, Steve, illus. see Pfeffer, Wendy & Pfeffer.
Jenkins, Steve, illus. see Pfeffer, Wendy.
Jenkins, Steve, illus. see Pringle, Laurence.
Jenkins, Steve, illus. see Rockwell, Anne.
Jenkins, Steve, illus. see Sayre, April Pulley.
Jenkins, Steve, illus. see Ward, Jennifer.
Jenkins, Steve, illus. see Worth, Valerie.
Jenkins, Steve, jt. auth. see Page, Robin.
Jenkins, Steve & Page, Robin. Animals Upside Down: A Pull, Pop, Lift & Learn Book! Jenkins, Steve, illus. (p. 84)
—Creature Features: Twenty-Five Animals Explain Why They Look the Way They Do. Jenkins, Steve, illus. (p. 380)
—Flying Frogs & Walking Fish: Leaping Lemurs, Tumbling Toads, Jet-Propelled Dragonflies, & More Surprising Ways That Animals Move. (p. 610)
—How Many Ways Can You Catch a Fly? Jenkins, Steve, illus. (p. 811)
—How to Clean a Hippopotamus: A Look at Unusual Animal Partnerships. (p. 816)
—How to Swallow a Pig: Step-By-Step Advice from the Animal Kingdom. Jenkins, Steve, illus. (p. 822)
—I See a Kookaburra! Discovering Animal Habitats Around the World. (p. 845)
—My First Day: What Animals Do on Day One. Jenkins, Steve, illus. (p. 1206)
—Time for a Bath. Jenkins, Steve, illus. (p. 1751)
—Time to Eat. Jenkins, Steve, illus. (p. 1753)
—Time to Sleep. Jenkins, Steve, illus. (p. 1753)
Jenkins, Steve, et al. Que Harias con una Cola Como Esta? (p. 1423)
Jenkins, Steven. Spider House: Battle for the Wall. (p. 1626)
Jenkins, Steven, illus. see Page, Robin.
Jenkins, Susan Padgett. Daddy Comes Back. (p. 398)
Jenkins, T. L. On the Bed & off the Bed. (p. 1289)
Jenkins, Toye L. Way God Made Me: A Self Image Book for Girls. (p. 1864)
Jenkins, Tranise. My Best Friend Snuff. (p. 1196)
Jenkins, Ward, illus. see Bardhan-Quallen, Sudipta.
Jenkins, Ward, illus. see Chatzky, Jean.
Jenkins, Ward, illus. see Chronicle Books Staff.
Jenkins, Ward, illus. see Phelps, Michael & Abrahamson, Alan.
Jenkins, Zeretha. Walking by Faith: An Afro-American Trilogy. (p. 1854)
Jenkins-Greaves, Shenita. Raptown U. S. A. Rappers. (p. 1439)
Jenkinson, Allison. My Friend the Bear. (p. 1209)
Jenkins-Tate, Nesha L. 10 Love Poems to Empower Young Souls: A Gift Book to Encourage Young People You Love. (p. 1993)
Jenks, Andrew. Andrew Jenks: My Adventures as a Young Filmmaker. (p. 72)
Jenks, Deneen, jt. auth. see Noguchi, Rick.
Jenks, Patricia. I'm Only a Little Bunny. Lehto, Christine, illus. (p. 859)
Jenkyns, Brenda. Ever After. (p. 541)
Jenne, Ed, illus. see Rutter, Michael.
Jennenga, John, illus. see Albers, Megan & Albers, Christine.
Jenner, Caryn. DK Adventures: in the Shadow of the Volcano: In the Shadow of the Volcano. (p. 455)
—First Flight: The Story of the Wright Brothers. Vol. 4 (p. 595)
—Pocahontas, Level 2. (p. 1375)
—Welcome to China. (p. 1873)
Jenner, Caryn & Dorling Kindersley Publishing Staff. In the Shadow of the Volcano. (p. 867)
—Thomas Edison - The Great Inventor, Level 4. (p. 1738)
Jenner, Caryn & Garrett, Leslie. First Flight, Level 4: The Story of the Wright Brothers. (p. 595)
Jenner, Kendall & Jenner, Kylie. Rebels: The Story of Lex & Livia. (p. 1451)
Jenner, Kendall Nicole, et al. Rebels, City of Indra: The Story of Lex & Livia. (p. 1451)
Jenner, Kylie, jt. auth. see Jenner, Kendall.
Jenner, Loreial, illus. see Pulford, Elizabeth.
Jenness, Diamond. American Aborigines: Their Origin & Antiquity; A Collection of Papers by Ten Authors, Assembled & Edited by Diamond Jenness. (p. 59)
—American Aborigines, Their Origin & Antiquity; A Collection of Papers by Ten Authors. (p. 59)
Jennett, Pamela. Discoverers & Inventors Reader's Theater: Develop Reading Fluency & Test Comprehension Skills, Vol. 2245 Hults, Alaska, ed. (p. 448)
—Human Body. (p. 825)
—Life Science. (p. 1013)
—Native American Peoples. Rous, Sheri, ed. (p. 1234)
—Physical Science. (p. 1353)
—Traditional Manuscript Handwriting. (p. 1776)
—Writing Makeovers 5-6: Improving Skills - Adding Style. Rous, Sheri, ed. (p. 1965)
Jennett, Pamela, ed. see Flores, Debra, et al.
Jennett, Pamela, ed. see Lewis, Dawn & Jacks, Cyndie.
Jennett, Pamela, ed. see Morton, Debra & Stover, Elizabeth.
Jennett, Pamela & Marchant, Sherry. Electing Our President: The Process to Elect the Nation's Leader. Jennett, Pamela, ed. (p. 508)
Jennette, Mairead. Ten Green Bottles. (p. 1718)
Jennewein, Daniel, illus. see Jennewein, Lenore.
Jennewein, Daniel, illus. see Vernick, Audrey.
Jennewein, James & Parker, Tom S. RuneWarriors: Sword of Doom. (p. 1497)
—RuneWarriors. (p. 1497)
—Shield of Odin. (p. 1566)
—Ship of the Dead. (p. 1567)
Jennewein, Lenore. Chick-O-Saurus Rex. Jennewein, Daniel, illus. (p. 299)
Jennicrai, Susanna. Button & Bow: Friends Forever. (p. 248)
Jennie Lyon Wood. Bath Time Bears Have So Much Fun. Kristie Kryssing, illus. (p. 144)
Jennifermayormaynot. Muck in My Cup. (p. 1188)
Jennings, Arleen Naish. God Is in the Rain. (p. 689)
Jennings, Bob, et al. Birds of the Great Plains. (p. 192)
Jennings, C. S., illus. see Dahl, Michael & Nickel, Scott.
Jennings, C. S., illus. see Hirschmann, Kris.
Jennings, C. S., illus. see Katschke, Judy.
Jennings, C. S., illus. see Nickel, Scott, et al.
Jennings, C. S., illus. see Nickel, Scott.
Jennings, Carol E. Marshall & Satchmo. (p. 1096)
Jennings, Christopher S. Hello, Texas! Walker, David, illus. (p. 765)
Jennings, Coleman, jt. auth. see Jennings, Coleman A.
Jennings, Coleman A. & Jennings, Coleman. Theatre for Young Audiences: 20 Great Plays for Children. Jennings, Coleman A., ed. (p. 1728)
Jennings, Gary. Aztec. (p. 122)
—Aztec Autumn. (p. 122)
Jennings, Jason. Hit the Ground Running: A Manual for New Leaders. (p. 785)
Jennings, Jerry. Guitarist's Link to Sight Reading: #1 Guide to Understanding Studio Charts. (p. 731)
Jennings, Karen, jt. auth. see Pierce, Mark.
Jennings, Ken. Ancient Egypt. Lowery, Mike, illus. (p. 68)
—Greek Mythology. (p. 720)
—Greek Mythology. Lowery, Mike, illus. (p. 720)
—Human Body. Lowery, Mike, illus. (p. 825)
—Maps & Geography. Lowery, Mike, illus. (p. 1090)
—U. S. Presidents. Lowery, Mike, illus. (p. 1807)
Jennings, L. N. Seven Splinters. (p. 1555)
Jennings, Linda. Animal Tales for Bedtime. Biro, Val, illus. (p. 80)
—Duna y Dan. Chapman, Jane, illus. (p. 490)
—Little Puppy Lost Edgson, Alison, illus. (p. 1034)
—Tom's Tail. Warnes, Tim, tr. (p. 1765)
Jennings, Madeleine & Drewe, James. Tai Chi Step-By-Step. (p. 1695)
Jennings, Marlis, jt. auth. see Collins, Yozette Yogi.
Jennings, Patrick. Barb & Dingbat's Crybaby Hotline. (p. 137)
—Bat & Rat. Cordell, Matthew, illus. (p. 143)
—Ears of Corn: An Ike & Mem Story. Alter, Anna, illus. (p. 494)
—Lightning Bugs. Alter, Anna, illus. (p. 1016)
—We Can't All Be Rattlesnakes. (p. 1866)
—Wish Riders. (p. 1940)
Jennings, Paul. Don't Look Now 3: Haircut & Just a Nibble. Weldon, Andrew, illus. (p. 468)
Jennings, Paulla. Strawberry Thanksgiving. Peters, Ramona, illus. (p. 1666)
Jennings, Peter & Brewster, Todd. Century for Young People: 1936-1961: Defining America (p. 287)
—Century for Young People, 1961-1999: Changing America (p. 287)
Jennings, R. W., illus. see Finkelstein, Chaim.
Jennings, Randy, illus. see Blake, Colleen H. Robley.
Jennings, Randy, illus. see Campbell, Mari.
Jennings, Randy, illus. see Fox-Lee, Kyme & Fox-Lee, Susan.
Jennings, Randy, illus. see Fox-Lee, Susan & Fox-Lee, Kyme.
Jennings, Randy, illus. see Greenberg, Carmel.
Jennings, Randy, illus. see Prindle, Twyla.
Jennings, Randy, jt. auth. see Campbell, Mari.
Jennings, Richard W. Orwell's Luck. (p. 1305)
—Scribble. (p. 1533)
Jennings, Rosemary. Cuevas de Murcielagos (Inside Bat Caves) (p. 390)
—Eagles. (p. 492)
—I Can Grow Plants! (p. 835)
—Inside Bat Caves. (p. 876)
Jennings, Sharon. Batnapped. (p. 144)
—Bats in the Garbage Mardon, John, illus. (p. 145)
—Bats in the Graveyard. (p. 145)
—Bats on Horseback. (p. 145)
—Bearcub & Mama. Watt, Mélanie, illus. (p. 151)
—Bye-Bye Pie. (p. 249)
—Chanukah Noel: A True Story Newland, Gillian & Second Story Press Staff, illus. (p. 291)
—C'mere, Boy! Spires, Ashley, illus. (p. 336)
—Dancing on the Edge. Doherty, Catherine, illus. (p. 403)
—Franklin & the Cookies. Gagnon, Celeste et al, illus. (p. 630)
—Franklin & the Scooter. Gagnon, Celeste et al, illus. (p. 630)
—Franklin Stays Up. Jeffrey, Sean et al, illus. (p. 630)
—Franklin the Detective. Gagnon, Celeste et al, illus. (p. 630)
—Franklin's Pond Phantom. McIntyre, Sasha et al, illus. (p. 631)
—Franklin's Trading Cards. Jeffrey, Sean et al, illus. (p. 631)
—Happily Ever Afternoon. Lightburn, Ron, illus. (p. 744)
—Home Free (p. 792)
—Jingle Bats. Malloy, Kalle, illus. (p. 918)
—No Monsters Here Ohi, Ruth, illus. (p. 1259)
—Pump! (p. 1416)
—Sleep Tight, Mrs. Ming. (p. 1588)
Jennings, Sharon & Bourgeois, Paulette. Classic Franklin Story: Franklin's Thanksgiving. Clark, Brenda, illus. (p. 328)
—Franklin Goes to the Hospital. Clark, Brenda, illus. (p. 630)
—Franklin's Neighborhood. Clark, Brenda, illus. (p. 631)
—Franklin's Trading Cards. Jeffrey, Sean et al, illus. (p. 631)
—Franklin's Valentines. Clark, Brenda, illus. (p. 631)
Jennings, Sharon, et al. Franklin the Detective. Gagnon, Céleste, illus. (p. 630)
—Franklin's Library Book. Gagnon, Céleste, illus. (p. 631)
Jennings, Sharon, et al, adapted by. Franklin & the Computer. (p. 630)
—Franklin & the Duckling. (p. 630)
—Franklin & the Stopwatch. (p. 630)
—Franklin & the Tin Flute. (p. 630)
—Franklin Snoops. (p. 630)
—Franklin's Picnic. (p. 631)
—Franklin's Pond Phantom. (p. 631)
Jennings, Steven J. Bodacious Adventures of Joe & Barb. (p. 206)
Jennings, Sue. Creative Play with Children at Risk. (p. 380)
—Creative Storytelling with Children at Risk. (p. 380)
Jennings, Sue & Bodle, Katharine. Developing Early Literacy Skills: Practical Ideas & Activities. (p. 431)
Jennings, Sue, et al. Role Play Cards for Social Skills: Increasing Confidence. (p. 1485)
Jennings, Terri & Gold, Paul Daniel. Cadbury's Big Move. (p. 250)
Jennings, Terry. Aire (Air) (p. 31)
—Amazing Aquarium. (p. 53)
—Bird Paradise. (p. 190)
—Bird Watch (p. 190)
—Bugs & Slugs (p. 237)
—Camouflage. (p. 257)
—Clay. (p. 330)
—Electricidad y Magnetismo (Electricity & Magnetism) (p. 509)
—Forces. (p. 617)
—Glass. (p. 682)
—Hot & Cold. (p. 801)
—Light & Dark. (p. 1014)
—Magnets. (p. 1076)
—Mammal Kingdom. (p. 1084)
—Materials. (p. 1104)
—Metal. (p. 1130)
—Plastic. (p. 1370)
—Reptile Park. (p. 1461)
—Rocas y Suelos (Rocks & Soils) (p. 1481)
—Trucks. (p. 1791)
—Wood. (p. 1949)
Jennings, Terry, jt. auth. see Oxlade, Chris.
Jennings, Terry Catasús. Gopher to the Rescue! A Volcano Recovery Story O'Keefe, Laurie, illus. (p. 702)
—Sounds of the Savanna Saroff, Phyllis, illus. (p. 1615)
—Women's Liberation Movement, 1960-1990. (p. 1946)
—Women's Liberation Movement, 1960-1990. Harrington, A. Page, ed. (p. 1946)
Jennings, Terry J. Construction Vehicles. (p. 360)
—Earthquakes & Tsunamis. (p. 497)
—Electricity. (p. 509)
—Extreme Weather. (p. 557)
—Forces. (p. 617)
—Hot & Cold. (p. 801)
—Light & Dark. (p. 1014)
—Magnets. (p. 1076)
—Massive Mountains. (p. 1103)
—Sound. (p. 1615)
—Violent Volcanoes. (p. 1843)
—Weather: Rain. (p. 1869)
—Weather: Wind. (p. 1869)
Jennings, Terry J., jt. auth. see Oxlade, Chris.
Jennison, Christopher. Baseball Math: Grandslam Activities & Projects. (p. 141)
Jennison, Christopher, jt. auth. see Gregorich, Barbara.
Jennison, Nancy. Integrating Test Prep into Reading & Writing Workshops: Classroom-Tested Lessons & Activities That Teach Students the Skills They Need to Become Successful Readers & Writers-And Excel on the Tests. (p. 879)
Jennison, Peter S. Roadside History of Vermont. (p. 1477)
Jennkrist, K. Not So Snow White. (p. 1267)
Jenny, Christine, illus. see Birch, Beverley.
Jenny, Lindley, photos by see Learn As You Grow.
Jens, Charlene. Ookie Gets a New Best Friend. (p. 1298)
Jensema, Carl. Vision Screen 9000: Vision Testing. (p. 1845)
Jensema, Carl, des. MyTTY Phone Messenger. (p. 1227)
Jensema, Marissa. ASL Songs for Kids - 1: With Songs in American Sign Language. (p. 106)
Jensen, Angelina, jt. auth. see Scribner, Meagen.
Jensen, Astrid, illus. see Gabel, Ngareta.
Jensen, Barb E. Horse Named Summertime. (p. 799)
Jensen, Belinda. Blizzard! A Bel the Weather Girl Book. Kurilla, Renee, illus. (p. 199)
—Clouds! A Bel the Weather Girl Book. Kurilla, Renee, illus. (p. 335)
—Hail! A Bel the Weather Girl Book. Kurilla, Renee, illus. (p. 735)
—Hurricane! A Bel the Weather Girl Book. Kurilla, Renee, illus. (p. 829)
—Thunderstorms: A Bel the Weather Girl Book. Kurilla, Renee, illus. (p. 1746)
—Tornadoes: A Bel the Weather Girl Book. Kurilla, Renee, illus. (p. 1770)
Jensen, Brandi Ann & Courtright, Jordan K. Hilarious & Brave Adventures of Hog & Dog. (p. 779)
Jensen, Brian, illus. see Dahl, Michael & Ziegler, Mark.
Jensen, Brian, illus. see Dahl, Michael.
Jensen, Brian, illus. see Loewen, Nancy.
Jensen, Brian, jt. auth. see Dahl, Michael.
Jensen, Carolyn P. Favorite Bible Stories: Reproducible Activity Book. (p. 578)
—Graded Bulletin Boards for Sunday School. (p. 705)
—Jumbo Bible Bulletin Boards: Spring & Summer - Preschool & Primary. (p. 933)
—Seasonal Bulletin Boards: Fall. (p. 1538)
—Seasonal Bulletin Boards: Spring. (p. 1538)
—Seasonal Bulletin Boards: Summer. (p. 1538)
—Seasonal Bulletin Boards: Winter. (p. 1538)
Jensen, Daniel Loran, jt. auth. see Jensen, Rebecca Ridges.
Jensen, Danielle L. Stolen Songbird. (p. 1652)
Jensen, Derrick. Mischief in the Forest: A Yarn Yarn. McMillan, Stephanie, illus. (p. 1150)
Jensen, Diane Mastromarino. Girl's Guide to Loving Yourself: A book about falling in love with the one person who matters most... you - UPDATED EDITION - (p. 680)
Jensen, Donald D., jt. auth. see Williams, Eli.
Jensen, Edward C., rev. Trees to Know in Oregon (p. 1784)
Jensen, Elizabeth. Elnsame Drache. Sommerfeld, Monika, tr. (p. 507)
Jensen, Eric. Student Success Secrets. (p. 1669)
Jensen, Frode M., jt. auth. see Jones, Vernie O.
Jensen, Hans, illus. see Somerville, Louisa.
Jensen, Hay R. Home with Honor: A Vietnam P.O.W. Tells How to Conquer Adversity Through Courage, Honor & Faith. Vol. 1 (p. 793)
Jensen, Ivan. Mary Rode to Bethlehem on Me. (p. 1101)
Jensen, Jakob Hjort, illus. see Bennicke, Rune Brandt.
Jensen, James P., ed. see Loe, Erlend.
Jensen, Jeremy, jt. auth. see Lazar, Michelle.
Jensen, Joel, et al. Tiny Hamster Is a Giant Monster. (p. 1756)
Jensen, Jon. Adventures in the Desert. (p. 15)
Jensen, Jon, jt. auth. see Miller, Ed. L.
Jensen, Joyce, jt. auth. see Lohof, Arle.
Jensen, Karl, et al. Flowers for Grandma. (p. 608)
Jensen, Kathryn. Splash! (p. 1629)
Jensen, Kimberly. Always the Elf. Harmon, Glenn, illus. (p. 51)
Jensen, Lars, et al. Donald Duck Adventures Clark, John, ed. (p. 466)
—Uncle Scrooge - How Green Was My Lettuce. Clark, John, ed. (p. 1812)
Jensen, Leyah, illus. see Capucilli, Alyssa Satin.
Jensen, Leyah, photos by see Capucilli, Alyssa Satin.
Jensen, Lillian. Treasury of Modern Mother Goose Rhymes (p. 1783)
Jensen, Lisa. If My Hair Were Like Spagetti. Jensen, Lisa, illus. (p. 853)
Jensen, Marie-Louise. Between Two Seas. (p. 173)
—Drama Club. (p. 480)
Jensen, Marion. Almost Super. (p. 48)
—Searching for Super. (p. 1537)
Jensen, Melissa. Falling in Love with English Boys. (p. 567)
—Fine Art of Truth or Dare. (p. 589)
Jensen, Michael & King, David Powers. Woven. (p. 1962)
Jensen, Natalie Mahina, jt. auth. see Moen Cabanting, Ruth.
Jensen, Nathaniel P., illus. see Boeholt, V. A.
Jensen, Nathaniel P., illus. see Storad, Conrad J.
Jensen, Ned. Sam: Set Of 6. (p. 1506)
Jensen, Niels R. Maine. (p. 1077)
—Maryland. (p. 1101)
—Michigan. (p. 1135)
—Minnesota. (p. 1147)
—New Hampshire. (p. 1244)
—New York. (p. 1247)
—Ohio. (p. 1281)
—Rhode Island. (p. 1468)
—Vermont. (p. 1837)
—Virginia. (p. 1844)
Jensen, Olivia. Thomas & the Bully. (p. 1738)
Jensen, Pamela. Reverently, Quietly: Sacrament Meeting Activity Book. (p. 1466)
Jensen, Patricia. I Am Sick. Hantel, Johanna, illus. (p. 833)
—Mess. (p. 1129)
—Mess. Lewis, Anthony, illus. (p. 1129)
—My House. (p. 1211)
—My House. Becker, Wayne, illus. (p. 1211)
Jensen, Patricia & Demar, Regier. Good Food. Clar, David Austin & Hantel, Johanna, illus. (p. 698)
Jensen, Peder Skytte. Anton & Rosita: All Roads Lead to Rome. (p. 90)
Jensen, Rebecca Ridges. My Heavenly Father Loves Me. (p. 1211)
Jensen, Rebecca Ridges & Jensen, Daniel Loran. Creation-From the Book of Moses. (p. 379)
Jensen, Richard. Discovering U. S. History (p. 450)
Jensen Shaffer, Jody. Vampires & Light Gervasio, illus. (p. 1832)
Jensen Shaffer, Jody, jt. auth. see Weakland, Mark.
Jensen Shaffer, Jody, et al. Monster Science. Gervasio & Aón, Carlos, illus. (p. 1168)
Jensen, Stephanie L. Purple Watermelon. (p. 1419)
Jensen, Steve, jt. auth. see Eareckson Tada, Joni.
Jensen, Sydell A. Christian Alphabet. (p. 311)
Jensen, Travis. Left-Handed Stories. (p. 987)
Jensen, Valerie K. Romeo & Juliet: The Coloring Book. (p. 1486)

J

Jenson, Jeff. X-Factor. Ranson, Arthur, illus. (p. 1967)
Jenson, Jeff, et al. Before Tomorrowland. Case, Jonathan, illus. (p. 158)
Jenson-Elliot, Cythnia. Ancient Chinese Dynasties. (p. 68)
Jenson-Elliott, Cindy. Arctic Communities Past & Present (p. 96)
—Camping (p. 257)
—Desert Communities Past & Present (p. 428)
—Fly Fishing (p. 609)
—Pirates! (p. 1363)
—Weeds Find a Way. Fisher, Carolyn, illus. (p. 1871)
Jenson-Elliott, Cindy, jt. auth. see Jenson-Elliott, Cynthia L.
Jenson-Elliott, Cindy & Mebane, Jeanie. Wild Outdoors. (p. 1930)
Jenson-Elliott, Cindy, et al. Who Lived Here? (p. 1916)
Jenson-Elliott, Cynthia L. & Jenson-Elliott, Cindy. Life under the Pirate Code (p. 1013)
—Most Famous Pirates (p. 1177)
—Pirate Ships Ahoy! (p. 1363)
—Pirates' Tools for Life at Sea (p. 1364)
Jenson-Elliott, Cynthia L. & Sautter, Aaron. Most Famous Pirates. (p. 1177)
Jensz, Penny, illus. see Boylan, Eleanor.
Jentsch, Joyce Harp, illus. see Jentsch, R. D.
Jentsch, R. D. Froggy & Friends Go to the Creek Jentsch, Joyce Harp, illus. (p. 640)
Jeon, JinSeok. One Thousand & One Nights (p. 1297)
Jeon, Keuk-jin, jt. auth. see Geuk-jin, Jeon.
Jeong, Gu-mi. Dad's Favorite Cookie: Japan. Cowley, Joy, ed. (p. 399)
Jeong, HaJin, illus. see Kim, Cecil.
Jeong, Jini. Crayon Road: Imagination - Lines. Cowley, Joy, ed. (p. 377)
Jeong, SoYun. Lulu the Shy Piglet. Orsolini, Laura, illus. (p. 1065)
Jepperson, Richard. Two Fires in the Night: The Third Part of the Crazy Horse Chronicles. Mundie, Ken, illus. (p. 1803)
Jeppesen, Ryan, illus. see Butler, David.
Jepsen, D. R. Fabulous Fred Gets the Cheese. (p. 560)
—Fred's Exciting Night. (p. 633)
Jepson, Beth, illus. see Caldwell, J. Lynn.
Jepson, Edgar. Admirable Tinker: Child of the World. (p. 13)
—Admirable Tinker: Child of the World. Eckerson, Margaret, illus. (p. 13)
Jepson, Gill. Out of Time: The Secret of the Swan. (p. 1311)
—Out of Time 2: Raven's Hoard. (p. 1311)
Jepson, Jeanette. Adventures of Theodore Tortoise - Claude's Big Adventure: Claude's Big Adventure. (p. 24)
Jepson, Maud. Illustrated Biology (p. 857)
Jepson, Tim. Florence & Tuscany. (p. 606)
Jepson-Gilbert, Anita. Maria & the Stars of Nazca (Maria y las Estrellas de Nazca) Casis, Carmen A., tr. (p. 1093)
—Maria & the Stars of Nazca (Maria y las Estrellas de Nazca) Osban, Rodger, illus. (p. 1093)
Jer, Baant. Dekok & the Begging Death: A Detective Novel. Smittenaar, H. G., tr. from DUT. (p. 424)
Jeralds, Scott, illus. see Dahl, Michael.
Jeram, Anita. Bunny My Honey. Jeram, Anita, illus. (p. 242)
—I Love My Little Storybook. Jeram, Anita, illus. (p. 842)
—Inés del Revés. (p. 873)
—Me Gusta Mi Libro de Cuentos. Mlawer, Teresa, tr. (p. 1116)
Jeram, Anita, illus. see Hest, Amy.
Jeram, Anita, illus. see King-Smith, Dick.
Jeram, Anita, illus. see McBratney, Sam.
Jerde, Susan, illus. see Gunn, Barbara.
Jerde, Susan, illus. see Jones, Shelley V. & Gunn, Barbara.
Jerde, Susan, illus. see Sprick, Marilyn, et al.
Jeremiah, illus. see Labadie, Sally.
Jeremiah, Omari. Paper Boy Four: L. O. E. P. S. Worst Nightmare. Rollins, Berni, illus. (p. 1322)
—Paperboy 3: The School of Doom. Rollins, Bernie, illus. (p. 1323)
Jeremiatt, Omani. Paper Boy. Rollins, Bernie, illus. (p. 1322)
Jermann, David, illus. see Bolton, Michael.
Jermyn, Deborah. Crime Watching: Investigating Real Crime TV. (p. 382)
Jermyn, Leslie, jt. auth. see Foley, Erin.
Jermyn, Leslie, jt. auth. see Ngcheong-Lum, Roseline.
Jermyn, Leslie, jt. auth. see Sheehan, Sean.
Jermyn, Leslie, jt. auth. see South, Coleman.
Jermyn, Leslie & Conboy, Fiona. Mexico. (p. 1131)
Jermyn, Leslie & Wong, Winnie. Guyana. (p. 733)
—Uruguay. (p. 1826)
Jermyn, Leslie & Yong, Jui Lin. Belize. (p. 162)
—Paraguay. (p. 1323)
Jerome, Barb, illus. see Schield, Allie Schield.
Jerome, Elaine, illus. see Costales, Amy.
Jerome, Elaine, illus. see Ruiz-Flores, Lupe.
Jerome, Janice. Dust of Flour. . . Beyond the Family Tree. (p. 490)
Jerome, Jerome K. & Klapka, Jerome. Tres Hombres en una Barca. (p. 1784)
Jerome, Karen A., illus. see Bahr, Mary.
Jerome, Karen A., illus. see Luchsinger, Dena.
Jerome, Karen A., illus. see McMahon, Patricia & McCarthy, Conor Clarke.
Jerome, Kate Boehm. Atomic Universe: The Quest to Discover Radioactivity. (p. 113)
—Charleston, SC: Cool Stuff Every Kid Should Know. (p. 292)
—Chef down at the Zoo. (p. 297)
—Cincinnati, Oh: Cool Stuff Every Kid Should Know. (p. 319)
—Forces That Move. (p. 617)
—How Many Ants in an Anthill? (p. 811)
—Massachusetts: What's So Great about This State? (p. 1102)
—Miniature Golf Madness. (p. 1146)
—More Science of You. (p. 1174)
—North Carolina: What's So Great about This State? (p. 1265)
—Number Know-How. (p. 1271)
—Pennsylvania: What's So Great about This State? (p. 1338)
—Science at the Aquarium. (p. 1525)
—Tampa, Fl: Cool Stuff Every Kid Should Know. (p. 1704)
Jerome, Kate Boehm & National Geographic Learning Staff. Exploring Space. (p. 553)
—Fighting Disease. (p. 585)
—Protecting the Planet. (p. 1412)
—Thinking It Through. (p. 1734)
—Understanding the Brain. (p. 1816)
—Using Energy. (p. 1828)
—Volcanoes & Earthquakes. (p. 1849)
Jerome, Louie. Peter & the Black Dog. (p. 1346)
Jerrold, Walter, ed. Big Book of Nursery Rhymes. Robinson, Charles, illus. (p. 179)
(Jerry) Deal, Gerald R. Famous Dog Chowski. (p. 569)
Jerry, Spinelli. Blue Ribbon Blues. (p. 203)
—Loser. (p. 1054)
—Stargirl. (p. 1642)
—Wringer. (p. 1963)
Jerwa, Brandon. G. I. Joe Master & Apprentice vol II. Stevens, Chris & Udon, illus. (p. 651)
—Union of the Snake. (p. 1818)
Jeschke, Stefanie, illus. see Holzwarth, Werner.
Jeschonek, Robert. Pinstriped Finger's My Only Friend. (p. 1361)
Jeskins, John, et al. IGCSE Revision Guide for Mathematics. (p. 855)
Jesner, Alois, illus. see Badegruber, Bernie.
Jesness, Jerry. Teaching English Language Learners K-12: A Quick-Start Guide for the New Teacher. (p. 1710)
Jeso, Isabella. Bitney Adventures. (p. 194)
Jesperson, Per. Wonder & Magic: The David Tales. (p. 1947)
Jesrani, Asha. Shirley the Poppy Fairy & the Little Girl Lucky. (p. 1567)
Jess Golden, Jess, illus. see Silverman, Erica & Rucker, Justin.
Jess Golden, Jess, illus. see Silverman, Erica.
Jessa, Azra. Ramadhan & Eid-Ul-Fitr. Jessa, Azra, illus. (p. 1437)
Jesse, Janeen. Nail Book: Professional Secrets of Personal Nail Care. (p. 1227)
Jesse, Mary. Abbey & Friends M Is for Manners. Cherif, Jennifer, illus. (p. 2)
Jessee, Diana, illus. see Cooper, Ann Goode & Bowlin, William Harrison.
Jessee, Diana, illus. see Cooper, Ann Goode.
Jessell, Tim. Boardwalk Mystery. Dunn, Robert, illus. (p. 205)
—Boxcar Children. (p. 216)
—Falcon. (p. 565)
—Mystery of the Fallen Treasure. (p. 1225)
—Return of the Graveyard Ghost. (p. 1464)
Jessell, Tim, illus. see Abbott, Tony.
Jessell, Tim, illus. see Armstrong, Alan W.
Jessell, Tim, illus. see Armstrong, Alan.
Jessell, Tim, illus. see Finch, Kate.
Jessell, Tim, illus. see Haven, Paul.
Jessell, Tim, illus. see Ingle, Annie & Klimo, Kate.
Jessell, Tim, illus. see Kelly, David A.
Jessell, Tim, illus. see Klimo, Kate.
Jessell, Tim, illus. see Lee, Stan.
Jessell, Tim, illus. see MacLachlan, Patricia.
Jessell, Tim, illus. see Pyron, Bobbie.
Jessell, Tim, illus. see Stoudemire, Amar'e.
Jessell, Tim, illus. see Worth, Bonnie & Klimo, Kate.
Jessell, Tim, jt. auth. see Abbott, Tony.
Jessen, Lynn Lillard & Lillard, Paula Polk. Montessori from the Start: The Child at Home, from Birth to Age Three. (p. 1170)
Jesset, Aurore. Loopy. Korthues, Barbara, illus. (p. 1052)
—Loopy. Jesset, Aurore & Korthues, Barbara, illus. (p. 1052)
—Loquillo. Korthues, Barbara, illus. (p. 1052)
Jessi Swanson And Jessica Swanson & Swanson, Jessica. Adventurous Day for Lucy. (p. 25)
Jessica Hoel. Adam B Brave. Samantha Nowak, illus. (p. 11)
JessT, Grant, illus. see Segal, Andrew.
Jessum, Jeffrey E. Diary of a Social Detective: Real-life tales of mystery, intrigue & interpersonal Adventure. (p. 435)
Jessup, Dylan. We're All Americans. (p. 1875)
Jessup, J. W. Chaim: The Colossus of Rhodes. (p. 288)
—Yeshua Codex. (p. 1971)
Jessup, Lynne, as told by. Ramayana. (p. 1437)
Jessup, VonDa. Wanda the Witch at the Happy Haunted House. (p. 1856)
Jestice, Phyllis G. Ancient Egyptian Warfare. (p. 69)
—Ancient Persian Warfare. (p. 70)
Jesus, Opal De. Golden Apple Kingdom (p. 694)
Jeswald, Mary J. Crazy Adventure of Nicholas Mouse. Trimble, Anne M., illus. (p. 377)
Jeter, Derek. Hit & Miss. (p. 785)
Jeter, Derek & Mantell, Paul. Contract. (p. 361)
Jeter, Joseph C. Unknown Soldier. (p. 1821)
Jethani, Rita. Baby has a Burp. (p. 126)
Jett, Cindy. Harry the Happy Caterpillar Grows: Helping Children Adjust to Change. Voerg, Kathy, illus. (p. 751)
Jett, Stephen C. & Roberts, Lisa. France. (p. 627)
Jeune, Marie Carole. Rita & the Parrot. Saincilus, Larimer, illus. (p. 1475)
Jeunese, Gallimard & Salvador, Ana. Draw with Joan Miró. (p. 481)
Jeunesse, Gallimard, jt. auth. see Bour, Laura.
Jeunesse, Gallimard, jt. auth. see Houbre, Gilbert.
Jeunesse, Gallimard, jt. auth. see Mettler, René.
Jeunesse, Gallimard, tr. see Millet, Claude, et al.
Jeunesse, Gallimard & De Bourgoing, Pascale. Dogs. Galeron, Henri, illus. (p. 462)
Jeunesse, Gallimard & Delafosse, Claude. Butterflies. Heliadore, illus. (p. 247)
Jeunesse, Gallimard & Peyrols, Sylvaine. Human Body. Peyrols, Sylvaine, illus. (p. 825)
—Ladybugs & Other Insects. Peyrols, Sylvaine, illus. (p. 971)
Jeunesse, Gallimard, et al. Dinosaurs. Prunier, James & Galeron, Henri, illus. (p. 443)
Jevons, Chris, illus. see North, Laura.
Jewel. Sweet Dreams. Bates, Amy June, illus. (p. 1689)
—That's What I'd Do. Bates, Amy June, illus. (p. 1727)
Jewel, Judy. Sole Shoes: Nate the Skate in Search of His Mate. (p. 1607)
Jewell, Beverly. My Name Is Jeromy Russ Cardona, illus. (p. 1215)
Jewell, Helen M. Women in Dark Age & Early Medieval Europe C. 500-1200. (p. 1945)
—Women in Late Medieval & Reformation Europe, 1200-1550. (p. 1945)
Jewell, JoAnn Wyatt. Wintertime on Bushytail Lane. (p. 1939)
Jewell, Kim. Misery's Fire. (p. 1150)
Jewell, Laura. Ty Gets His Wings. (p. 1804)
Jewell, M. B. Tales of Amanda O' (p. 1702)
Jewell, Roe. Flight to Andolin: Journeys of a Reluctant Heroine. (p. 604)
Jewell, Sandra. Paula Peacock Discovers She Is Unique. (p. 1330)
Jewell, Teresa. How Charlie Mouse Learned about Cystic Fibrosis. (p. 805)
Jewell, Yvonne. Carla the Confused Caterpillar. (p. 270)
Jewett, Anne, illus. see Rando, Licia.
Jewett, Eleanore M. Big John's Secret. Chapman, Frederick T., illus. (p. 182)
Jewett, Sarah Orne. Betty Leicester: A Story for Girls. (p. 172)
—Betty Leicester's Christmas. (p. 172)
—Country of the Pointed Firs. (p. 372)
—White Heron. Alvord, Douglas, illus. (p. 1913)
Jewett, Sophie. God's Troubadour, the Story of Saint Francis of Assisi (Yesterday's Classics) (p. 692)
Jewish Lights Publishing Staff. New Jewish Baby Album: Creating & Celebrating the Beginning of a Spiritual Life - A Jewish Lights Companion. (p. 1245)
Jewitt, Kathryn. 3D Theater: Oceans. Dogi, Fiametta, illus. (p. 1992)
Jewitt, Kathryn, jt. auth. see Weber, Belinda.
Jewitt, Kathryn & Dogi, Fiametta. 3D Theater: Dinosaurs. (p. 1992)
—3D Theater: Rainforest. (p. 1992)
—Wild Animals: Play Look & Find in Amazing 3-D Pop Ups. (p. 1928)
Jewl, Terry. Pixies in Home Sweet Home. (p. 1365)
Jeyaveeran, Ruth, illus. see Krishnaswami, Uma.
Jezernik, Bozidar. Wild Europe: The Balkans in the Gaze of Western Travellers. (p. 1929)
JFA Productions Staff, jt. auth. see Cardero, Patrick.
JG Ferguson Publishing Company, creator. Computers. (p. 355)
J.G. Ferguson Publishing Company Staff. Music. (p. 1193)
J.G. Ferguson Publishing Company Staff, contrib. by. Fashion. (p. 575)
—Health Care. (p. 757)
—Publishing. (p. 1414)
Ji, Zhaohua & Xu, Cui. No! That's Wrong! Ji, Zhaohua & Xu, Cui, illus. (p. 1260)
Jian, Li. Horse & the Mysterious Drawing: A Story in English & Chinese. (p. 799)
—Ming's Adventure with the Terracotta Army. Wert, Yijin, tr. (p. 1146)
—Snake Goddess Colors the World: A Chinese Tale Told in English & Chinese. (p. 1596)
—Water Dragon: A Chinese Legend. (p. 1862)
Jian, Li, illus. see Wert, Yijin, tr.
Jiang, Emily. Summoning the Phoenix: Poems & Prose about Chinese Musical Instruments Chu, April, illus. (p. 1675)
Jiang, Eva. Eric Loved Fire Trucks. (p. 533)
Jiang, Helga. Clay Charm Magic! 25 Amazing, Teeny-Tiny Projects to Make with Polymer Clay. (p. 330)
Jiang, Ji-Li. Red Kite, Blue Kite. Ruth, Greg, illus. (p. 1454)
—Red Scarf Girl: A Memoir of the Cultural Revolution. (p. 1455)
Jiang, Mingyan. Stella Doggy: Book One of Stella's Awesome Adventures. (p. 1647)
Jianmei, Wang. America: My Horn, Your Country. (p. 58)
Jigsaw Nursery Rhymes. Blow, Wind, Blow. (p. 202)
—Jack & Jill. (p. 902)
—Old King Cole. (p. 1284)
—Rub-a-Dub-Dub. (p. 1493)
Ji-Li, Jiang. Red Scarf Girl: A Memoir of the Cultural Revolution. (p. 1455)
Jillette, Beatrice & Brennan, Peta, eds. True Tales & Prized Pictures: The 1890's Photographs & Journals of two New Hampshire Brothers. (p. 1793)
Jilson, Emily. Five Little Mice: A Collection of Children's Poems. (p. 600)
Jim Connelly, illus. see Bradford James Nolan.
Jim, Madsen, et al. NIV Adventure Bible (p. 1257)
Jim, Strawn, jt. auth. see Chuck, Stump.
Jimena Pinto-Krowjiline, illus. see Brannon, Pat.
Jimenez, Adan, jt. auth. see Tsang, Evonne.
Jimenez, Alberto, tr. see Cronin, Doreen.
Jiménez, Alberto, tr. see Recheis, Kèathe, et al.
Jimenez, Angeles. Macarena la Anguila. Gil, Sabina, illus. (p. 1067)
Jimenez, Angels, jt. auth. see Navarro, Paula.
Jimenez, Empar, jt. auth. see Jimenez, Nuria.
Jiménez, Francisco. Mariposa. Silva, Simon, illus. (p. 1094)
Jiménez, Juan Ramón. Canta Pajaro Lejano. (p. 262)
—Mi Primer Libro de Poemas. (p. 1133)
—Platero & I/Platero y Yo: A Dual-Language Book. Appelbaum, Stanley, ed. (p. 1370)
—Platero y Yo. (p. 1370)
—Platero y Yo (Platero & I) (p. 1370)
Jimenez, Leticia Serrano, illus. see Avila, Juan Casas.
Jimenez, Nuria & Jimenez, Empar. Splash! Water. Curto, Rosa M., illus. (p. 1629)
Jimenez, Phil. Paradise Found. (p. 1323)
Jimenez, Phil & Winick, Judd. Death & Return of Donna Troy. (p. 420)
Jimenez, Resu, illus. see Lopez, Minia.
Jiménez Rioja, Alberto, jt. auth. see Cronin, Doreen.
Jimenez Rioja, Alberto, tr. see Cronin, Doreen.
Jimenez Rioja, Alberto, tr. see Ganeri, Anita, et al.
Jimenez, Ruben D., tr. see Dicicco, Joe.
Jimenez, Vita. What Kind of Sound? (p. 1891)
Jimenz, Jim, illus. see Manning, Matthew K. & Poe, Edgar Allen.
Jimerson, Maxine Newman. Childhood Obesity. (p. 302)
Jimerson, Maxine Newman, jt. auth. see Marcovitz, Hal.
Jiminez, Elizabeth. Lalo. (p. 972)
Jimmie, Elsie, jt. auth. see Cook, Jean G.
Jimmy. My Kayak Lives in a Tree at the Beach (p. 1211)
Jimmy, Mary, illus. see Nicholai, Rachel, et al.
Jin, Chris & Trimmer, Christian. Simon's New Bed. Van der Paardt, Melissa, illus. (p. 1577)
Jin, Hong Gang, see Gang Jin, Hong.
Jin, Hong Gang, et al. Crossing Paths: Living & Learning in China. Wittlinger, Laurie A., photos by. (p. 385)
—Shifting Tides: Culture in Contemporary China. Wittlinger, Laurie A., photos by. (p. 1566)
Jin, Katherine, illus. see Collins, P. J. Sarah.
Jin, Susie Lee. It's Bedtime for Little Monkeys. (p. 896)
Jingling, Kathy, ed. Barnabas & His Great Mission for Christ. Tobar, Malena, illus. (p. 139)
—Bernabe y su Gran Mision por Cristo. Oyola, Milta, tr. from ENG. (p. 167)
Jingwen, Zhu, tr. see Tang, Sanmu.
Jinkins, Lisa Heath. PB & J Otter Noodle Stories: Busy Day. (p. 1331)
Jinks, Catherine. Abused Werewolf Rescue Group. (p. 7)
—Babylonne. (p. 128)
—Eglantine. (p. 506)
—Eloise. (p. 516)
—Elysium. (p. 517)
—Eustace. (p. 540)
—Evil Genius. (p. 546)
—Genius Squad. (p. 661)
—Genius Wars. (p. 661)
—How to Catch a Bogle. Watts, Sarah, illus. (p. 815)
—Living Hell. (p. 1041)
—Pagan in Exile. (p. 1317)
—Pagan's Vows. de Sève, Peter, illus. (p. 1318)
—Plague of Bogles. (p. 1366)
—Reformed Vampire Support Group. (p. 1456)
—Vacaciones Horribles. Cicero, Julian, illus. (p. 1829)
Jinks, Elizabeth Emily. Terrell/Terral Family History 1710-2003. (p. 1721)
Jinny, Johnson, jt. auth. see Martineau, Susan.
Jinshan Painting Academy, illus. see Kitze, Carrie A.
Jippes, Daan, et al. Donald Duck Family (p. 466)
—Walt Disney's Comics Clark, John, ed. (p. 1855)
—Walt Disney's Comics & Stories Clark, John, ed. (p. 1855)
—Walt Disney's Comics & Stories #703. (p. 1855)
Jirak, Tracey, illus. see Berthiaume, Donna M.
Jirankova-Limbrick, Martina, illus. see Edwards, Amelia.
Jiries, Nariman. Grace-A-Lena Learns the Meaning of Self-Esteem. (p. 704)
Jiron, Betsy. Sing for Me. (p. 1579)
JiSeung, Kook. Ouch! It Stings! JiSeung, Kook, illus. (p. 1307)
JIST Publishing Editors. Young Person's Occupational Outlook Handbook. (p. 1979)
JIST Publishing Editors, jt. auth. see Burkhardt, Mary Sue.
JIST Publishing Editors, ed. Young Person's Character Education Handbook. (p. 1979)
JIST Publishing Staff. Instructor's Guide for Creating Your High School Portfolio & Creating Your High School Resume. (p. 878)
JIST Publishing Staff, creator. Young Person's Career Skills Handbook. (p. 1979)
JIST Works. People at Work! Second Edition: A Student's A-Z Guide to 350 Jobs. (p. 1339)
—Young Person's Occupational Outlook Handbook, Fifth Edition. (p. 1979)
JIST Works, Inc. Staff & Department of Labor Staff. Exploring Careers: A Young Person's Guide to 1,000 Jobs. (p. 551)
Jitchotvisut, Donna M. Mittens for Christmas. (p. 1156)
Jitendra, Asha K., jt. ed. see Montague, Marjorie.
Jiya, Tapiwa. Epic of Goz. (p. 532)
Jjdenson. Kitty Crunch & Doggy Chow. (p. 963)
J'Lynn. Who's Your Daddy (p. 1921)
JN Productions Staff, tr. see Watase, Yuu & Caselman, Lance.
Jno-Lewis, Jason. Thank You Book: A Thank-You Goes a Long Way. (p. 1725)
Jo Berkus, jt. auth. see Jaynie R. Wood, M. s.
Jo, Eun-Ha. Bijoux Park, Sang-Sun, illus. (p. 185)
Jo, Eun-hwa, illus. see Kim, Soo-hyeon.
Jo, Eun-sook. Ah I'm Full: Food Chain. Cowley, Joy, ed. (p. 30)
Jo, Hyeon-suk, illus. see Brothers Grimm Staff.
Jo, Hyeon-suk, illus. see Brothers Grimm.
Jo, Kami. Toby Learns to Fly. (p. 1760)
Jo, Sinae, illus. see Choi, Na-mi.
Jo Tuttle, Mary. Tutties Touches. (p. 1799)
Joachim, David, jt. auth. see Schloss, Andrew.
Joachim, Jean C. Ancient Egypt Dot-to-Dot. Harrison, Nancy, illus. (p. 68)
—Construction Vehicles. Salvucci, Richard J., illus. (p. 360)
Joachimowski, Paula L. Swamp Band Lullaby. McGrath, Ryan, illus. (p. 1688)
—Swamp Band Lullaby. (p. 1688)
Joan, Marler. Secrets of the Wind. (p. 1546)
Joan, Pere, illus. see Bas, Mercè Escardó I.
Joan, Pere, illus. see Escardo Bas, Mercè.
Joane', E'nea, illus. see Keonna-E'nea.
Joanna, Harris. He's My God!-(Book 2) Knowing God Through His Names - a Childrens' Devotional. Jen, Kallin, photos by. (p. 774)
Joanna, Turner, jt. auth. see Harris, Nicholas.
Joanne Beeker Clurman, jt. auth. see Hall, Noelle Chason.
Joanne, O'Sullivan. Bizarre Weather: Howling winds, pouring rain, blazing heat, freezing cold, huge hurricanes, violent earthquakes, tsunami's, tornadoes & more of nature's Fury. (p. 194)
Job. Yakari. (p. 1968)
—Yakari & the Coyote. Dérib, illus. (p. 1968)
—Yakari & the Grizzly. Dérib, illus. (p. 1968)
—Yakari in the Land of Wolves. (p. 1968)
—Yakari Vol. 10: the River of Forgetfulness. Dérib, illus. (p. 1968)
—Yakari Vol. 11: Yakari & Nanabozo. Derib, illus. (p. 1968)
Job & Dérib. Yakari & the White Fleece. (p. 1968)
Job, Barbara & Morley, Diane. Statistics. (p. 1644)
Job, Chris. BMX. (p. 204)
Job, et al. Yakari & the Beavers. (p. 1968)
Job, Rueben P. & Thompson, Marjorie J. Embracing the Journey: Participant's Book. (p. 517)

Jobes, Cecily. Bugs & Plants Need Each Other. (p. 237)
—Colony of Maryland. (p. 342)
Jobin, Matthew. Nethergrim. (p. 1242)
Jobling, Curtis. My Daddy: Mini Edition. (p. 1201)
—My Daddy: My Daddy Is the Best in the Universe! (p. 1201)
—My Daddy. Jobling, Curtis, illus. (p. 1201)
—Nest of Serpents. (p. 1242)
—Old MacDonald Had a Zoo. McLaughlin, Tom, illus. (p. 1284)
—Rage of Lions. (p. 1433)
—Rise of the Wolf. (p. 1475)
—Shadow of the Hawk. (p. 1557)
—Storm of Sharks. (p. 1656)
—War of the Werelords. (p. 1857)
Jobling, Curtis, illus. see Schertle, Alice.
Jobson, Gary. Winner's Guide to Optimist Sailing. (p. 1937)
Jocelyn, Marthe. ABC X 3: English - Espanol - Francais. Slaughter, Tom, illus. (p. 3)
—Day with Nellie. Jocelyn, Marthe, illus. (p. 415)
—Earthly Astonishments. (p. 497)
—Eats. Slaughter, Tom, illus. (p. 501)
—Folly. (p. 612)
—Hannah & the Seven Dresses. (p. 742)
—Hannah's Collections. (p. 743)
—Home for Foundlings. (p. 792)
—Mable Riley: A Reliable Record of Humdrum, Peril, & Romance. (p. 1067)
—Mayfly. (p. 1113)
—One Some Many. Slaughter, Tom, illus. (p. 1297)
—Over Under. Slaughter, Tom, illus. (p. 1314)
—Ready for Autumn. (p. 1447)
—Ready for Spring. (p. 1447)
—Ready for Summer. (p. 1447)
—Ready for Winter. (p. 1447)
—Same Same. Slaughter, Tom, illus. (p. 1507)
—Scribbling Women: True Tales from Astonishing Lives. (p. 1533)
—Sneaky Art: Crafty Surprises to Hide in Plain Sight. Jocelyn, Marthe, illus. (p. 1597)
—What We Hide. (p. 1895)
—Which Way? Slaughter, Tom, illus. (p. 1911)
—Would You. (p. 1962)
Jocelyn, Marthe, illus. see Gleick, Beth.
Jocelyn, Marthe & Jocelyn, Nell. Ones & Twos. (p. 1298)
—Where Do You Look? (p. 1907)
Jocelyn, Marthe & Scrimger, Richard. Viminy Crowe's Comic Book. Dávila, Claudia, illus. (p. 1842)
Jocelyn, Marthe, ed. First Times: Stories Selected by Marthe Jocelyn. (p. 597)
Jocelyn, Marthe, selected by. Secrets. (p. 1544)
Jocelyn, Nell, jt. auth. see Jocelyn, Marthe.
Jocelyn, Sawyer, illus. see Lorenzen, Margaret Brownell.
Jocham, Tammy. Smiley Meets Twinkle. (p. 1594)
Jock, illus. see Aaron, Jason.
Jodie, Dias, illus. see Keen, Marian.
Jodorowsky, Alexandro. Son of the Gun: Saint. Vol. 2 (p. 1611)
Joe & Trish. Adventures of Sasha, the Six-Fingered Cat. (p. 22)
Joe, Anna Rose. Common Snipe. Afcan, Paschal, ed. (p. 349)
—Tukutukuaraller. Afcan, Paschal, ed. (p. 1796)
Joe Kent, illus. see Delena Deatherage.
Joe, O'Brien. Alfie Green & the Magical Gift. Jean, Texier, illus. (p. 37)
Joe, Saqamaw Mi'sel. Muinijj Becomes a Man. McQuane, Antonia, illus. (p. 1189)
Joe, Staton, et al. Crossovers (p. 385)
Joe Thomson-Swift. Magic Stone. (p. 1073)
Joel, Billy. Goodnight, My Angel: A Lullabye. Gilbert, Yvonne, illus. (p. 701)
Joelson. Oliver Mccoy - the Vegetable Boy. (p. 1285)
Joffo, Joseph. Bag of Marbles: The Graphic Novel. (p. 132)
—Bag of Marbles: The Graphic Novel. Gauvin, Edward, tr. (p. 132)
Jofre, Paola. Lilliput Blasts Off! (p. 1017)
Joggerst, Anita & Williamson, Don. Best Garden Plants for Missouri. (p. 169)
Johanek, Durrae. What I Saw in Yellowstone: A Kid's Guide to Wonderland. Cauble, Christopher, photos by. (p. 1887)
Johann David Wyss Staff. Swiss Family Robinson. (p. 1691)
Johannen, Kevin C., jt. auth. see Phillips, Carey R.
Johannes, Avril & Branham, Jan. Bunny an Alaskan Hare. (p. 242)
—Eeny, Meeny, Miney, Moe, Four Alaskan Ravens. Tessama, C., illus. (p. 505)
Johannes, Shelley, illus. see Clairmont, Patsy.
Johannes, Shelley, illus. see Cogswell, Jackie Chirco.
Johannes, Shelley, illus. see McKenna, Susan.
Johansen, Bruce E. Iroquois. (p. 888)
Johansen, H. L. How to Draw the Life & Times of Calvin Coolidge. (p. 818)
Johansen, Hanna. Henrietta & the Golden Eggs. Barrett, John S., tr. from GER. (p. 767)
Johansen, Hanna & Barrett, John S. Duck & the Owl. Bhend, Käthi, illus. (p. 488)
Johansen, Heidi. What I Look Like When I Am Angry. (p. 1886)
—What I Look Like When I am Angry / Cómo me veo cuando estoy Enojado. (p. 1886)
—What I Look Like When I Am Happy: N. (p. 1887)
—What I Look Like When I Am Happy. (p. 1887)
—What I Look Like When I am Happy / Cómo me veo cuando estoy Contento. (p. 1887)
Johansen, Heidi Leigh. How to Draw the Life & Times of Calvin Coolidge. (p. 818)
—My Book of Trucks. (p. 1199)
—My Food. (p. 1208)
—What I Look Like When I Am Angry. (p. 1886)
Johansen, K. V. Black Box. (p. 195)
—Nightwalker (p. 1255)
—Shadow Road (p. 1558)
—Torrie & the Pirate Queen. Delezenne, Christine, illus. (p. 1770)
—Torrie & the Snake-Prince. Delezenne, Christine, illus. (p. 1770)
—Treason in Eswy (p. 1781)
—Warden of Greyrock (p. 1858)
Johansen, Mila. 101 Theatre Games: For Drama Teachers, Classroom Teachers & Directors. (p. 2000)
—50 Scenes to Go: And 20 Monologues to Show. (p. 1997)
Johansen, Tesia. Christmas Secret. Johnson, Gary & Johansen, Tesia, illus. (p. 315)
Johansen, Zdenka. When You Give of Yourself. (p. 1905)
Johanson, Anna, illus. see Snyder, Susan.
Johanson, Chris. Auto Engine Performance & Driveability. (p. 117)
—Auto Heating & Air Conditioning. (p. 117)
—Auto Heating & Air Conditioning Technology. (p. 117)
Johanson, Chris & Duffy, James E. Automatic Transmissions & Transaxles. (p. 117)
—Manual Drive Trains & Axles: Teaching Package. (p. 1089)
—Manual Drive Trains & Axles. (p. 1089)
Johanson, Chris & Stockel, Martin T. Auto Brakes. (p. 117)
—Auto Suspension & Steering. (p. 117)
—Auto Suspension & Steering Technology. (p. 117)
Johanson, Chris, et al. Auto Fundamentals. (p. 117)
Johanson, Paula. Biofuels: Sustainable Energy in the 21st Century. (p. 188)
—Breast Cancer Prevention. (p. 225)
—Cobalt. (p. 336)
—Early British Poetry: "Words That Burn" (p. 493)
—Fake Foods: Fried, Fast, & Processed: The Incredibly Disgusting Story. (p. 565)
—Fish: From the Catch to Your Table. (p. 598)
—HIV & AIDS. (p. 786)
—Jobs in Sustainable Agriculture. (p. 919)
—Lithium. (p. 1023)
—Love Poetry: How Do I Love Thee? (p. 1060)
—Making Good Choices about Fair Trade. (p. 1081)
—Making Good Choices about Nonrenewable Resources. (p. 1081)
—Money-Making Opportunities for Teens Who Like Pets & Animals. (p. 1164)
—Muscular Dystrophy. (p. 1192)
—What Is Energy? (p. 1889)
—What's in Your Food? Fast Food. (p. 1898)
—Will Hobbs. (p. 1932)
—World Poetry: Evidence of Life. (p. 1958)
—World Poetry- Evidence of Life. (p. 1958)
Johanson, Paula, jt. auth. see Conti, Nicolette.
Johanson, Rhonda. Great Tempo Race. (p. 718)
Johanson, Ryan & Blansten, Gern. Pasquinading Poesy. (p. 1326)
Johanson, Sarah Margaret. Caillou: The Magic of Compost. Sevigny, Eric, illus. (p. 251)
—Caillou - I Can Brush My Teeth. Brignaud, Pierre, illus. (p. 251)
—Happy Thanksgiving! Brignaud, Pierre, illus. (p. 747)
Johansson, Anna, illus. see Ely, Kosa.
Johansson, Cecilia. Just Like Mommy. (p. 939)
Johansson, Cecilia, illus. see Bee, William.
Johansson, Cecilia, illus. see McKain, Kelly.
Johansson, Cecilia, illus. see Taplin, Sam.
Johansson, J. R. Cut Me Free. (p. 396)
—Insomnia. (p. 878)
—Mania. (p. 1087)
—Paranoia. (p. 1324)
Johansson, Philip. Coral Reef: A Colorful Web of Life. (p. 366)
—Desert: Discover This Dry Biome. (p. 428)
—Dry Desert: A Web of Life. (p. 487)
—Forested Taiga: A Web of Life. (p. 618)
—Frozen Tundra: A Web of Life. (p. 645)
—Grasslands: Discover This Wide Open Biome. (p. 712)
—Lakes & Rivers: A Freshwater Web of Life. (p. 972)
—Marshes & Swamps: A Wetland Web of Life. (p. 1096)
—Seashore: A Saltwater Web of Life. (p. 1538)
—Taiga: Discover This Forested Biome. (p. 1695)
—Temperate Forest: A Web of Life. (p. 1717)
—Temperate Forest: Discover This Wooded Biome. (p. 1717)
—Tropical Rain Forest: A Web of Life. (p. 1789)
—Tropical Rain Forest: Discover This Wet Biome. (p. 1789)
—Tundra: Discover This Frozen Biome. (p. 1796)
—What You Can Do about Carpal Tunnel Syndrome & Other Repetitive Strain Injuries. (p. 1896)
—Wide Open Grasslands: A Web of Life. (p. 1927)
Johari, Harish, illus. see Sperling, Vatsala.
Johari, Harish & Sperling, Vatsala. How Ganesh Got His Elephant Head. Weltevrede, Pieter, illus. (p. 809)
—How Parvati Won the Heart of Shiva. Weltevrede, Pieter, illus. (p. 811)
Johari, Sandeep, illus. see Sperling, Vatsala.
Johmann, Carol A. Lewis & Clark Expedition: Join the Corps of Discovery to Explore Uncharted Territory. (p. 1004)
John A. MacDonald. Pachung. (p. 1317)
John and Wendy, illus. see Andrews, Alexa.
John & Wendy, illus. see Krulik, Nancy E.
John & Wendy, illus. see Krulik, Nancy.
John and Wendy, illus. see Krulik, Nancy.
John and Wendy Staff, illus. see Krulik, Nancy E.
John and Wendy Staff, illus. see Krulik, Nancy.
John, Antony. Elemental. (p. 510)
—Five Flavors of Dumb. (p. 600)
—Imposter. (p. 862)
—Renegade. (p. 1460)
John, Antony & Barnes, John. Five Flavors of Dumb. (p. 600)
John, Archambault, jt. auth. see Bill, Martin.
John Blake. Pound a Poem. (p. 1389)
John Blake Publishing Staff. Pound a Poem: The Winning Entries from the National Schools Poetry Competition. Sayers, Myrna, illus. (p. 1389)
John, Clement. Best Friends: A Bedtime Story. (p. 169)
John, Deere & Berg, Ron. Touchdown for Danny Dozer. Running Press Staff, ed. (p. 1772)
John, Deere & Hill, Dave. Johnny Tractor's Fun Farm Festival. Running Press Staff, ed. (p. 923)
John, Gee. Octopus. (p. 1278)
—Tiger Sharks. (p. 1748)
John, Hatchard. Hedge of Thorns. (p. 761)
John, James "Jerry". Fee the Flea. (p. 580)
—Grandpa's Little White Truck Goes on a Picnic. (p. 710)
John, Jory. Goodnight Already! Davies, Benji, illus. (p. 701)
—I Love You Already! Davies, Benji, illus. (p. 843)
—I Will Chomp You! Shea, Bob, illus. (p. 848)
—I'm No Monster! Shea, Bob, illus. (p. 859)
John, Jory, jt. auth. see Barnett, Mac.
John, Kaliski, ed. see Crawford, Margaret & Kaliski, John.
John, Karen. Heavenly Treasures. (p. 761)
John Knapp, II. Pillar of Pepper & Other Bible Rhymes. Turner-Deckert, Dianne, illus. (p. 1359)
John, Louise. I Can Hear! Elkerton, Andy, illus. (p. 835)
—My Chair. Elkerton, Andy, illus. (p. 1200)
—My Mom Can't See. Elkerton, Andy, illus. (p. 1214)
—Small Elkerton, Andy, illus. (p. 1591)
John, Margaret. Little Belly Monster Makes French Toast. Kim, Sarah, illus. (p. 1024)
John, Matthew, illus. see Rosinsky, Natalie M.
John, Matthew, illus. see Rosinsky, Natalie M. & Picture Window Books Staff.
John, P. Lugar Seguro. (p. 1064)
John, Patricia St., see St. John, Patricia.
John Paul II, pseud. My Dear Young Friends: Pope John Paul II Speaks to Youth on Life, Love, & Courage. Vitek, John, ed. (p. 1201)
John, Peter. First Christmas Tree; Ts'eba Tthadala: The Young Spruce Tree. (p. 593)
John R Neill, illus. see Baum, L. Frank.
John, Rebecca Mary. Musings of a Young Girl. (p. 1194)
John, Roberta. Dibe Lizhini Jiiligo Bee Shanah IDLI/Proud to Be a Blacksheep. Thomas, Peter A., tr. from ENG. (p. 435)
—Red Is Beautiful: Chih Nizhoni. Ruffenach, Jessie, ed. (p. 1454)
John, Scott, text. Becoming A Student of the Game. (p. 156)
John Taylor, Jeannie St. Penguin's Special Christmas Tree. (p. 1337)
John the Beloved. Book of Revelations: An Inspired Translation (p. 211)
John, Victoria. Dolphins: Level N (p. 464)
John, Wivina. His Love for Me Is Strong. (p. 781)
Johnathan, Kuehl, illus. see Reich, J. J.
Johns, Ann, illus. see Hay, Sam.
Johns, Barbara. Heart Adventures with PuppyGirl. (p. 759)
Johns, Chris & Carney, Elizabeth. Face to Face with Cheetahs. (p. 560)
Johns, Dick, illus. see Mayer, Marvin S.
Johns, Eric. Giraffe Tree & Other Tall Stories. (p. 677)
—Home Front. (p. 792)
—Mindreaders. (p. 1145)
Johns, Geoff. Jsa: Black Reign. Vol. 8 (p. 930)
—No Fear. (p. 1258)
—Red Zone Copiel, Olivier, illus. (p. 1455)
—Rogue War. Faucher, Wayne, illus. (p. 1485)
—Teen Titans (p. 1714)
—Thing: Freakshow. (p. 1732)
—Titans Around the World. (p. 1758)
Johns, Geoff, jt. auth. see Goyer, David S.
Johns, Geoff, jt. auth. see Kramer, Don.
Johns, Geoff, jt. auth. see Waid, Mark.
Johns, Geoff & Busiek, Kurt. Up, up, & Away! (p. 1824)
Johns, Geoff & Champagne, Keith. Mixed Signals. (p. 1156)
Johns, Geoff & Gibbons, Dave. Recharge. (p. 1451)
Johns, Geoff & Goyer, David S. Savage Times (p. 1516)
Johns, Geoff & Heinberg, Allan. Crisis of Conscience (p. 383)
Johns, Geoff & Paceho, Carlos. Revenge of the Green Lanterns. (p. 1466)
Johns, Geoff & Raab, Ben. Beast Boys & Girls. (p. 152)
Johns, Geoff, et al. 52 (p. 1997)
—Jsa: All Stars. (p. 930)
—Power Girl. (p. 1389)
—Teen Titans: Family Lost (p. 1714)
Johns, Isabel G. I'm Happy Being Me. Stegall, Joel E., illus. (p. 859)
Johns, Linda. Crazy Fruit Salad. (p. 377)
—Postcard Clues. (p. 1387)
—Rocket Boy Grows Up. (p. 1482)
—Three Shapely Pigs. (p. 1743)
—Three Shapley Pigs. (p. 1743)
—Uniquely Washington (p. 1818)
Johns, Linda & Jones, Melanie Davis. I Can Do It! I Can Bowl!/I Can Ski/I Can Do It All. Boles, Terry, illus. (p. 835)
Johns, Michael-Anne. Celeb Fact Files! The 411 on All Your Faves. (p. 283)
—Class Acts: Your Favorite Stars in School. (p. 327)
—Hangin' with Lindsay Lohan. (p. 742)
—School Cool. (p. 1522)
Johns, Michael-Anne. Today's Coolest Stars. (p. 1761)
Johns, Michael-Anne, jt. auth. see Morreale, Marie.
Johns, Phillip. Little Levi & Uncle Donut. (p. 1030)
Johns, Rebecca. Julie Forgets Annie. (p. 932)
Johns, W. E. Biggles' Secret Assignments. (p. 185)
Johnsen, Erin L. Adventures of the Big Dog & the Little Dog: They First Meet! Nishii, illus. (p. 23)
Johnson, A. E., tr. see Perrault, Charles.
Johnson, Adam, jt. auth. see Gordon, Barry.
Johnson, Alaya. Goblin King. Gandy, Meg, illus. (p. 688)
Johnson, Alaya Dawn. Detective Frankenstein. Ota, Yuko, illus. (p. 431)
—Goblin King Gandy, Meg & Olson, Meagan, illus. (p. 688)
—Love Is the Drug. (p. 1060)
—Summer Prince. (p. 1674)
Johnson, Alberta & Johnson, Errick C. Stanley & the Jellybeans. (p. 1639)
—Twelve Roses for Ann. (p. 1800)
Johnson, Alexandra, jt. auth. see Oliver, Martin.
Johnson, Ali C. My Two Little Hands Book. (p. 1220)
—Where Do I Belong. (p. 1907)
Johnson, Alice. Believe & You're There (4 vol. Set) (p. 161)
Johnson, Alice W. Believe & You're There: When Esther Saved (p. 161)
—Believe & You're There: When David Slew Goliath (p. 161)
—Believe & You're There: When Daniel Was Delivered (p. 161)
Johnson, Alice W. & Warner, Allison H. Believe & You're There at the Miracles of Jesus. Nelson, Holly, illus. (p. 161)
—Believe & You're There When Ammon Was a Missionary. Harston, Jerry, illus. (p. 161)
—Believe & You're There When Lehi Left Jerusalem. Harston, Jerry, illus. (p. 161)
—Believe & You're There When the Night Was Bright As Day. Harston, Jerry, illus. (p. 161)
—Believe & You're There When the Prince of Peace Was Born. Harston, Jerry, illus. (p. 161)
—Believe & You're There When the Stone Was Rolled Away. Nelson, Holly, illus. (p. 161)
—Believe & You're There When the White Dove Descended. Nelson, Holly, illus. (p. 161)
Johnson, Allen, Jr. Dead House. McMorris, Kelley, illus. (p. 416)
—My Brother's Story. McMorris, Kelley, illus. (p. 1199)
Johnson, Allen L. Kayaking Around Iceland: Adventures with Grandchildren. (p. 946)
—Willmore Horseback Adventure: Adventures with Grandchildren (p. 1934)
Johnson, Allen LeRoy. Sweden through the Eyes of a Six-year-old: Adventures with Grandchildren (p. 1689)
Johnson, Amber W., illus. see Adams, Tonya.
Johnson, Amy. Princess & the Frog. (p. 1402)
—Tales of the Forest. (p. 1702)
Johnson, Amy Crane. Cinnamon & the April Shower. Mommaerts, Robb, illus. (p. 321)
—Home for Pearl Squirrel. Mommaerts, Robb, illus. (p. 792)
—Lewis Cardinal's First Winter. Mommaerts, Robb, illus. (p. 1004)
—Mason Moves Away. Mommaerts, Robb, illus. (p. 1102)
—Mason Moves Away/Mason se Muda: A Solomon Raven Story: un cuento del cuervo Salomon de la Vega, Eida, tr. (p. 1102)
Johnson, Andi. Hailey Snowstorm. (p. 735)
—Little Molly Yo-Yo. (p. 1032)
—Rollerskate Kate. (p. 1485)
Johnson, Andi, illus. see Popper, Garry & Volke, Gordon.
Johnson, Andi, illus. see Popper, Garry.
Johnson, Andrea N. Mommy & Me. (p. 1162)
Johnson, Andrew, illus. see Holden, J. T.
Johnson, Angela. All This & Heaven Too: Heaven; The First Part Last; Sweet, Hereafter. (p. 46)
—Bird. (p. 190)
—Certain October. (p. 287)
—Cool Moonlight. (p. 364)
—Daddy Calls Me Man. Mitchell, Rhonda, illus. (p. 398)
—Day Ray Got Away. LaMarca, Luke, illus. (p. 414)
—First Part Last. (p. 596)
—Heaven (p. 761)
—Heaven. (p. 761)
—I Dream of Trains. Long, Loren, illus. (p. 838)
—In Daddy's Arms, I Am Tall. (p. 863)
—Julius. Pilkey, Dav, illus. (p. 932)
—Just Like Josh Gibson. Peck, Beth, illus. (p. 939)
—Looking for Red. (p. 1051)
—Lottie Paris & the Best Place. Fischer, Scott M., illus. (p. 1057)
—Lottie Paris Lives Here. Fischer, Scott M., illus. (p. 1057)
—Sweet, Hereafter (p. 1689)
—Sweet, Hereafter. (p. 1689)
—Sweet Smell of Roses. Velasquez, Eric, illus. (p. 1690)
—Violet's Music. Huliska-Beith, Laura & Laura, Huliska-beith, illus. (p. 1843)
—Wind Flyers. Long, Loren, illus. (p. 1935)
Johnson, Ann, et al. Iowa Birds (p. 886)
Johnson, Annabel. Rock Candy Dream. (p. 1482)
Johnson, Annabel & Johnson, Edgar. Wilderness Bride. (p. 1931)
Johnson, Anne. Catch the Wind. (p. 279)
—Cat's Cradle. (p. 281)
Johnson, Anne Akers. Anillos. (p. 76)
—Fancy Friendship Bracelets. Johnson, Anne Akers, ed. (p. 570)
—Juegos con una Cuerda. (p. 931)
—Knitting: Learn to Knit Six Great Projects. (p. 965)
—Loop Loom Bracelets: Make Super-Stretchy Beaded Bracelets. (p. 1052)
—Make Your Own Washi Tape Stickers. (p. 1080)
—Origami. (p. 1303)
—Pulseras Rusticas. (p. 1416)
—Trenzas Locas. (p. 1784)
—Twirly Q's: Make Irresistible Cardboard Creations. (p. 1802)
Johnson, Anne Akers, jt. auth. see Chorba, April.
Johnson, Anne Akers, jt. auth. see Steele-Saccio, Eva.
Johnson, Anne Akers & Klutz Editors. Brilliant Bead Rings. (p. 228)
Johnson, Anne Akers & Murphy, Pat. Paper Flying Dragons: Design & Build Your Own Fantastic Flyers. Klutz Editors, ed. (p. 1322)
Johnson, Anne Akers, ed. Bead Loom Bracelets. (p. 149)
Johnson, Anne & Mortenson. Catch the Sun. (p. 279)
Johnson, Anne E. Trouble at the Scriptorium. (p. 1789)
Johnson, Anne Janette. Scopes Monkey Trial. (p. 1530)
—Warren Buffett. (p. 1858)
Johnson, Anne Janette & Raham, Gary. Fossils. (p. 623)
Johnson, Annie P., jt. auth. see Johnson, Russell W.
Johnson, Annie P. & Johnson, Russell. My Florida Alphabet. Hume, John, illus. (p. 1208)
Johnson, Antonia. Bianca's Light. (p. 175)
Johnson, Arden, illus. see Alderson, Sue Ann.
Johnson, Barbara. Who Said It's Poetry: Just Feel It. (p. 1917)
Johnson, Bee, illus. see Brown, Carron.
Johnson, Ben. Motocross. (p. 1179)
Johnson, Betsy, illus. see Halfmann, Janet.
Johnson, Betty. Farm Animals for Kids: Amazing Pictures & Fun Fact Children Book. (p. 573)
Johnson, Bill, illus. see Wolfson, Steve.
Johnson, Bill, photos by see Glebink, Bruce.
Johnson, Bob. Lost Mine of the Mechanical Spider. Johnson, Bob, illus. (p. 1056)
Johnson, Bonnie. No Matter What. (p. 1259)

J

Johnson, Brad & Brown, Greg. Brad Johnson: Play with Passion. (p. 221)
Johnson, Brandon, illus. see Bonner, Gayle.
Johnson, Brian. Creative Haven Abstract Designs Coloring Book. (p. 379)
Johnson, Britt, ed. see Durant, Sybrina, et al.
Johnson, Britt, ed. see Johnson, Sandi, et al.
Johnson, Britt, ed. see Johnson, Sandi.
Johnson, Bruce. We Both Read-About Dogs. (p. 1866)
—We Both Read-about Dogs. (p. 1866)
—We Read Phonics-A Day at the Zoo. Johnson, Meredith, illus. (p. 1868)
—We Read Phonics-Big Cats (Nonfiction) (p. 1868)
Johnson, Bruce, illus. see Benson, Linda Sue.
Johnson, Bruce, jt. auth. see Johnson, Odette.
Johnson, Bruce & Johnson, Meredith. Day at the Zoo. (p. 412)
Johnson, Bruce & McKay, Sindy. We Both Read Bilingual Edition-About Dogs/Acerca de Los Perros. (p. 1866)
—We Both Read-Zoo Day. Johnson, Meredith, illus. (p. 1866)
Johnson, Bryant. Bone Wars: The Game of Ruthless Paleontology. (p. 209)
Johnson, Bud. Break the Code: Cryptography for Beginners. (p. 224)
—Chirpy: Chirpy's First Time Flying. (p. 308)
Johnson, C. Homecoming. (p. 793)
Johnson, C. J. Coco & Petal: A Tweet Love Story. (p. 337)
Johnson, C. M. Cjs' Bible Adventure: CJs' first Adventure. (p. 326)
Johnson Cadwell, Warwick, illus. see Atinuke.
Johnson, Calvin. Buzzy the Vegetarian Vulture. Ciresi-Abremski, M. Kathleen, illus. (p. 249)
Johnson, Cara. Children of the Trees: The Dream Travelers - Book Four. (p. 302)
—Dream Travelers, Book Two: The Butterfly Voyage. (p. 484)
—Falling Awake - the Remembering: The Dream Travelers Companion. (p. 566)
—Looking Forward Back: The Dream Travelers Book Three. (p. 1051)
Johnson, Carl, jt. auth. see Johnson, Gwen.
Johnson, Carl & Johnson, Gwen. Diggin' the Big'un. Johnson, Gwen, illus. (p. 439)
—Dreamland Friends. Johnson, Gwen, illus. (p. 484)
Johnson, Carl R., Jr. Twelve Things a Leader Can Do to Influence Others More Effectively: The Essential Guide to Being a More Effective Leader. (p. 1800)
Johnson, Carol Ann, illus. see Laird, Donivee Martin.
Johnson, Carol V. Somerset Dreams. (p. 1609)
Johnson, Carole. Pennie the Piglet. (p. 1337)
Johnson, Carolyn M. Using Internet Primary Sources to Teach Critical Thinking Skills in the Sciences (p. 1828)
Johnson, Carolyn W. Sano Comes to the Farm (p. 1511)
Johnson, Catherine LeAnn, illus. see DeMico, Judy.
Johnson, Cathy Ann, illus. see Scholastic, Inc. Staff & Giovanni, Nikki.
Johnson, Cathy Jo. What's in a Name? Learning the Special Names of God. (p. 1897)
Johnson, Cecilia. In Stone Series: Secrets in Stone. (p. 865)
Johnson, Celeste. Beez Brothers: Baby Brother Has Autism. (p. 158)
Johnson, Celeste, illus. see Alpers, Jody.
Johnson, Celia, ed. 100 Great Poems for Girls. (p. 1998)
Johnson, Charles & Adelman, Bob. Life Remembering Martin Luther King, Jr. His Life & Crusade in Pictures. (p. 1012)
Johnson, Charles & Johnson, Elisheba. Adventures of Emery Jones, Boy Science Wonder: Bending Time. Johnson, Charles, illus. (p. 17)
Johnson, Charles D., jt. auth. see Dennison, John A.
Johnson, Chelsea, illus. see Stelten, Gene.
Johnson, Cheryl. Marlow. Ciesinki, Izabela, illus. (p. 1096)
Johnson, Christine. Claire de Lune. (p. 326)
—Deep in Alaska. Johnson, Gary R., illus. (p. 423)
—Gathering Dark. (p. 658)
—Nocturne. (p. 1262)
Johnson, Christine, ed. see Gray, Claudia, et al.
Johnson, Christopher L. I Don't Have Crooked Legs. (p. 837)
Johnson, Christopher/ Patrick. Reflection of God: Our Destiny As His Image. (p. 1456)
Johnson, Cindy B. Frantic the Frog. Lane, Cody R., illus. (p. 631)
Johnson, Claudia. Issues of Class in Jane Austen's Pride & Prejudice. (p. 893)
—Justice in Arthur Miller's The Crucible. (p. 940)
—Women's Issues in Alice Walker's the Color Purple. (p. 1946)
Johnson, Claudia, ed. see Mancini, Candice.
Johnson, Claudia & Mancini, Candice. Justice in Arthur Miller's - The Crucible. (p. 940)
Johnson, Claudia Durst. Race in the Poetry of Langston Hughes. Greenhaven Press Editors, ed. (p. 1431)
—Slavery & Racism in the Narative Life of Freddrick Douglass. (p. 1588)
Johnson, Claudia Durst & Johnson, Vernon. Understanding the Odyssey: A Student Casebook to Issues, Sources, & Historic Documents (p. 1816)
Johnson, Claudia, ed. Class Conflict in F. Scott Fitzgerald's The Great Gatsby. (p. 327)
—Colonialism in Joseph Conrad's Heart of Darkness. (p. 342)
—Issues of Class in Jane Austen's Pride & Prejudice. (p. 893)
—Women's Issues in Nathaniel Hawthorne's The Scarlett Letter. (p. 1946)
Johnson, Colette. Redneck Goes to Rome. (p. 1456)
Johnson, Cornelius. Escape from Ketan (p. 535)
Johnson, Craig. Dance & Donuts with Dad. (p. 402)
Johnson, Craig, illus. see Johnson, Joy.
Johnson, Craig Alan. Wave Watcher. (p. 1864)
Johnson, Crockett. Barnaby & Mr. O'Malley. (p. 139)
—Harold & the Purple Crayon. Johnson, Crockett, illus. (p. 749)
—Harold & the Purple Crayon Board Book. Johnson, Crockett, illus. (p. 749)
—Harold at the North Pole. Johnson, Crockett, illus. (p. 749)
—Harold et le Crayon Violet: The French Edition of Harold & the Purple Crayon. (p. 749)
—Harold's ABC Board Book. Johnson, Crockett, illus. (p. 749)
—Magic Beach. (p. 1071)
Johnson, Crockett, illus. see Cook, Bernadine.
Johnson, Crockett, illus. see Krauss, Ruth & Krauss.
Johnson, Crockett, illus. see Krauss, Ruth.
Johnson, Crockett & Baker, Liza. Harold & the Purple Crayon: Under the Sea. (p. 749)
Johnson, Crystal. Shaheed & His Rainbow. (p. 1558)
Johnson, Curtis, photos by see Rustad, Mark & Utter, Mark.
Johnson, Cynthia. Worldmark Conflict & Diplomacy. (p. 1960)
Johnson, Cynthia & Baker, Lawrence W. Bowling, Beatniks, & Bell-Bottoms: Pop Culture of 20th- & 21st-Century America (p. 216)
Johnson, Cynthia Brantley, ed. see Dickens, Charles.
Johnson, D. B. Four Legs Bad, Two Legs Good! (p. 625)
—Henry Hikes to Fitchburg. (p. 768)
—Henry Hikes to Fitchburg. Johnson, D. B., illus. (p. 768)
—Henry Works. (p. 769)
—Magritte's Marvelous Hat. Johnson, D. B., illus. (p. 1076)
Johnson, D. B., jt. auth. see Pinkwater, Daniel M.
Johnson, D. C. & Rowan, Ron. Secret of MeadowBrook Orphanage. (p. 1542)
Johnson, D. C. & Turner, Sandra. Let's Be Friends. Johnson, D. C. & Johnson, Darnell, illus. (p. 994)
Johnson, Dana A., jt. auth. see Morrison, Danette W.
Johnson, Darlington. Layla the Ladybug - "Honesty" (p. 981)
Johnson, Darnell, illus. see Johnson, D. C. & Turner, Sandra.
Johnson, Darrin Jon. Easter Hamster. (p. 499)
—Hamster Day. (p. 739)
Johnson, David. Boy Who Drew Cats. Johnson, David, illus. (p. 219)
—Bremen Town Musicians. (p. 226)
—Crystal Quest. (p. 387)
—Toby the Blow Fish: A Fish on A Quest & Learns A Life Lesson. (p. 1760)
Johnson, David, illus. see Andersen, Hans Christian.
Johnson, David, illus. see Bryant, Jen.
Johnson, David, illus. see Spinelli, Eileen.
Johnson, David A., illus. see Carlson, Drew.
Johnson, David Leslie, jt. auth. see Blakley-Cartwright, Sarah.
Johnson, Dawn M. I Have a Chuck. Klein, Ellen Marie, illus. (p. 839)
Johnson, Deacon, jt. auth. see Johnson, Deacon.
Johnson, Deacon & Johnson, Deacon. Unprincess: A Bedtime Story for Kids. Johnson, Deacon, illus. (p. 1822)
Johnson, Deanna. Blarron Creek Chronicles. (p. 198)
Johnson, Debbie. Dreams: Your Window to Heaven. (p. 484)
Johnson, Deborah C., illus. see Lockwood, Penny.
Johnson, Deborah C., illus. see Lopresti, Tony.
Johnson, Dell, illus. see Peterson, Brandon.
Johnson, Denise. Teaching Literacy in Fourth Grade. (p. 1710)
Johnson, Denise Donna. Veridical Circle. (p. 1837)
Johnson, Dennis. Tree That Went Sailing. (p. 1783)
Johnson, Diane, jt. auth. see Andres, Ken.
Johnson, Diane, jt. auth. see Andrews, Ken.
Johnson, Dirk. Purdue University Coloring & Activity Adventure Book. (p. 1419)
Johnson, Dolores. Children's Book of Kwanzaa: A Guide to Celebrating the Holiday. (p. 303)
—Onward: A Photobiography of African-American Polar Explorer Matthew Henson. (p. 1298)
Johnson, Dolores, illus. see Linderman, Dianne.
Johnson, Dolores & Schomp, Virginia. Harlem Reanissance. (p. 748)
Johnson, Dolores Uselman, illus. see Boyer, Melody.
Johnson, Dolores Uselman, illus. see Rosie, Maura & Gavlik, Sherry.
Johnson, Don. Tale of Billy the Bit. (p. 1699)
Johnson, Donald Knute, compiled by. Southport Secrets. (p. 1617)
Johnson, Donald-Brian, et al. Ceramic Arts Studio: The Legacy of Betty Harrington (p. 287)
Johnson, Donna. Giant Called Corp. (p. 673)
—Story of the Little Red Leaf. Johnson, Emily, illus. (p. 1661)
Johnson, Donna T., illus. see Gibbons, Joyce.
Johnson, Donnie. Little Flying Boy. (p. 1027)
Johnson, Doris M. Cookie Crumb Trail. Taylor, Jennifer Louise, illus. (p. 361)
Johnson, Dorothea, et al. Children's Tea & Etiquette: Brewing Good Manners in Young Minds. Peterson, Dawn, illus. (p. 304)
Johnson, Dorothy M. Bloody Bozeman: The Perilous Trail to Montana's Gold. (p. 201)
—Man Who Shot Liberty Valance: And A Man Called Horse, the Hanging Tree, & Lost Sister. (p. 1086)
Johnson, Drew, illus. see Ruka, Greg.
Johnson, Drew, et al. Junior Worldmark Encyclopedia of the States (p. 936)
Johnson, Duane, tr. see Hirano, Kohta.
Johnson, Duane A. Narrow Pathway to Success. (p. 1229)
Johnson, E. Harper, illus. see Rose, Mary Catherine.
Johnson, E. Pauline. Lost Island. Atanas, illus. (p. 1056)
—Lost Island. Matsoureff, Atanas, illus. (p. 1056)
Johnson, Earl L. Best of the West Hawkins, Grace M., ed. (p. 171)
Johnson, Earl L. & Hawkins, Grace. World's Greatest Working Trucks: The Best of the Northeast. Vol. 5 (p. 1960)
Johnson, Edgar, jt. auth. see Johnson, Annabel.
Johnson, Edward. Wonder-Working Providence of Sion's Saviour in New England. (p. 1947)
Johnson, Edward Augustus. History of Negro Soldiers in the Spanish American War: American Blacks in the Spanish American War. (p. 784)
Johnson, Elana. Abandon: A Possession Novel. (p. 2)
—Possession. (p. 1387)
—Surrender: A Possession Novel. (p. 1686)
—Surrender. (p. 1686)
Johnson, Eldon. King's Christmas List (p. 960)
Johnson, Elijah, illus. see Jordan, Pasquel.
Johnson, Elisheba, jt. auth. see Johnson, Charles.
Johnson, Elizabeth. And Then Nicholas Sang: The Story of the Trisagion Hymn. (p. 71)
—Hair: Do It Yourself! (p. 735)
Johnson, Emily, illus. see Johnson, Donna.
Johnson, Emily & Fontichiaro, Kristin. Know What to Ask: Forming Great Research Questions. (p. 965)
Johnson, Eric, illus. see Johnson, Joanna.
Johnson, Erin. Her Cold Revenge. (p. 769)
Johnson, Errick C., jt. auth. see Johnson, Alberta.
Johnson, Errol. What's That Sound? (p. 1899)
Johnson, Esther A. Princess & the Garden. Taylor, Carolyn, illus. (p. 1402)
Johnson, et al. Glencoe Keyboarding with Computer Applications: MS Office XP Professional Edition, Student Manual. (p. 683)
Johnson, Etta. Local & State Government. (p. 1044)
—Symbols of the United States. (p. 1693)
—United States Government. (p. 1819)
Johnson, F. Craig & Kattman, Robert, eds. Successful Applications of Quality Systems in K-12 Schools. (p. 1672)
Johnson, Felicia P. Shuck Shuck Shuck. (p. 1571)
Johnson, Fiona, illus. see Stockley, Corinne, et al.
Johnson, Fiona, illus. see Wertheim, Jane, et al.
Johnson, Florence. Christmas ABC. Wilkin, Eloise, illus. (p. 312)
Johnson, Fran. Mystery House. (p. 1224)
Johnson, G. B. Against the Grain. (p. 29)
Johnson, G. Francis. Has Anybody Lost a Glove? Tokunbo, Dimitrea, illus. (p. 752)
Johnson, Gabriel. Heroes of Dreams: A Heroic Dream Begins. (p. 773)
Johnson, Gail. Chasing the Sun. (p. 294)
Johnson, Gail & Grell, Jane. African & Caribbean Celebrations. Green, Toby, ed. (p. 27)
Johnson, Gary, illus. see Johansen, Tesla.
Johnson, Gary M. Adventures of MolarMan: Oral Health Bilingual (English/Spanish) Coloring Workbook. (p. 20)
Johnson, Gary R., illus. see Johnson, Christine.
Johnson, Gee. All I Can Be. (p. 44)
—Octopus. Johnson, Gee, illus. (p. 1278)
—Orcas. (p. 1302)
—Polar Bears. (p. 1379)
—Polar Bears. Johnson, Gee, illus. (p. 1379)
Johnson, Gee, illus. see Fleischer, Jayson.
Johnson, Gee & Fleischer, Jayson. Bald Eagles. (p. 133)
Johnson, Gee & Sánchez, Lucia M. Pulpo. (p. 1416)
Johnson, Gee & Zorzi, Gina. Tiger Sharks. (p. 1748)
Johnson, Gee, et al Sea Turtles. Dibble, Traci, illus. (p. 1536)
Johnson, George Ann, illus. see Persons, Marjorie Kiel.
Johnson, Gerald J. J. Bessie's Little Mouse Day Care. Miltenberger, Dave & Miltenberger, Jeri, illus. (p. 168)
—Betty, the Chubby Butterfly. Miltenberger, Jeri and Dave, illus. (p. 172)
—Boy Called Tiny Tim. (p. 217)
—Buffy Bunny. Miltenberger, Jeri & Miltenberger, Dave, illus. (p. 236)
—Ellie Saves the Day Funke, Peggy, illus. (p. 514)
—Misty's Christmas Present Miltenberger, Jeri & Miltenberger, Dave, illus. (p. 1155)
—Mouse Family Christmas Bousum, Julie, illus. (p. 1182)
—Officer Buck MacDuck. Miltenberger, Dave & Jeri, illus. (p. 1280)
Johnson, Gerald Jj. Miss Spinny, the Spider. Miltenberger, Jeri & Miltenberger, Dave, illus. (p. 1152)
Johnson, Gillian. My Sister Gracie. (p. 1218)
—Thora: A Half-Mermaid Tale. Johnson, Gillian, illus. (p. 1740)
—Thora. Johnson, Gillian, illus. (p. 1740)
—Thora & the Green Sea-Unicorn. Johnson, Gillian, illus. (p. 1740)
—Thora & the Incredible Crystals. (p. 1740)
Johnson, Gillian, illus. see Kelly, Katy.
Johnson, Gillian, illus. see Maybarduk, Linda.
Johnson, Gillian, illus. see Scrimger, Richard.
Johnson, Grace. Little Fish Who Was Afraid to Swim. (p. 1027)
Johnson, Grant. Big Tree Bob. (p. 184)
Johnson, Greg, jt. auth. see Ross, Michael.
Johnson, Gregg. Bedroom Bible College Manual: BBC Manual. (p. 156)
Johnson, Gretchen, illus. see Sandusky, Thomas & Hill, Kathy.
Johnson, Gwen. Story of Two-Toed Sam or How the Outer Banks Were Formed. (p. 1662)
Johnson, Gwen, jt. auth. see Johnson, Carl.
Johnson, Gwen & Johnson, Carl. Treasure of Diamond's Shoal. (p. 1782)
Johnson, H. E. Sequoia Secret Place: Redeeming the Stolen Kingdom. (p. 1552)
Johnson, Hal. Fearsome Creatures of the Lumberwoods: 20 Chilling Tales from the Wilderness. Mead, Tom, illus. (p. 579)
—Immortal Lycanthropes. White, Teagan, illus. (p. 861)
Johnson, Harriet McBryde. Accidents of Nature. (p. 8)
—Too Late to Die Young: Nearly True Tales from a Life. (p. 1766)
Johnson Harris, Brenda J. It's a Zoo in my Backyard! (p. 896)
Johnson, Harvell. What about Johnson? Howard, Vanetta, ed. (p. 1878)
Johnson, Heather Domjan. Itsy Bitsy Water Cycle. (p. 900)
—Itsy Bitsy Water Cycle Audiobook. (p. 900)
Johnson, Howard David, illus. see Laliberte, Michelle.
Johnson, J. Wellman's Lot Book I. (p. 1874)
—You Don't Have to Be Beautiful Introducing Lillian Samuelson Johnston-Swanson. (p. 1975)
Johnson, J. Angelique. Bats (p. 144)
—Eco-Family's Guide to Living Green Poling, Kyle, illus. (p. 502)
—Eco-Neighbor's Guide to a Green Community Poling, Kyle, illus. (p. 502)
—Eco-Shopper's Guide to Buying Green Poling, Kyle, illus. (p. 502)
—Eco-Student's Guide to Being Green at School Poling, Kyle, illus. (p. 502)
—Getting a Pet, Step by Step (p. 669)
—Making a Jack-O'-Lantern, Step by Step. (p. 1080)
—Raccoons (p. 1430)
—Red Foxes (p. 1454)
—Truth about Fairies Farias, Carolina, illus. (p. 1794)
Johnson, J. Angelique & Dunn, Mary R. Nocturnal Animals. (p. 1262)
Johnson, J. Angelique & Porter, Esther. Earth Matters. (p. 496)
Johnson, J. Bradley. Surround Yourself with Essential Vacation Spanish. (p. 1686)
—Surround Yourself with Spanish: Beginner Level. (p. 1686)
—Surround Yourself with Spanish Conversations (p. 1686)
Johnson, J. J. This Girl Is Different (p. 1735)
Johnson, Jack E., et al. Glencoe Keyboarding with Computer Applications: Lessons 1-80. (p. 683)
—Glencoe Keyboarding with Computer Applications. (p. 683)
Johnson, Jacqueline, jt. auth. see Young, Jeanna Stolle.
Johnson, Jacqueline, jt. auth. see Young, Jeanna.
Johnson, Jacqueline & Young, Jeanna Stolle. Princess Charity's Courageous Heart Aranda, Omar, illus. (p. 1403)
—Princess Faith's Mysterious Garden Aranda, Omar, illus. (p. 1403)
Johnson, Jacqueline Kinney, jt. auth. see Young, Jeanna Stolle.
Johnson, Jacqueline Kinney, jt. auth. see Young, Jeanna.
Johnson, Jacqueline Kinney & Young, Jeanna. Princess Grace & Poppy (p. 1404)
Johnson, Jacquitta. My First Day of School. (p. 1206)
Johnson, Jaime Gardner. Ghost of Donley Farm Klein, Laurie Allen, illus. (p. 671)
Johnson, Jake, illus. see Grim, Katie.
Johnson, Jaleigh. Mark of the Dragonfly. (p. 1095)
Johnson, James. Sidney Gets a House. (p. 1573)
—Sugar & Spice. (p. 1672)
Johnson, James A. Beast & the Backpack. (p. 152)
—Terror & the Talking Stick: Sundown Stories II. (p. 1722)
Johnson, James Ray. Timmy Wee Pee & Castle Friends. (p. 1755)
Johnson, Jan. Hallie & Grace: In the Beginning, God... (p. 737)
Johnson, Jane. Are You Ready for Bed? Hansen, Gaby, illus. (p. 97)
—Legends of the Shadow World: The Secret Country; the Shadow World; Dragon's Fire. Stower, Adam, illus. (p. 990)
—Little Bunny's Bathtime! (p. 1025)
—Little Bunny's Bedtime. Hansen, Gaby, illus. (p. 1025)
—Princesa y el Pintor. Johnson, Jane, illus. (p. 1402)
—Secret Country. Stower, Adam, illus. (p. 1540)
—Very Pretty Story. (p. 1838)
Johnson, Janet. Life on the Water: A Commercial Fishermen's Tale on Lake Superior. (p. 1012)
Johnson, Janie, compiled by. Up from the Cotton Fields. (p. 1824)
Johnson, Jann A. Wisdom Weaver/Bina'nitin Bidziilgo Atl'óhí. Manavi, Lorraine Begay, tr. from ENG. (p. 1939)
Johnson, Jared, illus. see Hurst, Joshua.
Johnson, Jason. How We See Things. (p. 823)
Johnson, Jay. Ten Little Pumpkins. (p. 1719)
Johnson, Jay, illus. see Denega, Danielle.
Johnson, Jay, illus. see Heling, Kathryn & Hembrook, Deborah.
Johnson, Jay, illus. see Karr, Lily.
Johnson, Jay B., illus. see Fisch, Sarah & Bridwell, Norman.
Johnson, Jay B., illus. see Karr, Lily.
Johnson, Jean. Cat (p. 277)
—Storm. (p. 1655)
Johnson, Jeanyne. Mysteryville: A Union Soldier. (p. 1226)
Johnson, Jeff, illus. see Dixon, Chuck.
Johnson, Jeff A., jt. auth. see Johnson, Tasha A.
Johnson, Jen Cullerton. Seeds of Change. Sadler, Sonia Lynn, illus. (p. 1547)
Johnson, Jennifer. Gettysburg: The Bloodiest Battle of the Civil War. (p. 670)
—Pickett's Charge at Gettysburg: A Bloody Clash in the Civil War. (p. 1354)
Johnson, Jennifer, illus. see Saffer, Barbara.
Johnson, Jennifer Hunt, jt. auth. see Hansen, Holly T.
Johnson, Jennifer Hunt & Hansen, Holly T. Christmas Memories (p. 314)
—Family Folklore (p. 568)
—Father Remembers (p. 577)
—Grandma Remembers (p. 708)
—Grandpa Remembers (p. 709)
—Mother Remembers (p. 1178)
—My Memories (p. 1214)
—Remembering Grandma (p. 1459)
—Remembering Grandpa (p. 1459)
—Your Memories (p. 1981)
Johnson, Jeremiah Sullivan, jt. auth. see Sullivan, John Jeremiah.
Johnson, Jeremy. Unusual & Awesome Jobs in Sports: Pro Team Mascot, Pit Crew Member, & More. (p. 1823)
Johnson, Jerome A., illus. see Mitchell, Gloria.
Johnson, Jessica. Socks. (p. 1605)
Johnson, Jessica, illus. see D'Ath, Justin.
Johnson, Jim. Hammer & the Nail. (p. 739)
Johnson, Jim, illus. see Johnson, Sandi, et al.
Johnson, Jim, illus. see Johnson, Sandi.
Johnson, Jinny. 1000 Things You Should Know about Birds. (p. 2001)
—Alligator. Rosewarne, Graham, illus. (p. 47)
—Animal Planet Atlas of Animals. (p. 79)
—Animal Planet - Atlas of Animals. (p. 79)
—Animal Planet - Wild World: An Encyclopedia of Animals. (p. 79)
—Animal Tracks & Signs: Track over 400 Animals from Big Cats to Backyard Birds. (p. 80)
—Ant. Sanzi, Desiderio, illus. (p. 88)
—Armored Dinosaurs. (p. 99)
—Beagle. (p. 149)
—Beaver. (p. 154)
—Birds. (p. 191)
—Boxer. (p. 217)
—Brachiosaurus & Other Dinosaur Giants. Rosewarne, Graham, illus. (p. 221)

—Brown Bear. (p. 231)
—Bulldog. (p. 240)
—Butterfly. Woods, Michael, illus. (p. 247)
—Caribou. (p. 269)
—Cats & Kittens. (p. 281)
—Children's Dinosaur Encyclopedia. (p. 303)
—Chimpanzee. Rosewarne, Graham, illus. (p. 306)
—Clash of the Dinos: Watch Dinosaurs Do Battle! (p. 327)
—Coral Reef Life. (p. 366)
—Coyote. (p. 374)
—Dandelion. Rosewarne, Graham, illus. (p. 403)
—Deep Sea Life. (p. 423)
—Dino Wars: Discover the Deadliest Dinosaurs, Bloodiest Battles, & Super Survival Strategies of the Prehistoric World. (p. 441)
—Dinosaur Giants. (p. 442)
—Dogs & Puppies. (p. 462)
—Duck. Woods, Michael, illus. (p. 488)
—Elephant. Rosewarne, Graham, illus. (p. 511)
—Flying Reptiles. (p. 610)
—Fox. Rosewarne, Graham, illus. (p. 625)
—Frog. Rosewarne, Graham, illus. (p. 639)
—German Shepherd. (p. 666)
—Golden Retriever. (p. 695)
—Gray Wolf. (p. 713)
—Guinea Pig. (p. 731)
—Guinea Pigs. (p. 731)
—Hamster & Gerbil. (p. 739)
—Hamsters & Gerbils. (p. 740)
—Iguanodon & Other Plant-Eating Dinosaurs. Rosewarne, Graham, illus. (p. 856)
—Kitten. (p. 962)
—Labrador Retriever. (p. 970)
—Mighty Killers. (p. 1140)
—Mountain Lion. (p. 1181)
—Oak Tree. Rosewarne, Graham, illus. (p. 1274)
—Ocean Life. (p. 1276)
—Parrot. Woods, Michael, illus. (p. 1325)
—Peaceful Plant Eaters. (p. 1332)
—Polar Bear. Rosewarne, Graham, illus. (p. 1378)
—Polar Sea Life. (p. 1379)
—Poodle. (p. 1383)
—Pteranodon & Other Flying Reptiles. Rosewarne, Graham, illus. (p. 1413)
—Puppy. (p. 1418)
—Rabbit. (p. 1429)
—Rabbits. (p. 1429)
—Raccoon. (p. 1430)
—Rats & Mice. (p. 1440)
—Sea Otter. (p. 1535)
—Seashore Life. (p. 1538)
—Speedy Dinosaurs. (p. 1624)
—Triceratops & Other Horned & Armored Dinosaurs. Rosewarne, Graham, illus. (p. 1785)
—Tricerratops & Other Horned & Armored Dinosaurs. Rosewarne, Graham, illus. (p. 1786)
—Tyrannosaurus & Other Mighty Hunters. Rosewarne, Graham, illus. (p. 1805)
—Velociraptor & Other Speedy Killers. Rosewarne, Graham, illus. (p. 1835)
—What's It Like to Be... Ant? Sanzi, Desiderio, illus. (p. 1898)
—What's It Like to Be... Butterfly? Sanzi, Desiderio, illus. (p. 1898)
—Yorkshire Terrier. (p. 1972)
Johnson, Jinny, jt. auth. see Dicker, Katie.
Johnson, Jinny, jt. auth. see Ganeri, Anita.
Johnson, Jinny, jt. auth. see Goldsmith, Mike.
Johnson, Jinny, jt. auth. see Llewellyn, Claire.
Johnson, Jinny, jt. auth. see Morris, Neil.
Johnson, Jinny, jt. auth. see Walters, Martin.
Johnson, Jinny & Bull, Peter. Explorers: Insects & Creepy-Crawlies. (p. 551)
Johnson, Jinny & Humphries, Tudor. How Fast Is a Cheetah? (p. 809)
Johnson, Jinny & Woods, Michael. How Big Is a Whale? (p. 805)
Johnson, Jinny, ed. Animal Planet Wild World: An Encyclopedia of Animals. (p. 79)
Johnson, Joanna. Phoebe's Sweater. Johnson, Eric, illus. (p. 1351)
Johnson, JoAnne. Pen Pals. (p. 1336)
Johnson, Joanne Gail. Donkey & the Racehorse. Ferris, Carole Anne, illus. (p. 466)
Johnson, Joe, tr. see Giardino, Vittorio.
Johnson, Joe, tr. see Grahame, Kenneth & Plessix, Michel.
Johnson, Joe, tr. see Grahame, Kenneth.
Johnson, John, illus. see Douglas, Babette.
Johnson, John Norton, jt. auth. see Krohn, Gretchen.
Johnson, Joshua C. Raccoon in My Room. (p. 1430)
Johnson, Joy. Harry the Woodpecker's Search for a Home. Johnson, Craig, illus. (p. 751)
Johnson, Joy, jt. auth. see Grollman, Earl A.
Johnson, Judith. Scary Play. (p. 1520)
Johnson, Judith Margaret. Feeling Great with Jasper State: Eat Your Green Things Every Day. Johnson, Patrick Henry, illus. (p. 580)
Johnson, Judy K. What Is It Like to Be Blind? (p. 1889)
Johnson, Julia. Humpy Grumpy Saves the Day! (p. 827)
—Leopard Boy. Lewis, Marisa, illus. (p. 992)
—One Humpy Grumpy Camel. Stacey International Staff, ed. (p. 1295)
—Pearl Diver. Stacey International Staff, ed. (p. 1333)
Johnson, Julia & Climent, Henry. Arabian Star. (p. 94)
Johnson, Julia & Hirst, Carla. Peacock & the Mermaid. (p. 1332)
Johnson, Julie Tallard. Teen Psychic: Exploring Your Intuitive Spiritual Powers. (p. 1713)
Johnson, K. Ii. Pig Farm: Adventures of Sal & Snapper. (p. 1357)
Johnson, Kandy, jt. auth. see Kids for Health Staff.
Johnson, Kandy & Kids for Health Staff. Health Education Adventure Video Series, Kids for Health: Fifth Grade Facilitator's Manual. (p. 758)
—Health Education Adventure Video Series, Kids for Health: First Grade Facilitator's Manual. (p. 758)
—Health Education Adventure Video Series, Kids for Health: Sixth Grade Facilitator's Manual. (p. 758)
—Health Education Adventure Video Series, Kids for Health: Third Grade Facilitator's Manual. (p. 758)
—Health Education Adventure Video Series, Kids for Health: Fourth Grade Facilitator's Manual. (p. 758)
—Health Education Adventure Video Series, Kids for Health: Kindergarten Facilitator's Manual. (p. 758)
—Health Education Adventure Video Series, Kids for Health: Second Grade Facilitator's Manual. (p. 758)
—Health Education Adventure Video Series, Kids for Health: Fourth Grade Facilitator's Manual/DVD. (p. 758)
—Health Education Adventure Video Series, Kids for Health: Fifth Grade Facilitator's Manual/DVD Set. (p. 758)
—Health Education Adventure Video Series, Kids for Health: First Grade Facilitator's Manual/DVD Set. (p. 758)
—Health Education Adventure Video Series, Kids for Health: Sixth Grade Facilitator's Manual/DVD Set. (p. 758)
—Health Education Adventure Video Series, Kids for Health: Third Grade Facilitator's Manual/DVD Set. (p. 758)
—Health Education Adventure Video Series, Kids for Health: Kindergarten Facilitator's Manual/DVD Set. (p. 758)
—Health Education Adventure Video Series, Kids for Health: Second Grade Facilitator's Manual/DVD Set. (p. 758)
Johnson, Karen, illus. see Gordon, Lynn & Chronicle Books Staff.
Johnson, Karen, illus. see Gordon, Lynn.
Johnson, Karrissa. What Would We Do Without the Color Blue? (p. 1895)
Johnson, Katherine. Nutrition Education for Kids: Health Science Series. (p. 1274)
Johnson, Kathleen A. Voice Came to Me. (p. 1847)
Johnson, Kathleen Jeffrie. Fast & Brutal Wing. (p. 576)
Johnson, Kathryn T. & Balczon, Mary-Lynne J. Sexual Dictionary: Terms & Expressions for Teens & Parents. St. John, Charlotte, ed. (p. 1556)
Johnson, Kathy. Let's Take a Walk in the Rain. Peer, Kate, illus. (p. 1001)
Johnson, Keith. Communicate in Writing: A Functional Approach to Writing Through Reading Comprehension. (p. 349)
Johnson, Ken & Myers, Bill. The Big Lie: A Star in the Breaking / The Not-so-Great Escape. (p. 1728)
Johnson, Kendall. Classroom Crisis: Quick & Proven Techniques for Stabilizing Your Students & Yourself. (p. 329)
Johnson, Kenneth W. & Cutnell, John D. Physics: Exploring Physics with PASCO Technology. (p. 1353)
Johnson, Kenny Ray, illus. see Hughes, Donna L.
Johnson, Kent R. & Strand, Vibeke. Implementing the Arthritis Foundation Life Improvement Series through Partnerships: A Step-by-Step Guide. (p. 862)
Johnson, Keri, jt. auth. see Johnson, Linda Carlson.
Johnson, Kevin. Pray: Talk to the King of the Universe (p. 1393)
—Stick: Glue Yourself to Godly Friends (p. 1649)
—Total Devotion: 365 Days to Hang Tight with Jesus. (p. 1771)
Johnson, Kevin, jt. auth. see McDowell, Josh.
Johnson, Kevin D. Around Every Corner. (p. 100)
Johnson, Kevin, frwd. Out of the Corner of My Eye. (p. 1311)
Johnson, Kevin Wayne. Give God the Glory! Know God & Do the Will of God Concerning Your Life (Study Guide) Know God & Do the Will of God Concerning Your Life - STUDY GUIDE Hallagen Ink, ed. (p. 681)
Johnson, Kim, illus. see Krulik, Nancy.
Johnson, Kim Howard & Cleese, John. True Brit. (p. 1792)
Johnson, Kimberli Anne, illus. see Webster, Raelyn & Rasmussen, Kenneth L.
Johnson, Kimberly. Things in Your Head: The Adventures of Bulu. (p. 1733)
Johnson, Kimberly P. Adventures of the Itty Bitty Bunny. (p. 23)
—Not Again, Mr. Cat! Smith, Landa, illus. (p. 1267)
Johnson, Kris, photos by see Muir, Kerry.
Johnson, Krista M., illus. see O'Reilly, Gillian.
Johnson, Kristel. Even When We Are Apart. (p. 541)
Johnson, Kristi. Grilled Pizza Sandwich & Other Vegetarian Recipes. (p. 724)
—Monkey Pudding & Other Dessert Recipes (p. 1165)
—Peanut Butter & Jelly Sushi & Other Party Recipes (p. 1332)
—Reindeer Crunch & Other Christmas Recipes. (p. 1457)
Johnson, Kristin. Endurance Expedition. (p. 527)
Johnson, Kristin & Cummins, Mimi. Christmas Cookies Are for Giving: Recipes, Stories & Tips for Making Heartwarming Gifts. (p. 313)
Johnson, Kristin F. Ho Chi Minh: North Vietnamese President. (p. 786)
—Orphan Trains. (p. 1304)
Johnson, Kylie. Fit for a Princess. (p. 599)
Johnson, Lafayette, Jr. & Liberty, Dendron. Tyler's Wise Old Tree. (p. 1805)
Johnson, Lakishi. Smiles. (p. 1594)
Johnson, Larry, illus. see Hovland, Stephenie M.
Johnson, Larry, illus. see Medearis, Michael & Medearis, Angela Shelf.
Johnson, Larry, illus. see Sherrow, Victoria.
Johnson, Larry, illus. see Swain, Gwenyth.
Johnson, Larry, illus. see Walter, Mildred Pitts.
Johnson, Laureen, tr. see Carroll, Lewis, pseud.
Johnson, Lauren. Beastly Basketball Garcia, Eduardo, illus. (p. 152)
Johnson, Lauren, illus. see Goyer, Deb.
Johnson, Layne. Grandparent Poems. (p. 709)
Johnson, Layne, illus. see Garland, Sherry.
Johnson, Layne, illus. see Knowlton, Laurie Lazzaro.
Johnson, Layne, illus. see Markle, Sandra.
Johnson, Layne, illus. see Osornio, Catherine L.
Johnson, Layne, illus. see Pulver, Robin.
Johnson, Layne, illus. see Spradlin, Michael P.
Johnson, Layne, illus. see Thomas, Peggy.
Johnson, Layne, illus. see Walsh, Barbara.
Johnson, Layne, jt. auth. see Markle, Sandra.
Johnson, Leona. Strengthening Family & Self: Teaching Package Teacher's Resource Guide. (p. 1667)
—Strengthening Family & Self: Teaching Package Teacher's Annotated Edition. (p. 1667)
—Strengthening Family & Self: Teaching Package Teacher's Resource Portfolio. (p. 1667)
—Strengthening Family & Self. (p. 1667)
Johnson, Liliane & Dufton, Jo S. Children's Chillers & Thrillers. Bruhn, Joan Z., illus. (p. 303)
Johnson, Lincoln. Hal the Hound: The Happiest Day Yet. (p. 736)
Johnson, Linda. Adventures of Mike the Mouse: The Best Smell in the Whole Wide World/Tail One in A Series. (p. 20)
—Fortunate Puppy. (p. 623)
Johnson, Linda & Hodges, Quae. 21st Century Parables: A Child's Book. (p. 1996)
Johnson, Linda Carlson & Johnson, Keri. 9.11 Helping the Heroes: A Salvation Army Story. (p. 1993)
Johnson, Linda Louisa. Beachcombers 911. (p. 149)
—Family Secrets. (p. 568)
—Needle in a Haystack. (p. 1239)
Johnson, Linda Rene'. Prissy, Where Are You? (p. 1407)
Johnson, Lindsay Lee. Ten Moonstruck Piglets. Cneut, Carll, illus. (p. 1719)
—Worlds Apart. (p. 1960)
Johnson, Lisa. All Hallows' Eve: The Story of the Halloween Fairy. Johnson, Tucker, illus. (p. 44)
Johnson, Lois Walfrid. Burnt Cookies. (p. 244)
—Creeping Shadows. (p. 381)
—Disappearing Stranger. (p. 446)
—Disaster on Windy Hill. (p. 446)
—Grandpa's Stolen Treasure. (p. 710)
—Heart of Courage. (p. 759)
—Hidden Message. (p. 776)
—Invisible Friend (p. 885)
—Mysterious Hideaway. (p. 1223)
—Mystery of the Missing Map. (p. 1225)
—Mystery of the Silver Coins (p. 1226)
—Raiders from the Sea. (p. 1433)
—Raider's Promise. (p. 1433)
—Runaway Clown. (p. 1496)
—Trouble at Wild River. (p. 1789)
—Vanishing Footprints. (p. 1833)
Johnson, Lori. Cell Function & Specialization (p. 286)
—Prodigal Penguin. (p. 1409)
Johnson, LouAnne. Muchacho. (p. 1188)
Johnson, Lucille M. Titus the Magnificent: The Adventures of Titus. (p. 1758)
Johnson, Lydia Sue. Chester, the Pink Elephant. (p. 298)
Johnson, Lynn E. Bear with the Purple Hat. (p. 151)
Johnson, Maerryane. I Am Still the Same Aubrey! (p. 834)
Johnson, Maggie & Wintgens, Alison. Can I Tell You about Selective Mutism? A Guide for Friends, Family & Professionals. Gallow, Robyn, illus. (p. 258)
—Selective Mutism Resource Manual. (p. 1549)
Johnson, Mar. Jack the Mighty Steed. (p. 903)
Johnson, Marcella, illus. see Black, Chuck.
Johnson, Margaret. Gone! Level Starter/Beginner American English. (p. 697)
—Gone! Starter/Beginner. (p. 697)
—New Zealand Level 2 Elementary/Lower-Intermediate. (p. 1249)
—Selfish & the Blue Box. (p. 1549)
—Seven Magical Tooth Fairies. (p. 1554)
Johnson, Margaret M. New Irish Table: 70 Contemporary Recipes. Hirsheimer, Christopher, photos by. (p. 1245)
Johnson, Mariana Ruiz. I Know a Bear. (p. 840)
Johnson, Marion. Caillou, What's That Noise. CINAR Corporation Staff, illus. (p. 251)
—School Bus. (p. 1522)
Johnson, Marion L. Streak: Black Cat & the Grumpy Grandpa. (p. 1666)
Johnson, Mark. Little Fish Lou. (p. 1027)
Johnson, Marlys. Careers in the Movies. (p. 268)
—Understanding Exercise Addiction. (p. 1815)
Johnson, Marlys H. Careers in the Movies. (p. 268)
Johnson, Marsha Deveaux. Power Angels on Assignment: Cinnamon Comes to Earth. (p. 1389)
Johnson, Martha, jt. auth. see Lansky, Bruce.
Johnson, Martin, jt. auth. see Cook, Sherry.
Johnson, Mary J. Super Smart Information Strategies: Your Fascinating Family History. (p. 1682)
Johnson, Mary L. Flinthills Frannie (p. 604)
Johnson, Maureen. 13 Little Blue Envelopes. (p. 1995)
—Bermudez Triangle. (p. 167)
—Devilish. (p. 432)
—Girl at Sea. (p. 678)
—Key to the Golden Firebird. (p. 950)
—Last Little Blue Envelope. (p. 978)
—Madness Underneath. (p. 1070)
—Name of the Star. (p. 1228)
—On the Count of Three. (p. 1290)
—Scarlett Fever. (p. 1520)
—Shadow Cabinet. (p. 1557)
—Suite Scarlett. (p. 1673)
Johnson, Melinda & Johnson, Mindy. Tinker Bell: An Evolution. (p. 1755)
Johnson, Meredith, ed. see Jane, Pamela.
Johnson, Meredith, ed. see Pingry, Patricia A.
Johnson, Meredith, illus. see Adams, Michelle Medlock.
Johnson, Meredith, illus. see Burke, Michelle Prater.
Johnson, Meredith, illus. see Cashman, Mary & Whipple, Cynthia.
Johnson, Meredith, illus. see Horlacher, Bill & Horlacher, Kathy.
Johnson, Meredith, illus. see Horlacher, Kathy & Horlacher, Bill.
Johnson, Meredith, illus. see Johnson, Bruce & McKay, Sindy.
Johnson, Meredith, illus. see Johnson, Bruce.
Johnson, Meredith, illus. see Lang, Andrew.
Johnson, Meredith, illus. see Latta, Sara L.
Johnson, Meredith, illus. see McGuire, Leslie.
Johnson, Meredith, illus. see McKay, Sindy.
Johnson, Meredith, illus. see Meiners, Cheri J.
Johnson, Meredith, illus. see Pearce, Valarie.
Johnson, Meredith, illus. see Pingry, Patricia A.
Johnson, Meredith, illus. see Raum, Elizabeth.
Johnson, Meredith, illus. see Ross, Dev.
Johnson, Meredith, illus. see Ryan, Karlene Kay.
Johnson, Meredith, illus. see Sears, Gale.
Johnson, Meredith, illus. see Shively, Julie.
Johnson, Meredith, illus. see Walsh, Sheila.
Johnson, Meredith, illus. see Willson, Sarah.
Johnson, Meredith, jt. auth. see McKay, Sindy.
Johnson, Meredith, jt. illus. see Johnson, Bruce.
Johnson, Meredith, tr. see Jane, Pamela.
Johnson, Michael. Iroquois: People of the Longhouse. (p. 888)
—Native Tribes of North America (p. 1235)
—Native Tribes of the Plains & Prairie. (p. 1235)
Johnson, Michael, jt. auth. see Thorne, Paul.
Johnson, Michael & Burkinshaw, Jane. Native Tribes of the North & Northwest Coast. (p. 1235)
Johnson, Michael & Clarke, Duncan. Native Tribes of the Great Basin & Plateau. (p. 1235)
—Native Tribes of the Southeast. (p. 1235)
Johnson, Michael & Yenne, Bill. Native Tribes of California & the Southwest. (p. 1235)
Johnson, Michael E. Barley & Betsy: Journey #1 A cat & dog's great adventure to the Mall. Atchley, Kendra, illus. (p. 139)
Johnson, Michelle. Stories of a Child's Heart: Ella's Instrument & Who You Are. (p. 1654)
Johnson, Mike. Galileo Seven Part 1. (p. 653)
—Galileo Seven Part 2. (p. 653)
—Star Trek. (p. 1641)
—Where No Man Has Gone Before Part 1. (p. 1909)
Johnson, Mike, illus. see Carder, Ken & LaRoy, Sue.
Johnson, Mike & Scott, Mairghread. Transformers Prime: Rage of the Dinobots: Rage of the Dinobots. (p. 1778)
Johnson, Milton, illus. see Haugaard, Erik Christian.
Johnson, Mimi Evelyn. Day in the Life of Div. (p. 413)
Johnson, Mindy, jt. auth. see Johnson, Melinda.
Johnson, Miri & Wachtel, Aleina, eds. 'Twas the Night Before... A Collection of Short Stories by Orchard Middle School Students. (p. 1799)
Johnson, Mo. Noah's Garden: When Someone You Love Is in the Hospital. Josse, Annabelle, illus. (p. 1262)
Johnson Mockler, Nicole. Alex Has Had Enough! Mockler, Sean, illus. (p. 36)
Johnson, Mukkove. Christmas Is about Jesus: An Advent Devotional. (p. 314)
Johnson, Myrna. Let's Take a Hike. (p. 1001)
Johnson, Nancy. Sweet-Sounding Place: A Civil War Story. (p. 1690)
Johnson, Nancy, jt. auth. see Hann, Harry Henry.
Johnson, Nancy Carole. Pierre, the Turtle Who Went to College. (p. 1357)
Johnson, Nancy Jo, photos by see Dolphin, Laurie.
Johnson, Nancy Pelander. 44 Animals of the Bible. Hight, Lloyd R., illus. (p. 1997)
Johnson, Nathan. Jujutsu: Winning Ways. James, Adam, ed. (p. 932)
—Karate: Winning Ways. James, Adam, ed. (p. 943)
—Kickboxing & MMA: Winning Ways. James, Adam, ed. (p. 951)
—Kung Fu: Winning Ways. James, Adam, ed. (p. 968)
—Martial Arts for Children: Winning Ways. James, Adam, ed. (p. 1097)
Johnson, Ned & Eskelsen, Emily Warner. Conquering the SAT: How Parents Can Help Teens Overcome the Pressure & Succeed. (p. 358)
Johnson, Nerissa & Parra, Angelo. Teen Reflections, Then & Now. (p. 1713)
Johnson, Nevlynn L., Sr. Faith, Courage & Wisdom: A Journey to Manhood. (p. 565)
Johnson, Nick, illus. see Solomon, Steven.
Johnson, Nikki, illus. see Anderson, Jeannine.
Johnson, Nikki, illus. see Dey, Joy M.
Johnson, Odette & Johnson, Bruce. Apples, Alligators & Also Alphabets (p. 92)
Johnson, Pamela. David & Goliath. (p. 410)
—Jonah & the Whale. (p. 925)
—Joseph & His Brothers. (p. 926)
Johnson, Pamela, illus. see Berendes, Mary.
Johnson, Pamela, illus. see Dussling, Jennifer.
Johnson, Pamela, illus. see Edwards, Roberta.
Johnson, Pamela, illus. see Kamma, Anne.
Johnson, Pamela, illus. see Matero, Robert.
Johnson, Pamela, illus. see Trice, Linda.
Johnson, Pamela Ford, illus. see Kamma, Anne.
Johnson, Pamela G., illus. see Rappoport, Bernice.
Johnson, Patricia. Make Your Own Magic Soil: Life's Lessons on Sustainable Living. (p. 1080)
Johnson, Patrick, illus. see Ali, Maryum.
Johnson, Patrick Henry, illus. see Johnson, Judith Margaret.
Johnson, Paul, illus. see Fogle, Robin.
Johnson, Paul Brett. Fearless Jack. Johnson, Paul Brett, illus. (p. 579)
—Jack Outwits the Giants. (p. 903)
Johnson, Paul F. & Halfman, Patti. 50 Quick Play Vocabulary Games. (p. 1997)
Johnson, Pauletta Cox. Come under the Mushroom. (p. 347)
Johnson, Penny. 50 Amazing Things Kids Need to Know about Science. (p. 1997)
Johnson, Pete. Help! I'm a Classroom Gambler. (p. 765)
—How to Train Your Parents. (p. 822)
—Vampire Fighters. (p. 1832)
—Vampire Hunters. (p. 1832)
Johnson, Peter. Amazing Adventures of John Smith, Jr. Aka Houdini. (p. 52)
—Life & Times of Benny Alvarez. (p. 1008)
—What Happened. (p. 1885)
Johnson, Phyllis. Ben's Dreams. (p. 165)
—Betsy Star Ballerin. (p. 172)
—Four Baby Goats. (p. 624)
Johnson, Quinn. Kung-Fu Panda Digest: Noodle Cart Capers: Noodle Cart Capers. (p. 968)
—Richie Rich Digest: Just Desserts! Vol. 3 (p. 1470)

J

Johnson, Quinn, jt. auth. see Anderson, Matt.
Johnson, R. Kikuo. Shark King. (p. 1562)
—Shark King. Loeffler, Trade & Johnson, R. Kikuo, illus. (p. 1562)
Johnson, Rachel N. No Ordinary Princess. Hill, Jessie, illus. (p. 1259)
Johnson, Rafer. Great Athletes (p. 713)
Johnson, Ramona. All Steamed Up. (p. 45)
Johnson, Randy & Allan, Nancy P. Dispatch to Custer: The Tragedy of Lieutenant Kidder. Vol. 1 (p. 453)
Johnson, Rebecca. Chernobyl's Wild Kingdom: Life in the Dead Zone. (p. 298)
—Clown Fish Finds a Friend. Parish, Steve, illus. (p. 335)
—Cranky Crocodile. Parish, Steve, illus. (p. 376)
—Little Dolphin's Big Leap. Parish, Steve, illus. (p. 1027)
—Proud Pelican's Secret. Parish, Steve, illus. (p. 1412)
—Sea Turtle's Clever Plan. Parish, Steve, illus. (p. 1536)
—Tree Frog Hears a Sound. Parish, Steve, illus. (p. 1783)
—When Lunch Fights Back: Wickedly Clever Animal Defenses. (p. 1903)
Johnson, Rebecca L. Acids & Bases. (p. 9)
—Amazing Dna. (p. 54)
—Amazing DNA. Desrocher, Jack & Fairman, Jennifer, illus. (p. 54)
—Aparato Digestivo. Translations.com Staff, tr. (p. 91)
—Aparato Digestivo (the Digestive System) Translations.com Staff, tr. (p. 91)
—Chemical Changes. (p. 297)
—Crunching Numbers. (p. 386)
—Daring Cell Defenders. (p. 406)
—Decoding Data. (p. 422)
—Ernest Shackleton: Gripped by the Antarctic. (p. 534)
—Genetics. (p. 660)
—Investigating Climate Change: Scientists' Search for Answers in a Warming World. (p. 884)
—Journey into an Estuary. Saroff, Phyllis V., illus. (p. 928)
—Journey into the Deep: Discovering New Ocean Creatures. (p. 928)
—Journey into the Ocean. Saroff, Phyllis V., illus. (p. 928)
—Machines - Simple & Compound. (p. 1068)
—Microquests: Complete Set. (p. 1136)
—Microquests: Classroom Set. (p. 1136)
—Microquests Desrocher, Jack & Fairman, Jennifer, illus. (p. 1136)
—Mighty Animal Cells. Desrocher, Jack & Fairman, Jennifer, illus. (p. 1139)
—Muscular System. (p. 1192)
—Nanotechnology. (p. 1229)
—Powerful Plant Cells. (p. 1390)
—Powerful Plant Cells. Desrocher, Jack & Fairman, Jennifer, illus. (p. 1390)
—Puzzling Out Patterns. (p. 1421)
—Respiration & Circulation. (p. 1463)
—Satellites. (p. 1515)
—Sistema Muscular. Translations.com Staff, tr. (p. 1581)
—Sizing up Shapes. (p. 1583)
—Ultra-Organized Cell Systems. (p. 1810)
—Ultra-Organized Cell Systems. Desrocher, Jack & Fairman, Jennifer, illus. (p. 1810)
—Understanding Global Warming. (p. 1815)
—Your Digestive System. (p. 1980)
—Your Muscular System. (p. 1981)
—Zombie Makers: True Stories of Nature's Undead. (p. 1988)
Johnson, Rebecca L. & National Geographic Learning Staff. Bones & Muscles. (p. 209)
—Global Warming. (p. 684)
—Looking at Cells. (p. 1050)
—Magic of Light & Sound. (p. 1073)
—Peering into Darkness. (p. 1335)
—Robert Ballard: Discovering Underwater Treasures. (p. 1478)
—San Francisco Earthquake. (p. 1510)
—Surviving Volcanoes & Glaciers. (p. 1687)
—Sylvia Earle: Protecting the Seas. (p. 1692)
—Tracking Animal Migrators. (p. 1775)
—You & Your Genes. (p. 1973)
Johnson, Rebecca L. & Schifini, Alfredo. From Cells to Systems. (p. 642)
Johnson, Rebecca L., et al. Ocean Exploration. (p. 1276)
—Paul Sereno: Digging for Dinosaurs. (p. 1330)
—Weather & Climate. (p. 1869)
Johnson, Regan. Hold on to Your Tail: Letters from Camp Lizard. Johnson, Regan, illus. (p. 788)
—Little Bunny Kung Fu. Johnson, Regan, illus. (p. 1025)
Johnson, Regan, illus. see Guzman, Lila.
Johnson, Rhonda & Paladin, Frank. Little Garden. Amber, Holly & Davidsson, Ashton, illus. (p. 1028)
Johnson, Rich & James, Robert F. Outdoor Life's Disaster Survival Guide. (p. 1312)
Johnson, Richard. Don't Cry, Sly! (p. 467)
—Giant Turnip. (p. 674)
—Lion Book of Five-Minute Bible Stories. (p. 1020)
—Little Red Hen & the Grains of Wheat. (p. 1034)
—Little Red Hen & the Grains of Wheat: Big Book English Only. (p. 1035)
—Three Little Pigs. (p. 1742)
Johnson, Richard, illus. see Barkaw, Henniette.
Johnson, Richard, illus. see Barkow, Henriette.
Johnson, Richard, illus. see Goodwin, John.
Johnson, Richard, illus. see Grierson, Ruth.
Johnson, Richard, illus. see Joslin, Mary.
Johnson, Richard, illus. see Knight, Richard John & Walker, Richard.
Johnson, Richard, illus. see Knight, Richard.
Johnson, Richard, illus. see Pirotta, Saviour.
Johnson, Richard, illus. see Wang, Margaret.
Johnson, Richard, illus. see Zolkower, Edie Stoltz.
Johnson, Richard, jt. auth. see Rivera-Ashford, Roni Capin.
Johnson, Richard, jt. illus. see Barkow, Henriette.
Johnson, Richard A., illus. see Goodwin, John.
Johnson, Richard & Barkow, Henriette. Little Red Hen & the Grains of Wheat. (p. 1035)
Johnson, Richard G., illus. see Bowman, Crystal.
Johnson, Richard G., illus. see Wargin, Kathy-jo.
Johnson, Richard, tr. Jack & the Beanstalk. (p. 902)
Johnson, Rick, illus. see Auer, Chris.
Johnson, Robert. British History 1870-1918: The Emergence of a Nation. (p. 229)
—European History 1870-1918: The Rise of Nationalism. (p. 540)
Johnson, Robin. Bobsleigh, Luge, & Skeleton. (p. 206)
—California Gold Rush! (p. 253)
—Conquering Everest. (p. 358)
—Famous People of the War of 1812. (p. 569)
—Great Depression. (p. 715)
—How Does Sound Change? (p. 809)
—Ice Hockey & Curling. (p. 850)
—Jaguar. Crabtree, ed. (p. 905)
—Jonas Brothers. (p. 925)
—Katy Perry. (p. 946)
—Kristen Stewart. (p. 967)
—March on Washington. (p. 1091)
—Mississippi: America's Mighty River. (p. 1154)
—Oceans Inside Out. (p. 1277)
—Olympic Heroes & Zeroes. (p. 1287)
—Paralympic Sports Events. (p. 1324)
—Pearl Harbor. (p. 1333)
—Pompeii. (p. 1382)
—Rain Forests Inside Out. (p. 1435)
—Rihanna. (p. 1472)
—Robert Pattinson. (p. 1479)
—Rodeo. (p. 1484)
—Show Jumping. (p. 1570)
—Take off Track & Field. (p. 1697)
—Takedown Wrestling. (p. 1697)
—Titanic. (p. 1757)
—Understanding Roman Myths. (p. 1816)
—Urals. (p. 1825)
—What Are Light Waves? (p. 1879)
—What Are Shadows & Reflections? (p. 1879)
—What Are Sound Waves? (p. 1879)
—What Is Precipitation? (p. 1890)
—What Is Temperature? (p. 1890)
—What Is Weather? (p. 1891)
—What Is Wind? (p. 1891)
—Why Mirabeau Lamar Matters to Texas. (p. 1925)
—Word Wizard's Book of Adjectives. (p. 1951)
—Word Wizard's Book of Adverbs. (p. 1951)
—Word Wizard's Book of Homonyms. (p. 1951)
—Word Wizard's Book of Nouns. (p. 1951)
—Word Wizard's Book of Prefixes & Suffixes. (p. 1951)
Johnson, Robin, jt. auth. see Corporate Contributor Staff.
Johnson, Robin, jt. auth. see Crabtree Publishing Co. Staff.
Johnson, Robin, jt. auth. see Crabtree Staff.
Johnson, Robin, jt. auth. see Kalman, Bobbie.
Johnson, Robin, jt. auth. see Miller, Reagan.
Johnson, Robin & Kalman, Bobbie. Conoce China. (p. 358)
—Conoce India. (p. 358)
—Conoce Perú. (p. 358)
—Spotlight on China. (p. 1634)
—Spotlight on India. (p. 1634)
—Spotlight on Peru. (p. 1634)
Johnson, Robyn. Enchanted Dolls' House. Johnson, Robyn, illus. (p. 523)
Johnson, Roland. Jeremya Jones: A King's Kid. (p. 913)
Johnson, Rose. Discoveries in Chemistry That Changed the World (p. 448)
—Discoveries in Earth & Space Science That Changed the World (p. 448)
—Discoveries in Life Science That Changed the World (p. 448)
—Discoveries in Medicine That Changed the World (p. 448)
—Discoveries in Physics That Changed the World (p. 448)
Johnson, Rossiter, ed. Stories of Childhood. (p. 1654)
—Stories of Comedy. (p. 1654)
Johnson, Russell, jt. auth. see Johnson, Annie P.
Johnson, Russell W. & Johnson, Annie P. My Florida Facts. Swing, Michael, illus. (p. 1208)
Johnson, S. & Evans, C. Starting Gardening. (p. 1644)
Johnson, S. K. Billy & Bob. (p. 187)
Johnson, Sabin W. Jolly Shop. (p. 924)
Johnson, Sally. Alfabeto Animal. (p. 37)
Johnson, Samuel. Book of Hymns. (p. 211)
—Elementa Philosophica. (p. 510)
—Elements Ethica: Or, the First Principals of Moral Philosophy. (p. 510)
—English & Hebrew Grammar. (p. 529)
—History of Rasselas, Prince of Abyssinia. (p. 784)
—History of Rasselas, Prince of Abyssinia. Emerson, Oliver Farrar, ed. (p. 784)
—Hymns of the Spirit. (p. 831)
—Introduction to the Study of Philosophy. (p. 882)
—Lectures, Essays & Sermons. (p. 987)
—Oriental Religions & Their Relation to Universal Religion (p. 1303)
—Samuel Johnson — A History of My Journey: From Life on the Farm to Many Adventures Worldwide & Back Home. (p. 1509)
Johnson, Sandi. 1 - Dorp the Scottish Dragon: Scotland Johnson, Britt & Durant, Sybrina, eds. (p. 1990)
—3 - Dorp the Scottish Dragon: Book 3 - Hollywood - the Movie Bk. 3 Johnson, Britt & Durant, Sybrina, eds. (p. 1991)
—4 - Dorp the Scottish Dragon: New York Christmas. Bk. 4 Durant, Sybrina, ed. (p. 1992)
—5 - Dorp the Scottish Dragon: In the Bermuda Triangle Brundige, Britt & Durant, Sybrina, eds. (p. 1992)
—Baseball Billy. Johnson, Britt, ed. (p. 141)
—Black Ridge Mountain. Durant, Sybrina, ed. (p. 196)
—Cats on Vacation. Durant, Sybrina, ed. (p. 281)
—Chip Dude from Outer Space. Johnson, Britt, ed. (p. 308)
—Cowgirls Dream. Perritt, Jordona, illus. (p. 374)
—Dingbat: El Gato Voluntario. Johnson, Britt, ed. (p. 440)
—Dittle's Christmas Wish. Durant, Sybrina, ed. (p. 454)
—Harold the Hopping Hamster. Johnson, Britt, ed. (p. 749)
—Haunted Dog House. Brundige, Britt & Durant, Sybrina, eds. (p. 753)
—Jim Elephant: The Nasty Bug (p. 917)
—Lost Island. Johnson, Britt & Durant, Sybrina, eds. (p. 1056)
—My Teacher Is an Alien. Durant, Sybrina, ed. (p. 1220)
—Peaceful Lion. Johnson, Britt, ed. (p. 1332)
—Red Hot Dot's Fire Safety Book: Fire Safety. Durant, Sybrina, ed. (p. 1454)
—White Wolf at Dawn. Johnson, Britt, ed. (p. 1914)
Johnson, Sandi & Fehr, Flora. Zemo to the Rescue: Dorp 7 Rock Band. (p. 1986)
Johnson, Sandi, et al. Haunted Doghouse II: Halloween Night Durant, Sybrina, ed. (p. 753)
—Legend of the Blue Unicorn: Land of OSM. Johnson, Britt, ed. (p. 989)
Johnson, Sandra, adapted by. Shoobie (p. 1568)
Johnson, Sarah Knights. Maker's Instructions: Helping Children to Explore & Understand the Ten Commandments. (p. 1080)
—Talking with God. (p. 1704)
Johnson, Scott A. Deadlands. (p. 417)
—Mayor's Guide: The Stately Ghosts of Augusta. (p. 1113)
Johnson, Shane. How to Draw Avatar: The Last Airbender. (p. 816)
—OLIVIA Paints a Mural. (p. 1287)
Johnson, Shane L. Chickens & the Eggs. (p. 300)
—Need for Speed. (p. 1239)
—Olivia & Her Ducklings. (p. 1286)
—OLIVIA & the Christmas Present. (p. 1286)
—OLIVIA & the Dog Wash. (p. 1286)
—OLIVIA & the Easter Egg Hunt. (p. 1286)
—Olivia & the Ice Show: A Lift-The-Flap Story. (p. 1286)
—OLIVIA & the Snow Day. (p. 1286)
—OLIVIA Builds a House. (p. 1286)
—OLIVIA la Princesa. (p. 1286)
—OLIVIA Leads a Parade. (p. 1286)
—Olivia the Princess. (p. 1287)
—OLIVIA Trains Her Cat. (p. 1287)
—Princess for a Day: A Pop-Up Storybook. (p. 1403)
—Star of the Show. (p. 1641)
Johnson, Shane L., illus. see Black, Allyson.
Johnson, Shane L., illus. see Black, Jake.
Johnson, Shane L., illus. see Bryant, Megan E.
Johnson, Shane L., illus. see Evans, Cordelia.
Johnson, Shane L., illus. see Falconer, Ian, et al.
Johnson, Shane L., illus. see Golden Books.
Johnson, Shane L., illus. see Hiranandani, Veera.
Johnson, Shane L., illus. see Oliver, Ilanit.
Johnson, Shane L., illus. see Romay, Alexis, tr.
Johnson, Shane L., illus. see Shaw, Natalie.
Johnson, Shane L., illus. see Snider, Brandon T.
Johnson, Shane L., illus. see Stuart, Wrigley.
Johnson, Shane L., illus. see Testa, Maggie.
Johnson, Shane L., jt. auth. see Brallier, Max.
Johnson, Shane L., jt. illus. see Mawhinney, Art.
Johnson, Shane L. & Mawhinney, Art. Deep Freeze. (p. 423)
Johnson, Shane L., ed. Avatar: The Last Airbender. (p. 118)
Johnson, Sharon. Midnight's Destiny. (p. 1139)
Johnson, Sharon, illus. see Nash, Myrna Lee.
Johnson, Sheri. Kids in the Medieval World (p. 954)
—Medieval Plague (p. 1119)
Johnson, Sheri A. Cockapoo: A Cross Between a Cocker Spaniel & a Poodle (p. 337)
—Girls' Guide to Fairies: Everything Irresistible about the Fair Folk. (p. 680)
—Girl's Guide to Mermaids: Everything Alluring about These Mythical Beauties. (p. 680)
—Girls' Guides to Everything Unexplained. (p. 680)
Johnson, Sidra. Mesha's Great Big World. Johnson, Sidra, illus. (p. 1129)
Johnson, Sloan. Fairy Catchers. (p. 563)
Johnson, Sonia M. Tyler's Third Grade Science Project. (p. 1805)
Johnson, Spencer. Quién Se Ha Llevado Mi Queso? Para Niños: Una Forma Sorprendente de Cambiar y Ganar ! (p. 1427)
—ValueTales Treasury: Stories for Growing Good People. Andreasen, Dan, illus. (p. 1831)
—Who Moved My Cheese? An A-Mazing Way to Change & Win! For Kids. Pileggi, Steve, illus. (p. 1917)
—¿Quién Se Ha Llevado Mi Queso? Para Jovenes: ¡Una Forma Sorprendente de Cambiar y Ganar! (p. 1427)
Johnson, Staz, illus. see Brook, Henry.
Johnson, Staz, illus. see Stoker, Bram.
Johnson, Stephen. Dance, Dance, Dance! (p. 402)
Johnson, Stephen, jt. auth. see Johnson, Stephen T.
Johnson, Stephen, ed. From the Holocaust to Healing the World. (p. 644)
Johnson, Stephen R. & Farrar-Hunter, Patricia A. Exploring Transportation. (p. 554)
Johnson, Stephen T. A Is for Art: An Abstract Alphabet. Johnson, Stephen T., illus. (p. 1)
—Alphabet School. Johnson, Stephen T., illus. (p. 50)
—My Little Blue Robot. Johnson, Stephen T., illus. (p. 1212)
—My Little Pink Princess Purse. Johnson, Stephen T., illus. (p. 1212)
—My Little Red Fire Truck. Johnson, Stephen T., illus. (p. 1213)
Johnson, Stephen T. & Johnson, Stephen. City by Numbers. (p. 323)
—City by Numbers. Johnson, Stephen T., illus. (p. 323)
Johnson, Steve. Holt Biology: Online Edition Upgrade. (p. 789)
—Holt Biology: Enhanced Online Edition. (p. 789)
—How to Be a Receptionist. (p. 814)
—Photocabulary. (p. 1353)
Johnson, Steve, illus. see Angelou, Maya.
Johnson, Steve, illus. see Bohrer, Maria.
Johnson, Steve, illus. see George, Jean Craighead.
Johnson, Steve, illus. see Gutman, Dan.
Johnson, Steve, illus. see Hanson, Warren.
Johnson, Steve, illus. see Hill, Karen.
Johnson, Steve, illus. see Keillor, Garrison.
Johnson, Steve, illus. see Krull, Kathleen.
Johnson, Steve, illus. see Larson, Deborah Jo.
Johnson, Steve, illus. see Mora, Pat, et al.
Johnson, Steve, illus. see Oppel, Kenneth.
Johnson, Steve, illus. see Osborne, Mary Pope.
Johnson, Steve, illus. see Palatini, Margie.
Johnson, Steve, illus. see Panahi, H. L.
Johnson, Steve, illus. see Paolilli, Paul & Brewer, Dan.
Johnson, Steve, illus. see Rusch, Elizabeth.
Johnson, Steve, illus. see Salten, Felix.
Johnson, Steve, illus. see Scieszka, Jon.
Johnson, Steve, illus. see Smucker, Anna.
Johnson, Steve, jt. auth. see Cutnell, John D.
Johnson, Steve & Hansen. Duerme, Pequeño. (p. 489)
Johnson, Steve & Kennedy, Deirdre. Pre-Algebra: Student Edition with Study Guide & Practice Workbook. (p. 1394)
Johnson, Sue, illus. see Honey, Elizabeth.
Johnson, Sue & Evans, Cheryl. Starting Gardening. Gower, Teri, illus. (p. 1644)
Johnson, Susan. Government to Government: Models of Cooperation Between States & Tribes. (p. 704)
Johnson, Susan & Johnson, Wil. Making Collages. (p. 1080)
Johnson, Susana M. Our Very Special Brother. (p. 1310)
Johnson, Sylvia A. Cobras. (p. 337)
—Crows. (p. 386)
—Shaking the Foundation: Charles Darwin & the Theory of Evolution. (p. 1559)
—Spanish Conquest of Mexico. (p. 1621)
Johnson, T. Beach Club: Magic Beach (p. 149)
—Seasons of the Year. (p. 1538)
Johnson, Tamaris, illus. see Williams, Lee.
Johnson, Tami. Arriba y Abajo. (p. 101)
—Cerca y Lejos. (p. 287)
—Encima y Debajo. (p. 524)
—Girls' Ice Hockey: Dominating the Rink (p. 680)
Johnson, Tami & Capstone Press Staff. Above & Below (p. 6)
—In & Out (p. 863)
—Near & Far (p. 1238)
—Up & Down (p. 1824)
Johnson, Tammie D. Tammie's Tales: An ABC Cat Series Featuring Simon, the S Cat. (p. 1704)
Johnson, Tasha A. & Johnson, Jeff A. Child Care Alphabet Book of Early Learning. (p. 301)
—Child Care Alphabet Book of Manipulatives. (p. 301)
Johnson, Temeka & Phillips, Quency. Decisions, Decisions, Decisions. (p. 421)
Johnson, Tera. Berkeley's Barn Owl Dance. Howells, Tania, illus. (p. 167)
Johnson, Terri. What Really Happened in Colonial Times: A Collection of Historical Biographies. Dixon, Darla, illus. (p. 1893)
Johnson, Terri, jt. auth. see Cook, Sherry.
Johnson, Terri, creator. Blackline Maps of World History: The Complete Set - Revised (p. 197)
—Wonders of Old: A Blank Timeline Book of World History. (p. 1948)
Johnson, Terry. Growing New Plants. (p. 726)
—Legal Rights (p. 988)
Johnson, Terry David. As I Sat on My Grandpa's Knee. (p. 105)
Johnson, Terry Lynn. Ice Dogs. (p. 850)
Johnson, Thaddeus. Unison High Senior High School. (p. 1818)
Johnson, Thomas M., jt. auth. see Weinand, Margaret.
Johnson, Tiffany & Benchmark Education Co., LLC Staff. I. (p. 831)
—Kids Have Fun. (p. 954)
Johnson, Tim. Lost Dutchman in Cochise County? Incidents & Coincidences. (p. 1055)
Johnson, Tim, jt. auth. see Nichols, Rod.
Johnson, Timothy, jt. auth. see Chatfield, Carl.
Johnson, Tina Marie. Heaven Dolly: I Dare You! (p. 761)
—Heaven Dolly: Little Miss Attitude. (p. 761)
Johnson, Tony. How Bobo Became King. (p. 805)
Johnson, Tora, jt. auth. see DeStrulle, Arlene.
Johnson, Trol. Cabbit: Safety Is the Key. (p. 250)
Johnson, Troy, ed. see Akyroyd, Clarrissa.
Johnson, Troy, ed. see Carew-Miller, Anna.
Johnson, Troy, ed. see Corrigan, Jim.
Johnson, Troy, ed. see Glatzer, Jenna.
Johnson, Troy, ed. see Keating, Susan.
Johnson, Troy, ed. see Orr, Tamra.
Johnson, Troy, ed. see Patrick, Bethanne.
Johnson, Troy, ed. see Staeger, Rob.
Johnson, Troy, ed. see Williams, Colleen Madonna Flood.
Johnson, Troy, ed. see Williams, Colleen.
Johnson, Tucker, illus. see Johnson, Lisa.
Johnson, Vargie. Alexander the Great the All-Powerful: What Made Them Famous? (p. 36)
—Catherine the Great the Victorious: What Made Them Famous? (p. 280)
—Charles Darwin, the Discoverer: What Made Them Famous? (p. 292)
—Eric the Red the Fearless: What Made Them Famous? (p. 533)
—Ferdinand Magellan the Explorer: What Made Them Famous? (p. 582)
—Joan of Arc the Messenger: What Made Them Famous? (p. 919)
—Marco Polo the Adventurer: What Made Them Famous? (p. 1092)
Johnson, Varian. Great Greene Heist. (p. 716)
Johnson, Vernon. Corruption in William Shakespeare's Hamlet. (p. 368)
—Power in William Shakespeare's Macbeth. (p. 1389)
Johnson, Vernon, jt. auth. see Johnson, Claudia Durst.
Johnson, Vernon, ed. Power in William Shakespeare's Macbeth. (p. 1389)
Johnson, Veronica E. Donkey Ride. (p. 466)
Johnson, Vic. Day by Day with James Allen. (p. 412)
Johnson, Vickey L. Monster Mix-Up. (p. 1168)
Johnson, Vickie, illus. see Allen, Lisa & Sharp, Julis.
Johnson, Vickie, illus. see Thorne, K. C.
Johnson, Victoria. Lemonade Standoff. (p. 991)
Johnson, Vincent L. Daddy's Good Cookin' Pavlova, Vera, illus. (p. 399)
—Of Corn Silk & Black Braids. Crockett, Linda, illus. (p. 1279)
Johnson, Virginia. Don't (p. 466)
—Hands-on Math, Grades K-1: Manipulative Activities for the Classroom. Hamaguchi, Carla, ed. (p. 741)
—Officer Rick & the Raccoon — a True Story. (p. 1280)
Johnson, Virginia, illus. see Jam, Teddy.

Johnson, Wil, jt. auth. see Johnson, Susan.
Johnson, William. Every Second Something Happens: Poems for the Mind & Senses. Hall, Melanie W., illus. (p. 543)
Johnson, William C. Little Tree. (p. 1037)
Johnson, William R. William's First Day of Kindergarten. (p. 1933)
—William's First Day of Kindergarten (Coloring Book) Coloring Book. (p. 1933)
—William's First Hair Cut. (p. 1933)
—William's First Haircut (Coloring Book) (p. 1934)
Johnson, Wyletta. Your Precious Eyes. (p. 1981)
Johnson, Young, et al. Princess Hope & the Hidden Treasure Aranda, Omar, illus. (p. 1404)
Johnson, Yuki, tr. see Ohkami, Mineko.
Johnson, Yuki N., tr. see Milky, D. J. & Kujiradov, Misaho.
Johnson, Yuki N., tr. see Milky, D. J., et al.
Johnson, Yuki N., tr. from JPN. Tramps Like Us (p. 1778)
Johnson-Carrigan, Ettarose. Old Rugged: How the Tree Became the Cross. (p. 1284)
Johnson-Choong, Shelly. Jewelry Box. (p. 917)
—Light to Come Home By. (p. 1015)
—Sand Dollar Promise. (p. 1510)
Johnson-Crouse, Donna C. Whispering Kids Club: The Ruby Ring. (p. 1912)
Johnson-Farris, Nancy. Critters & Bugs of Africa. (p. 384)
—Critters & Bugs of the Great Sonoran Desert. (p. 384)
Johnson-Hall, Wanda. You Can Be: Yes! He Can! (p. 1973)
Johnson-Isaacs, Cally, illus. see Shields, Gillian.
Johnson-McCue, Joyce. Gizmo's Great Adventure. (p. 681)
Johnson-Petrov, Arden, illus. see Harrison, David L.
Johnson-Shelton, Nils. Dragon King. (p. 477)
—Invisible Tower. (p. 886)
—Otherworld Chronicles #2: the Seven Swords. (p. 1307)
—Seven Swords. (p. 1555)
Johnson-Shelton, Nils, jt. auth. see Frey, James.
Johnson-Simon. Anaya Visits the James E Lewis Museum of Art at Morgan State University. (p. 67)
Johnson-Stefanidou, Catherine. Kid's Box Levels 1-2 Monty's Alphabet Book. (p. 953)
Johnston, Alexa. Sir Edmund Hillary: An Extraordinary Life. (p. 1580)
Johnston, Alexander. American Political History (p. 62)
—Connecticut. (p. 357)
—Genesis of a New England State. (p. 660)
—History of American Politics. (p. 783)
—History of the United States for Schools. (p. 785)
—Representative American Orations to Illustrate American Political History (p. 1461)
—United States: It's History & Constitution. (p. 1819)
Johnston, Andrew M. Hegemony & Culture in the Origins of NATO Nuclear First Use, 1945-1955. (p. 762)
Johnston, Ann. Quilter's Book of Design, Second Edition. (p. 1428)
Johnston, Annabelle, ed. see Melvin, J. C.
Johnston, Annie. Mary Ware, the Little Colonel's Chum Barry, Etheldred B., illus. (p. 1101)
Johnston, Annie Fell. Georgina of the Rainbows (Illustrated Ed. (p. 665)
—Little Colonel. (p. 1026)
—Little Colonel's Chum: Mary Ware (il. (p. 1026)
—Quilt That Jack Built; and, How He W. (p. 1428)
—Story of Dago. (p. 1658)
—Two Little Knights of Kentucky (Illustra. (p. 1804)
Johnston, Annie Fellows. Gate of the Giant Scissors. (p. 658)
—Giant Scissors. (p. 674)
—Giant Scissors. Barry, Etheldred B., illus. (p. 674)
—In the Desert of Waiting the Legend of Camel Back Mountain. (p. 865)
—Little Colonel. (p. 1026)
—Little Colonel's Chum: Mary Ware. (p. 1026)
—Little Colonel's Chum: Mary Ware. (p. 1026)
—Little Colonel's Hero. (p. 1026)
—Little Colonel's Hero. Barry, Etheldred B., illus. (p. 1026)
—Little Colonel's House Party. Meynell, Louis, illus. (p. 1026)
—Mary Ware the Little Colonel's Chum. Barry, Etheldred B., illus. (p. 1101)
—Mildred's Inheritance, Just Her Way & Ann's Own Way. Horne, Diantha W., illus. (p. 1142)
—Story of the Red Cross As Told to the Little Colonel. Goss, John, illus. (p. 1662)
Johnston, Antony. F-Stop. (p. 559)
—Julius. (p. 932)
Johnston, Antony, jt. auth. see Horowitz, Anthony.
Johnston, Becky, jt. auth. see Neuschwander, Angel.
Johnston, Brenda A. & Pruitt, Pamela. Struggle for Freedom & Henry Box Brown: A Read along Book. McCluskey, John A., ed. (p. 1668)
Johnston, Brian, ed. see Ibsen, Henrik.
Johnston, Camille. Gifted Book. Donahue, Linda, illus. (p. 675)
Johnston, Carol Shaw. Lily & Sophie: Sisters & Best Friends. (p. 1017)
Johnston, Carrie Lynn. Sir Bear Knight. (p. 1580)
Johnston, Cassandra, jt. auth. see Stumpff, April D.
Johnston, Cathy & Pecsenye, Jessica. Hamilton College College Prowler off the Record. (p. 739)
Johnston, Charles H. Famous Discoverers & Explorers of Amer. (p. 569)
Johnston, Charles H. L. Famous Frontiersmen & Heroes of the Border: Their Adventurous. (p. 569)
Johnston, Cindy. Zip, Burp & Hula. (p. 1987)
Johnston, Coleen. Unusual Mammals from A to Z. (p. 1823)
Johnston, Darcie. Is This Normal? More Girls' Questions, Answered by the Editors of the Care & Keeping of You. (p. 890)
Johnston, David, jt. auth. see Johnston, Kayla.
Johnston, E. K. Prairie Fire. (p. 1392)
—Story of Owen: Dragon Slayer of Trondheim. (p. 1659)
Johnston, Gail. Shaggy Pony & the Spotted Pup. (p. 1558)
—Whispers in the Mist. (p. 1912)
Johnston, Ginny & Cutchins, Judy. Ice Age Giants of the South. (p. 850)
Johnston, Jack. Ice Cream Hotel. (p. 850)
—Vineyard Book. Manion, Moira, illus. (p. 1843)
Johnston, James D. Adventures of Lucas & Celi: Lucas Stows Away. (p. 20)
Johnston, Jan. Amélie the Most Amazing Butterfly: I Do So Love Being a Butterfly ... (p. 58)
—Cruiser & the Night Noises. Eugenia, Maria, illus. (p. 386)
—Lisa Finds a Playful Tree Elf: No! I Am Not a Fairy! (p. 1022)
—Ruby - the Naughty Little Black Kitten: Hello! My Name Is Ruby ... (p. 1493)
Johnston, Jan, jt. auth. see Ziefert, Harriet.
Johnston, Jeanna. My Busy Day at the Ranch. (p. 1199)
Johnston, Jeffry W. Fragments. (p. 627)
Johnston, Jillian S., illus. see Powell, Gary Allison.
Johnston, Joe. Snag & Me - Christmas Miracle in Blanchard Forks. Johnston, Joe, illus. (p. 1595)
Johnston, Johanna. They Led the Way: 14 American Women. Hollinger, Deanne, illus. (p. 1732)
Johnston, Joseph A. Snag & Me & Mr Handy Henry's Show in St Louis. (p. 1595)
Johnston, Julie. Adam & Eve & Pinch-Me. (p. 11)
—Hero of Lesser Causes. (p. 772)
—Little Red Lies. (p. 1035)
—Very Fine Line. (p. 1838)
Johnston, K. E. M. Witness Tree & the Shadow of the Noose: Mystery, Lies, & Spies in Manassas. (p. 1942)
Johnston, Kathy. Get That Grasshopper! (p. 668)
Johnston, Kayla & Johnston, David. Butterflies in My Belly. (p. 247)
Johnston, Kurt, et al. My Friends (p. 1209)
—My School (p. 1218)
Johnston, Lisa Harp, illus. see Waszak, Madonna.
Johnston, Lissa. Brief Political & Geographic History of North America: Where Are... New France, New Netherland, & New Sweden. (p. 228)
Johnston, Lissa J. & Núñez Cabeza de Vaca, Alvar. Crossing a Continent: The Incredible Journey of Cabeza de Vaca. (p. 385)
Johnston, Lissa Jones. Alabama. (p. 33)
Johnston, Lynn, jt. auth. see Cruikshank, Beth.
Johnston, Marianne. Daniel Boone. (p. 405)
—Davy Crockett. (p. 411)
—Dealing with Anger / Qué hacer con la Ira. (p. 418)
—Dealing with Anger/Que Hacer con la Ira. De Leon, Mauricio Velzaquez, tr. from ENG. (p. 418)
—Dealing with Bullying / Qué hacer con los Bravucones. (p. 418)
—Dealing with Bullying/Que Hacer con Los Bravucones. Velazquez De Leon, Mauricio, tr. from ENG. (p. 418)
—Dealing with Fighting / Qué hacer con las Peleas. (p. 418)
—Dealing with Fighting/Que Hacer con Las Peleas. Velazquez De Leon, Mauricio, tr. from ENG. (p. 418)
—Dealing with Insults / Qué hacer con los Insultos. (p. 418)
—Dealing with Insults/Que Hacer con Los Insultos. Velazquez De Leon, Mauricio, tr. from ENG. (p. 418)
—Dealing with Jealousy / Qué hacer con los Celos. (p. 418)
—Dealing with Teasing / Qué hacer con las Burlas. (p. 418)
—Johnny Appleseed. (p. 923)
—Paul Bunyan. (p. 1330)
Johnston, Mark, jt. auth. see Spizman, Robyn Freedman.
Johnston, Mark & Spizman, Robyn Freedman. Secret Agents Strike Back. (p. 1540)
Johnston, Michael, jt. auth. see De la Cruz, Melissa.
Johnston, Patches. Mark's Mixed-up Months. (p. 1095)
Johnston, Paul F., jt. auth. see Lunis, Natalie.
Johnston, Phillip, illus. see Kropp, Joseph P.
Johnston, Richard M. Dukesborough Tales. (p. 489)
Johnston, Robert D. Making of America: The History of the United States from 1492 to the Present. (p. 1082)
Johnston, Shaun. Father, in a Far Distant Time I Find You: Utopian novel exploring the impact of evolutionary theory on human Nature. (p. 577)
Johnston, Shawn. Tale from the Forest of Fairshaw: The Big Fish Story. (p. 1699)
Johnston, Shelagh, jt. auth. see Napoli, Donna Jo.
Johnston, Steve. Other Side of Nowhere. (p. 1306)
Johnston, Tamra L. Libby the Little Leprechaun: And the Majestic Roller Coaster. (p. 1005)
—Libby the Little Leprechaun: Exploring the Opposite Side of South Africa. (p. 1005)
—Libby the Little Leprechaun. (p. 1005)
Johnston, Teresa. My Tooth Is Loose, Dr. Moose! (p. 1220)
—My Tooth Is Loose, Dr. Moose! Sendelbach, Brian, illus. (p. 1220)
—Thanksgiving for Emily Ann. Newton, Vanessa Brantley, illus. (p. 1726)
Johnston, Tony. 10 Fat Turkeys. Deas, Rich, illus. (p. 1993)
—10 Fat Turkeys. Deas, Richard F., illus. (p. 1993)
—Any Small Goodness. Colón, Raúl, illus. (p. 90)
—Bone by Bone by Bone. (p. 208)
—Cat, What Is That? Minor, Wendell, illus. (p. 278)
—Desert Dog Weatherford, Robert, illus. (p. 429)
—Desert Song Young, Ed, illus. (p. 429)
—First Grade, Here I Come! Sweet, Melissa & Walker, David, illus. (p. 595)
—Hanging Out. DiTerlizzi, Tony, illus. (p. 742)
—Isabel's House of Butterflies. Guevara, Susan, illus. (p. 891)
—Laugh-Out-Loud Baby. Gammell, Stephen, illus. (p. 980)
—Levi Strauss Gets a Bright Idea: A Fairly Fabricated Story of a Pair of Pants. Innerst, Stacy, illus. (p. 1004)
—My Abuelita. Morales, Yuyi, illus. (p. 1195)
—Noel. Chee, Cheng-Khee, illus. (p. 1262)
—P Is for Pinata. Parra, John, illus. (p. 1316)
—Sequoia. Minor, Wendell, illus. (p. 1552)
—Spoon in the Bathroom Wall. (p. 1631)
—Sticky People. (p. 1650)
—Uncle Rain Cloud. VandenBroeck, Fabricio, illus. (p. 1812)
—Voice from Afar: Poems of Peace. Guevara, Susan, illus. (p. 1848)
—Winter Is Coming. LaMarche, Jim, illus. (p. 1938)
Johnston, Tony & Davenier, Christine. Cat with Seven Names. (p. 278)
Johnston, Tony & Mazellan, Ron. Harmonica. Mazellan, Ron, illus. (p. 749)
Johnston, William. Limpy. (p. 1018)
Johnston, William R. Fabergé Menagerie. (p. 559)
Johnston-Brown, A. M. Chronicles of Pleasant Grove. (p. 317)
—Chronicles of Pleasant Grove (Glossary of Terms) (p. 317)
—Life at Pleasant Grove. (p. 1008)
Johnstone, Anne Grahame, illus. see Kingsley, Charles.
Johnstone, Catherine, ed. Women of Southwest Detroit: An Anthology of Prose & Poetry. (p. 1946)
Johnstone, Drummond & Wakefield, Chris. Numbers Game, Theparent Booklet: It's a Real Cure for Maths Fright. (p. 1272)
Johnstone, G. L. Sleep Tight Nancy... (p. 1588)
Johnstone, Ian. Circles of Stone. (p. 321)
—The Bell Between Worlds. (p. 1728)
Johnstone, Jan. Tom the Grocery Trolley. (p. 1764)
Johnstone, Jill & Spraggett, Daphne. Tu Puedes Cambiar el Mundo (p. 1795)
Johnstone, Leslie, jt. auth. see Levine, Shar.
Johnstone, Michael. Cars. (p. 272)
—Christmas Hugs. (p. 314)
—My Special Friend. (p. 1219)
—Together Forever. (p. 1762)
Johnstone, Michael, et al. Trains. (p. 1777)
Johnstone, Robb. Hockey. (p. 786)
—Louisiana. (p. 1058)
Johnston-Thomas, Lee Ann. Hidden Treasure of the Forgotten Pharaoh. (p. 776)
Johri, Shaan Mohammad, illus. see Johri, Subia Ali.
Johri, Subia Ali. Snackman & His Son Johri, Shaan Mohammad, illus. (p. 1595)
Joicey, Celia & Nothdruft, Dennis. How to Draw Like a Fashion Designer: Inspirational Sketchbooks, Tips from Top Designers. (p. 818)
Joihnson, Robert, compiled by. Lenin, Stalin & Communist Russia: The Myth & Reality of Communism. (p. 991)
Joiner, D. Wayne, Sr. Dudley Gloworm & the Saving Light. Joiner, D. Wayne, Sr., illus. (p. 489)
Joiner, Mica. Petunia Pollie & Her Prolific Purse. (p. 1349)
Joiner, Sara K. After the Ashes. (p. 28)
Joines, M. Hidden Chamber Beneath the Great Sphinx: Portal Key Quest. (p. 775)
Jojean. Twilight in the Vineyard. (p. 1801)
Jojo. Landon Wants a Puppy. (p. 974)
Jok, illus. see Biskup, Agnieszka.
Jok, illus. see Weakland, Mark.
Jok, Diego, illus. see Biskup, Agnieszka.
Jok, Diego, illus. see Weakland, Mark.
Jokisch, Kimberly. I Have Two Homes. (p. 839)
Jökulsson, Illugi. FC Barcelona: More Than a Club. (p. 578)
—Manchester United: The Biggest & the Best. (p. 1086)
—Messi. (p. 1129)
—Real Madrid: The Most Successful Club in the World. (p. 1448)
Jokulsson, Illugi. Ronaldo. Jokulsson, Illugi, ed. (p. 1487)
Jökulsson, Illugi. Stars of the World Cup. (p. 1643)
—Stars of Women's Soccer. (p. 1643)
—Stars of World Soccer. (p. 1643)
—U. S. Men's Team: New Stars on the Field. (p. 1806)
—Zlatan. (p. 1987)
Jolby. Monsters under Bridges. (p. 1169)
Joles, Alonso Sennell. Mejor Novio del Mundo. Estrada, Pau, illus. (p. 1124)
Jolet, Stefan, illus. see De Las Casas, Dianne.
Joliffe, Angela, jt. auth. see Clayden, Julie.
Jolin, Dominique. Toupie Veut Jouer. (p. 1773)
Jolin, Paula. In the Name of God. (p. 866)
Joline Anderson, Jennifer. Bigfoot & Yeti. (p. 185)
Jolis, Annie, jt. auth. see Meyer, Jared.
Jolivert, Immaculine. Lamb Who Counted Clouds. Gillen, Rosemarie, illus. (p. 972)
Jolivet, Joëlle. 10 Little Penguins. (p. 1993)
Jolivet, Joelle. Almost Everything. Siegel, Alexis, tr. from FRE. (p. 48)
—Zoo - Ology. Jolivet, Joelle, illus. (p. 1988)
Jolivet, Joëlle, illus. see Fromental, Jean-Luc.
Jolivet, Joëlle, illus. see Lamb, Charles & Lamb, Mary.
Jolivet, Joëlle, illus. see Marceau, Fani.
Jolley, Alana L. If You Give a Padre a Peppertree. (p. 854)
Jolley, Dan. Agent Mongoose & the Hypno-Beam Scheme. Wendt, Matt, illus. (p. 29)
—Alex Unlimited Volume 1: The Vosarak Code. (p. 36)
—Alien Adventure on Planet J. Wendt, Matt, illus. (p. 40)
—Alien Incident on Planet J. Wendt, Matt, illus. (p. 40)
—Attack of the Mutant Meteors. Witt, David, illus. (p. 113)
—Escape from Pyramid X. Wendt, Matt, illus. (p. 535)
—Guan Yu: Blood Brothers to the End [A Chinese Legend]. Randall, Ron, illus. (p. 728)
—Hero Twins: Against the Lords of Death. (p. 772)
—Hero Twins: Against the Lords of Death [A Mayan Myth]. Witt, David, illus. (p. 772)
—My Boyfriend Bites Martinez, Alitha E., illus. (p. 1199)
—My Boyfriend Is a Monster - My Boyfriend Bites. Martinez, Alitha E., illus. (p. 1199)
—Odysseus: Escaping Poseidon's Curse. (p. 1278)
—Odysseus: Escaping Poseidon's Curse. Yeates, Thomas, illus. (p. 1278)
—Pigling: A Cinderella Story [A Korean Tale]. Timmons, Anne, illus. (p. 1358)
—Shipwrecked on Mad Island. Huddleston, Courtney, illus. (p. 1567)
—Smoking Mountain: The Story of Popocatépetl & Iztaccíhuatl [an Aztec Legend]. Witt, David, illus. (p. 1595)
—Time Travel Trap. Wendt, Matt, illus. (p. 1753)
—Toy Story: The Mysterious Stranger. Moreno, Chris, illus. (p. 1774)
—Vampire Hunt. Titus, Gregory, illus. (p. 1832)
—Wrapped up in You. Nourigat, Natalie, illus. (p. 1962)
Jolley, Dan, jt. auth. see Croall, Marie P.
Jolley, Dan, jt. auth. see Hunter, Erin.
Jolley, Dan & Croall, Marie P. Agent Mongoose & the Attack of the Giant Insects. (p. 29)
—Agent Mongoose & the Attack of the Giant Insects. Wendt, Matt, illus. (p. 29)
Jolley, Dan & Hunter, Erin. Rise of Scourge. Kurkoski, Bettina, illus. (p. 1474)
—Warrior's Refuge Barry, James L., illus. (p. 1859)
Jolley, Dan & Nelson, O. T. Girl Who Owned a City: The Graphic Novel. Jones, Joëlle, illus. (p. 679)
Jolley, Mack, illus. see Brown, Toni Sorenson.
Jolley, Mike. I'll See You in the Morning. Moriuchi, Mique, illus. (p. 856)
Jolley, Tyler H., jt. auth. see Ficklin, Sherry D.
Jolliffe, Angela, illus. see Williams, Brenda.
Jolliffe, Angela, illus. see Clayden, Julie.
Jolliffe, Susan Rennick. Lady Ginny's Tea Parties (p. 970)
Jolliffe, Susan Rennick, illus. see Andrews, Jan.
Jolly, Alison. Ny Aiay Ako: Ako the Aye-Aye. Rasamimanana, Hantanirina, tr. (p. 1274)
Jolly, Judy. Happy Baptism Day. (p. 744)
Jolly, Karen. Singing Goat. (p. 1579)
Joly, Dominique, jt. auth. see Equipo Staff.
Joly, Dominique, jt. auth. see Héliadore.
Joly, Fanny. Atencion, Bebe Atacal Capdevila, Roser, illus. (p. 111)
—Bebe? Que Mala Idea! Capdevila, Roser, illus. (p. 155)
Joma, illus. see Bofill, Francesc.
Jo-Marie. Adi's World. (p. 12)
Jon Scieszkas Trucktown, et al. Take a Trip with Trucktown! Gordon, David et al, illus. (p. 1696)
Jonach, Ingrid. When the World Was Flat (and We Were in Love) (p. 1905)
Jonaitis, Alice, ed. see Blassingame, Wyatt.
Jonaitis, Alice, ed. see Seuss, Dr.
Jonas. JONAS #5: about Face. (p. 925)
—Three's a Crowd. (p. 1744)
Jonas, Ann, illus. see Sayre, April Pulley.
Jonas, Anne. Little Elephants. (p. 1027)
—Little Penguins. (p. 1033)
—Ulises y Casimiro. (p. 1809)
Jonas, Debbie Sue. Key Lime Candies Clubt in Two Turtles' Tales. (p. 950)
Jonas, Gennevive. Mary Loves Butterflies. Barrett, Karish, illus. (p. 1100)
Jonas, J. J. Conflagration: A Ten-Minute Dramatic Duet. (p. 357)
—Last of the Lotto Laity: A Ten-Minute Comedy Monologue. (p. 978)
—Lifescripts: Dramatic Monologue. (p. 1013)
—Revenge of the Coach's Daughter: A Ten-Minute Comedy Monologue. (p. 1465)
—Running on Empty: A Ten-Minute Dramatic Monologue. (p. 1497)
—Twitcher: A Ten-Minute Dramatic Duet. (p. 1803)
Jonason, Dave, illus. see Ellis, Libby.
Jonas-Simpson, Christine. Ethan's Butterflies: A Spiritual Book for Parents & Young Children after a Baby's Passing. Friis, Karen, illus. (p. 539)
Jonath, Leslie. Postmark Paris: A Story in Stamps. (p. 1388)
Jonath, Leslie & Christy, Jana. In Your Dreams. (p. 868)
Jonath, Leslie & Nash, Josh. On the Go. (p. 1290)
Jonathan Siruno, illus. see Pottle, Robert.
Jonell, Bob. Katie the Cricket. Prince, Brian, illus. (p. 945)
—Penny the Chinstrap Penguin Prince, Brian, illus. (p. 1338)
Jonell, Lynne. Bravemole. (p. 223)
—Emmy & the Home for Troubled Girls. Bean, Jonathan, illus. (p. 520)
—Emmy & the Incredible Shrinking Rat. (p. 520)
—Emmy & the Incredible Shrinking Rat. Bean, Jonathan, illus. (p. 520)
—Emmy & the Rats in the Belfry. Bean, Jonathan, illus. (p. 520)
—Grasshopper Magic. Dorman, Brandon, illus. (p. 711)
—Hamster Magic. Dorman, Brandon, illus. (p. 740)
—Secret of Zoom. (p. 1543)
—Sign of the Cat. (p. 1574)
—Wild Water Magic. Dorman, Brandon, illus. (p. 1930)
Jones, A. I Can Make a Shoe for You. (p. 836)
—Not One, Not Two, Not Even a Few. (p. 1267)
—Responsibility. (p. 1463)
Jones, Aaron, illus. see Drake, Karen.
Jones, Abigail. Still a Family. (p. 1650)
Jones, Alan & Ellis, Jane. My Life As a Plant - Russian: Activity & Coloring Book for Plant Biology. Khvostova, Ekaterina, tr. (p. 1212)
Jones, Alexandra. Moon Magic. (p. 1172)
Jones, Alexandria. Rico & Pencil Boy's 911 Adventure. (p. 1470)
—Rico & Pencil Boy's Adventure. (p. 1470)
—Rico & Pencil Boy's Circus Adventure. (p. 1470)
Jones, Alice Eley. Carpentry & Woodworking Tools of Hope Plantation. Jackson, April Eley & DeShazo, Sharon B., illus. (p. 271)
Jones, Allan. Burning Sky. (p. 244)
—In the Zone. (p. 868)
—Six Crowns: Fair Wind to Widdershins. Chalk, Gary, illus. (p. 1582)
—Six Crowns: Full Circle. Chalk, Gary, illus. (p. 1582)
—Six Crowns: Sargasso Skies. Chalk, Gary, illus. (p. 1582)
—Six Crowns: the Ice Gate of Spyre. Chalk, Gary, illus. (p. 1582)
—Six Crowns: Trundle's Quest. Chalk, Gary, illus. (p. 1582)
—Tyrant King. (p. 1805)
Jones, Allan Frewin. Blood Stone (p. 200)
—Fire over Swallowhaven. Chalk, Gary, illus. (p. 590)
—Legend of the Anaconda King. (p. 989)
—Legend of the Pharaoh's Tomb. (p. 989)
—Legends of the Golden Elephant. (p. 990)
—Skull Stone File. (p. 1586)
—Trundle's Quest. Chalk, Gary, illus. (p. 1793)
—Wreckers. (p. 1962)
Jones., Amber, illus. see Ken Lindstrom To Ken Lindstrom.
Jones, Amy Robin. Mary McLeod Bethune. (p. 1101)
Jones, Andrea. Spitting Twins. Kulka, Joe, illus. (p. 1629)
Jones, Andrea Koehle. Wish Trees. (p. 1940)
Jones, Andrea R. Garrison, et al. Abernathy the Basset Hound. (p. 5)
Jones, Andy, jt. auth. see Dinn, Philip.
Jones, Angela. Bird Lady. Newell, Brian, illus. (p. 190)
Jones, Angela & Jones, Sourou. Crowder Pea, Don't Bite! Naba, Dajana, illus. (p. 386)

J

Jones, Anita. My 15 Dogs: A 55-Year Journey of Love. (p. 1195)
Jones, Ann. Kabul in Winter: Life Without Peace in Afghanistan. (p. 941)
Jones, Ann, illus. see Hodson, Sally.
Jones, Anna. Goodnight, Mouse: A Peek-A-Boo Adventure. (p. 701)
—Scrub-a-Dub Froggy: Bath Mitt & Book Set. (p. 1533)
Jones, Anna, illus. see Agnew, Kate.
Jones, Anna, illus. see Forde, Patricia & Agnew, Kate.
Jones, Anna, illus. see Froeb, Lori C., ed.
Jones, Anna, illus. see Reasoner, Charles & Taylor, Jane.
Jones, Anna, illus. see Reasoner, Charles.
Jones, Anna, illus. see Rivers-Moore, Debbie.
Jones, Anne Marie. Mother Hen's Family Time Rhymes for Thought Book II. (p. 1178)
Jones, Anthony S. Little Puppy Du. (p. 1034)
Jones, Arthur T. Just Let God Be God. (p. 939)
Jones, Ashton & Gangemi, Alicia. I Am Special: Daily Gratitude & Affirmations for Children. (p. 834)
Jones, Ayanna, illus. see Walter-Goodspeed, Dee Dee.
Jones, B. J. Let's Color Korea - Everyday Life in Traditional. (p. 995)
Jones, B. J., ed. see Nahm, Andrew C.
Jones, B. J., jt. auth. see Rhie, Gene S.
Jones, Bandi. To Be Me. (p. 1758)
Jones, Barbara. Academic Word Power 4. (p. 7)
Jones, Barry, illus. see Poe, Edgar Allen.
Jones, Barry, illus. see Shelley, Mary & Shelley, Mary.
Jones, Barry, illus. see Stoker, Bram.
Jones, Bedo. Adventures of Rodeo Duck. (p. 22)
Jones, Beverley & Lodge, Maureen. Ready-to-Use Independent Reading Management: Reproducible, Skill-Building Activity Packs That Engage Kids in Meaningful, Structured Reading & Writing... While You Work in Small Groups. (p. 1448)
Jones, Bill, illus. see Fasbinder, Susie.
Jones, Bill, illus. see Weber, Ken.
Jones, Birdy. Mister Cool. Lynch, Tara, illus. (p. 1155)
Jones, Blake. Kevin the ninja kid Collection 1. (p. 950)
Jones, Bob, illus. see Diroma, Joseph.
Jones, Brandy. Petunia: The Plump Princess (p. 1349)
Jones, Branson, illus. see Jones, Linda.
Jones, Brenda. Adventures of Murphy the Mouse. Moore, Dwain, illus. (p. 21)
—Kids Sunday Notes: I Will Follow God's Plan for Me. (p. 955)
Jones, Brenda, illus. see Choyce, Lesley.
Jones, Brenda, illus. see Connors, Stompin' Tom.
Jones, Brenda, illus. see Hull, Maureen.
Jones, Brenda, illus. see Kessler, Deirdre.
Jones, Brenda, illus. see MacDonald, Hugh.
Jones, Brenda, illus. see O'Brien, Gerry.
Jones, Brenda, illus. see Smiley, Norene.
Jones, Brenn. Character Building Book: Set 4: Inspirational Role Models (p. 291)
—Learning about Equal Rights from the Life of Ruth Bader Ginsburg. (p. 984)
—Learning about Love from the Life of Mother Teresa. (p. 984)
—Learning about Public Service from the Life of John F. Kennedy Jr. (p. 984)
—Learning about Resilience from the Life of Lance Armstrong. (p. 984)
—Learning about Teamwork from the Lives of Sir Edmund Hillary & Tenzing Norgay. (p. 984)
Jones, Brenna, jt. auth. see Jones, Stan.
Jones, Brian and Brad. Righteous Heroes. (p. 1472)
Jones, Brian T., illus. see Bardhan-Quallen, Sudipta.
Jones, Brian T., illus. see Dunsmuir, Tom.
Jones, Brittany. Drake the Dragon King. Grimes, Kristopher, illus. (p. 480)
Jones, Bruce. Captain America Legends: What Price Glory. Rude, Steve, illus. (p. 263)
—Episode IV: A New Hope Barreto, Eduardo, illus. (p. 532)
—Formula 1 Sticker Activity Book. (p. 620)
—Incredible Hulk Youngquist, Jeff, ed. (p. 869)
—Kingpin: Thug. Youngquist, Jeff, ed. (p. 960)
Jones, Bruce & Austen, Chuck. Call of Duty: The Precinct Vol. 2 Mandrake, Tom & Zezelj, Danijel, illus. (p. 254)
Jones, Bruce Patrick. Action Stars Paper Dolls. Jones, Bruce Patrick, illus. (p. 10)
—Celebrity Scenes: Fun & Games with Hollywood Stars. (p. 285)
Jones, Bryan. Go Hokies Go: An Interactive Book Featuring Virginia Tech University. Bowman, Hootie, illus. (p. 686)
—Restoration & Revelations. (p. 1464)
Jones, Bryan E. Somebody Stole My Yawn! Embry, Stacey, illus. (p. 1609)
Jones, Bryony. Fabulous Fruit. (p. 560)
—Very Tasty Vegetables. (p. 1839)
Jones, Bryony, ed. see Carter, Andrew.
Jones, Bryony, jt. auth. see Smallwood, Sally.
Jones, Buck. Buck Jones in Ride 'Em Cowboy. (p. 234)
—Buck Jones Rangers-Cowboys Collection. (p. 234)
Jones, Buck, illus. see Artell, Mike.
Jones, Buck, illus. see Horsfall, Jacqueline.
Jones, Buck, illus. see McDowell, Josh & Johnson, Kevin.
Jones, Buck, illus. see Moore, Arden.
Jones, Buck, illus. see Pierce, Terry.
Jones, Buck, illus. see Tait, Chris.
Jones, C. Ashley. Draconic Destiny: Birth Rite. (p. 476)
Jones, C. Denise West & Darby, Stephania Pierce. Koko & Friends: Born to Play-Destined to Win! Jones, C. Denise West & Darby, Stephania Pierce, illus. (p. 966)
Jones, Callie Carol Rodgers. Good Cry. (p. 697)
—Sweet Potato Pie. (p. 1690)
Jones, Cameron. Insider's Guide to Lacrosse (p. 878)
Jones, Carl. Rudy the Rangifer & Why Her Nose Turned Orange. (p. 1494)
Jones, Carl L. Aaron Burrd, the Paranoid Bird with Acute Acrophobi. Vicki, Jones, ed. (p. 2)
Jones, Carl L., Sr. Joint Jerome Jones. (p. 924)
Jones, Carmen S. Grammar Minutes: 100 Minutes to Better Basic Skills. Ly, Dorothy, ed. (p. 706)
Jones, Carol. Lake of the Lost. (p. 972)
Jones, Carolyn. Theodora Bear Spurll, Barbara, illus. (p. 1729)
Jones, Carrie. Captivate. (p. 264)
—Endure. (p. 527)
—Entice. (p. 531)
—Need. (p. 1239)
—Sarah Emma Edmonds Was a Great Pretender: The True Story of a Civil War Spy. Oldroyd, Mark, illus. (p. 1514)
Jones, Carrie, jt. auth. see Hall, Megan Kelley.
Jones, Carrie, et al. After Obsession. (p. 28)
Jones, Carroll. Grandma Battles the Mouse. Giovannini, Jody, illus. (p. 708)
Jones, Caryn Gracey & Compass Point Books Staff. Teens in Brazil (p. 1715)
Jones, Caryn Gracey, et al. Teens in Venezuela (p. 1715)
Jones, Casey, illus. see Wald, Mark.
Jones, Cede. King Cobra / Cobra Real. (p. 958)
Jones, Chamira, illus. see Russell-Gilmer, Phyllis A.
Jones, Channing, illus. see Beckstrand, Karl.
Jones, Charisse, jt. auth. see Unlocking the Truth Staff.
Jones, Charisse & Shorter-Gooden, Kumea. Shifting: The Double Lives of Black Women in America. (p. 1566)
Jones, Charlotte Foltz. King Who Barked. Yayo, illus. (p. 959)
—Westward Ho! Eleven Explorers of the American West. (p. 1876)
Jones, Cheri. Adventures of a Mermaid Princess. (p. 16)
Jones, Cheryl. Where Are My Shoes? (p. 1906)
Jones, Cheryl & Joseph, Rahzheena. Jojo the Dappled Dachshund. Simmons, Ann, illus. (p. 924)
Jones, Chris. Cameron Jack & the Ghosts of World War 2. (p. 256)
—Cameron Jack & the Key to the Universe. (p. 256)
Jones, Chris B., illus. see Ballen, Karen.
Jones, Chris B., illus. see Clark, Katie Lea.
Jones, Chris B., illus. see Clark, Katie.
Jones, Chris B., illus. see Kolpin, Molly Erin.
Jones, Chris B., illus. see Kolpin, Molly, et al.
Jones, Chris B., illus. see Kolpin, Molly.
Jones, Chris B., illus. see McKnight, Marty.
Jones, Chris B., illus. see Reina, Mary.
Jones, Christianne C. Acampar Ruiz, Carlos, tr. from ENG. (p. 7)
—Babysitter Trover, Zachary, illus. (p. 129)
—Back to School Haugen, Ryan, illus. (p. 130)
—Beauty & the Beast Muehlenhardt, Amy Bailey, illus. (p. 154)
—Bella's Boat Surprise Sullivan, Mary, illus. (p. 162)
—Camping in Green Ouren, Todd, illus. (p. 257)
—Carta de Paula Ruiz, Carlos, tr. from ENG. (p. 272)
—Chicken Little Hermanson, Kyle, illus. (p. 300)
—Cuarto para Dos Ruiz, Carlos, tr. (p. 388)
—Dani el Dinosaurio Lozano, Clara, tr. from ENG. (p. 404)
—Elf Boogie. Randall, Emma, illus. (p. 512)
—Eric No Juega Ruiz, Carlos, tr. (p. 533)
—Gallinita Roja Abello, Patricia, tr. from ENG. (p. 653)
—Guillo el Gusano. Lozano, Clara, tr. from ENG. (p. 730)
—Hello, Goodbye, & a Very Little Lie Battuz, Christine, illus. (p. 764)
—How the Camel Got Its Hump Rooney, Ronnie, illus. (p. 813)
—John Henry Robledo, Sol, tr. (p. 922)
—John Henry Peterson, Ben, illus. (p. 922)
—Lacey Walker, Nonstop Talker Watson, Richard, illus. (p. 970)
—Lifeguard Skeens, Matthew, illus. (p. 1013)
—Little Red Hen Magnuson, Natalie, illus. (p. 1034)
—Messy One Martinez-Neal, Juana, illus. (p. 1130)
—Morning Mystery Simard, Remy, illus. (p. 1175)
—Pollita Pequeñita Abello, Patricia, tr. from ENG. (p. 1381)
—Pruebalo Ruiz, Carlos, tr. (p. 1413)
—Rah-Rah Ruby! Doerrfeld, Cori, illus. (p. 1433)
—Rapunzel: A Retelling of the Grimms' Fairy Tale Muehlenhardt, Amy Bailey, illus. (p. 1439)
—Reindeer Dance. Randall, Emma, illus. (p. 1457)
—Santa Shimmy. Randall, Emma, illus. (p. 1513)
—Secret Scooter Sullivan, Mary, illus. (p. 1543)
—Snowman Shuffle. Randall, Emma, illus. (p. 1601)
—Stone Soup Chambers-Goldberg, Micah, illus. (p. 1652)
Jones, Christianne C., jt. auth. see Blackaby, Susan.
Jones, Christianne C. & Kipling, Rudyard. How the Camel Got Its Hump Rooney, Ronnie, illus. (p. 813)
Jones, Christopher, illus. see Baltazar, Art, et al.
Jones, Christopher, illus. see Weisman, Greg, et al.
Jones, Chuck, illus. see Kipling, Rudyard.
Jones, Cloteal Mae. Five Little Ducks Went to the Forest: The Work Book. (p. 600)
—Five Little Ducks Went to the Forest. (p. 600)
Jones, Clyde, jt. auth. see Phillips, Carleton J.
Jones, Connie. On the Farm with Kaden & Moxie. (p. 1290)
Jones, Constance A. & Ryan, James D. Encyclopedia of Hinduism. (p. 525)
Jones, Constance & Ryan, James Daniel. Encyclopedia of Hinduism. Melton, J. Gordon, ed. (p. 525)
Jones, Cory, illus. see Big Idea Entertainment, LLC.
Jones, Cory, illus. see Schmidt, Troy.
Jones Crabbe, Ann. T J & His Friend: It's Just a Baby Thing. (p. 1694)
Jones, Daisy. I Always Knew We Were Rich! You Were Looking at the Checkbook... While I Was Looking at our Blessings. (p. 831)
Jones, Damon S. My Colorful Day. (p. 1200)
Jones, Dani, illus. see Guard, Anara.
Jones, Dani, illus. see Holub, Joan.
Jones, Dani, illus. see Smith, J. D.
Jones, Dani, jt. auth. see Smith, J. D.
Jones, Darlene. Silhouette (A Glimpse into My World) (p. 1575)
Jones, Darryl. Jane Austen. (p. 908)
Jones, Darynda. Death & the Girl He Loves. (p. 420)
—Death, Doom, & Detention. (p. 420)
Jones, David. Baboon. (p. 124)
—Mighty Robots: Mechanical Marvels That Fascinate & Frighten. (p. 1140)
—Monks in Space: Trapped in a Fatal Orbit. (p. 1166)
Jones, David & Kimpton, Laurence. Quick Revision KS3 Geography. (p. 1427)
Jones, David C. One Person to Another: Smoking, Chewing Tobacco & Young Peopole. (p. 1296)
Jones, Davy, illus. see Dussling, Jennifer.
Jones, Davy, jt. auth. see Cobb, Annie.
Jones, Debbie Knatt. Maurice ... As Read to the Students in Room D183 & D184. (p. 1110)
Jones, Deborah, illus. see Baxter, Nicola.
Jones, Deborah, jt. auth. see Baxter, Nicola.
Jones, Debra. Christmas & the Little Dolls. Bullock Jr., Michael A., illus. (p. 312)
Jones, Debra M. What in the World Should I Be. Collier, Kevin, illus. (p. 1888)
Jones, Dee. Winston Wonders about Capacity: A mathematical Story. Klaus, Machelle, illus. (p. 1937)
Jones, Denise West & Darby, Stephania Pierce. Koko & Friends: Friends? Oh, Really!!! Jones, Denise West & Darby, Stephania Pierce, illus. (p. 966)
Jones, Dennis. Adventures of the Fruitiebears: Book 2 Fruitiecars. (p. 23)
—Fruitiebears: Yorkies Birthday Today: Book 1. (p. 645)
—Life of Socks. (p. 1012)
Jones, Dennis, illus. see Zondervan Bibles Staff.
Jones, Dennis, illus. see Zondervan Publishing Staff.
Jones, Dennis, illus. see Zondervan, A.
Jones, Dennis G., illus. see Zondervan Publishing Staff.
Jones, Destry. What We Like. (p. 1895)
Jones, Diana Wynne. Castle in the Air (p. 276)
—Castle in the Air. (p. 276)
—Chronicles of Chrestomanci. (p. 317)
—Conrad's Fate: Read-Along/Homework Pack (p. 358)
—Conrad's Fate. (p. 358)
—Dogsbody. (p. 463)
—Earwig & the Witch. Zelinsky, Paul O., illus. (p. 498)
—Enchanted Glass. (p. 523)
—Fire & Hemlock. (p. 590)
—House of Many Ways. (p. 803)
—Howl's Moving Castle (p. 824)
—Howl's Moving Castle. (p. 824)
—Merlin Conspiracy. (p. 1128)
—Mixed Magics: Four Tales of Chrestomanci. (p. 1156)
—Pinhoe Egg. (p. 1359)
—Tale of Time City. (p. 1700)
—Unexpected Magic: Collected Stories. (p. 1817)
Jones, Diana Wynne, illus. see Miyazaki, Hayao.
Jones, Diana Wynne & Jones, Ursula. Islands of Chaldea. (p. 892)
Jones, Don. When the Firewood Comes. (p. 1904)
Jones, Don, illus. see Anderson, David A.
Jones, Donald M., photos by. Buffalo Country: America's National Bison Range. (p. 235)
Jones, Donnie. Nine Seconds to a Championship: The Story of LSU's Meteroic Rise to a National Championship Through the Eyes of A. (p. 1256)
Jones, Doris McKinney. Introducing Banana Anna & Friends. (p. 882)
Jones, Doug, illus. see Broslavick, Chris & Pichler, Tony.
Jones, Doug, illus. see Charlesworth, Liza.
Jones, Doug, illus. see Rosen, Michael J. & Kassoy, Ben.
Jones, Doug, illus. see Tomblin, Mark.
Jones, Douglas B., illus. see Cordsen, Carol Foskett.
Jones, Douglas B., illus. see Thimmesh, Catherine.
Jones, DuPre. Adventures of Gremlin. Gorey, Edward, illus. (p. 18)
Jones, Edward Huws, ed. Unbeaten Tracks: 8 Contemporary Pieces for Trumpet & Piano. (p. 1811)
Jones, Eileen. Classworks Fiction & Poetry Year 3. (p. 329)
—Classworks Literacy: Year 5. (p. 329)
Jones, Elisabeth & Jones, Lis. Walk in the Wild Woods. Coplestone, Jim, illus. (p. 1853)
Jones, Elizabeth McDavid. Peril at King's Creek: A Felicity Mystery. Tibbles, JeanPaul, illus. (p. 1343)
Jones, Elizabeth Orton, illus. see Field, Rachel.
Jones, Elizabeth Orton, illus. see Hunt, Mabel Leigh.
Jones, Elwynn. Frank's Frantic Friday. (p. 631)
Jones, Emily, illus. see Ster, Caroline Rose.
Jones, Ena. Clayton Stone, at Your Service. (p. 330)
Jones, Erasmus W. Young Captives: A Story of Judah & Babylon. Hayne, Mark, illus. (p. 1978)
Jones, Eric, illus. see Walker, Landry Q.
Jones, Eric, illus. see Walker, Landry Q. & Mason, Joey.
Jones, Eric, jt. auth. see Hodgson, Louise.
Jones, Erik. God Is in the Refrigerator. (p. 689)
Jones, Erik, illus. see King, Kimberly.
Jones, Ernest. Great Mix Up. (p. 717)
Jones, Eula V., jt. auth. see Harris, Valerie F.
Jones, F. Thomas. Backstep Forward. (p. 130)
Jones, Faith. Sprouting Wings (p. 1635)
Jones, Francisco Lancaster, tr. see Haque, Mary Baca.
Jones, Frewin. Charmed Return. (p. 294)
—Destiny's Path. (p. 431)
—Emerald Flame. (p. 517)
—Enchanted Quest. (p. 523)
—Faerie Path: The Immortal Realm. Bk. 4 (p. 562)
—Faerie Path. (p. 562)
—Lost Queen. (p. 1056)
—Seventh Daughter. (p. 1555)
—Warrior Princess. (p. 1859)
—Warrior Princess #2: Destiny's Path. (p. 1859)
Jones, Gail. House of Breathing. (p. 803)
Jones, Gareth. Imaginarium. (p. 860)
Jones, Gareth P. Clan of the Scorpion. Finlayson, Luke, illus. (p. 326)
—Constable & Toop. (p. 359)
—Dinosaurs Are Having a Party! Parsons, Garry, illus. (p. 444)
—Eye of the Monkey. Finlayson, Luke, illus. (p. 557)
—Ninja Meerkats (#3): Escape from Ice Mountain. Finlayson, Luke, illus. (p. 1256)
—Ninja Meerkats (#4): Hollywood Showdown. Finlayson, Luke, illus. (p. 1256)
—Ninja Meerkats (#5): the Tomb of Doom. Finlayson, Luke, illus. (p. 1256)
—Ninja Meerkats (#6): Big City Bust-Up. Finlayson, Luke, illus. (p. 1256)
—Ninja Meerkats (#7) the Ultimate Dragon Warrior. Finlayson, Luke, illus. (p. 1256)
—Ninja Meerkats (#8) Outback Attack. Finlayson, Luke, illus. (p. 1256)
Jones, Gareth P., jt. auth. see MacHado, CJ.
Jones, Garry L. Straight Out of Hell 2, The True Character of a Man. (p. 1664)
Jones, Gerard, jt. auth. see Toriyama, Akira.
Jones, Geriant H., jt. auth. see Graham, Ian.
Jones, Gillian, jt. auth. see Duris, Joan.
Jones, Glenda. Tree Who Wanted to Touch the Stars. (p. 1784)
Jones, Gordon, jt. auth. see McDonnell, Flora.
Jones, Graham. How They Lived in Bible Times. Deverell, Richard, illus. (p. 814)
Jones, Gregory Burgess, illus. see Barlics, Brian.
Jones Gunn, Robin, see Gunn, Robin Jones.
Jones, Gwen Angharad, tr. see McAllister, Angela.
Jones, Gwyneth. Hidden Ones. (p. 776)
Jones, H. Lena. Trapped on Planet Liska. (p. 1779)
Jones, Harriett E. & Long, Dani L. Principles of Insurance: Life, Health, & Annuities: Book One (Korean) (p. 1406)
—Principles of Insurance: Life, Health, & Annuities: Book Two (Korean) (p. 1406)
Jones, Helen. Poco - a Chiropractic Story. (p. 1375)
Jones, Helen, illus. see Thompson, Lisa.
Jones, Helen, jt. auth. see Hall, Betty L.
Jones, Helga. Venezuela. (p. 1835)
Jones, Henrietta, illus. see Seyfert, Ella Male.
Jones, Hettie, jt. auth. see Marley, Rita.
Jones, Heulwen. O'Grady's Well. (p. 1280)
Jones, Hugh. Present State of Virginia. (p. 1396)
—Shortenglish Grammar: An Accidence to the English Tongue. (p. 1569)
Jones, Huw Vaughan. Ar ôl y Parti. (p. 94)
—Mynd I'r Siop. (p. 1222)
—Pwdin Siocled. (p. 1421)
Jones, J. Just Bugs: Learning the Short U Sound. (p. 938)
—My First ABC & Number Coloring Book. (p. 1204)
Jones, J. J. Flute Tudor & the Secret Order. (p. 608)
Jones, J. Sydney, et al. Crusades Biography. (p. 386)
—Crusades Primary Sources. (p. 386)
Jones, Jac. In Chatter Wood. Jones, Jac, illus. (p. 863)
Jones, Jac, illus. see Morden, Daniel.
Jones, Jac, illus. see Weston, Simon.
Jones, Jac, jt. auth. see Doyle, Malachy.
Jones, Jac, jt. auth. see Jones, Meinir Pierce.
Jones, Jac, tr. see Morden, Daniel.
Jones, Jac, et al. Dianc. (p. 434)
Jones, Jack. Rusty's Life. (p. 1498)
Jones, Jack Jr. Marriah's Easter Egg Hunt. (p. 1096)
Jones, Jada. Nishell: Holding Back. (p. 1257)
Jones, Jada & Kuskowski, Alex. Kiki: Bein' Good. (p. 955)
Jones, James Lucas, ed. see Guggenheim, Marc.
Jones, James Lucas, ed. see Naifeh, Ted.
Jones, James Lucas & Torres, J., eds. Yo Gabba Gabba: Comic Book Time. (p. 1971)
Jones, Jan, illus. see Cramer, Gayle Shaw.
Jones, Jan Naimo, illus. see Keene, Carolyn.
Jones, Jan Naimo, illus. see Mitchell, Barbara.
Jones, Jan Naimo, illus. see Welch, Catherine A.
Jones, Jan Naimo, tr. see Mitchell, Barbara.
Jones, Janey Louise. Cloudberry Castle. (p. 334)
—Secrets of Sophia Musgrove: Dancing & Deception. No. 1 (p. 1545)
Jones, Jasmine. Coach Carter. (p. 336)
—Head over Heels. (p. 756)
Jones, Jasmine, adapted by. Head over Heels. (p. 756)
—Importance of Being Gordo. (p. 862)
—Just Like Lizzie. (p. 939)
—Lizzie Loves Ethan. (p. 1043)
—Oh, Brother! (p. 1280)
Jones, Jasmine & Alfonsi, Alice. My Second Way Cool (p. 1218)
Jones, Jason. Twas the Fourth Night before Christmas: Modern Myths-the First Tale. (p. 1799)
Jones, Jeannelle. Henry's Adventure. (p. 769)
Jones, Jen. Accessory Parties: Planning a Party That Makes Your Friends Say Cool! (p. 8)
—Are You a Good Friend? (p. 97)
—Ashley Goes Viral. Franco, Paula, illus. (p. 106)
—Becoming a Pop Star (p. 156)
—Beyoncé Knowles. (p. 173)
—Bone-Chilling Ghost Stories (p. 208)
—Braiding Hair: Beyond the Basics (p. 221)
—Brooke's Big Decision: #8 (p. 230)
—Brooke's Big Decision Adams, Liz, illus. (p. 230)
—Brooke's Quest for Captain (p. 230)
—Brooke's Quest for Captain: # 2 (p. 230)
—Bullies (p. 240)
—Cancer, Scorpio, & Pisces: All about the Water Signs. (p. 261)
—Cheer All-Stars: Best of the Best (p. 295)
—Cheer Competitions: Impressing the Judges (p. 296)
—Cheer Gear (p. 296)
—Cheer Professionals: Cheer as a Career. (p. 296)
—Cheer Skills (p. 296)
—Cheer Spirit: Revving up the Crowd (p. 296)
—Cheer Squad: Building Spirit & Getting Along (p. 296)
—Cheerleaders in Action (p. 296)
—Cheerleading (p. 296)
—Cheers, Chants, & Signs: Getting the Crowd Going. (p. 296)
—Competition for Gaby (p. 352)
—Competition for Gaby: # 4 (p. 352)
—Cool Crafts with Cardboard & Wrapping Paper: Green Projects for Resourceful Kids (p. 363)
—Cool Crafts with Flowers, Leaves, & Twigs: Green Projects for Resourceful Kids (p. 363)
—Cool Crafts with Newspapers, Magazines, & Junk Mail: Green Projects for Resourceful Kids (p. 363)
—Cool Crafts with Seeds, Beans, & Cones: Green Projects for Resourceful Kids (p. 363)
—Costume Parties: Planning a Party That Makes Your Friends Say Wow! (p. 368)
—Delaney vs. the Bully. Franco, Paula, illus. (p. 424)
—Dog Days for Delaney. Franco, Paula, illus. (p. 461)
—Faith & the Camp Snob (p. 565)
—Faith & the Camp Snob: # 1 (p. 565)
—Faith & the Dance Drama: #5 (p. 565)

—Faith & the Dance Drama Adams, Liz, illus. (p. 565)
—Figure Skating for Fun! (p. 586)
—Game Night Parties: Planning a Bash That Makes Your Friends Say Yeah! (p. 654)
—Gemini, Libra, & Aquarius: All about the Air Signs. (p. 660)
—Girls' Guide to Vampires: Everything Enchanting about These Immortal Creatures. (p. 680)
—Girls' Guide to Werewolves: Everything Charming about These Shape-Shifters (p. 680)
—Girls' Guide to Wizards: Everything Magical about These Spellbinders. (p. 680)
—Girls Guide to Zombies: Everything Vital about These Undead Monsters. (p. 680)
—Gymnastics Competitions: On Your Way to Victory Doyle, Renee, illus. (p. 734)
—Gymnastics Essentials: Safety & Equipment Doyle, Renee, illus. (p. 734)
—Gymnastics Events: Floor, Vault, Bars, & Beam (p. 734)
—Gymnastics Skills: Beginning Tumbling (p. 734)
—Gymnastics Training & Fitness: Being Your Best. (p. 734)
—How Much Do You Know about Bullying? (p. 811)
—Judy Blume: Fearless Storyteller for Teens. (p. 931)
—Lissa & the Fund-Raising Funk (p. 1022)
—Lissa & the Fund-Raising Funk: # 3 (p. 1022)
—Lissa on the Sidelines: #6 (p. 1022)
—Lissa on the Sidelines Adams, Liz, illus. (p. 1022)
—Looking Great (p. 1051)
—Maren Loves Luke Lewis. Franco, Paula, illus. (p. 1092)
—Maren's New Family. Franco, Paula, illus. (p. 1092)
—New Ashley. Franco, Paula, illus. (p. 1243)
—Oprah Winfrey: Celebrity with Heart. (p. 1301)
—Pampering Parties: Planning a Party That Makes Your Friends Say Ahhh (p. 1320)
—Perfect Parties (p. 1342)
—Planning Perfect Parties: The Girls' Guide to Fun, Fresh, Unforgettable Events. (p. 1368)
—Reader's Guide to Gary Soto's Taking Sides. (p. 1444)
—Save Our Squad, Gaby: #7 (p. 1516)
—Save Our Squad, Gaby Adams, Liz, illus. (p. 1516)
—Sean "Diddy" Combs: A Biography of a Music Mogul. (p. 1537)
—Sleepover Girls. Franco, Paula, illus. (p. 1589)
—Team Cheer. (p. 1710)
—Throwing Parties (p. 1745)
—Willow's: Spring Break Adventure. Franco, Paula, illus. (p. 1934)
—Willow's Boy-Crazy Birthday. Franco, Paula, illus. (p. 1934)
Jones, Jen & Capstone Press Editors. Fashion Careers: Finding the Right Fit (p. 575)
Jones, Jen & Capstone Press Staff. Fashion Design: The Art of Style (p. 575)
—Fashion Design School: Learning the Skills to Succeed. (p. 575)
Jones, Jen & Sirrine, Carol. Re-Craft: Unique Projects That Look Great (And Save the Planet) (p. 1441)
Jones, Jen & Wittrock, Jeni. Friendship Quizzes. (p. 639)
Jones, Jennie. Surgeon - Craftsman: Laurence Knight Groves, M. D. 1922-2007. (p. 1685)
Jones, Jennifer Berry. Who Lives in the Snow? Powell, Consie, illus. (p. 1916)
Jones, Jenny. Shadowsong. (p. 1558)
Jones, Jenny B. Charmed Life (p. 294)
—In Between: A Katie Parker Production (Act I) (p. 863)
—So Not Happening (p. 1602)
—So over My Head (p. 1602)
Jones, Jeremy V. Keeper: The Tim Howard Story. (p. 947)
—Toward the Goal: The Kaka Story (p. 1773)
—Toward the Goal: The Kaká Story (p. 1773)
Jones, Jill. Broken/Open. (p. 230)
—Screens Jets Heaven: New & Selected Poems. (p. 1533)
Jones, Joanna, jt. auth. see Cartwright, Nancy.
Jones, Joëlle, illus. see Jolley, Dan & Nelson, O. T.
Jones, Joff, illus. see Nettles Jr, J. H.
Jones, John Beauchamp. Adventures of Col. Gracchus Vanderbomb. (p. 17)
—Books of Visions. (p. 212)
—Freaks of Fortune: Or the History of Ned Lorn. (p. 631)
—Life & Adventures of a Country Merchant. (p. 1007)
—Monarchist. (p. 1163)
—Rebel War Clerk's Diary at the Confederate States Capital. (p. 1451)
—Rural Sports: A Poem. (p. 1497)
—Secession, Coercion & Civil War. (p. 1539)
—Spanglers & Tingles: The Rival Belles. (p. 1620)
—War Path. (p. 1858)
—Western Merchant. (p. 1876)
—Wild Southern Scenes. (p. 1930)
—Wild Western Scenes. (p. 1930)
Jones, John Lawrence, photos by see Windling, Terri.
Jones, John R., illus. see McMullan, Kate.
Jones, Joy, jt. auth. see Newsom, Mary T.
Jones, Joyce Adams. Remembering the Marches in Selma, Alabama. (p. 1460)
Jones, Joyce Elaine. For Such a Journey. (p. 616)
Jones, Juan Luis, illus. see Cabrera, Mirna Y. & Esquenazi, Martha E., eds.
Jones, Juanita. Mr. Nice Guy. (p. 1185)
Jones, Judith. You're from Where Grandma? (p. 1982)
Jones, Julie. Problem at Pepperpine Zoo. Jones, Julie, illus. (p. 1408)
Jones, Julie Brangers. Can I Fly? (p. 258)
Jones, Julienne, illus. see Jackson, Bobby L.
Jones, K. L., illus. see Burroughs, Edgar Rice.
Jones, K. L., illus. see Helfand, Lewis.
Jones, K. L., illus. see Welsh, C. E. L.
Jones, Kadeem. Healthy Fractions: Develop Understanding of Fractions & Numbers. (p. 758)
—Look Out for the Poison Dart Frog! (p. 1050)
Jones, Karen. Adventures of Señorita Rita: Running of the Bulls. Rodriguez, Cristian, illus. (p. 22)
—Around the World from a to Z. (p. 100)
—Stories from the Television Show Imagination Way. (p. 1654)
—Vital Skills: How to Use Your Spiritual Gifts. (p. 1846)
Jones, Karen A. Light Pole Books: Reading Series (p. 1015)
Jones, Karen Lee. Giggle with Friends from Imagination Way. (p. 676)
Jones, Kari. Out of Season (p. 1311)
—Storm Tide (p. 1656)
Jones, Karl. Chinese New Year Activity Book. Simpson, Steve, illus. (p. 307)
—Day of the Dead Activity Book. Simpson, Steve, illus. (p. 414)
—Thanksgiving Activity Book. Chou, Joey, illus. (p. 1725)
—Which Dude Are You? (p. 1911)
Jones, Katherine. Forbidden Tree. (p. 616)
Jones, Kelley, illus. see Disney Book Group Staff & Miller, Bryan Q.
Jones, Kelly. Mama. Kewley, Ken, illus. (p. 1084)
—Unusual Chickens for the Exceptional Poultry Farmer. Kath, Katie, illus. (p. 1823)
Jones, Ken, ed. see Dahle, Lele, et al.
Jones, Kevin. Lamb Named Ewe. (p. 972)
Jones, Kia. Adventures of Shamya & Friends: The Thanksgiving Day Wish. (p. 22)
Jones, Kim P. Maggie & the Halloween Bandit. (p. 1071)
Jones, Kimberly & Jones, Laura. Morning Zoo. (p. 1175)
Jones, Kimberly K. Genie Scheme. (p. 661)
—Sand Dollar Summer. (p. 1510)
Jones, Kip. Power of Bystanders: Willie Bohanon & Friends Learn to Handle Bullying Like a B. O. S. S. Isely, Chad, illus. (p. 1389)
—Power of Self-D: Willie Bohanon & Friends Learn the Power of Self-Determination. Isely, Chad, illus. (p. 1389)
Jones, Kirk. Lisa the Ministering Mole: Meet the Mole. Jones, Kirk, illus. (p. 1022)
Jones, Kolin, jt. auth. see Jones, Ryan.
Jones, Kristen Wyrick, jt. auth. see Wyrick, June Gray.
Jones, Kurt. Tree Tale. (p. 1783)
Jones, Kym. Misadventures of the Tweevils: Bath Time. (p. 1150)
Jones, L. Diane. Bully Busters. (p. 241)
—My Buddy & Me. (p. 1199)
Jones, Lara. Bestario. (p. 171)
—Me Gusta Mi Orinal. (p. 1116)
—Me Gustan Los Besos y Abrazos. (p. 1116)
Jones, Lara, illus. see Finch, Keith.
Jones, Lara, illus. see Little, Penny.
Jones, Latoya. My Learning Rhythms: Book 1. (p. 1211)
—My Learning Rhythms: Book 3. (p. 1211)
—My Learning Rhythms: Book 4. (p. 1211)
Jones, Laura, jt. auth. see Jones, Kimberly.
Jones, Lauren V., ed. see Chaple, Glenn F.
Jones, Leanne. It's Cool to Be Clever: The story of Edson C. Hendricks, the genius who invented the design for the Internet. Mah, Anna, illus. (p. 896)
Jones, Lee. Whimper. (p. 1911)
Jones, Leslie. ADV of Callaway. (p. 13)
Jones, Linda. Alphabet Anatomy: Meet the Capital Letters. Jones, Branson & Mikle, Toby, illus. (p. 49)
Jones, Linda 'Amias'. LiquidPlastic. (p. 1021)
Jones, Linda Gale, jt. auth. see Cosman, Madeline Pelner.
Jones, Lis, jt. auth. see Jones, Elisabeth.
Jones, Lisa A. Black Dog. (p. 195)
Jones, Liz. Noah's Bed. Copplestone, Jim, illus. (p. 1261)
Jones, Lloyd. Mister Pip. (p. 1155)
Jones, Lois. Use It up, Wear It Out. (p. 1827)
Jones, Lois S. Development of Christian Symbolism Jones, Preston, ed. (p. 432)
Jones, Lonetha. Big Brother's Missing Shoes. (p. 180)
Jones, Lori M. Riley's Heart MacHine. Hammond, Julie, illus. (p. 1472)
Jones, Lorraine. Super Science Projects about Weather & Natural Forces. (p. 1681)
Jones, Loyal. Preacher Joke Book: Religious Anecdotes from the Oral Tradition. (p. 1394)
Jones, Loyal, jt. ed. see Wheeler, Billy Edd.
Jones, Loyal & Wheeler, Billy E. Hometown Humor: More than 300 Jokes from the Porch Swings, Barber Shops, Corner Cafes, & Beauty Parlors of America. (p. 794)
Jones, Loyal & Wheeler, Billy Edd. Curing the Cross-Eyed Mule: Appalachian Mountain Humor. Hall, Wendell E., illus. (p. 392)
—More Laughter in Appalachia: Southern Mountain Humor. Hall, Wendell E., illus. (p. 1174)
Jones, Lucinda. Moody: What Moody Likes to Do. (p. 1171)
Jones, Lynda. Hurricane Disaster. (p. 829)
—Mrs. Lincoln's Dressmaker: The Unlikely Friendship of Elizabeth Keckley & Mary Todd Lincoln. (p. 1187)
Jones, Lynn. Citizenship Studies for OCR GCSE Short Course. (p. 323)
Jones, M. B., jt. auth. see Jones, M. b.
Jones, M. b. & Jones, M. B. Manners Are Free. (p. 1088)
Jones M.A., Yvette. I Know I Love You. (p. 840)
Jones, Marcia Thornton. Very Haunted Holiday. (p. 1838)
Jones, Marcia Thornton, jt. auth. see Dadey, Debbie.
Jones, Marcia Thornton & Dadey, Debbie. Dragons Do Eat Homework. Dreidemy, Joëlle, illus. (p. 479)
—Ghosts Do Splash in Puddles. Dreidemy, Joëlle, illus. (p. 672)
—Guys & Ghouls. Francis, Guy, illus. (p. 733)
—Other Side of Magic. (p. 1306)
—Red, White, & Boo! Francis, Guy, illus. (p. 1455)
—This Side of Magic. Stower, Adam, illus. (p. 1737)
—Wizards Do Roast Turkeys. Dreidemy, Joëlle, illus. (p. 1943)
Jones, Marcie. Mama Cat. (p. 1084)
Jones, Margaret. Nat. (p. 1230)
Jones, Margaret, illus. see Ifans, Rhiannon.
Jones, Margaret, illus. see Thomas, Gwyn.
Jones, Mark. Blissed Out! An Adventure in Consciousness. (p. 199)
Jones, Mark, illus. see Elkins, Stephen.
Jones, Mark, illus. see Turnbull, Elizabeth J.
Jones, Mark, illus. see Turnbull, Elizabeth.
Jones, Mark, jt. auth. see Parkin, Lance.
Jones, Marla F. Ponder Learns to Be Thankful. (p. 1382)
Jones, Marlis. Wyn Melangell. (p. 1966)
—Y Brenin a'r Gath. (p. 1968)
Jones, Marlis & Jên, Ruth. Cuddio'r Colur. (p. 389)
Jones, Mary, et al. Cambridge Checkpoint Science Coursebook 7. (p. 255)
—Cambridge Checkpoint Science Workbook 7. (p. 255)
Jones, Mary Noble. Itsy Rabbit & Friends: Itsy's First Adventure. Jones, Mary Noble, illus. (p. 900)
Jones Med, Marquita J. Marvette Made Fun of Me. (p. 1099)
Jones, Meinir Pierce & Jones, Jac. Taid Ar Binnau. (p. 1695)
Jones, Melanie Davis. Balls. Bronson, Linda, illus. (p. 135)
—Big Machines. Gay-Kassel, Doreen, illus. (p. 182)
—Field Day. Molnar, Albert, illus. (p. 583)
—I Can Ski! (p. 836)
—I Can Ski! Boles, Terry, illus. (p. 836)
Jones, Melanie Davis, jt. auth. see Johns, Linda.
Jones, Michael. Finding Imagine Nation. (p. 588)
Jones, Michael J. Travis Loses His Way. (p. 1781)
Jones, Michael P. Whales—The Gentle Giants: Calendar 1988. (p. 1878)
Jones, Michelle, jt. auth. see Hirsch, Jennifer.
Jones, Milo. Snow Friends. Lewis, Stephen, illus. (p. 1599)
Jones, Molly. 21st-Century Education & Careers: Options & Strategies. (p. 1996)
—Choosing Tree. (p. 310)
—First Amendment: Freedom of Speech, the Press, & Religion. (p. 592)
—Frequently Asked Questions about Slander & Libel in the Digital Age. (p. 636)
—Medieval Knights. (p. 1119)
—Something in the Air. Welch, Sheila Kelly, illus. (p. 1610)
—Top 10 Tips for Planning for a Career. (p. 1768)
Jones, Monica C. 25 Candy Canes for Jesus. (p. 1996)
Jones, Morris. Is There Life Beyond Earth? (p. 890)
—Out of This World: Rockets & Astronauts. (p. 1311)
Jones, Morris & Rohr, Ian. Encyclopedia of World Animals. (p. 525)
Jones, Nancy. Grandpaws. (p. 710)
Jones, Natalya. George Washington Carver: Peanut Scientist. (p. 664)
Jones, Nathan, illus. see Gray, Susannah.
Jones, Nathan Smith. Boy Who Ate America. Nelson, Casey, illus. (p. 219)
Jones, Nick. Food-head Makes a Pie. (p. 613)
Jones, Nicky. Toby Fletcher's Fly-Away Tree. (p. 1760)
Jones, Noah, illus. see Boelts, Maribeth.
Jones, Noah, illus. see Demas, Corinne.
Jones, Noah, illus. see Florian, Douglas.
Jones, Noah Z. Little Red Quacking Hood. (p. 1035)
—Moldylocks & the Three Beards. Jones, Noah Z., illus. (p. 1160)
Jones, Noah Z., illus. see Bardhan-Quallen, Sudipta.
Jones, Noah Z., illus. see Bennett, Kelly.
Jones, Noah Z., illus. see Bloom, Amy Beth.
Jones, Noah Z., illus. see Boelts, Maribeth.
Jones, Noah Z., illus. see Carris, Joan Davenport.
Jones, Noah Z., illus. see Carris, Joan.
Jones, Noah Z., illus. see Demas, Corinne.
Jones, Noah Z., illus. see Moser, Lisa.
Jones, Noah Z., illus. see Palatini, Margie.
Jones, Noah Z., illus. see Singer, Marilyn.
Jones, Noah Z., jt. auth. see Jones, Noah Z.
Jones, Noah Z. & Jones, Noah Z. Princess Pink & the Land of Fake-Believe #2: Little Red Quacking Hood (a Branches Book) Jones, Noah Z., illus. (p. 1405)
Jones, Nona C. When the Soul Won't Let Go: No-Nonsense Answers to a Broken Woman's Questions. (p. 1905)
Jones, Otis. Geonopolis, the Shapely City of Geometry. (p. 663)
Jones, P. T. Floating Boy & the Girl Who Couldn't Fly. (p. 605)
Jones, Patrick. Always Faithful. (p. 51)
—Barrier. (p. 140)
—Body Shot. (p. 207)
—Bridge. (p. 227)
—Cheated. (p. 295)
—Combat Zone. (p. 346)
—Controlled. (p. 361)
—Doing Right. (p. 463)
—Drift: Nissan Skyline. (p. 485)
—Freedom Flight. (p. 634)
—Gamble. (p. 654)
—Guarding Secrets. (p. 728)
—Head Kick. (p. 756)
—My Dog-Walking Business: Work with Money (p. 1202)
—Nailed. (p. 1227)
—Out of the Tunnel. (p. 1311)
—Outburst. (p. 1312)
—Raising Heaven. (p. 1437)
—Returning to Normal. (p. 1465)
—Side Control. (p. 1573)
—Slammed: Honda Civic. (p. 1587)
—Stolen Car. (p. 1652)
—Taking Sides. (p. 1698)
—Target. (p. 1706)
—Tear Collector. (p. 1711)
—Triangle Choke. (p. 1785)
—Ultimate Fighting: The Brains & Brawn of Mixed Martial Arts. (p. 1809)
Jones, Patrick & Chartier, Brent. At All Costs. (p. 110)
—Collateral Damage. (p. 339)
—Franchise. (p. 627)
Jones, Paul, illus. see Takhar, Jodi.
Jones, Penny & Norris, Aaron. Bangu the Flying Fox: A Dreamtime Story of the Yuin People of Wallaga Lake. (p. 136)
Jones, Penri. Dan Leuad Llyn. (p. 402)
Jones, Peter. Complete Guides Human Body. (p. 353)
—French Revolution: 1787-1804. (p. 636)
Jones, Peter B., ed. Harvest of Tales: Short Stories & Essays up to 325 Words. (p. 751)
Jones, Phil, illus. see Clark, Ruth E.
Jones, Phill. Disability Rights. (p. 446)
—Reproduction & Cloning. (p. 1461)
—Sickle Cell Disease. (p. 1572)
—Viruses. (p. 1844)
Jones, Phillip. Genetic Code. (p. 660)
—Kingdoms of Life. (p. 960)
Jones, Phillip & Marzilli, Alan. Freedom of Information. (p. 634)
Jones, Pia. Sometimes I Feel... (p. 1610)
Jones, Pixy. Teen Dumb Come. (p. 1713)
Jones, Preston, ed. see Jones, Lois S.
Jones, Rachel. Adventures of AJ & Hunter: Lost in the Back Yard. sheltrown, karen, illus. (p. 16)
Jones, Ralph E. Adventures of Kele: Boy of the Rock Shelter. (p. 19)
Jones, Randy, illus. see Leacock, Elspeth & Buckley, Susan.
Jones, Rebecca C. Captain John Smith's Big & Beautiful Bay Shute, Linda, illus. (p. 264)
—Matthew & Tillie. Peck, Beth, illus. (p. 1109)
—Mystery of Mary Surratt: The Plot to Kill President Lincoln (p. 1224)
Jones, Rena. Dinner Date for Dilly. Nielson, Ginger, illus. (p. 441)
—Pony Strings & Critter Things. Nielson, Ginger, illus. (p. 1383)
Jones, Rene'. New Friend for Dilly. Nielson, Ginger, illus. (p. 1244)
Jones, Rhonda Jo. Making Hayley. (p. 1081)
Jones, Richard. Liberation of Aunt Jemima: A Poetic Tribute to the Spiritual Woman. (p. 1005)
Jones, Richard, illus. see Casanova, Mary.
Jones, Richard & Santillan, Jorge. Manga Animals. (p. 1087)
—Manga Dinosaurs. (p. 1087)
—Manga Dragons. (p. 1087)
—Manga Martial Arts Figures. (p. 1087)
—Manga Superheroes. (p. 1087)
Jones, Rob, illus. see Tenbeth, Kate.
Jones, Rob Lee. Mathematics 1 for Young Catholics. (p. 1108)
Jones, Rob Lloyd. 1001 Pirate Things to Spot. Gower, Teri, illus. (p. 2002)
—Flip Flap Cars. (p. 604)
—Look Inside an Airport. (p. 1049)
—Look Inside Cars. (p. 1049)
—Look Inside Space. (p. 1049)
—Look Inside Sports. (p. 1049)
—Martin Luther King Jr. Le Rolland, Leonard, illus. (p. 1097)
—Martin Luther King, Jr. (p. 1097)
—See Inside Famous Buildings. Ablett, Barry, illus. (p. 1546)
—See Inside Houses Long Ago. (p. 1546)
—See Inside Pirate Ships. Muhle, Jorg, illus. (p. 1546)
—See Inside the Second World War. Pritelli, Maria Cristina, illus. (p. 1546)
—Story of Football. (p. 1658)
—Story of Islam. Chisholm, Jane, ed. (p. 1658)
—Story of Pirates. Dutrait, Vincent, illus. (p. 1659)
—Story of Robin Hood. Marks, Alan, illus. (p. 1659)
—Wild Boy. (p. 1929)
—Wild Boy & the Black Terror. (p. 1929)
Jones, Rob Lloyd, jt. auth. see George, Isabel.
Jones, Rob Lloyd & Gower, Teri. 1001 Pirate Things to Spot. (p. 2002)
Jones, Robert. Captain Bob & Crime Fighter Mike in the Case of the Dangerous Realm of Dirty Socks! (p. 263)
Jones, Robert, jt. auth. see Isbell, Susan.
Jones, Robert S., illus. see Flegal, Daphna & Smith, Betsi H.
Jones, Robert S., illus. see Flegal, Daphna, ed.
Jones, Ron, ed. Jesus: Passages from the Gospel Records. (p. 914)
Jones, Rosemarie, ed. see Jones, Ryan & Jones, Kolin.
Jones, Rosemary. Mouse House. (p. 1182)
Jones, Rufus Matthew. St. Paul the Hero. (p. 1638)
Jones, Ruth Fosdick. Boy of the Pyramids: A Mystery of Ancient Egypt. Morse, Dorothy Bayley, illus. (p. 218)
Jones, Ryan. King James: Believe the Hype - The Lebron James Story. (p. 958)
Jones, Ryan, illus. see Honigsberg, Peter John.
Jones, Ryan & Jones, Kolin. Bad Boys Club: The Case of the Missing Homework. Jones, Rosemarie, ed. (p. 131)
Jones, Sally Lloyd. Lift-the-Flap Bible. Moroney, Tracey, illus. (p. 1014)
Jones, Sam. Yolo. (p. 1972)
Jones, Sandie, jt. auth. see Baldwin, Rich.
Jones, Sandra. Sasha's Little Red Box: An Adoption Story. (p. 1515)
Jones, Sandra O. Voice on the Wind: I Know about the Apple... do You? (p. 1848)
Jones, Sandy. Anya's Gift: A Tale of Two Christmases Yourell, Pam, illus. (p. 90)
Jones, Sarah. Film. (p. 586)
Jones, Seth, illus. see Stamey, Marsha.
Jones, Shelley Lynn. Story of Corey & Alice. (p. 1657)
Jones, Shelley V. & Gunn, Barbara. Read Well Magazine Unit 20: Slanted Text. (p. 1443)
—Shells on the Shore: Read Well Level K Unit 14 Storybook. Jerde, Susan, illus. (p. 1565)
Jones, Shelley V. & Sprick, Marilyn. Turtle in the Tuba: Read Well Level K Unit 8 Storybook. McDonnell, Kevin, illus. (p. 1798)
Jones, Sherilyn. Can't Keep up with the Joneses: Created to Be. Jones, Sherilyn, illus. (p. 262)
Jones, Sherryl. WELCOME to GOD's ACRE Room for No More Sherryl Jones. (p. 1873)
Jones, Simon, tr. see Zuffi, Stefano.
Jones, Smokey. Dinky the Donkey. (p. 440)
Jones, Sourou, jt. auth. see Jones, Angela.
Jones, Stan & Jones, Brenna. Story of Me. Spector, Joel, illus. (p. 1659)
Jones, Stephanie. Bedtime. (p. 156)
—Puddin' Spot: Series Title: by the Way Series. (p. 1414)
Jones, Stephanie, illus. see Litchfield, Jo & Sanchez Gallego, Maria Isabel.
Jones, Stephanie, jt. illus. see Durber, Matt.
Jones, Stephanie, jt. illus. see Litchfield, Jo.
Jones, Stephanie, des. 1-2-3 Look & Say Chunky Flashcards. (p. 1990)
—First Words Look & Say Flashcards. (p. 597)
Jones, Stephen A. So What Did the People Find? (p. 1602)
Jones, Stephen Anderton. America Is Good. (p. 59)
Jones, Stephen B. Scratch the Boatyard Cat. (p. 1532)
Jones, Steve. Audio Cd: Used with ... Jones-College Oral Communication 4. (p. 114)
—College Oral Communication 4 (p. 340)

J

Jones, Steven. Journey to Excellence: An Introduction to E4. (p. 928)
Jones, Steven, jt. auth. see Hughes, Mair Wynn.
Jones, Steven E. Ballad of Blue Eagle. Jones, Steven E., Jr., illus. (p. 134)
—Blue Eagle Meets Double Trouble. Jones, Steven E., Jr., illus. (p. 202)
Jones, Steven E., Jr., illus. see Jones, Steven E.
Jones, Susan. Solar Power of the Future: New Ways of Turning Sunlight into Energy. (p. 1607)
Jones, Susan, jt. auth. see Jones, Susan.
Jones, Susan & Jones, Susan. Until We Meet Again. (p. 1823)
Jones, Susan Smith & Warren, Dianne. Vegetable Soup - The Fruit Bowl. Lindman, Amy Sorvaag, illus. (p. 1834)
Jones, Suzanne, jt. ed. see Jones, Suzanne Whitmore.
Jones, Suzanne Whitmore & Jones, Suzanne, eds. Growing up in the South. Jones, Suzanne Whitmore, tr. (p. 726)
Jones, Sydney. Destiny & Damnation. (p. 431)
Jones, T. Llew. Storiau Cwm-Pen-Llo. (p. 1654)
Jones, T. S. Everything but the Ring. (p. 544)
Jones, T. W. Derth. (p. 427)
Jones, Tambor & Benchmark Education Co., LLC Staff. Cole & Rose. (p. 339)
Jones, Tammy. At the Shore. (p. 111)
—Big Pet, Little Pet. (p. 183)
—Count Around the Room. (p. 369)
—Count at the Baseball Field. (p. 369)
—Count on Me. (p. 369)
—I Am Active. (p. 832)
—I Go! (p. 838)
—I Like the Spring! (p. 841)
—I Like to Play Sports. (p. 841)
—In the Water. (p. 867)
—Jobs Around Town. (p. 919)
—Look at the Coins. (p. 1049)
—Look at the Shapes. (p. 1049)
—Look at the Sky. (p. 1049)
—Look at the Weather. (p. 1049)
—My Family. (p. 1202)
—My Home. (p. 1211)
—My Pet. (p. 1217)
—My Town. (p. 1220)
—We Can Use Coins. (p. 1866)
—We Go to School. (p. 1867)
—We Have Fruit. (p. 1867)
—We Like Birthdays. (p. 1867)
—What Has Stripes? (p. 1886)
—What Is the Time? (p. 1890)
Jones, Tammy & Smith, Carrie. Katy's First Day of School. (p. 946)
—primer día de escuela de Katy: Fiction-tp-Fact Big Book. Bowles, Janice, illus. (p. 1400)
Jones, Tayari. Leaving Atlanta. (p. 986)
Jones, Terence Graham Parry, see Fairgray, Richard & Jones, Terry.
Jones, Terence Graham Parry, see Jones, Terry.
Jones, Teresa Chin. Tales of the Monkey King. Harris, Miki, illus. (p. 1702)
Jones, Terri. Nanny Mouse's Tales: Raindrops & Rainbows. (p. 1229)
Jones, Terry. Animal Tales. Foreman, Michael, illus. (p. 80)
—Fairy Tales. Foreman, Michael, illus. (p. 564)
—Fantastic Stories. Foreman, Michael, illus. (p. 572)
—Ferbey Four. (p. 581)
—Saga of Erik the Viking. Foreman, Michael, illus. (p. 1502)
Jones, Terry, jt. auth. see Fairgray, Richard.
Jones, Terry & Foreman, Michael, trs. Fairy Tales & Fantastic Stories. Jones, Terry & Foreman, Michael, illus. (p. 564)
Jones, Theodore. April Fools' Day: What a Joke! (p. 93)
—Celebrating Day of the Dead. (p. 284)
—Halloween's Spooky History. (p. 739)
Jones, Thomas Rumsey. Boris: The Bengal Tiger. Eguiguren, India J. & Eguiguren, A. R., illus. (p. 214)
Jones, Tiara. Sins of Saints. (p. 1580)
Jones, Tim. Wild Critters. Walker, Tom, photos by. (p. 1929)
Jones, Tim, illus. see Murphy, Stuart J.
Jones, Tim, illus. see Murphy, Stuart J. & Mlawer, Teresa.
Jones, Tina C. Mothballs, Mothballs All in the Hall: Memories of a Great World War II Hero. Jones, Tina C. & Balogh, Jared, illus. (p. 1177)
Jones, Toni Stokes, jt. auth. see Harmon, Deborah A.
Jones, Tonwen & Parkin, Megan. Glam My Watch: 12 Cool Watch Straps to Make & Wear. (p. 682)
Jones, Tony. Divine Intervention: Encountering God Through the Ancient Practice of Lectio Divina. (p. 454)
Jones, Traci L. Silhouetted by the Blue. (p. 1575)
—Standing Against the Wind. (p. 1639)
Jones, Tracy. Whales & Dolphins. (p. 1878)
Jones, Ursula. Lost King Trilogy: Part 1. (p. 1056)
—Princess Who Had No Kingdom. (p. 1406)
—Princess Who Had No Kingdom. Gibb, Sarah, illus. (p. 1406)
—Star Turn. (p. 1641)
Jones, Ursula, jt. auth. see Jones, Diana Wynne.
Jones, V. C. Anna Banana Goes to Louisiana. (p. 85)
—Anna Banana Goes to Montana. (p. 85)
—When You're Sick. (p. 1906)
Jones, V. M. Juggling with Mandarins. (p. 932)
—Out of Reach (p. 1311)
—Prince of the Wind. (p. 1401)
Jones, V. M. & Tulloch, Scott. Echo & Hush. (p. 502)
Jones, V. S. Vernon, tr. see Aesop.
Jones, Val. Who Wants Broccoli? Jones, Val, illus. (p. 1918)
Jones, Vanessa. I Dreamed It Snowed in Afric. (p. 838)
—Santa's Secret. (p. 1513)
Jones, Veda Boyd. Jazz Age Poet: A Story about Langston Hughes. Kiwak, Barbara, illus. (p. 911)
—John F. Kennedy. (p. 921)
Jones, Vernie O. & Jensen, Frode M. Journey Through Grammar Land, Parts 1 And 2. (p. 928)
—Journey Through Grammar Land, Parts 1 & 2 Tests & Answers. (p. 928)
Jones, Vernon. Aesop's Fables. Rackham, Arthur, illus. (p. 25)
Jones, Vickie E. Many Worlds of Sachsawan. (p. 1089)
Jones, Victoria Garrett. Amelia Earhart: A Life in Flight. (p. 58)
—Marian Anderson: A Voice Uplifted. (p. 1093)
—Pocahontas: A Life in Two Worlds. (p. 1375)
Jones, Viola & Hasan, Heather. Archimedes: Innovative Mathematician, Engineer, & Inventor. (p. 95)
Jones, Viola & Wainwright, Tabitha. Living with an Illness in the Family. (p. 1042)
Jones, Viola & Willett, Edward. Conquering Negative Body Image. (p. 358)
Jones, Viola & Wolny, Philip. Primary Source Investigation of the Underground Railroad. (p. 1400)
Jones, W. Glyn, ed. see Zeruneith, Keld.
Jones, Wendy & Blackwell, Su. Fairy-Tale Princess: Seven Classic Stories from the Enchanted Forest. (p. 564)
Jones, Wendy Lou. Bastian - Defender of Golden Downs. (p. 143)
—Last Knight of Golden Downs. (p. 978)
—Quest for Golden Downs. (p. 1426)
Jones, William. Arte de la Manipulacion. (p. 103)
Jones, Willie. Demonology. (p. 426)
Jones Yang, Dori. Daughter of Xanadu. (p. 409)
Jones, Yevad. Sea Quill. (p. 1535)
Jones, Yira. Stella Strawberry: the Fruit of Love: Fruity Friends. (p. 1647)
Jones, Zach, illus. see Gray, Susannah.
Jones-Cisneros, Tiffany. Blaxicana It's a ed World. (p. 198)
Jones-Nelson, Wanda. Adventure on the Tyler City Trail. (p. 14)
Jones-Sorge, Jennifer Elaine. Monsters, Monsters, Monsters! The Power in Me Is Bigger Then Any Monster I've Ever Met! (p. 1169)
Jones-Taylor, Audree V. All about Me & My Abc's. (p. 43)
Jong, Meindert De, see DeJong, Meindert.
Jongerius, Hella & Schouwenberg, Louise. Hella Jongerius. (p. 763)
Jongkuch, Deng. Story of Hope: The Journey of a Lost Boy of Sudan. (p. 1658)
Joni, Rasa, illus. see Long, Ilana.
Jonke, Tim, illus. see Hunt, Angela Elwell.
Jonniaux, Isabelle, illus. see Girard, Franck.
Jonquet, François. Gilbert & George: Intimate Conversations with François Jonquet. Hutchinson, Mark & Taylor, Michael, trs. from FRE. (p. 676)
Jons, Christianne, jt. auth. see Knox, Barbara.
Jonsberg, Barry. Admission. (p. 13)
—Being Here. (p. 161)
—Blacky Blasts Back! On the Tail of the Tassie Tiger. (p. 198)
—Categorical Universe of Candice Phee. (p. 279)
—Croc Called Capone. (p. 384)
—Dog That Dumped on My Doona. (p. 461)
—Dreamrider. (p. 484)
—Ironbark. (p. 888)
Jonsdottir, Aslaug, illus. see Magnason, Andri Snaer.
Jonson, Ben. Volpone or the Fox. Barish, Jonas A., ed. (p. 1849)
Jonson, Wilfrid. Magic Tricks & Card Tricks. (p. 1074)
Jönsson, Maria. Astrid the Fly. Reiss, Christina, tr. from SWE. (p. 109)
Joo, Mi-hwa. I Am a Little Monk: Thailand. Cowley, Joy, ed. (p. 832)
—Where the Winds Meet: Mongolia. Cowley, Joy, ed. (p. 1909)
Joo, Soon-kyo, illus. see Jeong, Gu-mi.
Joosse, Barbara. Evermore Dragon. Cecil, Randy, illus. (p. 542)
—Lovabye Dragon. Cecil, Randy, illus. (p. 1059)
Joosse, Barbara M. Friends (Mostly) Milian, Tomaso, illus. (p. 638)
—Higgledy-Piggledy Chicks. Chrustowski, Rick, illus. (p. 777)
—Mama, Do You Love Me? (p. 1084)
—Please Is a Good Word to Say. Plecas, Jennifer, illus. (p. 1373)
—Roawr! Jutte, Jan, illus. (p. 1478)
—Sleepover at Gramma's House. Jutte, Jan, illus. (p. 1589)
Joosse, Barbara M. & Lavallee, Barbara. Papa, Do You Love Me? Lavallee, Barbara, illus. (p. 1322)
Joost, Trudy, illus. see Otto, Gina.
Jooste, Zonia, et al. Mathematics Matters Grade 4. (p. 1108)
—Mathematics Matters Grade 4 Afrikaans Translation. (p. 1108)
—Mathematics Matters Grade 4 Learner's Book. (p. 1108)
—Mathematics Matters Grade 4 Learner's Book Afrikaans Translation. (p. 1108)
—Mathematics Matters Grade 5 Learner's Book Arikaans Translation. (p. 1108)
Joosten, Michael. Dance & Choreography. (p. 402)
Jopling, Heather. Not-So-Only Child. (p. 1267)
Jordan, Anna Louise. Lo Que Hacen Los EMT/What EMTs Do. (p. 1044)
—What Does an EMT Do? (p. 1884)
Jordan, Anne. Perspectives on Religious Issues. (p. 1344)
—Thinking about God & Morality. (p. 1734)
—Truth, Spirituality, & Contemporary Issues. (p. 1794)
Jordan, Anne Devereaux. Civil War. (p. 325)
—Slavery & Resistance. (p. 1588)
Jordan, Annie Laurie. Bogwaddle Pond. La Grange, Myrtle, illus. (p. 207)
Jordan, Apple. Bunny Surprise. (p. 242)
—Bunny Surprise (Disney/Pixar Toy Story) RH Disney Staff, illus. (p. 242)
—Cake to Bake. (p. 252)
—Cake to Bake (Disney Princess) Laguna, Fabio & Cagol, Andrea, illus. (p. 252)
—Cat: Why Do Cats Purr? & Other True Facts. (p. 277)
—Empty Full. (p. 521)
—Fairy-Tale Fall. (p. 564)
—Fairy-Tale Fall. Legramandi, Francesco, illus. (p. 564)
—Fast Kart, Slow Kart. (p. 576)
—Guess Who Bites. (p. 729)
—Guess Who Changes. (p. 729)
—Guess Who Grabs. (p. 729)
—Guess Who Hops. (p. 729)
—Guess Who Sniffs. (p. 729)
—Guess Who Soars. (p. 729)
—Noisy Quiet. (p. 1263)
—Oh, Brother! (p. 1280)
—Oh, Brother! RH Disney Staff, illus. (p. 1280)
—Open Shut. (p. 1299)
—Princess Can! (p. 1403)
—Princess Can! (Disney Princess) RH Disney Staff et al, illus. (p. 1403)
—Smooth Rough. (p. 1595)
—Spooky Adventure (Disney/Pixar Toy Story) RH Disney Staff, illus. (p. 1631)
—Sweetest Spring. Matta, Gabriella & Legramandi, Francesco, illus. (p. 1690)
Jordan, Apple, jt. auth. see McMahon, Kara.
Jordan, Apple, jt. auth. see RH Disney Staff.
Jordan, Apple & Amerikaner, Susan. Game On! Random House Disney Staff, illus. (p. 654)
Jordan, Apple & Rau, Dana Meachen. My Bones & Muscles. (p. 1198)
—My Brain. (p. 1199)
—My Heart & Blood. (p. 1210)
—My Lungs. (p. 1213)
—My Skin. (p. 1219)
—My Stomach. (p. 1219)
Jordan, Apple & RH Disney Staff. Barbie: On Your Toes. Wolcott, Karen, illus. (p. 138)
—Driving Buddies. Disney Storybook Artists Staff, illus. (p. 485)
Jordan, Apple J. Winter Wishes. Marrucchi, Elisa, illus. (p. 1938)
Jordan, Apple, told to. Dog: Best in Show. (p. 460)
Jordan, Ashley. Gabriella's Butterfly Garden: Understand & Apply Properties of Operations. (p. 652)
—Gabriella's Butterfly Garden. (p. 652)
—Maddie's Map Adventure. (p. 1069)
Jordan, Bernice. God Guides Us - Textbook: Footsteps of Faith - Old Testament Volume 4: Footsteps of Faith - Old Testament Volume 4. (p. 689)
Jordan, Bernice C. Who Is Jesus Christ? - Textbook: Footsteps of Faith New Testament Volume 1 (p. 1916)
Jordan, Brian. I Told You I Can Play! (p. 846)
Jordan, Carol, illus. see Truly Blessed Ink.
Jordan, Carrie, illus. see Lee Bates, Katharine & Gamwell, Calvert.
Jordan, Cedar, jt. auth. see Layne, Casey.
Jordan, Charles, illus. see Fontes, Justine.
Jordan, Charles, illus. see Heinrichs, Ann.
Jordan, Charles, jt. auth. see Fontes, Justine.
Jordan, Christina. I Wish I Were a Furry Ferret. Utomo, Gabhor, illus. (p. 849)
—I Wish I Were a Howler Monkey. Utomo, Gabhor, illus. (p. 849)
—I Wish I Were a Humpback Whale. Utomo, Gabhor, illus. (p. 849)
—I Wish I Were a Komodo Dragon. Utomo, Gabhor, illus. (p. 849)
—I Wish I Were a Speedy Cheetah. Utomo, Gabhor, illus. (p. 849)
—I Wish I Were an Enormous Elephant. Utomo, Gabhor, illus. (p. 849)
Jordan, Christopher. ABC. (p. 3)
—Baseball Animals. (p. 141)
—Baseball Opposites. (p. 141)
—Hockey 123. (p. 786)
—Hockey ABC. (p. 786)
—Hockey Animals. (p. 786)
—Hockey Colors. (p. 786)
—Hockey Colours. (p. 786)
—Hockey Opposites. (p. 786)
—Hockey Shapes. (p. 786)
—NASCAR 123. (p. 1230)
—NASCAR Colors. (p. 1230)
—NASCAR Shapes. (p. 1230)
Jordan, Claire. Fanakapan & the Fairies - a Children's Fairy Story. Skou, Nick, illus. (p. 570)
Jordan, Dana Hall. Clang Went the Cymbals: An Onomatopoeia Alphabet Book. Burma, Willingham, illus. (p. 326)
Jordan, Daniel. Joni. (p. 925)
Jordan, David. U. S. Air Force. (p. 1806)
—U. S. Navy. (p. 1807)
Jordan, Deloris. Baby Blessings: A Prayer for the Day You Are Born. Ransome, James E., illus. (p. 125)
—Did I Tell You I Love You Today? Evans, Shane W., illus. (p. 436)
—Dream Big: Michael Jordan & the Pursuit of Excellence. Root, Barry, illus. (p. 483)
—Dream Big: Michael Jordan & the Pursuit of Olympic Gold. Root, Barry, illus. (p. 483)
—Michael's Golden Rules. Nelson, Kadir, illus. (p. 1135)
Jordan, Deloris & Jordan, Roslyn M. Salt in His Shoes: Michael Jordan in Pursuit of a Dream. Nelson, Kadir, illus. (p. 1505)
Jordan, Denise. Juneteenth (p. 934)
—Walter Dean Myers: A Biography of an Award-Winning Urban Fiction Author. (p. 1856)
Jordan, Denise M. Muhammad Ali: Meet the Champion. (p. 1189)
—Walter Dean Myers: A Biography of an Award-Winning Urban Fiction Author. (p. 1856)
Jordan, Devin. Dragon's Pearl. Di Bartolo, Jim, illus. (p. 479)
Jordan, Dream. Bad Boy. (p. 131)
—Hot Girl. (p. 801)
Jordan, Erin L. Women, Power, & Religious Patronage in the Middle Ages. (p. 1946)
Jordan, Evora. Annie Love: A Hannah Gray Dog Story. (p. 87)
Jordan, Helene J. Cómo Crece una Semilla. Fiol, Maria A., tr. (p. 350)
—How a Seed Grows. Krupinski, Loretta, illus. (p. 804)
Jordan, Howard. Mommat & Me. (p. 1162)
Jordan, Jacqueline. Encounters with Fear: Short Stories about Young Teens. (p. 524)
Jordan, Jami. How to Rhyme: Similes, Metaphors, & PUNCHLINES! Vol. 4 (p. 821)
Jordan, Jennifer. Silly Tilly Witch: And Other Stories. Guile, Gill, illus. (p. 1576)
Jordan, Jennifer L. If No One's Looking. (p. 853)
Jordan, Joe. Cape May Point: The Illustrated History From 1875-Present (p. 262)
Jordan, Keith. Don't Stress the Process: The College Plan. (p. 468)
Jordan, L. W. Santa Heads South: Casey's Christmas Surprise. Lasson, Matt, illus. (p. 1512)
Jordan, Lana. Sleepytime Ponies Trick a Trickster. Allen, Kd & Giraud, Teresa, illus. (p. 1590)
Jordan, Laura. My Kitten, Mycat. (p. 1211)
Jordan, Mark. Courage the Monkey. (p. 372)
Jordan, Mary Ellen & Weldon, Andrew. Lazy Daisy, Cranky Frankie: Bedtime on the Farm. Weldon, Andrew, illus. (p. 981)
Jordan, Matt Dukes. Weirdo Deluxe: The Wild World of Pop Surrealism & Lowbrow Art. (p. 1873)
Jordan, Meredith & Abramson, Andra Serlin. Kids Meet the Snakes. (p. 954)
Jordan, Pasquel. Little Edward Pumpernickel. Johnson, Elijah, illus. (p. 1027)
Jordan, Pat. Adventures of King Arthur: From the Every Teacher's Friend Classroom Plays Series. (p. 19)
—Alice in Wonderland: From the Every Teacher's Friend Classroom Plays Series. (p. 39)
—Classic Literature for Teens: Every Teachers Friend Classroom Plays. Alliger, Richard, illus. (p. 328)
—Little Women, or the March Girls of New England: From the Every Teacher's Friend Classroom Plays Series. (p. 1038)
—Mini-Myths: Eleven Short Plays & Mimes of Favorite Greek & Roman Myths. (p. 1146)
—Mini-Myths for Pre-Teens & Teens: Every Teacher's Friend Classroom Plays. Vol. 2 Alliger, Richard, illus. (p. 1146)
—Mother Goose Plays: From Every Teacher's Friend Classroom Plays Vol. 4: Mother Goose Plays. (p. 1178)
—Oliver Twist: From the Every Teacher's Friend Classroom Plays Series. (p. 1286)
—Plays from Around the World: Every Teacher's Friend Classroom Plays. Alliger, Richard, illus. (p. 1373)
—Secret Garden: From the Every Teacher's Friend Classroom Plays Series. (p. 1541)
Jordan, Richard, jt. auth. see Kelly, Douglas F.
Jordan, Robert. Conan Chronicles (p. 355)
—Further Chronicles of Conan. (p. 650)
—Hunt Begins. Keegan, Charles, illus. (p. 828)
—New Threads in the Pattern. (p. 1247)
Jordan, Rosa. Goatnappers. (p. 687)
—Last Wild Place (p. 979)
—Lost Goat Lane (p. 1055)
—Wild Spirits. (p. 1930)
Jordan, Roslyn M., jt. auth. see Jordan, Deloris.
Jordan, Sandra, jt. auth. see Greenberg, Jan.
Jordan, Sandra & Greenberg, Jan. Action Jackson. Parker, Robert Andrew, illus. (p. 10)
Jordan, Sara. Fonetica Funky y Algo Mas (p. 612)
Jordan, Sara, jt. auth. see Ayotte-Irwin, Tracy.
Jordan, Sara & Brudzynski, Jack. Funky Phonics Learn to Read. (p. 649)
Jordan, Sara & Gomez, Patricia. Bilingual Beginners: English-Spanish (p. 186)
Jordan, Sarah, jt. auth. see Piven Borgenicht Jordan.
Jordan, Sherryl. Raging Quiet. (p. 1433)
—Time of the Eagle. (p. 1752)
Jordan, Shirley. American Flag: Moments in History. (p. 60)
—America's Greatest Natural Disaster. (p. 64)
—America's Greatest Natural Disasters. (p. 64)
—Benjamin Brown & the Great Steamboat Race. Kemly, Kathleen, illus. (p. 164)
—Benjamin Brown & the Great Steamboat Race. Chayka, Doug & Kemly, Kathleen, illus. (p. 164)
—Boys. (p. 220)
—California Gold Rush: Moments in History. (p. 253)
—Cars. (p. 272)
Jordan, Shirley J. Egypt (p. 506)
—Hatshepsut: First Female Pharaoh (p. 752)
Jordan, Sid, illus. see Hillert, Margaret.
Jordan, Sophie. Firelight. (p. 592)
—Hidden. (p. 775)
—Uninvited. (p. 1818)
—Unleashed. (p. 1821)
—Vanish. (p. 1833)
Jordan, Stephanie. Is the Moon God's? Houston, Melissa, illus. (p. 890)
Jordan, Taylor. Movin' on In. Wummer, Amy, illus. (p. 1183)
Jordan, Terry W. Carson Goes to Work with Dad. (p. 272)
Jordan, Tonya Y. Just Beyond My Heart Lies My Soul. (p. 938)
Jordan, Walton C. Are You Looking for a Miracle? (p. 97)
Jordan-Bellamy, Shirley. Baby Glen Backyard Safari. (p. 126)
—Baby Glen Bedtime Story. (p. 126)
—Baby Glen First Day of School. (p. 126)
—Baby Glen's Bath Time. (p. 126)
—Baby Glen's Trip to See the City. (p. 126)
—Baby See, Baby Do. (p. 128)
—Balls. (p. 135)
—Bear & His Honey. (p. 150)
—Butterfly. (p. 247)
—Dark. (p. 407)
—It's Halloween Baby Glen. (p. 897)
—Lisa's Dog, Sandy. (p. 1022)
—Moving Slowly. (p. 1184)
—My Turtle. (p. 1220)
—Nail Biting. (p. 1227)
—Rain. (p. 1434)
—Special Christmas for Baby Glen. (p. 1623)
—Toys. (p. 1774)
—Trip to the Barbershop. (p. 1787)
—Trip to the Dentist. (p. 1787)
—Twins. (p. 1802)
Jordan-Bychkov, Terry G. Australia. (p. 116)
Jordan-Fenton, Christy & Pokiak-Fenton, Margaret. Fatty Legs: A True Story. Amini-Holmes, Liz, illus. (p. 577)
—Not My Girl. Grimard, Gabrielle, illus. (p. 1267)
—Stranger at Home: A True Story. Amini-Holmes, Liz, illus. (p. 1665)
—When I Was Eight. Grimard, Gabrielle, illus. (p. 1903)

Jordan-Fenton, Christy, et al. Fatty Legs: A True Story. Amini-Holmes, Liz, illus. (p. 577)
Jordano, Kimberly & Adsit, Kim. Bookmaking Bonanza Cernek, Kim, ed. (p. 212)
—Jumping into Journals: Guided Journaling for Beginning Readers & Writers. Cernek, Kim, ed. (p. 934)
Jordano, Kimberly & Corcoran, Tebra. Down on the Farm. Fisch, Teri L., ed. (p. 474)
—Going Buggy! Fisch, Teri L., ed. (p. 692)
—Oceans of Fun. Fisch, Teri L., ed. (p. 1277)
—Rain Forest Adventures. Fisch, Teri L., ed. (p. 1434)
—Soaring into Space. Fisch, Teri L., ed. (p. 1603)
—Super Senses. Fisch, Teri L., ed. (p. 1681)
—Weather Wonders. Fisch, Teri L., ed. (p. 1870)
—Zipping Around the Zoo. Fisch, Teri L., ed. (p. 1987)
Jordan-Tegtmeier, Jennifer. Small Shady Tree. (p. 1592)
Jorden, Edwin W. Cookie Paws. Waywell, Valerie J., illus. (p. 361)
—Cookie Paws/Spreadin' the Sweetness. Waywell, Valerie J., illus. (p. 361)
Jordison, P. B. Maggie to the Rescue. (p. 1071)
—Voices in the Attic. (p. 1848)
Jordom, Deloris M., jt. auth. see Falconer, Ian.
Jorge, Gutiérrez Sahagún, illus. see Equipo Staff.
Jorgensen, David. Three Little Pigs. (p. 1742)
Jorgensen, David, illus. see Andersen, Hans Christian.
Jorgensen, David, illus. see Potter, Beatrix.
Jorgensen, David, illus. see Roberts, Tom & Asbjornsen, Peter Christen.
Jorgensen, David, illus. see Williams, Margery.
Jorgensen, Katrina. Food, Football, & Fun! Sports Illustrated Kids' Football Recipes. (p. 613)
—Football Cookbooks. (p. 615)
—Football Fuel: Recipes for Before, During, & after the Big Game. (p. 615)
—Football Party Recipes: Delicious Ideas for the Big Event. (p. 615)
—Football Tailgating Recipes: Tasty Treats for the Stadium Crowd. (p. 615)
Jorgensen, Norman. Fine Mess. (p. 589)
—In Flanders Fields. Harrison-Lever, Brian, illus. (p. 863)
Jorgensen, Norman & Harrison-Lever, Brian. Call of the Osprey. (p. 254)
—In Flanders Fields. (p. 863)
Jorgenson, Norman. In Flanders Fields. Harrison-Lever, Brian, illus. (p. 863)
Jorisch, Stéphane, illus. see Bourgeois, Paulette & Paulette, Bourgeois.
Jorisch, Stéphane, illus. see Carroll, Lewis, pseud.
Jorisch, Stéphane, illus. see Compestine, Ying Chang.
Jorisch, Stéphane, illus. see Gauthier, Bertrand.
Jorisch, Stéphane, illus. see Gingras, Charlotte.
Jorisch, Stéphane, illus. see Heos, Bridget.
Jorisch, Stéphane, illus. see Kaplan, Michael B.
Jorisch, Stéphane, illus. see Lear, Edward.
Jorisch, Stéphane, illus. see Orgill, Roxane.
Jorisch, Stéphane, illus. see Papineau, Lucie.
Jorisch, Stéphane, illus. see Tibo, Gilles.
Jorisch, Stéphane, illus. see Trout Fishing in America Staff, et al.
Jorisch, Stephane, illus. see Uegaki, Chieri.
Jorisch, Stéphane, illus. see Vigneault, Gilles.
Jorisch, Stéphane, illus. see Wayland, April Halprin.
Jorisch, Stéphane, illus. see Yolen, Jane.
Jorisch, Stéphane, jt. illus. see Trout Fishing in America Staff.
Jortberg, Charles A. Big Machines: Kids & Computers. (p. 182)
Jos, Luis Telleria, illus. see Maneru, Maria, et al.
José, Cañas Torregrosa, jt. auth. see Canas, José.
José, F. Sionil. Molave & the Orchid & Other Children's Stories. (p. 1160)
José, Martí, jt. auth. see Martí, José.
Josef, Marion. We Thank God Col/Act Bk. (p. 1868)
Josep, Tort, jt. auth. see Tort, Pep.
Joseph, A. Valentine. Forest Is Our Home. (p. 618)
Joseph, Albert, illus. see Mesibere, Ellen.
Joseph, Annette. Tear from the Corner of Her Eye. Coleman-Grider, Angelee, ed. (p. 1711)
Joseph, Beverly L. Don't Forget about Me. Swope, Brenda, illus. (p. 467)
Joseph, Bruchac. Eagle Song. (p. 492)
Joseph, Caldwell. Pig Did It. (p. 1357)
Joseph, Clara A. B., jt. ed. see Ortiz, Gaye Williams.
Joseph, Coppinger. American Practical Brewer & Tanner. (p. 62)
Joseph, Costa & Christopher, Romero. Puffs In: Christmas in Puffville. Rachel, Drapkin, illus. (p. 1415)
Joseph, Curtis. Fairy Tales of the Forbidden & Untold. (p. 564)
Joseph, Curtis M. Max Baxter. (p. 1111)
—Order of Godalming: Max Baxter (p. 1302)
Joseph, Danielle. Pure Red. (p. 1419)
—Shrinking Violet. (p. 1571)
Joseph, Debbie, illus. see Mathias, Adeline.
Joseph, Doug. Last Bye: Book Three of the Millennial Teleport Trilogy. (p. 977)
Joseph, E. T. Larry Light up Sneakers. (p. 976)
Joseph, Frank S. To Love Mercy. (p. 1759)
Joseph, Jessica, et al. Suny Albany College Prowler off the Record: Inside State University of New York. (p. 1679)
Joseph, Joan Marie. Who Made the Stars? (p. 1916)
Joseph, Jonathan. Marxism & Social Theory. (p. 1100)
Joseph, Kurt. I Am Respectful. (p. 833)
—I Am Respectful / Soy Respetuoso. (p. 833)
Joseph, L. Marie. First Generation White Collar: A practical guide on how to get ahead & not just get by with your Money. (p. 595)
Joseph, Leonard. Rascacielos: Por dentro y por fuera (Skyscrapers: Inside & Out) (p. 1439)
—Skyscrapers: Inside & Out. (p. 1587)
Joseph, Lila. Boy Who Could Talk to Animals. (p. 219)
Joseph, Lilliana, tr. see Degn, Bibi.
Joseph, Lynn. Color de Mis Palabras. (p. 342)
—Color de Mis Palabras. Rioja, Alberto Jiménez, tr. (p. 342)
—Color of My Words. (p. 343)
—Flowers in the Sky. (p. 608)
Joseph M. Martin. Light Before Christmas. (p. 1015)
Joseph, Natalie. Visit the Washington Monument. (p. 1845)
Joseph, O'Day E. I Like Wind! Foster, Ron, illus. (p. 841)
Joseph, Patricia. Animals from Aa to Zz. (p. 82)
Joseph, Patricia, illus. see Cooper, Glenessa.
Joseph, Patricia L. Look At. (p. 1048)
—This Is Bb. (p. 1735)
Joseph, Patrick, illus. see Heling, Kathryn & Hembrook, Deborah.
Joseph, Rahzheena, jt. auth. see Jones, Cheryl.
Joseph, Robin, illus. see DiPucchio, Kelly.
Joseph, Taylor S., compiled by. Your Stories, Volume 1. (p. 1981)
Joseph, Thomas. Crosswords (p. 385)
—Large Print Crosswords (p. 975)
Joseph, Tiffani & Keller, Carolyn. Temple University College Prowler off the Record. (p. 1718)
Josephine Breglia. Adventures of Poke Sa' Baar. (p. 21)
Josephine, Paker, jt. auth. see Equipo Staff.
Josephine, Wall, illus. see Hall, Susan Liberty.
Josephs, Alison, illus. see Sullivan, Maureen.
Josephs, Alison, jt. auth. see Sullivan, Maureen.
Josephs, Ben. Where Dinosaurs Walked (p. 1906)
Josephs, Ben & Capstone Press Staff. Where Dinosaurs Walked (p. 1906)
Josephs, Mary. All Aboard Noah's Ark! Bratun, Katy, illus. (p. 42)
Josephs, Rudy & Barba, Rick. Gemini Agent. (p. 660)
Joseph-Samuel, Dennese H. God Is H. I. T. S. Happily Interested in Teenager's Services. (p. 689)
Josephson, Judith Pinkerton. Bold Composer: A Story about Ludwig Van Beethoven. Kiwak, Barbara, illus. (p. 208)
—Louis Armstrong. (p. 1058)
—Nelson Mandela. (p. 1240)
—Walt Disney: Genius of Entertainment. (p. 1855)
—Who Was Sitting Bull? And Other Questions about the Battle of Little Bighorn. (p. 1919)
—Why Did Cherokees Move West? And Other Questions about the Trail of Tears. (p. 1923)
—Why Did Cherokees Walk West? And Other Questions about the Trail of Tears. (p. 1923)
Josephson, Judith Pinkerton, jt. auth. see Fine, Edith Hope.
Josh Green, illus. see Ingram, Doreen.
Joshi, Bhabika. Mortals: Hayden Roux Chronicles. (p. 1176)
Joshi, Jagdish, illus. see Dayal, Mala.
Joshua, Aaron. There Was a Man & He Was Mad. (p. 1730)
Joshua, Benson Benson Joshua, illus. see Benson, Lyn.
Joshua, Elder, jt. auth. see Elder, Joshua.
Josiah, Iris. Tiny Bird. (p. 1756)
—Tiny Bird's Alphabet Book. (p. 1756)
—Tiny Goat. (p. 1756)
—Tiny Goat's Alphabet Book. (p. 1756)
—Tiny Hen. (p. 1756)
—Tiny Hen's Alphabet Book. (p. 1756)
—Tiny Pig. (p. 1756)
—Tiny Pig's Alphabet Book. (p. 1756)
—Tiny Rabbit. (p. 1756)
—Tiny Rabbit's Alphabet Book. (p. 1756)
Josie, Melinda, illus. see Thomas, Penny.
Joslin. Minstrel's Tale. (p. 1148)
Joslin, Irene, illus. see Becker, Michele Joy.
Joslin, Irene, illus. see Eisenberg, Kristy.
Joslin, Irene, illus. see Neely, Judith.
Joslin, Mary. Bible Promises for a Little Boy. Mhasane, Ruchi, illus. (p. 176)
—Bible Promises for a Little Girl. Mhasane, Ruchi, illus. (p. 176)
—Fourth Wise Man. Johnson, Richard, illus. (p. 625)
—Lion Book of Day-by-Day Prayers. Hall, Amanda, illus. (p. 1020)
—Lion Classic Wisdom Stories. Balit, Christina, illus. (p. 1020)
—Lion Day-by-Day Bible. Hall, Amanda, illus. (p. 1020)
—Paraclete Treasury of Angel Stories. Temporin, Elena, illus. (p. 1323)
—Saint Francis: The Good Man of Assisi. Wisenfeld, Alison, illus. (p. 1503)
—Story of Christmas. Massari, Alida, illus. (p. 1657)
Joslin, Mary & Ray, Jane. Lion Classic Christmas Stories. (p. 1020)
Joslin, Sesyle. What Do You Say, Dear? Sendak, Maurice, illus. (p. 1883)
Joslin, Steve. Working Class Meets the Carpenter. (p. 1952)
Joss, Julia. Blue Hooves & a Broken Wing. (p. 203)
Josse, Annabelle, illus. see Johnson, Mo.
Jossem, Carol, illus. see Laird, Donivee M.
Jossen, Penelope, jt. auth. see Willis, Jeanne.
Jostand, Jeffrey Jay. Sedrick the Snake. Llamas, Kristin, illus. (p. 1546)
Jotave, Jazmin Velasco, illus. see Sandoval, Jaime Alfonso, et al.
Joubert, Beverly, jt. auth. see Joubert, Dereck.
Joubert, Beverly, photos by see Joubert, Dereck.
Joubert, Beverly & Joubert, Dereck. African Animal Alphabet. (p. 27)
—Face to Face with Lions. (p. 560)
Joubert, Dereck. Face to Face with Elephants. Joubert, Beverly, photos by. (p. 560)
—Face to Face with Lions. Joubert, Beverly, photos by. (p. 560)
Joubert, Dereck, jt. auth. see Joubert, Beverly.
Joubert, Dereck & Joubert, Beverly. Face to Face with Leopards. (p. 560)
Joucla, Peter. Absurd Black & Comic Sketches. (p. 7)
Jougla, Frederic. Tricked on Halloween: Rina & Jax's Stories. Jougla, Karina, illus. (p. 1786)
Jougla, Karina, illus. see Jougla, Frederic.
Joule, Beau. Infidels: The Solution to Muslim Terror. (p. 873)
Joura, Brian. Carolina Panthers. (p. 270)
Jourdan, Diego, jt. auth. see Schmidt, Andy.
Jourdenais, Norma Jean, illus. see Gould, Roberta.
Jourdenais-Martin, Norma Jean, illus. see Carreiro, Carolyn.
Jouvet. Anne et L'Ordinateur. (p. 85)
Jovanovic, Katarina. King Has Goat Ears Beha, Philippe, illus. (p. 958)
Jovanovic, Vanja Vuleta, illus. see Stehlik, Tania Duprey.
Joven, John. Wounded Lion: A Tale from Spain. (p. 1962)
Joven, John, illus. see Barchers, Suzanne I.
Joven, John, illus. see Dinardo, Jeff.
Jovinelly, Joann. Coping with Bipolar Disorder & Manic-Depressive Illness. (p. 365)
—Crafts & Culture of a Medieval Cathedral. (p. 375)
—Crafts & Culture of a Medieval Guild. (p. 375)
—Crafts & Culture of the Ancient Greeks. (p. 375)
—Crafts & Culture of the Aztecs. (p. 375)
—Crafts & Culture of the Romans. (p. 376)
—Oil: The Economics of Fuel. (p. 1282)
Jovinelly, Joann, jt. auth. see Leonard, Basia.
Jovinelly, Joann & Netelkos, Jason. Crafts & Culture of a Medieval Cathedral. (p. 375)
—Crafts & Culture of a Medieval Guild. (p. 375)
Joy, Amy. Princess & the Pepperoni Pizza: A What Happens Next? (p. 1403)
Joy, Angela. My Dog. Slater, Nicola, illus. (p. 1202)
Joy, Angelica. My Cat Merigold. Bolle, Frank, illus. (p. 1200)
Joy, Berry. Fun & Easy Way to Be Good. (p. 647)
—Help Me Good about Being Greedy. (p. 765)
—Help Me Good about Being Messy. (p. 765)
—Mine & Yours. (p. 1145)
Joy, Brenda. Kaweah's Journey to New Mexico. (p. 946)
Joy, Christine. Dream Quest. (p. 483)
Joy, Delgado. Zooprise Party / Fiesta Zoorpresa Activity Book / Actividades. Joy, Delgado, illus. (p. 1990)
Joy, Eliza. Blue Monkey. (p. 203)
—Yellow Dolphin. (p. 1970)
Joy, Elvis, illus. see Cherian, Raichel & Cherian, Raichel.
Joy, Judith Bourassa. Doorway Through Space: Winner of Mayhaven Award for Children's Fiction. (p. 470)
Joy, Linda. Little Wave & the Mission of Laura Hawksbill. (p. 1037)
—Little Wave & the Mystery of the Lost Whale. (p. 1037)
Joy, Mama. Galactic Primer Vol 1: An Intergalactic Journey of Tongue-Twisting Creatures Using the Earth Alphabet. (p. 652)
Joy, N. Secret Olivia Told Me. Devard, Nancy, illus. (p. 1543)
Joy, Susan. My 1st Wacky ABCs. (p. 1195)
Joyal, Kristen. Baking with Mommy Cookbook: Recipes for Kid-Size Ovens 10th Anniversary Edition. (p. 133)
—Gardening with Mommy. (p. 656)
Joyal, Lisa. Swahili for Beginners (p. 1688)
Joyart, B., illus. see Hope, Rinnah Y.
Joyce. Sally & Lil Ranch Critters. (p. 1505)
Joyce, Alexandria. Trail of the Caribou: A Tale of Dire Wolves in the Time of the Ice Age. (p. 1776)
Joyce, B. Big Easy & His Quest for the Stars. (p. 181)
Joyce, Bridget & Furman, Eric. Tonka Rescue Trucks! Dean Kleven Studios & Finley, Shawn, illus. (p. 1765)
Joyce, Carol. Just Friends. (p. 938)
Joyce, Caroline, jt. auth. see Joyce, Samantha.
Joyce, Dru, II. Beyond Championships Teen Edition: A Playbook for Winning at Life (p. 173)
Joyce, Gare. Northern Dancer: King of the Racetrack (p. 1265)
Joyce, Graham. Exchange. (p. 547)
Joyce, Irma. Never Talk to Strangers. Buckett, George, illus. (p. 1243)
Joyce, Jaime. Bullet Proof! The Evidence That Guns Leave Behind. (p. 240)
—Fatal Fall: Was It an Accident or Murder? (p. 577)
—Going Ballistic: Who Pulled the Trigger in a Gangland Massacre? (p. 692)
Joyce, James. Cats of Copenhagen. Sorrow, Casey, illus. (p. 281)
Joyce, Jeffrey. Pablo's Paper Crafts: Shapes & Their Attributes. (p. 1317)
—Pablo's Paper Crafts. (p. 1317)
—Week with Nate. (p. 1871)
—Who Was Neil Armstrong? (p. 1919)
Joyce, John. Black John the Bogus Pirate - Cartoon Workbook of Marine Beasts. Joyce, John, illus. (p. 196)
Joyce, Julie. What Should You Do? Safety Tips for Kids. (p. 1893)
Joyce, Kelley A. Amos the Elf & His Magical Pajamas. Beckman, Jeff & Aguirre, Diego, illus. (p. 65)
Joyce, Melaine. Cinderella. (p. 320)
—Snow White. (p. 1599)
Joyce, Melanie. Goldilocks. (p. 696)
Joyce, Peter, illus. see Hennessy, B. G.
Joyce, Peter, illus. see Hennessy, Barbara G.
Joyce, Rita. Deer of the Dawn. (p. 423)
—Johnny Peppertoes. (p. 923)
—Wandawillie. (p. 1856)
Joyce, S. E. Silas Saves the Friendly Crab: A Low Country Tale. (p. 1575)
Joyce, Samantha & Joyce, Caroline. Fluffy's Story Part 1 Fluffy's Journey. Moore, Debra, illus. (p. 608)
Joyce, Sandie May. Aunt Sandie Goes to School - the Comics. (p. 115)
—Crying Princess. (p. 387)
—Little Miss Alice & the Bookworm. (p. 1031)
Joyce, Sophie, illus. see Bedford, William.
Joyce, Susan. ABC Nature Riddles. DuBosque, Doug, illus. (p. 3)
Joyce, William. Bean, a Stalk & a Boy Named Jack. Joyce, William & Callicutt, Kenny, illus. (p. 150)
—Big Time Olie. Joyce, William, illus. (p. 184)
—Billy's Booger. (p. 187)
—Billy's Booger. Joyce, William, illus. (p. 187)
—Day with Wilbur Robinson. Joyce, William, illus. (p. 415)
—Dinosaur Bob. (p. 441)
—E. Aster Bunnymund & the Warrior Eggs at the Earth's Core! Joyce, William, illus. (p. 491)
—Fantastic Flying Books of Mr. Morris Lessmore. (p. 571)
—Fantastic Flying Books of Mr. Morris Lessmore. Joyce, William & Bluhm, Joe, illus. (p. 571)
—George Shrinks. Joyce, William, illus. (p. 663)
—Lost Snowman. (p. 1056)
—Man in the Moon. Joyce, William, illus. (p. 1085)
—Numberlys. Joyce, William & Ellis, Christina, illus. (p. 1271)
—Sandman. Joyce, William, illus. (p. 1511)
—Sandman & the War of Dreams. Joyce, William, illus. (p. 1511)
—Santa Calls Stationery Set. (p. 1511)
—Toothiana: Queen of the Tooth Fairy Armies. Bk. 3 Joyce, William, illus. (p. 1768)
—True Story of E. Astor Bunnyman. (p. 1793)
Joyce, William, jt. auth. see Moonbot.
Joyce, William & Geringer, Laura. Nicholas St. North & the Battle of the Nightmare King Joyce, William, illus. (p. 1251)
Joyful Noise, ed. see Morgan, Beverly.
Joyner, A. Bernard. Out of the Mouths of Babes! A Book of Childrenrsquo;s Poetry. (p. 1311)
Joyner, Andrew. Boris #4: Boris Sees the Light (a Branches Book) (p. 214)
—Boris for the Win. (p. 214)
—Boris Gets a Lizard. (p. 214)
—Boris on the Move (p. 214)
—Boris on the Move. (p. 214)
—Boris Sees the Light. (p. 214)
—Boris - Sees the Light. (p. 214)
Joyner, Andrew, illus. see Dubosarsky, Ursula.
Joyner, Andrew, illus. see Friend, Peter.
Joyner, Andrew, illus. see Gwynne, Phillip.
Joyner, Andrew, illus. see Ormerod, Jan.
Joyner, Holly, jt. auth. see Luce, Pat.
Joyner, Louise, illus. see Gwynne, Phillip.
Joyner, Melinda Bramlett. Boogie Dog & Guine. (p. 210)
Joyner, Rick. Harvest. (p. 751)
Joynes, Gary, illus. see Rand, Casey & Heinemann Library Staff.
Joynt, Amanda, jt. auth. see Sullivan, Mike.
JoySoul Corporation, illus. see Monson, Lois.
Jozefowicz, Chris. Auto Technician. (p. 117)
—Video Game Developer. (p. 1841)
—Video Games. (p. 1841)
Jozev. Claws of Darkness. (p. 330)
—Journal of the Vampire Hunter: Claws of Darkness. Vol. 4 (p. 927)
—Journal of the Vampire Hunter: Claws of Darkness. Vol. 3 Zhao, Yun, tr. (p. 927)
Jozsa, Orsolya. Meaning & Perspective in Tom Stoppard's Three Plays - Rosencrantz & Guildenstern Are Dead, Jumpers, Dogg's Hamlet Cahoot's MacBeth. (p. 1117)
J.s., Monroe-Daley. Is for Arizona. (p. 889)
Juan, Ana. Night Eater. (p. 1253)
—Pet Shop Revolution. (p. 1345)
—Pet Shop Revolution. Juan, Ana, illus. (p. 1345)
Juan, Ana, illus. see Cunnane, Kelly.
Juan, Ana, illus. see Geeslin, Campbell.
Juan, Ana, illus. see Valente, Catherynne M.
Juan, Farias, jt. auth. see Farias, Juan.
Juan, Felipe Herrera. Coralito's Bay: Bahia de Coralito. (p. 366)
Juarbe, Cynthia. Callie the Caterpillar Collects Coins. (p. 254)
Juarez, Adriana, illus. see Gallagher, Diana G.
Juarez, Amanda, jt. auth. see Gasca, Theresa.
Juarez, Christine. Afghanistan (p. 26)
—Canada (p. 260)
—China (p. 306)
—Countries (p. 372)
—Egypt (p. 506)
—England (p. 529)
—India (p. 870)
—Japan (p. 909)
—Kenya (p. 949)
—Mexico (p. 1131)
—United States of America (p. 1820)
—United States of America. (p. 1820)
Juarez, Fernando, illus. see Richards, Kitty.
Juaristi, Felipe & Felipe, Juaristi. Loro de Haydn. (p. 1053)
Juback, Wendy L. Sorry about Your Luck, Chuck. (p. 1614)
Jubb, Kendahl Jan, illus. see Patent, Dorothy Hinshaw.
Jubb, Mike. Ghost of My Pussycat's Bottom. (p. 671)
Jubert, Hervé. Dance of the Assassins. Bell, Anthea, tr. from FRE. (p. 402)
JUBERT, Herve. Devil's Tango. Bell, Anthea, tr. from FRE. (p. 432)
Jubilee Jr., Thomas. Same As James. Baker, David, illus. (p. 1507)
Juby, Susan. Alice MacLeod, Realist at Last. (p. 39)
—Another Kind of Cowboy. (p. 88)
—Getting the Girl: A Guide to Private Investigation, Surveillance, & Cookery. (p. 669)
—Miss Smithers. (p. 1152)
—Truth Commission. (p. 1794)
Juckes, Deborah Sioux. Meesha, Guardian of Grand Mountain: Book One of the Guardian Series. McCleary, Twila, illus. (p. 1120)
Judah, Nathan, illus. see Fanning, Meghan.
Judah, Susan, illus. see Sherlock, Philip.
Judal. Vampire Game (p. 1832)
—Vampire Game Hiroe, Ikoi, tr. from JPN. (p. 1832)
—Vampire Game Coffman, Patrick, tr. from JPN. (p. 1832)
Judal, illus. see Coffman, Patrick, tr.
Judal, jt auth. see Judal.
Judal & Judal. Vampire Game Judal & Judal, illus. (p. 1832)
—Vampire Game. Judal & Judal, illus. (p. 1832)
Judal, creator. Vampire Game (p. 1832)
Judd. Guardian Angels. (p. 728)
Judd, Christopher M. Bearable Moments. (p. 151)
Judd, Joshua. Multiprotocol Routers for SANS. (p. 1190)
Judd, Lissa Elaine. Slightly Larger Book of Kick-Arse Poetry. (p. 1590)
—Small Book of Kick-Arse Poetry. (p. 1592)
Judd, Mary Catherine. Classic Myths. (p. 328)
—Classic Myths. MacDonall, Angus, illus. (p. 328)
Judd, Merlynne. Circle of Friendship. (p. 321)
Judd, Philip, et al. Learning with Computers. (p. 986)
Judd-Leisten, Betty. Tell It for a Toll, Toll It for a Tale. (p. 1716)
Jude, Connie, illus. see Sanderson, Ana.
Jude, Conny, illus. see Evans, Cheryl & Smith, Lucy.
Jude, T. B's Story. (p. 233)
Jude, Tracey. Mr. Topaz Takes a Walk. (p. 1186)
Judge, Chris. Brave Beast. (p. 223)

J

—Brian & the Vikings. (p. 226)
—Great Explorer. (p. 715)
—Lonely Beast. Judge, Chris, illus. (p. 1046)
—Tin. Judge, Chris, illus. (p. 1755)
Judge, Emma. Ink Stained Hands. (p. 874)
Judge, Kathleen, illus. see Taylor, Yuval, ed.
Judge, Lita. Bird Talk: What Birds Are Saying & Why. Judge, Lita, illus. (p. 190)
—Born in the Wild: Baby Mammals & Their Parents. Judge, Lita, illus. (p. 214)
—Born to Be Giants: How Baby Dinosaurs Grew to Rule the World. Judge, Lita, illus. (p. 214)
—Flight School. Judge, Lita, illus. (p. 604)
—Good Morning to Me! Judge, Lita, illus. (p. 698)
—How Big Were Dinosaurs? Judge, Lita, illus. (p. 805)
—Red Hat. Judge, Lita, illus. (p. 1454)
—Red Sled. Judge, Lita, illus. (p. 1455)
Judge, Lita, illus. see James, Helen Foster.
Judge, Lita, jt. auth. see Chapman, Todd.
Judith Anne Moody. Golden Eye & the Killer Cat. (p. 694)
Judith Brown Lamb. Gaudy Goosey Gander. (p. 658)
Judith Mader. I Went to Safety Town! (p. 848)
Judowitz, Chani, illus. see Gerstenblit, Rivke.
Judowitz, Yoel, illus. see Ornstein, Esther.
Judson, Clara Ingram. Jerry & Jean Detectors. Gregory, Dorothy Lake, illus. (p. 913)
—Mary Jane: Her Book. (p. 1100)
—Mary Jane: Her Visit. White, Frances, illus. (p. 1100)
—Mary Jane - Her Book. White, Frances, illus. (p. 1100)
—Mary Jane - Her Visit. White, Frances, illus. (p. 1100)
Judson, Karen. Abraham Lincoln: This Nation Shall Have a New Birth of Freedom. (p. 6)
—Animal Testing. (p. 80)
—Biological & Chemical Warfare. (p. 189)
—Religion & Government: Should They Mix? (p. 1458)
—Resolving Conflicts: How to Get along When You Don't Get Along. (p. 1463)
—United States Constitution: Its History, Bill of Rights, & Amendments. (p. 1819)
Judson, Kathryn. Trouble Pug. (p. 1790)
Judy, jt. auth. see Greer, Terri Gregory.
Judy, Beth. Medicinal Plants of North America: A Flora Delaterre Coloring Book. (p. 1119)
Judy, Bridell. Going Wild with Eloise Butler. (p. 693)
Judy Delton Family Trust Staff & Delton, Judy. Angel's Mother's Baby. Weber, Jill, illus. (p. 75)
Judy Kohl. Little Heavenly Poems. (p. 1029)
Judybee. Danny Strikes Out in Americ: A R. E. A. d Book. Kecskés, Anna, illus. (p. 406)
—Queen Amina of Zari: Queens of Africa Book 1. LittlePinkPebble, illus. (p. 1424)
—Queen Esther: Queens of Africa Book 4. LittlePinkPebble, illus. (p. 1424)
—Queen Idi: Queens of Africa Book 5. LittlePinkPebble, illus. (p. 1424)
—Queen Maked: Queens of Africa Book 2. LittlePinkPebble, illus. (p. 1425)
—Queen Moremi: Queens of Africa Book 3. LittlePinkPebble, illus. (p. 1425)
—Zoo Crew Play Ball. LittlePinkPebble, illus. (p. 1989)
JudyBee, tr. see Jâho.
Judæus, Philo. Works of Philo Judeaus, the Contemporary of Josephus (p. 1953)
—Works of Philo Judzus, the Contemporary of Josephus Yonge, Charles Duke, tr. (p. 1953)
Jue, Thea. Remember the Love. Lenz, Mary, illus. (p. 1459)
Juel, Connie, jt. auth. see Hiebert, Elfrieda H.
Juel, Connie, et al. Ready Readers: Collection. (p. 1447)
—Ready Readers: Set 1 Collection. (p. 1447)
—Ready Readers: Set 2 Collection. (p. 1447)
—Ready Readers: Set 3 Collection. (p. 1447)
—Ready Readers: Nonfiction Favorites. (p. 1447)
Juettner, Bonnie. 100 Native-Americans Who Shaped American History. (p. 1998)
—Abortion. (p. 5)
—Blackmail & Bribery. (p. 197)
—Child Abuse. (p. 301)
—Childhood Obesity. (p. 302)
—Climate Change. (p. 332)
—Diet & Disease. (p. 437)
—Genies. (p. 661)
—Global Warming. (p. 684)
—Griffins. (p. 724)
—Hybrid Cars. (p. 831)
—Molecules. (p. 1160)
—Motion. (p. 1179)
—Phoenix. (p. 1351)
—Photosynthesis. (p. 1353)
—Seed Vault. (p. 1547)
Juettner, Bonnie, jt. auth. see Uschan, Michael V.
Juettner, Bonnie, et al. Dementia. (p. 425)
Jugran, Jan. Baby Dolphins. Larranaga, Ana Martin, illus. (p. 126)
—Goodnight Faces: A Book of Masks. Larranaga, Ana Martin, illus. (p. 701)
—Hugs. Larranaga, Ana Martin, illus. (p. 825)
—Ibaby - Rub-a-Dub-Dub. Larranaga, Ana Martin, illus. (p. 849)
—Three Little Duckies. Parsons, Jackie & Larranaga, Ana Martin, illus. (p. 1742)
Juhasz, Brenda, illus. see Juhasz, Mike.
Juhasz, George, illus. see Miles, Victoria, et al.
Juhasz, George, illus. see Oppenheim, Shulamith.
Juhasz, George, illus. see Owen, Leslie E.
Juhasz, Mike. Posey & Mosey Go Camping. Juhasz, Brenda, illus. (p. 1387)
Juhasz, Victor, illus. see Elissa Grodin.
Juhasz, Victor, illus. see Grodin, Elissa.
Juhasz, Victor, illus. see Kimmelman, Leslie.
Juhasz, Victor, illus. see Scillian, Devin.
Juhasz, Victor, illus. see Shoulders, Debbie & Shoulders, Michael.
Juhasz, Victor, illus. see Wilbur, Helen L.
Juhasz, Victor, illus. see Young, Judy & A12.
Juhasz, Victor, illus. see Young, Judy.
Juhl, Jerry, jt. auth. see Henson, Jim.
Juillard, André, illus. see Sente, Yves.
Juillard, Andre, jt. auth. see Sente, Yves.
Jukes, Carlisle E. Rhino & the Rat: The Delightful Story of Coco & Max. (p. 1467)
Jukes, Geoffrey & O'Neill, Robert John. World War II: The Eastern Front 1941-1945. (p. 1959)
Jukes, Mavis. Es Cosa de Chicas. (p. 534)
—Like Jake & Me. (p. 1017)
—New Kid. (p. 1245)
Jukes, Mavis, et al. Be Healthy! It's a Girl Thing: Food, Fitness, & Feeling Great. Ziss, Debra, illus. (p. 148)
Jule, Allyson, ed. see Pedersen, Bettina Tate.
Jules. Bubble's World: Isabella's Magic Dream. (p. 233)
—Bubble's World: Book Five Frogs & Fairies. (p. 233)
—Bubble's World: Book Four Enchanted England. (p. 233)
—Bubble's World. (p. 233)
Jules, Jacqueline. Abuela's Birthday. Smith, Kim, illus. (p. 7)
—Before We Eat: A Thank You Prayer. Iwai, Melissa, illus. (p. 159)
—Duck for Turkey Day. Mitter, Kathryn, illus. (p. 488)
—Freddie Ramos Makes a Splash Bk. 4. Benitez, Miguel, illus. (p. 632)
—Freddie Ramos Makes a Splash. Benitez, Miguel, illus. (p. 632)
—Freddie Ramos Springs into Action. Benitez, Miguel, illus. (p. 632)
—Freddie Ramos Takes Off Benitez, Miguel, illus. (p. 632)
—Freddie Ramos Zooms to the Rescue. Benitez, Miguel, illus. (p. 632)
—Happy Hanukkah Lights. Shapiro, Michelle, illus. (p. 745)
—Marigold Mess. Smith, Kim, illus. (p. 1094)
—Missing Mouse. Smith, Kim, illus. (p. 1152)
—My Family Adventure. Smith, Kim, illus. (p. 1202)
—Never Say a Mean Word Again: A Tale from Medieval Spain. Bernhard, Durga Yael, illus. (p. 1243)
—Noah & the Ziz. Kahn, Katherine Janus, illus. (p. 1261)
—Picnic at Camp Shalom. Melmon, Deborah, illus. (p. 1355)
—Picture Perfect. Smith, Kim, illus. (p. 1355)
—Princess & the Ziz. Kahn, Katherine Janus, illus. (p. 1403)
—Sarah Laughs. Ugliano, Natascia, illus. (p. 1514)
—Sofia Martinez. (p. 1605)
—What a Way to Start a New Year! A Rosh Hashanah Story. Stead, Judy, illus. (p. 1878)
—Ziz & the Hanukkah Miracle. Kahn, Katherine Janus, illus. (p. 1987)
Jules, Jacqueline & Benitez, Miguel. Freddie Ramos Takes Off. (p. 632)
Jules, Jacqueline & Hechtkopf, Jacqueline. Abraham's Search for God. Ugliano, Natascia, illus. (p. 7)
—Going on a Hametz Hunt. Brown, Rick, illus. (p. 692)
—Goodnight Sh'ma. Hall, Melanie W., illus. (p. 701)
—Miriam in the Desert. Ugliano, Natascia, illus. (p. 1149)
—Noah & the Ziz. Kahn, Katherine Janus, illus. (p. 1261)
—Picnic at Camp Shalom. Melmon, Deborah, illus. (p. 1355)
—Ziz & the Hanukkah Miracle. Kahn, Katherine Janus, illus. (p. 1987)
Jules, Laurie. Tales from a Magical Kingdom. (p. 1701)
Jules, Prud'homme, illus. see Leblanc, Louise.
Julia, Alvarez. Before We Were Free. (p. 159)
—How Tia Lola Came to Visit Stay. (p. 814)
Julian, Alison. 12 Days of Christmas. (p. 1994)
Julian, Alison, illus. see Hoffmann, E. T. A.
Julian, Russell. Busy Dog. (p. 246)
—Happy Cockerel. (p. 745)
Julian, Russell, illus. see Balfour, Melissa.
Julian, Russell, illus. see Bedford, David.
Julian, Russell, illus. see Freedman, Claire.
Julian, Russell, illus. see Harris, Trudy.
Julian, Russell, illus. see Puttock, Simon.
Julian, Russell, illus. see Tebbs, Victoria.
Julian, Sarah. My Daddy's in Heaven & I'm Still Here. (p. 1201)
—My Friend's Daddy Passed Away & I Don't Know What to Say. (p. 1209)
—My Friend's Mommy Passed Away & I Don't Know What to Say. (p. 1209)
—My Mommy's in Heaven & I'm Still Here. (p. 1214)
Julian, Sean, illus. see Rooney, Anne.
Julian, Sean, illus. see Roth, Carol.
Julian, Sean, jt. auth. see Roth, Carol.
Julian, Sean, jt. auth. see Smith, Ian.
Juliana, M., Sr., jt. auth. see McGrade, Francis.
Juliao, David S. Pais Mas Hermoso del Mundo. (p. 1319)
Julich, Jennifer, jt. auth. see DiLorenzo, Michael A.
Julich, Jennifer, jt. auth. see DiLorenzo, Michael.
Julich, Jenniffer, illus. see Bennett-Boltinghouse, Jo Ann.
Julich, Jenniffer, illus. see Bryan, Jennifer Liu & Kendle, Hazel Cole.
Julich, Jenniffer, illus. see Dachman, Adam.
Julich, Jenniffer, illus. see DiLorenzo, Michael A.
Julich, Jenniffer, illus. see Farrell, Bill.
Julich, Jenniffer, illus. see Greene, John McBride.
Julich, Jenniffer, illus. see Lile, Linda L.
Julie, illus. see Charest, Jocelyne.
Julie A. Kircher, jt. auth. see Nena L. Kircher.
Julie, Aunt. Paddleduck! Julie, A Little Girl from Texas. (p. 1317)
—State Symbols of Texas - Paddleduck #8. (p. 1644)
Julie, Danneberg. First Day Jitters. (p. 594)
Julie Marie. Adventures of Fred the Five Pound Note. (p. 18)
Julie Shelton. World of Vampires Part 1: The Huntress. (p. 1957)
Julien, Terry, illus. see Beveridge, Amy.
Julien, Terry, illus. see Holder, Jennifer.
Julieta, Irla, illus. see Garza, Ben.
Julings, Emma, photos by see Miles, Lisa.
Julio, Susan, jt. auth. see Rhodes, Immacula A.
Julio, Susan & Rhodes, Immacula A. Numbers & Counting: 10 Ready-to-Go Games That Help Children Learn & Practice Early Math Skills-Independently. (p. 1272)
Julio, Susan & Schooler, Cindy. Interactive Bible Bulletin Boards: Winter. (p. 879)
Julius, Jessica. New Reindeer Friend. (p. 1247)
—New Reindeer Friend (Disney Frozen) RH Disney Staff, illus. (p. 1247)
Julius, Jessica, jt. auth. see Posner-Sanchez, Andrea.
Julius, Jessica, jt. auth. see RH Disney Staff.
Julius, Nicholas. Mythfitz: Unee the Unicorn. (p. 1227)
Julivert, Maria Angeles. Birds. (p. 191)
—Trees. (p. 1784)
Julivert, Maria Angels. Vida de Las Plantas. (p. 1840)
Jull Costa, Margaret, tr. see Galdós, Benito Pérez.
Jullien, Jean, illus. see Taylor, Sean.
Jumbo, Sheyenne & Willett, Mindy. Come & Learn with Me Macintosh, Tessa, photos by. (p. 347)
Junaid, Bushra, illus. see Badoe, Adwoa.
Junaid, Bushra, illus. see Warner, Jody Nyasha.
Juncar, Nicola. Legend of Thornton Wood. (p. 989)
June, Cathy, illus. see Russ-Ayon, Angela.
June, Kimberly. It's No Fun Sucking Your Thumb. (p. 897)
June-Bug. Sweetbread & Tattletale. (p. 1690)
Jung, Mike. Geeks, Girls, & Secret Identities. Maihack, Mike, illus. (p. 659)
Jung, Scott. Verdades bíblicas eternas (Timeless Bible Truths) (p. 1836)
—Verdades bíblicas eternas (Timeless Bible Truths) - Bilingual. (p. 1836)
Jung, Shirley, illus. see Phillips, Clifton.
Jung, Tori. Have Fun with Math. Chung, Haley, illus. (p. 754)
—Math Game 3 Chung, Haley, illus. (p. 1106)
Jung, Wook Jin, illus. see Rau, Dana Meachen.
Junge, Alexandra. Night-Time Tale. Connolly, Kate, tr. from GER. (p. 1254)
Jung-Hüttl, Angelika, jt. auth. see Edmaier, Bernhard.
Jungle Factor Staff, illus. see VIZ Media Staff.
Jungle Factor Staff & Media Staff. Complete Pokémon Jungle Factor Staff, illus. (p. 353)
Jungman, Ann. Footballing Frog. Burnett, Seb, illus. (p. 615)
—Lucy & the Big Bad Wolf. Littlewood, Karin, illus. (p. 1063)
—Vlad the Drac. Thompson, George, illus. (p. 1846)
—Vlad the Drac Returns. (p. 1846)
—Vlad the Drac Superstar. Thompson, George, illus. (p. 1846)
—Vlad the Drac, Vampire. (p. 1846)
Jungman, Ann, jt. auth. see Welvaert, Scott R.
Jungman, Ann & Quarto Generic Staff. Most Magnificent Mosque. Fowles, Shelley, illus. (p. 1177)
—Vlad the Drac: The Adventures of a Vegetarian Vampire. (p. 1846)
Junior League of Tyler, Texas Staff, contrib. by. Ring Around the Rosie: A Collection of Children's Recipes. (p. 1473)
Juniper, Tony, jt. auth. see Burnie, David.
Junjie, Cheng, illus. see Li, Ma, et al.
Junkerman, Kelly, jt. auth. see Rogers, Kenny.
Junor, Amy. Dino-School - Alphabet. Wood, Hannah, illus. (p. 441)
—Dino-School: Colours. Wood, Hannah, illus. (p. 441)
—My Giant Fold-Out Bright Bugs. (p. 1209)
—My Giant Fold-Out Wild Animals. (p. 1209)
—Skate! Level 4. (p. 1583)
Junyk, Myra. 10 Greatest Presidents. (p. 1993)
—10 Mightiest Rivers. (p. 1993)
—10 Most Defining Moments of the Civil War. (p. 1993)
Jupin, David Perez. Love. (p. 1059)
Jupo, Frank. Nothing to Wear but Clothes. (p. 1268)
—Time to Spare: The Story of Man's Leisure Hours. (p. 1753)
Juraszek, Barbara, tr. see Morgan, Bernard P.
Juravel, Rabbi. Journey with Rabbi Juravel: The Great Escape & Other Stories (p. 929)
—Journey with Rabbi Juravel: Adventure in the Sky & other Stories (p. 929)
—Parsha with Rabbi Juravel: Shemos. Toron, Eli, illus. (p. 1325)
—Parsha with Rabbi Juravel: Bereishis. Toron, Eli, illus. (p. 1325)
Jurevicius, Nathan. Adventures of Scarygirl. (p. 22)
Jurevicius, Nathan, illus. see Thompson, Lisa.
Jurgens, Dan. Spiral (p. 1628)
—Spiral. Bennett, Joe et al, illus. (p. 1628)
—Thor: The Death of Odin. Bennett, Joe, illus. (p. 1739)
—Thor: Gods & Men. Eaton, Scot & Robinson, Roger, illus. (p. 1739)
Jurgens, Dan, et al. Thor: Gods on Earth Vol. 3 Raney, Tom & Bennett, Davis, illus. (p. 1739)
Jurinich, Anna, illus. see Davis, Elena.
Jurksaitis, Dinah, ed. see Croft, Steven.
Jurmain, Suzanne. Forbidden Schoolhouse: The True & Dramatic Story of Prudence Crandall & Her Students. (p. 616)
—Secret of the Yellow Death: A True Story of Medical Sleuthing. (p. 1543)
Jurmain, Suzanne Tripp. George Did It. Day, Larry, illus. (p. 663)
—Worst of Friends: Thomas Jefferson, John Adams, & the True Story of an American Feud. Day, Larry, illus. (p. 1961)
Jury, Walter & Fine, Sarah. Burn. (p. 243)
—Scan. (p. 1519)
Jury, Walter, et al. Scan. (p. 1519)
Jusaitis, J. Journey to Anderswelt. (p. 928)
Juscik, Andy. Tear Catchers. (p. 1711)
Jusid, Carolina, tr. see Gnojewski, Carol.
Jusino, Cindy M. Toodle's Big Race: Interactive for Children That Don't Like to Sit Still! Studio, Gau Family, illus. (p. 1767)
Juslin, Lee. Nurse Frosty & the Four Paws Retirement Home. (p. 1273)
—Nurse Frosty & the Wond'ear'ful Adventure. (p. 1273)
—Nurse Frosty Saves the Day. (p. 1273)
Just, John, illus. see Kick, J. D.
"Just Right" Authors and Artists, "Just Right". Merry Christmas Stories. (p. 1129)
Juster, Norton. Alberic the Wise & Other Journeys. Gnoli, Domenico, illus. (p. 34)
—Annotated Phantom Tollbooth. Feiffer, Jules, illus. (p. 87)
—Casello Magico. (p. 275)
—Hello, Goodbye Window. Raschka, Chris, illus. (p. 764)
—Neville. Karas, G. Brian, illus. (p. 1243)
—Odious Ogre. Feiffer, Jules, illus. (p. 1278)
—Phantom Tollbooth. (p. 1349)
—Phantom Tollbooth. Feiffer, Jules, illus. (p. 1349)
Juster, Norton, jt. auth. see Nanus, Susan.
Justesen, Kim Williams. Deepest Blue. (p. 423)
—Hey Ranger! Kids Ask Questions about Rocky Mountain National Park. Newhouse, Judy, illus. (p. 774)
—Kiss, Kiss, Bark! (p. 961)
Justice, Joseph. Lawyer's Week Before Christmas Alikhan, Salima, illus. (p. 981)
Justice, Laura M. & Sofka, Amy E. Engaging Children with Print: Building Early Literacy Skills Through Quality Read-Alouds. (p. 529)
Justice, Laura M. & Vukelich, Carol, eds. Achieving Excellence in Preschool Literacy Instruction. (p. 9)
Justice, Lee. Words Every 4th Grader Needs to Know! Academic Vocabulary Practice! (p. 1951)
—Words Every Fifth Grader Needs to Know! Academic Vocabulary Practice. (p. 1951)
Justice, Lee S. Words Every 3rd Grader Needs to Know! (p. 1951)
—Words Every Second Grader Needs to Know! Academic Vocabulary Practice. (p. 1951)
Justice, Lee S. & Benchmark Education Co., LLC. Chicago World's Fair Of 1893: Bigger, Brighter, & Better! (p. 299)
Justice, Margot E. Tails of Windswept Farm. (p. 1695)
Justice, Robert H. Rainbow Chicken Feed. (p. 1435)
Justice, Tonya. Millie Mathison's Imagination: Cowboys, Indians, & no Red Cards. (p. 1144)
Justice, W. Shelton. Miss Fluffy a Special Cat. (p. 1151)
Justice, William E. Kodoku. Rivera, Hanae, illus. (p. 966)
Justin McGovern, illus. see Kelly McGovern Lu.
Justine, jt. auth. see Fontes, Ron.
Justine, Clovacco. Meerkats. (p. 1120)
Justine, Torode, jt. illus. see Scott, Peter.
Justinen, Kim, illus. see Thomas, Jerry D.
Justis, Jon. Pumpkin & the Great Dragon Caper. (p. 1416)
Justus, Barbara & Starbird, Caroline. Day Papa Came Home Newman, Timothy, ed. (p. 414)
Justus, Fred. Jumbo Vocabulary Development Yearbook: Grade 1. (p. 933)
—Jumbo Vocabulary Development Yearbook: Grade 2. (p. 933)
—Jumbo Vocabulary Fun Yearbook. (p. 933)
Juta, Jason, illus. see Colich, Abby.
Juta, Jason, illus. see Sautter, A. J.
Jutte, Jan, illus. see Joosse, Barbara M.
Jutte, Jan, illus. see Kuyper, Sjoerd.
Juttner, Joan. Balderdash: A Halloween Story. (p. 134)
Juventud Staff & Grosschmid, Pablo - Ecjegoyen. Regionalismos de la Lengua. (p. 1457)
Juventud Staff & Martin, A - Weissmann. Diccionario Portugues - Espanol. (p. 435)
Juwayriyah, Umm & Ayed, Juwayriyah. Hind's Hands: A Story about Autism. Apple, Emma, illus. (p. 780)
Juwell & Precious. Runaway. (p. 1496)
Juwell, et al. Ab-Solute Truth. (p. 2)
Ju-Yeon, Rhim. President Dad. (p. 1397)
—President Dad. Ju-Yeon, Rhim, illus. (p. 1397)
Ju-Young Im, Joy, illus. see Roberts, Deborah.
Juzwiak, Rich. Addictive Personality. (p. 11)
—Lifehouse. (p. 1013)
Juzwiak, Richard. Addictive Personality. (p. 11)
—Frequently Asked Questions about Peer Pressure. (p. 636)
—Lifehouse. (p. 1013)

K

K. B. Kendricks. Travis Taylor & the Dragon Quest. (p. 1781)
K. Elizabeth, Sterling. Austin's First Puppy. (p. 116)
K. Hall. Adventures of Ranald the Rugby Player: The First Game. (p. 22)
K, J. My Sister Says the Strangest Things. (p. 1218)
K, Mark, illus. see V, Larry.
K. Maurice Strickland. I Want to Be a Bucket. (p. 847)
K, Miller Mace. Not Without Power: Lost in Africa. (p. 1267)
K, T. Natural Healing Self Empowerment: The Ultimate Self Help Health Guide (p. 1235)
K, U. Palomino. (p. 1320)
K., Ulf. Hieronymus B., 1997-2007. (p. 777)
K/H (Kyb). Grade K Know Your Body Student Workbook. (p. 705)
K/H (Pathways). Kindergarten Stepping Stones: Kindergarten the Bravest Dog Ever - The True Story of Balto Trade Book. (p. 957)
—Pathways: Grade 6 Dr. Rabbit Trade Book. (p. 1328)
—Pathways: Grade 4 Where the Waves Break: Life at the Edge of the Sea Trade Book. (p. 1328)
K/H (Pegasus). Random House Book of Poetry. (p. 1438)
Kaaberbol, Lene. Heartbreak Island. (p. 760)
—Serpent Gift. (p. 1552)
—Shamer's Daughter. (p. 1559)
Kaaris, illus. see Lu, Marie.
Kaarsholm, Preben, ed. City Flicks: Indian Cinema & the Urban Experience. (p. 323)
Kababik, Dana. From Bulb to Flower. (p. 642)
—From Seed to Flower. (p. 643)
Kaback, Suzy, illus. see Power, Brenda, et al.
Kabaji, Egara. When the Dead Met the Living (p. 1904)
Kabakov, Vladimir. R Is for Russia. Das, Prodeepta, illus. (p. 1429)
—R Is for Russia. Das, Prodeepta, photos by. (p. 1429)
Kabana, Joni. Torina's World: A Child's Life in Madagascar. (p. 1769)
Kabat, Vicki Marsh. Will You Still Love Me? (p. 1932)
Kabat-Zinn, Jon. Arriving at Your Own Door: 108 Lessons in Mindfulness. (p. 101)
Kabaya, Kosuke. Android Angels. (p. 72)
Kabbalah Learning Center Staff, ed. see Berg, Rav P. S.

Full bibliographic information is available on the Title Index page number referenced in parentheses at the end of each entry

Kabbani, Muhammad. Naqshbandi Sufi Tradition Guidebook of Daily Practice & Devotions (p. 1229)
Kabbani, Muhammad Hisham, jt. auth. see Kabbani, Shaykh Muhamma.
Kabbani, Shaykh Muhamma & Kabbani, Muhammad Hisham. Links of Light: The Golden Chain: A Child's Version of the Naqshbandi Sufi Way. Sperling, Karima & Sperling, Alia, illus. (p. 1019)
Kabei, Yukako. Dead Sleep Eternally in the Wilderness (p. 417)
Kabel, Amy. Hank's Visit to the Doggie Store. (p. 742)
Kabir, Shohag. Mice & Squirrel. (p. 1134)
KaBOOM!. Go Out & Play! Favorite Outdoor Games from KaBOOM! Rose, Julianna, illus. (p. 687)
Kaboom! Staff, jt. auth. see Rosen, Michael J.
Kacer, Kathy. Diary of Laura's Twin (p. 435)
—Hiding Edith: A True Story (p. 777)
—Magician of Auschwitz Newland, Gillian, illus. (p. 1075)
—Shanghai Escape (p. 1559)
—To Hope & Back: The Journey of the St. Louis (p. 1759)
—Underground Reporters: A True Story (p. 1815)
Kacer, Kathy, ed. We Are Their Voice: Young People Respond to the Holocaust (p. 1866)
Kacer, Stephen, illus. see Painter, Grace.
Kacev, Glenda. Bal Yoga for Kids. (p. 133)
Kachlany, Scott C. Infectious Diseases of the Mouth. (p. 873)
Kachmann, Rudy. Kid Scripts: Just What the Doctor Ordered. Lynch, Dan, illus. (p. 951)
Kachmar, Lilliam, jt. auth. see Steele, John F.
Kachur, Matthew. Making Maps: Set Of 6. (p. 1081)
—Making Maps & Cómo hacer un Mapa: 6 English, 6 Spanish Adaptations. (p. 1081)
—Miracle Material: Set Of 6. (p. 1148)
—Miracle Material & un material Milagroso: 6 English, 6 Spanish Adaptations. (p. 1148)
—Our Current World: Set Of 6. (p. 1308)
—Our Current World & Nuestro mundo Eléctrico: 6 English, 6 Spanish Adaptations. (p. 1308)
—Slave Trade. Schwarz, Philip, ed. (p. 1588)
Kachur, Matthew, jt. auth. see Sterngass, Jon.
Kachur, Matthew & Sterngass, Jon. Mexican-American War. (p. 1131)
Kachurek, Sandra J. Francisco Pizarro: Explorer of South America. (p. 628)
—George W. Bush. (p. 663)
Kacvinsky, Katie. Awaken. (p. 120)
—Middle Ground. (p. 1137)
Kaczka, Fallon. What about Oysters. (p. 1879)
Kaczmarczyk, Kyle J. Misadventures of Silent Boy - Volume II: the Stupid Strikes Back. (p. 1150)
Kaczmarskyj, Vera, tr. see Mak, Olha.
Kadair, Deborah. I Spy in the Louisiana Sky Kadair, Deborah, illus. (p. 846)
—Today Is Monday in Kentucky (p. 1760)
Kadair, Deborah & Downing, Johnette. Today Is Monday in New York (p. 1760)
—Today Is Monday in Texas (p. 1760)
Kadair, Deborah Ousley. Down in Louisiana (p. 474)
—Grandma's Gumbo Kadair, Deborah Ousley, illus. (p. 708)
—I Spy in the Texas Sky Kadair, Deborah Ousley, illus. (p. 846)
Kadair, Deborah Ousley, jt. auth. see Downing, Johnette.
Kadair, Deborah Ousley & Kralovansky, Susan Holt. There Was a Tall Texan Who Swallowed a Flea (p. 1730)
Kadavy, Paul D., compiled by. 101 Classic Books for All Ages (p. 1999)
Kade, J. V. Bot Wars. (p. 215)
—Meta-Rise. (p. 1130)
Kade, Stacey. Body & Soul. (p. 207)
—Ghost & the Goth. (p. 670)
—Project Paper Doll: the Hunt. (p. 1410)
—Project Paper Doll the Rules. (p. 1410)
—Trials. (p. 1785)
Kadence, Sam. Evolution. (p. 546)
—Evolution [Library Edition]. (p. 546)
—On the Right Track. (p. 1291)
—Unicorns & Rainbow Poop. (p. 1818)
Kader, Nino, retold by. To the Prince of Persia: Timeless Advice on Money, Love, War & More. (p. 1759)
Kaderli, Janet. Patchwork Trail. Arnold, Patricia, illus. (p. 1328)
Kadilak, Kathy. Tommy Finds His Forever Home. (p. 1765)
Kadmon, Christina, illus. see Weigelt, Udo.
Kadmon, Cristina, illus. see Horn, Peter.
Kadohata, Cynthia. Cracker! The Best Dog in Vietnam. (p. 375)
—Half a World Away. (p. 736)
—Kira-Kira. (p. 961)
—Million Shades of Gray. (p. 1144)
—Outside Beauty. (p. 1313)
—Thing about Luck. (p. 1732)
—Thing about Luck. Kuo, Julia, illus. (p. 1732)
—Weedflower. (p. 1871)
Kadono, Eiko. Grandpa's Soup. Ichikawa, Santomi, illus. (p. 710)
Kadono, Eiko & Miyazaki, Hayao. Kiki's Delivery Service (p. 955)
Kadylak, Shirley. Cody's New Pet. (p. 338)
Kaeden Corp. Staff, ed. see Evans, Karen & Urmston, Kathleen.
Kaeden Corp. Staff, ed. see Frankford, Marilyn.
Kaeden Corp. Staff, ed. see Geddes, Diana E.
Kaeden Corp. Staff, ed. see Urmston, Kathleen & Evans, Karen.
Kaeden Corp. Staff, ed. see Yannone, Deborah.
Kaelberer, Angie P., jt. auth. see Kaelberer, Angie Peterson.
Kaelberer, Angie Peterson. Big Show. (p. 183)
—Cool Pro Wrestling Facts. (p. 364)
—Fabulous, Freaky, Unusual History of Pro Wrestling (p. 560)
—Kickboxing (p. 951)
—Triple H (p. 1787)
—U. S. Army Humvees (p. 1806)
Kaelberer, Angie Peterson & Kaelberer, Angie P. U. S. Army Special Operations (p. 1806)
—U. S. Navy SEALs. (p. 1807)
Kaelberer, Angie Peterson & Peterson Kaelberer, Angie. Hulk Hogan: Pro Wrestler Terry Bollea (p. 825)
—McMahons: Vince McMahon & Family. (p. 1114)
—Nature Boy: Pro Wrestler Ric Flair (p. 1236)
Kaelberer, Angie Peterson & Raij, Emily. Pro Wrestling Superstars. (p. 1408)
Kaemmerlen, Cathy. Buzz on Honeybees Coates, Kathy, illus. (p. 248)
Kaergel, Julia. Fingerprints: Let's Make Art with Everyday Things. (p. 589)
Kaergel, Julia, illus. see Dorrie, Doris & Dörrie, Doris.
Kaeser, Gigi, photos by see Beard, Jean J. & Gillespie, Peggy, eds.
Kaesshaefer, Charles. Lost Princess. (p. 1056)
Kaetler, Sarah, tr. Bible Stories from the German Classic Biblische Geschichten. (p. 176)
Kafer, Kathy & Benchmark Education Co. Staff. Analytical Arguments about Folklore. (p. 67)
—Opinions about Difficult Times Portrayed in Literature. (p. 1300)
Kafer, Kathy, et al. Opinions about the Voting Age. (p. 1300)
Kafka, Franz. Carta al Padre. Cristancho M, Jose Martin, tr. (p. 272)
—Metamorfosis. (p. 1130)
—Metamorfosis/la Condena/en la Colonia Penitenciaria. Kovacsics Meszaros, Marta, tr. (p. 1130)
—Metamorphosis. Bloom, Harold, ed. (p. 1130)
Kafka, Rebecca. Alef Is for Abba. Basaluzzo, Constanza, illus. (p. 35)
Kafka, Tina. Cloning. (p. 333)
—Folk Art. (p. 611)
—Gay Rights. (p. 659)
—Genetic Engineering. (p. 660)
—Graphic Design. (p. 710)
Kagan, Miguel. Match Mine: Language Builder. (p. 1104)
Kagan, Miguel, jt. auth. see Kagan, Spencer.
Kagan, Spencer & Kagan, Miguel. Kagan Cooperative Learning. (p. 941)
Kagawa, Julie. Eternity Cure. (p. 539)
—Forever Song. (p. 619)
—Immortal Rules. (p. 861)
—Iron Daughter. (p. 888)
—Iron King. (p. 888)
—Iron King the Iron Daughter. (p. 888)
—Iron Knight. (p. 888)
—Iron Legends. (p. 888)
—Iron Queen. (p. 888)
—Iron Traitor. (p. 888)
—Lost Prince. (p. 1056)
—Rogue. (p. 1484)
—Talon. (p. 1704)
Kagayame, Johnny & Sherman, Josepha. Discovering the Construct of Time. (p. 449)
Kagda, Falaq. India. (p. 870)
Kagda, Falaq & Koh, Magdalene. Hong Kong. (p. 795)
Kagda, Falaq & Latif, Zawiah Abdul. Algeria. (p. 38)
Kagda, Sakina & Cooke, Barbara. Norway. (p. 1266)
Kagda, Sakina & Latif, Zawiah Abdul. Lithuania. (p. 1023)
Kageler, Len, jt. auth. see Robbins, Duffy.
Kagesaki, Yuna, jt. auth. see Kai, Tohru.
Kageyama, Naoyuki, jt. auth. see Takahashi, Kazuki.
Kageyama, Naoyuki & Takahashi, Kazuki. Semifinals Begin! Kageyama, Naoyuki, illus. (p. 1550)
Kagiliery, Theodore. Angelo & Peter. (p. 74)
Kagna, Barbara. Magic of Masara. Gonzalez, Ashley, illus. (p. 1073)
Kagume, Krista, jt. auth. see Bezener, Andy.
Kagume, Krista, jt. contrib. by see Smalling, Curtis.
Kahalewai, Marilyn. Whose Slippers Are Those? Kobayashi, Gavin, illus. (p. 1922)
Kahan, Alex. Entrepreneurship: Create Your Own Business. Crosier, Mike, illus. (p. 531)
Kahan, Bob, ed. see DC Comics Staff.
Kahan, Bob, ed. see DC Comics Staff, et al.
Kahan, Bob, ed. see Delano, Jamie.
Kahan, Bob, ed. see Dixon, Chuck, et al.
Kahan, Bob, ed. see Ennis, Garth.
Kahan, Bob, ed. see Fox, Gardner & DC Comics Staff.
Kahan, Bob, ed. see Gaiman, Neil, et al.
Kahan, Bob, ed. see Gaiman, Neil.
Kahan, Bob, ed. see Morrison, Grant.
Kahan, Bob, ed. see Starlin, Jim.
Kahan, Bob, ed. see Thomas, Roy, et al.
Kahan, Bob, ed. see Wagner, Matt & Seagle, Steven.
Kahan, Jane, jt. auth. see Feierabend, John M.
Kahanek, Kristine Elizabeth. Katie & the Magic Umbrella: A Stormy Adventure. (p. 944)
Kahaner, Ellen. Everything You Need to Know about Growing up Female. (p. 545)
Kahaney, Amelia. Brokenhearted. (p. 230)
—Invisible: A Brokenhearted Novel. (p. 885)
—Invisible. (p. 885)
Kahaney, Phyllis, ed. see Aharoni, Nesta A. & Aharoni, Nesta.
Kahate, Ruta. 5 Spices, 50 Dishes: Simple Indian Recipes Using Five Common Spices. Cushner, Susie, photos by. (p. 1992)
Kahla, Robert. Mr. X from Planet X: And Other Animules. (p. 1187)
Kahler, A. R. Immortal Circus: Final Act: The Final Act (p. 861)
—Martyr. (p. 1098)
Kahler, A. R., jt. auth. see Destiny, A.
Kahler, Janet C. 1918 Covered Wagon Adventure. (p. 2002)
Kahlo, Frida, illus. see Bernier-Grand, Carmen T.
Kahn, Ada P. Encyclopedia of Stress & Stress-Related Diseases. (p. 525)
—Encyclopedia of Work-Related Illnesses, Injuries & Health Issues. (p. 525)
Kahn, Ada P. & Doctor, Ronald M. Phobias. (p. 1351)
Kahn, Colleen Alyssa. Peadoaks (p. 1332)
Kahn, doc, Robert. Bobby & Mandee's Good Touch/Bad Touch: Children's Safety Book. Hardie, Chris, illus. (p. 206)
Kahn, Elithe Manuha'aipo. HA Breathe! Hawaiian Meditative Contemplation. (p. 734)
Kahn, J. Retour du Jedi (p. 1464)
Kahn, Katherine, illus. see Rouss, Sylvia A.
Kahn, Katherine, illus. see Rouss, Sylvia.
Kahn, Katherine, jt. auth. see Rouss, Sylvia A.
Kahn, Katherine Janus, illus. see Gellman, Ellie B.
Kahn, Katherine Janus, illus. see Jules, Jacqueline & Hechtkopf, Jacqueline.
Kahn, Katherine Janus, illus. see Jules, Jacqueline.
Kahn, Katherine Janus, illus. see Lehman-Wilzig, Tami.
Kahn, Katherine Janus, illus. see Rouss, Sylvia A.
Kahn, Katherine Janus, illus. see Rouss, Sylvia A. & Lanton, Sandy.
Kahn, Katherine Janus, illus. see Rouss, Sylvia A. & Turndorf, Genene Levy.
Kahn, Katherine Janus, illus. see Rouss, Sylvia.
Kahn, Michàéle. Ordenador Nada Ordinario. Trapero, Florentino & Lapointe, Claude, trs. (p. 1302)
Kahn, Robert, et al. Bobby & Mandee's Too Solid for Suicide. (p. 206)
Kahn, Sarah. Creepy Crawlies. Scott, Peter David, illus. (p. 381)
—Little Book of Cats & Kittens: Internet-Linked. (p. 1025)
Kahn, Sarah, ed. 50 Horses & Ponies to Spot. Jackson, Ian, illus. (p. 1997)
Kahn, William A. Student's Guide to Successful Project Teams. (p. 1669)
Kahrs, Christina, jt. auth. see Gibbs, Noni.
Kahrs, Evelyn. I Can Find God. (p. 835)
—I Can Find God in My City. (p. 835)
Kai, illus. see Summers, Terry.
Kai Dotlich, Rebecca. All Aboard! Lowery, Mike, illus. (p. 41)
—What Can a Crane Pick Up? Lowery, Mike, illus. (p. 1880)
Kai, Naleighna. Every Woman Needs a Wife. (p. 543)
Kai, Tohru & Kagesaki, Yuna. Chibi Vampire (p. 299)
Kaida, Garrett, illus. see Ulz, Ivan.
Kaider, Azi Sabi. Angela's Sunflower. (p. 74)
Kail, Leanna. Owl Who Couldn't Whoo. Rottinger, Amy, illus. (p. 1315)
Kaili, Sorano. Monochrome Factor (p. 1166)
Kain, Bob. Chirp Book. Kain, Bob & Owlkids Books Inc. Staff, illus. (p. 308)
—Laugh with Chirp: Jokes, Riddles, Tongue Twisters, & More! Kain, Bob & Owlkids Books Inc. Staff, illus. (p. 980)
—Play with Chirp: Puzzles, Mazes, Games, & More! Kain, Bob & Owlkids Books Inc. Staff, illus. (p. 1371)
—Read with Chirp: Read along with Pictures. Kain, Bob & Owlkids Books Inc. Staff, illus. (p. 1443)
—Travel with Chirp: Comics, Jokes, Games, & More Travelling Fun! Kain, Bob & Owlkids Books Inc. Staff, illus. (p. 1780)
Kain, Bob, illus. see Chirp Magazine Editors.
Kain, Bob & Becker, Helaine. Read with Chirp: Read along with Pictures. Kain, Bob & Owlkids Books Inc. Staff, illus. (p. 1443)
Kain, Daniel L. Problem-Based Learning for Teachers, Grades 6-12. (p. 1408)
Kain, Jamie. Good Sister. (p. 700)
Kain, Karen. Nutcracker. Kupesic, Rajka, illus. (p. 1274)
Kain, Kathleen. All about Holidays: With Inspector McQ. Mahan, Ben, illus. (p. 42)
—All about Holidays. Mahan, Ben, illus. (p. 42)
—All about Pets. Miyake, Yoshi, illus. (p. 43)
Kain, P. G. Dramatic Pause. (p. 480)
—Famous for Thirty Seconds. (p. 569)
—Social Experiments of Dorie Dilts: The School for Cool. (p. 1604)
—Social Experiments of Dorie Dilts: Dumped by Popular Demand. (p. 1604)
Kain, P. G. & Frost, Michael. Picture Perfect. (p. 1356)
Kain, Roger. Xtreme Vocals. (p. 1967)
Kain, Wallace M. Nunca Riddle: A Young Woman Proves Herself in the Amazon Rain Forest. (p. 1273)
—Red Column: A Young Woman's Capture, Imprisonment & Escape in the Amazon Jungle. (p. 1453)
Kainen, Dan. Ocean: A Photicular Book. (p. 1276)
Kainen, Dan & Kaufmann, Carol. Safari: A Photicular Book. (p. 1501)
Kaino, Kim, illus. see McNutt, Nan.
Kainz, Howard P. Natural Law: A Reevaluation. (p. 1235)
Kaiser, Amy L. If I Lived in the Jungle. (p. 853)
—If I Lived in the Ocean. (p. 853)
Kaiser, Andy. Waking the Dreamer: Transhuman #1. (p. 1853)
Kaiser, Carducci, et al. Shyness: The Ultimate Teen Guide. (p. 1572)
Kaiser, Cecily. On the First Night of Chanukah. Schatell, Brian, illus. (p. 1290)
Kaiser, Lisa, illus. see Dalton, William.
Kaiser, Lori. Florence Flamingo Gets the Flu. Kaiser, Lori, illus. (p. 606)
—George Washington. Kaiser, Lori, illus. (p. 664)
—Gigi the Greedy Giraffe. Kaiser, Lori, illus. (p. 676)
—Megan the Moody Moose. Kaiser, Lori, illus. (p. 1124)
Kaishaku. Eternal Alice Rondo (p. 539)
Kaishaku, jt. auth. see Kaishaku.
Kaishaku & Kaishaku. Eternal Alice Rondo (p. 539)
Kaizer, Judy. Smitten the Kitten. (p. 1594)
Kajencki, AnnMarie Francis. Count Casimir Pulaski: From Poland to America, a Hero's Fight for Liberty. (p. 369)
Kajikawa, Kimiko. Tsunami! Young, Ed, illus. (p. 1795)
Kajumulo, Alex. Soccer Monster: Mwalimu Wa Soca. (p. 1603)
Kakakios, Melissa. I Love Taekwondo: My First Taekwondo Books. (p. 843)
—Spirit of Courage: My First Tae Kwon Do Books. (p. 1628)
Kakinouchi, Narumi. My Codename Is Charmer (p. 1200)
Kakinuma, Hideki & Senno, Knife. Mecha (p. 1118)
Kakkar, Renu. Granny's Return from Heaven as an Incredible Car. (p. 710)
Kako, Franco, illus. see Bolte, Mari.
Kako, Satoshi, illus. see Matsuoka, Kyoko.
Kakugawa, Frances. Wordsworth Dances the Waltz. DeSica, Melissa, illus. (p. 1952)
Kakugawa, Francis. Wordsworth the Poet. Goto, Scott, illus. (p. 1952)
Kakurai, Missile, jt. auth. see Kikuchi, Hideyuki.
Kala & Kol. Where Your Love Is: For Peace Is in This Place. (p. 1910)
Kalafatis, John, illus. see Smith, Jacquelyn.
Kalagayan, Elly, des. Say & Do R Artic Bingo: Bgo42. (p. 1518)
Kalahele, Imaikalani, illus. see Eyre, David.
Kalahele, Imaikalani, jt. auth. see Eyre, David.
Kalaichelvan, Kalai. WiMax Explained; System Fundamentals. (p. 1935)
Kalaidjian, Walter. Understanding Poetry. (p. 1816)
Kalal, Dan, illus. see Miller, Connie Colwell.
Kalan, Robert. Jump, Frog, Jump! Barton, Byron, illus. (p. 934)
Kalanovic, Dubravka, illus. see Ross, Mandy.
Kalantary, Tanya. So Can You! (p. 1602)
Kalar, Bonnie. Ann Paints & Plays. Spreen, Kathe, illus. (p. 85)
—At Dawn. Spreen, Kathe, illus. (p. 110)
—At the Lake. Spreen, Kathe, illus. (p. 111)
—At the Pond. Spreen, Kathe, illus. (p. 111)
—At the Zoo. Spreen, Kathe, illus. (p. 111)
—Beth & Thad. Spreen, Kathe, illus. (p. 171)
—Bird & the Shirt. Spreen, Kathe, illus. (p. 190)
—Burt. Spreen, Kathe, illus. (p. 244)
—Chuck & the Chick. Spreen, Kathe, illus. (p. 318)
—Clair at Home. Spreen, Kathe, illus. (p. 326)
—Clown. Spreen, Kathe, illus. (p. 335)
—Cook & the Crook. Spreen, Kathe, illus. (p. 361)
—Crows. Spreen, Kathe, illus. (p. 386)
—Dream. Spreen, Kathe, illus. (p. 483)
—Early Phonetic Readers - Set A Spreen, Kathe, illus. (p. 494)
—Fran & the Doll. Spreen, Kathe, illus. (p. 627)
—Fred. Spreen, Kathe, illus. (p. 632)
—Gail Sails. Spreen, Kathe, illus. (p. 652)
—Gay & Jay Play. Spreen, Kathe, illus. (p. 658)
—Good Day. Spreen, Kathe, illus. (p. 697)
—Jack. Spreen, Kathe, illus. (p. 902)
—Joan's Coat. Spreen, Kathe, illus. (p. 919)
—Josh & the Fish. Spreen, Kathe, illus. (p. 926)
—Kirk & the Deer. Spreen, Kathe, illus. (p. 961)
—Lew & His New Cap. Spreen, Kathe, illus. (p. 1004)
—Mark at the Farm. Spreen, Kathe, illus. (p. 1095)
—Mike. Spreen, Kathe, illus. (p. 1141)
—Miss Lane's Class. Spreen, Kathe, illus. (p. 1151)
—Neal Camps Out. Spreen, Kathe, illus. (p. 1238)
—Rose & the Mole. Spreen, Kathe, illus. (p. 1489)
—Scouts. Spreen, Kathe, illus. (p. 1532)
—Sheep & the Bee. Spreen, Kathe, illus. (p. 1564)
—Stan & His Sled. Spreen, Kathe, illus. (p. 1639)
—Trip. Spreen, Kathe, illus. (p. 1787)
—Trip to the Beach. Spreen, Kathe, illus. (p. 1787)
Kalasea, illus. see Declus, Jennifer.
Kalb, Chris, illus. see Ray, Rachael.
Kalbag, Asha & Sheikh-Miller, Jonathan. Homework on Your Computer. (p. 794)
Kalber, Zoe. New Baby. (p. 1243)
Kalda, Sam, illus. see Fitzgerald, F. Scott.
Kaldor, Connie. Duck in New York City. Fil and Julie Staff, illus. (p. 488)
—Poodle in Paris. Fil and Julie Staff, illus. (p. 1383)
Kaldor, Connie & Campagne, Carmen. Lullaby Berceuse: A Warm Prairie Night. Deines, Brian, illus. (p. 1064)
Kale, Ann Stephanian. Artie - The Ugly Frog. Kale, Ann Stephanian, illus. (p. 104)
—Marco & Princess Gina. Kale, Ann Stephanian, illus. (p. 1092)
Kalechofsky, Roberta. Boy, a Chicken & the Lion of Judah: How An Became a Vegetarian. (p. 217)
Kalender, Oznur, illus. see Kaplan, Osman.
Kalep, Elvy. Air Babies. (p. 31)
Kaler, Amy. Running after Pills: Politics, Gender, & Contraception in Colonial Zimbabwe. (p. 1497)
—Running after Pills: Politics, Gender, & Contraception in Colonial Zimbabwe. (p. 1497)
Kaler, David, et al. Action Heroes Archives Mastroserio, Rocke, illus. (p. 10)
Kaleta, Don. Puppy Scents: The Kids' Guide to Puppy Care. Habel, Helen, illus. (p. 1418)
Kaleta, Magda & Gerngross, Günter. Join Us for English Level 2 Pupil's Book with CD-ROM Polish Edition. (p. 924)
Kalicicki, Missy & Ketner, Abi. Branded. (p. 222)
Kalinowski, Delphine. Frog's Fruit Stand. (p. 641)
—Weather Report. (p. 1870)
Kallor, Susan D. Other Side of God: Psychological Crisis, Altered States, Alternate Realities, Dreams, Meditation, Parallel Worlds, Death, Personal Growth & Transformation):the Eleven Gem Odyssey of Being. (p. 1306)
Kalis, Jennifer, illus. see Erhard, Lorie.
Kalis, Jennifer, illus. see Friedman, Laurie B.
Kalis, Jennifer, illus. see Friedman, Laurie.
Kalis, Jennifer, illus. see Ikids Staff.
Kalis, Jennifer, illus. see King, Bart.
Kalis, Jennifer, illus. see O'Connor, Jane.
Kalis, Jennifer, illus. see Tuchman, Laura.
Kalis, Jennifer, illus. see Wood, Anita.
Kalish, Leah & Fatus, Sophie. Yoga Planet: 50 Fun Activities for a Greener World. (p. 1972)
Kaliski, John, jt. auth. see Crawford, Margaret.
Kalkipsakis, Thalia. Catch Me If You Can. Oswald, Ash, illus. (p. 279)
—Dancing Queen. Oswald, Ash, illus. (p. 403)
—Go Girl! #10: Basketball Blues. Oswald, Ash, illus. (p. 686)
—Holy Crushamoly. (p. 791)
—It's Not Me, It's You. (p. 898)
—Netball Dreams. (p. 1242)
—Silhouette. (p. 1575)
—Sink or Swim. (p. 1579)
—Sister Spirit. Oswald, Ash, illus. (p. 1581)
—Worst Gymnast. Oswald, Ash, illus. (p. 1961)
Kalkowski, John. Red Cell. (p. 1453)
Kallai, Kriszta Nagy, illus. see Howie, Vicki.
Kallai, Nagy, illus. see Ross, Mandy.
Kallai Nagy, Krisztina, illus. see Hartman, Bob.
Kallai Nagy, Krisztina, illus. see Jackson, Antonia.

K

Kallai Nagy, Krisztina, illus. see Ross, Mandy.
Kallan, Stuart A. Gas Crisis. (p. 657)
Kallander, Susan & Boomgaarden, Larry. Up in Smoke. (p. 1824)
Kallanovic, Dubravka, illus. see Poltier, Anton.
Kallas, Randi & Dougherty, Mike, eds. Rochester, Minnesota: A Visual & Historic Journey. (p. 1481)
Kallen, Stuart. Animation. (p. 84)
—Burj Khalifa: The Tallest Tower in the World. (p. 243)
—Sculpture. (p. 1533)
Kallen, Stuart A. African Mythology. Greenhaven Press Editors, ed. (p. 27)
—Aftermath of the Sandinista Revolution. (p. 28)
—Artist's Tools. (p. 104)
—Atlantis. (p. 112)
—Beatles. (p. 153)
—Bono. (p. 209)
—Burj Khalifa: The Tallest Tower in the World. (p. 243)
—Che Guevara: You Win or You Die. (p. 295)
—Claude Monet. (p. 329)
—Communication with the Dead. (p. 349)
—Crop Circles. (p. 385)
—Digital Cameras & Camcorders. (p. 439)
—Does Equality Exist in America? (p. 460)
—Elon Musk & Tesla. (p. 516)
—Gwen Stefani. (p. 733)
—Harlem Renaissance. (p. 749)
—Haunted Houses. (p. 753)
—Heroin: Drugs. (p. 773)
—History of Free Blacks in America. (p. 784)
—History of Latin Music. (p. 784)
—History of R&B & Soul Music. Greenhaven Press Editors, ed. (p. 784)
—History of Reggae. (p. 784)
—History of World Music. (p. 785)
—How Should the World Respond to Global Warming? (p. 812)
—Information Revolution. (p. 874)
—Instruments of Music. (p. 879)
—IPods & MP3 Players. (p. 886)
—Is Factory Farming Harming America? (p. 889)
—Jeff Bezos & Amazon. (p. 911)
—John F. Kennedy Assassination. (p. 921)
—K-Pop: Korea's Musical Explosion. (p. 941)
—Life During the Crusades. (p. 1010)
—Loch Ness Monster. (p. 1044)
—Marcus Garvey & the Back to Africa Movement. (p. 1092)
—Mark Zuckerberg & Facebook. (p. 1095)
—Matt Groening the Simpsons: The Simpsons. (p. 1109)
—Medieval Food & Customs. (p. 1119)
—National Security. (p. 1233)
—Nuclear & Toxic Waste. (p. 1269)
—Open the Jail Doors — We Want to Enter: The Defiance Campaign Against Apartheid Laws, South Africa 1952. (p. 1299)
—Pablo Picasso. (p. 1316)
—Photography. (p. 1353)
—Postmodern Art. (p. 1388)
—Primary Sources. (p. 1400)
—Race to Discover the AIDS Virus: Luc Montagnier vs Robert Gallo. (p. 1431)
—Rain Forests. Cothran, Helen, ed. (p. 1434)
—Renaissance Art. (p. 1460)
—Running Dry: The Global Water Crisis. (p. 1497)
—Spontaneous Human Combustion. (p. 1631)
—Time Travel. (p. 1753)
—Toxic Waste. (p. 1774)
—Travel Guide to Harlem Renaissance. (p. 1780)
—Twentieth-Century Immigration to the United States. (p. 1801)
—Vampire History & Lore. (p. 1832)
—Voodoo. (p. 1850)
—Water, Water Everywhere? Protecting a Diminishing Resource in a Warming World. (p. 1863)
—We Are Not Beasts of Burden: Cesar Chavez & the Delano Grape Strike, California, 1965-1970. (p. 1865)
—Werewolves. (p. 1875)
—What Are the Most Serious Threats to National Security? (p. 1880)
—What Energy Sources Should. (p. 1884)
—Wireless Society. (p. 1939)
—Women of the Civil Rights Movement. (p. 1946)
Kallen, Stuart A., jt. auth. see Boekhoff, P. M.
Kallen, Stuart A., jt. auth. see Boekhoff.
Kallen, Stuart A., jt. auth. see Greenhaven Press Editors.
Kallen, Stuart A. & Cothran, Helen, eds. Are Privacy Rights Being Violated? (p. 96)
Kallen, Stuart A., ed. Alternative Rock. (p. 50)
—History of American Pop. (p. 783)
—History of Classical Music. (p. 783)
—History of Latin Music. (p. 784)
—History of Rock & Roll. (p. 784)
—What Energy Sources Should Be Pursued? (p. 1884)
Kallen, Stuart K. Aliens. (p. 41)
—search for extraterrestrial Life. (p. 1537)
Kallet, Marilyn. One for Each Night: Chanukah Tales & Recipes. (p. 1295)
Kallevig, Christine P. Nature Fold-along Stories: Quick & Easy Origami Tales about Plants & Animals. (p. 1236)
—Sun, the Moon, & the Origami Grammie. (p. 1676)
Kallgren, Beverly H. Duck Named Goose. (p. 488)
Kallio, Jamie. Aliens. (p. 41)
—Angel Island Immigration: A History Perspectives Book. (p. 73)
—Bigfoot. (p. 184)
—Haunted Houses. (p. 753)
—Mayflower Compact. (p. 1113)
—What's Great about Alabama? (p. 1897)
—What's Great about Virginia? (p. 1897)
Kallmaker, Karin. Dawning. (p. 412)
—Night Vision. (p. 1254)
—Warming Trend. (p. 1858)
Kallmeyer-Mehlhorn, Margarete. Wondrous Ball of Yarn: A Facsimile of the Previously Unpublished Manuscript. (p. 1949)
Kallus, Ryder. Ryder the Red-Nosed Engine. (p. 1499)
Kalman, Bobbi. ABCs of Endangered Animals. (p. 4)
Kalman, Bobbie. ABCs of Animals. (p. 4)
—ABCs of Continents. (p. 4)
—ABCs of Endangered Animals. (p. 4)
—ABCs of Habitats. (p. 4)
—ABCs of Insects. (p. 4)
—ABCs of Oceans. (p. 4)
—ABCs of Plants. (p. 4)
—ABCs of the Environment. (p. 4)
—Abeilles. Briere, Marie-Josee, tr. from ENG. (p. 4)
—Animal Community. (p. 77)
—Animal Families. (p. 77)
—Animal Life Cycles: Growing & Changing. (p. 78)
—Animal Mothers. (p. 78)
—Animales Crecen y Cambian. (p. 80)
—Animals Grow & Change. (p. 82)
—Animals Move Like This. (p. 83)
—Animals Without Backbones. (p. 84)
—Are You Like Me? (p. 97)
—Arms & Legs, Fingers & Toes: Brazos, Piernas y Dedos. (p. 100)
—Arms & Legs, Fingers & Toes. (p. 100)
—At School. (p. 110)
—Ayudantes de Mi Comunidad. (p. 121)
—Baby Animal Names: Nombres de Animales Bebé. (p. 124)
—Baby Animal Names. (p. 124)
—Baby Animals in Cities. (p. 124)
—Baby Animals in Desert Habitats. (p. 124)
—Baby Animals in Forest Habitats. (p. 124)
—Baby Animals in Grassland Habitats. (p. 124)
—Baby Animals in Land Habitats. (p. 124)
—Baby Animals in Mountain Habitats. (p. 124)
—Baby Animals in Northern Forests. (p. 124)
—Baby Animals in Ocean Habitats. (p. 124)
—Baby Animals in Rainforest Habitats. (p. 124)
—Baby Animals in Rivers. (p. 124)
—Baby Animals in Savanna Habitats. (p. 124)
—Baby Animals in Water Habitats. (p. 124)
—Baby Animals in Wetland Habitats. (p. 124)
—Baby Animals on Islands. (p. 124)
—Baby Apes. (p. 125)
—Baby Bears. (p. 125)
—Baby Birds. (p. 125)
—Baby Bunnies. (p. 125)
—Baby Carnivores. (p. 125)
—Baby Cats. (p. 125)
—Baby Chipmunks. (p. 125)
—Baby Deer. (p. 125)
—Baby Elephants. (p. 126)
—Baby Foxes. (p. 126)
—Baby Giraffes. (p. 126)
—Baby Horses. (p. 126)
—Baby Lemurs. (p. 127)
—Baby Mammals. (p. 127)
—Baby Marsupials. (p. 127)
—Baby Pets. (p. 127)
—Baby Pigs. (p. 127)
—Baby Polar Bears. (p. 127)
—Baby Primates. (p. 127)
—Baby Raccoons. (p. 127)
—Baby Reptiles. (p. 127)
—Baby Rodents. (p. 128)
—Baby Wolves. (p. 128)
—Bath. (p. 144)
—Bébés Cochons. (p. 155)
—Bébés Lapins. (p. 155)
—Bébés Loups. (p. 155)
—Bébés Ours Polaires. (p. 155)
—Bébés Renards. (p. 155)
—Bébés Tamias. (p. 155)
—Big Science Ideas. (p. 183)
—Body Talk. (p. 207)
—Bomberos Al Rescate. (p. 208)
—Brazos, Piernas y Dedos. (p. 224)
—Breakfast Blast: Step-by-Step Recipes. (p. 224)
—Cadenas Alimentarias del Bosque. (p. 250)
—Camiones Robustos. (p. 256)
—Camouflage: Changing to Hide. (p. 257)
—Camouflage Changing to Hide. (p. 257)
—Can It Fly? (p. 258)
—Canada: The Land. (p. 260)
—Canada: The Culture. (p. 260)
—Canada - The People. (p. 260)
—Castors. Briere, Marie-Josee, tr. from ENG. (p. 277)
—Caterpillars to Butterflies. (p. 280)
—China: The Land. (p. 306)
—China: The People. (p. 306)
—China - The Culture. (p. 306)
—China - The People. (p. 306)
—Ciclo de Vida de la Abeja. (p. 318)
—Ciclo de Vida de la Lombriz de Tierra. (p. 319)
—Ciclo de Vida de la Mariposa. (p. 319)
—Ciclo de Vida de la Mariposa. Reiach, Margaret Amy, illus. (p. 319)
—Ciclo de Vida de la Rana. (p. 319)
—Ciclo de Vida del Árbol. (p. 319)
—Ciclo de Vida del Mosquito. (p. 319)
—Ciclos de Vida de los Animales: Crecimiento y Cambios. (p. 319)
—Clothes I Wear. (p. 334)
—Colonial Women. (p. 342)
—Communication Then & Now. (p. 349)
—Community Helpers Then & Now. (p. 350)
—Como Se Adaptan los Animales? (p. 351)
—Comunidad de Mi Escuela. (p. 355)
—Conoce Australia. (p. 358)
—Conoce Canadá. (p. 358)
—Crezco y Cambio. (p. 382)
—Dauphins. (p. 410)
—Delicious Desserts. (p. 425)
—Dragons de Komodo. (p. 479)
—Earth's Coasts. (p. 498)
—Earth's Mountains. (p. 498)
—Earth's Rivers. (p. 498)
—Emergency Workers Are on Their Way! (p. 518)
—Endangered Baby Animals. (p. 526)
—Endangered Elephants. (p. 526)
—Endangered Komodo Dragons. (p. 526)
—Endangered Rhinoceros. (p. 527)
—Endangered Sea Turtles. (p. 527)
—Endangered Tigers. (p. 527)
—Esta Es Mi Casa. (p. 538)
—Esta Es Mi Familia. (p. 538)
—Everglades National Park. (p. 542)
—Explore Earth's Five Oceans. (p. 550)
—Explore Earth's Seven Continents. (p. 550)
—Extreme Wakeboarding. (p. 557)
—Familias de Animales. (p. 567)
—Famille des Dauphins. (p. 568)
—Farm Animals. (p. 573)
—Field Events in Action. (p. 583)
—Field Events in Action. Crabtree, Marc & Rouse, Bonna, illus. (p. 583)
—Firefighters to the Rescue! (p. 592)
—Food & Farming Then & Now. (p. 613)
—Food Chains & You. (p. 613)
—Forest Food Chains. (p. 618)
—Forest Habitat. (p. 618)
—Fotosíntesis: De la Luz del Sol al Alimento. (p. 624)
—Fotosíntesis: De la Luz Del Sol Al Alimento. (p. 624)
—Frogs & Other Amphibians. (p. 641)
—Gorilles de Montagne. (p. 703)
—Grenouilles et Autres Amphibiens. (p. 723)
—Guinea Pigs & Other Rodents. (p. 731)
—Habitat de Bosque. (p. 734)
—Helpers in My Community. (p. 766)
—Hip-Hop Dancers. (p. 780)
—Hippocampes. (p. 781)
—Hogares de los Seres Vivos. (p. 787)
—Homes of Living Things. (p. 793)
—Hospital Workers in the Emergency Room. (p. 801)
—How & What Do Animals Eat? (p. 804)
—How & What Do Animals Learn? (p. 804)
—How & Why Do Animals Adapt? (p. 804)
—How & Why Do Animals Build Homes? (p. 804)
—How & Why Do Animals Change As They Grow? (p. 804)
—How & Why Do Animals Move? (p. 804)
—How Are They the Same? (p. 805)
—How Are We the Same & Different? (p. 805)
—How Do Animals Change? (p. 806)
—How Do Animals Communicate? (p. 806)
—How Do Animals Hide? (p. 806)
—How Do Baby Animals Learn? (p. 806)
—How Do Living Things Find Food? (p. 807)
—How Do Plants Help Us? (p. 807)
—How Does It Feel? (p. 808)
—How Does It Look? (p. 809)
—How Does It Move? (p. 809)
—I Am a Living Thing. (p. 832)
—I Am Growing & Changing. (p. 833)
—I Am Growing & Changing / Crezco y Cambio. (p. 833)
—I Can Count: Sé Contar. (p. 835)
—I Can Count. (p. 835)
—I Can Do It! (p. 835)
—I Can Write a Book about Butterflies. (p. 837)
—I Can Write a Book about Countries. (p. 837)
—I Can Write a Book about Culture. (p. 837)
—I Can Write a Book about How to Be Healthy & Happy. (p. 837)
—I Can Write a Book Called If I Could Talk to Animals... (p. 837)
—I Eat a Rainbow: Me Como un Arco Iris. (p. 838)
—I Eat a Rainbow. (p. 838)
—I Have Feelings: Tengo Sentimientos. (p. 839)
—I Have Feelings. (p. 839)
—I Like Riding. (p. 841)
—I Like to Play. (p. 841)
—I Move Like This. (p. 844)
—India: The Land. (p. 870)
—India: The People. (p. 870)
—India: The Culture. (p. 870)
—India - The People. (p. 870)
—Insect Eaters. (p. 875)
—Introducción a los Accidentes Geográficos. (p. 882)
—Is It a Living Thing? (p. 889)
—Is It Big or Small? (p. 889)
—Is It the Same or Different? (p. 889)
—It Is My Birthday. (p. 894)
—It Looks Like a Dog. (p. 894)
—Japan: The Land. (p. 909)
—Japan: The People. (p. 909)
—Japan: The Culture. (p. 909)
—Japan the Land. (p. 909)
—Japan - The People. (p. 909)
—L'Alimentation des Animaux. (p. 972)
—Las Cadenas Alimentarias y Tú. (p. 976)
—Las Costas de la Tierra. (p. 976)
—Las Plantas Son Seres Vivos. (p. 977)
—Life Cycle Rouse, Bonna, illus. (p. 1008)
—Life Cycle of a Beaver. (p. 1008)
—Life Cycle of a Butterfly. (p. 1008)
—Life Cycle of a Frog. (p. 1009)
—Life Cycle of a Honeybee. (p. 1009)
—Life Cycle of A Lion. (p. 1009)
—Life Cycle of a Mosquito. (p. 1009)
—Life Cycle of a Sea Horse. (p. 1009)
—Life Cycle of an Earthworm. (p. 1009)
—Life Cycle of an Emperors. (p. 1009)
—Living Things in My Back Yard. (p. 1042)
—Living Things Need Water. (p. 1042)
—Lunch Munch: Step-by-Step Recipes. (p. 1065)
—Me Como un Arco Iris. (p. 1115)
—Metamorfosis: Cuerpos Que Cambian. (p. 1130)
—Metamorphosis: Changing Bodies. (p. 1130)
—Mexico: The Land. (p. 1131)
—Mexico: The People. (p. 1131)
—Mexico: The Culture. (p. 1131)
—Mexico - The Land. (p. 1131)
—Mexico - The People. (p. 1131)
—Mi Cuerpo Sano. (p. 1132)
—MIS Sentidos Me Ayudan. (p. 1150)
—Montañas de la Tierra. (p. 1170)
—Moustiques. Briere, Marie-Josee, tr. from ENG. (p. 1182)
—Multicultural Meals: Step-by-Step Healthy Recipes for Kids. (p. 1190)
—My Backyard Community. (p. 1196)
—My Big & Small Pets. (p. 1197)
—My Community Long Ago. (p. 1200)
—My Culture. (p. 1200)
—My Dog Likes Me. (p. 1202)
—My Family Community. (p. 1202)
—My Funny Cat. (p. 1209)
—My Healthy Body. (p. 1210)
—My School Community. (p. 1218)
—My Senses Help Me. (p. 1218)
—My Toys Have Shapes. (p. 1220)
—Nations of the Plains. (p. 1234)
—Nature's Cleaners. (p. 1237)
—Night Animals. (p. 1252)
—Nombres de Animales Bebé. (p. 1263)
—Océanos de la Tierra. (p. 1277)
—Oiseaux. (p. 1282)
—Photosynthesis: Changing Sunlight into Food. (p. 1353)
—Places in My Community. (p. 1366)
—Planche Nautique Extrême. (p. 1366)
—Plantes. (p. 1369)
—Plants Are Living Things. (p. 1370)
—Qué Es el Reino Animal? (p. 1423)
—?Que Son Las Plantas? (p. 1424)
—?Qué Son los Reptiles? (p. 1424)
—Ranas y Otros Anfibios. (p. 1438)
—Rapping about Animal Homes. (p. 1439)
—Rapping about Being a Girl. (p. 1439)
—Rapping about Bodies of Water. (p. 1439)
—Rapping about Directions on Earth. (p. 1439)
—Rapping about the Air Around Us. (p. 1439)
—Rapping about What Animals Eat. (p. 1439)
—Refugee Child: My Memories of the 1956 Hungarian Revolution. Bedell, Barbara, illus. (p. 1456)
—Refugee Child Activity Guide. (p. 1456)
—Regne Animal. (p. 1457)
—Reptile Rap. (p. 1461)
—Ríos de la Tierra. (p. 1473)
—Rodent Rap. (p. 1484)
—Santa Claus. (p. 1511)
—School Days Then & Now. (p. 1522)
—Sé Contar. (p. 1534)
—Seres Vivos de Mi Jardín. (p. 1552)
—Seres Vivos de mi Jardín. (p. 1552)
—Spotlight on Argentina. (p. 1634)
—Spotlight on Brazil. (p. 1634)
—Spotlight on Canada. (p. 1634)
—Spotlight on Egypt. (p. 1634)
—Spotlight on France. (p. 1634)
—Spotlight on Indonesia. (p. 1634)
—Spotlight on Italy. (p. 1634)
—Spotlight on Japan. (p. 1634)
—Spotlight on Kenya. (p. 1634)
—Spotlight on Russia. (p. 1634)
—Spotlight on South Africa. (p. 1634)
—Spotlight on South Korea. (p. 1634)
—Spotlight on the Philippines. (p. 1634)
—Super Snacks: Step-by-Step Recipes. (p. 1682)
—Tadpoles to Frogs. (p. 1695)
—Tengo Sentimientos. (p. 1720)
—These Are My Friends. (p. 1731)
—This Is My Family. (p. 1736)
—This Is My Home. (p. 1736)
—Tiburones Espectaculares. (p. 1747)
—Tierra y el Sol. (p. 1748)
—Today Is a Great Day! (p. 1760)
—Tortues de Mer. Briere, Marie-Josee, tr. from ENG. (p. 1771)
—Tough Trucks. (p. 1773)
—Toys & Games Then & Now. (p. 1774)
—Travel Then & Now. (p. 1780)
—Vers de Terre. (p. 1837)
—Veterinarians Help Keep Animals Healthy. (p. 1839)
—Veterinarios Cuidan la Salud de los Animales. (p. 1839)
—Visual Dictionary of a Colonial Community. (p. 1846)
—Visual Dictionary of a Pioneer Community. (p. 1846)
—Visual Dictionary of Christmas Long Ago. (p. 1846)
—Visual Dictionary of the Old West. (p. 1846)
—Visual Dictionary of Victorian Life. (p. 1846)
—Volcanes de la Tierra. (p. 1848)
—Volcanoes on Earth. (p. 1849)
—Volcans. (p. 1849)
—Warm-Blooded or Cold-Blooded? (p. 1858)
—Water Changes. (p. 1862)
—We Are the Earth. (p. 1865)
—What Are Dinosaurs? (p. 1879)
—What Are Earth's Biomes? (p. 1879)
—What Are Food Chains & Webs? (p. 1879)
—What Are My Jobs? (p. 1879)
—What Are Natural Structures? (p. 1879)
—What Are Nature's Copycats? (p. 1879)
—What Are Opposites in Nature? (p. 1879)
—What Are These Animals Doing? (p. 1880)
—What Color Is It? (p. 1881)
—What Comes Next? (p. 1881)
—What Do I Need? (p. 1882)
—What Do I See? (p. 1882)
—What Is a Bat (p. 1888)
—What Is a Biome? (p. 1888)
—What Is a Carnivore? (p. 1888)
—What Is a Cat? (p. 1888)
—What Is a Food Chain? (p. 1888)
—What Is a Herbivore? (p. 1888)
—What Is a Top Predator? (p. 1888)
—What Is a Vertebrate? (p. 1888)
—What Is a Vertibrate? (p. 1888)
—What Is an Ocean? (p. 1889)
—What Is an Omnivore? (p. 1889)
—What Is Climate? (p. 1889)
—What Is Culture? (p. 1889)

—What Is Hatching? (p. 1889)
—What Is It? (p. 1889)
—What Is It Made From? (p. 1889)
—What Is Pollination? (p. 1890)
—What Is Religion? (p. 1890)
—What Is Super Nature? (p. 1890)
—What Is Symmetry in Nature? (p. 1890)
—What Kind of Coverings Do Animals Have? (p. 1891)
—What Kind of Living Thing Is It? (p. 1891)
—What Senses Do Animals Have? (p. 1893)
—What Shape Is It? (p. 1893)
—What Shapes the Land? (p. 1893)
—What Time Is It? (p. 1894)
—When I Am Happy. (p. 1902)
—Where Am I? (p. 1906)
—Where Do Animals Live? (p. 1906)
—Where Does Our Food Come From? (p. 1907)
—Where Is It? (p. 1908)
—Where on Earth Are Deserts? (p. 1909)
—Where on Earth Are Forests? (p. 1909)
—Where on Earth Are Mountains? (p. 1909)
—Where on Earth Are Rivers? (p. 1909)
—Which Season Is It? (p. 1911)
—Who Am I? (p. 1914)
—Why & Where Are Animals Endangered? (p. 1922)
—Why Do Animals Become Extinct? (p. 1923)
—Why Do Animals Migrate? (p. 1923)
—Wild & Pet Puppies. (p. 1928)
—Wonderful Whales. (p. 1948)
—Yo soy un Ser Vivo. (p. 1971)
—Yo soy un ser Vivo. (p. 1971)
—¿Cómo Encuentran Alimento los Animales? (p. 350)
—¿Cómo Se Esconden los Animales? (p. 351)
—¿Cómo Se Mueve? (p. 351)
—¿Como Se Siente Al Tocarlo? (p. 351)
—¿Cómo se siente al Tocarlo? (p. 351)
—¿De Qué Color Es? (p. 416)
—¿Donde Esta? (p. 466)
—¿Dónde Está? (p. 466)
—¿Dónde Estoy? (p. 466)
—¿Dónde Viven Los Animales? (p. 466)
—¿Es Grande O Pequeño? (p. 534)
—¿Es Igual O Diferente? (p. 534)
—¿Esto Es un Ser Vivo? (p. 538)
—¿Qué Aspecto Tiene? (p. 1423)
—¿Qué Es el Ciclo de Vida? (p. 1423)
—¿Qué Es el Tiempo? (p. 1423)
—¿Qué Forma Tiene? (p. 1423)
—¿Qué forma Tiene? (p. 1423)
—¿Qué Hacen Estos Animales? (p. 1423)
—¿Qué le Da Forma a la Tierra? (p. 1424)
—¿Qué Necesito? (p. 1424)
—¿Qué Sigue? (p. 1424)
—¿Qué Son Las Estructuras Naturales? (p. 1424)
—¿Qué Son Las Plantas? (p. 1424)
—¿Qué Son Las Redes y Cadenas Alimentarias? (p. 1424)
—¿Qué Son los Biomas? (p. 1424)
—¿Qué Son los Reptiles? (p. 1424)
—¿Qué Son los Seres Vivos? (p. 1424)
Kalman, Bobbie, jt. auth. see Aloian, Molly.
Kalman, Bobbie, jt. auth. see Bishop, Amanda.
Kalman, Bobbie, jt. auth. see Crossingham, John.
Kalman, Bobbie, jt. auth. see Dyer, Hadley.
Kalman, Bobbie, jt. auth. see Johnson, Robin.
Kalman, Bobbie, jt. auth. see Lundblad, Kristina.
Kalman, Bobbie, jt. auth. see MacAulay, Kelley.
Kalman, Bobbie, jt. auth. see McAuley, Kelly.
Kalman, Bobbie, jt. auth. see Nickles, Greg.
Kalman, Bobbie, jt. auth. see Sjonger, Rebecca.
Kalman, Bobbie, jt. auth. see Smithyman, Kathryn.
Kalman, Bobbie, jt. auth. see Walker, Niki.
Kalman, Bobbie & Aloian, Molly. Autos de Carrera: Enciendan Sus Motores! (p. 117)
—Ciclo de Vida de Los Insectos. (p. 319)
—Ciclo de Vida de los Insectos. (p. 319)
—Cuerpo de Los Insectos. (p. 390)
—Cuerpo de los Insectos. (p. 390)
—Famous Native North Americans. (p. 569)
—Insectos Que Trabajan en Equipo. (p. 875)
—Insectos Utiles y Daninos. (p. 875)
—Océans Polaires. (p. 1277)
—Polar Oceans. (p. 1379)
—Spectacular Sharks. (p. 1624)
—Tiburones Espectaculares. (p. 1747)
—Underground Habitats. (p. 1814)
—Volcanoes on Earth. (p. 1849)
Kalman, Bobbie & Bishop, Amanda. Ciclo de Vida Del León. (p. 319)
—Félins. (p. 581)
—Life in a Pueblo. (p. 1010)
—Nations of the Southwest. (p. 1234)
—Terres Humides. (p. 1721)
Kalman, Bobbie & Burns, Kylie. Cadenas Alimentarias de los Pantanos. (p. 250)
—Endangered Bears. (p. 526)
—Wetland Food Chains. (p. 1877)
Kalman, Bobbie & Crossingham, John. Baloncesto Espectacular. (p. 135)
—Batter up Baseball. (p. 145)
—Extreme Climbing. (p. 556)
—Extreme Motocross. (p. 556)
—Extreme Skydiving. (p. 557)
—Extreme Sports. (p. 557)
—Fútbol para Patear. (p. 651)
—Gymnastique. (p. 734)
—Habitats Terrestres. (p. 735)
—Hábitats Terrestres. (p. 735)
—Hogares de los Insectos. (p. 787)
—Huddle up Football. (p. 824)
—Insect Homes. (p. 875)
—Kick It Soccer. (p. 951)
—Land Habitats. (p. 973)
—Life Cycle of a Raccoon. Bedell, Barbara, illus. (p. 1009)
—Ours. (p. 1310)
—Phoques et les Otaries. Briere, Marie-Josee, tr. from ENG. (p. 1352)
—Slam Dunk Basketball. (p. 1587)
—Trabajo en Equipo en el Fútbol Americano. (p. 1774)
Kalman, Bobbie & Dyer, Hadley. Australian Outback Food Chains. (p. 116)
—Chimpanzés. Briere, Marie-Josee, tr. from ENG. (p. 306)
—Endangered Chimpanzees. (p. 526)
—Endangered Manatees. (p. 526)
—Léopards. (p. 993)
—Savanes. (p. 1516)
—Savanna Food Chains. (p. 1516)
—Turno al bate en el Béisbol. (p. 1798)
Kalman, Bobbie & Jeffrey, Gary. Gallipoli & the Southern Theaters. (p. 653)
Kalman, Bobbie & Johnson, Robin. Ciclo de Vida Del Pinguino Emperador. (p. 319)
—Ciclo de Vida del Pinguino Emperador. (p. 319)
—Endangered Butterflies. (p. 526)
—Endangered Penguins. (p. 527)
—Koalas & Other Marsupials. (p. 966)
—Koalas et Autres Marsupiaux. (p. 966)
—Life Cycle of an Emperor Penguin. (p. 1009)
—Life Cylce of an Emperor Penguin. (p. 1010)
—Manchots. (p. 1087)
—Spotlight on Australia. (p. 1634)
Kalman, Bobbie & Langille, Jacqueline. Mammiferes Marins. (p. 1085)
—?Que Son los Anfibios? (p. 1424)
—Rongeurs. (p. 1487)
—¿Qué Es el Ciclo de Vida? (p. 1423)
—¿Qué Son los Anfibios? (p. 1424)
Kalman, Bobbie & Larin, Allison. Poissons. Briere, Marie-Josee, tr. from ENG. (p. 1377)
Kalman, Bobbie & Levigne, Heather. Chauves-Souris. (p. 295)
—Primates. (p. 1400)
—Que es un Caballo? (p. 1423)
—¿Qué Es un Caballo? (p. 1423)
—¿Qué Son los Murciélagos? (p. 1424)
Kalman, Bobbie & Lundblad, Kristina. Animales Llamados Mamiferos. (p. 81)
—Animals Called Mammals. (p. 82)
—Endangered Bats. (p. 526)
—Endangered Mountain Gorillas. (p. 527)
—Mammifères. (p. 1085)
Kalman, Bobbie & MacAulay, Kelley. Cadenas Alimentarias del Desierto. (p. 250)
—Changing Seasons. (p. 290)
—Cobayos. Crabtree, Marc, photos by. (p. 336)
—Cochons D'Inde. (p. 337)
—Desert Food Chains. (p. 429)
—Earth & the Sun. (p. 495)
—Earth's Oceans. (p. 498)
—Extreme Snowboarding. (p. 557)
—Fantásticos Vehiculos Para la Construccion. (p. 572)
—Guinea Pigs. Crabtree, Marc, illus. (p. 731)
—Introducing Landforms. (p. 882)
—Karate in Action. (p. 943)
—Meadow Food Chains. (p. 1116)
—Surf des Neiges Extrême. (p. 1685)
Kalman, Bobbie & Macaulay, Kelly. Mers Tropicales. Briere, Marie-Josee, tr. from ENG. (p. 1129)
Kalman, Bobbie & Miller, Reagan. Cochons D'Inde et Autres Rongeurs. (p. 337)
Kalman, Bobbie & Sjonger, Rebecca. Amazing Octopus. (p. 55)
—Animal Life Cycles: Growing & Changing. (p. 78)
—Ciclo del Agua. (p. 319)
—Cycle de L'eau. Briere, Marie-Josee, tr. from ENG. (p. 396)
—écrevisses. (p. 503)
—Everyday Insects. (p. 543)
—Explore Africa. (p. 550)
—Explore Antarctica. (p. 550)
—Explore Asia. (p. 550)
—Explore Australia & Oceania. (p. 550)
—Habitat de Sabana. (p. 734)
—Insect Defenses. (p. 875)
—Insectos Comunes. (p. 875)
—L'Afrique. (p. 971)
—L'Antarctique. (p. 975)
—Las Plantas de Distintos Habitats. (p. 977)
—L'Asie. (p. 977)
—Life Cycle of a Crayfish. (p. 1009)
—Life Cycle of a Salmon. (p. 1009)
—Life in the Far North. (p. 1011)
—L'Océanie. (p. 1044)
—Metamorphosis: Changing Bodies. (p. 1130)
—Photosynthesis: Changing Sunlight into Food. (p. 1353)
—Plants in Different Habitats. (p. 1370)
—Saumons. Briere, Marie-Josee, tr. from ENG. (p. 1516)
—Savanna Habitat. (p. 1516)
—Water Cycle. (p. 1862)
Kalman, Bobbie & Smithyman, Kathryn. Araignées. (p. 94)
—Ciclo de Vida de la Araña. (p. 318)
—Ciclo de Vida de la Rana. Rouse, Bonna, illus. (p. 319)
—Foret. (p. 618)
—Grenouilles. Briere, Marie-Josee, tr. from ENG. (p. 723)
—Vie des Oiseaux. Briere, Marie-Josee, tr. from ENG. (p. 1841)
Kalman, Bobbie & Sotzek, Hannelore. ¿Que Es un Perro? (p. 1423)
—¿Qué Es un Perro? (p. 1423)
Kalman, Bobbie & Thal, Karuna. Rorquals. (p. 1488)
Kalman, Bobbie & Walker, Niki. Conoce los Estados Unidos de América. (p. 358)
—Conoce México. (p. 358)
—Spotlight on Mexico. (p. 1634)
—Spotlight on the United States of America. (p. 1634)
Kalman, Bobbie, et al. Arbres. (p. 95)
—Autos de Carrera: ¡enciendan Sus Motores! (p. 117)
—Koalas. (p. 966)
—Loups. (p. 1059)
—Pieuvres. (p. 1357)
—Requins. (p. 1462)
—Turno al Bate en el Béisbol. (p. 1798)
Kalman, Esther. Tchaikovski Descubre America. (p. 1708)
Kalman, Israel. How to Stop Being Teased & Bullied Without Really Trying (p. 821)
Kalman, Izzy C. Bullies to Buddies - How to Turn Your Enemies into Friends! How to Turn Your Enemies into Friends! Kalman, Lola, illus. (p. 240)
Kalman, Lola, illus. see Kalman, Izzy C.
Kalman, Maira. Ah-Ha to Zig-Zag: 31 Objects from Cooper Hewitt, Smithsonian Design Museum. (p. 30)
—Fireboat: The Heroic Adventures of John J. Harvey. (p. 591)
—Fireboat: The Heroic Adventures of the John J. Harvey. Kalman, Maira, illus. (p. 591)
—Looking at Lincoln. Kalman, Maira, illus. (p. 1051)
—Smartypants: Pete in School. (p. 1593)
—Smartypants (Pete in School) Kalman, Maira, illus. (p. 1593)
—Thomas Jefferson: Life, Liberty & the Pursuit of Everything. Kalman, Maira, illus. (p. 1739)
—What Pete Ate from A to Z. (p. 1892)
Kalman, Maira, illus. see Handler, Daniel.
Kalman, Maira, illus. see Snicket, Lemony, pseud.
Kalmanovitz, Manuel, tr. see Stewart, Mark.
Kalmbach, Nicole. Lilly J, What Did I Say? (p. 1017)
Kalmenoff, Matthew, illus. see Bosco, Antoinette.
Kalmenoff, Matthew, illus. see Wright, A. Gilbert.
Kalna-Dubinyuk, Arynova, jt. auth. see Yespolov, Johnson.
Kalnes, Stephanie, creator. Viking Adventure: History-in-a-Box-Board-Game (p. 1842)
Kalodner, Cynthia R. Too Fat or Too Thin? A Reference Guide to Eating Disorders (p. 1766)
Kalomas, Alice & Kerr, Lenora. Sir Wrinkles. Utomo, Gabhor, illus. (p. 1580)
—Sir Wrinkles Goes to School. Utomo, Gabhor, illus. (p. 1580)
Kalpart, illus. see Davis, Melissa.
Kalpart, illus. see Prignano, Barbara.
Kalpart, illus. see Risselada, Melissa.
Kalpart Designs, illus. see Alexander, Carol.
Kalpish Ratna. Nyagrodha. Pandya, Yamini, illus. (p. 1274)
Kaltenborn, Karl, illus. see McGee, Helen.
Kaltenhauser, Bettina & van Swol-Ulbrich, Hilly. When Abroad - Do As the Local Children Do: Ori's Guide for Young Expats. (p. 1901)
Kalthoff, Robert. Viking Life. (p. 1842)
Kaltovich, Edith Rusconi. Adventures of Juan, the Fox: Argentine Tales & Fables. (p. 19)
Kalvitis, David. Greatest Dot-to-Dot Book in the World (p. 719)
—Greatest Dot-to-Dot Super Challenge Book 5 (p. 719)
—Greatest Dot-to-Dot Super Challenge Book 6. (p. 719)
—Greatest Newspaper Dot-to-Dot! Puzzles (p. 720)
—Greatest Newspaper Dot-to-Dot! Puzzles: Volume 5. (p. 720)
—Greatest Newspaper Dot-to-Dot! Puzzles: Volume 6. (p. 720)
Kalvitis, David R. Greatest Dot-to-Dot Super Challenge Book 8. (p. 719)
—Greatest Newspaper Dot-to-Dot Puzzles (p. 720)
—Greatest Newspaper Dot-To-Dot Puzzles, Vol. 1 (p. 720)
Kalvoda, LeAnn, illus. see Holmes, Wayne & Pelletier, Christine.
Kalvoda, Mike. Piper. Gregory, Raven & Kolasinski, Ken, eds. (p. 1361)
Kalyan, Srivi, illus. see Rajan, Vithal.
Kalz, Jill. Amusement Park Adventure. Cerato, Mattia, illus. (p. 66)
—Christmas Chaos: Hidden Picture Puzzles Yamasaki, James, illus. (p. 313)
—Colors. Banks, Timothy, illus. (p. 344)
—Dairy Products. (p. 400)
—Dolphins. (p. 464)
—Eagles. (p. 492)
—Fall. (p. 566)
—Farm Adventure. Cerato, Mattia, illus. (p. 573)
—Fire Station. (p. 591)
—Fruits. (p. 645)
—Giraffes. (p. 677)
—Grains. (p. 706)
—Halloween Hide & Seek: Hidden Picture Puzzles Borlasca, Hector, illus. (p. 737)
—I Hate to Read: Belle Pepper. (p. 839)
—Loons. (p. 1052)
—Meats & Protein. (p. 1118)
—Mona Lisa. (p. 1163)
—Mount Everest. (p. 1180)
—My First Arabic Phrases TransPerfect Translations Staff, tr. (p. 1204)
—My First French Phrases Translations.com Staff, tr. (p. 1206)
—My First Japanese Phrases TransPerfect Translations Staff, tr. (p. 1207)
—My First Mandarin Chinese Phrases Translations.com Staff, tr. (p. 1207)
—My First Mandarin Chinese Phrases Advocate-Art Staff & Translations.com Staff, trs. (p. 1207)
—My First Russian Phrases TransPerfect Translations Staff, tr. (p. 1207)
—My First Spanish Phrases Translations.com Staff, tr. (p. 1208)
—My First Spanish Phrases Advocate-Art Staff & Translations.com Staff, trs. (p. 1208)
—No Snow for Christmas Erkocak, Sahin, illus. (p. 1260)
—Northern Lights. (p. 1266)
—Out-Of-This-World Aliens: Hidden Picture Puzzles Smith, Simon, illus. (p. 1311)
—Parrots. (p. 1325)
—Pretty Princess Party: Hidden Picture Puzzles Epstein, Len & Pullan, Jack, illus. (p. 1398)
—Robins. (p. 1480)
—School Adventure. Cerato, Mattia, illus. (p. 1522)
—School Shake-Up: Hidden Picture Puzzles Holgate, Douglas, illus. (p. 1523)
—Seek It Out. Epstein, Len & Smith, Simon, illus. (p. 1548)
—Seek It Out. Smith, Simon & Epstein, Len, illus. (p. 1548)
—Spring. (p. 1634)
—Summer. (p. 1673)
—Tuckerbean Mahan, Benton, illus. (p. 1795)
—Tuckerbean at the Movies Mahan, Benton, illus. (p. 1795)
—Tuckerbean in the Kitchen Mahan, Benton, illus. (p. 1795)
—Tuckerbean on the Moon Mahan, Benton, illus. (p. 1795)
—Vegetables. (p. 1834)
—Victoria Falls. (p. 1840)
—Water. (p. 1862)
—Winter. (p. 1937)
—Woodpeckers. (p. 1949)
—Zoo Adventure. Cerato, Mattia, illus. (p. 1988)
—Zoo Hideout: Hidden Picture Puzzles Smith, Simon & Chiacchiera, Moreno, illus. (p. 1989)
Kalz, Jill, jt. auth. see Gray-Wilburn, Renée.
Kalz, Jill, jt. auth. see Mayesky.
Kalz, Jill, jt. auth. see Rustad, Martha E. H.
Kalz, Jill, jt. auth. see Skog, Jason.
Kam, Jennifer Wolf. Devin Rhodes Is Dead. (p. 432)
Kam, Kathleen, illus. see Lum, Leimomi o. Kamahae Kuamoo Mookini.
Kamachi, Kazuma. Certain Magical Index. Haimura, Kiyotaka, illus. (p. 287)
Kamalei, A. Me Thinks I See Strange Things. (p. 1116)
Kamat Tarkar, Poorwa Yeshwant. Cornelius Sign: & the Season Queen Business (p. 367)
Kamata, Suzanne. Gadget Girl: The Art of Being Invisible. (p. 652)
—Screaming Divas. (p. 1533)
Kamatani, Yuhki, creator. Nabari No Ou. (p. 1227)
Kamateros, Litsa & Morfonios, Nia. Sarah's Socks: My World of Autism. (p. 1514)
Kamau, G. How Porcupine Got His Spines. (p. 812)
—Why Beetles Roll Cowdung. (p. 1922)
Kambadais, George, illus. see Deneen, Brendan.
Kamberg, Mary-Lane. Bono: Fighting World Hunger & Poverty. (p. 209)
—Bono Fighting World Hunger & Poverty. (p. 209)
—Career As an Athletic Trainer. (p. 266)
—Evan Williams, Biz Stone, Jack Dorsey, & Twitter. (p. 540)
—Frequently Asked Questions about Financial Literacy. (p. 636)
—Getting a Job in Law Enforcement, Security, & Corrections. (p. 668)
—I Have Been Bullied—Now What? (p. 839)
—Kawasaki: World's Fastest Bike. (p. 946)
—Margaret Peterson Haddix. (p. 1092)
—North Carolina Basketball. (p. 1265)
—Saltwater Fishing. (p. 1506)
—Special Ops: Snipers (p. 1623)
—Sports Concussions. (p. 1632)
—Stephen Hawking. (p. 1648)
—Teen Pregnancy & Motherhood. (p. 1713)
—Truth about Heroin: World's Fastest Bike. (p. 1794)
—Working As a Mechanic in Your Community. (p. 1952)
Kamerer, Justin, illus. see Martin, Michael & Martin, Michael J.
Kamerling, Yvonne. TLC for Teenagers & their Parents: Inspirational Quotes, Poetry, Touching Stories. (p. 1758)
Kames, Lord, jt. auth. see Home, Henry.
Kami, Y. Z., illus. see Bronn, Charles Heil.
Kamijyo, Akimine. Samurai Deeper Kyo (p. 1509)
—Samurai Deeper Kyo Forbes, Jake T., ed. (p. 1509)
—Samurai Deeper Kyo Kamijyo, Akimine, illus. (p. 1509)
—Samurai Deeper Kyo Smith, Alexander O., tr. from JPN. (p. 1509)
Kamijyo, Akimine & Akimine, Kamijyo. Samurai Deeper Kyo (p. 1509)
Kamijyo, Akimine, creator. Samurai Deeper Kyo (p. 1509)
Kamin, Rachel & The Association of Jewish Libraries Staff. 2011 Sydney Taylor Book Award: Quest for the Best. (p. 2003)
Kaminker, Laura. Everything You Need to Know about Dealing with Sexual Assault. (p. 545)
Kamins, Julie Firstenberg. Why Am I at the Red Table? Long, Carlos, illus. (p. 1922)
Kaminski, Heide A. W. ADHD & ME: Activity Book for Exploring Childhood ADHD. (p. 12)
Kaminski, Karol, illus. see Ashour, Monica.
Kaminski, Karol, illus. see Monchamp, Genny.
Kaminski, Karol, illus. see Schmauss, Judy Kentor.
Kaminski, Karol, jt. illus. see Williams, Ted.
Kaminski, Mary. Raising Reptiles: Divide Within 100. (p. 1437)
Kaminski, Tom. Miss Olivia, the Little Red Poodle: Her First Big Adventure. Fallon, Lisa, illus. (p. 1151)
Kaminsky, Jef, illus. see Mahoney, Daniel J.
Kaminsky, Jef, illus. see McAnulty, Stacy.
Kaminsky, Jeff. Poppy & Ella. (p. 1385)
Kaminsky, Kristy & Domboski, Brian. Ashlee & Jessica Simpson. (p. 106)
Kaminsky, Marty. Uncommon Champions: Fifteen Athletes Who Battled Back. (p. 1812)
Kamio, Yoko. Boys over Flowers (p. 220)
—Boys over Flowers Kamio, Yoko, illus. (p. 220)
—Boys over Flowers: Volume 4. Kamio, Yoko, illus. (p. 220)
—Boys over Flowers. Kamio, Yoko, illus. (p. 220)
—Hana Yori Dango. (p. 740)
—Hana Yori Dango. Kamio, Yoko, illus. (p. 740)
Kamisar, Yale, jt. auth. see Hook, Sue Vander.
Kamke, Bridget. Story of the Infinipede. Ospital, Geneveive, illus. (p. 1661)
Kamkwamba, William, jt. auth. see Mealer, Bryan.
Kamkwamba, William & Mealer, Bryan. Boy Who Harnessed the Wind. Zunon, Elizebeth, illus. (p. 219)
Kamma, Anne. If You Lived at the Time of Squanto. Johnson, Pamela Ford, illus. (p. 854)
—If You Lived When There Was Slavery in America. Johnson, Pamela, illus. (p. 854)
—If You Lived When Women Won Their Rights. Johnson, Pamela, illus. (p. 854)
—If You Lived with the Hopi. (p. 854)
—If You Lived with the Indians of the Northwest Coast. (p. 854)
Kammeraad, Kevin. Tomato Collection. (p. 1764)
Kammeraad, Kevin & Kammeraad, Stephanie. Curious Glimpse of Michigan. Kammeraad, Kevin & Hipp, Ryan, illus. (p. 394)
Kammeraad, Stephanie, jt. auth. see Kammeraad, Kevin.
Kammerer, Heitiare. Pa'a Pono. (p. 1316)
Kamofonas, Mary Katherine. In the Doghouse. (p. 865)
Kamon. Hooty & the Magic Power. Krit, Joey, illus. (p. 796)

K

—Playtoon & the Antpod. Krit, Joey, illus. (p. 1373)
Kampakis, Kari. 10 Ultimate Truths Girls Should Know (p. 1994)
Kampff, Joseph. Beyonce: Singer, Songwriter, & Actress. (p. 173)
—Erie Canal: Joining the Hudson River & Lake Erie. (p. 533)
—Louis Sachar. (p. 1058)
—Walt Disney. (p. 1855)
—What Are Weather Instruments? (p. 1880)
—What Degree Do I Need to Pursue a Career in Education? (p. 1881)
Kampia, Judy. God's Great Book: A Complete Collection of Bible Stories & Activities for All Ages. (p. 691)
Kampman, Marcella. Inanna, Goddess of Love: Great Myths & Legends from Sumer. (p. 868)
Kamuro, Koreaki. Hanky Panky. (p. 742)
Kanaan. Literati: A Revolution of Living. (p. 1023)
Kanady, Mary Ellen Murdock. Mommy & Me. (p. 1162)
Kanae, Billy, illus. see Markrich, Mike & Bourke, Bob.
Kanagy, Audrey Ann Zimmerman, illus. see Stoltzfus, Sherman Matthew.
Kanagy, Jeremy. Making of a King. (p. 1082)
Kanai, P'ninah and Kari. Welcome to Kanoo Zoo! (p. 1873)
Kanako, illus. see Horowitz, Anthony & Johnston, Antony.
Kanako, illus. see Horowitz, Anthony.
Kananen, Barbara L. Fairies in My Garden. (p. 563)
Kanarek, Michael, illus. see Corrado, Diane.
Kanary, Robert. How Tortoise Helped Jack Rabbit Win Too: A Read Out Loud Story Book for Adults & Children. (p. 823)
—How Tortoise Helped Jack Rabbit Win Too. (p. 823)
Kanata, Konami. Chi's Sweet Home. (p. 308)
—Chi's Sweet Home 11. (p. 308)
Kandel, Megan. Let's Celebrate Ohio. (p. 995)
Kander, Beth & Kenyon, Bret. Glubbery Gray, the Knight-Eating Beast Labbé, Jesse, illus. (p. 685)
Kandimba, V. T. Folktales from Zimbabwe: Short Stores. (p. 611)
Kandimba, Vt. Folk Tales from Zimbabwe. (p. 611)
Kandinsky, Wassily. Concerning the Spiritual in Art (p. 355)
Kane, Barbara, jt. auth. see Chorba, April.
Kane, Barbara, ed. Paper Stained Glass: Color-by-Number Art for Your Windows. (p. 1323)
Kane, Barry, photos by see Kane, Tracy.
Kane, Barry & Kane, Tracy. Fairy Houses ... Everywhere! (p. 563)
Kane, Bob. Batman in the Sixties. Khan, Jenette, ed. (p. 144)
—Comic con & Labor Day. Nguyen, Dustin, illus. (p. 348)
—Month of Waters & Independence Day. Nguyen, Dustin, illus. (p. 1170)
—Sandwich Day & Our Family Album. Nguyen, Dustin, illus. (p. 1511)
—Tropical Getaway & Bird Watching. Nguyen, Dustin, illus. (p. 1789)
Kane, Bob & DC Comics Staff, creators. Batman: The Greatest Stories Ever Told. (p. 144)
Kane, Bob, creator. Batman: War Games Outbreak- Act 1. (p. 144)
—Batman in the Forties. (p. 144)
Kane, Brenden, illus. see Hartley, Susan.
Kane, Brian. Jazz Style & Technique for All Treble Clef Instruments. (p. 911)
—Singing Tongue Twisters A-Z: Fifty Fun Filled Wacky Warm-ups to Improve Pronunciation, Vocal Range, & Technique. (p. 1579)
Kane, Brian J. Creative Jazz Sight Reading. (p. 379)
—Jazz Style & Technique for Saxophone. (p. 911)
Kane, Christy. Tales of the Sisters Kane. (p. 1703)
Kane, Darlene. Missing Hannah: Based on a True Story of Sudden Infant Death. (p. 1152)
Kane, Doug. Ariel's Journey. (p. 98)
Kane, Gil, illus. see Lee, Stan.
Kane, Gil, jt. illus. see Andru, Ross.
Kane, Gil, et al. Thor Epic Collection: A Kingdom Lost. (p. 1739)
Kane, Gillian. Witch Who Liked to Wear Pink. Povey, Andrea, illus. (p. 1941)
Kane, Herb K., jt. illus. see Feher, Joseph.
Kane, James. Tom & Katie's Greatest Adventure. (p. 1762)
Kane, John, photos by see Pilobolus.
Kane, Karen. Chimpanzees. Ellis, Gerry, illus. (p. 306)
Kane, Kim. Esther's Rainbow. Acton, Sara, illus. (p. 538)
—Family Forest. Masciullo, Lucia, illus. (p. 568)
Kane, Kimberly Brougham. Every Time You Call Me Mommy-an Adoption Blessing. (p. 543)
Kane, Kristen. K Is for Keystone: A Pennsylvania Alphabet. Knorr, Laura, illus. (p. 941)
Kane, Linda Lee. Matty's Adventures in Numberland. (p. 1110)
Kane, P. B. & Kane, Paul. Rainbow Man. (p. 1435)
Kane, Paul, jt. auth. see Kane, P. B.
Kane, Sharon. Kitty & Me. Kane, Sharon, illus. (p. 963)
—Little Mommy. Kane, Sharon, illus. (p. 1032)
Kane, Tim. Monster Mega Trucks: ... & Other Four-Wheeled Creatures. (p. 1167)
Kane, Tracy. Fairy Houses & Beyond! Kane, Barry, photos by. (p. 563)
—Fairy Houses Trilogy. (p. 563)
—Magic of Color. Kane, Tracy, illus. (p. 1073)
Kane, Tracy, jt. auth. see Kane, Barry.
Kaneda, Mario. Girls Bravo. (p. 679)
—Girls Bravo Kaneda, Mario, illus. (p. 679)
Kanefield, Teri. Girl from the Tar Paper School: Barbara Rose Johns & the Advent of the Civil Rights Movement. (p. 678)
—Guilty? Crime, Punishment, & the Changing Face of Justice. (p. 730)
Kaneko, Amanda Bullard. Darza the Little Dragon. Hildebrandt, Lowell, illus. (p. 409)
Kaneko, Shinya. Culdcept Kaneko, Shinya, illus. (p. 390)
Kanekuni, Daniel, illus. see Ide, Laurie Shimizu.
Kanell, Beth, jt. auth. see Dugger, Elizabeth L.
Kanellos, Nicolás. Mexican American Theatre: Then & Now. (p. 1130)
Kanemitsu, Dan, tr. see Shigeno, Suichi.
Kanemoto, Dan, illus. see Silverhardt, Lauryn.
Kaner, Etta. And the Winner Is... Amazing Animal Athletes. Anderson, David, illus. (p. 71)
—Animal Groups: How Animals Live Together. Stephens, Pat, illus. (p. 78)
—Animals Migrating: How, When, Where & Why Animals Migrate. Stephens, Pat, illus. (p. 83)
—Earth-Friendly Buildings, Bridges & More: The Eco-Journal of Corry Lapont. MacEachern, Stephen, illus. (p. 496)
—Friend or Foe: The Whole Truth about Animals People Love to Hate. Anderson, David, illus. (p. 637)
—Have You Ever Seen a Duck in a Raincoat? Szuc, Jeff, illus. (p. 754)
—Have You Ever Seen a Hippo with Sunscreen? Szuc, Jeff, illus. (p. 754)
—Have You Ever Seen a Stork Build a Log Cabin? Szuc, Jeff, illus. (p. 754)
—Have You Ever Seen an Octopus with a Broom? Szuc, Jeff, illus. (p. 754)
—How Animals Defend Themselves. Stephens, Pat, illus. (p. 804)
—Who Likes the Rain? Lafrance, Marie, illus. (p. 1916)
—Who Likes the Snow? Lafrance, Marie, illus. (p. 1916)
—Who Likes the Sun? Lafrance, Marie, illus. (p. 1916)
—Who Likes the Wind? Lafrance, Marie, illus. (p. 1916)
—Word Catchers for Reading & Spelling. (p. 1950)
Kanesata, Yukio, illus. see Takemoto, Novala.
Kaneshiro, Scott, illus. see Armitage, Kimo.
Kanevsky, Polly. Here Is the Baby. Yoo, Taeeun, illus. (p. 770)
—Sleepy Boy. Anderson, Stephanie, illus. (p. 1589)
Kaneyoshi, Izumi. Doubt!! (p. 473)
—Doubt!! Kaneyoshi, Izumi, illus. (p. 473)
Kanfush, Philip M. Emma's Wetlands Adventure: The Story of the Monastery Run Impovement Project Wetlands at Saint Vincent. (p. 520)
Kang, Andrea, illus. see Hutton, John.
Kang, Hildi. Chengli & the Silk Road Caravan. (p. 297)
Kang, Lydia. Catalyst. (p. 278)
—Control. (p. 361)
Kang, Mi-Sun. Lazy Man/the Spring of Youth. (p. 981)
—Snail Lady/the Magic Vase. (p. 1596)
Kang, Mi-Sun, jt. illus. see Kim, Yon-Kyong.
Kang, Mi-Sun & Kim, Yon-Kyong. Brave Hong Gil-Dong/the Man Who Bought the Shade of a Tree. (p. 223)
—Faithful Daughter Sim Cheong/the Little Frog Who Never Listened. (p. 565)
Kang, Morim. 10, 20, & 30 (p. 1993)
Kang, Setha, jt. auth. see Kimmel, Eric A.
Kang Won, Kim. Invu Na, Lauren, tr. from KOR. (p. 886)
—Queen's Knight Kang Won, Kim, illus. (p. 1425)
—Queen's Knight. (p. 1425)
Kangira, Jairos. Creatures Great & Small: A Collection of Short Stories. (p. 380)
Kania, Matt, illus. see Peterson, Sheryl.
Kaniecki, Larry. Ho Ho the Elf. (p. 786)
Kanietzko, Bryan. Avatar: The Last Airbender. Vol. 2 (p. 118)
Kanietzko, Bryan & Dante DiMartino, Michael. Avatar: The Last Airbender. (p. 118)
Kanietzko, Bryan & Dimartino, Michael Dante. Avatar. (p. 118)
Kanietzko, Bryan & DiMartino, Michael Dante, creators. Avatar: the Last Airbender: Volume 6. (p. 118)
Kanigher, Bob & Kubert, Joe. Enemy Ace Archives (p. 527)
Kanigher, Robert. Sgt. Rock. (p. 1556)
—War That Time Forgot. (p. 1858)
Kanigher, Robert, jt. auth. see Haney, Bob.
Kanigher, Robert & Broome, John. Flash. Infantino, Carmine & Giella, Joe, illus. (p. 602)
Kanitsch, Christine, illus. see Williams, Jonnie.
Kaniut, Larry, ed. Tales from the Edge: True Adventures in Alaska. (p. 1701)
Kanji, Sheneeza. Amazing Canadian Kids! What They're Doing to Make A Difference & How You Can Too! (p. 54)
Kankey, Andrew T. Penelope & Mrs Grace: A Swine Mystery. (p. 1336)
Kann, Alice G. Tales from Time & Beyond the Stars (p. 1702)
Kann, Bob. Belle & Bob la Follette: Partners in Politics. (p. 162)
—Cordelia Harvey: Civil War Angel. (p. 366)
—Recipe for Success: Lizzie Kander & Her Cookbook. (p. 1451)
Kann, Elizabeth, jt. auth. see Kann, Victoria.
Kann, Rachel. 10 for Everythin: Redux. (p. 1993)
Kann, Victoria. Aqualicious. Kann, Victoria, illus. (p. 93)
—Cherry Blossom. (p. 298)
—Cherry Blossom. Kann, Victoria, illus. (p. 298)
—Crazy Hair Day. (p. 377)
—Emeraldalicious. Kann, Victoria, illus. (p. 518)
—Fairy House. (p. 563)
—Fairy House. Kann, Victoria, illus. (p. 563)
—Flower Girl. (p. 607)
—Flower Girl. Kann, Victoria, illus. (p. 607)
—Goldidoodles. Kann, Victoria, illus. (p. 695)
—Goldilicious. Kann, Victoria, illus. (p. 696)
—Love, Pinkalicious. Kann, Victoria, illus. (p. 1060)
—Merry Pinkmas! Kann, Victoria, illus. (p. 1129)
—Mother's Day Surprise. Kann, Victoria, illus. (p. 1178)
—Perfectly Pink Collection. Kann, Victoria, illus. (p. 1342)
—Pink of Hearts. Kann, Victoria, illus. (p. 1360)
—Pink or Treat! (p. 1360)
—Pink or Treat! Kann, Victoria, illus. (p. 1360)
—Pinkadoodles. Kann, Victoria, illus. (p. 1360)
—Pinkafy Your World. Kann, Victoria, illus. (p. 1360)
—Pinkalicious: School Rules! Kann, Victoria, illus. (p. 1360)
—Pinkalicious: The Pinkamazing Storybook Collection. (p. 1360)
—Pinkalicious: Crazy Hair Day. Kann, Victoria, illus. (p. 1360)
—Pinkalicious: Pinkie Promise. Kann, Victoria, illus. (p. 1360)
—Pinkalicious: The Royal Tea Party. Kann, Victoria, illus. (p. 1360)
—Pinkalicious: Pink Around the Rink. Kann, Victoria, illus. (p. 1360)
—Pinkalicious. Kann, Victoria, illus. (p. 1360)
—Pinkalicious & the Cupcake Calamity. (p. 1360)
—Pinkalicious & the Cupcake Calamity. Kann, Victoria, illus. (p. 1360)
—Pinkalicious & the New Teacher. Kann, Victoria, illus. (p. 1360)
—Pinkalicious & the Perfect Present. (p. 1360)
—Pinkalicious & the Perfect Present. Kann, Victoria, illus. (p. 1360)
—Pinkalicious & the Pink Drink. (p. 1360)
—Pinkalicious & the Pink Drink. Kann, Victoria, illus. (p. 1360)
—Pinkalicious & the Pink Parakeet. Kann, Victoria, illus. (p. 1360)
—Pinkalicious & the Pink Pumpkin. Kann, Victoria, illus. (p. 1360)
—Pinkalicious & the Pinkatastic Zoo Day. (p. 1360)
—Pinkalicious & the Pinkatastic Zoo Day. Kann, Victoria, illus. (p. 1360)
—Pinkalicious & the Sick Day. Kann, Victoria, illus. (p. 1360)
—Pinkalicious & the Snow Globe. Kann, Victoria, illus. (p. 1360)
—Pinkalicious - Cherry Blossom. Kann, Victoria, illus. (p. 1360)
—Pinkalicious Cupcake Cookbook. Kann, Victoria, illus. (p. 1360)
—Pinkalicious - Eggstraordinary Easter. Kann, Victoria, illus. (p. 1360)
—Pinkalicious - Puptastic! Kann, Victoria, illus. (p. 1360)
—Pinkalicious - Soccer Star. Kann, Victoria, illus. (p. 1360)
—Pinkalicious Take-Along Storybook Set. Kann, Victoria, illus. (p. 1360)
—Pinkalicious - Teeny Tiny Pinky Library (p. 1360)
—Pinkalicious - Thanksgiving Helper. Kann, Victoria, illus. (p. 1360)
—Pinkalicious - Tutu-Rrific! Kann, Victoria, illus. (p. 1360)
—Pink-a-Rama. Kann, Victoria, illus. (p. 1359)
—Pinkatastic Giant Sticker Book. Kann, Victoria, illus. (p. 1360)
—Pinkerrific Playdate. Kann, Victoria, illus. (p. 1360)
—Pinkie Promise. Kann, Victoria, illus. (p. 1360)
—Princess of Pink Slumber Party. (p. 1404)
—Princess of Pink Slumber Party. Kann, Victoria, illus. (p. 1404)
—Princess of Pink Treasury. Kann, Victoria, illus. (p. 1404)
—Puptastic! Kann, Victoria, illus. (p. 1418)
—Puptastic! (p. 1419)
—Purpledoodles. Kann, Victoria, illus. (p. 1419)
—Royal Tea Party. (p. 1492)
—School Lunch. Kann, Victoria, illus. (p. 1523)
—School Rules! Kann, Victoria, illus. (p. 1523)
—Silverlicious. Kann, Victoria, illus. (p. 1577)
—Soccer Star. (p. 1603)
—Soccer Star. Kann, Victoria, illus. (p. 1603)
—Tickled Pink. Kann, Victoria, illus. (p. 1747)
—Tutu-Rrific! (p. 1799)
Kann, Victoria & Kann, Elizabeth. Pinkalicious. Kann, Victoria, illus. (p. 1360)
—Purplicious. Kann, Victoria, illus. (p. 1419)
Kannenberg, Stacey. Let's Get Ready for First Grade! (p. 997)
—Let's Get Ready for Kindergarten! (p. 997)
—Let's Get Ready for Kindergarten! Spanish/English Edition. Sin Fronteras (Without Borders) et al, trs. (p. 997)
Kanner, Bernice. Are You Normal about Sex, Love, & Relationships? (p. 97)
Kanner, Robert. What Has a Pointed Head & Eats Lizards? Daff, Russ, illus. (p. 1886)
—What Has Armor & a Tail Club? Daff, Russ, illus. (p. 1886)
—What Weighs 70,000 Pounds & Swallows Stones? Daff, Russ, illus. (p. 1895)
Kanninen, Barbara. Atomic Energy. (p. 113)
—Story with Pictures. Reed, Lynn Rowe, illus. (p. 1663)
Kanno, Aya. Otomen. Kanno, Aya, illus. (p. 1307)
Kano, illus. see Rucka, Greg & Brubaker, Ed.
Kano, illus. see Spencer, Nick.
Kano, Ayumi. Sea View (Yaoi) (p. 1536)
Kano, Shiuko. Kiss All the Boys (p. 961)
—Priceless Honey. (p. 1398)
Kano, Shiuko, et al. Yakuza in Love Kano, Shiuko, illus. (p. 1968)
Kano, Yasuhiro. Pretty Face Kano, Yasuhiro, illus. (p. 1398)
Kansil, J. Q. Conversations with Opa: Sharing Wisdom about the Universe & Lesser Things. (p. 361)
Kant, Tanya. How a Caterpillar Grows into a Butterfly. Franklin, Carolyn, illus. (p. 804)
—How an Egg Grows into a Chicken. Franklin, Carolyn, illus. (p. 804)
—Migration of a Butterfly. Franklin, Carolyn, illus. (p. 1141)
—Migration of a Whale. Bergin, Mark, illus. (p. 1141)
Kantar, Andrew. Game Face. Keleher, Fran, illus. (p. 654)
Kantjas, Linda, illus. see Szymanski, Lois.
Kantjas, Linda, photos by see Szymanski, Lois.
Kantner, Seth. Pup & Pokey. Hill, Beth, illus. (p. 1417)
Kanto, Erik & Kanto, Ilona. Your Face Tells All: Learn the Wisdom of the Chinese Art of Face Reading. (p. 1980)
Kanto, Ilona, jt. auth. see Kanto, Erik.
Kantor, Melissa. Amanda Project. (p. 52)
—Better Than Perfect. (p. 172)
—If I Have a Wicked Stepmother, Where's My Prince? (p. 853)
—Maybe One Day. (p. 1113)
Kantor, Michael, et al. Broadway: The American Musical. (p. 230)
Kantor, Stuart. Call Me Collective. (p. 254)
Kantor, Stuart & Storey, William. Tao of Composition: The Eight-Fold Path to Analytical Enlightenment. (p. 1705)
Kantor, Susan, ed. Read-Aloud African-American Stories: 40 Selections from the World's Best-Loved Stories for Parent & Child to Share. (p. 1442)
Kantorek, Keith A. Soldier's Choice. (p. 1607)
Kantorovitz, Sylvie. Very Tiny Baby. (p. 1839)
—Very Tiny Baby. Kantorovitz, Sylvie, illus. (p. 1839)
—Zig & the Magic Umbrella. (p. 1986)
Kantorovitz, Sylvie, illus. see Hays, Anna Jane.
Kantrowitz, David. Reckless Faith. (p. 1451)
Kantrowitz, David, illus. see Pillsbury, Samuel H.
Kantrowitz, Joseph & Moran, Jeffrey B. Discovering Thermodynamics. (p. 450)
Kantz, Bill, illus. see Tompkins, Robyn Lee.
Kantz, John, illus. see Acosta, Robert.
Kanu, Rosslyn. Give Mommy Some Love. (p. 681)
—Little Girl Called Princess: Princess Where Are You? (p. 1028)
Kanut, Larry. Alaska's Fun Bears: Coloring & Activity Book Kanut, Larry, illus. (p. 34)
Kanyer, Laurie A. 25 Things to Do When Grandpa Passes Away, Mom & Dad Get Divorced, or the Dog Dies: Activities to Help Children Suffering Loss or Change. Williams, Jenny, illus. (p. 1996)
Kanzaka, Hajime. Silver Beast Araizumi, Rui, illus. (p. 1576)
—Slayers Araizumi, Rui, illus. (p. 1588)
—Slayers: The Sorcerer of Atlas Araizumi, Rui, illus. (p. 1588)
—Slayers: The Battle of Saillune Araizumi, Rui, illus. (p. 1588)
—Slayers - Vezendi's Shadow Araizumi, Rui, illus. (p. 1588)
Kanzaka, Hajime & Yoshinaka, Shoko. Super-Explosive Demon Story: Return (p. 1680)
—Super-Explosive Demon Story: City of Lost Souls (p. 1680)
Kanzaki, Masaomi. Street Fighter II - The Manga (p. 1666)
Kanzlemar, Joseph. Biblical Creation Authenticated. (p. 176)
—Biblical Creation Authenticated - Youth Edition. (p. 176)
Kanzler, Janine. Things Are Not As They Seem. (p. 1733)
Kanzler, John. Rock-a -Bye Baby. Tiger Tales Staff, ed. (p. 1481)
Kanzler, John, illus. see Asch, Frank & Asch, Frank.
Kanzler, John, illus. see Asch, Frank.
Kanzler, John, illus. see Bateman, Teresa.
Kanzler, John, illus. see Cooper, Ilene.
Kanzler, John, illus. see Hamilton, Martha & Weiss, Mitch.
Kanzler, John, illus. see Harrison, David L.
Kanzler, John, illus. see Hess, Nina.
Kanzler, John, illus. see Lofting, Hugh.
Kanzler, John, illus. see Stohs, Anita Reith.
Kanzler, John, tr. see Hess, Nina.
Kanzler, John, tr. see Stohs, Anita Reith.
Kanzler, John, jt. Big Rock Candy Mountain. (p. 183)
Kao, Sleepless. Duet. (p. 489)
—Monchan's Bag. (p. 1163)
Kao, Sleepless, illus. see Lolley, Sarah.
Kaopio, Matthew. Hawaiian Family Legends. (p. 755)
Kapal, Khyati. Express Yourself! Writing Persuasive Essays. (p. 555)
Kapai, Tommy. Cuzzies Find the Rainbow's End. Henry, Mike, illus. (p. 396)
—Cuzzies Meet the Motuhoa Shark. Henry, Mike, illus. (p. 396)
Kapaku, David. I Love You; I Love You More. (p. 843)
Kapart, illus. see Howard, Cheryl L.
Kapatos, Elizabeth, illus. see Outram, Richard.
Kapchinske, Pam. Hey Diddle Diddle: A Food Chain Tale Rogers, Sherry, illus. (p. 774)
Kapica, Dan. Mangrove Seed Chronicles: Learning to Trust. (p. 1087)
Kaplan, Amy. Well-Balanced Tale. (p. 1874)
Kaplan, Andrew. Marvelous Math Writing Prompts: 300 Engaging Prompts & Reproducible Pages That Motivate Kids to Write about Math - And Help You Meet the New NCTM Standards! (p. 1099)
Kaplan, Andrew & DeBold, Carol. Math on Call: A Mathematics Handbook. (p. 1106)
Kaplan, Arie. American Pop: Hit Makers, Superstars, & Dance Revolutionaries. (p. 62)
—Awesome Inner Workings of Video Games. (p. 121)
—Biggest Names of Video Games. (p. 185)
—Blogs: Finding Your Voice, Finding Your Audience. (p. 200)
—Brain-Boosting Benefits of Gaming. (p. 221)
—Dating & Relationships: Navigating the Social Scene. (p. 409)
—Dracula: The Life of Vlad the Impaler. (p. 476)
—Epic Evolution of Video Games. (p. 532)
—Gratitude. (p. 712)
—New Kid from Planet Glorf Bradley, Jessica, illus. (p. 1245)
—Social Intelligence. (p. 1604)
—Swashbuckling Scoundrels: Pirates in Fact & Fiction. (p. 1689)
Kaplan, Arie, jt. auth. see Shaw!, Scott.
Kaplan, Asli. What, Why & How? (p. 1895)
—What, Why, & How? (p. 1895)
Kaplan, Bruce Eric. Cousin Irv from Mars. Kaplan, Bruce Eric, illus. (p. 373)
—Meaniehead. Kaplan, Bruce Eric, illus. (p. 1116)
—Monsters Eat Whiny Children. Kaplan, Bruce Eric, illus. (p. 1169)
Kaplan, Coach Bobby. Bball Basics for Kids: A Basketball Handbook. (p. 147)
Kaplan, Debbie. Davie Learns a Lesson about Karma. (p. 411)
—Grandpa Went Away. (p. 709)
—When I Was Big. Osadchuk, Keit, illus. (p. 1903)
Kaplan, Dori, tr. see Gitchel, Sam & Foster, Lorri.
Kaplan, Elizabeth, jt. auth. see Brill, Marlene Targ.
Kaplan, Elizabeth, jt. auth. see Price-Groff, Claire.
Kaplan, Gisela T., jt. auth. see Rajendra, Vijeya.
Kaplan, Gloria. Ride the White Horse. (p. 1471)
Kaplan, Harold. Poetry, Politics, & Culture: Argument in the Work of Eliot, Pound, Stevens, & Williams. (p. 1376)
Kaplan, Howard S. John F. Kennedy: A Photographic Story of a Life. (p. 921)
Kaplan, Isabel. Hancock Park. (p. 740)
Kaplan, Kathy Walden. Crow Story: A Tale from the Oak Grove. (p. 386)
—Dog of Knots. (p. 461)
Kaplan, Leslie. Cinco de Mayo. (p. 319)
Kaplan, Leslie C. Art & Religion in Ancient Egypt. (p. 101)
—Chinese New Year. (p. 307)
—Cinco de Mayo. (p. 319)
—Flag Day. (p. 601)
—Home Life in Ancient Egypt. (p. 792)
—Independence Day. (p. 870)
—Land & Resources in Ancient Egypt. (p. 973)
—Land & Resources of Ancient Egypt. (p. 973)
—Martin Luther King Jr. Day. (p. 1098)
—Politics & Government in Ancient Egypt. (p. 1381)
—Primary Source Guide to Argentina. (p. 1399)
—Primary Source Guide to Canada. (p. 1399)
—Primary Source Guide to Iran. (p. 1399)
—Prmiary Source Guide to Greece. (p. 1408)
—Technology of Ancient Egypt. (p. 1711)
—Veterans Day. (p. 1839)
—Veteran's Day. (p. 1839)

Kaplan, Louise J. Cultures of Fetishism. (p. 391)
Kaplan, Madeline. Planet Earth Gets Well. (p. 1367)
Kaplan, Michael B. Betty Bunny Didn't Do It. Jorisch, Stéphane, illus. (p. 172)
—Betty Bunny Loves Chocolate Cake. Jorisch, Stéphane, illus. (p. 172)
—Betty Bunny Loves Easter. Jorisch, Stéphane, illus. (p. 172)
—Betty Bunny Wants a Goal. Jorisch, Stéphane, illus. (p. 172)
—Betty Bunny Wants Everything. Jorisch, Stéphane, illus. (p. 172)
Kaplan, Osman. Animal Wonders of the Sky. Kalender, Oznur, illus. (p. 80)
—Animal Wonders of the Water. Kalender, Oznur, illus. (p. 80)
—Giants of the World. Kalender, Oznur, illus. (p. 674)
—Wonders of the Land. Kalender, Oznur, illus. (p. 1949)
Kaplan, Richard, et al. Santa, NASA y el Hombre en la Luna. Palumbo, Debi, illus. (p. 1513)
Kaplan, Robert D. Balkan Ghosts: A Journey Through History. (p. 134)
Kaplan, Sarah Pitt. Pompeii: City of Ashes. (p. 1382)
Kaplan, Suki R. Around the World with Littlest Cat: Great Britain. (p. 101)
Kaplan-Maxfield, Thomas. Memoirs of a Shape-Shifter. (p. 1125)
Kaplan-Taylor, Maeve. At the Movies with Maeve. (p. 111)
Kaplon, Pat Allen. Betsy's Choice. (p. 172)
Kaploun, Uri, tr. see Rabbi Schneur Zalman of Liadi.
Kaplow, Julie, jt. auth. see Pincus, Donna.
Kapoor, Natalya. My Favorite Time of Day. (p. 1203)
Kaposy, Jeremy, illus. see O'Meara, Stephen James.
Kapovich, Katia. Gogol in Rome. (p. 692)
Kappely, Sarah & Priddy, Roger. ABC. (p. 3)
Kappes, Serena. Alex Rodriguez: Hot Corner, Hot Shot. (p. 36)
Kappler, Kathleen. Whitney's School Morning. (p. 1914)
Kaputa, Christine C. Bad Kitty! (p. 132)
—Jungle Gym Me & Him! (p. 935)
Kara & Woo, SooJung. Legend. (p. 988)
Kara, György, illus. see Hee, Lee Yun.
Kara, György, illus. see Hyong, Lee Chi.
Kara Higgins. Johnny Depp. (p. 923)
Kara, M., et al, eds. Abstract Machine Models for Parallel & Distributed Computing. (p. 7)
Karagulleyan, Rachelle. Mo, the Mischievous Mongoose. (p. 1157)
Karakida, Toshihiko, illus. see Kumon Staff.
Karalius, Kimberly. Love Fortunes & Other Disasters. (p. 1059)
Karam, P. Andrew. Artificial Intelligence. (p. 104)
Karam, P. Andrew & Stein, Ben P. Light & Sound. (p. 1014)
—Matter & Energy. (p. 1109)
—Planetary Motion. (p. 1368)
—Radioactivity. (p. 1433)
Karamanides, Dimitra. Pythagoras: Pioneering Mathematician & Musical Theorist of Ancient Greece. (p. 1421)
Karamanides, Dimitra, jt. auth. see Coakley, Louis C.
Karandeev, Oleg. Dmitri: The Kind Storyteller Book One of Five. Ciesinska, Izabela, illus. (p. 456)
—Dmitri II: The Kind Storyteller Book Two of Five. Ciesinska, Izabela, illus. (p. 456)
Karanja, Geoffrey Gacheru, illus. see Mbuthia, Waithira.
Karaperkova, Holly. Square? A Rectangle! (p. 1636)
Karapetian, Marjam. Bilingual Content Dictionary: English to Korean. (p. 186)
—Bilingual Content Dictionary: English to Spanish. (p. 186)
—Bilingual Content Dictionary: English to Armenian. (p. 186)
—Bilingual Content Dictionary: English to Mandarin Chinese. (p. 186)
—Bilingual Content Dictionary: English to Korean: Social Studies - American History Through 1776. (p. 186)
—Bilingual Content Dictionary: English to Spanish: Social Studies - American History Through 1776. (p. 186)
—Bilingual Content Dictionary: English to Armenian: Social Studies - American History Through 1776. (p. 186)
—Bilingual Content Dictionary: English to Mandarin Chinese: Social Studies - American History Through 1776. (p. 186)
Karapetkova, Holly. Dance. (p. 402)
—Desert Dwellers. (p. 429)
—Goodbye Friends. (p. 700)
—Katydid? Katy Didn't! (p. 946)
—Knock! Knock! (p. 965)
—Landing at Ellis Island. (p. 974)
—Las Serpientes en el Tercer Grado. (p. 977)
—Number Chants. (p. 1271)
—Riding with Paul Revere. (p. 1471)
—Seconds, Minutes, & Hours. (p. 1540)
Karapetkova, Holly, jt. auth. see Feldman, Jean R.
Karapetkova, Holly, jt. auth. see Feldman, Jean.
Karapetkova, Holly & Moreta, Gladys. Stop Arguing! Reese, Bob, illus. (p. 1653)
Karapetkova, Holly & Picou, Lin. Ouch! Stitches. Reese, Bob, illus. (p. 1307)
Karapetkova, Holly & Robertson, J. Jean. ?un Cuadrado? ! un Rectangulo! A Square? a Rectangle! (p. 1810)
Karapetkova, Holly & Robins, Maureen. Stop Arguing! Reese, Bob, illus. (p. 1653)
Karas, G., illus. see Hort, Lenny.
Karas, G. Brian. As an Oak Tree Grows. Karas, G. Brian, illus. (p. 105)
—Atlantic. (p. 112)
—Atlantic. Karas, G. Brian, illus. (p. 112)
—Case of the Missing Monkey. (p. 274)
—Case of the Puzzling Possum. (p. 275)
—On Earth. Karas, G. Brian, illus. (p. 1288)
—Switching on the Moon: A Very First Book of Bedtime Poems. (p. 1692)
Karas, G. Brian, illus. see Appelt, Kathi.
Karas, G. Brian, illus. see Applegate, Katherine.
Karas, G. Brian, illus. see Beeler, Selby B.
Karas, G. Brian, illus. see Billingsley, Franny.
Karas, G. Brian, illus. see Bluemle, Elizabeth.
Karas, G. Brian, illus. see Cline-Ransome, Lesa.
Karas, G. Brian, illus. see Eaton, Deborah J.
Karas, G. Brian, illus. see Elya, Susan Middleton.
Karas, G. Brian, illus. see Fleming, Candace.
Karas, G. Brian, illus. see Flor Ada, Alma.
Karas, G. Brian, illus. see Harper, Jessica.
Karas, G. Brian, illus. see Hort, Lenny.
Karas, G. Brian, illus. see Jenkins, Emily.
Karas, G. Brian, illus. see Juster, Norton.
Karas, G. Brian, illus. see McDonald, Megan.
Karas, G. Brian, illus. see McNamara, Margaret.
Karas, G. Brian, illus. see Michaels, Anna.
Karas, G. Brian, illus. see Mills, Claudia.
Karas, G. Brian, illus. see Rylant, Cynthia.
Karas, G. Brian, illus. see Stanley, Diane.
Karas, G. Brian, illus. see Zolotow, Charlotte.
Karas, Phyllis. Hate Crime. (p. 752)
Karas, Roma, illus. see Moore, Lilian.
Karasov, Corliss, jt. auth. see Field, Nancy.
Karasyov, Carrie, jt. auth. see Kargman, Jill.
Karasyov, Carrie & Kargman, Jill. Jet Set. (p. 916)
—Summer Intern. (p. 1674)
Kar-Ben Publishing, creator. Jerusalem Artists Wrapping Paper. (p. 914)
Karcher, Angie. Where the River Grins: The History of Evansville, Indiana. (p. 1909)
Kärcher, Gabriele. Games for Kids on Horseback: 13 Ideas for Fun & Safe Horseplay. (p. 655)
Karchut, Darby. Gideon's Spear. (p. 674)
—Griffin Rising. (p. 724)
—Hound at the Gate. (p. 802)
Karcz, Katherine, illus. see Craig, Deborah Anne.
Karcz, Katherine, illus. see Levitt, Paul M., et al.
Karczewski, Deborah. Cheerleader Meets the Goth: A Ten-Minute Comedy Monologue. (p. 296)
Kardec, Allan. Spirits' Book: Modern English Edition. (p. 1629)
Karden, Laura. Summit Climbing Guide. (p. 1675)
Kardong, Kenneth V. Introduction to Biological Evolution. (p. 882)
Kardy, Glenn. Kana de Manga: the Fun, Easy Way to Learn the ABCs of Japanese: The Fun, Easy Way to Learn the ABCs of Japanese. (p. 942)
—Kanji de Manga: The Comic Book That Teaches You How to Read & Write Japanese! Vol. 1 (p. 942)
—Kanji de Manga Volume 3: the Comic Book That Teaches You How to Read & Write Japanese! The Comic Book That Teaches You How to Read & Write Japanese! (p. 942)
Karen & Kary. Little Wizard. (p. 1038)
Karen Bisset. Rahab's Story. (p. 1433)
Karen, Frantz. Children's Parables: Earthly Stories with Heavenly Lessons for Children. (p. 304)
Kares, P. S. Hole-in-the-Wall with the Prairie Orphans. (p. 788)
—Prairie Orphans' Journey. (p. 1392)
Karesh, Sara E. & Hurvitz, Mitchell M. Encyclopedia of Judaism. (p. 525)
Karesh, Tracy Ann. Brave Little Soldier. (p. 223)
Karevold, Alison. KenKarta: Battle of the Onoxmon. Malone, Susan Mary, ed. (p. 948)
Kargbo, Mariatu. Mr Byrd's Bird. (p. 1184)
Kargbo, Ms Mariatu. Three Themne Titi Girls. (p. 1744)
Kargman, Jill, jt. auth. see Karasyov, Carrie.
Kargman, Jill & Karasyov, Carrie. Bittersweet Sixteen. (p. 194)
Karia, Roopal. Why & What of Epilepsy: A Book for Children & Teens. Mittal, Shiekha, illus. (p. 1922)
Karim, Archbishop Cyril Aphrem. In the Tree House. (p. 867)
Karim, Joseph & Karim, Silvana. What Does Happy Look Like? Karim, Joseph & Karim, Silvana, illus. (p. 1884)
Karim, Silvana, jt. auth. see Karim, Joseph.
Karim-Kincey, Rabiyah A. Nommo Rhyme & Reason. (p. 1263)
Kariya, Tetsu. Oishinbo: Izakaya—Pub Food: A la Carte. Hanasaki, Akira, illus. (p. 1282)
Karkevandian, Parisa. No Way Out. (p. 1261)
Karki, Ajay, jt. auth. see Thapaliya, Bishnu Prasad.
Karkowsky, Nancy. Ten Commandments: Text. (p. 1718)
Karl, Linda, illus. see Depken, Kristen L.
Karl, Linda, illus. see Golden Books Staff.
Karl, Linda, illus. see Man-Kong, Mary.
Karl, Linda, illus. see Masino, Brian.
Karl, Mary Elleen. Buddy in Winter: Lost & Found. Karl, Therese, illus. (p. 235)
Karl, Therese, illus. see Karl, Mary Elleen.
Karla, Nicolee, illus. see Bonacci, Ross.
Karle, Vincent & Blondel, Jean-Vincent. Descent into Paradise & a Place to Live. Little, Melanie, ed. (p. 428)
Karli, Land. Baby, Don't Cry. (p. 126)
Karlik, Danielle. Kaylee Chronicles: First Day Fright. (p. 946)
Karlin, Ann. Another Time - Another Place. Mazo, Chaim, ed. (p. 88)
Karlin, Ann Bell. Eight Bedtime Stories for Jewish Children. Mazo, Chaim, ed. (p. 507)
Karlin, Barbara. Cinderella. Marshall, James, illus. (p. 320)
Karlin, Wade. Pumas. (p. 1416)
Karlitz, Gail. Author. (p. 117)
—FBI Agent. (p. 578)
—Virtual Apprentice: FBI Agent. (p. 1844)
Karlitz, Gail, jt. auth. see Reeves, Diane Lindsey.
Karlitz, Gail & Honig, Debbie. Growing Money: A Complete Investing Guide for Kids. Lewis, Stephen, illus. (p. 726)
Karlon, Ann Lee, ed. see Etingoff, Kim.
Karlsson, Val. Egypt. (p. 506)
—Protectors. (p. 1412)
Karmaga, Ramanda, illus. see Henderson, Jason & Salvaggio, Tony.
Karman, Janice, jt. auth. see Bagdasarian, Ross.
Karmel, Annabel. First Meals: Fast, Healthy, & Fun Foods to Tempt Infants & Toddlers. (p. 596)
—Mom & Me Cookbook: Have Fun in the Kitchen! (p. 1161)
—My Favorite Recipes. (p. 1203)
—Toddler Cookbook. (p. 1761)
Karn, Mike, illus. see Snyder, Vicki & West, Lois.
Karner, Julie. Biography of Vanilla. (p. 189)
—Plague & Pandemic Alert! (p. 1366)
—Plague & Pandemic Alert! Disaster Alert! (p. 1366)
—Roald Amundsen: The Conquest of the South Pole. (p. 1477)
—Space Disaster & Meteorite Alert! (p. 1619)
Karnosh, Ami. Let's Eat: A Book about Food. (p. 996)
Karnovsky, Susan, jt. auth. see Lago, Mary Ellen.
Karol, Leslee. Sylvie the Littlest Guardian Angel: Cassie Makes a Friend. (p. 1693)
Karolides, Nicholas J., jt. auth. see Green, Jonathon.
Karp, Cindy, illus. see Marx, Trish.
Karp, Cindy, photos by see Marx, Trish.
Karp, Jesse. Those That Wake. (p. 1740)
—What We Become. (p. 1895)
Karp, Ken. Will You Wear a Blue Hat? (p. 1932)
Karp, Ken, photos by see Ackerman, Jill & Bryan, Beth.
Karpen, Cheryl. Eat Your Peas for the Holidays. (p. 501)
Karper, Deborah, ed. see Pedrow, Debra A.
Karpes, H. R. Morris... the Downside-Up Bat. (p. 1176)
Karpinske, Stephanie & Chihak, Sheena, eds. Disney the Magic Kitchen Cookbook. (p. 453)
Karpinski, David. Sarah's Christmas Presence. (p. 1514)
Karr, D. A. Legend of Pendyne: The King, the Horse, the Boy, & the Legend. (p. 988)
Karr, Justin. Drug Abuse. (p. 486)
—Gun Control. (p. 731)
Karr, Kathleen. 7th Knot (p. 1993)
—Born for Adventure (p. 214)
—Boxer. (p. 217)
—Exiled: Memoirs of a Camel (p. 548)
—Great Turkey Walk. (p. 719)
—Seventh Knot (p. 1555)
—Worlds Apart (p. 1960)
Karr, Leona, compiled by. Make Way for Miracles. (p. 1079)
Karr, Lily. Christmas Present for Me! McDonald, Jill, illus. (p. 315)
—Easter Bunny's Basket. Poling, Kyle, illus. (p. 499)
—Easter Parade! (p. 499)
—Easter Parade! Richards, Kirsten, illus. (p. 499)
—Five Bouncing Bunnies. Rogers, Jacqueline, illus. (p. 600)
—Five Little Puppies Jumping on the Bed! Zenz, Aaron, illus. (p. 601)
—My Easter Bunny! Johnson, Jay B., illus. (p. 1202)
—My Pumpkin. Marts, Doreen Mulryan, illus. (p. 1217)
—My Santa Claus. Johnson, Jay, illus. (p. 1218)
—Noah's Ark. Berg, Michelle, illus. (p. 1261)
—Pretty Princess: A Vanity Table Book. Waters, Erica-Jane, illus. (p. 1398)
—Spooky Boo: A Halloween Adventure. Poling, Kyle, illus. (p. 1631)
Karr, Lily, jt. auth. see Scholastic, Inc. Staff.
Karr, Susan Schott. Scream Machines: All about Roller Coasters. Ruben, Paul L., photos by. (p. 1532)
Karras, Demetra. Ayasha: You're Never Too Little to Dream Big. (p. 121)
Karre, Andrew. High Heat. (p. 777)
Karre, Andrew, ed. see Singleton, Linda Joy.
Karre, Andrew, ed. see Stolarz, Laurie Faria.
Karre, Andrew, jt. auth. see Carr, Elias.
Karre, Elizabeth. All You Are. (p. 46)
—Blind Curve: Acura Integra. (p. 199)
—Calling the Shots. (p. 254)
—Campaign. (p. 257)
—Certain Signals. (p. 287)
—Fight. (p. 585)
—No Regrets. (p. 1260)
Karre, Nancy. On Herman's Pond. (p. 1289)
Karres, Erika V. Shearin. Mean Chicks, Cliques, & Dirty Tricks: A Real Girl's Guide to Getting Through It All. (p. 1116)
—Mean Chicks, Cliques, & Dirty Tricks: A Real Girl's Guide to Getting Through the Day with Smarts & Style. (p. 1116)
Karsh, Efraim. Arab-Israeli Conflict: The 1948 War. (p. 94)
Karsky, A. K., illus. see Wojciechowska, Maia.
Karson, Jill. Club Drugs. (p. 335)
Karson, Jill, jt. auth. see Szumski, Bonnie.
Karson, Jill, ed. Civil Rights. (p. 324)
—Leaders of the Civil Rights Movement. (p. 981)
Karst, Ken. Area 51: Enduring Mysteries. (p. 97)
—Area 51. (p. 97)
—Bermuda Triangle. (p. 167)
—Bigfoot. (p. 184)
—Enduring Mysteries: Area 51. (p. 527)
—Enduring Mysteries: Atlantis. (p. 527)
—Enduring Mysteries: Bermuda Triangle. (p. 527)
—Enduring Mysteries: Loch Ness Monster. (p. 527)
—Loch Ness Monster. (p. 1044)
Karst, Patrice. Invisible String. Stevenson, Geoff, illus. (p. 886)
—Smile That Went Around the World. (p. 1594)
—Smile That Went Around the World (Revised) New Updated Edition. Christy, Jana, illus. (p. 1594)
Karsten, Margo & Karsten, Steven. Story of Sugar Cookie. (p. 1660)
Karsten, Steven, jt. auth. see Karsten, Margo.
Kartinyeri, Doris. Bush Games & Knucklebones. McInerney, Kunyi June-Anne, illus. (p. 244)
Karvonen, Tanjah, tr. see Banting, Erinn.
Karvonen, Tanjah, tr. see Craats, Rennay.
Karvonen, Tanjah, tr. see Cruickshank, Don.
Karvonen, Tanjah, tr. see Foran, Jill.
Karvonen, Tanjah, tr. see Howse, Jennifer.
Karvonen, Tanjah, tr. see Kissock, Heather.
Karvonen, Tanjah, tr. see LeClair, Danielle.
Karvonen, Tanjah, tr. see Lomberg, Michelle.
Karvonen, Tanjah, tr. see McIntyre, Sandra.
Karvonen, Tanjah, tr. see Morrison, Jessica.
Karvonen, Tanjah, tr. see Pezzi, Bryan.
Karvonen, Tanjah, tr. see Pratt, Laura.
Karvonen, Tanjah, tr. see Rebus, Anna.
Karvonen, Tanjah, tr. see Webster, Christine.
Karvonen, Tanjah, tr. see Wiseman, Blaine.
Karvonen, Tanjah, tr. see Yasuda, Anita.
Karwoski, Gail & Gootman, Marilyn E. Thank You, Trees! Balouch, Kristen, illus. (p. 1725)
Karwoski, Gail Langer. Julie the Rockhound Downey, Lisa, illus. (p. 932)
—Quake! Disaster in San Francisco 1906 Papp, Robert, illus. (p. 1422)
—River Beds: Sleeping in the World's Rivers McLennan, Connie, illus. (p. 1475)
—SeaMan: The Dog Who Explored the West with Lewis & Clark Watling, James, illus. (p. 1536)
—Search & Rescue Dogs (p. 1537)
—Terriers: Loyal Hunting Companions (p. 1721)
—Tsunami: The True Story of an April Fools' Day Disaster. MacDonald, John, illus. (p. 1795)
—Water Beds: Sleeping in the Ocean McLennan, Connie, illus. (p. 1862)
—When Hurricane Katrina Hit Home. Marshall, Julia, illus. (p. 1902)
Karwoski, Gail Langer, et al. Dogs on the Job. (p. 463)
Karwowski, Chris. Coalition of Malice Young, Steve, illus. (p. 336)
—Incredible Shrinking Allowance. Young, Steve, illus. (p. 869)
Karwowski, Chris & Serwacki, Anita. Word Up Vol. 3. Young, Steve, illus. (p. 1951)
Karwowski, Chris, et al. WordGirl - Fashion Disaster Young, Steve, illus. (p. 1951)
Kary, jt. auth. see Karen.
Karyn, Henley. I Learn about God. (p. 840)
Kasbarian, Lucine. Greedy Sparrow: An Armenian Tale Zaikina, Maria, illus. (p. 720)
Kaschula, Janet. Rosie the African Elephant. (p. 1490)
Kasdan, Mallory. Ella. Chin, Marcos, illus. (p. 513)
Kasdepke, Grzegorz. Beast in My Belly. Kozlowski, Tomasz, illus. (p. 152)
Kaserman & Haberkern, E. United States of America (p. 1820)
Kaserman, James & Kaserman, Sarah Jane. How the Pirates Saved Christmas. (p. 813)
Kaserman, Sarah Jane, jt. auth. see Kaserman, James.
Kasey, Debra C. Little Cloud That Could. (p. 1026)
Kashatus, William C. Past Present & Personal: A Guide for doing local history in Luzerne County, Pennsylvania. (p. 1327)
Kashman, Nancy & Mora, Janet. Sensory Connection: Sensory & Communication Strategies That Work (p. 1551)
Kashyap, Keshni. Tina's Mouth: An Existential Comic Diary. Araki, Mari, illus. (p. 1755)
Kasischke, Laura. Boy Heaven. (p. 218)
—Feathered. (p. 579)
Kaske, Anne, jt. auth. see Graf, Mike.
Kasko, John & Fabbri, Freddie. Breaking Benjamin: The Road to Platinum. Kasko, John, photos by. (p. 225)
Kaslik, Ibi. Skinny. (p. 1585)
Kasner, Kurt. Beyond the Hole in the Universe: Crisis in the World Next Door. Kasner, Kurt, illus. (p. 174)
—Through a Hole in the Universe: An Odyssey in the World Next Door. (p. 1744)
Kasnett, Yitzchak. Student's Guide to the Cohens of Tzefat. (p. 1669)
Kasony_O'Malley, Michael R. Irish Tale: Tom Moore & the Seal Woman. Rowland, Michael J., illus. (p. 888)
Kaspar, Anna. Look at Pluto & Other Dwarf Planets. (p. 1048)
—What's a Bird? (p. 1896)
—What's a Bird? Qué Es un Ave? (p. 1896)
—What's a Fish? (p. 1896)
—What's a Fish? Qué Es un Pez? (p. 1896)
—What's a Mammal? (p. 1896)
—What's a Mammal? Qué Es un Mamífero? (p. 1896)
—What's a Reptile? (p. 1896)
—What's a Reptile? Qué Es un Reptil? (p. 1896)
—What's an Amphibian? (p. 1896)
—What's an Amphibian? Qué Es un Anfibio? (p. 1896)
—What's an Insect? (p. 1896)
—What's an Insect? Qué Es un Insecto? (p. 1896)
Kaspar, Anna & Yablonski, Judy. How Plant & Animal Cells Differ (p. 812)
Kasparavicius, Kestutis, illus. see Maar, Paul.
Kasparek, Jonathan & Malone, Bobbie. Voices & Votes: How Democracy Works in Wisconsin. (p. 1848)
Kasparek, Jonathan, et al. Voices & Votes: How Democracy Works in Wisconsin. (p. 1848)
Kasparov, Garry. Checkmate! My First Chess Book. (p. 295)
Kaspee. Taming of the Halloween Monster: The Saga of the Gallant Platoon. McCarthy, Mary Toia, illus. (p. 1704)
Kasper, Beth. Billy's Secret. (p. 187)
Kasper, Catherine. Field Stone: Poems. (p. 584)
Kasper, Kathy. Mary Jean Learns to Shine. (p. 1100)
Kass, Daniele L., ed. City Trail: A Skip-Counting Tale. (p. 324)
Kass, Ed. D. Playground Time: A Skip-Counting Rhyme. (p. 1372)
Kass, Pnina Moed. Real Time. (p. 1449)
Kassab, Selena, illus. see Asher, Penny & Booker, Ricki.
Kassandra, ed. IV Antología Nuevo Milenio: Narració y Poesía. Carrillo, Azalea & Morrissey, Kay, photos by. (p. 900)
—V antología nuevo Milenio: Narración (Cuentos) y Poesía. Ramírez, Antonio & Morrissey, Kay, photos by. (p. 1829)
Kasschau, Richard A., et al. Understanding Psychology. (p. 1816)
Kassel, Roger de. Mr P & the Bully Birds. (p. 1186)
—Mr P & the Red Poppy. (p. 1186)
—Mr P & the Silver Red Bag. (p. 1186)
—Mr P & the Sticky Gum. (p. 1186)
Kassian, Mary. Vertically Inclined: Climbing Higher with God Member. (p. 1837)
Kassian, Olena, illus. see Roemer, Heidi.
Kassinger, Ruth. Iron & Steel: From Thor's Hammer to the Space Shuttle. (p. 888)
Kassirer, Sue. feria musical de Matematicas: Math Matters en Espanol. Smath, Jerry, illus. (p. 582)
—Learn to Write. (p. 984)
—Que Sigue, Nina? Math Matters en Espanol. O'Rourke, Page Eastburn, illus. (p. 1424)
—Thar She Blows! Whaling in The 1860s. Fridell, Pat, illus. (p. 1726)
Kassnoff, David. Special Ops: Weapons & Gear (p. 1623)
—Transformers, Robots, & Cyborgs. (p. 1778)

K

—What Degree Do I Need to Pursue a Career in Information Technology & Information Systems? (p. 1881)
—Working As a Physical Therapist in Your Community. (p. 1952)
Kasso, Martin. Sharks. Jeffris, Matt, illus. (p. 1562)
Kasson, Joseph E. Making of the Star of Texas. (p. 1082)
Kassouf, Jeff. Girls Play to Win Soccer. (p. 680)
Kassoy, Ben, jt. auth. see Rosen, Michael J.
Kast, Edie. Heroic Animals. (p. 773)
Kastan, Bill, illus. see Coughlin, Denise.
Kastan Karakochuk, Stephanie. Release Me into the Midnight Sky. (p. 1458)
Kastan, Marina, jt. ed. see Kasten, David Scott.
Kasten, David Scott & Kastan, Marina, eds. William Shakespeare. Harrington, Glenn, illus. (p. 1933)
Kasten, Nancy. First Feather (p. 595)
Kasten, Victoria. Mighty Stallion. (p. 1140)
—Mighty Stallion 2 Fury's Journey. (p. 1140)
—Mighty Stallion 3 Glory's Legend. (p. 1140)
—Mighty Stallion 4 Dancer's Dream. (p. 1140)
—Mighty Stallion 5 A Stallion's Heart. Briggs, Scott, photos by. (p. 1140)
Kasten, Wendy C., et al. Living Literature: Using Children's Literature to Support Reading & Language Arts. (p. 1041)
Kaster, Jeffrey. What Catholic Teens Should Know about Homosexuality. Larking, Jean K., ed. (p. 1881)
Kaster, Jeffrey & Kaster, Liz. What Catholic Teens Should Know about How Far to Go. Larkin, Jean, ed. (p. 1881)
Kaster, Liz, jt. auth. see Kaster, Jeffrey.
Kaster, Pam. Molly the Pony: A True Story. (p. 1161)
Kastigar, Jessica. King of Hearts. (p. 958)
Kastl, Christine, illus. see Viswanath, Shobha.
Kastner, Bernice. Space Mathematics. (p. 1619)
Kästner, Erich. Dot & Anton. Bell, Anthea, tr. from GER. (p. 472)
—Emil & the Detectives. Stahl, J. D., tr. (p. 518)
—Emil & the Detectives. Martin, W. & Stahl, J. D., trs. (p. 518)
—Flying Classroom. Bell, Anthea, tr. from GER. (p. 609)
—Kleine Grenzverkehr (p. 963)
Kastner, Erich. Lisa & Lottie. (p. 1022)
Kastner, Janet. Snake Fence: A Novel. (p. 1596)
Kastner, Jill, illus. see Hobbs, Will.
Kastner, Jill, illus. see Nolan, Lucy.
Kastner, Jill, illus. see Rylant, Cynthia.
Kasun, Mike, illus. see Tuzee, John & Tuzee, Diane.
Kasunick, Heather, illus. see Glenn, Joshua & Larsen, Elizabeth Foy.
Kasunick, Heather, illus. see Larsen, Elizabeth Foy & Glenn, Joshua.
Kasy, Frank, illus. see Liepelt, Juanita.
Kasza, Keiko. Badger's Fancy Meal. (p. 132)
—Badger's Fancy Meal. Kasza, Keiko, illus. (p. 132)
—Dia de Campo de Don Chancho. (p. 433)
—Dog Who Cried Wolf. Kasza, Keiko, illus. (p. 462)
—Estofado del Lobo. (p. 538)
—Finders Keepers. Kasza, Keiko, illus. (p. 587)
—Mas Poderoso. (p. 1102)
—Mightiest. (p. 1139)
—Mother for Choco. (p. 1177)
—My Lucky Birthday. Kasza, Keiko, illus. (p. 1213)
—My Lucky Day. (p. 1213)
—My Lucky Day. Kasza, Keiko, illus. (p. 1213)
—No Te Rias, Pepe. (p. 1260)
—Rat & the Tiger. (p. 1440)
—Ready for Anything! Kasza, Keiko, illus. (p. 1447)
—Secretos de Abuelo Sapo. (p. 1544)
—Silly Goose's Big Story. Kasza, Keiko, illus. (p. 1576)
—When the Elephant Walks. Kasza, Keiko, illus. (p. 1904)
Kaszonyi, Janet, illus. see Wagner, Elaine.
Katar, Al. Captain Scratch: Island of Sirmarj. (p. 264)
—Captain Scratch: The Island of Sirmarj. (p. 264)
Katayama, Kyoichi. Yami No Matsuei. Kazui, Kazumi, illus. (p. 1968)
Katayama, Mits, illus. see Parenting Press & Kennedy-Moore, Eileen.
Katcher, Brian. Almost Perfect. (p. 48)
—Improbable Theory of Ana & Zak. (p. 862)
—Playing with Matches. (p. 1372)
Katcher, Ruth, jt. auth. see Monceaux, Morgan.
Katchur, Matthew & Sterngass, Jon. Spanish Settlement in North America: 1822-1898. Overmyer-Velazquez, Mark, ed. (p. 1621)
Kate, Alejandria. How the Strawberry Got Its Seeds. (p. 813)
Kate Breding. Revolution of Cool. (p. 1466)
Kate Greenaway, illus. see Bret Harte, Harte & Bret Harte.
Kate, Lauren. Fallen. (p. 566)
—Fallen in Love. (p. 566)
—Oscuros. (p. 1305)
—Pasión. (p. 1326)
—Passion. (p. 1326)
—Rapture. (p. 1439)
—Teardrop. (p. 1711)
—Torment. (p. 1769)
—Tormento. (p. 1770)
—Waterfall. (p. 1863)
Kate, Maggie, ed. Glitter Roses Stickers. (p. 684)
Kate Smith Designs. Who's Playing on the Farm? (p. 1921)
—Who's Playing Outdoors? (p. 1921)
Kateley, John. Last Rabbit. (p. 978)
Kater, Mary, ed. see Benett, Janet M.
Kates, Steven A., jt. ed. see Tsaloun, Katya.
Katey, Miss. Jelly Bean: A Puppy's Tale. (p. 912)
Kath, Katie, illus. see Anderson, Shannon.
Kath, Katie, illus. see Jones, Kelly.
Kath, Katie, illus. see Meehan, Thomas.
Kath, Katie, illus. see Mills, Claudia.
Kath, Katie, illus. see Ziefert, Harriet.
Kath, Natalie. Summer I Lost It (p. 1674)
Katherine, Cullen. Earth Science: The People Behind the Science. (p. 496)
Katherine Cullen, PH D & Cullen, Katherine E. Biology: The People Behind the Science. (p. 189)
Katherine, Paterson. Great Gilly Hopkins. (p. 716)
—Lyddie. (p. 1066)
Katheryn, Shelly. Legends of the New Worlds: In the Beginning. (p. 990)
Kathie, Gabriel, illus. see Hawkesworth, Asha.
Kathleen, Jo Ann. Buddy Can't Tie Shoes. (p. 234)
—NATALIA, O' MIA, WHITE LACES & SHOES. (p. 1230)
Kathleen, Judith. Attila's Wobbly Birthday Box (p. 114)
Kathleen, King. I Love You All the Way to God. (p. 843)
Kathrens, Ginger. Cloud's Legacy: The Wild Stallion Returns. (p. 335)
Kathryn Aartman-Weed. Little Brown Bear. (p. 1025)
Kaths, Kathy, illus. see Hoover, T. A.
Kathuria, Rohit, illus. see Abdul Kalam, A. P. J.
Kathy, jt. auth. see Kiester, Rob.
Kathy, Lucius. Our Dearest Little One. (p. 1308)
Kathy, Newell-Worby, illus. see Sharon, Janusz.
Katic, Marija, jt. auth. see Kern, Dale.
Katie, Byron & Wilhelm, Hans. Tiger-Tiger, Is It True? Four Questions to Make You Smile Again. (p. 1748)
Katie, Harlin. Master Painter. (p. 1103)
Katirgis, Jane. Baby Backyard Animals. (p. 125)
—Baby Farm Animals. (p. 126)
—Baby Forest Animals. (p. 126)
—Baby Grassland Animals. (p. 126)
—Baby Snow Animals. (p. 128)
—Baby Zoo Animals. (p. 128)
—Back & Front. (p. 130)
—Big & Little. (p. 177)
—Celebrating First Lady Michelle Obama in Pictures. (p. 284)
—Celebrating President Barack Obama in Pictures. (p. 285)
—Celebrating the Inauguration of Barack Obama in Pictures. (p. 285)
—Celebrating the Obama Family in Pictures. (p. 285)
—Day & Night. (p. 412)
—Over & Under. (p. 1313)
—STEM Jobs in Food & Nutrition. (p. 1647)
—STEM Jobs with Cars. (p. 1647)
—Tall & Short. (p. 1704)
—Up & Down. (p. 1824)
Katirgis, Jane & Czech, Jan M. Endangered Rhinos. (p. 527)
Katirgis, Jane & Droham, Michele Ingber. Fearsome Forest Fires. (p. 579)
Katirgis, Jane & Drohan, Michele Ingber. Awful Avalanches. (p. 121)
—Eerie Earthquakes. (p. 505)
—Frightening Floods. (p. 639)
—Scary Tsunamis. (p. 1521)
Katirgis, Jane & Green, Carl R. Endangered Giant Pandas. (p. 526)
—Endangered Gorillas. (p. 526)
—Endangered Tigers. (p. 527)
Katirgis, Jane & Harkrader, Lisa. Endangered Orangutans. (p. 527)
Katirgis, Jane & Ingber Drohan, Michele. Volatile Volcanoes. (p. 1848)
Katirgis, Jane & Reiter, Chris. Endangered Blue Whales. (p. 526)
Katis, Alex. Africa: People, Places, & Cultures. (p. 26)
Katis, Alex, jt. auth. see Katis, Alexandria.
Katis, Alexandria & Katis, Alex. Washington D. C. (p. 1860)
Katis, Michael. Cheech the Pup: With Illustrations by Sharyn Crownover. (p. 295)
Katner, Etta. More Word Catchers for Reading & Spelling. (p. 1175)
Kato, Etsuo. King Who Saved the Dove. Yasui, Koji, illus. (p. 959)
Kato, Gary, illus. see Kellogg, Richard.
Kato, Haruhi, illus. see Makura, Sho.
Kato, Shakila Maria Inviolata & Kato, Sharifa Maria Inviolata. Adventures by the Magic Bicycle. (p. 15)
Kato, Sharifa Maria Inviolata, jt. auth. see Kato, Shakila Maria Inviolata.
Kato, Sharleen L. Lifespan Development. (p. 1013)
—Teaching. (p. 1709)
Kato, Yukiko. In the Meadow. Sakai, Komako, illus. (p. 866)
Katrak, N., jt. auth. see Edom, Helen.
Katrana, Carol. Charlie, the Christmas Camel: A Christmas Story to Remember. (p. 293)
Katris Gonis, Theofania. Icon for Christmas: Sophia's Gift: an Icon Christmas Story to Color. Deshamais, Margo, illus. (p. 851)
Kats, Jewel. Cinderella's Magical Wheelchair: An Empowering Fairy Tale. Kinra, Richa, illus. (p. 320)
—Hansel & Gretel: A Fairy Tale with a down Syndrome Twist. Lenart, Claudia, illus. (p. 743)
—Miss Popular Steals the Show: Girls in Wheelchairs Rule! Stenton, Murray, illus. (p. 1152)
—Princess & the Ruby: An Autism Fairy Tale. Kinra, Richa, illus. (p. 1403)
—Reena's Bollywood Dream: A Story about Sexual Abuse. (p. 1456)
—Snow White's Seven Patches: A Vitiligo Fairy Tale. Goodfellow, Dan, illus. (p. 1600)
—Teddy Bear Princess: A Story about Sharing & Caring. Arts, Richa Kinra, illus. (p. 1712)
Katschke, Judy. All about the Dragons. Style Guide Staff, illus. (p. 43)
—Bring on Spring! Elsom, Clare, illus. (p. 228)
—Facts about Flirting. (p. 561)
—First Grade Feast!/By Judy Katschke ; Illustrated by Clare Elsom. Elsom, Clare, illus. (p. 595)
—I Love My Mami! Aikins, Dave, illus. (p. 842)
—Phonics Comics. Baumann, Marty, illus. (p. 1352)
—Ready, Set, Boo! Elsom, Clare, illus. (p. 1447)
—Shrek the Third. (p. 1571)
—Shrek the Third: King for a Day, Ogre for Life. (p. 1571)
—Teeny Genie. Jennings, C. S., illus. (p. 1715)
Katschke, Judy, jt. auth. see Shultz, Charles M.
Katschke, Judy, jt. auth. see Williams, Ted.
Katschke, Judy & Nickle, John. Ant Bully: Movie Novel. (p. 88)
Katschke, Judy, et al. April Fools' Rules. (p. 93)
—Bye-Bye Boyfriend (p. 249)
—Shore Thing. (p. 1569)
Katsoris, Nick. Growing up with Loukoumi. (p. 727)
—Loukoumi. (p. 1059)
—Loukoumi & the Schoolyard Bully. (p. 1059)
—Loukoumi's Gift. (p. 1059)
—Loukoumi's Good Deeds. (p. 1059)
Katsu, Aki. Psychic Academy Box (p. 1413)
—Vision of Escaflowne (p. 1845)
Katsu, Aki, creator. Psychic Academy (p. 1413)
Katsumoto, Sayaka, tr. see Campbell, Mari.
Katsura, Hoshino, jt. auth. see Hoshino, Katsura.
Katsura, Masakazu. Bitter Summer. Katsura, Masakazu, illus. (p. 194)
—Close-Up Katsura, Masakazu, illus. (p. 334)
—Cut Scenes Katsura, Masakazu, illus. (p. 396)
—Fade Out Katsura, Masakazu, illus. (p. 562)
—IS (p. 888)
—IS Katsura, Masakazu, illus. (p. 888)
—I"S (p. 888)
—I's: Iori. Vol. 1 Katsura, Masakazu, illus. (p. 888)
—I's: Itsuki. Vol. 2 Katsura, Masakazu, illus. (p. 888)
—Len's Story (p. 991)
—Mix Down Katsura, Masakazu, illus. (p. 1156)
—Off-Line. Katsura, Masakazu, illus. (p. 1279)
—Preproduction. Katsura, Masakazu, illus. (p. 1396)
—Recall Vol. 3. Katsura, Masakazu, illus. (p. 1451)
—Rough Cut Katsura, Masakazu, illus. (p. 1491)
—Spinoff Katsura, Masakazu, illus. (p. 1628)
—Video Girl Ai: Flashback (p. 1841)
—Video Girl Ai Katsura, Masakazu, illus. (p. 1841)
—Video Girl Ai: Retake Katsura, Masakazu, illus. (p. 1841)
—Video Girl Ai: Cutting Room Katsura, Masakazu, illus. (p. 1841)
—Video Girl Ai: Farewell Scene Katsura, Masakazu, illus. (p. 1841)
Katsura, Masakazu & Masakazu Staff. IS Katsura, Masakazu, illus. (p. 888)
Katsura, Masakazu & Oshii, Mamoru. Ghost in the Shell 2: Innocence Katsura, Masakazu & Oshii, Mamoru, illus. (p. 671)
Katsuura, Jaden. Glimpses. (p. 683)
Kattan, Nicola, jt. auth. see Kattan, Peter.
Kattan, Peter & Kattan, Nicola. Kindergarten Sudoku: 4x4 Sudoku Puzzles for Kids. (p. 957)
—More Kindergarten Sudoku: 4x4 Classic Sudoku Puzzles for Kids. (p. 1174)
Kattman, Robert, jt. ed. see Johnson, F. Craig.
Katula, Bob. Larry y el Increible Ataque de los Tapa Oidos. (p. 976)
Katz, Alan. Are You Quite Polite? Silly Dilly Manners Songs. Catrow, David, illus. (p. 97)
—Born to Be Funny! (p. 214)
—Day the Mustache Took Over. Easler, Kris, illus. (p. 414)
—Don't Say That Word! Catrow, David, illus. (p. 468)
—Going, Going, Gone! And Other Silly Dilly Sports Songs. Catrow, David, illus. (p. 692)
—I'm Still Here in the Bathtub: Brand New Silly Dilly Songs. Catrow, David, illus. (p. 860)
—Let's Get a Checkup! Lemaitre, Pascal, illus. (p. 996)
—Me! Me! Mine! Lemaitre, Pascal, illus. (p. 1116)
—Mosquitoes Are Ruining My Summer! And Other Silly Dilly Camp Songs. Catrow, David, illus. (p. 1177)
—On Top of the Potty: And Other Get-up-and-Go Songs. Catrow, David, illus. (p. 1292)
—Oops! Koren, Edward, illus. (p. 1299)
—Poems from under My Bed: LOL Halloween Rhymes. LaCoste, Gary, illus. (p. 1376)
—Poems I Wrote When No One Was Looking. Koren, Edward, illus. (p. 1376)
—Ricky Vargas: The Funniest Kid in the World. Curtis, Stacy, illus. (p. 1470)
—Smelly Locker: Silly Dilly School Songs. Catrow, David, illus. (p. 1593)
—Stalling. Smith, Elwood H., illus. (p. 1639)
—Too Much Kissing! And Other Silly Dilly Songs about Parents. Catrow, David, illus. (p. 1767)
—Where Did They Hide My Presents? Silly Dilly Christmas Songs. Catrow, David, illus. (p. 1906)
Katz, Alan & Moreton, Daniel. Karate Pig. (p. 943)
Katz, Andrew & Gohari, Omid. Brandeis University College Prowler off the Record. (p. 222)
Katz, Anne. Girl in the Know: Your Inside-and-Out Guide to Growing Up. Melnychuk, Monika, illus. (p. 678)
Katz, Avi, illus. see Dran, Ruth.
Katz, Avi, illus. see Ganz, Yaffa.
Katz, Avi, illus. see Gordon, Ellen.
Katz, Avi, illus. see Greenspan, Shari Dash.
Katz, Avi, illus. see Mermelstein, Yael.
Katz, Avi, illus. see Metter, Bert & Metter, Bertram.
Katz, Avi, illus. see Orgad, Dorit.
Katz, Avi, illus. see Perlowitz, Rebecca & Becky, Morah.
Katz, Avi, illus. see Ramsay, Elizabeth.
Katz, Avi, illus. see Reiss, I.
Katz, Avi, illus. see Seltzer, Sara Leah.
Katz, Aya. Ping & the Snirkelly People. (p. 1359)
Katz, Bebe Weinberg. Best Friend for Claudia. (p. 169)
—Princess Claudia & the Freckles. (p. 1403)
Katz, Ben & Nyman, Debbie. 10 Greatest Sports Dynasties. (p. 1993)
Katz, Bobbi. Partner Poems for Building Fluency: 25 Original Poems with Research-Based Lessons That Help Students Improve Their Fluency & Comprehension. (p. 1325)
—Pocket Poems. Hafner, Marylin, illus. (p. 1375)
Katz Cooper, Sharon. Aprender de los Fósiles. (p. 93)
—Learning from Fossils (p. 985)
—Streets & Alleys (p. 1667)
—Usar el Agua (p. 1826)
—Usar el Aire (p. 1826)
—Usar la Tierra (p. 1826)
—Usar las Plantas. (p. 1827)
—Usar las Rocas. (p. 1827)
—Using Air (p. 1828)
Katz Cooper, Sharon, jt. auth. see Cooper, Sharon Katz.
Katz, Danny. Little Lunch Four. Vane, Mitch, illus. (p. 1031)
Katz, David. DC Super Heroes Colors, Shapes & More! (p. 416)
Katz, David, illus. see Friend, Robyn & Cohen, Judith.
katz, david A., illus. see cohen, judith L. & friend, robyn.
Katz, David A., illus. see Cohen, Judith Love & Friend, Robyn C.
Katz, David A., illus. see Cohen, Judith Love.
katz, david A., illus. see friend, robyn C. & cohen, Judith Love.
Katz, David Arthur, illus. see Bozak, Kristin & Cohen, Judith Love.
Katz, David Arthur, illus. see Franks, Sharon E. & Cohen, Judith Love.
Katz, David Arthur, illus. see Friend, Robyn C.
Katz, David Arthur, illus. see Friend, Robyn C. & Cohen, Judith Love.
Katz, David Arthur, illus. see Ghez, Andrea Mia & Cohen, Judith Love.
Katz, David Bar. DC Super Heroes ABC 123. (p. 416)
—My First Wonder Woman Book: Touch & Feel. (p. 1208)
—Super Heroes Book of Opposites. (p. 1680)
Katz, David Bar, jt. auth. see Bookworks, Downtown.
Katz, Elizabeth Jamie. Princess, the Pearls & the Pekingese: Celebrate Christmas. (p. 1406)
Katz, Eric, jt. auth. see Bluestein, Jane.
Katz, Farley. Journal of a Schoolyard Bully - Cyberbully. (p. 927)
Katz, Jennifer A. Era of Courting. (p. 533)
Katz, Jon. Lenore Finds a Friend: A True Story from Bedlam Farm. Katz, Jon, photos by. (p. 991)
—Meet the Dogs of Bedlam Farm. Katz, Jon, photos by. (p. 1122)
Katz, Julie & Merberg, Julie. Turn the Key: Who Do You See? McQueen, Lucinda, illus. (p. 1797)
Katz, Karen. Babies on the Bus. Katz, Karen, illus. (p. 124)
—Baby at the Farm. Katz, Karen, illus. (p. 125)
—Baby Loves Fall! A Karen Katz Lift-The-Flap Book. Katz, Karen, illus. (p. 127)
—Baby Loves Spring! Katz, Karen, illus. (p. 127)
—Baby Loves Summer! Katz, Karen, illus. (p. 127)
—Baby Loves Winter! A Karen Katz Lift-The-Flap Book. Katz, Karen, illus. (p. 127)
—Baby's Box of Family Fun! Katz, Karen, illus. (p. 128)
—Baby's Colors. Katz, Karen, illus. (p. 129)
—Baby's Day. Katz, Karen, illus. (p. 129)
—Baby's Numbers. Katz, Karen, illus. (p. 129)
—Baby's Shapes. Katz, Karen, illus. (p. 129)
—Beddy-Bye, Baby. Katz, Karen, illus. (p. 156)
—Best-Ever Big Brother. (p. 169)
—Best-Ever Big Sister. (p. 169)
—Buzz, Buzz, Baby! Katz, Karen, illus. (p. 248)
—Can You Say Peace? Katz, Karen, illus. (p. 259)
—Colors of Us. Katz, Karen, illus. (p. 345)
—Counting Christmas. Katz, Karen, illus. (p. 371)
—Counting Kisses: Lap Edition. Katz, Karen, illus. (p. 371)
—Counting Kisses. Katz, Karen, illus. (p. 371)
—Daddy & Me. Katz, Karen, illus. (p. 398)
—Daddy Hugs. Katz, Karen, illus. (p. 398)
—Daddy Hugs 1 2 3. Katz, Karen, illus. (p. 398)
—Grandpa & Me. Katz, Karen, illus. (p. 709)
—How Does Baby Feel? A Karen Katz Lift-The-Flap Book. Katz, Karen, illus. (p. 808)
—I Can Share! (p. 836)
—I Can Share. Katz, Karen, illus. (p. 836)
—Mommy Hugs: Lap Edition. Katz, Karen, illus. (p. 1162)
—Mommy Hugs. Katz, Karen, illus. (p. 1162)
—My Big Boy Undies. (p. 1197)
—My Big Girl Undies. (p. 1197)
—My First Chinese New Year. Katz, Karen, illus. (p. 1206)
—My First Kwanzaa. Katz, Karen, illus. (p. 1207)
—No Biting! (p. 1257)
—No Hitting! (p. 1258)
—No Hitting! Katz, Karen, illus. (p. 1258)
—Now I'm Big! Katz, Karen, illus. (p. 1269)
—Nutcracker Twinkle Toes. (p. 1274)
—Peek-a-Baby. Katz, Karen, illus. (p. 1334)
—Potty for Me! Katz, Karen, illus. (p. 1388)
—Princess Baby. Katz, Karen, illus. (p. 1403)
—Princess Baby, Night-Night. Katz, Karen, illus. (p. 1403)
—Princess Baby on the Go. Katz, Karen, illus. (p. 1403)
—Roar, Roar, Baby! Katz, Karen, illus. (p. 1478)
—Rosie Goes to Preschool. (p. 1490)
—Shake It up, Baby! Katz, Karen, illus. (p. 1558)
—Ten Tiny Babies. Katz, Karen, illus. (p. 1719)
—Ten Tiny Tickles. Katz, Karen, illus. (p. 1719)
—Twinkle Toes. (p. 1802)
—What Does Baby Say? Katz, Karen, illus. (p. 1884)
—Where Are Baby's Easter Eggs? Katz, Karen, illus. (p. 1906)
—Where Is Baby's Beach Ball? Katz, Karen, illus. (p. 1908)
—Where Is Baby's Belly Button? (p. 1908)
—Where Is Baby's Belly Button? Katz, Karen, illus. (p. 1908)
—Where Is Baby's Birthday Cake? Katz, Karen, illus. (p. 1908)
—Where Is Baby's Christmas Present? Katz, Karen, illus. (p. 1908)
—Where Is Baby's Dreidel? Katz, Karen, illus. (p. 1908)
—Where Is Baby's Pumpkin? Katz, Karen, illus. (p. 1908)
—Where Is Baby's Puppy? Katz, Karen, illus. (p. 1908)
—Where Is Baby's Valentine? Katz, Karen, illus. (p. 1908)
—Where Is Baby's Yummy Tummy? Katz, Karen, illus. (p. 1908)
—Wiggle Your Toes: A Karen Katz Book to Pull, Fluff, & Wiggle. Katz, Karen, illus. (p. 1928)
—Zoom, Zoom, Baby! A Karen Katz Lift-The-Flap Book. Katz, Karen, illus. (p. 1989)
—¡Cu-Cú, Bebé! Katz, Karen, illus. (p. 387)
—¿Dónde Está el Ombliguito? Ziegler, Argentina Palacios, tr. (p. 466)
Katz, Karen, illus. see Bauer, Marion Dane.
Katz, Karen, illus. see Brown, Margaret Wise.
Katz, Karen, illus. see Shelton, Jayne C.
Katz, Karen, illus. see Suen, Anastasia.
Katz, Karen A., et al. What Does Being Jewish Mean? Read-Aloud Responses to Questions Jewish Children Ask about History, Culture, & Religion. (p. 1884)
Katz, Karen & Bauer, Marion Dane. Baby's Box of Fun! A Karen Katz Lift-the-Flap Gift Set - Where Is Baby's Bellybutton? - Where Is Baby's Mommy? - Toes, Ears, & Nose! Katz, Karen, illus. (p. 128)

Katz, Karin Jill. There's a Fly in My Soup. (p. 1730)
Katz, Leon. Fables: A Collection for Youth. (p. 559)
—Greek Myths: Puppet Plays for Children from Ovid's Metamorphoses. (p. 720)
Katz, Michelle V., jt. auth. see Lewis, Jaime.
Katz, Myrna, jt. auth. see Kirshblum, Helen Fried Frommer.
Katz, Nevin. Constructing the Earth: Middle & High School. Norris, Jill, ed. (p. 359)
Katz, Susan. Oh, Theodore! Guinea Pig Poems. Schuett, Stacey, illus. (p. 1281)
—President's Stuck in the Bathtub: Poems about the Presidents. Neubecker, Robert, illus. (p. 1397)
Katz, Susan B. ABC, Baby Me! Padron, Alicia, illus. (p. 3)
—ABC School's for Me! Munsinger, Lynn, illus. (p. 3)
—My Mama Earth. Launay, Melissa, illus. (p. 1214)
—My Mama Hung the World for Me. Newey, Gail, illus. (p. 1214)
Katz, T. Miss L'eau. (p. 1151)
Katz, Tova, illus. see Blitz, Shmuel.
Katz, Tova, illus. see Leon, Sarah & Elsikowitz, Michal.
Katz, Tova, illus. see Pruzansky, Binyomin.
Katz, Tova, jt. auth. see Blitz, Shmuel.
Katz, Vladimir. Timeline of the Life of George Washington. (p. 1754)
Katz, Welwyn W. Come Like Shadows. Springett, Martin, illus. (p. 347)
—Sun God, Moon Witch. (p. 1676)
Katz, Welwyn Wilton. Beowulf Gal, Laszlo, illus. (p. 166)
Katz, William Loren. Black Indians: A Hidden Heritage. (p. 196)
Katz, William Loren & Crawford, Marc. Lincoln Brigade: A Picture History. (p. 1018)
Katz, Yoni, prod. Virtual I'Shana Tovah. (p. 1844)
Katzen, Mollie. Honest Pretzels: And 64 Other Amazing Recipes for Kids Who Love to Cook. (p. 794)
—Salad People & More Real Recipes: A New Cookbook for Preschoolers & Up. (p. 1504)
—Vegetable Dishes I Can't Live Without. Katzen, Mollie, illus. (p. 1834)
Katzen, Mollie & Willett, Walter. Eat, Drink, & Weigh Less: A Flexible & Delicious Way to Shrink Your Waist Without Going Hungry. (p. 501)
Katzenstein, Jason A., illus. see Peymani, Christine.
Katzler, Eva. Florentine & Pig. Mikhail, Jess, illus. (p. 606)
Katzman, Nicole, jt. auth. see Lehman-Wilzig, Tami.
Katzwinkle, William, et al. Walter the Farting Dog Goes on a Cruise. Colman, Audrey, illus. (p. 1856)
Kauble, Christa. Little Acorn. Natural Resources Conservation Service (U.S.), ed. (p. 1023)
Kauchak, Therese. Real Beauty: 101 Ways to Feel Great about You. Yoshizumi, Carol, illus. (p. 1448)
Kauenhofen, Jessica. My First A B C Book. Kauenhofen, Jessica, illus. (p. 1203)
Kaufeldt, Martha. Teachers Change Your Bait! Brain-Compatible Differentiated Instruction. (p. 1709)
Kauffin, Karlynn, illus. see Gaskins, Melda.
Kauffman, Christopher G. Faith's Star. Jenkins, Jacqueline, illus. (p. 565)
Kauffman, Dorothy. Computer Age. (p. 354)
—How the Earth Gets Its Shape. (p. 813)
—Inside the Human Body. (p. 877)
—Letters from Canada & Mexico. (p. 1002)
—Math Every Day. (p. 1106)
—Measurement All over the World. (p. 1117)
—Science Lab. (p. 1526)
—Two Villages: Two Hundred Years Apart. (p. 1804)
—Use Your Senses. (p. 1827)
—Weather. (p. 1869)
Kauffman, Dorothy & Apple, Gary. English Dictionary for the Content Areas. (p. 529)
Kauffman, Dorothy, et al. English Dictionary. (p. 529)
—Oxford Picture Dictionary for the Content Areas. (p. 1315)
Kauffman, Judy. Lord God Made Them All. (p. 1052)
Kauffman, Margaret, illus. see Hambleton, Anne.
Kauffman, Scott. Francis Marion: Swamp Fox of South Carolina. (p. 628)
Kauffman, Tracy. Gwendolyn's Wish. (p. 733)
Kauffman Yaun, Debra. People: Learn to Draw Step by Step. (p. 1339)
Kauflin, Chris. Smiletown's Big Snow Day. (p. 1594)
Kaufman, Amie & Spooner, Meagan. These Broken Stars. (p. 1731)
—This Shattered World. (p. 1737)
Kaufman, Angelika, illus. see Nöstlinger, Christine.
Kaufman, Burton I. Carter Years. (p. 272)
Kaufman, Elliott, photos by. Alphabet Everywhere. (p. 49)
—Numbers Everywhere. (p. 1272)
Kaufman, Gabriel. Basketball in the Big Ten Conference. (p. 143)
—Saltwater Crocodile: The World's Biggest Reptile. (p. 1506)
—Sporting Events: From Baseball to Skateboarding. (p. 1632)
Kaufman, Gershen, et al. Defiendete! Desarrolla Tu Poder Personal y Autoestima. (p. 424)
Kaufman Goodstein, Phyllis & Verdick, Elizabeth. Stand up to Bullying! (Upstanders to the Rescue!) (p. 1639)
Kaufman, Jeanne. Young Henry & the Dragon. Tessler, Daria, illus. (p. 1978)
Kaufman, Kenneth C., tr. see Salten, Felix.
Kaufman, Lance. Eyes of Sedona: An Anthropomorphical Pictorial of Red Rock Country. (p. 558)
—Mummy Mountain Story. (p. 1191)
Kaufman, Mary Bee, illus. see Peterson, Sara Budinger.
Kaufman, Mervyn D. Christopher Columbus (p. 316)
—Ferdinand Magellan (p. 581)
Kaufman, Michael, jt. auth. see Kaufman, Michael T.
Kaufman, Michael T. & Kaufman, Michael. 1968. (p. 2002)
Kaufman, Nancy R. Kaufman Speech Praxis Workout Book. (p. 946)
Kaufman, Sarah. Big, Brave Sis. (p. 179)
Kaufman, Sashi. Other Way Around. (p. 1306)
Kaufman, Seufert. Wee Wilhelmina & Her Magic Marbles. (p. 1871)
Kaufman, Shirley, tr. see Daleski, Gil.
Kaufman, Sue. Diary of a Mad Housewife: A Novel. (p. 434)
Kaufman, Yaki, illus. see Penina, M.
Kaufman Yaun, Debra. Drawing - Faces & Features: Learn to Draw Step by Step. (p. 481)
Kaufmann, Angelika, illus. see Lobe, Mira & Kovács, Cécile.
Kaufmann, Angelika, illus. see Nöstlinger, Christine.
Kaufmann, Anne. Glenn Gould: Sketches of Solitude. Koci, Rudin, illus. (p. 683)
Kaufmann, Carol, jt. auth. see Kainen, Dan.
Kaufmann, Helen L. Story of Beethoven. Meadowcroft, Enid Lamonte, ed. (p. 1657)
—Story of Mozart. Meadowcroft, Enid Lamonte, ed. (p. 1659)
Kaufmann, Kelli. Ned Redd, World Traveler: A Search-And-Find Adventure. Boyd, Aaron, illus. (p. 1239)
Kaufmann, Nancy. Bye, Bye! Spetter, Jung-Hee, illus. (p. 249)
Kaufmann, Paola. Sister. (p. 1581)
Kaulbach, Kathy, illus. see Bellingham, Brenda.
Kaulbach, Kathy R., illus. see Morgan, Lori.
Kaulen, Diane Bouman. In the Wake of Suicide: A Child's Journey. McAdoo, Grami & McAdoo, O'Pa, illus. (p. 867)
Kaupp, Rosemarie. Amberella Tales: Amberella in the City. (p. 57)
—Amberella Tales: Amberella & Double Double Trouble. (p. 57)
Kaur, Bal, illus. see Kaur, K. S.
Kaur, Harliv & Kaur, Jasmine, compiled by. My Gurmukhi Khajana: A Gurmat Based Primer. (p. 1210)
Kaur, Jasmine, jt. compiled by see Kaur, Harliv.
Kaur, K. S. Horncastles & the Magnopeus Medicine. Kaur, Bal, illus. (p. 798)
Kaur, Prabhjot. Daddoo's Day Out. (p. 398)
Kaur-Singh, Kanwaljit. Sikhism. (p. 1575)
Kaus, Cathy. Bean Bandit (p. 150)
Kaushal, Tara, jt. auth. see Balsavar, Deepa.
Kaut, Ellis. Duende del Carpintero. (p. 489)
Kaut, Joy. Matilda Moose Learns about Being Unique. (p. 1109)
Kautza, Jeremy. Geometry Student Activity Book. Matthews, Douglas L., ed. (p. 663)
Kauzlarich, David. Sociological Classics: A Prentice Hall Pocket Reader. (p. 1605)
Kauzlarich, Jane. Quack: A Two Jane Creation. (p. 1422)
Kavan, Barbara. Trainman: Gaining Acceptance ... & Friends ... Through Special Interests. (p. 1777)
Kavanagh, Charlene Kate. Going Home: The Lost Story of Chief the Fire Dog. (p. 692)
Kavanagh, Herminie Templeton. Darby O'Gill & the Crocks of Gold: And Other Irish Tales. Schluenderfritz, Ted, illus. (p. 406)
Kavanagh, Jack. Larry Bird: Hall of Fame Basketball Superstar. (p. 976)
Kavanagh, James. African Wildlife Nature Activity Book. Leung, Raymond, illus. (p. 28)
—Arctic Wildlife Nature Activity Book. Leung, Raymond, illus. (p. 96)
—Australian Wildlife. Leung, Raymond, illus. (p. 116)
—Birds Nature Activity Book. Leung, Raymond, illus. (p. 191)
—Dinosaurs Nature Activity Book. Leung, Raymond, illus. (p. 445)
—Ducks Nature Activity Book. Leung, Raymond, illus. (p. 488)
—Freshwater Fishing: A Waterproof Folding Guide to What a Novice Needs to Know. Leung, Raymond, illus. (p. 637)
—Grasslands Wildlife: A Folding Pocket Guide to Familiar Species Found in Prairie Grasslands. Leung, Raymond, illus. (p. 712)
—Great Lakes Wildlife Nature Activity Book. Leung, Raymond, illus. (p. 717)
—Hawaii Trees & Wildflowers: A Folding Pocket Guide to Familiar Species. Leung, Raymond, illus. (p. 755)
—In God's Kitchen. Belisle, John, illus. (p. 863)
—Mammals Nature Activity Book. Leung, Raymond, illus. (p. 1085)
—My First Arctic Nature. Leung, Raymond, illus. (p. 1204)
—My First Deserts Nature. Leung, Raymond, illus. (p. 1206)
—My First Forests Nature. Leung, Raymond, illus. (p. 1206)
—My First Grasslands Nature. Leung, Raymond, illus. (p. 1206)
—My First Seashores Nature. Leung, Raymond, illus. (p. 1207)
—My First Wetlands Nature. Leung, Raymond, illus. (p. 1208)
—Pond Life Nature Activity Book. Leung, Raymond, illus. (p. 1382)
—Seashore Wildlife. Leung, Raymond, illus. (p. 1538)
—Southwest Desert Wildlife Nature. Leung, Raymond, illus. (p. 1617)
—World of Bears. (p. 1956)
—World of Sharks. (p. 1957)
—World of Snakes. (p. 1957)
—World of Wild Cats. (p. 1957)
—World of Wild Dogs. (p. 1957)
Kavanagh, Peter. I Love My Mama. Chapman, Jane, tr. (p. 842)
Kavanagh, Peter, illus. see Bradman, Tony.
Kavanagh, Peter, illus. see Green, Sylvia.
Kavanagh, Peter, illus. see Lindsay, Elizabeth.
Kavanagh, Peter, illus. see Taylor, Dereen.
Kavanagh, Peter, illus. see Wilson, Jacqueline.
Kavanagh, Peter, jt. auth. see Adeney, Anne.
Kavanagh, Peter, jt. auth. see Graves, Sue.
Kavanagh, Shannon & Davie, Rob. Safari Jeff & Shannon Visit Africa. (p. 1502)
Kavanagh, Shannon & McKay, Jeffrey. Safari Jeff & Shannon Visit South America. (p. 1502)
Kavanagh, Terry, jt. auth. see Mackie, Howard.
Kavanagh, Terry & Harris, Joseph. Powerless! Larsen, Eric et al, illus. (p. 1391)
Kavanagh, Terry, et al. X-Man: Dance with the Devil. Skroce, Steve et al, illus. (p. 1967)
Kavanaugh, Dorothy. Central Mississippi River Basin: Arkansas, Iowa, Missouri (p. 287)
—Feeling Unloved? Girls Dealing with Feelings. (p. 580)
—Hassled Girl? Girls Dealing with Feelings. (p. 752)
—Islamic Festivals & Celebrations. (p. 891)
—Morocco. (p. 1176)
—Morocco. Rotberg, Robert I., ed. (p. 1176)
—Moses. (p. 1176)
—Muslim World: An Overview. (p. 1194)
—Sudan. (p. 1672)
—Sudan & Southern Sudan. Rotberg, Robert I., ed. (p. 1672)
—War in Afghanistan: Overthrow of the Taliban & Aftermath Musteen, Jason R., ed. (p. 1857)
Kavanaugh, Dorothy, jt. auth. see Friedenthal, Lora.
Kavanaugh, Dorothy, jt. auth. see Gallagher, Jim.
Kavanaugh, Dorothy, jt. auth. see Logan, John.
Kavanaugh, Kieran, ed. see Teresa of Avila.
Kavanaugh, Missy & Gurman, Sarah, texts. Babies. (p. 123)
—Farm Animals. (p. 573)
—Horses. (p. 800)
—Sea Creatures. (p. 1534)
Kavasch, E. Barrie. Dream Catcher. Holland, Gay W., illus. (p. 483)
Kaveney, Roz. From Alien to the Matrix: Reading Science Fiction Film. (p. 641)
Kavin, Kim. Native Americans: Discover the History & Cultures of the First Americans with 15 Projects. Hetland, Beth, illus. (p. 1234)
Kavlin, Miriam. Kaleidoscope. (p. 941)
Kawa, Cosei, illus. see Hosford, Kate.
Kawa, Cosei, illus. see Perlov, Betty Rosenberg.
Kawa, Dominic. Sasha Is a Good Citizen. (p. 1515)
Kawa, Katie. Baby Koalas. (p. 127)
—Baby Penguins. (p. 127)
—Baby Seals. (p. 128)
—Barack Obama: First African American President. (p. 137)
—Bulldozers. (p. 240)
—Claire's Clothing Drive: Represent & Solve Problems Involving Subtraction. (p. 326)
—Colorful Goldfish: Peces Dorados Brillantes. (p. 344)
—Colorful Goldfish. (p. 344)
—Cranes: Grúas. (p. 376)
—Cranes. (p. 376)
—Cuddly Rabbits: Conejos Encantadores. (p. 389)
—Cuddly Rabbits. (p. 389)
—Curious Cats: Gatos Curiosos. (p. 392)
—Curious Cats. (p. 392)
—Diggers: Excavadoras. (p. 439)
—Diggers. (p. 439)
—Ducklings. (p. 488)
—Dump Trucks: Camiones de Volteo. (p. 489)
—Dump Trucks. (p. 489)
—Exploring Food Chains & Food Webs (p. 552)
—Fawns. (p. 578)
—Fearless Honey Badger. (p. 579)
—Forest Food Chains (p. 618)
—Freaky Space Stories. (p. 632)
—Furry Hamsters: Hámsteres Peludos. (p. 650)
—Furry Hamsters. (p. 650)
—Hockey's Greatest Records (p. 787)
—I Feel Happy. (p. 838)
—I Feel Lonely. (p. 838)
—I Feel Mad. (p. 838)
—I Feel Sad. (p. 838)
—I Feel Scared. (p. 838)
—I Feel Worried. (p. 838)
—Lambs. (p. 972)
—Loaders: Palas Cargadoras. (p. 1044)
—Loaders. (p. 1044)
—Lovable Dogs: Perros Adorables. (p. 1059)
—Lovable Dogs. (p. 1059)
—Meadow Food Chains (p. 1116)
—Mujeres en Los Deportes (Women in Sports). (p. 1189)
—My First Trip on an Airplane: Mi Primer Viaje en Avión. (p. 1208)
—My First Trip on an Airplane. (p. 1208)
—My First Trip to a Baseball Game: Mi Primer Partido de Béisbol. (p. 1208)
—My First Trip to A Baseball Game. (p. 1208)
—My First Trip to a Baseball Game. (p. 1208)
—My First Trip to the Aquarium: Mi Primera Visita Al Acuario. (p. 1208)
—My First Trip to the Aquarium. (p. 1208)
—My First Trip to the Bank: Mi Primera Visita Al Banco. Livingston, Jessica, illus. (p. 1208)
—My First Trip to the Bank. Livingston, Jessica, illus. (p. 1208)
—My First Trip to the Beach: Mi Primer Viaje a la Playa. (p. 1208)
—My First Trip to the Beach. (p. 1208)
—My First Trip to the Dentist: Mi Primera Visita Al Dentista. Livingston, Jessica, illus. (p. 1208)
—My First Trip to the Dentist. Livingston, Jessica, illus. (p. 1208)
—My First Trip to the Doctor. Livingston, Jessica, illus. (p. 1208)
—My First Trip to the Doctor / Mi Primera Visita Al MéDico. (p. 1208)
—My First Trip to the Farm: Mi Primera Visita a una Granja. (p. 1208)
—My First Trip to the Farm. (p. 1208)
—My First Trip to the Fire Station. (p. 1208)
—My First Trip to the Fire Station /Mi Primera Visita A la EstacióN de Bomberos. (p. 1208)
—My First Trip to the Library: Mi Primera Visita a la Biblioteca. Livingston, Jessica, illus. (p. 1208)
—My First Trip to the Post Office: Mi Primera Visita Al Correo. Livingston, Jessica, illus. (p. 1208)
—My First Trip to the Post Office. Livingston, Jessica, illus. (p. 1208)
—My First Trip to the Zoo: Mi Primera Visita Al Zoológico. Livingston, Jessica, illus. (p. 1208)
—My First Trip to the Zoo. Livingston, Jessica, illus. (p. 1208)
—Oliver's Orchard: Perform Multi-Digit Arithmetic (p. 1286)
—Playful Parakeets: Pericos Juguetones. (p. 1372)
—Playful Parakeets. (p. 1372)
—Science of Gymnastics. (p. 1527)
—Staying Fit with Sports! (p. 1645)
—Tapeworms. (p. 1705)
—Tractors. (p. 1775)
—Tractors / Tractores. (p. 1775)
—We Need Bacteria. (p. 1867)
—Women in Sports. (p. 1946)
Kawa, Katie, jt. auth. see Mills, Nathan.
Kawachi, Izumi. Enchanter. (p. 523)
Kawahara, Kazune. High School Debut. (p. 778)
Kawahara, Reki. Accel World (p. 7)
—Aincrad. (p. 30)
Kawahara, Yumiko. Dolls. Kawahara, Yumiko, illus. (p. 464)
Kawai, Chigusa. Alice the 101st (p. 39)
—Esperanca. (p. 536)
Kawai, Ritsuko. Balloon Adventure. Kawai, Ritsuko, illus. (p. 135)
—Ham-Ham Party Vol. 1. Kawai, Ritsuko, illus. (p. 739)
—Hamtaro Gets Lost & Other Stories. Kawai, Ritsuko, illus. (p. 740)
—Hamtaro Pop-Up Playset. Kawai, Ritsuko, illus. (p. 740)
—Hamtaro Postcard Book. Kawai, Ritsuko, illus. (p. 740)
—Let's Play!: A Playground for Ham-Ham. Vol. 4 Kawai, Ritsuko, illus. (p. 999)
—Little Lost Caterpillar Kawai, Ritsuko, illus. (p. 1031)
Kawalae, Aaron A, illus. see Kawalae, Kekaulelenaeole A.
Kawalae, Kekaulelenaeole A. Kohala Kuamoo. Kawalae, Aaron A, illus. (p. 966)
Kawane, Michelle. Little Dragon Who Wasn't Small after All: Adventures with Mathius Mccloud. (p. 1027)
Kawanishi, Mikio. Amazing Effects. (p. 54)
Kawanishi, Mikio, illus. see Sugamoto, Junichi.
Kawar, Mary, jt. auth. see Frick, Sheila M.
Kawarajima, Koh. Nouveis Logic. (p. 1268)
Kawasaki, Beth, ed. see Inada, Koji & Sanjo, Riku.
Kawasaki, Beth, jt. auth. see Oda, Eiichiro.
Kawasaki, Shauna Mooney. My Family Can Be Forever: Sharing Time Activities. (p. 1202)
Kawasaki, Shauna Mooney, illus. see Carabine, Sue & Adams, Jennifer.
Kawasaki, Shauna Mooney, illus. see Carabine, Sue & Smith, Johanna.
Kawashita, Mizuki. Ichigo 100% (p. 851)
—Ichigo 100% Sweet Little Sister (p. 851)
Kawecki, Daniel. Mad Moose. (p. 1069)
Kay. Tiny Turtle's Holiday Sleeptime Stories Collection. (p. 1757)
Kay, Alan. Breaking the Rules. (p. 225)
Kay, Alan N. Crossroads at Gettysburg. (p. 385)
—No Girls Allowed. (p. 1258)
Kay, Antony L. Turbojet - History & Development, 1930-1960: USSR, USA, Japan, France, Canada, Sweden, Switzerland, Italy & Hungary Vol. 2 (p. 1797)
Kay, Betty Carlson. Civil War from A to Z: Two Points of View. (p. 325)
Kay Campbell, Lindsay. Different, but Oh So Lovely. (p. 438)
Kay, Carl, jt. auth. see Clark, Tim.
Kay, Cassandra. Week in the Life of Mertyle. (p. 1871)
Kay, Devora. Sleep Sheep Story. (p. 1588)
Kay, Elizabeth. Felix y el Mundo Al Reves. Batlles, Camila, tr. (p. 581)
—Fury. (p. 650)
Kay, Francesca. One Busy Book. Glynn, Chris, illus. (p. 1294)
Kay, Helen. First Teddy Bear. Detwiler, Susan, illus. (p. 597)
Kay, Jill. Caterpillars & Butterflies. (p. 280)
—Fernando Exercises! (p. 582)
—Fernando Exercises! Tell & Write Time. (p. 582)
Kay, Jim, illus. see Almond, David, et al.
Kay, Jim, illus. see McGavin, George.
Kay, Jim, illus. see Ness, Patrick.
Kay, Karin. Floppy Cat. (p. 606)
Kay, Keith. Optical Illusions. (p. 1301)
Kay, Kimberly. Courage to Face an Ogre. (p. 372)
Kay, L. M. Frederick's Birthday Surprise. (p. 633)
Kay, Nicole, tr. see Nekrasov, Andrei.
Kay, Nicole, tr. see Nosov, Nikolai.
Kay, Nicole, tr. see Olesha, Yuri.
Kay, Regina. I Just Want to Be Liked. Kinard, Brandi, illus. (p. 840)
Kay, Ross. Go Ahead Boys & Simon's Mine. (p. 686)
—Go Ahead Boys & Simon's Mine. Owen, R. Emmett, illus. (p. 686)
—Go Ahead Boys & the Racing Motorboat. (p. 686)
—Go Ahead Boys & the Racing Motor-Boat. (p. 686)
Kay, Sjoukje, jt. auth. see Kay, Sjoukje.
Kay, Sjoukje & Kay, Sjoukje. Donut Yogi. Vita, Ariela, illus. (p. 469)
Kay, Stan. Fraggle Rock Classics Volume 1. Christy, Stephen et al, eds. (p. 627)
Kay, Stephanie. Let's Go to the Parade! Understand Place Value. (p. 997)
Kay, Susan. Abby & Gabby Tales. (p. 2)
—Raspus. VonRecht, illus. (p. 1440)
Kay, Terry. To Whom the Angel Spoke: A Story of the Christmas Blyth, Eileen, illus. (p. 1759)
Kay, Verla. Civil War Drummer Boy. Day, Larry, illus. (p. 325)
—Hornbooks & Inkwells. Schindler, S. D., illus. (p. 798)
—Whatever Happened to the Pony Express? Root, Kimberly Bulcken & Root, Barry, illus. (p. 1896)
Kaya, Rahime. Prophet Muhammad: The Seal of All Prophets. (p. 1411)
Kayaalp, Suzan. Adventures of Lucky the Duck. (p. 20)
—Inch Worm Inch Worm. Merrifield, Monarca, illus. (p. 868)
Kayani, M. S. Assalamu Alaykum. Hewitt, Ibrahim, ed. (p. 107)
Kaye, Bernard. Coconut for Christmas. (p. 337)
Kaye, Cathryn Berger, et al. Going Blue: A Teen Guide to Saving Our Oceans, Lakes, Rivers, & Wetlands. (p. 692)
—Make a Splash! A Kid's Guide to Protecting Our Oceans, Lakes, Rivers, & Wetlands. (p. 1079)
Kaye, Christian Thomas. Rachel the Homely Rabbit: A Story about Kindness. Albright, Audrey, illus. (p. 1432)
Kaye, Daniel, jt. auth. see Zenescope Entertainment Staff.
Kaye, Danny. Danny Kaye's Stories from Far Away Places. Bevans Marks And Barrow, illus. (p. 405)
—Danny Kaye's Stories from Many Lands. (p. 406)
Kaye, Deborah. Stubby the Frog: Three Journeys Beyond the Pond (p. 1668)
Kaye, Donna M., illus. see Stein, Ethel.
Kaye, Edward B., ed. see Purcell, John M.
Kaye, Elizabeth, jt. auth. see Curran, Abbey.
Kaye, Jacqueline, jt. auth. see Gordon, Keith.
Kaye, Jacqueline, jt. auth. see Senior, Trevor.
Kaye, Kathy. Imagine That! (p. 861)

K

Kaye, Kathy, et al. Secrets Volume 17 Erotic Nights - the Secrets Collection: The Best in Women's Erotic Romance: Erotic Nights. Vol. 17 (p. 1546)
Kaye, Leon. Cooking on the Street: A Comedy Monologue. (p. 362)
—Eat a Can: A Comedy Skit (p. 501)
Kaye, Mandy. Dream in the Sky. (p. 483)
—Tommy's Gap. (p. 1765)
Kaye, Marilyn. Gloss. (p. 685)
—Gloss - Summer Scandal (p. 685)
—Jill's Happy Un-Birthday: The after School Club. (p. 917)
—Penelope. (p. 1336)
—Teammates. (p. 1710)
—Valentine's Day Surprise: The after School Club. (p. 1830)
Kaye, Megan. Do You Know Who You Are? Singer, Allie, ed. (p. 458)
Kaye, Peggy. Games with Books: 28 of the Best Children's Books & How to Use Them to Help Your Child Learn. (p. 655)
Kaye, Rosalind Charney, illus. see Cone, Molly.
Kaye, Rosalind Charney, illus. see Manushkin, Fran.
Kaye, Rosalind Charney, illus. see Schuman, Burt E.
Kaye, Shannie. Funny Bunny. (p. 649)
—O, Little Star. (p. 1274)
Kaye, Shelley. Saving Private Woods. (p. 1517)
Kaye, Teri, ed. Christmas Crafts on a Budget: Over 100 Project Ideas. (p. 313)
Kaye, Terry, et al. Hebrew Through Prayer Siegel, Adam, ed. (p. 761)
Kayganich, Bob, illus. see Driscoll, Laura.
Kayganich, Bob, illus. see Edwards, Roberta.
Kayl, Bradley, jt. auth. see Gossett, Christian.
Kayla Taylor. Fatal Elements: Book 1. (p. 577)
Kayler, Ralph. Tea Party in the Tree Tops. (p. 1708)
Kaylor, Emiko, illus. see Peterson, Hiromi & Omizo, Naomi.
Kaylor, J. Garcia. Animal Magic Coloring Pages. (p. 78)
Kaymer, Lin. Who Is Mackie Spence? (p. 1916)
Kaynak, Kate. Accused: The Fourth Ganzfield Novel. (p. 8)
—Minder: A Ganzfield Novel. (p. 1145)
Kays, Judy. ABC Rhymes by Grammy. (p. 3)
Kayser, Eric. Champion: Graphic Novel Series. (p. 249)
Kayser, Eric, creator. Champion: Graphic Novel Series (p. 249)
Kayser, Megan. Finishing What I Didn't Start. (p. 589)
Kazaleh, Mike, jt. auth. see Shawl, Scott.
Kazaleh, Mike, jt. auth. see Shaw, Scott.
Kazem, Halima, jt. auth. see Fordyce, Deborah.
Kazemi, Elham & Hintz, Allison. Intentional Talk: How to Structure & Lead Productive Mathematical Discussions. (p. 879)
Kazenbroot, Nelly. Down the Chimney with Googal & Googolplex. (p. 474)
—Down the Chimney with Googol & Googolplex (p. 474)
—Over the Rainbow with Googol & Googolplex (p. 1314)
—Under the Sea with Googol & Googolplex (p. 1814)
—Under the Sea with Googol & Googolplex. (p. 1814)
Kazeroid, Sibylle, tr. see Sellier, Marie.
Kazeroid, Sibylle, tr. from FRE. Liu & the Bird: A Journey in Chinese Calligraphy. Louis, Catherine, illus. (p. 1039)
Kazimierski, Diana. Star. (p. 1640)
Kazimirova, Karina, ed. see AZ Books Staff.
Kazlow, Samuel, ed. Astronomy: Understanding Celestial Bodies. (p. 109)
Kazmi, Ummul Baneen. Alisha's Heavenly Adventures: It's Magic! (p. 41)
Kazmierczak, Jean. National Chrome 2: The Good, the Bad & the Indifferent. (p. 1231)
Kazmierski, Stephen, photos by see Muntean, Michaela.
Kazui, Kazumi, illus. see Katayama, Kyoichi.
Kazuko, illus. see Rogers, Paul.
Kazumi, Yuana. Flower of the Deep Sleep Schilling, Christine, tr. (p. 607)
Kazunas, Ariel. Jupiter. (p. 937)
—Mercury. (p. 1127)
—Neptune. (p. 1241)
—Saturn. (p. 1515)
—Uranus. (p. 1825)
—Venus. (p. 1836)
Kazunas, Ariel, jt. auth. see Simon, Charnan.
Kazunas, Ariel & Simon, Charnan. Super Cool Science Experiments: Erosion. (p. 1679)
Kazunis, Ariel, jt. auth. see Simon, Charnan.
Kazuya, Minekura. Wild Adapter (p. 1928)
Keable, Ruth. Jesus A True Story. (p. 915)
Keach, James, jt. auth. see Seymour, Jane.
Keaggy, Sarah, illus. see Gentry, Nancy.
Keaggy, Sarah, illus. see Robertson, Robbin Davis.
Keaggy, Sarah, illus. see Rogers, Lauren.
Keaggy, Sarah, illus. see Young, Dawn.
Kean, Edward. Howdy Doody in Funland. Seiden, Art, illus. (p. 823)
—Howdy Doody in the Wild West. Seiden, Art, illus. (p. 823)
—Howdy Doody's Lucky Trip. McNaught, Harry, illus. (p. 823)
Keane, Claire. Once upon a Cloud. (p. 1292)
Keane, Dave. First Day Frights. Keane, Dave, illus. (p. 594)
—Haunted Toolshed. Keane, Dave, illus. (p. 754)
—Monster School: First Day Frights. Keane, Dave, illus. (p. 1168)
—Monster School: The Spooky Sleepover. Keane, Dave, illus. (p. 1168)
—Sloppy Joe. Brunkus, Denise, illus. (p. 1591)
—Spooky Sleepover. (p. 1631)
Keane, David. Who Wants a Tortoise? Campbell, K. G., illus. (p. 1918)
Keane, Erin. Copycats. (p. 366)
Keane, Jerome. Ellie's Bad Hair Day. De Dios, Susana, illus. (p. 514)
Keane, Michael. Night Santa Got Lost: How NORAD Saved Christmas. Garland, Michael, illus. (p. 1254)
—What You Will See Inside a Catholic Church. (p. 1896)
Keane, Sarah. Around the World in Twenty-Eight Pages. (p. 101)
—Cuckoo, Cuckoo: A Folktale from Mexico (p. 389)
—Hare & the Tortoise: An Aesop's Fable Retold by Sarah Keane. (p. 748)
—My Foot Fell Asleep. (p. 1209)
—Town Mouse & the Country Mouse: An Aesop Fable Retold by Sarah Keane. (p. 1773)
Keane, Terence M., ed. see Foa, Edna B.
Keane-Dawes, Jennifer M., ed. see Hole, Lois.
Keaney, Brian. Haunting of Nathaniel Wolfe. (p. 754)
—Jacob's Ladder. (p. 904)
—Nathaniel Wolfe & the Bodysnatchers. (p. 1231)
Kear, Angela A. Mommy & Me Go to Swimming Lessons. (p. 1162)
Kearby, Mike. Texas Tales Illustrated: The Revolution. White, Mack, illus. (p. 1724)
—Texas Tales Illustrated—1A: The Revolution. White, Mack, illus. (p. 1724)
—Trail Drives White, Mack, illus. (p. 1776)
Kearins, Krit. Surf's up Penny. (p. 1685)
Kearney, Brendan, illus. see Candlewick Press Staff & Arnold, Nick.
Kearney Cooper, Nicole. Time for Bed: Andrew & April's Adventures. Broadnax, Charles, illus. (p. 1751)
Kearney, Elfric Leofwine, jt. auth. see Carroll, Lewis, pseud.
Kearney, G. M. Apple Trees of Tschlin. (p. 92)
Kearney, Jennifer, illus. see King, Ken.
Kearney, Meg. Girl in the Mirror. (p. 678)
—Secret of Me. (p. 1542)
—Trouper. Lewis, E. B., illus. (p. 1790)
Kearney, Rena. Mimi Fairy's Purple Hair. (p. 1145)
Kearney, Tom. Buckeyes Big Game. (p. 234)
Kearney, Tom John. Cougars Big Game. (p. 369)
Kearns, Ann. Dell's Discovery. (p. 425)
Kearns, Trevor Conan, jt. auth. see Books, D. W. J.
Kearns, Zannah & Quarto Generic Staff. No Use Crying. (p. 1260)
Keary, Annie & Keary, Eliza. Tales of the Norse Warrior Gods: The Heroes of Asgard. Brock, C. E., illus. (p. 1702)
Keary, Eliza, jt. auth. see Keary, Annie.
Keast, Ellen Frances. Rainy Week. (p. 1436)
—Snowy Week. (p. 1601)
Keast, Jennifer H. Dora the Explorer (Giant First Play-a-Sound) (p. 471)
—Mickey Mouse Clubhouse (Giant First Play-a-Sound) (p. 1136)
Keaster, Diane. Tawny-The Beauty. Page, Debbie, illus. (p. 1707)
Keaster, Diane W. Chickadee - the Traveler Page, Debbie, illus. (p. 299)
—Darby - the Cow Dog Page, Debbie et al, illus. (p. 406)
—Goldie - the Wise Page, Debbie, illus. (p. 695)
—Leroy - the Stallion Page, Debbie, illus. (p. 993)
—Sonny - the Spectacular. Becker, Toni, illus. (p. 1612)
Keat, Nawuth & Kendall, Martha. Alive in the Killing Fields: Surviving the Khmer Rouge Genocide. (p. 41)
Keates, Colin, photos by see Symes, R. F. & Harding, Robert.
Keathley, Betty Higdon. Hannah's Pink World. (p. 743)
Keathley, Christian. Cinephilia & History, or the Wind in the Trees. (p. 321)
Keathley, Margaret. Color Story. (p. 343)
Keathley, Margaret S. Star's Angel. (p. 1643)
Keating, Alison, jt. auth. see Canetti, Yanitzia.
Keating, Alison, tr. see Canetti, Yanitzia.
Keating, Brian. Amazing Animal Adventures Around the World (p. 53)
—Amazing Animal Adventures Around the World. (p. 53)
—Amazing Animal Adventures at the Poles (p. 53)
—Amazing Animal Adventures in Rivers (p. 53)
—Amazing Animal Adventures in the Desert (p. 53)
—Amazing Animal Adventures on Islands (p. 53)
Keating, Dan & Porter, Chip. Great Lakes Salmon & Trout Fishing: The Complete Troller's Guide. (p. 717)
Keating, Eliza. Folk of Feodora's Lane: There Is a Lane....... (p. 611)
Keating, Frank. George: George Washington, Our Founding Father. Wimmer, Mike, illus. (p. 663)
—Theodore. Wimmer, Mike, illus. (p. 1729)
Keating, Jess. How to Outrun a Crocodile When Your Shoes Are Untied. (p. 821)
—How to Outswim a Shark Without a Snorkel. (p. 821)
Keating, Laurel. Find Scruncheon & Touton 2: All Around Newfoundland Keating, Nancy, illus. (p. 587)
—Search for Scruncheon & Touton Keating, Nancy, illus. (p. 1537)
Keating, Nancy, illus. see Browne, Susan Chalker.
Keating, Nancy, illus. see Keating, Laurel.
Keating, Nancy, illus. see Moore, Angela.
Keating, Nancy, illus. see Pynn, Susan.
Keating, Nancy, illus. see Trottier, Maxine.
Keating, Susan. Archimedes: Ancient Greek Mathematician. (p. 95)
—Jesus Christ: Influential Religious Leader. (p. 915)
—Native American Rivalries. Johnson, Troy, ed. (p. 1234)
Keating, Susan K. Archimedes: Ancient Greek Mathematician. (p. 95)
—Isadora Duncan: American Dancer. (p. 891)
—Jesus Christ. (p. 915)
Keating, Susan Katz. Saudi Arabia (p. 1516)
—Saudi Arabia. (p. 1516)
Keating, T. P. Bleeding Hearts: the Diary of a Country Vampire. (p. 199)
Keatinge, Joe. Hell Yeah! Volume 1: Last Days on Earth TP: Last Days on Earth TP. (p. 763)
Keating-Velasco, Joanna. In His Shoes, A Short Journey Through Autism. (p. 863)
Keating-Velasco, Joanna L. Is for Autism, F Is for Friend: A Kid's Book on Making Friends with a Child Who Has Autism. (p. 889)
Keaton, Bobby J. Closet Monster. (p. 334)
Keaton, Kelly. Beautiful Evil. (p. 153)
—Darkness Becomes Her. (p. 408)
—Wicked Within. (p. 1927)
Keaton, Pam, illus. see Hall, Lisa.
Keaton, Skeet. Adventures of Jd Losey. (p. 19)
Keats Curtis, Jennifer. Animal Helpers: Sanctuaries (p. 78)
—Kali's Story: an Orphaned Polar Bear Rescue Gomes, John, illus. (p. 942)
Keats Curtis, Jennifer Keats. Animal Helpers Aquariums: Aquariums (p. 78)
Keats, Ezra Jack. Jennie's Hat. (p. 912)
—Jennie's Hat. Keats, Ezra Jack, illus. (p. 912)
—John Henry: An American Legend. (p. 922)
—John Henry: an American Legend 50th Anniversary Edition. (p. 922)
—Kitten for a Day. (p. 962)
—Letter to Amy. (p. 1002)
—Louie. (p. 1058)
—Louie. Keats, Ezra Jack, illus. (p. 1058)
—Pet Show! (p. 1345)
—Peter's Chair. (p. 1347)
—Peter's Chair. Keats, Ezra Jack, illus. (p. 1347)
—Regards to the Man in the Moon. (p. 1457)
—Snowy Day. (p. 1601)
—Whistle for Willie. (p. 1912)
Keats, Felicity. Dancing Pencils. (p. 403)
Keats, John. Bright Star: Selected Poems. Chalk, Miriam, ed. (p. 228)
Keats, John & Prosek, James. Bird, Butterfly, Eel. Prosek, James, illus. (p. 190)
Keay, Ben. Perfect Solution. Hsu, Florence, illus. (p. 1342)
Keay, Claire, illus. see Lanton, Sandy.
Keay, Claire, illus. see Levins, Sandra.
Keay, Claire, illus. see Metzger, Steve.
Keay, Claire, illus. see Patterson, Colleen A. & Miles, Brenda.
Keay, Claire, illus. see Straus, Susan Farber.
Keay, Loralee. Ear Muffs for Phoebe. (p. 492)
Keba, Jamila, illus. see Magnolia, B.
Kebbe, Jonathan. Shredder. Nayler, Sarah, illus. (p. 1571)
Kebbi, Yann. Americanine: A Haute Dog in New York. (p. 64)
Keck, Chad. Vital Skills: How to Be a Campus Missionary. (p. 1846)
Keck, Christine M., jt. auth. see Elson, William H.
Keck, Gayle, jt. auth. see Beach, Byron.
Keck, Thomas D. Fifth Cup Haggadah. (p. 584)
Keckler, Ben. From Here to There. Davis, Dick, illus. (p. 642)
—Incredibly Lonely, That's Me. Davis, Dick, illus. (p. 870)
Kecskés, Anna, illus. see Judybee.
Kecskés, Anna, illus. see Zuggo, Violeta & Zuggo, Jutka.
KecskTs, Anna, illus. see Kisson, Nisha.
Keddy, Brian, illus. see Williamson, Liza.
Keding, Dan. Stories of Hope & Spirit: Folktales from Eastern Europe. (p. 1655)
Kee, Ed, jt. creator see Forsythe, Gary.
Keeble, Helen. Fang Girl. (p. 571)
—No Angel. (p. 1257)
Keeble, Susan, illus. see Todino, Grace.
Keeble, Susan, illus. see Tondino-Gonguet, Grace.
Keedle, Jayne. Americans from the Caribbean & Central America. (p. 64)
—Ellen Ochoa. (p. 514)
—Jonas Brothers. (p. 925)
—Mexican Americans. (p. 1131)
—Oprah Winfrey. (p. 1301)
—Rachael Ray. (p. 1431)
—Volcanoes. (p. 1849)
—West African Americans. (p. 1876)
—Zac Efron. (p. 1984)
Keedle, Jayne, jt. auth. see Prokos, Anna.
Keefe, Susan. Toby's Tails. (p. 1760)
Keefer, Nick T. Pear-A-Dise. Bowser, Sean T., illus. (p. 1333)
Keegan, Anna. United States Constitution & the Bill of Rights: The Law of the Land. (p. 1819)
Keegan, Anne. Cat for Claire. (p. 278)
Keegan, Charles, illus. see Jordan, Robert.
Keegan, Coral, illus. see Keegan, Orsolya.
Keegan, John. Winston Churchill: A Life. (p. 1937)
Keegan, Jonathan, illus. see Bunting, Eve.
Keegan, Kyle, et al. Chasing the High: A Firsthand Account of One Young Person's Experience with Substance Abuse. (p. 294)
Keegan, Orsolya. Who Is Baby Hoo Hoo? Keegan, Coral, illus. (p. 1915)
Keegan, Shannon. Legend of the Sea Fairies. (p. 989)
Keel, Charlene, jt. auth. see Gates, J. Gabriel.
Keel, Pamela K. Eating Disorders. (p. 501)
Keeler, Patricia, illus. see Virtue, Doreen.
Keeler, Patricia A. & Leitao, Júlio T. Drumbeat in Our Feet Keeler, Patricia A., illus. (p. 487)
Keeler, Renee. Seasons. (p. 1538)
Keeler Robinson, Elizabeth, jt. auth. see Robinson, Elizabeth Keeler.
Keeley, Catherine. Secrets of Phantom Valley. (p. 1545)
Keeley, Hannah. Hannah Keeley's Total Mom Makeover: The Six-Week Plan to Completely Transform Your Home, Health, Family, & Life. (p. 742)
Keeley, Holly M. Journey of a Grape. (p. 928)
Keeley, Jennifer. Containing the Communists: America's Foreign Entanglements. (p. 360)
Keeley, Jenny Conner. Hollow: A Kansas Fairytale. (p. 789)
Keeley, Rose. Apple Gang. (p. 92)
Keeling, Annie E. Andrew Golding A Tale of the Great Plague. (p. 72)
Keeling, Evan. CrumbSnatchers. (p. 386)
Keeling, Jodie. You Can't Make Me Go to School! (p. 1974)
Keels, Steve. NLT TruthQuest Inductive Student Bible. (p. 1257)
—Truth Quest Survival Guide: The Quest Begins! Vorm, Dan, ed. (p. 1794)
—Truthquest Inductive Student Bible: New Living Translation with Black Expedition Case. (p. 1794)
Keels, Steve, ed. see Cote, Keith.
Keels, Steve, ed. see Wilson, Ronald.
Keels, Steve, jt. auth. see Perry, Jason.
Keels, Steve, ed. TruthQuest Inductive Student Bible. (p. 1794)
Keels, Steve, et al. Truth Quest Inductive Student Bible. (p. 1794)
Keely, Jack, illus. see Branzel, Sylvia.
Keely, Jack & Van Osten, Carson. Cartooning 1: Learn the Basics of Cartooning. (p. 273)
Keen, Annette, ed. see Routenburg, Rise' & Wasser, Barbara.
Keen, Dan, jt. auth. see Bonnet, Robert L.
Keen, Karl D. They Call Me Chief. (p. 1732)
Keen, Lisa. Out Law: What LGBT Youth Should Know about Their Legal Rights. (p. 1311)
Keen, Marian. Lexi & Hippocrates: Find Trouble at the Olympics. Jodie, Dias & Wendy, Watson, illus. (p. 1004)
Keen, Richard A. Skywatch West: The Complete Weather Guide. (p. 1587)
Keen, Sophie. Baby's First Lullabies. (p. 129)
Keen, Sophie, illus. see Helman, Laura.
Keen, Sophie, illus. see Howell, Gill.
Keenan, Brona, illus. see Rose, M. E.
Keenan, Edward. Art of the Possible: An Everyday Guide to Politics. McLaughlin, Julie, illus. (p. 102)
Keenan, Margaret. Dogs. (p. 462)
Keenan, Penny. Cooking with Ginger: Ginger Gets Lost Book I. Murray, Carol, illus. (p. 362)
Keenan, Sheila. As the Crow Flies. Duggan, Kevin, illus. (p. 105)
—Dogs of War. Fox, Nathan, illus. (p. 463)
—Looking for Leprechauns. Meisel, Paul, illus. (p. 1051)
—Outstanding Americans. (p. 1313)
Keenan, Sheila, jt. auth. see MacAulay, David.
Keenan, Sheila, jt. auth. see Scholastic, Inc. Staff.
Keenan, Sheila & Stine, R. L. Scary Summer. Haspiel, Dean et al, illus. (p. 1521)
Keenan, Tanya. Cappella. (p. 263)
Keenan-Bolger, Andrew & Wetherhead, Kate. Jack & Louisa - Act 1. Webster, Kyle T., illus. (p. 902)
Keene, Brian. Last Zombie: Neverland TP: Neverland TP. (p. 979)
Keene, Carloyn, jt. auth. see Keene, Carolyn.
Keene, Carolyn. Action! (p. 10)
—Apple Bandit. Jones, Jan Naimo, illus. (p. 92)
—April Fool's Day. Pamintuan, Macky, illus. (p. 93)
—Babysitting Bandit. Pamintuan, Macky, illus. (p. 129)
—Bad Times, Big Crimes. (p. 132)
—Best of Nancy Drew Classic Collection Vol. 1. (p. 170)
—Best of Nancy Drew Classic Collection: The Hidden Staircase; The Ghost of Blackwood Hall; The Thirteenth Pearl (p. 170)
—Bike Race Mystery. Casale, Paul, illus. (p. 185)
—Buggy Breakout. Pamintuan, Macky, illus. (p. 236)
—Bungalow Mystery (p. 242)
—Bunny-Hop Hoax. Jones, Jan Naimo, illus. (p. 242)
—Butterfly Blues. Francis, Peter, illus. (p. 247)
—California Schemin' (p. 253)
—Camp Creepy. Pamintuan, Macky, illus. (p. 257)
—Candy Is Dandy. Jones, Jan Naimo, illus. (p. 261)
—Cape Mermaid Mystery. Pamintuan, Macky, illus. (p. 262)
—Case of the Sneaky Snowman. Pamintuan, Macky, illus. (p. 275)
—Cat Burglar Caper. Pamintuan, Macky, illus. (p. 277)
—Chick-Napped! Pamintuan, Macky, illus. (p. 299)
—Cinderella Ballet Mystery. Pamintuan, Macky, illus. (p. 320)
—Circus Scare. Pamintuan, Macky, illus. (p. 322)
—Close Encounters. (p. 333)
—Club Dread. (p. 335)
—Clue in the Jewel Box Tandy, Russell H., illus. (p. 335)
—Cooking Camp Disaster. Pamintuan, Macky, illus. (p. 361)
—Cupcake Chaos. Pamintuan, Macky, illus. (p. 392)
—Curse of the Arctic Star. (p. 394)
—Dance Off. Pamintuan, Macky, illus. (p. 402)
—Dangerous Plays. (p. 404)
—Designed for Disaster. Pamintuan, Macky, illus. (p. 430)
—Dollhouse Mystery. Jones, Jan Naimo, illus. (p. 464)
—Double Take. Pamintuan, Macky, illus. (p. 473)
—Dressed to Steal. (p. 485)
—Earth Day Escapade. Pamintuan, Macky, illus. (p. 495)
—En Garde. (p. 522)
—False Notes. (p. 567)
—Fashion Disaster. Pamintuan, Macky, illus. (p. 575)
—Fishing for Clues. (p. 599)
—Flower Show Fiasco. Pamintuan, Macky, illus. (p. 607)
—Framed. (p. 627)
—Getting Burned. (p. 669)
—Ghost Stories. (p. 671)
—Gold Medal Murder. (p. 693)
—Green with Envy: Book Two in the Eco Mystery Trilogy. (p. 722)
—Green-Eyed Monster: Book One in the Eco Mystery Trilogy. (p. 721)
—Halloween Hoax. Pamintuan, Macky, illus. (p. 737)
—Hidden Staircase (p. 776)
—High Risk. (p. 778)
—Identity Revealed. (p. 852)
—Identity Theft. (p. 852)
—Intruder. (p. 883)
—Kitten Caper. Jones, Jan Naimo, illus. (p. 962)
—Lights, Camera ... Cats! Pamintuan, Macky, illus. (p. 1016)
—Lights, Camera ... Cats! Pamintuan, Macky, illus. (p. 1016)
—Magician's Secret. (p. 1075)
—Make-a-Pet Mystery. Pamintuan, Macky, illus. (p. 1078)
—Mall Madness. Pamintuan, Macky, illus. (p. 1083)
—Mardi Gras Masquerade. (p. 1092)
—Model Menace: Book Two in the Model Mystery Trilogy. (p. 1157)
—Model Suspect: Book Three in the Model Mystery Trilogy. (p. 1157)
—Murder on the Set. (p. 1192)
—Musical Mess. Pamintuan, Macky, illus. (p. 1194)
—Mystery at Lilac Inn. (p. 1223)
—Mystery at Malachite Mansion. (p. 1223)
—Mystery of the Midnight Rider. (p. 1225)
—Nancy Drew & the Clue Crew Pamintuan, Macky, illus. (p. 1228)
—Nancy Drew & the Clue Crew Collection: Sleepover Sleuths; Scream for Ice Cream; Pony Problems; the Cinderella Ballet Mystery; Case of the Sneaky Snowman. Pamintuan, Macky, illus. (p. 1229)
—Nancy Drew Cookbook: Clues to Good Cooking. (p. 1229)

—Nancy Drew Diaries: Curse of the Arctic Star; Strangers on a Train; Mystery of the Midnight Rider; Once upon a Thriller. (p. 1229)
—Once upon a Crime. (p. 1292)
—Once upon a Thriller. (p. 1293)
—Orchid Thief. (p. 1302)
—Pageant Perfect Crime: Book One in the Perfect Mystery Trilogy. (p. 1318)
—Perfect Cover. (p. 1341)
—Perfect Escape (p. 1341)
—Pit of Vipers. (p. 1364)
—Pony Problems. Pamintuan, Macky, illus. (p. 1382)
—Pool Party Puzzler. Francis, Peter, illus. (p. 1383)
—Princess Mix-Up Mystery Pamintuan, Macky, illus. (p. 1404)
—Pumpkin Patch Puzzle. Pamintuan, Macky, illus. (p. 1416)
—Race Against Time. (p. 1430)
—Real Fake. (p. 1448)
—Riverboat Ruse (p. 1476)
—Riverboat Ruse. (p. 1476)
—Sabotage at Willow Woods. (p. 1500)
—Sabotage Surrender: Book Three in the Sabotage Mystery Trilogy. (p. 1500)
—Scarlet Macaw Scandal. Frost, Michael, illus. (p. 1520)
—Scream for Ice Cream. Pamintuan, Macky, illus. (p. 1532)
—Secret at Mystic Lake. (p. 1540)
—Secret Identity (p. 1541)
—Secret of the Old Clock (p. 1542)
—Secret of the Scarecrow. Pamintuan, Macky, illus. (p. 1543)
—Secret of the Spa (p. 1543)
—Secret Sabotage (p. 1543)
—Seeing Green: Book Three in the Eco Mystery Trilogy. (p. 1548)
—Serial Sabotage: Book Two in the Sabotage Mystery Trilogy. (p. 1552)
—Singing Suspects. Jones, Jan Naimo, illus. (p. 1579)
—Ski School Sneak. Pamintuan, Macky, illus. (p. 1584)
—Sleepover Sleuths. Pamintuan, Macky, illus. (p. 1589)
—Snowman Surprise. Casale, Paul, illus. (p. 1601)
—Stage Fright. (p. 1638)
—Stalk, Don't Run. (p. 1638)
—Stolen Bones. (p. 1652)
—Stolen Relic. (p. 1652)
—Stop the Clock. (p. 1653)
—Strangers on a Train. (p. 1665)
—Taste of Danger. (p. 1707)
—Thanksgiving Thief. Pamintuan, Macky, illus. (p. 1726)
—Ticket Trouble. Pamintuan, Macky, illus. (p. 1747)
—Time Thief. Pamintuan, Macky, illus. (p. 1752)
—Trade Wind Danger. (p. 1776)
—Trails of Treachery. (p. 1776)
—Treasure Trouble. Pamintuan, Macky, illus. (p. 1782)
—Troubled Waters. (p. 1790)
—Uncivil Acts. (p. 1811)
—Unicorn Uproar. Pamintuan, Macky, illus. (p. 1818)
—Valentine's Day Secret. Pamintuan, Macky, illus. (p. 1830)
—Wedding Day Disaster. Pamintuan, Macky, illus. (p. 1870)
—Where's Nancy? (p. 1910)
—Without a Trace. (p. 1942)
—Without a Trace - A Race Against Time - False Notes - High Risk Set (p. 1942)
—Zoo Crew. Pamintuan, Macky, illus. (p. 1988)
Keene, Carolyn, jt. auth. see Dixon, Franklin W.
Keene, Carolyn, jt. auth. see Magoon, Kekla.
Keene, Carolyn & Dixon, Franklin W. Danger Overseas. (p. 404)
—Terror on Tour. (p. 1722)
Keene, Carolyn & Drew, Nancy. Lights, Camera... (p. 1016)
Keene, Carolyn & Frost, Michael. Stop the Clock (p. 1653)
Keene, Carolyn & Keene, Carloyn. Lost Files of Nancy Drew. (p. 1055)
Keene, Carolyn & Whelan, Patrick. Danger on the Great Lakes. (p. 404)
Keene, Daniel. Terminus & Other Plays. (p. 1721)
Keene, Frances W., jt. auth. see Hyde, Margaret O.
Keene, Michael. Judaism. (p. 930)
—Religious Education. (p. 1458)
—Religious Education. (p. 1458)
—Through the Mist. Heims, Freya, ed. (p. 1745)
Keene, Michael, jt. auth. see Hairston, Maxine.
Keener, A. E. My Name Is Charlie. (p. 1215)
Keener, Cathy Beddow. Jazzy Bunny Gets Floppy-Ear-itis. (p. 911)
Keener, Joan N. God Thought of It First. Petrova, Valeria, illus. (p. 690)
Keeney, Scott. Sappho Does Hay(na)ku. (p. 1514)
Keeney, Stephen S. Spencer the Adventurer & the Castle of Bran. (p. 1625)
Keens-Douglas, Richardo. Tales from the Isle of Spice. Bourbonniere, Sylvie, illus. (p. 1701)
Keep, Richard. Clatter Bash! A Day of the Dead Celebration Keep, Richard, illus. (p. 329)
—Thump from Upstairs: Starring Mr. Boo & Max Keep. Richard, illus. (p. 1745)
Keep, Richard, jt. auth. see Lowery, Linda.
Keep, Virginia, illus. see Gates, Josephine Scribner.
Keepin, William, et al. Divine Duality: The Power of Reconciliation Between Women & Men. (p. 454)
Keeping, Charles, illus. see Garfield, Leon & Blishen, Edward.
Keeping, Charles, illus. see Noyes, Alfred.
Keeran, Daniel. Who Are Homeless People? A Drawing Book of Stories for Children. (p. 1914)
Kees Csa, Cecile Marie. Patrick & Puppy Wuppy: Life in Grade Two. (p. 1329)
Keeshig-Tobias, Lenore. Emma & the Trees. Keeshig-Tobias, Polly, illus. (p. 519)
Keeshig-Tobias, Polly, illus. see Keeshig-Tobias, Lenore.
Keesler, Karen, illus. see Duksta, Laura.
Keeter, Hunter. American Air Forces in the Vietnam War. (p. 59)
—American Ground Forces in the Vietnam War. (p. 61)
—U. S. Homeland Security Forces. (p. 1806)
—U. S. Marine Corps. (p. 1806)
Keeter, Susan, illus. see Altman, Alexandra Jessup.
Keeter, Susan, illus. see Duncan, Alice Faye.
Keeter, Susan, illus. see Malaspina, Ann.
Keeter, Susan, illus. see McKissack, Patricia C.
Keeter, Susan, illus. see Merlo, Maria.
Keeter, Susan, illus. see Turner, Glennette Tilley.
Keevil, Tyler. Fireball. (p. 591)
Keevish, Michele C. When a Stranger Says Hello. (p. 1901)
Keffer, Ann. Seventh Chair. (p. 1555)
Keffer, Ken, jt. auth. see Tornio, Stacy.
Keffer, Lindy, jt. auth. see Keffer, Lois.
Keffer, Lois & Keffer, Lindy. Bible Brain Benders. (p. 175)
Kegel, Stan, jt. auth. see Lederer, Richard.
Kegel-Coon, Veronica. For the Love of a Game. (p. 616)
—Stranger in Treatenville. (p. 1665)
Kegerreis, Carl. Tibby & His Friend's Big Secret. (p. 1747)
Kegley, Charles W., Jr. & Wittkopf, Eugene R. World Politics: Trend & Transformation. (p. 1958)
Kegley, David E. Where Does Rain Come From? (p. 1907)
Kehe, David & Kehe, Peggy Dustin. Conversation Strategies: Pair & Group Activities for Developing Communicative Competence. (p. 361)
Kehe, Peggy Dustin, jt. auth. see Kehe, David.
Kehew, George & Kehew, Roger. Brett the Collector. (p. 226)
Kehew, Roger, jt. auth. see Kehew, George.
Kehl, Drusilla, illus. see Levinson, Robin K.
Kehl, Esther. Amazing Action Alphabet Activities. Carlson, Andy, illus. (p. 52)
Kehl, R., jt. auth. see Edens, Cooper.
Kehm, Greg. Olympic Swimming & Diving. (p. 1288)
Kehn, Regina, illus. see Ende, Michael & Michael, Ende.
Kehne, Carroll Harrison, Jr. Buried Treasure, a Pirate's Tale (p. 243)
Kehnemui Donnelly, Susan. Al-Rihlah Al-Mudhishah: Jawlah Fi Al-Mamlakah Wa-Aramku Al-Saudiyah. (p. 33)
Kehner, George B. Date Rape Drugs. (p. 409)
Kehoe, John, et al. Mind Power for Children: The Guide for Parents & Teachers. (p. 1145)
Kehoe, Lindy. Home on a Giggle. (p. 792)
Kehoe, Stasia Ward. Sound of Letting Go. (p. 1615)
Kehoe, Tim. Furious Jones & the Assassin's Secret. (p. 650)
—Top Secret Toys. Francis, Guy, illus. (p. 1769)
—Unusual Mind of Vincent Shadow. Francis, Guy & Wohnoutka, Mike, illus. (p. 1823)
—Vincent Shadow: Toy Inventor. Francis, Guy & Wohnoutka, Mike, illus. (p. 1842)
Kehret, Peg. Abduction! (p. 4)
—Animals Welcome: A Life of Reading, Writing & Rescue. (p. 84)
—Backstage Fright. (p. 130)
—Bone Breath & the Vandals. (p. 208)
—Dangerous Deception. (p. 404)
—Deadly Stranger. (p. 418)
—Desert Danger. (p. 429)
—Escaping the Giant Wave. (p. 535)
—Flood Disaster. (p. 605)
—Ghost Dog Secrets. (p. 670)
—Ghost Followed Us Home. (p. 670)
—Ghost's Grave. (p. 672)
—Peg Kehret Thrill-Ogy. (p. 1335)
—Race to Disaster. (p. 1431)
—Runaway Twin. (p. 1496)
—Screaming Eagles. (p. 1533)
—Secret Journey. (p. 1541)
—Shelter Dogs: Amazing Stories of Adopted Strays. Farrar, Greg, photos by. (p. 1565)
—Stolen Children. (p. 1652)
—Tell It Like It Is: Fifty Monologs for Talented Teens (p. 1716)
—Trapped. (p. 1779)
Kehret, Peg & the Cat, Pete. Spy Cat. (p. 1636)
—Stranger Next Door. (p. 1665)
—Trapped! (p. 1779)
Kei, Rose. Emotion & Spirit in Harmony: The ABC's of Emotion. Smith, Penny, ed. (p. 520)
Keido, Ippo, jt. auth. see Stone, Kazuko G.
Keierleber, Tricia. She Is not your real Mommy! (p. 1564)
Keighery, Chrissie. I Heart You, Archie de Souza. (p. 839)
—Invisible Me. (p. 885)
—Love Is the New Black. (p. 1060)
—Outside In. (p. 1313)
—Waiting for It. (p. 1852)
—Whisper. (p. 1912)
Keil, James. Tiger & the Poachers. (p. 1748)
Keil, Melissa. Life in Outer Space (p. 1010)
Keil, Patricia. Mary Dannie. (p. 1100)
Keilbart, L. S. One. Benson, Barbara, illus. (p. 1293)
Keillor, Garrison. Cat, You Better Come Home. Johnson, Steve & Fancher, Lou, illus. (p. 278)
—Old Man Who Loved Cheese. (p. 1284)
Keilty, Derek. Back up the Beanstalk. Myler, Terry, illus. (p. 130)
Keily, Kevin. Horse Called el Dorado. (p. 799)
Keimig, Candice, illus. see Andrews, Alexa.
Keimig, Candice, illus. see Baltzer, Rochelle.
Keimig, Candice, illus. see Elston, Heidi M. D.
Keimig, Candice, illus. see Gunderson, Megan M.
Keimig, Candice, illus. see O'Brien, Bridget.
Keino, illus. see Gunderson, Jessica.
Keino, illus. see Patterson, James & Papademetriou, Lisa.
Keiran, Monique. Pachyrhinosaurus: The Mystery of the Horned Dinosaur (p. 1317)
Keiser, Cody. Baby Animals. (p. 124)
—Fleas. (p. 603)
—Is It Hot or Is It Cold? Describe & Compare Measurable Attributes. (p. 889)
—Thurgood Marshall: Civil Rights Leader. (p. 1746)
Keiser, Debbie Triska, jt. auth. see McGee, Brenda Holt.
Keiser, Frances R. Annie the River Otter: The Adventures of Pelican Pete. Keiser, Hugh M., illus. (p. 87)
Keiser, Hugh M., illus. see Keiser, Frances R.
Keiser, Melissa. My Airplane Book-Colors. (p. 1195)
—My Airplane Book-Counting. (p. 1195)
Keiser, Paige, illus. see Adams, Diane.
Keiser, Paige, illus. see Adams, Michelle Medlock.
Keiser, Paige, illus. see Barber, Alison.
Keiser, Paige, illus. see Pelley, Kathleen T.
Keiser, Tammy L., illus. see Maisel, Grace Ragues & Shubert, Samantha.
Keiser, Tammy L., illus. see Rossoff, Donald.
Keiser, Tammy L., illus. see Schram, Peninnah.
Keister, Douglas. Regalo de Fernando. Keister, Douglas, photos by. (p. 1457)
Keita, Fatou, tr. see Asare, Meshack.
Keith, Barbara Benson. Girls & Boys of Mother Goose. (p. 679)
—Mosaic Zoo: An ABC Book. Keith, Barbara Benson, illus. (p. 1176)
Keith, Baxter. Judas Kiss. (p. 930)
Keith, Brooke. Chrissie's Shell. Bausman, Mary, illus. (p. 311)
Keith, David. Hands Across Time. (p. 741)
Keith, Donna. I Love You All the Same Edgson, Allison, illus. (p. 843)
—I Love You Even When Edgson, Allison, illus. (p. 843)
Keith, Doug. B Is for Baseball: Alphabet Cards. (p. 122)
Keith, Doug, illus. see Adler, Kathy.
Keith, Doug, illus. see Cohlene, Terri.
Keith, Doug, illus. see Okimoto, Jean Davies.
Keith, Doug, illus. see Tompert, Ann.
Keith, Gill, compiled by. Finances: Managing Money God's Way. (p. 587)
Keith, Helen, jt. auth. see Costello, Dee.
Keith, Kody. Horace the Horse Threw a Shoe. (p. 797)
Keith, Patty J. Hank the Honking Goose Learns to Listen. Wright, Brent A., illus. (p. 742)
—I Wish I Was a Mallard but God Made Me a Pekin Instead. Keith, Patty J., photos by. (p. 849)
—Will You Be My Friend? Even If I Am Different from You. Keith, Patty J., photos by. (p. 1932)
Keith, Sarah A. Chalk-It-up: 22 Awesome Outdoor Games Kids Draw with Chalk. MacLeod, Kit, ed. (p. 288)
Keith, Ted. Matt Kenseth. (p. 1109)
Keithahn, Mary Nelson, ed. see Horman, John D., et al.
Keithley, Laura Lee. Ellie's Big Day. Holliday, Holly, illus. (p. 514)
Keithline, Brian, illus. see Redwine, Connie.
Keithly, Bryan. Princess Tarang. (p. 1405)
—Timmy Wren. (p. 1755)
Keitz, Roderick K. North Pole Chronicles (p. 1265)
Keitzmueller, Christian, illus. see Schatz, Dennis & Bonadonna, Davide.
Keizer, Garret, et al, contrib. by. Twelve Seasons of Vermont: A Vermont Life Book. (p. 1800)
Kekewich, Deborah. Balloons. (p. 135)
Kelahan, Renee. Agua, the Mysterious Portuguese Water Dog. (p. 30)
Kelaita, Lynda. Some Houses Are White. (p. 1609)
Kelbaugh, Duncan, jt. auth. see Beck, Alison.
Kelbaugh, Duncan & Beck, Alison. Best Garden Plants for Atlantic Canada. (p. 169)
Kelbly, Kelly. Stuck in the Middle. (p. 1668)
Kelborne, Wenna. Stinkozimus. (p. 1651)
Kelby, Tom. Nathaniel's Journey: The King's Armory. Yaeger, Mark, illus. (p. 1231)
Kelch, Kalle. Grab Your Boarding Pass: A Daily Devotional for Juniors/Earliteens. (p. 704)
Kelder, Karin H. Study & Master Physical Science Grade 10 Learner's Book. (p. 1670)
—Study & Master Physical Science Grade 10 Learner's Book Afrikaans Translation. (p. 1670)
Keleher, Fran, illus. see Kantar, Andrew.
Kelemen, Pal. Medieval American Art, a Survey in Two Volumes (p. 1119)
Kelemen, Violet. Misty Finds a Family. (p. 1155)
Kelesides, Tom, jt. auth. see Dye, Troy.
Kelfher, Brian, jt. auth. see Nolen, Jerdine.
Kelin, Daniel. Marshall Island Legends & Stories. Nashton, Nashon, illus. (p. 1096)
Kelin, John, ed. see Salandria, Vincent J.
Kell, Harley, illus. see Kell, Nancy.
Kell, Nancy. Pearls of Wisdom; Pearl Makes Pono. Kell, Harley, illus. (p. 1333)
Kellaher, Karen. Grammar Games & Activities Kids Can't Resist! 40 Super-Cool Crosswords, Codes, Mazes & More That Teach the Essential Rules of Grammar. (p. 706)
Kellas, Lydia. Our English 3 Student Book: Volume 0, Part 0: Integrated Course for the Caribbean. (p. 1308)
Kellas, Lydia, jt. auth. see Lucantoni, Peter.
Kellas, Lydia, et al. Our English. (p. 1308)
—Our English 4. (p. 1308)
Kelleher, Damian. Planes. Robson, Matthew, illus. (p. 1367)
Kelleher, Kathie, illus. see Cunningham, Sheila S.
Kelleher, Kathie, illus. see Neme, Laurel.
Kelleher, Kathie, illus. see Rossi, Sophia.
Kelleher, Michael, illus. see Campbell, Jan-Ives.
Kelleher, Victor. Big Big Book of Gibblewort the Goblin King, Stephen Michael, illus. (p. 178)
—Dogboy. (p. 462)
—Gibblewort the Goblin King. Stephen Michael, illus. (p. 674)
—Goblin at the Beach. King, Stephen Michael, illus. (p. 688)
—Goblin at the Zoo. King, Stephen Michael, illus. (p. 688)
—Goblin in the Bush. King, Stephen Michael, illus. (p. 688)
—Goblin in the City. King, Stephen Michael, illus. (p. 688)
—Goblin in the Snow. King, Stephen Michael, illus. (p. 688)
—Goblin on the Reef. King, Stephen Michael, illus. (p. 688)
—Return of Gibblewort the Goblin King, Stephen Michael, illus. (p. 1464)
Kellem-Kellner, Blynda, illus. see Miller-Gill, Angela.
Kellen, Susan. My Name Is Ed or Betty. (p. 1215)
Kellenbarger, Sandy Hurst. Magic Gnomes. (p. 1072)
—Magic Gnomes Treasure Hunt. (p. 1072)
Keller, Alex. Rebellion. (p. 1451)
Keller, Bill. Tree Shaker: The Life of Nelson Mandela. (p. 1783)
—Tree Shaker: The Story of Nelson Mandela. (p. 1783)
Keller, Carolyn, jt. auth. see Cooper, Amy.
Keller, Carolyn, jt. auth. see Cyr, Jessica.
Keller, Carolyn, jt. auth. see Florence, Sylvia.
Keller, Carolyn, jt. auth. see Joseph, Tiffani.
Keller, Carolyn, jt. auth. see Marshall, Ashley.
Keller, Carolyn, jt. auth. see Palmer, Amy.
Keller, Carolyn, jt. auth. see Sandoval, Kate.
Keller, Carolyn, jt. auth. see Thomas, Jesse.
Keller, Carolyn, jt. auth. see Todd, Danielle.
Keller, Carolyn, jt. auth. see Woolsey, Matthew.
Keller, Carolyn & Seaman, Jim. Allegheny College College Prowler off the Record. (p. 46)
Keller, Charles. Knock-Knocks. Hoffman, Sanford, illus. (p. 965)
—Super Silly Riddles. Winter, Dave, illus. (p. 1681)
Keller, Charles & Rosenbloom, Joseph. Gigantic Book of Giggles. (p. 676)
Keller, Dick, illus. see Keller, Irene.
Keller, Elinoar & Peleg-Segal, Naama. Just Like I Wanted. Gordon-Noy, Aya, illus. (p. 939)
Keller, Ellen. Kids Are Citizens. (p. 952)
Keller, Ellen & Schifini, Alfredo. Kids Manage Money. (p. 954)
Keller, Gailya Len. Secret of Smiley's Woods. (p. 1542)
Keller, George. Squirrelly Whirly & the Haunted House. (p. 1637)
Keller, Holly. Bed Full of Cats. (p. 156)
—Farfallina & Marcel. Keller, Holly, illus. (p. 573)
—Hat. (p. 752)
—Hat. Keller, Holly, illus. (p. 752)
—Help! A Story of Friendship. Keller, Holly, illus. (p. 765)
—Miranda's Beach Day. Keller, Holly, illus. (p. 1149)
—Pearl's New Skates. Keller, Holly, illus. (p. 1333)
—Sophie's Window. Keller, Holly, illus. (p. 1613)
—Van. (p. 1832)
—What I See. (p. 1887)
Keller, Holly, illus. see Pfeffer, Wendy.
Keller, Irene. Santa Visits the Thingumajigs. Keller, Dick, illus. (p. 1513)
—Thingamajig Book of Manners. Keller, Dick, illus. (p. 1733)
—Thingamajig Books of Do's & Don'ts. Keller, Dick, illus. (p. 1733)
Keller, Jeff, Jr. Ricky Climbs Pikes Peak. Gilman, Christopher, illus. (p. 1470)
Keller, Jennifer, illus. see Amidon Lusted, Marcia.
Keller, Jennifer K., illus. see Yasuda, Anita.
Keller, Jessica. Mia's Marvelous Musical Group. (p. 1134)
Keller, John E. Emperor's Elephant. (p. 521)
Keller, Kristin Thoennes. Booker T. Washington: Innovative Educator (p. 212)
—Camping. (p. 257)
—From Apples to Applesauce (p. 642)
—From Maple Trees to Maple Syrup (p. 643)
—From Oranges to Orange Juice (p. 643)
—From Peanuts to Peanut Butter (p. 643)
—From Wheat to Bread (p. 644)
—Responsibility (p. 1463)
Keller, Laurie. Arnie the Doughnut. Keller, Laurie, illus. (p. 100)
—Arnie - The Doughnut. Keller, Laurie, illus. (p. 100)
—Birdy's Smile Book. Keller, Laurie, illus. (p. 192)
—Bowling Alley Bandit. Keller, Laurie, illus. (p. 216)
—Do unto Otters: A Book about Manners. Keller, Laurie, illus. (p. 457)
—Invasion of the Ufonuts. Keller, Laurie, illus. (p. 883)
—Open Wide: Tooth School Inside. Keller, Laurie, illus. (p. 1299)
—Scrambled States of America. (p. 1532)
—Scrambled States of America. Keller, Laurie, illus. (p. 1532)
—Scrambled States of America Talent Show. Keller, Laurie, illus. (p. 1532)
Keller, Laurie, illus. see Wulffson, Don.
Keller, Matt, illus. see Burkum, Rachel.
Keller, Matthew M., illus. see Gibbons, Erin, ed.
Keller, Nora Okja. Fox Girl. (p. 626)
Keller, R W. Biology Level I Laboratory Workbook. (p. 189)
—Biology Pre-Level 1. (p. 189)
—Chemistry Pre-Level I Laboratory Workbook. (p. 297)
—Physics Level I Laboratory Workbook. (p. 1353)
Keller, Rebecca W. Biology Level I. (p. 189)
—Chemistry Pre-Level I. Moneymaker, Janet, illus. (p. 297)
—Physics Level I. (p. 1353)
—Pre-Level I Physics Laboratory Workbook. (p. 1394)
—Real Science-4-kids Chemistry Level I Student Textbook. (p. 1449)
—Real Science-4-Kids PreLevel I Biology Student Textbook. (p. 1449)
Keller, Susanna. Age of Exploration. (p. 29)
—Meet the Ape. (p. 1122)
—Meet the Elephant. (p. 1122)
—Meet the Giraffe. (p. 1122)
—Meet the Lion. (p. 1123)
—Meet the Panda. (p. 1123)
—Meet the Sea Lion. (p. 1123)
—True Story of Christopher Columbus. (p. 1793)
—True Story of Lewis & Clark. (p. 1793)
—True Story of Paul Revere's Ride. (p. 1793)
Keller, Susanna & Levy, Janey. Primary Source Investigation of the Alamo. (p. 1400)
Keller, William B. Olivia & the Mystery. (p. 1286)
Kellerhals-Stewart, Heather. Brave Highland Heart. (p. 223)
—SAR: Powderhounds (p. 1514)
—Skookum Sal, Birling Gal. Blaine, Janice, illus. (p. 1586)
Kellerman, Aliza, jt. auth. see Kellerman, Faye.
Kellerman, Faye. Garden of Eden & Other Criminal Delights. (p. 656)
—Stone Kiss. (p. 1652)
—Street Dreams. (p. 1666)
Kellerman, Faye, jt. auth. see Kellerman, Jonathan.
Kellerman, Faye & Kellerman, Aliza. Prism. (p. 1407)
Kellerman, Jonathan & Kellerman, Faye. Double Homicide. (p. 473)
Kellermann, Alan. You, Me & the Birds. (p. 1976)
Keller-Miller, LeAnn Marie. When I Grow Up: An A-Z Poem Book for Children & Their Dreams. (p. 1903)
Kelley, Aimee & Lauer, Brett Fletcher. Bartlett's Words for the Wedding. (p. 140)
Kelley, Ann. Burying Beetle (p. 244)
—Inchworm. (p. 868)
Kelley, Barbara, jt. auth. see Elwell, Telva.
Kelley, C. April. Ostrom, Bob, illus. (p. 93)
—Atlanta Braves. (p. 112)

K

—August. Ostrom, Bob, illus. (p. 115)
—Boston Celtics. (p. 215)
—Boston Red Sox. (p. 215)
—Chicago Cubs. (p. 299)
—December. Ostrom, Bob, illus. (p. 421)
—February. Ostrom, Bob, illus. (p. 580)
—January. Ostrom, Bob, illus. (p. 908)
—July. Ostrom, Bob, illus. (p. 933)
—June. Ostrom, Bob, illus. (p. 934)
—Los Angeles Lakers. (p. 1053)
—March. Ostrom, Bob, illus. (p. 1091)
—May. Ostrom, Bob, illus. (p. 1112)
—Miami Heat. (p. 1134)
—New York Knicks. (p. 1248)
—New York Yankees. (p. 1248)
—November. Ostrom, Bob, illus. (p. 1268)
—October. Ostrom, Bob, illus. (p. 1277)
—Philadelphia Phillies. (p. 1350)
—San Antonio Spurs. (p. 1510)
—September. Ostrom, Bob, illus. (p. 1551)
—St. Louis Cardinals. (p. 1638)
Kelley, Charlie. Buddy the Beagle: 2010 Christmas Edition. (p. 235)
Kelley, D. G., illus. see Allan, David & Brown, Vinson.
Kelley, Dawn Ann & Kelley, James G. Legacy. (p. 987)
Kelley, Donald R., jt. auth. see Smith, Bonnie G.
Kelley, Ellen A. Buckamoo Girls. Curry, Tom, illus. (p. 234)
—My Life as a Chicken. Slack, Michael H., illus. (p. 1211)
Kelley, Emily. Christmas Around the World. Oeltjenbruns, Joni, illus. (p. 312)
—Navidad Alrededor del Mundo. Translations.com Staff, tr. (p. 1237)
Kelley, Gail & Hershberger, Carol. Come Mime with Me: A Guide to Preparing Scriptural Dramas for Children. (p. 347)
Kelley, Gary, illus. see de Maupassant, Guy.
Kelley, Gary, illus. see Frisch, Aaron.
Kelley, Gary, illus. see Lewis, J. Patrick.
Kelley, Gary, illus. see Rappaport, Doreen.
Kelley, Gerald, illus. see Anderson, AnnMarie.
Kelley, Gerald, illus. see Blane, Francisco.
Kelley, Gerald, illus. see Bredeson, Carmen.
Kelley, Gerald, illus. see Fuerst, Jeffrey B.
Kelley, Gerald, illus. see Galbraith, Kathryn O.
Kelley, Gerald, illus. see Green, Carl R. & Sanford, William R.
Kelley, Gerald, illus. see Silverstein, Alvin, et al.
Kelley, Gerald, illus. see Smith, Carrie.
Kelley, Gerald, illus. see Stewart, Melissa.
Kelley, Gerald, illus. see Stiefel, Chana.
Kelley, Gerald, illus. see Stone, Tanya Lee.
Kelley, Gina Grimes. Littlest Monster. (p. 1039)
Kelley, Gloria. Beverly Babes & Guys: Alicia's Thirtee. (p. 173)
Kelley, J. A. Meteor Showers. (p. 1130)
Kelley, James E. & Buckley, James. Baseball. (p. 140)
Kelley, James G., jt. auth. see Kelley, Dawn Ann.
Kelley, Jane. Book of Dares for Lost Friends. (p. 211)
—Desperate Adventures of Zeno & Alya. (p. 430)
—Girl Behind the Glass. (p. 678)
—Nature Girl. (p. 1236)
Kelley, Jennifer. Ways Things Move. (p. 1865)
Kelley, Jesse, et al. Visions. (p. 1845)
Kelley, K. C. AFC East. (p. 26)
—AFC West. (p. 26)
—Astronauts! (p. 109)
—BASE Jumping. (p. 140)
—Basketball Superstars 2015. (p. 143)
—Bungee Jumping. (p. 242)
—Dallas Cowboys. (p. 401)
—Drag Racing. (p. 476)
—Football: Dynamic Duos. (p. 615)
—Freestyle Skiing. (p. 635)
—Gliding. (p. 683)
—Hang Gliding. (p. 742)
—Hottest NASCAR Machines. (p. 802)
—How Spies Work. (p. 812)
—Marine Biologists! (p. 1094)
—Mountain Biking. (p. 1180)
—NASCAR. (p. 1230)
—Pit Stop Secrets. (p. 1364)
—Quarterbacks. (p. 1423)
—Running Backs. (p. 1497)
—Skateboard Stars. (p. 1583)
—Skateboarding. (p. 1583)
—Smokin' Race Cars. (p. 1594)
—Stand-up Paddleboarding. (p. 1639)
—Stunt Bicycle Riding. (p. 1670)
—Surfing. (p. 1685)
—Surf's Up! (p. 1685)
—Ultralight Aircraft. (p. 1810)
Kelley, K. C., jt. auth. see Child's World Staff, The.
Kelley, K. C., jt. auth. see Child's World Staff.
Kelley, K. C., jt. auth. see Eliason, Mike.
Kelley, K. C., jt. auth. see Roshell, Starshine.
Kelley, K. C., jt. auth. see Scholastic, Inc. Staff.
Kelley, K. C. & Buckley, James. Paramedic (p. 1324)
Kelley, Kevin M. Up down All Around. (p. 1824)
Kelley, Khris. Ringo the Helpful Raccoon. Crisenbery, Casey, illus. (p. 1473)
Kelley, Lisa. Nutty. (p. 1274)
Kelley, Louise. Stretch the Giraffe. (p. 1667)
Kelley Ludovici, Joanne Dzioba. Maggie Stone Becomes Morning Starr. (p. 1071)
Kelley, Lynn. First Boykin Spaniels: The Story of Dumpy & Singo. Gardiner, Lisa, illus. (p. 593)
Kelley, Maria Felicia. Buz Words: Discovering Words in Pairs. Kelley, Maria Felicia, illus. (p. 248)
Kelley, Marty. Fame, Fortune, & the Bran Muffins of Doom. Kelley, Marty, illus. (p. 567)
—Messiest Desk. (p. 1130)
—Spring Goes Squish: A Vibrant Volume of Vociferous Vernal Verse. (p. 1635)
—Winter Woes. (p. 1938)
Kelley, Marty, illus. see Benoit, Brian.
Kelley, Matt. Crosswind: A Spirit-Drawn Experience. (p. 385)
—Crosswind: A Spirit-Driven Experience. (p. 385)
Kelley, Michelle. Different Places, Different Words. (p. 438)
—Just Like You. (p. 939)
—Places I Go. (p. 1366)
—Rules, Rules, Rules! (p. 1495)
—Rules, Rules, Rules. (p. 1495)
Kelley, Patrick, illus. see Driscoll, Christ.
Kelley, Patrick, illus. see Luongo, Jane.
Kelley, Patrick, illus. see Stone, Elaine Murray.
Kelley, R. A. Why Doesn't Daddy Feel so Well? (p. 1924)
Kelley, Tracey. Assassination of John F. Kennedy. (p. 107)
Kelley, Trevor, jt. auth. see Simon, Leslie.
Kelley, True. Dog Who Saved Santa. Kelley, True, illus. (p. 462)
—Pierre-Auguste Renoir - Paintings That Smile. (p. 1357)
—Quién Fue Pablo Picasso? Kelley, True & Harrison, Nancy, illus. (p. 1427)
—School Lunch. Kelley, True, illus. (p. 1523)
—Where Is Mount Rushmore? (p. 1908)
—Where Is Mount Rushmore? Groff, David & Hinderliter, John, illus. (p. 1908)
—Who Is Dolly Parton? (p. 1915)
—Who Is Dolly Parton? Harrison, Nancy et al, illus. (p. 1915)
—Who Was Abigail Adams? (p. 1918)
—Who Was Abigail Adams? O'Brien, John, illus. (p. 1918)
—Who Was Pablo Picasso? Kelley, True & Harrison, Nancy, illus. (p. 1919)
—Who Was Roald Dahl? (p. 1919)
—Who Was Roald Dahl? Marchesi, Stephen & Harrison, Nancy, illus. (p. 1919)
Kelley, True, illus. see Edwards, Roberta.
Kelley, True, illus. see Hill, Susanna Leonard.
Kelley, True, illus. see Hodgkins, Fran & Hodgkins.
Kelley, True, illus. see Hodgkins, Fran.
Kelley, True, illus. see Kimmelman, Leslie.
Kelley, True, illus. see Reid, Margarette S.
Kelley, W. Michael. Humongous Book of Algebra Problems: Translated for People Who Don't Speak Math. (p. 827)
Kelley, Walter P. "I Love You" Story. McGregor, Tony L., illus. (p. 844)
Kelli Hunter Beamon. Mommy, I Want to Be a Cheerleader! (p. 1162)
Kellie, Kerrie. Benjamin's Journey. (p. 165)
—Sleep over Adventure. (p. 1588)
Kellingley, Krystina. Mistflower - the Loneliest Mouse. (p. 1155)
Kellis, Michael. Grubkins. (p. 727)
Kellner, Brian. Brandon: Book One of the Wizard Rift Series. Kellner, Joanne, ed. (p. 222)
Kellner, Joanne, ed. see Kellner, Brian.
Kellogg, Catherine Berry. Moose Who Ate My Fort: Stories from Bella Sage. (p. 1173)
Kellogg, Elijah. Ark of Elm Island. (p. 99)
—Ark of Elm Island by Rev Elijah Kellogg. (p. 99)
—Charlie Bell, the Waif of Elm Island by Rev Elijah Kellogg. (p. 292)
—Lion Ben of Elm Island. (p. 1020)
—Young Shipbuilders of Elm Island by Rev Elijah Kellogg. (p. 1979)
Kellogg, Garland. Things They Never Taught You in School. (p. 1733)
Kellogg, Richard. Barry Baskerville Solves a Case. Kato, Gary, illus. (p. 140)
Kellogg, Steven. Johnny Appleseed. Cohn, Amy, ed. (p. 923)
—Missing Mitten Mystery. Kellogg, Steven, illus. (p. 1152)
—Mysterious Tadpole. Kellogg, Steven, illus. (p. 1223)
—Paul Bunyan. Kellogg, Steven, illus. (p. 1330)
—Pied Piper's Magic. Kellogg, Steven, illus. (p. 1356)
—Pinkerton, Behave! (p. 1360)
—There Was an Old Woman Who Swallowed a Fly. (p. 1730)
Kellogg, Steven, illus. see Coots, J. Fred.
Kellogg, Steven, illus. see Gillespie, Haven & Coots, J. Fred.
Kellogg, Steven, illus. see Guarino, Deborah.
Kellogg, Steven, illus. see Haseley, Dennis.
Kellogg, Steven, illus. see Kinerk, Robert.
Kellogg, Steven, illus. see MacLachlan, Patricia.
Kellogg, Steven, illus. see Mahy, Margaret.
Kellogg, Steven, illus. see Massie, Diane Redfield.
Kellogg, Steven, illus. see McNulty, Faith.
Kellogg, Steven, illus. see Noble, Trinka Hakes.
Kellogg, Steven, illus. see Nodset, Joan L.
Kellogg, Steven, illus. see Schwartz, David M.
Kellogg, Steven, illus. see Schwartz, David M. & Schwartz, David.
Kellogg, Steven, illus. see Ward, B. J.
Kellogg, Steven, jt. auth. see Guarino, Deborah.
Kellogg, Steven, jt. auth. see Kinerk, Robert.
Kellogg, Steven, tr. see Gillespie, Haven & Coots, J. Fred.
Kells, Deanne. Jamestown Community. (p. 907)
—Mesa Verde Communities. (p. 1129)
Kellum Enterprises, 1st. ADVENTURES of Diggle, Boogle & Lolo: Diggle Loses Lolo. (p. 17)
Kellum, Rebecca L. Conceited Little Girl. (p. 355)
Kelly, Allison, et al. Castle That Jack Built. (p. 277)
Kelly, Allison Palmer. Power of Words. (p. 1390)
Kelly, Ann. Ready ... Set ... GOLF! An Essential Guide for Young Golfers. (p. 1447)
Kelly, Annette. Max's Magical Journey. (p. 1112)
Kelly, Apryl, jt. auth. see Small, Amare.
Kelly, Becky. Fairy Kisses. (p. 563)
—Night Before Christmas. (p. 1252)
Kelly, Becky, illus. see Fallon, Kathy Reilly & Pellegrino, Frank.
Kelly, Bernadette. Balancing Act (p. 133)
—Courage to Ride (p. 372)
—If Wishes Were Horses (p. 854)
—Leap of Faith (p. 982)
—Making Waves (p. 1082)
—Ridgeview Riding Club (p. 1471)
—Team Challenge (p. 1710)
Kelly, Bernadette & Ward, Krista. Naughty Norton Alger, Liz, illus. (p. 1237)
—Norton Saves the Day Alger, Liz, illus. (p. 1266)
—Norton's First Show Alger, Liz, illus. (p. 1266)
—Pony Tales. Alger, Liz, illus. (p. 1383)
—Who Stole Norton? Alger, Liz, illus. (p. 1917)
Kelly, Bill. You Ought to Know: A Guy's Guide to Sex. (p. 1976)
Kelly, Camryn. Hot Chocolate with God: Just Me & Who God Created Me to Be. (p. 801)
Kelly, Camryn, et al. Hot Chocolate with God: Just Me & My Friends & Family. (p. 801)
Kelly, Cathy, illus. see Gould, Ellen.
Kelly, Cheryl. Adam the Adventurous Ant. (p. 11)
Kelly, Christopher M., jt. auth. see Northcutt, Wendy.
Kelly, Claire. Nellie in the News. Hicks, Faith, illus. (p. 1240)
Kelly, Cooper, illus. see Gamble, Adam & Adams, David J.
Kelly, Cooper, illus. see Gamble, Adam & Jasper, Mark.
Kelly, Cooper, illus. see Gamble, Adam, et al.
Kelly, Cooper, illus. see Gamble, Adam.
Kelly, Cooper, illus. see Gamble, Jasper, et al.
Kelly, Cooper, illus. see Jasper, Mark & Gamble, Adam.
Kelly, Cooper, illus. see Jasper, Mark.
Kelly, Cooper, illus. see Tougias, Michael, et al.
Kelly, Cooper, jt. auth. see Gamble, Adam.
Kelly, Cooper, jt. auth. see Jasper, Mark.
Kelly, David A. All-Star Joker. Meyers, Mark, illus. (p. 45)
—Astro Outlaw. (p. 109)
—Astro Outlaw. Meyers, Mark, illus. (p. 109)
—Babe Ruth & the Baseball Curse. Jessell, Tim, illus. (p. 123)
—Ballpark Mysteries #10: the Rookie Blue Jay. Meyers, Mark, illus. (p. 135)
—Ballpark Mysteries #8: the Missing Marlin. Meyers, Mark, illus. (p. 135)
—Ballpark Mysteries #9: the Philly Fake. Meyers, Mark, illus. (p. 135)
—Fenway Foul-Up. Meyers, Mark, illus. (p. 581)
—L. A. Dodger. Meyers, Mark, illus. (p. 969)
—Miracle Mud: Lena Blackburne & the Secret Mud That Changed Baseball. Dominguez, Oliver, illus. (p. 1148)
—Missing Marlin. (p. 1152)
—Philly Fake. (p. 1351)
—Pinstripe Ghost. Meyers, Mark, illus. (p. 1361)
—Rookie Blue Jay. (p. 1487)
—San Francisco Splash. (p. 1510)
—San Francisco Splash. Meyers, Mark, illus. (p. 1510)
—Tiger Trouble. Meyers, Mark, illus. (p. 1748)
—Tiger Troubles. (p. 1748)
—Wrigley Riddle. (p. 1963)
—Wrigley Riddle. Meyers, Mark, illus. (p. 1963)
Kelly, Deborah. Bouncing Ball. Perry, Georgia, illus. (p. 216)
—Jam for Nana. Stewart, Lisa, illus. (p. 906)
Kelly, Diana. Tamla Bear & the Magic Goblin. Walker, Jack, illus. (p. 1704)
Kelly, Doris Holik. Mystery of the Copper Turtle. (p. 1225)
Kelly, Dorothy A. Developing a Sense of Self: A Workbook of Tenets & Tactics for Adolescent Girls. (p. 431)
Kelly, Dot Hutchinson. Meet Moses Mcrae. (p. 1121)
Kelly, Douglas F. & Jordan, Richard. New Life in the Wasteland: 2nd Corinthians on the Cost & Glory of Christian Ministry. (p. 1246)
Kelly Edwards Elementary School (Williston, S.C.) Staff, contrib. by. ABCs of Williston History. (p. 4)
Kelly, Elaine A. & Carl, Jean R. Among the Buildings That Touch the Sky: Philadelphia. Noone, Cathleen L., illus. (p. 65)
Kelly, Erin. Mystery at the Eiffel Tower: Paris, France. (p. 1224)
Kelly, Erin, jt. auth. see Kelly, Jill.
Kelly, Erin Entrada. Blackbird Fly. Peterschmidt, Betsy, illus. (p. 197)
Kelly, Evelyn. Coping with Schizophrenia. (p. 365)
—Skeletal System (p. 1584)
Kelly, Evelyn B. Alzheimer's Disease. (p. 51)
Kelly, Evelyn B. & Wilker, Ian. Tuberculosis & Superbugs: Examining TB & Bacterial Infections. (p. 1795)
Kelly, Evelyn B. & Wilson, Claire. Influenza & Bird Flu: Examining the Flu. (p. 873)
—Investigating Influenza & Bird Flu: Real Facts for Real Lives. (p. 884)
Kelly, Evelyn B., et al. Investigating Tuberculosis & Superbugs: Real Facts for Real Lives. (p. 885)
—Tuberculosis & Superbugs: Examining TB & Bacterial Infections. (p. 1795)
Kelly, Everett. Tiny Tom. (p. 1757)
Kelly, Frances & Murray, Penny. Star-Crossed: 18 Tales of Bittersweet Love. (p. 1640)
Kelly, Geoff. How to Draw Krappy Kartoons Really Well. (p. 817)
Kelly, Geoff, illus. see Cohen, Bernard.
Kelly, Harold G. How the Dinosaurs Disappeared. (p. 813)
—Inside the Sun. (p. 877)
—Sol por dentro (Inside the Sun) (p. 1606)
Kelly, Helen. Double Trouble. Whitby, Charlotte, illus. (p. 473)
—Lost in Translation. Whitby, Charlotte, illus. (p. 1056)
—Ruby's Misadventure. Whitby, Charlotte, illus. (p. 1493)
Kelly, Helen, jt. auth. see Harding, David.
Kelly, Irene. Even an Octopus Needs a Home. Kelly, Irene, illus. (p. 541)
—Even an Ostrich Needs a Nest: Where Birds Begin. (p. 541)
—It's a Butterfly's Life. (p. 895)
—It's a Hummingbird's Life. (p. 895)
—Small Dog's Big Life: Around the World with Owney. (p. 1592)
Kelly, Jack. Benjamin Franklin. Tafalla, Ortiz, illus. (p. 164)
Kelly, Jacqueline. Curious World of Calpurnia Tate. (p. 394)
—Evolucion de Calpurnia Tate. (p. 546)
—Evolución de Calpurnia Tate. (p. 546)
—Evolution of Calpurnia Tate. (p. 546)
Kelly, Jacqueline & Grahame, Kenneth. Return to the Willows. Young, Clint, illus. (p. 1465)
Kelly, Jamie, jt. auth. see Benton, Jim.
Kelly, Jamie & Benton, Jim. Never Underestimate Your Dumbness. (p. 1243)
Kelly, Jason. No Fish in My Dish. (p. 1258)
Kelly, Jennifer. Jackson Jones: The Tale of a Boy, an Elf, & a Very Stinky Fish. (p. 904)
Kelly, Jill & Kelly, Erin. Hot Chocolate with God Devotional: More Real Questions & Answers from Girls Just Like You. (p. 801)
Kelly, Jo. Deer Tales of Drummond Island. (p. 423)
Kelly, Joan. Let Me Tell You an African Tale: How the Leopard Got His Spots. (p. 994)
Kelly, Joan Jackson. Let Me Tell You an African Tale: A Goat, a Dog, & a Donkey. (p. 994)
Kelly, Joan L. Dna Connection: Tannenhauser's Theory. (p. 456)
Kelly, Jo'Anne, illus. see Oliviero, Jamie.
Kelly, Jodi. At the Race: Count to Tell the Number of Objects. (p. 111)
Kelly, Joe. Deadpool Classic - Volume 4. Harris, Steven et al, illus. (p. 418)
—Four Eyes: Forged in Flames. Vol. 1 (p. 625)
—Golden Perfect. (p. 695)
—Justice League Elite (p. 940)
Kelly, Joe, jt. auth. see Starkings, Richard.
Kelly, Joe & Mahnke, Doug. Obsidian Age (p. 1275)
Kelly, Joe & Turner, Michael. Superman - Godfall. (p. 1683)
Kelly, Joe & Weisenfeld, Aron. Black & White (p. 195)
Kelly, Joe, et al. Candor. (p. 261)
—Infinite Crisis. (p. 873)
—Megamind Movie Prequel. (p. 1124)
Kelly, John, illus. see Goodhart, Pippa & Goodheart, Pippa.
Kelly, John, illus. see Goodhart, Pippa.
Kelly, John, illus. see Platt, Richard.
Kelly, John, illus. see Taylor, Thomas.
Kelly, John, illus. see Tincknell, Cathy.
Kelly, John P. & Costa, Paul. Power to Get Wealth. (p. 1390)
Kelly, Joseph, illus. see Kerrin, Jessica Scott & Kerrin, Jessica.
Kelly, Joseph, illus. see Kerrin, Jessica Scott.
Kelly, Joseph, illus. see Parker, Marjorie Blain.
Kelly, Judy, illus. see Everson, Hobart G.
Kelly, Julia, illus. see Brenner, Harriett A.
Kelly, Kachelle. Pretty Painful. (p. 1398)
Kelly, Karen. Angel Tree. (p. 74)
Kelly, Kate. Early Civilizations: Prehistoric Times to 500 C. E. (p. 493)
—Medicine Becomes a Science, 1840-1999. (p. 1119)
—Medicine Today: 2000 to the Present. (p. 1119)
—Middle Ages, 500-1450 C. E. (p. 1137)
—Old World & New: Early Medical Care, 1700-1840. (p. 1285)
—Scientific Revolution & Medicine, 1450-1700. (p. 1528)
Kelly, Kate, jt. auth. see Zeman, Anne.
Kelly, Katherine, text. Albert Bear & the Big Celebration. (p. 34)
Kelly, Kathy & Feder, Debbie. Jelly Bean's Art Museum Adventure. (p. 912)
Kelly, Katy. Big on Plans. Rex, Adam, illus. (p. 183)
—Busy Like You Can't Believe. Rex, Adam, illus. (p. 246)
—Here's the Thing about Me. Rex, Adam, illus. (p. 771)
—Melonhead. Johnson, Gillian, illus. (p. 1125)
—Melonhead & the Big Stink. (p. 1125)
—Melonhead & the Big Stink. Johnson, Gillian, illus. (p. 1125)
—Melonhead & the Undercover Operation. Johnson, Gillian, illus. (p. 1125)
—Melonhead & the Vegalicious Disaster. Johnson, Gillian, illus. (p. 1125)
—Melonhead & the We-Fix-It Company. Johnson, Gillian, illus. (p. 1125)
—Working Myself to Pieces & Bits. Ferguson, Peter, illus. (p. 1953)
Kelly, Keith. Peace Comes to Ajani. Kelly, Keith, illus. (p. 1331)
Kelly, Kelley R. Sundays with Daddy. Cook, Jeffrey, illus. (p. 1676)
Kelly, Kevin Vincent. Hattie Mcdimple Makes a Wish. (p. 753)
Kelly, Kiva A. Pink P. A. M., Pancakes & Poodles: The Joy in Having Caring Friends, Second Edition. (p. 1360)
Kelly, L. Meme's Christmas Stories. (p. 1125)
Kelly, L. J. R. Blanket & Bear, a Remarkable Pair. Tanaka, Yoko, illus. (p. 198)
Kelly, Laurene. Still Waving. (p. 1650)
Kelly, Leslie A., illus. see Anderson, William.
Kelly, Lisa. Many Adventures of Elysse: Her Journey Begins. (p. 1089)
Kelly, Lucas, illus. see Leonard, Krystian.
Kelly, Lynda. Arab Dream Horse, Not. (p. 94)
—Blister Parkin & the Bullies. (p. 199)
—Magazine-Page Pony. (p. 1071)
—Most Horrible Pony! (p. 1177)
Kelly, Lynne. Chained. (p. 288)
—Maths Wizard. (p. 1108)
—Simple Concepts in Physics: Motion. (p. 1577)
—Simple Concepts in Physics: Sound & Light. (p. 1577)
Kelly, Maeve, illus. see Doolan, Catherine.
Kelly, Maoliosa. My Bike Ride: Band 02A/Red A. Roberts, Ley Honor, illus. (p. 1197)
—My Party. (p. 1216)
—My Party. Lumb, Steve, photos by. (p. 1216)
—What Am I? Band 00/Lilac. Blake, Beccy, illus. (p. 1879)
Kelly, Margo. Who R U Really? (p. 1917)
Kelly, Mark. Mousetronaut: Based on a (Partially) True Story. Payne, C. F., illus. (p. 1182)
—Mousetronaut Goes to Mars. Payne, C. F., illus. (p. 1182)
Kelly, Martin. Color Train, Color Train! Luiz, Fernando, illus. (p. 343)
—Skeleton Stretch. (p. 1584)
Kelly, Martin & Adamac, Matt. Three Little Kittens. (p. 1742)
Kelly, Martin & Kelly, Melissa. Government. (p. 704)
Kelly, Martin & Legris, Phil. Itsy Bitsy Spider. (p. 900)
Kelly, Mary. On English Costume. (p. 1288)
Kelly, Mary B., illus. see Horsfall, Jacqueline.
Kelly, Marylee A. Quest to Obsidia: The Second Peter Mcfall Adventure. (p. 1426)
Kelly, Matthew. Why Am I Here? A Story about Becoming The-Best-Version-of-Yourself! Mitchell, Hazel, illus. (p. 1922)
Kelly McGovern Lu. Be Kind to the Earth: A Little Kid's Guide to Reducing your Carbon Footprint. Justin McGovern, illus. (p. 148)

Kelly, Melissa, jt. auth. see Kelly, Martin.
Kelly, Michael, jt. text see Mayer, Kirsten.
Kelly, Mij. Achoo! Good Manners Can Be Contagious! McQuillan, Mary, illus. (p. 9)
—Bed of Your Own. McQuillan, Mary, illus. (p. 156)
—Bump. Allan, Nicholas, illus. (p. 241)
—Have You Seen My Potty? McQuillan, Mary, illus. (p. 754)
—I Hate Everyone. Palmer, Ruth, illus. (p. 838)
—One More Sheep. Ayto, Russell, illus. (p. 1296)
—Preschool Time. McQuillan, Mary, illus. (p. 1396)
—Where Giants Hide. Collins, Ross, illus. (p. 1907)
—Wheres My Darling Daughter. McEwen, Katharine, illus. (p. 1910)
Kelly, Mij & Fuge, Charles. Friendly Day. (p. 637)
Kelly, Miles, jt. auth. see Parker, Steve.
Kelly, Neil & Dorling Kindersley Publishing Staff. Glow in the Dark - Marvel Heroes: Sticker Book. (p. 685)
—Marvel Heroes. (p. 1098)
Kelly, Nigel & Tames, Richard. Point of Impact Series (p. 1377)
Kelly, Nikki. Lailah. (p. 972)
Kelly, P. Coping with Diabetes. (p. 365)
Kelly, Pat. Coping with Diabetes. (p. 365)
—Coping with Schizophrenia. (p. 365)
Kelly, Rachel, jt. ed. see Esiri, Allie.
Kelly, Regina Anne. Energy Supply & Renewable Resources. (p. 528)
Kelly, Richard, ed. see Dickens, Charles.
Kelly, Robert, illus. see Boehm, Patricia.
Kelly, Ryan, illus. see Carey, Mike.
Kelly, Ryan, jt. auth. see Carey, Mike.
Kelly, Shannon, ed. Lyme Disease. (p. 1066)
Kelly, Sharon L. C. M. Coco's Vineyard Vacation: Double Fun on Martha's Vineyard. Galbraith, Alison L., illus. (p. 337)
Kelly, Sheila, jt. auth. see Rotner, Shelley.
Kelly, Sheila M., jt. auth. see Rotner, Shelley.
Kelly, Sophia. What a Beast! A Look-It-Up Guide to the Monsters & Mutants of Mythology. (p. 1878)
Kelly, Stephen M. Prince Chester & the Salamander King (p. 1401)
—Symbala's River. (p. 1693)
Kelly, Susan. Spanish Do Nows. (p. 1621)
Kelly, Susan & Rose, Deborah Lee. Jimmy the Joey: The True Story of an Amazing Koala Rescue. Kelly, Susan, photos by. (p. 918)
Kelly, Terri B. Mary Slessor: Missionary Mother. (p. 1101)
Kelly, Tess. Buko's Journey. (p. 240)
Kelly, Theresa. Aloha Cove Set (p. 48)
—Tony the Pony: Bugs Are Not Bad. Sampson, Jody, illus. (p. 1766)
—Tony the Pony. Sampson, Jody, illus. (p. 1766)
Kelly, Thomas E. Fox & the Young Rooster. Ward, Kelly, illus. (p. 626)
Kelly, Timothy, jt. see Cary, Michael.
Kelly, Tom. Finn's Going. (p. 589)
Kelly, Veronica & Goody, Wendy. One Hundred First Communions. Pruitt, Ginny, illus. (p. 1295)
Kelly, Victoria, ed. see Chandpai - Dhamrai Bangladeshi Students Staff.
Kelm, Tracy Martin. Light. (p. 1014)
Kelman, Ari & Fetter-Vorm, Jonathan. Battle Lines: A Graphic History of the Civil War. Fetter-Vorm, Jonathan, illus. (p. 146)
Kelman, Janet Harvey. Stories from the Crusades (Yesterday's Classics) (p. 1654)
Kelman, Jennifer. Mrs Pinkelmeyer & Moopus Mcglinden Prance into New York City. (p. 1187)
Kelman, Louise & Kelman, Suzanne. Big Purple Undies. Dowling, Jane, ed. (p. 183)
Kelman, Marcy. Annie's Solo Mission. Song, Aram, illus. (p. 87)
—Doc Mcstuffins Doc's Mobile Clinic. Disney Storybook Artists Staff, illus. (p. 459)
Kelman, Marcy, jt. auth. see Disney Book Group Staff.
Kelman, Marcy & Disney Book Group Staff. Ahoy, Izzy! Disney Storybook Art Team, illus. (p. 30)
—Hoppy Clubhouse Easter. Disney Storybook Art Team, illus. (p. 797)
—Minnie's Bow-Tastic Sticker Collection. Disney Storybook Art Team, illus. (p. 1148)
—Out of the Box. Disney Storybook Art Team, illus. (p. 1311)
—Sofia the First Sofia's Royal Sticker Collection. Disney Storybook Art Team, illus. (p. 1605)
—Trick or Treasure? Disney Storybook Artists Staff, illus. (p. 1786)
Kelman, Suzanne, jt. auth. see Kelman, Louise.
Kelner, Toni L. P., jt. ed. see Harris, Charlaine.
Kelsey, Amanda, illus. see Hartley, James.
Kelsey, Amanda, illus. see Winter, Isobelle.
Kelsey, Avonelle. Grandma Says Kelsey, Avonelle, illus. (p. 708)
—Iroquois Medicine Woman. Kelsey, Avonelle, illus. (p. 888)
Kelsey, Dawn M., jt. auth. see Mese, John R.
Kelsey, Elin. Not Your Typical Book about the Environment. Hanmer, Clayton & Owlkids Books Inc. Staff, illus. (p. 1267)
—Wild Ideas. Kim, Soyeon, illus. (p. 1929)
—You Are Stardust. Kim, Soyeon, illus. (p. 1973)
Kelsey, Elin & Owlkids Books Inc. Staff. Strange New Species: Astonishing Discoveries of Life on Earth. (p. 1665)
Kelsey, Juliet Grey. Nettie by the Sea Stories: Set I. (p. 1242)
Kelsey, Linda J. Big Fish. Kelsey-Livin, Barbara, illus. (p. 181)
Kelsey, Marybeth. Recipe for Robbery. (p. 1451)
Kelsey, Stacy. Meet the Pro's with Sproket the Moto Dog (p. 1123)
—Sproket the Moto Dog (p. 1635)
Kelsey-Livin, Barbara. Mighty Beasts. (p. 1140)
—Monkey & the Frog. (p. 1165)
Kelsey-Livin, Barbara, illus. see Kelsey, Linda J.
Kelso, Brendan. Shakespeare's a Midsummer Night's Dream for Kids: 3 Short Melodramatic Plays for 3 Group Sizes. Lopez, Shana, illus. (p. 1559)
Kelso, Brendan P. Shakespeare's Julius Caesar for Kids: 3 Short Melodramatic Plays for 3 Group Sizes. Sidaris-Green, Hannah, ed. (p. 1559)
Kelso, Mary Jean. Adventures of Andy & Spirit: Book 1. Snider, K. C., illus. (p. 16)
—Andy & Spirit Go to the Fair. Snider, K. C., illus. (p. 72)
—Andy & Spirit in Search & Rescue. Snider, Kc, illus. (p. 72)
—Andy & Spirit in the Big Rescue. Snider, K. C., illus. (p. 72)
—Andy & Spirit Meet the Rodeo Queen. Snider, K. C., illus. (p. 72)
—Birds in the Flower Basket. Hammond, Julie, illus. (p. 191)
—Christmas Angel. Snider, K. C., illus. (p. 312)
—Cowboy James. Snider, K. C., illus. (p. 374)
—One Family's Christmas. Snider, K. C., illus. (p. 1295)
—Rv Mouse. Snider, K. C., illus. (p. 1499)
Kelso, Mary Jean & Hammond, Julie. Birds in the Flower Basket. (p. 191)
Kelso, Mary Jean & Snider, K. C. Rv Mouse. (p. 1499)
Kelso, Susan. OUCH or AHHH - The Choice IS Easy! Serpentelli, John, illus. (p. 1307)
Kelson, Ellen, illus. see Rosen, Michael J. & Kaboom! Staff.
Keltgen, Gina. Once upon a Star. (p. 1293)
Keltie, Helen. Mysterious Lake: Otriana. (p. 1223)
Kelton, Elmer. Bowie's Mine. (p. 216)
Kelton, G F. Land of Cigam. (p. 973)
Kelty, Colleen A. Spencer the Spectacular. (p. 1625)
Kelty, Colleen Alyce. I Guess I'll Be Swope, Brenda, illus. (p. 838)
Keltz, Karen. Sally Jo Survives Sixth Grade: A Journal. Carrigg, Susan, illus. (p. 1505)
Kelzke, Sheila. Chris the Little Christmas Tree. (p. 311)
Kemarskaya, Oksana. Planet Earth Projects. (p. 1367)
Kemarskaya, Oksana, illus. see De Anda, Diane.
Kemarskaya, Oksana, illus. see Slingerland, Janet.
Kemarskaya, Oksana, illus. see Troupe, Thomas Kingsley.
Kemble, Mai S. I'm So Not Wearing a Dress! (p. 860)
—Moon & the Night Sweeper. (p. 1171)
—Moon & the Night Sweeper. Kemble, Mai S., illus. (p. 1171)
Kemble, Mai S., illus. see Guerras Safia.
Kemble, Mai S., illus. see Khan, Hana.
Kemble, Mai S., illus. see Morrison, Kevin.
Kemble, Mai S., illus. see Urdahl, Catherine.
Kemeny, Esther. On the Shores of Darkness: The Memoir of Esther Kemeny Haller, Heather, ed. (p. 1291)
Kemer, Eric, jt. auth. see Gardner, Robert.
Kemler, Nancy. Dragon Box: The Key to Magic. (p. 476)
Kemly, Kathleen, illus. see Bruhn, Aron.
Kemly, Kathleen, illus. see Callahan, Sean.
Kemly, Kathleen, illus. see Jordan, Shirley.
Kemly, Kathleen, illus. see Lehmann, Charles.
Kemly, Kathleen, illus. see McDonald, Rae A.
Kemly, Kathleen, illus. see Ochiltree, Dianne.
Kemly, Kathleen, illus. see Smucker, Anna Egan.
Kemly, Kathleen Hadam, illus. see Bruhn, Aron.
Kemmerer, Brigid. Sacrifice. (p. 1501)
—Secret. (p. 1540)
—Spirit. (p. 1628)
Kemmerer, Susan. Apples: Daily Spelling Drills for Secondary Students. (p. 92)
—Research in Increments. (p. 1462)
—Word Artist. (p. 1950)
Kemmetmueller, Donna Jean. My Muslim Friend: A Young Catholic Learns about Islam. Jacobsen, Laura, illus. (p. 1215)
Kemnitz, Dianna. Another Lesson for Jack. (p. 88)
—King Eli Speaks to Jack. (p. 958)
—Meet Jack & His New Friend. (p. 1121)
—Mia, Jack & Nurse Olivi. (p. 1133)
—New Hat for Jack. (p. 1245)
—Sing with Jack. (p. 1579)
Kemoun, Hubert Ben & Grenier, Christian. Half & Half-Voyage into Space. Moutarde & Blanchin, Matthieu, illus. (p. 736)
Kemp, Albert W. Industrial Mechanics: Answer Key. (p. 872)
—Industrial Mechanics: Transparencies. (p. 872)
Kemp, Anna. Dogs Don't Do Ballet. Ogilvie, Sara, illus. (p. 462)
—Great Brain Robbery. Smith, Alex T., illus. (p. 714)
—Rhinos Don't Eat Pancakes. Ogilvie, Sara, illus. (p. 1467)
—Worst Princess. Ogilvie, Sara, illus. (p. 1961)
Kemp, Beth. Grammar for GCSE English. Gould, Mike & Higgins, Paul, eds. (p. 706)
Kemp, Dane. Imaginary Tales. (p. 860)
Kemp, Dina. Milo & Unico Adventures. (p. 1144)
Kemp, Edward. Woodard's Crest: Keeper of the Scroll. (p. 1949)
Kemp, Ellwood W. Streams of History: Ancient Rome (Yesterday's Classics) (p. 1666)
—Streams of History: Ancient Greece (Yesterday's Classics) (p. 1666)
—Streams of History: Early Civilizations (Yesterday's Classics) (p. 1666)
—Streams of History. (p. 1666)
Kemp, Henry Lucia. Now I Know My Numbers, Colors, Shapes & More. (p. 1269)
Kemp, Hill. Capitol Offense. (p. 263)
Kemp, Hill & Kemp, Siena. Lucky Penny. (p. 1063)
Kemp, Jane, jt. auth. see Walters, Clare.
Kemp, Jane & Walters, Clare. Cat. West, Linzi, illus. (p. 277)
—Outdoor Fun & Games for Kids: Over 100 Activities for 3-11 Year Olds. (p. 1312)
Kemp, Kathie, illus. see Erwin, Wesley.
Kemp, Kristen. Healthy Sexuality. (p. 759)
Kemp, Kristin. Amazing Americans: Rosa Parks (p. 52)
—Amazing Americans: Thurgood Marshall (p. 52)
—Boy in the Striped Pajamas: An Instructional Guide for Literature (p. 218)
—Of Mice & Men: An Instructional Guide for Literature (p. 1279)
Kemp, Loraine, illus. see Hancock, Lyn.
Kemp, Marion, jt. auth. see Lane, Sheila Mary.
Kemp, Marion, et al. All Together. Barnes-Murphy, Rowan, illus. (p. 46)
Kemp, Mary Kay. Adventures of Jimmy Joe & Tippy Toe: Show & Tell. (p. 19)
Kemp, Michelle. Flutter by Butterfly. (p. 609)
Kemp, Moira. Hey Diddle Diddle. Kemp, Moira, illus. (p. 774)
—I'm a Little Teapot. Kemp, Moira, illus. (p. 858)
—Knock at the Door. Kemp, Moira, illus. (p. 965)
—Pat-a-Cake, Pat-a-Cake. Kemp, Moira, illus. (p. 1327)
—Round & Round the Garden. Kemp, Moira, illus. (p. 1491)
Kemp, Moira, illus. see Price, Mathew.
Kemp, Richard. Atlas Visual del Mundo. Delf, Brian, illus. (p. 113)
Kemp, Robert. Conspirators. (p. 359)
—Heart is Highland. (p. 759)
—Henrietta, M.D. (p. 767)
—King of Scots. (p. 959)
—Other Dear Charmer. (p. 1306)
—Saxon Saint. (p. 1518)
—Venom for Two. (p. 1836)
Kemp, Siena, jt. auth. see Kemp, Hill.
Kemp, Steve. Who Pooped in the Park? Great Smoky Mountains National Park. Rath, Robert, illus. (p. 1917)
Kemp, Steve, ed. see Horstman, Lisa.
Kemp, Thomas Jay. Virtual Roots 2. 0: A Guide to Genealogy & Local History of the World Wide Web. (p. 1844)
Kempe, Barbara, ed. see Snyder, R. Bradley & Engelsgjerd, Marc.
Kemper, Bitsy. Budgeting, Spending & Saving. (p. 235)
—Earning Income. (p. 494)
—France. (p. 627)
—Growing Your Money. (p. 727)
—Out & about at the Baseball Stadium Trover, Zachary, illus. (p. 1310)
—Out & about at the Dentist Trover, Zachary, illus. (p. 1310)
—Out & about at the Greenhouse Trover, Zachary, illus. (p. 1310)
—Out & about at the Theater Trover, Zachary, illus. (p. 1310)
—Philippines. (p. 1350)
—Right to Privacy: Interpreting the Constitution. (p. 1472)
—Sweden. (p. 1689)
—United Kingdom. (p. 1818)
Kemper, Sherrill. Hodgepodge of Blessings. (p. 787)
Kempf, Molly & Robin, Emily. Blake Lively: Traveling to the Top! (p. 198)
Kempshall, Paddy. Hobbit: An Unexpected Journey. (p. 786)
—Hobbit - An Unexpected Journey: The World of Hobbits. (p. 786)
—Hobbit - An Unexpected Journey. (p. 786)
Kempshall, Paddy, jt. auth. see Houghton Mifflin Harcourt Publishing Company Staff.
Kempster, Rachel, jt. auth. see Leder, Meg.
Kempter, Christa. Benito y Melosa (Wally & Mae) Weldin, Frauke, illus. (p. 164)
—Uncle Rabbit's Busy Visit. Weldin, Frauke, illus. (p. 1812)
—Wally & Mae. Weldin, Frauke, illus. (p. 1855)
Kempter, Christa, jt. auth. see Rosenberg, Natascha.
Kempter, Christa & Weldin, Frauke. Wally & Mae. (p. 1855)
Kempton, Alexa, ed. see Calza, Gian Carlo.
Kempton, Clive & Atkin, Alan. Rip-Roaring Round Book. Pascoe, Jed, illus. (p. 1473)
Kempton, Linda. Jessica Sweetapple & the Battle. (p. 914)
Ken, Akamatsu. Love Hina Rymer, Nan, tr. from JPN. (p. 1059)
Ken, Davidson. Jimmy Was a Fly. (p. 918)
Ken, Hills. Historia del Mundo. (p. 782)
Ken Lindstrom To Ken Lindstrom. Ollie & Grampa Go to the Zoo: How the Polar Bear Got to the Zoo. Jones., Amber, illus. (p. 1287)
Ken, Rand. Kitty Letters. (p. 963)
Kenah, Katharine. Amazing Creations. (p. 54)
—Best Chef in Second Grade. Carter, Abby, illus. (p. 168)
—Best Seat in Second Grade. Carter, Abby, illus. (p. 171)
—Best Teacher in Second Grade. Carter, Abby, illus. (p. 171)
—Big Beasts. (p. 178)
—Ferry Tail. Wong, Nicole, illus. (p. 582)
—Lost in the Leaf Pile. (p. 1055)
—Nature's Amazing Partners. (p. 1237)
—Predator Attack!, Level 3. (p. 1394)
—Pumpkin Fair Problem. (p. 1416)
—Scholastic Reader Level 1: the Saturday Triplets #3: Teacher Trouble! Lyon, Tammie, illus. (p. 1522)
—Scholastic Reader Level 1: the Saturday Triplets #2: the Pumpkin Fair Problem. Lyon, Tammie, illus. (p. 1522)
—Teacher Trouble! (p. 1709)
Kenah, Katharine, jt. auth. see Domnauer, Teresa.
Kenan, Randall. James Baldwin. (p. 907)
Kenan, Tessa. "What Did He Say?" A Book about Quotation Marks. (p. 1882)
Kendal, Penny. Broken. (p. 230)
Kendall, Bradford, illus. see Dahl, Michael.
Kendall, Bradford, illus. see Preece, Philip.
Kendall, Bradford, illus. see Strange, Jason.
Kendall, Bridget. Bond & the Big Green Hill. (p. 208)
Kendall, Carol & Li, Yao-Wen. Sweet & Sour: Tales from China. Felts, Shirley, illus. (p. 1689)
Kendall, Carolyn. Phibby & Ribby. (p. 1350)
Kendall, Diane & Marsh, Merle. Carousel Kids. York, Susanne, photos by. (p. 271)
Kendall, Gideon, illus. see Hulme, John & Wexler, Michael.
Kendall, Gideon, illus. see McCallum, Ann.
Kendall, Gideon, illus. see Nielsen, Jennifer A.
Kendall, Gideon, illus. see Plourde, Lynn.
Kendall, Gideon, illus. see Ring, Susan.
Kendall, Gillian Murray. Garden of Darkness. (p. 656)
Kendall, Jack. Magic Apple Tree. Bostrom, Sally, illus. (p. 1071)
Kendall, Jackie. Man Worth Waiting For: How to Avoid a Bozo. (p. 1086)
Kendall, Jane. Tennessee Rose. (p. 1720)
Kendall, Jane, illus. see Harrison, David L.
Kendall, Jane F. Maestoso Petra. Sanderson, Ruth, illus. (p. 1070)
—Tennessee Rose. Sheckels, Astrid, illus. (p. 1720)
Kendall, Julie. Vital Skills: How to Make Wise Decisions. (p. 1846)
Kendall, Martha, jt. auth. see Keat, Nawuth.
Kendall, Martha E. Erie Canal. (p. 533)
—Susan B. Anthony: Fighter for Women's Voting Rights. (p. 1688)
Kendall, Monica, illus. see Glatzer, Jenna.
Kendall, Penny. Sleepy Baby. (p. 1589)
—Socks. (p. 1605)
Kendall, Peter, illus. see Majid, Ellisha.
Kendall, R. T. Between the Times: Malachi: God's Last Prophet of the Old Testament. (p. 173)
—Just Say Thanks: Cultivating Gratitude Deepens Intimacy with God. (p. 939)
Kendall, R. T., jt. auth. see Rosen, David.
Kendall, Russell, illus. see Waters, Kate.
Kendall, Sara, jt. auth. see Burkhardt, Jason.
Kendall, Sara & Burkhardt, Jason. Backdoor Trio: Don't Look Back. (p. 130)
—Backdoor Trio: Floats Their Boat. (p. 130)
—Backdoor Trio: Walks in the Garden. (p. 130)
—Backdoor Trio: Babble on about Babylon. (p. 130)
Kendall, Sarita H. Al Rescate de Omacha. (p. 32)
Kendall, Stan P. Samson Gets a Family. (p. 1509)
Kendall, Sydney. Turn for de Wurst. (p. 1797)
Kendle, Hazel Cole, jt. auth. see Bryan, Jennifer Liu.
Kendra, Bratko. Mr. Mouse Right! (p. 1185)
Kendree, McLean. Pandora's Vase (p. 1321)
Kendree, McLean, illus. see O'Hearn, Michael.
Kendrick, Charles L. Adventures of Lowboy & Friski. (p. 20)
Kendrick, D., illus. see Rosenbloom, Joseph & Artell, Mike.
Kendrick, D., illus. see Simon, Seymour.
Kendrick, Evelyn R. Molly & Bailey Make New Friends (p. 1160)
Kendrick, Karolyn. Chemistry in Medicine: Set Of 6. (p. 297)
—Chemistry in Medicine: Text Pairs. (p. 297)
Kendrick, Robert. Treasure Quest: Journey to the Jungle. (p. 1782)
Kendrick-TaZiyah, Brandi, illus. see Lollino, Jessica.
Kenealy, Cindy Brouse. Away in a Manger: An ABC Book on the Birth of Jesus Christ. (p. 120)
Kenerly, Ken. Milly's What Ifs... (p. 1144)
Kenison, Misti. Egypt - The Tiny Traveler: A Book of Shapes. (p. 506)
—France - The Tiny Traveler: A Book of Colors. (p. 627)
Kenkmann, Andrea. 1000 First Words in German. Lacome, Susie, illus. (p. 2001)
Kenley, Holli. Another Way: A Novel. (p. 88)
Kenna, Diane, illus. see Wales, Dirk.
Kenna, Kara. Let's Get Creative. (p. 996)
—PLAY-DOH: Farm Friends. (p. 1371)
—PLAY-DOH: Jungle Friends. (p. 1371)
—PLAY-DOH: Old MacDonald Had a Farm. (p. 1371)
—PLAY-DOH: the Wheels on the Bus. (p. 1371)
—PLAY-DOH: Trucks. (p. 1371)
—PLAY-DOH: Twinkle, Twinkle, Little Star. Kenna, Kara, illus. (p. 1371)
—Whose Ears? Nelson, Judy, illus. (p. 1921)
—Whose Eyes? Nelson, Judy, illus. (p. 1921)
—Whose Feet? Nelson, Judy, illus. (p. 1921)
—Whose Nose? Nelson, Judy A., illus. (p. 1922)
Kenna, Kara, illus. see Boyd, Michele.
Kennaley, Blair. People Have a Lot of Wacky Feelings. (p. 1339)
Kennan, Audrey, jt. auth. see Krech, Bob.
Kennard, Carol King. I Can Be Quiet! (p. 835)
Kennard, Michaela, illus. see Gibson, Ray.
Kennard, Thomas, illus. see Knoebel, Suzanne B.
Kennaway, Adrienne, illus. see Hadithi, Mwenye.
Kennaway, Adrienne, illus. see Hadithi, Mweyne.
Kennaway, Adrienne, illus. see Kennaway, Mwalimu & Hadithi, Mwenye.
Kennaway, Adrienne, illus. see Moss, Miriam.
Kennaway, Adrienne, jt. auth. see Hadithi, Mwenye.
Kennaway, James. Tunes of Glory. (p. 1797)
Kennaway, Mwalimu & Hadithi, Mwenye. Awkward Aardvark. Kennaway, Adrienne, illus. (p. 121)
Kenneally, Cath. All Day, All Night. (p. 44)
Kenneally, Miranda. Breathe, Annie, Breathe. (p. 226)
—Catching Jordan. (p. 279)
—Jesse's Girl. (p. 914)
—Racing Savannah. (p. 1432)
—Things I Can't Forget. (p. 1733)
Kenneally, Miranda, jt. auth. see Anderson, E. Kristin.
Kenneally, Miranda, jt. ed. see Anderson, E. Kristin.
Kennedy, Ai, tr. see Saiga, Reiji & Inoue, Sora.
Kennedy, Allan, illus. see Milligan, Jean F.
Kennedy, Anne, illus. see Bellenson, Evelyn.
Kennedy, Anne, illus. see Charlesworth, Liza & Scholastic, Inc. Staff.
Kennedy, Anne, illus. see Fliess, Sue.
Kennedy, Anne, illus. see Hapka, Catherine, pseud.
Kennedy, Anne, illus. see Marie, Lynne.
Kennedy, Anne, illus. see Muldrow, Diane & Golden Books Staff.
Kennedy, Anne, illus. see Ringler, Matt.
Kennedy, Anne, illus. see Schade, Susan.
Kennedy, Anne, illus. see Spinelli, Eileen.
Kennedy, Anne V., jt. auth. see Kennedy, Anne Vittur.
Kennedy, Anne Vittur. Farmer's Away! Baa! Neigh! Kennedy, Anne Vittur, illus. (p. 574)
—Ragweed's Farm Dog Handbook. Kennedy, Anne Vittur, illus. (p. 1433)
Kennedy, Anne Vittur & Kennedy, Anne V. One Shining Star (p. 1296)
Kennedy, Annie, illus. see Herman, Emmi S.
Kennedy Associates Staff, jt. auth. see Ronzio, Robert.
Kennedy, Brian. Growing up Hockey: The Life & Times of Everyone Who Ever Loved the Game. (p. 726)
Kennedy, Bryan. Charlie's Favorite Christmas. (p. 293)
Kennedy, Cam, illus. see Stevenson, Robert Louis.
Kennedy, Caroline. Family Christmas. Muth, Jon J. & Maestro, Laura Hartman, illus. (p. 568)
—Family of Poems: My Favorite Poetry for Children. Muth, Jon J., illus. (p. 568)
—Poems to Learn by Heart. Muth, Jon J., illus. (p. 1376)
—Poems to Share. Muth, Jon J., illus. (p. 1376)

K

Kennedy, Caroline & Sampson, Ana. Poems to Learn by Heart. Muth, Jon J., illus. (p. 1376)
Kennedy, Catherine, illus. see Herbertson, Lisa.
Kennedy, Cecilia. Whatever Life You Wear (p. 1896)
Kennedy Center Staff. Chasing George Washington. Hoyt, Ard, illus. (p. 294)
—Teddy Roosevelt & the Treasure of Ursa Major. Hoyt, Ard, illus. (p. 1712)
—Unleashed: The Lives of White House Pets. Hoyt, Ard, illus. (p. 1821)
Kennedy, Claire. After Hours. (p. 28)
Kennedy, Dana & Wilson, Etta. Children's Bible Stories. Dolce, Ellen, illus. (p. 303)
Kennedy, David. My Name Is Myshkin: A Philosophical Novel for Children. (p. 1215)
—Roads. (p. 1477)
Kennedy, David, et al. American Pageant. (p. 62)
Kennedy, Debi. Angry Monster Book. Kennedy, Debi, illus. (p. 75)
Kennedy, Deirdre, jt. auth. see Johnson, Steve.
Kennedy, Donna. Furples Aren't Purple. (p. 650)
—Little Lost Lamborgimme. (p. 1031)
—Three Little Bats. (p. 1742)
Kennedy, Doug, illus. see Bardoe, Cheryl.
Kennedy, Doug, illus. see Kennedy, Kim.
Kennedy, Doug, illus. see San Souci, Robert D.
Kennedy, Doug, jt. auth. see Kennedy, Kim.
Kennedy, Douglas, jt. auth. see Kennedy, Pamela.
Kennedy, Edward. My Senator & Me: A Dog's-Eye View of Washington, D. C. Small, David, illus. (p. 1218)
Kennedy, Edward M. My Senator & Me: A Dog's-Eye View of Washington, D. C. Small, David, illus. (p. 1218)
Kennedy, Emily. Daniel Boone. (p. 405)
Kennedy, Emma. Case of the Fatal Phantom Marc, Sylvain, illus. (p. 274)
—Case of the Frozen Hearts. (p. 274)
—Case of the Putrid Poison Marc, Sylvain & Dorman, Brandon, illus. (p. 275)
—Wilma Tenderfoot: the Case of the Fatal Phantom. Marc, Sylvain, illus. (p. 1934)
—Wilma Tenderfoot - The Case of the Frozen Hearts. Marc, Sylvain et al, illus. (p. 1934)
Kennedy, Geno. Tiny Takes a Trip. Engler, Lori, illus. (p. 1756)
Kennedy, Graham, illus. see Bingham, Jane & Sansom, Fiona.
Kennedy, Graham, illus. see Mackenzie, Carine.
Kennedy, Graham, illus. see MacKenzie, Carine.
Kennedy, Graham, illus. see Mackenzie, Carine.
Kennedy, Graham, illus. see Morris, Neil.
Kennedy, Gregory, jt. auth. see Ogle, Jennifer.
Kennedy, Gregory, jt. auth. see Putnam, Caleb.
Kennedy, Gregory, jt. auth. see Roedel, Michael.
Kennedy, Gregory, jt. auth. see Smalling, Curtis G.
Kennedy, Gregory, jt. auth. see Smalling, Curtis.
Kennedy, Gregory & Arnold, Keith A. Birds of Texas. (p. 192)
Kennedy, Gregory & Bell, Brian H. Birds of Washington State. (p. 192)
Kennedy, Gregory, et al. Compact Guide to Oklahoma Birds. (p. 351)
Kennedy, Hugh J. Flowers & the Fairies. (p. 608)
Kennedy, J. Aday. Buster Bear & Uncle B. Movshina, Marina, illus. (p. 245)
—Cobbledom's Curse. Foster, Jack, illus. (p. 336)
—Itcha Itcha Goo Goo Blues. Foster, Jack, illus. (p. 895)
—Juggerum. Morris, Alexander, illus. (p. 932)
—Stella, the Fire Farting Dragon. Foster, Jack, illus. (p. 1647)
Kennedy, J. Aday & Foster, Jack. Klutzy Kantor. (p. 964)
Kennedy, James. Order of Odd-Fish. (p. 1302)
Kennedy, John. Puppet Mania! The World's Most Incredible Puppet Making Book Ever! (p. 1417)
Kennedy, Kelly. Who's There? 501 Side-Splitting Knock-Knock Jokes from Highlights. (p. 1921)
Kennedy, Kelly, illus. see Brown, Jordan D.
Kennedy, Kelly, illus. see Charlesworth, Liza & Scholastic, Inc. Staff.
Kennedy, Kelly, illus. see Fleming, Maria & Charlesworth, Liza.
Kennedy, Kelly, illus. see Haselhurst, Maureen.
Kennedy, Kelly, illus. see Lucero, Jaime.
Kennedy, Kelly, illus. see Martin, Justin McCory.
Kennedy, Kelly, illus. see Menotti, Andrea.
Kennedy, Kelly, illus. see Schwartz, Linda.
Kennedy, Kelly, illus. see Slater, Teddy.
Kennedy, Kelly, illus. see Teagarden, Janine.
Kennedy, Kelly, illus. see Whitney, Brooks.
Kennedy, Kendra. French Toast the Early Morning Adventure. (p. 636)
—Why Wolf Has Big Feet. (p. 1927)
Kennedy, Kevin. Ten Dollar Words for Kids. Fife, Jay, illus. (p. 1718)
Kennedy, Kim. Misty Gordon & the Mystery of the Ghost Pirates. (p. 1155)
—Pirate Pete. Kennedy, Doug & Kennedy, Roy D., illus. (p. 1362)
—Pirate Pete's Talk Like a Pirate. Kennedy, Doug, illus. (p. 1362)
Kennedy, Kim & Kennedy, Doug. Hee-Haw-Dini & the Great Zambini. (p. 762)
Kennedy, Kimberling Galeti. Hey, Don't Forget the Sunscreen! Sun Safety & Protection for Your Skin. (p. 774)
—Why You Should Laugh Three Times a Day. (p. 1927)
Kennedy, Kirk. Mr. Blue Butterfly. Nazario, Rafael, illus. (p. 1184)
Kennedy, Laura. Pat's Vat Goes Splat: A Lesson in Honesty. (p. 1329)
Kennedy, Lauren, et al. Arizona State University College Prowler off the Record. (p. 99)
Kennedy, Leo B. Devin & the Greedy Ferret. (p. 432)
Kennedy, Leola. There's a Reason. (p. 1731)
Kennedy, Linda. I Love You More... (p. 843)
Kennedy, Marge. Pets at the White House. (p. 1348)
—Scholastic News Nonfiction Readers: Let's Visit the White House (p. 1522)
—See Inside the White House. (p. 1546)
—Story of the White House. (p. 1662)
—Time to Eat at the White House. (p. 1753)
—Who Works at the White House? (p. 1919)
Kennedy, Marge, jt. auth. see Kennedy, Marge M.
Kennedy, Marge M. & Kennedy, Marge. Having Fun at the White House. (p. 755)
—Story of the White House. (p. 1662)
Kennedy, Marlane. Blizzard Night. (p. 200)
—Disaster Strikes #1: Earthquake Shock. (p. 446)
—Disaster Strikes #2: Tornado Alley. (p. 446)
—Disaster Strikes #3: Blizzard Night. (p. 446)
—Dog Days of Charlotte Hayes. (p. 461)
—Earthquake Shock. (p. 497)
—Me & the Pumpkin Queen. (p. 1115)
—Tornado Alley. (p. 1770)
—Volcano Blast. (p. 1848)
Kennedy, Michelle. Big Book of Happy: 500 Games & Activities for Ages 2 to 6. (p. 179)
Kennedy, Mike. Derek Jeter. (p. 427)
—Football. (p. 615)
—Ice Hockey. (p. 850)
—Infinite City. (p. 873)
—Language of Chaos. Velasco, Francisco Ruiz, illus. (p. 975)
—Lebron James. (p. 987)
—Lone Wolf 2100 Volume 1: Shadows on Saplings: Shadows on Saplings. Velasco, Francisco Ruiz, illus. (p. 1046)
—Michael Phelps. (p. 1134)
—Pattern Storm. (p. 1329)
—Shaun White. (p. 1563)
—Thrill of the Hunt. (p. 1744)
—Tony Hawk. (p. 1766)
Kennedy, Mike, ed. see Harrison, Geoffrey C. & Scott, Thomas F.
Kennedy, Mike, ed. see Stewart, Mark.
Kennedy, Mike, jt. auth. see Stewart, Mark.
Kennedy, Mike & Stewart, Mark. Meet the Astros. (p. 1122)
—Meet the Bears. (p. 1122)
—Meet the Cardinals. (p. 1122)
—Meet the Colts. (p. 1122)
—Meet the Cowboys. (p. 1122)
—Meet the Cubs. (p. 1122)
—Meet the Dodgers. (p. 1122)
—Meet the Patriots. (p. 1123)
—Meet the Rays. (p. 1123)
—Meet the Red Sox. (p. 1123)
—Meet the Steelers. (p. 1123)
—Meet the Vikings. (p. 1123)
—Meet the Yankees. (p. 1123)
—Soccer in Africa. (p. 1603)
—Soccer in Asia. (p. 1603)
—Soccer in Central America. (p. 1603)
—Soccer in Eastern Europe. (p. 1603)
—Soccer in North America. (p. 1603)
—Soccer in South America. (p. 1603)
—Soccer in the British Isles. (p. 1603)
—Soccer in Western Europe. (p. 1603)
Kennedy, Nancy B. Even the Sound Waves Obey Him: Bible Stories Brought to Life with Science. Regan, Dana, illus. (p. 541)
—Make It, Shake It, Mix It Up: 44 Bible Stories Brought to Life with Science. Cannell, Jon, illus. (p. 1079)
Kennedy, Pamela. Easter Celebration: Traditions & Customs from Around the World. (p. 499)
—Easter in the Garden. Wenzel, David T., illus. (p. 499)
—Five Minute Devotions for Children: Celebrating God's World As a Family. Wummer, Amy, illus. (p. 601)
—Granny's Cozy Quilt of Memories: Remembering Grandmother's Love Through Her Lasting Gift. Wummer, Amy, illus. (p. 710)
—Moving Day for Sam: A Story about Change. Petrov, Anton, illus. (p. 1183)
—My Big Book of 5-Minute Devotions: Celebrating God's World. Wummer, Amy, illus. (p. 1197)
—Prayers at Eastertime. Britt, Stephanie, illus. (p. 1393)
—Sister for Matthew. (p. 1581)
—Two Homes for Tyler: A Story about Understanding Divorce. Wummer, Amy, illus. (p. 1803)
Kennedy, Pamela & Brady, Anne Kennedy. Five-Minute Bible Devotions for Children: Stories from the New Testament. Wummer, Amy, illus. (p. 601)
Kennedy, Pamela & Britt, Stephanie. Easter Basket of Prayers. (p. 499)
Kennedy, Pamela & Kennedy, Douglas. More Five-Minute Devotions for Children: Celebrating God's World As a Family. Wummer, Amy, illus. (p. 1174)
Kennedy, Patricia Moran. Loving Tree A Story of Love, Loss, & Transformation for All Ages. (p. 1061)
Kennedy, Paul E. Fun with Whales Stencils. (p. 649)
Kennedy, Philip. Modern Introduction to Theology: New Questions for Old Beliefs. (p. 1158)
Kennedy, Richard. Crazy in Love. (p. 377)
—Porcelain Man. (p. 1386)
Kennedy, Richard, illus. see Dillon, Eilis.
Kennedy, Richard, illus. see Sleigh, Barbara.
Kennedy, Robert. Drake. (p. 479)
Kennedy, Robert F., Jr. Robert Smalls: The Boat Thief. Fancy, Patrick, illus. (p. 1479)
—Saint Francis of Assisi: A Life of Joy. Nolan, Dennis, illus. (p. 1503)
Kennedy, Roy D., illus. see Bardoe, Cheryl.
Kennedy, Roy D., illus. see Kennedy, Kim.
Kennedy, Ryan, jt. auth. see Edwards, Hazel.
Kennedy, Sam, illus. see Burchett, Jan & Vogler, Sara.
Kennedy, Seamus, illus. see O' Byrne, Lorraine.
Kennedy, Shawn. Funny Cryptograms. (p. 649)
Kennedy Shea, Bobby, jt. auth. see Shea, Bobby Kennedy.
Kennedy, Steven. Crescent City Collection: Marimba Tunes from the Big Easy for Grades 4 - 8. Holl, Brent, ed. (p. 381)
Kennedy, Tammy Helena. Jingles Lost Her Jingle. (p. 919)
Kennedy, Tim, compiled by. Road Less Traveled: Seventh Grade Reader. (p. 1476)
Kennedy Tosten, S. Troy's Amazing Universe: A for Aliens. (p. 1790)
Kennedy, Triona. Benny Bunny. (p. 165)
Kennedy, Victor, illus. see McEwan, Jamie.
Kennedy, X. J. City Kids: Street & Skyscraper Rhymes Beha, Philippe, illus. (p. 323)
—Owlstone Crown. (p. 1315)
Kennedy-Moore, Eileen, jt. auth. see Elman, Natalie Madorsky.
Kennedy-Moore, Eileen, jt. auth. see Parenting Press.
Kennell, Julie, illus. see Wellings, Chris R.
Kennelly, Sean. All Around America. (p. 43)
—American Inventors & Innovators. (p. 62)
—American Inventors & Innovators. Flowerpot Press, ed. (p. 62)
Kennelly, Sean & Carpenter, Dan. Amazing America: An Adventure into American History. (p. 52)
—Amazing America. Flowerpot Press, ed. (p. 52)
—Great Americans. (p. 713)
—Great Americans. Flowerpot Press, ed. (p. 713)
Kennemore, Tim. Alice's Birthday Pig. Spoor, Mike, illus. (p. 40)
—Alice's Shooting Star. (p. 40)
—Alice's World Record. (p. 40)
—Alice's World Record. Spoor, Mike, illus. (p. 40)
Kenner, Crystal R. King of All Tickle Bugs & Other Stories. (p. 958)
Kenner, Harold, jt. auth. see Collins, Anthony.
Kennerson, Vern. Love Stories for Children. Falk, Cathy Kennerson, illus. (p. 1060)
Kenneth, G., jt. auth. see West, Patty Old.
Kennett, Chris, illus. see Smith, Geof.
Kenney, Amanda. Dragon's Heart. (p. 479)
Kenney, Bob. Albert the Machine. (p. 34)
Kenney, Cindy. Cool Hand Cuke: A Lesson in Giving Vol. 5 Moore, Michael, illus. (p. 363)
—Easter Carol (p. 499)
—God's World & Me: Boz's Big Book of Bible Fun. (p. 692)
—How in the World? Moore, Michael & Big Idea Design Staff, illus. (p. 810)
—Junior Asparagus. (p. 936)
—Laura Carrot. (p. 980)
—Project Precious Paws (p. 1410)
—Veggie Tales I Can! And So Can You! (p. 1834)
—Veggietales Bible Storybook (p. 1834)
—Where Is God When I'm Scared? (p. 1908)
Kenney, Cindy, jt. auth. see Big Idea, Inc. Staff.
Kenney, Cindy, jt. auth. see Peterson, Doug.
Kenney, Cindy & Peterson, Doug. Snooze Brothers: A Lesson in Responsibility Moore, Michael, illus. (p. 1598)
Kenney, Cindy, et al. Frog Wars (p. 640)
—Knight to Remember (p. 964)
—Peas & Thank You! (p. 1333)
—Veggietown Voyage Moore, Michael, illus. (p. 1834)
Kenney, Dave. Northern Lights: The Stories of Minnesota's Past. (p. 1266)
Kenney, Dave, et al. Northern Lights: The Stories of Minnesota's Past. (p. 1266)
Kenney, Karen. Civic Responsibilities. (p. 324)
—Economics Through Infographics. Stankiewicz, Steven, illus. (p. 503)
—Government in Your City or Town. (p. 704)
—Illegal Immigration. (p. 856)
—State Government. (p. 1644)
—US History Through Infographics. Westlund, Laura, illus. (p. 1826)
Kenney, Karen L. Firefighters at Work. Dumm, Brian Caleb, illus. (p. 591)
—Girls Play to Win Skiing & Snowboarding. (p. 680)
—Nurses at Work. Dumm, Brian Caleb, illus. (p. 1273)
—Police Officers at Work. Dumm, Brian Caleb, illus. (p. 1380)
—Teachers at Work. Dumm, Brian Caleb, illus. (p. 1709)
Kenney, Karen Latchana. Energy. (p. 528)
—Magnets. (p. 1076)
Kenney, Karen Latchana. Ancient Aztecs. (p. 68)
—Bald Eagle. Hunt, Judith A., illus. (p. 133)
—Bea on Broadway: A Story about New York. (p. 149)
—Boho Fashion. Kubley, Ashley Newsome, illus. (p. 207)
—Buzz with the Bees. Hedicker, Lisa, illus. (p. 248)
—Canada. (p. 260)
—Cool School Cheerleading: Fun Ideas & Activities to Build School Spirit. (p. 364)
—Cool School Clubs: Fun Ideas & Activities to Build School Spirit. (p. 364)
—Cool School Dance: Fun Ideas & Activities to Build School Spirit. (p. 364)
—Cool School Music: Fun Ideas & Activities to Build School Spirit. (p. 364)
—Cool School Volunteering: Fun Ideas & Activities to Build School Spirit. (p. 364)
—David Karp: The Mastermind Behind Tumblr. (p. 411)
—Domestic Violence. (p. 465)
—Ellis Island. Hunt, Judith A., illus. (p. 515)
—Harsh or Heroic? The Middle Ages. (p. 751)
—Hide with the Ladybugs. Hedicker, Lisa, illus. (p. 777)
—Hop with the Grasshoppers. Hedicker, Lisa, illus. (p. 796)
—Hunt with the Fireflies. Hedicker, Lisa, illus. (p. 828)
—Iran. (p. 886)
—Librarians at Work. Dumm, Brian Caleb, illus. (p. 1005)
—Lincoln Memorial. Hunt, Judith A., illus. (p. 1018)
—Lonesome Star: A Story about Texas. (p. 1046)
—Mail Carriers at Work. Dumm, Brian Caleb, illus. (p. 1077)
—March with the Ants. Hedicker, Lisa, illus. (p. 1091)
—Memorial Day. Hunt, Judith A., illus. (p. 1125)
—Mount Rushmore. Hunt, Judith A., illus. (p. 1180)
—National Geographic Kids Everything World War I. (p. 1232)
—Our Nation's Pride Hunt, Judith A., illus. (p. 1309)
—Pizza Pie in the Sky: A Story about Illinois. (p. 1365)
—Science of Car Racing (p. 1527)
—Science of Color: Investigating Light. (p. 1527)
—Science of Race Cars: Studying Forces & Motion. (p. 1527)
—Science of Roller Coasters: Understanding Energy. (p. 1527)
—Science of Stars: Exploring Matter. (p. 1527)
—Shop Tech: The Science of Cars (p. 1568)
—Skin Care & Makeup Tips & Tricks. Heschke, Elena, illus. (p. 1585)
—Spin with the Spiders. Hedicker, Lisa, illus. (p. 1627)
—Spoils of War. (p. 1630)
—Stephen Hawking: Extraordinary Theoretical Physicist. (p. 1648)
—Strength Training for Teen Athletes: Exercises to Take Your Game to the Next Level (p. 1667)
—Sunshine Champs: A Story about Florida. (p. 1678)
—Super Simple Art to Wear: Fun & Easy-to-Make Crafts for Kids. (p. 1681)
—Super Simple Clay Projects: Fun & Easy-to-Make Crafts for Kids. (p. 1681)
—Super Simple Crafts (p. 1681)
—Super Simple Glass Jar Art: Fun & Easy-to-Make Crafts for Kids. (p. 1681)
—Super Simple Jewelry: Fun & Easy-to-Make Crafts for Kids. (p. 1681)
—Super Simple Magnets: Fun & Easy-to-Make Crafts for Kids. (p. 1681)
—Super Simple Masks: Fun & Easy-to-Make Crafts for Kids. (p. 1681)
—Teen Pregnancy. (p. 1713)
—Thrilling Sports Cars. (p. 1744)
—US History Through Infographics. Westlund, Laura, illus. (p. 1826)
—What Makes Medical Technology Safer? (p. 1892)
—What Makes Vehicles Safer? (p. 1892)
—White House. Hunt, Judith A., illus. (p. 1913)
Kenney, Karen Latchana, jt. auth. see Hunt, Sara R.
Kenney, Karen Latchana & Friedman, Richard D. Korematsu v. the United States: World War II Japanese-American Internment Camps. (p. 967)
Kenney, Rebecca. Silent. (p. 1575)
—Where I Belong. (p. 1908)
Kenney, Sean. Amazing ABC: An Alphabet Book of Lego Creations. Kenney, Sean, illus. (p. 52)
—Cool Cars & Trucks. Kenney, Sean, illus. (p. 363)
—Cool Castles. (p. 363)
—Cool City. Kenney, Sean, illus. (p. 363)
—Cool Creations in 101 Pieces. Kenney, Sean, illus. (p. 363)
—Cool Creations in 35 Pieces. Kenney, Sean, illus. (p. 363)
—Cool Robots. Kenney, Sean, illus. (p. 364)
—Totally Cool Creations. Kenney, Sean, illus. (p. 1771)
Kennington, Tammy. Beluga Whales. (p. 163)
—Blue Sharks. (p. 203)
—Bull Sharks. (p. 240)
—Penguins. (p. 1337)
—Protein Group. (p. 1412)
Kennis, Don. Monsters Have Big Feet. Gowens, Kyle & Richmond, Bob, illus. (p. 1169)
Kennison, Ruth, jt. auth. see Hochman, David.
Kennon, Caroline. Helen Keller in Her Own Words. (p. 763)
Kennon, Michou. Beyoncé. (p. 173)
—Queen Latifah. (p. 1424)
Kennon, Michou, jt. auth. see Salazar, Sam.
Kenny, Allison. Starring Celia. Rose, Thorina, illus. (p. 1642)
Kenny, Chantal Lacourcière. Kids Can Press French & English Phrase Book. Hendry, Linda, illus. (p. 953)
Kenny, Cindy. Larry Cucumber: I Can. (p. 976)
Kenny, Mary Ann. MoonChild: A Celebration of Menstruation. (p. 1172)
Kenny, Michael Daedalus. Little Miss Sunshine in: Here Comes the Sun! (p. 1032)
—Mr. Strong: Good Thing I Came Along. Corbera, Gabriel, illus. (p. 1186)
Kenny, Natalie. Earth Day: Taking Care of Our Planet. (p. 495)
Kenny, Paraic & Bozzone, Donna M. Stages of Cancer Development. (p. 1638)
Kenny, Robert F. Teaching TV Production in a Digital World: Integrating Media Literacy (p. 1710)
Kenoyer, Jonathan M. & Heuston, Kimberley Burton. Ancient South Asian World. (p. 70)
Kenoyer, Jonathan Mark & Heuston, Kimberley Burton. Ancient South Asian World. (p. 70)
Kenrick, Joanna. Tears of a Friend. (p. 1711)
Kenshole, Fiona. Let's Go to the Rainforest. Wright, Craig, ed. (p. 997)
Kensington, Mary Jane, jt. auth. see Moore, Marian.
Kensley, Karen. Gods in Pods. (p. 691)
Kent, Alex. Big Ted's Guide to Tapping: Positive EFT Emotional Freedom Techniques for Children. Smith, Jen, illus. (p. 184)
Kent, Allegra. Ballerina Swan. McCully, Emily Arnold, illus. (p. 134)
Kent, Carrie, contrib. by. Baby Sing & Sign: A Play-Filled Language Development Program for Hearing Infants & Toddlers, Second Edition. (p. 128)
Kent, Daniel T. Muhammad Ali & Laila Ali. (p. 1189)
Kent, Deborah. American Revolution: From Bunker Hill to Yorktown. (p. 63)
—Changing Face of America: Hispanic Roots, Hispanic Pride. (p. 290)
—Cuba. (p. 388)
—Cuban Refugees: Cuban Roots, American Freedoms. (p. 388)
—Diego Rivera: Painting Mexico. (p. 437)
—Dorothy Day: Friend to the Forgotten. (p. 471)
—Elizabeth Cady Stanton: Woman Knows the Cost of Life. (p. 513)
—Franklin Delano Roosevelt: Nothing to Fear! (p. 630)
—Frida Kahlo: An Artist Celebrates Life. (p. 637)
—Great Civil War Draft Riots. (p. 714)
—Hawai'i. (p. 755)
—Hawaii's Road to Statehood. (p. 755)
—Idaho (Revised Edition) (p. 852)
—Inuit: A Proud People. (p. 883)
—James A. Garfield. (p. 906)
—Jimmy Carter. (p. 918)
—Mario Molina: Chemist & Nobel Prize Winner. (p. 1094)
—Mexico. (p. 1131)
—Middle Eastern Migration (p. 1137)
—Migrant Farmworkers: Hoping for a Better Life. (p. 1140)
—New Hampshire (Revised Edition) (p. 1245)
—New Jersey. (p. 1245)
—Oregon (Revised Edition) (p. 1303)
—Phillis Wheatley: First Published African-American Poet. (p. 1351)

—Snake Pits, Talking Cures, & Magic Bullets: A History of Mental Illness. (p. 1596)
—Statue of Liberty. (p. 1645)
—Ukraine. (p. 1808)
—Utah (Revised Edition) (p. 1829)
—Vietnam War: From Da Nang to Saigon. (p. 1841)
—Virginia. (p. 1844)
—Washington D. C. (p. 1860)
—Washington, DC (Revised Edition) (p. 1860)
—What Is Braille? (p. 1889)
—What Is It Like to Be Blind? (p. 1889)
—What Is It Like to Be Deaf? (p. 1889)
—What Is Sign Language? (p. 1890)
—Witchcraft Trials: Fear, Betrayal, & Death in Salem. (p. 1941)
Kent, Deborah, jt. auth. see Taylor, Charlotte.
Kent, Donald H., tr. see Trudel, Marcel.
Kent, Elizabeth. Enchanted Adventures of the Caroline Kemps. (p. 523)
Kent, Evelyn, jt. auth. see Schloss, Eva.
Kent, Jack. There's No Such Thing as a Dragon. (p. 1731)
Kent, Jack, illus. see Folsom, Michael & Elting, Mary.
Kent, Jacqueline C. Business Builders in Cosmetics. (p. 244)
—Business Builders in Fashion. (p. 244)
—Molly Pitcher. (p. 1161)
—Phillis Wheatley. (p. 1350)
Kent, Jennifer McGrath. Chocolate River Rescue (p. 309)
—Gadzooks: The Christmas Goose Murphy, Ivan, illus. (p. 652)
—White Cave Escape (p. 1912)
Kent, Lindsay, jt. auth. see Dorling Kindersley Publishing Staff.
Kent, Lorna. At the Beach. (p. 110)
—At the Zoo. (p. 111)
—Baby's First ABC Book. (p. 129)
—Baby's First Animal Book. (p. 129)
—Baby's First Board Books: On the Move; Animals; My Home; Playtime. (p. 129)
—Baby's First Counting Book. (p. 129)
—Baby's First Toys Book. (p. 129)
—Baby's First Word Book. (p. 129)
—In My House. (p. 864)
—In the Garden. (p. 866)
—In the Park. (p. 867)
—On the Move. (p. 1291)
—Word Magic: Magnetic Sentence Builder. (p. 1950)
Kent, Lou. Chessmaster Biz Secrets: For Wealth, Power & Success. (p. 298)
Kent, Neville. Secrets of the Forest - the Time Zone. (p. 1545)
Kent, Peter, illus. see Brookes, Olivia.
Kent, Peter, illus. see Martin, Peter.
Kent, Renee Holmes. Adventures in Misty Falls (p. 15)
—Best Friends Forever? (p. 169)
—Cassie, You're a Winner! (p. 276)
—Girl Talk (p. 679)
—J. J. Navajo Princess (p. 901)
—Robyn Flies Home (p. 1481)
—Robyn to the Rescue (p. 1481)
—Tell the Truth, Cassie (p. 1717)
Kent, Rockwell, illus. see Shephard, Esther.
Kent, Rose. Kimchi & Calamari. (p. 957)
—Rocky Road. (p. 1484)
Kent, Su. Living in Spain. Hampton, David, photos by. (p. 1041)
Kent, Susan. Learning How to Be Kind to Others. (p. 985)
—Learning How to Feel Good about Yourself. (p. 985)
—Learning How to Say Safe at School. (p. 985)
—Learning How to Say You Are Sorry. (p. 985)
Kent, Trilby. Medina Hill. (p. 1120)
—Stones for My Father. (p. 1653)
Kent, V. E. & Vaughn, James. Magic of Mrs. Magee. (p. 1073)
Kent, Zachary. Alexander Hamilton: Creating a Nation. (p. 36)
—Andrew Carnegie: Industrialist & Philanthropist. (p. 72)
—Civil War: From Fort Sumter to Appomattox. (p. 325)
—Connecticut. (p. 357)
—Dolley Madison: The Enemy Cannot Frighten a Free People. (p. 464)
—Genghis Khan: Invincible Ruler of the Mongol Empire. (p. 661)
—James Madison: Creating a Nation. (p. 907)
—John Adams: Creating a Nation. (p. 921)
—Julius Caesar: Ruler of the Roman World. (p. 933)
—Mysterious Disappearance of Roanoke Colony in American History. (p. 1223)
—Story of Henry Ford & the Automobile: Cornerstones of Freedom. (p. 1658)
—World War I: From the Lusitania to Versailles. (p. 1958)
Kentawy, Al. Sunset Tales from the New Iraq: Share the stories of four lives, changed forever in Iraq. (p. 1677)
Kentera, Kim, creator. Look What I Did Today: Preschool Journal. (p. 1050)
—Look What I Did Today: Infant/Toddler Journal. (p. 1050)
Kentley, Eric, jt. auth. see Hawcock, David.
Kentley, Eric, et al. Pop-Up Book of Ships. (p. 1384)
Kentor Schmauss, Judy, jt. auth. see Sohn, Emily.
Kenward, Jean, et al. Egg Poems & Fox Poems. (p. 506)
Kenward, Jean, et al, selected by. Egg Poems & Fox Poems. (p. 506)
Kenworthy, Mary. Tid Bit. (p. 1747)
Kenyon, Bret, jt. auth. see Kander, Beth.
Kenyon, David Grayson, illus. see Demuth, Patricia Brennan.
Kenyon, Dolores. History of Complex Numbers - A Genealogy. (p. 783)
Kenyon, John. Spain. (p. 1620)
Kenyon, Karen Smith. Charles Dickens: A Biography. (p. 292)
Kenyon, Linda. Rainforest Bird Rescue: Changing the Future for Endangered Wildlife. (p. 1436)
Kenyon, Sherrilyn. Illusion. (p. 857)
—Infamous. (p. 873)
—Inferno. (p. 873)
—Infinity Ahn, JiYoung, illus. (p. 873)
—Infinity. (p. 873)
—Invincible. (p. 885)
Kenyon, Sherrilyn, see Macgregor, Kinley, pseud.
Kenyon, Tony, illus. see Schmicker, Michael.
Kenyon, Tony, illus. see Symes, Ruth Louise.
Keogh, Josie. Christmas: Navidad. Alamán, Eduardo, tr. from SPA. (p. 312)
—Christmas. (p. 312)
—Halloween. (p. 737)
—Halloween. Alamán, Eduardo, tr. from SPA. (p. 737)
—Hanukkah. (p. 743)
—Hanukkah: Janucá. Alamán, Eduardo, tr. from SPA. (p. 744)
—St. Patrick's Day: Dia de San Patricio. Alamán, Eduardo, tr. from SPA. (p. 1638)
—St. Patrick's Day. (p. 1638)
—Thanksgiving: Día de Acción de Gracias. Alamán, Eduardo, tr. from ENG. (p. 1725)
—Thanksgiving. (p. 1725)
—Trip to the Firehouse: De Visita en la Estación de Bomberos. (p. 1787)
—Trip to the Firehouse. (p. 1787)
—Trip to the Grocery Store: De Visita en la Tienda. (p. 1787)
—Trip to the Grocery Store. (p. 1787)
—Trip to the Hospital. (p. 1787)
—Trip to the Hospital / de visita en el Hospital. Alamán, Eduardo, tr. from ENG. (p. 1787)
—Trip to the Library: De Visita en la Biblioteca. (p. 1787)
—Trip to the Library. (p. 1787)
—Trip to the Police Station. (p. 1787)
—Trip to the Post Office. (p. 1787)
—Valentine's Day: Día de San Valentín. Alamán, Eduardo, tr. from SPA. (p. 1830)
—Valentine's Day. (p. 1830)
Keogh, Josie & Alamán, Eduardo. Trip to the Police Station: De Visita en la Estación de Policía. (p. 1787)
—Trip to the Post Office: De Visita en el Correo. (p. 1787)
Keoke, Emory Dean. American Indian Contributions to the World. (p. 61)
Keoke, Emory Dean & Porterfield, Kay Marie. American Indian Contributions to the World. (p. 61)
—Food, Farming, & Hunting. (p. 613)
—Medicine. (p. 1119)
Keonna-E'nea. Momzilla Joane', E'nea, illus. (p. 1163)
Keough, Kevin. Snoozy Dog: And Curly Cat Too! (p. 1598)
Keough, Rob. Gem Lakes. (p. 659)
—Wolf Summer. (p. 1944)
Kephart, Beth. Heart Is Not a Size. (p. 759)
—House of Dance. (p. 803)
—Nothing but Ghosts. (p. 1268)
—One Thing Stolen. (p. 1297)
—Small Damages. (p. 1592)
—Undercover. (p. 1814)
Keplinger, Kody. DUFF: Designated Ugly Fat Friend. (p. 489)
—Lying Out Loud: A Companion to the DUFF. (p. 1066)
—Midsummer's Nightmare. (p. 1139)
—Shut Out. (p. 1572)
—Swift Boys & Me. (p. 1690)
Kepnes, Caroline. Stephen Crane. (p. 1648)
Kerbel, Deborah. Girl on the Other Side. (p. 678)
—Lure. (p. 1066)
Kerber, Kathy, illus. see Nelson, Sheila K.
Kerber, Kathy, jt. auth. see Mead, Purnima.
Kerby, Johanna. Little Pink Pup. Kerby, Johanna, photos by. (p. 1033)
Kerby, Mona. Amelia Earhart. (p. 58)
—Owney, the Mail-Pouch Pooch. Barasch, Lynne, illus. (p. 1315)
—Robert E. Lee: Commander of the Confederate Army. (p. 1479)
Kerchner, Janet Hall, illus. see RAZ.
Keren Weaver Graphics, illus. see Price, Melissa.
Kerick, Mia. Intervention [Library Edition]. (p. 881)
—Not Broken, Just Bent [Library Edition]. (p. 1267)
—Red Sheet. (p. 1455)
—Us Three. (p. 1826)
Kerins, Tony, illus. see Randall, Ronne.
Kerisel, Françoise. Diogenes' Lantern. Mansot, Fédérick, tr. from FRE. (p. 445)
Kerkow, Larry. Angel Goes to Sea. (p. 73)
Kerl, Mary Ann. Cut Me Some Slack, Lord: Reflections for Teen Males. (p. 396)
Kerley, Barbara. Cool Drink of Water. (p. 363)
—Dinosaurs of Waterhouse Hawkins: An Illuminating History of Mr. Warehouse Hawkins, Artist & Lecturer. Selznick, Brian, illus. (p. 445)
—Extraordinary Mark Twain (According to Susy) Fotheringham, Edwin, illus. (p. 555)
—"Extrodinary" Mark Twain (According to Susy) Fotheringham, Edwin, illus. (p. 557)
—Home for Mr. Emerson. Fotheringham, Edwin, illus. (p. 792)
—Little Peace. (p. 1033)
—One World, One Day. (p. 1297)
—Those Rebels, John & Tom. Fotheringham, Edwin, illus. (p. 1740)
—Walt Whitman: Words for America. Selznick, Brian, illus. (p. 1856)
—What to Do about Alice? (p. 1894)
—What to Do about Alice? How Alice Roosevelt Broke the Rules, Charmed the World, & Drove Her Father Teddy Crazy! Fotheringham, Edwin, illus. (p. 1894)
—With a Friend by Your Side. (p. 1942)
—World Is Waiting for You. (p. 1956)
—You & Me Together: Moms, Dads, & Kids Around the World. (p. 1973)
—You & Me Together: Moms, Dads, & Kids Arounds the World. (p. 1973)
Kerlikowske, Elizabeth. Before the Rain. (p. 158)
Kerline, Joni M. Sebastian Breaks for Freedom (p. 1539)
Kerline-Nowak, Joni. Sebastian Breaks for Freedom (p. 1539)
Kermani, Arax. Wyrm (p. 1966)
Kermeen, Frances. Myrtles Plantation: The True Story of America's Most Haunted House. (p. 1222)
Kern. Kern Alphabet Deck & Book Set. (p. 949)
Kern, Adrienne, illus. see Fischel, Emma.
Kern, Betty. Nutrition & Activity Journal for Teenaged Girls. (p. 1274)
Kern, Corbyn, illus. see Schwartz, Linda.
Kern, Dale & Katic, Marija. Imagine. (p. 860)
Kern, Debb, illus. see Williams, Noele.
Kern, Deborah J. Learning to Trust God. (p. 986)
Kern, Donna. Animal Alphabet. Kern, Donna, illus. (p. 76)
—Kern Alphabet Card Games. Kern, Donna, illus. (p. 949)
Kern, Jennifer. Patterning & Sequencing. (p. 1329)
Kern, Kimberly, ed. see Jasnoch, Dorothy.
Kern, Merilee A. Making Healthy Choices: A Story to Inspire Fit, Weight-Wise Kids (Boys' Edition) (p. 1081)
—Making Healthy Choices: A Story to Inspire Fit, Weight-Wise Kids (Girls' Edition) (p. 1081)
Kern, Peggy. Little Peach. (p. 1033)
—No Way Out. (p. 1261)
—Test. (p. 1723)
Kern, Shelly, illus. see Adams, Wayne.
Kernaghan, Eileen. Alchemist's Daughter. (p. 35)
—Dance of the Snow Dragon. (p. 402)
—Snow Queen. (p. 1599)
Kernaghan, Eileen, jt. auth. see Faragher, Nick.
Kernahan, C., jt. auth. see Kernahan, J. C.
Kernahan, J. C. & Kernahan, C. Tom, Dot & Talking Mouse & Other Bedtime Stories. (p. 1763)
KERNAN. Steps to English (p. 1648)
—Steps to English: Grade 2. (p. 1648)
Kernan, Doris. Steps to English. (p. 1648)
Kernan, Elizabeth. Counting at the Store: Learning to Count from 6 To 10. (p. 370)
—Dolly Takes a Drive. (p. 464)
—Fred's Bread. (p. 633)
—Harriet Tubman: A Lesson in Bravery. (p. 750)
—How Long Is It? Learning to Measure with Nonstandard Units. (p. 810)
—Meet Firefighter Jen. (p. 1121)
—Patty's Pictures. (p. 1330)
Kernan, Martin James. Danger Dolphin. Finley, Thomas Murray, illus. (p. 403)
—Entertaining Elephant. Finley, Thomas Murray, illus. (p. 531)
Kernen, Steven, illus. see McClure, C. R.
Kerner, Stuart, et al. Religions to Inspire - Hinduism. (p. 1458)
Kerner, Susan. Always by My Side Haywood, Ian Benfold, illus. (p. 51)
Kerney, Kelly. Born Again. (p. 214)
Kerns, Ann. Australia in Pictures. (p. 116)
—Did Castles Have Bathrooms? And Other Questions about the Middle Ages. (p. 436)
—I Date Dead People. Görrissen, Janina, illus. (p. 837)
—I Date Dead People. Gorman, Mike & Görrissen, Janina, illus. (p. 837)
—Romania in Pictures. (p. 1486)
—Seven Wonders of Architecture. (p. 1555)
—Troy. (p. 1790)
—Was There Really a Gunfight at the O. K. Corral? And Other Questions about the Wild West. Thompson, Colin W., illus. (p. 1859)
—Who Will Shout If Not Us? Student Activists & the Tiananmen Square Protest, China, 1989. (p. 1919)
—Wizards & Witches. (p. 1943)
Kerns, Kim A. Moose on the Loose: Moose Capades Book 1. (p. 1173)
Kerns, Kristen. Tommy Fakes the Flu. Barrett, Casey, illus. (p. 1764)
Kerr, B. Modern Persona: Valhalla High School. (p. 1158)
Kerr, Christine. Bloom's How to Write about J. D. Salinger. (p. 201)
Kerr, Cora. Love Lessons on Bird Beach. (p. 1060)
Kerr, Donald. Smell of Powder: A History of Duelling in New Zealand. Elliot, David, illus. (p. 1593)
Kerr, Eleanor. To Get to Me. Rossell, Judith, illus. (p. 1759)
Kerr, Esme. Girl with the Glass Bird. (p. 679)
Kerr, George, illus. see Burgess, Thornton W.
Kerr, George, tr. see Burgess, Thornton W.
Kerr, Gordon. Story of Robinson Crusoe. (p. 1659)
Kerr, Harold. Pout or Purpose? A Simple Approach for Understanding Your Purpose Pie & Improving Your Life. (p. 1389)
Kerr, J. B. Food - Ethical Debates in What We Eat. (p. 613)
Kerr, Jim. How to Improve at Cricket. (p. 820)
—Polar Regions (p. 1379)
—Sports. (p. 1632)
Kerr, Judith. Creatures: A Celebration of the Life & Work. (p. 380)
—Crocodile under the Bed. (p. 384)
—Cuando Hitler Robó el Conejo Rosa. (p. 388)
—En la Batalla de Inglaterra. (p. 522)
—Goodbye Mog. Kerr, Judith, illus. (p. 701)
—Goose in a Hole. (p. 702)
—Goose in a Hole. Kerr, Judith, illus. (p. 702)
—Judith Kerr Treasury. (p. 931)
—Mog & Bunny. Kerr, Judith, illus. (p. 1160)
—Mog & the Baby. Kerr, Judith, illus. (p. 1160)
—Mog & the Granny. (p. 1160)
—MOG & the V. E. T. Kerr, Judith, illus. (p. 1160)
—Mog & the Vet. (p. 1160)
—Mog in the Dark. (p. 1160)
—Mog in the Dark. Kerr, Judith, illus. (p. 1160)
—Mog on Fox Night. (p. 1160)
—Mog on Fox Night. Kerr, Judith, illus. (p. 1160)
—Mog the Forgetful Cat. Kerr, Judith, illus. (p. 1160)
—Mog's Amazing Birthday Caper. Kerr, Judith, illus. (p. 1160)
—Mog's Bad Thing. (p. 1160)
—Mog's Christmas. (p. 1160)
—One Night in the Zoo. Kerr, Judith, illus. (p. 1296)
—Tiger Who Came to Tea. (p. 1748)
—Tiger Who Came to Tea. Kerr, Judith, illus. (p. 1748)
—Twinkles, Arthur & Puss. (p. 1802)
—Twinkles, Arthur & Puss. Kerr, Judith, illus. (p. 1802)
—When Hitler Stole Pink Rabbit. (p. 1902)
—When Willy Went to the Wedding. (p. 1905)
Kerr, Kathleen, jt. auth. see Glaspey, Terry.
Kerr, Lenora, jt. auth. see Kalomas, Alice.
Kerr, M. E., pseud. If I Love You, Am I Trapped Forever? (p. 853)
—I'll Love You When You're More Like Me. (p. 856)
—Slap Your Sides. (p. 1588)
—Snakes Don't Miss Their Mothers. (p. 1596)
—Someone Like Summer. (p. 1609)
—Son of Someone Famous. (p. 1611)
—Your Eyes in Stars. (p. 1980)
Kerr, Mike. Mike & a Lynx Named Kitty. Vitt, Karren, illus. (p. 1141)
Kerr, Norbert L., jt. auth. see Baron, Robert S.
Kerr, P. B., pseud. Day of the Djinn Warriors. (p. 414)
—Eye of the Forest. (p. 557)
—Five Fakirs of Faizabad. (p. 600)
—Grave Robbers of Genghis Khan. (p. 712)
—One Small Step. (p. 1297)
Kerr, Pat. Down to Earth. (p. 474)
Kerr, Philip, see Kerr, P. B., pseud.
Kerr, Sophie. Kid's Guide to Sewing: 16 Projects You'll Love to Make & Use. (p. 954)
Kerr, Valerie. Adventures of Selwyn & Robert: Saving Whako the White Lion. (p. 22)
—Adventures of Selwyn & Robert. (p. 22)
—My World Within: Fun with Animals. (p. 1222)
—My World Within: Up in the Clouds. (p. 1222)
Kerrigan, Brooke, illus. see Beck, Carolyn.
Kerrigan, Brooke, illus. see McLeod, Heather.
Kerrigan, Brooke, illus. see Slavens, Elaine.
Kerrigan, Michael. Biological & Germ Warfare Protection. (p. 189)
—Coastlines. (p. 336)
—Department of Homeland Security. (p. 427)
—Egyptians. (p. 507)
—Greeks. (p. 721)
—Mesopotamians. (p. 1129)
—National Guard. (p. 1233)
—Police Crime Prevention. (p. 1380)
—Romans. (p. 1486)
—War Against Drugs. (p. 1857)
Kerrigan, William, ed. see Milton, John.
Kerrin, Jessica, jt. auth. see Kerrin, Jessica Scott.
Kerrin, Jessica Scott. Blazing Ahead! Kelly, Joseph, illus. (p. 199)
—In High Gear! Kelly, Joseph, illus. (p. 863)
—Martin Bridge: Onwards & Upwards! Kelly, Joseph, illus. (p. 1097)
—Out of Orbit! Kelly, Joseph, illus. (p. 1311)
—Sky's the Limit! Kelly, Joseph, illus. (p. 1587)
—Sound the Alarm! Kelly, Joseph, illus. (p. 1615)
Kerrin, Jessica Scott & Kerrin, Jessica. Martin Bridge: On the Lookout! Kelly, Joseph, illus. (p. 1097)
—Ready for Takeoff! Kelly, Joseph, illus. (p. 1447)
Kerrod, Robin. Dawn of the Space Age. (p. 412)
—Exploring Nature: Whales & Dolphins. (p. 552)
—Exploring Science: Weather an Amazing Fact File & Hands-On Project Book. (p. 553)
—Exploring Science: Volcanoes & Earthquakes - an Amazing Fact File & Hands-On Project Book. (p. 553)
—Find Out about Astronomy. (p. 587)
—Find Out about the Sea: With 20 Projects & More Than 260 Pictures. (p. 587)
—Find Out about Weather: With 15 Projects & More Than 260 Pictures. (p. 587)
—New Materials. (p. 1246)
—Space. (p. 1618)
—Space Stations. (p. 1620)
—Transportation. (p. 1779)
—Whales & Dolphins. (p. 1878)
Kerrod, Robin, jt. auth. see Herrod, Robin.
Kerrod, Robin & Parker, Steve. Find Out about the Body. (p. 587)
Kerry, Mary. Saving the Scrolls. (p. 1517)
Kerschner, Stacie. Remember Love. (p. 1459)
Kersey, R.W., tr. see De Sede, Gerard & de Sede, Sophie.
Kersey, W.T., tr. see De Sede, Gerard & de Sede, Sophie.
Kershaw, Linda. Alberta Wayside Wildflowers. Kershaw, Linda, illus. (p. 35)
Kershaw, Linda & Resnicek, Tony. Trees of Michigan. (p. 1784)
Kershaw, Linda J. Manitoba Wayside Wildflowers. (p. 1087)
Kershner, Gerry. Lancaster Landmarks Coloring Book. Kershner, Gerry, illus. (p. 973)
Kershner, Tad. Body Double: Understanding Physical Changes. (p. 207)
—Living with ADHD. (p. 1042)
Kerstein, Lauren H. Week of Switching, Shifting, & Stretching: How to Make My Thinking More Flexible. (p. 1871)
Kersting, Chris A. Shepherds Went with Haste: A Little Dog's Christmas Miracle. (p. 1565)
—Shepherds Went with Haste. (p. 1565)
Kerston, Caroline. Hollywood Harry. (p. 789)
Kertell, Lynn Maslen. Alphabet. Maslen, John R. & Hendra, Sue, illus. (p. 49)
—Bob Books: First Stories. Sullivan, Dana, illus. (p. 205)
—Buddy to the Rescue. (p. 235)
—Buddy to the Rescue. Hendra, Sue, illus. (p. 235)
—Cupcake Surprise! (p. 392)
—Cupcake Surprise! Hendra, Sue, illus. (p. 392)
—I Can Ride! (p. 836)
—I Can Ride! Hendra, Sue, illus. (p. 836)
—My School Trip. (p. 1218)
—My School Trip. Hendra, Sue, illus. (p. 1218)
—Pre-Reading Skills. Hendra, Sue & Maslen, John R., illus. (p. 1394)
—Rhyming Words. Sullivan, Dana, illus. (p. 1468)
Kertell, Lynn Maslen, jt. auth. see Maslen, Bobby Lynn.
Kertesz, Susan. Harvey. (p. 752)
Kervegant, Fflon, jt. auth. see Baker, David.
Kerven, Rosalind. Coyote Girl. (p. 374)
—Sparrow, the Crow & the Pearl. Williamson, Melanie, illus. (p. 1622)
Kerven, Rosalind & Quarto Generic Staff. Fairy-Spotter's Handbook. Anderson, Wayne, illus. (p. 564)
Kerwin, Betsy. Adventures of Floret the Woodland Fairy: The Adventures Begin. (p. 18)
Kerz, Anna. Better Than Weird (p. 172)
—Gnome's Eye (p. 685)
—Mealworm Diaries (p. 1116)
Kesead, Melissa. Commotion in the Ocean: A Collection of Ocean Related Poetry for Children. (p. 349)

—Walter the Dreamer in the Enchanted Wood. Bryan, Tayler, illus. (p. 1856)
Kesecker, Jennifer. Adventures of Mr. Feeny & Cinnamon. Thomas, James, illus. (p. 20)
Kesel, Barbara. Coming Home McNiven, Steve et al, illus. (p. 348)
—First Smith, Andy et al, illus. (p. 592)
—First: Ragnarok Smith, Andy et al, illus. (p. 592)
—Fluttershy. Fleecs, Tony, illus. (p. 609)
—Flying Solo. Middleton, Joshua et al, illus. (p. 610)
—Going to Ground McNiven, Steve et al, illus. (p. 693)
—Meridian McNiven, Steve et al, illus. (p. 1127)
—Minister of Cadador McNiven, Steve et al, illus. (p. 1147)
—Mystery of Sheristan Cucca, Vincenzo et al, illus. (p. 1225)
—Radiant Perez, George et al, illus. (p. 1432)
—Solus. Perez, George et al, illus. (p. 1608)
—Taking the Skies McNiven, Steve et al, illus. (p. 1698)
Kesel, Karl. Human Torch: Burn. Young, Skottie, illus. (p. 826)
Kesel, Karl, illus. see Wolfman, Marv.
Keselman, Gabriela. Marc Just Couldn't Sleep. Villamuza, Noemi, illus. (p. 1091)
—Mejor Amigo. (p. 1124)
Keselman, Porter Gabr. Ponete Los Zapatos. (p. 1382)
Kesey, Ken. One Flew over the Cuckoo's Nest. Sacco, Joe, illus. (p. 1295)
Kesinger, Brian. Coloring with Your Octopus: A Coloring Book for Domesticated Cephalopods. (p. 344)
Kesler, Matt, illus. see Moore, Clement C.
Kespert, Deborah. 3-D Chillers: Vampires, Zombies, & Werewolves. (p. 1991)
—Genius! The Most Astonishing Inventions of All Time. (p. 661)
Kespert, Deborah & Baker, David. Space Academy: How to Fly Spacecraft Step by Step. (p. 1618)
Kess, Ollie Garrett. Cutie Curlie Claire. (p. 396)
Kessel, Joyce K. Halloween. Carlson, Nancy, illus. (p. 737)
—Halloween. Translations.com Staff, tr. from ENG. (p. 737)
—Squanto & the First Thanksgiving. Donze, Lisa, illus. (p. 1636)
—Squanto y el Primer Día de Acción de Gracias. Translations.com Staff, tr. from ENG. (p. 1636)
Kessel, Kristin. Martha Graham. (p. 1097)
Kessel, Margaret May, illus. see Kessel, Quinta Cattell.
Kessel, Quinta Cattell. Mama Is A Mammal. Kessel, Margaret May, illus. (p. 1084)
Kessel, William B. & Wooster, Robert, eds. Encyclopedia of Native American Wars & Warfare. (p. 525)
Kesselman, Marc, jt. auth. see Kesselman, Robin.
Kesselman, Robin & Kesselman, Marc. Nerdel's ABC Book. Martinez, Natali, illus. (p. 1241)
Kesselman-Turkel, Judi & Peterson, Franklynn. Research Shortcuts. (p. 1462)
—Secrets to Writing Great Papers. (p. 1546)
—Spelling Simplified. (p. 1625)
—Vocabulary Builder: The Practically Painless Way to a Larger Vocabulary. (p. 1847)
Kesselring, Mari. Alabama. (p. 33)
—April. Dumm, Brian Caleb, illus. (p. 93)
—Arizona. (p. 98)
—August. Collier-Morales, Roberta, illus. (p. 115)
—Cyber Poser. Epelbaum, Mariano, illus. (p. 396)
—December. Billin-Frye, Paige, illus. (p. 421)
—Delaware. (p. 424)
—February. Billin-Frye, Paige, illus. (p. 580)
—Florida. (p. 606)
—Georgia. (p. 665)
—How to Analyze the Works of Franklin D. Roosevelt. (p. 814)
—How to Analyze the Works of William Shakespeare. (p. 814)
—How to Analyze the Works of Winston Churchill. (p. 814)
—Idaho. (p. 851)
—January. Billin-Frye, Paige, illus. (p. 908)
—July. Collier-Morales, Roberta, illus. (p. 933)
—June. Collier-Morales, Roberta, illus. (p. 934)
—March. Dumm, Brian Caleb, illus. (p. 1091)
—May. Dumm, Brian Caleb, illus. (p. 1112)
—Months of the Year (p. 1170)
—November. Rooney, Ronnie, illus. (p. 1268)
—October. Rooney, Ronnie, illus. (p. 1277)
—Selfie Sabotage. Epelbaum, Mariano, illus. (p. 1549)
—September. Rooney, Ronnie, illus. (p. 1551)
—Techie Cheater. Epelbaum, Mariano, illus. (p. 1711)
Kesselring, Susan. 5 Steps to Drawing Machines at Work. DeSantis, Susan, illus. (p. 1992)
—Eat a Rainbow: Healthy Foods. Avakyan, Tatevik, illus. (p. 501)
—Grow a Garden: Sustainable Foods. Avakyan, Tatevik, illus. (p. 726)
—Make a Meal Plan: Smart Food Shopping. (p. 1078)
—National Day Traditions Around the World. Chavarri, Elisa, illus. (p. 1231)
Kesselring, Susan, jt. auth. see Lindeen, Mary.
Kesselring, Susan Temple. Robert Frost. (p. 1479)
Kessen, Virginia. Children's Worship Activities, Year 2. (p. 304)
Kessey, K.O. Rhythms of African Drums: Rhymes & Lyrics for School Children & Youngsters. (p. 1468)
Kessler, Brad. Firebird. Van Nutt, Robert, illus. (p. 591)
—John Henry. Jackson, Barry, illus. (p. 922)
Kessler, Brad & Harris, Joel Chandler. Brer Rabbit & Boss Lion. Mayer, Bill, illus. (p. 226)
Kessler, Colleen. Math Problem Solvers: Using Word Problems to Enhance Mathematical Problem Solving. (p. 1107)
—Project Guide to Electricity & Magnetism. (p. 1410)
—Project Guide to Forces & Motion. (p. 1410)
—Project Guide to Light & Optics. (p. 1410)
—Project Guide to Reptiles & Birds. (p. 1410)
—Project Guide to the Solar System. (p. 1410)
Kessler, Colleen & Benchmark Education Co. Staff. Galileo's Gift. (p. 653)
—Rodrigo & the Dogs. (p. 1484)
Kessler, Cristina. Best Beekeeper of Lalibela: A Tale from Africa. Jenkins, Leonard, illus. (p. 168)
—Hope Is Here! Castillo, Marcos, illus. (p. 796)
Kessler, David A. Your Food Is Fooling You: How Your Brain Is Hijacked by Sugar, Fat, & Salt. (p. 1980)
Kessler, Deirdre. Born: A Foal, Five Kittens & Confederation Jones, Brenda, illus. (p. 214)
—Lobster in My Pocket Jones, Brenda, illus. (p. 1044)
Kessler, Deirdre & Montgomery, L. M. Anne of Green Gables Smith, David Preston, illus. (p. 86)
Kessler, Ethel & Kessler, Leonard. Night Story. (p. 1254)
Kessler, Jackie Morse. Breath. (p. 225)
—Hunger. (p. 827)
—Loss. (p. 1054)
—Rage. (p. 1433)
Kessler, James H., jt. auth. see Bennett, Andrea T.
Kessler, Kathryn. Marvin Discovers Snow. (p. 1099)
Kessler, Leonard. That's Not Santa! (p. 1727)
Kessler, Leonard, jt. auth. see Kessler, Ethel.
Kessler, Leonard P. Mr. Pine's Purple House. Kessler, Leonard P., illus. (p. 1186)
—Mrs. Pine Takes a Trip. Kessler, Leonard P., illus. (p. 1187)
Kessler, Liz. Emily Windsnap & the Castle in the Mist. (p. 519)
—Emily Windsnap & the Castle in the Mist. Ledwidge, Natacha, illus. (p. 519)
—Emily Windsnap & the Castle in the Mist. Ledwidge, Natacha & Gibb, Sarah, illus. (p. 519)
—Emily Windsnap & the Land of the Midnight Sun. (p. 519)
—Emily Windsnap & the Land of the Midnight Sun. Gibb, Sarah & Ledwidge, Natacha, illus. (p. 519)
—Emily Windsnap & the Monster from the Deep. (p. 519)
—Emily Windsnap & the Monster from the Deep. Gibb, Sarah, illus. (p. 519)
—Emily Windsnap & the Ship of Lost Souls. Gibb, Sarah, illus. (p. 519)
—Emily Windsnap & the Siren's Secret. (p. 519)
—Emily Windsnap: Two Magical Mermaid Tales. Gibb, Sarah, illus. (p. 519)
—Four Sparkling Underwater Adventures. Gibb, Sarah & Ledwidge, Natacha, illus. (p. 625)
—Has Anyone Seen Jessica Jenkins? (p. 752)
—North of Nowhere. (p. 1265)
—Philippa Fisher & the Dream-Maker's Daughter. (p. 1350)
—Philippa Fisher & the Fairy Godsister. (p. 1350)
—Philippa Fisher's Fairy Godsister. (p. 1350)
—Poppy the Pirate Dog. Phillips, Mike, illus. (p. 1385)
—Poppy the Pirate Dog & the Missing Treasure. Phillips, Mike, illus. (p. 1385)
—Poppy the Pirate Dog's New Shipmate. Phillips, Mike, illus. (p. 1385)
—Tail of Emily Windsnap. (p. 1695)
—Tail of Emily Windsnap. Gibb, Sarah, illus. (p. 1695)
—Year Without Autumn. (p. 1969)
Kessler, MacKenzie. Murphy the Lonely Robot/Cecil the Lonely Pterodactyl. (p. 1192)
Kessler, Mario, illus. see Hubner, Franz.
Kessler, Ramon Wilke. Treasure Trove of Pirate Stories: A Collection of Best Pirate Stories for Young People. Scott, A. O., illus. (p. 1782)
Kessler, Rikki, ed. see Alexander, Carol & DiCamillo, Kate.
Kessler, Rikki, ed. see Alexander, Carol.
Kessler, Rikki, ed. see Christopher, Garrett & McDonald, Megan.
Kessler, Rikki, ed. see Christopher, Garrett.
Kessler, Rikki, ed. see Kirsch, Suzanne.
Kessler, Rikki, ed. see Kleinman, Estelle.
Kessler, Rikki, ed. see Searl, Duncan, et al.
Kessler, Rikki, ed. see Searl, Duncan.
Kessler, Rikki, ed. see Stevens, Garrett.
Kessler, Siglint, illus. see Fiedler, Christamaria.
Kessler, Susie. Where's the Christmas Angel? (p. 1910)
Kessler, Tim. When God Made the Dakotas. Morin, Paul, illus. (p. 1902)
Kest, Kristin, illus. see Bonnett-Rampersaud, Louise.
Kest, Kristin, illus. see Dennard, Deborah.
Kest, Kristin, illus. see Diaz, Katacha.
Kest, Kristin, illus. see Dunphy, Madeleine.
Kest, Kristin, illus. see Díaz, Katacha.
Kest, Kristin, illus. see Galvin, Laura Gates & Soundprints Editorial Staff.
Kest, Kristin, illus. see Galvin, Laura Gates.
Kest, Kristin, illus. see Giancamilli, Vanessa.
Kest, Kristin, illus. see Random House Staff.
Kest, Kristin, illus. see Salas, Laura Purdie.
Kest, Kristin, illus. see Slade, Suzanne.
Kest, Kristin, jt. auth. see Dennard, Deborah.
Kestell, Diane. I'm Their Mom. (p. 860)
Kesterson, Casie. Goldfish in the Chandelier. Hovland, Gary, illus. (p. 695)
Kestler, Justin, ed. see Cisneros, Sandra & SparkNotes Staff.
Kestler, Justin, ed. see Hesse, Hermann & SparkNotes Staff.
Kestler, Justin, ed. see Wilde, Oscar & SparkNotes Staff.
Keswick, Kitty. Freaksville. Cox, Val, illus. (p. 631)
Ketch, jt. auth. see Ketchedjian, Armen G.
Ketch, Ann. Lightning Bugs. Hood, Joyce, illus. (p. 1016)
—There Goes Peanut Butter! Totire, Valerie, illus. (p. 1729)
Ketchedjian, Armen G. & Ketch. Golden Apples. (p. 694)
Ketchell, Maureen. Five & a Half Mystery. (p. 599)
Ketchen, Susan. Born That Way. (p. 214)
—Made That Way. (p. 1070)
Ketchum, Holly. D Mouse's Christmas Adventure. Coyle, Charissa B., illus. (p. 398)
Ketchum, Ron. Rochestrivia: 2,000 Amazing questions & answers all about Rochester NY, it's people & surrounding Towns. (p. 1481)
Ketchum, Sally. Bread Garden. Harvey, Michael C., illus. (p. 224)
Ketchum, William C., Jr., jt. auth. see Panchyk, Richard.
Ketel, Debbie M. One Baby Mountain Goat. Horstman, Lisa, illus. (p. 1293)
Ketelsen, David P., jt. auth. see Phillips, Jane E.
Ketner, Abi, jt. auth. see Kalicicki, Missy.
Ketteman, Helen. Armadillo Chili. Terry, Will, illus. (p. 99)
—Goodnight, Little Monster Leick, Bonnie, illus. (p. 701)
—If Beaver Had a Fever O'Malley, Kevin, illus. (p. 852)
—Senorita Gordita. Terry, Will, illus. (p. 1550)
—Swamp Song Goembel, Ponder, illus. (p. 1688)
—There Once Was a Cowpoke Who Swallowed an Ant. Terry, Will, illus. (p. 1730)
—Three Little Gators. Terry, Will, illus. (p. 1742)
—Waynetta & the Cornstalk: A Texas Fairy Tale. Greenseid, Diane, illus. (p. 1865)
Ketter, Mamie. AJ the African Grey Visits the Zoo, Book #3. (p. 32)
—AJ, the African Grey Visits the Zoo, Book# 3, Coloring Book. (p. 32)
Ketter-Brust, Sandra. Sir Guinness of Wildridge. (p. 1580)
Kettle, Jenny. Monster Hunting. (p. 1167)
Kettle, Phil, jt. auth. see Arena, Felice.
Kettle, Shey. Girl Pirates. Thomas, Meredith, illus. (p. 678)
—Surf Girls. Thomas, Meredith, illus. (p. 1685)
Kettles, Nick. All-Seeing Boy & the Blue Sky of Happiness: A Children's Parable. Hallam, Serena Sax, illus. (p. 45)
Keun, Irmgard. Child of All Nations. Hofmann, Michael, tr. from GER. (p. 301)
Keuren, David K. Van, see Brown, Joanne.
Keusal, Eugene L. Story of Cardinal George: The Boy Who Wanted to be a Priest. the God Who Wanted Him to be a Prince. Ferrara, Madeleine, illus. (p. 1657)
Keuss, Jeff & Sloth, Lia. Character in Motion! Athlete Series. (p. 291)
Kevin, Henkes. Chrysanthemum. (p. 317)
Kevin, Henkes, jt. auth. see Henkes, Kevin.
Kevin Williamson & Julie Plec, jt. auth. see Smith, L. J.
Kevtherev. Riddle Tails: The Golden Fruit. (p. 1471)
Kew, Trevor. Breakaway (p. 224)
—Sidelined (p. 1573)
—Trading Goals (p. 1776)
Kewley, Ken, illus. see Jones, Kelly.
Key, Carolyn. Bunny Who Didn't Think It Was Funny. (p. 242)
Key, Francis Scott. Star Spangled Banner. (p. 1641)
—Star Spangled Banner. Minger, Nancy, illus. (p. 1641)
Key, Janet Rhyme. Rosa in Bloom. (p. 1488)
Key, Pamela, illus. see Coniglio, John.
Key, Pamela, illus. see Fairchild, Simone.
Key, Pamela Marie. Kitty Fantastic in Monroe's Art Adventure. (p. 963)
Key, Pamela Marie, illus. see Fairchild, Simone.
Key, Watt. Alabama Moon. (p. 33)
—Dirt Road Home. (p. 446)
—Fourmile (p. 625)
—Fourmile. (p. 625)
Keyama, Hiroshi Hata, illus. see Hood, Karen Jean Matsko.
Keyama, Hiroshi Hata, tr. see Hood, Karen Jean Matsko.
Keyes, Anna. Pharaohs, Pyramids & Mummies: Set Of 6. (p. 1350)
—Pharaohs, Pyramids Mummies & Faraones, pirámides y Momias: 6 English, 6 Spanish Adaptations. (p. 1350)
—World War II: 6 English, 6 Spanish Adaptations: by the Numbers & Los números de la Segunda Guerra Mundial. (p. 1959)
—World War II by the Numbers: Set Of 6. (p. 1959)
Keyes, Charlotte E. & Emerson, Ralph Waldo. Experimenter: A Biography of Ralph Waldo Emerson. (p. 549)
Keyes, Daniel. Flores para Algernon. (p. 606)
Keyes, Diane. Spirit of the Snowpeople. Stevens, Helen, illus. (p. 1628)
Keyes, Eric, 3rd, et al. Light in the Dark Marie, Paula Braxton, illus. (p. 1015)
Keyes, Joan Ross, jt. auth. see Buckley, Elizabeth.
Keyes, Joan Ross, jt. auth. see Santamaria, Jenni Currie.
Keyes, Joan Ross, jt. auth. see Stamper, Judith Bauer.
Keyes, Joan Ross, see Stamper, Judith Bauer & Ross Keyes, Joan.
Keyes, Joseph W. Sparrows of Saint Thomas. (p. 1622)
Keyes, Morgan. Darkbeast. (p. 408)
—Darkbeast Rebellion. (p. 408)
Keyes, Pamela. Legend of Zamiel Zimbalist: Book Two of the Connedim Series. (p. 989)
—Rune of Zachary Zimbalist: Book One of the Connedim Series. (p. 1497)
Keyes, Ralph. Courage to Write: How Writers Transcend Fear. (p. 372)
Keyes, Shirley. Diffee, the White Deer. (p. 437)
Keyes, Tina Misrasi, illus. see Hege, Lynnita.
Keyishan, Elizabeth. Todo lo que necesitas saber sobre el cigarillo (Everything You Need to Know about Smoking) (p. 1761)
Keyishian, Elizabeth. Everything You Need to Know about Smoking. (p. 546)
—Smoking. (p. 1595)
Keyishian, Elizabeth, jt. auth. see Stollers, Veronica.
Keylock, Andy, illus. see Waddell, Martin.
Keylock, Joanna Murray. Pupazzo's Colorful World. Pelayo, Ruben, tr. (p. 1417)
Keylon, Joe, illus. see Bloom, Stephanie.
Keylor, William R. & McGuire, Michael. Encyclopedia of the Modern World: 1900 to the Present Set (p. 525)
Keys, Dalen. Just a Quilt? Sponaugle, Kim, illus. (p. 937)
Keys, Demetria M. Replacements. (p. 1461)
Keys, Larry. Hoodzville II: From Detention to Detective. (p. 795)
Keys, Larry, illus. see Stilton, Geronimo.
Keyser, Amber. Sneaker Century: A History of Athletic Shoes. (p. 1597)
Keyser, Amber J. Anatomy of a Pandemic (p. 67)
—Way Back from Broken. (p. 1864)
Keyser, Amber J., et al. Basics of Cell Life with Max Axiom, Super Scientist (p. 142)
—Decoding Genes with Max Axiom, Super Scientist (p. 422)
Keyser, Francois. Tiger Loses His Stripes. (p. 1748)
Keyser, Herbert. Chautauquan Searches Paris for the Best Tarte au Citron. (p. 295)
Keyser, Samuel Jay & Boyds Mills Press Staff. Pond God & Other Stories. Shetterly, Robert, illus. (p. 1382)
Keyser, William. Once upon A Night. Barnes, Trisha, illus. (p. 1293)
Keyser-Rogers, Marianne. Lighthouse Neighbors Are Coral Reefs. (p. 1015)
Keystone, David, jt. auth. see Jakab, Cheryl.
Keyworth, R. L. Do Pirates Like to Play Pattie Cake? A Pirate's Guide to Playing Nice. (p. 457)
—Gregory Giraffe's New Friends Adventure: Gregory Giraffe Is about to find some altogether different but new friends at his watering Hole. (p. 723)
Kezar, Wanda. It's a Scamp's Life! Derby, Sarah, illus. (p. 896)
Kezer, Claude D. Principles of Stage Combat Handbook. (p. 1406)
KG, Mav. Angeline: the Catacombs of Egypt. (p. 74)
KH Pathways. Kindergarten Stepping Stones: Jesus Is God's Best Gift Lapbook. (p. 957)
Kha, Dang, tr. see Crouch, Adele.
Khaiphus, Kosta Demetrius, ed. see Briefing Associates Staff.
Khairnar, Kishore, ed. see Carlson, Dale Bick.
Khairnar, Kishore, jt. auth. see Carlson, Dale Bick.
Khakdan, Wahed, jt. auth. see Mola, Astrid.
Khalifé, Fatima & Mouazen, Deema. If Your Mom Was… . What Will You Do? (p. 855)
Khalili, Davood. Developing Olympian Character (p. 431)
Khalsa, Dayal Kaur. My Family Vacation. (p. 1203)
Khalsa, Gurmukh Kaur. Bountiful, Beautiful, Blissful: Experience the Natural Power of Pregnancy & Birth with Kundalini Yoga & Meditation. (p. 216)
Khamis, Johnny. Costi & the Raindrop Adventure. Belanger, Damon, illus. (p. 368)
Khan, Aisha. Avicenna (Ibn Sina) Muslim Physician & Philosopher of the Eleventh Century. (p. 119)
—Historical Atlas of India. (p. 782)
—Historical Atlas of Kyrgyzstan. (p. 783)
Khan, Aisha Karen. What You Will See Inside a Mosque. Pepis, Aaron, photos by. (p. 1896)
Khan, Aliyah. Adventures of Solomon Spider: Solomon Sees the City. (p. 23)
Khan, Aziz, illus. see Reid, Struan.
Khan, Farheen. Ibrahim Khan & the Mystery of the Haunted Lake. (p. 849)
Khan, Geoffrey, et al, eds. NeoAramaic & Its Linguistic Context. (p. 1241)
Khan, Hana. Taylor's Birthday Party. Kemble, Mai S., illus. (p. 1708)
Khan, Hena. Golden Domes & Silver Lanterns: A Muslim Book of Colors. Amini, Mehrdokht, illus. (p. 694)
—How to Be a Know-It-All on Almost Any Subject You Can Think Of. (p. 814)
—How to Say What You Mean, Mean What You Say, & Get What You Want. (p. 821)
—Night of the Moon: A Muslim Holiday Story. Paschkis, Julie, illus. (p. 1254)
—Space Explorer's Guide to Earth's Neighborhood. (p. 1619)
Khan, Hena, jt. auth. see Borgenicht, David.
Khan, Hena & Dyson, Marianne J. Space Explorer's Guide to Out-Of-This-World Science. (p. 1619)
Khan, Jahangir & Pratt, Kevin. Learn Squash in a Weekend. Ward, Matthew, photos by. (p. 983)
Khan, Jenette, ed. see Kane, Bob.
Khan, Nafeesa. Pompom's Rainbow Day. (p. 1382)
Khan, Nahnatchka, jt. auth. see Howard, Lee.
Khan, Nicholai. Nicho the Tiger - Create Your World. (p. 1250)
Khan, R. So You Want to Buy A Dog. (p. 1602)
Khan, Ramla. Fairy Tale Baking: More Than 50 Enchanting Cakes,bakes, & Decorations. (p. 564)
Khan, Rukhsana. Big Red Lollipop. Blackall, Sophie, illus. (p. 183)
—Roses in My Carpets Himler, Ronald, illus. (p. 1490)
—Wanting Mor (p. 1857)
Khan, Rukhsana, et al. Many Windows: Six Kids, Five Faiths, One Community. (p. 1089)
Khan, S. Amazing Animal Facts & Lists. (p. 53)
Khan, Sarah. Birds Lift-the-Flap. Scott, Peter, illus. (p. 191)
—Creepy Crawlies Lift-the-Flap. Scott, Peter, illus. (p. 381)
—Dinosaur Quiz Cards. (p. 445)
—First Illustrated Science Dictionary. Robson, Kirsteen, ed. (p. 595)
—Little Book of Horses & Ponies. Lambert, Stephen, illus. (p. 1025)
—Night Sky Sticker Book. Clarke, Phillip, ed. (p. 1254)
—Pets Lift-the-Flap. (p. 1348)
—Word Puzzles. (p. 1951)
Khan, Sarah, ed. see Miles, Lisa.
Khan, Sarah, jt. auth. see Clarke, Phillip.
Khan, Sharaz. Zambo & the Haunted House. (p. 1984)
Khan, Sophie, illus. see Cottrell, Sue.
Khanbaghi, Aptin. Fire, the Star & the Cross: Minority Religions in Medieval & Early Modern Iran. (p. 591)
Khanduri, K. Great World Search. (p. 719)
—Tales of the trojan War. (p. 1703)
—Usborne Book of World Wildlife. (p. 1827)
Khanduri, K., jt. auth. see Claybourne, A.
Khanduri, Kamini. Great World Search. Hancock, David, illus. (p. 719)
—Usborne the Great World Search. Hancock, David, illus. (p. 1827)
Khanduri, Kamini, et al. Usborne Big Book of Picture Puzzles. Groebner, Dominic, illus. (p. 1827)
Khanlari, Parviz-Natel. Young Persons History of Iran. Yazdanfar, Farzin, tr. (p. 1979)
Khanlu, Nancy Yousefian. Trip into Space. (p. 1787)
Khanna, Balraj. Rajah: King of the Jungle. (p. 1437)
Khanna, Rachel. Oh the Places to Know: A Guide to Greenwich for Kids. (p. 1281)
Kharbanda, Priya. Flumpa & Bosly Learn the Magic Three Rs: Reduce, Reuse & Recycle. (p. 608)
Khare, Pratibha & Bekooy Khare, Catherine. Hindi Primer (p. 780)
Khatib, Ahmed. Al Mousou'a al Ilmiya al Mouysarah: Illustrated Children's Encyclopedia. (p. 32)
Khatreja, Himani, jt. auth. see Dorling Kindersley Publishing Staff.
Khatri, Meeta. Can You Sound Out with Me? (p. 259)
Khayyam, Omar. Quatrains of Omar Khayyam: Three Translations of the Rubaiyat. FitzGerald, Edward et al, trs. from PEO. (p. 1423)
Khee, Seah Wee, et al. Chemagic. (p. 297)
Kheirabadi, Masoud. Islam. (p. 891)

—Sri Satya Sai Baba. (p. 1637)
Kheirabadi, Masoud & Gritzner, Charles F. Iran. (p. 886)
Kheiriyeh, Rashin. There Was an Old Lady Who Swallowed a Fly. (p. 1730)
Kheiriyeh, Rashin, illus. see Kim, YeShil.
Kheneigar, Ahmed Abou. Muhammad: The Life of the Prophet - Based on Original Sources. Abou El Azm, Mohsen, illus. (p. 1189)
Kherdian, David. Come Back, Moon. Hogrogian, Nonny, illus. (p. 347)
Kheroufi, Allel. I Want to Fly: A Play for Children in Four Parts. (p. 848)
Khing, T. T. Where Is the Cake? (p. 1909)
Khmelnitsky, Igor. Chess Exam & Training Guide: Rate yourself & learn how to Improve. (p. 298)
Khodjibaev, Karim, tr. see Shookuhi, Aminjon.
Khodjibaeva, Moukhabbat, tr. see Shookuhi, Aminjon.
Khoo, Rowena. Where Is My Sock? (p. 1909)
Khory, Emil, illus. see Crotts, Barbara.
Khoury, Elias. Gate of the Sun. Davies, Humphrey, tr. (p. 658)
Khoury, Jessica. Kalahari. (p. 941)
—Origin. (p. 1304)
—Vitro. (p. 1846)
Khoury, Marielle D., jt. auth. see Du Bouchet, Paule.
Khoury, Marielle D. & du Bouchet, Paule. Bach. Voake, Charlotte, illus. (p. 129)
Khoury, Raymond. Sanctuary. (p. 1510)
Khu, Jannel. Let's Draw a Fire Truck with Shapes. (p. 995)
—Let's Draw a Fire Truck with Shapes/Vamos a dibujar un camión de bomberos usando Figuras. (p. 995)
—Let's Draw a House with Shapes. (p. 996)
—Let's Draw a House with Shapes/Vamos a dibujar una casa usando Figuras. (p. 996)
—Let's Draw a School Bus with Shapes. (p. 996)
—Let's Draw a School Bus with Shapes/Vamos a dibujar un autobus escolar usando Figuras. (p. 996)
Khu, Jannell. Dogs. (p. 462)
—Spiders. (p. 1627)
—Spiders / Arañas. (p. 1627)
—Spiders/Aranas. Beullens, Nathalie, tr. (p. 1627)
Khu, Jannell, jt. auth. see Schimel, Kate.
Khuc, Mimi & Nguyen, Thanh-Trieu. Here & Now Meditation: A Quick & Effective Way to Overcome Suffering. (p. 769)
Khulekani, Magubane. Angels Salvation. (p. 75)
Khvostova, Ekaterina, tr. see Jones, Alan & Ellis, Jane.
Khzouz, Medlaine. Suzie Time. (p. 1688)
Kiah Odom, Danayla Odom-West. Emily's Way. (p. 519)
Kiani, Sabra. Billy Ben's Fantastic Pictures. (p. 187)
Kiarie, Vivian W. Waltz, the Weasel & the Lair. (p. 1856)
Kiaulevicius, Rolandas, illus. see Glassman, Bruce.
Kibbe, Pat. Mrs. Kiddy & the Moonbooms. (p. 1187)
Kibble, George Anthon. Bilwok: Dawn of the Trolls. (p. 188)
Kibera, Ngumi. Shaza's Trials. (p. 1564)
Kibuishi, Kazu. Amulet Boxed Set (p. 66)
—Copper. (p. 365)
—Daisy Kutter: The Last Train. Kibuishi, Kazu, illus. (p. 400)
—Escape from Lucien. (p. 535)
—Explorer: The Hidden Doors. (p. 551)
—Explorer: The Mystery Boxes. (p. 551)
—Explorer - The Lost Islands. (p. 551)
—Last Council. (p. 977)
—Lost Islands. (p. 1056)
—Prince of the Elves. (p. 1401)
—Stonekeeper. (p. 1653)
—Stonekeeper's Curse. (p. 1653)
Kibuishi, Kazu, ed. see Matte, Johane, et al.
Kibuishi, Kazu, ed. Explorer: The Lost Islands. (p. 551)
—Explorer: The Mystery Boxes. (p. 551)
Kick, J. D. Amazing Tale of Archie the Alligator. Just, John, illus. (p. 56)
—Goose Tale—Downside up. Just, John, illus. (p. 702)
Kick The Ball. Celticology Trivia Challenge: Boston Celtics Basketball. (p. 286)
—Lakerology Trivia Challenge: Los Angeles Lakers Basketball. (p. 972)
Kickbusch, Consuelo Castillo. Journey to the Future: A Roadmap for Success for Youth. (p. 929)
Kickbusch, Ilona, et al. Globalization, Women, & Health in the 21st Century. (p. 685)
Kickingbird, Samantha, illus. see Chovanetz, Tabatha Moran.
Kicklighter, Clois E. Architecture: Residential Drafting & Design. (p. 95)
—Architecture. (p. 95)
—Modern Masonry. (p. 1158)
Kicklighter, Clois E., jt. auth. see Brown, Walter C.
Kicklighter, Clois E., jt. auth. see Wagner, Willis H.
Kicklighter, Clois E. & Kicklighter, Joan C. Architecture: Residential Drafting & Design. (p. 95)
—Residential Housing & Interiors: Teaching Package Instructor's Resource. (p. 1463)
—Residential Housing & Interiors: Teaching Package Powerpoint Presentations. (p. 1463)
—Residential Housing & Interiors: Teaching Package Instructor's Resource Portfolio. (p. 1463)
—Residential Housing & Interiors: Teaching Package PowerPoint Presentations Individual License. (p. 1463)
—Residential Housing & Interiors. (p. 1463)
—Upholstery Fundamentals. (p. 1825)
Kicklighter, Joan C., jt. auth. see Kicklighter, Clois E.
Kicksee, John, illus. see Thomas, Keltie.
Kid, Penelope. Teach Me to Love. Goffe, Toni, illus. (p. 1708)
—Teach Me to Pray. Goffe, Toni, illus. (p. 1708)
Kidd, Bruce. Tom Longboat (p. 1763)
Kidd, Chip. Go: A Kidd's Guide to Graphic Design. (p. 685)
Kidd, Diane, illus. see Weitekamp, Margaret A. & DeVorkin, David.
Kidd, Diane, illus. see Weitekamp, Margaret.
Kidd, Dorothy. Tina's Tail (p. 1755)
Kidd, Erin. Cowgirl. (p. 374)
Kidd, J. S. & Kidd, Renee A. Science & Society Set. (p. 1525)
Kidd, Jessica A. Zachary Zoom. (p. 1984)
Kidd, Melissa J. Jonathan Jumps. (p. 925)
Kidd, Paul T. Father Christmas Adventures: Unexpected Tales of Christmas Magic. (p. 577)
Kidd, Pennie. Oops! Beardshaw, Rosalind, illus. (p. 1299)
Kidd, Renee A. Air Pollution: Problems & Solutions. (p. 31)
—New Genetics: The Study of Lifelines. (p. 1244)
—Nuclear Power: The Study of Quarks & Sparks. (p. 1270)
—Potent Natural Medicines: Mother Nature's Pharmacy. (p. 1388)
Kidd, Renee A., jt. auth. see Kidd, J. S.
Kidd, Rob. Day of the Shadow. (p. 414)
—Jack Sparrow: The Siren Song. Orpinas, Jean-Paul, illus. (p. 903)
—Quest for the Sword of Cortes (p. 1426)
Kidd, Ron. Bookee Presents Colors, Shapes & Sounds. Nord, Mary, illus. (p. 212)
—Magical Circus Train. Boyd, Patti, illus. (p. 1074)
Kidd, Ronald. Monkey Town: The Summer of the Scopes Trial. (p. 1165)
—Undercover Kid: The Comic Book King. Sklar, Andy, illus. (p. 1814)
—Year of the Bomb. (p. 1969)
Kidd, Ronald, et al. Chasing George Washington. Hoyt, Ard, illus. (p. 294)
Kidd, Sabrina. Examining Hurricanes. (p. 547)
Kidd, Sue Monk. Firstlight: The Early Inspirational Writings. (p. 598)
Kidd, Tom, illus. see Card, Orson Scott.
Kidd, Virginia Bates. Children's Escape. (p. 303)
Kidde, Rita. What Do School Secretaries Do? (p. 1882)
—What Do School Secretaries Do? (¿Qué Hacen los Secretarios de la Escuela?) de la Vega, Eida, ed. (p. 1882)
—What Do Teachers Do? (p. 1882)
—What Do Teachers Do? (¿Qué Hacen los Maestros?) de la Vega, Eida, ed. (p. 1882)
—What Does a Janitor Do? (p. 1883)
—What Does a Janitor Do? (¿Qué Hace el Conserje?) de la Vega, Eida, ed. (p. 1883)
—What Does the Principal Do? (p. 1884)
—What Does the Principal Do? (¿Qué Hace el Director?) de la Vega, Eida, ed. (p. 1884)
Kidde, Rita & Wilson, Antoine. Mourning a Death in the Family. (p. 1181)
Kidder, Clark. Emily's Story: The Brave Journey of an Orphan Train Rider. (p. 519)
Kidder, Harvey. Ajedrez Infantil: Diviertete Con el Juego Mas Inteligente! Osorio, Sergio, illus. (p. 32)
Kidder, Lisa & Kidder, Lisa Damian. Glee Totally Unofficial: The Ultimate Guide to the Smash-Hit High School Musical. Triumph Books Staff, ed. (p. 683)
Kidder, Lisa Damian, jt. auth. see Kidder, Lisa.
Kidder, Tracy & French, Michael. Mountains Beyond Mountains (Adapted for Young People) The Quest of Dr. Paul Farmer, a Man Who Would Cure the World. (p. 1181)
Kiddies, jt. auth. see Maria, Nony.
Kidney, Christine. Medieval London. (p. 1119)
Kidnie, Margaret Jane. Taming of the Shrew. (p. 1704)
Kido, Yukiko, illus. see Ziefert, Harriet.
Kidpressions!. Sea Creature Creations: A Hand Print Discovery Book. Uting, Justin, illus. (p. 1534)
Kids, Belly. More Than a Woman. Coley, Mike, ed. (p. 1175)
Kids Can Learn Franklin Staff, ed. Early Reading. (p. 494)
—Printing. (p. 1407)
—Ready for Printing. (p. 1447)
—Ready for School. (p. 1447)
Kids Can Press Staff. First Phonics. (p. 596)
—Franklin & the Big Small Case. (p. 630)
—Franklin & the Wonder. (p. 630)
—Franklin, the Little Bubble. (p. 630)
—Franklin's Partner. (p. 631)
—Franklin's Picnic. (p. 631)
—Math Stories - Addition. (p. 1107)
—Numbers. (p. 1271)
—Printing Practice. (p. 1407)
—This Is Daniel Cook at the Farm. (p. 1735)
—This Is Daniel Cook at the Fire Station. Li, Karen, ed. (p. 1735)
—This Is Daniel Cook on a Hike. Li, Karen, ed. (p. 1735)
—This Is Daniel Cook on a Plane. (p. 1735)
Kids Can Press Staff & Becker, Helaine. Zoobots: Wild Robots Inspired by Real Animals Ries, Alex, illus. (p. 1989)
Kids Can Press Staff & Forbes, Scott. How to Make a Planet: A Step-by-Step Guide to Building the Earth. Camden, Jean, illus. (p. 820)
Kids Can Press Staff & Shannon, Rosemarie. Alphabet Mazes. (p. 49)
Kids Can Press Staff, ed. Franklin & the Duckling. (p. 630)
—Franklin & the Stopwatch. (p. 630)
Kids Can Read Staff, ed. Franklin's Pond Phantom. (p. 631)
Kids for Health Staff, jt. auth. see Johnson, Kandy.
Kids for Health Staff & Johnson, Kandy. Health Education Adventure Video Series, Kids for Heath: Kindergarten Facilitator's Manual/VHS Set (p. 758)
Kids Write On, jt. creator see Ray, Cindy.
Kidscan Staff. Franklin's Day with Dad. (p. 631)
—Franklin's Rocket Team. (p. 631)
KidsLabel Staff. Christmas. (p. 312)
KidsLabel Staff & Fujimoto, Makoto. Spot 7 Spooky. (p. 1633)
KidsLabel Staff, creator. Spot 7 Animals. (p. 1633)
Kidwell, Justina. Enchanted Garden & the Curse of the Evil Witch: The Kent Boys' Adventures. (p. 523)
—Haunted Tree House, the Ghost Town, & the Dark Reaper: The Kent Boys' Adventures (p. 754)
Kidwell, Leigh-Anne. Year i Lost My Popularity! (p. 1969)
Kidz Bop Kids Staff & Bryan, Bethany. Kidz Bop Plus One: Join the Kidz Bop Kidz as They Hit the Road to Find Their Newest Member. (p. 955)
—Rockin' Fill-In Story: Play along with the Kidz Bop Stars - And Have a Totally Jammin' Time! (p. 1483)
Kidz Bop Kids Staff & Potts, Kimberly. Kidz Bop - Be a Pop Star! Start Your Own Band, Book Your Own Gigs, & Become a Rock & Roll Phenom! (p. 955)
Kidzfirst. Bible Studies for Children: Acts (KOREAN) (p. 176)
Kidzup Productions Staff. ABC Theater. (p. 3)
—Addition & Subtraction. (p. 12)
—I'm Learning Spanish. (p. 859)
—I'm Learning to Multiply. (p. 859)
Kidzup Productions Staff, jt. auth. see Audio.
Kieber-King, Cynthia. Habitat Spy Wald, Christina, illus. (p. 734)
Kiedrowski, Steve, illus. see Hoch, Jeff.
Kiefe, Raab. Exploring Matter & Energy: Physical Science. (p. 552)
Kiefe, Raab, jt. auth. see Raab.
Kiefer, Janet Kennedy. Curious Freckles. (p. 393)
—Freckles. (p. 632)
Kiefer, Janet Kennedy & Barrett, Jill. Can I Play with You? Freckles Book 2. (p. 258)
Kiefer, Karen, illus. see Morrison, Susan.
Kiefer, Karen, tr. see Morrison, Susan.
Kiefer, Katja, illus. see Mörchen, Roland.
Kiefer, Kit. Jake the Grizz & the World's Fastest Snowboard. (p. 906)
Kiefer, Lorraine, jt. auth. see Beck, Alison.
Kiefer, Velma, et al. Fellowship, Enjoying God: New Testament Volume 41: 1, 2 & 3 John & Jude. Vol. 41 Henkel, Vernon et al, illus. (p. 581)
Kieffer, Elise Lael. Littlest Star. Leist, Kara Suzanne, illus. (p. 1039)
Kieffer, Jean-Francois. Adventures of Loupio, Volume 3: The Tournament. Chevrier, Janet, tr. (p. 20)
Kieffer, Jean-Francois & Ponsard, Christine. Illustrated Parables of Jesus. (p. 857)
Kieffer, Jean-Francois, et al. Illustrated Gospel for Children. (p. 857)
Kieffer, Steve, jt. auth. see Rugg, Michael.
Kiefl, Mike, tr. see Inui, Sekihiko.
Kiefl, Mike, tr. from JPN. Qwan Shimizu, Aki, illus. (p. 1429)
Kiehm, Eve Begley. B Is for Bagpipes: A Scotland Alphabet. Rutherford, Alexa, illus. (p. 122)
Kiejna, Magdalenea, illus. see Martini, T. J.
Kiel, Casey K., illus. see Carlson, Geri L.
Kiel, Casey Kizer, illus. see Moore, Angela Hays.
Kiel, Gerald. Adventures of the Super Cousins. (p. 23)
Kielburger, Craig. Lessons from a Street Kid Antonello, Marisa & Laidley, Victoria, illus. (p. 993)
Kieley, Rob, illus. see Eggleton, Jill.
kieliszewski, sheila. Superhero. (p. 1683)
Kiely, Brendan. Gospel of Winter. (p. 703)
Kiely, Kevin. SOS Lusitania. (p. 1614)
Kiely, Orla. Colors. Kiely, Orla, illus. (p. 344)
—Creatures. (p. 380)
—Numbers. Kiely, Orla, illus. (p. 1271)
—Shapes. (p. 1560)
Kiely, Richard & Rea-Dickins, Pauline. Program Evaluation in Language Education. (p. 1410)
Kiely, Rob, illus. see Hinkler Books Staff.
Kiem, Elizabeth. Dancer, Daughter, Traitor, Spy. (p. 402)
—Hider, Seeker, Secret Keeper. (p. 777)
Kiendl, Maly M. At the Door: Adapted & Illustrated by Maly M. Kiendle, Based on a Children's Story Book by Katherine M. Yates. (p. 111)
Kienzle, Ed. Last Buffalo. (p. 977)
Kienzle, Jackie. It's a Monkey's Life. (p. 895)
Kieper, Rienhold Richard. Blue Thunder One. (p. 203)
—Ten Letters for Our Children. (p. 1718)
—Tomahawk. (p. 1764)
Kier, Jenny Paul. If God Had a Bod. (p. 852)
Kiernan, Caitlin R. & Tierney, Kathleen. Cherry Bomb. (p. 298)
Kiernan, Celine. Into the Grey. (p. 881)
Kiernan, Denise. Fractions & Decimals: Familiar & Flexible Games with Dozens of Variations That Help Struggling Learners Practice & Really Master Basic Fraction & Decimal Facts. (p. 627)
—Multiplication & Division: Familiar & Flexible Games with Dozens of Variations That Help Struggling Learners Practice & Really Master Multiplication & Division Facts. (p. 1190)
Kiernan, Denise & Mitchell, Cindi. Motivating Math Homework: 80 Reproducible Practice Pages That Reinforce Key Math Skills. (p. 1179)
Kiernan, Kathy, ed. see Powers, Retha.
Kiernan, Kenny. Save the Day! (p. 1516)
Kiernan, Kenny, illus. see King, Trey.
Kiernan, Kenny, illus. see Salane, Jeffrey.
Kiernan, Kenny, illus. see Scholastic, Inc. Staff & King, Trey.
Kiernan, Kenny, illus. see Steele, Michael Anthony.
Kiernan, Kenny, jt. auth. see King, Trey.
Kiernan, Kristy. Catching Genius. (p. 279)
Kiernan, Linda. Sam & Friends: A Collection of Recollections of Life with a Knothead. (p. 1506)
—Sam & Friends. (p. 1506)
Kiernan, Tim. Liams Luck & Finnegans Fortune. (p. 1004)
Kiers, Erin L. I Have Chakras Just Like You. (p. 839)
Kiesbye, Stefan. Alaska Gas Pipeline. (p. 34)
—Body Piercing & Tattoos. (p. 207)
—Can Busy Teens Succeed Academically? (p. 258)
—Cheating. (p. 295)
—Cliques. (p. 333)
—Disasters. (p. 447)
—Drunk Driving. (p. 487)
—How Should the U. S. Proceed in Afghanistan? (p. 812)
—Identity Theft. (p. 852)
—Is Parenthood a Right or a Privilege? (p. 889)
—Is There a New Cold War? (p. 890)
—Nuclear & Toxic Waste. (p. 1269)
—Polygamy. (p. 1381)
Kiesbye, Stefan, ed. see Gerdes, Louise I.
Kiesbye, Stefan & Minamide, Elaine. How Should One Cope with Death? (p. 812)
Kiesbye, Stefan, ed. DNA Databases. (p. 456)
—Polygamy. (p. 1381)
Kiesler, Kate, illus. see Fletcher, Ralph J. & Fletcher, Ralph.
Kiesler, Kate, illus. see George, Kristine O'Connell.
Kiesler, Kate, illus. see Horowitz, Ruth.
Kieslich, Anita Hilliker. Friends Forever: Adventures of Henderson. (p. 638)
Kiesling Garrett, Doris. Butterfly Book das Schmetterling Buch. (p. 247)
Kiesling, Ralph W. Exploration (p. 550)
Kiester, Rob & Kathy. Tool in the Master's Hand. (p. 1767)
Kightley, Rosalinda. Sophie's Ballet Show: A Sparkly Pop-up Extravaganza! (p. 1613)
Kightley, Rosalinda, illus. see Cole, Joanna.
Kightley, Rosalinda, illus. see Grover, Lorie Ann.
Kightley, Rosalinda, illus. see Watt, Fiona.
Kightly, Rosalinda, illus. see Wang, Margaret.
Kihm, Steve. Lost Candy Bar. (p. 1055)
Kiick, Lisa. Bailey & Friends. Stouch, Ryan, illus. (p. 133)
Kij, Krysia. Becoming a Butterfly. (p. 156)
Kijinski, Paul. Camp Limestone. (p. 257)
Kiker, Jean. Jumping Lizard Tales. (p. 934)
—Story of Misty: The star who became the most famous star of All. (p. 1659)
Kikuchi, Hideyuki & Kakurai, Missile. Sword of Shibito 1 (p. 1692)
Kilabuk, Elisha. Qalupalik Ang, Joy, illus. (p. 1422)
Kiland, Taylor Baldwin. Careers in the US Navy. (p. 268)
—U. S. Navy & Military Careers. (p. 1807)
Kiland, Taylor Baldwin, jt. auth. see Gray, Judy Silverstein.
Kiland, Taylor Baldwin & Bledsoe, Glen. Military Helicopters: Heroes of the Sky. (p. 1143)
Kiland, Taylor Baldwin & Souter, Gerry. Armored Tanks: Battlefield Dominance. (p. 100)
—Military Rifles: Combat Ready. (p. 1143)
Kiland, Taylor Baldwin & Stein, R. Conrad. Careers in the US Marine Corps. (p. 268)
Kiland, Taylor Baldwin & Teitelbaum, Michael. Military Humvees: Armored Mobility. (p. 1143)
—Military Submarines: Sea Power. (p. 1143)
Kiland, Taylor Baldwin, et al. Fighter Planes: Masters of the Sky. (p. 585)
—Military Helicopters: Heroes of the Sky. (p. 1143)
Kilby, Don. At a Construction Site. Kilby, Don, illus. (p. 110)
—In the City. Kilby, Don, illus. (p. 865)
—In the Country. Kilby, Don, illus. (p. 865)
—On the Road. (p. 1291)
—On the Road. Kilby, Don, illus. (p. 1291)
Kilby, Don, illus. see Bennet, Amy.
Kilby, Jak, illus. see A&C Black Staff & Ganeri, Anita.
Kilby, Janice Eaton, et al. Libro de Trucos de Magia del Aprendiz de Brujo: Ingeniosos Trucos de Magia y Sorprendentes Ilusiones para Divertir A Tus Amigos. (p. 1006)
Kilby, Keith. Broken Halo. (p. 230)
Kilby, Tracie. Gymnastics Gina. (p. 734)
Kile, Joan. God's Fig Tree. Ragland, Teresa, illus. (p. 691)
—God's Fruit Tree. Ragland, Teresa, illus. (p. 691)
—God's Mustard Seed: Volume 1 Ragland, Teresa, illus. (p. 691)
—God's Protecting Angels. Ragland, Teresa, illus. (p. 691)
—God's Rugged Cross. Ragland, Teresa, illus. (p. 691)
Kileff, Mary Carol. King of Bozark. (p. 958)
Kilen, Josh. Tell Me a Story: Sean Ryanis & the Impossible Chase. (p. 1716)
—Tell Me a Story: The Super Hero Chronicles - Birth of Moonlight. (p. 1716)
—Tell Me a Story. (p. 1716)
Kiley, Christian Kennedy. Little Trixie's Big Adventure. (p. 1037)
Kiley, Kieran, jt. auth. see Byerly, Robbie.
Kilgannon, Amy. Missy Moo & Bailey Too Go down the Shore. MacKay, Mark, illus. (p. 1154)
Kilgore, James. Pedagogic Logic. (p. 1334)
Kilgore, Lee. Mr. Munch Adventures: Six Short Stories (p. 1185)
—Riddle of the Rustled Reindeer: A Christmas Mystery. (p. 1470)
—Widga's Quest (p. 1927)
Kilgore, Mary & Kilgore, Mitchell. Where Is My Mommy? Coping When a Parent Leaves (and Doesn't Come Back) Pillo, Cary, illus. (p. 1908)
Kilgore, Mitchell, jt. auth. see Kilgore, Mary.
Kilgour, Mary Cameron. Me May Mary. (p. 1116)
Kilgras, Heidi. Peanut. Reed, Mike, illus. (p. 1332)
Kilgras, Heidi & Parker, Jessie. Barbie - Horse Show Champ. Wolcott, Karen, illus. (p. 138)
Kilgus, Walter C. Bess Takes a Ride. (p. 168)
Kilham, Chris. Hot Plants: Nature's Proven Sex Boosters for Men & Women. (p. 802)
Kilic, Vanessa. Snow Globe Book. (p. 1599)
Kilimo, R. The Donkey Who Wanted to Be a Lion. (p. 1728)
Kilkelly, Francis. Bo & Blu in the Garden. (p. 204)
Kilkka, Mary. Meet the Nydees (p. 1123)
Killaire, B. M. Adventures of Betty & Bo-Bob: A Tale of One & a Half Frogs. Kwik, Penny Shannon, ed. (p. 16)
Killam, Catherine D. Sweeet Old Lady Coloring & Activity Book. Svensson, Richard, illus. (p. 1689)
—Sweeet Old Lady down the Street. Svensson, Richard, illus. (p. 1689)
Killam, Douglas. Literature of Africa (p. 1023)
Killcoyne, Hope, ed. Great Authors of Popular Fiction. (p. 713)
Killcoyne, Hope L., ed. see Masters, Susan Rowan.
Killcoyne, Hope L., ed. see Sheely, Robert.
Killcoyne, Hope Lourie. Anne Frank: Heroic Diarist of the Holocaust. (p. 85)
—History of Music. (p. 784)
—Hockey & Its Greatest Players (p. 786)
—Key Figures of the Vietnam War. (p. 950)
Killcoyne, Hope Lourie, ed. History of Music. (p. 784)
—Science: Its History & Development. (p. 1524)
Kille, Steve, illus. see Soling, Cevin.
Killebrew, Joyce Louise. Triumphant Queen Leah - the Ultimate African American Fairy Tale Picture Book. (p. 1788)
Killeen, Gretel. My Life Is a Wedgie. (p. 1212)
Killeen, James. Top of the Class! Martinez, Heather, illus. (p. 1769)
Killeen, Jared & Nash, Kevin. Bard College College Prowler off the Record. (p. 138)

K

Killen, Nicola. Animal Noises. (p. 79)
—Animal Numbers. (p. 79)
—Animal Opposites. (p. 79)
—Fluff & Billy. (p. 608)
—I Got a Crocodile. (p. 838)
—Stop Sticking, Stan! (p. 1653)
—Things That Go. (p. 1733)
Killgore, James. Passage (p. 1326)
Killian, Beth. Boy Trouble. (p. 219)
—Everything She Wants. (p. 545)
Killian, Bette, jt. auth. see Goldenburg, Dorothea.
Killian, Brandon. Seesaw Book. (p. 1548)
Killian, Maryellen. Energy for Earth. (p. 528)
Killian, Pat. Put It Together: Analyze, Compare, Create, & Compose Shapes. (p. 1420)
Killian, Rick & Yaxley, Trevor. Making of the Ten Commandments. (p. 1082)
Killian, Sue, illus. see Whelahan, Marlene.
Killingbeck, Dale. Michigan Triumphs & Tragedies (p. 1135)
Killinger, Jerry & Killinger, LaDonna. Heating & Cooling Essentials. (p. 761)
—Heating & Cooling Essentials Instructor's Manual. (p. 761)
Killinger, LaDonna, jt. auth. see Killinger, Jerry.
Killingworth, Gerald. Lord of the Silver Hand. (p. 1052)
Killion, Kathleen. Glass Heart. Lang, Gary, illus. (p. 682)
Killpack, David C., illus. see Franklin, Carl J.
Kilman, Nancy. Lockgate Mystery: Level O (p. 1045)
Kilmer, Jim. Adventures with Grandp. (p. 25)
Kilmer, Nidra N., illus. see Parsa, Mona.
Kilner, Dorothy. Life & Perambulations of a Mouse. (p. 1007)
Kilodavis, Cheryl. My Princess Boy. DeSimone, Suzanne, illus. (p. 1217)
Kilpatrick, Cathy. Creepy Crawlies. (p. 381)
—Creepy Crawlies. Jacquemier, Sue, ed. (p. 381)
—Creepy Crawlies Kid Kit. (p. 381)
Kilpatrick, Irene. Foofa's Happy Book. (p. 614)
—Let's Use Our Imaginations! Giles, Mike, illus. (p. 1001)
—Meet the Gabba Gang. (p. 1122)
—Welcome to Gabba Land! (p. 1873)
Kilpatrick, Leanne. One Night on Earth: The Story of Christmas. (p. 1296)
—Two by Two: Noah's Story in Rhyme. McCullough, Marilyn, illus. (p. 1803)
Kilpatrick, Paul, jt. auth. see Acosta, Robert.
Kilpatrick, Sheila. Anastasia's Rain. (p. 67)
Kilpin, Veronica Paula Marie. Fairy Play. (p. 563)
Kilworth, Garry. Attica. (p. 114)
—Hundred-Towered City. (p. 827)
—Jigsaw. (p. 917)
Kim, Aerim. Tiny Bud. Kim, Lindsey, illus. (p. 1756)
Kim, Alex, illus. see Van Vleet, Carmella.
Kim, Alex, illus. see Yasuda, Anita.
Kim, Allen. American History Kim, Nicole, illus. (p. 61)
Kim, Ayoung M. Asian. Woman. Alone. (p. 106)
Kim, Bo Young, illus. see Markel, Michelle.
Kim, Boo Young, illus. see O'Donnell, Kevin & Gon, Zang Sung.
Kim, Byung-Gyu & Hao, K. T. 100th Customer. Ferri, Giuliano, illus. (p. 1999)
Kim, Cecil. Friendship Quilt. Jeong, HaJin, illus. (p. 639)
—I Can't Sleep: Imagination - Bedtime. Cowley, Joy, ed. (p. 837)
—Little Moon's Christmas: Imagination - Objects. Cowley, Joy, ed. (p. 1032)
—Mommy & Daddy Love You. Ladecka, Anna, illus. (p. 1162)
—Nicknames. Han, SooJin, illus. (p. 1251)
—One Little Bean: Observation - Life Cycle. Cowley, Joy, ed. (p. 1295)
—Three Pig Sisters. Park, Keun, illus. (p. 1743)
Kim, Cecil & Kim, Joo-Kyung. Happy Hat. (p. 746)
Kim, Chuck, et al. X-Men - Curse of the Mutants: Mutants vs. Vampires. Hernandez Walta, Gabriel et al, illus. (p. 1967)
Kim, Daeshin. Horse with Wings: And Other Songs for Children Sung by Characters from Shakespeare with CD. (p. 800)
Kim, Derek Kirk. Vanishing Point. Kim, Derek Kirk, illus. (p. 1833)
Kim, Derek Kirk, illus. see Yang, Gene Luen.
Kim, Dong-soo, illus. see Lee, Mi-Ae.
Kim, Eric, jt. auth. see Torres, J.
Kim, F. S. Blueberry Muffin's Book: An Adventure in Blue. (p. 204)
—Constellations. (p. 359)
—Dig Deep! Looking for Dinosaurs. (p. 438)
Kim, Flora. Constellations. (p. 359)
Kim, Glenn, illus. see Lynch, Mike & Barr, Brandon.
Kim, H. Y. Michelle. Art Play-Ground A-1: A Complete & Self-Contained Curriculum for Art Education. (p. 102)
—Art Play-Ground A-2: A Complete & Self-Contained Curriculum for Art Education. (p. 102)
—Art Play-Ground A-3: A Complete & Self-Contained Curriculum for Art Education. (p. 102)
—Art Play-Ground B-1: A Complete & Self-Contained Curriculum for Art Education. (p. 102)
—Art Play-Ground C-1: A Complete & Self-Contained Curriculum for Art Education. (p. 102)
—Art Play-Ground C-2: A Complete & Self-Contained Curriculum for Art Education. (p. 102)
—Art Play-Ground C-3: A Complete & Self-Contained Curriculum for Art Education. (p. 102)
—Art Play-Ground E-1: A Complete & Self-Contained Curriculum for Art Education. (p. 102)
—Art Play-Ground E-2: A Complete & Self-Contained Curriculum for Art Education. (p. 102)
—Art Play-Ground E-3: A Complete & Self-Contained Curriculum for Art Education. (p. 102)
—Art Play-Ground F-1: A Complete & Self-Contained Curriculum for Art Education. (p. 102)
—Art Play-Ground F-2: A Complete & Self-Contained Curriculum for Art Education. (p. 102)
—Art Play-Ground F-3: A Complete & Self-Contained Curriculum for Art Education. (p. 102)
Kim, Hanmin & Lee, Sera. Tiptoe Tapirs. (p. 1757)
Kim, HoJeong. Kanga & Anger. Kim, SookKyeong, illus. (p. 942)
Kim, Hy. Complete Book of Multiplication & Division: Grades 2-3. Applebaum, Teri L. & Rous, Sheri, eds. (p. 352)
—Complete Book of Multiplication & Division: Basic Facts & Advanced Number Theories. Applebaum, Teri L. & Rous, Sheri, eds. (p. 352)
—Math Cycles: Problems & Quizzes that Strengthen Math Skills. (p. 1105)
Kim, Hyun-Joo, tr. see Armand, Villavert.
Kim, IhHyeon, illus. see Lee, HaeDa.
Kim, In-sook, jt. auth. see Jang, Ki-hwa.
Kim, Intae, photos by. Wind Drawing. (p. 1935)
Kim, Isabel Joy & Prasad, Siona. Tangled in Beauty: Contemplative Nature Poems. Kim, Isabel Joy, illus. (p. 1705)
Kim, Ja Youn. Song of Pots. Kim, Seung Ae, tr. (p. 1611)
Kim, Jay Jiyeon, illus. see Shariati, Karen Allison.
Kim, Jeehyun, illus. see Cook, William.
Kim, JeongHo. Oh That Snow! Ok, SeoJeong, illus. (p. 1281)
Kim, Jessica, tr. see Hyung, Min-Woo.
Kim, Ji-Hyuk, illus. see Howland, Leila.
Kim, Jin-Woo, illus. see Olmstead, Kathleen & Andersen, Hans Christian.
Kim, Ji-yeon, illus. see Choi, Eun-gyu.
Kim, JiYu. Wise Boy, Hwang, YoSeob, illus. (p. 1940)
—Zippy the Runner. Seon, JeongHyeon, illus. (p. 1987)
Kim, Joo-Kyung, jt. illus. see Kim, Cecil.
Kim, Joung Un, illus. see Carter, Candace.
Kim, Joung Un, illus. see Franco, Betsy & Franco-Feeney, Betsy.
Kim, Joung Un, illus. see Held, George.
Kim, Joung Un, illus. see McDonald, Megan.
Kim, Julie, illus. see Kim, Ju-Ri.
Kim, Julie, illus. see Park, Je-Sung.
Kim, Julie, illus. see Park, Se-Jung.
Kim, Julie J., illus. see Bramwell, Wendie & Normand, Bridgid.
Kim, Julie J., illus. see Meachen Rau, Dana.
Kim, Julie J., illus. see Pfeffer, Wendy.
Kim, Julie J., tr. see Bramwell, Wendie & Normand, Bridgid.
Kim, Jung-cho, jt. auth. see Choi, Young-Jin.
Kim, Jung-Su, jt. auth. see Park, Sang-Sun.
Kim, Ju-Ri. Sweety Kim, Julie, illus. (p. 1690)
Kim, Kang Won. INVU Kim, Kang Won, illus. (p. 886)
—Queen's Knight (p. 1425)
Kim, KyeMahn, illus. see Kim, YunYeong.
Kim, Lindsey, illus. see Kim, Aerim.
Kim, Maria. JookaPooka & Friends ABC. (p. 925)
Kim, Maryellen. Ribbon Girls—Wind, Weave, Twist & Tie: Dress up Your Room * Show Team Spirit * Create Pretty Presents. (p. 1469)
Kim, Melissa. Learning about the Endocrine & Reproductive Systems. (p. 985)
Kim, Melissa & Fitch, Jada. Snowy Owl Story (p. 1601)
Kim, Melissa L. Endocrine & Reproductive Systems. (p. 527)
—Learning about the Endocrine & Reproductive Systems. (p. 985)
Kim, Michelle. Art Play-Ground B-2. (p. 102)
—Art Play-Ground B-3. (p. 102)
—Art Play-Ground D-1. (p. 102)
—Art Play-Ground D-2. (p. 102)
—Art Play-Ground D-3. (p. 102)
Kim, Nicole, illus. see Kim, Allen.
Kim, Patti. Here I Am Sánchez, Sonia, illus. (p. 770)
Kim, Raeshin. Legend of Goo-Shu: Journal 1. (p. 988)
Kim, Regina Hurh, ed. see Hex, Kathleen.
Kim, Ryan Woorahm. Gordie's New Face. (p. 702)
Kim, Sarah, illus. see John, Margaret.
Kim, Sarah, tr. from KOR. Chrono Code Choi, Il-Ho, illus. (p. 317)
Kim, Seong, tr. see Crouch, Adele.
Kim, Seung Ae, tr. see Kim, Ja Youn.
Kim, Seyoung. Boy Princess: Volume 3. (p. 218)
—Boy Princess. (p. 218)
Kim, Soo-hyeon. There It Is! Observation - Objects. Cowley, Joy, ed. (p. 1730)
—What Does the Bee See? Observation - Parts & Whole. Cowley, Joy, ed. (p. 1884)
Kim, Sook. Zzim! 3 (p. 1990)
Kim, SookKyeong, illus. see Kim, HoJeong.
Kim, Soyeon, illus. see Kelsey, Elin.
Kim, Soyeon, illus. see Thornhill, Jan.
Kim, So-yeong, illus. see Perrault, Charles.
Kim, Sue. How Does a Seed Grow? A Book with Foldout Pages. Tilde, photos by. (p. 808)
Kim, Sung-Min, illus. see Seo & So, Chong-O.
Kim, Sunyoung, jt. auth. see Metzler, Chris.
Kim, Susan & Klavan, Laurence. Brain Camp. Hicks, Faith Erin, illus. (p. 221)
—Guardians. (p. 728)
—Wanderers: A Wasteland Novel. (p. 1856)
—Wanderers. (p. 1856)
—Wasteland. (p. 1860)
Kim, Tae-yeon. Mango Trees: Philippines. Cowley, Joy, ed. (p. 1087)
Kim, Tong-Song, illus. see Tae-Jun, Lee, et al.
Kim, Violet, illus. see McGrath, Barbara Barbieri.
Kim, Violet, illus. see Wright, Maureen.
Kim, YeShil. My Best Buddy. Tanco, Miguel, illus. (p. 1196)
—Tortoise & Hare. Kheiriyeh, Rashin, illus. (p. 1771)
—Very Best Teacher. Moriuchi, Mique, illus. (p. 1837)
—We Are Proud of You. The Pope Twins, illus. (p. 1865)
Kim, YoeongAh. Shooting Stars Soccer Team. Lee, Hyeongjin, illus. (p. 1568)
Kim, Yon-Kyong. Mr. Moon & Miss Sun/the Herdsman & the Weaver. (p. 1185)
—Ogres' Magic Clubs - the Tiger & the Dried Persimmons. (p. 1280)
—Woodcutter & the Heavenly Maiden & the Fire Dogs. (p. 1949)
Kim, Yon-Kyong, jt. illus. see Kang, Mi-Sun.
Kim, Yon-Kyong, jt. illus. see Pak, Mi-Sun.
Kim, Yon-Kyong & Kang, Mi-Sun. Son of the Cinnamon Tree/the Donkey's Egg. (p. 1611)
Kim, Yoon-Kyung. Id_Entity (p. 852)
—iD_eNTITY (p. 852)
Kim, Yoon-Kyung, illus. see Son, Hee-Joon.
Kim, Young, illus. see Meyer, Stephenie.
Kim, Young-Ah. So Lonely. Shin, Ji-Soo, illus. (p. 1602)
Kim, Youngsun, illus. see Allen, Nancy Kelly.
Kim, Youn-Kyung, illus. see Son, Hee-Joon.
Kim, YunYeong. Brown Bear's Dream. Kim, KyeMahn, illus. (p. 231)
Kimani, Kamande. Why the Hyena Has Short Hind Legs. Therrian, John, illus. (p. 1926)
Kimaya. All the Flavours of Love. (p. 45)
Kimball, Allan. Big Bend Guide. McMullin, Marcus, illus. (p. 178)
Kimball, Amelia. Inside Out. (p. 877)
Kimball, Angela. Of All the Silly Things. (p. 1279)
Kimball, Cheryl. Horse Showing for Kids: Training, Grooming, Trailering, Apparel, Tack, Competing, Sportsmanship. (p. 800)
Kimball, Marrae. Secret Combination to Middle School; Real Advice from Real Kids, Ideas for Success, & Much More! (p. 1540)
Kimball, Michael D. Alligator Bay: A Beary Tale. (p. 47)
Kimball, Nick. Noah's Story. (p. 1262)
Kimball, Paige, jt. auth. see Eshleman, William.
Kimball, Richard. Shadows of the Men with Green Faces. (p. 1558)
Kimball, Virginia. Day for Doughnuts: April 19, 1775. (p. 412)
Kimber, Murray, illus. see Hovey, Kate.
Kimber, Murray, illus. see Noyes, Alfred.
Kimberl, Karen. Tea Party for All Seasons. (p. 1708)
Kimberly, Anne. Dark Well of Decision. (p. 408)
Kimberly, Neuburger. Take the Fear Out of Intermediate Algebra (p. 1697)
Kimberly Vogel. Everyone's Price: Book 4 of Rae's Story. (p. 544)
Kimble, George J. Poetry for the Road (p. 1376)
Kimble, Maggie T. Peep Learns to Sing. (p. 1335)
Kimble-Ellis, Sonya. Beyoncé: Entertainer. (p. 173)
—Bill Cosby: Entertainer & Activist. (p. 186)
—Sancastle Kids: A Maya Adventure. (p. 1510)
Kimbles, Samuel L., jt. ed. see Singer, Thomas.
Kimbrell, Grady, et al. Entering the World of Work. (p. 531)
Kimbrell, Lara. Where Does My Dadda Go? (p. 1907)
Kimbrough, Ariah. Angel Is My Name. (p. 73)
Kimbrough, Lawrence. Bible Promises for Kids. (p. 176)
—Bible Promises for Teens. (p. 176)
Kime, Steve. Rollin on Route 66: Get on Your Bike to Ride & Make New Friends! (p. 1485)
Kimes, Valerie. Case of the Missing Valentines: A Super Sleuths Mystery. (p. 274)
—Peevee Plunkett the Magnificent Mouse. (p. 1335)
—Treelove. (p. 1784)
Kimiko. Cucu, Papa, Noel! (p. 389)
Kimiko, jt. auth. see Kimiko, Mitsuko.
Kimiko, Mitsuko. Avion. (p. 120)
Kimiko, Mitsuko & Kimiko. Gato. (p. 658)
—Lobo. (p. 1044)
Kimiko, Mitsuko & Mitsuko, Kimiko -. Elefante. (p. 510)
Kimjin. Kingdom of the Winds. (p. 960)
Kimla, Lenka J. I Love My Mommy. Golds, Alexandra Kimla, illus. (p. 842)
Kimlan, Lanie & Alvergue, Anne. Truth about Ecstasy. (p. 1794)
Kimmel, Allison Crotzer. Montgomery Bus Boycott. (p. 1170)
—Prepped & Punked: Bringing 1980s & 1990s Flair to Your Wardrobe (p. 1396)
—Primary Source History of Slavery in the United States. (p. 1400)
Kimmel, Allison Crotzer, jt. auth. see Mortensen, Lori.
Kimmel, E. Cody. In the Eye of the Storm. Snow, Scott, illus. (p. 866)
—West on the Wagon Train. Snow, Scott, illus. (p. 1876)
Kimmel, Elizabeth Cody. #1 Forever Four. Mingus, Cathi, illus. (p. 1991)
—As Far as the Eye Can Reach: Lewis & Clark's Westward Quest. (p. 105)
—Boxtrolls: A Novel. (p. 217)
—Crossing Over. (p. 385)
—In the Eye of the Storm. Snow, Scott, illus. (p. 866)
—Ladies First: 40 Daring American Women Who Were Second to None. (p. 970)
—Ladies First: 40 Daring American Women Who Were Second to None. (p. 970)
—Leading Ladies Mingus, Cathi, illus. (p. 982)
—Legend of the Ghost Dog. (p. 989)
—Lily B. on the Brink of Cool. (p. 1018)
—Lily B. on the Brink of Paris. (p. 1018)
—Mi Pinguino Oliver. Lewis, H. B., illus. (p. 1133)
—My Penguin Osbert. Lewis, H. B., illus. (p. 1216)
—My Penguin Osbert Book & Toy Gift Set. Lewis, H. B., illus. (p. 1216)
—My Penguin Osbert in Love. Lewis, H. B., illus. (p. 1216)
—ParaNorman: A Novel. (p. 1324)
—ParaNormaN. (p. 1324)
—ParaNorman. (p. 1324)
—Reinvention of Moxie Roosevelt. (p. 1457)
—Secret of the Mountain Dog. (p. 1542)
—Stories from New York Mingus, Cathi, illus. (p. 1654)
—Suddenly Supernatural 4: Crossing Over. (p. 1672)
—Suddenly Supernatural: Scaredy Kat. (p. 1672)
—Suddenly Supernatural: School Spirit. (p. 1672)
—Suddenly Supernatural: Unhappy Medium. (p. 1672)
—Taste of Freedom: Gandhi & the Great Salt March. Ferri, Guiliano, illus. (p. 1707)
—Unhappy Medium. (p. 1817)
Kimmel, Elizabeth Cody & Buck, Lewis. My Penguin Osbert in Love Lewis, H. B., illus. (p. 1216)
Kimmel, Eric. Runaway Tortilla. Brooks, Erik, illus. (p. 1496)
Kimmel, Eric A. Anansi & the Magic Stick. Stevens, Janet, illus. (p. 67)
—Anansi Series. Stevens, Janet, illus. (p. 67)
—Anansi's Party Time. Stevens, Janet, illus. (p. 67)
—Bar Mitzvah: A Jewish Boy's Coming of Age. Weihs, Erika, illus. (p. 137)
—Bernal & Florinda: A Spanish Tale. Rayevsky, Robert, illus. (p. 167)
—Brass Serpent. Miller, Joanna, illus. (p. 222)
—Brother Wolf, Sister Sparrow: Stories about Saints & Animals. Winch, John, illus. (p. 231)
—Cactus Soup Huling, Phil, illus. (p. 250)
—Castle of Cats: A Story from Ukraine. Krenina, Katya, illus. (p. 277)
—Chanukkah Guest. Carmi, Giora, illus. (p. 291)
—Even Higher! A Rosh Hashanah Story by I. L. Peretz. Weber, Jill, illus. (p. 541)
—Fisherman & the Turtle (p. 599)
—Flying Canoe: A Christmas Story. San Souci, Daniel, illus. (p. 609)
—Frog Princess: A Tlingit Legend from Alaska. Litzinger, Rosanne, illus. (p. 640)
—Golem's Latkes Jasinski, Aaron, illus. (p. 696)
—Hanukkah Bear. Wohnoutka, Mike, illus. (p. 744)
—Hayyim's Ghost. (p. 756)
—Hayyim's Ghost. Binus, Ari, illus. (p. 756)
—Hershel & the Hanukkah Goblins. Hyman, Trina Schart, illus. (p. 774)
—Hiss-S-S-S! (p. 781)
—Horn for Louis. Bernardin, James, illus. (p. 798)
—Jack & the Giant Barbecue Manders, John, illus. (p. 902)
—Joha Makes a Wish: A Middle Eastern Tale Rayyan, Omar, illus. (p. 920)
—Joseph & the Sabbath Fish. Peluso, Martina, illus. (p. 926)
—Lady in the Blue Cloak: Legends from the Texas Missions. Guevara, Susan, illus. (p. 971)
—Little Red Hot Huliska-Beith, Laura, illus. (p. 1035)
—Los Tres Cabritos Gilpin, Stephen, illus. (p. 1054)
—Mcelderry Book of Greek Myths. Montserrat, Pep, illus. (p. 1114)
—Medio Pollito: A Spanish Tale Docampo, Valeria, illus. (p. 1120)
—Moby Dick: Chasing the Great White Whale. Glass, Andrew, illus. (p. 1157)
—Mysterious Guests: A Sukkot Story. Krenina, Katya, illus. (p. 1223)
—Onions & Garlic: An Old Tale. Arnold, Katya, illus. (p. 1298)
—Scarlett & Sam: Escape from Egypt. Stevanovic, Ivica, illus. (p. 1520)
—Spotlight for Harry. Madsen, Jim, illus. (p. 1633)
—Story of Esther. Weber, Jill, illus. (p. 1658)
—Three Cabritos Gilpin, Stephen, illus. (p. 1741)
—Three Little Tamales Docampo, Valeria, illus. (p. 1743)
—Three Princes. Fisher, Leonard Everett, illus. (p. 1743)
—Tuning Up: A Visit with Eric Kimmel. Childers, Basil, photos by. (p. 1797)
—Why the Snake Crawls on Its Belly. Davis, Allen, illus. (p. 1926)
—Wonders & Miracles: A Passover Companion. Kimmel, Eric A., illus. (p. 1948)
Kimmel, Eric A., illus. see Hesse, Karen.
Kimmel, Eric A. & Kang, Setha. Rolling Stone: And Other Read Aloud Stories. Kuon, Vuthy, illus. (p. 1485)
Kimmel, Eric A. & Korelitz, Jean Hanff. Great Texas Hamster Drive Whatley, Bruce, illus. (p. 718)
Kimmel, Eric A. & Trueman, Matthew. Simon & the Bear: A Hanukkah Tale. (p. 1577)
Kimmel, Haven. Kaline Klattermaster's Tree House. Brown, Peter, illus. (p. 942)
Kimmel, Heidi. West Point. (p. 1876)
Kimmel, Janine L., jt. auth. see Ceccarelli, David.
Kimmel, Jordan L. Magic Gown. (p. 1072)
Kimmel, Smith Robert. War with Grandpa. (p. 1858)
Kimmelman, Leslie. Ben Lost a Tooth. (p. 163)
—Dog Named Honey. (p. 461)
—Everybody Bonjours! McMenemy, Sarah, illus. (p. 543)
—Hello, My New Baby... With Love from Your Big Brother or Big Sister. Jabar, Cynthia, illus. (p. 764)
—Hot Dog! Eleanor Roosevelt Throws a Picnic. Juhasz, Victor, illus. (p. 801)
—How Do I Love You? McCue, Lisa, illus. (p. 807)
—In the Doghouse: An Emma & Bo Story. Kelley, True, illus. (p. 865)
—Little Red Hen & the Passover Matzah. Meisel, Paul, illus. (p. 1035)
—Mind Your Manners, Alice Roosevelt! Gustavson, Adam, illus. (p. 1145)
—Round the Turkey: A Grateful Thanksgiving. Cote, Nancy, illus. (p. 1491)
—Sam & Charlie (and Sam Too!) Tambellini, Stefano & Owl, William, illus. (p. 1506)
—Sam & Charlie (and Sam Too) at Camp! Owl, William, illus. (p. 1506)
—Shabbat Puppy Zollars, Jaime, illus. (p. 1556)
—Star Pictures. (p. 1641)
—Three Bully Goats. Terry, Will, illus. (p. 1741)
—Trick Arrr Treat: A Pirate Halloween. Monlongo, Jorge, illus. (p. 1786)
—Very Crowded Sukkah (p. 1837)
Kimmelman, Leslie A. Everybody Says Shalom. (p. 543)
Kimmelman, Leslie & Shepherd, Jodie. How Do You Feel? (p. 808)
Kimmich, Ian. Antonio Gates. (p. 90)
—Steve Nash. (p. 1649)
Kimmons, Janet M. Jewel in the Attic & the Adventures of Tiger. Farmer, Zoe, illus. (p. 917)
Kimpton, Ann Kaczkowski, jt. auth. see Kimpton, Paul.
Kimpton, Diana. Pony Crazed 08: Princess Ellie Solves A Mystery. (p. 1382)
—Pony-Crazed Princess: Princess Ellie's Mystery. Finlay, Lizzie, illus. (p. 1382)
—Pony-Crazed Princess Super Special: Princess Ellie's Summer Vacation. Finlay, Lizzie, illus. (p. 1382)
—Princess Ellie Solves a Mystery. Finlay, Lizzie, illus. (p. 1403)
—Princess Ellie to the Rescue. Finlay, Lizzie, illus. (p. 1403)
—Princess Ellie's Moonlight Mystery. (p. 1403)
—Princess Ellie's Royal Jamboree No. 11. Finlay, Lizzie, illus. (p. 1403)
—Princess Ellie's Secret No. 2. Finlay, Lizzie, illus. (p. 1403)
—Princess Ellie's Snowy Ride No. 9. Finlay, Lizzie, illus. (p. 1403)

—Princess Ellie's Snowy Ride. Finlay, Lizzie, illus. (p. 1403)
—Princess Ellie's Treasure Hunt No. 10. Finlay, Lizzie, illus. (p. 1403)
—Surprise for Princess Ellie. (p. 1686)
—Surprise for Princess Ellie. Finlay, Lizzie, illus. (p. 1686)
Kimpton, Laurence, jt. auth. see Jones, David.
Kimpton, Paul & Kimpton, Ann Kaczkowski. Dog Tags: A Boy & His Bugle in America During WWII. (p. 461)
—Starting Early: A Boy & His Bugle in America During WWII. (p. 1644)
—Summer of Firsts: WWII Is Ending, but the Music Adventures Are Just Beginning. (p. 1674)
Kimura & North, Lucy. One Stormy Night. Abe, Hiroshi, illus. (p. 1297)
—One Sunny Day Abe, Hiroshi, illus. (p. 1297)
Kimura, ken. 999 Frogs Wake Up. (p. 2001)
Kimura, ken, jt. illus. see Murakami, Yasunari.
Kimura, ken & Murakami, Yasunari. 999 Tadpoles. (p. 2001)
Kimura, Rie, jt. auth. see Jackson, Patrick.
Kimura, Tomo, jt. auth. see Hino, Matsuri.
Kimura, Tomo, jt. auth. see Tanemura, Arina.
Kimura, Yuichi. On the Seesaw Bridge. Hata, Kowshiro, illus. (p. 1291)
Kimvall, Jacob. Graffiti Coloring Book: Characters. (p. 705)
Kin, Pamphil. Gorilla Princess. (p. 703)
Kinard, Brandi, illus. see Kay, Regina.
Kinard, Kami. Boy Prediction: Notes & Observations of Tabitha Reddy. (p. 218)
—Boy Project: Notes & Observations of Kara McAllister. (p. 218)
Kinarney, Tom, illus. see Muldoon, Kathleen M. & Wallace, Susan Helen.
Kinarney, Tom, illus. see Wallace, Susan Helen.
Kinast, Susan. Play from A to Z. (p. 1371)
Kincade, Chris. Encountering Aliens: Eyewitness Accounts Mallea, Cristian, illus. (p. 524)
Kincaid, Angela, illus. see Reed, Natasha.
Kincaid, C. A. Deccan Nursery Tales: Or, Fairy Tales from the South. (p. 421)
Kincaid, S. J. Catalyst. (p. 278)
—Insignia. (p. 878)
—Vortex. (p. 1850)
Kincaid, Tracy. Adventures of Casey the Lost Suitcase. (p. 17)
Kincaide, Drakeman R. Recipes for Fireside Romance. (p. 1451)
Kincannon, Karla M. Creativity & Divine Surprise: Finding the Place of Your Resurrection. Kincannon, Karla M., illus. (p. 380)
Kinch, Devon. Pretty Penny Comes up Short. (p. 1398)
Kinch, Michael. Blending Time. (p. 199)
—Fires of New SUN: A Blending Time Novel. (p. 592)
—Rebels of New SUN. (p. 1451)
Kincheloe, Larry. Master's Garden. (p. 1103)
Kincy, Karen. Bloodborn. (p. 200)
—Other. (p. 1306)
Kindberg, Sally. Draw It! 100 Wacky Things to Doodle & Draw! (p. 480)
—Draw It! Monsters: 100 Spooky Things to Doodle & Draw! (p. 481)
Kindberg, Sally, illus. see Turner, Tracey.
Kindberg, Sally, jt. auth. see Turner, Tracey.
Kinde, Christa. Hidden Deep (p. 775)
Kindel, Gerde, jt. auth. see Lawall, Gilbert.
Kinder, Cando. Birth of Whale Read-Along. (p. 192)
Kinder, Connie & Virden, Carole. Dash's Pause: An Adventure in Being Found. (p. 409)
Kinder, Hermann & Hilgemann, Werner. Penguin Atlas of World History: From the French Revolution to the Present. Vol. 2 (p. 1336)
Kinderman, Robert W. & Moore, Trudy E. Kelly Kapers: Adventures of Kelly & Her Family. Moore, Trudy E., illus. (p. 948)
Kindersley, Anabel, jt. photos by see Kindersley, Barnabas.
Kindersley, Barnabas & Kindersley, Anabel, photos by. Celebraciones. (p. 283)
Kindert, Jennifer, illus. see Scholastic, Inc. Staff & Black, Sonia.
Kindert, Jennifer C., illus. see Ford, Bernette G.
Kindert, Jennifer C., illus. see Smith, Icy.
Kindig, Tess. Luv @ First Site. (p. 1066)
Kindig, Tess Eileen. Slam Dunk Set (p. 1587)
Kindl, Patrice. Goose Chase. (p. 702)
—Keeping the Castle. (p. 947)
—Lost in the Labyrinth. (p. 1055)
—Owl in Love. (p. 1315)
—School for Brides: A Story of Maidens, Mystery, & Matrimony. (p. 1522)
Kindle Hodson, Victoria, jt. auth. see Hart, Sura.
Kindle Hodson, Victoria, jt. auth. see Willis, Mariaemma.
Kindle, Karen. Using Read-Alouds to Teach Vocabulary: Research-Based Strategies & Model Lessons for Using Fiction & Nonfiction Books to Build Children's Vocabulary & Improve Their Reading, Writing, & Speaking Skills. (p. 1828)
Kindler, Jennifer. Rita's Fairytale. (p. 1475)
Kindlon, Dan. Cuidado con los Ninos Consentidos! (p. 390)
Kindt, Kathleen G., illus. see Brasch, Pamela.
Kindt, Matt. Super Spy. (p. 1682)
Kindt, Matt, illus. see Fox, Annie.
Kindt, Rita, illus. see Ward, Terri & Ward, Tom.
Kinelski, Marilyn D. Am I Important? (p. 51)
Kinerk, Robert. Clorinda. Kellogg, Steven, illus. (p. 333)
—Clorinda Plays Baseball! Kellogg, Steven, illus. (p. 333)
—Clorinda Takes Flight. Kellogg, Steven, illus. (p. 333)
—Oh, How Sylvester Can Pester! And Other Poems More or Less about Manners. Kozjan, Drazen, illus. (p. 1280)
Kinerk, Robert & Kellogg, Steven. Clorinda. Kellogg, Steven, illus. (p. 333)
King, A. S. Ask the Passengers. (p. 106)
—Dust of 100 Dogs. (p. 490)
—Everybody Sees the Ants. (p. 543)
—Glory O'Brien's History of the Future. (p. 685)
—I Crawl Through It. (p. 837)
—Please Ignore Vera Dietz. (p. 1373)
—Reality Boy. (p. 1449)
King, Alice (Ali). Daisy the Different Dolphin. (p. 400)
King, Alyson. Joyful Jumping. (p. 930)
King, Andy, photos by see Walker, Sally M.
King, Andy, photos by see Walker, Sally M. & Feldmann, Roseann.
King, Annie J. Granny Annie Lives at the Airport! (p. 710)
King, Anthea. Where Do Butterflies Go ... ?? (p. 1906)
King, Aven. Doctor's Tools. (p. 459)
—Harp Seals. (p. 749)
—My Mexican Heritage. (p. 1214)
King, B. B., jt. auth. see Boynton, Sandra.
King, B. J. Through a Dog's Eye: A Dog's Tale. (p. 1744)
King, Bart. Bart's King Sized Book of Fun (p. 140)
—Big Book of Girl Stuff Kalis, Jennifer, illus. (p. 179)
—Big Book of Gross Stuff. Miller, Russell, illus. (p. 179)
—Big Book of Superheroes (p. 179)
—Cute! A Guide to All Things Adorable (p. 396)
—Pocket Guide to Boy Stuff. (p. 1375)
—Pocket Guide to Brilliance. (p. 1375)
—Pocket Guide to Girl Stuff. (p. 1375)
—Pocket Guide to Magic. (p. 1375)
—Pocket Guide to Mischief. Brown, Brenda, illus. (p. 1375)
King, Bart & Sabatino, Chris. Big Book of Boy Stuff (p. 179)
King, Bill. Stinkin' Thinkin' Stinks: A Kid's Guide to the Lighter Side of Life. (p. 1651)
King, Bonnie. Left Behind: Marion's Story. (p. 987)
King, C. Jigsaw World Atlas. (p. 917)
King, Caro. Seven Sorcerers. (p. 1555)
—Shadow Spell. (p. 1558)
King, Caro & Bowater, Charlie. Seven Sorcerers. (p. 1555)
King, Carole & King, E. Gregory. Hollow Weens. (p. 789)
King, Carrie. Joni-Pip. Boddy, James & Moon, Paul, illus. (p. 925)
—Life in the Wood with Joni-Pip. (p. 1011)
King, Cheryl, illus. see Eagan, Mary.
King, Chris, illus. see Bingham, Jane.
King, Chris, illus. see Colson, Mary.
King, Chris, illus. see Deverell, Christine.
King, Chris, illus. see Hile, Lori.
King, Chris, jt. illus. see Deverell, Richard.
King, Clayton. 40 Days of Purity for Guys. (p. 1997)
—True Love Project: How the Gospel Defines Your Purity. (p. 1792)
King, Clive. Town That Went South. (p. 1773)
King, Colin. Jigsaw Atlas of North America. (p. 917)
King, Colin, illus. see Amery, Heather, et al.
King, Colin, illus. see Baxter, Nicola.
King, Colin, illus. see Bingham, Jane.
King, Colin, illus. see Bone, Emily.
King, Colin, illus. see Daynes, Katie.
King, Colin, illus. see Mason, Conrad.
King, Colin, illus. see Turnbull, Stephanie.
King, Colin, jt. auth. see Bone, Emily.
King, Colin, jt. auth. see Daynes, Katie.
King, Colin, jt. auth. see Elliot, Jane.
King, Colin, jt. auth. see Elliott, Jane.
King, Colin, jt. auth. see Frith, Alex.
King, Colin, jt. auth. see Patchett, F.
King, Colin, jt. ed. see Elliot, Jane.
King, Corinne & Fenton, Corinne. Queenie: One Elephant's Story. Gouldthorpe, Peter, illus. (p. 1425)
King, Daren. Frightfully Friendly Ghosties. Roberts, David, illus. (p. 639)
—Frightfully Friendly Ghosties: School of Meanies. Roberts, David, illus. (p. 639)
King, Darrell. Dirty South. (p. 446)
King, Dave, photos by see Dorling Kindersley Publishing Staff.
King, Dave, photos by see Gardner, Charlie & Dorling Kindersley Publishing Staff.
King, Dave, photos by see Parker, Steve.
King, Dave, photos by see Sirett, Dawn & Dorling Kindersley Publishing Staff.
King, Dave, photos by see Whittington, Melanie & Holtz, Lara Tankel, eds.
King, David C. Arkansas. (p. 99)
—Azerbaijan. (p. 121)
—Blackfeet. (p. 197)
—Civil War & Reconstruction. (p. 325)
—Delaware. (p. 424)
—Dorothea Lange: Photographer of the People. (p. 471)
—First People: An Illustrated History of American Indians. (p. 596)
—Franklin Pierce. (p. 630)
—Greenland. (p. 723)
—Haida. (p. 735)
—Have Fun with the Presidents: Activities, Projects, & Fascinating Facts. (p. 754)
—Herbert Hoover. (p. 769)
—Huron. (p. 829)
—Inuit. (p. 883)
—Iowa. (p. 886)
—Kyrgyzstan. (p. 969)
—Mohawk. (p. 1160)
—Monaco. (p. 1163)
—Mozambique. (p. 1184)
—Navajo. (p. 1237)
—Nez Perce. (p. 1249)
—Ojibwe. (p. 1282)
—Oman. (p. 1288)
—Powhatan. (p. 1391)
—Projects about Ancient Egypt. (p. 1410)
—Projects about the Ancient Aztecs. (p. 1410)
—Rwanda. (p. 1499)
—Seminole. (p. 1550)
—Sioux. (p. 1580)
—United Arab Emirates. (p. 1818)
—Virginia. (p. 1844)
—Westward Expansion. (p. 1876)
King, David C. & American Heritage, American. Colonies & Revolution. (p. 342)
King, David C. & Bass, Elissa. Arkansas. (p. 99)
King, David C. & Dorling Kindersley Publishing Staff. Charles Darwin: A Photographic Story of a Life. (p. 292)
King, David C. & Fitzgerald, Brian. Delaware. (p. 424)
King, David C. & Fitzgerald, Stephanie. Virginia. (p. 1844)
King, David C. & McGeveran, William. New Jersey. (p. 1245)
King, David C. & Orr, Tamra B. Taiwan. (p. 1696)
King, David C., et al. Delaware. (p. 424)
—New Jersey. (p. 1245)
King, David Powers, jt. auth. see Jensen, Michael.
King, Dedie. I See the Sun in Afghanistan. Vahidi, Mohd, tr. (p. 845)
—I See the Sun in Mexico Inglese, Judith, illus. (p. 845)
—I See the Sun in Russia. Ossipova, Irina, tr. (p. 845)
King, Deja. Bitch. (p. 194)
—Ride Wit' Me: A Novel. (p. 1471)
King, Dexter Scott & Wiley, Ralph. Growing up King: An Intimate Memoir. (p. 727)
King, Diane. Elijah & the Talking Tree. (p. 512)
King, Dianne. Hezekiah's Boots. (p. 775)
King, Dr. Dorothy. What Is Ethnophobia? (p. 1889)
King, E. Gregory, jt. auth. see King, Carole.
King, Elaine. Alaskan Honeymoon Adventure. (p. 34)
King, Elizabeth. Quinceanera: Celebrating Fifteen. King, Elizabeth, photos by. (p. 1428)
King, Emily. Clopper & the Lost Boy Olson, Ed, illus. (p. 333)
—Clopper & the Night Travelers. Olson, Ed, illus. (p. 333)
—Clopper the Christmas Donkey Olson, Ed, illus. (p. 333)
—Mrs. Twiggenbotham Goes to a Party. (p. 1188)
—Mrs. Twiggenbotham Goes to Town. (p. 1188)
King, Emmett. Kitten Grows. (p. 962)
King, Eva. Dear Sweetie, I'm Okay: Helping Children Understand Death. (p. 419)
King Farris, Christine. My Brother Martin: A Sister Remembers Growing up with the Rev. Dr. Martin Luther King Jr. Soentpiet, Chris K., illus. (p. 1199)
King, Frances. Roundabout Boy. (p. 1491)
King, Frank. Nina & Skeezix: The Problem of the Lost Ring. (p. 1256)
—Tee Tee Peetum. (p. 1713)
King, Geoff. American Independent Cinema. (p. 61)
King, Glynda T. Skippy the Flea Is off to see the President. (p. 1586)
King, H. Elizabeth. Kemo Shark. (p. 948)
King, Hazel. Carbohydrates for a Healthy Body (p. 265)
King, Ian, jt. auth. see Schuler, Lou.
King Iii, Dudley Allen. Skye's High Fly'n Adventures: How Skye Gets His Name. (p. 1587)
King, J. Eric & Graham, Greg. Byron Carmichael Book One: The Human Corpse Trade. Mizer, Lindsay, ed. (p. 249)
King, J. R. Arianna Kelt & the Renegades of Time: Deluxe Edition, Wizards of Skyhall Book 2. (p. 98)
—Arianna Kelt & the Renegades of Time: Signature Edition, Wizards of Skyhall Book 2. (p. 98)
—Arianna Kelt & the Wizards of Skyhall: Deluxe Edition, Wizards of Skyhall Book 1. (p. 98)
—Arianna Kelt & the Wizards of Skyhall. (p. 98)
King James Bible Staff. Christmas Is Here. Castillo, Lauren, illus. (p. 314)
—Love Is ... Halperin, Wendy Anderson, illus. (p. 1060)
King, Jane. Creepy Cafeteria. (p. 381)
—Monster Bash. (p. 1166)
—Welcome to Chillsville Elementary. (p. 1873)
King, Janet, illus. see King, Philip.
King, Jeremy Jordan. Dark Rites. (p. 408)
—In Stone: A Grotesque Faerie Tale. (p. 865)
King, Jerry. Tommy the Turtle. (p. 1765)
King, Jerry, illus. see Lewis, J. Patrick.
King, Jessie Marion, illus. see Wilde, Oscar.
King, Jo. Flight of Fancy. (p. 604)
King, Joseph, illus. see Menges, Thais D.
King, Joy. Hooker to Housewife. (p. 795)
King, Juaness. Prodigal's Quest. (p. 1409)
King, Judy. When Summer Comes Again. King, Judy, illus. (p. 1904)
King, Julia. Bingo Explores the Farm. (p. 188)
—Bingo's Big Adventure: A Cat's Tale. (p. 188)
King, Karen. Sparkle the Seahorse. Hicks, Angie, illus. (p. 1622)
—Unicorn Magic. Hicks, Angie, illus. (p. 1818)
King, Kathleen, jt. auth. see Priddy, Roger.
King, Katina. Ride Wit' Me: A Young Adult Urban Tale. (p. 1471)
King, Kellie. Once a Caterpillar. (p. 1292)
King, Kelly. Vital Skills: How to Manage Your Money. (p. 1846)
—Vital Skills: How to Have a Balanced Life. (p. 1846)
King, Ken. Sunflower. Kearney, Jennifer, illus. (p. 1676)
King, Kerrigan. At the Aquarium. (p. 110)
King, Kimberly. God Is in the Window. Jones, Erik, illus. (p. 689)
King, Kirsty. My New Friends. (p. 1216)
King, Kristin. Project: Noah's Ark. (p. 1410)
King, Lisa. Gingerbread Baby in Search of a Family. (p. 677)
—Lurkey the Proud Turkey. (p. 1066)
King, M. Gknobin. Rowell, Coralynn, illus. (p. 682)
King, M. C. Truth or Dare. (p. 1794)
King, M. G. Librarian on the Roof: A True Story. Gilpin, Stephen, illus. (p. 1005)
—Librarian on the Roof! A True Story. Gilpin, Stephen, illus. (p. 1005)
King, Martin Luther, III. My Daddy, Dr. Martin Luther King, Jr. Ford, A. G., illus. (p. 1201)
King, Martin Luther, Jr. I Have a Dream Nelson, Kadir, illus. (p. 839)
—I Have a Dream. (p. 839)
King, Meet Martin Luther, Jr. Meet Martin Luther King Jr. (p. 1121)
King, Michael & Thornhill, Chris. Niklas Luhmann's Theory of Politics & Law. (p. 1255)
King, Michael Riano, Jr. Let's Learn Together. (p. 998)
King, Michelle L. Barrett's Unusual Ice Cream Party. (p. 140)
—Mr. Percy's Mysterious Glasses. (p. 1186)
King, Mike. I Is for Indy. Rodgers, John, illus. (p. 839)
King, Ms Marcy Cockerille. Orpies Learn to Read. (p. 1305)
King, Paul, Sr. Hobo & His Dog. (p. 786)
King, Paulk, Sr. Hero. (p. 772)
—What has happened to America. (p. 1886)
King, Penny. Adventure Stories. (p. 14)
King, Peter. Changels: The Crucible. (p. 290)
King, Philip. Bluey, the Little Drip. King, Janet, illus. (p. 204)
KING, R. O. N. S. emerald Fire. (p. 517)
—Kiss-diamond. (p. 961)
—Soul-pearl. (p. 1614)
—trilogy of magical Tales. (p. 1786)
King, Rachel. Technical Support. (p. 1711)
King, Rebecca E. B. Unji Finds A Friend. (p. 1821)
King, Ronnie L. Star the White Stallion & the Secret of the Light. (p. 1641)
King, Rosemary. Peanut Brittle. (p. 1332)
King, Ruth. Healing Rage: Women Making Inner Peace Possible. (p. 757)
King, Sally. Desert Blooms. (p. 428)
King, Seth David. Substitute Teacher Named Mr King. Clark, Matthew Levi, illus. (p. 1671)
King, Sharie. 40 Days of Purity for Girls. (p. 1997)
King, Sharon. Junior Alien Zone: Creative Experiences for Hands of All Ages! (p. 936)
—Oops Was Bullied? Hey, Why Did You Hurt Me That Way? LaRoe, Misty Bailey, illus. (p. 1299)
King Sprools, Wendy. Brothers Are Forever. (p. 231)
King Sr., Billy. Story. (p. 1656)
King, Stephen. Carrie. (p. 271)
—Drawing of the Three (p. 482)
—Drawing of the Three. Hale, Phil, illus. (p. 482)
—Gunslinger. (p. 732)
—Gunslinger. Whelan, Michael, illus. (p. 732)
—Long Road Home. (p. 1047)
—Resplandor. (p. 1463)
—Waste Lands Dameron, Ned, illus. (p. 1860)
—Wizard & Glass McKean, Dave, illus. (p. 1942)
King, Stephen, jt. auth. see Farris, John.
King, Stephen Michael. Mutt Dog! King, Stephen Michael, illus. (p. 1194)
—You: A Story of Love & Friendship. King, Stephen Michael, illus. (p. 1972)
King, Stephen Michael, illus. see Daly, Cathleen.
King, Stephen Michael, illus. see Fienberg, Anna.
King, Stephen Michael, illus. see French, Jackie.
King, Stephen Michael, illus. see Kelleher, Victor.
King, Stephen Michael, illus. see Wild, Margaret.
King, Steve. Stone Dragon. (p. 1652)
King, Steve, illus. see Canning, Laura A.
King, Sue, illus. see Bowman, Lucy.
King, Sue, illus. see Watt, Fiona.
King, Susan. Place for Me Beneath the Se. (p. 1365)
King, Tara Calahan, illus. see Munson, Derek.
King, Terri. Midwinter's Tail. (p. 1139)
King, Terrie. Six-Toed Dog & the Big-Headed Puppy. (p. 1583)
King, Thomas. Coyote Columbus Story Monkman, William Kent, illus. (p. 374)
—Coyote Solstice Tale Clement, Gary, illus. (p. 374)
King, Travis, illus. see Ikids Staff.
King, Trey. Count Our Friends! (p. 370)
—Cragger's Revenge. (p. 376)
—Detective Chase McCain- Save That Cargo! Primeau, Chuck, illus. (p. 431)
—Follow That Easter Egg! (p. 612)
—Halloween Rescue! Wang, Sean, illus. (p. 738)
—Last Laugh! Kiernan, Kenny, illus. (p. 978)
—Legend Begins. (p. 988)
—Lego City: Detective Chase McCain - Save That Cargo! (p. 990)
—LEGO City: Follow That Easter Egg! Wang, Sean, illus. (p. 990)
—LEGO DC Comics Super Heroes - Friends & Foes! Wang, Sean, illus. (p. 990)
—Lego DC Superheroes: Friends & Foes. (p. 990)
—Mystery on the Lego Express. (p. 1226)
—Mystery on the Lego Express. Wang, Sean, illus. (p. 1226)
—Need for Speed! (p. 1239)
—Save the Day! Kiernan, Kenny, illus. (p. 1516)
—Star Wars: a Very Vader Valentine's Day. Cook, Katie, illus. (p. 1641)
—Treasure Time! (p. 1782)
King, Trey, jt. auth. see Hasbro.
King, Trey, jt. auth. see Scholastic, Inc. Staff.
King, Trey, jt. auth. see Universal Books (Panama) Staff.
King, Trey, jt. auth. see Universal.
King, Trey & Kiernan, Kenny. Cops, Crocs, & Crooks! (p. 366)
—Lego City. (p. 990)
King, Valerie. Gift of Fate. (p. 675)
King, Veronica. Moon Is Laughing. (p. 1172)
—Sun Is Sleepy. (p. 1676)
King, Vickie. Search Dogs & You, a Wilderness Safety Guide from American Search Dogs. (p. 1537)
King, W. B., illus. see Garis, Howard Roger.
King, Wanda Fulbright. Fundamentals: Living it Out, Study of Bk of James, Fac Guide. (p. 649)
—Fundamentals: Living it Out Study of Book of James, Oldr Child Bk. (p. 649)
King, Wesley. Incredible Space Raiders from Space! (p. 869)
—Vindico. (p. 1843)
King, William. Vintner's Kitchen: Celebrating the Wines of Oregon. Schafer, Rick, photos by. (p. 1843)
King, Zelda. Battle of the Little Bighorn: Both Sides of the Story. (p. 146)
—Class Surprise. (p. 327)
—Dolphins. (p. 464)
—Examining Backyard Habitats. (p. 547)
—Examining Desert Habitats. (p. 547)
—Examining Forest Habitats. (p. 547)
—Examining Meadow Habitats. (p. 547)
—Examining Pond Habitats. (p. 547)
—Examining Tide Pool Habitats. (p. 547)
—Lemonade Stand. (p. 991)
—Let's Bake a Cake. (p. 994)
—Manatees. (p. 1086)
—Orcas. (p. 1302)
—Sea Otters. (p. 1535)
—Seals. (p. 1536)

K

—Story of Our Numbers: The History of Arabic Numerals. (p. 1659)
—Try It with Triangles: Learning to Put Triangles Together to Form Other Shapes. (p. 1794)
—Try it with Triangles: Learning to Put Triangles Together to Form Other Shapes. (p. 1794)
—Walruses. (p. 1855)
—Where's That Cat? (p. 1910)
King, Zola. Whatever Became of Charlie Caterpillar? (p. 1896)
King- Bennett, Dawn. Locket. (p. 1045)
King-Cason, Jermaine & McCollum, Nicole. From a Caterpillar to a Butterfly. (p. 641)
Kinger, Rachit. Zapp: The Squirrel Who Wanted to Fly. (p. 1985)
Kingfisher Editors. Animal Babies in Rain Forests. (p. 76)
—Animal Babies in Seas. (p. 76)
—At the Zoo. (p. 111)
—Baby Animals at Night. (p. 124)
—Baby Animals at the Zoo. (p. 124)
—Baby Animals in the Forest. (p. 124)
—Baby Animals - In the Sea. (p. 124)
—Baby Animals in the Snow. (p. 124)
—Baby Animals Pets. (p. 125)
—First Encyclopedia of Animals. (p. 594)
—In Grasslands. (p. 863)
—Joke a Day: 365 Guaranteed Giggles. Trimmer, Tony & Chatterton, Martin, illus. (p. 924)
—Kingfisher Children's Encyclopedia. (p. 960)
—Kingfisher First Encyclopedia. (p. 960)
—Kingfisher History Encyclopedia. (p. 960)
—Kingfisher Illustrated Pocket Dictionary. (p. 960)
—Who's That? Eating. (p. 1921)
—Who's That? Jumping. (p. 1921)
—Who's That? Roaring. (p. 1921)
—Zoo on the Move (p. 1989)
Kingfisher Editors, ed. see Weber, Vicky.
Kingfisher Editors, jt. auth. see Taylor, Charles.
Kingfisher Editors & Banes, Graham L. Kingfisher Encyclopedia of Life: Minutes, Months, Millennia-How Long Is a Life on Earth? (p. 960)
Kingfisher Editors & Dods, Emma. Surprising Facts about the Human Body. Aspinall, Marc, illus. (p. 1686)
Kingfisher Editors & Murrell, Deborah. Lift & Explore: Dinosaurs. Bull, Peter, illus. (p. 1014)
—Lift & Explore: Oceans. Bull, Peter, illus. (p. 1014)
Kingfisher Editors, ed. Animal Babies Around the House. (p. 76)
—Kingfisher Book of Classic Boy Stories. (p. 960)
—Kingfisher Book of Classic Girl Stories. (p. 960)
—Puzzling Puzzles: What Shape Is This? Book + (p. 1421)
Kingfisher Editors, et al. Wow, I Didn't Know That! Surprising Facts about Animals. Aspinall, Marc, illus. (p. 1962)
Kingfisher Publications, Inc. Staff, ed. see Taylor, Charles.
Kingfisher Publications, Inc. Staff, jt. auth. see Stanley, Mandy.
Kingfisher Publications, Inc. Staff, creator. Animal Babies in Ponds & Rivers. (p. 76)
—Animal Babies on Mountains. (p. 76)
Kingfisher Publications, Inc. Staff, ed. Animal Babies in Grasslands. (p. 76)
—Animal Babies in Towns & Cities. (p. 76)
—Kingfisher First Encyclopedia of Animals. (p. 960)
Kingfisher, Rupert. Madame Pamplemousse & Her Incredible Edibles. Hellard, Sue, illus. (p. 1069)
—Madame Pamplemousse & the Enchanted Sweet Shop. (p. 1069)
King-Hanna, Shirley. Ghost Child of Camay Lane (p. 670)
Kinghorn, Harriett. Classic to Contemporary: Famous Artists by Activities. (p. 328)
Kings, Gary & Ginger, Richard. Funky Junk: Recycle Rubbish into Art! Green, Barry, illus. (p. 649)
Kingsbury, Karen. Always Daddy's Princess Docampo, Valeria, illus. (p. 51)
—Brave Young Knight Grimard, Gabrielle, illus. (p. 223)
—Far Flutterby Bell, Jennifer A., illus. (p. 572)
—Let's Go on a Mommy Date Andreasen, Dan, illus. (p. 997)
—Let's Have a Daddy Day Andreasen, Dan, illus. (p. 998)
—Maggie's Miracle. (p. 1071)
—Princess & the Three Knights Grimard, Gabrielle, illus. (p. 1403)
—Red Gloves Collection. (p. 1454)
—Whatever You Grow up to Be DoCampo, Valeria, illus. (p. 1896)
—Whatever You Grow up to Be Docampo, Valeria, illus. (p. 1896)
Kingsbury, Karen, jt. auth. see Mackall, Dandi Daley.
Kingsbury, Karen & Smith, Alex. Go Ahead & Dream. Banning, Greg, illus. (p. 686)
Kingsbury, Robert. Assassination of James A. Garfield. (p. 107)
Kingscourt / McGraw-Hill. Mix & Match Flip Book Numbers 1-10 (Maths Links Plus) (p. 1156)
Kingscourt/McGraw-Hill. Meanie's Party Big Big Book - Story Chest. (p. 1116)
—Seven Fat Cats Big Big Book - Story Chest. (p. 1554)
—Super Smile Shop. (p. 1682)
Kingsland, L. W., tr. see Andersen, Hans Christian.
Kingsland, L. W., tr. see Holm, Anne.
Kingsland, Robin. Blame It on the Bard! (p. 198)
—Crabtree Chronicles: Frankie & the Fuhrer Hodder Children's Books. Vol. 3 (p. 375)
—Crabtree Chronicles. (p. 375)
—Porky Pies: Wolves, Squeals & Dodgy Deals: A Play with Songs for School Performances. (p. 1386)
—Porky Pies. (p. 1386)
Kingsley, Charles. Glaucus: The Wonders of the Shore. (p. 682)
—Glaucus or the Wonders of the Shore. (p. 682)
—Heroes: Or Greek Fairy Tales for My Children. (p. 772)
—Heroes. Robinson, T. H., illus. (p. 772)
—Heroes of Greek Mythology. Squire, M H & Mars, E., illus. (p. 773)
—Madam How & Lady Why: Or First Lessons in Earth Lore for Children. (p. 1069)
—Ther Water Babies. Johnstone, Anne Grahame, illus. (p. 1729)
—Water Babies: A Fairy Tale for a Land-Baby. Goble, Warwick, illus. (p. 1862)
—Water Babies. (p. 1862)
Kingsley, Charles, jt. auth. see Kingsley, Charles.
Kingsley, Charles & Kingsley, Charles. Water-Babies: A Fairy Tale for a Land-Baby. (p. 1862)
Kingsley, Kate. Everything but the Truth. (p. 544)
—Kiss & Break Up. (p. 961)
—Pretty on the Outside. (p. 1398)
—Too Cruel for School: Young, Loaded & Fabulous. (p. 1766)
Kingsley, Kaza. Dragon's Eye. (p. 479)
—Dragon's Eye. Grant, Melvyn, illus. (p. 479)
—Erec Rex: The Dragon's Eye. Payne, John, ed. (p. 533)
—Erec Rex: the Monsters of Otherness. (p. 533)
—Monsters of Otherness. Grant, Melvyn, illus. (p. 1169)
—Search for Truth. Jacobus, Tim, illus. (p. 1537)
—Secret of Ashona. Ng, James, illus. (p. 1542)
—Three Furies. Mohrbacher, Peter, illus. (p. 1742)
—Three Furies. Ng, James & Mohrbacher, Peter, illus. (p. 1742)
Kingsley, Linda Kurtz. Bringing up Sophie. (p. 229)
—Bringing up Sophie. Kingsley, Linda Kurtz, illus. (p. 229)
—Signs of Jays. Kingsley, Linda Kurtz, illus. (p. 1574)
Kingsley, M. t., et al. Best Worst Summer Ever. (p. 171)
Kingsley, Mike. Haunted House. (p. 753)
—Treasure of King Midas. (p. 1782)
Kingsley, Nellie F., jt. auth. see Beebe, Katherine.
Kingsley, Ron D. Stories from the Life of Ronnie Kaye: Monsters. (p. 1654)
Kingsley, Salome. Two Wishes for Natty's Birthday. (p. 1804)
Kingsley, Shawn. Uncle Jesus. (p. 1811)
King-Smith, Dick. All Pigs Are Beautiful. Jeram, Anita, illus. (p. 45)
—Catlady. Eastwood, John, illus. (p. 280)
—Dinosaur Trouble. Bruel, Nick, illus. (p. 443)
—Funny Frank. Eastwood, John, illus. (p. 650)
—Golden Goose. Kronheimer, Ann, illus. (p. 694)
—Lady Lollipop. Barton, Jill, illus. (p. 971)
—Merman. (p. 1128)
—Spider Sparrow. (p. 1626)
—Stray. (p. 1666)
—Three Terrible Trins. (p. 1744)
—Titus Rules! Eastwood, John, illus. (p. 1758)
—Twin Giants. Grey, Mini, illus. (p. 1802)
—Water Horse. Parkins, David, illus. (p. 1862)
King-Smith, Dick & Fox Busters Ltd. Staff. Smasher. Bernal, Richard, illus. (p. 1593)
Kingston, Anna. Life Cycle of a Pelican. (p. 1009)
—Life Cycle of the Poison Dart Frog. (p. 1009)
—Life Cycle of the Sea Turtle. (p. 1009)
—Respecting the Contributions of African Americans. (p. 1463)
—Respecting the Contributions of Asian Americans. (p. 1463)
—Respecting the Contributions of Latino Americans. (p. 1463)
—Respecting the Contributions of LGBT Americans. (p. 1463)
Kingston, Anna & Viegas, Jennifer. Heart in 3D. (p. 759)
Kingston, Mary. Fantastic Far-Flung Facts for Fun. (p. 571)
Kingston, W. Aventuras en la Selva. (p. 119)
Kingston, W. H. G. In the Rocky Mountains. (p. 867)
Kingston, W. H. G., tr. see Verne, Jules.
Kingston, William H. In the Eastern Seas. (p. 866)
Kingston, William Henry Giles, tr. Swiss Family Robinson. Wyss, Johann David, illus. (p. 1691)
Kingstone, Peter. Readings in Latin American Politics: Challenges to Democratization. (p. 1447)
Kini, Kanyika, illus. see Ravishankar, Anushka.
Kinkade, Sheila. My Family. Little, Elaine, photos by. (p. 1202)
Kinkade, Thomas. Amanda's Story. (p. 52)
—Away in a Manger. (p. 120)
—Katherine's Story. (p. 944)
—Lizabeth's Story (p. 1042)
—Sister Knows Your Heart. (p. 1581)
Kinkade, Thomas, illus. see Public Domain Staff.
Kinkade, Thomas & Tamar, Erika. Rose's Story. (p. 1490)
Kinkade, Thomas, contrib. by. Lifepac Elective Drawing Basics (p. 1013)
Kinkead-Weekes, Mark, ed. see Lawrence, D. H.
Kinmont, Ritchie. Every Kid Needs Things That Fly Casey, Robert, photos by. (p. 542)
Kinmonth, Patrick, jt. auth. see Testino, Mario.
Kinnaird, Ross, illus. see Holt, Sharon.
Kinnaird, Ross, illus. see Kyi, Tanya Lloyd.
Kinnaird, Ross, illus. see McMillan, Dawn.
Kinnaird, Ross, illus. see Shapiro, Stephen.
Kinnaird, Ross, jt. auth. see Christie, Peter.
Kinnaird, Ross, jt. auth. see McMillan, Dawn.
Kinnaird, Sara Jane, jt. auth. see Black Fox, Barbara.
Kinnaman, Gary. Angels Dark & Light. (p. 75)
—Winning Your Spiritual Battles. (p. 1937)
Kinnaman, Scott A. Worshiping with Angels & Archangels: An Introduction to the Divine Service. Kirchhoff, Arthur, illus. (p. 1961)
Kinnear, Kay. Deedee's Easter Surprise. Park, Julie, illus. (p. 422)
Kinneman, D. Michael, illus. see Hees, Miriam.
Kinney, Cyndi, ed. see Donner, Candie.
Kinney, Cyndi, ed. see Hagen, Debra.
Kinney, Cyndi, ed. see Smith, Kim.
Kinney, Cyndi, ed. see Sutton, Pam.
Kinney, Cyndi & Trout, Judy. State History for ALL 50 States - 100 Lapbooks & Lapbook Journals & Study Guides. (p. 1644)
Kinney, Dick, jt. auth. see Barks, Carl.
Kinney, Donald, et al. to Z: Global Edition. (p. 1759)
Kinney, Jeff. Cabin Fever. (p. 250)
—Cabin Fever. (p. 250)
—Carnet de Bord de Greg Heffley. Zimmerman, Natalie, tr. (p. 270)
—Diario de Greg, un Renacuajo. Morán, Esteban, tr. (p. 434)
—Diary of a Wimpy Kid. (p. 435)
—Dias de Perros. (p. 435)
—Dog Days. (p. 461)
—Hard Luck. (p. 748)
—Last Straw. (p. 978)
—Ley de Rodrick. Morán, Esteban, tr. (p. 1004)
—Long Haul. (p. 1047)
—Long Haul. Kinney, Jeff, illus. (p. 1047)
—Rodrick Rules. (p. 1484)
—Rodrick Rules. (p. 1484)
—Third Wheel. (p. 1734)
—Ugly Truth. (p. 1808)
—Ugly Truth. (p. 1808)
—Wimpy Kid Do-It-Yourself Book. (p. 1935)
—Wimpy Kid Movie Diary. (p. 1935)
—¡Esto Es el Colmo! Morán, Esteban, tr. (p. 538)
Kinney, Jessica. Pig Scramble. Brannen, Sarah S., illus. (p. 1357)
Kinney, Jo Hannah, illus. see Enos, Barbara.
Kinney, Kendall. Tiger Tails. (p. 1748)
Kinney, Monica & Ehrich, Meghen. Using Google Apps. (p. 1828)
Kinney, Patrick. Who Is Jeff Kinney? Hinderliter, John, illus. (p. 1916)
Kinney, Sarah. Nancy Drew & the Clue Crew #3: Enter the Dragon Mystery. Goldberg, Stan, illus. (p. 1228)
—Nancy Drew & the Clue Crew - Enter the Dragon Mystery. Goldberg, Stan, illus. (p. 1228)
Kinney, Sarah, jt. auth. see Petrucha, Stefan.
Kinney, Sarah & Petrucha, Stefan. Secret Sand Sleuths. Goldberg, Stan, illus. (p. 1543)
Kinney, Sarah, et al. Walt Disney's Vacation Parade Clark, John, ed. (p. 1856)
Kinney, Scott. Kozmik. O'Reilly, Sean Patrick, ed. (p. 967)
Kinney, Tom, ed. see Tenpas, Steve.
Kinney-Petrucha, Margo, jt. auth. see Petrucha, Stefan.
Kinra, Richa. Princess Panda Tea Party: A Cerebral Palsy Fairy Tale. (p. 1405)
Kinra, Richa, illus. see Barth, Amy.
Kinra, Richa, illus. see Kats, Jewel.
Kinra, Richa, illus. see Lawson, Brandi.
Kinra, Richa, illus. see MacLean, Betty.
Kinra, Richa, illus. see Morris, Kirkland.
Kinra, Richa, illus. see Singal, Sudesh.
Kinra, Richa, illus. see Vance, Colleen.
Kinross, Robin. No! Go Away! (p. 1258)
Kinsel, Kate & Maughan, Jennifer. Flashback. (p. 602)
Kinsella, Audrey. Dingle: The Helpful Ice Cream Cone Delivery Dog. (p. 440)
Kinsella, John. Doppler Effect. (p. 470)
Kinsella, John, ed. see Mengham, Rod.
Kinsella, John & Ryan, Tracy. Conspiracies. (p. 359)
Kinsella, John, ed. ABC of Theory & Praxis. (p. 3)
Kinsella, Pat, illus. see Biskup, Agnieszka.
Kinsella, Pat, illus. see Collins, Terry, et al.
Kinsella, Pat, illus. see Collins, Terry.
Kinsella, Pat, illus. see Gunderson, Jessica & Collins, Terry.
Kinsella, Pat, illus. see Gunderson, Jessica.
Kinsella, Pat, illus. see Raum, Elizabeth, et al.
Kinsella, Pat, illus. see Raum, Elizabeth.
Kinsella, Sophie, illus. see Oliver, A. J.
Kinsella, Sophie, pseud. Finding Audrey. (p. 587)
Kinser, Kathy. Doomed to Disappear? Endangered Species: Set Of 6. (p. 470)
—Everglades: Set Of 6. (p. 542)
Kinsey, Thomas D., ed. see Heller, Pete.
Kinsey-Warnock, Natalie. Gifts from the Sea. Pederson, Judy, illus. (p. 675)
—Lumber Camp Library. Bernardin, James, illus. (p. 1065)
—Nora's Ark. McCully, Emily Arnold, illus. (p. 1264)
—True Colors. (p. 1792)
Kinsinger, Mary Ann, jt. auth. see Fisher, Suzanne Woods.
Kinsler, Gwen Blakley, see Blakley Kinsler, Gwen.
Kinsley, James, ed. see Austen, Jane & Stabler, Jane.
Kinsley, James, ed. see Austen, Jane, et al.
Kinsley, Sean, illus. see Horton, Elizabeth.
Kinsman, Josephine. Ginger's New Tail. (p. 677)
Kinsman, Naomi. Shades of Truth (p. 1557)
Kinsner, Kathy. Amazing Plants. (p. 55)
—Amazon: Set Of 6. (p. 56)
—Animals at the Extremes: Set Of 6. (p. 82)
—Animals at the Extremes & Animales en los Extremos: 6 English, 6 Spanish Adaptations. (p. 82)
—Doomed to Disappear? Endangered Species & Condenadas a desaparecer? Especies en peligro de Extinción: 6 English, 6 Spanish Adaptations. (p. 470)
—Everglades. (p. 542)
—Fabric Around the World: Small Book. (p. 559)
—Fabric Around the World. (p. 559)
—Relationships in Nature & Relaciones en la Naturaleza: 6 English, 6 Spanish Adaptations. (p. 1457)
Kinstle Nocera, Suzanne, illus. see Rode, Maureen.
Kinstler, Everett Raymond, jt. auth. see Vadeboncoeur, Jim, Jr.
Kinton, P. D. Wishing for Wizards & Chips for Te. (p. 1940)
Kintz, Elizabeth. Magic Hose. (p. 1072)
Kinzer, Stephen. Overthrow: America's Century of Regime Change from Hawaii to Iraq. (p. 1314)
Kinzy, Ryan, jt. auth. see Kinzy, Ryan.
Kinzy, Ryan & Kinzy, Ryan. New Frontier: The Cielo Space Chronicles. Bk. 1 (p. 1244)
Kiosse, Connie. Best of Friends, Two Sisters, One Journey. (p. 170)
Kipiniak, Chris, jt. auth. see Chilman-Blair, Kim.
Kiplagat, Linet. Bible Abc: My Memory Verse Book. (p. 175)
Kipling, Joe. Blinded by the Light. (p. 199)
Kipling, John Lockwood, jt. illus. see Kipling, Rudyard.
Kipling, Rudyard. Brave Little Seal. Hale, Nathan, illus. (p. 223)
—Bridge Builders. (p. 227)
—Captains Courageous. (p. 264)
—Collection of Rudyard Kipling's Just So Stories. Sis, Peter, illus. (p. 340)
—Como el Leopardo Obtuvo Sus Manchas: Y Otros Cuentos de Animales. Calderon, Catalina, tr. (p. 350)
—Complete Children's Short Stories. (p. 352)
—Crocodile, Crocodile. Mogensen, Jan & Schroeder, Binnette, illus. (p. 384)
—Elephant's Child: From the Just So Stories. Raglin, Tim, illus. (p. 512)
—Elephant's Child. Patterson, Geoffrey, illus. (p. 512)
—Hijo del Elefante. Mogensen, Jan, illus. (p. 779)
—How the Camel Got His Hump: The Graphic Novel Rodriguez, Pedro, illus. (p. 812)
—How the Camel Got His Hump. Raglin, Tim, illus. (p. 812)
—How the Elephant Got His Trunk: The Graphic Novel Rodriguez, Pedro, illus. (p. 813)
—How the Leopard Got His Spots: The Graphic Novel Rodriguez, Pedro, illus. (p. 813)
—How the Leopard Got His Spots. Lohstoeter, Lori, illus. (p. 813)
—How the Leopard Got His Spots. Rodriguez, Pedro, illus. (p. 813)
—How the Rhinoceros Got His Skin: The Graphic Novel Rodriguez, Pedro, illus. (p. 813)
—How the Rhinoceros Got His Skin: The Graphic Novel Rodriguez, Pedro, illus. (p. 813)
—How the Rhinoceros Got His Skin. Raglin, Tim, illus. (p. 813)
—If: A Father's Advice to His Son. Smith, Charles R., Jr., photos by. (p. 852)
—Jungle Book: A Classic Story about Uniqueness. (p. 935)
—Jungle Book: Rikki-Tikki-Tavi Moves In. Madsen, Jim, illus. (p. 935)
—Jungle Book. (p. 935)
—Jungle Book. Rowe, John, ed. (p. 935)
—Jungle Book. Daily, Don, illus. (p. 935)
—Jungle Book. Corvino, Lucy, illus. (p. 935)
—Jungle Book. Drake, W. H., Jr., illus. (p. 935)
—Jungle Book. Ingpen, Robert R., illus. (p. 935)
—Jungle Book. Detmold, Edward J. & Detmold, Maurice, illus. (p. 935)
—Jungle Books. (p. 935)
—Just So Comics: Tales of the World's Wildest Beasts. Rodriguez, Pedro, illus. (p. 939)
—Just So Stories Wallace, Ian, illus. (p. 939)
—Just So Stories: For Little Children. Set (p. 939)
—Just So Stories: For Little Children. Set Salter, Safaya, illus. (p. 939)
—Just So Stories. (p. 939)
—Just So Stories. Lewis, Lisa, ed. (p. 939)
—Just So Stories. Latimer, Alex, illus. (p. 939)
—Just So Stories. Ingpen, Robert R., illus. (p. 939)
—Just So Stories. Montefiore, Jan & Plotz, Judith, eds. (p. 939)
—Just So Stories. Gleeson, J. M. & Bransom, Paul, illus. (p. 939)
—Kim. (p. 956)
—Kim. Trivedi, Harish & Montefiore, Jan, eds. (p. 956)
—Land & Sea Tales for Scouts & Scout. (p. 973)
—Libro de la Selva. (p. 1006)
—Libro de la Selva. López, Javier Alfonso, tr. (p. 1006)
—Mowgli Knows Best Hale, Nathan, illus. (p. 1184)
—Puck of Pook's Hill. (p. 1414)
—Rikki-Tikki-Tavi. Jones, Chuck, illus. (p. 1472)
—Rikki-Tikki-Tavi & Toomai of the Elephants. (p. 1472)
—Rudyard Kipling: The Complete Children's Short Stories. (p. 1494)
—Stalky & Co. (p. 1639)
—Storyteller Book: The Jungle Book. Thome, Jenny, illus. (p. 1663)
—White Seal. Jones, Chuck, illus. (p. 1913)
Kipling, Rudyard, jt. auth. see Jones, Christianne C.
Kipling, Rudyard, jt. auth. see Manguel, Alberto.
Kipling, Rudyard, jt. auth. see Robson.
Kipling, Rudyard & Busch, Jeffrey. Jungle Books. (p. 935)
Kipling, Rudyard & Kipling, John Lockwood. Jungle Book. (p. 935)
Kipling, Rudyard & Landolf, Diane Wright. Jungle Book. Rowe, John, illus. (p. 935)
Kipling, Rudyard & Pinkney, Jerry. Rikki-Tikki-Tavi. (p. 1472)
—Rikki-Tikki-Tavi. Pinkney, Jerry, illus. (p. 1472)
Kipling, Rudyard & Solari, Maria J. Libro de la Selva. Puerta, Carlos, tr. (p. 1006)
Kipling, Rudyard, et al. Mejores Relatos Fantasmagóricos. (p. 1124)
Kiplinger Pandy, Lori. Flying Hugs & Kisses. (p. 610)
Kiplinger Pandy, Lori, illus. see Collins, Arda.
Kiplinger Pandy, Lori, illus. see McWilliams Pittard, Irene.
Kiplinger Pandy, Lori, illus. see Sample, Jewel.
Kippur, Yom, jt. auth. see Hashanah, Rosh.
Kira, Rick. Noah & the Unicorns. (p. 1261)
—Omed's Camels. (p. 1288)
Kiraithe, Jackie. Magic Links: Manual. Gonzales, Linda, ed. (p. 1072)
Kiraz, George. Syriac Alphabet for Children. (p. 1693)
Kirberger, Jesse, jt. auth. see Kirberger, Kimberly.
Kirberger, Kimberly & Kirberger, Jesse. I Don't Know What I Want but I Want to Be Happy. (p. 837)
Kirby, Chris. Lost Squad. (p. 1056)
Kirby, David. Evidence of Harm: Mercury in Vaccines & the Autism Epidemic: A Medical Controversy. (p. 546)
Kirby, Jack. Essential Fantastic Four (p. 537)
—Essential Uncanny X-Men (p. 537)
—Kamandi Archives (p. 942)
Kirby, Jack, illus. see Lee, Stan, et al.
Kirby, Jack, illus. see Waid, Mark.
Kirby, Jack, jt. text see Marvel Comics Staff.
Kirby, Jack & Ditko, Steve. Incredible Hulk (p. 869)
Kirby, Jack & Wood, Dave. Challengers of the Unknown - Archives (p. 289)
Kirby, Jack, et al. Captain America vs. the Red Skull. (p. 263)
Kirby, Jack, text. Captain America by Jack Kirby Omnibus. (p. 263)
Kirby, Jessi. Golden. (p. 694)
—In Honor. (p. 863)
—Moonglass. (p. 1172)
—Things We Know by Heart. (p. 1734)
Kirby, Matthew. Spider Stories. (p. 1626)
Kirby, Matthew J. Arctic Code. (p. 96)
—Cave of Wonders. (p. 282)
—Clockwork Three. (p. 333)
—Icefall. (p. 851)
—Lost Kingdom. (p. 1056)
—Quantum League #1: Spell Robbers. (p. 1422)

Kirby, Pamela F. What Bluebirds Do. (p. 1880)
—What Bluebirds Do. Kirby, Pamela F., photos by. (p. 1880)
Kirby, Peter. Child Labour in Britain, 1750-1870 (p. 301)
Kirby, Robert. Kirby Soup for the Soul. Bagley, Pat, illus. (p. 961)
Kirby, Ruth M. Claudius Saves the Pumpkin Patch. Larson, Lisa K., illus. (p. 329)
Kirby, Stan. Captain Awesome & the Easter Egg Bandit. O'Connor, George, illus. (p. 263)
—Captain Awesome & the Missing Elephants. (p. 263)
—Captain Awesome & the New Kid. (p. 263)
—Captain Awesome & the New Kid. O'Connor, George, illus. (p. 263)
—Captain Awesome & the Ultimate Spelling Bee. (p. 263)
—Captain Awesome & the Ultimate Spelling Bee. O'Connor, George, illus. (p. 263)
—Captain Awesome Collection: A MI-TEE Boxed Set: Captain Awesome to the Rescue!; Captain Awesome vs. Nacho Cheese Man; Captain Awesome & the New Kid; Captain Awesome Takes a Dive. O'Connor, George, illus. (p. 263)
—Captain Awesome Gets Crushed. (p. 263)
—Captain Awesome Gets Crushed. O'Connor, George, illus. (p. 263)
—Captain Awesome Goes to Superhero Camp. O'Connor, George, illus. (p. 263)
—Captain Awesome Saves the Winter Wonderland. (p. 263)
—Captain Awesome Saves the Winter Wonderland. O'Connor, George, illus. (p. 263)
—Captain Awesome, Soccer Star. (p. 263)
—Captain Awesome, Soccer Star. O'Connor, George, illus. (p. 263)
—Captain Awesome Takes a Dive. (p. 263)
—Captain Awesome Takes a Dive. O'Connor, George, illus. (p. 263)
—Captain Awesome to the Rescue! (p. 263)
—Captain Awesome to the Rescue! O'Connor, George, illus. (p. 263)
—Captain Awesome vs. Nacho Cheese Man. (p. 263)
—Captain Awesome vs. Nacho Cheese Man. O'Connor, George, illus. (p. 263)
—Captain Awesome vs. the Evil Babysitter. O'Connor, George, illus. (p. 263)
—Captain Awesome vs. the Spooky, Scary House. (p. 263)
—Captain Awesome vs. the Spooky, Scary House. O'Connor, George, illus. (p. 263)
Kirby, Susan E. No-Fuss Christmas. (p. 1258)
Kirby-Payne, Ann, jt. auth. see Clarke, Julie.
Kirchel, Karen. Irrepressible Lucie Archer. (p. 888)
Kirchen, Jeannie. Why Barry Bear Skipped His Bath. (p. 1922)
Kircher, Jean. Bertie Can't Fly. (p. 168)
Kirchhoff, Art, illus. see Bergt, Carolyn.
Kirchhoff, Art, illus. see Nielsen, Pamela & Luhmann, Edward Q.
Kirchhoff, Arthur, illus. see Kinnaman, Scott A.
Kirchhoff, Liz M. Teaching Social Media: The Can-Do Guide (p. 1710)
Kirchmeier, Jenn-Ann. Tails of Brinkley the Berner: The Beginning. (p. 1695)
Kirchner, Don E. Matter of Time: A True Story. (p. 1109)
Kirchner, Janette. I Love You So Much. (p. 844)
Kirchoff, Arthur, illus. see Meyer, Kay L.
Kirgiss, Crystal & Lyon, Christopher. Teenager's Daily Prayer Book. Publications International Ltd. Staff, ed. (p. 1714)
Kirgiss, Crystal & Zondervan Publishing Staff. What's up with Boys? Everything You Need to Know about Guys (p. 1900)
Kirihara, Idumi. Hitohira. (p. 786)
Kirk, Amanda. Food, Agriculture, & Natural Resources. (p. 613)
—Information Technology. (p. 874)
—Internet & Media. (p. 880)
Kirk, Amanda, jt. auth. see Matters, Print.
Kirk & Rossiter, Sofia. Story of the Great Pumpkin Man. (p. 1661)
Kirk, Andrea Cope, illus. see McLelland, Michael J.
Kirk, Andrew. Understanding Thoreau's Civil Disobedience. (p. 1816)
Kirk B. Gradin. Jadhu Ram & the Thirsty Forest. (p. 905)
Kirk, Bill. Brainy Refrain: The Sum of Our Parts Book 4. Ruble, Eugene, illus. (p. 222)
—Circulation Celebration: The Sum of Our Parts Series. Ruble, Eugene, illus. (p. 321)
—Great Gobs of Gustation- the Sum of Our Parts. Ruble, Eugene, illus. (p. 716)
—Ins & Outs of Air: The Sum of Our Parts Series. Ruble, Eugene, illus. (p. 875)
—Muscles Make Us Move. Ruble, Eugene, illus. (p. 1192)
—My Grandma's Kitchen Rules. Movshina, Marina, illus. (p. 1210)
—My Tooth Is Loose: The Sum of Our Parts. Ruble, Eugene, illus. (p. 1220)
—Skin We're In: The Sum of Our Parts Series. Ruble, Eugene, illus. (p. 1585)
—There's a Beetle in My Bed. Brown, Suzy, illus. (p. 1730)
—There's a Spider in My Sink! Brown, Suzy, illus. (p. 1731)
—Tissue Tantra: The Sum of Our Parts Series Book 9. Ruble, Eugene, illus. (p. 1757)
Kirk, Brett & Kirk, Hayley S. Brave Heart: Lessons Learnt from Life. (p. 223)
Kirk, Connie Ann. Sky Dancers Hale, Christy, illus. (p. 1586)
—Student's Guide to Jane Austen. (p. 1669)
—Student's Guide to Robert Frost. (p. 1669)
Kirk, Courtney. There's a Zebra in My Pocket. (p. 1731)
Kirk, Daniel. Elf Realm: The High Road. (p. 512)
—Elf Realm: The Road's End. (p. 512)
—Honk Honk! Beep Beep! Kirk, Daniel, illus. (p. 795)
—Library Mouse. (p. 1006)
—Library Mouse: Home Sweet Home. (p. 1006)
—Library Mouse: A Museum Adventure. (p. 1006)
—Library Mouse: A World to Explore. (p. 1006)
—Library Mouse: A Friend's Tale. No. 2 (p. 1006)
—Library Mouse. (p. 1006)
—Library Mouse - A Friend's Tale. (p. 1006)
—Ten Thank-You Letters. Kirk, Daniel, illus. (p. 1719)
—Ten Things I Love about You. Kirk, Daniel, illus. (p. 1719)
—Thing about Spring. (p. 1732)
—You Are Not My Friend, but I Miss You. (p. 1973)
Kirk, Daniel, illus. see Lewis, Kevin.
Kirk, Daniel, illus. see Schlein, Miriam.
Kirk, Daniel, illus. see Stevenson, Robert Louis.
Kirk, Daniel, jt. auth. see Lewis, Kevin.
Kirk, David. Bedtime Story. (p. 157)
—Captain Sunny Patch. (p. 264)
—Happy Heartwood Day. (p. 746)
—Miss Spider's Sunny Patch Surprise. (p. 1152)
—Miss Spider's Tea Party. (p. 1152)
—Nova's Christmas Creation. (p. 1268)
—Oh So Brave Dragon. Kirk, David, illus. (p. 1281)
—Oh So Tiny Bunny. Kirk, David, illus. (p. 1281)
Kirk, David & Scholastic / LeapFrog. Miss Spider's Tea Party. (p. 1152)
Kirk, Donald. Hinsdale: The Summer Of '58. (p. 780)
Kirk, E. J. Step into Narnia: A Journey Through the Lion, the Witch & the Wardrobe. (p. 1648)
Kirk, Ellen. Human Footprint: Everything You Will Eat, Use, Wear, Buy, & Throw Out in Your Lifetime. (p. 826)
—My Plane Book. (p. 1217)
Kirk, Emily. Rubber Ducks Don't Grow Up. (p. 1493)
Kirk, Franklyn W., et al. Instrumentation: Text. (p. 879)
—Instrumentation: Workbook. (p. 879)
—Instrumentation: Answer Key. (p. 879)
—Instrumentation: Resource Guide. (p. 879)
Kirk, Hayley S. Divine Clementine. (p. 454)
Kirk, Hayley S., jt. auth. see Kirk, Brett.
Kirk, Heather. Drop of Rain. (p. 486)
—My First Picture Alphabet. (p. 1207)
—My First Picture Numbers. (p. 1207)
Kirk, Heather, illus. see Harvey, Keith.
Kirk, Heather, jt. auth. see Harvey, Keith.
Kirk, Jacqueline, illus. see Rosenblatt, Danielle.
Kirk, Janice. Christmas Redwood. Kirk, Janice, illus. (p. 315)
Kirk, Karly. All My Cousins: Understand & Apply Properties of Operations. (p. 45)
Kirk, Katie. Eli, No! (p. 512)
Kirk, Leonard, illus. see Parker, Jeff.
Kirk, Lori Grant. Heart for Jesus. (p. 759)
—Light of the Firefly. (p. 1015)
Kirk, Maria L., illus. see MacDonald, George, ed.
Kirk, Maria L., illus. see MacDonald, George.
Kirk, Maria L., illus. see Spyri, Johanna & Stork, Elisabeth P.
Kirk, Peggy. Pukka Blue. (p. 1415)
Kirk, Ruth Lynn. Charlie Ate My Hat! (p. 292)
Kirk, Susan Van. Importance of Being Earnest. (p. 862)
Kirk, Tim, illus. see Beahm, George.
Kirk, Tim, illus. see Black, Cassandra.
Kirk, Trish. I Think There's a Bear Out There. (p. 846)
Kirkby, Joanne & Cooper, Sharon. Mosaic Picture Sticker Book. (p. 1176)
Kirkby, Mandy. Pick Your Brains about Scotland. Williams, Caspar, illus. (p. 1354)
—Pick Your Brains about Spain. (p. 1354)
Kirkeby, Jennifer. Dot & Tot of Merryland - (p. 472)
—Harriet & Walt. (p. 749)
Kirker, Solveig. Florida Pod. (p. 607)
Kirkham, Aileen. Collaborative Bridges: People, Places & Things. (p. 339)
Kirkham, Rian, jt. auth. see Kirkham, Tyler.
Kirkham, Teresa. Tattle Tom. (p. 1707)
Kirkham, Tyler & Kirkham, Rian. My Best Friend's a Booger. O'Reilly, Sean Patrick, ed. (p. 1196)
Kirkland, Jane. Take a Backyard Bird Walk. Easter, Dennis, illus. (p. 1696)
—Take a Beach Walk. Burke, Dorothy et al, eds. (p. 1696)
—Take a City Nature Walk. (p. 1696)
—Take a Tree Walk. (p. 1696)
—Take a Walk with Butterflies & Dragonflies (p. 1696)
—Take a Winter Nature Walk. (p. 1696)
Kirkland, Jo. Donald the Donkey. (p. 466)
Kirkland, Joseph. Captain of Company K. (p. 264)
Kirkland, Justin B. Jb Pumpernikel vs the Sock Monster. (p. 911)
Kirkland, Katherine, illus. see Bowman, Crystal.
Kirkland, Katherine, illus. see Hallinan, P. K.
Kirkland, Katherine, illus. see Winters, Kay.
Kirkland, Kim M. Car Cars Go Zoom Zoom Zoom. (p. 265)
—Mi Mi's Mini Tea Party. Swope, Brenda, illus. (p. 1132)
Kirkland, Kyle. Frontiers of Science (p. 644)
Kirkland, S. M. Higher Honor. (p. 779)
Kirkle, Diane Luise. Rachel Serves a Stew. Batson, Susann, illus. (p. 1432)
Kirkman, Françoise Dudal, jt. auth. see Di Vecchio, Jerry Anne.
Kirkman, Kelly, illus. see Swensen, Karen & Ronquillo, Karen.
Kirkman, Robert. Boy from Earth. (p. 217)
—Eight Is Enough. (p. 507)
—Genesis (p. 660)
—Marvel Knights 2099. (p. 1098)
—Masters of the Universe: He-Man's Icons of Evil. Neves, Diogenes & Walker, Cory, illus. (p. 1103)
—Super Dinosaur. (p. 1679)
—Super Dinosaur Volume 2 TP. (p. 1679)
—Tales of the Realm. (p. 1702)
Kirkman, Robert, jt. auth. see Brown, Bruce.
Kirkman, Robert & Casey, Joe. Haunt. (p. 753)
Kirkman, Robert & Ottley, Ryan. Invincible. (p. 885)
Kirkman, Steve & McAlister, Kerrie. Maths in Practice Workbook 2 & Hotmaths Bundle. (p. 1108)
Kirkova, Milena, illus. see Accord Publishing Staff.
Kirkova, Milena, illus. see Boniface, William.
Kirkova, Milena & Hannigan, Paula. When I'm Big. (p. 1903)
Kirkpatrick, Brenna. My Motorcycle & Me: A Trip in the Mountains. (p. 1215)
Kirkpatrick, Karen, illus. see Rodenbur, Susan.
Kirkpatrick, Katherine. Between Two Worlds. (p. 173)
—Escape Across the Wide Sea. (p. 534)
—Mysterious Bones: The Story of Kennewick Man. Stevenson, Emma, illus. (p. 1222)
—Snow Baby: The Arctic Childhood of Robert E. Peary's Daring Daughter. (p. 1598)
—Snow Baby: The Arctic Childhood of Admiral Robert E. Peary's Daring Daughter. (p. 1598)
Kirkpatrick, Katrina, illus. see Gifune, Greg F.
Kirkpatrick, Kevin. Francisco's Friends: The Pachyderm Predicamen. (p. 628)
Kirkpatrick, Larry D., jt. auth. see Eisenkraft, Arthur.
Kirkpatrick, Naida. Sumerians. (p. 1673)
Kirkpatrick, Patricia. John Keats. Delessert, Etienne, illus. (p. 922)
Kirkpatrick, Patricia, jt. auth. see Angelou, Maya.
Kirkpatrick, Rob. Alexi Lalas: Sensación del Fútbol Soccer (Soccer Sensation) (p. 37)
—Alexi Lalas: Soccer Sensation / Sensación del Fútbol Soccer. (p. 37)
—Cobi Jones: Estrella del Fútbol Soccer (Soccer Star) (p. 336)
—Cobi Jones: Soccer Star / Estrella del Fútbol Soccer. (p. 336)
—Dale Earnhardt Jr: NASCAR Road Racer. (p. 401)
—Dale Earnhardt Jr: Piloto de NASCAR (NASCAR Road Racer) (p. 401)
—Dale Earnhardt Jr: NASCAR Road Racer / Piloto de NASCAR. (p. 401)
—Dale Earnhardt Jr. NASCAR Road Racer/Piloto de NASCAR. (p. 401)
—Dale Earnhardt Jr. , NASCAR Road Racer/Piloto de NASCAR. De Leon, Mauricio Velzaquez, tr. (p. 401)
—Doug Flutie: International Football Star. (p. 473)
—Doug Flutie: Estrella Internacional de Fútbol Americano (International Football Star) (p. 473)
—Evander Holyfield: Campeón de los Pesos Pesados (Heavyweight Champion) (p. 540)
—Evander Holyfield: Heavyweight Champion / Campeón de los Pesos Pesados. (p. 540)
—Florence Griffith Joyner: Olympic Runner. (p. 606)
—Grant Hill: Basketball All-Star. (p. 710)
—Grant Hill: Basketball Star/Estrella del Basketball. (p. 710)
—Grant Hill: Estrella del Basketball (Basketball All-Star) (p. 710)
—Hot Shots (p. 802)
—Jeff Gordon: Campeón de NASCAR (NASCAR Champion) (p. 911)
—Jeff Gordon: NASCAR Champion / Campeón de NASCAR. (p. 911)
—Kobe Bryant: Campeón de Slam Dunk (Slam Dunk Champion) (p. 966)
—Kobe Bryant: Slam Dunk Champion / Campeón de Slam Dunk. (p. 966)
—Kobe Bryant, Slam Dunk Champion/Campeon del Slam Dunk. De Leon, Mauricio Velzaquez, tr. (p. 966)
—Mark Mcgwire: The Home Run King. (p. 1095)
—Mark Mcgwire: Record Breaker/Rompe Records. (p. 1095)
—Mark Mcgwire: Rompe Récords (Record Breaker) (p. 1095)
—Mia Hamm: Soccer Star. (p. 1133)
—Michael Jordan: Basketball Superstar. (p. 1134)
—Oscar de la Hoya: Boxeador de Medalla de Oro (Gold-Medal Boxer) (p. 1305)
—Oscar de la Hoya: Gold-Medal Boxer / Boxeador de Medalla de Oro. (p. 1305)
—Oscar de la Hoya, Gold Medal Boxer/Boxeador de Medalla de Oro. De Leon, Mauricio Velzaquez, tr. (p. 1305)
—Power Players (p. 1390)
—Sammy Sosa: Home Run Hitter/Bateador de home Runs. (p. 1508)
—Sammy Sosa: Bateador de Home Runs (Home-Run Hitter) (p. 1508)
—Sammy Sosa, Home Run Hitter/Bateador de Home Runs. De Leon, Mauricio Velzaquez, tr. (p. 1508)
—Tara Lipinski: Super Ice-Skater. (p. 1706)
—Terrell Davis: Corredor de Superbowl (Super Bowl Running Back) (p. 1721)
—Wayne Gretzky: Hockey All-Star. (p. 1865)
Kirkpatrick, Robert. Bob Cousy. (p. 205)
Kirkpatrick, Robin, tr. see Alighieri, Dante.
Kirkpatrick, Taylor. Worthwhile. Lynch, Jason, illus. (p. 1962)
Kirkpatrick, Teresa. Adventures of Four Friends on Vacation (p. 18)
—Roscoe's Forest Adventures. (p. 1489)
Kirkpatrick-Bertels, Malinda. Just Pete. (p. 939)
Kirkup, Mary. More Tales of Granny Grunt. (p. 1175)
—Tales of Granny Grunt. (p. 1702)
Kirkwood. Looking for God. (p. 1051)
Kirkwood, Edith Brown. Animal Children: The Friends of the Forest & the Plain. Ross, M. T., illus. (p. 77)
Kirkwood, G. M. Short Guide to Classical Mythology. (p. 1569)
Kirkwood, Ian. Rob & the Black Mill. (p. 1478)
Kirkwood, James. P. S. Your Cat Is Dead. (p. 1316)
Kirkwood, Jeff. Adventures of Little Mouse. (p. 19)
Kirkwood, Neville A. Jungle Heroes. (p. 935)
Kirkwood, Robert. Looking for Happiness. (p. 1051)
Kirkwood, Roger. Antarctica. (p. 88)
Kirmes, William. Year the Snow Didn't Melt. (p. 1969)
Kirmse, Marguerite, illus. see Davis, Lydia & Ollivant, Alfred.
Kirmse, Marguerite, illus. see Knight, Eric.
Kirn, Walter. Mission to America. (p. 1153)
Kir-on, Callanitte. 3-D Files: Prisoner on the Loose. (p. 1991)
Kirouac Bn, Nicole. I Am Unique. (p. 834)
Kirov, Erica. Chalice of Immortality. (p. 288)
—Magickeepers: The Eternal Hourglass. Fortune, Eric, illus. (p. 1075)
—Magickeepers: The Pyramid of Souls. Bk. 2 Williams, Eric, illus. (p. 1075)
Kirrane, Danielle. Fish Who Swam Too Far. (p. 598)
Kirsch, Alexis, tr. see Allen, Peter, ed.
Kirsch, Alexis, tr. from JPN. Jing: King of Bandits Twilight Tales Kumakura, Yuichi, illus. (p. 918)
Kirsch, Amanda. Honor Bound. (p. 795)
Kirsch, Dieter, jt. auth. see Derkow-Disselbeck, Barbara.
Kirsch - Gambrell, Deneen. No Music for Mouseville. (p. 1259)
Kirsch, R. A. Big One: (A Bicycle Tale) (p. 183)
Kirsch, Suzanne. Flush. Friedland, Joyce & Kessler, Rikki, eds. (p. 608)
Kirsch, Vincent X. Freddie & Gingersnap. Kirsch, Vincent X., illus. (p. 632)
—Freddie & Gingersnap Find a Cloud to Keep. Kirsch, Vincent X., illus. (p. 632)
Kirsch, Vincent X., illus. see Ferris, Jeri Chase.
Kirsch, Vincent X., illus. see Miller, Pat.
Kirsch, Vincent X., illus. see Rockliff, Mara.
Kirshblum, Helen Fried Frommer & Katz, Myrna. Always up Front. (p. 51)
Kirshenblatt, Shane. Dorothy Gale - Journey to Oz. (p. 471)
Kirshner, Judith Russi, et al. Gordon Matta-Clark. (p. 702)
Kirst, Kat, jt. auth. see Kirst, Kathleen.
Kirst, Kathleen & Kirst, Kat. Surviving My Family. House, Nancy, ed. (p. 1687)
Kirsten, A. We Bring the Zoo to You. (p. 1866)
Kirszner, Laurie G. Brief Holt Handbook for UCF. (p. 227)
—Casebook: A Good Man Is Hard to Find. (p. 275)
Kirszner, Laurie G. & Mandell, Stephen R. Brief Holt Handbook with APA Update Card. (p. 227)
Kirton, Enid. Of Boys & Girls: Caribbean Storyteller Classics. (p. 1279)
Kirton, Pamela T., illus. see Garr, Hillary.
Kirwan, Wednesday. Baby Loves to Boogie! Kirwan, Wednesday, illus. (p. 127)
—Baby Loves to Rock! Kirwan, Wednesday, illus. (p. 127)
—Baby Loves to Rock! & Baby Loves to Boogie! 2-Pack. Kirwan, Wednesday, illus. (p. 127)
Kirwan, Wednesday, illus. see Higgins, Melissa.
Kirwan, Wednesday, illus. see Inches, Alison.
Kirwan, Wednesday, illus. see Long, Greg & Edmundson, Chris.
Kiryakova, Niya, illus. see Hunt, Angela.
Kiser, Christina. Cora's Way-A Story of Kindness. (p. 366)
Kiser, Dolores White. Marriage of White Rabbit. (p. 1096)
Kiser, Penny & Bell, Margie, eds. Paris Moderne: Art Deco Works from the Musee d'Art Moderne de la Ville de Paris. (p. 1324)
Kishel, Ann-Marie. Chickens & Chicks. (p. 300)
—Cows & Calves. (p. 374)
—Dogs & Puppies. (p. 462)
—Government Services. (p. 704)
—Jane Addams: A Life of Cooperation. (p. 908)
—Our Leaders. (p. 1309)
—Pigs & Piglets. (p. 1358)
—Recycle. (p. 1452)
—Reduce. (p. 1456)
—Reuse. (p. 1465)
—Rosa Parks: A Life of Courage. (p. 1489)
—Rosa Parks: Una Vida de Valentia. Translations.com Staff, tr. (p. 1489)
—Thomas Jefferson: A Life of Patriotism. (p. 1739)
—Thomas Jefferson: Una Vida de Patriotismo. Translations.com Staff, tr. (p. 1739)
—Turtles & Hatchlings. (p. 1799)
—U. S. Symbols. (p. 1807)
—What Is Government? (p. 1889)
Kishel, Ann-Marie, jt. auth. see Rivera, Sheila.
Kishel, Ann-Marie & Rivera, Sheila. Hexagon. (p. 774)
—Nurse. (p. 1273)
—Oval. (p. 1313)
—Server. (p. 1552)
—Trapezoid. (p. 1779)
Kishimoto, Jon Wayne, illus. see Ronay, Laura.
Kishimoto, Masashi. Art of Naruto: Uzumaki. Wall, Frances, ed. (p. 102)
—Beauty Is the Beast. Kishimoto, Masashi, illus. (p. 154)
—Boy Ninja Kishimoto, Masashi, illus. (p. 218)
—Bridge of Courage. Kishimoto, Masashi, illus. (p. 227)
—Cell Seven Reunion. Kishimoto, Masashi, illus. (p. 286)
—Coward. Kishimoto, Masashi, illus. (p. 373)
—Last Chance Kishimoto, Masashi, illus. (p. 977)
—Naruto Vol. 14. Kishimoto, Masashi, illus. (p. 1229)
—Naruto Vol. 64. Kishimoto, Masashi, illus. (p. 1229)
—Naruto: The First Test. Kishimoto, Masashi, illus. (p. 1229)
—Naruto: The Forest of Death. Kishimoto, Masashi, illus. (p. 1229)
—Naruto. Kishimoto, Masashi, illus. (p. 1229)
—Naruto 28. Kishimoto, Masashi, illus. (p. 1229)
—Naruto 49. (p. 1230)
—Naruto 51. (p. 1230)
—Naruto Anime Profiles (p. 1230)
—Naruto: Chapter Book , Vol. 16: Trapped. Kishimoto, Masashi, illus. (p. 1230)
—Naruto Illustration Book. Kishimoto, Masashi, illus. (p. 1230)
—Naruto - The Official Fanbook. Cunningham, Andrew, tr. from JPN. (p. 1229)
—Official Character Data Book. Kishimoto, Masashi, illus. (p. 1280)
—Secret Plan. Kishimoto, Masashi, illus. (p. 1543)
—Tenth Question Kishimoto, Masashi, illus. (p. 1720)
—Tests of a Ninja. Kishimoto, Masashi, illus. (p. 1723)
—Worst Job Kishimoto, Masashi, illus. (p. 1961)
—Zatch Bell. (p. 1985)
Kishimoto, Masashi, et al. Tekkon Kinkreet. Olsen, Lillian, tr. from JPN. (p. 1716)
Kishimoto, Seishi. O-Parts Hunter. Kishimoto, Seishi, illus. (p. 1274)
Kishimoto, Yuko. God Will Take Care of You. (p. 690)
Kishiro, Yukito. Angel of Victory Kishiro, Yukito, illus. (p. 74)
—Battle Angel Alita Kishiro, Yukito, illus. (p. 145)
—Battle Angel Alita Last Order: Angel of Protest. Vol. 4 Kishiro, Yukito, illus. (p. 145)
—Battle Angel Alita - Last Order Kishiro, Yukito, illus. (p. 145)
—Battle Angel Alita: Last Order Volume 16. (p. 145)
—Fallen Angel Kishiro, Yukito, illus. (p. 566)
—Killing Angel Kishiro, Yukito, illus. (p. 956)
Kishkan, Dan. Porcupines, Politicians & Plato. Lister, Judy, illus. (p. 1386)
Kisinger, E. Jean. Firebug & the Mind Spark. Marta, Diana M., illus. (p. 591)
Kisko, Stephen. Sailing the Puddles. (p. 1503)
Kisner, Kathy. Relationships in Nature: Set Of 6. (p. 1457)
Kiss, Andrew, illus. see Drake, Jane & Love, Ann.

Kiss, Andrew, illus. see Ruurs, Margriet.
Kiss, Gergely, illus. see Frohlich, Anja.
Kiss, Kay. Mr B T Bumblebee. (p. 1184)
Kissane, sheela. Easter Bunny Visits Easterville. Lavery, Breanne, ed. (p. 499)
Kissell, Casey. Awaiting Your Arrival. (p. 120)
Kisseloff, Jeff. Who Is Baseball's Greatest Pitcher? (p. 1915)
Kisseloff, Jeff & Wells, Rosemary. Ruby's Tea for Two. (p. 1494)
Kissinger, Katie. All the Colors We Are/Todos Los Colores de Nuestra Piel: The Story of How We Get Our Skin Color/la Historia de Por Que Tenemos Diferentes Colores de Piel. (p. 45)
Kissock, Heather. Algonquin. (p. 38)
—Algonquins: Les Autochtones du Canada. Karvonen, Tanjah, tr. from ENG. (p. 38)
—American Indian Art & Culture (p. 61)
—Comanche: American Indian Art & Culture. (p. 346)
—Comanche. (p. 346)
—Extreme Sports. (p. 557)
—Horseback Riding. (p. 800)
—Insects. (p. 875)
—Military Vehicles. (p. 1143)
—Moon. (p. 1171)
—Parthenon. (p. 1325)
—Planets. (p. 1368)
—Pyramids. (p. 1421)
—Rainbow. (p. 1435)
—Robert Munsch. (p. 1479)
—Seasons. (p. 1538)
—Stars. (p. 1643)
—Structural Wonders. (p. 1668)
—Sun. (p. 1675)
—Taj Mahal. (p. 1696)
—Underwater Life. (p. 1817)
Kissock, Heather, ed. see Craats, Rennay.
Kissock, Heather, ed. see Crats, Rennay & Rediger, Pat.
Kissock, Heather, ed. see Hamilton, Lynn A.
Kissock, Heather, ed. see Nault, Jennifer.
Kissock, Heather, ed. see Ring, Susan.
Kissock, Heather, jt. auth. see Aspen-Baxter, Linda.
Kissock, Heather, jt. auth. see Baker, David.
Kissock, Heather, jt. auth. see Baldwin, Douglas.
Kissock, Heather, jt. auth. see Banting, Erinn.
Kissock, Heather, jt. auth. see Diemer, Lauren.
Kissock, Heather, jt. auth. see Howse, Jennifer.
Kissock, Heather, jt. auth. see Hurtig, Jennifer.
Kissock, Heather, jt. auth. see Koopmans, Carol.
Kissock, Heather, jt. auth. see Matthews, Sheelagh.
Kissock, Heather, jt. auth. see Morrison, Jessica.
Kissock, Heather, jt. auth. see Rebus, Anna.
Kissock, Heather, jt. auth. see Richardson, Gillian.
Kissock, Heather, jt. auth. see Webster, Christine.
Kissock, Heather & Aspen-Baxter, Linda. Cows. (p. 374)
—Ducks. (p. 488)
—Goats. (p. 687)
—Llamas. (p. 1043)
—Pigs. (p. 1358)
—Ponies. (p. 1382)
Kissock, Heather & McGill, Jordan. Apache: American Indian Art & Culture. (p. 91)
—Apache. (p. 91)
—Tigua: American Indian Art & Culture. (p. 1749)
—Tigua. (p. 1749)
Kissock, Heather & Small, Rachel. Caddo: American Indian Art & Culture. (p. 250)
—Caddo. (p. 250)
—Cherokee: American Indian Art & Culture. (p. 298)
—Cherokee. (p. 298)
Kissock, Heather, ed. Disasters. (p. 447)
—Eiffel Tower. (p. 507)
—Entertainment. (p. 531)
—Lion, the Bear, & the Fox: Is It Better to Cooperate or Compete? (p. 1020)
—Parthenon. (p. 1325)
—Pyramids. (p. 1421)
—Taj Mahal. (p. 1696)
—Trends. (p. 1784)
Kisson, Nisha. Leah - the Fairy of the Lime Tree. KecskTs, Anna, illus. (p. 982)
Kiste, Tori Lynn, illus. see Barnett, Wm.
Kiszko, Martin. Green Poems for a Blue Planet. (p. 722)
Kiszkurno, Irene, tr. see Luetkemeyer, Jenny.
Kit, Oscar. Timeline of the Life of Thomas Jefferson. (p. 1754)
Kita, Joe, ed. Men's Health Best Abs. (p. 1126)
Kita, Suzanne. Three Whales: Who Won the Heart of the World. Sundram, Steve, illus. (p. 1744)
Kitakata, Kenzo. Ashes. Shimokawa, Emi, tr. from JPN. (p. 105)
—Winter Sleep. Schilling, Mark, tr. from JPN. (p. 1938)
Kitami, Yoko. Cactus. (p. 250)
Kitamura, Satoshi. Colours. Kitamura, Satoshi, illus. (p. 346)
—Comic Adventures of Boots. Kitamura, Satoshi, illus. (p. 348)
—Cuando los Borregos No Pueden Dormir. Kitamura, Satoshi, illus. (p. 388)
—Me & My Cat? Kitamura, Satoshi, illus. (p. 1115)
—Millie's Marvellous Hat. (p. 1144)
—Pececito Juega a las Escondidas. (p. 1333)
—Por el Hilo se Saca el Ovillo. Kitamura, Satoshi, illus. (p. 1385)
—Pot-San's Tabletop Tales. Kitamura, Satoshi, illus. (p. 1388)
—UFO Diary. Kitamura, Satoshi, illus. (p. 1807)
—When Sheep Can't Sleep (Cuando los Borregos no Pueden Dormir) (p. 1904)
Kitamura, Satoshi, illus. see Agard, John & Quarto Generic Staff.
Kitamura, Satoshi, illus. see Agard, John.
Kitamura, Satoshi, illus. see Bee, Sarah.
Kitamura, Satoshi, illus. see Jenkins, Martin.
Kitamura, Satoshi, illus. see Oram, Hiawyn.
Kitch, Anne E. Anglican Family Prayer Book. (p. 75)
—Bless This Way. Conahan, Carolyn Digby, illus. (p. 199)
—Cómo Participar en la Liturgia: Un Libro de Para los Ninos Anglicanos-Episcopales. Martell, Oswald Perez, tr. (p. 351)
—What We Do in Advent: An Anglican Kids' Activity Book. Perez, Dorothy Thompson, illus. (p. 1895)
—What We Do in Church: An Anglican Child's Activity Book. Perez, Dorothy Thompson, illus. (p. 1895)
—What We Do in Lent: A Child's Activity Book. Perez, Dorothy Thompson, illus. (p. 1895)
Kitchel, JoAnn E., illus. see Celenza, Anna Harwell.
Kitchel, JoAnn E., illus. see Rottmann, Erik.
Kitchel, Samantha. Beauty in the Beasts. (p. 154)
Kitchell, Joann E., illus. see Celenza, Anna Harwell.
Kitchen, Bert, illus. see Ericsson, Jennifer A.
Kitchen, Bert, illus. see Hooper, Meredith.
Kitchen, David. Adventures of Chesed & Cadence. (p. 17)
—Adventures of David & Freddie Boo. (p. 17)
Kitchen, James D., jt. auth. see Faber, David.
Kitchen, Martha T., tr. see Matthiessen, F. O.
Kitchen, Rebecca, et al. Geography Key Stage - Collins Geographical Enquiry (p. 662)
Kitchen, Willie. Stoic Eyes. (p. 1651)
Kitchens, Jennifer. Who Made the Stars? A Collection of Bedtime Stories. (p. 1916)
Kitching, Laura, illus. see Henry, A.
Kitchings, Taylor. Yard War. (p. 1968)
Kite, Justin. Even Tigers Need to Sleep. (p. 541)
Kite, L. Patricia. Building the Three Gorges Dam (p. 239)
—Leeches. (p. 987)
—Maya Angelou. (p. 1112)
—Silkworms. (p. 1575)
—Unicellular Organisms. (p. 1818)
Kite, Lorien. Chinese: We Came to North America. (p. 307)
—Life in a Rain Forest. (p. 1010)
Kithinji, Gerald, et al. Of Friends, Money & Gossip: 3 Stories & a Play. (p. 1279)
Kitner-Mainello, Shirley. Snooty the Reading Dog: Snooty Helps Miss Em Teach Reading. (p. 1598)
—We'll Love You Forever. (p. 1874)
Kitoh, Moiro. Ours. Nieh, Camellia, tr. from JPN. (p. 1310)
Kitora, Tetsuo, illus. see Paz Lozano, Octavio.
Kitrilakis, Thalia. Biting Sun. Rosenwasser, Rena, ed. (p. 194)
Kitson, Barry, illus. see Spencer, Nick.
Kittay, Matthew & Mason, Chris. Brown University College Prowler off the Record. (p. 232)
Kittell DiOrio, Kathy, illus. see Gilkey, Gail.
Kittinger, Jo S. Breath of Hope. Galey, Chuck, illus. (p. 225)
—Cuando sea Grande: When I Grow Up. Lucas, Margeaux, illus. (p. 388)
—Cuando Sea Grande. Lucas, Margeaux, illus. (p. 388)
—George Washington Carver. (p. 664)
—Going to the Beach. Warren, Shari, illus. (p. 693)
—Helping a Hero. Galey, Chuck, illus. (p. 766)
—House on Dirty-Third Street Gonzalez, Thomas, illus. (p. 803)
—Jane Goodall. (p. 908)
—Lunch with Punch. (p. 1065)
—Rosa's Bus: The Ride to Civil Rights. Walker, Steven, illus. (p. 1489)
Kittinger, Jo S., et al. Aliento de Esperanza. Galey, Chuck, illus. (p. 41)
Kittle, Katrina. Reasons to Be Happy. (p. 1450)
Kittle, Randall D. Biblical Foundation: A Bible Study Series for Developing a Solid Foundational Understanding of Biblical Christianity. (p. 176)
Kittle, Sharon K., jt. auth. see Kittle, Sharon K.
Kittle, Sharon K. & Kittle, Sharon K. Really Read Book. (p. 1450)
Kittleson, Gail. Celebrate Easter. (p. 283)
Kittredge, Caitlin. Coffin Hill - Dark Endeavors Miranda, Inaki, illus. (p. 338)
—Iron Thorn. (p. 888)
—Mirrored Shard: the Iron Codex Book Three. (p. 1149)
—Nightmare Garden: the Iron Codex Book Two. (p. 1255)
Kittredge, Frances. Neeluk: An Eskimo Boy in the Days of the Whaling Ships. Rock, Howard, illus. (p. 1240)
Kittredge, James M. Three Little Explorers Reyes, Glendalys, illus. (p. 1742)
Kitts, Wendy. Sable Island: The Wandering Sandbar (p. 1500)
Kittscher, Kristen. Wig in the Window. (p. 1927)
Kitunga, Demere. Lupompo & the Baby Monkey. (p. 1066)
Kitz, Judith. Grandma Wants You To. (p. 708)
Kitze, Carrie A. I Don't Have Your Eyes. Williams, Rob, illus. (p. 837)
—We See the Moon. Jinshan Painting Academy, illus. (p. 1868)
Kitzmiller, Brenda. Muddy Mud — an Easy to Read Beginning Reader Book. (p. 1189)
Kitzmüller, Christian, illus. see Gordon, David George.
Kiuchi, Tatsuro, illus. see Garland, Sherry.
Kivel, Lee. Lonely Train. Tucci, Al, illus. (p. 1046)
Kivestu, Patty & Pearson, Carey. Rags to Riches: A Dog's Tale of Hope & Friendship. (p. 1433)
Kiwak, Barbara, illus. see Dority, Victoria & Andes, Mary Lou.
Kiwak, Barbara, illus. see Glavich, Mary Kathleen.
Kiwak, Barbara, illus. see Jablonski, Patricia Edward.
Kiwak, Barbara, illus. see Jones, Veda Boyd.
Kiwak, Barbara, illus. see Josephson, Judith Pinkerton.
Kiwak, Barbara, illus. see Mobin-Uddin, Asma.
Kiwak, Barbara, illus. see Wallace, Susan Helen.
Kiwak, Barbara, tr. see Glavich, Mary Kathleen.
Kiwus, Steve. Babes, Beasts, & Brawn: Sculpture of the Fantastic. (p. 123)
Kiyosaki, Kim. Rich Woman: A Book on Investing for Women. (p. 1469)
Kiyosaki, Robert T. Rich Dad Poor Dad for Teens. (p. 1469)
—Rich Dad's Escape from the Rat Race: How to Become a Rich Kid by Following Rich Dad's Advice. (p. 1469)
Kiyosaki, Robert T., jt. auth. see Sutton, Garrett.
Kiyosaki, Robert T. & Lechter, Sharon L. Rich Dad's Escape from the Rat Race: How to Become a Rich Kid by Following Rich Dad's Advice. Hoseley, Rantz, illus. (p. 1469)
—Rich Dad's Prophecy: Why the Biggest Stock Market Crash in History Is Still Coming... & How You Can Prepare Yourself & Profit from It! (p. 1469)
—Rich Dad's Success Stories: Real Life Success Stories from Real Life People Who Followed the Rich Dad Lessons. (p. 1469)
—Secrets about Money: That You Don't Learn in School! (p. 1544)
Kiyuduki, Satoko. Ga - Geijutsuka Art Design Class (p. 652)
—Shoulder-a-Coffin Kuro (p. 1570)
Kizer, Amber. Matter of Days. (p. 1109)
—Pieces of Me. (p. 1356)
—Speed of Light. (p. 1624)
—Wildcat Fireflies: A Meridian Novel. (p. 1931)
Kizer, Andy. To the Overcomers. (p. 1759)
Kizer, Drew. Make Your Stand. (p. 1080)
Kizer, Fran, illus. see Stone, Sandra J.
Kizer, Linda M. Plug, the Lonely Little Fire Hydrant. (p. 1374)
Kizer Whitt, Kelly. Solar System Forecast Allen Klein, Laurie, illus. (p. 1607)
Kizlauskas, Diana, illus. see Monge, Marlyn & Wolfe, Jaymie Stuart.
Kizlik, S. B. & BarCharts Inc., Staff. Algebra (p. 38)
KJA Artists Staff, illus. see Candlewick Press Staff.
KJA Artists Staff, illus. see Graf, Mike & Snedden, Robert.
Kjartansson, Stefan. Sometimes I Work in Atlanta: What I Do When I'm Not with You. (p. 1610)
Kjeldsen, Neil, jt. auth. see Robinson, Garrick.
Kjelgaard, Jim. Big Red. (p. 183)
—Eleven Novels by Jim Kjelgaard Including: The Spell of the White Sturgeon, the Lost Wagon, Trading Jeff & His Dog, Double. (p. 512)
—Story of Geronimo. Meadowcroft, Enid Lamonte, ed. (p. 1658)
Kjellberg, B. Apple Acres: The Farm. (p. 92)
Kjellberg Publishers. Courtnee: A Farm Girl (p. 373)
—Sandy: A City Girl (p. 1511)
Kjellberg Publishing. Abe: A Farm Boy (p. 4)
Kjelle, Marylou. Antoine Lavoisier: Father of Modern Chemistry. (p. 89)
—John Dalton & the Atomic Theory. (p. 921)
—Katherine Paterson. (p. 944)
—Line Dances Around the World. (p. 1019)
—Trends in Hip-Hop Dance. (p. 1784)
Kjelle, Marylou Morano. Alabama: A MyReportLinks. Com Book. (p. 33)
—Alex Rodriguez: Professional Baseball Player. (p. 36)
—Ann M. Martin. (p. 85)
—Arkansas: A MyReportLinks. Com Book. (p. 99)
—Ashlee Simpson. (p. 106)
—Bill Gates: Microsoft Founder & Philanthropist. (p. 186)
—Boston Massacre. (p. 215)
—Brittany Murphy. (p. 230)
—Conquering Disease. (p. 358)
—Dwayne the Rock Johnson. (p. 491)
—Extreme Skateboarding with Paul Rodriquez JR. (p. 556)
—Francis Scott Key. (p. 628)
—Hilary Duff. (p. 779)
—Jacques Cartier. (p. 905)
—Jesse Mccartney. (p. 914)
—John Hancock. (p. 922)
—Kid's Guide to Landscape Design. (p. 953)
—Korea. (p. 967)
—L. M. Montgomery. (p. 969)
—Lion. (p. 1019)
—Lion Paperback. (p. 1020)
—Louis Pasteur: Fighter Against Contagious Disease. (p. 1058)
—Meet Our New Student from Korea. (p. 1122)
—Mixtures & Compounds. (p. 1156)
—Natasha Bedingfield. (p. 1230)
—Pre-Columbian America. (p. 1394)
—Project Guide to Wind, Weather, & the Atmosphere. (p. 1410)
—Properties of Gases. (p. 1411)
—Properties of Liquids. (p. 1411)
—Properties of Metals. (p. 1411)
—Properties of Salts. (p. 1411)
—Properties of Solids. (p. 1411)
—S. E. Hinton: Author of the Outsiders. (p. 1499)
—Saigon. (p. 1503)
—Steve Jobs: Visionary Founder of Apple. (p. 1649)
—Teen Guide to Buying Mutual Funds. (p. 1713)
Kjersgaard, Carly. Muffins' New Beginning. (p. 1189)
Kjesbo, Rynette, jt. auth. see Eisenberg, Rebecca.
Kjesbo, Rynette, jt. auth. see Neal, Angie.
Kladder, Jeri. Story Hour: 55 Preschool Programs for Public Libraries. (p. 1657)
Kladstrup, Kristin. Garden Princess. (p. 656)
—Gingerbread Pirates. Tavares, Matt, illus. (p. 677)
Klages, Ellen. Green Glass Sea. (p. 722)
—White Sands, Red Menace. (p. 1913)
Klam, Cheryl. Pretty One. (p. 1398)
Klam, Cheryl, jt. auth. see Gabel, Claudia.
Klammer, Lynn. God & Me! 2: Ages 2-5 (p. 688)
—Gotta Have God 2: Ages 2-5 Heiser, Aline, illus. (p. 704)
Klanot, Khaya Dawn. Just Hanging Out, a Collection of Poems for Kids. Pirnot, Karen Hutchins, illus. (p. 938)
Klanot, Makenna Karen, illus. see Pirnot, Karen Hutchins.
Klanot, Sameon Clay, illus. see Pirnot, Dr Karen Hutchins & Pirnot, Karen Hutchins.
Klanot, Taryn Lane, illus. see Pirnot, Karen Hutchins.
Klapka, Jerome, jt. auth. see Jerome, Jerome K.
Klar, Jeremy. French Revolution, Napoleon, & the Republic: Liberte, égalité, Fraternité. (p. 636)
—Louisiana Purchase & Westward Expansion. (p. 1059)
Klar, Jeremy & Byers, Ann. Primary Source Investigation of the Trail of Tears. (p. 1400)
Klar, Jeremy & Lily, Henrietta M. Josef Mengele. (p. 926)
Klar, Jeremy, ed. French Revolution, Napoleon, & the Republic: Liberté, Égalité, Fraternité. (p. 636)
Klare, Roger. Gregor Mendel: Genius of Genetics. (p. 723)
Klass, David. Firestorm. (p. 592)
—Grandmaster. (p. 709)
—Home of the Braves. (p. 792)
—Stuck on Earth. (p. 1669)
—Timelock. (p. 1754)
—Whirlwind. (p. 1912)
—You Don't Know Me. (p. 1975)
Klass, David & Klass, Perri. Second Impact. (p. 1539)
Klass, Myleene. Things to Make & Do with Your Children: 150 Activities That You & Your Child Will Love. (p. 1733)
Klass, Perri, jt. auth. see Klass, David.
Klassen, Barnett -, jt. auth. see Barnett, Mac.
Klassen, Joanne. Tools of Transformation: Write Your way to New Worlds of Possibility-in just 5 Minutes. (p. 1767)
Klassen, Jon. I Want My Hat Back. Klassen, Jon, illus. (p. 847)
—This Is Not My Hat. Klassen, Jon, illus. (p. 1736)
Klassen, Jon, illus. see Barnett, Mac.
Klassen, Jon, illus. see Kooser, Ted.
Klassen, Jon, illus. see Snicket, Lemony, pseud.
Klassen, Jon, illus. see Stutson, Caroline.
Klassen, Jon, illus. see Wood, Maryrose.
Klassen, Kirsten L. Katelyn's Affection. (p. 944)
Klaus, Gustav. James Kelmam. (p. 907)
Klaus, Machelle, illus. see Jones, Dee.
Klaus, Sandra. Mustafas Geheimnis: Ein Moslemischer Junge auf der Suche nach Gott. (p. 1194)
—Surrounded by Headhunters. (p. 1686)
—Tainata na Mustapha. (p. 1696)
Klause, Annette Curtis. Blood & Chocolate. (p. 200)
—Freaks: Alive, on the Inside! (p. 631)
—Silver Kiss. (p. 1576)
Klausmeier, Jesse. Open This Little Book. Lee, Suzy, illus. (p. 1299)
Klausner, Julie. Art Girls Are Easy. (p. 102)
Klauss, Anja, illus. see Elschner, Geraldine.
Klauss, Lucas. Everything You Need to Survive the Apocalypse. (p. 546)
Klautsch, Kathy. Pumpkin Fairy. (p. 1416)
Klavan, Andrew. Hostage Run (p. 801)
—Last Thing I Remember (p. 979)
—Long Way Home (p. 1047)
—Nightmare City (p. 1255)
Klavan, Laurence, jt. auth. see Kim, Susan.
Klawitter, Pamela Amick. Centers on the Go: Fun, Creative Activity Folders to Take to Your Seat. VanBlaricum, Pam, ed. (p. 287)
—Critical Thinking Social Studies: Creative Puzzles to Challenge the Brain. Vol. 414 Schwartz, Linda, ed. (p. 383)
—Language Critical Thinking, Grades 5-8: Creative Puzzles to Challenge the Brain. Vol. 412 Schwartz, Linda, ed. (p. 975)
—Math Critical Thinking, Grades 5-8: Creative Puzzles to Challenge the Brain. Vol. 413 Schwartz, Linda, ed. (p. 1105)
—Pick a Project. Clark, Kimberly, ed. (p. 1354)
Klay, Sharon Joy. Denny Grows a Giant Pumpkin. (p. 426)
Klco, Gene. Loon Chick's First Flight. Klco, Gene, photos by. (p. 1052)
Kleback, Amanda. Hoo Hoo's Song. Kleback, Amanda & Kleback, Brian, illus. (p. 795)
Kleback, Brian, illus. see Kleback, Amanda.
Klebanow, Barbara & Fischer, Sara. American Holidays: Exploring Traditions, Customs, & Backgrounds. (p. 61)
Kleczka, John A. Flick the Butterfly: Flick & Mom Go to Grandma's. (p. 603)
Klee, Paul, jt. auth. see Vry, Silke.
Klee, Sheila. Working Together Against Violence in School. (p. 1953)
Kleeman, Terry & Barrett, Tracy. Ancient Chinese World. (p. 68)
Kleemann, Linda. Larry the Turtle When Everyone Helps, Everyone Wins! Malkowski, Melissa, illus. (p. 976)
Klees, Amy. 100 Ways I Love to Read. (p. 1999)
Klehr, Dawn. Cutting Room Floor. (p. 396)
Kleid, Neil, illus. see Talen, Hunter.
Kleid, Neil, jt. text see DeMatteis, J. M.
Kleid, Rodney. Shoshone. (p. 1569)
Kleiman, Andrew, jt. auth. see McIntosh, Kenneth.
Kleiman, Deanna. Jacob's Journey, Living with Type 1 Diabetes. Brieger, Ms. Kirsten, illus. (p. 904)
Kleiman, Deanna M. My Twin Brother. Greenes, Shimra, illus. (p. 1220)
Kleiman, Zalman, illus. see Lehman, Marcus.
Klein. Operation Firestorm. (p. 1300)
Klein, A. M. Doctor Dwarf & Other Poems for Children. (p. 459)
Klein, Abby. April Fool's Surprise. McKinley, John, illus. (p. 93)
—Camping Catastrophe! McKinley, John, illus. (p. 257)
—Don't Sit on My Lunch! Mckinley, John & McKinley, John, illus. (p. 468)
—Easter Egg Hunt. (p. 499)
—Giant Swing. (p. 674)
—Halloween Fraidy-Cat. McKinley, John, illus. (p. 737)
—Halloween Parade. McKinley, John, illus. (p. 738)
—Homework Hassles. McKinley, John, illus. (p. 794)
—King of Show-and-Tell. McKinley, John, illus. (p. 959)
—Looking for Leprachauns. McKinley, John, illus. (p. 1051)
—One Hundredth Day of School! McKinley, John, illus. (p. 1295)
—Penguin Problem. (p. 1337)
—Pumpkin Elf Mystery. McKinley, John, illus. (p. 1416)
—Reading Race. McKinley, John, illus. (p. 1446)
—Ready, Freddy! #26: the Giant Swing. McKinley, John, illus. (p. 1447)
—Ready, Set, Snow! McKinley, John, illus. (p. 1447)
—Save the Earth! (p. 1516)
—Save the Earth! McKinley, John, illus. (p. 1516)
—Second Grade Rules! McKinley, John, illus. (p. 1539)
—Shark Attack! McKinley, John, illus. (p. 1562)
—Stop That Hamster! McKinley, John, illus. (p. 1653)
—Thanks for Giving. McKinley, John, illus. (p. 1725)
—Thanksgiving Turkey Trouble. McKinley, John, illus. (p. 1726)
—Tooth Trouble. (p. 1768)
—Tooth Trouble. McKinley, John, illus. (p. 1768)
Klein, Abby, jt. auth. see Klein, Joel.
Klein, Abby & Mckinley, John. Show & Tell. (p. 1570)
Klein, Adria F. Arnold Schwarzenegger. (p. 100)
—Barack Obama. (p. 137)
—Big Train: Takes a Trip. Cameron, Craig, illus. (p. 184)
—Big Train. Cameron, Craig, illus. (p. 184)

—Big Train Takes a Trip Cameron, Craig, illus. (p. 184)
—Circus Train Cameron, Craig, illus. (p. 322)
—Circus Train & the Clowns Cameron, Craig, illus. (p. 322)
—City Train Cameron, Craig, illus. (p. 324)
—City Train in Trouble Cameron, Craig, illus. (p. 324)
—Freight Train Cameron, Craig, illus. (p. 635)
—Full Freight Train Cameron, Craig, illus. (p. 646)
—Hank Hammer Rowland, Andrew, illus. (p. 742)
—Hank Hammer & the Puppy Rowland, Andrew, illus. (p. 742)
—Max & Buddy Go to the Vet Gallagher-Cole, Mernie, illus. (p. 1110)
—Max & the Adoption Day Party Gallagher-Cole, Mernie, illus. (p. 1110)
—Max Aprende la Lengua de Senas Robledo, Sol, tr. from ENG. (p. 1111)
—Max Celebra el Ano Nuevo Chino Robledo, Sol, tr. from ENG. (p. 1111)
—Max Come Al Aire Libre Robledo, Sol, tr. from ENG. (p. 1111)
—Max Goes Shopping Gallagher-Cole, Mernie, illus. (p. 1111)
—Max Goes to School. Gallagher-Cole, Mernie, illus. (p. 1111)
—Max Goes to the Barber. Gallagher-Cole, Mernie, illus. (p. 1111)
—Max Goes to the Dentist. Gallagher-Cole, Mernie, illus. (p. 1111)
—Max Goes to the Doctor Gallagher-Cole, Mernie, illus. (p. 1111)
—Max Goes to the Farm Gallagher-Cole, Mernie, illus. (p. 1111)
—Max Goes to the Farmers' Market Gallagher-Cole, Mernie, illus. (p. 1111)
—Max Goes to the Fire Station Gallagher-Cole, Mernie, illus. (p. 1111)
—Max Goes to the Grocery Store Gallagher-Cole, Mernie, illus. (p. 1111)
—Max Goes to the Library. Gallagher-Cole, Mernie, illus. (p. 1111)
—Max Goes to the Nature Center Gallagher-Cole, Mernie, illus. (p. 1111)
—Max Goes to the Playground Gallagher-Cole, Mernie, illus. (p. 1111)
—Max Goes to the Recycling Center Gallagher-Cole, Mernie, illus. (p. 1111)
—Max Goes to the Zoo Gallagher-Cole, Mernie, illus. (p. 1111)
—Max Se Queda a Dormir Robledo, Sol, tr. from ENG. (p. 1111)
—Max Stays Overnight Gallagher-Cole, Mernie, illus. (p. 1111)
—Max Va a la Biblioteca Lozano, Clara, tr. (p. 1111)
—Max Va a la Escuela Lozano, Clara, tr. (p. 1111)
—Max Va a la Peluqueria Lozano, Clara, tr. (p. 1111)
—Max Va Al Dentista Lozano, Clara, tr. (p. 1111)
—Max Va Al Doctor. Lozano, Clara, tr. from ENG. (p. 1111)
—Max Va de Paseo Robledo, Sol, tr. from ENG. (p. 1111)
—Max y la Fiesta de Adopcion Robledo, Sol, tr. from ENG. (p. 1111)
—Max's Fun Day Gallagher-Cole, Mernie, illus. (p. 1112)
—Sammy Saw Rowland, Andrew, illus. (p. 1508)
—Sammy Saw & the Campout Rowland, Andrew, illus. (p. 1508)
—Sophie Screwdriver Rowland, Andrew, illus. (p. 1613)
—Sophie Screwdriver & the Classroom Rowland, Andrew, illus. (p. 1613)
—Steve Jobs. (p. 1649)
—Tia Tape Measure Rowland, Andrew, illus. (p. 1746)
—Tia Tape Measure & the Move Rowland, Andrew, illus. (p. 1746)
—Tool School. Rowland, Andrew, illus. (p. 1767)
—Train Time. (p. 1777)
—Train Time. Cameron, Craig, illus. (p. 1777)
Klein, Adria F. & Gallagher-Cole, Mernie. Max Va Al Doctor. Lozano, Clara, tr. from ENG. (p. 1111)
—Max Va Al Zoologico. Lozano, Clara, tr. from ENG. (p. 1111)
Klein, Alina. Rape Girl. (p. 1439)
Klein Bernstein, Sandy. Door in the Sky. (p. 470)
Klein, Bradley S., ed. see Takemori, Lianne K.
Klein, Carol Swartout. Painting for Peace in Ferguson. (p. 1318)
Klein, David, illus. see Ellis, Warren.
Klein, David, jt. auth. see Hughes, Theodore E.
Klein, Dvora. Eleanor Roosevelt. (p. 508)
Klein, Ellen Marie, illus. see Johnson, Dawn M.
Klein, Ellery. Complete Idiot's Guide to Playing the Fiddle. (p. 353)
Klein, Frederick C. For Love of the Cubs: An A-to-Z Primer for Fans of All Ages. Anderson, Mark, illus. (p. 616)
—For the Love of the Cubs: An A to Z Primer for Cubs Fans of All Ages. Anderson, Mark, illus. (p. 616)
—For the Love of the Cubs: An A-to-Z Primer for Cubs Fans of All Ages. Anderson, Mark, illus. (p. 616)
Klein, Fredrick C. For the Love of the Red Sox: An A-to-Z Primer for Red Sox Fans of All Ages. Anderson, Mark, illus. (p. 616)
Klein, Hilary Dole. Day with a Chef. (p. 414)
Klein, Jacky & Klein, Suzy, texts. What Is Contemporary Art? a Guide for Kids. (p. 1889)
Klein, Janet A. Angelic Beginnings: What are Angels? (p. 74)
Klein, Jean-Louis, illus. see Frattini, Stephane.
Klein, Jean-Louis, photos by see Tracqui, Valérie.
Klein, Jen. Jillian Cade: Fake Paranormal Investigator. (p. 917)
Klein, Jennifer. Sir Bumble. (p. 1580)
Klein, Jennifer & Gray, Kevan. University of Pennsylvania College Prowler off the Record. (p. 1821)
Klein, Joel & Klein, Abby. Night I Saved the Universe: From the Files of the Galactic Police Department. (p. 1253)
Klein, Judith Anne. Tuxedo Flyer. (p. 1799)
Klein, Laurie, illus. see Nelson, Amanda.
Klein, Laurie Allen, illus. see Halfmann, Janet.
Klein, Laurie Allen, illus. see Johnson, Jaime Gardner.
Klein, Laurie Allen, illus. see McGranaghan, John.
Klein, Laurie Allen, illus. see Ring, Susan.
Klein, Laurie Allen, illus. see Whit, Kelly.
Klein, Laurie Allen, illus. see Whitt, Kelly Kizer.
Klein, Laurie Allen, illus. see Wlodarski, Loran.
Klein, Laurie Allen, illus. see Yardi, Robin.
Klein, Lisa. Cate of the Lost Colony. (p. 279)
—Love Disguised. (p. 1059)
—Two Girls of Gettysburg. (p. 1803)
Klein, Marissa. Rosie Wants to Be a Fireman. Hagel, Brooke, illus. (p. 1490)
Klein, Michael. Masorah to Targum Onqelos. (p. 1102)
Klein, Nadav & Varacalli, Lauren. Amherst College College Prowler off the Record. (p. 65)
Klein, Nancy, illus. see Beall, Pamela Conn & Nipp, Susan Hagen.
Klein, Nancy Spence, illus. see Beall, Pamela Conn & Nipp, Susan Hagen.
Klein, Nic, jt. illus. see Alixe, Pascal.
Klein, Nic, jt. illus. see Pacheco, Carlos.
Klein, Pamela. Swing! Tanis, Joel E., illus. (p. 1691)
Klein, Peter. Mudpoo & the Magic Tree Stump. De Montignie, Leon, illus. (p. 1189)
—(True) Adventures of Mudpoo. deMontignie, Leon, illus. (p. 1791)
Klein, Rebecca T. Career Building Through Using Digital Publishing Tools. (p. 266)
—Careers for Tech Girls in Science. (p. 267)
—Frequently Asked Questions about Texting, Sexting, & Flaming. (p. 636)
—School Integration: Brown V. Board of Education of Topeka. (p. 1523)
—Your Legal Rights in School (p. 1981)
Klein, Robert, et al. Walt Disney's Comics & Stories #691. Clark, John, ed. (p. 1855)
Klein, Samara Q. Lite'N Up! Laugh Yourself Skinny. Dardik, Helen, illus. (p. 1022)
Klein, Sheri R. Art & Laughter. (p. 101)
Klein, Steve. Power of Early Speed. (p. 1389)
Klein, Susan. Through a Ruby Window: A Martha's Vineyard Childhood. (p. 1744)
Klein, Suzy, jt. text see Klein, Jacky.
Klein, Ted. Rhode Island. (p. 1468)
Klein, Todd, jt. auth. see Miller, Frank.
Kleinberg, Naomi. 1, 2, 3 Count with Me. Moroney, Christopher, illus. (p. 1990)
—Abby Cadabby Makes a Wish. Mathieu, Joe, illus. (p. 2)
—Abby's Pink Party. Brannon, Tom, illus. (p. 2)
—Circle of Friends (Sesame Street) Brannon, Tom, illus. (p. 321)
—Elmo & Abby's Wacky Weather Day (Sesame Street) Brannon, Tom, illus. (p. 515)
—Elmo's Alphabet Soup (Sesame Street) Brannon, Tom, illus. (p. 515)
—Elmo's Christmas Snowman (Sesame Street) Brannon, Tom, illus. (p. 515)
—Elmo's Daddy. Womble, Louis, illus. (p. 515)
—Elmo's Furry Friend (Sesame Street) Moroney, Christopher, illus. (p. 515)
—Elmo's Little Dreidel (Sesame Street) Moroney, Christopher, illus. (p. 515)
—Elmo's Mommy. Womble, Louis, illus. (p. 516)
—Elmo's Monster Mash. Moroney, Christopher, illus. (p. 516)
—Elmo's Rockin' Rhyme Time! (Sesame Street) Brannon, Tom, illus. (p. 516)
—Elmo's Walk in the Woods. Brannon, Tom, illus. (p. 516)
—Firsts! Moroney, Christopher, illus. (p. 598)
—Grouches Are Green. Mathieu, Joe, illus. (p. 725)
—Have Yourself a Furry Little Christmas. Womble, Louis, illus. (p. 754)
—In Elmo's Easter Parade. Moroney, Christopher, illus. (p. 863)
—Is My Face Red! A Book of Colorful Feelings. Mathieu, Joe, illus. (p. 889)
—Lovies. Moroney, Christopher, illus. (p. 1061)
—My Fuzzy Valentine. Womble, Louis, illus. (p. 1209)
—Over on Sesame Street (Sesame Street) A Counting Rhyme. Brannon, Tom, illus. (p. 1313)
—Plant a Tree for Me! Mathieu, Joe, illus. (p. 1368)
—Sesame Beginnings: It's Time! (Sesame Street) Moroney, Christopher, illus. (p. 1553)
—Sesame Beginnings: Oops! (Sesame Street) Moroney, Christopher, illus. (p. 1553)
—Who Are the People in Your Neighborhood? Mathieu, Joe, illus. (p. 1914)
Kleinberg, Naomi, jt. auth. see Random House Editors.
Klein-Carroll, Theodora. Tippy & the Runaway Cloud. (p. 1757)
—Tippy the Raindrop. (p. 1757)
Kleine, Rg. Olseau. (p. 1282)
Kleiner, Mariela. Meet Einstein. Garofoli, Viviana, illus. (p. 1121)
Kleiner, Susan M. & O'Connell, Jeff. Powerfood Nutrition Plan: The Guy's Guide to Getting Stronger, Leaner, Smarter, Healthier, Better Looking, Better Sex with Food! (p. 1390)
Kleinhenz, Sydnie M. Elephants (p. 511)
—Elephants [Scholastic]. (p. 512)
Kleinhenz, Sydnie M., jt. auth. see Meltzer Kleinhenz, Sydnie.
Kleinhenz, Sydnie Meltzer. Trabajar y Jugar. Reasor, Mick, illus. (p. 1774)
Klein-Higger, Joni. Ten Tzedakah Pennies. Leff, Tova, illus. (p. 1719)
Klein-Higger, Joni, jt. auth. see Tesh, Jane.
Kleinman, Andi, illus. see Gowey, Christine Ann.
Kleinman, Bertha A., jt. auth. see Abts, Stacey.
Kleinman, Estelle. Al Capone Does My Shirts. Friedland, Joyce & Kessler, Rikki, eds. (p. 32)
—Bloomability. Friedland, Joyce & Kessler, Rikki, eds. (p. 201)
—City of Ember. Friedland, Joyce & Kessler, Rikki, eds. (p. 323)
—Penderwicks: A Study Guide. Friedland, Joyce & Kessler, Rikki, eds. (p. 1336)
—Tears of a Tiger. Friedland, Joyce & Kessler, Rikki, eds. (p. 1711)
Kleinman, Kathryn. Birthday Cakes. (p. 192)
Kleinman, Liza & Gideon, Brook. Azalea, Unschooled (p. 121)
Kleinmartin, Hex. Seward's Folly & Alaska. (p. 1555)
Kleinmartin, Hex, et al. Rhode Island. (p. 1468)
—Texas. (p. 1723)
—Washington. (p. 1859)
Kleinova, Pavla, illus. see Ruzicka, Oldrich.
Kleinsorge, Mary. Go the Extra Mile. (p. 687)
—Tanya's Lasagna. (p. 1705)
Kleinsorge, Stephanie. Mom & I Adventure to Italy. (p. 1161)
Kleist, Nick. Super Sports Numbers: Understand Place Value. (p. 1682)
Kleman, Jamie. Uncovered. (p. 1812)
Klemek, Ryan, illus. see Gavin, Fred.
Klement, Jon. Rush & the Grey Fox: Ready to Rumble. (p. 1498)
—Smerd's Book of ABC's. (p. 1593)
Klemer, Amy Wade. Scary Snake Monster. (p. 1520)
Klemetz, Leticia, tr. see Alexander, J. H.
Klemm, Rebecca & Rebecca Klemm Charitable Foundation. NumbersAlive! Books for Young Travelers. (p. 1272)
Klemp, Harold. Days of Soul Journal. (p. 415)
—Eternal Dreamer. (p. 539)
—Language of Soul: Keys to Living a More Meaningful Life. (p. 975)
Klemp, Joan, ed. see Davis, James.
Klempner, Rebecca. Dozen Daisies for Raizy: A Shavuos Story. Chava, illus. (p. 474)
Klemstein, Stacey. Silver Spoon. (p. 1577)
Klenovsky, Daniel & Cabala, Edith. Fruto del Espiritu: Mensajes para Ninos. (p. 646)
Klepacki, Linda M., jt. auth. see Scherrer, David L.
Klepack, Hal. Cuba's Military, 1990-2005: Revolutionary Soldiers During Counter-Revolutionary Times. (p. 388)
Klepeis, Alicia. Africa. (p. 26)
—Bizarre Things We've Called Medicine. (p. 194)
—Goblins. (p. 688)
—Mountains, Monsoons, & Mules. (p. 1181)
—Understanding Saudi Arabia Today. (p. 1816)
—Understanding Turkey Today. (p. 1816)
—Vampires: The Truth Behind History's Creepiest Bloodsuckers. (p. 1832)
Klepeis, Alicia & Ventura, Gabriela Baeza. Francisco's Kites. Undercuffler, Gary, illus. (p. 628)
Klepeis, Alicia Z. World's Strangest Foods. (p. 1961)
Klepper, Mark A. Fatherhood. (p. 577)
Klerk, Judith De, see De Klerk, Judith.
Klett, David. Adventures of Willy & Billy: The Lake Lure Chronicles - Book 1. Bk. 1 Lang, Carole, illus. (p. 24)
Klett, David E. Rachel & the Wizard of Lake Lure: The Lake Lure Chronicles - Book 2. (p. 1431)
Kletter, Dana, jt. auth. see Beaton, Clare.
Kletzky, Shanna. New Friends for Lulu: Friends Come in All Colors, Shapes & Sizes! (p. 1244)
Klevanksy, Rhonda, ed. 999 Amazing Animal Facts: Featuring Whales, Elephants, Bears, Wolves, Monkeys, Turtles, Snakes, Birds, Bees, Ants & Many, Many More. (p. 2001)
Klevansky, Rhonda. Exploring Nature: Big Cats. (p. 552)
Kleven, Dean. Little Einsteins. (p. 1027)
Kleven, Elisa. Dancing Deer & the Foolish Hunter. (p. 402)
—Glasswings: A Butterfly's Story. (p. 682)
—Monster in the House. (p. 1167)
—Puddle Pail. Kleven, Elisa, illus. (p. 1414)
—Sun Bread. (p. 1676)
—Welcome Home, Mouse. Kleven, Elisa, illus. (p. 1873)
Kleven, Elisa, illus. see Chronicle Books Staff & Thong, Roseanne.
Kleven, Elisa, illus. see Durango, Julia.
Kleven, Elisa, illus. see Jaskol, Julie & Lewis, Brian.
Kleven, Elisa, illus. see Weber, Elka.
Klevgaard, Cady. Sam & Rexie. (p. 1506)
Kleyla, Mary Pat. Identity Unknown. (p. 852)
Kleyn, Diana. Taking Root: Conversion Stories for Children. (p. 1698)
Kleyn, Diana, jt. auth. see Beeke, Joel R.
Kleyn, Diana & Beeke, Joel. Truths of God's Word. (p. 1794)
Kleypas, Tracy D. Wagon: A Child's Discovery of the World & Her Journey Through It. (p. 1852)
Klick, Gloria, illus. see Wood, Barbie.
Klick, Kenn. Little Coyote Tales. (p. 1026)
Kliczkowski, H., ed. see Cormand, Bernat.
Kliever, S. I. Slave's Quest. (p. 1588)
Kligge, Elizabeth, illus. see Hillson, Ted.
Klim, Christopher. Firecracker Jones Is on the Case. (p. 591)
Kliman, Gilbert. My Personal Story about Hurricanes Katrina & Rita: A Guided Activity Workbook for Middle & High School Students. (p. 1216)
Kliman, Gilbert, et al. My Personal Story about Tropical Storm Stan: A Guided Activity Workbook for Children, Adolescents & Families. (p. 1216)
Kliman, Susie. Jonathon's Thongs. Erlich, Esther, illus. (p. 925)
Klimchuk, Karen. Manuel Makes a Map! (p. 1089)
Klimek, Cheyenne. Belle's Monster. (p. 163)
Klimes, Jan, illus. see Ruzicka, Oldrich & Sanza, Silvie.
Klimes, Jan, illus. see Ruzicka, Oldrich.
Klimit, Gustav. Coloring Book Gustav Klimt. (p. 344)
Klimko, Andrew, illus. see Ross, Jay.
Klimo, Kate. Barry. (p. 140)
—Buddy. (p. 234)
—Centauriad #2: a Gathering of Wings. (p. 287)
—Dash. (p. 409)
—Dog Diaries: Togo. No. 4 Jessell, Tim, illus. (p. 461)
—Dog Diaries #3: Barry. Jessell, Tim, illus. (p. 461)
—Dog Diaries #5: Dash. Jessell, Tim, illus. (p. 461)
—Dragon in the Driveway. Shroades, John, illus. (p. 477)
—Dragon in the Sock Drawer. Shroades, John, illus. (p. 477)
—Dragon Keepers #3: the Dragon in the Library. Shroades, John, illus. (p. 477)
—Dragon Keepers #4: the Dragon in the Volcano. Shroades, John, illus. (p. 477)
—Dragon Keepers #5: the Dragon in the Sea. Shroades, John, illus. (p. 477)
—Dragon Keepers #6: the Dragon at the North Pole. Shroades, John, illus. (p. 477)
—Ginger. (p. 676)
—Stubby. Jessell, Tim, illus. (p. 1668)
—Sweetie Jessell, Tim, illus. (p. 1690)
—Togo. (p. 1762)
—Twinky the Dinky Dog. (p. 1802)
—Twinky the Dinky Dog. Fleming, Michael, illus. (p. 1802)
Klimo, Kate, jt. auth. see Ingle, Annie.
Klimo, Kate, jt. auth. see Worth, Bonnie.
Klimpton, Diana. Amy Wild, Animal Talker - the Musical Mouse. (p. 66)
—Amy Wild, Animal Talker - the Secret Necklace 1. (p. 66)
Kline, C. A. Fright Night Series: Elizabeth Kind & the Strange Things. (p. 639)
—Fright Night Series. (p. 639)
Kline, C. A. & Lauder, M. F. Halloween Night. (p. 738)
Kline, Daniel & Strom, Kay Marshall. Hand in Hand. (p. 740)
Kline, Daniel T., ed. Medieval Literature for Children. (p. 1119)
Kline, Jason. Public Forum Debate. (p. 1414)
Kline, Joel. Cookie's Colorful World. Borsch, Kim, illus. (p. 361)
Kline, Karen E. Bell That Wouldn't Ring. Spencer, Monica, illus. (p. 162)
Kline, Lisa Williams. Floods. (p. 605)
—Write Before Your Eyes. (p. 1963)
Kline, Lpc. Flutter Flies Away: A Book about Rules. (p. 609)
Kline, Michael. Wordplay Cafe: Cool Codes, Priceless Punzles & Phantastic Phonetic Phun. Kline, Michael, illus. (p. 1951)
Kline, Michael, illus. see Friestad, Kathleen M., et al.
Kline, Michael, illus. see Hauser, Jill Frankel.
Kline, Michael, illus. see Littlefield, Cindy A.
Kline, Michael, illus. see Mehra, Heather & McManama, Kerry.
Kline, Michael, illus. see Mitchell, Mari Rutz.
Kline, Michael, illus. see Ollen, Rebecca.
Kline, Michael, illus. see Press, J.
Kline, Michael, illus. see Trumbauer, Lisa.
Kline, Michael P. Wordplay Cafe. (p. 1951)
Kline, Michael P., illus. see Cook, Deanna F.
Kline, Michael P., illus. see Temperley, Howard.
Kline, Nancy. Ohio. (p. 1281)
Kline, Spencer. Adventures of Fujimori-San. Brown, E. Jackie, illus. (p. 18)
Kline, Suzy. Herbie Jones. (p. 769)
—Horrible Harry & the Dead Letters. Remkiewicz, Frank et al, illus. (p. 798)
—Horrible Harry & the Dragon War. (p. 798)
—Horrible Harry & the Dragon War. Remkiewicz, Frank, illus. (p. 798)
—Horrible Harry & the Goog. Remkiewicz, Frank, illus. (p. 798)
—Horrible Harry & the Goog. Remkiewicz, Frank & Frank, Remkiewicz, illus. (p. 798)
—Horrible Harry & the Hallway Bully. (p. 798)
—Horrible Harry & the Hallway Bully. Wummer, Amy, illus. (p. 798)
—Horrible Harry & the Holidaze. Remkiewicz, Frank, illus. (p. 798)
—Horrible Harry & the June Box. Wummer, Amy, illus. (p. 798)
—Horrible Harry & the Locked Closet. Remkiewicz, Frank, illus. (p. 798)
—Horrible Harry & the Missing Diamond. Wummer, Amy, illus. (p. 798)
—Horrible Harry & the Mud Gremlins. Remkiewicz, Frank, illus. (p. 798)
—Horrible Harry & the Scarlet Scissors. Wummer, Amy, illus. (p. 798)
—Horrible Harry & the Triple Revenge. Remkiewicz, Frank, illus. (p. 798)
—Horrible Harry Cracks the Code. Remkiewicz, Frank, illus. (p. 798)
—Horrible Harry Goes Cuckoo. Wummer, Amy, illus. (p. 798)
—Horrible Harry Goes to Sea: Puffine Chapters. (p. 798)
—Horrible Harry Goes to Sea: Puffine Chapters. Remkiewicz, Frank, illus. (p. 798)
—Horrible Harry on the Ropes Wummer, Amy, illus. (p. 798)
—Horrible Harry on the Ropes. Remkiewicz, Frank & Wummer, Amy, illus. (p. 798)
—Horrible Harry Takes the Cake. Remkiewicz, Frank, illus. (p. 798)
Kline, Suzy & Remkiewicz, Frank. Horrible Harry Bugs the Three Bears. Remkiewicz, Frank & Remkiewicz, illus. (p. 798)
Kline, Tom. God's Love in Action: The Amazing Gift of Jesus. Weber, Penny, illus. (p. 691)
Kline, Trish. Earth Academy 7, Purple Book One: Journey to Earth. (p. 495)
—Earth Academy 7, Red Book One: The Aliens Are Coming! (p. 495)
—Fang Gang: KA Reader 4. (p. 571)
—Super Hero: KA Reader 1. (p. 1680)
Kline, Trish & Donev, Mary. Busy Preschooler's Guide to Learning. (p. 246)
—Celebration of Letters A & B: Busy Preschoolers. (p. 285)
—Coming Home: KA Reader 8. (p. 348)
—Day at the Zoo: KA Reader 3. (p. 412)
—Don't Frown, Clown! KA Reader 9. (p. 467)
—Ghost Hunter & the Ghost of the Amazon Warrior. Droney, John, illus. (p. 670)
—Hoops in the Coop: KA Reader 7. (p. 795)
—It's a Party! KA Reader 2. (p. 896)
—Scary Day in the Forest: KA Reader 5. (p. 1520)
—Where Can Lost Bee Be? KA Reader 6. (p. 1906)
Klineman, Harvey, illus. see Ganz, Yaffa.
Klineman, Harvey, illus. see Hodes, Loren.
Klineman, Harvey, jt. auth. see Shollar, Leah Perl.
Kling, Andrew. Cell Phones. (p. 286)
Kling, Andrew A. British Monarchy. (p. 230)
—Cloud Computing. (p. 334)
—Surveillance. (p. 1686)
—Web 2.0: Basiswissen in 50 x 2 Minuten. (p. 1870)
Kling, Andrew A., ed. see Busby, Barbara Sheen.
Kling, Andrew A., jt. auth. see Taylor, Robert.
Kling, Andrew A., ed. Age of Exploration. (p. 29)
Kling, Kevin. Big Little Brother. Monroe, Chris, illus. (p. 182)
—Big Little Mother. Monroe, Chris, illus. (p. 182)
Kling, Leslie, illus. see Chandler, Bill & Chandler, Marie.
Klingbeil, Kendall, illus. see Torrel, Wendy.
Klingel, Cynthia, jt. auth. see Klingel, Cynthia Fitterer.
Klingel, Cynthia, jt. auth. see Klingel/Noyed.
Klingel, Cynthia & Noyed, Robert B. Ears / Los Oidos. (p. 494)

K

—Ears (Los Oidos). (p. 494)
—Ears/Los Oidos. (p. 494)
—Eyes. (p. 558)
—Eyes / Los Ojos. (p. 558)
—Eyes/Los Ojos. (p. 558)
—Feet. (p. 580)
—Feet / Los Pies. (p. 580)
—Feet/Los Pies. (p. 581)
—Hair. (p. 735)
—Hair / el Cabello. (p. 736)
—Hair/el Cabello. (p. 736)
—Hands. (p. 741)
—Hands / Las Manos. (p. 741)
—Hands/Las Manos. (p. 741)
—Mouth. (p. 1182)
—Mouth / la Boca. (p. 1182)
—Mouth/la Boca. (p. 1182)
—Nose. (p. 1266)
—Nose / la Nariz. (p. 1266)
—Nose/la Nariz. (p. 1266)
—Skin. (p. 1585)
—Skin / la Piel. (p. 1585)
—Skin/la Piel. (p. 1585)
Klingel, Cynthia Fitterer. Ack! There's a Bug in My Ear! (And Other Sayings That Just Aren't True) Cole, Mernie & Gallagher-Cole, Mernie, illus. (p. 9)
Klingel, Cynthia Fitterer & Klingel, Cynthia. Alexander Graham Bell: Inventor. (p. 36)
—Amelia Earhart: Aviation Pioneer. (p. 58)
—Go Fly a Kite! (and Other Sayings We Don't Really Mean) Gallagher-Cole, Mernie, illus. (p. 686)
—You Let the Cat Out of the Bag! (and Other Crazy Animal Sayings) Cole, Mernie, illus. (p. 1975)
—You're Clean as a Whistle! (And Other Silly Sayings) Cole, Mernie & Gallagher-Cole, Mernie, illus. (p. 1982)
Klingel, Deanna K. Avery's Battlefield. (p. 119)
—Avery's Crossroad. (p. 119)
Klingel, Deb. Jelly Bean Green Thing. (p. 912)
Klingel/Noyed & Klingel, Cynthia. Thomas Edison: Inventor. (p. 1738)
Klingensmith, Ryan Lee & Klingensmith, Sherri Ann. Starlight Blue: A New Baby. Rollinger, Marsha, illus. (p. 1642)
Klingensmith, Sherri Ann, jt. auth. see Klingensmith, Ryan Lee.
Klinkenborg, Verlyn. Rural Life. (p. 1497)
Klinkerman, Anthonette. Battle of the Grandmas. (p. 146)
Klinting, Lars. Beaver the Tailor: A How-to Picture Book. Klinting, Lars, illus. (p. 155)
—Castor Jardinero. (p. 277)
—Castor Pintor. (p. 277)
—Castor Sastre. (p. 277)
Klio Burrell, Carol. Welcome to the Tribe! (p. 1874)
Klio Burrell, Carol, tr. see Magnet, Julien.
Klippenstein, Blaine. Andrea's Fiddle. Jedele, Christie, illus. (p. 72)
Kliros, Thea, illus. see Andersen, Hans Christian.
Kliros, Thea, illus. see Burnett, Frances Hodgson.
Kliros, Thea, illus. see Domain Public Staff.
Kliros, Thea, illus. see Dover Staff.
Kliros, Thea, illus. see Garis, Howard Roger.
Kliros, Thea, illus. see Grahame, Kenneth.
Kliros, Thea, illus. see Hoffmann, E. T. A.
Kliros, Thea, illus. see Spyri, Johanna & Blaisdell, Robert.
Kliros, Thea, illus. see Stevenson, Robert Louis.
Kliros, Thea, illus. see Stoker, Bram.
Kliros, Thea, illus. see Twain, Mark, pseud, et al.
Kliros, Thea, illus. see Williams, Margery.
Klise, James. Art of Secrets. (p. 102)
—Love Drugged. (p. 1059)
Klise, Kate. Circus Goes to Sea. Klise, M. Sarah, illus. (p. 322)
—Dying to Meet You. Klise, M. Sarah, illus. (p. 491)
—Far from Normal. (p. 572)
—Grammy Lamby & the Secret Handshake. Klise, Kate & Klise, M. Sarah, illus. (p. 706)
—Greetings from the Graveyard. Klise, M. Sarah, illus. (p. 723)
—Grounded. (p. 725)
—Hollywood, Dead Ahead. (p. 789)
—Hollywood, Dead Ahead. Klise, M. Sarah, illus. (p. 789)
—Homesick. (p. 793)
—Little Rabbit & the Meanest Mother on Earth. Klise, M. Sarah, illus. (p. 1034)
—Over My Dead Body. Klise, M. Sarah, illus. (p. 1313)
—Phantom of the Post Office. (p. 1349)
—Phantom of the Post Office. Klise, M. Sarah, illus. (p. 1349)
—Pop Goes the Circus! Klise, M. Sarah, illus. (p. 1384)
—Regarding the Bathrooms: A Privy to the Past. Klise, Kate & Klise, M. Sarah, illus. (p. 1457)
—Regarding the Sink: Where, Oh Where, Did Waters Go? Klise, M. Sarah, illus. (p. 1457)
—Shall I Knit You a Hat? A Christmas Yarn. Klise, M. Sarah, illus. (p. 1559)
—Stand Straight, Ella Kate: The True Story of a Real Giant. Klise, M. Sarah, illus. (p. 1639)
—Till Death Do Us Bark. (p. 1750)
—Till Death Do Us Bark. Klise, M. Sarah, illus. (p. 1750)
—Why Do You Cry? Not a Sob Story. Klise, M. Sarah, illus. (p. 1924)
Klise, Kate, jt. auth. see Klise, Kate.
Klise, Kate & Klise, Kate. Regarding the Bees: A Lesson, in Letters, on Honey, Dating, & Other Sticky Subjects. Klise, M. Sarah, illus. (p. 1457)
Klise, Kate & Klise, M. Sarah. Greatest Star on Earth. Klise, M. Sarah, illus. (p. 720)
—Loch Ness Punster. Klise, M. Sarah, illus. (p. 1044)
—Regarding the Trees: A Splintered Saga Rooted in Secrets. (p. 1457)
—Show Must Go On! (p. 1570)
—Till Death Do Us Bark. Klise, Kate & Klise, M. Sarah, illus. (p. 1750)
Klise, M. Sarah, illus. see Klise, Kate & Klise, Kate.
Klise, M. Sarah, illus. see Klise, Kate.
Klise, M. Sarah, jt. auth. see Klise, Kate.
Klistoff, Lorin. Literacy Activities - Science. (p. 1022)
Klistoff, Lorin, ed. see Crane, Kathy Dickerson.
Klitzner, Irene. Sean Michael K. Whistles the Wrong Way! Who, Carrie Lou, illus. (p. 1537)
Klitzner, Irene & Adams, Peggy. Today Is My Birthday & I Have Nothing to Wear! Lou Who, Carrie, illus. (p. 1760)
Klivans, Elinor. Cupcakes! Ruffenach, France, photos by. (p. 392)
Klobuchar, Lisa. 1963 Birmingham Church Bombing: The Ku Klux Klan's History of Terror. (p. 2002)
—Africans of the Ghana, Mali, & Songhai Empires. (p. 28)
—Badgers & Other Mustelids. (p. 132)
—Cockatiels & Other Parrots. (p. 337)
—Elizabeth Blackwell: With Profiles of Elizabeth Garrett Anderson & Susan la Flesche Picotte. (p. 513)
—How Did They Do That? (p. 806)
—Iran-Contra Affair: Political Scandal Uncovered (p. 886)
—Third Parties: Influential Political Alternatives (p. 1734)
—USA in Our World. (p. 1826)
Klobuchar, Lisa, jt. auth. see Sohn, Emily.
Klocek-Lim, Christine. Disintegrate. (p. 451)
Klock, Kimberly, illus. see Kountz, Charity.
Kloczko, Edouard. Magical World of Tolkien. Camprubi, Krystal, illus. (p. 1075)
Klodt, Louise. Door to Kandalaura: Book One of the Kandalaura Chronicles. (p. 470)
Kloefkorn, William. Alvin Turner As Farmer. (p. 51)
Kloepfer, John. Empire State of Slime. DeGrand, Ned & DeGrand, David, illus. (p. 521)
—Galaxy's Most Wanted. Edwards, Nick, illus. (p. 653)
—Into the Dorkness. Edwards, Nick, illus. (p. 881)
—Nothing Left to Ooze. DeGrand, David, illus. (p. 1268)
—Sludgment Day. (p. 1591)
—Sludgment Day. Wolfhard, Steve, illus. (p. 1591)
—Undead Ahead. Wolfhard, Steve, illus. (p. 1813)
—Zombie Chasers. Wolfhard, Steve, illus. (p. 1988)
—Zombie Chasers #7: World Zombination. DeGrand, David, illus. (p. 1988)
—Zombie Chasers - Zombies of the Caribbean. DeGrand, David, illus. (p. 1988)
Kloet, Chris, ed. see Renshaw, Amanda.
Klofkorn, Lisa, illus. see Ahouse, Jeremy John & Barber, Jacqueline.
Klofkorn, Lisa, illus. see Barber, Jacqueline, et al.
Klofkorn, Lisa, illus. see Barber, Jacqueline.
Klofkorn, Lisa, illus. see Erickson, John & Willard, Carolyn.
Klofkorn, Lisa, illus. see Gould, Alan.
Klofkorn, Lisa, illus. see Kopp, Jaine.
Klofkorn, Lisa, illus. see Sutter, Debra, et al.
Klontz, Mary-Hannah & Kuntz, Ron. There's Noel in Rat. (p. 1731)
Kloran, Francis M. BLN: Babel Loth Nion. (p. 200)
Klose, Liz, jt. auth. see Beck, Alison.
Klose, Liz & Peters, Laura. Roses for Ontario. (p. 1490)
Kloser, David. Stepping up to the Plate: Inspiring Interviews with Major Leaguers. (p. 1648)
Kloske, Geoffrey. Once upon a Time, the End: Asleep in 60 Seconds. (p. 1293)
—Once upon a Time, the End: Asleep in 60 Seconds. Blitt, Barry, illus. (p. 1293)
Klossner, John, illus. see Schwartz, Barry L. & Levine, Mark H.
Kloster, Kaia L. Rainy Day Duck. (p. 1436)
Klosterman, Lorrie. Drug-Resistant Diseases & Superbugs. (p. 486)
—Endocrine System. (p. 527)
—Excretory System. (p. 547)
—Facts about Caffeine. (p. 561)
—Facts about Drug Dependence to Treatment. (p. 561)
—Facts about Drugs & the Body. (p. 561)
—Immune System. (p. 861)
—Leukemia. (p. 1003)
—Meningitis. (p. 1126)
—Nervous System. (p. 1241)
—Rabies. (p. 1430)
—Reproductive System. (p. 1461)
—Skin. (p. 1585)
—Vision Disorders. (p. 1844)
Klostermann, Penny Parker. There Was an Old Dragon Who Swallowed a Knight. Mantle, Ben, illus. (p. 1730)
Klotz, Bryan, illus. see Shragg, Karen I.
Klubien, Jorgen, illus. see Burton, Tim & Disney Book Group Staff.
Kluever, Karen T. Synago Friends for the Journey Student. (p. 1693)
Kluever, Karen Trogdon, jt. auth. see Hamby, Joe.
Klug, Dave, illus. see Cobb, Vicki.
Klug, Dave, illus. see Dyson, Marianne J.
Klug, David, illus. see Bryan, Sarah Jane & Bellenson, Suzanne.
Klug, David, illus. see Conlon, Mara.
Klug, Eric. Monster in My Closet. Klug, Eric, illus. (p. 1167)
Klug, Frances Marie. Stories from Heaven Klug, Frances Marie, ed. (p. 1654)
—Stories from Heaven. (p. 1654)
Klug, Kirsten. Healthy Smiles! (p. 759)
—Oregon Is Fun! Rain or Sun! Skorpen, Neal, illus. (p. 1303)
Klug, Leigh A., illus. see Shields, Kathleen J.
Kluge, Christine Boyka. Stirring the Mirror. (p. 1651)
Kluger, Garry M. Till Death or Whatever Do Us Part. Landes, William-Alan, ed. (p. 1750)
Kluger, Jeffrey. Freedom Stone. (p. 635)
—Splendid Solution: Jonas Salk & the Conquest of Polio. (p. 1630)
Kluger, Steve. My Most Excellent Year: A Novel of Love, Mary Poppins, & Fenway Park. (p. 1214)
Klund, Barbara, illus. see Glossop, Jennifer.
Klunder, Barbara. Other Goose: Recycled Rhymes for Our Fragile Times... (p. 1306)
Klusza, Maureen, illus. see Napoli, Donna Jo & DeLuca, Doreen.
Kluth, Paula & Kluth, Victoria. A Is for All Aboard!" Littlejohn, Brad, illus. (p. 1)
Kluth, Paula & Schwarz, Patrick. Pedro's Whale (p. 1334)
Kluth, Victoria, jt. auth. see Kluth, Paula.
Klutz, contrib. by. SlingChute. (p. 1590)
Klutz Editors. Books in a Cup; Grape. (p. 212)
—Cootie Catcher Book. (p. 365)
—Design Your Own Charm Watch. (p. 430)
—Doodlewire. (p. 470)
—Encyclopedia of Immaturity (p. 525)
—Encyclopedia of Immaturity: How to Never Grow Up. (p. 525)
—Encyclopedia of My Immaturity: Your Own Personal Stinky Diary Ah. (p. 525)
—Face Painting. (p. 560)
—Paper Fashions. (p. 1322)
—Rule the World: 119 Shortcuts to Total World Domination. (p. 1495)
—Shrink & Link Jewelry: Make Mix-and-Match Shrink Art Jewelry with over 50 Traceable Designs. (p. 1571)
Klutz Editors, ed. see Cassidy, John.
Klutz Editors, ed. see Chorba, April.
Klutz Editors, ed. see Hannigan, Paula.
Klutz Editors, ed. see Johnson, Anne Akers & Murphy, Pat.
Klutz Editors, ed. see Pilkey, Dav.
Klutz Editors, jt. auth. see Grossblatt, Ben.
Klutz Editors, jt. auth. see Haab, Sherri.
Klutz Editors, jt. auth. see Johnson, Anne Akers.
Klutz Editors, jt. auth. see Murphy, Pat.
Klutz Editors, jt. auth. see Phillips, Karen.
Klutz Editors, jt. auth. see Sherman, Michael.
Klutz Editors, jt. auth. see Steele-Saccio, Eva.
Klutz Editors, jt. auth. see Steele-Staccio, Eva.
Klutz Editors & Boyle, Brendan. Klutz Book of Inventions. Cassidy, John, ed. (p. 963)
Klutz Editors & Burton, Bonnie, eds. Fingerprint Fabulous: Create Sweet & Sparkly Thumbprint Art. (p. 589)
Klutz Editors & Dzwonik, Cristian. Amigas para Siempre. Esteve, Laura, tr. (p. 65)
—De las 1000 y una Actividades. (p. 416)
Klutz Editors, contrib. by. Klutz Kwiz Gizmo. (p. 964)
—Shrinky Dinks Refill (p. 1571)
—Window Art Deluxe Refill Set. (p. 1936)
Klutz Editors, ed. Draw Star Wars Rebels. (p. 481)
—Fuzzy Little Monkeys. (p. 651)
—Glossy Bands: Stretchy Bracelets to Share with Your Friends. (p. 685)
—Little Letters (p. 1030)
—Most Amazing Thumb Doodles Book: In the History of the Civilized World. (p. 1177)
—My Style Studio: Design & Trace Your Own Fashions. (p. 1219)
—Paper Fashions Fancy. (p. 1322)
—Scoubidou. (p. 1532)
—Shrinky Dinks. (p. 1571)
—TRIPtivities. (p. 1787)
—Why I Love My Dad. (p. 1925)
—Window Art. (p. 1936)
Klutz Editors, et al. Dress up Your Own Paper Pups. (p. 485)
Klutz Labs Scientists Staff, jt. auth. see Murphy, Pat.
Klutz Press Staff. Arte en Ventanas. (p. 103)
—Books-in-a-Cup: Orange. (p. 212)
—libro del body Crayon. (p. 1006)
—Monsters. (p. 1168)
Klutz Press Staff, ed. see Steele-Staccio, Eva.
Klutz Press Staff, jt. auth. see Stein, David.
Klutz Press Staff & Rose, Amber. Monsters. (p. 1168)
Klutz Press Staff, contrib. by. Extra Stuff for Window Art. (p. 555)
—Klutz Extra Stuff: Building Cards Castles - How to Build Castles. (p. 964)
—Wishing Stars. (p. 1940)
Klutz Press Staff, creator. Magnetic A to Z. (p. 1075)
—Mi Vida Segun Yo. (p. 1133)
Klutz Press Staff, ed. Most Incredible, Outrageous, Packed-to-The Gills, Bulging-at-the-Seams Sticker Book You've Ever Seen. (p. 1177)
Kluver, Cayla. Legacy. Isern, Carol, tr. (p. 987)
—Queen's Choice. (p. 1425)
Kluzek, Stan & Coldwell, Andrew. READ IT Home Reading Senior Level: U.S. Version. (p. 1443)
K.M. Mohr, John Kelley and. Waking Dalifi. (p. 1853)
Kmiec, Douglas W. Can a Catholic Support Him? Asking the Big Questions about Barack Obama. (p. 258)
Kmiec, Irka. Princess Ella Bell. (p. 1403)
—Princess Ella Bella. (p. 1403)
Knaak, Richard A., jt. auth. see Lee, Myung.
Knaak, Richard A., tr. see Lee, Myung-Jin.
Knaak, Richard A. & Jae-hwan, Kim. Shadows of Ice. (p. 1558)
K'naan, jt. auth. see Sol.
Knab, Christopher & Day, Bartley F. Music Is Your Business: The Musician's FourFront Strategy for Success. Cook, Sue D., ed. (p. 1193)
Knaggs, Robin A. I Am a Squirmy Wormy. (p. 832)
Knapczyk, Dennis. Teaching Self-Discipline: A self-monitoring Program. (p. 1710)
Knapik-Kick, Kathryn. Many Tales of Sammy the Cat. (p. 1089)
Knapke, Debra, jt. auth. see Beck, Alison.
Knapke, Debra & Beck, Alison. Annuals for Ohio. (p. 87)
—Best Garden Plants for Ohio. (p. 169)
—Perennials for Ohio. (p. 1341)
Knapman, Tim. Cowboy Can Be Kind. (p. 373)
—Friendliest Ballerina. Rovolio, Jimothy, illus. (p. 637)
—Princesses Love to Share! Rovolio, Jimothy, illus. (p. 1406)
Knapman, Timothy. Great Easter Egg Scramble. Walker, David, illus. (p. 715)
—Guess What I Found in Dragon Wood. Millward, Gwen, illus. (p. 729)
—Let's Read!/Little Ogre's Surprise Supper. Cort, Ben, illus. (p. 1000)
—Pirate Who Said Please. (p. 1363)
—Soon. Benson, Patrick, illus. (p. 1613)
Knapp, Brent W. Animal Alphabet: From Alligator to Zebra. (p. 76)
—Discovering My ABC's: My First Introduction to the Alphabet. (p. 449)
—Learning My ABC's: Introducing the Alphabet. (p. 985)
Knapp, Cheryl, illus. see Drake, Michelle.
Knapp, J. Richard. Bobby's Story: An Amazing Story of Teen Courage. (p. 206)
Knapp, Jennifer F. Walk with Ovid. (p. 1854)
Knapp, Jodi. Adventures of Kelly & Lucky: The Beginning. (p. 19)
Knapp, Kate. Ruby Red Shoes. (p. 1493)
Knapp, Rene & Berger, Marjorie B. Little Lost Allygator. (p. 1030)
—Little Lost Allygator. Kurt D Williams and Jeff Baker, illus. (p. 1031)
Knapp, Ron. Bloodsucking Creatures. (p. 201)
—Connecticut: A MyReportLinks. Com Book. (p. 357)
—Fighting U. S. Generals of World War II. (p. 586)
—Indiana: A MyReportLinks.com Book. (p. 871)
—Mummy Secrets Uncovered. (p. 1191)
—North Dakota: A MyReportLinks. Com Book. (p. 1265)
—Tennessee: A MyReportLinks. Com Book. (p. 1720)
Knapp, Ruthie. Who Stole Mona Lisa? McElmurry, Jill, illus. (p. 1917)
Knapp, Susan. Bells Goes to the Fair. Whitehurst, John et al, illus. (p. 163)
Knapp, Vincent, photos by see Hoppen, Kelly.
Knapp-Fisher, H. C. Outline of World History: For Boys & Girls. (p. 1313)
Knapp-Grosz, Tamara & Loyd, Elizabeth. Some Things Are Made to Smoke. McCue, Patrick, illus. (p. 1609)
Knapps, Susan Wadino. Baby Bear to the Rescue! (p. 125)
Knapsey, Kath, jt. auth. see Carr, Roger Vaughan.
Knauer, Kelly, ed. see Time for Kids Magazine Staff.
Knauf, Barbara. When I Was Little in the Old Country: Childhood Memories of a German Grandmother. (p. 1903)
Knaupp, Andrew, illus. see Rich, J. Milton.
Knaus, Jill, tr. see Krakow, Amy.
Knaus, Patricia. Letters from Space. The Mousekins Staff, illus. (p. 1002)
Knebel, Arthur & Udelhoven, Hermann-Josef. Modern Era through World War II: From the 18th Century To 1945. (p. 1158)
Kneblik, Debi. Shipwreck of Knottingburg. (p. 1567)
Knecht, Alicia. Sparky & Millie's Ocean Adventure. (p. 1622)
Knecht, Eileen. Christine's Christmas Crib. (p. 312)
Knecht, F. J. Child's Bible History. Schumacher, Philip, tr. (p. 304)
Knechtel, Crystal, jt. auth. see Knechtel, Mark.
Knechtel, Mark & Knechtel, Crystal. Pollywog Pickle's Great Big Plan. (p. 1381)
Kneece, Mark & Serling, Rod. Will the Real Martian Please Stand Up? McHargue, Dove & Ellis, Rich, illus. (p. 1932)
Kneen, Maggie. Chocolate Moose. (p. 309)
—Christmas Surprise. Kneen, Maggie, illus. (p. 315)
—First Christmas: An Angel Came to Nazareth. (p. 593)
—Some Pig! A Charlotte's Web Picture Book. (p. 1609)
—Two by Two: The Story of Noah & the Ark. (p. 1803)
Kneen, Maggie, illus. see Bell, Michael D.
Kneen, Maggie, illus. see Brodien-Jones, Christine.
Kneen, Maggie, illus. see Godden, Rumer.
Kneen, Maggie, illus. see Rylant, Cynthia.
Kneen, Maggie, illus. see White, E. B.
Kneen, Maggie, illus. see Wood, A. J.
Kneen, Maggie, jt. auth. see Wood, Amanda.
Kneep, Maggie, illus. see Randall, Ronne.
Kneff, Steff F. Emlyn & the Gremlin: Emlyn & the Gremlin Series. Spooner, Luke, illus. (p. 519)
Kneib, Martha. Benin. (p. 164)
—Chad. (p. 288)
—Christopher Columbus: Master Italian Navigator in the Court of Spain. (p. 316)
—Historical Atlas of the American Revolution. (p. 783)
—Kareem Abdul-Jabbar. (p. 943)
—Meningitis. (p. 1126)
—Turkey: A Primary Source Cultural Guide. (p. 1797)
Kneib, Martha, jt. auth. see Pietrzyk, Leslie.
Kneidel, Sally. Creepy Crawlies & the Scientific Method: More Than 100 Hands-On Science Experiments for Children. (p. 381)
Kneisley, Amy. Gentle Elephant. Tina, Dunnier, illus. (p. 661)
Knelman, Martin. Mike's World: The Life of Mike Myers. (p. 1141)
Knesek, Marian. Sage & the Peacock. Buehrle, Jackie, illus. (p. 1502)
—Zane & the Armadillo. Leipsic, Regina, illus. (p. 1984)
Knets, Peggy L. In the Eyes of a Boy, Forgiveness, the News, Climate Change & the Olympics. (p. 866)
Kneupper, Setch, illus. see Specter, Baron.
Kneupper, Setch, illus. see Spector, Baron.
Knevels, Gertrude. Wonderful Bed. Chamberlin, Emily Hall, illus. (p. 1948)
Knibbs, Carl. Tickly Ogre. (p. 1747)
Knickelbine, Scott. Great Peshtigo Fire: Stories & Science from America's Deadliest Fire. (p. 717)
Knickerbocker, Peggy, jt. auth. see Hirsheimer, Christopher.
Knickerbocker, S. J. King of the Ball. (p. 959)
Knickerbocker-Silva, Heather. Tinkle, Tinkle When I Go to the Potty. (p. 1756)
Knife, Ivan M. Uses the. Black Thursday. (p. 197)
Kniffe, Sen'no. Eden (p. 504)
Kniffe, Sophie & De Bourgoing, Pascale. Weather. (p. 1869)
Kniffke, Sophie, et al. Coche. (p. 337)
—Tiempo. (p. 1747)
Knight, Andrew. Dead Beckoning. (p. 416)
—Monster in the Loch. (p. 1167)
Knight, Arabella. Susie in Servitude. (p. 1688)
Knight, Aya. Chronicles of Kale: Dawn of Retribution. (p. 317)
Knight, Barbara. Cowboys with penny the mustang Pony. (p. 374)
—Lost Boy. (p. 1055)
—Rescue, with Penny the Mustang Pony. (p. 1462)
Knight, Barbara Maxine. Storm. (p. 1655)
Knight, Betty. Sailwind the Seabird. Aton, Barbara, illus. (p. 1503)
Knight, Bob & Hammel, Bob. Knight: My Story. (p. 964)
Knight, C. R., illus. see Du Chaillu, Paul.
Knight, Charles R. Charles R. Knight: Autobiography of an Artist. Ottaviani, Jim, ed. (p. 292)
Knight, Chris. Body of Jesus. (p. 207)

—Karen Bighead: The Story of a Little Girl with a Big Head. (p. 943)
—Piggy's Party. (p. 1358)
—Skaggy the Scarecrow: A Halloween Story. (p. 1583)
—Statue. (p. 1644)
Knight, Christo. Adventures of Charlz from Marz: Book I Going Home. (p. 17)
Knight, Christopher. World Is Black & White. (p. 1956)
Knight, Christopher G., photos by see Lasky, Kathryn.
Knight, Clayton & Royce, Ralph. We Were There at the Normandy Invasion. (p. 1868)
Knight, Dahna. Cartoon Chef: Zoo Animals. (p. 272)
Knight, Deborah Janet. Puzzling Picnic. Hauvette, Marion, illus. (p. 1421)
Knight, Deidre Denise. Wash Cloth & the Turtle. Milosevic, Tamara, illus. (p. 1859)
Knight, Diedre. Beanie's Backyard. (p. 150)
Knight, Eric. Lassie Come-Home. Kirmse, Marguerite, illus. (p. 977)
Knight, Erin. Chemistry Around the House. (p. 297)
—Steroids. (p. 1649)
Knight, Ernie C. Bean Heads, Another Batch. (p. 150)
Knight, Geof. Cosmetic Procedures. (p. 368)
—Plastic Pollution. (p. 1370)
Knight, Georgia. Little House Mouse. Knight, Georgia, illus. (p. 1029)
Knight, Grover. Ahzar's Travels & Life Lessons - Meet Ahzar: Book One. (p. 30)
Knight, Hilary. Eloise Throws a Party! Lyon, Tammie, illus. (p. 516)
—Firefly in a Fir Tree: A Carol for Mice. Knight, Hilary, illus. (p. 592)
—Night Before Christmas. (p. 1252)
Knight, Hilary, illus. see MacDonald, Betty.
Knight, Hilary, illus. see Thompson, Kay & Brenner, Marie.
Knight, Hilary, jt. see Thompson, Kay.
Knight, Hilary, jt. auth. see Fry, Sonali.
Knight, Hilary, jt. auth. see McClatchy, Lisa.
Knight, Hilary, jt. auth. see Thompson, Kay.
Knight, Hilary, et al. Nina in That Makes Me Mad! (p. 1256)
Knight, J. A. Ben & Ken: The Odd Job Men. (p. 163)
Knight, J. Redice, creator. Chinaberry Tree: Growing up in Rural Southern Mississippi during the Great Depression - A Sequel to Nubbin Ridge- (p. 307)
Knight, Joan MacPhail. Charlotte in Giverny. Sweet, Melissa, illus. (p. 293)
—Charlotte in Paris. Sweet, Melissa, illus. (p. 293)
Knight, Jovannah. Heavenly Message. (p. 761)
Knight, Karsten. Afterglow. (p. 28)
—Embers & Echoes. (p. 517)
—Wildefire. (p. 1931)
Knight, Khadijah. My Muslim Faith. (p. 1215)
Knight, Linsay. Australia's Greatest People & Their Achievements. (p. 116)
Knight, Linsay, ed. Stories for Eight Year Olds. Jellett, Tom, illus. (p. 1654)
—Stories for Nine Year Olds. Jellett, Tom, illus. (p. 1654)
—Stories for Seven Year Olds. Jellett, Tom, illus. (p. 1654)
—Stories for Six Year Olds. Jellett, Tom, illus. (p. 1654)
Knight, M. J. Why Should I Care about Nature? (p. 1926)
Knight M J. Why Should I Switch off the Light? (p. 1926)
Knight, M. J. Why Should I Switch off the Light? (p. 1926)
—Why Should I Turn off the Tap? (p. 1926)
Knight M J. Why Should I Walk More Often? (p. 1926)
Knight, M. J. Why Should I Walk More Often? (p. 1926)
Knight M J. Why Shouldn't I Drop Litter? (p. 1926)
Knight, M. J. Why Shouldn't I Drop Litter? (p. 1926)
Knight, Margy Burns. Talking Walls: Discover Your World. O'Brien, Anne Sibley, illus. (p. 1704)
—Talking Walls. O'Brien, Anne Sibley, illus. (p. 1704)
—Who Belongs Here? An American Story. O'Brien, Anne Sibley, illus. (p. 1914)
Knight, Margy Burns, see Burns Knight, Margy.
Knight, Michael T., illus. see Chatlos, Timothy J.
Knight, Nelson & Knight, Suzanne. ABCs of Southern Virginia University. (p. 4)
Knight, P. B. Little Orange & Red Butterfly (p. 1032)
—Secret Passage (p. 1543)
Knight, Patricia. Mussolini & Fascism. (p. 1194)
Knight, Paul. Abbabuwas Mountain. (p. 2)
Knight, Paula, illus. see Brown, J. A.
Knight, Paula, illus. see Law, Felicia.
Knight, Richard. Winter Shadow. Johnson, Richard, illus. (p. 1938)
Knight, Richard, et al. Finn at Clee Point. Hurst, Oliver, illus. (p. 589)
Knight, Richard John & Walker, Richard. Winter Shadow. Johnson, Richard, illus. (p. 1938)
Knight, Russell & Williams, Tim. University of Puget Sound College Prowler off the Record. (p. 1821)
Knight, S. Black Magic. (p. 196)
Knight, Sheryn. Meet Diplodocus. (p. 1120)
—Meet Scipionyx. (p. 1122)
Knight, Suzanne, jt. auth. see Knight, Nelson.
Knight, Tom. Little Red Riding Hood. (p. 1035)
Knight, Tom S. It's an Itty Bitty Part of Life. (p. 896)
Knight, Tori, ed. see Niedworok, Claudio O.
Knight, Vanessa, illus. see De Charleroy, Charles, Jr.
Knight, Vanessa, illus. see Howard, Jim & Welsh-Howard, Paula.
Knight, Vanessa, illus. see Miller, Jennifer.
Knight, Vanessa, illus. see Morgan, Margaret.
Knight Whittley, Karen. God Hears My Prayers Too! A Tiny Book of Prayer for Little Ones. (p. 689)
Knight-Mudie, Karen. Yams from Yandilla. (p. 1968)
Knighton, Kate. 50 Easter Things to Make & Do. (p. 1997)
—50 Science Things to Make & Do. (p. 1997)
—Why Shouldn't I Eat Junk Food? Larkum, Adam, illus. (p. 1926)
Knighton, Kate, ed. see Caudron, Chris & Childs, Caro.
Knighton, Kate, jt. auth. see Andrews, Georgina.
Knighton, Kate, retold by. Phantom of the Opera. (p. 1349)
Knights, David. Stumpy the Tree. (p. 1670)
Knights, Harry B. Angel's Star. (p. 75)
—Luigi & the Lost Wish Calico World Entertainment Staff, illus. (p. 1064)
—Maiden Voyage of Kris Kringle Calico World Entertainment Staff, illus. (p. 1077)
Knights, Nancy. Gracie's Hill. Norie, Rooney, illus. (p. 705)
Knijpenga, Siegwart. Stories of the Saints: A Collection for Children. (p. 1655)
Knipe, Sally J. Angel with the Broken Wings. (p. 74)
Knipping, Jutta, illus. see Schultze, Miriam.
Knipping, Rod, jt. auth. see Roberts, Emrys.
Knisley, Eric. Adventures of Furlington Mackelthwaite. (p. 18)
Knisley, Lucy. Heart: Seed Snow Circuit. (p. 759)
Kniss, Michelle. If Every Day Was a Summer Day. Kniss, Michelle, illus. (p. 852)
Knittel, John. Everything You Need to Know about the Dangers of Computer Hacking. (p. 546)
Knittel, John & Soto, Michael. Everything You Need to Know about the Dangers of Computer Hacking. (p. 546)
Knittel, Patty. Red Coats & Scimitars. (p. 1453)
Knizia, Reiner, des. Rheinlander. (p. 1467)
Knk Adventures. Ruth & Her Shepherd. (p. 1498)
Knobel, Andy. New York Knicks. (p. 1248)
—New York Mets. (p. 1248)
Knoblock, Julie, illus. see Wilson, Tony.
Knoch, Frank. Big Rescue: The Greenwood Forest Series Meierhofer, Brian, illus. (p. 183)
Knock Knock. Breakups & Rejections: Lines for All Occasions. (p. 225)
—Excuses & Lies: Lines for All Occasions. (p. 548)
—Insults & Comebacks: Lines for All Occasions. (p. 879)
—Pickups & Come-Ons: Lines for All Occasions. (p. 1355)
—Savvy Convert's Guide to Choosing a Religion. (p. 1518)
Knoebel, Suzanne B. Dr. Tootsie: A Young Girl's Dream. Armour, Steven & Kennard, Thomas, illus. (p. 475)
Knoke, Paul. Storm on Godfather Mountain: A True Story. (p. 1656)
Knold, Nijlon, illus. see Branning, Debe.
Knoll, Amos. Flower That Could Not Talk. (p. 607)
Knoll, Linda L. Patient for Pumpkins. (p. 1328)
Knoner, Beverly. Big Tall Tree. (p. 184)
Knope, Liz. Carter Visits the U. S. Capitol. (p. 272)
Knopf, Heather, illus. see Prichard, Diana.
Knopf, Susan. Welcome to Merriweather Farm. Walstead, Curt, illus. (p. 1873)
Knopf, Susan & Ballinger, Bryan. Barney Backhoe Loves to Build. (p. 139)
Knopp, Justin Douglas. Epica: The Ballad of the Nwyrrin. (p. 532)
Knopp, Sue, creator. Study Guide for Wolf Journal: A Novel. (p. 1670)
Knorr, Laura, illus. see Crane, Carol.
Knorr, Laura, illus. see Dunham, Terri Hoover.
Knorr, Laura, illus. see Kane, Kristen.
Knorr, Laura, illus. see Prieto, Anita C.
Knorr, Laura, illus. see Ulmer, Wendy K.
Knorr, Laura, illus. see Ulmer, Wendy.
Knoten, Erinn. Nickelas the Lost Nickel. (p. 1251)
Knotoff, Karenann. Island of Rouge. (p. 892)
Knott, Cheryl, jt. auth. see Laman, Tim.
Knott, Joan. Merry Christmas, Marushka! Frohliche Weihnachten, Marie! Knott, Marie, ed. (p. 1129)
Knott, Marie, ed. see Knott, Joan.
Knott, Marie, ed. Why Waabooz Has Long Ears. (p. 1926)
Knott, Simon, illus. see Correll, Stephanie.
Knott, Stephen, illus. see Allman-Varty, Faye.
Knott, Stephen F. Reagan Years. (p. 1448)
Knott, Stephen F. & Chidester, Jeffrey L. Reagan Years. (p. 1448)
Knotts, Bob. All Around Florida: Regions & Resources (p. 43)
—Florida Native Peoples (p. 607)
—Florida Plants & Animals (p. 607)
—People of Florida (p. 1339)
—Sports Superstars: 8 of Today's Hottest Athletes. (p. 1633)
—Uniquely Florida (p. 1818)
Knotts, Joe. Case of the Stolen Twins. (p. 275)
—Mystery of the Small Tower. (p. 1226)
Knotts, Reigan. Book. (p. 210)
Knotz, Sarah, illus. see Baloyra, Patricia.
Knowelden, Martin, illus. see Gilpin, Daniel.
Knowlden, Kelly. Battle. (p. 145)
Knowlden, Martin. Kids' Cookbook: Over 50 Fun Recipes for Kids to Cook. Heap, Will & Dunne, Kevin, photos by. (p. 953)
Knowlen, Maralee Burdick. Ian's Christmas Tree. (p. 849)
Knowles, Amy. Working in a School Store. (p. 1952)
Knowles, Daniel S. Mouse. (p. 1181)
—Rodent. (p. 1484)
Knowles, Elizabeth & Smith, Martha. Discovering Florida Through Literature. (p. 449)
—Talk about Books! A Guide for Book Clubs, Literature Circles, & Discussion Groups, Grades 4-8 (p. 1703)
Knowles, Harry, et al. Ain't It Cool? Hollywood's Redheaded Stepchild Speaks Out. (p. 30)
Knowles, Heather. Learn to Draw Tangled. (p. 983)
Knowles, Heather, jt. auth. see RH Disney Staff.
Knowles, Jo. Jumping off Swings. (p. 934)
—Lessons from a Dead Girl. (p. 993)
—Living with Jackie Chan. (p. 1042)
—Read Between the Lines. (p. 1443)
—See You at Harry's. (p. 1547)
Knowles, Johanna. Huntington's Disease. (p. 829)
—Jacques Cousteau. (p. 905)
—Pearl. (p. 1333)
Knowles, Johanna, et al. Junior Drug Awareness: Over-the-Counter Drugs. (p. 936)
Knowles, Jon. Facts of Life: A Guide for Teens & Their Families. (p. 561)
Knowles, Kent. Lucius & the Storm. Knowles, Kent, illus. (p. 1062)
Knowles, Trudy. Kids Behind the Label: An Inside Look at ADHD for Classroom Teachers. (p. 952)
Knowlton, Charlotte, illus. see Knowlton, Laurie Lazzaro.
Knowlton, Dwight. Little Red Racing Car: A Father/Son/Car Story. Knowlton, Dwight, illus. (p. 1035)
Knowlton, Jack. Geography from A to Z: A Picture Glossary. (p. 662)
Knowlton, Judith M. Twelve Christmas Gifts: ... from Cushing, Maine. (p. 1800)
Knowlton, Laurie. I Know a Librarian Who Chewed on a Word Leonhard, Herb, illus. (p. 840)
—N 2 Deep. (p. 1227)
—Pirates Don't Say Please! Tans, Adrian, illus. (p. 1363)
Knowlton, Laurie Lazzaro. African Giants. Tusan, Stan, illus. (p. 27)
—Come on Down. Brown, Kevin, illus. (p. 347)
—Cowgirl Alphabet Knowlton, Charlotte & Coates, Kathy, illus. (p. 374)
—Hide & Seek. (p. 776)
—My Valentine for Jesus Erdogan, Buket, illus. (p. 1221)
—Young Man's Dance. Johnson, Layne, illus. (p. 1979)
Knowlton, Laurie Lazzaro, et al. Catholic Book of Bible Stories Ettlinger, Doris, illus. (p. 280)
Knowlton, Mary Lee. Turkmenistan. (p. 1797)
—Uzbekistan. (p. 1829)
Knowlton, MaryLee. Colonia de Jamestown. (p. 341)
—Iraq. (p. 887)
—Safety Around Water. (p. 1502)
—Safety at Home. Andersen, Gregg, photos by. (p. 1502)
—Safety at School. Andersen, Gregg, photos by. (p. 1502)
—Safety at the Playground. Andersen, Gregg, photos by. (p. 1502)
Knowlton, MaryLee, jt. auth. see Riehecky, Janet.
Knowlton, MaryLee & Dowdy, Penny. Safety at School. Andersen, Gregg, photos by. (p. 1502)
—Safety at the Playground. Andersen, Gregg, photos by. (p. 1502)
Knox, Anna Mae, illus. see Hutton, Galia.
Knox, Barbara. ABC under the Sea: An Ocean Life Alphabet Book (p. 3)
—Abraham Lincoln. Saunders-Smith, Gail, ed. (p. 6)
—Baby Animals 1, 2, 3: A Counting Book of Animal Offspring (p. 124)
—Edinburgh Castle: Scotland's Haunted Fortress. (p. 504)
—Flood! The 1993 Midwest Downpours. (p. 605)
—Forbidden City: China's Imperial Palace. (p. 616)
—George Washington. Saunders-Smith, Gail, ed. (p. 664)
—Maine. (p. 1077)
—Under the Sea 1, 2, 3: Counting Ocean Life (p. 1814)
—Vermont. (p. 1837)
Knox, Barbara, jt. auth. see Doering, Amanda.
Knox, Barbara & Jons, Christianne. Jackie Robinson. (p. 903)
Knox, Barbara & Schuette, Sarah L. Animal Babies ABC: An Alphabet Book of Animal Offspring (p. 76)
Knox, Barbara J. Castle Dracula: Romania's Vampire Home. (p. 276)
—Hearst Castle: An American Palace. (p. 759)
Knox, Dahk. Zander, Friend of the Se. (p. 1984)
Knox, Dahk, ed. see Dorris, Peggy.
Knox, E. C. Don't Call Me Honey! Call Me Cherry Pie. Knox, E. C., illus. (p. 467)
Knox, Elizabeth. Dreamhunter. (p. 484)
—Dreamquake. (p. 484)
—Mortal Fire. (p. 1176)
Knox, Joy, compiled by. Croppin' Dictum: Travel & Holiday. (p. 385)
—Croppin' Dictum: Big, Strong Titles. (p. 385)
—Croppin' Dictum. (p. 385)
Knox, Lorna Ann. I Came from Joy: Spiritual Affirmations & Activities for Children. (p. 834)
Knox nee Ramsamugh, Lorna. Fire the Wolf & His Magical Kingdom (p. 591)
Knox, Regina. Clintonville Abduction. (p. 333)
Knox, Susi Grell, illus. see Boone, Sheila.
Knox, Thomas W. Young Nimrods Around the World. (p. 1979)
Knox-Henry, Kheri. Invisible Car. (p. 885)
Knuckles, Tiffany S., jt. auth. see Smyers, David D.
Knudsen, Anders. Antoine de la Mothe Cadillac: French Settlements at Detroit & Louisiana. (p. 89)
—Sir John Franklin: The Search for the Northwest Passage. (p. 1580)
Knudsen, Michelle. Argus. Wesson, Andrea, illus. (p. 98)
—Big Mean Mike. Magoon, Scott, illus. (p. 182)
—Bugged! Sims, Blanche, illus. (p. 236)
—Carl the Complainer. Cocca-Leffler, Maryann, illus. (p. 269)
—Caso de Vivian la Vampira. Wummer, Amy, illus. (p. 276)
—Caso de Vivian la Vampira (the Case of Vampire Vivian) Wummer, Amy, illus. (p. 276)
—Dragon of Trelian. (p. 477)
—Easter Fun. Starace, Tom, illus. (p. 499)
—Evil Librarian. (p. 546)
—Fish & Frog: Brand New Readers. Petrone, Valeria, illus. (p. 598)
—Fish & Frog Big Book: Brand New Readers. Petrone, Valeria, illus. (p. 598)
—Library Lion. (p. 1006)
—Library Lion. Hawkes, Kevin, illus. (p. 1006)
—Marilyn's Monster. Phelan, Matt, illus. (p. 1094)
—Moldy Mystery. Gott, Barry, illus. (p. 1160)
—Mother's Day Ribbons. Wallace, John, illus. (p. 1178)
—Princess of Trelian. (p. 1405)
—Slimy Story. Billin-Frye, Paige, illus. (p. 1590)
Knudsen, Michelle & Yoon, Salina. Happy Easter! Yoon, Salina, illus. (p. 745)
Knudsen, Shannon. Alice Ray & the Salem Witch Trials. Palmer, Ruth, illus. (p. 39)
—Climbing Orangutans. (p. 333)
—Easter Around the World. Erickson, David, illus. (p. 499)
—Eggs, Legs, Wings: A Butterfly Life Cycle Smith, Simon, illus. (p. 506)
—Fairies & Elves. (p. 562)
—Fantastical Creatures & Magical Beasts. (p. 572)
—From Egg to Butterfly. (p. 642)
—From Iron to Car. (p. 643)
—From Tadpole to Frog. (p. 643)
—Giants, Trolls, & Ogres. (p. 674)
—Guatemala. (p. 728)
—I'll Haunt You! - Meet a Ghost. Bucchen, Chiara, illus. (p. 856)
—I'M All Wrapped Up! - Meet a Mummy. Kurilla, Renee, illus. (p. 858)
—Leif Eriksson. Oldroyd, Mark, illus. (p. 991)
—Mermaids & Mermen. (p. 1128)
—Police Officers. (p. 1380)
—Postal Workers. (p. 1387)
—Rise Above. (p. 1474)
—Seed, Sprout, Fruit: An Apple Tree Life Cycle Smith, Simon, illus. (p. 1547)
—Testing the Truth. (p. 1723)
—When Were the First Slaves Set Free During the Civil War? And Other Questions about the Emancipation Proclamation. (p. 1905)
—When Were the First Slaves Set Free During the Civil War? And Other Questions about the Emancipation Proclamation. (p. 1905)
Knudsen, Sherilyn. Smart Way to Be. Bodily, Michael, illus. (p. 1593)
Knudson, Dana, illus. see Griner, Jack.
Knudson, Jason, illus. see O'Donnell, Liam.
Knudson, Michelle. Bugged! (p. 236)
—Case of Vampire Vivian. Wummer, Amy, illus. (p. 275)
Knudson, Mike. Cool Campers. (p. 362)
Knudson, Mike & Wilkinson, Steve. Dancing Dudes. Curtis, Stacy, illus. (p. 402)
—Raymond & Graham - Bases Loaded. (p. 1441)
—Raymond & Graham Rule the School. Curtis, Stacy, illus. (p. 1441)
Knudson, R. R. Babe Didrikson: Athlete of the Century. Lewin, Ted, illus. (p. 123)
—Babe Didrikson. (p. 123)
Knudson, Shannon. Climbing Orangutans. (p. 333)
Knudtsen, Ken. My Monkey's Name Is Jennifer. (p. 1214)
Knudtsen, Ken, illus. see Ferrara, Brian.
Knussen, Oliver, jt. auth. see Sendak, Maurice.
Knutson, Barbara. Love & Roast Chicken: A Trickster Tale from the Andes Mountains. Knutson, Barbara, illus. (p. 1059)
Knutson, Barbara, illus. see Lowery, Linda.
Knutson, Barbara, illus. see McDunn, Linda L.
Knutson, Eric. I Never Get Scared. Stensen, Cindy, illus. (p. 844)
Knutson, Janette C., jt. auth. see Hemmel, David Lee.
Knutson, Jeff. Business of Skateboarding: From Board to Boardroom. (p. 245)
Knutson, Jeffrey. Business of Skateboarding: From Board to Boardroom. (p. 245)
Knutson, Lori. Ghost of Northumberland Strait. (p. 671)
Knutson, Shanna. Can God Talk to Me? (p. 258)
Knutsson, Catherine. Shadows Cast by Stars. (p. 1558)
Knuvers, Onno, illus. see Fuerst, Jeffrey B.
Ko, Erik, jt. auth. see Lewis, Corey.
Ko, Jung-wook. Mother to the Poor: The Life of Blessed Teresa of Calcutta. Park, Seung-bum, illus. (p. 1178)
Koba, Susan & Tweed, Anne. Hard-To-Teach Biology Concepts, Revised 2nd Edition: Designing Standards-Based Instruction Through the Lens of NGSS. (p. 748)
Kobak, Carrie, illus. see Foley, Sue.
Kobald, Irena. My Two Blankets. Blackwood, Freya, illus. (p. 1220)
Kobar, Christopher, jt. auth. see Hindmarch, Will.
Kobasa, Paul A. Personal & Household Items. (p. 1344)
Kobasic, Kevin, illus. see Defalco, Tom & McDaniel, Scott.
Kobasic, Kevin, illus. see Random House.
Kobayashi, Gavin, illus. see Kahalewai, Marilyn.
Kobayashi, Jin. School Rumble. (p. 1523)
Kobayashi, Mayumi, tr. see Furuyama, Kan & Taniguchi, Jiro.
Kobayashi, Mayumi, tr. see Marukawa, Tomohiro.
Kobayashi, Mayumi, tr. see Tomizawa, Hitoshi.
Kobayashi, Michelle, tr. see Tsuda, Masami.
Kobayashi, Michelle, tr. from JPN. Kare Kano Tsuda, Masami, illus. (p. 943)
Kobayashi, Tatsuyoshi. Thomas Edison: Genius of the Electric Age. (p. 1738)
Kobayashi, Tatsuyoshi, illus. see Kurosawa, Tetsuya.
Kobayashi, Tatsuyoshi, illus. see Sugaya, Atsuo.
Kobayashi, Yoko, tr. see Morinaga, Ai.
Kobayashi, Yoko, tr. see Tomizawa, Hitoshi.
Kobel, Peter. Silent Movies: The Birth of Film & the Triumph of Movie Culture. (p. 1575)
Kober, Clayton. Adventures of Garth: Garth's Close Encounter. (p. 18)
Kober, Shahar. Dreidel, Dreidel, Dreidel. (p. 484)
Kober, Shahar, illus. see Cohen, Deborah Bodin.
Kober, Shahar, jt. auth. see Leiter, Richard.
Kobernick, J. W. Mary Margaret & the Magical Mall. (p. 1100)
Kobert, Michael Gilead & Donato, Dona. Who Goes with That Nose? The Wild Adventures of Juicy Coppertoes. Fuller, Laurie, illus. (p. 1915)
Kobler, Florian, ed. see Andersen, Hans Christian.
Kobliner Shaw, Beth & Shaw, Jacob. Jacob's Eye Patch. Feiffer, Jules, illus. (p. 904)
Kobus, Joanne. Mr Frog's Bad Day. (p. 1185)
Kocandrle, Mirek. Pop/Rock: Sounds & Vibes of the 20th Century, Second Edition. (p. 1385)
Koceich, Matt. My Texas. (p. 1220)
Kocek, Sara. Promise Me Something. (p. 1411)
Koch, Carla, illus. see Wilson, M. Leonora.
Koch, Chris L. Living the Lord's Prayer. (p. 1041)
Koch, Christian, et al, eds. Gulf Yearbook 2004. (p. 731)
Koch, Claus. Three Little Wolves & the Big Bad Boar. (p. 1743)
Koch, Dott Clarke. Jacob's House. Koch, William, ed. (p. 904)
Koch, Edward R. Relay. (p. 1458)
Koch, Janet Marie. Hallie's Best Birthday. (p. 737)
Koch, Janie, jt. auth. see Heitzmann, Connie.
Koch, Joann. Annie's World. (p. 87)
Koch, Kamla Devi, et al. Teen Stories: Personal Stories for Students Who Are Beginning to Read. (p. 1714)
Koch, Miriam. Digby Differs. Garlid, Ann, tr. from GER. (p. 438)

Koch, Nobu, illus. see Lindoff, Hannah.
Koch, Patricia. High in the Sky. (p. 777)
Koch, Theresa F. Gift of Laughter. (p. 675)
Koch, William, ed. see Koch, Dott Clarke.
Kochalka, James. Best Little Ghost in the World! (p. 170)
—Cute Manifesto. (p. 396)
—Dragon Puncher Book 1. (p. 477)
—Dragon Puncher Book 2: Dragon Puncher Island: Dragon Puncher Island. (p. 477)
—Glorkian Warrior Delivers a Pizza. Kochalka, James, illus. (p. 685)
—Happy Apples (p. 744)
—Johnny Boo Book 5: Johnny Boo Does Something! Johnny Boo Does Something! (p. 923)
—Mean Little Boy. (p. 1116)
—Monkey vs. Robot & the Crystal of Power. (p. 1165)
—Twinkle Power. (p. 1802)
Kochan, Vera. What If Your Best Friend Were Blue? Garófoli, Viviana, illus. (p. 1887)
Kochanoff, Peggy. Be a Beach Detective: Solving the Mysteries of Seas, Sands & Surf (p. 147)
—You Can Be a Nature Detective. (p. 1973)
Kochel, Marcia Agness, jt. auth. see Baxter, Kathleen A.
Koch-Gotha, Fritz, illus. see Sixtus, Albert.
Kochner, Donna Rose Porta. Through the Night. (p. 1745)
Kochnevitz, Jane, illus. see Dowley, Tim.
Kochnez, Jane, illus. see Dowley, Tim.
Koci, Rudin, illus. see Kaufmann, Anne.
Kocialski, Trish. Forces of Evil. (p. 617)
Kocienda, Genevieve. Aliens: Is Anybody Out There? Low Intermediate Book with Online Access. (p. 41)
—Blizzards: Killer Snowstorms. (p. 200)
—Catch a Wave: the Story of Surfing Beginning Book with Online Access. (p. 279)
—Do Not Disturb: the Importance of Sleep High Beginning Book with Online Access. (p. 457)
—Madagascar Low Intermediate Book with Online Access. (p. 1069)
—Magic of Music Low Intermediate Book with Online Access. (p. 1073)
—Only in America Low Intermediate Book with Online Access. (p. 1298)
—Sushi Nation Low Intermediate Book with Online Access. (p. 1688)
—Three in One: The Challenge of the Triathlon. (p. 1742)
—Water: Vital for Life. (p. 1862)
—Weird Animals Low Intermediate Book with Online Access. (p. 1872)
Kocin, Paul J. & Uccellini, Louis W. Northeast Snowstorms (p. 1265)
Kock, Carl, illus. see Hillert, Margaret.
Kockere, Geert De. Willy. Cneut, Carll, illus. (p. 1934)
Kocsis, J. C., illus. see Gephart, Donna.
Kocsis, Konrád Hayward. Adventures of the Krusaders & the Legend of Wilde Island. (p. 23)
Kodaira, Hiromi, jt. auth. see Uchiyama, Akira.
Kodaira, Machiyo, illus. see Newman, Lesléa.
Kodansha. Tokyo Mew Mew a la Mode Ikumi, Mia, illus. (p. 1762)
Kodera, Craig, illus. see Handleman, Philip.
Kodera, Craig, illus. see Sutcliffe, Jane.
Kodiath, Alex. Elephant Escapes to an Island. (p. 511)
Kodish, Debora, ed. see Cheung, Shu Pui, et al.
Kodman, Stanislawa, illus. see Havill, Juanita.
Kodman, Stanislawa, illus. see Havill, Juanita.
Koefler, Leatha, illus. see Toler, Violet M.
Koehler, Ed, illus. see Burgdorf, Larry.
Koehler, Ed, illus. see Busch, Melinda Kay.
Koehler, Ed, illus. see Hartman, Sara.
Koehler, Ed, illus. see Marxhausen, Joanne.
Koehler, Ed, illus. see Molski, Carol.
Koehler, Ed, illus. see Stohs, Anita Reight.
Koehler, Ed, illus. see Stohs, Anita Reith.
Koehler, Fred. How to Cheer up Dad. (p. 816)
Koehler, Hanne Lore & Laraya-Coutts, Corie. Tale of a Malipayon Warrior. (p. 1699)
Koehler, Manfred, jt. auth. see Ross, Michael.
Koehler, Mary. Children are Happy Story CD with Animals from the Southwest. (p. 302)
Koehler, Max. Journey to the Sun (p. 929)
Koehler, Susan. Animal Trainer. (p. 80)
—Clima. (p. 332)
—Race Car Crew Chief. (p. 1430)
—Treasure Hunter. (p. 1781)
Koehler-Pentacoff, Elizabeth. Jackson & Bud's Bumpy Ride: America's First Cross-Country Automobile Trip. Hargis, Wes, illus. (p. 904)
—John Muir & Stickeen: An Alaskan Adventure. Swanson, Karl, illus. (p. 922)
Koehn, Wendel. Love Problematic: And Other Stories. (p. 1060)
—Wendel Plants Potatoes. (p. 1875)
Koel, Leonard. Carpentry: Workbook. (p. 271)
—Carpentry: Answer Key. (p. 271)
—Carpentry. (p. 271)
—Concrete Formwork: Text. (p. 355)
—Concrete Formwork: Answer Key. (p. 355)
Koeller, Carol, illus. see Adams, Michelle Medlock.
Koeller, Carol, illus. see Cleveland, Alexandra, et al.
Koeller, Carol, illus. see Nemiroff, Marc A. & Annunziata, Jane.
Koeller, Carol, illus. see Riggs, Sandy.
Koeller, Carol, illus. see Taylor-Butler, Christine.
Koeller, Carol, illus. see Wilmes, Liz & Wilmes, Dick.
Koeller, Carol, tr. see Nemiroff, Marc A. & Annunziata, Jane.
Koeller, Kim & La France, Robert. Chinese, Indian & Thai Cuisine Passport: Part of the Award Winning Let's Eat Out! Series. (p. 307)
—Multi-Lingual Phrase Passport: Part of the Award Winning Let's Eat Out! Series. (p. 1189)
Koellhoffer, Tara. Ecstasy & Other Club Drugs. (p. 503)
—Inhalants & Solvents. (p. 874)
—Science News for Kids, 6-Volume Set. (p. 1527)
Koellhoffer, Tara & Banas, Sharon L. Being Fair & Honest. (p. 161)
Koellhoffer, Tara, ed. Computers & Technology. (p. 355)
—Environment. (p. 531)
—Food & Nutrition. (p. 613)
—France. (p. 627)
—Space & Astronomy. (p. 1618)
Koellhoffer, Tara, et al. Prozac & Other Antidepressants. (p. 1413)
Koelsch, Michael, illus. see Christopher, Matt.
Koelsch, Michael, illus. see Grogan, John.
Koelsch, Michael, illus. see Wells, Rosemary & Rosemary, Wells.
Koelsch, Michael, tr. see Christopher, Matt.
Koerner, Sandy, et al. Water Adventures Around the World (p. 1862)
Koenig, Albert. Wood, Hay, & Pigs. Compton, Donna, illus. (p. 1949)
Koenig, Emily C. North America. (p. 1264)
Koenig, Emily Grace. Tallest Leprechaun: A Tall Tale of Terrible Teasing. (p. 1704)
Koenig, Faydra. Two Homes for Daniel. (p. 1803)
Koenig, Harold G. Medicine, Religion & Health: Where Science & Spirituality Meet. (p. 1119)
Koenig, Jenaya. Jumping Animals! Relate Addition & Subtraction to Length. (p. 934)
Koenig, Sharolett. Is This Really Good, or Am I Just Starved? Rhonda Ghent's Camp Recipes. (p. 890)
Koenigsberg, Phyllis & Winkler, Ziporah, creators. Color My Alef Bet. (p. 343)
Koenig-Wilson, LaNell. Alexander Graham Cracker Goes to the Moon. (p. 36)
Köenings, N. S. Blue Taxi. (p. 203)
Koepnick, Lutz P., jt. auth. see Eckmann, Sabine.
Koepp, Patricia. Mittens' Magical Mittens: Listen, Read & Sing Along. (p. 1156)
—Mr. Mittens' Magical Mittens: Listen, Read & Sing Along. (p. 1185)
Koeppel, Ruth. At the Seashore. McBee, Scott, illus. (p. 111)
—Dora Carryalong Treasury. Hall, Susan, illus. (p. 470)
—In the Wild. McBee, Scott, illus. (p. 868)
—Nick Jr. Wonder Pets Adventures: Book & Magnetic Playset. (p. 1251)
Koerner, Henry. Early Works of Henry Koerner 1945-1957. (p. 494)
Koerner, Jason L. Two Princesses & the Dark Chocolate Castle. (p. 1804)
Koerner, Miranda Pike. Blue Mermaid. (p. 203)
Koerper, Ruby Cavanaugh. Elaine of Palo Alto Farm: Cavanaugh Koerper Collection of Children's Stories. (p. 508)
—Freddie the Frog: Cavanaugh Koerper Collection of Children's Stories. (p. 632)
—Pedro of Palestine: A Christmas Story for Children: Cavanaugh Koerper Collection of Children's Stories. (p. 1334)
—Pedro of Palo Alto Farm: Cavanaugh Koerper Collection of Children's Stories. (p. 1334)
—Three Little Ghosts: Cavanaugh Koerper Collection of Children's Stories. (p. 1742)
Koers, Diane. Microsoft Excel 2003 Fast & Easy. (p. 1136)
—Microsoft Word 2003 Fast & Easy. (p. 1137)
Koertge, Ron. Coaltown Jesus. (p. 336)
—Lies, Knives, & Girls in Red Dresses. Dezsö, Andrea, illus. (p. 1007)
—Now Playing: Stoner & Spaz II. (p. 1269)
—Shakespeare Makes the Playoffs. (p. 1559)
—Stoner & Spaz. (p. 1653)
Koertge, Ronald. Arizona Kid. (p. 98)
—Boy Girl Boy. (p. 218)
—Brimstone Journals. (p. 228)
—Deadville. (p. 418)
—Margaux with an X. (p. 1092)
—Shakespeare Bats Cleanup. (p. 1559)
—Shakespeare Makes the Playoffs. (p. 1559)
—Strays. (p. 1666)
—Where the Kissing Never Stops. (p. 1909)
Koertge, Ronald, jt. auth. see Heppermann, Christine.
Koestler, Larry & Scheff, William. Lehigh University College Prowler off the Record. (p. 991)
Koestler-Grack, Rachel. Elie Wiesel: Witness for Humanity. (p. 512)
—Katie Couric: Groundbreaking TV Journalist. (p. 945)
Koestler-Grack, Rachel A. Abraham Lincoln. (p. 6)
—Annie Oakley. (p. 87)
—Assassination of Robert F. Kennedy. (p. 107)
—Brett Favre. (p. 226)
—Choctaw: Stickball Players of the South. (p. 309)
—Daily Life in a Southern Trading Town: New Orleans. (p. 399)
—Daily Life in a Southwestern Settlement: San Antonio. (p. 399)
—Department of Homeland Security. (p. 427)
—Eleanor of Aquitaine: Heroine of the Middle Ages. (p. 508)
—Ferdinand Magellan. (p. 581)
—Helen Keller. (p. 762)
—Hernando Cortes & the Fall of the Aztecs. Goetzmann, William H., ed. (p. 772)
—House of Representatives. (p. 803)
—Iroquois: Longhouse Builders (p. 888)
—Johnstown Flood Of 1889. (p. 924)
—Kent State Tragedy. (p. 949)
—Kirby Puckett. (p. 961)
—Kofi Annan: Guiding the United Nations. (p. 966)
—Leonardo Da Vinci: Artist, Inventor, & Renaissance Man. (p. 992)
—Marie Curie: Scientist. (p. 1093)
—Moon Landing. (p. 1172)
—Mount Rushmore. (p. 1180)
—Nathan Hale: Courageous Spy. (p. 1231)
—Neil Armstrong. (p. 1240)
—Northern Colonial Town: Plymouth. (p. 1265)
—Pilgrims. (p. 1358)
—Queen Latifah. (p. 1424)
—Space Shuttle Columbia Disaster. (p. 1619)
—Spirit of St. Louis. (p. 1628)
—Stonewall Jackson. (p. 1653)
—Tom Brady. (p. 1762)
—Vasco Da Gama & the Sea Route to India. Goetzmann, William H., ed. (p. 1833)
—William Tecumseh Sherman. (p. 1933)
Koestler-Grack, Rachel A., jt. auth. see Shields, Charles J.
Koestler-Grack, Rachel A. & Woog, Adam. Calamity Jane. (p. 252)
Koff, Deborah, illus. see Andersdatter, Karla Margaret.
Koffman, Donna Carol. Different Kinds of Special. Biggar, Breanne, illus. (p. 438)
Koffsky, Ann, illus. see Wasserman, Sand.
Koffsky, Ann D. Frogs in the Bed: My Passover Seder Activity Book. (p. 641)
—Kayla & Kugel. (p. 946)
—Kayla & Kugel's Almost-Perfect Passover. (p. 946)
—My Jewish Holiday Fun Book. (p. 1211)
—Noah's Swim-A-Thon. (p. 1262)
—Shabbat Shalom, Hey! (p. 1556)
Koffsky, Ann D., illus. see Abraham, Michelle Shapiro.
Koffsky, Ann D., illus. see Halper, Sharon D.
Koffsky, Ann D., illus. see Halper, Sharon.
Koffsky, Ann D., jt. auth. see Abraham, Michelle Shapiro.
Kofman, Victoria. Guni-Pi Academy, Math & Logic: Hands-On Textbook for 4 - 7 Year Olds. (p. 732)
—Guni-Pi Academy, Math & Logic: Hands-on Textbook for 4 - 7 Year Olds - Non-Laminated. (p. 732)
Koford, Adam. Book of Mormon on Trial Activity Learning Book. (p. 211)
Koford, Adam, illus. see Rich, J. Milton.
Kofsky, Ann, illus. see Ochs, Carol.
Kofsky, Kristen, illus. see Pierce, Terry.
Kofsky, Kristen, illus. see Williams, Laura E.
Kofsky, Kristen, jt. auth. see Pierce, Terry.
Kogawa, Joy. Naomi's Road Ohi, Ruth, illus. (p. 1229)
—Naomi's Tree Ohi, Ruth, illus. (p. 1229)
Koge Donbo. Pita-Ten (p. 1364)
Koge, Donbo, creator. Pita-Ten (p. 1364)
Koge-donb. Kamichama Karin (p. 942)
Koge-Donbo. Di Gi Charat (p. 433)
—Kamichama Karin (p. 942)
—Pita-Ten Official Fan Book. Koge-Donbo, illus. (p. 1364)
Koge-Donbo, creator. Kamichama Karin (p. 942)
Koger, Danny K. Misadventures of Carson & C J Crenshaw: In Search of the Book of Life. (p. 1150)
Kogge, Michael. Rebellion Begins. (p. 1451)
—Star Wars Rebels. (p. 1641)
—Star Wars Rebels: Battle to the End. (p. 1641)
Kogge, Michael, jt. auth. see Disney Book Group Staff.
Kogler, Jennifer. Otherworldlies. (p. 1307)
Kogler, Jennifer A., jt. auth. see Kogler, Jennifer Anne.
Kogler, Jennifer Anne. Death Catchers. (p. 420)
—Ruby Tuesday. (p. 1493)
—Siren's Cry. (p. 1580)
Kogler, Jennifer Anne & Kogler, Jennifer A. Otherworldlies. (p. 1307)
Kogo, Yoshi, illus. see Clements, Andrew.
Kogon, Stephen. Max Mooth—Cyber Sleuth & the Case of the Zombie Virus. (p. 1111)
Koh, Angeline, jt. auth. see Heale, Jay.
Koh, Frederick. 10 Mightiest Conquerors. (p. 1993)
—10 Most Compelling News Images. (p. 1993)
—10 Most Fascinating Cities. (p. 1994)
—10 Most Outstanding Entrepreneurs. (p. 1994)
—Danger at Work. (p. 403)
Koh, Jennifer Pretious. Zindi's Journey: Finding Gem. (p. 1987)
Koh, Magdalene, jt. auth. see Kagda, Falaq.
Koh, Magdalene, jt. auth. see Mansfield, Stephen.
Koh, Magdalene, jt. auth. see Sheehan, Sean.
Kohake, Beverly. Funny Bunny. (p. 649)
—Red Dragon Kite. (p. 1453)
Kohara, Kazuno. Ghosts in the House! Kohara, Kazuno, illus. (p. 672)
—Here Comes Jack Frost. Kohara, Kazuno, illus. (p. 770)
—Little Wizard. (p. 1038)
—Midnight Library. Kohara, Kazuno, illus. (p. 1139)
Kohart, Georgia. Heritage of the Heart Teaching Companion. (p. 771)
Kohen, E. Italy. (p. 895)
Kohen, Elizabeth. Spain. (p. 1620)
Kohen, Elizabeth, jt. auth. see Gan.
Kohen, Elizabeth & Graff, Marie Louise. Spain. (p. 1620)
Kohen, Gabriela. Circus: Spanish Superbook. (p. 322)
Kohen Winter & Fuller, Barbara. Greece. (p. 720)
Kohen-Klieman, Clarita, tr. see Gile, John.
Kohl, Carly, tr. see Crouch, Adele.
Kohl, Katrin M., jt. auth. see Trim, John.
Kohl, MaryAnn F. & Potter, Jean. Storybook Art: Hands-On Art for Children in the Styles of 100 Great Picture Book Illustrators. Davis, Katheryn & Van Slyke, Rebecca, illus. (p. 1663)
Kohl, MaryAnn F. & Solga, Kim. Great American Artists for Kids: Hands-On Art Experiences in the Styles of Great American Masters. (p. 713)
Kohl, MaryAnn F. & Zaborowski, Barbara. Action ART: Hands-On Active Art Adventures. (p. 10)
Kohl, T. Michelle. Magical Adventures of Bailey Boo the Cockatoo: When the Family's Away, the Parrots Will Play! (p. 1074)
Kohlenberger, John R., III, et al. Truth Quest Inductive Student Bible. (p. 1794)
Kohler, Christine. No Surrender Soldier. (p. 1260)
—Turkey in the News: Past, Present, & Future. (p. 1797)
Kohler, Dean Ellis & VanHecke, Susan. Rock 'n' Roll Soldier: A Memoir. (p. 1482)
Kohler, Lucartha. Women Working in Glass (p. 1946)
Kohler, Michelle, illus. see Tapler, Judy.
Kohler, Ursula, illus. see Haxhia, Miranda.
Kohles, Deniese. Heaven Has a Secret for You. (p. 761)
Kohlhepp, Michael. Within the Hearthstone: Book 1: the Trea. (p. 1942)
Kohlhepp, Michael G. Within the Hearthstone Book 2: The Fountain of Balance. (p. 1942)
Kohlmann, Krista. Mapsume: Unscramble the Hero. (p. 1091)
Kohlsaat, Caroline, jt. auth. see Baker, Clara Belle.
Kohn, Arnie, illus. see Spizzirri, Linda, ed.
Kohn, George C. Dictionary of Wars. (p. 436)
Kohn, George Childs. Dictionary of Historic Documents. (p. 436)
Kohner, Elaine, illus. see Arsenault, Jane & Cedor, Jean.
Kohout, Rosemary, ed. see Pence, Shari A.
Kohuth, Jane. Anne Frank's Chestnut Tree. (p. 86)
—Anne Frank's Chestnut Tree. Sayles, Elizabeth, illus. (p. 86)
—Duck Sock Hop. Porter, Jane, illus. (p. 488)
—Ducks Go Vroom. Garófoli, Viviana, illus. (p. 488)
—Ducks Go Vroom. Garófoli, Viviana, illus. (p. 488)
Koike, Kazuo. Samurai Executioner (p. 1509)
—Shinobi with Extending Fists (p. 1567)
Koike, Kazuo & Kojima, Goseki. Serving in the Dark (p. 1553)
Koizim, Jessica. Geometry. (p. 662)
—Mathematical Thinking Expressing Ideas Strategies. (p. 1107)
—Mathematical Thinking Linking Math. (p. 1107)
Koja, Kathe. Blue Mirror. (p. 203)
—Buddha Boy. (p. 234)
—Kissing the Bee. (p. 962)
—Straydog. (p. 1666)
—Talk. (p. 1703)
Koja, Stephan. Gustav Klimt: A Painted Fairy Tale. (p. 733)
Koji, Jeanette, illus. see Blume, Rebecca.
Kojima, Goseki, jt. auth. see Koike, Kazuo.
Kok, Gemma. Explore. (p. 550)
—Explore (Printed in black & White) (p. 550)
—Scribble. (p. 1533)
—Scribble (Printed in black & White) (p. 1533)
Kok Hoong Derek, Wong. Little Genius. (p. 1028)
Koka. Adventures of Popoki: The Curious Kitten with a Crooked Tail. Koka, illus. (p. 21)
Kokash, Elena, ed. see AZ Books Staff.
Kokino, Olga. Journalism Student Activity Book: Student Activities Book. Matthews, Douglas L., ed. (p. 927)
Kokkinos, Nikos, jt. auth. see Jacobson, David M.
Kokoro, Natsume. Lovephobia Volume 2. (p. 1061)
Koksal, Erin. Bedtime for Abble. (p. 156)
Kokubo, Naomi, tr. see Hamazaki, Tatsuya.
Kokubo, Naomi, tr. see Higuchi, Daisuke.
Kokubo, Naomi, tr. see Izumi, Kaneyoshi.
Kol, jt. auth. see Kala.
Kola, Pamela, ed. East African How Stories. (p. 498)
—East African Why Stories. (p. 498)
Kola, Sari & Nystrom, Kim. Panamaris Move to Brazil. (p. 1320)
Kolanovic, Dubravka. Wipe-Clean Colours. Kolanovic, Dubravka, illus. (p. 1939)
Kolanovic, Dubravka, illus. see Andersen, Hans Christian.
Kolanovic, Dubravka, illus. see Cabral, Jeane.
Kolanovic, Dubravka, illus. see Conway, David.
Kolanovic, Dubravka, illus. see Davidson, Susanna.
Kolanovic, Dubravka, illus. see Dodd, Sarah J.
Kolanovic, Dubravka, illus. see Freedman, Claire.
Kolanovic, Dubravka, illus. see Gray, Joanna.
Kolanovic, Dubravka, illus. see Pasquali, Elena.
Kolanovic, Dubravka, illus. see Patterson, Ellie.
Kolanovic, Dubravka, illus. see Piper, Sophie.
Kolanovic, Dubravka, illus. see Ritchie, Alison.
Kolanovic, Dubravka, jt. auth. see Dodd, Sarah J.
Kolar, Bob. Big Kicks. Kolar, Bob, illus. (p. 182)
—Stomp, Stomp! A Dino Romp. (p. 1652)
Kolar, Bob, illus. see Cuyler, Margery.
Kolar, Bob, illus. see Kontis, Alethea.
Kolar, Bob, illus. see Masurel, Claire.
Kolar, Bob, illus. see Slater, David Michael.
Kolar, Bob, illus. see Soltis, Sue.
Kolar, Bob, jt. auth. see Masurel, Claire.
Kolar, Marsha. Little Brave Bear. Di Marco, Audrey, illus. (p. 1025)
Kolars, Frank. Long Trail: The Story of Buffalo Bill. Micale, Albert, illus. (p. 1047)
Kolasinski, Ken, ed. see Kalvoda, Mike.
Kolb, Andrew. Edmund Unravels. Kolb, Andrew, illus. (p. 504)
Kolb, Carolyn G. Fun Seeker's New Orleans: The Ultimate Guide to One of the World's Hottest Cities. (p. 648)
Kolb, Joseph J. Reservation Dreams. (p. 1463)
Kolb, Robin, ed. see Hassler-Scoop, Jill K., et al.
Kolberg, Sue, ed. see Erickson, Byron, et al.
Kolby, Jeff. Master the LSAT Ultimate Prep. (p. 1103)
Kolcavova, Klara, jt. auth. see Ruzicka, Oldrich.
Kolczynski, Sean. Night Before Middle School! (p. 1253)
Kolding, Richard Max, illus. see Mueller, Virginia.
Kolding, Richard Max, illus. see Seese, Ellen.
Kole, Andre. Tricks & Twists. (p. 1786)
Kole MacLean, Christine. Mary Margaret Running Scared. (p. 1100)
Kole, Nicholas, illus. see Disney Book Group Staff, et al.
Kole, Ted & Genet, John, eds. Katoufs in Nursery Rhymes: Mother Goose. Princess Marie, illus. (p. 945)
—Katoufs in Nursery Rhymes Chapbook: Mother Goose. (p. 945)
Kolehmainen, Aili, tr. see Bowman, James Cloyd, et al.
Kolesnikow, Tassia. Sexually Transmitted Diseases. (p. 1556)
Kolich, Heather N. Pawnee. (p. 1331)
Kolins, Scott. Excalibur Visionaries (p. 547)
Kolitsky, Joy, illus. see Sullivan, Michael.
Kolka, Diane & Clarke, Steve. Religions to Inspire - Buddhism. (p. 1458)
—Religions to Inspire - Christianity. (p. 1458)
—Religions to InspiRE for KS3: Roman Catholic Christianity. (p. 1458)
Koll, Hilary, jt. auth. see Mills, Steve.
Koll, Hilary, et al. Using Math in the ER. (p. 1828)
—Using Math to Build a Skyscraper. (p. 1828)
—Using Math to Design a Roller Coaster. (p. 1828)
—Using Math to Survive in the Wild. (p. 1828)
Kollabora, Inc. Super Simple Jewelry: 10 Modern, Versatile Pieces to Make in 30 Minutes or Less. (p. 1681)
Kollár, Daniel. Slovakia. (p. 1591)
Kollar, J. P. Three Tomato Brand. (p. 1744)

Kollas, Candace. Birthday Fairy: A Fairyland Tradition. (p. 192)
Koller, jt. auth. see Koller, Jackie French.
Koller, Christopher. Paradeisos (p. 1323)
Koller, Jackie French. No Such Thing. Lewin, Betsy, illus. (p. 1260)
—One Monkey Too Many. Munsinger, Lynn, illus. (p. 1296)
—Someday. (p. 1609)
—Wizard Named Nell. Guay, Rebecca, illus. (p. 1943)
—Wizard's Apprentice. Guay, Rebecca, illus. (p. 1943)
—Wizard's Scepter. (p. 1943)
Koller, Jackie French & Koller. Horace the Horrible: A Knight Meets His Match Urbanovic, Jackie, illus. (p. 797)
Kollin, Dani. My Very Own Dreidel: A Pop-up Hanakkah Celebration! Howard, Juliet, illus. (p. 1221)
Kollman, Carrie, illus. see Compton, Dawn.
Kollmar, Elizabeth M. Hooked on Rubber Band Jewelry: 12 Off-the-Loom Designs for Bracelets, Necklaces, & Other Accessories. (p. 795)
Kollmer, Jen, jt. auth. see Flaherty, Somer.
Kolloch, Brigitte, jt. auth. see Zoller, Elisabeth.
Kolloch, Brigitte, jt. auth. see Zöller, Elisabeth.
Kolnik, Paul, photos by see Morris, Ann.
Kolodny, Cynthia. We Like Puddles. Sagasti, Miriam, illus. (p. 1867)
Kolodny, Nancy J. Beginner's Guide to Eating Disorders Recovery. (p. 159)
Kolodziej, Vivian. Corinne's Big Decision. (p. 367)
—Mystery in Glen Cove. (p. 1224)
Kolosov, Jacqueline. Along the Way. (p. 48)
Kolpin, Amanda, jt. auth. see Kolpin, Molly.
Kolpin, Amanda & Kolpin, Molly. Story of the Civil War (p. 1660)
Kolpin, Molly. American Black Bears (p. 60)
—Barbara Park Byers, Michael, illus. (p. 137)
—Barn Spiders (p. 139)
—Bears. (p. 151)
—Biggest Battles of the Civil War (p. 185)
—Black Widow Spiders (p. 197)
—Chiweenie: A Cross Between a Chihuahua & a Dachshund (p. 308)
—Daddy Long-Leg Spiders (p. 398)
—Eerie Haunted Places (p. 505)
—Favorite Horses: Breeds Girls Love (p. 578)
—Galapagos Penguins (p. 653)
—Giant Pandas (p. 674)
—Great Women of the Civil War (p. 719)
—Grizzly Bears (p. 724)
—My Silly Body. (p. 1218)
—Newts (p. 1249)
—Polar Bears (p. 1379)
—Puggle: A Cross Between a Pug & a Beagle (p. 1415)
—Salamanders (p. 1504)
—Shel Silverstein Byers, Michael, illus. (p. 1564)
—Tarantulas (p. 1706)
—Tour of Your Digestive System. Jones, Chris B., illus. (p. 1773)
—Tour of Your Nervous System. Jones, Chris B., illus. (p. 1773)
—Trapdoor Spiders (p. 1779)
—Velociraptor: Clawed Hunter Dove, Jason, illus. (p. 1835)
—Why Do I Burp? (p. 1923)
—Why Do I Hiccup? (p. 1923)
—Why Do I Sneeze? (p. 1923)
—Why Do I Yawn? (p. 1923)
Kolpin, Molly, jt. auth. see Kolpin, Amanda.
Kolpin, Molly & Bratton, Donna Bowman. Crazy about Horses (p. 377)
—Crazy about Horses: Everything Horse Lovers Needs to Know (p. 377)
Kolpin, Molly & Kolpin, Amanda. Story of the Civil War (p. 1660)
Kolpin, Molly Erin. Tour of Your Digestive System Jones, Chris B., illus. (p. 1773)
—Tour of Your Nervous System Jones, Chris B., illus. (p. 1773)
Kolpin, Molly, et al. Designer Dogs. (p. 430)
—First Graphics: Body Systems. Jones, Chris B., illus. (p. 595)
—Your Favorite Authors. Byers, Michael, illus. (p. 1980)
Kolter, Roberto, photos by see Kornberg, Arthur.
Koltun, Amy, illus. see Carroll, Jonathan.
Koltz, Tony, jt. auth. see Zinni, Tony.
Kolvanovic, Dubravka, illus. see Tiger Tales, ed.
Komada, Yoshihiro, et al. Flesh for the Beast. Pannone, Frank, ed. (p. 603)
Komai, Asuka. October Moon. (p. 1277)
Komaiko, Leah. Annie Bananie. Cornell, Laura, illus. (p. 86)
Komalasari, Arie. Kiki the Orangutan: The Big Banana Festival. (p. 955)
Komarck, Michael, illus. see Hunt, Darleen L.
Komarnitsky, Kara. Grimalkin's Secret. (p. 724)
Komarudin. Golden Feather: A Jataka Tale: A Story & Coloring Book. (p. 694)
Komatsu, Eiko, jt. illus. see Nishiyama, Akira.
Komatsu, Narumi & Suzuki, Ichiro. Ichiro on Ichiro. Gabriel, Philip, tr. (p. 851)
Komatsu, Yoshio, photos by see Nishiyama, Akira & Komatsu, Eiko, illus.
Komechak, Marilyn Gilbert. Paisano Pete: Snake-Killer Bird. Eckhardt, Jason C., illus. (p. 1319)
Komendat, Tiffany. ... When along Came Chad the Cheetah. (p. 1901)
Komiya, Teruyuki. Life-Size Aquarium. Miyakoshi, Junko, tr. from JPN. (p. 1013)
—Life-Size Farm. (p. 1013)
—More Life-Size Zoo: An All-New Actual-Size Animal Encyclopedia. Miyakoshi, Junko, tr. (p. 1174)
Komorn, Julie, adapted by. Out of the Dark. (p. 1311)
Komorn, Julie & Lenhard, Elizabeth, adapted by. Light of Meridian. (p. 1015)
Komorova, Nadia, illus. see Ritt, Sharon I.
Kompelein, Tracy. 1, 2, 3, It's Easy for Me! (p. 1990)
—I Can Add, It's Not So Bad! (p. 834)
—I Can Measure Weight at Any Rate. (p. 836)
—I Can Subtract, It's Not an Act! (p. 836)
—Lets Compare, If You Dare! (p. 995)
—Skip Count by 2, Now Can You? (p. 1585)
—Skip Count by 5, Its No Jive! (p. 1585)
—We Have the Skills to Know U. S. Bills! (p. 1867)
Kompelien, Tracy. 2-D Shapes Are Behind the Drapes! (p. 1991)
—3-D Shapes Are Like Green Grapes! (p. 1991)
—Ahi to Ziti: Food from A to Z. (p. 30)
—Calico in the Window. (p. 253)
—Can You Count More Than Before? (p. 258)
—Castle Is Cold, Ancient & Old! (p. 276)
—Duck Bills. Haberstroh, Anne, illus. (p. 488)
—Dwight & the Magic Kite. (p. 491)
—Elephant Trunks. Nobens, C. A., illus. (p. 511)
—Elephant Trunks. Nobens, Cheryl A., illus. (p. 511)
—Ella Is Right, Smart & Bright! (p. 514)
—Fly Paper. Haberstroh, Anne, illus. (p. 609)
—I Can Divide, I Need No Guide! (p. 835)
—I Can Measure Length, It Has No Strength! (p. 836)
—I Can Multiply, It's Not a Lie! (p. 836)
—I Can Tell Time with a Rhyme! (p. 836)
—I Know about Money, It Is So Funny! (p. 840)
—I Know Fractions by Their Actions! (p. 840)
—I Know the Days in Many Ways! (p. 840)
—I See a Pattern, What Can I Learn? (p. 845)
—Leap Frog. Haberstroh, Anne, illus. (p. 982)
—Lets All Assume, We Can Measure Volume! (p. 994)
—Lets Sort, Its a Real Sport! (p. 1000)
—Lion Manes. Nobens, C. A., illus. (p. 1020)
—Lion Manes. Haberstroh, Anne, illus. (p. 1020)
—Mole with a Goal. (p. 1160)
—Monarch Butterfly. Chawla, Neena, illus. (p. 1163)
—Octopus's Garden. (p. 1278)
—Pickle Is Dilly, Cool & Chilly! (p. 1354)
—Scott the Astronaut. (p. 1531)
—Skip Count by 10, Lets Do It Again! (p. 1585)
—Spider Web. Haberstroh, Anne, illus. (p. 1626)
—There Is Order on the Border! (p. 1730)
—Thumb & His Chum. (p. 1745)
—Why Are You Sad & Blue? (p. 1922)
—Why Is Today Cloudy & Gray? (p. 1925)
—Yaks Relax. (p. 1968)
—Yell & Scream for Your Team! (p. 1969)
—You Can Estimate, Thats Really Great! (p. 1974)
—Zebra Stripes. Nobens, C. A., illus. (p. 1985)
—Zebra Stripes. Nobens, Cheryl A., illus. (p. 1985)
Kompelien, Tracy, jt. auth. see ABDO Publishing Company Staff.
Komroff, Manuel. Big City, Little Boy. (p. 180)
Komura, Ayumi. Mixed Vegetables. Komura, Ayumi, illus. (p. 1156)
—Mixed Vegetables, Vol. 8. Komura, Ayumi, illus. (p. 1156)
Konagaya, Kiyomi. Beach Feet. Saito, Masamitsu, illus. (p. 149)
Konami, Kanata. Chi's Sweet Home. (p. 308)
—Chi's Sweet Home 9. (p. 308)
Konatich, James, illus. see Dutta-Yean, Tutu & Maire, Lucy Bedoya.
Koncerak, Veronica. Bubble That Never Popped. (p. 233)
Konda, Cynthia. Okasan & Me: Japanese American Educational Program. (p. 1282)
Kondeatis, Christos. Scenes from the Life of Jesus Christ: A Three-Dimensional Bible Storybook. Kondeatis, Christos, illus. (p. 1521)
Kondonassis, Yolanda. Our House Is Round: A Kid's Book about Why Protecting Our Earth Matters. Brush, Joan, illus. (p. 1309)
Kondor, Karen. How to Trap a Leprechaun. (p. 822)
Kondrat, Lauren. Mischievous Mort. (p. 1150)
Kondrchek, Jamie. Day in the Life (Un Dia en la Vida) Vega, Eida de la, tr. (p. 413)
—My Favorite Time of Day (Mi Hora Preferida del Dia) Vega, Eida de la, tr. from ENG. (p. 1203)
Kondrchek, Jamie & Rasemas, Joe. On My Way to School (De Camino a la Escuela) Vega, Eida de la, tr. (p. 1289)
—What Day Is It? (Que Dia Es Hoy?) Vega, Eida de la, tr. (p. 1881)
—What Should I Wear Today? (Que Ropa Me Pondre Hoy?) Vega, Eida de la, tr. (p. 1893)
Konecny, John, illus. see Boodey, Erin.
Konecny, John, illus. see Dewane, Patrick Ryan.
Konecny, John, illus. see Raffaelli, Sean & Dreske, Erin.
Konecny, John, illus. see Thieme-Baeseman, Rebecca.
Konecny, John, illus. see Waisanen, Emily.
Konecny, Linda. Dave's First Christmas. (p. 410)
Konen, Leah. after Girls. (p. 28)
Kong, Anja & Sunkara, Naveena. Battle Of: Secret of the Taj. (p. 146)
Kong, Emilie, illus. see Freeman, Don.
Kongyin. Gooby & the Dreamwalker. (p. 697)
—Sungrass. (p. 1677)
Konieczko, Craig. Intervention: Putting Yourself Between a Friend & Addiction. (p. 881)
—Recovery from Drug Addiction. (p. 1452)
Konieczny, Margaret. Ten Finger Prints in the Butter. (p. 1718)
Konieczny, Vladimir. Struggling for Perfection: The Story of Glenn Gould. (p. 1668)
—Struggling for Perfection: The Story of Glenn Gould. Wysotski, Chrissie, illus. (p. 1668)
Konietzko, Bryan, jt. auth. see DiMartino, Michael Dante.
Konietzko, Bryan, jt. creator see DiMartino, Michael Dante.
Konietzko, Bryan & DiMartino, Michael Dante. Avatar: The Last Airbender. (p. 118)
Konietzko, Bryan, et al. Avatar: The Last Airbender. Marshall, Dave, ed. (p. 118)
König, Hans J. Geheime Mission. (p. 659)
—Mysteriose Konzert. (p. 1222)
Konigbagbe, Olutobi. Joy in the Morning. (p. 929)
Konigsberg, Bill. Openly Straight. (p. 1300)
—Porcupine of Truth. (p. 1386)
Konigsburg, E. L. About the B'nai Bagels. Konigsburg, E. L., illus. (p. 6)
—E. L. Konigsburg Newbery Collection: From the Mixed-Up Files of Mrs. Basil E. Frankweiler; Jennifer, Hecate, Macbeth, William Mckinley, & Me, Elizabeth; the View from Saturday. (p. 492)
—From the Mixed-Up Files of Mrs. Basil E. Frankweiler. (p. 644)
—George. Konigsburg, E. L., illus. (p. 663)
—Jennifer, Hecate, Macbeth, William McKinley, & Me, Elizabeth. (p. 912)
—Journey to an 800 Number. (p. 928)
—My Father's Daughter. (p. 1203)
—Mysterious Edge of the Heroic World. (p. 1223)
—Outcasts of 19 Schuyler Place. (p. 1312)
—Sabato di Gloria. (p. 1499)
—Second Mrs. Giaconda. (p. 1539)
—Second Mrs. Gioconda. (p. 1539)
—Silent to the Bone. (p. 1575)
—T-Backs, T-Shirts, Coat, & Suit. (p. 1693)
—Throwing Shadows. (p. 1745)
—View from Saturday. (p. 1841)
Konigsburg, E. L. & Haley, Gail E. Altogether, One at a Time. Mayer, Mercer et al, illus. (p. 50)
Königslöw, Andrea Wayne von, see von Königslöw, Andrea Wayne.
Konings, Neeltje, tr. see Berner, Rotraut Susanne.
Koniver, Laura. From the Ground Up. Koniver, Laura, illus. (p. 644)
—Jake, A Guinea Pig Finds Adventure. (p. 905)
—Together We Sleep. (p. 1762)
Konlee, Mark & LeBeau, Conrad. Immune Restoration Handbook (p. 861)
Könnecke, Ole. Anton & the Battle. Chidgey, Catherine, tr. from GER. (p. 90)
—Big Book of Animals of the World. Könnecke, Ole, illus. (p. 178)
—Big Book of Words & Pictures. Könnecke, Ole, illus. (p. 179)
Könnecke, Ole & Chidgey, Catherine. Anton Can Do Magic. Könnecke, Ole, illus. (p. 90)
Konnikova, Svetlana. Grapette, the Runaway Who Rolled Away: A Timeless Tale of Love & Family: A Child Discovering the World. Smishliaev, Anatoli, illus. (p. 710)
Kono, Erin Eitter. Caterina & the Best Beach Day. (p. 279)
—Caterina & the Lemonade Stand. (p. 279)
—Caterina & the Perfect Party. (p. 279)
—Twelve Days of Christmas in Wisconsin. (p. 1800)
Kono, Erin Eitter, illus. see Brimner, Larry Dane.
Konomi, Takeshi. Prince of Tennis Konomi, Takeshi, illus. (p. 1401)
—Prince of Tennis. Brown, Urian, ed. (p. 1401)
—Prince of Tennis. Konomi, Takeshi, illus. (p. 1401)
—Prince of TennisTM Yamazaki, Joe, tr. from JPN. (p. 1401)
Konopka, Annie. Tale of A Parkie Princess. (p. 1699)
Konopka, Jan, illus. see Williams, Rachel.
Konrad, Dee C. Grammar Handbook. (p. 706)
Konrad, Marla Stewart. Getting There. (p. 669)
—Grand. (p. 707)
—Just Like You: Beautiful Babies Around the World Wang, Lin, illus. (p. 939)
—Mom & Me. (p. 1161)
Konrath, J. A. Bloody Mary. (p. 201)
Konstam, Angus. America Speaks (p. 59)
Konstantinov, Vitali, illus. see Welborn, Amy.
Konsul, Mike. Auggie the Doggie & Pat the Cat. (p. 115)
Kontis, Alethea. Alpha Oops! The Day Z Went First. Kolar, Bob, illus. (p. 48)
—Alphaoops! H Is for Halloween. Kolar, Bob, illus. (p. 50)
—Dearest (p. 419)
—Enchanted. (p. 523)
—Hero. (p. 772)
Kontis, Alethea, jt. auth. see Carroll, Lewis, pseud.
Kontler, Laszlo. History of Hungary. (p. 784)
Kontzias, Bill. Look & See: A What's-Not-The-Same-Game. Kontzias, Bill, photos by. (p. 1048)
Konye, Paul, illus. see Ashforth, Kate.
Konye, Paul, illus. see Rushby, Pamela.
Konye, Paul, jt. auth. see Mitchell, Julie.
Konzen, Lisa M. Good News for Naaman. Snyder, Joel, illus. (p. 699)
Koo, Rob. Great Buddhist Stories. (p. 714)
—More Great Buddhist Stories. (p. 1174)
Kool, Jason. Hunter's Legacy: Cause. (p. 828)
Kooistra, Alex, illus. see Bersma, Danielle & Visscher, Marjoke.
Kook, Ima. Big Bang Theory: The Bang That Created Our Universe. (p. 178)
—Binary Numbers: Learning to Count with 0's And 1's. (p. 188)
—Einstein's Theory of Relativity: Go Too Fast & Strange Things Happen. (p. 507)
—Newton's Laws: They Tell How Things Move. (p. 1249)
Koolen, Maayken. Kidnapping of Mona Lisa. (p. 952)
Koolish, Lynn, et al. Wonderful Colorful Wonder Wheel of Color: Activities, Stickers, Poster & More. (p. 1948)
Koon, Adam, jt. ed. see Mendenhall, Emily.
Koon, Cheng Puay, illus. see Humphreys, Neil.
Koon-Chiu, Lo, illus. see Hume, Lotta Carswell & Lo, Koon-Chiu.
Koontx, Jayne. California Central Coast Coloring Book. (p. 253)
Koontz, Dean. Every Day's a Holiday: Amusing Rhymes for Happy Times. Parks, Phil, illus. (p. 542)
—Robot Santa: The Further Adventures of Santa's Twin. Parks, Phil, illus. (p. 1480)
—Santa's Twin. Parks, Phil, illus. (p. 1513)
—Watchers. (p. 1861)
Koontz, Dean, jt. auth. see Nichols, Leigh, pseud.
Koontz, Dean, see Nichols, Leigh, pseud.
Koontz, Jennifer. Charlie's Great Adventure. (p. 293)
Koontz, Robin. Apples, Apples Everywhere! Learning about Apple Harvests Takvorian, Nadine, illus. (p. 92)
—Binoculars. (p. 188)
—Cinderella Zelda. Koontz, Robin, illus. (p. 320)
—Computer Mouse. (p. 355)
—Hide & Seek Moon: The Moon Phases Davidson, Chris, illus. (p. 776)
—Light in the Real World. (p. 1015)
—Los Tres Carneros y el Ogro / the Three Billy Goats & Gruff. (p. 1054)
—Paul Bunyan. Koontz, Robin, illus. (p. 1330)
—Pequeña Lagartija, ¡el Cielo Se Está Cayendo! / Lizzie Little, the Sky Is Falling! (p. 1341)
—Pick a Perfect Pumpkin: Learning about Pumpkin Harvests Takvorian, Nadine, illus. (p. 1354)
—Robin Hood. Koontz, Robin, illus. (p. 1479)
—Rumpelstiltskin. Koontz, Robin, illus. (p. 1495)
—Run... It's a Bee! Koontz, Robin, illus. (p. 1496)
—Three Billy Goats & Gruff. Koontz, Robin, illus. (p. 1741)
—Traje Nuevo Del Rey. (p. 1777)
—TV Remotes. (p. 1799)
—Water Goes Round: The Water Cycle Davidson, Chris, illus. (p. 1862)
—What Was Hurricane Katrina? (p. 1894)
—What Was Hurricane Katrina? Hinderliter, John & McVeigh, Kevin, illus. (p. 1894)
—Zelda la Cenicienta. (p. 1986)
Koontz, Robin, jt. auth. see Koontz, Robin Michal.
Koontz, Robin Michal. Apples, Apples Everywhere! Learning about Apple Harvests Takvorian, Nadine, illus. (p. 92)
—Composting: Nature's Recyclers Harrad, Matthew, illus. (p. 354)
—Connecticut: The Constitution State. (p. 358)
—Erosion: Changing Earth's Surface Harrad, Matthew, illus. (p. 534)
—Hide & Seek Moon: The Moon Phases Davidson, Chris, illus. (p. 776)
—King's New Clothes. Koontz, Robin Michal, illus. (p. 960)
—Leaps & Creeps: How Animals Move to Survive. (p. 982)
—Learning about Africa. (p. 984)
—Lizzie Little, the Sky Is Falling! Koontz, Robin Michal, illus. (p. 1043)
—Maine: The Pine Tree State. (p. 1077)
—Movers & Makers: How Animals Build & Use Tools to Survive. (p. 1183)
—New Hampshire: The Granite State. (p. 1245)
—Pick a Perfect Pumpkin: Learning about Pumpkin Harvests Takvorian, Nadine, illus. (p. 1354)
—Rhode Island: The Ocean State. (p. 1468)
—Robin Hood. Koontz, Robin Michal, illus. (p. 1479)
—Screams & Songs: How Animals Communicate to Survive. (p. 1533)
—Sniffs & Stinks: How Animals Use Odor to Survive. (p. 1597)
—Spits & Squirts: How Animals Squirt to Survive. (p. 1629)
—Vermont: The Green Mountain State. (p. 1837)
—Water Goes Round: The Water Cycle Davidson, Chris, illus. (p. 1862)
—West Virginia: The Mountain State. (p. 1876)
—What's Great about Missouri? (p. 1897)
Koontz, Robin Michal, illus. see Dunn, Richard & Sprick, Jessica.
Koontz, Robin Michal & Elliott, Rebecca. Butterfly Spring. (p. 248)
Koontz, Robin Michal & Koontz, Robin. What's the Difference Between a Butterfly & a Moth? Dacey, Bandelin et al, illus. (p. 1899)
Koopmans, Andy. Harlem Renaissance. (p. 749)
—History of the Blues. (p. 784)
—Rwanda. (p. 1499)
—Rwanda. Rotberg, Robert I., ed. (p. 1499)
Koopmans, Anna. Sioux. (p. 1580)
Koopmans, Carol. Caring for Your Gerbil. (p. 269)
—Gerbil. (p. 666)
Koopmans, Carol & Kissock, Heather. Aboriginal Peoples. (p. 5)
Koopmans, Loek. Frog, Bee & Snail Look for Snow (p. 640)
Koopmans, Loek, illus. see Mason, Jane B.
Koopmans, Loek, tr. see Mason, Jane B.
Koops, Sheena. Voice of the Valley (p. 1848)
Koorang, Mundara. Little Platypus & the Fire Spirit. (p. 1033)
—Little Platypus & the Fire Spirit. Koorang, Mundara, illus. (p. 1033)
Kooser, Ted. House Held up by Trees. Klassen, Jon, illus. (p. 803)
Koosman, Melissa. Fall of Apartheid in South Africa. (p. 566)
—Meet Our New Student from South Africa. (p. 1122)
Koosmann, Melissa. Recipe & Craft Guide to South Africa. (p. 1451)
Kootstra, Kara. Boy in Number Four. Thomson, Regan, illus. (p. 218)
Kootz, Russell & Seidman, David. Understanding Civil Rights. (p. 1815)
Kopald, Sue-Anne, illus. see Thomasson, Merry F.
Kopan, Alice Orphanos, jt. auth. see Meek, Janis P.
Kopanic, Michael J., ed. see Culen, Konstantin.
Kopczynski, Megan. Anastasia Rose Sleeps in Her Own Room Stasiuk, Max, illus. (p. 67)
Kopec, Mary Kate. Awesome Adventures of Randi Raindrop. (p. 120)
Kopelke, Lisa. Younger Brother's Survival Guide. Kopelke, Lisa, illus. (p. 1979)
Kopelke, Lisa, illus. see De La Hoya, Oscar.
Kopervas, Gary, illus. see Wilcox, Jean K. & Cameron, E. Jane.
Kopetz, Mark. Red Herrings at Rock Island: A Door County Mystery. (p. 1454)
Kopito, Janet Baine, ed. see Dodge, Mary Mapes.
Kopka, Deborah. Norway. (p. 1266)
Kopka, Deborah L. Norway. (p. 1266)
Kopler, Joe, illus. see Garrett, Kelsey.
Kopley, Richard. Remarkable David Wordsworth. Fazio, Michael, illus. (p. 1458)
Koponen, Libby. Blow Out the Moon. (p. 202)
—Floods. (p. 605)
—Ireland. (p. 887)
—North America. (p. 1264)
—South America. (p. 1616)
Kopp, Claire B., jt. ed. see Brownell, Celia A.
Kopp, J. J. Aurora, Daughter of the Dawn: A Story of New Beginnings. Will, Clark Moor, illus. (p. 116)
Kopp, Jaine. Algebraic Reasoning: Professor Arbegla Introduces Variables & Functions. (p. 38)
—Early Adventures in Algebra: Featuring Zero the Hero. Klofkorn, Lisa, illus. (p. 493)
Kopp, Megan. Anacondas (p. 66)
—Avalanches. (p. 118)

K

—Black Widow Spiders. (p. 197)
—Campana de la Libertad. (p. 257)
—Chickens. (p. 300)
—Cobras (p. 337)
—Energy from Wind: Wind Farming. (p. 528)
—Football. (p. 615)
—Gallinas. (p. 653)
—Gallinas/Megan Kopp. (p. 653)
—Hockey. (p. 786)
—How Do Insects Move? (p. 807)
—How Do Insects Protect Themselves? (p. 807)
—How Do Insects Work Together? (p. 807)
—How to Write a Drama. (p. 822)
—How to Write Science Fiction. (p. 823)
—Islands Inside Out. (p. 892)
—Liberty Bell with Code. (p. 1005)
—Light Works. (p. 1015)
—Living in a Sustainable Way: Green Communities. (p. 1041)
—Mexico. (p. 1131)
—Migration. (p. 1141)
—Milky Way & Other Galaxies (p. 1143)
—Montana: The Treasure State. (p. 1170)
—NASCAR. (p. 1230)
—Nebraska: The Cornhusker State. (p. 1239)
—Nevada: The Silver State. (p. 1242)
—New Hampshire: The Granite State. (p. 1245)
—New Jersey: The Garden State. (p. 1245)
—Ovejas. (p. 1313)
—Parasites. (p. 1324)
—Prairie Dogs. (p. 1392)
—Reality Television. (p. 1449)
—Real-Life Vampires (p. 1448)
—Rhinos. (p. 1467)
—Rivers & Lakes Inside Out. (p. 1476)
—Saudi Arabia. (p. 1516)
—Scary Folktales (p. 1520)
—Sheep. (p. 1564)
—South Dakota: Mount Rushmore State. (p. 1617)
—Suzanne Collins. (p. 1688)
—Understanding Chinese Myths. (p. 1815)
—Understanding Native American Myths. (p. 1816)
—United States. (p. 1819)
—What Do Insects Eat? (p. 1882)
Kopp, Megan, jt. auth. see Crabtree Staff.
Koppelhus, Eva B., jt. auth. see Currie, Philip J.
Koppens, Judith. Good-Bye, Fish. van Lindenhuizen, Eline, illus. (p. 697)
—Seesaw. van Lindenhuizen, Eline, illus. (p. 1548)
Kopper, Lisa, illus. see Greaves, Margaret.
Kopper, Lisa, illus. see Hallworth, Grace.
Kopper, Lisa, tr. see Greaves, Margaret.
Koppes, Steven N. Killer Rocks from Outer Space: Asteroids, Comets, & Meteorites. (p. 956)
Kopple, Deborah. Spear of Golden Grass: Short Stories by Norwalk High School Honors English Students. (p. 1623)
Kopple, Deborah, ed. Heads in the Ground: Short Stories by Norwalk High School Honor's English Students. (p. 757)
Kopplin, Carolin, ed. see Fury, David Arthur.
Kops, Deborah. Ancient Rome: A MyReportLinks. com Book. (p. 70)
—Discover Ancient Rome. (p. 447)
—Exploring Exoplanets. (p. 552)
—Exploring Space Robots. (p. 553)
—Great Molasses Flood: Boston 1919. (p. 717)
—Great Molasses Flood. (p. 717)
—Humpback Whale: Help Save This Endangered Species! (p. 827)
—Machu Picchu. (p. 1068)
—Native Americans of the Plains: Set Of 6. (p. 1234)
—Native Americans of the Plains: Text Pairs. (p. 1234)
—Palenque. (p. 1319)
—Racial Profiling. (p. 1432)
—Were Early Computers Really the Size of a School Bus? And Other Questions about Inventions. (p. 1875)
—Were Potato Chips Really Invented by an Angry Chef? And Other Questions about Food. (p. 1875)
—Zachary Taylor: America's 12th President. (p. 1984)
Kor, Eva Mozes & Buccieri, Lisa Rojany. Surviving the Angel of Death: The True Story of a Mengele Twin in Auschwitz. (p. 1687)
Kor, Eva Mozes, et al. Surviving the Angel of Death: The Story of a Mengele Twin in Auschwitz. (p. 1687)
Koraido, Beth S. On the Farm with Grandma Gert. (p. 1290)
—Summers with Grampa Gus. (p. 1675)
Koralek, Jenny. Coat of Many Colors. Baynes, Pauline, illus. (p. 336)
—Moses Basket. Baynes, Pauline, illus. (p. 1176)
—Story of Queen Esther. Holderness, Grizelda, illus. (p. 1659)
—War Games. (p. 1857)
Korantema, Jwajiku. I'm African & Proud. (p. 858)
Korb, Rena. Awesome Air. Reibeling, Brandon, illus. (p. 120)
—Crazy about Clouds. Reibeling, Brandon, illus. (p. 377)
—Digging on Dirt. Reibeling, Brandon, illus. (p. 439)
—Discovering Giganotosaurus. Dawson, Ted, illus. (p. 449)
—Discovering Ichthyosaurs. Dawson, Ted, illus. (p. 449)
—Groovy Gravity. Reibeling, Brandon, illus. (p. 725)
—Radical Rocks. Reibeling, Brandon, illus. (p. 1432)
—Science Rocks! CD + Book Set. Reibeling, Brandon, illus. (p. 1527)
—Wild Water Cycle. Reibeling, Brandon, illus. (p. 1930)
Korb, Rena B. Discovering Brachiosaurus. Dawson, Ted, illus. (p. 449)
—Discovering Pteranodon. Dawson, Ted, illus. (p. 449)
—Discovering Tyrannosaurus Rex. Dawson, Ted, illus. (p. 450)
—Discovering Velociraptor. Dawson, Ted, illus. (p. 450)
—Pulling down the Walls: The Struggle of African American Performers. (p. 1416)
Korb, Rena B. & Weinhaus, Anthony J. My Brain. Simard, Remy, illus. (p. 1199)
—My Mouth. Simard, Remy, illus. (p. 1215)
—My Muscles. Simard, Remy, illus. (p. 1215)
—My Nose. Simard, Remy, illus. (p. 1216)
—My Spine. Simard, Remy, illus. (p. 1219)
—My Stomach. Simard, Remy, illus. (p. 1219)
Korba, Joanna. Cindy Eller Plays Ball: A Modern-Day Cinderella Tale. (p. 321)
—Demeter & Persephone: A Myth from Ancient Greece. (p. 425)
—Fox & the Cheese Queen. (p. 626)
—Rough-Face Girl: A Native American Cinderella Tale. (p. 1491)
—Sleepless Beauty. (p. 1589)
—Yeh-shen: A Cinderella Tale from China. (p. 1969)
Korba, Joanna & Benchmark Education Co., LLC. Pluto, the Planet That Was. (p. 1374)
—Who Are You? Fabbri, Daniele, illus. (p. 1914)
Korba, Joanne. Two Golden Geese. (p. 1803)
—Wild Weather. (p. 1930)
Korbel, Wendy. Gus: Adventures on the Farm. (p. 732)
Korczak, Janusz. Kaytek the Wizard. Lloyd-Jones, Antonia, tr. from POL. (p. 946)
Korczak, Janusz & Lourie, Richard. King Matt the First: A Novel. Lourie, Richard, tr. from POL. (p. 958)
Korda, Lerryn. Into the Wild. Korda, Lerryn, illus. (p. 881)
—It's Vacation Time. Korda, Lerryn, illus. (p. 899)
—Millions of Snow. Korda, Lerryn, illus. (p. 1144)
—So Cozy. Korda, Lerryn, illus. (p. 1602)
Korda, Lerryn, jt. auth. see Korda, Lerryn.
Korda, Lerryn & Korda, Lerryn. Rocket to the Moon. Korda, Lerryn & Korda, Lerryn, illus. (p. 1483)
Kordey, Igor, illus. see Macan, Darko.
Kordich, Melinda, illus. see Baumann, Jessica.
Korelitz, Jean Hanff. Interference Powder (p. 879)
Korelitz, Jean Hanff, jt. auth. see Kimmel, Eric A.
Korell, Jennifer. Day at the Beach with Shrimp & Friends. (p. 412)
Koren, Edward. Very Hairy Harry. (p. 1838)
—Very Hairy Harry. Koren, Edward, illus. (p. 1838)
Koren, Edward, illus. see Katz, Alan.
Koren, Robert. Moon in the Man. (p. 1172)
Korenblit, Michael & Janger, Kathleen. Until We Meet Again: A True Story of Love & Survival in the Holocaust. (p. 1823)
Korhel, Erik. My Tooth Fell in My Soup: And Other Poems. Baker, Celia M., illus. (p. 1220)
Korhonen, Kari, et al. Uncle Scrooge #355. Clark, John, ed. (p. 1812)
—Walt Disney's Comics & Stories #705. (p. 1855)
Korkos, Alain, illus. see Pinet, Michele.
Korman, Gordon. 6th Grade Nickname Game. (p. 1992)
—Born to Rock. (p. 214)
—Chasing the Falconers. (p. 294)
—Climb. (p. 332)
—Collision Course (p. 341)
—Contest. (p. 360)
—Dragonfly Effect (the Hypnotists #3) (p. 478)
—Emperor's Code. (p. 521)
—Escape. (p. 534)
—Everest: The Climb. (p. 542)
—Everest Book One: the Contest. (p. 542)
—Everest Book Three: the Summit. (p. 542)
—Everest Book Two: the Climb. (p. 542)
—Framed. (p. 627)
—Hideout. (p. 777)
—Hypnotists. (p. 831)
—Hypnotists Book 2: Memory Maze. (p. 831)
—Island Trilogy. (p. 892)
—Jackpot: A Swindle Mystery. (p. 904)
—Jackpot. (p. 904)
—Jake, Reinvented. (p. 906)
—Juvie Three. (p. 941)
—Masterminds. (p. 1103)
—Medusa Plot. (p. 1120)
—Memory Maze. (p. 1126)
—One False Note. (p. 1295)
—Pop. (p. 1384)
—Schooled. (p. 1523)
—Search. (p. 1537)
—Showoff. (p. 1571)
—Son of the Mob. (p. 1611)
—Summit. (p. 1675)
—Swindle. (p. 1691)
—This Can't Be Happening at MacDonald Hall! (p. 1735)
—Titanic. (p. 1757)
—Ungifted. (p. 1817)
—Unleashed. (p. 1821)
—Unsinkable (p. 1822)
—Unstoppable - Flashpoint. (p. 1823)
—Zoobreak. (p. 1989)
Korman, Justine. 101 Dalmatians. Langley, Bill & Dias, Ron, illus. (p. 1999)
—Poky Little Puppy's First Christmas. Korman, Justine, illus. (p. 1378)
—Spring Is Here, Grumpy Bunny! McQueen, Lucinda, illus. (p. 1635)
Korman, Justine, jt. auth. see Fontes, Justine.
Korman, Susan. Bad Deal. (p. 131)
—Birds of a Feather. (p. 191)
—Box Turtle at Silver Pond Lane: Smithsonians Backyard. Marchesi, Stephen, illus. (p. 216)
—Box Turtle at Silver Pond Lane. Marchesi, Stephen, illus. (p. 216)
—Continental Drift. (p. 360)
—Groundhog at Evergreen Road. (p. 725)
—Groundhog at Evergreen Road. Bond, Higgins, illus. (p. 725)
—Overexposed. (p. 1314)
—Rachael Ray. (p. 1431)
—Swordfish Returns. Stegos, Daniel, illus. (p. 1692)
—Swordfish Returns. Stegos, Daniel J., illus. (p. 1692)
—They Came from Upstairs. (p. 1732)
Korman, Susan, ed. see Thayer, Robert Scott.
Korman, Susan, jt. auth. see Titan Books Staff.
Korman, Susan J. Bad Deal. (p. 131)
—Overexposed. (p. 1314)
Kormos, Lawrence. It Happened One Night in the Barn. Purdy, Joanne, illus. (p. 894)
Kormos, Lawrence A. Fate of Old Joe Malone. (p. 577)
—There Is A Place I Go. (p. 1730)
—What Is Love Mama? (p. 1889)
Korn, David M. Young King Arthur in Brooklyn. (p. 1979)
Kornacki, Christine, illus. see Hardie, Jill.
Kornberg, Arthur. Germ Stories. Alaniz, Adam, illus. (p. 666)
Kornell, Max. Bear with Me. Kornell, Max, illus. (p. 151)
—Me First. Kornell, Max, illus. (p. 1115)
Korneski, Kelly. Compassionate Chipmunk. (p. 352)
—Grumpy Kitty. (p. 727)
—Pretty Bunny. (p. 1398)
Korngold, Jamie. Sadie & the Big Mountain. Fortenberry, Julie, illus. (p. 1501)
—Sadie, Ori, & Nuggles Go to Camp. Fortenberry, Julie, illus. (p. 1501)
—Sadie's Almost Marvelous Menorah. Fortenberry, Julie, illus. (p. 1501)
—Sadie's Lag Ba'Omer Mystery. Fortenberry, Julie, illus. (p. 1501)
—Seder in the Desert. Finkelstein, Jeff, photos by. (p. 1546)
Korngold, Jamie S. Mazel Tov! It's a Boy: Mazel Tov! It's a Girl. Finkelstein, Jeff, illus. (p. 1113)
—Sadie's Sukkah Breakfast. Fortenberry, Julie, illus. (p. 1501)
Kornher-Stace, Nicole. Archivist Wasp: A Novel. (p. 95)
Kornprobst, Jacques & Laverne, Christine. Living Mountains: How & Why Volcanoes Erupt. (p. 1041)
Korobkina, Katya, illus. see Boutenko, Victoria.
Korobov, Kristine. Allison Marisa Burbank Gets into Trouble. Mahanov, Tanya, ed. (p. 47)
Koroknay, Tom. Lyman Boats: America's Lapstake Classic: Legend of the Lakes. (p. 1066)
Korotky, V. Yvonne. Abbey's Story. (p. 2)
Korr, Mary. Winston the water Dog: Portuguese water dog tales book One. (p. 1937)
Korrell, Emily B. Awesome Adventures at the Smithsonian: The Official Kids Guide to the Smithsonian Institution. (p. 120)
Korringa, Olivia. Miss Olivia Series: Lessons to Start Your Child on the Right Path of Speaking English Correctly. (p. 1151)
Korrow, Chris. Organic Bug Book. Korrow, Chris, illus. (p. 1303)
Korschunow, Irina. Zorrito Abandonado. (p. 1990)
Kort, Michael. Brief History of Russia. (p. 227)
—Russia. (p. 1498)
Kort, Michael G. Central Asian Republics. (p. 287)
—Handbook of the Middle East. (p. 740)
Korte, Steve. Cat Crime Club Baltazar, Art, illus. (p. 277)
—DC Super-Pets Character Encyclopedia Baltazar, Art, illus. (p. 416)
—Mxy's Magical Mayhem. Levins, Tim, illus. (p. 1195)
Korten, Gerri. Parakeets & the Ginkgo Tree at Hide Park. (p. 1323)
Kortenkamp, Steve. Asteroids, Comets, & Meteoroids (p. 108)
—Demoting Pluto: The Discovery of the Dwarf Planets. (p. 426)
—Dwarf Planets (p. 491)
—Future Explorers: Robots in Space. (p. 651)
—NASA (p. 1230)
—Planets of Our Solar System (p. 1368)
—Show Me Space: My First Picture Encyclopedia (p. 1570)
—Space Life (p. 1619)
—Space Robots (p. 1619)
—Space Shuttles (p. 1619)
—Space Stations (p. 1620)
—Space Tourism (p. 1620)
—Space Travelers (p. 1620)
—Spacecraft (p. 1620)
—Working in Space (p. 1953)
Kortenkamp, Steve, jt. auth. see Krumm, Brian.
Korth, Melanie. Hummingbird: Learns Compassion. (p. 826)
—Javelina: Finds Contentment. (p. 910)
—Roadrunner: Finds a Friend. (p. 1477)
—Songbirds. (p. 1611)
Korthues, Barbara, illus. see Jesset, Aurore.
Korthues, Barbara, illus. see Stalder, Päivi.
Kortvely, Zolton. Stories of a Lost Sock. (p. 1654)
Korty, Carol. Plays from African Folktales. Landes, William-Alan, ed. (p. 1373)
—Silly Soup. Landes, William-Alan, ed. (p. 1576)
—Writing Your Own Plays: Creating, Adapting, Improvising. (p. 1965)
Koruda, Yousuke, jt. auth. see Hajime, Yatate.
Korwitts, Maryanna. I Am Me, You Are Thee. (p. 833)
Korzeniowski, Samson, ed. see Jasnoch, Dorothy.
Korzenlowski, Samson O., ed. see Jasnoch, Dorothy.
Kos, Eric J., jt. auth. see Evanovsky, Dennis.
Kosaka, Fumi, illus. see Rylant, Cynthia.
Kosaka, Fumi, illus. see Weeks, Sarah.
Kosara, Tori. Big Kid Shoes. Borlasca, Hector, illus. (p. 182)
—Hibernation. (p. 775)
Kosara, Tori, jt. auth. see Arlon, Penelope.
Kosara, Tori, jt. auth. see Kosara, Victoria.
Kosara, Victoria. Graduation Party. Durk, Jim, illus. (p. 705)
Kosara, Victoria & Kosara, Tori. Marcel & Paddy Save the Day. (p. 1091)
Koscielniak, Bruce. About Time: A First Look at Time & Clocks. (p. 6)
Kosemund, Brandi. Sister Dog. (p. 1581)
Kosgei, William. Talented & Gifted: African Writers Series. (p. 1701)
Koshi, Rikdo. Excel Saga. Koshi, Rikdo, illus. (p. 547)
Koshiba, Tetsuya. Remote. (p. 1460)
Koshiba, Tetsuya, illus. see Amagi, Seimaru.
Koshiyama, Masayo, creator. Journal 10+ A Tool for Documenting Life. (p. 927)
Kosir, Ana, illus. see Glover, Darryl.
Kositchek, Gloria. Dream Prom (p. 483)
Kosits, Andrew, illus. see Maxson, H. A. & Young, Claudia H.
Kositsky, Lynne. Claire by Moonlight. (p. 326)
—Minerva's Voyage. (p. 1146)
—Plagues of Kondar. (p. 1366)
—Thought of High Windows. (p. 1740)
Koski, Mary, jt. auth. see Collins, Lori.
Koski, Mary B. Color, Color, Where Are You, Color? Mason, Janeen, illus. (p. 342)
—Impatient Pamela Asks: Why Are My Feet So Huge? Brown, Dan, illus. (p. 862)
—Impatient Pamela Calls 9-1-1. Brown, Dan, illus. (p. 862)
Koski, Rozanne, illus. see Caza, Sheila.
Koski, Rozanne, illus. see Erb, Diane.
Kosko, S. J. Logan, a Prairie Dog: Springtime Adventures in a Wish-Ton-Wish Borough. (p. 1045)
Koslowski, Rich. King. (p. 958)
Kosmal, Mariana, tr. see Levine, Karen.
Kosmo, Lisa, jt. auth. see Broadbent, Tom.
Kosofsky, Chaim. Much, Much Better. (p. 1188)
Koss, Amy Goldman. Cheat. (p. 295)
—Gossip Times Three. (p. 703)
—Kailey. Howe, Philip, illus. (p. 941)
—Not-So-Great Depression. (p. 1267)
—Poison Ivy. (p. 1377)
—Side Effects. (p. 1573)
Kossuth, Kornel. English for Common Entrance 13+ Practice Book. (p. 530)
Kostadinov, Petar. Speechless Thunder. (p. 1624)
Kostakis, Will. First Third. (p. 597)
Kostecke, Nancy, illus. see Appelhof, Mary, et al.
Kostecki-Shaw, Jenny Sue. Luna & Me: The True Story of a Girl Who Lived in a Tree to Save a Forest. Kostecki-Shaw, Jenny Sue, illus. (p. 1065)
—My Travelin' Eye. Kostecki-Shaw, Jenny Sue, illus. (p. 1220)
—Same, Same but Different. Kostecki-Shaw, Jenny Sue, illus. (p. 1507)
Kostelyk, Jason, illus. see Nesci, Andrea Lynn & Nesci, Jim.
Koster, Amy Sky. Cuddly Princess Pals. (p. 389)
Koster, Gloria. Mitzi's Mitzvah. Conger, Holli, illus. (p. 1156)
—Peanut-Free Café. (p. 1332)
Koster, Lorraine. Students Beware: Life Does Not Begin At 21. (p. 1669)
Kostic, Dimitri, illus. see Winter, Barbara.
Kostick, Conor. Edda. (p. 503)
—Epic. (p. 532)
—Saga. (p. 1502)
Kostigen, Thomas M. Extreme Weather: Surviving Tornadoes, Tsunamis, Hailstorms, Thunder Snow, Hurricanes, & More! (p. 557)
Kostman, Samuel, ed. see Chaitkin, Carol.
Kostro, Ed. Mystery of Madera Canyon. (p. 1224)
Kostyal, K. M. Trial by Ice: A Photobiography of Sir Ernest Shackleton. (p. 1785)
Kostyal, Karen. 1862 - Fredericksburg: A New Look at a Bitter Civil War Battle. Epstein, Lori, photos by. (p. 2002)
Kostyal, Karen & Colonial Williamsburg Foundation Staff. 1776: A New Look at Revolutionary Williamsburg. Renda, Lori Epstein, photos by. (p. 2002)
Koszowski, Allen, illus. see Lumley, Brian.
Kotchman, Susan C. With Love, from Grandma. (p. 1942)
Kote, Genevieve, illus. see Schusterman, Michelle.
Kote, Geneviève, jt. auth. see Schusterman, Michelle.
Kotecki, Jason. Stupid Swimming Lessons: Kim & Jason Annual #3. (p. 1670)
Kotecki, Nathan. Pull down the Night. (p. 1415)
—Suburban Strange. (p. 1671)
Kotler, Arkady, illus. see Kranzler, Gershon.
Kotler, Elina, illus. see Kranzler, Gershon.
Kotoyoshi, Yumisuke, illus. see Akahori, Satoru.
Kotrous, Chad, illus. see Goode, Teresa.
Kotsiovos, Jean, jt. auth. see Biz Kid$.
Kotsut, Rafat. LEGO City: Space Escape Comic Reader. Ameet Studio Staff, illus. (p. 990)
—Space Escape Comic Reader. (p. 1619)
Kott, Jennifer & Streiffert, Kristi. Nicaragua. (p. 1250)
Kottak, Conrad Phillip. Anthropology: The Exploration of Human Diversity, with Student Atlas & PowerWeb. (p. 89)
Kottmeyer, William, ed. see Ware, Kay & Sutherland, Lucille.
Kottmeyer, William A. Basic Goals in Spelling (p. 141)
—Basic Goals in Spelling: Grade 5. (p. 141)
—Basic Goals in Spelling. (p. 141)
—Basic Goals in Spelling (Pupil Edition) (p. 142)
—Conquests in Reading. (p. 358)
Kotzwinkle, William. Trouble in Bugland: A Collection of Inspector Mantis Mysteries. Servello, Joe, illus. (p. 1789)
Kotzwinkle, William & Murray, Glenn. Walter Canis Inflatus: Walter the Farting Dog, Latin-Language Edition. Dobbin, Rob, tr. from ENG. (p. 1856)
—Walter el Perro Pedorrero. Bohorquez, Eduardo, tr. from ENG. (p. 1856)
—Walter le Chien Qui Pete. Choquette, Michel, tr. from ENG. (p. 1856)
—Walter the Farting Dog: Trouble at the Yard Sale. Colman, Audrey, illus. (p. 1856)
—Walter the Farting Dog: Trouble at the Yard Sale. Coleman, Audrey & Audrey, Colman, illus. (p. 1856)
Kotzwinkle, William & Pearson Education Staff. PLAR2: Et Extra Terrestrial Book & Cd-Rom. (p. 1370)
Kotzwinkle, William, et al. Rough Weather Ahead for Walter the Farting Dog. Colman, Audrey, illus. (p. 1491)
—Walter the Farting Dog: Banned from the Beach. Colman, Audrey, illus. (p. 1856)
—Walter the Farting Dog: Banned from the Beach. Coleman, Audrey, illus. (p. 1856)
—Walter the Farting Dog Goes on a Cruise. Coleman, Audrey, illus. (p. 1856)
Kou, Christopher D., ed. see Haggard, H. Rider.
Koubena, Elizabeth. Trouble with Harry. (p. 1790)
Kouga, Yun. Crown of Love. (p. 386)
—Earthian (p. 497)
—Earthian. Kouga, Yun, illus. (p. 497)
—Loveless Kouga, Yun, illus. (p. 1061)
Kouga, Yun, et al. Loveless (p. 1061)
Kouguell, Susan. Savvy Screenwriter: How to Sell Your Screenplay (And Yourself) Without Selling Out! (p. 1518)
Koumjian, Gay Melanie. Mojo's Mojo. (p. 1160)
Koumpouras, Sally. Comprehension Crosswords Grade 5 Adams Marks, Elizabeth, illus. (p. 354)
Kountz, Charity. Jason, Lizzy & the Snowman Village. Klock, Kimberly, illus. (p. 910)
Koupelis, Theo. In Quest of the Solar System. (p. 864)

—In Quest of the Stars & Galaxies. (p. 864)
Kouris, Kiki. Kittens of Color. (p. 963)
Kouse, Patrick, illus. see Wolfe, Jacqueline A.
Kousky, Vern. Otto the Owl Who Loved Poetry. Kousky, Vern, illus. (p. 1307)
Koutsky, Jan Dale. My Grandma, My Pen Pal. Koutsky, Jan Dale, illus. (p. 1210)
Kovac, Stefan Patrik, tr. see Krcmár, Karol.
Kovac, Tommy. Wonderland #1. (p. 1948)
—Wonderland #2: The Tulgey Wood & the Treacle Well. (p. 1948)
Kovach, John. Bob Ehrlich: His Historical Campaign for Governor & How a Young Girl Made a Difference. (p. 205)
Kovacik, Charles F. & Steinke, Theodore R., eds. South Carolina: An Atlas. (p. 1616)
Kovács, Cécile, jt. auth. see Lobe, Mira.
Kovacs, Charles. Age of Revolution. (p. 29)
—Ancient Greece. (p. 69)
—Botany (p. 215)
Kovacs, Deborah. Catie Copley. Williams, Jared T., illus. (p. 280)
—Catie Copley's Great Escape. Williams, Jared T., illus. (p. 280)
Kovacs, Deborah & Preller, James. Meet the Authors & Illustrators. (p. 1122)
Kovacs, Lawrence. Inca: Discover the Culture & Geography of a Lost Civilization with 25 Projects. Rizvi, Farah, illus. (p. 868)
Kovacs, Nicola. Digging Deep. (p. 439)
Kovacs, Vic. Cowboy's Life. (p. 374)
—Native Americans in the West. (p. 1234)
—Outlaws & Sheriffs. (p. 1312)
Kovacs, Victoria. Christmas/Easter Flip-Over Book. Krome, Mike, illus. (p. 316)
—Creation/Noah Flip-Over Book. Krome, Mike, illus. (p. 379)
—David/Esther Flip-Over Book. Krome, Mike, illus. (p. 411)
—Jesus' Miracles/Martha Flip-Over Book. Krome, Mike & Ryley, David, illus. (p. 916)
—Joseph/the Good Samaritan Flip-Over Book. Krome, Mike, illus. (p. 926)
—Joshua/Rahab Flip-Over Book. Ryley, David, illus. (p. 927)
—Miriam/Daniel Flip-Over Book. Krome, Mike & Ryley, David, illus. (p. 1149)
—Samuel/the Little Maid Flip-Over Book. Krome, Mike, illus. (p. 1509)
Kovacsics Meszaros, Marta, tr. see Kafka, Franz.
Kovalcik, Terry, illus. see Evans, Mary.
Kovalev, Neil. Kaylee Can Cook: Number Names & Count Sequence. (p. 946)
Kovalevich, Denise, ed. see Holt, Madeline.
Kovalkova-McKenna, Svetlana. Vasilisa & the Queen of Asps. (p. 1833)
Kovalkova-McKenna, Svetlana & McKenna, Alexandra. Fairy Book. (p. 563)
Kovalkova-McKenna, Svetlana & McKenna, Konstantin. Oberon. (p. 1275)
Kovalski, Maryann. Jenny & Joanna Album. (p. 913)
—Omar on Board (p. 1288)
—Omar on Board Kovalski, Maryann, illus. (p. 1288)
—Omar on Ice. (p. 1288)
—Omar's Halloween (p. 1288)
—Pizza for Breakfast. (p. 1365)
—Take Me Out to the Ballgame (p. 1696)
Kovanchak, Danielle. It's about Time. (p. 896)
Kovar, Ben, illus. see Dahl, Michael.
Kovatch, Sarah. Record Breaking Woman. (p. 1452)
—Special Helpers. (p. 1623)
Kovatch, Sarah & Crumpler, Rebecca Lee. Rebecca Lee Crumpler. (p. 1450)
Kovatch, Sarah, text. Giving up Grapes. (p. 681)
Kove, Torill, illus. see Hovland, Henrik & Bartlett, Don.
Kovel, Ralph M. & Kovel, Terry H. Kovels' Buyers' Guide to 20th-Century Costume Jewelry. (p. 967)
—Kovels' Dealing with Disaster: How to Protect Your Collection from Theft, Fire & Natural Disasters & How to Handle as Disaster If It Strikes. (p. 967)
—Kovels' Numbers. (p. 967)
Kovel, Terry H., jt. auth. see Kovel, Ralph M.
Kovner, Vladimir, tr. from ENG. Prilaskaite L'va: Amerikanskiye i Angliiskiye Stikhi Dlya Detei. Braslavskii, Felix, illus. (p. 1399)
Kovolenko, Petro, tr. from ENG. Free at Last: Breaking the Cycle of Family Curses. (p. 634)
Kowalchuk, Lacon. Harrison's Dream. (p. 750)
Kowalchyk, Gayle, jt. see Barden, Christine H.
Kowalchyk, Gayle, et al. My First Pop Songs, Book 1: Eleven Favorite Pop Songs for the Beginning Pianist. (p. 1207)
Kowalik, Susie. Lumen: The Star That Shone for the Visit of the Composer-Conductor. (p. 1065)
Kowalski, Bernard. Alexis & Ralph the Dragon (p. 37)
—Alexis & Ralph the Dragon. Phillips, Dawn, illus. (p. 37)
Kowalski, Eli. Kushka, the Dog Named Cat. (p. 968)
Kowalski, Emma. American Idol. (p. 61)
—America's Next Top Model. (p. 64)
—Project Runway. (p. 1410)
—Run's House. (p. 1497)
—Story of Konvict Muzik. (p. 1658)
—Story of Mosley Music Group. (p. 1659)
—Story of Roc-A-Fella Records. (p. 1659)
Kowalski, Gary A. Earth Day: An Alphabet Book. Baviera, Rocco, illus. (p. 495)
Kowalski, Kathiann M. Affirmative Action. (p. 26)
—Alternative Energy Sources. (p. 50)
—Attack of the Superbugs: The Crisis of Drug-Resistant Diseases. (p. 114)
—Balancing Act: A Look at Checks & Balances. (p. 133)
—Be Smart about Credit: Credit & Debt Management. (p. 149)
—Be Smart about Investing: Planning, Saving, & the Stock Market. (p. 149)
—Be Smart about Shopping: The Critical Consumer & Civic Financial Responsibility. (p. 149)
—Checks & Balances: A Look at the Powers of Government. (p. 295)
—Evolution on Trial: From the Scopes Monkey Case to Inherit the Wind. (p. 547)
—Free Trade. (p. 634)
—Global Warming. (p. 684)
—It's Your World! A Crash Course in Social Studies (p. 899)
—Judges & Courts: A Look at the Judicial Branch. (p. 930)
—Lemon V. Kurtzman & the Separation of Church & State Debate. (p. 991)
—National Health Care. (p. 1233)
—Order in the Court: A Look at the Judicial Branch. (p. 1302)
—Poverty in America: Causes & Issues. (p. 1389)
—Pro/con Look at Homeland Security: Safety vs. Liberty After 9/11. (p. 1408)
—Taxes. (p. 1707)
Kowalski, William. Just Gone (p. 938)
—Way It Works (p. 1864)
Kowen, Dorothy. Gift of Gold. Mathew, Gillian, illus. (p. 675)
—Thando Rocker. Sherrell, Craig, illus. (p. 1725)
Kowitt, H. N. Jinx of the Loser. (p. 919)
—Loser List. (p. 1054)
—Revenge of the Loser. (p. 1466)
—Take Me to Your Loser. (p. 1696)
Kowitt, Holly. Dracula's De-Composition Book. (p. 476)
—Loser List. (p. 1054)
—Off-The-Hook Big Book of Really Dumb School Jokes. (p. 1279)
—Revenge of the Loser. (p. 1466)
—Too Funny! 234 Laugh-Out-Loud Jokes. (p. 1766)
Kowtaluk, Helen, et al. Food for Today (p. 613)
Koyose, Junji, illus. see Nakagawa, Chihiro.
Koystal, K. M. Aves. (p. 119)
Koz, Paula Goodman, illus. see Olswanger, Anna.
Kozak, Diane, compiled by. Kaleidoscope Project. (p. 942)
Koziara, Colleen. Thirteen Silver Moons. Koziara, Colleen, illus. (p. 1735)
Kozjan, Drazen, illus. see Castrovilla, Selene.
Kozjan, Drazen, illus. see Kinerk, Robert.
Kozjan, Drazen, illus. see McGhee, Alison.
Kozleski, Lisa. James Madison. (p. 907)
—Leeward Islands Henderson, James D., ed. (p. 987)
—Leeward Islands. (p. 987)
—Pledge of Allegiance: Story of One Indivisible Nation. Moreno, Barry, ed. (p. 1374)
Kozloff, Joyce & Kushner, Robert, contrib. by. Joyce Kozloff: Boys' Art (p. 930)
Kozlowski, Darrell J. Colonialism. (p. 342)
Kozlowski, Darrell J., jt. auth. see Books, D. W. J.
Kozlowski, Michal. Louis the Tiger Who Came from the Sea. Walker, Sholto, illus. (p. 1058)
Kozlowski, Tomasz, illus. see Kasdepke, Grzegorz.
Kozlowsky, M. P. Dyerville Tales. Thompson, Brian, illus. (p. 491)
—Juniper Berry. Madrid, Erwin, illus. (p. 936)
Kozuszek, Rebecca. Betty Beagle. (p. 172)
Kozyrev, Joann Rishel. Sound Bites: Pronunciation Activities. (p. 1615)
Kraal, David. Gesta De Salomon. (p. 667)
—Solomons Quest. (p. 1608)
Kraatz, Jeramey. Cloak Society. (p. 333)
—Fall of Heroes. (p. 566)
—Villains Rising. (p. 1842)
Krackow, Eric T. Have an Abominably Good Day (p. 754)
—Lollipop Monster (p. 1046)
—Lollipop Monster Meets Clem the Klutz (p. 1046)
—Lollipop Monster's Christmas (p. 1046)
Krackow, Eric T., illus. see Ginn, Jennifer.
Krackow, Eric T. & Krackow, Krackow. Bill the Snowman (p. 187)
Krackow, Krackow, jt. auth. see Krackow, Eric T.
Kraegel, Kenneth. King Arthur's Very Great Grandson. Kraegel, Kenneth, illus. (p. 958)
—Song of Delphine. Kraegel, Kenneth, illus. (p. 1611)
Kraemer, Lillian Rosa. Wheelchair Adventures of Jeannie & the Wallpaper Children. Drown, Eleanor J., illus. (p. 1900)
Kraevskaya, Tatiyana. Wings for Little Turtle. (p. 1936)
Krafft, Melody A. Finding Me. (p. 588)
Kraft, Andrea. Gracie Blue Knows a Secret (p. 705)
—Gracie Blue Knows a Secret Kraft, Joe, illus. (p. 705)
Kraft, Betsy Harvey. Mother Jones: One Woman's Fight for Labor. (p. 1178)
Kraft, Ellen Christiansen. Alphabet Hide & Seek. (p. 49)
—Chinese Take-Out Stickers. (p. 308)
—Doodle Design & Draw DREAM ROOMS. (p. 469)
—Emoticon Stickers. (p. 520)
—Fiesta! Stickers. (p. 584)
—Get Well! Stickers. (p. 668)
—Graduation Day Stickers. (p. 705)
—Thank You Stickers. (p. 1725)
Kraft, Ellen Christiansen, jt. auth. see Sun, Jennie.
Kraft, Eric. Gold Rush! Set Of 6. (p. 694)
—Gold Rush! & ¡la fiebre del Oro! 6 English, 6 Spanish Adaptations. (p. 694)
—Transcontinental Railroad: Set Of 6. (p. 1778)
—Transcontinental Railroad & el ferrocarril Transcontinental: 6 English, 6 Spanish Adaptations. (p. 1778)
Kraft, Erik P. Lenny & Mel. Kraft, Erik P., illus. (p. 991)
—Lenny & Mel after-School Confidential. Kraft, Erik P., illus. (p. 991)
—Lenny & Mel's Summer Vacation. Kraft, Erik P., illus. (p. 991)
Kraft, Jason, illus. see Hamilton, Libby.
Kraft, Jason, illus. see O'Ryan, Ray.
Kraft, Joe, illus. see Kraft, Andrea.
Kraft, Lauri, illus. see Johnson, Sandi.
Kraft, Tamera & Colkmire, Lance. Kid Konnection: Kids Entering the Presence of God (p. 951)
Kragen, Emma. Twelve Dogs of Christmas. (p. 1800)
Krager, Sharon. Bethany's Birthday Wish for a Fish. (p. 171)
—Ethan Scott's Little Red Box. (p. 539)
—Sierra & the Bright Pink Umbrella. (p. 1573)
Kragh, Abby. Thomas, Berkley, & the Missing Socks. (p. 1738)
Krahe, Elena Gallo, tr. see Lacombe, Benjamin.
Krahe, Elena Gallo, tr. see Puybaret, Eric.
Krahn, Fernando. Quien Ha Visto las Tijeras? (p. 1427)
Krahulik, Mike, illus. see Holkins, Jerry.
Krailing, Tessa. Cabrita Revoltosa. (p. 250)
—Ladron de Gatos. (p. 970)
—Mano Verde. (p. 1088)
Krajenbrink Hulin, Yvonne. My Magic Box of Shapes. (p. 1213)
Krajenbrink Hulin, Yvonne, illus. see Holst, Jerome Alphonse.
Krakauer, Steve & Skindzier, Jon. Syracuse University College Prowler off the Record. (p. 1693)
Krakow, Amy. Matt & the Monster Do to Mexico - la Mutt y la Monster Van a Mexi. Knaus, Jill, tr. (p. 1109)
—Matt & the Monster 60 Sking & Snowboarding. Williams, Steve, illus. (p. 1109)
Krakower, Harold. Adventures of Jacob & Mr Ludicus. (p. 19)
—Sugarland: Princess Sarafina. (p. 1673)
—Sugarland: Josh & his magic Bed. (p. 1673)
—Sugarland: Sarah's Dance Recital. (p. 1673)
—Sugarland: Volume 2 Trouble in Sugarland. (p. 1673)
—Sugarland. (p. 1673)
Kralapp, Karl E. Fish Food. Kralapp, Karl E., illus. (p. 598)
Kralick, Evelyn. Famous Fossils: Measure Lengths in Standard Units. (p. 569)
Kraljic, Helena. cuento del lobo. (p. 389)
Krall, Dan. Great Lollipop Caper. Krall, Dan, illus. (p. 717)
—Sick Simon. Krall, Dan, illus. (p. 1572)
Krall, Dan, illus. see Crow, Kristyn.
Krall, Dan, illus. see Sauer, Tammi.
Kralovansky, Susan. Crocodile or Alligator? (p. 384)
—Frog or Toad? (p. 640)
—Monkey or Ape? (p. 1165)
—Moth or Butterfly? (p. 1177)
—Salamander or Lizard? (p. 1504)
—Twelve Cowboys Ropin' Kralovansky, Susan, illus. (p. 1800)
—Whale or Fish? (p. 1877)
—What Would You Do in a Library? (p. 1895)
—What Would You Do with a Database? (p. 1895)
—What Would You Do with a Dictionary? (p. 1895)
—What Would You Do with a Thesaurus? (p. 1895)
—What Would You Do with an Atlas. (p. 1895)
—What Would You Do with an Encyclopedia? (p. 1895)
Kralovansky, Susan Holt, jt. auth. see Kadair, Deborah Ousley.
Kram, T. Gooey Desserts & Messy Shirts Poetry F. (p. 702)
Kramek, Oren, illus. see Lagos, Alexander & Lagos, Joseph.
Kramek, Oren, illus. see Lagos, Joseph & Lagos, Alexander.
Kramer, Adam. Monkey of the Month Kramer, David, illus. (p. 1165)
Kramer, Alan. Bajo el mar con Jacques Cousteau & under the Sea with Jacques Cousteau. (p. 133)
—Completely Cool Clothing Company. (p. 353)
—Counting at the Zoo. (p. 370)
—Escape de la extinción & Path from Extinction. (p. 534)
—In Search of Numbers. (p. 864)
—Jack & the Beanstalk Trial. (p. 902)
—Jackie Robinson: Breaking Baseball's Barriers. Leon, Karen, illus. (p. 904)
—No Math Day at School. (p. 1259)
—Ogs Discover Fire & Other Stuff. (p. 1280)
—Path from Extinction. (p. 1328)
—Ramses & Nefertari. (p. 1438)
—Three Little Pigs Wise up & the Princess Prince & the Vegetables. (p. 1743)
—Under the Sea with Jacques Cousteau. (p. 1814)
—Wright Brothers at Kitty Hawk. (p. 1963)
Kramer, Alan & Kramer, Candice. Brer Rabbit Hears a Big Noise in the Woods: An African /American Folktale. (p. 226)
—Fifth Grade Votes. Leon, Karen, illus. (p. 584)
—Isaac Newton: The World in Motion. (p. 890)
—Star-Spangled Banner Story. (p. 1641)
Kramer, Alan & Romer, Ruth. Wizard of Wherever. (p. 1943)
Kramer, Andrew. Pajama Pirates. Lammle, Leslie, illus. (p. 1319)
Kramer, Ann. Anne Frank: The Young Writer Who Told the World Her Story. (p. 85)
—Drugs. (p. 487)
—Egyptian Myth: A Treasury of Legends, Art, & History. (p. 507)
—Eleanor of Aquitaine: The Queen Who Rode off to Battle. (p. 508)
—Mandela: The Hero Who Led His Nation to Freedom. (p. 1087)
—Mandela: The Rebel Who Led His Nation to Freedom. (p. 1087)
—Women & War. (p. 1945)
Kramer, Barbara. Alexander Graham Bell. (p. 36)
—Beyoncé: Singer, Songwriter, & Actress. (p. 173)
—Dave Thomas: Honesty Pays. (p. 410)
—Gloria Estefan: Never Give Up. (p. 685)
—Jimmy Carter: A Life of Service. (p. 918)
—Lance Armstrong: Determined to Beat the Odds. (p. 973)
—Life of George Washington Carver: Inventor & Scientist. (p. 1012)
—Mahalia Jackson: The Voice of Gospel & Civil Rights. (p. 1076)
—Michael J. Fox: Courage for Life. (p. 1134)
—National Geographic Kids Readers: Sonia Sotomayor. (p. 1232)
—National Geographic Readers: Cleopatra. (p. 1233)
—National Geographic Readers: Pope Francis. (p. 1233)
—Neil Armstrong: Meet the Famous Astronaut. (p. 1240)
—Oprah Winfrey: Reaching Out to Others. (p. 1301)
—Toni Morrison: A Biography of a Nobel Prize-Winning Writer. (p. 1765)
Kramer, Barbara, jt. auth. see National Geographic Kids Staff.
Kramer, Berri, photos by. Mbali: A story from South Africa. (p. 1114)
Kramer, Brandie, illus. see Tirabassi, Maren C.
Kramer, Candice. Ben Franklin's Visit: A When Machine Play. (p. 163)
—Cesar Chavez Comes to Visit. (p. 288)
—Clara Barton: Angel of the Battlefield. (p. 326)
—De visita con Benjamin Franklin & Ben Franklin's Visit A When Machine Play. (p. 416)
—Eleanor Roosevelt & Marian Anderson. (p. 508)
—Matthew Henson at the North Pole. (p. 1109)
—Matthew Henson en el Polo Norte & Matthew Henson at the North Pole. (p. 1109)
—Why Coyote Stopped Imitating His Friends. Leon, Karen, illus. (p. 1923)
Kramer, Candice, jt. auth. see Kramer, Alan.
Kramer, Candice, jt. auth. see Romer, Ruth.
Kramer, Connie, photos by see Cooke, Brandy.
Kramer, Daniel Elihu. Coyote Tales. (p. 374)
Kramer, David, illus. see Ginn, Jennifer.
Kramer, David, illus. see Kramer, Adam.
Kramer, Don & Johns, Geoff. Black Vengeance. Champagne, Keith, illus. (p. 197)
Krämer, Eva-Maria. Get to Know Dog Breeds: The 200 Most Popular Breeds. (p. 668)
Kramer, Gerri Freid, et al. Eating Disorders. (p. 501)
Kramer, Jaap, illus. see Prins, Piet.
Kramer, Jaap, illus. see Vogelaar, Alie.
Kramer, Janice. Christmas Baby. Rooney, Ronnie, illus. (p. 312)
Kramer, Jennifer E. Good Luck Charlie. Moores, Jeff, illus. (p. 698)
Kramer, Jennifer Evans. Ocean Hide & Seek Phillips, Gary R., illus. (p. 1276)
Kramer, Jon. Learning about Simple Machines with Graphic Organizers. (p. 984)
Kramer, Joyce. Gingerbread Man Goes to Kindergarten. (p. 677)
Kramer, K. Out on the Farm with Farmer Jack. (p. 1311)
Kramer, Lance. Great Ancient China Projects: You Can Build Yourself. Weinberg, Steven, illus. (p. 713)
Kramer, Marie. Grandchildren of the Pioneers. (p. 707)
Kramer, Mark. Santa Claws: A True Story. (p. 1511)
Kramer, Nash. How Many Pets Do You Have? (p. 811)
—Night Animals. (p. 1252)
—What Goes Fastest? (p. 1885)
—Where Did My Grandparents Come From? (p. 1906)
—Why Do You Change in Winter? (p. 1924)
Kramer, Pat. Totem Poles for Kids: A Kids Own SuperGuide. Kramer, Pat, photos by. (p. 1772)
Kramer, Paul. Do Not Dread Wetting the Bed. (p. 457)
—Louie the Lobster Mobster. (p. 1058)
—Maggie Goes on a Diet. (p. 1071)
Kramer, Paul M. Are You Afraid of the Doctor? (p. 97)
—Divorce Stinks. (p. 455)
Kramer, Saunders B., jt. auth. see Chester, Michael.
Kramer, Sharon. Chester Jester Finds His Smile. (p. 298)
Kramer, Stacy & Thomas, Valerie. Karma Bites. (p. 944)
Kramer, Stephen. Hidden Worlds: Looking Through a Scientist's Microscope. (p. 776)
—Hidden Worlds: Looking Through a Scientist's Microscope. Kunkel, Dennis, photos by. (p. 776)
Kramer, Susan. Yoga for all Kids, Preschoolers to Teens. (p. 1972)
Kramer, Sydelle. Who Was Daniel Boone? (p. 1918)
—Who Was Daniel Boone? Ulrich, George, illus. (p. 1918)
—Who Was Ferdinand Magellan? Wolf, Elizabeth, illus. (p. 1918)
—Who Was Ferdinand Magellan? Wolf, Elizabeth & Harrison, Nancy, illus. (p. 1918)
—¿Quién Fue Fernando de Magallanes? (Who Was Ferdinand Magellan?) Wolf, Elizabeth, illus. (p. 1427)
Kramer, Sydelle, jt. auth. see Mannis, Celeste Davidson.
Kramin, Valerie, illus. see Bugg, Ann T.
Krammer, Arnold. Hitler in Paris: How a Photograph Shocked a World at War (p. 786)
Kranking, Kathy. Gone! Dino Extinction. (p. 697)
—In the Spotlight: Animal Superstars. (p. 867)
—Mini & Mighty: Teeny Tiny Animals. (p. 1146)
Kranking, Kathy & Carrano, Matthew T. Swimming with Saurs. (p. 1691)
Kranowitz, Carol. Goodenoughs Get in Sync: Five Different Ways SPD Can Affect You & Me! (p. 701)
Kranowitz, Carol & Newman, Joye. In Sync Activity Cards: Simple, Fun Activity Cards to Help Every Child Develop, Learn, & Grow! (p. 865)
Kranowitz, Carol Stock. Goodenoughs Get in Sync: A Story for Kids about the Tough Day When Filibuster Grabbed Darwin's Rabbit's Foot.. Wylie, T. J., illus. (p. 701)
Krantz, Grover S. Only A Dog: One of America's best known anthropologists contemplates his beloved Wolfhound. (p. 1298)
Krantz, Hazel. In the Garden of the Caliph. (p. 866)
Kranz, Jonathan David. Our Brothers at the Bottom of the Bottom of the Sea. (p. 1308)
Kranz, Linda. All about Me: A Keepsake Journal for Kids. (p. 42)
—Love You When. (p. 1061)
—More about Me: Another Keepsake Journal for Kids. (p. 1173)
—My Nature Book: A Journal And. (p. 1215)
—Only One You. (p. 1298)
—Only One You. Mlawer, Teresa, tr. from ENG. (p. 1298)
—Through My Eyes: A Journal for Teens. (p. 1745)
—You Be You. (p. 1973)
—You Be You. Mlawer, Teresa, tr. from ENG. (p. 1973)
Kranz, Linda & Cool Springs Press Publications Staff. Let's Rock! (p. 1000)
Kranz, Peter M. Dinosaurs of the District of Columbia. (p. 445)
Kranz, Rachel. exploración del Espacio. (p. 549)
—Montaña Santa Helena: Set Of 6. (p. 1170)
—Mount St. Helens. (p. 1180)
—Mount St. Helens & la montaña Santa Helena: 6 English, 6 Spanish Adaptations (p. 1180)
—Opening Night. (p. 1300)
—Our Solar System & el sistema Solar: 6 English, 6 Spanish Adaptations (p. 1310)
—sistema Solar: Set Of 6. (p. 1581)
—Space Exploration & la exploración del Espacio: 6 English, 6 Spanish Adaptations (p. 1619)
Kranzler, Gershon. Seder in Herlin: And Other Stories. Kotler, Arkady & Kotler, Elina, illus. (p. 1546)
Krapp, JoAnn Vergona. Missing Treasure Means Trouble. Rivera, Roberta, illus. (p. 1153)

K

Krapp, Kristine M., jt. auth. see Nelson, M. Rae.
Kras, Sara L. & Kras, Sara Louise. Kangaroos (p. 942)
—Koalas (p. 966)
—Platypuses (p. 1370)
—Wombats (p. 1945)
Kras, Sara Louise. Antigua & Barbuda. (p. 89)
—Cambodia. (p. 255)
—Everglades. (p. 542)
—Galapagos Islands. (p. 653)
—Horse Riding. (p. 800)
—Hunted: Polar Prey. (p. 828)
—Japan in Colors (p. 909)
—Kangaroos (p. 942)
—Kenya in Colors (p. 949)
—Koalas (p. 966)
—Platypuses (p. 1370)
—Steam Engine. (p. 1646)
—Wombats (p. 1945)
Kras, Sara Louise, jt. auth. see Kras, Sara L.
Kras, Sara Louise, jt. auth. see McDaniel, Melissa.
Kras, Sara Louise & Capstone Press Staff. Kenya: A Question & Answer Book (p. 949)
Kras, Sarah Louise. Horse Riding. (p. 800)
Kraselsky, Rebeca. Las Medidas del Tiempo. Aymez, Carla, illus. (p. 976)
Kraselsky, Rebeca & Ferreiro, Natalia. Ojo Multiple: Del Espejo y Otros Secretos. (p. 1282)
Krasinski, Jay. Who Works at the Store? (p. 1919)
Krasinski, Norma. I Am the One That Reads. (p. 834)
—I Am Their Reading Hero. (p. 834)
—Please, Please, Read to Me. (p. 1373)
—Tyler Story. (p. 1805)
Krasinski, Norma & Marx, Donald. Kids Reading to Kids: The Phenomenon. (p. 955)
Kraske, Robert. Harry Houdini. (p. 750)
—Mae Jemison: Space Pioneer. (p. 1070)
—Queen Elizabeth of England. (p. 1424)
Krasner, Barbara. Career As an Event Coordinator (p. 266)
—Goldie Takes a Stand: Golda Meir's First Crusade. Garrity-Riley, Kelsey, illus. (p. 695)
—Goldie Takes a Stand! Golda Meir's First Crusade. Garrity-Riley, Kelsey, illus. (p. 695)
—Native Nations of the Great Basin & Plateau. (p. 1235)
—Native Nations of the Northeast. (p. 1235)
Krasner, Jonathan B., et al. History of the Jewish People: A Story of Tradition & Change (p. 785)
Krasner, Nick. My Bed Is a Spaceship: The Globbus. White, Charlotte, illus. (p. 1196)
Krasner, Steven. Play Ball Like the Hall of Famers: Tips for Kids from 19 Baseball Greats Neely, Keith, illus. (p. 1371)
—Play Ball Like the Pros: Tips for Kids from 20 Big League Stars (p. 1371)
Krasnesky, Thad. I Always, Always Get My Way. Parkins, David, illus. (p. 831)
—That Cat Can't Stay. Parkins, David, illus. (p. 1726)
Krasnow, David, ed. see Parker, Lew.
Krass. Sojourner Truth. (p. 1606)
Krassa, Victoria, illus. see Unobagha, Uzo.
Krasulja, Zorica, illus. see Smith, Linda.
Kraszewski. Surf Angel. (p. 1685)
Kratky, Lada J., tr. see White, Amy.
Kratt, Chris & Kratt, Martin. Wild Predators (Wild Kratts) Random House, illus. (p. 1930)
—Wild Reptiles: Snakes, Crocodiles, Lizards, & Turtles (Wild Kratts) Random House, illus. (p. 1930)
—Wild Sea Creatures: Sharks, Whales & Dolphins! (p. 1930)
Kratt, Martin, jt. auth. see Kratt, Chris.
Kratter, Paul. Living Rain Forest: An Animal Alphabet. Kratter, Paul, illus. (p. 1041)
Kratter, Paul, illus. see Nagda, Ann Whitehead.
Kratz, Jessica R. Sleigh Bells in Springtime: Frogs Calling. (p. 1590)
Kratz, Marilyn. Umpire in a Skirt: The Amanda Clement Story. Curriel, Hector, illus. (p. 1810)
Kratzert, Barbara & Probst, Sharon Patrice. Bobby Bubblebug in the Bubblegum Tree Forest. (p. 206)
Krauczyk, Sabine & Allaire, Caroline. Let's Look at the Vegetable Garden. (p. 999)
Kraul, Walter. Earth, Water, Fire & Air: Playful Explorations in the Four Elements. Maclean, Donald, tr. from GER. (p. 497)
—Earth, Water, Fire, & Air: Playful Explorations in the Four Elements. (p. 497)
Kraulis, Julie. Armadillo in Paris. (p. 99)
—Whimsy's Heavy Things. Kraulis, Julie, illus. (p. 1911)
Kraus, Daniel. Monster Variations. (p. 1168)
—Rotters. (p. 1491)
—Scowler. (p. 1532)
Kraus, Daniel, jt. auth. see del Toro, Guillermo.
Kraus, Franz, jt. auth. see Walton, Rick.
Kraus, Jeanne. Cory's Stories: A Kid's Book about Living with ADHD. Martin, Whitney, illus. (p. 368)
—Get Ready for Jetty! My Journal about Adhd & Me. (p. 668)
Kraus, Jeanne R. Annie's Plan: Taking Charge of Schoolwork & Homework. Beyl, Charles, illus. (p. 87)
Kraus, Joanna H. Night of Tamales & Roses. Caravela, Elena, illus. (p. 1253)
Kraus, Nicola, jt. auth. see McLaughlin, Emma.
Kraus, Robert. Daddy Long Ears' Halloween. (p. 398)
—Leo, el Retaño Tardío. Mlawer, Teresa, tr. (p. 992)
—Whose Mouse Are You? Aruego, Jose, illus. (p. 1921)
Krause, Claudia. Word Wheels. (p. 1951)
Krause, George, photos by see Dowell, Frances O'Roark.
Krause, John & Chua, Maria. Poco Loco (p. 1375)
Krause, Maria. Alhambra: Create Your Own Castle!—Sticker Book. (p. 38)
—Hokusai Coloring Book. (p. 787)
Krause, Robert. President's Counting Book: The Future Generations of America. (p. 1397)
Krause, Scott. Development of Good Health: Help & Healing for All Complaints. (p. 432)
Krause, Ute. Nick & the Nasty Knight. (p. 1251)
—No Ordinary Family! (p. 1259)
—Oscar & the Very Hungry Dragon. (p. 1305)
Krauskopf, Sharma. Moose Family Close Up. Holdsworth, Henry, photos by. (p. 1173)
Krauss, jt. auth. see Krauss, Ruth.
Krauss, jt. auth. see Ruth, Krauss.
Krauss, Dan, photos by see Kopp, Jaine.
Krauss, Gene. Awesome Performance Music & Tracks. (p. 121)
Krauss, Peter. Sojourner Truth: Antislavery Activist. Huggins, Nathan I., ed. (p. 1606)
Krauss, Ruth. Backward Day. Simont, Marc, illus. (p. 130)
—Bears. Sendak, Maurice, illus. (p. 151)
—Big & Little. Szilagyi, Mary, illus. (p. 177)
—Carrot Seed. Johnson, Crockett, illus. (p. 271)
—Goodnight Goodnight Sleepyhead. Dyer, Jane, illus. (p. 701)
—Growing Story. Oxenbury, Helen, illus. (p. 726)
—Happy Egg. Johnson, Crockett, illus. (p. 745)
—I Can Fly. Blair, Mary, illus. (p. 835)
Krauss, Ruth & Krauss. Carrot Seed. Johnson, Crockett, illus. (p. 271)
Krauss, Trisha, illus. see Candlewick Press Staff.
Krauss, Trisha, illus. see Candlewick Press, Candlewick.
Krauss, Trisha, illus. see Child, Lauren.
Krautwurst, Terry, et al. Science Smart: Cool Projects for Exploring the Marvels of the Planet Earth. (p. 1528)
Kravanek, J. Elise, illus. see Draper, Melissa J.
Kravetz, Jonathan. Boll Weevils. (p. 208)
—Cockroaches. (p. 337)
—How to Deal with Bullies. (p. 816)
—How to Deal with Fighting. (p. 816)
—How to Deal with Jealousy. (p. 816)
—Learning about Energy with Graphic Organizers. (p. 984)
—Learning about Plant Growth with Graphic Organizers. (p. 984)
—Locusts. (p. 1045)
—Mosquitoes. (p. 1176)
—Stink Bugs. (p. 1651)
—Ticks. (p. 1747)
Kravetz, Nathan. Horse of Another Color. (p. 799)
—Monkey's Tale. (p. 1166)
Kravetz, Stacy. Fosters: Keep Your Frenemies Close. (p. 624)
Kravitz, Cathy. Art Box. (p. 101)
—Dog's Day. (p. 462)
—What We Can Do: A Book about Global Warming. (p. 1895)
Kravitz, Danny. In the Shadow of Lady Liberty: Immigrant Stories from Ellis Island. (p. 867)
—Journey to America: A Chronology of Immigration in the 1900s. (p. 928)
—Surviving the Journey: The Story of the Oregon Trail (p. 1687)
—Untold Story of Henry Knox: The Man Who Saved Boston. (p. 1823)
—Untold Story of Washington's Surprise Attack: The Daring Crossing of the Delaware River. (p. 1823)
Kravitz, Danny, jt. auth. see Baker, Brynn.
Kravitz, Danny & Burgan, Michael. What You Didn't Know about the American Revolution. (p. 1896)
Kravitz, Robert J. Collector's Guide to Fractional Currency: The Pocket Change of the Union Soldier. (p. 340)
Krawczyk, Sabine, illus. see Biard, Philippe, et al.
Krawczyk, Sabine, jt. auth. see Allaire, Caroline.
Krawczyk, Sabine, jt. auth. see Delafosse, Claude.
Krawczyk, Sabine & Allaire, Caroline. Let's Look under the Stone. Krawczyk, Sabine, illus. (p. 999)
Krawczyk, Sabine & Delafosse, Claude. Let's Look at Insects. Krawczyk, Sabine, illus. (p. 999)
Krawczyk, Sabine & Sautai, Raoul. Insects. Krawczyk, Sabine, illus. (p. 875)
Krawiec, Richard. Yao Ming: Gentle Giant of Basketball. (p. 1968)
Kray, Peter. Monster. (p. 1166)
Kray, Robert C., illus. see Hansen, Amy S.
Kraynak, George, illus. see Falk, Elsa.
Krcmár, Karol. Kirigami Greeting Cards: The Art of Paper Cutting & Folding. Simekova, Jela, ed. (p. 961)
—Kirigami Paper Kingdom: The Art of Paper Cutting & Folding. Simekova, Jela, ed. (p. 961)
Krebs, Betsy & Pitcoff, Paul. On Your Own as a Young Adult Facilitator's Guide. (p. 1292)
—On Your Own as a Young Adult, Workbook: Self-Advocacy Case Studies. (p. 1292)
Krebs, Brian. Spam Nation: The Inside Story of Organized Cybercrime - From Global Epidemic to Your Front Door. (p. 1620)
Krebs, Laurie. Day in the Life of a Colonial Indigo Planter. (p. 413)
—Day in the Life of a Colonial Lighthouse Keeper. (p. 413)
—Day in the Life of a Colonial Miller. (p. 413)
—Day in the Life of a Colonial Shipwright. (p. 413)
—Nos Fuimos Todos de Safari: Una Aventura de Números Por Tanzania. Cairns, Julia, illus. (p. 1266)
—Off We Go to Mexico. Corr, Christopher, illus. (p. 1279)
—Sube y Baja Por Los Andes: Un Cuento de un Festival Peruano. Fronty, Aurélia, illus. (p. 1671)
—Up & down the Andes: A Peruvian Festival Tale. Fronty, Aurélia, illus. (p. 1824)
—Up & down the Andes. Fronty, Aurélia, illus. (p. 1824)
—Vamos Todos de Safari: Un Recorrido Numerico por Tanzania, Africa. Cortes, Eunice, tr. (p. 1831)
—We All Went on Safari: A Counting Journey Through Tanzania. Cairns, Julia, illus. (p. 1865)
—We're Riding on a Caravan: An Adventure on the Silk Road. Cann, Helen, illus. (p. 1875)
—We're Roaming in the Rainforest. Wilson, Anne, illus. (p. 1875)
—We're Sailing down the Nile: A Journey Through Egypt. Wilson, Anne, illus. (p. 1875)
—We're Sailing to Galapagos: A Week in the Pacific. Restelli, Grazia, illus. (p. 1875)
Krebs, Laurie & Barefoot Books. 1,2, 3, Partons en Safari! Cairns, Julia, illus. (p. 1994)
Krebs, Laurie & Blackstone, Stella. Nos Vamos a Mexico! Una Aventura Bajo el Sol. Canetti, Yanitzia James, tr. from ENG. (p. 1266)
Krebs, Laurie & Cairns, Julia. We All Went on Safari: A Counting Journey Through Tanzania. Cairns, Julia, illus. (p. 1865)
Krebs, Laurie & Cis, Valeria. Beeman. Cis, Valeria, illus. (p. 157)
Krebs, Laurie & Corr, Christopher. Off We Go to Mexico! An Adventure in the Sun. (p. 1279)
Krebs, Patricia. On Your Mark, Get Set, Go! (p. 1292)
Krebs, Patricia, illus. see Gilbert, Marcie.
Krebs, Robert E. Basics of Earth Science: Spheres & Forces (p. 142)
Krech, Bob. Fractions & Decimals: Mini-Lessons, Games, & Activities to Review & Reinforce Essential Math Concepts & Skills. (p. 627)
—Math Word Problems Made Easy: Surefire Strategies-With 100+ Guided & Independent Practice Problems-That Give Kids the Tools to Tackle All Kinds of Word Problems. (p. 1107)
—Rebound (p. 1451)
Krech, Bob & Grabell, Jeff. Algebra Readiness: Mini-Lessons, Games, & Activities to Review & Reinforce Essential Math Concepts & Skills. (p. 38)
Krech, Bob & Kennan, Audrey. Multiplication & Division: Mini-Lessons, Games, & Activities to Review & Reinforce Essential Math Concepts & Skills. (p. 1190)
Krech, Bob & Krecht, R.J. Love Puppies & Corner Kicks. (p. 1060)
Krech, Bob & Novelli, Joan. 50 Fill-In Math Word Problems - Algebra Readiness: Engaging Story Problems for Students to Read, Fill-In, Solve, & Sharpen Their Math Skills. (p. 1997)
—50 Fill-In Math Word Problems - Time & Measurement: Engaging Story Problems for Students to Read, Fill-In, Solve, & Sharpen Their Math Skills. (p. 1997)
—Algebra: Engaging Story Problems for Students to Read, Fill-In, Solve, & Sharpen Their Math Skills. (p. 38)
—Fractions & Decimals: Engaging Story Problems for Students to Read, Fill-In, Solve, & Sharpen Their Math Skills. (p. 627)
—Multiplication & Division: Engaging Story Problems for Students to Read, Fill-In, Solve, & Sharpen Their Math Skills. (p. 1190)
Krech, Bob, et al. Addition & Subtraction: Mini-Lessons, Games, & Activities to Review & Reinforce Essential Math Concepts & Skills. (p. 12)
—Geometry & Measurement: Mini-Lessons, Games, & Activities to Review & Reinforce Essential Math Concepts & Skills. (p. 662)
Krecht, R.J., jt. auth. see Krech, Bob.
Krecskay, Stephen, illus. see Thompson, Yvonne.
Kredel, Fritz, illus. see Kaufmann, Helen L.
Kredel, Fritz, illus. see Twain, Mark, pseud, tr.
Kredell, Janine. Jesus, the Brother of James & Jude, & the Savior of the World. (p. 916)
Kredensor, Diane. Aloha! (p. 48)
—Ollie & Moon: Aloha! (p. 1287)
Kreder, Mary Ellen DeLuca, jt. auth. see Kreder Sr., Edward G.
Kreder Sr., Edward G. & Kreder, Mary Ellen DeLuca. Sparkle's Journey. Vanden Berg, Myra, illus. (p. 1622)
Kreeft, Peter. Socratic Logic: A Logic Text Using Socratic Method, Platonic Questions, & Aristotelian Principles. (p. 1605)
Krefta, Ben. Step by Step Manga. (p. 1647)
Kregel Publishing, jt. auth. see Kregel Publishing.
Kregel Publishing & Kregel Publishing. Jumbo Bible Activity Book (p. 933)
Kreger, Claire. Homes: From Start to Finish. Carney, Patrick, illus. (p. 793)
Krehbiel, Angie, illus. see Unruh, Cindy.
Kreib, jt. auth. see Krieb.
Kreider, Alan, as told by. Missio Dei #16, Spanish: Tomillos en la Legnua Y Testimonio. (p. 1153)
Kreider, Karen. Aladdin. Baker, Darrell, illus. (p. 33)
Kreidler, Shannon. Adventures of Sally the Squirrel: Interactive... Educational & Earn Gold Stars. (p. 22)
Kreie, Chris. Don't Wobble on the Wakeboard! Santillan, Jorge H., illus. (p. 469)
—I Couldn't Land a Bunny Hop Santillan, Jorge H., illus. (p. 837)
—There Are No Figure Eights in Hockey Santillan, Jorge H., illus. (p. 1729)
—Who Wants to Play Just for Kicks? Santillan, Jorge H., illus. (p. 1918)
Kreie, Chris & Maese, Fares. Shot Clock Slam. Aburto, Jesus & Esparza, Andres, illus. (p. 1569)
Kreie, Chris, et al. Battle for Home Plate Aburto, Jesus, illus. (p. 145)
—Battle for Home Plate Aburtov, Jesus Aburto, illus. (p. 145)
Kreilein, Debra. Tombstone Treasure Mystery. (p. 1764)
Kreinberg, Sylvia, illus. see Giulieri, Anne.
Kreinberg, Sylvia, photos by see Dale, Jay.
Kreinberg, Sylvia, photos by see Giulieri, Anne.
Kreiner, Anna. Being Afraid. (p. 161)
—Let's Talk about Being Afraid. (p. 1001)
—Todo lo que necesitas saber sobre la violencia en la escuela (Everything You Need to Know about Violence in School) (p. 1761)
Kreisel, C. Mae. Aggi Pursued. (p. 29)
Kreisler, Ken, jt. auth. see Rotner, Shelley.
Kreisman, Rachelle. Back off, Sneezy! A Kids' Guide to Staying Well. Haggerty, Tim, illus. (p. 130)
—Start Sweating! A Kids' Guide to Being Active. Haggerty, Tim, illus. (p. 1643)
—What's That Smell? A Kids' Guide to Keeping Clean. Haggerty, Tim, illus. (p. 1899)
—You Want Me to Eat That? A Kids' Guide to Eating Right. Haggerty, Tim, illus. (p. 1976)
Kreitz, Tina. Rocky the Sea Turtle. Triplett, Chris Harper, illus. (p. 1484)
Kreitzer, Dora. Summer in Connecticut. (p. 1674)
Kreitzer, Jerry, jt. auth. see Levine, David.
Krejca, Gary, illus. see Gillis, Jennifer Blizin.
Krejca, Gary, illus. see Pearson, Mary E.
Krejcova, Zdenka, illus. see Selucky, Oldrich.
Krejewski, Sandra. Kitty Kitty. (p. 963)
—Little Hermit Crab. (p. 1029)
—Numbers with Attitude. (p. 1272)
Krekula, Nathan L. Rooney the Blue-Tailed Mouse. (p. 1488)
Krelle, Ginger R., jt. auth. see Brown, Patrica A.
Krell-Oishi, Mary. Scenes Keep Happening: More Real-Life Snapshots of Teen Lives (p. 1521)
Kreloff, Elliot. Counting Duckies. (p. 371)
—Matching Puzzle Cards - Numbers. (p. 1104)
—My Little Baby. (p. 1212)
—No More TV, Sleepy Cat. (p. 1259)
—Tic & Tac Clean Up. (p. 1747)
—Where's Your Nose. (p. 1911)
Kreloff, Elliot, illus. see Conroy, Melissa.
Kreloff, Elliot, illus. see Danis, Naomi.
Kreloff, Elliot, illus. see Ochiltree, Dianne.
Kreloff, Elliot, illus. see Ziefert, Harriet & Johnston, Jan.
Kreloff, Elliot, illus. see Ziefert, Harriet & Nagel, Karen.
Kreloff, Elliot, illus. see Ziefert, Harriet.
Kreloff, Elliot, jt. auth. see Ziefert, Harriet.
Krementz, Jill. Very Young Rider. Krementz, Jill, photos by. (p. 1839)
Kremer, Kevin. Are You Smarter Than a Flying Teddy? Teddy Roosevelt Returns to North Dakota! Ely, Dave, illus. (p. 97)
—Most Amazing Halloween Ever. Ely, Dave, illus. (p. 1177)
—Santa's Our Substitute Teacher. Ely, Dave, illus. (p. 1513)
—Year Our Teacher Won Super Bowl. Ely, Dave, illus. (p. 1969)
Kremer, Kevin, jt. auth. see Pohl, Dora.
Kremer, Kevin R. Are You Smarter Than a Flying Gator? Gator Mikey over Florida! Ely, Dave, illus. (p. 97)
Kremer, Roberta S., ed. Broken Threads: The Destruction of the Jewish Fashion Industry in Germany & Austria. (p. 230)
Kremer, Shelly. Coco the Coconut Crab. (p. 337)
Krempel, Ulrich. Niki's World: Niki de Saint Phalle. (p. 1255)
Kremsner, Cynthia, illus. see Dannenbring, Cheryl.
Krenek, Randy. Adventures of Li'l Otto in Calico Grotto. (p. 19)
Krenina, Katya. Birds' Gift: A Ukrainian Easter Story. (p. 191)
—Spider's Gift: A Ukrainian Christmas Story. (p. 1627)
Krenina, Katya, illus. see Kimmel, Eric A.
Krenner, Digna. Twin Who Ran Away: Life of St. Benedict. (p. 1802)
Krensky, Stephen. Anansi & the Box of Stories. Reeves, Jeni, illus. (p. 67)
—Arthur & the 1,001 Dads. (p. 103)
—Big Bad Wolves at School. (p. 178)
—Big Bad Wolves at School. Sneed, Brad, illus. (p. 178)
—Bogeyman. (p. 207)
—Bokuden & the Bully: [A Japanese Folktale]. Noll, Cheryl, illus. (p. 208)
—Bokuden & the Bully. Noll, Cheryl Kirk, illus. (p. 208)
—Breaking into Print: Before & after the Invention of the Printing Press. Christensen, Bonnie, illus. (p. 225)
—Bubble Trouble. Pickering, Jimmy, illus. (p. 233)
—Bunny Money. Bolam, Emily, illus. (p. 242)
—Calamity Jane. Carlson, Lisa, illus. (p. 252)
—Case of the Missing Mice: A Simon Mystery. (p. 274)
—Case of the Missing Pail. (p. 274)
—Casey Jones. (p. 275)
—Casey Jones. Schroder, Mark, illus. (p. 275)
—Chaucer's First Winter. Cole, Henry, illus. (p. 295)
—Constitution. (p. 359)
—Creatures from the Deep. (p. 380)
—Dangerous Crossing: The Revolutionary Voyage of John Quincy Adams. Harlin, Greg, tr. (p. 404)
—Davy Crockett: A Life on the Frontier. Bandelin, Debra & Dacey, Bob, illus. (p. 411)
—Davy Crockett A Life on the Frontier. Dacey, Bob & Bandelin, Debra, illus. (p. 411)
—Declaration of Independence. (p. 422)
—Deep Dish on Pizza! Guidera, Daniel, illus. (p. 422)
—Dragon Emperor: A Chinese Folktale. (p. 477)
—Dragons. (p. 478)
—Emancipaton Proclamation. (p. 517)
—George Washington's First Victory. Hearn, Diane Dawson, illus. (p. 665)
—Ghosts. (p. 672)
—Great Moon Hoax. Bisaillon, Josée, illus. (p. 717)
—High Score & Lowdown on Video Games! Burroughs, Scott, illus. (p. 778)
—How Coyote Stole the Summer: A Native American Folktale. Dupre, Kelly, illus. (p. 806)
—How Coyote Stole the Summer: [A Native American Folktale]. Dupre, Kelly, illus. (p. 806)
—How Santa Lost His Job. Schindler, S. D., illus. (p. 812)
—I Am So Brave! Gillingham, Sara, illus. (p. 834)
—I Can Do It Myself! Gillingham, Sara, illus. (p. 835)
—I Know a Lot! Gillingham, Sara, illus. (p. 840)
—John Henry. Oldroyd, Mark, illus. (p. 922)
—Last Christmas Tree. Campion, Pascal, illus. (p. 977)
—Lion & the Hare. Reeves, Jeni, illus. (p. 1019)
—Lizzie Newton & the San Francisco Earthquake. (p. 1043)
—Lizzie Newton & the San Francisco Earthquake. Tugeau, Jeremy, illus. (p. 1043)
—Locked in the Library! (p. 1045)
—Magic Pomegranate: A Jewish Folktale. (p. 1073)
—Malarkey & the Big Trap. Shortley, Michele, illus. (p. 1083)
—Mike Fink. (p. 1141)
—Mike Fink. Reeves, Jeni, illus. (p. 1141)
—Milo the Really Big Bunny. Suber, Melissa, illus. (p. 1144)
—Monster Chronicles (p. 1166)
—Monster Chronicles Set II: Complete Library. (p. 1166)
—Monster Chronicles Set II Classroom Library. (p. 1167)
—Mother's Day Surprise Ember, Kathi, illus. (p. 1178)
—Nellie Bly: A Name to Be Reckoned With. Guay, Rebecca, illus. (p. 1240)
—Noah's Bark. Girard, Roger, illus. (p. 1261)
—Now I Am Big! Gillingham, Sara, illus. (p. 1269)
—On My Own Folklore: Complete Set. (p. 1289)
—On My Own Folklore: Classroom Set. (p. 1289)
—Once upon a Time in the Woods. Shortley, Michele, illus. (p. 1293)
—Open Wide! Burks, James, illus. (p. 1299)

—Paul Bunyan. (p. 1330)
—Pecos Bill. (p. 1334)
—Pecos Bill. Tong, Paul, illus. (p. 1334)
—Pins & Needles. Litten, Kristyna, illus. (p. 1361)
—Pins & Needles Share a Dream. Litten, Kristyna, illus. (p. 1361)
—Play Ball, Jackie! Morse, Joe, illus. (p. 1371)
—Sacagawea. Magnuson, Diana, illus. (p. 1500)
—Snack Attack. Curtis, Stacy, illus. (p. 1595)
—Tale of la Llorona: A Mexican Folktale. (p. 1699)
—Three Little Pigs' Sledding Adventure. Shortley, Michele, illus. (p. 1743)
—Too Many Leprechauns: Or How That Pot O' Gold Got to the End of the Rainbow. Andreasen, Dan, illus. (p. 1766)
—Trucks. Lola & Ivanke, illus. (p. 1791)
—Vampires. (p. 1832)
—Watchers in the Woods. (p. 1861)
—Werewolves. (p. 1875)
—What Do You See? A Lift-the-Flap Book about Endangered Animals. Schimler, Amy, illus. (p. 1883)
—Youngest Fairy Godmother Ever. Bluthenthal, Diana Cain, illus. (p. 1979)
—Zombies. (p. 1988)
Krensky, Stephen, jt. auth. see Morrissey, Dean.
Krensky, Stephen & Brown, Marc. Arthur Plays the Blues. (p. 104)
Krensky, Stephen & Dorling Kindersley Publishing Staff. Benjamin Franklin. (p. 164)
—Biography Barack Obama: A Photographic Story of Life. (p. 188)
Krensky, Stephen & Sarfatti, Esther. Arturo y la Carrera por la Lectura. (p. 105)
Krensky, Stephen, et al. Arturo y el Concurso de Poesia. (p. 105)
Krensky, Stephen, text. Arthur Makes the Team. (p. 104)
Krentz, Jayne Ann. Truth or Dare. (p. 1794)
Krenzer, Rolf. Jesus Is Risen. Maloney, Linda M., tr. from GER. (p. 915)
Krepela, Rebecca. Vernon, Drake & Chomp. (p. 1837)
Kreple, Pat. 4 Dog Tales. (p. 1992)
Kresge, S., ed. see Hayek, F. A.
Kreske, Damian P., et al. Junior Drug Awareness: How to Say No to Drugs. (p. 936)
Kress, Adrienne. Outcast. (p. 1312)
Kress, Camille. High Holy Days. Kress, Camille, illus. (p. 777)
—Purim! Kress, Camille, illus. (p. 1419)
—Tree Trunk Seder. Kress, Camille, illus. (p. 1784)
Kress, Dave. Thomas Pynchon. (p. 1739)
Kress, Stephen W. Project Puffin: How We Brought Puffins Back to Egg Rock. (p. 1410)
Kress, Stephen W., jt. auth. see Salmansohn, Pete.
Kressley, Carson. You're Different & That's Super. Lee, Jared, illus. (p. 1982)
Kretzer, Joyce B. Shane & the Jackadoo: A Butcher Hollow Fantasy. (p. 1559)
Kretzer, Kimberly. Mystic Valley Adventures of Kody & Kory: The Journey Begins. (p. 1226)
Kretzmann, Jane. Eddie & Harry. Ditewig, Diann, illus. (p. 503)
Kretzmer, Alissa. Brandy's Day at the Beach. (p. 222)
Kreuger, Jim & Averdonz, N. R. My Double-Edged Life Padilla, Ariel, illus. (p. 1202)
Kreutzer, Rudolph. Forty-Two Studies for Violin. Singer, Edmund, ed. (p. 623)
Kreye, Eric & Youngberg, Norma. Under the Blood Banner. (p. 1813)
Krezel, Cindy. 101 Kid-Friendly Plants: Fun Plants & Family Garden Projects. (p. 1999)
—Kids' Container Gardening: Year-Round Projects for Inside & Out. Curtis, Bruce, photos by. (p. 953)
Kricher, John C. Dinosaurs. Morrison, Gordon, illus. (p. 444)
—Seashores. Peterson, Roger Tory, ed. (p. 1538)
Krick, Robert K. Civil War: Gettysburg & Other Eastern Battles, 1863-1865. (p. 325)
Krider, Dave. Do Animals Go to Heaven? (p. 456)
Krieb & Kreib. We're off to Find the Witch's House. Alley, R. W., illus. (p. 1875)
Krieg, Katherine. Attack on Pearl Harbor: A History Perspectives Book. (p. 114)
—Claude Monet. Morrow, J. T., illus. (p. 329)
—Congress. (p. 357)
—How Many Days? (p. 811)
—How Many Hours? (p. 811)
—How Many Minutes? (p. 811)
—How Many Months? (p. 811)
—How Many Seconds? (p. 811)
—How Many Weeks? (p. 811)
—How Many Years? (p. 811)
—Marie Curie: Physics & Chemistry Pioneer. (p. 1093)
—President & Cabinet. (p. 1396)
—Supreme Court. (p. 1684)
—Thomas Edison: World-Changing Inventor. (p. 1738)
Krieger, Emily. Funny Fill-In - My Space Adventure. Sipple, Dan, illus. (p. 649)
—Myths Busted! Just When You Thought You Knew What You Knew... Cocotos, Tom Nick, illus. (p. 1227)
—National Geographic Kids Funny Fill-In: My Ancient Egypt Adventure. (p. 1232)
—National Geographic Kids Funny Fill-In: My Dinosaur Adventure. Sipple, Dan, illus. (p. 1232)
—National Geographic Kids Myths Busted!: Just When You Thought You Knew What You Knew ... No. 2 Cocotos, Tom Nick, illus. (p. 1232)
—National Geographic Kids Myths Busted! 2: Just When You Thought You Knew What You Knew ... Cocotos, Tom Nick, illus. (p. 1232)
Kriesberg, Daniel A. Think Green, Take Action: Books & Activities for Kids (p. 1734)
Kriescher, Jeanette "Netty". Big Message from a Little Book: A Color-Blind World. (p. 182)
Krietzman, Ariel, illus. see Stalder, Erika.
Krilanovich, Nadia. Chicken, Chicken, Duck! Krilanovich, Nadia, illus. (p. 300)
—Moon Child. Sayles, Elizabeth, illus. (p. 1172)
Krill, Richard M. Greek & Latin in English Today. (p. 720)
Krinard, Susan. Dark of the Moon. (p. 408)
Krings, Antoon. Droles de Petites Betes. (p. 485)
—Duendecillo Membrillo. Krings, Antoon, illus. (p. 489)
—Gilberto Mariposa. (p. 676)
—Mireille L Abeille. (p. 1149)
—Ursula Libelula. Krings, Antoon, illus. (p. 1826)
Krinsky, Ed. Pip, Veronica & the Harmonica. Evans, Casey, illus. (p. 1361)
Krinsky, Lee. Longest Fall. (p. 1047)
Krinsky, Rivkah. Touch of Shabbat: A Touch & Feel Book. Becker, Boruch, illus. (p. 1772)
Kripke, Dorothy Karp. Let's Talk about God. Tripp, Christine, tr. (p. 1001)
Kris, Alison E., illus. see Scholastic, Inc. Staff & Cannon, Nick.
Kris Hirschmann. Whale Shark. (p. 1877)
Krischke, Nikki, ed. see Bumcrot, Curt & Bumcrot, Jenny.
Krise, Carrie. Even Little Ones Are in God's Care. (p. 541)
Krise, Gale. It's a Colorful Candy Birthday. (p. 895)
Krisher, Trudy. Affectionate Farewell: the Story of Old Abe & Old Bob. Dodson, Bert, illus. (p. 26)
—Fallout. (p. 567)
Krishna, McArthur & Spalding, Bethany Brady. Girls Who Choose God: Stories of Strong Women from the Book of Mormon. Peterson, Kathleen, illus. (p. 681)
—Girls Who Choose God. Peterson, Kathleen, illus. (p. 681)
Krishnamurti, J. Que Estas Haciendo con Tu Vida: Comentarios Sobre el Vivir para Jovenes. (p. 1423)
Krishnaswami, Uma. Ants Have a Picnic. (p. 90)
—árbol Más Feliz: Un Cuento Sobre Yoga. Jeyaveeran, Ruth, illus. (p. 94)
—Big Party. (p. 183)
—Bringing Asha Home Jeyaveeran, Ruth & Akib, Jamel, illus. (p. 229)
—Broken Tusk: Stories of the Hindu God Ganesha. (p. 230)
—Chachaji's Cup. Sitaraman, Soumya, illus. (p. 288)
—Grand Plan to Fix Everything. Halpin, Abigail, illus. (p. 707)
—Hooray! 100 Days. (p. 795)
—Learn to Estimate. (p. 984)
—Out of the Way! Out of the Way! Krishnaswamy, Uma, illus. (p. 1311)
—Problem with Being Slightly Heroic. Halpin, Abigail, illus. (p. 1408)
Krishnaswami, Uma & Bhabha, Shiraaz. Closet Ghosts. Bhabha, Shiraaz, illus. (p. 334)
Krishnaswamy, Uma, illus. see Krishnaswami, Uma.
Krisp, Caleb. Anyone but Ivy Pocket. Cantini, Barbara, illus. (p. 91)
Kristen, Judith. Everybody Loves Mookie. Daly, Sue V., illus. (p. 543)
—My Name Is Henley: My life & times as a rescued Dog. (p. 1215)
—Once upon a Time in Liverpool. Cash, Eric, illus. (p. 1293)
Kristen, Mantooth. Danny Goes to the Doctor. Kristen, Mantooth, illus. (p. 405)
Kristiansen, Kate. Black Dog White Dog. (p. 196)
Kristiansen, Teddy, illus. see Gaiman, Neil.
Kristiansson, Leif. Not My Fault. Stenberg, Dick, illus. (p. 1267)
Kristie Kryssing, illus. see Jennie Lyon Wood.
Kristie Smith-Armand M.Ed Ctvl. Adventures of Abby Diamond: Out of Sight. (p. 16)
Kristie Smith-Armand M.Ed Tvl. Adventures of Abby Diamond: Abby Diamond in Teenage Wizard & Secrets in the Attic. (p. 16)
Kristina Simmons. Winter Beauty. (p. 1938)
Kristine, Gerber, compiled by. Council Bluffs Remembered. (p. 369)
Kristine, Jaime. Oh, You Hero! (p. 1281)
Kristo, Jancie, et al. Nonfiction in Focus: A Comprehensive Framework for Helping Students Become Independent Readers & Writers of Nonfiction, K-6. (p. 1263)
Kristof Pincheira, Kyra, illus. see Cassell, Jody.
Kriszt-Mohn, Beti. First Football ABC Pretzel Book. (p. 595)
Kriszt, Ann Marie. Bestis Friends. (p. 171)
Krit, Joey, illus. see Kamon.
Krittendon, Kim, illus. see Johnson, Sandi, et al.
Krivinskas, Carol Italiano. Barnyard Babies to the Rescue. (p. 139)
Krivitzky, Nathan & Nathan, Krivitzky. Always Late Nate. O'Connell, Dave, illus. (p. 51)
Kriyananda, Swami. Time Tunnel: A Tale for All Ages & for the Child in You. (p. 1753)
Krizmanic, Tatjana, illus. see Fordham, Walter.
Krizmanic, Tatjana, illus. see Simms, Laura.
Krizner, L. J. Peter Stuyvesant: New Amsterdam, & the Origins of New York. (p. 1347)
Krizner, L. J. & Sita, Lisa. Peter Stuyvesant: New Amsterdam & the Origins of New York. (p. 1347)
Krmer, Eva-Maria. Get to Know Dog Breeds: The 200 Most Popular Breeds. (p. 668)
Krock, Libby Carruth, illus. see St. Jean, Alan.
Kroeger, Mary Kay, jt. auth. see Borden, Louise.
Kroeger, Vanesa, illus. see Fernandez, Cecilia Fau.
Kroelinger, Melanie. Ocean: A Lullaby Book. (p. 1276)
Krog, Hazlitt, jt. auth. see Shulman, Mark.
Kroha, Kristin V. Sophie's Magic Underwear. (p. 1613)
Krohberger, Dawn. Jack Out of the Box: Self-Esteem Elevation for Children. (p. 903)
Krohmer, Randolph W. Reproductive System. (p. 1461)
Krohn, Genendel. I Wish I Were a King. Pelleg, Tirtsa, illus. (p. 849)
—Miracle of the Rock & other Stories: Timeless Tales from the Lives of Our Sages. Pelleg, Tirtsa, illus. (p. 1148)
—When We Left Yerushalayim: Stories of the Churban Beis HaMikdash. (p. 1905)
—Who Is the Builder? Pelleg, Tirtsa, illus. (p. 1916)
Krohn, Gretchen & Johnson, John Norton. Scales of the Silver Fish. Haring, Mary, illus. (p. 1519)
Krohn, Katherine. 1918 Flu Pandemic Williams, Keith et al, illus. (p. 2002)
—Biography Gwen Stefani. (p. 189)
—Earth-Shaking Facts about Earthquakes with Max Axiom, Super Scientist Smith, Tod G. & Milgram, Al, illus. (p. 497)
—Encountering Bigfoot: Eyewitness Accounts Byers, Michael, illus. (p. 524)
—Fortune-Telling. (p. 623)
—Jane Goodall: Animal Scientist Martin, Cynthia & Timmons, Anne, illus. (p. 908)
—Jennifer Lawrence: Star of the Hunger Games. (p. 913)
—Mystery of Haunted Houses. (p. 1224)
—Unsolved Mystery of Haunted Houses. (p. 1822)
Krohn, Katherine, jt. auth. see Krohn, Katherine E.
Krohn, Katherine & Milgrom, Al. Whirlwind World of Hurricanes with Max Axiom, Super Scientist. (p. 1912)
Krohn, Katherine E. Calico Dresses & Buffalo Robes: American West Fashions from the 1840s to the 1890s. (p. 253)
—Earth-Shaking Facts about Earthquakes with Max Axiom, Super Scientist. Smith, Tod G. & Milgrom, Al, illus. (p. 497)
—Everything You Need to Know about Birth Order. (p. 545)
—Everything You Need to Know about Living on Your Own. (p. 545)
—Jennifer Lawrence: Star of the Hunger Games. (p. 913)
—Jonas Salk & the Polio Vaccine Milgrom, Al, illus. (p. 925)
—Madam C. J. Walker & New Cosmetics Dominquez, Richard et al, illus. (p. 1069)
—Michael Jackson: Ultimate Music Legend. (p. 1134)
—Oprah Winfrey: Global Media Leader. (p. 1301)
—Oprah Winfrey. (p. 1301)
—Sojourner Truth: Freedom Fighter (p. 1606)
—Stephenie Meyer: Dreaming of Twilight. (p. 1648)
—Vera Wang: Enduring Style. (p. 1836)
—You & Your Parents' Divorce. (p. 1973)
Krohn, Katherine E., jt. auth. see McLaughlin, Jerry.
Krohn, Katherine E. & Krohn, Katherine. Evelyn Cisneros: Prima Ballerina. (p. 541)
Krohn, Katherine E., et al. Refreshing Look at Renewable Energy with Max Axiom, Super Scientist. (p. 1456)
—Whirlwind World of Hurricanes with Max Axiom, Super Scientist (p. 1912)
Krohn, Katherine, et al. Refreshing Look at Renewable Energy with Max Axiom, Super Scientist. (p. 1456)
Krohn, Kathryn T. Sarah's Most Perfect Day. Sage, Trina, illus. (p. 1514)
Krohn, Terry L. Power of the Scepter. (p. 1390)
Krokos, Dan. False Future. (p. 567)
—False Memory. (p. 567)
—False Sight. (p. 567)
—Planet Thieves. (p. 1368)
Kroll, Belinda. Catching the Rose: Second Edition. (p. 279)
Kroll, Francis Lynde. Young Crow Raider: Young Heroes Library. Geer, Charles H., illus. (p. 1978)
—Young Sand Hills Cowboy: Young Heroes Library. Geer, Charles H., illus. (p. 1979)
—Young Sioux Warrior. Geer, Charles H., illus. (p. 1979)
Kroll, Henry. Philosopher's Stone. (p. 1351)
Kroll, Jennifer. Cutting Edge: Breakthroughs in Technology (p. 396)
—Mighty Macros: Little Things, Big Results. (p. 1140)
—Mighty Micros: Little Things Big Results. (p. 1140)
—Their Eyes Were Watching God: An Instructional Guide for Literature (p. 1728)
Kroll, Jeri. Coat of Cats. James, Ann, illus. (p. 336)
—Mickey's Little Book of Letters. (p. 1136)
Kroll, Jeri & James, Ann. Coat of Cats. (p. 336)
Kroll, Jon. Tales of a Hippy Kid: Road Trippin' & Skinny Dippin' GN: Road Trippin' & Skinny Dippin' GN. (p. 1702)
Kroll, Linda. Winter, Awake! Lieberherr, Ruth, illus. (p. 1938)
Kroll, Olivia. Riley's Vegetable Garden: Count to Tell the Number of Objects. (p. 1472)
Kroll, Sherri. Petal-Topia Presents: A Bullied Girl's/ Bullied Boy's Story. (p. 1346)
Kroll, Steve. Nina in That Makes Me Mad! (p. 1256)
Kroll, Steven. Barbarians! Byrd, Robert, illus. (p. 137)
—Biggest Christmas Tree Ever. Bassett, Jeni, illus. (p. 185)
—Biggest Easter Basket Ever. Bassett, Jeni, illus. (p. 185)
—Biggest Pumpkin Ever. Bassett, Jeni, illus. (p. 185)
—Biggest Pumpkin Surprise Ever. Bassett, Jeni, illus. (p. 185)
—Biggest Snowman Ever. Bassett, Jeni, illus. (p. 185)
—Biggest Valentine Ever. Bassett, Jeni, illus. (p. 185)
—Ellis Island: Doorway to Freedom. (p. 515)
—Hand-Me-Down Doll Andreasen, Dan, illus. (p. 740)
—Hanukkah Mice Shapiro, Michelle, illus. (p. 744)
—Jungle Bullies Nguyen, Vincent, illus. (p. 935)
—Patches Lost & Found Gott, Barry, illus. (p. 1328)
—Pooch on the Loose: A Christmas Adventure Garland, Michael, illus. (p. 1383)
—Stuff! Reduce, Reuse, Recycle Cox, Steve, illus. (p. 1670)
—Super-Dragon Holgate, Doug, illus. (p. 1679)
—Sweet America: An Immigrant's Story. (p. 1689)
—Tyrannosaurus Game Schindler, S. D., illus. (p. 1805)
—When I Dream of Heaven: Angelina's Story. (p. 1902)
Kroll, Steven & Bassett, Jeni. Poisson d'Avril. (p. 1377)
Kroll, Steven & Droll. Pooch on the Loose: A Christmas Adventure Garland, Michael, illus. (p. 1383)
Kroll, Virginia. Equal Shmequal. O'Neill, Philomena, illus. (p. 533)
—Good Neighbor Nicholas: A Concept Book. Cote, Nancy, illus. (p. 698)
—I Wanted to Know All about God. Jenkins, Debra Reid, illus. (p. 848)
—Let There Be Llamas! Lombardo, Irina, illus. (p. 994)
—Makayla Cares about Others. Cote, Nancy, illus. (p. 1078)
—Mosquito LePlatt, Betsy, illus. (p. 1176)
—On the Way to Kindergarten. Schlossberg, Elizabeth, illus. (p. 1292)
—Selvakumar Knew Better. Li, Xiaojun, illus. (p. 1550)
—She Is Born. (p. 1564)
—Thanksgiving Bowl O'Neill, Philomena, illus. (p. 1726)
Kroll, Virginia L. Christmas Cow. (p. 313)
—Especially Heroes. Ladwig, Tim, illus. (p. 536)
—Forgiving a Friend. Billin-Frye, Paige, illus. (p. 619)
—New Friends, True Friends, Stuck-Like-Glue Friends. Rosely, Rose, illus. (p. 1244)
Kroll, Woodrow. God's Guide for Life's Choices. (p. 691)
Krols, Birgit. Extreme Hotels (p. 556)
Krome, Mike, illus. see Kovacs, Victoria.
Kromer, Christiane, illus. see Howard, Elizabeth Fitzgerald.
Kromer, Christiane, illus. see Silver, Gail.
Kromhout, Rindert. 1 2 3 Little Donkey. Nagelkerke, Bill, tr. from DUT. (p. 1990)
Krommenacker, Mark. Dave the Duck Gets Active (p. 410)
Krommes, Beth, illus. see Martin, Jacqueline Briggs.
Krommes, Beth, illus. see Nicholls, Judith, ed.
Krommes, Beth, illus. see Nicholls, Judith.
Krommes, Beth, illus. see Sidman, Joyce.
Krommes, Beth, illus. see Swanson, Susan Marie.
Krommes, Beth, illus. see White, Dianne.
Krone, Mike, illus. see Sperry, Amanda.
Krone, Thelma Smith. Nosey. (p. 1266)
—Sadie. Snader, Gregory, illus. (p. 1501)
Kroneberger, Abigail Grace. Sensory Room Kids Get in Sync. Kroneberger, Abigail Grace, illus. (p. 1551)
Kroner, David & Du Houx, Ramona. Seasons. Du Houx, E. M. Cornell, illus. (p. 1538)
Kronheim, Joseph Martin. My First Picture Book. (p. 1207)
Kronheimer, Ann. Delicious Doodles: Super Sweet Designs to Complete & Create. (p. 425)
—Pretty Princesses: Beautiful Princesses to Color! (p. 1398)
Kronheimer, Ann, illus. see Austen, Jane.
Kronheimer, Ann, illus. see Chapman, Linda.
Kronheimer, Ann, illus. see King-Smith, Dick.
Kronheimer, Ann, jt. auth. see Metzger, Steve.
Kronstadt, Jonathan. Ocean Extremes: Life in the Darkest Depths & under the Ice. (p. 1276)
Kronzek, Allan Zola & Kronzek, Elizabeth. Diccionario del Mago. Paula Vicens, Ines Belasategui, tr. (p. 435)
Kronzek, Elizabeth, jt. auth. see Kronzek, Allan Zola.
Kropf, Latifa Berry. Happy Birthday, World: A Rosh Hashanah Celebration. Carlson, Lisa, illus. (p. 745)
—It's Hanukkah Time! Cohen, Tod, photos by. (p. 897)
—It's Purim Time! Cohen, Tod, photos by. (p. 898)
—It's Seder Time! Cohen, Tod, illus. (p. 898)
—It's Shofar Time! Cohen, Tod, photos by. (p. 898)
—It's Sukkah Time! Cohen, Tod, photos by. (p. 899)
—It's Time Set. Cohen, Tod, photos by. (p. 899)
Kropik, Linda Kristine. Christopher the Choo Choo Train. Haezer, Jane, illus. (p. 317)
Kropp, Alex. Hacker! (p. 735)
—Turf Wars. (p. 1797)
Kropp, Joseph. Bowlegs' Bounty. (p. 216)
Kropp, Joseph P. Hickok's Gold. (p. 775)
—Nathan Meets His Monsters. Johnston, Phillip, illus. (p. 1231)
Kropp, Paul. Against All Odds. Melanson, Matt, illus. (p. 29)
—Avalanche. (p. 118)
—Behind the Door. (p. 160)
—Countess & Me (p. 370)
—Countess & Me. (p. 370)
—Crash. (p. 376)
—Edge Is Burning. Doherty, Catherine, illus. (p. 504)
—Foul Shot. Doherty, Catherine, illus. (p. 624)
—Home Run. (p. 792)
—I Didn't Do It! Doherty, Catherine, illus. (p. 837)
—Kid Is Lost. Melanson, Matt, illus. (p. 951)
—Lunatico y su Hermana Libertad. (p. 1065)
—My Broken Family. (p. 1199)
—One Stormy Night. (p. 1297)
—Running the Bases: Definitely Not a Book about Baseball. (p. 1497)
—Scarface. (p. 1520)
—Shooting the Rapids. (p. 1568)
—Student Narc. Melanson, Matt, illus. (p. 1669)
—Tag Team. (p. 1695)
—Winner! (p. 1936)
Kropp, Paul & Doherty, Catherine. Juvie. (p. 941)
Kropp, Paul & Jamison, Lori. HIP Readers' Theater Plays. (p. 780)
Krosoczka, Jarrett J. Annie Was Warned. (p. 87)
—Baghead. Krosoczka, Jarrett J., illus. (p. 132)
—Frog Who Croaked. Krosoczka, Jarrett J., illus. (p. 640)
—Good Night, Monkey Boy. Krosoczka, Jarrett J., illus. (p. 699)
—Lunch Lady & the Author Visit Vendetta. (p. 1065)
—Lunch Lady & the Bake Sale Bandit. (p. 1065)
—Lunch Lady & the Cyborg Substitute. (p. 1065)
—Lunch Lady & the Field Trip Fiasco. (p. 1065)
—Lunch Lady & the League of Librarians. (p. 1065)
—Lunch Lady & the Mutant Mathletes. (p. 1065)
—Lunch Lady & the Picture Day Peril. (p. 1065)
—Lunch Lady & the Schoolwide Scuffle. (p. 1065)
—Lunch Lady & the Summer Camp Shakedown. (p. 1065)
—Lunch Lady & the Video Game Villain. (p. 1065)
—Lunch Lady y el Sustituto Cibernetico. (p. 1065)
—Max for President. (p. 1111)
—Ollie the Purple Elephant. (p. 1287)
—Peanut Butter & Jellyfish. (p. 1332)
—Platypus Police Squad: Last Panda Standing. Krosoczka, Jarrett J., illus. (p. 1370)
—Platypus Police Squad: The Ostrich Conspiracy. Krosoczka, Jarrett J., illus. (p. 1370)
—Punk Farm. (p. 1417)
—Punk Farm on Tour. (p. 1417)
Krosoczka, Jarrett J., illus. see Good, Jason.
Krosoczka, Jarrett J., illus. see Perl, Erica S.
Krosoczka, Jarrett J., illus. see Thompson, Lauren.
Krossing, Karen. Bog (p. 207)
—Cut the Lights (p. 396)
—Pure (p. 1419)
—Take the Stairs (p. 1697)
—Yo-Yo Prophet (p. 1972)
Kroupa, Robert J. Just Like You. (p. 939)
Kroupa, Susan. Bed-Bugged. (p. 156)
Krouskop, Adrienne. Bakers Moon. (p. 133)
Kroutil Artists, creator. Elements: A Fun, Easy to Learn, Introduction to the Elements in Character! (p. 510)
—Elements & Their Electron Configurations: Build the Atoms from Actinum to Zirconium. (p. 510)
Krovatin, Christopher. Entombed. (p. 531)
—Mountain of Bones. (p. 1181)
—Terror Cove. (p. 1722)
—Venomous. Yates, Kelly, illus. (p. 1836)
Krovatin, Dan, illus. see Nichols, Joan K.
Krpan, Cathy Marks. 10 Most Phenomenal Modern Buildings. (p. 1994)
Kruckvich, Francis. Blue Chequered Harlequin. (p. 202)

K

Kruckvich, Francis, text. Hero & a Great Man. (p. 772)
Krudop, Walter Lyon, illus. see Burleigh, Robert.
Krudop, Walter Lyon, illus. see Peacock, Louise.
Krudwig, Vickie L. We Are the Noochew - A Brief History of the Ute People & their Colorado Connection. (p. 1866)
Krudwig, Vickie L., creator. Silly Circles Sketch Pad. (p. 1575)
Krueger, Anton. Sunnyside Sal. (p. 1677)
Krueger, Carol. Smelly Skunks. (p. 1593)
Krueger, Diane. Blessly's Carrotnog Christmas Book & Coloring Book. Krueger, Diane & Westenbroek, Ken, illus. (p. 199)
Krueger, Jennifer, jt. auth. see Allen, Kathy.
Krueger, Jenny, jt. auth. see Allen, Kathy.
Krueger, Jenny & Allen, Kathy. Science of a Rock Concert: Sound in Action (p. 1527)
Krueger, Jim, jt. auth. see Rogers, Bud.
Krueger, Jim & Rogers, Bud. Argon Deception Padilla, Ariel, illus. (p. 98)
—Child of Destiny Padilla, Ariel, illus. (p. 301)
Krueger, Jim & Zondervan Publishing Staff. Betrayal of Trust Rogers, Bud, ed. (p. 171)
Krueger, Joseph A. Where Is Jesus? (p. 1908)
Krueger, K. S. Traegonia: The Ember Rune. (p. 1776)
Krueger, Kathryn L. Road to Grandma's House. (p. 1477)
Krueger, S. L., jt. auth. see Brzycki, M. L.
Krueger, Susan Heidi. Tempest. (p. 1717)
Krueger, Susan L. & Bernadkin, Mila. Addie Slaughter: The Girl Who Met Geronimo. (p. 11)
Krueger, T. W. Donkeys Are Special & So Are You! Bohart, Lisa, illus. (p. 466)
Krug, Christine Suguitan. Favorite Action Bible Verses. (p. 578)
Krug, Jane, jt. auth. see Gast, Christy.
Krug, Ken. No, Silly! Krug, Ken, illus. (p. 1260)
Krug, R. Lyding. Treasure of Ferson Creek. (p. 1782)
Kruger, Jim. Paradise X Ross, Alex & Braithwaite, Doug, illus. (p. 1323)
Kruger, Kat. Night Has Claws. (p. 1253)
Kruger, Leanne Flett. Taking Care of Mother Earth. Hamelin, Marie-Micheline, illus. (p. 1698)
Kruger, Malia. Naughty Elepaio. Furchgott, Eve, illus. (p. 1237)
Kruger, Mark H. Overpowered. (p. 1314)
—Overtaken. (p. 1314)
Krugler, David F. This Is Only a Test: How Washington D. C. Prepared for Nuclear War. (p. 1736)
Kruglik, Gerald, jt. auth. see Bottner, Barbara.
Kruh, David. Top of the World, Ma! A Ten-Minute Comedy Duet. (p. 1769)
Kruijff, Geert-Jan M. & Oehrle, Richard T., eds. Resource-Sensitivity, Binding & Anaphora (p. 1463)
Kruk, Halya. Littlest One. Morchiladze, Manana, illus. (p. 1039)
Krukar, Jeff, et al. Melting Down: A Comic for Kids with Asperger's Disorder & Challenging Behavior (the Orp Library) (p. 1125)
Krul, J. T. Lost Spark. (p. 1056)
Krulik, Nancy. All's Fair. (p. 48)
—All's Fair. John and Wendy Staff, illus. (p. 48)
—Any Way You Slice It. (p. 90)
—Any Way You Slice It. John and Wendy Staff, illus. (p. 90)
—Attack of the Tighty Whities! (p. 114)
—Attack of the Tighty Whities! Blecha, Aaron, illus. (p. 114)
—Bad Rap John and Wendy Staff, illus. (p. 132)
—Be Careful What You Sniff For Braun, Sebastien, illus. (p. 148)
—Be Careful What You Sniff For. (p. 148)
—Be Nice to Mice! John and Wendy Staff, illus. (p. 149)
—Burp or Treat... Smell My Feet! (p. 244)
—Burp or Treat ... Smell My Feet! Super Special. Blecha, Aaron, illus. (p. 244)
—Camp Rules! John and Wendy Staff, illus. (p. 257)
—Can You Get an F in Lunch? (p. 259)
—Catch That Wave. (p. 279)
—Catch That Wave. Braun, Sebastien, illus. (p. 279)
—Collection of Katie: Books 1-4. John and Wendy, illus. (p. 340)
—Dance Your Pants Off! (p. 402)
—Dance Your Pants Off! Blecha, Aaron, illus. (p. 402)
—Doggone It! (p. 462)
—Doggone It! John and Wendy Staff, illus. (p. 462)
—Dogs Don't Have Webbed Feet Braun, Sebastien, illus. (p. 462)
—Don't Be Such a Turkey! John and Wendy Staff, illus. (p. 467)
—Don't Mess with the Ninja Puppy! (p. 468)
—Don't Mess with the Ninja Puppy! Braun, Sebastien, illus. (p. 468)
—Drat! You Copycat! (p. 480)
—Eww! What's on My Shoe? (p. 547)
—Eww! What's on My Shoe? Blecha, Aaron, illus. (p. 547)
—Flower Power John and Wendy Staff, illus. (p. 607)
—Follow That Furball. (p. 612)
—Follow That Furball. Braun, Sebastien, illus. (p. 612)
—Free the Worms! John & Wendy, illus. (p. 634)
—Free the Worms! John and Wendy Staff, illus. (p. 634)
—Friends for Never John and Wendy Staff, illus. (p. 638)
—Get Lost! (p. 667)
—Get Lost! John and Wendy Staff, illus. (p. 667)
—Girls Don't Have Cooties John and Wendy Staff, illus. (p. 680)
—Go Fetch! (p. 686)
—Go Fetch! Braun, Sebastien, illus. (p. 686)
—Going Batty. (p. 692)
—Going Batty. John and Wendy Staff, illus. (p. 692)
—Going Overboard! John and Wendy Staff, illus. (p. 692)
—Gotcha! Gotcha Back! John and Wendy Staff, illus. (p. 704)
—Hair Today, Gone Tomorrow! John and Wendy Staff, illus. (p. 736)
—Hey! Who Stole the Toilet? (p. 774)
—Hey! Who Stole the Toilet? Blecha, Aaron, illus. (p. 774)
—Holly's Jolly Christmas. John and Wendy Staff, illus. (p. 789)
—Horsing Around John and Wendy Staff, illus. (p. 800)
—How Do You Pee in Space? (p. 808)
—How Do You Pee in Space? Blecha, Aaron, illus. (p. 808)
—How I Survived Middle School: Madame President. (p. 810)
—I Hate Rules! (p. 839)
—I Hate Rules! John and Wendy Staff, illus. (p. 839)
—I Heard a Rumor. Martini, Angela, illus. (p. 839)
—Ice-Cream Dreams. Martinez, Heather, illus. (p. 850)
—I'm Game! John and Wendy Staff, illus. (p. 859)
—It's Snow Joke. John and Wendy Staff, illus. (p. 898)
—Karate Katie John and Wendy Staff, illus. (p. 943)
—Katie Kazoo Christmas. John and Wendy Staff, illus. (p. 945)
—Katie Kazoo, Switcheroo: A Collection of Katie. John and Wendy, illus. (p. 945)
—Keep on Burpin' Blecha, Aaron, illus. (p. 947)
—Let the Burping Begin. Blecha, Aaron, illus. (p. 994)
—Lice Check Blecha, Aaron, illus. (p. 1007)
—Lice Check. (p. 1007)
—Love Stinks! John and Wendy Staff, illus. (p. 1060)
—Major League Mess-Up. John and Wendy Staff, illus. (p. 1078)
—My Pops Is Tops! John and Wendy Staff, illus. (p. 1217)
—Nice Snowing You! (p. 1250)
—Nice Snowing You! Braun, Sebastien, illus. (p. 1250)
—No Biz Like Show Biz John and Wendy Staff, illus. (p. 1257)
—No Bones about It. John and Wendy Staff, illus. (p. 1257)
—No Messin' with My Lesson. John and Wendy Staff, illus. (p. 1259)
—Oh, Baby! John and Wendy Staff, illus. (p. 1280)
—On Thin Ice. John and Wendy Staff, illus. (p. 1292)
—On Your Mark, Get Set, Laugh! John and Wendy Staff, illus. (p. 1292)
—Open Wide John and Wendy Staff, illus. (p. 1299)
—Prom! The Complete Guide to a Truly Spectacular Night. Johnson, Kim, illus. (p. 1411)
—Puppy Love. (p. 1418)
—Quiet on the Set! John and Wendy Staff, illus. (p. 1428)
—Red, White, & - Achoo! John and Wendy Staff, illus. (p. 1455)
—Red, White, And—Achoo! (p. 1455)
—Ripped at the Seams. (p. 1474)
—Rootin' Tootin' Cow Dog #8. Braun, Sebastien, illus. (p. 1488)
—Royal Pain in the Burp #15. Blecha, Aaron, illus. (p. 1492)
—She's Got the Beat. (p. 1566)
—'Snot Funny! Blecha, Aaron, illus. (p. 1598)
—Something's Fishy John and Wendy Staff, illus. (p. 1610)
—Super Burp! Blecha, Aaron, illus. (p. 1679)
—Super Special: Going Overboard! (p. 1682)
—Three Burps & You're Out! (p. 1741)
—Three Cheers For... Who? John and Wendy Staff, illus. (p. 1741)
—Tip-Top Tappin' Mom! (p. 1757)
—Tip-Top Tappin' Mom! John and Wendy Staff, illus. (p. 1757)
—Trouble Magnet. Blecha, Aaron, illus. (p. 1790)
—Twelve Burps of Christmas. (p. 1800)
—Twelve Burps of Christmas. Blecha, Aaron, illus. (p. 1800)
—Vote for Suzanne. John and Wendy Staff, illus. (p. 1850)
—Wet & Wild! #5 Blecha, Aaron, illus. (p. 1877)
—What's Black & White & Stinks All Over? Blecha, Aaron, illus. (p. 1896)
—Whirlwind Vacation. John and Wendy Staff, illus. (p. 1912)
—Who's Afraid of Fourth Grade? John and Wendy Staff, illus. (p. 1920)
—Witch Switch. John and Wendy, illus. (p. 1941)
—World's Worst Wedgie. Blecha, Aaron, illus. (p. 1961)
—Write On! John and Wendy Staff, illus. (p. 1963)
Krulik, Nancy E. Dogs Don't Have Webbed Feet. (p. 462)
—Flower Power. John and Wendy Staff, illus. (p. 607)
—Rootin' Tootin' Cow Dog. (p. 1488)
—Royal Pain in the Burp. (p. 1492)
—'Snot Funny! (p. 1598)
—Something's Fishy. John & Wendy, illus. (p. 1610)
Krulikowski, Claire. Rapture. (p. 1439)
Krulikowski, Linda. Snakes of New England. (p. 1597)
Krull, Kathleen. Albert Einstein. Kulikov, Boris, illus. (p. 34)
—Benjamin Franklin. Kulikov, Boris, illus. (p. 164)
—Boy Named FDR: How Franklin D. Roosevelt Grew up to Change America. Johnson, Steve & Fancher, Lou, illus. (p. 218)
—Boy on Fairfield Street: How Ted Geisel Grew up to Become Dr. Seuss. (p. 218)
—Boy on Fairfield Street: How Ted Geisel Grew up to Become Dr. Seuss. Johnson, Steve & Fancher, Lou, illus. (p. 218)
—Boy Who Invented TV: The Story of Philo Farnsworth. Couch, Greg, illus. (p. 219)
—Brothers Kennedy: John, Robert, Edward. Bates, Amy June, illus. (p. 231)
—Charles Darwin. Kulikov, Boris, illus. (p. 292)
—Cosechando Esperanza: La Historia de César Chávez. Campoy, F. Isabel & Flor Ada, Alma, trs. (p. 368)
—Dolley Madison: Parties Can Be Patriotic! Fancher, Lou & Johnson, Steve, illus. (p. 464)
—Harvesting Hope: The Story of Cesar Chavez. Morales, Yuyi, illus. (p. 752)
—Houdini: World's Greatest Mystery Man & Escape King. Velasquez, Eric, illus. (p. 802)
—How to Trick or Treat in Outer Space. Brewer, Paul, illus. (p. 822)
—Isaac Newton. Kulikov, Boris, illus. (p. 890)
—Jim Henson: the Guy Who Played with Puppets. Johnson, Steve & Fancher, Lou, illus. (p. 917)
—Kubla Khan: The Emperor of Everything. Byrd, Robert, illus. (p. 968)
—Leonardo Da Vinci. Kulikov, Boris, illus. (p. 992)
—Lives of the Artists: Masterpieces, Messes (and What the Neighbors Thought) Hewitt, Kathryn, illus. (p. 1040)
—Lives of the Athletes: Thrills, Spills (and What the Neighbors Thought) Hewitt, Kathryn, illus. (p. 1040)
—Lives of the Explorers: Discoveries, Disasters (and What the Neighbors Thought) Hewitt, Kathryn, illus. (p. 1040)
—Lives of the Musicians: Good Times, Bad Times (and What the Neighbors Thought) Hewitt, Kathryn, illus. (p. 1040)
—Lives of the Pirates: Swashbucklers, Scoundrels (Neighbors Beware!) Hewitt, Kathryn, illus. (p. 1040)
—Lives of the Presidents: Fame, Shame (And What the Neighbors Thought) Hewitt, Kathryn, illus. (p. 1040)
—Lives of the Scientists: Experiments, Explosions (And What the Neighbors Thought) Hewitt, Kathryn, illus. (p. 1040)
—Louisa May's Battle: How the Civil War Led to Little Women. Beccia, Carlyn & Marinov, Marin, illus. (p. 1058)
—M Is for Music. Innerst, Stacy, illus. (p. 1067)
—Marie Curie. (p. 1093)
—Pocahontas: Princess of the New World. Diaz, David, illus. (p. 1375)
—Road to Oz: Twists, Turns, Bumps, & Triumphs in the Life of L. Frank Baum. Hawkes, Kevin, illus. (p. 1477)
—Sacajawea. Collins, Matt, illus. (p. 1500)
—Sigmund Freud. (p. 1574)
—Sonia Sotomayor: I'll Be the Judge of That! Dominguez, Angela N., illus. (p. 1612)
—They Saw the Future: Oracles, Psychics, Scientists, Great Thinkers, & Pretty Good Guessers. Brooker, Kyrsten, illus. (p. 1732)
—What Was the Boston Tea Party? (p. 1895)
—What Was the Boston Tea Party? Mortimer, Lauren & Bennett, James, illus. (p. 1895)
—What Was the March on Washington? (p. 1895)
—What Was the March on Washington? Tomkinson, Tim, illus. (p. 1895)
—What's New? the Zoo! A Zippy History of Zoos. Hall, Marcellus, illus. (p. 1898)
—Wilma Unlimited. Diaz, David, illus. (p. 1934)
—Woman for President: The Story of Victoria Woodhull. Dyer, Jane, illus. (p. 1945)
Krull, Kathleen & Brewer, Paul. Beatles Were Fab (and They Were Funny) Innerst, Stacy, illus. (p. 153)
—Fartiste. Kulikov, Boris, illus. (p. 575)
—Lincoln Tells a Joke: How Laughter Saved the President (and the Country) Innerst, Stacy, illus. (p. 1018)
Krum, Atticus. Taming. Donaera, Patrizia, illus. (p. 1704)
Krum, Ronda, illus. see Derico, Laura Ring.
Krumenaker, Larry, ed. Characteristics & the Life Cycle of Stars: An Anthology of Current Thought. (p. 291)
Krumenauer, Heidi. Brett Favre. (p. 226)
—Flo-Rida. (p. 605)
—Harry Styles of One Direction: Harry Styles. (p. 751)
—Jimmie Johnson. (p. 918)
—Joe Flacco. (p. 920)
—Lady Gaga. (p. 970)
—Lorde. (p. 1052)
—Michael Strahan. (p. 1134)
—Rihanna. (p. 1472)
—Sean Kingston. (p. 1537)
Krumm, Brian. Little Rock Nine: A Primary Source Exploration of the Battle for School Integration (p. 1036)
—Shuttle in the Sky: The Story of the Space Shuttle Columbia. (p. 1572)
Krumm, Brian & Kortenkamp, Steve. Exploring Space & Beyond. (p. 553)
Krump, Katy. Drippy Face. (p. 485)
Krumrey, Melanie. Bagels, Buddy, & Me: A Story about Gluten Intolerance & Celiac Disease. (p. 132)
Krumwiede, Lana. Archon. (p. 95)
—Freakling. (p. 631)
—Just Itzy. Pizzoli, Greg, illus. (p. 938)
—True Son. (p. 1792)
Krupic, Janice. Felicia's Family Divorces. (p. 581)
Krupin, Connie G., illus. see Mark, Yudel.
Krupinski, Loretta, illus. see Jordan, Helene J.
Krupinski, Loretta, illus. see Maestro, Betsy.
Krupinski, Tiffany J. Pangi the Penguin. (p. 1321)
Krupnek, Joann J., illus. see Eddy, Catherine J.
Krupp, Marian N., illus. see Patterson, Sherri, et al.
Krupp, Vicki Levy, jt. auth. see Gelman, Judy.
Kruse, Anne. Takota's Dream. (p. 1698)
Kruse, Donald W. Cluck, Cluck, Cluck Splash! Crank, Donny, illus. (p. 335)
—Fleas, Please. Crank, Donny, illus. (p. 603)
—Gorilla Soup! (p. 703)
—Jasper Has Left the Building! Crank, Donny, illus. (p. 910)
—That's Not A Pickle! Howarth, Craig, illus. (p. 1727)
—That's Not a Pickle! Part 2 Pt. 2. Howarth, Craig, illus. (p. 1727)
—There's a Goof on My Roof. Crank, Donny, illus. (p. 1730)
—Where's the Gold. Shipman, Josie, illus. (p. 1911)
Kruse, Jan, et al. Walt Disney's Spring Fever Volume 3. (p. 1856)
Kruse, Jason T., illus. see Greenberger, Robert & Loughridge, Lee.
Kruse, Lynn. New Neighbor. (p. 1246)
Kruse, Nancy. Treasure Hunt: A Book of Clues for Parties. (p. 1781)
Kruse, Robyn A. Sammy the Sea Turtle Litteral, Christopher, illus. (p. 1508)
Krush, Beth, illus. see Cleary, Beverly.
Krush, Beth, illus. see Emery, Anne.
Krush, Beth, illus. see Enright, Elizabeth.
Krush, Beth, illus. see Norton, Mary.
Krush, Beth, illus. see Sorensen, Virginia.
Krush, Joe, illus. see Enright, Elizabeth.
Krush, Joe, illus. see Norton, Mary.
Krush, Joe, illus. see Sorensen, Virginia.
Krusi, Carolynne, ed. see Beisswenger, Iffer & Eldred, Margaret.
Krusinski, Lorraine. It's Hip to Be Square. (p. 897)
Kruss, James. Wake up, It's Easter! Wilson, David Henry, tr. from GER. (p. 1853)
Krutop, Lee. Ocean Creatures. (p. 1276)
Krutop, Lee, creator. Go Out to Play. (p. 687)
Kruusval, Catarina. Ellen's Apple Tree. Sandin, Joan, tr. from SWE. (p. 514)
—Franny's Friends. Sandin, Joan, tr. from SWE. (p. 631)
Krych, Elizabeth. Magnetic Learning - Safari. (p. 1075)
Krygler, Leora. Juvenile Court: A Judge's Guide for Young Adults & Their Parents. (p. 941)
Krygsman, Joan, illus. see Priest, Robert.
Krykorka, Vladyana. Arctic Sea (p. 96)
—Arctic Sky (p. 96)
—Arctic Stories (p. 96)
Krykorka, Vladyana, illus. see Bushey, Jeanne.
Krykorka, Vladyana, illus. see Kusugak, Michael Arvaarluk & Kusugak, Michael.
Krykorka, Vladyana, illus. see Kusugak, Michael.
Krykorka, Vladyana, illus. see Page, P. K.
Krykorka, Vladyana, illus. see Page, P. K. & Ellis, Sarah.
Krykorka, Vladyana Langer, illus. see Kusugak, Michael Arvaarluk & Kusugak, Michael.
Krymski, Walter A. Adventures of Peter Pangler Puncker: Discovering the Pumping Heart. (p. 21)
Krys, Michelle. Hexed. (p. 774)
Krysac, L. C., ed. Gravitational, Electric, & Magnetic Forces: An Anthology of Current Thought. (p. 712)
—Sound & Electromagnetic Waves: An Anthology of Current Thought. (p. 1615)
Krysko, Kenneth L., jt. auth. see MacKenzie-Krysko, Claudia.
Krystek, Lee. Cardboard Rocket. (p. 265)
Krystoforski, Andrej, illus. see Elliott, George.
Krystoforski, Andrej, illus. see Gorrell, Gena K.
Krystoforski, Andrej, illus. see MacLeod, Elizabeth.
Krystoforski, Andrej, illus. see Moore, Christopher.
Krystoforski, Andrej, illus. see Thomas, Cameron.
Krystosek, Richard. Chicken Scratch. (p. 300)
Kryzanowsky, Sari. Grandmother's Tales: Book One. (p. 709)
K's Art. Fondos. (p. 612)
Kshir, Donna M. & Potter, Sandra Dawn. I Was A Teen Abuser: One Boy's Struggle to Gain Self-Control. (p. 848)
—Three Little Golden Retrievers. (p. 1742)
K-Town Youth Empowerment Network Youth Council, et al. Be True to You: Celebrating the Youth Things that Make Us Unique. (p. 149)
Ku, Grace. When Grace Was. (p. 1902)
Ku, Min Sung, illus. see Kupperberg, Paul & Loughridge, Lee.
Ku, Min Sung, illus. see Lemke, Donald B.
Ku, Min Sung, illus. see Montroll, John.
Ku, Min Sung, illus. see Simon, Jenne.
Kuang, Miao, illus. see Jay, Eric.
Kubasta, Vojtech, illus. see Green, Roger Lancelyn, ed.
Kubena, Jake, jt. auth. see Augustin, Byron.
Kubert, Adam. Return to Weapon X (p. 1465)
Kubert, Adam, illus. see Millar, Mark & Austen, Chuck.
Kubert, Adam, illus. see Youngquist, Jeff, ed.
Kubert, Adam & Bachalo, Chris. World Tour. (p. 1958)
Kubert, Adam & Finch, David. Return of the King (p. 1464)
Kubert, Adam & Kubert, Andy. Tomorrow People (p. 1765)
Kubert, Adam, et al. Hellfire & Brimstone (p. 763)
Kubert, Andy, jt. auth. see Vaughan, Brian K.
Kubert, Andy, jt. illus. see Kubert, Adam.
Kubert, Andy, jt. illus. see Quesada, Joe.
Kubert, Andy & Ferry, Pasqual. Ultimate Comics Iron Man Ultimate Collection. (p. 1809)
Kubert, Andy, et al. Captain America: Land of the Free. (p. 263)
Kubert, Joe. Adventures of Yaakov & Isaac. (p. 24)
—Yossel: April 19, 1943. Abuli, Enrique Sanchez, tr. (p. 1972)
Kubert, Joe, jt. auth. see Kanigher, Bob.
Kubesh, Katie & Belletto, Kimm. HOCPP 1056 Renaissance. (p. 787)
Kublak, Shannon. God Called a Girl: How Mary Changed Her World — And You Can Too. (p. 688)
Kubic, Ginger, illus. see Bonk, John J.
Kubic, Ginger, illus. see Butler, Dori Hillestad.
Kubick, Dana, illus. see French, Vivian.
Kubick, Dana, illus. see Wood, David.
Kubik, Dorothy. Adventures of Elbert & Leopoldina. James, Annie, illus. (p. 17)
Kubik, Jeff. Wimbledon. (p. 1935)
Kubinyi, Laszlo, illus. see Hunter, Erin.
Kubinyi, Laszlo, illus. see Lewis, J. Patrick.
Kubinyi, Laszlo, illus. see Riggs, Kate.
Kubinyi, Laszlo, illus. see Roberts, Tom.
Kubish, Shelagh & Craig, Lee, eds. Pumpkin Carving (p. 1416)
Kubit, Glenna. Art Is ... Elements & Principles If Design. (p. 102)
Kubke, Jane. Bull Riding. (p. 240)
Kubke, Jane & Kubke, Jessica. Bull Riding. (p. 240)
Kubke, Jessica, jt. auth. see Kubke, Jane.
Kubler, Annie. Baa Baa, Black Sheep! (p. 123)
—Baa, Baa, Black Sheep! (p. 123)
—Dingle Dangle Scarecrow. (p. 440)
—Dinosaur Diner. (p. 442)
—Dive in, Ducky! (p. 454)
—Dress Up! (p. 485)
—Head, Shoulders... (p. 756)
—Head, Shoulders, Knees & Toes. (p. 756)
—Hey Diddle Diddle. (p. 774)
—Hickory Dickory Dock. (p. 775)
—Hop a Little, Jump a Little! (p. 796)
—Humpty Dumpty. (p. 827)
—If You're Happy. (p. 855)
—I'm a Little Teapot. (p. 858)
—Incey Wincey Spider. (p. 868)
—Itsy Bitsy Spider. (p. 900)
—Itsy, Bitsy Spider. (p. 900)
—Mary Had a Little Lamb. (p. 1100)
—Mixed up Caterpillar. (p. 1156)
—My First Signs. (p. 1208)
—Pat-A-Cake! (p. 1327)
—Pat-A-Cake! Nursery Rhymes. (p. 1327)
—Peek-A-Boo! Nursery Games. (p. 1334)
—Pinocchio. (p. 1360)
—Play Time, Puppy! (p. 1371)
—Pussy Cat, Pussy Cat. (p. 1420)
—Ride On! (p. 1471)
—Ring Around a Rosie. (p. 1473)
—Row, Row, Row Your Boat. (p. 1492)
—See Saw! Nursery Songs. (p. 1547)
—See You Later Alligator. (p. 1547)
—Sleep Tight, Teddy! (p. 1588)
—Teddy Bear, Teddy Bear. (p. 1712)
—Ten Little Fingers. (p. 1719)
—This Little Piggy. (p. 1737)
—Twinkle, Twinkle, Little Star. (p. 1802)
—Wee Willie Winkie. (p. 1871)
—What Can I Feel? (p. 1880)
—What Can I Hear? (p. 1880)

—What Can I Look? (p. 1880)
—What Can I Smell? (p. 1880)
—What Can I Taste? (p. 1880)
—What's the Time, Mr. Wolf? (p. 1900)
—Wheels on the Bus (p. 1901)
—Wheels on the Bus: Go Round & Round. (p. 1901)
—Wheels on the Bus Kubler, Annie, illus. (p. 1901)
—Work Out! (p. 1952)
Kubler, Annie, illus. see Mlawer, Teresa, tr.
Kubler, Annie & Adams, Pam. Down by the Station. (p. 474)
Kubler, Annie & Nascimbeni, Barbara. Little Miss Muffet. (p. 1031)
Kubler, Annie, tr. Wheels on the Bus Go Round & Round. (p. 1901)
Kubley, Ashley Newsome, illus. see Kenney, Karen Latchana.
Kubley, Ashley Newsome, illus. see Watson, Stephanie.
Kubo, Shirley, tr. see Yazawa, Ai.
Kubo, Taito. Bleach, Volume 43: Kingdom of Hollows. (p. 199)
Kubo, Tite. Bleach. (p. 199)
—Bleach. Kubo, Tite, illus. (p. 199)
—Bleach. Wall, Frances, ed. (p. 199)
—Zombie Powder. Kubo, Tite, illus. (p. 1988)
Kubo, Tite & Caselman, Lance. Bleach. Kubo, Tite, illus. (p. 199)
—Broken Coda. Kubo, Tite, illus. (p. 230)
Kubuitsile, Lauri. Uganda. (p. 1808)
—Uganda. Rotberg, Robert I., ed. (p. 1808)
Kubus, Patricia Goskowski. Amanda Helps Becky Say Farewell. (p. 52)
Kuc, Jessica. Mawby the Christmas Pony. (p. 1110)
Kucej, Kristine. Sheldon Zab the Crab. Lester, Roseanna, illus. (p. 1564)
Kucharik, E. NT y Salmos Pequenas Bendiciones. (p. 1269)
Kucharik, Elena, illus. see Barnhill, Carla.
Kucharik, Elena, illus. see Bostrom, Kathleen Long.
Kucharik, Elena, illus. see Bowman, Crystal.
Kucharik, Elena, illus. see Mackall, Dandi Daley & Bostrom, Kathleen Long.
Kucharik, Elena, illus. see Mackall, Dandi Daley.
Kucharski, Linda. Sneak the Sneaker. (p. 1597)
Kuchler, B. L. That's Life. (p. 1727)
Kuchler, Bonnie Louise, compiled by. Just Kids: Pictures, Poems & Other Silly Animal Stuff Just for Kids! (p. 939)
Kuchman, D. S. Krystal Steps: The Journey Begins. (p. 968)
Kuck, Anna. Seven Holy Sleepers: Amazing Saints. (p. 1554)
Kuczenski, Tyler & Schumacher, Dan. Twelve Little Piggies. (p. 1800)
Kuczmarski, Susan Smith. Sacred Flight of the Teenager: A Parent's Guide to Stepping Back & Letting Go. (p. 1500)
Kudela, Katy R. Bilingual Picture Dictionaries. (p. 186)
—My First Book of Arabic Words Translations.com Staff, tr. (p. 1205)
—My First Book of French Words (p. 1205)
—My First Book of German Words (p. 1205)
—My First Book of Greek Words Translations.com Staff, tr. (p. 1205)
—My First Book of Hindi Words Translations.com Staff, tr. (p. 1205)
—My First Book of Italian Words Translations.com Staff, tr. (p. 1205)
—My First Book of Japanese Words Translations.com Staff, tr. (p. 1205)
—My First Book of Korean Words Translations.com Staff, tr. (p. 1205)
—My First Book of Mandarin Chinese Words (p. 1205)
—My First Book of Polish Words Translations.com Staff, tr. (p. 1205)
—My First Book of Portuguese Words Translations.com Staff, tr. from ENG. (p. 1205)
—My First Book of Russian Words Translations.com Staff, tr. (p. 1205)
—My First Book of Spanish Words (p. 1205)
—My First Book of Vietnamese Words Translations.com Staff, tr. (p. 1205)
—Pebble First Guide to Penguins. (p. 1333)
—Pebble First Guide to Snakes. (p. 1333)
—Pebble First Guide to Songbirds. (p. 1333)
Kudela, Katy R. & Translations.com Staff. My First Book of Japanese Words (p. 1205)
Kuderick, Madeleine. Kiss of Broken Glass. (p. 961)
Kuderka, Michael S. Essential Reference of Domestic Brewers & Their Bottled Brands - DBBB. (p. 537)
Kudina Steinberg, Ganna V. Princess Conspiracy: an Inspector Poopchyk Mystery. (p. 1403)
Kudlinski, Kathleen. Christopher Columbus: Young Explorer. (p. 317)
—Dr. Seuss: Young Author & Artist. Henderson, Meryl, illus. (p. 475)
—Franklin Delano Roosevelt: Champion of Freedom. Henderson, Meryl, illus. (p. 630)
—Harriet Tubman. Brown, Robert, illus. (p. 749)
—Joan of Arc. (p. 919)
—Mother Teresa: Friend to the Poor. (p. 1178)
—Sojourner Truth: Voice for Freedom. Wooden, Lenny, illus. (p. 1606)
Kudlinski, Kathleen, jt. auth. see Kudlinski, Kathleen V.
Kudlinski, Kathleen V. Boy, Were We Wrong about Dinosaurs! Schindler, S. D., illus. (p. 219)
—Boy, Were We Wrong about the Solar System! Rocco, John, illus. (p. 219)
—Boy, Were We Wrong about the Weather! Serra, Sebastià, illus. (p. 219)
—Helen Keller: A Light for the Blind. Diamond, Donna, illus. (p. 762)
—Helen Keller. (p. 762)
—My Lady Pocahontas (p. 1211)
—Rebel with a Cause: The Daring Adventure of Dicey Langston, Girl Spy of the American Revolution. Faber, Rudy, illus. (p. 1451)
—Sunset Switch. Burnett, Lindy, illus. (p. 1677)
—What Do Roots Do? Schuppert, David, illus. (p. 1882)
Kudlinski, Kathleen V. & Kudlinski, Kathleen. Gandhi: Young Nation Builder. (p. 655)
Kudo, Takeo, jt. auth. see Burton, Leon H.
Kuechenmeister, Mary & Ferguson, Brinker. Sam & the Silver Stones. (p. 1506)
Kuedee, Jaycee. How to Draw Minnesota's Sights & Symbols. (p. 818)
—How to Draw Mississippi's Sights & Symbols. (p. 818)
—How to Draw Missouri's Sights & Symbols. (p. 818)
—How to Draw Montana's Sights & Symbols. (p. 818)
Kueffner, Sue. Orangutans. (p. 1302)
Kueffner, Sue & Kueffner, Susan. Orangutans. (p. 1302)
Kueffner, Susan. Orangutans. (p. 1302)
—Pandas. (p. 1321)
Kueffner, Susan, jt. auth. see Kueffner, Sue.
Kuefler, Joseph. Beyond the Pond. Kuefler, Joseph, illus. (p. 174)
Kuehl, William Aksel. Aksel's Field Guide to Monsters. (p. 32)
Kuehn, Stephanie. Charm & Strange. (p. 294)
—Complicit. (p. 354)
—Delicate Monsters. (p. 425)
Kuehnel, Judy Lyons. Archie & Abigail. (p. 95)
—Autumn of Aunt Charlotte. (p. 118)
Kuehnert, Stephanie. I Wanna Be Your Joey Ramone. (p. 847)
Kueker, Donald. Christmas Story According Luke. (p. 315)
—Easter Story According to Matthew. (p. 499)
Kuelnad, Marlon. Little People's Little Happenings. (p. 1033)
Kueng, Christian Roulland. Three Genie Brothers. (p. 1742)
Kuenzler, Lou. How the Elephant Got His Trunk. (p. 813)
—Magical Animals at Bedtime: Tales of Guidance & Inspiration for You to Read with Your Child - To Comfort & Enlighten. Weale, Andrew, illus. (p. 1074)
Kuenzler, Lou & Powell, Jillian. Fox & the Stork. Newton, Jill, illus. (p. 626)
—Town Mouse & the Country Mouse. Newton, Jill, illus. (p. 1773)
Kuepfer, Sharon (Durksen) Schnupp. Little Prairie Girl: Are We Rich ... or Poor? (p. 1033)
Kuerner, Karl J., illus. see McLellan, Richard A.
Kuettel, Nina, tr. see Streit, Jakob.
Kuffner, Trish. Arts & Crafts Busy Book: 365 Art & Craft Activities to Keep Toddlers & Preschoolers Busy. (p. 104)
—Arts & Crafts Busy Book: 365 Art & Craft Activities to Keep Toddlers & Preschoolers Busy. Lansky, Bruce, ed. (p. 104)
—Wiggle & Giggle Busy Book: 365 Fun, Physical Activities for Toddlers & Preschoolers. McGinnis, Megan, ed. (p. 1927)
Kuga, Cain. Cowboy Bebop: Shooting Star Nakamura, Yuki, tr. from JPN. (p. 373)
—Cowboy Bebop Shooting Star Kuga, Cain, illus. (p. 373)
Kuga, Cain, illus. see Yadate, Hajime.
Kugel, Bruriah. Effy Helps Out. Gerstein, Yoni, illus. (p. 505)
Kughn, Heather. I Love You a Little Bit More. (p. 843)
Kügler, Carson, jt. auth. see Kügler, Tina.
Kügler, Carson, jt. illus. see Kügler, Tina.
Kügler, Tina, illus. see Shirtliffe, Leanne.
Kügler, Tina & Kügler, Carson. In Mary's Garden. Kügler, Tina & Kügler, Carson, illus. (p. 864)
—Snail & Worm: Meet My Friend. (p. 1595)
Kuhl, Debra. Black Bert the Pirate (p. 195)
—Sammy's Magic Carpet Ride (p. 1508)
Kuhlman, Evan. Brother from a Box. Bruno, Iacopo, illus. (p. 231)
—Great Ball of Light. Holmes, Jeremy, illus. (p. 713)
—Last Invisible Boy. Coovert, J. P., illus. (p. 978)
Kuhlman, Thomas, et al. Beauty of Thy House: The History, Art & Architecture of Saint Cecilia Cathedral Omaha. (p. 154)
Kuhlmann, Torben. Lindbergh: The Tale of a Flying Mouse. (p. 1019)
Kuhn, Andy, illus. see Lynch, Brian.
Kuhn, Betsy. Force Born of Truth: Mohandas Gandhi & the Salt March, India, 1930. (p. 616)
—Gay Power! The Stonewall Riots & the Gay Rights Movement 1969. (p. 659)
—Prying Eyes: Privacy in the Twenty-First Century. (p. 1413)
—Race for Space: The United States & the Soviet Union Compete for the New Frontier. (p. 1431)
Kuhn, Donna. Santa Trout. (p. 1513)
Kuhn, Douglas W., illus. see Kuhn, Tom B.
Kuhn, Douglas Wolcik. Animals' Christmas Gift. Cimino, Nicole C., ed. (p. 82)
—Summer of the Monarch Butterflies. (p. 1674)
—Uncle Kyle's Magic Kite. Kuhn, Douglas Wolcik, illus. (p. 1812)
Kuhn, Dwight, illus. see Pascoe, Elaine.
Kuhn, Dwight, illus. see Schwartz, David M. & Schy, Yael.
Kuhn, Dwight, photos by see Pascoe, Elaine.
Kuhn, Dwight, photos by see Schwartz, David M.
Kuhn, Dwight, photos by see Schwartz, David M. & Schy, Yael.
Kuhn, Dwight, photos by see Schwartz, David M., et al.
Kuhn, Dwight, photos by see Schy, Yael & Schwartz, David.
Kuhn, Gerald. Cadkey V21 Cookbook. (p. 250)
Kuhn, Glenda. Delilah Dances One Step at a Time. (p. 425)
Kuhn, Jerry. KeyCreator Cookbook. (p. 950)
Kuhn, Jesse, illus. see Cook, Sherry & Johnson, Martin.
Kuhn, Jesse, illus. see Cook, Sherry & Johnson, Terri.
Kuhn, Krystyna. Game. (p. 654)
Kuhn, Pamela J. Bible Crafts on a Shoestring Budget: Boxes & Containers. (p. 175)
—Bible Crafts on a Shoestring Budget: Paper Plates & Cups. (p. 175)
—Bible Crafts on a Shoestring Budget: Craft Sticks & Clothespins. (p. 175)
—Bible Crafts on a Shoestring Budget: Paper Sacks & Cardboard Tubes. (p. 175)
—More Instant Bible Lessons: Jesus' Disciples. (p. 1174)
—More Instant Bible Lessons: Walking with Jesus. (p. 1174)
—More Instant Bible Lessons: Wisdom from God's Word. (p. 1174)
Kuhn, Pamela J., jt. auth. see Domeij, Scott.
Kuhn, Pamela J., jt. auth. see Pearson, Mary R.
Kuhn, Pamela J., jt. auth. see Pelfrey, Wanda B.
Kuhn, Pamela J., jt. auth. see Sanders, Nancy I.
Kuhn, Tom B. Little Chick: Learns to Trust in the Lord Kuhn, Douglas W., illus. (p. 1026)
Kuhnke, Larry. Cloud 9. (p. 334)
Kuhns, Jennifer. Hailey's Dream. Sneed, Patty, illus. (p. 735)
Kuhoric, James Anthony & Bradshaw, Nick. Army of Darkness: Shop 'Til You Drop Dead Collection. (p. 100)
Kuhtz, Cleo & Martell, Hazel. Ancient Greek Civilization. D'Ottavi, Francesca, illus. (p. 69)
Kuhtz, Russell, ed. Chemistry: Understanding Substance & Matter. (p. 297)
Kuijer, Guus. Libro de Todas las Cosas. (p. 1006)
Kuijer, Guus & Nieuwenhuizen, John. Book of Everything. (p. 211)
Kuijpers, Justin. Dragon Myth & the Mysterious Eyeball. (p. 477)
Kuiper, Kathleen, ed. 100 Most Influential Painters & Sculptors of the Renaissance. (p. 1998)
—Ancient Egypt: From Prehistory to the Islamic Conquest. (p. 68)
—Britannica Guide to Theories & Ideas That Changed the Modern World. (p. 229)
—Islamic: Art, Literature, & Culture. (p. 891)
—Mesopotamia: The World's Earliest Civilization. (p. 1129)
—Pre-Columbian America: Empires of the New World. (p. 1394)
Kuipers, Alice. Best-Ever Bookworm Book. Murguia, Bethanie Deeney, illus. (p. 169)
—Lost for Words. (p. 1055)
Kuipers, Jennifer L. Lynn's Magic Trunk: An Adventure in King Arthur's Court. (p. 1066)
Kuipers, Ken. A. D. A Study of Church History. (p. 1)
Kuivila, Janet. Gamma Girls of Chagrin Falls: Lillie, Rose & Irisa. (p. 655)
Kujawinski, Peter, jt. auth. see Halpern, Jake.
Kujiradov, Misaho, jt. auth. see Milky, D. J.
Kukahiko, Puni, illus. see Honda, Liana.
Kukathas, Uma. Global Food Crisis. (p. 684)
—Minimum Wage. (p. 1147)
—Native American Rights. (p. 1234)
—Personal Liberty. (p. 1344)
Kuker, Debbie F. Susie Q Where Are You? (p. 1688)
Kukla, Amy. Thomas Jefferson: Life, Liberty, & the Pursuit of Happiness. (p. 1739)
Kuklin, Susan. Beyond Magenta: Transgender Teens Speak Out. (p. 174)
—Beyond Magenta: Transgender Teens Speak Out. Kuklin, Susan, photos by. (p. 174)
—No Choirboy: Murder, Violence, & Teenagers on Death Row. (p. 1258)
Kukolax, Andy. Ultralight Wildflower Guide to the Central Montana Rocky Mountains: Wildflower Montana. (p. 1810)
Kukreja, Julie, illus. see Harrah, Judith.
Kula, Cheryl. Play Day with Daddy. Trolenberg, Karl, illus. (p. 1371)
Kulagina, Alla V., ed. see Marshall, Bonnie.
Kulak, Jeff, illus. see Crossingham, John.
Kulak, Jeff, illus. see deCarufel, Laura.
Kulak, Jeff, illus. see Elton, Sarah.
Kulak, Jeff, illus. see Glassbourg, Michael.
Kulak, Jeff, illus. see Williams, Ann-Marie.
Kulavis, Allyson. Fossil-Icious. (p. 623)
—Insect-O-Mania! (p. 875)
—Sea-Sational. (p. 1535)
—Space-Tacular! (p. 1620)
Kule, Elaine A. Beginning Again: Immigrating to America. Thermes, Jennifer, illus. (p. 159)
—Celebrate Chinese New Year. (p. 283)
—Celebrate Thanksgiving Day. (p. 284)
Kulhavy, Carolyn. Charlie's Unforgettable Journey. (p. 293)
Kulick, Don & Meneley, Anne. Fat: The Anthropology of an Obsession. (p. 576)
Kulick Triscila, Verne. Joel & the Magic Toy Tree. (p. 920)
Kulig, Ann & Skulski, Monica Fitch. Garbage Can Day. (p. 655)
Kuligowski, Stephanie. 22nd Century: Future of Space. (p. 1996)
—Colonizacion de Texas / the Colonization of Texas. (p. 342)
—Colonization of Texas: Missions & Settlers. (p. 342)
—Dangerous Catch! - Deep Sea Fishers. (p. 404)
—Fearless! Stunt People. (p. 579)
—Leonardo Da Vinci: Renaissance Artist & Inventor. (p. 992)
—Renaissance: A Rebirth of Culture. (p. 1460)
—Salle: Early Texas Explorer. (p. 1505)
—Salle: Uno de los Primeros Exploradores de Texas. (p. 1505)
—Unsolved! Mysterious Events. (p. 1822)
—Wild Work! Animal Trainers. (p. 1931)
Kuligowski, Stephanie, jt. auth. see Cohn, Jessica.
Kuligowski, Stephanie, jt. auth. see Greathouse, Lisa.
Kuligowski, Stephanie, jt. auth. see Isecke, Harriet.
Kuligowski, Stephanie, jt. auth. see Paris, Stephanie.
Kuligowski, Stephanie, jt. auth. see Rice, Katie.
Kulihin, Vic, illus. see Higgins, Nadia.
Kulihin, Vic, illus. see Savage, Jeff.
Kulikov, Boris, illus. see Banks, Kate.
Kulikov, Boris, illus. see Bryant, Jennifer.
Kulikov, Boris, illus. see Downes, Patrick.
Kulikov, Boris, illus. see Fern, Tracey E.
Kulikov, Boris, illus. see Fleming, Candace.
Kulikov, Boris, illus. see Heller, Linda.
Kulikov, Boris, illus. see Hennessy, B. G.
Kulikov, Boris, illus. see Krull, Kathleen & Brewer, Paul.
Kulikov, Boris, illus. see Krull, Kathleen.
Kulikov, Boris, illus. see Lithgow, John.
Kulikov, Boris, illus. see Stone, Tanya Lee.
Kulikovsky-Romanoff, Grand Duchess Olga Alexandrovna. Adventures of Three White Bears. (p. 24)
Kulis, Stephen Stanley, jt. auth. see Marsiglia, Flavio Francisco.
Kulka, Joe. Christmas Coal Man. Kulka, Joe, illus. (p. 313)
—My Crocodile Does Not Bite. (p. 1200)
—Rope (p. 1488)
—Vacation's Over! Return of the Dinosaurs. Kulka, Joe, illus. (p. 1830)
—Wolf's Coming! Kulka, Joe, illus. (p. 1944)
Kulka, Joe, illus. see Brimner, Larry Dane.
Kulka, Joe, illus. see Brown, Marcy & Haley, Dennis.
Kulka, Joe, illus. see Enderle, Dotti.
Kulka, Joe, illus. see Jones, Andrea.
Kulka, Joe, illus. see Orshoski, Paul.
Kulka, Joe, illus. see Plourde, Lynn.
Kulkarni, Suresh. Wise King & Other Stories. (p. 1940)
Kull, Cyndi. I Spy. (p. 846)
Kulling, Monica. All Aboard! Elijah McCoy's Steam Engine. Slavin, Bill, illus. (p. 41)
—Eat My Dust! Henry Ford's First Race. Walz, Richard, illus. (p. 501)
—Francis Scott Key's Star-Spangled Banner. (p. 628)
—Francis Scott Key's Star-Spangled Banner. Walz, Richard, illus. (p. 628)
—Going Up! Elisha Otis's Trip to the Top. Parkins, David, illus. (p. 693)
—In the Bag! Margaret Knight Wraps It Up. Parkins, David, illus. (p. 865)
—It's a Snap! George Eastman's First Photograph. Slavin, Bill, illus. (p. 896)
—Listen Up! Alexander Graham Bell's Talking Machine. Walz, Richard, illus. (p. 1022)
—Making Contact! Marconi Goes Wireless. Rudnicki, Richard, illus. (p. 1081)
—Merci Mister Dash! Melo, Esperanca, illus. (p. 1127)
—Mister Dash & the Cupcake Calamity. Melo, Esperanca, illus. (p. 1155)
—When Emily Carr Met Woo Griffiths. Dean, illus. (p. 1902)
Kulling, Monica, jt. auth. see Walker, Nan.
Kulling, Monica & Walker, Nan. Messiest Room on the Planet. Smath, Jerry, illus. (p. 1130)
Kulman, Andrea M. Adventures of Charlie & Doo-Doo: Not a Baby Anymore (p. 17)
Kulman, Randy. Train Your Brain for Success: A Teenager's Guide to Executive Functions. (p. 1777)
Kulot, Daniela. Lio de Cordones. (p. 1019)
Kulp, Donald. Money Puppies: America's #1 Money Management Book for Kids. (p. 1164)
Kulp, Jodee, ed. see McConnell, Mac.
Kulp, Jodee, illus. see Smythe, Cheryl, et al.
Kulper, Kendall. Drift & Dagger. (p. 485)
—Salt & Storm. (p. 1505)
Kulsa, Wha. Childs Play: Positive Affirmations for Children to Sing & Dramatize. Gardner, Stephen, illus. (p. 305)
Kumakura, Yuichi. Jing: King of Bandit (p. 918)
—Jing: King of Bandits Vol. 6 (p. 918)
—Jing: King of Bandits Vol. 6 Kumakura, Yuichi, illus. (p. 918)
—Jing: King of Bandits Twilight Tales Kumakura, Yuichi, illus. (p. 918)
—Jing, King of Bandits (p. 918)
—Jing, King of Bandits Kumakura, Yuichi, illus. (p. 918)
—Jing, King of Bandits: Twilight Tales Kumakura, Yuichi, illus. (p. 918)
Kumakura, Yuichi, illus. see Kirsch, Alexis, tr.
Kumanchik, Cynthia. Deception. (p. 421)
Kumar, Asha, jt. auth. see Kumar, Monica.
Kumar, Jai Robert, jt. auth. see Kumar, Krishna.
Kumar, Krishna & Kumar, Jai Robert. Redhead from Alpha Centauri. (p. 1455)
Kumar, Manisha, jt. auth. see Kumar, Monica.
Kumar, Monica. Jay & Juhi: Taj Mahal Kee Saahsik Khoj. Aggarwal, Madhu, tr. (p. 910)
Kumar, Monica & Kumar, Asha. Great Desert Adventure. (p. 715)
Kumar, Monica & Kumar, Manisha. Diwali: A Festival of Lights & Fun. Sona & Jacob, illus. (p. 455)
Kumar, Naresh. Dusk Society. (p. 490)
Kumar, Naresh, illus. see Helfand, Lewis.
Kumar, Naresh, illus. see Stevenson, Robert Louis.
Kumar, Navina Magesh. Haley's Wish. (p. 736)
Kumar, Nishanth. Book of the Heavens. (p. 212)
Kumar, Pradyumna. How the Firefly Got Its Light. (p. 813)
Kumar, Vinay, illus. see Holland, Trish.
Kumar, Vinod, illus. see Doyle, Arthur.
Kumar, Vinod, illus. see Verne, Jules.
Kumara, Mark. Tr-Youth Truth: Knowledge, Apprehens. (p. 1774)
Kumasi, Akili, et al. Fun Meals for Fathers & Sons: Recipes & Activities for Bonding & Mentoring. (p. 648)
Kumata, Michelle Reiko, illus. see Noguchi, Rick & Jenks, Deneen.
Kumiega, Michelle. Bunnies Who Learn Not to Bully. (p. 242)
—Greedy Bunny. (p. 720)
Kumin, Maxine. Lizzie! (p. 1043)
—Oh, Harry! Moser, Barry, illus. (p. 1280)
—What Color Is Caesar? Friend, Alison, illus. (p. 1881)
Kumiski, John A. Fishing Florida's Space Coast: An Angler's Guide. (p. 599)
Kummer, Mark, illus. see Everett, Melissa.
Kummer, Mark, illus. see Fitzpatrick, Joe.
Kummer, Patricia K. Africa. (p. 26)
—Asia. (p. 106)
—Athletic Trainer. (p. 112)
—Calendar. (p. 252)
—Changing Climate of Asia. (p. 290)
—Changing Climate of North America. (p. 290)
—Currency. (p. 394)
—Enchantment of the World: Tibet. (p. 523)
—Food of Thailand. (p. 613)
—Great Barrier Reef. (p. 714)
—Great Lakes. (p. 716)
—Jordan. (p. 925)
—Singapore. (p. 1579)
—Sports Medicine Doctor. (p. 1633)
—Syria. (p. 1693)
—Working Horses. (p. 1952)
Kummer, Patricia K., jt. auth. see Schwabacher, Martin.
Kummer, Patricia K., jt. auth. see Shirley, David.
Kummerer, Erma. Someday I'll Ride a Train. (p. 1609)
Kumon. My Book of Numbers 1-120. (p. 1199)
—My Book of Numbers 1-30. (p. 1199)
—My First Book of Lowercase Letters. (p. 1205)
—My First Book of Uppercase Letters. (p. 1205)
—What Does Baby See? (p. 1884)

K

Kumon, creator. Let's Color! (p. 995)
Kumon Editors, ed. My Book of Rhyming Words Long Vowels. (p. 1199)
Kumon Publishing, creator. ABC's Write & Wipe! Lowercase Letters. (p. 4)
—Addition Grade 2: Kumon Math Workbooks. (p. 12)
—Animals Lion & Mouse (p. 83)
—Easy Telling Time Write & Wipe! (p. 500)
—More Let's Color! (p. 1174)
—More Let's Cut Paper! (p. 1174)
—More Let's Fold! (p. 1174)
—My Book of Alphabet Games Ages 4, 5, 6. (p. 1198)
—My Book of Amazing Crafts: Ages 5-6-7. (p. 1198)
—My Book of Coloring: Ages 2-3-4. (p. 1199)
—My Book of Coloring at the Zoo: Ages 3, 4, 5. (p. 1199)
—My Book of Sentences: Ages 6,7, 8. (p. 1199)
—My Book of Simple Addition. (p. 1199)
—My Book of Simple Multiplication. (p. 1199)
—My Book of Simple Sentences: Learning about Nouns & Verbs. (p. 1199)
—My Book of Simple Subtraction (p. 1199)
—My Book of Subtraction (p. 1199)
—My Book of Writing Words: Learning about Consonants & Vowels. (p. 1199)
Kumon Publishing, ed. Amazing Mazes. (p. 55)
—Focus on Multiplication & Division with Decimals. (p. 611)
—Focus on Multiplication Numbers 1-10. (p. 611)
—Focus on Reducing & Calculating Fractions. (p. 611)
—Multiplication & Division with Decimals. (p. 1190)
—My Book of Amazing Tracing. (p. 1199)
—My Book of Number Games 1-150. (p. 1199)
—My Book of Number Games 1-70. (p. 1199)
kumon publishing, ed. My Book of Pasting. (p. 1199)
Kumon Publishing, ed. My Book of Rhyming Words. (p. 1199)
—My Book of Rhyming Words & Phrases. (p. 1199)
—My First Book of Cutting. (p. 1205)
—My First Book of Mazes. (p. 1205)
—Paper Playtime Vehicles. (p. 1323)
—Subtraction, Grade 2. (p. 1671)
—Velocity, Proportion & Ratio. (p. 1835)
Kumon Publishing North America, creator. ABC's Write & Wipe! Uppercase Letters. (p. 4)
—My Book of Easy Crafts. (p. 1199)
—My Book of Easy Mazes, Ages 2-3-4. (p. 1199)
—My Book of Easy Telling Time: Learning about Hours & Half-Hours. (p. 1199)
—My Book of Pasting: Jigsaw Puzzles. (p. 1199)
—My Book of Telling Time: Learning about Minutes. (p. 1199)
—Numbers 1-30 Write & Wipe! (p. 1272)
Kumon Staff. Let's Cut Paper! (p. 995)
—Let's Fold! (p. 996)
—Let's Sticker & Paste! (p. 1000)
—My Book of Mazes Around the World. Karakida, Toshihiko & Murakami, Yoshiko, illus. (p. 1199)
Kumuhana High, Kukulu. Hala Grove of Wakiu (p. 736)
Kun Rong, Yap, illus. see Dahl, Michael.
Kunardi, Marco, illus. see Ventrillo, James & Ventrillo, Nick.
Kunce, Craig. Spring Is for Gardening. (p. 1635)
Kunda, Shmuel. Boruch Learns His Brochos. Kunda, Shmuel, illus. (p. 214)
Kundalic, Damir, illus. see Inglis, Karen.
Kundiger, Donovan & Kundiger, Marion. Catbird? Chomphootung, Rassamee, illus. (p. 278)
Kundiger, Marion, jt. auth. see Kundiger, Donovan.
Kundiger, Marion S. Izzie of Fergus Falls: A Minnesota Childhood in The 1880s. Kundiger, Marion S., illus. (p. 901)
Kung, Annie, tr. see Hao, K. T.
Kung, Annie, tr. Auntie Tigress & Other Favorite Chinese Folk Tales. Wang, Eva, illus. (p. 115)
Kung, Edward, ed. see Advance Cal-Tech Inc. Staff.
Kung, Isabella, illus. see Blackaby, Tom & Osborne, Rick.
Kunhardt, Dorothy. Junket Is Nice. Kunhardt, Dorothy, illus. (p. 936)
—Kitty's New Doll. (p. 963)
—Now Open the Box. Kunhardt, Dorothy, illus. (p. 1269)
—Pat the Bunny: First Books for Baby (p. 1327)
—Pat the Bunny. Golden Books Staff, illus. (p. 1327)
Kunhardt, Dorothy, ed. Pinocchio. (p. 1360)
Kunhardt, Katharine. Let's Count the Puppies. (p. 995)
Kunieda, Saika. Future Lovers (p. 651)
Kunjufu, Jawanza. Culture of Respect. (p. 391)
Kunjufu, Jawanza & Prescott, Folami. Kindergarten: Self-Esteem Through Culture Leads to Academic Excellence. (p. 957)
—Self-Esteem Through Culture Leads to Academic Excellence. (p. 1549)
—SETCLAE, Fifth Grade: Self-Esteem Through Culture Leads to Academic Excellence. (p. 1554)
—SETCLAE, First Grade: Self-Esteem Through Culture Leads to Academic Excellence. (p. 1554)
—SETCLAE, Fourth Grade: Self-Esteem Through Culture Leads to Academic Excellence. (p. 1554)
—SETCLAE, Second Grade: Self-Esteem Through Culture Leads to Academic Excellence. (p. 1554)
—SETCLAE, Seventh Grade: Self-Esteem Through Culture Leads to Academic Excellence. (p. 1554)
—SETCLAE, Sixth Grade: Self-Esteem Through Culture Leads to Academic Excellence. (p. 1554)
—SETCLAE, Third Grade: Self-Esteem Through Culture Leads to Academic Excellence. (p. 1554)
Kunkel, Dennis, illus. see Siy, Alexandra.
Kunkel, Dennis, photos by see Cobb, Vicki.
Kunkel, Dennis, photos by see Kramer, Stephen.
Kunkel, Dennis, photos by see Latta, Sara L.
Kunkel, Dennis, photos by see Siy, Alexandra.
Kunkel, Jeff, jt. auth. see Robinson, Hilda.
Kunkel, Kristen, jt. auth. see Blackwell-Burke, Melissa.
Kunkel, Mike. Archie Babies. Mawhinney, Art, illus. (p. 95)
—Billy Batson & the Magic. Kunkel, Mike, illus. (p. 187)
—Billy Batson & the Magic of Shazam! Kunkel, Mike, illus. (p. 187)
—Brother vs. Brother! Kunkel, Mike, illus. (p. 231)
—Herobear & the Kid Vol. 1 the Inheritance. Kunkel, Mike, illus. (p. 772)
—Inheritance. (p. 874)
—Magic Words! Kunkel, Mike, illus. (p. 1074)
—Perilous Peril! Kunkel, Mike, illus. (p. 1343)
—World's Mightiest Mortal! Kunkel, Mike, illus. (p. 1960)
Kuno, Dorothy. Micah. (p. 1134)
Kunoth, Joanne Kamara, illus. see Kunoth, Mark.
Kunoth, Mark. Eastern Anmatyerr Colouring Book. Purvis, Jedda Ngwarai & Purvis, Joy Pitjara, trs. (p. 499)
Kunoth, Mark & Turner, Margaret. Alyawarr Colouring Book. Turner, Margaret Petyerr, tr. (p. 51)
Kunoth, Mark, et al. Kaytetye Colouring Book. (p. 946)
Kunsang, Erik Pema, tr. see Padmasambhava.
Kunsang, Erik Pema, tr. see Tsogyal, Yeshe.
Kunstler, James Howard. Aladdin & the Magic Lamp. Couch, Greg, illus. (p. 33)
—Annie Oakley. Warter, Fred, illus. (p. 87)
—Davy Crockett. Brodner, Steve, illus. (p. 411)
—Johnny Appleseed. Olson, Stan, illus. (p. 923)
Kuntz, Lynn. Firefly. (p. 592)
—Roman Colosseum. (p. 1485)
Kuntz, Ron, jt. auth. see Klontz, Mary-Hannah.
Kuntz, Ron L. Doodlin Ducks. (p. 470)
Kunz, Barbara & Kunz, Kevin. Reflexology: Healing at Your Fingertips. (p. 1456)
Kunz, C. A. Childe. Kunz, Robert & Kunz, Stephanie, illus. (p. 302)
Kunz, Chris. Million Paws Puppy. Whitby, Charlotte, illus. (p. 1144)
Kunz, Chris, jt. auth. see Black, Jess.
Kunz, Chris, jt. auth. see Irwin, Bindi.
Kunz, Joseph C., Jr., ed. see Holmes, Oliver Wendell, Sr.
Kunz, Kevin, jt. auth. see Kunz, Barbara.
Kunz, Robert, illus. see Kunz, C. A.
Kunz, Stephanie, illus. see Kunz, C. A.
Kunze, Lauren & Onur, Rina. Ivy. (p. 901)
—Rivals. (p. 1475)
—Scandal. (p. 1519)
—Secrets. (p. 1544)
Kunze, Nansi. Dangerously Placed. (p. 404)
—Kill the Music. (p. 956)
Kunzinger, Bob. Infant: A Tale from Prague. (p. 873)
Kunzler-Behncke, Rosemarie. Where in the World Is God? Maloney, Linda M., tr. from GER. (p. 1908)
Kuo, Jane C. M. Open for Business: Lessons in Chinese Commerce for the New Millennium (p. 1299)
Kuo, Julia. Everyone Eats. Kuo, Julia, illus. (p. 544)
Kuo, Julia, illus. see Gilbert, Melissa.
Kuo, Julia, illus. see Grigg-Saito, Katrina.
Kuo, Julia, illus. see Kadohata, Cynthia.
Kuola. Kuola & Iosepa. (p. 968)
Kuon, Vuthy, illus. see Epner, Paul.
Kuon, Vuthy, illus. see Kimmel, Eric A. & Kang, Setha.
Kuon, Vuthy, illus. see Lavette, Lavaille.
Kuon, Vuthy, jt. auth. see Epner, Paul.
Kupchella, Rick. Girls Can! Make it Happen. Brown, Marilyn, illus. (p. 679)
—Tell Me What We Did Today. Hanson, Warren, illus. (p. 1717)
Kuper, Simon. Magnum Soccer. Magnum Editors Staff, ed. (p. 1076)
Kuper, Tonya. Anomaly. (p. 87)
Kuperman, Joshua & Kuperman, Laura. Little Lost Cricket. (p. 1031)
Kuperman, Laura, jt. auth. see Kuperman, Joshua.
Kuperman, Marina. Turtle Feet, Surfer's Beat. (p. 1798)
Kupesic, Rajka. White Ballets. (p. 1912)
Kupesic, Rajka, illus. see Kain, Karen.
Kupfer, Wendy. Let's Hear It for Almigal. Lyon, Tammie, illus. (p. 998)
Kuphal, Shirley M. Flavor's Wild Wish. (p. 603)
Kuplenk, Martina. Angelettes. (p. 74)
Kupperberg, Alan, et al. Essential Defenders - Volume 7. (p. 537)
Kupperberg, Paul. Alaska Highway. (p. 34)
—Careers in Robotics. (p. 268)
—Creation of Spider-Man. (p. 379)
—Critical Perspectives on the Great Depression. (p. 383)
—Dr. Psycho's Circus of Crime Schoening, Dan, illus. (p. 475)
—How Do We Know the Nature of Disease. (p. 808)
—Hubble & the Big Bang. (p. 824)
—Hurricanes. (p. 830)
—Influenza Pandemic Of 1918-1919. (p. 873)
—Jerry Yang. (p. 914)
—John Glenn. (p. 921)
—John Glenn: The First American in Orbit & His Return to Space. (p. 922)
—Primary Source History of the Colony of New York. (p. 1400)
—Rodeo Clowns. (p. 1484)
—Scooby-Doo & the Night of the Undead! (p. 1529)
—Scooby-Doo in over the Boardwalk. (p. 1529)
—Scooby-Doo in Read All about It! (p. 1529)
—Spy Satellites. (p. 1636)
—Tragedy of the Titanic: When Disaster Strikes! (p. 1776)
—Tragedy of the Titanic. (p. 1776)
Kupperberg, Paul & Loughridge, Lee. Kid Who Saved Superman Ku, Min Sung, illus. (p. 952)
—Meteor of Doom McManus, Shawn, illus. (p. 1130)
—Shadow Masters. Burchett, Rick, illus. (p. 1557)
Kupperberg, Paul, ed. Critical Perspectives on the Great Depression. (p. 383)
Kupperberg, Paul, et al. Bat-Mite's Big Blunder Schigiel, Gregg, illus. (p. 143)
—Super-Villain Showdown Doescher, Erik, illus. (p. 1682)
Kupperman, Michael, illus. see Snicket, Lemony, pseud.
Kupperstein, Joel. Biology: Overhead Transparencies - Student Reproducibles - Assessment Tools. Hults, Alaska, ed. (p. 189)
Kuprin, Alexander. To Chekhov's Memory. (p. 1758)
Kuracka, Vicki. When the Sun Sleeps. (p. 1905)
Kurchan, Rodolfo, et al. Giant Book of Hard-to-Solve Word Puzzles/Giant Book of Hard-to-Solve Mind Puzzles: Flip Book. Sterling Publishing Company Staff, ed. (p. 673)
Kurchinski, Alessandra. Disney Story. (p. 453)
Kurchinski, Catherine Celli. Hurray for the Yoder Barn! (p. 829)
Kurd, Tariq. Gordon the Goblin in Oh My! Is That a Pork Pie? Robertson, Laura, illus. (p. 702)
Kureishy, Simala. Lore of Love Series: Bismi & the Secret of the Kohinoor. (p. 1053)
Kurelek, William & Engelhart, Margaret S. They Sought a New World: The Story of European Immigration to North America. Kurelek, William, illus. (p. 1732)
Kurian, George Thomas. Encyclopedia of the World's Nations & Cultures (p. 525)
—Timetables of World Literature. (p. 1754)
Kuricheva, Natasha, illus. see Regan, Patrick.
Kurihashi, Shinsuke & Asamiya, Kia. Record of the Last Hero Kurihashi, Shinsuke, illus. (p. 1452)
Kurilla, Renee, illus. see Bellisario, Gina.
Kurilla, Renee, illus. see Bullard, Lisa.
Kurilla, Renee, illus. see Emerson, Sharon.
Kurilla, Renee, illus. see Engle, Margarita.
Kurilla, Renee, illus. see Jensen, Belinda.
Kurilla, Renee, illus. see Knudsen, Shannon.
Kurilovitch, Mike. Silly Sisters. (p. 1576)
Kurimoto, Kaoru. Battle of Nospherus. Smith, Alexander O., tr. from JPN. (p. 146)
—Leopard Mask. Smith, Alexander O. & Alexander, Elye J., trs. from JPN. (p. 993)
—Seven Magi. Yanagisawa, Kazuaki, illus. (p. 1554)
—Warrior in the Wilderness. Smith, Alexander O., tr. from JPN. (p. 1858)
Kurisu, Jane, illus. see Baillie, Marilyn.
Kurisu, Jane, illus. see Colgan, Lynda.
Kurisu, Jane, illus. see Dunleavy, Deborah.
Kurisu, Jane, illus. see Helmer, Marilyn.
Kurisu, Jane, illus. see Sadler, Judy Ann & Sadler, Judy.
Kurisu, Jane, illus. see Suzuki, David & Vanderlinden, Kathy.
Kurisu, Jane, illus. see Warwick, Ellen & Di Salle, Rachel.
Kurisu, Jane, illus. see Yes Magazine Editors.
Kurisu, Jane, tr. see Dunleavy, Deborah.
Kuriyan, Priya, jt. auth. see Chadha, Radhika.
Kurkela, Cassidy S., illus. see Kurkela, Robert W.
Kurkela, Robert W. Lilies on the Moon. Kurkela, Cassidy S., illus. (p. 1017)
Kurki, Kim & National Wildlife Federation Staff. National Wildlife Federation's World of Birds: A Beginner's Guide. (p. 1234)
Kurkoski, Bettina, illus. see Jolley, Dan & Hunter, Erin.
Kurkoski, Bettina M., illus. see Hunter, Erin.
Kurkosky, Tina. Bunny Brothers. (p. 242)
Kurkowiak, Anne, jt. auth. see Mills, Nathan.
Kurland, Michael, ed. My Sherlock Holmes: Untold Stories of the Great Detective. (p. 1218)
Kurlander, Keith. Tommy the Fishboy. Belominsky, Alex, illus. (p. 1765)
Kurlansky, Mark. Cod's Tale. Schindler, S. D., illus. (p. 338)
—Frozen in Time: Clarence Birdseye's Outrageous Idea about Frozen Food. (p. 645)
—Girl Who Swam to Euskadi: Euskadiraino Igerian Joan Zen Neska. Kurlansky, Mark, illus. (p. 679)
—Story of Salt. (p. 1659)
—Story of Salt. Schindler, S. D., illus. (p. 1659)
—World Without Fish. Stockton, Frank, illus. (p. 1959)
Kuroda, Yosuke. Scryed Toda, Yasunari, illus. (p. 1533)
—Scryed Yasunari, Toda, illus. (p. 1533)
Kuroda, Yosuke, jt. auth. see Hajime, Yatate.
Kuroda, Yosuke & Hayashiya, Shizuru. Onegai Teacher (p. 1298)
Kurokawa, Mitsuhiro. Dinosaur Valley. (p. 443)
Kurosaki, Yoshisuke, illus. see Sakade, Florence & Hayashi, Yoshio.
Kurosaki, Yoshisuke, illus. see Sakade, Florence.
Kurosaki, Yoshisuke, jt. auth. see Sakade, Florence.
Kurosawa, Tetsuya. Thomas Edison: Genius of the Electric Age. Kobayashi, Tatsuyoshi, illus. (p. 1738)
Kurowski, Kathryn. Year Round Project-Based Activities for STEM PreK-K. (p. 1969)
Kurson, Ken, jt. auth. see Faber, David.
Kurstedt, Rosanne. And I Thought about You. Carletta-Vietes, Lisa, illus. (p. 71)
Kurt D Williams and Jeff Baker, illus. see Knapp, Rene & Berger, Marjorie B.
Kurt, Robert, jt. auth. see Andersen, Hans Christian.
Kurtagich, Dawn. Dead House. (p. 416)
Kurth, Steve. Iron Man: War of the Iron Man. (p. 888)
Kurth, Steve, illus. see Ellis, Warren.
Kurth, Steve, illus. see Fontes, Justine & Fontes, Ron.
Kurth, Steve, illus. see Storrie, Paul D.
Kurti, Richard. Monkey Wars. (p. 1165)
Kurty, G. Thomas the Treemaker: a Short Story about a Tall Tale. (p. 1739)
Kurtz, Barbara. Hummingbird's Story: How I Came to Be. (p. 827)
—Sebastian's Neighborhood: A Hummingbird's Story. Naughton, Christine, ed. (p. 1539)
Kurtz, Bob, jt. auth. see Lenburg, Jeff.
Kurtz, Carmen. Brun. (p. 232)
—Habeis Visto un Huevo? (p. 734)
—Veva. (p. 1839)
—Veva y el Mar. (p. 1839)
Kurtz, Chris. Adventures of a South Pole Pig. (p. 16)
—Pup Who Cried Wolf. Francis, Guy, illus. (p. 1417)
Kurtz, Jane. Anna Was Here. (p. 85)
—Celebrating Georgia: 50 States to Celebrate. Canga, C. B., illus. (p. 284)
—Celebrating New Jersey. Canga, C. B., illus. (p. 285)
—Celebrating Ohio. Canga, C. B., illus. (p. 285)
—Celebrating Pennsylvania: 50 States to Celebrate. Canga, C. B., illus. (p. 285)
—Do Kangaroos Wear Seatbelts? Rossi, Ino, ed. (p. 457)
—In the Small, Small Night. Isadora, Rachel, illus. (p. 867)
—Jane Kurtz & YOU (p. 908)
—Johnny Appleseed. Haverfield, Mary, illus. (p. 923)
—Lanie Hirsch, Jennifer, ed. (p. 975)
—Lanie's Real Adventures England, Tamara, ed. (p. 975)
—Lanie's Real Adventures. Papp, Robert, illus. (p. 975)
—Lemon Sand. (p. 991)
—Martin's Dream. Bates, Amy June, illus. (p. 1098)
—Mister Bones: Dinosaur Hunter. Haverfield, Mary, illus. (p. 1155)
—Mister Bones Dinosaur Hunter. Haverfield, Mary, illus. (p. 1155)
—River Friendly, River Wild. Brennan, Neil, illus. (p. 1475)
Kurtz, John. Claus Kids Christmas Coloring Book. (p. 329)
—Claus Kids Stickers. (p. 329)
—Claus Kids Super Sticker Book: A Year-Round Christmas Celebration. (p. 329)
—Disney Princess: Look & Find. (p. 452)
—Fairy Tale Treasury. (p. 564)
—FLIP OUTS — Bird Bash: Color Your Own Cartoon! (p. 605)
—FLIP OUTS — Funny Farm: Color Your Own Cartoon! (p. 605)
—JATS Fairytale Classics - Goldilocks & the Three Bears. Kurtz, John, illus. (p. 910)
—JATS Fairytale Classics - Jack & the Beanstalk. Kurtz, John, illus. (p. 910)
—Kooky Birds Coloring Book. (p. 967)
—Santa Claus Christmas Paper Dolls. (p. 1511)
—Silly Snowmen Coloring Book. (p. 1576)
—Unicorn Fun Coloring Book. (p. 1818)
—What Belongs? Baby Looney Tunes. Shively, Julie, illus. (p. 1880)
—What to Doodle? at School. (p. 1894)
—What to Doodle? Jr. —My World. (p. 1894)
—World Around Us! Smelling. (p. 1954)
—World Around Us! Tasting. (p. 1954)
—World Around Us! Touch. (p. 1954)
Kurtz, John, illus. see Lee, Quinlan B.
Kurtz, John, illus. see Marshall, Hallie.
Kurtz, John, illus. see Shively, Julie.
Kurtz, John, illus. see Weinberg, Jennifer Liberts.
Kurtz, John, jt. auth. see Phillips, Jillian.
Kurtz, John & Activity Books Staff. Claus Kids Activity Book. (p. 329)
Kurtz, John & Kurtz, Sandrina. Big & Little Farm Coloring Book: Featuring Romy the Cow. (p. 177)
—Chef Lorenzo's Foods Around the World Coloring Book. (p. 297)
—Storyland: Mr. Rodento Cleans House: A Story Coloring Book. (p. 1663)
Kurtz, Kevin. Day in the Deep Hunter, Erin E., illus. (p. 413)
—Day in the Salt Marsh Powell, Consie, illus. (p. 413)
—Day on the Mountain Hunter, Erin E., illus. (p. 414)
—Día en la Profundidad Hunter, Erin E., illus. (p. 433)
—What Makes Sports Gear Safer? (p. 1892)
Kurtz Kingsley, Linda. Blue Skies for Lupe. (p. 203)
Kurtz, Pauline. Deutsche Haus. (p. 431)
Kurtz, Rob. Meet the Robots. (p. 1123)
—Power of the Seventh Ring. (p. 1390)
—Robot Galaxy #4: the New Warriors: The New Warriors. (p. 1480)
—Robots to the Rescue! (p. 1481)
—Seamus McNamus: The Goat Who Would Be King. (p. 1536)
Kurtz, Rob & Oprisko, Kris. Battle Begins. (p. 145)
—Brotherhood Returns. (p. 231)
Kurtz, Sandrina, jt. auth. see Kurtz, John.
Kurtz, Scott. Dork Ages. (p. 471)
—Pvp at Large (p. 1421)
—Rides Again (p. 1471)
Kurumada, Masami. Knights of the Zodiac (p. 964)
—Knights of the Zodiac: Saint Seiya (p. 964)
—Knights of the Zodiac: The Knights Of Athena. Vol. 1 (p. 964)
—Knights of the Zodiac. Kurumada, Masami, illus. (p. 964)
—Knights of the Zodiac (Saint Seiya) Kurumada, Masami, illus. (p. 964)
Kurup, Prakash, illus. see Mehta, Poonam V.
Kurup, Sindhu. Baby Bear's Favorite Food Pyramid. (p. 125)
Kurusa. Streets Are Free. Englander, Karen, tr. (p. 1667)
Kurusa, Monika. Lorn & the Gnatters Amado, Elisa, tr. from SPA. (p. 1046)
Kuryla, Mary, jt. auth. see Yelchin, Eugene.
Kurz, Ron. Inner Music Experience. (p. 875)
Kurzawa, Greg. Gideon's Wall. (p. 674)
Kurzweil, Allen. Leon & the Champion Chip. Bertholf, Bret, illus. (p. 992)
—Leon & the Spitting Image. Bertholf, Bret, illus. (p. 992)
Kurzweil, Allen & Kurzweil, Max. Potato Chip Science: 29 Incredible Experiments. (p. 1388)
Kurzweil, Max, jt. auth. see Kurzweil, Allen.
Kurzyca, Krystyna Emilia, illus. see Anderson, Al.
Kurzyca, Krystyna Emilia, illus. see Davidow, Shelley.
Kusaka, Hidenori. Best of Pokemon Adventures - Yellow. Mato, illus. (p. 170)
—Black & White Yamamoto, Satoshi, illus. (p. 195)
—Black & White. Yamamoto, Satoshi, illus. (p. 195)
—Diamond & Pearl-Platinum. Yamamoto, Satoshi, illus. (p. 434)
—Heart Gold & Soul Silver (p. 759)
—Heartgold & Soulsilver (p. 760)
—Pokemon Yamamoto, Satoshi, illus. (p. 1377)
—Pokemon Adventures (p. 1377)
—Pokémon Adventures Kusaka, Hidenori, illus. (p. 1377)
—Pokemon Adventures Yamamoto, Satoshi, illus. (p. 1377)
—Pokemon Adventures. (p. 1377)
—Pokemon Adventures. (p. 1377)
—Pokémon Adventures. Mato, illus. (p. 1377)
—Pokemon Adventures. Kusaka, Hidenori, illus. (p. 1377)
—Pokémon Adventures. Kusaka, Hidenori, illus. (p. 1377)
—Pokémon Adventures. Yamamoto, Satoshi, illus. (p. 1377)
—Pokemon Adventures (p. 1378)
—Pokémon Adventures Mato, illus. (p. 1378)
—Pokemon Adventures Kusaka, Hidenori, illus. (p. 1378)
—Pokemon Adventures. Kusaka, Hidenori, illus. (p. 1378)
—Pokémon Adventures: Diamond & Pearl - Platinum. (p. 1378)
—Pokemon Adventures: Diamond & Pearl - Platinum. Yamamoto, Satoshi, illus. (p. 1378)
—Pokemon Adventures: Diamond & Pearl - Platinum. Vol. 7 Yamamoto, Satoshi, illus. (p. 1378)

—Pokémon Adventures: Diamond & Pearl - Platinum. Vol. 3 Satoshi, Yamamoto, illus. (p. 1378)
—Pokémon Adventures: Diamond & Pearl - Platinum. Vol. 6 Yamamoto, Satoshi, illus. (p. 1378)
—Pokémon Adventures - Black & White Yamamoto, Satoshi, illus. (p. 1378)
—Pokémon Adventures - Black & White Yamamoto, Satoshi, illus. (p. 1378)
—Pokémon Adventures: Black & White, Vol. 7. Yamamoto, Satoshi, illus. (p. 1378)
—Pokémon Adventures: Diamond & Pearl/Platinum Yamamoto, Satoshi, illus. (p. 1378)
—Pokémon Adventures - Diamond & Pearl/Platinum. Yamamoto, Satoshi, illus. (p. 1378)
—Pokémon Adventures - Diamond & Pearl-Platinum (p. 1378)
—Pokemon Adventures - Platinum Vol. 1. (p. 1378)
—Pokemon Adventures, Vol. 27. (p. 1378)
—Pokémon Adventures, Vol. 27. Mato, illus. (p. 1378)
—Pokémon Adventures, Vol. 29. Yamamoto, Satoshi, illus. (p. 1378)
—Pokémon Black & White. (p. 1378)
—Pokémon Black & White. Yamamoto, Satoshi, illus. (p. 1378)
—Pokémon Black & White, Vol. 16. Yamamoto, Satoshi, illus. (p. 1378)
—Pokémon XY, Vol. 1. Yamamoto, Satoshi, illus. (p. 1378)
—Pokmon Adventures. Yamamoto, Satoshi, illus. (p. 1378)
—Pokmon Adventures - Black & White. Yamamoto, Satoshi, illus. (p. 1378)
Kusaka, Hidenori & Harukaze, Santa. Pokemon Pocket Comics: Black & White. (p. 1378)
Kushii, Tetsuo, illus. see Gilpin, Rebecca.
Kushii, Tetsuo, illus. see Helbrough, Emma.
Kushii, Tetsuo, illus. see Patchett, Fiona.
Kushii, Tetsuo, illus. see Pearcey, Alice.
Kushii, Tetsuo, illus. see Turnbull, Stephanie.
Kushner, Elisabeth. Purim Superhero. Byrne, Mike, illus. (p. 1419)
Kushner, Ellen, jt. ed. see Black, Holly.
Kushner, Jill Menkes. Johnny Depp: Movie Megastar. (p. 923)
—Who on Earth Is Dian Fossey? Defender of the Mountain Gorillas. (p. 1917)
Kushner, Jill Menkes, jt. auth. see Glasser, Judith M.
Kushner, Lawrence & Schmidt, Gary. In God's Hands. Baek, Matthew J., illus. (p. 863)
Kushner, Malcolm. California Squisine: Healthy Food That's Fast & Fun for Kids. (p. 253)
Kushner, Marina. Truth about Caffeine: How Companies That Promote it Deceive Us & What We Can Do about It (p. 1794)
Kushner, Robert, jt. contrib. by see Kozloff, Joyce.
Kushner, Sam. Cinderell. (p. 320)
Kushner, Sarah, illus. see Shoemaker, Craig.
Kushner, Tony. Brundibar. Sendak, Maurice, illus. (p. 232)
Kusinitz, Nat, illus. see Bunnell, Jacinta.
Kuskin, Karla. Boy Had a Mother Who Bought Him a Hat. Hawkes, Kevin, illus. (p. 218)
—I Do Not Understand Art. (p. 837)
—Lullaway of Rockabye. (p. 1064)
—Roar & More. (p. 1478)
—So, What's It Like to Be a Cat? Lewin, Betsy, illus. (p. 1602)
Kuskin, Karla, illus. see Fox, Paula.
Kuskowski, Alex. Bears. (p. 151)
—Biggest, Baddest Book of Caves. (p. 185)
—Calves. (p. 255)
—Cool Body Basics: Healthy & Fun Ways to Care for Your Body. (p. 362)
—Cool Breads & Biscuits. (p. 362)
—Cool Cake Mix Cupcakes: Fun & Easy Baking Recipes for Kids! (p. 362)
—Cool Crocheting for Kids: A Fun & Creative Introduction to Fiber Art. (p. 363)
—Cool Dips & Drinks. (p. 363)
—Cool East Coast Cooking: Easy & Fun Regional Recipes. (p. 363)
—Cool Eating: Healthy & Fun Ways to Eat Right. (p. 363)
—Cool Embroidery for Kids: A Fun & Creative Introduction to Fiber Art. (p. 363)
—Cool Filled Cupcakes: Fun & Easy Baking Recipes for Kids! (p. 363)
—Cool Fun Cupcakes: Fun & Easy Baking Recipes for Kids! (p. 363)
—Cool Gulf Coast Cooking: Easy & Fun Regional Recipes. (p. 363)
—Cool Healthy Muffins: Fun & Easy Baking Recipes for Kids! (p. 363)
—Cool Home Cooking. (p. 363)
—Cool Knitting for Kids: A Fun & Creative Introduction to Fiber Art. (p. 363)
—Cool Main Dishes. (p. 363)
—Cool Midwest Cooking: Easy & Fun Regional Recipes. (p. 364)
—Cool Needle Felting for Kids: A Fun & Creative Introduction to Fiber Art. (p. 364)
—Cool Outdoor Arts & Crafts: Great Things to Do in the Great Outdoors. (p. 364)
—Cool Pacific Coast Cooking: Easy & Fun Regional Recipes. (p. 364)
—Cool Punch Needle for Kids: A Fun & Creative Introduction to Fiber Art. (p. 364)
—Cool Refashioned Hardware: Fun & Easy Fashion Projects. (p. 364)
—Cool Refashioned Jeans: Fun & Easy Fashion Projects. (p. 364)
—Cool Refashioned Odds & Ends: Fun & Easy Fashion Projects. (p. 364)
—Cool Refashioned Scarves & Ties: Fun & Easy Fashion Projects. (p. 364)
—Cool Refashioned Sweaters: Fun & Easy Fashion Projects. (p. 364)
—Cool Refashioned T-Shirts: Fun & Easy Fashion Projects. (p. 364)
—Cool Relaxing: Healthy & Fun Ways to Chill Out. (p. 364)
—Cool Savory Muffins: Fun & Easy Baking Recipes for Kids! (p. 364)
—Cool Sewing for Kids: A Fun & Creative Introduction to Fiber Art. (p. 364)
—Cool Sides & Salads. (p. 364)
—Cool Sleeping: Healthy & Fun Ways to Sleep Tight. (p. 364)
—Cool Soups & Stews. (p. 364)
—Cool Southern Cooking: Easy & Fun Regional Recipes. (p. 364)
—Cool Sweet Muffins: Fun & Easy Baking Recipes for Kids! (p. 364)
—Cool Thinking: Healthy & Fun Ways to Train Your Brain. (p. 364)
—Cool Treats & Sweets. (p. 364)
—Cool Western Cooking: Easy & Fun Regional Recipes. (p. 364)
—Down & Out (p. 474)
—Flock of Sheep: Animal Groups on the Farm. (p. 605)
—Foals. (p. 610)
—Gaggle of Geese: Animal Groups on Lakes & Rivers. (p. 652)
—Herd of Deer: Animal Groups in the Forest. (p. 769)
—Know Your Numbers: School. (p. 965)
—Know Your Numbers: Sports. (p. 965)
—Line Up (p. 1019)
—Lions. (p. 1021)
—Magnificent Macaws. Nobens, C. A., illus. (p. 1076)
—Mini Animal Marvels. (p. 1146)
—Miniature Mammals. (p. 1146)
—Miniature Reptiles. (p. 1146)
—Monkeys. (p. 1165)
—Penguins. (p. 1337)
—Portly Potbellied Pigs. Nobens, C. A., illus. (p. 1386)
—Puppies. (p. 1417)
—School of Fish: Animal Groups in the Ocean. (p. 1523)
—Science Experiments with Gravity & Motion. (p. 1525)
—Science Experiments with Light. (p. 1525)
—Science Experiments with Liquid. (p. 1525)
—Science Experiments with Magnets. (p. 1525)
—Science Experiments with Sight & Sound. (p. 1525)
—Stargazing. (p. 1642)
—Streak of Tigers: Animal Groups in the Jungle. (p. 1666)
—Super Simple African Art: Fun & Easy Art from Around the World. (p. 1681)
—Super Simple American Art: Fun & Easy Art from Around the World. (p. 1681)
—Super Simple Australian Art: Fun & Easy Art from Around the World. (p. 1681)
—Super Simple Bar Cookies: Easy Cookie Recipes for Kids! (p. 1681)
—Super Simple Butterfly Gardens: A Kid's Guide to Gardening. (p. 1681)
—Super Simple Chinese Art: Fun & Easy Art from Around the World. (p. 1681)
—Super Simple Classic Cookies: Easy Cookie Recipes for Kids! (p. 1681)
—Super Simple European Art: Fun & Easy Art from Around the World. (p. 1681)
—Super Simple Fairy Gardens: A Kid's Guide to Gardening. (p. 1681)
—Super Simple Gardening. (p. 1681)
—Super Simple Hanging Gardens: A Kid's Guide to Gardening. (p. 1681)
—Super Simple Healthy Cookies: Easy Cookie Recipes for Kids! (p. 1681)
—Super Simple Holiday Cookies: Easy Cookie Recipes for Kids! (p. 1681)
—Super Simple Indian Art: Fun & Easy Art from Around the World. (p. 1681)
—Super Simple Indoor Gardens: A Kid's Guide to Gardening. (p. 1681)
—Super Simple Japanese Art: Fun & Easy Art from Around the World. (p. 1681)
—Super Simple Kitchen Gardens: A Kid's Guide to Gardening. (p. 1681)
—Super Simple Mediterranean Art: Fun & Easy Art from Around the World. (p. 1681)
—Super Simple Mexican Art: Fun & Easy Art from Around the World. (p. 1681)
—Super Simple Native American Art: Fun & Easy Art from Around the World. (p. 1681)
—Super Simple No-Bake Cookies: Easy Cookie Recipes for Kids! (p. 1681)
—Super Simple Phonograph Projects: Inspiring & Educational Science Activities. (p. 1681)
—Super Simple Salad Gardens: A Kid's Guide to Gardening. (p. 1681)
—Super Simple Scandinavian Art: Fun & Easy Art from Around the World. (p. 1681)
—Super Simple South & Central American Art: Fun & Easy Art from Around the World. (p. 1681)
—Super Simple Specialty Cookies: Easy Cookie Recipes for Kids! (p. 1681)
—Super Simple Telegraph Projects: Inspiring & Educational Science Activities. (p. 1681)
—Super Simple Telephone Projects: Inspiring & Educational Science Activities. (p. 1681)
—Tia: Fitting In. (p. 1746)
—Tigers. (p. 1749)
—Tricky Tarantulas. Nobens, C. A., illus. (p. 1786)
—Zeal of Zebras: Animal Groups on an African Safari. (p. 1985)
—Zebras. (p. 1985)
Kuskowski, Alex, jt. auth. see Jones, Jada.
Kuskowski, Alex & Craig, Diane. Super Simple Aircraft Projects: Inspiring & Educational Science Activities. (p. 1681)
—Super Simple Automobile Projects: Inspiring & Educational Science Activities. (p. 1681)
—Super Simple Camera Projects: Inspiring & Educational Science Activities. (p. 1681)
Kusky, Timothy. Climate Change: Shifting Glaciers, Deserts, & Climate Belts. (p. 332)
—Coast. (p. 336)
—Encyclopedia of Earth & Space Science (p. 525)
—Floods: Hazards of Surface & Groundwater Systems. (p. 605)
—Landslides: Mass Wasting, Soil, & Mineral Hazards. (p. 974)
—Tsunamis: Giant Waves from the Sea. (p. 1795)
Kusky, Timothy & Kusky, Timothy M. Asteroids & Meteorites: Catastrophic Collisions with Earth. (p. 108)
Kusky, Timothy M. Encyclopedia of Earth Science. (p. 525)
Kusky, Timothy M., jt. auth. see Kusky, Timothy.
Kusmierski, Janet & Colin, Paul. Snowman's Big Job. (p. 1601)
Kusugak, Michael. Littlest Sled Dog Krykorka, Vladyana, illus. (p. 1039)
—T Is for Territories: A Yukon, Northwest Territories, & Nunavut Alphabet. (p. 1694)
Kusugak, Michael, jt. auth. see Kusugak, Michael Arvaarluk.
Kusugak, Michael, jt. auth. see Munsch, Robert.
Kusugak, Michael Arvaarluk & Kusugak, Michael. My Arctic 1, 2, 3. Krykorka, Vladyana Langer & Krykorka, Vladyana, illus. (p. 1196)
Kusunoki, Kei, illus. see Ohashi, Kaoru.
Kusunoki, Kei, jt. auth. see Ohashi, Kaoru.
Kusunoki, Kei & Ohashi, Kaoru. Diabolo. (p. 433)
Kuszewski, Ivy. Hopi. (p. 797)
Kutner, Laura, jt. auth. see Slade, Suzanne.
Kutner, Merrily. Down on the Farm. Hillenbrand, Will, illus. (p. 474)
—Zombie Nite Cafe. Long, Ethan, illus. (p. 1988)
Kutner, Richard, tr. see Pommaux, Yvan.
Kutner, Richard, tr. from FRE. Suspended Castle: a Philemon Adventure: A TOON Graphic. Fred, illus. (p. 1688)
—Wild Piano. Fred, illus. (p. 1930)
Kutschbach, Doris. Art: A World of Words in 12 Languages. (p. 101)
—Art Detective: Spot the Difference! (p. 101)
—Art Treasure Hunt: I Spy with My Little Eye. (p. 103)
—Great Art Treasure Hunt: I Spy Red, Yellow, & Blue. (p. 713)
Kutschbach, Doris, illus. see Aston, Paul, tr.
Kutschbach, Doris & Goldner, Rahel. Hundertwasser: Create Your Own City. (p. 827)
Kutscher, Eric, ed. Cacophony! an Anthology: An Anthology. (p. 250)
Kutscher, Marc, ed. Revolution of the Undertones: A Teen Anthology (p. 1466)
Kutscher, Scott & Lyon, Abby. Suny Binghamton College Prowler off the Record: Inside State University of New York. (p. 1679)
Kutsuwada, Chie, illus. see Shakespeare, William.
Kutsuwada, Chie, illus. see Tsunetomo, Yamamoto & Wilson, William Scott.
Kuumba, Mshindo, illus. see Pitt, Roosevelt, Jr.
Kuykendall, Anna. Otter & the Troll. Britton, Terre, illus. (p. 1307)
Kuykendall, Roger. All Day September. (p. 44)
Kuykendoll, Kim. Adventures of the Coral Way Gang. (p. 23)
Kuyper, Sjoerd. Swan's Child. Jutte, Jan, illus. (p. 1689)
Kuyper, Tony, photos by see Flood, Nancy Bo.
Kuyper, Vicki J. & Baker Publishing Group Staff. Jesus Speaks to Teens. (p. 916)
Kuypers, Janet I. Etc. (p. 539)
Kuzio, Daisy Williams. All about Annie: (A True Story) (p. 42)
Kuzma, Gregory. On the Field from Denver, Colorado... the Blue Knights! One Member's Experience of the 1994 Summer National Tour. (p. 1290)
Kuzma, Jakub, illus. see Anderson, Eric B.
Kuzmunich, Shirley. Watching over Everything. (p. 1861)
Kuznick, Peter J., jt. auth. see Stone, Oliver.
Kvale, Anthony, creator. Head1Liners board Game. (p. 756)
Kvalvasser, Leonid. Eagle - Proud Bird. (p. 492)
Kvarnstrom, Todd M. King of Pete's Pond. (p. 959)
Kvasnosky, Laura McGee. Big Picture. Kvasnosky, Laura McGee, illus. (p. 183)
—Keeping Secrets. Kvasnosky, Laura McGee, illus. (p. 947)
—Really Truly Bingo. Kvasnosky, Laura McGee, illus. (p. 1450)
—Runaways. (p. 1497)
—Runaways. Kvasnosky, Laura McGee, illus. (p. 1497)
—Zelda & Ivy & the Boy Next Door. Kvasnosky, Laura McGee, illus. (p. 1986)
—Zelda & Ivy - Big Picture. Kvasnosky, Laura McGee, illus. (p. 1986)
—Zelda & Ivy - Keeping Secrets. Kvasnosky, Laura McGee, illus. (p. 1986)
—Zelda & Ivy One Christmas. Kvasnosky, Laura McGee, illus. (p. 1986)
—Zelda & Ivy - The Runaways. Kvasnosky, Laura McGee, illus. (p. 1986)
Kvatum, Lia. Saving Yasha: The Incredible True Story of an Adopted Moon Bear. Pokrovskaya, Liya, photos by. (p. 1518)
Kveta, illus. see Banner, Melanie Jane.
Kveta, tr. see Banner, Melanie Jane.
Kwag, Jin-yeong, illus. see Hsu, Yi Ling.
Kwakkenbos, Frans, illus. see Janssen-Mathes, Mieke M. E.
Kwalwasser, Eugene I. Beyond the Tears: Helping Jewish Kids Cope with Death. (p. 174)
K'wan Staff. Eve. (p. 541)
Kwapisz, Gary, jt. auth. see Dixon, Chuck.
Kwapong, Ohene. 12 Steps to Getting Admitted into Colleges & Universities in the United States. (p. 1994)
Kwarta, Darlene. Walking with King Tut. (p. 1854)
Kwarta, James. Decomposers. (p. 422)
—Science of Soil. (p. 1527)
Kwas, Susan Estelle, illus. see Ryder, Joanne.
Kwasney, Karl, illus. see Hood, Ann & Altmann, Scott.
Kwasney, Karl, illus. see Hood, Ann.
Kwasney, Michelle D. Blue Plate Special. (p. 203)
Kwasny, Karl, illus. see Hood, Ann.
Kwasny, Karl, illus. see Legrand, Claire.
Kwasny, Karl, illus. see Segel, Jason & Miller, Kirsten.
Kwaymullina, Ambelin. Interrogation of Ashala Wolf. (p. 881)
Kwaymullina, Ambelin, illus. see Morgan, Sally.
Kwaymullina, Ezekiel. Wonderful Whisper. Pignataro, Anna, illus. (p. 1948)
Kwek, Karen. Welcome to Jamaica. (p. 1873)
Kwek, Karen & Haque, Jameel. Pakistan. (p. 1319)
Kwek, Karen & Massé, Johanna. South Korea. (p. 1617)
Kwiat, Ernie. Abby Caddaby up & Down. (p. 2)
—Sesame Street Boo! Guess Who, Elmo! (p. 1553)
Kwiat, Ernie, illus. see Sesame Workshop Staff.
Kwiat, Ernie, illus. see Sesame Workshop.
Kwiat, Ernie, jt. auth. see Wax, Wendy.
Kwiatkowski, Gerhard & Lanczkowski, Günter. Religionen: Von Alten Naturreligionen bis zu Modernen Sekten, Ursprung und Geschichte aller Religionen (p. 1458)
Kwik, Penny Shannon, ed. see Killaire, B. M.
Kwint, Marius, ed. see Brown Reference Group PLC.
Kwitney, Alisa. Vertigo Visions: Artwork from the Cutting Edge of Politics. (p. 1837)
Kwon, Elisa, illus. see Schreiber, Ellen.
Kwon, Min. Snow Biz (p. 1598)
Kwon, Nahyun, jt. ed. see Alexander, Linda B.
Kwon, Yeong-mook, illus. see Jo, Eun-sook.
Kwon, Yoon-duck. My Cat Copies Me. Kwon, Yoon-duck, illus. (p. 1200)
Kwong, Alvina, illus. see Estes-Hill, Katrina.
Kwong, Julia, jt. auth. see Huffman, Ivy.
Kwong-Chiu, Chiu. In the Forbidden City. Steinhardt, Nancy S., ed. (p. 866)
Kyber, Manfred. Fables & Fairytales to Delight All Ages: Books One to Three with 'Mantao the Jester King' (p. 559)
—Mantao the Jester King: A Fairytale from Tibet. Fairall, Barbara, tr. (p. 1088)
—Three Candles of Little Veronica. (p. 1741)
Kyber, Manfred. Fables & Fairytales to Delight All Ages Book Two: Gossamer Kingdoms (p. 559)
Kyelberg, Hope, jt. auth. see Heckler, Naomi.
Kyi, Tanya Lloyd. 50 Body Questions: A Book That Spills Its Guts. Kinnaird, Ross, illus. (p. 1997)
—50 Burning Questions: A Sizzling History of Fire. Kinnaird, Ross, illus. (p. 1997)
—50 Poisonous Questions: A Book with Bite. Kinnaird, Ross, illus. (p. 1997)
—50 Underwear Questions: A Bare-All History. Kinnaird, Ross, illus. (p. 1997)
—Anywhere but Here. (p. 91)
—Burn: The Life Story of Fire. (p. 243)
—Canadian Boys Who Rocked the World Bagley, Tom, illus. (p. 260)
—Canadian Girls Who Rocked the World Bagley, Tom, illus. (p. 260)
—Crystal Connection. (p. 387)
—Denver. (p. 427)
—DNA Detective. Crump, Lil, illus. (p. 456)
—Houston. (p. 804)
—Jared Lester, Fifth Grade Jester. Newbigging, Martha, illus. (p. 909)
—Kentucky. (p. 949)
—Lowdown on Denim. Hanmer, Clayton, illus. (p. 1061)
—Maryland. (p. 1101)
—My Time as Caz Hazard (p. 1220)
—Nova Scotia (p. 1268)
—Rescues! (p. 1462)
—Seeing Red: The True Story of Blood. Rolston, Steve, illus. (p. 1548)
—Truth (p. 1793)
—Truth. (p. 1793)
—When the Worst Happens: Extraordinary Stories of Survival. Parkins, David, illus. (p. 1905)
Kyi, Tanya Lloyd & Fernández, Queta. Verdad (p. 1836)
Kyle, Amarie. Navajo. (p. 1237)
Kyle, Bradley. Pick-a-WooWoo - Herbie & the Tune: Deep within every moment, there Is pure Joy. Evans, Gabriel, illus. (p. 1354)
Kyle, Carolyn. Let There Be Light. (p. 994)
Kyle, Margaret, illus. see Chapman, Patricia.
Kyle, Margaret, illus. see Payne-Krzyzanowski, Anna, et al.
Kyle, Margaret & Sinclair, Donna. Family Story Bible Colouring Book. (p. 568)
Kyle, Tracey C. Gazpacho for Nacho (p. 659)
Kyle, William, et al. Real Science: Assessment Book. (p. 1449)
—Real Science: Student Edition. (p. 1449)
—Real Science: Activity Journal. (p. 1449)
—Real Science: Teacher's Edition. (p. 1449)
—Real Science: Teacher Resource Book. (p. 1449)
—Real Science: Science Connection Center. (p. 1449)
—Real Science: Activity Journal Teacher's Edition. (p. 1449)
—Real Science: Alternate Activities Blackline Masters. (p. 1449)
—Real Science: Process Skills Handbook Blackline Masters. (p. 1449)
Kyler, Inge Logenburg. Search for a House. (p. 1537)
Kyne, Peter B. Jarron Azul. (p. 909)
—Three Godfathers. (p. 1742)
Kyong-Nan, Nani, illus. see Suyenaga, Ruth, et al.
Kyong-Nan, Nani, illus. see Suyenaga, Ruth.
Kyoung-Sim, Jeong, illus. see So-Un, Kim.
Kyoung-Sim, Jeong, jt. auth. see So-Un, Kim.
Kypta, Judith. Abby Ding Glove & ... Friends. Kypta, Judith, illus. (p. 2)
Kyriacou, Kyriacos. BELCH the Nastiest Gnome in the World. (p. 161)
Kyriakou, Marie. Mike the Little Bean: Christmas with Mike. (p. 1141)
—Mike the Little Bean: Flying to the Beach! (p. 1141)
—Mike the Little Bean: I'm Gonna Tickle You! (p. 1141)
Kyriazis, Ilias. Falling for Lionheart. (p. 566)
Kyrja. Rupert's Tales: A Book of Bedtime Stories. Osborn, Tonia Bennington, illus. (p. 1497)
—Rupert's Tales: The Wheel of the Year Activity Book. Osborn, Tonia Bennington, illus. (p. 1497)
—Rupert's Tales: The Wheel of the Year - Samhain, Yule, Imbolc, & Ostara. Osborn, Tonia Bennington, illus. (p. 1497)
Kyrja, et al. Rupert's Tales: The Wheel of the Year Beltane, Litha, Lammas, & Mabon. (p. 1497)
Kysiak, Penelope Ann. You Can't Steal One's Wishes (p. 1975)
Kyung-ah, Choi. Snow Drop Dyer, Sarah, tr. (p. 1599)
—Snow Drop. (p. 1599)

K

Kyungu Mordi, Nicku. Next Generation: Know Before You Grow. (p. 1249)
—Next Generation: Do You Know Who You Are? (p. 1249)

L

L. Prince Cloud & Princess Evergreen (p. 1401)
L. A. Goal Members, contrib. by. Disabled Fables: Aesop's Fables Retold & Illustrated by Artists with Developmental Disabilities (p. 446)
L and L Enterprises, ed. see Williams, Rose.
L & M Trustam. Turn Left for Christmas. (p. 1797)
L. DeVere Burton, jt. auth. see Cram101 Textbook Reviews Staff.
L, Jay'. Unlikely Love. (p. 1821)
L, Jessica & Skindzier, Jon. Grove City College College Prowler off the Record. (p. 725)
L, Joe, illus. see May, Maggie.
L., Small Juanita. Clarissa: A Dolly Head Adventure. (p. 327)
L. Wright, Sean & Nash, Kevin. Villanova University College Prowler off the Record. (p. 1842)
la Bédoyère, Guy De, see De la Bédoyère, Guy.
La Bee, Jesse M. First Day of School for Randy Willie Bumble Bee. (p. 594)
La Bella, Laura. Angelina Jolie: Goodwill Ambassador for the United Nations. (p. 74)
—Blood Pressure Basics. (p. 200)
—Building Apps. (p. 239)
—California: Past & Present. (p. 253)
—Careers for Tech Girls in Video Game Development. (p. 267)
—Careers in Crisis Management & Hostage Negotiation. (p. 267)
—Careers in Painting & Wall Covering. (p. 268)
—Careers in Web Development. (p. 268)
—Carl Edwards: NASCAR Driver. (p. 269)
—Carrie Underwood. (p. 271)
—Connecticut: Past & Present. (p. 358)
—Curiosity. (p. 392)
—Dating Violence. (p. 409)
—Discovering the Songhay Empire. (p. 450)
—How Commodities Trading Works. (p. 806)
—How Consumer Credit & Debt Work. (p. 806)
—How Do I Use a Database? (p. 807)
—How Globalization Works. (p. 809)
—How Taxation Works. (p. 812)
—Hulu & Jason Kilar (p. 825)
—Kanye West. (p. 943)
—Living in a Violent Household. (p. 1041)
—Marissa Meyer. (p. 1094)
—My Chemical Romance. (p. 1200)
—Not Enough to Drink: Pollution, Drought, & Tainted Water Supplies. (p. 1267)
—Nuremberg Trials. (p. 1273)
—Oxygen Elements. (p. 1316)
—Philip Pullman. (p. 1350)
—Safety & the Food Supply. (p. 1502)
—Search & Rescue Swimmers. (p. 1537)
—Search-and-rescue Swimmers. (p. 1537)
—Stalking. (p. 1639)
—Top STEM Careers in Technology. (p. 1769)
—What Degree Do I Need to Pursue a Career in Bookkeeping & Accounting? (p. 1881)
—Women & Sports. (p. 1945)
—World Financial Meltdown. (p. 1955)
La Beree, Brian. Herbert the Tadpole in the Big Change: Color-Me Version. (p. 769)
La Beree, Brian, illus. see Bodrogi, Michael.
La Clair, Claire. School Crossing Guard. (p. 1522)
La Coccinella. Animals at Play. (p. 82)
—At Night. (p. 110)
—Circus of Colors! (p. 322)
—Fairy Tales. (p. 564)
—Farm Animals. (p. 573)
—Guess Who? (p. 729)
—Happy Birthday, Elephant! (p. 744)
—Here Comes Leo Lion. (p. 770)
—Little Star. (p. 1036)
—Look & See: Let's Count! (p. 1048)
—Look & See: Mommy, Where Are You? (p. 1048)
—Look & See: the Green Caterpillar. (p. 1048)
—Look & See: What Am I? (p. 1048)
—Look & See: What Do I Eat? (p. 1048)
—Look & See: What Sound Do You Make? (p. 1048)
—Look & See: Wheels on the Go! (p. 1048)
—Look at Me. (p. 1048)
—Wild Animals. (p. 1928)
La Farge, John. Gospel Story in Art. (p. 703)
—Great Masters. (p. 717)
—Higher Life in Art. (p. 779)
—One Hundred Masterpieces of Painting. (p. 1295)
—Reminiscences of the South Seas. (p. 1460)
La Farge, Oliver. Cochise of Arizona. (p. 337)
La Fave, Kim, illus. see Evans, Hubert.
La Fave, Kim, illus. see Henry, Tom.
La Flamme Beighey, Carole. Waddodles of Hollow Lake: The Mighty Oak. (p. 1852)
La Fon-Cox, Angelique. Tale of Kooshla & Saboo: The Great Dinosaur Discovery. (p. 1699)
La Fontaine, Jean De. Falcon & the Little Dog. (p. 565)
La Fontaine, Jean de, jt. auth. see Larned, W. T.
La France, Robert, jt. auth. see Koeller, Kim.
la Giorgia, Giancarlo. Canadian War Heroes: Ten Profiles in Courage. (p. 260)
La Grange, Myrtle, illus. see Jordan, Annie Laurie.
La Guardia, Anton, jt. auth. see LaGuardia, Anton.
la Jara, Fatima de, see de la Jara, Fatima.
La Jars, David. One, Two, Red & Blue. (p. 1297)
La Madrid, Enriquee, tr. see Salenas, Bobbi.
la Mare, Walter de, see de la Mare, Walter.
La Paz, Myrna J. De, see De La Paz, Myrna J.
La Pierre, Yvette. Ghana in Pictures. (p. 670)
—Neandertals: A Prehistoric Puzzle. (p. 1238)
La Plante, Clare. Teen's Guide to Working. (p. 1715)
La Porte, Mary Ellen. Almost Christmas Story. (p. 48)
La Prade, Erik. Swatches. Snyder, Don, photos by. (p. 1689)
La Ramee, Louise De, see De La Ramee, Louise.
La Raso, Carlo, jt. auth. see Smith, Charles R., Jr.
La Ray, Marina, illus. see James, Eric.
La Rose, Melinda. Jake & the Neverland Pirates: X Marks the Croc! Batson, Alan, illus. (p. 906)
La Rue, Coco. Dog Rules. May, Kyla, illus. (p. 461)
—New Pig in Town. May, Kyla, illus. (p. 1246)
La Rue, Mabel Guinnip. Letter to Popsey: A Story Parade Picture Book. Lenski, Lois, illus. (p. 1002)
la Valette, Desiree, et al. Keith Haring: I Wish I Didn't Have to Sleep! (p. 948)
La Valley, Josanne. Vine Basket. (p. 1843)
la Vega, Eida de, see de la Vega, Eida, tr.
Laab, Sandy. Sing Me a Song! Songs Designed to Musically & Emotionally Nourishinfants, Toddlers, & their Parents. (p. 1579)
Laaker, Terry. Charlie the Spy: Charlie's Great Adventure #6. (p. 293)
Laaker, Terry, illus. see Goody, C. A.
Laar-Yond C.T. Six Fingers & the Blue Warrior. Playcrib, illus. (p. 1582)
Labadie, Sally. Tanner's Turtle. Jeremiah, illus. (p. 1705)
Labadie, Sally Zolkosky. Schoolhouse Mouse. (p. 1524)
LaBaff, Stephanie. Draw Aliens & Space Objects in 4 Easy Steps: Then Write a Story. LaBaff, Tom, illus. (p. 480)
Labaff, Stephanie. Draw Aliens & Space Objects in 4 Easy Steps: Then Write a Story. LaBaff, Tom, illus. (p. 480)
LaBaff, Stephanie. Draw Animals in 4 Easy Steps: Then Write a Story. LaBaff, Tom, illus. (p. 480)
Labaff, Stephanie. Draw Animals in 4 Easy Steps: Then Write a Story. LaBaff, Tom, illus. (p. 480)
LaBaff, Stephanie. Draw Cartoon People in 4 Easy Steps: Then Write a Story. LaBaff, Tom, illus. (p. 480)
Labaff, Stephanie. Draw Cartoon People in 4 Easy Steps: Then Write a Story. LaBaff, Tom, illus. (p. 480)
LaBaff, Stephanie. Draw Pirates in 4 Easy Steps: Then Write a Story. LaBaff, Tom, illus. (p. 481)
—Draw Princesses in 4 Easy Steps: Then Write a Story. LaBaff, Tom, illus. (p. 481)
Labaff, Stephanie. Draw Princesses in 4 Easy Steps: Then Write a Story. LaBaff, Tom, illus. (p. 481)
LaBaff, Stephanie. Draw Superheroes in 4 Easy Steps: Then Write a Story. LaBaff, Tom, illus. (p. 481)
LaBaff, Stephanie, illus. see Calhoun, Yael.
LaBaff, Stephanie, illus. see Gardner, Robert & Conklin, Barbara Gardner.
LaBaff, Stephanie, illus. see Gardner, Robert.
LaBaff, Stephanie, illus. see Goodstein, Madeline P.
LaBaff, Stephanie, illus. see Rybolt, Thomas R. & Mebane, Robert C.
LaBaff, Tom, illus. see Benbow, Ann & Mably, Colin.
LaBaff, Tom, illus. see Calhoun, Yael.
LaBaff, Tom, illus. see Gardner, Robert & Conklin, Barbara Gardner.
LaBaff, Tom, illus. see Gardner, Robert.
LaBaff, Tom, illus. see Goodstein, Madeline P.
LaBaff, Tom, illus. see LaBaff, Stephanie.
LaBaff, Tom, illus. see Labaff, Stephanie.
LaBaff, Tom, illus. see LaBaff, Stephanie.
LaBaff, Tom, illus. see Murphy, Patricia J.
LaBaff, Tom, illus. see Rybolt, Thomas R. & Mebane, Robert C.
LaBaff, Tom, illus. see Wingard-Nelson, Rebecca.
Labairon, Cassandra Sharri. Arizona. (p. 98)
—Connecticut. (p. 357)
—Kansas. (p. 942)
—Kentucky. (p. 949)
Labaky, Lordys. Visual Dictionary of Botany. (p. 1846)
Laban, Elizabeth. Tragedy Paper. (p. 1776)
Laban, Terry. Donald Duck Adventures Clark, John, ed. (p. 465)
Laban, Terry, et al. Uncle Scrooge Clark, John, ed. (p. 1812)
LaBarge, Shain. Sage Looks for a Job: A Group of Frogs Who Discuss Work. Safariland Friends Join in the Conversation with a Surprising Twist of Sage's Identity. (p. 1502)
LaBarr, Annetta. Sand Dollar Club: Ms. Sarah's Surprise. (p. 1510)
Labastida, Roberta. My Ancestor's Village. (p. 1196)
Labat, Yancey, illus. see Borgenicht, David & Khan, Hena.
Labat, Yancey, illus. see Borgenicht, David & Lurie, Alexander.
Labat, Yancey, illus. see Borgenicht, David, et al.
Labat, Yancey, illus. see Menotti, Andrea.
Labat, Yancey C. Fun Foods for Holidays! (p. 647)
—It's Party Time! (p. 898)
—Let's Have a Cookout! (p. 998)
—Pizza-Zazz & Lotsa Pasta. (p. 1365)
—Rise & Shine! It's Breakfast Time! (p. 1474)
—S'mores, Shakes & Chocolate Cakes: Chocolate, Chocolate All Day Long. (p. 1595)
Labat, Yancey C., illus. see Doyle, Bill.
Labat, Yancey C., illus. see Gaylord, Susan Kapuscinski & Jabbour, Joyce.
Labatt, Mary. Friend for Sam. Sarrazin, Marisol, illus. (p. 637)
—Lake Monster Mix-Up. Rioux, Jo-Anne, illus. (p. 972)
—Mummy Mayhem. Rioux, Jo-Anne, illus. (p. 1191)
—Pizza for Sam. Sarrazin, Marisol, illus. (p. 1365)
—Puppy Is for Loving Liwska, Renata, illus. (p. 1418)
—Sam at the Seaside. Sarrazin, Marisol, illus. (p. 1506)
—Sam Finds a Monster. Sarrazin, Marisol, illus. (p. 1506)
—Sam Goes Next Door. Sarrazin, Marisol, illus. (p. 1506)
—Sam Goes to School. Sarrazin, Marisol, tr. (p. 1506)
—Sam's First Halloween. Sarrazin, Marisol, illus. (p. 1509)
—Sam's Snowy Day. Sarrazin, Marisol, illus. (p. 1509)
—Witches' Brew. Rioux, Jo-Anne, illus. (p. 1941)
Labatt, Mary, jt. auth. see Butcher, Kristin.
LaBaum, Jessie. Thomas, the Wandering Cat. (p. 1739)
Labay, Laura. How the Little Gray Woman Found Her Rainbow. (p. 813)
Labbé, Jesse, illus. see Kander, Beth & Kenyon, Bret.
Labbe, Jesse & Coffey, Anthony. Fight for Amity. Morrissey, Paul, ed. (p. 585)
Labeda, Patricia R. Miko & the Mystery Friend. Labeda, Patricia R., illus. (p. 1142)
Labella, Susan. Animal Survivors (p. 80)
—Animales Migratorios: En el Agua. (p. 81)
—Chameleons & Other Animals with Amazing Skin. (p. 289)
—Como Migran los Animales. (p. 351)
—How Animals Migrate. (p. 804)
—Maryland. (p. 1101)
—Migrating Animals of the Water. (p. 1140)
—Nevada. (p. 1242)
—Oklahoma. (p. 1282)
—Oregon. (p. 1302)
—Rhode Island. (p. 1468)
—Washington. (p. 1859)
—West Virginia. (p. 1876)
Labella, Susan, jt. auth. see LaBella, Susan.
LaBella, Susan & Labella, Susan. Cómo Migran los Animales. (p. 351)
—Migrating Animals of the Water. (p. 1140)
Labenne, Jonathan A. Annual Bear Dance. (p. 87)
Labensohn, Judy, et al. Jewish Sports Stories for Kids. (p. 917)
LaBerge, Margaret M. Sara Safety, Personal Safety: Kid's Activity Book. Lucas, Stacey L. & Lopresti, Sarah H., illus. (p. 1514)
—Sara Safety, School Safety: Kid's Activity Book. Seager, Maryann et al, illus. (p. 1514)
—Sara Safety, School Safety Pamphlet. Lucas, Stacey L. et al, illus. (p. 1514)
Laberge, Monique. Biochemistry. (p. 188)
Laberis, Stephanie & Coloring Books Staff. Mix & Match ZOO ANIMALS. (p. 1156)
Laberje, Reji. Max Explores Chicago. Fenech, Liza, illus. (p. 1111)
—Max Explores New York. Fenech, Liza, illus. (p. 1111)
—Max Explores San Francisco. Fenech, Liza, illus. (p. 1111)
—Max Explores Seattle. Fenech, Liza, illus. (p. 1111)
—Max Explores the Beach. Fenech, Liza, illus. (p. 1111)
Laber-Warren, Emily. Walk in the Woods: Into the Field Guide. (p. 1853)
Laber-Warren, Emily & Goldman, Laurie. Walk on the Beach: Into the Field Guide. (p. 1853)
Labosh, Kathy. Child with Autism Learns the Faith: The Sunday School Guide. (p. 301)
Labossiere, Julie. Amy Goes Surfing. Brown, Dwayne, illus. (p. 66)
—Amy Plays the Violin. Brown, Dwayne, illus. (p. 66)
—Amy Volunteers. Brown, Dwayne, illus. (p. 66)
LaBounty, David. Eye of the Deer. (p. 557)
Labov, Steven L., ed. Rescue & Prevention: Defending Our Nation (p. 1462)
Laboy, Gloria J. Freddie Learns Obedience. (p. 632)
—Sally Learns Honesty. (p. 1505)
LaBrant, Kenneth R. Uncle Kenny's Crazy Bedtime Stories. (p. 1812)
Labrecque, Candida. Riverside Walk with Grandma. Labrecque, Candida & Labrecque, Candida, illus. (p. 1476)
Labrecque, Ellen. Air Sports (p. 31)
—Amazing Bike Tricks (p. 54)
—Arctic Tundra (p. 96)
—Basketball. (p. 143)
—Caves (p. 282)
—Chicago Bulls. (p. 299)
—Cliff Diving. (p. 332)
—Cool Board Tricks (p. 362)
—Dallas Mavericks. (p. 401)
—Deep Oceans (p. 423)
—Earth's Last Frontiers (p. 498)
—Fighting Crime (p. 585)
—George Washington Carver (p. 664)
—How Did That Get to My House? Music. (p. 806)
—Impressive Dance Moves (p. 862)
—Islands (p. 892)
—Jim Thorpe: An Athlete for the Ages. (p. 918)
—Jumping Gymnastics. (p. 934)
—Jungle Worlds (p. 935)
—Living Beside a River. (p. 1040)
—Living Beside the Ocean. (p. 1040)
—Living in a City. (p. 1041)
—Living in a Desert. (p. 1041)
—Living in a Valley. (p. 1041)
—Living on a Mountain. (p. 1041)
—Magic Johnson. (p. 1072)
—Mountain Tops (p. 1181)
—NFC East. (p. 1249)
—NFC West. (p. 1249)
—Pakistan. (p. 1319)
—Pittsburgh Penguins. (p. 1364)
—Places We Live. (p. 1366)
—Rope Sports (p. 1488)
—Running. (p. 1497)
—Sky Surfing. (p. 1587)
—Special Forces (p. 1623)
—Speed: Get Quick! (p. 1624)
—Stamina: Get Stronger & Play Longer! (p. 1639)
—Strength: Build Muscles & Climb High! (p. 1667)
—Valleys (p. 1831)
—What's Your Story, Sacagawea? (p. 1900)
—Whitewater Kayaking. (p. 1914)
—Who Was Winston Churchill? Hoare, Jerry & Harrison, Nancy, illus. (p. 1919)
—Windsurfing. (p. 1936)
Labrecque, Ellen & Hunter, Nick. Try This at Home! (p. 1794)
Labrecque, Ellen & Oxlade, Chris. Learning about Landforms (p. 984)
Labrecque, Ellen C. BMX Racers. (p. 204)
LaBree Stute, Lela. Freedom Pugs! (p. 634)
—My Name Is Ingah, I Am A Pug. (p. 1215)
—Summer Pugs. (p. 1674)
—Sunnyset Pugs. (p. 1677)
—Sunshine Pugs. (p. 1678)
—Three Pugs & a Trout. (p. 1743)
—Three Pugs & One Vacation. (p. 1743)
—Wonder Pugs. (p. 1947)
LaBrie, Aimie. E. B. White. (p. 491)
Labriola, Mark E. Little Pine Tree. (p. 1033)
LaBrot, Matthew, jt. auth. see Hale, Daniel J.
LaBrot, Matthew & Daniel, Hale. Green Streak. (p. 722)
Labuda, Scott A. Color of People. Franfou Studio, illus. (p. 343)
Lacaille, Link. Roots, Rock, Rap & Reggae (p. 1488)
LaCaille, Link. Smoken Careers: Roots, Rock, Rap & Reggae Book 2 (p. 1594)
Lacamara, Laura. Dalia's Wondrous Hair / el Maravilloso Cabello de Dalia. Baeza Ventura, Gabriela, tr. from SPA. (p. 401)
Lacámara, Laura. Floating on Mama's Song: Flotando con la Canción de Mamá. Morales, Yuyi, illus. (p. 605)
Lacámara, Laura, illus. see Luna, James & Villarroel, Carolina.
Lacámara, Laura, illus. see Ruiz-Flores, Lupe.
Lacapa, Michael, illus. see Ortiz, Simon J.
Lacapa, Michael, jt. auth. see Ortiz, Simon J.
Lacapra, Dominick. History & Reading: Tocqueville, Foucault, French Studies. (p. 783)
Lacasse, Michael. George & His Special New Friends. (p. 663)
Lacasse, Monique. Good Morning to You. (p. 698)
Lacca, Victor. Heyden Hushbunny & the Great Jellybean Caper. (p. 775)
Lace, William W. Benjamin Franklin. (p. 164)
—Blacks in Film. (p. 197)
—Captain James Cook. (p. 264)
—Christianity. (p. 312)
—Curse of King Tut. (p. 394)
—Elizabethan England. (p. 513)
—Hindenburg Disaster Of 1937. (p. 780)
—Indian Ocean Tsunami Of 2004. (p. 871)
—Jesus of Nazareth. (p. 916)
—Joan of Arc & the Hundred Years' War in World History. (p. 919)
—King Arthur. (p. 958)
—LaDanian Tomlinson. (p. 970)
—Mummification & Death Rituals of Ancient Egypt. (p. 1191)
—Nolan Ryan: Hall of Fame Baseball Superstar. (p. 1263)
—Oliver Cromwell & the English Civil War in World History. (p. 1285)
—Roberto Clemente, Baseball Hall of Famer. (p. 1479)
—Sir Francis Drake. (p. 1580)
—Unholy Crusade: The Ransacking of Medieval Constantinople. (p. 1817)
Lacek, Carolyn. Destiny Awakened. (p. 431)
Lacey, Barbara, jt. auth. see Lacey, Bill.
Lacey, Bill & Lacey, Barbara. Alamo. (p. 33)
Lacey, Josh. Sultan's Tigers. (p. 1673)
Lacey, Josh & Pakenham, Sarah. Island of Thieves. (p. 892)
Lacey, Mike, illus. see Fabiny, Sarah.
Lacey, Mike, illus. see Jeffery, Gary & Petty, Kate.
Lacey, Mike, illus. see Jeffrey, Gary.
Lacey, Mike, illus. see Pollack, Pamela D. & Belviso, Meg.
Lacey, Mike, illus. see West, David.
Lacey, Minna. Big Book of Big Machines. (p. 179)
—Big Book of Big Ships. Chisholm, Jane, ed. (p. 179)
—Guitar for Beginners. (p. 731)
—Look Inside Science. (p. 1049)
—Nelson. Cuzik, David, illus. (p. 1240)
—Story of the Olympics. (p. 1661)
Lacey, Minna, ed. see Amery, Heather.
Lacey, Minna, jt. auth. see Firth, Alex.
Lacey, Minna, jt. auth. see Frith, Alex.
Lacey, Minna & Davidson, Susanna. Gladiators. Cerisier, Emmanuel, illus. (p. 682)
Lacey, Minna & Gilpin, Rebecca. 50 Christmas Things to Make & Do. (p. 1997)
Lacey, Minna, ed. 50 Fairy Things to Make & Do. (p. 1997)
Lacey, Robert. Great Tales from English History: Captain Cook, Samuel Johnson, Queen Victoria, Charles Darwin, Edward the Abdicator, & More. Vol. 3 (p. 718)
—Great Tales from English History: A Treasury of True Stories about the Extraordinary People-Knights & Knaves, Rebels & Heroes, Queens & Commoners-Who Made Britain Great. (p. 718)
Lacey, Saskia. Foods for the Future. (p. 614)
—Hidden by Time. (p. 775)
Lacey, T. Jensen. Comanche. (p. 346)
Lacey, Theresa Jensen & Rosier, Paul C. Blackfeet. (p. 197)
Lach, Hope Carlin. Mr. Contrareloj. (p. 1184)
—Mr. Counter Clockwise. (p. 1184)
Lach, William. Can You Hear It? (p. 259)
Lach, William, jt. auth. see van Gogh, Vincent.
LaChanze. Little Diva. Pinkney, Brian, illus. (p. 1026)
Lachenmeyer, Nathaniel. Boo! Book. Cecconi, Nicoletta, illus. (p. 209)
—Broken Beaks. Ingpen, Robert R., illus. (p. 230)
—Eureka! Jack, Colin, illus. (p. 540)
—Origami Master. Sogabe, Aki, illus. (p. 1304)
—Scarlatti's Cat. Beccia, Carlyn, illus. (p. 1520)
Lachner, Elizabeth. Bioengineering. (p. 188)
—Herbivores & Carnivores. (p. 769)
—History of Electricity. (p. 784)
—Magnetic Forces. (p. 1075)
Lachocki, Dezyeriusz. Long Road to Wayne. (p. 1047)
Lachtman, Ofelia Dumas. Pepita & the Bully: Pepita y la Peleonera. Baeza Ventura, Gabriela, tr. (p. 1340)
—Pepita on Pepper Street/Pepita en la Calle Pepper. Monsivais, Maria Estela, tr. from ENG. (p. 1340)
—Pepita Packs Up: Pepita Empaca. Ventura, Gabriela Baeza, tr. from ENG. (p. 1340)
—Trouble with Tessa. (p. 1790)
—Truth about las Mariposas. (p. 1794)
Lachuk, Dani, illus. see Wallace, Susan Helen & Jablonski, Patricia E.
Lacivita, Michael J. Rag Man, Rag Man. (p. 1433)
Lackey, Jennifer. Biography of Wheat. (p. 189)
—Jacques Cartier: Exploring the St. Lawrence River. (p. 905)
Lackey, Mercedes. Alta. (p. 50)

Lackey, Mercedes & Edghill, Rosemary. Conspiracies. (p. 359)
—Dead Reckoning. (p. 417)
—Legacies (p. 987)
—Shadow Grail #3: Sacrifices. (p. 1557)
—Shadow Grail #4: Victories. (p. 1557)
Lackey, Mercedes, ed. Hunter. (p. 828)
Lackner, Michelle Myers, jt. auth. see North American Bear Center.
Lacktman, Maija. Adventures of Moleby. (p. 20)
LaClair, Teresa. Americans Move West (1846-1860) (p. 64)
—Americans Move West (1846-1860) Rakove, Jack N., ed. (p. 64)
—Northern Colonies: Freedom to Worship (1600-1770) (p. 1265)
—Northern Colonies: Freedom to Worship (1600-1770) Rakove, Jack N., ed. (p. 1265)
—Southern Colonies: The Search for Wealth (1600-1770) (p. 1617)
—Southern Colonies: The Search for Wealth (1600-1770) Rakove, Jack N., ed. (p. 1617)
Lacle, Tony. Man Called Avalon. (p. 1085)
Lacombe, Benjamin. Genealogia de una Bruja. Krahe, Elena Gallo, tr. (p. 660)
—Melodia en la Ciudad. Krahe, Elena Gallo, tr. from FRE. (p. 1125)
Lacombe, Benjamin, illus. see Oliver, Lauren & Chester, H. C.
Lacombe, Benjamin, illus. see Williams, Brenda.
Lacombe, Benjamin, jt. auth. see Williams, Brenda.
Lacome, Julie. Walking Through the Jungle Big Book. Lacome, Julie, illus. (p. 1854)
Lacome, Susie, illus. see Baxter, Nicola.
Lacome, Susie, illus. see Budds, Sam.
Lacome, Susie, illus. see Campaniello, Don.
Lacome, Susie, illus. see Dopffer, Guillaume.
Lacome, Susie, illus. see Kenkmann, Andrea.
LaCompte, Angie. I Am a Scientist. (p. 832)
—Math for Fun. (p. 1106)
Laconi, Kristin. Karma the Kangaroo Takes the Court. (p. 944)
Lacont'e. Overcoming Obstacles. (p. 1314)
LaCoste, Gary. First Word Search: Phonics Word Search. (p. 597)
—First Word Search: Words to Learn. (p. 597)
—Phonics Fun. (p. 1352)
LaCoste, Gary, illus. see Hovanec, Helene.
LaCoste, Gary, illus. see Katz, Alan.
LaCoste, Gary, illus. see Mullarkey, Lisa.
LaCoste, Gary, illus. see Murray, Carol.
LaCoste, Michael, ed. Design Denied: The Dynamics of Withholding Good Design & its Ethical Implications: The Dynamics of Withholding Good Design & its Ethical ImplicationsThe Withholding of Good Design & its Ethical Implications (p. 429)
LaCour, Nina. Disenchantments. (p. 450)
—Everything Leads to You. (p. 545)
—Hold Still. (p. 788)
Lacoursiere, Patrick. Dream Songs Night Songs: From China to Senegal. Bourbonnière, Sylvie, illus. (p. 483)
—Dream Songs Night Songs: From Mali to Louisiana. Bourbonnière, Sylvie, illus. (p. 483)
Lacoursiere, Suzanne, jt. auth. see Dumont, C.
Lacoursiere, Suzanne, jt. auth. see Dumont, Claire.
Lacroix, Cynthia, jt. creator see Cordier, Séverine.
LaCroix, Debbie Bernstein. It's Almost Time. Chalek, Sarah, illus. (p. 896)
Lacroix, Nitya. Massage. (p. 1102)
Lacroix, Paul, see Jacob, P. L., pseud.
Lacruz, Javier, tr. see Hinton, S. E. & Hinton, Susan E.
Lacy, Kendra. Drachen. (p. 476)
—Stone Garden. (p. 1652)
Lacy, Lauren, illus. see Chocolate Cupcake Staff.
Lacy, Mariscott. Would-Be Butterfly. (p. 1962)
Lacy, Sandy Allbee. Pepe & Lupita & the Great Yawn Jar. Schrom, Garren, illus. (p. 1340)
Ladage, Cindy, jt. auth. see Aumann, Jane.
Ladage, Cindy & Aumann, Jane. My Name Is Huber. (p. 1215)
Ladbrooke, Sheree. Big Alien School. (p. 177)
Ladd, Ann Frances. Phonics: 12 Book Reading Program. (p. 1351)
Ladd, Debbie. Don't Pick Your Nose (p. 468)
—Ethan the Ending Eater. Nakasone, Shaun, illus. (p. 539)
—Nurse Robin's Hats. Nakasone, Shaun, illus. (p. 1273)
—Puddles. Morejon, Tom, illus. (p. 1414)
—What If. (p. 1887)
Ladd, Karol. Glad Scientist Explores the Human Body. (p. 682)
—Glad Scientist Learn about the Weather. (p. 682)
Ladd, London, illus. see Farris, Christine King.
Ladd, London, illus. see Frank, John.
Ladd, London, illus. see VanHecke, Susan.
Ladd, London, illus. see Vanhecke, Susan.
Ladd, Mike. Rooms & Sequences. (p. 1488)
Laddy, Lee, jt. auth. see Lipson, Amy Kron.
Laddy, Lee & Lipson, Amy Kron. Rufus Rules! from Underdog to Top Dog - a Playful Journey of Acceptance. (p. 1494)
Lade, Linda. Peter Bunny: Adventures in the Kudzu Pat. (p. 1346)
Ladeane, Symone. Caterpillar That Would Be a Rainbow. (p. 279)
LaDeane, Symone. E Is for Exercise. (p. 492)
—Momma, Where Will You Be? (p. 1162)
—Night Lights. (p. 1253)
Ladecka, Anna, illus. see Kim, Cecil.
Laden, Nina. Daddy Wrong Legs. (p. 399)
—Grow Up! (p. 726)
—Once upon a Memory. Liwksa, Renata, illus. (p. 1293)
—Peek-A Boo! (p. 1334)
—Peek-A Who? Matching Game. (p. 1335)
—Peek-A Zoo! (p. 1335)
—Who Loves You, Baby? (p. 1916)
Laden, Nina, illus. see Myers, Walter Dean.
Lader, Curt. Painless American History. (p. 1318)
Ladew, Donald. Troop 402: A Novel. (p. 1788)
Ladewski, Paul & Smallwood, John. Playmaker. (p. 1373)
Ladig, Kim. Ellie's Lake House. (p. 514)
Ladin - Bramet, Lisa. I Was Told That Angels Don't Need Friends. (p. 848)
Ladin, Marc J. Playground Bully Blues. Margolis, Al, illus. (p. 1372)
LaDoux, Rita C. Oklahoma. (p. 1283)
LaDow, William. Conversations with a Winner — the Ray Nichels Story. (p. 361)
LaDuca, Michael, illus. see Gehret, Jeanne.
LaDuca, Michael, illus. see Seidler, Rena.
Ladwig, Tim. Lord's Prayer. (p. 1053)
Ladwig, Tim, illus. see Carlstrom, Nancy White.
Ladwig, Tim, illus. see Grimes, Nikki.
Ladwig, Tim, illus. see Hearth, Amy Hill.
Ladwig, Tim, illus. see Kroll, Virginia L.
Ladwig, Tim, illus. see Neale, J. M.
Ladwig, Tim, illus. see Norris, Jeannine Q.
Ladwig, Tim, illus. see Wangerin, Walter, Jr.
Ladwig, Tim, illus. see Weatherford, Carole Boston.
Lady Bird Johnson Wildflower Center Staff, Lady Bird Johnson, compiled by. Exploring the Native Plant World Grades 1-2: Changes. (p. 554)
—Exploring the Native Plant World Pre-K-K: Patterns & Shapes. (p. 554)
Lady Jan, jt. auth. see Paul.
Lady Josephine, illus. see Hassan, Masood.
Ladybird. Alice in Wonderland. (p. 39)
—Black Beauty. (p. 195)
Ladybird Books Staff. Blanca Nieves y los Siete Enanos. (p. 198)
—Caperucita Roja. (p. 262)
—Cenicienta. (p. 286)
—Cinderella. (p. 320)
—Jack y los Frijoles Magicos. (p. 903)
—Mago de Oz. (p. 1076)
—My Counting Book. (p. 1200)
—Noah's Ark. (p. 1261)
—Nursery Rhymes. (p. 1273)
—Three Little Pigs. (p. 1742)
Ladybird Books Staff, illus. see Candlewick Press Staff.
Ladybird Books Staff, illus. see Candlewick Press, Candlewick.
Ladybird Books Staff, jt. auth. see Read, Lorna.
Ladybird Books Staff, jt. auth. see Yates, Irene.
Ladybird Books Staff & Candlewick Press Staff. Peppa Pig & the Muddy Puddles. Ladybird Books Staff, illus. (p. 1340)
Lael, Anita. Little Brick House. Gresham, Della, illus. (p. 1025)
Laezman, Rick. 100 Hispanic Americans Who Shaped American History. (p. 1998)
Lafan, Algie, illus. see Dingler, Jay.
Lafantasie, Shilo. House of Love. (p. 803)
Lafarge, Kelly, illus. see Lawson, Barbara.
LaFave, Kim, illus. see Bourgeois, Paulette & Bourgeois, Paulette.
LaFave, Kim, illus. see Bourgeois, Paulette.
Lafave, Kim, illus. see Campbell, Nicola I.
LaFave, Kim, illus. see Campbell, Nicola.
LaFave, Kim, illus. see Ellis, Sarah.
LaFave, Kim, illus. see Harris, Dorothy Joan.
Lafave, Kim, illus. see Lunn, Janet.
LaFave, Kim, illus. see McBay, Bruce.
LaFave, Kim, illus. see McFarlane, Sheryl.
LaFave, Kim, illus. see Thompson, Richard & Spicer, Maggee.
LaFave, Kim, illus. see Waterton, Betty.
LaFaye, A. Keening. (p. 946)
—Nissa's Place. (p. 1257)
—Stella Stands Alone. (p. 1647)
—Walking Home to Rosie Lee. Shepherd, Keith D., illus. (p. 1854)
—Water Steps. (p. 1863)
—Worth. (p. 1962)
—Year of the Sawdust Man. (p. 1969)
Lafayette, David P. Peril in the West. (p. 1343)
Lafayette, Madame De, see De Lafayette, Madame.
LaFehr, Raymond Michael. Female Code. (p. 581)
LaFer, Jenni. Ben Dhere! Don Dhat! Tall Tales from the Island of Gullah. Weitzel, Erica, illus. (p. 163)
LaFerriere, Suzanne, illus. see Castle, Jan And Kare.
Lafette, Jordan. Kites: Shapes in the Air: Reason with Shapes & Their Attributes (p. 962)
LaFever, Greg, illus. see Mackall, Dandi Daley.
LaFevers, R. L. Basilisk's Lair. Murphy, Kelly, illus. (p. 142)
—Flight of the Phoenix Bk. 1. Murphy, Kelly, illus. (p. 604)
—Forging of the Blade. (p. 619)
—Theodosia & the Eyes of Horus. Tanaka, Yoko, illus. (p. 1729)
—Theodosia & the Serpents of Chaos. Tanaka, Yoko, illus. (p. 1729)
—Theodosia & the Staff of Osiris. Tanaka, Yoko, illus. (p. 1729)
—Unicorn's Tale. (p. 1818)
—Unicorn's Tale. Murphy, Kelly, illus. (p. 1818)
—Wyverns' Treasure. (p. 1966)
—Wyverns' Treasure. Murphy, Kelly, illus. (p. 1966)
LaFevers, Robin. Dark Triumph (p. 408)
—Dark Triumph. (p. 408)
—Grave Mercy (p. 712)
—Grave Mercy. (p. 712)
—Mortal Heart. (p. 1176)
Lafferty, Peter. How Things Are Made. (p. 814)
Laffin, Ima. Knock-Knock Jokes. (p. 965)
—Monster Jokes. (p. 1167)
—More Monster Jokes. (p. 1174)
Laffon, Martine & De Chabaneix, Hortense. Book of How. Azam, Jacques, illus. (p. 211)
Laffon, Martine, et al. Poem in Your Pocket for Young Poets. (p. 1375)
Laflamme, Essie. Caring for Mama Bear: A Story of Love. Crane-Yvon, Marie, illus. (p. 269)
Laflamme, Mark. Guys Named Jack. (p. 733)
LaFleur, David, illus. see McMullan, Kate.
Lafleur, Denis. Koal's Not Happy. (p. 966)
LaFleur, James & Massie, Gordon. Order Of 5ive: The Complete First Season. Dalglish, Rich, ed. (p. 1302)
LaFleur, John & Dubin, Shawn. Dreary & Naughty: The ABCs of Being Dead (p. 484)
—Dreary & Naughty: Friday the 13th of February. (p. 484)
—Misadventures of Dreary & Naughty (p. 1150)
LaFleur, Richard & Tillery, Brad. Ovid Vocabulary Cards for AP Selections. (p. 1314)
LaFleur, Suzanne. Eight Keys. (p. 507)
—Listening for Lucca. (p. 1022)
—Love, Aubrey. (p. 1059)
Lafond, Pascale. Story of Jesus. Flowerpot Press, ed. (p. 1658)
—Story of Moses. Flowerpot Press, ed. (p. 1659)
—Story of Noah. Flowerpot Press, ed. (p. 1659)
LaFontaine, Bruce. Adventures of Ulysses. (p. 24)
—All about the Weather. (p. 43)
—Big Book of Space Exploration to Color. (p. 179)
—BOOST the Story of the Wright Brothers Coloring Book. (p. 213)
—Classic Cars Coloring Book. (p. 327)
—Classic Cars of the Fifties. (p. 327)
—Constellations of the Night Sky. (p. 359)
—Construction Trucks Stained Glass Coloring Book. (p. 360)
—Famous Trains. (p. 570)
—Famous Trains Stickers. (p. 570)
—Famous Women Aviators. (p. 570)
—History of Trucks. (p. 785)
—International Space Station Coloring Book. (p. 880)
—Locomotives Stickers. (p. 1045)
—Luxury Cars Coloring Book. (p. 1066)
—Railroad Engines from Around the World Coloring Book. (p. 1434)
—Shiny Fast Cars Stickers. (p. 1567)
—Shiny Fire Engines Stickers. (p. 1567)
—Shiny Trucks Stickers. (p. 1567)
—Sports Cars. (p. 1632)
—Tanks & Armored Vehicles. (p. 1705)
—Warriors Through the Ages. (p. 1859)
—Wigwams, Longhouses & Other Native American Dwellings. (p. 1928)
Lafortune, Claude. Wonderful Story of Christmas. (p. 1948)
LaFosse, Michael. Making Origami Cards Step by Step. (p. 1082)
—Making Origami Science Experiments Step by Step. (p. 1082)
LaFosse, Michael G. Making Origami Cards Step by Step. (p. 1082)
—Making Origami Masks Step by Step. (p. 1082)
—Making Origami Puzzles Step by Step. (p. 1082)
—Making Origami Science Experiments Step by Step. (p. 1082)
—Origami Activities: Create Secret Boxes, Good-Luck Animals, & Paper Charms with the Japanese Art of Origami. (p. 1303)
Laframboise, Tammy. Popsy in Ballet My Way. (p. 1385)
Lafrance, Daniel, jt. auth. see McKay, Sharon E.
Lafrance, David, illus. see Chiasson, Herménéglide.
LaFrance, Debbie, illus. see Redmond, Pamela Woods.
Lafrance, Marie. Princess & the Giant: A Tale from Scotland. (p. 1402)
Lafrance, Marie, illus. see Barchers, Suzanne I.
Lafrance, Marie, illus. see Farmer, Bonnie.
Lafrance, Marie, illus. see Gadot, A. S.
Lafrance, Marie, illus. see Kaner, Etta.
Lafrance, Marie, illus. see Nolan, Janet.
LaFrentz, Pamela Daley. Foiled Money. (p. 611)
Laganke, Traci Smith. Way Home. (p. 1864)
Lagares, Luciano, illus. see Gemmen, Heather.
Lagarrigue, Jerome, illus. see Grimes, Nikki.
Lagarrigue, Jerome, illus. see Harrington, Janice N.
Lagarrigue, Jerome, illus. see Weatherford, Carole Boston.
Lagarrigue, Jerome, illus. see Wiles, Deborah.
Lagarrigue, Jerome, illus. see Wilson, Edwin Graves, ed.
Lagarrigue, Jerome Lagarrigue, illus. see Weatherford, Carole Boston.
Lagartos, M. L., et al. Entre Amigos. (p. 531)
Lagasse, Emeril. Emeril's There's a Chef in My Soup! Recipes for the Kid in Everyone. Yuen, Charles, illus. (p. 518)
Lagasse, Paul. Seeing Through Clouds: The Story of an Airship Apprentice. (p. 1548)
Lagerborg, Mary Beth, jt. auth. see Wilson, Mimi.
Lagercrantz, Rose. My Happy Life. Eriksson, Eva, illus. (p. 1210)
—When I Am Happiest. Eriksson, Eva, illus. (p. 1902)
Lagerloeff, Selma. What the Shepherd Saw. Dusikova, Maja, illus. (p. 1893)
Lagerlöf, Selma. Christ Legends. (p. 311)
—Christ Legends: & Other Stories. (p. 311)
—Further Adventures of Nils. (p. 650)
—Further Adventures of Nils. Howard, Velma Swanston, tr. (p. 650)
—Holy Night. Wikland, Ilon, illus. (p. 791)
—Wonderful Adventures of Nils. (p. 1948)
—Wonderful Adventures of Nils. Howard, Velma Swanston, tr. (p. 1948)
Lageson, David R., et al. Roadside Geology of Wyoming. (p. 1477)
Lagneau, Mary. Blessed Jacint: Patron for Children for Tummy Troubles. Gillen, Rosemarie, illus. (p. 199)
Lago, Alexis, illus. see Silva Lee, Alfonso.
Lago, Angela. Juan Felizario Contento: El Rey de los Negocios. (p. 930)
Lago, Angela, illus. see Dinesen, Isak.
Lago, Mary Ellen. Missouri. (p. 1154)
Lago, Mary Ellen & Karnovsky, Susan. Missouri. (p. 1154)
Lago, Ray, illus. see Croall, Marie P.
Lago, Ray, illus. see Scott, Walter.
Lago, Shelby. Henry's Unlikely Friend. (p. 769)
Lagonegro, Melissa. Barbie in Princess Power - Saving the Day! (p. 138)
—Beautiful Brides. Marrucchi, Elisa, illus. (p. 153)
—Big Friend, Little Friend. (p. 181)
—Big Friend, Little Friend. RH Disney Staff, illus. (p. 181)
—Cars - The Spooky Sound. (p. 272)
—Cinderella. (p. 320)
—Cinderella (Diamond) Step into Reading (Disney Princess) RH Disney Staff, illus. (p. 320)
—Friends for a Princess. (p. 638)
—Frozen - A Tale of Two Sisters. (p. 645)
—Go, Go, Go! (p. 686)
—Go, Go, Go! Cohee, Ron, illus. (p. 686)
—Little Mermaid Junior Novelization (Disney Princess) RH Disney Staff, illus. (p. 1031)
—Mater's Birthday Surprise. (p. 1104)
—Mater's Birthday Surprise (Disney/Pixar Cars) RH Disney Staff, illus. (p. 1104)
—Monster Games. RH Disney Staff, illus. (p. 1167)
—Monsters Get Scared of the Dark, Too (Disney/Pixar Monsters, Inc.) RH Disney Staff, illus. (p. 1169)
—Monsters University. (p. 1169)
—Puppy Problems! (p. 1418)
—Puppy Problems! RH Disney Staff, illus. (p. 1418)
—Saving the Day! (p. 1517)
—Sealed with a Kiss. Marrucchi, Elisa, illus. (p. 1536)
—Secret Agent Mater. RH Disney Staff, illus. (p. 1540)
—Spooky Sound. Cohee, Ron, illus. (p. 1631)
—Tale of Two Sisters. Random House Disney Staff, illus. (p. 1701)
—Travel Like a Princess. (p. 1780)
—Travel Like a Princess (Disney Princess) RH Disney Staff et al, illus. (p. 1780)
Lagonegro, Melissa, jt. auth. see Arps, Melissa.
Lagonegro, Melissa, jt. auth. see RH Disney Staff.
Lagonegro, Melissa & Redbank, Tennant. Five Toy Tales. (p. 601)
Lagonegro, Melissa & RH Disney Staff. Ballerina Princess. Harding, Niall, illus. (p. 134)
—Dream for a Princess. Saichann, Alberto, illus. (p. 483)
—Friends for a Princess. Harchy, Atelier Philippe, illus. (p. 638)
—Horse to Love: An Enchanted Stables Story. Disney Storybook Artists Staff, illus. (p. 800)
—Just Keep Swimming. Harchy, Atelier Philippe, illus. (p. 939)
—Old, New, Red, Blue! (p. 1284)
—Roadwork! Mawhinney, Art, illus. (p. 1477)
Lagonegro, Melissa, et al. Sharing & Caring. RH Disney Staff et al, illus. (p. 1561)
Lagos, Alexander, jt. auth. see Lagos, Joseph.
Lagos, Alexander & Lagos, Joseph. Sons of Liberty Kramek, Oren & Walker, Steve, illus. (p. 1613)
Lagos, Joseph, jt. auth. see Lagos, Alexander.
Lagos, Joseph & Lagos, Alexander. Sons of Liberty: Death & Taxes. Walker, Steve & Kramek, Oren, illus. (p. 1613)
Lagoutaris, Maria Mamakas, jt. auth. see Mamakas, Stavroula.
Lago-Weed, Melissa. Hairys: Don't Talk to Strangers. (p. 736)
Lagrange, Jacques, ed. see Foucault, Michel & Davidson, Arnold I.
Lagrange, Tiffany. My Abc Blue Book. LaGrange, Tiffany, illus. (p. 1195)
—My Abc Pink Book. LaGrange, Tiffany, illus. (p. 1195)
LaGrange, Tiffany, illus. see Bender, Randy L.
LaGrange, Tiffany, illus. see Bootsma, Verner.
LaGrange, Tiffany, illus. see Falcon, David.
LaGrange, Tiffany, illus. see Howell, Julie Ann.
LaGrange, Tiffany, illus. see Howell, Julie.
LaGrange, Tiffany, illus. see Lagrange, Tiffany.
LaGrange, Tiffany, illus. see Medley, Shari.
LaGrange, Tiffany, illus. see Reeves, Pamela.
LaGrange, Tiffany, illus. see Shaber, Mark.
LaGrange, Tiffany, illus. see Snyder, Karen.
LaGrange, Tiffany, illus. see Stilwell, Norma Minturn.
LaGrange, Tiffany, illus. see Tarsy, Jean.
Lagron, Camille. Tatian. (p. 1707)
Lagrou, Patrick. Born among the Dolphins. (p. 214)
Lagrow, Victoria. Adventures of the Magical Hubcap Kid. (p. 23)
LaGuardia, Anton & La Guardia, Anton. War Without End: Israelis, Palestinians, & the Struggle for a Promised Land. (p. 1858)
Laguatan, Alwen & Buada, Joselito. Kobi. (p. 966)
Laguda, Kardy. Daisy & the Unicorn. Bell, Diana, illus. (p. 400)
Lague, Peter, jt. auth. see Naidoo, Mathevan.
Laguin, Ursula K. Telling: A Novel. (p. 1717)
Laguna, Fabio. Sherman's Awesome Adventure. (p. 1566)
Laguna, Fabio, illus. see Capozzi, Suzy.
Laguna, Fabio, illus. see David, Erica.
Laguna, Fabio, illus. see Jordan, Apple.
Laguna, Fabio, illus. see Posner-Sanchez, Andrea.
Laguna, Fabio, illus. see Random House.
Laguna, Fabio, illus. see RH Disney Staff & Posner-Sanchez, Andrea.
Laguna, Fabio, illus. see RH Disney Staff & Weingartner, Amy.
Laguna, Fabio, illus. see Titan Books Staff, et al.
Laguna, Sofie. Fighting Bones: 1836 Do You Dare? (p. 585)
Lagunilla, Cheryl, told to. ABC's of Tennis. (p. 4)
LaHaye, Tim, jt. auth. see Jenkins, Jerry B.
LaHaye, Tim & Jenkins, Jerry B. Dejados Atrás. (p. 424)
—John's Story: The Last Eyewitness. (p. 924)
—Mark's Story: The Gospel According to Peter. (p. 1095)
Lahdensuo, Debbie, illus. see Teys, Jo-Anne.
Lahey, Cindy. Nose Medicine. (p. 1266)
Lahey, Thomas A. King of the Pygmies. (p. 959)
Lahman, Lois E., compiled by. Reuben & the Fire (p. 1465)
Lahr, Joy Jenks. BJ Visits the Farm. (p. 194)
LAHRING, Heinjo, jt. auth. see Lahring, Heinjo.
Lahring, Heinjo & LAHRING, Heinjo. Water & Wetland Plants of the Prairie Provinces: A Field Guide for Alberta, Saskatchewan, Manitoba, & the Northern United States. (p. 1862)
Lai, Ben, illus. see Waid, Mark, et al.
Lai, Hsin-Shih, illus. see Andersen, Hans Christian.
Lai, Hsin-Shih, illus. see Bell, Anthea, ed.
Lai, Rozalli. Lethal Light. (p. 994)
Lai, Thanhhà. Inside Out & Back Again. (p. 877)
—Listen, Slowly. (p. 1022)
Laible MBA, Steve William, ed. see Nevis, Lance.

Laible, Steve William, ed. see Beggs, Melissa.
Laible, Steve William, ed. Dandylion. Berry, VacieAnna, illus. (p. 403)
Laidlaw, Jill. Cities. (p. 322)
—Energy. (p. 528)
—Water. (p. 1862)
Laidlaw, Jill, jt. auth. see Pitamic, Maja.
Laidlaw, Jill A. Cities. (p. 322)
—Energy. (p. 528)
—Frida Kahlo. (p. 637)
—Quick Expert: Ancient Egypt. (p. 1427)
—Roman City Guidebook. (p. 1485)
—Visit Egypt! (p. 1845)
Laidlaw, Rob. 5 Elephants (p. 1992)
—Cat Champions: Caring for Our Feline Friends. (p. 277)
—No Shelter Here: Making the World a Kinder Place for Dogs. (p. 1260)
—On Parade: The Hidden World of Animals in Entertainment (p. 1289)
—Saving Lives & Changing Hearts: Animal Sanctuaries & Rescue Centers (p. 1517)
—Wild Animals in Captivity (p. 1928)
Laidley, Victoria, illus. see Kielburger, Craig.
Laletta, Luann. Tonka the Special Puppy. (p. 1765)
LAIKA. Boxtrolls: Make Your Own Boxtroll Punch-Out Activity Book. (p. 217)
LAIKA & Fox, Jennifer. Boxtrolls: Meet the Boxtrolls. (p. 217)
Lailah, Daniel, photos by see Schapira, Leah & Dwek, Victoria.
Lai-Ma, jt. auth. see Lai-Ma.
Lai-Ma & Lai-Ma. Monster of Palapala Mountain. Lai-Ma, illus. (p. 1168)
Laine, Grannie. Good Night, Block Island. (p. 699)
Lainez, René Colato. From North to South. Cepeda, Joe, illus. (p. 643)
—From North to South/Del Norte Al Sur. Cepeda, Joe, illus. (p. 643)
—I Am Rene, the Boy. Graullera, Fabiola, illus. (p. 833)
—Juguemos Al Futbol y Al Football!/Let's Play Futbol & Football! (p. 932)
—My Shoes & I. Broeck, Fabricio Vanden, illus. (p. 1218)
—Playing Loteria Mexicana: El Juego de la Loteria Mexicana. Arena, Jillayne, illus. (p. 1372)
—René Has Two Last Names/René Tiene Dos Apellidos. Lainez, René Colato & Graullera Ramírez, Fabiola, illus. (p. 1460)
—Señor Pancho Had a Rancho. Smith, Elwood, illus. (p. 1550)
—Señor Pancho Had a Rancho & Old MacDonald Had a Farm. Smith, Elwood H., illus. (p. 1550)
—Tooth Fairy Meets el Ratón Pérez. Lintern, Tom, illus. (p. 1768)
—Waiting for Papá/Esperando a Papá. Accardo, Anthony, illus. (p. 1853)
Laing, Amy Wilson. Ginger Helps Spikey. (p. 677)
Laing, David. Forest Shadows. (p. 618)
—Forest Spirit. (p. 618)
Laing, Ishmael. Better Now or Then? (p. 172)
Laing, Marilyn. Why the Turtle & the Snail Carried their Houses on Their Back. (p. 1926)
Laing, Robin. Whisky Muse: Collected & Introduced by Robin Laing. Dewar, Bob, illus. (p. 1912)
Laing, Sarah, illus. see Jansen, Adrienne, ed.
Laing, Zhivargo, jt. auth. see Burrows, David M.
Lair, Diane, jt. auth. see Diane Lair, Lair.
Lairamore, Dawn. Ivy & the Meanstalk. (p. 901)
—Ivy's Ever After. (p. 901)
Laird, Charlton. Webster's New World Thesaurus. (p. 1870)
Laird, Chynna. Dark Water. (p. 408)
Laird, Chynna T. Don't Rush Me! For Siblings of Children with Sensory Processing Disorder (SPD) (p. 468)
—I'm Not Weird, I Have Sensory Processing Disorder (SPD) Alexandra's Journey. (p. 859)
Laird, Donivee M. Ula Li'i & the Magic Shark. Jossem, Carol, illus. (p. 1809)
—Will Wai Kula & the Three Mongooses. Jossem, Carol, illus. (p. 1932)
Laird, Donivee Martin. Magic Shark Learns to Cook. Johnson, Carol Ann, illus. (p. 1073)
Laird, Elizabeth. Beautiful Bananas Pichon, Liz, illus. (p. 153)
—Beautiful Bananas. Pichon, Liz, tr. (p. 153)
—Betrayal of Maggie Blair. (p. 171)
—Little Piece of Ground. Neal, Bill, illus. (p. 1033)
—Lost Riders (p. 1056)
—Oranges in No Man's Land. (p. 1302)
—Red Sky in the Morning. (p. 1455)
—Secrets of the Fearless (p. 1545)
—Shahnameh: The Persian Book of Kings. Adl, Shirin, illus. (p. 1558)
—Shahnameh. Adl, Shirin, illus. (p. 1558)
—Two Crafty Jackals: The Animal Fables of Kalilah & Dimnah. Sadig bai Afshar & Beg, Sadiqi, illus. (p. 1803)
Laird, Elizabeth, jt. auth. see Vincent, Jenny.
Laird, Elizabeth & Davison, Roz. Jungle School. Sim, David, illus. (p. 935)
Laird, Elizabeth & Quarto Generic Staff. Ogress & the Snake: And Other Stories from Somalia. Fowles, Shelley, illus. (p. 1280)
Laird, Johnna M. Southwest: New Mexico, Oklahoma, Texas (p. 1617)
Laird, Judie. I Don't Want to Play the Piano! (p. 838)
—Jane's Special Day. (p. 908)
—Lori Takes Piano Lessons. (p. 1053)
Laird, Lisa, tr. see Tracqui, Valérie.
Laird, Lisa J. I'm the Only One Who Loves Cliff the Goat. (p. 860)
Laird, Peter, jt. auth. see Eastman, Kevin B.
Laisney, Sarah. Ice Flowers & Pomegranates (p. 850)
Lait, Alain le. It's So Good (p. 899)
Laiug, Naucie, illus. see Ashley, Jane, IV.
Laiz, Jana. Elephants of the Tsunami. Cafiero, Tara, illus. (p. 512)
—Thomas & Autumn. Lamb, Melody, illus. (p. 1737)
Lajeunesse, Nicolas, illus. see Fournier, Chantal.
Lajic, Maïté, illus. see Mariolle, Mathieu.
Lajiness, Katie. Adam Sandler. (p. 11)
—Pharrell Williams. (p. 1350)
Lake, A. J. Book of the Sword. (p. 212)
—Circle of Stone. (p. 321)
—Coming of Dragons: The Darkest Age. (p. 348)
Lake, Autumn. Terrible Day. (p. 1721)
Lake, Darlene A. Leaf Collecting & Preserving Made Easy. (p. 982)
Lake, Donna C. Big Sister. (p. 183)
Lake, James H., ed. see Shakespeare, William.
Lake, Jay. Rocket Science. (p. 1483)
Lake, Julie. Galveston's Summer of the Storm. (p. 654)
Lake, Mary. Piccolo. Collier, Kevin Scott, illus. (p. 1354)
Lake, Nick. Betrayal of the Living. (p. 171)
—Blood Ninja. (p. 200)
—Hostage Three. (p. 801)
—In Darkness. (p. 863)
—Revenge of Lord Oda. (p. 1465)
—There Will Be Lies. (p. 1730)
Lake, Oliver, illus. see Belle, Trixie & Caruso-Scott, Melissa.
Lake, Oliver, illus. see Mack, Tracy, et al.
Lake, Sam. Sticker Picture Atlas of the World. (p. 1650)
Lake, Susan. Ebony & the Five Dwarfs. (p. 502)
Laker, Rosalind, pseud. Venetian Mask. (p. 1835)
Lakes, Lofton & Metu. Dream Team. (p. 484)
Lakeshore Learning Materials Staff. Is Your Mama a Llama? Big Book Theme Packet. (p. 890)
Lakeshore Learning Materials Staff, contrib. by. Big Book of Learning Songs. (p. 179)
—Big Surprise: A Homophone Story (p. 184)
—Big Surprise: A Homophone Story Big Book. (p. 184)
—Game: A Multiple Meaning Story (p. 654)
—Game: A Multiple Meaning Story Big Book. (p. 654)
—Great Race: A Synonym Story (p. 718)
—Great Race: A Synonym Story Big Book. (p. 718)
—Partner Reading Book Set. (p. 1325)
—Read & Learn Nonfiction: Maps, Charts, & Graphs (p. 1442)
—Read & Learn Nonfiction: Bold Words & Glossaries (p. 1442)
—Read & Learn Nonfiction: Photos, Captions, & Diagrams (p. 1442)
—Read & Learn Nonfiction: Maps, Charts, & Graphs Big Book. (p. 1442)
—Read & Learn Nonfiction: Bold Words & Glossaries Big Book. (p. 1442)
—Read & Learn Nonfiction: Photos, Captions, & Diagrams Big Book. (p. 1442)
—Read-along Alphabet Chants: Big Book. (p. 1442)
—Read-along Alphabet Chants: Student Books. (p. 1442)
—Reading Comprehension Mystery Readers (p. 1445)
—Spanish Alphabet Big Book. (p. 1620)
—Spanish Emergent Readers: Set of 8 Books. (p. 1621)
—Special Gift: An Antonym Story (p. 1623)
—Special Gift: An Antonym Story Big Book. (p. 1623)
—Storyteller Complete Library: CD Version. (p. 1663)
Lakhani, Anisha. Schooled. (p. 1523)
Lakhous, Amara. Clash of Civilizations over an Elevator in Piazza Vittorio. Goldstein, Ann, tr. from ITA. (p. 327)
Lakin, Patricia. Abigail Adams: First Lady of the American Revolution. Bandelin, Debra & Dacey, Bob, illus. (p. 5)
—Abigail Adams: First Lady of the American Revolution. Dacey, Bob & Bandelin, Debra, illus. (p. 5)
—Albert Einstein: Genius of the Twentieth Century. Daniel, Alan & Daniel, Lea, illus. (p. 34)
—Amelia Earhart: Amelia Earhart: More Than A Flier. Daniel, Alan & Daniel, Lea, illus. (p. 58)
—Bruno & Lulu's Playground Adventures. Edmunds, Kirstie, illus. (p. 232)
—Clara Barton: Spirit of the American Red Cross. Sullivan, Simon, illus. (p. 326)
—Clara Barton Spirit of the American Red Cross. Sullivan, Simon, illus. (p. 326)
—Max & Mo Go Apple Picking. Floca, Brian, illus. (p. 1110)
—Max & Mo Make a Snowman. Floca, Brian, illus. (p. 1110)
—Max & Mo's First Day at School. Floca, Brian, illus. (p. 1110)
—Max & Mo's Halloween Surprise. Floca, Brian, illus. (p. 1110)
—Muddy, Mud, Bud. Atkinson, Cale, illus. (p. 1189)
—Steve Jobs: Thinking Differently. (p. 1649)
Lakin, Patricia, et al. Amelia Earhart: More Than a Flier. Daniel, Alan & Daniel, Lea, illus. (p. 58)
Lakin, Sunny. Family for Anca. (p. 568)
Lakritz, Deborah. Joey & the Giant Box. Byrne, Mike, illus. (p. 920)
—Say Hello, Lily. Avilés, Martha, illus. (p. 1518)
Laks Gorman, Jacqueline. Alcalde (Mayor) (p. 35)
—Bus Drivers / Conductores de Autobuses. Andersen, Gregg, photos by. (p. 244)
—Firefighters / Bomberos. Andersen, Gregg, photos by. (p. 591)
—Gobernador (Governor) (p. 688)
—Juez (Judge) (p. 931)
—Librarians. Andersen, Gregg, photos by. (p. 1005)
—Librarians / Bibliotecarios. Andersen, Gregg, photos by. (p. 1005)
—Miembro del Congreso (Member of Congress) (p. 1139)
—Police Officers / Policías. Andersen, Gregg, photos by. (p. 1380)
—Vicepresidente (Vice President) (p. 1840)
Laks Gorman, Jacqueline, jt. auth. see Gorman, Jacqueline Laks.
Laks, Shan. Tale of Brave Ritchie: Be Aware of Strangers; Beat the Bullies & Exercise Changes Health. (p. 1699)
Laky, Esther. Just Fairy Tales. (p. 938)
Lal, Anupa, tr. Premchand Selected Stories. (p. 1395)
Lal, Neeta. Whisker Cats: Life on the Farm. (p. 1912)
Lal, Ranjit. Caterpillar Who Went on a Diet & Other Stories. (p. 279)
Lal, Sunandini Arora, jt. auth. see Seward, Pat.
Lalana, Fernando. Secreto de la Arboleda. (p. 1544)
Lalana, Fernando & Almarcegui, Jose María. Bomba. (p. 208)
Lale, Tim. We Can Trust the Bible: Helping Children Understand Where the Bible Came From. (p. 1866)
Lalliberete, Louise-Andree, illus. see Wishinsky, Frieda.
Lalliberté, Louise-Andrée, illus. see Wishinsky, Frieda.
Lalliberte, Mario. Match, Sort & Play. (p. 1104)
Lalliberte, Michelle. Marijuana: A MyReportLinks. com Book. (p. 1094)
—Seven Wonders of the Ancient World: A MyReportLinks.com Book. Johnson, Howard David, illus. (p. 1555)
—What Are the 7 Wonders of the Ancient World? (p. 1879)
Lalicki, Tom. Danger in the Dark: A Houdini & Nate Mystery. (p. 403)
—Shots at Sea: A Houdini & Nate Mystery. (p. 1569)
Lalla, C. R. Wiggles & Wags Tale: Coming Home. (p. 1928)
Lalla, Christine, photos by see Oxlade, Chris.
Lallemand, Orianne. Wolf Who Didn't Want to Walk. Thuillier, Eleonore, illus. (p. 1944)
—Wolf Who Wanted to Change His Color. Thuillier, Eleonore, illus. (p. 1944)
—Wolf Who Wanted to Travel the World. Thuillier, Eleonore, illus. (p. 1944)
Lalley, Kristine. Busy Bees. (p. 245)
—How Many Legs? Learning to Multiply Using Repeated Addition. (p. 811)
—How Many Legs? Learning to Multiply Using Repeated Action. (p. 811)
—Show & Tell. (p. 1570)
Lalli, Judy. I Like Being Me: Poems for Children about Feeling Special, Appreciating Others, & Getting Along. Mason-Fry, Douglas L., photos by. (p. 841)
L'Allier, Peter Wesley Thomas. Rotten Robbie & the Legend of Wanabinoo. (p. 1490)
Lallouz, Michele. Adventures of Cali. Nielson, Ginger, illus. (p. 17)
Lally, Cory, illus. see Serino, Robert.
Lalonde, Carolyn. Hide Tommy Turkey. Lalonde, Johnathan, illus. (p. 777)
LaLonde, Deanna L., illus. see Ell, Flynn J.
Lalonde, Johnathan, illus. see Lalonde, Carolyn.
Lalor, Liz. Homeopathic Guide to Partnership & Compatibility: Understanding Your Type & Finding Love. (p. 793)
Lalwani, Shalaka. Mrs. Mulberry's Winter (p. 1187)
Lam, Fiona Tinwei. Rainbow Rocket. (p. 1436)
Lam, Laura. Pantomime. (p. 1321)
Lam, Maple, illus. see Cordell, Ryan & Cordell, Evie.
LaMachia, Dawn. Inclined Planes at Work. (p. 869)
—Levers at Work. (p. 1004)
—Pulleys at Work. (p. 1416)
—Screws at Work. (p. 1533)
—Wedges at Work. (p. 1871)
—Wheels & Axles. (p. 1900)
—Wheels & Axles at Work. (p. 1900)
LaMachia, John. So What Is Patriotism Anyway? (p. 1602)
—So What Is Tolerance Anyway? (p. 1602)
Lamadrid, Enrique R. Amadito & the Hero Children: Amadito y Los Niños Héroes. Córdova, Amy, illus. (p. 51)
—Amadito & the Hero Children: Amadito y los Ninos Héroes. Cordova, Amy, illus. (p. 51)
Lamadrid, Enrique R., tr. see Anaya, Rudolfo A.
Lamadrid, Enrique R., tr. see Anaya, Rudolfo A. & Anaya, Rudolfo.
Lamadrid, Enrique R., tr. see Anaya, Rudolfo.
Lamadrid, Enrique R. & Arellano, Juan Estevan. Juan the Bear & the Water of Life: La Acequia de Juan del Oso. Córdova, Amy, illus. (p. 930)
Laman, Judi-Lynn. 10 Most Bizarre Animal Habits. (p. 1993)
Laman, Judi-Lynn, jt. auth. see Gunby, Shirley.
Laman, Tim, photos by see Lawler, Janet.
Laman, Tim & Knott, Cheryl. Face to Face with Orangutans. (p. 560)
Lamana, Julie T. Three Little Bayou Fishermen. (p. 1742)
—Upside down in the Middle of Nowhere. (p. 1825)
Lamanna, Paolo, illus. see Colfer, Eoin & Donkin, Andrew.
Lamar, Brad A. Megalith Union. Adasikov, Igor, illus. (p. 1124)
Lamar, Gail Renfroe. Moon of the Wishing Night. Mask, Cynthia, illus. (p. 1172)
Lamar, Lloyd. Pond. (p. 1382)
Lamar, Melvin. Call to Be Different. (p. 254)
Lamar, William W., jt. auth. see Campbell, Jonathan A.
LaMarca, Luke, illus. see Berry, Lynne.
LaMarca, Luke, illus. see Johnson, Angela.
LaMarche, Jim. Elves & the Shoemaker. (p. 517)
LaMarche, Jim, illus. see Brown, Margaret Wise.
LaMarche, Jim, illus. see Clements, Andrew.
LaMarche, Jim, illus. see Hanson, Warren.
LaMarche, Jim, illus. see Johnston, Tony.
LaMarche, Jim, illus. see Melmed, Laura Krauss.
LaMarche, Jim, illus. see Napoli, Donna Jo.
LaMarche, Jim, illus. see Rubel, David.
LaMarche, Jim, illus. see Wells, Rosemary.
LaMarche, Una. Like No Other. (p. 1017)
Lamarche, Una. Like No Other. (p. 1017)
Lamaro, Glenda. Max Goes to Kindy. Ratyna, Linda, illus. (p. 1111)
La-Marr, Chiquita. Sally's Adventures. (p. 1505)
Lamartina-Lens, Iride, ed. see Clua, Guillem.
Lamas, Blanca Rosa, tr. see Romanelli, Serena.
LaMaster, Melissa. Appaloosa Tales with a Christmas Spirit. (p. 92)
Lamb. Bianca the Dancing Crocodile. Skon, Sandy, illus. (p. 175)
Lamb, Albert. Tell Me the Day Backwards. McPhail, David, illus. (p. 1716)
Lamb, Amy And Chris. Our World Series: Friends around our Home. (p. 1310)
Lamb, Braden. Adventure Time. Paroline, Shelli, illus. (p. 14)
Lamb, Braden, illus. see North, Ryan.
Lamb, Branden, illus. see Monroe, Caleb & Paroline, Shelli.
Lamb, Branden, illus. see Monroe, Caleb.
Lamb, Branden, jt. auth. see Monroe, Caleb.
Lamb, Branden, jt. auth. see North, Ryan.
Lamb, Branden & Boom Studios Staff. Ice Age: Where There's Thunder. Paroline, Shelli, illus. (p. 850)
Lamb, Charles. Adventures of Ulysses. (p. 24)
—Tales from Shakespeare (p. 1701)
Lamb, Charles & Lamb, Mary. Shakespeare Cuenta. (p. 1559)
—Tales from Shakespeare: "Othello" Strang, Kay, ed. (p. 1701)
—Tales from Shakespeare: "King Lear" Strang, Kay, ed. (p. 1701)
—Tales from Shakespeare: "Twelfth Night" Strang, Kay, ed. (p. 1701)
—Tales from Shakespeare: "A Midsummer Night's Dream" Strang, Kay, ed. (p. 1701)
—Tales from Shakespeare. (p. 1701)
—Tales from Shakespeare. Jolivet, Joëlle, illus. (p. 1701)
—Ten Tales from Shakespeare. (p. 1719)
Lamb, Enelle. Christopher Collin & the True Okemus - the Adventure Begins. (p. 316)
Lamb, Harold A. Marching Sands. (p. 1092)
Lamb II, James. Jimmy Jimmy el Cordero Salto Cumple Phil el Pato. (p. 918)
Lamb, Iner. Relics of Ancient America. (p. 1458)
Lamb, Janie, illus. see Renshaw, Douglas.
Lamb, Jim. Ryan the Lion Finds His Roar. Schallmo, Carolyn, illus. (p. 1499)
Lamb, Jody. Easter Ann Peters' Operation Cool. (p. 499)
Lamb, Jowana. Makhi & the Run Away Elephant. (p. 1080)
Lamb, Karen, illus. see Rowsell, Cyrilla & Vinden, David.
Lamb, Lee. Oak Island Family: The Restall Hunt for Buried Treasure. (p. 1274)
—Oak Island Family: The Restall Hunt for Buried Treasure (Large Print 16pt) (p. 1274)
Lamb, Lenny. Facing Your Fears: Greener Grass Volume 4. (p. 561)
—Moving Blues: Greener Grass. (p. 1183)
—Truth about Lying: Greener Grass Volume 3. (p. 1794)
Lamb, Mary. Mrs. Leicester's School, 1809. (p. 1187)
Lamb, Mary, jt. auth. see Lamb, Charles.
Lamb, Melody, illus. see Laiz, Jana.
Lamb, Michael, illus. see Lamb, Phillip C.
Lamb, Pamela. No Everyday Dragon. (p. 1258)
—Seeking Sarah. (p. 1548)
Lamb, Phillip C. Ace Canary & Dud Clutch. Lamb, Michael, illus. (p. 8)
Lamb, Ros, et al. New Livewire (p. 1246)
Lamb, Rosy. Paul Meets Bernadette. Lamb, Rosy, illus. (p. 1330)
Lamb, Sally Ann, illus. see Roddie, Shen & Quarto Generic Staff.
Lamb, Sandra, illus. see Coulman, Valerie.
Lamb, Stacey. 123 Sticker Book. (p. 2000)
—ABC. (p. 3)
—ABC Coloring Book with Stickers. (p. 3)
—Colors Sticker Coloring Book. (p. 345)
—Shapes Sticker Book. Lamb, Stacey, illus. (p. 1561)
—Wipe Clean 123 Book. (p. 1939)
—Wipe Clean Alphabet Book. (p. 1939)
—Wipe Clean First Letters. (p. 1939)
—Wipe Clean Ready for Writing. (p. 1939)
—Wipe-Clean Doodles. (p. 1939)
—Wipe-Clean Dot-To-Dot. (p. 1939)
—Wipe-Clean Mazes. (p. 1939)
Lamb, Stacey, illus. see Bowman, Crystal.
Lamb, Stacey, illus. see Taplin, Sam.
Lamb, Stacey, et al. My First Christmas Activity Book. (p. 1206)
Lamb, Stacy. First Puzzles. (p. 596)
Lamb, Steven. Eliot. (p. 513)
Lamb, Susan Condie, illus. see Houston, Gloria M.
Lamb, Susan Condie, illus. see Stutson, Caroline.
Lamb, T. S., illus. see Oddo, Jennifer M.
Lamb, Tanya. Kyle's One Day Adventures. (p. 969)
Lamb, Victoria. Witchfall. (p. 1941)
—Witchrise. (p. 1941)
—Witchstruck. (p. 1942)
Lamballe, Jérôme. Curious Story of Pablo Picasslug. (p. 394)
Lambdin, Victor R., illus. see Hall, Jennie.
Lambe, Jennifer Holloway. Kudzu Chaos Lyne, Alison Davis, illus. (p. 968)
Lambe, Mona. Yintin Tales. (p. 1971)
Lambe, Steve, illus. see Golden Books Staff & Smith, Geof.
Lambe, Steve, illus. see Golden Books Staff.
Lamberson, Karen, jt. auth. see Lamberson, Scott.
Lamberson, Scott & Lamberson, Karen. Professor Clark the Science Shark: Going Home. (p. 1409)
—Professor Clark the Science Shark: The Beginning. (p. 1409)
—Professor Clark the Science Shark: the Encounter: Book 3. (p. 1409)
Lambert, Alan & Scott-Hughes, Brian. Junior Drama Workshop. (p. 936)
Lambert, Alix. Russian Prison Tattoos: Codes of Authority, Domination, & Struggle (p. 1498)
Lambert, Andy, jt. auth. see McNaney, Lowell.
Lambert, Angela. Animals. (p. 81)
Lambert, Barbara, ed. see Van Slyke, Marge.
Lambert, Carol D. New Dawn. (p. 1244)
Lambert, Carol Davis. When Day Is Done. (p. 1901)
Lambert, Celeste, illus. see Lambert, George J.
Lambert, Chad, jt. auth. see Anderson, Matt.
Lambert, Cheryl A. Bird That Couldn't Sing. (p. 190)
Lambert, Clercina. Indifferent Twin: Outside Beauty Will Fade Away but Inside Beauty Will Last for a Lifetime. (p. 872)
Lambert, David. Dinosaur. (p. 441)
Lambert, Deborah. Adjectives. (p. 13)
—Adverbs. (p. 25)
—Nouns. (p. 1268)
—Pronouns. (p. 1411)
—Verbs. (p. 1836)
Lambert, George J. 8 Boys & 8 Beasts Lambert, Celeste, illus. (p. 1993)
—There's a Barn up Ahead, There's a Barn! (p. 1730)
Lambert, Haley. Fishy Tales: The Bark Is Worse Than the Byten. (p. 599)
Lambert, Hines. Hunting Deer. (p. 829)
—Hunting Ducks. (p. 829)
—Hunting Moose & Elk. (p. 829)
—Hunting Quail & Pheasants. (p. 829)
—Hunting Rabbits. (p. 829)
—Hunting Turkeys. (p. 829)
Lambert, Janet. Big Deal: Cinda Hollister Story. (p. 181)
—Boy Wanted. (p. 219)
—Cinda. (p. 319)
—Extra Special: A Patty & Ginger Story. (p. 555)
—Fly Away Cinda: A Cinda Hollister Story. (p. 609)

—Hi Neighbor: A Sugar Bradley Story. (p. 775)
—Just Jenifer. (p. 938)
—Love to Spare: Cinda Hollister Story. (p. 1060)
—On Her Own. (p. 1289)
—Spring Fever. (p. 1635)
—Summer Madness. (p. 1674)
—Sweet As Sugar: A Sugar Bradley Story. (p. 1689)
—Triple Trouble. (p. 1787)
—We're Going Steady: A Patty & Ginger Story. (p. 1875)
—Where the Heart Is: A Christy Drayton Story. (p. 1909)
Lambert, Jeffrey. Before Christmas Was Called Christmas. (p. 158)
Lambert, Jonathan, illus. see Faulkner, Keith & Tyger, Rory.
Lambert, Jonathan, illus. see Faulkner, Keith.
Lambert, Jonathan, illus. see Goldhawk, Emma.
Lambert, Joyce. Slick 'n Slide. Metzger, Jan, illus. (p. 1590)
Lambert, Kate. Can I Tell You about Epilepsy? A Guide for Friends, Family & Professionals. Hellier, Scott, illus. (p. 258)
Lambert, Kelly. Sounds of a Coo. (p. 1615)
Lambert, Kristina. Lily's Treasure Map. (p. 1018)
Lambert, Lorene. Forgotten Explorer? The Story of Amerigo Vespucci. Mickle, Jed, illus. (p. 619)
Lambert, Mark John. 10 Most Incredible Landforms. (p. 1994)
Lambert, Martha. I Won't Get Lost. (p. 849)
Lambert, Megan. Crow of His Own. Costello, David, illus. (p. 386)
Lambert, Megan Dowd. Crow of His Own. Costello, David & Costello, David Hyde, illus. (p. 386)
Lambert, Monica & Algozzine, Bob. Strategies That Make Learning Fun. (p. 1666)
Lambert, Nat. Brain Busting Workout. Green, Barry, illus. (p. 221)
—Brain Workout. Green, Barry, illus. (p. 222)
Lambert, Noelle. Can I Play Too? (p. 258)
Lambert, Page, ed. see Swick, Carmen D.
Lambert, Patricia. Blue Ribbon Chicken. (p. 203)
Lambert, Roy. Lamb, the Hip Cat Daddy. (p. 972)
Lambert, Sally Anne, illus. see Fleming, Candace.
Lambert, Sally Anne, illus. see Macomber, Debbie & Carney, Mary Lou.
Lambert, Sally Anne, illus. see Tegen, Katherine Brown.
Lambert, Sally Anne, illus. see Tegen, Katherine.
Lambert, Sally Anne & Hodgson, Karen J. Teeny-Weeny Walking Stick. (p. 1715)
Lambert, Shirley. Tales of Beaver Hollow: The Magic Flute (p. 1702)
Lambert, Stephen, illus. see Birch, Beverley.
Lambert, Stephen, illus. see Crebbin, June.
Lambert, Stephen, illus. see Khan, Sarah.
Lambert, Stephen, illus. see MacCaughrean, Geraldine, et al.
Lambert, Stephen, illus. see Wood, A. J.
Lambert, Steve, et al. Microsoft(r) Office Access 2007. (p. 1136)
Lambert, Susan Dodd. Clarence the Clam. Modugno, Tina, illus. (p. 327)
Lambert, Teres. Mommy, Do You Love Me? (p. 1162)
Lamberth, Christine, ed. see Gugliuzza, Susan M.
Lamberti, B. J. Nelson Paige under the Turquoise Sky. (p. 1241)
Lambeth, Amy. Body. (p. 206)
Lamblase, Lauren, illus. see Conkling, Keri.
Lambil, Willy, illus. see Cauvin, Raoul.
Lambil, Willy & Raoul, Cauvin. Blues in Black & White. (p. 204)
Lambillion, Paul. Staying Cool. (p. 1645)
Lambke, Bryan & Lambke, Tom. I Just Am. (p. 840)
Lambke, Tom, jt. auth. see Lambke, Bryan.
Lambo, Don, illus. see Mulcahy, Lucille.
Lamborn, Florence, tr. see Lindgren, Astrid.
Lambson, Elizabeth, illus. see Gill, Janie S.
Lambson, Elizabeth, illus. see Spaht-Gill, Janie.
Lamedman, Debbie. Teen Drama Student's Guide to Laying the Foundation for A. (p. 1713)
—Twenty 10-Minute Plays For Teens By Teens (p. 1801)
—Ultimate Audition Book for Teens: 111 Monologues from Classical Theater, 2 Minutes & Under. Vol. II (p. 1809)
—Ultimate Audition Book for Teens: 111 Monologues from Classical Literature, 2 Minutes & Under Vol. III (p. 1809)
—Ultimate Audition Book for Teens IV: 111 One Minute Monologues. (p. 1809)
Lamensdorf, Len. Flying Dragon. (p. 609)
Lamere, Jill. King's Crown. (p. 960)
—Upside Down. Lamere, Jill, illus. (p. 1825)
—Wishing Star. (p. 1940)
Lamerton, Todd. Tale from Flurryville: The Berg's Big Surprise. (p. 1699)
Lamia, Mary C. Emotions! Making Sense of Your Feelings. (p. 520)
—Understanding Myself: A Kid's Guide to Intense Emotions & Strong Feelings. (p. 1816)
Lamichhane, Priyanka, ed. see U. S. National Geographic Society Staff.
Lamichhane, Shiva. Golden Ball in a Piggy Bank. (p. 694)
Laminack, Lester. Saturdays & Teacakes. (p. 1515)
—Three Hens & a Peacock Cole, Henry, illus. (p. 1742)
Laminack, Lester & Laminack, Lester L. Cracking Open the Author's Craft: Teaching the Art of Writing. (p. 375)
Laminack, Lester L. Jake's 100th Day of School Love, Judy, illus. (p. 906)
—Saturdays & Teacakes Soentpiet, Chris K., illus. (p. 1515)
—Snow Day! Gustavson, Adam, illus. (p. 1598)
—Three Hens & a Peacock Cole, Henry, illus. (p. 1742)
Laminack, Lester L., jt. auth. see Laminack, Lester.
Lamison, C., jt. auth. see Shulman, Mark.
Lamkin, Robert J. Tommy's Train. (p. 1765)
Lamm, C. Drew. Screech Owl at Midnight Hollow. Snyder, Joel, illus. (p. 1533)
—Woodchuck at Blackberry Road. Davis, Allen, illus. (p. 1949)
Lamm, Drew. Sea Lion Swims. Cohen, Jessie, photos by. (p. 1534)
Lamm, Drew C. Cottontail at Clover Crescent. (p. 369)
—Cottontail at Clover Crescent. Davis, Allen, illus. (p. 369)
Lammers, Elizabeth A. & McKinney, Dan. Pierre's Stupendous Birthday Bash. Epstein, Gabriela, illus. (p. 1357)
—Tale of the Black Igloo: Another Adventure of Pepe & Pierre Epstein, Gabriela, illus. (p. 1700)
Lammertink, Ilona. Don't Be Afraid to Say No! Georger, Lucie, illus. (p. 466)
Lamming, George. In the Castle of My Skin. (p. 865)
Lammle, Leslie. Once upon a Saturday. Lammle, Leslie, illus. (p. 1293)
—Princess Wannabe. Lammle, Leslie, illus. (p. 1406)
Lammle, Leslie, illus. see Kramer, Andrew.
Lamond, Margete & Zak, Drahos. Frankenstein. (p. 629)
Lamond, Peter. Rainforest Family & Those Terrible Toads. Purnell, Teresa, illus. (p. 1436)
Lamonica, Lisa. On Halloween, I Love You As Big As the Moon. (p. 1289)
—You & Me As Big As the Se. (p. 1973)
Lamonica, Tracey. Adventures of Sammie: The Rescue. (p. 22)
Lamont, Jess. Peter's Garden. (p. 1347)
Lamont, Kelton. Super K: The Attack of the Popcorn Chicken. (p. 1680)
Lamont, Priscilla. Nursery Rhyme Crimes: Little Bo Peep. (p. 1273)
Lamont, Priscilla, illus. see Barkow, Henriette.
Lamont, Priscilla, illus. see Dowdy, Linda Cress.
Lamont, Priscilla, illus. see George, Jean Craighead.
Lamont, Priscilla, illus. see McKay, Hilary.
Lamont, Priscilla, illus. see Pasquali, Elena.
Lamont, Priscilla, illus. see Rosen, Michael & Quarto Generic Staff.
Lamont, Priscilla, illus. see Stauffacher, Sue.
Lamont, Priscilla, illus. see Zoehfeld, Kathleen Weidner.
Lamont, Tracey. Adventures of Speedy & Creedy: The Surprise. (p. 23)
—Adventures of Speedy & Creedy: Mrs. Smith's Kitchen. (p. 23)
Lamore, Garretta, jt. auth. see Noensie, Pamela.
La'more, Sheila. Runt: The Omega Wolf. (p. 1497)
Lamoreaux, M. A., illus. see Andersen, Hans Christian.
Lamoreaux, M. A., illus. see Stone Arch Books Staff.
Lamoreaux, Michelle, illus. see Andersen, Hans Christian.
Lamoreaux, Michelle, illus. see Capstone Press Staff.
Lamoreaux, Michelle, illus. see Graydon, Shari.
Lamoreaux, Michelle, illus. see Snowe, Olivia.
Lamoreaux, Michelle, illus. see Stone Arch Books Staff.
Lamoreaux, Robert D. Winning or Losing: The Financial & Retirement Race. (p. 1937)
Lamorisse. Ballon Rouge. (p. 135)
LaMothe, Karin Elaine. Angels' Lullaby. (p. 75)
LaMothe, Kimerer L. Nietzsche's Dancers: Isadora Duncan, Martha Graham, & the Revaluation of Christian Values. (p. 1251)
LaMotta, Margo. Bath Time Bubbles. (p. 144)
Lamotte, Andree, jt. auth. see Calais-Germain, Blandine.
Lamotte, Kathleen. Horsetrailer Mystery. (p. 800)
LaMountain, Jackie. God Did! Mrs. I's Lyrics for Little Ones. (p. 688)
Lamour, Frantz. Notre Pere un Tresor Non Exploite. (p. 1268)
Lampard, Frank. Frankie vs. the Cowboy's Crew. (p. 630)
—Frankie vs. the Mummy's Menace. (p. 630)
—Frankie vs. the Pirate Pillagers. (p. 630)
—Frankie vs. the Rowdy Romans. (p. 630)
Lampe, Ramona. Blue Ribbon Chickens. (p. 203)
—Calves in the Kitchen. (p. 255)
—Ruby, the Diva Clydesdale. (p. 1493)
—Santa & the Clydesdales. (p. 1511)
Lampe, Roberta Seiwert. Air Dog First Class. (p. 31)
—Bath & the Three Bears. (p. 144)
—Farm Girls' Revenge. (p. 574)
—Pig Wish. (p. 1357)
—Prairie Dog Pet. (p. 1392)
—Santa Fun Book One. (p. 1511)
—Santa Fun, Book Three. (p. 1511)
—Santa Fun, Book Two. (p. 1512)
—Spiders' Web. (p. 1627)
—Two Farm Cats. (p. 1803)
Lampen, John. Peace Kit. (p. 1331)
Lamperd, Laurel. Battle for Boodicuttup Creek. (p. 145)
Lamphere Slaughter, Sharyn. Anjelina Bobalina Concerto Juarez Small. (p. 84)
Lamphere-Slaughter, Sharyn. Droopy Drawers & the Peg Leg Pirate. (p. 485)
Lampkin, Laveta M. Where Is Grandmother? Nicely, Darthy, illus. (p. 1908)
Lampkins, Antonia. Favorite Things. (p. 578)
—Global Friends. (p. 684)
—My First Book Collection. (p. 1205)
Lampley, David Gerald. Shorty's Dilemm. (p. 1569)
Lampley, Titra. Jazzy Dolls & Swaggro's Get's Revenge on Bullies. (p. 911)
Lamplighter Staff. Boys of Grit Who Became Men Of. (p. 220)
—Boys of Grit Who Changed. (p. 220)
—Clean Your Boots Sir? (p. 330)
—Fireside Readings. (p. 592)
—Hidden Hand. (p. 775)
—Highland Chairman. (p. 779)
—Inheritance. (p. 874)
—Me & Nobbles. (p. 1115)
—Melody the Story of a Child. (p. 1125)
—Nobody Loves Me. (p. 1262)
—Probable Sons. (p. 1408)
—Stephen Soldier of the Cross. (p. 1648)
—Stick to the Raft. (p. 1650)
—Tales of the Restoration. (p. 1703)
—Teddys Button Hardcover. (p. 1713)
—Tom Gillies. (p. 1763)
—Tom Watkins Mistake. (p. 1764)
—True Princess. (p. 1792)
—What Is Her Name. (p. 1889)
Lampman, Annette. Nicole's Wish. (p. 1251)
Lampman, Evelyn Sibley. Shy Stegosaurus of Cricket Creek. Buel, Hubert, illus. (p. 1572)
Lamprell, Klay. Paris (p. 1324)
Lamprell, Klay, jt. auth. see Lonely Planet Publications Staff.
Lamprell, Klay & Lonely Planet Publications Staff. New York City: Everything You Ever Wanted to Know (p. 1248)
Lamprell, Penny, jt. auth. see Pinnington, Andrea.
Lamprey, L. Masters of the Guild. (p. 1103)
Lampshire Hayden, Gwendolen. Really Truly Stories #1/9 (p. 1450)
—Really Truly Stories #2/9. (p. 1450)
Lampson, Rosalie. Give Mom a Minute. (p. 681)
Lamson, Deborah Ann. Nativity Lighting. (p. 1235)
Lamson, Martha. Oliver. (p. 1285)
Lamson, Sharon, jt. auth. see Tuitel, Johnnie.
Lamstein, Sarah Marwil. Big Night for Salamanders. Benioff, Carol, illus. (p. 182)
—Hunger Moon. (p. 828)
Lamut, Sonja, illus. see Toscano, Charles.
LaMuth, John E. Ultimate Guide to Family Values: A Grand Unified Theory of Ethics & Morality. (p. 1809)
Lamuth, Nancy. Lucky & Me. Thomas, Richard A., illus. (p. 1062)
Lamy, Matt. Dead Strange: The Bizarre Truths Behind 50 World-Famous Mysteries. (p. 417)
—Dead Strange. (p. 417)
Lanagan, Margo. Brides of Rollrock Island. (p. 227)
—Red Spikes. (p. 1455)
—Tender Morsels. (p. 1719)
—White Time. (p. 1913)
—Yellowcake: Stories. (p. 1970)
—Yellowcake. (p. 1970)
Lanan, Jessica, illus. see Schoettler, Joan.
Lancaster, Cindy Clark. Flowers in the Desert. (p. 608)
Lancaster, Clay. American Bungalow, 1880-1930. (p. 60)
Lancaster, Derek, illus. see Wixom, Jason Kay & Wixom, Tedi Tuttle.
Lancaster, Gwen, et al. Working with Children's Phonology. Evershed-Martin, Susanna, ed. (p. 1953)
Lancaster, J. A. Joe Parker's Prophecy of Zargala. (p. 920)
Lancaster, Janie. Julie & the Lost Fairy Tale. (p. 932)
Lancaster, Juliana. PBIS- Building Big Things. (p. 1331)
—PBIS- Lift, Spin, Drop & Fall. (p. 1331)
—PBIS- Planetary Forecaster. (p. 1331)
Lancaster, Melinda. Tyler & the Spider. Gillen, Rosemarie, illus. (p. 1805)
Lancaster, Scott B. Fair Play: Making Organized Sports a Great Experience for Your Kids. (p. 562)
Lancaster, Shannon E. Becky: The Budding Ballerina. (p. 156)
Lancaster, Susan. Caves & the Skull. (p. 282)
—Diamond Talisman. (p. 434)
—Hell's Gate. (p. 765)
Lance, Charlotte. Really Super Hero. Lance, Charlotte, illus. (p. 1450)
Lance, John & Narvarro. Priscilla Holmes & the Case of the Glass Slipper. (p. 1407)
Lance, Scott. Pourman's Library. (p. 1389)
Lancett, Peter. Bridge of Dark Tears (p. 227)
—Bridge of Dark Tears. (p. 227)
—Danger in the Dark (p. 403)
—Dark Candle (p. 407)
—Dark Candle. (p. 407)
—Dark Dreams (p. 407)
—Dark Garden (p. 407)
—Dark Garden. (p. 407)
—Dark Glass (p. 407)
—Dark Machine (p. 407)
—Dark Machine. (p. 407)
—Dark Music (p. 407)
—Dark Music. (p. 407)
—Dark River (p. 408)
—Dark River. (p. 408)
—Dark Side of Magic (p. 408)
—Dark Waters of Time (p. 408)
—Dark Words (p. 408)
—Dark Words. (p. 408)
—Day Is Dark (p. 413)
—Day Is Dark. (p. 413)
—Dying for the Dark (p. 491)
—Dying for the Dark. (p. 491)
—Gun Dog. (p. 732)
—Killer in the Dark (p. 956)
—Killer in the Dark. (p. 956)
—Past Is Dark (p. 1327)
—Past Is Dark. (p. 1327)
—Playing the Dark Game (p. 1372)
—Playing the Dark Game. (p. 1372)
—Seeing Red (p. 1548)
—Seeing Red. (p. 1548)
—Shadow in the Dark (p. 1557)
Lanchais, Aurelie, et al. I Can Fly, What Am I? (p. 835)
—Kto A? (p. 968)
—What Am I? (p. 1879)
—Who Am I? (p. 1914)
Lanczkowski, Günter, jt. auth. see Kwiatkowski, Gerhard.
Land, Autumn. Monarch & the Monarch. (p. 1163)
Land Eagle, illus. see Packard, Mary.
Land, Fiona, illus. see Ackerman, Jill & Smith, Justine.
Land, Fiona, illus. see Ackerman, Jill.
Land, Fiona, illus. see Bird, Nicola.
Land, Fiona, illus. see Smith, Justine & Ackerman, Jill.
Land, Greg. Crossover. (p. 385)
Land, Greg, illus. see Edginton, Ian.
Land, Greg, illus. see Marz, Ron.
Land, Greg, illus. see Rucka, Greg, et al.
Land, Greg, jt. illus. see Dodson, Terry.
Land, Linda C. Mysterious Traveling Trunk. (p. 1223)
Land Management Bureau (U.S.), jt. ed. see Interior Dept. (U.S.).
Land of Milk and Honey Staff. ABC God Loves Me. (p. 3)
Land, Richard, jt. auth. see Strack, Jay.
Landa, Gertrude, jt. auth. see Naomi, Aunt.
Landa, Mariasun. Cuando Los Gatos Se Sienten Tan Solos. (p. 388)
Landa, Norbert. Little Bear & the Wishing Tree Mendez, Simon, illus. (p. 1024)
—Secret House of Papa Mouse. Turk, Hanne, illus. (p. 1541)
Landa, Norbert, jt. auth. see Baeuerle, Patrick A.
Landau, Abraham, et al. Branded on My Arm & in My Soul: A Holocaust Memoir. (p. 222)
—Branded on My Arm & in My Soul: The Holocaust Memoir of Abraham Landau. (p. 222)
Landau, Donna, illus. see MansBach, Sara.
Landau, Elaine. Alamo: Would You Join the Fight? (p. 33)
—Alcohol. (p. 35)
—Alligators & Crocodiles: Hunters of the Night. (p. 47)
—American Flag. (p. 60)
—American Quarter Horses Are My Favorite! (p. 63)
—American Shorthairs Are the Best! (p. 63)
—Annie Oakley: Wild West Sharpshooter. (p. 87)
—Appaloosas Are My Favorite! (p. 92)
—Arabians Are My Favorite! (p. 94)
—Are the Drums for You? (p. 96)
—Assassins, Traitors, & Spies. (p. 107)
—Assassins/Traitors/Spies. (p. 107)
—Asthma. (p. 108)
—Bald Eagle. (p. 133)
—Bats: Hunters of the Night. (p. 145)
—Battle of Gettysburg: Would You Lead the Fight? (p. 146)
—Beagles Are the Best! (p. 150)
—Beluga Whales. (p. 163)
—Best Cats Ever (p. 168)
—Best Dogs Ever (p. 169)
—Beyoncé: R & B Superstar. (p. 173)
—Big Cats: Hunters of the Night. (p. 180)
—Big Snakes: Hunters of the Night. (p. 184)
—Bill Pickett: Wild West Cowboy. (p. 186)
—Billy the Kid: Wild West Outlaw. (p. 187)
—Bites & Stings. (p. 194)
—Boston Tea Party: Would You Join the Revolution? (p. 215)
—Boston Terriers Are the Best! (p. 215)
—Boxers Are the Best! (p. 217)
—Broken Bones. (p. 230)
—Bulldogs Are the Best! (p. 240)
—Bumps, Bruises, & Scrapes. (p. 241)
—Burns. (p. 244)
—California Gold Rush: Would You Go for the Gold? (p. 253)
—Cavities & Toothaches. (p. 282)
—Celebrate the First Thanksgiving with Elaine Landau. (p. 284)
—Celebrate the Founding of America with Elaine Landau. (p. 284)
—Celebrating Columbus Day. (p. 284)
—Celebrating Earth Day. (p. 284)
—Celebrating St. Patrick's Day. (p. 285)
—Celebrating Veterans Day. (p. 285)
—Chickenpox. (p. 300)
—Cigarettes. (p. 319)
—Civil Rights Movement in America. (p. 325)
—Cocker Spaniels Are the Best! (p. 337)
—Common Cold. (p. 349)
—Crazy Horse: American Indian Leader. (p. 377)
—Creepy Spiders. (p. 381)
—Dachshunds Are the Best! (p. 398)
—Date Violence. (p. 409)
—Deadly High-Risk Jobs. (p. 417)
—Declaration of Independence: American History. (p. 422)
—Declaration of Independence. (p. 422)
—Dia de Accion de Gracias: Un Momento para Agradecer. Cinquemani, Romina C., tr. from ENG. (p. 433)
—Dia de Colon: Celebramos a un Explorador Famoso. (p. 433)
—Dia de San Valentin: Caramelos, Amor y Corazones. (p. 433)
—Discovering a New World: Would You Sail with Columbus? (p. 448)
—Dyslexia. (p. 491)
—Earaches. (p. 492)
—Easter: Parades, Chocolates, & Celebration. (p. 499)
—Egyptian Maus Are the Best! (p. 506)
—Ellis Island. (p. 515)
—Emancipation Proclamation: Would You Do What Lincoln Did? (p. 517)
—Emperor Penguins. (p. 521)
—Explore Colonial Jamestown with Elaine Landau. (p. 550)
—Exploring Ancient China with Elaine Landau. (p. 551)
—Exploring Ancient Egypt with Elaine Landau. (p. 551)
—Exploring Ancient Greece with Elaine Landau. (p. 551)
—Exploring Ancient Rome with Elaine Landau. (p. 551)
—Exploring the World of the Aztecs with Elaine Landau. (p. 554)
—Exploring the World of the Vikings. (p. 554)
—Family Therapy. (p. 568)
—Fearsome Alligators. (p. 579)
—Fever. (p. 583)
—Fierce Cats. (p. 584)
—Fleeing to Freedom on the Underground Railroad: The Courageous Slaves, Agents, & Conductors. (p. 603)
—Food Allergies. (p. 613)
—Food Poisoning & Foodborne Diseases. (p. 614)
—Friendly Foes: A Look at Political Parties. (p. 638)
—General Washington Crosses the Delaware: Would You Join the American Revolution? (p. 660)
—George Washington Crosses the Delaware: Would You Risk the Revolution? (p. 664)
—Gold Rush in California: Would You Catch Gold Fever? (p. 694)
—Golden Retrievers Are the Best! (p. 695)
—Great Battle of Gettysburg: Would You Stand & Fight? (p. 714)
—Great Danes Are the Best! (p. 715)
—Harp Seals: Animals of the Snow & Ice. (p. 749)
—Head Lice. (p. 756)
—Head-to-Toe Health (p. 756)
—Healthy Diet. (p. 759)
—History of Energy. (p. 784)
—Hunters of the Night. (p. 829)
—Is Singing for You? (p. 890)
—Is the Clarinet for You? (p. 890)
—Is the Flute for You? (p. 890)
—Is the Guitar for You? (p. 890)

L

—Is the Saxophone for You? (p. 890)
—Is the Trumpet for You? (p. 890)
—Is the Violin for You? (p. 890)
—Jefferson's Louisiana Purchase: Would You Make the Deal of the Century? (p. 912)
—Jesse James: Wild West Train Robber. (p. 914)
—Killer Bees. (p. 956)
—Labrador Retrievers Are the Best! (p. 970)
—Lincoln's Emancipation Proclamation: Would You Sign the Great Document? (p. 1019)
—Lipizzans Are My Favorite! (p. 1021)
—Louisiana Purchase: Would You Close the Deal? (p. 1059)
—Maine Coons Are the Best! (p. 1077)
—Manx Are the Best! (p. 1089)
—Mastiffs Are the Best! (p. 1103)
—Meet Ben Franklin with Elaine Landau. (p. 1120)
—Meth: America's Drug Epidemic. (p. 1130)
—Mexico. (p. 1131)
—Miniature Schnauzers Are the Best! (p. 1146)
—Morgan Horses Are My Favorite! (p. 1175)
—National Anthem. (p. 1231)
—Newfoundlands Are the Best! (p. 1249)
—Nosebleeds. (p. 1266)
—Oil Spill! Disaster in the Gulf of Mexico. (p. 1282)
—Oregon Trail. (p. 1303)
—Owls: Hunters of the Night. (p. 1315)
—Persians Are the Best! (p. 1344)
—Pink Eye. (p. 1359)
—Pit Bulls Are the Best! (p. 1364)
—Polar Bears: Hunters of the Snow & Ice. (p. 1379)
—Pomeranians Are the Best! (p. 1382)
—Poodles Are the Best! (p. 1383)
—Popcorn! Lies, Brian, illus. (p. 1384)
—President, Vice President, & Cabinet: A Look at the Executive Branch. (p. 1397)
—Pugs Are the Best! (p. 1415)
—Raccoons: Scavengers of the Night. (p. 1430)
—Ragdolls Are the Best! (p. 1433)
—Rashes. (p. 1439)
—Ready to Make Music (p. 1448)
—Revolutionary War Begins: Would You Join the Fight? (p. 1466)
—Rottweilers Are the Best! (p. 1491)
—Sacco & Vanzetti. (p. 1500)
—Saint Bernards Are the Best! (p. 1503)
—Salem Witchcraft Trials: Would You Join the Madness? (p. 1504)
—Scary Sharks. (p. 1520)
—Schizophrenia. (p. 1521)
—Sense of Hearing. (p. 1551)
—Sense of Touch. (p. 1551)
—Shetland Ponies Are My Favorite! (p. 1566)
—Shih Tzus Are the Best! (p. 1566)
—Siamese Are the Best! (p. 1572)
—Sinister Snakes. (p. 1579)
—Snow Leopards: Hunters of the Snow & Ice. (p. 1599)
—Snowy Owls: Hunters of the Snow & Ice. (p. 1601)
—Sphynx Are the Best! (p. 1626)
—Sprains & Strains. (p. 1634)
—Start of the Revolutionary War: Would You Fight for Independence? (p. 1643)
—Statue of Liberty. (p. 1645)
—Strep Throat. (p. 1667)
—Suicide Bombers: Foot Soldiers of the Terrorist Movement. (p. 1673)
—Taylor Lautner: Twilight's Fearless Werewolf. (p. 1708)
—Triangle Shirtwaist Factory Fire. (p. 1785)
—Tyrannosaurus Rex. Landau, Elaine, illus. (p. 1805)
—Underground Railroad: Would You Help Them Escape? (p. 1815)
—Velociraptor. Landau, Elaine, illus. (p. 1835)
—Volcanoes. (p. 1849)
—Warts. (p. 1859)
—Washington Monument. (p. 1860)
—What Is Christmas? (p. 1889)
—What Is Halloween? (p. 1889)
—What Is St. Patrick's Day? (p. 1890)
—What Is Thanksgiving? (p. 1890)
—What Is the 4th of July? (p. 1890)
—What Is Valentine's Day? (p. 1891)
—What Is Veterans Day? (p. 1891)
—Witness the Boston Tea Party with Elaine Landau. (p. 1942)
—Witness the Salem Witchcraft Trials. (p. 1942)
—Wounded Knee Massacre. (p. 1962)
—Wyatt Earp: Wild West Lawman. (p. 1966)
—Yorkshire Terriers Are the Best! (p. 1972)
—Your Pet Cat. Landau, Elaine, illus. (p. 1981)
—Your Pet Hamster. (p. 1981)
Landau, Helena Von, illus. see Stein, Evaleen.
Landau, Jeff. Saying Goodbye to Sophie. (p. 1519)
Landau, Jennifer. Bipolar Disorder. (p. 190)
—Dealing with Bullies, Cliques, & Social Stress. (p. 418)
—Dr. Seuss. (p. 475)
—Endometriosis. (p. 527)
—How to Beat Psychological Bullying. (p. 815)
—Jane Lynch (p. 908)
—Jeff Bezos & Amazon. (p. 911)
—Pesticides & Your Body. (p. 1345)
—Right Words: Knowing What to Say & How to Say It. (p. 1472)
—Smart Strategies for Sharing, Subletting, & Renting an Apartment. (p. 1593)
—Vincent Van Gogh: Master of Post-Impressionist Painting. (p. 1843)
Landau, Natasha. Misha Loves to Sing. (p. 1150)
Landau, Orna. Leopardpox! Sadie Is Having the Funniest Sick Day Ever! Hoffmann, Omer, illus. (p. 993)
Landaw, Jonathan. Prince Siddhartha: The Story of Buddha. Brooke, Janet, illus. (p. 1401)
Landeman, Tanya. Little Egg. (p. 1027)
Landen, Cynthia & Phillips, Lorrie. Elson Readers, Primer. (p. 516)
Lander, Donna, jt. ed. see Friedman, Randee.
Landers, Ace. Anakin: Space Pilot. White, David A., illus. (p. 66)
—Anakin to the Rescue. (p. 66)
—Anakin to the Rescue! White, David A., illus. (p. 66)
—Arctic Blast. White, Dave, illus. (p. 96)
—Armed for Battle. (p. 99)
—Cave Race! White, Dave, illus. (p. 282)
—Darth Maul's Mission. White, David A., illus. (p. 409)
—Emmet's Guide to Being Awesome. Scholastic, Inc. Staff, illus. (p. 520)
—Empire Strikes Out. (p. 521)
—Hot Wheels: Race to Win! (p. 802)
—Hot Wheels: Wild Rides. White, Dave, illus. (p. 802)
—Lego Official Movie Handbook. (p. 990)
—LEGO Star Wars: Yoda's Secret Missions. (p. 990)
—Lego Star Wars: The Yoda Chronicles Trilogy. (p. 990)
—My Race Car. White, David A., illus. (p. 1217)
—Padawan Menace. (p. 1317)
—Power Rangers Megaforce - Mega Mission. (p. 1390)
—Power Rangers Megaforce: Robo Knight! Scholastic, Inc. Staff, illus. (p. 1390)
—Power Rangers Samurai: Official Guide. (p. 1390)
—Race for Treasure. White, Dave, illus. (p. 1431)
—Shark Attack. (p. 1562)
—Start Your Engines. White, Dave, illus. (p. 1643)
—Vader's Secret Missions. Ameet Studio, Ameet, illus. (p. 1830)
—Yoda Chronicles Trilogy. (p. 1972)
—Yoda's Secret Missions Ameet Studio (Firm) Staff, illus. (p. 1972)
Landers, Ace, jt. auth. see Ackerman, Jill.
Landers, Ace, jt. auth. see Santos, Ray.
Landers, Ace, jt. auth. see Scholastic, Inc. Staff.
Landers, Ace & Cartwheel Editors. I Am a Garbage Truck. Scholastic, Inc. Staff, ed. (p. 832)
Landers, Ace & Doodle Pictures Studio Staff. Save the Galaxy! Hyland, Greg, illus. (p. 1516)
Landers, Gail J. Late for the Race. (p. 979)
Landers, Jeri. Journey of Bushky Bushybottom. Landers, Jeri, illus. (p. 928)
Landers, Melissa. Alienated. (p. 41)
—Invaded. (p. 883)
Landers, Terri. Ways to Play with Words! A Collection of Word Games & Activities. (p. 1865)
Landes, David. 3 Little Fish. (p. 1991)
Landes, S. H., tr. see Aristophanes.
Landes, S. H., tr. see Euripides.
Landes, S. H., tr. see Landes, William-Alan, ed.
Landes, S. H., tr. see Molière.
Landes, S. H., tr. see Strindberg, August.
Landes, William Alan, ed. see Hezlep, William.
Landes, William-Alan. Aladdin n' His Magic Lamp. (p. 33)
—Alice n' Wonderland. (p. 39)
—Ambassador. (p. 56)
—Jack 'n the Beanstalk: Playscript. (p. 903)
—Peter 'n the Wolf: Acting Edition. (p. 1346)
—Rapunzel 'n the Witch. (p. 1439)
—Rhyme Tyme: Playscript. (p. 1468)
—Rumpelstiltskin: Playscript. (p. 1495)
—Rumpelstiltskin. (p. 1495)
Landes, William-Alan, ed. see Addison, Joseph.
Landes, William-Alan, ed. see Aeschylus.
Landes, William-Alan, ed. see Alvarez Quintero, Serafin & Alvarez Quintero, Joaquin.
Landes, William-Alan, ed. see Aristophanes.
Landes, William-Alan, ed. see Barker, Granville.
Landes, William-Alan, ed. see Barrie, J. M.
Landes, William-Alan, ed. see Brooke, Iris.
Landes, William-Alan, ed. see Brooke, Rupert.
Landes, William-Alan, ed. see Chekhov, Anton.
Landes, William-Alan, ed. see Crawford, David W.
Landes, William-Alan, ed. see Davis, R. I.
Landes, William-Alan, ed. see Dickens, Charles.
Landes, William-Alan, ed. see Euripides.
Landes, William-Alan, ed. see Fass, Gertrude.
Landes, William-Alan, ed. see France, Anatole.
Landes, William-Alan, ed. see Galsworthy, John.
Landes, William-Alan, ed. see Gilbert, William S.
Landes, William-Alan, ed. see Goldsmith, Oliver.
Landes, William-Alan, ed. see Gorky, Maxim.
Landes, William-Alan, ed. see Ibsen, Henrik.
Landes, William-Alan, ed. see Kluger, Garry M.
Landes, William-Alan, ed. see Korty, Carol.
Landes, William-Alan, ed. see Langner, Lawrence.
Landes, William-Alan, ed. see Lillo, George.
Landes, William-Alan, ed. see Marlowe, Christopher.
Landes, William-Alan, ed. see McCaslin, Nellie.
Landes, William-Alan, ed. see Molière.
Landes, William-Alan, ed. see Morton, Carlos.
Landes, William-Alan, ed. see Pinero, Arthur Wing.
Landes, William-Alan, ed. see Pirandello, Luigi.
Landes, William-Alan, ed. see Plautus, Titus Maccius.
Landes, William-Alan, ed. see Potter, Jonathan.
Landes, William-Alan, ed. see Racine, Jean.
Landes, William-Alan, ed. see Reyburn, Stanley S.
Landes, William-Alan, ed. see Rowe, Nicholas.
Landes, William-Alan, ed. see Ryback, Jeffrey W.
Landes, William-Alan, ed. see Sabato, George F.
Landes, William-Alan, ed. see Schnitzler, Arthur.
Landes, William-Alan, ed. see Shakespeare, William.
Landes, William-Alan, ed. see Shaw, George Bernard.
Landes, William-Alan, ed. see Sheridan, Richard Brinsley.
Landes, William-Alan, ed. see Sinclair, Jean.
Landes, William-Alan, ed. see Sitarz, Paula Gaj.
Landes, William-Alan, ed. see Sophocles, et al.
Landes, William-Alan, ed. see Sophocles.
Landes, William-Alan, ed. see Strindberg, August.
Landes, William-Alan, ed. see Strong, Austin.
Landes, William-Alan, ed. see Synge, John M.
Landes, William-Alan, ed. see Terence.
Landes, William-Alan, ed. see Thistle, Louise.
Landes, William-Alan, ed. see Tibbets, Mike.
Landes, William-Alan, ed. see Wheeler, Jacque & Laughlin, Haller.
Landes, William-Alan, ed. see Wilde, Oscar.
Landes, William-Alan, jt. auth. see Brooke, Iris.
Landes, William-Alan, jt. auth. see Crawford, David W.
Landes, William-Alan, jt. auth. see Evans, Mary.
Landes, William-Alan, jt. ed. see Ibsen, Henrik.
Landes, William-Alan, photos by see Wheeler, Jacque & Laughlin, Haller.
Landes, William-Alan, tr. see Plautus, Titus Maccius.
Landes, William-Alan & Lasky, Mark A. Grandpa's Bedtime Story. (p. 709)
Landes, William-Alan & Standish, Marilyn. Wizard of Oz. (p. 1943)
Landes, William-Alan, ed. Everyman. (p. 544)
—Ghosts. Ibsen, Henrik & Landes, S. H., trs. from NOR. (p. 672)
—Punch & Judy. Cruikshank, George, illus. (p. 1416)
—Wild Duck. Ibsen, Henrik, illus. (p. 1929)
Landes, William-Allan, ed. see Howard, Vernon.
Landes, William-Allan, ed. see Synge, John M.
Landes, Willian-Alan, ed. see Gilbert, William S.
Landfair, Barton, jt. auth. see Martin, Debra.
Landgraf, James, Jr. Monsters Monsters Go Away. Warrick, Jessica, illus. (p. 1169)
Landgraf, Kenneth, illus. see Defoe, Daniel.
Landinez, Jairo Linares, illus. see Arrieta, Luisa Noguera.
Landinez, Jairo Linares, illus. see Silva, Luna.
Landis, Beth, ed. see Dorling Kindersley Publishing Staff.
Landis, Mary. David & Susan at the Little Green House. (p. 410)
Landis, Mary M. Winter Days with the Treelo Triplets. (p. 1938)
Landman, Tanya. Goldsmith's Daughter. (p. 696)
—I Am Apache. (p. 832)
—Mary's Penny. Holland, Richard, illus. (p. 1101)
Landman, Yael & Hill, Barbara. Fred's Wish for Fish. Stein, Laurie, illus. (p. 633)
Landmann, Bimba. Fate of Achilles. (p. 577)
—Genius of Leonardo. (p. 661)
—I Am Marc Chagall. Landmann, Bimba, illus. (p. 833)
—In Search of the Little Prince: The Story of Antoine de Saint-Exupéry. (p. 865)
—Incredible Voyage of Ulysses. (p. 869)
Landmann, Bimba, illus. see Visconti, Guido.
Landmark, Ken, illus. see Dahl, Michael.
Landolf, Diane Wright. Barbie: Thumbelina. Random House Audio Publishing Group Staff, illus. (p. 138)
—Hog & Dog. Harris, Jennifer Beck, illus. (p. 787)
—Hooray for Halloween! Wolcott, Karen, illus. (p. 796)
—Thumbelina. Ulkutay Design Group & Choi, Allan, illus. (p. 1745)
Landolf, Diane Wright, jt. auth. see Kipling, Rudyard.
Landolfi, Meghan Ann. Washington, D. C. (p. 1860)
Landolt, Gredna, illus. see Diaz, Katacha.
Landon, Angela. Innkeeper's Wife: A Christmas Story. (p. 875)
—What Is Freedom? How Does It Ring? (p. 1889)
Landon, Kristen. Life in the Pit. (p. 1011)
—Limit. (p. 1018)
Landon, Lucinda. Meg Mackintosh & the Mystery at Red Herring Beach: A Solve-It-Yourself Mystery. (p. 1124)
—Meg Mackintosh & the Stage Fright Secret: A Solve-It-Yourself Mystery. (p. 1124)
—Meg Mackintosh Solves Seven American History Mysteries: A Solve-It-Yourself Mystery. (p. 1124)
—Meg Mackintosh's Mystery Writing Handbook: For Young Authors & Illustrators. (p. 1124)
Landon, Melissa, ed. Biology: Understanding Living Matter. (p. 189)
Landon, Rocky & MacDonald, David. Native American Thought of It: Amazing Inventions & Innovations. (p. 1234)
L&ostroke, et al. Omstigning. (p. 1288)
Landowne, Youme. Mali under the Night Sky: A Lao Story of Home. (p. 1083)
—Selavi, That Is Life: A Haitian Story of Hope. Landowne, Youme, illus. (p. 1549)
Landowne, Youme & Horton, Anthony. Pitch Black. (p. 1364)
Landreth, Christina. Tommy Picks Flowers. (p. 1765)
Landreth, Jane. Bible Prayers for Bedtime. (p. 176)
Landreth, Jane, jt. auth. see Sumner, Tracy M.
Landreth, Jane, et al. Bedtime Bible Stories. (p. 156)
Landreth, Kenneth. Crazy Book about a Crazy Trip. (p. 377)
Landrón, José Rafael, jt. auth. see Landrón, Rafael.
Landrón, Rafael & Landrón, José Rafael. Beba y la Isla Nena: Beba & the Little Island. Ordóñez, Maria Antonia, illus. (p. 155)
Landry, Barbara. Day at the Zoo. (p. 412)
Landry, Cornell P. Goodnight Nola: An Endearing Bedtime Book for All Ages. Schmitt, Louis J., illus. (p. 701)
—Happy JazzFest! (p. 746)
Landry, Cristy. Garret's Science Project, Why Does Matter Matter? (p. 657)
—Kona's Science Project. (p. 967)
—Mariah's Science Project, Is My Grandma a Fossil? (p. 1093)
—Martha's Market, Aisle One. (p. 1097)
—Martha's Market Aisle Three. (p. 1097)
Landry, Deb. Sticks Stones & Stumped the Play & Teacher's Guide. (p. 1650)
Landry, Douglas, illus. see Maxfield, Deanna.
Landry, Jennifer, jt. auth. see Defelice, Jennie.
Landry, Jennifer, jt. auth. see DeFelice, Jennie.
Landry, Jennifer, jt. auth. see Defelice, Jennie.
Landry, Leo. Eat Your Peas, Ivy Louise! (p. 501)
—Grin & Bear It. Landry, Leo, illus. (p. 724)
—Space Boy. Landry, Leo, illus. (p. 1618)
—Trick or Treat. (p. 1786)
—What's up, Chuck? (p. 1900)
Landry, Leo, illus. see Ault, Kelly.
Landry, Leo, illus. see Post, Peggy, et al.
Landsman, Julie, jt. ed. see Haynes, David.
Landstrom, Lee Ann & Shragg, Karen. Nature's Yucky! Gross Stuff That Helps Nature Work Bergum, Constance Rummel, illus. (p. 1237)
—Nature's Yucky! 2: The Desert Southwest. Rogge, Rachel, illus. (p. 1237)
Landstrom, Lee Ann & Shragg, Karen I. Nature's Yucky! 3: The Eastern United States. Rogge, Rachel, illus. (p. 1237)
Landstrom, Lena. Four Hens & a Rooster. Sandin, Joan, tr. from SWE. (p. 625)
—Hippo's Tale. Sandin, Joan, tr. from SWE. (p. 781)
—New Hippos. Sandin, Joan, tr. from SWE. (p. 1245)
Landstrom, Olaf, illus. see Lindgren, Barbro.
Landstrom, Olof, illus. see Bottner, Barbara & Kruglik, Gerald.
Landstrom, Olof, illus. see Cohen, Peter.
Landstrom, Olof, illus. see Landstrom, Lena.
Landstrom, Olof, illus. see Lindgren, Barbro & Lindgren, B. L.
Landstrom, Olof, illus. see Lindgren, Barbro.
Landstrom, Olof, tr. see Bottner, Barbara & Kruglik, Gerald.
Landstrom, Olof, et al. Boo & Baa Have Company. Sandin, Joan, tr. from SWE. (p. 209)
Landwehr, James M. Exploring Surveys & Information from Samples. (p. 553)
Landwehr, Karen A., jt. auth. see Baker, Larry S.
Landy, Adrienne. Rudy the Shy Car. Seivwright, Leonard, illus. (p. 1494)
Landy, Derek. And He's the Good Guy. Percival, Tom, illus. (p. 71)
—Dark Days. (p. 407)
—Faceless Ones. (p. 561)
—Playing with Fire. (p. 1372)
—Scepter of the Ancients. Percival, Tom, illus. (p. 1521)
Landy, Derek, jt. auth. see Landy, Derek.
Landy, Derek & Landy, Derek. Faceless Ones: A California Gothic. Bastida, Xohana, tr. (p. 561)
Lane. Step by Step Noah's Ark. (p. 1647)
Lane, Alison Hoffman. Uncle Arnel & the Awful, Angry Alligator. (p. 1811)
—Uncle Arnel & the Swamp Witch Thompson, Egil, illus. (p. 1811)
Lane, Amy. Triane's Son Fighting. (p. 1785)
—Triane's Son Learning. (p. 1785)
—Triane's Son Reigning. (p. 1785)
Lane, Andrew. Black Ice. (p. 196)
—Death Cloud. (p. 420)
—Fire Storm. (p. 591)
—Rebel Fire. (p. 1450)
—Snake Bite. (p. 1596)
Lane, Andy. Glendale: Nashville's Magical Park. Sloan, Michael, illus. (p. 683)
Lane, Angela. Mommy, there's a giraffe in my Room. (p. 1162)
Lane, Anne Kelly. Powder Mill Gates. (p. 1389)
Lane, Arnetta L. I Am. (p. 831)
—Nine Steps of Bedtime. (p. 1256)
Lane, Barry. 51 Wacky We Search Reports: Facing the Facts with Fun. (p. 1997)
Lane, Bonnie. Bob the Inchworm & the Four Seasons. (p. 205)
Lane, Brian, et al. Ecology. (p. 502)
—Eyewitness Books - Crime & Detection. Crawford, Andy, photos by. (p. 558)
Lane, Bruce Courand. Friendly Little Martian. (p. 638)
Lane, Bryan. Stepbrothers. (p. 1648)
—Stepbrothers the New Arrival. (p. 1648)
Lane, Chloe. Package Design. (p. 1317)
Lane, Chloe, jt. auth. see Dugan, Christine.
Lane, Chris, illus. see Weaver, Janice.
Lane, Cody R., illus. see Johnson, Cindy B.
Lane County Mathematics Project Staff. Problem Solving in Mathematics. (p. 1408)
Lane, Dakota. Gothic Lolita: A Mystical Thriller. Lane, Dakota, illus. (p. 704)
—Orpheus Obsession. (p. 1305)
Lane, Darrell A. Off Guard: Honest Security for Honest America. (p. 1279)
Lane, Deborah. Fishing with Mom. (p. 599)
Lane, Deborah Jean. I Am an Individual. (p. 832)
Lane Durbin, Deborah, jt. auth. see Attaway-Young, Andrea.
Lane, Frederick A. Flag for Lafitte: Story of the Battle of New Orleans. Vosburgh, Leonard, illus. (p. 602)
Lane Gross, Ila. Uncommon Tales Around the World: Global Understanding/Cultural Literacy. (p. 1812)
Lane Holm, Sharon, illus. see Hall, Pamela.
Lane, Jean E. Lil & Mewe Journey to the Ocean of Runa. (p. 1017)
Lane, Jeanette & Cole, Joanna. Magic School Bus in the Bat Cave. Cuddy, Robbin & Cole, Joanna, illus. (p. 1073)
Lane, Jeanette, et al. Magic School Bus Gets Caught in a Web. Enik, Ted, illus. (p. 1073)
Lane, Jessica E. Fletcher: The Quickest Chicken Catcher. (p. 603)
—Secret of the Swans. (p. 1543)
Lane, Jill. Blossom, Alex & the Renaissance Rabbit: A Novel. (p. 202)
Lane, Kathleen. Nana Takes the Reins Home, Sarah, illus. (p. 1228)
—Protectors of the Universe. (p. 1412)
Lane, Kathleen, et al. Nana Cracks the Case! Horne, Sarah, illus. (p. 1228)
Lane, Kim, illus. see Gibson, Ray.
Lane, Kim, illus. see Rogers, Kirsteen.
Lane, Kim, illus. see Watt, Fiona.
Lane, Kimberly. Latin American Art. (p. 979)
Lane, Kimberly & Charlesbridge Publishing Staff. Asian Art. (p. 106)
Lane, L. E. Mysterious Golden Seed. (p. 1223)
Lane, Larry. Alphabet Soup. (p. 50)
Lane, Leena. Angels among Us. Baboni, Elena, illus. (p. 75)
—Birds & Beasties. (p. 191)
—Christmas Fun: Bible Activity Book. Bishop, Roma, illus. (p. 314)
—Christmas Fun: My First Bible Activity BK. Bishop, Roma, illus. (p. 314)
—Christopher Bear's Anytime Prayers. (p. 316)
—Climb up the Tree with Zacchaeus. Reynolds, Annette, ed. (p. 333)
—Come to the Party with Jesus. Reynolds, Annette, ed. (p. 347)
—Easter Days: My First Bible Activity Book. (p. 499)
—Friends of God: My First Bible Activity BK. Bishop, Roma, illus. (p. 638)

—Kids Bible. Chapman, Gillian, illus. (p. 952)
—My First Bible. Chapman, Gillian, illus. (p. 1204)
—Old Testament Stories. Bishop, Roma, illus. (p. 1285)
—Sail in the Boat with Jesus. Reynolds, Annette, ed. (p. 1503)
—Stand up & Walk with Jesus. Reynolds, Annette, ed. (p. 1639)
—Star of Wonder. Baboni, Elena, illus. (p. 1641)
—Stories of Jesus. Bishop, Roma, illus. (p. 1655)
Lane, Leena & Boshof, Penny. My Little Yellow Book: First Steps in Bible Reading. (p. 1213)
Lane, Leena & Chapman, Gillian. Step by Step Christmas Creche. (p. 1647)
Lane, Leonie. Fork Tongue Freimon. (p. 620)
—Retford Witch Catchers. (p. 1464)
Lane, Lindsey. Evidence of Things Not Seen. (p. 546)
Lane, Lori & Winsor, Kathy. Nana's Quilt: Stitched in St. John'S, Newfoundland & Labrador Costello, Jim, illus. (p. 1228)
—Poppy & Allie: Hooked on St. John's, Newfoundland Costello, Jim, photos by. (p. 1385)
Lane, M. J., jt. auth. see Lane, M. j.
Lane, M. j. & Lane, M. J. Where in the World Is Snickers? (p. 1908)
Lane, Marion T. Patriots of African Descent in the Revolutionary War: Part 1. (p. 1329)
Lane, Melaina. Chubs. . Another Day at School. (p. 318)
Lane, Melissa. Little Tornadoes. (p. 1037)
Lane, Mike. Close-Up Magic. Mostyn, David, illus. (p. 334)
—Magic Tricks: Packed with Dozens of Dazzling Tricks to Learn in Simple Steps! (p. 1074)
—Mind Magic. Mostyn, David, illus. (p. 1145)
Lane, Mike, jt. auth. see Egan, Kate.
Lane, Mitchell. Contemporary African-American Collection (p. 360)
Lane, Nancy, illus. see Benson, Linda.
Lane, Nancy, illus. see Blaisdell, Molly.
Lane, Nancy, illus. see Graham-Barber, Lynda.
Lane, Nancy, illus. see Havill, Juanita.
Lane, Nancy, illus. see Wax, Wendy.
Lane, Nickel. Book Making for Everyone. (p. 210)
—Ferret Crusaders: Quest of the Wish A Pod. (p. 582)
—Maggy, the Cow that Jumped over the Moon. (p. 1071)
Lane, Queen. It's Christmas Time (Babytown Storybook) (p. 896)
Lane, Queen & Boykin, Brian. No No Baby (Babytown Storybook) (p. 1259)
Lane, Ranae, illus. see Comley, Kathryn.
Lane, Rob, ed. see Shirt, Virginia.
Lane, Ronald. Avina's Song: A Children's Story. (p. 120)
Lane, Sandra & Miles, Brenda. Moment You Were Born: A NICU Story for You & Your Preemie. Hehenberger, Shelly, illus. (p. 1161)
Lane, Sharmen. Why Am I Special? (p. 1922)
Lane, Sheila Mary & Kemp, Marion. Start Here. Birch, Linda, illus. (p. 1643)
Lane, Sondra. Showin' Out to God's Glory. (p. 1571)
Lane, Stewart F. Let's Put on a Show! Theatre Production for Novices. (p. 1000)
Lane, Tracy & Benchmark Education Co., LLC Staff. Shade Lake. (p. 1556)
—Snail in May. (p. 1595)
Lane, Travis. Redhaze: Trilogy. (p. 1455)
Lane, W. Seth. Riley Rabbit's Quest to the Ark. (p. 1472)
Lane, Yancey. Amanda Younger: Girl Detective. (p. 52)
Lane, Yvet-Renee. Cambridge Checkpoints VCE Media 2005. (p. 255)
Laner, Melissa, ed. see Soentgen, Beate, et al.
Laney, Dawn. Down Syndrome. (p. 474)
—Hunting. (p. 829)
Laney, Mark. Land & Resources of Colorado. (p. 973)
Lanford, Mickey. Inside Passage to Death: A Mystery Novel. (p. 877)
Lanford, Susan. Vital Skills: How to Take Care of Yourself. (p. 1846)
Lang, A. G., jt. auth. see Amos, H. D.
Lang, Alex & Burns, Adam. University of Iowa College Prowler off the Record. (p. 1820)
Lang, Allison, illus. see Cohen, Pamela June.
Lang, Andrew. Andrew Lang's Blue, Red, Green & Yellow Fairy Books. (p. 72)
—Andrew Lang's Brown, Orange, Olive & Lilac Fairy Books. (p. 72)
—Andrew Lang's Complete Fairy Book Series: Traditional Folk Tales & Fairy Stories from Around the World. (p. 72)
—Andrew Lang's Pink, Grey, Violet & Crimson Fairy Books. (p. 72)
—Blue Fairy Book. (p. 202)
—Blue Fairy Book. Lang, Andrew, ed. (p. 202)
—Book of Romance. (p. 211)
—Crimson Fairy Book. (p. 383)
—Green Fairy Book. (p. 721)
—Grey Fairy Book. (p. 723)
—Hut in the Forest: A Tale about Being Kind to Animals. Johnson, Meredith, illus. (p. 830)
—Lilac Fairy Book. (p. 1017)
—Olive Fairy Book. Lang, Andrew, ed. (p. 1285)
—Orange Fairy Book. (p. 1301)
—Pink Fairy Book. (p. 1359)
—Prince Prigio. (p. 1401)
—Prince Ricardo of Pantouflia. (p. 1401)
—Queen & the Mouse: A Story about Friendship. Lohmann, Renate, illus. (p. 1424)
—Red Fairy Book. (p. 1454)
—Red Fairy Book. Lang, Andrew, ed. (p. 1454)
—Red Romance Book; Tales of Knights. (p. 1455)
—Strange Story Book. (p. 1665)
—Tales of Troy: Ulysses the Sacker of Cities. (p. 1703)
—Tales of Troy & Greece. Ford, H. J., illus. (p. 1703)
—Violet Fairy Book. (p. 1843)
—Yellow Fairy Book. (p. 1970)
Lang, Andrew, ed. see Lang, Leonora Blanche.
Lang, Andrew & Ford, H. J. Tale of the Cid: And Other Stories of Knights & Chivalry. Ford, H. J., illus. (p. 1700)
Lang, Andrew, ed. Arabian Nights. (p. 94)
—Blue Fairy Book. (p. 202)
—Book of Romance. Ford, H. J., illus. (p. 211)
—Brown Fairy Book. (p. 232)
—Chronicles of Pantouflia: Prince Prigio; Prince Ricardo of Pantouflia. (p. 317)
—Crimson Fairy Book. (p. 383)
—Green Fairy Book. (p. 721)
—Grey Fairy Book. (p. 723)
—Lilac Fairy Book. (p. 1017)
—Olive Fairy Book. (p. 1285)
—Orange Fairy Book. (p. 1301)
—Pink Fairy Book. (p. 1359)
—Red Book of Animal Stories 1899. Ford, Henry J., illus. (p. 1453)
—Red Fairy Book. (p. 1454)
—Yellow Fairy Book. (p. 1970)
Lang, Annie J. Who Let the Kids Out. (p. 1916)
Lang, Aubrey. Baby Black Bear Lynch, Wayne, photos by. (p. 125)
—Baby Elephant Lynch, Wayne, photos by. (p. 126)
—Baby Fox Lynch, Wayne, illus. (p. 126)
—Baby Fox. Lynch, Wayne, photos by. (p. 126)
—Baby Grizzly Lynch, Wayne, photos by. (p. 126)
—Baby Ground Squirrel Lynch, Wayne, photos by. (p. 126)
—Baby Koala Lynch, Wayne, photos by. (p. 127)
—Baby Lion Lynch, Wayne, photos by. (p. 127)
—Baby Mountain Sheep Lynch, Wayne, photos by. (p. 127)
—Baby Owl Lynch, Wayne, photos by. (p. 127)
—Baby Polar Bear Lynch, Wayne, photos by. (p. 127)
—Baby Porcupine Lynch, Wayne, photos by. (p. 127)
—Baby Sea Turtle Lynch, Wayne, illus. (p. 128)
—Baby Seal Lynch, Wayne, photos by. (p. 128)
—Baby Sloth Lynch, Wayne, photos by. (p. 128)
Lang, Aubrey & Lynch, Wayne. Baby Elephant (p. 126)
Lang Books(Editors) Staff, ed. Christmas. (p. 312)
—Christmas Ideals 2004 (p. 314)
—Friendship. (p. 639)
—Friendship Ideals 2004. (p. 639)
—Greatest Gift. (p. 719)
—Thanksgiving Ideals 2004. (p. 1726)
—Treasury of Faith & Inspiration. (p. 1782)
Lang, Carol, et al. Character in Motion! Real Life Stories Series 3rd Grade Student Workbook. (p. 291)
Lang, Carole, illus. see Klett, David.
Lang, Cay. Taking the Leap: Building a Career as a Visual Artist. (p. 1698)
Lang, Cecily, illus. see Mora, Pat.
Lang, Constance. Drawings of Henry Fromm - Chris's Journey. (p. 482)
Lang, C.S. Score Reading Exercises (p. 1530)
Lang, Diane. Vulture Verses: Love Poems for the Unloved. Gallegos, Lauren, illus. (p. 1851)
Lang, Diane & Buchanan, Michael. Fat Boy Chronicles. (p. 577)
Lang, Elizabeth. First Aid Basics. (p. 592)
—In the Garden. (p. 866)
—Sports Safety. (p. 1633)
Lang, Elliott. Peafowls, Peacocks & Peahens Including Facts & Information about Blue, White, Indian & Green Peacocks Breeding, Owning, Keeping & Raising Pe. (p. 1332)
Lang, Gail M. Horticulture. (p. 801)
Lang, Gary, illus. see Killion, Kathleen.
Lang, George. Pixy's Holiday Journey. (p. 1365)
Lang, Glenna. Looking Out for Sarah. Lang, Glenna, illus. (p. 1051)
Lang, Glenna, illus. see Frost, Robert.
Lang, Glenna, illus. see Longfellow, Henry Wadsworth.
Lang, Glenna & Wunsch, Marjory. Genius of Common Sense: Jane Jacobs & the Story of the Death & Life of Great American Cities. (p. 661)
Lang, Glenna W. & Wunsch, Marjory. Genius of Common Sense: Jane Jacobs & the Story of the Death & Life of Great American Cities. (p. 661)
Lang, Gordon. Everyday Encounters: Face to Face with Jesus. (p. 543)
Lang, Heather. Original Cowgirl: The Wild Adventures of Lucille Mulhall. Beaky, Suzanne, illus. (p. 1304)
—Queen of the Track: Alice Coachman, Olympic High-Jump Champion. Cooper, Floyd, illus. (p. 1425)
Lang, J. Stephen. Bible Trivia. (p. 176)
Lang, Kathy. Spaced Out Gerbil. Cotton, Sue Lynn, illus. (p. 1620)
Lang, Lang. Lang Lang: Playing with Flying Keys. (p. 974)
Lang, Leonora Blanche. Book of Saints & Heroes. Lang, Andrew, ed. (p. 211)
Lang, Leslie, ed. see Wicks, Valerie.
Lang, Margaret & Perez, Isabelle. Modern French Grammar: A Practical Guide. (p. 1158)
—Modern French Grammar. (p. 1158)
Lang, Mark, illus. see Bodger, Joan.
Lang, Mark, illus. see Bogart, Jo Ellen.
Lang, Max, illus. see Lang, Suzanne.
Lang, Rocky. Lara Takes Charge: For Kids with Diabetes, Their Friends, & Siblings Huss, Sally, illus. (p. 975)
Lang, Samuel E. Slim Tiny & Raul Go on a Diet. (p. 1590)
Lang, Suzanne. Families, Families, Families! Lang, Max, illus. (p. 567)
Lang, Tiffany. Mango Leaves Strings in Your Teeth. (p. 1087)
Lang, Valerie E. Jet's Day: A Whisker Team Story. (p. 916)
Langan, Bob, illus. see Ambrosio, Michael.
Langan, John. Search for Safety. (p. 1537)
Langan, John & Langan, Paul. Bluford High #13: Search for Safety. (p. 204)
Langan, Paul. Bluford 06 Payback. (p. 204)
—Bluford 08 Blood Is Thicker. (p. 204)
—Bully (p. 241)
—Bully. (p. 241)
—Fallen. (p. 566)
—Payback. (p. 1331)
—Promises to Keep (p. 1411)
—Schooled. (p. 1523)
—Shattered. (p. 1563)
—Summer of Secrets. Langan, Paul, ed. (p. 1674)
—Survivor (p. 1687)
Langan, Paul, ed. see Schraff, Anne.
Langan, Paul, jt. auth. see Folan, Karyn Langhorne.
Langan, Paul, jt. auth. see Langan, John.
Langan, Paul, jt. auth. see Langhorne Folan, Karyn.
Langan, Paul, jt. auth. see Langhorne, Karyn.
Langan, Paul & Alirez, Ben. Brothers in Arms. Langan, Paul, ed. (p. 231)
Langan, Paul & Blackwell, D. M. Blood Is Thicker. (p. 200)
—Blood Is Thicker. Langan, Paul, ed. (p. 200)
Langan, Paul & Schraff, Anne. Summer of Secrets. (p. 1674)
Langbert, Enid W., ed. Right to a Fair Trial. (p. 1472)
Langcaon, Jeff. My Grandpa's Battleship Missouri Tour. (p. 1210)
Langcaon, Jeff, jt. auth. see Ide, Laurie S.
Langdale, Mark Roland. Professor Doppeganger & the Fantastical Cloud Factory. (p. 1409)
Langdo, Bryan. Tornado Slim & the Magic Cowboy Hat (p. 1770)
Langdo, Bryan, illus. see Annunziata, Jane & Nemiroff, Marc.
Langdo, Bryan, illus. see Hardin, Melinda.
Langdo, Bryan, illus. see Levins, Sandra.
Langdo, Bryan, illus. see Malone, Jean M.
Langdo, Bryan, illus. see Minarik, Else Holmelund.
Langdo, Bryan, illus. see Neuschwander, Cindy.
Langdo, Bryan, illus. see Trinco, Trish.
Langdo, Bryan, jt. illus. see Hirschmann, Kris.
Langdon, Katie, jt. auth. see Parker, Linda.
Langdon, Lorie, jt. auth. see Corp, Carey.
Langdon, Sharon, jt. auth. see Arlington, Jane.
Langdown, Leanne Shea. My Happy Gift. McKay, Traci, illus. (p. 1210)
Lange, Brenda. Antonio Lopez de Santa Anna. (p. 90)
—Edward Stratemeyer. (p. 505)
—Genghis Khan. (p. 661)
—Muammar Qaddafi: President of Libya. Schlesinger, Arthur M., Jr., ed. (p. 1188)
—Nefertiti. (p. 1240)
—Stock Market Crash Of 1929: The End of Prosperity. (p. 1651)
—Triangle Shirtwaist Factory Fire. (p. 1785)
Lange, Donna. Contraception & Pregnancy. Forman, Sara & McDonnell, Mary Ann, eds. (p. 361)
—Contraception & Pregnancy. McDonnell, Mary Ann & Forman, Sara, eds. (p. 361)
—Juvenile Court System. Albers, Lisa et al, eds. (p. 941)
—On the Edge of Disaster: Youth in the Juvenile Court System. (p. 1290)
—On the Edge of Disaster: Youth in the Juvenile Court System. (p. 1290)
Lange, Erin Jade. Butter. (p. 247)
—Dead Ends. (p. 416)
Lange, Ian. Ice Age Mammals of North America: A Guide to the Big, the Hairy, & the Bizarre Norton, Dorothy S., illus. (p. 850)
Lange, Jessica. It's about a Little Bird. (p. 896)
Lange, Karen. 1607: A New Look at Jamestown. Block, Ira, photos by. (p. 2002)
—Nevermore: A Photobiography of Edgar Allan Poe. (p. 1243)
Lange, Kelly. Dead File. (p. 416)
Lange, Nikki Bataille. My Little Pony: A Very Minty Christmas. LoRaso, Carlo, illus. (p. 1213)
Lange, Sue. Perpetual Motion Club. (p. 1343)
Lange, Willem. Favor Johnson: A Christmas Story. Dodson, Bert, illus. (p. 577)
—White-Footed Mouse. Dodson, Bert, illus. (p. 1913)
Langeland, Deirdre. Be Careful, Kangaroo! Ordaz, Frank, illus. (p. 148)
—Be Careful, Kangaroo!, Level 1. (p. 148)
—Kangaroo Island: A Story of an Australian Mallee Forest. (p. 942)
Langeler, Gerard. Let's Make Faces. Grindell, Joan & Grindell, Mark, illus. (p. 999)
Langelier-Lebeda, Suzanne, illus. see Torgan, Keith & Siesel, Barbara.
Langely, Andrew. Should We Eat Animals? (p. 1570)
Langen, Annette. Felix & the Flying Suitcase Adventure. Droop, Constanza, illus. (p. 581)
—Felix Explores Planet Earth. Droop, Constanza, illus. (p. 581)
—Felix Travels Back in Time. Droop, Constanza, illus. (p. 581)
—Felix's Christmas Around the World. Droop, Constanza, illus. (p. 581)
—Letters from Felix: A Little Rabbit on a World Tour. Droop, Constanza, illus. (p. 1002)
—Our Very Own Christmas. Tolman, Marije, illus. (p. 1310)
Langen, Annette & Gerhmann, Katja. Angry Little Knight. Gerhmann, Katja, illus. (p. 75)
Langer, Justin, jt. auth. see Carbon, Sally.
Langevin, Don, ed. Giant Tomatoes. (p. 674)
Langford, Alan, jt. auth. see Green, Roger Lancelyn.
Langford, Alton, illus. see Birch, Vanessa Giancamilli.
Langford, Anne. Meditation for Little People. Bethards, David, illus. (p. 1120)
Langford, Jane. Hero. Vince, Dawn, illus. (p. 772)
—Old Red Hat. Axworthy, Anni, illus. (p. 1284)
Langford, Lynn F. God's Gals: Lessons in Forgiveness, Courage, Serving, & Sharing. (p. 691)
Langford, Norman F. King Nobody Wanted. (p. 958)
—King Nobody Wanted. Lear, John, illus. (p. 958)
Langford, Sarah, jt. auth. see Gerdner, Linda.
Langford, Virginia. Monty Says Mice Are Nice. (p. 1170)
Langham, Tony. Creepy Crawly Calypso. Harter, Debbie, illus. (p. 381)
Langham, Tony, jt. auth. see Sherab, Chodzin.
Langham, Tony & Harter, Debbie. Creepy Crawly Calypso. (p. 381)
—Mira Quien Toca Calipso! Harter, Debbie, illus. (p. 1148)
Langhans, Bob. Disney's DuckTales: the Gold Odyssey: The Gold Odyssey. Clark, John, ed. (p. 453)
Langhorne Folan, Karyn & Langan, Paul. Breaking Point. (p. 225)
Langhorne, Karyn & Langan, Paul. Breaking Point. (p. 225)
Langhorne, Mary Jo, ed. Developing an Information Literacy Curriculum: A How-to-Do-It Manual for Librarians. (p. 431)
Langill, Jill. Sweet Tea for Frankenstein. (p. 1690)
Langille, Elaine, illus. see Hann, Harry Henry & Johnson, Nancy.
Langille, Jacqueline, jt. auth. see Kalman, Bobbie.
Langille, Rob, illus. see Stewart, Andrew.
Langley, Andrew. 100 Things You Should Know about the Wild West. (p. 1999)
—Ancient Medicine (p. 70)
—Bridging the Energy Gap (p. 227)
—Bush, Blair, & Iraq: Days of Decision Della-Rovere, Cynthia, illus. (p. 244)
—Cape Town. (p. 262)
—Chris Hadfield & Living on the International Space Station. (p. 311)
—Codes & Codebreaking. (p. 338)
—Diggers. (p. 439)
—Every Building Has a History (p. 542)
—Every Place Has a History (p. 543)
—Glass. (p. 682)
—Helicopters. (p. 763)
—Hitler & Kristallnacht: Days of Decision (p. 786)
—Hundred Days Offensive: The Allies' Push to Win World War I. (p. 827)
—Hurricane: Perspectives on Storm Disasters (p. 829)
—Israel in Our World. (p. 893)
—Metal. (p. 1130)
—Navigators: Rainforest. (p. 1238)
—Pakistan in Our World. (p. 1319)
—Paper Products. (p. 1323)
—Pirates. (p. 1363)
—Planes. (p. 1367)
—Plastic. (p. 1370)
—Sally Ride & the Shuttle Missions. (p. 1505)
—September 11: Attack on America Langley, Andrew, illus. (p. 1551)
—St. Petersburg. (p. 1638)
—Stories of Women in World War II: We Can Do It! (p. 1655)
—Submarines. (p. 1671)
—Tiananmen Square: Massacre Crushes China's Democracy Movement (p. 1746)
—Wartime Spies. (p. 1859)
—Wool. (p. 1950)
—World War II (p. 1959)
—You Wouldn't Want to Be a Viking Explorer! Voyages You'd Rather Not Make. Antram, David, illus. (p. 1977)
Langley, Andrew, jt. auth. see de Souza, Philip.
Langley, Andrew, jt. auth. see Dorling Kindersley Publishing Staff.
Langley, Andrew, jt. auth. see Hubbard, Ben.
Langley, Andrew, jt. auth. see Vickers, Rebecca.
Langley, Andrew, jt. ed. see Oxford Analytica Staff.
Langley, Andrew, et al. Days of Decision. (p. 415)
Langley, Bill, illus. see Ferguson, Don.
Langley, Bill, illus. see Korman, Justine.
Langley, C. Kevin. Brer Rabbit Comic. (p. 226)
Langley, Gene, illus. see Herron, Edward A.
Langley, Jan. Captain & Harry: A Trembling Tail of Thieves. Robinson, Susan, illus. (p. 263)
—Captain & Harry Haunting Tail. (p. 263)
Langley, Jonathan, illus. see Rosen, Michael.
Langley, Jonathan, illus. see Walters, Clare & Kemp, Jane.
Langley, Jonathan, jt. auth. see Root, Betty.
Langley, Jonathan, jt. auth. see Rosen, Michael.
Langley, Judy. God's World & Me from A to Z. Coker, Carla, illus. (p. 692)
Langley, Karen. Three Little Words. Blaskovich, Dominique, illus. (p. 1743)
Langley, Leonora. Let the Children Sing. (p. 994)
Langley, Myrtle. Eyewitness - Religion. (p. 558)
Langley, Myrtle & Dorling Kindersley Publishing Staff. Religion. (p. 1458)
Langley, Noel. Desbaroilda, the Waltzing Mouse. Ardizzone, Edward, illus. (p. 428)
—Land of Green Ginger. Ardizzone, Edward, illus. (p. 973)
Langley, Wanda. Faces Behind Beauty. (p. 561)
—Women of the Wind: Early Women Aviators. (p. 1946)
Langlieb, David & Burns, Adam. Haverford College College Prowler off the Record. (p. 754)
Langlois, Annie. Evasion d'Alfred le Dindon. Beaulieu, Jimmey, illus. (p. 541)
—Mia, Matt & the Lazy Gator. Cummins, Sarah, tr. from FRE. (p. 1133)
—Mia, Matt & the Turkey Chase Cummins, Sarah, tr. from FRE. (p. 1133)
—Victorine et la Pièce D'or. Beshwaty, Steve, tr. (p. 1840)
Langlois, Florence. Extraordinary Gift. Goodman, John, tr. from FRE. (p. 555)
Langlois, Linda. Pygmy Palm: A Book of Trials & Courage. (p. 1421)
Langlois, Suzane, illus. see Sydor, Colleen.
Langlois, Suzane, jt. auth. see Trudel, Sylvain.
Langlois, Suzanne. Mia, Matt & the Turkey Chase. Cummins, Sarah, tr. from FRE. (p. 1133)
Langmuir, Erika & Thomson, Ruth. Looking at Paintings: An Introduction to Fine Art for Young People. (p. 1051)
Langner, Lawrence. Another Way Out. Landes, William-Alan, ed. (p. 88)
Langner, Mark Eugene. One Window. (p. 1297)
Langridge, Roger. Family Reunion. Langridge, Roger & Mebberson, Amy, illus. (p. 568)
—Forks & Hope Vol. 1. (p. 620)
—Meet the Muppets. Langridge, Roger, illus. (p. 1123)
—Muppet Show Comic Book: The Treasure of Peg-Leg Wilson. Langridge, Roger, illus. (p. 1191)
—Muppet Show Comic Book - Muppet Mash. Langridge, Roger, illus. (p. 1191)
—On the Road. Langridge, Roger, illus. (p. 1291)
—Ships & Sealing Wax. Langridge, Roger, illus. (p. 1567)
—Snarked (p. 1597)
Langridge, Roger, text. Muppets Omnibus. (p. 1191)
Langrish, Bob. Horses & Friends Poster Book. (p. 800)
Langrish, Bob, jt. auth. see Hiley, Lisa.
Langrish, Bob, photos by see McFarland, Cynthia.
Langrish, Bob, et al, photos by. Dream Horses. (p. 483)
Langrish, Katherine. Shadow Hunt. (p. 1557)
—Troll Blood. Stevens, Tim & Wyatt, David, illus. (p. 1788)

—Troll Fell. (p. 1788)
—Troll Mill. (p. 1788)
Langsam, Miriam. Velcro Interactive Phonics Instruction Book. (p. 1835)
Langstaff, John & Wiseman, Ann Sayre. Making Music: Create & Play 70 Musical Instruments Using Stuff from Around Your House. (p. 1081)
Langston, Elizabeth. Whisper Falls. (p. 1912)
Langston, James. Maximus the Musical Elephant. (p. 1112)
Langston, Laura. Abuelita, te Acuerdas? Gardiner, Lindsey, illus. (p. 7)
—Exit Point (p. 548)
—Finding Cassidy. (p. 588)
—Hannah's Touch (p. 743)
—Hot New Thing (p. 802)
—Last Ride (p. 978)
—Perfect Blue (p. 1341)
—Taste of Perfection (p. 1707)
—Trouble with Cupid (p. 1790)
Langston, Mandy & Nash, Kevin. University of Kentucky College Prowler off the Record. (p. 1820)
Langston, Steven. Pigeon in the Pool. (p. 1357)
Langston, Thomas, et al. George Washington (p. 664)
Langston, W. R. Why I Like My Grandma's House. (p. 1925)
Langston-George, Rebecca. All Dolled Up: Bringing 1920s & 1930s Flair to Your Wardrobe (p. 44)
—For the Right to Learn: Malala Yousafzai's Story. Bock, Janna, illus. (p. 616)
—For the Right to Learn. Bock, Janna, illus. (p. 616)
—Primary Source History of the Dust Bowl. (p. 1400)
—Telling Tales: Writing Captivating Short Stories. (p. 1717)
Langston-George, Rebecca, et al. Encounter. (p. 524)
—Fashion Forward (p. 575)
—Primary Source History. (p. 1400)
Langstrom, Angela Chapman. And God Said See, I Told You So! A True Story of Faith & Adoption. (p. 71)
Langteau, Scott. Sofa Boy. Vernon, Rion, illus. (p. 1605)
Langton, Bruce, illus. see Hall, Rebecca.
Langton, Bruce, illus. see Herzog, Brad.
Langton, Bruce, illus. see Himle, Lisa.
Langton, Bruce, illus. see Pierce, Patricia A.
Langton, Bruce, illus. see Schonberg, Marcia.
Langton, Bruce, illus. see Shoulders, Michael.
Langton, Bruce, illus. see Wargin, Kathy-jo.
Langton, Bruce, tr. see Pierce, Patricia A.
Langton, Jane. Dragon Tree. (p. 478)
—Fledgling. (p. 603)
—Mysterious Circus. (p. 1223)
Langton, Jane P. Saint Francis & the Wolf. Plume, Ilse, illus. (p. 1503)
Langton, Roger, illus. see Baxter, Nicola.
Langton, Roger, illus. see Dowley, Tim.
Langton, Roger, illus. see Lindvall, Ella K.
Langton, Roger, jt. auth. see Baxter, Nicola.
Langton, Roger W., illus. see Rock, Lois.
Language 911 Staff, contrib. by. Basic Japanese for Travelers. (p. 142)
Language Works Staff. Early Morning (p. 494)
—Language Works: Crocodile. Vol. I (p. 975)
—Message of the Dance. (p. 1129)
—Peter & the Wolf. (p. 1346)
—Red Hen. (p. 1454)
—Red Jack. (p. 1454)
—Rhyme Time. (p. 1468)
—Stone Soup. (p. 1652)
Langwith, Jacqueline. Adoption. Greenhaven Press Editors & Gale Editors, eds. (p. 13)
—Alcoholism. (p. 35)
—Alternative Medicine. (p. 50)
—Cerebral Palsy. Gale Editors, ed. (p. 287)
—Childhood Obesity. (p. 302)
—Cloning. (p. 333)
—College. (p. 340)
—Death & Dying. (p. 420)
—Depression. (p. 427)
—Discrimination. (p. 450)
—Hepatitis. (p. 769)
—Juvenile Crime. Gale, ed. (p. 941)
—Lung Cancer. Gale Editors, ed. (p. 1065)
—Mood Disorders. (p. 1171)
—Pandemics. Greenhaven Press Editors, ed. (p. 1321)
—Renewable Energy. (p. 1460)
—Role of the Government. (p. 1485)
—Sports Injuries. Greenhaven Press Editors & Gale, A. G., eds. (p. 1632)
—Violence. (p. 1843)
Langwith, Jacqueline & Des Chenes, Elizabeth, eds. Drug Abuse. (p. 486)
Langwith, Jacqueline, ed. Bioterrorism. (p. 190)
—Cloning. (p. 333)
—Hpv. (p. 824)
—Stem Cells. (p. 1647)
Langworthy, John Luther. Aeroplane Boys Flight. (p. 25)
—Aeroplane Boys on the Wing: Aeroplane Chums in the Tropics. (p. 25)
—Airplane Boys among the Clouds: Or, Young Aviators in a Wreck. (p. 31)
Lanier, Renee Comeaux. Ruby's Reading Tree. (p. 1494)
Lanier, Sidney. Bob: The Story of Our Mocking Bird. (p. 205)
—Boy's King Arthur. Wyeth, N. C., illus. (p. 220)
Lanier, Wendy. Abortion. (p. 5)
—Avalanches. (p. 118)
—Life Cycles. (p. 1009)
—Pebble First Guide to Texas Symbols (p. 1333)
—What Was the Missouri Compromise? And Other Questions about the Struggle over Slavery. (p. 1895)
Lanier, Wendy & Nelson, Robin. What Was the Missouri Compromise? And Other Questions about the Struggle over Slavery. (p. 1895)
Lanier, Wendy H. Life During the Great Depression. (p. 1010)
—Life During World War II. (p. 1010)
Lanigan-Schmidt, Therese. Ghosts of New York City (p. 672)
Lanino, Deborah, illus. see Hopkinson, Deborah.
Lanisek, Bill. Tony the Pony. (p. 1766)
Lank, Annytsya, tr. see Crouch, Adele.
Lankford, J. R. Jesus Thief: A Novel. (p. 916)
Lankford, Mary D. Christmas USA. Dugan, Karen, illus. (p. 316)
Lankford, Ronald D. Iraq War. (p. 887)
—Is China's Economic Growth a Threat to America? Greenhaven Press Editors, ed. (p. 889)
—Should the Rich Pay Higher Taxes? Greenhaven Press Editors, ed. (p. 1570)
—Should the Rich Pay Higher Taxes? Greenhaven Press Editors & Gale Editors, eds. (p. 1570)
Lankford, Ronald D. & Lankford, Ronnie D. Greenhouse Gases. (p. 723)
Lankford, Ronald D., ed. Should the Voting Age Be Lowered? (p. 1570)
Lankford, Ronnie D. Are America's Wealthy Too Powerful? (p. 96)
—Censorship. (p. 287)
—Green Cities. (p. 721)
—Gun Violence. (p. 732)
—Junk Food. (p. 936)
—Polygamy. (p. 1381)
—Prostitution. (p. 1412)
Lankford, Ronnie D., ed. see Fankford, Ronald, Jr.
Lankford, Ronnie D., jt. auth. see Lankford, Ronald D.
Lankford, Ronnie D., ed. Foreign Oil Dependence. (p. 617)
—What Is the Future of the U. S. Economy? (p. 1890)
Lankford, Ronnie D., Jr., ed. Greenhouse Gases. (p. 723)
Lankford, T. R. Sweet Te. (p. 1690)
Lanksy, Bruce. Rolling in the Aisles: A Collection of Laugh-Out-Loud Poems. Carpenter, Stephen, illus. (p. 1485)
Lannen, Jon Jon. Giraffe That Taught Me How to Laugh. (p. 677)
Lannin, Ann. Child from Nowhere. (p. 301)
Lanning, Andrea J. Imposturous Egg. Lanning, Andrea J., illus. (p. 862)
Lanning, Andy, jt. auth. see Abnett, Dan.
Lanning, Jerry. Making Grade. (p. 1081)
—Making Grade - Grade 1: Easy Popular Pieces for Young Pianists. (p. 1081)
Lanning, Rosemary, tr. see de Beer, Hans, pseud.
Lanphear, Dave, illus. see Martin, Gary, et al.
Lanqcaon, Jeff. Grandpa's Magic Banyan Tree. (p. 710)
Lanquetin, Anne-Sophie, illus. see Yolen, Jane & Stemple, Heidi E. Y.
Lansana, Quraysh Ali & Lightfoot, Toni Asante. Sixth Wave. (p. 1583)
Lansdale, Joe R. All the Earth, Thrown to the Sky. (p. 45)
Lansdale, John L., et al. Something Wicca This Way Comes Romberger, James et al, illus. (p. 1610)
Lansdowne, Marcella. Adventures of Patty & Annabel: Apache Lake & the Chakras. (p. 21)
—Adventures of Patty & Annabel: The Monsoon & the Auric Field. (p. 21)
—Adventures of Patty & Annabel: The Javelinas & Releasing the Cords. (p. 21)
Lanser, Amanda. Adapting to Climate Change. (p. 11)
—America at War by the Numbers. (p. 59)
—American Revolution by the Numbers. (p. 63)
—Boa Constrictor. (p. 205)
—Boa Constrictor Paperback. (p. 205)
—Civil War by the Numbers. (p. 325)
—Food Science: You Are What You Eat. (p. 614)
—Ötzi the Iceman. (p. 1307)
—Pope Francis: Spiritual Leader & Voice of the Poor. (p. 1384)
—School Lunches: Healthy Choices vs Crowd Pleasers. (p. 1523)
—What's Great about Massachusetts? (p. 1897)
—What's Great about Texas? (p. 1897)
—World War I by the Numbers. (p. 1959)
—World War II by the Numbers. (p. 1959)
Lansford, Tom. Communism. (p. 349)
—Conflict Resolution. (p. 357)
—Democracy. (p. 425)
—Dictatorships. Greenhaven Press Staff, ed. (p. 436)
—Immigration. (p. 861)
—Presidential Election Process. (p. 1397)
—Voting Rights. (p. 1850)
—War in Iraq. (p. 1857)
Lansford, Tom & Watson, Robert P. George W. Bush. (p. 663)
Lansford, Tom & Woods, Thomas E., Jr. Exploring American History: From Colonial Times to 1877 (p. 551)
Lansford, Tom, ed. Presidential Election Process. (p. 1397)
—Voting Rights. (p. 1850)
Lansing, Sandra J. Imprints: Collected Stories. Lanyon, Mary-Justine, ed. (p. 862)
Lansky, Bruce. Bad Case of the Giggles. Carpenter, Stephen, illus. (p. 131)
—Early Birdy Gets the Worm: A PictureReading Book for Young Children. Bolton, Bill, illus. (p. 493)
—Early Birdy Gets the Worm. Wummer, Amy, illus. (p. 493)
—I Hope I Don't Strike Out! & Other Funny Sports Poems. Carpenter, Stephen, illus. (p. 839)
—Monkey See, Monkey Do. Bolton, Bill, illus. (p. 1165)
—Monkey See, Monkey Do at the Zoo. Wummer, Amy, illus. (p. 1165)
—Peter Peter Pizza Eater. Carpenter, Stephen, illus. (p. 1347)
—Polar BRRRR Delivers. Wummer, Amy, illus. (p. 1379)
—What I Did on My Summer Vacation: Kids' Favorite Funny Poems about Summer Vacation. Carpenter, Stephen, illus. (p. 1886)
Lansky, Bruce, ed. see Kuffner, Trish.
Lansky, Bruce, ed. see Mooser, Stephen.
Lansky, Bruce & Carpenter, Stephen. My Teacher's in Detention: Kids' Favorite Funny School Poems. (p. 1220)
Lansky, Bruce & Johnson, Martha. Girls to the Rescue (p. 681)
Lansky, Bruce & Meadowbrook Press Staff. Mary Had a Little Jam: And Other Silly Rhymes. Carpenter, Stephen, illus. (p. 1100)
Lansky, Bruce & Pottle, Robert. Tinkle, Tinkle, Little Tot: Songs & Rhymes for Toilet Training. Blake, Anne Catharine, illus. (p. 1756)
Lansky, Bruce & Wiechmann, Angela, eds. Rolling in the Aisles (Revision) A Collection of Laugh-Out-Loud Poems. Carpenter, Stephen, illus. (p. 1485)
Lansky, Bruce, ed. Danger! Thin Ice: 9 Inspiring Stories about Clever & Courageous Girls from Around the World. (p. 404)
—Dinner with Dracula. Gordon, Mike & Gordon, Carl, illus. (p. 441)
—Fishing for Trouble: 8 Inspiring Stories about Clever & Courageous Girls from Around the World. (p. 599)
—Girls Save the Day: The 25 Most Popular Stories about Clever & Courageous Girls from Around the World. (p. 680)
—Hidden Courage: 10 Inspiring Stories about Clever & Courageous Girls from Around the World. (p. 775)
—I've Been Burping in the Classroom: And Other Silly Sing-along Songs. Carpenter, Stephen, illus. (p. 900)
—Lion on the Prowl: 10 Inspiring Stories about Clever & Courageous Girls from Around the World. (p. 1020)
—Miles of Smiles. Carpenter, Stephen, illus. (p. 1142)
—Royal Joust: 10 Inspiring Stories about Clever & Courageous Girls from Around the World. (p. 1492)
—Stormy Flight: 8 Inspiring Stories about Clever & Courageous Girls from Around the World. (p. 1656)
—Where There's Smoke, There's Fire! 10 Inspiring Stories about Clever & Courageous Girls from Around the World. (p. 1910)
Lansley, Oliver. Holly & Ivan's Christmas Adventure. (p. 789)
Lanthier, Jennifer. Legend of the Lost Jewels. (p. 989)
—Mystery of the Martello Tower. (p. 1225)
—Stamp Collector Thisdale, Francois, illus. (p. 1639)
Lantier, Patricia. Arkansas. (p. 99)
—Harriet Tubman: Conductor on the Underground Railroad. (p. 750)
—Kentucky. (p. 949)
—Rachel Carson: Fighting Pesticides & Other Chemical Pollutants. (p. 1431)
—Wisconsin. (p. 1939)
Lantier, Patricia, tr. see Marie, Christian.
Lantier, Patricia & Michael Horn, Geoffrey. Sojourner Truth: Speaking up for Freedom. (p. 1606)
Lantier-Sampon, Patricia. Arkansas. (p. 99)
—Kentucky. (p. 949)
—Louisiana. (p. 1058)
—Tennessee. (p. 1720)
—Wisconsin. (p. 1939)
Lantigua, Lizette M. Mission Libertad. (p. 1153)
Lantigua, Yanette. Mariana y el Albiqueno. Martinez, Tito, illus. (p. 1093)
Lanting, Frans, illus. see Esbaum, Jill.
Lanting, Fred. Canine Hip Dysplasia & Other Orthopedic Disorders. (p. 261)
Lantis, Lora, jt. auth. see Roy, Brenda.
Lanton, Sandy. Littlest Levine. Keay, Claire, illus. (p. 1039)
—Lots of Latkes: A Hanukkah Story. Redenbaugh, Vicki Jo, illus. (p. 1057)
Lanton, Sandy, jt. auth. see Rouss, Sylvia A.
Lantos, James, ed. Benjamin Franklin. (p. 164)
—Love: Vintage Images of America's Living Past. (p. 1059)
Lantz, Francess L. Current Affairs. (p. 394)
—Sea for Yourself. (p. 1534)
Lantz, Hays B., Jr. Rubrics for Assessing Student Achievement in Science Grades K-12. (p. 1493)
Lantz, Peggy, jt. auth. see Hale, Wendy.
Lantz, Peggy Sias & Hale, Wendy A. Coastlines of Florida. (p. 336)
—Coral Reefs of Florida. (p. 366)
—Oceans of Florida. (p. 1277)
—Wetlands of Florida. (p. 1877)
Lanyon, Mary-Justine, ed. see Lansing, Sandra J.
Lanz, Helen. Grow Your Own Lettuce. (p. 726)
—Grow Your Own Potatoes. (p. 726)
—Grow Your Own Strawberries. (p. 726)
—Grow Your Own Tomatoes. (p. 726)
—Having the Energy. (p. 755)
—How Shall We Travel? (p. 812)
—Reduce, Reuse, Recycle. (p. 1456)
—Shopping Choices. (p. 1569)
—What Shall We Eat? (p. 1893)
—Wonderful Water. (p. 1948)
Lanz, Helen, jt. auth. see Barraclough, Sue.
Lanza, Barbara. Glitter Tattoos Angels. (p. 684)
—How to Draw & Paint Enchanting Fairies. (p. 816)
—Time to Fly: A Fairy Lane Book. Lanza, Barbara, illus. (p. 1753)
Lanza, Janet, jt. auth. see Flahive, Lynn K.
Lanza, Janet & Flahive, Lynn. Blooming Category Activities. (p. 201)
Lanza, Janet R. & Flahive, Lynn K. Blooming Speech & Language Activities. (p. 201)
Lanza, Janet R., et al. Artic to Go. (p. 104)
Lanza, Marco, photos by see Gioffre, Rosalba, et al.
Lanza, Susan E. Nurturing Nuggets for Dementia Caregivers: 25 Supportive Strategies in Caring for Persons with Dementia. (p. 1273)
Lanzing, Jackson, jt. auth. see Server, David.
Lanzing, Jackson & Server, David. Penguins of Madagascar Volume 1 TP. (p. 1337)
Lanzrein, Helen. All Things Bright & Beautiful: A Collection of Prayer & Verse. (p. 46)
Lao, Samantha. Scared Panda. (p. 1519)
Laouénan, Christine. Stand Up! How to Stay True to Yourself. Moloney, Kate, ed. (p. 1639)
LaPadula, Thomas. My Giant Tractor. (p. 1209)
Lapadula, Thomas, illus. see Awdry, W.
Lapadula, Thomas, illus. see Golden Books.
Lapadula, Thomas, illus. see Lovitt, Chip.
Lapadula, Thomas, illus. see Random House.
LaPadula, Tom. Learn to Draw Planes, Choppers & Watercraft. (p. 983)
Lapadula, Tom. Tough Trucks. (p. 1773)
LaPadula, Tom, illus. see Banks, Steven.
LaPadula, Tom, illus. see Beechen, Adam.
LaPadula, Tom, illus. see McVeigh, Mark, et al.
LaPadula, Tom, illus. see Walter Foster Creative Team.
LaPadula, Tom & Shellly, Jeff. All about Drawing: Cool Cars, Fast Planes & Military Machines. (p. 42)
LaPadula, Tom & Shelly, Jeff. All about Drawing Cool Cars, Fast Planes & Military Machines: Learn How to Draw More Than 40 High-Powered Vehicles Step by Step. (p. 42)
Lapallo, Connie. Dark Enough to See the Stars in a Jamestown Sky. (p. 407)
LaPenta, Marilyn. Artful Snacks. (p. 103)
—Cool Cookies. (p. 363)
Lapenta, Marilyn. Fall Shakes to Harvest Bakes. (p. 566)
—Spring Spreads to Nutty Breads. (p. 1635)
—Summer Sips to Chill Dips. (p. 1675)
LaPenta, Marilyn. Super 'Wiches. (p. 1682)
—Way Cool Drinks. (p. 1864)
Lapenta, Marilyn. Winter Punches to Nut Crunches. (p. 1938)
Lapham, Lewis. 30 Satires. (p. 1996)
Lapham, Steven Sellers & Walton, Eugene. Philip Reid Saves the Statue of Freedom. (p. 1350)
Lapham, Thea Rozetta & Conroy, Erin Brown. Free to See: How Helen Keller's Friendship, Courage & Compassion Freed a Young Girl's Imagination & Taught Her to See with Her Heart & Mind. (p. 634)
Lapid, Koty. Wild Virtual Enchanted Garden. (p. 1930)
Lapidot, Gila. Shakel Shakelovitz Finds a Treasure. (p. 1558)
Lapierre, Bob. Endepandans! Pyès Teyat an Sis Planch. (p. 527)
LaPierre, Karina, illus. see Dellasega, Cheryl.
Lapierre, Steeve, jt. auth. see Meunier, Sylvain.
Lapin Feeblebunny. Gang That Couldn't Think Straight. (p. 655)
Lapine, James, jt. auth. see Talbott, Hudson.
Lapinksy, Terri, jt. auth. see Blohm, Judith M.
Laplander, Cheryl. Maximillion. (p. 1112)
Laplante, Carole. Magic Is in You. Byrne-Walker, Mary Ann, illus. (p. 1072)
—Night Noises. Byrne-Walker, Mary Ann, illus. (p. 1253)
LaPlante, Walter. Conserving the Great Lakes. (p. 359)
—Plants & Animals of the Great Lakes. (p. 1369)
—Presidential Seal. (p. 1397)
—Sea Anemones. (p. 1534)
—Sitting Bull. (p. 1582)
—Tecumseh. (p. 1712)
—Waterways of the Great Lakes. (p. 1864)
—What Happens When I Flush the Toilet? (p. 1886)
—What Makes Fire Burn? (p. 1892)
LaPoint, Crystal Godfrey. When My Mommy Cries: A Story to Help Families Cope with Sadness (Book with CD) Eldridge, Crystal, illus. (p. 1904)
Lapointe, Claude, illus. see Kahn, Michaéle.
Lapointe, Claude, tr. see Kahn, Michaéle.
LaPorta, Joann. Unexpected Visitor: A Journey of Hilarious & Sometimes Embarrassing Moments. (p. 1817)
LaPorte, Tom. Hembree Heiroglyphs. (p. 766)
—Hembree Hopefuls: A Hembree Elementary Story. (p. 766)
Lapp, Diane, et al. Teaching Literacy in First Grade. (p. 1710)
Lappan, Glenda. Connected Mathematics (p. 357)
Lappan, Glenda & Prentice Hall Staff. Connected Mathematics (p. 357)
Lappe, S. M. Street Painting: A Guide for Young Artists. (p. 1666)
Lappi, Megan. Birds. (p. 191)
—C. S. Lewis. (p. 250)
—Church: Pioneers of Canada. (p. 318)
—Decomposers. (p. 422)
—Fossils. (p. 624)
—Mount Everest: The Highest Mountain in the World. (p. 1180)
—Mount Everest. (p. 1180)
—Sahara Desert: The Largest Desert in the World. (p. 1503)
—Sahara Desert. (p. 1503)
—Will Hobbs. (p. 1932)
Lapsley, Sarah. Learning about Cows. Williams, Glenn, illus. (p. 984)
Lapthorn, Nicholas, jt. auth. see Chambers, Catherine.
Lapucci, Carlo. Fiabe toscane di maghi, fate, animali, diavoli e Giganti: Volume 2. (p. 583)
—Fiabe toscane di maghi, fate, animali, diavoli e Giganti: Edizione economica. Volume I. (p. 583)
Lapytski, Kristina, jt. auth. see Lapytski, Serge.
Lapytski, Serge & Lapytski, Kristina. Heart of a Lion! E-Hare. (p. 759)
LaQuay, Kate, jt. auth. see LoGiudice, Carolyn.
LaQuay, Kate, jt. auth. see Logiudice, Carolyn.
LaQuay, Kate & LoGiudice, Carolyn. Spotlight on Vocabulary Antonyms Level 1 (p. 1634)
LaQuay, Kate & Logiudice, Carolyn. Spotlight on Vocabulary Associations Level 1 (p. 1634)
—Spotlight on Vocabulary Attributes Level 1 (p. 1634)
Lar Rieu, Barry, text. Penguin Paradise. (p. 1337)
Lara, David, illus. see Fleischman, Sid.
Lara, Enrique & Garcia, Luis. Leaves. (p. 986)
Lara, Jose Luis Trueba. Descubre la historia de los Ninos. Cortes, Osvaldo, illus. (p. 428)
—Descubrelas Diez Maravillas. (p. 428)
Lara, Mike. Boy & a Horse. (p. 217)
Lara, Sahai. My Loveable Little Monster. Hunt, Jim, illus. (p. 1213)
Larable, Gayle. Is My Dad Still My Dad? (p. 889)
Larade, April, illus. see May, Maggie.
LaRamee-Jones, Shanda, jt. auth. see McDougall, Carol.
LaRamee-Jones, Shanda & McDougall, Carol. Baby Talk (p. 128)
Laraya-Coutts, Corie, jt. auth. see Koehler, Hanne Lore.
Larbalestier, Justine. How to Ditch Your Fairy. (p. 816)
—Liar. (p. 1005)
—Magic's Child. (p. 1075)
—Razorhurst. (p. 1441)
Larbalestier, Justine, jt. ed. see Black, Holly.
Larbalestier, Justine & Brennan, Sarah Rees. Team Human. (p. 1710)
Larbi, George A., jt. ed. see Bangura, Yusuf.
Larcenet, Manu, illus. see Sfar, Joann & Trondheim, Lewis.
Larcher, Jean. Optical & Geometrical Allover Patterns: 70 Original Drawings. (p. 1301)
Larcom. March. (p. 1091)

Larcombe, Jennifer Rees. Best Boat Ever Built. Björkman, Steve, illus. (p. 168)
—Dance to the Music. (p. 402)
—Danger on the Lonely Road. Björkman, Steve, illus. (p. 404)
—Lost in Jerusalem! Björkman, Steve, illus. (p. 1055)
—Stone of Evil. (p. 1652)
—Terrible Giant. Björkman, Steve, illus. (p. 1721)
—Walls That Fell down Flat. Björkman, Steve, illus. (p. 1855)
Larcombe, Tony. Who Ate Monica the Japonica. (p. 1914)
Lard, Mary Anne, illus. see Bender, Esther.
Lardone, Lilia. Caballero Negro. (p. 250)
—Papiros. (p. 1323)
Lardot, Christopher, illus. see Brocklehurst, Ruth.
Lardy, Philippe, illus. see Nelson, Marilyn.
LaReau, Jenna, illus. see Janeczko, Paul B., ed.
LaReau, Jenna, illus. see LaReau, Kara.
LaReau, Kara. No Slurping, No Burping! A Tale of Table Manners. Bové, Lorelay, illus. (p. 1260)
—Rocko & Spanky Call It Quits. LaReau, Jenna, illus. (p. 1483)
—Ugly Fish. Magoon, Scott, illus. (p. 1808)
Laredo, Elizabeth. Jump Rope Book. Cooper, Martha, photos by. (p. 934)
Large, Nathan, tr. see Nordqvist, Sven.
Large, Tori. Illustrated Dictionary of Math: Internet-Linked. (p. 857)
—Usborne Illustrated Dictionary of Math. (p. 1827)
—Usborne Illustrated Dictionary of Math. Constantine, Adam, illus. (p. 1827)
—Usborne Illustrated Dictionary of Math. Rogers, Kirsteen, ed. (p. 1827)
Large, Tori, jt. auth. see Rogers, Kirsteen.
Largen, Velda L. & Bence, Deborah L. Good Food. (p. 698)
—Guide to Good Food: Resource Portfolio. (p. 730)
—Guide to Good Food: Teaching Package Teacher's Wraparound Edition. (p. 730)
—Guide to Good Food: Teaching Package Exam View(r) Text Generator Software. (p. 730)
—Guide to Good Food Recipe. (p. 730)
LaRiccia, Mike, illus. see Dauer, Marty.
Larichev, Andrei Borisovich. Boy Who was President. Moresco, Jamie, ed. (p. 219)
Larimore, Walt, et al. Lintball Leo's Not-So-Stupid Questions about Your Body Phillips, Mike, illus. (p. 1019)
Larimore, Walter L. Bryson City Tales: Stories of a Doctor's First Year of Practice in the Smoky Mountains. (p. 233)
—Hazel Creek: A Novel. (p. 756)
Larin, Allison, jt. auth. see Kalman, Bobbie.
Lark, Casi, photos by see Schindel, John.
Lark Crafts Staff, jt. ed. see Momu, Nathalie.
Lark, Liz. Yoga for Kids. Park, Clare, photos by. (p. 1972)
Lark, Liz, jt. auth. see Spilling, Michael.
Larkee, Tom, compiled by. Here We Rec: Clarence Radtke & his Hometown. (p. 771)
Larkin, Catherine, illus. see Mahony, Mary.
Larkin, Eric, illus. see Martin, Jacqueline Briggs.
Larkin, Jean. Absolutely Advent! Getting Ready for Christmas 2007. (p. 7)
—Days of Faith: Student Planner & Assignment Book/Primary Teacher Supplement 2005-2006. (p. 415)
—First Eucharist: Activities for Intermediate Grades. (p. 594)
—First Reconciliation: Activities for Intermediate Grades. (p. 596)
—Totally Lent! A Kid's Journey to Easter 2007. (p. 1771)
—Totally Lent! A Child's Journey to Easter 2007. (p. 1771)
Larkin, Jean, ed. see Buell, Jean.
Larkin, Jean, ed. see Dotterweich, Kass.
Larkin, Jean, ed. see Hakes, Matthew.
Larkin, Jean, ed. see Kaster, Jeffrey & Kaster, Liz.
Larkin, Jean, ed. see Meister, Deborah.
Larkin, Jean, ed. Celebrate with Jesus: A Child's Book of the Sacraments. Swisher, Elizabeth et al, illus. (p. 284)
—First Eucharist: Activities for Primary Grades. (p. 594)
—Prayers & Guidelines for Young Catholics. (p. 1393)
—Sacred Stories: A Child's Bible Book. (p. 1500)
Larkin, Jean K. Absolutely Advent! Getting Ready for Christmas 2005. (p. 7)
Larkin, Jean K., ed. see Crain, Michael.
Larkin, Jean K., ed. see Hakes, Matthew.
Larkin, Jean K., ed. see Meister, Deborah.
Larkin, Jean K., ed. see Pfeifer, Alice Ann.
Larkin, Jean K., ed. see Savitskas, Margaret & Behe, Mary.
Larkin, Jean K., ed. see Savitskas, Margaret.
Larkin, Jean K., ed. see Stanley, Barb.
Larkin, Jean K., ed. see Thiele, Christine.
Larkin, Jillian. Diva. (p. 454)
—Ingenue. (p. 874)
—Vixen. (p. 1846)
Larkin, Jim & Rambo, Lee Elliot. Books for Oliver. Brown, Dan, illus. (p. 212)
Larkin, John. Pause. (p. 1331)
—Shadow Girl. (p. 1557)
Larkin, Judy. Strategic Reputation Risk Management. (p. 1666)
Larkin, Paige A., illus. see Stroud-Peace, Glenda.
Larkin, Peter. Terrain Seed Scarcity: Poems from a Decade. (p. 1721)
Larkin, Rochelle, ed. Beauty & the Beast & Other Stories. (p. 154)
—Little Mermaid & Other Stories. (p. 1031)
Larkin, Susan. All the Ways I Love You. Trotter, Stuart, illus. (p. 46)
Larkin, Tanya. Cooking Throughout American History Set 2 (p. 362)
—Jacques Marquette & Louis Jolliet: Explorers of the Mississippi. (p. 905)
—What Was Cooking in Abigail Adams' White House? (p. 1894)
—What Was Cooking in Dolley Madison's White House? (p. 1894)
—What Was Cooking in Edith Roosevelt's White House? (p. 1894)
—What Was Cooking in Julia Grant's White House? (p. 1894)
—What Was Cooking in Martha Washington's Presidential Mansion? (p. 1894)
—What Was Cooking in Mary Todd Lincoln's White House? (p. 1894)
Larking, Jean K., ed. see Kaster, Jeffrey.
Larkins, Mona, illus. see Day-Bivins, Pat.
Larkins, Mona, illus. see Robinson, Linda M.
Larkins, Mona, illus. see Thomas, Kate.
Larkum, A., illus. see Daynes, Katie.
Larkum, A., jt. auth. see Claybourne, A.
Larkum, Adam, illus. see Dalby, Elizabeth.
Larkum, Adam, illus. see Daynes, Katie.
Larkum, Adam, illus. see Firth, Alex.
Larkum, Adam, illus. see Gilpin, Rebecca.
Larkum, Adam, illus. see Helbrough, Emma.
Larkum, Adam, illus. see Knighton, Kate.
Larkum, Adam, illus. see Meredith, Sue.
Larkum, Adam, illus. see Turnbull, Stephanie.
Larmoyeux, Mary, jt. auth. see Bradford, Amy L.
Larned, Phillip, illus. see Larned, S.
Larned, S. Magic Muffin Larned, Phillip, illus. (p. 1072)
Larned, W. T. & La Fontaine, Jean de. Reynard the Fox & Other Fables. Rae, John, illus. (p. 1467)
Larner, Bob, jt. auth. see Davis, Darren G.
Larner, Eric. Adventure of Paperman - Journey into Night. Schmolze, Ian, illus. (p. 14)
Larocco. Literature for Life & Work. (p. 1023)
LaRoche, Amelia. Care for a Pet Parrot. (p. 266)
LaRoche, Amelia. Amusing Animal Jokes to Tickle Your Funny Bone. (p. 66)
—April Fool's Day Jokes to Tickle Your Funny Bone. (p. 93)
—Fowl Chicken Jokes to Tickle Your Funny Bone. (p. 625)
—Ho-Ho-Ho Christmas Jokes to Tickle Your Funny Bone. (p. 786)
—Recipe & Craft Guide to France. (p. 1451)
—We Visit Turkey. (p. 1868)
LaRoche, Amy. Chimaera. (p. 306)
Laroche, Bridget, illus. see Valeska, Jon & Fripp, Jean.
Laroche, Giles. If You Lived Here: Houses of the World. (p. 854)
Laroche, Giles, illus. see Prince, April Jones.
LaRoche, Loretta. Lighten Up! with Loretta (p. 1015)
Laroche, M. Perplexing Problems of Pea & Friends. (p. 1343)
LaRochelle, David. 1+1=5: And Other Unlikely Additions. Sexton, Brenda, illus. (p. 1991)
—Arlo's ARTrageous Adventure! Includes 50 Flaps to Flip. (p. 99)
—Best Pet of All. Wakiyama, Hanako, illus. (p. 171)
—End. Egielski, Richard, illus. (p. 526)
—How Martha Saved Her Parents from Green Beans. Fearing, Mark, illus. (p. 811)
—It's a Tiger! Tankard, Jeremy, illus. (p. 896)
—Moo! Wohnoutka, Mike, illus. (p. 1171)
Larocque, Gisele, tr. see Dumont, Claire & Lacoursiere, Suzanne.
LaRocque, Greg. Crybaby: Extinction. Castillo, Cesar & Burruss, Melissa, illus. (p. 387)
LaRoe, Locki & Salazar, Sharon. Willie the Charismatic Kangaroo: The Beginning... (p. 1934)
LaRoe, Misty Bailey, illus. see King, Sharon.
Laronde, Gary, illus. see Bauld, Jane Scoggins.
LaRosa, James, jt. auth. see Seles, Monica.
Larosa, Lewis. In the Beginning. (p. 865)
Larosa, Marjanita. Mosquit: The Very Disobedient Mosquito. (p. 1176)
LaRosa, Paula & Benchmark Education Co., LLC Staff. I Am Pat. (p. 833)
—Time to Tug. (p. 1753)
Larose, Ella. Best Rainbow Ever! (p. 171)
Larose, Melinda. Jake & the Never Land Pirates: Treasure of the Tides. (p. 905)
—Jake & the Never Land Pirates: After a While, Crocodile. (p. 905)
—Surfin' Turf. (p. 1685)
LaRose, Melinda, jt. auth. see Disney Book Group Staff.
LaRose, Melinda & Disney Book Group Staff. Birthday Bash! Disney Storybook Art Team, illus. (p. 192)
—Bucky Makes a Splash! Disney Storybook Artists Staff, illus. (p. 234)
—Croc Takes the Cake. Disney Storybook Artists Staff, illus. (p. 384)
—Jake & the Never Land Pirates after a While, Crocodile. Disney Storybook Artists Staff, illus. (p. 905)
—Jake & the Never Land Pirates Treasure of the Tides. Disney Storybook Artists Staff, illus. (p. 905)
—Jake Hatches a Plan, Pre-Level 1. Disney Storybook Art Team, illus. (p. 906)
—Let's Get Jumping! Disney Storybook Art Team, illus. (p. 997)
—Save Me, Smee! Disney Storybook Artists Staff, illus. (p. 1516)
—X Marks the Croc!, Pre-Level 1. Disney Storybook Art Team, illus. (p. 1967)
LaRose, Melinda, et al. Follow That Sound! (p. 612)
Larousse Editors. Larousse Pocket Student Dictionary: Spanish-English / English-Spanish. (p. 976)
—Larousse Pocket Student Dictionary French-English/English-French. (p. 976)
—Larousse Student Dictionary French-English/English-French. (p. 976)
—Larousse Student Dictionary Spanish-English/English-Spanish. (p. 976)
Larousse Editors, jt. ed. see Cabot, Paloma.
Larousse Editors, ed. Larousse College Dictionary. (p. 975)
Larousse Mexico Staff. Ingles para Todos Gramatica. (p. 874)
Larousse Mexico Staff, ed. Buenas Noche. Desplanche, Vincent, illus. (p. 235)
—Historias de Princesas y Hadas. (p. 782)
—Los Dinosaurios. (p. 1053)
Larousse Staff. Diccionario Basico Escolar. (p. 435)
—Mon premier Larousse du Monde. (p. 1163)
Larousse Staff, ed. Larousse College Dictionary. (p. 975)
LaRoy, Sue, jt. auth. see Carder, Ken.
Laroyster, Angela. Puppy. (p. 1418)
Larra, Mariano José de. Articulos de Larra. (p. 104)
Larranaga, Ana. Matching Puzzle Cards - Animals. (p. 1104)
Larranaga, Ana, illus. see Ikids Staff.
Larranaga, Ana, illus. see Powell, Richard.
Larranaga, Ana, illus. see Schultz, Lucy & Shultz, Lucy.
Larranaga, Ana M. Buggy Buddies - Noisy Home. (p. 236)
—Pull & Play - Opposites. Martin, Ana I., illus. (p. 1415)
Larranaga, Ana Martin. Counting. (p. 370)
Larrañaga, Ana Martin. I Love You All Day Long. (p. 843)
Larranaga, Ana Martin. Noisy Beach. Larranaga, Ana Martin, illus. (p. 1262)
—Noisy Park. Larranaga, Ana Martin, illus. (p. 1263)
—Noisy Town. (p. 1263)
Larrañaga, Ana Martin, illus. see Hill, Susanna Leonard.
Larranaga, Ana Martin, illus. see Ikids Staff.
Larrañaga, Ana Martin, illus. see Innovative Kids Staff.
Larranaga, Ana Martin, illus. see Jugran, Jan.
Larrañaga, Ana Martin, illus. see Page, Liza & Innovative Kids Staff.
Larranaga, Ana Martin, illus. see Rivers-Moore, Debbie.
Larrañaga, Ana Martin, illus. see Root, Phyllis.
Larranaga, Ana Martin, illus. see Thalia.
Larrañaga, Martin & Innovative Kids Staff. I Love You, Little One. (p. 843)
Larrew, Brekka Hervey. Apple Pie Calzones & Other Cookie Recipes (p. 92)
—Banana-Berry Smoothies & Other Breakfast Recipes (p. 135)
—Cheesecake Cupcakes & Other Cake Recipes. (p. 296)
—Golden Retrievers (p. 695)
—Labradoodles (p. 970)
—Shih Tzus (p. 1566)
Larrick, Nancy. Rain, Hail, Sleet & Snow. Yap, Weda, illus. (p. 1435)
Larrison, Joanne. Week That Led to Easter. Williams, Jenny, illus. (p. 1871)
Larrivee, Barbara & Cooper, James M. Educator's Guide to Teacher Reflection. (p. 505)
Larroca, Salvador, illus. see Jemas, Bill & Watson, Andi.
Larroca, Salvador, illus. see Peyer, Tom.
Larrondo, Valérie & Desmarteau, Claudine. Mama Fue Pequena Antes de Ser Mayor. (p. 1084)
Larry, H. I. Blockbuster. (p. 200)
—Boot Camp. (p. 213)
—Deep Waters. Oswald, Ash, illus. (p. 423)
—Fossil Fury. (p. 623)
—Frozen Fear. Oswald, Ash, illus. (p. 645)
—Horror House. (p. 799)
—Lunar Strike. (p. 1065)
—Mind Games. Oswald, Ash, illus. (p. 1145)
—Poison Island. Oswald, Ash, illus. (p. 1377)
—River Rampage. (p. 1476)
—Shock Music. (p. 1568)
—Sky High. (p. 1586)
—Swamp Race. (p. 1688)
—Tomb of Doom. (p. 1764)
—Volcanic Panic. (p. 1848)
—Zac Blasts Off. (p. 1984)
—Zac Climbs High. (p. 1984)
—Zac Runs Wild. (p. 1984)
—Zac Strikes Out. (p. 1984)
—Zac's Bank Bust. (p. 1984)
—Zac's Quicksand. (p. 1984)
—Zac's Skate Break. (p. 1984)
—Zac's Sticky Fix. (p. 1984)
Larry, Loyie, jt. auth. see Brissenden, Constance.
Larry Sweitzer. Ghost, the Eggheads, & Babe Ruth's Piano: A Novel. (p. 672)
Larrypoet. Green, the Fairy: Cici & the Fairy. (p. 722)
Larsa, Angela. Norman PhartEphant. (p. 1264)
Larsen, Aaron & Perrin, Christopher. Latin for Children, Primer B. (p. 979)
—Latin for Children, Primer B Answer Key. (p. 979)
Larsen, Alison. My Turtle. Larsen, Alison, illus. (p. 1220)
—Thomas the Turtle. (p. 1739)
—Thomas the Turtle's Adventures. (p. 1739)
—What Makes You Smile? Larsen, Alison, illus. (p. 1892)
Larsen, Andrew. Bella & the Bunny. Endle, Kate, illus. (p. 162)
—Charlie's Dirt Day Hudon-Verrelli, Jacqueline, illus. (p. 293)
—Imaginary Garden. Luxbacher, Irene, illus. (p. 860)
—In the Tree House. Petricić, Dušan, illus. (p. 867)
—Luck of Jude (p. 1062)
Larsen, Angela. Travel to Tomorrow: Book One of the Fifties Chix Series. (p. 1780)
Larsen, Angela Sage. Fifties Chix: till the End of Time (p. 584)
—Fifties Chix: Broken Record (Book 4) (p. 585)
—Fifties Chix: Keeping Secrets (Book 2) (p. 585)
—Fifties Chix: Third Time's a Charm (Book 3) (p. 585)
—Petalwink Learns to Fly. Larsen, Angela Sage, illus. (p. 1346)
Larsen, Becca. Buying & Selling. (p. 248)
Larsen, C. S. All Pooped Out: And Other Gross Expressions. Blecha, Aaron, illus. (p. 45)
—Chronicles of Marvin Archibald Trekker: Boy Magician Book 1 - Penguins of Choice. (p. 317)
—Crust & Spray: Gross Stuff in Your Eyes, Ears, Nose, & Throat. Slack, Michael H., illus. (p. 387)
Larsen, Carolyn. 101 Bible Stories for Toddlers. (p. 1999)
—Abraham, Isaac, & Jacob. (p. 6)
—Bible Stories for Tiny Tots. Incrocci, Rick, illus. (p. 176)
—Egypt to the Promised Land. (p. 506)
—For Girls Only! Devotions. Sutherland, Leah, illus. (p. 615)
—Jesus: His Last Days. (p. 914)
—Little Angels Bible Storybook. Incrocci, Rick, illus. (p. 1023)
—Little Boys Bible Storybook for Fathers & Sons. Turk, Caron, illus. (p. 1025)
—Little Girls Bible Storybook for Fathers & Daughters. Turk, Caron, illus. (p. 1028)
—My 123 Bible Storybook. Turk, Caron, illus. (p. 1195)
—My ABC Bible Storybook. Turk, Caron, illus. (p. 1195)
—Prayers for Little Boys. Turk, Caron, illus. (p. 1393)
—Prayers for Little Girls. Turk, Caron, illus. (p. 1393)
—Princess Stories: Real Bible Stories of God's Princesses. Eliseev, Sergey, illus. (p. 1405)
—Stories about Jesus for Little Ones. Incrocci, Rick, illus. (p. 1654)
—Teachings of Jesus. (p. 1710)
—What Does the Bible Say about That? Incrocci, Rick, illus. (p. 1884)
Larsen, Carolyn & Baker Publishing Group Staff. My Bedtime Bible. Incrocci, Rick, illus. (p. 1196)
Larsen, Chris T. Real Love: An Enchanting Journey of the Heart. (p. 1448)
Larsen, Chuck, ed. see Ahlman, Larry.
Larsen, Claire A. God's Great Covenant, Old Testament 1. (p. 691)
—God's Great Covenant, Old Testament 2: A Bible Course for Children. (p. 691)
Larsen, Dan. Samson. (p. 1509)
Larsen, Dan, illus. see Wood, Francis Eugene.
Larsen, Dan, illus. see Wood, Francis.
Larsen, Dean. Fish Dreams. (p. 598)
Larsen, Donna R. In My Own Backyard. Reilly, Michelle, illus. (p. 864)
Larsen, Elizabeth. Buster Hardings: Buster Makes New Friends. (p. 245)
—Kendra's Decision. (p. 948)
—Open House at Buster's New School: Season 1, Book 2: Buster Hardings (p. 1299)
—Party for Buster & Haylee! (p. 1326)
Larsen, Elizabeth Foy, jt. auth. see Glenn, Joshua.
Larsen, Elizabeth Foy & Glenn, Joshua. Unbored: The Essential Field Guide to Serious Fun. Kasunick, Heather & Reusch, Mister, illus. (p. 1811)
Larsen, Eric, illus. see Falk, Laine.
Larsen, Eric, illus. see Kavanagh, Terry & Harris, Joseph.
Larsen, Erik. Last Rites. (p. 978)
—Resurrection. (p. 1464)
—Savage Dragon - Dragon War. (p. 1516)
—Savage Dragon on Trial TP. (p. 1516)
—Savage Dragon: United We Stand TP: United We Stand TP. (p. 1516)
—Terminated. (p. 1721)
—Worlds at War (p. 1960)
Larsen, Erik, et al. Image Comics. (p. 860)
—Spider-Man: The Vengeance of Venom. (p. 1626)
Larsen, Grey & Grey Larsen. Toolbox Exercises for Finger Coordination: A Supplement to the Book the Essential Tin Whistle Toolbox (p. 1767)
—Toolbox Tune Collection: A Supplement to the Book the Essential Tin Whistle Toolbox. (p. 1767)
Larsen, Henrik. Analysing the Foreign Policy of Small States in the EU: The Case of Denmark. (p. 67)
Larsen, Jen. Future Perfect. (p. 651)
Larsen, Jill. There's a Moose on the Loose Coloring Book. (p. 1731)
Larsen, Kirsten. Dora & the Baby Crab. Roper, Robert, illus. (p. 470)
—Dora's Perfect Pumpkin. Miller, Victoria, illus. (p. 471)
—Ghost Town Mystery. Smath, Jerry, illus. (p. 672)
—It's Sharing Day! Zalme, Ron, illus. (p. 898)
—Tara Pays Up! Billin-Frye, Paige, illus. (p. 1706)
—Whoa! UFO! Gott, Barry, illus. (p. 1919)
Larsen, Kirsten, et al. Mater & the Easter Buggy. Disney Storybook Art Team, illus. (p. 1104)
Larsen, Laurel. One Night in the Everglades. Turley, Joyce Mihran, illus. (p. 1296)
Larsen, Laurie. Chronicles of Casey V. (p. 317)
Larsen, Mylisa. Instructions for Bedtime. Cole, Babette, illus. (p. 878)
Larsen, Patti. Sassafras. (p. 1515)
Larsen, Ramonita. Yes, I Can Do It/Si, lo Puedo Hacer. Larsen, Ramonita, illus. (p. 1970)
Larsen, Randall J. Our Own Worst Enemy: Asking the Right Questions about Security to Protect You, Your Family, & America. (p. 1309)
Larsen, Sharon G. Parable of the Chocolate Chips. (p. 1323)
Larsen, Wayne. A. Y. Jackson: A Love for the Land. (p. 2)
Larson, Abigail, illus. see Herz, Henry, et al.
Larson, Amanda, illus. see Gildea, Kathy.
Larson, Angela. Anthony Smoochiano: First Loves. (p. 89)
—Bobbie Burple: Frog Song. (p. 206)
—Harry Hiccers: Friends of A Feether. (p. 750)
—Norman PhartEphant: The coloring Book. (p. 1264)
Larson, Ann K. Terrifying Tub Tornado. (p. 1722)
Larson, Beverly. Toca y Siente las Historias de la Biblia. Pineda, Nancy, tr. (p. 1760)
Larson, Caleb A., illus. see Larson, Melissa J.
Larson, Chuck. Heroes among Us: Firsthand Accounts of Combat from America's Most Decorated Warriors in Iraq & Afghanistan. Larson, Chuck, ed. (p. 772)
Larson, Cynthia. Karen Kimball: And the Dream Weaver's Web. (p. 943)
Larson, D. J. Pigsley Brew. Larson, D. J., illus. (p. 1358)
Larson, Daniel T. Nature of Matter. (p. 1236)
Larson, Deborah Jo. One Frozen Lake. Johnson, Steve & Fancher, Lou, illus. (p. 1295)
Larson, Elaine M., et al. I Am Utterly Unique: Celebrating the Strengths of Children with Asperger Syndrome & High-Functioning Autism. Strand, Vivian, illus. (p. 834)
Larson, Elaine Marie. Chameleon Kid: Controlling Meltdown Before He Controls You. (p. 289)
—Kaleidoscope Kid: Focusing on the Strengths of Children with Asperger Syndrome & High-Functioning Autism. Strand, Vivian, illus. (p. 941)
Larson, Eric. How Did Carpet Get in This House? Burns, William G., ed. (p. 806)
Larson, Eric, ed. see Schwartz, Linda.
Larson, Eric, ed. see Sylvester, Diane.
Larson, Frank. Baloney on Wry: Humorous Essays. (p. 135)
Larson, Heidi. Love the Lord Your God! (p. 1060)
Larson, Hope. Chiggers. Larson, Hope, illus. (p. 301)
—Mercury. Larson, Hope, illus. (p. 1127)
Larson, Hope, illus. see L'Engle, Madeleine.
Larson, J. E., illus. see Shecter, Vicky Alvear.
Larson, Jason. Me & My Safety. (p. 1115)
Larson, Jeanette, ed. see Yorinks, Adrienne.
Larson, Jeanette & Yorinks, Adrienne. Hummingbirds: Facts & Folklore from the Americas. Yorinks, Adrienne, illus. (p. 826)
Larson, Jennifer. Category Cut-Ups Workbook with CD-ROM: Bk335. Prince, Audrey & Webber, Thomas, eds. (p. 279)
Larson, Jennifer S. Delicious Vegetarian Main Dishes. Cohen, Brie, photos by. (p. 425)

L

—Do I Need It? or Do I Want It? Making Budget Choices. (p. 457)
—Meaty Main Dishes. Cohen, Brie, photos by. (p. 1118)
—Mighty Bison. (p. 1140)
—Perfect Pizza Recipes. Cohen, Brie, photos by. (p. 1342)
—Super Pasta & Rice Dishes. Cohen, Brie, photos by. (p. 1680)
—Tasty Sandwiches. Cohen, Brie, photos by. (p. 1707)
—What Can You Do with Money? Earning, Spending, & Saving. (p. 1881)
—What Is Money, Anyway? Why Dollars & Coins Have Value. (p. 1890)
—Where Do We Keep Money? How Banks Work. (p. 1907)
—Who's Buying? Who's Selling? Understanding Consumers & Producers. (p. 1920)
—Yummy Soup & Salad Recipes. Cohen, Brie, photos by. (p. 1983)
Larson, Jennifer S., photos by see Cornell, Karl A.
Larson, Joan, illus. see Olsen, Sylvia.
Larson, K. D. That Place. (p. 1726)
Larson, Karen. Changing Matter. (p. 290)
Larson, Karl, et al. Truth about Violence. (p. 1794)
Larson, Katherine, illus. see Ahern, Dianne.
Larson, Katherine, illus. see Hall, Rebecca.
Larson, Katherine, illus. see Wargin, Kathy-jo.
Larson, Kirby. Dash. (p. 409)
—Duke. (p. 489)
—Fences Between Us: The Diary of Piper Davis. (p. 581)
—Friendship Doll. (p. 639)
—Hattie Big Sky. (p. 752)
—Hattie Ever After. (p. 752)
Larson, Kirby & Nethery, Mary. Two Bobbies: A True Story of Hurricane Katrina, Friendship, & Survival. Cassels, Jean, illus. (p. 1803)
—Two Bobbies. Cassels, Jean, illus. (p. 1803)
Larson, Kirby, et al. Lucky Dog: Twelve Tales of Rescued Dogs. (p. 1062)
Larson, Kirsten. Ghost Town Mystery. (p. 672)
—Science Fair Success! (p. 1526)
—Using the Scientific Method. (p. 1828)
Larson, Kirsten W. Mutants in Nature. (p. 1194)
—Super Powers in Nature. (p. 1680)
—Vampires in Nature. (p. 1832)
—West: Arizona, California, Nevada. (p. 1876)
—Zombies in Nature. (p. 1988)
Larson, Lisa K., illus. see Kirby, Ruth M.
Larson, Lyn. Ghana. (p. 670)
—New Zealand. (p. 1249)
—Switzerland. (p. 1692)
Larson, M. A. Pennyroyal Academy. (p. 1338)
Larson, Maria Burgaleta, illus. see Charney, Steve & Goldbeck, David.
Larson, Mark. Adventures of Pinky, the Pink Flamingo. (p. 21)
Larson, Mark H. & Boone, Robert S. Moe's Cafe: 48 Decidedly Different Creative Writing Prompts. (p. 1160)
Larson, Mary Kay. Tales of Tillie Terwillie: Who Does Tillie Love? (p. 1703)
Larson, Mary L., et al. Keyboarding First: Student Manual. (p. 950)
Larson, Melissa J. It's Your Ball after All. Larson, Caleb A., illus. (p. 899)
Larson, Michael J. Nature's Christmas Story. (p. 1237)
Larson, Nancy. Lesson Planner Instruction. Saxon Publishers Staff, tr. (p. 993)
—Saxon Lesson Planner & Teacher Resource CD's & Books. Saxon Publishers Staff, tr. (p. 1518)
—Teacher Resource Instruction. Saxon Publishers Staff, tr. (p. 1709)
Larson, Pamela Ali, jt. auth. see Larson, Paul Cliff.
Larson, Paul. Four Spheres of the Earth. (p. 625)
Larson, Paul Cliff & Larson, Pamela Ali. Mississippi Escapade: Reliving the Grand Excursion Of 1854. (p. 1154)
Larson, Rachel. Jesse Strong & Courageous Runaway: There Comes A Time When the Roads of Destiny Will No Longer Wait... (p. 914)
Larson, Randy. Bunches of Grammar Fun - Binder 3. (p. 242)
Larson, Robert. Pick-a-WooWoo - Robbie the Butterfly: An enlightening story of Transformation Pocock, Aaron, illus. (p. 1354)
Larson, Roland E. Passport to Algebra & Geometry: (c)2004. (p. 1327)
Larson, Ron. Elementary & Intermediate Algebra. (p. 510)
—Middle School Math, Course 2. (p. 1138)
—Precalculus. (p. 1394)
—Precalculus Advanced Placement. (p. 1394)
—Study & Solutions Guide: Used with ... Larson-Precalculus. (p. 1670)
—Trigonometry Advanced Placement Version. (p. 1786)
—Trigonometry Computer Solutions. (p. 1786)
—Trigonometry IG. (p. 1786)
Larson, Ron, jt. auth. see Hostetler, Robert P.
Larson, Ron & Edwards, Bruce H. Brief Calculus: An Applied Approach. (p. 227)
—Calculus: An Applied Approach. (p. 252)
Larson, Ron & Hostetler, Robert P. Algebra for College Students. (p. 38)
—Internet Algebra & Trigonometry 3.0 Online Learning Environment & Web Passcard: Used with ... Larson-Algebra & Trigonometry. (p. 880)
—Internet Precalculus 3.0 Online Learning Environment: Used with ... Larson-Precalculus. (p. 880)
—Precalculus. (p. 1394)
—Trigonometry. (p. 1786)
Larson, Ron, et al. Algebra 1: Concepts & Skills. (p. 38)
—Algebra 1. (p. 38)
—Algebra 2. (p. 38)
—Calculus (p. 252)
—College Algebra: A Concise Course. (p. 340)
—College Algebra: Concepts & Models. (p. 340)
—College Algebra. (p. 340)
—Geometry: Applying, Reasoning, Measuring. (p. 662)
—Mathematics. (p. 1107)
—McDougall Littell Middle School Math Course 3. (p. 1114)
—Passport to Mathematics (p. 1327)
—Precalculus with Limits: A Graphing Approach. (p. 1394)
—Trigonometry: A Graphing Approach. (p. 1786)
Larson, Sara B. Defy. (p. 424)
—Ignite. (p. 856)
Larson, Scott, illus. see Miller, Connie Colwell.
Larson, Susan. Sam (a Pastoral) (p. 1506)
Larsson, Carl. Family: Paintings from a Bygone Age. (p. 568)
—Farm: Paintings from a Bygone Age (p. 573)
Larter, John, illus. see Blaylock, Josh.
Lartey, Ben. Last Hero of Foreverland. (p. 978)
LaRue, Athena Mariah, illus. see Stanley, Dan.
LaRue, Jane. New Home for Humphrey. (p. 1245)
—Oscar's Eyes. (p. 1305)
—To Ride the Wild Wind. (p. 1759)
Larue, Ravyn. Sophie Browne Isn't Dead. (p. 1613)
Larwick, Valerie. Cat Named Frenchy Blue: Arrow Yellow Dog of the great Northwest. (p. 278)
Larwood, Kieran. Freaks. (p. 631)
L.A.S., Alex. Magnificent Sir Johnny & Santa Claus. (p. 1076)
LaSala, Paige. Pig Kissing. Gullotti, Pat, illus. (p. 1357)
Lasalle, Janet, illus. see Hillert, Margaret.
Lasaracina, Barbara. Mermaid Tears: A Magical Sea Tale. Peer, Nancy, illus. (p. 1128)
Lasarus, Gwen. Hud Hen Hanes. (p. 824)
—Ram. (p. 1437)
Lasater, Amy. This Is the Hill. Gerber, Patric, illus. (p. 1736)
Lascaris, Alexia, jt. auth. see Melean, Mary.
Lascaro, Rita. Down on the Farm. (p. 474)
Lascarso, Laura. Counting Backwards. (p. 370)
Lasconi, Diego, tr. see Masurel, Claire.
Lascurain, Anna. Apollo in the Moon House. (p. 92)
Lascurain, Guadalupe Aleman. Domadora de Miedos. Arte y Cultura, A.C Staff, illus. (p. 465)
Lasenby, Jack. Aunt Effie & the Island That Sank. (p. 115)
—Because We Were the Travellers. (p. 155)
—Taur. (p. 1707)
Laser, Tammy & Watson, Stephanie. Eating Disorders. (p. 501)
Lash, Batton. Mister Negativity: And Other Tales of Supernatural Law. (p. 1155)
Lash, Batton, et al. Scrapyard Detectives: Collected Cases. (p. 1532)
Lash, Jill. He Knows You. (p. 756)
Lashawn Graves, M. Ed. Listen & Embrace When Children Care. (p. 1022)
Lashbrook, Marilyn. God, Please Send Fire. Sharp, Chris, illus. (p. 690)
—I May Be Little. Britt, Stephanie McFetridge, illus. (p. 844)
—Out on a Limb. Britt, Stephanie McFetridge, illus. (p. 1311)
—Who Needs a Boat? Britt, Stephanie McFetridge, illus. (p. 1917)
LaShea, Riley. Bleeding Through Kingdoms: Cinderella's Rebellion. (p. 199)
Lasher, Kathy. Heinrich Streudleman Climbs Mt. Baker. (p. 762)
Lasher, Mary Ann, illus. see Baglio, Ben M.
Lasher, Mary Ann, jt. auth. see Baglio, Ben M.
Lasher, Olga Rivera. Historieta (the Storyteller) (p. 783)
Lasher, Shelby. Spiky the Grumpy Porcupine. (p. 1627)
Lashley, Beverly. One Can Never Have Too Many Cats!! Morrow, Jason, illus. (p. 1294)
Lashley, Ken & Pichelli, Sara. Women of Marvel. (p. 1946)
Lashley, Steven. E. Buggouts: The Buggouts learning Club. Hunter, Laura E., ed. (p. 236)
Lashnits, Tom. Columbia River. (p. 346)
—Maya Lin. (p. 1112)
—Recep Tayyip Erdogan: Prime Minister ofTurkey. Schlesinger, Arthur M., Jr., ed. (p. 1451)
Lasi, Cindy. B C d Is for Down. (p. 122)
Lask, Bryan & Watson, Lucy. Can I Tell You about Eating Disorders? A Guide for Friends, Family & Professionals. (p. 258)
Lask, I. M., tr. see Simhoni, S.
Laskas, Gretchen Moran. Miner's Daughter. (p. 1146)
Laske, Ernest. Life in Monkey Town. (p. 1010)
Laskey, Andrew, jt. auth. see Heighton, Mary Beth.
Laskey, Paul. Fire Observation Towers of New York State. (p. 590)
Laskey, Shannon, illus. see Anton, Carrie, ed.
Laskey, Shannon, illus. see Cindrich, Sharon.
Laskey, Shannon, illus. see Falligant, Erin, ed.
Laskey, Shannon, illus. see Madison, Lynda.
Laskey, Shannon, jt. auth. see Calkhoven, Laurie.
Laski, Deirdre. Hidden in the Next Step. (p. 775)
Laskin, Pamela, et al. Animal Crackers & Their Friends (p. 77)
Laskin, Pamela L. Getting to Know You. (p. 670)
Lasky, David, illus. see Bell, Cece.
Lasky, David, illus. see Young, Frank.
Lasky, Kathryn. Ashes. (p. 105)
—Before I Was Your Mother. Pham, LeUyen, illus. (p. 158)
—Blazing West, the Journal of Augustus Pelletier, the Lewis & Clark Expedition 1804. (p. 199)
—Blood Secret. (p. 200)
—Broken Song. (p. 230)
—Burning. (p. 244)
—Capture. (p. 265)
—Chasing Orion. (p. 294)
—Christmas after All. (p. 312)
—Coming of Hoole. (p. 348)
—Dancing Through Fire. (p. 403)
—Double Trouble Squared. (p. 473)
—Escape. (p. 534)
—Exile. (p. 548)
—Extra. (p. 555)
—Felix Takes the Stage. Gilpin, Stephen, illus. (p. 581)
—First Collier. (p. 593)
—Frost Wolf. (p. 644)
—Golden Tree. (p. 695)
—Hannah. (p. 742)
—Hatchling. (p. 752)
—Hawksmaid: The Untold Story of Robin Hood & Maid Marian. (p. 755)
—Horses of the Dawn #1: the Escape. (p. 800)
—Interrupted Journey: Saving Endangered Sea Turtles. Knight, Christopher G., photos by. (p. 881)
—John Muir: America's First Environmentalist. (p. 922)
—Journey. (p. 927)
—Journey to the New World: The Diary of Remember Patience Whipple, Mayflower 1620. (p. 929)
—Lone Wolf. (p. 1046)
—Lost Tales of Ga'Hoole. Huang, Kathryn, illus. (p. 1056)
—Lucy. (p. 1063)
—Marie Antoinette: Princess of Versailles, Austria-France 1769. (p. 1093)
—May. (p. 1112)
—My Uncle Eats Carrots on the Roof. (p. 1220)
—Night Journey. (p. 1253)
—One Beetle Too Many: The Extraordinary Adventures of Charles Darwin. Trueman, Matthew, illus. (p. 1294)
—Outcast. (p. 1312)
—Pirate Bob. Clark, David, illus. (p. 1362)
—Poodle & Hound. Vane, Mitch, illus. (p. 1383)
—Rescue. (p. 1462)
—Rise of a Legend. (p. 1474)
—River of Wind. (p. 1476)
—Shadow Wolf. (p. 1558)
—Shadows in the Water. (p. 1558)
—Shattering. (p. 1563)
—Siege. (p. 1573)
—Spiders on the Case. Gilpin, Stephen, illus. (p. 1627)
—Spirit Wolf. (p. 1629)
—Spirit Wolf. Cowdrey, Richard, illus. (p. 1629)
—Star Rise. (p. 1641)
—Star Wolf. (p. 1642)
—Sugaring Time. (p. 1673)
—To Be a King. (p. 1758)
—Tumble Bunnies. Hafner, Marylin, illus. (p. 1796)
—Untitled Historical #1: Picturebook Series. (p. 1823)
—Untitled Middle Grade Fiction. (p. 1823)
—Untitled Middle Grade Novel. (p. 1823)
—Vision of Beauty: The Story of Sarah Breedlove Walker. (p. 1844)
—Vision of Beauty: The Story of Sarah Breedlove Walker. Bennett, Nneka, illus. (p. 1844)
—Voice in the Wind. (p. 1848)
—Voice of Her Own: A Story of Phillis Wheatley, Slave Poet. (p. 1848)
—Voice of Her Own: The Story of Phillis Wheatley, Slave Poet. Lee, Paul, illus. (p. 1848)
—War of the Ember. (p. 1857)
—Watch Wolf. (p. 1861)
—Wolves of the Beyond. (p. 1945)
Lasky, Mark A., jt. auth. see Landes, William-Alan.
Lasky, Melvin, jt. auth. see Lasky, Melvin J.
Lasky, Melvin J. & Lasky, Melvin. Media Warfare: The Americanization of Language. (p. 1118)
Lasky, Ricki & Siqueiros, Paula. Brave Adventures of Captain Courage: The Bully. (p. 223)
Lasley, Tony, illus. see Reinoso, Marta.
Lasota, Mary. Kitty Piper Angel Cat: I Almost Lost My Best Friend. (p. 963)
—Kitty Piper, Angel Cat, Book: Sweet Lucy. (p. 963)
—Kitty Piper, Angel Cat, Book: A tribute to Scooter. (p. 963)
—Kitty Piper, Angel Cat, Book 2: The Venusians Have Landed. (p. 963)
—Kitty Piper, Angel Cat, Book 3, A Surprise for Ashley. (p. 963)
Lass, David A. Angelfish: Understanding & Keeping Angelfish. (p. 74)
Lassen, Christian R., illus. see Book Company Staff.
Lassen, Christian Riese. Moon Dance. (p. 1172)
Lasser, Jessica. Stormy the Cloud. (p. 1656)
Lasser, Olivier. Charlotte et l'nie du Destin. (p. 293)
Lasserre, Philippe & Schutte, Hellmut. Strategies for Asia Pacific: Building the Business in Asia, Third Edition. (p. 1666)
Lasseter, John. Disney/Pixar a Bug's Life Read-along. (p. 453)
Lasseter, Rollin, ed. History: All Ye Lands. (p. 783)
Lassieur, Allison. Albert Einstein: Genius of the Twentieth Century. (p. 34)
—Ancient India. (p. 69)
—Ancient Mesopotamia. (p. 70)
—At Battle in the Civil War: An Interactive Battlefield Adventure. (p. 110)
—At Battle in World War I: An Interactive Battlefield Adventure. (p. 110)
—Attack on Pearl Harbor: An Interactive History Adventure. (p. 114)
—Attack on Pearl Harbor [Scholastic]: An Interactive History Adventure. (p. 114)
—Battle of Bull Run: An Interactive History Adventure (p. 146)
—Battle of Bull Run: An Interactive History Adventure. (p. 146)
—Benjamin Banneker: Astronomer & Mathematician (p. 164)
—Building the Empire State Building: An Interactive Engineering Adventure (p. 239)
—Building the Great Wall of China: An Interactive Engineering Adventure (p. 239)
—Buses in Action (p. 244)
—Can You Survive Being Lost at Sea? An Interactive Survival Adventure (p. 259)
—Can You Survive the Titanic? An Interactive Survival Adventure (p. 259)
—Clara Barton: Angel of the Battlefield. Bascle, Brian, illus. (p. 326)
—Colonial America: An Interactive History Adventure (p. 341)
—Dairy. (p. 400)
—Dust Bowl: An Interactive History Adventure (p. 490)
—Eleanor Roosevelt: Activist for Social Change. (p. 508)
—Fruits. (p. 645)
—Grains. (p. 706)
—Harlem Renaissance: An Interactive History Adventure. (p. 749)
—Is Atlantis Real? (p. 889)
—Is the Bermuda Triangle Real? (p. 890)
—Is the Loch Ness Monster Real? (p. 890)
—Life as a Viking: An Interactive History Adventure. (p. 1008)
—Life as a Viking. (p. 1008)
—Lords of the Sea: The Vikings Explore the North Atlantic Barnett, Charles, III et al, illus. (p. 1052)
—Louisiana. (p. 1058)
—Meats & Proteins. (p. 1118)
—Middle Ages: An Interactive History Adventure (p. 1137)
—Moon Exposed: The Moon (p. 1172)
—Navajo: A Proud People. (p. 1237)
—Race to the Moon: An Interactive History Adventure (p. 1431)
—Storm Tracker: Measuring & Forecasting Weather (p. 1656)
—Subways in Action. (p. 1671)
—Underground Railroad: An Interactive History Adventure (p. 1814)
—Unsolved Historical Mysteries. (p. 1822)
—Vegetables. (p. 1834)
—Viaje del Mayflower. McDonnell, Peter, illus. (p. 1839)
—Violent Crime (p. 1843)
—Westward Expansion: An Interactive History Adventure (p. 1876)
—Wild West: An Interactive History Adventure (p. 1930)
Lassieur, Allison, jt. auth. see Eugster, Rachel.
Lassieur, Allison, jt. auth. see Hanel, Rachael.
Lassieur, Allison & Doeden, Matt. Civil War Experience: An Interactive History Adventure (p. 325)
Lassieur, Allison & Otfinoski, Steven. You Choose: History (p. 1975)
Lassieur, Allison, et al. World War II Experience: An Interactive History Adventure (p. 1959)
—You Choose: Battlefields. (p. 1975)
Lassiter, Erin & Garcia, Jolanda. EarTwiggle's Adventure 1: The Treasure Hunt. (p. 498)
Lassiter, Gianna Bari. Rosy Proses: Whimsical Verses & Sanity Journal for Big People Who Have Little People in Their Lives. (p. 1490)
Lassiter, Nancy. Proud Racer: Blind Faith. (p. 1412)
Lassiter, Rhiannon. Shadows. (p. 1558)
—Supernatural. (p. 1684)
—Void: Hex; Shadows; Ghosts. (p. 1848)
Lassiter, Rhiannon, ed. see Hoffman, Mary.
Lasslett, Sally, et al. Jump Start 9 & 10: Health & Physical Education. (p. 934)
Lasson, Matt, illus. see Jordan, L. W.
Lasswell, Barbara. Different Ways (p. 438)
Last, Ian & Smith, Diana. How to Draw. (p. 816)
Last, Mary. Ghost of Dark Swamp Road. (p. 671)
Last, Shari. Heroes in Action. (p. 773)
—Let's Mix! (p. 999)
—Meet the Heroes. (p. 1122)
—Meet the Mixels. (p. 1123)
Last, Shari, jt. auth. see Dorling Kindersley Publishing Staff.
Last, Shari & Dorling Kindersley Publishing Staff. Meet the Mixels, Level 1. (p. 1123)
—Mixels - Let's Mix! (p. 1156)
Laster, Brenda, illus. see Rucker, David.
Lastoka, Mariann. Pete & Patricia Prairie Dog & their Pack of Prairie Pups. Carpenter, Debra, illus. (p. 1346)
Lastrapes, Tracy. Silly Sally Sue Eats BlackEyed Peas. (p. 1576)
Laswell, Wendy Jo. Gone Hunting. (p. 697)
Lat. Kampung Boy. Lat, illus. (p. 942)
Latae, Lamura. Rooney Crooney's Second Chance. (p. 1488)
Lataif, Nicole. I Forgive You: Love We Can Hear, Ask for, & Give. Betz, Katy, illus. (p. 838)
—Siempre Tú: Un Libro Sobre Tu Cuerpo y Tu Alma. Pérez, Karen H., tr. from ENG. (p. 1573)
Latell, Brian. After Fidel: Raul Castro & the Future of Cuba's Revolution. (p. 28)
Laterra, Joann. Halloween Crossing. (p. 737)
Latham, Donna. Amazing Biome Projects: You Can Build Yourself. Rizvi, Farah, illus. (p. 54)
—Amazing Biome Projects. Rizvi, Farah, illus. (p. 54)
—Backyard Biology: Investigate Habitats Outside Your Door with 25 Projects. Hetland, Beth, illus. (p. 130)
—Bridges & Tunnels: Investigate Feats of Engineering with 25 Projects. Vaughn, Jen, illus. (p. 227)
—Canals & Dams: Investigate Feats of Engineering with 25 Projects. Christensen, Andrew, illus. (p. 260)
—Cells, Tissues, & Organs (p. 286)
—Earth's Biomes De Angelis, Maurizio, illus. (p. 498)
—Ecology De Angelis, Maurizio et al, illus. (p. 502)
—Ellen Ochoa: Reach for the Stars! (p. 514)
—Fire Dogs. (p. 590)
—Garbage: Investigate What Happens When You Throw It Out with 25 Projects. Hetland, Beth, illus. (p. 655)
—Hurricane! The 1900 Galveston Night of Terror. (p. 829)
—Music: Investigate the Evolution of American Sound. Stone, Bryan, illus. (p. 1193)
—Norah Jones. (p. 1264)
—Respiration & Photosynthesis. (p. 1463)
—Skyscrapers: Investigate Feats of Engineering with 25 Projects. Christensen, Andrew, illus. (p. 1587)
—Space: Surviving in Zero-G. (p. 1618)
—Superfast Rockets. (p. 1683)
—Superfast Trucks. (p. 1683)
Latham, Donna & Heinemann Library Staff. Earth's Biomes De Angelis, Maurizio, illus. (p. 498)
—Ecology De Angelis, Maurizio et al, illus. (p. 502)
Latham, Frank. Jed Smith: Trail Blazer of the West. McHugh, Michael J., ed. (p. 911)
Latham, Frank Brown. Fighting Quaker: The Southern Campaigns of General Nathaniel Greene. Vosburg, L., illus. (p. 586)
Latham, Hugh, tr. see Sehlin, Gunhild.
Latham, Irene. Don't Feed the Boy. Graegin, Stephanie, illus. (p. 467)
—Leaving Gee's Bend. (p. 986)
—Summer in Antarctica. Wadham, Anna, illus. (p. 1674)
Latham, Jean Lee. Carry on, Mr. Bowditch. (p. 271)
Latham, Jennifer. Scarlett Undercover. (p. 1520)
Latham, Karen, illus. see Wargin, Kathy-jo.
Latham, Rebecca, illus. see Wargin, Kathy-jo.
Latham, Sarah, illus. see Valenzuela, Anabelle.
Latham, William. Scary Stories of Stamford. (p. 1521)
Lathan, Betty Jean. Are You Sure That's My Child? (p. 97)
—Sierra, the Unwanted Cat. (p. 1573)
Lathan, Edward. My Glasses Are a Friend to Me. (p. 1210)
Lathbury, Mary A. Child's Story of the Bible. (p. 305)

Lathrop, Brandy. Jalen Goes to Mars. (p. 906)
Lathrop, Dorothy P., illus. see Mare, Walter de La.
Latif, Zawiah Abdul, jt. auth. see Hassig, Susan M.
Latif, Zawiah Abdul, jt. auth. see Heale, Jay.
Latif, Zawiah Abdul, jt. auth. see Kagda, Falaq.
Latif, Zawiah Abdul, jt. auth. see Kagda, Sakina.
Latif, Zawiah Abdul, jt. auth. see Levy, Patricia.
Latif, Zawiah Abdul, jt. auth. see Sheehan, Sean.
Latif, Zawiah Abdul, jt. auth. see Wilcox, Jonathan.
Latimer, Alex. Boy Who Cried Ninja Latimer, Alex, illus. (p. 219)
—Boy Who Cried Ninja. (p. 219)
—Lion vs Rabbit Latimer, Alex, illus. (p. 1020)
—Penguin's Hidden Talent (p. 1337)
Latimer, Alex, illus. see Kipling, Rudyard.
Latimer, Alex, illus. see Loory, Ben.
Latimer, Brenda. I See God. (p. 845)
Latimer, Clay. Game Day: From the Locker Room to the Press Box (and Everything in Between) (p. 654)
—Muhammad Ali. (p. 1189)
—VIP Pass to a Pro Baseball Game Day: From the Locker Room to the Press Box (and Everything in Between) (p. 1843)
—VIP Pass to a Pro Basketball Game Day: From the Locker Room to the Press Box (and Everything in Between) (p. 1843)
—VIP Pass to a Pro Football Game Day: From the Locker Room to the Press Box (and Everything in Between) (p. 1843)
—VIP Pass to a Pro Hockey Game Day: From the Locker Room to the Press Box (and Everything in Between) (p. 1843)
Latimer, Kiki. Heal of the Hand. Griffeth, Bunny, illus. (p. 757)
Latimer, Mariam. Choose to Reuse. (p. 310)
Latimer, Miriam. Emily's Tiger. (p. 519)
—Little Red Riding Hood. (p. 1035)
—Shrinking Sam. Latimer, Miriam, illus. (p. 1571)
—Wheelie Girl. (p. 1900)
Latimer, Miriam, illus. see Bewley, Elizabeth.
Latimer, Miriam, illus. see Harvey, Matt.
Latimer, Miriam, illus. see Oppenheim, Joanne F.
Latimer, Miriam, illus. see Oppenheim, Joanne F. & Barefoot Books Staff.
Latimer, Miriam, illus. see Oppenheim, Joanne F. & Barefoot Books.
Latimer, Miriam, illus. see Sperring, Mark.
Latimer, Miriam, illus. see Traditional Staff.
Latimer, Miriam, illus. see White, Kathryn.
Latimer, Miriam, jt. auth. see Harvey, Matt.
Latimer, Miriam & Ginnings, Miriam. Wheelie Girl. Ginnings, Miriam, illus. (p. 1900)
Latimer, Muriam, jt. auth. see Oppenheim, Joanne F.
Latimer, Tamara. Peddar Zaskq... in this Moment. (p. 1334)
Latimor, Miriam. Emily's Tiger. Latimor, Miriam, illus. (p. 519)
Latina, Paul A. Places You'll Go: While at the University of Florida. (p. 1366)
Latno, Mark. Paper Boomerang Book: Build Them, Throw Them, & Get Them to Return Every Time. (p. 1322)
LaTondre, Richard. Grandpa's Cat. (p. 709)
Latorre, Adolfo, illus. see Taylor, Vincent.
LaTorre, Donald R., et al. Calculus Concepts: An Informal Approach to the Mathematics of Change. (p. 252)
Latou, Pierre. Where Do Big Machines Work? (p. 1906)
—Who Eats Who in A Food Chain? (p. 1915)
—Who Works Here? (p. 1919)
—Why Can Plants Grow in the Desert? (p. 1923)
LaTreill, Donna. Vinedresser: Two Keys to Reaping the Best Harvest from Your Spiritual & Physical Vineyards. (p. 1843)
Latsch, Oliver, tr. see Funke, Cornelia.
Latsch, Oliver, tr. from GER. Pirate Pig. (p. 1363)
Latta, Jan. Charlie the Cheetah. (p. 293)
—Elisa la Elefanta. (p. 513)
—Ella the Elephant. (p. 514)
—Gerardo el Guepardo. (p. 666)
—Koby el Koala. (p. 966)
—Koby the Koala. (p. 966)
—Leonor la leona (Lisa the Lion) (p. 992)
—Lisa the Lion. (p. 1022)
—Rudy el Rinoceronte. (p. 1494)
—Rudy the Rhinoceros. (p. 1494)
—Timba el Tigre. (p. 1750)
—Timba the Tiger. (p. 1750)
Latta, Leslie Jay. Patches' Day Out. (p. 1328)
Latta, Nigel. Into the Darklands: Unveiling the Predators among Us. (p. 881)
Latta, Ruth. Revenant & Other Stories for Hallowe'en. (p. 1465)
Latta, Sara. Scared Stiff: Everything You Need to Know about 50 Famous Phobias. Gates, G. E., illus. (p. 1519)
Latta, Sara L. All about Earth: Exploring the Planet with Science Projects. (p. 42)
—Bones: Dead People Do Tell Tales. (p. 209)
—Cybercrime: Data Trails Do Tell Tales. (p. 396)
—DNA & Blood: Dead People DO Tell Tales. (p. 456)
—DNA & Blood: Dead People Do Tell Tales. (p. 456)
—Good, the Bad, the Slimy: The Secret Life of Microbes. Kunkel, Dennis, photos by. (p. 700)
—Ice Scientist: Careers in the Frozen Antarctic. (p. 850)
—Investigate Steroids & Performance Drugs. (p. 884)
—Keep Out! Invasive Species (p. 947)
—Lava Scientist: Careers on the Edge of Volcanoes. (p. 980)
—Microwave Man: Percy Spencer & His Sizzling Invention. (p. 1137)
—Polar Scientists: Studying the Antarctic. (p. 1379)
—Positive Reaction! A Crash Course in Science (p. 1387)
—Stella Brite & the Dark Matter Mystery. Johnson, Meredith, illus. (p. 1647)
—Volcanologists: Examining Active Volcanoes. (p. 1849)
—What Happens in Fall? (p. 1886)
—What Happens in Spring? (p. 1886)
—What Happens in Summer? (p. 1886)
—What Happens in Winter? (p. 1886)
—What You Can Do about Allergies. (p. 1895)
—Who Fixed Babies' Hearts? Vivien Thomas. (p. 1915)
—Who Invented Basketball? James Naismith. (p. 1915)
—Who Invented the Ferris Wheel? George Ferris. (p. 1915)
—Why Is It Fall? (p. 1925)
—Why Is It Spring? (p. 1925)
—Why Is It Summer? (p. 1925)
—Why Is It Winter? (p. 1925)
—Woman Who Invented Windshield Wipers: Mary Anderson & Her Wonderful Invention. (p. 1945)
—¿Qué Pasa en el Invierno? What Happens in Winter? (p. 1424)
—¿Qué Pasa en el Otoño? What Happens in Fall? (p. 1424)
—¿Qué Pasa en el Verano? What Happens in Summer? (p. 1424)
—¿Qué Sucede en la Primavera? What Happens in Spring? (p. 1424)
Latta, Sara L. & Anderson, Mary. Woman Who Invented Windshield Wipers: Mary Anderson & Her Wonderful Invention. (p. 1945)
Latta, Sara L., et al. Nature's Invaders. (p. 1237)
Latta, Susan M. Reconstruction Era. (p. 1452)
Lattak, Cheryl. Puppy Tales. Rimes, Nicole, illus. (p. 1418)
Latter, Kym & Stroud, Cassie. Trouble with Bear Hugs: A Story about Asthma. (p. 578)
Lätti, Leo, illus. see Bach, Nancy.
Lätti, Leo, illus. see Cerulli, Claudia.
Lattimore, Deborah Nourse. Mystery at Midnight Museum. (p. 1223)
Lattimore, Eleanor Frances. Little Pear. Lattimore, Eleanor Frances, illus. (p. 1033)
—Little Pear & His Friends. Lattimore, Eleanor Frances, illus. (p. 1033)
Latty, Jasmin. Oh, My Boring Toes! (p. 1280)
Latushkin, Valentin, illus. see Laud, Valerie.
Latushko, Julia, ed. see AZ Books Staff.
Latyk, Olivier, illus. see Hausfater, Rachel.
Latyk, Olivier, illus. see Hausfater-Douieb, Rachel.
Latyk, Olivier, illus. see Rees, Douglas.
Latz, Martin E. Gain the Edge! Negotiating to Get What You Want. (p. 652)
Latza, Jodi. Rhyming on Rushmore: From A to Z. (p. 1468)
Lau, Barbara & Nesbitt, Kris. Sokita Celebrates the New Year: A Cambodian American Holiday. Chatterley, Cedric N., photos by. (p. 1606)
Lau, Benny, illus. see Benny.
Lau, D. C., ed. see Mencius.
Lau, D. C., tr. see Mencius.
Lau, Ding Kin, jt. auth. see Ma, Wing Shing.
Lau, Kevin, illus. see Roman, Steven A.
Lau, Ruth, jt. auth. see Berg, Elizabeth.
Laub, Frima. Between the Shadows. Uhlig, Elizabeth, illus. (p. 173)
—Between the Shadows. Laub, Frima & Uhlig, Elizabeth, illus. (p. 173)
Laubach, Frank. Story of Jesus: Part 1. Woodworth, Ralph, ed. (p. 1658)
—Story of Jesus: Part 2. Woodworth, Ralph, ed. (p. 1658)
Laubach, Melody. Words & Thoughts. (p. 1951)
Laube, Greta L. B., jt. auth. see Hawkins, Frank C.
Laube, Sigrid. Flower Ball. Boehm, Philip, tr. from GER. (p. 607)
Laubenstein, Sharon. Something about Sally. (p. 1609)
Lauber, Leah F. Soccer Dreams: My True Adventure Following the U. S. Women's National Soccer Team, As a Fan & 12-Year Old Junior Reporter for the St. Petersburg Times During the History-Making 1999 FIFA Women's World Cup! (p. 1603)
Lauber, Patricia. True-or-False Book of Dogs. Schanzer, Rosalyn, illus. (p. 1792)
—What You Never Knew about Beds, Bedrooms, & Pajamas. Manders, John, illus. (p. 1896)
—What You Never Knew about Fingers, Forks, & Chopsticks. Manders, John, illus. (p. 1896)
Laubscher, André, illus. see Schermbrucker, Reviva.
Laud, Julia, illus. see Brewer, Heather.
Laud, Valerie. Picture Book Dictionary: The Essential Source for Bilingual Families, English-Spanish Edition. Latushkin, Valentin, illus. (p. 1355)
Laudati, Joe. Faela: A Fairy's Tale. (p. 562)
Laudec, illus. see Cauvin, Raoul.
Laudec, Calvinaoul, illus. see Cauvin, Raoul.
Lauder, M. F., jt. auth. see Kline, C. A.
Lauer, Brett Fletcher, jt. auth. see Kelley, Aimee.
Lauer, Lucy S. Horse Named Kat. (p. 799)
Laufer, Liora. Callirobics: Advanced Handwriting Exercises with Music from Around the World. (p. 254)
Laufer, Peter. Hecho en Mexico. Reyes, Victor, tr. (p. 761)
Laufer, Tiffany A. Porch Dream. (p. 1386)
Laufer, William. Holes in My Toes. (p. 788)
Lauffray, Mathieu, illus. see Dorison, Xavier.
Laugesen, Malene R., illus. see Cummins, Julie.
Laughbaum, Steve, illus. see Sparkman, Winette.
Laughead, Mike, illus. see Fliess, Sue.
Laughead, Mike, illus. see Guard, Anara.
Laughead, Mike, illus. see Perritano, John.
Laughead, Mike, illus. see Suen, Anastasia & Heck, Claudia M.
Laughead, Mike, illus. see Suen, Anastasia.
Laughing Elephant Publishing Staff. Puppy Dog's ABC. (p. 1418)
—Truth about Santa Claus. (p. 1794)
Laughing Elephant Publishing Staff, jt. auth. see Anonymous.
Laughing Elephant Publishing Staff, jt. compiled by see Poltarnees, Welleran.
Laughing Elephant Publishing Staff, compiled by. By the Sea. (p. 249)
Laughing Elephant Publishing Staff, creator. Cats' Christmas ABC. (p. 281)
Laughing Elephant Publishing Staff, ed. Green Tiger's Book of Children's Poetry. (p. 722)
—Truth about Snow People. (p. 1794)
Laughing Gravy Design Staff, illus. see Ward-Johnson, Chris & Gould, William.
Laughing Gravy Design Staff, illus. see Ward-Johnson, Chris.
Laughlin, Florence. Little Leftover Witch. (p. 1030)
Laughlin, Haller, jt. auth. see Wheeler, Jacque.
Laughlin, Kara L. Beautiful Bags for the Crafty Fashionista (p. 153)
—Bomb-Sniffing Dogs. (p. 208)
—Fun Things to Do with Egg Cartons (p. 648)
—Fun Things to Do with Paper Cups & Plates (p. 648)
—Guide Dogs. (p. 730)
—Hip Hair Accessories for the Crafty Fashionista (p. 780)
—Marvelous Memories: Paper Keepsake Creations (p. 1099)
—Police Dogs. (p. 1380)
—Search-And-Rescue Dogs. (p. 1537)
—Seizure-Alert Dogs. (p. 1549)
—Therapy Dogs. (p. 1729)
Laughlin, Kara L., jt. auth. see Ventura, Marne.
Laughlin, Kara L., et al. Fashion Craft Studio. (p. 575)
—Paper Creations. (p. 1322)
Laughlin, Rosemary. John D. Rockefeller: Oil Baron & Philanthropist. (p. 921)
—Ludlow Massacre Of 1913-14. (p. 1064)
—Pullman Strike of 1894: American Labor Comes of Age. (p. 1416)
Laughlin, Sako, tr. see Saito, Ryusuke & Takidaira, Jiro.
Laughter, Jim. Strangers in the Stable. WillowRaven, Aidana, illus. (p. 1665)
Launay, Melissa, illus. see Katz, Susan B.
Launchbury, Jane. Witch & Wizard Stories. (p. 1941)
Laune, Paul, illus. see Avery, Al.
Laune, Paul, illus. see Dixon, Franklin W.
Laune, Paul, illus. see Peckham, Howard Henry.
Laune, Paul, illus. see Stevenson, Augusta.
Laune, Paul, illus. see Striker, Fran.
Launier, Veronique. Deliverance. (p. 425)
Launier, Veronique, jt. auth. see Launier, Véronique.
Launier, Véronique & Launier, Veronique. Redemption. (p. 1455)
Laura Beth. Two Girls 2 Cats: A Magical Mystery (p. 1803)
Laura Grey Wahl. Magic Town of Stuart Easterly. (p. 1074)
Laura, Huliska-beith, illus. see Johnson, Angela.
Laura Lee, Cundiff, illus. see Foresman, Timothy.
Laura Lee Hope. Bunny Brown & His Sister Sue at Aunt Lu's City Home. (p. 242)
—Moving Picture Girls at Oak Farm. (p. 1184)
—Six Little Bunkers at Cowboy Jack's. (p. 1582)
—Six Little Bunkers at Grandma Bell's. (p. 1582)
Lauré, Jason, jt. auth. see Blauer, Ettagale.
Laureano, C. E. Beneath the Forsaken City. (p. 164)
Laurel Associates. Kidnapped Study Guide: The Complete Adventures of David Balfour. (p. 952)
Laurel Associates Inc, ed. see Suter, Joanne.
Laurel Associates Inc. & Saddleback Educational Publishing Staff, eds. Writing 1 (p. 1964)
—Writing 2 (p. 1964)
Laurel Associates Inc. Staff, ed. see Bevington, David.
Laurel Associates Inc. Staff, ed. see Dickens, Charles.
Laurel Associates Inc. Staff, ed. see Dumas, Alexandre.
Laurel Associates Inc. Staff, ed. see Hugo, Victor Marie.
Laurel Associates Inc. Staff, ed. see Suter, Joanne.
Laurel Associates Inc. Staff, ed. see Verne, Jules.
Laurel Associates Inc. Staff, ed. Spelling Steps 1 (p. 1625)
—Spelling Steps 4 (p. 1625)
Laurel Carter, Anne. Shepherd's Granddaughter. (p. 1565)
Laurel Corona. Jewish Americans. (p. 917)
Laurel, Hylton. Cowboy Frog. Laurel, Hylton, illus. (p. 374)
Laurel, Jaime M. & Romulo, Liana. My First Book of Tagalog Words: Filipino Rhymes & Verses. (p. 1205)
Lauren, Jessica. Piggy Wiggy, Yum Yum: My Healthy Future! (p. 1358)
Lauren, Jill. That's Like Me! (p. 1727)
Lauren, Sonja. Covered Smile: A True Story. (p. 373)
Lauren, Whitney. Vanessa & Johnny: The Cabinets. (p. 1833)
Laurence, Alexander. Five Fingers Make a Fist. (p. 600)
Laurence, Daniel. Captain & Matey Set Sail. Muñoz, Claudio, illus. (p. 263)
Laurence, Jo. How to Be a Wizard at Nursery Rhymes. Ford, Kate, illus. (p. 815)
—How to Be a Wizard at Phonics. (p. 815)
—How to Sparkle at Alphabet Skills. (p. 821)
—How to Sparkle at Nursery Rhymes. (p. 821)
—How to Sparkle at Phonics. (p. 821)
—How to Sparkle at Prediction Skills. (p. 821)
Laurence, Laurence, illus. see Appleby, Danny & Pirie, Lauren.
Laurence, Margaret. Olden Days Coat. Wood, Muriel, illus. (p. 1285)
Laurence, Margaret & James Lorimer and Company Ltd. Staff. Six Darn Cows Blades, Ann, illus. (p. 1582)
Laurence, Yep. Dragonwings. (p. 479)
Laurendeau, Jason. BASE Jumping: The Ultimate Guide (p. 140)
Laurens, Jennifer. Falling for Romeo. (p. 566)
—Magic Hands. (p. 1072)
Laurent, Karine. Coo Is in Love Alastra, Stephanie, illus. (p. 361)
Laurente, Lourdes, illus. see Bradley, Adrian.
Laurenti, Jeffrey. Being Fulfilled: How You Can Achieve Unlimited Wealth in Every Area of Your Life! (p. 161)
Laurentine, Florianne Daphne. Mystery Chronicles: The Unknown Masterpiece & the Case of the Practical Joker. (p. 1224)
—Mystery Chronicles: The Amazing Chocolate Mystery & the Case of the Phantom Cat. (p. 1224)
Lauridsen, Craig. Stop Motion Handbook: Using GarageBand & IStopMotion. (p. 1653)
Laurie, jt. auth. see Burnham.
Laurie, Caple, illus. see Linden, Joanne.
Laurie, Cook. Amelia Asks Why. (p. 57)
Laurie Douglas, Inez. No One Heard His Cry. (p. 1259)
Laurie, Jane, illus. see McHugh, Maura.
Laurie, Peter. Mauby & the Hurricane. (p. 1110)
Laurie, Rona. Actor's Art & Craft. (p. 10)
—Auditioning: A Practical Guide for the Would-Be Actor & Drama Student. (p. 115)
Laurie, Victoria. Curse of Deadman's Forest. (p. 394)
—Demons Are a Ghoul's Best Friend: A Ghost Hunter Mystery. (p. 426)
—Oracles of Delphi Keep. (p. 1301)
—When Would You Want to Know? (p. 1905)
Laurin, Anthony. Mally. (p. 1084)
Laurita, Susan. CREATION Curriculum CD: Genesis 1, Psalm 139. (p. 379)
Lauritano, Michael, illus. see Older, Jules.
Lauso, Judith, illus. see Mazeroski, Kelly.
Laut, Phil, ed. see Combs, Jeffery.
Lauter, Paul. Selections from Walt Whitman & Emily Dickinson. (p. 1549)
Lauter, Richard. Little Women. (p. 1038)
Lauter, Richard, illus. see Alcott, Louisa May.
Lauter, Richard, illus. see Burnett, Frances Hodgson.
Lauter, Richard, illus. see Twain, Mark, pseud.
Lauter, Richard, tr. see Twain, Mark, pseud.
Lauterbach, B. L. Home-Grown Experiences. (p. 792)
Lauture, Denize. Father & Son. Green, Jonathan, illus. (p. 577)
Lauture, Mireille B. Bobo, Chen Odasye A / Bobo, the Sneaky Dog: Mancy's Haitian Folktale Collection. Minckler, Kathleen L., illus. (p. 206)
—Gade Yon Kado Remi Jwenn / Remi's Magical Gift: Mancy's Haitian Folktale Collection. (p. 652)
—Konpè Kochon Pran Nan Mer: Mancy's Haitian Folktale Collection. (p. 967)
—Loulou, Gason Vanyan! / Loulou, the Brave! (p. 1059)
—Mancy's Haitian Folktale Collection: Father Misery. Minckler, Kathleen L., illus. (p. 1087)
Lauve, Celia, illus. see Collins, David R.
Lauzon, Christi. Where's Owen Goin'? (p. 1910)
Laval, Anne-Marie. Mountain Biking. (p. 1180)
—Windsurfing & Kite Surfing. (p. 1936)
Laval, Thierry. Colors. (p. 344)
—Numbers. (p. 1271)
Lavallee, Barbara, illus. see Brown, Tricia.
Lavallee, Barbara, illus. see Cobb, Vicki.
Lavallee, Barbara, illus. see Schertle, Alice.
Lavallee, Barbara, illus. see Stihler, Cherie B.
Lavallee, Barbara, jt. auth. see Cobb, Vicki.
Lavallee, Barbara, jt. auth. see Joosse, Barbara M.
Lavandeira, Sandra, illus. see Campoy, F. Isabel.
Lavandeira, Sandra, illus. see Flor Ada, Alma.
Lavandeira, Sandra, illus. see Walsh, Maria Elena.
Lavandeira, Sandra, illus. see White, Amy.
Lavant, Joseph, as told by. Book of Context: God Still Speaks (p. 211)
Lavar, Vanda, illus. see Walsh, Christopher.
Lavarello, Jose Maria. Cuentame un Cuento (p. 389)
Lavarello, Jose Maria, illus. see Ramon, Elisa.
Lavarello, Jose Maria, illus. see Zubizarreta, Paxti.
Lavarello, Jose Mo, jt. auth. see Viza, Monserrat.
Lavash, Donald. Journey Through New Mexico History Hardc. (p. 928)
Lavash, Donald R. Journey Through New Mexico History: The Land of Enchantment. (p. 928)
Lavelett, Lucille. Through the Years at Monument, Colorado (p. 1745)
Lavelle, Mary T. Watcher. (p. 1861)
Lavelle, Sheila. Clever Dog, Webster. (p. 331)
LaVelle, Steven. Just Passing Through: A Grown-Up Book for Kids. (p. 939)
Laven, Zp. Benjamin's Big Lesson. Craft, Donna, illus. (p. 165)
Lavender, Bee & Rossini, Maia, eds. Mamaphonic: Balancing Motherhood & Other Creative Acts. (p. 1084)
Lavender, Todd. Farmer Fred & His Hen So Red. Lavender, Todd, illus. (p. 574)
Lavender, Todd, illus. see Freeman, J. Miller.
Lavender, William. Just Jane: A Daughter of England Caught in the Struggle of the American Revolution. (p. 938)
Lavene, Jim, jt. auth. see Lavene, Joyce.
Lavene, Joyce & Lavene, Jim. Wicked Weaves. (p. 1927)
Laver, Sarah, 8th, illus. see Jeffs, Stephanie.
Laverde, Arlene. Alaska's Three Little Pigs. Dwyer, Mindy, illus. (p. 34)
Laverdunt, Damien. Small & Tall Tales of Extinct Animals. Rajcak, Hélène, illus. (p. 1591)
Laverne, Christine, jt. auth. see Kornprobst, Jacques.
Lavers, Ralph, illus. see Grant, Joan Marshall.
Laverty, Neil. Bebe's Big Adventure: A Bebe & Muckle Book. Diana Cox, illus. (p. 155)
Lavery, Breanne, ed. see Kissane, sheela.
Lavery, Brian, jt. auth. see Steele, Philip.
Lavette, Lavaille. Adventures of Roopster Roux: That's Not Punny Nguyen, Duke, ed. (p. 22)
—Adventures of Roopster Roux: You're So Victor Vain Kuon, Vuthy, illus. (p. 22)
Lavi, Yifat. Fish Also Fade: Illustrated by: Oren Somech. (p. 598)
Lavigne, Guy. Obsession de Jerome Delisle. (p. 1275)
—Pas de Quartier pour les Poires. (p. 1326)
Lavigne, Guy & Godbout, Real. Dans la Peau de Bernard. (p. 406)
—Maison du Pendu. (p. 1077)
Lavigne, Mark Hunter. Aventures de Matilda la Fée des Dents: Premier Épisode. (p. 119)
Lavin, Christine. Amoeba Hop. Feeney, Betsy Franco, illus. (p. 65)
Lavin, Christine & Franco-Feeney, Betsy. Hole in the Bottom of the Sea. McHugh, Patricia & Feeney, Kathryn, eds. (p. 788)
Lavin, Paul J., jt. auth. see Brave M.A., Kathryn A.
Lavis, Rose Brenda. Christopher's New Suit. (p. 317)
—Here Comes Trouble & Double Trouble. (p. 770)
Lavis, Steve, illus. see Dickson, John & Pasquali, Elena.
Lavis, Steve, illus. see Roddie, Shen.
Lavohn, Jodi. Sam's Adventure. (p. 1509)
LaVoice, Patricia. Helmets & Hoses, Toes & Noses. (p. 765)
Lavoie, Jennifer. Andy Squared. (p. 73)
—Meeting Chance. (p. 1123)
—Tristan & Elijah. (p. 1787)
Lavoie, Rejean. Des Legumes Pour Frank Einstein. Begin, Jean-Guy, illus. (p. 427)

L

Lavonne, Victoria. Twas the Night at the Capitol: A Narrative Featuring the First African American Family. (p. 1799)
LaVoy, Geri. What about Me God? (p. 1878)
Lavreys, Debbie, illus. see Grimm, Jacob, et al.
Lavreys, Debbie, illus. see Van Der Linden, Elly.
Lavy, Sharon A. Ella's Surprise: A Child's Tale from the Ohio Valley. (p. 514)
Law, Bibiana. Campylobacteriosis. (p. 258)
Law, David. Flight of the Mantids. (p. 604)
Law, Felicia. Alice the Armadillo: A Tale of Self Discovery. Messina, Lilli, illus. (p. 39)
—Alphabet. Knight, Paula, illus. (p. 49)
—Atlas of Southwest & Central Asia QTA Media Staff et al, illus. (p. 113)
—Atlas of Southwest & Central Asia. Elliott, Rebecca et al, illus. (p. 113)
—Atlas of the Far East & Southeast Asia QTA Media Staff et al, illus. (p. 113)
—Atlas of the Far East & Southeast Asia. Elliott, Rebecca et al, illus. (p. 113)
—Benjamin the Bear: A Tale of Selfishness. Spoor, Mike, illus. (p. 165)
—Buildings & Structures. (p. 239)
—Cairo the Camel: A Tale of Responsibility. Danson, Lesley, illus. (p. 252)
—Caught in the Rapids. (p. 282)
—Colors. Knight, Paula, illus. (p. 344)
—Darwin the Dolphin: A Tale of Bravery & Courage. Danson, Lesley, illus. (p. 409)
—Electricity. (p. 509)
—Escape from the Volcano. (p. 535)
—Family. Knight, Paula, illus. (p. 568)
—Feelings. Knight, Paula, illus. (p. 580)
—Florence the Flamingo: A Tale of Pride. Messina, Lilli, illus. (p. 606)
—Hudson the Hippo: A Tale of Self-Control. Danson, Lesley, illus. (p. 824)
—Kimberly the Koala: A Tale of Independence. Danson, Lesley, illus. (p. 957)
—Limpopo the Lion: A Tale of Laziness & Lethargy. Messina, Lilli, illus. (p. 1018)
—Lost in the Cave. (p. 1055)
—Materials. (p. 1104)
—Numbers. Knight, Paula, illus. (p. 1271)
—Olivia the Orangutan: A Tale of Helpfulness. Spoor, Mike, illus. (p. 1287)
—Shapes. Knight, Paula, illus. (p. 1560)
—Simple Machines. (p. 1577)
—Size. Knight, Paula, illus. (p. 1583)
—Trouble in Space. (p. 1790)
—Zanzibar the Zebra: A Tale of Individuality. Messina, Lilli, illus. (p. 1985)
Law, Felicia, jt. auth. see Bailey, Gerry.
Law, Felicia, jt. auth. see Foster, Karen.
Law, Felicia & Way, Steve. Castaway Code: Sequencing in Action. Law, Felicia et al, illus. (p. 276)
—Crocodile Teeth: Geometric Shapes in Action. Spoor, Mike & Mostyn, David, illus. (p. 384)
—Mirage in the Mist: Measurement in Action. Spoor, Mike & Mostyn, David, illus. (p. 1149)
—Mirage in the Mist: Measurements in Action. Spoor, Mike & Mostyn, David, illus. (p. 1149)
—Mystery of Nine: Number Place & Value in Action. Spoor, Mike & Mostyn, David, illus. (p. 1225)
—Storm at Sea: Sorting, Mapping, & Grids in Action. Spoor, Mike & Mostyn, David, illus. (p. 1655)
—Weather. (p. 1869)
Law, Ingrid. Savvy. (p. 1518)
—Scumble. (p. 1534)
—Switch. (p. 1691)
Law, Janice. Capitol Cat & Watch Dog Unite Lady Freedoms. Eckhardt, Jason C., illus. (p. 263)
Law, Jenny, illus. see Donohue, Moira Rose.
Law, Jerel. Spirit Fighter (p. 1628)
—Truth Runner (p. 1794)
Law, Jessica. Farmer's Life for Me. McDonald, Jill, illus. (p. 574)
—Hole in the Bottom of the Sea. McDonald, Jill, illus. (p. 788)
Law, Karina. Handwriting. (p. 741)
—Homework (p. 794)
Law, Karina & Collins Easy Learning Staff. Handwriting (p. 741)
Law, Karina, et al. Collins Primary Literacy (p. 341)
Law, Martin. IGCSE Mathematics. (p. 855)
Law, Ohm. Mice of the Bear Traps Field. (p. 1134)
Law, Preston E. Drummer Boy for the Bonnie Blue: Marching Through Maryland, Virginia, & Pennsylvania with Robert E. Lee's Army. (p. 487)
Law, Stephanie Pui-Mun, illus. see Baker, Kage.
Law, Stephen, jt. ed. see Burns, Elizabeth.
Lawall, Gilbert & Kindel, Gerde. Phaedra of Seneca. (p. 1349)
Lawati, A. Jungle Adventure of Chimpoo. (p. 935)
Lawes, Alexander. Peter & the Enchanted Cavern. (p. 1346)
Lawhead, Stephen R. Arthur. (p. 103)
—Dragon King Trilogy: n the Hall of the Dragon King; The Warlords of Nin; The Sword & the Flame. (p. 477)
—Sword & the Flame. (p. 1692)
—Tale of Anabelle Hedgehog. (p. 1699)
—Tale of Jeremy Vole. (p. 1699)
—Tale of Timothy Mallard. (p. 1700)
—Warlords of Nin. (p. 1858)
Lawhorn, Mary Joyce. When Annie Dreams. (p. 1901)
Lawler, Graham. Introducing Algebra 2: Specialising & Generalising. (p. 882)
Lawler, Janet. If Kisses Were Colors. Jay, Alison, illus. (p. 853)
—Love Is Real. Brown, Anna, illus. (p. 1060)
—Ocean Counting. Skerry, Brian, photos by. (p. 1276)
—Rain Forest Colors. Laman, Tim, photos by. (p. 1434)
—Silly Skeletons: A Not-So-Spooky Pop-Up Book. (p. 1576)
—Snowzilla Haley, Amanda, illus. (p. 1601)
Lawler, Janet & Moore, Clement C. Tyrannoclaus. Shroades, John, illus. (p. 1805)
Lawler, Lillian B. Latin Club. (p. 979)
Lawler, Mary. Marcus Garvey: Black Nationalist Leader. Wagner, Heather Lehr & Huggins, Nathan I., eds. (p. 1092)
Lawless, Freda. Shauna's Chance. (p. 1563)
Lawless, Laura, jt. auth. see Bybee, Linda.
Lawless, Mary Ann. Proud Christmas Tree. McCool, Arlene, illus. (p. 1412)
Lawless, Robert E. Student's Guide to Financial Literacy (p. 1669)
Lawless, Tony. Lawless in Vietnam. (p. 981)
Lawley, Baker. Stealing the Show: Book One of the Such Sweet Sorrow Trilogy. (p. 1646)
Lawley, Lacy. Life Cycle of a Tree. (p. 1009)
Lawlis, Frank. Mending the Broken Bond: The 90-Day Answer to Repairing Your Relationship with Your Child. (p. 1126)
Lawlor, Ashley. Ashley & the First Day of School. (p. 106)
Lawlor, Laurie. Biggest Pest on Eighth Avenue. Fisher, Cynthia, illus. (p. 185)
—He Will Go Fearless. (p. 756)
—Muddy As a Duck Puddle & Other American Similes. Long, Ethan, illus. (p. 1188)
—Muddy as a Duck Puddle & Other American Similes. Long, Ethan, illus. (p. 1188)
—Rachel Carson & Her Book That Changed the World. Beingessner, Laura, illus. (p. 1432)
—Shadow Catcher: The Life & Work of Edward S. Curtis. (p. 1557)
—Two Loves of Will Shakespeare. (p. 1804)
—Wind on the River. (p. 1935)
Lawlor, Michelle. Kelly Clarkson. (p. 948)
—Missy Elliot. (p. 1154)
Lawn, John, illus. see Brandt, Keith & Macken, JoAnn Early.
Lawner, Elizabeth K., jt. auth. see Mosatche, Harriet S.
Lawrason, June, illus. see Little, Jean.
Lawrence, Antoinette & Lewis, Terry. I Remember. (p. 844)
—My Dad, My Granddad, & Me. (p. 1201)
Lawrence, Ava. Button for a Crown. Ford, Christina, illus. (p. 248)
Lawrence, Barry C. In Search of River Phoenix: The Truth Behind the Myth. (p. 864)
Lawrence, Blythe. Girls' Gymnastics. (p. 680)
—Great Moments in Olympic Gymnastics. (p. 717)
Lawrence, C. H. Aladdin or, the Wonderful Lamp. (p. 33)
Lawrence, C. H., illus. see Perrault, Charles.
Lawrence, Caroline. Assassins of Rome. (p. 107)
—Case of the Deadly Desperados: Western Mysteries, Book One. (p. 274)
—Dolphins of Laurentum. (p. 465)
—Fugitive from Corinth. (p. 646)
—P. K. Pinkerton & the Deadly Desperados. (p. 1316)
—P. K. Pinkerton & the Pistol-Packing Widows. (p. 1316)
—Piratas de Pompeya. (p. 1362)
—Pirates of Pompeii. (p. 1364)
—Secrets of Vesuvius. (p. 1546)
—Sirens of Surrentum. (p. 1581)
Lawrence CCS, Mary, et al. Clinotes 5th Edition. (p. 333)
Lawrence, Cherry. David & the Blue Racer. (p. 410)
Lawrence, D. H. Being Alive: Selected Poems. (p. 161)
—Rainbow. Kinkead-Weekes, Mark et al, eds. (p. 1435)
—Rocking-Horse Winner. (p. 1483)
Lawrence, D. H. & Pearson Education Staff. British & American Short Stories. (p. 229)
Lawrence, David. Chocolate Teapot: Surviving at School. (p. 309)
—Home Run. (p. 792)
Lawrence, David, illus. see Platt, Richard.
Lawrence, David, et al. Niño Escarabajo. (p. 1257)
Lawrence, David L. New Adventure of Geoffrey & Chongo: Book 2. (p. 1243)
Lawrence, David M. Huntington's Disease. (p. 829)
Lawrence, David M. & Millonzi, Kara A. Incorporation of a North Carolina Town. (p. 869)
Lawrence, David P. Skill & Practice Masters in Algebra Using the Ti-84. (p. 1584)
—Ti-84 Easy Warm Ups in Algebra One. (p. 1746)
Lawrence, Debbie & Lawrence, Richard. God's Design for Heaven & Earth: Our Weather & Water. (p. 691)
—Heat & Energy: God's Design for the Physical World. (p. 760)
—Machines & Motion: God's Design for the Physical World. (p. 1068)
—Our Planet Earth. (p. 1309)
—Properties of Ecosystems. (p. 1411)
Lawrence, Diane. Oblit. (p. 1275)
Lawrence, Dionne L. Story of Her?! (p. 1658)
Lawrence, Donna. Miracle of Susie the Puppy That Changed the Law. Coble, Lynn Bemer, ed. (p. 1148)
—Susie's Tale Hand with Paw We Changed the Law. Coble, Lynn Bemer, ed. (p. 1688)
Lawrence, Duane. Sammy Squirrel & Rodney Raccoon. Clover, Gordon, illus. (p. 1508)
Lawrence, Elden. Peace Seekers: Indian Christians & the Dakota Conflict. (p. 1331)
Lawrence, Elizabeth. Celebrate Christmas. (p. 283)
—Celebrating Hanukkah. (p. 284)
—I See Circles. (p. 845)
—I See Ovals. (p. 845)
—I See Rectangles. (p. 845)
Lawrence, Elizabeth K. Celebrate Thanksgiving. (p. 284)
Lawrence, Ellen. Air. (p. 31)
—Amazing Plant Bodies: Tiny to Gigantic. (p. 55)
—Baking & Crushing: A Look at Metamorphic Rock. (p. 133)
—Bird's Life. (p. 191)
—Butterfly's Life. (p. 248)
—Celebrations & Special Days. (p. 285)
—Chameleon's Life. (p. 289)
—Clothes We Wear. (p. 334)
—Color. (p. 342)
—Comets, Meteors, & Asteroids: Voyagers of the Solar System. (p. 348)
—Cooking with Sunshine: How Plants Make Food. (p. 362)
—Dirt. (p. 446)
—Dirt or Soil: What's the Difference? (p. 446)
—Dirty Air. (p. 446)
—Dragonfly's Life. (p. 478)
—Earth: Our Home in the Solar System. (p. 495)
—Enormous Ears & Soft Brown Hair (Moose) (p. 531)
—Everybody Needs Water. (p. 543)
—Extreme Trees. (p. 557)
—Famous Rocks. (p. 569)
—Fog, Mist, or Haze? (p. 611)
—Food We Eat. (p. 614)
—Freaky Plant Facts: Extreme Greens. (p. 632)
—Frog's Life. (p. 641)
—From Bird Poop to Wind: How Seeds Get Around. (p. 642)
—Garbage Galore. (p. 655)
—Giant Egg & Fluffy Feathers (Ostrich) (p. 673)
—Global Warming. (p. 684)
—Healing Plants. (p. 757)
—How are Rain, Snow, & Hail Alike? (p. 805)
—How Do Animals Help Make Soil? (p. 806)
—How Do People Use Rocks? (p. 807)
—How Do Volcanoes Make Rock? A Look at Igneous Rock. (p. 807)
—How Do Water & Wind Change Rock? A Look at Sedimentary Rock. (p. 807)
—How Plants Clean the Air. (p. 812)
—How We Get Around. (p. 823)
—Is Sand a Rock? (p. 889)
—Is Soil All the Same? (p. 890)
—Jupiter: The Giant of the Solar System. (p. 937)
—Kangaroo's Life. (p. 942)
—Light. (p. 1014)
—Liquids & Solids. (p. 1021)
—Magnets. (p. 1076)
—Mars: The Dusty Planet. (p. 1096)
—Meat-Eating Plants: Toothless Wonders. (p. 1118)
—Mercury: The High-Speed Planet. (p. 1127)
—Moon: Our Neighbor in Space. (p. 1171)
—Motion. (p. 1179)
—Neptune: The Stormiest Planet. (p. 1241)
—Place to Call Home. (p. 1365)
—Pluto & the Dwarf Planets. (p. 1374)
—Poison Petals: Don't Eat! (p. 1377)
—Poisoned Rivers & Lakes. (p. 1377)
—Polluted Oceans. (p. 1381)
—Prickly Plants: Stuck! (p. 1398)
—Rocks & Minerals. (p. 1483)
—Saturn: The Ringed Wonder. (p. 1515)
—Snake's Life. (p. 1597)
—Sound. (p. 1615)
—Spider's Life. (p. 1627)
—Spiny Back & Green Scaly Skin (Iguana) (p. 1628)
—Sun: The Star of Our Solar System. (p. 1675)
—Time for School. (p. 1751)
—Time to Play. (p. 1753)
—Tiny Beak & Spiky Feathers (Cockatiel) (p. 1756)
—Tiny Fingers & Fuzzy Orange Hair (Orangutan) (p. 1756)
—Tiny Paws & Big Black Eyes (Giant Panda) (p. 1756)
—Uranus: The Sideways-Spinning Planet. (p. 1825)
—Venus: The Hot & Toxic Planet. (p. 1836)
—Water. (p. 1862)
—Water Plants. (p. 1863)
—What Are Clouds? (p. 1879)
—What Are Rocks Made Of? (p. 1879)
—What Is Climate? (p. 1889)
—What Is Lightning? (p. 1889)
—What Is Soil Made Of? (p. 1890)
—What Is the Rock Cycle? (p. 1890)
—What Is the Water Cycle? (p. 1890)
—What Is Weather? (p. 1891)
—What Lily Gets from Bee: And Other Pollination Facts. (p. 1891)
—Why Do Most Plants Need Soil? (p. 1924)
—Wolf's Life. (p. 1944)
Lawrence, Eve Pollard. My Friend Eddie. (p. 1209)
Lawrence, Frances. Lauren Meets a New Friend in the Schoolyard. (p. 980)
Lawrence, George, illus. see Weaver, Anne H.
Lawrence, Gregory. Christmas Surprise (p. 315)
Lawrence Hall of Science. Foss animals two by two spanish big Book. (p. 623)
—Foss animals two by two spanish science Stories. (p. 623)
—Foss fabric spanish big Book. (p. 623)
—Foss fabric spanish science Stories. (p. 623)
—Foss levers & pulleys science Stories. (p. 623)
—Foss trees spanish big Boo. (p. 623)
—Foss trees spanish science Stories. (p. 623)
—FOSS WOOD & PAPER SPANISH BIG BOOK. (p. 623)
—FOSS WOOD & PAPER SPANISH SCIENCE STORIES. (p. 623)
Lawrence, Hilary R. Adventures of Little Ted. (p. 20)
Lawrence, Iain. Buccaneers. (p. 234)
—Cannibals. (p. 261)
—Convicts. (p. 361)
—Giant-Slayer. (p. 674)
—Lord of the Nutcracker Men. (p. 1052)
—Winter Pony. (p. 1938)
Lawrence, Jack, illus. see Titan Comics, Titan.
Lawrence, Jacob, jt. auth. see Handford, S. A.
Lawrence, James. Buck Rogers in the 25th Century Herman, Daniel, ed. (p. 234)
Lawrence, Jim, illus. see Lieber, Larry & Parkhouse, Steve.
Lawrence, John. This Little Chick. (p. 1737)
—This Little Chick. Lawrence, John, illus. (p. 1737)
Lawrence, John, illus. see Butterworth, Christine.
Lawrence, John, illus. see Pullman, Philip.
Lawrence, John, illus. see Stevenson, Robert Louis.
Lawrence, John, illus. see Waddell, Martin.
Lawrence, Josephine. Rainbow Hill. (p. 1435)
Lawrence, Katherine. Jean-Claude Van Damme. (p. 911)
—Labor Legislation: The Struggle to Gain Rights for America's Workforce. (p. 969)
—Laurence Yep. (p. 980)
—Life in the Desert. (p. 1011)
Lawrence, Katherine Drobot. Jean-Claude Van Damme. (p. 911)
—Laurence Yep. (p. 980)
—Life in the Desert. (p. 1011)
Lawrence, Kelly. Unconditional. (p. 1812)
Lawrence, Kelsey. Rune. (p. 1497)
Lawrence, Kenneth. Korah's Travels: The Saga of an Israelite Family. (p. 967)
Lawrence, L. S. Escape by Sea. (p. 534)
Lawrence, Lane & Ridgway, Tom. Buying Goods & Services. (p. 248)
Lawrence, Linda. Crosswords for Kids (p. 385)
—Crosswords for Kids Reardon, Will, ed. (p. 385)
Lawrence, Maggie. Element of Fun. (p. 510)
Lawrence, Margaret. Earthshakers, Top Blowers & High Rollers. (p. 498)
Lawrence, Mary. Que Es Ese Sonido? Adams, Lynn, illus. (p. 1423)
—¿Qué es Ese Sonido? (What's That Sound?) Adams, Lynn, illus. (p. 1423)
Lawrence, Michael. Crack in the Line. (p. 375)
—Curse of the Poltergoose. (p. 395)
—Iron, the Switch & the Broom Cupboard. (p. 888)
—Jack & the Broomstick: From a Jack to a King. Ross, Tony, illus. (p. 902)
—Jack & the Giant Killer / Jackwitch. Ross, Tony, illus. (p. 902)
—Jack Four's Jackdaws & Jack of the Gorgons. Ross, Tony, illus. (p. 903)
—Jack in the Box? And Tall-Tale Jack. Ross, Tony, illus. (p. 903)
—Jiggy & the Witchfinder. (p. 917)
—Jiggy the Vampire Slayer: A Bloodcurdling Caper! (p. 917)
—Jiggy's Magic Balls - A Medieval Mess! (p. 917)
—Kid Swap. (p. 951)
—Killer Underpants. (p. 956)
—Meanest Genie. (p. 1116)
—Neville the Devil. Nadler, Ellis, illus. (p. 1243)
—Nudie Dudie. (p. 1270)
—Rudie Dudie. (p. 1494)
—Ryan's Brain. (p. 1499)
—Small Eternities. (p. 1592)
—Snottle. (p. 1598)
—Toilet of Doom. (p. 1762)
—Underwood See. (p. 1817)
Lawrence, Michael & Nadler, Ellis. One for All & All for Lunch. (p. 1295)
Lawrence, Mike. Macaroni Disaster! (p. 1067)
Lawrence, Mike, illus. see Rusch, Elizabeth.
Lawrence, Muriel, illus. see Roberts, Helen M.
Lawrence, P. Anthony. Jessie & Fumbling Giant. (p. 914)
Lawrence, Paul. Communicator Mathematics#8482; Content Series - Concepts of Fractions & Decimals Teacher Guide: W/DVD Book F. (p. 349)
—Communicator Mathematics#8482; Content Series — Fraction Addition & Subtraction Teacher Guide: W/DVD Book G. (p. 349)
—Communicator Mathematics#8482; Content Series Fractions & Decimals - Decimals Multiplication & Division Teacher Guide: W/DVD Book J. (p. 349)
—Communicator Mathematics#8482; Content Series - Whole Number Addition & Subtraction Teacher Guide: W/DVD Book C. (p. 349)
—Communicator Mathematics#8482; Content Series - Whole Numbers: Multiplication & Division Beyond Facts Teacher Guide: W/DVD Book E. (p. 349)
—Communicator Mathematics#8482; Content Series - Whole Numbers: Understanding & Mastering Multiplication & Division Facts Teacher Guide: W/DVD Book D. (p. 349)
—Communicator Mathematics#8482; Content Series- Decimal Addition & Subtraction Teacher Guide I: W/DVD Book I. (p. 349)
—Communicator Mathematics#8482; Fractions Multiplacation & Division Teacher Guide: W/DVD Book H. (p. 349)
—Communicator#8482; Mathematics Content Series— Decimal Multiplication & Division: Book J Student Pak. (p. 349)
—Communicator#8482; Mathematics Content Series- Concepts of Fractions & Decimals: Book F Student Pak. (p. 349)
—Communicator#8482; Mathematics Content Series-Decimal Addition & Subtraction: Book I Student Pak. (p. 349)
—Communicator#8482; Mathematics Content Series- Fraction Multiplication & Division: Book H Student Pak. (p. 349)
—Communicator#8482; Mathematics Content Series- Perspective on Numbers Assessment: Book B Student Pak. (p. 349)
—Communicator#8482; Mathematics Content Series- Whole Number Addition & Subtraction: Book C Student Pak. (p. 349)
—Communicator#8482; Mathematics Content Series- Whole Numbers: Multiplication & Division Beyond Facts: Book E Student Pak. (p. 349)
—Communicator#8482; Mathematics Content Series- Whole Numbers: Understanding & Mastering Multiplication & Division Facts: Book D Student Pak. (p. 349)
Lawrence, Paul R. Question Quest HSPA Math Algebra Companion (p. 1426)
—Question Quest HSPA Math Geometry Companion. (p. 1426)
—Question Quest HSPA Math - Level A (p. 1426)
Lawrence, Richard. Our Universe. (p. 1310)
Lawrence, Richard, jt. auth. see Lawrence, Debbie.
Lawrence, Theo. Mystic City. (p. 1226)
—Toxic Heart. (p. 1774)
—Toxic Heart: a Mystic City Novel. (p. 1774)
Lawrence, Treat. You're the Detective! 23 Solve-Them-Yourself Mysteries. Borowick, Kathleen, illus. (p. 1982)
Lawrence, Trisha. Princess's Crown: A Magnetic Storybook. Barnard, Lucy, illus. (p. 1406)
Lawrence-Loughlin, Amy. For the Love of Gus: A True Rescue to Riches Tale. (p. 616)
Lawrenson, Diana. Your Hair Is Dead. Hobbs, Leigh, illus. (p. 1980)
Lawrenson, Judith. Petunia the Pirate of Port Royal Sound. (p. 1349)
Lawrey, Derek, illus. see Hetherington, Lisa.
Lawrie, Chris, jt. illus. see Lawrie, Robin.
Lawrie, Gabrielle, jt. auth. see Waterhouse, Raymond.

Lawrie, Robin. Ballerina Biker. (p. 134)
—First among Losers. (p. 593)
—Gone Green. (p. 697)
—Great Irish Legends for Children. (p. 716)
—Paintball Panic. (p. 1318)
—Radar Riders. (p. 1432)
—Treetop Trauma. (p. 1784)
Lawrie, Robin, illus. see Ashe, Susan.
Lawrie, Robin, illus. see Burnett, Frances Hodgson.
Lawrie, Robin, illus. see Carroll, Yvonne.
Lawrie, Robin, illus. see Huws, Emily.
Lawrie, Robin, jt. auth. see Platt, Richard.
Lawrie, Robin & Lawrie, Chris. Chain Reaction. (p. 288)
—Fear 3.1. (p. 579)
—Muddy Mayhem. (p. 1189)
—Winged Avenger. (p. 1936)
Lawrinson, Julia. Loz & Al. (p. 1061)
Laws, Gordon D. & Laws, Lauren M. Northwest Territories. (p. 1266)
Laws, Jamie Lynn. Cameron & the Mysterious Shack. (p. 256)
Laws, John Muir. Sierra Birds: A Hiker's Guide. (p. 1573)
Laws, Lauren M., jt. auth. see Laws, Gordon D.
Lawson, Archie B., as told by. View from the Cockpit: Looking Up. (p. 1841)
Lawson, Barbara. Huff the Magicless Dragon Swope, Brenda, illus. (p. 824)
—Three Little Pigs Go to School. (p. 1743)
—Ugly Black Bird Lafarge, Kelly, illus. (p. 1808)
Lawson, Brandi. Soap Bubble Frog. Kinra, Richa, illus. (p. 1603)
Lawson, Carol S., ed. Your Turn! Stories of Renewal. (p. 1981)
Lawson, Cheri. Chip the Buffalo: Based on a True Story. Lawson, J., illus. (p. 308)
Lawson, Devin, illus. see Holmes, Kimberly.
Lawson, Dorie McCullough. Posterity: Letters of Great Americans to Their Children. (p. 1388)
—Tex: A Book for Little Dreamers. (p. 1723)
Lawson, Glenn. No More Rivers to Cross. (p. 1259)
Lawson, Greg, photos by. Natural States. (p. 1236)
Lawson, Gwendolynn. Jane's Secret Angel. (p. 908)
Lawson, Helen. Spaceship Saga & Other Stories: Read a Play - Book 1. (p. 1620)
Lawson, Henry. Henry Lawson Treasury. Davis, Oslo, illus. (p. 768)
Lawson, J., illus. see Lawson, Cheri.
Lawson, J. B. Harbor Island: A Logan Adventure Story. (p. 747)
Lawson, J. C. Litany of the Elves. (p. 1022)
Lawson, Janet. Alberts & Me. (p. 35)
Lawson, Jennifer. Our New Solar System: A Puppet Show. (p. 1309)
—Secret Tea Party at the Zoo. (p. 1544)
Lawson, Jessica. Actual & Truthful Adventures of Becky Thatcher. Bruno, Iacopo, illus. (p. 10)
—Nooks & Crannies. Andrewson, Natalie, illus. (p. 1264)
—Sharing & Making Friends. (p. 1561)
Lawson, Jessica & Twain, Mark. Tom Sawyer Collection: The Adventures of Tom Sawyer; the Adventures of Huckleberry Finn; the Actual & Truthful Adventures of Becky Thatcher. Bruno, Iacopo, illus. (p. 1763)
Lawson, Jim & Dooney, Michael. Paleo: Tales of the Late Cretaceous. (p. 1319)
Lawson, Jon Arno. Man in the Moon-Fixer's Mask. Tjia, Sherwin, illus. (p. 1085)
Lawson, JonArno. Black Stars in a White Night Sky. Tjia, Sherwin, illus. (p. 197)
—Down in the Bottom of the Bottom of the Box. (p. 474)
—Man in the Moon-Fixer's Mask. Tjia, Sherwin, illus. (p. 1085)
—Think Again. Morstad, Julie, illus. (p. 1734)
—Voweller's Bestiary: From Aardvark to Guineafowl. (p. 1850)
Lawson, JonArno & Smith, Sydney. Sidewalk Flowers (p. 1573)
Lawson, Julia & Goodman, Polly. Games. (p. 654)
—Music. (p. 1193)
—Weather. (p. 1869)
Lawson, Julie. Cougar Cove (p. 369)
—Ghosts of the Titanic. (p. 672)
—Klondike Cat. Mombourquette, Paul, illus. (p. 963)
Lawson, Kay. Human Polity: A Comparative Introduction to Political Science. (p. 826)
Lawson, Keri, photos by see Taylor,
Lawson, Kristan. Darwin & Evolution for Kids: His Life & Ideas with 21 Activities. (p. 409)
Lawson, Michael S. Grandpa Mike Talks about God. (p. 709)
Lawson, Peter. Tractor. (p. 1775)
Lawson, Peter, illus. see Baxter, Nicola.
Lawson, Peter, illus. see Goldsack, Gaby & Dawson, Peter.
Lawson, Peter, illus. see Goldsack, Gaby.
Lawson, Peter, illus. see Noonan, Julia.
Lawson, Peter, illus. see Wolfe, Jane & Baxter, Nicola.
Lawson, Peter & Smith, Kathryn. Animal Ambulance. (p. 76)
Lawson, Polly. Sam Luckless. (p. 1506)
Lawson, Polly, tr. see Grimm, Jacob & Grimm, Wilhelm K.
Lawson, Polly, tr. see Grimm, Wilhelm K. & Grimm, Jacob.
Lawson, Polly, tr. see Lindgren, Astrid.
Lawson, Rob. Duke Finds a Home. (p. 489)
Lawson, Robert. Great Wheel. Lawson, Robert, illus. (p. 719)
—Just for Fun: A Collection of Stories & Verses. (p. 938)
—Mr. Revere & I. (p. 1186)
—Rabbit Hill. (p. 1429)
—Rabbit Hill. Lawson, Robert, illus. (p. 1429)
Lawson, Robert, illus. see Gray, Elizabeth Janet.
Lawson, Robert, illus. see Leaf, Munro.
Lawson, Robert, illus. see Novara, Joe.
Lawson, Robert, illus. see Teal, Val.
Lawson, Sandra. Best Baker in the World! (p. 168)
Lawson, Shandy. Loop. (p. 1052)
Lawson, Sue. Ferret Boy. (p. 582)
Lawson, Sylvia J. Little Eagle & God's Green World. (p. 1027)
Lawson, Tanya. Pawpaw Harry & the Baby Squirrel. (p. 1331)
Lawson-Goins, Helen. Surprise in the Garden. (p. 1686)
Lawson-Miller, Barb. I Love Daddy Because... (p. 842)
—I Love Mommy Because... (p. 842)
Lawson-Williams, BerNadette. Blossom Bee's Golf Adventures. (p. 202)
Lawton, Caroline, jt. auth. see Bayley, Kimberly.
Lawton, Clive A. Hiroshima: The Story of the First Atom Bomb. (p. 781)
Lawton, Diana. Paulie the Penguin Meets Sammy the Seal. (p. 1331)
Lawton, Natasha, illus. see Esiri, Allie & Kelly, Rachel, eds.
Lawton, Val. New York. (p. 1247)
—Ohio. (p. 1281)
—West Virginia. (p. 1876)
Lawton, Val, illus. see Clark, CoraMarie.
Lawton, Wendy. Daughters of the Faith Set #2. (p. 410)
—La Sombra de Su Mano (p. 969)
Lawton, Wendy G. Almost Home: A Story Based on the Life of the Mayflower's Mary Chilton. (p. 48)
—Captive Princess: A Story Based on the Life of Young Pocahontas. (p. 264)
—Hallelujah Lass: A Story Based on the Life of Salvation Army Pioneer Eliza Shirley. (p. 737)
—Ransom's Mark: A Story Based on the Life of the Pioneer Olive Oatman. (p. 1438)
—Shadow of His Hand: A Story Based on the Life of Holocaust Survivor Anita Dittman. (p. 1557)
Lawton, Wendy G., jt. auth. see Moody Publishing Staff.
Lawton, Wilbur. Boy Aviators' Polar Dash or Facing Death in the Antarctic. (p. 217)
Laxer, James. Empire (p. 521)
—Oil (p. 1282)
—Tecumseh Rudnicki, Richard, illus. (p. 1712)
Lay, Eddie. Mystery of the Hats. (p. 1225)
Lay, Kathryn. Crown Me! (p. 386)
—Extreme Senses: Animals with Unusual Senses for Hunting Prey. Wald, Christina, illus. (p. 556)
—Hearing Their Prey: Animals with an Amazing Sense of Hearing. Wald, Christina, illus. (p. 759)
—Josh's Halloween Pumpkin Bratun, Katy, illus. (p. 926)
—Seeing Their Prey: Animals with an Amazing Sense of Sight. Wald, Christina, illus. (p. 1548)
—Smelling Their Prey: Animals with an Amazing Sense of Smell. Wald, Christina, illus. (p. 1593)
—Substitutes: An Up2U Action Adventure. Calo, Marcos, illus. (p. 1671)
—Tasting Their Prey: Animals with an Amazing Sense of Taste. Wald, Christina, illus. (p. 1707)
—Touching Their Prey: Animals with an Amazing Sense of Touch. Wald, Christina, illus. (p. 1772)
Lay, L. Clark, jt. auth. see Lay, Steven R.
Lay, Richard & Zarrinnaal, Laura Nienhaus. Green Kid's Guide to Composting. (p. 722)
—Green Kid's Guide to Garden Pest Removal. (p. 722)
—Green Kid's Guide to Preventing Plant Diseases. (p. 722)
—Green Kid's Guide to Soil Preparation. (p. 722)
—Green Kid's Guide to Watering Plants. (p. 722)
Lay, Steven R. & Lay, L. Clark. Prelude to Algebra. (p. 1395)
Layboum, Emma. Dungeon Dragon. (p. 490)
Laybourne, Emmy. Monument 14. (p. 1170)
—Savage Drift. (p. 1516)
—Sky on Fire. (p. 1587)
—Sweet. (p. 1689)
Layburn, Joe. Runaways. Williams, John, illus. (p. 1497)
Layden, Joe & Preller, James. NFL: Super Bowl - Behind the Scenes. (p. 1249)
—Super Bowl Super Touchdowns. (p. 1679)
Layden, Joseph. Rising Stars, NFL. (p. 1475)
Layden, Joseph Lyon. Other Side of Yore. (p. 1306)
Layfield, David. Marxism & Environmental Crises. (p. 1100)
Layfield, Eleanor Newman, jt. auth. see Newman, Gerald.
Layman, Curt. Christmas Cheese. (p. 313)
Layman, John. Red Sonja/Claw the Unconquered: Devil's Hands. (p. 1455)
Layne, Adriana. To be the First One. (p. 1758)
Layne, Carmela C. I See Many Colors Around My House: Los Colores que Veo Por Mi Casa. Layne, Carmela C., ed. (p. 845)
Layne, Casey & Jordan, Cedar. Back Alley Pupsters: Zac & Roxie for the Win. Fischer, Shan, illus. (p. 130)
Layne, Deborah, illus. see Layne, Steven L.
Layne, Deborah & Layne, Stephen L. T Is for Teachers: A School Alphabet. Ettlinger, Doris, illus. (p. 1693)
Layne, Deborah & Layne, Steven. P Is for Princess: A Royal Alphabet. Papp, Robert & Papp, Lisa, illus. (p. 1316)
Layne, Deborah Dover, jt. auth. see Layne, Steven L.
Layne, Stephen L., jt. auth. see Layne, Deborah.
Layne, Steven. Principal's Night Before Christmas Rice, James, illus. (p. 1406)
Layne, Steven, jt. auth. see Layne, Deborah.
Layne, Steven, et al. W Is for Windy City: A Chicago City Alphabet. Hays, Michael, illus. (p. 1851)
Layne, Steven L. Love the Baby Hoyt, Ard, illus. (p. 1060)
—Mergers (p. 1127)
—My Brother Dan's Delicious Galey, Chuck, illus. (p. 1199)
—Number 1 Teacher: A School Counting Book. Ettlinger, Doris & Layne, Deborah, illus. (p. 1271)
—Over Land & Sea: The Story of International Adoption Bower, Jan, illus. (p. 1313)
—Paradise Lost (p. 1323)
—Preacher's Night Before Christmas Benioff, Carol, illus. (p. 1394)
—Share with Brother Hoyt, Ard, illus. (p. 1561)
—Stay with Sister Hoyt, Ard, illus. (p. 1645)
—Teachers' Night Before Halloween Hoyt, Ard, illus. (p. 1709)
—This Side of Paradise (p. 1737)
—Thomas's Sheep & the Spectacular Science Project Board, Perry, illus. (p. 1739)
Layne, Steven L. & Layne, Deborah Dover. T Is for Teacher: A School Alphabet. Ettlinger, Doris, illus. (p. 1693)
Layne, Steven L., et al. T Is for Teachers: A School Alphabet. Ettlinger, Doris, illus. (p. 1693)
Layos, Alexandra. Almost True Horse Tale. Bauer, Dana, illus. (p. 48)
—Timeless: Blue Ribbon Days #2 (p. 1754)
Layson, Annelex Hofstra, jt. auth. see Viola, Herman J.
Layton, Bob, jt. auth. see Stern, Roger.
Layton, Dan. Adventures in the Kingdom, the Dreamer. (p. 15)
Layton, Dian. Armor of Light. (p. 99)
—Rescued from the Dragon. (p. 1462)
—Seeker's Great Adventure. (p. 1548)
Layton, Geoff. Germany - The Third Reich, 1933-1945 for AQA. (p. 666)
—Weimar & the Rise of Nazi Germany, 1918-33. (p. 1872)
Layton, George. Trick & Other Stories (p. 1786)
Layton, Lesley, et al. Singapore. (p. 1579)
Layton, Mary Evans. Bobby's Piano. (p. 206)
Layton, Neal. Colours. (p. 346)
—Go Wild with ... Designs. (p. 687)
—Go Wild with Noises. (p. 687)
—Go Wild with ... Opposites. (p. 687)
—Hot Hot Hot. Layton, Neal, illus. (p. 801)
—Story of Things: From the Stone Age to the Modern Age in 10 Pop-Up Spreads. (p. 1662)
Layton, Neal, illus. see Cleary, Brian P.
Layton, Neal, illus. see Cowell, Cressida.
Layton, Neal, illus. see Davies, Nicola.
Layton, Neal, illus. see Hegley, John.
Layton, Neal, illus. see McGough, Roger.
Layton, Neal, illus. see Oldfield, Jenny.
Layton, Neal, jt. auth. see Cowell, Cressida.
Layton, Neal, tr. see Cleary, Brian P.
Layton, Neal & Cowell, Cressida. Cheer up Your Teddy Bear, Emily Brown! (p. 296)
Layton, Neil. Go Wild with Colors. (p. 687)
—Go Wild with Opposites. (p. 687)
—Go Wild with Patterns. (p. 687)
Layton, Rebecca, jt. auth. see Rega, Joseph.
Layton, Roxanne A. Eddie Saves Cats. (p. 503)
—Henry & His Amazing MacHine. (p. 767)
—Keep Goin' Owen! (p. 946)
—Tommy's Happy Place. (p. 1765)
Laz, Ashley Ann. Totally Washi! More Than 45 Super Cute Washi Tape Crafts for Kids. (p. 1771)
Lazar, Carole. Lucy Unstrung. (p. 1063)
Lazar, Ligia, illus. see Tudosa-Fundureanu, Lucia.
Lazar, Michelle & Jensen, Jeremy. Tuned in to Learning: Social Skills & Pragmatics for Autism & Related Needs Vol. 1 (p. 1796)
Lazar, Ralph, jt. auth. see Swerling, Lisa.
Lazar, Tara. Monstore. Burks, James, illus. (p. 1169)
Lazaro, Georgina. Jose. Sanchez, Maria, illus. (p. 926)
—Juana Ines. Preza, Bruno Gonzalez, illus. (p. 930)
—Julia: Cuando Los Grandes Eran Pequenos. Marichal, Poli, illus. (p. 932)
—Pablo. Donoso, Marcela, illus. (p. 1316)
Lázaro, Georgina & Moreiro, Enrique S. Federico García Lorca. Moreiro, Enrique S., illus. (p. 580)
Lázaro León, Georgina & Genovés, Graciela. Jorge Luis Borges. Genovés, Graciela, illus. (p. 926)
Lázaro León, Georgina & Yockteng, Rafael. Gabriel García Márquez: Gabito. Yockteng, Rafael, illus. (p. 652)
Lazarri, Andrea. Vocabulary To Go. (p. 1847)
Lazarus, Emma. English Spelling & Spelling Reform. (p. 530)
Lazdowski, Ken. Prayer of the Child Mystic. Lee, Gail, illus. (p. 1393)
Lazear, Jonathon. Come On, Get Happy. (p. 347)
Lazear, Suzanne. Fragile Destiny. (p. 627)
—Innocent Darkness. (p. 875)
LaZebnik, Claire. Epic Fail. (p. 532)
—Last Best Kiss. (p. 977)
—Trouble with Flirting. (p. 1790)
—Wrong about the Guy. (p. 1965)
Lazer, Hank. Elegies & Vacations. (p. 510)
Lazewnik, Libby. Burglar & Other Stories. (p. 243)
—Jumping In: And Other Stories. (p. 934)
—Out of the Woods. Scheinberg, Shepsil, illus. (p. 1311)
—Three Cheers for Shira! (p. 1741)
Lazewnik, Sara, illus. see Finkelstein, Ruth.
Laznicka, Mike, illus. see Edgers, Geoff.
Lazo, Dorina. Children of the San Joaquin Valley. Hires, Josh, photos by. (p. 302)
Lazo Gilmore, Dorina K. Cora Cooks Pancit. Valiant, Kristi, illus. (p. 366)
Lazo, Jeanne Rae. If Looks Could Kill. (p. 853)
Lazoo Publishing Staff. All about Faces. Miyakoshi, Junko, tr. from JPN. (p. 42)
—Colors! (p. 344)
—Hidden Animals! (p. 775)
—Holes! A Coloring Book. Oku, Makiko, tr. (p. 788)
—Imagine That! A Coloring Book for Growing Young Minds. Miyakoshi, Junko, tr. (p. 861)
—Stickers! An Activity Book with Stickers. Miyakoshi, Junko, tr. (p. 1650)
Lazoo Publishing Staff & ZOO, La. Let's Color! A Coloring Book Like No Other. Miyakoshi, Junko, tr. (p. 995)
—Squiggles! A Drawing Book. Oku, Makiko, tr. (p. 1637)
Lazor, Stephanie. Life on the Equator. (p. 1012)
Lazurek, Michelle S. Daddy, Am I Beautiful? Stott, Apryl, illus. (p. 398)
—Mommy, Am I Strong? Spinks, Scott, illus. (p. 1162)
Lazzarino, Graziana, et al. Prego! An Invitation to Italian: Student Prepack with Bind-In Card. (p. 1395)
Lazzaro, Toni Lyn. As I Took a Walk Through History. (p. 105)
Lazzati, Laura, illus. see Weakland, Mark.
Lazzell, R. H., illus. see McCormick, Scott.
Lazzell, R. H., illus. see Mccormick, Scott.
Lazzell, R. H., illus. see McCormick, Scott.
LBCL & Emberley, Ed. Picture Pie: A Drawing Book & Stencil. Vol. 2 Emberley, Ed, illus. (p. 1356)
Lcg. Pencil Monster! (p. 1336)
LD COACH. TEH Learns to Read: Opposites (p. 1715)
—TEH Learns to Read: Basic Words (p. 1715)
—TEH Learns to Read: Action Words (p. 1715)
—TEH Learns to Read: Elementary Words (p. 1715)
—TEH Learns to Read: More Action Words (p. 1715)
—TEH Learns to Read: Mixed Sight Words—Group A (p. 1715)
—TEH Learns to Read: Pronouns & Possessive Adjectives (p. 1715)
—TEH Learns to Read: Beginning Words & Written Characters (p. 1715)
Le Berre, Carole. François Truffaut at Work. (p. 628)
Le Blanc, Lennie. Minnesota Summer. (p. 1147)
Le Bloas-Julienne, Renee. Shark: Silent Hunter. Bios Agency, photos by. (p. 1562)
Le Carré, John. Spy Who Came in from the Cold (p. 1636)
Lê, Christine & Lê, Michel. Hawai'i Snowman. (p. 755)
Le Clézio, J. M. G. Lullaby. Lemoine, Georges, illus. (p. 1064)
Le Compte, David & Rolland, Carol. Eugene Stillwell Wants to Know! Padrick, Kendell, ed. (p. 540)
Le Duc, Michel, et al. Ciudad a Tu Alcance. Marti, Nuria, tr. (p. 324)
Le Fanu, J. Sheridan. Madam Crowl's Ghost & the Dead Sexton. (p. 1069)
Le Feuvre, Amy. Harebell's Friend. (p. 748)
—His Big Opportunity. (p. 781)
—Teddy's Button. (p. 1713)
Le Fevebvre, Severine, illus. see Twain, Mark, pseud.
Le Feyer, Diane, illus. see Alexander, Heather.
Le Feyer, Diane, illus. see Burchett, Jan & Vogler, Sara.
Le Gall, Frank. Freedom! Balthazar, Flore, illus. (p. 634)
—Miss Annie: 6Pack Set. Balthazar, Flore, illus. (p. 1151)
—Miss Annie: Single Copy Set. Balthazar, Flore, illus. (p. 1151)
—Miss Annie. Balthazar, Flore, illus. (p. 1151)
—Rooftop Cat. Balthazar, Flore, illus. (p. 1487)
Le Gall, Frank & Doo, Robin. Freedom! Balthazar, Flore, illus. (p. 634)
Le Gallienne, Richard. Book Bills of Narcissus. (p. 210)
Le Grand, Claire, illus. see Husar, Stephane.
Le Gras, Gilbert. Joaquin & Olivier en Haute Mer! On the High Seas. (p. 919)
LE GRECCO, SILVIA, jt. auth. see Equipo Staff.
Le Guillou, Philippe. Jesús. Pérez, Berta Herreros, tr. (p. 914)
Le Guin, Ursula K. Catwings. (p. 281)
—Catwings. Schindler, S. D., illus. (p. 281)
—Catwings Return. (p. 281)
—Catwings Return. Schindler, S. D., illus. (p. 281)
—Daughter of Odren. (p. 409)
—Farthest Shore. (p. 575)
—Gifts. (p. 675)
—Jane on Her Own. Schindler, S. D., illus. (p. 908)
—Powers. (p. 1391)
—Tehanu. (p. 1715)
—Tom Mouse. (p. 1763)
—Tombs of Atuan. (p. 1764)
—Very Far Away from Anywhere Else. (p. 1838)
—Voices. (p. 1848)
—Wizard of Earthsea. (p. 1943)
—Wonderful Alexander & the Catwings. Schindler, S. D., illus. (p. 1948)
Le Guin, Ursula K., et al. Diverse Energies Buckell, Tobias & Monti, Joe, eds. (p. 454)
Le, Guo. Dragon's Tears. (p. 479)
Le, Guo, illus. see Gregory, Manju.
Le Huche, Magali, illus. see Webb, Steve.
Le Jars, David. Por Aqui y Por Alli. (p. 1385)
—Uno, Dos, Hola y Adios. (p. 1822)
Le Lait, Alain. Parapluie: Fabulous French Songs for Children. (p. 1324)
Le, Le Pham. From Where the Wind Blows. Arbuthnot, Nancy, tr. (p. 644)
Le, Leonard Rolland, illus. see Dowswell, Paul.
Le, Loanne, illus. see Chedekel, Evelyn.
Le Mair, Henriette Willebeek, illus. see Milne, A. A.
Le May Doan, Catriona & McGoogan, Ken. Going for Gold. (p. 692)
Le Messurier, Mark. Cognitive Behavioral Training: A How-To Guide for Successful Behavior. (p. 338)
Lê, Michel, jt. auth. see Lê, Christine.
Lê, Minh. Let Me Finish! Roxas, Isabel, illus. (p. 994)
Le Normand, Bruno. Palace of Versailles. Heinrich, Christian, illus. (p. 1319)
Le Pere, Leslie, illus. see Robbins, Tom.
Le Queux, William. House of Whispers. (p. 803)
Le Ray, Marina. Row, Row, Row Your Boat ; and, Ride, Ride, Ride Your Bike. (p. 1492)
Le Ray, Marina, illus. see James, Eric.
Le Ray, Marina, illus. see Matthews, Rupert.
Le Ray, Marina, illus. see Reasoner, Charles & Taylor, Jane.
Le Ray, Marina, illus. see Reasoner, Charles.
le Riche, Tim. Alberta's Oil Patch: The People, Politics & Companies. (p. 35)
Le Riche, Timothy. Billionaires of Canada: The Power Elite & Their Influence on Canada. (p. 187)
Le Rolland, L. & Smith, Alastair. Classroom Jokes. (p. 329)
Le Rolland, Leonard, illus. see Clarke, Phillip.
Le Rolland, Leonard, illus. see Dalby, Elizabeth.
Le Rolland, Leonard, illus. see Howell, Laura, ed.
Le Rolland, Leonard, illus. see Jones, Rob Lloyd.
Le Saux, Alain - Solotareff, jt. auth. see Solotareff, Gregoire.
Le Sueur, William Dawson. W. I. MacKenzie. (p. 1851)
Le Tord, Bijou. Bird or Two: A Story about Henri Matisse. Le Tord, Bijou, illus. (p. 190)
—Mountain Is to Climb. Le Tord, Bijou, illus. (p. 1181)
Le Verrier, Renee & Frank, Samuel. Treasure Hunt for Mama & Me: Helping Children Cope with Parental Illness. Taylor, Adam, illus. (p. 1781)
Lea, Audry. Scott the Dot. (p. 1531)
Lea, Corinne, illus. see Powell, Gregg E.
Lea, Henry Charles. Moriscos of Spain: Their Conversion & Expulsion (p. 1176)
Lea, Larry, et al. Larry Learns to Listen (p. 976)
Lea, Ruth Ann. Granny Grace. (p. 710)
Lea, Sienna. Stealing the Moon: Revelations of the Deep Shadow Self. (p. 1646)
Leach, Cheryl. Sally to the Rescue. (p. 1505)
Leach, Craig. Beyond the Gathering. (p. 174)
Leach, Emma, illus. see Child, Jeremy.
Leach, Michael. Badger. (p. 132)
—Deer. (p. 423)
—Fox. (p. 625)
—Hare. (p. 748)
—Hedgehog. (p. 761)
—Otter. (p. 1307)

L

Leach, Norman. Canadian Peacekeepers: Ten Stories of Valour in War-Torn Countries. (p. 260)
Leach, Sara. Count Me In (p. 369)
—Jake Reynolds: Chicken or Eagle? (p. 906)
—Warm Up (p. 1858)
Leacock, Elspeth. Exxon Valdez Oil Spill. (p. 557)
Leacock, Elspeth, jt. auth. see Buckley, Susan.
Leacock, Elspeth & Buckley, Susan. Places in Time: A New Atlas of American History. Jones, Randy, illus. (p. 1366)
Leacock, Elspeth & Schifini, Alfredo. West. (p. 1876)
Leadbeater, Tim. Islamic Empires, 600-1650. (p. 891)
Leadbeater, Tim & Clare, John. Islamic Empires, 600-1650. (p. 891)
Leadbetter, Lesley. Harold the Owl Who Couldn't Sleep. Leszek, Cedryll, illus. (p. 749)
Leader, Christine. You Can't Make a Dinosaur Out of Three Dead Horses. Leader, Christine, illus. (p. 1974)
Leader, Jessica. Nice & Mean. (p. 1250)
LeaderTreks Staff. Student Leaders Start Here. (p. 1669)
LeaderTreks Staff, creator. Grassroots. (p. 712)
Leadlove, Ben, illus. see Lowe, Tom.
Leaf, Autumn. Coto, Child of the Ocean. (p. 369)
Leaf, Brian. Defining Breaking Dawn: Vocabulary Workbook for Unlocking the SAT, ACT, GED, & SSAT. (p. 424)
—Name That Movie! A Painless Vocabulary Builder. (p. 1228)
—Top 50 Skills for a Top Score: ACT English, Reading, & Science. (p. 1769)
Leaf, Christina. American Shorthairs. (p. 63)
—Baby Cheetahs. (p. 125)
—Baby Ducks. (p. 126)
—Baby Elephants. (p. 126)
—Baby Gorillas. (p. 126)
—Baby Lions. (p. 127)
—Baby Orangutans. (p. 127)
—Baby Owls. (p. 127)
—Baby Pigs. (p. 127)
—Baby Sea Otters. (p. 128)
—Baby Seals. (p. 128)
—Baby Sheep. (p. 128)
—Baby Tigers. (p. 128)
—Birmans. (p. 192)
—Brown Bats. (p. 231)
—Gray Squirrels. (p. 713)
—Gray Wolves. (p. 713)
—Great-Horned Owls. (p. 716)
—Jackrabbits. (p. 904)
—Jeff Kinney. (p. 912)
—Laura Ingalls Wilder. (p. 980)
—Porcupines. (p. 1386)
—Roald Dahl. (p. 1477)
Leaf, Claudia. Radical Will. (p. 1432)
Leaf, Munro. Brushing Your Teeth Can Be Fun: And Lots of Other Good Ideas for How to Grow up Healthy, Strong, & Smart. (p. 233)
—How to Speak Politely & Why. (p. 821)
—Manners Can Be Fun. (p. 1088)
—Noodle. Bemelmans, Ludwig, illus. (p. 1263)
—Reading Can Be Fun. (p. 1445)
—Story of Ferdinand: 75th Anniversary Edition. (p. 1658)
—Story of Ferdinand. Lawson, Robert, illus. (p. 1658)
—Wee Gillis. Lawson, Robert, illus. (p. 1871)
Leah. Alligator Named Ally (p. 47)
Leah, Carole. God's World: Book 1 A Biblebased Reading Project (p. 692)
Leahy, Sandy & Tarentino, Kathy. Hibernating House. (p. 775)
Leak, Nancy M., illus. see Penn, Audrey.
Leake, Diyan. Bomberos. (p. 208)
—Canals (p. 260)
—Dentistas. (p. 426)
—Dentists (p. 427)
—Doctors (p. 459)
—Feet (p. 580)
—Firefighters (p. 591)
—Lakes (p. 972)
—Legs (p. 991)
—Los Bomberos (p. 1053)
—Los Veterinarios (p. 1054)
—Maestros. (p. 1070)
—Médicos. (p. 1119)
—Oceans & Seas (p. 1277)
—People in the Community (p. 1339)
—Police Officers (p. 1380)
—Policía (p. 1380)
—Ponds (p. 1382)
—Rivers & Streams (p. 1476)
—Tails (p. 1695)
—Teachers (p. 1709)
—Veterinarios. (p. 1839)
—Vets (p. 1839)
—Water, Water Everywhere! (p. 1863)
—Wings (p. 1936)
Leake, Kate, illus. see Zobel-Nolan, Allia.
Leake, Trish. Christmas Dream. (p. 313)
Leal, Ann Haywood. Also Known As Harper. (p. 50)
Leal, Joao, tr. see Cunha, Francisco.
Leal, Luis, compiled by. Cuentos Mexicanos - de los origenes a la Revolucion. (p. 390)
Leal, Mireya Fonseca, ed. see Quiroga, Horacio.
Leal, Mireya Fonseca, ed. see Tolstoy, Leo.
Leamon, Kevin. Oh No. Not Again! (p. 1281)
Lean, Chris Mac. BearWild. (p. 152)
Lean, Sarah. Dog Called Homeless. (p. 461)
—Hero. (p. 772)
—Hundred Horses. (p. 827)
Leance. Her Uniqueness -She Was Her- (p. 769)
Leaney, Cindy. It's Your Turn Now: Politeness. Wilks, Peter, tr. (p. 899)
—Pollution. (p. 1381)
Leanoard, James & Nash, Kevin. University of San Diego College Prowler off the Record. (p. 1821)
LeapForg Staff/Nickelodeon, jt. auth. see Nickelodeon Staff.
LeapFrog Schoolhouse Staff. Read-It-All Books: 2nd Grade & Up. (p. 1443)
—Read-It-All Books. (p. 1443)
LeapFrog Staff. Disney Lion King - U. K. (p. 451)
—Disney Princess Stories - France. (p. 453)
—Disney Princess Stories - Latin America. (p. 453)
—Imagination Desk Counting Day at the Beach. (p. 860)
—Leap Track Assessment & Instruction System Guide. (p. 982)
—LeapPad Grade 1 Getting Starter Kit. (p. 982)
—LeapPad Grade 2 Getting Starter Kit. (p. 982)
—LeapPad Kindergarten Getting Starter Kit. (p. 982)
—Links Program, for Use with Harcourt Brace - Grade 1: Die Cut Cards. (p. 1019)
—Lots & Lots of Honeypots. (p. 1057)
—Ozzie & Mack. (p. 1316)
—Pirates: The Treasure of Turtle Island. (p. 1363)
—Sing-along Read-along: Early Reading Set. (p. 1578)
—T. Rex's Mighty Roar: Une belle journee pour Rugir. (p. 1694)
—T. Rex's Mighty Roar. (p. 1694)
LeapFrog Staff & Partnership Staff, compiled by. Jay Jay the Jet Plane: U.K. (p. 910)
LeapFrog Staff, compiled by. I Know My ABC's! - U. K. (p. 840)
—Once upon a Time - U. K. (p. 1293)
—Tad Goes Shopping - U. K. (p. 1695)
—Tad's Silly Number Farm - U. K. (p. 1695)
Lear, E., jt. auth. see Lear, Edward.
Lear, Edward. Buho y la Gatita. (p. 237)
—Duck & the Kangaroo. Wattenberg, Jane, illus. (p. 488)
—Nonsense Botany & Nonsense Alphabets. (p. 1263)
—Nonsense Drolleries: The Owl & the Pussy-Cat, the Duck & the Kangaroo. Foster, William, illus. (p. 1263)
—Nonsense Poems. (p. 1263)
—Nonsense Song. (p. 1263)
—Nonsense Songs & Stories 1888. (p. 1263)
—Owl & the Pussycat. Jorisch, Stephane, illus. (p. 1314)
—Owl & the Pussycat. Jorisch, Stéphane, illus. (p. 1314)
—Owl & the Pussy-Cat & Other Stories. (p. 1314)
—Table & the Chair. Ebbeler, Jeffrey, illus. (p. 1694)
Lear, Edward, jt. auth. see Galdone, Paul.
Lear, Edward, jt. illus. see Gorey, Edward.
Lear, Edward & Campbell, Lori M. Complete Nonsense Books of Edward Lear. (p. 353)
Lear, Edward & Lear, E. Owl & the Pussy-Cat. (p. 1314)
Lear, Edward & Mortimer. Owl & the Pussycat. Mortimer, Anne, illus. (p. 1315)
Lear, John, illus. see Langford, Norman F.
Lear, Ruth, illus. see Hench, Larry.
Leardi, Jeanette. Great Pyramid: Egypt's Tomb for All Time. (p. 718)
—Making Cities Green. (p. 1080)
—Protecting Our Oceans: Set Of 6. (p. 1412)
—Protecting Our Oceans: Text Pairs. (p. 1412)
—Southern Sea Otters: Fur-Tastrophe Avoided. (p. 1617)
Leardi, Jeannette. Brain. (p. 221)
Learn As You Grow. God Loves You So Much... Reuben, Borgen & Jenny, Lindley, photos by. (p. 689)
Learner, Vickie, illus. see Howard-Hess, Susan.
Learning Co Bks Staff. Best Gift Ever. (p. 170)
—Lucky for Us! (p. 1062)
—New Friend. (p. 1244)
—Night Noises. (p. 1253)
—Reader Rabbit Comprehensive Workbook: Preschool. (p. 1444)
—Reader Rabbit Comprehensive Workbook: First Grade. (p. 1444)
—Reader Rabbit Comprehensive Workbook: Kindergarten. (p. 1444)
—Starry, Starry Night. (p. 1642)
Learning Company Books Staff. Learning with Curious George Pre-K Reading. (p. 986)
Learning Company Books Staff, ed. Bounty Hunter. (p. 216)
—Carmen Sandiego USA Adventures. (p. 270)
—Carmen Sandiego World Adventures. (p. 270)
—Mighty Math: Money & Decimals. (p. 1140)
—Reader Rabbit: Phonics. (p. 1444)
—Reader Rabbit: Alphabet. (p. 1444)
—Reader Rabbit: ABC Order. (p. 1444)
—Reader Rabbit: Rhyming Words. (p. 1444)
—Reader Rabbit: Writing Mechanics. (p. 1444)
—Reader Rabbit: Reading Comprehension. (p. 1444)
—Reader Rabbit 1st Grade Workbook. (p. 1444)
—Reader Rabbit Fun with ABC's. (p. 1444)
—Reader Rabbit Fun with Colors. (p. 1444)
—Reader Rabbit Fun with Crayons: 1-2-3. (p. 1444)
—Reader Rabbit Fun with Paint: Shapes. (p. 1444)
—Reader Rabbit Kindergarten Workbook. (p. 1444)
—Reader Rabbit Math: Addition & Subtraction. (p. 1444)
—Reader Rabbit Preschool Workbook. (p. 1444)
—Reader Rabbit Spelling Challenge. (p. 1444)
—Ride to Rescue. (p. 1471)
—Westward Bound! (p. 1876)
Learning Company, Inc. Staff. Achieve!: First Grade: Building Skills for School Success. (p. 8)
—Achieve!: Pre-Kindergarten: Building Skills for School Success. (p. 9)
—Learning with Curious George Kindergarten Math. (p. 986)
—Let's Learn 1st Grade Math. (p. 998)
—Let's Learn 1st Grade Reading. (p. 998)
—Pre-K Math. (p. 1394)
—Reader Rabbit Let's Learn Kindergarten Math. (p. 1444)
—Reader Rabbit Let's Learn Kindergarten Reading. (p. 1444)
Learning Company, Inc Staff & Houghton Mifflin Harcourt Children's Group Staff, creators. Learning with Curious George Kindergarten Reading. (p. 986)
Learning Company Staff. Achieve!: Kindergarten: Building Skills for School Success. (p. 9)
Learning Express Llc. Catholic High School Entrance Exams. (p. 280)
Learning Fun, Early & Priddy, Roger. Things That Go. (p. 1733)
Learning Made Easy LLC. Learn to Write the Alphabet. (p. 984)
Learning Works, creator. Ancient Egypt. (p. 68)
LearningExpress Staff. U. S. Constitution in 15 Minutes a Day. (p. 1806)
Lears, Laurie. Ian's Walk: A Story about Autism. Ritz, Karen, illus. (p. 849)
—Stay Away from Rat Boy! Hansen, Red, illus. (p. 1645)
Leary, Catherine, illus. see Scelsa, Greg.
Leary, Catherine, illus. see Williams, Rozanne Lanczak.
Leary, Jackson, jt. auth. see Leary, Sean.
Leary, Sean & Leary, Jackson. Go, Racecars Go! (p. 687)
Leary, Timothy. Start Your Own Religion. (p. 1643)
Leary, Vicki. Roberto el R?ipido: Rapid Robert. (p. 1479)
Leary's. Leary Tales. (p. 986)
Lease, Janice. Manny the Marmot. (p. 1088)
—Marigold Little Squirrel in a Cactus Patch. (p. 1094)
—Pellina the Pelican. (p. 1336)
Lease, Janice M. Rudy the Roadrunner. Lease, Janice m, illus. (p. 1494)
Lease, Janice m, illus. see Lease, Janice M.
Leaser, David. Betrock's Essential Guide to Palms. (p. 172)
Leaser, Marcia K. Frizzeldee's Catastrophe: Watch out for that Tree. (p. 639)
Leasman, Nancy Packard, illus. see Tanner, Dawn Leasman.
Leath, Patricia. I'd Like to Go to Sleep & Dream. (p. 851)
Leatham, Alan D. Four Cats, Five Monkeys, Absurd Birds & Other Fanciful Stuff. (p. 624)
Leatham, Marc Vincent. Race. (p. 1430)
—Story of the Five Squirrels. Leatham, Marc Vincent, illus. (p. 1661)
Leather, Harry & Leather, Jan. Cambridge Checkpoints VCE Biology Unit 3 2005. (p. 255)
Leather, Jan, jt. auth. see Leather, Harry.
Leatherdale, Mary, jt. auth. see Leatherdale, Mary Beth.
Leatherdale, Mary Beth & Charleyboy, Lisa. Urban Lives: Native Americans in the City. (p. 1825)
Leatherdale, Mary Beth & Leatherdale, Mary. My Class & Me: Kindergarten. Ritchie, Scot, illus. (p. 1200)
Leatherman, Diane. Abigail Before the Revolution. (p. 5)
Leatherman, Greg & Harris Wilson, P. Moving the Clouds: Tales of Priscilla. (p. 1184)
Leathers, Dan. Polar Bears on the Hudson Bay. (p. 1379)
—Snows of Kilimanjaro. (p. 1601)
Leathers, Daniel. Johnstown Flood 1889. (p. 924)
—Tornado Outbreak 1985. (p. 1770)
Leathers, Philippa. Black Rabbit. Leathers, Philippa, illus. (p. 196)
—How to Catch a Mouse. Leathers, Philippa, illus. (p. 815)
Leathers, Rain. Purple Mountain. (p. 1419)
Leavell, Tracy. Lily. (p. 1017)
Leaver, Trisha. Secrets We Keep. (p. 1546)
Leaver, Trisha & Currie, Lindsay. Creed. (p. 380)
Leavey, Peggy Dymond. Deep End Gang. (p. 423)
—Path Through the Trees. (p. 1328)
—Treasure at Turtle Lake. (p. 1781)
—Trouble at Turtle Narrows. (p. 1789)
Leavey, Peggy Dymond, jt. auth. see Guest, Jacqueline.
Leavitt, Amie. Amanda Bynes. (p. 52)
—Backyard Vegetable Garden for Kids. (p. 131)
—Miley Cyrus. (p. 1142)
—Raven-Symone. (p. 1441)
—Threat to the Yangtze River Dolphin. (p. 1741)
Leavitt, Amie J., jt. auth. see Leavitt, Amie Jane.
Leavitt, Amie Jane. Abigail Breslin. (p. 5)
—Amelia Earhart. (p. 58)
—Anatomy of a Plane Crash (p. 67)
—Anatomy of a Volcanic Eruption (p. 67)
—Ancient Athens. (p. 68)
—Backyard Flower Garden for Kids. (p. 131)
—Battle of the Alamo: An Interactive History Adventure (p. 146)
—Bill of Rights. (p. 186)
—Bill of Rights in Translation: What It Really Means. (p. 186)
—Bill of Rights in Translation [Scholastic]: What It Really Means. (p. 186)
—Bizarre Things We've Eaten. (p. 194)
—Bruno Mars. (p. 232)
—Care for a Pet Chimpanzee. (p. 266)
—Care for a Pet Chinchilla. (p. 266)
—Care for a Pet Mouse. (p. 266)
—Care for a Pet Sugar Glider. (p. 266)
—Care for a Pet Tarantula. (p. 266)
—Christopher Columbus. (p. 316)
—Ciara. (p. 318)
—Daredevil's Guide to Storm Chasing (p. 406)
—Daredevil's Guide to Swimming with Sharks (p. 406)
—Day by Day with Miley Cyrus. (p. 412)
—Design Your Family Tree. (p. 430)
—Discovering the Kingdom of Benin. (p. 449)
—Dylan & Cole Sprouse. (p. 491)
—Elizabeth Blackwell. (p. 513)
—George Washington Carver. (p. 664)
—Harriet Tubman. (p. 749)
—Helen Keller. (p. 762)
—Helping People with Disabilities & Special Needs Through Service Learning (p. 766)
—History of the Republican Party. (p. 785)
—Keith Urban. (p. 948)
—Miranda Cosgrove. (p. 1149)
—Nancy Pelosi. (p. 1229)
—Physical Computing & Makerspaces. (p. 1353)
—Rhine River. (p. 1467)
—Robert Downey Jr. (p. 1478)
—Southwestern Recipes. (p. 1618)
—Taylor Lautner. (p. 1708)
—Toby Keith. (p. 1760)
—U. S. Navy by the Numbers (p. 1807)
—United States Immigration Services. (p. 1819)
—United States Laws of Citizenship. (p. 1819)
—Vo-Tech Track to Success in Architecture & Construction. (p. 1846)
—We Visit Morocco. (p. 1868)
—Western Recipes. (p. 1876)
—What It's Like to Be Miley Cyrus. Vega, Eida de la, tr. (p. 1891)
—What It's Like to Be the Jonas Brothers: Que Se Siente Al Ser Los Hermanos Jonas. Vega, Eida de la, tr. (p. 1891)
—Who Really Created Democracy? (p. 1917)
—Who Really Discovered Electricity? (p. 1917)
Leavitt, Amie Jane, jt. auth. see Dougherty, Terri.
Leavitt, Amie Jane, jt. auth. see Murray, Robb.
Leavitt, Amie Jane, jt. auth. see Schuh, Mari C.
Leavitt, Amie Jane & Leavitt, Amie J. Battle of the Alamo: An Interactive History Adventure. (p. 146)
Leavitt, Amy. Yoga Fitness. (p. 1972)
Leavitt, Caroline. Girls in Trouble: A Novel. (p. 680)
—Samurai Martin, Cynthia, illus. (p. 1509)
Leavitt, Lindsey. Chapel Wars. (p. 291)
—Going Vintage. (p. 693)
—Princess for Hire. (p. 1403)
—Sean Griswold's Head. (p. 1537)
Leavitt, Loralee. Candy Experiments. (p. 261)
—Candy Experiments 2. (p. 261)
Leavitt, Martine. Blue Mountain. (p. 203)
—Heck Superhero! (p. 761)
—Heck Superhero. (p. 761)
—Heck, Superhero. (p. 761)
—Keturah & Lord Death. (p. 949)
—My Book of Life by Angel. (p. 1199)
—Tom Finder (p. 1763)
Leavitt, Martine, jt. auth. see Bates, Martine.
Leavy, Diana C. Backstroke the Sea Otter & the Perfect Day. (p. 130)
Leavy, Una. O'Brien Book of Irish Fairy Tales & Legends. Field, Susan, illus. (p. 1275)
—Tomas No Quiere Zapatos. (p. 1764)
Lebachen, Medyhne. Hilhairyass Poems: By a Six Year Old Adult. Payne, Mark, illus. (p. 779)
LeBar, Anna, illus. see LeBar, Stephen.
LeBar, Stephen. Terry the Tiny Parrot My Granny & Me. LeBar, Anna, illus. (p. 1722)
LeBaron, Cecilia. Cap. (p. 262)
—Map. (p. 1089)
—Nat & Tab. (p. 1230)
—Sam & Val. (p. 1506)
LeBaron, Sarah & Dawson, Kai. Oberlin College College Prowler off the Record. (p. 1275)
LeBaron, Taylor, et al. Cutting Myself in Half: 150 Pounds Lost, One Byte at a Time. (p. 396)
Lebbon, Tim. Contagion. (p. 360)
Lebbon, Tim, jt. auth. see Golden, Christopher.
LeBeau, Conrad, jt. auth. see Konlee, Mark.
Lebedev, Aleksandr. Bible Stories. (p. 176)
Lebedev, Aleksandr, illus. see Brierley, Jane.
Lebedev, Vladimir, illus. see Marshak, Samuil.
Lebell, Gene. Toughest Man Alive. (p. 1773)
Leber, Nancy. Rain Forest Animals (p. 1434)
—Solids: Text Pairs. (p. 1608)
—Sounds All Around Us (p. 1615)
—What Plants & Animals Need (p. 1892)
Leber, Nancy & Capstone Press Editors. What Plants & Animals Need (p. 1892)
Leber, Nancy & Capstone Press Staff. Rain Forest Animals (p. 1434)
—Sounds All Around Us (p. 1615)
Leber, Nancy Jolson, et al. Picture Sorting for Phonemic Awareness: Reproducible Picture Cards with Hands-On Sorting Games & Activities. (p. 1356)
Leberer, Sigrid. Adventures of the Three Best Friends. (p. 23)
Leberer, Sigrid, jt. auth. see Franke, Kristina.
Lebihan, Kara & Allwright, Deborah. Mrs Vickers' Knickers. Allwright, Deborah, illus. (p. 1188)
Leblanc, A. J. Donnie & His First Surf Lesson. (p. 466)
—Donnie the Little Knee Boarder. (p. 466)
Leblanc, André. Red Piano. Werner, Justine, tr. from FRE. (p. 1454)
LeBlanc, Andre, illus. see Hoth, Iva.
LeBlanc, Avis Lyons. To Ride a Dragonfly. (p. 1759)
Leblanc, Catherine. How to Defeat Dragons. Garrigue, Roland, illus. (p. 816)
—How to Demolish Dinosaurs. Garrigue, Roland, illus. (p. 816)
—How to Get Rid of Ghosts. Garrigue, Roland, illus. (p. 820)
—How to Mash Monsters. Garrigue, Roland, illus. (p. 820)
—How to Outwit Witches. Garrigue, Roland, illus. (p. 821)
—How to Pulverize Pirates. Garrigue, Roland, illus. (p. 821)
—How to Ward off Wolves. Garrigue, Roland, illus. (p. 822)
Leblanc, Denise. Mr. Blue, I Have a Question for You. (p. 1184)
LeBlanc, Ellen Lieb. Tea & Cookie. Pape, Wendy Fehrle, illus. (p. 1708)
LeBlanc, Giselle, illus. see Hall, Raelene.
Leblanc, Louise. Bon, la Brute et le Vampire. (p. 208)
—Ca Suffit, Sophie! (p. 250)
—Leo's Midnight Rescue Cummins, Sarah, tr. from FRE. (p. 993)
—Leo's Midnight Rescue. Prud'homme, Jules, illus. (p. 993)
—Leo's Poster Challenge Prud'homme, Jules & Cummins, Sarah, trs. from FRE. (p. 993)
—Leo's Skiing Surprise Cummins, Sarah, tr. from FRE. (p. 993)
—Leo's Skiing Surprise. Prud'homme, Jules, illus. (p. 993)
—Maddie on TV Cummins, Sarah, tr. from FRE. (p. 1069)
—Maddie Stands Tall Cummins, Sarah, tr. from FRE. (p. 1069)
—Maddie Stands Tall. Cummins, Sarah, tr. from FRE. (p. 1069)
—Maddie Surfs for Cyber Pals Cummins, Sarah, tr. from FRE. (p. 1069)
—Maddie Surfs for Cyber-Pals. Gay, Marie-Louise, illus. (p. 1069)
—Maddie Surfs for Cyber-Pals. Cummins, Sarah, tr. from FRE. (p. 1069)
—Maddie's Big Test Cummins, Sarah, tr. from FRE. (p. 1069)
—Maddie's Big Test. Cummins, Sarah, tr. from FRE. (p. 1069)
—Sophie Est en Orbite. Gay, Marie-Louise, tr. (p. 1613)
—Tombeau en Peril Brochard, Philippe, illus. (p. 1764)
Leblanc, Louise & Prud'homme, Jules. Vampires Sortent de L'ombre. (p. 1832)
LeBlanc, Marc, illus. see Rogers-Busboom, Kimberly.
Leblanc, Margaret. Ms. Maddy Comes to Town. (p. 1188)
LeBlanc, Margaret Ann. Mexico Adventure: Book Three of Ms. Maddy Series (p. 1131)
Leblanc, Margaret Ann. Ms Maddy & the Lake Adventure. (p. 1188)
LeBlanc, Nancy, illus. see Gardner, Graham.
LeBlanc, Natalie, jt. auth. see Denis, Erik.
Leblanc, P. J. New Brother for Snowflake. (p. 1243)

LeBlanc, Rebecca, ed. see Tobin, Richard K.
LeBlanc, Steven A., jt. auth. see Register, Katherine E.
LeBlanc, Terry. Learning to Recycle with Terry the Trashman. (p. 986)
Lebloas-Julienne, Renee. Dolphin. (p. 464)
Leblond, Michaël. New York in Pajamarama. Bertrand, Frederique, illus. (p. 1248)
Lebost, Diana. Mr. Kite & the Perilous Flight: Izzy & Daisy. Ersoz, Sahin, illus. (p. 1185)
LeBoutillier, Linda. Food Long Ago & Today (p. 613)
—Unusual & Awesome Jobs Using Technology: Roller Coaster Designer, Space Robotics Engineer, & More. (p. 1823)
LeBoutillier, Nate. Basketball. (p. 143)
—Best of Everything Baseball Book (p. 170)
—Best of Everything Basketball Book (p. 170)
LeBoutillier, Nate. Dallas Cowboys. (p. 401)
LeBoutillier, Nate. Day in the Life of a Garbage Collector (p. 413)
—Day in the Life of a Zookeeper (p. 413)
Leboutillier, Nate. Denver Broncos. (p. 427)
—Eiffel Tower. (p. 507)
LeBoutillier, Nate. Gymnastics. (p. 733)
LeBoutillier, Nate. Miami Dolphins. (p. 1133)
LeBoutillier, Nate. NBA: a History of Hoops: the Story of the Denver Nuggets. (p. 1238)
—NBA: a History of Hoops: the Story of the Minnesota Timberwolves. (p. 1238)
—NBA: a History of Hoops: the Story of the Oklahoma City Thunder. (p. 1238)
—NBA: a History of Hoops: the Story of the Utah Jazz. (p. 1238)
Leboutillier, Nate. New England Patriots. (p. 1244)
—New York Giants. (p. 1248)
—Pittsburgh Steelers. (p. 1365)
LeBoutillier, Nate. Play Basketball Like a Pro: Key Skills & Tips (p. 1371)
—Running Back Can't Always Rush Santillan, Jorge H., illus. (p. 1497)
Leboutillier, Nate. San Francisco 49ers. (p. 1510)
—Seattle Supersonics. (p. 1539)
—St. Louis Rams. (p. 1638)
—Story of the Boston Celtics. (p. 1660)
LeBoutillier, Nate. Story of the Chicago Bears. (p. 1660)
Leboutillier, Nate. Story of the Chicago Bulls. (p. 1660)
LeBoutillier, Nate. Story of the Chicago White Sox. (p. 1660)
LeBoutillier, Nate. Story of the Cleveland Cavaliers. (p. 1660)
LeBoutillier, Nate. Story of the Cleveland Indians. (p. 1660)
—Story of the Denver Nuggets. (p. 1660)
Leboutillier, Nate. Story of the Denver Nuggets. (p. 1660)
Leboutillier, Nate. Story of the Detroit Lions. (p. 1660)
Leboutillier, Nate. Story of the Detroit Pistons. (p. 1660)
LeBoutillier, Nate. Story of the Detroit Tigers. (p. 1660)
Leboutillier, Nate. Story of the Golden State Warriors. (p. 1661)
LeBoutillier, Nate. Story of the Green Bay Packers. (p. 1661)
Leboutillier, Nate. Story of the Houston Rockets. (p. 1661)
LeBoutillier, Nate. Story of the Kansas City Royals. (p. 1661)
—Story of the Los Angeles Dodgers. (p. 1661)
Leboutillier, Nate. Story of the Los Angeles Lakers. (p. 1661)
—Story of the Milwaukee Bucks. (p. 1661)
LeBoutillier, Nate. Story of the Minnesota Timberwolves. (p. 1661)
—Story of the Minnesota Twins. (p. 1661)
Leboutillier, Nate. Story of the Minnesota Twins. (p. 1661)
LeBoutillier, Nate. Story of the Minnesota Vikings. (p. 1661)
Leboutillier, Nate. Story of the New Jersey Nets. (p. 1661)
—Story of the New York Knicks. (p. 1661)
LeBoutillier, Nate. Story of the Oklahoma City Thunder. (p. 1661)
Leboutillier, Nate. Story of the Philadelphia 76ers. (p. 1662)
LeBoutillier, Nate. Story of the Pittsburgh Pirates. (p. 1662)
—Story of the Portland Trail Blazers. (p. 1662)
Leboutillier, Nate. Story of the Sacramento Kings. (p. 1662)
—Story of the San Antonio Spurs. (p. 1662)
LeBoutillier, Nate. Story of the Seattle Mariners. (p. 1662)
—Story of the Tampa Bay Rays. (p. 1662)
—Story of the Toronto Blue Jays. (p. 1662)
—Story of the Utah Jazz. (p. 1662)
Leboutillier, Nate. Story of the Utah Jazz. (p. 1662)
LeBoutillier, Nate. Swimming. (p. 1691)
—Ultimate Guide to Pro Baseball Teams (p. 1809)
—Ultimate Guide to Pro Basketball Teams (p. 1809)
—Volleyball. (p. 1849)
Leboutillier, Nate. Washington Redskins. (p. 1860)
Lebovics, Dania. Baby Chronicles: My Very Own Story: From Pre-Natal to Pre-School. Quach, Lam, illus. (p. 125)
LeBow, Michael. Sally Sall & the Case of the Tic Monster: A Book for Kids Who Tic. Barnett, Thora, illus. (p. 1505)
LeBox, Annette. Peace Is an Offering. Graegin, Stephanie, illus. (p. 1331)
—Salmon Creek Reczuch, Karen, illus. (p. 1505)
Lebredo, Raquel, jt. auth. see Jarvis, Ana C.
LeBreton, Heather. Rhyming with the Little Ones LeBreton, Zachary, illus. (p. 1468)
LeBreton, Sue. Whale Shark. (p. 1877)
LeBreton, Zachary, illus. see LeBreton, Heather.
Lebron, Karen. My Big Book of Numbers. Lonsdale, Mary, illus. (p. 1197)
LeBrun, Barbie. Porter Horse Finds Blackbeard's Treasure. (p. 1386)
Lebrun, Jessica. Rainbow's Mist. (p. 1436)
Lebscky, Ibi. Albert. Cardoni, Paolo, illus. (p. 34)
—Amadeus. Cardoni, Paolo, illus. (p. 51)
—Leonardo. Cardoni, Paolo, illus. (p. 992)
—Marie. Cardoni, Paolo, illus. (p. 1093)
—Pablito. Cardoni, Paolo, illus. (p. 1316)
—William. Cardoni, Paolo, illus. (p. 1933)
LeBuis, Peter. Character Building Songs (p. 291)
Lebuis, Peter, jt. auth. see Marie-France, Marcie.
Lecaye, Olga. Ratoncito Perez. (p. 1440)
—Sombra Del Oso. (p. 1608)
Lecesne, James. Absolute Brightness. (p. 7)
—Trevor. (p. 1785)
Lecher, Doris. New House for Charlie. (p. 1245)
Lechermeier, Philippe. Hilo de Hada. Rozarena, P., tr. from FRE. (p. 780)
—Secret Lives of Princesses. Dautremer, Rébecca, illus. (p. 1541)
Lechermeier, Philippe & Dautremer, Rebecca. Princesas/ Princesses: Mini Album. (p. 1402)
Lechler, Louan, illus. see Wooten, Terry.
Lechner, Diane, et al, texts. Jesus Comes to Us. (p. 915)
Lechner, John. Clever Stick. Lechner, John, illus. (p. 331)
—Sticky Burr: Adventures in Burrwood Forest. Lechner, John, illus. (p. 1650)
Lechner, Judith. Maya: Set Of 6. (p. 1112)
—Maya: Text Pairs. (p. 1112)
—Our New Fish Tank: Learning to Estimate & Round Numbers to the Nearest Ones, Tens, & Hundreds Places. (p. 1309)
Lechon, Daniel, illus. see Brammer, Ethriam Cash.
Lechón, Daniel, illus. see De Anda, Diane.
Lechon, Daniel, illus. see Mora, Pat.
Lechter, Sharon L., jt. auth. see Kiyosaki, Robert T.
Lecia, Balian, illus. see Lorna, Balian.
Lecis, Alessandro & Shirtliffe, Leanne. I Am Not Little Red Riding Hood. Wolfsgruber, Linda, illus. (p. 833)
Leck, Henry H., et al. Creating Artistry Through Choral Excellence. (p. 378)
Leck, James. Adventures of Jack Lime. (p. 19)
Leckey, Carl. Pop up & Go. (p. 1384)
LeClair, Danielle. Sidney Crosby: Ma Vie. Karvonen, Tanjah, tr. from ENG. (p. 1573)
LeClaire, Allen, ed. Modern Young's Literal Translation, New Testament W/Psalms & Proverbs. (p. 1159)
Leclaire, Danielle. Sidney Crosby. (p. 1573)
Leclerc, Caroline, ed. see Quarto Generic Staff.
Leclerc, Caroline, jt. ed. see Delpech, Sylvie.
LeClerc, Regis L. Tim, Tobbie, & the Train. (p. 1750)
L'Ecole des loisirs/LeapFrog, jt. auth. see McKee, David.
LeCompte, David & Padrick, Kendell. Eugene Stillwell Wants to Know! (p. 540)
—Eugene Stillwell Wants to Know! Part III. (p. 540)
LeCompte, Jeff. Christmas Miracle at Firehouse Seven. (p. 314)
Lecomte, Eva. Paula the Waldensian. (p. 1331)
Lecor, Tex, jt. auth. see Rossignol, Manon Éléonor.
LeCornu, J. Aerial Navigation: La Navigation Aerienne: a Documentary & Anecdotal History. LeCornu, J., ed. (p. 25)
Lecoy, Denise. Looking after Me. Hamelin, Marie-Micheline, illus. (p. 1050)
LeCraw, Cynthia, retold by. Tale of the Wonderful Tar Baby. (p. 1700)
Lecreux, Michele & Gallais, Celia. Boy's Book of Adventure: The Little Guidebook for Smart & Resourceful Boys. Millet, Esao & Millet, Jocelyn, illus. (p. 220)
—Girl's Book of Adventure: The Little Guidebook for Smart & Resourceful Girls. Millet, Esao & Millet, Jocelyn, illus. (p. 679)
LeCron, Helen Cowles. Animal Etiquette Book of Rhymes. Day, Maurice, illus. (p. 77)
Leday, Linda. Sammy the Scarecrow. (p. 1508)
Ledbetter, Darril & Graham, Leland. Reading Bridge Enriching Classroom Skills: 6th Grade. Willie, Kirsten et al, eds. (p. 1445)
—Reading Bridge Enriching Classroom Skills: 7th Grade. Willie, Kirsten et al, eds. (p. 1445)
—Reading Bridge Enriching Classroom Skills: 8th Grade. Willie, Kirsten et al, eds. (p. 1445)
Ledbetter, Ebonie. Media Bias. (p. 1118)
Ledbetter, John'el, illus. see Curry, Cicero.
Ledbetter, Mary Ellen. You Say I Say. (p. 1976)
Ledbetter, Penny. Frog's Lily Pad. (p. 641)
Ledbetter, Penny S. Mushroom's Day Away. Garrett, Caroline S., illus. (p. 1193)
Ledeaux, Lola. If A Dog Could Blog. (p. 852)
Leder, Jane Mersky & Donovan, Sandy. Keep Your Cool! What You Should Know about Stress. Desrocher, Jack, illus. (p. 947)
Leder, Meg & Kempster, Rachel. Big Me, Little You Book. (p. 182)
Lederer, Richard, jt. auth. see Ertner, Jim.
Lederer, Richard & Ertner, Jim. Animal Cracker Uppers Jr. (p. 77)
—Cleverly Comical Animal Jokes. (p. 331)
—Rip Roaring Animal Jokes. (p. 1473)
Lederer, Richard & Gibbs Smith Publisher Staff. Presidential Trivia: The Feats, Fates, Families, Foibles, & Firsts of Our American Presidents Art Parts & Black Eye Design, illus. (p. 1397)
Lederer, Richard & Kegel, Stan. Hilarious Holiday Humor. (p. 779)
Lederer, Ryan. Adventures of Captain Candy. (p. 17)
Lederer, Susan. I Can Do That. Loehr, Jenny, illus. (p. 835)
Lederer, Suzy. I Can Say That. Loehr, Jenny, illus. (p. 836)
Lederhos, Anne, illus. see Abel, Melanie.
Lederhos, Lynn. Return to Her Roots: Revelations from a Young Girl's Journey Home. (p. 1465)
Lederman, Marsha, illus. see Shepard, Betty Bruce.
Lederman, Todd. Notch Ear's Sacrifice. Lederman, Todd, illus. (p. 1267)
Ledesma Vazquez, Jorge, tr. see Minch, John, et al.
Ledford, Jan Roadarmel, jt. auth. see Calaway, Bernie L.
Ledford, Mary"Aunt Sissy"Ledlowtranette. Cowboy Will & the Magic Rope. (p. 374)
Ledgard, Edna, compiled by. Snake Prince & Other Stories: Burmese Folk Tales. (p. 1596)
Ledgard, J. M., tr. see Jalonen, Riitta.
Ledger, Bill, illus. see Fuerst, Jeffrey B.
Ledger, Bill, illus. see Grudzina, Rebecca.
Ledger, Bill, illus. see Harris, Brooke.
Ledger, Faye, illus. see Hall, Shirley.
Ledger, Kate. Lost Tooth Rescue. (p. 1056)
—Twin Magic: School Bully, Beware! (p. 1802)
Ledger, Sally. Henrik Ibsen. (p. 767)
Ledgerwood, Maja. Pocahontas: Princess of Faith & Courage. (p. 1375)
Ledray, Michael. Fifi Loves You! (p. 584)
Ledson, Sidney. Give Your Child Genius IQ: A Program for Busy Parents. (p. 681)
Ledu, Stephanie. We Both Read-the Horse Lover's Book. Hudrisier, Cecile, illus. (p. 1866)
Ledu, Stéphanie. We Both Read-The Horse Lover's Book. Hudrisier, Cecile, illus. (p. 1866)
Leduc-Lenmark, MaryAlice. Meet Mister Muttley. Speas, Joann, illus. (p. 1121)
Ledu-Frattini, Stephanie. Tiger. Uhlig, Elizabeth, tr. from FRE. (p. 1748)
Ledwidge, Asher. Black Family: Towards More Self-Love. (p. 196)
Ledwidge, Maria. My Salvation Birthday. (p. 1218)
Ledwidge, Michael, jt. auth. see Patterson, James.
Ledwidge, Natacha, illus. see Kessler, Liz.
Ledwon, Peter. Mia's Secret. Ledwon, Peter & Mets, Marilyn, illus. (p. 1134)
Ledwon, Peter, illus. see Lohans, Alison.
Ledyard, Addie, illus. see Coolidge, Susan.
Ledyard, Addie, jt. auth. see Coolidge, Susan.
Lee, Adrienne. Aztec Warriors (p. 122)
—Gladiators (p. 682)
—Knights Martin, Cynthia, illus. (p. 964)
—Legendary Warriors. Martin, Cynthia, illus. (p. 989)
—Samurai Martin, Cynthia, illus. (p. 1509)
—Vikings Martin, Cynthia, illus. (p. 1842)
Lee, Alan, illus. see Sutcliff, Rosemary.
Lee, Alfonso Silva, see Silva Lee, Alfonso.
Lee, Amy Sue. Lou Lou & Lenny's Boat Ride. (p. 1057)
Lee, Anais, illus. see Tucker, Seletha Marie Head.
Lee, Anais, illus. see V, Vasanthi.
Lee, Anita Lynn. Kenny's Amazing Adventures. (p. 949)
Lee, Ann. Charming, Alarming, Disarming. (p. 294)
Lee, Anne. When You Are Camping. Lee, Anne, illus. (p. 1905)
Lee, Anne, illus. see Young, Patrick.
Lee, April. Helping at School. (p. 766)
—How We Get Around Town. (p. 823)
Lee, Audrey. Once upon a Storytime at Christmas (p. 1293)
—Once upon a Storytime at Christmas - 1. (p. 1293)
Lee Badtke, Danica. Day Care. (p. 412)
Lee, Barbara R. Pookey the Pony. (p. 1383)
Lee Bates, Katharine & Gamwell, Calvert. America the Beautiful: A Pop-up Book about the Famous Song by Katharine Lee Bates. Jordan, Carrie, illus. (p. 59)
Lee Bates, Katherine. America the Beautiful. (p. 59)
Lee, Becca. Skilda the Skunk. (p. 1584)
Lee, Bennie. Adventures of Sarah. (p. 22)
Lee, Betsy B. Buggy That Boogied Away. Lee, Sarah Ann, illus. (p. 236)
—Funny Dolch Word Book # 1: Un Libro Comico # 1 de la Palabra de Dolch. Davis, Pollyanna S., tr. (p. 649)
—Whoa, Wiggle-Worm: A Little Lemon Book about an Overly Active Child Varnedoe, Catharine E., illus. (p. 1919)
Lee, Bill, illus. see Thompson, Richard & Thompson, Ofa.
Lee, Bin. One (p. 1293)
Lee, Bin, illus. see Spinelli, Eileen.
Lee, Bonnie. Go Go Sadie. Taylor, Erin, illus. (p. 686)
—Welcome. (p. 1873)
Lee, Bowen Lyam. Shining Light in My Cat's Eye. Lee, Bowen Lyam, illus. (p. 1566)
Lee, Brenda Donaloio, ed. see Lee, George Douglas.
Lee, Brett, jt. auth. see Panckridge, Michael.
Lee, Brian. Bouncey the Elf & Friends - Bedtime St. (p. 216)
—Castle. (p. 276)
—Construction Site. (p. 360)
—Pirate Ship. (p. 1363)
—World of Dinosaurs. (p. 1956)
Lee, Brian, illus. see Harris, Nicholas.
Lee, Brian, jt. auth. see Saper, Lee.
Lee, Briant H. & Wedwick, Daryl M. Corrugated Cardboard Scenery. (p. 368)
Lee, Britney, illus. see RH Disney Staff & Wooster, Devin Ann.
Lee, Brittany. Rollins College. Moore, Kim & Burns, Adam, eds. (p. 1485)
Lee, Brittney, illus. see Anderson, Jodi Lynn.
Lee, Calee M. I Love You! Tharp, Tricia, illus. (p. 843)
Lee, Carol & Bell, Donna. Saying Goodbye to Hare: A Story about Death & Dying to Be Used with Children. Ages 5-9. (p. 1519)
Lee, Carol Ann. Anne Frank & the Children of the Holocaust. (p. 86)
Lee, Carol Ann, jt. auth. see Van Maarsen, Jacqueline.
Lee, Carolyn A. My World & Me: The & Me Collection. (p. 1221)
Lee, Cathy & Uhlmann, Chris. Worship Dramas for Children & Adults. (p. 1961)
Lee, Cecelia In. Alphabets. (p. 50)
Lee, Celeste & Herndon, Ryan, compiled by. Guinness World Records: Bizarre Bug Records. (p. 731)
—Guinness World Records, Top 10. (p. 731)
Lee, Charlotte, jt. auth. see Gura, Timothy.
Lee, Chi-ching, illus. see Ahlstrom, Peter, ed.
Lee, Chris. Becoming a Sant: A Guidebook for Parents & Santa's Helpers. (p. 156)
Lee, Claudia, jt. auth. see Park, Devin.
Lee, Cora. Great Motion Mission: A Surprising Story of Physics in Everyday Life. Rolston, Steve, illus. (p. 717)
Lee, Cora & O'Reilly, Gillian. Great Number Rumble: A Story of Math in Surprising Places. Gray, Virginia, illus. (p. 717)
Lee, Cory. Velociraptor. (p. 1835)
Lee Coy, Amy. Duke Devlin the Daring Dogie. (p. 489)
Lee, Cyl. More Ridiculous Riddles. (p. 1174)
—Really Silly Jokes. (p. 1450)
—Ridiculous Riddles. (p. 1471)
Lee, D. Clarence. Mystery of the Red Creek Valley Kidnapper: Second Edition. (p. 1226)
Lee, Dakota. Flash of Freedom. (p. 602)
Lee, Danielle. JumpStart Your Future: A Guide for the College-Bound Christian. (p. 934)
Lee, Darrien. 16 Going on 21. (p. 1995)
—Grown in Sixty Seconds. (p. 727)
Lee, David. Colony of Delaware. (p. 342)
—Comanche. (p. 346)
—Danny & the Portal of the World: Danny Falls into a Portal, Meets His Relatives & Returns Home Again. Lee, David, illus. (p. 405)
—Danny & the Trip to Outer Space: This Book Is Written & Illustrated by 8 Year Old Author, David T. Lee. It Contains 16 Chapters, 6,500 Words & 6 Full Color Illustrations. It Is the Sequel of Danny & the Portal of the World. Lee, David, illus. (p. 405)
—Ellie's Family Album. (p. 514)
Lee, Day's. Fragrant Garden. Bellemare, Josee, illus. (p. 627)
Lee, Deborah Baptiste & Atcheson-Melton, Patty. In the Shade of the Spade: This Tale in a Poetry Format Takes Us on a Journey. the Illustrations Are Bright & Whimsical. You Can Almost Hear Music. Baptiste, Annette Green, illus. (p. 867)
Lee, Dennis. Bubblegum Delicious. (p. 233)
—Cat & the Wizard. (p. 277)
—Garbage Delight. (p. 655)
Lee, Desmond, tr. see Plato.
Lee, Dom, illus. see Mochizuki, Ken.
Lee, Dom, illus. see Yoo, Paula.
Lee, Dom, jt. auth. see Mochizuki, Ken.
Lee, Donya. Colorless Cupcakes Caper. (p. 344)
Lee, Dora & Palmer, Dora. Biomimicry: Inventions Inspired by Nature. Thompson, Margot, illus. (p. 190)
Lee, Dwight R., jt. auth. see Crain, Cynthia D.
Lee, Edith. Romeo & Julie Square. (p. 1486)
Lee, Eldon, jt. auth. see Lee, Todd.
Lee, Ella Dolbear. Wonderful Story of Jesus. (p. 1948)
Lee, Etrulia R. Phonics Is My Way Series (p. 1352)
Lee, Eun. Antique Gift Shop (p. 89)
Lee, Eunice. Antique Gift Shop (p. 89)
Lee, Evelyn. Bluestem Horizon: A Story of a Tallgrass Prairie. Brauckmann-Towns, Krista, illus. (p. 204)
—Buffalo Prairie. (p. 235)
—Buffalo Prairie. Brauckmann-Towns, Krista, illus. (p. 235)
—Buffalo Prairie. Brauckman-Towns, Krista, illus. (p. 236)
Lee Follen, Eliza. Pedler of Dust Sticks. (p. 1334)
—Piccolissima. (p. 1354)
—Talkative Wig. (p. 1703)
—What the Animals Do & Say. (p. 1893)
Lee, Fonda. Zeroboxer. (p. 1986)
Lee, Foxglove. Tiffany & Tiger's Eye. (p. 1748)
Lee, Fran. Backyard Birding for Kids Lee, Fran, illus. (p. 131)
Lee, Fran, illus. see Drinkard, Lawson.
Lee, Fran, illus. see Elton, Candice & Elton, Richard.
Lee, Frances. Fun with Chinese Cooking. (p. 648)
Lee, Frances Cook, illus. see Dymock, Melissa.
Lee, Frank. Creating the Cover for Your Graphic Novel. (p. 379)
—Drawing Action in Your Graphic Novel. (p. 481)
—Drawing the Heroes in Your Graphic Novel. (p. 482)
—Drawing the Villains in Your Graphic. (p. 482)
—Penciling, Inking, & Coloring Your Graphic Novel. (p. 1336)
—Telling the Story in Your Graphic Novel. (p. 1717)
Lee, Frank, illus. see Longnecker, Steve.
Lee, G. I Want My Kitty Cat Tv! Scott, E., illus. (p. 847)
Lee, Gail, illus. see Lazdowski, Ken.
Lee, Gentry, jt. auth. see Clarke, Arthur C.
Lee, George Douglas. Oppy Stops the Hopping Popper. Lee, Brenda Donaloio, ed. (p. 1301)
—Twyla the Truffle Pig. Lee, Brenda Donaloio, ed. (p. 1804)
—Wolf Who Cried Boy. Lee, Brenda Donaloio, ed. (p. 1944)
Lee, George L. Worldwide Interesting People: 162 History Makers of African Descent. (p. 1961)
Lee, George T., illus. see Hannaford, Linda S.
Lee, Georgia. Tour the U. S. Capitol. (p. 1773)
Lee, Gia. Hurricane Hound. Davis, Jason, illus. (p. 829)
Lee, Gi-eun, ed. see Nahm, Andrew C.
Lee, Ginger. Tessa T's Treasures (p. 1723)
Lee, Gisela. China (p. 306)
Lee, Gisela, jt. auth. see Conklin, Wendy.
Lee, Glenda. Alexander's Tree. (p. 37)
Lee, Glenn. Forever Four! Clever! Clever! Meets Battle Girl & the Staff of Power! (p. 619)
Lee, Glenn E. Origin of the Forever Four! F4 Clever! Clever! Lee, Imani K., illus. (p. 1304)
Lee, Grace, illus. see Disney Book Group Staff & Hapka, Catherine.
Lee, Grace, illus. see Disney Book Group Staff & Scollon, Bill.
Lee, Grace, illus. see Disney Book Group Staff, et al.
Lee, Grace, illus. see Hapka, Catherine, pseud & Disney Book Group Staff.
Lee, Grace, illus. see Posner-Sanchez, Andrea.
Lee, Grace, illus. see Saxon, Victoria.
Lee Green Pope. Enchanted Toy Shop. (p. 523)
Lee, H. Chuku. Beauty & the Beast. Cummings, Pat, illus. (p. 154)
Lee, HaeDa. Ida's Present. Kim, IhHyeon, illus. (p. 852)
Lee, Han, illus. see Anderson, Pamela.
Lee, HaNa & Park, KangHo. Heavenly Executioner Chiwoo (p. 761)
Lee, Hanlim, illus. see Anderson, Pamela Dell.
Lee, Haylen, illus. see Woods, Shirley.
Lee, Helen. Guide's Greatest Escape from Crime Stories. (p. 730)
—Where in the World? Stories from Everywhere: Daily Devotions for Juniors. (p. 1908)
Lee, Helen J., ed. Spot-the-Difference Picture Puzzles. (p. 1633)
Lee, Ho Baek. While We Were Out. Lee, Ho Baek, illus. (p. 1911)
Lee, Ho Baek, illus. see Park, Linda Sue.
Lee, Hope H. What Colors Did You Eat Today? (p. 1881)
Lee Hope, Laura. Bobbsey Twins in the Great West. (p. 206)
Lee, Hoseok M. Different Kind of Fle. (p. 438)
Lee, Howard. Day at the Zoo. Reasoner, Charles, illus. (p. 412)
—Jamshid & the Lost Mountain of Light. (p. 907)
Lee Humphrey, Robert, ed. Culture & Costumes: Symbols of Their Period (p. 391)
Lee, Huy Voun, illus. see Jacobs, Paul DuBois & Swender, Jennifer.
Lee, Huy Voun, illus. see Sayre, April Pulley.

L

Lee, Huy Voun, illus. see Wardlaw, Lee.
Lee, Huy Voun, illus. see Ziefert, Harriet.
Lee, Huy Voun, jt. auth. see Yeh, Kat.
Lee, Hye Ran, illus. see Burnett, Frances Hodgson.
Lee, Hyeongjin, illus. see Kim, YeoongAh.
Lee, Hyeon-joo, illus. see Kim, Soo-hyeon.
Lee, Hye-Seong. Call of Samuel: From 1 Samuel 3:1-10. (p. 254)
Lee, Hyun Se. Armageddon 1 (p. 99)
Lee, Hyun Young. Something for School. Lee, Hyun Young, illus. (p. 1610)
Lee, Ilchi. Meridian Exercise for Self-Healing Book 1: Classified by Common Symptoms (p. 1127)
—Meridian Exercise for Self-Healing Book 2: Classified by Common Symptoms (p. 1127)
Lee, Imani K. Clever! Clever! & the Book of Forever. (p. 331)
Lee, Imani K., illus. see Lee, Glenn E.
Lee, Ingrid. Cat Found. (p. 278)
—Dragon Tide Meister, Soizick, illus. (p. 478)
—George Most Wanted Denis, Stephane, illus. (p. 663)
—George Most Wanted. Denis, Stephane, illus. (p. 663)
—George, the Best of All! Denis, Stephane, illus. (p. 663)
—Maybe Later Grimard, Gabrielle, illus. (p. 1113)
—Thief Girl (p. 1732)
—True Story of George Denis, Stephane, illus. (p. 1793)
—True Story of George. Denis, Stephane, illus. (p. 1793)
Lee, Ioe, illus. see Cole, Bob.
Lee, J. A. Trials of Edward Finlay. (p. 1785)
Lee, J. H., creator. Boo Paper Doll Set. (p. 210)
Lee, J. Marie. 4Jellybean Junction. (p. 1992)
—4Teen Jellybean. (p. 1992)
Lee, Jack, illus. see Lee, Patty.
Lee, Jack, jt. auth. see Lee, Patty.
Lee, Jackie. Coconut. (p. 337)
—Cranberry. (p. 376)
—Pumpkin. (p. 1416)
Lee, Jacqueline. Twirled Paper. (p. 1802)
Lee, Jacqui, illus. see Lloyd, Jennifer.
Lee, Jae. Fantastic Four: 1234. (p. 571)
Lee, James, ed. South America in Charts & Graphs. (p. 1616)
Lee, James V., ed. see Fischer, John J.
Lee, Jamie. Washaka: The Bear Dreamer. (p. 1859)
Lee, Janet. Emma. (p. 519)
Lee, Janet K., illus. see Carroll, Lewis, pseud & Kontis, Alethea.
Lee, Janice. Ethan's First Day of School. (p. 539)
Lee, Janice G. Adventures of Chewy & Tonk. (p. 17)
Lee, Jared, illus. see Colandro, Lucille.
Lee, Jared, illus. see Doyle, Bill.
Lee, Jared, illus. see Fontes, Justine.
Lee, Jared, illus. see James, Steven.
Lee, Jared, illus. see Kressley, Carson.
Lee, Jared, illus. see Martin, Justin McCory.
Lee, Jared, illus. see Metzger, Steve.
Lee, Jared, illus. see Thaler, Mike.
Lee, Jared, tr. see Fontes, Justine.
Lee, Jared D. Dentist from the Black Lagoon. (p. 426)
Lee, Jared D., illus. see Colandro, Lucille.
Lee, Jared D., illus. see Doyle, Bill.
Lee, Jared D., illus. see Metzger, Steve.
Lee, Jared D., illus. see Thaler, Mike.
Lee, Jc. Clara's Red Balloon. Park, Kathy, illus. (p. 326)
Lee, Jeanie. Baby Farm Friends. (p. 126)
Lee, Jeannie, jt. illus. see Whitten, Samantha.
Lee, Jee-Hyung. Demon Diary Lim, Kara, illus. (p. 426)
Lee, Jeffrey Lyndon. Locked in the Box. (p. 1045)
Lee, Jen SookFong, jt. auth. see Conlin, Christy Ann.
Lee, Jenn Manley, illus. see Thielbar, Melinda.
Lee, Jennifer. Illinois Confederacy of Illinois, Missouri, Wisconsin, Iowa, & Oklahoma. (p. 857)
Lee, Jenny. Elvis & the Underdogs: Secrets, Secret Service, & Room Service. Light, Kelly, illus. (p. 517)
—Elvis & the Underdogs. Light, Kelly, illus. (p. 517)
Lee, Jihyeon. Pool. (p. 1383)
Lee, Jill. Beautiful Surprise Beneath. (p. 154)
Lee, Jim, illus. see Azzarello, Brian, et al.
Lee, Jim, illus. see Claremont, Chris & Simonson, Louise.
Lee, Jisun, illus. see Blackaby, Susan.
Lee, Jisun, illus. see Donahue, Jill Lynn.
Lee, Joe, illus. see Cole, Bob.
Lee, Joe, illus. see Harris, M. S. Ed Rebecca a. & Harris, M. S. Ed.
Lee, Joe, illus. see Markette, Paul Scott.
Lee, Joe, illus. see Quinn, Patricia O. & Stern, Judith M.
Lee, Joe, illus. see Tait, Elena.
Lee, John R. & Hopkins, Virginia. What Your Doctor May Not Tell You about Menopause: The Breakthrough Book on Natural Hormone Balance. (p. 1896)
Lee, John R., et al. Breast Cancer: How Hormone Balance Can Help Save Your Life. (p. 225)
Lee, Johnie. Courtney. (p. 373)
Lee, Jonathan. Remember the Lost Sheep. (p. 1459)
—So I Could Fly Free. (p. 1602)
Lee, Jong-Kyu, jt. auth. see Shin, Hwan.
Lee, Jong-Kyu & Shin, Hwan. Evil's Return (p. 546)
Lee, Jordan, jt. auth. see Spencer, Anne.
Lee, Joshua. Mysterious Quest of Johnathan Davis. (p. 1223)
Lee, Josie D. & Myers, Glenice. Reno & the Rodeo. (p. 1460)
Lee, Judith, jt. ed. see Slade, Joseph W., III.
Lee, Julia Elizabeth. Seahorses Down Under. Weiser, Robert, ed. (p. 1536)
Lee, Jumin, illus. see Heinrichs, Cynthia.
Lee, Jung Hwa. Adrenalin (p. 13)
—Adrenalin Lee, Jung Hwa, illus. (p. 13)
Lee, Justin. Everything You Need to Know about Cystic Fibrosis. (p. 545)
—How to Draw African Animals. (p. 816)
—How to Draw Animals of the Rain Forest. (p. 816)
—How to Draw Fish. (p. 817)
—How to Draw Sharks. (p. 818)
—How to Draw Whales. (p. 819)
—Respiratory System. (p. 1463)
Lee, K. D. What's a Girl to Do? (p. 1896)
Lee, Kanani K. M. & Wallenta, Adam. Incredible Plate Tectonics Comic: The Adventures of Geo (p. 869)
Lee, Kang-Woo. Rebirth (p. 1451)
—Rebirth Lee, Kang-Woo, illus. (p. 1451)
—Rebirth Ryu, Youngju, tr. from JPN. (p. 1451)
—Rebirth. (p. 1451)
Lee, Kang-Woo, illus. see Woo, et al.
Lee, Karen. ABC Safari Lee, Karen, illus. (p. 3)
—Instrument for Eddie. The, Tienny, illus. (p. 879)
—Mushy Mashed Bananas. Lee, Karen, illus. (p. 1193)
Lee, Karen, illus. see Fisher, Doris & Sneed, Dani.
Lee, Karen, illus. see Ingalls, Ann.
Lee, Karen, illus. see Sneed, Dani & Fisher, Doris.
Lee, Karin. Zangadoo Kangaroo & the Mysterious Boomerang. Porterfield, Scott, illus. (p. 1985)
Lee, Kary, illus. see Nyikos, Stacy.
Lee, Kathryn, tr. see Christen, Dennis H.
Lee, Kathy. Captive in Rome. (p. 264)
—Hall of Mirrors. (p. 737)
—No Means No. (p. 1259)
—Phoebe's Fortune. (p. 1351)
—River Rapids. (p. 1476)
—Rome in Flames. (p. 1486)
—Runaway Train. (p. 1496)
—Space Invaders. (p. 1619)
Lee, Katie, illus. see Armour, Michael C.
Lee, Katie, illus. see Jay, Lorraine A.
Lee, Katie, illus. see Ring, Elizabeth.
Lee, Katie Bertoch. Ma Ma's Hair Is Everywhere. (p. 1067)
Lee, Keith Russell. Power Faith & Living. (p. 1389)
Lee, Kendra. Best Friends Forever! (p. 169)
Lee, Ki-Hoon. Phantom Cho, Seung-Yup, illus. (p. 1349)
Lee, Kim, illus. see Webb, Carla.
Lee, Kim & Benchmark Education Co., LLC Staff. Pop! Pop! Pop! (p. 1384)
Lee, Kimberly Fekany. Cell Scientists: From Leeuwenhoek to Fuchs. (p. 286)
—Cells (p. 286)
—Looking Inside Cells. (p. 1051)
Lee, Kong, illus. see Morrissey, Tricia.
Lee, Kyanna Shanae. Stepdad? No Thanks...! (p. 1648)
Lee, Laura. Little Laura & the Birthday Surprise. Huey, Debbie & Viray, Sherwin, illus. (p. 1030)
—Snail Race at Penny's Place. (p. 1596)
Lee, Lavina. Handel's World. (p. 740)
Lee, LaWanda. Word of Essence: Poetry by LawWanda Lee. (p. 1951)
Lee, Leslie W., jt. illus. see Lee, Melicent Humason.
Lee, Linda, illus. see Strong, Frances Dinkins.
Lee, Linda, jt. auth. see Haymond, Mary.
Lee, Lindsay Wilder. Legend of Tooth Boy. (p. 989)
Lee, Lori K. Bonnie the Honeybee & the Case of the Butterfly Blues. (p. 209)
Lee, Lucas Taekwon. Legend of Baeoh: How Baeoh Got His Stripes. Forward, Max, illus. (p. 988)
Lee, Lynne. Bramble'S Story. (p. 222)
Lee, Mackenzi. This Monstrous Thing. (p. 1737)
Lee, Mahogony. Mr. & Mrs. Ladybug's Morning Walk. (p. 1184)
Lee, Margaret. Adventures of Sebastian the Helpful Seagull. (p. 22)
—Tsumiki (p. 1795)
Lee, Margaret A. Grandpa, What Are Lasers? (p. 709)
Lee, Marie G. September 4 Jellybean (p. 1551)
—September 4 TeenJellybean Junction (p. 1551)
Lee, Marie Myung-Ok. Somebody's Daughter. (p. 1609)
Lee, Mark. Twenty Big Trucks in the Middle of the Street. Cyrus, Kurt, illus. (p. 1801)
—Veinte Camiones Grandes en Medio de la Calle. Cyrus, Kurt, illus. (p. 1834)
Lee, Martin, et al. 40 Elaboration Activities That Take Writing from Bland to Brilliant! (p. 1997)
—40 Elaboration Activities That Take Writing from Bland to Brilliant! Lee, Martin, illus. (p. 1997)
Lee, Mary. Cuando Los Dientes Falsos de Abuela Volan. (p. 388)
—My Airforce Mom. (p. 1195)
—When Grandma's False Teeth Fly. (p. 1902)
Lee, Mary Ellen. Danny & Life on Bluff Point: Lost in the Dark. (p. 405)
—Danny & Life on Bluff Point: Blizzard of '95 revised Edition. (p. 405)
Lee, Mary R. Island Dog Books. (p. 892)
Lee, Maxine. Big Whoop! (p. 184)
—Pi-Rat! Lee, Maxine, illus. (p. 1353)
Lee, Maxine, illus. see Wharton, Ellie.
Lee, Melicent Humason & Lee, Leslie W. Indians of the Oaks. (p. 872)
Lee, Mi-Ae. Twinkle Twinkle: Insect Life Cycle. Cowley, Joy, ed. (p. 1802)
Lee, Michael. Chandler Park Drive. (p. 289)
Lee, Michelle. Myth & Magic of Nemadji Indian Pottery: History, Identification & Value Guide: Nemadji Indian Pottery. (p. 1227)
Lee, Michelle, jt. ed. see Hetzel, D. June.
Lee, Milly. Landed. Choi, Yangsook, illus. (p. 974)
Lee, Mini. Ms. Behaviour. (p. 1188)
Lee, Mykle, ed. see Lumpkin, Kenya.
Lee, Mykle, jt. auth. see S., LaTisha.
Lee, Myung. Ragnarok - Seeds of Betrayal (p. 1433)
Lee, Myung & Knaak, Richard A. Ragnarok: Revenge of the Valkyrie (p. 1433)
—Ragnarok - Seeds of Betrayal (p. 1433)
Lee, Myung Jin. Lights Out (p. 1016)
—Ragnarok Lee, Myung Jin, illus. (p. 1433)
Lee, Myung-Jin. Ragnarok: Twilight of Terror Knaak, Richard A., tr. from KOR. (p. 1433)
Lee, Myung-Jin, creator. Ragnarok: Memories of Shadow (p. 1433)
—Ragnarok Boxed Set Collection (p. 1433)
Lee, Na Hyeon. Traveler of the Moon Lee, Na Hyeon, illus. (p. 1780)
Lee, Nancy. Baby Chipmunks & Backyard Friends. (p. 125)
—Hoover's Funny Little Kids. (p. 796)
—Hoover's Summer Tale. (p. 796)
—Rescued by the Great Tow Truck. (p. 1462)
Lee, Nate. Don't Miss the Bus. (p. 468)
—Invitation & 5 Other Dramas for Tweens. (p. 886)
—Joy in the Morning: Easy Dramas, Speeches, & Recitations for Children. (p. 929)
—Pushing the Boundaries: And Five Other Dramas for Tweens. (p. 1420)
—Sleep on It! And Five Other Dramas for Tweens. (p. 1588)
—Words from the Cross & 5 Other Dramas for Tweens. (p. 1951)
Lee, Newman. Creepy Kitchen. Elizabeth, Neering, ed. (p. 381)
Lee, Nicole. Night Ward: Welcome to Amity House. (p. 1254)
Lee, Nikita, illus. see Meredith, Amberley.
Lee, Otha. Mrs. Lee's Stories about God's First People. (p. 1187)
—Mrs. Lee's Stories about Jesus. (p. 1187)
Lee, P. Janet. Ella Elephant: And Her Fear of Mice. (p. 513)
Lee, Pascal. Mission: Mars. (p. 1153)
Lee, Pat. DrawbotZ. (p. 481)
Lee, Patricia Mary. Pick-a-WooWoo - the Star Who Lost Her Sparkle: Sprinkle here & Sparkle ther. We work with love because we Care. Evans, Gabriel, illus. (p. 1354)
Lee, Patty. Three Dogs & a Horse Named Blue. Lee, Jack, illus. (p. 1742)
—Wild Animals: What Is That I Ask? Lee, Jack, illus. (p. 1928)
Lee, Patty & Lee, Jack. Biblical: Who Is That I Ask? a Children's Poetry Book. (p. 176)
Lee, Paul, illus. see Farshtey, Greg.
Lee, Paul, illus. see Golenbock, Peter.
Lee, Paul, illus. see Lasky, Kathryn.
Lee, Paul, jt. auth. see Farshtey, Greg.
Lee, Penny. Schoolio: Pets, Projects & Pandemonium. (p. 1524)
Lee, Philip Yungkin. 250 Essential Chinese Characters for Everyday Use (p. 2001)
Lee, Prema. Maki's Journey Begins. (p. 1082)
Lee, Puck Hee. Wizard Monk of Kamayut & Six Other True Stories. (p. 1943)
Lee, Quentin Daschel. Demon Within. (p. 426)
Lee, Quickjen. Off*Beat (p. 1279)
Lee, Quinlan B. Beach Day. Haefele, Steve, illus. (p. 149)
—Christmas Angel. Kurtz, John, illus. (p. 312)
—Christmas Tree for Me: A New Holiday Tradition for Your Family. Basaluzzo, Constanza, illus. (p. 316)
—Circus Comes to Town. (p. 322)
—Great Day for Soccer. (p. 715)
—Phonics: 12 Book Reading Program (p. 1351)
—Sail Away. (p. 1503)
—Star Wars: Phonics Boxed Set. (p. 1641)
—Super Spies. (p. 1682)
—Valentine Surprise. Haefele, Steve, illus. (p. 1830)
Lee, Quinlan B. & Bridwell, Norman. Clifford's Best School Day. Haefele, Steve, illus. (p. 332)
—Happy St. Patrick's Day, Clifford! Haefele, Steve, illus. (p. 746)
Lee, R. Lacey Learns: Love & Beauty. (p. 970)
Lee, R. Denzil. Found in the Forest. (p. 624)
Lee, Raymond, jt. auth. see Sherman, M. Zachary.
Lee, Rex. Rann Braden Circus Showman A Circus Adve. (p. 1438)
Lee, Richard B., jt. auth. see Opini, Bathseba.
Lee, Roslyn, illus. see Harper, Julie-Ann.
Lee, Ru. Witch Class Lee, Ru, illus. (p. 1941)
Lee, Rudolph, illus. see Burks, Catherine.
Lee, Sally. Abigail Adams (p. 5)
—Allosaurus. (p. 47)
—Ankylosaurus (p. 84)
—Apatosaurus. (p. 91)
—Arnold Schwarzenegger: From Superstar to Governor. (p. 100)
—Castles & Palaces (p. 277)
—Delicious Dairy Group Poling, Kyle, illus. (p. 425)
—Diplodocus (p. 445)
—Eleanor Roosevelt. (p. 508)
—Food Safety (p. 614)
—Freddie Prinze, Jr: From Shy Guy to Movie Star. (p. 632)
—George W. Bush (p. 663)
—Gloria Estefan: Superstar of Song. (p. 685)
—Healthy Snacks, Healthy You! Swift, Gary, illus. (p. 759)
—Healthy Snacks, Healthy You! [Scholastic]. Swift, Gary, illus. (p. 759)
—Hillary Clinton (p. 779)
—Holiday Histories. (p. 788)
—Iguanodon. (p. 856)
—Kings & Queens (p. 960)
—Knights (p. 964)
—Laura Bush (p. 980)
—Little Paleontologist. (p. 1033)
—Mad Scientists: The Not-So-Crazy Work of Amazing Scientists (p. 1069)
—Martha Washington. (p. 1097)
—Megalosaurus. (p. 1124)
—Pebble First Guide to Dinosaurs (p. 1333)
—Powerful Protein Group Swift, Gary, illus. (p. 1390)
—Princes & Princesses (p. 1401)
—Royalty. (p. 1492)
—Sam Walton: Business Genius of Wal-Mart. (p. 1507)
—School Long Ago & Today (p. 1523)
—Short History of Christmas. (p. 1569)
—Short History of Halloween. (p. 1569)
—Short History of Thanksgiving. (p. 1569)
—Short History of Valentine's Day. (p. 1569)
—Staying Safe Online (p. 1645)
—William Jefferson Clinton (p. 1933)
Lee, Sally, jt. auth. see Aboff, Marcie.
Lee, Sally, jt. auth. see Asselin, Kristine Carlson.
Lee, Sally, jt. auth. see Raatma, Lucia.
Lee, Sally & Edison, Erin. Presidential Biographies. (p. 1397)
Lee, Sandra. Semi-Homemade Cool Kids Cooking. (p. 1550)
Lee, Sang-Eun. Love or Money (p. 1060)
Lee, SangEun, creator. 13th Boy (p. 1995)
Lee, Sarah Ann, illus. see Lee, Betsy B.
Lee, Sera, jt. auth. see Kim, Hanmin.
Lee, Seung-Ah, tr. see Eun-Ha, Jo.
Lee, Shari. Mandie's & Mindie's Adventure under the Sea (p. 1087)
Lee, Sharon. Max. (p. 1110)
—Tale of the Selfish Shellfish. (p. 1700)
Lee, Sharon Alberta. Mickey of Las Vegas. (p. 1136)
Lee, Shell. Teenie's Treehouse Adventures: The Magic Begins. (p. 1714)
Lee, Shelley R. Before I Knew You. Lee, Shelley R., ed. (p. 158)
Lee, Silver Ann. Amazing Bedtime Stories. (p. 54)
Lee, Sonja. Sauce. (p. 1516)
Lee, Soo, illus. see Goh, Colin & Woo, Yen Yen.
Lee, So-Young. Arcana (p. 95)
—Arcana. (p. 95)
—Arcana. Lee, So-Young, illus. (p. 95)
Lee, So-Young, creator. Model (p. 1157)
Lee, Spider. Hair Ball. Eckstrom, Nathaniel, illus. (p. 736)
Lee, Spike, jt. auth. see Lee, Tonya Lewis.
Lee, Spike & Lee, Tonya Lewis. Giant Steps to Change the World. Qualls, Sean, illus. (p. 674)
—Please, Baby, Please. Nelson, Kadir, illus. (p. 1373)
Lee, Stacey. Under a Painted Sky. (p. 1813)
Lee, Stan. Balder the Brave. (p. 134)
—Boyhood of Thor! (p. 220)
—Challenge! (p. 288)
—Essential Daredevil Romita, John, illus. (p. 536)
—Fantastic Four (p. 571)
—Fantastic Four. (p. 571)
—Fantastic Four Omnibus (p. 571)
—Incredible Hulk Vol. 2 Kane, Gil et al, illus. (p. 869)
—Marvel Masterworks: Captain America. Vol. 6 Morrow, Gray et al, illus. (p. 1099)
—Quest for the Mystic Mountain! (p. 1426)
—Spider-Man. (p. 1626)
—Stan Lee's How to Draw Superheroes. (p. 1639)
—Superhero Christmas. Jessell, Tim, illus. (p. 1683)
—Thor (p. 1739)
—Thor: Tales of Asgard. (p. 1739)
—To the Death! (p. 1759)
—When Speaks the Dragon! (p. 1904)
Lee, Stan, jt. auth. see Conway, Gerry.
Lee, Stan, jt. auth. see Wald, Mark.
Lee, Stan & Moore, Stuart. Convergence. Tong, Andie, illus. (p. 361)
Lee, Stan, et al. Amazing Spider-Man Youngquist, Jeff, ed. (p. 55)
—Amazing Spider-Man Romita, John & Lieber, Larry, illus. (p. 55)
—Doctor Strange Ditko, Steve et al, illus. (p. 459)
—Golden Treasury of Klassic Krazy Kool Kids Komics. Yoe, Craig, ed. (p. 695)
—Ka-Zar. Kirby, Jack et al, illus. (p. 941)
—Marvel Weddings. (p. 1099)
—Spider-Man: Am I an Avenger? (p. 1626)
Lee, Stephen J. Europe, 1890-1945. (p. 540)
—Gladstone & Disraeli. (p. 682)
Lee, Stephi. Where Do My Prayers Go? Zareba, Lukasz, illus. (p. 1907)
Lee, Steven. TruthQuest: In the Beginning. (p. 1794)
Lee, Sun Hee Teresa. How to Analyze the Films of Tim Burton. (p. 814)
Lee, Sungun, et al, creators. Korean Language I: Easy to Learn (p. 967)
Lee, Susan, illus. see Hurley, Wes.
Lee, Susie & Skindzier, Jon. MIT College Prowler off the Record: Inside Massachusetts Institute of Technology. (p. 1155)
Lee, Suzy. Mirror. (p. 1149)
—Shadow. (p. 1557)
—Wave. (p. 1864)
—Zoo. Lee, Suzy, illus. (p. 1988)
Lee, Suzy, illus. see Klausmeier, Jesse.
Lee, Suzy, illus. see Waber, Bernard.
Lee, T. S. Lincoln Story: The Boy Who Embraced a Nation. (p. 1018)
—Martin Luther King, Jr. Story: The Boy Who Broke Barriers with Faith. (p. 1098)
—Obama Story: The Boy with the Biggest Dream! Shin, Janet Jaywan, tr. from KOR. (p. 1275)
—Oprah Winfrey Story: The First Oprah Winfrey Comic Biography. (p. 1301)
—Stephen Hawking Story: The First Stephen Hawking Comic Biography. (p. 1648)
—Stephen Spielberg Story: The First Stephen Spielberg Comic Biogrhaphy. (p. 1648)
—Thomas Edison Story: The First Thomas Edison Comic Biography. (p. 1738)
Lee, T. S., jt. auth. see Ahn, H. M.
Lee, Tae E., illus. see Pulido, Brian.
Lee, Tammie. House. (p. 802)
Lee, Tanith. Black Unicorn. (p. 197)
—Piratica: Being a Daring Tale of a Singular Girl's Adventure upon the High Seas. (p. 1364)
Lee, Thomas. Battle at Otter Lake. (p. 145)
—Cooties. (p. 365)
—My Grandma Is A Mermaid. (p. 1210)
Lee, Tiffany A. Meadow City Presents: A New Friend. (p. 1116)
Lee, Todd & Lee, Eldon. From California to North 52 Degrees: Cariboo Experiences. (p. 642)
Lee, Tony. Clemson Tigers. (p. 331)
—Excalibur: The Legend of King Arthur. Lee, Tony & Hart, Sam, illus. (p. 547)
—Gloom. (p. 685)
—Greatest Rivalries in Sports. (p. 720)
—Outlaw: The Legend of Robin Hood. Hart, Sam & Fujita, Artur, illus. (p. 1312)
Lee, Tony, jt. auth. see Chilman-Blair, Kim.
Lee, Tonya Lewis, jt. auth. see Lee, Spike.
Lee, Tonya Lewis & Lee, Spike. Please, Puppy, Please. Nelson, Kadir, illus. (p. 1373)
Lee, Tricia Ting, illus. see Libby, Lori Ann.
Lee, Tzexa Cherta, jt. auth. see Coburn, Jewell Reinhart.
Lee, Vanessa. Beauty Queen & the School Nerd. (p. 154)
Lee, Vanessa Rose. Funny Jimmy. (p. 650)
—Haunted House of Riddles. Gillen, Rosemarie, illus. (p. 753)
Lee, Vin, creator. Crazy Love Story (p. 377)

—One (p. 1293)
Lee, Virginia, illus. see Clayton, Sally Pomme.
Lee, Wan & Benchmark Education Co., LLC Staff. Fish Wish. (p. 598)
Lee Wardlaw. Seventh-Grade Weirdo. (p. 1555)
Lee, Wei-Chun, illus. see Tidwell, Susan.
Lee, Wendy W., illus. see Schram, Peninnah & Davis, Rachayl Eckstein.
Lee, Williams, illus. see Brouillette, Peter.
Lee Wilson, Diane. To Ride the God's Own Stallion. (p. 1759)
Lee, Witness. Entrenamiento para Ancianos: El Ancianato y la Manera Ordenada Por Dios (1), Libro 9. (p. 531)
—Holy Word for Morning Revival: Ephesians 4:1-6:24 (p. 791)
—Holy Word for Morning Revival: Keeping the Principles of the Body (p. 791)
Lee, WonKyeong. Chirping Band. Jang, EunJoo, illus. (p. 308)
—Green River. Yang, HyeWon, illus. (p. 722)
Lee, Xiongpao, illus. see Allen, C. William.
Lee, Y. J. Little Moon Princess. Lee, Y. J., illus. (p. 1032)
Lee, Y. S. Agency 3: The Traitor in the Tunnel. (p. 29)
—Body at the Tower. (p. 207)
—Rivals in the City. (p. 1475)
Lee, Yawtsong, tr. see Shanghai Animation Studio Staff & Tang, Sanmu.
Lee, Yiting. Mr White. (p. 1187)
Lee, Youjung. Let's Be Perverts: Volume 4. (p. 994)
—Passionate Two-Face (p. 1327)
Lee, Young Shin, jt. auth. see Rogers, Bud.
Lee, Young Shin & Rogers, Buddy. Fights, Flights, & the Chosen Ones Burner, Brett & Earls, J. S., eds. (p. 586)
Lee, Young Yuu, creator. Kill Me, Kiss Me (p. 956)
Lee, Youngran. Click. (p. 331)
—Romance Papa (p. 1486)
Lee, Yuan, illus. see Mann, Elizabeth.
Lee, YunHee. Angel Diary (p. 73)
Lee, Zaina. Sun Takes a Holiday. (p. 1676)
Lee/Sinonexus, Emma /Fung-Ing. Learn Mandarin through Chinese Proverbs. (p. 983)
LeeAnn, Jodi & Luker, Myrna. Teddy in a Shoebox. (p. 1712)
Leebaert, Derek. To Dare & to Conquer: Special Operations & the Destiny of Nations, from Achilles to Al Qaeda. (p. 1758)
Leebrick, Kristal. Lucky Buckeye: A Story about Ohio. (p. 1062)
Lee-Browne, Patrick, jt. tr. see Merz, Caroline.
Leech, Bonnie. Geometry's Great Thinkers: The History of Geometry. (p. 663)
—Gregor Mendel's Genetic Theory: Understanding & Applying Concepts of Probability. (p. 723)
—Mesopotamia: Creating & Solving World Problems. (p. 1129)
—Names of Numbers: Learning How Numbers Are Represented with Words. (p. 1228)
Leech, Bonnie Coulter. Circles & Spheres. (p. 321)
—Geometry's Great Thinkers: The History of Geometry. (p. 663)
—Gregor Mendel's Genetic Theory: Understanding & Applying Concepts of Probability. (p. 723)
—Mesopotamia: Creating & Solving Word Puzzles. (p. 1129)
—Mesopotamia: Creating & Solving Word Problems. (p. 1129)
—Polygons. (p. 1381)
—Prisms. (p. 1407)
—Quadrilaterals. (p. 1422)
—Triangles. (p. 1785)
Leech, Carlyle & Leech, Thirma. Ha-Ha Farm. (p. 734)
Leech, Christopher & Pattison, Mark. Your 'Body Bitz' & What They Are Doing Right Now. (p. 1980)
Leech, Jacob, illus. see Guerrero, Rhonda.
Leech, John, illus. see Dickens, Charles.
Leech, Richard W. Adventures of Button Broken Tail (p. 17)
Leech, Thirma, jt. auth. see Leech, Carlyle.
Leedahl, Shelley A. Bone Talker Slavin, Bill, illus. (p. 209)
Leeder, Teresa. Silly Boy. (p. 1575)
Leedham, Jacalyn, jt. auth. see Hanke, Maureen.
Leedom, Karen L. Is for Astoria. Bailey, Sally, illus. (p. 889)
Leeds, Constance. Unfortunate Son. (p. 1817)
Leeds, Marjorie M., illus. see Terrill Holdman, Shirley.
Leeds, Robert X. Christmas Tails. Stetz, Ken, illus. (p. 316)
—HOW to Almost MAKE A MILLION DOLLARS: I Almost Did it. You Can Almost Do It Too! (p. 814)
—HOW to almost MAKE A MILLION DOLLARS: I almost did it. You can almost do it Too! (p. 814)
Leedy, Loreen. Crazy Like a Fox. Leedy: A Simile Story. (p. 377)
—Crazy Like a Fox. Leedy, Loreen, illus. (p. 377)
—Edible Pyramid: Good Eating Every Day. Leedy, Loreen, illus. (p. 504)
—Follow the Money! (p. 612)
—Great Graph Contest. Leedy, Loreen, illus. (p. 716)
—It's Probably Penny. Leedy, Loreen, illus. (p. 898)
—Jack & the Hungry Giant: Eat Right with Myplate. (p. 902)
—Look at My Book! How Kids Can Write & Illustrate Terrific Books. (p. 1048)
—Look at My Book! How Kids Can Write & Illustrate Terrific Books. Leedy, Loreen, tr. (p. 1048)
—Mapping Penny's World. Leedy, Loreen, illus. (p. 1090)
—Monster Money Book. Leedy, Loreen, illus. (p. 1168)
—My Teacher Is a Dinosaur: And Other Prehistoric Poems, Jokes, Riddles & Amazing Facts (p. 1220)
—Seeing Symmetry. Leedy, Loreen, illus. (p. 1548)
—Shocking Truth about Energy. Leedy, Loreen, illus. (p. 1568)
—Subtraction Action. Leedy, Loreen, illus. (p. 1671)
Leedy, Loreen, jt. auth. see Leedy, Loreen.
Leedy, Loreen & Leedy, Loreen. Jack & the Hungry Giant: Eat Right with Myplate. (p. 902)
Leedy, Loreen & Schuerger, Andrew. Amazing Plant Powers: How Plants Fly, Fight, Hide, Hunt, & Change the World. (p. 55)
—Messages from Mars. Leedy, Loreen, illus. (p. 1129)
Leedy, Loreen & Street, Pat. There's a Frog in My Throat! 440 Animal Sayings a Little Bird Told Me. Leedy, Loreen, illus. (p. 1730)
Leedy, Nancy. Leah's Pet Bird Beba. (p. 982)
lee-Epstein, michael, jt. auth. see epstein, brad M.
Leeflang-Oudenarden, C., illus. see Van Walsum-Quispel, J. M.
Leek, Kenny, illus. see Markels, Bobby.
Lee-Karlon, Ann, ed. see Etingoff, Kim.
Lee-Karlon, Ann, ed. see Indovino, Shaina Carmel.
Lee-Karlon, Ann, ed. see Indovino, Shaina.
Leeke, John, tr. see da Vignola, Giacomo Barozzi.
Leeks, David, illus. see Cullen, Dave & Williams, Simon.
Leeks, David, illus. see Cullen, Dave.
Leeks, David, illus. see Richard, John.
Leeming, Joseph. Fun with String: A Collection of String Games, Useful Braiding & Weaving, Knot Work & Magic with String & Rope. Pont, Charles E., illus. (p. 649)
Leeper, Angela. Juneteenth: A Day to Celebrate Freedom from Slavery. (p. 934)
Leeper, Chris, illus. see Grey, Chelsea Gillian.
Leeper, Christopher, ed. see Grey, Chelsea Gillian.
Leeper, Christopher, illus. see Galvin, Laura Gates.
Leeper, Christopher, illus. see Galvin, Laura.
Leeper, Christopher, illus. see Shriver, Chelsea & Grey, Chelsea Gillian.
Leeper, Christopher J., illus. see Galvin, Laura Gates.
Leeper, Christopher J., illus. see Grey, Chelsea Gillian.
Leeper, Christopher J., illus. see Shriver, Chelsea & Grey, Chelsea Gillian.
Leeper, Christopher J., tr. see Galvin, Laura Gates.
Leeper, Christopher J., tr. see Shriver, Chelsea & Grey, Chelsea Gillian.
Leer, Rebecca, illus. see Hayes, Joe.
Lees, Caroline. Silly Sea Stories. (p. 1576)
Lees, Gemma. Smart Stories for Clever Kids. (p. 1593)
Lees, Harry H., illus. see Burt, Olive Woolley.
Lees, Patricia. Kingdom of Youu. (p. 960)
Lees, Sophie. Brad Pitt: Reluctant Leading Man. (p. 221)
Leese, Jennifer. Uniquely Maryland (p. 1818)
Leese, Jennifer L. B. Two Spots Bakery. (p. 1804)
Leese, Joan, et al. Three Plays for Women. (p. 1743)
Leese, Peter. Britain Since 1945: Aspects of Identity. (p. 229)
Leese, Vickie. When God Created Little Girls... (p. 1902)
Leeson, Christine. Just for You! Ellis, Andy, illus. (p. 938)
—Molly & the Storm. Hansen, Gaby, illus. (p. 1160)
Leeson, Cole. Arctic. (p. 95)
—Tidal Flat/Coastal. (p. 1747)
—Wetland/Swamp. (p. 1877)
Leeson, Robert. All the Gold in the World. Leplar, Anna, illus. (p. 45)
Leeson, Tom and Pat, et al, photos by. Cascade Babies. (p. 273)
Leet, Karen M. Food Intruders: Invisible Creatures Lurking in Your Food. (p. 613)
—Gross Pranks (p. 725)
—Sarah's Courage: A Kentucky Frontier Kidnapping. (p. 1514)
—This Book Might Blow You Away: A Collection of Amazing Weather Trivia (p. 1735)
—Yard Monsters: Invisible Creatures Lurking in Your Backyard (p. 1968)
Leet, Karen M., jt. auth. see Swanson, Jennifer.
Lee-Tai, Amy. Place Where Sunflowers Grow. Hoshino, Felicia, illus. (p. 1366)
Leeth, Dawna. Pipa & the Puppy Parlor. (p. 1361)
Lee-Thompson, Ann. Opera World: An Overture for Young People. (p. 1300)
Leeuwen, Jean Van, see Van Leeuwen, Jean.
Leeuwen, Joke van, jt. auth. see Leeuwen, Joke Van.
Leeuwen, Joke Van & Leeuwen, Joke van. Eep! Leeuwen, Joke van, illus. (p. 505)
Lefall, Kathy. Stargaze. (p. 1642)
Lefcourt, Jack. Four Thousand Years of Jewish History: Then & Now. (p. 625)
Lefebure, Ingrid, illus. see Canale, Allison.
Lefebvre, Gail. Week at Snug Bend. (p. 1871)
Lefebvre, Jason. Too Much Glue. Retz, Zac, illus. (p. 1767)
Lefebvre, Patrick, photos by see Eisenberg, Rebecca & Kjesbo, Rynette.
Lefeuvre, Amy. Probable Sons. (p. 1408)
Lefèvre, A. M. Hugan Fach Goch. (p. 824)
—Pws Esgid Uchel. (p. 1421)
Lefevre-Garros. Wright Brothers. (p. 1963)
Lefèvre-Garros, J. P. Wright Brothers Uderzo, M., illus. (p. 1963)
Leff, Tova, illus. see Fajnland, Leibel.
Leff, Tova, illus. see Klein-Higger, Joni.
Leff, Tova, illus. see Rotman, Risa.
Leff, Tova, illus. see Sitner, Nechama.
Leff, Tova, illus. see Steiner, Nancy.
Leff, Valerie Ann. Better Homes & Husbands. (p. 172)
Leffert, Nancy, jt. auth. see Roehlkepartain, Jolene L.
Leffert, Nancy, jt. auth. see Scales, Peter C.
Leffler, Silke. Andersen's Fairy Tales. (p. 72)
Leffler, Silke, illus. see Laube, Sigrid.
Leffler, Silke, illus. see Rylance, Ulrike.
Leffler, Silke, jt. auth. see Janisch, Heinz.
Leffler, Silke & Janisch, Heinz. "I Have a Little Problem," Said the Bear. (p. 839)
—"I Have a Little Problem," Said the Bear. Leffler, Silke, illus. (p. 839)
Lefkon, Wendy, et al, eds. Birnbaum's Walt Disney World. Wright, Alex, illus. (p. 192)
—Walt Disney World Without Kids: The Official Guide for Fun-Loving Adults. (p. 1855)
Lefkowits, John. Adventures of Weezy, the One-Eyed Pug: Book 1: How Weezy Lost His Eye & Came to His Senses. Seroya, Tea, illus. (p. 24)
Leflore, Henry. Aftermath: The Curse of the Blue Flamed Meteor. (p. 28)
LeFlore, Lyah B. Can't Hold Me Down. Warfield, D. L., illus. (p. 262)
—World Is Mine. Warfield, D. L., illus. (p. 1956)
LeFlur, Shine, jt. auth. see LeFlur, Shine.
LeFlur, Shine & LeFlur, Shine. Elephant for Jotto. (p. 511)
LeFrak, Karen. Best in Show. Day, Andrew, illus. (p. 170)
—Jake the Philharmonic Dog. Baranski, Marcin, illus. (p. 906)
Lefrak, Karen, jt. auth. see LeFrak, Karen.
LeFrak, Karen & Lefrak, Karen. Jake the Ballet Dog. Baranski, Marcin, illus. (p. 906)
Lefranc, Karin & Parker, Tyler. I Want to Eat Your Books. (p. 848)
Lefrancois, Viateur. Coureurs des Bois a Clark City. Arseneau, Philippe & Drouin, Julie Saint-Onge, illus. (p. 373)
LeFroy, Joy & Frylinck, Diana. Pipeline C. Y. O'Connor Built. Duke, Marion, illus. (p. 1361)
Lefroy, Joy, et al. Catalpa Escape. (p. 278)
Leftheri, Eleftheria-Garyfallia, illus. see Atkins, Jill.
Leftridge, Alan. Going to Glacier National Park. (p. 693)
Legacy Press Staff. God's Girls! Fun & Faith for Ages 9-12. (p. 691)
—Gotta Have God: Devotions for Boys. (p. 704)
Legacy Press Staff & Davis, Mary J. My Praise Journal: A Celebration of Psalms for Kids. (p. 1217)
Legall, D. Antoinette. Gift for God. (p. 675)
Légaré, Gisèle, jt. auth. see L'Heureux, Christine.
Légaré, Gisèle & L'Heureux, Christine. Good Night! Brignaud, Pierre, illus. (p. 699)
Legay, Gilbert. Atlas de los Indios Norteamericanos. (p. 112)
Legend, Bobby. Hunt for Ned October: The Novel. (p. 828)
—Hunt for Ned October. (p. 828)
Legendre, Philippe. I Can Draw! Dinosaurs, Dragons & Prehistoric Creatures. (p. 835)
Legendre, Philippe, illus. see Osle, Janessa.
Legendre, Philippe, jt. auth. see Walter Foster Creative Team Staff.
Legendre, Philippe, jt. auth. see Walter Foster Creative Team.
Léger, Diane Carmel. Emily Carr's Attic Léger, Michael, illus. (p. 518)
—Who's in Maxine's Tree? Gait, Darlene, illus. (p. 1920)
leger, Jarett, illus. see Leleux, Skip.
Léger, Michael, illus. see Léger, Diane Carmel.
LeGette, M. L. Unicorn Girl. (p. 1818)
Legg, Barbara, illus. see Buchholz, Erwin.
Legg, Brook. Healing Rhythms of Home: 30 Days of Devotion for the Homeschool Mom. (p. 757)
Legg, Gerald. Birds of Prey. Hersey, Bob, illus. (p. 191)
—Minibeasts. (p. 1146)
—X-Ray Picture Book of Incredible Creatures. Salariya, David & Scrace, Carolyn, illus. (p. 1967)
Legg, Gerald & Weston, Steve. World of Animal Life. (p. 1956)
—World of Insect Life. (p. 1956)
—World of Plant Life. (p. 1957)
Legge, Barbara, ed. see Hartley, James.
Legge, David, illus. see Watts, Frances.
Legge, James. Hsiao King or Classic of Filial Piet. (p. 824)
—Hsiao King or Classic of Filial Piety. (p. 824)
Leggitt, Linda, ed. see Gregory, Charles, II.
Leggitt, Marjorie, illus. see Graf, Mike.
Leggitt, Marjorie, illus. see Padilla-Gamino, Jacqueline L.
Leggitt, Marjorie & Padilla-Gamino, Jacqueline L. Kupe & the Coral (Kupe e te To'a) (p. 968)
Legler, Caroline. Super Words Early Reading Program (p. 1682)
Legnazzi, Claudia, illus. see Montes, Graciela.
Lego, et al. Fire Truck to the Rescue! (p. 591)
Legramandi, Francesco. Cinderella. (p. 320)
Legramandi, Francesco, illus. see David, Erica.
Legramandi, Francesco, illus. see Jordan, Apple.
Legramandi, Francesco, illus. see Posner-Sanchez, Andrea.
Legramandi, Francesco, illus. see Random House Disney Staff & Redbank, Tennant.
Legramandi, Francesco, illus. see RH Disney Staff.
Legramandi, Francesco, illus. see Weinberg, Jennifer Liberts.
Legramandi, Francesco, illus. see Wrecks, Billy.
Legrand, Claire. Cavendish Home for Boys & Girls. Watts, Sarah, illus. (p. 282)
—Year of Shadows. Kwasny, Karl, illus. (p. 1969)
LeGrand, Eric & Yorkey, Mike. Believe: The Victorious Story of Eric LeGrand. (p. 161)
Legrand, H J, III. Paddle Tail's First Winter Adventure. Fair, Patricia Anne, illus. (p. 1317)
LeGrand, Hank, 3rd. Paddle Tail. Merrison, Stacy, illus. (p. 1317)
Legrand, Martine & Delvaux, Nancy. ¡una nalgada por Favor! (p. 1811)
Legris, Phil, jt. auth. see Kelly, Martin.
Lehane, Pearse. Train That Never Came. (p. 1777)
Lehavi, Tali. Power of Infinite Goodness Activity Book. (p. 1389)
Lehfeldt, Elizabeth A. Black Death. (p. 195)
Lehman, A. C., illus. see Roy, Lillian Elizabeth.
Lehman, Barbara. Museum Trip. (p. 1193)
—Rainstorm. (p. 1436)
—Red Book. Lehman, Barbara, illus. (p. 1453)
—Secret Box. (p. 1540)
—Trainstop. (p. 1777)
Lehman, Barbara, illus. see Graham-Barber, Lynda.
Lehman, David. Great American Prose Poems: From Poe to the Present. (p. 713)
Lehman, Denise, illus. see Lee, Shelley R.
Lehman, Emil. Israel: Idea & Reality. (p. 893)
Lehman, Helena. Language of God in History. (p. 975)
—Language of God in Humanity. (p. 975)
—Language of God in Prophecy. (p. 975)
—Language of God in the Universe. (p. 975)
Lehman, Jacques. Adventures of Pepe Pandejo. (p. 21)
Lehman, John, et al. Canine Classics Pomplun, Tom & Lehman, John, eds. (p. 261)
Lehman, Julie. Kyle in His Compost Pile: The Story of a Red Wiggler. (p. 969)
Lehman, Marcus. 5 Novelettes by Marcus Lehman Slipcased: Adopted Princess, Bustenai, Out of the Depths, Rabenu Gershom & Unpaid Ransom. Mindel, Nissan, tr. from GER. (p. 1992)
Lehman, Paul, et al. Compact Guide to New Jersey Birds. (p. 351)
Lehman, Robert, jt. auth. see Metzger, Julie.
Lehman, Seth. Color Pets. (p. 343)
Lehman, Theodore H. Defying Odds. (p. 424)
Lehmann, Charles. Dios Lo Hizo para Ti! La Historia de la Creacion. Kemly, Kathleen, illus. (p. 445)
—God Made It for You! The Story of Creation. Kemly, Kathleen, illus. (p. 689)
Lehmann, Christian. Ultimate Game. Rodarmor, William, tr. (p. 1809)
Lehmann, Marcus & Zucker, Pearl. Akiva: The Story of Rabbi Akiva & His Times. (p. 32)
Lehmann, Peter, jt. ed. see Stastny, Peter.
Lehmann, R' Marcus, contrib. by. Family y Aguilar. (p. 569)
Lehman-Wilzig, Tami. Green Bible Stories for Children. Bernhard, Durga, illus. (p. 721)
—Green Bible Stories for Children. Bernhard, Durga Yael, illus. (p. 721)
—Hanukkah Around the World. Wehrman, Vicki, illus. (p. 744)
—Keeping the Promise: A Torah's Journey. Orback, Craig, illus. (p. 948)
—Passover Around the World. Wolf, Elizabeth, illus. (p. 1327)
—Stork's Landing. Shuttlewood, Anna, illus. (p. 1655)
—Tasty Bible Stories: A Menu of Tales & Matching Recipes. Kahn, Katherine Janus, illus. (p. 1707)
—Zvuvi's Israel. Topaz, Ksenia, illus. (p. 1990)
Lehman-Wilzig, Tami & Katzman, Nicole. Nathan Blows Out the Hanukkah Candles. Tugeau, Jeremy, illus. (p. 1231)
Lehmkuhl, Pat. Starlight, Star Bright: (the Starlight Books, 3) (p. 1642)
Lehmkuhl, Pat, illus. see Hill, Janet Muirhead.
Lehndorff, Betsy & Peters, Laura. Best Garden Plants for Colorado. (p. 169)
Lehner, Montserrat. Legend of the Açaí: Retold & Illustrated by Montserrat Lehner. (p. 989)
Lehner-Rhoades, Shirley, illus. see Nazareth, Melanie.
Lehnert, R. B. Adventures of Billy Butterfly. Garcia, Marc Khayam, illus. (p. 16)
Lehoczky, Martin. Silver Tube. (p. 1577)
Lehoczky, Sandor & Rusczyk, Richard. Art of Problem Solving: The Basics. Vol. 1 (p. 102)
Lehrhaupt, Adam. Warning - Do Not Open This Book! Forsythe, Matthew, illus. (p. 1858)
Lehrman, Maggie. Cost of All Things. (p. 368)
Lehti, Kauko. Beautiful Animal Stories for Good Children. (p. 153)
Lehto, Christine, illus. see Jenks, Patricia.
Lei, Vicki. Creepy Caterpillar. (p. 381)
—Mr Grumpy. (p. 1185)
Lei, Xu. Grave Robbers' Chronicles Vol 1-6 Box Set. Mok, Kathy, tr. (p. 712)
Leialoha, Steve, illus. see Willingham, Bill & Jean, James.
Leialoha, Steve, illus. see Willingham, Bill.
Leib, Michael S., illus. see Giffen, Keith.
Leibel, Blake. United Free Worlds #3. (p. 1818)
Leibenkop, T. Sovereign of the Northern Winds. (p. 1618)
Leiber, Fritz. Creature from Cleveland Depths. (p. 380)
—Gonna Roll the Bones. Wiesner, David, illus. (p. 697)
Leibold, Anna. Time-Out Hero: Raggedy Dolls in Danger, Second Edition. (p. 1752)
Leibold, Jay. Secret of the Ninja. Nugent, Suzanne & Marron, Jose, illus. (p. 1542)
Leibovici, Danielle. With You Always. Gabrielov, Julia, illus. (p. 1942)
Leibowitz, Julie. Finding Your Place: A Teen Guide to Life in a Blended Family. (p. 588)
Leicester, Mal. Can I Tell You about Tourette Syndrome? A Guide for Friends, Family & Professionals. (p. 258)
—Early Years Stories for the Foundation Stage: Ideas & Inspiration for Active Learning. (p. 494)
Leichner, Jeannine Timko. Joy Joy the Mass: Our Family Celebration. (p. 929)
—Making Things Right: The Sacrament of Reconciliation. Davidson, Kevin, illus. (p. 1082)
Leicht, Martin & Neal, Isla. Mothership. (p. 1179)
—Stranger Thing. (p. 1665)
—World Forgot. (p. 1955)
Leichter, Albert. Augusta County, Staunton, & Waynesboro Virginia Find-A-Word Puzzles. (p. 115)
—Case of the Missing Menorah: A Chanukah Play (p. 274)
—Staunton Treasures Past & Present Connect the Dots. (p. 1645)
Leick, Bonnie, illus. see Carey, Becky.
Leick, Bonnie, illus. see Conly, Jane Leslie.
Leick, Bonnie, illus. see Cooper, Lynne.
Leick, Bonnie, illus. see Huggins-Cooper, Lynn.
Leick, Bonnie, illus. see Jeffers, Dawn.
Leick, Bonnie, illus. see Ketteman, Helen.
Leick, Bonnie, illus. see McKy, Katie.
Leick, Bonnie, illus. see Pearson, Anthony.
Leick, Bonnie, illus. see Send-up, Maurice.
Leidemer, Adam, illus. see Ritner, Amelia.
Leidenfrost, Lisa. At the Edge of the Village: Musings of a Missionary Wife. (p. 111)
Leider, Rick Allen. Robots: Explore the World of Robots & How They Work for Us. (p. 1481)
Leiderman, Lucy. Lives of Magic. (p. 1040)
Leidtke, Leila. If I Were President. (p. 853)
Leifer, Lyon. How to Play the Bansuri: A Manual for Self-Instruction Based on the Teaching of Devendra Murdeshwar (p. 821)
Leige, Ottis Dale. Poems of Inspiration. (p. 1376)
Leigh, A. Giant Giraffes: Learning the Soft G Sound. (p. 673)
—It Grows in Spring: Learning the GR Sound. (p. 894)
Leigh, Anita L. Willow's Gift (p. 1934)
Leigh, Autumn. Apple Tree. (p. 92)
—Circulatory System. (p. 321)
—Diamondback Rattlesnake. (p. 434)
—Diamondback Rattlesnake / Cascabel Diamantada. (p. 434)
—Door to Door. (p. 470)
—Far-Out Friends. (p. 572)
—Flying Without Wings: Amazing Animal Adaptations. (p. 610)
—From Caterpillar to Butterfly: A Life Cycle. (p. 642)
—From the Farm to the Table. (p. 644)
—Making History: A Horse Sock Puppet. (p. 1081)
—manzano (the Apple Tree) (p. 1089)
—My Teacher. (p. 1219)
—Niagara Falls. (p. 1250)
—On the Ball: Learning to Identify the Place Values of Ones & Tens. (p. 1289)
—Penguin Colony. (p. 1336)

—Penguin Colony / una Colonia de Pingüinos. (p. 1336)
—Primary Source Guide to India. (p. 1399)
—Signs on the Road: Learning to Identify the Four Basic Geometric Shapes. (p. 1574)
—Spots & Stripes. (p. 1634)
—Trip Through Our Solar System. (p. 1787)
—Warning: Volcano! the Story of Mt. St. Helens. (p. 1858)
Leigh, Autumn, jt. auth. see Roza, Greg.
Leigh, Britt. Ten Commandments for Kissing Gloria Jean. (p. 1718)
Leigh, Brittany. New Friend in Jungletown. (p. 1244)
Leigh, David S. Ichiro Suzuki. (p. 851)
Leigh, Heather. Hey Little Baby! Côté, Geneviève, illus. (p. 774)
Leigh, Jennifer Austin. Laid or Loved? The Secrets Guys Wish You Knew about Being a Dream Girl Instead of a Just-In-His-Jeans Girl. (p. 972)
Leigh, Lora. Nauti Nights (p. 1237)
Leigh, Lora, et al. Magical Christmas Cat. (p. 1074)
Leigh, Nila K. Learning to Swim in Swaziland; A child's-eye view of a southern African Country. (p. 986)
—Learning to Swim in Swaziland - A Child's-Eye View of a Southern African Country (PDF Download) (p. 986)
Leigh, Peter. Livewire Classics the Half Brothers. (p. 1040)
—Livewire Plays Doing Macbeth. (p. 1040)
—Livewire Plays I Never Done Nothing. (p. 1040)
—Livewire Youth Fiction the Lie. (p. 1040)
Leigh, Rob, illus. see Wagner, Matt.
Leigh, S. Dream Pony. (p. 483)
—Puzzle Dungeon. (p. 1420)
—Puzzle Farm. (p. 1421)
—Puzzle Jungle. (p. 1421)
—Puzzle Ocean. (p. 1421)
—Puzzle Planet. (p. 1421)
—Puzzle School. (p. 1421)
—Puzzle Town. (p. 1421)
—Runaway Pony. (p. 1496)
—Uncle Pete's Pirate Adventure. (p. 1812)
Leigh, Savanah-Rose. Trunks & Amelia. (p. 1793)
Leigh, Sharon. Tiramisu: My Little Lamb. (p. 1757)
Leigh, Susan K. God, I Need to Talk to You About Bad Manners. (p. 689)
—God, I Need to Talk to You about Bad Words. Clark, Bill, illus. (p. 689)
—God I Need to Talk to You About Bedtime. (p. 689)
—God, I Need to Talk to You about Bullying. Clark, Bill, illus. (p. 689)
—God, I Need to Talk to You about Disrespect. (p. 689)
—God, I Need to Talk to You about Greed. Clark, Bill, illus. (p. 689)
—God I Need to Talk to you About Homework. (p. 689)
—God, I Need to Talk to You about Laziness. (p. 689)
—God I Need to Talk to you About Video Games. (p. 689)
—God, I Need to Talk to You about Whining. Clark, Bill, illus. (p. 689)
—God I Need to Talt To you About Healthy Eating. (p. 689)
—Luther: Echoes of the Hammer. (p. 1066)
Leigh, Susannah. Ciudad Enigma: Lumen Puzzles Infantiles. (p. 324)
—Ile Fantastique: Fantastic Island. Gemmell, Kathy & Irving, Nicole, eds. (p. 856)
—Isla Enigma: Lumen Puzzles Infantiles. (p. 891)
—Puzzle Castle. Waters, Gaby, ed. (p. 1420)
—Puzzle Dinosaurs. Tyler, Jenny, ed. (p. 1420)
—Puzzle Dungeon. Haw, Brenda, illus. (p. 1421)
—Puzzle Farm. Waters, Gaby, ed. (p. 1421)
—Puzzle Mountain. Waters, Gaby, ed. (p. 1421)
—Puzzle Mountain. Haw, Brenda, illus. (p. 1421)
—Puzzle Ocean. Haw, Brenda, illus. (p. 1421)
—Puzzle Palace. Tyler, Jenny, ed. (p. 1421)
—Puzzle Pirates. Tyler, Jenny, ed. (p. 1421)
—Puzzle Pirates. Haw, Brenda, illus. (p. 1421)
—Puzzle Planet. Waters, Gaby, ed. (p. 1421)
—Puzzle Pyramid. Haw, Brenda, illus. (p. 1421)
—Puzzle School. Haw, Brenda, illus. (p. 1421)
—Puzzle Town. Waters, Gaby, ed. (p. 1421)
—Puzzle Train. Waters, Gaby, ed. (p. 1421)
—Puzzle Train. Haw, Brenda, illus. (p. 1421)
—Puzzle World: Combined Volume. Waters, Gaby, ed. (p. 1421)
—Uncle Pete the Pirate. (p. 1812)
—Uncle Pete's Pirate Adventure. Stowell, Louie, ed. (p. 1812)
Leigh, Susannah, ed. see Bates, Michelle.
Leigh, Susannah, et al. Young Puzzle Adventures: Combined Volume. (p. 1979)
Leigh, Suzie. Glitter Man. (p. 684)
Leigh, Tom. Pinocchio: A Tale of Honesty. (p. 1360)
Leigh, Tom, illus. see Albee, Sarah, et al.
Leigh, Tom, illus. see Albee, Sarah.
Leigh, Tom, illus. see Balsley, Tilda & Fischer, Ellen.
Leigh, Tom, illus. see Marbury, Stephanie.
Leigh, Tom, illus. see Voigt, Cynthia.
Leigh-Anna Tehan. Beyond All Imagination: The First Souvenir. Paul Reising, illus. (p. 173)
Leigh-Crawford, Lynda. Hovis the Hedgehog: Bonfire Night. (p. 804)
Leighfield, D. K. Abel's Song. (p. 4)
Leighton, Davis L. & Strickland, Karen L. Three Little Dinosaurs. (p. 1742)
Leighton, Douglas. Canadian Rockies (p. 260)
Leighton, Lisa. Dressed for Battle. (p. 485)
Leighton, Margaret. Bride of Glory: The Story of Elizabeth Bacon Custer, 1842-1933. (p. 227)
Leighton, Marian. George Washington. Salvador, Martin, illus. (p. 664)
Leighton, Maxinne Rhea. Ellis Island Christmas. Nolan, Dennis, illus. (p. 515)
Leighton, Michael S. Law & Disorder. (p. 981)
Leighton, Noreen. Mr Tilly & the Christmas Lights. Wilson, Lorna, illus. (p. 1186)
—Mr Tilly & the Halloween Mystery. Wilson, Lorna, illus. (p. 1186)
Leighton, Robert. Bravest Boy in the Camp A Story of Adven. (p. 223)
Leighton, Robert, illus. see Albee, Sarah.
Leighton, Robert, et al. Brainiest Insaniest Ultimate Puzzle Book! 250 Wacky Word Games, Mystifying Mazes, Picture Puzzles, & More to Boggle Your Brain. (p. 222)
Leighton-Porter, Wendy. Shadow of Camelot. (p. 1557)
—Shadow of the Norman Arrow. (p. 1557)
Leija-Sysak, Viviana. My House Is Full of Light. (p. 1211)
Leijs, Tommie, illus. see Vinsh, Aara J.
Leijten, Aileen, illus. see Bloom, Susan & Bertram, Debbie.
Leijten, Aileen, illus. see Dotlich, Rebecca Kai.
Leijten, Aileen, illus. see Marsoli, Lisa Ann.
Leiman, Sondra. Atlas of Great Jewish Communities: A Voyage Through History. (p. 112)
Leimbach, Judy & Eckert, Sharon. Detective Club: Mysteries for Young Thinkers. (p. 431)
—Math Extension Units (p. 1106)
Leimbach, Judy & Leimbach, Kathy. Math Extension Units (p. 1106)
Leimbach, Kathy, jt. auth. see Leimbach, Judy.
Leinberger, Judy. Man Who Talks with Eagles. (p. 1086)
Leipe, Ulla. Lo Que los Ninos Quieren Saber. Limmer, Hannes, illus. (p. 1044)
Leiper, Esther M., illus. see Sundberg, Norma J.
Leipold, Judith. Destiny's Wild Ride, a Tall Tale of the Legendary Hub Hubbell. White, David, illus. (p. 431)
—Hoops. Giddens, Jake, illus. (p. 795)
Leipsic, Regina, illus. see Knesek, Marian.
Leist, Christina. Jack the Bear. (p. 903)
Leist, Christina, illus. see Schwartz, Virginia Frances.
Leist, Christina, illus. see Winters, Karl-Lynn.
Leist, Kazue Lene, illus. see Kieffer, Elise Lael.
Leisure Arts, creator. Cool Stuff Teach Me to Quilt. (p. 364)
—Rubber Band Loom Crafts. (p. 1493)
—Rubber Band Loom Fun! (p. 1493)
—Scrapbooking with Your Kids: The Ultimate Guide to Kid-Friendly Crafting. (p. 1532)
Leisure Arts Staff, ed. Quilter's Mix & Match Blocks: A Comprehensive Handbook. (p. 1428)
Leitao, Júlio T., jt. auth. see Keeler, Patricia A.
Leitch, Cecil. Golf for Girls. (p. 696)
Leitch, Wayne. Way of Assurance. (p. 1864)
Leitch, Will. Catch. (p. 278)
Leite, Eleni. Boy, Have I Got Problems. (p. 218)
—Jesus, Awesome Power, Awesome Love. (p. 915)
—Jesus in the Spotlight. (p. 915)
—Jesus, to Eternity & Beyond. (p. 916)
—Wrong Way Jonah. (p. 1965)
Leite, Eleni, tr. see Arthur, Kay & Domeij, Scott.
Leite, Karen. Miracle Named Angel. (p. 1148)
Leiter, Andrew S. Chameleon Chronicles Merola, Marcelo & Nichx, illus. (p. 289)
Leiter, Richard & Kober, Shahar. Flying Hand of Marco B. (p. 610)
Leiter, Sharon. Critical Companion to Emily Dickinson: A Literary Reference to Her Life & Work. (p. 383)
Leiterman, Robert S. Operation Redwood Quest: Search for Answers. (p. 1300)
—Yeti or Not, Here We Come! Bigfoot in the Redwoods. (p. 1971)
Leith, Marcus, photos by see Blake, Peter.
Leitha, Dan. Welcome to Life after Eden. (p. 1873)
Leithart, Peter J. Wise Words: Family Stories That Bring the Proverbs to Life. (p. 1940)
Leithauser, Jessica. Maps Show Us the Way. (p. 1090)
Leitikow, Greg & Varacalli, Lauren. Colorado College College Prowler off the Record. (p. 343)
Leitten, Amanda. Transportation Then & Now. (p. 1779)
Leitten, Emily. Lava. (p. 980)
Leiva, Miriam A., et al. Algebra 1: Explorations & Applications. (p. 38)
Lejeune, Leah. Sam & Jo: In the Adventure in the Woods. (p. 1506)
LeJeune, Shonda. Love Is... (p. 1060)
Lekander, Lance, illus. see Tait, Chris.
Lekich, John. Prisoner of Snowflake Falls (p. 1407)
Lekuton, Joseph Lemasolai. Facing the Lion: Growing up Maasai on the African Savanna. (p. 561)
Lekuton, Joseph Lemasolai & Viola, Herman. Facing the Lion: Growing up Maasai on the African Savanna. (p. 561)
Leland, April. Best Christmas Present Ever. (p. 168)
Leland, Debbie. Daddy's Love. Rife, Ann Hollis, illus. (p. 399)
—Little Prairie Hen. Ann Hollis Rife, illus. (p. 1033)
Leland, Dorothy Kupcha. Balloon Boy of San Francisco. (p. 135)
Leland, Toni M. Christa Joins a Horse Club: Second in Christa Duncan Series. Leland, Toni M., illus. (p. 311)
LeLarge, Blandine. Fashion Design Lookbook: More Than 50 Creative Tips & Techniques for the Fashion-Forward Artist. (p. 575)
LeLeu, Lisa. Diggity the Dog Puppet Show Play Set. (p. 439)
—Frenchy the Frog Story Starter: Puppet Show Book Story Starter. (p. 636)
—Miss Moo-Moo the Cow: Puppet Show Play Set with 2 books & Crayons. (p. 1151)
—Miss Moo-Moo the Cow Story Starter: Puppet Book Story Starter. (p. 1151)
—Percilla the Gorilla Gift Set: Puppet Book Gift Set with 2 Books. (p. 1341)
—Scooter the Cat Gift Set: Puppet Book Gift Set with 2 Books. (p. 1529)
—Scooter the Cat Story Teller: Puppet Book Story Starter. (p. 1529)
Leleu, Sinead & Greck-Ismair, Michaela. German Pen Pals Made Easy: A Fun Way to Write German & Make a New Friend. (p. 666)
Leleux, Skip. Courage in the Swamp. leger, Jarett & Mayeaux, Alicia, illus. (p. 372)
Lelievre, Barclay, ed. see East, Mike, et al.
Lelivelđ, Alette Wells. Remember Me. (p. 1459)
Leloup, Geneviève, illus. see Reidy, Jean.
Leloup, Roger. Curious Trio. (p. 394)
—Daughter of the Wind. (p. 409)
—Dragon of Hong Kong - Yoko Tsuno (p. 477)
—Morning of the World. (p. 1175)
—On the Edge of Life. (p. 1290)
—Prey & the Ghost. (p. 1398)
—Time Spiral. (p. 1752)
—Yoko Tsuno Vol. 8: The Devil's Organ. (p. 1972)
LeMae, Katie. Color Bunch Goes to the Zoo. (p. 342)
Lemaire, Bonnie, illus. see Cotton, Peter B.
LeMaistre, Gretchen, photos by. Boo ABC: A to Z with the World's Cutest Dog. (p. 209)
LeMaitre, George D. Crucified under Pontius Pilate. (p. 386)
LeMaitre, Pascal. Pinocchio. (p. 1360)
Lemaitre, Pascal, illus. see Beaty, Andrea.
Lemaitre, Pascal, illus. see Elkins, J. Theron.
Lemaitre, Pascal, illus. see Heilbroner, Joan.
Lemaitre, Pascal, illus. see Katz, Alan.
LeMaitre, Pascal, illus. see McGhee, Alison.
LeMaitre, Pascal, illus. see McMullan, Kate.
Lemaitre, Pascal, illus. see Morrison, Toni & Morrison, Slade.
Lemaitre, Pascal, illus. see Muntean, Michaela.
Lemaitre, Pascal, illus. see Ray, J. Hamilton.
Lemaitre, Pascal, illus. see Roth, Judith.
Leman, Amber. Wilma & the Water Hose. (p. 1934)
Leman, Kevin, II. My Firstborn, There's No One Like You. (p. 1208)
—My Middle Child, There's No One Like You. (p. 1214)
—My Only Child, There's No One Like You. (p. 1216)
Leman, Nora. Alpha Building Crew. Hartmann, April, illus. (p. 48)
Lemanski, Mike, illus. see Oxlade, Chris.
Lemardele, Stephane, tr. see Marois, Andre.
Lemaresquier, D. & Pivard, G. Story of a Conquest: The Bayeux Tapestry Narrated to Children. (p. 1657)
LeMaster, David. Sir Saddlesore & the Dragon: One-Act Children's Comedy Play. (p. 1580)
LeMaster, David J. Abe Lincoln & Elvis: Comedy Skit (p. 4)
—Dinner & a Murder: A Full-Length Play. (p. 441)
—Homeland Insecurity: A Comedy Skit (p. 793)
—Paper, Rock, Scissors, Bomb! A Ten-Minute Comedy Duet. (p. 1323)
—Shakespeare, Horny Toads & Banana Peels: Ten-Minute Comedy Duet. (p. 1559)
Lemaster, Karen Frisbie. Little Bill the Bengal Kitten: The Black Smoke Kitten. (p. 1024)
Lemaster, Kevin. Corn for Tomorrow: A Story from Glengary. Lemaster, Michael, illus. (p. 367)
Lemaster, Michael, illus. see Lemaster, Kevin.
Lemay, Alan. Tonopah Range: Western Stories. (p. 1765)
LeMay, DiDi. Freddy's French Fries Fiasco. (p. 633)
Lemay, Didi. Winter Solstice Celebration. Campbell, Jacquie, illus. (p. 1938)
Lemay, Heather. Melvin the Mossasaurus. (p. 1125)
LeMay, Meagan, illus. see Magnuson, James.
Lemay, Violet. 100 Pablo Picassos. (p. 1998)
—Southern Baby. Lemay, Violet, illus. (p. 1617)
Lemay, Violet, illus. see Froeb, Lori.
Lemay, Violet, illus. see Puck & Pohlen, Jerome.
Lemay, Violet, illus. see Puck.
Lemay, Violet, illus. see Shea, Tess & Pohlen, Jerome.
Lember, Barbara Hirsch, photos by see Christian, Peggy.
Lemberg, David S. & Canby, Courtlandt. Encyclopedia of Historic Places (p. 525)
Lemberger, Evelyn. Furmin & Clyde Think Positive. (p. 650)
Lembo, Margaret Ann. Color Your Life with Crystals! Your First Guide to Crystals, Colors & Chakras. (p. 343)
Lemelin, Linda, tr. see Plourde, Josee.
Lement, Wendy. Keri Tarr - Cat Detective. Burrows, Jeffrey Scott, illus. (p. 949)
Lemieux, Aurora, jt. adapted by see Sprick, Marilyn.
Lemieux, Carlotta & Hacker, Carlotta. E. Cora Hind (p. 492)
Lemieux, Jean. Fil de la Vie. Casson, Sophie, illus. (p. 586)
—Toby & the Mysterious Creature. Cummins, Sarah, tr. from FRE. (p. 1760)
—Toby Laughs Last Cummins, Sarah, tr. from FRE. (p. 1760)
—Toby Laughs Last. Cummins, Sarah, tr. from FRE. (p. 1760)
—Toby Shoots for Infinity Cummins, Sarah, tr. from FRE. (p. 1760)
—Toby Shoots for Infinity. Casson, Sophie, illus. (p. 1760)
—Toby Shoots for Infinity. Cummins, Sarah, tr. from FRE. (p. 1760)
—Toby's Best Friend. Cummins, Sarah, tr. from FRE. (p. 1760)
—Toby's Very Important Question Cummins, Sarah, tr. from FRE. (p. 1760)
—Toby's Very Important Question. Casson, Sophia, illus. (p. 1760)
—Toby's Very Important Question. Cummins, Sarah, tr. from FRE. (p. 1760)
Lemieux, Jean & Casson, Sophie. Toby & the Mysterious Creature Cummins, Sarah, tr. from FRE. (p. 1760)
Lemieux, Michele. What's That Noise? (p. 1899)
Leming, Mary Gail Cowan. Mailbox Surprise: A Cursive Handwriting Book for Students, Teachers, & Parents. (p. 1077)
Lemire, Jeff. Tales from the Farm. Lemire, Jeff, illus. (p. 1701)
Lemire, Lillie. Young Witch's Magical Adventure. (p. 1979)
Lemire, Roger. Pumpkin & Lumpkin. (p. 1416)
Lemke, Amy J. Dinosaurs for Breakfast Bradley, Jessica, illus. (p. 444)
—Snorkeling with Sea-Bots Bradley, Jessica, illus. (p. 1598)
—Too Short for the Court Harpster, Steve, illus. (p. 1767)
Lemke, Amy J. & Lemke, Donald B. Frank 'n' Beans Bradley, Jessica, illus. (p. 629)
—My Little Bro-Bot Bradley, Jessica, illus. (p. 1212)
Lemke, Donald. Awakening Glass House Graphics Staff, illus. (p. 120)
—Batman Classic: Batman Versus the Riddler. Gordon, Steven E. & Gordon, Eric A., illus. (p. 144)
—Batman Classic: Battle in the Batcave. (p. 144)
—Batman - Nightmare in Gotham City. Tong, Andie, illus. (p. 144)
—Batman - The Penguin's Arctic Adventure. Roberts, Jeremy, illus. (p. 144)
—Batman Versus the Riddler. (p. 144)
—Batman - Who Is Clayface? Gordon, Steven E. & Gordon, Eric A., illus. (p. 144)
—Batman - Winter Wasteland. Gordon, Steven E. & Gordon, Eric A., illus. (p. 144)
—Book-O-Beards. Lentz, Bob, illus. (p. 210)
—Book-O-Hats. Lentz, Bob, illus. (p. 210)
—Book-O-Masks. Lentz, Bob, illus. (p. 210)
—Coldfinger: Zinc Alloy. Holgate, Douglas, illus. (p. 339)
—Diver Down Glass House Graphics Staff, illus. (p. 454)
—Nightmare in Gotham City. (p. 1255)
—Penguin's Arctic Adventure. (p. 1337)
—Revealed! Holgate, Douglas, illus. (p. 1465)
—Revealed! Zinc Alloy Holgate, Douglas, illus. (p. 1465)
—Super Zero Holgate, Douglas, illus. (p. 1682)
—Superman: A Giant Attack. (p. 1683)
—Superman: Glowing Kryptonite & Illustrated Book. (p. 1683)
—Superman - A Giant Attack. Ferguson, Lee, illus. (p. 1683)
—Superman Versus the Silver Banshee. (p. 1684)
—Superman vs. the Silver Banshee. Smith, Andy, illus. (p. 1684)
—Who Is Clayface? (p. 1915)
—Winter Wasteland. (p. 1938)
Lemke, Donald, jt. auth. see Sherman, M. Zachary.
Lemke, Donald & Lemke, Donald B. Apollo 13 Mission Tucker, Keith, illus. (p. 91)
Lemke, Donald & Loughridge, Lee. Puppet Master's Revenge. Burchett, Rick, illus. (p. 1417)
Lemke, Donald B. Amazing Mini-Mutts Baltazar, Art, illus. (p. 55)
—Awakening (p. 120)
—Book-O-Teeth. Lentz, Bob, illus. (p. 210)
—Brave Escape of Ellen & William Craft. Barnett, Charles, III et al, illus. (p. 223)
—Chameleon Cage Match! Eliopoulos, Chris, illus. (p. 289)
—Coldfinger Holgate, Douglas, illus. (p. 339)
—Diver Down (p. 454)
—Drop In Majado, Caio et al, illus. (p. 485)
—Finland: A Question & Answer Book (p. 589)
—Investigating the Scientific Method with Max Axiom, Super Scientist Smith, Tod G. & Milgrom, Al, illus. (p. 885)
—Invincible Boy-Bot. (p. 885)
—Schoolchildren's Blizzard. (p. 1523)
—Spokes on the Water Holgate, Douglas, illus. (p. 1630)
—Steve Jobs, Steve Wozniak, & the Personal Computer Milgrom, Al & Smith, Tod G., illus. (p. 1649)
—Steve Jobs, Steve Wozniak, & the Personal Computer Smith, Tod G. & Milgrom, Al, illus. (p. 1649)
—Superman. Ku, Min Sung, illus. (p. 1683)
—Wheelies of Justice Holgate, Douglas, illus. (p. 1900)
—Wonder Woman. Ku, Min Sung, illus. (p. 1947)
—Zinc Alloy vs Frankenstein Holgate, Douglas, illus. (p. 1987)
Lemke, Donald B., jt. auth. see Lemke, Amy J.
Lemke, Donald B., jt. auth. see Lemke, Donald.
Lemke, Donald B. & Loughridge, Lee. Mad Hatter's Movie Madness Schigiel, Gregg, illus. (p. 1069)
—Puppet Master's Revenge Burchett, Rick, illus. (p. 1417)
Lemke, Donald B. & Pattison, Ronda. Captured off Guard: The Attack on Pearl Harbor St. Aubin, Claude, illus. (p. 265)
Lemke, Donald B., et al. Emperor of the Airwaves DC Comics Staff, illus. (p. 520)
—Emperor of the Airwaves. (p. 520)
—Fun House of Evil (p. 648)
—Lecciones Sobre la Seguridad en el Trabajo Científico. Smith, Tod G., illus. (p. 987)
—Lessons in Science Safety with Max Axiom, Super Scientist Smith, Tod G., illus. (p. 994)
—Lessons in Science Safety with Max Axiom, Super Scientist Anderson, Bill & Smith, Tod G., illus. (p. 994)
—Wrath of the Weather Wizard Doescher, Erik, illus. (p. 1962)
Lemke, Horst. Places & Faces. (p. 1366)
Lemke, Horst, illus. see Bond, Susan.
Lemke, Horst, illus. see Van der Linde, Polly & Van der Linde, Tasha.
Lemke, Nancy. Southern Coast Missions in California. (p. 1617)
Lemley, Ronald W. Wee Bannock: A Scottish Fairy Tale. (p. 1871)
Lemmens, Mary Jo. Christina Aguilera. (p. 312)
—Cypress Hill. (p. 397)
—Jennifer Lopez. (p. 913)
Lemmens, Maryjo. Cypress Hill. (p. 397)
—Jennifer Lopez. (p. 913)
—Xzibit. (p. 1967)
Lemmens, Riske. Box Full of Monsters. (p. 216)
—Little Dragon. (p. 1027)
Lemmens, Riske & Dutta, Kunal, texts. Box Full of Monsters: Kutia Plot Me Monstra. (p. 216)
Lemmerz, Claudia Baumgaertner. My Book about Musical Instruments. (p. 1198)
Lemmo, Peter S., jt. auth. see Greenblatt, Miriam.
Lemmon, Steven B. From the Backseat. (p. 644)
Lemna, Don. Out in Left Field. Collins, Matt, illus. (p. 1311)
—When the Sergeant Came Marching Home. (p. 1905)
Lemniscates. Silence. (p. 1575)
Lemoine, Georges, illus. see Le Clézio, J. M. G.
Lemon, Emily. Little Hands. (p. 1028)
Lemon, Philip & Bevan, Teleri. Barking Mad. (p. 139)
Lemon, Willie Sells. Everything God Made Gives. (p. 544)
—Obeying God Cause It's Right. (p. 1275)
—Prayer Changes Things. (p. 1393)
—Things Happen When You Disobey God. (p. 1733)
Lemonde, Connie. Short Stories: For the Young & Young at Heart. (p. 1569)
—Uphill & Downhill & Everywhere in Between. (p. 1825)
LeMonde', Stephanie. Misty Forest. (p. 1155)
LeMonds, James. Deadfall: Generations of Logging in the Pacific Northwest. (p. 417)
Lemonick, Michael. Science Alive #2. (p. 1524)
Lemonick, Michael D. Science Alive (p. 1524)
Lemos, Lauren M. If I Could Have a Puppy. (p. 852)
—Tooth Fairy Troubles. (p. 1768)
Lemu, B.Aisha. Animals in Islam. (p. 83)
Lemus, Kristina, illus. see Mau, Connie.
Lenagh, Cecilia. Brujita Fregona. (p. 232)
Lenahan, Joe. Fire House. (p. 590)
Lenahan, John. Shadowmagic. (p. 1558)
—Sons of Macha. (p. 1613)

Lenain, Thierry. Little Zizi. Zolinsky, Daniel, tr. from FRE. (p. 1038)
Lenam, Salva. Aseo de Kiko. (p. 105)
—Dibuja y Pinta. Roman, Santi, illus. (p. 435)
—Kiko le Pican los Ojitos. Roman, Santi, illus. (p. 956)
—Kiko No Quiere Comer. Roman, Santi, illus. (p. 956)
—Kiko Ya Se Viste Solo. Roman, Santi, illus. (p. 956)
—¡Hoy Empieza la Escuela!, Kiko. Roman, Santi, illus. (p. 824)
Lenard, Alexander, tr. see Milne, A. A. & Soman, David.
Lenard, Steve. Mysterious Maze #1: The Search for the Skeleton Key. (p. 1223)
Lenart, Claudia, illus. see Kats, Jewel.
Lenburg, Jeff. Genndy Tartakovsky. (p. 661)
—Hayao Miyazaki. (p. 755)
—John Lasseter. (p. 922)
—Matt Groening. (p. 1109)
—Tex Avery. (p. 1723)
—Walt Disney. (p. 1855)
—Walter Lantz. (p. 1856)
—William Hanna & Joseph Barbera. (p. 1933)
Lenburg, Jeff & Kurtz, Bob. Career Opportunities in Animation. (p. 267)
Lender, Mark Edward, jt. auth. see Martin, James Kirby.
Lendler, Ian. Stratford Zoo Midnight Revue Presents Macbeth. Giallongo, Zack, illus. (p. 1666)
—Undone Fairy Tale. Martin, Whitney, illus. (p. 1817)
Lendroth, Susan. Calico Dorsey: Mail Dog of the Mining Camps. Gustavson, Adam, illus. (p. 253)
—Maneki Neko: The Tale of the Beckoning Cat. Otoshi, Kathryn, illus. (p. 1087)
—Old Manhattan Has Some Farms: (E-I-E-I-Grow!) Endle, Kate, illus. (p. 1284)
Lendway, Andy, illus. see Grocki, Jennifer.
Lenehan, Mary, illus. see Mott, Professor.
Lenero, Carmen. Frida Kahlo. Mesquita, Camila, illus. (p. 637)
Lenerville, Karen. Keeper of the Sword: The Quest for Home. (p. 947)
L'Enfant, Julie, anno. Sketches by Anton Gag. (p. 1584)
Lenfest, Kevyn & Mandelbaum, Jolie. University of Vermont College Prowler off the Record. (p. 1821)
Leng, Qin. Not Just Another Princess Story. (p. 1267)
Leng, Qin, illus. see Cole, Kathryn.
Leng, Qin, illus. see Foggo, Cheryl.
Leng, Qin, illus. see Hainnu, Rebecca & Ziegler, Anna.
Leng, Qin, illus. see Lloyd, Jennifer & Osmond, Claudia.
Leng, Qin, illus. see Lloyd, Jennifer.
Leng, Qin, illus. see MacLeod, Elizabeth, et al.
Leng, Qin, illus. see Noah, Jennifer.
Leng, Qin, illus. see Potter, Ellen.
Leng, Qin, illus. see Sulurayok, Matilda.
Leng, Qin, illus. see Tsiang, Sarah.
Leng, Qin, illus. see Uluadluak, Donald.
Lengacher, Janice. My Imaginary Other. (p. 1211)
L'Engle, Madeleine. Acceptable Time. (p. 8)
—And Both Were Young. (p. 71)
—Arruga en el Tiempo. (p. 101)
—Camilla. (p. 256)
—Dragons in the Waters. (p. 479)
—House Like a Lotus. (p. 803)
—Many Waters. (p. 1089)
—Meet the Austins. (p. 1122)
—Moon by Night. (p. 1172)
—Moon by Night. (p. 1172)
—Other Dog. Davenier, Christine, illus. (p. 1306)
—Ring of Endless Light Bk. 4. (p. 1473)
—Ring of Endless Light. (p. 1473)
—Swiftly Tilting Planet. (p. 1690)
—Troubling a Star. (p. 1790)
—Wind in the Door. (p. 1935)
—Wrinkle in Time. (p. 1963)
—Wrinkle in Time. (p. 1963)
—Wrinkle in Time. Larson, Hope, illus. (p. 1963)
—Wrinkle in Time Quintet. (p. 1963)
—Wrinkle in Time Trilogy. (p. 1963)
—Young Unicorns. (p. 1979)
Lengyel, Emil. Siberia. (p. 1572)
Lenhard, Elizabeth. Ball of Clay That Rolled Away Wolff, Jason, illus. (p. 134)
—Bridge Between Worlds. (p. 227)
—Different Path. (p. 438)
—Disappearance. (p. 446)
—Drop-Dead Gorgeous. (p. 485)
—Finding Meridian. (p. 588)
—It's a Purl Thing. (p. 896)
—Power of Five. (p. 1389)
Lenhard, Elizabeth, jt. adapted by see Komorn, Julie.
Lenhard, Elizabeth, jt. auth. see Destiny, A.
Lenhard, Elizabeth, jt. auth. see Miller, Sibley.
Lenhard, Elizabeth, adapted by. Disappearance. (p. 446)
—Return of a Queen. (p. 1464)
Lenhardt, Lisa M. Good Morning Son. (p. 698)
—Good Morning Sun. (p. 698)
Lenhart, Crystal. One Nation under God: A Family Study of Biblical Israel. (p. 1296)
Lenhart, Kristin & Passamani, Julia. Notre Dame Spirit. Mountford, Katie, illus. (p. 1268)
Lenihan, Eddie. Eddie Lenihan's Irish Tales of Mystery. Clarke, Alan, illus. (p. 503)
Lenington, Paula. Forgotten Birthday. Olan, Agnieszka, illus. (p. 619)
LenKaltis-Thompson, Kristen. Momo Kitty, Maddy Girl, & the Strange Little Creature (p. 1163)
Lenker, David "Papa". Skin They're In. (p. 1585)
Lenkiewicz, Isaac, illus. see Crumpton, Nick.
Lenkov, Peter. R. I. P. D. Volume 1 (2nd Edition) Thorpe, Patrick, ed. (p. 1429)
Lenman, Jamie, illus. see Turner, Tracey.
Lennard, Daric. My Name Is Berta. (p. 1215)
Lennard, John. Poetry Handbook: A Guide to Reading Poetry for Pleasure & Practical Criticism. (p. 1376)
Lennard, Kate. Brains. Gulliksen, Eivind, illus. (p. 222)
Lennard, Steve. Colour & Learn Fractions. (p. 346)
Lennhoff, Andrew, illus. see Stone, Amy Wingrove.
Lennicx, Michael, illus. see Fremont, Eleanor.
Lennie, Charles. Apatosaurus. (p. 91)
—Bulldozers. (p. 240)
—Concrete Mixers. (p. 355)
—Cranes. (p. 376)
—Dump Trucks. (p. 489)
—Excavators. (p. 547)
—Loaders. (p. 1044)
—Pteranadon. (p. 1413)
—Stegosaurus. (p. 1646)
—Triceratops. (p. 1785)
—Tyrannosaurus Rex. (p. 1805)
—Velociraptor. (p. 1835)
Lennie, Charles, jt. auth. see ABDO Publishing Company Staff.
Lennie, Charles, et al. Apatosaurus. (p. 91)
—Pteranodon. (p. 1413)
—Stegosaurus. (p. 1646)
—Tiranosaurio Rex. (p. 1757)
—Velociraptor. (p. 1835)
Lennon, Andrew J. & Lennon, Jeffrey L. Things Can Get Better. (p. 1733)
Lennon, Christy G. Let's Make Nana B. Dragon a Grandmother. (p. 999)
Lennon, Jeffrey L., jt. auth. see Lennon, Andrew J.
Lennon, Joan. Ely Plot. (p. 517)
—Ice Road. (p. 850)
—Ice Road. Wyatt, David, illus. (p. 850)
Lennon, John. Real Love: The Drawings for Sean. (p. 1448)
Lennon, Liz. I Am Kind. (p. 833)
—I Can Help. (p. 835)
—I Don't Hit. (p. 837)
—I Keep Clean. (p. 840)
Lennon, Margie. Snowball's Sheepdog Adventures: Summer. (p. 1600)
Lennon, Maria T. Confessions of a So-Called Middle Child. (p. 356)
—Watch Out, Hollywood! More Confessions of a So-Called Middle Child. (p. 1861)
Lennon, Pat. Is for Ark. (p. 889)
Lennon, Stella, et al. Amanda Project (p. 52)
—Revealed. (p. 1465)
Lennon, Tom. When Love Comes to Town. (p. 1903)
Lennox, Lisa. Crack Head. (p. 375)
Leno, Jay. If Roast Beef Could Fly. Whitehead, S. B., illus. (p. 854)
Leno, Katrina. Half Life of Molly Pierce. (p. 736)
Lenoir, Jane, illus. see Sargent, Daina.
Lenoir, Jane, illus. see Sargent, Dave & Sargent, David M., Jr.
Lenoir, Jane, illus. see Sargent, Dave & Sargent, David, Jr.
Lenoir, Jane, illus. see Sargent, Dave & Sargent, Pat.
Lenoir, Jane, illus. see Sargent, Dave, et al.
Lenoir, Jane, illus. see Sargent, Dave.
Lenoir, Jane, illus. see Sargent, David M.
Lenoir, Jane, illus. see Sargent, Pat L.
Lenoir, Jane, illus. see Sargent, Pat.
Lenoir, Jane, jt. auth. see Sargent, Daina.
Lenoir, Sue, illus. see Sargent, Dave, et al.
LeNois, Margaret. Don't Go Alone. (p. 467)
Lenore, Vikki. I Can Count To 100. (p. 835)
Lenox, August, illus. see Beecher, Elizabeth.
Lensch, Chris. Coral Reef: Hide & Seek. (p. 366)
Lensch, Chris, illus. see Doering Tourville, Amanda.
Lensch, Chris, illus. see Finn, Carrie & Picture Window Books Staff.
Lensch, Chris, illus. see Finn, Carrie, et al.
Lensch, Chris, illus. see Finn, Carrie.
Lensch, Chris, illus. see Perez, Jessica.
Lensch, Chris, illus. see Tourville, Amanda Doering.
Lenski, jt. auth. see Lenski, Lois.
Lenski, Lois. Bound Girl of Cobble Hill. (p. 216)
—Cowboy Small. Lenski, Lois, illus. (p. 374)
—Little Airplane. (p. 1023)
—Little Airplane. Lenski, Lois, illus. (p. 1023)
—Policeman Small. Lenski, Lois, illus. (p. 1380)
Lenski, Lois, illus. see La Rue, Mabel Guinnip.
Lenski, Lois, illus. see Lovelace, Maud Hart.
Lenski, Lois & Lenski. Strawberry Girl. Lenski, Lois, illus. (p. 1666)
Lenski, Susan, ed. see Lewis, Jill & Lenski, Susan Davis.
Lenski, Susan Davis, jt. auth. see Lewis, Jill.
Lensky, Mordechai. Physician Inside the Warswa Ghetto. (p. 1353)
Lensmire, Lynn E. Chaucer's Toy Box. (p. 295)
Lent, Blair, illus. see Mosel, Arlene.
Lent, Colleen Van. Web Design with Html5. (p. 1870)
Lent, Patricia & Fosnot, Catherine Twomey. Trades, Jumps, & Stops: Early Algebra. (p. 1776)
Lente, Fred Van. Captain America: First Vengeance. Marvel Comics Staff, illus. (p. 263)
—Marvel Zombies Walker, Kev, illus. (p. 1099)
—Pack: Part 1. (p. 1317)
—Pack: Part 2. (p. 1317)
—Substitute. (p. 1671)
Lente, Fred Van, jt. auth. see David, Peter.
Lentin, Alana. Racism & Ethnic Discrimination. (p. 1432)
Lentini, Joe. Mickey the Monster: He's Just Misunderstood. (p. 1136)
—Mickey the Monster's New Adventure: The Mysterious Fence. (p. 1136)
Lenton, Steven. Five Christmas Penguins. (p. 600)
—Teddy Bear, Teddy Bear: And Other Favorite Nursery Rhymes. (p. 1712)
Lenton, Steven, illus. see Boyce, Frank Cottrell & Boyce, Frank Cottrell.
Lenton, Steven, illus. see Boyce, Frank Cottrell.
Lenton, Steven, illus. see Corderoy, Tracey.
Lentz, Bob, illus. see Glaser, Jason.
Lentz, Bob, illus. see Lemke, Donald B.
Lentz, Bob, illus. see Lemke, Donald.
Lentz, Bob, illus. see Sautter, Aaron.
Lentz, Bob, illus. see Sutcliffe, Jane.
Lentz, Bob, illus. see Welvaert, Scott R.
Lenz, Adrienne. Glitter Ball: Princess Jewels. (p. 683)
Lenz, Dave. Jack Crow: Indian Healer. (p. 903)
Lenz, Mario, ed. Case Retrieval Nets as a Model for Building Flexible Information Systems (p. 275)
Lenz, Mary, illus. see Jue, Thea.
Lenz Mulligan Rights and Co. Staff & Chronicle Books Staff. Little Dino. (p. 1026)
Lenz Mulligan Rights and Co. Staff, et al. Little Penguin. (p. 1033)
Lenz, Siegfried. Lehmanns Erzählungen (p. 991)
Lenzi, Danielle E. My Search for Prince Charming's Normal Brother. (p. 1218)
Lenzlinger, Jorg, jt. auth. see Steiner, Gerda.
Lenzo, Caroline, jt. auth. see Hughes, Melissa.
Leo. Group (p. 725)
Leo & LEO, Inc Staff. Aldebaran Vol. 1 LEO, Inc Staff, illus. (p. 35)
Leo, Domenic. Messengers: The Secret of the Orbs. (p. 1129)
LEO, Inc Staff. Antares (p. 88)
—Other (p. 1306)
LEO, Inc Staff, jt. auth. see Leo.
Leo, Veronica. Three Silver Coins: A Story from Tibet. (p. 1743)
Leograndis, Denise. Launching the Writing Workshop: A Step-by-Step Guide in Photographs. (p. 980)
Leokum, Arkady, et al. Weird & Wacky Facts. (p. 1872)
Leon, Andrew. House on the Corner: First Person Edition. (p. 803)
Leon, Carol Boyd. Dayenu! A Passover Haggadah for Families & Children. Connelly, Gwen, illus. (p. 415)
Leon, Gabriela, illus. see Del Angel, Varinia.
Leon, George D. Story of Electricity: With 20 Easy-to-Perform Experiments. (p. 1658)
Leon, Georgina Lazaro. Conoce a Gabriela Mistral: Get to Know Gabriela Mistral. Palacios, Sara Helena, illus. (p. 358)
—Mejor Es Mi Papa. Alvarez, David, illus. (p. 1124)
—Niña y la Estrella. Perez-Moliere, Marnie, illus. (p. 1256)
León, Georgina Lázaro. ¡Viva la Tortuga! Torres, Walter, illus. (p. 1846)
Leon, John Paul, illus. see Tieri, Frank.
Leon, Karen, illus. see Flounders, Anne.
Leon, Karen, illus. see Higgins, Kitty.
Leon, Karen, illus. see Howard, Annabelle.
Leon, Karen, illus. see Kramer, Alan & Kramer, Candice.
Leon, Karen, illus. see Kramer, Alan.
Leon, Karen, illus. see Kramer, Candice.
Leon, Karen, illus. see Meissner, David.
Leon, Karen, illus. see Wall, Suzy.
Leon, Loni. Can you Imagine... Leon, Loni & Huston, Kyle, illus. (p. 259)
Leon, Richard, ed. see McDevitt, Bradley.
Leon, Sarah & Elsikowitz, Michal. Story of Chanukah. Katz, Tova, illus. (p. 1657)
León, Vicki. Colony of Seals: The Captivating Life of a Deep Sea Diver. (p. 342)
—Pod of Killer Whales: The Mysterious Life of the Intelligent Orca. Foott, Jeff, photos by. (p. 1375)
Leon, Vicki. Raft of Sea Otters: The Playful Life of a Furry Survivor. (p. 1433)
—Rainbow of Parrots. (p. 1435)
—Secrets of Tidepools: The Bright World of the Rocky Shoreline. (p. 1546)
Leon, Vicki, ed. see Berger, Bruce.
Leon, Vicki, ed. see Hall, Howard.
Leon, Vicki, ed. see Hamilton, Jean.
León, Vicki, ed. see Hunt, Joni Phelps & London Town Press Staff.
León, Vicki, ed. see Hunt, Joni Phelps.
Leonard, Barbara, illus. see Ross, Kathy.
Leonard, Barry, contrib. by. Rock a Bye Baby. (p. 1481)
Leonard, Barry, ed. Alice in Wonderland. (p. 39)
—Alphabet Connections: English-Spanish: 26 Picture Cards. (p. 49)
—Drawing Trucks & Diggers: A Book of 10 Stencils. (p. 482)
—Helping Your Child Succeed in School: With Activities for Children. (p. 766)
—Humpty Dumpty & Other Rhymes. (p. 827)
—Little Tin Soldier. (p. 1037)
—Mary Had a Little Lamb & Other Rhymes. (p. 1100)
—Mary, Mary, Quite Contrary & Other Rhymes. (p. 1100)
—NASCAR Jumbo Coloring & Activity Book (p. 1230)
—Pinocchio. (p. 1360)
—Rock-a-Bye, Baby & Other Rhymes. (p. 1481)
—See-Saw Margery Daw & Other Rhymes. (p. 1547)
—Sleeping Beauty. (p. 1589)
—Squishy Shapes: Dinosaurs. (p. 1637)
—Symbols of the US Government: Ben's Activity Book. (p. 1693)
—Three Little Pigs. (p. 1743)
—Treasure Trove of an Ancient Egyptian Child. (p. 1782)
—Ugly Duckling. (p. 1808)
—Wee Willie Winkie & Other Rhymes. (p. 1871)
Leonard, Basia & Jovinelly, Joann. Bipolar Disorder. (p. 190)
Leonard, Basia & Roberts, Jeremy. Truth about Prescription Drugs. (p. 1794)
Leonard, Clavon. Dawn of My Deliverance. (p. 411)
Leonard, David, illus. see Christopher, Matt.
Leonard, David, illus. see Parry, Rosanne.
Leonard, David, illus. see Spinelli, Eileen.
Leonard, David, illus. see Stier, Catherine.
Leonard, Debra R. Lubby Lubby Story. (p. 1062)
Leonard, Elise. Killer Lunch Lady. (p. 956)
—Monday Morning Blitz. (p. 1163)
—Scared Stiff. (p. 1519)
Leonard, Erskine, illus. see Pozdol, MaryBeth.
Leonard, Herb, illus. see Sutcliffe, Jane.
Leonard, Julia Platt. Cold Case. (p. 338)
—Cold Case. Mauro, Tony, illus. (p. 338)
Leonard, Kaycee, illus. see Bassler, Joni.
Leonard, Kiri Ostergaard. Vikings of Legend & Lore Paper Dolls. (p. 1842)
Leonard, Krystian. Shining Scars. Kelly, Lucas, illus. (p. 1566)
Leonard, Marcia. I Feel Angry. Bartholomew, illus. (p. 838)
—I Feel Happy. Bartholomew, illus. (p. 838)
—I Feel Sad. Bartholomew, illus. (p. 838)
—I Feel Scared. Bartholomew, illus. (p. 838)
—Me Gusta el Desorden. Translations.com Staff, tr. from ENG. (p. 1116)
—Me Gusta el Desorden; I Like Mess. (p. 1116)
—Mi Dia de Campamento. Translations.com Staff, tr. from ENG. (p. 1132)
—Mi Dia de Campamento; My Camp Out. (p. 1132)
—Saltar, Brincar, Correr. Translations.com Staff, tr. from ENG. (p. 1505)
—Saltar, Brincar, Correr; Hop, Skip, Run. (p. 1505)
Leonard, Mary T. Three Best Friends. Russell, Terry, illus. (p. 1741)
Leonard, Michael, illus. see Rhema, Dan.
Leonard, Nellie M. Grand Daddy Whiskers, M. D. (p. 707)
Leonard, Niall. Crusher. (p. 387)
—Incinerator. (p. 869)
—Shredder. (p. 1571)
Leonard, Scott A. Myths & Legends of Ancient Britain & Ireland. (p. 1227)
—Myths & Legends of Ancient Greece. (p. 1227)
—Myths & Legends of China. (p. 1227)
—Myths & Legends of Scandinavia. (p. 1227)
—Myths & Legends of South Asia & Southeast Asia. (p. 1227)
Leonard, Sue, ed. Kitchen Science: With over 50 Fantastic Experiments. (p. 962)
Leonard, Terry, illus. see Weisner, Candace.
Leonard, Tom, illus. see Brenner, Barbara.
Leonard, Tom, illus. see Cooper, Sharon Katz.
Leonard, Tom, illus. see Dunphy, Madeleine.
Leonard, Tom, illus. see Pallotta, Jerry.
Leonard, Tom, jt. illus. see Daly, Catherine.
Leonard, Wendy. Human Anatomy: The Fun, Visual Way to Teach Yourself about Anything & Everything. Ferguson-Jones, Philip, illus. (p. 825)
Leonardi, Rick, illus. see Blackman, Haden.
Leonardi, Rick, illus. see Defalco, Tom.
Leonardo & Harris, Godfrey. Leonardo's "Quotebook" Thoughts by & about Leonardo Da Vinci. (p. 992)
Leonardo, Victoria. Midwest Region. (p. 1139)
—Northeast Region. (p. 1265)
—Pacific Northwest Region. (p. 1317)
Leone, Anthony. Great Adventure with a Cub Named Troy. (p. 713)
Leone, Daniel A., ed. Is the World Heading Toward an Energy Crisis? (p. 890)
Leone, Dee. Bizz & Buzz Make Honey Buns. Maritie, illus. (p. 194)
Leone, Elaine H. Grandies. (p. 707)
—Grandy Goose Rhymes. (p. 710)
Leone, Jason. Enchantress of Caratunk. Manna, Elizabeth, photos by. (p. 523)
Leone, Laura. Choosing a Career in Information Science. (p. 310)
Leone, Sergio, illus. see Hughes, Virginia.
Leonetti, Mike. My Leafs Sweater. (p. 1211)
—Wendel & the Great One. Banning, Greg, illus. (p. 1875)
Leong, Sonia, illus. see Shakespeare, William & Appignanesi, Richard.
Leonhard, Herb. Faerie Garden Coloring Book. (p. 562)
—Sir Norman & the Dreaming Dragon. Leonhard, Herb, illus. (p. 1580)
Leonhard, Herb, illus. see Davis, David.
Leonhard, Herb, illus. see Hill, Janet Muirhead.
Leonhard, Herb, illus. see Knowlton, Laurie.
Leonhard, Herb, illus. see Morgan, Connie & Morgan, Connie Collins.
Leonhard, Herb, illus. see Peck, Jan.
Leonhard, Herb, illus. see Reish, Kathleen.
Leonhard, Herb, illus. see Richardson, Steve.
Leonhard, Herb, illus. see Stengel, Joyce A.
Leonhard, Herb, illus. see Sutcliffe, Jane.
Leonhard, Herb, illus. see Watts, James.
Leonhardt, Alice. Why the Ocean Is Salty. (p. 1926)
Leonhardt, Alice & Hart, Alison. Return of the Gypsy Witch. Burleson, Joe, illus. (p. 1464)
Leoni, Cristiana. In Caesar's Rome with Cicero. Cappon, Manuela, illus. (p. 863)
—In Pericles' Athens with Socrates. Cappon, Manuela, illus. (p. 864)
—New York in the 1930s with La Guardia. (p. 1248)
Leoni, Gail. Chalk Dust. (p. 288)
—Shudders! Horrible Things Kids Love to Be Afraid Of. (p. 1571)
Leoni, Maria Teresa Zanobini. Leonardo Da Vinci. (p. 992)
Leoni, Nancy. Toby Goes to Camp Leoni, Nancy, illus. (p. 1760)
Leonidou, Niki, illus. see Poulter, J. R.
Leonori, Ann, tr. see D'Adamo, Francesco.
Leopold, Astara Ladyvienna. Stardream Chronicles (p. 1642)
Leopold, Nikia Speliakos Clark. Adam's Crayons. Nemett, Barry & Nemett, Laini, illus. (p. 11)
Leopold, Patricia, jt. ed. see Gay, Oonagh.
Leota, Kealaulaokamamo. Zhaka. (p. 1986)
Leotti-Bachem, Janice. Everglades. (p. 542)
Lepage, Catherine, illus. see Macavinta, Courtney & Pluym, Andrea Vander.
Lepage, Michaele. Year at Santa's Workshop. (p. 1969)
Lepage, Michaele L. I Wish I Had a Tail. Lovass-Nagy, Nicole, illus. (p. 848)
LePage, Michaele L. & Lovass-Nagy, Nicole. Year at the North Pole. (p. 1969)
LePan, Don. Animals. Taback, Simms, illus. (p. 81)
Lepard, Jenina. Diamonds in the Rough. (p. 434)
Lepell, Rachel. Time Dance. (p. 1751)
Lepere, J. Mindseed. (p. 1145)
Lepetit, Angie. Three Cheers for Trees! A Book about Our Carbon Footprint. (p. 1741)
—Trash Magic: A Book about Recycling a Plastic Bottle (p. 1780)
Leplar, Anna, illus. see Grahame, Kenneth.
Leplar, Anna, illus. see Leeson, Robert.
Leplar, Anna C., illus. see Adams, Georgie.
LePlatt, Betsy, illus. see Kroll, Virginia.
L'Eplattenier, Michelle, illus. see Neuls, Lillian.
Lepley, Kathy, illus. see Hocker, Katherine M.
Lepley, Lynne. Scrumptious Scriptures. (p. 1533)

L

Lepora, Nathan. Chromium. (p. 317)
—Inside Atoms & Molecules. (p. 876)
—Molybdenum. (p. 1161)
Lepore, James. World I Never Made. (p. 1955)
LePorte, Christine, ed. see Pratt, Gary Thomas.
Lepp, Bil. King of Little Things Wenzel, David T., illus. (p. 959)
Lepp, Bil, jt. auth. see Lepp, Paul.
Lepp, Kevin, illus. see Figley, Marty Rhodes.
Lepp, Kevin, tr. see Figley, Marty Rhodes.
Lepp, Kristin. Libby Louanne & the Amazing Hospital Mystery. (p. 1005)
Lepp, Paul & Lepp, Bil. Monster Stick & Other Appalachian Tall Tales. Brewer, Terry, illus. (p. 1168)
Lepp, Royden. Barnabas Helps a Friend Lepp, Royden, illus. (p. 139)
—Happy Birthday Barnabas Lepp, Royden, illus. (p. 744)
Leppanen, Debbie. Trick-or-Treat: A Happy Haunter's Halloween. Carpenter, Tad, illus. (p. 1786)
Leppard, Laura Jennifer. Duchess of Sao Paulo. (p. 487)
Leppard, Lois Gladys. Mandie & the Cherokee Legend. (p. 1087)
—Mandie & the Graduation Mystery. (p. 1087)
—Mandie & the Night Thief (p. 1087)
—Mandie Collection. (p. 1087)
—Mandie Collection. (p. 1087)
—Mysterious Teacher. (p. 1223)
—New Horizons. (p. 1245)
—Secret Garden. (p. 1541)
Leppman, Elizabeth & Andrews, David. Business Without Borders: Globalization (p. 245)
Leppman, Elizabeth J. Australia & the Pacific. (p. 116)
Leprechaun, Seamus T. o'Shea Chronicles. (p. 1305)
Lepretre, Jean-Marc, illus. see Vandewiele, Agnes.
Lepri, Nancy, illus. see Weber, Saul.
Lepri, Nancy Carty. Tiny Angel. (p. 1756)
Leprince de Beaumont, Marie. Bella y la Bestia. (p. 162)
Leprince de Beaumont, Marie & Perrault, Charles. Beauty & the Beast & Other Fairy Tales. (p. 154)
Lerangis, Peter. Big Production (p. 183)
—Code. (p. 338)
—Colossus Rises Lerangis, Peter, illus. (p. 346)
—Colossus Rises. (p. 346)
—Colossus Rises. Norstrand, Torstein & Reagan, Mike, illus. (p. 346)
—Colossus Rises. Reagan, Mike & Norstrand, Torstein, illus. (p. 346)
—Curse of the King. Norstrand, Torstein, illus. (p. 395)
—Dead of Night. (p. 417)
—Fall Musical (p. 566)
—Journals: The Key. (p. 927)
—Lost in Babylon. (p. 1055)
—Lost in Babylon. Norstrand, Torstein, illus. (p. 1055)
—Seven Wonders Journals: The Key. (p. 1555)
—Seven Wonders Journals: The Select & the Orphan. (p. 1555)
—Seven Wonders Journals. (p. 1555)
—Sword Thief. (p. 1692)
—Tomb of Shadows. (p. 1764)
—Tomb of Shadows. Norstrand, Torstein, illus. (p. 1764)
—Too Hot! (p. 1766)
—Viper's Nest. (p. 1844)
—Whoa! Amusement Park Gone Wild! Talbot, Jim, illus. (p. 1919)
—Wow! Blast from the Past! Talbot, Jim, illus. (p. 1962)
—Wtf. (p. 1965)
Lerangis, Peter, jt. auth. see Mazer, Harry.
Lerasle, Magdeleine. Songs from a Journey with a Parrot: Lullabies & Nursery Rhymes from Portugal & Brazil. Fronty, Aurélia, illus. (p. 1612)
Leray, Marjolaine & Ardizzone, Sarah. Little Red Hood. Ardizzone, Sarah, tr. from FRE. (p. 1035)
Leray, Merrill. House of Lady Chase. (p. 803)
—Kidnapping. (p. 952)
Lerch, Kathryn W., ed. Words of War: Wartime Memories from the American Revolution Through the Iraq War (p. 1952)
Lerch, Steffie, illus. see Gipson, Morrell.
LeReau, Kara. Otto: The Boy Who Loved Cars. Magoon, Scott, illus. (p. 1307)
Lerer, Seth, jt. auth. see Grahame, Kenneth.
Lerner, Adrienne. Alzheimer's Disease. (p. 51)
—Climate Change. (p. 332)
—Suicide in Arthur Miller's Death of a Salesman. (p. 1673)
Lerner, Adrienne, ed. Leukemia. (p. 1003)
Lerner, Adrienne Wilmoth, jt. auth. see Lerner, Alicia Cafferty.
Lerner, Alicia Cafferty. Marriage. (p. 1096)
Lerner, Alicia Cafferty & Lerner, Adrienne Wilmoth. Freedom of Expression. (p. 634)
Lerner, Bernice, ed. see Clifford, Kathleen & Uy, Megan Black.
Lerner, Brenda Wilmoth, jt. auth. see Lerner, K. Lee.
Lerner, Carol. Plants that Make You Sniffle & Sneeze. (p. 1370)
Lerner, Claire & Parlakian, Rebecca. Everyday Ways to Support Your Baby's & Toddler's Early Learning. (p. 544)
Lerner Classroom & Zuehlke, Jeffrey. Grand Canyon. (p. 707)
Lerner Classroom Staff & Bullard, Lisa. Everglades. (p. 542)
Lerner Classroom Staff & Piehl, Janet. Great Lakes. (p. 716)
Lerner Classroom Staff & Zuehlke, Jeffrey. Rocky Mountains. (p. 1484)
Lerner Group Staff. Create a Story. (p. 378)
Lerner, Harry. Tenacity Well Directed: The Inside Story of How a Publishing House Was Created & Became a Sleeping Giant in Its Field-Well, Not Exactly. (p. 1719)
Lerner, K. Lee & Lerner, Brenda Wilmoth. Biotechnology: Changing Life Through Science. (p. 190)
Lerner, K. Lee, et al. U-X-L Doomed: The Science Behind Disasters. (p. 1807)
—UXL Encyclopedia of Water Science (p. 1829)
Lerner Publishing Group Staff. Animal Predators: Complete Set. (p. 79)
—Animal Predators: Classroom Set. (p. 79)
—Civil Rights Struggles Around the World (p. 325)
—Work People Do: Classroom Set. (p. 1952)
Lerner Publishing Group Staff, ed. Time Nature's Wonders: The Science & Splendor of Earth's Most Fascinating Places. (p. 1752)
Lerner, Sharon. DC Board Books. (p. 415)
—DC Board Books (Large) (p. 415)
—DC Board Books (Small) (p. 415)
Lerner, Sharon & Sewell, Anna. Black Beauty. Jeffers, Susan, illus. (p. 195)
LernerClassroom Editors, ed. Amazing Athletes Set V: Classroom Library. (p. 53)
—Country Explorers: Complete Set. (p. 372)
—Early Bird Earth Science: Classroom Set. (p. 493)
—Graphic Myths & Legends: Classroom Set. (p. 711)
—Graphic Myths & Legends Complete Set. (p. 711)
—Mitos Y Leyendas en Vinetas; Graphic Myths & Legends: Complete Set. (p. 1156)
—Science Solves It! en Espanol: Complete Set. (p. 1528)
—Science Solves It! en Espanol: Classroom Set. (p. 1528)
—Twisted Journeys (p. 1802)
—Twisted Journeys Classroom Set. (p. 1802)
Leroe, Ellen. Dear Big V. (p. 418)
Lerot-Calvo, Florence, illus. see Galan, Christian.
Leroux, Gaston. Fantasma de la Opera. (p. 571)
—Graphic Horror Espinosa, Rod, illus. (p. 711)
—Phantom of the Opera. (p. 1349)
—Phantom of the Opera. Howell, Troy, illus. (p. 1349)
—Phantom of the Opera. Espinosa, Rod, illus. (p. 1349)
Leroy, Robert & Ripley's Believe It or Not Editors. Ripley's Search for the Shrunken Heads: And Other Curiosities. (p. 1474)
Leroy-Bennett, Veronique. First French: Chez Moi. (p. 595)
—First French: An Introduction to Commonly Used French Words & Phrases about Animal Friends, with 400 Lively Photographs. (p. 595)
LeRoye, Dee. Crossfire. (p. 385)
Lersch, Jean. Old Testament Servants of God: Faith for Life2 Course Three. Janssen, Patricia E., ed. (p. 1285)
—Scrapbook: Faith for Life2 Course Three. Janssen, Patricia E., ed. (p. 1532)
Lersch, N. Scrantz. Bob Loves Letters. (p. 205)
Lervold, Erik, illus. see Reynolds, Aaron.
Les Becquets, Diane. Season of Ice. (p. 1538)
—Stones of Mourning Creek (p. 1653)
Les, Papa. Gio the Friendly T-Rex & Friends: Hide-and-Seek. (p. 677)
Lesa, Ropeti F. Being a Boy in Samoa in the 1950s. Asuao, Kelcey, illus. (p. 160)
Lesaux, Nonie K., jt. auth. see Stanos, Dimi.
Lescarbeau, Nicole. Ellie's Allies. (p. 514)
Leschnikoff, Nancy, illus. see Meredith, Susan.
Leschnikoff, Nancy & Wood, Helen, des. Illustrated Fairy Tales. (p. 857)
Lescroart, John. Oath. (p. 1275)
—Second Chair. (p. 1539)
—Suspect. (p. 1688)
Lescuyer, Moira. Little Life Reminders. (p. 1030)
Lesczynski, Jim. Walton Street Tycoons. (p. 1856)
Leseberg, Bambi. Rollo's Rescue. (p. 1485)
Lesh, Bruce A., jt. see Finkelman, Paul.
Leshem, Yossi, jt. auth. see Vogel, Carole Garbuny.
Leske, Steven. Dragon & Sir Richard. (p. 476)
Lesler, Rebecca. Magic Stone: Return of Two Kings. (p. 1073)
—Truth of the Magic Stone (p. 1794)
Lesley, J. Coins of Power. (p. 338)
Lesley, Sharon. Red Scarf & Other Stories. (p. 1455)
—Red Scarf & Other Stories, Activity Book. (p. 1455)
Lesley, Simon. Funky Scales for Flute. (p. 649)
Leslie, Clare Walker. Curious Nature Guide: Explore the Natural Wonders All Around You. (p. 394)
Leslie, Clare Walker, jt. auth. see Gerace, Frank E.
Leslie, Dawn Marie. Orthify. (p. 1305)
Leslie, Emma. Captives: Or, Escape from the Druid Council. (p. 265)
—For Merrie England: A Tale of the Weavers of Norfolk. Taylor, R., illus. (p. 616)
—From Bondage to Freedom: A Tale of the Times of Mohammed. Symmons, Sheeres, illus. (p. 642)
—Glaucia the Greek Slave: A Tale of Athens in the First Century. Felter & Butterworth & Heath, illus. (p. 682)
—Gytha's Message: A Tale of Saxon England. Staniland, C., illus. (p. 734)
—Martyr's Victory: A Story of Danish England. Stacey, W., illus. (p. 1098)
—Out of the Mouth of the Lion: Or, the Church in the Catacombs. Felter and Gunston & Butterworth and Heath, illus. (p. 1311)
—Sowing Beside All Waters: A Tale of the World in the Church. Morgin, W. J. & W., E., illus. (p. 1618)
Leslie, H. Steve, jt. auth. see Leslie, Natalie Johnson.
Leslie, Jennifer, jt. auth. see Millman, Isaac.
Leslie, Lashawn. Thundermonsters. (p. 1746)
Leslie, Lawrence J. With Trapper Jim in the North Woods. (p. 1942)
Leslie, M. A. Tristen & the Magic Shop. Leslie, M. A., illus. (p. 1787)
Leslie, Melissa, illus. see Ferraro, Lynn.
Leslie, Natalie Johnson & Leslie, H. Steve. Surviving School Violence. (p. 1687)
Leslie, Robyn. Rinny & the Trail of Clues. (p. 1473)
Leslie, Roger. Isak Dinesen: Gothic Storyteller. (p. 891)
—Success Express for Teens: 50 Life-Changing Activities. (p. 1672)
Leslie, Sherrie L. Apple A Day: The Adventures of Grannie Annie & Pickles #1. (p. 92)
Leslie-Pelecky, Diandra. Physics of Nascar: The Science Behind the Speed. (p. 1353)
Lesnick, Tina, illus. see Nettrour, Nelani.
Lesnie, Phil, illus. see Millard, Glenda.
LeSourd, Nancy. Adventures in Jamestown (p. 15)
—Attack at Pearl Harbor (p. 113)
—Escape on the Underground Railroad (p. 535)
—Secrets of Civil War Spies (p. 1545)
LeSourd, Nancy & Zondervan Publishing Staff. Early Reader's Bible: A Bible to Read All by Yourself! (p. 494)
Lespérance, Colette. Baby's First Christmas. (p. 129)
Less, Sally, illus. see Irvin, Christine.
Lessa, Charlotte F. My Bible Storybook. (p. 1197)
Lessa, M. S. W., jt. auth. see Lessa, Nicholoas.
Lessa, Nicholoas & Lessa, M. S. W. Living with Alcoholism & Drug Addiction. (p. 1042)
Lessac, Frané. Island Counting 1 2 3. Lessac, Frané, illus. (p. 892)
Lessac, Frané, illus. see Cotten, Cynthia.
Lessac, Frané, illus. see Greenwood, Mark.
Lessac, Frané, illus. see Melmed, Laura Krauss.
Lessac, Frané, illus. see Quarto Generic Staff.
Lessac, Frané, illus. see Rockwell, Anne F.
Lessac, Frané, illus. see Wilson, Barbara K.
Lessac, Frané, illus. see Zelver, Patricia.
Lessac, Frané, jt. auth. see Greenwood, Mark.
Lessem, Don. Armored Dinosaurs. Bindon, John, illus. (p. 99)
—Carnivoros Gigantes. Translations.com Staff, tr. from ENG. (p. 270)
—Deadliest Dinosaurs. Bindon, John, illus. (p. 417)
—Dinosaurios Acorazados. Translations.com Staff, tr. (p. 443)
—Dinosaurios Con Plumas. Translations.com Staff, tr. from ENG. (p. 443)
—Dinosaurios Mas Rapidos. Translations.com Staff, tr. from ENG. (p. 443)
—Dinosaurios Pico de Pato. Translations.com Staff, tr. (p. 443)
—Dinosaurs. (p. 443)
—Fastest Dinosaurs. Bindon, John, illus. (p. 576)
—Gigantes Marinos de la Época de los Dinosaurios. Translations.com Staff, tr. from ENG. (p. 676)
—Gigantes Voladores de la Epoca de los Dinosaurios. Translations.com Staff, tr. from ENG. (p. 676)
—Herbívoros Gigantes. Translations.com Staff, tr. (p. 769)
—Horned Dinosaurs. Bindon, John, illus. (p. 798)
—Los Dinosaurios Más Inteligentes. Translations.com Staff, tr. from ENG. (p. 1053)
—Los Dinosaurios Más Pequeños. Translations.com Staff, tr. (p. 1053)
—National Geographic Kids Ultimate Dinopedia: The Most Complete Dinosaur Reference Ever. Tempesta, Franco, illus. (p. 1232)
—Smartest Dinosaurs. Bindon, John, illus. (p. 1593)
Lessing, Edeltraut B. Amber & Flax. (p. 56)
Lessman, Steve. D-Day: American Character. (p. 397)
Lessnick, Jaden. Kira's Dream. (p. 961)
Lessoff, Alan. Where Texas Meets the Sea: Corpus Christi & Its History. (p. 1909)
Lestelle, Wende. Science Mouse. (p. 1526)
Lester, Alison. Bibs & Boots. Lester, Alison, illus. (p. 177)
—Circus Horse. Harvey, Roland, illus. (p. 322)
—Green As a Bean. (p. 721)
—Growl Like a Tiger. (p. 727)
—Happy & Sad. Lester, Alison, illus. (p. 744)
—Magic Beach. Lester, Alison, illus. (p. 1071)
—Noni the Pony. Lester, Alison, illus. (p. 1263)
—Noni the Pony Goes to the Beach. Lester, Alison, illus. (p. 1263)
—One Clucky Hen. (p. 1294)
—Run Like a Rabbit. (p. 1496)
—Running with the Horses. (p. 1497)
—Snow Pony. (p. 1599)
—Sophie Scott Goes South. (p. 1613)
Lester, Alison & Harvey, Roland. Silver Horse Switch. (p. 1576)
Lester, Anna. Stories of Fairies. Gower, Teri, illus. (p. 1655)
—Stories of Fairytale Castles. Lo Cascio, Maria Cristina, illus. (p. 1655)
Lester, Brian. Kansas City Chiefs. (p. 943)
—R U In? Using Technology Responsibly. (p. 1429)
—San Francisco 49ers. (p. 1510)
—Seattle Seahawks. (p. 1539)
Lester, Frank K. Teaching Mathematics Through Problem Solving: Prekindergarten-Grade 6. (p. 1710)
Lester, Helen. All for Me & None for All. Munsinger, Lynn, illus. (p. 44)
—Batter up Wombat. Munsinger, Lynn, illus. (p. 145)
—Hooway for Wodney Wat Munsinger, Lynn, illus. (p. 796)
—Hurty Feelings. Munsinger, Lynn, illus. (p. 830)
—It Wasn't My Fault. Munsinger, Lynn, illus. (p. 894)
—Listen, Buddy. Munsinger, Lynn, illus. (p. 1022)
—Loch Mess Monster. Munsinger, Lynn, illus. (p. 1044)
—Me First. Munsinger, Lynn, illus. (p. 1116)
—Miss Nelson Is Missing! Munsinger, Lynn, illus. (p. 1151)
—Mochila de Lin Flor Ada, Alma, tr. from ENG. (p. 1157)
—Porcupine Named Fluffy. Munsinger, Lynn, illus. (p. 1386)
—Sheep in Wolf's Clothing. Munsinger, Lynn, illus. (p. 1564)
—Tacky & the Haunted Igloo. Munsinger, Lynn, illus. (p. 1694)
—Tacky & the Winter Games. Munsinger, Lynn, illus. (p. 1694)
—Tacky Goes to Camp. (p. 1694)
—Tacky Goes to Camp. Munsinger, Lynn, illus. (p. 1694)
—Tacky in Trouble. Munsinger, Lynn, illus. (p. 1694)
—Tacky the Penguin. Munsinger, Lynn, illus. (p. 1694)
—Tackylocks & the Three Bears. Munsinger, Lynn, illus. (p. 1694)
—Tacky's Christmas. Munsinger, Lynn, illus. (p. 1694)
—Wizard, the Fairy, & the Magic Chicken: A Story about Teamwork. Munsinger, Lynn, illus. (p. 1943)
—Wodney Wat's Wobot. Munsinger, Lynn, illus. (p. 1943)
Lester, Helen & Munsinger, Lynn. Happy Birdday, Tacky! Lester, Helen & Munsinger, Lynn, illus. (p. 744)
—Laugh-Along Lessons 5-Minute Stories. (p. 980)
Lester, J. D. Grandma Calls Me Gigglepie. Nakata, Hiroe, illus. (p. 708)
—Mommy Calls Me Monkeypants. Nakata, Hiroe, illus. (p. 1162)
Lester, James D., Jr. & Lester, James D., Sr. Research Paper Handbook: Your Complete Guide. (p. 1462)
Lester, James D., Sr., jt. auth. see Lester, James D., Jr.
Lester, Julius. Day of Tears. (p. 414)
—Guardian. (p. 728)
—Let's Talk about Race. Barbour, Karen, illus. (p. 1001)
—Old African. Pinkney, Jerry, illus. (p. 1283)
—Pharaoh's Daughter: A Novel of Ancient Egypt. (p. 1349)
—Tales of Uncle Remus: The Adventures of Brer Rabbit. Pinkney, Jerry, illus. (p. 1703)
—To Be a Slave. Feelings, Tom, illus. (p. 1758)
—When Dad Killed Mom. (p. 1901)
Lester, Margot Carmichael, jt. auth. see Peha, Steve.
Lester, Marnie. Ariel's Charm. (p. 98)
Lester, Mary Frances, ed. see Windeatt, Mary Fabyan & Ignatz, Marie.
Lester, Mike, illus. see Bennett, Artie.
Lester, Mike, illus. see Calvert, Deanna.
Lester, Mike, illus. see Collins, Suzanne.
Lester, Mike, illus. see Rothman, Cynthia Anne.
Lester, Mike, illus. see Snodgrass, Lady Cecily.
Lester, Natasha. What Is Left over, After. (p. 1889)
Lester, R. A. Clearview Stories (p. 330)
Lester, Roseanna, illus. see Kucej, Kristine.
Lester, Roseanna, illus. see Thomas, Amy T.
Lester, Sharon. Boy Who Wouldn't Sit Still! Smith, Jeff, illus. (p. 219)
Lester, Stephanie. Year Round Project-Based Activities for STEM Grd 1-2. (p. 1969)
Lester, Vivian. Wee-Dolph, the Tiniest Reindeer. Wiggs, Sue, illus. (p. 1871)
Lester, Vivian & Luhrs, Jeannece Jackson. Alphabet Alive Lesson Plans Books. (p. 49)
Lestrade, Agnès de & Frank-McNeil, Julia. Phileas's Fortune: A Story about Self-Expression. Docampo, Valeria, illus. (p. 1350)
Lestrade, Ursula & Hachette Children's Books Staff. Werewolf Hunter's Guide. (p. 1875)
Lesueur, James W. Indian Legends. (p. 871)
Lesynski, Loris. Cabbagehead. Lesynski, Loris, illus. (p. 250)
—Crazy about Basketball! Rasmussen, Gerry, illus. (p. 377)
—Crazy about Hockey! Rasmussen, Gerry, illus. (p. 377)
—Crazy about Soccer. Rasmussen, Gerry, illus. (p. 377)
—Gatomagico. Canetti, Yanitzia, tr. from ENG. (p. 658)
—I Did It Because... How a Poem Happens. Martchenko, Michael, illus. (p. 837)
—Shoe Shakes. Martchenko, Michael, illus. (p. 1568)
—Zigzag: Zoems for Zindergarten. Lesynski, Loris, illus. (p. 1986)
Lesynski, Loris & Martchenko, Michael. Boy Soup. (p. 219)
Leszczynski, Diana. Fern Verdant & the Silver Rose. (p. 582)
Leszek, Cedryll, illus. see Leadbetter, Lesley.
Le-Tan, Pierre, illus. see Gash, Amy.
Le-Tan, Pierre, illus. see Metaxas, Eric.
Le'Taxione. Bully's Behavior. (p. 241)
Letcher, MaKayla. Dog & the Frog: The Change. Pope, T., illus. (p. 461)
Letchford, Clive, jt. auth. see Affleck, Judith.
Letendre, Peter A. If I Could Be a Doughnut. (p. 852)
Leth, Kate. Adventure Time Vol. 4. (p. 15)
Lethbridge, Lucy. Napoleon. (p. 1229)
—True Stories of Pirates. (p. 1792)
Lethcoe, Jason. Amazing Adventures from Zoom's Academy. Lethcoe, Jason, illus. (p. 52)
—Capture of the Crimson Cape. Lethcoe, Jason, illus. (p. 265)
—Geheimnisvolle Mr. Spines - Wings Altmann, Scott, illus. (p. 659)
—No Place Like Holmes (p. 1260)
—Song Altmann, Scott, illus. (p. 1611)
—You Wish. (p. 1976)
—Zoom's Academy. (p. 1989)
Lethem, Jonathan, ed. see Dick, Philip K.
Letherby, Gayle. Feminist Research in Theory & Practice. (p. 581)
Letizia, Kenneth M. Go Ask Ally: Wearing Seat Belts Doesn't Change Lives, Not Wearing Them Does. (p. 686)
Leto, Frank & Scelsa, Greg. Let's Go to the Market. Faulkner, Stacey, ed. (p. 997)
LeTourneau, Anthony, illus. see Wiens, Patti.
LeTourneau, Anthony Alex. Hanni & Beth: Safe & Sound. (p. 743)
LeTourneau, Anthony Alex, illus. see Beyers, Andrea.
LeTourneau, Anthony Alex, illus. see Clark, Patricia Nikolina.
LeTourneau, Anthony Alex, illus. see Duncan, Karen & Issa, Kate Hannigan.
LeTourneau, Anthony Alex, jt. illus. see Bone, Thomas H.
Letourneau, Armand. Etymology of First Names. American-French Genealogical Society Staff, ed. (p. 540)
Letourneau, Cameron. Skyriders. (p. 1587)
LeTourneau, Marie, illus. see Paquette, Ammi-Joan.
LeTourneau, Marie, illus. see Wolff, Ferida & Savitz, Harriet May.
LeTourneau, Marie & Baty, Danielle Reed. Mice of Bistrot des Sept Frères. (p. 1134)
—Mice of Bistrot des Sept Frères. LeTourneau, Marie, illus. (p. 1134)
Letria, Andre. Donkey Reads (p. 466)
Letria, Andre, illus. see Letria, José Jorge.
Letria, Andre, illus. see Mejuto, Eva.
Letria, José Jorge. If I Were a Book. Letria, Andre, illus. (p. 853)
Let's Draw Studio Staff, illus. see Chanda, J-P.
Letscher, Lance. Perfect Machine. (p. 1342)
Lette, Lauren Britt. Kiwi's First Day of School. (p. 963)
Lettera, Janine Hamel. My First Day of School. (p. 1206)
Lettich, Sheldon, et al. Max: Best Friend, Hero, Marine. (p. 1110)
Lettrick, Robert. Frenzy. (p. 636)
—Murk. Disney Storybook Art Team, illus. (p. 1192)
Letts, Amelia. What Happens at an Orchard? Perform Multi-Digit Arithmetic. (p. 1886)
Letts, Jason. Inevitable. Hocking, Amanda, ed. (p. 873)
Léturgie, Jean & Fauche, Xavier. Daily Star. Morris, illus. (p. 400)
Leube, Karen, tr. see Häusler, Thomas.
Leuck, Laura. Goodnight, Baby Monster. (p. 701)
—Jeepers Creepers: A Monstrous ABC. Parkins, David, illus. (p. 911)
—My Beastly Brother. Nash, Scott, illus. (p. 1196)
—My Creature Teacher. Nash, Scott, illus. (p. 1200)
—Santa Claws. Grimly, Gris, illus. (p. 1511)
Leuck, Laura, jt. auth. see Chronicle Books Staff.
Leue, Mary, ed. see Barry, Jack.
Leue, Mary, illus. see Barry, Jack.

Leue, Mary, photos by see Barry, Jack.
Leuenberger, Constance J. New Kindergarten: Teaching, Reading, Writing, & More - A Mentor Teacher Shares Insights, Strategies, & Lessons That Give Kids a Strong Start in Building the Essential Skills They'll Need for Learning Success. (p. 1245)
Leuenroth, Stephanie. Hantavirus Pulmonary Syndrome. (p. 743)
Leung, Andrew, illus. see Masters, Elaine.
Leung, Bryce, jt. auth. see Shen, Kristy.
Leung, Erika. Dinosaur Hunt. (p. 442)
Leung, Helen. Toni. (p. 1765)
Leung, Hilary, illus. see Bruins, David.
Leung, Hilary, illus. see Leung, Peyton.
Leung, Peyton. Pirate Girl's Treasure. Leung, Hilary, illus. (p. 1362)
Leung, Raymond, illus. see Kavanagh, James.
Leunk, Thea. Fossils & Faith: Finding Our Way Through the Creation Controversy. (p. 624)
—Which Way to God? A Christian Look at World Religions. (p. 1911)
Leusted, Marcia Amidon & Amidon Lusted, Marcia. Money-Making Opportunities for Teens Who Like to Write. (p. 1164)
Leutwiler, Anita, illus. see Ravishankar, Anushka.
Levandowski, Barbara. Adventures of Muffin & Alexander: Let the Explorations Begin. (p. 21)
—Adventures of Muffin & Alexander: A New Home, a New Beginning. (p. 21)
—Adventures of Muffin & Alexander: The Please & Thank You Tea Party. (p. 21)
Levasseur, Jody Rogers. Forever Star. (p. 619)
LeVasseur, Michal L., jt. auth. see Jacobs, Heidi Hayes.
Leveen, Tom. Manicpixiedreamgirl. (p. 1087)
—Party. (p. 1325)
—Random. (p. 1438)
—Shackled: The Truth Doesn't Always Set You Free. (p. 1556)
—Sick. (p. 1572)
—Zero. (p. 1986)
Levene, Anna. My Friend Has Asthma. (p. 1209)
—My Friend Has Diabetes. (p. 1209)
—My Friend Has Epilepsy. (p. 1209)
—My Friend Is Deaf. (p. 1209)
Levene, Rebecca. Captain Cook. Cuzik, David, illus. (p. 264)
Levene, Rebecca, ed. Three Musketeers. Tavares, Victore, illus. (p. 1743)
Levenson, George. Bread Comes to Life: A Garden of Wheat & a Loaf to Eat. Thaler, Shmuel, photos by. (p. 224)
Leventhal-Belfer, Laurie. Why Do I Have To? A Book for Children Who Find Themselves Frustrated by Everyday Rules. Montaini-Klovdahl, Luisa, illus. (p. 1923)
Leventis, Kelly, jt. auth. see DiGuardo, Maggie.
Leveque, Anne-Claire. Mira Que Paso! (p. 1148)
Lever, Casey. Headgames. (p. 756)
Leverett S. Lyon. Elements of Debating. (p. 510)
Leverich, Jean. Abortion. (p. 5)
—Juvenile Justice. (p. 941)
Levering, Ralph B. Cold War, 1945-1991. Eisenstadt, Abraham S. & Franklin, John Hope, eds. (p. 339)
Levering, Vicki. Postcards from the Pound. (p. 1388)
Levering-Duff, Judy. Barnaby Wetzel, Boy Wizard. (p. 139)
—Medallion of Tiben: Book Two of the Adventures of Princess Isabella. (p. 1118)
LeVerrier, Renee. Four Friends. (p. 625)
Levert, Mireille. Nuits de Rose. (p. 1270)
—Princess Who Had Almost Everything. Masse, Josée, illus. (p. 1406)
LeVert, Mireille, illus. see Brown, Greg.
Levert, Mireille, illus. see Dyer, Heather.
LeVert, Suzanne. Botswana. (p. 215)
—Facts about Antidepressants. (p. 561)
—Facts about Nicotine. (p. 561)
—How States Make Laws. (p. 812)
—Louisiana. (p. 1058)
—Sierra Leone. (p. 1573)
—State Courts. (p. 1644)
—State Government. (p. 1644)
LeVert, Suzanne & Hendricks, Jeff. Ecstasy. (p. 503)
LeVert, Suzanne & Orr, Tamra. Massachusetts. (p. 1102)
LeVert, Suzanne & Whiting, Jim. Facts about Steroids. (p. 561)
Leverton, Yossi, ed. see Altein, Chani.
Leverton, Yossi, ed. see Benenfeld, Rikki.
Leverton, Yossi, ed. see Hodakov, Levi.
Leverton, Yossi, ed. see Levy, Leah.
Leverton, Yossi, ed. see Peysin, Shainy.
Leverton, Yossi, ed. see Simhaee, Rebeka.
Leveson, Sarah. From Tree to Book. (p. 644)
Levesque, Andy. Walden Vision Quest. (p. 1853)
Levesque, Catherine, jt. text see Noblet, Jean-François.
Levesque, Dawn Renee. Women Who Walk with the Sky. du Houx, Ramona, illus. (p. 1946)
Levesque, Haude, illus. see Brooklyn, Isabella.
LeVesque, Sherry, photos by see Cavanaugh, Wendy.
Levesque, Suzanne, tr. from ENG. Secret de Sindbad. (p. 1540)
Levete. Monster Trucks 6-Pack. (p. 1168)
Levete, Sarah. Afghanistan War: Frontline Soldiers & Their Families. (p. 26)
—Catastrophic Weather. (p. 278)
—Coming of Age. (p. 348)
—Death. (p. 420)
—Destroying the Oceans. (p. 431)
—Explaining Cerebral Palsy. (p. 549)
—Explaining Deafness. (p. 549)
—Food Around the World. (p. 613)
—Games Around the World. (p. 654)
—Habitats & Wildlife in Danger. (p. 734)
—Jungle Crash! (p. 935)
—Life in the Rain Forest. (p. 1011)
—Make an Animation! (p. 1079)
—Paper. (p. 1322)
—Race to Fix the Global Economy. (p. 1431)
—Rain Forest. (p. 1434)
—Rubber. (p. 1493)
—Save the Oceans. (p. 1516)
—Science Fact or Fiction? You Decide! (p. 1526)
—Taking Action Against Family Breakups. (p. 1698)
—Taking Action Against Internet Crime. (p. 1698)
—Tale of One Well in Malawi. (p. 1699)
—Toxins in the Food Chain. (p. 1774)
—Understanding the Heart, Lungs, & Blood. (p. 1816)
—Vietnam War: Frontline Soldiers & Their Families. (p. 1841)
—Wool. (p. 1950)
Levete, Sarah, jt. auth. see Ganeri, Anita.
Levey, Judith S. Scholastic First Dictionary. (p. 1522)
Levey, Michael. Book of the Holy Light. (p. 212)
Levey, Richard, jt. auth. see Ball, Jacqueline.
Levey, Richard H. Dust Bowl! The 1930s Black Blizzards. (p. 490)
Levey, Richard H., jt. auth. see Ball, Jacqueline.
Levi, Kevin B. Shred. (p. 1571)
Levigne, Heather. Arts Martiaux. Briere, Marie-Josee, tr. from ENG. (p. 105)
Levigne, Heather, jt. auth. see Kalman, Bobbie.
Levigne, Michelle. Commonwealth Universe: Modern Era. (p. 349)
Levin, Amy. Astronauts (p. 109)
—Bear's Year (p. 152)
—Hard Workers (p. 748)
—Vet (p. 1839)
Levin, Amy & Capstone Press Staff. Astronauts (p. 109)
—Bear's Year (p. 152)
—Hard Workers (p. 748)
—Vet (p. 1839)
Levin, Betty. Shoddy Cove. (p. 1568)
—Thorn. (p. 1740)
—Unmaking of Duncan Veerick. (p. 1821)
Levin, Daniel T. & Hammer, David. Becoming a Responsive Science Teacher: Focusing on Student Thinking in Secondary Science. (p. 156)
Levin, David H. Bridge Puzzles for Children: Simple Card Play Problems to Introduce Them to This Wonderful Game. Vol. 1 (p. 227)
Levin, Debra, ed. General Hospitals Planning & Design. (p. 660)
Levin, Freddie. 1-2-3 Draw Dogs. (p. 1990)
—1-2-3 Draw Horses. Levin, Freddie, illus. (p. 1990)
—1-2-3 Draw Mythical Creatures: A Step-by-Step Guide. Levin, Freddie, illus. (p. 1990)
—1-2-3 Draw Ocean Life. (p. 1990)
—ABC Fun Stained Glass Jr. Coloring Book. (p. 3)
—ABC Stained Glass Coloring Book. (p. 3)
—Chanukah Coloring Book. (p. 291)
—Glitter Hanukkah Stickers. (p. 684)
—Goodnight Stained Glass Coloring Book. (p. 701)
—Noah's Ark Stained Glass Coloring Book. (p. 1261)
—Outer Space Activity Book. (p. 1312)
—People. (p. 1339)
—Princesses. (p. 1406)
Levin, Freddie, illus. see Martin, Jannelle.
Levin, Freddie, illus. see Murray, Carol.
Levin, Freddie & Gordon, Freddie. 1-2-3 Draw Baby Animals. Levin, Freddie, illus. (p. 1990)
Levin, Gail, jt. see Levin, Herbert.
Levin, Herbert & Levin, Gail. Distant Bells: Twelve Melodies Arranged for Resonator Bells & Piano. (p. 453)
—Symphonics R Us. (p. 1693)
Levin, Ina. Journey to Athens: Grades 4-6. (p. 928)
—Olympic Experience in the School: Grades 1-3. (p. 1287)
—Olympic Experience in the School: Grades 4-6. (p. 1287)
Levin, Ina & Siskind, Ellyn. Journey to Athens: Grades 1-3. (p. 928)
Levin, Jack. Domestic Terrorism. (p. 465)
Levin, Jack E. & Levin, Mark R. George Washington: The Crossing. (p. 664)
Levin, Jonathan, ed. Walt Whitman. Burke, Jim, illus. (p. 1856)
Levin, Judith. Anxiety & Panic Attacks. (p. 90)
—Careers Creating Search Engines. (p. 267)
—Depression & Mood Disorders. (p. 427)
—Hammurabi. (p. 739)
—Ichiro Suzuki. (p. 851)
—Mariano Rivera. (p. 1093)
—Tattoos & Indigenous Peoples. (p. 1707)
Levin, Judith N. Careers Creating Search Engines. (p. 267)
Levin, Judy. Christopher Paul Curtis. (p. 317)
—Life at a High Altitude. (p. 1008)
—Timeline of the Abolitionist Movement. (p. 1754)
Levin, Judy & Draper, Allison Stark. Christopher Paul Curtis. (p. 317)
Levin, Kate, illus. see O'Connor, Jane.
Levin, Lon. I'm Going to Read (Level 4) The Small Potatoes Club. (p. 859)
—Small Potatoes Club. Levin, Lon, illus. (p. 1592)
Levin, Lon, illus. see Emerson, Carl.
Levin, Mark. Kids in Print: Publishing A School Newspaper. (p. 954)
Levin, Mark & Flackett, Jennifer. Family Hitchcock. (p. 568)
Levin, Mark R., jt. auth. see Levin, Jack E.
Levin, Michael. Start to Finish: Word Searches. (p. 1643)
Levin, Michael H. Start to Finish - Word Searches, Grades 3-4. (p. 1643)
Levin, Peter. Write Great Essays! Reading & Essay Writing for Undergraduates & Taught Postgraduates. (p. 1963)
Levin, Sue, jt. auth. see Skotko, Brian.
Levin, Vadim. Silly Horse. Wolfson, Tanya & Zunshine, Tatiana, trs. from RUS. (p. 1576)
Levine, Aaron D. Cloning. (p. 333)
Levine, Abby. Gretchen Groundhog, It's Your Day! Cote, Nancy, illus. (p. 723)
—This Is the Dreidel. Billin-Frye, Paige, illus. (p. 1736)
—This Is the Matzah. Billin-Frye, Paige, illus. (p. 1736)
Levine, Anna. Jodie's Hanukkah Dig. Topaz, Ksenia, illus. (p. 919)
—Jodie's Passover Adventure. Topaz, Ksenia, illus. (p. 919)
—Jodie's Shabbat Surprise. Topaz, Ksenia, illus. (p. 919)
Levine, Arthur A. Gold Medal Winter. (p. 693)
—Monday Is One Day. Hector, Julian, illus. (p. 1163)
—Very Beary Tooth Fairy. Brannen, Sarah S., illus. (p. 1837)
Levine, Barbara G., jt. auth. see Mogil, H. Michael.
Levine, Bdette M. Talking Baseball. (p. 1703)
Levine, Becky. For Life & Liberty: Causes & Effects of the Declaration of Independence (p. 615)
Levine, Becky, jt. auth. see Hall, Brianna.
Levine, Becky D. Hounds: Loyal Hunting Companions (p. 802)
Levine, Becky D., et al. Hunting Dogs: Loyal Hunting Companions. (p. 829)
Levine, Caroline Anne. Jay Grows an Alien. (p. 910)
Levine, Cory. Ghost Ship. Brown, Alan, illus. (p. 671)
Levine, Cory, jt. auth. see Smith, Brian.
Levine, Daniel U., jt. auth. see Ornstein, Allan C.
Levine, David & Kreitzer, Jerry. Peer Partners Handbook: Helping Your Friends Live Free from Violence, Drug Use, Teen Pregnancy & Suicide: a Guide to Students in Leadership Programs. (p. 1335)
Levine, Deborah A. & Riley, JillEllyn. Icing on the Cake. (p. 851)
—Kitchen Chaos. (p. 962)
Levine, Diana. Dancing Waves. (p. 403)
Levine, Ellen. Darkness over Denmark: The Danish Resistance & the Rescue of the Jews. (p. 408)
—Henry's Freedom Box: A True Story from the Underground Railroad. Nelson, Kadir, illus. (p. 769)
—In Trouble. (p. 868)
—Rachel Carson. (p. 1431)
Levine, Ellen & Megarry, Tim. Seababy: A Little Otter Returns Home. Van Zyle, Jon, illus. (p. 1536)
Levine, Ellen S., jt. auth. see Grambs, David L.
Levine, Gail C., jt. auth. see Levine, Gail Carson.
Levine, Gail Carson. Betsy Red Hoodie. Nash, Scott, illus. (p. 172)
—Betsy Who Cried Wolf. Nash, Scott, illus. (p. 172)
—Dave at Night. (p. 410)
—Ella Enchanted. (p. 513)
—Ella Enchanted. (p. 514)
—Enchanted Collection Box Set: Ella Enchanted, the Two Princesses of Bamarre, Fairest. (p. 523)
—Ever. (p. 541)
—Fairest. (p. 562)
—Fairy Haven & the Quest for the Wand. Christiana, David, illus. (p. 563)
—Forgive Me, I Meant to Do It: False Apology Poems. Schmid, Paul & Cordell, Matthew, illus. (p. 619)
—Pais de Nunca Jamas y el Secreto de la Hadas. Pombo, Juan Manuel, tr. (p. 1319)
—Princess Tales Elliott, Mark, illus. (p. 1405)
—Stolen Magic. (p. 1652)
—Tale of Two Castles. Call, Greg, illus. (p. 1700)
—Two Princesses of Bamarre. (p. 1804)
—Wish. (p. 1940)
—Writer to Writer: From Think to Ink. (p. 1964)
—Writing Magic: Creating Stories That Fly. (p. 1965)
Levine, Gail Carson & Levine, Gail C. Ella Enchanted. (p. 514)
—Fairest. (p. 562)
—Fairy's Return & Other Princess Tales. (p. 565)
—Writing Magic: Creating Stories That Fly. (p. 1965)
Levine, Gussie. Big Red Umbrella. (p. 183)
Levine, Harold. Vocabulary for the High School Student. (p. 1847)
Levine, Harold, et al. Vocabulary for the College-Bound Student. (p. 1847)
LeVine, Harry, III. Great Explainer: The Story of Richard Feynman. (p. 715)
Levine, Jason. Creature in the Patch. (p. 380)
Levine, Jennifer, illus. see Fabrikant, Amy.
Levine, Julia Pimsleur. Little Pim: Animals. (p. 1033)
—Little Pim - Feelings. (p. 1033)
—Little Pim: Numbers. (p. 1033)
Levine, Julia Pimsleur & Little Pim Corporation Staff. Little Pim: Colors. (p. 1033)
Levine, Karen. Hana's Suitcase: A True Story (p. 740)
—Hana's Suitcase Anniversary Album (p. 740)
—Hana's Suitcase on Stage (p. 740)
—Maleta de Hana: Un Relato Veridico. Kosmal, Mariana, tr. from ENG. (p. 1083)
Levine, Karen R. Daddy's Picture. Stasuyk, Max, illus. (p. 399)
Levine, Karen Rae. All about Color Blindness. (p. 42)
Levine, Kristin. Best Bad Luck I Ever Had. (p. 168)
—Lions of Little Rock. (p. 1021)
—Paper Cowboy. (p. 1322)
Levine, Lenora D., illus. see Gomes, Linda Nunes.
Levine, Mark H., jt. auth. see Schwartz, Barry L.
Levine, Martha Peaslee. Stop That Nose! White, Lee, illus. (p. 1653)
Levine, Mathea. I'm Lucy: A Day in the Life of a Young Bonobo. Brickner, Marian, illus. (p. 859)
Levine, Melvin D., contrib. by. Developing Minds Library (p. 431)
Levine, Michael K. Broken Windows, Broken Business: How the Smallest Remedies Reap the Biggest Rewards. (p. 230)
Levine, Michelle. Allergies. (p. 46)
—Amphibians. (p. 65)
—Asthma. (p. 108)
—Autism. (p. 117)
—Cerebral Palsy. (p. 287)
—Down Syndrome. (p. 474)
—Fish. (p. 598)
—Giant Pandas. (p. 674)
—Greeks: Life in Ancient Greece. Hiti, Samuel, illus. (p. 721)
—Jumping Kangaroos. (p. 934)
—Let's Look at Sea Otters. (p. 999)
—Mammals. (p. 1085)
—Red Foxes. (p. 1454)
—Reptiles. (p. 1461)
—Speedy Cheetahs. (p. 1624)
—Vehicles of the Vietnam War (p. 1834)
Levine, Michelle & Waxman, Laura. Let's Look at Sea Otters. (p. 999)
—Let's Look at Snails. (p. 999)
Levine, Michelle & Waxman, Laura Hamilton. Ambulances on the Move. (p. 57)
Levine, Phyllis. At the Skylight with Matilda. (p. 111)
—Matilda. (p. 1109)
—Matilda's Way. (p. 1109)
Levine, Rhoda. He Was There from the Day We Moved In. Gorey, Edward, illus. (p. 756)
—Three Ladies Beside the Sea. Gorey, Edward, illus. (p. 1742)
Levine, Robyn, illus. see Gabriel, Camila.
Levine, Sara. Bone by Bone: Comparing Animal Skeletons. Spookytooth, T. S., illus. (p. 208)
—Tooth by Tooth: Comparing Fangs, Tusks, & Chompers. Spookytooth, T. S., illus. (p. 1768)
Levine, Sara (Veterinarian). Tooth by Tooth. Spookytooth, T. S., illus. (p. 1768)
Levine, Shar. Animals. (p. 81)
—Bathtub Science. (p. 144)
—Plants: Flowering Plants, Ferns, Mosses, & Other Plants. (p. 1369)
Levine, Shar & Johnstone, Leslie. Scary Science: 25 Creepy Experiments. Spires, Ashley, illus. (p. 1520)
—Ultimate Guide to Your Microscope. (p. 1809)
—Volcanoes! (p. 1849)
Levine, Stuart P. Animals. (p. 81)
Levine, Susan Sachs. Harriett's Homecoming: A High-Flying Tour of Cincinnati. Burchwell, Erin, illus. (p. 750)
—Packard Takes Flight: A Bird's-Eye View of Columbus, Ohio. Burchwell, Erin McCauley, illus. (p. 1317)
Levine, Whitney Joy. Tiniest Reindeer. (p. 1755)
Levinge, Vivian & Corley, Suzanne. I've Always Wanted a Monkey. (p. 900)
Levinger, Elma Ehrli. Story of the Jew for Young People. (p. 1661)
Levins Morales, Ricardo, illus. see Ortiz, Teresa, et al.
Levins, Sandra. Bumblebee Bike. Keay, Claire, illus. (p. 241)
—Do You Sing Twinkle? A Story about Remarriage & New Family. Langdo, Bryan, illus. (p. 458)
—Eli's Lie-O-Meter: A Story about Telling the Truth. Ebbeler, Jeffrey, illus. (p. 513)
—Was It the Chocolate Pudding? A Story for Little Kids about Divorce. Langdo, Bryan, illus. (p. 1859)
Levins, Tim, illus. see Bird, Benjamin & Siegel, Jerry.
Levins, Tim, illus. see Bird, Benjamin.
Levins, Tim, illus. see Bright, J. E.
Levins, Tim, illus. see Korte, Steve.
Levins, Tim, illus. see Sautter, Aaron.
Levins, Tim, illus. see Weissburg, Paul.
Levinson, Cynthia. Watch Out for Flying Kids! (p. 1861)
—We've Got a Job: The 1963 Birmingham Children's March (p. 1877)
—Youngest Marcher: The Story of a Young Civil Rights Activist. Brantley-Newton, Vanessa, illus. (p. 1979)
Levinson, Cynthia Y. We've Got a Job: The 1963 Birmingham Children's March (p. 1877)
Levinson, Debra. Italy's Best with Kids: Extraordinary Places to Sleep, Eat & Play. (p. 895)
Levinson, Lara. Zachary's Dinnertime Van Wright, Cornelius, illus. (p. 1984)
Levinson, Marilyn. Rufus & Magic Run Amok (p. 1494)
Levinson, Nancy Smiler. Cars: A Holiday House Reader, Level 2. Rogers, Jacqueline, tr. (p. 272)
—Prairie Friends. Schuett, Stacey, illus. (p. 1392)
—Rain Forests. Hearn, Diane Dawson, illus. (p. 1434)
Levinson, Robin. Reyna & the Jade Star. (p. 1467)
Levinson, Robin K. Miriam's Journey: Discovering a New World. (p. 1149)
—Shoshana & the Native Rose. Kehl, Drusilla, illus. (p. 1569)
Levinthal, David. Who Pushed Humpty Dumpty? And Other Notorious Nursery Tale Mysteries. Nickle, John, illus. (p. 1917)
Levis, Caron. Stuck with the Blooz. Davis, Jon, illus. (p. 1669)
Leviskiy, Olga, illus. see Vojta, Pat Stemper.
Levison, Doug, jt. auth. see Dwyer, Joe.
Levison, Jesse. U Is for Underwear. (p. 1805)
Levitas, Alex, illus. see Alexandria, Chris.
Levitas, Alexander, illus. see Benatar, Raquel.
Levitas, Alexander, illus. see Brandeis, Batsheva.
Levitas, Alexander, illus. see Cohen, R. G.
Levitas, Ruth. Inclusive Society? Social Exclusion & New Labour. (p. 869)
Levithan, David. Another Day. (p. 87)
—Are We There Yet? (p. 96)
—Boy Meets Boy. (p. 218)
—Every Day. (p. 542)
—Every You, Every Me. Farmer, Jonathan, photos by. (p. 543)
—Every You, Every Me. Levithan, David & Farmer, Jonathan, photos by. (p. 543)
—Hold Me Closer: The Tiny Cooper Story. (p. 787)
—How They Met & Other Stories. (p. 814)
—Love Is the Higher Law. (p. 1060)
—Marly's Ghost. Selznick, Brian, illus. (p. 1096)
—Realm of Possibility. (p. 1450)
—Two Boys Kissing. (p. 1803)
—What We Remember, What We Forget: The Best Young Writers & Artists in America. Levithan, David, ed. (p. 1895)
—Wide Awake. (p. 1927)
Levithan, David, ed. see Melissa, De La Cruz, et al.
Levithan, David, jt. auth. see Cohn, Rachel.
Levithan, David, jt. auth. see Green, John.
Levithan, David & Ehrenhaft, Daniel. 21 Proms. (p. 1996)
Levithan, David & Merrell, Billy. Full Spectrum: A New Generation of Writing about Gay, Lesbian, Bisexual, Transgender, Questioning, & Other Identities. (p. 646)
Levithan, Ed., David. 21 Proms. (p. 1996)
Levitin, Sonia. Boom Town. Smith, Cat Bowman, illus. (p. 213)
—Junk Man's Daughter. Porfirio, Guy, illus. (p. 936)
Levitsky, Alexander, ed. see Matthiessen, F. O.
Levitsky, Alexander & Matthiessen, F. O. James Family: A Group Biography. (p. 907)
LeVitt, J. A. Ghsots of Whitner. LeVitt, Mike, illus. (p. 673)
LeVitt, Mike, illus. see LeVitt, J. A.
Levitt, Paul M., et al. Weighty Word Book. Stevens, Janet, illus. (p. 1872)
—Weighty Words, Too. Karcz, Katherine, illus. (p. 1872)
Levitt, Steve. Journey to the MountainA Roots Tale. (p. 929)
Levitt, Susan. Teen Feng Shui: Design Your Space, Design Your Life. (p. 1713)

L

Levitz, Paul. Ghost Stories. (p. 671)
Levitz, Paul & Conway, Gerry. Justice Society (p. 940)
Levivier, Juliette. Prayers Around the Crib. Gravier, Anne, illus. (p. 1393)
Levoy, Myron. Alan & Naomi. (p. 33)
Levy, Barbara Soloff. Dinosaurs Dot-to-Dot. (p. 444)
—Dot-To-Dot Fun. (p. 472)
—Drawing on the Go! Animals. (p. 482)
—Drawing on the Go! Lots of Things. (p. 482)
—How to Draw. (p. 816)
—How to Draw Ballet Pictures. (p. 817)
—How to Draw Bible Figures. (p. 817)
—How to Draw Christmas Pictures. (p. 817)
—How to Draw Circus Pictures. (p. 817)
—How to Draw Dogs. (p. 817)
—How to Draw Faces. (p. 817)
—How to Draw for All Seasons. (p. 817)
—How to Draw Forest Animals. (p. 817)
—How to Draw Halloween Pictures. (p. 817)
—How to Draw Mother Goose Characters. (p. 818)
—How to Draw Musical Instruments. (p. 818)
—How to Draw Pets. (p. 818)
—How to Draw Sports. (p. 818)
—I Can Draw Dinosaurs. (p. 835)
—I Can Draw Wizards, Dragons & Other Magical Creatures. (p. 835)
—Incredible Dot-To-Dot Book. (p. 869)
—Little Farm Follow-the-Dots. (p. 1027)
—Little Zoo Animal Mazes. (p. 1038)
—Pets Follow-the-Dots. (p. 1348)
—Sea Creatures: How to Draw with Simple Shapes. (p. 1534)
—Ultimate Dot-to-Dot Book. (p. 1809)
—Who's Who in the Zoo? Dot-to-Dot Fun. (p. 1921)
Levy, Barbara Soloff & Activity Books. Drawing on the Go! People. (p. 482)
—Drawing on the Go! under the Sea. (p. 482)
Levy, Barbara Soloff & Dover Publications Inc. Staff. I Can Draw Dogs. (p. 835)
Levy, Barbara Soloff & Drawing Staff. ART START Animals: How to Draw with Simple Shapes. (p. 103)
—ART START Funny Characters: How to Draw with Simple Shapes. (p. 103)
—How to Draw Aquarium Animals. (p. 816)
—How to Draw Pirates: Captain, Crew, Ships & More. (p. 818)
—How to Draw Princesses & Other Fairy Tale Pictures. (p. 818)
—You Can Draw Animals. (p. 1974)
Levy, Barrie. In Love & in Danger: A Teen's Guide to Breaking Free of Abusive Relationships. (p. 864)
Levy, Barry. How the Rules Were Made. (p. 813)
Levy, Carol L. Elphy Grey. (p. 516)
Levy, David B., illus. see Inches, Alison.
Levy, David B., illus. see Santomero, Angela C.
Levy, Debbie. Imperfect Spiral. (p. 862)
—Richard Wright: A Biography. (p. 1470)
—Signing of the Magna Carta. (p. 1574)
—Slaves on a Southern Plantation. (p. 1588)
—We Shall Overcome: The Story of a Song. Brantley-Newton, Vanessa, illus. (p. 1868)
—Year of Goodbyes: A True Story of Friendship, Family & Farewells. (p. 1969)
Levy, Debbie & Panza, Rosana. Dozer's Run: A True Story of a Dog & His Race. Opie, David, illus. (p. 474)
Levy, Didier & Rapaport, Gilles. Ernesto. (p. 534)
Levy, Duncan. Happy about Animals: An 8-Year-Old's View on Sharing the Earth. (p. 744)
—Happy about Animals: An 8-Year-Old's View (Now 11) on Sharing the Earth. (p. 744)
Levy, Elizabeth. Hare-Raising Tale. Gerstein, Mordicai, illus. (p. 748)
—Mixed-Up Mask Mystery: A Fletcher Mystery. Gerstein, Mordicai, illus. (p. 1156)
—Principal's on the Roof. Gerstein, Mordicai, illus. (p. 1406)
—Vampire State Building. Comport, Sally Wern, illus. (p. 1832)
Levy, Elizabeth & Brunkus, Denise. Mystery of the Missing Dog. (p. 1225)
Levy, Elizabeth & Coville, Bruce. Dragon of Doom. Gerstein, Mordicai & Coville, Katherine, illus. (p. 477)
Levy, Elizabeth & Havlan, J. R. Westward, Ha-Ha! 1800-1850. McFeeley, Dan, illus. (p. 1876)
Levy, Emily, rev. Strategies for Study Success: Highlighting I. (p. 1666)
Levy, Gavin, ed. 112 Acting Games: A Comprehensive Workbook of Theatre Games for Developing Acting Skills (p. 2000)
Levy, Janey. 20 Fun Facts about the Presidency. (p. 1995)
—20 Fun Facts about Women of the Middle Ages. (p. 1995)
—Alopecia Areata. (p. 48)
—Architecture of Frank Lloyd Wright: Understanding the Concepts of Parallel & Perpendicular. (p. 95)
—Arkansas: Past & Present. (p. 99)
—At Sea on a Viking Ship: Solving Problems of Length & Weight Using the Four Math Operations. (p. 110)
—Battle of the Alamo. (p. 146)
—Breaking the Code with Cryptography: Analyzing Patterns. (p. 225)
—Careers in Criminal Profiling. (p. 267)
—City of Pompeii. (p. 324)
—Dale Earnhardt, Jr. (p. 401)
—Discovering Coral Reefs. (p. 449)
—Discovering Mountains. (p. 449)
—Discovering Rain Forests. (p. 449)
—Discovering the Arctic Tundra. (p. 449)
—Discovering the Tropical Savanna. (p. 450)
—Edwin Visits Earth. (p. 505)
—Esophageal Cancer. (p. 536)
—Freestyle Motocross. (p. 635)
—Genocide in Darfur. (p. 661)
—Great Pyramid of Giza: Measuring Length, Area, Volume, & Angles. (p. 718)
—Illegal Immigration & Amnesty: Open Borders & National Security. (p. 857)
—Iran & the Shia. (p. 886)
—Islamic Art: Recognizing Geometric Ideas in Art. (p. 891)
—Jenny in the Jungle. (p. 913)
—Journey along the Erie Canal: Dividing Multidigit Numbers by a One-Digit Number Without Remainders. (p. 927)
—Juneteenth: Celebrating the End of Slavery. (p. 934)
—Keeping Time Through the Ages: The History of Tools Used to Measure Time. (p. 948)
—Kurt Busch. (p. 968)
—Language Development Writing Process. (p. 975)
—Life During the Gold Rush. (p. 1010)
—Life in a Rain Forest Ecosystem. (p. 1010)
—Life on a Wagon Train. (p. 1012)
—Magna Carta. (p. 1075)
—Making Good Choices about Conservation. (p. 1081)
—Mapping America's Westward Expansion: Applying Geographic Tools & Interpreting Maps. (p. 1090)
—Mapping Australia. (p. 1090)
—Mexico. (p. 1131)
—Michigan: Past & Present. (p. 1135)
—Motocross. (p. 1179)
—Motocross. (p. 1179)
—Motocross Races. (p. 1179)
—Motocross Superstars. (p. 1179)
—Motocross Tricks. (p. 1179)
—Native American Art from the Pueblos. (p. 1234)
—Native Americans in Texas. (p. 1234)
—Piggies Picnic. (p. 1358)
—Play Ball! (p. 1371)
—Primary Source Guide to Kenya. (p. 1399)
—Racing Through History: Stock Cars Then to Now. (p. 1432)
—Recipes for a Medieval Feast: Working Flexibly with Fractions. (p. 1451)
—Recipes for a Medieval Feast: Medieval Feast: Working Flexibly with Fractions. (p. 1451)
—Refugee Workers. (p. 1456)
—Renaissance Paintings: Using Perspective to Represent Three-Dimensional Objects. (p. 1460)
—Silk Road: Using A Map Scale to Measure Distances. (p. 1575)
—Silk Road: Using a Map Scale to Measure Distances. (p. 1575)
—Spanish Explorers of North America. (p. 1621)
—Supercross. (p. 1683)
—Tiny Bugs up Close. (p. 1756)
—UFOs. (p. 1807)
—Wampanoag of Massachusetts & Rhode Island. (p. 1856)
—What Lives on a Prairie? (p. 1892)
—What Would I Wear? (p. 1895)
—William Penn: Shaping a Nation. (p. 1933)
—World of Microbes: Bacteria, Viruses, & Other Microorganisms. (p. 1957)
—World's Worst Earthquakes. (p. 1961)
—World's Worst Fires. (p. 1961)
—World's Worst Floods. (p. 1961)
—World's Worst Hurricanes. (p. 1961)
—World's Worst Tsunamis. (p. 1961)
—World's Worst Volcanic Eruptions. (p. 1961)
Levy, Janey, jt. auth. see Keller, Susanna.
Levy, Janey, jt. auth. see Sahgal, Lara.
Levy, Janey, jt. auth. see Schimel, Kate.
Levy, Janey & Donnell, Kerri. Missions of Texas. (p. 1154)
Levy, Janice. Alley Oops. Decker, C. B., illus. (p. 47)
—Diva Duck Dreams. Madden, Colleen M., illus. (p. 454)
—Diva Duck Goes to Hollywood. Madden, Colleen M., illus. (p. 454)
—Diva Duck Travels the World. Madden, Colleen M., illus. (p. 454)
—Finding the Right Spot: When Kids Can't Live with Their Parents. Martin, Whitney, illus. (p. 588)
—Flip-Flop & the Absolutely Awful New Baby. Madden, Colleen M., illus. (p. 605)
—Flip-Flop & the BFFs. Madden, Colleen M., illus. (p. 605)
—Flip-Flop & the Bully Frogs Gruff. Madden, Colleen M., illus. (p. 605)
—Gonzalo Grabs the Good Life. Slavin, Bill, illus. (p. 697)
—I Remember Abuelito/Yo Recuerdo a Abuelito: A Day of the Dead Story / un Cuento del Dia de los Muertos. Arisa, Miguel, tr. (p. 844)
—Runaway Radish/El Rabano Que Escapo. de la Vega, Eida, tr. (p. 1496)
—School Rules for Diva Duck. Madden, Colleen M., illus. (p. 1523)
—Showtime for Flip-Flop. Madden, Colleen M., illus. (p. 1571)
Levy, Janice & Arisa, Miguel. I Remember Abuelito: A Day of the Dead Story. Lopez, Loretta, illus. (p. 844)
Levy, Joan & Levy, Norman, creators. Ultimate ACT Test Preparation. (p. 1809)
Levy, Joanne. Small Medium at Large. (p. 1592)
Levy, Joel. Phobiapedia. (p. 1351)
Levy, Leah. Waiting Wall. Rosenfeld, D. L. & Leverton, Yossi, eds. (p. 1853)
Levy, Marianne. Ellie May Is Totally Happy to Share Her Place in the Spotlight. (p. 514)
Levy, Marilyn. Checkpoints. (p. 295)
Levy, Matthys & Salvadori, Mario. Earthquakes, Volcanoes, & Tsunamis: Projects & Principles for Beginning Geologists. (p. 498)
Levy, Max. Brief Jewish Biographies in Biblical, Post-Biblical & Talmudical Times. (p. 227)
Levy, Meredith. Interactive. (p. 879)
—Interactive Level 1 Workbook with Downloadable Audio. (p. 879)
—Interactive Level 3 Workbook with Downloadable Audio. (p. 879)
Levy, Michael. Inspiring Story of Little Goody Two Shoes. (p. 878)
—Joys of Live Alchemy. (p. 930)
Levy, Michelle. Not after Everything. (p. 1266)
Levy, Nathan, jt. auth. see Michels, Dia.
Levy, Nathan, jt. auth. see Segal, Kevin.
Levy, Norman, jt. creator see Levy, Joan.
Levy, P., et al. Scotland. (p. 1530)
Levy, Pamela R., illus. see Baker, Ginger.
Levy, Pamela R., illus. see Nelson, Steve & Rollins, Jack.
Levy, Pamela R., illus. see Shreeve, Elizabeth.
Levy, Pat, jt. auth. see Sheehan, Sean.
Levy, Patricia. From Punk Rock to Perestroika: The Mid 1970s to the Mid 1980s. (p. 643)
—From Speakeasies to Stalinism: The 1920s to the Mid-1930s. (p. 643)
—Holocaust. (p. 789)
—Ireland. (p. 887)
—Modern Eras Uncovered: From Beatlemania to Watergate. (p. 1158)
—Modern Eras Uncovered: From Punk Rock to Perestroika. (p. 1158)
—Modern Eras Uncovered: From Compact Discs to the Gulf War. (p. 1158)
—Modern Eras Uncovered: From the World Wide Web to September 11. (p. 1158)
Levy, Patricia, jt. auth. see Sheehan, Sean.
Levy, Patricia & Bahrawi, Nazry. Puerto Rico. (p. 1415)
Levy, Patricia & Bosco, Don. Tibet. (p. 1747)
Levy, Patricia & Latif, Zawiah Abdul. Sudan. (p. 1672)
Levy, Patricia & Nevins, Debbie. Ireland. (p. 887)
Levy, Patricia & Sheehan, Sean. From Compact Discs to the Gulf War: The Mid 1980s to the Early 1990s. (p. 642)
—From the World Wide Web to September 11: The Early 1990s to 2001. (p. 644)
—Modern Eras Uncovered: From the World Wide Web to September 11. (p. 1158)
Levy, Patricia & Spilling, Michael. Belarus. (p. 161)
—Liberia: By Patricia Levy & Michael Spilling. (p. 1005)
Levy, Patricia & Wong, Winnie. Ghana. (p. 670)
Levy, Patricia, et al. Switzerland. (p. 1692)
Levy, Robert. Not Just Mustard & Ketchup/ No Solo Mostaza y Salsa de Tomate. (p. 1267)
Levy, Rochel. Moshe Goes to Yeshiva. David, Racheli, illus. (p. 1176)
Levy, Ruth, illus. see Morris, Ting & Morris, Neil.
Levy, Shaun, illus. see Fiddick, Calay.
Levy, Stuart. Karma Club (p. 944)
Levy, Talia. Scratch & Sketch Trace-Along Doodle Mania: An Art Activity Book for Imaginative Artists of All Ages. Zschock, Martha Day, illus. (p. 1532)
Lew, Kristi. 15 Lanthanides & the 15 Actinides. (p. 1995)
—Antibiotics. (p. 89)
—Argon. (p. 98)
—Bat Spit, Maggots, & Other Amazing Medical Wonders (p. 143)
—Biochemistry. (p. 188)
—Chemical Reactions. (p. 297)
—Clot & Scab: Gross Stuff about Your Scrapes, Bumps, & Bruises. Slack, Michael H., illus. (p. 334)
—Cool Biology Activities for Girls (p. 362)
—Dwarf Planet Pluto. (p. 491)
—Egg Donation: The Reasons & the Risks. (p. 506)
—Electricity & Magnetism. (p. 509)
—Evolution: The Adaptation & Survival of Species. (p. 546)
—Exterminator: Wiping Out the World's Most Infectious Diseases. (p. 555)
—Farts, Vomit, & Other Functions That Help Your Body (p. 575)
—Fishing the Flats. (p. 599)
—Heredity. (p. 771)
—I Have an Eating Disorder, Now What? (p. 839)
—Iodine. (p. 886)
—Laurie Halse Anderson. (p. 980)
—Mercury. (p. 1127)
—Monsters, Beasts, & Demons in America. (p. 1169)
—Mosquito-Borne Illnesses. (p. 1176)
—North Carolina: Past & Present. (p. 1264)
—Ohio: Past & Present. (p. 1281)
—Powering up a Career in Nanotechnology. (p. 1391)
—Respiratory System. (p. 1463)
—Science Experiments That Fly & Move: Fun Projects for Curious Kids (p. 1525)
—Truth about Cancer: Understanding & Fighting a Deadly Disease. (p. 1794)
—Truth about Oxycodone & Other Narcotics. (p. 1794)
—Volt. (p. 1849)
Lew, Kristi, jt. auth. see Corrick, James A.
Lew, Kristi & Lewandowski, Laura C. Goodbye, Gasoline: The Science of Fuel Cells (p. 701)
—Human Organs (p. 826)
—Itch & Ooze: Gross Stuff on Your Skin. Slack, Michael H., illus. (p. 895)
Lewallen, Shirley Ann & Svensson, Schery Kay, eds. Muffin Tree. (p. 1189)
Lewandowski, James E. Christmas Box: An Eerie Tale of the Perfect Gift. (p. 313)
—Road Hunter in the Land between the Rivers: A Soldier's Story of the Iraq War. (p. 1476)
Lewandowski, Laura C., jt. auth. see Lew, Kristi.
Lewandowski, Lisa & Trost, Shannon. Darcy Daisy & the Firefly Festival: Learning about Bipolar Disorder & Community. Shaw-Peterson, Kimberly, illus. (p. 406)
Lewelin, Kelvin. Cruelty Has a Human Heart. (p. 386)
Lewellen, Emily, illus. see Curatola Knowles, Carmela N.
Lewellen, LaRose. Grasp on Reality: Breaking It down for Our Teens. (p. 711)
Lewellyn, Claire. Ladybug. Mendez, Simon, illus. (p. 971)
Lewellyn, Natalie. Nutty to Meet You! Dr. Peanut Book #1. (p. 1274)
Lewers, Rob & Murphy, Ed. Hidden Hurt: How to Beat Bullying in Schools. (p. 775)
Lewicki, Krys Val. Thanksgiving Day in Canada. Auml, Ana, illus. (p. 1726)
Lewin, Betsy. Good Night, Knight. Lewin, Betsy, illus. (p. 699)
—Scholastic Reader Level 1: Groundhog Day. (p. 1522)
—Thumpy Feet. (p. 1746)
—Thumpy Feet. Lewin, Betsy, illus. (p. 1746)
—Where Is Tippy Toes? Lewin, Betsy, illus. (p. 1909)
—You Can Do It! (p. 1974)
—You Can Do It! Lewin, Betsy, illus. (p. 1974)
Lewin, Betsy, illus. see Cronin, Doreen & Jiménez Rioja, Alberto.
Lewin, Betsy, illus. see Cronin, Doreen & Simon and Schuster/LeapFrog Staff.
Lewin, Betsy, illus. see Cronin, Doreen.
Lewin, Betsy, illus. see Koller, Jackie French.
Lewin, Betsy, illus. see Kuskin, Karla.
Lewin, Betsy, illus. see Silverman, Erica.
Lewin, Betsy, illus. see Weeks, Sarah.
Lewin, Betsy, illus. see Winthrop, Elizabeth.
Lewin, Betsy, jt. auth. see Cronin, Doreen.
Lewin, Betsy, jt. auth. see Lewin, Ted.
Lewin, Betsy, jt. auth. see Silverman, Erica.
Lewin, Betsy, jt. auth. see Weeks, Sarah.
Lewin, Rhoda. Reform Jews of Minneapolis. (p. 1456)
Lewin, Russ, ed. see Gardner, Jane P.
Lewin, Russ, ed. see Gardner, Jane.
Lewin, Ted. Animals Work. Lewin, Ted, illus. (p. 84)
—At Gleason's Gym. Lewin, Ted, illus. (p. 110)
—Can You See Me? Lewin, Ted, illus. (p. 259)
—How Much? Visiting Markets Around the World. Lewin, Ted, illus. (p. 811)
—I See & See. (p. 845)
—Look! Lewin, Ted, illus. (p. 1047)
—Lost City: The Discovery of Machu Picchu. Lewin, Ted, illus. (p. 1055)
—What Am I? Where Am I? (p. 1879)
—What Am I? Where Am I? Lewin, Ted, illus. (p. 1879)
Lewin, Ted, illus. see Bartone, Elisa.
Lewin, Ted, illus. see Bauer, Marion Dane.
Lewin, Ted, illus. see Bunting, Eve.
Lewin, Ted, illus. see Chaconas, Dori.
Lewin, Ted, illus. see Helfer, Ralph.
Lewin, Ted, illus. see Knudson, R. R.
Lewin, Ted, illus. see Love, Maryann Cusimano.
Lewin, Ted, illus. see O'Dell, Scott.
Lewin, Ted, illus. see Oberman, Sheldon.
Lewin, Ted, jt. auth. see Lewin, Ted.
Lewin, Ted & Lewin, Betsy. Balarama: A Royal Elephant. Lewin, Ted & Lewin, Betsy, illus. (p. 133)
—How to Babysit a Leopard: And Other True Stories from Our Travels Across Six Continents. (p. 814)
Lewin, Ted & Lewin, Ted. Can You See Me? (p. 259)
Lewin, Terry. God Remembered Us. Gumm, Susan Kathleen, illus. (p. 690)
Lewinski, Marcel. Great Decisions 2005. Rohan, Karen M., ed. (p. 715)
Lewis. Tomboy Terror in Bunk 109. (p. 1764)
—Want to Trade Two Brothers for a Cat? (p. 1856)
Lewis, A. David. Some New Kind of Slaughter: Or, Lost in the Flood (And How We Found Home Again) mpMann, illus. (p. 1609)
Lewis, Adam. Life in India. (p. 1010)
Lewis, Alan K. I Grew up on a Farm. Fletcher, Bob, illus. (p. 838)
Lewis, Alaric. When Someone You Love Has Cancer: A Guide to Help Kids Cope. Alley, R. W., illus. (p. 1904)
Lewis, Alexandra. Ultimate Jump Rope Book. (p. 1809)
Lewis, Ali. Timber Creek Station. (p. 1750)
Lewis, Amos L. Pearls of Wisdom Study Guide & Devotional. (p. 1333)
Lewis, Andre. Pay to Play (p. 1331)
Lewis, Angela, ed. Child Sexual Abuse. (p. 301)
Lewis, Ann. Atlantis. (p. 112)
Lewis, Anna. City Doodles - Chicago. Chaffin, Daniel, illus. (p. 323)
Lewis, Anna M. Women of Steel & Stone: 22 Inspirational Architects, Engineers, & Landscape Designers. (p. 1946)
Lewis, Anne. Atlantis. (p. 112)
—Dragonchild. (p. 478)
Lewis, Anne G. Perfect Tree for Christmas. Stahlberg, Carina, illus. (p. 1342)
Lewis, Anne Gillespie, ed. see Rydaker, Ewa.
Lewis, Anne Margaret. Fly Blanky Fly. Chavarri, Elisa, illus. (p. 609)
—Hidden Pumpkins. DeWildt, Jim, illus. (p. 776)
—Runaway Mitten. Zenz, Aaron, illus. (p. 1496)
—Runaway Pumpkin. Zenz, Aaron, illus. (p. 1496)
—Sleeping Bear: Journey of the Cub Book 1. (p. 1589)
—Sleeping Bear: The Legend. Grant, Sarah, illus. (p. 1589)
—Tears of Mother Bear. Fritz, Kathleen Cheney, illus. (p. 1711)
—What Am I? Easter. Mills, Tom, illus. (p. 1879)
—What am I? Christmas. Mills, Tom, illus. (p. 1879)
—What Am I? Florida. Mills, Tom, illus. (p. 1879)
—What Am I? Halloween. Mills, Tom, illus. (p. 1879)
—What am I? Illinois. Mills, Tom, illus. (p. 1879)
—What Am I? New Jersey. DeWildt, Jim, illus. (p. 1879)
—What Am I? Passover. Mills, Tom, illus. (p. 1879)
—What Am I? Texas. Mills, Tom, illus. (p. 1879)
Lewis, Anne Margaret & Campbell, Janis. Hidden Michigan. Popko, Wendy, illus. (p. 776)
Lewis, Anthony. Bath or Bed? (p. 144)
—Carrots or Peas? (p. 271)
—Five Little Ducks. (p. 600)
—Humpty Dumpty: Asl. (p. 827)
—Jack & Jill. (p. 902)
—Little Jungle Explorers. (p. 1029)
—Little Ocean Explorers. (p. 1032)
—Little Snow Explorers. (p. 1036)
—Little Space Explorers. (p. 1036)
—Meal Time. (p. 1116)
—Old MacDonald. (p. 1284)
—Play Time. (p. 1371)
—Teddy or Train? (p. 1712)
—Wheels on the Bus: Asl. (p. 1901)
—Wind or Rain? (p. 1935)
Lewis, Anthony, illus. see Bauer, Marion Dane.
Lewis, Anthony, illus. see Brooks, Susie.
Lewis, Anthony, illus. see Chancellor, Deborah.
Lewis, Anthony, illus. see Danziger, Paula, et al.
Lewis, Anthony, illus. see Davidson, Alice Joyce.
Lewis, Anthony, illus. see Goodhart, Pippa.
Lewis, Anthony, illus. see James, Anne.
Lewis, Anthony, illus. see Jensen, Patricia.
Lewis, Anthony, illus. see Murrell, Deborah & Brooks, Susie.
Lewis, Anthony, illus. see Murrell, Deborah.
Lewis, Anthony, illus. see Nilsen, Anna.
Lewis, Anthony, illus. see Piper, Sophie.
Lewis, Anthony, illus. see Powell, Marie.
Lewis, Anthony, illus. see Rock & Piper, Sophie.

Lewis, Anthony, illus. see Slater, Teddy.
Lewis, Anthony, illus. see Wargin, Kathy-jo.
Lewis, Ashley. Roads to Rodeos. (p. 1477)
Lewis, Axel. Arctic Adventure (p. 95)
—Canyon Chaos (p. 262)
—Desert Disaster (p. 429)
—Rain Forest Rampage. (p. 1434)
—Robot Races (p. 1480)
Lewis, Barbara A. Kid's Guide to Service Projects: Over 500 Service Ideas for Young People Who Want to Make a Difference. (p. 953)
—What Do You Stand For? For Teens: A Guide to Building Character. Espeland, Pamela, ed. (p. 1883)
—What Do You Stand for? a Kid's Guide ToBuilding Character. (p. 1883)
—What Do You Stand For? - For Kids: A Guide to Building Character. Lisovskis, Marjorie, ed. (p. 1883)
Lewis, Barbara A. & Free Spirit Publishing Staff. What Do You Stand For? Character Building. (p. 1883)
Lewis, Benjamin E., illus. see Scheve, Janice Rose.
Lewis, Beverly. Eight Is Enough. (p. 507)
—Girls Only! (p. 680)
—Holly's Heart. (p. 789)
—Holly's Heart Collection (p. 789)
—In Jesse's Shoes: Appreciating Kids with Special Needs. Nikiel, Laura Gibbons, illus. (p. 864)
—SummerHill Secrets. (p. 1675)
—What Is God Like? Querin, Pamela, illus. (p. 1889)
—What Is Heaven Like? Querin, Pamela, illus. (p. 1889)
Lewis, Beverly & Querin, Pamela. Annika's Secret Wish. (p. 87)
Lewis, Bisa. Let's Potty! Floyd, John, Jr., illus. (p. 1000)
Lewis, Bisa, as told by. How Flowers Get Their Colors. (p. 809)
Lewis, Brenda Ralph. Crabs & Mollusks. (p. 375)
—Firefighters. (p. 591)
—Hostage Rescue with the FBI. (p. 801)
—Lizards. (p. 1043)
—Meat-Eating Dinosaurs. (p. 1118)
—Plant-Eating Dinosaurs. (p. 1369)
—Poisonous Snakes. (p. 1377)
—Prehistoric Creatures in the Sea & Sky. (p. 1395)
—Sharks. (p. 1562)
—Small & Deadly Dinosaurs. (p. 1591)
—Wilderness Rescue with the U. S. Search & Rescue Task Force. (p. 1931)
Lewis, Brian, jt. auth. see Jaskol, Julie.
Lewis, Brooke & Varacalli, Lauren. Dickinson College College Prowler off the Record. (p. 436)
Lewis, Bryan. Tiny World You Can't See. (p. 1757)
Lewis, Buddy, illus. see Cole, Burton.
Lewis, C. A. Harold the Sparrow & His Bellybutton. (p. 749)
Lewis, C. Robbie. Rapunzel. (p. 1439)
Lewis, C. S. Armoire Magique. (p. 99)
—Chronicles of Narnia. Baynes, Pauline, illus. (p. 317)
—Horse & His Boy. Baynes, Pauline, illus. (p. 799)
—Las Cronicas de Narnia. Baynes, Pauline, illus. (p. 976)
—Last Battle. Baynes, Pauline, illus. (p. 977)
—Leon, la Bruja y el Ropero. (p. 992)
—Lion, the Witch & the Wardrobe. Baynes, Pauline, illus. (p. 1020)
—Lion, the Witch & the Wardrobe. Humphries, Tudor, illus. (p. 1020)
—Magician's Nephew. Baynes, Pauline, illus. (p. 1075)
—Magician's Nephew. Baynes, Pauline & Van Allsburg, Chris, illus. (p. 1075)
—Neveu du Magicien. (p. 1243)
—Prince Caspian: The Return to Narnia. Baynes, Pauline, illus. (p. 1401)
—Prince Caspian. (p. 1401)
—Prince Caspian. Baynes, Pauline, illus. (p. 1401)
—Principe Caspian. Gallart, Gemma, tr. (p. 1406)
—Prinz Kaspian Von Narnia. (p. 1407)
—Silberne Sessel. (p. 1575)
—Silla de Plata Gallart, Gemma, tr. (p. 1575)
—Silver Chair. Baynes, Pauline, illus. (p. 1576)
—Voyage of the Dawn Treader. Baynes, Pauline, illus. (p. 1850)
Lewis, C. S., jt. auth. see Baynes, Pauline.
Lewis, C. S., jt. auth. see Peacock, Ann.
Lewis, C. S. & Orem, Hiawyn. Lion, the Witch & the Wardrobe. Humphries, Tudor, illus. (p. 1020)
Lewis, C. S., et al. Cuatro Amigos. (p. 388)
Lewis, Calvin, Jr & Wilhite, Susan L. It Comes in the Night: Speaking Eagle, Book One. (p. 893)
Lewis, Carole. Back on Track. (p. 130)
—Choosing to Change: The First Place Challenge. (p. 310)
—First Place: Lose Weight & Keep It off Forever. (p. 596)
—First Place Food Exchange Pocket Guide. (p. 596)
—First Place Group Starter Kit. (p. 596)
—Life That Wins. (p. 1013)
—Life under Control. (p. 1013)
—Living in Grace (p. 1041)
—Living the Legacy. (p. 1041)
—Making Wise Choices. (p. 1082)
—New First Place Favorites. (p. 1244)
—Pathway to Success. (p. 1328)
—Pressing on to the Prize. (p. 1397)
—Seeking God's Best. (p. 1548)
Lewis, Carole & Symank, Cara. Mother-Daughter Legacy: How a Mother's Love Shapes a Daughter's Life. (p. 1177)
Lewis, Carolyn. Hairy Beary Book Two: The Great Waterfall Bk. 2,Vol. 2 DeVince, James, ed. (p. 736)
Lewis, Carolyn & DeVince, James. Hairy Beary Adventure Series DeVince, James, ed. (p. 736)
—Hairy Beary Book Three: The Blue Ribbon Hero DeVince, James, ed. (p. 736)
Lewis, Caryl & Lolfa, Y. lawn Boi? (p. 849)
Lewis, Catherine. Thrice Told Tales: Three Mice Full of Writing Advice. Swarte, Joost, illus. (p. 1744)
Lewis, Cerise D. Be Encouraged: Words of Encouragement to Change Your Outlook on Life (p. 148)
Lewis, Charlotte, jt. auth. see Mills, Nathan.
Lewis, Cindi. Banjo Backwards. (p. 136)
Lewis, Cindy (Didas). Sugar Spigot. (p. 1673)
—Time to Head South with Cindy the Canadian Goose (p. 1753)
Lewis, Clarajane. House on the Hill. (p. 803)
Lewis, Clare. Amphibian Body Parts. (p. 65)
—Animal Body Parts. (p. 76)
—Around the World (p. 100)
—Bird Body Parts. (p. 190)
—Bug Body Parts. (p. 236)
—Clothes Around the World (p. 334)
—Entertainment Through the Years: How Having Fun Has Changed in Living Memory. (p. 531)
—Families Around the World (p. 567)
—Fish Body Parts. (p. 598)
—Games Around the World (p. 654)
—History in Living Memory. (p. 783)
—Homes Around the World (p. 793)
—Mammal Body Parts. (p. 1084)
—Reptile Body Parts. (p. 1461)
—Schools Around the World (p. 1524)
—Shopping Around the World (p. 1569)
Lewis, Clare, jt. auth. see Beaumont, Holly.
Lewis, Corey. Seedless OGN. (p. 1547)
—Sharknife. (p. 1562)
Lewis, Corey & Ko, Erik. Rival Schools. (p. 1475)
Lewis, Cynthia, illus. see Cobb, Vicki.
Lewis, D. Geraint. Shorter Welsh Dictionary. (p. 1569)
Lewis, Daisy. Pequeno Don Cisco. (p. 1341)
Lewis, Dana, tr. see Fujishima, Kosuke.
Lewis, Dana, tr. see Samura, Hiroaki.
Lewis, Dana & Fujishima, Kosuke. Oh My Goddess! (p. 1280)
Lewis, Darlene. Don't Be Stupid, Advice for Young People & a Few Old Fools. (p. 467)
Lewis, David. Body Language of Children: How Children Talk Before They Can Speak. (p. 207)
Lewis, David, tr. see Miyazaki, Hayao.
Lewis, David & Dugas, Lisa, eds. Hill House Speaks. (p. 779)
Lewis, Dawn, jt. auth. see Jacks, Cyndie.
Lewis, Dawn & Jacks, Cyndie. Plants. Jennett, Pamela & Rous, Sheri, eds. (p. 1369)
Lewis, Deborah Shaw, jt. auth. see Lewis, Gregg.
Lewis, Doreen. Bubblegum Babes' Guide to Sixth Grade. (p. 233)
Lewis, E. B. Everlasting Embrace. (p. 542)
Lewis, E. B., illus. see Bass, Hester & Anderson, Walter Inglis.
Lewis, E. B., illus. see Bass, Hester.
Lewis, E. B., illus. see Curtis, Gavin.
Lewis, E. B., illus. see Grimes, Nikki.
Lewis, E. B., illus. see Howard, Elizabeth Fitzgerald.
Lewis, E. B., illus. see Kearney, Meg.
Lewis, E. B., illus. see Lyons, Kelly Starling.
Lewis, E. B., illus. see Michelson, Richard.
Lewis, E. B., illus. see Noble, Trinka Hakes.
Lewis, E. B., illus. see Nolen, Jerdine.
Lewis, E. B., illus. see Norman, Geoffrey.
Lewis, E. B., illus. see Raven, Margot Theis.
Lewis, E. B., illus. see Rodman, Mary Ann.
Lewis, E. B., illus. see Sanders, Nancy I.
Lewis, E. B., illus. see Slate, Joseph.
Lewis, E. B., illus. see Smith, Hope Anita.
Lewis, E. B., illus. see Stiegemeyer, Julie.
Lewis, E. B., illus. see Tarpley, Natasha Anastasia.
Lewis, E. B., illus. see Wong, Janet S.
Lewis, E. B., illus. see Woodson, Jacqueline.
Lewis, E. B. & Public Domain Staff. This Little Light of Mine. (p. 1737)
Lewis, Earl, illus. see Rodman, Mary Ann.
Lewis, Earl, illus. see Woodson, Jacqueline.
Lewis, Earl B., illus. see Goodman, Susan E.
Lewis, Earl B., illus. see San Souci, Robert D.
Lewis, Earl B., jt. auth. see Carbone, Elisa.
Lewis, Edwina. Who Eats? Parker, Ant, illus. (p. 1915)
—Who Jumps? Parker, Ant, illus. (p. 1916)
—Who Plays? Parker, Ant, illus. (p. 1917)
—Who Swims? Parker, Ant, illus. (p. 1917)
Lewis, Elfyn. Scruff & Friends. (p. 1533)
Lewis, Elisa. Priodas Branwen. (p. 1407)
Lewis, Elizabeth Foreman. Young Fu of the Upper Yangtze. Low, William & Cobalt Illustrations Studio Staff, illus. (p. 1978)
Lewis, Ellen Parry. Unremarkable Girl. (p. 1822)
Lewis, Eric. Garbage Flowers: Green & Groovy Crafts. (p. 655)
Lewis, Evelyn L. & Turner, Carolyn S. Housing Decisions: Resource Portfolio. (p. 804)
—Housing Decisions: Teaching Package Teacher's Annotated Edition. (p. 804)
—Housing Decisions. (p. 804)
Lewis, Fiona. Dreaming in Color. (p. 484)
Lewis, Floyd. Foundered Mule. (p. 624)
Lewis, Gail. Oriental Cats. (p. 1303)
Lewis, Gill. Moon Bear. Gottardo, Alessandro, illus. (p. 1171)
—One White Dolphin. Aparicio, Raquel, illus. (p. 1297)
—Wild Wings. Onoda, Yuta, illus. (p. 1930)
Lewis, Gregg & Lewis, Deborah Shaw. Gifted Hands: The Ben Carson Story (p. 675)
Lewis, H. B., illus. see Kimmel, Elizabeth Cody & Buck, Lewis.
Lewis, H. B., illus. see Kimmel, Elizabeth Cody.
Lewis, Harriet, jt. auth. see Raphael, Akili.
Lewis, Herschell Gordon. Hot Appeals or Burnt Offerings: Do's & Don'ts for Twenty-First Century Fundraising. (p. 801)
Lewis, J. M. Adventures of Gabby & Coyote Girl. (p. 18)
Lewis, J. Patrick. And the Soldiers Sang. Kelley, Gary, illus. (p. 71)
—Arithme-Tickle: An Even Number of Odd Riddle-Rhymes. Remkiewicz, Frank, illus. (p. 98)
—Big Is Big & Little, Little: A Book of Contrasts. Barner, Bob, illus. (p. 182)
—Black Swan/White Crow. Manson, Christopher, illus. (p. 197)
—Blackbeard the Pirate King. (p. 197)
—Brothers' War: Civil War Voices in Verse. Civil War Photographers Staff, photos by. (p. 231)
—Castles: Old Stone Poems. (p. 277)
—Earth & Me, Our Family Tree: Nature's Creatures. Canyon, Christopher, illus. (p. 495)
—Earth & Us-Continuous: Earth's Past & Future. Canyon, Christopher, illus. (p. 495)
—Earth & You - A Closer View: Nature's Features. Canyon, Christopher, illus. (p. 495)
—Edgar Allan Poe's Pie: Math Puzzlers in Classic Poems. Slack, Michael, illus. (p. 504)
—Everything Is a Poem: the Best of J. Patrick Lewis. Pritelli, Maria Cristina, illus. (p. 545)
—Face Bug. Murphy, Kelly, illus. (p. 560)
—First Dog. Bowers, Tim, illus. (p. 594)
—Freedom Like Sunlight: Praisesongs for Black Americans. (p. 634)
—Galileo's Universe. Curry, Tom, illus. (p. 653)
—God Made the Skunk: And Other Animal Poems. King, Jerry, illus. (p. 690)
—Good Ship Crocodile. Felix, Monique, illus. (p. 700)
—Harlem Hellfighters. Kelley, Gary, illus. (p. 748)
—House. Innocenti, Roberto, illus. (p. 803)
—If You Were a Chocolate Mustache. Cordell, Matthew, illus. (p. 854)
—Just Joking Animal Riddles. (p. 938)
—Last Resort. Innocenti, Roberto, illus. (p. 978)
—Michelangelo's World. (p. 1135)
—Monumental Verses. (p. 1171)
—Once upon a Tomb: A Collection of Gravely Humorous Verses. Bartram, Simon, illus. (p. 1293)
—Please Bury Me in the Library. Stone, Kyle M., illus. (p. 1373)
—Self-Portrait with Seven Fingers: The Life of Marc Chagall in Verse. Chagall, Marc, illus. (p. 1549)
—Skywriting: Poems to Fly. Kubinyi, Laszlo, illus. (p. 1587)
—Snowflake Sisters. Desimini, Lisa, illus. (p. 1600)
—Spot the Plot: A Riddle Book of Book Riddles. Munsinger, Lynn, illus. (p. 1633)
—Stolen Smile. Kelley, Gary, illus. (p. 1652)
—Swan Song. Wormell, Chris, illus. (p. 1688)
—Swan Song. Wormell, Christopher, illus. (p. 1688)
—That's What Friends Are For. Denise, Christopher, illus. (p. 1727)
—Tugg & Teeny: That's What Friends Are For. Denise, Christopher, illus. (p. 1796)
—Tugg & Teeny. Denise, Christopher, illus. (p. 1796)
—Tugg & Tweeny - Jungle Surprises Denise, Christopher, illus. (p. 1796)
—Under the Kissletoe: Christmastime Poems. Shepperson, Rob, illus. (p. 1813)
—Underwear Salesman: And Other Jobs for Better or Verse. Bloch, Serge, illus. (p. 1817)
—What's Looking at You Kid? (p. 1898)
—When Thunder Comes: Poems for Civil Rights Leaders. Christie, R. Gregory et al, illus. (p. 1905)
—World Rat Day: Poems about Real Holidays You've Never Heard Of. Raff, Anna, illus. (p. 1958)
—World's Greatest. Graves, Keith, illus. (p. 1960)
—Wren & the Sparrow. Nayberg, Yevgenia, illus. (p. 1962)
Lewis, J. Patrick, tr. see Lewis, Patrick J.
Lewis, J. Patrick & Florian, Douglas. Poem-Mobiles: Crazy Car Poems. Holmes, Jeremy, illus. (p. 1375)
Lewis, J. Patrick & Innocenti, Roberto. último Refugio. (p. 1810)
Lewis, J. Patrick & Lyon, George Ella. Voices from the March on Washington. (p. 1848)
Lewis, J. Patrick & Nesbitt, Kenn. Bigfoot Is Missing! MinaLima, illus. (p. 185)
Lewis, J. Patrick & Thompson, John. Freedom Like Sunlight. (p. 634)
Lewis, J. Patrick & Yolen, Jane. Last Laughs: Animal Epitaphs. Timmins, Jeffrey Stewart, illus. (p. 978)
—Take Two! A Celebration of Twins. Blackall, Sophie, illus. (p. 1697)
Lewis, J. Patrick, et al. First Dog's White House Christmas. Bowers, Tim, illus. (p. 594)
Lewis, J. S., jt. auth. see Benz, Derek.
Lewis, Jackie. Jam! Tales from the World of Roller Derby. Beaton, Jill, ed. (p. 906)
Lewis, Jaime & Katz, Michelle V. Mahazor Katan: Machzor Katan: High Holiday Prayer Book for Families with Young Children. (p. 1076)
Lewis, Jan. 123: Turn the Wheels Learn to Count! (p. 2000)
—Baby's First Book of Prayers. (p. 129)
—Baby's First Stories of Jesus. (p. 129)
—Baby's Story Book: Bible. (p. 129)
—Emperor's New Clothes. (p. 521)
—First Fairy Tales: Cinderella. (p. 594)
—First Fairy Tales: Puss in Boots. (p. 594)
—First Fairy Tales: Sleeping Beauty. (p. 594)
—First Fairy Tales: The Ugly Duckling. (p. 594)
—First Fairy Tales: Three Little Pigs. (p. 594)
—First Fairy Tales Aladdin & the Lamp. (p. 594)
—First Fairy Tales Goldilocks & the Three Bears. (p. 594)
—First Fairy Tales Little Red Riding Hood. (p. 594)
—First Fairy Tales Snow White. (p. 594)
—Let's Look & See: Farm. (p. 998)
—Look & Learn with Little Dino: Busy Day. (p. 1048)
—Look & Learn with Little Dino: Count 123. (p. 1048)
—Look & Learn with Little Dino: Action Words. (p. 1048)
—Look & Learn with Little Dino: Colour Fun. Lewis, Jan, illus. (p. 1048)
—Love from Santa (p. 1059)
—Mother Goose Action Rhymes: Old MacDonald Had a Farm; One, Two, Buckle My Shoe; Round & Round the Garden; This Little Pig. (p. 1177)
—Mother Goose Rhymes: One, Two, Buckle My Shoe. (p. 1178)
—Mother Goose Rhymes: Round & Round the Garden. (p. 1178)
—My First 123. (p. 1203)
—My First ABC. (p. 1204)
—My First Animals. (p. 1204)
—My First Colours. (p. 1206)
—My First Words. (p. 1208)
—My Little Nursery Rhymes. (p. 1212)
—My Mother Goose Collection: Action Rhymes. (p. 1214)
—My Mother Goose Collection: Best Ever Rhymes. (p. 1214)
—Old Macdonald Had a Farm - Mother Goose Rhymes. (p. 1284)
—Performance. (p. 1343)
—Pied Piper of Hamelin. (p. 1356)
—School. (p. 1522)
—School Trip. (p. 1523)
—Sports Day. (p. 1632)
—The Princess & the Pea. (p. 1728)
—Words: Turn the Wheels, Find the Pictures. (p. 1951)
Lewis, Jan, illus. see Armadillo Publishing Staff.
Lewis, Jan, illus. see Cassidy, Anne.
Lewis, Jan, illus. see Read, Lorna & Ladybird Books Staff.
Lewis, Jan, illus. see Rees, Lesley.
Lewis, Jan, illus. see Taylor, Sean.
Lewis, Jan, illus. see Tucker Slingsby Ltd., Staff.
Lewis, Janaka Bowman. Brown All Over. (p. 231)
Lewis, Jeff & Byrns, Adam. University of New Hampshire College Prowler off the Record. (p. 1821)
Lewis, Jenn, illus. see Brown, Derrick.
Lewis, Jennifer & Williams, Tim. Mount Holyoke College College Prowler off the Record. (p. 1180)
Lewis, Jesse, illus. see Foster, D. S.
Lewis, Jill. Don't Read This Book! Allwright, Deborah, illus. (p. 468)
—Mom in a Million. Gulbis, Stephen, illus. (p. 1161)
—Something Delicious. Pye, Ali, illus. (p. 1609)
—Something Missing. Pye, Ali, illus. (p. 1610)
—Ug-a-Lug: Four Cavemen & a Prehistoric Pencil. Rickerty, Simon, illus. (p. 1808)
Lewis, Jill & Blue Bananas. Coconut Jack. Waters, Erica-Jane, illus. (p. 337)
Lewis, Jill & Lenski, Susan Davis. Reading Success for Struggling Adolescent Learners. Lenski, Susan & Lewis, Jill, eds. (p. 1446)
Lewis, Jill & Pye, Ali. Something Different. Pye, Ali, illus. (p. 1609)
Lewis, Joan Lane. See with Me. Hough, Hannah Bliss, illus. (p. 1547)
Lewis, JoAnn & Addams, Kelly. Kissing Frogs. (p. 962)
Lewis, Joshua, jt. auth. see Clare, Cassandra.
Lewis Jr, Daryl M. 3Ds' Christmas. (p. 1992)
Lewis, Judith. Not Like Any Bird I've Ever Heard. (p. 1267)
Lewis, K. E., illus. see Broyles, Anne.
Lewis, K. E., illus. see Rusch, Elizabeth.
Lewis, K., Parker. How to Draw the Life & Times of Richard M. Nixon. (p. 819)
lewis, k. s. YELLOW ANGELS DANCING on A RED TOOTHBRUSH: a Charlie Travel Adventure Story. (p. 1970)
Lewis, K. S., jt. auth. see Lewis, K. s.
Lewis, K. s. & Lewis, K. S. Happiness: A Charlie Travel Adventure Story. (p. 744)
Lewis, Karianna. Gladyus & the Voodoo Priestess. (p. 682)
Lewis, Kellie, illus. see Schaefer, Lola M.
Lewis, Kelly. Johan & the Dragon. (p. 920)
Lewis, Kevin. Dinosaur, Dinosaur. Kirk, Daniel, illus. (p. 442)
—Kj's Adventures. (p. 963)
—Not Inside This House! Ercolini, David, illus. (p. 1267)
—Tugga-Tugga Tugboat. Kirk, Daniel, illus. (p. 1796)
Lewis, Kevin, jt. auth. see Disney Book Group Staff.
Lewis, Kevin, jt. auth. see Slaughter, Nathan E.
Lewis, Kevin & Kirk, Daniel. My Truck Is Stuck! Kirk, Daniel, illus. (p. 1220)
Lewis, Kim. Emma's Lamb. (p. 520)
—Hooray for Harry. (p. 796)
—Seymour & Henry. Lewis, Kim, illus. (p. 1556)
Lewis, Kim, illus. see McBratney, Sam.
Lewis, Kim, illus. see Shaw, Janet.
Lewis, Kimberly, illus. see Whitecap Books Staff.
Lewis, Kristin. Mikaylah: A Little Girl with a Big Heart. (p. 1141)
Lewis, Kurt. Improbable Barnsy & the Pocket Full of Teeth. (p. 862)
Lewis, L. D. Rory: The Little 'Dragon' Lizard. (p. 1488)
Lewis, L. W. Poodles Tigers Monsters & You. Harris, Lorrayne R., illus. (p. 1383)
Lewis, Larry. Laddie's Tales & Travels. (p. 970)
Lewis, Linda. All for the Love of That Boy. (p. 44)
—Loving Two Is Hard to Do. (p. 1061)
—My Heart Belongs to That Boy. (p. 1210)
—We Hate Everything but Boys. (p. 1867)
—We Love Only Older Boys. (p. 1867)
Lewis, Lisa. Tsunaxen's Journey. (p. 1795)
Lewis, Lisa, ed. see Kipling, Rudyard.
Lewis, Liza. Noisy Car: Press the Wheel for Some Noisy Fun! (p. 1263)
—Noisy Tractor: Press the Wheel for Some Noisy Fun! (p. 1263)
—Noisy Train: Press the Wheel for Some Noisy Fun! (p. 1263)
—Noisy Truck: Press the Wheel for Some Noisy Fun! (p. 1263)
Lewis, Lorinne. Junior & Callie's Awesome Adventure. (p. 936)
Lewis, Maggie. Morgy Coast to Coast. Chesworth, Michael, illus. (p. 1175)
Lewis, Marion. Kaugjagjuk. Smith, Kim, illus. (p. 946)
Lewis, Marisa, illus. see Johnson, Julia.
Lewis, Mark. Is There Life after Boys? (p. 890)
Lewis, Mark J. Classification of Living Organisms. (p. 328)
—North Dakota: Past & Present. (p. 1265)
Lewis, Marla. Rescued: Benny's Story. (p. 1462)
Lewis, Marla, jt. auth. see Falletta, Bernadette.
Lewis, Maud. Christmas with the Rural Mail BB (p. 316)
Lewis, Megan. Girl Who Could Fly. (p. 679)
Lewis, Meharry H. Mary Lena Lewis Tate - Vision! The Woman Who Compassed a Man (p. 1100)
Lewis, Melinda. Bulls-Eye Bob & the Backyard Buddies. (p. 241)
Lewis, Michael. Great Pirate Christmas Battle Jaskiel, Stan, illus. (p. 717)
Lewis, Michael S., jt. auth. see Mitchard, Jacquelyn.
Lewis, Michelle. President Pickler's Pockets. (p. 1397)
—Whoa, Willy! (p. 1919)
Lewis, Naomi. Tales from Hans Christian Andersen. Clark, Emma Chicester, illus. (p. 1701)
Lewis, Naomi, jt. auth. see Andersen, Hans Christian.

Lewis, Naomi, tr. see Andersen, Hans Christian.
Lewis, Naomi C., illus. see Ellis, Julie.
Lewis, Norma. Connecting the Coasts: The Race to Build the Transcontinental Railroad (p. 358)
Lewis, Olive. Three Shades of Blackness. (p. 1743)
Lewis, Ophelia S. My Dear Liberia: Recollections, Poetic Memoirs from My Heart. (p. 1201)
Lewis, Orane. Miss Henn & Family. Vest, Dianne, illus. (p. 1151)
Lewis, Oscar, jt. auth. see Holt, Stephen.
Lewis, Paeony. I'll Always Love You. Ives, Penny, illus. (p. 856)
Lewis, Patrick J. Heroes & She-Roes: Poems of Amazing & Everyday Heroes. Lewis, J. Patrick & Cooke, Jim, trs. (p. 772)
Lewis, Paul Owen. Frog Girl. (p. 640)
—Storm Boy Lewis, Paul Owen, illus. (p. 1655)
—Storm Boy. (p. 1655)
Lewis, Peyton. Diary of Maggie, A Madison Mouse. (p. 435)
Lewis, Philip, jt. auth. see Stent, Amanda.
Lewis, Phyllis. Legend of the Aneeka. (p. 989)
Lewis, R. C. Stitching Snow. (p. 1651)
Lewis, R. J., illus. see Van Scoyoc, Pam.
Lewis, Rachel. Cook's Coloring Book: Simple Recipes for Beginners Lewis, Rachel, illus. (p. 362)
Lewis, Rebecca, illus. see Williams, Barbara A.
Lewis, Regina N. Smallest Forest. Moore, P. M., illus. (p. 1592)
—Smallest Schoolhouse. Moore, P. M., illus. (p. 1592)
—Smallest Toy Store, A Christmas Story. Moore, Phyllis M., illus. (p. 1592)
Lewis, Richard. Cave: An Evocation of the Beginnings of Art. Crawford, Elizabeth, illus. (p. 282)
—Demon Queen. (p. 426)
—Killing Sea. (p. 956)
—Monster's Proof. (p. 1169)
—Play, Said the Earth to Air. Neilson, Heidi, illus. (p. 1371)
—Tree Lives. Baen, Noah, illus. (p. 1783)
Lewis, Rob. Brothers & Sisters. (p. 231)
—Friends. (p. 638)
—Whats up Jac. (p. 1900)
Lewis, Robert, illus. see Feasel, PaPa.
Lewis, Robert Ellsworth. Search of Far Horizons. (p. 1537)
Lewis, Robin Baird, illus. see Stinson, Kathy.
Lewis, Roger, jt. auth. see Trevitt, Roger.
Lewis, Rose. Fruit Smoothie. (p. 645)
Lewis, Rose A. Sweet Dreams. Corace, Jen, illus. (p. 1689)
Lewis, Rose & Zong, Grace. Orange Peel's Pocket. (p. 1302)
Lewis, Samantha, jt. auth. see Hadkins, Helen.
Lewis, Samantha, jt. auth. see Sullivan, Lauren M.
Lewis, Samantha & Benchmark Education Co., LLC Staff. I Am Lib. (p. 833)
Lewis, Sarah. Kids' Baking: 60 Delicious Recipes for Children to Make. (p. 952)
Lewis, Siân. Billy Jones Dog Star. Roberts, Maggy, tr. (p. 187)
—Dilyn Declan. (p. 440)
—Dim Mwnci'n y Dosbarth. Glynn, Chris, illus. (p. 440)
—Josh in the Jungle. Roberts, Gill, illus. (p. 926)
Lewis, Siân, jt. auth. see Vaisey, Gill.
Lewis, Siân & Thomas, Rhianedd. Cris Croes. (p. 383)
Lewis, Siân, et al. Cartwnio gydag Elwyn Ioan. (p. 273)
Lewis, Simon. Adventures in the Air. (p. 15)
—Desperate Escapes. (p. 430)
—Survival at Sea. (p. 1686)
Lewis, Simon, illus. see Townsend, John.
Lewis, Sophie, tr. see Gripari, Pierre.
Lewis, Stephen, illus. see Charlesworth, Liza.
Lewis, Stephen, illus. see Jones, Milo.
Lewis, Stephen, illus. see Karlitz, Gail & Honig, Debbie.
Lewis, Stephen, illus. see Slater, Teddy & Scholastic, Inc. Staff.
Lewis, Steve, Sr. Course of a Horse. (p. 373)
Lewis, Steven & Parker, Shelley. Return to Allapatria. (p. 1465)
Lewis, Stevie, illus. see Banks, Angelica.
Lewis, Stevie, illus. see Gutknecht, Allison.
Lewis, Stewart. Secret Ingredient. (p. 1541)
—You Have Seven Messages. (p. 1975)
Lewis, Sue. Month-by-Month Crafts. (p. 1170)
Lewis, Sue & Abrams, Suzanne. Sight Word Puzzles & Activities. Rous, Sheri, ed. (p. 1574)
Lewis, Sue & Stern, Amy. Picture Sorting Hamaguchi, Carla, ed. (p. 1356)
—Vowel Puzzles & Activities Cernek, Kim, ed. (p. 1850)
—Word Family Puzzles & Activities Cernek, Kim, ed. (p. 1950)
—Word Sorting Hamaguchi, Carla, ed. (p. 1951)
Lewis, Suford, ed. see Bujold, Lois McMaster.
Lewis, Susan Grant. Education in Africa. Rotberg, Robert I. & Ojakorotu, Victor, eds. (p. 505)
Lewis, Suzanne. Penguin Named Patience: A Hurricane Katrina Rescue Story. Anchin, Lisa, illus. (p. 1337)
Lewis, Sylvia. Beautiful Decay. (p. 153)
Lewis, T. Caroline's Beautiful Pictures. (p. 270)
—I am who I say I Am. (p. 834)
Lewis, T., illus. see Tharp, Barbara, et al.
Lewis, Terence. Bani a Butterfly Adventure. (p. 136)
Lewis, Terry, jt. auth. see Lawrence, Antoinette.
Lewis, Tracy. Little Girl Beautiful. (p. 1028)
Lewis, Tracy M., jt. auth. see Phelan, Thomas W.
Lewis, Wayne, illus. see Lougher, Jenny.
Lewis, Wendy. Sabrina the Girl with A Hole in Her Heart. Lucas, Diane, illus. (p. 1500)
—Sabrina, the Girl with a Hole in Her Heart. (p. 1500)
Lewis, Wendy, jt. auth. see Lewis, Wendy A.
Lewis, Wendy A. Cheetah Ross, Graham, illus. (p. 296)
—Fire on the Water: The Red-Hot Career of Superstar Rower Ned Hanlan (p. 590)
—Lacrosse Warrior: The Life of Mohawk Lacrosse Champion Gaylord Powless (p. 970)
Lewis, Wendy A. & Lewis, Wendy. Fire on the Water: The Red-Hot Career of Superstar Rower Ned Hanlan. (p. 590)
—Lacrosse Warrior: The Life of Mohawk Lacrosse Champion Gaylord Powless (p. 970)
Lewis-Brown, Alscess. Mosquito Get in Trouble Too. Hatfield, Cynthia, illus. (p. 1176)
Lewis-Cook, Ashley. Beautiful Me! (p. 153)
Lewis-Domenech, Shanty. Toot (p. 1767)
Lewis-Long, Carla. Why I'm So Special: A Book about Surrogacy. (p. 1925)
Lewis-MacDougall, Patricia Ann, illus. see Qitsualik-Tinsley, Rachel & Qitsualik-Tinsley, Sean.
Lewis-MacDougall, Patricia Ann, illus. see Wishinsky, Frieda.
Lewison, Wendy Cheyette. L Is for Liberty. Hines, Laura Freeman, illus. (p. 969)
—My First Garden. Sakamoto, Miki, illus. (p. 1206)
—Prince & the Potty. Motoyama, Keiko, illus. (p. 1401)
—Raindrop, Plop! Paparone, Pamela, tr. (p. 1436)
—Silly Milly. (p. 1576)
—Silly Milly. Westcott, Nadine Bernard, illus. (p. 1576)
—Two Is for Twins. Nakata, Hiroe, illus. (p. 1803)
Lewisson, Helene. Hem: The Duckbill Dinosaur. (p. 766)
Lewis-Tilden, Thomasine E., jt. auth. see Tilden, Thomasine E. Lewis.
Lewis-Wells, Helen. Sad Duck. (p. 1501)
Lewman, David. Case File #1 First Contact. Spaziante, Patrick, illus. (p. 273)
—Case File #4 Rabbids Go Viral. Spaziante, Patrick, illus. (p. 273)
—Case of the Missing Moola. (p. 274)
—Case of the Mystery Meat Loaf. (p. 274)
—Case of the Plagued Play. (p. 275)
—Case of the Ruined Ram. (p. 275)
—Case of the Vanished Squirrel. Moore, Harry, illus. (p. 275)
—Chuckle & Cringe: SpongeBob's Book of Embarrassing Stories. (p. 318)
—Double Trouble: The Case of the Missing Spatula - The Case of the Vanished Squirrel. Moore, Harry, Jr., illus. (p. 473)
—Lovestruck! Fruchter, Jason, illus. (p. 1061)
—New Developments Spaziante, Patrick, illus. (p. 1244)
—Oh, Barnacles! SpongeBob's Handbook for Bad Days. Style Guide Staff, illus. (p. 1280)
—Soccer Star!/Estrella de Futbol! (SpongeBob SquarePants) Gomez, Yuliana, tr. (p. 1603)
—Spongebob Jokepants. (p. 1630)
—SpongeBob, Soccer Star! Reed, Stephen, illus. (p. 1630)
—Spongebob's Slap Shot. (p. 1631)
—SpongeBob's Slap Shot. Moore, Harry, illus. (p. 1631)
Lewman, David, jt. auth. see Eliot, Chip.
Lewman, David, jt. auth. see Golden Books Staff.
Lewman, David, jt. auth. see O'Ryan, Ellie.
Lewman, David & Gomez, Yuliana. Batter up!/¡a Batear!(SpongeBob SquarePants) Random House, illus. (p. 145)
Lew-McCabe, Minette. Make Your Own Hawaii Landmarks. (p. 1080)
Lewolt, Bruce. Bible by Heart: The Ultimate Bible Study & Memorization System. (p. 175)
Lewolt, Bruce, jt. auth. see Daugherty, Steven R.
Lew-Vriethoff, Joanne, illus. see Ashman, Linda.
Lew-Vriethoff, Joanne, illus. see Cleary, Brian P.
Lew-Vriethoff, Joanne, illus. see Craver, Marcella Marino.
Lew-Vriethoff, Joanne, illus. see Schafer, Milton.
Lew-Vriethoff, Joanne, illus. see Spinelli, Eileen.
Lewy, Faye Tillis, ed. see Moskowitz, Nachama Skolnik.
Lewy, Faye Tillis, jt. auth. see Person, Hara.
Lexa, Katrina & Skindzier, Jon. Hampton University College Prowler off the Record. (p. 739)
Ley, Mary. Tri-Son: The Little Triathlete. Ley, Mary, illus. (p. 1785)
Ley, Willy, ed. see Rockwell, Carey.
Ley, Willy, jt. auth. see Rockwell, Carey.
Leybas, Veronica A. Let's Imagine. (p. 998)
Leyhane, Vici, illus. see Pratt, Leonie.
Leyhane, Vici, illus. see Watt, Fiona.
Leysen, An. Princess Who Could Not Sleep. (p. 1406)
Leyson, Leon. Boy on the Wooden Box: How the Impossible Became Possible... On Schindler's List. (p. 218)
Leyssenne, Mathieu, illus. see Hamilton, Libby.
Leyva, Barbara. Henry & the Magic Window. Leyva, Barbara, illus. (p. 767)
Leyva, Juan Camilo, illus. see Delisle, Annette Gonzalez.
Lezin, Katya. Knight Swan. (p. 964)
LeZotte, Ann Clare. T4. (p. 1694)
Lhamo, Choki, photos by see Hawley, Michael.
L'Heureux, Christine. Baby Caillou, I'm Growing! Brignaud, Pierre, illus. (p. 125)
—Caillou: I Love You. Brignaud, Pierre, illus. (p. 251)
—Caillou: No More Diapers. Brignaud, Pierre, illus. (p. 251)
—Caillou & the Big Bully. Brignaud, Pierre, illus. (p. 251)
—Caillou, Ma Maman. (p. 251)
—Caillou Meets a Princess. Brignaud, Pierre, illus. (p. 251)
—Caillou, Mon Papa. (p. 251)
—Moves Around. Brignaud, Pierre, illus. (p. 1183)
—Play with Me. Brignaud, Pierre, illus. (p. 1371)
L'Heureux, Christine, jt. auth. see Légaré, Gisèle.
L'Heureux, Christine & Légaré, Gisèle. Caillou: My Nightlight Book. Brignaud, Pierre, illus. (p. 251)
L'Heureux, J. J. Good Day Book. (p. 697)
L'Hirondelle, Cheryl, illus. see Griggs, Terry.
L'Homme, Erik. Tales of a Lost Kingdom: A Journey into Northwest Pakistan. Place, François, illus. (p. 1702)
Lhomme, Sandrine, illus. see Galliez, Roxane Marie.
Lhomme, Sandrine & Piu, Amandine. Sammy the Snail's Amazing Day Lhomme, Sandrine, illus. (p. 1508)
L'Hommedieu, Arthur John. Children of the Sun. L'Hommedieu, Arthur John, illus. (p. 302)
—Our Solar System. (p. 1310)
Li, Amanda. Hot Dogs & Dinosnores. Eccles, Jane, illus. (p. 801)
Li, Amanda & Pan MacMillan, Pan. Christmas Cracker Jokes. (p. 313)
Li, Deborah. Tricia & the Blue Cap. (p. 1786)
Li, Edward. Attack of the Unstoppables. (p. 114)
Li, Helen, tr. see Howard, Monique.
Li, John, jt. auth. see Mills, Nathan.
Li, Judith L. Ellie's Log: Exploring the Forest Where the Great Tree Fell. Herring, M. L., illus. (p. 514)
Li, Karen, ed. see Kids Can Press Staff.
Li, Kit Shan. Dim Sum: A Pocket Guide. (p. 440)
Li, Luchen, jt. auth. see Schultz, Jeffrey.
Li, Ma, et al. Chinese Fables & Folktales (III) Junjie, Cheng, illus. (p. 307)
Li, Maggie. Bug Detective. (p. 236)
Li, Moying. Snow Falling in Spring: Coming of Age in China During the Cultural Revolution. (p. 1599)
Li, Oswald, jt. auth. see Du, Sharon.
Li, Peter, et al, eds. Culture & Politics in China: An Anatomy of Tiananmen Square. (p. 391)
Li, Richard T. Golden Lotus: Life of a Bound-Feet Peasant Mother in the Chinese Cultural Revolution. (p. 695)
Li, Wenfang. Extreme Sports. (p. 557)
Li, Xiaojun, illus. see Kroll, Virginia.
Li, Yao-Wen, jt. auth. see Kendall, Carol.
Li, Yishan, illus. see Novik, Naomi.
Li, Yishan, illus. see Poe, Edgar Allen & Morvan, Jean-David.
Li, Yishan, jt. auth. see Southgate, Anna.
Li, Zheng, jt. auth. see Ma, Zheng.
Liang, Kuan, jt. auth. see Yung, Kao.
Liang, Kuan & Yung, Kao. Magic Lover's Tower (p. 1072)
Liang, Xiao Long, illus. see Chen, Wei Dong.
Liang, Xiao Long, illus. see Dong Chen, Wei.
Liang, Xiao Long, jt. auth. see Chen, Wei Dong.
Liano, Dante, jt. auth. see Menchú, Rigoberta.
Liano, Dante, et al. Honey Jar Unger, David, tr. from SPA. (p. 794)
Liao, Jimmy. When the Moon Forgot. (p. 1905)
Liao, Jimmy, illus. see Oram, Hiawyn.
Liao, Jimmy, illus. see Taylor, Sean.
Liao, Yan. Famous People of China. (p. 569)
—Famous People of China. Wang, Jianwei, ed. (p. 569)
—Food & Festivals of China. Wang, Jianwei, ed. (p. 613)
Liao, Yivian, illus. see Hale, Linda.
Liardon, Roberts & Goldberg, Olly. God's Generals for Kids, Volume 3: John Alexander Dowie. (p. 691)
Liardon, Roberts & Goldenberg, Olly. God's Generals for Kids, Volume 2: Smith Wigglesworth. (p. 691)
—God's Generals for Kids, Volume 4: Maria Woodworth-Etter. (p. 691)
Lias, Joe. Wood Rats Dragging Their Long Tales. (p. 1949)
Liautaud, Judy. Lulu Turns on the Night Light. Liautaud, Judy, illus. (p. 1065)
Libal, Angela. Fingerprints, Bite Marks, Ear Prints. Noziglia, Carla Miller & Siegel, Jay A., eds. (p. 589)
—Forensic Anthropology. Noziglia, Carla Miller & Siegel, Jay A., eds. (p. 617)
—Science. (p. 1524)
Libal, Autumn. Can I Change the Way I Look? A Teen's Guide to the Health Implications of Cosmetic Surgery, Makeovers, & Beyond. (p. 258)
—Chained: Youth with Chronic Illness. (p. 288)
—Chronic Illness. Albers, Lisa et al, eds. (p. 317)
—Cuban Americans: Exiles from an Island Home (p. 388)
—Deaf & Hard of Hearing. Albers, Lisa et al, eds. (p. 418)
—Dental Care. Noyes, Nancy & Forman, Sara, eds. (p. 426)
—Discrimination & Prejudice. Garcia, Victor, ed. (p. 450)
—Dissociative Disorders. McDonnell, Mary Ann & Esherick, Donald, eds. (p. 453)
—Drug Therapy & Dissociative Disorders. (p. 487)
—Drug Therapy & Impulse Control Disorders. (p. 487)
—Drug Therapy & Postpartum Disorders. (p. 487)
—Drug Therapy & Psychosomatic Disorders. (p. 487)
—Emotional Disturbance. Albers, Lisa et al, eds. (p. 520)
—Exercise for Fitness & Weight Loss. Garcia, Victor, ed. (p. 548)
—Fast Food & the Obesity Epidemic. Garcia, Victor, ed. (p. 576)
—Fats, Sugars, & Empty Calories: The Fast Food Habit. (p. 577)
—FDA & Psychiatric Drugs: Drugs & Psychology for the Mind & Body (p. 578)
—Folk Proverbs & Riddles. (p. 611)
—Health Implications of Cosmetic Surgery, Makeovers, & Body Alterations. McDonnell, Mary Ann & Forman, Sara, eds. (p. 758)
—Impulse-Control Disorders. McDonnell, Mary Ann & Esherick, Donald, eds. (p. 862)
—Intellectual Disabilities. Albers, Lisa et al, eds. (p. 879)
—My Name Isn't Slow: Youth with Mental Retardation. (p. 1215)
—Ocean Inside: Youth Who Are Deaf & Hard of Hearing. (p. 1276)
—Postpartum Disorders. McDonnell, Mary Ann & Esherick, Donald, eds. (p. 1388)
—Psychosomatic Disorders. McDonnell, Mary Ann & Esherick, Donald, eds. (p. 1413)
—Runaway Train: Youth with Emotional Disturbance. (p. 1496)
—Runaway Train: Youth with Emotional Disturbance. (p. 1496)
—Social, Monetary, & Moral Costs of Prisons. (p. 1604)
—Women in the Hispanic World. (p. 1946)
—Women in the Mediterranean World. (p. 1946)
—Women in the World of Russia. (p. 1946)
Libal, Autumn, jt. auth. see Ford, Jean.
Libal, Autumn & Hovius, Christopher. Taking Care of Your Smile: A Teen's Guide to Dental Care. (p. 1698)
Libal, Autumn & Indovino, Shaina Carmel. Estonia. (p. 538)
Libal, Joyce. Antidepressants & Social Anxiety: A Pill for Shyness? (p. 89)
—Antidepressants & Suicide: When Treatment Kills. (p. 89)
—California. (p. 253)
—Drug Therapy an Substance-Related Disorders. (p. 487)
—Drug Therapy & Mental Disorders Due to a Medical Condition. (p. 487)
—Drug Therapy for Mental Disorders Caused by a Medical Condition. (p. 487)
—Finding My Voice: Youth with Speech Impairment. (p. 588)
—Finding My Voice: Youth with Speech Impairment. (p. 588)
—Folk Games. (p. 611)
—Getting Ready for the Fair: Crafts, Projects, & Prize-Winning Animals. (p. 669)
—House Between Homes: Youth in the Foster Care System. (p. 803)
—Mental Disorders Due to a Medical Condition. McDonnell, Mary Ann & Esherick, Donald, eds. (p. 1126)
—Migrant Youth: Falling Between the Cracks. (p. 1140)
—Military & Elite Forces Officer. Riggs, Ernestine G. & Gholar, Cheryl, eds. (p. 1142)
—New England. (p. 1244)
—Protective Services. Albers, Lisa et al, eds. (p. 1412)
—Somebody Hear Me Crying: Youth in Protective Services. (p. 1609)
—Somebody Hear Me Crying: Youth in Protective Services. (p. 1609)
—Southern. (p. 1617)
—Speech Impairment. Albers, Lisa et al, eds. (p. 1624)
—Substance-Related Disorders. McDonnell, Mary Ann & Esherick, Donald, eds. (p. 1671)
—Texas. (p. 1723)
Libal, Joyce & Simons, Rae. Professional Athlete & Sports Official. Riggs, Ernestine G. & Gholar, Cheryl, eds. (p. 1409)
Libal, Joyce, compiled by. Mid-Atlantic Cooking. (p. 1137)
Libbrecht, Kenneth. Secret Life of a Snowflake: An up-Close Look at the Art & Science of Snowflakes. Sorenson, Vanessa, illus. (p. 1541)
Libby, Alisa M. King's Rose. (p. 961)
Libby, Jay. Xandoria the Saga Collection. (p. 1967)
Libby, Kathryn. Cursive Connections: Modern Style. (p. 395)
Libby, Lori Ann. Adventures of Henry Hamper & the Flying Fish. Lee, Tricia Ting, illus. (p. 18)
Libby-Larson, Yvonne, jt. auth. see Herr, Judy.
Liberman, Sherri. Historical Atlas of Azerbaijan. (p. 782)
—Historical Atlas of the Industrial Age & the Growth of America's Cities. (p. 783)
—Lynee Reid Banks. (p. 1066)
Liberman, W. L., jt. auth. see Ejersbo, Jakob.
Liberston, Jody. Nathan Hale: Heroe de la guerra de Independencia. (p. 1231)
Liberto, Lorenzo. Matt the Rat & His Magic Cloud / Raton Mateo y Su Nube Magica: A Day at School / un Dia de Escuela. Gomez, Rocio, ed. (p. 1109)
—Matt the Rat & His Sister Maggie (Raton Mateo y Su Hermana Maggie) When I Grow Up (Cuando Yo Crezca) Gomez, Rocio, ed. (p. 1109)
—Matt the Rat Fights Back / Ratón Mateo se Defiende. Gomez, Rocio, tr. from ENG. (p. 1109)
—Save the Planet / Salva el Planeta. Gomez, Rocio, tr. (p. 1517)
Liberto, Lorenzo, et al. Matt the Rat's Incredible Creations / Las Creaciones Increíbles de Ratón Mateo. Torres, Irving, illus. (p. 1109)
—Practice Makes Perfect / la Práctica Hace al Maestro. Torres, Irving, illus. (p. 1392)
Liberts, Jennifer. Cake Monster. VanTuyle, David, illus. (p. 252)
Libertson, Jody. Nathan Hale: Hero of the American Revolution. (p. 1231)
—Nathan Hale: Héroe revolucionario / Hero of the American Revolution. (p. 1231)
—Nathan Hale: Héroe revolucionario (Nathan Hale: Hero of the American Revolution) (p. 1231)
Liberty, Anita. Center of the Universe: Yep, That Would Be Me. (p. 287)
Liberty, Dendron, jt. auth. see Johnson, Lafayette, Jr.
Liberty, Jesse, et al. Introduction to Computer Science Using Java. (p. 882)
Libhart, Virginia B. Carrie's Dream. (p. 271)
Libonn, Jula, illus. see Brown, Sam E.
Libra, Anna. How Do My Cuts Heal? An Inside Look at the Circulatory System. (p. 807)
—Why Does Loud Music Hurt My Ears? An Inside Look at the Ear. (p. 1924)
—Why Does My Head Hurt? An Inside Look at the Nervous System. (p. 1924)
—Why Does My Stomach Ache? An Inside Look at the Digestive System. (p. 1924)
—Why Does That Taste Bad? An Inside Look at the Tongue. (p. 1924)
Libra, Michael W. Dragons of Draegoni: Dragon Black's Revenge Book 2. (p. 479)
Librado. Thank You Jesus. (p. 1725)
Library, jt. auth. see Bozzo, Linda.
Library, jt. auth. see Feinstein, Stephen.
Library, jt. auth. see Gordon, Sherri Mabry.
Library, jt. auth. see Jankowski, Susan.
Library, jt. auth. see Mullarkey, Lisa.
Library, jt. auth. see Scherer, Glenn.
Library, jt. auth. see Wingard-Nelson, Rebecca.
Library, jt. auth. see Wroble, Lisa A.
Library, jt. auth. see Wyckoff, Edwin Brit.
Library Association Staff, jt. auth. see Bozzo, Linda.
Library Association Staff, jt. auth. see Carson, Mary Kay.
Library Association Staff, jt. auth. see Dodson, Peter.
Library Association Staff, jt. auth. see Llimós, Anna.
Library Association Staff, jt. auth. see Niven, Felicia Lowenstein.
Library Of Congress, creator. Wizard of Oz Coloring Book. (p. 1943)
Libre, Madeline. Who's Untying My Shoelaces? (p. 1921)
Libretto, Ellen V. General Slocum Steamboat Fire of 1904. (p. 660)
Libritos Mios staff, et al. Spanish Emergent Reader 1: Mira como Juego; ¡Curitas!; Los Animales del Zoológico; Construyendo una Casa; la Alberca; ¡Agua y Jabónl; Me Visto; Mi Gato Elias, Annette, tr. (p. 1621)
LIBSA Staff, ed. Animales. (p. 80)
—Mascotas. (p. 1102)
—Mis Juguetes. (p. 1150)
—Transportes. (p. 1779)
Libster, Bernard. Bonsai Bear. Cheung, Aries, illus. (p. 209)
Libura, Krystyna, jt. auth. see Urrutia, Maria Christina.
Liburdi, Mariana, creator. Happy Hearts. (p. 746)
Licari, Peter J., jt. auth. see Flanagan, Artie.
Licata, Annette, jt. auth. see Hensley, Wendie.
Licata, Renora. Todo lo que necesitas saber sobre la ira (Everything You Need to Know about Anger) (p. 1761)

Licata, Rosemarie, jt. auth. see Reizer, Edwina.
Licata, Rosemarie & Reizer, Edwina. Betsy & Her Buttons. (p. 172)
—Hare & the Hound. (p. 748)
Licciardi, Paula. Wasting Calvin's Time. (p. 1860)
Liccioni, Tina. Clownfish/el Pez Payaso: An English/Spanish Bilingual Book. Vesazquez, Gloria, tr. (p. 335)
Lichfield, Walter C. Fanciful Bear Stories for Small Kids & Factual Bear Stories for Big Kids. (p. 570)
Lichfield, Wilma B. Pocketful of Melodies. (p. 1375)
Lichius, Ben. Rise of the Guardians: Hidden Truth & Other Stories: Hidden Truth & Other Stories. (p. 1475)
Licht, S. Goodbye, Pacifier! Edelstein, Racheli, illus. (p. 701)
—Goodbye, Thumb-Sucking! Edelstein, Racheli, illus. (p. 701)
Licht, Sharon. Return of Chancellor Paddywack: A Sequel to Magic Marmalade, A Tale of the Moonlight Fairies. Browne, James, illus. (p. 1464)
Lichtenberg, Georg Christoph. Algunos Aforismos. (p. 38)
Lichtenberg, Tamara. Lily's Rose. (p. 1018)
Lichtenheld, Tom. Bridget's Beret. Lichtenheld, Tom, illus. (p. 227)
—Cloudette. Lichtenheld, Tom, illus. (p. 334)
—E-Mergency! Lichtenheld, Tom, illus. (p. 492)
—Everything I Know about Cars. Lichtenheld, Tom, illus. (p. 545)
—Everything I Know about Pirates. Lichtenheld, Tom, illus. (p. 545)
—What Are You So Grumpy About? Lichtenheld, Tom, illus. (p. 1880)
—What Mess? (p. 1892)
Lichtenheld, Tom, illus. see Barton, Chris.
Lichtenheld, Tom, illus. see Ferry, Beth.
Lichtenheld, Tom, illus. see Fields-Meyer, Ezra.
Lichtenheld, Tom, illus. see Holub, Joan.
Lichtenheld, Tom, illus. see Raposo, Joe.
Lichtenheld, Tom, illus. see Rinker, Sherri Duskey.
Lichtenheld, Tom, illus. see Rosenthal, Amy Krouse.
Lichtenheld, Tom, illus. see Smallcomb, Pam.
Lichtenheld, Tom, jt. auth. see Rinker, Sherri Duskey.
Lichtenheld, Tom, jt. auth. see Rosenthal, Amy Krouse.
Lichter, Nick. Road of Souls: Reflections on the Mississippi. (p. 1477)
Lichtman, Wendy. Secrets, Lies, & Algebra. (p. 1545)
—Writing on the Wall. (p. 1965)
Lichtwardt, Rita. Barbie - A Perfect Christmas. (p. 138)
Lickel, Lisa J. German Girl. Hendricks, Brenda K., illus. (p. 666)
—Potawatomi Boy. Hendricks, Brenda K., illus. (p. 1388)
Lickens, Alice V. Dance to the Boogaloo? (p. 402)
Licker, Laura. Frogs & Dragons (p. 641)
Licker, Lori. Writing-Right with Professor Pendleton Pencil. (p. 1965)
Lickona, Judy, jt. auth. see Lickona, Tom.
Lickona, Tom & Lickona, Judy. Sex, Love & You: Making the Right Decision. (p. 1556)
Licos, Ruffino S. Our Four Loaves of Bread. (p. 1308)
Lida, Toshitsugu, illus. see Bones & Nobumoto, Keiko.
Lida, Toshitsugu, illus. see Bones.
Lida, Xing, illus. see Sloan, Christopher.
Lidard, Kelly, illus. see Seeley, Bonnie L.
Lidard, Kelly, photos by see Seeley, Bonnie L.
Lidberg, Micah. Rise & Fall. (p. 1474)
Lidbury, Alan, jt. auth. see Storey, Tony.
Liddell, Daniel, illus. see Boule, Mary Null.
Liddell, Daniel & Basta, Mary. Native Americans of North America (p. 1234)
Liddell, Joshua & Liddell, Kentrell. Little Kid, Big Fears. (p. 1029)
—My Pet Elephant & Best Friend, TARU. (p. 1217)
Liddell, Kentrell, jt. auth. see Liddell, Joshua.
Liddell, Louise A. & Gentzler, Yvonne S. Building Life Skills. (p. 239)
Liddell, Louise A. & Samuels, Carolee S. Clothes & Your Appearance. (p. 334)
Liddell, Louise A., et al. Clothes & Your Appearance. (p. 334)
Liddell, Mary. Little Machinery: A Critical Facsimile Edition. (p. 1031)
Liddiment, Carol. Wooden Sword: A Jewish Folktale from Afghanistan. (p. 1949)
Liddiment, Carol, illus. see MacDonald, Margaret Read & Taibah, Nadia Jameel.
Liddle. Ears. (p. 494)
—Reading for Concepts: Book A. (p. 1446)
—Reading for Concepts: Book B. (p. 1446)
—Reading for Concepts: Book C. (p. 1446)
—Reading for Concepts: Book D. (p. 1446)
Liddle, Sharon. Eli - the Bi-Polar Bear. Maximilian Press Staff, ed. (p. 512)
Liddle-Pirouet, Leasal. I Love You More Than Ice Cream Dipped in Sprinkles. (p. 843)
Liddy, G. Gordon, et al. Fight Back! Tackling Terrorism, Liddy Style. (p. 585)
Liddy, Michael. Kid's Cooking in the Kitchen. (p. 953)
Lide, Emily. Zimbabwe. (p. 1986)
Lidell, Alex. Cadet of Tildor. (p. 250)
Lidh, Jessica. Number 7. (p. 1271)
Lidner, D. B. A,B, C's of Firefighting & Fire Safety. (p. 2)
Lie, Vivian, illus. see Masters, H.
Lieb, Josh. I Am a Genius of Unspeakable Evil & I Want to Be Your Class President. (p. 832)
—Ratscalibur. (p. 1440)
Liébana, Luisa Villar. Misterio Del Dragón de Ojos de Fuego. Urberuaga, Emilio, illus. (p. 1155)
Liebeck, Lisa, illus. see Rembisz, Linda.
Liebenow, Todd. Sensational Shadows. Washburn, Sue, ed. (p. 1551)
Liebenow, Todd & VonSeggen, Liz. Join the Hall of Faith. (p. 924)
Liebenow, Todd, et al. Beyond Words 2. (p. 174)
—Plug into the Power. Guibord, Charity, illus. (p. 1374)
Lieber, Dave. Dog of My Nightmares: Stories by Texas Columnist Dave Lieber. (p. 461)
Lieber, Larry, illus. see Lee, Stan, et al.
Lieber, Larry & Heck, Don. Invincible Iron Man (p. 885)
Lieber, Larry & Parkhouse, Steve. Captain Britain: Siege of Camelot. Lawrence, Jim et al, illus. (p. 263)
Lieber, Steve, illus. see Rucka, Greg & Brubaker, Ed.
Lieberherr, Ruth, illus. see Kroll, Linda.
Lieberherr, Ruth, illus. see Mellon, Nancy.
Lieberman, A. J. Martian Manhunter: The Others among Us. Barrionuevo, Al, illus. (p. 1097)
—Silver Six. Rawlings, Darren, illus. (p. 1577)
Lieberman, Alicia F. & Van Horn, Patricia. Psychotherapy with Infants & Young Children: Repairing the Effects of Stress & Trauma on Early Attachment. (p. 1413)
Lieberman, Channah. Happy Birthday to Me! - Boys' Edition. Argoff, Patti, illus. (p. 745)
—Happy Birthday to Me! Girls' Edition. Argoff, Patti, illus. (p. 745)
Lieberman, Dan & Rahimi, Joey. Carnegie Mellon University College Prowler off the Record. (p. 270)
Lieberman, David J. How to Change Anybody: Proven Techniques to Reshape Anyone's Attitude, Behavior, Feelings, or Beliefs. (p. 815)
Lieberman Hackelberg, Lori. Shep & the Wounded Soldier. (p. 1565)
Lieberman, Leanne. Book of Trees (p. 212)
—Gravity (p. 712)
—Lauren Yonofsky Hates the Holocaust (p. 980)
—Off Pointe (p. 1279)
Lieberman, Naomi. Shabbos, Shabbos I Love You. Rosenfeld, D. L., ed. (p. 1556)
Lieberman, Paulette (Peshe Razel) Fein. Jewish Plays for Children: For successful educational fun & fundraising Purposes. (p. 917)
Lieberman, Sylvia. Archibald's Swiss Cheese Mountain. Wendell, Jeremy, illus. (p. 95)
Liebermann, Jude. Modern Myth: Nada's Secret. (p. 1158)
Liebert, Burt. Kid from the Other Side. Liebert, Marjorie, illus. (p. 951)
Liebert, Emily. Those Secrets We Keep. (p. 1740)
Liebert, Marjorie, illus. see Liebert, Burt.
Liebig, Nelda Johnson. Carrie & the Boarding House. (p. 271)
Liebler, M. L. Moon a Box. (p. 1171)
Liebling, A. J. Liebling - World War II Writings: The Road Back to Paris/Mollie & Other War Pieces/Uncollected War Journalism/Normandy Revisited. Hamill, Pete, ed. (p. 1007)
Liebman, Dan. Bombero. (p. 208)
—I Want to Be a Builder. (p. 847)
—I Want to Be a Chef. (p. 847)
—I Want to Be a Librarian. (p. 847)
—I Want to Be a Mechanic. (p. 847)
—I Want to Be a Soldier. (p. 847)
—Infirmiere. Lior, Tsipora, tr. from ENG. (p. 873)
—Je Veux Etre Medecin. Lior, Tsipora, tr. from ENG. (p. 911)
—Pilote. Lior, Tsipora, tr. from ENG. (p. 1359)
—Piloto. (p. 1359)
—Policier. Lior, Tsipora, tr. from ENG. (p. 1380)
—Pompier. Lior, Tsipora, tr. from ENG. (p. 1382)
—Vaquero. (p. 1833)
—Veterinaire. Lior, Tsipora, tr. from ENG. (p. 1839)
Liebman, Dan, jt. auth. see Liebman, Daniel.
Liebman, Dan & Liebman, Daniel. President. (p. 1396)
—Presidente. (p. 1397)
Liebman, Daniel, jt. auth. see Liebman, Dan.
Liebman, Daniel & Liebman, Dan. Guardian de Zoologico. (p. 728)
—I Want to Be a Builder. (p. 847)
—I Want to Be a Librarian. (p. 847)
—I Want to Be a Mechanic. (p. 847)
—I Want to Be a Musician. (p. 847)
—I Want to Be a Soldier. (p. 847)
—I Want to Be a Zookeeper. (p. 847)
—Quiero Ser Bibliotecario. (p. 1428)
—Quiero Ser Constructor. (p. 1428)
—Quiero Ser Mecanico. (p. 1428)
—Quiero Ser Musico. (p. 1428)
Liebman, Hollis Lance. Core Fitness (p. 367)
Liebman, Simean, illus. see Arthur, Anne.
Liechty, Anna L., jt. auth. see Wezeman, Phyllis Vos.
Liechty, Anna L., jt. auth. see Wezeman, Phyllis Vos.
Lieder, Rick, illus. see Frost, Helen.
Lieder, Rick, photos by see Frost, Helen.
Liederbach, Tom, jt. auth. see Barulich-Liederbach, Terri.
Liefeld, Rob, illus. see Nicieza, Fabián.
Liefeld, Rob, illus. see Simonson, Louise.
Liefeld, Rob, et al. X-Force: Under the Gun. (p. 1967)
Lieffering, Jan, illus. see Lynette, Rachel.
Liegey, Daniel, illus. see Michels-Gualtieri, Zaydek G.
Liegey, Daniel, illus. see Michels-Gualtieri, Zaydek G. & Michels-Gualtieri, Akaela S.
Lienas, Gemma. Callejon Slin Salida. (p. 254)
Liening, Cathy. B. I. B. L. E. Be Involved Bible Learners Everyone: A Children's Bible Study. (p. 122)
Liepelt, Juanita. Blue: The Luckiest Dog in the World. Kasy, Frank, illus. (p. 202)
Liepke, Peter, photos by see Roos, Stephen.
Lierman, Jane. Cursive Writing Practice - Inspiring Quotes: Reproducible Activity Pages with Motivational & Character-Building Quotes That Make Handwriting Practice Meaningful. (p. 395)
—Standards-Based Map Activities: Easy & Engaging Lessons, Activities, & Practice Pages That Build Key Map & Geography Skills. (p. 1639)
Lies, Anne. Earthquake in Haiti. (p. 497)
—Oprah Winfrey: Media Mogul. (p. 1301)
Lies, Brian. Bats at the Ballgame. (p. 145)
—Bats at the Beach. (p. 145)
—Bats at the Library. (p. 145)
—Bats at the Library. Lies, Brian, illus. (p. 145)
—Bats in the Band. Lies, Brian, illus. (p. 145)
Lies, Brian, illus. see Bateman, Donna M.
Lies, Brian, illus. see Beck, W. H.
Lies, Brian, illus. see Landau, Elaine.
Lies, Brian, illus. see Livingston, Irene.
Lies, Brian, illus. see Springman, I. C.
Lies, Brian, illus. see Weiss, Ellen.
Liese, Charles, illus. see Meyer, Franklyn E.
Liess, Claudia. Stranger on Planet Earth. (p. 1665)
Liess, Claudia Schmidt. But Where Is Dad? (p. 246)
—Harry the Hamster: Learns a Lesson. (p. 751)
—Henry the Magical, Mythical Dragon. (p. 768)
Liessner, Richard. Foot Prince. Liessner, Richard, illus. (p. 614)
Liest, Christina, illus. see Hughes, Vi.
Lietaert, Kelly Jean. I Wish I Was Big. (p. 849)
Lietha, Dan, et al. Dinosaur Pak & Stak. (p. 442)
Liette, Chad. Downy Duck. (p. 474)
Lieurance, Suzanne. Ancient Maya: A MyReportLinks. com Book. (p. 70)
—Locket: Surviving the Triangle Shirtwaist Fire. (p. 1045)
—Lucky Baseball: My Story in a Japanese-American Internment Camp. (p. 1062)
—Mexico: A MyReportLinks. com Book. (p. 1131)
—Philippines: A MyReportLinks. com Book. (p. 1350)
—Prohibition Era in American History. (p. 1410)
—Triangle Shirtwaist Fire & Sweatshop Reform in American History. (p. 1785)
—Weapons & Strategies of the Civil War: A MyReportLinks. com Book. (p. 1869)
—Write a Romance in 5 Simple Steps. (p. 1963)
Liew, Sonny. Liquid City Volume 2 OGN. Liew, Sonny & Tju, Lim Cheng, eds. (p. 1021)
Liew, Sonny, illus. see Friesen, Ray.
Liew, Sonny, illus. see Yang, Gene Luen.
Life Changing Books, creator. Teenage Bluez 2 (p. 1714)
Life, Kay, illus. see Bunting, Eve.
Life, Kay, tr. Keys & Clues for Benny. (p. 950)
Life Lab Science Program Staff, jt. auth. see Cohen, Whitney.
Life Magazine Editors. Greatest Unsolved Mysteries of All Time: 50 Baffling Cases from the Files. (p. 720)
—LIFE Wonders of the World. (p. 1013)
—Picture Puzzle: Can You Spot the Differences? Adams, Mark, ed. (p. 1356)
Life Magazine Editors, creator. Remembering Elvis: 30 Years Later. (p. 1459)
Life Publishers International Staff, tr. see Peretti, Frank E.
Life Publishers International Staff, tr. see Puppet Prod.
Liff, Stewart. Managing Your Government Career: Success Strategies That Work. (p. 1086)
Liflander, Pamela. Gray's Anatomy. (p. 713)
Lifton, Betty Jean. Taka-Chan & I: A Dog's Journey to Japan by Runcible. Hosoe, Eikoh, photos by. (p. 1696)
Ligasan, Darryl, illus. see Barber, Barbara E.
Liggett, Diane T. & Mack, James A. Awesome Arizona Places for Curious Kids. (p. 121)
Liggett, Kim. Blood & Salt. (p. 200)
Light, Amorah. Sierra's Journey Home. (p. 1573)
Light, Bridget, jt. auth. see Craig, Jonathan.
Light Brown, Cynthia. Amazing Kitchen Chemistry Projects. (p. 54)
Light, Carol. Chickensing Big Book. Light, Carol, illus. (p. 300)
—Chickensing Little Book. Light, Carol, illus. (p. 300)
—Chickensing Story Book Reader. Light, Carol, illus. (p. 301)
—Oops, a Curious Horse Story Telling Board. (p. 1299)
Light, Carol, illus. see Gansle, Sherry.
Light, Douglas. Senses. (p. 1551)
Light, Douglas B. Cells, Tissues, & Skin. (p. 286)
Light, John. Are These Rhymes Nonsense? (p. 96)
—Dotty. (p. 472)
—Flower. (p. 607)
—Flower. Evans, Lisa, illus. (p. 607)
—Julie's Problem. (p. 932)
—Making a Splash! (p. 1080)
—Neighbours Are a Nuisance! (p. 1240)
Light, John & Light, Marilyn. TT Triangle. (p. 1795)
Light, Kayte. Nicholas & the Spirit of Love. (p. 1250)
Light, Kelly. Louise Loves Art. Light, Kelly, illus. (p. 1058)
Light, Kelly, illus. see Lee, Jenny.
Light, Kelly, illus. see Orshoski, Paul.
Light, Kelly, illus. see Rosenthal, Amy Krouse.
Light, Kelly, illus. see Soderberg, Erin.
Light, Marilyn, jt. auth. see Light, John.
Light, Steve. Boats Go. (p. 205)
—Christmas Giant. Light, Steve, illus. (p. 314)
—Diggers Go. (p. 439)
—Have You Seen My Dragon? Light, Steve, illus. (p. 754)
—I Am Happy: A Touch-and-Feel Book of Feelings. Light, Steve, illus. (p. 833)
—Planes Go. (p. 1367)
—Trains Go. (p. 1777)
—Trucks Go. (p. 1791)
—Zephyr Takes Flight. Light, Steve, illus. (p. 1986)
Light, Steve, illus. see Light, Steven.
Light, Steven. Have You Seen My Monster? Light, Steve, illus. (p. 754)
Light, The, jt. auth. see Chilton, Pamela.
Lightbourn-Rowe, Melanie. Things I Wish You Knew. (p. 1733)
Lightburn, Ron. Frankenstink! A Cautionary Tale. (p. 629)
Lightburn, Ron, illus. see Becker, Helaine.
Lightburn, Ron, illus. see Gregory, Nan.
Lightburn, Ron, illus. see Jennings, Sharon.
Lightburn, Ron, illus. see Lightburn, Sandra.
Lightburn, Ron, illus. see Manson, Ainslie.
Lightburn, Sandra. Pumpkin People Lightburn, Ron, illus. (p. 1416)
Lightender, J. Quicksilver Project: Forbidden Portals. (p. 1427)
Lightfoot, D. J. Trail Fever: The Life of a Texas Cowboy. Bobbish, John, illus. (p. 1776)
Lightfoot, Dale. Iraq. (p. 887)
Lightfoot, Gordon. Canadian Railroad Trilogy Wallace, Ian, illus. (p. 260)
Lightfoot, Joanne. Cat & the Fat Suit. (p. 277)
Lightfoot, Martha. Lion's Share. (p. 1021)
Lightfoot, Martha, illus. see Archer, Mandy.
Lightfoot, Toni Asante, jt. auth. see Lansana, Quraysh Ali.
Lighthipe, Mindy. Mother Monarch (p. 1178)
Lightman, Benjamin, jt. auth. see Lightman, Marjorie.
Lightman, Marjorie & Lightman, Benjamin. A to Z of Greek & Roman Women. (p. 2)
Lightner, Laura. FirstFires. Messina, Linda, illus. (p. 598)
Lightstone, Alexander. Dog IQ: Design 1. 0: A Story of Dogs & Computers. (p. 461)
Lightwood, Donald. Long Revenge. (p. 1047)
Ligi, Raffaella, illus. see Davidson, Susanna.
Lignell, Brent, illus. see Lignell, Kirk.
Lignell, Kirk. Listen to the Raindrops: Featuring the Storm Song. Lignell, Brent, illus. (p. 1022)
Lignor, Amy, ed. see Callsen, Terri.
Liguori, Anthony J. Vienna & Venture: Tales from the Equine Side. (p. 1841)
Liguori, Kathy, illus. see Losey, Tori.
Liguori Publications, creator. Every Day of Advent & Christmas, Year C: A Book of Activities for Children. (p. 542)
—Every Day of Lent & Easter, Year C: A Book of Activities for Children. (p. 542)
Liguori, Tara. Silly Milly Is a Princess. (p. 1576)
Lihoreau, Tim & Fry, Stephen. Stephen Fry's Incomplete & Utter History of Classical Music. (p. 1648)
Lihou, Gavin. Revenge of the Cannibal Chickens. Ross Kennedy, illus. (p. 1465)
Liittschwager, David, photos by see Waters, Alice & Duane, Daniel.
Lijewski, Christy. Next Exit (p. 1249)
—Replay (p. 1461)
Lijun, Yang, tr. see Way, Charles.
Likens, Arthur Dale. Wounded White Dove. (p. 1962)
Likins, Kim. Charlie's Perfect Day. Magalinska, Ingrid, illus. (p. 293)
—Charlie's Special Friends. (p. 293)
Lil Gems & Black, Magenta. Tutu's Lil Gems. (p. 1799)
Lilagan, Kenneth D., illus. see Boodey, David M.
Lile, Linda L. Nonnie, What's God? Julich, Jenniffer, illus. (p. 1263)
Lileng, Kimberly, ed. see Cadeau, Michelle.
Liles, Modesta. Fun Careers from a to Z. (p. 647)
Liles, R. D. Princess & the Troll. (p. 1403)
Liles, Rebecca. My Daddy's a Soldier (p. 1201)
—My Mommy's a Soldier (p. 1214)
Lilibeth, Ethel. Princesses Take Baths Too! (p. 1406)
Lilienstein, Jennel. Birthday! (p. 192)
—Day at the Beach. (p. 412)
—First Ball Game/Sports! (p. 593)
—Trip to the Zoo. (p. 1787)
Lilienthal, Alfred N. What Price Israel? 1953-2003. (p. 1893)
Liliom, Laura. You Are a Really Good Friend of Mine. Vagharshyan, Lilit, illus. (p. 1973)
Lilje, Karen, illus. see Orford, Margie.
Liljeblad, Fredrik. Democracy at Work. (p. 425)
—Voting. (p. 1850)
Liljeblad, Lynn, illus. see Sherayko, Peter.
Lill, Debra, illus. see Robb, Laura.
Lillard, David. West Virginia: A MyReportLinks. Com Book. (p. 1876)
—William Henry Harrison: A MyReportLinks. Com Book. (p. 1933)
Lillard, Paula Polk, jt. auth. see Jessen, Lynn Lillard.
Lillegard, Dee. Papas el Martes (p. 1322)
—Sitting in My Box Agee, Jon, illus. (p. 1582)
Lillehaug-Collins, Yvonne. Little Dragon. (p. 1027)
Lilley, Andrew, Sr. Story of Old Dog. (p. 1659)
Lillian, Miss. Jonah's Kids. (p. 925)
Lillibridge, Serenity. Rise of Trinity. (p. 1475)
Lillis, Holly. Place to Call Home (p. 1365)
Lillis, Rebecca. Yonah: Daughter of the Wind. (p. 1972)
Lillis, Sonya. Fuzzy Bacon. (p. 651)
—God's Kids: Being a Light in a Dark World. (p. 691)
—God's Kids: Growing up Holy in an Unholy World (p. 691)
—God's Kids: Great Bit Thoughts for Young Minds. (p. 691)
Lillo, George. London Merchant: The History of George Barnwell. Landes, William-Alan, ed. (p. 1046)
Lilly, Alexandra. Spanish Colonies in America. (p. 1621)
Lilly, Evangeline. Squickerwonkers. Fraser-Allen, Johnny, illus. (p. 1636)
Lilly, Kenneth, illus. see Hansard, Peter.
Lilly, Kenneth, illus. see Taylor, Barbara.
Lilly, Marsha W. Math to Hand: A Mathematics Handbook. (p. 1107)
Lilly, Matthew, illus. see Bailey, Jacqui.
Lilly, Melinda. Color. Thompson, Scott M., illus. (p. 342)
—Dirty & Clean. Thompson, Scott M., illus. (p. 446)
—Energy. Thompson, Scott M., photos by. (p. 528)
—Gravity. Thompson, Scott M., illus. (p. 712)
—Hot & Cold. (p. 801)
—Make It Grow. Thompson, Scott M., illus. (p. 1079)
—Misiones Espanolas (Spanish Missions) Capaldi, Gina, illus. (p. 1150)
—Rocks. (p. 1483)
—Rocks. Thompson, Scott M., photos by. (p. 1483)
—San Agustin (St Augustine) Rhine, Karen C., illus. (p. 1510)
—Solid, Liquid, & Gas. Thompson, Scott M., illus. (p. 1607)
—Sound up & Down. Thompson, Scott M., illus. (p. 1615)
—Sun & Moon. Thompson, Scott M., photos by. (p. 1676)
—Water & Ice. (p. 1862)
Lilly, Stephanie. Amazing Adventures of Ethan-Tyrannosaurus-Rex: The Escape from Raptor Forest. (p. 52)
Lilly, Suzanne. Untellable. (p. 1823)
Lilly, T. S. Upgrade. (p. 1824)
Lilly, Teresa Ives. I Don't Want to be a Pirate. (p. 838)
Lily, Henrietta M., jt. auth. see Klar, Jeremy.
Lily, Henrietta M. & Harmon, Daniel E. Frequently Asked Questions about Alcohol Abuse & Binge Drinking. (p. 636)
Lim, Andrew. Tales from the Kopitiam. (p. 1701)
Lim, Annalees. 10-Minute Seasonal Crafts for Autumn. (p. 1993)
—Fun with Fabric. (p. 648)
—Fun with Nature. (p. 648)
—Fun with Paint. (p. 649)
—Fun with Paper. (p. 649)
Lim, Bee Ling, jt. auth. see Goh, Sui Noi.

L

Lim, Charlotte. Attack of the Swordfish & Other Singapore Tales: Text by Charlotte Lim: Illustrations by Alicia Tan Yen Ping: Creative Directing by Ruby Lim-Yang. (p. 114)
Lim, Hwei, illus. see Noah, Jennifer & Giroux, Chris.
Lim, Jun, jt. auth. see Dhillon, Natasha C.
Lim, Kara, illus. see Jee-Hyung, Lee.
Lim, Kara, illus. see Lee, Jee-Hyung.
Lim, Rebecca. Astrologer's Daughter. (p. 109)
—Sweet Life. (p. 1690)
Lim, Robin. Indonesia. (p. 872)
Lim, Ron, illus. see Disney Book Group Staff & Thomas, Rich.
Lim, Ron, illus. see Marvel Book Group & Wong, Clarissa S.
Lim, Ron, illus. see Rieber, John Ney.
Lim, Ron, illus. see Wyatt, Chris.
Lim, Ron, jt. illus. see Bagley, Mark.
Lima, Graca, illus. see Rozen, Beti.
Lima, Rick. Redd: The Beta Fish. (p. 1455)
Lima, Sidney, illus. see McGregor, Don.
Lima, Sidney, jt. auth. see McGregor, Don.
Lima, Thais Clemente. God Is Good to Me. (p. 689)
Limb, Lisa. Wishing Wheelchair. (p. 1941)
Limb, Sue. Girl, 15, Charming but Insane. (p. 678)
Limbaugh, Kathryn Adams, jt. auth. see Limbaugh, Rush H., III.
Limbaugh, Rush H., III. Rush Revere & the Brave Pilgrims: Time-Travel Adventures with Exceptional Americans. (p. 1498)
—Rush Revere & the First Patriots: Time-Travel Adventures with Exceptional Americans. (p. 1498)
Limbaugh, Rush H., III & Limbaugh, Kathryn Adams. Rush Revere & the American Revolution. (p. 1498)
—Rush Revere & the American Revolution. Hiers, Christopher, illus. (p. 1498)
Limburg, Joanne. Woman Who Thought Too Much: A Memoir. (p. 1945)
Lime, Harry. Spider-Man 3: Meet the Heroes & Villains. Gordon, Steven E., illus. (p. 1626)
Limeres. Alaska Fishing: The Ultimate Angler's Guide. (p. 34)
Limke, Jeff. Arthur & Lancelot: The Fight for Camelot - An English Legend. Yeates, Thomas, illus. (p. 103)
—Isis & Osiris: To the Ends of the Earth. Witt, David, illus. (p. 891)
—Isis & Osiris: To the Ends of the Earth - An Egyptian Myth. Witt, David, illus. (p. 891)
—Isis & Osiris. (p. 891)
—Jason: Quest for the Golden Fleece, a Greek Myth. Seeley, Tim & Schulz, Barbara, illus. (p. 910)
—Jason. (p. 910)
—King Arthur: Excaliber Unsheathed. Yeates, Thomas, illus. (p. 958)
—King Arthur: Excalibur Unsheathed. Yeates, Thomas, illus. (p. 958)
—King Arthur. (p. 958)
—Rey Arturo: La Espada Excalibur Desenvainada; King Arthur: Excalibur Unsheathed. (p. 1467)
—Rey Arturo: La Espada Excalibur Desenvainada: Una Leyenda Inglesa. Translations.com Staff, tr. from ENG. (p. 1467)
—Theseus: Battling the Minotaur. (p. 1732)
—Theseus: Battling the Minotaur. McCrea, John, illus. (p. 1732)
—Thor & Loki: In the Land of Giants - A Norse Myth. Randall, Ron, illus. (p. 1739)
—Thor & Loki. (p. 1739)
—Treasure of Mount Fate. Hilinski, Clint, illus. (p. 1782)
—Tristan & Isolde: The Warrior & the Princess. (p. 1787)
—Tristan & Isolde: The Warrior & the Princess - A British Legend. Randall, Ron, illus. (p. 1787)
Limmer, Hannes, illus. see Leipe, Ulla.
Limon, Cyndi. Hello, My Name Is Boots. (p. 764)
Limon, Helen. Om Shanti Babe. (p. 1288)
Limón, José E., ed. see Arkham, Thomas.
Limón, José E., ed. see DePietro, Frank.
Limón, José E., ed. see Palmer, Bill.
Lin, Albert, illus. see Smith, Michael.
Lin, Alex. Little Detective. (p. 1026)
Lin, Amy. Book Sale: Represent & Solve Subtraction Problems. (p. 212)
Lin, Chris. Mandy & Pandy Play Let's Count. Villalta, Ingrid, illus. (p. 1087)
—Mandy & Pandy Play Sports. Villalta, Ingrid, illus. (p. 1087)
—Mandy & Pandy Say Ni Hao Ma? Villalta, Ingrid, illus. (p. 1087)
—Mandy & Pandy Say Ni Hao Ma? Teach Kids Chinese the Fun & Easy Way. (p. 1087)
—Mandy & Pandy Visit China. Villalta, Ingrid, illus. (p. 1087)
Lin, Grace. Bringing in the New Year. (p. 229)
—Dim Sum for Everyone! Lin, Grace, illus. (p. 440)
—Dumpling Days. (p. 490)
—Fortune Cookie Fortunes. Lin, Grace, illus. (p. 623)
—Kite Flying. (p. 962)
—Ling & Ting: Not Exactly the Same! (p. 1019)
—Ling & Ting Share a Birthday. (p. 1019)
—Ling & Ting: Twice As Silly. (p. 1019)
—Red Thread: An Adoption Fairy Tale. Lin, Grace, illus. (p. 1455)
—Starry River of the Sky. (p. 1642)
—Thanking the Moon: Celebrating the Mid-Autumn Moon Festival. (p. 1725)
—Ugly Vegetables. (p. 1808)
—Where the Mountain Meets the Moon. (p. 1909)
—Year of the Dog. (p. 1969)
—Year of the Rat. (p. 1969)
Lin, Grace, illus. see Park, Frances & Park, Ginger.
Lin, Grace, illus. see Thong, Roseanne.
Lin, Grace, illus. see Tucker, Kathy & Hong, Lily Toy.
Lin, Grace, illus. see Tucker, Kathy.
Lin, Grace, illus. see Wang, Xiaohong.
Lin, Grace, illus. see Yee, Paul.
Lin, Grace & Mckneally, Ranida T. Our Seasons. Lin, Grace, illus. (p. 1310)
Lin, Joyce, tr. frog in the Well. Caprio, Pattie, illus. (p. 640)
Lin, Kelly Jenkins. Mr. Astley's Blueberries. Fiddy, Samantha Lane, illus. (p. 1184)
Lin, Melanie, illus. see Paladin, Frank.
Lin, Yali, illus. see Thielbar, Melinda.
Lin, Yoming S. Alexander Graham Bell & the Telephone. (p. 36)
—Charles Darwin & Evolution. (p. 292)
—Curies & Radioactivity. (p. 392)
—Defeating Depression. (p. 423)
—Fahrenheit, Celsius, & Their Temperature Scales. (p. 562)
—Galileo & the Telescope. (p. 653)
—Isaac Newton & Gravity. (p. 890)
Lin, Yu-Chin. Vision of the Other Side Volume 1 (p. 1845)
Lin, Zhimin. China under Reform. (p. 307)
—China under Reform. Wang, Jianwei, ed. (p. 307)
Linardi, Franca, jt. auth. see Ciccone, Tizania.
Linardi, Franca, jt. auth. see Ciccone, Tiziana.
Linares, Jairo. Pinocho. (p. 1361)
Linares, Jairo, illus. see Panamericana Staff, ed.
Linares, Luisa-Ma. Ponga un Tigre en Su (Put a Tiger in Your Bed) (p. 1382)
Linari, Adrian. Los Cuentos de Aguara. (p. 1053)
Linaweaver, Brad, jt. auth. see Hatch, Richard.
Linch, Tanya. Owl, the Aat & the Roar. (p. 1315)
Lincoln Collier, James. Corn Raid. (p. 367)
—Worst of Times. (p. 1961)
Lincoln, Dallas Ford. Sawmill Sant. (p. 1518)
Lincoln, Emma, jt. auth. see Lincoln, Ray.
Lincoln, Hazel. Little Snow Bear Lincoln, Hazel, illus. (p. 1036)
Lincoln, Jacqueline Michelle. Adventures of Sheila the Awesome (Aussie) Dog. (p. 22)
Lincoln, James. Rainbow Jars. Smith, Jacqui, illus. (p. 1435)
Lincoln, Jerri. Little Unicorn Who Could Coloring Book. (p. 1037)
Lincoln, Jerri Kay. Dancing with Unicorns. (p. 403)
Lincoln, Margarette. Pirate's Handbook: How to Become a Rogue of the High Seas. (p. 1363)
Lincoln, Nan. Cecily's Summer. Wynne, Patricia J., illus. (p. 283)
Lincoln, Peggy. Oh, Dear! (p. 1280)
Lincoln, Ray & Lincoln, Emma. Dog in a Box: The Story of Free vs. Crated Champ. (p. 461)
Lind, Alan, jt. auth. see Luther, Jacqueline.
Lind, Amy, et al. Greenwood Encyclopedia of Women's Issues Worldwide (p. 723)
Lind, Jenny. Navajo Coyote Tales (p. 1237)
Lind, Karen K. Exploring Science in Early Childhood Education. (p. 553)
Lind, Kathleen. Best Friends. Lind, Kathleen & Simonis, Cheryl, illus. (p. 169)
Linda Bartlett & Wen Marcec. Keby the Earth-Friendly Bear. (p. 946)
Linda Cole Design Ltd Staff, creator. Chick Pea & the Changing Leaves. (p. 299)
Linda, Graves, illus. see Yolen, Jane.
Linda, Miiller. Grandma's Blessing X 2. (p. 708)
Linda (Mimi') Wise. Come Grow with Me: Inspirational Poems for Children. (p. 347)
Linda, Miss. Miss Viola's Kitchen. (p. 1152)
Linda, Winder. Glitter: My First Book of Shapes Numbers Colors & the Alphabet Gods Way. (p. 683)
Lindahl, Ben. World Outside My Door. (p. 1958)
Lindahl, Inger. Bertil & the Bathroom Elephants. Dyssegaard, Elisabeth Kallick, tr. (p. 168)
Lindahl, Kay. How Does God Listen? Maloney, Cynthia, photos by. (p. 808)
Lindahl, Larry, photos by see Andres, Dennis Michael.
Lindaman, Jane. Zip It! Carlson, Nancy, illus. (p. 1987)
Lindaman, Jane, jt. auth. see Allen, Susan.
Lindberg, Eric, jt. auth. see Thomas, Doni Zasloff.
Lindberg, Tod. Political Teachings of Jesus. (p. 1380)
Lindbergh, Anne M. People in Pineapple Place. (p. 1339)
—Worry Week. Hawkes, Kevin, illus. (p. 1961)
Lindbergh, Charles A., Jr. Spirit of St Louis. (p. 1628)
Lindbergh, Reeve. Homer: The Library Cat. Wilsdorf, Anne, illus. (p. 793)
—My Little Grandmother Often Forgets. Brown, Kathryn, illus. (p. 1212)
—Nobody Owns the Sky. Paparone, Pamela, illus. (p. 1262)
Lindblad, Stefan, illus. see Orme, David.
Lindbo, David L., et al, texts. Soil! Get the Inside Scoop. (p. 1606)
Linde, Barbara. Climates of the World: Identifying & Comparing Mean, Median, & Mode. (p. 332)
—Coyotes & Wolves Are Not Pets! (p. 375)
—Cyberspace Research. (p. 396)
—Heroes of the US Air Force. (p. 773)
—Managing Your Money: Understanding Math Operations Involving Decimals & Integers. (p. 1086)
—Mapping Europe. (p. 1090)
—Math in Our Solar System: Applying Problem-Solving Strategies. (p. 1106)
—Olympic Wrestling. (p. 1288)
—Thurgood Marshall. (p. 1746)
Linde, Barbara, jt. auth. see Sohn, Emily.
Linde, Barbara & Benchmark Education Co. Staff. Opinions about Matthew Brady. (p. 1300)
Linde, Barbara & Linde, Barbara M. Coyotes & Wolves Are Not Pets! (p. 375)
—Mapping Europe. (p. 1090)
Linde, Barbara M. Appaloosas. (p. 92)
—Arabian Horses. (p. 94)
—Becoming a Supreme Court Justice. (p. 156)
—Bizarre Life Cycle of a Cuckoo. (p. 194)
—Bizarre Life Cycle of A Kangaroo. (p. 194)
—Building Washington, D. C. Measuring the Area of Rectangular Shapes. (p. 239)
—Building Washington, DC: Measuring the Area of Rectangular Shapes. (p. 239)
—Climates of the World: Identifying & Comparing Mean, Median, & Mode. (p. 332)
—Clydesdales. (p. 336)
—Daniel Radcliffe. (p. 405)
—Deforestation & Desertification: Set Of 6. (p. 424)
—Deforestation & Desertification: Text Pairs. (p. 424)
—Earth Measuring Its Changes: Set Of 6. (p. 496)
—Earth: Measuring Its Changes: Text Pairs. (p. 496)
—Ecological Disasters: Set Of 6. (p. 502)
—Ecological Disasters: Text Pairs. (p. 502)
—Famous Horses. (p. 569)
—Heroes of the US Army. (p. 773)
—Horses in History. (p. 800)
—I Show Respect. Mones, Marc, illus. (p. 845)
—I Show Respect Lap Book. Mones, Marc, illus. (p. 845)
—I Take Turns. Patton, Julia, illus. (p. 846)
—I Take Turns Lap Book. Patton, Julia, illus. (p. 846)
—I Will Find a Way. Evans, Antony, illus. (p. 848)
—I Will Find a Way Lap Book. Evans, Antony, illus. (p. 848)
—Jealous of Josie. Poole, Helen, illus. (p. 911)
—Jealous of Josie Lap Book. Poole, Helen, illus. (p. 911)
—Jesse Jackson. (p. 914)
—Life Cycle of a Crocodile. (p. 1009)
—Life Cycle of a Honeybee. (p. 1009)
—Life Cycle of an Opossum. (p. 1009)
—Living in a Community. (p. 1041)
—Malcolm X. (p. 1083)
—Managing Your Money: Understanding Math Operations Involving Decimals & Integers. (p. 1086)
—Mapping Africa. (p. 1090)
—Mapping Asia. (p. 1090)
—Martin Luther King Jr. (p. 1097)
—Math in Our Solar System: Applying Problem-Solving Strategies. (p. 1106)
—Miniature Horses. (p. 1146)
—Olympic Wrestling. (p. 1288)
—Origami: Identifying Right Angles in Geometric Figures. (p. 1303)
—Pollution. (p. 1381)
Linde, Barbara M.. Pollution. (p. 1381)
Linde, Barbara M. Power of Storms. (p. 1389)
—Price of a Pioneer Journey: Adding & Subtracting Two-Digit Dollar Amounts. (p. 1398)
—Quarter Horses. (p. 1422)
—Rosa Parks. (p. 1488)
—Shopping Trip: Learning to Add Dollars & Cents up to $10. 00 Without Regrouping. (p. 1569)
—Slavery in Early America. (p. 1588)
—Snakes Are Not Pets! (p. 1596)
—Strip Mining. (p. 1667)
—Taylor Swift. (p. 1708)
—Tent Caterpillars. (p. 1720)
—Traveling Around the United States: Learning to Add 2 Three-Digit Numbers Without Regrouping. (p. 1780)
—Water on Earth. (p. 1863)
—Weather & Climate. (p. 1869)
—What Happened at Area 51? (p. 1885)
—When Floods Flow. (p. 1902)
—When Hurricanes Howl. (p. 1902)
—Working at the Farmer's Market: Solving Money Problems Involving the Four Math Operations. (p. 1952)
—Working at the Post Office: Learning to Subtract 2 Three-Digit Numbers Without Renaming. (p. 1952)
Linde, Barbara M., jt. auth. see Linde, Barbara.
Linde, Barbara M. & Benchmark Education Co. Staff. Monsters among Us? (p. 1169)
—Mysteries Set in Stone. (p. 1222)
Linde, Hermann, illus. see Goethes Fairy Tale Staff.
Linde, Polly Van der, see Van der Linde, Polly.
Linde, Tasha Van der, see Van der Linde, Polly & Van der Linde, Tasha.
Lindeen, Carol K. Ballenas. (p. 134)
—Básico de la Tierra. Translation Services Staff & Translations.com Staff, trs. from ENG. (p. 142)
—Básico de las Rocas. Translation Services Staff & Translations.com Staff, trs. from ENG. (p. 142)
—Brachiosaurus Hughes, Jon, illus. (p. 221)
—Corals (p. 366)
—Dolphins [Scholastic]. (p. 465)
—Farm Tools over Time (p. 574)
—Freshwater Fishing (p. 637)
—From Coast to Coast (p. 642)
—Let's Do Karate! (p. 995)
—Let's Ride Bikes! (p. 1000)
—Life in a Desert (p. 1010)
—Life in a Pond (p. 1010)
—Look at Gravity (p. 1048)
—Native American Powwows (p. 1234)
—Police Cars (p. 1380)
—Seres Vivos y No Vivos. Translations.com Staff, tr. from ENG. (p. 1552)
—Sharks [Scholastic]. (p. 1563)
—Sky at Night (p. 1586)
—Sólidos, Líquidos y Gases. Translation Services Staff & Translations.com Staff, trs. from ENG. (p. 1607)
—Solids, Liquids, & Gases (p. 1608)
—Velociraptor [Scholastic]. Hughes, Jon, illus. (p. 1835)
—Water Basics Saunders-Smith, Gail, ed. (p. 1862)
—What Is a Museum? (p. 1888)
—Who Makes Our Laws? (p. 1917)
—¡Vamos a Jugar al Básquetbol! (p. 1831)
Lindeen, Carol K. & Capstone Press Editors. Caballitos de Mar. Saunders-Smith, Gail, ed. (p. 250)
—Pulpos. Saunders-Smith, Gail, ed. (p. 1416)
Lindeen, Carol K. & Capstone Press Staff. Corales. Saunders-Smith, Gail, ed. (p. 366)
—Farm Tools over Time (p. 574)
—Focas. Saunders-Smith, Gail, ed. (p. 610)
—From Coast to Coast (p. 642)
—Look at Gravity (p. 1048)
—My Heart (p. 1210)
—Native American Powwows (p. 1234)
—Sky at Night (p. 1586)
—Velociraptor. Saunders-Smith, Gail, ed. (p. 1835)
—What Is a Museum? (p. 1888)
—Who Makes Our Laws? (p. 1917)
Lindeen, Carol K & Lugtu, Carol J. Ambulances (p. 57)
—Ambulancia. (p. 57)
—Apatosaurus Hughes, Jon, illus. (p. 91)
—Clown Fish (p. 335)
—Corals (p. 366)
—Dolphins (p. 464)
—Fire Trucks (p. 591)
—Giant Ripper Lizard (p. 674)
—Jellyfish (p. 912)
—Let's Downhill Ski! (p. 995)
—Let's Ice-Skate! (p. 998)
—Let's Swim! (p. 1000)
—Life in a Desert (p. 1010)
—Life in a Forest (p. 1010)
—Life in a Polar Region (p. 1010)
—Life in a Pond Saunders-Smith, Gail, ed. (p. 1010)
—Life in a Rain Forest (p. 1010)
—Life in a Stream (p. 1010)
—Life in a Wetland (p. 1010)
—Life in an Ocean (p. 1010)
—Living & Nonliving (p. 1040)
—My Bones (p. 1198)
—My Bones Saunders-Smith, Gail, ed. (p. 1198)
—My Brain Saunders-Smith, Gail, ed. (p. 1199)
—My Heart Saunders-Smith, Gail, ed. (p. 1210)
—My Muscles Saunders-Smith, Gail, ed. (p. 1215)
—Natural & Human-Made (p. 1235)
—Octopuses (p. 1278)
—Police Cars (p. 1380)
—Rescue Boats (p. 1462)
—Rescue Boats (Barcos de Rescate) (p. 1462)
—Rock Basics (p. 1482)
—Sea Horses (p. 1534)
—Sea Turtles (p. 1536)
—Sea Turtles [Scholastic]. (p. 1536)
—Soil Basics (p. 1606)
—Solids, Liquids, & Gases (p. 1608)
—Velociraptor Hughes, Jon, illus. (p. 1835)
—Whales (p. 1878)
—Whales [Scholastic]. (p. 1878)
Lindeen, Carol K. & Sullivan, Jody. Under the Sea (8 book Set) [NASCO]. (p. 1814)
Lindeen, Carol K., et al. Ambulances (p. 57)
—Braquiosaurio/Brachiosaurus Saunders-Smith, Gail, ed. (p. 222)
Lindeen, Mary. Airplanes. (p. 32)
—All about Boats (p. 42)
—Ashes to Ashes: Uncovering Pompeii. (p. 106)
—At the Beach. (p. 110)
—At the Pond. (p. 111)
—Digital Safety Smarts: Preventing Cyberbullying. (p. 440)
—Elephants. (p. 511)
—Fall! (p. 566)
—Fire Trucks. (p. 591)
—Forest Doubles. (p. 618)
—Friday. Gonzalez, Javier A., illus. (p. 637)
—Garbage Trucks. (p. 655)
—Getting Ready for Bed. (p. 669)
—Giraffes. (p. 677)
—Glaciers. (p. 682)
—Graders. (p. 705)
—Griz Finds Gold: A Story about California. (p. 724)
—Halloween! (p. 737)
—Happy Groundhog Day! (p. 745)
—Helicopters. (p. 763)
—History Rocks! (p. 785)
—How Things Change (p. 814)
—If the Shoe Fits. (p. 854)
—In the Sky. (p. 867)
—In the Woods. (p. 868)
—Investigating the Carbon Cycle. (p. 885)
—Investigating the Rock Cycle. (p. 885)
—It's a Dog's Life (p. 895)
—Jane Goodall: Friend of the Apes. Soud, illus. (p. 908)
—Leading the Way (p. 982)
—Lend a Hand. (p. 991)
—Let's Play Basketball. (p. 1000)
—Let's Play Football! (p. 1000)
—Let's Play Hockey! (p. 1000)
—Let's Play Soccer. (p. 1000)
—Letter Aa: Things at School Set (p. 1001)
—Lions. (p. 1021)
—Lugares Donde Vive la Gente (p. 1064)
—Marie Curie: Scientist. Soud, illus. (p. 1093)
—Merry Christmas! (p. 1128)
—Monday. Gonzalez, Javier A., illus. (p. 1163)
—Monkeys. (p. 1165)
—Natural States. (p. 1236)
—Parks of the U. S. A. (p. 1325)
—Parques de Los EUA (p. 1325)
—Penguins. (p. 1337)
—Polar Bears. (p. 1379)
—Rain Forests. (p. 1434)
—Saturday. Gonzalez, Javier A., illus. (p. 1515)
—Saving Money. (p. 1517)
—Ships. (p. 1567)
—Smart Online Communication: Protecting Your Digital Footprint. (p. 1593)
—Snowplows. (p. 1601)
—Spring! (p. 1634)
—St. Patrick's Day. (p. 1638)
—Story of Corn (p. 1657)
—Summer! (p. 1673)
—Sunday. Gonzalez, Javier A., illus. (p. 1676)
—Then & Now (p. 1729)
—Thursday. Gonzalez, Javier A., illus. (p. 1746)
—Tractors. (p. 1775)
—Trains. (p. 1777)
—Trucks. (p. 1791)
—Tuesday. Gonzalez, Javier A., illus. (p. 1796)
—Visit to the Aquarium. (p. 1845)
—Visit to the Firehouse. (p. 1845)
—Visit to the Library. (p. 1845)
—Visit to the Market. (p. 1845)
—Wednesday. Gonzalez, Javier A., illus. (p. 1871)
—Week. Gonzalez, Javier A., illus. (p. 1871)
—Welcome to Mexico (p. 1873)
—Welcome to Mexico! (p. 1873)
—Welcome to North America (p. 1873)
—Where People Live (p. 1909)

—Winter! (p. 1937)
—Wonder Readers. (p. 1947)
—Wonder Readers: Social Studies. (p. 1947)
Lindeen, Mary, ed. see Cecchini, Marie E.
Lindeen, Mary, ed. see Fisher, Ann Richmond.
Lindeen, Mary, ed. see Storey, Melinda.
Lindeen, Mary, ed. see Tucker, Mary.
Lindeen, Mary & Capstone Press Editors. Letter Aa: Things at School (p. 1001)
Lindeen, Mary & Capstone Press Staff. Letter Oo: How Things Change (p. 1002)
Lindeen, Mary & Eunjoo, Jang. Helping Others. (p. 766)
Lindeen, Mary & Kesselring, Susan. Being Safe around Water. McGeehan, Dan & Moore, David, Jr., illus. (p. 161)
—Being Safe at Home. McGeehan, Dan & Moore, David, Jr., illus. (p. 161)
—Being Safe in Your Neighborhood. McGeehan, Dan & Moore, David, illus. (p. 161)
—Being Safe on Wheels. McGeehan, Dan & Moore, David, illus. (p. 161)
—Being Safe with Fire. McGeehan, Dan & Moore, David, illus. (p. 161)
—Being Safe with Weather. McGeehan, Dan & Moore, David, illus. (p. 161)
Lindeen, Mary & Peggy, Nille. Playing Together. (p. 1372)
Lindelauf, Benny. Nine Open Arms. (p. 1256)
Lindeman, Carolynn. Musical Children: Engaging Children in Musical Experiences. (p. 1194)
Lindeman, Craig. Big Black Dog & the Big Blue Se. Shoop, Johanna, illus. (p. 178)
Lindemann, Kara, ed. see Robins, Jeannie.
Lindemann, Lindy. Cat's Tale, One Cat's Search for the Meaning of Life. Wheeler, Jody, illus. (p. 281)
—Kicklighter Shadow & Beeples Book: The Beeples' Birthday Bash. (p. 951)
—Kicklighter Shadow & the Beeples. White, David, illus. (p. 951)
Lindemer, C. R. Beauly, the Donkey-Mooing Beltie. Bouthyette, Valerie, illus. (p. 153)
Lindemood, Kimmer & Pelletier, Ingrid. Ghost of Island Lake. (p. 671)
Linden, Becca, jt. auth. see Botnick, Julie.
Linden, Carol. Susie Q Kitten, Is That Your Sister? (p. 1688)
Linden, Dianne. Peacekeepers. (p. 1332)
—Shimmerdogs (p. 1566)
Linden, Joanne. Ben & Zip: Two Short Friends. Goldsmith, Tom, illus. (p. 163)
—Fiddleheads to Fir Trees: Leaves in All Seasons. Laurie, Caple, illus. (p. 583)
—Shih Tzus (p. 1566)
—Yorkshire Terriers (p. 1972)
Linden, Martijn van der, illus. see Rinck, Maranke.
Lindenbaum, Pija. Bridget & the Moose Brothers. Board, Kjersti, tr. from SWE. (p. 227)
—Mini Mia & Her Darling Uncle. Dyssegaard, Elisabeth Kallick, tr. from SWE. (p. 1146)
—When Owen's Mom Breathed Fire. Dyssegaard, Elisabeth Kallick, tr. (p. 1904)
Lindenbaum, Pija, illus. see Lindgren, Astrid.
Linder, Bertram L., ed. see Baker, Paul R. & Hall, William H.
Linder, Don. Where Do Things Go When I Close My Eyes? (p. 1907)
Linder, Dorothy Perilo. Vegetable Collection: Recipes & Rhymes to Conquer Kids of All Ages. (p. 1834)
Linder, Karen A. Jack the Curly Black Dog: Goes to the Beach. (p. 903)
Linder, Kim And Joe. Story of Nastyman. (p. 1659)
Linder, Nani Aki. All about Me Look at Me I'm a Star: Children's Workbook. (p. 43)
Linderman, Dianne. Entrepreneurial Kids' Books: Books That Inspire, Teach & Entertain Johnson, Dolores, illus. (p. 531)
—How to Become an Entrepreneurial Kid (p. 815)
—My Cookie Business. Johnson, Dolores, illus. (p. 1200)
—My Fishing Business. Johnson, Dolores, illus. (p. 1208)
—My Pony Ride Business. Johnson, Dolores, illus. (p. 1217)
Linderman, Frank B., et al. Big Jinny: The Story of a Grizzly Bear. Lochrie, Elizabeth, illus. (p. 182)
Linderoth, Joel. Almost & Always: Adult Lessons Hidden in 10 Children's Poems. (p. 48)
Lindert, Reyna & Anthony, Michelle. My First Signs. (p. 1208)
Lindgren, Alan. Courage of the Flame: Ballads, Sonnets & Other Gardens of Poetry with Prose Writings. Lindgren, Alan, ed. (p. 372)
Lindgren, Astrid. Brothers Lionheart. Morgan, Jill, tr. from SWE. (p. 231)
—Calf for Christmas. Lawson, Polly, tr. from SWE. (p. 252)
—Do You Know Pippi Longstocking? Dyssegaard, Elisabeth Kallick, tr. (p. 458)
—Ferien auf Saltkroken. (p. 582)
—Happy Times in Noisy Village. Wikland, Ilon, illus. (p. 747)
—Mio, My Son. Wikland, Ilon, illus. (p. 1148)
—Mirabelle. Dyssegaard, Elisabeth Kallick, tr. from SWE. (p. 1148)
—Pippa Mediaslargas. (p. 1362)
—Pippi Goes on Board. (p. 1362)
—Pippi in the South Seas. (p. 1362)
—Pippi in the South Seas. Turner, Marianne, tr. from SWE. (p. 1362)
—Pippi Langstrumpf geht an Bord. (p. 1362)
—Pippi Longstocking. (p. 1362)
—Pippi Longstocking. Nunally, Tina, tr. (p. 1362)
—Pippi Longstocking. Lamborn, Florence, tr. from SWE. (p. 1362)
—Pippi Moves In. Nunnally, Tiina, tr. from SWE. (p. 1362)
—Rasmus & the Vagabond. Bothmer, Gerry, tr. from SWE. (p. 1439)
—Seacrow Island. (p. 1536)
Lindgren, Astrid & Crampton, Patricia. Red Bird. Tornqvist, Marit, illus. (p. 1453)
Lindgren, Astrid & Nyman, Ingrid. Pippi Won't Grow Up. Nunnally, Tiina, tr. from SWE. (p. 1362)
Lindgren, Astrid & Vang Nyman, Ingrid. Pippi Fixes Everything. Nunnally, Tiina, tr. from SWE. (p. 1362)
Lindgren, Astrid & Wiberg, Harald. Tomten (p. 1765)
Lindgren, B. L., jt. auth. see Lindgren, Barbro.
Lindgren, Barbro. Benito y el Chupon. Landstrom, Olaf, illus. (p. 164)
—Benny's Had Enough! Dyssegaard, Elisabeth Kallick, tr. from SWE. (p. 165)
—Julia Wants a Pet. Dyssegaard, Elisabeth Kallick, tr. (p. 932)
Lindgren, Barbro, jt. auth. see Liniers.
Lindgren, Barbro & Lindgren, B. L. Oink, Oink Benny. Dyssegaard, Elisabeth Kallick, tr. from SWE. (p. 1282)
Lindgren, Laura, tr. see Schmidt, Hans-Christian.
Lindholm, Marjorie & Lindholm, Peggy. Columbine Survivor's Story. (p. 346)
Lindholm, Megan, jt. auth. see Brust, Steven.
Lindholm, Peggy, jt. auth. see Lindholm, Marjorie.
Lindin, Kerri & Pecsenye, Jessica. University of Rochester College Prowler off the Record. (p. 1821)
Lindley, Nancy & Peters, Laura. Roses for Michigan (p. 1490)
Lindley, Thomas, photos by see Steiner, Joan.
Lindman. Flicka, Ricka, Dicka & the Little Dog. Lindman, illus. (p. 603)
—Flicka, Ricka, Dicka & the Strawberries. Lindman, illus. (p. 603)
—Flicka, Ricka, Dicka & the Three Kittens. Lindman, illus. (p. 603)
—Flicka, Ricka, Dicka & Their New Skates: Updated Edition with Paperdolls. Lindman, illus. (p. 603)
—Flicka, Ricka, Dicka Bake a Cake. Lindman, illus. (p. 603)
Lindman, Amy Sorvaag, illus. see Jones, Susan Smith & Warren, Dianne.
Lindman, Maj. Flicka, Ricka, Dicka & the New Dotted Dresses. (p. 603)
—Flicka, Ricka, Dicka & the New Dotted Dresses. Lindman, Maj, illus. (p. 603)
—Flicka, Ricka, Dicka & Their New Skates. Lindman, Maj, illus. (p. 603)
—Flicka, Ricka, Dicka Go to Market. Lindman, Maj, illus. (p. 603)
Lindmark, Margaret, illus. see Contreras, Kathleen.
Lindmark, Margaret, illus. see Lipp, Frederick.
Lindmark, Margaret, jt. auth. see Contreras, Kathleen.
Lindner, April. Catherine. (p. 280)
—Jane. (p. 907)
—Love, Lucy. (p. 1060)
Lindner, Brooke. Dance with Brobee! (p. 402)
—Diego's Halloween Party. Mawhinney, Art, illus. (p. 437)
—Hooray for School! Going to School with Nick Jr. Hall, Susan & Hall, Susan, illus. (p. 796)
Lindner, Brooke, jt. auth. see Barrie, J. M.
Lindner, Ellen, illus. see Poe, Marshall.
Lindner, Heidi, ed. Animals, Animals, Animals. (p. 82)
—Great Games for Small Children (p. 716)
—Off We Go Outside! (p. 1279)
—Wintertime. (p. 1939)
Lindo, Elvira. Manolito Four-Eyes Emilio, Urberuaga & Urberuaga, Emilio, illus. (p. 1088)
—Manolito Four-Eyes: the 2nd Volume of the Great Encyclopedia of My Life: The 2nd Volume of the Great Encyclopedia of My Life Urberuaga, Emilio, illus. (p. 1088)
—Manolito Gafotas Urberuaga, Emilio, illus. (p. 1088)
Lindoff, Hannah. Mary's Wild Winter Feast. Koch, Nobu & Rizal, Clarissa, illus. (p. 1101)
Lindon, David A. Lost Children of the Namuh & the Chamber of Souls - the First of a Trilogy. (p. 1055)
Lindop, Christine. Jack the Hero. Wright, Craig, ed. (p. 903)
—Where Is It? Wright, Craig, ed. (p. 1908)
Lindop, Christine, ed. see Bassett, Jennifer & Stewart, Sue.
Lindop, Christine, ed. see Hopkins, Andy & Potter, Joc.
Lindop, Christine, jt. ed. see Oxford University Press Staff.
Lindop, Edmund & DeCapua, Sarah. America in the 1950s. (p. 59)
Lindop, Edmund & Goldstein, Margaret. America in the 1920s. (p. 59)
—America in the 1930s. (p. 59)
—America in the 1940s. (p. 59)
—America in the 1960s. (p. 59)
Lindop, Laurie. Cave Sleuths. (p. 282)
—Dynamic Modern Women Series (p. 491)
—Venturing the Deep Sea. (p. 1836)
Lindquist, Jennie D. Crystal Tree. Chalmers, Mary, illus. (p. 387)
—Little Silver House. Williams, Garth, illus. (p. 1036)
Lindquist, K. Margaret. Tyler Poncho's Amalgamated Menagerie. (p. 1805)
Lindquist, Kaeti. Tyler Poncho's Amalgamated Menagerie. (p. 1805)
Lindquist, N. J. Best of Friends (p. 170)
—Friends in Need. (p. 638)
—Friends Like These. (p. 638)
—In Time of Trouble. (p. 868)
—More Than Friends: Circle of Friends. Vol. 4 (p. 1175)
Lindro, illus. see Hughes, Lynn Gordon.
Lindroth, David, ed. see Facts on File, Inc. Staff, et al.
Lindroth, Malin & Martini, Clem. Train Wreck & Too Late. Little, Melanie, ed. (p. 1777)
Lindsay, Alan, jt. auth. see Anfuso, Dennis.
Lindsay and Crouse Staff, jt. auth. see Rodgers and Hammerstein Organization Staff.
Lindsay, Anne, photos by see Wong, Janet S.
Lindsay, Bruce. Hometown Weekly: Good News for a Change: Humorous Tales from Parley Grove. (p. 794)
Lindsay, Courtney B. ABC Scream, It's Halloween! (p. 3)
Lindsay, Debbie. Itty-Bitty Icky Committee/Heroes of the Heart. (p. 900)
Lindsay, Elizabeth. Annie Saves the Day. Eastwood, John, illus. (p. 87)
—Annie to the Rescue. Kavanagh, Peter, illus. (p. 87)
—Bugs & Butterflies. (p. 237)
—Dancing Magic. (p. 403)
—Ghost in the House. (p. 670)
—Ready to Fly. (p. 1447)
—Stardust Surprise. (p. 1642)
—Unicorn Dreams (Book 1) (p. 1818)
—Wands & Charms (Book 2) (p. 1856)
Lindsay, Fitzroy A. My Daddy Came Home Long after the War. (p. 1201)
—Two Aliens Looking in My Window. (p. 1803)
Lindsay, Jabari. Gangs: Deal with It Before Wrong Seems Right (p. 655)
Lindsay, Jeanne Warren & Brunelli, Jean. Nurturing Your Newborn: Young Parents' Guide to Baby's First Month. (p. 1273)
Lindsay, Kristine. Basic Math Practice 5 - Rounding, Reasonableness & Estimating. (p. 142)
—Basic Reading Series - Binder 3. (p. 142)
—Basic Vocabulary - 1. (p. 142)
—Basic Vocabulary 2. (p. 142)
—Coupon Math. (p. 372)
Lindsay, Liddy. Opera a to Z: A Beginner's Guide to Opera. (p. 1300)
Lindsay, Linda. People Heaven. (p. 1339)
Lindsay, Marion, illus. see Baguley, Elizabeth.
Lindsay, Marion, illus. see Webb, Holly.
Lindsay, Marion, jt. auth. see Webb, Holly.
Lindsay, Maud. More Mother Stories. Sanborn, F. C. & Railton, Fanny, illus. (p. 1174)
—Mother Stories. (p. 1178)
—Mother Stories. Ives, Sarah Noble, illus. (p. 1178)
Lindsay, Norene. Dream Catchers. (p. 483)
—Pathfinder Instructor's Guide, Third Edition: Exploring Career & Educational Paths. (p. 1328)
—Pathfinder, Third Edition: Exploring Career & Educational Paths. (p. 1328)
Lindsay, Norman. Magic Pudding: The Adventures of Bunyip Bluegum. (p. 1073)
—Magic Pudding. (p. 1073)
—Magic Pudding. Lindsay, Norman, illus. (p. 1073)
Lindsay, Ryan K. Rainbow Dash. Fleecs, Tony, illus. (p. 1435)
Lindsay, Sarah. Nelson Comprehension Pupil Book Yellow Jackman, John, ed. (p. 1240)
Lindsay, Sierra. Spindly the Spider. Lindsay, Sierra, illus. (p. 1628)
Lindsay, William. Eyewitness - Prehistoric Life. (p. 558)
—Prehistoric Life. (p. 1395)
Lindsey, Audrey. Against the Dawn (p. 29)
Lindsey, Brooklyn. Confessions of a Not-So-Supermodel: Faith, Friends, & Festival Queens (p. 356)
Lindsey, Brooklyn, jt. auth. see Oestreicher, Mark.
Lindsey, Cameron. 10 Best Animal Camouflages. (p. 1993)
—10 Most Dangerous Geographic Locations. (p. 1993)
—10 Most Terrifying Experiences. (p. 1994)
Lindsey, Cath, illus. see Carthew, Mark.
Lindsey, Chad. Greatest Father. (p. 719)
Lindsey, David. Animosity. (p. 84)
Lindsey, Jason. Beyond the Science Lab. MacLure, Ashley, illus. (p. 174)
Lindsey, Jeffrey. EMT-Paramedic Premium Edition Flashcard Book W/CD. (p. 521)
Lindsey, Jessica, illus. see Burt, Vickie.
Lindsey, Jessica, illus. see Burt, Vicky.
Lindsey, Johanna. Heir. (p. 762)
Lindsey, Julie Anne. Deceived. (p. 421)
—Reinventing Chloe. (p. 1457)
Lindsey, Kathleen D. Sweet Potato Pie. Riley-Webb, Charlotte, illus. (p. 1690)
Lindsey, Lynn. Little Lamb. (p. 1030)
Lindsey, Marta. Grandes Migraciones de la Ballena Gris Gabriel, Andrea, illus. (p. 707)
—Little Gray's Great Migration Gabriel, Andrea, illus. (p. 1028)
Lindsey, Mary. Ashes on the Waves. (p. 105)
—Fragile Spirits. (p. 627)
—Shattered Souls. (p. 1563)
Lindsey, Maurice, illus. see Gadson, Cynthia.
Lindsey, Michael, illus. see deSouza, Sabrina.
Lindsey, Ms. Elanna T. Scoo Scoo, Bo Bo & the Dragonfly. Compton, Brian L., illus. (p. 1529)
Lindsey, Norman. Magic Pudding. (p. 1073)
Lindsey Reeves, Diane. Career Ideas for Teens in Education & Training. (p. 266)
—Career Ideas for Teens in Transportation, Distribution, & Logistics. (p. 267)
Lindsey, Robin, photos by see Peterson, Brenda.
Lindsey, Stephanie. Crabs in a Bucket. (p. 375)
Lindskold, Jane. Wolf Hunting. (p. 1943)
Lindskold, Jane, jt. auth. see Weber, David.
Lindskoog, Kathryn & Hunsicker, Ranelda Mack, eds. Faerie Gold: Treasures from the Lands of Enchantment. (p. 562)
Lindskoog, Kathryn, ed. Little Women. Chitouras, Barbara, illus. (p. 1038)
Lindsley, David, jt. auth. see Nunes, Rachel.
Lindsley, Jennifer, illus. see Downing, Johnette.
Lindstrom, Brita, illus. see Turley, Sandy.
Lindstrom, C. G., jt. auth. see Wallis, Mary Alice.
Lindstrom, Charlotte, jt. auth. see Wallace, MaryAlice.
Lindstrom, Eva, illus. see Lindahl, Inger.
Lindstrom, Florence M. Meeting New Friends. (p. 1123)
Lindstrom, Karin. Tiny Life on Plants. (p. 1756)
Lindstrom, Ken. Grandpa, Is There Really a Santa Claus? (p. 709)
Lindvall, Ella K. Bible in Pictures for Toddlers. Langton, Roger, illus. (p. 175)
—Biblia en Cuadros para Niños Pequeños (p. 176)
—Read-Aloud Bible Stories (p. 1442)
Lindwall, Erika. Moose & the Goose. Lindwall, Erika, illus. (p. 1173)
Lindy J. & Hubbard, Bobbie. Story of Becky & Zippy. (p. 1657)
Line Art Staff, illus. see Marsh, Carole.
Line, Deirdre. All in the Dark. (p. 44)
Lineback, Mandy & Gritzner, Jason. Bolivia. (p. 208)
Linebarger, Paul M. A. Psychological Warfare. (p. 1413)
Lineberger, Judy, illus. see D'Agata, Tabatha Jean.
Lineburg, P. R. Simple Animation: Make Your Own Cartoons. (p. 1577)
Linehan, Jess Golden. Martin Mixed-Up at the Beach. (p. 1098)
Lineker, Gary. More of Gary Lineker's Favourite Football Stories. (p. 1174)
Linenthal, Peter. Look at Baby's House! (p. 1048)
—Look at the Animals! (p. 1049)
—Look Look Outside! (p. 1049)
Linenthal, Peter, illus. see Morris, Ann.
Linenthal, Peter, photos by see Morris, Ann.
Liner, Robin. Your Own Little Silly Mcgilly. Rogers, Madalyn V., illus. (p. 1981)
Linforth, Veda. More Toy Shop Tales. (p. 1175)
Ling, Bettina. Indiana. (p. 871)
—Willa Cather: Author & Critic. (p. 1933)
Ling, L. M. ZOEY LEE Schoolyard Scuffle. (p. 1987)
Ling, Lei & Benchmark Education Co., LLC Staff. Home for Moles. (p. 792)
—I See Nat. (p. 845)
Ling, Mary, jt. auth. see Basman, Michael.
Ling, Nancy Tupper. Double Happiness. Chau, Alina, illus. (p. 473)
Lingard, Darren, illus. see Hile, Lori.
Lingard, Joan. Odd Girl Out. (p. 1278)
Lingas, Leo, illus. see Downey, Glen.
Lingemann, Linda. Beluga Passage. Weiman, Jon, illus. (p. 163)
Lingen, Marissa. Chinese Immigration. (p. 307)
Lingen, Marissa, jt. auth. see Moreno, Barry.
Lingenfelser, Lynda L. Adventures of Lizah Lizard: The Laughing, Lovable Lizard. (p. 20)
—Lizah Lizard: Koco's Tale. (p. 1042)
Lingenfelter, Andrea, tr. see Mian, Mian.
Lingenfelter, Jim, illus. see Meister, Cari.
Lingenfelter, Libby. Watermelon Story. (p. 1864)
Lingle, Lise. One for You & One for Me. (p. 1295)
Lingo, Susan L. Collect-n-Make Crafts for Kids. Stoker, Bruce, ed. (p. 339)
—Collect-n-Play Games for Kids. Stoker, Bruce, ed. (p. 339)
—Hope Finders. Barr, Marilynn G. & Jeffery, Megan E., illus. (p. 796)
—Joy Builders. Barr, Marilynn G. & Jeffery, Megan E., illus. (p. 929)
—Peace Makers. Barr, Marilynn G. & Jeffery, Megan E., illus. (p. 1331)
—Power Boosters. Barr, Marilynn G. & Jeffery, Megan E., illus. (p. 1389)
—Preschool Bible Message Make-n-Takes: 50 Fun Crafts with Lively Messages for Preschoolers. (p. 1396)
—Quick-Quiz Talk Starters: 30 Fast 'n Fun Quizzes - & More - to Get Kids Talking about God & Faith. (p. 1427)
Lingo, Susan L., jt. auth. see Route 52 Staff.
LinguiSystems. Preschool Phonology Cards. (p. 1396)
Liniers. Big Wet Balloon (El Globo Grande y Mojado) Liniers, illus. (p. 184)
—Escrito y Dibujado Por Enriqueta: TOON Level 3. (p. 535)
—Globo Grande y Mojado) Liniers, illus. (p. 184)
—Written & Drawn by Henrietta. (p. 1965)
Liniers & Lindgren, Barbro. What There Is Before There Is Anything There: A Scary Story Amado, Elisa, tr. from SPA. (p. 1894)
Liniers, Ricardo. Big Wet Balloon. Liniers, Ricardo, illus. (p. 184)
Lininger, Dianne. Kingdom of Cydinah. (p. 959)
Lininger, Linda, jt. auth. see Anderson, Jean.
Link, Amy. My Mommy Wears a Wig. (p. 1214)
Link, Arthur S., et al. Concise History of the American People. (p. 355)
Link, C. Edward. Little Motorcycle. Serfass, Jim, illus. (p. 1032)
Link, Eric Carl & Salem Press Staff. Red Badge of Courage, by Stephen Crane. (p. 1453)
Link, Kelly. Pretty Monsters. (p. 1398)
Link, Kelly, jt. auth. see Beagle, Peter S.
Link, Kelly, jt. ed. see Grant, Gavin J.
Link, Kelly & Grant, Gavin J., eds. Monstrous Affections: An Anthology of Beastly Tales. (p. 1169)
Link, Theodore. Annie Oakley: Wild West Sharpshooter. (p. 87)
—Argentina: A Primary Source Cultural Guide. (p. 98)
—Communism: A Primary Source Analysis. (p. 349)
—George Armstrong Custer: General of the U. S. Cavalry. (p. 663)
—George Armstrong Custer: General de la caballeria Estadounidense. (p. 663)
—George Armstrong Custer: General of the U. S. Cavalry / General de la caballeria Estadounidense. (p. 663)
—George Armstrong Custer: General de la caballeria estadounidense (George Armstrong Custer: General of the U. S. Cavalry) (p. 663)
—George Armstrong Custer. (p. 663)
Link, Theodore & McCarthy, Rose. Argentina: A Primary Source Cultural Guide. (p. 98)
Linka, Catherine. Girl Called Fearless. (p. 678)
—Girl Undone: A Novel. (p. 679)
Linke, Donald Q., Jr., illus. see Benett, Janet M.
Linke, Glenn Colin. Gargantuan Boy. (p. 657)
Linke, Marcus V. Professor & the Haunted Museum. (p. 1409)
Linke, Uwe. In the Meadow, Boldt, Fabienne & Wensell, Ulises, illus. (p. 866)
—Knights of the Castle. Muller, Daniel, illus. (p. 964)
—Princess Parade. (p. 1405)
Linker, Julie. Disenchanted Princess. (p. 450)
Linkerhand, Antje, jt. auth. see Barth, Katrin.
Linklater, Eric. Pirates in the Deep Green Sea. (p. 1363)
—Wind on the Moon. Bentley, Nicolas, illus. (p. 1935)
Linko, Gina. Indigo. (p. 872)
Linkov, Igor & Ramadan, Abou Bakr, eds. Comparative Risk Assessment & Environmental Decision Making (p. 351)
Linkowski, Tami Leli. Lynn Can Fly Selover, Lisa & Selover, Arthur, illus. (p. 1066)
—Lynn Was a Cow Who Could Ski. (p. 1066)
Linn, Dennis, et al. What Is My Song? Miranda, Francisco, illus. (p. 1890)
Linn, Jennifer. Hungry Spider. (p. 828)
Linn, Laurent, jt. illus. see Nelson, Mary Beth.
Linn, Leigh Ann. Drowsy Eels on Banana Peels. (p. 486)
Linn, Margot. Big Red Blanket. Jacobson, David, illus. (p. 183)
—Can You Play? Bolam, Emily, illus. (p. 259)
—Harry's Bath. Chwast, Seymour, illus. (p. 751)
—I Won't Go to Bed! Baruffi, Andrea, illus. (p. 849)

L

—I'm Going to New York to Visit the Lions. Roitman, Tanya, illus. (p. 859)
—Pizza & Other Stinky Poems. Haley, Amanda, illus. (p. 1365)
—Silly Pig. Rader, Laura, illus. (p. 1576)
—Sometimes I Share. Nicklaus, Carol, illus. (p. 1610)
—Take My Picture. Hoffman, Sanford, illus. (p. 1696)
—Who Spilled the Milk?, Level 1. Gradisher, Martha, illus. (p. 1917)
Linnamagi, Anne, jt. auth. see Voskoboinikov, Valery.
Linney, Graham F. Seaside Adventure of Carrot, Pea, & Friends. (p. 1538)
Linney, Susan. Martin Luther King, Jr: With a Discussion of Responsibility. (p. 1098)
Linnihan, Ellen. Stranded at Sea (p. 1664)
Linscott, Caroline. Watercolor 1: Learn the Basics of Watercolor Painting. (p. 1863)
Linsdell, Jo, illus. see Rochelle, Maria.
Linseman, Daniel. Shroobear's First Swim: Book I of the Shroobear Short Stories. (p. 1571)
Linser, Joseph Michael & Hopkins, Eva. Dawn: Behind the Scenes. (p. 411)
Linsley, Barbara. I Can Help on Farm. (p. 836)
Linsley, Paul, illus. see Linsley, Sonja Paschal.
Linsley, Paul Adam, illus. see Linsley, Sonja Paschal.
Linsley, Sonja Paschal. Conifer Court Competition. Linsley, Paul, illus. (p. 357)
—May I Have the First Dance? Linsley, Paul Adam, illus. (p. 1112)
Linsner, Joseph Michael. Three Tiers. (p. 1744)
Lint, Charles De, see de Lint, Charles.
Lintern, Fiona. Study Guide for OCR Psychology. (p. 1670)
Lintern, Tom, illus. see Laínez, René Colato.
Lintner, Tommy. BIG RED's Clucking Good Time: Short Stories & Poetry for Kids of All Ages. (p. 183)
Linton, Chandra S. Colors, Colors, Colors, A World Filled with Colors, Who Made Them? (p. 345)
Linton, J. D., illus. see Bunyan, John.
Linton, J. Tells & Linton, S. B. Colors Outside. (p. 345)
Linton, Jonathan, illus. see Evans, Richard.
Linton, S. B., jt. auth. see Linton, J. Tells.
Linton, Sara. Misfortune Cookie. (p. 1150)
Linton, Vera, illus. see Howell, Kathy.
Lintz, Roy K. Leadership in Our Society. (p. 981)
Linus, Benjamin. Spring, Summer, Fall, Winter. (p. 1635)
Linville, S. Olga, illus. see Anjou, Colette.
Linz, Kathryn. Jim Brandon's Adventures. (p. 917)
Linz, Peter, jt. auth. see Moore, Clement C.
Linzy, Jan, jt. auth. see Pata, Sharae.
Lion, David C. Habitats (p. 734)
—Home in the Swamp. (p. 792)
—Vida en el Pantano. (p. 1840)
—Vida en la Pradera. (p. 1840)
Lionel/Bovier, contrib. by. Doug Aitken: Man As House (p. 473)
Liong-A-Kong, Mireille. Going-Natural: How to Fall in Love with Nappy Hair. (p. 692)
Lionheart, Amelia. Can Snow Leopards Roar? (p. 258)
—Dolphin Heptad. (p. 464)
Lionni, Leo. Alexander & the Wind-Up Mouse. (p. 36)
—Color of His Own. Lionni, Leo, illus. (p. 343)
—Colors, Numbers, Letters. (p. 345)
—Extraordinary Egg. (p. 555)
—Fish Is Fish. (p. 598)
—Frederic. (p. 633)
—Frederick. Mlawer, Teresa, tr. (p. 633)
—Geraldine, the Music Mouse. (p. 666)
—Greentail Mouse. (p. 723)
—Inch by Inch. (p. 868)
—Inch by Inch. Lionni, Leo, illus. (p. 868)
—It's Mine! (p. 897)
—Let's Make Rabbits. Lionni, Leo, illus. (p. 999)
—Let's Play. (p. 999)
—Little Blue & Little Yellow. (p. 1024)
—Nadarin. Mlawer, Teresa, tr. from SPA. (p. 1227)
—Nicolas, Where Have You Been? (p. 1251)
—Pezzettino. (p. 1349)
—Pezzettino. Lionni, Leo, illus. (p. 1349)
—Six Crows. (p. 1582)
—Su Propio Color. Mlawer, Teresa, tr. from ENG. (p. 1670)
—Sueno de Matias. (p. 1672)
—Swimmy 50th Anniversary Edition. (p. 1691)
—Theodore & the Talking Mushroom. (p. 1729)
—Tico & the Golden Wings. (p. 1747)
—Tillie & the Wall. (p. 1750)
—Tillie & the Wall. Lionni, Leo, illus. (p. 1750)
—What? (p. 1878)
—When? (p. 1901)
—Where? (p. 1906)
—Who? (p. 1914)
Lior, Tsipora, tr. see Liebman, Dan.
Liora, Iimma. Flick. (p. 603)
—Flick Goes Bush. (p. 603)
—Flick Goes under the Sea! (p. 603)
Liotta, Clayton, illus. see Morris, Dick, et al.
Lipan, Linda. Jeremiah's Journey. (p. 913)
Lipara, Laura. Gramma Shares Her Faith: Cain & Abel. (p. 706)
Lipari, Laura. Gramma Shares Her Faith: Adam & Eve. (p. 706)
Liparulo, Robert. Gatekeepers (p. 658)
—House of Dark Shadows (p. 803)
—Watcher in the Woods (p. 1861)
—Whirlwind (p. 1912)
Lipchenko, Oleg, illus. see Carroll, Lewis, pseud.
Lipchenko, Oleg, selected by. Humpty Dumpty & Friends: Nursery Rhymes for the Young at Heart. (p. 827)
Lipe, Barbara, illus. see Roberts, Mary.
Lipe, Riki. Hanging with Yum-Yum & Yuck. (p. 742)
Liphardt, Linda. Secret in the Old Barn. (p. 1541)
Lipinski, Maureen. Cleopatra Ascending. (p. 331)
Lipka, Francine. Balloon Babies Inside Our Rainbows. (p. 135)
Lipking, Ron, illus. see Perry, Phyllis J.
Lipkowitz, Daniel. Dark Side. (p. 408)
—LEGO Book. (p. 990)
Lipkowitz, Daniel, jt. auth. see Dorling Kindersley Publishing Staff.
Lipkowitz, Daniel, jt. auth. see Farshtey, Greg.
Lipkowitz, Daniel & Dorling Kindersley Publishing Staff. Lego Batman Visual Dictionary. (p. 990)
—LEGO Ideas Book. (p. 990)
Lipkowitz, Daniel & Farshtey, Greg. Lego Play Book. (p. 990)
Lipner, Joseph & Yasgur, Abigail. Max Said Yes! The Woodstock Story. Mendes, Barbara, illus. (p. 1111)
Lipow, Dan, photos by see Martin, Bill, Jr. & Sampson, Michael.
Lipp, Frederick. Fatima. Lindmark, Margaret, illus. (p. 577)
—Running Shoes. Gaillard, Jason, illus. (p. 1497)
Lipp, Frederick J. Bread Song. Gaillard, Jason, tr. (p. 224)
—Tea Leaves. Coloma, Lester, tr. (p. 1708)
Lipp, Tony, illus. see Reid, Robin L.
Lippert, David. Born Talking. (p. 214)
Lippert, Margaret H., jt. auth. see Paye, Won-Ldy.
Lippincott, Gary, illus. see Yolen, Jane.
Lippincott, Gary A., illus. see Chester, Laura.
Lippincott, Gary A., illus. see Coville, Bruce.
Lippincott, Kristen. DK Eyewitness Books: Astronomy: Astronomy. (p. 456)
Lippincott, Kristen, jt. auth. see Dorling Kindersley Publishing Staff.
Lippman, David & Muschal, Frank. Energy from Hydrogen. (p. 528)
Lippman, Peter. Ice Cream Truck. (p. 850)
—Mini Express. (p. 1146)
Lippman, Peter & Gikow, Louise. Land of Dinosaurs. (p. 973)
Lippmann, Wilfried. Gift of Eye. (p. 675)
Lipschultz, Wes. All about the Moon. (p. 43)
—Is It Hot or Cold? Learning to Use a Thermometer. (p. 889)
Lipscomb, William N. & Chemistry. Boron Hydrides. (p. 214)
Lipscombe, Nick, illus. see Butterfield, Moira.
Lipsey, Jennifer. I Love to Draw! (p. 843)
Lipsey, Sheila E. House of Cars: Book 1 Fairley High Series. (p. 803)
Lipson, Amy Kron, jt. auth. see Laddy, Lee.
Lipson, Amy Kron & Laddy, Lee. Penelope Pratt's Hats: A Young Girl's Dilemma Turns Rhyme to Reason. (p. 1336)
Lipson, Eden Ross. Applesauce Season. Gerstein, Mordicai, illus. (p. 93)
Lipson, Greta Barclay. Two Sides to Every Story. Hierstein, Judith, illus. (p. 1804)
Lipsyte, Robert. Brave. (p. 223)
—Center Field. (p. 287)
—Chief. (p. 301)
—Contender. (p. 360)
—Heroes of Baseball: The Men Who Made It America's Favorite Game. (p. 773)
—One Fat Summer. (p. 1295)
—Raiders Night. (p. 1433)
—Twin Powers. (p. 1802)
—Twinning Project. (p. 1802)
—Warrior Angel. (p. 1858)
—Yellow Flag. (p. 1970)
Lipton, Gladys C. Spanish Beginner's Bilingual Dictionary. (p. 1621)
Lipton, Lauren. It's about Your Husband. (p. 896)
Lipton, Lenny, jt. auth. see Yarrow, Peter.
Liput, Andrew L. Who Put the Snarfdoodle in My Lunch Box? (p. 1917)
Li-Qiong, Yu. New Year's Reunion: A Chinese Story. Cheng-Liang, Zhu, illus. (p. 1247)
Lisa Byers, illus. see Robyn Washburn.
Lisa Catanzarite. What the World Is Like to Bea Moore: Dear Santa. (p. 1894)
Lisa Darby And Rachel Darby. When Balloons Go Bye-Bye. (p. 1901)
Lisa LeLeu, 6th. Alphie's Alphabet Act. (p. 50)
Lisa Maria. Princess of the King. (p. 1404)
Lisa-Marie. Victoria & Her Friends in the Forest. (p. 1840)
Lisansky, Sue. Cinderella. (p. 320)
Lisboa, David M. World Best Jokes. (p. 1954)
Lisbona, Margie Taylor. Rock & Rhino Learn Responsibility. Roberts, J. P., illus. (p. 1481)
Lisech, Howard, jt. auth. see Harris, Janice L.
Lisette, Soleil, illus. see De Las Casas, Dianne & Eliana, Kid.
Lishak, Antony. Animal Welfare. (p. 80)
—Drugs. (p. 487)
—Racism. (p. 1432)
Lishinski, Ann King. Let Your Light Shine. Morello, Charles, ed. (p. 994)
Lishinski, Jamie, illus. see Lishinski, Ann King.
Lisi, Branden. Count on the Farm. Lisi, Margaret, illus. (p. 369)
Lisi, Charlotte. I Am Special. Ortega, David, illus. (p. 834)
Lisi, Margaret, illus. see Lisi, Branden.
Lisi-Neumann, Kathleen, et al. Engaging Parents As Literacy Partners: A Reproducible Toolkit with Parent How-To Pages, Recordkeeping Forms, & Everything You Need to Engage Families & Tap Their Power As Reading Coaches. (p. 529)
Liska, Eliska, illus. see Buble, Brandee.
Liska, Eliska, illus. see Weber, Lori.
Lisker, Sonia, illus. see Blume, Judy.
Lisl. Dictionary with a Difference. (p. 436)
Lisle, Andria, jt. auth. see Plumley, Amie.
Lisle, Andria & Plumley, Amie Petronis. Sewing School 2: Lessons in Machine Sewing; 20 Projects Kids Will Love to Make. (p. 1556)
Lisle, Chris. Bedtime Stories for Girls. (p. 157)
Lisle, Holly. Ruby Key (p. 1493)
Lisle, Janet, jt. auth. see Lisle, Janet Taylor.
Lisle, Janet Taylor. Black Duck. (p. 196)
—Crying Rocks. (p. 387)
Lisle, Janet Taylor & Lisle, Janet. Highway Cats. (p. 779)
Lisle, Rebecca. Amethyst. Hess, Paul, illus. (p. 65)
—Curse of the Ravens. (p. 395)
—Dog in the Diamond Collar. Archbold, Tim, illus. (p. 461)
—Toad Prince. (p. 1760)
Lisman, Jaclyn, jt. auth. see Ekberg, Jodi.
Lisovskis, Marjorie, ed. see Lewis, Barbara A.
Lisovskis, Marjorie, jt. auth. see Verdick, Elizabeth.
Lisowski, Gabriel, illus. see Chaikin, Miriam.
Lispector, Clarice. Misterio do Coelho Pensante. (p. 1155)
Lispi, Robert. Buddy Hawk: Story of Buddy Hawk. (p. 235)
Liss, David. Randoms. (p. 1438)
Liss, Ira, illus. see Hein, Simeon.
Lissberger, Susan. Aa You Are Amazing Zz You Are Zzzzzz Best. (p. 2)
Lissiat, Amy, illus. see Thompson, Colin.
Lissiat, Amy, jt. auth. see Thompson, Colin.
Liss-Levinson, Nechama & Baskette, Molly Phinney. Remembering My Grandparent: A Kid's Own Grief Workbook in the Christian Tradition. (p. 1459)
—Remembering My Pet: A Kid's Own Spiritual Workbook for When a Pet Dies. (p. 1459)
Lissner, Caren. Carrie Pilby. (p. 271)
Lisson, Deborah. Red Hugh: The Kidnap of Hugh O'Donnell. (p. 1454)
List, Gloria A. Heart That Finds His Way: More on the Line. Sturcke, Otto, illus. (p. 760)
Lista, Michael. Bloom (p. 201)
Lister, Adrian. Ice Age Tracker's Guide. Ursell, Martin, illus. (p. 850)
Lister, Jessica, jt. auth. see Mia, Tjalaminu.
Lister, John C. Good Manners for Very Young Children with Rio the Rat. Britt, Rachel, illus. (p. 698)
Lister, Judy, illus. see Kishkan, Dan.
Lister, Mary. Winter King, Summer Queen. Mayo, Diana, illus. (p. 1938)
Lister, Ralph, jt. auth. see Tompert, Ann.
Lister, Tresina. Itty Bitty Birdie. Greengaard, Alex, illus. (p. 900)
Listinsky, Tamara. Important Little Things to Teach Your Children. (p. 862)
Listokin, David, illus. see Switzer, Vern.
Liszt, Franz. Danse Macabre & Other Piano Transcriptions. Glover, Daniel, ed. (p. 406)
Litchfield & Allman. Animales (Animals) (p. 80)
Litchfield, Felicity. Primeros Numeros. (p. 1401)
Litchfield, J. My Food. (p. 1208)
—Very First Numbers. (p. 1838)
Litchfield, J., jt. auth. see Brooks, F.
Litchfield, J., jt. auth. see Brooks, Felicity.
Litchfield, J. & Brooks, F. Dinosaurs. (p. 443)
—Everyday Words in German. (p. 544)
—Farm. (p. 573)
—Rescue Vehicles. (p. 1462)
Litchfield, Jo. Animals. (p. 81)
—At Home. (p. 110)
—Baby Brother Look & Say. (p. 125)
—Baby Sister Look & Say. (p. 128)
—Beach. (p. 149)
—Bit-Bot & the Blob. (p. 193)
—Box of Trucks. (p. 216)
—Christmas. Litchfield, Jo, illus. (p. 312)
—Farm. (p. 573)
—First Book of Christmas Carols. (p. 593)
—First Picture 123. (p. 596)
—First Picture Abc. (p. 596)
—First Picture Nursery Rhymes. (p. 596)
—First Words Look & Say. Litchfield, Jo, illus. (p. 597)
—Home. Litchfield, Jo & Allen, Francesca, illus. (p. 791)
—Jobs. Litchfield, Jo & Allen, Francesca, illus. (p. 919)
—Things That Move. (p. 1733)
—Town. (p. 1773)
—Usborne Book of Everyday Words. Treays, Rebecca et al, eds. (p. 1827)
—Usborne Book of Everyday Words in French. (p. 1827)
—Usborne Lift-The-Flap Nitivity. Allman, Howard, photos by. (p. 1827)
—Very First ABC. (p. 1838)
—Very First Words in Spanish. (p. 1838)
—Weather. Maynard, Marc, illus. (p. 1869)
Litchfield, Jo, illus. see Brooks, Felicity & MacKinnon, Mairi.
Litchfield, Jo, illus. see Brooks, Felicity, ed.
Litchfield, Jo, illus. see Brooks, Felicity.
Litchfield, Jo, illus. see Durber, Matt.
Litchfield, Jo, illus. see Young, Caroline & Brooks, Felicity.
Litchfield, Jo, jt. auth. see Brooks, Felicity.
Litchfield, Jo & Allen, Francesca. First Picture Fairytales. MMStudios, photos by. (p. 596)
—First Picture Nursery Rhymes With. (p. 596)
Litchfield, Jo & Brooks, F. Tractors. (p. 1775)
—Trains. (p. 1777)
—Trucks. (p. 1791)
Litchfield, Jo & Brooks, Felicity. Building Site. (p. 239)
—Diggers. (p. 439)
—Everyday Words Sticker Book. (p. 544)
Litchfield, Jo & Jones, Stephanie. First 1,2,3. Allman, Howard, photos by. (p. 592)
Litchfield, Jo & Sanchez Gallego, Maria Isabel. 123. Jones, Stephanie, illus. (p. 2000)
Litchfield, Jo, contrib. by. Goldilocks & the Three Bears. (p. 696)
Litchfield, Jo, des. Usborne Everyday Words French Flashcards. (p. 1827)
Litchfield, Judie, ed. see Conyers, Tom.
Litchford, David O. Nephi Was an Eagle. (p. 1241)
Litchman, Kristin E., ed. Let's Dance! Dances for Children from America's Melting Pot, Dance Program for Pre-School & Elementary School Children. (p. 995)
Litchmore, Michael. MB Force: Heroes at the Best! (p. 1114)
Lite, Lori. Affirmation Weaver: A Believe in Yourself Story Designed to Help Children Increase Self-Esteem While Decreasing Stress & Anxiety. (p. 26)
—Angry Octopus: An Anger Management Story Introducing Active Progressive Muscular Relaxation & Deep Breathing. (p. 75)
—Boy & a Bear: The Children's Relaxation Book. Hartigan, Meg, illus. (p. 217)
—Boy & a Turtle: A Relaxation Story Teaching Young Children Visualization Techniques to Increase Creativity While Lowering Stress & Anxiety Lev. (p. 217)
—Bubble Riding: A Relaxation Story Designed to Teach Children Visualization Techniques to Increase Creativity While Lowering Stress & Anxiety. (p. 233)
—Buenas Noches Oruga: Una Historia para la Relajación Que Ayuda a Los Niños a Controlar la Ira y el Estrés para Que Se Queden Dormidos Sosegadamente. (p. 235)
—Caleta de la Nutria Marina: Un Cuento para la Ansiedad Infantil, Enseña la Relajación, la Respiración Profunda para Reducir la Ansiedad, el Estrés y la Ira, a la Vez Que Fomenta el Sueño Sosegado. (p. 252)
—Children's Wellness Curriculum: Lessons, Stories & Techniques Designed to Decrease Bullying, Anxiety, Anger & Obesity While Promoting Self-Esteem & Healthy Food Choices. (p. 304)
—Goodnight Caterpillar: A Children's Relaxation Story to Improve Sleep, Manage Stress, Anxiety, Anger. (p. 701)
—Montando Burbujas: Un Cuento con Ejercicios de Relajación para Niños, Diseñada para Enseñar a Los Niños Técnicas de Visualización para Aumentar la Creatividad Mientras Disminuyen Sus Niveles de Ansiedad y de Estrés. (p. 1170)
—Niño y la Tortuga: Un Cuento para Promover la Relajación. (p. 1257)
—Pulpo Enojado: Un Cuento Sobre Cómo Controlar la Ira Que Enseña la Relajación Muscular Activa y Progresiva, y la Respiración: un Cuento Sobre Cómo Controlar la Ira Que Enseña la Relajación Muscular Activa y Progresiva, y la Respiración. (p. 1416)
—Sea Otter Cove: A Relaxation Story, Introducing Deep Breathing to Decrease Anxiety, Stress & Anger While Promoting Peaceful Sleep. (p. 1535)
—Tejedor de Afirmaciones: Un Cuento Que Aumenta la Autoestima en Los Niños, Creer en Ellos Mismos, Mientras Que Reducen Sus Estrés y Su Ansiedad. (p. 1715)
Lites, B. James & Lites, James R. Lessons in Peer Pressure For Kids All over the World. (p. 993)
Lites, James R., jt. auth. see Lites, B. James.
Lith, Daan van der. Study & Master Mathematics Grade 11 Learner's Book. (p. 1670)
—Study & Master Mathematics Grade 11 Learner's Book Afrikaans Translation. (p. 1670)
Lithgow, John. Carnival of the Animals. Kulikov, Boris, illus. (p. 270)
—I Got Two Dogs. Neubecker, Robert, illus. (p. 838)
—I'm a Manatee. Hoyt, Ard, illus. (p. 858)
—Lithgow Palooza! 101 Ways to Entertain & Inspire Your Kids. (p. 1023)
—Mahalia Mouse Goes to College. Oleynikov, Igor, illus. (p. 1076)
—Marsupial Sue Presents the Runaway Pancake. Davis, Jack E., illus. (p. 1096)
—Micawber. Payne, C. F., illus. (p. 1134)
—Never Play Music Right Next to the Zoo. Hernandez, Leeza, illus. (p. 1243)
Lithgow, John & Davis, Jack E. Marsupial Sue. (p. 1096)
—Marsupial Sue Presents the Runaway Pancake. (p. 1096)
Lithgow, John & Payne, C. F. Remarkable Farkle McBride. (p. 1458)
Litke, Erin. Crystal Shards. (p. 387)
Litrel, Suzanne. Jackie Tempo & the House of Wisdom. (p. 904)
Litrel, Suzanne M. Jackie Tempo & the Emperor's Seal. (p. 904)
Littell, William Adams. Guillaume. (p. 730)
Litten, Kristyna. Hong Kong & Macau: a 3D Keepsake Cityscape. Litten, Kristyna, illus. (p. 795)
—Rome: a 3D Keepsake Cityscape. Litten, Kristyna, illus. (p. 1486)
Litten, Kristyna, illus. see Berger, Samantha.
Litten, Kristyna, illus. see Krensky, Stephen.
Litten, Kristyna, illus. see Liu, Cynthea.
Litten, Kristyna, illus. see Pitman, Gayle E.
Litteral, Christopher, illus. see Kruse, Robyn A.
Littke, Lael. Searching for Selene. (p. 1537)
Littke, Lael, jt. auth. see Turley, Richard E.
Littke, Lael, jt. auth. see Turley, Richard.
Little Airplane Productions, illus. see Selig, Josh.
Little Airplane Productions & Fogarty, Alexandria. Baby Beaver Rescue. (p. 125)
Little Airplane Productions & Scanlon, Michael. Off to School! (p. 1279)
Little Airplane Productions Staff, illus. see Scanlon, Michael.
Little, Ashley. New Normal (p. 1246)
Little, Awen. Sid y Bwystfil Bwyta Sanau. (p. 1573)
Little Bear, Shena. How the lone wolf got her Name. (p. 813)
Little Bee Books Staff. On the Move: A Touch-and-Feel Book. (p. 1291)
Little Bee Books Staff, jt. auth. see Saunders, Katie.
Little Bee Books Staff & Brook-Piper, Holly. Fun with Colors. Max and Sid Staff, illus. (p. 648)
Little, Billee Kae. Ennis & His Friends. (p. 530)
Little, Brown and Company Staff, ed. see Bartlett's.
Little, Celeste. At the Park with Tommy & Scales. Motz, Mike, illus. (p. 111)
—Scales. Motz, Mike, illus. (p. 1519)
Little, Christiana. Southwestern University College Prowler off the Record. (p. 1618)
Little, Cynthia. Mom's Imaginary Child. (p. 1163)
Little, Eddy. Too Big for Just One. (p. 1766)
Little, Elaine, photos by see Kinkade, Sheila.
Little, Frances Delanoy. Ancient Stories from the Dardanelles 1924. (p. 70)
Little, Gary, illus. see Lohof, Arle & Jensen, Joyce.
Little Golden Books Staff. Three Bears. Rojankovsky, Feodor, illus. (p. 1741)
Little Golden Books Staff, jt. auth. see Shealy, Dennis.
Little Grandma. Apple Stew. (p. 92)
Little, Greta D., ed. see Cranch, Christopher Pearse.
Little, Jean. Birthday Girl. Lawrason, June, illus. (p. 192)
—Do Not Open until Christmas (p. 457)
—Do Not Open until Christmas: Short Stories (p. 457)
—Emma's Strange Pet. Plecas, Jennifer, illus. (p. 520)
—Forward, Shakespeare! (p. 623)

—Hey World, Here I Am! Truesdell, Sue, illus. (p. 774)
—I Gave My Mom a Castle Denton, Kady MacDonald, illus. (p. 838)
—I Know an Old Laddie. (p. 840)
Little, Jeanette, illus. see Hunter, Ryan Ann.
Little, Jennifer. My Brother Is Such a Slob! (p. 1199)
Little, Judy. Yody & Bippy the Boo: Friends for Life. (p. 1972)
Little, Kelli Ann, illus. see Polark, Kelly.
Little, Kimberley Griffiths. Circle of Secrets. (p. 321)
—Healing Spell. (p. 757)
—Last Snake Runner. (p. 978)
—Time of the Fireflies. (p. 1752)
Little, Lorna. Mark of the Wagari. Lyndon, Janice, illus. (p. 1095)
Little, Lucretia. I Rode a Bumblebee. (p. 844)
—Slip. (p. 1590)
Little, Melanie. Apprentice's Masterpiece: A Story of Medieval Spain. (p. 93)
Little, Melanie, ed. see Karle, Vincent & Blondel, Jean-Vincent.
Little, Melanie, ed. see Lindroth, Malin & Martini, Clem.
Little, Melanie, ed. see Livingston, Billie & Adderson, Caroline.
Little, Melanie, ed. What My Father Gave Me: Daughters Speak. (p. 1892)
Little Monster Records, et al. All Together Now. (p. 46)
Little, Paul D. Christmas Chips. (p. 313)
Little, Penny. Baby Bear's Birthday Hiccups! Jones, Lara, illus. (p. 125)
—Blackest Hole in Space. Vigla, Vincent, illus. (p. 197)
Little People of America, Inc Staff, jt. see Fisher-Price Staff.
Little Pickle Press & DiOrio, Rana. What Does It Mean to Be Global? Hill, Chris, illus. (p. 1884)
Little Pim Corporation Staff, jt. auth. see Levine, Julia Pimsleur.
Little, Richard. We Love Purple! (p. 1867)
—We Love Red! (p. 1867)
—We Love Yellow! (p. 1867)
Little, Robert. Fun Day in Mrs. Walker's Class. Galey, Chuck, illus. (p. 647)
—Grandma's Biscuits. Richmond, Jamea, illus. (p. 708)
—Jamaal's Lucky Day. Fitzpatrick, Audrey, illus. (p. 906)
Little, Stephen R. Home Tree. (p. 793)
—Mighty Locomotive. (p. 1140)
Little, Thomas Hamilton & Ogle, David B., eds. Legislative Branch of State Government: People, Process, & Politics (p. 990)
Little, Troy. Harvest of Revenge. (p. 751)
—Powerpuff Girls Volume 1. (p. 1391)
Littlechild, George. This Land Is My Land Littlechild, George, illus. (p. 1737)
Littlechild, George, illus. see Van Camp, Richard.
Littlefield, jt. auth. see Littlefield, Cindy A.
Littlefield, Angie & Littlefield, Jennifer. 10 Deadliest Plants. (p. 1993)
Littlefield, Cindy A. Awesome Ocean Science: Investigating the Secrets of the Underwater World. (p. 121)
—Awesome Ocean Science. (p. 121)
—Crafts Across America. Caputo, Jim, illus. (p. 375)
—Pop-Out & Paint Dogs & Cats. (p. 1384)
—Pop-Out & Paint Farm Animals. (p. 1384)
—Pop-Out & Paint Horse Breeds: Create Paper Models of 10 Different Breeds. (p. 1384)
—Sea Life Games & Puzzles: 100 Brainteasers, Word Games, Jokes & Riddles, Picture Puzzles, Matches & Logic Tests. Kline, Michael et al, illus. (p. 1534)
Littlefield, Cindy A. & Littlefield. Horse Games & Puzzles for Kids: 102 Brainteasers, Word Games, Jokes & Riddles, Picture Puzzlers, Matches & Logic Tests for Horse-Loving Kids. (p. 799)
Littlefield, Cynthia, jt. auth. see Disney Book Group Staff.
Littlefield, Eireann. Maisie the Animal Minder: Maisie & Ben. Haynes, Penny, illus. (p. 1077)
Littlefield, Holly. Rooftop Adventure of Minnie & Tessa, Factory Fire Survivors. Trover, Zachary et al, illus. (p. 1487)
—Rooftop Adventure of Minnie & Tessa, Factory Fire Survivors. Hammond, Ted & Carbajal, Richard, illus. (p. 1487)
Littlefield, Jennifer, jt. auth. see Littlefield, Angie.
Littlefield, Sophie. Oliver Wendell Holmes Jr: The Supreme Court & American Legal Thought. (p. 1286)
—Unforsaken. (p. 1817)
Littlefield, Sophie W. & Wiecek, William. Oliver Wendell Holmes Jr: The Supreme Court & American Legal Thought. (p. 1286)
Littlehales, Bates, jt. auth. see Simmons, Rulon E.
Littlehawk. Ghost in the Closet. (p. 670)
Littlejohn, Andrew, jt. auth. see Hicks, Diana.
Littlejohn, Andrew & Hicks, Diana. Primary Colours (p. 1399)
—Primary Colours Pupil's (p. 1399)
Littlejohn, Anna, illus. see Upham, Linda.
Littlejohn, Brad, illus. see Kluth, Paula & Kluth, Victoria.
Littlejohn, Carol, jt. auth. see Thomas, Cathlyn.
Littlejohn, E. G. Texas History Stories. (p. 1724)
Littlejohn, Randy. Air Warfare of the Future. (p. 31)
—Life in Outer Space. (p. 1011)
—Timeline of the Slave Trade in America. (p. 1754)
LittlePinkPebble, illus. see Judybee.
Littler, Phil, illus. see Guillain, Adam & Guillain, Charlotte.
Littlest Pet Shop Staff. Littlest Pet Shop Blythe's Big Adventure: Panorama Sticker Storybook. (p. 1039)
Littleton, Mark. Stories Jesus Told. Moroney, Trace, illus. (p. 1654)
Littlewolf, Grandmother. Mr. Feathers & the Geow-Lud-Mo-Sis-Eg. (p. 1185)
Littlewood, Graham. Restless Owl & Other Stories. Preston, Carole, illus. (p. 1464)
Littlewood, Karin. Immi's Gift Littlewood, Karin, illus. (p. 861)
Littlewood, Karin, illus. see Bateson-Hill, Margaret.
Littlewood, Karin, illus. see Beake, Lesley.
Littlewood, Karin, illus. see Cornwell, Nikki.
Littlewood, Karin, illus. see Dunmore, Helen.
Littlewood, Karin, illus. see Faundez, Anne.
Littlewood, Karin, illus. see Grindley, Sally.
Littlewood, Karin, illus. see Hoffman, Mary.
Littlewood, Karin, illus. see Jungman, Ann.
Littlewood, Karin, illus. see Moore, Genevieve.
Littlewood, Karin & Quarto Generic Staff. Star Girl. (p. 1640)
Littlewood, Kathryn. Bite-Sized Magic: A Bliss Novel. McGuire, Erin, illus. (p. 194)
—Bliss. (p. 199)
—Dash of Magic: A Bliss Novel. McGuire, Erin, illus. (p. 409)
Littlewood, Peter. Rain Forest Destruction. (p. 1434)
—Why Are the Rainforests Being Destroyed? (p. 1922)
Littlewort, Lizza, illus. see Orford, Margie.
Littman, Sarah Darer. Backlash. (p. 130)
—Confessions of a Closet Catholic. (p. 356)
—Life, After. (p. 1007)
—Purge. (p. 1419)
—Want to Go Private? (p. 1856)
Litton, Jonathan. ABC Alphabet Fun. (p. 3)
—Baby Animals Sticker Activities. Isherwood, Matthew, illus. (p. 125)
—Hoot: A Hide-And-Seek Book of Counting. Galloway, Fhiona, illus. (p. 796)
—I Like to Squeak! How Do You Speak? Galloway, Fhiona, illus. (p. 841)
—Mesmerizing Math. Flintham, Thomas, illus. (p. 1129)
—One, Two, Baa, Moo: A Pop-Up Book of Counting. Verrall, Lisa, illus. (p. 1297)
—Planet Pop-Up: Monkey on the Moon. Anderson, Nicola, illus. (p. 1368)
—Planet Pop-Up: Shark Makes a Splash! Anderson, Nicola, illus. (p. 1368)
—Planet Pop-Up: Sheep Rules the Roost! Anderson, Nicola, illus. (p. 1368)
—Planet Pop-Up: Tiger Takes Off. Anderson, Nicola, illus. (p. 1368)
—Roar: A Big-Mouthed Book of Sounds! Galloway, Fhiona, illus. (p. 1478)
—Snap: A Peek-Through Book of Shapes. Galloway, Fhiona, illus. (p. 1597)
—Surprise: A Book of Christmas Shapes. Galloway, Fhiona, illus. (p. 1685)
—Tall & Short: A Peek-Through Book of Opposites. Galloway, Fhiona, illus. (p. 1704)
Littrell, J. J., et al. From School to Work: Teaching Package Teacher's Resource Guide. (p. 643)
—From School to Work: Teaching Package Teacher's Resource Portfolio. (p. 643)
—From School to Work. (p. 643)
Littrell, John M. & Peterson, Jean S. Portrait & Model of a School Counselor. (p. 1386)
Litvin, Gary, jt. auth. see Litvin, Maria.
Litvin, Gary, ed. 800 Questions in Calculus: 25 Years of Continental Mathematics League Contests. (p. 2001)
Litvin, Maria & Litvin, Gary. 175 Multiple-Choice Questions in Java. (p. 2000)
Litwiller, Bonnie H., ed. see Yeatts, Karol, et al.
Litwin, Eric. I Love My White Shoes. Dean, James, illus. (p. 842)
—Nuts: Bedtime at the Nut House. Magoon, Scott, illus. (p. 1274)
—Nuts: Sing & Dance in Your Polka Dot Pants. Magoon, Scott, illus. (p. 1274)
—Pete the Cat & His Four Groovy Buttons. Dean, James, illus. (p. 1346)
—Pete the Cat Saves Christmas. Dean, James, illus. (p. 1346)
—Rocking in My School Shoes. Dean, James, illus. (p. 1483)
Litwin, Eric & Dean, James. I Love My White Shoes. (p. 842)
Litwin, Eric, ed. Rocking in My School Shoes. (p. 1483)
Litwin, Laura Baskes. Diego Rivera: Legendary Mexican Painter. (p. 437)
—Dorothea Lange: A Life in Pictures. (p. 471)
—E. B. White: Beyond Charlotte's Web & Stuart Little. (p. 491)
—Life of Benjamin Banneker: Astronomer & Mathematician. (p. 1011)
—Reader's Guide to Zora Neale Hurston's Their Eyes Were Watching God. (p. 1444)
—Write Horror Fiction in 5 Simple Steps. (p. 1963)
—Zora Neale Hurston: I Have Been in Sorrow's Kitchen. (p. 1990)
Litwin, Mike. Big Cowhuna. Litwin, Mike, illus. (p. 180)
—Crown of the Cowibbean. Litwin, Mike, illus. (p. 386)
—Lost in Bermooda. Litwin, Mike, illus. (p. 1055)
Litwin, Mike, illus. see Fosberry, Jennifer.
Litwin, Stephanie K. Raising Otter. (p. 1437)
Litz, Amanda. Sam & Pam Can & You Can Too! We Can Count. Garcia, Cynthia, illus. (p. 1506)
—Sam & Pam Can & You Can Too! We Can Help Our Mom. Garcia, Cynthia, illus. (p. 1506)
—Sam & Pam Can & You Can Too! We Can Ride Our Bikes. Garcia, Cynthia, illus. (p. 1506)
Litz, Mamie Saebz, illus. see McGrew, Michael.
Litzenberg, Corinne. Sand Lady: A Cape May Tale (p. 1510)
Litzenberg, Corinne M. Grandpa's Basement (p. 709)
—Sand Lady: An Ocean City, Maryland, Tale (p. 1510)
Litzenberger, Mona. Humble the Bumblebee. (p. 826)
Litzgus, Hazel. Where the Meadowlark Sang: Cherished Scenes from an Artist's Childhood (p. 1909)
Litzinger, Rosanne, illus. see Hershenhorn, Esther.
Litzinger, Rosanne, illus. see Kimmel, Eric A.
Litzinger, Rosanne, illus. see Nishizuka, Koko.
Litzinger, Rosanne, illus. see Paul, Ann Whitford.
Litzinger, Rosanne, illus. see Shulman, Lisa.
Litzinger, Rosanne, illus. see Stewig, John Warren.
Liu, Aimee. Gaining: The Truth about Life after Eating Disorders. (p. 652)
Liu, Carol & Caldarone, Marybeth Sidoti. Arlene on the Scene. (p. 99)
Liu, Cynthea. Bike on, Bear! Litten, Kristyna, illus. (p. 185)
—Wooby & Peep: A Story of Unlikely Friendship. Peterson, Mary, illus. (p. 1949)
Liu, Davy. Fire Fish: Fins Refined by Fire. (p. 590)
—Giant Leaf: Take a Giant Leaf of Faith. Liu, Davy, illus. (p. 673)
Liu, Eleanor. Lao Li & His Beancurd. (p. 975)
Liu, Jenny, ed. see Lu, Tina.
Liu, Julia. Gus, the Dinosaur Bus. Lynn, Bei, illus. (p. 732)
Liu, Kimi, illus. see Trujillo, Rafael E.
Liu, Liana. Memory Key. (p. 1126)
Liu, Marjorie M. Black Widow: The Name of the Rose. Acuña, Daniel, illus. (p. 197)
Liu, Na, jt. auth. see Martinez, Andrés Vera.
Liu, Na, jt. auth. see Martinez, Andrés Vera.
Liu, Peter, jt. auth. see Helsel, Larry D.
Liu, Siyu, illus. see Protopopescu, Orel O.
Liu, Siyu, tr. see Protopopescu, Orel O.
Liu, Wei. Mom, Little Lake Girl Again Says: My School Days in China. (p. 1161)
Liu, Xuemei, ed. see Huancai, Yang, et al.
Liu-Perkins, Christine. At Home in Her Tomb: Lady Dai & the Ancient Chinese Treasures of Mawangdui. (p. 110)
—At Home in Her Tomb: Lady Dai & the Ancient Chinese Treasures of Mawangdui. Brannen, Sarah S., illus. (p. 110)
Liván, Paco. Thing That Hurts Most in the World. Olmos, Roger, illus. (p. 1732)
—What a Snout! Prieto, Iván, illus. (p. 1878)
LiveABC (Firm) Staff & McGraw-Hill Companies Staff, contrib. by. McGraw-Hill's Spanish Illustrated Dictionary. (p. 1114)
LiveLearn, Robert, illus. see Richter, Debra A.
Lively, Crystal. Welcome to Brookesville. (p. 1873)
Lively, Deborah Dreher. Hateya Sam. (p. 752)
—Vanishing Treasure of the Virungas. (p. 1833)
—Walkabout Sam. (p. 1854)
Lively, Jim. Through the Eyes of Emma. (p. 1745)
Lively, Joe. Notes of a Time Traveler: Our Forgotten Folk Heritage. (p. 1268)
Lively, Judy. Hanny Bonz. (p. 743)
Lively, Penelope & Gliori, Debi. Goldilocks & the Three Bears. (p. 696)
Liverman, Debra, ed. Daily Journal Prompts. (p. 399)
Livermore, Edward. Phebe the Blackberry Girl. (p. 1350)
, Liverpool Football Club, Liverpool Football Club. Official Liverpool FC Sticker Colouring Book. (p. 1280)
Liverpool Football Club Staff. Official Liverpool FC Sticker Activity Book. (p. 1280)
—Official Liverpool FC Ultimate Junior Reds' Book. (p. 1280)
Livers, Dee. Maxwell, the Day-Maker. (p. 1112)
Liversidge, Cassie. Ice Cream! Grow Your Own Ingredients. (p. 850)
—Pasta Sauce! Grow Your Own Ingredients. (p. 1327)
Livesey, Margot. Banishing Verona: A Novel. (p. 136)
Livesey, Robert, illus. see Smith, A. G.
Livesey, Robert & Smith, A. G. Great War (p. 719)
Living Language Staff. Living Language Irish (p. 1041)
Living Stone Arts, prod. Crossing Tract (p. 385)
Living Stream Ministry Staff. Hymns: #1-1348. (p. 831)
—Hymns: 100 Selected. (p. 831)
—Hymns #1-1348. (p. 831)
Living the Good News Staff. First Reconciliation & Beyond Child's Book. Mueller, Steve, ed. (p. 596)
—Growing a Grateful, Generous Heart Children's Papers Grades 3-4: Stewardship Resources for Children andTheir Families. (p. 726)
—Growing a Grateful, Generous Heart Children's Papers Grades 1-2: Stewardship Resources for Children & Their Families. (p. 726)
—Growing a Grateful, Generous Heart Children's Papers Preschool/Kindergarten: Stewarship Resources for Children & Their Families. (p. 726)
—Kids in Common: A Children's Book of Common Prayer. (p. 954)
Living the Good News Staff, prod. First Eucharist & Beyond: Ongoing Initiation into Communion with Christ. (p. 594)
Livingood, Allen. No Luck at All. (p. 1258)
Livingston, A. A. B. Bear & Lolly: Off to School. Chou, Joey, illus. (p. 122)
—B. Bear & Lolly: Catch That Cookie! Chou, Joey, illus. (p. 122)
Livingston, Amee. Cup of Tea for Tiger & Me. (p. 392)
Livingston, Billie & Adderson, Caroline. Trouble with Marlene & Film Studies. Little, Melanie, ed. (p. 1790)
Livingston, Eric. Brandon Marlowe & the Spirit Snatcher. (p. 222)
Livingston, Esther, creator. Never Alone: 10 Years As Missionaries to Korea. (p. 1242)
Livingston, Francis, illus. see Brandt, Keith & Macken, JoAnn Early.
Livingston, Francis, illus. see Santrey, Laurence & Macken, JoAnn Early.
Livingston, Irene. Finklehopper Frog. Lies, Brian, illus. (p. 589)
Livingston, Jessica, illus. see Kawa, Katie.
Livingston, Joshua. Sun Rays: Tales for Children of Every Age. Roth, Judy Langemo, illus. (p. 1676)
Livingston, Juwuan. One Word for Good. (p. 1297)
Livingston, Lesley. Darklight. (p. 408)
—Descendant. (p. 428)
—Starling. (p. 1642)
—Tempestuous. (p. 1718)
—Transcendent. (p. 1778)
—Wondrous Strange. (p. 1949)
Livingston, Luna. Vanessa. (p. 1833)
Livingston, Mary A., jt. auth. see Livingston, Timothy J.
Livingston, Mary A. & Shufelberger, Amanda. Buddy & the Magic Chicken Tree Livingston, Tim, illus. (p. 234)
Livingston, Myra Cohn. Calendar. Hillenbrand, Will, illus. (p. 252)
Livingston, Phyllis, jt. auth. see Chastain, Zachary.
Livingston, Phyllis, jt. auth. see Hunter, David.
Livingston, Phyllis, jt. auth. see McIntosh, Kenneth.
Livingston, Phyllis, jt. auth. see Nelson, Sheila.
Livingston, R. E. Super Scamper & Jayden's Big Adventure. (p. 1680)
Livingston, Sara J. Picture on the Wall: The Ultimate Love Story. (p. 1355)
Livingston, Tim, illus. see Livingston, Mary A. & Shufelberger, Amanda.
Livingston, Timothy J. & Livingston, Mary A. FireStorm in the Forest: When a Forest Burns. Livingston, Timothy J., illus. (p. 592)
Livingston, Todd. Odd Squad (p. 1278)
Livingston, Todd & Tinnell, Robert. Castle of Shadows (p. 277)
Livingstone Corporation Staff, jt. prod. see Tyndale House Publishers Staff.
Livingstone, Ian. Deathtrap Dungeon. (p. 420)
Livingstone, Ian, jt. auth. see Jackson, Steve.
Livoti, Carol & Topp, Elizabeth. Stress-Free Pregnancy Guide: A Doctor Tells You What to Really Expect (p. 1667)
Livre, Hachette, jt. auth. see Goscinny, René.
Livsey, John. '38: The Great Hurricane in Quonochontaug, Rhode Island. (p. 1996)
—Letters to Mary. (p. 1002)
Livshits, Larisa. Seven Little Brothers. Wilson, Phil, illus. (p. 1554)
Livy, jt. auth. see Curry, Jane Louise.
Liwksa, Renata, illus. see Laden, Nina.
Liwska, Renata. Red Wagon. Liwska, Renata, illus. (p. 1455)
Liwska, Renata, illus. see Cronin, Doreen.
Liwska, Renata, illus. see Labatt, Mary.
Liwska, Renata, illus. see Underwood, Deborah.
Liwska, Renata, jt. auth. see Cronin, Doreen.
Liz Collard. Jeremiah, the Schoolhouse Dog. (p. 913)
Liz, Pichon. Three Horrid Little Pigs. Liz, Pichon, illus. (p. 1742)
Liz Smith And Kate Spohrer. Jangelle the Adhd Angel - Training the Dunelm Way. (p. 908)
Liz Warren, illus. see Harris-Wyrick, Wayne.
Liza, Behles, illus. see Lorenzen, Margaret Brownell.
Lizana, Lorenzo, illus. see Bain, Michelle.
Lizana, Robert V. Two Weeks Before Christmas. (p. 1804)
Lizano, Marc, illus. see Dauvillier, Loïc & Salsedo, Greg.
Lizardi-Rivera, Carmen, tr. see Loya, Olga.
Lizatovic, Josip, illus. see Weir, Liz.
Lizb. My Clean Teeth. (p. 1200)
Lizzy Anne's Adventures Staff & Zarrella, Sharon. Lizzy Anne's Adventures Vasudevan, Vidya, illus. (p. 1043)
Ljungberg, Jon, illus. see Toews, Rita Y.
Ljungberg, Jon, illus. see Toews, Rita.
Ljungklist, Laura, jt. auth. see Ljungkvist, Laura.
Ljungkvist, Laura. Follow the Line to School. (p. 612)
—Line Can Be ... (p. 1019)
—Pepi Sings a New Song. Ljungkvist, Laura, illus. (p. 1340)
Ljungkvist, Laura, illus. see Fox, Mem.
Ljungkvist, Laura & Ljungklist, Laura. Follow the Line. Ljungkvist, Laura, illus. (p. 612)
Llama, Gram. Bunny Fuzz Mystery. (p. 242)
Llamas, Kristin, illus. see Jostand, Jeffrey Jay.
Llanas, Sheila. Jonas Salk: Medical Innovator & Polio Vaccine Developer. (p. 925)
Llanas, Sheila Griffin. Armadillos. (p. 99)
—Bald Eagles. (p. 133)
—Beauty Poetry: She Walks in Beauty. (p. 154)
—Buffaloes. (p. 236)
—Caleb Davis Bradham: Pepsi-Cola Inventor. (p. 252)
—Colonel Harland Sanders: KFC Creator. (p. 341)
—Contemporary American Poetry: Not the End, but the Beginning. (p. 360)
—Contemporary American Poetry- Not the End, but the Beginning. (p. 360)
—Coyotes. (p. 374)
—Daniel Radcliffe (p. 405)
—Dave Thomas: Wendy's Founder. (p. 410)
—Easy Breakfasts from Around the World. (p. 500)
—Easy Lunches from Around the World. (p. 500)
—Easy Vegetarian Foods from Around the World. (p. 500)
—Ettore Boiardi: Chef Boyardee Manufacturer. (p. 540)
—Gray Wolves. (p. 713)
—Grizzly Bears. (p. 724)
—Hip-Hop Stars (p. 780)
—Hip-Hop Stars [Scholastic]. (p. 780)
—How to Analyze the Works of Suzanne Collins. (p. 814)
—John Pemberton: Coca-Cola Developer. (p. 922)
—Modern American Poetry: Echoes & Shadows. (p. 1158)
—Modern American Poetry- Echoes & Shadows. (p. 1158)
—Nature Poetry: Make Me a Picture of the Sun. (p. 1236)
—Picture Yourself Writing Fiction: Using Photos to Inspire Writing (p. 1356)
—Taylor Lautner (p. 1708)
—Tom Monaghan: Domino's Pizza Innovator. (p. 1763)
—Underground Railroad: A History Perspectives Book. (p. 1814)
—Walt Whitman. (p. 1856)
—Who Reached the South Pole First? (p. 1917)
—Women of the U. S. Army: Pushing Limits (p. 1946)
—Women of the U. S. Navy: Making Waves (p. 1946)
—Zac Efron (p. 1984)
Llanas, Sheila Griffin, jt. auth. see Peterson-Hilleque, Victoria.
Llanes, Adrian & Llanes, Christi. There's a Monster in My Closet. (p. 1731)
Llanes, Christi, jt. auth. see Llanes, Adrian.
Llanes, Rene. Topper: The Miracle of the Scrubby Little Christmas Tree. (p. 1769)
Llano, Gabriella, jt. auth. see Vazquez, Tiziana.
Llapashtica, Mentor, illus. see Brezinova, Ivona.
Llc, Books, ed. Story of Tracy Beaker: List of Tracy Beaker Returns Episodes, the Dare Game. (p. 1662)
Llewellyn, Bridget McGovern. One Child, One Planet: Inspiration for the Young Conservationist. Sams, Carl R., 2nd & Stoick, Jean, photos by. (p. 1294)
Llewellyn, Claire. And Everyone Shouted, Pull! A First Look at Forces & Motion. Abel, Simone, illus. (p. 71)
—Apples. (p. 92)
—Asi Nace un Arbol. Mendez, Simon, illus. (p. 106)
—Asi Nace un Pato. Mendez, Simon, illus. (p. 106)
—Asi Nace una Mariposa. Giraldo, Maria Cristina, tr. (p. 106)
—Asi Nace una Rana. Mendez, Simon, illus. (p. 106)
—Bad Dog, Digby! East, Jacqueline, illus. (p. 131)
—Banarse! Aprender Sobre Higiene Personal. (p. 136)
—Best Book of Bugs. (p. 168)
—Best Book of Sharks. (p. 168)
—Boo-Hoo, Baby! Lovsin, Polona, illus. (p. 209)
—Caliente y Frio. (p. 253)
—Cat Nap East, Jacqueline, illus. (p. 278)

L

—City Animals. (p. 323)
—Como Nacen los Bebes? Aprender Sobre Sexualidad. Gordon, Mike, illus. (p. 351)
—Day & Night. (p. 412)
—Dia y Noche. (p. 433)
—Diminuto y Enorme. (p. 440)
—Duck. Mendez, Simon, tr. (p. 488)
—Estoy Sano? Aprender Sobre Alimentacion y Actividad Fisica. Gordon, Mike, illus. (p. 538)
—Explorers: Reptiles. Bull, Peter, illus. (p. 551)
—Fight Air Pollution. (p. 585)
—Food Webs: Who Eats What? (p. 614)
—Forests (p. 618)
—Go Away, Baby! Lovsin, Polona, illus. (p. 686)
—Good Night, Baby! Lovsin, Polona, illus. (p. 699)
—Hearing. (p. 759)
—How Animals Grow. (p. 804)
—How Plants Grow. (p. 812)
—Is It for Me? Lovsin, Polona, illus. (p. 889)
—Let's Recycle. (p. 1000)
—Life of Plants. (p. 1012)
—Me Hace Bien o Mal? Aprender Sobre Medicamentos, Drogas y Salud. Gordon, Mike, illus. (p. 1116)
—Metal. (p. 1130)
—Moon. (p. 1171)
—New Pet. East, Jacqueline, illus. (p. 1246)
—Oceans (p. 1277)
—Paper. (p. 1322)
—Plants & Animals. (p. 1369)
—Plants & Humans. (p. 1369)
—Plants of the World. (p. 1370)
—Plastic. (p. 1370)
—Protect Natural Habitats. (p. 1412)
—Saints & Angels: Popular Stories of Familiar Saints. (p. 1504)
—Saints & Angels. (p. 1504)
—Sand! Beard, Lauren, illus. (p. 1510)
—Save Energy. (p. 1516)
—Sea. (p. 1534)
—Sea Animals. (p. 1534)
—Seeing. (p. 1548)
—Smelling & Tasting. (p. 1593)
—Snakes. (p. 1596)
—Sound. (p. 1615)
—Sound & Hearing. (p. 1615)
—Splash! Beard, Lauren, illus. (p. 1629)
—Stop Water Waste. (p. 1654)
—Tierra y Mar. (p. 1748)
—Touching. (p. 1772)
—Tree. Mendez, Simon, tr. (p. 1783)
—Watch Out! Around Town. Gordon, Mike, illus. (p. 1861)
—Watch Out! at Home. Gordon, Mike, illus. (p. 1861)
—Watch Out! on the Road. Gordon, Mike, illus. (p. 1861)
—Why Should I Eat Well? Gordon, Mike, illus. (p. 1926)
—Why Should I Listen? Gordon, Mike, illus. (p. 1926)
—Wood. (p. 1949)
—Your Body. (p. 1980)
—Your Food. (p. 1980)
—Your Hair. (p. 1980)
—Your Teeth. (p. 1981)
Llewellyn, Claire & Feldman, Thea. Kingfisher Readers L2: Amazing Animal Senses. (p. 960)
—Kingfisher Readers L2: in the Rainforest. (p. 960)
—Kingfisher Readers L4: Rivers. (p. 960)
Llewellyn, Claire & Holden, Arianne. It's Great to Play & Fun to Learn: A Stimulating Play-And-Learn Book with over 130 Amazing Facts, Exercises & Projects, & More Than 5000 Bright Action-Packed Photographs. (p. 897)
Llewellyn, Claire & Johnson, Jinny. Explorers: Big Cats. Bull, Peter, illus. (p. 551)
Llewellyn, Claire & O'Shea, Clare. Cooking with Fruits & Vegetables. (p. 362)
—Cooking with Meat & Fish. (p. 362)
Llewellyn, Claire, et al. Spiders: Deadly Predators. (p. 1627)
—Spiders - Kingfisher Readers: Deadly Predators. (p. 1627)
Llewellyn, Sam. Darksolstice. (p. 409)
—Well Between the Worlds. (p. 1874)
Llewellyn, Tom. Shadow of Seth: A Seth Anomundy Murder Mystery. (p. 1557)
Llewelyn, Claire. Exercise. (p. 548)
—Healthy Eating. (p. 758)
—Hygiene & Health. (p. 831)
—Stay Safe! (p. 1645)
Llewhellin, Gareth, illus. see Granger, Trudi.
Llewhellin, Gareth, illus. see Reasoner, Charles.
Llimós, Anna. Earth-Friendly Christmas Crafts in 5 Easy Steps. (p. 496)
—Earth-Friendly Clay Crafts in 5 Easy Steps. (p. 496)
—Earth-Friendly Crafts from Recycled Stuff in 5 Easy Steps. (p. 496)
—Earth-Friendly Papier-Mâché Crafts in 5 Easy Steps. (p. 496)
—Earth-Friendly Wood Crafts in 5 Easy Steps. (p. 496)
—Easy Bead Crafts in 5 Steps. (p. 500)
—Easy Cardboard Crafts in 5 Steps. (p. 500)
—Easy Clay Crafts in 5 Steps. (p. 500)
—Easy Cloth Crafts in 5 Steps. (p. 500)
—Easy Earth-Friendly Crafts in 5 Steps. (p. 500)
—Easy Paper Crafts in 5 Steps. (p. 500)
—Fairy Tale Adventure Crafts. (p. 564)
—Haunted House Adventure Crafts. (p. 753)
—Medieval Castle Adventure Crafts. (p. 1119)
—Pirate Ship Adventure Crafts. (p. 1363)
—Space Adventure Crafts. (p. 1618)
Llimós, Anna, jt. auth. see Llimos Plomer, Anna.
Llimós, Anna & Library Association Staff. Fairy Tale Adventure Crafts. (p. 564)
—Medieval Castle Adventure Crafts. (p. 1119)
—Pirate Ship Adventure Crafts. (p. 1363)
—Space Adventure Crafts. (p. 1618)
Llimós Plomer, Anna. Earth-Friendly Christmas Crafts in 5 Easy Steps. (p. 496)
—Earth-Friendly Clay Crafts in 5 Easy Steps. (p. 496)
—Earth-Friendly Crafts from Recycled Stuff in 5 Easy Steps. (p. 496)
—Earth-Friendly Papier-Mâché Crafts in 5 Easy Steps. (p. 496)
—Earth-Friendly Wood Crafts in 5 Easy Steps. (p. 496)
—Haunted House Adventure Crafts. (p. 753)
Llimos Plomer, Anna. Paper. (p. 1322)
Llimos Plomer, Anna & Llimós, Anna. Madera y Corcho. Casanova, Jose Maria, illus. (p. 1070)
Llimos Plomer, Anna & Parramon's Editorial Team Staff. Clay. (p. 330)
—Wood & Cork. (p. 1949)
Llongueras, Joan & Masnou, Merce. Kadingir: El Cetro de Zink. (p. 941)
Llorente, Maria Isabel Molina. Misterio del Hombre Que Desaparecio. (p. 1155)
Llorente, Pilar Molina. Aura Gris. (p. 116)
Llorente, Pilar Molina & Molina Llorente, Pilar. Mensanje de Maese Zamaor. (p. 1126)
Llosa, Mario Vargas, see Vargas Llosa, Mario.
Lloyd, A. R. Kine. (p. 958)
Lloyd, A. Wallis. Monster-Musical. (p. 1168)
Lloyd, Alicia. When the Monsters Are Quiet. Rottinger, Amy, illus. (p. 1904)
Lloyd, Alison. Year of the Tiger. (p. 1969)
Lloyd, Anna, illus. see Weaver, Ruth.
Lloyd, Ashley. Red Matkovich, Gregory, illus. (p. 1453)
Lloyd, Christopher. What on Earth? Wallbook of Natural History. Forshaw, Andy, illus. (p. 1892)
—What on Earth? Wallbook of the Natural World: From the Dawn of Life to the Present Day. Forshaw, Andy, illus. (p. 1892)
Lloyd, Elizabeth. Piggyon. (p. 1358)
Lloyd, Glynis, jt. auth. see Dyer, Dorothy.
Lloyd, Helen. New Zealand Art Activity Book: 100+ Ideas for Creative Kids. (p. 1249)
Lloyd, Henry Demarest. Man: The Social Creator. (p. 1085)
—Newest England: A County Without Strikes. (p. 1249)
—Sovereign People. (p. 1618)
Lloyd, Hugh. Among the River Pirates. Fogel, Seymour, illus. (p. 65)
—Held for Ransom: A Skippy Dare Mystery Story. Fogel, Seymour, illus. (p. 762)
—Lonesome Swamp Mystery: A Hal Keen Mystery Story. Salg, Bert, illus. (p. 1046)
—Lost Mine of the Amazon. Salg, Bert, illus. (p. 1056)
Lloyd, James, illus. see Bondy, Halley.
Lloyd, Janet E. Joy & Wonder in All God's Works: Year B. (p. 929)
Lloyd, Jennifer. Best Thing about Kindergarten. Leng, Qin, illus. (p. 171)
—Ella's Umbrellas. Spires, Ashley, illus. (p. 514)
—Murilla Gorilla & the Hammock Problem. Lee, Jacqui, illus. (p. 1192)
—Murilla Gorilla & the Lost Parasol. Lee, Jacqui, illus. (p. 1192)
—Murilla Gorilla, Jungle Detective. George, Kallie, ed. (p. 1192)
—Taffy Time. Lee, Jacqui, illus. (p. 1695)
Lloyd, Jennifer & Osmond, Claudia. Smudge's Mark. Leng, Qin, illus. (p. 1595)
Lloyd, Jennifer & Wakelin, Kirsti Anne. Looking for Loons. (p. 1051)
Lloyd, Jon. View of America's Future by America's. (p. 1842)
Lloyd Jones, Rob. Crusaders. (p. 386)
—See Inside Ancient Egypt. Hancock, David, illus. (p. 1546)
—Story of Spying. (p. 1660)
Lloyd Jones, Rob, retold by. Robin Hood. (p. 1479)
Lloyd, Megan. Davy Crockett Gets Hitched. (p. 411)
Lloyd, Megan, illus. see Branley, Franklyn M.
Lloyd, Megan, illus. see Branley, Franklyn M. & Branley.
Lloyd, Megan, illus. see Edwards, Pamela Duncan.
Lloyd, Megan, illus. see Hershenhorn, Esther.
Lloyd, Megan, illus. see Miller, Bobbi.
Lloyd, Megan, illus. see Shore, Diane Z.
Lloyd, Megan, illus. see Shore, Diane ZuHone.
Lloyd, Megan, illus. see Spinelli, Eileen.
Lloyd, Megan, illus. see White, Becky.
Lloyd, Megan, illus. see White, Linda Arms.
Lloyd, Megan, illus. see White, Linda.
Lloyd, Megan Wagner. Finding Wild. Halpin, Abigail, illus. (p. 588)
Lloyd, Natalie. Snicker of Magic. (p. 1597)
—Want More? Life. (p. 1856)
Lloyd, Patricia. I Love Me 2! (p. 842)
Lloyd, Saci. Carbon Diaries 2015. (p. 265)
—Carbon Diaries 2017. (p. 265)
—Momentum. (p. 1162)
Lloyd, Sam. Crunchy Croc. (p. 386)
—Farty Fred. (p. 575)
—Grumpy Gertie. (p. 727)
—Shape Sorters - Numbers Lloyd, Sam, illus. (p. 1560)
—Turn It up, Doris! (p. 1797)
—What's in Your Tummy Mummy? Lloyd, Sam, illus. (p. 1898)
Lloyd, Sam, illus. see Sperring, Mark.
Lloyd, Sam, jt. auth. see Lloyd, Sam R.
Lloyd, Sam R. Two Little Aliens. (p. 1803)
—Whose Tail? (p. 1922)
—Yucky Mucky Manners. (p. 1983)
—Yummy Yummy! Food for My Tummy. Tickle, Jack, illus. (p. 1983)
Lloyd, Sam R. & Lloyd, Sam. Happy Dog, Sad Dog (p. 745)
—Mr. Pusskins: A Love Story. Lloyd, Sam R. & Lloyd, Sam, illus. (p. 1186)
—Mr. Pusskins & Little Whiskers: Another Love Story. Lloyd, Sam R. & Lloyd, Sam, illus. (p. 1186)
Lloyd, Sandra Mackenzie, ed. Patriots, Pirates, Heroes & Spies: Stories from Historic Philadelphia. (p. 1329)
Lloyd, Sophie. Behind Brown Eyes. (p. 160)
Lloyd, Stacey. Prairie Pet. (p. 1392)
Lloyd, Stacy K. Friends & Letters. (p. 638)
—Girl & Her Dog. (p. 678)
Lloyd, Sue. How to Be Brilliant at Recording in Geography. (p. 815)
—Jolly Phonics Letter Sound Strips (Print Letters) Stephen, Lib, illus. (p. 924)
Lloyd, Sue, jt. auth. see Molzan, Janet.
Lloyd, Sue, jt. auth. see Wernham, Sara.
Lloyd, Sue & Wernham, Sara. Finger Phonics Big Books 1-7: Set of 7 Big Books (precursive Letters) Vol. 7 Stephen, Lib, illus. (p. 589)
—Finger Phonics Big Books 1-7 (print Letters) Set of 7 Big Books (p. 589)
—Jolly Phonics Sound Stories (US Ed, in Print Letters) Stephen, Lib, illus. (p. 924)
—Jolly Phonics Word Book (Print Letters) (p. 924)
Lloyd, Sylvia. Little Turtle's Tale. (p. 1037)
Lloyd, Tanner. Days of Sorrow & Joy. (p. 415)
Lloyd-Caldwell, Marian. Dancing Watermelon Babies & Mr Mouse's Good Deed. (p. 403)
Lloyd-Diviny, Karen, illus. see Morecroft, Richard & MacKay, Alison.
Lloyd-Diviny, Karen, illus. see Morecroft, Richard, et al.
Lloyd-Jones, Antonia, tr. see Korczak, Janusz.
Lloyd-Jones, Emily. Deceptive: An Illusive Novel. (p. 421)
—Illusive. (p. 857)
Lloyd-Jones, Sally. Baby's Hug-a-Bible. Gévry, Claudine, illus. (p. 129)
—Biblia para Niños - Historias de Jesús: Cada historia susurra Su Nombre (p. 176)
—Bunny's First Spring McPhail, David, illus. (p. 242)
—Goldfish on Vacation. Muradov, Roman, illus. (p. 695)
—How to Be a Baby: By Me, the Big Sister. Heap, Sue, illus. (p. 814)
—How to Be a Baby... by Me, the Big Sister. Heap, Sue, illus. (p. 814)
—How to Get a Job - By Me, the Boss. Heap, Sue, illus. (p. 820)
—Jesus Storybook Bible: Every Story Whispers His Name Jago, illus. (p. 916)
—Jesus Storybook Bible Deluxe Edition (p. 916)
—Just Because You're Mine. Endersby, Frank, illus. (p. 938)
—My Promise Rainbow: And the Story of Noah's Ark. (p. 1217)
—Old MacNoah Had an Ark. Newton, Jill, illus. (p. 1284)
—Poor Doreen: a Fishy Tale. Boiger, Alexandra, illus. (p. 1383)
—Thoughts to Make Your Heart Sing (p. 1740)
—Time to Say Goodnight. Chapman, Jane, illus. (p. 1753)
—Tiny Bear's Bible Oleynikov, Igor, illus. (p. 1756)
—Ultimate Guide to Grandmas & Grandpas! Emberley, Michael, illus. (p. 1809)
Lloyd-Jones, Sally & Dyer, Jane. House That's Your Home. (p. 804)
Lluch, Alex. Big Bugs, Small Bugs: If You Could Be a Bug, Which Bug Would You Be? Defenbaugh, David, illus. (p. 180)
—Do I Look Good in Color? Defenbaugh, David, illus. (p. 457)
Lluch, Alex A. Alexander, It's Time for Bed! Defenbaugh, David, illus. (p. 36)
—Alphabet: I Like to Learn the ABCs! Defenbaugh, David, illus. (p. 49)
—Alphabet Wipe-Off Activities: Endless Fun to Get Ready for School! (p. 50)
—Animal Alphabet: Slide & Seek the ABCs. (p. 76)
—Animal Alphabet: Slide & Seek the ABCs. Defenbaugh, David, illus. (p. 76)
—Animal Numbers: Slide & Seek Counting. (p. 79)
—Animal Numbers: Slide & Seek The 123s. (p. 79)
—Baby's First 100 Plus Words. (p. 129)
—I Like to Learn Alphabet: Zoo Clues. (p. 841)
—I Like to Learn Colors: Curious Penguin. (p. 841)
—I Like to Learn Numbers: Hungry Chameleon. (p. 841)
—I Like to Learn Opposites: Amazing Bugs. (p. 841)
—Kindergarten Learning While Having Fun! (p. 957)
—Let's Leap Ahead 1st Grade Trivia. (p. 998)
—Let's Leap Ahead 2nd Grade Trivia. (p. 998)
—Let's Leap Ahead 2nd Grade Trivia Notepad: The Game of 300 Questions for You & Your Friends! (p. 998)
—Let's Leap Ahead 3rd Grade Trivia. (p. 998)
—Let's Leap Ahead 3rd Grade Trivia Notepad: The Game of 300 Questions for You & Your Friends! (p. 998)
—Let's Leap Ahead 4th Grade Trivia. (p. 998)
—Let's Leap Ahead Alphabet. (p. 998)
—Let's Leap Ahead - Alphabet Play & Learn! (p. 998)
—Let's Leap Ahead Colors & Shapes. (p. 998)
—Let's Leap Ahead Kindergarten. (p. 998)
—Let's Leap Ahead Kindergarten School Games. (p. 998)
—Let's Leap Ahead Kindergarten Wipe-Off. (p. 998)
—Let's Leap Ahead Numbers. (p. 998)
—Let's Leap Ahead - Numbers Play & Learn! (p. 998)
—Let's Leap Ahead Phonics. (p. 998)
—Let's Leap Ahead: Phonics, Colors & More Play & Learn! (p. 998)
—Let's Leap Ahead Pre-K. (p. 998)
—Let's Leap Ahead - Pre-K Fun Pad! (p. 998)
—Let's Leap Ahead Pre-K School Games. (p. 998)
—Let's Leap Ahead Pre-K Wipe-Off. (p. 998)
—Lose up to 10 Pounds in 2 Weeks. (p. 1054)
—Math - Make Learning Fun! (p. 1105)
—Numbers - I Like to Count from 1 to 10! Defenbaugh, David, illus. (p. 1272)
—Numbers Wipe-Off Activities: Endless Fun to Get Ready for School! (p. 1272)
—Pre-K Learning While Having Fun! (p. 1394)
—Read & Write - Make Learning Fun! (p. 1443)
—Touch the Red Button. (p. 1772)
—Trace & Learn The 123s. (p. 1774)
—Trace & Learn the ABCs: And Have Fun Playing Peek-A-Boo Who? Defenbaugh, David, illus. (p. 1774)
—Zoo Clues Animal Alphabet: Learn with Me the ABCs. (p. 1988)
—Zoo Clues Animal Alphabet. (p. 1988)
Lluch, Constantino. Capital de Provincia. (p. 262)
Lluch, Emily, jt. auth. see Lluch, Isabel B.
Lluch, Isabel. Fabulous Book of Me! The Ultimate Girls' Guide Journal & Keepsake That's All about You! (p. 559)
Lluch, Isabel B. Ultimate Girls' Guide Journal to Feel Confident, Pretty & Happy. (p. 1809)
Lluch, Isabel B. & Lluch, Emily. B. F. F. Best Friends Forever: Have Fun, Share, & Laugh While Getting to Know Your Best Friends! (p. 122)
—B. F. F. - Best Friends Forever: Fun Questions & Quizzes for You & Your Best Friends. (p. 122)
—B. F. F. Quizzes. (p. 122)
—Girls' Guide to Caring for Your Body: Everything You Need to Know - Questions & Answers about Growing Up. (p. 680)
—iGirl - B. F. F. Quizzes for You & Your Friends. (p. 856)
—iGirl - My B. F. F. S. (p. 856)
—iGirl - My Diary. (p. 856)
—iGirl - My Keepsake. (p. 856)
Llull, Maria. I-Ballers: Little Books for Big Minds. (p. 834)
Llywelyn, Morgan. Cave of Secrets. (p. 282)
—Grania: She-King of the Irish Seas. (p. 710)
Lo, Beth, illus. see Lo, Ginnie.
Lo, Beth, jt. auth. see Lo, Ginnie.
Lo Bianco, Nick, illus. see Shultz, Charles M. & Katschke, Judy.
Lo Bianco, Peter, illus. see Shultz, Charles M. & Bailer, Darice.
Lo Bianco, Peter, illus. see Shultz, Charles M. & Katschke, Judy.
Lo Cascio, Maria Cristina, illus. see Burrin, Angela M.
Lo Cascio, Maria Cristina, illus. see Lester, Anna.
Lo, Catherine. How It Ends. (p. 810)
Lo, Chi. Phantom of the China Economic Threat: Shadow of the Next Asian Crisis. (p. 1349)
Lo, Erika, jt. auth. see Maccarone, Grace.
Lo Famia, Jon, illus. see Dickens, Charles.
Lo, Ginnie. Mahjong All Day Long. Lo, Beth, illus. (p. 1076)
Lo, Ginnie & Lo, Beth. Auntie Yang's Great Soybean Picnic. (p. 115)
Lo, Koon-Chiu, jt. auth. see Hume, Lotta Carswell.
Lo, Malinda. Adaptation. (p. 11)
—Ash. (p. 105)
—Huntress. (p. 829)
—Inheritance. (p. 874)
Lo, Monica. Old Testament Heroines of the Faith. Diehl, Nichole, illus. (p. 1284)
Lo Raso, Carlo. Watch Me Draw the Backyardigans' Incredible Adventures. (p. 1861)
Lo Raso, Carlo, illus. see Mattern, Joanne & Toohey, Cathy.
Lo Raso, Carlo, illus. see Weinberg, Jennifer Liberts.
Lo, Rich. Father's Chinese Opera. Lo, Rich, illus. (p. 577)
Lo, Talthau, photos by see Lo, Yer Jenny.
Lo, Yer Jenny. Disobedient Ducklings. Lo, Talthau, photos by. (p. 453)
Loader, Mair. Meistrgopïau. (p. 1124)
—Yr Haen Fathemateg. (p. 1982)
Loader, Mandy. Amazing Young Sports People, Level 1 (p. 56)
—Amazing Young Sports People Level 1 Beginner/Elementary. (p. 56)
Loane, Cormac. Team Woodwind: Flute. (p. 1710)
Loane, Cormac, jt. see Duckett, Richard.
Lobato, Arcadio. Volando por las Palabras. (p. 1848)
Lobb, Nancy. 16 Extraordinary Americans with Disabilities. (p. 1995)
—16 Extraordinary Native Americans. (p. 1995)
—16 Extraordinary Young Americans. (p. 1995)
Löbbecke, Eric, illus. see Thomson, Jimmy.
Lobby, Mackenzie. Babe Didrikson Zaharias: Groundbreaking All-Around Athlete. (p. 123)
Lobby, Mackenzie & Gitlin, Martin. Minnesota Vikings. (p. 1147)
Lobdell, Chanel Mickayla. Tale of Phoebe & Leonardo. Cain, Mary, illus. (p. 1700)
Lobdell, Scott. Deadliest Stunt. Henrique, Paulo, illus. (p. 417)
—Deadly Strategy Henrique, Paulo, illus. (p. 418)
—Dude Ranch O' Death! Henrique, Paulo, illus. (p. 489)
—Flesh & Blood (p. 603)
—Haley Danelle's Top Eight! Henrique, Paulo, illus. (p. 736)
—Hardy Boys #18: D. A. N. G. E. R. Spells the Hangman! Henrique, Paulo, illus. (p. 748)
—Hardy Boys #19: Chaos at 30,000 Feet! Henrique, Paulo, illus. (p. 748)
—Identity Theft. Rendon, Daniel, illus. (p. 852)
—Live Free, Die Hardy! Henrique, Paulo, illus. (p. 1039)
—Mad House. Rendon, Daniel, illus. (p. 1069)
—Ocean of Osyria. Rendon, Daniel, illus. (p. 1276)
—Opposite Numbers. Rendon, Daniel et al, illus. (p. 1300)
—Shhhhhh! Henrique, Paulo, illus. (p. 1566)
—Word Up! Henrique, Paulo, illus. (p. 1951)
Lobdell, Scott & Coney, Malachy. Darkness: Origins Volume 4 TP: Origins Volume 4 TP. (p. 408)
Lobdell, Scott, et al. X-Force: Phalanx Covenant. Cruz, Roger et al, illus. (p. 1967)
—X-Men: X-Cutioner's Song. Peterson, Brandon et al, illus. (p. 1967)
Lobdell-Bulson, Jodi. Toddler Room: Free Play. (p. 1761)
Lobe, Mira & Kovács, Cécile. Hoppelpopp & the Best Bunny. Kaufmann, Angelika, illus. (p. 797)
Lobel, Adrianne, jt. auth. see Lobel, Arnold.
Lobel, Anita. 10 Hungry Rabbits: Counting & Color Concepts. Bowers, Tim, illus. (p. 1993)
—10 Hungry Rabbits. (p. 1993)
—Animal Antics: A to Z. Lobel, Anita, illus. (p. 76)
—Hello, Day! Lobel, Anita, illus. (p. 763)
—Lena's Sleep Sheep. (p. 991)
—Nini Here & There. (p. 1256)
—No Pretty Pictures: A Child of War. (p. 1260)
—Potatoes, Potatoes. (p. 1388)
—Taking Care of Mama Rabbit. (p. 1698)
Lobel, Anita, illus. see Davidson, Rebecca Piatt.
Lobel, Anita, illus. see Henkes, Kevin.
Lobel, Anita, illus. see Lobel, Arnold.
Lobel, Arnold. Arnold Lobel Treasury. (p. 100)
—Days with Frog & Toad. Lobel, Arnold, illus. (p. 415)
—Días con Sapo y Sepo. (p. 435)
—Frog & Toad Are Friends. Lobel, Arnold, illus. (p. 640)
—Frog & Toad Collection Lobel, Arnold, illus. (p. 640)
—Frog & Toad Storybook Treasury. Lobel, Arnold, illus. (p. 640)
—Historias de Ratones. (p. 782)
—Mago de Los Colores. (p. 1076)
—On Market Street. Lobel, Anita, illus. (p. 1289)
—Saltamontes Va Da Viage. (p. 1505)
—Sapo y Sepo, Inseparables. Lobel, Arnold, illus. (p. 1514)
—Sapo y Sepo Son Amigos. Lobel, Arnold, illus. (p. 1514)
—Sopa de Raton. (p. 1613)
—Tio Elefante. (p. 1757)
Lobel, Arnold, illus. see Young, Miriam.

Lobel, Arnold & Lobel, Adrianne. Frogs & Toads All Sang. Lobel, Arnold & Lobel, Adrianne, illus. (p. 641)
—Odd Owls & Stout Pigs: A Book of Nonsense. Lobel, Arnold & Lobel, Adrianne, illus. (p. 1278)
Lobel, Arnold & Rylant, Cynthia. Friendship Stories You Can Share. Howard, Arthur, illus. (p. 639)
Lobel, Gill. Little Bear's Special Wish. Hansen, Gaby, illus. (p. 1024)
—Where's My Cuddly? Braun, Sebastien, illus. (p. 1910)
Lobel, Gillian. Little Honey Bear & the Smiley Moon Warnes, Tim, illus. (p. 1029)
Lobiondo, Christine. Red Rock Capers. (p. 1455)
Lobo, Chris. Brand New Day: (of School) (p. 222)
Lobo, Julia. Eek! That's Creepy! Look & Find. Cavallini, Linda, illus. (p. 505)
—Guess How Much I Miss You. (p. 729)
Lobos, Anya Luz. Más Tenue Que la Brisa. (p. 1102)
Locatelli, Ellen. Filastrocche Italiane- Italian Nursery Rhymes. (p. 586)
Loccisano, Rina. Baby Dario Eats His First Carrot. Baker, David, illus. (p. 125)
—Baby Dario Is Born. Baker, David, illus. (p. 125)
Loccisano, Rina Fuda. Little Rina Meets Baby Brother. Prouix, Denis, illus. (p. 1035)
—Meatball 1 & Meatball 2. (p. 1118)
Lochhead, Joyce N. Adventures of Mr Figaro Tailhead. (p. 20)
Lochmandy, Sandy. Kids & Critters on an Adventure. (p. 952)
Lochrie, Elizabeth, illus. see Linderman, Frank B., et al.
Lochstoer, Christian, jt. auth. see Ylvis.
Lochte, Hilary. W. E. B. du Bois. (p. 1851)
Lock, Brian. Chicken Lips & Rocket Ships (p. 300)
—There's a Hippo in My Bathtub. (p. 1731)
Lock, David. Animals at Home, Level 1. (p. 82)
Lock, Deborah. Big Trucks. (p. 184)
—Mega Machines. (p. 1124)
—Pirate Attack! (p. 1362)
—Submarines & Submersibles, Level 1. (p. 1671)
—Train Travel. (p. 1777)
Lock, Deborah, jt. auth. see Dorling Kindersley Publishing Staff.
Lock, Deborah, jt. auth. see Hayden, Kate.
Lock, Deborah & Dorling Kindersley Publishing Staff. 10 Minutes a Day: Math, Grade 1. (p. 1993)
—Big Trucks. (p. 184)
—Math, Grade 3. (p. 1106)
—Train Travel, Level 1. (p. 1777)
Lock, Deborah & Hayden, Kate. Astronaut Living in Space, Level 2. (p. 109)
Lock, Deborah, et al. Homes Around the World. (p. 793)
Lock, Joan. Famous Trials. (p. 570)
Lock, Kath. Short Pants: Band 14/Ruby. Grimwood, Tracie, illus. (p. 1569)
Lock, Peter. Space Quest. (p. 1619)
Lock, Peter, jt. auth. see Patenaude, Jeremy.
Lockaby, Angie. Tad the Turtle It's Okay to Be Different. (p. 1695)
Lockard, Donna Lee. Sasha the Tortoise's Summer Vacation. (p. 1515)
Lockard, Lynn. Gone Batty!!! (p. 697)
Locke, Barbara K., illus. see Bouton, Warren Hussey.
Locke, Barbara Kauffmann, illus. see Bouton, Warren Hussey.
Locke, Betty. Campfire Tales: Spooky Tales for Halloween. (p. 257)
—Luge Mountain: A Happy Story about Christmas. (p. 1064)
—Pied Piper of Ellington County: A Modern Pied Piper Story. (p. 1356)
Locke, Elsie. Canoe in the Mist. (p. 261)
Locke, Gary, illus. see Romano, Ray.
Locke, Gary, illus. see Sayre, April Pulley.
Locke, Ian. Cracking Christmas. Rowe, Alan, illus. (p. 375)
Locke, Juliane. England's Jane: the Story of Jane Austen. (p. 529)
Locke, Margo, illus. see Doolittle, Sara.
Locke, Pamela K. Centaur's Door. (p. 287)
Locke, Scott Martin. Philosophy of the Worker & Adventure in Learning. (p. 1351)
Locke, Sue. Back-To-School Crafts. (p. 130)
—Back-to-School Crafts. (p. 130)
Locke, Terry. Spencer Hurley & the Aliens: Book One: the Abduction Hucks, Robin, ed. (p. 1625)
—Spencer Hurley & the Aliens: Book One: the Abduction. Hucks, Robin, ed. (p. 1625)
Locker, Thomas. Cloud Dance. (p. 334)
—John Muir: America's Naturalist. (p. 922)
—Walking with Henry: The Life & Works of Henry David Thoreau. (p. 1854)
Locker, Thomas, illus. see Comora, Madeleine.
Locker, Thomas, illus. see Foehner, Ashley & Irving, Washington.
Locker, Thomas, jt. auth. see Baron, Robert C.
Locker, Thomas, jt. auth. see Bruchac, Joseph.
Locker, Thomas & Christiansen, Candace. Water Dance. (p. 1862)
Locker, Thomas & Foehner, Ashley P. Rip Van Winkle. Locker, Thomas, illus. (p. 1473)
Lockerd, Jodi. Nocturnal Animals: Represent & Solve Problems Involving Multiplication. (p. 1262)
Lockett, Eve. Tales of Grace: 50 Five-Minute Stories for All-Age Talks, Sermons & Assemblies. Doggett, Sue, ed. (p. 1702)
Lockhart, Barbara. Mosey's Field Crow. Heather, illus. (p. 1176)
Lockhart, Barbara M. Circle the Moon. Grunden, Kimberly, illus. (p. 321)
Lockhart, Charlotte F. Discover Intensive Phonics for Yourself (p. 447)
—Discover Intensive Phonics for Yourself: Student Involvement Material. (p. 447)
—Discover Intensive Phonics for Yourself Adult Manual (p. 447)
Lockhart, David, illus. see Coolidge, Olivia E.
Lockhart, E. Boy Book: A Study of Habits & Behaviors, Plus Techniques for Taming Them. (p. 217)
—Boyfriend List: 15 Guys, 11 Shrink Appointments, 4 Ceramic Frogs & Me, Ruby Oliver. (p. 220)
—Disreputable History of Frankie Landau-Banks. (p. 453)
—Dramarama. (p. 480)
—Fly on the Wall: How One Girl Saw Everything. (p. 609)
—Real Live Boyfriends: Yes. Boyfriends, Plural. If My Life Weren't Complicated, I Wouldn't Be Ruby Oliver. (p. 1448)
—Treasure Map of Boys: Noel, Jackson, Finn, Hutch, Gideon - And Me, Ruby Oliver. (p. 1782)
—We Were Liars. (p. 1868)
Lockhart, E., et al. How to Be Bad. (p. 815)
Lockhart, Howard M. Consequences. (p. 358)
Lockhart, Kendra. Favorite Hat. (p. 578)
—Marvelous Misadventures of Magnificent Madelaine. (p. 1099)
Lockhart, Laurie. Twas Christmas Day Morning. (p. 1799)
Lockhart, Linda J. Little Angel Dressed in Red. (p. 1023)
Lockheart, Susanna. If You Love a Christmas Tale. (p. 854)
Lockie, Mark. Biometric Technology (p. 190)
Lockley, Belinda. Sometimes I Think of the Fish in the Sea. (p. 1610)
Lockman, Darcy. Softball for Fun! Lockman, Darcy, illus. (p. 1606)
Lockman, Vic. Catechism for Young Children Coloring Book. Lockman, Vic, illus. (p. 279)
Locks, Gil. Coming Back to Earth: The Central Park Guru Becomes an Old City Jew. (p. 348)
Lockspeiser, Nancy Flanders. Flexible You: 21 Stretches a Day for a 9-Lives Body: a Cat's Quick Guide to Stretching & Self-Massage. Lockspeiser, Nancy Flanders, illus. (p. 603)
Lockwood, Barbara. Bible Crafts on a Shoestring Budget. (p. 175)
Lockwood, Brad. Bill Gates: Profile of a Digital Entrepreneur. (p. 186)
—Domestic Spying & Wiretapping. (p. 465)
—Ketamine: Dangerous Hallucinogen. (p. 949)
—Oxycontin: From Pain Relief to Addiction. (p. 1315)
Lockwood, C. C., photos by see Baker, David G. & Stewart, Margaret Taylor.
Lockwood, Cara. Moby Clique. (p. 1157)
—Scarlet Letterman. (p. 1520)
—Wuthering High: At Boarding School, No One Can Hear Your Scream. (p. 1966)
Lockwood, Cate. Science Lab Tools. (p. 1526)
Lockwood, Julie L., jt. auth. see Goldstein, Natalie.
Lockwood, Mark W. Learn About... Texas Birds. Ivy, Elena T., illus. (p. 982)
Lockwood, Penny. Boo's Bad Day. Johnson, Deborah C., illus. (p. 213)
Lockwood, Sophie. Ants. (p. 90)
—Bees. (p. 157)
—Beetles. (p. 158)
—Butterflies. (p. 247)
—Dragonflies. (p. 478)
—Experiment with Heat. (p. 549)
—Experiment with Rocks. (p. 549)
—Flies. (p. 604)
—Grasshoppers. (p. 711)
—Moths. (p. 1179)
—Super Cool Science Experiments: Heat. (p. 1679)
—Super Cool Science Experiments: Rocks. (p. 1679)
—Super Cool Science Experiments: Minerals. (p. 1679)
—Super Cool Science Experiments: Electricity. (p. 1679)
Lockwood, Vicki. Magnificent Lizzie Brown (p. 1076)
—Magnificent Lizzie Brown & the Devil's Hound (p. 1076)
—Magnificent Lizzie Brown & the Fairy Child. Hans, Stephanie, illus. (p. 1076)
—Magnificent Lizzie Brown & the Ghost Ship. Hans, Stephanie, illus. (p. 1076)
—Magnificent Lizzie Brown & the Mysterious Phantom (p. 1076)
—Magnificent Lizzie Brown & the Mysterious Phantom Hans, Stephanie, illus. (p. 1076)
Lockyer, John. Measuring & Sharks (p. 1117)
Lockyer, John & Holden, Pam. Making a Movie (p. 1080)
Lockyer, John & Irving, Dianne. Elapsed Time at the Olympics (p. 508)
Lockyer, Roger. Tudor & Stuart Britain: 1485-1714. (p. 1796)
Locricchio, Matthew. 2nd International Cookbook for Kids (p. 1991)
—Cookiing of Mexico. (p. 361)
—Cooking of Brazil. (p. 362)
—Cooking of Italy. (p. 362)
—Cooking of Thailand. (p. 362)
—International Cookbook for Kids (p. 880)
Locsinto, Lucas, illus. see Swanepoel, Sharon.
Locurto, Ian N. Christmas Penny. (p. 315)
Loday, Gyelsey, photos by see Hawley, Michael.
Lodding, Linda Ravin. Busy Life of Ernestine Buckmeister. Beaky, Suzanne, illus. (p. 246)
—Gift for Mama. Jay, Alison, illus. (p. 675)
LoDestro, Christine. Littlest Cloud. (p. 1039)
Lodge, Ali. Leopard & the Sky God. (p. 992)
Lodge, Ali, illus. see Baxter, Nicola.
Lodge, Ali, illus. see Billam, Rosemary.
Lodge, Ali, illus. see Golding, Elizabeth.
Lodge, Ali, illus. see Lodge, Yvette.
Lodge, Ali, jt. auth. see Lodge, Alison.
Lodge, Alison & Lodge, Ali. Clever Chameleon. Lodge, Alison, illus. (p. 331)
Lodge, Bernard. Custard Surprise. Bowers, Tim, illus. (p. 395)
Lodge, Bernard, illus. see Siegen-Smith, Nikki, ed.
Lodge, David, ed. see James, Henry.
Lodge, Henry Cabot. Boston. (p. 215)
—Democracy of the Constitution & Other Essays. (p. 425)
—Early Memories. (p. 494)
—Frontier Town & Other Essays. (p. 644)
—Senate of the United States. (p. 1550)
Lodge, Jo. 1, 2, 3, ¡Ya! Lodge, Jo, illus. (p. 1990)
—Ali Baba & the Forty Thieves. (p. 39)
—Bump! Little Owl. (p. 241)
—Casa del Senor Coc/ The House of Mr Coc. (p. 273)
—Colour & Stick, Mr Croc. (p. 346)
—Come & Play, Mr Croc. (p. 347)
—Cosy Cuddlers: Cow (p. 369)
—Cosy Cuddlers: Horse (p. 369)
—Cosy Cuddlers: Pig. (p. 369)
—Cosy Cuddlers: Sheep (p. 369)
—Farm. (p. 573)
—Flip Flap, Mr Croc: A Mix & Match Book. (p. 604)
—Happy Birthday, Mr Croc! (p. 745)
—Happy Snappy! A Mr. Croc Book about Feeling. (p. 746)
—Imita Al Senor Coc/ Imitate Mr Coc. (p. 861)
—Land Ahoy, Mr Croc. (p. 973)
—Little Roar's Five Butterflies. (p. 1035)
—Little Roar's Red Boots. (p. 1035)
—Little Roar's Round Balloon. (p. 1035)
—Little Roar's Starry Pyjamas. (p. 1036)
—Oops! Little Chick. (p. 1299)
—Pets. (p. 1348)
—Ready or Not Mr Croc? (p. 1447)
—Ready, Steady, Go, Mr Croc. (p. 1447)
—Sleepy or Not, Mr Croc? (p. 1590)
—Snappy Green. (p. 1597)
—Splat! Little Cow. (p. 1629)
—Square Window: A Mr. Croc Book about Shapes. (p. 1636)
—Stomp! Little Dinosaur. (p. 1652)
—Wiggle, Jump, Stomp, Mr. Croc. (p. 1927)
Lodge, Jo & Nosy Crow Staff. Icky Sticky Monster Pop-Up. Lodge, Jo, illus. (p. 851)
Lodge, Joan L. Barry Bowling Ball. (p. 140)
—Minky's Forest Adventures. (p. 1147)
Lodge, Katherine. Let's Find Mimi: At Home. (p. 996)
—Let's Find Mimi: On Holiday. (p. 996)
—Let's Find Mimi: Around the World. (p. 996)
Lodge, Katherine, illus. see Miranda, Anne.
Lodge, Maureen, jt. auth. see Jones, Beverley.
Lodge, Vivienne E., ed. see Reid, Siuna A.
Lodge, Vivienne E., ed. see Reid, Siuna Ann.
Lodge, Yvette. Noah's Ark: Baby's First Pop-up! Lodge, Ali, illus. (p. 1261)
—Rainbow Duck. Abel, Simone, illus. (p. 1435)
Lodico, Cheryl. Wacky World of Winnie & Willie. (p. 1852)
Lodico, Cheryl Madeleine. Ice Princess Trilogy. (p. 850)
Lodien, Jennie, des. Cat Tales. (p. 278)
—Doggie Diary: The story of our Dog. (p. 462)
—I Am Chosen: Hearts. (p. 832)
—I Am Chosen: Brights. (p. 832)
—Life on a Leash: My Dog's Story. (p. 1012)
LoDolce, Jodi. Johnny's Adventure at Sea. (p. 923)
Lodwick, Sarah, illus. see Spangenberg, Greg.
Loe, Deborah M., jt. auth. see Frederick, Daniel R.
Loe, Erlend. Naiv. Super: En norsk-engelsk Lesebok. Jensen, James P., ed. (p. 1228)
Loe, Vanessa. Marble Magic. (p. 1091)
Loeb, Jason & Green, Robert. Education. (p. 505)
Loeb, Jeph. Absolute Power. Merino, Jesus, illus. (p. 7)
—Batman - Hush (p. 144)
—Blue. Sale, Tim, illus. (p. 202)
—Power. (p. 1389)
—Supergirl. (p. 1683)
—Superman & Batman - Public Enemies (p. 1683)
—Witching Hour. (p. 1941)
—Yellow. Sale, Tim, illus. (p. 1969)
—Yellow, Blue & Gray. (p. 1970)
Loeb, Jeph, jt. auth. see Azzarello, Brian.
Loeb, Jeph, jt. auth. see Williams, Loeb Lee.
Loeb, Jeph & Sale, Tim. Long Halloween. (p. 1047)
—When in Rome. Research & Education Association Editors & Starkings, Richard, illus. (p. 1903)
Loeb, Lisa. Lisa Loeb's Silly Sing-Along: The Disappointing Pancake & Other Zany Songs. O'Rourke, Ryan, illus. (p. 1022)
Loeb, Lisa & O'Rourke, Ryan. Lisa Loeb's Songs for Movin' & Shakin': the Air Band Song & Other Toe-Tapping Tunes. (p. 1022)
Loebel, Bonnie, illus. see Perry, Shelly.
Loebel-Fried, Caren, illus. see Beamer, Winona Desha, et al.
Loebel-Fried, Caren Keala, illus. see Beamer, Winona Desha & Beamer-Trapp, Kaliko.
Loebel-Fried, Caren, retold by. Hawaiian Legends of Dreams. (p. 755)
Loeffelholz, Sarah. Can You Just Imagine. (p. 259)
Loeffelholz, Sarah, illus. see Robey, Stephanie.
Loeffler, Sherry. Guardian Angel. (p. 728)
Loeffler, Trade, illus. see Johnson, R. Kikuo.
Loeffler, Trade, illus. see Spiegelman, Nadja.
Loeffler, Trade, jt. auth. see Spiegelman, Nadja.
Loehle, Richard, illus. see Lowery, Lawrence F.
Loehr, Jenny, illus. see Carlson, Lavelle.
Loehr, Jenny, illus. see Lederer, Susan.
Loehr, Jenny, illus. see Lederer, Suzy.
Loehr, Mallory. Baby Faces. Newton, Vanessa Brantley, illus. (p. 126)
—Dragon Egg. Wittwer, Hala, illus. (p. 477)
—Unicorn Wings. Silin-Palmer, Pamela, illus. (p. 1818)
Loehr, Patrick. Mucumber McGee & the Half-Eaten Hot Dog. Loehr, Patrick, illus. (p. 1188)
Loendorf, Lawrence L. & Stone, Nancy Medaris. Two Hawk Dreams. (p. 1803)
Loening, Grover, jt. auth. see Sutton, Felix.
Loeper, John J. Galloping Gertrude: By Motorcar In 1908. Chironna, Ronald, illus. (p. 653)
Loesch, Joe. Joshua - Victory Through God: As Told by God's Animals. Cox, Brian T., illus. (p. 927)
—Lions, Lions Everywhere: The Story of Daniel as told by God's Animals. Hutchinson, Cheryl, ed. (p. 1021)
—Tuskegee Airmen: Raiders of the Skies with Buffalo Biff & Farley's Raiders. Hutchinson, Cheryl, ed. (p. 1799)
Loesch, Uwe. Anticipation: The End Is Where We Start From. Nadin, Mihai, ed. (p. 89)
Loeschnig, L. V. Experimentos Sencillos de Geologia y Biologia. (p. 549)
—Experimentos Sencillos de Quimica. (p. 549)
Loesser, Frank. I Love You! A Bushel & a Peck. Wells, Rosemary, illus. (p. 843)
—I Love You! A Bushel & A Peck. Wells, Rosemary, illus. (p. 843)
Loever, Charmaine. David's Big Break. Bohman, Natasha, illus. (p. 411)
Loew, Patty. Native People of Wisconsin, Revised Edition. (p. 1235)
Loew, Patty, et al. Native People of Wisconsin. (p. 1235)
Loewen, Ann E. Fast for My Feet. (p. 576)
Loewen, Nancy. Action! Writing Your Own Play Beacon, Dawn, illus. (p. 10)
—Airplanes. (p. 32)
—Amazing Science - Planets Yesh, Jeff, illus. (p. 55)
—Baby Wants Mama Melmon, Deborah, illus. (p. 128)
—Backyard Bugs Reibeling, Brandon, illus. (p. 131)
—Believe Me, Goldilocks Rocks! The Story of the Three Bears As Told by Baby Bear. Avakyan, Tatevik, illus. (p. 161)
—Believe Me, Goldilocks Rocks! The Story of the Three Bears as Told by Baby Bear. Avakyan, Tatevik, illus. (p. 162)
—BIG Problem (and the Squirrel Who Eventually Solved It) Understanding Adjectives & Adverbs. (p. 183)
—Brightest in the Sky: The Planet Venus Yesh, Jeff, illus. (p. 228)
—Busy Buzzers: Bees in Your Backyard. Reibeling, Brandon, illus. (p. 246)
—Chirp, Chirp! Crickets in Your Backyard. Peterson, Rick, illus. (p. 308)
—Cyclops Tells All: The Way EYE See It Pentney, Ryan, illus. (p. 397)
—Cyclops Tells All: The Way Eye See It. Pentney, Ryan, illus. (p. 397)
—Dalmatians. (p. 401)
—Duckster Ducklings Go to Mars: Understanding Capitalization. (p. 488)
—Dwarf Planets: Pluto, Charon, Ceres, & Eris Yesh, Jeff, illus. (p. 491)
—Farthest from the Sun: The Planet Neptune Yesh, Jeff, illus. (p. 575)
—Frankly, I Never Wanted to Kiss Anybody! The Story of the Frog Prince As Told by the Frog. Alonso, Denis, illus. (p. 631)
—Frankly, I Never Wanted to Kiss Anybody! The Story of the Frog Prince, As Told by the Frog. Alonso, Denis, illus. (p. 631)
—Frankly, I Never Wanted to Kiss Anybody! The Story of the Frog Prince As Told by the Frog. Alonso, Denis & Tayal, Amit, illus. (p. 631)
—Frog, Frog? Frog! Understanding Sentence Types Rainey, Merrill, illus. (p. 640)
—Garden Wigglers: Earthworms in Your Backyard. Peterson, Rick, illus. (p. 656)
—German Shepherds. (p. 666)
—Girl Talk: Questions & Answers about Daily Dramas, Disasters, & Delights. Mora, Julissa, illus. (p. 679)
—Good-Bye, Jeepers: What to Expect When Your Pet Dies Lyles, Christopher, illus. (p. 697)
—Gordon Grizwald's Grumpy Goose Greathouse, Justin, illus. (p. 702)
—Helen of Troy Tells All: Blame the Boys Gilpin, Stephen, illus. (p. 763)
—Hungry Hoppers: Grasshoppers in Your Backyard. Reibeling, Brandon, illus. (p. 828)
—If You Were a Conjunction Gray, Sara, illus. (p. 854)
—If You Were a Homonym or a Homophone Gray, Sara, illus. (p. 855)
—If You Were a Preposition. Gray, Sara, illus. (p. 855)
—If You Were a Pronoun Gray, Sara, illus. (p. 855)
—If You Were an Antonym Gray, Sara, illus. (p. 855)
—If You Were an Interjection. Gray, Sara, illus. (p. 855)
—In the Money: A Book about Banking Fitzpatrick, Brad, illus. (p. 866)
—It's All about You: Writing Your Own Journal Lyles, Christopher & Ouren, Todd, illus. (p. 896)
—Just the Facts: Writing Your Own Research Report Beacon, Dawn, illus. (p. 940)
—Just the Facts: Writing Your Own Research Report Beacon, Dawn & Lyles, Christopher, illus. (p. 940)
—Just the Facts [Scholastic]: Writing Your Own Research Report. Beacon, Dawn, illus. (p. 940)
—Largest Planet: Jupiter Yesh, Jeff, illus. (p. 975)
—Last Day of Kindergarten Yoshikawa, Sachiko, illus. (p. 977)
—Lemons & Lemonade: A Book about Supply & Demand. Fitzpatrick, Brad & Jensen, Brian, illus. (p. 991)
—Let's Trade: A Book about Bartering. Jensen, Brian, illus. (p. 1001)
—Living Lights: Fireflies in Your Backyard. Reibeling, Brandon, illus. (p. 1041)
—Make Me Giggle: Writing Your Own Silly Story Doerrfeld, Cori, illus. (p. 1079)
—Make Me Giggle: Writing Your Own Silly Story Doerrfeld, Cori & Lyles, Christopher, illus. (p. 1079)
—Nearest to the Sun: The Planet Mercury Yesh, Jeff, illus. (p. 1239)
—Night Fliers: Moths in Your Backyard. Reibeling, Brandon, illus. (p. 1253)
—No Kidding, Mermaids Are a Joke! The Story of the Little Mermaid As Told by the Prince. Tayal, Amit, illus. (p. 1258)
—No Kidding, Mermaids Are a Joke! The Story of the Little Mermaid, As Told by the Prince. Tayal, Amit & Alsonso, Denis, illus. (p. 1258)
—No Lie, I Acted Like a Beast: The Story of Beauty & the Beast as Told by the Beast. Bernardini, Cristian, illus. (p. 1258)
—No Lie, I Acted Like a Beast! The Story of Beauty & the Beast As Told by the Beast Bernardini, Cristian, illus. (p. 1258)
—Once upon a Time: Writing Your Own Fairy Tale Lyles, Christopher, illus. (p. 1293)
—Other Side of the Story. Bernardini, Cristian & Guerlais, Gérald, illus. (p. 1306)
—Other Side of the Story. Guerlais, Gérald & Bernardini, Cristian, illus. (p. 1306)
—Our Home Planet: Earth Yesh, Jeff, illus. (p. 1309)
—Pandora Tells All: Not the Curious Kind Pentney, Ryan, illus. (p. 1321)
—Ringed Giant: The Planet Saturn Yesh, Jeff, illus. (p. 1473)

L

—Save, Spend, or Donate? A Book about Managing Money. Fitzpatrick, Brad & Jensen, Brian, illus. (p. 1516)
—Saying Good-Bye to Uncle Joe: What to Expect When Someone You Love Dies Lyles, Christopher, illus. (p. 1519)
—Scarlett the Cat to the Rescue: Fire Hero Sorra, Kristin, illus. (p. 1520)
—Seeing Red: The Planet Mars Yesh, Jeff, illus. (p. 1548)
—Seriously, Snow White Was SO Forgetful! The Story of Snow White As Told by the Dwarves Guerlais, Gérald, illus. (p. 1552)
—Seriously, Snow White Was So Forgetful! The Story of Snow White as Told by the Dwarves. Guerlais, Gérald, illus. (p. 1552)
—Share a Scare: Writing Your Own Scary Story Lyles, Christopher, illus. (p. 1561)
—She Sells Seashells & Other Tricky Tongue Twisters Wu, Donald, illus. (p. 1564)
—Show Me a Story: Writing Your Own Picture Book Lyles, Christopher, illus. (p. 1570)
—Sideways Planet: Uranus Yesh, Jeff, illus. (p. 1573)
—Sincerely Yours: Writing Your Own Letter Lyles, Christopher, illus. (p. 1578)
—Stubborn as a Mule & Other Silly Similes. Watkins, Adam, illus. (p. 1668)
—Talking Turkey & Other Clichés We Say Watkins, Adam, illus. (p. 1703)
—Taxes, Taxes! Where the Money Goes. Fitzpatrick, Brad, illus. (p. 1707)
—Ups & Downs: A Book about the Stock Market. Fitzpatrick, Brad, illus. (p. 1825)
—Walt Whitman. Day, Rob, illus. (p. 1856)
—Ways to Say It (p. 1865)
—Words, Wit, & Wonder: Writing Your Own Poem Lyles, Christopher, illus. (p. 1952)
—Writer's Toolbox Lyles, Christopher, illus. (p. 1964)
—Writer's Toolbox: Learn How to Write Letters, Fairy Tales, Scary Stories, Journals, Poems, & Reports Lyles, Christopher et al, illus. (p. 1964)
—Writing Outstanding Opinion Pieces. (p. 1965)
—Writing Powerful Persuasive Pieces. (p. 1965)
—You're Toast & Other Metaphors We Adore Wu, Donald, illus. (p. 1982)
Loewen, Nancy, jt. auth. see Dahl, Michael.
Loewen, Nancy, jt. auth. see Gunderson, Jessica.
Loewen, Nancy, jt. auth. see Meister, Cari.
Loewen, Nancy, jt. auth. see Shaskan, Trisha Speed.
Loewen, Nancy, jt. auth. see Whiting, Jim.
Loewen, Nancy & Braun, Eric. Trust Me, Jack's Beanstalk Stinks! The Story of Jack & the Beanstalk as Told by the Giant. Guerlais, Gérald & Bernardini, Cristian, illus. (p. 1793)
Loewen, Nancy & Dahl, Michael. If You Were an Antonym Gray, Sara, illus. (p. 855)
Loewen, Nancy & Gunderson, Jessica. Other Side of the Story. Bernardini, Cristian & Guerlais, Gérald, illus. (p. 1306)
Loewen, Nancy & Skelley, Paula. Besties, Sleepovers, & Drama Queens: Questions & Answers about Friends. Mora, Julissa, illus. (p. 171)
—Clothing of the World. (p. 334)
—Food of the World. (p. 613)
—Girl Talk. Mora, Julissa, illus. (p. 679)
—Go Go Global. (p. 686)
—Homes of the World. (p. 793)
—Lunch Lines, Tryouts, & Making the Grade: Questions & Answers about School. Mora, Julissa, illus. (p. 1065)
—People of the World. (p. 1339)
—Siblings, Curfews, & How to Deal: Questions & Answers about Family Life. Mora, Julissa, illus. (p. 1572)
—Tangles, Growth Spurts, & Being You: Questions & Answers about Growing Up. Mora, Julissa, illus. (p. 1705)
Loewen, Nancy & Speed Shaskan, Trisha. Other Side of the Story. Jatkowska, Ag et al, illus. (p. 1306)
Loewen, Nancy, et al. Language on the Loose. (p. 975)
—Other Side of the Myth Gilpin, Stephen & Pentney, Ryan, illus. (p. 1306)
—Other Side of the Story. Avakyan, Tatevik et al, illus. (p. 1306)
—Other Side of the Story. Guerlais, Gérald & Bernardini, Cristian, illus. (p. 1306)
Loewer, Jean, illus. see Loewer, Peter.
Loewer, Peter. Moonflower Loewer, Jean, illus. (p. 1172)
Loewer, Peter, jt. auth. see Jenkins, Jean.
LoFaro, Jerry, illus. see Goldenburg, Dorothea & Killian, Bette.
LoFaro, Jerry, illus. see Publications International Ltd. Staff, ed.
Lofficier, Jean-Marc, jt. auth. see Lofficier, Randy.
Lofficier, Randy. If Your Possum Go Daylight. OKeefe, Raven, illus. (p. 855)
Lofficier, Randy & Lofficier, Jean-Marc. Robonocchio. Pijuán Aragón, Miren, tr. (p. 1480)
—Robonocchio. Martiniere, Stephan, illus. (p. 1480)
Loffredo, Edward. Adventures of the First Buffarillo. (p. 23)
Lofland-Brown, Sandra. Cancer Is Tough, Be Tougher: With Your Attitude, Motivation, & Faith. (p. 260)
Loftin, Nancy. Sloppy Al. (p. 1591)
Loftin, Nikki. Nightingale's Nest. (p. 1255)
—Wish Girl. (p. 1940)
Lofting, Hugh. Animal Talk. Kanzler, John, illus. (p. 80)
—Doctor Dolittle's Magical Cure. Kanzler, John, illus. (p. 459)
—Historia del Doctor Dolittle. (p. 782)
—Porridge Poetry Huber, Joyce, illus. (p. 1386)
—Story of Doctor Dolittle: Animal Talk. Kanzler, John, illus. (p. 1658)
—Story of Doctor Dolittle: The Circus Crocodile. Kanzler, John, illus. (p. 1658)
—Story of Doctor Dolittle. (p. 1658)
—Story of Doctor Dolittle, Original Version. Lofting, Hugh, illus. (p. 1658)
—Voyages of Doctor Dolittle. (p. 1851)
—Voyages of Doctor Dolittle. Corvino, Lucy, illus. (p. 1851)
—Voyages of Doctor Dolittle. McKowen, Scott, illus. (p. 1851)
Lofting, Hugh, jt. auth. see Chwast, Seymour.
Loftis, Chris & Lowenthal, Gary T. I Want It Now: Helping Children Deal with Frustration & Disappointment. Moore, Darryl, illus. (p. 847)
Loftis, Cory, illus. see Bach, Shelby.
Loftis, John, ed. see Sheridan, Richard Brinsley.
Lofton, Maseyree. It Just Gets Better with Time. (p. 894)
Loftus, David, photos by see Oliver, Jamie.
Loftus, Jennifer. Buying & Selling at the Yard Sale. (p. 248)
Loftus, Tracy. Lucky Pup & Miss Millie Go Home. (p. 1063)
Logan, Ashley. Laugh Oh My Soul. (p. 980)
Logan, Beth J. Cats at the Beach Stickers. (p. 281)
Logan, Bob. Rocket Town. (p. 1483)
Logan, Christopher. Daphne. (p. 406)
Logan, Debra Kay. Language Arts: Biographies Across the Curriculum, Grades 4-6. (p. 974)
Logan, Denise. Dynamic Art Projects for Children. (p. 491)
Logan, Desiree, illus. see Parker, Lisa L. Gray.
Logan, Dottie Colegrove. Picnic on the Beach: Nana & Me Series, Book Three. (p. 1355)
Logan, Erika. Tick Tribe. (p. 1747)
Logan, J. Gavin. Plum Bunny. (p. 1374)
Logan, John. Unloved Guy's Guide: How to Deal. (p. 1821)
Logan, John & Kavanaugh, Dorothy. Guys' Guide to Love. (p. 733)
Logan, June. Billy & His Underwater Adventures. (p. 187)
Logan, Laura. Jesus Loves Me. (p. 915)
Logan, Laura, illus. see Bastianich, Lidia Matticchio.
Logan, Laura, illus. see Bodach, Vijaya.
Logan, Laura, illus. see Feigh, Alison.
Logan, Laura, illus. see Hodgman, Ann.
Logan, Laura, illus. see Plourde, Lynn.
Logan, Laura, illus. see Spinelli, Eileen.
Logan, Michael. Nation-Building. (p. 1231)
Logan, Stephanie, jt. auth. see Noah, Ian.
Logan, Wanda. Caesar, a Story about a Dog. (p. 250)
—Traces of Love. (p. 1775)
Loggia, Wendy. Aurora: The Perfect Party. Studio IBOIX, illus. (p. 116)
Loggia, Wendy & Disney Book Group Staff. Aurora: The Perfect Party. Disney Storybook Art Team, illus. (p. 116)
Loggia, Wendy & Roberts, Christa. Employee Handbook. (p. 521)
Loggins, Kenny. Moose N' Me. Nash, Joshua, illus. (p. 1173)
Loggins, Thelma Puckett. Little Moo Moo's Afraid. (p. 1032)
Loggins, Trace. Farm Life, City Life. (p. 574)
Logie, Daniel, jt. auth. see Nelson, Linda.
Logie, Mark. Storm Troopers Tz9. (p. 1656)
Logiudice, Carolyn. US History Reading Comrehension Book. (p. 1826)
LoGiudice, Carolyn, jt. auth. see LaQuay, Kate.
LoGiudice, Carolyn & LaQuay, Kate. Spotlight on Vocabulary Antonyms Level 2 (p. 1634)
Logiudice, Carolyn & LaQuay, Kate. Spotlight on Vocabulary Associations Level 2 (p. 1634)
LoGiudice, Carolyn & LaQuay, Kate. Spotlight on Vocabulary Multiple-Meaning Words Level 2 (p. 1634)
—Spotlight on Vocabulary Roots, Prefixes & Suffixes Level 2 (p. 1634)
—Spotlight on Vocabulary Word Origins Level 2 (p. 1634)
LoGiudice, Carolyn & McConnell, Nancy. Room 28 a Social Language Program. (p. 1488)
Logsted, Greg. Alibi Junior High. (p. 39)
—Something Happened. (p. 1610)
Logue, C. Robert & Logue, Michael. From the Top of the Mountain. (p. 644)
Logue, Damien. Favorite Foods: Classify & Count Objects in Each Category. (p. 578)
Logue, Mary. Sleep Like a Tiger. Zagarenski, Pamela, illus. (p. 1588)
Logue, Mary, jt. auth. see Hautman, Pete.
Logue, Michael, jt. auth. see Logue, C. Robert.
Logue, Stephanie. Mango's Revenge. Murphy, Chris, illus. (p. 1087)
Loh, Martin, illus. see Lyons, Kay.
Loh, Martin, jt. auth. see Lyons, Kay.
Loh, Virginia Shin-Mui, jt. auth. see James, Helen Foster.
Lohan, Tara & Clarke, Tony, eds. Water Consciousness: How We All Have to Change to Protect Our Most Critical Resource. (p. 1862)
Lohans, Alison. Laws of Emotion. (p. 981)
—Picturing Alyssa. (p. 1356)
—Waiting for the Sun Mets, Marilyn & Ledwon, Peter, illus. (p. 1853)
Loh-Hagan, Virginia. Acupuncturist. (p. 10)
—Art Show. (p. 103)
—Band. (p. 136)
—Ethical Hacker. (p. 539)
—Extreme BASE Jumping. (p. 556)
—Extreme BMX Freestyle. (p. 556)
—Extreme Kite Surfing. (p. 556)
—Extreme Rock Climbing. (p. 556)
—Extreme Skateboarding. (p. 556)
—Extreme Sky Diving. (p. 557)
—Extreme Snow Skiing. (p. 557)
—Extreme Snowboarding. (p. 557)
—Ghost Hunter: Odd Jobs. (p. 670)
—Mortician. (p. 1176)
—Odor Tester. (p. 1278)
—Parade Float Designer: Odd Jobs. (p. 1323)
—Sound Effects Artist. (p. 1615)
Lohlein, Henning. All Better! Bernd, Penners, illus. (p. 44)
Löhlein, Henning, illus. see Löhlein, Susanne.
Löhlein, Susanne. Hamster Monster. Löhlein, Henning, illus. (p. 740)
Lohman, Patricia. Luke's Noun Book. (p. 1064)
Lohmann, Raychelle Cassada. Anger Workbook for Teens: Activities to Help You Deal with Anger & Frustration. (p. 75)
Lohmann, Raychelle Cassada & Taylor, Julia V. Bullying Workbook for Teens: Activities to Help You Deal with Social Aggression & Cyberbullying. (p. 241)
Lohmann, Renate. Lucky Boots. (p. 1062)
Lohmann, Renate, illus. see Andersen, Hans Christian.
Lohmann, Renate, illus. see Hirsch, Jennifer.
Lohmann, Renate, illus. see Lang, Andrew.
Lohmann, Stephanie, illus. see McCurdy, Steve.
Lohnes, Marilyn. ABC Literacy Storytimes: Storytimes to Promote Literacy & Learning. Neu, Debra, illus. (p. 3)
—F Is for Fiddlehead: A New Brunswick Alphabet. Tooke, Susan, illus. (p. 559)
Lohof, Arle & Jensen, Joyce. My Story as Told by Sacagawea. Little, Gary, illus. (p. 1219)
Lohr, Ruth. First Coloradans: Native Americans in Colorado. (p. 593)
Lohr, Steve. Digital Revolutionaries: The Men & Women Who Brought Computing to Life. (p. 440)
Lohr, Tyrel, illus. see Waschak, Jay, et al.
Lohre, Mike. Six Degrees of Lebron James: Connecting Basketball Stars. (p. 1582)
Lohse, Joyce B. Emily Griffith: Opportunity's Teacher. (p. 519)
—General William Palmer: Railroad Pioneer. (p. 660)
—Justina Ford, Medical Pioneer. (p. 940)
—Unsinkable: The Molly Brown Story. (p. 1822)
Lohse, Otha Zackariah Edward, illus. see Burgan, Michael & Hoena, Blake A.
Lohse, Otha Zackariah Edward, illus. see Olson, Kay Melchisedech & Melchisedech Olson, Kay.
Lohse, Otha Zackariah Edward, illus. see Olson, Kay Melchisedech.
Lohstoeter, Lori, illus. see Kipling, Rudyard.
Lohstoeter, Lori, illus. see McBrier, Page.
Lohstoeter, Lori, illus. see Soto, Gary.
Loiodice, Lisa M. Through His Eyes. (p. 1745)
Lois, Veals. 10 Commandments. (p. 1993)
Loisillier, Maud & Morel, Diane. Planet of Jade. Smith, Owen & Collins Smith, Anne, trs. (p. 1367)
Loisillier, Maud, et al. Planet of Jade. (p. 1367)
Loiske, Jennifer. Black Diamond. (p. 195)
Loiske, Jennifer, et al. Tales of an Old Wizard. (p. 1702)
Lokaisingh, Jasmine. Tales of Mme. Bovarie Vache & Mr. P. Huggins: In Huggsie's Birthday. (p. 1702)
Loker, Aleck. Fearless Captain: The Adventures of John Smith. (p. 579)
—Murder of Joseph Henry Ching: A Legend Examined. (p. 1192)
Loker, Aleck, text. Matter of Space. (p. 1109)
Lokere, Jillian. Cells: An Anthology of Current Thought. (p. 286)
—Genetics: Unlocking the Secrets of Life. (p. 661)
Lokere, Jillian, ed. Cells: An Anthology of Current Thought. (p. 286)
Loki, illus. see Gormally, Eleanor.
Loki, jt. auth. see Chihak, Sheena.
Lokko, CNN. Adventures of Elizabeth Sam. (p. 17)
Lokus, Rex, illus. see Cooper, Sharon Katz.
Lokus, Rex, jt. auth. see Verne, Jules.
Lola, illus. see Bryant, Megan E. & O'Ryan, Ellie.
Lola, illus. see Krensky, Stephen.
Lolfa, Y., jt. auth. see Lewis, Caryl.
Lollar, Cathy, illus. see Quantrell, Angie.
Lolley, Kimberley Frederick. Granny Has a Mo-Ped. (p. 710)
Lolley, Sarah. Emilie & the Mighty Om. Kao, Sleepless, illus. (p. 518)
Lollino, Jessica. Lily & the Big Italian Wedding. Lollino, Jessica, ed. (p. 1018)
—Little Lily Mays & the Daddy Dilemma. Kendrick-TaZiyah, Brandi, illus. (p. 1030)
Lollino, Jessica, ed. see Byers, Shaunette.
Lollis, Sylvia & Hogan, Joyce W. Should We Have Pets? A Persuasive Text. (p. 1570)
Loman, Karen L., jt. auth. see Arens, Amanda B.
Lomando, Suzanne. My, Buddy Bear, Tales: Buddy Bear's First Storybook. (p. 1199)
Lomas, Graham. Smoky the Mischievous Kitten. (p. 1595)
Lomask, Milton. Charles Carroll & the American Revolution. Polseno, Jo, illus. (p. 292)
—Invention & Technology. (p. 883)
Lomax M.Ed., L. E. Saint Called Nicholas: The Christmas Legends Series, Vol. I. (p. 1503)
Lomba, Ana. Boucle d'or et les Trois Ours. Wenzel, Dominique, tr. (p. 215)
—Petit Chaperon Rouge. Wenzel, Dominique, tr. (p. 1348)
Lombana, J. P., jt. auth. see Paul, Ruth.
Lombard, Ernest. Remember the Seagulls: A Modern Fable. (p. 1459)
Lombard, Jenny. Drita, My Homegirl. (p. 485)
Lombardi, Elizabeth L. Jonathan's Journey. (p. 925)
Lombardi, Janet, jt. auth. see Eubanks, Toni.
Lombardi, Kristine. Barbie What Shall I Be. Mattel, illus. (p. 138)
—It's a Surprise Playhouse Storybook. Mattel Inc. Staff, illus. (p. 896)
Lombardi, Kristine, jt. auth. see Reader's Digest Editors.
Lombardi, Kristine, jt. auth. see Reader's Digest Staff.
Lombardi, Kristine A. Lovey Bunny. (p. 1061)
Lombardi, Kristine & Disney Storybook Artists Staff. Disney Cars Carry along Treasury. (p. 451)
—Disney Princess Special Celebrations. (p. 453)
Lombardi, Mary. Grandpa's Chair. (p. 709)
Lombardi, Tom. My Summer on Earth. (p. 1219)
Lombardo, Allison. Navigating Your Freshman Year. (p. 1238)
Lombardo, Cindy, ed. Capturing Character: Orrville Ohio. (p. 265)
Lombardo, Constance. Stunt Cat to the Stars. Lombardo, Constance, illus. (p. 1670)
Lombardo, G. Where the Trees Grow Gumballs. (p. 1909)
Lombardo, Irina, illus. see Amadeo, Diana M.
Lombardo, Irina, illus. see Kroll, Virginia.
Lombardo, Mary A. Mastering Math Through Magic, Grades 2-3 (p. 1103)
—Poetry & Pop-Ups: An Art-Enhanced Approach to Writing Poetry (p. 1376)
Lombardo, Michelle. Balancing the Energy Equation: One Step at a Time! Herron, Mark, illus. (p. 133)
—OrganWise Guys Pepto's Place Activity Book. Herron, Mark, illus. (p. 1303)
—Pepto's Place: Where Every Portion Size Is OrganWise! Herron, Mark, illus. (p. 1340)
Lomberg, Michelle. Avoiding Gridlock. Schwartzenberger, Tina, ed. (p. 120)
—Caring for Your Horse. (p. 269)
—Caring for Your Spider. (p. 269)
—Grand Canyon: Wonders of the World. (p. 707)
—Grand Canyon: The Largest Canyon in the United States. (p. 707)
—Grand Canyon. (p. 707)
—Horse. (p. 799)
—Iroquois. (p. 888)
—Mars. (p. 1096)
—Ojibwa. (p. 1282)
—Ojibwés: Les Autochtones du Canada. Karvonen, Tanjah, tr. from ENG. (p. 1282)
—Spider. (p. 1626)
Lomberg, Michelle, jt. auth. see Aspen-Baxter, Linda.
Lomberg, Michelle & Gillespie, Katie. Horse. (p. 799)
—Spider. (p. 1626)
Lome, Emilio Angel. Lottery of Riddles. Martinez, Enrique, illus. (p. 1057)
Lomenech Gill, Olivia, illus. see Morpurgo, Michael & Morpurgo, Clare.
Lommel, Cookie. Mary Church Terrell: Speaking Out for Civil Rights. (p. 1100)
—Russell Simmons. (p. 1498)
Lomofsky, Lynne, illus. see Schermbrucker, Reviva.
Lomurno, Inez Regina. Love at Christmas I, II, & III. (p. 1059)
Lon Rogers. Between Season. (p. 173)
Lonaytis, Olga, illus. see Grimm, Jacob & Grimm, Wilhelm K.
Lonborg, Rosemary. Helpin' Bugs. Houghton, Diane R., illus. (p. 766)
Lonczak, Heather Suzanne. Mookey the Monkey Gets over Being Teased. Ramsey, Marcy Dunn, illus. (p. 1171)
Lond, Lara. Dvorets: Prikliucheniya Zhikasana Tarresa. (p. 491)
Lond, Laura. My Sparkling Misfortune. Alekseyeva, Alla, illus. (p. 1219)
—Palace: The Adventures of Jecosan Tarres. (p. 1319)
Londa And Pop-Pop. On Christmas Day. Harrell, Symear, illus. (p. 1288)
Londner, Renee. Stones for Grandpa. Aviles, Martha, illus. (p. 1653)
London, Adam. Lucky the Rubber Ducky. Atherton, Jim, illus. (p. 1063)
London, Alex. Guardian. (p. 728)
—Proxy. (p. 1413)
London Burlington Fine Arts Staff. Catalogue of an Exhibition of Objects of Indigenous American Art. (p. 278)
London, C. Alexander. Blood in the Water. (p. 200)
—Divided We Fall. (p. 454)
—Honor Bound. (p. 795)
—Prisoners of War. (p. 1407)
—Semper Fido. (p. 1550)
—Strays. (p. 1666)
—We Are Not Eaten by Yaks. (p. 1865)
—We Dine with Cannibals. (p. 1867)
—We Give a Squid a Wedgie. Duddle, Jonny, illus. (p. 1867)
—Wild Ones. (p. 1930)
London, C. Alexander & Scholastic, Inc. Staff. Mission Hindenburg. (p. 1153)
London, Ellen. Bangladesh. (p. 136)
London, Gerri, jt. auth. see Diersch, Sandra.
London, H. B., jt. auth. see Wiseman, Neil B.
London, J. A. After Daybreak. (p. 28)
—Darkness Before Dawn. (p. 408)
London, Jack. Brown Wolf & Other Stories. (p. 232)
—Call of the Wild: A Bed Book First Edition Classic. (p. 254)
—Call of the Wild No. 15. Villagran, Ricardo, illus. (p. 254)
—Call of the Wild: Prestwick House Literary Touchstone Edition. (p. 254)
—Call of the Wild. (p. 254)
—Call of the Wild. Clift, Eva, tr. (p. 254)
—Call of the Wild. Green, John, illus. (p. 254)
—Call of the Wild. Moser, Barry, illus. (p. 254)
—Call of the Wild. Corvino, Lucy, illus. (p. 254)
—Call of the Wild. Terrazzini, Daniela Jaglenka, illus. (p. 254)
—Call of the Wild & White Fang. McKowen, Scott, illus. (p. 254)
—Call of the Wild - Spotlight Edition. Grudzina, Douglas, ed. (p. 254)
—Colmillo Blanco. (p. 341)
—Faith of Men. (p. 565)
—House of Pride & Other Tales of Hawaii. (p. 803)
—Jack London. (p. 903)
—Jack London/the Call of the Wild. Carillo, Fred, illus. (p. 903)
—Llamada de la Naturaleza. (p. 1043)
—Llamada de la Selva. (p. 1043)
—Michael Brother of Jerry. (p. 1134)
—Mutiny of the 'ElsinoreApos. (p. 1194)
—Quimera del Oro. (p. 1428)
—Rumbo Oeste y Otros Cuentos. (p. 1495)
—Sea Wolf (p. 1536)
—Timeless Classics Low Level: Call of the Wild (p. 1754)
—White Fang. (p. 1912)
—White Fang: With a Discussion of Resilience. Walker, Karen, illus. (p. 1913)
—White Fang. (p. 1913)
—White Fang. Andreasen, Dan, illus. (p. 1913)
—White Fang. Martin, Cynthia, illus. (p. 1913)
—White Fang. Guillope, Antoine, illus. (p. 1913)
—White Fang Study Guide. (p. 1913)
London, Jack, jt. auth. see Francis, Pauline.
London, Jack & Access Matrix Staff. Call of the Wild. (p. 254)
London, Jack & Alex, Nino. Call of the Wild. (p. 254)
London, Jack & Gascoigne, Martin. Call of the Wild. Gascoigne, Martin, illus. (p. 254)
London, Jack, et al. Jack London Pomplun, Tom, ed. (p. 903)
London, Jesse Lev. Epigramme. (p. 532)
London, Jonathan. Desolation Canyon. London, Sean, illus. (p. 430)
—Flamingo Sunset Rodanas, Kristina, illus. (p. 602)
—Froggy Builds a Tree House. (p. 640)
—Froggy Builds a Tree House. Remkiewicz, Frank, illus. (p. 640)
—Froggy Builds a Tree House. (p. 641)
—Froggy Eats Out. (p. 641)

—Froggy Eats Out. Remkiewicz, Frank, illus. (p. 641)
—Froggy Gets a Doggy. Remkiewicz, Frank, illus. (p. 641)
—Froggy Gets Dressed Remkiewicz, Frank, illus. (p. 641)
—Froggy Goes to Camp. Remkiewicz, Frank, illus. (p. 641)
—Froggy Goes to Hawaii. (p. 641)
—Froggy Goes to Hawaii. Remkiewicz, Frank, illus. (p. 641)
—Froggy Goes to School. Remkiewicz, Frank, illus. (p. 641)
—Froggy Goes to the Doctor. (p. 641)
—Froggy Goes to the Doctor. Remkiewicz, Frank, illus. (p. 641)
—Froggy Is the Best. Remkiewicz, Frank, illus. (p. 641)
—Froggy Plays in the Band. Remkiewicz, Frank, illus. (p. 641)
—Froggy Plays in the Band. Remkiewicz, Frank & Frank, Remkiewicz, illus. (p. 641)
—Froggy Rides a Bike. Remkiewicz, Frank, illus. (p. 641)
—Froggy's Baby Sister. Remkiewicz, Frank, illus. (p. 641)
—Froggy's Best Babysitter. Remkiewicz, Frank, illus. (p. 641)
—Froggy's Birthday Wish. Remkiewicz, Frank, illus. (p. 641)
—Froggy's Day with Dad. Remkiewicz, Frank, illus. (p. 641)
—Froggy's Halloween. Remkiewicz, Frank, illus. (p. 641)
—Froggy's Sleepover. Remkiewicz, Frank, illus. (p. 641)
—Froggy's Worst Playdate. Remkiewicz, Frank, illus. (p. 641)
—Giving Thanks. Manchess, Gregory, illus. (p. 681)
—Gone Again Ptarmigan. Van Zyle, Jon, illus. (p. 697)
—Here Comes Doctor Hippo: A Little Hippo Story. Eduar, Gilles, illus. (p. 770)
—Here Comes Firefighter Hippo. Eduar, Gilles, illus. (p. 770)
—Hippos Are Huge! Trueman, Matthew, illus. (p. 781)
—Honey Paw & Lightfoot. Van Zyle, Jon, illus. (p. 794)
—I'm a Truck Driver. Parkins, David, illus. (p. 858)
—Lion Who Had Asthma. Westcott, Nadine Bernard, illus. (p. 1020)
—Little Lost Tiger Spirin, Ilya, illus. (p. 1031)
—Little Penguin: The Emperor of Antarctica Olson, Julie, illus. (p. 1033)
—Little Puffin's First Flight. Zyle, Jon Van, illus. (p. 1034)
—Little Swan Rodanas, Kristina, illus. (p. 1037)
—My Big Rig Garofoli, Viviana, illus. (p. 1197)
—Ollie's First Year. Van Zyle, Jon, illus. (p. 1287)
—Plane Goes Ka-Zoom! Roche, Denis, illus. (p. 1367)
—Seasons of Little Wolf. Van Zyle, Jon, illus. (p. 1538)
London, Jonathan & Remkiewicz, Frank. Froggy Plays T-Ball. Remkiewicz, Frank, illus. (p. 641)
—Froggy Rides a Bike. Remkiewicz, Frank & Remkiewicz, F., illus. (p. 641)
London, Jude. Powering Our Planet. (p. 1391)
London, Kelli. Beware of Boys. (p. 173)
—Cali Boys. (p. 253)
—Reality Check. (p. 1449)
—Star Power. (p. 1641)
—Uptown Dreams. (p. 1825)
London, Kelli, jt. auth. see Simone, Ni-Ni.
London, Lewis. Wesley Owl. (p. 1876)
London, Matt. 8th Continent. (p. 1993)
—Born to Be Wild. (p. 214)
—Welcome to the Jungle. (p. 1874)
London, Matt & Cordill, Lloyd. My Left or Yours?: #1 Hold on to Your Planet! (p. 1211)
London, Olivia. Meet the Ponies of Ponyville. (p. 1123)
—My Little Pony: Welcome to the Everfree Forest! (p. 1213)
—My Little Pony: Meet the Ponies of Ponyville. (p. 1213)
—My Little Pony: Welcome to Equestria! (p. 1213)
—Welcome to Equestria! (p. 1873)
—Welcome to Rainbow Falls! (p. 1873)
—Welcome to the Crystal Empire! (p. 1874)
London, Olivia, jt. auth. see Reader's Digest Staff.
London, S. Keith & Osleeb, Rebecca. Defined Mind Vocabulary Accelerator: Music-Driven Vocabulary & Comprehension Tools for School / Test / SAT Prep (p. 424)
London, Sean, illus. see London, Jonathan.
London Town Press Staff, jt. auth. see Hunt, Joni Phelps.
London, Victoria. Emily Cobbs & the Naked School: A Gifted Girls Series. Bk. 1 (p. 518)
—Emily Cobbs Collection (p. 518)
—Emily Cobbs Collection: A Gifted Girls Series. Bk. 1 & Bk. 2 (p. 518)
—Emily Cobbs Collection 1: A Gifted Girls Series. Bk. 1 & Bk. 2 (p. 518)
—Jackie Green Collection 1: A Gifted Girls Series. (p. 903)
Londoño, Patricia Torres. Amelia Earhart. (p. 58)
Londt, Claire, et al. English Matters for Zambia Basic Education Grade 3 Pupil's Book. (p. 530)
—English Matters Grade 1. (p. 530)
Lonechild, Michael, illus. see Wiebe, Rudy.
Lonely Planet Publications Staff. Adventures in Busy Places: Packed Full of Activities & over 250 Stickers. (p. 15)
—Adventures in Cold Places. (p. 15)
—Adventures in Noisy Places: Packed Full of Activities & over 250 Stickers (p. 15)
—Adventures in Smelly Places: Packed Full of Activities & over 250 Stickers (p. 15)
—Adventures in Wild Places: Packed Full of Activities & over 750 Stcikers. (p. 16)
—Africa: Everything You Ever Wanted to Know (p. 26)
—Asia: Everything You Ever Wanted to Know (p. 106)
—Australia: Everything You Ever Wanted to Know (p. 116)
—Europe: Everything You Ever Wanted to Know (p. 540)
—How to Be a Dinosaur Hunter (p. 814)
—How to Be a World Explorer (p. 815)
—Not for Parents China: Everything You Ever Wanted to Know (p. 1267)
—Not for Parents Extreme Planet (p. 1267)
—Not for Parents Great Britain: Every Thing You Wanted to Know (p. 1267)
—South America: Everything You Ever Wanted to Know (p. 1616)
—U. S. A. Everything You Ever Wanted to Know (p. 1805)
—World Search - Amazing Jobs (p. 1958)
—World Search - Busy Places (p. 1958)
—World Search - Incredible Animals (p. 1958)
Lonely Planet Publications Staff, jt. auth. see Brake, Mark.
Lonely Planet Publications Staff, jt. auth. see Lamprell, Klay.
Lonely Planet Publications Staff & Lamprell, Klay. Londres - Grandes Secretos para Pequenos Viajeros (p. 1046)
—Mi Primera Lonely Planet Nueva York (p. 1133)
—Not for Parents London: Everything You Ever Wanted to Know (p. 1267)
—Not for Parents Rome: Everything You Ever Wanted to Know (p. 1267)
—Paris: Everything You Ever Wanted to Know (p. 1324)
—Roma - Grandes Secretos para Pequenos Viajeros (p. 1485)
Lonergan Iorio, John, illus. see Sera, Lucia.
Lonergan, Lei-Seu. Great Paper Toy Book. (p. 717)
Lonergan, Paula Hines. Titan of a Man: A Coach of the Famous '71 Titans Who Inspired Generations of Young People. (p. 1757)
Lonewolf, S. William. Thunder Fox's Long Hair: (a True Story) (p. 1746)
Long, Angela Pullam. Salvador the Spy in the Case of the Missing Cats. (p. 1506)
Long, Carlos, illus. see Kamins, Julie Firstenberg.
Long, Chad M. Lycan Journal. (p. 1066)
Long, Chad Michael. Lycan Journal. (p. 1066)
Long, Christopher E. Hero Worship. (p. 772)
Long, Christopher E. & Warner, Gertrude Chandler. Tree House Mystery Bloodworth, Mark, illus. (p. 1783)
Long, Claire Nicole. Dreaming of Dolphins. (p. 484)
Long, Cliff. Broadside Ben & the Big Brass Cannon. (p. 230)
Long, Corey, illus. see Robinson, Vickie J.
Long, Cynthia. Sage for the Ages. (p. 1502)
Long, Dani L., jt. auth. see Jones, Harriett E.
Long, Dave, illus. see Filipi, Carmen.
Long, Debbie. Short Stories with Imagination: The Imagination Series. (p. 1569)
Long, Denise. Survivor Kid: A Practical Guide to Wilderness Survival. (p. 1687)
Long, DeWayne Lee, illus. see Parker, Robert H.
Long, Dorian. What Are Polygons? Reason with Shapes & Their Attributes. (p. 1879)
Long, Dustin. Daytona 500. (p. 415)
—Greatest Comebacks in Sports. (p. 719)
—NASCAR Racing. (p. 1230)
Long, Earlene R., jt. auth. see Wissinger, Tamera Will.
Long, Ethan. Big Cat. (p. 180)
—Book That Zack Wrote. (p. 212)
—Chamelia. (p. 289)
—Chamelia & the New Kid in Class. (p. 289)
—Clara & Clem in Outer Space. (p. 326)
—Clara & Clem Take a Ride. (p. 326)
—Clara & Clem Take a Ride. Long, Ethan, illus. (p. 326)
—Clara & Clem Take a Ride (HC) Long, Ethan, illus. (p. 326)
—Clara & Clem under the Sea. Long, Ethan, illus. (p. 326)
—Croaky Pokey! Long, Ethan, illus. (p. 384)
—Draw with Scribbles & Ink: Draw & Paint Your Own Masterpieces! (p. 481)
—Fright Club. (p. 639)
—Good Night! (p. 699)
—Hi! (p. 775)
—In, over & on the Farm. Long, Ethan, illus. (p. 864)
—It's Pooltime! (p. 898)
—Me & My Big Mouse (p. 1115)
—Ms. Spell. (p. 1188)
—My Dad, My Hero. Long, Ethan, illus. (p. 1201)
—One Drowsy Dragon. (p. 1294)
—Pig Has a Plan. (p. 1357)
—Pig Has a Plan. Long, Ethan, illus. (p. 1357)
—Rick & Rack & the Great Outdoors. (p. 1470)
—Scribbles & Ink. (p. 1533)
—Scribbles & Ink Doodles for Two. (p. 1533)
—Scribbles & Ink, Out of the Box. Long, Ethan, illus. (p. 1533)
—Scribbles & Ink, the Contest. (p. 1533)
—Soup for One. (p. 1615)
—Up, Tall & High! Long, Ethan, illus. (p. 1824)
—Wing Wing Brothers: Carnival de Math. Long, Ethan, illus. (p. 1936)
—Wing Wing Brothers Carnival de Math. Long, Ethan, illus. (p. 1936)
—Wing Wing Brothers Geometry Palooza! Long, Ethan, illus. (p. 1936)
—Wing Wing Brothers Math Spectacular! (p. 1936)
Long, Ethan, illus. see Amato, Mary.
Long, Ethan, illus. see Carr, Jan.
Long, Ethan, illus. see Elliott, David.
Long, Ethan, illus. see Kutner, Merrily.
Long, Ethan, illus. see Lawlor, Laurie.
Long, Ethan, illus. see Maccarone, Grace.
Long, Ethan, illus. see Nesbitt, Kenn.
Long, Ethan, illus. see Paul, Ann Whitford.
Long, Ethan, illus. see Slater, Teddy.
Long, Ethan, illus. see Spurr, Elizabeth.
Long, Ethan, illus. see Stegman-Bourgeois, Karen M.
Long, Ethan, illus. see Urey, Gary.
Long, Ethan, illus. see Watson, Tom.
Long, Ethan, illus. see Ziefert, Harriet.
Long, Ethan, jt. auth. see Long, Heather.
Long, Ethan, tr. see Paul, Ann Whitford.
Long, Eula. Pirate's Doll: The Story of the China Poblana. (p. 1363)
Long, Greg & Edmundson, Chris. Yeti, Turn Out the Light! Kirwan, Wednesday, illus. (p. 1971)
Long, Hayley. Lottie Biggs Is Not Tragic. (p. 1057)
Long, Heather & Long, Ethan. Max & Milo Go to Sleep! Long, Ethan, illus. (p. 1110)
—Max & Milo the Mixed-Up Message. Long, Ethan, illus. (p. 1110)
Long, Ilana. Ziggy's Big Idea. Joni, Rasa, illus. (p. 1986)
Long, James D. & Williams, Robert L. Making It till Friday: Your Guide to Effective Classroom Management. (p. 1081)
Long, Jamey. Possum's Date Which Will Live in Infamy: Pearl Harbor. (p. 1387)
—Possum's Renaissance Man: Leonardo Da Vinci. (p. 1387)
Long, Jamey M. Possum's Band of Merry Men & the Tales of Robin Hood. (p. 1387)
—Possum's Bible Story: Noah's Ark. (p. 1387)
—Possum's Bible Story: The Gospel According to John. (p. 1387)
—Possum's Bible Story: Moses & the Exodus from Egypt. (p. 1387)
—Possum's Big Apple: NYC & the Events of September 11 2001. (p. 1387)
—Possum's by the Dawn's Early Light: The Star Spangled Banner. (p. 1387)
—Possum's Christmas Tale. (p. 1387)
—Possum's Day at School. (p. 1387)
—Possum's Expedition: Lewis & Clark & Sacagawea. (p. 1387)
—Possum's First in Flight: The Wright Brothers. (p. 1387)
—Possum's Good Apple John Chapman & the Legend of Johnny Appleseed. (p. 1387)
—Possum's Happy Easter. (p. 1387)
—Possum's I Have Not yet Begun to Fight: John Paul Jones & the Bonhomme Richard. (p. 1387)
—Possum's Lady Liberty: The Story of Liberty Enlightening the World. (p. 1387)
—Possum's Land down Under. (p. 1387)
—Possum's Man on the Moon: The Eagle Has Landed. (p. 1387)
—Possum's Prehistoric Adventure. (p. 1387)
—Possum's Pyramid & the Tomb of King Tut. (p. 1387)
—Possum's Remember the Alamo & the Legend of Davy Crockett. (p. 1387)
—Possum's War Between the States: The American Civil War. (p. 1387)
—Possum's Wild West & the Gunfight at the O. K. Corral. (p. 1387)
Long, Jan. Azule & the White Hummingbird: The Birth of the White Hummingbird. (p. 122)
Long, Janice, compiled by. In the Deep Woods Cookbook. (p. 865)
Long, John. Big Picture Book. Choo, Brian, illus. (p. 183)
—Big Picture Book of Environments. (p. 183)
—Big Picture Book of Human Civilisation: From Cave Paintings to Hadron Collider - A Guided Tour. (p. 183)
—Dinosaurs. (p. 443)
—Gogo Fish! The Story of the Western Australian State Fossil Emblem. Long, John & Ruse, Jill, illus. (p. 692)
—Journey to the Dawn of Time: Return to Devil's Roost. (p. 929)
Long, John & Ruse, Jill. Gogo Fish! The Story of the Western Australian State Fossil Emblem. Long, John, illus. (p. 692)
Long, John, ed. Dinosaurs. (p. 443)
Long, Julie Anne. Notorious Countess Confesses: Pennyroyal Green Series. (p. 1268)
—Ways to Be Wicked. (p. 1865)
Long, Julie Whidden. Portraits of Courage: Stories of Baptist Heroes. (p. 1387)
Long, Kathy. Christopher SAT Straight up in Bed. Cantor, Patricia, illus. (p. 317)
Long, Laurel. Twelve Days of Christmas. (p. 1800)
—Twelve Days of Christmas. Long, Laurel, illus. (p. 1800)
Long, Laurel, illus. see Ryan, Brittney.
Long Liang, Xiao, illus. see Chen, Wei Dong.
Long Liang, Xiao, illus. see Dong Chen, Wei.
Long, Lisa, ed. see Stansberry, Don & Cluster Springs Elementary School Staff.
Long, Loren. Drummer Boy. Long, Loren, illus. (p. 487)
—Let's Doodle, Otis! Long, Loren, illus. (p. 995)
—Let's Go, Otis! Long, Loren, illus. (p. 997)
—Otis. Long, Loren, illus. (p. 1307)
—Otis & the Puppy. Long, Loren, illus. (p. 1307)
—Otis & the Scarecrow. Long, Loren, illus. (p. 1307)
—Otis & the Tornado. (p. 1307)
—Otis & the Tornado. Long, Loren, illus. (p. 1307)
—Otis Christmas. Long, Loren, illus. (p. 1307)
—Otis Loves to Play. Long, Loren, illus. (p. 1307)
—Otis's Busy Day. Long, Loren, illus. (p. 1307)
Long, Loren, illus. see Berk, Ari.
Long, Loren, illus. see de Seve, Randall.
Long, Loren, illus. see de Sève, Randall, et al.
Long, Loren, illus. see de Sève, Randall.
Long, Loren, illus. see Johnson, Angela.
Long, Loren, illus. see Obama, Barack.
Long, Loren, illus. see Piper, Watty & Penguin / LeapFrog.
Long, Loren, illus. see Piper, Watty.
Long, Loren, illus. see Scieszka, Jon.
Long, Loren, illus. see Weller, Frances Ward.
Long, Loren, jt. auth. see Bildner, Phil.
Long, Loren, jt. auth. see Whitman, Walt.
Long, Loren & Bildner, Phil. Blastin' the Blues. Long, Loren, illus. (p. 198)
—Great Balls of Fire. Long, Loren, illus. (p. 713)
—Home of the Brave. Long, Loren, illus. (p. 792)
—Horsin' Around. Long, Loren, illus. (p. 800)
—Magic in the Outfield. Long, Loren, illus. (p. 1072)
—Water, Water Everywhere. Long, Loren, illus. (p. 1863)
Long, Lynette. Great Graphs & Sensational Statistics: Games & Activities That Make Math Easy & Fun. (p. 716)
—Groovy Geometry: Games & Activities That Make Math Easy & Fun. (p. 725)
—Math Smarts: Tips, Tricks, & Secrets for Making Math More Fun! McGuinness, Tracy, illus. (p. 1107)
—Painless Geometry. (p. 1318)
—Wacky Word Problems: Games & Activities That Make Math Easy & Fun. (p. 1852)
Long, Lynette, jt. auth. see Denecke, Edward J., Jr.
Long, Mark A. Bad Fads. Fee, Jim, illus. (p. 131)
Long, Martha, illus. see Ramirez, Jeannette.
Long, Mary Evelyn Curton. First Christmas Gift. (p. 593)
Long, Matthew & Long, Thomas. Any Bear Can Wear Glasses: The Spectacled Bear & other Curious Creatures. Long, Sylvia, illus. (p. 90)
Long, May, illus. see Partin, Charlotte Corry.
Long, Melinda. How I Became A Pirate. Shannon, David, illus. (p. 810)
—How I Became a Pirate. Shannon, David, illus. (p. 810)
—Pirates Activity Book. Shannon, David, illus. (p. 1363)
—Pirates Don't Change Diapers. Shannon, David, illus. (p. 1363)
—Twelve Days of Christmas in South Carolina. Mai-Wyss, Tatjana, illus. (p. 1800)
Long, Michelle. Mckayla, the Girl with the Special Hug, Makes A Friend. (p. 1114)
Long, Olivia. Billy Bumble Is Missing! Long, Olivia, illus. (p. 187)
—Boy & the Dog. Long, Olivia, illus. (p. 217)
—Dandelion Queen. Long, Olivia, illus. (p. 403)
—Diary of a Dog. Long, Olivia, illus. (p. 434)
—Elephant Who Forgot. Long, Olivia, illus. (p. 511)
—Horse of a Different Color. Long, Olivia, illus. (p. 799)
—Hortense, the Happy Hippo. Long, Olivia, illus. (p. 801)
—Impossible Peacock. Long, Olivia, illus. (p. 862)
—There's a Dinosaur in My Bathtub! Long, Olivia, illus. (p. 1730)
—Thunderbirds & Thunderbeings. Long, Olivia, illus. (p. 1746)
—Too Many Kittens. Long, Olivia, illus. (p. 1766)
—Why Don't Cats Lay Eggs? Long, Olivia, illus. (p. 1924)
Long, Paul, jt. auth. see Harris, Rita.
Long, Paulette Rich, illus. see Condenzio, Mary.
Long, Paulette Rich, illus. see Paiva, Johannah Gilman.
Long, Rachael Freeman. Black Rock Desert Trilogy: Valley of Fire: Book II. (p. 196)
Long, Robert. Inside the Chrysanthemum: New Japanese Fables. (p. 877)
—New Aesop Fables for Children Volume I. (p. 1243)
—New Aesop Fables for Children Volume II. (p. 1243)
Long, Ruth Frances. Treachery of Beautiful Things. (p. 1781)
Long, Samantha Gail. Don't Let the Bedbugs Bite Byers, Bradley, illus. (p. 468)
Long, Sara. nexos Multimedia: Used with ... Long-Nexos: Introductory Spanish. (p. 1249)
Long, Sharon J. Let Me Be Me. (p. 994)
Long, Susan Hill. Whistle in the Dark. (p. 1912)
Long, Sylvia. Sylvia Long's Thumbelina. (p. 1693)
—Twinkle, Twinkle, Little Star: A Traditional Lullaby. Long, Sylvia, illus. (p. 1802)
Long, Sylvia, illus. see Aston, Dianna Hutts & Hutts Aston, Dianna.
Long, Sylvia, illus. see Aston, Dianna Hutts.
Long, Sylvia, illus. see Aston, Dianna.
Long, Sylvia, illus. see Long, Matthew & Long, Thomas.
Long, Sylvia, illus. see Ward, Jennifer.
Long, Taillefer, illus. see Binkow, Howard.
Long, Tammy J. Like a Fish. (p. 1017)
Long, Thomas, jt. auth. see Long, Matthew.
Long, Trish. If You Can Survive High School, You Can Survive Anything! (p. 854)
Long, Trishia. How I Met Bigfoot. (p. 810)
Long, Tyler. Wires Fleming, Christopher, illus. (p. 1939)
Long, William. Secrets of the Woods. (p. 1546)
Longabough, Kristen, illus. see Goss, Michael Anthony.
Longacre, Tracy Ardella. Very Merry Ferret Christmas. (p. 1838)
Longbotham, Lori. Luscious Chocolate Desserts. Meppem, William & Manville, Ron, photos by. (p. 1066)
Longe, Bob. Little Giant Book: Card Tricks. (p. 1028)
Longenecker, Brenda, jt. auth. see Longenecker, Jeff.
Longenecker, Jeff & Longenecker, Brenda. Adventures of Critterville: The Beginning of Critterville. (p. 17)
Longfello, Henry Wadsworth. Paul Revere's Ride. Vachula, Monica, illus. (p. 1330)
Longfellow, Henry Wadsworth. Children's Hour. Lang, Glenna, illus. (p. 303)
—Children's Own Longfellow & the Golden Legend. (p. 304)
—Paul Revere's Ride: The Landlord's Tale. Santore, Charles, illus. (p. 1330)
—Paul Revere's Ride: The Landlord's Tale. Encarnacion, Elizabeth, ed. (p. 1330)
—Song of Hiawatha. (p. 1611)
Longfellow, Henry Wadsworth & Remington, Frederic. Song of Hiawatha. (p. 1611)
Longfellow, Henry Wadsworth & Revere, Paul. Paul Revere's Ride. (p. 1330)
Longfoot, Stephanie, illus. see Taylor, Caroline.
Longford, Elizabeth, jt. auth. see Longford, Elizabeth.
Longford, Elizabeth & Longford, Elizabeth. Pilgrimage of Passion: The Life of Wilfrid Scawen Blunt. (p. 1358)
Longhi, Katya, illus. see Heos, Bridget & Powell, Marie.
Longhi, Katya, illus. see Heos, Bridget.
Longhi, Katya, illus. see Perkins, Wendy.
Longhi, Phoebe. Steampunk Coloring & Activity Book: Containing Illustrations, Recipes, Formulas & Other Activities to Entertain & Entice Creativity for the Prevention of Ennui & General Malaise among the Youth of Today & Their Progenitors. (p. 1646)
Longhi, Sarah & Van Zile, Susan. Social Studies Graphic Organizers & Mini-Lessons. (p. 1604)
Longhine, Laura, ed. see Youth Communication.
Longino, Gina M. Livvie & Buggles. Longino, Gina M., illus. (p. 1042)
Longley, Joshua. Barnaby's Buccaneers. (p. 139)
Longman, Mary, illus. see Cuthand, Beth.
Longman Publishing Staff. My Second Handwriting. (p. 1218)
—People Who Came (p. 1340)
Longman Publishing Staff & Dallas, Donald. My First Handwriting. (p. 1206)
Longmeyer, C. M. My Life As a Third Grade Werewolf. Blanding, Dexter, illus. (p. 1212)
—My Life As a Third Grade Zombie. Blanding, Dexter, illus. (p. 1212)
Longmire, Lynda, jt. auth. see Gosule, Bette.
Longmore, Nickolai, illus. see Rock, Michelle L.
Longmore, Nickolai, illus. see Snider, Lori L.
Longmore, Sandra. Saving the Lost Children. (p. 1517)
Longnecker, Steve. Steve Longenecker's Wilderness Emergency Medical Aid Book for Kids & Their Adults. Lee, Frank, illus. (p. 1649)
Longo, Cheryl. Love, Limits, & Lessons: A Parent's Guide to Raising Cooperative Kids. (p. 1060)
Longo, Jason. Otto's Colorful Campus Tour - Syracuse University A-Z. (p. 1307)
Longo, Jason, illus. see Giroir, Constance H.
Longo, Jennifer. Six Feet over It. (p. 1582)
Longo, Kaitlin. Secret in Olivia's Garden. (p. 1541)
Longo, Sharon. My Friend Daniel Doesn't Talk. (p. 1209)
Longoria, Dora. Beans a la Charr. (p. 150)
Longoria, Eugene R., Jr. Junior y la Llorona en la Montana de Nieve. (p. 936)
Longoria, Madelín G. Verdeazul. (p. 1836)

L

Longship, Burns & Price, Robin. Beowuff & the Horrid Hen. (p. 166)
Longshore, Katherine. Brazen. (p. 224)
—Gilt. (p. 676)
—Manor of Secrets. (p. 1088)
—Tarnish. (p. 1706)
Long-Solis, Janet, jt. auth. see Vargas, Luis Alberto.
Longson, D. M. Scunner. (p. 1534)
Longstaff, Abie. Fairytale Hairdresser: And How Rapunzel Got Her Prince! Beard, Lauren, illus. (p. 565)
—Fairytale Hairdresser & Cinderella. Beard, Lauren, illus. (p. 565)
—Fairytale Hairdresser & Sleeping Beauty. Beard, Lauren, illus. (p. 565)
—Rumplestiltskin. Romanet, Caroline, illus. (p. 1495)
Longstreet, Barbara, et al. Woodsey School Kids Thanksgiving Feast. (p. 1950)
Longstreet, Olivia. Edgar's Moon. (p. 504)
Longstreet, Roxanne, see Caine, Rachel, pseud.
Longstreth, Galen Goodwin. Yes, Let's. Wicks, Maris, illus. (p. 1970)
Longus. ADVENTURES of SILVANA & the MAGIC UNICORN. (p. 23)
Longwood, Marc, photos by see Gleeson, Bill.
Longworth, Holly. Philippines. (p. 1350)
Lonsdale, Cathy. Bill the Brush Turkey. (p. 187)
Lonsdale, Mary. First Words Sticker Book. (p. 597)
—My Prayers for Everyday. (p. 1217)
—Whatever the Weather: When the Snow Comes. (p. 1896)
Lonsdale, Mary, illus. see Lebron, Karen.
Lonvig, Asbjorn, jt. auth. see Nygaard, Orla.
Look, Lenore. Alvin Ho: Allergic to Girls, School, & Other Scary Things. Pham, LeUyen, illus. (p. 51)
—Alvin Ho: Allergic to Camping, Hiking, & Other Natural Disasters. Pham, LeUyen, illus. (p. 51)
—Alvin Ho: Allergic to Babies, Burglars, & Other Bumps in the Night. Pham, LeUyen, illus. (p. 51)
—Alvin Ho: Allergic to Birthday Parties, Science Projects, & Other Man-Made Catastrophes. Pham, LeUyen, illus. (p. 51)
—Alvin Ho: Allergic to the Great Wall, the Forbidden Palace, & Other Tourist Attractions. Pham, LeUyen, illus. (p. 51)
—Alvin Ho: Allergic to Babies, Burglars, & Other Bumps in the Night. Pham, LeUyen, illus. (p. 51)
—Alvin Ho: Allergic to Dead Bodies, Funerals, & Other Fatal Circumstances. Pham, LeUyen, illus. (p. 51)
—Alvin Ho: Allergic to the Great Wall, the Forbidden Palace, & Other Tourist Attractions. Pham, LeUyen, illus. (p. 51)
—Brush of the Gods. So, Meilo, illus. (p. 232)
—Henry's First-Moon Birthday. (p. 769)
—Ruby Lu, Brave & True. (p. 1493)
—Ruby Lu, Brave & True. Wilsdorf, Anne, illus. (p. 1493)
—Ruby Lu, Empress of Everything. Wilsdorf, Anne, illus. (p. 1493)
—Ruby Lu, Star of the Show. Choi, Stef, illus. (p. 1493)
—Uncle Peter's Amazing Chinese Wedding. Heo, Yumi, illus. (p. 1812)
Look, Lenore & Wilsdorf, Anne. Ruby Lu, Brave & True. Wilsdorf, Anne, illus. (p. 1493)
Lookadoo, Justin. 97: Random Thoughts about Life, Love & Relationships. (p. 1998)
Loomis, Jennifer A. Wildlife in the Rocky Mountains. Loomis, Jennifer A., photos by. (p. 1931)
Looney, Bill. Flood of Noah: Legends & Lore of Survival. (p. 605)
Looney, Bill, illus. see Golden, William Lee.
Looney, Bill, illus. see Oard, Beverly & Oard, Michael.
Looney, Bill, illus. see Townsend, Stephanie Z.
Looney, Bill, illus. see Vance, Vince.
Looney, Michael. Battle of the Bulge: The Untold Story of Hofen. Vol. III (p. 146)
Loonin, Meryl. Overweight America. (p. 1314)
—Public Art. Greenhaven Press Editors, ed. (p. 1414)
Loop, Mary Ann. Mary Ann's Flying Basket. Eding, Bob, illus. (p. 1100)
Looper, Amy, jt. ed. see Carls, Beth.
Looper, Grace W. Great-Grandpa's Hidden Treasure. (p. 716)
—Molasses Making Time. (p. 1160)
Loopstra, Esther Dawn, illus. see Shaskan, Trisha Speed.
Loory, Ben. Baseball Player & the Walrus. Latimer, Alex, illus. (p. 141)
Loos, Jody C. Alex the Alien: Train Ride. (p. 36)
—Alex the Alien: Bubble Magic. (p. 36)
—Alex the Alien: The Cars of Mars. (p. 36)
Loos, Pamela. Hart Crane. Bloom, Harold, ed. (p. 751)
—Norman Mailer. Bloom, Harold, ed. (p. 1264)
—Reader's Guide to Lorraine Hansberry's a Raisin in the Sun. (p. 1444)
—Reading Sounder. (p. 1446)
—Reading the Giver. (p. 1446)
Loos, Pamela, ed. see Bloom, Harold.
Loos, Pamela, jt. ed. see Bloom, Harold.
Lootens, Ann. Birthday Surprise. Faas, Linde, illus. (p. 193)
Looye, Juliette. Ruby Bridges. (p. 1493)
Looye, Juliette, text. I Live in the Desert. (p. 841)
—I Live near a Canyon. (p. 841)
—I Live near a River. (p. 841)
—I Live near a Wetland. (p. 841)
—I Live on an Island. (p. 841)
—I Live on the Earth. (p. 841)
LoParco, Chris, illus. see St. Pierre-Ford, Hillary & Ford, Xander.
Lopata-Kurzweil, Ruti. Story of Colors: And Much More! (p. 1657)
Lopatin, Dmitry, tr. see Lopatina, Irina.
LoPatin, Norman, jt. auth. see Clement, Ben.
Lopatina, Irina. Tales from the Frog Forest. Lopatin, Dmitry, tr. (p. 1701)
Lopatka, Michael. Nuclear Power Facility Virtual Field Trip. (p. 1270)
—Scuba Divers Sign Language: A Guide to Underwater Communications of Tropical Reef Inhabitants. (p. 1533)
Loper, Ami M. Miracle of Life. Loper, Carol J., illus. (p. 1148)
Loper, Carol J., illus. see Loper, Ami M.
Loper, Kathleen. Angelina Katrina: Bugs in My Backyard. Waltz, Dan, illus. (p. 74)
—Angelina Katrina: Builds Troy Snowman. Waltz, Dan, illus. (p. 74)
Lopes, Marilyn/Jansen. Amaryllis of Hawaii Big Coloring Book: Drawings of Hawaii to Color. (p. 52)
—Amaryllis of Hawaii Pocket Coloring Book: Drawings of Hawaii to Color. (p. 52)
Lopes, Tom, illus. see Baker, Rosalie.
Lopez, Adrian R. Adrian. (p. 13)
Lopez, Alex, illus. see Braun, Eric.
Lopez, Andre. Emily's Electricity Experiments. (p. 519)
Lopez, Antonio Castro, illus. see Hayes, Joe.
Lopez, Armida. Some Say. (p. 1609)
Lopez, Ayesha, illus. see Braun, Eric & Gunderson, Jessica.
López, Barbara J. Pepper's Wish. (p. 1340)
Lopez, Bolivar. Z Finds a Kite. (p. 1984)
Lopez, C. Pellicer. Juan y Sus Zapatos. (p. 930)
—Julieta y Su Caja de Colores. (p. 932)
López, Casimiro de la Cruz, illus. see Endredy, James.
López, Casimiro de la Cruz, tr. see Endredy, James.
Lopez, Cece. Mini Munchkin Mania Mini Series Presents: Mini Munchkin in the Mirror. (p. 1146)
Lopez, Cheyene. Billy's Wish: Where Dreams Are Wishes of Christmas. (p. 188)
—Captain Blue Wonder: The Adventures of Captain Blue Wonder. Lopez, Cheyene & Lopez, Patricia, illus. (p. 263)
—Christmas Year Without Snow. (p. 316)
—Jolly House: From the Lands of Jolly Happy Holidays. Lopez, Cheyene, illus. (p. 924)
—Little Town of Christmas: The Town That's Always Christmas. (p. 1037)
—Pocket of Rainbows: Volume II the Rainbow Series. (p. 1375)
—Snow Feather: The Magic of Dreams. Lopez, Patricia, illus. (p. 1599)
Lopez, Cheyene Montana. Blue Sky Rainbows: A Series of Children's Stories of the World of Dreams & Imaginations (p. 203)
—Celebration America (p. 285)
Lopez, Chris. Carta de Acordes de Guitarra la Primera Etapa: Aprenda Como Tocar las Acordes Mas Comunes de Guitarra! (p. 272)
—First Stage Guitar Book: Learn How to Play Guitar Easily & Quickly! (p. 597)
—"First Stage" Guitar Book: Learn How to Play Guitar Easily & Quickly! (p. 597)
—First Stage Guitar Chord Chart: Learn How to Play the Most Commonly Played Guitar Chords! (p. 597)
—Guitar Book: For Those Who Have Just Landed on the Planet Earth! Learn How to Play Guitar. (p. 731)
—Libro de Guitarra la Etapa Siguiente: Aprenda Como Tocar Patrones y Tabs de la Escala Facil y Rapidamente! (p. 1006)
—Libro de Guitarra la Primera Etapa: Aprenda Como Tocar la Guitarra Facil y Rapidamente! (p. 1006)
—Next Stage Guitar Book: Learn How to Play Scale Patterns & Tabs Easily & Quickly! (p. 1249)
—Pre-Stage Guitar Book: Learn How to Get a Grip on Your First Guitar!- Learn How to Play Guitar. (p. 1394)
Lopez, Christopher P. Absolute Truth about Lying. Racine, Victoria, illus. (p. 7)
Lopez, Claudia Navarro, illus. see Chavez, Ricardo & Aguilera, Gabriela.
Lopez, Daniela. Maria Makes 10: Understanding Addition. (p. 1093)
Lopez, David. Blank Generation. (p. 198)
Lopez, David, illus. see Anderson, Julie.
Lopez, David Mark. Maddie's Magic Markers: Ride Like an Indian. (p. 1069)
—Run Like a Fugitive. (p. 1496)
—Walk Like an Egyptian. (p. 1853)
Lopez Dekker, Anna. Everwhere. (p. 542)
Lopez, Delano. Amazing Solar System Projects: You Can Build Yourself. (p. 55)
Lopez, Delano & Braley, Shawn. Amazing Solar System Projects. (p. 55)
Lopez, Denise M. If God Was a Superhero. (p. 852)
López, Diana. Ask My Mood Ring How I Feel. (p. 106)
Lopez, Diana. Ask My Mood Ring How I Feel. (p. 106)
Lopez, Diana. Choke. (p. 309)
—Confetti Girl. (p. 356)
López Dominguez, Xan, illus. see Sánchez, Gloria.
López Dominguez, Xan, tr. see Sánchez, Gloria.
Lopez, Eddie, ed. see Bumpers, Katrina B.
Lopez, Gerry. Surf Is Where You Find It. (p. 1685)
Lopez, Horacio. Funcion de Teatro. Wright, Douglas, illus. (p. 649)
López, Javier Alfonso, tr. see Kipling, Rudyard.
Lopez, Jessica. Big Mouth's Bubble Gum. Lopez, Jessica, illus. (p. 182)
—Big Mouth's Icecream. Lopez, Jessica, illus. (p. 182)
Lopez, Jill, jt. auth. see Blake, Christine.
Lopez, Joe. Solemates. (p. 1607)
Lopez, Jose Javier. Puerto Rico. Gritzner, Charles F., ed. (p. 1415)
Lopez, Jose M., tr. see Munsch, Robert.
Lopez, Jose Miguel, tr. see Olmstead, Mary.
Lopez, Khrystle M. & Lopez, Yolanda C. Princess Khrystle & the Monster Cancer: An informative fairytale version about brain cancer in Children. (p. 1404)
Lopez, Lois. Grandpape. (p. 709)
Lopez, Loretta. Que Suppresa de Cumpleanos! (p. 1424)
Lopez, Loretta, illus. see Elya, Susan Middleton.
Lopez, Loretta, illus. see Levy, Janice & Arisa, Miguel.
Lopez, Loretta, illus. see Levy, Janice.
Lopez, Lorraine. Call Me Henri. (p. 254)
Lopez, Luz-Maria, illus. see Moore, Elizabeth & Couvillon, Alice.
Lopez, Lyle, illus. see Dzidrums, Christine.
Lopez, Maria Lorena. Bird's Party, Birds in the Tropical Dry Forest. (p. 192)
Lopez, Max. How Do Microscopes Work? (p. 807)
Lopez, Minia. Amigos en el Bosque. Jimenez, Resu, illus. (p. 65)
—Friends in the Forest. Jimenez, Resu, illus. (p. 638)
—Plumas en la Pradera. Cantalapiedra, Jose, illus. (p. 1374)
López Narváez, Concha. Arbol de los Pajaros Sin Vuelo. (p. 94)
López Nárvaez, Concha & Concha, López Narváez. Cernicalo Porque. (p. 287)
López, Nivio, illus. see Almena, Fernando & Artigot, Manuel.
López, Nivio, tr. see Almena, Fernando & Artigot, Manuel.
Lopez Ortega, Jose. Why We Suffer, the Story of Balaam & the Talking Donkey. (p. 1926)
López, Oscar J. Sing along with Abuelita Rosa: Hispanic Lullabies = Canciones de Cuna. (p. 1579)
Lopez, Patricia. Dog Named Pom Pom & Friends. Lopez, Patricia, illus. (p. 461)
Lopez, Patricia, illus. see Lopez, Cheyene.
Lopez, Patricia A. Carly & Boey. (p. 270)
—Corky & Pirate Dan (p. 367)
—Imaginations of Wonders (p. 860)
Lopez, Paul, illus. see Hong, Denise & Hong, Andrew.
Lopez, Paul, illus. see Howell, Trisha Adelena.
Lopez, Paul, illus. see Robinson, Fay.
Lopez, Paul, illus. see Schoberle, Cecile.
Lopez, Paul, illus. see Winkelman, Barbara Gaines.
López, Rafael, illus. see Brown, Monica.
López, Rafael, illus. see Campoy, F. Isabel & Howell, Theresa.
López, Rafael, illus. see Engle, Margarita.
López, Rafael, illus. see Mora, Pat, et al.
López, Rafael, illus. see Mora, Pat.
López, Rafael, illus. see Ryan, Pam Muñoz.
López, Rafael, illus. see Vamos, Samantha R.
López, Rafael, jt. auth. see Mora, Pat.
López, Samuel Salinas & Altamirano, Ignacio M. Disfraz y Clemencia. (p. 450)
Lopez, Shana, illus. see Kelso, Brendan P.
Lopez, Shana, illus. see Kelso, Brendan.
Lopez, Sixto. Snarloff Duwaki's Adventures. (p. 1597)
Lopez, Susana. Best Family in the World. Wensell, Ulises, illus. (p. 169)
Lopez, Suzanne. Get Smart with your Heart: The Intelligent Guide to Love, Lust, & Lasting Relationships. (p. 668)
Lopez, Tony. False Memory. (p. 567)
—Meaning Performance: Essays on Poetry. (p. 1117)
Lopez, Victoria. Little King: An Aztec Tale. (p. 1030)
Lopez, Willie, illus. see Simmons, Lynn Sheffield.
Lopez, Xan, illus. see Gómez Cerda, Alfredo.
Lopez, Yolanda C., jt. auth. see Lopez, Khrystle M.
Lopez-Izquierdo, Nieves, tr. see Sutherland, Lin.
Lopez- Jackson, Lillian. Eight 8 Short Stories for Children. (p. 507)
Lopilato, Elizabeth H. Marshmello Mountain. (p. 1096)
Lopiz, Violeta, illus. see Alcolea, Ana.
Lopresti, Aaron, illus. see Bedard, Tony.
Lopresti, Aaron, jt. auth. see Claremont, Chris.
LoPresti, Angeline Sparagna. Place for Zero. Hornung, Phyllis, illus. (p. 1365)
Lopresti, Kirsten. Bright Coin Moon: A Novel. (p. 228)
Lopresti, Sarah H., illus. see LaBerge, Margaret M.
Lopresti, Tony. My Cat. Johnson, Deborah C., illus. (p. 1200)
Lopshire, Robert. I Want to Be Somebody New! Lopshire, Robert, illus. (p. 848)
Lopuszynski, Barbara. Angel & Brie. (p. 73)
Loran. My Friends Call Me Rocky: Book I Rocky's Rescue Book Ii Runaway Rocky. (p. 1209)
Lorang, C. J. Where Are My Shoes. (p. 1906)
Loranger, Marc J. Diamond in the Rough. (p. 434)
—Down There. (p. 474)
LoRaso, Carlo, illus. see Lange, Nikki Bataille.
Lorbiecki, Marybeth. Circles. (p. 321)
—Circles. Holm, Sharon, illus. (p. 321)
—Escaping Titanic: A Young Girl's True Story of Survival Lorbiecki, Marybeth & Heinzen, Kory S., illus. (p. 535)
—Jackie's Bat. Pinkney, Brian, illus. (p. 904)
—Planet Patrol: A Kids' Action Guide to Earth Care. Meyers, Nancy, illus. (p. 1368)
—Prairie Dogs. (p. 1392)
—Things Natural, Wild, & Free: The Life of Aldo Leopold. (p. 1733)
—Triangles. Holm, Sharon, illus. (p. 1785)
Lorbiecki, Marybeth, jt. auth. see Dunlap, Julie.
Lorbiecki, Marybeth & Eastman, Seth. Painting the Dakota: Seth Eastman at Fort Snelling. (p. 1318)
Lorca, Federico Garcia, see Garcia Lorca, Federico.
Lord, Bette Bao. In the Year of the Boar & Jackie Robinson. (p. 868)
—In the Year of the Boar & Jackie Robinson. Simont, Marc, illus. (p. 868)
Lord, Bruce & Richards, Elisabeth. Humpty Dumpty Was Pushed: And Other Cracked Tales. (p. 827)
Lord, Cynthia. Half a Chance. (p. 736)
—Handful of Stars. (p. 740)
—Happy Birthday Hamster. Anderson, Derek, illus. (p. 744)
—Hot Rod Hamster. Anderson, Derek, illus. (p. 802)
—Hot Rod Hamster & the Awesome ATV Adventure! Anderson, Derek, illus. (p. 802)
—Hot Rod Hamster & the Haunted Halloween Party! Anderson, Derek, illus. (p. 802)
—Hot Rod Hamster & the Haunted Halloween Party. Anderson, Derek & Paprocki, Greg, illus. (p. 802)
—Hot Rod Hamster & the Wacky Whatever Race! Anderson, Derek, illus. (p. 802)
—Jelly Bean. (p. 912)
—Jelly Bean. McGuire, Erin, illus. (p. 912)
—Monster Truck Mania! Anderson, Derek, illus. (p. 1168)
—Rules. (p. 1495)
—Touch Blue. (p. 1772)
Lord, Emery. Open Road Summer. (p. 1299)
—Start of Me & You. (p. 1643)
Lord, Gabrielle. Black Ops Hunted: Conspiracy 365. (p. 196)
—Black Ops Missing: Conspiracy 365. (p. 196)
—Conspiracy 365 April. (p. 359)
—Conspiracy 365 August. (p. 359)
—Conspiracy 365 December. (p. 359)
—Conspiracy 365 February. (p. 359)
—Conspiracy 365 - January. (p. 359)
—Conspiracy 365 July. (p. 359)
—Conspiracy 365 June. (p. 359)
—Conspiracy 365 March. (p. 359)
—Conspiracy 365 May. (p. 359)
—Conspiracy 365 November. (p. 359)
—Conspiracy 365 October. (p. 359)
—Conspiracy 365 September. (p. 359)
—Malice. (p. 1083)
—Revenge. (p. 1465)
Lord, Grant. Tales of Rex Riley Aged 10 & a Bit, It's A Dog's Life. (p. 1702)
Lord, Janet. Albert the Fix-It Man Paschkis, Julie, illus. (p. 34)
—Here Comes Grandma! Paschkis, Julie, illus. (p. 770)
—Where Is Catkin? Paschkis, Julie, illus. (p. 1908)
Lord, Jennifer Fallin. Pipersville: And the troll that lost his big Toe. (p. 1362)
Lord, Jeremy, illus. see Saxby, Claire.
Lord, Jill Roman. If Jesus Came to Visit Me. Graef, Renee, illus. (p. 853)
—If Jesus Lived Inside My Heart. Wummer, Amy, illus. (p. 853)
—If Jesus Walked Beside Me. Wummer, Amy, illus. (p. 853)
—If Jesus Walked Beside Me. Graef, Renee, illus. (p. 853)
Lord, John Vernon, jt. auth. see Burroway, Janet.
Lord, Kenniston. Pirates of Peary Village. (p. 1363)
Lord, Leonie, illus. see Hart, Caryl.
Lord, Leonie, illus. see Robinson, Michelle.
Lord, Leonie, illus. see Waddell, Martin.
Lord, Leonie, jt. auth. see Hart, Caryl.
Lord, Michelle. Animal School: What Class Are You? Garland, Michael, illus. (p. 79)
—Naturaleza Recicla¿lo Haces Tú? Morrison, Cathy, illus. (p. 1236)
—Nature Recycles: How about You? Morrison, Cathy, illus. (p. 1236)
—Quick Quarterback Harpster, Steve, illus. (p. 1427)
—Song for Cambodia Arihara, Shino, illus. (p. 1611)
—Tide Pool Trouble Harpster, Steve, illus. (p. 1747)
Lord, Michelle & Hoshino, Felicia. Little Sap & Monsieur Rodin (p. 1036)
Lord, Nancy. Beluga Days: Tracking a White Whale's Truths. (p. 163)
Lord, Pia. Adventures of M M , Music Mouse. (p. 20)
—Cato the Caterpillar. (p. 280)
—Day the Sun Went Out. (p. 414)
—Night the Moon Went Out. Thompson, Karin, illus. (p. 1254)
Lord, Raymond. Fox on a Cold Tin Roof. (p. 626)
—Usher. (p. 1828)
Lord, Richard. Germany. (p. 666)
Lord, Richard A., jt. auth. see Frank, Nicole.
Lord, Roberta. Reflections: French Version. (p. 1456)
—Reflections: English Version. (p. 1456)
—Reflections: Albanian Version. (p. 1456)
Lord, Suzanne. Music from the Age of Shakespeare: A Cultural History (p. 1193)
Lord Tennyson, Alfred. Enoch Arden & Other Poems. (p. 530)
—Lady of Shalott. Côté, Geneviève, illus. (p. 971)
Lord Tennyson, Alfred, see Lord Tennyson, Alfred.
Lore, Erin. Timmy the Dragon. (p. 1755)
Lore, Mark & Lore, Matthew. Flying Rubberneckers: High-Flying Fun for the Airport & Plane. Zimmerman, Robert, illus. (p. 610)
Lore, Matthew, jt. auth. see Lore, Mark.
Lore, Pittacus. Fall of Five. (p. 566)
—I Am Number Four: The Lost Files: the Legacies. (p. 833)
—I Am Number Four: The Lost Files - The Legacies. (p. 833)
—I Am Number Four: The Lost Files: Secret Histories. (p. 833)
—I Am Number Four: The Lost Files - Secret Histories. (p. 833)
—I Am Number Four. (p. 833)
—I Am Number Four - The Lost Files Hidden Enemy (p. 833)
—Power of Six. (p. 1389)
—Revenge of Seven. (p. 1465)
—Rise of Nine. (p. 1474)
Loren, Josephina. Cody Helps at the Race: Subtract Within 20. (p. 338)
Lorencz, Bill, illus. see RH Disney Staff.
Loreno, Rose, et al. In the Garden. (p. 866)
Lorente, Mariano J., jt. auth. see Ibañez, Vincente Blasco.
Lorentz, Dayna. No Dawn Without Darkness. (p. 1258)
—No Easy Way Out. (p. 1258)
—No Safety in Numbers. (p. 1260)
—Pack. (p. 1317)
Lorentzen, Bent. Dragon's Moon. (p. 479)
—Krona: Dragons of Nistala. (p. 968)
Lorenz, Albert. Exceptionally, Extraordinarily Ordinary First Day of School. (p. 547)
—Renovated Fairy Tales: As Told by the Boy Who Drew Flies. (p. 1460)
Lorenz, Albert, illus. see Armstrong, Jennifer.
Lorenz Books Staff. Ultimate Animal Sticker Book: With 100 Amazing Stickers. (p. 1809)
—Ultimate Bird Sticker Book: With 100 Amazing Stickers. (p. 1809)
Lorenz Books Staff, creator. Patterns (p. 1329)
Lorenz, Catherine, jt. auth. see Harris, John.
Lorenz, Colton. I Am a New York City. (p. 832)
Lorenz, Geoff & Vogt, Janet, creators. Music Out of a Hat, Grades 4-6: 7 Card Games for Classroom Fun! (p. 1193)
Lorenz, Geoff, et al, creators. Ultimate Music Game Book; Grades K-6+ (p. 1809)
Lorenz Guest, Donna. Enchanted Ride. (p. 523)
Lorenz, Jinye. Ryong's Story: Extended Version of Grandfather, the Tiger & Ryong. Lorenz, Virginia O., ed. (p. 1499)
Lorenz, Jinye, Sr. Grandfather, the Tiger & Ryong. Lorenz, Virginia O., Sr., ed. (p. 707)
Lorenz, Nancy. Strength of Ballerinas. (p. 1667)
Lorenz, Patricia. Great American Outhouse Stories: The Hole Truth & Nothing Butt. (p. 713)
Lorenz, Virginia O., ed. see Lorenz, Jinye.
Lorenz, Virginia O., Sr., ed. see Lorenz, Jinye, Sr.

Lorenzen, Margaret Brownell. Petunia Patch Pockets & the Golden Locket. Jocelyn, Sawyer & Liza, Behles, illus. (p. 1349)
Lorenzen, Margartet. Slinky Slithertail & the Talent Show. Sawyer, Jocelyn, illus. (p. 1590)
Lorenzetti, Doreen, illus. see Barth, Linda J.
Lorenzetti, Doreen, illus. see Solomon, Sharon.
Lorenzi, Natalie Dias. Flying the Dragon. (p. 610)
Lorenzo, Alejandro. Mateo's Progress/Jornadas de Mateo: Tales for Children of All Ages/Cuentos para Niños de Todas las Edades. (p. 1104)
Lorenzo, Amanda. Clovis Escapes!: Runt Farm. Bks. 3 Walker, Mark Evan, illus. (p. 335)
Lorenzo, Gloria, illus. see Correa, Alvaro.
Lorenzo, Lucia Ann. Lucky, My Best Friend. (p. 1063)
Lorenzo, Mike. Allison's Summer Of '53. (p. 47)
Lorenzo, Rafel Fernandez. Ladron de Voces. (p. 970)
Lorenzo, Rose, et al. Dog's Life. (p. 463)
—Families. (p. 567)
Lorey, Dean. Monster Law. (p. 1167)
Lori A. Smolin, ed. Eating Right: An Introduction to Human Nutrition. (p. 501)
Loria, Laura. Air Force. (p. 31)
—Bones in Your Body (p. 209)
—Eyes in Your Body (p. 558)
—Marine Force Recon. (p. 1094)
—Show Horses. (p. 1570)
—Solving Real World Problems with Electrical Engineering. (p. 1608)
—What Is a Constellation? (p. 1888)
—What Is Citizenship? (p. 1889)
—What Is Magnetism? (p. 1889)
—What Is the Judicial Branch? (p. 1890)
—Wolfgang Amadeus Mozart (p. 1944)
Lorig, Steffanie. Oodles de Doodles. (p. 1298)
Lorig, Steffanie & Jacobs, Jeanean. Chill & Spill: A Place to Put It down & Work It Out. (p. 305)
Lorimer, Colin. Uxb. Warner, Chris, ed. (p. 1829)
Lorimer, Janet. Bad Luck Play (p. 132)
—Beasts. (p. 152)
—Ben Cody's Treasure (p. 163)
—Boneyard (p. 209)
—Bugged! (p. 236)
—Danger on Ice (p. 404)
—Deadly Game (p. 417)
—Death Grip (p. 420)
—Empty Eyes (p. 521)
—Eye for an Eye (p. 557)
—Flashback (p. 602)
—Kula'i Street Knights (p. 968)
—Look to the Light (p. 1050)
—Murray's Nightmare (p. 1192)
—Mystery Quilt (p. 1226)
—No Place Like Home (p. 1260)
—Ring of Fear (p. 1473)
—Ruby's Terrible Secret. (p. 1494)
—Scavenger Hunt (p. 1521)
—Strange but True Book 2 (p. 1665)
—Student Bodies. (p. 1669)
—Tiger Lily Code (p. 1748)
—Tuesday Raven (p. 1796)
—Tug-of-War (p. 1796)
—Woman Who Loved a Ghost (p. 1945)
Lorimer, Lawrence, jt. auth. see Riley, Peter.
Lorinc, John. Cities. (p. 322)
Lorini, Andrea. Bunny's Easter Surprise. (p. 242)
—Diplodocus. (p. 445)
—Easter Egg Party. Rigo, Laura, illus. (p. 499)
—Spooky Castle. (p. 1631)
—Stegosaurus. (p. 1646)
—T-Rex. (p. 1694)
—Triceratops. (p. 1785)
—Trick or Treat. (p. 1786)
Lorioz, Jacques Loïc, tr. see Downie, Mary Alice & Rawlyk, George.
Lorna, Balian. Aminal Lorna, Balian & Lecia, Balian, illus. (p. 65)
Lorne, Patrick, photos by see Tracqui, Valérie.
Lornie, June, illus. see Carroll, Lewis, pseud.
Lornsen, Boy. Bosque en Peligro. (p. 214)
Lorrah, Jean & Howlett, Winston A. Prophecies. (p. 1411)
Lorraine. Adventures of Ruthy: Ruthy Gets Lost. (p. 22)
Lorraine, Florido. Dezzer the Gasser. Shami, Susan & Crossman, Keith, eds. (p. 433)
Lorraine, Loria. Wild about Manners. Bonnie, Spino, illus. (p. 1928)
—Wild about Manners. Spino, Bonnie, illus. (p. 1928)
Lorraine, Nancy. Butterfly Adventure. Herron, Dorothy, illus. (p. 247)
—Tatty, the Lonely Monarch. Herron, Dorothy, illus. (p. 1707)
Lorsch-Saltzman, Laurie. Josh & George. (p. 926)
Lorton, Barbara. Sidney Seagull Marks Lighthouses & Buoys of the Chesapeake. (p. 1573)
Lorton, Sylvia. Johnny's Wish. (p. 924)
los Santos, Marisa de, see de los Santos, Marisa.
Losa, Ann, illus. see Gillis, Jennifer Blizin.
Losacano, Connie. Now I Can Hear! (p. 1269)
Losada, Basilio. Cristobal Colon. (p. 383)
—Isabel la Catolica. (p. 890)
—Lazarillo de Tormes. (p. 981)
Losantos, Cristina. Beauty & the Beast: La Bella y la Bestia. (p. 154)
—Beauty & the Beast (La Bella y la Bestia) (p. 154)
—Bella y la Bestia. (p. 162)
Losantos, Cristina, illus. see Cela, Jaume.
Loser, Barry, jt. auth. see Smith, Jim.
Loser, Barry & Smith, Jim. I Am Not a Loser. (p. 833)
Losey, Tori. Ducks of Congress Park. Liguori, Kathy, illus. (p. 488)
Losh, Eric, illus. see Reffett, Frances.
Loski, Krystle C. Ode to Me & My Day. (p. 1278)
Losli, Joy. Little Red Sailboat. (p. 1035)
Lossani, Chiara. Nacimiento de las Estaciones: El Mito de Demetery Persefone. Monaco, Octavia, illus. (p. 1227)
Lossani, Chiara & van Gogh, Vincent. Vincent Van Gogh & the Colors of the Wind. Monaco, Octavia, illus. (p. 1843)
Lostimolo, Stephanie, illus. see Griffin, Lydia.
Lostorto, Eric. Rounding Rescue, a Rounding Numbers Story. Cotton, Sue Lynn, illus. (p. 1491)
Losure, Mary. Backwards Moon. (p. 130)
—Fairy Ring: Or Elsie & Frances Fool the World. (p. 564)
—Wild Boy: The Real Life of the Savage of Aveyron. Ering, Timothy Basil, illus. (p. 1929)
Loter, Inc., illus. see Golden Books.
Loter Inc. Staff, illus. see Amerikaner, Susan & Disney Book Group Staff.
Loter, Inc. Staff, illus. see Disney Book Group Staff & Ritchey, Kate.
Loter Inc. Staff, illus. see Higginson, Sheila Sweeny & Disney Book Group Staff.
Loter Inc. Staff, illus. see Reader's Digest Editors & Mitter, Matt.
Loter Inc. Staff, illus. see Reader's Digest Staff & Rhodes, Lilly.
Loter Inc. Staff, illus. see Scollon, Bill.
Loter, John, illus. see Mackerel, Seymour & RH Disney Staff.
Loter, John, illus. see Reader's Digest Editors & Mitter, Matt.
Lotersztain, Ileana, jt. auth. see Baredes, Carla.
Lotfy, Evelyn. Ms. Plant & Friends. (p. 1188)
Loth, Sebastian. Clementine. (p. 330)
—Remembering Crystal. (p. 1459)
Lotherington, John, ed. see Grossel, David, et al.
Loti, Pierre. Story of A Child. (p. 1657)
—Story of a Child. (p. 1657)
Lotlikar, Anita M. Goodnight Singapur. (p. 701)
Lotorto - Soroka, Mary. Catiana Makes a Family. (p. 280)
Lotorto-Soroka, Mary. Memoirs of a Cat: Interpreted for Humans Too! (p. 1125)
—Who Needs Spots Anyways? (p. 1917)
Lott, Cheryl Lynn. My Firefly Friends. (p. 1203)
Lott, Ruth. BK's Big Move Across the Country: From Philadelphia to Los Angeles. (p. 194)
Lott, Sheena, illus. see Ellis, Sarah & Suzuki, David.
Lott, Sheena, illus. see McFarlane, Sheryl.
Lott, Sheena, illus. see Sproule, Gail.
Lotto, Lisa Marie. Oh How We Feel When We Are Sick with the Flu: Oh the Things We See When We Go to the Park. (p. 1280)
Lottridge, Celia. Listening Tree (p. 1022)
—Mother Goose. Clement, Gary et al, illus. (p. 1177)
—One Watermelon Seed Patkau, Karen, illus. (p. 1297)
—Ticket to Curlew (p. 1747)
Lottridge, Celia Barker. Home Is Beyond the Mountains (p. 792)
—Stories from Adam & Eve to Ezekiel Clement, Gary, illus. (p. 1654)
—Stories from the Life of Jesus Wolfsgruber, Linda, illus. (p. 1654)
—Wings to Fly (p. 1936)
Lottridge, Celia Barker & Chan, Harvey. Music for the Tsar of the Sea. (p. 1193)
Lotz, Anne Graham & Graham Lotz, Anne. Heaven God's Promise for Me Bryant, Laura J., illus. (p. 761)
Lotz, Dana. What It's Like to Still Be a Kid. (p. 1891)
Lotz, Dana R. Kids' Tales. (p. 955)
Lotz, Louis. Sweet Life: A Taste of God in the Ordinary. (p. 1690)
Lotz, Nancy & Phillips, Carlene. Marie Antoinette & the Decline of French Monarchy. (p. 1093)
Lou, Cindy. King of Ing Wants to Sing. (p. 959)
Lou, Lizzie. Covered in Chocolate: Child-centered Recipes, Chocolate-inspired Curriculum. (p. 373)
Lou Who, Carrie, illus. see Klitzner, Irene & Adams, Peggy.
Louchard, Anto. Plume dans le Whisky. (p. 1374)
Louck, Cheryl. ABC's of Motocross. Zielinski, Dave, photos by. (p. 4)
Loucks-Christenson, Lisa. Waiting Room to Heaven Presents: The Eagle Nest Coffee Bar & Cafe. Loucks-Christenson, Lisa, photos by. (p. 1853)
Loufane. Lola. (p. 1045)
Loufane, illus. see Boonen, Stefan.
Loufane, illus. see Robberecht, Thierry.
Lough, Amber. Blind Wish. (p. 199)
—Fire Wish. (p. 591)
Lough, Erin & Duke, Mave Lough. Spirit Tree at Toomer's Corner. (p. 1628)
Lough, Whitney. Smoke Hole Adventure. Cosner, Jeff, illus. (p. 1594)
Loughead, Deb. Caught in the Act (p. 282)
—Frappée Par la Foudre (p. 631)
—Pocketful of Fur. Birke, Lisa, tr. (p. 1375)
—Sidetracked (p. 1573)
—Snowball Effect (p. 1600)
—Time & Again (p. 1751)
Loughead, Deb & Shipley, Jocelyn. Cleavage: Breakaway Fiction for Real Girls (p. 330)
Loughead, Cordelia. Tales of the Magpie. (p. 1702)
Lougher, Jenny. Ted & His New Trousers. (p. 1712)
—Ted & the Combine Harvester. Lewis, Wayne, illus. (p. 1712)
Loughlin, Patrick. Academy All-Stars. Hart, James, illus. (p. 7)
—Banana Kick. (p. 136)
—Chip & Chase. Ziersch, Nahum, illus. (p. 308)
—State Showdown. Hart, James, illus. (p. 1644)
—Try Time. (p. 1795)
—World Domination. Hart, James, illus. (p. 1954)
Loughlin, Patrick & Maxwell, Glenn. Lucky Break. (p. 1062)
Loughlin, Peter J. Law School Bible: How Anyone Can Become a Lawyer... Without Ever Setting Foot in a Law School!... Unless You Really Want To. (p. 981)
Loughran, Donna. Carnival Coins: How Will We Count Our Money? (p. 270)
—Day at Mini-Golf: What's the Length? (p. 412)
—Field of Play: Measuring Distance, Rate, & Time. (p. 584)
—Finding the Treasure: Coordinate Grids. (p. 588)
—Garden Club: Operations with Fractions. (p. 656)
—Herding a Hundred: Counting the Sheep. (p. 769)
—Hidden Ducks: Describing & Interpreting Data. (p. 775)
—How Long Is It? (p. 810)
—Living in the Tundra. (p. 1041)
—Look for Them: Where Are the Shapes? (p. 1049)
—Look for Them. (p. 1049)
—On the Playground: How Do You Build Place Value? (p. 1291)
—Picnic Fun: Hot Dog Operations. (p. 1355)
—Save Now, Buy Later: Finding Unit Prices. (p. 1516)
—Ship Shape: Making Shapes Fly. (p. 1567)
—Stir It Up: Mixing Decimals. (p. 1651)
—Tending the Tide Pool: The Parts Make a Whole. (p. 1719)
—Time Ticks By: How Do You Read a Clock? (p. 1753)
—Toy Tally: How Many Toys Are There? (p. 1774)
—Uniquely Louisiana (p. 1818)
—Winning the Game: Putting Miles in Their Place. (p. 1937)
—Year at the Fairgrounds: Finding Volume. (p. 1969)
Loughran, Donna, jt. auth. see Brunner-Jass, Renata.
Loughran, Kelley. Crab Called Mouse. (p. 375)
Loughran, P. J. Turning 15 on the Road to Freedom: My Story of the 1965 Selma to Montgomery March. (p. 1798)
Loughrey, Anita. Explaining Diabetes. (p. 549)
—Mouse's Summer Muddle. Howarth, Daniel, illus. (p. 1182)
—Owl's Winter Rescue. Howarth, Daniel, illus. (p. 1315)
—Rabbit's Spring Adventure. Howarth, Daniel, illus. (p. 1430)
—Squares. (p. 1636)
—Squirrel's Fall Search. (p. 1637)
—Triangles. (p. 1785)
Loughrey, Eithne. Annie Moore: New York City Girl. (p. 87)
—Annie Moore: The Golden Dollar Girl. (p. 87)
—Annie Moore: First in Line for America. (p. 87)
Loughrey, Stephen. Hopper's Day at the Zoo. (p. 797)
Loughridge, Lee, jt. auth. see Bright, J. E.
Loughridge, Lee, jt. auth. see Dahl, Michael.
Loughridge, Lee, jt. auth. see Fein, Eric.
Loughridge, Lee, jt. auth. see Greenberger, Robert.
Loughridge, Lee, jt. auth. see Hoena, Blake A.
Loughridge, Lee, jt. auth. see Kupperberg, Paul.
Loughridge, Lee, jt. auth. see Lemke, Donald B.
Loughridge, Lee, jt. auth. see Lemke, Donald.
Loughridge, Lee, jt. auth. see Pasko, Martin.
Loughridge, Lee, jt. auth. see Sonneborn, Scott.
Loughridge, Lee, jt. auth. see Sutton, Laurie S.
Loughridge, Lee & Hoena, Blake A. Cosmic Bounty Hunter Burchett, Rick, illus. (p. 368)
Loughridge, Stuart, illus. see Gerdner, Linda & Langford, Sarah.
Louhi, Kristiina, illus. see Jalonen, Riitta.
Louie, Ai-Ling. Vera Wang Queen of Fashion; Amazing Chinese American: Biographies of Amazing Asian Americans. (p. 1836)
—Yo-Yo & Yeou-Cheng Ma, Finding Their Way: Amazing Asian Americans. Peng, Cathy, illus. (p. 1971)
Louie, Hilary, jt. auth. see Pang, Evelyn.
Louie, Mary. Amazing Amand. (p. 52)
Louie, Ron, illus. see Arita, Vera.
Louie, Wes, illus. see Montgomery, R. A.
Louie, Wes, jt. illus. see Semionov, Vladimir.
Louis, Catherine. My Little Book of Chinese Words. Bradley, MaryChris, tr. (p. 1212)
Louis, Catherine, illus. see Kazeroid, Sibylle, tr.
Louis, Catherine, illus. see Sellier, Marie.
Louis, Dominique, illus. see RH Disney Staff.
Louis HéMon Staff. Maria Chapdelaine. (p. 1093)
Louis, Margareth Belledent. When I Make It to Heaven. (p. 1903)
Louis, Robb. Monster in the Moat. (p. 1167)
Louis, Ron & Copeland, David. How to Succeed with Women. (p. 821)
Louis, Sachar. There's a Boy in the Girls' Bathroom. (p. 1730)
Louis, Stevenson Robert, jt. auth. see Stevenson, Robert Louis.
Louis, Wm. Roger, ed. Burnt Orange Britannia: Adventures in History & the Arts. (p. 244)
—Resurgent Adventures with Britannia: Personalities, Politics & Culture in Britain. (p. 1464)
Louise, Cristina & McIlroy, Michelle. Where Is Paco Now? Louise, Cristina & McIlroy, Michelle, illus. (p. 1909)
Louise, Finnoula. Cookies Cookies: A Year of Holiday Treats. Louise, Finnoula, illus. (p. 361)
Louise, Karen, illus. see Winton, Tim.
Louise, Kate. Upside-Down Fish. Matine, Laura, illus. (p. 1825)
Louise, Kate, jt. auth. see Ormand, Kate.
Louise, Landes-Levi. Sweet on My Lips: The Love Poems of Mirabai. (p. 1690)
Louise, Märtha. Why Kings & Queens Don't Wear Crowns. Sevig-Fajardo, Mari Elise, tr. from NOR. (p. 1925)
Louise, T. See You in My Dreams. (p. 1547)
Louise, Verna & McKinney, Doris. Tales & Rhymes for Children: Cute Little Stories for Kids. (p. 1701)
Louissaint, Louis, illus. see Heurtelou, Maude.
Loulan, Joann & Worthen, Bonnie. Periodo: Guina de una Joven. Dyrud, Chris Wold & Quackenbush, Marcia, illus. (p. 1343)
LouLou, illus. see Skinner, Tina.
Loundagin, Choeleen. Inner Champion: A Mental Toughness Training Manual for Figure Skaters. (p. 875)
Lounsberry, Alice. Garden Book for Young People. (p. 656)
Lounsbury, Pete. Jesus & the Blind Man. (p. 915)
Lounsbury, Thomas RaynesFord. Early Literary Career of Robert Browning. (p. 493)
—Life & Times of Tennyson from 1809-1850. (p. 1008)
—Shakespeare & Voltaire. (p. 1559)
—Shakespeare as a Dramatic Artist (p. 1559)
—Standard of Usage in English. (p. 1639)
Loupy, Christophe. Hugs & Kisses. Tharlet, Eve, illus. (p. 825)
—Hugs & Kisses. James, J. Alison, tr. from GER. (p. 825)
Loupy, Christophe & Tharlet, Eve. Puppy Love: A Litter of Puppy Stories. Tharlet, Eve, illus. (p. 1418)
Lourdes-Pitt, H. H. Brett Favre. (p. 226)
Lourie, Peter. Hidden World of the Aztec. (p. 776)
—Manatee Scientists: Saving Vulnerable Species. (p. 1086)
—On the Texas Trail of Cabeza de Vaca. (p. 1291)
—On the Trail of Lewis & Clark: A Journey up the Missouri River. (p. 1291)
—On the Trail of Sacagawea. (p. 1291)
Lourie, Richard, jt. auth. see Korczak, Janusz.
Loutchinina, Ekaterina, tr. see Uralskaia, Valeria, et al.
Louth, Jack, jt. auth. see Sanchez, Alex.
Louthain, J. A. Arne the Elephant: Terrorized by Evil Mice. Eberbach, Andrea, illus. (p. 57)
Louv, Barbara. Choose a Career in Science. (p. 310)
Loux, Lynn Crosbie. Day I Could Fly. Porfirio, Guy, illus. (p. 413)
Loux, Matthew. Legend of Old Salty Jarrell, Randal C., ed. (p. 988)
—Salt Water Taffy: Caldera's Revenge! (p. 1505)
—Salt Water Taffy: Caldera's Revenge! Pt. 2 (p. 1505)
—Truth about Dr. True. (p. 1794)
Lovasclo, Jane. Casey & Bella Go to New York. Jasuna, Aija, illus. (p. 275)
Lovasik, Lawrence G. Buen San Jose. (p. 235)
—Child's Prayer Treasury. (p. 305)
—Diez Mandamientos. (p. 437)
—Los Angeles. (p. 1053)
—St. Joseph Catholic Children's Bible. (p. 1638)
Lovasik, Lawrence G. & Winkler, J. Book of Saints (p. 211)
Lovasik, Lorenzo G. Primer Libro de los Santos: La Historia de Sus Vidas y Sus Ejemplos. (p. 1400)
Lovass-Nagy, Nicole, illus. see Lepage, Michaele L.
Lovass-Nagy, Nicole, jt. auth. see LePage, Michaele L.
Lovato, David C. Little Old Man. (p. 1032)
Lovato, Demi. Stay Strong. (p. 1645)
Love. Why Do I Take Vitamins? a Book for Children with Autism. (p. 1923)
Love, Andrea. Quiggly J. 's Super Secret Pirate Adventure. (p. 1428)
Love, Angela. 'Gwyngallion' Guardian of Little Children Lost in the Woods. (p. 733)
Love, Ann. Fishing. (p. 599)
—Yes You Can! Your Guide to Becoming an Activist. (p. 1971)
Love, Ann, jt. auth. see Drake, Jane.
Love, Ann & Drake, Jane. Kids Book of the Far North. Bouchard, Jocelyne, illus. (p. 952)
—Kids Book of the Night Sky. Collins, Heather, tr. (p. 952)
—Sweet! The Delicious Story of Candy. Dávila, Claudia, illus. (p. 1689)
—Talking Tails: The Incredible Connection Between People & Their Pets. Slavin, Bill, illus. (p. 1703)
Love, Ann, et al. Talking Tails: The Incredible Connection Between People & Their Pets. (p. 1703)
Love, Berna. Arkansas Indians: Learning & Activity Book. (p. 99)
Love, D. Anne. Defying the Diva. (p. 424)
—Of Numbers & Stars: The Story of Hypatia. Paparone, Pamela & Paparone, Pam, illus. (p. 1279)
—Picture Perfect. (p. 1356)
—Puppeteer's Apprentice. (p. 1417)
—Secret Prince. (p. 1543)
—Semiprecious. (p. 1550)
Love, Donna. Awesome Ospreys: Fishing Birds of the World. Turley, Joyce Mihran, illus. (p. 121)
—Glaciers Are Melting! Bersani, Shennen, illus. (p. 682)
—Henry the Impatient Heron Wald, Christina, illus. (p. 768)
—Loons: Diving Birds of the North Turley, Joyce Mihran, tr. (p. 1052)
—Totally Out There Gd Glacier Natl Park. Mihran, Turley Joyce, illus. (p. 1771)
—Wild Life of Elk. Wald, Christina, illus. (p. 1929)
Love, Emily. Beginning of Freedom. (p. 159)
Love, Jeremy, illus. see McKeever, Sean, et al.
Love, Jessica, jt. auth. see Hill, Chelsie.
Love, Judy. Praise Be & Rainbows. (p. 1393)
Love, Judy, illus. see Bunting, Eve.
Love, Judy, illus. see Danneberg, Julie.
Love, Judy, illus. see Gill, Shelley.
Love, Judy, illus. see Grambling, Lois G.
Love, Judy, illus. see Laminack, Lester L.
Love, Judy, illus. see Paschen, Elise.
Love, Katie. Fruit to Live By... (p. 645)
Love, Makada H. Harold's Adventures. Holt, Lindsey, illus. (p. 749)
Love, Mary. Mama's House. (p. 1084)
Love, Mary A. Learning Through Symbolism & Celebrations. Flournoy, L. Diana, illus. (p. 985)
Love, Mary Elise. I Think I'll Rest a While. (p. 846)
Love, Maryann Cusimano. Sleep, Baby, Sleep. van Lieshout, Maria, illus. (p. 1588)
—Tú Eres Mi Te Quiero. Ichikawa, Satomi, illus. (p. 1795)
—You Are My I Love You. Ichikawa, Satomi, illus. (p. 1973)
—You Are My Miracle. Ichikawa, Satomi, illus. (p. 1973)
—You Are My Wonders. Ichikawa, Satomi & Lewin, Ted, illus. (p. 1973)
Love, Maryann Cusimano & Ichikawa, Satomi. You Are My Wish. (p. 1973)
Love, Nicole M. Cool Cougar! Cool Cougar! Cool Cougar! & the Puma Dance. (p. 363)
Love, Pamela. Cub Explores. Sykes, Shannon, illus. (p. 388)
—Dos pies suben, dos pies Bajan: Two Feet up, Two Feet Down. Chapman, Lynne, illus. (p. 472)
—Dos Pies Suben, Dos Pies Bajan. Chapman, Lynne, illus. (p. 472)
—Lighthouse Seeds. Warner, Linda, illus. (p. 1015)
—Moose's Morning. Sochor, Lesia, illus. (p. 1173)
—Two Feet up, Two Feet Down. Chapman, Lynne, illus. (p. 1803)
Love, Roger & Frazier, Donna. Set Your Voice Free: How to Get the Singing or Speaking Voice You Want. (p. 1554)
Love, Terrence, illus. see Copeland, Edna D. & Love, Valerie L.
Love, Tiffany. Surviving Financial Disasters: Bankruptcy, Foreclosure, Auto Repossession, Eviction, Excessive Debts & More. (p. 1687)
Love, Timothy, jt. auth. see Park, Louise.
Love, Valerie L., jt. auth. see Copeland, Edna D.
Lovecraft, H. P. At the Mountains of Madness. (p. 111)
Lovecraft, H. P. & Culbard, Ian N. J. At the Mountains of Madness. (p. 111)

L

Loveday, Roy. Inscribed Across the Landscape: The Cursus Monuments of Great Britain. (p. 875)
Lovegrove, Emily. Help! I'm Being Bullied. (p. 765)
Lovegrove, James. Kill Swap. (p. 956)
—Lord of Fire (Five Lords of Pain Book 5) (p. 1052)
—Lord of Tears (Five Lords of Pain Book 3) (p. 1052)
—Lord of the Mountain (Five Lords of Pain Book 1) (p. 1052)
—Lord of the Typhoon (Five Lords of Pain Book 4) (p. 1052)
—Lord of the Void (Five Lords of Pain Book 2) (p. 1052)
Lovegrove, Ray. Health: Ethical Debates in Modern Medicine. (p. 757)
—Health - Ethical Debates in Modern Medicine. (p. 757)
Lovegrove, Ross & Antonelli, Paola. Supernatural: The Work of Ross Lovegrove. (p. 1684)
Loveheart, Lucy, illus. see Clibbon, Meg & Meg, Mighty.
Loveheart, Lucy, illus. see Meg, Magic.
Lovejoy, Brenda, illus. see Napthine, Margaret.
Lovejoy, Robert. Golden Dog Book of Fairy Tales & Animal Stories. (p. 694)
Lovejoy, Sharon. Little Green Island with a Little Red House: A Book of Colors & Critters. (p. 1028)
—Running Out of Night. (p. 1497)
Lovelace, Eloise. Elvin's Friends. (p. 517)
—I Was a Boy Just Like You. (p. 848)
—Your Ema Loves You. (p. 1980)
Lovelace, Kelley. Ready Set Go Organic. (p. 1447)
Lovelace, Maud Hart. Betsy-Tacy. Lenski, Lois, illus. (p. 172)
—Betsy-Tacy Treasury: The First Four Betsy-Tacy Books. (p. 172)
Lovelace, Victoria. Animal Crackers & Alphabet Soup. (p. 77)
Lovelady, W. f. Adventures of Johnny Saturday: Back to the Drawing Board. (p. 19)
Loveland, Seymour. Illustrated Bible Story Book: New Testament. Winter, Milo, illus. (p. 857)
—Illustrated Bible Story Book - Old Testament. Winter, Milo, illus. (p. 857)
Loveland-Coen, Victoria. I Love You Mom Coupon Book: 28 Ways to Show Mom You Appreciate Her Every Day Stillwell, Jennifer, illus. (p. 843)
Loveless, Antony. Air War. (p. 31)
—Apache Helicoper Pilot. (p. 91)
—Apache Helicoper Pilots. (p. 91)
—Bodyguards. (p. 207)
—Bomb & Mine Disposal Officers. (p. 208)
—Fighter Pilots. (p. 585)
—Nuclear Submariners. (p. 1270)
—Tank Warfare. (p. 1705)
—Test Pilots. (p. 1723)
Loveless, Antony & Crewe, Sabrina. War Correspondents. (p. 1857)
Loveless, Antony & Nixon, James. Infantry Soldiers. (p. 873)
Loveless, Antony & Oxlade, Chris. Support Helicopter Pilots. (p. 1684)
Loveless, Antony & Tisdale, Rachel. Police Officers. (p. 1380)
Loveless-Hill, Tracie. I Too Matter. (p. 847)
Lovell, Brandy. Crazy Colours. Mitchell, Tina, illus. (p. 377)
Lovell, David. Survey of U. S. History to 1945 Student Activity Book. Matthews, Douglas L., ed. (p. 1686)
Lovell, Edith, illus. see Guzman, Maria Del C.
Lovell, H. N. Wootie's Delightful Picnic. (p. 1950)
—Wootie's Great Adventure: Escape to Freedom. (p. 1950)
Lovell, Katie. Christmas Stencil Cards. (p. 315)
Lovell, Katie, illus. see Brooks, Felicity.
Lovell, Katie, illus. see Watt, Fiona.
Lovell, Nadine. Children Around the World: Passport to Adventure. (p. 302)
Lovell, Patty. Have Fun, Molly Lou Melon. Lovell, Patty & Catrow, David, illus. (p. 754)
Lovell, Whitney. Game of the Season. (p. 654)
Lovelock, Brian, illus. see Holt, Sharon.
Lovelock, Brian, illus. see Huber, Raymond.
Lovelock, Brian, illus. see Sutton, Sally.
Lovelock, James, jt. auth. see Davies, Nicola.
Lovelock-Brown, Emma. Moons Time to Shine. (p. 1173)
Loven, Beth Glick, illus. see Prior, R. W.
Loveridge, Matt, illus. see Ipcizade, Catherine, et al.
Loveridge, Matt, illus. see Lubar, David.
Loveridge, Matt, illus. see Wissinger, Tamera Will.
Loveridge, Pamela. Buzzy Bee. (p. 249)
—Knife of Blood. (p. 964)
—Man in the Moon. (p. 1085)
—Mr Foo. (p. 1185)
—Tooth Fairy Who Lost a Tooth. (p. 1768)
Loverly, L. What Shall I Pretend to be Today. (p. 1893)
Loves, June. Flight Series (p. 604)
—Mi Angel de la Guarda. (p. 1132)
—Pets (p. 1348)
Lovett, Danny. Jesus Is Awesome. (p. 915)
Lovett, Darrell. Hi, I'm Alex. (p. 775)
—My Dog Tony. (p. 1202)
Lovett, Darrell F. Darrell's Lake Franklin. (p. 409)
Lovett, Louise Sheppa. Happy Day. (p. 745)
Lovett, Nate, illus. see Golden Books Staff.
Lovett, Nate, illus. see Golden Books.
Lovett, Nate, jt. auth. see Brown, Peggy.
Lovett, Tracy M. Buck's Rodeo. Lovett, Tracy M., illus. (p. 234)
Lovett, Vienna. Mission from God. (p. 1153)
Lovhaug, Lewis J. Angel Armor: Just a Boy. (p. 73)
—Angel Armor: The Cassandra Conflict. (p. 73)
Lovik, Thomas A. Unterwegs! Video for Deutsch Heute: Used with ... Lovik-Vorsprung: an Introduction to the German Language & Culture for Communication. (p. 1823)
Lovillo, Pilar Ortiz, tr. see Abodehman, Ahmed.
Loving, Vikki. Wildly Austin: Austin's Landmark Art. Cestaro, Gregg, photos by. (p. 1931)
Loving, Winifred "Oyoko". My Grandma Loves to Play. (p. 1210)
Lovins, Jennifer O. Opihi Baby. (p. 1300)
Lovitt, Chip. My Big Dump Truck. LaPadula, Thomas, illus. (p. 1197)
—My Red Fire Truck. LaPadula, Thomas, illus. (p. 1217)
—Skate Parks: On a Roll! (p. 1583)
Lovric, Michelle. Mourning Emporium. (p. 1181)
—Undrowned Child. (p. 1817)
Lovsin, Polona, illus. see Llewellyn, Claire.
Lovvorn, Ann R. Chocolate Puddles. Reece, James A., illus. (p. 309)
—Purple Frogs & Pumpkin Seeds. Ingram, Jan, illus. (p. 1419)
Low, A. M. Popular Scientific Recreations - Science. (p. 1385)
Low, Alan M., illus. see Wacker, Eileen.
Low, Alice. Blueberry Mouse. Friend, David Michael, tr. (p. 204)
—Fastest Game on Two Feet: And Other Poems about How Sports Began. O'Brien, John A., illus. (p. 576)
—Summer. McKie, Roy, illus. (p. 1673)
Low, Chen-Chen-Chen. Lizzie May & Oshin. (p. 1043)
—Lizzie May & the Shoelaces. (p. 1043)
—Lizzie May the Immortal. (p. 1043)
Low, Dene. Petronella Saves Nearly Everyone: The Entomological Tales of Augustus T. Percival. (p. 1348)
Low, Elizabeth Cothen. Big Book of Seasons, Holidays, & Weather: Rhymes, Fingerplays, & Songs for Children (p. 179)
—Big Book of Seasons, Holidays, & Weather: Rhymes, Fingerplays, & Songs for Children. (p. 179)
Low, Emma & Wood, Mary. Cambridge Primary Mathematics Stage 5 Learner's Book. (p. 255)
Low, Gennita. Squirrel Came to Stay: Adventures of MikiSquirrel. (p. 1637)
Low, Jennifer, jt. auth. see Low, Jennifer A.
Low, Jennifer A. & Low, Jennifer. Kitchen for Kids: 100 Amazing Recipes Your Children Can Really Make (p. 962)
Low, Jessica & Nash, Kevin. Bentley College College Prowler off the Record. (p. 165)
Low, Mary & Coutellier, Connie. Creek Stompin' & Gettin' into Nature: Environmental Activities That Foster Youth Development. (p. 380)
Low, Rachel. Girl's Guide to DIY Fashion: Design & Sew 5 Complete Outfits * Mood Boards * Fashion Sketching * Choosing Fabric * Adding Style. (p. 680)
Low, Robert. Peoples of the Savanna. (p. 1340)
Low, Susan. Just Draw! (p. 938)
Low, Vicki. Cave of Secrets. Rooth, Mike, illus. (p. 282)
—First Emperor. Mayhew, Sara E., illus. (p. 594)
Low, William. Chinatown. (p. 307)
Low, William, illus. see Barron, T. A.
Low, William, illus. see Hall, Bruce Edward & Hall, Bruce.
Low, William, illus. see Lewis, Elizabeth Foreman.
Low, William, illus. see O'Reilly, Bill.
Low, William, illus. see Rockliff, Mara.
Low, William, tr. see Hall, Bruce Edward & Hall, Bruce.
Low, William & Cobalt Illustrations Studio Staff. Daytime Nighttime. Low, William & Cobalt Illustrations Studio Staff, illus. (p. 415)
—Machines Go to Work. Low, William & Cobalt Illustrations Studio Staff, illus. (p. 1068)
—Old Penn Station. Low, William & Cobalt Illustrations Studio Staff, illus. (p. 1284)
Low, Yvonne. Kyoodoz Algebra Solutions Book. (p. 969)
—Kyoodoz Pre-Algebra Maven. (p. 969)
Lowden, Stephanie. Time of the Eagle: A Story of an Ojibwe Winter. (p. 1752)
Lowden, Stephanie Golightly. Time of the Eagle: A Story of an Ojibwe Winter. (p. 1752)
Lowdermilk, Charity. Fifth Rule. (p. 584)
—Treasure. (p. 1781)
Low-Dumond, Sabrina. Weakling Willie. (p. 1869)
Low-DuMond, Sabrina. Weakling Willie. (p. 1869)
Lowe, Brodie. Werewolf on My Street. (p. 1875)
Lowe, Clint. Lincoln Mcsweeney: In the Streets of London & New York. (p. 1018)
Lowe, David, illus. see Schwaeber, Barbie Heit.
Lowe, Doug. PowerPoint 2003 for Dummies(r). (p. 1391)
Lowe, E. Van. Never Slow Dance with a Zombie. (p. 1243)
Lowe, Frank Allen, illus. see Riddle, Sharon Kay & Sanders, Nancy/Ida.
Lowe, Greg, photos by see Myall, Julia.
Lowe, Isabel, illus. see Price, Hugh.
Lowe, Jackie, jt. auth. see Marion Nash Jackie Lowe Staff.
Lowe, Jason, jt. auth. see Dickinson, Gill.
Lowe, Jason, photos by see Phaidon Press Editors, ed.
Lowe, Jason, photos by see Rosenbaum, Stephanie.
Lowe, John C., jt. auth. see Honeyman-Lowe, Gina.
Lowe, Joy L., jt. auth. see Matthew, Kathryn I.
Lowe, Joy L. & Matthew, Kathryn I. Colonial America in Literature for Youth: A Guide & Resource Book. (p. 341)
Lowe, Julian. My Aunt Is in the Army Reserve. (p. 1196)
Lowe, Lana. Three Little Girls & the Giant Sea Turtle. Beaumont, Peter, illus. (p. 1742)
Lowe, Leigh. Prima Latina Student Book: Introduction to Christian Latin. (p. 1399)
Lowe, Le'Marqunita. Tall Tall Giraffe. (p. 1704)
Lowe, Marilyn & Gordon, Edwin. Music Moves for Piano. (p. 1193)
—Music Moves for Piano Preparatory Book. (p. 1193)
Lowe, Marilyn, et al. Music Moves for Piano Boogies & Blues. (p. 1193)
—Music Moves for Two. (p. 1193)
Löwe, Michael. Tribal Fusion. (p. 1785)
Lowe, Nakesha. It's All about Me. (p. 896)
—Just Leave Me Alone. (p. 939)
Lowe, Natasha. Courage of Cat Campbell. (p. 372)
—Power of Poppy Pendle. (p. 1389)
Lowe, Pamela Fleming. Missouri Then & Now. (p. 1154)
Lowe, Ruby Hasegawa, et al. O Kamehameha IV: Alexander Liholiho. (p. 1274)
Lowe, Tom. Louie the Loon & the Moon. Leadiove, Ben, illus. (p. 1058)
Lowe, Tony, illus. see Falk, Nicholas.
Lowe, Vicky, illus. see MacLean, Christine Kole & Maclean, Christine.
Lowe, Wes, illus. see Branson, Eve.
Lowe, Wes, illus. see Carr, Simonetta.
Lowe, Wesley. Griffin's Gauntlet. (p. 724)
Lowe, Wesley, illus. see Castaldo, Nancy.
Lowe, Wesley, illus. see Houran, Lori Haskins.
Lowe, Wesley, illus. see Richardson, Steve.
Lowe, Wesley, illus. see Stamper, Judith Bauer.
Lowe, Wesley, illus. see Zoehfeld, Kathleen Weidner.
Lowe, Wesley, illus. see ¿Ládo¿U, F¿Lák¿'.
Lowel, Margaret. Weather Tools: A Content Area Reader-science. (p. 1870)
Lowell, Barbara. George Ferris, What a Wheel! Hoare, Jerry, illus. (p. 663)
Lowell Gallion, Sue. Rick & Rachel Build a Research Report. Chung, Chi, illus. (p. 1470)
Lowell, James Russell. Four Poems. (p. 625)
—New Letters. (p. 1246)
Lowell, Jax Peters. No More Cupcakes & Tummy Aches. (p. 1259)
Lowell, Pamela. Returnable Girl. (p. 1465)
—Returnable Girl. (p. 1465)
Lowell, Shelley. This Is the Land of Two Suns: Paintings & Poetry Lowell, Shelley, illus. (p. 1736)
Lowell, Sophia. Glee: Summer Break: An Original Novel. (p. 682)
—Glee - The Beginning. (p. 682)
Lowell, Sophia, jt. auth. see The Creators of Glee.
Lowell, Susan. Dusty Locks & the Three Bears. Cecil, Randy, illus. (p. 490)
—Great Grand Canyon Time Train. Shroades, John / W., illus. (p. 716)
—I Am Lavina Cumming: A Novel of the American West. (p. 833)
—Josefina Javelina: A Hairy Tale. MacPherson, Bruce, illus. (p. 926)
—Tortoise & the Jackrabbit: La Tortuga y la Liebre. Harris, Jim, illus. (p. 1771)
—Tres Pequenos Jabalies: The Three Little Javelinas. Harris, Jim, illus. (p. 1784)
—Very Hairy Christmas. Harris, Jim, illus. (p. 1838)
Lowenstein, Anna, illus. see Pasiadis, Vanessa.
Lowenstein, Felicia. All about Sign Language: Talking with Your Hands. (p. 43)
—What Does a Doctor Do? (p. 1883)
—What Does a Police Officer Do? (p. 1883)
—What Does a Teacher Do? (p. 1884)
—What Does a Veterinarian Do? (p. 1884)
Lowenstein, Sallie. Sir Kyle & Lady Madeline. (p. 1580)
—Waiting for Eugene. Lowenstein, Sallie, illus. (p. 1852)
Lowenstein, Sallie Claire. Waiting for Eugene. (p. 1852)
Lowenthal, Ambur & Werner, Joe. Shirley's Cakes (p. 1567)
Lowenthal, Gary T., jt. auth. see Loftis, Chris.
Lowe-Phelps, Karla. Yama the Llama: Off to Jerusalem. (p. 1968)
—Yama, the Llama: Off to Bethlehem. (p. 1968)
Lower, Catherine, jt. auth. see Thuma, Cynthia.
Lower, Steven S. Refleksshuns Uv Uh Colleeg Grajuwhat. (p. 1456)
Lowery, Ellen. Bird Might Be Most Anywhere. (p. 190)
Lowery, Endora Dial. Lucky Louisa. (p. 1062)
Lowery, Janette Sebring. Poky Little Puppy. Tenggren, Gustaf, illus. (p. 1378)
Lowery, Lawrence. Clouds, Rain, Clouds Again. (p. 335)
Lowery, Lawrence F. Animals Two by Two. (p. 84)
—Dark As a Shadow. Goldsborough, June, illus. (p. 407)
—How Does a Plant Grow? Smith, Phil, illus. (p. 808)
—How Does the Wind Blow? (p. 809)
—How Tall Was Milton? Smith, Phil, illus. (p. 812)
—Light & Color: I Wonder Why. Wood, Muriel, illus. (p. 1014)
—Look & See. (p. 1048)
—Looking for Animals. (p. 1051)
—Michael's Racing Machine. Loehle, Richard, illus. (p. 1135)
—Our Very Own Tree. (p. 1310)
—Rubber vs. Glass: I Wonder Why. Smith, Phil, illus. (p. 1493)
—Sounds Are High, Sounds Are Low: I Wonder Why. Fraser, Betty, illus. (p. 1615)
—Spenser & the Rocks: I Wonder Why. (p. 1625)
—Tommy's Turtle. (p. 1765)
—Tree by Diane's House. (p. 1783)
—Up, Up in a Balloon. (p. 1824)
—What Can an Animal Do? Pfloog, Jan, illus. (p. 1880)
—What Does an Animal Eat? Reusswig, William, illus. (p. 1884)
—What Makes Different Sounds? (p. 1892)
Lowery, Linda. Aunt Clara Brown: Official Pioneer. Porter, Janice Lee, illus. (p. 115)
—Day of the Dead. Knutson, Barbara, illus. (p. 414)
—Dia de los Muertos. Translations.com Staff, tr. (p. 433)
—Earth Day. Bergherr, Mary, illus. (p. 495)
—Martin Luther King Jr. Day. Mitchell, Hetty, illus. (p. 1098)
—Native Peoples of California. (p. 1235)
—Native Peoples of the Plains. (p. 1235)
—Native Peoples of the Southeast. (p. 1235)
—Truth & Salsa (p. 1794)
Lowery, Linda & Keep, Richard. Chocolate Tree: [A Mayan Folktale]. Porter, Janice, illus. (p. 309)
—Tale of la Llorona: A Mexican Folktale. Porter, Janice Lee, illus. (p. 1699)
Lowery, Marie Hayes. Beau & Friends. (p. 153)
—Bruce & Swish: A Christmas Tale of Holiday Wishes & Dreams. (p. 232)
Lowery, Mark A. Magic Time, Time Is Magical. (p. 1074)
Lowery, Mike, illus. see Bulion, Leslie.
Lowery, Mike, illus. see Howie, Betsy.
Lowery, Mike, illus. see Jennings, Ken.
Lowery, Mike, illus. see Kai Dotlich, Rebecca.
Lowery, Mike, illus. see Murray, Laura.
Lowery, Mike, illus. see Nesbo, Jo.
Lowery, Mike, illus. see Ryan, Candace.
Lowery, Mike, illus. see Ward, D. J.
Lowery, Paul. Do You Know Where Sea Turtles Go? (p. 458)
—Do You Know Where Sea Turtles Go? Thomas, Tim, illus. (p. 458)
Lowery, Rae. Case of the Pack-Rat Park. (p. 274)
—Charlie & the Case of the Big Bully: The Adventures of Charlie #4 (p. 292)
Lowery, Will. Peyton Heart of a Child Series Kokomo the Sleeping Monkey. (p. 1349)
Lowery, Zoe. African American Experience: From Slavery to the Presidency Set. (p. 27)
—American Revolution: Life, Liberty, & the Pursuit of Happiness. (p. 63)
—American Revolution. (p. 63)
—Barack Obama & a "Post-Racial Society" (p. 137)
—Key Figures of the Wars in Iraq & Afghanistan. (p. 950)
—Technology of the Modern World. (p. 1712)
Lowery, Zoe & MacBain, Jenny. Primary Source Investigation of the Salem Witch Trials. (p. 1400)
Lowery, Zoe & Roberts, Jeremy. Oscar Schindler. (p. 1305)
Lowery, Zoe, ed. American Revolution. (p. 63)
—Barack Obama & the Idea of a Postracial Society. (p. 137)
—Democracy. (p. 425)
—Key Figures of the Wars in Iraq & Afghanistan. (p. 950)
Lowes, Sarah. Snow Queen. Clara, Miss, illus. (p. 1599)
Lowes, Tom. Casey's Four Holiday Celebrations. (p. 275)
Lowes, Tom, illus. see Cantor, Joanne.
Lowes, Tom, illus. see Stormer, Kate.
Lowitz, Anson, jt. auth. see Lowitz, Sadyebeth.
Lowitz, Leza & Oketani, Shogo. Jet Black & the Ninja Wind. (p. 916)
Lowitz, Sadyebeth & Lowitz, Anson. Mr Key's Song: The Star Spangled Banner. (p. 1185)
Lowory, Brigid. Guitar Highway Rose. (p. 731)
Lowrey, Becky. Chirps. (p. 308)
Lowrey, Chris. Wonec Adventures: The Gift of Giving. (p. 1949)
Lowrey, Janette Sebring. Poky Little Puppy. Tenggren, Gustaf, illus. (p. 1378)
—Where Is the Poky Little Puppy? Tenggren, Gustaf, illus. (p. 1909)
Lowrey-Christian, Jane. Quackless Duck Finds His Pals. (p. 1422)
—Quakless Duck Prays for a New Voice. (p. 1422)
Lowrie, D. L. Hope When Believers Struggle: Studies in Mark's Gospel. (p. 797)
Lowrie, Paul. Hooray for Minnesota Lakes. (p. 796)
—Hooray for Minnesota Winters. (p. 796)
Lowrie, Paul, jt. auth. see Nicholaus, Bret.
Lowry, Amy & Aesop. Fox Tails: Four Fables from Aesop. (p. 626)
Lowry, Brigid. Follow the Blue. (p. 612)
—Guitar Highway Rose. (p. 731)
—Juicy Writing: Inspiration & Techniques for Young Writers. (p. 932)
—Things You Either Hate or Love. (p. 1734)
—Triple Ripple: A Fabulous Fairytale. (p. 1787)
Lowry, Dave. In the Dojo: A Guide to the Rituals & Etiquette of the Japanese Martial Arts. (p. 866)
Lowry, Judith, illus. see Santiago, Chiori.
Lowry, Lois. Anastasia Asusordenes. (p. 67)
—Anastasia at Your Service. (p. 67)
—Anastasia Esta al Mando. (p. 67)
—Anastasia off Her Rocker. (p. 67)
—Anastasia, por Supuesto. Bustelo, Ana, tr. (p. 67)
—Anastasia Tiene las Respuetas. Bustelo, Ana, tr. (p. 67)
—Anastasia Tiene Problemas. Amechazurra, G., illus. (p. 67)
—Anastasia Vive Aqui. Alonso, Juan Ramon, illus. (p. 67)
—Birthday Ball. Feiffer, Jules, illus. (p. 192)
—Compte les Etoiles. (p. 354)
—Crow Call. (p. 385)
—Crow Call. Ibatoulline, Bagram, illus. (p. 385)
—Gathering Blue. (p. 658)
—Giver (p. 681)
—Giver. (p. 681)
—Giver. Ibatoulline, Bagram, illus. (p. 681)
—Giver Quartet. (p. 681)
—Giver Quartet Boxed Set. (p. 681)
—Gooney Bird & All Her Charms. Thomas, Middy, illus. (p. 702)
—Gooney Bird & the Room Mother. Thomas, Middy, illus. (p. 702)
—Gooney Bird Greene. Middy Chilman, Thomas, illus. (p. 702)
—Gooney Bird Is So Absurd. Thomas, Middy, illus. (p. 702)
—Gooney Bird on the Map. Thomas, Middy, illus. (p. 702)
—Gooney the Fabulous. (p. 702)
—Gossamer. (p. 703)
—Like the Willow Tree: The Diary of Lydia Amelia Pierce, Portland, Maine 1918. (p. 1017)
—Messenger. (p. 1129)
—Number the Stars: And Related Readings. (p. 1271)
—Number the Stars. (p. 1271)
—Passeur. (p. 1326)
—Silent Boy. (p. 1575)
—Son. (p. 1611)
—Summer to Die. Oliver, Jenni, illus. (p. 1675)
—Willoughbys. (p. 1934)
—Willoughbys. Lowry, Lois, illus. (p. 1934)
Lowry, Lois & Rohmann, Eric. Bless This Mouse. Lowry, Lois & Rohmann, Eric, illus. (p. 199)
Lowry, Mark & Bolton, Martha. Piper's Great Adventures. Myers, Kristen, illus. (p. 1362)
Lowry, Mark & Greene, Buddy. Mary, Did You Know? Bond, Denny, illus. (p. 1100)
Lowry, Patrick & Dunn, Carole. Atchison at 150: A Look Back, 1854 - 2004. (p. 111)
Lowry-Manning, Lil. Color God Love: A Bible Study Designed to Excite Children Ages 6-12. (p. 342)
Lowthert, Carrie. Minkie & Emily. (p. 1147)
Loxton, Daniel. Ankylosaur Attack. Loxton, Daniel & Smith, Jim W. W., illus. (p. 84)
—Evolution. Loxton, Daniel, illus. (p. 546)
—Plesiosaur Peril Loxton, Daniel & Smith, Jim W. W., illus. (p. 1374)
—Pterosaur Trouble. Loxton, Daniel & Smith, Jim W. W., illus. (p. 1414)
Loxton, Howard. Cats: An Eyewitness 3-D Book. (p. 280)
Loy, Jessica. Weird & Wild Animal Facts. Loy, Jessica, illus. (p. 1872)
Loy, John. Burger Versus Burrito. (p. 243)
Loy, Nikki, illus. see Page, Nick & Page, Claire.
Loya, Olga. Magic Moments: Bilingual Latin American Tales. Lizardi-Rivera, Carmen, tr. from SPA. (p. 1072)
Loyd, Elizabeth, jt. auth. see Knapp-Grosz, Tamara.
Loyd, Mark. Big Ben: A Little Known Story. Loyd, Mark, illus. (p. 178)
Loyd, Todd. Dark Ride. (p. 408)

Loye, David. Grandfather's Garden: Bedtime Stories for Little & Big Folk. (p. 707)
Loye, Scott. Moon Ring. (p. 1172)
Loyle, Larry & Brissenden, Constance. As Long As the Rivers Flow Holmlund, Heather D., illus. (p. 105)
Loyola, Mother Mary. King of the Golden City: An Allegory for Children. Davis, John Watson, illus. (p. 959)
—King of the Golden City Study Edition, an Allegory for Children. (p. 959)
Lozada, Edwin A., ed. Field of Mirrors: An Anthology of Philippine American Writers. (p. 584)
Lozano Carbayo, Pilar. Retratos. (p. 1464)
Lozano, Clara, tr. see Jones, Christianne C.
Lozano, Clara, tr. see Klein, Adria F.
Lozano, Clara, tr. see Klein, Adria F. & Gallagher-Cole, Mernie.
Lozano, Dawn. Lily Pad's Adventures Series: Lily Pad Goes to the Park. (p. 1018)
—Lily Pad's Adventures Series: Lily Pad Is Growing Up. (p. 1018)
Lozano, Gustavo Vazquez, et al. Luis Suarez. (p. 1064)
Lozano, Hector, illus. see McChesney, Terry.
Lozano, José. Little Chanclas. (p. 1026)
—Once Around the Block (Una Vuelta a la Manzana) Crosthwaite, Luis Humberto, tr. (p. 1292)
Lozano, Juan Antonio. Animales Entreversos. Garcia, Humberto, illus. (p. 81)
Lozano, Luciano, illus. see Davies, Nicola.
Lozano, Luciano, illus. see MacCuish, Al.
Lozano, Luciano, illus. see Nesquens, Daniel & Schimel, Lawrence.
Lozano, Neal. Can God See Me in the Dark? Hatke, Ben, illus. (p. 258)
—Will You Bless Me? Hatke, Ben, illus. (p. 1932)
Lozano, Omar, illus. see Comeau, Joey.
Lozano, Omar, illus. see Sonneborn, Scott.
Lozano, Tammy Lynn. Livingston's Lessons: Learn to Share. (p. 1042)
Lozier Jackson, Beverly. Mommy, Is God a Super Hero? (p. 1162)
Lozzi, Annette. Mystery of the Vanishing Chickens. Storey, Lela Belle, illus. (p. 1226)
Lstarte. Sam the Slug. (p. 1507)
Lu, Catherine. Just & Unjust Interventions in World Politics: Public & Private. Whitman, Jim, ed. (p. 937)
Lu, Jia. Geography of China. (p. 662)
—Geography of China. Wang, Jianwei, ed. (p. 662)
Lu, Marie. Champion. (p. 289)
—Evertree. (p. 542)
—Legend. (p. 988)
—Legend: the Graphic Novel. Kaaris, illus. (p. 989)
—Legend Trilogy Boxed Set (p. 989)
—Prodigy. (p. 1409)
—Young Elites. (p. 1978)
Lu, Tina. Mystery of the Starry Night. Liu, Jenny, ed. (p. 1226)
Lu, Wang Du. Crouching Tiger, Hidden Dragon (p. 385)
Luadzers, Darcy. Virgin S.e.x: A Girl's No-Regrets Guide to Happy, Healthy Sex... the First Time & Every Time. (p. 1844)
—Virgin Sex for Girls: A No-Regrets Guide to Safe & Healthy Sex. (p. 1844)
—Virgin Sex for Guys: A No-Regrets Guide to Safe & Healthy Sex. (p. 1844)
Lubach, Peter, illus. see Bowman, Donna H.
Lubach, Peter, illus. see Dinardo, Jeff.
Lubach, Vanessa. Jane Eyre. (p. 908)
Lubach, Vanessa, illus. see Brontë, Emily.
Lubach, Vanessa, illus. see Stevenson, Robert Louis.
Luban, Marianne. Priest. (p. 1399)
Lubanski, Paul, jt. auth. see Lubanski, Paul.
Lubanski, Paul & Lubanski, Paul. Bonky, a Moose & the Magic Hockey Stick. (p. 209)
Lubar, David. Attack of the Vampire Weenies: And Other Warped & Creepy Tales. (p. 114)
—Battle of the Red Hot Pepper Weenies: And Other Warped & Creepy Tales. (p. 147)
—Beware the Ninja Weenies: And Other Warped & Creepy Tales. (p. 173)
—Big Stink. (p. 184)
—Bully Bug: A Monsterrific Tale. (p. 241)
—Curse of the Campfire Weenies: And Other Warped & Creepy Tales. (p. 394)
—Dead Guy Spy. (p. 416)
—Dinosaur Disaster. (p. 442)
—Dinosaur Disaster. Loveridge, Matt, illus. (p. 442)
—Dog Days. (p. 461)
—Dunk. (p. 490)
—Enter the Zombie. (p. 531)
—Extremities: Stories of Death, Murder, & Revenge. (p. 557)
—Gloomy Ghost. (p. 685)
—Goop Soup. (p. 702)
—Hidden Talents. (p. 776)
—Hyde & Shriek: A Monsterrific Tale. (p. 831)
—In the Land of the Lawn Weenies: And Other Warped & Creepy Tales. (p. 866)
—Invasion of the Road Weenies. (p. 883)
—Meltdown Madness. (p. 1125)
—Meltdown Madness. Loveridge, Matt, illus. (p. 1125)
—My Rotten Life. (p. 1218)
—Numbed! (p. 1270)
—Punished! (p. 1417)
—Sleeping Freshmen Never Lie. (p. 1589)
—Sophomores & Other Oxymorons. (p. 1614)
—Stage Fright. Loveridge, Matt, illus. (p. 1638)
—Stranger Things. (p. 1665)
—Stranger Things. Loveridge, Matt, illus. (p. 1665)
—True Talents. (p. 1793)
—Unwilling Witch: A Monsterrific Tale. (p. 1823)
—Vanishing Vampire: A Monsterrific Tale. (p. 1833)
—Wavering Werewolf: A Monsterrific Tale. (p. 1864)
—Wipeout of the Wireless Weenies: And Other Warped & Creepy Tales. (p. 1939)
—Wipeout of the Wireless Weenies. (p. 1939)
—Wizards of the Game. (p. 1943)
Lubawy, Susan. World View: A Global Study of Geography, History & Culture (p. 1958)
Lubbe, Angela C. Don't Forget about Us. (p. 467)
Lubben, Amy & Williams, Rozanne Lanczak. Build-a-Skill Instant Books Word Families-Long Vowels. Shiotsu, Vicky & Faulkner, Stacey, eds. (p. 238)
—Build-a-Skill Instant Books Word Families-Short Vowels. Shiotsu, Vicky & Faulkner, Stacey, eds. (p. 238)
Lubber, William. Pirateology: The Pirate Hunter's Companion. Steer, Dugald A., ed. (p. 1363)
—Pirateology Handbook: A Course in Pirate Hunting. Steer, Dugald A. & Twist, Clint, eds. (p. 1363)
Lubber, William & Steer, Dugald A. Pirateology Guidebook & Model Set. (p. 1363)
Lubera, Logan, illus. see Bowyer, Clifford B.
Luberoff, William, illus. see Cavanaugh, Karen.
Luberto, Bradley. Clide & Druce: A Repulsive Tale of Trolls & Toy Money. (p. 332)
Lubitsky, Maribeth Jenkins, illus. see Angelo, Tony.
Lubka, S. Ruth. Pupniks: The Story of Two Space Dogs (p. 1417)
Lublin, Nancy, et al. Do Something! A Handbook for Young Activists. (p. 457)
Lubner, Susan. Horse's Tale: A Colonial Williamsburg Adventure. Moore, Margie, illus. (p. 800)
—Upside of Ordinary. (p. 1825)
Lubotsky, Dana, jt. reader see Beach, John.
Luca, Bogdan, illus. see Macdonald, Kelly.
Luca, Daniela De, see De Luca, Daniela.
Lucado, Denalyn, jt. auth. see Lucado, Max.
Lucado, Jenna, jt. auth. see Lucado, Max.
Lucado, Max. Best of All. Martinez, Sergio, illus. (p. 170)
—Christmas Story for Children (p. 315)
—En el Ojo de la Tormenta (p. 522)
—Every Day Deserves a Chance: Wake up & Live! (p. 542)
—Experiencing the Heart of Jesus: Knowing His Heart, Feeling His Love (p. 549)
—God's Story, Your Story: When His Becomes Yours (p. 692)
—Hat for Ivan. Wenzel, David, illus. (p. 752)
—Hermie & Friends: A Hermie & Friends Scrapbook & Photo Album. (p. 771)
—It's Not about Me: Live Like You Mean It (p. 897)
—Itsy Bitsy Christmas: You're Never Too Little for His Love (p. 900)
—Just in Case You Ever Wonder (p. 938)
—Max Lucado Children's Treasury: A Child's First Collection (p. 1111)
—Next Door Savior (p. 1249)
—Oak Inside the Acorn Angelini, George, illus. (p. 1274)
—One Hand, Two Hands (p. 1295)
—Plunge! Come Thirsty (p. 1374)
—Punchinello & the Most Marvelous Gift: And, Your Special Gift. Martinez, Sergio, illus. (p. 1416)
—Punchinello & the Most Marvelous Gift. Martinez, Sergio, illus. (p. 1416)
—Song of the King. Gillies, Chuck, illus. (p. 1611)
—Tallest of Smalls Monescillo, Maria, illus. (p. 1704)
—Tell Me the Story: A Story for Eternity. DiCianni, Ron, illus. (p. 1716)
—You Are Mine. Martinez, Sergio, illus. (p. 1973)
—You Are Special. Martinez, Sergio, illus. (p. 1973)
Lucado, Max, jt. auth. see Strack, Jay.
Lucado, Max & Bishop, Jenna Lucado. You Were Made to Make a Difference (p. 1976)
Lucado, Max & Lucado, Denalyn. Lucado Treasury of Bedtime Prayers: Prayers for Bedtime & Every Time of Day! (p. 1062)
Lucado, Max & Lucado, Jenna. Redefining Beautiful: What God Sees When God Sees You (p. 1455)
Lucado, Max & Schmidt, Troy. Buzby, the Misbehaving Bee. (p. 248)
—Flo, the Lyin' Fly. (p. 605)
—Webster, the Scaredy Spider. (p. 1870)
Lucado, Max & Smith, Brian. Turn: Remembering Our Foundations. (p. 1797)
Lucado, Max, creator. Hermie: A Common Caterpillar. (p. 771)
Lucado, Max, et al. Story for Children Bianchi, Fausto, illus. (p. 1657)
—Story for Children: A Storybook Bible. Bianchi, Fausto, illus. (p. 1657)
—Story for Children Bible (p. 1657)
—Story for Kids: Discover the Bible from Beginning to End (p. 1657)
—Your Special Gift. Wenzel, David T. & Wenzel, David, illus. (p. 1981)
Lucado, Max, et al, contrib. by. Hermie Learning Every Day. (p. 771)
Lucan, Dawn. Adventure Memories for Girls. (p. 14)
—Daily Adventure Memories. (p. 399)
—Memories of my Childhood. (p. 1126)
—My Challenge Memories. (p. 1200)
Lucantoni, Peter & Kellas, Lydia. International English Workbook 1. (p. 880)
Lucarelli, Ariana. Volcanoes: Shaping Earth. (p. 1849)
Lucarelli, Marco. Finding Shapes at the Fair: Identify & Describe Shapes. (p. 588)
Lucarelli, Sue, jt. auth. see Curtiss, A. B.
Lucas, Alexander, Jr. O. G. Like Me: Inner Thoughts from an Urban Mind. (p. 1274)
Lucas, Ana Cristina Llompart, tr. see Brocklehurst, Ruth.
Lucas, Andrew. Cataclysm on Cloudholme. (p. 278)
Lucas, Ann Lawson, tr. see Collodi, Carlo.
Lucas, Bruce. Drawing Shapes: Shapes & Their Attributes. (p. 482)
—North America on the Map. (p. 1264)
Lucas, Cedric, jt. auth. see Miller, William.
Lucas, Christopher J. American Higher Education: A History. (p. 61)
Lucas, D J, jt. auth. see Grindley, Sally.
LUCAS, David. Christmas at the Toy Museum. LUCAS, David, illus. (p. 312)
Lucas, David. Letter for Bear. (p. 1002)
—Lying Carpet. Lucas, David, illus. (p. 1066)
—Peanut. Lucas, David, illus. (p. 1332)
—Robot & the Bluebird. Lucas, David, illus. (p. 1480)
LUCAS, David. Skeleton Pirate. (p. 1584)
Lucas, David, illus. see Oram, Hiawyn.
Lucas, Debra. Our Moon. (p. 1309)
Lucas, Derek. Why We Need Hospitals. (p. 1926)
Lucas, Diane, illus. see Anderson, Debra.
Lucas, Diane, illus. see Black, Angie.
Lucas, Diane, illus. see Boudreau, Hélène.
Lucas, Diane, illus. see E.A. Budd.
Lucas, Diane, illus. see Lewis, Wendy.
Lucas, Diane, illus. see Rininger, Alyce.
Lucas, Diane, illus. see Roy Shah, Amita.
Lucas, Diane, illus. see Tatro, MaryAnn.
Lucas, Edward Verall. Forgotten Tales of Long Ago. (p. 620)
Lucas, Eileen. Aaron Burr Treason Trial. (p. 2)
—Cracking the Wall: The Struggles of the Little Rock Nine. Anthony, Mark, illus. (p. 375)
—Little Rock Nine Stand up for Their Rights. Gustavson, Adam, illus. (p. 1036)
—More Than the Blues? Understanding & Dealing with Depression. (p. 1175)
Lucas, Eugene F. New SAT: A Book-LET with Video CD: What It Should Mean to You. (p. 1247)
Lucas, George. Guerre des Etoiles (p. 728)
—Star Wars Episode 2: Attack of the Clones. (p. 1641)
Lucas, George, jt. auth. see Reinhart, Matthew.
Lucas, Ian & Medoza, Chris. Million Year Meal. Cruz, Cheryl, illus. (p. 1144)
Lucas, James, illus. see Simon, Francesca.
Lucas, James E., illus. see Simon, Francesca.
Lucas, Kath, jt. auth. see Durant, Alan.
Lucas, Kristen. Maddy & Scooter: Unlikely Friends. (p. 1069)
Lucas, Lawrence R. Purity. (p. 1419)
Lucas, Lexie. Adventures of Little Boy Brown. (p. 19)
Lucas, Margeaux, illus. see Clay, Kathryn.
Lucas, Margeaux, illus. see Dadey, Debbie.
Lucas, Margeaux, illus. see Golding, Theresa Martin.
Lucas, Margeaux, illus. see Kittinger, Jo S.
Lucas, Margeaux, illus. see Lucas, Sally.
Lucas, Margeaux, illus. see Meachen Rau, Dana & Franco-Feeney, Betsy.
Lucas, Margeaux, illus. see Morton, Carlene.
Lucas, Margeaux, illus. see Nesbitt, Kenn.
Lucas, Margeaux, illus. see Parker, David.
Lucas, Margeaux, illus. see Stone, Tanya Lee.
Lucas, Margeaux, illus. see Williams, Rozanne Lanczak.
Lucas, Margeaux, jt. auth. see Lucas, Sally.
Lucas, Matthew. Roar in the Pinelands. (p. 1478)
Lucas, Nancy T. Peppy's Coral Kingdom. (p. 1340)
Lucas, Nicole A. Sammy Bo Bo Hammy. (p. 1507)
Lucas, Ronne Kay. How the Cactus Got Its Thorns. (p. 812)
Lucas, Sally. Dancing Dinos at the Beach. (p. 402)
—Dancing Dinos at the Beach. Lucas, Margeaux, illus. (p. 402)
Lucas, Sally & Lucas, Margeaux. Dancing Dinos Go to School. (p. 402)
Lucas, Scott. Lies Nostalgia & Cow Gas. (p. 1007)
Lucas, Spencer G., jt. auth. see Guggenheim, Jaenet.
Lucas, Stacey L., illus. see LaBerge, Margaret M.
Lucas, Stephanie M. Miss Annabelle Twinkle Toes. (p. 1151)
Lucas, Vivien. Mathematical Team Games: Enjoyable Activities to Enhance the Curriculum. (p. 1107)
—Puzzle a Day: A Collection of Mathematical Problems for Every Day of the Year. (p. 1420)
Lucasfilm, jt. auth. see Reinhart, Matthew.
Lucasfilm Ltd. Clone Wars (p. 333)
Lucco, Kristine, illus. see Manzione, Lisa.
Luce, Catherine. Milk Horse. Snider, K. C., illus. (p. 1143)
Luce, Clare Boothe, jt. auth. see Shaw, Tucker.
Luce, Pat & Joyner, Holly. How a Bill Becomes a Law: A Complete Tool Kit with Background Information, Primary Sources, & More to Help Students Build Reading & Writing Skills-And Deepen Their Understanding of How Our Government Works. (p. 804)
Luce, Philip. Gotno Tale. (p. 704)
Luce, Willard. Jerry Lindsey: Explorer to the San Juan. Collett, Farrell R., illus. (p. 913)
Lucent Books, ed. see Abramovitz, Melissa.
Lucent Books, ed. see Pearce, Q. L.
Lucent Books, ed. Meningitis. (p. 1126)
—Skateboarding. (p. 1583)
Lucent Books Staff. Selena Gomez. (p. 1549)
Lucent Books Staff, ed. see Hillstrom, Kevin.
Lucent Books Staff, ed. see Mackay, Jenny.
Lucente-Rizzo, Susan, jt. auth. see Macrae, Tammy Vallieres.
Lucerne, Sam. Theocracies. (p. 1729)
Lucero, Erik Kristofer. Ki-Ky the Cat. (p. 951)
Lucero, Jaime. Bilingual Bingo: Easy-to-Make Reproducible Games-in English & Spanish-That Reinforce Key Vocabulary for Emergent Readers & English Language Learners. (p. 186)
—One Little Egg. Kennedy, Kelly, illus. (p. 1295)
Lucero, Jamie, et al. Amazing Word Power: 100 Words Every 4th Grader Should Know. (p. 56)
Lucero, Jessica, illus. see Marquitz, Tim.
Lucero, Len & Tracy, Kristina. How to Roll Like Chris P. Bacon. (p. 821)
Lucero, Sharon. Princess Smile. (p. 1405)
Luces-Tucker, Max. Bobby & Chrissy: One Gift. (p. 206)
Lucey, Donna M. Photographing Montana, 1894-1928: The Life & Work of Evelyn Cameron. (p. 1353)
Lucey, Marcia T. Puzzles & Activities for Children Ages 5-7: Year B. (p. 1421)
—Puzzles & Activities for Children Ages 7-10: Year B. (p. 1421)
Lucey, Marcia T., ed. Catholic Corner: Puzzles & Activities: Year C, Ages 5-7. Radtke, Becky, illus. (p. 280)
Luchesi, Dennis. Benji Rabbit. (p. 165)
Luchsinger, Dena. Sometimes Smart Is Good/A Veces Es Bueno Ser Listo. Jerome, Karen A., illus. (p. 1610)
Luchsinger, Linda, illus. see Poet, Jonny.
Lucht, Susan & Wilson, Mollie. Olden Days of Medina: A Children's Guide to Medina History. Allman, Cynthia, illus. (p. 1285)
Lucía, Baquedano Azcona, jt. auth. see Baquedano, Lucia Azcona.
Lucia, Doriane. Story of Lilly & Lou: Based on a True Story. DeVito, Anthony T., illus. (p. 1658)
Lucia Kemp, Henry. Now I Know My Alphabet & Phonics. (p. 1269)
—Now I Know My Word Families & Sight Words. (p. 1269)
Luciani, Brigitte. Carnival. Tharlet, Eve, illus. (p. 270)
—How Will We Get to the Beach? Tharlet, Eve, illus. (p. 823)
—Hubbub. Gauvin, Edward, tr. from FRE. (p. 824)
—Meeting. Burrell, Carol, tr. from FRE. (p. 1123)
—Peace & Quiet. Burrell, Carol, tr. (p. 1331)
—What a Team! Gauvin, Edward, tr. from FRE. (p. 1878)
Luciani, Brigitte & Tharlet, Eve. How Will We Get to the Beach?/Como Iremos a la Playa? An English-Spanish Guessing-Game Story. (p. 823)
Luciano, Sonia. Mr. I Forgot. (p. 1185)
Lucier, Makila. Death-Struck Year. (p. 420)
Lucie-Smith, Edward, et al, comments. David Remfry: Dancers. (p. 411)
Lucini, Carmen, illus. see Plaza, José María & María, Plaza José.
Lucini, Chata, illus. see Gisbert, Joan Manuel.
Lucini, Chata, jt. auth. see Mateos, Pilar.
Lucio, Mick. Kings for a Day: A Western. (p. 960)
Lucio, Miguel Martinez, ed. see Alonso Benito, L. E.
Luck, Carolyn, ed. see Harte, Lawrence & Sutton, Kyle.
Luck, Gail. Bumduggle Davis Beats the Boobrats or the Inauguration of the Motherless Club. (p. 241)
—Bumduggle Davis Bites off More Than He Can Chew: Or You Can't Make an Omelette Without Breaking Eggs. (p. 241)
—Bumduggle Davis Joins the Dots: Or It's All There in Black & White. (p. 241)
Lück, Stefanie. Carla's Worlds. (p. 270)
Lucke, Deb. Book of Time Outs: A Mostly True History of the World's Biggest Troublemakers. Lucke, Deb, illus. (p. 212)
—Sneezenesia. (p. 1597)
Lucke, Deb, illus. see Gunderson, Jessica.
Lucke, Deb, illus. see Pulver, Robin.
Lucke, Karen. Simmer Diaries: Lost & Found. (p. 1577)
Luckemeyer, Norma, illus. see Witschen, Kay.
Lucken, Eve M. Tree, the Crazy Leaf, & Me. (p. 1783)
Luckett, Kathy. Little Library Literacy: Does your Father Snore? Afrikaans. van Heerden, Marjorie, illus. (p. 1030)
—Little Library Literacy: Does your Father Snore? Sesotho. van Heerden, Marjorie, illus. (p. 1030)
—Little Library Literacy: Does your Father Snore? Setswana. van Heerden, Marjorie, illus. (p. 1030)
—Little Library Literacy: Does your Father Snore? Tsonga. van Heerden, Marjorie, illus. (p. 1030)
—Little Library Literacy: Does your Father Snore? Venda. van Heerden, Marjorie, illus. (p. 1030)
Luckey, Bud, illus. see RH Disney Staff.
Luckhurst, Matthew. Paul Bunyan & Babe the Blue Ox: The Great Pancake Adventure. (p. 1330)
Luckiesh, Matthew. Language of Color. (p. 975)
Luckritz, Gratti C. Christopher's Duck. (p. 317)
Lucks, Naomi. Makeda (Queen of Sheba) (p. 1080)
Lucky, A. E. Kyle the Detective (p. 969)
Lucky (The Cat). My 9 8 7 6 5 4 3 2 1 Lives: A Cat's Tail of Her near Death & Life Experiences. (p. 1195)
LuckySports. Adventures in SportsLand - the Golf Bully (with accompanying CD) The Golf Bully. (p. 15)
Lucot, Erica, illus. see Pursh, Eric.
Lucy Cousins, illus. see Cousins, Lucy.
Lucy Fitch Perkins. Dutch Twins. (p. 490)
Luddy, Karon. Spelldown: The Big-Time Dreams of a Small-Town Word Whiz. (p. 1625)
Ludeke, Amalia H., jt. auth. see Ludeke, Kenneth L.
Ludeke, Kenneth L. & Ludeke, Amalia H. Day with Anion, an Ion Science. (p. 414)
Luder, Doreen. Dax the Last Dragon. (p. 412)
Ludgate, Kevin. Pilgrim Village: A Thanksgiving Diorama (p. 1358)
Ludin, Marine, illus. see Saïd.
Ludlam, Jamie, illus. see Whitaker, Sue.
Ludlow, Patricia, illus. see Augustine, Peg.
Ludlow, Patricia, illus. see Cooper, Gilly Cameron.
Ludlow, Patricia D., illus. see McCaughrean, Geraldine.
Ludlow, Susan, jt. auth. see Mills, Nathan.
Ludman, Mark D. & Wynbrandt, James. Encyclopedia of Genetic Disorders & Birth Defects. (p. 525)
Ludvigsen, Henning, illus. see Clark, Stuart.
Ludvik, Elizabeth. Butterflies & Dragon Tears: A Pacific Northwest Quileute Legend Come to Life for Children. Forrest, Amber, illus. (p. 247)
—Toymakers New Job: The Story of Why Santa Claus Dedicated His Life to Serving the Children Around the World. Forrest, Amber, illus. (p. 1774)
Ludwig, Ashley. You Tickle My Heart: and other ways you make me laugh. (p. 1976)
Ludwig, Dellena. Where Did Dinosaurs Come From? (p. 1906)
Ludwig, Elisa. Pretty Crooked. (p. 1398)
—Pretty Sly. (p. 1398)
—Pretty Wanted. (p. 1398)
Ludwig, Elisa, jt. auth. see Abrams, Dennis.
Ludwig, Sabine. Story of the Little Pig Who Couldn't Say No. Wilharm, Sabine, illus. (p. 1661)
Ludwig, Trudy. Better Than You. Gustavson, Adam, illus. (p. 172)
—Confessions of a Former Bully. (p. 356)
—Confessions of a Former Bully. Adams, Beth, illus. (p. 356)
—Gifts from the Enemy. Orback, Craig, illus. (p. 675)
—Invisible Boy. Barton, Patrice, illus. (p. 885)
—Just Kidding. Gustavson, Adam, illus. (p. 939)
—Mi Enemiga Secreta. Hernandez, Aurora, tr. (p. 1132)
—My Secret Bully. Marble, Abigail, illus. (p. 1218)
—Sorry! Manning, Maurie J., illus. (p. 1614)
—Too Perfect. Fields, Lisa, illus. (p. 1767)
—Trouble Talk. Prevost, Mikela, illus. (p. 1790)
Ludy, Mark. Jujo: The Youngest Tribesman. Ludy, Mark, illus. (p. 932)
—Noah: A Wordless Picture Book. (p. 1261)
Ludy, Mark, illus. see Matott, J. P. & Baker, Margaret.
Ludy, Mark, illus. see Matott, Justin.

L

Lue Sue, Majella, illus. see O'Connell, Rebecca.
Luebbermann, Mimi. Heirloom Tomato Cookbook. Holmes, Robert & Mills, Dan, photos by. (p. 762)
Luebering, J. E., ed. 100 Most Influential Writers of All Time. (p. 1998)
Luebke, Gayle M. There's A Bug in My Bed. (p. 1730)
—When I Grow Up. (p. 1902)
Luebke, Rose. Beagle Bailey Looks for a Job. (p. 150)
Luebs, Robin. Please Pick Me up, Mama! Luebs, Robin, illus. (p. 1373)
Luebs, Robin, illus. see Moore, Raina.
Luebs, Robin, illus. see Ruddell, Deborah.
Luebs Shepherd, Rajean. C Is for Cornhusker: A Nebraska Alphabet. Appleoff, Sandy, illus. (p. 250)
Lueck, Andrew M. Chicabee. (p. 299)
Luecke, Richard A. & Patterson, James G. How to Become a Better Negotiator (p. 815)
Luedecke, Bev, illus. see Hall, Kirsten.
Luedeke, Lisa. Smashed. (p. 1593)
Lueders, Tamara Devitre. Hoagie, the Hockey Turtle. (p. 786)
Luedke, Robert James. Eye Witness: A Fictional Tale of Absolute Truth. (p. 558)
Luedtke, Courtney. Baby Boo: The Happy Beginning. (p. 125)
Lueer, Carmen A., illus. see Nees, Diane L.
Luenebrink, Judy, illus. see George, Elizabeth.
Luenn, Nancy. Gift for Abuelita/Un Regalo para Abuelita: Celebrating the Day of the Dead/En Celebration del Dia de los Muertos. Chapman, Robert, illus. (p. 675)
Lueth, Nathan, illus. see Barlow, Steve & Skidmore, Steve.
Lueth, Nathan, illus. see Mikkelsen, Jon.
Luetkemeyer, Jenny. Jesus, I Trust in You! The Story of Saint Faustina, Missionary of Divine Mercy. Kiszkurno, Irene & Chacon, Cesar, trs. (p. 915)
Luevano, Raul, illus. see Gifford, Dorinda.
Luevano, Richard. Uncle Bun Bun's Abc's of the Animal World. (p. 1811)
Luff, Barbara K. Tea Time. (p. 1708)
Luff, Ian, jt. auth. see Banham, Dale.
Lufkin, Raymond, illus. see Holt, Stephen & Lewis, Oscar.
Lüftner, Kai. Lily Loves. Drews, Judith, illus. (p. 1018)
Lugaro, Maria. Stardust from Meteorites: An Introduction to Presolar Grains. (p. 1642)
Lugibihl, Robert. Pandora: Love & War. (p. 1321)
Luginbuhl, Susan. Puppies from Heaven. (p. 1418)
Lugira, Aloysius M. & Palmer, Martin. World Religions (p. 1958)
Lugo, Patricia, jt. auth. see Woods, Jeanne.
Lugo, Patrick, illus. see Fusco, John.
Lugthart, Kim, ed. Historical Maps of Montana: Educator's Edition. (p. 783)
Lugtu, Carol J. Clown Fish [Scholastic]. (p. 335)
Lugtu, Carol J., jt. auth. see Lindeen, Carol K.
Lugtu, Carol J., et al. Under the Sea (p. 1814)
Luh, Shu Shin. Economy of China: The History of Culture of China. (p. 503)
—Economy of China. (p. 503)
—Economy of China. Wang, Jianwei, ed. (p. 503)
—People of China. (p. 1339)
—People of China. Wang, Jianwei, ed. (p. 1339)
Luhmann, Edward Q., jt. auth. see Nielsen, Pamela.
Luhrs, Henry, illus. see Hale, Helen.
Luhrs, Jeannece Jackson, jt. auth. see Lester, Vivian.
Lui, Tai-lok, jt. auth. see Chiu, Stephen.
Luigart-Stayner, Becky, photos by see McDermott, Nancie.
Luigart-Staynes, Becky, photos by see McDermott, Nancie.
Luiken, Nicole. Dreamfire. (p. 484)
—Dreamline. (p. 484)
—Frost. (p. 644)
Luirette, William Blaine. Frank the Snowman. (p. 629)
Luis, Olaizola José, jt. auth. see Luis, Olaizola José.
Luis, Olaizola José & Luis, Olaizola José. Micaela No Sabe Jugar. (p. 1134)
Luisa, Gioffre-Suzuki, illus. see Asselin, Kristine Carlson.
Luiso, Lisa. What Daddy Sees in San Francisco. (p. 1881)
—What Mommy Sees in San Francisco. (p. 1892)
Luiso, Lisa, jt. auth. see Allvord, Crash.
Luiz, Fernando. Babies Love the Little Things. (p. 124)
—How to Be a Princess: A Girly Girl Book. (p. 814)
Luiz, Fernando, illus. see Kelly, Martin.
Luizada, A., illus. see Simhoni, S.
Lujan Ed.D., Nan. Snoozles. Montgomery, Samantha, illus. (p. 1598)
Luján, Jorge. Colors! / ¡Colores! Simon, John Oliver & Parfitt, Rebecca, trs. (p. 345)
—Doggy Slippers Amado, Elisa, tr. from SPA. (p. 462)
—Numeralia Ouriou, Susan, tr. from SPA. (p. 1272)
—Rooster Gallo. Amado, Elisa, tr. (p. 1488)
Luján, Jorge, jt. auth. see Lujan, Jorge Elias.
Lujan, Jorge, tr. see Jeffers, Oliver.
Lujan, Jorge Elias. Gitana de las Flores. Monroy, Manuel, illus. (p. 681)
—Vaca Roja. Nava, Francisco, illus. (p. 1829)
Lujan, Jorge Elias & Luján, Jorge. Winter Afternoon (Tarde de Invierno) Amado, Elisa, tr. (p. 1938)
Luján, Jorge, et al. Palabras Manzana. Marín, Manuel, illus. (p. 1319)
Lujan, Michael L., creator. Mentoring Minds' Smart Chart: 1st Grade. (p. 1127)
—Mentoring Minds' Smart Chart: 2nd Grade. (p. 1127)
—Mentoring Minds' Smart Chart: 3rd Grade. (p. 1127)
—Mentoring Minds' Smart Chart: 4th Grade. (p. 1127)
—Mentoring Minds' Smart Chart: 5th Grade. (p. 1127)
—Mentoring Minds' Smart Chart: 6th Grade. (p. 1127)
—Mentoring Minds' Smart Chart: Head Start. (p. 1127)
—Mentoring Minds' Smart Chart: Kindergarten. (p. 1127)
—Mentoring Minds' Smart Chart: Birth - 3 Years. (p. 1127)
—Mentoring Minds' Smart Chart: Pre-Kindergarten. (p. 1127)
Lujan, Tonita, illus. see Clark, Ann Nolan.
Luk, Hoenie W., jt. auth. see Wong, Pindy Y.
Lukachko, Mary Louise. Peter the Blue Penguin. (p. 1347)
Lukacs, Krisztian. Bud & Barnie: 2 Tales. (p. 234)
—Bud & Barnie: Let's Paint! (p. 234)
Lukas, Catherine. Bears. (p. 151)
—Hooray for Mother's Day! Cavender, Bernie, illus. (p. 796)
Lukas, Catherine & Artifact Group, The. Trouble on the Train. (p. 1790)
Lukas, Mary, illus. see Drogo, Susette.
Lukatz, Casey, illus. see Chobanian, Elizabeth & American Girl Publishing Staff, eds.
Lukatz, Casey, illus. see Chobanian, Elizabeth, ed.
Lukatz, Casey, illus. see Maring, Therese, ed.
Lukavics, Amy. Daughters unto Devils. (p. 410)
Luke, Jacqueline. Yellow Pea in the Pod. (p. 1970)
Luke, Melinda. Green Dog. Manning, Jane K., illus. (p. 721)
—Perro Verde; the Green Dog. (p. 1344)
Luke, Pauline. Amber Pash on Pink. (p. 57)
lukel, Onur, illus. see Pierro, Rita.
Luker, Lynne M. Mr Mushroom's Busy Day: Little Forest People. (p. 1185)
Luker, Myrna, jt. auth. see LeeAnn, Jodi.
Luker, Penny. Green Book. (p. 721)
Lukes, Bonnie L. Henry Wadsworth Longfellow: America's Beloved Poet. (p. 768)
—John Adams: Public Servant. (p. 921)
—Soldier's Courage: The Story of Stephen Crane. (p. 1607)
—Woodrow Wilson & the Progressive Era. (p. 1949)
Lukes, Jessica, jt. auth. see Weiss, Carrie.
Lukesh, Jean A. Lucky Ears: The True Story of Ben Kuroki, World War II Hero. (p. 1062)
—My Favorite Dog & Cat Story: My Favorite Dog Story/My Favorite Cat Story. Lukesh, Ronald E., illus. (p. 1203)
—Nebraska Adventure. (p. 1239)
—Sky Rider: Story of Evelyn Sharp, World War II WASP. (p. 1587)
Lukesh, Ronald E., illus. see Lukesh, Jean A.
Lukic, Dragan. Friend to Friend. Vuchic-Radovich, Sladjana, tr. (p. 637)
Lukitsh, Joanne. Julia Margaret Cameron. (p. 932)
Lukjanenko, Anna, ed. see AZ Books Staff.
Lukkarinen, Ritva. Amy. Vainio, Pirkko, illus. (p. 66)
Lulu.com, ed. see Mistretta, Jay Francis.
Lum, Bernice, illus. see Biskup, Agnieszka, et al.
Lum, Bernice, illus. see Biskup, Agnieszka.
Lum, Bernice, illus. see Hartley, Steve.
Lum, Bernice, illus. see Murphy, Stuart J.
Lum, Bernice, illus. see Swanson, Jennifer Ann.
Lum, Bernice, illus. see Swanson, Jennifer, et al.
Lum, Bernice, illus. see Swanson, Jennifer.
Lum, Bernice, illus. see Warwick, Ellen.
Lum, Bernice, illus. see Weakland, Mark Andrew.
Lum, Bernice, illus. see Weakland, Mark.
Lum, Bernice, tr. see Warwick, Ellen.
Lum, J., illus. see Torres, J.
Lum, Kate. Princesses Are Not Just Pretty. Hellard, Sue, illus. (p. 1406)
Lum, Kwei-lin. Chinatown Paper Dolls. (p. 307)
—Twisted Fairy Tales Paper Dolls. (p. 1802)
—Voodoo Paper Dolls. (p. 1850)
Lum, Kwei-lin, et al. Speakeasy Paper Dolls: Fabulous Flappers & More from the Roaring Twenties. (p. 1623)
Lum, Leimomi o. Kamahae Kuamoo Mookini. Legend of Kuamo'o Mo'okini & Hamumu the Great Whale. Kam, Kathleen, illus. (p. 988)
Lum, Misha Anne. Sleepy Time, Baby Mine (p. 1590)
Lumb, Steve, illus. see Afzal, Uz.
Lumb, Steve, photos by see Kelly, Maoliosa.
Lumer, Marc. When Miracles Happened- Wondrous Stories of Tzaddikim. (p. 1903)
Lumer, Marc, illus. see Altein, Chani.
Lumer, Marc, illus. see Blitz, Shmuel & Zakon, Miriam Stark.
Lumer, Marc, illus. see Burston, Chaim & Naiditch, Dov.
Lumer, Marc, illus. see Segal, Nechamy.
Lumley, Brian. House of the Temple. Clark, Alan M. & Koszowski, Allen, illus. (p. 803)
—Nonesuch & Others. (p. 1263)
Lumley, Jemima. Journey Home from Grandpa's. Fatus, Sophie, illus. (p. 928)
Lumley, Jemima & Penner, Fred. Journey Home from Grandpa's. Fatus, Sophie, illus. (p. 928)
Lumley, Stef, photos by see Dickins, Rosie.
Lumpkin, Kenya. Quechning the Fire: Many Waters Cannont Quench Love. Lee, Mykle & Shefield, April, eds. (p. 1424)
Lumpkin, Susan, jt. auth. see Seidensticker, John.
Lumry, Amanda & Hurwitz, Laura. Adventures of Riley: Dolphins in Danger. McIntyre, Sarah, illus. (p. 22)
—Adventures of Riley: Mission to Madagascar. McIntyre, Sarah, illus. (p. 22)
—Amazon River Rescue. McIntyre, Sarah, illus. (p. 56)
—Operation Orangutan. (p. 1300)
—Polar Bear Puzzle. (p. 1379)
—Polar Bear Puzzle. (p. 1379)
—Project Panda. (p. 1410)
—Riddle of the Reef. (p. 1470)
—South Pole Penguins. (p. 1617)
—Survival of the Salmon. (p. 1686)
—Tigers in Terai. McIntyre, Sarah, illus. (p. 1749)
Lumry, Amanda, et al. Safari in South Africa. (p. 1502)
Lumsden, Colin. Apostles. (p. 92)
—Hebrews Men of Faith. (p. 761)
—John the Baptist. (p. 923)
—Miracles of Jesus. (p. 1149)
—Parables of Jesus. (p. 1323)
—People in the Life of Jesus. (p. 1339)
—People in the Life of Paul. (p. 1339)
—Story of Mary. (p. 1659)
—Story of Paul. (p. 1659)
—Story of Peter. (p. 1659)
Lumsden, Matt, illus. see Burggraaf, Deborah.
Luna, Abuela. Another Voice Sings in the Forest. Pecos NM After School Program Staff, illus. (p. 88)
—How the Earth Heard Music. Pecos,, 4th & 5th grade Art Students, & 5th grade Art Students, illus. (p. 813)
Luna, Arcadio. Al Reves Esta Bien. Cicero, Julian, illus. (p. 32)
Luna, Danielle. Precious & Loved. (p. 1394)
Luna, Gayla. Rafting on the South China Sea. (p. 1433)
Luna, James & Villarroel, Carolina. Runaway Piggy/El Cochinito Fugitivo. Lacámara, Laura, illus. (p. 1496)
Luna, James, et al. Place Where You Live / El Lugar donde Vives. Muraida, Thelma, illus. (p. 1366)
Luna, Jose'. Queso y la Rata: With English Subtitles. Luna, Jose', illus. (p. 1426)
Luna, Lauren, illus. see Houston, Alecia.
Luna, Margarita, illus. see Baranda, Maria.
Luna, Margarita, illus. see Estrada, Jorge Antonio.
Luna, Pilar P. Hello, Sunny Day! (p. 765)
Luna, Rachel Nickerson. Haunting of Captain Snow. (p. 754)
—Murder Aboard the California Girl. (p. 1192)
—Strange Disappearance of Agatha Buck. (p. 1665)
Luna Rising Editors. Great Southwest Activity Book. (p. 718)
Luna, Sagrario & Alcott, Louisa May. Mujercitas. González, Ángel Luis, tr. (p. 1189)
Luna, Tom. Spots on the Jaguar: A Counting Book. Luna, Tom & Alvarez, Laura, illus. (p. 1634)
Lunablau, Jani. Little Snowflake. (p. 1036)
Lunch Lab LLC, Lunch Lab, illus. see Candlewick Press, Candlewick.
Lunch Lab Staff, illus. see Candlewick Press Staff.
Lunchbox Lessons Staff, creator. Neighborhood Naturalist. (p. 1240)
Lund, Brian, illus. see Verstraete, Larry.
Lund, Celia. Square Sails & Dragons. (p. 1636)
Lund, Charles. Math Games & Activies with Cards. (p. 1106)
—Math games & Activities with Dice. (p. 1106)
—Math in the Cards. (p. 1106)
—Place Mat Math (p. 1365)
Lund, Deb. All Aboard the Dinotrain. Fine, Howard, illus. (p. 42)
—All Day Long: A Book of Partner Prayers. Conahan, Carolyn Digby, illus. (p. 44)
—Dinosailors. Fine, Howard, illus. (p. 441)
—Dinosoaring. Fine, Howard, illus. (p. 445)
Lund, Deborah. Me & God: A Book of Partner Prayers. Conahan, Carolyn Digby, illus. (p. 1115)
Lund, Deborah S. Tell Me My Story, Mama. Nakata, Hiroe, illus. (p. 1716)
—Waiting for Me. (p. 1852)
Lund, Evelyn. It Happened on Alphabet Street. (p. 894)
Lund, Flauna. Indigo. (p. 872)
Lund, J. L. Temple of Kahmahrgx. (p. 1718)
Lund, Jillian. Have You Ever Seen a Jackalope? (p. 754)
Lund, Laurel. When Glory Got Her Glow Back: A Glowworm's Tail. (p. 1902)
Lund, Nancy, jt. auth. see Guilard, Pamela.
Lund, Nancy M., illus. see Haller, Christine A.
Lund, Wendy E. Fly Away Balloon. (p. 609)
Lundberg, Constance. Why We Need Water. (p. 1926)
Lundbergh, Holger, tr. from SWE. Swedish Folk Tales Bauer, John, illus. (p. 1689)
Lundblad, Kristina, jt. auth. see Kalman, Bobbie.
Lundblad, Kristina & Kalman, Bobbie. Animales llamados Peces. (p. 81)
—Animals Called Fish. (p. 82)
Lunde, Darrin. Dirty Rats? Gustavson, Adam, illus. (p. 446)
—Discovering a New Animal with a Scientist. (p. 448)
—Hello, Bumblebee Bat. Wynne, Patricia J., illus. (p. 763)
—Meet the Meerkat. Wynne, Patricia J., illus. (p. 1123)
Lunde, Darrin P. After the Kill. Stock, Catherine, illus. (p. 28)
—Hello, Mama Wallaroo. Wynne, Patricia J., illus. (p. 764)
—Monkey Colors. Wynne, Patricia J., illus. (p. 1165)
Lunde, Darrin P. & Stock, Catherine. Hello, Baby Beluga. Wynne, Patricia J., illus. (p. 763)
Lunde, Stein Erik. My Father's Arms Are a Boat. Dickson, Kari, tr. from NOR. (p. 1203)
Lundebrek, Amy. Under the Night Sky Rich, Anna, illus. (p. 1813)
Lunden, Vickie. From Horses to Unicorns. (p. 643)
Lundgren, Jodi & Second Story Press Staff. Leap (p. 982)
Lundgren, Julie. Eagles. (p. 492)
—Hawks. (p. 755)
—Kites. (p. 962)
—Owls. (p. 1315)
—Vultures. (p. 1851)
Lundgren, Julie, jt. auth. see Lundgren, Julie.
Lundgren, Julie & Lundgren, Julie. Owls. (p. 1315)
Lundgren, Julie K. Animal Adaptations. (p. 76)
—Animal Habitats. (p. 78)
—Apple Trees & the Seasons. (p. 92)
—Bringing up Bamboo. (p. 229)
—Butterflies & Moths. (p. 247)
—Camping. (p. 257)
—Chickens. (p. 300)
—Desert Dinners: Studying Food Webs in the Desert. (p. 429)
—Earth: The Living Planet. (p. 495)
—Eating & the Digestive System. (p. 501)
—Frogs & Toads. (p. 641)
—Hiking. (p. 779)
—How Do Humans Depend on Earth? (p. 807)
—How Do Plants Grow? (p. 807)
—How Ecosystems Work. (p. 809)
—I Look Like My Mother. (p. 841)
—Life Cycles (p. 1009)
—Moon: Earth's Satellite. (p. 1171)
—Plant Adaptations. (p. 1368)
—Plant Life Cycles. (p. 1369)
—Plants As Food, Fuel, & Medicine. (p. 1370)
—Plants Make Their Own Food. (p. 1370)
—Reproduction in Plants. (p. 1461)
—Run, Swim, Fly. (p. 1496)
—Seeds, Bees, & Pollen. (p. 1547)
—Skeletons & Exoskeletons. (p. 1584)
—Squirrels. (p. 1637)
—STEM Jobs with the Environment. (p. 1647)
—Sun: Energy for Our Solar System. (p. 1675)
—Sunflowers. (p. 1676)
—What Do Critters Do in the Winter? (p. 1882)
—What's on the Food Chain Menu? (p. 1899)
—Who Do I Look Like? A Book about Animal Babies. (p. 1915)
—Why Plants Become Extinct. (p. 1925)
—¿Cómo Crecen Las Plantas? / How Do Plants Grow? (p. 350)
Lundin, Maria, tr. see Forssberg, Manne.
Lundin, Stephen C., jt. auth. see Hagerman, Carr.
Lundin, Stephen C., et al. Fish! for Life: A Remarkable Way to Achieve Your Dreams. (p. 598)
—Fish! Sticks: A Remarkable Way to Adapt to Changing Times & Keep Your Work Fresh. (p. 598)
Lundquist, David R., photos by see Peterson, Cris.
Lundquist, Jean M. Recycling, Step by Step (p. 1453)
Lundquist, Jeanne L., jt. auth. see Lundquist, Joegil K.
Lundquist, Jenny. Opal Crown. (p. 1299)
—Plastic Polly. (p. 1370)
—Princess in the Opal Mask. (p. 1404)
—Seeing Cinderella. (p. 1548)
Lundquist, Joegil K. English from the Roots up I: Help for Reading, Writing, Spelling & S. A. T. Scores. (p. 530)
Lundquist, Joegil K. & Lundquist, Jeanne L. English from the Roots up Volume II: Help for Reading, Writing, Spelling, & S. A. T. Scores (p. 530)
—English from the Roots up, Volume II: Help for Reading, Writing, Spelling & S. A. T. Scores. (p. 530)
Lundquist, Mary. Cat & Bunny. Lundquist, Mary, illus. (p. 277)
Lundquist, Mary, illus. see DiPucchio, Kelly.
Lundquist, Mary, illus. see Hood, Susan.
Lundquist, Robert, illus. see Griffiths, Deborah.
Lundsten, Apryl. Girls' Life Guide to Being a Style Superstar! Parett, Lisa, illus. (p. 680)
—Smart Girl's Guide to Parties: How to Be a Great Guest, Be a Happy Hostess, & Have Fun at Any Party. Anton, Carrie, ed. (p. 1592)
Lundstrom, Norma Niemi. Chubby Girl. (p. 317)
Lundy, Charlotte. Thank You, God. Waldrep, Evelyn L., ed. (p. 1725)
—Thank You, Jesus. Waldrep, Evelyn L., ed. (p. 1725)
—Thank You, Peter. Waldrep, Evelyn L., ed. (p. 1725)
—Thank You, Ruth & Naomi. Waldrep, Evelyn L., ed. (p. 1725)
Lundy, Kathleen Gould. In a Class of Her Own. Alward, Jeff, illus. (p. 863)
Lundy, Miranda & Mcnaughton, Phoebe. Sacred Number: The Secret Quality of Quantities. Lundy, Miranda et al, illus. (p. 1500)
Luneau, Terri Robert. Big Woods Bird: An Ivory-Bill Story. Bennett, Trevor, illus. (p. 184)
Lunelli, Giuliano, illus. see Perrault, Charles.
Lunetta, Demitria. In the After. (p. 865)
—In the End. (p. 866)
Lunge-Larsen, Lise. Adventures of Thor the Thunder God. Madsen, Jim, illus. (p. 24)
—Gifts from the Gods: Ancient Words & Wisdom from Greek & Roman Mythology. Hinds, Gareth, illus. (p. 675)
—Race of the Birkebeiners. Azarian, Mary, illus. (p. 1431)
Lunianski, Stephanie. Luke's Perfect Day. (p. 1064)
Lunievicz, Joe. Open Wounds. (p. 1299)
Luning, Barbara. Quilted Zoo. (p. 1428)
Lunis, Natalie. arte de hacer tarjetas y Regalos: Set Of 6. (p. 103)
—Backyard Scientist. (p. 131)
—Baking Bread. (p. 133)
—Black Spiny-Tailed Iguana: Lizard Lightning! (p. 197)
—Blue-Ringed Octopus: Small but Deadly. (p. 203)
—Box Jellyfish: Killer Tentacles. (p. 216)
—Bugs All Around. (p. 237)
—California Sea Lion: Fast & Smart! (p. 253)
—Capybara: The World's Largest Rodent. (p. 265)
—Cars. (p. 272)
—Cars & Los Carros: 6 English, 6 Spanish Adaptations (p. 272)
—Cheetah: Speed Demon! (p. 296)
—Chihuahua: Señor Tiny. (p. 301)
—Comfort Dogs. (p. 348)
—Coyote: The Barking Dog. (p. 374)
—Crawling Crabs. (p. 377)
—Crows. (p. 386)
—Dachshund: The Hot Dogger. (p. 398)
—Deadly Black Widows. (p. 417)
—Dinero: Set Of 6. (p. 440)
—Eerie Inns. (p. 505)
—Electric Animals. (p. 508)
—Fun with Fingerprints. (p. 648)
—Furry Ferrets. (p. 650)
—German Shepherd: Super Smart. (p. 666)
—Giant Weta: The World's Biggest Grasshopper. (p. 674)
—Glow-in-the-Dark Animals. (p. 685)
—Gooey Jellyfish. (p. 702)
—Gravity-Defying Animals. (p. 712)
—Green Iguanas. (p. 722)
—Green Tree Frogs: Colorful Hiders. (p. 722)
—Greyhound: Canine Blur! (p. 723)
—Growing a Kitchen Garden & un jardín en la Cocina: 6 English, 6 Spanish Adaptations (p. 726)
—Haunted Caves. (p. 753)
—Hippopotamus. (p. 781)
—Hippo—River Horse. (p. 781)
—Historia de Las Celebraciones: Set Of 6. (p. 782)
—History Behind the Holidays & la historia de las Celebraciones: 6 English, 6 Spanish Adaptations (p. 783)
—Household Inventions: From Toilets to Toasters. (p. 804)
—Howler Monkey: Super Loud. (p. 823)
—Humpback Whale: The Singer. (p. 827)
—Hyena: Who's Laughing? (p. 831)
—Inside the Spider's Web. (p. 877)
—Inside the Tarantula's Burrow. (p. 877)
—Jack Russell Terrier: Bundle of Energy. (p. 903)
—jardín en la Cocina. (p. 909)
—Katydids: Leaf Look-Alikes. (p. 946)
—Killer Whale: The World's Largest Dolphin. (p. 956)
—Komodo Dragon: The World's Biggest Lizard. (p. 966)
—Las Plantas y Los Animales: Set Of 6. (p. 977)
—Leggy Centipedes. (p. 990)
—Lifeguard Dogs. (p. 1013)
—Los Carros: Set Of 6. (p. 1053)
—Los Colores: Set Of 6. (p. 1053)
—Los Volcanes: Set Of 6. (p. 1054)
—Making a Bug Habitat. (p. 1080)
—Making a Terrarium. (p. 1080)
—Making a Weather Station. (p. 1080)

—Making Great Greeting Cards Gifts & el arte de hacer tarjetas y Regalos: 6 English, 6 Spanish Adaptations (p. 1081)
—Making Ice Cream. (p. 1081)
—Miniature Horses. (p. 1146)
—Mockingbird: Noisy Mimic. (p. 1157)
—Money & el Dinero: 6 English, 6 Spanish Adaptations (p. 1164)
—Ocean Monsters. (p. 1276)
—Ostrich: The World's Biggest Bird. (p. 1306)
—Peregrine Falcon: Dive, Dive, Dive! (p. 1341)
—Pet-Sized Dinos. (p. 1345)
—Plant & Animal Partners & Las plantas y los Animales: 6 English, 6 Spanish Adaptations (p. 1368)
—Portuguese Man-of-War: Floating Misery. (p. 1387)
—Potbellied Pigs. (p. 1388)
—Prickly Sea Stars. (p. 1398)
—Pronghorn: Long-Distance Runner! (p. 1411)
—Red Kangaroo: The World's Largest Marsupial. (p. 1454)
—See-Through Animals. (p. 1547)
—Shape-Shifting Animals. (p. 1560)
—Sky Terrors. (p. 1587)
—Slimy Sea Slugs. (p. 1590)
—Spooky Schools. (p. 1631)
—Squirting Squids. (p. 1637)
—Squishy Sponges. (p. 1637)
—Stinging Scorpions. (p. 1651)
—Stormy Weather And ¡Tormentas! 6 English, 6 Spanish Adaptations Hanner, Albert, illus. (p. 1656)
—T. Rex Named Sue: Sue Hendrickson's Huge Discovery. (p. 1694)
—Three-Toed Sloths: Green Mammals. (p. 1744)
—Tiny Titanosaurs: Luis Chiappe's Dinosaur Nests. (p. 1757)
—Tragic Theaters. (p. 1776)
—Tricky Tree Frogs. (p. 1786)
—Tut's Deadly Tomb. (p. 1799)
—Volcanoes. (p. 1849)
—Watching the Night Sky. (p. 1861)
—Wiggly Earthworms. (p. 1928)
—¡Tormentas! Hanner, Albert, illus. (p. 1770)
Lunis, Natalie & Johnston, Paul F. Lost Cities. (p. 1055)
Lunis, Natalie & Pushies, Fred J. Takedown of Osama Bin Laden. (p. 1697)
Lunis, Natalie & Sereno, Paul C. Supercroc: Paul Sereno's Dinosaur Eater. (p. 1683)
Lunis, Natalie & Taylor, Troy. Haunted Capital. (p. 753)
Lunis, Natalie & White, Nancy. Being a Scientist. (p. 160)
—Exploring Everyday Wonders. (p. 552)
—Investigating Rocks. (p. 885)
—Popcorn Science. (p. 1384)
—Savage Slashers. (p. 1516)
—World of Change. (p. 1956)
Lunn, Corey, illus. see Night & Day Studios.
Lunn, Janet. Amos's Sweater Lafave, Kim, illus. (p. 65)
—Double Spell. (p. 473)
—Laura Secord: A Story of Courage. Newhouse, Maxwell, illus. (p. 980)
—One Hundred Shining Candles. Grater, Lindsay, illus. (p. 1295)
Lunn, John. Aquanauts. (p. 93)
—Mariner's Curse. (p. 1094)
Lunn, Naomi, illus. see McCormack, Chris.
Lunney, Linda Hayward. Monster Bug. Palmisciano, Diane, tr. (p. 1166)
Lunny, June C. Spirit of the Yukon. (p. 1628)
Lunsford, Gary. Georgia Is on My Mind: A Tale of a Guardian Angel. (p. 665)
Lunsford, Judy. Sally & the Buccaneers. (p. 1505)
Lunsford, Russell. Benjamin Nathan Tuggle: Adventurer: Daniel Boone & the Settlement of Boonesborough, Kentucky. (p. 165)
Lunsford, Susie. Magical Wishing Well Forest Series. (p. 1075)
Lunsk, Robert. Kippy Berryfoote. (p. 961)
Luntz, Frank I. Words That Work: It's Not What You Say, It's What People Hear. (p. 1952)
Lunzer, Lee. Betty Grable Paper Dolls. Lunzer, Lee, illus. (p. 172)
Lunzer, Lee, illus. see Valliant, Regina.
Luo, Keyi. Colorful Childhood. (p. 344)
Luo, Shiyin Sean, illus. see Goss, Leon.
Luongo, Charlotte. Evolution. (p. 546)
—Plate Tectonics. (p. 1370)
Luongo, Jane. Jake's First Word. Kelley, Patrick, illus. (p. 906)
Luongo, Ruth E. Beautiful, Big & Bright: The Journey of Sunny Sunflower Seed. (p. 153)
Lupa, Mary R. Stacy Takes the Train to School. Andriyevskaya, Yevgeniya, illus. (p. 1638)
Luper, Eric. Chocolate Lab. (p. 309)
—Darwin's Dos & Don'ts. (p. 409)
—Gumball's Ghost Stories. (p. 731)
—Gumball's Summer Journal That He Definitely Finished All on His Own. Reed, Stephen, illus. (p. 731)
—Hey Bro, Did Ya Know? (p. 774)
—Jeremy Bender vs. the Cupcake Cadets. (p. 913)
—Miss Simian's Ironclad Rules for School. (p. 1152)
—Seth Baumgartner's Love Manifesto. (p. 1554)
Lupica, Mike. Batboy. (p. 143)
—Big Field. (p. 181)
—Fantasy League. (p. 572)
—Game Changers. (p. 654)
—Heat. (p. 760)
—Heavy Hitters. (p. 761)
—Hero. (p. 772)
—Hot Hand. (p. 801)
—Long Shot. (p. 1047)
—Million-Dollar Throw. (p. 1144)
—Miracle on 49th Street. (p. 1148)
—Only Game. (p. 1298)
—Play Makers. (p. 1371)
—Qb 1. (p. 1422)
—Safe at Home. (p. 1502)
—Shoot-Out. (p. 1568)
—Summer Ball. (p. 1673)
—Travel Team. (p. 1780)
—Travel Team & the Big Field. (p. 1780)
—True Legend. (p. 1792)
—Two-Minute Drill. (p. 1804)
—Underdogs. (p. 1814)
Lupini, Valerie Rolfe. Whistle (p. 1912)
Lupo, Tamar. BMX: X Games. (p. 204)
—Caring for Your Mouse. (p. 269)
—Moto X: X Games. (p. 1179)
—Passover. (p. 1327)
—Warren Buffett. (p. 1858)
Lupo, Tamar & Hudak, Heather C. BMX: X Games. (p. 204)
—Moto X: X Games. (p. 1179)
Luppens, Michel & Béha, Philippe. What Do the Fairies Do with All Those Teeth? (p. 1882)
Lupton, David. Goodbye Brecken. (p. 700)
Lupton, Ellen & Lupton, Julia. D. I. Y. - Kids. (p. 397)
Lupton, Hugh. Demeter & Persephone. Hénaff, Carole, illus. (p. 425)
—Gingerbread Man. Mayo, Diana, illus. (p. 677)
—Orpheus & Eurydice. Hénaff, Carole, illus. (p. 1305)
—Pirican Pic & Pirican Mor. Heo, Yumi, illus. (p. 1364)
—Riddle Me This! Riddles & Stories to Sharpen Your Wits. Fatus, Sophie, illus. (p. 1470)
—Riddle Me This! Riddles & Stories to Challenge Your Mind. Fatus, Sophie, illus. (p. 1470)
—Story Tree: Tales to Read Aloud. Fatus, Sophie, illus. (p. 1663)
—Story Tree. Fatus, Sophie, illus. (p. 1663)
—Tales of Mystery & Magic. Baruzzi, Agnese, illus. (p. 1702)
—Tales of Wisdom & Wonder. Sharkey, Niamh, illus. (p. 1703)
—Theseus & the Minotaur. Hénaff, Carole, illus. (p. 1732)
Lupton, Hugh & Morden, Daniel. Adventures of Odysseus. Balit, Christina, illus. (p. 21)
Lupton, Hugh, et al. Adventures of Achilles. Henaff, Carole, illus. (p. 16)
—Adventures of Odysseus. (p. 21)
Lupton, Julia, jt. auth. see Lupton, Ellen.
Luque, Paco Diaz. Hawkeye: Blindspot. (p. 755)
Luraschi, Anna. Nutcracker. (p. 1274)
Luraschi, Anna, illus. see Chandler, Samuel.
Luraschi, Anna, illus. see Taplin, Sam.
Lurie, Alexander, jt. auth. see Borgenicht, David.
Lurie, Craig. Butterflies, Ladybugs, & Bumble Bees & the wonderful world this could Be .... (p. 247)
Lurie, Ian. Unfun Parent: Keeping your kids safe Online. (p. 1817)
Lurie, Susan. Swim, Duck, Swim! Head, Murray, photos by. (p. 1690)
Luscier, Kim. Steven Learns about Temper Tantrums (p. 1649)
Luse, Renate E., et al. Destined to be an American. (p. 430)
Lusen, Aron. Dead Samurai (p. 417)
—Dead Samurai. (p. 417)
Lush, Debbie, illus. see Bloom, Valerie.
Lush, Debbie, jt. auth. see Rock, Lois.
Lush, Nella. Gracie & Belle Never Again! (p. 705)
Luskin, Fred. Perdonar es Sanar! Liberese de los rencores y experimente los beneficios saludables que trae el Perdon. (p. 1341)
Lusted, Greg & Lusted, Marcia Amidon. Nuclear Power Plant. (p. 1270)
Lusted, Marcia. Surviving Accidents & Crashes. (p. 1687)
—Understanding Palestine Today. (p. 1816)
Lusted, Marcia Amidon. 2004 Indian Ocean Tsunami. (p. 2003)
—2011 Japan Disasters. (p. 2003)
—Advertising to Children. (p. 25)
—African Americans in the Military. (p. 27)
—African Americans in the Military. Hill, Marc Lamont, ed. (p. 27)
—Air Commandos: Elite Operations. (p. 31)
—Alabama: The Heart of Dixie. (p. 33)
—Alaska: The Last Frontier. (p. 34)
—America's Colonization & Settlement. (p. 64)
—Apple: The Company & Its Visionary Founder, Steve Jobs. (p. 92)
—Army Delta Force: Elite Operations. (p. 100)
—Army Rangers: Elite Operations. (p. 100)
—Banned Books. (p. 136)
—Battle of Bunker Hill: A History Perspectives Book. (p. 146)
—Blake Shelton: Country Singer & TV Personality. (p. 198)
—Booboo Stewart: Twilight's Breakout Idol. (p. 210)
Lüsted, Marcia Amidon. California Gold Rush: A History Perspectives Book. (p. 253)
Lusted, Marcia Amidon. Capture & Killing of Osama Bin Laden. (p. 265)
Lüsted, Marcia Amidon. Careers for Tech Girls in Engineering. (p. 267)
Lusted, Marcia Amidon. Chernobyl Disaster. (p. 298)
—Chilean Miners' Rescue. (p. 305)
—Cosmetic Surgery. (p. 368)
—D. B. Cooper Hijacking. (p. 397)
—District of Columbia: The Nation's Capital. (p. 454)
—Entertainment. (p. 531)
—Fight for Women's Suffrage. (p. 585)
—Georgia: The Peach State. (p. 665)
—Greece. (p. 720)
—Hawaii: The Aloha State. (p. 755)
—How to Analyze the Works of Stephen King. (p. 814)
—Idaho: The Gem State. (p. 852)
—Illinois: The Prairie State. (p. 857)
—Iowa: The Hawkeye State. (p. 886)
—Justin Timberlake: Musician, Actor, & Dancer. (p. 940)
—Marine Force Recon: Elite Operations. (p. 1094)
—Mark Zuckerberg: Facebook Creator. (p. 1095)
—Maryland: The Old Line State. (p. 1101)
—Mighty Military Ships. (p. 1140)
—Missouri: The Show-Me State. (p. 1154)
—Montana: The Treasure State. (p. 1170)
—Natural Disasters. (p. 1235)
—Netflix: The Company & Its Founders. (p. 1242)
—Nevada: The Silver State. (p. 1242)
—North Dakota: The Peace Garden State. (p. 1265)
—Nuclear Energy. (p. 1269)
—Obesity & Food Policing. (p. 1275)
—Ohio: The Buckeye State. (p. 1281)
—One Direction: Breakout Boy Band. (p. 1294)
—Oregon: The Beaver State. (p. 1303)
—Oregon Trail. (p. 1303)
—Pennsylvania: The Keystone State. (p. 1338)
—Poverty. (p. 1389)
—Puerto Rico: The Isle of Enchantment. (p. 1415)
—Revolution & the New Nation: 1750-Early 1800s. (p. 1466)
—Science of Motorcycle Racing (p. 1527)
—Sinking of the Titanic: A History Perspectives Book. (p. 1580)
—Social Networking: Myspace, Facebook, & Twitter. (p. 1604)
—Spain. (p. 1620)
Lüsted, Marcia Amidon. Supporting the Elderly Through Service Learning (p. 1684)
Lusted, Marcia Amidon. Surviving Natural Disasters. (p. 1687)
—Suzanne Collins: Words on Fire. (p. 1688)
—Three Mile Island Nuclear Disaster. (p. 1743)
—Tiananmen Square Protests. (p. 1746)
—US National Guard. (p. 1826)
—Utah: The Beehive State. (p. 1829)
—Virginia: The Old Dominion. (p. 1844)
Lüsted, Marcia Amidon. Vo-Tech Track to Success in Human Services. (p. 1847)
—What You Need to Know about Your Status As an Immigrant under the Law. (p. 1896)
Lusted, Marcia Amidon. Wisconsin: The Badger State. (p. 1939)
Lüsted, Marcia Amidon. Working As a Plumber in Your Community. (p. 1952)
Lusted, Marcia Amidon. Wyoming: The Equality State. (p. 1966)
—Your Legal Rights As an Immigrant. (p. 1981)
Lusted, Marcia Amidon, jt. auth. see Lusted, Greg.
Lusted, Marcia Amidon & Thain, Gerald J. Tinker v. Des Moines: The Right to Protest in Schools. (p. 1756)
Luster, Bonnie. Adventures of Mrs. Tibbles & Her Toys: Spots. (p. 21)
Luster, Hope. Friends till the End. (p. 639)
Luster, Lori. Cool Cat: Bringing 1940s & 1950s Flair to Your Wardrobe (p. 363)
Luster, Lori, et al. Fashion Forward: Creating Your Look with the Best of Vintage Style (p. 575)
Lustig, Harriet & Lustig, Laurence. Young Folks' Cook Book. (p. 1978)
Lustig, John, et al. Walt Disney's Comics & Stories #690. Clark, John, ed. (p. 1855)
Lustig, Laurence, jt. auth. see Lustig, Harriet.
Lustig, Lindsey Beth. Snail's Trail. (p. 1596)
Lustig, Loretta. Little Red Hen: A Tale about Cooperation. (p. 1034)
Luterman, Lillian & Bloom, Jennifer. In! College Admissions & Beyond: The Experts' Proven Strategy for Success. (p. 863)
Luthardt, Kevin. Flying! Luthardt, Kevin, illus. (p. 609)
—Larabee Luthardt, Kevin, illus. (p. 975)
—Peep! Luthardt, Kevin, illus. (p. 1335)
—When Edgar Met Cecil Luthardt, Kevin, illus. (p. 1902)
Luthardt, Kevin, illus. see Adams, Diane.
Luthardt, Kevin, illus. see Walker, Sally M.
Luthardt, Kevin, jt. auth. see Luthardt, Kevin.
Luthardt, Kevin & Luthardt, Kevin. Larabee. (p. 975)
Luther Gulick, jt. auth. see Gulick, Luther.
Luther, Jacqueline. Polar Bear Cub. Trachock, Cathy, illus. (p. 1378)
Luther, Jacqueline, ed. see Nussbaum, Ben.
Luther, Jacqueline, jt. auth. see Galvin, Laura Gates.
Luther, Jacqueline & Lind, Alan. Black Bear Cub. Trachock, Cathy, illus. (p. 195)
Luthi, Morgan, illus. see Carlson, Bryce.
Luthi, Morgan, illus. see Wheeler, Shannon & Torres, J.
Luthi, Morgan, illus. see Wheeler, Shannon, et al.
Luthringer, Chelsea. So What Is Citizenship Anyway? (p. 1602)
—So What Is Justice Anyway? (p. 1602)
Luthringer, Melisande, illus. see Walter Foster Custom Creative Team.
Lütje, Susanne & Zabini, Eleni. Best Daddy in the World. (p. 168)
—Best Mama in the World. (p. 170)
Luton, Mildred. Christmas Time in the Mountains. Peattie, Gary, illus. (p. 316)
Luton, Susan. Bilingual Beginning Skills, Grades PreK-1. (p. 186)
Lutterbach, Johanna. Little Orly & the Cricket. Polchlopek, Mary Ann, illus. (p. 1032)
Luttrel, Bill. Redheaded Robbie's Christmas Story. Melanson, Luc, illus. (p. 1455)
Luttrell, Ida Harbis. Road to Randado: The Life Story of Former Texas Ranger Pell Harbison & His Pioneer Ancestors (p. 1477)
Luttrell, Wanda. Let's Explore Kentucky. (p. 996)
Luttrull, Polly, jt. auth. see Chafin, T. A.
Lutz, A. Fowler. Stories of the Child Jesus from Many Lands. (p. 1655)
Lutz, Barbara. My Cat. (p. 1200)
Lutz, Donald S. Colonial Origins of the American Constitution: A Documentary History. (p. 341)
Lutz II, William. Frog from Anoratum. (p. 640)
Lutz Ii, William. Prisoner of Castle Windward. (p. 1407)
Lutz II, William. Quest of Brothers. (p. 1426)
—Seeking Mason. (p. 1548)
Lutz, Kimberly S. Meet Maddie Paddywak. (p. 1121)
Lutz, Lisa, jt. auth. see Spellman, David.
Lutz, Nancie Anne. Patsy & Freckles Make Christmas Cookies. Lutz, Nancie Anne, illus. (p. 1329)
—Patsy Ann Back Again. Lutz, Nancie Anne, illus. (p. 1329)
—Patsy Ann Paperdoll: Including Photographs of Patsy's Original Clothes. Lutz, Nancie Anne, illus. (p. 1329)
Lutz, Suzanne, jt. auth. see FLH Students.
Lutz, W. Bryant. Hercules the Mighty Steed Meets Ginger the Sparrow: A Diversity Book- Allows Everyone to Feel Special & Good about Each Other. (p. 769)
Luu, Cindy, illus. see Roney, Carley.
Luv A. Lamb. Meet the Luv A Lambs: 2009 Edition. (p. 1123)
Luvd, U. R. Camp Gumbo. (p. 257)
Lux, Eldon, illus. see Rey, Carol.
Lux, Josephine Kei & Doerflinger, Marion. Daydreaming Daisy Part of the Daydreamer's Club Series. (p. 415)
Luxa, Sue. Cabin in Cripple Creek. (p. 250)
—Denver Days. (p. 427)
—One Golden Summer. (p. 1295)
Luxbacher, Irene. 123 I Can Build! Luxbacher, Irene, illus. (p. 2000)
—123 I Can Collage! Luxbacher, Irene, illus. (p. 2000)
—123 I Can Draw! Luxbacher, Irene, illus. (p. 2000)
—123 I Can Make Prints! Luxbacher, Irene, illus. (p. 2000)
—123 I Can Paint! Luxbacher, Irene, illus. (p. 2000)
—123 I Can Sculpt! Luxbacher, Irene, illus. (p. 2000)
—Jumbo Book of Art. Luxbacher, Irene, illus. (p. 933)
—Jumbo Book of Outdoor Art. Luxbacher, Irene, illus. (p. 933)
—Mattoo, Let's Play! Luxbacher, Irene, illus. (p. 1110)
—Mr. Frank (p. 1185)
Luxbacher, Irene, illus. see Larsen, Andrew.
Luxenberg, Alan. Palestine Mandate & the Creation of Israel, 1920-1949. (p. 1320)
Luxenberg, Alan H. Radical Islam. (p. 1432)
Luxich, Matt, illus. see Hovanec, Helene.
Luxich, Matt, illus. see Nickel, Scott.
Luykx, Th. D., illus. see Wyler, Rose & McSpadden, Warren W.
Luz, Oscar. Payton's Plane Figures: Understand Concepts of Area. (p. 1331)
Luz Uribe, Maria. Primer Pajaro de Piko-Niko. (p. 1400)
Luzio-Poitras, Linda Di. Kitchi's Christmas Wish. (p. 962)
LuzMarie. Suicidal Beauty (p. 1673)
Luzzati, Emanuele. Three Little Owls. Yeoman, John, tr. from ITA. (p. 1742)
Luzzatto, Caroline. Interplanetary Avenger. (p. 880)
LV Studio, illus. see Golden Books.
LV Studio Staff, illus. see Golden Books Staff.
Ly, Dorothy, ed. see Jones, Carmen S.
Ly, Thu Hà, illus. see Song Hà.
Ly, Youme Nguy?n, illus. see Silver, Gail.
Lya, Maria. Wise Parrot & a Plan to Save the Forest: A Plan to Save the Forest. (p. 1940)
Lyall, Dennis, illus. see Rife, Douglas M. & Capaldi, Gina.
Lyall, Dennis, illus. see Stewart, Whitney.
Lyall, Dennis, illus. see Wulffson, Don L.
Lyall, Maureen. Magus & the Blue Fairy. (p. 1076)
Lyday, Kevin J. Albert's Shell. (p. 35)
Lydia Jane. Fifth Moon: The First Installment in the Gates Trilogy. (p. 584)
Lydon, Jeff. Donald Dent. Behles, Liza, illus. (p. 465)
Lye, Michael, illus. see Aspland, G.
Lye, Michael, illus. see Aspland, Gordon.
Lye, Michael, illus. see Hare, Ralph.
Lyen, Taylor Samuel. Pembroke: The Adventures of Arthur Bacterium & Patty Virus. (p. 1336)
Lyford, Cabot. Arthur the Moose. Lyford, Cabot, illus. (p. 104)
Lyford, Joan. Daisybelle & Dash, a Bedtime Story. (p. 401)
Lyga, Barry. Archvillain. (p. 95)
—Astonishing Adventures of Fanboy & Goth Girl. (p. 108)
—Blood of My Blood. (p. 200)
—Boy Toy. (p. 219)
—Game. (p. 654)
—Goth Girl Rising. (p. 704)
—Hero Type. (p. 772)
—I Hunt Killers. (p. 839)
—Mad Mask. (p. 1069)
—Mangaman. Doran, Colleen, illus. (p. 1087)
—Wolverine Young Readers Novel. (p. 1944)
Lyga, Barry & DeFranco, Robert. After the Red Rain. (p. 28)
Lyle, Anthony. Peculiar, Perplexing Mr. Pickle. (p. 1334)
Lyle, Avis, illus. see Inman, George, Jr., et al.
Lyle, Cindy. Creation Chronicles - the Dragon Within. (p. 379)
Lyle, Kevin, illus. see Caudron, Chris & Childs, Caro.
Lyle, Maryann, ed. see James, Richard E., III.
Lyle, Patrice. Case of the Invisible Witch. (p. 274)
Lyles, Brian & Lyles, Jason. LEGO Neighborhood Book: Build Your Own Town! (p. 990)
Lyles, Christopher, illus. see Loewen, Nancy.
Lyles, Jason, jt. auth. see Lyles, Brian.
Lyles, Tanya. Frog That Needed an Umbrella. (p. 640)
Lyles, Whitney. Love Off-Limits. (p. 1060)
—Party Games. (p. 1326)
Lyle-Soffe, Shari. Horse of Course. Ruble, Eugene, illus. (p. 799)
—Misadventures of Rooter & Snuffle. Collier, Kevin Scott, illus. (p. 1150)
—Nothing Stops Noah. Collier, Kevin Scott, illus. (p. 1268)
—On the Go with Rooter & Snuffle. Collier, Kevin Scott, illus. (p. 1290)
—Shoo Cat. Foster, Jack, illus. (p. 1568)
—Trouble Finds Rooter & Snuffle. Collier, Kevin Scott, illus. (p. 1789)
Lyman, Mitzi, illus. see Yager, Jan.
Lyman Schremmer, Patty. Women of the Green Mountain State: 25 Vermont Women You Should Know. Greenleaf, Lisa, illus. (p. 1946)
Lyn, Jami, illus. see Wahn, Udo.
Lynch, Amy. Smart Girl's Guide to Understanding Her Family: Feelings, Fighting & Figuring It Out. Scheuer, Lauren, illus. (p. 1592)
Lynch, Annabelle, jt. auth. see Bird, Julia.
Lynch, Brendan Denis. Document. (p. 459)
Lynch, Brian. Leonardo. Campbell, Ross, illus. (p. 992)
—Michelangelo. Kuhn, Andy, illus. (p. 1135)
—Minions: The Junior Novel. (p. 1147)
—Raphael. Urru, Franco, illus. (p. 1439)
Lynch, Brian & Waltz, Tom. Donatello. Schiti, Valerio, illus. (p. 466)
Lynch, Casey. Mighty Mike Builds a Ball Field. Lynch, Kelly, illus. (p. 1140)
—Mighty Mike Builds a Library. Lynch, Kelly, illus. (p. 1140)
—Mighty Mike Repairs a Playground. Lynch, Kelly, illus. (p. 1140)
—Mighty Mike Saves a School Bus. Lynch, Kelly, illus. (p. 1140)
Lynch, Casey, illus. see Lynch, Kelly.

L

Lynch, Catherine Carrasco. Mi Abuelita. (p. 1132)
Lynch, Chris. Alive & Kicking. (p. 41)
—Angry Young Man. (p. 75)
—Casualties of War. (p. 277)
—Cyberia. (p. 396)
—Free-Fire Zone. (p. 634)
—Freewill. (p. 635)
—Gravedigger's Cottage. (p. 712)
—Hit Count. (p. 785)
—Hothouse. (p. 802)
—I Pledge Allegiance. (p. 844)
—Iceman. (p. 851)
—Inexcusable. (p. 873)
—Kill Switch. (p. 956)
—Killing Time in Crystal City. (p. 956)
—Little Blue Lies. (p. 1024)
—Me, Dead Dad, & Alcatraz. (p. 1115)
—Monkey See, Monkey Don't. (p. 1165)
—Pieces. (p. 1356)
—Prime Evil. (p. 1400)
—Right Fight. (p. 1472)
—Shadow Boxer. (p. 1557)
—Sharpshooter. (p. 1563)
—Sins of the Fathers. (p. 1580)
—Slot Machine. (p. 1591)
—Vietnam #1: I Pledge Allegiance. (p. 1841)
—Walking Wounded. (p. 1854)
—World War II Book 1: the Right Fight. (p. 1959)
—World War II Book 2: Dead in the Water. (p. 1959)
Lynch, Christopher. Totally Chill: A Stress Management Workbook for Kids with Social, Emotional, or Sensory Sensitivities: My Complete Guide to Staying Cool. (p. 1771)
Lynch, Dan, illus. see Kachmann, Rudy.
Lynch, David. Catching the Big Fish: Meditation, Consciousness, & Creativity. (p. 279)
Lynch, David, jt. auth. see Morris, Bill.
Lynch, Denise A. PB & J. (p. 1331)
Lynch, Diane M., ed. Between You & Me, God: Prayers by Catholic Kids. (p. 173)
Lynch, Emily S., illus. see Reinert, Linda M.
Lynch, Wayne. —Celebrate the Season! Twelve Short Stories for Advent & Christmas. (p. 284)
—Family Ties: Thirteen Short Stories. (p. 568)
—Friend 2 Friend: Twelve Short Stories. (p. 637)
—Now You're Cooking! Ten Short Stories with Recipes. (p. 1269)
Lynch, Edward P., jt. auth. see Davies, Will.
Lynch, Emily S., illus. see Reinert, Linda M.
Lynch, Emma. Brazil (p. 224)
—China (p. 306)
—Harriet Tubman. (p. 749)
—Indonesia (p. 872)
—Italy (p. 894)
—Kenya (p. 949)
Lynch, Emma, et al. Martin Luther King Jr. (p. 1098)
Lynch, F. Michael. I Don't Want to Share a Bedroom. (p. 838)
—I Will Always Need You. (p. 848)
Lynch, Fred D., et al. My Changes (p. 1200)
Lynch, Jack & Salem Press Staff. Canterbury Tales, by Geoffrey Chaucer. (p. 262)
Lynch, James. Corporate Compassion: Succeeding with Care. (p. 368)
Lynch, Jane, et al. Marlene, Marlene, Queen of Mean. Tusa, Tricia, illus. (p. 1095)
Lynch, Janet Nichols. Addicted to Her. (p. 11)
—Messed Up. (p. 1129)
—My Beautiful Hippie. (p. 1196)
—Peace Is a Four-Letter Word. (p. 1331)
—Racing California. (p. 1432)
Lynch, Jason. Everyone Has Hope. Hale, Cole, illus. (p. 544)
Lynch, Jason, illus. see Kirkpatrick, Taylor.
Lynch, Jay. Mo & Jo: Fighting Together Forever. Haspiel, Dean, illus. (p. 1157)
—Otto's Orange Day. Mouly, Francoise, ed. (p. 1307)
—Otto's Orange Day. Cammuso, Frank, illus. (p. 1307)
Lynch, Jay, jt. auth. see Cammuso, Frank.
Lynch, Jay, jt. auth. see Haspiel, Dean.
Lynch, Jay & Cammuso, Frank. Otto's Orange Day. (p. 1307)
Lynch, Jay & Haspiel, Dean. Mo & Jo: Fighting Together Forever. (p. 1157)
—Mo & Jo Fighting Together Forever. (p. 1157)
Lynch, Joseph. Pockets. Yamasaki, Katie, illus. (p. 1375)
Lynch, Josh, illus. see Hooper, M.
Lynch, Judy. Making Word Walls Work: A Complete, Systematic Guide with Routines, Grade-Perfect Word Lists, & Reproducible Word Cards to Help All Children Master High-Frequency Words. (p. 1082)
Lynch, Katherine E. & Radclyffe, eds. OMGQueer. (p. 1288)
Lynch, Kelly. Mighty Mike Builds a Nature Trail. Lynch, Casey, illus. (p. 1140)
—Mighty Mike Does What's Right! Lynch, Casey, illus. (p. 1140)
Lynch, Kelly, illus. see Lynch, Casey.
Lynch, Kelly Ann. He Said Yes: The Story of Father Mychal Judge. Oatman, M. Scott, illus. (p. 756)
Lynch, Kendra. Sweet Dreams Little. (p. 1689)
Lynch, Keven R. What's a Buffalo Soldier? The Historical Adventures of Amber & Trevor. (p. 1896)
Lynch, Lauren Boehm. Working As a Team: Down to the End of the Road & Back. DeBroeck, Sarah, illus. (p. 1952)
—Yellow Butterfly. DeBroeck, Sarah, illus. (p. 1970)
Lynch, Marietta & Perry, Patricia. No More Monkeys: A Photographic Version of the Children's Finger Game. (p. 1259)
Lynch, Mary D., tr. see Birmelin, Immanuel.
Lynch, Michael. Bolshevik & Stalinist Russia, 1918-56. (p. 208)
—Reaction & Revolutions: Russia, 1894-1924. (p. 1442)
Lynch, Michelle. Penguin Baby. Washington, Joi, illus. (p. 1336)
Lynch, Michelle, jt. auth. see Fleischer, Jayson.
Lynch, Michelle, jt. auth. see Taylor, Trace.
Lynch, Michelle & Taylor, Trace. Cobras. Taylor, Trace, illus. (p. 337)
Lynch, Mike & Barr, Brandon. When the Sky Fell. Kim, Glenn, illus. (p. 1905)
Lynch, P. J. Boy Who Fell off the Mayflower, or John Howland's Good Fortune. Lynch, P. J., illus. (p. 219)
Lynch, P. J., illus. see Andersen, Hans Christian & Lewis, Naomi.
Lynch, P. J., illus. see Andersen, Hans Christian.
Lynch, P. J., illus. see Dickens, Charles.
Lynch, P. J., illus. see Dillon, Patrick.
Lynch, P. J., illus. see Henry, O.
Lynch, P. J., illus. see Hest, Amy.
Lynch, P. J., illus. see Peet, Mal & Graham, Elspeth.
Lynch, P. J., illus. see Stockton, Frank Richard.
Lynch, P. J., illus. see Wells, Rosemary.
Lynch, P. J., illus. see Wojciechowski, Susan.
Lynch, P. J., illus. see Wood, Douglas.
Lynch, P. J., jt. auth. see Wilde, Oscar.
Lynch, Patricia. Tales of Irish Enchantment. Baker, Sara, illus. (p. 1702)
Lynch, Patricia Ann, jt. auth. see Roberts, Jeremy.
Lynch, Patricia Ann & Roberts, Jeremy. Native American. (p. 1234)
Lynch, Priscilla. Using Big Books & Predictable Books. (p. 1828)
Lynch, Ryan. Just a Pup: And Other Poems for Children. (p. 937)
Lynch, Sharon Boylan. Nimbles of Nimbus. (p. 1256)
Lynch, Sheri. Be Happy or I'll Scream! My Deranged Quest for the Perfect Husband, Family, & Life. (p. 148)
Lynch, Stephanie, illus. see Young, Rachel & Young, Jackie.
Lynch, Stephen D. Travels of Kui, the African Spurred Tortoise. Richard, Keisha Luana, illus. (p. 1780)
Lynch, Stephen M. All Alone in the Dark. (p. 43)
Lynch Street, Nancy, told to. In Search of Red Buddha: Higher Education in China after Mao Zedong. (p. 864)
Lynch, Suzanne. Bones, for Wishing. (p. 209)
Lynch, Tara, illus. see Jones, Birdy.
Lynch, Todd, jt. auth. see Breckenridge, Trula.
Lynch, Tom, illus. see Coy, John & Reonegro, Antonio.
Lynch, Wayne. Arctic. Lynch, Wayne, photos by. (p. 95)
—Arctic A to Z. (p. 95)
—Arctic Alphabet: Exploring the North from A to Z. Lynch, Wayne, photos by. (p. 96)
—Everglades. Lynch, Wayne, photos by. (p. 542)
—Falcons. Neidigh, Sherry, illus. (p. 566)
—Sonoran Desert. (p. 1612)
—Vultures. Neidigh, Sherry, illus. (p. 1851)
—Wayne Lynch's Canadian Rockies Wildlife for Kids. (p. 1865)
—Whose Baby Is This? (p. 1921)
—Whose Bottom Is This? (p. 1921)
—Whose Eyes Are These? (p. 1921)
—Whose Feet Are These? (p. 1921)
—Whose House Is This? (p. 1921)
—Whose Nose Is This? (p. 1922)
—Whose Tail Is This? (p. 1922)
—Whose Teeth Are These? (p. 1922)
—Whose Tongue Is This? (p. 1922)
Lynch, Wayne, illus. see Lang, Aubrey.
Lynch, Wayne, jt. auth. see Evert, Laura.
Lynch, Wayne, jt. auth. see Lang, Aubrey.
Lynch, Wayne, photos by see Lang, Aubrey.
Lynch, Wayne, contrib. by. Vultures. (p. 1851)
Lynch, Wayne, photos by. Sonoran Desert. (p. 1612)
Lynch, Zachary. Life of St. Patrick: Enlightener of the Irish. (p. 1012)
Lynde, Stan. Pardners (p. 1324)
Lyndon, Janice, illus. see Little, Lorna.
Lyndon, Tracy S., illus. see Hubbs, M. E.
Lyne, Alison, illus. see Hébert-Collins, Sheila.
Lyne, Alison, illus. see Simmons, Lynn.
Lyne, Alison D., illus. see Vidrine, Beverly Barras.
Lyne, Alison Davis, illus. see Bethea, Nikole.
Lyne, Alison Davis, illus. see Hébert-Collins, Sheila.
Lyne, Alison Davis, illus. see Lambe, Jennifer Holloway.
Lyne, Alison Davis, illus. see Simmons, Lynn Sheffield.
Lyne, Alison Davis, illus. see Vidrine, Beverly Barras.
Lyne, Alison Davis & Burrows, Mark. Little Things Aren't Little ... When You're Little Lyne, Alison Davis, illus. (p. 1037)
Lyne, Jennifer H. Catch Rider. (p. 279)
Lyne, William Rayford. Galisteo: Thothmes III's Colony in America, C. 1626 B. C. : the Tanoan-Egyptian Djed Festival Stone. Lyne, William Rayford, illus. (p. 653)
Lynellen Sullivan & Bryan Castle. Poppers to the Rescue: Book 1 of the Popcorn Series. (p. 1384)
Lynes, William. Pirates, Scoundrels, & Kings. (p. 1364)
Lynette, Rachel. Abominable Snowman. (p. 5)
—Ana Dodson: Advocate for Peruvian Orphans. (p. 66)
—Anacondas. (p. 66)
—Area 51. (p. 97)
—Ben & Bailey Build a Book Report. Chewning, Randy, illus. (p. 163)
—Bicycles Before the Store. McGeehan, Dan, illus. (p. 177)
—Bluntnose Sixgill Sharks & Other Strange Sharks (p. 204)
—Burial Grounds. (p. 243)
—Capybaras. (p. 265)
—Caves. (p. 282)
—Deep-Sea Anglerfish & Other Fearsome Fish (p. 423)
—Drugs. (p. 487)
—Electrical Experiments: Electricity & Circuits (p. 509)
—Experiments with Light: Light Energy (p. 549)
—Footballs Before the Store. McGeehan, Dan, illus. (p. 615)
—Frank & Fiona Build a Fictional Story. Lieffering, Jan, illus. (p. 628)
—Giant River Otters. (p. 674)
—Gold Rush. (p. 694)
—Gravity: Forces & Motion (p. 712)
—Great Wall of China. (p. 719)
—How to Deal with Competitiveness. (p. 816)
—How to Deal with Discrimination. (p. 816)
—How to Deal with Feeling Left Out. (p. 816)
—How to Deal with Hurt Feelings. (p. 816)
—How to Deal with Lying. (p. 816)
—How to Deal with Secrets. (p. 816)
—Jaguars. (p. 905)
—Jennifer Aniston. (p. 912)
—Jesse & Jasmine Build a Journal. Aon, Carlos, illus. (p. 914)
—Kinkajous. (p. 961)
—Leah & Leshawn Build a Letter. Cox, Steve, illus. (p. 982)
—Let's Throw a Christmas Party! (p. 1001)
—Let's Throw a Hanukkah Party! (p. 1001)
—Let's Throw a St. Patrick's Day Party! (p. 1001)
—Let's Throw a Thanksgiving Party! (p. 1001)
—Let's Throw a Valentine's Day Party! (p. 1001)
—Let's Work It Out: What to Do When Your Family Has to Cut Costs. (p. 1001)
—Louisiana Purchase. (p. 1058)
—Magnets: Magnetism (p. 1076)
—Meriwether Lewis & William Clark. (p. 1127)
—Miles Davis. (p. 1142)
—Mountain Food Chains (p. 1180)
—Oregon Trail. (p. 1303)
—Pencils Before the Store. McGeehan, Dan, illus. (p. 1336)
—Pink River Dolphins. (p. 1360)
—Piranhas. (p. 1362)
—Plants (p. 1369)
—Producing Meat (p. 1409)
—Rats. (p. 1440)
—Real Deal: Drugs Hardback. (p. 1448)
—River Food Chains (p. 1475)
—Sacagawea. (p. 1500)
—Scorpions. (p. 1530)
—Soda Pop Before the Store. McGeehan, Dan, illus. (p. 1605)
—South American Tapirs. (p. 1616)
—Squirrel Monkeys. (p. 1637)
—Super Colon Saves the Day! Gallagher-Cole, Mernie, illus. (p. 1679)
—Super Parentheses Saves the Day! Gallagher-Cole, Mernie, illus. (p. 1680)
—Tarantulas. (p. 1706)
—Three-Toed Sloths. (p. 1744)
—Tim Burton: Filmmaker. (p. 1750)
—Toilet Paper Before the Store. McGeehan, Dan, illus. (p. 1762)
—Transcontinental Railroad. (p. 1778)
—Trolls. (p. 1788)
—Urban Legends. (p. 1825)
—Vampire Bats. (p. 1831)
—What Makes Us a Family? Living in a Nontraditional Family. (p. 1892)
—What to Do When Your Family Can't Afford Health Care. (p. 1894)
—What to Do When Your Family Has to Cut Costs. (p. 1894)
—What to Do When Your Family Is in Debt. (p. 1894)
—What to Do When Your Family Is on Welfare. (p. 1894)
—What to Do When Your Family Loses Its Home. (p. 1894)
—Who Lives in a Deep, Dark Cave? (p. 1916)
—Who Lives in a Wet, Wild Rain Forest? (p. 1916)
—Who Lives on a Towering Mountain? (p. 1916)
—Who Lives on the Icy, Cold Tundra? (p. 1916)
Lynette, Rachel, jt. auth. see Miller, Tori.
Lynette, Rachel & Hile, Kevin. ESP. (p. 536)
Lynette, Shannon. Place with No Name. (p. 1366)
Lynetter, Rachel. Ashley Shuyler: Founder of AfricAid. (p. 106)
—Julia Butterfly Hill: Saving the Ancient Redwoods. (p. 932)
—Witches. (p. 1941)
Lynn, Adele B. EQ Interview: Finding Employees with High Emotional Intelligence. (p. 533)
Lynn, Auntie. Magical Scarecrows Special RSPCA Edition: For the Magical Scarecrows Let's Make Magic program with the RSPCA's Million Paws Walk ~ 2010. Thomas, Jean et al, illus. (p. 1075)
Lynn, Bei, illus. see Liu, Julia.
Lynn, Catherine. Great Sock Adventure. (p. 718)
Lynn, Cheryl. Kayla's Day at the Park. (p. 946)
Lynn, Debbie. Angel George Series James Needs a Miracle. Norberg, Ken, illus. (p. 73)
Lynn, Deidre. Treasure Delight: A Sweet Story about the Joy in Sharing. Morris, Jessica, illus. (p. 1781)
Lynn, Diana & Arroyo, George. Dog's Scratch: Los Perritos Se Rascan. (p. 463)
Lynn, Diana & Arroyo, George, creators. Dogs Scratch: Les Chiens Se Grattent. (p. 463)
Lynn, Elizabeth B. Forget the Vet. Meyer, Ashley M., illus. (p. 619)
Lynn, Erin. Speed Demon. (p. 1624)
Lynn, Galsterer, illus. see Haller, Reese.
Lynn, Harris Deanna. Taters of the Ozarks (softcover) The Feud. (p. 1707)
Lynn, Jeffrey. Adventures of Pablo. . the Ecuadorian Panda. (p. 21)
Lynn, Jennifer. Homeschool on a Battlefield. (p. 793)
Lynn, Joseph. Color of My Words. (p. 343)
Lynn, Kelly. Princess Transformation (p. 1406)
Lynn, Michaela & Chrisemer, Michael. Baby Greens: A Live-Food Approach for Children of All Ages. (p. 126)
Lynn, Michelle. Fall Leaves. (p. 566)
—Sasha Discovers There Is a Job for Everyone. (p. 1515)
Lynn, Richard & Nova Blue. Historic Savannah, GA Coloring Book. Claughton, Dena, ed. (p. 782)
Lynn, Rick, illus. see Conant, Susan Sens.
Lynn, Ronny, illus. see Fancy, Robin Lyn & Welch, Vala Jeanne.
Lynn Rund, Jennifer. Me & My Bossy Big Sister... the Babysitter. (p. 1115)
Lynn, Sarah. 1-2-3 Va-Va-Vroom! A Counting Book Griffo, Daniel, illus. (p. 1990)
—Boulder Brothers: Meet Mo & Jo. Collet-Derby, Pierre, illus. (p. 216)
—Tip-Tap Pop Docampo, Valeria, illus. (p. 1757)
Lynn, Saundra. Am I Like the Weather? (p. 51)
Lynn Sauthoff, Taryn & Williams, Tim. Rutgers New Brunswick College Prowler off the Record. (p. 1498)
Lynn, Shannon. Tooth Fairy Trouble Hits Tinsel Tooth Town. (p. 1768)
Lynn, Steve & Rogers, Aïda, eds. Writing South Carolina. (p. 1965)
Lynn, Tammy. Happy Birthday Puppy: An I See Puppy Book. Stewart, Elaine, ed. (p. 745)
Lynn, Tracy. Snow: A Retelling of Snow White & the Seven Dwarfs. (p. 1598)
Lynn, Vicki, concept. Hilda Is Here. (p. 779)
Lynne, Douglas. Contemporary United States: 1968 to the Present. (p. 360)
Lynne, Kaycee. Something Good! (p. 1610)
Lynne, Kimberlee. Frog & the Mouse. (p. 640)
Lynne Paxton, Vicki. Here Comes DudLee. (p. 770)
Lynne Rounds, Sharon. Gootzes Go to Giza. (p. 702)
Lynne Virgin, Kay. Ember the Dragon: Hero of the Day. (p. 517)
—Ember the Dragon & the Birthday Surprise. (p. 517)
Lynne, Zoe. That Witch! (p. 1726)
—That Witch! [Library Edition]. (p. 1726)
Lynnes, Gina, jt. auth. see Hemry, Melanie.
Lynott, Vicky, jt. auth. see Fredericks, Anthony D.
Lyon, Abby, jt. auth. see Alter, Austin.
Lyon, Abby, jt. auth. see Amboba, Ethan.
Lyon, Abby, jt. auth. see Collins, Elizabeth.
Lyon, Abby, jt. auth. see Dearing, Kate.
Lyon, Abby, jt. auth. see Fackrell, Caitlin.
Lyon, Abby, jt. auth. see Fraser, Alison.
Lyon, Abby, jt. auth. see Hopkins, Adrianna.
Lyon, Abby, jt. auth. see Kutscher, Scott.
Lyon, Anna, jt. auth. see Moore, Paula.
Lyon, Annabel. All-Season Edie (p. 45)
Lyon, Belinda, illus. see Baxter, Nicola.
Lyon, Benn, jt. auth. see Lyon, George Ella.
Lyon, Carol, illus. see Hamilton, Martha & Weiss, Mitch.
Lyon, Chris, illus. see Butterfield, Moira.
Lyon, Chris, illus. see Castor, Harriet.
Lyon, Chris, illus. see Young, Caroline & Castor, Harriet.
Lyon, Chris, illus. see Young, Caroline.
Lyon, Christopher, jt. auth. see Kirgiss, Crystal.
Lyon, David. Flight of the Buzby Bee. Lyon, David, illus. (p. 604)
Lyon, Elizabeth. Manuscript Makeover: Revision Techniques No Fiction Writer Can Afford to Ignore. (p. 1089)
Lyon, George Ella. All the Water in the World. Tillotson, Katherine, illus. (p. 46)
—My Friend, the Starfinder. Gammell, Stephen, illus. (p. 1209)
—No Dessert Forever! Catalanotto, Peter, illus. (p. 1258)
—Pirate of Kindergarten. Avril, Lynne, illus. (p. 1362)
—Planes Fly! Wiggins, Mick, illus. (p. 1367)
—Sleepsong. Catalanotto, Peter, illus. (p. 1589)
—Sonny's House of Spies. (p. 1612)
—Trucks Roll! Frazier, Craig, illus. (p. 1791)
—What Forest Knows. (p. 1884)
—Where I'm From. (p. 1908)
—Which Side Are You On? The Story of a Song. Cardinale, Christopher, illus. (p. 1911)
—You & Me & Home Sweet Home. Anderson, Stephanie, illus. (p. 1973)
Lyon, George Ella, jt. auth. see Lewis, J. Patrick.
Lyon, George Ella & Anderson, Stephanie. Weaving the Rainbow. Anderson, Stephanie, illus. (p. 1870)
Lyon, George Ella & Catalanotto, Peter. Mother to Tigers. (p. 1178)
Lyon, George Ella & Lyon, Benn. Boats Float! Wiggins, Mick, illus. (p. 205)
Lyon, Greg. Walk, Walk. (p. 1854)
Lyon, Harold C., Jr. Angling in the Smile of the Great Spirit: Six Centuries of Wisdom from the Anglers of Lake Winnipesaukee (p. 75)
—Angling in the Smile of the Great Spirit: Six Centuries of Wisdom from the Master Anglers of Lake Winnipesaukee (p. 75)
Lyon, Jane & Bailey, Karen. Primerica: A Home for the Brave. (p. 1400)
Lyon, Lea, illus. see Beckwith, Kathy.
Lyon, Lea, illus. see Faruqi, Reem.
Lyon, Lea, illus. see Moss, Peggy.
Lyon, Lea, illus. see Penn, Audrey.
Lyon, Lea, jt. auth. see Moss, Peggy.
Lyon, Lea, jt. auth. see Petrillo, Genevieve.
Lyon, Lea07/, illus. see Petrillo, Genevieve.
Lyon, Nathan W. & Ellis, Kevin L. Sam the Clam. (p. 1507)
Lyon, Robin. Spanish Missions of Arizona. (p. 1621)
—Spanish Missions of New Mexico. (p. 1621)
Lyon, Tammie. Olive & Snowflake (p. 1285)
Lyon, Tammie, illus. see Bauer, Marion Dane.
Lyon, Tammie, illus. see Bostrom, Kathleen Long.
Lyon, Tammie, illus. see Chapman, Kelly.
Lyon, Tammie, illus. see Dennis, Robert.
Lyon, Tammie, illus. see Froeb, Lori.
Lyon, Tammie, illus. see Fry, Sonali & Knight, Hilary.
Lyon, Tammie, illus. see Grogan, John.
Lyon, Tammie, illus. see Hapka, Catherine, pseud.
Lyon, Tammie, illus. see Kenah, Katharine.
Lyon, Tammie, illus. see Knight, Hilary.
Lyon, Tammie, illus. see Kupfer, Wendy.
Lyon, Tammie, illus. see Manushkin, Fran.
Lyon, Tammie, illus. see McClatchy, Lisa & Knight, Hilary.
Lyon, Tammie, illus. see McClatchy, Lisa & Thompson, Kay.
Lyon, Tammie, illus. see McClatchy, Lisa.
Lyon, Tammie, illus. see McClure, Wendy.
Lyon, Tammie, illus. see McNamara, Margaret & Thompson, Kay.
Lyon, Tammie, illus. see Nolan, Allia Zobel.
Lyon, Tammie, illus. see O'Hair, Margaret.
Lyon, Tammie, illus. see Perry, Anne M.
Lyon, Tammie, illus. see Skultety, Nancy.
Lyon, Tammie, illus. see Stier, Catherine.
Lyon, Tammie, illus. see Thompson, Kay & McClatchy, Lisa.
Lyon, Tammie, illus. see Weiss, Ellen.
Lyon, Tammie, jt. auth. see Manushkin, Fran.
Lyon, Tammie, jt. auth. see Parker, David.
Lyon, Tammie, jt. auth. see Ransom, Candice.
Lyon, Tammie Speer. Hickory Dickory Dock! (p. 775)
—Mary Had a Little Lamb. (p. 1100)
—Now I Lay Me down to Sleep. (p. 1269)

—This Little Piggy. (p. 1737)
Lyon, Tammie Speer, illus. see Fry, Sonali & Knight, Hilary.
Lyon, Tammie Speer, illus. see McClatchy, Lisa & Knight, Hilary.
Lyon, Tammie Speer, illus. see McClatchy, Lisa & Thompson, Kay.
Lyon, Tammie Speer, illus. see McClatchy, Lisa.
Lyon, Tammie Speer, illus. see Thompson, Kay.
Lyon, Tammie Speer, illus. see Weiss, Ellen.
Lyon, Tammie Speer, illus. see Welch, Willy.
Lyona, illus. see Balmes, Santi.
Lyons, Belinda. Meet My Air Force Mommy. (p. 1121)
Lyons, C. J. Broken. (p. 230)
—Watched. (p. 1861)
Lyons, Deborah. Edward Hopper: Summer at the Seaside. (p. 505)
Lyons, Eric. God Made Animals. (p. 689)
—God Made Insects. (p. 689)
Lyons, Fergus. Muckeen & the Big Freeze. (p. 1188)
—Muckeen & the UFO. (p. 1188)
—Shoestring Soup. (p. 1568)
Lyons, I. J. April's Pond. (p. 93)
Lyons, Jack. Pyruko: The New Logic Puzzle That's Not for Squares. (p. 1421)
Lyons, Jane & Bailey, Karen. Skipingo Home: A Thoroughbred's Second Chance. Gordon, Susie, illus. (p. 1586)
Lyons, Jayne. 100% Hero. (p. 1998)
—100% Wolf. Rivas, Victor, illus. (p. 1999)
Lyons, Kathy, jt. auth. see Patten, Elizabeth.
Lyons, Kay. Malaysian Children's Favourite Stories. Loh, Martin, illus. (p. 1083)
Lyons, Kay & Loh, Martin. Malaysian Children's Favourite Stories. (p. 1083)
Lyons, Kay, et al. Asian Children's Favorite Stories: A Treasury of Folktales from China, Japan, Korea, India, the Philippines, Thailand, Indonesia & Malaysia. Yee, Patrick, illus. (p. 106)
Lyons, Kelly Starling. Ellen's Broom. Minter, Daniel, illus. (p. 514)
—Hope's Gift. Tate, Don, illus. (p. 797)
—NEATE Book: Eddie's Ordeal. Vol. 4 (p. 1239)
—One Million Men & Me. Ambush, Peter, illus. (p. 1296)
—Tea Cakes for Tosh. Lewis, E. B., illus. (p. 1708)
Lyons, Lewis. Rescue at Sea with the U. S. & Canadian Coast Guards. (p. 1462)
Lyons, Maggie. Dewi & the Seeds of Doom. (p. 432)
—Vin & Dorky Duet. (p. 1842)
Lyons, Mary E. Letters from a Slave Boy: The Story of Joseph Jacobs. (p. 1002)
—Letters from a Slave Girl: The Story of Harriet Jacobs. (p. 1002)
—Poison Place. (p. 1377)
—Roy Makes a Car. Widener, Terry, illus. (p. 1492)
Lyons, Mary E., ed. Feed the Children First: Irish Memories of the Great Hunger. (p. 580)
Lyons, P. J., jt. auth. see Zondervan.
Lyons, Sandy Lyons. Michigan's Most Haunted: A Ghostly Guide to the Great Lakes State. (p. 1135)
Lyons, Sarah. Fairy stories about sally & Mignonette. (p. 564)
Lyons, Shelly. If I Were a Movie Star Rooney, Ronnie, illus. (p. 853)
—If I Were a Veterinarian Rooney, Ronnie, illus. (p. 853)
—If You Were a Question Mark Gray, Sara, illus. (p. 855)
—If You Were a Question Mark [LTD Commodities]. Gray, Sara, illus. (p. 855)
—If You Were a Question Mark [Readers World]. Gray, Sara, illus. (p. 855)
—If You Were an Apostrophe [Readers World]. Gray, Sara, illus. (p. 855)
—If You Were an Exclamation Point Gray, Sara, illus. (p. 855)
—If You Were an Exclamation Point [LTD Commodities]. Gray, Sara, illus. (p. 855)
—If You Were an Exclamation Point [Readers World]. Gray, Sara, illus. (p. 855)
—My Neighborhood. (p. 1215)
—People in My Neighborhood. (p. 1339)
—Places in My Neighborhood. (p. 1366)
—Safety in My Neighborhood. (p. 1502)
—Signs in My Neighborhood. (p. 1574)
—Transportation in My Neighborhood. (p. 1779)
Lyons, Shelly, jt. auth. see Blaisdell, Molly.
Lyons, Shelly & Blaisdell, Molly. If You Were an Apostrophe Gray, Sara, illus. (p. 855)
Lyons, Stefanie. Dating Down. (p. 409)
Lyons Stroud, Patricia. Seven Keys to Adventure. (p. 1554)
Lyons, Suzanne. Electricity Adds Up: Set Of 6. (p. 509)
—Electricity Adds up & Electricidad Lógica: 6 English, 6 Spanish Adaptations. (p. 509)
—Gravity: Set Of 6. (p. 712)
—Oops! Why Did I Do That? Set Of 6. (p. 1299)
—Pete Discovers Gravity: Set Of 6. (p. 1346)
—Pete Discovers Gravity. (p. 1346)
Lyons, Theresa. Eating My ABC's. (p. 501)
Lyons, Wendy Ackerman. Girl Who Reached for the Star. Sayles, John, illus. (p. 679)
Lyons-Reid, Nashika. My Brother the Superhero. (p. 1199)
Lyra, Rael, illus. see Giffen, Keith, et al.
Lyrrek, E. Dawne. Page Turns 12 & Comes of Age. (p. 1318)
Lysaght, Richard. Black Bag Mystery. Wolfhound Publishing Editors, ed. (p. 195)
Lyssenko, Taras. Wendy's Fear of Heights. (p. 1875)
Lyster, R. Iona. Believers in Christ: New Testament Volume 29 Ephesians: God's Workamanship. Volume 29 Willoughby, Yuko, illus. (p. 162)
Lyster, R. Iona, et al. Inspiration of the Scriptures: New Testament Volume 33: 1 & 2 Timothy, Titus, Philemon. Hertzler, Frances & Olson, Ed, illus. (p. 878)
Lythgoe, James. Up Is the Best Place to Be. (p. 1824)
Lytle, Robert A. Pirate Party. Williams, Bill, illus. (p. 1362)
Lytrelle, Chenise. Kaleidoscope: A Collection of Poetry. (p. 941)
Lyttle, Marcy. Catching Fireflies: Family Night Devotional Fun. Irwin, Kendra, illus. (p. 279)
Lyttleton, Kay. Jean Craig in New York. (p. 911)
Lytton, Deborah. Silence. (p. 1575)
Lyver, Patti. Did You Ever See Gulls? (p. 437)
Lyzenga, Antonia Babauta. Happy Island. (p. 746)

M

M a. Stuck. Proulx, Denis, illus. (p. 1668)
M. A. Benjamin. When I Pray: The Lord's Prayer. (p. 1903)
M, Akiko, tr. see Downie, David.
M. Alvarado. We Are Different, but the Same. (p. 1865)
M. Eugenia Coeymans. Universe of the Aurus. (p. 1820)
M F Feierabend, J. Olivia Ponty & Friends to the Rescue. (p. 1287)
M. Gebert, Shirley. Lucky Lucy. (p. 1062)
M, Gracie. Walk on the Ceiling. (p. 1854)
M. J. Studios Staff, illus. see Nichols, V.
M. Kurkoski, Bettina. My Cat Loki (p. 1200)
M. L. Tyndall. Reliance. (p. 1458)
M, Patty. Seven Beagles. (p. 1554)
M, Pierce, illus. see Wing, Natasha.
M. Ward. Evergreens Go to the Park. (p. 542)
Ma, Hermione & Fu, Jennifer. Revolving Resort. (p. 1467)
Ma, Ian, jt. auth. see Wallach, Joel Dennis.
Ma, Jyoti & Devi, Chandra. Sparkling Together: Starbright & His Earthling Friends. (p. 1622)
Ma, Karin & Taylor, Nicole. Differentiating Assessment in the Reading Workshop: Templates, Checklists, How-To'S, & Student Samples to Streamline Ongoing Assessments So You Can Plan & Teach More Effectively. (p. 438)
Ma, Wenhai. Tang Monk Disciples Monkey King: English/Chinese. (p. 1705)
—Tang Monk Disciples Monkey King. (p. 1705)
Ma, Wenhai, illus. see Do, Kim-Thu, tr.
Ma, Wing Shing. Invading Sun. (p. 883)
—Storm Riders: Invading Sun. Vol. 1 (p. 1656)
—Storm Riders. (p. 1656)
—Tale of No Name (p. 1699)
Ma, Wing Shing & Lau, Ding Kin. Chinese Hero: Tales of the Blood Sword. Vol. 3 Yang, Sue & Stone, Benjamin, eds. (p. 307)
Ma, Winnie, illus. see Sturup, Signe.
Ma, Yamin. Chinese Made Easy for Kids: Text Book. (p. 307)
—Chinese Made Easy for Kids. (p. 307)
Ma, Zheng & Li, Zheng. Chinese Fables & Folktales (I) She, Liu & Rujin, Ma, illus. (p. 307)
—Chinese Fables & Folktales (II) Wei, Miao & Xianoqing, Pan, illus. (p. 307)
—Stories Behind Chinese Idioms (I) Taixi, Su & Xiaoming, Wang, illus. (p. 1654)
—Stories Behind Chinese Idioms (II) Youzhi, He & Xiaofang, Ding, illus. (p. 1654)
—Stories Behind Chinese Idioms (III) She, Liu & Xiaoqing, Pan, illus. (p. 1654)
Maa'Dhoor, Lilian, illus. see Hernandez, Eufemia.
Maag, John W. & Jackson, Michael C. Codey's Monsters (p. 338)
Maalos, text. Baruch & Berel. (p. 140)
Maar, Paul. Canguro Aprende a Volar (Kangaroo Learns to Fly) (p. 261)
—Puerta Olvidada. (p. 1414)
—Viaje de Lisa. Kasparavicius, Kestutis, illus. (p. 1839)
Maarsen, Jacqueline Van, see Van Maarsen, Jacqueline.
Maartman, Ben. Lost Treasures of Yucatan: A Belizean Saga. (p. 1057)
Maas, Alice E. Baby Jesus Visits the Temple. Miyake, Yoshi, illus. (p. 126)
Maas, Dorothy, illus. see Work, Rhoda O.
Maas, Jason/A, illus. see Reisman, Dave.
Maas, Mark. Harold the Hark Angel. (p. 749)
Maas, Rita, photos by see Scott-Goodman, Barbara.
Maas, Sarah J. Assassin's Blade. (p. 107)
—Court of Thorns & Roses. (p. 373)
—Crown of Midnight. (p. 386)
—Heir of Fire. (p. 762)
—Queen of Shadows. (p. 1425)
—Throne of Glass. (p. 1744)
Maas, Susan Thogerson. Picture Imperfect. (p. 1355)
Maass, Mary Kurnick, illus. see Eastwick, Ivy O.
Maass, Robert. A Is for Autumn. Maass, Robert, photos by. (p. 1)
Maass, Sarah. Appaloosa Horse (p. 92)
—Percheron Horse (p. 1341)
Mabbitt, Will. Unlikely Adventures of Mabel Jones. Collins, Ross, illus. (p. 1821)
Mabee, Andrea. Dory Glory: Building A Boat from Stem to Stern. Mabee, Andrea, photos by. (p. 472)
Maberry, Jonathan. Bits & Pieces. (p. 194)
—Dust & Decay. (p. 490)
—Fire & Ash. (p. 590)
—Flesh & Bone. (p. 603)
—Orphan Army. (p. 1304)
—Rot & Ruin (p. 1490)
—Rot & Ruin. (p. 1490)
—Rot & Ruin Collection: Rot & Ruin; Dust & Decay; Flesh & Bone, Fire & Ash. (p. 1490)
Maberry, Maranda. Stamps & Doodles for Girls. (p. 1639)
Maberry, Maranda, illus. see Miller, Sara.
Mabey, Coline, illus. see Gevry, C. C.
Mabian, Mercy. Little Crying Hearts: A Play. (p. 1026)
Mabie, H. W., ed. Heroes Every Child Should Know (Yesterday's Classics) (p. 772)
Mabie, Hamilton Wright. Fairy Tales Every Child Should Know. (p. 564)
—Fairy Tales Every Child Should Know a Selection of the Best Fairy Tales of All Time & of All Authors. (p. 564)
—Heroes Every Child Should Know. (p. 772)
—Heroines That Every Child Should Know: T. (p. 773)
—Legends That Every Child Should Know: A Selection of the Great Legends of All Times for Young People. (p. 990)
—Legends That Every Child Should Know. (p. 990)
—Myths That Every Child Should Know. (p. 1227)
—Norse Stories Retold from the Eddas. (p. 1264)
Mabie, Hamilton Wright, ed. Fairy Tales Every Child Should Know. (p. 564)
—Heroes Every Child Should Know. (p. 772)
Mabie, Hamilton Wright, et al, eds. Childhood's Favorites & Fairy Stories. (p. 302)
Mabille, Christine. Potato-Kid & the Adventure: Treasures Within (p. 1388)
Mabire, Grégoire, illus. see Baguley, Elizabeth.
Mabire, Grégoire, jt. auth. see Albout, Corrine.
Mableton, Barry & Ching, Jacqueline. Camping. (p. 257)
Mableton, Barry & Gettelman, Elizabeth. Basketball: Girls Rocking It. (p. 143)
Mably, Colin, jt. auth. see Benbow, Ann.
Mabry, Virginia. Jolly Ollie from Olney. (p. 924)
Mabry-Gordon, Sherri, jt. auth. see Gordon, Sherri Mabry.
MAC, jt. auth. see Mac.
Mac an Ghaill, Mairtin, jt. auth. see Haywood, Chris.
Mac & MAC. Anna Smudge: Professional Shrink. (p. 85)
Mac, Carrie. Beckoners (p. 156)
—Charmed (p. 294)
—Crush (p. 386)
—Droughtlanders (p. 486)
—Jacked (p. 903)
—Pain & Wastings (p. 1318)
—Retribution. (p. 1464)
—Storm. (p. 1655)
—Way Back (p. 1864)
Mac, Cola. Rhyming on Time. Bey, Charles, illus. (p. 1468)
Mac, Gi Gi. Poetry Stories for the Rug Rat the Ankle Biter & the Bun in the Oven. (p. 1376)
Mac Iver, Kathi. Ghosts of the Mining District. (p. 672)
Mac, Janie. Moon over Americ. (p. 1172)
—Moon over Canada. (p. 1172)
—Moon over Florida. (p. 1172)
—Moon over Michigan. (p. 1172)
Mac Killian, Caroline. Travels of the Zephyr: An Interactive Journey Around the World. (p. 1780)
Mac, Sami, illus. see Vanorny-Barcus, LaVina.
Mac, Toby, et al. Bajo Dios. (p. 133)
Mac Uistin, Liam. Táin: Ireland's Epic Adventure. Teskey, Donald, illus. (p. 1696)
Macadam, Heather Dune. Will & the Magic Mirror. Macadam, Winn, illus. (p. 1932)
MacAdam, Ian Paul, illus. see Rath, Tom H.
MacAdam, Lea. You & Rules in Your Family. (p. 1973)
—You & the Rules in Your Family. (p. 1973)
MacAdam, Lea, jt. auth. see Towne, Isobel.
MacAdam, Reegory, illus. see Rath, Tom H.
Macadam, Winn, illus. see Macadam, Heather Dune.
Macalino, Damien. What If an Alligator Ate an Avalanche. Paj, Eduardo, illus. (p. 1887)
Macaluso, Jennifer. Where Do the Bubbles Go? O'Shaughnessy, Nancy, illus. (p. 1907)
Macan, Darko. Soldier X. Kordey, Igor, illus. (p. 1607)
MacAndrew, Richard. Black Pearls Starter/Beginner. (p. 196)
—Little Trouble in Amsterdam, Level 2. (p. 1037)
—Little Trouble in California. (p. 1037)
—Little Trouble in California Level Starter/Beginner (p. 1037)
—Little Trouble in California Level Starter/Beginner American English Edition. (p. 1037)
Macaraeg, Diane. Last Meal. (p. 978)
Macardle, Donald W. & Schindler, Anton Felix. Beethoven As I Knew Him. (p. 158)
Macari, Mario Duilio, ed. Funny Riddles for Kids: Squeaky Clean Easy Kid Riddles Drawn As Funny Kid's Cartoons in A Cool Comicbook Style. (p. 650)
MacArthur, Collin. Inside a Drag Racer. (p. 876)
—Inside a Formula 1 Car. (p. 876)
—Inside a High-Speed Train. (p. 876)
—Inside a Speedboat. (p. 876)
MacArthur, John. Gospel According to the Apostles Butcher, Sam, illus. (p. 703)
—My Faith & Prayer Journal. (p. 1202)
MacArthur, John F., Jr. Experiencing the Passion of Christ. (p. 549)
MacAulay, David. Black & White. (p. 195)
—Building Big (p. 239)
—Building Big. (p. 239)
—Building Big. MacAulay, David, illus. (p. 239)
—Built to Last. (p. 240)
—Castle: Revised & in Full Color. (p. 276)
—Cathedral: The Story of Its Construction. (p. 280)
—Mosque. (p. 1176)
—Way We Work: Getting to Know the Amazing Human Body. (p. 1864)
MacAulay, David & Keenan, Sheila. Castle: How It Works. (p. 276)
—Castle: How It Works. (p. 276)
—Eye: How It Works. (p. 557)
—Jet Plane. (p. 916)
—Jet Plane: How It Works. (p. 916)
—Toilet: How It Works. (p. 1762)
Macaulay, Doug, et al. Garden Bugs of Alberta: Gardening to Attract, Repel & Control. Briere, Charity, illus. (p. 656)
Macaulay, Ellen. Arkansas. (p. 99)
—Louisiana. (p. 1058)
Macaulay, John. Alcoholism. (p. 35)
MacAulay, Kelley. How Are Plants Helpful? (p. 805)
—How Do Plants Survive? (p. 807)
—Récifs Coralliens. (p. 1451)
—What Are Flowers? (p. 1879)
—What Are Leaves? (p. 1879)
—Why Do We Need Air? (p. 1924)
—Why Do We Need Rocks & Minerals? (p. 1924)
—Why Do We Need Soil? (p. 1924)
—Yoga in Action. (p. 1972)
—Zebras. (p. 1985)
MacAulay, Kelley, jt. auth. see Kalman, Bobbie.
MacAulay, Kelley & Kalman, Bobbie. Backyard Habitats. (p. 131)
—Cambios del Estado del Tiempo: Las Tormentas. (p. 255)
—Caniches. (p. 261)
—Caniches o Poodles. (p. 261)
—Caniches o Poodles. Crabtree, Marc, photos by. (p. 261)
—Changing Weather: Storms. (p. 290)
—Cocker Spaniel. (p. 337)
—Cocker Spaniel. Crabtree, Marc, photos by. (p. 337)
—Cocker Spaniels. Crabtree, Marc, photos by. (p. 337)
—Cool Construction Vehicles. (p. 363)
—Coral Reef Food Chains. (p. 366)
—Dálmatas. Crabtree, Marc, photos by. (p. 401)
—Dalmatians. Crabtree, Marc, photos by. (p. 401)
—Desert Habitat. (p. 429)
—Dolphins & Other Marine Mammals. (p. 465)
—Endangered Zebras. (p. 527)
—Extreme Mountain Biking. (p. 556)
—Extreme Skiing. (p. 556)
—Fantasticos Vehiculos para la Construccion. (p. 572)
—Goldfish. Relach, Margaret Amy & Crabtree, Marc, illus. (p. 695)
—Grassland Habitat. (p. 712)
—Habitat de Desierto. (p. 734)
—Habitat de Pastizal. (p. 734)
—Habitats de Jardin. (p. 735)
—Hábitats de Jardín. (p. 735)
—Karaté. (p. 943)
—Labrador Retrievers. (p. 970)
—Labrador Retrievers. Crabtree, Marc, photos by. (p. 970)
—Los Dálmatas: Un Libro de Bobbie Kalman. (p. 1053)
—Parakeets. (p. 1323)
—Perros Labrador. (p. 1344)
—Perros Labrador. Crabtree, Marc, photos by. (p. 1344)
—Perruches. (p. 1344)
—Ponies. Crabtree, Marc, illus. (p. 1382)
—Poodles. Crabtree, Marc, photos by. (p. 1383)
—Prairie Food Chains. (p. 1392)
—Rabbits. Crabtree, Marc, illus. (p. 1429)
—Reptiles. (p. 1461)
—Reptiles de Todo Tipo. (p. 1461)
—Reptiles of All Kinds. (p. 1461)
—Taekwondo in Action. Crabtree, Marc, photos by. (p. 1695)
—Tempêtes. Briere, Marie-Josee, tr. from ENG. (p. 1718)
—Toundra. (p. 1773)
—Tropical Oceans. (p. 1789)
—Tundra Food Chains. (p. 1796)
—Vélo de Montagne Extrême. (p. 1835)
MacAulay, Kelley, et al. Labradors. (p. 970)
—Lapins. (p. 975)
—Poissons Rouges. (p. 1377)
—Poneys. (p. 1382)
Macaulay, Kelly, jt. auth. see Kalman, Bobbie.
Macaulay, Margaret C., ed. Stories from Chaucer: Re-Told from the Canterbury Tales. (p. 1654)
Macauley, Jo. Inferno (p. 873)
—New World (p. 1247)
—Plague (p. 1366)
—Plague. (p. 1366)
—Secrets & Spies (p. 1544)
—Treason (p. 1781)
—Treason. (p. 1781)
Macauley, Michael. Inheritance Almanac. Vaz, Mark Cotta, ed. (p. 874)
Macauley, Myron Christian. Modern Man in Search of Soul. (p. 1158)
Macavinta, Courtney & Pluym, Andrea Vander. Respect: A Girl's Guide to Getting Respect & Dealing When Your Line Is Crossed. Lepage, Catherine, illus. (p. 1463)
Macaw, Grant. Vigil's End. (p. 1842)
MacBain, Jennifer. Gertrude Elion: Nobel Prize Winner in Physiology & Medicine. (p. 667)
MacBain, Jenny. Salem Witch Trials: A Primary Source History of the Witchcraft Trials in Salem, Massachusetts. (p. 1504)
MacBain, Jenny, jt. auth. see Lowery, Zoe.
MacBain-Stephens, Jennifer. Women's Suffrage: Giving the Right to Vote to All Americans. (p. 1947)
Macbain-Stephens, Jennifer. Women's Suffrage: Giving the Right to Vote to All Americans. (p. 1947)
MacBeth, Sybil. Praying in Color. (p. 1393)
MacBride, Roger Lea. Little Farm in the Ozarks. (p. 1027)
MacCall, Terry, jt. auth. see Bryce, Frank.
MacCallum, Jess. Swimming with the Fishes. (p. 1691)
Maccaro, Janet. Breaking the Grip of Dangerous Emotions: Don't Break down - Break Through! (p. 225)
Maccarone, Grace. Bunny Race! Long, Ethan, illus. (p. 242)
—Cowboy. Müller, Hildegard, illus. (p. 373)
—Day with Miss Lina's Ballerinas. (p. 415)
—Day with Miss Lina's Ballerinas. Davenier, Christine, illus. (p. 415)
—Gingerbread Family: A Scratch-and-Sniff Book. Gardner, Louise, illus. (p. 677)
—Miss Lina's Ballerinas. Davenier, Christine, illus. (p. 1151)
—Miss Lina's Ballerinas & the Wicked Wish. Davenier, Christine, illus. (p. 1151)
—Peter Rabbit's Happy Easter. McPhail, David, illus. (p. 1347)
—Princess Tales: Once upon a Time in Rhyme with Seek-and-Find Pictures. de Marcken, Gail, illus. (p. 1405)
—Six Super Easy-To-Read Stories. (p. 1582)
—Three Bears ABC. Hibbert, Hollie, illus. (p. 1741)
—Three Little Pigs Count To 100. Pistacchio, illus. (p. 1743)
—Turkey Day. Manders, John, illus. (p. 1797)
Maccarone, Grace, ed. see Scholastic, Inc. Staff.
Maccarone, Grace, jt. auth. see Bridges, Ruby.
Maccarone, Grace, jt. auth. see Panzieri, Lucia.
Maccarone, Grace, jt. auth. see Schneider, Antonie.
Maccarone, Grace & Lo, Erika. Dinosaurs: 4 Favorite Stories! (p. 444)
Maccarone, Sandra F. Meeting Challenges: American Readers. (p. 1123)
MacCarthy, Patricia. Moon Forest. (p. 1172)
—Ocean Parade: A Counting Book. MacCarthy, Patricia, illus. (p. 1276)
MacCarthy, Patricia, illus. see Musgrove, Marianne.
MacCaughrean, Geraldine, et al. Reloj de Mi Abuela. Lambert, Stephen, illus. (p. 1458)
Macceca, Michael L. World of Plants. (p. 1957)
Macceca, Michael L. & Doak, Robin S. World of Plants (p. 1957)

Macceca, Stephanie. George Washington Carver: Agriculture Pioneer. (p. 664)
—Tornado Trouble. (p. 1770)
MacColl, Gail. Book of Cards for Kids. (p. 211)
MacColl, Michaela. Always Emily. (p. 51)
—Nobody's Secret. (p. 1262)
—Prisoners in the Palace: How Princess Victoria Became Queen with the Help of Her Maid, a Reporter, & a Scoundrel. (p. 1407)
—Revelation of Louisa May. (p. 1465)
MacColl, Michaela & Chronicle Books Staff. Novel of Intrigue & Romance. (p. 1268)
MacColl, Michaela & Nichols, Rosemary. Rory's Promise. (p. 1488)
MacConnel, Kim. Collection of Applied Design. (p. 339)
MacCoon, Nancy. Backyard Wonders. Watkins, Courtney, illus. (p. 131)
MacCormick SEcure Center, Residents. Another Sad Inning: Incarcerated Youth Reveal Their Trials, Tribulations & Loves. MacCormick Secure Center, Residents, illus. (p. 88)
MacCormick Secure Center, Residents, illus. see MacCormick SEcure Center, Residents.
MacCracken, Joan. Trisba & Sula: A Miskitu Folktale from Nicaragua (Una Leyenda de los Miskitos de Nicaragua) Macdonald, Isabel et al, trs. (p. 1787)
MacCuish, Al. Operation Alphabet. Lozano, Luciano, illus. (p. 1300)
Maccuish, Isla, jt. ed. see Gallagher, Belinda.
MacCullough, Carolyn. Always a Witch. (p. 51)
—Once a Witch. (p. 1292)
MacCurtain, Fionnuala. Story of Tomás Mac Curtáin. (p. 1662)
MacDangereuse, T. T. Epic Tales from Adventure Time: Queen of Rogues. Houghton, Christopher, illus. (p. 532)
—Epic Tales from Adventure Time: the Untamed Scoundrel. Houghton, Christopher, illus. (p. 532)
Macdangereuse, T. T. Queen of Rogues. (p. 1425)
—Untamed Scoundrel. (p. 1823)
MacDonald, Alan. Alien Attack! Baines, Nigel, illus. (p. 40)
Macdonald, Alan. Dirty Bertie: Burp! Roberts, David, illus. (p. 446)
—Dirty Bertie: Worms! Roberts, David, illus. (p. 446)
MacDonald, Alan. Fangs! Roberts, David, illus. (p. 571)
—Fleas! Roberts, David, illus. (p. 603)
—Germs! Roberts, David, illus. (p. 667)
—Pig in a Wig. Hess, Paul, illus. (p. 1357)
—Scaredy Mouse. Warnes, Tim, illus. (p. 1519)
—Superhero School: The Revenge of the Green Meanie. Baines, Nigel, illus. (p. 1683)
—Worms! Roberts, David, illus. (p. 1961)
MacDonald, Alan & Roberts, David. Dirty Bertie. (p. 446)
Macdonald, Alastair. First Christmas. Nassief, Adel, illus. (p. 593)
—Primera Navidad. Canetti, Yanitzia, tr. from ENG. (p. 1400)
MacDonald, Allison, jt. ed. see Carmichael, Tricia.
MacDonald, Alysha. Noodles - a Lunchtime Adventure. Swaim, Mike, illus. (p. 1264)
MacDonald, Anne Louise. Ghost Horse of Meadow Green. (p. 670)
—Memory Stone Ouellet, Joanne, illus. (p. 1126)
—Seeing Red. (p. 1548)
MacDonald, Anne Louise & Wahl, Charis. Seeing Red. (p. 1548)
MacDonald, Annie. Bubbles for Poppo. (p. 233)
Macdonald, Annie. Poppo's Memory Book: A Child's Guide to Remember & S. M. I. L. E. after Loss. (p. 1385)
MacDonald, Annie. Poppo's Very Best Trick. (p. 1385)
—What's up with Poppo? (p. 1900)
MacDonald, Bailey. Secret of the Sealed Room: A Mystery of Young Benjamin Franklin. (p. 1543)
—Wicked Will: A Mystery of Young William Shakespeare. (p. 1927)
MacDonald, Barry. Everything Real Justin Bieber Fans Should Know & Do. (p. 545)
MacDonald, Bernell. One Day the Animals Talked: Short Stories. Gardner, Rita, illus. (p. 1294)
MacDonald, Betty. Happy Birthday, Mrs. Piggle-Wiggle. Boiger, Alexandra, illus. (p. 745)
—Hello, Mrs. Piggle-Wiggle. Knight, Hilary & Boiger, Alexandra, illus. (p. 764)
—Mrs. Piggle-Wiggle. Knight, Hilary & Boiger, Alexandra, illus. (p. 1187)
—Mrs. Piggle-Wiggle's Magic. Knight, Hilary & Boiger, Alexandra, illus. (p. 1187)
—Nancy & Plum. GrandPré, Mary, illus. (p. 1228)
MacDonald, Betty & Canham, Anne MacDonald. Happy Birthday, Mrs. Piggle-Wiggle. Boiger, Alexandra, illus. (p. 745)
MacDonald, Betty Bard. Hello, Mrs Piggle Wiggle. (p. 764)
—Mrs. Piggle-Wiggle. (p. 1187)
—Mrs. Piggle-Wiggle. Boiger, Alexandra, illus. (p. 1187)
—Mrs. Piggle-Wiggle's Magic. (p. 1187)
—Nancy & Plum. GrandPré, Mary, illus. (p. 1228)
—Squeaky Door. (p. 1636)
MacDonald, Beverley. Written in Blood: A Brief History of Civilisation (With All the Gory Bits Left In) Weldon, Andrew, illus. (p. 1965)
MacDonald, Bruce, illus. see Hamilton, Martha & Weiss, Mitch.
MacDonald, Clarke, illus. see Bellingham, Brenda.
MacDonald, Daniel & Escobar, Michael. Chess for Kids! Everything You Need to Learn & Play. (p. 298)
MacDonald, David, jt. auth. see Ipellie, Alootook.
MacDonald, David, jt. auth. see Landon, Rocky.
MacDonald, David W., ed. Encyclopedia of Mammals (p. 525)
MacDonald, Dawn. Beyond Darkness. (p. 173)
Macdonald, Eric, jt. auth. see Mcfaul, Jason.
Macdonald, Fiona. Amazing Archaeologists: True Stories of Astounding Archaeological Discoveries (p. 53)
MacDonald, Fiona. Ancient Egyptians: Dress, Eat, Write & Play Just Like the Egyptians. (p. 69)
—Ancient Egyptians: An Epic Lost Civilisation Brought Vividly to Life. (p. 69)
Macdonald, Fiona. Ancient Greece. (p. 69)
—Ancient Rome. (p. 70)
MacDonald, Fiona. Aztec & Maya Worlds. (p. 122)
—Aztecs: Dress, Eat, Write & Play Just Like the Aztecs. (p. 122)
—Be a Suffragist! A Protest Movement That's Rougher Than You Expected. Antram, David, illus. (p. 148)
Macdonald, Fiona. Celtic Myths & Legends (p. 286)
MacDonald, Fiona. Celtic World. (p. 286)
Macdonald, Fiona. Courageous Circumnavigators: True Stories of Around-The-World Adventurers (p. 373)
MacDonald, Fiona. Design. (p. 429)
Macdonald, Fiona. Do You Want to Be a Roman Soldier? (p. 458)
MacDonald, Fiona. Edwin Hubble. (p. 505)
—Egyptian Mummy. (p. 507)
Macdonald, Fiona. Egyptians. (p. 507)
MacDonald, Fiona. Equal Opportunities (p. 533)
—Equal Opportunities. (p. 533)
Macdonald, Fiona. Hands-On History! Ancient Japan: Step Back to the Time of Shoguns & Samurai, with 15 Step-By-Step Projects & over 330 Exciting Pictures. (p. 741)
MacDonald, Fiona. Hands-On History! Aztec & Maya: Rediscover the Lost World of Ancient Central America, with 450 Exciting Pictures & 15 Step-By-Step Projects. (p. 741)
—Hands-On History! the Celts: Step into the World of the Celtic Peoples, with 15 Step-By-Step Projects & over 400 Exciting Pictures. (p. 741)
—History of Culture. (p. 784)
—How to Be a Medieval Knight. Bergin, Mark, illus. (p. 814)
—How to Be a Roman Soldier. Hewetson, Nicholas, illus. (p. 815)
—How to Be a Roman Soldier. Hewetson, Nicholas J., illus. (p. 815)
—How to Be a Samurai Warrior. James, John, illus. (p. 815)
—How to Be an Aztec Warrior. Antram, Dave & Bergin, Mark, illus. (p. 815)
—How to Be an Aztec Warrior. Bergin, Mark & Antram, Dave, illus. (p. 815)
—How to Be an Aztec Warrior. Bergin, Mark & Antram, David, illus. (p. 815)
—I Wonder Why Greeks Built Temples: And Other Questions about Ancient Greece. (p. 849)
—Inside the Beagle with Charles Darwin. Bergin, Mark, illus. (p. 877)
Macdonald, Fiona. Killer Animals: You Wouldn't Want to Meet! (p. 956)
MacDonald, Fiona. Knights & Castles. (p. 964)
—Knights, Castles, & Warfare in the Middle Ages. (p. 964)
Macdonald, Fiona. Medieval Chronicles: Vikings, Knights, & Castles. Antram, David, illus. (p. 1119)
MacDonald, Fiona. Meet a Body Snatcher! Criminals & Murderers You'D Rather Avoid. (p. 1120)
—Monarchs in the Middle Ages. (p. 1163)
Macdonald, Fiona. Murderous Mythical Creatures. (p. 1192)
—Nasty Pirates: You Wouldn't Want to Meet! (p. 1230)
MacDonald, Fiona. Plague & Medicine in the Middle Ages. (p. 1366)
—Religion. (p. 1458)
—Romans: Dress, Eat, Write & Play Just Like the Romans. (p. 1486)
Macdonald, Fiona. Romans. (p. 1486)
MacDonald, Fiona. Shipwrecks. (p. 1567)
Macdonald, Fiona. Shipwrecks. (p. 1567)
MacDonald, Fiona. Solving the Mysteries of the Pyramids. (p. 1608)
—Step into the Aztec & Maya Worlds. (p. 1648)
Macdonald, Fiona. Top 10 Worst Ruthless Warriors. Antram, David, illus. (p. 1768)
—Top 10 Worst Wicked Rulers. Antram, David, illus. (p. 1768)
MacDonald, Fiona. Travel & Trade in the Middle Ages. (p. 1780)
—Viking Raiders. (p. 1842)
—Vikings: Dress, Eat, Write & Play Just Like the Vikings. (p. 1842)
Macdonald, Fiona. Vikings. (p. 1842)
—World in the Time Of ... (p. 1956)
MacDonald, Fiona. You Wouldn't Want to Be a Crusader! A War You'd Rather Not Fight. Bergin, Mark, illus. (p. 1976)
Macdonald, Fiona. You Wouldn't Want to Be a Medieval Knight! Armor You'd Rather Not Wear. Antram, David, illus. (p. 1976)
—You Wouldn't Want to Be a Samurai! A Deadly Career You'd Rather Not Pursue. Antram, David, illus. (p. 1977)
—You Wouldn't Want to Be a Slave in Ancient Greece! A Life You'd Rather Not Have. Antram, David, illus. (p. 1977)
MacDonald, Fiona. You Wouldn't Want to Be a Suffragist! A Protest Movement That's Rougher Than You Expected. Antram, David, illus. (p. 1977)
Macdonald, Fiona. You Wouldn't Want to Be an Aztec Sacrifice: Gruesome Things You'd Rather Not Know. Antram, David, illus. (p. 1977)
—You Wouldn't Want to Be in a Medieval Dungeon! Prisoners You'd Rather Not Meet. (p. 1977)
—You Wouldn't Want to Be in a Medieval Dungeon! Prisoners You'd Rather Not Meet. Antram, David, illus. (p. 1977)
—You Wouldn't Want to Be Joan of Arc! A Mission You Might Want to Miss. Antram, David, illus. (p. 1977)
MacDonald, Fiona. You Wouldn't Want to Be Mary Queen of Scots: A Ruler Who Really Lost Her Head. Antram, David, illus. (p. 1977)
—You Wouldn't Want to Be Mary Queen of Scots. Antram, David, illus. (p. 1977)
Macdonald, Fiona. You Wouldn't Want to Live Without Clocks & Calendars! Antram, David, illus. (p. 1977)
—You Wouldn't Want to Live Without Dentists! Antram, David, illus. (p. 1977)
—You Wouldn't Want to Live Without Toilets! Antram, David, illus. (p. 1977)
MacDonald, Fiona. You Wouldn't Want to Meet a Body Snatcher! Criminals & Murderers You'd Rather Avoid. (p. 1977)
Macdonald, Fiona. You Wouldn't Want to Sail with Christopher Columbus! (Revised Edition) (p. 1977)
MacDonald, Fiona. You Wouldn't Want to Work on a Medieval Cathedral! A Difficult Job That Never Ends. (p. 1977)
Macdonald, Fiona. You Wouldn't Want to Work on a Medieval Cathedral! A Difficult Job That Never Ends. (p. 1977)
MacDonald, Fiona, jt. auth. see Jacobs, Pat.
Macdonald, Fiona, jt. auth. see MacDonald, Fiona.
Macdonald, Fiona, jt. auth. see Malam, John.
Macdonald, Fiona, jt. auth. see Steele, Philip.
MacDonald, Fiona & Bergin, Mark. How to Be a Medieval Knight. (p. 814)
MacDonald, Fiona & Donnelly, S. E. How to Be a Samurai Warrior. James, John, illus. (p. 815)
MacDonald, Fiona & Geyer, Flora. Mao Zedong: The Rebel Who Led a Revolution. (p. 1089)
MacDonald, Fiona & Macdonald, Fiona. You Wouldn't Want to Be a Victorian Servant! A Thankless Job You'd Rather Not Have. Antram, David, illus. (p. 1977)
—You Wouldn't Want to Be in a Medieval Dungeon! Prisoners You'd Rather Not Meet. Antram, David, illus. (p. 1977)
MacDonald, Fiona & Millard, Anne. Mummies: Discover the Fascinating World of Mummies, Tombs, Mysterious Gods & Treasure Troves. (p. 1190)
MacDonald, Fiona & Steele, Philip. Raiders of the North: Discover the Dramatic World of the Celts & Vikings. (p. 1433)
MacDonald, Fiona & Weaver, Clare. Human Rights. (p. 826)
Macdonald, Fiona, et al. Incredible Ancient History Book Box: Includes Fascinating Facts, 120 Step-by-Step Projects & over 3000 Amazing Pictures (p. 869)
—Ultimate Adventurers (p. 1809)
MacDonald, Frances. Sang's Adventures 1/2/3. (p. 1511)
—Screaming Tunnel. (p. 1533)
MacDonald, George. At the Back of the North Wind. (p. 110)
—Carasoyn. (p. 265)
—Cross Purposes & Shadows. (p. 385)
—Day Boy & the Night Girl. (p. 412)
—Double Story. (p. 473)
—Elect Lady. (p. 508)
—George MacDonald Original Works Series 8: Unspoken Sermons (Series 1, 2, 3), Wilfrid Cumbermede, Thomas Wingfold, St. George & St. Michael, Poetical Works Vol. I, Poetical Works Vol. II (p. 663)
—George MacDonald's Fantasy Novels for Children Including: The Princess & the Goblin, the Princess & Curdie & at the Ba. (p. 663)
—Golden Key: Classic fairy Tales. McCabe, Steve, illus. (p. 695)
MacDonald George. Gutta Percha Willie: The Working Genius. (p. 733)
MacDonald, George. History of GuttaPercha Willie. (p. 784)
—History of Gutta-Percha Willie. (p. 784)
—Home Again: (A Duplex Edition with the Elect Lady) (p. 791)
—Home Again. (p. 791)
—Light Princess. (p. 1015)
—Light Princess & Other Fairy Stories. (p. 1015)
—Malcolm. (p. 1083)
—Phantastes, a Faerie Romance. (p. 1349)
—Princess & Curdie. (p. 1402)
—Princess & Curdie. Stratton, Helen, illus. (p. 1402)
—Princess & the Goblin. (p. 1402)
—Princess & the Goblin. Hughes, Arthur, illus. (p. 1402)
—Princess & the Goblin. Kirk, Maria L. & Hughes, Arthur, illus. (p. 1402)
—Princess Treasury. (p. 1406)
—Ranald Bannermans Boyhood. (p. 1438)
—Stephen Archer & Other Tales. (p. 1648)
—Wise Woman. (p. 1940)
MacDonald, George & Heo, Yumi. Lady Hahn & Her Seven Friends. Heo, Yumi, illus. (p. 970)
MacDonald, George, ed. Princess & Curdie. Kirk, Maria L. & Hughes, Arthur, illus. (p. 1402)
—Princess & the Goblin. (p. 1402)
MacDonald, Hugh. Crosby & Me McNevin, Dale, illus. (p. 385)
—I Is for Island: A Prince Edward Island Alphabet. Jones, Brenda, illus. (p. 839)
—Morgan's Boat Ride Bald, Anna, illus. (p. 1175)
Macdonald, Isabel, tr. see MacCracken, Joan.
MacDonald, Jake. Juliana & the Medicine Fish. (p. 932)
MacDonald, James. Dale Earnhardt, Jr. Racing's Living Legacy. (p. 401)
—Dale Earnhardt, Sr. The Intimidator. (p. 401)
—Hockey Skills: How to Play Like a Pro. (p. 787)
—Levi, Adventures of a Police Dog. (p. 1004)
MacDonald, James, 1st, tr. see Potter, Beatrix.
MacDonald, Jerry. Red Eyes & Crazy Jake. (p. 1453)
MacDonald, Joan Vos. Religion & Free Speech Today: A Pro/con Debate. (p. 1458)
—Tanzania. (p. 1705)
—Tanzania. Rotberg, Robert I., ed. (p. 1705)
MacDonald, John. Child's Play in Poetry. (p. 305)
MacDonald, John, illus. see Karwoski, Gail Langer.
MacDonald, John A. Pachung. (p. 1317)
MacDonald, Judy, illus. see Galvin, Laura Gates.
Macdonald, Kelly. They Shoot! They Score! Life's Lessons on Ice. Luca, Bogdan, illus. (p. 1732)
MacDonald, Kimber. The Misfits, Level 3. Swain, Wilson, illus. (p. 1728)
Macdonald, Laurianne. Once upon a Christmas Secret. (p. 1292)
MacDonald, Lisa Lynn. Can't Get Me! (p. 262)
MacDonald, Margaret. Animal Habitats. (p. 78)
—Bargaining at the Market. (p. 139)
—Big Cities. (p. 180)
—Boots & Shoes. (p. 213)
—Caves. (p. 282)
—Deciduous & Evergreen Trees. (p. 421)
—Energy from the Sun. (p. 528)
—Family Tree. (p. 569)
—Fire. (p. 590)
—Glass. (p. 682)
—Homes of the Past. (p. 793)
Macdonald, Margaret. How Can You Re-Use an Egg Carton? (p. 805)
MacDonald, Margaret. How Do Plants Grow? (p. 807)
—I Want to Buy a Rabbit. (p. 848)
—Job Quiz. (p. 919)
—Kitchen Machines. (p. 962)
—Leisure in the Past. (p. 991)
—Meat-Eating Plants. (p. 1118)
—Rain. (p. 1434)
—Rivers of the World. (p. 1476)
—Rules on the Soccer Field. (p. 1495)
—Scooters & Skates. (p. 1529)
—Skit Book: 101 Skits from Kids. Scull, Marie-Louise, illus. (p. 1586)
—Spring Plants. (p. 1635)
—Tell Me about the Continents. (p. 1716)
—Toys Long Ago. (p. 1774)
—What Are Houses Made Of? (p. 1879)
—What Do New Clothes Cost? (p. 1882)
—What Do People Do in Winter? (p. 1882)
—What Does the Referee Do? (p. 1884)
Macdonald, Margaret. What Keeps Me Healthy? (p. 1891)
MacDonald, Margaret. What Season Is It? (p. 1893)
Macdonald, Margaret. What Things Did Your Parents Play With? (p. 1894)
MacDonald, Margaret. What to Do When You Are Lost. (p. 1894)
Macdonald, Margaret. When Does This Tree Grow Best? (p. 1902)
—Where Am I? (p. 1906)
—Where Can You Eat This Food? (p. 1906)
—Who Can Save Power? (p. 1914)
MacDonald, Margaret. Working as a Team. (p. 1952)
MacDonald, Margaret, jt. auth. see MacDonald, Margaret Read.
MacDonald, Margaret & Smart Apple Media Staff. Animal Coverings. (p. 77)
MacDonald, Margaret Read. Algarabia en la Granja. Fatus, Sophie, illus. (p. 38)
—Bat's Big Game. Nobati, Eugenia, illus. (p. 145)
—Earth Care: World Folktales to Talk About. (p. 495)
—Farmyard Jamboree. Fatus, Sophie, illus. (p. 575)
—Fat Cat: A Danish Folktale. Paschkis, Julie, illus. (p. 577)
—Five-Minute Tales: More Stories to Read & Tell When Time Is Short. (p. 601)
—Ghost Stories from the Pacific Northwest. (p. 671)
—Give up, Gecko! Melmon, Deborah, illus. (p. 681)
—Little Rooster's Diamond Button Book & DVD Set Terry, Will, illus. (p. 1036)
—Party Croc! A Folktale from Zimbabwe. Sullivan, Derek, illus. (p. 1326)
—Peace Tales: World Folktales to Talk About. (p. 1331)
—Pickin' Peas. Cummings, Pat, illus. (p. 1354)
—Shake-It-Up Tales! Stories to Sing, Dance, Drum, & Act Out. (p. 1558)
—Squeaky Door. DePalma, Mary Newell, illus. (p. 1636)
—Surf War! A Folktale from the Marshall Islands. Valério, Geraldo, illus. (p. 1685)
—Too Many Fairies: A Celtic Tale Mitchell, Susan, illus. (p. 1766)
—Tuck-Me-In Tales: Bedtime Stories from Around the World. (p. 1795)
—Tuck-Me-In Tales: Bedtime Stories from Around the World. Davis, Yvonne, illus. (p. 1795)
—Tunjur! Tunjur! Tunjur! A Palestinian Folktale Arzoumanian, Alik, illus. (p. 1797)
MacDonald, Margaret Read & Jaeger, Winifred. Round Book: Rounds Kids Love to Sing. Davis, Yvonne LeBrun, illus. (p. 1491)
MacDonald, Margaret Read & Macdonald, Margaret. Farmyard Jamboree. (p. 575)
MacDonald, Margaret Read & Talbah, Nadia Jameel. How Many Donkeys? An Arabic Counting Tale. Liddiment, Carol, illus. (p. 811)
MacDonald, Maryann. Christmas Cat. Bates, Amy June, illus. (p. 313)
—How to Hug Christy, Jana & Mitchell, Jana Christy, illus. (p. 820)
—No Room for Francie. Richards, Virginia Helen, illus. (p. 1260)
—Odette's Secrets. (p. 1278)
—Pink Party Stead, Judy, illus. (p. 1360)
—Starring Francie O'Leary. Richards, Virginia Helen, illus. (p. 1642)
MacDonald, Maryann & Ingalls, Ann. Little Piano Girl: The Story of Mary Lou Williams, Jazz Legend. Potter, Giselle, illus. (p. 1033)
MacDonald, Mercia. Mammals on a Mission: 1. the Big Cat... 2. the Little Lamb... 3. the Cheeky Colt... (p. 1085)
MacDonald, Mindy. 7 Days of Creation. (p. 1992)
—9 Fruits Alive. (p. 1993)
—Jesus & the 12 Dudes Who Did. (p. 915)
—My Bible Storybook. (p. 1197)
—Noah's Crew Came 2 By 2. (p. 1262)
MacDonald, Ranald, jt. auth. see Eggins, Heather.
MacDonald, Ross. Henry's Hand. (p. 769)
MacDonald, Ross, illus. see Burleigh, Robert.
MacDonald, Ross, illus. see Cook, Sally & Charlton, James.
MacDonald, Ross, illus. see Henson, Heather.
MacDonald, Ross, illus. see McGhee, Alison.
MacDonald, Ross, illus. see Nobleman, Marc Tyler.
Macdonald, Ross, illus. see Sewell, Anna, et al.
MacDonald, Ross, illus. see Swift, Jonathan, et al.
MacDonald, Stella, illus. see Fitzmaurice, Gabriel.
MacDonald, Stella, illus. see Thomas, Debbie.
Macdonald, Stella, jt. auth. see Fitzmaurice, Gabriel.
MacDonald, Steven. Just Clowning Around: Two Stories. McPhail, David, illus. (p. 938)
Macdonald, Stuart. Information for Innovation: Managing from an Information Perspective. (p. 874)
MacDonald, Suse. Alphabet Animals: A Slide-and-Peek Adventure. MacDonald, Suse, illus. (p. 49)
—Circus Opposites: An Interactive Extravaganza! MacDonald, Suse, illus. (p. 322)
—Dino Shapes. MacDonald, Suse, illus. (p. 441)
—Fish, Swish! Splash, Dash! Counting Round & Round. MacDonald, Suse, illus. (p. 598)
—Shape by Shape. MacDonald, Suse, illus. (p. 1560)

MacDonald, Tom. Secret of the Tree: Marcus Speer's Ecosentinel. Stieber, Joel, illus. (p. 1543)
MacDonald, William Colt. Riddle of Ramrod Ridge. (p. 1470)
MacDonall, Angus, illus. see Judd, Mary Catherine.
MacDougal, P. Paullette. Waiting for MacArthur. (p. 1852)
MacDougall, Larry, illus. see Qitsualik, Rachel A.
MacDougall, Larry, illus. see Robey, Katharine Crawford.
MacDowell, Diane. Adventures of Timkin: The Early Years. (p. 24)
MacDowell, Maureen. Tomorrow Is the First Day of School. Hergenrother, Max, illus. (p. 1765)
Macduff, J. R. Story of a Dewdrop. (p. 1657)
Mace, Aubrey. My Fairy Grandmother. (p. 1202)
Mace, Virginia. South Africa. (p. 1616)
MacEachern, Robyn. Cyberbullying: And Ctrl Alt Delete It Charette, Geraldine, illus. (p. 396)
Maceachern, Sally. New Cultural Atlas of the Islamic World. (p. 1244)
MacEachern, Stephen, illus. see Acer, David.
MacEachern, Stephen, illus. see Hunter, Dette.
MacEachern, Stephen, illus. see Kaner, Etta.
MacEachern, Stephen, illus. see Scandiffio, Laura.
MacEachern, Stephen, illus. see Thomas, Keltie.
MacEachern, Stephen, tr. see Thomas, Keltie.
Macejko, Jeanne Anne. Million Chameleons. (p. 1144)
MacElroy, Mary H. Work & Play in Colonial Days. (p. 1952)
Macenski, Geraldine. Healthy, Happy Gigil (p. 758)
Macey, Rune. Bloodlink to Sorcery/Seven Deadly Sins. (p. 201)
—Tales of Terror. (p. 1702)
—What If. . . a Black Cat Crosses. . . (p. 1887)
Macfarlan, Allan A. Living Like Indians: A Treasury of North American Indian Crafts, Games & Activities. (p. 1041)
Macfarlane, John. Stormstruck! (p. 1656)
MacFarlane, John, illus. see Mayerhofer, Felix.
Macfarlane, Katherine. Father of the Atom: Democritus & the Nature of Matter. (p. 577)
MacFarlane, Katherine. Jeweler's Art. (p. 917)
MacFarlane, Linda, jt. auth. see MacFarlane, Stuart.
MacFarlane, Stuart & MacFarlane, Linda. Secret Diary of Adrian Cat. (p. 1540)
MacGillivray, Alex. Understanding Rachel Carson's Silent Spring. (p. 1816)
Macgoye, Marjorie Oludhe. Black Hand Gang. (p. 196)
MacGregor, Bailey. What's for Lunch? Classify & Count Objects in Each Category. (p. 1897)
MacGregor, Cynthia. Divorce Helpbook for Teens. (p. 455)
—How Do You Feel Today? (p. 808)
—Jigsaw Puzzle Family: The Stepkids' Guide to Fitting It Together. (p. 917)
—Recycling a Can. (p. 1453)
—Refuse to Use. (p. 1456)
—Think for Yourself: A Kid's Guide to Solving Life's Dilemmas & Other Sticky Problems. Farias, Susan Norberg, illus. (p. 1734)
MacGregor, Doug. Doug MacGregor's Cartoons: A Twenty-five Year Retrospective. (p. 473)
—Incredible Tongue Twister That Swallowed My Sister: Another Santa Story by Doug MacGregor. MacGregor, Doug, illus. (p. 869)
MacGregor, Doug, creator. Ochre the Smoker: A fantastic Fable. (p. 1277)
Macgregor, Eloise. Roadrunner. (p. 1477)
—Sidewinder. (p. 1573)
MacGregor, Fiona, et al. Collins Primary Science - Student's Book Stage 3. (p. 341)
MacGregor, Helen. Gnasher, Delta & the Biscuits. (p. 685)
MacGregor, Jill. Swim Safe Little Seals. (p. 1691)
MacGregor, Joanne. Rock Steady. (p. 1482)
MacGregor, K. G. Just This Once. (p. 940)
—Worth Every Step. (p. 1962)
MacGregor, Kim. Button, Buckle, Tie. Snider, Sharon & Reny, Todd, trs. (p. 248)
—Yummy Yummy Nummy Nummy, Should I Put This in My Tummy? (p. 1983)
—Yummy Yummy Nummy Nummy, Should I Put This in My Tummy? Ioannou, Gregory Phillip, ed. (p. 1983)
Macgregor, Kinley, pseud & Furth, Robin. Knight of Darkness. (p. 964)
MacGregor, Lucy. Choosing a Career as an Entrepreneur. (p. 310)
—Everything You Need to Know about Social Anxiety. (p. 546)
MacGregor, Mariam. Let's Talk! Leadership for Kids: Questions to Get Things Started. (p. 1001)
MacGregor, Megan, jt. auth. see MacGregor, Rob.
MacGregor, Rob & MacGregor, Megan. Star Power: Astrology for Teens. (p. 1641)
MacGregor, Rose. Princess Bendy. (p. 1403)
MacGregor, Roy. Attack on the Tower of London. (p. 114)
—Complete Screech Owls. (p. 353)
—Complete Screech Owls, Volume 2 (p. 353)
—Face-Off at the Alamo. (p. 560)
—Forever: The Annual Hockey Classic Deines, Brian, illus. (p. 619)
—Ghost of the Stanley Cup. (p. 671)
—Highest Number in the World. Despres, Genevieve, illus. (p. 779)
—Kindergarten Caper: The Screech Owls Prequel. (p. 957)
—Murder at the Winter Games (p. 1192)
—Mystery at Lake Placid. (p. 1223)
—Night They Stole the Stanley Cup. (p. 1254)
—Panic in Pittsburgh. (p. 1321)
—Peril at the World's Biggest Hockey Tournament. (p. 1343)
—Screech Owls' Reunion (p. 1533)
—Secret of the Deep Woods (p. 1542)
—Sudden Death in New York City. (p. 1672)
—Trouble at the Top of the World. (p. 1789)
MacGuire, Maxine. Maddie & the Naughty Elf: Santa Learns a Lesson (p. 1069)
MacHado, Ana Maria. Ah, Pajarita Si Yo Pudiera. (p. 30)
Machado, Ana Maria. Aunque Parezca Mentira. (p. 115)
MacHado, Ana Maria. Barbero y el Coronel. Coll, Ivar Da, illus. (p. 138)
—Buen Coro. (p. 235)
—De carta en Carta. Basulto, Rita, illus. (p. 416)
—Del Otro Lado Hay Secretos. (p. 424)
—Del otro Mundo. (p. 424)
—Delantal Que el Viento Lleva. (p. 424)
—Deseo Loco. (p. 428)
—Eso No Me lo Quita Nadie. (p. 536)
Machado, Ana Maria. Me in the Middle Unger, David, tr. from POR. (p. 1116)
MacHado, Ana Maria. Mi Reino Por un Caballo. (p. 1133)
—Pimienta en la Cebecita. (p. 1359)
—Tiririca, Jararaca y Perereca. Faria, Rosana, illus. (p. 1757)
—Todo al Mismo Tiempo Ahora. (p. 1761)
Machado, Ana Maria. What a Party! Amado, Elisa, tr. from POR. (p. 1878)
—Wolf Wanted Amado, Elisa, tr. from POR. (p. 1944)
Machado, Ana Maria, jt. auth. see MacHado, Ana Maria.
MacHado, Ana Maria & Machado, Ana Maria. Camilon, Comilon. (p. 256)
MacHado, Ana Maria & Machado, Ana Maria. From Another World Baeta, Luisa, tr. from POR. (p. 642)
MacHado, Ana Maria & Machado, Ana Maria. Juego del Cambia-Cambia. Valverde, Mikel, illus. (p. 931)
Machado, Antonio. Antologia Poetica de Machado. (p. 89)
—Antonio Machado para Ninos. Puebla, Teo, illus. (p. 90)
—Yo Voy Sonando Caminos. (p. 1971)
MacHado, Cj & Jones, Gareth P. Even Cowgirls Brush Their Teeth. (p. 541)
Machado, Eduardo & Domitrovich, Michael. Tastes Like Cuba: An Exile's Hunger for Home. (p. 1707)
MacHado, et al. Pavo Que Abria y Cerraba la Cola. (p. 1331)
Machado, Maria Clara & Clara, Machado Maria. Pluft, el Fantasmita. (p. 1374)
Machajewski, Sarah. Cesar Chavez in His Own Words. (p. 288)
—Cherokee People. (p. 298)
—Colony of Georgia. (p. 342)
—Cool Careers Without College for People Who Love to Cook & Eat. (p. 363)
—Death Rituals. (p. 420)
—Discovering STEM at the Restaurant. (p. 449)
—Freaky Science Discoveries. (p. 632)
—Great Fire of London. (p. 716)
—Kid's Life During the American Civil War (p. 954)
—Kid's Life in Colonial America (p. 954)
—Killer Bees. (p. 956)
—Life of a Honey Badger. (p. 1011)
—Malcolm X in His Own Words. (p. 1083)
—Mark Pincus & Zynga. (p. 1095)
—Musical Genius: Ludwig Van Beethoven. (p. 1194)
—My Dad Is a Nurse. (p. 1201)
—Our Country's Symbols. (p. 1308)
—Pearls. (p. 1333)
—Saving the Endangered Green Sea Turtle. (p. 1517)
—Standing in the President's Shoes. (p. 1639)
—We Need Plants. (p. 1867)
—What Are State & Local Government? (p. 1879)
—What Are State & Local Governments? (p. 1879)
Machajewski, Sarah, jt. auth. see Mills, Nathan.
Machajewski, Sarah, jt. auth. see Smith, Bill D.
MacHale, D. J. Black. (p. 194)
—Black Water. (p. 197)
—Blood. (p. 200)
—East of the Sun, West of the Moon. Flesher, Vivienne, illus. (p. 498)
—Guide to the Territories of Halla. Ferguson, Peter, illus. (p. 730)
—Light. (p. 1014)
—Lost City of Faar. (p. 1055)
—Merchant of Death. (p. 1127)
—Merchant of Death; The Lost City of Faar. (p. 1127)
—Monster Princess. Boiger, Alexandra, illus. (p. 1168)
—Never War. (p. 1243)
—Pendragon: The Merchant of Death; The Lost City of Fear; The Never War; The Reality Bug; Black Water. (p. 1336)
—Pilgrims of Rayne. (p. 1359)
—Quillan Games. (p. 1428)
—Raven Rise. (p. 1441)
—Reality Bug. (p. 1449)
—Rivers of Zadaa. (p. 1476)
—Soldiers of Halla. (p. 1607)
—Storm. (p. 1655)
—Strike. (p. 1667)
—Sylo. (p. 1692)
MacHale, Des. Puzzleology: Tough Puzzles for Kids. (p. 1421)
MacHale, D.J. Project Alpha. (p. 1410)
—Strike: The SYLO Chronicles #3. (p. 1667)
MacHalek, Bj. Adventures of a Noble Duchess: Duchess on Yard Patrol. (p. 16)
Machas, Dimi. Tsaani: The Grizzly Bear Story. (p. 1795)
Machen Pritchard, M. Ann. Phil the Pill & Friends: Making Positive Choices. Machen Pritchard, M. Ann, illus. (p. 1350)
Machen, Sherry Ann. Hannah & Friends. (p. 742)
Macheske, Felicia. Awesome Arms. (p. 121)
—Big & Blubbery: Walrus. (p. 177)
—Blue & Bumpy: Blue Crab. (p. 202)
—Bright & Beautiful: Butterfly. (p. 228)
—Flying Flippers: Sea Turtle. (p. 610)
—Lanky Legs. (p. 975)
—Quick & Quiet: Dragonfly. (p. 1427)
Machetto, Augusto, jt. auth. see Mulazzi, Paola.
Machetto, Augusto, et al. Disney Fairies Graphic Novel #6: A Present for Tinker Bell. Urbano, Emilio et al, illus. (p. 451)
—Tinker Bell & the Day of the Dragon Melaranci, Elisabetta et al, illus. (p. 1755)
—Tinker Bell & the Lucky Rainbow. Dalena, Antonello et al, illus. (p. 1755)
Machiavelli, Niccolò. Prince. (p. 1401)
—Prince. Bull, George, tr. from ITA. (p. 1401)
Macho, Geri. Beautiful Mouse (p. 154)
MacHoka, Rebecca. Dog Sisters: One Missing Sister. (p. 461)
Machon, Daphne E. Charlee's New Glasses. (p. 291)
Macht, Heather. You May Just Be a Dinosaur Gillard, Jason, illus. (p. 1976)
Macia, Raquel Garcia, illus. see Bari, Ellen.
Macias, Elva. Busca un Magico Lunar. Gedovius, Juan, illus. (p. 244)
Maciborski, Charmaine, illus. see Prendergast, R. L.
Macielski, Ellen. Little Raccoon's Adventures. (p. 1034)
Maciel, Amanda. Tease. (p. 1711)
Maciel, Amanda, jt. auth. see Cohen, Sasha.
MacInnis, Katherine. Kelsar. (p. 948)
MacInnis, Katherine Grace. Kelsar. (p. 948)
Macintosh, Tessa, photos by see André, Julie-Ann, et al.
Macintosh, Tessa, photos by see Highway, Tomson, et al.
Macintosh, Tessa, photos by see Jumbo, Sheyenne & Willett, Mindy.
Macintosh, Tessa, photos by see McLeod, Tom & Willett, Mindy.
Macintosh, Tessa, photos by see Willett, Mindy & Enyagotailak, Darla.
Macintosh, Tessa, photos by see Willett, Mindy & Enzoe, Pete.
MacIntyre, R. P. Blue Camaro. (p. 202)
—Crying Jesus. (p. 387)
—Feeding at Nine. (p. 580)
—Revved. (p. 1467)
—Yuletide Blues (p. 1983)
MacIntyre, R. P., ed. see Chan, Marty.
MacIntyre, R P, ed. see Truckey, Don.
MacIver, Juliette. Toucan Can. Davis, Sarah, illus. (p. 1772)
—Yak & Gnu. Chapman, Cat, illus. (p. 1968)
Mack. Baby, Where Are You? (p. 128)
—Legend of the Lonesome Bear: Level O (p. 989)
Mack, B. P. Animalphabet. (p. 81)
Mack, Cassandra. Cool, Confident & Strong: 52 Power Moves for Girls. (p. 363)
Mack, Crystal. Pentrals. (p. 1338)
Mack, Dave. What Lives in a Marsh? (p. 1891)
Mack, Dave L. In the Soil. (p. 867)
Mack, David. Daredevil: End of Days. Janson, Klaus & Sienkiewicz, Bill, illus. (p. 406)
—Kabuki Volume 1: Circle of Blood: Circle of Blood. (p. 941)
Mack, David, illus. see Gandhi, Arun, et al.
Mack, Dinah. Daddy, Look What I Can Do! (p. 398)
—Mommy, Look What I Can Do! (p. 1162)
—Mommy, Where Are You? (p. 1162)
—Vicks, the Polar Bear Cub. (p. 1840)
Mack, Gail. Horses. (p. 800)
—Kickboxing. (p. 951)
—Stars. (p. 1643)
Mack, Gerhard, et al. Roman Signer. (p. 1486)
Mack, Harry. Treasure Mystery Clues. (p. 1782)
Mack, Iris Marie. Mama Says, Money Doesn't Grow on Trees! (p. 1084)
Mack, James. Be a Great Babysitter! (p. 148)
Mack, James A., jt. auth. see Liggett, Diane T.
Mack, James & Mack, Jim. Journals & Blogging (p. 927)
Mack, Jeff. Ah Ha! (p. 30)
—Clueless Mcgee. Mack, Jeff, illus. (p. 336)
—Clueless McGee & the Inflatable Pants Mack, Jeff, illus. (p. 336)
—Clueless Mcgee Gets Famous. Mack, Jeff, illus. (p. 336)
—Duck in the Fridge (p. 488)
—Frog & Fly. (p. 639)
—Good News, Bad News. (p. 699)
—Hippo & Rabbit. Mack, Jeff, illus. (p. 781)
—Hippo & Rabbit in Brave Like Me. Mack, Jeff, illus. (p. 781)
—Hush Little Polar Bear. Mack, Jeff, illus. (p. 830)
—Look! Mack, Jeff, illus. (p. 1047)
—Things I Can Do. Mack, Jeff, illus. (p. 1733)
—Who Needs a Bath? Mack, Jeff, illus. (p. 1917)
—Who Wants a Hug? Mack, Jeff, illus. (p. 1918)
Mack, Jeff, illus. see Bentley, Dawn.
Mack, Jeff, illus. see Bunting, Eve.
Mack, Jeff, illus. see Galbraith, Kathryn O.
Mack, Jeff, illus. see Henson, Heather, et al.
Mack, Jeff, illus. see Howe, James.
Mack, Jeff, illus. see Mortensen, Lori.
Mack, Jeff, illus. see Sauer, Tammi.
Mack, Jeff, tr. see Henson, Heather, et al.
Mack, Jeff, tr. see Howe, James.
Mack, Jim. Hip-Hop. (p. 780)
Mack, Jim, jt. auth. see Mack, James.
Mack, Julia. God's Very Special People: An Activity Book for Children Who Grieve. (p. 692)
Mack, Karen. Magical Adventures of Sun Beams. (p. 1074)
—Who Makes the Sound? (p. 1917)
Mack, Kathryn, illus. see Carl, Dave.
Mack, Kelvin. Bullies Need Friends Too. (p. 240)
Mack, Lizzie. Friend or Flirt? Quick Quizzes about Your Crush. (p. 637)
—Sink or Swim? Quick Quizzes about Summer Camp. (p. 1579)
Mack, Lorna B. Lorna's Whale. (p. 1053)
Mack, Lorrie. DK Adventures: Ballet Academy: Ballet Academy. (p. 455)
Mack, Lorrie, jt. auth. see Dorling Kindersley Publishing Staff.
Mack, Lorrie & Dorling Kindersley Publishing Staff. Arctic & Antarctic. (p. 96)
—Ballet Academy. (p. 134)
—Weather. (p. 1869)
Mack, Michele. Henry Fickle & the Secret Laboratory. (p. 768)
Mack, Molly. Bugs, Pests, & Plants. (p. 237)
—Life of Paul Revere. (p. 1012)
Mack, Nancy. Teaching Grammar with Playful Poems: Engaging Lessons with Model Poems by Favorite Poets That Motivate Kids to Learn Grammar. (p. 1710)
Mack, Paulette. Cookout at Grandma's House: The Adventures of Mielle & Cheeky. (p. 362)
Mack, Phillip. Missy Finds a Home. (p. 1154)
Mack, Rachel. Kiss Goodnight: When My Daddy Had a Stroke. (p. 961)
Mack, Rodney. Adventures of Jimmy & Charlie. (p. 19)
Mack, Stan & Champlin, Susan. Fight for Freedom. (p. 585)
—Road to Revolution! Mack, Stan, illus. (p. 1477)
Mack, Steve. AmazErasers: Drive-Thru. (p. 52)
—AmazErasers: Sweet Shoppe. (p. 52)
—Leaves Fall All Around. (p. 986)
Mack, Steve, illus. see Berkowitz, Jacob.
Mack, Steve, illus. see Cleary, Brian P.
Mack, Steve, illus. see Friedman, Maya.
Mack, Steve, illus. see Goebel, Jenny.
Mack, Steve, illus. see Miles, Brenda.
Mack, Steve, illus. see Newman, Vivian.
Mack, Steve, illus. see Wagenbach, Debbie.
Mack, Steve, jt. auth. see Flash Kids Editors.
Mack, Tracy & Citrin, Michael. Fall of the Amazing Zalindas. (p. 566)
Mack, Tracy, et al. Cinderella: Les Petits Fairytales. Lake, Oliver, illus. (p. 320)
—Snow White: Les Petits Fairytales. Lake, Oliver, illus. (p. 1599)
Mack, Travis, illus. see Spencer, Mignon.
Mack, W. C. Athlete vs. Mathlete. (p. 112)
—Athlete vs. Mathlete: Double Dribble. (p. 112)
—Time-Out. (p. 1752)
Mack, William. Pondo Takes a Stand. (p. 1382)
Mack, Winnie. After All, You're Callie Boone. (p. 28)
Mackall, Dandi. Fantastic Gifts of Fall. (p. 571)
—Super Gifts of Spring: Easter. (p. 1680)
—Wonderful Gifts of Winter. Blackmore, Katherine, illus. (p. 1948)
Mackall, Dandi Daley. Bed Time Blessings. Kucharik, Elena, illus. (p. 156)
—Bob's Great Escape Wolf, Claudia, illus. (p. 206)
—Buckskin Bandit. (p. 234)
—Cinnamon Lake Mysteries Set (p. 321)
—Crazy in Love. (p. 377)
—Dark Horse. (p. 407)
—Double Trouble Wolf, Claudia, illus. (p. 473)
—Easter Colors Sticker Book. Fyffe, Brian, illus. (p. 499)
—Easter Is for Me! (p. 499)
—Finds a Home (p. 588)
—Friendly Foal. (p. 638)
—Gaggle of Geese & a Clutter of Cats. Hohn, David, illus. (p. 652)
—Gift Horse. (p. 675)
—Girl Named Dan. Graef, Renee, illus. (p. 678)
—God Loves Me More Than That. (p. 689)
—God Made Polliwogs & Puppy Dogs. (p. 690)
—Horse Named Bob Wolf, Claudia, illus. (p. 799)
—Horsefeathers Set (p. 800)
—I'll Talk to God about That. (p. 856)
—Jesus lo Hizo por Mi. Petrov, Anton, illus. (p. 915)
—Kids' Rules for Life: A Guide to Life's Journey from Those Just Starting Out. (p. 955)
—Legend of Ohio. LaFever, Greg, illus. (p. 988)
—Legend of St. Nicholas: A Story of Christmas Giving Cowdrey, Richard, illus. (p. 988)
—Little Shepherd. (p. 1036)
—Mad Dog. (p. 1069)
—Natalie: School's First Day of Me Blakeslee, Lys, illus. (p. 1230)
—Natalie & the Bestest Friend Race Blakeslee, Lys, illus. (p. 1230)
—Natalie & the Downside-Up Birthday Blakeslee, Lys, illus. (p. 1230)
—Natalie & the One-of-a-Kind Wonderful Day! Blakeslee, Lys, illus. (p. 1230)
—Natalie Really Very Much Wants to Be a Star Blakeslee, Lys, illus. (p. 1230)
—Natalie Wants a Puppy Blakeslee, Lys, illus. (p. 1230)
—No, No Noah! Kucharik, Elena, illus. (p. 1259)
—Perfect Pony Wolf, Claudia, illus. (p. 1342)
—Please Reply! (p. 1373)
—Rudy Rides the Rails: A Depression Era Story. Ellison, Chris, illus. (p. 1494)
—Runaway. (p. 1496)
—Secrets of Tree Taylor. (p. 1546)
—Shepherd's Christmas Story. Catalano, Dominic, illus. (p. 1565)
—Silence of Murder. (p. 1575)
—Story of the Easter Robin Vojtech, Anna, illus. (p. 1661)
—Thank You for Thanksgiving. Walker, John, illus. (p. 1725)
—That's My Colt: An Easter Tale. Ellison, Chris, illus. (p. 1727)
—There's a Baby in There! Whitt, Carlynn, illus. (p. 1730)
—Unhappy Appy. (p. 1817)
—Wild Cat. (p. 1929)
—Wonder of Christmas. Hill, Dave, illus. (p. 1947)
—You & Your Horse: How to Whisper Your Way into Your Horse's Life. O'Connor, Jeff, illus. (p. 1973)
Mackall, Dandi Daley, adapted by. Pastorcito: Para ninos de 4-7 Anos. (p. 1327)
Mackall, Dandi Daley & Bostrom, Kathleen Long. Bedtime Stories & Prayers. Kucharik, Elena, illus. (p. 157)
Mackall, Dandi Daley & Kingsbury, Karen. Gift of the Christmas Cookie: Sharing the True Meaning of Jesus' Birth Chabrian, Deborah L., illus. (p. 675)
Mackall, Debbie, illus. see Mackall, Deborah.
Mackall, Deborah. Be Still! The Story of a Little Bird & How He Found His Purpose. Mackall, Deborah, illus. (p. 149)
—What Happens When I'm Asleep? Mackall, Debbie, illus. (p. 1886)
Mackan, Paul. Dream Girl, Dream! A Story for Children to Share with Groan-Ups (p. 483)
MacKay, Alison, jt. auth. see Morecroft, Richard.
MacKay, Andrew. Young Lions Roar. (p. 1979)
Mackay, Anne-Marie, creator. Magus Deck: Your Gateway to Balhundorra. (p. 1076)
Mackay, Barbara. Starters: Three Practice Tests for Cambridge English. (p. 1643)
Mackay, David. What in the World? (p. 1887)
MacKay, Elly. Butterfly Park. (p. 248)
—If You Hold a Seed. (p. 854)
—Shadow Chasers. (p. 1557)
MacKay, Elly, illus. see Holland, Loretta.
MacKay, Elly, illus. see Skrypuch, Marsha Forchuk.
Mackay, Hugh, illus. see Perry, Laurie.
Mackay, J. A. Rockin' Roly Poly. (p. 1483)
MacKay, Jennifer. Amnesia. (p. 65)
Mackay, Jennifer. Bipolar Disorder. Abramovitz, Melissa, ed. (p. 190)
MacKay, Jennifer. Columbine School Shootings. (p. 346)

M

—Forensic Art. (p. 617)
—Forensic Biology. (p. 617)
—James Cameron. Greenhaven Press Editors, ed. (p. 907)
Mackay, Jennifer. Online Schools. Greenhaven Press, ed. (p. 1298)
MacKay, Jennifer. Phobias. (p. 1351)
—Soccer. (p. 1603)
—Tim Tebow. Greenhaven Press Editors, ed. (p. 1750)
Mackay, Jennifer, jt. auth. see Mackay, Jennifer.
MacKay, Jennifer, jt. auth. see Taylor, Robert.
MacKay, Jennifer, jt. ed. see Gale Editor.
MacKay, Jennifer, jt. ed. see Greenhaven Press Editors.
Mackay, Jennifer & Mackay, Jennifer. Art of Songwriting. Greenhaven Press Editors, ed. (p. 102)
MacKay, Jennifer, ed. Bullying. (p. 241)
—Gangs. (p. 655)
—Roller Coasters. (p. 1485)
—Track & Field. (p. 1775)
Mackay, Jenny. Cryptology. (p. 387)
MacKay, Jenny. Do Haunted Houses Exist? (p. 457)
—Figure Skating. (p. 586)
—Fingerprints & Impression Evidence. (p. 589)
Mackay, Jenny. Hindu Mythology. Lucent Books Staff, ed. (p. 780)
—Taekwondo. Greenhaven Press Staff, ed. (p. 1695)
Mackay, John, illus. see Ross, Kendric.
Mackay, John L. Haggai, Zechariah & Malachi: God's Restored People. (p. 735)
MacKay, Lisa. Nick Finds a Home. (p. 1251)
Mackay, Louis, illus. see Carson, Mary Kay.
MacKay, Mark, illus. see Kilgannon, Amy.
Mackel, Kathy. Boost. (p. 213)
—MadCat. (p. 1069)
Macken, JoAnn Early. Animals I See at the Zoo/Animales Que Veo en el Zoológico (p. 82)
—Animals I See at the Zoo/Animales Que Veo en el Zoológico Coffey, Colleen & Carrillo, Consuelo, trs. (p. 82)
—Animals That Live in... Complete Series (p. 84)
—Animals That Live in the Desert;Animales del desierto Complete Series (p. 84)
—Animals That Live on the Farm;Animales que viven en la granja Complete Series (p. 84)
—Autumn. (p. 118)
—Autumn (Otoño). (p. 118)
—Autumn/Otoño. (p. 118)
—Baby Says Moo! Walker, David, illus. (p. 128)
—Beaches. (p. 149)
—Bighorn Sheep: Carneros de Canada. (p. 185)
—Bighorn Sheep. (p. 185)
—Bike Riding. (p. 185)
—Black Bears: Osos Negros. (p. 195)
—Black Bears. (p. 195)
—Building a House (p. 238)
—Building a Road Saunders-Smith, Gail, ed. (p. 238)
—Building a Skyscraper Saunders-Smith, Gail, ed. (p. 238)
—Chickens. (p. 300)
—Chickens;Las Gallinas. (p. 301)
—Condors. (p. 356)
—Condors;Cóndor. (p. 356)
—Construction Tools (p. 360)
—Coral Reefs. (p. 366)
—Coral Reefs (Arrecifes de Coral) (p. 366)
—Cougars. (p. 369)
—Cougars;Puma. (p. 369)
—Cows. (p. 374)
—Cows;Las Vacas. (p. 374)
—Coyotes. (p. 375)
—Coyotes;Coyotes. (p. 375)
—Deer: Venados. (p. 423)
—Deer. (p. 423)
—Demolition (p. 426)
—Deserts. (p. 429)
—Digging Tunnels Saunders-Smith, Gail, ed. (p. 439)
—Dinosaur Museum. (p. 442)
—Elk. (p. 513)
—Elk;Venado. (p. 513)
—Flip, Float, Fly: Seeds on the Move. Paparone, Pam, illus. (p. 605)
—Gary Paulsen: Voice of Adventure & Survival. (p. 657)
—Gila Monsters. (p. 676)
—Gila Monsters;Monstruos de Gila. (p. 676)
—Goats. (p. 687)
—Goats;Las Cabras. (p. 688)
—Golden Eagles. (p. 694)
—Golden Eagles;Águila Real. (p. 694)
—Guinea Pigs. (p. 731)
—Gymnastics. (p. 733)
—Horses. (p. 800)
—Horses;Los Caballos. (p. 800)
—Jackrabbits. (p. 904)
—Jackrabbits;Liebres Americanas. (p. 904)
—Karate. (p. 943)
—Kittens. (p. 963)
—Lagos. (p. 971)
—Lakes. (p. 972)
—Lakes/Lagos. (p. 972)
—Life Cycle of a Bat. (p. 1008)
—Life Cycle of a Cicada. (p. 1009)
—Life Cycle of a Dragonfly. (p. 1009)
—Life Cycle of a Flamingo. (p. 1009)
—Life Cycle of a Hummingbird. (p. 1009)
—Life Cycle of a Moth. (p. 1009)
—Monkeys: Los Monos. (p. 1166)
—Monkeys (Los Monos) (p. 1166)
—Montanas. (p. 1170)
—Montañas. (p. 1170)
—Moose. (p. 1173)
—Moose;Alces. (p. 1173)
—Mountain Goats. (p. 1180)
—Mountain Goats;Cabra Montés. (p. 1180)
—Mountains. (p. 1181)
—Nurses. (p. 1273)
—Ocean Floors. (p. 1276)
—Ocean Floors (Fondos Oceánicos) (p. 1276)
—Opossums. (p. 1300)
—Opossums;Zarigüeyas. (p. 1300)
—Owls. (p. 1315)
—Owls;Búhos y Lechuzas. (p. 1315)
—Parakeets. (p. 1323)
—Penguins/Los Pingüinos. (p. 1337)
—Pigs. (p. 1358)
—Pigs;Los Cerdos. (p. 1358)
—Plains. (p. 1366)
—Porcupines. (p. 1386)
—Porcupines;Puercoespines. (p. 1386)
—Puppies. (p. 1417)
—Rabbits. (p. 1429)
—Rattlesnakes. (p. 1440)
—Rattlesnakes;Serpientes de Cascabel. (p. 1440)
—Read, Recite, & Write Cinquains. (p. 1443)
—Read, Recite, & Write Concrete Poems. (p. 1443)
—Read, Recite, & Write Haiku. (p. 1443)
—Read, Recite, & Write List Poems. (p. 1443)
—Rios. (p. 1473)
—Ríos (Rivers) (p. 1473)
—Rivers: Rios. (p. 1476)
—Rivers. (p. 1476)
—Road Signs. (p. 1477)
—Roadrunners. (p. 1477)
—Roadrunners;Correcaminos. (p. 1477)
—Sanitation Workers. (p. 1511)
—Sea Lions/los Leones Marinos. (p. 1535)
—Seas. (p. 1538)
—Sheep. (p. 1564)
—Sheep;Las Ovejas. (p. 1564)
—Simple Machines. (p. 1577)
—Snakes/Las Serpientes. (p. 1597)
—Spring. (p. 1634)
—Spring (Primavera) (p. 1635)
—Spring/Primavera. (p. 1635)
—Summer. (p. 1673)
—Summer (Verano) (p. 1675)
—Swimming. (p. 1691)
—Teachers. (p. 1709)
—Tigers: Los Tigres. (p. 1749)
—Tigers (Los Tigres) (p. 1749)
—Toys. (p. 1774)
—Veterinarians. (p. 1839)
—Vultures. (p. 1851)
—Vultures;Buitres. (p. 1851)
—Waiting Out the Storm. Gaber, Susan, illus. (p. 1853)
—Wetlands. (p. 1877)
—Winter. (p. 1937)
—Winter (Invierno) (p. 1938)
Macken, JoAnn Early, jt. auth. see Brandt, Keith.
Macken, JoAnn Early, jt. auth. see Sabin, Francene.
Macken, JoAnn Early, jt. auth. see Sabin, Louis.
Macken, JoAnn Early, jt. auth. see Santrey, Laurence.
Macken, JoAnn Early & Early Macken, JoAnn. Beaches (Playas) (p. 149)
—Beaches/Playas. (p. 149)
—Coral Reefs/Arrecifes de Coral. (p. 366)
—Ocean Floors/Fondos Oceánicos. (p. 1276)
—Rivers/Rios. (p. 1476)
—Summer/Verano. (p. 1675)
—Wetlands: Terrenos Pantanosos. (p. 1877)
—Wetlands/ Pantanos. (p. 1877)
—Winter/Invierno. (p. 1938)
Macken, Ultan. Story of Daniel O'Connell. (p. 1658)
Mackenzie, Anne L., jt. auth. see MacKenzie, Anne L.
MacKenzie, Anne L. & Mackenzie, Anne L. Let's Recycle! (p. 1000)
MacKenzie, C. A. Search for a Golden Eagle. (p. 1537)
MacKenzie, Carine. Baby Moses. (p. 127)
—Barnabas: The Encourager. Apps, Fred, illus. (p. 139)
—Beautiful Garden. (p. 153)
—Bible Heroes Daniel. (p. 175)
Mackenzie, Carine. Bible Heroes Elijah. (p. 175)
—Bible Heroes Esther. (p. 175)
MacKenzie, Carine. Bible Heroes Gideon. (p. 175)
Mackenzie, Carine. Bible Heroes Joseph. (p. 175)
MacKenzie, Carine. Bible Heroes - Noah. (p. 175)
—Bible Heroes Paul. (p. 175)
—Bible Heroes Peter. (p. 175)
Mackenzie, Carine. Bible Heroes Ruth. (p. 175)
MacKenzie, Carine. Bible Stories for Bedtime. (p. 176)
—Christian Focus Story Bible. (p. 311)
—Colour the Bible: Hosea-Malachi. Bk. 3 (p. 346)
—Colour the Bible: Genesis-2 Chronicles. (p. 346)
—Colour the Bible: Romans-2Thessalonians. (p. 346)
—Daniel: The Praying Prince. Apps, Fred, illus. (p. 404)
—David: The Fearless Fighter. (p. 410)
—David the Fugitive: True Friendship. (p. 411)
—David the Shepherd: A Man of Courage. (p. 411)
—David the Soldier: True Friendship. (p. 411)
—Elias Siervo de Dios/Hacia Milagros. (p. 512)
—Elijah: God's Miracle Man. (p. 512)
Mackenzie, Carine. Esther: The Brave Queen. McLaren, Duncan, illus. (p. 538)
MacKenzie, Carine. Famous Bible Stories: Adam & Eve. (p. 569)
—Foolish Farmer. (p. 614)
—Gideon: Soldier of God. McLaren, Duncan, illus. (p. 674)
—Glorifying God: Obedient Lives from the Bible. (p. 685)
Mackenzie, Carine. God Has Power. (p. 689)
MacKenzie, Carine. God Is Everywhere. (p. 689)
Mackenzie, Carine. God Is Everywhere. (p. 689)
MacKenzie, Carine. God Is Faithful. (p. 689)
—God Is Kind. (p. 689)
—God Knows Everything. (p. 689)
—God Never Changes. (p. 690)
—God, the Ten Commandments & Jesus. (p. 690)
—Hannah: The Mother Who Prayer. McLaren, Duncan, illus. (p. 742)
—How God Changes People: Conversion Stories from the Bible. (p. 809)
—How to Handle Your Life. (p. 820)
—Jesus Files. (p. 915)
—John: The Baptist. McLaren, Duncan, illus. (p. 921)
Mackenzie, Carine. Jonah: The Runaway Preacher. McLaren, Duncan, illus. (p. 924)
—Jonah & the Big Fish. Apps, Fred, illus. (p. 925)
—Jonathan: The Faithful Friend. Apps, Fred, illus. (p. 925)
MacKenzie, Carine. Joseph's Coat. (p. 926)
Mackenzie, Carine. Joshua: The Brave Leader. McLaren, Duncan, illus. (p. 926)
—Little Hands Life of Jesus. Cosco, Rafaella, illus. (p. 1029)
MacKenzie, Carine. Little Hands Story Bible. Cosco, Raffaella, illus. (p. 1029)
—Long Journey. (p. 1047)
Mackenzie, Carine. Lost Coin. (p. 1055)
—Martha & Mary: Friends of Jesus. McLaren, Duncan, illus. (p. 1097)
MacKenzie, Carine. Mary: Mother of Jesus. McLaren, Duncan, illus. (p. 1100)
—Mary - Bible Heroes. (p. 1100)
Mackenzie, Carine. Missing Sheep. (p. 1153)
—Moses: God's Leader. (p. 1176)
—Moses the Child: Kept by God. Kennedy, Graham, illus. (p. 1176)
MacKenzie, Carine. Moses the Leader: Used by God. Kennedy, Graham, illus. (p. 1176)
Mackenzie, Carine. Moses the Shepherd: Chosen by God. Kennedy, Graham, illus. (p. 1176)
—Moses the Traveller: Guided by God. Kennedy, Graham, illus. (p. 1176)
MacKenzie, Carine. My 1st Book about the Church. (p. 1195)
Mackenzie, Carine. My Bible Story Book. Apps, Fred, illus. (p. 1197)
MacKenzie, Carine. My First Book about Jesus. (p. 1205)
Mackenzie, Carine. My First Book of Bible Promises. (p. 1205)
MacKenzie, Carine. My First Book of Christian Values. (p. 1205)
—My First Book of Questions & Answers. (p. 1205)
—Naaman: The Soldier. Apps, Fred, illus. (p. 1227)
—Noah: Rescue Plan. Apps, Fred, illus. (p. 1261)
—Noah's Ark. (p. 1261)
Mackenzie, Carine. Paul: God's Traveller. (p. 1330)
MacKenzie, Carine. Peter: The Apostle. McLaren, Duncan, illus. (p. 1346)
—Peter: The Fisherman. McLaren, Duncan, illus. (p. 1346)
—Proud Prayer. (p. 1412)
Mackenzie, Carine. Rebekah: The Mother of Twins. McLaren, Duncan, illus. (p. 1450)
—Runaway Son. (p. 1496)
MacKenzie, Carine. Ruth: The Harvest Girl. McLaren, Duncan, illus. (p. 1498)
Mackenzie, Carine. Ruth's Journey. Apps, Fred, illus. (p. 1499)
MacKenzie, Carine. Samuel: The Boy Who Listened. Apps, Fred, illus. (p. 1509)
Mackenzie, Carine. Samuel's Surprise. Apps, Fred, illus. (p. 1509)
—Sara y Abraham: La maravillosa Promesa. Foce, Natalia C., tr. from ENG. (p. 1514)
MacKenzie, Carine. Sarah & Abraham: The Wonderful Promise. Apps, Fred, illus. (p. 1514)
—Secreto de la Hermana Mayor, el Maria. (p. 1544)
Mackenzie, Carine. Selfish Servant. (p. 1549)
MacKenzie, Carine. Simon Peter: The Disciple. McLaren, Duncan, illus. (p. 1577)
—Special Birthday. Taylor, Roger, illus. (p. 1623)
Mackenzie, Carine. Talking to You. (p. 1703)
MacKenzie, Carine. Very Busy Week. (p. 1837)
—Wise Words to Follow: Words of wisdom from the book of Proverbs. (p. 1940)
—Wise Words to Obey: Words of wisdom from the book of Proverbs. (p. 1940)
—Wise Words to Trust: Words of wisdom from the book of Proverbs. (p. 1940)
—Wonderful Boat. (p. 1948)
MacKenzie, Carine, jt. auth. see Christian Focus Publications (CFP) Staff.
MacKenzie, Carine, jt. auth. see Mackenzie, Carine.
MacKenzie, Carine, jt. auth. see Taylor, Jane.
MacKenzie, Carine & Apps, Fred. Miriam: Big Sister's Secret. (p. 1149)
—Paul: Journeys of Adventure. (p. 1330)
Mackenzie, Carine & Galr, Cyhoeddiadau'r. 3 Hosea - Malachi. (p. 1991)
—4 Mathew - Actau. (p. 1992)
—6 1 Timotheus - Datguddiad. (p. 1992)
Mackenzie, Carine & MacKenzie, Carine. Jesus: The Real Story. Anderson, Jeff, illus. (p. 914)
Mackenzie, Carine & Ross, Neil M. Nehemiah: Builder for God. McLaren, Duncan, illus. (p. 1240)
Mackenzie, Carine, et al. Beibl y Bobl Bach: 69 o Storiau. (p. 160)
MacKenzie, Catherine. Amy Carmichael - Can Brown Eyes Be Made Blue? Ammassari, Rita, illus. (p. 66)
—Can You Imagine? (p. 259)
—Corrie Ten Boo - Are All of the Watches Safe? Ammassari, Rita, illus. (p. 368)
—Could Somebody Pass the Salt? Ammassari, Rita, illus. (p. 369)
—Dark Blue Bike at No 17: Tammy & Jake Learn about Friendship & Bullying. (p. 407)
MacKenzie, Catherine. Deep Black Pond at No 12. (p. 422)
MacKenzie, Catherine. Feelings. (p. 580)
—George Müller: Does Money Grow on Trees? (p. 663)
—Gladys Aylward - Are You Going to Stop? (p. 682)
Mackenzie, Catherine. God's Little Guidebooks - Creation: God Creates Light. (p. 691)
—God's Little Guidebooks - Creation: God Creates a Day of Rest. (p. 691)
—God's Little Guidebooks - Creation: God Creates New Life in Me. (p. 691)
—God's Little Guidebooks - Creation: God Creates Animals & People. (p. 691)
—God's Little Guidebooks - Creation: God Creates the Fish & Birds. (p. 691)
—God's Little Guidebooks - Creation: God Creates the Water & the Sky. (p. 691)
—God's Little Guidebooks - Creation: God Creates the Sun, Moon & Stars. (p. 691)
—God's Little Guidebooks - Creation: God Creates the Land, Seas & Plants. (p. 691)
MacKenzie, Catherine. Going to the Doctor. (p. 693)
—Greatest Gift: A Puzzle Book about the Birth of Jesus. (p. 720)
—Hearing. (p. 759)
—Helen Roseveare: What's in the Parcel? (p. 763)
—Hudson Taylor: An Adventure Begins. (p. 824)
Mackenzie, Catherine. I Can Say to God, I Love You. (p. 836)
—I Can Say to God, Please. (p. 836)
MacKenzie, Catherine. I Can Say to God, Thank You. (p. 836)
—Jesus Christ the Best King of All. (p. 915)
—Jesus Finds His People. Apps, Fred, illus. (p. 915)
—Jesus Helps His People. Apps, Fred, illus. (p. 915)
—Jesus Rescues His People. Apps, Fred, illus. (p. 916)
—Jesus Rose from the Dead - The Evidence. (p. 916)
—Jesus Saves His People. Apps, Fred, illus. (p. 916)
—Joni Eareckson Tada: Swimming Against the Tide. (p. 925)
—Lonely Grey Dog at No. 6: Tammy & Jake Learn about Love & Loyalty. (p. 1046)
—Mary & Joseph Love Jesus. Apps, Fred, illus. (p. 1100)
—My Bible ABC. (p. 1197)
—Richard Wurmbrand - A Voice in the Dark. (p. 1470)
—Scottish Highland. (p. 1532)
—Shepherds Find Jesus. Apps, Fred, illus. (p. 1565)
—Sight. (p. 1574)
—Simeon & Anna See Jesus. Apps, Fred, illus. (p. 1577)
—Smell. (p. 1593)
—Taste. (p. 1707)
—Touch. (p. 1772)
—What God Says: Creation. (p. 1884)
—What God Says: Holiness. (p. 1884)
—What God Says: Repenting. (p. 1884)
—What God Says: Salvation. (p. 1884)
—What God Says: Redemption. (p. 1884)
—What God Says: Resurrection. (p. 1884)
—What Is the Truth? (p. 1890)
—What Should I Do? (p. 1893)
—Wise Mean Help Jesus. Apps, Fred, illus. (p. 1940)
MacKenzie, Cerena & MacKenzie, Madison. Little Ponytail Girl. (p. 1033)
MacKenzie, Donald A. Scottish Fairy Tales. Green, John, illus. (p. 1532)
Mackenzie, Donald Alexander. Myths of Pre-Columbian America. (p. 1227)
MacKenzie, Donald M. Fish. (p. 598)
MacKenzie, Edie. Golden Retrievers. (p. 695)
MacKenzie, Emily. Wanted! Ralfy Rabbit, Book Burglar. (p. 1856)
MacKenzie, Fiona, ed. see Collins Staff.
MacKenzie, Joy, ed. see Frank, Marjorie.
MacKenzie, Julia, ed. see Bailey, Gauvin Alexander.
MacKenzie, Lachlan. Duke's Daughter: A Story of Faith & Love. Anderson, Jeff, illus. (p. 489)
MacKenzie, Madison, jt. auth. see MacKenzie, Cerena.
MacKenzie, Maryellen. Sneekie & Snookie: And the Honey Tree. (p. 1597)
MacKenzie, Robert. Jack & the Beanstalk. (p. 902)
MacKenzie, Ross. My Sailor Dad. (p. 1218)
—Zac & the Dream Stealers. (p. 1984)
Mackenzie, Thomas, illus. see Ransome, Arthur.
MacKenzie, W. R., jt. auth. see Caldwell, Tiffany.
MacKenzie-Krysko, Claudia & Krysko, Kenneth L. Adventures of Granville, Coming to America. Cotton, Sue Lynn, illus. (p. 18)
Mackerel, Seymour & RH Disney Staff. Fish School. Home, Philip & Loter, John, illus. (p. 598)
Mackerras, Alyce, jt. auth. see Chang, Peter.
Mackey, Bill, jt. auth. see Gamble, Adam.
MacKey, Cindy. Curious Abc's: An Alphabet for Non Linear Thinkers. (p. 392)
—Girl Who Blamed the World. Chiang, Shirley, illus. (p. 679)
—Hannah's Day of Revelations. (p. 743)
—My Sister Sophie. Tebbit, Jake, illus. (p. 1218)
MacKey, Cindy K. Curious Abc's: An Alphabet for Non Linear Thinkers. (p. 392)
Mackey Davis, Cathy. Postal Workers Then & Now. (p. 1387)
Mackey, Dean. Paper Planes That Really Fly. (p. 1323)
MacKey, Esther L. Little Bear & Honey Bee. Mackey, Kaitlin L., illus. (p. 1023)
—Meet Mickey. (p. 1121)
MacKey, Garry. Joey: The Christmas Kangaroo. (p. 920)
Mackey, Heather. Dreamwood. (p. 484)
Mackey, James, illus. see Shaskan, Trisha Speed.
Mackey, James, jt. auth. see Wallace, Karen.
Mackey, Kaitlin L., illus. see MacKey, Esther L.
Mackey, Lori. Money Mama & the Three Little Pigs. (p. 1164)
Mackey, R. Scott. Bugfish Experiment. (p. 236)
Mackey, Stephen. Miki. Mackey, Stephen, illus. (p. 1141)
—Miki & the Moon Blossom. (p. 1141)
—Pushka. (p. 1420)
—Pushka. Mackey, Stephen, illus. (p. 1420)
Mackey, Stewart. Aenon: The Heart of Hope. (p. 25)
Mackey, Weezie Kerr. Throwing Like a Girl (p. 1745)
Macki, Erik J., tr. see Pressler, Mirjam.
Mackie, Clare, illus. see Reidy, Hannah.
Mackie, Clare, illus. see Rosen, Michael.
Mackie, Dan. Greater Heights. (p. 719)
Mackie, Howard & Kavanagh, Terry. Gambit Classic - Volume 2. Janson, Klaus, illus. (p. 654)
Mackie, Howard, et al. X-Men - Age of Apocalypse Omnibus Companion. Dodson, Terry et al, illus. (p. 1967)
MacKie, Ian. Adventures of Hamish the Sea Eagle. Mackie, Marie-Anne, illus. (p. 18)
Mackie, Marie-Anne, illus. see MacKie, Ian.
Mackin, B., jt. auth. see Mackin, Bob.
Mackin, Bob & Mackin, B. Record-Breaking Baseball Trivia: Games, Puzzles, Quizzes. (p. 1452)
Mackin, Dan. Reflections of Paradise. (p. 1456)
Mackin, Joan Marie. It's Just the Moon. (p. 897)
MacKinnon, Andy, et al. Plants of the Pacific Northwest Coast: Washington, Oregon, British Columbia & Alaska. (p. 1370)

M

MacKinnon, Art. Chloe's Great Blue Adventure. (p. 308)
Mackinnon, Bernard. Boy Who Turned Green. (p. 219)
MacKinnon, Catherine-Anne. Animals Baby Flashcards. MacKinnon, Catherine-Anne, illus. (p. 82)
—Babies Baby Flashcards. (p. 123)
MacKinnon, Catherine-Anne, illus. see Watt, Fiona.
MacKinnon, Christopher. Canadian Sports Sites for Kids: Places Named for Speedsters, Scorers, & Other Sportsworld Citizens. (p. 260)
—Canadian Sports Sites for Kids: Places Named for Speedsters, Scorers, & Other Sportsworld Citizens (Large Print 16pt) (p. 260)
MacKinnon, Cynthia L., ed. Light at the Edge of Darkness. (p. 1015)
MacKinnon, J. Beyblade: Official Handbook. (p. 173)
Mackinnon, Mairi. Boy Who Cried Wolf. (p. 219)
MacKinnon, Mairi. Croc Gets a Shock. Blunt, Fred, illus. (p. 384)
Mackinnon, Mairi. Phonics Workbook 3. (p. 1352)
—Phonics Workbook 4. (p. 1352)
MacKinnon, Mairi. Usborne Animal Alphabet Activity Book. Horne, Sarah & Barker, Vicky, illus. (p. 1827)
MacKinnon, Mairi, ed. see Amery, Heather.
MacKinnon, Mairi, jt. auth. see Brooks, Felicity.
MacKinnon, Mairi, jt. auth. see Punter, Russell.
MacKinnon, Mairi, ed. Hare & the Tortoise. Howarth, Daniel, illus. (p. 748)
MacKinnon, Mark C., jt. auth. see Pulver, David L.
MacKinnon, Mary & Berg, N. Erpill the Caterpillar. (p. 534)
MacKinnon, Patsy, illus. see Coates, Jan.
MacKinstry, Elizabeth, illus. see Wiggin, Kate Douglas & Smith, Nora Archibald.
Mackintosh, David. Frank Show. (p. 629)
—Lucky. (p. 1062)
—Marshall Armstrong Is New to Our School. (p. 1096)
—Standing in for Lincoln Green. (p. 1639)
Mackintosh, Michelle, illus. see Badger, Meredith.
Mackintosh, Michelle, illus. see Fulton-Keats, Louise.
Mackler, Carolyn. Best Friend Next Door. (p. 169)
—Earth, My Butt, & Other Big Round Things. (p. 496)
—Guyaholic. (p. 733)
—Infinite in Between. (p. 873)
—Tangled. (p. 1705)
—Vegan Virgin Valentine. (p. 1834)
Mackler, Carolyn, jt. auth. see Asher, Jay.
Macklin, Karen, ed. see Flynn, Nancy.
MacKoul, Eva. Pig Who Didn't Want to Be Pink. (p. 1357)
Mackowiak Elson, Maya. Transformers: Rescue Bots: the Mystery of the Pirate Bell. (p. 1778)
MacLachlan, Emily, jt. auth. see MacLachlan, Patricia.
Maclachlan, James, jt. auth. see Collier, Bruce.
Maclachlan, Kate. Love My Enemy. (p. 1060)
MacLachlan, Marie. Granny Grotbag's Bedtime Stories. (p. 710)
MacLachlan, Patricia. Boxcar Children Beginning: The Aldens of Fair Meadow Farm. Jessell, Tim, illus. (p. 216)
—Boxcar Children Beginning - The Aldens of Fair Meadow Farm. Jessell, Tim, illus. (p. 216)
—Caleb's Story. (p. 252)
—Edward's Eyes. (p. 505)
—Fly Away. (p. 609)
—Grandfather's Dance. (p. 707)
—Iridescence of Birds: A Book about Henri Matisse. Hooper, Hadley, illus. (p. 887)
—Kindred Souls. (p. 957)
—Lala Salama: A Tanzanian Lullaby. Zunon, Elizabeth, illus. (p. 972)
—Moon's Almost Here! dePaola, Tomie, illus. (p. 1173)
—More Perfect Than the Moon. (p. 1174)
—Nora's Chicks. Brown, Kathryn, illus. (p. 1264)
—Prairie Days. Moser, Barry, illus. (p. 1392)
Maclachlan, Patricia. Sarah, Plain & Tall: 30th Anniversary Edition. (p. 1514)
MacLachlan, Patricia. Sarah, Plain & Tall. (p. 1514)
—Skylark. (p. 1587)
—Snowflakes Fall. Kellogg, Steven, illus. (p. 1600)
—True Gift: A Christmas Story. Floca, Brian, illus. (p. 1792)
—True Gift. Floca, Brian, illus. (p. 1792)
—Truth of Me. (p. 1794)
—Waiting for the Magic. Bates, Amy June, illus. (p. 1853)
—What You Know First. (p. 1896)
—White Fur Flying. (p. 1913)
—Word after Word after Word. (p. 1950)
—Your Moon, My Moon: A Grandmother's Words to a Faraway Child. Collier, Bryan, illus. (p. 1981)
MacLachlan, Patricia, jt. auth. see Charest, Emily MacLachlan.
MacLachlan, Patricia & Charest, Emily MacLachlan. Cat Talk. Moser, Barry, illus. (p. 278)
—I Didn't Do It. Schneider, Katy, illus. (p. 837)
—Once I Ate a Pie. (p. 1292)
—Once I Ate a Pie. Schneider, Katy, illus. (p. 1292)
MacLachlan, Patricia & MacLachlan, Emily. Painting the Wind. Schneider, Katy, illus. (p. 1318)
Maclaine, James. Bees & Wasps. (p. 158)
—Drawing, Doodling & Coloring Blue Book. (p. 481)
—Elephants IR. (p. 512)
—Lift-The-Flap General Knowledge IR. (p. 1014)
MacLaine, James. Snakes. Parker, Paul & Moor, Becka, illus. (p. 1596)
Maclaine, James. Tigers IR. (p. 1749)
MacLaine, James. Usborne Little Children's Travel Activity Book. Watt, Fiona, ed. (p. 1827)
—Wolves. Francis, John & Scott, Kimberley, illus. (p. 1944)
MacLaine, James, jt. auth. see Bowman, Lucy.
MacLaine, James & Bowman, Lucy. Usborne Little Boys' Activity Book. Watt, Fiona, ed. (p. 1827)
MacLaren, Dorothy H. Esopus Hodie, Aesop Today (p. 536)
Maclay, Elise. Reading the Wild. Doolittle, Bev, illus. (p. 1446)
MacLean, Alistair. Circus. (p. 322)
MacLean, Amber, illus. see Williams, Suzanne.
Maclean, Andrew, illus. see Davies, Helen Emanuel.
MacLean, Betty. Jiali's Traveling Heart. Kinra, Richa, illus. (p. 917)
MacLean, Christine. Even Firefighters Hug Their Moms. Reed, Mike, illus. (p. 541)
Maclean, Christine. Mary Margaret Meets Her Match. (p. 1100)
Maclean, Christine, jt. auth. see MacLean, Christine Kole.
MacLean, Christine Kole & Maclean, Christine. Mary Margaret & the Perfect Pet Plan. Lowe, Vicky, illus. (p. 1100)
MacLean, Colin. Julia Roberts: More Than a Pretty Woman. (p. 932)
—Leonardo DiCaprio: An Intimate Portrait. Vol. 1 (p. 992)
MacLean, Colin, illus. see Reader's Digest Staff.
Maclean, Donald, tr. see Kraul, Walter.
Maclean, Donald, tr. see Sehlin, Gunhild.
MacLean, Eva. Far Land. (p. 572)
Maclean, Fiona. Death or Victory: Tales of the Clan Maclean. Turnbull, Brian, illus. (p. 420)
MacLean, G. Helen of the Glen. (p. 763)
Maclean, Gerald. Rise of Oriental Travel: English Visitors to the Ottoman Empire, 1580-1720. (p. 1474)
MacLean, Heather. Moonicorn Fairies. (p. 1172)
—Mousecat & the Moonicorns on Halloween Night. (p. 1182)
MacLean, Jill. Hidden Agenda of Sigrid Sugden (p. 775)
—Present Tense of Prinny Murphy (p. 1396)
MacLean, John Patterson. Mound Builders; Being an Account of a Remarkable People That Once Inhabited the Valleys of the Ohio & Mississippi, Together with an Investigation into the Archaeology of Butler County, O. (p. 1180)
MacLean, Kenneth. I Love You Dad: Conversations with my Father. (p. 843)
MacLean, Kerry Lee. Just Me & My Mind. (p. 939)
—Moody Cow Learns Compassion. (p. 1171)
—Moody Cow Meditates. (p. 1171)
—Peacefully Piggy Meditation. MacLean, Kerry Lee, illus. (p. 1332)
MacLean, Kerry Lee, illus. see Alderfer, Lauren.
MacLean, Kerry Lee, creator. Pigs Ski over Colorado: The Top Ten Reasons Winter Is the Piggies Favorite Season. (p. 1358)
MacLean, Moira, illus. see Howie, Vickie.
MacLean, Moira, illus. see Reader's Digest Staff.
MacLean, Moira, illus. see Reynolds, Annette.
MacLean, Moira, illus. see Wright, Sally Ann.
MacLean, Moira, jt. auth. see Howie, Vickie.
MacLean, Moira, jt. auth. see Howie, Vicky.
MacLean, Ruth. Dr. Luke's Casebook. (p. 475)
—Happy Harvest: A Puzzle Book about Ruth. (p. 746)
—Man Who Ran: A Puzzle Book about Jonah. (p. 1086)
—Shepherd King: A Puzzle Book about David. (p. 1565)
MacLean, Sarah. Season. (p. 1538)
Maclear, Kyo. Good Little Book. Arbona, Marion, illus. (p. 698)
—Virginia Wolf. Arsenault, Isabelle, illus. (p. 1844)
Maclear, Kyo & Arsenault, Isabelle. Spork. Arsenault, Isabelle, illus. (p. 1631)
MacLellan, Erin. Run from the Nun! (p. 1496)
MacLelland, Edith Bennett. Grandma Tell Me a Story. (p. 708)
MacLennan, Cathy. Spooky Spooky Spooky! (p. 1631)
MacLennan, David. Santa's Stormy Christmas Eve. Parkinson, Cheryl, tr. (p. 1513)
MacLennan, Donald. Gaidhlig Blasad (A Taste of Gaelic) (p. 652)
Macleod, Brittany & Terri. 113 Things to Do By 13. (p. 2000)
MacLeod, Deirdre Day. Mexico's Central States. (p. 1131)
—Mexico's Northern States. (p. 1131)
MacLeod, Doug. Heather Fell in the Water. Smith, Craig, illus. (p. 760)
—I'm Being Stalked by a Moonshadow. (p. 858)
—My Extraordinary Life & Death. (p. 1202)
—Shiny Guys. (p. 1567)
MacLeod, Elizabeth. Alexander Graham Bell. Krystoforski, Andrej, illus. (p. 36)
—Bones Never Lie: How Forensics Helps Solve History's Mysteries. (p. 209)
—Chock Full of Chocolate. Bradford, June, illus. (p. 309)
—Eleanor Roosevelt: An Inspiring Life. (p. 508)
—Galloping Through History: Incredible True Horse Stories. (p. 653)
—George Washington Carver: An Innovative Life. (p. 664)
—Harry Houdini: A Magical Life. (p. 750)
—Harry Houdini. Mantha, John, illus. (p. 750)
—Helen Keller. Krystoforski, Andrej, illus. (p. 762)
—I Heard a Little Baa. Phillips, Louise, illus. (p. 839)
—Kids Book of Canada at War. Mantha, John, illus. (p. 952)
—Kids Book of Great Canadian Women. Mantha, John, illus. (p. 952)
—Kids Book of Great Canadians. Mantha, John, illus. (p. 952)
—Lucy Maud Montgomery. Mantha, John, illus. (p. 1063)
—Marie Curie: A Brilliant Life. (p. 1093)
—Marie Curie. Mantha, John, illus. (p. 1093)
—Mark Twain: An American Star. (p. 1095)
—Monster Fliers: From the Time of the Dinosaurs. Bindon, John, illus. (p. 1167)
—Royal Murder: The Deadly Intrigue of Ten Sovereigns. (p. 1492)
—Samuel de Champlain. Mantha, John, illus. (p. 1509)
—Secrets Underground: North America's Buried Past. (p. 1546)
—Thomas Edison. Krystoforski, Andrej, illus. (p. 1738)
—Why Do Cats Have Whiskers? (p. 1923)
—Why Do Horses Have Manes? (p. 1923)
—Wright Brothers. Krystoforski, Andrej, illus. (p. 1963)
MacLeod, Elizabeth, jt. auth. see Skreslet, Laurie.
MacLeod, Elizabeth, et al. History of Just about Everything: 180 Events, People & Inventions That Changed the World. Leng, Qin, illus. (p. 784)
MacLeod, Gavin, illus. see Reeve, Tim.
MacLeod, Ian, ed. Even More Talks for Children. (p. 541)
MacLeod, J. E. Waiting to Score. (p. 1853)
MacLeod, Jean. At Home in This World: A China Adoption Story. Su, Qin, illus. (p. 110)
MacLeod, Jilly. Great Inventions. (p. 716)
MacLeod, Kit, ed. see Keith, Sarah A.
Macleod, Robert. Vikingworld: The Age of Seafarers & Sagas. (p. 1842)
Macleod, Steve. 200010: Canadian Decades. (p. 2003)
—2000-10: Canadian Decades. (p. 2003)
—Anacondas. (p. 66)
—Dolphin. (p. 464)
—Elephants. (p. 511)
—Giant Panda. (p. 673)
—Gorilla. (p. 703)
—Jaguar. (p. 905)
—Panda Gigante. (p. 1320)
—Polar Bear. (p. 1378)
—Soy el Delfin. (p. 1618)
—Soy el Gorila. (p. 1618)
—Soy el Jaguar. (p. 1618)
—Soy el Oso Polar. (p. 1618)
—Soy el Tigre. (p. 1618)
—Tiger. (p. 1748)
MacLeod, Sue. Namesake (p. 1228)
Macleod, Una, jt. auth. see Taylor, Jane.
Macleod, William Christie. American Indian Frontier. (p. 62)
MacLure, Ashley, illus. see Lindsey, Jason.
MacIver, Juliette. Frog Who Lost His Underpants. Chapman, Cat, illus. (p. 640)
MacManus, Seumas. Donegal Fairy Stories. Verbeck, Frank, illus. (p. 466)
MacMaster, Eve B., contrib. by. Children's Illustrated Bible. (p. 303)
MacMenamin, John, illus. see Coon, Thomas & Coon, Helene.
MacMenamin, John, illus. see Raine, Bonnie.
MacMillan Art Publishing Staff, jt. auth. see Woolley, Steph.
Macmillan Audio Staff, jt. auth. see Woolley, Steph.
Macmillan Children's Books Staff. Football Jokes: Fantastically Funny Jokes for Football Fanatics (p. 615)
—Party Time Sticker Book: Over 250 Stickers. (p. 1326)
—Pirates Sticker Book: Over 250 Stickers. (p. 1364)
—Princesses Sticker Book: Over 250 Stickers. (p. 1406)
—Super Heroes Sticker Book: Over 250 Stickers. (p. 1680)
MacMillan Company Staff. Bin Weevils: The Secret Weevil Service Handbook. (p. 188)
MacMillan, Daniel. Golfing in Idaho & Montana. (p. 696)
MacMillan, Dianne M. Cheetahs. (p. 296)
—Chinese New Year. (p. 307)
—Diwali - Hindu Festival of Lights. (p. 455)
—Humpback Whales. (p. 827)
—Life in a Deciduous Forest. (p. 1010)
—Mardi Gras. (p. 1092)
—Martin Luther King, Jr. Day. (p. 1098)
—Mexican Independence Day & Cinco de Mayo. (p. 1131)
—Ramadan & Id Al-Fitr. (p. 1437)
MacMillan, Dianne M., jt. auth. see Freeman, Dorothy Rhodes.
MacMillan, Dustin. Place of Dreams. (p. 1365)
MacMillan, Eric G., illus. see MacMillan, Ian C.
MacMillan, Ian C. Khala Maninge - the Little Elephant That Cried a Lot: An African Fable. MacMillan, Eric G., illus. (p. 951)
MacMillan, Lesley. Draw Me a Picture. (p. 481)
—What Would You Be? Holcomb, Michele, illus. (p. 1895)
Macmillan Reference USA, ed. Space Sciences: 4 Volume Set (p. 1619)
Macmillan, Sue. Bouncy, Pouncy Puppy. Ward, Sarah, illus. (p. 216)
—Happy, Hoppy Bunny. Ward, Sarah, illus. (p. 746)
—Hoppy Frog's Fly Spy. Ward, Sarah, illus. (p. 797)
—Racing, Chasing Kitten. Ward, Sarah, illus. (p. 1432)
Macmillan/Mcgraw. Alternative Learning Strategies: Staff Development Videotapes. (p. 50)
—Cooperative Learning: Staff Development Videotapes. (p. 365)
MacNab, Chris. Weight Training. (p. 1872)
MacNab, Peter. Tall Tales from an Island. (p. 1704)
Macnair, Patricia. Everything You Need to Know about the Human Body. (p. 546)
Macnair, Patricia & Dixon, Dougal. Everything You Need to Know about Dinosaurs. (p. 545)
Macnaughton, Tina, illus. see Butler, M. Christina.
Macnaughton, Tina, illus. see Freedman, Claire.
Macnaughton, Tina, illus. see Goodwin, John.
Macnaughton, Tina, illus. see Piper, Sophie.
Macnaughton, Tina, illus. see Rivett, Rachel.
MacNeal, Noel. 10-Minute Puppets. (p. 1993)
MacNeal, Susan Elia. Infused: 100+ Recipes for Infused Liqueurs & Cocktails. Beisch, Leigh, photos by. (p. 874)
MacNeil, Ben. Farmer & His Animals. Smith, Charlie E. T., illus. (p. 574)
MacNeil, Chris, illus. see Wollman, Jessica.
MacNeil, Stephen. Woolies & Worms. Sandford, John, illus. (p. 1950)
MacNeill, Scott. How Things Work Vehicles - Motorcycle. (p. 814)
Macnow, Glen. Cal Ripken, Jr: Hall of Fame Baseball Superstar. (p. 252)
—Deion Sanders: Hall of Fame Football Superstar. (p. 424)
—Sports Great Allen Iverson. (p. 1632)
—Troy Aikman: Hall of Fame Football Superstar. (p. 1790)
Maco, Leonardo, jt. auth. see Carey, Mike.
Macomber, Debbie & Carney, Mary Lou. Truly Terribly Horrible Sweater... That Grandma Knit. Nguyen, Vincent, illus. (p. 1793)
—Yippy, Yappy Yorkie in the Green Doggy Sweater. Lambert, Sally Anne, illus. (p. 1971)
Maconachie, Roy, jt. auth. see Bowden, Rob.
Maconachie, Roy, photos by see Bowden, Rob.
Maconie, Robin. Alice & Her Fabulous Teeth! Fruisen, Catherine Myler, illus. (p. 39)
Macor, Jim. Frazier Fir, A Christmas Fable. Macor, Jim, illus. (p. 631)
MacPhaidan, Daire, tr. see Shaw, Elizabeth.
MacPhail, C. Get That Ghost to Go! Donnelly, Karen, illus. (p. 668)
MacPhail, C. & Cosson, M. J. Pirate, Big Fist, & Me Garvey, Brann, illus. (p. 1362)
MacPhail, Catherine. Collins Big Cat - Own Goal. Philips, Mike, illus. (p. 340)
—Copycat. Packer, Natalie, ed. (p. 366)
—Hide & Seek. (p. 776)
MacPhail, Cathy. Run, Zan, Run: Newly Rejacketed. (p. 1496)
MacPhee, Bill. Stella, Nothing Has Changed. (p. 1647)
MacPhee, K. M. Maths & English: Basics Manual for Young People. (p. 1108)
MacPhee, Ross, jt. auth. see Wynne, Patricia J.
MacPherson, Bruce, illus. see Coyle, Carmela Lavigna.
MacPherson, Bruce, illus. see Lowell, Susan.
Macpherson, Carol, illus. see Grandmother Littlewolf.
MacPherson, D. R. First Wave. (p. 597)
—Sport of Kings. (p. 1631)
MacPherson, Dwight L. Lil' Hellions. O'Reilly, Sean Patrick, ed. (p. 1017)
MacPherson, Georgia, jt. auth. see Gianakoulis, Theodore.
MacPherson, Lorry. Adventures of Super Keith! Alexander, Yvonne Rabdau, illus. (p. 23)
—Lynne Woke Up! Alexander, Yvonne Rabdau, illus. (p. 1066)
MacPherson, M. J. Magic Thread: Overcoming challenges during World War II, a young girl discovers secrets that change adversity into Adventure. (p. 1074)
MacPherson, Margaret. Nellie McClung: Voice for the Voiceless. (p. 1240)
Macquignon, Stephen, illus. see Harris-Wyrick, Wayne.
Macquignon, Stephen, illus. see Mayer, Marvin.
MacQuitty, Miranda. DK Eyewitness Books: Ocean: Ocean. (p. 456)
MacRae, Jock, illus. see Greenwood, Barbara.
MacRae, Sloan. Aaron Rodgers. (p. 2)
—Big-Game Hunting: Bears, Elk, & Other Large Animals. (p. 181)
—Boston Red Sox. (p. 215)
—Carmelo Anthony. (p. 270)
—Chad Ochocinco. (p. 288)
—Chicago Bears. (p. 299)
—Dallas Cowboys. (p. 401)
—David Wright. (p. 411)
—Deer Hunting. (p. 423)
—Evan Longoria. (p. 540)
Macrae, Sloan. Greatest Records in Sports (p. 720)
MacRae, Sloan. Green Bay Packers. (p. 721)
—Indianapolis Colts. (p. 871)
—Los Angeles Lakers. (p. 1053)
—Meet Ben Roethlisberger: Football's Big Ben. (p. 1120)
—Meet Dirk Nowitzki: Basketball's Blond Bomber. (p. 1120)
—Meet Eli Manning: Football's Unstoppable Quarterback. (p. 1121)
—Meet Manny Ramirez: Baseball's Grand Slam Hitter. (p. 1121)
—Meet Tony Parker: Basketball's Famous Point Guard. (p. 1123)
—Meet Vladimir Guerrero: Baseball's Super Vlad. (p. 1123)
—Miami Dolphins. (p. 1133)
—Minnesota Twins. (p. 1147)
—Minnesota Vikings. (p. 1147)
—New England Patriots. (p. 1244)
—New Orleans Saints. (p. 1246)
—New York Giants. (p. 1248)
—New York Mets. (p. 1248)
—New York Yankees. (p. 1248)
—Philadelphia Phillies. (p. 1350)
—Pittsburgh Steelers. (p. 1365)
—Rajon Rondo. (p. 1437)
—Respecting the Contributions of Disabled Americans. (p. 1463)
—San Antonio Spurs. (p. 1510)
—San Francisco 49ers. (p. 1510)
—Small-Game Hunting: Squirrels, Rabbits, & Other Small Animals. (p. 1592)
—St. Louis Cardinals. (p. 1638)
—Turkey Hunting. (p. 1797)
—Upland Hunting: Pheasant, Quail, & Other Game Birds. (p. 1825)
—Washington Redskins. (p. 1860)
—Waterfowl Hunting. (p. 1863)
Macrae, Tammy Vallieres & Lucente-Rizzo, Susan. Jeffrey Finds His Way. (p. 912)
MacRae, Tom. Opposite Odriozola, Elena, illus. (p. 1300)
—When I Woke up I Was a Hippopotamus. Collins, Ross, illus. (p. 1903)
MacReady, R. J. We Can Use a Map. (p. 1866)
Macri, Rebecca. Pip: A Very Special Little Caterpillar. (p. 1361)
Macri, Thomas. Spidey's New Costume. (p. 1627)
—Story of the X-Men. (p. 1662)
—Story of the X-Men Level 2 Reader. Olliffe, Pat, illus. (p. 1662)
—These Are the X-Men. (p. 1731)
—World of Reading: X-Men Days of Future Past: Level 3. Disney Book Group Staff, illus. (p. 1957)
—X-Men: Days of Future Past. (p. 1967)
Macri, Thomas, jt. auth. see Disney Book Group Staff.
Macro, Chris, jt. auth. see Hartley, Karen.
MacRobert, Virginia. Almost Cat-Astrophe & the Message. (p. 48)
Macveety, Sue Maney. Singing Sea/el Mar Que Canta. Zantay, Valerie, tr. (p. 1579)
MacVicar, Andrea. Tales of Zoftic. Morse, Patti, illus. (p. 1703)
MacVicar, Angus. Stranger at Xmas. (p. 1665)
Macy, Carolyn. Hawaiian Night Before Christmas Macy, Carolyn, illus. (p. 755)
—Oklahoma Night Before Christmas. (p. 1283)
Macy, Jesse. Comparative Free Government. (p. 351)
—Party Organization & Machinery. (p. 1326)
—Political Parties in the United States. (p. 1380)
Macy, Laura, jt. ed. see Sadie, Stanley.
Macy, Sue. Basketball Belles: How Two Teams & One Scrappy Player Put Women's Hoops on the Map. Collins, Matt, illus. (p. 143)
—Bull's Eye: A Photobiography of Annie Oakley. (p. 241)
—Bull's-Eye: A Photobiography of Annie Oakley. (p. 240)
—Bylines: A Photobiography of Nellie Bly. (p. 249)
—Freeze Frame: A Photographic History of the Winter Olympics. (p. 635)

—Roller Derby Rivals. Collins, Matt, illus. (p. 1485)
—Swifter, Higher, Stronger: A Photographic History of the Summer Olympics. (p. 1690)
—Wheels of Change: How Women Rode the Bicycle to Freedom (With a Few Flat Tires along the Way) (p. 1901)
Macy, Tana. Tap Shoes & Horse Shoes. Gardiner, Nancy, illus. (p. 1705)
Macy-Mills, Phyllis. Murphy Moose & Garrett Goose. Russell, Kay, illus. (p. 1192)
Maczulak, Anne. Green Technology Set, 8-Volumes. (p. 722)
—Renewable Energy: Sources & Methods. (p. 1460)
—Sustainability: Building Eco-Friendly Communities. (p. 1688)
Maczulak, Anne E. Biodiversity: Conserving Endangered Species. (p. 188)
—Conservation: Protecting Our Plant Resources. (p. 358)
—Infectious Diseases & Their Origins. (p. 873)
—Waste Treatment: Reducing Global Waste. (p. 1860)
—Where Microorganisms Live. (p. 1909)
Mada Design Inc, illus. see Chihak, Sheena & Loki.
Mada Design, Inc Staff, illus. see Strathearn, Chris.
Mada Design Staff, illus. see Sazaklis, John.
Mada Design Staff, illus. see Stephens, Sarah Hines.
Mada Design Staff, illus. see Sudduth, Brent & Meredith Books Staff.
Mada Design Staff, illus. see Teitelbaum, Michael.
Madagan, Denise. Around the Block with Mommy. (p. 100)
Madama, Khadi. Adventures of Jade Charme: A Follow-Along Book with Nine Exciting Adventures to Solve. (p. 19)
Madame M. Eerie Little Bedtime Stories. (p. 505)
—Trauma Queens/Trauma Kings. (p. 1780)
Madan, Fredric C. Greer Garson Paper Dolls. Madan, Fredric C. & Ernst, Clara, illus. (p. 723)
Madani, Hamed. Judicial Branch: Interpreting America's Laws. (p. 931)
—Supreme Court & the Judicial Branch: How the Federal Courts Interpret Our Laws. (p. 1684)
Madaras, Area, jt. auth. see Madaras, Lynda.
Madaras, Diana. Kitty Humbug's Christmas Tail. Madaras, Diana & Nielsen, Ric, illus. (p. 963)
Madaras, Lynda. Ready, Set, Grow! A What's Happening to My Body? Book for Younger Girls. Davick, Linda, tr. (p. 1447)
Madaras, Lynda & Davick, Linda. Ready, Set, Grow! A What's Happening to My Body? Book for Younger Girls. (p. 1447)
Madaras, Lynda & Gilligan, Paul. On Your Mark, Get Set, Grow! (p. 1292)
—On Your Mark, Get Set, Grow! A What's Happening to My Body? Book for Younger Boys. (p. 1292)
Madaras, Lynda & Madaras, Area. My Body, My Self for Boys. (p. 1198)
—My Body, My Self for Girls. (p. 1198)
—¿Que Pasa en Mi Cuerpo? El Libro para Muchachos: La Guía de Mayor Venta Sobre el Desarrollo, Escrita para Adolescentes y Preadolescentes. (p. 1424)
—¿Que Pasa en Mi Cuerpo? Libro para Muchachas: La Guía de Mayor Venta Sobre El Desarrollo Escrita para Adolescentes y Preadolescentes. (p. 1424)
Madaras, Lynda, et al. "What's Happening to My Body?" Book for Boys. (p. 1897)
—"What's Happening to My Body?" Book for Girls. (p. 1897)
—"What's Happening to My Body?" Book for Boys. (p. 1897)
Maday, Alice M., jt. auth. see Cleary, Brian P.
Maday, Gregory. Hunting with Grizzly Bears. (p. 829)
Madden, Alison, jt. auth. see Bunte, Joan.
Madden, Avery. Sport Talk with Avery. (p. 1631)
Madden, Colleen, illus. see Blumenstock, Jacqueline & Pool, David.
Madden, Colleen, illus. see Brunstetter, Wanda E.
Madden, Colleen, illus. see Gunderson, Jessica & Meister, Cari.
Madden, Colleen, illus. see Gunderson, Jessica Sarah.
Madden, Colleen, illus. see Gunderson, Jessica.
Madden, Colleen, illus. see Spurr, Elizabeth.
Madden, Colleen M., illus. see Brunstetter, Wanda E.
Madden, Colleen M., illus. see Enderle, Dotti.
Madden, Colleen M., illus. see Fine, Edith Hope & Halpin, Angela Demos.
Madden, Colleen M., illus. see Guard, Anara.
Madden, Colleen M., illus. see Javernick, Ellen.
Madden, Colleen M., illus. see Levy, Janice.
Madden, Gloria. Grandmothers Bedtime Stories: Book 5. (p. 709)
—Grandmothers Bedtime Stories. (p. 709)
—Grandmother's Bedtime Stories. (p. 709)
Madden, Jean Griffing. Digger Digs Digits. (p. 438)
Madden, Kerry. Gentle's Holler. (p. 661)
—Harper Lee. (p. 749)
—Jessie's Mountain. (p. 914)
Madden, Mathilde. Mad about the Boy. (p. 1068)
Madden, Matt, jt. auth. see Abel, Jessica.
Madden, Matt, tr. see Aristophane.
Madden, Michelle. Butterfly Garden. (p. 247)
Madden-Lunsford, Kerry. Nothing Fancy about Kathryn & Charlie. Madden-Lunsford, Lucy, illus. (p. 1268)
Madden-Lunsford, Lucy, illus. see Madden-Lunsford, Kerry.
Maddern, Eric. Cow on the Roof. Hess, Paul, illus. (p. 373)
—King & the Seed. Hess, Paul, illus. (p. 958)
—King with Horse's Ears. Hess, Paul, illus. (p. 959)
Maddern, Eric, jt. auth. see East, Helen.
Maddern, Eric & Quarto Generic Staff. Earth Story. Duff, Leo, illus. (p. 497)
Maddern, Eric & Williamson, Duncan. Death in a Nut. Hess, Paul, illus. (p. 420)
Maddex, Robert L. State Constitutions of the United States (p. 1644)
Maddin, John, jt. auth. see Walch, Michelle E.
Maddison, Kate. Incredible Charlotte Sycamore. (p. 869)
Maddison, Kevin, illus. see Fields, Sadie & Tango Books Staff.
Maddison, Kevin, illus. see Tango Books.
Maddison, Lucy, illus. see Dinneen, John.
Maddison, Lucy, illus. see Moses, Brian.
Maddison, Simon. Telecoms. (p. 1716)
Maddock, Lisa. Bridezilla Who Stole Christmas: A Teddy & Pip Story. (p. 227)
—Tale of Two Guinea Pigs. (p. 1700)
Maddock, Monika, illus. see Arena, Jacqueline.
Maddock, Monika, illus. see Mullins, Julie.
Maddock, Monika, illus. see Smith Dinbergs, Holly.
Maddock-Cowart, Donna. Anhinga Tree. Mann, William A., illus. (p. 76)
Maddocks, Maria. Two Little Ballerinas: A Girly Girl Book. (p. 1804)
Maddocks, Maria, illus. see Goodings, Christina.
Maddocks, Maria, illus. see Nolan, Allia Zobel.
Maddocks, Maria, illus. see Piggy Toes Press.
Maddocks, Maria, illus. see Piper, Sophie.
Maddocks, Maria, illus. see Wilding, Valerie.
Maddocks, Maria, illus. see Zobel-Nolan, Allia.
Maddocks, Steven. World Hunger. (p. 1955)
Maddox, Diana, jt. auth. see Maddox, Joseph.
Maddox, Jake. Back on the Beam Mourning, Tuesday, illus. (p. 130)
—Backup Goalie Tiffany, Sean, illus. (p. 130)
—Bad-Luck Basketball Ray, Mike, illus. (p. 132)
—Batter Up! Tiffany, Sean, illus. (p. 145)
—Beach Bully Aburtov, illus. (p. 149)
—Beach Bully Aburtov, Jesus, illus. (p. 149)
—Beach Bully. (p. 149)
—Behind the Plate Tiffany, Sean, illus. (p. 160)
—Blizzard! A Survive! Story Tiffany, Sean, illus. (p. 199)
—BMX Challenge Tiffany, Sean, illus. (p. 204)
—Board Battle Aburtov, Jesus Aburto, illus. (p. 205)
—Board Battle. (p. 205)
—Board Rebel. Tiffany, Sean, illus. (p. 205)
—Caught Stealing. Aburtov, Jesus Aburto, illus. (p. 282)
—Cheer Captain Pulsar Studios Staff, illus. (p. 295)
—Cheer Challenge. Mourning, Tuesday, illus. (p. 296)
—Cheer Choice Wood, Katie, illus. (p. 296)
—Cowboy Up Tiffany, Sean, illus. (p. 374)
—Cycling Champion Garcia, Eduardo, illus. (p. 397)
—Dance Team Dilemma Wood, Katie, illus. (p. 402)
—Dancing Solo Wood, Katie, illus. (p. 403)
—Definición por Penales. Heck, Claudia M., tr. from ENG. (p. 424)
—Disc Golf Drive Tiffany, Sean, illus. (p. 447)
—Diving off the Edge Tiffany, Sean, illus. (p. 455)
—Double-Axel Doubt (p. 472)
—Drive to the Hoop Pulsar Studios Staff, illus. (p. 485)
—En la línea de Ataque. Heck, Claudia M., tr. from ENG. (p. 522)
—Face-Off Tiffany, Sean, illus. (p. 560)
—Field Hockey Firsts Mourning, Tuesday, illus. (p. 584)
—Free Climb. Tiffany, Sean, illus. (p. 634)
—Free Throw Tiffany, Sean, illus. (p. 634)
—Full Court Dreams. Mourning, Tuesday, illus. (p. 646)
—Geocache Surprise Tiffany, Sean, illus. (p. 661)
—Go-Kart Rush. Tiffany, Sean, illus. (p. 686)
—Gold Medal Swim Garcia, Eduardo, illus. (p. 693)
—Gridiron Bully Tiffany, Sean, illus. (p. 723)
—Gridiron Showdown Ray, Mike, illus. (p. 723)
—Gymnastics Jitters Wood, Katie, illus. (p. 734)
—Half-Pipe Prize Mourning, Tuesday, illus. (p. 736)
—Heavyweight Takedown. (p. 761)
—Hockey Meltdown Tiffany, Sean, illus. (p. 786)
—Home-Field Football Tiffany, Sean, illus. (p. 792)
—Hoop Hotshot Tiffany, Sean, illus. (p. 795)
—Hoop Hustle. Aburto, Jesus, illus. (p. 795)
—Horseback Hopes Mourning, Tuesday, illus. (p. 800)
—Hunter's Code. Tiffany, Sean, illus. (p. 828)
—Impact Books Tiffany, Sean, illus. (p. 862)
—Jake Maddox. (p. 906)
—Jake Maddox. Tiffany, Sean, illus. (p. 906)
—Jake Maddox Girl Sport Stories. Wood, Katie, illus. (p. 906)
—Jake Maddox Girls Sport Stories. Wood, Katie, illus. (p. 906)
—Jake Maddox JV Ray, Mike, illus. (p. 906)
—Jake Maddox JV. Ray, Mike, illus. (p. 906)
—Jake Maddox Sports Stories (p. 906)
—Jump Serve. Mourning, Tuesday, illus. (p. 934)
—Karate Countdown Tiffany, Sean, illus. (p. 943)
—Kart Competition Aburtov, Jesus, illus. (p. 944)
—Kart Competition Aburtov, Jesus Aburto, illus. (p. 944)
—Kart Competition. (p. 944)
—Kart Crash Tiffany, Sean, illus. (p. 944)
—Lacrosse Attack. Tiffany, Sean, illus. (p. 970)
—Lanzador Bajo Presión. Heck, Claudia M., tr. from ENG. (p. 975)
—Legend of the Lure Tiffany, Sean, illus. (p. 989)
—Linebacker Block Tiffany, Sean, illus. (p. 1019)
—Motocross Double-Cross. Tiffany, Sean, illus. (p. 1179)
—Mountain Bike Hero Tiffany, Sean, illus. (p. 1180)
—Mr. Strike Out Tiffany, Sean, illus. (p. 1186)
—Off the Bench Tiffany, Sean, illus. (p. 1279)
—On Guard Tiffany, Sean, illus. (p. 1289)
—On the Line Tiffany, Sean, illus. (p. 1290)
—On the Speedway Tiffany, Sean, illus. (p. 1291)
—Outfield Outcast Ray, Mike, illus. (p. 1312)
—Over the Net Mourning, Tuesday, illus. (p. 1314)
—Paintball Blast. Tiffany, Sean, illus. (p. 1318)
—Paintball Invasion Tiffany, Sean, illus. (p. 1318)
—Paintball Problems Aburtov, Jesus Aburto, illus. (p. 1318)
—Paintball Problems. (p. 1318)
—Pit Crew Crunch Tiffany, Sean, illus. (p. 1364)
—Pitcher Pressure Tiffany, Sean, illus. (p. 1364)
—Playing Forward. Tiffany, Sean, illus. (p. 1372)
—Point Guard Prank Tiffany, Sean, illus. (p. 1377)
—Quarterback Comeback Tiffany, Sean, illus. (p. 1422)
—Quarterback Sneak Tiffany, Sean, illus. (p. 1423)
—Race Car Rival Tiffany, Sean, illus. (p. 1430)
—Rebelde de la Patineta Heck, Claudia, tr. from ENG. (p. 1451)
—Record Run Tiffany, Sean, illus. (p. 1452)
—Relay Race Breakdown Garcia, Eduardo, illus. (p. 1458)
—Running Back Dreams Tiffany, Sean, illus. (p. 1497)
—Running Rivals. Mourning, Tuesday, illus. (p. 1497)
—Second-Chance Soccer Ray, Mike, illus. (p. 1539)
—Shark Attack! Tiffany, Sean, illus. (p. 1562)
—Shipwreck! Tiffany, Sean, illus. (p. 1567)
—Skate Park Challenge Tiffany, Sean, illus. (p. 1583)
—Skateboard Save. Tiffany, Sean, illus. (p. 1583)
—Skateboard Struggle Tiffany, Sean, illus. (p. 1583)
—Skatepark Challenge. Tiffany, Sean, illus. (p. 1584)
—Skater's Secret Mourning, Tuesday, illus. (p. 1584)
—Skating Showdown Wood, Katie, illus. (p. 1584)
—Slam Dunk Shoes Tiffany, Sean, illus. (p. 1587)
—Slap-Shot Slump. (p. 1588)
—Snowboard Duel Tiffany, Sean, illus. (p. 1600)
—Snowboard Hero. (p. 1600)
—Soccer Shake-Up. Aburto, Jesus, illus. (p. 1603)
—Soccer Shootout Tiffany, Sean, illus. (p. 1603)
—Soccer Show-Off Wood, Katie, illus. (p. 1603)
—Soccer Spirit. Mourning, Tuesday, illus. (p. 1603)
—Softball Surprise Wood, Katie, illus. (p. 1606)
—Speed Camp Tiffany, Sean, illus. (p. 1624)
—Speed Receiver Tiffany, Sean, illus. (p. 1624)
—Speedway Switch. Tiffany, Sean, illus. (p. 1624)
—Stock Car Sabotage Tiffany, Sean, illus. (p. 1651)
—Stolen Bases. Mourning, Tuesday, illus. (p. 1652)
—Storm Surfer Mourning, Tuesday, illus. (p. 1656)
—Striker Assist Tiffany, Sean, illus. (p. 1667)
—Swimming the Distance. (p. 1691)
—Takedown. Tiffany, Sean, illus. (p. 1697)
—Tennis Liar Tiffany, Sean, illus. (p. 1720)
—Tennis Trouble. Mourning, Tuesday, illus. (p. 1720)
—Tiro Libre Heck, Claudia M., tr. from ENG. (p. 1757)
—Touchdown Triumph. Aburto, Jesus, illus. (p. 1772)
—Track & Field Takedown Garcia, Eduardo, illus. (p. 1775)
—Tramposo de BMX Heck, Claudia M., tr. from ENG. (p. 1778)
—Victory Vault Pulsar Studios Staff, illus. (p. 1840)
—Volcano! A Survive! Story. Tiffany, Sean, illus. (p. 1848)
—Volleyball Dreams Wood, Katie, illus. (p. 1849)
—Whitewater Courage Tiffany, Sean, illus. (p. 1914)
—Wild Hike. Tiffany, Sean, illus. (p. 1929)
—Wildcats Blitz Tiffany, Sean, illus. (p. 1931)
—Wildcats Slam Dunk Tiffany, Sean, illus. (p. 1931)
—Win or Lose. Tiffany, Sean, illus. (p. 1935)
—Windsurfing Winner Tiffany, Sean, illus. (p. 1936)
Maddox, Jake, jt. auth. see Stevens, Eric.
Maddox, Jake, jt. auth. see Suen, Anastasia.
Maddox, Jake, jt. auth. see Tiffany, Sean.
Maddox, Jake & Berne, Emma Carlson. Ballet Bullies Mourning, Tuesday, illus. (p. 134)
—Hoop Doctor Mourning, Tuesday, illus. (p. 795)
—Horseback Hurdles Wood, Katie, illus. (p. 800)
—Rebound Time Wood, Katie, illus. (p. 1451)
—Running Scared Wood, Katie, illus. (p. 1497)
—Soccer Surprise Wood, Katie, illus. (p. 1603)
Maddox, Jake & McMullan, Kate. Stop That Bull, Theseus! Zilber, Denis, illus. (p. 1653)
Maddox, Joseph & Maddox, Diana. See You in Hell. (p. 1547)
Maddox, Linda. Resonating the Sound. (p. 1463)
Maddox, Mike & Anderson, Jeff. Lion Graphic Bible: The Whole Story from Genesis to Revelation. Harrison, Steve, illus. (p. 1020)
Maddox, Nellie Hazel. Grandmother Nellie's Poems (p. 709)
Maddox, Nicklas. Big Tiny Spaceman (p. 184)
Maddox, Tony & Wen, Dref. Ffred ar y Dwr. (p. 583)
Madel, Dan. Cracker the Cat, Almost Caught. (p. 375)
Madelag. Selva Feliz * Happy Jungle. Alvarado, Andrea E., tr. (p. 1550)
Mademann Vaughan, Kathryn. My Day at the Zoo. Martin, Don, illus. (p. 1201)
Mader, C. Roger. Lost Cat. Mader, C. Roger, illus. (p. 1055)
—Tiptop Cat. Mader, C. Roger, illus. (p. 1757)
Mader, Jan. Let's Play Football! (p. 1000)
—Michigan. (p. 1135)
—My Brother Wants to Be Like Me. Palmer, Kate S., illus. (p. 1199)
—Time for a Bath! World of Discovery II. Maizel, Karen, illus. (p. 1751)
—Virginia. (p. 1844)
—¡Vamos a Jugar Al Fútbol Americano! (p. 1831)
Mader, Jan & Capstone Press Editors. Dolley Madison (p. 464)
—Elizabeth Blackwell (p. 513)
Mader, Jan & Capstone Press Staff. Betsy Ross (p. 172)
—Molly Pitcher (p. 1161)
Mader, Lothar, jt. auth. see Mader, Ph. D. Lothar.
Mader, Ph. D. Lothar & Mader, Lothar. Fartface: Stop Teasing Me, Bullyback... (p. 575)
Mader, Sylvia S. Biology: With Bound-In OLC Card. (p. 189)
—Biology. (p. 189)
—General & Human Biology. (p. 660)
Maderich, Robin. Faith & Honor. (p. 565)
Maderna, Victoria. Crazy Cows Stickers. (p. 377)
—Glow-In-the-Dark Tattoos Owls. (p. 685)
—Look & Find Letters to Color. (p. 1048)
—Look & Find Numbers to Color. (p. 1048)
—Look & Find Opposites to Color. (p. 1048)
—Look & Find Shapes to Color. (p. 1048)
—Make Your Own Plush Pals. (p. 1080)
—Playful Pictures — Animals. (p. 1372)
Maderna, Victoria & Stickers. Woodland Music Stickers. (p. 1949)
Madge, Amy. Adventures of Kwun-Gee & Uba Dooba Boy. (p. 19)
Madgwick, Wendy. First Science Library: Water Play. (p. 596)
—First Science Library: On the Move. (p. 596)
—First Science Library: Sound Magic. (p. 596)
—First Science Library: Light & Dark. (p. 596)
—First Science Library: Up in the Air. (p. 596)
—First Science Library: Super Materials. (p. 596)
—First Science Library: Animals & Plants. (p. 596)
—First Science Library: Magnets & Sparks. (p. 596)
Madhu, Kailash. Wise Tree & Meu: Mind & Spirit. (p. 1940)
Madia, Anita. What's for Breakfast, Mr. Fickle? (p. 1897)
Madian. Bald-Headed Chicken. (p. 134)
Madigan, L. K. Flash Burnout. (p. 602)
—Mermaid's Mirror. (p. 1128)
Madill, Douglas, illus. see Bissell, Sybil A.
Madill, Emily Elizabeth & Bzymek, Izabela. Grateful Jake. (p. 712)
Madison, Alan. Pecorino Plays Ball. Cantone, AnnaLaura, illus. (p. 1334)
—Pecorino's First Concert. Cantone, AnnaLaura, illus. (p. 1334)
—Velma Gratch & the Way Cool Butterfly. Hawkes, Kevin, illus. (p. 1835)
Madison, Amelia. Predators of Asia & Australia. (p. 1395)
—Predators of Europe & Africa. (p. 1395)
Madison, Bennett. September Girls. (p. 1551)
Madison, Chandler. Gorax & His Green Machine. (p. 702)
Madison, James H. Lynching in the Heartland: Race & Memory in America. (p. 1066)
Madison, James H., et al. Hoosiers & the American Story: A Student Guide. (p. 796)
Madison, Jennifer. Glass Stone: The Tales of the Chinese Checkerboard. (p. 682)
Madison, Lynda. All about You Quiz Book: Discover More about Yourself & How to Be Your Best! Laskey, Shannon, illus. (p. 43)
—Food & You: Eat Right, Being Strong & Feeling Great. (p. 613)
Madison, Mike. No Time to Nap. Peterson, Mary, illus. (p. 1260)
Madison, Paul. Purple Monkey. (p. 1419)
Madison, Richard & Cunningham, Mark. Molly Pitcher: The Woman Who Fought the War. (p. 1161)
Madison, Ron. Ned & the General: A Lesson about Deployment. Covolo, David, illus. (p. 1239)
—Ned & the World's Religions: As Seen Through the Eyes of Children. Covolo, David, illus. (p. 1239)
—Ned Learns to Say No: A Lesson about Drugs. Covolo, David, illus. (p. 1239)
Madison, Taylor. Boys We Love: Today's Top 30 Hottest Stars. (p. 220)
Madiwale, Frances. Special Creatures. (p. 1623)
Madkins, Dorenda W. Smiley Face: A Smile a Day Takes the Frown Away. (p. 1594)
Madkins, Doris J. God Made the Sun to Shine. (p. 690)
Madlener, Michael & Reeves, Patrick. Feed Your Fish. (p. 580)
Madl-Palfi, L. & Tujner-Marko, B. Kaspertheater Rund ums Jahr. (p. 944)
Madonia, Kristen-Paige. Fingerprints of You. (p. 589)
—Fingerprints of You. Ribera, Terry, illus. (p. 589)
—Invisible Fault Lines. (p. 885)
Madonna, jt. auth. see Ciccone, Madonna L.
Madonna, Colleen & Williams, Flood. Beautiful Diversity: The Geography of Mexico. (p. 153)
—Fiesta! the Festivals of Mexico. (p. 584)
—Spirit of a Nation: The People of Mexico. (p. 1628)
Madonna, Lenae. Lost & Found. Conde, Manuel, illus. (p. 1054)
Madonna, Marissa. There's a Hole in the Bucket! (p. 1731)
Madonna, pseud. Being Binah Fulvimari, Jeffrey, illus. (p. 161)
—Big-Sister Blues Fulvimari, Jeffrey, illus. (p. 183)
—Catch the Bouquet! (p. 279)
—Friends for Life! Fulvimari, Jeffrey, illus. (p. 638)
—Good-Bye, Grace? Fulvimari, Jeffrey, illus. (p. 697)
—New Girl Fulvimari, Jeffrey, illus. (p. 1244)
—Ready, Set, Vote! (p. 1447)
—Rose by Any Other Name. Fulvimari, Jeffrey, illus. (p. 1489)
Madonna, pseud & Fulvimari, Jeffrey. Runway Rose. (p. 1497)
Madore, Michele. Rudee Goes Bananas for Manners. Gravitt, Bill, illus. (p. 1494)
Madormo, John V. Homemade Stuffing Caper (p. 793)
Madou, Carol. When Pigs Can Fly! (p. 1904)
Madow, Michelle. Diamonds in the Rough. (p. 434)
—Secret Diamond Sisters. (p. 1540)
Madrian, Brigitte, ed. see Earl, C. F.
Madrian, Brigitte, ed. see Fischer, James.
Madrian, Brigitte, ed. see Thompson, Helen.
Madrid, Bo. Lunar Express. (p. 1065)
Madrid, Erwin, illus. see Feldman, Thea.
Madrid, Erwin, illus. see Hapka, Catherine, pseud.
Madrid, Erwin, illus. see Hennessy, B. G.
Madrid, Erwin, illus. see Howard, Ryan & Howard, Krystle.
Madrid, Erwin, illus. see Kozlowsky, M. P.
Madrid, Erwin, illus. see McDonald, Megan.
Madrid, Erwin, illus. see Wiley, Melissa.
Madrid-Branch, Michelle. Tummy Mummy. (p. 1796)
Madrigal, Antonio Hernandez. Erandi's Braids. dePaola, Tomie, illus. (p. 533)
Madrigal, Margarita. Open Door to Spanish: A Conversation Course for Beginners, Level 1. (p. 1299)
—Open Door to Spanish: A Conversation Course for Beginners, Level 2. Vol. 2 (p. 1299)
Madrzak, Carole. Arronna Crystal. (p. 101)
—In the Shadows of Bington Manor. (p. 867)
—Moonlight Dare. (p. 1172)
—Secrets Inside Bington Manor. (p. 1545)
Madsen, Chris. Bugs. (p. 237)
—Undersea Adventure. (p. 1815)
Madsen, Cindi. All the Broken Pieces. (p. 45)
Madsen, David A. Geometric Dimensioning & Tolerancing. (p. 662)
Madsen, David A., jt. auth. see Shumaker, Terence M.
Madsen, James, jt. auth. see Bullman, Carol.
Madsen, Jim, illus. see Carson, Mary Kay.
Madsen, Jim, illus. see DeVries, Catherine.
Madsen, Jim, illus. see Grey, C. R.
Madsen, Jim, illus. see Hamlisch, Marvin.
Madsen, Jim, illus. see Henry, Juliann.
Madsen, Jim, illus. see Kimmel, Eric A.
Madsen, Jim, illus. see Kipling, Rudyard.
Madsen, Jim, illus. see Lunge-Larsen, Lise.
Madsen, Jim, illus. see Manning, Peyton, et al.
Madsen, Jim, illus. see Napoli, Donna Jo.
Madsen, Jim, illus. see Stanley, George E.
Madsen, Jim, illus. see Stewart, Melissa.
Madsen, Jim, illus. see Young, Judy.
Madsen, Michael. American Badass. Naughton, Michael P. & Novak, Donna, eds. (p. 59)
Madsen, Michelle, illus. see Allie, Scott, et al.
Madsen, Michelle, illus. see Espenson, Jane, et al.

M

Madsen, Shane. Stevenson Chronicles: Deltom. (p. 1649)
Madsen, Susan Arrington. I Walked to Zion: True Stories of Young Pioneers on the Mormon Trail. (p. 847)
Madsen, W. J. Arkeepers: Episode One. (p. 99)
—Arkeepers: Episode Two. (p. 99)
Madson, Robin. No More Crackers, Please. (p. 1259)
Madu, Abraham. Road to take to School Is the Phonics Way: Companion Book for Students. (p. 1477)
Maduell, Andree'. Secret of the Dolphins. (p. 1542)
Madzel, D. E., illus. see Hayes, MJ.
Mae, Darcie. Sammy & Robert. (p. 1507)
—Sammy & Robert Discover the Ocean (p. 1507)
—Sammy & Robert Go Home for the Holidays. (p. 1507)
—Sammy & Robert's Animal Adventures. (p. 1507)
Maed, Mary Ann Graziani. Filled to Capacity. (p. 586)
Maeda, Matsuo, illus. see Arai, Shizuko.
Maeda, Shunshin. Ninja Baseball Kyuma! (p. 1256)
Maeda, Tomo. Beyond My Touch. (p. 174)
Maeda, Toshio. Adventure Kid - the Original Manga 1: User Friendly. Vol. 1 Maeda, Toshio, illus. (p. 14)
Maehl, Sarah & Nash, Kevin. Beloit College College Prowler off the Record. (p. 163)
Maekawa, Jun & Origami. Genuine Japanese Origami: 33 Mathematical Models Based upon √2. Hatori, Koshiro, tr. from JPN. (p. 661)
Maelor, Gwawr, et al. Neli Neidr. (p. 1240)
—Tân Yn y Jyngl. (p. 1705)
Maeno, Itoko, illus. see Paine, Penelope C.
Maerov, Jeff. Boca Buddies. Can't We Just Say Goodnight? (p. 206)
Maes, Adolfo P. Christ & the Children. (p. 311)
Maes, Ame, illus. see Munoz, Ruby.
Maes, Nicholas. Fortuna: A Felix Taylor Adventure. (p. 623)
—Laughing Wolf. (p. 980)
—Locksmith. (p. 1045)
—Transmigration. (p. 1779)
Maese, Fares, illus. see Renner, C. J., et al.
Maese, Fares, jt. auth. see Ciencin, Scott.
Maese, Fares, jt. auth. see Kreie, Chris.
Maese, Fares, jt. auth. see Tulien, Sean.
Maese, Fares & Shakespeare, William. Midsummer Night's Dream Esparza, Andres et al, illus. (p. 1139)
Maestas, Kathy. Sun's Not up but His Hair Is Sticking Out: Hope & Comfort Together. (p. 1677)
Maestas, Phillip. Adventures of Little Big-Foot. (p. 19)
Maestro, Betsy. Coming to America. Ryan, Susannah, illus. (p. 348)
—Liberty or Death: The American Revolution: 1763-1783. Maestro, Giulio, illus. (p. 1005)
—More Perfect Union: The Story of Our Constitution. Maestro, Giulio, illus. (p. 1174)
—New Americans: Colonial Times: 1620-1689. Maestro, Giulio, illus. (p. 1243)
—Story of Clocks & Calendars. Maestro, Giulio, illus. (p. 1657)
—What Is a Skeleton? (p. 1888)
—Why Do Leaves Change Color? Krupinski, Loretta, illus. (p. 1923)
Maestro, Betsy & Maestro, Giulio. Sea Full of Sharks. (p. 1534)
Maestro, Giulio, illus. see Maestro, Betsy.
Maestro, Giulio, illus. see Terban, Marvin.
Maestro, Giulio, jt. auth. see Maestro, Betsy.
Maestro, Laura Hartman, illus. see Kennedy, Caroline.
Maestro, Pepe. Blomeaestra. Guirao, David, illus. (p. 189)
—Gato con Botas. Zabala, Javier, illus. (p. 658)
—Hansel y Gretel (Colorin Colorado/That Is the End of the Story) Metola, Patricia, illus. (p. 743)
Mafera, Sandra. Cloud of Dauphin Island. (p. 334)
Maffini, Helen. Sammy's Next Move: Sammy the Snail Is a Travelling Snail Who Lives in Different Countries. (p. 1508)
Maffla, Jaime Garcia, compiled by. Antologia de la Poesia Colombiana E Hispanoamericana. (p. 89)
Mafi, Tahereh. Ignite Me. (p. 856)
—Shatter Me. (p. 1563)
—Unite Me: Fracture Me & Destroy Me. (p. 1818)
—Unravel Me. (p. 1822)
Maga, Timothy P. 1960s. (p. 2002)
Magabala Books Staff. Aussie Toddlers Can. Dellos, Kim, photos by. (p. 116)
—Australian Babies. (p. 116)
Magagna, Anna Marie, illus. see Mays, Blanche, ed.
Magalhaes, Roberto Carvalho de, jt. auth. see Brooke, Beatrice D.
Magalinska, Ingrid, illus. see Likins, Kim.
Magallanes, Alejandro, illus. see Baranda, Maria.
Magallanes, Alejandro, illus. see Guerra, Elisa Speckman.
Magallanes, Alejandro, illus. see Hernandez, Claudia, et al.
Magaril, Mikhail, illus. see Sanfield, Steve.
Magarino, Aurel. Evangelizando Por Medio De. (p. 541)
Magaro, Dan. Adventures of Fred & Daisymae. (p. 18)
Magazine, Stories for Children. Best of Stories for Children Volume 1. (p. 170)
Magaziner, Henry Jonas. Our Liberty Bell. O'Brien, John, illus. (p. 1309)
—Our Liberty Bell. O'Brien, John A., illus. (p. 1309)
Magaziner, Lauren. Only Thing Worse Than Witches. (p. 1298)
Magby, Meryl. American Bison. (p. 60)
—Bald Eagles. (p. 133)
—Bighorn Sheep. (p. 185)
—Black Bears. (p. 195)
—Hammerhead Sharks. (p. 739)
—Jellyfish. (p. 912)
—Lobsters. (p. 1044)
—Moose. (p. 1173)
—Mountain Goats. (p. 1180)
—Mountain Lions. (p. 1181)
—Mustangs. (p. 1194)
—Prairie Dogs. (p. 1392)
—Raccoons. (p. 1430)
—Sea Anemones. (p. 1534)
—Sea Urchins. (p. 1536)
—Sponges. (p. 1631)
—White-Tailed Deer. (p. 1913)
—Wild Turkeys. (p. 1930)
Magdalena-Brown, Maria, illus. see Irvin-Marston, Hope.
Magden, Loretta. Treetop Bird Family. Barringer, J. M., illus. (p. 1784)
Magedanz, Stacy. St. Augustine's Confessions: Over 300 Titles Aand 100 Million Sold! (p. 1637)
Magee, Christopher, illus. see Pellegrino, Victor C.
Magee, David. How Toyota Became #1: Leadership Lessons from the World's Greatest Car Company. (p. 823)
Magee, Dolunay. Perrey's Adventures. (p. 1343)
Magee, Elaine. Tell Me What to Eat If I Have Irritable Bowel Syndrome. (p. 1717)
—Tell Me What to Eat to Help Prevent Breast Cancer. (p. 1717)
Magee, Eric, jt. auth. see Moxon, Kay.
Magee, Helen. Ghost Called Clarence. (p. 670)
—What's French for Help, George? (p. 1897)
Magee, Kanika. Rain, Rain, Come Today. Crosson, Cierra, illus. (p. 1435)
—Where Is God at Midnight?? Thomas, Sonya, illus. (p. 1908)
Magee, Kanika A. M. Today I Got Saved Thomas, Sonya, illus. (p. 1760)
Magee, Lonnie. North to the Tallgrass, the Drive. (p. 1265)
Magee, Mary. Dog Who Adopted a Postman. (p. 462)
Magee, Melanie, illus. see Grant, Callie.
Magee, Wes. Blue, Where Are You? Suggs, Margaret, illus. (p. 203)
—Itsy Bitsy Spider & Itsy Bitsy Beetle. (p. 900)
—Little Dragon. Warburton, Sarah, illus. (p. 1027)
—Pet the Cat. (p. 1346)
—Who Likes Pancakes? (p. 1916)
Magellan, Marta. Those Colossal Cats. Weaver, Steve, illus. (p. 1740)
—Those Lively Lizards. Gersing, James & Weaver, Steve, illus. (p. 1740)
—Those Voracious Vultures. Weaver, Steve et al, illus. (p. 1740)
Magellan, Mauro. Max the Apartment Cat. Magellan, Mauro, illus. (p. 1111)
Magenta, Emma. Orlando on a Thursday. Magenta, Emma, illus. (p. 1304)
Magerl, Caroline, illus. see Herrick, Steven.
Magerl, Caroline, jt. auth. see Hathorn, Libby.
Magers, Ramona Hirsch. Walter's Discovery. Hirsch, Charmaine, illus. (p. 1856)
Maggart, Kaye Wiley & Prentice Hall Staff. Shining Star, Introductory Level. (p. 1566)
Maggi, María Elena. Great Canoe: A Karina Legend. (p. 714)
Maggi, Nicole. Forgetting. (p. 619)
Maggin, Elliot, et al. Superman in the Seventies. Swan, Curt & Giordano, Dick, illus. (p. 1683)
Maggin, Elliot S. Starwinds Howl: The Epic Story of Krypto the Superdog. (p. 1644)
Maggin, Elliot S., told to. Luthor's Gift. (p. 1066)
Maggio, Viqui. Baby Tease. (p. 128)
Maggiora, Linda Jean. Three Little Pigs. (p. 1742)
Maggiore, Angela T. Short Stories for Children. (p. 1569)
Maggiore, Evana. FASHION FENG SHUI the Power of Dressing with Intention: Transform Your Look & Your Life! (p. 575)
Maggiore, Lisa. Ava the Monster Slayer. Felten, Ross, illus. (p. 118)
Maggipinto, Donata. Everyday Celebrations: Savoring Food, Family & Life at Home. Ruffenach, France, photos by. (p. 543)
Maggs, William Alan. Jungle Adventures of Henry Littlejohn. (p. 935)
Magi, Aria. Lulilites: And the Star of Seven Rays. (p. 1064)
Magi, Jodi, illus. see Poulter, J. R.
Magic Eye, Inc. Staff. Harry Potter Magic Eye Book: 3D Magical Moments. (p. 751)
—Harry Potter Magic Eye Book: 3D Magical Creatures, Beasts & Beings. (p. 751)
Magic Eye Studios, illus. see Ambrosio, Stefano.
Magic Eye Studios, illus. see Porter, Alan J.
Magic Eye Studios Staff, illus. see Petrucha, Stefan.
Magic Wagon Staff. Flip-Flop Adventure. (p. 605)
—Presidents of the United States Bio-Graphics. (p. 1397)
Magic Wagon Staff & ABDO Publishing Company Staff. Climate Change. (p. 332)
—Famous Firsts: Animals Making History. (p. 569)
—I Wish I Were ... (p. 849)
—Planets. (p. 1368)
Magid, Jennifer. Angelina Jolie. (p. 74)
—Miley Cyrus/Hannah Montana. (p. 1142)
Magill, Frank N., ed. see Salem Press Staff.
Magill, Ron, photos by see Magellan, Marta.
Magill, Sharon L. Chloe Madison & the Beach Heists. (p. 308)
Maginn, Traci, illus. see McCord, Marianne.
Maglio-Macullar, Andrea, illus. see Piantedosi, John J.
Magloff, Lisa. Experiments with Heat & Energy. (p. 549)
Magnarelli, Margaret. Backstage Pass: Today's Hottest Stars. (p. 130)
Magnason, Andri Snaer. Story of the Blue Planet. D'Arcy, Julian Meldon, tr. (p. 1660)
Magnat, Julien, et al. Curse of the Cat People. Ellipsanime Staff & Dargaud Media Staff, illus. (p. 394)
Magnayon, Megan Coy. PuzzlePal Books: Pretty Pig. Cohen, Melissa, illus. (p. 1421)
Magnayon, Megan Coy, illus. see Cohen, Melissa.
Magner, Laura. Creativity Calendar. (p. 380)
—Researching Adventures: Challenging GLYPH-Making Activities. (p. 1463)
—Scientific Method in Fairy Tale Forest. (p. 1528)
Magness, Lee. Silver Dasher. (p. 1576)
Magness, Robert. Silent Knife, Holy Knife. Glon, Nancy, illus. (p. 1575)
Magness, Valerie. Special Book about Me! (p. 1623)
Magness, Vicki. Stephen: A Strong Man to Run a Race. (p. 1648)
—Victor the Victorious: And the Tale of Two Cities. (p. 1840)
Magnet, Julien. Planet of the Firebird. Klio Burrell, Carol, tr. (p. 1368)
Magnette, Paul, illus. see Scanlon, Liz Garton.
Magni, Aurora. 10 Marys & the Little Gabriel. Vignaga, Francesca Dafne, illus. (p. 1993)
Magniat, Jeffrey, illus. see Mattern, Joanne.
Magnier, Thierry & Hallenleben, Georg. Babel y el Angel. (p. 123)
Magnin, Joyce. Cake: Love, Chickens, & a Taste of Peculiar Ivanov, Alexsey & Ivanov, Olga, illus. (p. 252)
—Carrying Mason (p. 271)
Magninie, Betty, jt. auth. see Colville, Lucy.
Magnisi, Angelica, illus. see Magnisi, Sabrina.
Magnisi, Sabrina. Miss Sabrina's Learn the Hail Mary As You Color the Rosary: A Guide for Children 6 - 9 & Up! Magnisi, Sabrina & Magnisi, Angelica, illus. (p. 1152)
Magno, Carlos. Transformers: Movie Prequel: Rising Storm: Vol 1. (p. 1778)
Magno, Ryan, illus. see Robledo, Ronald J.
Magnolia, B. Beautiful Wild Rose Girl. Hugel, William K., ed. (p. 154)
Magnor, Mary, et al, texts. Jesus Teaches Us. (p. 916)
Magnum Editors Staff, ed. see Kuper, Simon.
Magnum Photos Staff, photos by see Boot, Chris.
Magnus, Erica, illus. see Brisson, Pat.
Magnus, Kellie. Little Lion Goes to School. Robinson, Michael, illus. (p. 1030)
Magnuson, Diana, illus. see Adams, Alison.
Magnuson, Diana, illus. see Ehrmantraut, Brenda.
Magnuson, Diana, illus. see Hillert, Margaret.
Magnuson, Diana, illus. see Krensky, Stephen.
Magnuson, Diana, illus. see Magoun, James.
Magnuson, Diana, illus. see Smithsonian Institution Staff.
Magnuson, Gregory. Crab & Will, a Tale of Shakespeare's Dog. (p. 375)
Magnuson, James. Emma's First Agate LeMay, Meagan, illus. (p. 520)
Magnuson, Natalie, illus. see Jones, Christianne C.
Magodia, Spruha. From the Other Side: Entwining Worlds. (p. 644)
Magona, Sindiwe. Ugly Duckling. Hinrichsen, Natalie, illus. (p. 1808)
Magone, Teresa. Little Bunny Has Belly Surgery. (p. 1025)
Magoo, Flossy. Upside down & Backwards. (p. 1825)
Magoon, Kekla. 37 Things I Love (in No Particular Order) (p. 1996)
—Abraham Lincoln. (p. 6)
—Camo Girl. (p. 256)
—Cesar Chavez: Crusader for Labor Rights. (p. 288)
—Fire in the Streets. (p. 590)
—Gun Control. (p. 732)
—How It Went Down. (p. 810)
—Media Censorship. (p. 1118)
—Nelson Mandela: A Leader for Freedom. (p. 1240)
—Rock & the River. (p. 1482)
—Salem Witch Trials. (p. 1504)
—Sex Education in Schools. (p. 1556)
—Shadows of Sherwood. (p. 1558)
—Today the World Is Watching You: The Little Rock Nine & the Fight for School Integration 1957. (p. 1761)
—Welfare Debate. (p. 1874)
—Zebulon Pike Expedition. (p. 1985)
Magoon, Kekla, jt. auth. see Shabazz, Ilyasah.
Magoon, Kekla & Keene, Carolyn. Strangers on a Train. (p. 1665)
Magoon, Scott. Boy Who Cried Bigfoot! Magoon, Scott, illus. (p. 219)
—Breathe. Magoon, Scott, illus. (p. 226)
Magoon, Scott, illus. see Harper, Charise Mericle.
Magoon, Scott, illus. see Holub, Joan.
Magoon, Scott, illus. see Knudsen, Michelle.
Magoon, Scott, illus. see LaReau, Kara.
Magoon, Scott, illus. see LeReau, Kara.
Magoon, Scott, illus. see Litwin, Eric.
Magoon, Scott, illus. see Rosenthal, Amy Krouse.
Magoon, Scott, illus. see Sauer, Tammi.
Magor, Dianne M. Ed. Lauren's Wish. (p. 980)
Magoun, James. There's a Bear in My Chair. Magnuson, Diana, illus. (p. 1730)
Magpie, ed. see Smith, Roy.
Magpie, Lance White, reader. Girl Who Loved Wild Horses. (p. 679)
Magram, Clara. John Legend. (p. 922)
Magram, Hannah Straus. Railroads of the West. (p. 1434)
Magrane, Mijares. Grandma Garcia: La Abuela Garcia - An Intimate Journey into the Past. (p. 708)
Magritte, Rene, jt. auth. see Rubin, Susan Goldman.
Magritte, Rene, jt. auth. see Venezia, Mike.
Magruder, Dan. Journey to See the King: Second Edition. (p. 929)
Magruder, Jana, jt. auth. see Jackson, Jack.
Magruder, Jana & Amberson, Mary. Brave Boy & a Good Soldier Educator Guide: John C. C. Hill & the Texas Expedition to Mier. (p. 223)
Magruder, Trula. Doll Dining. American Girl Editors, ed. (p. 463)
—Doll Play: Crafts, Games, & Fun for You & Your Doll. American Girl Editors, ed. (p. 463)
—What a Girl Loves Puzzle Book. Magruder, Trula, ed. (p. 1878)
Magruder, Trula, ed. see Brodman, Larisa.
Magruder, Trula, ed. see Smith, Keri.
Magruder, Trula, ed. see Walton, Rick.
Magruder, Trula, jt. ed. see American Girl Editors.
Magruder, Trula & American Girl Editors, eds. Design by Me Tropical: Fancy Art & Fun Display Ideas! (p. 429)
—Design by Me Wings: Fancy Art & Fun Display Ideas! Ingham, Julie, illus. (p. 429)
—Just Grandma & Me: The Fill-In, Tear-Out, Fold-Up Book of Fun for Girls & Their Grandmas. Peterson, Stacy, illus. (p. 938)
Magruder, Trula & David, Chris. Art Starts: Every Page Illustrated by You! (p. 103)
Magruder, Trula & Decaire, Camela, eds. Doll Crafts: Make Your Doll Accessories to Fill Her World! (p. 463)
Magruder, Trula, ed. Doll Parties. (p. 463)
—Doll School (Revised) (p. 463)
—Oodles of Horses: A Collection of Posters, Doodles, Cards, Stencils, Crafts, Stickers, Frames & Lots More for Girls Who Love Horses! Peterson, Stacy, illus. (p. 1298)
—Poster Puzzle Book: Puzzles to Solve & Posters to Share. (p. 1388)
Magsamen, Sandra. Baa, Moo, I Love You! A Book of Animal Sounds. (p. 123)
—Baby Love. (p. 127)
—Bedtime Bunny. (p. 156)
—Beecause I Love You. (p. 157)
—Boo, Boo, I Love You! (p. 209)
—Butterfly Kisses. (p. 248)
—Go to Sleepy, Little Sheepy. (p. 687)
—Good Morning, Sunshine! Magsamen, Sandra, illus. (p. 698)
—Good Night, My Love. (p. 699)
—Goodnight, Little One. Magsamen, Sandra, illus. (p. 701)
—I Love Shapes! (p. 843)
—I Love You Beary Much. (p. 843)
—I Love You, Honey Bunny. (p. 843)
—I Love You, Little Pumpkin! (p. 843)
—I Love You, Snugglesaurus! (p. 844)
—I Ruff You. (p. 845)
—Love Bug. (p. 1059)
—Merry Christmas, Little One! (p. 1128)
—Our Little Deer. (p. 1309)
—Peek-a-Boo, I Love You! (p. 1334)
—Peep, Peep, I Love You! (p. 1335)
—Twinkle, Twinkle, You're My Star. (p. 1802)
—Whooo Loves You? (p. 1920)
—You! (p. 1972)
—You're Purrfect to Me. (p. 1982)
—You're Tutu Cute! (p. 1982)
Magsamen, Susan. Classic Collection of Childhood Wonders: Favorite Adventures, Stories, Poems, & Songs for Making Lasting Memories. (p. 328)
—Classic Treasury of Childhood Wonders: Favorite Adventures, Stories, Poems, & Songs for Making Lasting Memories. (p. 328)
Maguire, Eden. Arizona. (p. 98)
—Jonas. (p. 925)
—Summer. (p. 1673)
Maguire, Eve, jt. auth. see Maguire, Suzanne.
Maguire, Gregory. Egg & Spoon. (p. 506)
—Leaping Beauty: And Other Animal Fairy Tales. Demarest, Chris L., illus. (p. 982)
—Matchless: An Illumination of Hans Christian Andersen's Classic the Little Match Girl. (p. 1104)
—Missing Sisters. (p. 1153)
—What-the-Dickens: The Story of a Rogue Tooth Fairy. (p. 1893)
Maguire, Gregory, ed. see Baum, L. Frank.
Maguire, Jake, illus. see Heneghan, Lou.
Maguire, K. C. Inside the Palisade. (p. 877)
Maguire, Kerry, illus. see Goodman, Susan E.
Maguire, Laurie E. Studying Shakespeare: A Guide to the Plays. (p. 1670)
Maguire, Suzanne & Maguire, Eve. Spellbound Chronicles - Blood Line. (p. 1625)
Maguire, Thomas Aquinas. Growling Place. (p. 727)
—Three Little Dreams (p. 1742)
Maguire, Thomas Aquinas, illus. see Andersen, Hans Christian.
Magusin, Matthew. Diary of a Nerd. the Start of Middle School. (p. 434)
Mah, Adeline Yen. Along the River: A Chinese Cinderella Novel. (p. 48)
—China: Land of Dragons & Emperors. (p. 306)
—China: Land of Dragons & Emperors. (p. 306)
—Chinese Cinderella. (p. 307)
—Chinese Cinderella & the Secret Dragon Society. (p. 307)
Mah, Anna, illus. see Jones, Leanne.
Mah, Derek, illus. see Slade, Arthur.
Mahabeer, Rishen. Anna & Timothy. (p. 85)
Mahadeo Rdh, Elizabeth. Teddy Visits the Dentist: Teddy Gets a Filling. Barth, Alexandra, illus. (p. 1713)
—Teddy Visits the Dentist. Barth, Alexandra, illus. (p. 1713)
Mahadevan, Madhavi S. Hanuman's Adventures in the Nether World: A 600 Year Old Classic Retold. Srivi, illus. (p. 744)
Mahaffey, James A. Nuclear Fission Reactors. (p. 1270)
Mahal, Susan, illus. see Athan, Polly, et al.
Mahalik, Cathy. Longest Hair Ever. (p. 1047)
Mahan, Alfred Thayer. From Sail to Steam: Recollections of Naval Life. (p. 643)
—Harvest Within. (p. 752)
—Major Operations of the Navies in the War of American Independence. (p. 1078)
—Naval Strategy. (p. 1237)
—Problem of Asia & Its Effects upon International Policies. (p. 1408)
—Retrospect & Prospect. (p. 1464)
—Sea Power in Its Relations to the War of 1812. (p. 1535)
—Types of Naval Officers: Drawn from the History of the British Navy. (p. 1805)
Mahan, Asa. Out of Darkness into Light: Or, the Hidden Life Made Manifest Through Facts of Observation & Experience: Facts Elucidated by the Word of God. Friedrich, Richard, ed. (p. 1311)
—Science of Moral Philosophy Vol. 5. Friedrich, Richard M., ed. (p. 1527)
Mahan, Asa & Hills, Aaron Merritt. Food for Lambs; Or, Leading Children to Christ. Friedrich, Richard, ed. (p. 613)
Mahan, Ben, illus. see Carlson, Melody.
Mahan, Ben, illus. see Kain, Kathleen.
Mahan, Ben, illus. see Marshall, Shelley.
Mahan, Ben, illus. see Pingry, Patricia A.
Mahan, Benton, illus. see Kalz, Jill.
Mahan, Benton, illus. see Scelsa, Greg & Debney, John.
Mahan, Benton, illus. see Williams, Rozanne Lanczak.
Mahan, S. A. Baby Sea Turtle. (p. 128)
Mahaney, Carolyn & Whitacre, Nicole Mahaney. Girl Talk: Mother-Daughter Conversations on Biblical Womanhood. (p. 679)
Mahaney, Ian. Solar Energy. (p. 1606)
—Tony Hawk: Skateboarding Champ. (p. 1766)
—Water Power. (p. 1863)
Mahaney, Ian F. Author (p. 117)
—Best Job Ever (p. 170)

—Climate Maps. (p. 332)
—Danny Harf: Wakeboarding Champion. (p. 405)
—Dave Mirra: Bicycle Stunt Champ. (p. 410)
—Electricity. (p. 509)
—Energy in Action (p. 528)
—Extreme Aircraft. (p. 556)
—Extreme off-Road Vehicles. (p. 556)
—Extreme Snow Vehicles. (p. 557)
—Extreme Submarines. (p. 557)
—Extreme Unmanned Vehicles. (p. 557)
—Extreme Watercraft. (p. 557)
—Heat. (p. 760)
—Light. (p. 1014)
—Math of Baseball. (p. 1106)
—Math of Basketball. (p. 1106)
—Math of Football. (p. 1106)
—Math of Hockey. (p. 1106)
—Math of Soccer. (p. 1106)
—Movie Star (p. 1183)
—Physical Maps. (p. 1353)
—Political Maps. (p. 1380)
—Road Maps. (p. 1476)
—Solar Energy. (p. 1606)
—Sound Waves. (p. 1615)
—Taig Khris: In-Line Skate Champion. (p. 1695)
—Taig Khris: In-Line Skating Champion. (p. 1695)
—Tony Hawk: Skateboarding Champion. (p. 1766)
—Topographic Maps. (p. 1769)
—Travis Pastrana: Motorcross Champion. (p. 1781)
—Water Power. (p. 1863)
—Weather Maps. (p. 1870)
Mahanov, Tanya, ed. see Korobov, Kristine.
Mahany, Patricia Shely. Baby Moses in a Basket. Grant, Margriet, illus. (p. 127)
—Charlie's Be Kind Day. Wasco, Cindy, illus. (p. 293)
Mahase, Compton & Morris, Mark. CXC Revision Guide for Chemistry. (p. 396)
Mahbab, Mustashrik, illus. see Shakespeare, William.
Maher, Adele. Franky Fox's Fun with English Readers Level A1. Maher, Adele & Cline, Mike, illus. (p. 631)
Maher, Alex. Safari de Diego. (p. 1502)
Maher, Alex, illus. see Ricci, Christine.
Maher, Alex, illus. see Stierle, Cynthia.
Maher, Allison. I, the Spy. (p. 846)
Maher, Bob, illus. see Edwards, Linda M.
Maher, Erin. Chinese Foods & Recipes. (p. 307)
—Traditions of the Crow People. (p. 1776)
Maher, Jack. Animal Instincts. (p. 78)
Maher, Liam. Blue Paint. Everett-Hawkes, Bonnie, illus. (p. 203)
—Golden Daffodils. Movshina, Marina, illus. (p. 694)
—Plumber & the Wishing Well. May, Gin, illus. (p. 1374)
Maher, Liam & May, Gin. Ghost Story. (p. 671)
Maher, Mickie Brandt. Master Stitchum & the Moon. Dousias, Spiro, illus. (p. 1103)
Maher, Terre, illus. see Nye, Naomi Shihab.
Maher-O'Keefe, Patricia. My Special Day. (p. 1219)
Mahfood, Jim, jt. auth. see Wagner, Matt.
Mahfouz, Sabrina, et al. National Theatre Connections 2014: Plays for Young People: Same; Horizon; the Wardrobe; Heritage; a Letter to Lacey; a Shop Selling Speech; Angels; Hearts; Pronoun; Tomorrow. Banks, Anthony, ed. (p. 1234)
Mahjouri. Science of Sleep. Mahjouri, illus. (p. 1527)
Mahle, Melissa & Dennis, Kathryn. Camp Secret. Wong, Liz, illus. (p. 257)
—Lost in Petra. (p. 1055)
Mahler, Jonathan. Ladies & Gentlemen, the Bronx Is Burning: 1977, Baseball, Politics, & the Battle for the Soul of a City. (p. 970)
Mahler, Nicolas. Van Helsing's Night Off. (p. 1833)
Mahler, Zdenek. New York: A Mod Portrait of the City. Fuka, Vladimír, illus. (p. 1247)
Mahmood, Kamaal Manzoor. Lost & Found. (p. 1054)
Mahmoodian, Maryam. Muslim Teens In: Pitfalls & Pranks. (p. 1194)
Mahmoud, Ghada Mohamed, tr. see Mayer, Cassie & Resl, Brigitte.
Mahmoud, Ghada Mohamed, tr. see Medina, Sarah.
Mahmoud, Zaki Naguib. Land & People of Egypt. (p. 973)
Mahmout, Ulfet & Thompson, Alan. My Life Story. (p. 1212)
Mahnke. Grammar Links 1 (p. 706)
Mahnke, Doug, jt. auth. see Kelly, Joe.
Mahnke, M. Kathleen & O'Dowd, Elizabeth. Audio Cd: Used with ... Mahnke-Grammar Links 2: A Theme-Based Course for Reference & Practice. (p. 114)
—Grammar Links 2 (p. 706)
—Grammar Links 2: A Theme-Based Course for Reference & Practice. (p. 706)
—Grammar Links Text 2 (p. 706)
Mahnke, M. Kathleen, et al. Grammar Links 2: A Theme-Based Course for Reference & Practice. (p. 706)
Mahomet, John, illus. see Ansong, Anthony.
Mahon, Amy & Gohari, Omid. Elon University College Prowler off the Record. (p. 516)
Mahon, Elaine. Preparing for First Reconciliation: A Guide for Families. (p. 1396)
Mahon, Matthew. Defenders of All Thats Fall. (p. 423)
Mahone, Austin. Just How It Happened - My Official Story. (p. 938)
Mahone, J. Stephen. Fury of Gabriel's Wings: Silent Screams, Diary of a Serial Killer (p. 650)
Mahoney, Anne, jt. auth. see Mahoney, Judy.
Mahoney, Daniel, illus. see Ranson, Erin.
Mahoney, Daniel, illus. see Young, Laurie.
Mahoney, Daniel J. I See a Monster. (p. 845)
—Monstergarten. Kaminsky, Jef, illus. (p. 1168)
Mahoney, Daniel J., illus. see Charlesworth, Liza & Scholastic, Inc. Staff.
Mahoney, Daniel J., illus. see Ranson, Erin.
Mahoney, Daniel J., illus. see Young, Laurie.
Mahoney, Ellen. Nellie Bly & Investigative Journalism for Kids: Mighty Muckrakers from the Golden Age to Today, with 21 Activities. (p. 1240)
Mahoney, Ellen, jt. auth. see Mitchell, Edgar.
Mahoney, Ellen Voelckers. Coping: A Specialized Title for Everyone Rosen, Roger, ed. (p. 365)
Mahoney, Emily Jankowski. 20 Fun Facts about Amphibian Adaptations. (p. 1995)
—Amethysts. (p. 65)
—Becoming a State Governor. (p. 156)
—Kate Middleton. (p. 944)
—Science of Soccer. (p. 1527)
Mahoney, Jan. Moose Tales. (p. 1173)
Mahoney, Jean. Sleeping Beauty Ballet Theatre. Seddon, Viola Anne, illus. (p. 1589)
—Swan Lake Ballet Theatre. Seddon, Viola Anne, illus. (p. 1688)
Mahoney, Judy. Teach Me Even More Spanish Book Box: Twenty-One Songs to Sing & a Story about Pen Pals. (p. 1708)
—Teach Me Everyday English V1 Girouard, Patrick, illus. (p. 1708)
—Teach Me Everyday French Vol 1 Girouard, Patrick, illus. (p. 1708)
—Teach Me Everyday German V. 1 Girouard, Patrick, illus. (p. 1708)
—Teach Me Everyday Italian: Celebrating the Seasons Girouard, Patrick, illus. (p. 1708)
—Teach Me Everyday Japanese V 1 Girouard, Patrick, illus. (p. 1708)
—Teach Me Everyday Korean V. 1 (p. 1708)
—Teach Me Everyday Spanish: Celebrating the Seasons Girouard, Patrick, illus. (p. 1708)
—Teach Me Everyday Spanish Vol 1 Girouard, Patrick, illus. (p. 1708)
Mahoney, Judy & Mahoney, Anne. Teach Me... French Spiritual Songs. (p. 1708)
Mahoney, Karen. Falling to Ash. (p. 567)
—Iron Witch. (p. 888)
—Stone Demon. (p. 1652)
—Wood Queen: An Iron Witch Novel. (p. 1949)
Mahoney, Kevin. Bobo the Amazing. (p. 206)
—Curly Jess & Her Big Math Mess. (p. 394)
—Darling Jordan. (p. 409)
Mahoney, Liana. Forest Green: A Walk Through the Adirondack Seasons. Henry, Maggie, illus. (p. 618)
Mahoney, Paula J., illus. see Petrie, Kathye Fetsko & Boyds Mills Press Staff.
Mahoney, Tammy. Eddie the Eagle Learns to Fly. (p. 503)
Mahony, J., jt. auth. see Dickens, Charles.
Mahony, Mary. Harry Scores A Hat Trick, Pawns, Pucks, & Scoliosis: The Sequel to Stand Tall, Harry. Pasternack, Susan, ed. (p. 751)
—School is Not for Me, Jeremy James Conor McGee. Frederick, Sarah, illus. (p. 1523)
Mahony, Terry. Principled Headship: A Teacher's Guide to the Galaxy. (p. 1406)
—Words Work! How to Change Your Language to Improve Behaviour in Your Classroom. (p. 1952)
Mahr, Aryeh. Mysteries of the Aleph Bets. (p. 1222)
Mahr, Aryeh, jt. auth. see Wein, Berel.
Mahr, Frank J. I Can Sleep Alone. Milstrey, Dawn Bourdeau, illus. (p. 836)
Mahtani, Nikhil & Mahtani, Sherina. What Do Dads Do? (p. 1882)
Mahtani, Sherina, jt. auth. see Mahtani, Nikhil.
Mahurin, Matt, illus. see Yolen, Jane & Dotlich, Rebecca Kai.
Mahy, Margaret. Boom, Baby, Boom Boom! Chamberlain, Margaret, illus. (p. 213)
—Boom, Baby, Boom, Boom! Chamberlain, Margaret, illus. (p. 213)
—Bubble Trouble. Dunbar, Polly, illus. (p. 233)
—Chocolate Porridge. Milne, Terry, illus. (p. 309)
—Don't Read This! And Other Tales of the Unnatural. (p. 468)
—Gargling Gorilla. Phillips, Mike, illus. (p. 657)
—Great Piratical Rumbustification & the Librarian & the Robbers. Blake, Quentin, illus. (p. 717)
—Green Bath. Kellogg, Steven, illus. (p. 721)
—Maddigan's Fantasia. (p. 1069)
—Magician of Hoad. (p. 1075)
—Man from the Land of Fandango. Dunbar, Polly, illus. (p. 1085)
—Mister Whistler. Bishop, Gavin, illus. (p. 1155)
—Portable Ghosts. (p. 1386)
—Shock Forest: And Other Stories. (p. 1568)
—Stop That Stew! Rigby, Deborah, illus. (p. 1653)
—Very Wicked Headmistress. Chamberlain, Margaret, illus. (p. 1839)
Mahy, Margaret, et al, contrib. by. Don't Read This! And Other Tales of the Unnatural. (p. 468)
Mai. Many Hands. (p. 1089)
Mai, Lily. Bertie Boom's Trip to the Moon. (p. 168)
Mai Long, illus. see Minh Quoc.
Mai, Resa. Toy for Chantelle. (p. 1774)
Mai, Vo-Dinh, illus. see Hanh, Thich Nhat & Parallax Press Staff.
Mai, Vo-Dinh, illus. see Hanh, Thich Nhat.
Maia, Chavez Larkin, illus. see Rubi, Nicholas.
Maiani, Patrik, Sr., creator. Beatles Letter Music (p. 153)
Maiben, Dina. Ready, Set... Go Alef Bet! (p. 1447)
Maiborada, Tanya, illus. see Malaspina, Ann.
Maiden, Cecil. Molliwumps. Price, Christine, illus. (p. 1160)
Maiden, D. W., photos by see Walls, Suzanne L.
Maidment, Mikaila, illus. see Brown, Rena Cherry.
Maidment, Stella. Cowboy Puzzles. (p. 374)
—Fairy Puzzles. Dogliani, Daniela, illus. (p. 564)
—Pirate Puzzles. Dogliani, Daniela, illus. (p. 1363)
—Princess Puzzles. Dogliani, Daniela, illus. (p. 1405)
Maidment, Stella, illus. see Whelan, Olwyn.
Maidment, Stella, jt. auth. see Bunkers, Traci.
Maidment, Stella, jt. auth. see Durkin, Kath.
Maidment, Stella, jt. auth. see Walker, Wendy.
Maidment, Stella & Wilde, Oscar. Star Child. Whelan, Olwyn, tr. (p. 1640)
Maidment, Stella, et al. Cyfres Stryd Hapus 1: Llyfr Dosbarth. (p. 397)
—Cyfres Stryd Hapus 1: Llyfr Gweithgareddau. (p. 397)
Maidwell, Sandra. Giselle. (p. 681)
—My Parents Are Aliens & I Don't Like Peanut Butter! (p. 1216)
—What about Judy? (p. 1878)
Maier, Gary B. Key Masters: The Tyrannosaur Rebellion. (p. 950)
Maier, Inger M. Ben's Flying Flowers. Bogade, Maria, illus. (p. 165)
—When Fuzzy Was Afraid: Of Losing His Mother. Candon, Jennifer, illus. (p. 1902)
—When Fuzzy Was Afraid of Big & Loud Things. Candon, Jennifer, illus. (p. 1902)
—When Lizzie Was Afraid: Of Trying New Things. Candon, Jennifer, illus. (p. 1903)
Maier, Kimberly. History Odyssey, Ancients - Level Three. (p. 783)
Maier, Paul. Real Story of the Flood. Barrett, Robert, illus. (p. 1449)
Maier, Paul L. Martin Luther a Man Who Change. (p. 1097)
—Real Story of the Creation. Barrett, Robert T., illus. (p. 1449)
—Real Story of the Exodus. Taylor, Gerad, illus. (p. 1449)
—Very First Christmas. (p. 1838)
—Very First Christmas. Ordaz, Francisco, illus. (p. 1838)
—Very First Easter. (p. 1838)
—Very First Easter. Ordaz, Francisco, illus. (p. 1838)
Maier, Thomas. Kennedys: America's Emerald Kings: a Five-Generation History of the Ultimate Irish-Catholic Family. (p. 948)
Maier, Ximena, illus. see Alcantara, Ricardo.
Maier, Ximena, illus. see Aldecoa, Josefina.
Maier, Ximena, illus. see Garcia Castellano, Ana.
Maier, Ximena, tr. see Aldecoa, Josefina.
Maihack, Mike. Target Practice. (p. 1706)
—Thief & the Sword. (p. 1732)
Maihack, Mike, illus. see Jung, Mike.
Maile, Ruby. Shapes. (p. 1560)
—What Do Animals Eat? (p. 1882)
—When Do You Sleep? (p. 1902)
—Why Are You Having A Party? (p. 1922)
—Why Do You Live Here? (p. 1924)
—Why Should I Eat Fruit? (p. 1926)
Maile, Tim, jt. auth. see Tuber, Douglas.
Mailer, Maggie, illus. see Howell, Alice O.
Mailey, Maria C., illus. see Goss, Leon.
Maillet, Kevin And Haylie. Scruzzels: Life on the Farm. (p. 1533)
Maillis, Nicole. How Did I Get Here? Safar, Lina, illus. (p. 806)
Maillu, David G. Julius Nyerere: Father of Ujamaa. (p. 933)
Maimone, Max Q. Justin Timberlake. (p. 940)
Maimone, Sofia. Exploring the Amazon River. (p. 553)
—Snow Leopards in Danger. (p. 1599)
Maimone, Sofia Z. Mary J. Blige. (p. 1100)
Main, Judith Lang. Is for Altar, B Is for Bible. (p. 889)
Main, June, jt. auth. see Eggen, Paul D.
Main, June & Eggen, Paul D. Developing Critical Thinking through Science: Hands-on Physical Science. Bk.1 (p. 431)
Main, Katy. Baby Animals of the North. (p. 124)
Main, Mary. Dr. Phil: Self-Help Guru & TV Superstar. (p. 475)
—Isabel Allende: Award-Winning Latin American Author. (p. 890)
Main, Mary & Thomason, Cathy. African-Americans in Law & Politics. (p. 27)
—African-Americans in Law & Politics. Hill, Marc Lamont, ed. (p. 27)
Main, Sally, jt. auth. see Poesch, Jessie.
Main Street Publishing, compiled by. Talent among Us: Trail of Tales (p. 1701)
Maine, Margarita. Mar Muy Mojado. (p. 1091)
Mainé, Margarita. Me Duele la Lengua. Decis, Anne, illus. (p. 1115)
Maine, Margarita. Montana para Pancho. Hilb, Nora, illus. (p. 1170)
Maines, Barbara. Reading Faces: And Learning about Human Emotions. (p. 1445)
Maines, David. Tales of the Resistance. (p. 1702)
Maines, Steven. Longinus: Book I of the Merlin Factor. (p. 1047)
Maio, Barbara, ed. see Williams, Rozanne Lanczak.
Malocco, Chris & Malocco, Kimberly. Things My Father Taught Me Through Sports. . . Playing the Game of Football. Cox, Tom, illus. (p. 1733)
—Things My Father Taught Me Through Sports... Playing the Game of Baseball: Playing the Game of Baseball. Cox, Tom, illus. (p. 1733)
Malocco, Kimberly, jt. auth. see Malocco, Chris.
Maione, Heather, illus. see Cuyler, Margery.
Maione, Heather, illus. see Hest, Amy.
Maione, Heather, illus. see McDonough, Yona Zeldis.
Maione, Heather, illus. see Mills, Claudia.
Maione, Heather Harms, illus. see Cuyler, Margery.
Maione, Heather Harms, illus. see Mills, Claudia.
Maione, Heather Harms, jt. auth. see Beard, Darleen Bailey.
Maiorano, Jamison, illus. see Cecca, John.
Mair, J. Samia. Amira's Totally Chocolate World. (p. 65)
—Colours of Islam. Adams, Shireen, illus. (p. 346)
—Great Race to Sycamore Street. (p. 718)
—Perfect Gift. Howarth, Craigh, illus. (p. 1342)
Maire, Lucy Bedoya, jt. auth. see Dutta-Yean, Tutu.
Mairi, Mackinnon. Fighter Planes. (p. 585)
—Phonics Workbook 1. (p. 1352)
—Phonics Workbook 2. (p. 1352)
Maisano, Lucy. Who Thought Learning Could be Fun: The Fun Book. (p. 1917)
Maisel, Gail. Feelings Can Be Friends. (p. 580)
Maisel, Grace Ragues & Shubert, Samantha. Year of Jewish Stories: 52 Tales for Children & Their Families. Keiser, Tammy L., illus. (p. 1969)
Maisner, Heather. Diary of a Princess: A Tale from Marco Polo's Travels. Moxley, Sheila, illus. (p. 434)
Maison, Jerome, photos by see Jacquet, Luc.
Maiste, Pila, illus. see Petrone, Epp.
Maithya, Susan M. Struffel Cares: Struffel's New Pet. (p. 1668)
Maitland, Frederic William, jt. auth. see Pollock, Frederick.
Maitland, Theresa E. Laurie, jt. auth. see Quinn, Patricia O.
Mai-Wyss, Tatjana, illus. see Bar-el, Dan.
Mai-Wyss, Tatjana, illus. see Barash, Chris.
Mai-Wyss, Tatjana, illus. see Gagliano, Eugene.
Mai-Wyss, Tatjana, illus. see Long, Melinda.
Mai-Wyss, Tatjana, illus. see Marshall, Linda Elovitz.
Mai-Wyss, Tatjana, illus. see Rodman, Mary Ann.
Mai-Wyss, Tatjana, illus. see Shahan, Sherry.
Mai-Wyss, Tatjana, illus. see Souders, Taryn.
Maizel, Karen, illus. see Bauer, Roger.
Maizel, Karen, illus. see Bowman, Crystal.
Maizel, Karen, illus. see Mader, Jan.
Maizel, Karen, illus. see Sheldon, Annette.
Maizel, Rebecca. Between Us & the Moon. (p. 173)
—Infinite Days. (p. 873)
—Stolen Nights. (p. 1652)
Maizels, Jennie. Pop-Up New York. Maizels, Jennie, illus. (p. 1384)
Maizes, Sarah. On My Way to Bed. Paraskevas, Michael, illus. (p. 1289)
—On My Way to School. Paraskevas, Michael, illus. (p. 1289)
—On My Way to the Bath. Paraskevas, Michael, illus. (p. 1289)
Majado, Caio, illus. see Hoena, Blake A.
Majado, Caio, illus. see Hoena, Blake A. & Tortosa, Wilson.
Majado, Caio, illus. see Lemke, Donald B.
Majado, Caio, illus. see Sherman, M. Zachary.
Majado, Caio, illus. see Terrell, Brandon.
Majado, Caio, jt. auth. see Manning, Matthew K.
Majado, Caio, jt. auth. see Terrell, Brandon.
Majewski, Anthony & "Max", Maximus. Dog's Work Too! From Max's Point of View. Majewski, Julie, illus. (p. 463)
Majewski, Anthony M. T. & Maximus. Color with Max! Activity & Coloring Book. Majewski, Julie, illus. (p. 343)
Majewski, Dawn, illus. see Bond, Juliet C.
Majewski, Dawn, illus. see McNamara, Joan.
Majewski, Julie, illus. see Majewski, Anthony &
Majewski, Julie, illus. see Majewski, Anthony M. T. & Maximus.
Majher, Patricia. Great Girls in Michigan History. (p. 716)
Majid, Ellisha. Sausage Went for a Walk. Kendall, Peter, illus. (p. 1516)
Major, Charles. Bears of Blue River. (p. 152)
Major, Christina, creator. Sombulus (p. 1608)
Major, Diane C. Augusta Tabor: Enterprising Pioneer. (p. 115)
Major, Gail Baccelli. What Do You See in Me I am Who I am. Major, Rebekah, illus. (p. 1883)
Major, Kevin. Ann & Seamus Blackwood, David, illus. (p. 84)
—Eh? To Zed: A Canadian Abecedarium. (p. 507)
—Far from Shore (p. 572)
—House of Wooden Santas George, Imelda, illus. (p. 803)
—House of Wooden Santas Pratt, Ned, photos by. (p. 803)
Major, Ralphine, jt. auth. see Major, Wayne A.
Major, Rebekah. Mama Wrex. Major, Rebekah, illus. (p. 1084)
Major, Rebekah, illus. see Major, Gail Baccelli.
Major, Roberta Olsen. Deluged. (p. 425)
—Royal Paines, Book Seven: The 24-Karat King: The 24-Karat King. (p. 1492)
—Royal Pains: The Bottle of DJINN. Bk. 4 (p. 1492)
—Royal Pains: The Ice Cream Crone. Bk. 5 (p. 1492)
—Royal Paines, Book Eight: The Bad Heir Day. (p. 1492)
Major, Roberta Olser. Royal Pains: The Good Knight Kiss. Bk. 3 (p. 1492)
Major, Sarah. Alphabet Tales. Major, Sarah, illus. (p. 50)
—C Collection. (p. 249)
—Easy-for-Me Level C Books. Major, Sarah, illus. (p. 500)
—Easy-for-Me Reading Teaching Manual: A Snap for the teacher...a Cinch for the Child. Major, Sarah, illus. (p. 500)
—Right-Brained Addition & Subtraction: A Forget Memorization Book. Major, Sarah, illus. (p. 1472)
—Right-Brained Place Value: A Forget Memorization Book. Major, Sarah, illus. (p. 1472)
—SnapWords Mini-Lessons: How to Teach Each SnapWord Integrating Spelling, Writing, & Phonics Concepts. Major, Sarah, illus. (p. 1597)
—Writing the Visual, Kinesthetic, & Auditory Alphabet. Major, Sarah, illus. (p. 1965)
Major, Wayne A. & Major, Ralphine. Piddle Diddle's Lost Hat: Adventures of Piddle Diddle, the Widdle Penguin. Wilkerson, Teresa, illus. (p. 1356)
Majors, Alexander. Seventy Years on the Frontier: Alexander Majors' Memoirs of a Lifetime on the Border. Ingraham, Prentiss, ed. (p. 1555)
Majors, Jj. Natty's Adventures. (p. 1235)
Majors, Kerri. This Is Not a Writing Manual: Notes for the Young Writer in the Real World. (p. 1736)
Majors, Reggie, jt. auth. see Gaines, Ann Graham.
Majumdar, Anuradha. Island of Infinity: Marina's Dream. (p. 892)
Mak, Alice, illus. see Tse, Brian.
Mak, D P. Invisible Pill. (p. 886)
Mak, Ding Sang, illus. see Morrissey, Tricia.
Mak, Kam. Chinatown. Mak, Kam, illus. (p. 307)
Mak, Olha. Stones under the Scythe. Kaczmarskyj, Vera, tr. from UKR. (p. 1653)
Maka, Stephen, photos by see Stewart, Melissa.
Make Believe Ideas. 1000 Hootiful Stickers. (p. 2001)
—1000 Stickers: Christmas. (p. 2001)
—Annie the Apple Pie Fairy. (p. 87)
—B Is for Breakdancing Bear Alphabet Sticker Activity Book. (p. 123)
—Bear Hugs. (p. 150)
—Best Book in the World Because I Made It. (p. 168)
—Bubble Buddies 123. (p. 233)
—Bubble Buddies ABC. (p. 233)
—Clara the Cookie Fairy Sticker Activity Book. (p. 326)
—Cootie Catcher Art. (p. 365)
—Cuddle Buddies Cat. (p. 389)
—Dot Art. (p. 472)
—Epic & Awesome. (p. 532)
—Even Pirates Poop. (p. 541)
—Even Princesses Poop. (p. 541)
—Fairies Scratch & Sniff Camilla the Cupcake Fairy. (p. 563)
—Fairies Scratch & Sniff Lola the Lollipop Fairy. (p. 563)
—First 100 Animals. (p. 592)
—First 100 Pretty Pink Words. (p. 592)
—Flower Friends Daisy's First Words. (p. 607)
—Flower Friends Poppy's Shapes. (p. 607)

—Flower Friends Primrose's Counting. (p. 607)
—Flower Friends Rosie's Colors. (p. 607)
—Goldilocks & the Three Bears. (p. 696)
—Guess What. (p. 729)
—Hey Diddle Diddle & Other Nursery Rhymes. (p. 774)
—I Love Felt ABC. (p. 842)
—I Love to Learn Math Games. (p. 843)
—I Love to Learn Math Puzzles. (p. 843)
—I Love to Learn Phonics Letter Sounds. (p. 843)
—I Love to Learn Phonics Read & Spell. (p. 843)
—Incy Wincy Spider. (p. 870)
—Izzy the Ice Cream Fairy Sticker Dolly Dress Up. (p. 901)
—Katie the Candy Cane Fairy Storybook. (p. 945)
—Little Red Riding Hood. (p. 1035)
—Make This Book. (p. 1079)
—Molly the Muffin Fairy. (p. 1161)
—My Best Ever: ABC Alphabet Book. (p. 1196)
—My Best Ever: Things That Go. (p. 1196)
—My Very First: on the Move (p. 1221)
—Noah. (p. 1261)
—Paulette the Pinkest Puppy. (p. 1331)
—Paulette the Pinkest Puppy in the World. (p. 1331)
—Paulette's Sticker Salon. (p. 1331)
—Quack-A-doodle-moo. (p. 1422)
—Secret Message Cards. (p. 1542)
—Strictly Pink Sticker Activity Fun. (p. 1667)
—Talk to the Door. (p. 1703)
—Think Bubbles. (p. 1734)
—Three Little Pigs. (p. 1742)
—Treasures Five-Minute Bedtime Stories. (p. 1782)
—Treasuries Five-Minute Fairy Tales. (p. 1782)
—Twinkle Twinkle Little Star. (p. 1802)
—Ultimate Sticker File: Dinosaurs. (p. 1810)
—Under the Sea. (p. 1814)
Make Believe Ideas, creator. Alphabet Book. (p. 49)
—BJ's Finger Puppet Book Assortment. (p. 194)
—Busy Baby 123: First Concepts. (p. 245)
—Busy Baby ABC: First Concepts. (p. 245)
—Busy Baby: First 100 Things That Go. (p. 245)
—Busy Baby Shapes: First Concepts. (p. 245)
—Emergency: Sticker Activity Book. (p. 518)
—Great Fairy Candy Store Sticker Activity Book. (p. 716)
—Lift Stick & Learn Baby Animals. (p. 1014)
—Lift Stick & Learn Horse & Pony. (p. 1014)
—Lift Stick & Learn Sticker Book Prepack. (p. 1014)
—Lots of Love. (p. 1057)
—Mouseton Abbey Sticker Activity Book. (p. 1182)
—My Fairy Dress up Book. (p. 1202)
—My Princess Dress up Book. (p. 1217)
—My Scrapbook about Me. (p. 1218)
—Pink Puppy Sticker Activity Book. (p. 1360)
—Touch & Learn 123 Casebound. (p. 1772)
—Touch & Learn ABC. (p. 1772)
—Touch & Learn Baby Animals Casebound. (p. 1772)
—Touch & Learn Tractors & Trucks Casebound. (p. 1772)
—Trace, Stick & Learn Wipe Clean ABC Activity Book. (p. 1774)
—Twinkle Book & Mouse Plush. (p. 1802)
—Udderly Book & Cow Plush. (p. 1807)
Make Believe Ideas, Ltd. Build Your Own Prayers: Magnetic Prayer Book. (p. 238)
—Shiny, Touchy, Smelly Creation. (p. 1567)
—Touch & Learn - God's Animals. (p. 1772)
Make Believe Ideas, Ltd., creator. Animals & Kittens Pack. (p. 82)
—Pets & Puppies Pack. (p. 1348)
—Read with Me: the Good Samaritan. (p. 1444)
—Read with Me: the Loaves & Fish. (p. 1444)
Make Believe Ideas Staff. Baby Fun 123. (p. 126)
—Baby Fun Colors. (p. 126)
Make Believe Ideas Staff, jt. auth. see Cox, Katie.
Make Believe Ideas Staff, jt. auth. see Down, Hayley.
Make Believe Ideas Staff, jt. auth. see Page, Claire.
Make Believe Ideas Staff, jt. auth. see Toms, Kate.
Make Believe Ideas Staff, jt. auth. see Wallace, Bruce.
Make-a-Wish Foundation Staff, ed. see Culpepper, Peter Ryan & Culpepper, Gina G. Felix.
Makee, Charles. Otherworld Tales: Irish the Demon Slayer. (p. 1307)
Makeeff, Cyndi Sue. Inky Winky Spider 1,2,3,4. Riley, Kevin, illus. (p. 874)
—Inky Winky Spider ABC's. Riley, Kevin, illus. (p. 874)
—Inky Winky Spider Colors by the Bay. Riley, Kevin, illus. (p. 874)
Makely, William, jt. auth. see Bollendorf, Robert F.
Makenzie, jt. auth. see Schaller, Tandy.
Makepeace, Jonathan, ed. see Anderson, Henry Morgan.
Maker, Don. Miranda's Magic. (p. 1149)
Maki, Jeffrey Stephen. Adventures of Jason Roy Mouse: The Fun Adventures of a Little Mouse Who Uses His Diabetes to His Great Advantage. Maki, Jeffrey Stephen, illus. (p. 19)
Maki, Julia A. All Hands on Deck! Dad's Coming Home! (p. 44)
—My Mom Hunts Submarines. (p. 1214)
Maki, Tab, illus. see Syrstad, Suzi.
Maki, Yoko. Aishiteruze Baby Maki, Yoko, illus. (p. 32)
Maki-Griffis, Linda R. In the Berry Patch. (p. 865)
Mäkinen, Kirsti. Kalevala: Tales of Magic & Adventure. Brooks, Kaarina, tr. from FIN. (p. 942)
Makinen, Merja. Novels of Jeanette Winterson. (p. 1268)
Makis, Sidney, illus. see Friend, Larry.
Makishi, Cynthia. Heinle Picture Dictionary for Children - Monkey Puppet. (p. 762)
Makishi, Cynthia, jt. auth. see O'Sullivan, Jill Korey.
Makofske, Leonard V. Adventures of Skipperjack: An Epic Fairy Tale. (p. 23)
Makosz, Rory. Latino Arts & Their Influence on the United States: Songs, Dreams, & Dances. (p. 979)
MAKOTO, Mizobuchi. Arceus & the Jewel of Life. MAKOTO, Mizobuchi, illus. (p. 95)
Makowski, Robin Lee. Cats. (p. 280)
—Dogs. (p. 462)
—Draw Anything You Like. (p. 480)
—Sea Creatures. (p. 1534)
Makso, Malisa. Inside & Outside. (p. 876)
Makuc, Lucy, illus. see Besel, Jennifer M.
Makuc, Lucy, illus. see Bolte, Mari.
Makumi, Joel. Return of Njega. (p. 1464)
Makura, Sho. Panda Man & the Treasure Hunt. Kato, Haruhi, illus. (p. 1320)
—Panda Man to the Rescue! Kato, Haruhi, illus. (p. 1320)
—Panda Man vs. Chiwanda. Kato, Haruhi, illus. (p. 1320)
Malagarriga, Carlos Fanlo, tr. see Gregoire, Fabian.
Malaghan, Michael. Lost Prophecies. (p. 1056)
Malaghan, Michael G. Greek Ransom. (p. 721)
Malak, Annabel. Cinderella. (p. 320)
—Goldilocks & the Three Bears. (p. 696)
Malak, Annabel, illus. see Biddle, Charles, Jr.
Malam, John. Ancient Egypt. Malam, John, illus. (p. 68)
—Ancient Greece. (p. 69)
—Ancient Rome. (p. 70)
—Be a Skyscraper Builder! A Hazardous Job You'd Rather Not Take. (p. 148)
—Be a Victorian Mill Worker! A Grueling Job You'd Rather Not Have. Antram, David, illus. (p. 148)
—Be a Worker on the Statue of Liberty! A Monument You'd Rather Not Build. Antram, David, illus. (p. 148)
—Bowl of Cornflakes. (p. 216)
—Buried Treasure. (p. 243)
—Columbus Reaches the Americas. (p. 346)
—Dig It: History from Objects (p. 438)
—Dinosaur Ultimate Sticker Book. (p. 443)
—Egyptians. (p. 507)
—Extreme Exploration. (p. 556)
—Fairies. (p. 562)
—Giants. (p. 674)
—Gladiator's Grave. (p. 682)
—Greeks. (p. 721)
—Grow Your Own Butterfly Farm (p. 726)
—Grow Your Own Cat Toy (p. 726)
—Grow Your Own Sandwich (p. 726)
—Grow Your Own Smoothie (p. 726)
—Grow Your Own Snack (p. 726)
—Grow Your Own Soup (p. 726)
—Guglielmo Marconi (p. 729)
—Gunpowder Plot. (p. 732)
—Hitler Invades Poland. (p. 786)
—How the Ancient Greeks Lived. (p. 812)
—How to Be a Pirate. Antram, Dave, illus. (p. 814)
—How to Be a Pirate. Bergin, Mark, illus. (p. 814)
—Hyenas. (p. 831)
—Hyenas - Scary Creatures. (p. 831)
—Journey of a Bar of Chocolate (p. 928)
—Journey of a Book (p. 928)
—Journey of a Bowl of Cornflakes (p. 928)
—Journey of a Glass of Milk (p. 928)
—Journey of a Toy (p. 928)
—Journey of a T-Shirt (p. 928)
—Killer Whales. (p. 956)
—Killer Whales - Scary Creatures. (p. 956)
—Leonardo Da Vinci: El Genio Que Definio el Renacimiento. P. López, Wendy, tr. from ENG. (p. 992)
—Library: From Ancient Scrolls to the Worldwide Web: A Building Works Book. Malam, John, illus. (p. 1005)
—Life in Ancient Rome (p. 1010)
—Live in Pompeii! A Volcanic Eruption You'd Rather Avoid. Antram, David, illus. (p. 1040)
—Man Walks on the Moon. (p. 1086)
—Martin Luther King. (p. 1097)
—Monsters. (p. 1168)
—Mummies. (p. 1190)
—Of the Night. (p. 1279)
—Pinnipeds. (p. 1360)
—Pompeii & Other Lost Cities. (p. 1382)
—Prehistoric Scary Creatures. (p. 1395)
—Pyramids. (p. 1421)
—Roger Hargreaves. (p. 1484)
—Romans. (p. 1486)
—Samurai. (p. 1509)
—Scary Creatures of the Night. (p. 1520)
—Terracotta Army & Other Lost Treasures. (p. 1721)
—Theater: From First Rehearsal to Opening Night! a Building Works Book. Malam, John, illus. (p. 1728)
—Titanic & Other Lost Ships. (p. 1757)
—Tutankhamun & Other Lost Tombs. (p. 1799)
—Vikings. (p. 1842)
—Warriors. (p. 1859)
—World War I: Armistice Day. (p. 1958)
—You Wouldn't Want to Be a 19th-Century Coal Miner in England! A Dangerous Job You'd Rather Not Have. Antram, David, illus. (p. 1976)
—You Wouldn't Want to Be a Ninja Warrior! Antram, David, illus. (p. 1976)
—You Wouldn't Want to Be a Ninja Warrior! A Secret Job That's Your Destiny. Antram, David, illus. (p. 1976)
—You Wouldn't Want to Be a Pirate's Prisoner! Horrible Things You'd Rather Not Know. Antram, David, illus. (p. 1976)
—You Wouldn't Want to... Be a Pirate's Prisoner! Antram, David, illus. (p. 1976)
—You Wouldn't Want to Be a Roman Galdiator! Antram, David, illus. (p. 1976)
—You Wouldn't Want to... Be a Roman Galdiator! Antram, David, illus. (p. 1976)
—You Wouldn't Want to Be a Secret Agent During World War II! A Perilous Mission Behind Enemy Lines. (p. 1977)
—You Wouldn't Want to Be a Skyscraper Builder! (p. 1977)
—You Wouldn't Want to Be a Skyscraper Builder! A Hazardous Job You'd Rather Not Take. (p. 1977)
—You Wouldn't Want to Be a Worker on the Statue of Liberty! A Monument You'd Rather Not Build. Antram, David, illus. (p. 1977)
—You Wouldn't Want to Sail in the Spanish Armada! An Invasion You'd Rather Not Launch. Antram, David, illus. (p. 1977)
Malam, John, jt. auth. see Scurman, Ike.
Malam, John & Dorling Kindersley Publishing Staff. Dinosaur. (p. 441)
Malam, John & Hincks, Gary. Extraordinary World: Highest, Longest, Deepest - An Exploration of the World's Most Fantastic Features. (p. 555)
Malam, John & Macdonald, Fiona. Pyramids. (p. 1421)
Malam, John & Molinaro, Fernando. Fairies. (p. 562)
Malam, John & Parker, Steve. Encyclopedia of Dinosaurs: And Other Prehistoric Creatures. (p. 525)
Malam, John & Smith, Karen Barker. You Wouldn't Want to Be a Mammoth Hunter! Dangerous Beasts You'd Rather Not Encounter. Antram, David, illus. (p. 1976)
Malam, John, et al. Children's Dinosaur Encyclopedia. (p. 303)
—Dinosaur Atlas. (p. 441)
Malam, John, reader. Moby Dick. (p. 1157)
—Treasure Island. (p. 1781)
Malam, John, retold by. Oliver Twist. (p. 1286)
Malan, Violette. Soldier King. (p. 1607)
Maland, Nick, illus. see Bergman, Mara.
Maland, Nick, illus. see Cave, Kathryn.
Maland, Nick, illus. see Davies, Nicola.
Maland, Nick, illus. see McKay, Hilary.
Malandrinos, Cheryl C. Little Shepherd. Ruble, Eugene, illus. (p. 1036)
Malara, Maria. Mysterious Places. (p. 1223)
Malara, Maria, jt. auth. see Downey, Glen R.
Malarek, Victor. Hey Malarek! The True Story of a Street Kid Who Made It. (p. 774)
Malaspina, Ann. Boston Tea Party. (p. 215)
—Chinese Revolution & Mao Zedong in World History. (p. 307)
—Chopin's World. (p. 310)
—Ethnic & Group Identity Movements: Earning Recognition. (p. 539)
—False Images, Deadly Promises: Smoking & the Media. (p. 567)
—Feraj & the Magic Lute: An Arabian Folktale. Peluso, Martina, illus. (p. 581)
—Finding Lincoln. Bootman, Colin, illus. (p. 588)
—Guinea Fowl & Rabbit Get Justice: An African Folktale. Wendland, Paula, illus. (p. 730)
—Harriet Tubman. (p. 749)
—Heart on Fire: Susan B. Anthony Votes for President. James, Steven, illus. (p. 760)
—Hunting of the Great Bear: A Native American Folktale. Maiborada, Tanya, illus. (p. 829)
—Iroquois: A Proud People. (p. 888)
—Jack & the Beanstalk: An English Folktale. Manning, Mary, illus. (p. 902)
—Lebanon. (p. 986)
—Mouse & the Wizard: A Hindu Folktale. Sylvaine, Jenny, illus. (p. 1182)
—Nathan & Nicole Learn about Nouns. Hamblin, George, illus. (p. 1231)
—New Jersey. (p. 1245)
—New Year Traditions Around the World. Chavarri, Elisa, illus. (p. 1247)
—People Could Fly: An African-American Folktale. Otero, Sole, illus. (p. 1339)
—Phillis Sings Out Freedom: The Story of George Washington & Phillis Wheatley. Keeter, Susan, illus. (p. 1350)
—Primary Source History of the Colony of Connecticut. (p. 1400)
—Signing of the Declaration of Independence. (p. 1574)
—Take a Closer Look at Your Bones. (p. 1696)
—Tooth Traditions Around the World. Chavarri, Elisa, illus. (p. 1768)
—Touch the Sky: Alice Coachman, Olympic High Jumper. Velasquez, Eric, illus. (p. 1772)
—Tsunamis. (p. 1795)
—Underground Railroad: The Journey to Freedom. (p. 1815)
—Vivian & Victor Learn about Verbs. Prater, Linda, illus. (p. 1846)
—What's Great about New York? (p. 1897)
—Yasmin's Hammer. Chayka, Doug, illus. (p. 1968)
Malaspina, Ann & Woog, Adam. Nubia. (p. 1269)
Malatesta, Resa. Jewel & Chin Chin's Adventure. (p. 916)
Malavolti, Angela. You Are a Twisting Tornado. Stiffler, Michael, illus. (p. 1973)
Malbrough, Michael, illus. see Malbrough, Page.
Malbrough, Page. Fire Proves Iron: Grounded Stars. Malbrough, Michael & Fisher, G. W., illus. (p. 590)
Malcher, Barbara. Tonia Baby Bee & Her First Friend. (p. 1765)
Malchik, Antonia E. Great Depression by the Numbers: Set Of 6. (p. 715)
Malchik, E. Great Depression by the Numbers & Los números de la Gran Depresión: 6 English, 6 Spanish Adaptations. (p. 715)
Malchow, Alex, jt. auth. see Malchow, Hal.
Malchow, Hal & Malchow, Alex. Sword of Darrow. (p. 1692)
Malcolm, Jahnna N. Pirate's Revenge. Comport, Sally Wern, illus. (p. 1364)
—Write Stuff. (p. 1964)
Malcolm, James. Anthology: Ants Odyssey. (p. 89)
Malczyk, Kathryn, tr. see Mattheis, Philipp.
Maldonado, Helen. Big Dog & His Family. (p. 181)
Maldonado, Lucia, jt. auth. see Maldonado, Virgilio.
Maldonado, Luis. Friends Having Fun. (p. 638)
Maldonado, Premier. Animales. (p. 80)
—Cuerpo. (p. 390)
Maldonado, Premier, creator. House-Casa: English-Español. (p. 803)
—House-Casa Coloring Book: English-Español. (p. 803)
—House-Casa Interactive Book: English-Español. (p. 803)
—Market-Mercado: English-Español. (p. 1095)
Maldonado, Torrey. Secret Saturdays. (p. 1543)
Maldonado, Torrey Maldonado. Secret Saturdays. (p. 1543)
Maldonado, Victor, jt. auth. see Rivera Lassén, Carmen.
Maldonado, Victor, jt. auth. see Rivera, Carmen.
Maldonado, Virgilio & Maldonado, Lucia. Snail & the Quail. (p. 1595)
Male, Alan, illus. see Bull, Schuyler M.
Male, Alan, illus. see Bull, Schuyler.
Malea. Princess Melia. (p. 1404)
Maleev, Alex, illus. see Bendis, Brian Michael.
Maleev, Alex, et al. Road to Civil War. (p. 1477)
Maleev, Alexander, illus. see Gale, Bob & Grayson, Devin K.
Málek, Jaromír, jt. auth. see Malek, Jaromír.
Malek, Jaromír & Málek, Jaromír. Egypt. (p. 506)
Malenfant, Isabelle, illus. see Galbraith, Bree.
Malenfant, Paul Chanel. Si Tu Allais Quelque Part. (p. 1572)
Malepart, Celine. When Pigs Fly: A Piggy Pop-up Book! (p. 1904)
Malepart, Celine, illus. see Richardson, Bill.
Malépart, Céline, illus. see Ross, Kathy.
Malépart, Céline, illus. see Stanké, Claudie.
Malépart, Céline, illus. see Tremblay, Alain Ulysse.
Malepart, Celine, tr. see Tremblay, Alain Ulysse.
Maleska, Eugene T., ed. see New York Times Staff.
Maletsky, Evan A., et al. Check What You Know: Intervention Practice Books. (p. 295)
Maletsky, Sophie. Sticky Fingers: DIY Duct Tape Projects. (p. 1650)
Maley, Adrienne Houk. 20 Fun Facts about Praying Mantises. (p. 1995)
Malhotra, Sonali. Iraq. (p. 887)
—Welcome to Iraq. (p. 1873)
Malia, Tara Campasano. Special Princess. (p. 1623)
Malik, Katherine. Giselle's Magical World (p. 681)
Malik, S. A. Omari's Flight: The Mercy of Love. (p. 1288)
Malin, David, jt. auth. see Roucoux, Katherine.
Malin, David & Roucoux, Katherine. Heaven & Earth: Unseen by the Naked Eye. (p. 761)
Malinow, Wendy, illus. see Schick-Jacobowitz, Jeannie, et al.
Malinowska-Sempruch, Kasia & Gallagher, Sarah, eds. War on Drugs, HIV/AIDS & Human Rights. (p. 1858)
Malinowski, Carrie. Hand-Me-Down Bear. (p. 740)
Malinowski, Judy & Malinowski, Mel. Snorkel Hawaii the Big Island: Guide to the beaches & snorkeling of Hawaii. (p. 1598)
—Snorkel Maui Lanai & Molokai: Guide to the beaches & snorkeling of Hawaii. (p. 1598)
Malinowski, Mel, jt. auth. see Malinowski, Judy.
Malison, Anna. Through Thick & Thin. (p. 1745)
Malisow, Ben. Terrorism. (p. 1722)
Maliszewski, Julia. Grandmas Got the Goodies. (p. 708)
Malizia, Laura. Nonna's Kitchen. (p. 1263)
Malk, Steven, jt. auth. see Harper, Charise Mericle.
Malkasian, Carter. Korean War. (p. 967)
Malkin, Arlene Swinson. Adventures with Grandma & Grandpa: The Secret of the Old Trunk. (p. 25)
Malkin, Lawrence. Krueger's Men: The Secret Nazi Counterfeit Plot & the Prisoners of Block 19. (p. 968)
Malkin, Nina. Looking for a Better World: What Every Person can DO! (p. 1051)
—Swear. (p. 1689)
—Swoon. (p. 1692)
Malkowski, Melissa, illus. see Kleemann, Linda.
Malkus, Alida Sims. Story of Good Queen Bess. Meadowcroft, Enid Lamonte, ed. (p. 1658)
—Story of Louis Pasteur. Meadowcroft, Enid Lamonte, ed. (p. 1659)
—We Were There at the Battle of Gettysburg. Vosburgh, Leonard, illus. (p. 1868)
Mallam, Sally. Dende Maro: The Golden Prince. (p. 426)
Mallam, Sally, illus. see Shah, Idries.
Mallat, Kathy. Brave Bear. (p. 223)
—Just Ducky. (p. 938)
Mallea, Cristian, illus. see Biskup, Agnieszka Józefina.
Mallea, Cristian, illus. see Biskup, Agnieszka.
Mallea, Cristian, illus. see Collins, Terry, et al.
Mallea, Cristian, illus. see Collins, Terry.
Mallea, Cristian, illus. see Kincade, Chris.
Mallea, Cristian, illus. see Wacholtz, Anthony.
Mallet, C. Claire. Disparition Chez les Lutins. Begin, Jean-Guy, illus. (p. 453)
Mallett, Joanne A. Shamus. (p. 1559)
Mallett, Keith, illus. see Winter, Jonah.
Mallett, Lisa, illus. see Golding, Elizabeth.
Mallette, Dania, illus. see Dimarco, Tony.
Mallette, Dania, illus. see _Meli, Ayani & D., Jessie.
Mallette, Herb, jt. auth. see Dunn, Ben.
Malley, Alex. Chris Hemsworth. (p. 311)
Malley, Barbara. Read Me A Rhyme Please. (p. 1443)
Malley, Gemma. Declaration. (p. 421)
—Declaration. (p. 421)
—Legacy. (p. 987)
—Returners. (p. 1465)
Mallick, April. Wisdom's Recipe. (p. 1939)
Mallick, David, tr. see Campbell, Mel.
Mallick, David, tr. see Olliges, Rob.
Mallick, Nita & Watson, Stephanie. Conquering Binge Eating. (p. 358)
Mallik, Romi. Love's Flame. (p. 1061)
Mallin, Jay. Al Sharpton: Community Activist. (p. 33)
Mallon, Lynn & Marshall, Jennifer. It Pays to Be Honest. (p. 894)
Mallonee, Dennis & Wilson, Shawn V. Adventures of Chrissie Claus: Volume 1 (p. 17)
Mallory, Alex. Wild. (p. 1928)
Mallory, Barbara. Shantelle: Angels, Stars & Faith. (p. 1559)
Mallory, Carolyn. Painted Skies Zhao, Amei, illus. (p. 1318)
Mallory, Edgar, illus. see Norfleet, Mary Crockett.
Mallory, Enid. Captain Fitz: FitzGibbon, Green Tiger of the War of 1812. (p. 264)
Mallory, Gail. Bear Went over the Mountain. (p. 151)
Mallory, H. P. Ghouls Rush In (p. 673)
Mallory II, Philip R. More Than a Mountain: My Year Cycling in France. (p. 1175)
Mallory, Kenneth. Adventure Beneath the Sea: Living in an Underwater Science Station. Skerry, Brian, photos by. (p. 14)
—Diving to a Deep-Sea Volcano. (p. 455)
—Home by the Sea: Protecting Coastal Wildlife. (p. 792)
Mallory, Marilynn H., illus. see Gove, Doris.
Mallory, Mark. Amelia Earhart: Queen of the Sky. (p. 58)
Mallory, Nicole. I Wish I Was an Alligator. (p. 849)

Mallory, Roger. From Layoff to Liftoff: A Beginner's Guide to Overcoming Job Trauma & Finding True Financial Freedom. (p. 643)
Malloy, Brian. Twelve Long Months. (p. 1800)
—Year of Ice: A Novel. (p. 1969)
Malloy, Chris. Wizard Academies - A Special Kind of Talent. (p. 1942)
Malloy, Devin. FootballTalk: Conversation Cards for the Entire Family. (p. 615)
—SpookyTalk: Conversation Cards for the Entire Family. (p. 1631)
—WeatherTalk: Conversation Cards for the Entire Family. (p. 1870)
Malloy, Kalie, illus. see Jennings, Sharon.
Mally, Sarah. Before You Meet Prince Charming: A Guide to Radiant Purity. Brandon, Dan & Weaver, Brandon, illus. (p. 159)
—Bright Lights Discipleship Notebook. (p. 228)
Mally, Sarah, et al. Making Brothers & Sisters Best Friends: How to Fight the Good Fight at Home. (p. 1080)
Malm, John, et al. Atlas de Dinosaurios: Dinosaur Atlas. (p. 112)
Malnor, Bruce, jt. auth. see Malnor, Carol L.
Malnor, Bruce & Malnor, Carol. Earth Heroes, Champions of the Wilderness. Hovemann, Anisa Claire, illus. (p. 496)
Malnor, Carol, jt. auth. see Malnor, Bruce.
Malnor, Carol & Fuller, Sandy F. BLUES Go Extreme Birding. Schroeder, Louise, illus. (p. 204)
Malnor, Carol L. On Kiki's Reef. Hunner, Trina L., illus. (p. 1289)
Malnor, Carol L. & Fuller, Sandy F. BLUES Go Birding Across America. Schroeder, Louise, illus. (p. 204)
—BLUES Go Birding at Wild America's Shores. Schroeder, Louise, illus. (p. 204)
Malnor, Carol L. & Hunner, Trina L. Molly's Organic Farm. Hunner, Trina L., illus. (p. 1161)
Malnor, Carol L. & Malnor, Bruce. Earth Heroes, Champions of Wild Animals. Hovemann, Anisa Claire, illus. (p. 496)
Malokas, Ann. Tag-a-long Trio: Zak, Lizze & Ben Too! Nicholas, Corasue, illus. (p. 1695)
Malone. Computerized Test Bank Ibm to Accompany Basic Concepts of Chemistry. (p. 355)
—Instructor's Manual & Test Bank to Accompany Basic Concepts of Chemistry. (p. 878)
Malone, Beni & White, Marian Frances. Sights Before Christmas Erdelji, Darka, illus. (p. 1574)
Malone, Bobbie. Learning from the Land: Wisconsin Land Use. (p. 985)
—Wisconsin: Our State, Our Story. (p. 1939)
Malone, Bobbie, jt. auth. see Holliday, Diane Young.
Malone, Bobbie, jt. auth. see Holliday, Diane.
Malone, Bobbie, jt. auth. see Kasparek, Jonathan.
Malone, Bobbie, jt. auth. see Rosebrough, Amy.
Malone, Bobbie & Oberle, Kori. Wisconsin: Our State, Our Story. (p. 1939)
Malone, D. L. 52 Purple Monkeys. (p. 1997)
Malone, Dan, jt. auth. see Moran, Theresa.
Malone, David P. Adventures of Benny the Bunnyduck: Escape from Chindia. (p. 16)
Malone, Geoffrey. Torn Ear. (p. 1770)
Malone, Henry. Portals to Cleansing. (p. 1386)
Malone, Janet, jt. auth. see Dumont, Thora.
Malone, Jean M. Miracle of Easter. Langdo, Bryan, illus. (p. 1148)
—No Room at the Inn: The Nativity Story. Langdo, Bryan, illus. (p. 1260)
Malone, Jen & Nall, Gail. You're Invited. (p. 1982)
Malone, Julio. Sammy Sosa en 9 Innings. (p. 1508)
—Sammy Sosa in 9 Innings. (p. 1508)
Malone, Kelly, jt. auth. see Stontz, Karen.
Malone, Kelly, et al. 50 Quick Play Listening Games. (p. 1997)
Malone, Kyle, illus. see Merilatt, James & Frainier, Tamara.
Malone, Ladawn. Master's Garden. (p. 1103)
Malone, Margaret Gay. Sweater for Duncan. Dey, Lorraine, illus. (p. 1689)
Malone, Marianne. Pirate's Coin. Call, Greg, illus. (p. 1363)
—Secret of the Key. Call, Greg, illus. (p. 1542)
—Secret of the Key: a Sixty-Eight Rooms Adventure. (p. 1542)
—Sixty-Eight Rooms. Triplett, Gina & Call, Greg, illus. (p. 1583)
—Stealing Magic. Call, Greg, illus. (p. 1646)
Malone, Nola. Home. (p. 791)
Malone, Nola Langner, illus. see Viorst, Judith.
Malone, Peter, illus. see Bridges, Shirin Yim.
Malone, Peter, illus. see Edwards, Richard.
Malone, Peter, illus. see Freedman, Russell.
Malone, Peter, illus. see Havemeyer, Janie.
Malone, Peter, illus. see Hockinson, Liz.
Malone, Peter, illus. see Maurer, Gretchen.
Malone, Peter, illus. see Pack, Mary Fisk.
Malone, Peter, illus. see Russell, Freedman.
Malone, Peter, illus. see Spinner, Stephanie.
Malone, Peter, jt. auth. see Clark, Margaret.
Malone, Peter & Prokofiev, Sergei. Sergei Prokofiev's Peter & the Wolf: With a Fully-Orchestrated & Narrated CD. Malone, Peter, illus. (p. 1552)
Malone, Richard & Shettleworth, Earle. Rediscovering S. P. Rolt Triscott: Monhegan Island Artist & Photographer. (p. 1455)
Malone, Susan Mary, ed. see Freedman, Anne.
Malone, Susan Mary, ed. see Karevold, Alison.
Malone, Susan Mary, ed. see Morton Cuthrell, Kimberly.
Malone, Susan Mary, ed. see Woodson, J. L.
Malone, Sydney, jt. auth. see Scholastic, Inc. Staff.
Malone, Tom. What's Important: A Roadmap for Loving God. (p. 1897)
Maloney, Alison. Grandmas' Book: For the Grandma Who's Best at Everything. Woodroffe, David, illus. (p. 708)
Maloney, Andrew. Master Song. (p. 1103)
—Verse of Valor. (p. 1837)
Maloney, Brenna. Ready Rabbit Gets Ready! (p. 1447)
—Ready Rabbit Gets Ready! Maloney, Brenna, illus. (p. 1447)
—This Is Mouse - An Adventure in Sewing: Make Mouse & Friends * Travel with Them from Africa to Outer Space. (p. 1736)
Maloney, Cynthia, photos by see Lindahl, Kay.
Maloney, George A. Discovering the Hidden Reality: A Journey into Christian Mystical Prayer. (p. 449)
Maloney, Jim. Directioner's Handbook: Because It's All about Loving One Direction. (p. 445)
—I Love Liam. Maloney, Jim, illus. (p. 842)
Maloney, Jim & Baxter, Nicola. One Direction: Test Your Super-Fan Status: Packed with Puzzles, Quizzes, Crosswords, & More! (p. 1294)
Maloney, Jim & Buster Books Staff. I Love Harry. Maloney, Jim, illus. (p. 842)
Maloney, Linda M., tr. see Krenzer, Rolf.
Maloney, Linda M., tr. see Kunzler-Behncke, Rosemarie.
Maloney, Linda M., tr. see Wensell, Paloma.
Maloney, Peter. Big Apple Mystery. (p. 177)
—Bump on the Head. (p. 241)
—Here Comes Summer! (p. 770)
Maloney, Peter & Zekausakas, Felicia. Late for the Library: Just Schoolin' Around Series. (p. 979)
Maloney, Peter & Zekauskas, Felicia. Lose That Tooth! (p. 1054)
—One Foot, Two Feet. Maloney, Peter & Zekauskas, Felicia, illus. (p. 1295)
—Thanks for Nothing! (p. 1725)
Maloney, Raelynn, jt. auth. see Wolfelt, Alan D.
Maloney, Ralph. Heavenly Flavors. (p. 761)
Maloof, Torrey. Analyze It! (p. 67)
—Climate. (p. 332)
—Earth & Moon. (p. 495)
—Extreme Weather. (p. 557)
—Looking Up! (p. 1051)
—People & the Planet. (p. 1339)
—Photosynthesis. (p. 1353)
—Rocks & Minerals. (p. 1483)
—Transferring Energy. (p. 1778)
—Understanding Elections, Levels K-2. (p. 1815)
—Water Cycle. (p. 1862)
—We Recycle. (p. 1868)
—Weathering & Erosion. (p. 1870)
—What's the Matter with Mr. Fuego? (p. 1899)
Malory, Thomas, jt. auth. see Hodges, Margaret.
Malot, Hector & Crewe-Jones, Florence. Nobody's Boy: Companion Story to Nobody's Girl. Gooch, Thelma & Gruelle, Johnny, illus. (p. 1262)
—Nobody's Girl: Companion Story to Nobody's Boy. Gooch, Thelma, illus. (p. 1262)
Malouf, Ranya. Blue Fish's Secret Wish. (p. 202)
Maloy, Jackie. Ancient Maya. (p. 69)
Maloza, Herve. Secret of Creation. (p. 1542)
Malpass, Peter. Housing & the Welfare State: The Development of Housing Policy in Britain. (p. 804)
Malpass, Suzanne M. Lab's Tale. Morgan, Trish, illus. (p. 970)
Malpica, Antonio. Querido Tigre Quezada. Castillo, Guillermo Graco, illus. (p. 1426)
Malpica, Tono. Mil Anos de Pepe Corcuena. Aranda, Amira, illus. (p. 1142)
Maltaite, Will, illus. see Peyo.
Maltbie, P. I. Bambino & Mr. Twain. Miyares, Daniel, illus. (p. 135)
Maltbie, P. I., et al. Claude Monet: The Painter Who Stopped the Trains. (p. 329)
Maltbie, Priscilla. Bambino & Mr. Twain. (p. 135)
Maltby, Ethel H. My Animal Story Book: A Treasury of Sunshine Stories for Children. Richardson, Frederick, illus. (p. 1196)
Maltby, Robert, ed. see Terence.
Maltby, Robert I. Diquan & the Book Monster (p. 445)
—My Money Got Gobbled (p. 1214)
Maltese, Donna K. Know Your Bible for Kids: All about Jesus. (p. 965)
—Know Your Bible for Kids: What Is That? My First Bible Reference for Ages 5-8. (p. 965)
Maltese, John. I Love You the Most. (p. 844)
Maltman Dinwoodie, Heather, illus. see Sellen, Sandi.
Malton, H. Mel. Pioneer Poltergeist. (p. 1361)
Malton, Mel. Drowned Violin. (p. 486)
Maltseff, Michele, jt. auth. see Gertha, Patricia.
Maltz, Harold & Maltz, Miriam, eds. Enlightenment. (p. 530)
Maltz, Miriam, jt. ed. see Maltz, Harold.
Maltz, Susan & Grahn, Barbara. Fork in the Road: A Career Planning Guide for Young Adults. (p. 620)
Malue, Jenna. Recycling Plastic: Understand Place Value. (p. 1453)
Malvasi, Meg Greene, jt. auth. see Greene, Meg.
Malven, Tim. Christmas That Almost Wasn't. (p. 316)
Malvern, Corinne, illus. see Jackson, Kathryn.
Malvern, Corinne, illus. see Moore, Clement C.
Malvezi, Irene, illus. see Nissen Samuels, Linda.
Mama Doo. Trevor's Adventure in Button Land (p. 1785)
—Zachary & the Magic Pumpkin Seeds (p. 1984)
Mama Jamie. I Will Call Myself Future. (p. 848)
Mamada, Mineko. Which Is Round? Which Is Bigger? Mamada, Mineko, illus. (p. 1911)
Mamah, Michael. Imp. (p. 862)
Mamakas, Stavroula & Lagoutaris, Maria Mamakas. Mama Lagoo: Bath Time Battle. (p. 1084)
Mamas, Michael. How to Be Your Own Psychotherapist: The Key to Your Own Psychological Health in a Nutshell. (p. 815)
Mamata, Sue, illus. see Harris, Amber.
Mamburay, Khadijah, jt. auth. see Mamburay, Yankuba.
Mamburay, Yankuba & Mamburay, Khadijah. Day at Grandma's Farm. (p. 412)
Mamet, Clara & Quaid, Jack. Solvit Kids. (p. 1608)
Mami, Itou. Maleficarum Vol. 1 (p. 1083)
Mamie, Cowser. Bird Left Behind. (p. 190)
Mamma Macs. Australian Animal Walkabout. (p. 116)
—Mick Mac Adoo's Australian Zoo. (p. 1135)
Mammano, Julie. Rhinos Who Play Baseball. Mammano, Julie, illus. (p. 1467)
—Rhinos Who Rescue. (p. 1467)
Mammay, Judith. It's Time. Fargo, Todd, illus. (p. 899)
—Knowing Joseph. (p. 965)
—Ryan's Victory. Fargo, Todd, illus. (p. 1499)
Mammina, David. Circle Stone Group: Book 1: the Beginning. (p. 321)
Mammo, Rebecca, ed. see Fesseha, Zewditu.
Mammola-Koravos, Beth A. Good Night God, Love Olivia. Bebirian, Helena, illus. (p. 699)
Man, John. Genghis Khan: Life, Death, & Resurrection. (p. 661)
Managhan, Patricia, jt. auth. see Monaghan, Patricia.
Manak, Dave, illus. see Gallagher, Mike.
Manalang, Dan. Ambrosia. Wong, Nichole, illus. (p. 57)
Manale, Shizumi & Marshall, Richard. Running with Cosmos Flowers: The Children of Hiroshima (p. 1497)
Manale, Steven Charles, illus. see de Mariaffi, Elisabeth.
Manar, Elizabeth P., jt. auth. see Hackney Blackwell, Amy.
Manarino, Mark, illus. see McKenna, Jacqueline & Manarino-Leggett, Priscilla.
Manarino-Leggett, Priscilla, jt. auth. see McKenna, Jacqueline.
Manary, Adria. More Mommy Magic: 506 Ways to Nurture Your Child. (p. 1174)
Manasau, Amos, illus. see Charles, Novalyn.
Manasau, Amos, illus. see Mesibere, Ellen.
Manasco, Hunter. Exceptional Children's Guide to Touch: Teaching Social & Physical Boundaries to Kids. Manasco, Katharine, illus. (p. 547)
—Way to A: Empowering Children with Autism Spectrum & Other Neurological Disorders to Monitor & Replace Aggression & Tantrum Behavior. Manasco, Katharine, illus. (p. 1864)
Manasco, Katharine, illus. see Manasco, Hunter.
Manatt, Kathleen. Architects. (p. 95)
—Nuclear Energy. (p. 1269)
—Robot Scientist. (p. 1480)
—Searching for Oil. (p. 1537)
—Volcanologist. (p. 1849)
Manatt, Kathleen G. Architects. (p. 95)
—Law & Order. (p. 981)
—Nuclear Energy. (p. 1269)
—Robot Scientist. (p. 1480)
—Searching for Oil. (p. 1537)
—Volcanologist. (p. 1849)
Manavi, Lorraine Begay, tr. see Browne, Vee.
Manavi, Lorraine Begay, tr. see Johnson, Jann A.
Manceau, Édouard. Race Owlkids Books Inc. Staff & Quinn, Sarah, trs. from FRE. (p. 1430)
—Tickle Monster. (p. 1747)
Mancek, Marjan, illus. see Brunel, Aude.
Mancell, Doris, illus. see Caraboolad, Arla.
Manchee, Michael, ed. see Manchee, William.
Manchee, William. Act Normal: A Stan Turner Mystery. Manchee, Michael, ed. (p. 9)
—Tarizon: Conquest Earth. (p. 1706)
—Tarizon the Liberator: Tarizon Trilogy Vol 1. (p. 1706)
Manchess, Gregory, illus. see Clifford, Barry.
Manchess, Gregory, illus. see Heinz, Brian J.
Manchess, Gregory, illus. see London, Jonathan.
Manchess, Gregory, illus. see Waldman, Stuart.
Manchester, Peter, jt. auth. see Ryan, Darlene.
Manchester, William. Arms of Krupp: The Rise & Fall of the Industrial Dynasty That Armed Germany. (p. 100)
Manci, Arlene. Grumpy Troll Rawcliffe, Lee, illus. (p. 727)
Mancil, Arlene. Angel Explains Christmas Blessings. McKinnon, Joy, illus. (p. 73)
—Garden Fairy. (p. 656)
Mancil, Julie A. Anna's Decision. (p. 85)
Mancini, Aly. Layne at Home. (p. 981)
Mancini, Candice. Child Soldiers. (p. 301)
—Civil Rights in Richard Wright's Native Son. (p. 324)
—Civil Rights in Richard Wright's Native Son. Johnson, Claudia, ed. (p. 324)
—Garbage & Recycling. (p. 655)
—Racism in the Autobiography of Malcolm X. (p. 1432)
Mancini, Candice, jt. auth. see Johnson, Claudia.
Mancini, Candice, ed. Racism in Harper Lee's To Kill a Mockingbird. (p. 1432)
Mancini, Joan. 25 Super Sight Word Songs & Mini-Books: Fun Songs Set to Favorite Tunes with Companion Read & Write Mini-Books That Teach Essential Sight Words. (p. 1996)
Mancini, Kristen Belmont. Bunny Named Boo. (p. 242)
Mancini, Robert, illus. see O'Brien, Tim.
Mancini-Wilson, Debbie. Color My World: An Interactive Poetry Book for Kids of All Ages. (p. 343)
Mancusi, Mari. Blood Coven Vampires, Volume 1. (p. 200)
—Boys That Bite. (p. 220)
—Gamer Girl. (p. 654)
—Girls That Growl (p. 681)
—Scorched. (p. 1530)
—Shattered. (p. 1563)
—Smoked. (p. 1594)
—Stake That (p. 1638)
Mancuso, Jackie Clark. Paris-Chien: Adventures of an Ex-Pat Dog. (p. 1324)
Mandala Publishing Staff. Buddha Altar. Waters, Kim, photos by. (p. 234)
Mandala Publishing Staff, jt. auth. see McElroy, Bonnie.
Mandanna, Sangu. Lost Girl. (p. 1055)
Mandara, Melissa. Who would you Be? (p. 1919)
Mandarino, Gene. What's Autism? (p. 1896)
Mandarino, Gene, illus. see Garrick, Lainie.
Mandel, Joey. Anxiety: Deal with It Before It Ties You up in Knots. (p. 90)
Mandel, Laurie, jt. auth. see Webber, Diane.
Mandel, Lee. Barf for Lunch. (p. 139)
—Frog Burgers. (p. 640)
Mandel, Mike, jt. selected by see Sultan, Larry.
Mandel, Peter. Bun, Onion, Burger. Eliopoulos, Chris, illus. (p. 241)
—Jackhammer Sam. Catrow, David, illus. (p. 903)
—Say Hey! A Song of Willie Mays. Tate, Don, illus. (p. 1518)
—Zoo Ah-Choooo. Smith, Elwood H., illus. (p. 1988)
Mandel, Ruth. How to Tell Your Children about the Holocaust. (p. 822)
Mandel, Scott & Udall, Anne J. Improving Test Scores: A Practical Approach for Teachers & Administrators. (p. 862)
Mandela, Nelson, ed. Favorite African Folktales. (p. 578)
Mandelbaum, Jolie, jt. auth. see Davis, Amy.
Mandelbaum, Jolie, jt. auth. see Lenfest, Kevyn.
Mandelbaum, Jolie, jt. auth. see Whitley, Jared.
Mandelkorn, Carole. Grandma, Will You Clap! Phillips, Laverne, illus. (p. 708)
Mandell, Muriel. Super Science Experiments. Garbot, Dave, illus. (p. 1680)
Mandell, Sabain. Www.AdorableDiapers.Com Presents How to Create Personalized Diapers for Kids! (p. 1966)
Mandell, Stephen R., jt. auth. see Kirszner, Laurie G.
Mander, Sanna, illus. see Slee, Natasha.
Manderly, Lorin. Lilith Celebrates Lammas. Drewes, Dan, illus. (p. 1017)
Manders, Jeff, illus. see Martin, David.
Manders, John. Really Awful Musicians. (p. 1449)
Manders, John, illus. see Berger, Samantha.
Manders, John, illus. see Crimi, Carolyn.
Manders, John, illus. see Daly, James & Zuckerman, Amy.
Manders, John, illus. see Demas, Corinne.
Manders, John, illus. see Dodds, Dayle Ann.
Manders, John, illus. see Friend, Catherine.
Manders, John, illus. see Griffin, Kitty & Combs, Kathy.
Manders, John, illus. see Hernandez, Keith.
Manders, John, illus. see Holland, Trish & Ford, Christine.
Manders, John, illus. see Hopkins, Jackie Mims.
Manders, John, illus. see Kimmel, Eric A.
Manders, John, illus. see Lauber, Patricia.
Manders, John, illus. see Maccarone, Grace.
Manders, John, illus. see Martin, David.
Manders, John, illus. see McClatchy, Lisa.
Manders, John, illus. see McMahon, P. J.
Manders, John, illus. see McMahon, Patricia.
Manders, John, illus. see Redmond, Shirley Raye.
Manders, John, illus. see Sanders, Rob.
Manders, John, illus. see Tripp, Jenny.
Manders, John, illus. see Wilbur, Helen L.
Mandeville, Terry M. Just Waiting for My Family. (p. 940)
Mandhardt, Laurie. Life of Jesus. (p. 1012)
Mandiela, Andri Zhina. Dark Diaspora. (p. 407)
Mandino, Og. Og Mandino's Great Trilogy: The Greatest Salesman in the World, the Greatest Secret in the World & the Greatest Miracle in the World. (p. 1280)
Mandl, Dave & Wilson, Peter L., eds. Wild Children: A Zine for Kids. (p. 1929)
Mandla. Garden Green Hills: And Finally Ants Run the Village. (p. 656)
Mandracchia, Charles, 8th. Showtoonz (p. 1571)
Mandracchia, Charles, creator. Wacky Wonder World. (p. 1852)
Mandrake, Tiffany. Flax the Feral Fairy. Chatterton, Martin, illus. (p. 603)
—Mal the Mischievous Mermaid. Chatterton, Martin, illus. (p. 1083)
—Nanda the Naughty Gnome. Chatterton, Martin, illus. (p. 1229)
—Tikki the Tricky Pixie. Chatterton, Martin, illus. (p. 1749)
—Weava the Wilful Witch. Chatterton, Martin, illus. (p. 1870)
Mandrake, Tom, illus. see Jones, Bruce & Austen, Chuck.
Mandy and Ness Staff, et al. George's Garden. (p. 665)
—Hattie's House: A First Book about Sound. (p. 753)
—Peter's Party. (p. 1347)
—Rosie's Room. (p. 1490)
Mandy Ross. Animal Exercises: Poems to Keep Fit. Rescek, Sanja, illus. (p. 77)
Mandy, Stanley. Bella: The Fairy Ball. Mandy, Stanley, illus. (p. 162)
—Bella: The Birthday Party. Mandy, Stanley, illus. (p. 162)
Mane, Carmen De Posadas, see De Posadas Mane, Carmen.
Manea, Elham. Regional Politics in the Gulf: Saudi Arabia, Oman, Yemen. (p. 1457)
Manell, Keane. Hall Pass to the Tenth Dimension. (p. 737)
Manen, Max Van, see Van Manen, Max.
Manera, Alexandria. Abigail Adams. (p. 5)
—Betsy Ross. (p. 172)
—Martha Washington. (p. 1097)
Manero, Elia, jt. auth. see Mendez, Raquel.
Manero Jimenez, Laura, tr. see Nicholson, William.
Manero, Laura, tr. see Nicholson, William.
Maneru, Maria, et al. Mis Primeros Relatos de Miedo. Jos Luis Telleria, illus. (p. 1150)
Maness, Branda Edwards. Animal Tales of Hawaii. (p. 80)
Maness, Patricia. Adventures of Ben & Golden. (p. 16)
Manetti, Francesco, illus. see Nayar, Nandini.
Manfre, Edward, et al. Great Beginnings. (p. 714)
Manfre, Joey, illus. see Swick, Carmen D.
Manfredi, Federica, illus. see de Campi, Alex.
Manfredi, Federica, illus. see De, Campialex.
Manfredi, Frederica, illus. see De Campi, Alex.
Manfredini, Becky. Get up & Move! A Content Area Reader-health. (p. 668)
Manga University, jt. auth. see Manga University Staff.
Manga University Staff. My First PC: The Comic Book That Teaches You about the Internet. (p. 1207)
Manga University Staff & Manga University. Manga Without Borders: Japanese Comic Art from All Four Corners of the World. (p. 1087)
Mangal, Melina. Mildred Taylor. (p. 1142)
Mangan, Anne & Moss, Joanne. Little Teddy Left Behind (p. 1037)
Mangan, Lucy. Inside Charlie's Chocolate Factory: The Complete Story of Willy Wonka, the Golden Ticket, & Roald Dahl's Most Famous Creation. (p. 876)
Mangano, Tom. Dora's World Adventure! (p. 471)
Mangano, Tom, illus. see Beinstein, Phoebe.
Mangano, Tom, illus. see Driscoll, Laura.
Mangano, Tom, illus. see Ricci, Christine.
Mangano, Tom, jt. auth. see Furman, Eric.
Mangels, Andy, et al. Dragon's Lair O'Reilly, Sean Patrick, ed. (p. 479)
Mangelsen, Thomas, photos by see Hirschi, Ron.
Mangelsen, Thomas D., illus. see Hirschi, Ron.
Mangelsen, Thomas D., photos by see Hirschi, Ron.
Mangelsen, Thomas D., photos by see Tye, Laurie.

Manger, Barbara & Smith, Janine. Mary Nohl: A Lifetime in Art. (p. 1101)
Mangiat, Jeff, illus. see Scott, L. K.
Mangiat, Jeffrey, illus. see Mattern, Joanne.
Mangieri, Catherine. Funny First Day. (p. 649)
—Powwow. (p. 1391)
—Using Measuring Tools. (p. 1828)
Mangieri, Catherine C. What Is a Rainbow? (p. 1888)
Mangin, John F. Squirt Blossom Jubilation. (p. 1637)
Manglobe, jt. auth. see Gotsubo, Masaru.
Manglobe & Gotsubo, Masaru. Samurai Champloo Gotsubo, Masaru, illus. (p. 1509)
Mangiou, Gabrielle, illus. see Ravishankar, Anushka.
Mangold, Sylvia Plimack, et al. Robert Mangold. (p. 1479)
Mangrum, Allison. African American Writers Who Inspired Change. (p. 27)
—Jobs from A to Z. Capaldi, Gina, illus. (p. 919)
Mangrum, Kaylea J. How to Draw, Step by Step, Using the Alphabet: Book 2. (p. 818)
—How to Draw Step-By-Step Using the Alphabet. Mangrum, Kaylea J., illus. (p. 818)
—How to Draw Step-By-Step with Special Kids. Mangrum, Kaylea J., illus. (p. 818)
Mangrum, Kaylea J., jt. auth. see Bartch, Lea.
Mangskau, Monica. My Grandpa the Super Hero. (p. 1210)
Mangual, Ines, jt. auth. see Berrios, Frank.
Manguel, Alberto & Kipling, Rudyard. Kipling: A Brief Biography. (p. 961)
Mangum, Ariana. Carlos, the Mouse Who Discovered Americ. (p. 270)
Mangum, James A. & Spires, Sidney. Fairy & the Chupacabra & Those Marfa Lights: A West Texas Fable. Mangum, James A., illus. (p. 563)
Mangum, James & Spires, Sidney. Silly Adventures of the Silly Name Gang: The Case of the Mixed-Up Families. Mangum, James, illus. (p. 1575)
Mangum, Kay Lynn. Love Like Lilly. (p. 1060)
—When the Bough Breaks. (p. 1904)
Mangum, Lisa. After Hello. (p. 28)
—Forgotten Locket. (p. 620)
—Golden Spiral. (p. 695)
—Hourglass Door. (p. 802)
Mangus, Robert. Legend of the Christmas Tree. (p. 989)
Manhardt, Laurie Watson. Friends of God: Catholic Bible Study for Children. Co, Aileen & Dayton, Melissa, illus. (p. 638)
Manheim, Ralph, tr. see Grimm, Wilhelm K.
Manheim, Ralph, tr. see Hoffmann, E. T. A.
Manheimer, Ann S. James Beckwourth: Legendary Mountain Man. (p. 907)
—Martin Luther King Jr: Dreaming of Equality. (p. 1098)
Manhire, Bill, jt. ed. see Callaghan, Paul.
Manhof, Errol. My Community. (p. 1200)
Mani, Anamika & Mani, Anu. Grooming Is Fun! (p. 725)
Mani, Anu, jt. auth. see Mani, Anamika.
Maniatis, Amy & Weil, Elizabeth. Crib Notes: A Random Reference for the Modern Parent. (p. 382)
Manifold, Delwyn, jt. auth. see Craig, Bobby.
Manikandan, illus. see Helfand, Lewis.
Manikoff, John, illus. see Sheppard, Caroline H.
Manion, Denaé. Sock Stealing Thieves! (p. 1605)
Manion, Jennifer. Safia AMA Jan. (p. 1502)
Manion, Moira, illus. see Johnston, Jack.
Manis, Shirley, jt. auth. see Manis, Shirley.
Manis, Shirley & Manis, Shirley. In a Scoop of Dirt: How Digging a Pond Changed North America's Prehistory. (p. 863)
Manison, Shelly A. Diamond Hero. (p. 434)
Manivong, Laura. Escaping the Tiger. (p. 535)
Manjrekar, Nima, jt. auth. see Datta, Aparajita.
Manjula Padmanabhan. Unprincess! (p. 1822)
Mankamyer, Laura. Adventures of the Stonycreek Gang. Mankamyer, Laura, illus. (p. 23)
Mankell, Henning. Bridge to the Stars. (p. 227)
—Journey to the End of the World. (p. 929)
—Secrets in the Fire. Stuksrud, Anne Connie, tr. from SWE. (p. 1544)
—Shadows in the Twilight. (p. 1558)
—When the Snow Fell. (p. 1905)
Mankita, Jay. Eat Like a Rainbow Coloring Book. (p. 501)
Man-Kong, Mary. Barbie: A Fairy Secret. Golden Books Staff, illus. (p. 138)
—Barbie & the Diamond Castle: A Storybook. Golden Books Staff, illus. (p. 138)
—Barbie & the Diamond Castle. Rainmaker Entertainment Staff & Rainmaker Entertainment, illus. (p. 138)
—Barbie & the Three Musketeers. Random House Staff, illus. (p. 138)
—Barbie as the Island Princess. (p. 138)
—Barbie -Fairy Secret. Random House Staff, illus. (p. 138)
—Barbie - Fashion Fairytale. Random House Value Publishing Staff, illus. (p. 138)
—Barbie Fun & Games (Barbie) Golden Books, illus. (p. 138)
—Barbie in a Christmas Carol. Random House Editors, illus. (p. 138)
—Barbie in a Mermaid Tale. Golden Books Staff, illus. (p. 138)
—Barbie in the 12 Dancing Princesses. (p. 138)
—Barbie Little Golden Book Favorites. Golden Books Staff, illus. (p. 138)
—Barbie Loves Horses (Barbie) Duarte, Pamela, illus. (p. 138)
—Barbie Loves Weddings. (p. 138)
—Barbie Pink Kit. Golden Books Staff, illus. (p. 138)
—Best Friends Rock! (p. 169)
—Boo-Tiful Halloween! Riley, Kellee, illus. (p. 210)
—Dazzling Duet. (p. 415)
—Dream Dancer. Golden Books, illus. (p. 483)
—Easter Stencil Fun! (Peter Cottontail) Karl, Linda, illus. (p. 499)
—Easter Surprises! Golden Books, illus. (p. 499)
—Fairy Dreams. (p. 563)
—Fairy Dreams. Random House Staff, illus. (p. 563)
—Fairy Surprises! Golden Books Staff, illus. (p. 564)
—Fairy-Tail Adventure. (p. 564)
—Fairy-Tail Adventure. Random House Staff, illus. (p. 564)
—Fairytale Favorites (Barbie) Random House Staff, illus. (p. 565)
—Feel the Music. (p. 580)
—Fin-Tastic Journey! Golden Books Staff, illus. (p. 586)
—Friends, Fashion, & Fun! (Barbie) Golden Books Staff & Das Group Staff, illus. (p. 638)
—Frosty the Snowman Pictureback (Frosty the Snowman) Random House, illus. (p. 645)
—Fun & Furry Friends (Barbie) (p. 647)
—Get Your Glam On! (Barbie) (p. 668)
—Hair-Tastic (Barbie) (p. 736)
—Happy, Jolly Fun! (Frosty the Snowman) Golden Books, illus. (p. 746)
—Here Comes Peter Cottontail Pictureback (Peter Cottontail) Random House, illus. (p. 770)
—Holiday Style (Barbie) (p. 788)
—Hoppy Easter! (Peter Cottontail) Karl, Linda, illus. (p. 797)
—I Can Be a Dance Star. Golden Books Staff, illus. (p. 835)
—I Can Be... a Fashion Designer. Golden Books Staff & An, Jiyoung, illus. (p. 835)
—I Can Be a Horse Rider. (p. 835)
—I Can Be a Horse Rider (Barbie) RH Disney Staff & An, Jiyoung, illus. (p. 835)
—I Can Be a Pastry Chef / I Can Be a Lifeguard. (p. 835)
—I Can Be a Pet Vet. An, Jiyoung, illus. (p. 835)
—I Can Be a Rock Star. Golden Books Staff, illus. (p. 835)
—I Can Be a Sports Star (Barbie) An, Jiyoung, illus. (p. 835)
—I Can Be a Teacher (Barbie) Golden Books Staff & Riley, Kellee, illus. (p. 835)
—I Can Be an Artist (Barbie) Fall, Brandon, illus. (p. 835)
—I Can Be... Anything I Want to Be. Golden Books Staff & An, Jiyoung, illus. (p. 835)
—It's Sparkle Time! (p. 899)
—Listen to Your Heart! (p. 1022)
—Magic of the Rainbow. (p. 1073)
—Magical Mermaid Adventure. (p. 1074)
—Magical Mermaid Adventure. (p. 1075)
—Mariposa. (p. 1094)
—Meet Bubble Kitty! Unten, Eren, illus. (p. 1120)
—Mermaid Style. (p. 1128)
—My Fabulous Friends! Golden Books Staff, illus. (p. 1202)
—On the Runway (Barbie) (p. 1291)
—Once upon a Dream. RH Disney Staff, illus. (p. 1292)
—Pop Star Dreams (Barbie) Golden Books Staff & Duarte, Pamela, illus. (p. 1384)
—Pretty Ponies (Barbie) (p. 1398)
—Princess Charm School (Barbie) Golden Books Staff, illus. (p. 1403)
—Princess in Training (Barbie) Golden Books Staff, illus. (p. 1404)
—Princess to the Rescue! (p. 1406)
—Purr-Fect Pets. Golden Books Staff, illus. (p. 1419)
—Purr-Fect Valentine! (Barbie) Golden Books, illus. (p. 1419)
—Sensational Style. Golden Books Staff, illus. (p. 1551)
—Sleeping Beauty. (p. 1589)
—Sleeping Beauty Step into Reading (Disney Princess) RH Disney Staff, illus. (p. 1589)
—Sleepover Fun! Glows in the Dark! - Over 30 Glow Stickers! (p. 1589)
—Sparkling Style. Golden Books Staff, illus. (p. 1622)
—Spook-Tacular Halloween! (Barbie) (p. 1631)
—Spooky Smells of Halloween. Garofoli, Viviana, illus. (p. 1631)
—Spring into Style. Golden Books Staff, illus. (p. 1635)
—Star Power. (p. 1641)
—Star Power. Random House Staff, illus. (p. 1641)
—Sweetest Halloween (Barbie) Golden Books Staff & Duarte, Pamela, illus. (p. 1690)
—Teachers' Pets (Disney Princess) Marrucchi, Elisa, illus. (p. 1709)
—Thumbelina. Golden Books Staff, illus. (p. 1745)
—Travel in Style (Barbie) (p. 1780)
—Wedding Party! (Barbie) Riley, Kellee, illus. (p. 1871)
—Welcome to My Dream House (Barbie) Golden Books Staff, illus. (p. 1873)
Man-Kong, Mary, jt. auth. see Golden Books Staff.
Man-Kong, Mary, jt. auth. see Random House.
Man-Kong, Mary & Hashimoto, Meika. Fashion Fairytale. Random House Editors, illus. (p. 575)
—Glimmer, Shimmer, & Shine! Golden Books Staff, illus. (p. 683)
Man-Kong, Mary & Inches, Alison. Pink Boots & Ponytails. Random House Staff, illus. (p. 1359)
Man-Kong, Mary & Random House. Surprise for a Friend (Barbie) (p. 1685)
Man-Kong, Mary & Roberts, Angela. Barbie Loves Ballet. Wolcott, Karen, illus. (p. 138)
Man-Kong, Mary & Tillworth, Mary. Barbie in a Mermaid Tale Golden Books Staff, illus. (p. 138)
—Perfect Christmas (Barbie) Golden Books Staff, illus. (p. 1341)
—Perfect Christmas Paint. Golden Books Staff, illus. (p. 1341)
—Princess Charm School (Barbie) Golden Books Staff, illus. (p. 1403)
—Princess Magic (Barbie) Golden Books Staff, illus. (p. 1404)
Man-Kong, Mary, et al. I Can Be a Pastry Chef/I Can Be a Lifeguard (Barbie) RH Disney Staff & Random House Staff, illus. (p. 835)
Mankowski, Sarah. Fallout: An original Screenplay. (p. 567)
Manley, Brenda Randazzo. Misfits of Millville. (p. 1150)
Manley, Candace. Skeeter's Dream. (p. 1584)
Manley, Claudia. Everything You Need to Know about Custody. (p. 545)
Manley, Claudia B. Competitive Track & Field for Girls. (p. 352)
—Crack & Your Circulatory System: The Incredibly Disgusting Story. (p. 375)
—Everything You Need to Know about Custody. (p. 545)
—Ultra Swimming. (p. 1810)
Manley, Claudia B., jt. auth. see Carroll, Myrna.
Manley, Claudia B., jt. auth. see Miller, Kat.
Manley, Craig. Rammarg Files. (p. 1438)
Manley, Curtis. Summer Nick Taught His Cats to Read. Berube, Kate, illus. (p. 1674)
Manley, Francis G. Tellin Twins: The Great Art Scam. (p. 1717)
Manley, Heather. Battle with the Bugs: An Imaginative Journey Through the Immune System. Swift, Jessica, ed. (p. 147)
—Heart Pumping Adventure: An Imaginative Journey Through the Circulatory System. (p. 760)
—Lucky Escape: An Imaginative Journey Through the Digestive System. (p. 1062)
Manley, Jeanette, illus. see Hassler, Jill K.
Manley, Molly. Nantucket Nanny. Marshall, Janet, illus. (p. 1229)
—On a Vineyard Veranda. Marshall, Janet, illus. (p. 1288)
Manley, Ruth. Plum-Rain Scroll. (p. 1374)
Mann. Instructor's Resource to Accompany Introductory Statistics. (p. 878)
—Instructor's Solutions Manual to Accompany Introdu Ctory Statistics. (p. 879)
—Test Bank to Accompany Introductory Statistics. (p. 1723)
Mann, Bethany, illus. see Stephens, Sarah Hines.
Mann, Bethany, jt. auth. see Stephens, Sarah Hines.
Mann, Charles C. Before Columbus: The Americas of 1491. (p. 158)
Mann, Clay, illus. see Carey, Mike.
Mann, Derek, illus. see Carroll, John.
Mann, Elissa, jt. auth. see Hanson, Anders.
Mann, Elizabeth. Brooklyn Bridge: The Story of the World's Most Famous Bridge & the Remarkable Family That Built It. Witschonke, Alan, illus. (p. 231)
—Empire State Building: When New York Reached for the Skies. Witschonke, Alan, illus. (p. 521)
—Great Pyramid: The Story of the Farmers, the God-King & the Most Astonding Structure Ever Built. Turco, Laura Lo, illus. (p. 718)
—Great Wall: The Story of Thousands of Miles of Earth & Stone That Turned a Nation into a Fortress. Witschonke, Alan, illus. (p. 719)
—Hoover Dam: The Story of Hard Times, Tough People & the Taming of a Wild River. Witschonke, Alan, illus. (p. 796)
—Little Man: A Novel. (p. 1031)
—Machu Picchu: The Story of the Amazing Inkas & Their City in the Clouds. Crehore, Amy, illus. (p. 1068)
—Panama Canal: The Story of How a Jungle Was Conquered & the World Made Smaller. Rangel, Fernando, illus. (p. 1320)
—Parthenon: The Height of Greek Civilization. Lee, Yuan, illus. (p. 1325)
—Roman Colosseum: The Story of the World's Most Famous Stadium & Its Deadly Games. Racz, Michael, illus. (p. 1485)
—Statue of Liberty: A Tale of Two Countries. Witschonke, Alan, illus. (p. 1645)
Mann, Elizabeth & Witschonke, Alan. Taj Mahal: A Story of Love & Empire. (p. 1696)
Mann, Elsa & Benchmark Education Co., LLC Staff. Hot, Hot, Hot. (p. 801)
—Jim & Jan. (p. 917)
Mann, Emma. Amelia's Star. (p. 58)
Mann, Gerre. Cora the Caterpillar. Brody, Joyce, illus. (p. 366)
Mann, Holly, jt. auth. see van Genechten, Guido.
Mann, Jennifer Ann. Sunny Sweet Can So Get Lost. (p. 1677)
—Sunny Sweet Is So Dead Meat. (p. 1677)
—Sunny Sweet Is So Not Sorry. (p. 1677)
Mann, Jennifer K. I Will Never Get a Star on Mrs. Benson's Blackboard. Mann, Jennifer K., illus. (p. 848)
—Two Speckled Eggs. Mann, Jennifer K., illus. (p. 1804)
Mann, Jennifer K., illus. see Shannon, George.
Mann, Juda, et al. My Vote Counts! (p. 1221)
Mann, Lawrence, illus. see Grasso, Julie Anne.
Mann, Margaret. Merlin's Island. Baker, Jennifer, illus. (p. 1128)
Mann, Rachel. Plants Grow from Seeds (p. 1370)
—Race to a Fire! (p. 1431)
—Sun & Rain (p. 1676)
Mann, Rachel & Capstone Press Staff. Plants Grow from Seeds (p. 1370)
—Race to a Fire! (p. 1431)
—Sun & Rain (p. 1676)
Mann, Scott. Daddy Keeps Us Free. Pannell, Nick, illus. (p. 398)
Mann, Seymour. Purple Automobile & the Newspaper Girl. (p. 1419)
Mann, T. L. Adventures of Magellan. (p. 20)
Mann, William A., illus. see Maddock-Cowart, Donna.
Manna, Anthony & Mitakidou, Christodoula. Orphan: A Cinderella Story from Greece. Potter, Giselle, illus. (p. 1304)
Manna, Anthony L. & Mitakidou, Christodoula. Mr. Semolina-Semolinus. Potter, Giselle, illus. (p. 1186)
Manna, Elizabeth, photos by see Leone, Jason, illus.
Manna, Giovanni. "Best friend" (Someone I Like) (p. 169)
—"Changing places" (Someone I Like) (p. 290)
—"I'm a river" (You & Me) (p. 858)
Manna, Giovanni, illus. see Blackstone, Stella.
Manna, Giovanni, illus. see Coward, Fiona.
Manna, Giovanni, illus. see Matthews, John.
Manna, Kirsti. Giggles & Goosebumples. (p. 676)
Manna, Sal, jt. auth. see Wojciechowska, Maia.
Mannari, Kaitlyn, et al. Out of Order. (p. 1311)
Mannering, G. R. Roses. (p. 1489)
Mannering, Rose. Boo's Beard. Straker, Bethany, illus. (p. 213)
—Spotty Dotty Daffodil. Straker, Bethany, illus. (p. 1634)
Manners, Jane. Clouds. (p. 335)
Manners, Richard. Girl Child Saturday. (p. 678)
Manners, Tyler. Continental Change of Heart. (p. 360)
Mannes, David M. Nahanni. (p. 1227)
Mannes, Jerry R. II. Zoopity: Adventures of the One Thinking Ant. (p. 1990)
Manni, Mia (Maio), illus. see Deluca, Laura.
Manning, Brennan. Posers, Fakers, & Wannabes: Unmasking the Real You. (p. 1387)
Manning, Clarice, illus. see Bruno, Daphnie.
Manning, Dennis & Crisalli, Joseph. Emeritus Peabody Mysteries. (p. 518)
—Turnip War. (p. 1798)
Manning, Eddie, illus. see McKay-Lawton, Toni.
Manning, Ella L. Ashleigh's Rainbow Garden. (p. 106)
—Macaretti. (p. 1067)
Manning, Jack. American Indian Homes (p. 62)
—Christmas Around the World. (p. 312)
—Christmas in France (p. 314)
—Christmas in Germany (p. 314)
—Christmas in Italy (p. 314)
—Christmas in Norway (p. 314)
—City Mayor (p. 323)
—Igloos (p. 856)
—Our Government (p. 1309)
—Pueblos (p. 1414)
—Serving on a Jury (p. 1553)
—State Governor (p. 1644)
—Tepees (p. 1721)
—Voting in Elections (p. 1850)
Manning, Jack, jt. auth. see Enderlein, Cheryl L.
Manning, Jane. Cat Nights. Manning, Jane, illus. (p. 278)
—Millie Fierce. Manning, Jane, illus. (p. 1144)
—Millie Fierce Sleeps Out. Manning, Jane, illus. (p. 1144)
Manning, Jane, illus. see Bardhan-Quallen, Sudipta.
Manning, Jane, illus. see Hopkins, Lee Bennett.
Manning, Jane, illus. see Jane, Pamela.
Manning, Jane, illus. see Kurtz, Jane.
Manning, Jane, illus. see Prelutsky, Jack.
Manning, Jane, illus. see Weeks, Sarah.
Manning, Jane K., illus. see Blackwood, Gary L.
Manning, Jane K., illus. see Luke, Melinda.
Manning, Jane K., illus. see McDonald, Megan.
Manning, Jane K., illus. see Schaefer, Lola M. & Miller, Heather Lynn.
Manning, Jane K., illus. see Weeks, Sarah & Weeks.
Manning, Jane K., illus. see Weeks, Sarah.
Manning, L. L. At the Roller Rink. (p. 111)
Manning, Lisa C. Falcons in the City. Manning, Lisa C., illus. (p. 566)
Manning, Mary, illus. see Copp, Raymond.
Manning, Mary, illus. see Everett, Melissa.
Manning, Mary, illus. see Malaspina, Ann.
Manning, Matthew, jt. auth. see Dorling Kindersley Publishing Staff.
Manning, Matthew K. Ali Baba & the Forty Thieves Osnaya, Ricardo, illus. (p. 39)
—Batman & the Flock of Fear. Vecchio, Luciano, illus. (p. 144)
—Catwoman's Nine Lives Vecchio, Luciano, illus. (p. 281)
—Green Lantern: An Origin Story. Baltazar, Art & Vecchio, Luciano, illus. (p. 722)
—Poisoned Planet Vecchio, Luciano, illus. (p. 1377)
—Scarecrow's Flock of Fear Vecchio, Luciano, illus. (p. 1519)
—Strong Cano, Fernando, illus. (p. 1668)
—Strong. (p. 1668)
—Superman: An Origin Story. Baltazar, Art & Vecchio, Luciano, illus. (p. 1683)
—Superman & the Poisoned Planet. Vecchio, Luciano, illus. (p. 1683)
Manning, Matthew K., jt. auth. see Dorling Kindersley Publishing Staff.
Manning, Matthew K. & Majado, Caio. Lockdown Ito, Leonardo, illus. (p. 1045)
Manning, Matthew K. & Poe, Edgar Allen. Fall of the House of Usher Jimenz, Jim & Calero, Dennis, illus. (p. 566)
Manning, Matthew K. & Sazaklis, John. DC Super Hero Origins. Vecchio, Luciano, illus. (p. 415)
Manning, Matthew K., et al. Attack of Professor Zoom! (p. 113)
—Little Green Men. (p. 1028)
—Rule of Three. Brizuela, Dario, illus. (p. 1495)
—Scarecrow, Doctor of Fear (p. 1519)
—Two-Face's Double Take. McManus, Shawn, illus. (p. 1803)
Manning, Maurie, illus. see Aboff, Marcie.
Manning, Maurie, illus. see Taylor-Butler, Christine.
Manning, Maurie J. Aunts Go Marching. (p. 116)
—Kitchen Dance. Manning, Maurie J., illus. (p. 962)
—Laundry Day. (p. 980)
Manning, Maurie J., illus. see Berry, Eileen M.
Manning, Maurie J., illus. see Farrell, John.
Manning, Maurie J., illus. see Hambrick, Sharon.
Manning, Maurie J., illus. see Ludwig, Trudy.
Manning, Maurie J., illus. see Pelley, Kathleen.
Manning, Maurie J., illus. see Rath, Tom & Reckmeyer, Mary.
Manning, Maurie J., illus. see Rosenbluth, Roz.
Manning, Maurie J., illus. see Taylor-Butler, Christine.
Manning, Maurie J., tr. see Hambrick, Sharon.
Manning, Maurie J., tr. see Pelley, Kathleen.
Manning, Mick. Cock-A-Doodle-Hoooooo! Granström, Brita, illus. (p. 337)
—Que Hay Debajo de la Cama? Cortes, Eunice, tr. (p. 1423)
—Secrets of Stonehenge. Granström, Brita, illus. (p. 1545)
—What Mr Darwin Saw. Manning, Mick & Granström, Brita, illus. (p. 1892)
—Woolly Mammoth. Granström, Brita, illus. (p. 1950)
Manning, Mick, illus. see Quarto Generic Staff.
Manning, Mick & Brita, Granström. Mi Primer Libro de Teatro. Granström, Brita, illus. (p. 1133)
Manning, Mick & Granström, Brita. Beatles. (p. 153)
—Charles Dickens: Scenes from an Extraordinary Life. (p. 292)
—Chomp, Chomp! (p. 309)
—Dino-Dinners. (p. 441)
—Dino-Dinners. Manning, Mick & Granström, Brita, illus. (p. 441)
—Drama School. (p. 480)
—Greek Hero. Manning, Mick & Granström, Brita, illus. (p. 720)
—How Did I Begin? (p. 806)
—Nature School. (p. 1236)
—Pharaoh's Egypt. Manning, Mick & Granström, Brita, illus. (p. 1350)
—Snap! (p. 1597)
—Supermama. (p. 1683)
—What Mr Darwin Saw. (p. 1892)
—Wild Adventures. (p. 1928)

Manning, Mick & Granstrom, Brita. Woolly Mammoth. (p. 1950)
Manning, Mick, et al. Teatro. (p. 1711)
Manning, Paul. Amazon River. (p. 56)
—Ganges. (p. 655)
—Mississippi. (p. 1154)
—Nile River. (p. 1255)
—Thames. (p. 1725)
—Yangtze. (p. 1968)
Manning, Peyton, et al. Family Huddle. Madsen, Jim, illus. (p. 568)
Manning, Phillip. Atoms, Molecules, & Compounds. (p. 113)
—Chemical Bonds. (p. 297)
—Gravity. (p. 712)
—Theory of Relativity. (p. 1729)
Manning, Russ, et al. Magnus, Robot Fighter 4000 A. D. (p. 1076)
Manning, Sara. Wally the Whale: A Tale about a Whale with Seizures. (p. 1855)
Manning, Sarra. Adorkable. (p. 13)
—French Kiss. (p. 635)
—French Kiss. (p. 636)
—Guitar Girl. (p. 731)
—Kiss & Make Up. (p. 961)
—Let's Get Lost. (p. 997)
—Pretty Things. (p. 1398)
—Sealed with a Kiss. (p. 1536)
Manning, Vicky. Lucy Goose & the Flying Seeds. (p. 1063)
Manning-Toonoo, Nina, tr. see Teevee, Ningeokuluk.
Mannino, Stephanie. Cool Careers Without College for People Who Love Crafts. (p. 362)
Mannion, James. Everything Guide to Government Jobs: A Complete Handbook to Hundreds of Lucrative Opportunities Across the Nation. (p. 544)
Mannion, Mary. Boy & the Fish. Fitzgerald, Brian, illus. (p. 217)
—Roaring Rory. Fitzgerald, Brian, illus. (p. 1478)
Mannion, Steve, illus. see Van Lente, Fred, et al.
Mannis, Celeste Davidson. One Leaf Rides the Wind. Hartung, Susan Kathleen, illus. (p. 1295)
Mannis, Celeste Davidson & Davidson, Mannis. Who Was William Shakespeare? O'Brien, John, illus. (p. 1919)
Mannis, Celeste Davidson & Kramer, Sydelle. Who Was William Shakespeare? O'Brien, John, illus. (p. 1919)
Mannon, L. J. Circle of the Hawk. (p. 321)
Mannone, Christine. Flowers for Pudding Street. Carolan, Christine, illus. (p. 608)
Mann's Miracles, creator. When the Hurricane Blew. (p. 1904)
Manny, illus. see storiesbypj.com.
Manolis, Kay. Abraham Lincoln: A Life of Honesty. (p. 6)
—Ambulances. (p. 57)
—Big Rigs. (p. 183)
—Blastoff! Readers - Body Systems (p. 198)
—Blizzards. (p. 200)
—Circulatory System. (p. 321)
—Color. (p. 342)
—Density. (p. 426)
—Digestive System. (p. 438)
—Energy. (p. 528)
—George Washington: A Life of Self-discipline. (p. 664)
—Gravity. (p. 712)
—Hurricanes. (p. 830)
—John F. Kennedy: A Life of Citizenship. (p. 921)
—Levers. (p. 1003)
—Matter. (p. 1109)
—Monster Trucks. (p. 1168)
—Motion. (p. 1179)
—Muscular System. (p. 1192)
—Nervous System. (p. 1241)
—Police Cars. (p. 1380)
—Pulleys. (p. 1415)
—Ramps. (p. 1438)
—Respiratory System. (p. 1463)
—Rosa Parks: A Life of Courage. (p. 1489)
—School Buses. (p. 1522)
—Screws. (p. 1533)
—Skeletal System. (p. 1584)
—Skid Steer Loaders. (p. 1584)
—Sound. (p. 1615)
—Taxis. (p. 1707)
—Temperature. (p. 1717)
—Thomas Jefferson: A Life of Patriotism. (p. 1739)
—Tow Trucks. (p. 1773)
—Wedges. (p. 1871)
—Wheels & Axles. (p. 1900)
Manolis, Tim, illus. see Biggs, Kathy.
Manoloff, Dennis. Omar Vizquel: The Man with the Golden Glove. Rains, Rob, ed. (p. 1288)
Manos, Helen. Samsara Dog. Vivas, Julie, illus. (p. 1509)
Manos, John. Big Ben Helps the Town. (p. 178)
—It's Earth Day! (p. 896)
—Mail Comes to Main Street. (p. 1077)
—Samantha Saves the Stream. (p. 1507)
Manousos, Dave. Life Is Good & Other Reasons for Rhyme. Manousos, Dave, illus. (p. 1011)
Manousos, Demetrius. Know Your Mass. Burbank, Addison, illus. (p. 965)
Manoy, Laureen. Where to Park Your Broomstick: A Teen's Guide to Witchcraft. (p. 1910)
Mansbach, Adam. Seriously, Just Go to Sleep. Cortés, Ricardo, illus. (p. 1552)
Mansbach, Adam & Zweibel, Alan. Benjamin Franklin: Huge Pain in My... (p. 165)
MansBach, Sara. Round & Round the Garden, Finger Games in English & Spanish. Arroyave, Heidy, tr. (p. 1491)
Manse, Whitney. What's Gramma Doing in Heaven? (p. 1897)
Manser, Martin H. Facts on File Dictionary of Proverbs. (p. 561)
—Facts on File Guide to Good Writing. Pickering, David H. & Curtis, Stephen, eds. (p. 561)
Mansfield, Andy. Follow the Star: A Pop-Up Christmas Journey. (p. 612)
Mansfield, Carol M. Jake & Jebadiah Visit the Veterinarian (p. 905)
Mansfield, Creina. My Nutty Neighbours. (p. 1216)
Mansfield, Katherine. Garden Party. (p. 656)
—Parties & Presents: Three Short Stories. (p. 1325)
—Parties & Presents, Level 2: Three Short Stories. (p. 1325)
Mansfield, Keith. Johnny Mackintosh & the Spirit of London. (p. 923)
—Johnny Mackintosh: Battle for Earth. (p. 923)
—Star Blaze. (p. 1640)
Mansfield, Monica. When You Have to Say Goodbye: Loving & Letting Go of Your Pet. Peterson, Lennie, illus. (p. 1905)
Mansfield, Phil, illus. see Gold, Rozanne.
Mansfield, Phil, photos by see Gold, Rozanne.
Mansfield, Richard. CSS Web Design for Dummies. (p. 387)
Mansfield, Stephen & Koh, Magdalene. Laos. (p. 975)
Mansilla, Lucio V. excursion a los indios Ranqueles. Sosnowski, Saul, ed. (p. 547)
Mansk, Anne. You Can Measure: A Content Area Reader-math. (p. 1974)
Mansmann, Leslie, illus. see Elder, Elizabeth.
Manson, Ainslie. Boy in Motion: Rick Hansen's Story. Benoit, Renné, illus. (p. 218)
—Roll On: Rick Hansen Wheels Around the World Lightburn, Ron, illus. (p. 1485)
Manson, Beverlie. Beverlie Manson's Fairies: A Celebration of the Seasons. (p. 173)
—Mermaid's Secret Diaries. (p. 1128)
Manson, Beverlie, illus. see Baxter, Nicola.
Manson, Beverly, jt. auth. see Baxter, Nicola.
Manson, Christopher. Good King Wenceslas. (p. 698)
Manson, Christopher, illus. see Child, Lydia Maria.
Manson, Christopher, illus. see Lewis, J. Patrick.
Manson, Christopher, illus. see Nikola-lisa, W.
Manson, Kayt. Molly Dolly - Dance with Me! Manson, Kayt, illus. (p. 1160)
Manson, Mary K. I Love You More. (p. 843)
Manson, Sheri. Bumpy & Boo Visits the Eye Doctor: Guess Who Needs Glasses? Cabrera, Marcela, illus. (p. 241)
Mansot, Fédérick, illus. see Kerisel, Françoise.
Mansot, Fédérick, tr. see Kerisel, Françoise.
Mansour, Vivian. Almohada. Aguirre, Alfredo, illus. (p. 48)
Mansour, Vivian, jt. auth. see Manzur, Vivian Mansour.
Mansur, Elisabeth Fahrni, illus. see Chandpai - Dhamrai Bangladeshi Students Staff.
Mansur, Motesem. Otis Best. Carroll, Jr., illus. (p. 1307)
—Terry Tornado Story: The Wake-up Call. (p. 1722)
Mantchev, Lisa. Eyes Like Stars: Theatre Illuminata, Act I. (p. 558)
—Perchance to Dream: Theatre Illuminata #2. (p. 1341)
—Sister Day! Sánchez, Sonia, illus. (p. 1581)
Mantell, Ahuva, illus. see Steinbock, Steven E.
Mantell, Paul. Arthur Ashe: Young Tennis Champion. Henderson, Meryl, illus. (p. 103)
—Dale Earnhardt: Young Race Car Driver. Henderson, Meryl, illus. (p. 401)
—Mountain Bike Mania. (p. 1180)
Mantell, Paul, jt. auth. see Jeter, Derek.
Mantell, Paul & Christopher, Matt. Snowboard Champ. (p. 1600)
Mantell, Paul, text. Cool As Ice: Cool As Ice: the #1 Sports Series for Kids. (p. 362)
—Nothin' but Net. (p. 1268)
Mantha, John, illus. see Chapman, Susan.
Mantha, John, illus. see Demuth, Patricia Brennan.
Mantha, John, illus. see Glossop, Jennifer.
Mantha, John, illus. see Hacker, Carlotta.
Mantha, John, illus. see Hancock, Pat.
Mantha, John, illus. see Hodge, Deborah.
Mantha, John, illus. see Holub, Joan.
Mantha, John, illus. see MacLeod, Elizabeth.
Mantha, John, illus. see O'Connor, Jim.
Mantha, John, illus. see Owens, Ann-Maureen & Yealland, Jane.
Mantha, John, illus. see Scandiffio, Laura.
Mantha, John, illus. see Shapiro, Stephen.
Mantha, John, illus. see Silvey, Diane.
Manthei, Jean-Marie. On Gratitude: The Journey a Photo Recovery Book Part 8. (p. 1289)
Mantilla, Maria Fernanda, illus. see Arciniega, Triunfo.
Mantla, Rosa, jt. auth. see Football, Virginia.
Mantle, Ben. Trick or Treat: 12 Board Books (p. 1786)
Mantle, Ben, illus. see Ferry, Beth.
Mantle, Ben, illus. see Klostermann, Penny Parker.
Mantle, Ben, illus. see Mills, J. Elizabeth.
Mantle, Ben, illus. see Tiger Tales Staff.
Mantle, Ben, illus. see Watt, Fiona.
Mantle, Ben, illus. see Webb, Steve.
Mantle, Ben, illus. see Wiley, Thom.
Mantlo, Bill. Avengers: Heart of Stone. Byrne, John et al, illus. (p. 118)
Mantlo, Bill, jt. auth. see Wolfman, Marv.
Mantlo, Mickey A. & Cook, Darren A. Tennis Shoes & Toe Clips (p. 1720)
Manton, Charlotte. Community of Lincoln. Stanley, Karen & Bornemeier, Pam, eds. (p. 350)
Manton, Jimmy, illus. see Demarco, Stacey.
Mantra Lingua Staff. Don't Bully Me. (p. 467)
Mantzke, Jurgen, illus. see Hartman, Moreta.
Manu, illus. see Nagpal, Saraswati.
Manuel, Ballesteros Pastor José, jt. auth. see Ballesteros, Jose Manuel.
Manuel, David, et al. From Sea to Shining Sea for Young Readers: 1787-1837. (p. 643)
Manuel, Gahete. Angeles de Colores. (p. 74)
Manuel, Infante Don Juan. Conde Lucanor. (p. 355)
Manuel, Lynn. Summer of the Marco Polo Charko, Kasia, illus. (p. 1674)
Manuel, Margaret. I See Me. (p. 845)
Manuel, Peter & Neely, Daniel. Reggae Scene: The Stars, the Fans, the Music. (p. 1457)
Manuel Reeves, Emily. Fiona Flamingo Has Lost Her Pink. (p. 589)
Manuelian, Peter Der, see Der Manuelian, Peter.
Manus, Morton, ed. see Alexander, Dennis, et al.
Manus, Ron, jt. auth. see Harnsberger, L. C.
Manus, Ron & Harnsberger, L. C. Alfred's Kid's Ukulele Course 2: The Easiest Ukulele Method Ever!, Book & CD. (p. 38)
—Alfred's Kid's Ukulele Course Notespeller 1 & 2: Music Reading Activities That Make Learning Even Easier! (p. 38)
—Easiest Guitar Method Ever! Vol. 2. Shelly, Jeff, illus. (p. 498)
—Guitar for Kids! Book & CD. (p. 731)
—Kid's Guitar Course 1: The Easiest Guitar Method Ever! Shelly, Jeff, illus. (p. 954)
Manus, Willard. Dog Called Leka. (p. 461)
Manushkid, Fran. Grandma Beatrice Brings Spring to Minsk. (p. 708)
Manushkin, Fran. Best Season Ever Lyon, Tammie, illus. (p. 171)
—Big Brothers Are the Best Richards, Kirsten, illus. (p. 180)
—Big Girl Panties. Petrone, Valeria, illus. (p. 181)
—Big Lie Lyon, Tammie, illus. (p. 182)
—Big Sisters Are the Best Richards, Kirsten, illus. (p. 183)
—Boo, Katie Woo! Lyon, Tammie, illus. (p. 209)
—Boss of the World Lyon, Tammie, illus. (p. 215)
—Cartwheel Katie. Lyon, Tammie, illus. (p. 273)
—Come, Let Us Be Joyful! The Story of Hava Nagila. Kaye, Rosalind Charney, illus. (p. 347)
—Cowgirl Katie Lyon, Tammie, illus. (p. 374)
—Elect Me! Demski, James, Jr., illus. (p. 508)
—Fly High, Katie Lyon, Tammie, illus. (p. 609)
—Goodbye to Goldie Lyon, Tammie, illus. (p. 701)
—Happy Day Lyon, Tammie, illus. (p. 745)
—Happy in Our Skin. Tobia, Lauren, illus. (p. 746)
—It Doesn't Need to Rhyme, Katie: Writing a Poem with Katie Woo Lyon, Tammie, illus. (p. 894)
—Katie & the Class Pet Lyon, Tammie, illus. (p. 944)
—Katie & the Fancy Substitute (p. 944)
—Katie Finds a Job Lyon, Tammie, illus. (p. 945)
—Katie Goes Camping Lyon, Tammie, illus. (p. 945)
—Katie in the Kitchen Lyon, Tammie, illus. (p. 945)
—Katie Saves Thanksgiving Lyon, Tammie, illus. (p. 945)
—Katie Saves the Earth Lyon, Tammie, illus. (p. 945)
—Katie Woo Lyon, Tammie, illus. (p. 945)
—Katie Woo & Friends Lyon, Tammie, illus. (p. 945)
—Katie Woo & Her Big Ideas Lyon, Tammie, illus. (p. 945)
—Katie Woo Book Club Kit. Lyon, Tammie, illus. (p. 945)
—Katie Woo Celebrates Lyon, Tammie, illus. (p. 945)
—Katie Woo, Don't Be Blue Lyon, Tammie, illus. (p. 945)
—Katie Woo, Every Day's an Adventure Lyon, Tammie, illus. (p. 945)
—Katie Woo Has the Flu Lyon, Tammie, illus. (p. 945)
—Katie Woo Loves School Lyon, Tammie, illus. (p. 945)
—Katie Woo Rules the School Lyon, Tammie, illus. (p. 945)
—Katie Woo Spring 2010 Lyon, Tammie, illus. (p. 945)
—Katie Woo: Star Writer. Lyon, Tammie, illus. (p. 945)
—Katie Woo, Super Scout. Lyon, Tammie, illus. (p. 945)
—Katie Woo Tries Something New. Lyon, Tammie, illus. (p. 945)
—Katie Woo, Where Are You? Lyon, Tammie, illus. (p. 945)
—Katie Woo's Big Idea Journal: A Place for Your Best Stories, Drawings, Doodles, & Plans Lyon, Tammie, illus. (p. 945)
—Katie Woo's Super Stylish Activity Book Alder, Charlie, illus. (p. 945)
—Katie's Happy Mother's Day. Lyon, Tammie, illus. (p. 945)
—Katie's Lucky Birthday Lyon, Tammie, illus. (p. 945)
—Katie's New Shoes Lyon, Tammie, illus. (p. 945)
—Katie's Noisy Music. Lyon, Tammie, illus. (p. 945)
—Keep Dancing, Katie (p. 946)
—Look at You, Katie Woo! Lyon, Tammie, illus. (p. 1049)
—Make-Believe Class Lyon, Tammie, illus. (p. 1079)
—Many Days, One Shabbat Monescillo, Maria, illus. (p. 1089)
—Moo, Katie Woo! Lyon, Tammie, illus. (p. 1171)
—Moving Day Lyon, Tammie, illus. (p. 1183)
—Nervous Night Lyon, Tammie, illus. (p. 1241)
—No More Teasing Lyon, Tammie, illus. (p. 1259)
—No Valentines for Katie Lyon, Tammie, illus. (p. 1260)
—Piggy Bank Problems Lyon, Tammie, illus. (p. 1358)
—Ready, Set, Oops! (p. 1447)
—Red, White, & Blue & Katie Woo! Lyon, Tammie, illus. (p. 1455)
—Shivers in the Fridge. Zelinsky, Paul O., illus. (p. 1567)
—Sincerely, Katie: Writing a Letter with Katie Woo Lyon, Tammie, illus. (p. 1578)
—Sophie & the Shofar. Kaye, Rosalind Charney, illus. (p. 1613)
—Star of the Show Lyon, Tammie, illus. (p. 1641)
—Stick to the Facts, Katie: Writing a Research Paper with Katie Woo Lyon, Tammie, illus. (p. 1649)
—Too Much Rain Lyon, Tammie, illus. (p. 1767)
—Tricky Tooth Lyon, Tammie, illus. (p. 1786)
—Tushy Book. Dockray, Tracy, illus. (p. 1799)
—What Do You Think, Katie? Writing an Opinion Piece with Katie Woo Lyon, Tammie, illus. (p. 1883)
—What Happens Next, Katie? Writing a Narrative with Katie Woo Lyon, Tammie, illus. (p. 1886)
—What's in Your Heart, Katie? Writing in a Journal with Katie Woo Lyon, Tammie, illus. (p. 1898)
—Who Needs Glasses? Lyon, Tammie, illus. (p. 1917)
Manushkin, Fran & Lyon, Tammie. Adiós a Goldie. Lyon, Tammie, illus. (p. 12)
—Basta de Burlas Lyon, Tammie, illus. (p. 143)
—Gran Mentira Lyon, Tammie, illus. (p. 707)
—Jefa Del Mundo Lyon, Tammie, illus. (p. 911)
Manville, Bill. Cool, Hip & Sober: 88 Ways to Beat Booze & Drugs. (p. 363)
Manville, Ron, photos by see Longbotham, Lori.
Manwiller, S. A. Adventures of Jack & Max: What Jack & Max Love. Manwiller, S. A., illus. (p. 19)
—Adventures of Jack & Max the Truliest Meaning of Christmas. Manwiller, S. A. & Overly, Kristen V., illus. (p. 19)
Manzak, Bonnie. Big Red Cat. (p. 183)
—Lairame's Birthday Surprise. (p. 972)
Manzanares, J. C. Have Sweet Dreams of Ice Cream. (p. 754)
Manzanero, Paula K. Who Is (Your Name Here)? The Story of My Life. Harrison, Nancy, illus. (p. 1916)
Manzano, Roberto. Synergos. Reese, Steven, tr. from SPA. (p. 1693)
Manzano, Sonia. Becoming Maria: Love & Chaos in the South Bronx. (p. 156)
—Box Full of Kittens. Phelan, Matt, illus. (p. 216)
—Miracle on 133rd Street. Priceman, Marjorie, illus. (p. 1148)
—No Dogs Allowed! Muth, Jon J., illus. (p. 1258)
—Revolution of Evelyn Serrano. (p. 1466)
Manzano, Sonia & Muth, Jon J. No Dogs Allowed! Muth, Jon J., illus. (p. 1258)
Manzel, Michael. Moby's Tale. (p. 1157)
Manzella, Teresa Ryan. How to Analyze the Music of Bob Dylan. (p. 814)
Manzione, Lisa. Let's Visit Jerusalem! Adventures of Bella & Harry. Lucco, Kristine, illus. (p. 1001)
—Let's Visit London! Adventures of Bella & Harry. Lucco, Kristine, illus. (p. 1001)
Manzur, Vivian Mansour & Mansour, Vivian. Vida Util de Pillo Polilla. Flores, Lupita, illus. (p. 1841)
Mao, Xian. Children's Version of 60 Classical Chinese Poems. (p. 304)
Maor, Eli. Facts on File Calculus Handbook. (p. 561)
Maoz, Baruch. Prophet on the Run. (p. 1411)
Mape, Michael, illus. see Baia, Edward.
Maple, James. Advanced Chemistry. (p. 13)
Maples, Mary Jane, jt. auth. see Collins, Tim.
Mapleson, Peter & Mapleson, Robyn. Bill the Bunyip. (p. 187)
Mapleson, Robyn, jt. auth. see Mapleson, Peter.
Mappin, Jennifer. Seven Continents of the World. Five Mile Press Staff, illus. (p. 1554)
Mappin, Jennifer, text. Lettering Book: A Totally Fun Approach to Lettering! (p. 1002)
Mapping Specialists. US & World Map Outlines (p. 1826)
Mapua, Jeff. Bill & Hillary Clinton. (p. 186)
—Career in Customer Service & Tech Support (p. 267)
—Extreme Motorsports. (p. 556)
—Hillary Clinton (p. 779)
—Ludwig Van Beethoven: Classical Composer of Passion & Power. (p. 1064)
—Ludwig Van Beethoven: Composer of the Classical & Romantic Eras. (p. 1064)
—Making the Most of Crowdfunding (p. 1082)
—Sitting Bull. (p. 1582)
—Taxation: Interpreting the Constitution. (p. 1707)
—What Is a Planet? (p. 1888)
Mara, Cate. Great Kieranski & the Bardbuy. (p. 716)
Mara, Sarah Robinson. Snug Little Island Hammond, Nancy Robinson, illus. (p. 1601)
Mara, Thalia. Steps in Ballet: Basic Exercises at the Barre, Basic Center Exercises, Basic Allegro Steps. Bobrizky, George, illus. (p. 1648)
Mara, Wil. Abraham Lincoln. (p. 6)
—Alexander Graham Bell. (p. 36)
—Amelia Earhart. (p. 58)
—American Entrepreneurship. (p. 60)
—Apatosaurus. (p. 91)
—Assassination of President John F. Kennedy. (p. 107)
—Bats. (p. 144)
—Benjamin Franklin. (p. 164)
—Betsy Ross. (p. 172)
—Burma. (p. 243)
—Cardinals. (p. 266)
—Chernobyl Disaster: Legacy & Impact on the Future of Nuclear Energy. (p. 298)
—Civil Unrest in the 1960s: Urban Riots & Their Aftermath. (p. 325)
—Clara Barton. (p. 326)
—Clint Eastwood. (p. 333)
—Clock. (p. 333)
—Community Connections: What Should I Do? (p. 350)
—Coyotes. (p. 374)
—Deep-Sea Exploration: Science, Technology, & Engineering. (p. 423)
—Deer. (p. 423)
—Ducks. (p. 488)
—Dwight Eisenhower. (p. 491)
—Environmental Protection. (p. 532)
—Extreme BMX. (p. 556)
—Extreme Motocross. (p. 556)
—Farmer. (p. 574)
—Four Oceans. (p. 625)
—Franklin D. Roosevelt. (p. 630)
—Frog in the Pond. Mendenhall, Cheryl, illus. (p. 640)
—From Cats' Eyes to... Reflectors. (p. 642)
—From Gecko Feet to Adhesive Tape. (p. 642)
—From Kingfishers to... Bullet Trains. (p. 643)
—From Sharks to... Swimsuits. (p. 643)
—George W. Bush. (p. 663)
—George Washington. (p. 664)
—Gerald Ford. (p. 666)
—Gunsmith. (p. 732)
—Gymnastics. (p. 733)
—Haiti. (p. 736)
—Harriet Tubman. (p. 749)
—Harry Truman. (p. 751)
—Helicopter Crew Chief. (p. 763)
—How Do Earthquakes Happen? (p. 807)
—How Do Waves Form? (p. 807)
—Information Security Analyst. (p. 874)
—Innkeeper. (p. 875)
—Iran. (p. 886)
—Jackie Robinson. (p. 903)
—James Cameron. (p. 907)
—James Garfield. (p. 907)
—John Adams. (p. 921)
—John F. Kennedy. (p. 921)
—John Muir. (p. 922)
—Karate. (p. 943)
—Kristallnacht: Nazi Persecution of the Jews in Europe. (p. 967)
—Laura Bush. (p. 980)
—Laura Ingalls Wilder. (p. 980)
—Martin Luther King Jr. (p. 1098)
—Mesopotamians. (p. 1129)
—Motor Transport Operator. (p. 1179)
—Oprah Winfrey. (p. 1301)

—Otters. (p. 1307)
—Oviraptor. (p. 1314)
—Oviraptors. (p. 1314)
—Owls. (p. 1315)
—Paul Revere. (p. 1330)
—People's Republic of China. (p. 1340)
—Peter Jackson. (p. 1346)
—Poland. (p. 1378)
—Rabbits. (p. 1430)
—Robins. (p. 1480)
—Robotics: From Concept to Consumer. (p. 1480)
—Romans. (p. 1486)
—Ronald Reagan. (p. 1486)
—Rosa Parks. (p. 1488)
—Rosa Parks: Mother of the Civil Rights Movement. (p. 1489)
—Rosa Parks. (p. 1489)
—Sam Walton: Rethinking Retail. (p. 1507)
—Sam Walton: The man Who Invented Walmart. (p. 1507)
—Schoolmaster. (p. 1524)
—Seven Continents. (p. 1554)
—Silversmith. (p. 1577)
—Singapore. (p. 1579)
—Soccer. (p. 1603)
—Stegosaurus. (p. 1646)
—Steven Spielberg. (p. 1649)
—Tee Ball. (p. 1713)
—Theodore Roosevelt. (p. 1729)
—Thomas Alva Edison. (p. 1737)
—Thurgood Marshall: Champion for Civil Rights. (p. 1746)
—Tiananmen Square Massacre. (p. 1746)
—Triceratops. (p. 1785)
—Trucks! (p. 1791)
—Trucks. (p. 1791)
—Tyrannosaurus Rex. (p. 1805)
—Velociraptors. (p. 1835)
—What Should I Do? At the Pool. (p. 1893)
—What Should I Do? If a Stranger Comes Near. (p. 1893)
—What Should I Do? If I See a Stray Animal. (p. 1893)
—What Should I Do? If There Is a Fire. (p. 1893)
—What Should I Do? In the Car. (p. 1893)
—What Should I Do? Near a Busy Street. (p. 1893)
—What Should I Do? On My Bike. (p. 1893)
—What Should I Do? On the Playground. (p. 1893)
—Why Do Volcanoes Erupt? (p. 1924)
—Why Does It Rain? (p. 1924)
—Why Is the Sky Blue? (p. 1925)
—Wind Turbine Service Technician. (p. 1935)
—Woodpeckers. (p. 1949)
Mara, Will. Beavers. (p. 155)
Marabini, Sergio. Arafat. (p. 94)
—Che Guevara. (p. 295)
—Juan D. Perón. (p. 930)
Marable, Justin. Noco. (p. 1262)
Marable, Manning & Mullings, Leith. Freedom: A Photographic History of the African American Struggle. (p. 634)
Marabout & Abrams Noterie Staff. Butterflies. (p. 247)
Maracle, Lee. Will's Garden. (p. 1934)
Marais, Vivian. Life in a Swamp: A Wetlands Habitat. (p. 1010)
Maraja. Alice in Wonderland Picture Book. (p. 39)
Maran Graphics Development Group Staff. Kids! Picture Yourself Crocheting. (p. 955)
MaranGraphics Development Group Staff. Kids! Picture Yourself Cooking. (p. 954)
—Kids! Picture Yourself Knitting. (p. 955)
Maranhas, Jayne Ellen. Claude's Shrinking Shell. Baker, David, illus. (p. 329)
Marano, John. Kody the Kid Cop: And the Case of the Missing Cat. (p. 966)
Marathon. When You're Having Fun (p. 1906)
Marathon, creator. Trouble in the Tropics. (p. 1790)
—When You're Having Fun (p. 1906)
Maraval-Hutin, Sophie. Bernadette: The Girl from Lourdes. (p. 167)
Marazano, Richard. Civilisation Ponzio, Jean-Michel, illus. (p. 326)
—Sons of Ares Ponzio, Jean-Michel, illus. (p. 1613)
Marble, Abigail, illus. see Amateau, Gigi.
Marble, Abigail, illus. see Ludwig, Trudy.
Marbury, Ja'Nitta. All Mixed Up. Marbury, Ja'Nitta, illus. (p. 45)
Marbury, Stephanie. Off to the Moon! Leigh, Tom, illus. (p. 1279)
Marbury, Stephon & Dean, Marshall. Adventures of Young Starbury: Practice Makes Perfect. Nakai, Ryan, illus. (p. 24)
Marc, Sylvain, illus. see Kennedy, Emma.
Marcamo, Thais. Vivencias & Despertar. Vilma Muises, ed. (p. 1846)
Marcantonio, Patricia Santos, et al. Red Ridin' in the Hood: And Other Cuentos. Alarcão, Renato, illus. (p. 1454)
Marceau, Fani. In This Book. Jolivet, Joelle, illus. (p. 868)
—Panorama: A Foldout Book. Jolivet, Joëlle, illus. (p. 1321)
Marcel, Cali. Edore, Foffey, & the Man Eating Ogre. (p. 504)
Marcellino, Fred, illus. see Babbitt, Natalie.
Marcellino, Fred, illus. see Perrault, Charles.
Marcellino, Fred, illus. see Seidler, Tor.
Marcello, Paul, jt. auth. see Morris, Rob.
Marcellus, Rhoald, illus. see Cosby, Andrew & Stokes, Johanna.
Marcero, Deborah, illus. see Heppermann, Christine & Koertge, Ronald.
Marcet, Jane. Mary's Grammar. (p. 1101)
March, Chloe, illus. see Haney Perez, Jessica.
March, El. Captain Leopold. (p. 264)
March, Guillermo, illus. see Bernabe, Marc.
March, J. D. Dance with the Devil. (p. 402)
March, Janet, photos by see Frender, Gloria.
March, John S. Talking Back to OCD: The Program That Helps Kids & Teens Say "No Way" - And Parents Say "Way to Go" (p. 1703)
March, Julia. Lego Chima: Power Up! (p. 990)
—Lego Ninjago: Ninja, Go! (p. 990)
March, Julia, jt. auth. see Dorling Kindersley Publishing Staff.
March, Michael. China. (p. 306)
—Japan. (p. 909)
Marchant, Jackie, jt. auth. see Trump, D.
Marchant, Peter, jt. told to see Appelbaum, Barbara G.
Marchant, Sherry, jt. auth. see Jennett, Pamela.
Marchesani, Laura. Baby Loves Colors. Alkins, Dave, illus. (p. 127)
—Baby's World: A First Book of Senses. Alkins, Dave, illus. (p. 129)
—I Love You More Than Chocolate. (p. 843)
—Who Says? Alkins, Dave, illus. (p. 1917)
Marchesani, Laura, jt. auth. see Alkins, Dave.
Marchesani, Laura, jt. auth. see Price Stern Sloan Staff.
Marchesani, Laura & Medina, Zenaides A., Jr. Pig & Pug. Jarvis, illus. (p. 1357)
Marchese, Allison Marie. Patty's Best Friend. (p. 1330)
Marchese, Stephen. Flights of Marceau: Week Two. (p. 604)
Marchesi, Stephen. Flights of Marceau: Week One. (p. 604)
—Glow-In-The-Dark Constellations. (p. 685)
Marchesi, Stephen, illus. see Belviso, Meg & Pollack, Pamela D.
Marchesi, Stephen, illus. see Brown, Joe.
Marchesi, Stephen, illus. see Buckley, James, Jr.
Marchesi, Stephen, illus. see Dubowski, Cathy East & Pascal, Janet.
Marchesi, Stephen, illus. see Edwards, Roberta.
Marchesi, Stephen, illus. see Kelley, True.
Marchesi, Stephen, illus. see Korman, Susan.
Marchesi, Stephen, illus. see McDonough, Yona Zeldis.
Marchesi, Stephen, illus. see Morgan, Ellen.
Marchesi, Stephen, illus. see Pollack, Pam & Belviso, Meg.
Marchesi, Stephen, illus. see Rottmann, Erik.
Marchesi, Stephen, illus. see Shaw, Maura D.
Marchesi, Stephen, illus. see Waldron, Ann.
Marchesi, Stephen, illus. see Weinberger, Kimberly.
Marchesi, Stephen, illus. see Whelan, Gloria.
Marchessault, Sara J. Pinky the Dreamer & Her Silver Jet. (p. 1360)
Marchetta, Melina. Finnikin of the Rock. (p. 589)
—Jellicoe Road. (p. 912)
—Looking for Alibrandi. (p. 1051)
—Piper's Son. (p. 1362)
—Quintana of Charyn: The Lumatere Chronicles. (p. 1428)
—Saving Francesca. (p. 1517)
Marchetti, Angela, illus. see Gorla, Stefano.
Marchetti, Dave. Nestle's Big Adventure. (p. 1242)
—Steve the Stickleback. (p. 1649)
Marchetti, Domenica. Glorious Soups & Stews of Italy. Meppem, William, photos by. (p. 685)
Marchetti, Matt. Annabel Aardvark Arrives at an Avalanche. (p. 85)
Marchi, C. You Can Grow Old with Me: A True Story. (p. 1974)
Marchi, Mary V. Web in the Halo: A Tale of a Spider Who Learns about Christmas. (p. 1870)
Marchi, Sergio. Emerald Table. (p. 517)
Marchini, Tracy. Hot Ticket. (p. 802)
Marchione, Margherita. Man of Peace: Pope Pius XII. (p. 1085)
—Pope Pius XII: Bilingual Coloring Book. Elliott, John, illus. (p. 1384)
Marchland-Martella, Nancy, jt. auth. see Nelson, J. Ron.
Marchon, Benoit. Good Night! Bravi, Soledad, illus. (p. 699)
—Spoonful: A Peek-A-Boo Book. Bravi, Soledad, illus. (p. 1631)
Marchon, Benoit & Rosa, Jean-Pierre. Descubrir la Biblia. Truong, Marcelino, illus. (p. 428)
Marchon, Blandine. Biblia: Los Grandes Relatos del Antiguo y del Nuevo Testamento. Millet, Claude & Millet, Denise, illus. (p. 176)
March-Settle, Michelle. Shining Star: A Journey for All Ages. (p. 1566)
Marchus, Linda. Gorilla Who Wanted to Dance. Marchus, Linda, illus. (p. 703)
Marciano, Daniel Darko. Thomas Blasts Off. (p. 1738)
Marciano, John Bemelmans. 9 Lives of Alexander Baddenfield. Blackall, Sophie, illus. (p. 1993)
—Madeline & Her Dog. (p. 1070)
—Madeline & the Cats of Rome. (p. 1070)
—Madeline & the Old House in Paris. (p. 1070)
—Madeline at the White House. (p. 1070)
—Madeline Loves Animals. (p. 1070)
—Madeline's Tea Party. (p. 1070)
—Nine Lives of Alexander Baddenfield. Blackall, Sophie, illus. (p. 1256)
—Tea Party. (p. 1708)
Marciniak, Christine. Always Ali. (p. 51)
—Honestly, Ali! (p. 794)
—Lights, Camera, Ali! (p. 1016)
—Reality Ali. (p. 1449)
—When Mike Kissed Emm. (p. 1903)
Marciniak, Kristin. Fascinating Military Submarines. (p. 575)
—Flu Pandemic Of 1918. (p. 608)
—Flu Pandemic of 1918 Paperback. (p. 608)
—Navy SEALs. (p. 1238)
—Navy Seals. (p. 1238)
—Oregon Trail & Westward Expansion: A History Perspectives Book. (p. 1303)
—Revolutionary War: Why They Fought. (p. 1466)
—Surviving in the Wilderness. (p. 1687)
—US Coast Guard. (p. 1826)
—What's Great about Illinois? (p. 1897)
—What's Great about Iowa? (p. 1897)
—What's Great about Pennsylvania? (p. 1897)
Marciniszyn, Alex, ed. see Siembieda, Kevin.
Marcionette, Jake. Just Jake Villa, Victor Rivas, illus. (p. 938)
—Just Jake - Dog Eat Dog Villa, Victor Rivas, illus. (p. 938)
Marcken, Gail De, see Cary, Bob.
Marco, Harvey, illus. see Niednagel, Jonathan P.
Marcola, Gabrielle. Bedding the Burglar. (p. 156)
Marcolina, P. J. My Friend Grows Feathers - the True Story of Jackie the Crow. (p. 1209)
Marconette, Gennifer, ed. see Jamison, Heather & Meckenstock, Shay.
Marconi, Gloria, illus. see Smith, Loretta.
Marconi, Martina. Birthday Wishes (p. 193)
Marcos, Crystal. Bellyache: A Delicious Tale. (p. 163)
—Headache: The Hair-Raising Sequel to Bellyache. (p. 756)
Marcos, Pablo, illus. see Boyd, Herb.
Marcos, Pablo, illus. see Burnett, Frances Hodgson.
Marcos, Pablo, illus. see Doyle, Arthur.
Marcos, Pablo, illus. see Haggard, H. Rider.
Marcos, Pablo, illus. see Hanft, Joshua E.
Marcos, Pablo, illus. see Marko, Eve.
Marcos, Subcomandante. Story of Colors (La Historia de los Colores) A Bilingual Folktale from the Jungles of Chiapas. Din, Anne Bar, tr. (p. 1657)
Marcos, Teri. Bethlehem's Gift. (p. 171)
Marcotte, Arline Seibert. Obeying Rules Brings Happiness. (p. 1275)
Marcotte, David A. Be Wary of Strangers. (p. 149)
Marcotte, Jennifer. Nightly Knight. (p. 1255)
—Noah's Star. (p. 1262)
Marcoux, Tom. Crystal Pegasus. (p. 387)
Marcovitz, Hal. Abortion. (p. 5)
—Alamo: Symbol of Freedom. Moreno, Barry, ed. (p. 33)
—Alamo. (p. 33)
—Aliens in Pop Culture. (p. 41)
—Ancient Greece. (p. 69)
—Ancient Rome. (p. 70)
—Angry Guy's Guide: How to Deal. (p. 75)
—Anime. (p. 84)
—Art Conservation. (p. 101)
—Asthma. (p. 108)
—Bald Eagle: The Story of Our National Bird. Moreno, Barry, ed. (p. 133)
—Bald Eagle. (p. 133)
—Barack. (p. 137)
—Benjamin Franklin: Scientist, Inventor, Printer, & Statesman. (p. 165)
—Bias in the Media. (p. 175)
—Bill Clinton. (p. 186)
—Biological & Chemical Warfare. (p. 189)
—Bipolar Disorder. (p. 190)
—Blindness. (p. 199)
—Bruce Coville. (p. 232)
—Can Renewable Energy Replace Fossil Fuels? (p. 258)
—Cause & Effect the American Revolution: The American Revolution. (p. 282)
—Cause & Effect the Fall of the Soviet Union: The Fall of the Soviet Union. (p. 282)
—Chris Daughtry. (p. 311)
—Confederate Flag: Controversial Symbol of the South. Moreno, Barry, ed. (p. 356)
—Cuban Americans. (p. 388)
—Declaration of Independence: Forming a New Nation. Moreno, Barry, ed. (p. 422)
—Declaration of Independence. (p. 422)
—Derek Jeter. (p. 427)
—Dictatorships. (p. 436)
—Do Ghosts Exist? (p. 457)
—Dr. Dre. (p. 475)
—Drug Abuse. (p. 486)
—Drug & Alcohol Abuse. (p. 486)
—EBooks. (p. 502)
—Eddie Murphy. (p. 503)
—Elliott Yamin. (p. 514)
—Ellis Island: The Story of a Gateway to America. Moreno, Barry, ed. (p. 515)
—Ellis Island. (p. 515)
—Energy Security. (p. 528)
—Exposing Torture: Centuries of Cruelty. (p. 554)
—Gangs. (p. 655)
—Guys from Jackass Go Out on Their Own. (p. 733)
—Health Care. (p. 757)
—Hepatitis. (p. 769)
—History of Slavery. (p. 784)
marcovitz, hal. How Serious a Problem Is Drug Use in Sports? (p. 812)
—How Serious a Threat Is Climate Change? (p. 812)
Marcovitz, Hal. Independence Hall: Birthplace of Freedom. Moreno, Barry, ed. (p. 870)
—Infectious Mononucleosis. (p. 873)
—Islam in Africa. Ojakorotu, Victor & Rotberg, Robert I., eds. (p. 891)
—Jackass. (p. 903)
—James Monroe. (p. 907)
—Jealous Guy's Guide: How to Deal. (p. 911)
—John Adams. (p. 921)
—John F. Kennedy. (p. 921)
—Jordin Sparks. (p. 925)
—Kellie Pickler. (p. 948)
—Kuwait. (p. 968)
—Larry Page, Sergey Brin, & Google. (p. 976)
—Lawrence Yep. (p. 981)
—LeBron James. (p. 987)
—Liberty Bell: Let Freedom Ring. (p. 1005)
—Life in Nazi Germany. (p. 1010)
—Life in the Time of Shakespeare. (p. 1011)
—Lincoln Memorial: Shrine to an American Hero. Moreno, Barry, ed. (p. 1018)
—Lincoln Memorial. (p. 1018)
—Lindsay Lohan. (p. 1019)
—Lonely Guy's Guide: How to Deal. (p. 1046)
—Madonna: Entertainer. (p. 1070)
—Manning Brothers. (p. 1088)
—Marijuana. (p. 1094)
—Maurice Sendak. (p. 1110)
—Meningitis. (p. 1126)
—Mexican Americans. (p. 1131)
—Michelle. (p. 1135)
—Nancy Pelosi: Politician. (p. 1229)
—Notorious B. I. G. (p. 1268)
—Obama Family Tree. (p. 1275)
—Obama Mania. (p. 1275)
marcovitz, hal. Online Gaming & Entertainment. (p. 1298)
—Online information & Research. (p. 1298)
Marcovitz, Hal. Organ & Body Donation. (p. 1303)
—Owen & Luke Wilson. (p. 1314)
—Pat Mora. (p. 1327)
—Phobias. (p. 1351)
—Poltergeists. (p. 1381)
—Puerto Ricans. (p. 1414)
—R. L. Stine. (p. 1429)
—Race Relations. (p. 1431)
—Religious Fundamentalism. (p. 1458)
—Rise of the Nazis. (p. 1475)
—Roaring Twenties. (p. 1478)
—Rock 'n Roll. (p. 1482)
—Rock 'N' Roll: Voice of American Youth. Moreno, Barry, ed. (p. 1482)
—Russian Americans. (p. 1498)
—Sacagawea: Guide for the Lewis & Clark Expedition. (p. 1500)
—Scott O'Dell. (p. 1531)
—Should Juveniles Be Tried As Adults? (p. 1569)
marcovitz, hal. Should Smoking Be Banned? (p. 1570)
Marcovitz, Hal. Statue of Liberty: A Beacon of Welcome & Hope. Moreno, Barry, ed. (p. 1645)
—Suicide. (p. 1673)
—Surrealism. (p. 1686)
—Teaching Intelligent Design. (p. 1710)
—Technology. (p. 1711)
—Teens & Career Choices. Developed in Association with the Gallup Organization Staff, ed. (p. 1714)
—Teens & Cheating. Developed in Association with the Gallup Organization Staff, ed. (p. 1714)
—Teens & Family Issues. (p. 1714)
—Teens & Family Issues. Developed in Association with the Gallup Organization Staff, ed. (p. 1714)
—Teens & Gay Issues. (p. 1714)
—Teens & LGBT Issues. Developed in Association with the Gallup Organization Staff, ed. (p. 1714)
—Teens & Race. (p. 1714)
—Teens & Race. Developed in Association with the Gallup Organization Staff, ed. (p. 1714)
—Teens & Sex. (p. 1715)
—Teens & Sex. Developed in Association with the Gallup Organization Staff, ed. (p. 1715)
—Teens & Suicide. (p. 1715)
—Teens & Suicide. Developed in Association with the Gallup Organization Staff, ed. (p. 1715)
—Teens & the Supernatural & Paranormal. (p. 1715)
—Teens & the Supernatural & Paranormal. Developed in Association with the Gallup Organization Staff, ed. (p. 1715)
—Teens & Voluntarism. (p. 1715)
—Teens & Volunteerism. Developed in Association with the Gallup Organization Staff, ed. (p. 1715)
—Teens, Religion & Values. Developed in Association with the Gallup Organization Staff, ed. (p. 1715)
—Teens, Religion, & Values. (p. 1715)
—Theodore Roosevelt. (p. 1729)
—U. S. Constitution: Government by the People. Moreno, Barry, ed. (p. 1806)
—Uncle Sam: International Symbol of America. Moreno, Barry, ed. (p. 1812)
—Venus & Serena Williams. (p. 1836)
—Vietnam War. (p. 1841)
—Washington Monument: Memorial to a Founding Father. Moreno, Barry, ed. (p. 1860)
—Washington Monument. (p. 1860)
—White House: The Home of the U. S. President. Moreno, Barry, ed. (p. 1913)
—White House. (p. 1913)
—Will Hobbs. (p. 1932)
—Yemen. (p. 1970)
Marcovitz, Hal, jt. auth. see ABDO Publishing Company Staff.
Marcovitz, Hal, jt. auth. see Foster, Brett.
marcovitz, hal, jt. auth. see Marcovitz, Hal.
Marcovitz, Hal & Ferry, Joseph. American Flag. (p. 60)
Marcovitz, Hal & Jimerson, Maxine Newman. Brain Trauma. (p. 222)
Marcovitz, Hal & marcovitz, hal. 1960s: Part of the Understanding American History Series. (p. 2002)
Marcovitz, Hal & Sheen, Barbara. Personality Disorders. (p. 1344)
Marcovitz, Hal & Snyder, Gail. Guys' Guide to Anger. (p. 733)
—Guys' Guide to Jealousy. (p. 733)
—Guys' Guide to Loneliness. (p. 733)
Marcovitz, Harold. Privacy Rights & the Patriot Act. (p. 1407)
Marcucci, Vince. Tutti Frutti. St Anthony, Gus, illus. (p. 1799)
Marcum, Lindsay A. God's Little Lydia Lu. (p. 691)
Marcus, Amy. Exploring Costa Rica with the Five Themes of Geography. (p. 551)
—Exploring Puerto Rico with the Five Themes of Geography. (p. 553)
—Exploring the Dominican Republic with the Five Themes of Geography. (p. 553)
Marcus, Barry David, jt. auth. see Voigt, Cynthia.
Marcus, Bernard. Malaria, Second Edition. (p. 1083)
Marcus, Cindy. Ultimate Young Actor's Guide: Getting the Role & Making It Shine. (p. 1810)
Marcus, Eric. Pessimisms: Famous (And Not So Famous) Observations, Quotations, Thoughts, & Ruminations on What to Expect When You're Expecting the Worst. (p. 1345)
Marcus, Hal, creator. Poker 6-7-8 Hold'Em Strategy Cards (p. 1378)
Marcus, Kimberly. Exposed. (p. 554)
Marcus, Leonard S. Golden Legacy: How Golden Books Won Children's Hearts, Changed Publishing Forever, & Became an American Icon along the Way. (p. 695)
—Randolph Caldecott: The Man Who Could Not Stop Drawing. Caldecott, Randolph, illus. (p. 1438)
—Side by Side: Five Favorite Picture-Book Teams Go to Work. (p. 1573)
—Ways of Telling: Conversations on the Art of the Picture Book. (p. 1865)
Marcus, Leonard S., jt. auth. see Schwartz, Amy.
Marcus, Leonard S., ed. Funny Business: Conversations with Writers of Comedy. (p. 649)
Marcus, Marcus. Bella Umbrella. (p. 162)
—Tiger & the Turtle. (p. 1748)
—Tigre y la Tortuga. (p. 1749)
Marcus, Mary Brophy. Sleep Disorders. (p. 1588)

Marcus, Mary J. Digger. (p. 438)
Marcus, Ms. Elena N. Devon: The Wild Adventures of Devon & Friends. (p. 432)
Marcus, Richard. What Will Happen in Eragon IV: Who Lives, Who Dies, Who Becomes the Third Dragon Rider & How Will the Inheritance Cycle Finally End? (p. 1895)
Marcuse, Aida E., tr. see Brown, Margaret Wise.
Marcuse, Aida E., tr. see Williams, Vera B.
Marcy Wirth's Second Grade Class, compiled by. Journey to Madagascar. (p. 929)
Mardani, Parisa. Nathan Sees a Monster But... . (p. 1231)
Marden, Kathleen & Stoner, Denise. Making Contact: Alien Abduction Case Studies (p. 1081)
Marder, Alan, illus. see Brutocao, W. J.
Marder, Larry. Beanworld: Tales of the Beanworld. Schutz, Diana, ed. (p. 150)
Marderosian, Mark, illus. see Herman, Gail.
Mardinly, Berdan. Fresh Tarhana Soup: Story in English & in Turkish. (p. 636)
—Fresh Tarhana Soup - English. Mardinly, Berdan, illus. (p. 636)
Mardon, John, illus. see Jennings, Sharon.
Mare, Walter de La. Three Mulla-Mulgars (the Three Royal Monkeys) Lathrop, Dorothy P., illus. (p. 1743)
Mare, Walter de la, see de la Mare, Walter.
Marek, Catherine. Luke's 1st Haircut. Mitchell, Hazel, illus. (p. 1064)
—Sara's 1st Haircut Mitchell, Hazel, illus. (p. 1514)
Marek, Claudia Craig, jt. auth. see St. Amand, R. Paul.
Marek, Hillary. smart ass guide to ridiculous Questions. (p. 1592)
Marek, Jane, illus. see Moreau, Chris.
Marek, Susan. Children's Guide to Chakras. (p. 303)
Maren, Julie, illus. see Aston, Dianna Hutts.
Maren, Julie, illus. see Chambers, Veronica.
Maresca, Beth Anne. Megan Owlet. (p. 1124)
Maresca, Wendi S. Alphabet Silly Time. (p. 50)
Marfa, Isabelle. Land & Resources of Texas: Shaping the Growth of the State. (p. 973)
Marfleet, Philip. Refugees in a Global Era. (p. 1456)
Margallo, Ramon. MANGER, the CROSS, & the EMPTY TOMB Christian Apologetics for Young Readers: A Short Story. (p. 1087)
Margaret. Curious George im Schokolade. (p. 393)
—Curious George und der Lastwa. (p. 393)
—Curious George und die Hundelb. (p. 393)
Margaret, jt. auth. see Rey, H. A.
Margaret, Amy. Franklin D. Roosevelt Library & Museum. (p. 630)
—George Bush Presidential Library. (p. 663)
—Gerald R. Ford Library & Museum. (p. 666)
—Halloween. (p. 737)
—Jimmy Carter Library & Museum. (p. 918)
—John F. Kennedy Library & Museum. (p. 921)
—Mission San Buenaventura. (p. 1153)
—Mission San Jose de Guadalupe. (p. 1153)
—Mission Santa Barbara. (p. 1153)
—Mission Santa Clara de Asis. (p. 1153)
—Presidents' Day. (p. 1397)
—Ronald Reagan Presidential Library. (p. 1487)
—Venus. (p. 1836)
Margaret, Amy & Nuñes, Sofia. Discovering Mission Santa Clara de Asís. (p. 449)
Margaret Bruce Clarke. Hunter's Marjory: A Story for Girls. (p. 828)
Margaret I. Pascuzzo. Anton Finds a Treasure. Bicking, Judith, illus. (p. 90)
Margaret Penrose. Dorothy Dale's Queer Holidays. (p. 471)
Margaret, R. Mead, jt. auth. see Miller, Reagan.
Margaret Scollan. Gods of Rome: Dei Romae. (p. 691)
Margaret, Tomlinson. Rescued Paws. (p. 1462)
Margaritas, Aki. Investigations in Geometry Using Cabri(r) Jr. & the Graphing Calculator. (p. 885)
Margeson, John, illus. see McEwan, Jamie.
Margeson, John, illus. see Rosen, Michael J.
Margeson, Susan & Dorling Kindersley Publishing Staff. Viking. (p. 1842)
Margiotta, Kristen, illus. see Castro, Adam-Troy.
Margles, Samantha. Earth's Solar System. (p. 498)
—Star Wars: Science Fair Book. (p. 1641)
—Star Wars: Science Fair Book. Scholastic, Inc. Staff, illus. (p. 1642)
Margolies, John & Orcutt, Georgia. Blue Ribbon USA: Prizewinning Recipes from State & County Fairs. (p. 203)
Margolin, Indrani, jt. auth. see Swartz, Larry.
Margolin, Phillip, jt. auth. see Silverstein, Shel.
Margolin, Phillip & Rome, Ami Margolin. Vanishing Acts. (p. 1833)
Margolis, Al, illus. see Dultz, Dorothy.
Margolis, Al, illus. see Faircloth, M. L.
Margolis, Al, illus. see Fontaine, Renee.
Margolis, Al, illus. see Ladin, Marc J.
Margolis, Al, illus. see Mastrud, Karen.
Margolis, Al, illus. see Rhode, Paul.
Margolis, Al, illus. see Rodhe, Paul & Wallas Reidy, Sarah.
Margolis, Al, illus. see Sanchez, Lorrie Christel & Blank, Carol.
Margolis, Al, illus. see Tait, Barbara.
Margolis, Al, illus. see Thorpe, Rochelle O'Neal.
Margolis, Alysia. Sit! Stay! Sign! Miller, Paton, illus. (p. 1582)
Margolis, Amy. Butterflies & Magical Wings (p. 247)
Margolis, Ida R., jt. auth. see Brazina, Rhonda.
Margolis, Leslie. Boys Are Dogs. (p. 220)
—Everybody Bugs Out. (p. 543)
—Fix. (p. 601)
—Girls Acting Catty. (p. 679)
—Girl's Best Friend. (p. 679)
—If I Were You. (p. 853)
—Monkey Business. (p. 1165)
—One Tough Chick. (p. 1297)
—Secrets at the Chocolate Mansion. (p. 1544)
—Vanishing Acts. (p. 1833)
Margolis, Lois, illus. see Spinelli, Jami.
Margot. Best Good Night Present Ever. (p. 170)
Marguerita, Ann. Fannie Annie & Her Little White Shoes. (p. 571)
Margulies, Nancy & Valenza, Christine. Visual Thinking: Tools for Mapping Your Ideas (p. 1846)
Margulies, Paul. What Julianna Could See. Zonneveld, Famke, illus. (p. 1891)
Margulies, Philip. Al-Qaeda: Osama Bin Laden's Army of Terrorists. (p. 32)
—Colony of North Carolina. (p. 342)
—Creutzfeldt-Jakob Disease. (p. 382)
—Deparatment of Energy. (p. 427)
—Department of Energy. (p. 427)
—Diphtheria. (p. 445)
—Down Syndrome. (p. 474)
—Everything You Need to Know about Rheumatic Fever. (p. 546)
—Exxon Valdez Oil Spill: When Disaster Strikes! (p. 557)
—Nuclear Nonproliferation. (p. 1270)
—Primary Source History of the Colony of North Carolina. (p. 1400)
—Strategic Defense Systems of the Future. (p. 1665)
Margulies, Philip, ed. Creation of Israel. (p. 379)
—Roaring Twenties. (p. 1478)
Margulies, Phillip. Al Qaeda: Osama bin Laden's Army of Terrorists. (p. 32)
—Creutzfeldt-Jakob Disease. (p. 382)
—Department of Energy. (p. 427)
—Diptheria. (p. 445)
—Down Syndrome. (p. 474)
—Exxon Valdez Oil Spill. (p. 557)
—Primary Source History of the Colony of North Carolina. (p. 1400)
—Strategic Defense Systems of the Future. (p. 1666)
—Timeline of the Continental Army. (p. 1754)
Margulies, Sheldon. Fascinating Body: How It Works. (p. 575)
Mari, Enzo, jt. auth. see Mari, Iela.
Mari, Ian Robert, photos by see Ratto, Linda Lee.
Mari, Iela & Mari, Enzo. Apple & the Butterfly. (p. 92)
Maria, jt. auth. see Scaglione, Dapos.
Maria, Miss Yvonne. Beautiful Black Mermaids of the Bayou (p. 153)
Maria Muirhead. Smoking = Problems: Flora-Lee's Journal. (p. 1595)
Maria, Nony & Kiddies. Old Fashioned Stories: South park little world of Adventures. (p. 1283)
María, Plaza José, jt. auth. see Plaza, José María.
Mariam, Sahra Mire - Umm. I Love Making Mummy Happy. (p. 842)
Marianne, Berkes. Over in the Jungle: A Rainforest Rhyme. Jeanette, Canyon, illus. (p. 1313)
Mariants, tr. see Terbay, Susan Handle.
Marichal, Poli, illus. see Lazaro, Georgina.
Mariconda, Barbara. Lucy at Sea. (p. 1063)
—Sort It Out! Rogers, Sherry, illus. (p. 1614)
—Voyage of Lucy P. Simmons. (p. 1850)
—Voyage of Lucy P. Simmons - The Emerald Shore. (p. 1850)
—¡Clasificalo! Rogers, Sherry, illus. (p. 327)
Marie, Anna. Hexon. (p. 774)
Marie, Anne, illus. see Ryan, Ann Marie.
Marie, Barbara. Snowy & Felix Find Christmas. (p. 1601)
Marie, Berri, illus. see Shadrick, Crystal Star.
Marie, Brandi. Lily White & the Necklace of Doom (p. 1018)
Marie, Carissa. Lonely Puppy. (p. 1046)
Marie, Cherry. President Eats Vegetables & So Do I! (p. 1397)
Marie, Christian. Little Beavers. (p. 1024)
—Little Dogs. (p. 1027)
—Little Giraffes. Lantier, Patricia, tr. from FRE. (p. 1028)
—Little Ladybugs. (p. 1030)
—Little Sheep. (p. 1036)
—Mariquita. (p. 1094)
—pequena Jirafa. (p. 1340)
Marie, Christina. Where Would I Live? (p. 1910)
Marie, Cynthia. Sister Aggie Goes Surfing. (p. 1581)
Marie, Dani. Tale of Prince George. (p. 1700)
Marie, E. Porcupine Connection: The Story of a Young Girl's Journey from Tragedy to Healing, with the Help of Her Forest Friends. (p. 1386)
Marie, J. Sophie, NO! Activity Book. (p. 1613)
Marie, Jacqueline. Felix the Wannabe Firefly. (p. 581)
Marie, Jessica. Keeping Broken Promises (p. 947)
Marie, Jill Jana. Anna Lee Enis Bee. (p. 85)
—Balloon Blessing. Zamboni, David, illus. (p. 135)
—Elsa Magda Val My Imaginary Pal. (p. 516)
—Zoo Rendezvous. Zamboni, David, illus. (p. 1989)
Marie, June. Harry the Plum Island Fisherman. (p. 751)
Marie, K. Beulah the Lunchroom Bully. Cook, Monique, illus. (p. 173)
Marie, Leann. Ghost of Oberlin. (p. 671)
Marie, Lynne. Hedgehog Goes to Kindergarten. Kennedy, Anne, illus. (p. 761)
Marie, Madeline, jt. auth. see Anton, Robert.
Marie, Paula Braxton, illus. see Keyes, Eric, 3rd, et al.
Marie, Sheryl. Rain-Drop & Peek-a-Boo: A Very Bunny Documentary. (p. 1434)
Marie, Tamara. Adventures of Madison. (p. 20)
Marie, Terri, jt. auth. see Marie, Terri.
Marie, Terri & Marie, Terri. Shack, Merry & a Cat Named Cha-Moan. (p. 1556)
Marie, Tina. Isabella Learns Her Manners. (p. 891)
—Isabella Learns Responsibility. (p. 891)
—Isabella Learns the Value of Money. (p. 891)
—Isabella Learns to Be Thankful. (p. 891)
—Isabella Learns to Share. (p. 891)
—Raccoon Round-Up at the Diamond R Ranch. (p. 1430)
Marie-France, Marcie. Bilingual Beginners: English-French Kit (p. 186)
—Bilingual Kids Beginners - English-French: Ready-to-Use Reproducible Worksheets & Exercises. Content-Based Units Making Language Acquisition Easy Fun. (p. 186)
Marie-France, Marcie & Lebuis, Peter. Additions Chansons et Activités (p. 12)
—Divisions Chansons et Activités (p. 455)
—Multiplications Chansons et Activités (p. 1190)
—Soustractions Chansons et Activités (p. 1616)
Marien, Donna. Waiting at the Bay: A Young Woman's Reflections on Journeys in the Sea of Life. (p. 1852)
Marier, Chuck, illus. see Gunn, Barbara.
Marii, Danila. My Tree & Me: A Journey Beyond the Rainbow. (p. 1220)
Mari?I?, ?Uro. How Children Grow. (p. 805)
Marika. Mary's Garden. (p. 1101)
Marillier, Juliet. Caller. (p. 254)
—Cybele's Secret. (p. 396)
—Raven Flight: A Shadowfell Novel. (p. 1441)
—Raven Flight. (p. 1441)
—Shadowfell. (p. 1558)
—Wildwood Dancing. (p. 1932)
Marimo, Ragawa, jt. auth. see Ragawa, Marimo.
Marin, Cheech. Captain Cheech. Ramirez, Orlando L., illus. (p. 263)
—Cheech the School Bus Driver. Ramirez, Orlando L., illus. (p. 295)
—Cheech y el Autobus Fantasma. Fabiancic, Miriam, tr. (p. 295)
Marin, Dale Diane. Friends Forever: A Rachel Beth Tale Borstel, Ian von, illus. (p. 638)
—Rachel Beth & the Day the Towers Came Down Marin, Liz, illus. (p. 1431)
Marin, Danny, illus. see Millsaps, Grace & Murphy, Ryan.
Marin, Doris Diana. Two Places at a Time. (p. 1804)
Marín, Guadalupe Rivera. My Papá Diego & Me (Mi Papa Diego y Yo) Memories of My Father & His Art (Recuerdos de Mi Padre y Su Arte) Rivera, Diego, illus. (p. 1216)
Marin, Liz, illus. see Marin, Dale Diane.
Marín, Manuel, illus. see Luján, Jorge, et al.
Marin Martinez, Juan M., ed. see Bécquer, Gustavo Adolpho.
Marin Martinez, Juan Maria, ed. Lazarillo de Tormes. (p. 981)
Marin, Mary Rodriguez, illus. see Baranda, Maria.
Marin, Victoria. Aiden's Waltz. (p. 30)
Marina, Budhos. Ask Me No Questions. (p. 106)
Marina J. Royer. Kitten Velvetliz Volume I the Fish & Veggies Eater - Economical Guide for Bringing up Your First Kitten. (p. 962)
Marinaro, Stacy. Annabelle & the Meteor. (p. 85)
—Carter Finds a Tiger. (p. 272)
—Carter Meets Ella the Elephant. (p. 272)
—Carter the Acorn Collecting Cutie. (p. 272)
—Cat who rules the Star Mice. (p. 278)
—If I Became a U. S. Marine. (p. 852)
—Mr. Robin's Ridiculous Birdhouse. (p. 1186)
—Nap Time. (p. 1229)
—Treasure Monkey. (p. 1782)
—Walrus King. (p. 1855)
Marine Debris Program (U.S.), Office of Response and Restoration, ed. Understanding Marine Debris: Games & Activities for Kids of All Ages: Marine Debris 101: Games & Activities for Kids of All Ages: Marine Debris 101. (p. 1815)
Marineau, Michele. Lean Mean Machines Ouriou, Susan, tr. from FRE. (p. 982)
—Road to Chlifa Ouriou, Susan, tr. (p. 1477)
Marinelli, Deborah A. Assassination of Abraham Lincoln. (p. 107)
Marinelli, Debra A. Assassination of Abraham Lincoln. (p. 107)
Marinello, Gina M. Simply Maggie M Manatee. (p. 1578)
Mariner, Tom, ed. Land. (p. 973)
Maring, Therese, ed. Top-Secret Code Book: Tricky, Fun Codes for You & Your Friends. Lukatz, Casey, illus. (p. 1769)
Marín-Guzman, Roberto & Zéraoui, Zidane. Arab Immigration in Mexico in the Nineteenth & Twentieth Centuries: Assimilation & Arab Heritage. (p. 94)
Marini, Enrico, illus. see Dufaux, Jean.
Marini, Enrico, jt. auth. see Desberg, Stephen.
Marini, Enrico & Dufaux, Jean. Rapaces (p. 1439)
Marini, Matt. Analytics: Sports Stats & More Ferrer, Al, ed. (p. 67)
Marini, Matthew. Special Forces (p. 1623)
Mariniello, Cecco, illus. see Suen, Anastasia.
Marino, Andy. Door. (p. 470)
—Uncrashable Dakota. (p. 1813)
Marino, Angie. Lemurs! Greene's 29 after school art students, K., illus. (p. 991)
Marino, Gianna. Following Papa's Song. (p. 612)
—Meet Me at the Moon. (p. 1121)
—Night Animals. Marino, Gianna, illus. (p. 1252)
—Too Tall Houses. (p. 1767)
Marino, Illustrator, Natalie, Natalie, illus. see Singer, Maurene, et al.
Marino, Jane. Babies in the Library! (p. 124)
Marino, Joe. Laugh until You Cry. (p. 980)
Marino, Kellie A. Marcella's Angel. (p. 1091)
Marino, Lia. Amelia & Gabby: More Than Just Sisters. Rankin, Shelly, illus. (p. 57)
Marino, Mary N. A, B, See It! (p. 1)
Marino, Michael. Magi Adventure. (p. 1071)
Marino, Michael F., illus. see Olson, Nancy.
Marino, Nan. Hiding Out at the Pancake Palace. (p. 777)
—Neil Armstrong Is My Uncle & Other Lies Muscle Man McGinty Told Me. (p. 1240)
Marino, Natalie, illus. see Arden, Lynne.
Marino, Natalie, illus. see Singer, Maurene, et al.
Marino, Peter. Dough Boy. (p. 473)
—Magic & Misery. (p. 1071)
Mariño, Ricardo. Lo Unico del Mundo. (p. 1044)
Marino, Rick. I Love You Very Muchly... (p. 844)
Marinov, Marin, illus. see Krull, Kathleen.
Marinsky, Jane. Just Perfect. (p. 939)
Marinsky, Jane, illus. see Sharpe, Leah Marinsky.
Mario. Arriving to Planet Noah. (p. 101)
Mariolle, Mathieu. Changing Moon. (p. 290)
—Changing Moon. MiniKim et al, illus. (p. 290)
—Even for A Dreamer Like Me. (p. 541)
—Even for a Dreamer Like Me. MiniKim et al, illus. (p. 541)
—Ferrets & Ferreting Out. MiniKim et al, illus. (p. 582)
—Ferrets & Ferreting Out. Buffiere, Mélanie & Lajic, Maïté, illus. (p. 582)
—Nola's Worlds MiniKim et al, illus. (p. 1263)
marion, designs, illus. see Crews, G.
Marion, Dominique & Shakespeare, William. Romeo & Juliet. Pelsuo, Martina, illus. (p. 1486)
Marion, L. K. Summer Holiday with Funny Bunny. (p. 1674)
Marion, Lucile. Sprinkles of Stardust. (p. 1635)
Marion Nash Jackie Lowe Staff & Lowe, Jackie. Spirals Series - Activities for Home Books (p. 1628)
Marion, Nino. Math for Welders: Answer Key. (p. 1106)
Mariotte, Jeff. Dark Vengeance Vol. 1: Summer, Fall. (p. 408)
—Dark Vengeance Vol. 2: Winter, Spring. (p. 408)
—Fall. (p. 566)
—Mirror Image. (p. 1149)
Mariotti, Celine Rose. Olivia Macallister, Who Are You? A Ghost Mystery Set in Maine. Tango-Schurmann, Ann, illus. (p. 1286)
Mariotti, Steve. Entrepreneurship: How to Start & Operate a Small Business. (p. 531)
—How to Start & Operate a Small Business: Exam View Text Bank - CD. (p. 821)
Mariposa Publishing Inc. Staff. Me Gusta el Invierno! (p. 1116)
Maris, Ron. Pwy Sy 'na? (p. 1421)
Mariscal, Blanca Lopez de, see de Mariscal, Blanca Lopez.
Mariscal, Javier, illus. see Summers, Kim.
Mariscal, Libia Barajas. Agente Oportuno: Cuando la Penicilina Entra en Accion. Mateo, Rosario, illus. (p. 29)
Mariscal, Libia Barajas, jt. auth. see Barajas Mariscal, Libia E.
Mariscal, Libia E. Barajas. Circulos y Calendarios. Bautista, Cisar Evangelis, illus. (p. 322)
Mariscal Vacas, Elisa & MARISCALACAS, ELISA, V. Tontos! Mariscal Vacas, Elisa, illus. (p. 1765)
MARISCALACAS, ELISA, V, jt. auth. see Mariscal Vacas, Elisa.
Maristella. One Step to Freedom. (p. 1297)
Maritie, illus. see Leone, Dee.
Marix Evans, Amina, tr. see Rooyackers, Paul.
Mariz, Rae. Unidentified. (p. 1818)
Marjama-Lyons, Jill, jt. auth. see Shomon, Mary J.
Marjoribanks, Karen, illus. see Thiel, Annie.
Marjorie, as told by. Flower Unfolds: Inspirational Teachings in Verse from Kwan Yin, Bodhisattva of Mercy & Compassion. (p. 607)
Marjorie, Leggitt, illus. see Graf, Mike.
Mark, Crilley. Brody's Ghost (p. 230)
Mark, Jan. Eyes Wide Open. (p. 558)
—Jetblack Sunrise: Poems about War & Conflict. (p. 916)
—Museum Book: A Guide to Strange & Wonderful Collections. Holland, Richard, illus. (p. 1192)
Mark, Jessica & Mark, Rebecca. Sky the Fly Explores Philadelphia. (p. 1587)
Mark, Juliet Y. Queendom of Evlantis. (p. 1425)
Mark R Borene, jt. auth. see Mark R. Borene, R. Borene.
Mark R. Borene, R. Borene & Mark R Borene. Welcome to the Farm: Book 2 of Welcome to the World. (p. 1874)
—Welcome to the Sky. (p. 1874)
Mark, Rebecca, ed. see Vaughan, Robert.
Mark, Rebecca, jt. auth. see Mark, Jessica.
Mark, Rebecca & Vaughan, Rob. Greenwood Encyclopedia of American Regional Cultures Piper, Paul, ed. (p. 723)
Mark, Steve, illus. see Espeland, Pamela & Verdick, Elizabeth.
Mark, Steve, illus. see Verdick, Elizabeth.
Mark Twain Media Staff, jt. auth. see Barden, Cindy.
Mark, Yudel. Jewish Pope: A Yiddish Tale. Goodman, Ruth Fisher, tr. from YID. (p. 917)
Markandaya, Kamala. Nectar in a Sieve. (p. 1239)
Markarian, Margie. Hilary Duff: Life in the Spotlight. (p. 779)
—Who Cleans Dinosaur Bones? Working at a Museum. (p. 1915)
—Who Scoops Elephant Poo? Working at a Zoo. (p. 1917)
Markarian, Marianne. Mariam's Easter Parade. Wasielewski, Margaret, illus. (p. 1093)
—Pesky Bird Wasielewski, Margaret M., illus. (p. 1345)
Markegard, Blake. Alberto Del Rio. (p. 35)
—John Cena. (p. 921)
—Miz. (p. 1156)
—Rey Mysterio. (p. 1467)
—Santino Marella. (p. 1513)
—Sheamus. (p. 1564)
—Zack Ryder. (p. 1984)
Markel, Marilyn, jt. auth. see Alarid, Carilyn.
Markel, Michelle. Brave Girl: Clara & the Shirtwaist Makers' Strike of 1909. Sweet, Melissa, illus. (p. 223)
—Dream Town. Reese, Rick, illus. (p. 484)
—Hillary Clinton. Pham, LeUyen, illus. (p. 779)
—Shark That Taught Me English/El Tiburon Que Me Enseno Ingles. Kim, Bo Young, illus. (p. 1562)
—Shark That Taught Me English/El Tiburon Que Me Enseno Ingles. Guerrero, Ernesto, tr. (p. 1562)
—Tyrannosaurus Math. Cushman, Doug, illus. (p. 1805)
Markel, Michelle & Rousseau, Henri. Fantastic Jungles of Henri Rousseau. Hall, Amanda, illus. (p. 571)
Markel, Rita J. Fall of the Roman Empire. (p. 566)
—Fidel Castro's Cuba. (p. 583)
—Guatemala in Pictures. (p. 728)
—Your Travel Guide to Ancient Rome. (p. 1981)
Markel, Rita J. & Poole, Rebecca. Jimi Hendrix. (p. 918)
Markell, Denis. Click Here to Start (A Novel) (p. 332)
—Hush, Little Monster. Iwai, Melissa, illus. (p. 830)
Markels, Bobby. How to Be a Human Bean. Leek, Kenny, illus. (p. 814)
Marken, Jon, ed. see Wood, Francis Eugene.
Marken, Jon, ed. see Wood, Francis Eusene.
Marker, Sherry. Plains Indian Wars. (p. 1366)
Markert, Jenny. Tigers. (p. 1749)
Markes, jt. auth. see Markes, Julie.
Markes, Julie. Shhhhh! Everybody's Sleeping. Parkins, David, illus. (p. 1566)
—Thanks for Thanksgiving. Barrette, Doris, illus. (p. 1725)
—Where's the Poop? Hartung, Susan Kathleen, illus. (p. 1911)
Markes, Julie & Markes. Good Thing You're Not an Octopus! Smith, Maggie, illus. (p. 700)
Markette, Paul Scott. I'm with Poppy!! Lee, Joe, illus. (p. 860)

Markey, Andrew C. Afterlife Phenomenon. (p. 28)
Markey, Kevin. Rainmaker. (p. 1436)
—Slumpbuster. Fitzgerald, Royce, illus. (p. 1591)
—Wall Ball. (p. 1854)
—Wing Ding. (p. 1936)
Markey, Neil. Woof! Spremulli, Pam, illus. (p. 1950)
Markey, Robert. Cool! Kids Making Mosaics in Brazil: Legal! Crianças Fazendo Mosaics No Brasil. Markey, Robert & Orfirer, Julie, eds. (p. 363)
Markham, E. A. Lambchops with Sally Goodman: The Selected Poems of Paul St. Vincent & Sally Goodman. (p. 972)
Markle, Sandra. Animal Heroes: True Rescue Stories. (p. 78)
—Animal Prey. (p. 79)
—Animal Scavengers (p. 79)
—Animales Carroneros; Animal Scavengers: Complete Set. (p. 80)
—Animales Carroneros; Animal Scavengers: Classroom Set. (p. 80)
—Animales Carroñeros (Animal Scavengers) Translations.com Staff, tr. (p. 80)
—Arachnid World (p. 94)
—Army Ants. (p. 100)
—Bad Burns. (p. 131)
—Bats: Biggest! Littlest! (p. 145)
—Battered Brains. (p. 145)
—Black Widows: Deadly Biters. (p. 197)
—Butterfly Tree Wu, Leslie, illus. (p. 248)
—Case of the Vanishing Golden Frogs. (p. 275)
—Case of the Vanishing Honeybees: A Scientific Mystery. (p. 275)
—Case of the Vanishing Little Brown Bats: A Scientific Mystery. (p. 275)
—Chocolate: A Sweet History. Harper, Charise Mericle, illus. (p. 309)
—Crab Spiders: Phantom Hunters. (p. 375)
—Crocodiles. (p. 384)
—Demonios de Tasmania. Translations.com Staff, tr. from ENG. (p. 426)
—Diving Beetles. (p. 454)
—Eagles. (p. 492)
—Family Dam. Hocking, Deborah, illus. (p. 568)
—Family Pack. Marks, Alan, illus. (p. 568)
—Faulty Hearts: True Survival Stories. (p. 577)
—Finding Home. Marks, Alan, illus. (p. 588)
—Fishing Spiders: Water Ninjas. (p. 599)
—Fledglings. (p. 603)
—Foxes. (p. 626)
—Great Monkey Rescue: Saving the Golden Lion Tamarins. (p. 717)
—Great White Sharks. (p. 719)
—Grizzly Bears. (p. 724)
—Harvestmen: Secret Operatives. (p. 752)
—Hip-Pocket Papa. Marks, Alan, illus. (p. 780)
—Hornets: Incredible Insect Architects. (p. 798)
—Hornets. (p. 798)
—How Many Baby Pandas? (p. 811)
—How Many Baby Pandas? / Scholastic Book Fair Edition. (p. 811)
—Hyenas. (p. 831)
—Insect World: Complete Library. (p. 875)
—Insect World: Classroom Library. (p. 875)
—Insects: Biggest! Littlest! Pollard, Simon, photos by. (p. 875)
—Jackals. (p. 903)
—Jumping Spiders: Gold-Medal Stalkers. (p. 934)
—Killer Whales. (p. 956)
—Las Hormigas Legionaria; Army Ants. (p. 976)
—Las Hormigas Legionarias. Translations.com Staff, tr. (p. 976)
—Leopard Seals. (p. 993)
—Leukemia. (p. 1003)
—Lobos. Translations.com Staff, tr. from ENG. (p. 1044)
—Locusts: Insects on the Move. (p. 1045)
—Long, Long Journey: The Godwit's Amazing Migration. Posada, Mia, illus. (p. 1047)
—Los Pulpos. Translations.com Staff, tr. from ENG. (p. 1054)
—Los Pulpos (Octopuses) (p. 1054)
—Lost Sight. (p. 1056)
—Luna Moths: Masters of Change. (p. 1065)
—Luna Moths. (p. 1065)
—Mites: Master Sneaks. (p. 1156)
—Mosquitoes. (p. 1176)
—Mosquitoes: Tiny Insect Troublemakers. (p. 1177)
—Mother's Journey. Marks, Alan, illus. (p. 1178)
—Mother's Journey. Marks, Alan, illus. (p. 1179)
—Mountain Lions. (p. 1181)
—Musk Oxen. (p. 1194)
—Octopuses. (p. 1278)
—Orb Weavers: Hungry Spinners. (p. 1302)
—Outside & Inside Dinosaurs. (p. 1313)
—Outside & Inside Mummies. (p. 1313)
—Outside & Inside Rats & Mice. (p. 1313)
—Owls. (p. 1315)
—Perritos de Las Praderas. Translations.com Staff, tr. from ENG. (p. 1343)
—Polar Bears. (p. 1379)
—Porcupines. (p. 1386)
—Powerful Medicine (p. 1390)
—Prairie Dogs. (p. 1392)
—Praying Mantises: Hungry Insect Heroes. (p. 1393)
—Praying Mantises. (p. 1393)
—Pulpos (Octopuses) Translations.com Staff, tr. (p. 1416)
—Race the Wild Wind: A Story of the Sable Island Horses. Johnson, Layne, illus. (p. 1431)
—Rattlesnakes. (p. 1440)
—Rescues! (p. 1462)
—Scorpions: Armored Stingers. (p. 1530)
—Sharks: Biggest! Littlest! Perrine, Doug, illus. (p. 1562)
—Sharks: Biggest! Littlest! Perrine, Doug, photos by. (p. 1562)
—Shattered Bones. (p. 1563)
—Skunks. (p. 1586)
—Snakes: Biggest! Littlest! McDonald, Joe, photos by. (p. 1596)
—Sneaky, Spinning Baby Spiders. (p. 1597)
—Snow School. Marks, Alan, illus. (p. 1599)
—Spiders: Biggest! Littlest! Pollard, Simon, photos by. (p. 1627)
—Tarantulas: Super-Sized Predators. (p. 1706)
—Tasmanian Devils. (p. 1707)
—Termites: Hardworking Insect Families. (p. 1721)
—Termites. (p. 1721)
—Thirsty, Thirsty Elephants. Vanden Broeck, Fabricio, illus. (p. 1734)
—Ticks: Dangerous Hitchhikers. (p. 1747)
—Toad Weather Gonzalez, Thomas, illus. (p. 1760)
—Vultures. (p. 1851)
—Waiting for Ice. Marks, Alan, illus. (p. 1852)
—What If You Had Animal Feet? McWilliam, Howard, illus. (p. 1887)
—What If You Had Animal Teeth? (p. 1887)
—What If You Had Animal Teeth? McWilliam, Howard, illus. (p. 1887)
—Wind Scorpions: Killer Jaws. (p. 1935)
—Wolf Spiders: Mothers on Guard. (p. 1944)
—Wolverines. (p. 1944)
—Wolves. (p. 1945)
—Zebras. (p. 1985)
—Zorrillos. Translations.com Staff, tr. from ENG. (p. 1990)
Markle, Sandra, jt. auth. see Chronicle Books Staff.
Markle, Sandra & Johnson, Layne. Race the Wild Wind: A Story of the Sable Island Horses. (p. 1431)
Markle, Sandra & Markle, William. Gone Forever: An Alphabet of Extinct Animals. Davalos, Felipe, illus. (p. 697)
Markle, William, jt. auth. see Markle, Sandra.
Marklew, Gilly, illus. see Waters, Fiona.
Marko, Cyndi. Birdy Snatchers. (p. 192)
—Bok! Bok! Boom! (p. 208)
—Bok! Bok! Boom! Marko, Cyndi, illus. (p. 208)
—Heroes on the Side. (p. 773)
—Heroes on the Side. Marko, Cyndi, illus. (p. 773)
—Kung Pow Chicken #1: Let's Get Cracking! (a Branches Book) Marko, Cyndi, illus. (p. 968)
—Kung Pow Chicken #2: Bok! Bok! Boom! (a Branches Book) Marko, Cyndi, illus. (p. 968)
—Kung Pow Chicken #3: the Birdy Snatchers (a Branches Book) Marko, Cyndi, illus. (p. 968)
—Kung Pow Chicken #3: the Birdy Snatchers (a Branches Book) - Library Edition. (p. 968)
—Kung Pow Chicken #4: Heroes on the Side (a Branches Book) Marko, Cyndi, illus. (p. 968)
—Let's Get Cracking! Marko, Cyndi, illus. (p. 996)
Marko, Eve. Clara Barton & the American Red Cross. Marcos, Pablo, illus. (p. 326)
Markova, Dawna. Como Desarrollar la Inteligencia de Sus Hijos. (p. 350)
Markovics, Joyce. Blizzard. (p. 199)
—Earthquake. (p. 497)
—French Bulldog: The Frenchie. (p. 635)
—Honey Bee's Hive: A Thriving City. (p. 794)
—Marte: Rocas y Polvo Rojos. (p. 1097)
—Measure It! (p. 1117)
—My Eyes Are Big & Red (Tree Frog) (p. 1202)
—My Legs Are Long & Strong (Ostrich) (p. 1211)
—My Nose Is Long & Fuzzy (Anteater) (p. 1216)
—My Skin Is Gray & Wrinkly (Walrus) (p. 1219)
—My Tail Is Long & Striped (Lemur) (p. 1219)
—Neptuno: Muy, Muy Lejos. (p. 1241)
—Papillon: Monsieur Butterfly. (p. 1323)
—Play with Shapes! (p. 1372)
—Sled Dogs. (p. 1588)
—Therapy Dogs. (p. 1729)
—Tierra: QuÉ Bien Se EstÁ en Casa. (p. 1748)
—Tsunami. (p. 1795)
Markovics, Joyce L. Angora Rabbit. (p. 75)
—Bat's Cave: A Dark City. (p. 145)
—Blitzed by a Blizzard! (p. 199)
—Caribou: And Reindeer, Too. (p. 269)
—China. (p. 306)
—City Colors: From Taxis to Skyscrapers. (p. 323)
—Earth: No Place Like Home. (p. 495)
—Farm Colors: From Purple Plums to Pink Pigs. (p. 573)
—Food Colors: From Blueberries to Beets. (p. 613)
—Great White Shark. (p. 719)
—Hedgehog. (p. 761)
—India. (p. 870)
—Jaguarundi: Otter Cat. (p. 905)
—Las Mariposas Monarca. (p. 976)
—Las Ranas de la Madera. (p. 977)
—Little Brown Bats. (p. 1025)
—Los Colores de la Ciudad: De Los Taxis a Los Rascacielos. (p. 1053)
—Los Colores de la Granja: De Las Ciruelas Moradas a Los Cerdos Rosados. (p. 1053)
—Los Colores de Las Estaciones: Cómo Cambian. (p. 1053)
—Los Colores de Los Alimentos: De Los Arándanos a la Remolacha. (p. 1053)
—Los Pequeños Murciélagos Café. (p. 1054)
—Mars: Red Rocks & Dust. (p. 1096)
—Mi Cola Es Larga y Rayada. (p. 1132)
—Mi Nariz Es Larga y Peluda. (p. 1133)
—Mi Piel Es Gris y Arrugada. (p. 1133)
—MIS Ojos Son Grandes y Rojos. (p. 1150)
—MIS Patas Son Largas y Fuertes. (p. 1150)
—Monarch Butterflies. (p. 1163)
—Neptune: Far, Far Away. (p. 1241)
—Oak Tree. (p. 1274)
—Patterns in the Desert. (p. 1329)
—Patterns in the Jungle. (p. 1329)
—Persians: Long-Haired Friends. (p. 1344)
—Pufferfish. (p. 1415)
—Ringtail: Miner's Cat. (p. 1473)
—Salvador. (p. 1506)
—Seasons' Colors: How They Change. (p. 1538)
—Shih Tzu: Lion Dog. (p. 1566)
—Sunflower. (p. 1676)
—Tasmanian Devil: Nighttime Scavenger. (p. 1707)
—Terremoto. (p. 1721)
—Tiny Invaders! Deadly Microorganisms (p. 1756)
—Today's Coast Guard Heroes. (p. 1761)
—Tormenta de Nieve. (p. 1770)
—Tsunami. (p. 1795)
—Vietnam. (p. 1841)
—Warthog. (p. 1859)
—Weddell Seal: Fat & Happy. (p. 1870)
—Wolverine: Super Strong. (p. 1944)
—Wood Frogs. (p. 1949)
Markovics, Joyce L. & Pushies, Fred J. Today's Army Heroes. (p. 1761)
Markovitch, Evegeny, illus. see Schreiber, Elisheva.
Markowitz, Darryl. Call of the Tree: Book One in the Faithwalker Series. Bukhari, Mary, ed. (p. 254)
—Dead Forest: Book Three in the Faithwalker Series. (p. 416)
Markowitz, Krista. Mrs Tipperwillow's Afterlife Adventures. (p. 1187)
Markowitz, Siri. HELP with RAISING YOUR NURSERY or PRESCHOOL CHILDREN - 26 great ideas for parents & preschool Teachers. (p. 766)
Markowitz, Susan Meredith. Bitsy the Beaver & Bitsy el Castor: 6 English, 6 Spanish Adaptations. (p. 194)
—Great Green Forest & el gran bosque Verde: 6 English, 6 Spanish Adaptations. (p. 716)
—Maggie Makes Macaroni & Maggie hace Macarrones: 6 English, 6 Spanish Adaptations. (p. 1071)
Markowitz-Meredith, Susan. Environmentally Friendly World: Set Of 6. (p. 532)
—Frances & the Fairy Dressmaker: Set Of 6. (p. 627)
—Stump Hill: Set Of 6. (p. 1670)
—What Is Form? (p. 1889)
—What Is Line? (p. 1889)
—What Is Space? (p. 1890)
Markowsky, Judy Kellogg. Shelterwood: Discovering the Forest. Giebfried, Rosemary, illus. (p. 1565)
Markrich, Mike & Bourke, Bob. Hanauma Bay. Kanae, Billy, illus. (p. 740)
Marks, A. Easy Piano Tunes. (p. 500)
—Piano Tunes for Children. (p. 1354)
Marks, Aaron. Transportation: Then & Now. (p. 1779)
Marks, Alan. Christmas Carol. (p. 313)
—Little Mermaid. (p. 1031)
—Stories of Knights. (p. 1655)
—Story of Heidi. (p. 1658)
Marks, Alan, illus. see Dolby, Karen.
Marks, Alan, illus. see Duble, Kathleen Benner.
Marks, Alan, illus. see East, Helen & Maddern, Eric.
Marks, Alan, illus. see Falkner, John Meade.
Marks, Alan, illus. see Jones, Rob Lloyd.
Marks, Alan, illus. see Markle, Sandra.
Marks, Alan, illus. see Milbourne, Anna.
Marks, Alan, illus. see Seabag-Montefiore, Mary.
Marks, Alan, illus. see Sebag-Montefiore, Mary.
Marks, Alan, illus. see Sewell, Anna.
Marks, Alan, illus. see Sims, Lesley.
Marks, Alan, illus. see Spyri, Johanna.
Marks, Alan, illus. see Wilde, Oscar.
Marks, Allison & Marks, Wayne. Og's Ark. Peluso, Martina, illus. (p. 1280)
Marks, Anthony. Christmas Tunes - Internet Referenced. (p. 316)
—Easy Guitar Tunes Internet Referenced. Abel, Simone, illus. (p. 500)
—Easy Piano Classics. Rogers, Kirsteen, ed. (p. 500)
—Usborne Farmyard Tales Songbook. Tyler, Jenny, ed. (p. 1827)
Marks, Anthony & Tingay, Graham. Romans. Jackson, Ian & Wood, Gerald, illus. (p. 1486)
—Romans II. (p. 1486)
—Romans - Internet Linked. (p. 1486)
Marks, Burton. Tanya Tinker & the Gizmo Gang. Smath, Jerry, illus. (p. 1705)
Marks, Darrell. Down on the Farm. (p. 474)
Marks, Dave. Writing Exposition: A Program for Expository Writing. (p. 1964)
Marks, Dea, jt. auth. see Sibley, Linda.
Marks, Ed. Ice Cream Collectibles (p. 850)
Marks, Graham. How It Works: Everyone Gets the Angel They Deserve. (p. 810)
—Radio Radio. (p. 1433)
—Zoo. (p. 1988)
Marks, Jeannette. Cheerful Cricket & Others. (p. 296)
Marks, Jeffrey Alan & Batonne, Eva. Techno-Noir. (p. 1711)
Marks, Jennifer L. Bobcats (p. 206)
—Cars & Trucks. (p. 272)
—Children (p. 302)
—Children. (p. 302)
—Christmas Fun: A Spot-It Challenge (p. 314)
—Clasificar Dinero/Sorting Money (p. 327)
—Clasificar Juguetes/Sorting Toys (p. 327)
—Clasificar por Tamaño. (p. 327)
—Clouded Leopards (p. 334)
—Fun & Games: A Spot-It Challenge (p. 647)
—Fun & Games. (p. 647)
—How to Make a Bouncing Egg (p. 820)
—Jaguars (p. 905)
—Mean Machines: A Spot-It Challenge (p. 1116)
—Parents (p. 1324)
—Parents. (p. 1324)
—People. (p. 1339)
—President Barack Obama (p. 1396)
—Presidente Barack Obama. (p. 1397)
—School. (p. 1522)
—School Times (p. 1523)
—School Times: A Spot-It Challenge (p. 1523)
Marks, Jennifer L., jt. auth. see Bruning, Matt.
Marks, Jennifer L., jt. auth. see Schuette, Sarah L.
Marks, Jennifer L. & Bruning, Matt. Clasificar/Sorting. (p. 327)
—Vamos a Ordenar por Colores. Ferrer, Martin Luis Guzman, tr. (p. 1831)
—Vamos a Ordenar/Sorting. (p. 1831)
Marks, Jennifer L., et al. Sorting by Size (p. 1614)
—Sorting Money (p. 1614)
Marks, John H. & Rogers, Virgil M. Beginner's Handbook to Biblical Hebrew. (p. 159)
Marks, Johnny. Rudolph The Red-Nosed Reindeer Recordable Story Book. (p. 1494)
Marks, Karl, jt. auth. see Indante, Dan.
Marks, Kathi. Butterflies are Special: The Most Beautiful Butterfly. (p. 247)
Marks, Mae. Chuggington: Icy Escapades. (p. 318)
Marks, Melanie. Phonics Comics: Spooky Sara - Level 3 Ball, Victoria, illus. (p. 1352)
—Phonics Comics: Super Sam - Level 3: Issue 1. Collins, Daryll, illus. (p. 1352)
Marks, Nancy Freeman. Just As You Are: The Story of Leon & Sam. Buchheim, Su Jen, illus. (p. 938)
Marks, Wayne, jt. auth. see Marks, Allison.
Marks, William C. Lawrence the Laughing Cookie Jar. Taylor, Josephine, illus. (p. 981)
Markstrom, Carol. Dance of the Desert. (p. 402)
Markun, Alan F. New Revolution. (p. 1247)
Markun, Patricia M. Little Painter of Sabana Grande. Casilla, Robert, illus. (p. 1033)
Markwardt, Richard A. Sometimes Life Just Doesn't Seem Fair. (p. 1610)
Marland, Hilary, jt. see Gijswijt-Hofstra, Marijke.
Marland, Michael. Ideas, Insights & Arguments: A Non-Fiction Collection. (p. 852)
Marland, Michael, jt. auth. see Bhinda, Madhu.
Marlar, Debra L. Morgan's Sleepover at Grandma's. (p. 1175)
Marlatt, Andrew. Economy of Errors: Satire Wire Gives Business the Business. (p. 503)
Marleau, Eve. Visit to the Doctor. Garton, Michael, illus. (p. 1845)
Marleau, Eve, jt. auth. see Askew, Amanda.
Marlee. Harry the Elephant & His New Found Friends. (p. 751)
Marler, Jerilyn. Lily Hates Goodbyes. Stoltenberg, Nathan, illus. (p. 1018)
Marler, Myrna Dee. Walter Dean Myers (p. 1856)
Marlet, Nico & Frawley, Keith. Book of Dragons. (p. 211)
Marlette, Andy, illus. see Baldwin, Laura.
Marlette, Andy, illus. see Bianchi, Mike & Novak, Marisol.
Marlette, Caroline D. Zachary. (p. 1984)
Marley, Bob, jt. auth. see Marley, Cedella.
Marley, Bob & Marley, Cedella. Every Little Thing: Based on the Song 'Three Little Birds' by Bob Marley. Brantley-Newton, Vanessa, illus. (p. 542)
Marley, Cedella. One Love. Brantley-Newton, Vanessa, illus. (p. 1296)
Marley, Cedella, jt. auth. see Marley, Bob.
Marley, Cedella & Marley, Bob. Every Little Thing: Based on the Song 'Three Little Birds' by Bob Marley. Brantley-Newton, Vanessa, illus. (p. 542)
—One Love: Based on the Song by Bob Marley. Newton, Vanessa, illus. (p. 1296)
Marley, David F. Daily Life of Pirates (p. 400)
Marley, Rita & Jones, Hettie. No Woman No Cry: My Life with Bob Marley. (p. 1261)
Marley, Ziggy. I Love You Too. Jatkowska, Ag, illus. (p. 844)
Marlgorz, Juliet. Elizabeth Cady Stanton & the Fight for Equal Rights. (p. 513)
Marlin Elementary Students, creator. Marlin Anthology: Exploring Our Horizons as Writers. (p. 1096)
Marlin, John. Mickey Mantle. (p. 1136)
Marlin, Kathryn, illus. see Bennett, Marian.
Marlin, Kathryn, illus. see Beveridge, Amy.
Marlin, Kathryn, illus. see Redford, Margorie & Rice, Courtney.
Marlin, Kathryn, illus. see Redford, Marjorie & Rice, Courtney.
Marlin, Kathryn, illus. see Redford, Marjorie.
Marlin, Kathryn, illus. see Shearer, Amelia.
Marlin, Peggy. Wackydoodle. (p. 1852)
Marlin, Therese. Cindyrella. (p. 321)
Marling, Karal Ann. Minnesota Hail to Thee! A Sesquicentennial History. (p. 1147)
Marlo Thomas and Friends Staff. Free to Be... You & Me. (p. 634)
Marlor, Tracy D. Jack's Journey to the Pond. (p. 904)
Marlow, Barb. Sweet Dreams! (p. 1689)
Marlow, Herb. Classroom Vandal. (p. 329)
—Hood River Home. Head, Pat, illus. (p. 795)
—Long Way Home. (p. 1047)
—Lost Kitten. Head, Pat, illus. (p. 1056)
—Sisters, Wild Dogs & Catfish Bait. Caffee, Julie, illus. (p. 1581)
—Student's Guide to Successful Writing. (p. 1669)
—Sundancer. Newberry, Loretta, illus. (p. 1676)
—Tiger's Den. Head, Pat, illus. (p. 1749)
Marlow, Layn. Hurry up & Slow Down. (p. 830)
—Witch with a Twitch. Dreidemy, Joëlle, illus. (p. 1941)
—You Make Me Smile. (p. 1976)
Marlow, Layn, illus. see Stewart, Amber.
Marlow, Patricia. What Fairy Tales Are All About: Grandma's Stories. (p. 1884)
Marlow, Susan K. Andi's Fair Surprise Gammelgaard, Leslie, illus. (p. 72)
—Andi's Indian Summer Gammelgaard, Leslie, illus. (p. 72)
—Andi's Pony Trouble Gammelgaard, Leslie, illus. (p. 72)
—Andi's Scary School Days Gammelgaard, Leslie, illus. (p. 72)
—Andrea Carter & the Dangerous Decision (p. 72)
—Andrea Carter & the Family Secret (p. 72)
—Andrea Carter & the Long Ride Home (p. 72)
—Andrea Carter & the San Francisco Smugglers: A Novel (p. 72)
—Andrea Carter & the Trouble with Treasure: A Novel (p. 72)
—Andrea Carter's Tales from the Circle C Ranch (p. 72)
—Heartbreak Trail: An Andrea Carter Book (p. 760)
—River of Peril (p. 1476)
—Thick As Thieves: An Andrea Carter Book (p. 1732)
Marlowe, Amy Bell. When Oriole Came to Harbor Light. (p. 1904)
—When Oriole Traveled Westward. (p. 1904)
Marlowe, Christie. Announcer. (p. 87)
—Car Mechanic. (p. 265)
—Chef. (p. 297)
—Cosmetologist. (p. 368)
—Dj. (p. 455)
—Dog Groomer. (p. 461)
—Presenting Yourself: Business Manners, Personality, & Etiquette. (p. 1396)

—Protecting Your Body: Germs, Super Bugs, Poison & Deadly Diseases. Stephens, Ronald, ed. (p. 1412)
Marlowe, Christopher. Doctor Faustus: Playscript. (p. 459)
—Edward II. Landes, William-Alan, ed. (p. 505)
—Jew of Malta. Landes, William-Alan, ed. (p. 916)
—Massacre at Paris. (p. 1102)
Marlowe, Christopher, jt. auth. see Shakespeare, William.
Marlowe, Dan J. Sixth Man. (p. 1583)
Marlowe, Paul. Knights of the Sea: A Grim Tale of Murder, Politics, & Spoon Addiction. (p. 964)
—Sporeville. (p. 1631)
Marlowe, Sam. Learning about Dedication from the Life of Frederick Douglass. (p. 984)
Marlowe, Sara. No Ordinary Apple: A Story about Eating Mindfully. Pascuzzo, Philip, illus. (p. 1259)
Marlowe, Susan B., illus. see Greene, Melanie W., et al.
Marman, Richard. Mcalister's Spark. Marman, Richard, illus. (p. 1114)
Marmell, Ari. Covenant's End: A Widdershins Adventure. (p. 373)
—Lost Covenant: A Widdershins Adventure. (p. 1055)
Marmon, Carol. When Mommy Bird Comes to Visit. (p. 1903)
Marmon, Jim. Alexander Barnaby Meadowlark. (p. 36)
Marois, Andre. Avis de Recherche. Lemardele, Stephane, tr. (p. 120)
Marois, Andrí. Chat Botti New York. (p. 294)
Marolt, Roger A. Dear Editor. (p. 419)
Maron, Margaret. Rituals of the Season. (p. 1475)
—Slow Dollar. (p. 1591)
—Winter's Child. (p. 1938)
Maron, Terra Rose. Cheyenne. (p. 299)
Maroney-Davoren, Danette. Completely Satisfied. (p. 353)
Maros, Steve. AKA Doctor: Second Wind. (p. 32)
Maros, Steven. AKA Doctor: Mandatory Minimum. (p. 32)
Maroudas, N. G. Adventures of Athena & Odysseus. (p. 16)
Maroulis, Danielle. Monk in the Trunk. (p. 1164)
Marovic, Mason A. Divorce & Me. (p. 455)
Marqina, Mignon. Shapes & Me: A Flip & Learn Book. (p. 1560)
Marquand, John P. Late George Apley. (p. 979)
Marquardt, Marie. Dream Things True: A Novel. (p. 484)
Marquardt, Michelle. Perfect Puppy. Murfield, Anna, illus. (p. 1342)
Marques, Jesus Velasco, et al, eds. Echoes of the Mexican-American War Fried, Mark, tr. (p. 502)
Marquess, Dana. Night of the Lighted Freedom - A Firefly Fantasy. (p. 1254)
Marquez, Athena. Leave It to Beaver's. (p. 986)
Marquez, Colleen D. C. Gift for Little Tree. (p. 675)
Marquez, David, illus. see Colak, Mirko & Hickman, Jonathan.
Marquez, David, illus. see Hester, Phil.
Marquez, Erick, illus. see Shaw-Lott, Karen.
Marquez, Francisca, illus. see Houran, Lori Haskins.
Márquez, Herón. George W. Bush. (p. 663)
—Peru in Pictures. (p. 1345)
—Russia in Pictures. (p. 1498)
Marquez, Sofia. Pepe Perez Mexican Mouse: Pepe Perez Comes to the United States: Book 1 (p. 1340)
—Pepe Perez Mexican Mouse: Pepe Perez Comes to the United States: Book 1 Marquez, Sofia, illus. (p. 1340)
Marquis, KariAnn, illus. see Greeley, David.
Marquis, Melanie. Bugbug & the Ants. (p. 236)
Marquis, Michelle. Mikey & the Mysterious Door. (p. 1141)
Marquith, M. Delmore. Flying Buddies of Texas. (p. 609)
Marquitz, Tim. Skulls. Milner, Isaac, ed. (p. 1586)
Marr, Andrew. Born in the Darkest Time of Year: Stories for the Season of the Christ Child. (p. 214)
—Creatures We Dream of Knowing: Stories of Our Life Together. (p. 380)
Marr, Ella J. Adventures of Curtis & Grammy. (p. 17)
Marr, Kendra Lynn. I Was Rufus. (p. 848)
Marr, M. A., jt. auth. see Armstrong, K. L.
Marr, Melissa. Bunny Roo, I Love You. White, Teagan, illus. (p. 242)
—Carnival of Souls. (p. 270)
—Challenge. Xian Nu Studio Staff, illus. (p. 288)
—Darkest Mercy (p. 408)
—Darkest Mercy. (p. 408)
—Desert Tales. (p. 429)
—Faery Tales & Nightmares. (p. 562)
—Fragile Eternity (p. 627)
—Fragile Eternity. (p. 627)
—Ink Exchange. (p. 874)
—Made for You. (p. 1070)
—Radiant Shadows. (p. 1432)
—Resolve. Xian Nu Studio, illus. (p. 1463)
—Sanctuary Diaz, Irene & Xian Nu Studio Staff, illus. (p. 1510)
—Untamed City - Carnival of Secrets. (p. 1823)
—Wicked Lovely. (p. 1927)
Marr, Melissa & Pratt, Tim, eds. Rags & Bones: New Twists on Timeless Tales. (p. 1433)
Marr, Melissa, et al. Enthralled: Paranormal Diversions. (p. 531)
—Love Is Hell. (p. 1060)
—Shards & Ashes. (p. 1561)
Marr, Nikki. Marty Misbehaves. (p. 1098)
Marr Osb, Andrew. From Beyond to Here: Merendael's Gift & Other Stories. (p. 642)
Marran, James F. Netherlands. (p. 1242)
Marranzino, Sami. Littlest Ladybug. Currey, Andrew K., illus. (p. 1039)
Marreel, Anne M. Kids in Court. (p. 954)
Marrell, Mar'ce. Ben & the Carrot Predicament. (p. 163)
Marren, Joe, jt. auth. see O'Shei, Tim.
Marrero, Alba. Diego's Busy Week: Learn the days of the week as you tag along with a boy named Diego. (p. 437)
Marrero, Carla. Magical Cat. (p. 1074)
Marrero, J., illus. see Paul, Brian.
Marrero Laurano, Edward A. Aliens & Angels: Secrets & Mysteries. (p. 41)
Marrero, Rafelito. Amar sin decir Nada. (p. 52)
Marrero, Rosa M. Nickolas Loves Toby. (p. 1251)
Marrero-Bond, Stephanie. Flor la Maripos. (p. 606)
Marrewa, Jennifer. Graphing Favorite Things. (p. 711)
—Graphing Favorite Things. Espinosa, Patrick, photos by. (p. 711)
—How Far Away? Comparing Trips. (p. 809)
—How Far Away? Comparing Trips. (p. 809)
—Making a Model with Solid Figures. (p. 1080)
—Measuring on a Treasure Hunt. (p. 1117)
—Midiendo para una Búsqueda Del Tesoro. (p. 1138)
—Midiendo para una Búsqueda Del Tesoro. McKinley, Kay, photos by. (p. 1138)
—Using Money on a Shopping Trip. (p. 1828)
—Using Money on a Shopping Trip. McKinley, Kay, photos by. (p. 1828)
—Vamos a Hacer Graficás de Nuestras Cosas Favoritas. (p. 1831)
—Vamos a Hacer Graficas de Nuestras Cosas Favoritas. Espinosa, Patrick, photos by. (p. 1831)
—Vamos a Hacer una Maqueta con Figuras Solidas. (p. 1831)
—Vamos a USAR DINERO en un Viaje de Compras. (p. 1831)
—Vamos a Usar Dinero en un Viaje de Compras. McKinley, Kay, photos by. (p. 1831)
—¿A qué distancia? Vamos a Comparar Viajes. (p. 1)
—¿A qué distancia? Vamos a Comparar Viajes. (p. 1)
Marrin, Albert. Black Gold: The Story of Oil in Our Lives. (p. 196)
—FDR & the American Crisis. (p. 578)
—Flesh & Blood So Cheap: The Triangle Fire & Its Legacy. (p. 603)
—Flesh & Blood So Cheap. (p. 603)
—Flesh & Blood So Cheap: the Triangle Fire & Its Legacy. (p. 603)
—Oh Rats! Mordan, C. B., illus. (p. 1281)
—Oh, Rats! The Story of Rats & People. (p. 1281)
—Thomas Paine: Crusader for Liberty: an Adventure in the History of Ideas. (p. 1739)
—Thomas Paine: Crusader for Liberty: How One Man's Ideas Helped Form a New Nation. (p. 1739)
—Virginia's General: Robert E. Lee & the Civil War. (p. 1844)
—Volcano Beneath the Snow: John Brown's War Against Slavery. (p. 1848)
—Years of Dust: The Story of the Dust Bowl. (p. 1969)
Marrion, Thom & Ward, Kyla. Buffy the Vampire Slayer: Welcome to Sunnydale Supplement. (p. 236)
Marriot, Pat, illus. see Dahl, Roald.
Marriott, Ashley & Paulsen, Marc. Dump Your Trainer: Looking to Lose Weight? Dump Your Trainer. (p. 489)
Marriott, Emma. Did Anything Good Come Out of World War II? (p. 436)
Marriott, Janice. Soldier in the Yellow Socks: Charles Upham - Our Finest Fighting Soldier. (p. 1607)
—Taking Off. (p. 1698)
—Thor's Tale: Adventure & Endurance in the Southern Ocean. (p. 1740)
Marriott, Pat, illus. see Dahl, Roald.
Marriott, Zoë. Name of the Blade. (p. 1228)
—Shadows on the Moon. (p. 1558)
—Swan Kingdom. (p. 1688)
Marro, Barbara. Smitty's Cave Adventures. (p. 1594)
Marron, Jose, illus. see Leibold, Jay.
Marron, Jose Luis, jt. illus. see Cannella, Marco.
Marrone, Amanda. Devoured. (p. 432)
—Master of Mirrors. (p. 1103)
—Multiplying Menace. (p. 1190)
—Revealers. (p. 1465)
—Shape-Shifter's Curse. (p. 1560)
—Slayed. (p. 1588)
—Uninvited. (p. 1818)
Marrone, Marc & Fernandez, Amy. Ask the Cat Keeper. (p. 106)
Marrone, Mario & Diamond, Nicola. Attachment & Intersubjectivity. (p. 113)
Marroquin, Feliciano. American Dream Journey. (p. 60)
Marroquin, Jose Manuel. Moro. (p. 1175)
Marroquin-Burr, Kristina. Learn to Draw Angry Birds Space. (p. 983)
Marrou, Elisabeth. Tell Me What Is That? (p. 1717)
Marrow, Lesley Mandel & Vacca, Richard T. Sadlier Phonics: Level A. (p. 1501)
—Sadlier Phonics: Level K. (p. 1501)
—Sadlier Phonics: Level B Grade 2. (p. 1501)
—Sadlier Phonics: Level C Grade 3. (p. 1501)
—Sadlier Phonics Reading: Level K. (p. 1501)
—Sadlier Phonics/Reading: Level B. (p. 1501)
—Sadlier Phonics/Reading: Level C. (p. 1501)
Marrs, Christie, creator. Perfect Gift: I B Hoofinit's Horse Tales. (p. 1342)
—Promise Keeper: I B Hoofinit's Horse Tales. (p. 1411)
Marrs, J. Pierce & Marrs, S. Nick. Andy Goes to the Aquarium. (p. 73)
Marrs, S. Nick, jt. auth. see Marrs, J. Pierce.
Marrucchi, Elisa, illus. see Golden Books Staff.
Marrucchi, Elisa, illus. see Jordan, Apple J.
Marrucchi, Elisa, illus. see Lagonegro, Melissa.
Marrucchi, Elisa, illus. see Man-Kong, Mary.
Marrucchi, Elisa, illus. see Posner-Sanchez, Andrea.
Marrucchi, Elisa, illus. see Random House Disney Staff.
Marrucchi, Elisa, illus. see Random House Editors & Posner-Sanchez, Andrea.
Marrucchi, Elisa, illus. see Weinberg, Jennifer & RH Disney Staff.
Marrucchi, Elisa, illus. see Weinberg, Jennifer.
Marrucchi, Elisa, illus. see Wrecks, Billy.
Marryat, jt. auth. see Akinyemi, Rowena.
Marryat, Captian. Children of the New Forest. (p. 302)
Marryat, Captian & Marryat, Frederick. Children of the New Forest. (p. 302)
Marryat, Frederick. Children of the New Forest (Yesterday's Classics) (p. 302)
—Masterman Ready. (p. 1103)
Marryat, Frederick, jt. auth. see Marryat, Captian.
Mars, E., illus. see Kingsley, Charles.
Mars, W. T., illus. see Meyer, Edith Patterson.
Marsalis, Dustin S. Alligator Astronauts Go to the Zipper Zoo. (p. 47)
Marsalis, Wynton. Jazz A-B-Z: An A to Z Collection of Jazz Portraits. Rogers, Paul, illus. (p. 910)
—Squeak, Rumble, Whomp! Whomp! Whomp! Rogers, Paul, illus. (p. 1636)
Marsaw, Roy. Swim, Swam, Swum. Harris, Phyllis, illus. (p. 1691)
Marschall, Ken, illus. see Tanaka, Shelley.
Marschell, Hannah, illus. see Goldman Marshall, Lauren.
Marschner, Janice. California's Arab Americans. (p. 253)
Marsden, Carolyn. Gold-Threaded Dress. (p. 694)
—Moon Runner. (p. 1172)
—My Own Revolution. (p. 1216)
—Starfields. (p. 1642)
—Take Me with You. (p. 1696)
—When Heaven Fell. (p. 1902)
—White Zone. (p. 1914)
Marsden, Carolyn & Matzigkeit, Philip. Sahwira: An African Friendship. (p. 1503)
Marsden, Carolyn & Niem, Thay. Buddha's Diamonds. (p. 234)
Marsden, Carolyn & Niem, Thay Phap. Buddha's Diamonds. (p. 234)
Marsden, John. Al Aranib (the Rabbits- Arabic Edition) Tan, Shaun, illus. (p. 32)
—Circle of Flight. (p. 321)
—Hamlet. (p. 739)
—Night Is for Hunting. (p. 1253)
Marsden, John, jt. auth. see Marsden, John.
Marsden, John & Marsden, John. Tomorrow, When the War Began. (p. 1765)
Marsden, Ken, illus. see Hansen, Jennifer.
Marsden, Peter. Taliban. (p. 1703)
Marsee', Angela Fultz. Samuel & the Rainbow. (p. 1509)
Marsee, Kimberly, illus. see Tucker, Terra.
Marsell-Jones, Connie. Abc's of Angels. (p. 4)
Marsh, Audrey, jt. auth. see Davison, Marion.
Marsh, Barry. Good Harbor Bay. (p. 698)
Marsh, Bobbi, illus. see Christensen, Bob.
Marsh, Bobbie, illus. see Dipinto, Michael J.
Marsh, Carol. Mimi & Papa's Everyday Amazing Almanac: 365 Days of Old-Time Newfangled Facts & Fun! (p. 1145)
Marsh, Carole. Abigail Adams. (p. 5)
—Adventure Diaries of Dharma, the Dedicated Doctor! (p. 14)
—Adventure Diaries of Felipe, the Fearless Firefighter! (p. 14)
—Adventure Diaries of Hannah, the Humanitarian Aid Worker! (p. 14)
—Adventure Diaries of Haz Matt, the Hazardous Materials Worker! (p. 14)
—Adventure Diaries of Li, the Excellent EMT! (p. 14)
—Adventure Diaries of P. J., the Photo-Journalist! (p. 14)
—Adventure Diaries of the Perils of Pauline, the Police Officer! (p. 14)
—Adventure Diaries of Vicki, the Volunteer! (p. 14)
—Adventure to the Eight Wonders of the World. (p. 15)
—Adventure to the Pioneer Prairie! (p. 15)
—Adventure to the Planet Mars! (p. 15)
—Africa: A Safari Through Its Amazing Nations! (p. 26)
—Alabama Current Events Projects: 30 Cool, Activities, Crafts, Experiments & More for Kids to Do to Learn about Your State! (p. 33)
—Alabama Geography Projects: 30 Cool, Activities, Crafts, Experiments & More for Kids to Do to Learn about Your State! (p. 33)
—Alabama Government Projects: 30 Cool, Activities, Crafts, Experiments & More for Kids to Do to Learn about Your State! (p. 33)
—Alabama History Projects: 30 Cool, Activities, Crafts, Experiments & More for Kids to Do to Learn about Your State! (p. 33)
—Alabama Native Americans: A Kid's Look at Our State's Chiefs, Tribes, Reservations, Powwows, Lore, & More from the Past & the Present. (p. 33)
—Alabama People Projects: 30 Cool, Activities, Crafts, Experiments & More for Kids to Do to Learn about Your State! (p. 33)
—Alabama Symbols & Facts Projects: 30 Cool, Activities, Crafts, Experiments & More for Kids to Do to Learn about Your State! (p. 33)
—Alaska Current Events Projects: 30 Cool, Activities, Crafts, Experiments & More for Kids to Do to Learn about Your State! (p. 34)
—Alaska Geography Projects: 30 Cool, Activities, Crafts, Experiments & More for Kids to Do to Learn about Your State! (p. 34)
—Alaska Government Projects: 30 Cool, Activities, Crafts, Experiments & More for Kids to Do to Learn about Your State! (p. 34)
—Alaska History Projects: 30 Cool, Activities, Crafts, Experiments & More for Kids to Do to Learn about Your State! (p. 34)
—Alaska People Projects: 30 Cool, Activities, Crafts, Experiments & More for Kids to Do to Learn about Your State! (p. 34)
—Alaska Symbols & Facts Projects: 30 Cool, Activities, Crafts, Experiments & More for Kids to Do to Learn about Your State! (p. 34)
—Alaska Wheel of Fortune: Game Book. (p. 34)
—Albert Einstein. (p. 34)
—Alexander Graham Bell. (p. 36)
—Alvar Nunez Cabeza de Vaca:Explorer & Survivor: Explorer & Survivor. (p. 51)
—Amelia Earhart. (p. 58)
—Andrew Jackson. (p. 72)
—Anne Hutchinson. (p. 86)
—Antonia C. Novello: First Female U. S. Surgeon General: First Female U. S. Surgeon General. (p. 90)
—Arizona Current Events Projects: 30 Cool, Activities, Crafts, Experiments & More for Kids to Do to Learn about Your State! (p. 98)
—Arizona Geography Projects: 30 Cool, Activities, Crafts, Experiments & More for Kids to Do to Learn about Your State! (p. 98)
—Arizona Government Projects: 30 Cool, Activities, Crafts, Experiments & More for Kids to Do to Learn about Your State! (p. 98)
—Arizona History Projects: 30 Cool, Activities, Crafts, Experiments & More for Kids to Do to Learn about Your State! (p. 98)
—Arizona People Projects: 30 Cool, Activities, Crafts, Experiments & More for Kids to Do to Learn about Your State! (p. 98)
—Arizona Symbols & Facts Projects: 30 Cool, Activities, Crafts, Experiments & More for Kids to Do to Learn about Your State! (p. 99)
—Arkansas Current Events Projects: 30 Cool, Activities, Crafts, Experiments & More for Kids to Do to Learn about Your State! (p. 99)
—Arkansas Geography Projects: 30 Cool, Activities, Crafts, Experiments & More for Kids to Do to Learn about Your State! (p. 99)
—Arkansas Government Projects: 30 Cool, Activities, Crafts, Experiments & More for Kids to Do to Learn about Your State! (p. 99)
—Arkansas History Projects: 30 Cool, Activities, Crafts, Experiments & More for Kids to Do to Learn about Your State! (p. 99)
—Arkansas Jeopardy! Answers & Questions about Our State! (p. 99)
—Arkansas "Jography" A Fun Run Thru Our State! (p. 99)
—Arkansas People Projects: 30 Cool, Activities, Crafts, Experiments & More for Kids to Do to Learn about Your State! (p. 99)
—Arkansas Symbols & Facts Projects: 30 Cool, Activities, Crafts, Experiments & More for Kids to Do to Learn about Your State! (p. 99)
—Australia: The Land down under for Mates of All Ages! (p. 116)
—Awesome Aquarium Mystery. (p. 121)
—Barack Obama: Biography FunBook. (p. 137)
—Barack Obama - America's 44th President. (p. 137)
—Barack Obama Presidential Coloring Book! (p. 137)
—Baseball Bully. (p. 141)
—Baskerville Basketball. (p. 142)
—Behemoth Blizzard Mystery. (p. 160)
—Ben Nighthorse Campbell. (p. 163)
—Benjamin Banneker. (p. 164)
—Best Book of Hispanic Biographies. (p. 168)
—Best Book of Native American Biographies. Corsey, Jenny, ed. (p. 168)
—BIG Book of Hispanic Activities. (p. 179)
—Big California Reproducible Activity Book. (p. 180)
—Big Florida Reproducible Activity Book! (p. 181)
—Big Illinois Reproducible Activity Book. (p. 182)
—Big Missouri Reproducible Big Activity Book. (p. 182)
—Big New Hampshire Reproducible Activity Book-New Version. (p. 182)
—Big New York Activity Book! (p. 182)
—Big Oklahoma Reproducible Activity Book! (p. 183)
—Big Tennessee Reproducible Activity Book! (p. 184)
—Breathtaking Mystery on Mt. Everest. (p. 226)
—California Current Events Projects: 30 Cool, Activities, Crafts, Experiments & More for Kids to Do to Learn about Your State! (p. 253)
—California Geography Projects: 30 Cool, Activities, Crafts, Experiments & More for Kids to Do to Learn about Your State! (p. 253)
—California Government Projects: 30 Cool, Activities, Crafts, Experiments & More for Kids to Do to Learn about Your State! (p. 253)
—California History Projects: 30 Cool, Activities, Crafts, Experiments & More for Kids to Do to Learn about Your State! (p. 253)
—California People Projects: 30 Cool, Activities, Crafts, Experiments & More for Kids to Do to Learn about Your State! (p. 253)
—California Symbols & Facts Projects: 30 Cool, Activities, Crafts, Experiments & More for Kids to Do to Learn about Your State! (p. 253)
—Canada: The Maple Leaf Melting Pot Country! (p. 260)
—Carol Moseley Braun. (p. 270)
—Case of the Crybaby Cowboy. (p. 274)
—Case of the Hunchback Hairdresser. (p. 274)
—Castaway Cheerleaders. (p. 276)
—Celebrating Hispanic Heritage: 20 Days of Activities, Reading, Recipes, Parties, Plays & More. (p. 285)
—Charles Drew: Dedicated Doctor. (p. 292)
—Charles Kettering: Patent Giant. (p. 292)
—Charles Lindbergh. (p. 292)
—Charles W. Dryden: Tuskegee Airman. (p. 292)
—China: A Great Wall Runs Thru It! (p. 306)
—Christmas: Activities, Crafts, Recipes & More! (p. 312)
—Christmas Recipes from the Past. (p. 315)
—Christmas Traditions Around the World. (p. 316)
—Clara Barton. (p. 326)
—Colonial Caper Mystery at Williamsburg. (p. 341)
—Colorado Current Events Projects: 30 Cool, Activities, Crafts, Experiments & More for Kids to Do to Learn about Your State! (p. 343)
—Colorado Experience Pocket Guide. (p. 343)
—Colorado Geography Projects: 30 Cool, Activities, Crafts, Experiments & More for Kids to Do to Learn about Your State! (p. 343)
—Colorado Government Projects: 30 Cool, Activities, Crafts, Experiments & More for Kids to Do to Learn about Your State! (p. 343)
—Colorado History Projects: 30 Cool, Activities, Crafts, Experiments & More for Kids to Do to Learn about Your State! (p. 343)
—Colorado Jeopardy! Answers & Questions about Our State! (p. 343)
—Colorado "Jography" A Fun Run Thru Our State! (p. 343)
—Colorado People Projects: 30 Cool, Activities, Crafts, Experiments & More for Kids to Do to Learn about Your State! (p. 343)
—Colorado Symbols & Facts Projects: 30 Cool, Activities, Crafts, Experiments & More for Kids to Do to Learn about Your State! (p. 343)
—Colorado's Big Activity Book. (p. 343)
—Condoleezza Rice. (p. 356)

—Connecticut Current Events Projects: 30 Cool, Activities, Crafts, Experiments & More for Kids to Do to Learn about Your State! (p. 358)
—Connecticut Experience Pocket Guide. (p. 358)
—Connecticut Geography Projects: 30 Cool, Activities, Crafts, Experiments & More for Kids to Do to Learn about Your State! (p. 358)
—Connecticut Government Projects: 30 Cool, Activities, Crafts, Experiments & More for Kids to Do to Learn about Your State! (p. 358)
—Connecticut History Projects: 30 Cool, Activities, Crafts, Experiments & More for Kids to Do to Learn about Your State! (p. 358)
—Connecticut Jeopardy! Answers & Questions about Our State! (p. 358)
—Connecticut "Jography" A Fun Run Thru Our State! (p. 358)
—Connecticut People Projects: 30 Cool, Activities, Crafts, Experiments & More for Kids to Do to Learn about Your State! (p. 358)
—Connecticut Symbols & Facts Projects: 30 Cool, Activities, Crafts, Experiments & More for Kids to Do to Learn about Your State! (p. 358)
—Connecticut's Big Activity Book. (p. 358)
—Cool Arkansas Coloring Book. (p. 362)
—Cool Colorado Coloring Book. (p. 363)
—Cool Connecticut Coloring Book. (p. 363)
—Cool Kansas Coloring Book. (p. 363)
—Counterfeit Constitution Mystery. (p. 370)
—Crazy Horse. (p. 377)
—Curse of the Acropolis: Athens, Greece. (p. 394)
—Curse of the Ancient Acropolis: Athens, Greece. (p. 394)
—Dear Alien: The Little Green Man Mystery. (p. 418)
—Dear Alien: the Little Green Man Mystery. (p. 418)
—Dear Bats: the Creepy Cave Caper Mystery. (p. 418)
—Dear Granny: The Spooky State Fair Fiasco. (p. 419)
—Dear Pirate, the Buried Treasure Mystery. (p. 419)
—Delaware Current Events Projects: 30 Cool, Activities, Crafts, Experiments & More for Kids to Do to Learn about Your State! (p. 424)
—Delaware Geography Projects: 30 Cool, Activities, Crafts, Experiments & More for Kids to Do to Learn about Your State! (p. 424)
—Delaware Government Projects: 30 Cool, Activities, Crafts, Experiments & More for Kids to Do to Learn about Your State! (p. 424)
—Delaware History Projects: 30 Cool, Activities, Crafts, Experiments & More for Kids to Do to Learn about Your State! (p. 424)
—Delaware People Projects: 30 Cool, Activities, Crafts, Experiments & More for Kids to Do to Learn about Your State! (p. 424)
—Delaware Symbols & Facts Projects: 30 Cool, Activities, Crafts, Experiments & More for Kids to Do to Learn about Your State! (p. 424)
—Dick Cheney: U. S. Vice President. (p. 435)
—Diego Rivera: Acclaimed Mural Painter: Acclaimed Mural Painter. (p. 437)
—Earthshaking Earthquake Mystery. (p. 498)
—Egypt: An Ancient Land of Lore, a Modern Land of Oil & More! (p. 506)
—Electricity: Common Core Lessons & Activities. (p. 509)
—Ellen Ochoa: First Hispanic American Woman in Space: First Hispanic American Woman in Space. (p. 514)
—False Paw! French for Kids. Beard, Chad, ed. (p. 567)
—Farm Days A-Z Coloring Book. Ford, Yvonne, illus. (p. 573)
—Father Junipero Serra: California Missions Founder: California Missions Founder. (p. 577)
—Ferdinand Magellan, World Voyager. (p. 582)
—Ferocious Forest Fire Mystery. (p. 582)
—First Woman President of the U. S. (p. 597)
—Florida Current Events Projects: 30 Cool, Activities, Crafts, Experiments & More for Kids to Do to Learn about Your State! (p. 607)
—Florida Experience Pocket Guide. (p. 607)
—Florida Geography Projects: 30 Cool, Activities, Crafts, Experiments & More for Kids to Do to Learn about Your State! (p. 607)
—Florida Government Projects: 30 Cool, Activities, Crafts, Experiments & More for Kids to Do to Learn about Your State! (p. 607)
—Florida History Projects: 30 Cool, Activities, Crafts, Experiments & More for Kids to Do to Learn about Your State! (p. 607)
—Florida People Projects: 30 Cool, Activities, Crafts, Experiments & More for Kids to Do to Learn about Your State! (p. 607)
—Florida Symbols & Facts Projects: 30 Cool, Activities, Crafts, Experiments & More for Kids to Do to Learn about Your State! (p. 607)
—Football Phantom. (p. 615)
—France: The Ooh-lala Country Everyone Loves! (p. 627)
—Frederick Douglass. (p. 633)
—From Russia with Love! Russian for Kids. Beard, Chad, ed. (p. 643)
—Gargoyle Golf Course. (p. 657)
—Garrett Morgan, Innovative Inventor. (p. 657)
—General Colin Powell. (p. 660)
—Georgia Current Events Projects: 30 Cool, Activities, Crafts, Experiments & More for Kids to Do to Learn about Your State! (p. 665)
—Georgia Geography Projects: 30 Cool, Activities, Crafts, Experiments & More for Kids to Do to Learn about Your State! (p. 665)
—Georgia Government Projects: 30 Cool, Activities, Crafts, Experiments & More for Kids to Do to Learn about Your State! (p. 665)
—Georgia Government: the Cornerstone of Everyday Life in Our State! The Cornerstone of Everyday Life in Our State! (p. 665)
—Georgia History Projects: 30 Cool, Activities, Crafts, Experiments & More for Kids to Do to Learn about Your State! (p. 665)
—Georgia Law: Make It, Don't Break It! (HC) Make It, Don't Break It! (HC) (p. 665)

—Georgia Native Americans: A Kid's Look at Our State's Chiefs, Tribes, Reservations, Powwows, Lore & More from the Past & the Present. (p. 665)
—Georgia People Projects: 30 Cool, Activities, Crafts, Experiments & More for Kids to Do to Learn about Your State! (p. 665)
—Georgia Symbols & Facts Projects: 30 Cool, Activities, Crafts, Experiments & More for Kids to Do to Learn about Your State! (p. 665)
—Georgia's Big Activity Book. (p. 665)
—Germany: The Country of Fairytale Castles & Cutting Edge Science! (p. 666)
—Geronimo. (p. 667)
—Ghost of Pickpocket Plantation. (p. 671)
—Ghost of the Golden Gate Bridge. (p. 671)
—Ghost of the Grand Canyon. (p. 671)
—Ghosts of Pickpocket Plantation. (p. 672)
—Giggling Ghost Girl Scout Mystery. (p. 676)
—Gosh Awful! Gold Rush Mystery. (p. 703)
—Granville Woods: Excellent Inventor. (p. 710)
—Greece: A Volcanic Land of Ancient Olympic Origins! (p. 720)
—Hanukkah: Activities, Crafts, Recipes & More! (p. 744)
—Harriet Beecher Stowe. (p. 749)
—Hawaii Current Events Projects: 30 Cool, Activities, Crafts, Experiments & More for Kids to Do to Learn about Your State! (p. 755)
—Hawaii Geography Projects: 30 Cool, Activities, Crafts, Experiments & More for Kids to Do to Learn about Your State! (p. 755)
—Hawaii Government Projects: 30 Cool, Activities, Crafts, Experiments & More for Kids to Do to Learn about Your State! (p. 755)
—Hawaii History Projects: 30 Cool, Activities, Crafts, Experiments & More for Kids to Do to Learn about Your State! (p. 755)
—Hawaii People Projects: 30 Cool, Activities, Crafts, Experiments & More for Kids to Do to Learn about Your State! (p. 755)
—Hawaii Symbols & Facts Projects: 30 Cool, Activities, Crafts, Experiments & More for Kids to Do to Learn about Your State! (p. 755)
—Henry Ford. (p. 768)
—Henry Hudson. (p. 768)
—Hernando de Soto: First Discovered the Mississippi River: First Discovered the Mississippi River. (p. 772)
—Heroes & Helpers. (p. 772)
—Heroes & Helpers Careers Book. (p. 772)
—Heroes & Helpers Coloring Book. (p. 772)
—Heroes & Helpers Resource Book for Teachers & Parents. (p. 772)
—Hispanic Heritage Coloring Book. (p. 781)
—Hispanic Trivia: The Hispanic Experience A to Z! (p. 781)
—Ho Lee Chow! Chinese for Kids. Beard, Chad, ed. (p. 786)
—Horrendous Hurricane Mystery. (p. 798)
—Idaho Current Events Projects: 30 Cool, Activities, Crafts, Experiments & More for Kids to Do to Learn about Your State! (p. 852)
—Idaho Geography Projects: 30 Cool, Activities, Crafts, Experiments & More for Kids to Do to Learn about Your State! (p. 852)
—Idaho Government Projects: 30 Cool, Activities, Crafts, Experiments & More for Kids to Do to Learn about Your State! (p. 852)
—Idaho History Projects: 30 Cool, Activities, Crafts, Experiments & More for Kids to Do to Learn about Your State! (p. 852)
—Idaho People Projects: 30 Cool, Activities, Crafts, Experiments & More for Kids to Do to Learn about Your State! (p. 852)
—Idaho Symbols & Facts Projects: 30 Cool, Activities, Crafts, Experiments & More for Kids to Do to Learn about Your State! (p. 852)
—Illinois Current Events Projects: 30 Cool, Activities, Crafts, Experiments & More for Kids to Do to Learn about Your State! (p. 857)
—Illinois Geography Projects: 30 Cool, Activities, Crafts, Experiments & More for Kids to Do to Learn about Your State! (p. 857)
—Illinois Government Projects: 30 Cool, Activities, Crafts, Experiments & More for Kids to Do to Learn about Your State! (p. 857)
—Illinois History Projects: 30 Cool, Activities, Crafts, Experiments & More for Kids to Do to Learn about Your State! (p. 857)
—Illinois Native Americans: A Kid's Look at Our State's Chiefs, Tribes, Reservations, Powwows, Lore, & More from the Past & the Present. (p. 857)
—Illinois People Projects: 30 Cool, Activities, Crafts, Experiments & More for Kids to Do to Learn about Your State! (p. 857)
—Illinois Symbols & Facts Projects: 30 Cool, Activities, Crafts, Experiments & More for Kids to Do to Learn about Your State! (p. 857)
—I'm Reading about Alaska. (p. 859)
—I'm Reading about Arizona. (p. 859)
—I'm Reading about Arkansas. (p. 859)
—I'm Reading about Connecticut. (p. 859)
—I'm Reading about Hawaii. (p. 859)
—I'm Reading about Kansas. (p. 859)
—I'm Reading about Maine. (p. 859)
—I'm Reading about Maryland. (p. 859)
—I'm Reading about Massachusetts. (p. 859)
—I'm Reading about Michigan. (p. 859)
—I'm Reading about Minnesota. (p. 859)
—I'm Reading about Mississippi. (p. 859)
—I'm Reading about Montana. (p. 859)
—I'm Reading about Nebraska. (p. 859)
—I'm Reading about Nevada. (p. 859)
—I'm Reading about New Hampshire. (p. 859)
—I'm Reading about New Jersey. (p. 859)
—I'm Reading about New Mexico. (p. 860)
—I'm Reading about New York. (p. 860)
—I'm Reading about North Dakota. (p. 860)
—I'm Reading about Oregon. (p. 860)
—I'm Reading about South Dakota. (p. 860)

—I'm Reading about Utah. (p. 860)
—I'm Reading about Vermont. (p. 860)
—I'm Reading about Washington. (p. 860)
—I'm Reading about Wyoming. (p. 860)
—I'm So Sad; I'm So Mad. (p. 860)
—India: Land of Six Senses & Intriguing Mystery! (p. 870)
—Indiana Coloring Book! (p. 871)
—Indiana Current Events Projects: 30 Cool, Activities, Crafts, Experiments & More for Kids to Do to Learn about Your State! (p. 871)
—Indiana Geography Projects: 30 Cool, Activities, Crafts, Experiments & More for Kids to Do to Learn about Your State! (p. 871)
—Indiana Government Projects: 30 Cool, Activities, Crafts, Experiments & More for Kids to Do to Learn about Your State! (p. 871)
—Indiana History Projects: 30 Cool, Activities, Crafts, Experiments & More for Kids to Do to Learn about Your State! (p. 871)
—Indiana Jeopardy! Answers & Questions about Our State! (p. 871)
—Indiana "Jography" A Fun Run Through Our State! (p. 871)
—Indiana People Projects: 30 Cool, Activities, Crafts, Experiments & More for Kids to Do to Learn about Your State! (p. 871)
—Indiana Symbols & Facts Projects: 30 Cool, Activities, Crafts, Experiments & More for Kids to Do to Learn about Your State! (p. 871)
—Industrial Revolution from Muscles to Machines! (p. 872)
—Industrial Revolution Reproducible Activity Book (HC) (p. 872)
—Iowa Current Events Projects: 30 Cool, Activities, Crafts, Experiments & More for Kids to Do to Learn about Your State! (p. 886)
—Iowa Geography Projects: 30 Cool, Activities, Crafts, Experiments & More for Kids to Do to Learn about Your State! (p. 886)
—Iowa Government Projects: 30 Cool, Activities, Crafts, Experiments & More for Kids to Do to Learn about Your State! (p. 886)
—Iowa History Projects: 30 Cool, Activities, Crafts, Experiments & More for Kids to Do to Learn about Your State! (p. 886)
—Iowa People Projects: 30 Cool, Activities, Crafts, Experiments & More for Kids to Do to Learn about Your State! (p. 886)
—Iowa Symbols & Facts Projects: 30 Cool, Activities, Crafts, Experiments & More for Kids to Do to Learn about Your State! (p. 886)
—It Really Is Greek to Me! Greek for Kids. Beard, Chad, ed. (p. 894)
—Italy: The Country of Amazing Fountains & Awesome Arts! (p. 895)
—Jamestown: America's First Permanent English Settlement. (p. 907)
—Japan: An Island Country of Endless Intrigue! (p. 909)
—Jefferson Davis, Civil War Hero. (p. 912)
—Jeopardy! (p. 913)
—Jimmy Carter. (p. 918)
—Job Tracks: 60 Great Careers & How to Get from Where You Are... to Where You Want to Go! (p. 919)
—Jography. (p. 920)
—John Adams. (p. 921)
—John C. Fremont. (p. 921)
—John Edwards: Vice Presidential Hopeful. (p. 921)
—John F. Kennedy. (p. 921)
—John Kerry: Successful Senator & 2004 Presidential Candidate. (p. 922)
—Jonas Salk. (p. 925)
—Kansas Current Events Projects: 30 Cool, Activities, Crafts, Experiments & More for Kids to Do to Learn about Your State! (p. 943)
—Kansas Geography Projects: 30 Cool, Activities, Crafts, Experiments & More for Kids to Do to Learn about Your State! (p. 943)
—Kansas Government Projects: 30 Cool, Activities, Crafts, Experiments & More for Kids to Do to Learn about Your State! (p. 943)
—Kansas History Projects: 30 Cool, Activities, Crafts, Experiments & More for Kids to Do to Learn about Your State! (p. 943)
—Kansas Jeopardy! Answers & Questions about Our State! (p. 943)
—Kansas "Jography" A Fun Run Thru Our State! (p. 943)
—Kansas People Projects: 30 Cool, Activities, Crafts, Experiments & More for Kids to Do to Learn about Your State! (p. 943)
—Kansas Symbols & Facts Projects: 30 Cool, Activities, Crafts, Experiments & More for Kids to Do to Learn about Your State! (p. 943)
—Kentucky Coloring Book. (p. 949)
—Kentucky Experience Pocket Guide. (p. 949)
—Kentucky Geography Projects: 30 Cool, Activities, Crafts, Experiments & More for Kids to Do to Learn about Your State! (p. 949)
—Kentucky Government Projects #4: 30 Cool Activities, Crafts, Experiments & More for Kids to Do! (p. 949)
—Kentucky History Projects #1: 30 Cool, Activities, Crafts, Experiments & More for Kids to Do! (p. 949)
—Kentucky Jeopardy! Answers & Questions about Our State! (p. 949)
—Kentucky "Jography" A Fun Run Thru Our State! (p. 949)
—Kentucky People Projects: 30 Cool, Activities, Crafts, Experiments & More for Kids to Do to Learn about Your State! (p. 949)
—Kentucky Symbols & Facts Projects: 30 Cool, Activities, Crafts, Experiments & More for Kids to Do to Learn about Your State! (p. 949)
—Kentucky's Big Activity Book. (p. 949)
—King George III. (p. 958)
—Kwanzaa: Activities, Crafts, Recipes & More! (p. 969)
—Legend of the Candy Cane. (p. 989)
—Let's Discover Florida! (p. 995)
—Let's Discover Georgia! (p. 995)
—Let's Discover Illinois! (p. 995)

—Let's Discover Indiana! (p. 995)
—Let's Discover Kansas! (p. 995)
—Let's Discover Kentucky! (p. 995)
—Let's Discover Louisiana! (p. 995)
—Let's Discover Maryland! (p. 995)
—Let's Discover Mississippi! (p. 995)
—Let's Discover Missouri! (p. 995)
—Let's Discover New Jersey! (p. 995)
—Let's Discover New York! (p. 995)
—Let's Discover North Carolina! (p. 995)
—Let's Discover Ohio! (p. 995)
—Let's Discover Oklahoma! (p. 995)
—Let's Discover Pennsylvania! (p. 995)
—Let's Discover Tennessee! (p. 995)
—Let's Discover Texas! (p. 995)
—Let's Discover Wisconsin! (p. 995)
—Lewis & Clark Go on a Hike. (p. 1004)
—Lords of Baltimore, Founders of Maryland. (p. 1052)
—Louisiana Coloring Book. (p. 1058)
—Louisiana Current Events Projects: 30 Cool, Activities, Crafts, Experiments & More for Kids to Do to Learn about Your State! (p. 1058)
—Louisiana Experience Pocket Guide. (p. 1058)
—Louisiana Geography Projects: 30 Cool, Activities, Crafts, Experiments & More for Kids to Do to Learn about Your State! (p. 1058)
—Louisiana Government Projects: 30 Cool, Activities, Crafts, Experiments & More for Kids to Do to Learn about Your State! (p. 1058)
—Louisiana History Projects: 30 Cool, Activities, Crafts, Experiments & More for Kids to Do to Learn about Your State! (p. 1058)
—Louisiana Jeopardy. (p. 1058)
—Louisiana Jography. (p. 1058)
—Louisiana Native Americans: A Kid's Look at Our State's Chiefs, Tribes, Reservations, Powwows, Lore, & More from the Past & the Present. (p. 1058)
—Louisiana People Projects: 30 Cool, Activities, Crafts, Experiments & More for Kids to Do to Learn about Your State! (p. 1058)
—Louisiana Purchase. (p. 1058)
—Louisiana Symbols & Facts Projects: 30 Cool, Activities, Crafts, Experiments & More for Kids to Do to Learn about Your State! (p. 1059)
—Louisiana's Big Activity Book. (p. 1059)
—Madcap Mystery of the Missing Liberty Bell. (p. 1069)
—Magnificant Michigan Coloring Book. (p. 1076)
—Magnificant Missouri Coloring Book. (p. 1076)
—Magnificent Mississippi Coloring Book. (p. 1076)
—Maine Current Events Projects: 30 Cool, Activities, Crafts, Experiments & More for Kids to Do to Learn about Your State! (p. 1077)
—Maine Geography Projects: 30 Cool, Activities, Crafts, Experiments & More for Kids to Do to Learn about Your State! (p. 1077)
—Maine Government Projects: 30 Cool, Activities, Crafts, Experiments & More for Kids to Do to Learn about Your State! (p. 1077)
—Maine History Projects: 30 Cool, Activities, Crafts, Experiments & More for Kids to Do to Learn about Your State! (p. 1077)
—Maine People Projects: 30 Cool, Activities, Crafts, Experiments & More for Kids to Do to Learn about Your State! (p. 1077)
—Maine Symbols & Facts Projects: 30 Cool, Activities, Crafts, Experiments & More for Kids to Do to Learn about Your State! (p. 1077)
—Marco Polo. (p. 1092)
—Marie Curie, Nobel Prize Winning Scientist. (p. 1093)
—Marvelous Maryland Coloring Book! (p. 1099)
—Maryland Current Events Projects: 30 Cool, Activities, Crafts, Experiments & More for Kids to Do to Learn about Your State! (p. 1101)
—Maryland Geography Projects: 30 Cool, Activities, Crafts, Experiments & More for Kids to Do to Learn about Your State! (p. 1101)
—Maryland Government Projects: 30 Cool, Activities, Crafts, Experiments & More for Kids to Do to Learn about Your State! (p. 1101)
—Maryland History Projects: 30 Cool, Activities, Crafts, Experiments & More for Kids to Do to Learn about Your State! (p. 1101)
—Maryland Jeopardy! Answers & Questions about Our State! (p. 1101)
—Maryland "Jography" A Fun Run Thru Our State! (p. 1101)
—Maryland People Projects: 30 Cool, Activities, Crafts, Experiments & More for Kids to Do to Learn about Your State! (p. 1101)
—Maryland Symbols & Facts Projects: 30 Cool, Activities, Crafts, Experiments & More for Kids to Do to Learn about Your State! (p. 1101)
—Massachusetts Current Events Projects: 30 Cool, Activities, Crafts, Experiments & More for Kids to Do to Learn about Your State! (p. 1102)
—Massachusetts Geography Projects: 30 Cool, Activities, Crafts, Experiments & More for Kids to Do to Learn about Your State! (p. 1102)
—Massachusetts Government Projects: 30 Cool, Activities, Crafts, Experiments & More for Kids to Do to Learn about Your State! (p. 1102)
—Massachusetts History Projects: 30 Cool, Activities, Crafts, Experiments & More for Kids to Do to Learn about Your State! (p. 1102)
—Massachusetts People Projects: 30 Cool, Activities, Crafts, Experiments & More for Kids to Do to Learn about Your State! (p. 1102)
—Massachusetts Symbols & Facts Projects: 30 Cool, Activities, Crafts, Experiments & More for Kids to Do to Learn about Your State! (p. 1102)
—Math for Girls Grades 3-6: The Book with the Number to Help Girls Love & Excel in Math! Beard, Chad, ed. (p. 1106)
—Meet Shirley Franklin, Mayor of Atlanta! (p. 1122)

For book reviews, descriptive annotations, tables of contents, cover images, author biographies & additional information, updated daily, subscribe to www.booksinprint2.com

2477

—Meriwether Lewis & William Clark: Explorers of the Uncharted West: Explorers of the Uncharted West. (p. 1128)
—Mexico: A Colorful Land of Exotic Culture! (p. 1131)
—Michelle Obama: Biography FunBook. (p. 1135)
—Michigan Classic Christmas Trivia. (p. 1135)
—Michigan Current Events Projects: 30 Cool, Activities, Crafts, Experiments & More for Kids to Do to Learn about Your State! (p. 1135)
—Michigan Experience Pocket Guide. (p. 1135)
—Michigan Geography Projects: 30 Cool, Activities, Crafts, Experiments & More for Kids to Do to Learn about Your State! (p. 1135)
—Michigan Government Projects: 30 Cool, Activities, Crafts, Experiments & More for Kids to Do to Learn about Your State! (p. 1135)
—Michigan History Projects: 30 Cool, Activities, Crafts, Experiments & More for Kids to Do to Learn about Your State! (p. 1135)
—Michigan Jeopardy! Answers & Questions about Our State! (p. 1135)
—Michigan "Jography" A Fun Run Thru Our State! (p. 1135)
—Michigan People Projects: 30 Cool, Activities, Crafts, Experiments & More for Kids to Do to Learn about Your State! (p. 1135)
—Michigan Symbols & Facts Projects: 30 Cool, Activities, Crafts, Experiments & More for Kids to Do to Learn about Your State! (p. 1135)
—Middle East: Ancient Countries of Current Events Headlines! (p. 1137)
—Minnesota Current Events Projects: 30 Cool, Activities, Crafts, Experiments & More for Kids to Do to Learn about Your State! (p. 1147)
—Minnesota Geography Projects: 30 Cool, Activities, Crafts, Experiments & More for Kids to Do to Learn about Your State! (p. 1147)
—Minnesota Government Projects: 30 Cool, Activities, Crafts, Experiments & More for Kids to Do to Learn about Your State! (p. 1147)
—Minnesota History Projects: 30 Cool, Activities, Crafts, Experiments & More for Kids to Do to Learn about Your State! (p. 1147)
—Minnesota People Projects: 30 Cool, Activities, Crafts, Experiments & More for Kids to Do to Learn about Your State! (p. 1147)
—Minnesota Symbols & Facts Projects: 30 Cool, Activities, Crafts, Experiments & More for Kids to Do to Learn about Your State! (p. 1147)
—Mission Possible Mystery at Space Center Houston. (p. 1153)
—Mississippi Big Activity Book. (p. 1154)
—Mississippi Current Events Projects: 30 Cool, Activities, Crafts, Experiments & More for Kids to Do to Learn about Your State! (p. 1154)
—Mississippi Experience Pocket Guide. (p. 1154)
—Mississippi Geography Projects: 30 Cool, Activities, Crafts, Experiments & More for Kids to Do to Learn about Your State! (p. 1154)
—Mississippi Government Projects: 30 Cool, Activities, Crafts, Experiments & More for Kids to Do to Learn about Your State! (p. 1154)
—Mississippi History Projects: 30 Cool, Activities, Crafts, Experiments & More for Kids to Do to Learn about Your State! (p. 1154)
—Mississippi Jeopardy. (p. 1154)
—Mississippi "Jography" A Fun Run Thru Our State! (p. 1154)
—Mississippi People Projects: 30 Cool, Activities, Crafts, Experiments & More for Kids to Do to Learn about Your State! (p. 1154)
—Mississippi Symbols & Facts Projects: 30 Cool, Activities, Crafts, Experiments & More for Kids to Do to Learn about Your State! (p. 1154)
—Missouri Current Events Projects: 30 Cool, Activities, Crafts, Experiments & More for Kids to Do to Learn about Your State! (p. 1154)
—Missouri Geography Projects: 30 Cool, Activities, Crafts, Experiments & More for Kids to Do to Learn about Your State! (p. 1154)
—Missouri Government Projects: 30 Cool, Activities, Crafts, Experiments & More for Kids to Do to Learn about Your State! (p. 1154)
—Missouri History Projects: 30 Cool, Activities, Crafts, Experiments & More for Kids to Do to Learn about Your State! (p. 1154)
—Missouri Jeopardy! Answers & Questions about Our State! (p. 1154)
—Missouri "Jography" A Fun Run Thru Our State! (p. 1154)
—Missouri Native Americans: A Kid's Look at Our State's Chiefs, Tribes, Reservations, Powwows, Lore, & More from the Past & the Present. (p. 1154)
—Missouri People Projects: 30 Cool, Activities, Crafts, Experiments & More for Kids to Do to Learn about Your State! (p. 1154)
—Missouri Symbols & Facts Projects: 30 Cool, Activities, Crafts, Experiments & More for Kids to Do to Learn about Your State! (p. 1154)
—Molly Pitcher. (p. 1161)
—Montana Current Events Projects: 30 Cool, Activities, Crafts, Experiments & More for Kids to Do to Learn about Your State! (p. 1170)
—Montana Geography Projects: 30 Cool, Activities, Crafts, Experiments & More for Kids to Do to Learn about Your State! (p. 1170)
—Montana Government Projects: 30 Cool, Activities, Crafts, Experiments & More for Kids to Do to Learn about Your State! (p. 1170)
—Montana History Projects: 30 Cool, Activities, Crafts, Experiments & More for Kids to Do to Learn about Your State! (p. 1170)
—Montana People Projects: 30 Cool, Activities, Crafts, Experiments & More for Kids to Do to Learn about Your State! (p. 1170)
—Montana Symbols & Facts Projects: 30 Cool, Activities, Crafts, Experiments & More for Kids to Do to Learn about Your State! (p. 1170)
—My First Book. (p. 1205)
—My First Book about Colorado. (p. 1205)
—My First Book about Connecticut. (p. 1205)
—My First Book about Indiana. (p. 1205)
—My First Book about Kansas. (p. 1205)
—My First Book about Louisiana. (p. 1205)
—My First Book about New Jersey. (p. 1205)
—My First Book about North Carolina. (p. 1205)
—My First Book about Pennsylvania. (p. 1205)
—My First Pocket Guide: Maryland. (p. 1207)
—My First Pocket Guide: Oklahoma. (p. 1207)
—My First Pocket Guide New Jersey. (p. 1207)
—Mystery at Area 51. Friedlander, Randolyn, illus. (p. 1223)
—Mystery at Big Ben. (p. 1223)
—Mystery at Cape Cod. (p. 1223)
—Mystery at Cape Cod. Friedlander, Randolyn, illus. (p. 1223)
—Mystery at Death Valley. (p. 1223)
—Mystery at Disney World. (p. 1223)
—Mystery at Dracula's Castle: Transylvania, Romania. (p. 1223)
—Mystery at Fort Sumter: First Shot Fired in the Civil War! (p. 1223)
—Mystery at Fort Sumter: The First Shot Fired in the Civil War. (p. 1223)
—Mystery at Fort Sumter. Friedlander, Randolyn, illus. (p. 1223)
—Mystery at Fort Thunderbolt. (p. 1223)
—Mystery at Grizzly Graveyard. (p. 1223)
—Mystery at Hollywood. (p. 1223)
—Mystery at Jamestown: First Permanent English Colony in America! (p. 1223)
—Mystery at Kill Devil Hills. (p. 1223)
—Mystery at Motown. Friedlander, Randolyn, illus. (p. 1223)
—Mystery at Mount Vernon: Home of America's First President George Washington. (p. 1223)
—Mystery at Mount Vernon. Friedlander, Randolyn, illus. (p. 1223)
—Mystery at Mt. Fuji: Tokyo, Japan. (p. 1223)
—Mystery at Rattlesnake Ridge. (p. 1223)
—Mystery at the Boston Marathon. (p. 1224)
—Mystery at the Eiffel Tower. (p. 1224)
—Mystery at the Kentucky Derby. (p. 1224)
—Mystery at the Mayan Ruins: Mexico. (p. 1224)
—Mystery at the Roman Coloseum. (p. 1224)
—Mystery at the Roman Colosseum. (p. 1224)
—Mystery at Yellowstone National Park: Volcano, Old Faithful, Bison, Grizzlies & More! (p. 1224)
—Mystery at Yellowstone National Park. (p. 1224)
—Mystery in Chocolate Town: Hershey, Pennsylvania. (p. 1224)
—Mystery in Chocolate Town Hershey, Pennsylvania. (p. 1224)
—Mystery in Hawaii: The 50th State. (p. 1224)
—Mystery in Hawaii: Red Hot Volcanoes, Whopper Waves, Luaus & Leis. (p. 1224)
—Mystery in Hawaii. Friedlander, Randolyn, illus. (p. 1224)
—Mystery in Las Vegas. (p. 1224)
—Mystery in New York City. (p. 1224)
—Mystery in the Amazon Rainforest: South America. (p. 1224)
—Mystery in the Rocky Mountains. (p. 1224)
—Mystery in the Twin Cities. Baker, Janice, ed. (p. 1224)
—Mystery of Blackbeard the Pirate. (p. 1224)
—Mystery of Blackbeard the Pirate. Marsh, Carole, photos by. (p. 1224)
—Mystery of Kill Devil Hills. (p. 1224)
—Mystery of the Alamo Ghost. (p. 1225)
—Mystery of the Ancient Pyramid: Cairo, Egypt. (p. 1225)
—Mystery of the Biltmore House. (p. 1225)
—Mystery of the Crystal Castle: Bavaria, Germany. (p. 1225)
—Mystery of the Graveyard of the Atlantic. (p. 1225)
—Mystery of the Haunted Ghost Town. (p. 1225)
—Mystery of the Lost Colony. (p. 1225)
—Mystery of the Missing Dinosaurs. (p. 1225)
—Mystery of the Missing Dinosaurs (Hardcover) (p. 1225)
—Mystery on Alaska's Iditarod Trail. (p. 1226)
—Mystery on California Mission Trail. (p. 1226)
—Mystery on the California Mission Trail. (p. 1226)
—Mystery on the California Mission Trail (Hardcover) (p. 1226)
—Mystery on the Freedom Trail. (p. 1226)
—Mystery on the Great Barrier Reef: Sydney, Australia. (p. 1226)
—Mystery on the Great Barrier Reef: Sydney, Australlia. (p. 1226)
—Mystery on the Great Barrier Reef. (p. 1226)
—Mystery on the Great Lakes: Haunted Lighthouses, Ghost Ships, Giant Sand Dunes. (p. 1226)
—Mystery on the Great Lakes. (p. 1226)
—Mystery on the Great Wall of China: Beijing, China. (p. 1226)
—Mystery on the Great Wall of China. (p. 1226)
—Mystery on the Mighty Mississippi. (p. 1226)
—Mystery on the Oregon Trail: Covered Wagons, Prairies & Pioneers. (p. 1226)
—Mystery on the Oregon Trail. (p. 1226)
—Mystery on the Oregon Trail. Friedlander, Randolyn, illus. (p. 1226)
—Mystery on the Underground Railroad. (p. 1226)
—Mystery on the Underground Railroad (Hardcover) (p. 1226)
—Native American Coloring Book. Corsey, Jenny, ed. (p. 1234)
—Nebraska Current Events Projects: 30 Cool, Activities, Crafts, Experiments & More for Kids to Do to Learn about Your State! (p. 1239)
—Nebraska Geography Projects: 30 Cool, Activities, Crafts, Experiments & More for Kids to Do to Learn about Your State! (p. 1239)
—Nebraska Government Projects: 30 Cool, Activities, Crafts, Experiments & More for Kids to Do to Learn about Your State! (p. 1239)
—Nebraska History Projects: 30 Cool, Activities, Crafts, Experiments & More for Kids to Do to Learn about Your State! (p. 1239)
—Nebraska People Projects: 30 Cool, Activities, Crafts, Experiments & More for Kids to Do to Learn about Your State! (p. 1239)
—Nebraska Symbols & Facts Projects: 30 Cool, Activities, Crafts, Experiments & More for Kids to Do to Learn about Your State! (p. 1239)
—Nevada Current Events Projects: 30 Cool, Activities, Crafts, Experiments & More for Kids to Do to Learn about Your State! (p. 1242)
—Nevada Geography Projects: 30 Cool, Activities, Crafts, Experiments & More for Kids to Do to Learn about Your State! (p. 1242)
—Nevada Government Projects: 30 Cool, Activities, Crafts, Experiments & More for Kids to Do to Learn about Your State! (p. 1242)
—Nevada History Projects: 30 Cool, Activities, Crafts, Experiments & More for Kids to Do to Learn about Your State! (p. 1242)
—Nevada People Projects: 30 Cool, Activities, Crafts, Experiments & More for Kids to Do to Learn about Your State! (p. 1242)
—Nevada Symbols & Facts Projects: 30 Cool, Activities, Crafts, Experiments & More for Kids to Do to Learn about Your State! (p. 1242)
—New Hampshire Geography Projects: 30 Cool, Activities, Crafts, Experiments & More for Kids to Do to Learn about Your State! (p. 1245)
—New Hampshire Government Projects: 30 Cool, Activities, Crafts, Experiments & More for Kids to Do to Learn about Your State! (p. 1245)
—New Hampshire History Projects: 30 Cool, Activities, Crafts, Experiments & More for Kids to Do to Learn about Your State! (p. 1245)
—New Hampshire People Projects: 30 Cool, Activities, Crafts, Experiments & More for Kids to Do to Learn about Your State! (p. 1245)
—New Hampshire Symbols & Facts Projects: 30 Cool, Activities, Crafts, Experiments & More for Kids to Do to Learn about Your State! (p. 1245)
—New Jersey Current Events Projects: 30 Cool, Activities, Crafts, Experiments & More for Kids to Do to Learn about Your State! (p. 1245)
—New Jersey Geography Projects: 30 Cool, Activities, Crafts, Experiments & More for Kids to Do to Learn about Your State! (p. 1245)
—New Jersey Government Projects: 30 Cool, Activities, Crafts, Experiments & More for Kids to Do to Learn about Your State! (p. 1245)
—New Jersey History Projects: 30 Cool, Activities, Crafts, Experiments & More for Kids to Do to Learn about Your State! (p. 1245)
—New Jersey Jeopardy! Answers & Questions about Our State! (p. 1245)
—New Jersey "Jography" A Fun Run Thru Our State! (p. 1245)
—New Jersey People Projects: 30 Cool, Activities, Crafts, Experiments & More for Kids to Do to Learn about Your State! (p. 1245)
—New Jersey Symbols & Facts Projects: 30 Cool, Activities, Crafts, Experiments & More for Kids to Do to Learn about Your State! (p. 1245)
—New Mexico Current Events Projects: 30 Cool, Activities, Crafts, Experiments & More for Kids to Do to Learn about Your State! (p. 1246)
—New Mexico Geography Projects: 30 Cool, Activities, Crafts, Experiments & More for Kids to Do to Learn about Your State! (p. 1246)
—New Mexico Government Projects: 30 Cool, Activities, Crafts, Experiments & More for Kids to Do to Learn about Your State! (p. 1246)
—New Mexico History Projects: 30 Cool, Activities, Crafts, Experiments & More for Kids to Do to Learn about Your State! (p. 1246)
—New Mexico People Projects: 30 Cool, Activities, Crafts, Experiments & More for Kids to Do to Learn about Your State! (p. 1246)
—New Mexico Symbols & Facts Projects: 30 Cool, Activities, Crafts, Experiments & More for Kids to Do to Learn about Your State! (p. 1246)
—New York Current Events Projects: 30 Cool, Activities, Crafts, Experiments & More for Kids to Do to Learn about Your State! (p. 1248)
—New York Geography Projects: 30 Cool, Activities, Crafts, Experiments & More for Kids to Do to Learn about Your State! (p. 1248)
—New York History Projects: 30 Cool, Activities, Crafts, Experiments & More for Kids to Do to Learn about Your State! (p. 1248)
—New York People Projects: 30 Cool, Activities, Crafts, Experiments & More for Kids to Do to Learn about Your State! (p. 1248)
—New York Pocket Guide. (p. 1248)
—New York Symbols & Facts Projects: 30 Cool, Activities, Crafts, Experiments & More for Kids to Do to Learn about Your State! (p. 1248)
—Nifty New Jersey Coloring Book. (p. 1252)
—Nifty New York Coloring Book. (p. 1252)
—Nifty North Carolina Coloring Book. (p. 1252)
—North Carolina Current Events Projects: 30 Cool, Activities, Crafts, Experiments & More for Kids to Do to Learn about Your State! (p. 1265)
—North Carolina Experience Pocket Guide. (p. 1265)
—North Carolina Geography Projects: 30 Cool, Activities, Crafts, Experiments & More for Kids to Do to Learn about Your State! (p. 1265)
—North Carolina Government Projects: 30 Cool, Activities, Crafts, Experiments & More for Kids to Do to Learn about Your State! (p. 1265)
—North Carolina History Projects: 30 Cool, Activities, Crafts, Experiments & More for Kids to Do to Learn about Your State! (p. 1265)
—North Carolina Jeopardy! Answers & Questions about Our State! (p. 1265)
—North Carolina "Jography" A Fun Run Through the Tarheel State! (p. 1265)
—North Carolina People Projects: 30 Cool, Activities, Crafts, Experiments & More for Kids to Do to Learn about Your State! (p. 1265)
—North Carolina Symbols & Facts Projects: 30 Cool, Activities, Crafts, Experiments & More for Kids to Do to Learn about Your State! (p. 1265)
—North Carolina's Big Activity Book. (p. 1265)
—North Dakota Current Events Projects: 30 Cool, Activities, Crafts, Experiments & More for Kids to Do to Learn about Your State! (p. 1265)
—North Dakota Geography Projects: 30 Cool, Activities, Crafts, Experiments & More for Kids to Do to Learn about Your State! (p. 1265)
—North Dakota Government Projects: 30 Cool, Activities, Crafts, Experiments & More for Kids to Do to Learn about Your State! (p. 1265)
—North Dakota History Projects: 30 Cool, Activities, Crafts, Experiments & More for Kids to Do to Learn about Your State! (p. 1265)
—North Dakota People Projects: 30 Cool, Activities, Crafts, Experiments & More for Kids to Do to Learn about Your State! (p. 1265)
—NYC-5 Boroughs: Activity Book. Baker, Janice, ed. (p. 1274)
—Obama Family - Life in the White House: President Barack Obama, First Lady Michelle Obama, First Children Malia & Sasha. (p. 1275)
—Of All the Gaul! Latin for Kids. Beard, Chad, ed. (p. 1279)
—Ohio Classic Christmas Trivia. (p. 1281)
—Ohio Current Events Projects: 30 Cool, Activities, Crafts, Experiments & More for Kids to Do to Learn about Your State! (p. 1281)
—Ohio Experience Book (HC) (p. 1281)
—Ohio Geography Projects: 30 Cool, Activities, Crafts, Experiments & More for Kids to Do to Learn about Your State! (p. 1281)
—Ohio Government Projects: 30 Cool, Activities, Crafts, Experiments & More for Kids to Do to Learn about Your State! (p. 1281)
—Ohio History Projects: 30 Cool, Activities, Crafts, Experiments & More for Kids to Do to Learn about Your State! (p. 1281)
—Ohio Native Americans: A Kid's Look at Our State's Chiefs, Tribes, Reservations, Powwows, Lore, & More from the Past & the Present. (p. 1281)
—Ohio People Projects: 30 Cool, Activities, Crafts, Experiments & More for Kids to Do to Learn about Your State! (p. 1281)
—Ohio Symbols & Facts Projects: 30 Cool, Activities, Crafts, Experiments & More for Kids to Do to Learn about Your State! (p. 1282)
—Ohio's Big Activity Book. (p. 1282)
—Oklahoma Current Events Projects: 30 Cool, Activities, Crafts, Experiments & More for Kids to Do to Learn about Your State! (p. 1283)
—Oklahoma Geography Projects: 30 Cool, Activities, Crafts, Experiments & More for Kids to Do to Learn about Your State! (p. 1283)
—Oklahoma Government Projects: 30 Cool, Activities, Crafts, Experiments & More for Kids to Do to Learn about Your State! (p. 1283)
—Oklahoma History Projects: 30 Cool, Activities, Crafts, Experiments & More for Kids to Do to Learn about Your State! (p. 1283)
—Oklahoma Jeopardy! Answers & Questions about Our State. (p. 1283)
—Oklahoma Jography! A Fun Run Thru Our State. (p. 1283)
—Oklahoma People Projects: 30 Cool, Activities, Crafts, Experiments & More for Kids to Do to Learn about Your State! (p. 1283)
—Oklahoma Symbols Projects: 30 Cool Activities, Crafts, Experiments & More for Kids to Do! (p. 1283)
—Oregon Current Events Projects: 30 Cool, Activities, Crafts, Experiments & More for Kids to Do to Learn about Your State! (p. 1303)
—Oregon Geography Projects: 30 Cool, Activities, Crafts, Experiments & More for Kids to Do to Learn about Your State! (p. 1303)
—Oregon Government Projects: 30 Cool, Activities, Crafts, Experiments & More for Kids to Do to Learn about Your State! (p. 1303)
—Oregon History Projects: 30 Cool, Activities, Crafts, Experiments & More for Kids to Do to Learn about Your State! (p. 1303)
—Oregon People Projects: 30 Cool, Activities, Crafts, Experiments & More for Kids to Do to Learn about Your State! (p. 1303)
—Oregon Symbols & Facts Projects: 30 Cool, Activities, Crafts, Experiments & More for Kids to Do to Learn about Your State! (p. 1303)
—Out-of-This-World Oklahoma Coloring Book! (p. 1311)
—Pass the Test! Civics & Economics. (p. 1326)
—Peachtree City Coloring Book! (p. 1332)
—Pennsylvania Current Events Projects: 30 Cool, Activities, Crafts, Experiments & More for Kids to Do to Learn about Your State! (p. 1338)
—Pennsylvania Geography Projects: 30 Cool, Activities, Crafts, Experiments & More for Kids to Do to Learn about Your State! (p. 1338)
—Pennsylvania Government Projects: 30 Cool, Activities, Crafts, Experiments & More for Kids to Do to Learn about Your State! (p. 1338)
—Pennsylvania History Projects: 30 Cool, Activities, Crafts, Experiments & More for Kids to Do to Learn about Your State! (p. 1338)
—Pennsylvania Jeopardy! Answers & Questions about Our State! (p. 1338)
—Pennsylvania "Jography" A Fun Run Thru Our State! (p. 1338)
—Pennsylvania People Projects: 30 Cool, Activities, Crafts, Experiments & More for Kids to Do to Learn about Your State! (p. 1338)
—Pennsylvania Symbols & Facts Projects: 30 Cool, Activities, Crafts, Experiments & More for Kids to Do to Learn about Your State! (p. 1338)
—Pennsylvania's Big Activity Book. (p. 1338)
—Phillis Wheatley. (p. 1350)
—Pocahontas. (p. 1375)
—Proud Pennsylvania Coloring Book. (p. 1412)
—Puzzle of the Indian Arrowhead. (p. 1421)
—Puzzle of the Shark Surfer Girl. (p. 1421)
—Quit Bossing Us Around! The Declaration of Independence. (p. 1428)

—Rachel Carson: Excellent Ecologist. (p. 1431)
—Rhode Island Current Events Projects: 30 Cool, Activities, Crafts, Experiments & More for Kids to Do to Learn about Your State! (p. 1468)
—Rhode Island Geography Projects: 30 Cool, Activities, Crafts, Experiments & More for Kids to Do to Learn about Your State! (p. 1468)
—Rhode Island Government Projects: 30 Cool, Activities, Crafts, Experiments & More for Kids to Do to Learn about Your State! (p. 1468)
—Rhode Island History Projects: 30 Cool, Activities, Crafts, Experiments & More for Kids to Do to Learn about Your State! (p. 1468)
—Rhode Island People Projects: 30 Cool, Activities, Crafts, Experiments & More for Kids to Do to Learn about Your State! (p. 1468)
—Rhode Island Symbols & Facts Projects: 30 Cool, Activities, Crafts, Experiments & More for Kids to Do to Learn about Your State! (p. 1468)
—Riddle of the Missing Puppies. (p. 1470)
—Riddle of the Oogli Boogli. (p. 1470)
—Rip-Roaring Mystery on the African Safari. (p. 1473)
—Roberto Clemente: Baseball Hero & Humanitarian: Baseball Hero & Humanitarian. (p. 1479)
—Roger Williams. (p. 1484)
—Russia: The Great Bear & Its Dramatic History! (p. 1498)
—Sacagawea: Native American Heroine: Native American Heroine. (p. 1500)
—Samuel Adams. (p. 1509)
—Say What When You Sneeze?! German for Kids. Beard, Chad, ed. (p. 1519)
—Secret of Eyesocket Island. (p. 1542)
—Secret of Skullcracker Swamp. (p. 1542)
—Secret Soccer Ball. (p. 1544)
—Sequoyah. (p. 1552)
—Sitting Bull. (p. 1582)
—Sojourner Truth. (p. 1606)
—Someone I Love Went off to War. (p. 1609)
—South America: A Continent of Countries of Amazing Proportions! (p. 1616)
—South Carolina Current Events Projects: 30 Cool, Activities, Crafts, Experiments & More for Kids to Do to Learn about Your State! (p. 1616)
—South Carolina Geography Projects: 30 Cool, Activities, Crafts, Experiments & More for Kids to Do to Learn about Your State! (p. 1616)
—South Carolina Government Projects: 30 Cool, Activities, Crafts, Experiments & More for Kids to Do to Learn about Your State! (p. 1616)
—South Carolina History Projects: 30 Cool, Activities, Crafts, Experiments & More for Kids to Do to Learn about Your State! (p. 1616)
—South Carolina People Projects: 30 Cool, Activities, Crafts, Experiments & More for Kids to Do to Learn about Your State! (p. 1616)
—South Carolina Symbols & Facts Projects: 30 Cool, Activities, Crafts, Experiments & More for Kids to Do to Learn about Your State! (p. 1616)
—South Dakota Current Events Projects: 30 Cool, Activities, Crafts, Experiments & More for Kids to Do to Learn about Your State! (p. 1617)
—South Dakota Geography Projects: 30 Cool, Activities, Crafts, Experiments & More for Kids to Do to Learn about Your State! (p. 1617)
—South Dakota Government Projects: 30 Cool, Activities, Crafts, Experiments & More for Kids to Do to Learn about Your State! (p. 1617)
—South Dakota History Projects: 30 Cool, Activities, Crafts, Experiments & More for Kids to Do to Learn about Your State! (p. 1617)
—South Dakota People Projects: 30 Cool, Activities, Crafts, Experiments & More for Kids to Do to Learn about Your State! (p. 1617)
—South Dakota Symbols & Facts Projects: 30 Cool, Activities, Crafts, Experiments & More for Kids to Do to Learn about Your State! (p. 1617)
—Story of Santa Claus. (p. 1659)
—Story of the Christmas Tree. (p. 1660)
—Tennessee Current Events Projects: 30 Cool, Activities, Crafts, Experiments & More for Kids to Do to Learn about Your State! (p. 1720)
—Tennessee Experience Pocket Guide. (p. 1720)
—Tennessee Geography Projects: 30 Cool, Activities, Crafts, Experiments & More for Kids to Do to Learn about Your State! (p. 1720)
—Tennessee Government Projects: 30 Cool, Activities, Crafts, Experiments & More for Kids to Do to Learn about Your State! (p. 1720)
—Tennessee History Projects: 30 Cool, Activities, Crafts, Experiments & More for Kids to Do to Learn about Your State! (p. 1720)
—Tennessee Jeopardy! Answers & Questions about Our State! Line Art Staff, illus. (p. 1720)
—Tennessee People Projects: 30 Cool, Activities, Crafts, Experiments & More for Kids to Do to Learn about Your State! (p. 1720)
—Tennessee Symbols & Facts Projects: 30 Cool, Activities, Crafts, Experiments & More for Kids to Do to Learn about Your State! (p. 1720)
—Terrific Tennessee Coloring Book! (p. 1721)
—Texas Current Events Projects: 30 Cool, Activities, Crafts, Experiments & More for Kids to Do to Learn about Your State! (p. 1724)
—Texas Geography Projects: 30 Cool, Activities, Crafts, Experiments & More for Kids to Do to Learn about Your State! (p. 1724)
—Texas Government Projects: 30 Cool, Activities, Crafts, Experiments & More for Kids to Do to Learn about Your State! (p. 1724)
—Texas History Projects: 30 Cool, Activities, Crafts, Experiments & More for Kids to Do to Learn about Your State! (p. 1724)
—Texas Native Americans: A Kid's Look at Our State's Chiefs, Tribes, Reservations, Powwows, Lore, & More from the

Past & the Present. Corsey, Jenny & Valentine, Teresa, eds. (p. 1724)
—Texas People Projects: 30 Cool, Activities, Crafts, Experiments & More for Kids to Do to Learn about Your State! (p. 1724)
—Texas Symbols & Facts Projects: 30 Cool, Activities, Crafts, Experiments & More for Kids to Do to Learn about Your State! (p. 1724)
—Texas's Big Activity Book. (p. 1724)
—Theodore Roosevelt. (p. 1729)
—Thomas Paine. (p. 1739)
—Transcontinental Railroad: The Big Race to the Golden Spike. (p. 1778)
—Treacherous Tornado Mystery. (p. 1781)
—U. S. Constitution. Beard, Chad, ed. (p. 1806)
—Uh, Oh, Amigo! Spanish for Kids. Beard, Chad, ed. (p. 1808)
—Underground Railroad: Path to Freedom. (p. 1815)
—United Kingdom: The Country of Ships, Sealing Wax, Cabbages & Kings! (p. 1819)
—Utah Current Events Projects: 30 Cool, Activities, Crafts, Experiments & More for Kids to Do to Learn about Your State! (p. 1829)
—Utah Geography Projects: 30 Cool, Activities, Crafts, Experiments & More for Kids to Do to Learn about Your State! (p. 1829)
—Utah Government Projects: 30 Cool, Activities, Crafts, Experiments & More for Kids to Do to Learn about Your State! (p. 1829)
—Utah History Projects: 30 Cool, Activities, Crafts, Experiments & More for Kids to Do to Learn about Your State! (p. 1829)
—Utah People Projects: 30 Cool, Activities, Crafts, Experiments & More for Kids to Do to Learn about Your State! (p. 1829)
—Utah Symbols & Facts Projects: 30 Cool, Activities, Crafts, Experiments & More for Kids to Do to Learn about Your State! (p. 1829)
—Vermont Current Events Projects: 30 Cool, Activities, Crafts, Experiments & More for Kids to Do to Learn about Your State! (p. 1837)
—Vermont Geography Projects: 30 Cool, Activities, Crafts, Experiments & More for Kids to Do to Learn about Your State! (p. 1837)
—Vermont Government Projects: 30 Cool, Activities, Crafts, Experiments & More for Kids to Do to Learn about Your State! (p. 1837)
—Vermont History Projects: 30 Cool, Activities, Crafts, Experiments & More for Kids to Do to Learn about Your State! (p. 1837)
—Vermont People Projects: 30 Cool, Activities, Crafts, Experiments & More for Kids to Do to Learn about Your State! (p. 1837)
—Vermont Symbols & Facts Projects: 30 Cool, Activities, Crafts, Experiments & More for Kids to Do to Learn about Your State! (p. 1837)
—Virginia Classic Christmas Trivia. (p. 1844)
—Virginia Current Events Projects: 30 Cool, Activities, Crafts, Experiments & More for Kids to Do to Learn about Your State! (p. 1844)
—Virginia Geography Projects: 30 Cool, Activities, Crafts, Experiments & More for Kids to Do to Learn about Your State! (p. 1844)
—Virginia Government Projects: 30 Cool, Activities, Crafts, Experiments & More for Kids to Do to Learn about Your State! (p. 1844)
—Virginia History Projects: 30 Cool, Activities, Crafts, Experiments & More for Kids to Do to Learn about Your State! (p. 1844)
—Virginia People Projects: 30 Cool, Activities, Crafts, Experiments & More for Kids to Do to Learn about Your State! (p. 1844)
—Virginia Symbols & Facts Projects: 30 Cool, Activities, Crafts, Experiments & More for Kids to Do to Learn about Your State! (p. 1844)
—Voracious Volcano Mystery. (p. 1850)
—War What Kids Should Know. (p. 1858)
—Washington Current Events Projects: 30 Cool, Activities, Crafts, Experiments & More for Kids to Do to Learn about Your State! (p. 1859)
—Washington D. C. Millionaire. (p. 1860)
—Washington D. C. Survivor. (p. 1860)
—Washington D. C. Wheel of Fortune. (p. 1860)
—Washington Geography Projects: 30 Cool, Activities, Crafts, Experiments & More for Kids to Do to Learn about Your State! (p. 1860)
—Washington Government Projects: 30 Cool, Activities, Crafts, Experiments & More for Kids to Do to Learn about Your State! (p. 1860)
—Washington History Projects: 30 Cool, Activities, Crafts, Experiments & More for Kids to Do to Learn about Your State! (p. 1860)
—Washington People Projects: 30 Cool, Activities, Crafts, Experiments & More for Kids to Do to Learn about Your State! (p. 1860)
—Washington Symbols & Facts Projects: 30 Cool, Activities, Crafts, Experiments & More for Kids to Do to Learn about Your State! (p. 1860)
—Way to Go Amigo!English for Kids! (p. 1864)
—West Virginia Current Events Projects: 30 Cool, Activities, Crafts, Experiments & More for Kids to Do to Learn about Your State! (p. 1876)
—West Virginia Geography Projects: 30 Cool, Activities, Crafts, Experiments & More for Kids to Do to Learn about Your State! (p. 1876)
—West Virginia Government Projects: 30 Cool, Activities, Crafts, Experiments & More for Kids to Do to Learn about Your State! (p. 1876)
—West Virginia History Projects: 30 Cool, Activities, Crafts, Experiments & More for Kids to Do to Learn about Your State! (p. 1876)
—West Virginia Native Americans: A Kid's Look at Our State's Chiefs, Tribes, Reservations, Powwows, Lore & More from the Past & the Present. (p. 1876)

—West Virginia People Projects: 30 Cool, Activities, Crafts, Experiments & More for Kids to Do to Learn about Your State! (p. 1876)
—West Virginia Symbols & Facts Projects: 30 Cool, Activities, Crafts, Experiments & More for Kids to Do to Learn about Your State! (p. 1876)
—What a Deal! The Louisiana Purchase. (p. 1878)
—What Was the Civil War All about Anyway? (p. 1895)
—When Did It Happen in the Civil War? (p. 1902)
—Where Did the Civil War Happen? (p. 1906)
—White House Christmas Mystery. (p. 1913)
—Who Were the Key Players in the Civil War? (p. 1919)
—Why Do We Hang Christmas Stockings. (p. 1924)
—Wild Water Mystery at Niagra Falls. (p. 1930)
—William Penn. (p. 1933)
—Wisconsin Current Events Projects: 30 Cool, Activities, Crafts, Experiments & More for Kids to Do to Learn about Your State! (p. 1939)
—Wisconsin Experience Pocket Guide. (p. 1939)
—Wisconsin Geography Projects: 30 Cool, Activities, Crafts, Experiments & More for Kids to Do to Learn about Your State! (p. 1939)
—Wisconsin Government Projects: 30 Cool, Activities, Crafts, Experiments & More for Kids to Do to Learn about Your State! (p. 1939)
—Wisconsin History Projects: 30 Cool, Activities, Crafts, Experiments & More for Kids to Do to Learn about Your State! (p. 1939)
—Wisconsin Jeopardy! Answers & Questions about Our State! (p. 1939)
—Wisconsin "Jography" A Fun Run Thru Our State! (p. 1939)
—Wisconsin People Projects: 30 Cool, Activities, Crafts, Experiments & More for Kids to Do to Learn about Your State! (p. 1939)
—Wisconsin Symbols & Facts Projects: 30 Cool, Activities, Crafts, Experiments & More for Kids to Do to Learn about Your State! (p. 1939)
—Wisconsin's Big Activity Book. (p. 1939)
—Wonderful Wisconsin Coloring Book. (p. 1948)
—Work Words: Job/Business/Career Words & Terms You Need to Know! (p. 1952)
—World War II: Reproducible Activity Book. (p. 1959)
—World War II Reproducible Activity Book (HC) (p. 1959)
—Would You Hire This Person? A Look at Getting Hired (or Not!)... from the Point of View of Your (Possible) Future Employer. (p. 1962)
—Wyoming Current Events Projects: 30 Cool, Activities, Crafts, Experiments & More for Kids to Do to Learn about Your State! (p. 1966)
—Wyoming Geography Projects: 30 Cool, Activities, Crafts, Experiments & More for Kids to Do to Learn about Your State! (p. 1966)
—Wyoming Government Projects: 30 Cool, Activities, Crafts, Experiments & More for Kids to Do to Learn about Your State! (p. 1966)
—Wyoming History Projects: 30 Cool, Activities, Crafts, Experiments & More for Kids to Do to Learn about Your State! (p. 1966)
—Wyoming Native Americans: A Kid's Look at Our State's Chiefs, Tribes, Reservations, Powwows, Lore & More from the Past to the Present. (p. 1966)
—Wyoming People Projects: 30 Cool, Activities, Crafts, Experiments & More for Kids to Do to Learn about Your State! (p. 1966)
—Wyoming Symbols & Facts Projects: 30 Cool, Activities, Crafts, Experiments & More for Kids to Do to Learn about Your State! (p. 1966)
—Young Patriot's Book of Puzzles, Games, Riddles, Stories, Poems, & Activities. (p. 1979)
—Zany Zoo MYST. (p. 1985)
Marsh, Carole & Marsh, Michael. Let's Discover Arkansas! (p. 995)
—Let's Discover California! (p. 995)
—Let's Discover Colorado! (p. 995)
—Let's Discover Connecticut! (p. 995)
Marsh, Charis. I Forgot to Tell You: Ballet School Confidential (Large Print 16pt) (p. 838)
—Love You, Hate You. (p. 1060)
—You're So Sweet: Ballet School Confidential (Large Print 16pt) (p. 1982)
Marsh, David. Into the Abyss. (p. 881)
Marsh, David, jt. auth. see Thorpe, Tony.
Marsh, Dilleen, tr. What Happens When People Die? (p. 1886)
Marsh, Emily Beata. Saint John Bosco: Champion for the Young. Alfano, Wayne, illus. (p. 1503)
Marsh, Graham & Quarto Generic Staff. Max & the Lost Note. (p. 1110)
Marsh, Jakob, illus. see Biesanz, Thomas.
Marsh, James. Super.Activ Skateboarding. (p. 1682)
Marsh, Jennifer & Williams, Barbara. Purple Pencil. (p. 1419)
Marsh, John, ed. You Work Tomorrow: An Anthology of American Labor Poetry, 1929-41. (p. 1976)
Marsh, Katherine. Jepp, Who Defied the Stars. (p. 913)
—Night Tourist. (p. 1254)
Marsh, Kathleen. My Mother Kept a Scrapbook: The True Story of a WWII POW. (p. 1214)
Marsh, Kathleen Marie & Sprangers, Heather. Sunrise Sunset. (p. 1677)
Marsh, Kathryn. Musical Playground: Global Tradition & Change in Children's Songs & Games. (p. 1194)
Marsh, Kay. Story of Bleulatoo: The Cat That Could Rhyme. (p. 1657)
Marsh, Kenneth L. & Marsh, Robin L., compiled by. Alaska Cache, the Works of Alaskan Artist Curt W. Wagner, Jr.: A Local Legacy of Beauty & Life Beneath the Mountain. (p. 34)
Marsh, Laura. Caterpillar to Butterfly. (p. 279)
—Elephants. (p. 511)
—Great Migrations Amazing Animal Journeys. (p. 717)
—Great Migrations - Amazing Animal Journeys. (p. 717)
—Great Migrations Butterflies. (p. 717)
—Lions. (p. 1021)
—Lizards. (p. 1043)

—National Geographic Readers: Caterpillar to Butterfly. (p. 1233)
—National Geographic Readers: Cheetahs. (p. 1233)
—National Geographic Readers: Halloween. (p. 1233)
—National Geographic Readers: Koalas. (p. 1233)
—National Geographic Readers: Lions. (p. 1233)
—National Geographic Readers: Lizards. (p. 1233)
—National Geographic Readers: Owls. (p. 1233)
—National Geographic Readers: Polar Bears. (p. 1233)
—National Geographic Readers: Red Pandas. (p. 1233)
—National Geographic Readers: Ugly Animals. (p. 1233)
—Take a Leap! (p. 1696)
—Toot's Tour of India. (p. 1768)
—Whales. (p. 1878)
Marsh, Laura, jt. auth. see Fernandez, Joyce.
Marsh, Laura, jt. auth. see U. S. National Geographic Society Staff.
Marsh, Laura & Carney, Elizabeth. National Geographic Readers: Planets. (p. 1233)
Marsh, Laura F. Big Enough. (p. 181)
—Steps to Liberty. Wright, John R., illus. (p. 1648)
—What's in a Tail? (p. 1897)
Marsh, Merle, jt. auth. see Kendall, Diane.
Marsh, Michael. Project Digger. (p. 1410)
Marsh, Michael, jt. auth. see Marsh, Carole.
Marsh, Mike. Elefant Hunters Part One: Shipwreck! Jain, Priti, illus. (p. 505)
—Grumblies Set a Trap. Jain, Priti, illus. (p. 727)
—Skyrats Capture the Grumblies! Jain, Priti, illus. (p. 1587)
Marsh, Nancy, illus. see DeVos, Janie.
Marsh, Naomi Fawn. Mr. Crabby Pants the Crab. (p. 1184)
Marsh, Richard Phillip. Mattress People Go to Bear Park. (p. 1110)
Marsh, Robert. Monster & Me Percival, Tom, illus. (p. 1166)
—Monster in the Outfield Percival, Tom, illus. (p. 1167)
—Monster Moneymaker Percival, Tom, illus. (p. 1168)
Marsh, Robin L., jt. compiled by see Marsh, Kenneth L.
Marsh, Savitri. I Am Only One & This Is How I Eat Spaghetti. (p. 833)
Marsh, Scott. Hannah & the Golden Swan. (p. 742)
Marsh, Thomas E. Official Guide to Collecting Applied Color Soda Bottles (p. 1280)
Marshack, D. L. I'm the Tooth Fairy: Amy's First Visit. (p. 860)
Marshak, Flo. Grandma Punch Is: A Woman, a Mother, a Grandma, a Professional & a Lesbian. (p. 708)
Marshak, Laura E., jt. auth. see Prezant, Fran Pollock.
Marshak, Samuil. Circus & Other Stories. Capus, Stephen, tr. from RUS. (p. 322)
Marshall, Alan David, ed. see Duchene-Marshall, Michele A.
Marshall, Ann, illus. see Fishman, Cathy Goldberg.
Marshall, Anne, ed. see Parker, Steve.
Marshall, Ashley & Keller, Carolyn. Texas a & M University College Prowler off the Record. (p. 1724)
Marshall, Bonnie. Snow Maiden & Other Russian Tales Kulagina, Alla V., ed. (p. 1599)
Marshall Bradley, Fern & Cole, Trevor. All-New Illustrated Guide to Gardening: Now All Organic! (p. 45)
Marshall, Carl & Marshall, David. Book of Myself: A Do-It-Yourself Autobiography in 201 Questions. (p. 211)
Marshall, Carly. Babysitter & Little Miss Bossy. (p. 129)
—Babysitter & Little Mr. Trouble Maker. (p. 129)
—Babysitter & the Critter Hunt. (p. 129)
—Babysitter & the Hot Rainy Days. (p. 129)
—Babysitter & the Six Pack. (p. 129)
—Babysitter Takes Us to Church. (p. 129)
Marshall, Carol. Vampire's Story: Bella's Diary. (p. 1832)
Marshall Cavendish. Attack on Pearl Harbor. (p. 114)
—Cooking of Brazil. (p. 362)
—Cooking of China. (p. 362)
—Cooking of Greece. (p. 362)
—Khmer Rouge. (p. 951)
—Lost Boys of Sudan. (p. 1055)
—Miller. (p. 1143)
Marshall Cavendish, jt. auth. see Anon.
Marshall Cavendish Benchmark, prod. Heavy/Light. (p. 761)
—Hot/Cold. (p. 802)
Marshall Cavendish Benchmark Staff. Cooking of France. (p. 362)
Marshall Cavendish Corporation Staff. Anatomy & Physiology: An Illustrated Guide. (p. 67)
—Ancient Egypt & the Near East: An Illustrated History. (p. 68)
—Ancient Greece: An Illustrated History. (p. 69)
—Ancient Rome: An Illustrated History. (p. 70)
—Final Victories. (p. 586)
—Global Chaos. (p. 684)
—Mammal Anatomy: An Illustrated Guide. (p. 1084)
—Terror & Triumph. (p. 1722)
Marshall Cavendish Corporation Staff, jt. auth. see Barker, Geoff.
Marshall Cavendish Corporation Staff, jt. auth. see Demi Staff.
Marshall Cavendish Corporation Staff, jt. auth. see Downing, David.
Marshall Cavendish Corporation Staff, jt. auth. see Mason, Paul.
Marshall Cavendish Corporation Staff, contrib. by. Animal & Plant Anatomy. (p. 76)
—Drugs & Society. (p. 487)
—Encyclopedia of Health. (p. 525)
—Exploring Mammals. (p. 552)
—Insects & Spiders of the World. (p. 876)
—Inventors & Inventions. (p. 884)
—Wildlife & Plants. (p. 1931)
—World & Its Peoples: Middle East, Western Asia, & Northern Africa. (p. 1954)
Marshall Cavendish Corporation Staff, ed. How It Works: Science & Technology. (p. 810)
Marshall Cavendish Reference Staff. Illustrated Dictionary of the Muslim World. (p. 857)
—Islamic Beliefs, Practices, & Cultures. (p. 891)
—Modern Muslim Societies. (p. 1158)
—Muslim World. (p. 1194)
—North American Wildlife. (p. 1264)

For book reviews, descriptive annotations, tables of contents, cover images, author biographies & additional information, updated daily, subscribe to www.booksinprint2.com

2479

Marshall Cavendish Reference Staff, contrib. by. Encyclopedia of Diseases & Disorders. (p. 525)
—Mammals of the Northern Hemisphere. (p. 1085)
—Mammals of the Southern Hemisphere. (p. 1085)
Marshall Cavendish Staff, jt. auth. see Mason, Paul.
Marshall, Dan, illus. see Rand, Carol.
Marshall, Dave, ed. see Aclin, Justin.
Marshall, Dave, ed. see Gelinas, Ben, et al.
Marshall, Dave, ed. see Konietzko, Bryan, et al.
Marshall, Dave, ed. see Yang, Gene Luen, et al.
Marshall, David. Brazil. (p. 224)
Marshall, David, jt. auth. see Marshall, Carl.
Marshall, David & Sayer, Geoff. Kenya. (p. 949)
Marshall, Deb. Orangutans. (p. 1302)
Marshall, Denise. Adventures of Hip Hop: Hip Hop & the Blueberry Pancakes. Champagne, Heather, illus. (p. 18)
—Adventures of Hip Hop: Hip Hop & the Yellow Hat. Schley, Cheri & Champagne, Heather, illus. (p. 18)
Marshall, Denise, illus. see Brothers Grimm Staff.
Marshall, Derek. What Is a Law? (p. 1888)
Marshall, Diana. Aboriginal Australians. (p. 5)
Marshall, Diana, ed. see Foran, Jill.
Marshall, Diana, ed. see Hamilton, Lynn A.
Marshall, Diana, ed. see Nault, Jennifer.
Marshall, Diana, ed. see Ring, Susan.
Marshall, Edward & Marshall, James. Fox & His Friends. (p. 626)
—Fox at School. (p. 626)
—Fox in Love. (p. 626)
—Fox on Wheels. (p. 626)
—Three by the Sea. (p. 1741)
Marshall, Felicia, illus. see Brown, Susan Taylor.
Marshall, Felicia, illus. see Figley, Marty Rhodes.
Marshall, Felicia, illus. see Gayle, Sharon.
Marshall, Felicia, illus. see McKissack, Patricia C.
Marshall, Felicia, illus. see Watts, Jeri Hanel.
Marshall, Felicity. Star. (p. 1640)
Marshall, G. Skies of Dawn. (p. 1584)
Marshall, George. Kingfisher Children's Illustrated Dictionary & Thesaurus. (p. 960)
Marshall, Gwendolyn. Saving Crystallia (p. 1517)
Marshall, H. Stories of Robin Hood Told to the Children (Yesterday's Classics) (p. 1655)
Marshall, H. E. Our Empire Story. Skelton, J. R., illus. (p. 1308)
—Our Island Story: A History of Britain for Boys & Girls, from the Romans to Queen Victoria. (p. 1309)
—Our Island Story. (p. 1309)
—Our Island Story (Yesterday's Classics) Forrest, A. S., illus. (p. 1309)
—Scotland's Story. (p. 1530)
—Scotland's Story (Yesterday's Classics) Skelton, J. R. et al, illus. (p. 1530)
—Stories of Beowulf Told to the Children (Yesterday's Classics) (p. 1654)
—Stories of Roland Told to the Children (Yesterday's Classics) (p. 1655)
—This Country of Ours. (p. 1735)
—This Country of Ours (Yesterday's Classics) (p. 1735)
Marshall, H. Keene, illus. see Rundstrom, Teressa.
Marshall, Hallie. Winnie the Pooh's Many Adventures Kurtz, John, illus. (p. 1937)
Marshall, Harriet C. Marathon Mama. (p. 1091)
Marshall, Heidi Amenda. Petra's Adventure in Nievenheim. Marshall, Heidi Amenda, illus. (p. 1348)
Marshall, Henrietta. Our Island Story Unabridged. (p. 1309)
Marshall, Ian, illus. see Turkovitz, Karen.
Marshall, Ingeborg. Beothuk of Newfoundland: A Vanished People. (p. 166)
Marshall, James. Complete Stories of Two Best Friends. (p. 353)
—George & Martha: One More Time Early Reader, No. 6 (p. 663)
—George & Martha: The Best of Friends Early Reader, No. 4 (p. 663)
—George & Martha Early Reader. (p. 663)
—George & Martha Two Great Friends Early Reader. (p. 663)
—Rise & Shine No. 5. (p. 1474)
—Round & Round (p. 1491)
—Swine Lake. (p. 1691)
—Three Little Pigs. (p. 1742)
—Wings: A Tale of Two Chickens. (p. 1936)
Marshall, James, illus. see Allard, Harry G., Jr.
Marshall, James, illus. see Allard, Harry.
Marshall, James, illus. see Karlin, Barbara.
Marshall, James, jt. auth. see Allard, Harry G., Jr.
Marshall, James, jt. auth. see Allard, Harry.
Marshall, James, jt. auth. see Blanchard, Jay.
Marshall, James, jt. auth. see Marshall, Edward.
Marshall, James, jt. auth. see Marshall, James.
Marshall, James & Marshall, James. George & Martha Book & CD (p. 663)
—Wings: A Tale of Two Chickens. (p. 1936)
Marshall, James Vance. More Stories from the Billabong. Firebrace, Francis, illus. (p. 1175)
—Stories from the Billabong. Firebrace, Francis, illus. (p. 1654)
Marshall, Jamie, illus. see Howell, Trisha Adelena.
Marshall, Jane. Boats. (p. 205)
—Fast Cars. (p. 576)
—Planes. (p. 1367)
—Rescue Vehicles. (p. 1462)
—Superbikes. (p. 1682)
—Trucks & Diggers. (p. 1791)
Marshall, Jane Garrett. Christmas Tree That Cried. Tomasek, Dean, illus. (p. 316)
Marshall, Janet, illus. see Manley, Molly.
Marshall, Jennifer, jt. auth. see Mallon, Lynn.
Marshall, Jill. Kave-Tina Rox. Childs, Sam, illus. (p. 946)
Marshall, Jillyann. Newlywed Club. (p. 1249)
Marshall, Jo. Leaf & the Rushing Waters: Twig Stories. Murray, D., illus. (p. 982)
—Leaf & the Sky of Fire: Twig Stories. Murray, D. W., illus. (p. 982)
Marshall, John A. Right On Book 1: Prevention Power. Osborn, Susan, ed. (p. 1472)
Marshall, Judy. Morning. Annelli, Nikki, illus. (p. 1175)
Marshall, Julia, illus. see Barbo, Theresa Mitchell & Webster, W. Russell.
Marshall, Julia, illus. see Downing, Johnette.
Marshall, Julia, illus. see Karwoski, Gail Langer.
Marshall, Julia, jt. auth. see Jablecki, Joseph S.
Marshall, Kate. Mokes, Mines & Mayhem. (p. 1160)
Marshall, Ken. Adventures of Maya & Grampa. (p. 20)
Marshall, Kenneth L. Adventures of Maya & Grandpa. (p. 20)
Marshall, Kevin, jt. auth. see Celentano, Suzanne C.
Marshall, Laurie, illus. see Venable, Alan.
Marshall, Linda, jt. auth. see Elovitz Marshall, Sylvia A.
Marshall, Linda Elovitz. Grandma Rose's Magic. Jatkowska, Ag, illus. (p. 708)
—Grandma Rose's Magic/By Linda Elovitz Marshall ; Illustrated by Ag Jatkowska. Jatkowska, Ag, illus. (p. 708)
—Kindergarten's Cool. Chatterton, Chris, illus. (p. 957)
—Mitzvah Magician. Engel, Christiane, illus. (p. 1156)
—Passover Lamb. Mai-Wyss, Tatjana, illus. (p. 1327)
—Shh..Shh..Shabbat. Golubeva, Evgenia, illus. (p. 1566)
—Talia & the Rude Vegetables. Assirelli, Francesca, illus. (p. 1703)
—Talia & the Very YUM Kippur. Assirelli, Francesca, illus. (p. 1703)
—Talia & the Very Yum Kippur. Assirelli, Francesca, illus. (p. 1703)
Marshall, Logan. Favorite Fairy Tales. (p. 578)
Marshall, Logan, compiled by. Favorite Fairy Tales. (p. 578)
Marshall, Margaret. Sing-A-Long with Me: A-Z & Letter Sounds Sing-A-Long. (p. 1578)
Marshall, Mark. Mapping Your Church Strategy. (p. 1090)
Marshall, Melanie. Ladybug. (p. 971)
Marshall, Monica. Joe Sacco. (p. 920)
Marshall, Natalie. Millie-Mae: In Autumn. (p. 1144)
—Monster, Be Good! (p. 1166)
—My Turn to Learn Colors. (p. 1220)
—My Turn to Learn Numbers. (p. 1220)
—My Turn to Learn Opposites. (p. 1220)
—My Turn to Learn Shapes. (p. 1220)
—Seaside Sandcastle! (p. 1538)
—This Little Piggy: A Fingers & Toes Nursery Rhyme Book. Marshall, Natalie, illus. (p. 1737)
—Tiny Creatures: Touch & Feel Book. (p. 1756)
—Zoo Fun: A Lift the Flap Guessing Book. (p. 1989)
Marshall, Natalie, illus. see Fletcher, Corina.
Marshall, Natalie, illus. see Ziefert, Harriet.
Marshall, Pam. De la Idea Al Libro. Translations.com Staff, tr. (p. 416)
—From Tree to Paper. (p. 644)
Marshall, Peter, et al. Mercy Clifton: Pilgrim Girl. (p. 1127)
—Nate Donovan: Revolutionary Spy. (p. 1230)
Marshall, Phillip, jt. auth. see Arcy, Sean.
Marshall, Phillip, jt. auth. see Stoddard, Rosie.
Marshall, Richard, jt. auth. see Manale, Shizumi.
Marshall, Richard D. Ed Ruscha. (p. 503)
Marshall, Rita. I Hate to Read! Delessert, Etienne, illus. (p. 839)
—I Still Hate to Read! Delessert, Etienne, illus. (p. 846)
Marshall, Rita & Chronicle Books Staff. Illustrated Treasury of Fairy Tales. Chronicle Books Staff, illus. (p. 858)
Marshall, Sandra K. Tom's Space Adventure. (p. 1765)
Marshall, Sarah. Learning Football with the Hokie Bird. (p. 985)
Marshall, Setsu, illus. see Rundstrom, Teressa.
Marshall, Shelley. Molly the Great Misses the Bus: A Book about Being on Time. Mahan, Ben, illus. (p. 1161)
—Molly the Great Respects the Flag: A Book about Being a Good Citizen. Mahan, Ben, illus. (p. 1161)
—Molly the Great Tells the Truth: A Book about Honesty. Mahan, Ben, illus. (p. 1161)
—Molly the Great's Messy Bed: A Book about Responsibility. Mahan, Ben, illus. (p. 1161)
—Super Ben Writes a Letter: A Book about Caring. Mahan, Ben, illus. (p. 1679)
—Super Ben's Brave Bike Ride: A Book about Courage. Mahan, Ben, illus. (p. 1679)
—Super Ben's Broken Cookie: A Book about Sharing. Mahan, Ben, illus. (p. 1679)
—Super Ben's Dirty Hands: A Book about Healthy Habits. Mahan, Ben, illus. (p. 1679)
Marshall, Stacey A. Captain Courage & the Fear-Squishing Shoes. Morse, Michelle, illus. (p. 264)
—Captain Courage & the World's Most Shocking Secret Book 2. Morse, Michelle, illus. (p. 264)
Marshall, Stephen A. Insects A to Z. (p. 876)
Marshall, Stephen A., jt. auth. see Worek, Michael.
Marshall, Stephen A. & Worek, Michael. Weird Insects. (p. 1872)
Marshall, Thurgood. Thurgood Marshall. (p. 1746)
Marshall, Todd, illus. see Dodson, Peter & Library Association Staff.
Marshall, Todd, illus. see Norman, Kim & American Museum of Natural History Staff.
Marshall, Wendolyn. Buzzbee Warnings about Drugs. (p. 249)
—Buzzbee Warnings about Strangers. (p. 249)
Marshall, Wendy. O'Clocks: Mr. O'Clock Goes to A Party. (p. 1277)
Marshall, William L., jt. ed. see Barbaree, Howard E.
Marshall, Wynne. Tree Monkeys. (p. 1783)
Marshall, Yvonne. Punishing Imogen. (p. 1417)
—Striping Kayla. (p. 1667)
Marshland, Brad. Imagicators & the Wind Between the Worlds. (p. 860)
Marsico, Katie. Alcohol Abuse. (p. 35)
—Alexander the Great: Ancient King & Conqueror. (p. 36)
—American Bullfrogs. (p. 60)
—Andrew Jackson. (p. 72)
—Arctic Fox (p. 96)
—Auto Technician. (p. 117)
—Baby Lobster Grows Up. (p. 127)
—Baby Lobster Grows Up. Marsico, Katie, illus. (p. 127)
—Ball Game Math. (p. 134)
—Black Widow Spiders. (p. 197)
—Bridges. (p. 227)
—Bullying. (p. 241)
—Cheetahs. (p. 296)
—Chesapeake Bay. (p. 298)
—Chimpanzees. (p. 306)
—Chinese New Year. Conger, Holli, illus. (p. 307)
—Choreographer. (p. 310)
—Colorado River. (p. 343)
—Cómo Crece una Mariquita. (p. 350)
—Conjunctions. Petelinsek, Kathleen, illus. (p. 357)
—Dancer. (p. 402)
—Darkest & the Brightest. (p. 408)
—Depression & Stress. (p. 427)
—Doctor. (p. 459)
—Doctors Without Borders. (p. 459)
—Drones. (p. 485)
—Drug Abuse. (p. 486)
—Eating Disorders. (p. 501)
—Egypt. (p. 506)
—Eleanor Roosevelt: First Lady & Human Rights Advocate. (p. 508)
—Elephants Have Trunks. (p. 512)
—Emperor Penguin (p. 520)
—Everglades. (p. 542)
—Falcons. (p. 566)
—Fidel Castro: Cuban President & Revolutionary. (p. 583)
—Fitness Math. (p. 599)
—Football. (p. 615)
—Garden Math. (p. 656)
—Geckos. (p. 659)
—Giraffes Have Long Necks. (p. 678)
—Good Manners at Home. Haslam, John, illus. (p. 698)
—Good Manners at School. Haslam, John, illus. (p. 698)
—Good Manners in a Restaurant. Haslam, John, illus. (p. 698)
—Good Manners in Public. Haslam, John, illus. (p. 698)
—Good Manners on the Phone. Haslam, John, illus. (p. 698)
—Good Manners on the Playground. Haslam, John, illus. (p. 698)
—Gulf of Mexico. (p. 731)
—Heroin. (p. 773)
—Highest & the Lowest. (p. 779)
—Hippopotamuses. (p. 781)
—HIV/AIDS. (p. 786)
—Horse Rescue. (p. 800)
—Hottest & the Coldest. (p. 802)
—How Do We Live Together? Coyotes. (p. 808)
—How Do We Live Together? Hawks. (p. 808)
—How to Analyze the Works of Andrew Lloyd Webber. (p. 814)
—I Cry. (p. 837)
—I Throw Up. (p. 846)
—Inclined Planes. Butler, Reginald, illus. (p. 869)
—Interjections. Petelinsek, Kathleen, illus. (p. 880)
—It's Cool to Learn about the United States Southeast. (p. 896)
—Jaguars. (p. 905)
—Kangaroo Joey Grows Up. (p. 942)
—Key Discoveries in Physical Science. (p. 950)
—King Cobras. (p. 958)
—Kitchen Math. (p. 962)
—Koala Bears. (p. 966)
—Komodo Dragon Hatchling Grows Up. (p. 966)
—Lady Gaga: Pop Singer & Songwriter. (p. 970)
—Ladybug Larva Grows Up. (p. 971)
—Ladybug Larva Grows Up. Marsico, Katie, illus. (p. 971)
—Leeches. (p. 987)
—Leopard Seal (p. 993)
—Levels. (p. 1003)
—Levers. Butler, Reginald, illus. (p. 1003)
—Lice. (p. 1007)
—Llama. (p. 1043)
—Lucretia Mott: Abolitionist & Women's Rights Leader. (p. 1063)
—Madame C. J. Walker. (p. 1069)
—Manatee Calf Grows Up. (p. 1086)
—Manatees. (p. 1086)
—Math on the Move. (p. 1106)
—Mississippi River. (p. 1154)
—Missouri River. (p. 1154)
—Money Math. (p. 1164)
—Montgomery Bus Boycott: Milestone of the Civil Rights Movement. (p. 1170)
—Mountains. (p. 1181)
—Narwhal (p. 1230)
—Oldest & the Newest. (p. 1285)
—Otters. (p. 1307)
—Peachick Grows Up. (p. 1332)
—Peachick Grows Up. Marsico, Katie, illus. (p. 1332)
—Plan Ahead! (p. 1366)
—Play Fair! (p. 1371)
—Please & Thank You! (p. 1373)
—Pliers. (p. 1374)
—Polar Bear (p. 1378)
—Prepositions. Petelinsek, Kathleen, illus. (p. 1396)
—Pronouns. Petelinsek, Kathleen, illus. (p. 1411)
—Puget Sound. (p. 1415)
—Pulleys. Butler, Reginald, illus. (p. 1415)
—Put Your Stuff Away! (p. 1420)
—Racism. (p. 1432)
—Red Cross. (p. 1453)
—Reindeer (p. 1457)
—Rio Grande. (p. 1473)
—Russia. (p. 1498)
—Saltwater Crocodiles. (p. 1506)
—Salvation Army. (p. 1506)
—Saws. (p. 1518)
—Scholastic News Nonfiction Readers: Life Cycles (p. 1522)
—Sharks. (p. 1562)
—Shopping Trip Math. (p. 1569)
—Skyscrapers. (p. 1587)
—Southeast. (p. 1617)
—Speak Up! (p. 1622)
—Speed Skating. (p. 1624)
—Step-by-Step Experiments with Insects. Ostrom, Bob, illus. (p. 1647)
—Step-by-Step Experiments with Life Cycles. Ostrom, Bob, illus. (p. 1647)
—Step-by-Step Experiments with Taste & Digestion. Ostrom, Bob, illus. (p. 1647)
—Stinky Sanitation Inventions. (p. 1651)
—Taking Turns! (p. 1698)
—Tape Measures. (p. 1705)
—Tennis. (p. 1720)
—Texas Polygamist Raid: Religious Freedom Versus Child Welfare. (p. 1724)
—Therapy Horses. (p. 1729)
—Trail of Tears: The Tragedy of the American Indians. (p. 1776)
—Trains. (p. 1777)
—Tremendous Technology Inventions. (p. 1784)
—Triangle Shirtwaist Factory Fire: Its Legacy of Labor Rights. (p. 1785)
—Turkey. (p. 1797)
—Unicef. (p. 1818)
—United States. (p. 1819)
—Use Your Indoor Voice! (p. 1827)
—War of 1812. (p. 1857)
—Warships. (p. 1859)
—Weather Math. (p. 1870)
—Wedges. Butler, Reginald, illus. (p. 1871)
—Wettest & the Driest. (p. 1877)
—What's It Like to Live Here? City. (p. 1898)
—What's It Like to Live Here? Fishing Village. (p. 1898)
—What's It Like to Live Here? Mining Town. (p. 1898)
—What's It Like to Live Here? Suburb. (p. 1898)
—White-Tailed Deer. (p. 1913)
—Wild Horses. (p. 1929)
—Wild Weather Days. (p. 1930)
—Women's Right to Vote: America's Suffrage Movement. (p. 1946)
—Woodrow Wilson. (p. 1949)
—Working at a Bank. (p. 1952)
—Working at a Computer Store. (p. 1952)
—Working at a Factory. (p. 1952)
—Working at a Grocery Store. (p. 1952)
—Working at a Park. (p. 1952)
—Working at a Restaurant. (p. 1952)
—Working at a School. (p. 1952)
—Working at the Airport. (p. 1952)
—Working at the Library. (p. 1952)
—Working at the Post Office. (p. 1952)
—Working on a Farm. (p. 1953)
—World Health Organization. (p. 1955)
—World War II: Why They Fought. (p. 1959)
—Your Healthy Plate: Dairy. (p. 1980)
—Your Healthy Plate - Dairy. (p. 1980)
—Your Healthy Plate: Fruits. (p. 1980)
—Your Healthy Plate - Fruits. (p. 1980)
—Your Healthy Plate: Oils & Fats. (p. 1980)
—Your Healthy Plate - Oils & Fats. (p. 1980)
—Your Healthy Plate: Protein. (p. 1980)
—Your Healthy Plate - Protein. (p. 1980)
—Your Healthy Plate: Vegetables. (p. 1980)
—Your Healthy Plate - Vegetables. (p. 1980)
—Zora Neale Hurston. (p. 1990)
Marsico, Katie, et al. Running. (p. 1497)
Marsiglia, Flavio Francisco & Kulis, Stephen Stanley. Diversity, Oppression, & Change: Culturally Grounded Social Work. (p. 454)
Marsocci, Joey & DeBlasio, Allison. How to Draw Steampunk: Discover the Secrets to Drawing, Painting, & Illustrating the Curious World of Science Fiction in the Victorian Age. Berry, Bob, illus. (p. 818)
Marsoli, Lisa Ann. Dinos are Big Babies & Dylan's Pets. Smitherton, Jeb, illus. (p. 441)
—Dinosaurs are Big Babies. Smitherton, Jeb, illus. (p. 444)
—Dylan's Pets from A to Z. Santat, Dan, illus. (p. 491)
—Harold Takes a Trip: Harold & the Purple Crayon. Chiang, Andy, illus. (p. 749)
—Harold's Birthday Surprise: Harold & the Purple Crayon. Murawski, Kevin, illus. (p. 749)
—Leaping Lily: A Ballet Story. Leijten, Aileen, illus. (p. 982)
—Let's Go to the Zoo. Smitherton, Jeb, illus. (p. 998)
—Let's Go to the Zoo & Leaping Lily. Smitherton, Jeb, illus. (p. 998)
—Minnierella. (p. 1148)
—Puppy Love. Durk, Jim, illus. (p. 1418)
—Rudolph the Red-Nosed Reindeer Pop-Up Book. Finch, Keith Andrew, illus. (p. 1494)
—Sofia the First: The Missing Necklace. (p. 1605)
—Tiggeriffic Band Harchy, Atelier Philippe, illus. (p. 1749)
Marsoli, Lisa Ann, jt. auth. see Disney Book Group Staff.
Marsoli, Lisa Ann & Bridwell, Norman. Snow Dog. Haefele, Steve, illus. (p. 1598)
Marsoli, Lisa Ann & Disney Book Group Staff. Doctoring the Doc. Disney Storybook Artists Staff, illus. (p. 459)
—Halloween Ball. Disney Storybook Art Team, illus. (p. 737)
—Mickey Mouse Clubhouse Minnie-Rella. Disney Storybook Artists Staff, illus. (p. 1136)
—Once upon a Princess. Disney Storybook Artists Staff & Disney Storybook Art Team, illus. (p. 1293)
—Sofia Takes the Lead, Level 1. Disney Storybook Artists Staff, illus. (p. 1605)
—Welcome to Royal Prep, Level 1. Disney Storybook Art Team, illus. (p. 1873)
Marsoli, Lisa Ann & RH Disney Staff. My Perfect Wedding. (p. 1216)
Marson, Janyce. Leo Tolstoy. (p. 992)
—Thomas Hardy. Bloom, Harold, ed. (p. 1738)
Marson, Janyce, jt. ed. see Bloom, Harold.
Marstall, Bob, illus. see Cleary, Beverly.
Marstall, Bob, illus. see Heinz, Brian.
Marstall, Bob, illus. see Pringle, Laurence.
Marstall, Robert, illus. see Strother, Ruth.
Marston, Carrie. Catch Me If You Can. (p. 279)
Marston, Daniel & O'Neill, Robert John. American Revolutionary War. (p. 63)
Marston, Elsa. Compassionate Warrior: Abd el-Kader of Algeria. (p. 352)
—Figs & Fate: Stories about Growing up in the Arab World Today. (p. 586)
—Olive Tree. Ewart, Claire, illus. (p. 1285)
—Santa Claus in Baghdad & Other Stories about Teens in the Arab World. (p. 1511)

—Songs of Ancient Journeys: Animals in Rock Art. (p. 1612)
Marston, Hope Irvin. Against the Tide: The Valor of Margaret Wilson. (p. 29)
—My Little Book of Manatees. Mirocha, Stephanie, illus. (p. 1212)
Marston, J. D., photos by. Poems for Pequenines (Poemas Para Pequenines) (p. 1376)
Marston, Ralph S., Jr. Living the Wonder of It All: Positive, Empowering Messages from the Daily Motivator. (p. 1041)
Marston, William Moulton. Wonder Woman. (p. 1947)
Marta, Diana M., illus. see Kisinger, E. Jean.
Marta, Karen, ed. Philippe Parreno & Johan Olander: Parade. (p. 1350)
Marta, Osorio, jt. auth. see Osorio, Marta.
Marta, Rivera Ferner, jt. auth. see Rivera Ferner, Marta.
Martchenko, Michael. Pigs. (p. 1358)
Martchenko, Michael, illus. see Lesynski, Loris.
Martchenko, Michael, illus. see Morgan, Allen.
Martchenko, Michael, illus. see Munsch, Robert.
Martchenko, Michael, illus. see Skrypuch, Marsha.
Martchenko, Michael, jt. auth. see Lesynski, Loris.
Martchenko, Michael, jt. auth. see Munsch, Robert.
Martchenko, Michael, jt. auth. see Skrypuch, Marsha Forchuk.
Martchenko, Michael, tr. see Morgan, Allen.
Martel, Janet Y. Taken in the Night: Second Edition. (p. 1697)
Martell, Hazel, jt. auth. see Kuhtz, Cleo.
Martell, Hazel Mary, et al. Big Book of Civilizations. (p. 179)
Martell, Oswald Perez, tr. see Kitch, Anne E.
Martell, Ray. Brox the Bungling Badger. (p. 232)
Martella, Liz. Izabella & her Wardrobe. (p. 901)
Martelli, Dawn. Like Me. Wharton, Jennifer Heyd, illus. (p. 1017)
Martelly, Ameline. Flor. (p. 606)
Marten, Luanne. There Was an Old Woman Who Lived in a Shoe. Marten, Luanne, illus. (p. 1730)
Marten, Luanne, illus. see StJohn, Amanda.
Marten, Luanne, illus. see Vogel, Julia.
Marten, Luanne Voltmer, illus. see Ziglar, Christy.
Martens, Elisabeth, jt. auth. see McLeod, Len.
Martens, Frederick H., tr. see Wilhelm, Richard, ed.
Martens, Helle, jt. auth. see Thydell, Johanna.
Martens, Kara. Two Missing Kids. (p. 1804)
Martens, Marianne, tr. see Perrin, Martine.
Martens, Marianne, tr. see Tashiro, Chisato.
Marter, Ian. Doctor Who & the Ark in Space. (p. 459)
Märtha Louise, Princess. Why Kings & Queens Don't Wear Crowns (with CD) Sevig-Fajardo, Mari Elise, tr. from NOR. (p. 1925)
Martha, Morales. Ariana Leaves San Francisco. Chiu, Bessie, illus. (p. 98)
Martha Stewart Living Magazine Staff. Martha Stewart's Favorite Crafts for Kids: 175 Projects for Kids of All Ages to Create, Build, Design, Explore, & Share. (p. 1097)
Marthal, Barbara G. Fighting for Freedom: A Documented Story. (p. 585)
Marthaller, Brent A. Lonely Christmas Tree. (p. 1046)
Marti, Jose. Jose Marti: Cuatro cuentos Infantiles. Martinez, Enrique & Graullera, Fabiola, illus. (p. 926)
—Jose Marti Seleccion. (p. 926)
—Meñique, las Aventuras del Niño Más Pequeñito. (p. 1126)
Martí, José & José, Martí. Zapaticos de Rosa. (p. 1985)
—Zapaticos de Rosa. Delacre, Lulu, illus. (p. 1985)
Martí, Mònica. Fiestas: Actividades Creativas para la Educacion Infantil. (p. 584)
—Invierno: Actividades Creativas para la Educacion Infantil. (p. 885)
—Otono: Actividades Creativas para la Educacion Infantil. (p. 1307)
—Primavera: Actividades Creativas para la Educacion Infantil. (p. 1400)
—Verano: Actividades Creativas para la Educacion Infantil. (p. 1836)
Marti, Nuria, tr. see Crist, James J. & Crist, J. J.
Marti, Nuria, tr. see Le Duc, Michel, et al.
Martian, Agent. Notes from Spaceship. (p. 1268)
Martin, A - Weissmann, jt. auth. see Juventud Staff.
Martin, Abigail M. Welcome to Applewood Place. (p. 1873)
Martin, Alice, illus. see Hunger, Bill.
Martin, Alison. Princess of Tabaria. (p. 1404)
Martin, Alison J. Charlie, the Brave Monkey. Martin, Alison J., illus. (p. 293)
Martin, Alixandra, illus. see DiVencenzo, Maria T.
Martin, Amie. Little One. (p. 1032)
Martin, Amy. As You Wake. (p. 105)
—In Your Dreams. (p. 868)
—Symphony City. (p. 1693)
Martin, Ana I., illus. see Larranaga, Ana M.
Martin, Andreu, tr. see Giraud, Jean & Charlier, Jean-Michel.
Martin, Andreu & Ribero, J. No Pidas Sardinas Fuera de Temporada. (p. 1259)
Martin, Angela. You Worry Me Tracey, You Really Do! (p. 1976)
Martin Anguita, Carmen & Carmen, Martin Anguita. Cuando Llega la Noche. Cortazar, Alicia Canas, illus. (p. 388)
—Cuéntame un Cuento, Que Voy a Comer. Cortazar, Alicia Canas, illus. (p. 389)
—Cumpleaños de Laika. Cortazar, Alicia Canas, illus. (p. 392)
—Marta y Mamá Juegan a Recordar. Cortazar, Alicia Canas, illus. (p. 1097)
—Marta y Su Dragón (Martha & Her Dragon) Cortazar, Alicia Canas, illus. (p. 1097)
—Primer Día de Colegio de David. Cortazar, Alicia Canas, illus. (p. 1400)
—Tarde en el Circo. Cortazar, Alicia Canas, illus. (p. 1706)
Martin, Ann M. Belle Teal. (p. 163)
—Belle Teale. (p. 163)
—Best Friends. (p. 169)
—Better to Wish. (p. 172)
—Bsls Box Set (p. 233)
—Claudia & Mean Janine. Telgemeier, Raina, illus. (p. 329)
—Claudia & the Phantom Phone Calls. (p. 329)
—Claudia y la Nueva Alumna. Peraire del Molino, C., tr. (p. 329)
—Claudia y la Triste Despedida. Peraire del Molino, Conchita, tr. (p. 329)
—Coming Apart. (p. 348)
—Corner of the Universe. (p. 367)
—Dawn on the Coast. (p. 412)
—Dawn y los Mensajes Aterradores. Peraire del Molino, Conchita, tr. (p. 412)
—Dog's Life: The Autobiography of a Stray. (p. 463)
—Error de Stacey. (p. 534)
—Everything for a Dog. (p. 544)
—Family Tree Book One: Better to Wish. (p. 569)
—Family Tree Book Three: Best Kept Secret. (p. 569)
—Here Today. (p. 770)
—Home Is the Place. (p. 792)
—Keeping Secrets. (p. 947)
—Kristy y el Niño Desaparecido. Peraire del Molino, C., tr. (p. 968)
—Kristy y el Pequeño Desastre. Peraire del Molino, C., tr. (p. 968)
—Kristy y el Secreto de Susan. (p. 968)
—Kristy y los Esnobs. (p. 968)
—Kristy's Great Idea. (p. 968)
—Kristy's Great Idea. Telgemeier, Raina, illus. (p. 968)
—Long Way Home. (p. 1047)
—Mala Suerte de Mary Anne. Peraire del Molino, Conchita, tr. (p. 1083)
—Mallory y el Gato Fantasma. Peraire del Molino, Conchita, tr. (p. 1084)
—Needle & Thread. (p. 1239)
—Needle & Thread. Andreasen, Dan, illus. (p. 1239)
—Rain Reign. (p. 1435)
—Secret Book Club. (p. 1540)
—September Surprises. (p. 1551)
—Special Delivery. (p. 1623)
—Stacey y el Anillo Perdido. (p. 1638)
—Summer Before. (p. 1674)
—Ten Good & Bad Things about My Life (So Far) (p. 1718)
—Ten Rules for Living with My Sister. (p. 1719)
—Tis the Season. (p. 1757)
—Truth about Stacey. (p. 1794)
—Truth about Stacey. Telgemeier, Raina, illus. (p. 1794)
—Upon a Midnight Clear. (p. 1825)
—Welcome to Camden Falls. (p. 1873)
Martin, Ann M., jt. auth. see Danziger, Paula.
Martin, Ann M. & Godwin, Laura. Doll People Selznick, Brian, illus. (p. 463)
—Doll People. (p. 463)
—Doll People. Selznick, Brian, illus. (p. 463)
—Doll People Set Sail. Helquist, Brett, illus. (p. 463)
—Meanest Doll in the World. Selznick, Brian, illus. (p. 1116)
—Runaway Dolls. Selznick, Brian, illus. (p. 1496)
Martin, Ann M. & Telgemeier, Raina. Mary Anne Saves the Day. (p. 1100)
Martin, Ann M., ed. Because of Shoe & Other Dog Stories. (p. 155)
—Because of Shoe & Other Dog Stories. Ivanov, Aleksey & Ivanov, Olga, illus. (p. 155)
—Because of Shoe & Other Dog Stories. Ivanov, Olga & Ivanov, Aleksey, illus. (p. 155)
Martin, Annabelle T. Superstars of the Boston Celtics. (p. 1684)
—Superstars of the Cleveland Cavaliers. (p. 1684)
—Superstars of the Los Angeles Lakers. (p. 1684)
Martin, Anne E. Flip Flops for Paige. (p. 605)
—Midnight Kitties. (p. 1139)
—Spike the Friendly Caterpillar. McCabb, Jamie, illus. (p. 1627)
—Tail & Two Kitties. Martin, Anne E., illus. (p. 1695)
—There's A Ladybug in My House. Martin, Anne E., illus. (p. 1731)
Martin, Ashley. How to Improve at Karate. (p. 820)
Martin, Ashley, jt. auth. see Brown, Heather E.
Martin, Ashley, jt. auth. see Drewett, Jim.
Martin, Ashley P. Shotokan Karate Bible: Beginner to Black Belt. (p. 1569)
Martin, Ashley P. & Walker, Andrew D. How to Improve at Fishing. (p. 820)
Martin, Benjamin. Revenge of the Akuma Clan. (p. 1465)
—Samurai Awakening. (p. 1509)
Martin, Bill, Jr. Baby Bear, Baby Bear, What Do You See? Carle, Eric, illus. (p. 125)
—Baby Bear, Baby Bear, What Do You See? Big Book. Carle, Eric, illus. (p. 125)
—Brown Bear & Friends. Carle, Eric, illus. (p. 231)
—Brown Bear & Friends Board Book Gift Set. Carle, Eric, illus. (p. 231)
—Brown Bear Book & CD Storytime Set. Carle, Eric, illus. (p. 231)
—Brown Bear, Brown Bear, What Do You See? (p. 231)
—Brown Bear, Brown Bear, What Do You See? Carle, Eric, illus. (p. 231)
—Oso Panda, Oso Panda, ¿Qué Ves Ahí? Mlawer, Teresa, tr. (p. 1305)
—Panda Bear, Panda Bear, What Do You See? Carle, Eric, illus. (p. 1320)
—Panda Bear, Panda Bear, What Do You See? 10th Anniversary Edition. Carle, Eric, illus. (p. 1320)
—Polar Bear Book & CD Storytime Set. Carle, Eric, illus. (p. 1378)
—Polar Bear, Polar Bear, What Do You Hear? Carle, Eric, illus. (p. 1379)
—Ten Little Caterpillars. Ehlert, Lois, illus. (p. 1719)
—Turning of the Year. Shed, Greg, illus. (p. 1798)
Martin, Bill, Jr., jt. auth. see Archambault, John.
Martin, Bill, Jr., jt. auth. see Sampson, Michael R.
Martin, Bill, Jr., jt. auth. see Sampson, Michael.
Martin, Bill, Jr. & Archambault, John. Chica Chica Bum Bum ABC. Ehlert, Lois, illus. (p. 299)
—Chicka Chicka ABC. Ehlert, Lois, illus. (p. 299)
—Chicka Chicka Boom Boom. Ehlert, Lois, illus. (p. 299)
Martin, Bill, Jr. & Priddy, Roger. Polar Bear, Polar Bear, What Do You Hear? Carle, Eric, illus. (p. 1379)
Martin, Bill, Jr. & Sampson, Michael. Chicka Chicka 1, 2, 3: Lap Edition. Ehlert, Lois, illus. (p. 299)
—Chicka Chicka 1, 2, 3. Ehlert, Lois, illus. (p. 299)
—I Love Our Earth. Lipow, Dan, photos by. (p. 842)
—I Love Our Earth / Amo Nuestra Tierra. Lipow, Dan, photos by. (p. 842)
—I Pledge Allegiance. Raschka, Chris, illus. (p. 844)
—Kitty Cat, Kitty Cat, Are You Going to School? Bryant, Laura J., illus. (p. 963)
—Kitty Cat, Kitty Cat, Are You Going to Sleep? Bryant, Laura J., illus. (p. 963)
—Kitty Cat, Kitty Cat, Are You Waking Up? Bryant, Laura J., illus. (p. 963)
—Trick or Treat? Meisel, Paul, illus. (p. 1786)
Martin, Bill, Jr., ed. Bill Martin Jr Big Book of Poetry. (p. 186)
Martin, Bill, Jr., et al. Chicka Chicka Boom Boom. Ehlert, Lois, illus. (p. 299)
—Chicka Chicka Box Box! Chicka Chicka Boom Boom; Chicka Chicka 1, 2, 3. Ehlert, Lois, illus. (p. 299)
—Little Squeegy Bug Corrigan, Patrick, illus. (p. 1036)
Martin, Bob. James' Night of Terror. Salinas, Alex, illus. (p. 907)
—Tony Stewart. (p. 1766)
Martin, Bobi. Muscles in Your Body (p. 1192)
—What Are Air Masses & Weather Fronts? (p. 1879)
—What Are Elections? (p. 1879)
—What Are Gems? (p. 1879)
—Working As an Electrician in Your Community. (p. 1952)
Martin, Bobi, ed. see Strelkoff, Tatiana.
Martin, Brenda Darnley. Freddie, Hector & Tish: The Treasure-Hunt Fish. (p. 632)
—Treasure Hunt Fish & Miss Bernadette's Wish. Ramos, Amy Jones, illus. (p. 1781)
Martin, Brian. Gold of Angel Island. McDonald, Kim, illus. (p. 693)
—Lost Ring. McDonald, Kim, illus. (p. 1056)
Martin, Brian, illus. see Smith, Bryan.
Martin, Bridgitt. Bunny & the Amazing Gift: God Cares for All His Creation. (p. 242)
Martin, Butch. Spook: (the adventures of a Wyoming ranch Cat) (p. 1631)
Martin, C. K. Kelly. Lighter Side of Life & Death. (p. 1015)
—My Beating Teenage Heart. (p. 1196)
Martin, C. L. Ducky Goes to the Dentist. (p. 488)
Martin, Candice J. Theo's Special Gift. Bonavita, Madison M., illus. (p. 1729)
Martin, Carme, jt. auth. see Martin, Carmen.
Martin, Carme & Herrero, Teresa. Gaudi. (p. 658)
Martin, Carmen & Martin, Carme. Vincent Van Gogh. (p. 1842)
Martin, Carol. Catharine Parr Traill: Backwoods Pioneer. (p. 280)
—Lighthouse. (p. 1015)
Martin, Caroline, illus. see Reader, Jenny.
Martin, Caroline Jane. Flow. (p. 607)
Martin, Carolyn. Book of Childhood Prayers. (p. 211)
—Metal Horse Figurines. (p. 1130)
Martin, Carrie Waddington. Ham the Astrochimp: Anything Is Possible. (p. 739)
Martin, Cecile L. K., illus. see Rash, Ron.
Martin, Chandra. Sintacs. (p. 1580)
Martin, Cheryl. Susie Lumpybothams: New & Improved. (p. 1688)
Martin, Cheryl Linn. Ukuleles Undercover. (p. 1809)
Martin, Chris. Build Your Own Web Site. (p. 238)
Martin, Chris, illus. see Yarney, Susan.
Martin, Christopher. Hodder Reading Project 5-6 Reader: Great Battles. (p. 787)
—War Poems. (p. 1858)
Martin, Claudia. Complete Guides Ocean Life. (p. 353)
—Farming. (p. 574)
—Helpers. (p. 766)
Martin, Colin. Welcome to Hell: One Man's Fight for Life Inside the Bangkok Hilton. (p. 1873)
Martin, Courtney, illus. see Coleman, Wim & Perrin, Pat.
Martin, Courtney A., illus. see Bardhan-Quallen, Sudipta.
Martin, Cynthia, illus. see Anderson, Bill & O'Donnell, Liam.
Martin, Cynthia, illus. see Biskup, Agnieszka & Schulz, Barbara.
Martin, Cynthia, illus. see Biskup, Agnieszka & Sohn, Emily.
Martin, Cynthia, illus. see Biskup, Agnieszka, et al.
Martin, Cynthia, illus. see Biskup, Agnieszka.
Martin, Cynthia, illus. see Braun, Eric.
Martin, Cynthia, illus. see Brezenoff, Steve.
Martin, Cynthia, illus. see Clay, Kathryn.
Martin, Cynthia, illus. see Conner, Daniel.
Martin, Cynthia, illus. see Doeden, Matt.
Martin, Cynthia, illus. see Dunn, Joeming W.
Martin, Cynthia, illus. see Engfer, Lee.
Martin, Cynthia, illus. see Fingeroth, Danny.
Martin, Cynthia, illus. see Gianopoulos, Andrea.
Martin, Cynthia, illus. see Glaser, Jason & Roley, Don.
Martin, Cynthia, illus. see Glaser, Jason.
Martin, Cynthia, illus. see Goodwin, Vincent & Shakespeare, William.
Martin, Cynthia, illus. see Gunderson, Jessica Sarah.
Martin, Cynthia, illus. see Hammer, Cully, et al.
Martin, Cynthia, illus. see Jacobson, Ryan.
Martin, Cynthia, illus. see Krohn, Katherine.
Martin, Cynthia, illus. see Leavitt, Caroline.
Martin, Cynthia, illus. see Lee, Adrienne.
Martin, Cynthia, illus. see London, Jack.
Martin, Cynthia, illus. see Martin, Michael & Martin, Michael J.
Martin, Cynthia, illus. see Niz, Xavier & Niz, Xavier W.
Martin, Cynthia, illus. see O'Donnell, Liam & Anderson, Bill.
Martin, Cynthia, illus. see Olson, Nathan & Glaser, Jason.
Martin, Cynthia, illus. see Olson, Nathan, et al.
Martin, Cynthia, illus. see Olson, Nathan.
Martin, Cynthia, illus. see Peterson, Christine.
Martin, Cynthia, illus. see Robbins, Trina.
Martin, Cynthia, illus. see Sautter, Aaron.
Martin, Cynthia, illus. see Sohn, Emily & Timmons, Anne.
Martin, Cynthia, illus. see Sohn, Emily.
Martin, Cynthia, illus. see Swift, Jonathan.
Martin, Cynthia, illus. see Temple, Bob.
Martin, Cynthia Bloom. Tryloc: The Quest. (p. 1795)
Martin, Dana, illus. see Mullarkey, John & Mullarkey, Lisa.
Martin, Dave & Watt, Nigel. Essential American West. (p. 536)
Martin, David. Christmas Tree. Sweet, Melissa, illus. (p. 316)
—Colony of Pennsylvania. (p. 342)
—Hanukkah Lights. Sweet, Melissa, illus. (p. 744)
—Let's Have a Tree Party! Manders, Jeff & Manders, John, illus. (p. 998)
—Peep & Ducky. Walker, David, illus. (p. 1335)
—Peep & Ducky Rainy Day. Walker, David, illus. (p. 1335)
—Three Little Bears Play All Day. Gutierrez, Akemi, illus. (p. 1742)
—Why Do Animals Hibernate? (p. 1923)
Martin, David Lozell. All for Pie, Pie for All. Gorbachev, Valeri, illus. (p. 44)
—Christmas Tree. Sweet, Melissa, illus. (p. 316)
—Hanukkah Lights. Sweet, Melissa, illus. (p. 744)
—Lucy & Bob: Brand New Readers. Martin, David Lozell, illus. (p. 1063)
—Piggy & Dad Play Big Book: Brand New Readers. Remkiewicz, Frank, illus. (p. 1358)
Martin, David Lozell, illus. see Mastromonaco, Pina.
Martin, Dawn. Fast Girls Finish Last: A Girl's Guide to Becoming a Virgin with Attitude! (p. 576)
Martin, Dawn L. Freeze Dance: A Story of the Dancing Cactus. (p. 635)
Martin, Debbie. Animal Homes. Baker, Alan, illus. (p. 78)
Martin, Debra & Landfair, Barton. Me & My Angels. (p. 1115)
Martin, Deirdre. Just a Taste (p. 937)
Martin, Denise R. Alicia's Dance. (p. 40)
Martin, Dick. Ozmapolitan of Oz. (p. 1316)
Martin, Dick, illus. see Hillert, Margaret.
Martin, D.M. Numbered! Numbered! Weighed! D!!!V!!ID!ED! (p. 1271)
Martin, Don, illus. see Mademann Vaughan, Kathryn.
Martin, Don, et al. They Call Me Fat Zoe: Helping Children & Families Overcome Obesity. Voerg, Kathy, illus. (p. 1732)
Martin, Donald R. "Rick". God Created You: A Guide to Temperament Therapy. (p. 688)
Martin, Dyna, ed. see Bertch, David P. & Bertch, Barbara A.
Martin, Ed, jt. auth. see Gauthier, James.
Martin Ed.D., Pamela. Include Me. (p. 869)
Martin, Elaine S. Bowman. Rooster's Fate: And Other Stories. Hackman, Evelyn, illus. (p. 1488)
Martin, Elena. Look at Both Sides. (p. 1048)
—Look Inside. (p. 1049)
—Seeing Is Believing. (p. 1548)
—Working Together (p. 1953)
—Working Together. (p. 1953)
Martin, Elena, jt. auth. see Trumbauer, Lisa.
Martin, Elizabeth. Marketing Identities Through Language: English & Global Imagery in French Advertising. (p. 1095)
Martin, Elizabeth B. I'm Not a Silly Goose. (p. 859)
Martin, Emily. Downpour. Shaughnessy, Mara, illus. (p. 474)
Martin, Emily Winfield. Day Dreamers: A Journey of Imagination. (p. 412)
—Dream Animals: A Bedtime Journey. (p. 483)
—Dream Animals. (p. 483)
—Oddfellow's Orphanage. (p. 1278)
—Wonderful Things You Will Be. (p. 1948)
Martin, Eugenio Alonso, notes. Lazarillo de Tormes. (p. 981)
Martín Fernández deelasco, Miguel, V, jt. auth. see De Velasco, Miguel Martin Fernandez.
Martin, Francesca. Cazadores de Miel. (p. 283)
Martin, Fred, illus. see Helmbuch, Carol Jo.
Martin, Gail Gaymer. Loving Care. (p. 1061)
Martin, Gary. 50 Classic Bible Stories. (p. 1997)
Martin, Gary, jt. auth. see Rogers, Bud.
Martin, Gary & Pennebaker, H. I. Professor Tyme's Timeless Tales: Revenge of the Sargasso Sea Ogre. (p. 1409)
Martin, Gary & Rogers, Bud. Raiders of Joppa Cariello, Sergio, illus. (p. 1433)
Martin, Gary & Zondervan Bibles Staff. Sword of Revenge Rogers, Bud, ed. (p. 1692)
Martin, Gary & Zondervan Publishing Staff. Heroes of God Cariello, Sergio, illus. (p. 773)
Martin, Gary, et al. Maiden of Thunder Cariello, Sergio & Lanphear, Dave, illus. (p. 1077)
Martin, Gary R. Welcome to the Professional World: Seven Success Principles for Entering the Workforce. (p. 1874)
Martin, George R. R. Ice Dragon. Royo, Luis, illus. (p. 850)
Martin, George R. R. & Avery, Ben. Hedge Knight. (p. 761)
—Sworn Sword (p. 1692)
Martin, George W. Battle of the Frogs & the Mice. Gwynne, Fred, illus. (p. 146)
Martin, Gina. Mother Moon: Magic Pool in the Sky. (p. 1178)
Martin, Harold. Brethren New Testament Commentary - 1 & 2 Timothy & Titus. (p. 226)
Martin, Harold S. Brethren New Testament Commentary - 2 Corinthians. (p. 226)
—Brethren New Testament Commentary - James & Jude. (p. 226)
Martin, Harold S., comment. Brethren New Testament Commentary - Colossians & Philemon. (p. 226)
Martin, Harvey. Shaggy Dog Story Book. (p. 1558)
Martin, Herbert. Catch A Falling Leaf. (p. 279)
Martin, Hope. Career Math. (p. 267)
Martin, Iain C. Complete Theory Fun Factory. (p. 353)
—Fun Factory Violin Book. (p. 647)
—Gettysburg: The True Account of Two Young Heroes in the Greatest Battle of the Civil War. (p. 670)
Martín, Inés, jt. tr. see Tamayo, José Luis.
Martin, Isabel. Airport Field Trip. (p. 32)
—Amphibians: A Question & Answer Book (p. 65)
—Animal Kingdom Questions & Answers (p. 78)
—Benjamin Banneker (p. 164)
—Birds: A Question & Answer Book (p. 191)
—Fire Station Field Trip. (p. 591)
—Fish: A Question & Answer Book (p. 598)
—Frederick Douglass (p. 633)
—Insects: A Question & Answer Book (p. 875)
—Jackie Robinson (p. 903)

—Let's Take a Field Trip. (p. 1001)
—Library Field Trip. (p. 1006)
—Mammals: A Question & Answer Book (p. 1085)
—Reptiles: A Question & Answer Book (p. 1461)
—Wilma Rudolph (p. 1934)
—Zoo Field Trip. (p. 1989)
Martin, Ivonne. Saga de la Mariposa. Eck, Bernhard, illus. (p. 1502)
Martin, J. Marshall. Bird. (p. 190)
Martin, J. P. Uncle. Blake, Quentin, illus. (p. 1811)
—Uncle Cleans Up. Blake, Quentin, illus. (p. 1811)
Martin, Jack & Serich, Mary. Pre-Apprentice Training: A Test Preparation Manual for the Skilled Trades. (p. 1394)
Martin, Jacqueline. English Legal System. (p. 530)
—Key Facts: Consumer Law. (p. 950)
Martin, Jacqueline Briggs. Alice Waters & the Trip to Delicious. (p. 39)
—Farmer Will Allen & the Growing Table. Larkin, Eric, illus. (p. 574)
—Finest Horse in Town. Gaber, Susan, illus. (p. 589)
—Lamp, the Ice, & the Boat Called Fish: Based on a True Story. Krommes, Beth, illus. (p. 972)
—Snowflake Bentley. (p. 1600)
—Snowflake Bentley. Azarian, Mary, illus. (p. 1600)
Martin, James E. Chartreuse Mongoose: Another Grandpa Ed's Bedtime Storybook. (p. 294)
Martin, James Kirby & Lender, Mark Edward. Respectable Army: The Military Origins of the Republic, 1763-1789. Franklin, John Hope & Eisenstadt, Abraham S., eds. (p. 1463)
Martin, James R., illus. see Graham, Baxter.
Martin, Jan, illus. see Orme, David.
Martin, Jane. Breathe Better, Live in Wellness. (p. 226)
—Spanish. Trotter, Stuart, illus. (p. 1620)
Martin, Janelle. Lexis, the Hiccupping Lion. (p. 1004)
Martin, Jann. This Babe So Small. (p. 1735)
Martin, Jannelle. ABC Math Riddles. Levin, Freddie, illus. (p. 3)
Martin, Jay. Baseball Magic. (p. 141)
Martin, Jayme. Skinny Little Tree. (p. 1585)
Martin, Jean, jt. auth. see Cooke, Andy.
Martin, Jean, jt. auth. see Homer.
Martin, Jean Ami, jt. auth. see Cooke, Andy.
Martin, Jean-Francois, illus. see Strady, Sophie.
Martin, Jeannette. Kwame's Sound: An Acoustical Engineering Story. (p. 968)
Martin, Jennifer C. Korean Americans. (p. 967)
Martin, Jenny. Tracked. (p. 1775)
Martin, Joan Watson. Inventing Chloe. (p. 883)
Martin, Joanna F. Betsey's Wishes. (p. 172)
Martin, JoElle. Bridge in the Forest (p. 227)
—Moonlight in the Forest. (p. 1172)
—Promise in the Forest (p. 1411)
Martin, John. Peter Puzzlemaker: A John Martin Puzzle-Book. Carlson, George Leonard, illus. (p. 1347)
—Willie the Jeep. (p. 1934)
Martin, John, ed. see Buzzy.
Martin, John, illus. see Stiegemeyer, Julie.
Martin, John David. My Little Farm Book. (p. 1212)
—My Little Wild Animal Book. (p. 1213)
—Time to Plant: Tests. (p. 1753)
—Time to Plant: Workbook. (p. 1753)
Martin, John, et al. Aesop's Fables in Rhyme for Little Philosophers. (p. 26)
Martin, John F., illus. see Sheely, Robert.
Martin, John F., illus. see Weber, Judith Eichler.
Martin, John Jeffries. Myths of Renaissance Individualism. (p. 1227)
Martin, Jonathan B. Titanic for Young Readers. (p. 1758)
Martin, Joseph M., et al. Sing & Celebrate! Sacred Songs for Young Voices. (p. 1579)
Martin, Joshua Rae. 3-D Fort Shapes (p. 1991)
Martin Jourdenais, Norma Jean, illus. see Gould, Roberta.
Martin, Joyce, illus. see Mock, Jean.
Martín, Juan Carlos. Poemamundi. (p. 1376)
Martin, Judith. Out of the Bag: The Paper Bag Players Book of Plays. Chwast, Seymour, illus. (p. 1311)
Martin, Judy, jt. auth. see Bentz, Laurice.
Martin, Julie, illus. see Rodgers, Denise.
Martin, Julie E. Freedom & Love. (p. 634)
Martin, Justin. Easy Reader Biographies: Alexander Graham Bell: A Famous Inventor. (p. 500)
—Easy Reader Biographies: George Washington: George Washington. (p. 500)
Martin, Justin McCory. 12 Fabulously Funny Folktale Plays: Super-Engaging Fractured Tales That Boost Fluency, Vocabulary & Comprehension. (p. 1994)
—Busy Honeybees. (p. 246)
—Deep-Sea Creatures. (p. 423)
—Dinosaurs. Gunson, Dave, illus. (p. 443)
—Earth. (p. 495)
—Mega-Deluxe Capitalization Machine. Phillips, Matt, illus. (p. 1124)
—Mystery of the Missing Socks. Kennedy, Kelly, illus. (p. 1225)
—Planet Without Pronouns. Lee, Jared, illus. (p. 1368)
—Planets. (p. 1368)
—Stars. (p. 1643)
—Sun. (p. 1675)
—Woodlands. (p. 1949)
Martin, K. F. Qwuedeviv Crew 52: We Come with Peas. (p. 1429)
Martin, Karen Jesse. Paper Mill Mangle: A Suzanne Sharp, RN, Mystery. (p. 1322)
Martin, Karla, jt. auth. see Heath, Kathy.
Martin, Katherine, jt. auth. see McCloud, Carol.
Martin, Kathy. Animals, Birds & the Alphabets. (p. 82)
Martin, Kathy E. What Do Those Two Numbers Mean? (p. 1882)
Martin, Kelly, ed. see Schwartz, Linda.
Martin, Kentrell. Shelly Goes to the Zoo. Rodriguez, Marc, illus. (p. 1565)
Martin, Kevin. Chomper the Stomper. (p. 310)
Martin, Kristina. Cozzi Dog Can't See. (p. 375)
Martin, L. Reptile Discovery Library Series (p. 1461)
Martin, L. & Beckett, G. Adventures of Timothy in Early New South Wales. (p. 24)
Martin, L. J. I Am an American. (p. 832)
Martin, LaJoyce. Silver Ghost. (p. 1576)
Martin, Lance. Little Hermit. (p. 1029)
Martín Larrañaga, Ana, illus. see Powell, Richard.
Martin, Laura, illus. see O' Byrne, Lorraine.
Martin, Laura C. Recycled Crafts Box: Sock Puppets, Cardboard Castles, Bottle Bugs & 37 More Earth-Friendly Projects & Activities You Can Create. (p. 1453)
Martin, Laura C. & Cain, David. Nature's Art Box: From T-Shirts to Twig Baskets, 65 Cool Projects for Crafty Kids to Make with Natural Materials You Can Find Anywhere. Cain, David, illus. (p. 1237)
Martin, Lee Anne. Color & Play: Sea Creatures. (p. 342)
Martin, Lily, ed. see UFA National Team.
Martin, Lisa. Holly the Deaf Dalmatian: Holly Gets A New Home. (p. 789)
Martin, Lisa & Martin, Valerie. Anton & Cecil, Book 2: Cats on Track. Murphy, Kelly, illus. (p. 89)
—Cats at Sea. (p. 281)
Martin, Louise, jt. auth. see Cooper, Gem.
Martin, Loyce, jt. auth. see Singleton, David.
Martin, Luanne, illus. see Ziglar, Christy.
Martin, Lyn, illus. see DeLand, M. Maitland.
Martin, Lynn & Hogg, Glenda. Funky Fairy Tales. (p. 649)
Martin, M. J., illus. see Danby, Aaron.
Martin, M. J. & Danby, Aaron. Elusive Mr. Zee. (p. 516)
Martin, M. T. Bulldozers. (p. 240)
—Cranes. (p. 376)
—Earth Movers. (p. 496)
Martin, Mabel. Talking with Hands. Witmer, Ruth, illus. (p. 1704)
Martin, Mairead S. Forgotten Little Penguin. (p. 619)
Martin, Manuela. Animales del Zoo. Susaeta Publishing, Inc., Staff, ed. (p. 81)
Martin, Manuela & Socolovsky, Gisela. Colores: Pequediccionario en Imagenes. Susaeta Publishing, Inc., Staff, ed. (p. 344)
Martin, Manuela & Susaeta, Equipo. 365 Advinanzas. Susaeta Publishing, Inc., Staff, ed. (p. 2001)
Martin, Marcos, illus. see Waid, Mark & Lee, Stan.
Martin, Marcos & Ramos, Humberto. Matters of Life & Death. (p. 1109)
Martin, Mari. Amazing Hairstyles Book. (p. 54)
Martin, Maria G. Christmas Crown. Stratman, Kay, illus. (p. 313)
Martin, Mark W. & Talbot, Ret. Complete Idiot's Guide to Saltwater Aquariums. (p. 353)
Martin, Martha. D-Day. (p. 397)
—Live It: Empathy. (p. 1040)
—Steeplechase. (p. 1646)
—Trail Riding. (p. 1776)
Martin, Martha M. Chipper, the Heroic Chipmunk. Matzen, Deon C., illus. (p. 308)
Martin, Mary. God Made Nuts. Derstine, Charlene, illus. (p. 690)
—Grandma's Goose. Hoover, Charity, illus. (p. 708)
Martin, Mary-Jane. Let Me Put It This Way. (p. 994)
Martin, Matthew. Adventure & Life -n- Times of Cleatus. (p. 14)
—Cleatus Goes Camping. (p. 330)
—Cleatus goes Drag Racing. (p. 330)
Martin, McDonald, illus. see Cantor, Don & Cantor, Michael.
Martin, Michael. Alien Abductions (p. 40)
—Bodyworx Vacation Bible School. (p. 207)
—Chinese Americans. (p. 307)
—Crop Circles (p. 385)
—Ghost Hunters (p. 670)
—Ghosts (p. 672)
—How to Survive a Tornado (p. 821)
—Mystery of Alien Abductions. (p. 1224)
—Mystery of Atlantis. (p. 1224)
—Near-Death Experiences (p. 1238)
—Persian Gulf War: Saddam's Failed Invasion. (p. 1344)
—Ricky Carmichael: Motocross Champion (p. 1470)
—Salem Witch Trials Bascle, Brian, illus. (p. 1504)
—Spy Gear (p. 1636)
—Spy Skills (p. 1636)
—TruthQuest Follywood VBS Kit. (p. 1794)
—Unsolved Mystery of Alien Abductions. (p. 1822)
—Unsolved Mystery of Atlantis. (p. 1822)
—Unsolved Mystery of Ghosts (p. 1822)
Martin, Michael & Capstone Press Staff. Atlantis (p. 112)
Martin, Michael & Ingram, Scott. California. (p. 253)
Martin, Michael & Martin, Michael J. Gladiators (p. 682)
—Harriet Tubman & the Underground Railroad Hoover, Dave & Anderson, Bill, illus. (p. 750)
—Knights Martin, Cynthia, illus. (p. 964)
—Pheasant Hunting. (p. 1350)
—Salem Witch Trials Kamerer, Justin & Bascle, Brian, illus. (p. 1504)
—World's Deadliest Snakes (p. 1960)
—World's Fastest Cars (p. 1960)
Martin, Michael, et al. Creature in the Lake. (p. 380)
—Unexplained Mysteries. (p. 1817)
Martin, Michael J. ESP - Extrasensory Perception. (p. 536)
—Harriet Tubman & the Underground Railroad Hoover, Dave & Anderson, Bill, illus. (p. 750)
—Teen Depression. (p. 1713)
Martin, Michael J., jt. auth. see Martin, Michael.
Martin, Michelle Nicole. Princess & Missy's Magical Adventures: The Crystal Heart. (p. 1402)
Martin, Mike. 365 Stories & Rhymes for Girls. (p. 2001)
Martin, Mildred A. Growing with the Millers. Burkholder, Edith, illus. (p. 727)
—Missionary Stories with the Millers. Burkholder, Edith, illus. (p. 1153)
—Wisdom & the Millers: Proverbs for Children. Burkholder, Edith, illus. (p. 1939)
Martin, Miles J., illus. see Jackson, Lora Z.
Martin, Molly. Princess Addison Gets Angry Florian, Mélanie, illus. (p. 1402)
—Princess Harper Gets Happy Florian, Mélanie, illus. (p. 1404)
—Princess Heart. Florian, Mélanie, illus. (p. 1404)
—Princess Sophia Gets Scared Florian, Mélanie, illus. (p. 1405)
—Princess Stella Gets Sad Florian, Mélanie, illus. (p. 1405)
Martin, Ms. Amalyn Persohn. Max & Mila at the Beach: A Sun Safety Guide for Kids. Danker, Jennifer Anne, illus. (p. 1110)
Martin, Nancy. Crazy Little Thing Called Death. (p. 377)
Martin, Nicholas. Fighting the Fangs: A Guide to Vampires & Werewolves. (p. 586)
Martin, Nicole. Werewolf. (p. 1875)
Martin, Norma. Don Martin Brain Games for Kids. (p. 465)
Martin, Oscar, Jr., creator. Birth of Jesus (p. 192)
—Civil Rights Leaders. (p. 324)
—Creation Story (p. 379)
—David & Goliath (p. 410)
—Doctors (p. 459)
—Famous Women (p. 570)
—History of Music (p. 784)
—Noah (p. 1261)
—Sports Legends (p. 1633)
—Story of Moses (p. 1659)
Martin, Paige. Daniel Keep Dreaming. Price, Ronnalda, ed. (p. 405)
Martin, Pat. Saints & Heroes of the Charles Bridge: The Lives of Extraordinary People. (p. 1504)
Martin, Pat, compiled by. Czech & Slovak Wit & Wisdom. (p. 397)
Martin, Patricia A. Fink. Gray Wolves. (p. 713)
—Manatees. (p. 1086)
Martin, Patricia A. Fink & Fink-Martin, Patricia A. California Condors. (p. 253)
Martin, Paul & Boisteau, Manu. Frankie Rocks the House: #2 (p. 630)
—Runaway Zombie! #8 (p. 1496)
Martin, Paul, et al. Beatrice's Spells: #3 (p. 153)
—Count Snobula Vamps It Up: #6 (p. 370)
—Horror Gets Slimed: #5 (p. 799)
—Sally Gets Silly: #7 (p. 1505)
—Von Skalpel's Experiment: #1. (p. 1850)
—Wolf Man Stu Bites Back: #4 (p. 1944)
Martin, Pauline, jt. auth. see Desbordes, Astrid.
Martin, Pedro, illus. see Davis, Kenneth C.
Martin, Pedro, illus. see Murphy, Stuart J.
Martin, Peter. Bible People Factfile. Buckingham, Matt, illus. (p. 176)
—Bible Stories for Boys. Bursi, Simona, illus. (p. 176)
—Jesus Detective: A Puzzle Search Book. Kent, Peter, illus. (p. 915)
Martin, Peter, illus. see Yung Dong, Venerable & Jacobs, Marjorie.
Martin, Priscilla. Big Fat Hare. (p. 181)
Martin, Rachael Lynn. McKenzie Drew: Adventures with David. (p. 1114)
Martin, Rafe. Banyan Deer: A Parable of Courage & Compassion. Wehrman, Richard, illus. (p. 137)
—Birdwing. (p. 192)
—World Before This One: A Novel Told in Legend. Nicholls, Calvin, illus. (p. 1954)
Martin Ramos, Juan Carlos & Carlos, Martin Ramos Juan. palabras que se lleva el viento. (p. 1319)
Martin, Rebecca. Blossoms on the Roof. (p. 202)
—Eyes for My Heart. (p. 558)
—Joanna's Journey. Yoder, Laura & Weaver, Lisa, illus. (p. 919)
—Treasure Hunt. (p. 1781)
Martin, Reed & Tichenor, Austin. Reduced Shakespeare: The Attention-Impaired Reader's Guide to the World's Best Playwright. (p. 1456)
Martin, RF. Tears of the Heart: A Modern Day Story in a 'Once upon a Time' Setting. (p. 1711)
Martin, Richard, illus. see Sewell, Anna.
Martin, Rob & Sellmeyer, Mark, des. Seasons: The Calendar Rummy Game. (p. 1538)
Martin, Robert. Bobby's Unexpected Birthday Party. (p. 206)
Martin, Robert, Jr. Vietnamese Children's Picture Dictionary: English-Vietnamese/Vietnamese-English. Voltaggio, Nicholas, illus. (p. 1841)
Martin, Robert Stanly, ed. see Hippocrene Books Staff.
Martin, Rod. Drama Games & Acting Exercises: 177 Games & Activities. (p. 480)
Martin, Roland. Greek Architecture. (p. 720)
Martin, Ron, jt. auth. see Olsen, Sylvia.
Martin, Rosa Maria, jt. auth. see Ellis, Martyn.
Martin, Rosa Maria & Ellis, Martyn. Aventura Nueva. (p. 119)
—Aventura Nueva - Rojo. (p. 119)
—Azul. (p. 122)
Martin, Rosemary. Rosie's Story. (p. 1490)
Martin, Russell & Nibley, Lydia. Mysteries of Beethoven's Hair. (p. 1222)
Martin, Ruth. Little Moose. Boey, Stephanie, illus. (p. 1032)
—Noisy Nature: in the Jungle. Pledger, Maurice, illus. (p. 1263)
—Noisy Nature: on the Farm. Pledger, Maurice, illus. (p. 1263)
Martin, Sandra. Mathopedia Level 1. (p. 1108)
—Mathopedia Level 2. (p. 1108)
Martin, Sara Hines. Shakin' up the Kingdom: Princess Lucinda Becomes the Queen. (p. 1559)
Martin, Sharon, jt. auth. see Davies, Caroline.
Martin, Shawn, illus. see Organ, Betty.
Martin, Sheila. Muddy Water. (p. 1189)
Martin, Sherri. Bye-Bye, Germs. (p. 249)
Martin, Sherry, illus. see Woods, Wendy.
Martin, Stephanie, illus. see Cooper, Afua.
Martin, Steve. Late for School. Payne, C. F., illus. (p. 979)
—Miss Pell Never Misspells: More Cool Ways to Remember Stuff. Remphry, Martin, illus. (p. 1152)
—Shopgirl. (p. 1568)
Martin, Steve & Chast, Roz. Alphabet from A to Y with Bonus Letter Z! (p. 49)
Martin, Steve & Scholastic, Inc. Staff. Boys' Book of Adventure: Are You Ready to Face the Challenge? (p. 220)
Martin, Steve, et al. I Wish I Knew That: Cool Stuff You Need to Know. (p. 848)
—Wacky & Wonderful World Through Numbers: Over 2,000 Figures & Facts. (p. 1852)
Martin, Stuart, illus. see David, Juliet.
Martin, Stuart, illus. see Dowley, Tim.
Martin, Stuart, illus. see Edgecombe, Jane.
Martin, Stuart, jt. auth. see Phillips, Gina.
Martin, Stuart, jt. auth. see Whiting, Sue.
Martin, Susan, illus. see Tuey.
Martin, Susi. Animal 123. (p. 76)
—Animal ABC. (p. 76)
Martin, T. H. Johnson House Mystery. (p. 924)
Martin, T. J. Why Do the Leaves Fall? (p. 1924)
Martin, T. Michael. End Games. (p. 526)
Martin, Tamara. Little Robin Redbreast: An Illustrated Poem. (p. 1036)
Martin, Tamara & Quebodeaux, Vernice. Flea & the Ant. (p. 603)
Martin, Tamra. My Wish, Our Little Oat. Tinker, Jason, illus. (p. 1221)
Martin, Ted. Area 51. (p. 97)
Martin, Terri. Adventures of Eddie the Emu. (p. 17)
Martin, Terry, ed. see Bertch, David P. & Bertch, Barbara A.
Martin, Terry, jt. auth. see Maynard, Christopher.
Martin, Timothy. Wimps Like Me. (p. 1935)
Martin, Tracy. How to Diagnose & Repair Automotive Electrical Systems. (p. 816)
Martin, Tyler. I Have a Question Williams, Toby, illus. (p. 839)
Martin, Valerie, jt. auth. see Martin, Lisa.
Martin, Vern. On Your Mark, Get Set, Live! (p. 1292)
Martin, Victor. Hood Legend. (p. 795)
Martin, W., tr. see Kästner, Erich.
Martin, W. D. Dragonfly Valley: When Best Plans Go Awry. (p. 478)
—Quest for the Cure: When Quitting Is Not an Option - Dragonfly Valley Series Book 2. (p. 1426)
Martin, W. Eric, jt. auth. see Bordessa, Kris.
Martin, W. Eric, jt. auth. see Formichelli, Linda.
Martin, W. Lyon. Aidan's First Full Moon Circle: A Magical Child Story. Martin, W. Lyon, illus. (p. 30)
—Ordinary Girl, A Magical Child. Martin, W. Lyon, illus. (p. 1302)
—Watchers. (p. 1861)
Martin, W. Lyon, illus. see Tucker, S. J. & Herring, Trudy.
Martin, Wendy. Art of the Short Story. (p. 102)
Martin, Whitney, illus. see Gallagher, Mary Collins.
Martin, Whitney, illus. see Kraus, Jeanne.
Martin, Whitney, illus. see Lendler, Ian.
Martin, Whitney, illus. see Levy, Janice.
Martin, Whitney, illus. see Spurr, Elizabeth.
Martin, William. Harvard Yard. (p. 751)
Martin, William C. Prophet with Honor: The Billy Graham Story. (p. 1411)
Martin, Yvonne. Mouse in the House. (p. 1182)
Martin-Duttmann, Robin. Zoo on the Moon. (p. 1989)
Martine, Victoria. 100 Dollar Sock. (p. 1998)
Martineau, Susan. 50 French Phrases: Games & Activities to Teach Language Essentials. Noyes, Leighton, illus. (p. 1997)
—Astonishing Art. Ursell, Martin, illus. (p. 108)
—Bubbles in the Bathroom. Noyes, Leighton, illus. (p. 233)
—Bugs in the Garden. Noyes, Leighton, illus. (p. 237)
—Crazy Contraptions. Ursell, Martin, illus. (p. 377)
—Dealing with Bullying. (p. 418)
—Fizz in the Kitchen. Noyes, Leighton, illus. (p. 601)
—Marvelous Magic. Ursell, Martin, illus. (p. 1099)
—Shadows in the Bedroom. Noyes, Leighton, illus. (p. 1558)
Martineau, Susan, jt. auth. see Bruzzone, Catherine.
Martineau, Susan, jt. auth. see Bushell, Nick.
Martineau, Susan, jt. auth. see Green, Jen.
Martineau, Susan, jt. auth. see Morgan, Philip.
Martineau, Susan, jt. auth. see Morgan, Sally.
Martineau, Susan & Bushell, Nick. Cool Circuits. (p. 363)
Martineau, Susan & James, Hel. All Kinds of Drinks. (p. 44)
—Bread, Rice, & Pasta. (p. 224)
—Fruits & Vegetables. (p. 645)
—Meat, Fish, & Eggs. (p. 1118)
—Milk, Butter, & Cheese. (p. 1143)
—Sweets & Snacks. (p. 1690)
Martineau, Susan & Jinny, Johnson. What's It Like to Be... Grasshopper? Sanzi, Desiderio, illus. (p. 1898)
Martineck, Michael J. Wrong Channel. (p. 1965)
Martinek, Frank V. Don Winslow Breaks the Spy Net. Warren, F., illus. (p. 465)
—Don Winslow Saves the Secret Formul. Warren, F., illus. (p. 465)
Martinek, Frank Victor. Don Winslow: Face to Face with the Scorpion. Warren, F., illus. (p. 465)
Martinek, Tom, jt. auth. see Sherman, M. Zachary.
Martinelli, Marjorie. Brain Quest Grade 2 Math. (p. 222)
Martinelli, Marjorie & Brain Quest Editors. Brain Quest Grade 1 Math. (p. 221)
Martinello, Marian L. Ready's Gifts. (p. 1448)
Martines, Donna, illus. see Spray, Michelle.
Martinez, A. Lee. Gil's All Fright Diner. (p. 676)
Martinez Alaniz, Eduardo. Hugo Sanchez. (p. 825)
Martínez, Alejandro Cruz. Mujer que Brillaba Aun Mas Que el Sol. (p. 1189)
Martinez, Alitha, illus. see Mayhall, Robin.
Martinez, Alitha, illus. see Quesada, Joe & Tieri, Frank.
Martinez, Alitha, jt. auth. see Triton, Mathias.
Martinez, Alitha E., illus. see Jolley, Dan.
Martinez, Alitha E., illus. see Mayhall, Robin.
Martinez, Alitha E., illus. see Tsang, Evonne.
Martinez, Andrés Vera, illus. see Delsante, Vito.
Martinez, Andres Vera & Liu, Na. Little White Duck: A Childhood in China. Martinez, Andres Vera, illus. (p. 1037)
Martínez, Andrés Vera & Liu, Na. Little White Duck: A Childhood in China. Martínez, Andrés Vera, illus. (p. 1037)
Martinez, Andrew, photos by see Erickson, Paul.
Martinez, Angel. Story of Natalie: Natalie gets prepare for a day of School. (p. 1659)
Martinez, April, illus. see Hays, K. D. & Weidman, Meg.
Martinez Aydelott, Carmen, tr. see Schwalm, Claudia.
Martínez B. de Quirós, Eladio, tr. see Grimm, Jacob, et al.

Martinez, Catalina, tr. see Downer, Ann & DOWNER, ANN.
Martinez, Claudia Guadalupe. Pig Park. (p. 1357)
—Smell of Old Lady Perfume. (p. 1593)
Martinez, Claudia Guadalupe. Smell of Old Lady Perfume. (p. 1593)
Martinez, David & Benchmark Education Co., LLC. My Whale of a Tale. (p. 1221)
Martinez, Demetria & Montoya-Read, Rosalee. Grandpa's Magic Tortilla. Casaus, Lisa May, illus. (p. 710)
Martinez, Diana Davila. School Named for Someone Like Me (Una Escuela Con un Nombre Como el Mio) (p. 1523)
Martinez, Edward, illus. see Medina, Jane.
Martinez, Edward, illus. see Parks, Carmen.
Martinez, Edward, jt. auth. see Parks, Carmen.
Martinez, Elsie & Stelly, Colette. Henriette Delille: Rebellious Saint Reppel, Phyllis, illus. (p. 767)
Martinez, Enrique, illus. see Alberto, Eliseo.
Martinez, Enrique, illus. see Alvarez, Leticia Herrera.
Martinez, Enrique, illus. see Boullosa, Carmen.
Martinez, Enrique, illus. see Diaz, Enrique Perez.
Martinez, Enrique, illus. see Lome, Emilio Angel.
Martinez, Enrique, illus. see Marti, Jose.
Martinez, Enrique, illus. see Martinez, Rafael.
Martinez, Enrique, illus. see Pi Andreu, Andrés.
Martinez, Enrique, illus. see Remolina, Tere.
Martinez, G. O. Count Von Ice Dela Cream & the Golden Ice Cream. (p. 370)
Martinez, Gayle Denise, illus. see Valdez, Joseph G.
Martinez, Genevieve. Master Potter: KK Makes a Choice. Simko, Danielle, illus. (p. 1103)
Martinez, Gil, illus. see Van Haeringen, Annemarie.
Martinez, Heather. Ice-Cream Dreams. (p. 850)
Martinez, Heather, illus. see Banks, Steven.
Martinez, Heather, illus. see Carbone, Courtney.
Martinez, Heather, illus. see Chanda, J-P.
Martinez, Heather, illus. see Chipponeri, Kelli.
Martinez, Heather, illus. see David, Erica.
Martinez, Heather, illus. see Golden Books Staff.
Martinez, Heather, illus. see Killeen, James.
Martinez, Heather, illus. see Krulik, Nancy.
Martinez, Heather, illus. see Miglis, Jenny.
Martinez, Heather, illus. see Random House.
Martinez, Heather, illus. see Reisner, Molly & Ostrow, Kim.
Martinez, Heather, illus. see Richards, Kitty.
Martinez, Heather, illus. see Wygand, Melissa.
Martinez, Ivanova, illus. see Flor Ada, Alma.
Martinez, J. Escape Artist. (p. 534)
Martinez, Jeny. Walk in the Park. (p. 1853)
Martinez, Jessica. Kiss Kill Vanish. (p. 961)
—Space Between Us. (p. 1618)
—Virtuosity. (p. 1844)
—Vow. (p. 1850)
Martinez, Jorge, illus. see Sommer, Carl.
Martinez Jover, Carmen. Twin Kangaroo Treasure Hunt, a Gay Parenting Story. Martinez, Rosemary, illus. (p. 1802)
Martinez, J-P Loppo, illus. see Derrick, Patricia & O'Neil, Shirley.
Martinez, J-P Loppo, illus. see Derrick, Patricia & Sibbett, Joyce.
Martinez, J-P Loppo, illus. see Derrick, Patricia.
Martinez, Katherine A., jt. auth. see Tompkins, Michael A.
Martinez, Kathleen. Identity in the Mirror. (p. 852)
Martinez, Kathleen & Edwards, Sue. Colossal Clubs: Activities-Based Curriculum for School-Age Programs. Edwards, Mark, illus. (p. 346)
Martinez, Leovigildo, illus. see Gollub, Matthew W.
Martinez, Leovigildo, illus. see Gollub, Matthew.
Martinez, Libby, jt. auth. see Mora, Pat.
Martinez, Lisa Bolivar & Martinez, Matthew. Good Night Miami. (p. 699)
Martinez, Mary Ann. 6 Disciplinas Espirituales: Expande las dimensiones de tu relacion con Dios. (p. 1992)
Martinez, Matthew, jt. auth. see Martinez, Lisa Bolivar.
Martinez, Maureen Cerminaro. Just Be Yourself! the Adventures of Ted the Pom-Poo. (p. 938)
Martinez, Michael, illus. see Williams, Justine.
Martinez, Michele. Most Wanted. (p. 1177)
Martinez, Migdalia Fonseca & Martinez-Radio, Jorge Baez. Maina. (p. 1077)
Martinez, Miguel Fernandez, illus. see Laban, Terry, et al.
Martinez, Natali, illus. see Kesselman, Robin & Kesselman, Marc.
Martínez, Rafael. Deseo de Aurelio. Martinez, Enrique, illus. (p. 428)
Martinez, Raul. Rooly & Flora's Reunion: A Story of Cuba. Prieto, Antonio, illus. (p. 1487)
Martinez, Rene. Journey of the Golden Sword. (p. 928)
Martinez Ricci, Andres, illus. see Higgins, Nadia.
Martinez, Rocio. De-Sastre Perfecto. (p. 416)
—Fox & the Crow. (p. 626)
—Gato Guille y Los Monstruos. (p. 658)
Martinez, Rocio, illus. see Ballesteros, Jose Manuel & Manuel, Ballesteros Pastor José.
Martinez, Rocio, illus. see Canas, José & José, Cañas Torregrosa.
Martinez, Rocio, illus. see Munrriz, Mercedes & Munárriz Guezala, Mercedes.
Martínez, Rocio, jt. auth. see Martinez, Rocio.
Martinez, Rocio & Martínez, Rocío. Matias Pierde Su Lapiz. (p. 1109)
Martinez, Rocio & Rocio, Martinez Pérez. Mi Primer Libro de Jardineria. (p. 1133)
Martinez, Roland. Angel with Red Wings. Graphic Manufacture, illus. (p. 74)
Martinez, Roland L. Evil Leaf. (p. 546)
Martinez, Rosemary, illus. see Martinez Jover, Carmen.
Martínez, Rueben. Once upon a Time: Traditional Latin American Tales. Unger, David, tr. from SPA. (p. 1293)
Martinez, Sergio, illus. see Eareckson Tada, Joni & Wolgemuth, Bobbie.
Martinez, Sergio, illus. see Hedstrom-Page, Deborah.
Martinez, Sergio, illus. see Lucado, Max.
Martinez, Sergio, illus. see Wilkinson, Bruce & Suggs, Robb.
Martinez, Sonia, illus. see Murphy, Sally.
Martinez, Tito, illus. see Lantigua, Yanette.
Martinez, Vendrell. Yo Las Queria (I Loved Them) (p. 1971)
Martinez, Victor. Parrot in the Oven. Scott, Steve, illus. (p. 1325)
Martinez Wood, Jamie. Latino Writers & Journalists. (p. 979)
Martinez y Luis San Vicente, Enrique, illus. see Sastrias, Marta.
Martinez-Neal, Juana, illus. see Elya, Susan Middleton.
Martinez-Neal, Juana, illus. see Garza, Lois Ann.
Martinez-Neal, Juana, illus. see Jones, Christianne C.
Martinez-Radio, Jorge Baez, jt. auth. see Martinez, Migdalia Fonseca.
Martin-Finks, Nancy. Custody Battle: A Workbook for Children. Barber, David L., illus. (p. 395)
Martin-Fluet, Marie T. Fairies' Century Celebration. (p. 563)
Martini, Angela, illus. see Bligh, Deirdre.
Martini, Angela, illus. see Criswell, Patti Kelley.
Martini, Angela, illus. see Falligant, Erin & American Girl Editors, eds.
Martini, Angela, illus. see Golosi, Rosanne.
Martini, Angela, illus. see Krulik, Nancy.
Martini, Angela, illus. see Lundsten, Apryl.
Martini, Angela, illus. see Stout, Shawn K.
Martini, Angela, illus. see Wasserman, Robin.
Martini, Clem. Judgment. (p. 930)
—Mob. (p. 1157)
—Plague. (p. 1366)
—Three Martini Lunch. (p. 1743)
Martini, Clem, jt. auth. see Lindroth, Malin.
Martini, Steve. Jury. (p. 937)
Martini, T. J. Christmas Lost & Found. Kiejna, Magdalenea, illus. (p. 314)
Martini, Teri. True Book of Indians. Heston, Charles, illus. (p. 1792)
Martinie, Sherri L., jt. auth. see Bay-Williams, Jennifer M.
Martiniere, Stephan, illus. see Lofficier, Randy & Lofficier, Jean-Marc.
Martin-James, Kathleen. Gentle Manatees. (p. 661)
—Harp Seals. (p. 749)
Martin-Jourdenais, Norma Jean, illus. see Blanchette, Peg & Thibault, Terri.
Martin-Laranaga, Ana, illus. see Powell, Richard.
Martin-Larranaga, Ana. Butterfly at Home. (p. 247)
—Butterfly in the Garden. (p. 248)
—Butterfly in the Town. (p. 248)
—Butterfly on the Farm. (p. 248)
Martinneau, Susan. Dinosaur Dishes & Fossil Food. Ursell, Martin, illus. (p. 442)
—Mad Machines & Dotty Devices. Ursell, Martin, tr. (p. 1069)
Martinneau, Susan, jt. auth. see Bruzzone, Catherine.
Martinneau, Susan & James, Hel. Meat Fish & Eggs. (p. 1118)
Martino, Alecia. Dewey's First Adventure. (p. 432)
Martino, Alfred C. Pinned: There Can Be Only One Winner... (p. 1360)
Martino, Anita, illus. see Spergel, Heather.
Martino, Wayne & Pallotta-Chiarolli, Maria. So What's a Boy? Addressing Issues of Masculinity & Schooling. (p. 1602)
Martins, Ann-Kathrin, illus. see Fowler, Leona.
Martins, E. V. Cookie Nana's Story Book: Featuring " Grumpy Granddad " (p. 361)
Martins, Isabel Minhós. My Neighbor Is a Dog. Herring, John, tr. from POR. (p. 1215)
—When I Was Born. Matoso, Madalena, illus. (p. 1903)
Martins, Isabel Minhós & Matoso, Madalena. Where Do We Go When We Disappear? (p. 1907)
Martins, Pam, jt. auth. see Hoffman, Mary.
Martins, Sharon. Murray. (p. 1192)
Martinsen, Sarah, illus. see Brown, Tricia.
Martinson, Jackie. Wishing Flower. (p. 1940)
Martinucci, Suzanne. At Space Camp (p. 110)
Martinusen-Coloma, Cindy. Ruby Unscripted (p. 1493)
Martirano, Ron. Book of Baseball Stuff: Great Records, Weird Happenings, Odd Facts, Amazing Moments & Cool Things. (p. 210)
Martirosian, Patty Ann, illus. see Bauer, Susan Wise.
Marton, Jirina, illus. see Cocks, Nancy.
Marton, Jirina, illus. see Pendziwol, Jean E.
Marton, Jirina, illus. see Rivera, Raquel.
Marton, Jirina, jt. auth. see Cocks, Nancy.
Martone, Ginny. Trapped in Dead Man's Cave. (p. 1779)
—Trouble at Big Bear Falls. (p. 1789)
—White Stallion. (p. 1913)
Martonyi, E. Andrew. Little Man in the Map: With Clues to Remember All 50 States. Olson, Ed, illus. (p. 1031)
Martorana, Cherie. Made You Laugh for Kids: Wacky Word Searches. (p. 1070)
Martorell, Antonio, illus. see Ada, Alma Flora.
Martos Sánchez, José Daniel, jt. auth. see Nesquens, Daniel.
Martowiredjo, Salim, illus. see Suyenaga, Joan.
Martres, Laurent, ed. see Till, Tom.
Marts, Doreen. Baxter the Tweeting Dog. (p. 147)
Marts, Doreen, illus. see Williamson, Rose.
Marts, Doreen Mulryan. Even Monsters Say Good Night. (p. 541)
Marts, Doreen Mulryan, illus. see Karr, Lily.
Marts, Doreen Mulryan, illus. see Stern, A. J.
Marty, Joyce D. I Was in School When...,Dane's Great Day. (p. 848)
Marty, Martin E. & Appleby, R. Scott. Glory & the Power: The Fundamentalist Challenge to the Modern World. (p. 685)
Marty, Martin E., intro. Spiritual Leaders & Thinkers. (p. 1629)
Marty the Dog Staff. I Am Found by Marty. (p. 833)
Martyn, Kim. All the Way: Sex for the First Time (p. 46)
Martyn, Marilyn. Phonics for Kids. (p. 1352)
Martyr, Paula, illus. see Brown, Michele.
Martz, John, illus. see Heidbreder, Robert.
Martz, Sandra, ed. If I Had My Life to Live over I Would Pick More Daisies. (p. 853)
—When I Am an Old Woman: Petite. (p. 1902)
—When I Am an Old Woman: Reading Card. (p. 1902)
—When I Am an Old Woman: Stationery. Garbutt, Lisa, illus. (p. 1902)
—When I Am an Old Woman I Shall Wear Purple: Petite Version. (p. 1902)
Martzowka, John M. Quilt of Heroes. (p. 1428)
Maruca, Mary. Brown vs. Board of Education National Historic Site. (p. 232)
Maruda, Trotsky. Line & Circle. (p. 1019)
—Line & Circle. Maruda, Trotsky, illus. (p. 1019)
Marudu, Trotsky. Line & Circle. (p. 1019)
Marudu, Trotsky, illus. see Menon, Radhika.
Marukawa, Tomohiro. World of Narue (p. 1957)
—World of Narue Kobayashi, Mayumi, tr. from JPN. (p. 1957)
Marunas, Nathaniel. NERF: Ultimate Blaster Book. (p. 1241)
Maruno, Jennifer. Cherry Blossom Winter. (p. 298)
—Kid Soldier. (p. 951)
—Totem (p. 1771)
—Warbird. (p. 1858)
—When the Cherry Blossoms Fell. (p. 1904)
Marunowski, Barbara L. My Cow Book. (p. 1200)
Marusak, Elaine. Truly Tales & Girl Fish Stories. (p. 1793)
Marusak, Elaine Truly. Truly Tales: Aunt Gertie & Uncle George's Haunted House. (p. 1793)
Marusic, Matko. Do Angels Cry? Tales of the War. (p. 456)
Maruszewski, Kelley. Matt Kenseth: Midwest Racing Sensation. (p. 1109)
Maruyama, Ed, photos by see Issaluk, Johnny.
Marvano, jt. auth. see Oppen, Mark van.
Marvel. Avengers: The Return of the First Avenger. (p. 118)
—Avengers: Age of Ultron: Avengers Save the Day. (p. 118)
—Avengers: Age of Ultron: Battle at Avengers Tower. (p. 118)
—Marvel Avengers Assemble: Built for Action. (p. 1098)
—Marvel Super Heroes Assemble! Tattoos, Fantastic Facts, & Amazing Activites. (p. 1099)
—Marvel's the Avengers Reading Adventures. (p. 1099)
—Marvel's the Avengers Storybook Collection. (p. 1099)
—These Are the Avengers. (p. 1731)
—This Is the Amazing Spider-Man. (p. 1736)
—This Is the Invincible Iron Man. (p. 1736)
Marvel, jt. auth. see Cho, Charles.
Marvel & Davis, Adam. Battle at Avengers Tower. (p. 145)
—Hulk to the Rescue. (p. 825)
Marvel & Palacios, Tomas. Friends & Foes. (p. 638)
Marvel & Wyatt, Chris. Age of Ultron. (p. 29)
—Marvel's Ant-Man: the Junior Novel. (p. 1099)
—Marvel's Avengers: Age of Ultron: the Deluxe Junior Novel. (p. 1099)
Marvel Artists Staff & Olliffe, Pat. Mighty Avengers. (p. 1139)
Marvel Avengers Staff. Avengers - Power Play. (p. 118)
Marvel Book Group. Ant-Man: Zombie Repellent: A Mighty Marvel Chapter Book. (p. 88)
—Avengers - Battle with Ultron, Level 2. (p. 118)
—Captain America: An Origin Story. (p. 263)
—Ultimate Spider-Man - Spider-Man vs Dracula. (p. 1810)
—World of Reading: Avengers the New Team: Level 1. (p. 1957)
—World of Reading: Hawkeye This Is Hawkeye. (p. 1957)
Marvel Book Group & Wong, Clarissa S. World of Reading Falcon: This Is Falcon: Level 1. Lim, Ron & Rosenberg, Rachelle, illus. (p. 1957)
Marvel Book Group & Wyatt, Chris. World of Reading: Hulk This Is Hulk. (p. 1957)
Marvel Book Group Staff. Ultimate Spider-Man Halloween. (p. 1810)
Marvel Book Group Staff & Disney Book Group Staff. Marvel Padded. Disney Book Group Staff, illus. (p. 1099)
Marvel Books Staff. Story of Wolverine. (p. 1663)
Marvel Books Staff & Disney Book Group Staff. Marvel Spider-Man. Disney Book Group Staff, illus. (p. 1099)
Marvel Books Staff & Strathearn, Chris. Marvel's Ant-Man. (p. 1099)
Marvel Books Staff & Wyatt, Chris. Guardians of the Galaxy. (p. 728)
Marvel Comics Staff. Art of Spider-Man Classic. (p. 102)
—Avengers Wegener, Scott, illus. (p. 118)
—Earth's Mightiest Heroes Avengers Scherberger, Patrick & Wegener, Scott, illus. (p. 498)
—Marvel Universe Roleplaying Game. Beazley, Mark, ed. (p. 1099)
—This Is Wolverine. (p. 1737)
Marvel Comics Staff, illus. see Fraction, Matt.
Marvel Comics Staff, illus. see Lente, Fred Van.
Marvel Comics Staff, jt. auth. see Matthews, Brett.
Marvel Comics Staff, jt. ed. see Beazley, Mark.
Marvel Comics Staff & Kirby, Jack, texts. Devil Dinosaur. (p. 432)
Marvel Comics Staff & Mayer, Kirsten. Age of Ultron: Avengers Save the Day. (p. 29)
Marvel Comics Staff, creator. Ultimate X-Men (p. 1810)
Marvel Comics Staff, et al. Marvel Monsters. (p. 1099)
—Wild Kingdom. (p. 1929)
Marvel Comics Staff, text. Art of Marvel Studios. (p. 102)
—Avengers: Official Index to the Marvel Universe. (p. 118)
—Captain America: The Art of Captain America - The First Avenger. (p. 263)
—Essential Peter Parker, the Spectacular Spider-Man (p. 537)
—Iron Man: Official Index to the Marvel Universe. (p. 888)
—Thor: Official Index to the Marvel Universe. (p. 1739)
—Women of Marvel: Celebrating Seven Decades. (p. 1946)
Marvel Comics, text. Annihilation Omnibus. (p. 87)
—Marvel's Agents of S. H. I. E. L. D. (p. 1099)
—Marvel's Iron Man 3. (p. 1099)
—Scary Stories. (p. 1520)
—Toy Story: Tales from the Toy Chest. (p. 1774)
Marvel, et al. Best of Wolverine (p. 171)
Marvel Illustrators, illus. see Castro, Nachie.
Marvel Illustrators, illus. see Rudnick, Elizabeth.
Marvel Illustrators, illus. see Siglain, Michael.
Marvel, Laura, ed. William Shakespeare. (p. 1933)
Marvel Press. Invincible Iron Man: An Origin Story. (p. 885)
Marvel Press Book Group, jt. auth. see Palacios, Tomas.
Marvel Press Group & Disney Book Group Staff. Flight of the Iron Spider! Based on the Hit TV Show from Marvel Animation. Disney Book Group Staff, illus. (p. 604)
—Iron Man Fights Back Disney Book Group Staff, illus. (p. 888)
—Marvel Super Heroes. Disney Book Group Staff, illus. (p. 1099)
Marvel Press Group Staff, et al. X-Men. Oliffe, Pat et al, illus. (p. 1967)
Marvel Press Staff & Palacios, Tomas. Suits of Armor. Disney Book Group Staff, illus. (p. 1673)
Marvel Press Staff, et al. Thor: the Dark World Junior Novel. Disney Book Group Staff, illus. (p. 1739)
Marvel, Robin. Awakening Consciousness: A Boy's Guide! (p. 120)
—Awakening Consciousness: A Girl's Guide. (p. 120)
Marvel, Saga, et al. Marvel Saga. (p. 1099)
Marvel Spider-Man Staff, jt. auth. see Teitelbaum, Michael.
Marvel Staff & Palacios, Tomas. Marvel's Ant-Man: Reader. (p. 1099)
Marven, Nigel, told to. Prehistoric Park. (p. 1395)
Marvin, Fred, illus. see Bogot, Howard I., et al.
Marvin, Isabel R. Bride for Anna's Papa. (p. 227)
—Tenth Rifle. Costner, Howard, illus. (p. 1720)
Marvin, Susan. Birthday Dreamz. (p. 192)
Marvis, Barbara. Day by Day with Beyonce. (p. 412)
—Day by Day with Lebron James. (p. 412)
Marvis, Barbara J. Charles Schulz. (p. 292)
—Famous People of Asian Ancestry (p. 569)
—Selena. (p. 1549)
Marwah, Gauri. Tikki Tikki Tembo. (p. 1749)
Marwood, Diane. Ant & the Grasshopper. (p. 88)
—Espresso Story Time: The Roman Treasure. (p. 536)
—Fox & the Crow. (p. 626)
—Kim's Top Hat. (p. 957)
—Lion & the Mouse. (p. 1020)
Marwood, Lorraine. Jamie Wins Again. Hocking, Geoff, illus. (p. 907)
—Ratwhiskers & Me. (p. 1440)
Marx, Christy. Battlefield Command Systems of the Future. (p. 147)
—Great Chicago Fire Of 1871. (p. 714)
—Great Chicago Fire of 1871. (p. 714)
—Jet Li. (p. 916)
—Life in the Ocean Depths. (p. 1011)
—Wachowski Brothers: Creators of the Matrix. (p. 1852)
Marx, David F. Doc Block. Phillips, Matt, illus. (p. 459)
Marx, Donald, jt. auth. see Krasinski, Norma.
Marx, Jeff. How to Win a High School Election: Advice & Ideas Collected from over 1,000 High School Seniors. (p. 822)
Marx, Mandy R. ATVs (p. 114)
—Great Vampire Legends (p. 719)
—Leatherback Turtles (p. 986)
—Maryland Colony. (p. 1101)
—Motocross Racing (p. 1179)
—Paintball (p. 1318)
—Peacocks (p. 1332)
—Skydiving (p. 1587)
—Stars of Pro Wrestling (p. 1643)
Marx, Mandy R., jt. auth. see McCarthy, Cecilia Pinto.
Marx, Mandy R. & Schuh, Mari. Sports Stars (p. 1633)
Marx, Monica, ed. see Doudna, Kelly.
Marx, Monica, ed. see Tuminelly, Nancy.
Marx, Pamela. Practical Plays: Grades 1-5. Moore, Cyd, illus. (p. 1392)
Marx, Patricia. Now I Will Never Go to Sleep. (p. 1269)
Marx, Trish. Everglades Forever: Restoring America's Great Wetland Karp, Cindy, illus. (p. 542)
—Friend Power. Senisi, Ellen B., photos by. (p. 637)
—Jeannette Rankin: First Lady of Congress. Andreasen, Dan, illus. (p. 911)
—Kindergarten Day USA & China. Senisi, Ellen B., photos by. (p. 957)
—Reaching for the Sun: Kids in Cuba. (p. 1442)
—Sharing Our Homeland: Palestinian & Jewish Children at Summer Peace Camp Karp, Cindy, illus. (p. 1561)
Marx, Trish & Senisi, Ellen B. Steel Drumming at the Apollo: The Road to Super Top Dog. (p. 1646)
Marx, Trish, et al. Elephants & Golden Thrones: Inside China's Forbidden City. (p. 511)
Marxhausen, Ben, illus. see Marxhausen, Joanne.
Marxhausen, Benjamin, illus. see Marxhausen, Joanne.
Marxhausen, Joanne. 3 In 1: A Picture of God. (p. 1991)
—Cielo Es un Lugar Maravilloso. Marxhausen, Benjamin & Koehler, Ed, illus. (p. 319)
—Heaven is a Wonderful Place. Marxhausen, Ben & Koehler, Ed, illus. (p. 761)
Marxhausen, Kim. Paper Paint & Print. (p. 1322)
Marxhausen, Kris. Faith the Flower Friend. (p. 565)
—Luke's Fishing Lessons. (p. 1064)
Mary, Agnes. Story of Sammie. (p. 1659)
Mary Barr. Ditch Dog the Hedge Cat. (p. 454)
Mary Connors, illus. see Claire Hamelin Bruyere.
Mary, Crosby. Snuggles. (p. 1601)
Mary E. Gale. Mountain Boy in the City. (p. 1180)
Mary Holland. Beavers' Busy Year (p. 155)
Mary Jean, illus. see Windeatt, Mary F.
Mary John Lewis. Pookie in Paris. (p. 1383)
Mary, Mize. Letters from Scamper. Shirley, Hoskins, illus. (p. 1002)
Mary, Ms. Little Lambie No-No's Great Escape. (p. 1030)
Mary, Nanette. Ashby, the Happy Little Elephant. (p. 105)
MaryAnn, Aunt. Spooky Journey down Riverside Drive the Night of the Full Moon. (p. 1631)
Maryann Pasda Diedwardo & Patricia J. Pasda. Pennsylvania Voices Book V: The Legacy of Allison. (p. 1338)
Marychild, H. D. Skater Sister. (p. 1584)
Mary-Todd, Jonathan. Giant. (p. 673)
—Lock-In. (p. 1045)
—Pig City. (p. 1357)
—Shot Down. (p. 1569)
—Snakebite. (p. 1596)
Maryvale Institute of Religious Education Staff & Catholic Church, Archdiocese of Birmingham (England) Staff, contrib. by. Gifted in the Spirit. (p. 675)
Marz, Ron. Angelus (p. 75)
—Artifacts (p. 104)
—Blood for Blood Cheung, Jim et al, illus. (p. 200)
—Blood on Snow Sears, Bart et al, illus. (p. 200)
—Chimera. Peterson, Brandon, illus. (p. 306)
—Conflict of Conscience. Cheung, Jim et al, illus. (p. 357)

—Crisis of Faith. Sears, Bart & Pennington, Mark, illus. (p. 383)
—Death & Dishonor Sears, Bart et al, illus. (p. 420)
—Divided Loyalties Cheung, Jim et al, illus. (p. 454)
—Dragon's Tale (p. 479)
—Enemies & Allies Smith, Matthew et al, illus. (p. 527)
—Far Kingdom Cheung, Jim et al, illus. (p. 572)
—First Born Deluxe Edition. (p. 593)
—From the Ashes. Land, Greg & Jay, Leisten, illus. (p. 644)
—Heaven & Earth. (p. 761)
—Mystic Traveler: The Demon Queen Peterson, Brandon et al, illus. (p. 1226)
—Path Sears, Bart et al, illus. (p. 1328)
—Path Traveler (p. 1328)
—Sanctuary Cheung, Jim et al, illus. (p. 1510)
—Scion: The Royal Wedding. Vol. 6 Cheung, Jim et al, illus. (p. 1529)
—Sojourn Land, Greg et al, illus. (p. 1606)
—Torchbearer. (p. 1769)
—Warrior's Tale Land, Greg et al, illus. (p. 1859)
—Witchblade Redemption (p. 1941)
—Witchblade: Redemption Volume 3 TP: Redemption Volume 3 TP. (p. 1941)
Marz, Ron & Poulton, Mark. Blade of Kumori GN. O'Reilly, Sean Patrick, ed. (p. 198)
Marz, Ron, et al. Progeny Volume 1 TP. (p. 1410)
Marzan, Jose, Jr., illus. see Vaughan, Brian K.
Marzan, Jose, Jr., illus. see Vaughan, Brian K. & Sudzuka, Goran.
Marzec, Robert P. Mid-Atlantic Region (p. 1137)
Marzel, Pépi, illus. see Groner, Judyth.
Marzel, Pepi, illus. see Sussman, Joni.
Marzilli, Alan. Affirmative Action. (p. 26)
—Capital Punishment. (p. 262)
—DNA Evidence. (p. 456)
—Drugs & Sports. (p. 487)
—Election Reform. (p. 508)
—Fetal Rights. (p. 582)
—Internet & Crime. (p. 880)
—Mental Health Reform. (p. 1126)
—Religion in Public Schools. (p. 1458)
—Stem Cell Research & Cloning. (p. 1647)
Marzilli, Alan, ed. see Hudson, David L., Jr.
Marzilli, Alan, ed. see Ruschmann, Paul.
Marzilli, Alan, jt. auth. see Hudson, David L., Jr.
Marzilli, Alan, jt. auth. see Jones, Phillip.
Marzilli, Alan, ed. Point/Counterpoint: Issues in Contemporary American Society. (p. 1377)
—Point/Counterpoint. (p. 1377)
Marzolf, Julie. Big Cats Are Not Pets! (p. 180)
—Gross Things about Your Pets. (p. 725)
Marzollo, Jean. C'est Moi l'Espion: Défis Suprêmes! Duchesne, Lucie, tr. (p. 288)
—C'est Moi l'Espion: Du Monde du Mystère. Wick, Walter, photos by. (p. 288)
—Christmas Tree. Wick, Walter, illus. (p. 316)
—Four Picture Riddle Books. Wick, Walter, illus. (p. 625)
—Funny Frog. (p. 650)
—Happy Birthday, Martin Luther King. Pinkney, J. Brian, illus. (p. 745)
—Help Me Learn Addition. Philips, Chad, photos by. (p. 765)
—Help Me Learn Addition. Phillips, Chad, photos by. (p. 765)
—Help Me Learn Numbers 0-20. Phillips, Chad, illus. (p. 765)
—Help Me Learn Numbers 0-20. Phillips, Chad, photos by. (p. 765)
—Help Me Learn Subtraction. Phillips, Chad, illus. (p. 765)
—Help Me Learn Subtraction. Phillips, Chad, photos by. (p. 765)
—I Spy: A Scary Monster. Wick, Walter, illus. (p. 846)
—I Spy a Balloon. Wick, Walter, illus. (p. 846)
—I Spy a Butterfly. Wick, Walter, illus. (p. 846)
—I Spy a Candy Can. Wick, Walter, illus. (p. 846)
—I Spy a Dinosaur's Eye. Wick, Walter, illus. (p. 846)
—I Spy a Funny Frog. Wick, Walter, illus. (p. 846)
—I Spy a Penguin. Wick, Walter, illus. (p. 846)
—I Spy a Skeleton. Wick, Walter, illus. (p. 846)
—I Spy Adventure: 4 Picture Riddle Books. Wick, Walter, illus. (p. 846)
—I Spy an Apple. Wick, Walter, illus. (p. 846)
—I Spy an Egg in a Nest. Wick, Walter, illus. (p. 846)
—I Spy Animals. (p. 846)
—I Spy Animals. Wick, Walter, illus. (p. 846)
—I Spy Letters. (p. 846)
—I Spy Letters. Wick, Walter, illus. (p. 846)
—I Spy Lightning in the Sky. Wick, Walter, illus. (p. 846)
—I Spy Little Hearts. Wick, Walter, illus. (p. 846)
—I Spy Little Toys. Wick, Walter, illus. (p. 846)
—I Spy Merry Christmas. Wick, Walter, illus. (p. 846)
—I Spy Nature: A Book of Picture Riddles. Wick, Walter, photos by. (p. 846)
—I Spy Numbers. (p. 846)
—I Spy Numbers. Wick, Walter, illus. (p. 846)
—I Spy Santa Claus. Wick, Walter, illus. (p. 846)
—I Spy School. (p. 846)
—I Spy Spectacular: A Book of Picture Riddles. Wick, Walter, illus. (p. 846)
—I Spy Thanksgiving. Wick, Walter, illus. (p. 846)
—Little Bunnies. Wick, Walter, illus. (p. 1025)
—Little Plant Doctor: The Story of George Washington Carver. Wilson-Max, Ken, illus. (p. 1033)
—Mama Mama - Papa Papa. Regan, Laura, illus. (p. 1084)
—Pierre the Penguin. Regan, Laura, illus. (p. 1357)
—Pumpkin. Wick, Walter, illus. (p. 1416)
—Scholastic Reader Level 1: I Spy School. Wick, Walter, illus. (p. 1522)
—School Bus. Wick, Walter, illus. (p. 1522)
—Shanna's Lost Shoe. (p. 1559)
—Sticker Book & Picture Riddles. Wick, Walter, illus. (p. 1650)
—to Z: A Book of Picture Riddles. Wick, Walter, illus. (p. 1759)
—Ultimate Challenger! A Book of Picture Riddles. Wick, Walter, illus. (p. 1809)
Marzollo, Jean & Scholastic / LeapFrog. I Spy Imagine That! Wick, Walter, illus. (p. 846)
Marzollo, Jean & Wick, Walter. I Spy a Dinosaur's Eye. (p. 846)
—I Spy Funny Teeth. (p. 846)
—School Bus. (p. 1522)
Marzon, Jose, jt. auth. see Vaughan, Brian K.
Marzot, Janet. Liebres Blancas. (p. 1007)
Marzullo, Re. Sped. (p. 1624)
Mas, Maribel, illus. see Barbot, Daniel.
Mas, Sylvie, jt. auth. see Zammarchi, Fabrice.
Masaaki, Aihara, jt. ed. see Sarris, Eno.
Masakazu Staff, jt. auth. see Katsura, Masakazu.
Masannak, Joachim. Wild Soccer Bunch, Book 2, Diego the Tornado: Diego the Tornado. Part, Michael, ed. (p. 1930)
Masar, Brenden. History of Punk Rock. (p. 784)
Mascarelli, Gloria & Mascarelli, Robert. Ceramics of China: 5000 B. C. to 1900 A. D. (p. 287)
Mascarelli, Robert, jt. auth. see Mascarelli, Gloria.
Mascie-Taylor, Heather, jt. auth. see Honnor, Sylvia.
Masciullo, Lucia, illus. see Fraillon, Zana.
Masciullo, Lucia, illus. see Kane, Kim.
Mase, Naokata. Rainy Trip Surprise. Perry, Mia Lynn, tr. (p. 1436)
Mase, Tina. Spencer: A Sense of Heritage. (p. 1625)
Masefield, John. Box of Delights. Masefield, Judith, illus. (p. 216)
—Jim Davis. (p. 917)
—Midnight Folk. Hilder, Rowland, illus. (p. 1138)
Masefield, Judith, illus. see Masefield, John.
Masel, Christy. Gorp's Dream: A Tale of Diversity, Tolerance, & Love in Pumpernickel Park. (p. 703)
Masel, Christy, illus. see Chessen, Sherri.
Masella, Rosalie Tagg. Adventures of Dingle Dee & Lingle Dee. Alemian, Kimberlee, illus. (p. 17)
Maselli, Christopher P. N. Attack of the Tremendous Truth! 12 Mystery Stories to Solve Using the Teachings of Jesus. (p. 114)
—Fruit Encounters of the God Kind: 12 Mystery Stories to Solve Using the Fruit of the Spirit. (p. 645)
—Gifts from Outer Space, Grades 3 - 6: 12 Mystery Stories to Solve Using Spiritual Gifts. (p. 675)
—Invasion of the Psalm Psnatchers: 12 Mystery Stories to Solve Using Wisdom from Psalms. (p. 883)
—Runaway Mission. (p. 1496)
—Secret of the Firm Foundations: 12 Mystery Stories to Solve Using the Foundations of Our Faith. (p. 1542)
—Smarter Than the Average Pair, Grades 3 - 6: 12 Mystery Stories to Solve Using Wisdom from Proverbs. (p. 1593)
Maser, Barry, jt. illus. see Moser, Barry.
Masera, Mariana. Zarabulli: Cantares de Alla y de Aqui. Cicero, Julian, illus. (p. 1985)
Masessa, Ed. Mixed-up Pups. (p. 1156)
—Scarecrow Magic. Myers, Matt, illus. (p. 1519)
Masheris, Bob, illus. see Donahue, Jill Urban.
Masheris, Bob, illus. see Riggs, Sandy.
Masheris, Bob, illus. see Urban Donahue, Jill.
Masheris, Robert, illus. see Hillert, Margaret.
Mashima, Hiro. Rave: Volume 2 (p. 1440)
—Rave: Volume 7 (p. 1440)
—Rave: Volume 9 (p. 1440)
—Rave: Volume 11 (p. 1440)
—Rave. (p. 1440)
—Rave Master (p. 1440)
—Rave Master Mashima, Hiro, illus. (p. 1440)
—Rave Master Dunn, Brian, tr. from JPN. (p. 1440)
—Rave Master Forsyth, Amy, tr. from JPN. (p. 1440)
—Rave Master Bourque, Jeremiah, tr. from JPN. (p. 1440)
—Rave Master. (p. 1440)
—Rave Master (p. 1441)
—Rave Master Mashima, Hiro, illus. (p. 1441)
—Rave Master. (p. 1441)
—Rave Master. Mashima, Hiro, illus. (p. 1441)
—Rave Master Volume 23 (p. 1441)
—Rave, Volume 8 (p. 1441)
Mashima, Hiro & Hiro, Mashima. Rave Master (p. 1441)
Mashima, Hiro, creator. Rave Master (p. 1441)
Mashonee, Jana & Galfas, Stephan. American Indian Story - the Adventures of Sha'kona. (p. 62)
Masi, P. J., illus. see Stevenson, Richard.
Masi, Sue. Journey Through Fantasy Forest. (p. 928)
Masiello, Ralph. Bug Drawing Book: Simple Steps Make Anyone an Artist. Masiello, Ralph, illus. (p. 236)
—Bug Drawing Book: Simple Steps to Make Anyone an Artist. Masiello, Ralph, illus. (p. 236)
—Ralph Masiello's Ancient Egypt Drawing Book. Masiello, Ralph, illus. (p. 1437)
—Ralph Masiello's Christmas Drawing Book. Masiello, Ralph, illus. (p. 1437)
—Ralph Masiello's Dinosaur Drawing Book. Masiello, Ralph, illus. (p. 1437)
—Ralph Masiello's Dragon Drawing Book. Masiello, Ralph, illus. (p. 1437)
—Ralph Masiello's Fairy Drawing Book. Masiello, Ralph, illus. (p. 1437)
—Ralph Masiello's Farm Drawing Book. Masiello, Ralph, illus. (p. 1437)
—Ralph Masiello's Halloween Drawing Book. Masiello, Ralph, illus. (p. 1437)
—Ralph Masiello's Ocean Drawing Book. Masiello, Ralph, illus. (p. 1437)
—Ralph Masiello's Robot Drawing Book. Masiello, Ralph, illus. (p. 1437)
Masiello, Ralph, illus. see Brockway, Stephanie.
Masiello, Ralph, illus. see Pallotta, Jerry.
Masiello, Ralph, illus. see Ryan, Pam Muñoz.
Masiello, Ralph, photos by see Pallotta, Jerry.
Masilela, Johnny. We Shall Not Weep. (p. 1868)
Masino, Brian. Cabbage Patch Kids: We Are All Best Friends. Karl, Linda, illus. (p. 250)
Mask, Cynthia, illus. see Lamar, Gail Renfroe.
Maskel, Hazel. 1001 Things to Spot on Vacation. (p. 2002)
Maskell, Hazel. Animal Picture Atlas. Edwards, Linda, illus. (p. 79)
—Big Book of Big Animals. (p. 179)
—Cycling IR. (p. 397)
Maskell, Hazel, jt. auth. see Bone, Emily.
Maskell, Hazell. Very First Words. (p. 1838)
Maskell, Philip Mo. King Milo & His Royal Court. (p. 958)
Maslen, jt. auth. see Maslen, Bobby Lynn.
Maslen, Bobby Lynn. Word Families Maslen, John R., illus. (p. 1950)
Maslen, Bobby Lynn, jt. auth. see Maslen, John R.
Maslen, Bobby Lynn & Kertell, Lynn Maslen. Sight Words, First Grade Maslen, John & Hendra, Sue, illus. (p. 1574)
—Sight Words Kindergarten Maslen, John & Hendra, Sue, illus. (p. 1574)
Maslen, Bobby Lynn & Maslen. Beginning Readers (p. 159)
Maslen, Bobby Lynn & Maslen, John R. Long Vowels (p. 1047)
Maslen, John, illus. see Maslen, Bobby Lynn & Kertell, Lynn Maslen.
Maslen, John R., illus. see Kertell, Lynn Maslen.
Maslen, John R., illus. see Maslen, Bobby Lynn.
Maslen, John R., jt. auth. see Maslen, Bobby Lynn.
Maslen, John R. & Maslen, Bobby Lynn. Advancing Beginners (p. 13)
—Compound Words Maslen, John R., illus. (p. 354)
Maslin, Mirabelle. Tracy. (p. 1776)
Maslyn, Stacie K., jt. auth. see Maslyn, Stacie K. B.
Maslyn, Stacie K. B. & Maslyn, Stacie K. Mad Maddie Maxwell Schettle, Jane, illus. (p. 1069)
Masnou, Merce, jt. auth. see Llongueras, Joan.
Masoff, Joy. African American Story: The Events That Shaped Our Nation & the People Who Changed Our Lives. (p. 27)
—Oh, Yikes! History's Grossest, Wackiest Moments. Sirrell, Terry, illus. (p. 1281)
—We Are All Americans: Understanding Diversity. (p. 1865)
Masoliver, Joaquín, jt. auth. see Masoliver, Juan Antonio.
Masoliver, Juan Antonio. Historias Breves para Leer (p. 782)
Masoliver, Juan Antonio & Masoliver, Joaquín. Historias Breves para Leer (p. 782)
Mason, Abi, illus. see Winbolt-Lewis, Martin.
Mason, Adrienne. Bats. Ogle, Nancy Gray & Ogle, Nancy, illus. (p. 144)
—Build It! Structures, Systems & You. Dávila, Claudia, illus. (p. 238)
—Change It! Solids, Liquids, Gases & You. Dávila, Claudia, illus. (p. 290)
—Drop of Doom. Cupples, Pat, illus. (p. 485)
—Lost & Found. Cupples, Pat, illus. (p. 1054)
—Motion, Magnets & More. Dávila, Claudia, illus. (p. 1179)
—Move It! Motion, Forces & You. Dávila, Claudia, illus. (p. 1183)
—Otters. Ogle, Nancy Gray & Ogle, Nancy, illus. (p. 1307)
—Owls. Ogle, Nancy Gray & Ogle, Nancy, illus. (p. 1315)
—Planet Ark: Preserving Earth's Biodiversity. Thompson, Margot, illus. (p. 1367)
—Secret Spies. Cupples, Patricia & Cupples, Pat, illus. (p. 1544)
—Skunks. Ogle, Nancy Gray & Ogle, Nancy, illus. (p. 1586)
—Snakes. Ogle, Nancy Gray & Ogle, Nancy, illus. (p. 1596)
—Touch It! Materials, Matter & You. Dávila, Claudia, illus. (p. 1772)
Mason, Albert. Ooshu, Dorothy, & the Old Lady. (p. 1299)
—Ooshu the Monkey Escapes from the Zoo. (p. 1299)
Mason, Albert D. Ooshu & Dorothy's Cricket. (p. 1299)
Mason, Alexis. Just an Ordinary Little Dog: Barnaby's Story. Bunch, Paul, illus. (p. 937)
Mason, Alfonso, illus. see Baker, Mary E.
Mason, Alfonso, illus. see Baker, Mary.
Mason & Marisa & Avery & Stella. Tale of Princess Fluffy & Prince Rupert. (p. 1700)
Mason, Anthony. Versailles. (p. 1837)
Mason, Antony. Art. (p. 101)
—Arte Contemporaneo: En los Tiempos de Warhol. (p. 103)
—Arte Impresionista: En Los Tiempos de Renoir. (p. 103)
—Arte Moderno: En los Tiempos de Picasso. (p. 103)
—arte Renacentista: En los tiempos de Miguel Angel. (p. 103)
—Literature. (p. 1023)
—Marc Chagall. (p. 1091)
—Music. (p. 1193)
—New Europe. (p. 1244)
—Performing Arts. (p. 1343)
Mason, Antony & Rembrandt Harmenszoon van Rijn. Rembrandt. (p. 1459)
Mason, Ashley. Everybody Is Somebody Special. (p. 543)
Mason, Bergetta, illus. see Mason, Craig.
Mason, Bonita. T-Bear the Most Special Bear. Hendricks, Sandy, illus. (p. 1693)
Mason, Caroline. Blacksmith's Cottage: A Pastoral War. (p. 197)
Mason, Casey. Unhinged. (p. 1817)
Mason, Catherine, jt. auth. see Waldman, Carl.
Mason, Chad. Wake up, Bertha Bear! Wallace, Chad, illus. (p. 1853)
Mason, Charlene. Landon's Backyard Adventures. (p. 974)
—Mr Wilson's Tree. (p. 1187)
—William's First Day of Preschool. (p. 1933)
Mason, Charles, photos by see Murphy, Claire Rudolf.
Mason, Cherie. Everybody's Somebody's Lunch Moore, Gustav, illus. (p. 543)
—Wild Fox: A True Story. Stammen, JoEllen McAllister, illus. (p. 1929)
Mason, Chris, jt. auth. see Biggers, Nikki.
Mason, Chris, jt. auth. see Coleman, Andrew.
Mason, Chris, jt. auth. see Kittay, Matthew.
Mason, Chris, jt. auth. see Olson, Remy.
Mason, Christine. Mystery of Nan Madol a Pacific Island Adventure. (p. 1225)
Mason, Christopher. California Colleges. Balzer, Jim et al, eds. (p. 253)
—Little Bunny Comfy Pants. (p. 1025)
Mason, Conrad. Dinosaurs IR. (p. 445)
—First World War. (p. 597)
—Polar Bears: Internet-Referenced. Howarth, Daniel, illus. (p. 1379)
—See Inside How Things Work. (p. 1546)
—See Inside Ships. King, Colin, illus. (p. 1546)
Mason, Conrad, illus. see Sims, Lesley, ed.
Mason, Conrad, illus. see Sims, Lesley.
Mason, Craig. Turtle Games. Mason, Bergetta, illus. (p. 1798)
Mason Crest Publishers Staff, jt. contrib. by see Ripley Publishing Staff.
Mason, David. Davey Mcgravy. Silverstein, Grant, illus. (p. 410)
Mason, David, jt. auth. see Hodson, Ann.
Mason, Dianne. Danny's Ghost. (p. 406)
Mason, Edward G., ed. see Frazetta, Frank.
Mason, Helen. Agricultural Inventions: At the Top of the Field. (p. 30)
—Chef. (p. 297)
—Costume Designer. (p. 368)
—Interior Designer. (p. 880)
—Landscape Designer. (p. 974)
—Makeup Artist. (p. 1080)
—Urban Planner. (p. 1825)
—Weird Nature. (p. 1872)
Mason, Helen, jt. auth. see Corporate Contributor Staff.
Mason, Helen, jt. auth. see Smith, Paula.
Mason, J. D. Don't Want No Sugar. (p. 469)
Mason, James, jt. auth. see Brooman, Josh.
Mason, James, jt. auth. see Purkis, Sallie.
Mason, James & Purkis, Sallie. Encounters. (p. 524)
—Invasions. (p. 883)
Mason, Jane B. Attack of the Cheetah Schoening, Dan, illus. (p. 113)
—Battle Bugs of Outer Space Baltazar, Art, illus. (p. 145)
—Black Manta & the Octopus Army Vecchio, Luciano, illus. (p. 196)
—Stella & the Berry Thief Koopmans, Loek, tr. (p. 1646)
—Super Hero Splash Down Baltazar, Art, illus. (p. 1680)
Mason, Jane B. & Hines-Stephens, Sarah. Cry Woof. (p. 387)
—Dead Man's Best Friend. (p. 417)
—Disguised & Dangerous. Phillips, Craig, illus. (p. 450)
—Let Sleeping Dogs Spy. Phillips, Craig, illus. (p. 994)
—Play Dead. (p. 1371)
Mason, Jane B. & Stephens, Sarah. Snowfall Surprise. (p. 1600)
Mason, Jane B. & Stephens, Sarah Hines. Bella Baxter & the Lighthouse Mystery. Shelley, John, illus. (p. 162)
—Dog & His Girl Mysteries #3: Cry Woof. (p. 461)
—Snowfall Surprise. (p. 1600)
Mason, Jane B., et al. Captain Cold's Arctic Eruption Doescher, Erik, illus. (p. 264)
—Ice & Flame (p. 850)
—Inkheart. (p. 874)
Mason, Janeen. Gift of the Magpie Mason, Janeen, illus. (p. 675)
—Ocean Commotion: Sea Turtles Mason, Janeen, illus. (p. 1276)
—Ocean Commotion: Life on the Reef Mason, Janeen, illus. (p. 1276)
—Ocean Commotion: Caught in the Currents Mason, Janeen, illus. (p. 1276)
Mason, Janeen, illus. see Berkes, Marianne Collins.
Mason, Janeen, illus. see Denver, John.
Mason, Janeen, illus. see Koski, Mary B.
Mason, Janeen, jt. auth. see Day, Jan.
Mason, Janeen, jt. auth. see Swinney, Geoff.
Mason, Joan, jt. auth. see Eller, Tracy.
Mason, Jo-Anne. Paddy, the Goat That Saved Rainbow Island. (p. 1317)
Mason, Joey, jt. auth. see Walker, Landry Q.
Mason, John, jt. auth. see Riel, Jörn.
Mason, Kate, jt. auth. see McKinney, Frank.
Mason, Kerry. Angel Baby. (p. 73)
Mason, Leah. Goldie: A Dog's Story. (p. 695)
Mason, Linda. Eye Candy: 50 Easy Makeup Looks for Glam Lids & Luscious Lashes. (p. 557)
Mason, Margaret. Inside All. Welch, Holly, illus. (p. 876)
Mason, Margaret H. These Hands. Cooper, Floyd, illus. (p. 1731)
Mason, Mark, illus. see Geiser, Traci Ferguson & Boylan, Maureen McCourt.
Mason, Mark, illus. see Heskett, Tracie.
Mason, Mark, illus. see McCullough, L. E.
Mason, Mark, illus. see Schwartz, Linda.
Mason, Mike. Blue Umbrella. (p. 203)
Mason, Mimi Canda. Lola's Cane. (p. 1046)
Mason, Miriam E. John Audubon: Young Naturalist. Morrison, Cathy, illus. (p. 921)
Mason, Otis Tufton. Aboriginal American Basketry: Studies in a Textile Art Without Machinery. (p. 5)
Mason, Paul. Are You Tough Enough? Body Systems (p. 97)
—Bike Mechanic: How to Be an Ace Bike Mechanic (p. 185)
—Boxing. (p. 217)
—Can You Lick Your Own Elbow? And Other Questions about the Human Body (p. 259)
—Caring for Critters. (p. 269)
—Cities in Crisis (p. 322)
—Could a Walrus Play the Saxophone? And Other Questions about Animals (p. 369)
—Cuba. (p. 388)
—Daily Life in Ancient Benin. (p. 399)
—Did Anything Good Come Out of the Cold War? (p. 436)
—Did the Romans Eat Chips? And Other Questions about History (p. 437)
—Dirt Biking: The World's Most Remarkable Dirt Bike Rides & Techniques (p. 446)
—Dogs. Elsom, Clare, illus. (p. 462)
—Earthquakes. (p. 497)
—España. (p. 536)
—Extreme Sports Stars. (p. 557)
—Extreme Storms. (p. 557)
—Extreme Zone: Forces & Motion (p. 557)
—Fishing: The World's Greatest Fishing Spots & Techniques (p. 599)
—Floods. (p. 605)
—Forests under Threat (p. 618)
—Formula 1. (p. 620)
—Francia. (p. 627)
—Frauds & Counterfeits. (p. 631)
—Grasslands under Threat (p. 712)
—Hiking & Camping: The World's Top Hikes & Camping Spots (p. 779)
—Horses & Ponies. Elsom, Clare, illus. (p. 800)
—How Big Is Your Clothing Footprint? (p. 805)

—How Big Is Your Energy Footprint? (p. 805)
—How Big Is Your Food Footprint? (p. 805)
—How Big Is Your Shopping Footprint? (p. 805)
—How Big Is Your Travel Footprint? (p. 805)
—How Big Is Your Water Footprint? (p. 805)
—How to Improve at Swimming. (p. 820)
—Improving Endurance. (p. 862)
—Improving Flexibility. (p. 862)
—Improving Speed. (p. 862)
—Improving Strength & Power. (p. 862)
—Indy Cars. (p. 873)
—Iraq (p. 887)
—Iraq War. (p. 887)
—Italia. (p. 894)
—Judo. (p. 931)
—Karting. (p. 944)
—Kayaking & Canoeing: The World's Best Paddling Locations & Techniques (p. 946)
—Know the Facts about Drinking & Smoking. (p. 965)
—London. Bowden, Rob & Cooper, Adrian, photos by. (p. 1046)
—Monster Trucks. (p. 1168)
—Monsters. (p. 1168)
—Motorcycles. (p. 1179)
—Mountain Biking. (p. 1180)
—Mountains under Threat (p. 1181)
—Ocean in Motion: Surfing & the Science of Waves (p. 1276)
—Oceans under Threat (p. 1277)
—Out & about with Your Senses. (p. 1310)
—Panning for Gold: Mixtures & Solutions (p. 1321)
—Passport to World Sports. (p. 1327)
—Pirate Adventures! (p. 1362)
—Polar Regions. (p. 1379)
—Rainforest Research Journal. (p. 1436)
—Religious Extremism. (p. 1458)
—Reports from the Front in WWII. (p. 1461)
—Rivers under Threat (p. 1476)
—Rock Climbing: The World's Hottest Climbing Locations & Techniques (p. 1482)
—Roller Coaster! Motion & Acceleration (p. 1485)
—Skateboarding: The World's Coolest Skate Spots & Techniques (p. 1583)
—Skiing. (p. 1584)
—Snowboarding. (p. 1600)
—Snowboarding: The World's Most Sizzling Snowboard Spots & Techniques (p. 1600)
—Snowboarding. (p. 1600)
—Sports Heroes of Ancient Greece. (p. 1632)
—Stock Cars. (p. 1651)
—Stories about Surviving Drug Addiction. (p. 1654)
—Surfing: The World's Most Fantastic Surf Spots & Techniques (p. 1685)
—Surfing. (p. 1685)
—Sydney. Bowden, Rob, photos by. (p. 1692)
—Tae Kwon Do. (p. 1695)
—Training for Sports (p. 1777)
—Tsunamis. (p. 1795)
—UFOs & Crop Circles. (p. 1808)
—Understanding Computer Safety. (p. 1815)
—Understanding Computer Search & Research. (p. 1815)
—Volcanoes. (p. 1849)
—Wackiest Machines Ever! Forms of Energy (p. 1852)
—Want to Be a Knight? (p. 1856)
—Wildfires. (p. 1931)
—Windsurfing: The World's Windiest Water Sport Spots & Techniques (p. 1936)
—Your Breathtaking Lungs & Rocking Respiratory System. (p. 1980)
—Your Growing Body & Remarkable Reproductive System. (p. 1980)
—Your Growling Guts & Dynamic Digestive System. (p. 1980)
—Your Hardworking Heart & Spectacular Circulatory System. (p. 1980)
—Your Mind-Bending Brain & Networking Nervous System. (p. 1981)
—Your Strong Skeleton & Amazing Muscular System. (p. 1981)
Mason, Paul, jt. auth. see Anniss, Matthew.
Mason, Paul, jt. auth. see Guillain, Charlotte.
Mason, Paul, jt. auth. see Hodge, Susie.
Mason, Paul, jt. auth. see Thorpe, Yvonne.
Mason, Paul & Barnham, Kay. Questions You Never Thought You'd Ask. (p. 1426)
Mason, Paul & Cavendish, Marshall. Indian Subcontinent. (p. 871)
Mason, Paul & Eason, Sarah. Free Running. (p. 634)
—Street Soccer. (p. 1667)
Mason, Paul & Hachette Children's Books Staff. Ghost Hunter's Guide. (p. 670)
—Vampire Hunter's Guide. (p. 1832)
Mason, Paul & Heinemann Library Staff. Cities in Crisis (p. 322)
—Forests under Threat (p. 618)
—Grasslands under Threat (p. 712)
—Mountains under Threat (p. 1181)
—Oceans under Threat (p. 1277)
—Rivers under Threat (p. 1476)
Mason, Paul & Hodge, Susie. Investigating UFOs & Aliens (p. 885)
Mason, Paul & Marshall Cavendish Corporation Staff. Iraq. (p. 887)
Mason, Paul & Marshall Cavendish Staff. Israel & Palestine. (p. 893)
Mason, Paul & Smart Apple Media Staff. Biking. (p. 186)
—Climbing & Abseiling. (p. 333)
Mason, Prue. Camel Rider. (p. 256)
Mason, Randy, jt. auth. see Smith, A. G.
Mason, Richard. Red Scarf: A Country Boy's Christmas Story. (p. 1455)
Mason, Roberta Black, illus. see Turner, Diane.
Mason, Roger. Mummies - Mysteries of the Past. (p. 1191)
—Space Race - Space Busters. (p. 1619)
Mason, Ruth, illus. see Baker, Mary E.
Mason, Ruth, illus. see Baker, Mary.
Mason, Shannon, ed. see Rowe, Papa.
Mason, Sue, illus. see Blackford, Andy.
Mason, Sue, illus. see Durant, Alan.
Mason, Sue, illus. see Goodhart, Pippa.
Mason, Sue, illus. see Harrison, Paul.
Mason, Theodore. South Pole Ponies. (p. 1617)
Mason, Tom. Magic of the Masters: Learn Tricks by David Copperfield, Harry Houdini & More! (p. 1073)
Mason, Tom, jt. auth. see Danko, Dan.
Mason, Tom & Danko, Dan. Christmas Surprise. Shannon, David et al, illus. (p. 315)
—Food Magic: How to Do Amazing Tricks with Ordinary Food! (p. 613)
—Lost Scrolls: Fire. Spaziante, Patrick, illus. (p. 1056)
—Where Did It Go? Magic: How to Make Things Change Places! (p. 1906)
Mason, Tom, et al. Disappearing Magic: How to Make Things Vanish into Thin Air! (p. 446)
—Funny Magic: How to Do Tricks That Make People Laugh! (p. 650)
—Honk That Horn! Shannon, David et al, illus. (p. 795)
—Shape-Shifting Magic: How to Turn One Thing into Another. (p. 1560)
—Who's That Truck? Shannon, David et al, illus. (p. 1921)
Mason, Tresor. Twisted Game Between Love & Lies. (p. 1802)
Mason, Turning Bear, illus. see Smith, Sandra S.
Mason-Fry, Douglas L., photos by see Lalli, Judy.
Maspons, Andrea. Las Medias de Carlota. (p. 976)
Masrud, Judy. Second Chance: A Tale of Two Puppies Pool, Cathy, illus. (p. 1539)
Mass, Aaron & Burns, Adam. Wake Forest University College Prowler off the Record. (p. 1853)
Mass, Wendy. 11 Birthdays. (p. 1994)
—13 Gifts. (p. 1995)
—Autumn: Poems, Songs, Prayers. (p. 118)
—Beauty & the Beast: The Only One Who Didn't Run Away. (p. 154)
—Candymakers. (p. 261)
—Celebrate Halloween. (p. 283)
—Every Soul a Star. (p. 543)
—Finally. (p. 587)
—Graceful. (p. 705)
—Heaven Looks a Lot Like the Mall. (p. 761)
—Jeremy Fink & the Meaning of Life. (p. 913)
—John Cabot: Early Explorer. (p. 921)
—Last Present. (p. 978)
—Leap Day. (p. 982)
—Mango-Shaped Space. (p. 1087)
—Pi in the Sky. (p. 1353)
—Rapunzel: The One with All the Hair. (p. 1439)
—Ray Bradbury: Master of Science Fiction & Fantasy. (p. 1441)
—Sleeping Beauty: The One Who Took the Really Long Nap. (p. 1589)
Mass, Wendy & Brawer, Michael. Archie Takes Flight. (p. 95)
—Space Taxi: Water Planet Rescue. (p. 1620)
—Space Taxi: Archie's Alien Disguise. (p. 1620)
—Space Taxi: Archie Takes Flight. Gravel, Élise, illus. (p. 1620)
Massachusetts Sabbath School Society Staff. Winnie Malone Written for the Mass S S Society, & Approved by the Committee of Publication. (p. 1937)
Massad, Diane. Go! STOP Go!: The Kidskills America Training Series. Vol. 3 (p. 687)
Massad, Diane P. Moving Right Along! The Kidskills America Training Series. (p. 1184)
Massad, Diane Patterson. Hang On! The Kidskills International Training Series. (p. 742)
—Making Muscles! The Kidskills America Training Series. (p. 1081)
—Up & Over! The Kidskills America Training Series. (p. 1824)
Massardier, Greg, illus. see Wyley, Enda.
Massardier, Greg, tr. see Wyley, Enda.
Massari, Alida, illus. see Joslin, Mary.
Massari, Alida, illus. see McAllister, Margaret.
Massari, Francesca. Everything You Need to Know about Cancer. (p. 545)
Massaro, Michael. Tony Towne & the Amazing Brain. (p. 1766)
—Tony Towne & the Fearful Summer. (p. 1766)
Massé, Johanna, jt. auth. see Kwek, Karen.
Masse, José, illus. see Xinran, Xinran, et al.
Masse, Josée, illus. see Bunting, Eve.
Masse, Josée, illus. see Levert, Mireille.
Masse, Josée, illus. see Natterson, Cara.
Masse, Josée, illus. see Singer, Marilyn.
Masse, Josee, illus. see Witte, Anna.
Masse, Josee, illus. see Xinran, Xinran & Mother's Bridge of Love Staff.
Masse, Josee, illus. see Ziefert, Harriet.
Masse, Josee, jt. auth. see Bailey, Linda.
Masse, Stephen V. Taste of Snow. (p. 1707)
Massenot, Véronique. Great Wave: A Children's Book Inspired by Hokusai. Pilorget, Bruno, illus. (p. 719)
—Journey on the Clouds: A Children's Book Inspired by Marc Chagall. Pilorget, Bruno, illus. (p. 928)
Massenot, Véronique & Hie, Vanessa. Three Musicians: A Children's Book Inspired by Pablo Picasso. (p. 1743)
Massey, Cal, illus. see Turner, Diane D.
Massey, Call, illus. see Turner, Diane D.
Massey, Carol. Not a Friend. (p. 1266)
Massey, Craig. Twig the Collie. (p. 1801)
Massey, David. Taken. (p. 1697)
—Torn. (p. 1770)
Massey, Ed. Jedlo, Defender of the Deep. (p. 911)
Massey, Ed, photos by see Massey, Wayland.
Massey, Eithne. Best-Loved Irish Legends: Mini Edition. Jackson, Lisa, illus. (p. 170)
—Blood Brother, Swan Sister: 1014 Clontarf - a Battle Begins. (p. 200)
—Silver Stag of Bunratty. (p. 1577)
—Where the Stones Sing: Who Are the Mysterious Voices in Christ Church? (p. 1909)
Massey, Gale. Healing Grief: Reflections to Nurture the Grieving Heart. (p. 757)
Massey, Jane. Animales de la Granja. (p. 80)
—Animales de la Selva. (p. 80)
—Mascotas. (p. 1102)
Massey, Jane, illus. see Dunbar, Joyce.
Massey, Jane, illus. see Freedman, Claire.
Massey, Jane, illus. see Haft, Sheryl.
Massey, Jane, illus. see Rawlinson, Julia.
Massey, Jane, illus. see Richards, Dawn.
Massey, Jane, illus. see Rock, Lois.
Massey, Jane, illus. see Warnes, Tim, et al.
Massey, Jane, tr. see Freedman, Claire.
Massey, K. J. Everyday Things with Morgan. Bowser, Katya, illus. (p. 544)
Massey, Kathy Hoeschen. You Laugh, I'll Drive: Giving yourself the green light to enjoy life — speed bumps & all — & stop worrying about Your (mile)age! (p. 1975)
Massey, Kay. What Do Animals Eat for Lunch? Canals, Sonia, illus. (p. 1882)
—What Do You See in the Sea? Canals, Sonia & O'Toole, Jeanette, illus. (p. 1883)
—What Is a Flower's Special Power? Canals, Sonia & O'Toole, Jeanette, illus. (p. 1888)
—Where Do Animals Hide? Canals, Sonia, illus. (p. 1906)
Massey, Mitch, illus. see Campbell, Jan-Ives.
Massey, Steve. Space, Stars & Planets. (p. 1619)
Massey, W. A. Joey an Ant's Story. (p. 920)
Massey, Wayland. Casper, the Friendly Service Dog. Massey, Ed, photos by. (p. 276)
Massicotte, Sylvie & Sottolichio, Rafael. Tu Rêves, Pitchounette? (p. 1795)
Massie, Diane Redfield. Baby Beebee Bird. Kellogg, Steven, illus. (p. 125)
Massie, Elizabeth. African American Educators. (p. 27)
—African American Educators. Hill, Marc Lamont, ed. (p. 27)
—Ameri-Scares: New York. (p. 58)
—Ameri-Scares: Virginia. (p. 58)
Massie, Elizabeth, jt. auth. see Favor, Lesli J.
Massie, Gordon, jt. auth. see LaFleur, James.
Massie, Rosemary. Rhymen the Rabbit: Save the Forest. (p. 1468)
—Rhymen the Rabbit: Meeting the Forest Ranger. (p. 1468)
Massingill, Robert, jt. auth. see Pitts, J. R.
Massingill, Robert, Jr. Adventures of John Henry. (p. 19)
Massini, Luca, illus. see Dalla Vecchia, Fabio Marco.
Massini, Sarah. Love Always Everywhere. (p. 1059)
Massini, Sarah, illus. see Blatt, Jane.
Massini, Sarah, illus. see Capucilli, Alyssa Satin.
Massini, Sarah, illus. see Hendry, Diana.
Massironi, Daniela. Frankie the Frog. (p. 630)
—Freddie the Fish. (p. 632)
Massivebrain.com, illus. see Strange, J. R.
Massman-Johnson, Tammy, jt. auth. see Strand, Jessica.
Masson, Annick, illus. see Callier, Marie-Isabelle.
Masson, Annick, illus. see Foccroulle, Luc.
Masson, J. Moussaieff. Cat Who Came in from the Cold: A Fable. (p. 278)
Masson, Lynne. Vegetable Patch. (p. 1834)
Masson, Sophie. Crystal Heart. (p. 387)
—Moonlight & Ashes. (p. 1172)
—Scarlet in the Snow. (p. 1520)
—Thomas Trew & the Hidden People. Dewan, Ted, illus. (p. 1739)
—Thomas Trew & the Horns of Pan. Dewan, Ted, illus. (p. 1739)
—Thomas Trew & the Island of Ghosts. Dewan, Ted, illus. (p. 1739)
—Thomas Trew & the Klint-King's Gold. Dewan, Ted, illus. (p. 1739)
—Thomas Trew & the Selkie's Curse. Dewan, Ted, illus. (p. 1739)
Mast, Dorcas R. God's Precious Gift. Zimmerman, Suzanne, illus. (p. 691)
Mast, Steven. God's Wonderful World: Science 5. (p. 692)
—God's Wonderful World: Science 5 Tests. (p. 692)
Mastel, Julie. Jesus Was with Me All Along: A Book about Divorce. (p. 916)
—Jesus Was with Me All Along: A Book about Bedwetting. (p. 916)
Master, Angel Michael. She Is a Gift from Jah. (p. 1564)
Master, Irfan. Beautiful Lie. (p. 153)
Master Merlin, jt. auth. see Steer, Dugald A.
Masterman, Lorrine A., jt. auth. see Hardy, Cindy.
Masters, Anthony. Ghost Stories to Tell in the Dark. (p. 671)
—Horror of the Heights Dennis, Peter, illus. (p. 799)
—Scary Tales to Tell in the Dark. (p. 1521)
Masters, Barbara. King Jack the Fourth. (p. 958)
Masters, Deborah. Magical Wisdom of Kids. (p. 1075)
Masters, Deborah, jt. auth. see Rabbin, Robert.
Masters, Elaine. Royal Waker-Upper. Leung, Andrew, illus. (p. 1492)
Masters, H. Pink Feathers,Murky Pools & a Witch: A Lellaland Adventure. Lie, Vivian, illus. (p. 1359)
Masters, Jane E. Indy. (p. 873)
Masters, M. Case of the Chocolate Snatcher: Can You Solve the Mystery #2. (p. 273)
—Case of the Mysterious Dognapper: Can You Solve the Mystery #4. (p. 274)
—Case of the Video Game Smugglers: Can You Solve the Mystery #3. (p. 275)
—Secret of the Long-Lost Cousin: Can You Solve the Mystery #1. (p. 1542)
Masters M.S. Ed., Margery. New York State Grade 4 Math Test. (p. 1248)
Masters, Nancy R. How Did That Get to My House? Water. (p. 806)
Masters, Nancy Robinson. Air Traffic Controller. (p. 31)
—Airplane. (p. 31)
—Airplanes. (p. 32)
—Drone Pilot. (p. 485)
—Extraordinary Patriots of the United States of America: Colonial Times to Pre-Civil War. (p. 555)
—Heavy Equipment Operator. (p. 761)
—How Did That Get to My House? Electricity. (p. 806)
—How Did That Get to My House? Telephone. (p. 806)
—How Did They Build That? House. (p. 806)
—How Did They Build That? Water Park. (p. 806)
—How Does It Fly? Glider. (p. 808)
—How Does It Fly? Hot Air Balloon. (p. 808)
—How Does It Fly? Propeller Plane. (p. 808)
—Jeans. (p. 911)
—Pararescue Jumper. (p. 1324)
—Salt. (p. 1505)
—Volcanic Eruptions. (p. 1848)
Masters, Neil. Aircrafts Coloring Book. (p. 31)
—Butterflies Coloring Book. (p. 247)
—Trucks Coloring Book. (p. 1791)
—Wild Animals Coloring Book. (p. 1928)
—Working Vehicles Coloring Book. (p. 1953)
Masters, Phil. Sinbad the Sailor. (p. 1578)
Masters, S. Ian's Visit with Gamma ... at the Beach. (p. 849)
Masters, Susan Rowan. Night Journey to Vicksburg. Killcoyne, Hope L., ed. (p. 1253)
—Vida Secreta de Hubie Hatzel. (p. 1841)
Masters, Tom. Blog to Book & Beyond: A New Path to Publishing Success. (p. 200)
Masters, William H. Love & Sex. Cart, Michael, ed. (p. 1059)
Masterson, Carla & Druckman, Mike. Memory Emory & His Hiding Places. (p. 1126)
Masterson, Carla Jo. What's on the Other Side of the Rainbow? The Secret of the Golden Mirror. Fochtman, Omra Jo, illus. (p. 1899)
Masterson, Jacqueline. Corrective Therapy. (p. 368)
—Punishment Camp. (p. 1417)
—Punishment Club. (p. 1417)
Masterson, Josephine. At the Hoover Dam. (p. 111)
—Nest for Robin. (p. 1242)
Masterson, Robert. Artificial Rats & Electric Cats: Communications from Transitional China, 1985-1986. (p. 104)
Mastin, Ian, illus. see Cross, John R.
Mastin, Marcus. Oscar Potter & His Late-Night Visitor. Peck, Jamie, illus. (p. 1305)
Mastnak, Rosemary. Cooking with Grandma. Mastnak, Rosemary, illus. (p. 362)
—Dancing with Grandma. Mastnak, Rosemary, illus. (p. 403)
Mastrangelo, Judy. What Do Bunnies Do All Day? (p. 1882)
—What Do Bunnies Do All Day? Mastrangelo, Judy, illus. (p. 1882)
Mastro, Jim. Talisman of Elam: Children of Hathor (p. 1703)
Mastro, M. L. Return to Baladah. (p. 1465)
Mastromarino, Diane. Being a Teen: Words of Advice from Someone Who's Been There. (p. 161)
Mastromarino, Diane, ed. Girl's Guide to Loving Yourself: A Book about Falling in Love with the One Person Who Matters Most - You. (p. 680)
Mastromonaco, Pina. King Bartholomew & the Jesters Riddle. Martin, David Lozell, illus. (p. 958)
Mastroserio, Rocke, illus. see Kaler, David, et al.
Mastrud, Karen. Fucious: The True Story of the Ugly Duckling. Margolis, Al, illus. (p. 646)
—Fucious. (p. 646)
Masu. Levi's Look'n for Things to Do in the Fall. (p. 1004)
Masumoto, Bryan, tr. see Akino, Matsuri.
Masura, Shauna. Digital Badges. (p. 439)
—Record It! Shooting & Editing Digital Video. (p. 1452)
Masurel, Claire. Cat & a Dog. Kolar, Bob, illus. (p. 277)
—Emily's Tea Party. Calitri, Susan, illus. (p. 519)
—iNo, Tito, No! - No, No, Titus! Lasconi, Diego, tr. (p. 875)
—Two Homes. (p. 1803)
—Two Homes. Denton, Kady MacDonald, illus. (p. 1803)
Masurel, Claire & Bond, Barbara Higgins. Penguins - Sticker Stories. Calitri, Susan & Bond, Barbara Higgins, illus. (p. 1337)
Masurel, Claire & Kolar, Bob. Gato y un Perro. Antreasyan, Andres, tr. (p. 658)
Mata, Julie. Kate Walden Directs: Bride of Slug Man. (p. 944)
—Kate Walden Directs: Night of the Zombie Chickens. (p. 944)
—Night of the Zombie Chickens. (p. 1254)
Mata, Nina, illus. see Wallace, Nancy K.
Matagrano, Joseph F. Forever Brothers. (p. 619)
Matalonis, Anne. Fox Behind the Chatterbox. McGhee, Chelsea, illus. (p. 626)
Matas, Carol. Burning Time (p. 244)
—Code Name Kris. (p. 338)
—Lisa's War. (p. 1022)
—Rosie in Los Angeles: Action! (p. 1490)
—Rosie in New York City: Gotcha! (p. 1490)
—Turned Away: The World War II Diary of Devorah Bernstein. (p. 1798)
—Whirlwind (p. 1912)
Matas, Carol & Nodelman, Perry. Of Two Minds. (p. 1279)
Matas, Toni. Comic Book Bible. Picanyol, illus. (p. 348)
—Discovering Jesus, the Light: Children's Bible. Picanyol, illus. (p. 449)
—Discovering Jesus, the Word: Children's Bible. Picanyol, illus. (p. 449)
—Saint Francis of Assisi, Messenger of Peace. Picanyol, illus. (p. 1503)
—St. Ignatius of Loyola, Leading the Way. Picanyol, illus. (p. 1638)
Mataya, David, illus. see Collins, David R.
Mataya, Marybeth. Are You My Bird? Williams, Matthew, illus. (p. 97)
—Are You My Cat? Williams, Matthew, illus. (p. 97)
—Are You My Dog? Williams, Matthew, illus. (p. 97)
—Are You My Rodent? Williams, Matthew, illus. (p. 97)
—Deep Ocean Food Chains. Adams, Hazel, illus. (p. 423)
—Grassland Food Chains. Adams, Hazel, illus. (p. 712)
—Luke & Leo Build a Limerick. Richard, Ilene, illus. (p. 1064)
Match Game Staff. Canada Scented Memory Game. (p. 260)
—Smelly Scented Memory Game. (p. 1593)
Matcheck, Diane. Untitled Novel. (p. 1823)
Matchett, Gillian. Adventures of Weston Super Cat with Activities. (p. 24)
Matchette, Dennis, photos by see Matchette, Katharine E.
Matchette, Katharine E. Discovering Oregon. Comfort, Mike & Baisley, Stephen, illus. (p. 449)
Mate, Rae, illus. see Bar-el, Dan.
Mate, Rae, illus. see Heidbreder, Robert.
Mateboer, Hans. Peter the Cruise Ship. (p. 1347)
—Peter the Cruise Ship - to Alaska. (p. 1347)
Mateer, Campbell Vonnie. Tree. (p. 1783)

Mateer, Eric. Paint Me Terrified. Mateer, Eric, illus. (p. 1318)
Matejko, Sonya. Things We All Know but too Afraid to Say. (p. 1733)
Matejovsky, Char. Shadow on the Moon: A Child's Guide to the Discovery of the Universe. Ream, Robaire, illus. (p. 1557)
Matens, Margaret H. & Armour, Christopher. Wisdom of Fishing. Matens, Margaret H., illus. (p. 1939)
Mateo, José Manual. Migrant. Pedro, Javier Martínez, illus. (p. 1140)
Mateo, Rosario, illus. see Caban, Jose Alberto.
Mateo, Rosario, illus. see Mariscal, Libia Barajas.
Mateos, Pilar. Capitanes de Plastico. (p. 262)
—Cuento Interrumpido. (p. 389)
—Molinete. (p. 1160)
Mateos, Pilar, jt. auth. see Mateos, Pilar.
Mateos, Pilar & Lucini, Chata. Lucas y Lucas. (p. 1062)
Mateos, Pilar & Mateos, Pilar. Historias de Ninguno. (p. 782)
Mater, Nadire. Voices from the Front: Turkish Soldiers on the War with the Kurdish Guerrillas. Altinay, Ayse Gül, tr. from TUR. (p. 1848)
Matero, Robert. Birth of a Humpback Whale. Johnson, Pamela, illus. (p. 192)
Maters, Ingrid, illus. see De Silva-Nijkamp, Tineke.
Mateu, Francesca, illus. see RH Disney Staff & Calmenson, Stephanie.
Mateusz, M. G. Treaty of Canandaigua 1794: A Primary Source Examination of the Treaty Between the United States & the Tribes of Indians called the Six Nations. (p. 1783)
Matevosyan, Naira. Kinkajou Who Saw Quite Well. (p. 961)
Matevosyan, Naira & Matevosyan, Richard. Turtlanium. (p. 1798)
Matevosyan, Richard, jt. auth. see Matevosyan, Naira.
Math Forum Staff. Dr. Math Explains Algebra: Learning Algebra Is Easy! Just Ask Dr. Math! (p. 475)
—Dr. Math Gets You Ready for Algebra: Learning Pre-Algebra Is Easy! Just Ask Dr. Math! (p. 475)
—Dr. Math Presents More Geometry: Learning Geometry Is Easy! Just Ask Dr. Math. (p. 475)
Math Forum Staff, jt. auth. see The Math Forum.
Math Montana Council of Teachers Staff. Columbus Returns! Math Activities for the Middle Grades. (p. 346)
Mathabane, Gail. Skwiza: A Memoir (p. 1586)
Mathabane, Mark, rev. Kaffir Boy: The True Story of A Black Youth's Coming of Age in Apartheid South Africa (p. 941)
Matharu, Taran. Novice. (p. 1268)
Matheis, Mickie. Berry Bitty Princess Pageant. Thomas, Laura, illus. (p. 167)
—Berry Lucky St. Patrick's Day. Thomas, Laura, illus. (p. 167)
—Berryella & Prince Berry Charming. Thomas, Laura, illus. (p. 168)
—Camp Berry. Thomas, Laura, illus. (p. 257)
—Gymnastics Fun. Thomas, Laura, illus. (p. 734)
—Merry Christmas, Strawberry Shortcake! Thomas, Laura, illus. (p. 1129)
—Scavenger Hunt Adventure. Design, Mada, illus. (p. 1521)
Matheny, B. K. Goodnight Baby (p. 701)
Matheny, Bill, et al. Alfred to the Rescue?! (p. 37)
—Bane on the Rampage! (p. 136)
—Bane's Breaking In! (p. 136)
—Batman Is on Fire! (p. 144)
—Batman Strikes! (p. 144)
—Batman Strikes. (p. 144)
—Catwoman Gets Busted by the Batman (p. 281)
—Frozen Solid by Mr. Freeze! (p. 645)
—Going... Batty! (p. 692)
—In the Clutches of the Penguin! (p. 865)
—Joker's Wild! (p. 924)
—Man-Bat's Sneak Attack! (p. 1085)
—Sanity Plea! (p. 1511)
—Scarface Is Gonna Go Boom! (p. 1520)
Matheny, Jean Sherlock, illus. see Paddock, Susan Star.
Matheny, Melody, illus. see Zito, Ann R.
Matheos, George P. Pure Magic. (p. 1419)
Mather, Anne D. & Weldon, Louise B. Character Building Day by Day: 180 Quick Read-Alouds for Elementary School & Home. Braun, Eric, ed. (p. 291)
Mather, Daniel. Case File #3 the Accidental Accomplice. (p. 273)
Mather, Daniel, illus. see Spinner, Stephanie.
Mather, David. Frog in the House. (p. 640)
Mather, Kelly. Five Keys to Wellness. Schneller, Lisa, illus. (p. 600)
Matherly, Ashley Page. Wonderful White Wintery Day: The Marvelous Misadventure of Katy Bear Fennewald, Joseph Grant, illus. (p. 1948)
Matheron, Annaliese. Ninja Nan & Her Merry Men. (p. 1256)
—Ninja Nan & Sidekick Grandad. (p. 1256)
—Ninja Nan Strikes Again. (p. 1256)
Mathers, Beth. Speaking of Me... Stepping Stones to a Better Life Teis, Kyra, illus. (p. 1623)
Mathers, Petra. McElderry Book of Mother Goose: Revered & Rare Rhymes. (p. 1114)
Mathers, Petra, illus. see Prelutsky, Jack.
Mathers, Petra, illus. see Schertle, Alice.
Mather-Smith, Charles, illus. see Arnov Jr., Boris & Mindlin, Helen Mather-Smith.
Mathes, Ben & Clack, Karin. Rowvotions: The Devotional Book of Rivers of the World. (p. 1492)
Mathes, Charles. In Every Moon There Is a Face. Graston, Arlene, illus. (p. 863)
Matheson, Anne. I Love to Sing. Cutting, David A., illus. (p. 843)
Matheson, Christie. Tap the Magic Tree. Matheson, Christie, illus. (p. 1705)
—Touch the Brightest Star. Matheson, Christie, illus. (p. 1772)
Matheson, Christie, jt. auth. see Strauss, Elisa.
Matheson, Dawn. Ruby Lee the Bumble Bee: A Bee's Bit of Wisdom. Cindy, Huffman, ed. (p. 1493)
—Ruby Lee the Bumble Bee: A Bee of Possibility. Barcita, Pamela, illus. (p. 1493)
—Ruby Lee the Bumble Bee: A Bee's Bit of Wisdom. Barcita, Pamela, illus. (p. 1493)
—Ruby Lee the Bumble Bee Critter Count Search & Find Game. Huffman, Cindy, ed. (p. 1493)
Matheson, Hughena. 10 Most Historic Speeches. (p. 1994)
Matheson, Jason. Buzzbomb: Adventures in the Forbidden Zone. Hope, Bill, illus. (p. 249)
Matheson, John. Ayla: An Archaeological Find, a Mysterious Bygone Civilization & an Enduring Love. (p. 121)
Matheson, Murdoch H. Building Wealth for Teens: Answers to Questions Teens Care About. (p. 239)
Matheson, Richard. Abu & the 7 Marvels. Stout, William, illus. (p. 7)
—What Dreams May Come. (p. 1884)
Matheson, Shirlee Smith. Fastback Beach (p. 576)
—Gambler's Daughter. (p. 654)
—Jailbird Kid. (p. 905)
—Keeper of the Mountains. (p. 947)
Mathew, Gillian, illus. see Kowen, Dorothy.
Mathews, Bill & Monger, J. W. H (Jim). Roadside Geology of Southern British Columbia (p. 1477)
Mathews, David George. We Can Do Anything! (p. 1866)
Mathews, Janice. Happy Jack: How Much Stuff Is Enough? (p. 746)
—Jack & the 10 Rules. (p. 902)
—Jack Gives Back. (p. 903)
—Jack, Jake, Jacque, & Jodie: The Get-Along Doggies. (p. 903)
Mathews, Jez. Pick Your Brains about Italy. (p. 1354)
Mathews, Joseph. Why Do Boys Make Girls Cry? (p. 1923)
Mathews, Leslie. Edgar Wants to Be Alone. Dumont, Jean-François, illus. (p. 504)
—I Am a Bear. Dumont, Jean-François, illus. (p. 831)
—Sheep Go on Strike. Dumont, Jean-François, illus. (p. 1564)
Mathews, Leslie, jt. auth. see Zoboli, Giovanna.
Mathews, Madge. Amelia Asks May I Have A Pet. Cook, Laurie, illus. (p. 57)
—Brandon's Really Bad, Really Good Day. Cook, Laurie, illus. (p. 222)
—Brandon's Really Big Birthday Surprise. Cook, Laurie, illus. (p. 222)
Mathews, Sarah. Farm Animals. (p. 573)
Mathews, Sarah & Mettler, René. Egg. Mettler, René, illus. (p. 506)
Mathews, Temple. New Kid. (p. 1245)
—Sword of Armageddon. (p. 1692)
—Sword of Armageddon. (p. 1692)
Mathewson, Christy. Catcher Craig. Relyea, Charles M., illus. (p. 279)
Mathewson, Robert F. How & Why Wonder Book of Reptiles & Amphibians. Sweet, Darrell & Allen, Douglas, illus. (p. 804)
Mathewson, Sherry. Barrier Stone. (p. 140)
Mathias, Adeline. How a Young Brave Survived. Hamilton, Penny, ed. (p. 804)
Mathias, M. R. Adventurion. (p. 25)
Mathieson, Karen. Duel or Duet: Book Two of the Rosemary Ridge Trilogy. (p. 489)
—Liza, Elizabeth: Book Three of the Rosemary Ridge Trilogy. (p. 1042)
—Thirteen Times Three: Book One of the Rosemary Ridge Trilogy. (p. 1735)
Mathieu, Jennifer. Devoted. (p. 432)
—Truth about Alice. (p. 1794)
Mathieu, Jill. Lenny the Lobster. (p. 991)
Mathieu, Joe, illus. see Albee, Sarah, et al.
Mathieu, Joe, illus. see Cox, Judy.
Mathieu, Joe, illus. see Dr. Seuss Enterprises Staff & Perkins, Al.
Mathieu, Joe, illus. see Golden Books Staff.
Mathieu, Joe, illus. see Greene, Stephanie.
Mathieu, Joe, illus. see Hayward, Linda.
Mathieu, Joe, illus. see Houran, Lori Haskins.
Mathieu, Joe, illus. see Hubbell, Patricia.
Mathieu, Joe, illus. see Kleinberg, Naomi.
Mathieu, Joe, illus. see Mitter, Matt.
Mathieu, Joe, illus. see November, Deborah, et al.
Mathieu, Joe, illus. see Numeroff, Laura Joffe.
Mathieu, Joe, illus. see Rabe, Tish.
Mathieu, Joe, illus. see Random House Staff.
Mathieu, Joe, illus. see Rodecker, Ron.
Mathieu, Joe, illus. see Seuss, Dr.
Mathieu, Joe, illus. see Surgal, Jon.
Mathieu, Joe, illus. see Urbanovic, Jackie.
Mathieu, Joe, illus. see Worth, Bonnie.
Mathieu, Joe, jt. auth. see Monica, Carol.
Mathieu, Joe, et al. Big Bird's Big Book. Mathieu, Joe, illus. (p. 178)
Mathieu, Joseph, illus. see Worth, Bonnie.
Mathieu, Middy, illus. see Fisher, Meaghan.
Mathieu, Middy, illus. see Hand, Renne.
Mathiews, Franklin K. Skyward Ho! (p. 1587)
Mathis, Bernard D., jt. auth. see Walker, John R.
Mathis, Kate. Moon over Monsters. (p. 1172)
Mathis, Leslie, illus. see Darlene, Cannon.
Mathis, Leslie, illus. see Fyne, Olga M.
Mathis, Leslie, illus. see Hazelwood, K. D.
Mathis, Leslie, illus. see Patterson, Eric.
Mathis, Leslie, illus. see Wolfe, Carolyn.
Mathis, May. Coffee, Pie & a Place to Die. (p. 338)
Mathis, Pamela. Sound Town the Story of Words. (p. 1615)
Mathis, Rev. Catherine. It's Your Big Day. (p. 899)
Mathis, Sharon Bell. Hundred Penny Box. Dillon, Diane & Dillon, Leo, illus. (p. 827)
—Hundred Penny Box. Dillon, Leo & Dillon, Diane, illus. (p. 827)
Mathis, Tabitha. Princess & the Tyger. (p. 1403)
Mathis, Teresa, illus. see Eagan, Robynne.
Mathis, Toby. Tax-Wise Business Ownership. (p. 1707)
Mathisen, Michael. Abby & the Helping Mommy. Estill, Amy, illus. (p. 2)
Mathison, Anne. I Love My Hair. Flowerpot Press, ed. (p. 842)
Mathison, Sandra, jt. auth. see Freeman, Melissa.
Mathson, Patricia L. Bless This Day: 150 Everyday Prayers for Grades 1 to 5. (p. 199)
Mathus, Don, et al, contrib. by. Fit to Serve. (p. 599)
Matic, Mia. Ocean Blue: Delphi Island. (p. 1276)
Matijasevich, Astrid, illus. see Eggleton, Jill.
Matine, Laura, illus. see Louise, Kate.
Matinkhah, Sue Ann. Plant a Tree & Watch It Grow. (p. 1368)
Matirko, M. John. Apex. (p. 91)
Matison, Jimbo. I'm Going to Catch My Tail! (p. 859)
Matisse, Henri, jt. auth. see Friedman, Samantha.
Matisse, Henri, jt. auth. see Parker, Marjorie Blain.
Matiuzzo, Nick, illus. see Sullivan-Ringe, Laurie.
Matje, Martin, illus. see Gershator, Phillis.
Matje, Martin, illus. see Pennypacker, Sara.
Matje, Martin, illus. see Yorinks, Arthur.
Matkovich, Gregory, illus. see Lloyd, Ashley.
Matlin, Marlee. Deaf Child Crossing. (p. 418)
Matlin, Marlee & Cooney, Doug. Leading Ladies. (p. 982)
—Nobody's Perfect. (p. 1262)
Matlock, Mark. Don't Buy the Lie: Discerning Truth in a World of Deception (p. 467)
—Wisdom On... Friends, Dating, & Relationships (p. 1939)
—Wisdom On... Making Good Decisions (p. 1939)
Mato, illus. see Kusaka, Hidenori.
Matoh, Sanami. Fake (p. 565)
—Fake Matoh, Sanami, illus. (p. 565)
—Fake Rymer, Nan, tr. from JPN. (p. 565)
Matos, Rebecca. Matter Is Everywhere: Solids, Liquids, & Gases. (p. 1109)
—Measuring Matter: Solids, Liquids, & Gases. (p. 1117)
—This Is Matter: Solids, Liquids, & Gases. (p. 1736)
Matoso, Madalena, illus. see Martins, Isabel Minhós.
Matoso, Madalena, illus. see Minhós Martins, Isabel.
Matoso, Madalena, jt. auth. see Martins, Isabel Minhós.
Matott, J. P. & Baker, Margaret. When I Was a Girl ... I Dreamed. Ludy, Mark, illus. (p. 1903)
Matott, Justin. When I Was a Boy... I Dreamed. Ludy, Mark, illus. (p. 1903)
Matov, G. Tales of Tzaddikim. Weinbach, Shaindel, tr. (p. 1703)
Matranga, Cindy. It Never Rains in Sunny California. (p. 894)
Matray, James I., ed. see Cottrell, Robert C.
Matray, James I., ed. see Davenport, John C.
Matray, James I., ed. Arbitrary Borders: Political Boundaries in World History. (p. 94)
Matray, James Irving. Korea Divided: The Thirty-Eighth Parallel & the Demilitarized Zone. (p. 967)
Matricardi, Luca, illus. see Mounts, Samia.
Matrishon, Maible. Island Experiences - Adventures in Bocas Del Toro, on the Caribbean Coast of Panama. (p. 892)
Matsakis, Cynthia. Sister Sun, Brother Storm. Silver, Jane, illus. (p. 1581)
Matsen, Bradford. Extreme Dive under the Antarctic Ice. (p. 556)
—Go Wild in New York City. Corio, Paul et al, illus. (p. 687)
—Incredible Hunt for the Giant Squid. (p. 869)
—Incredible Quest to Find the Titanic. (p. 869)
—Incredible Record-Setting Deep-Sea Dive of the Bathysphere. (p. 869)
—Incredible Search for the Treasure Ship Atocha. (p. 869)
—Incredible Submersible Alvin Discovers a Strange Deep-Sea World. (p. 869)
Matsi, Maria. Week in the Life of the Chromasomas. (p. 1871)
Matsick, Anni, illus. see Cavnar, Gracie.
Matson, Carole. Jesus Loves Dirt Bikes Too!! (p. 915)
Matson, Cheri. Moleys Yacolt Garden. (p. 1160)
Matson, Don, illus. see Macken, JoAnn Early.
Matson, Erik. Robobattlepets - Home Invasion. (p. 1480)
Matson, Gienna, jt. auth. see Roberts, Jeremy.
Matson, Laurie. Jaz-O & 'G' in Key West. Matson, Laurie, illus. (p. 910)
Matson, Lynne. Nil. (p. 1255)
—Nil Unlocked. (p. 1255)
Matson, Morgan. Amy & Roger's Epic Detour. (p. 66)
—Second Chance Summer. (p. 1539)
—Since You've Been Gone. (p. 1578)
Matson, Rob. Pickles Eyrie. (p. 1354)
Matsoureff, Atanas, illus. see Johnson, E. Pauline.
Matsubuchi, Akemi, photos by see Hole, Jim.
Matsuda, Christine. Goodnight Little One: Bedtime Around the World. Ishida, Jui, illus. (p. 701)
Matsuhashi, Toshimitsu, photos by see Komiya, Teruyuki.
Matsumoto, David, jt. auth. see Brousse, Michel.
Matsumoto, Lisa. Adventures of Gary & Harry: A Tale of Two Turtles. Furuya, Michael, illus. (p. 18)
Matsumoto, Natsumi. St. Dragon Girl. Matsumoto, Natsumi, illus. (p. 1637)
Matsumoto, Nina. Yokaiden 1. (p. 1972)
Matsumoto, Reiko Odate. Princess with the Magic Bowl: As retold from the Japanese folk tale By. (p. 1406)
—Sweet Potato. (p. 1690)
Matsumoto, Tomo. Beauty Is the Beast. Matsumoto, Tomo, illus. (p. 154)
Matsunaga, Aya, tr. see Tomino, Yoshiyuki.
Matsunaga, Judd. King's Kids Coloring Book. Fleming, Jesse, photos by. (p. 960)
Matsunaga, Judd & Fleming, Jesse. King's Kids Coloring Book. (p. 960)
Matsunari, Yumi, tr. see Coerr, Eleanor.
Matsunari, Yumi, tr. see Yasuda, Yuri & Yasuda, Yuri Old tales of Japan.
Matsuo, Marta. Lies Are a Gentleman's Manners. (p. 1007)
Matsuoka, Kyoko. Where Is Little Toko. (p. 1908)
—Where Is Little Toko? Kako, Satoshi, illus. (p. 1908)
Matsuoka, Mei. Footprints in the Snow. Matsuoka, Mei, illus. (p. 615)
Matsuoka, Mei, illus. see Bently, Peter.
Matsuoka, Yoko, illus. see Barton, Jen.
Matsushita, Yoko. Descendants of Darkness. Matsushita, Yoko, illus. (p. 428)
—Descendants of Darkness 8 Matsushita, Yoko, illus. (p. 428)
—Yami No Matsuei. Matsushita, Yoko, illus. (p. 1968)
—Yami No Matsuei. Ury, David, tr. from JPN. (p. 1968)
Matsushita, Yoko, et al. Descendants of Darkness. Matsushita, Yoko, illus. (p. 428)
—Yami No Matsuei. Matsushita, Yoko, illus. (p. 1968)
Matsutani, Miyoko. Peek-A-Boo. Segawa, Yasuo, illus. (p. 1334)
Matsuura, Richard & Matsuura, Ruth. Ali'i Kai. Chao, Linus, illus. (p. 41)
—Angels Masquerading on Earth. Chao, Linus, illus. (p. 75)
—Birthday Wish. Chao, Linus, illus. (p. 193)
—Fruit, the Tree & the Flower. (p. 645)
—Gift from Santa. Chao, Linus, illus. (p. 675)
—Hawaiian Christmas Story. Chao, Linus, illus. (p. 755)
—Kalani & Primo. Chao, Linus, illus. (p. 941)
Matsuura, Ruth, jt. auth. see Matsuura, Richard.
Matsuura, Tokihiko. Tuxedo Gin (p. 1799)
—Tuxedo Gin. Matsuura, Tokihiko, illus. (p. 1799)
Matsuzawa, Mari, jt. auth. see Arisawa, Mamizu.
Matsuzawa, Yoji, photos by see Sakanakun.
Matsuzuki, Kou. Happy Cafe (p. 745)
Matt, jt. auth. see Dave.
Matt and Dave. Supercool Snotman Baines, Nigel, illus. (p. 1682)
Matt & Dave. Yuck's Amazing Underpants. Baines, Nigel, illus. (p. 1983)
—Yuck's Big Booger Challenge. Baines, Nigel, illus. (p. 1983)
—Yuck's Mega Magic Wand. Baines, Nigel, illus. (p. 1983)
—Yuck's Pet Worm. Baines, Nigel, illus. (p. 1983)
—Yuck's Robotic Butt Blast. Baines, Nigel, illus. (p. 1983)
—Yuck's Slime Monster. Baines, Nigel, illus. (p. 1983)
Matt, Andrew, tr. see Perego, Jeanne.
Matt, Collins, illus. see Adler, David A. & Adler, Michael S.
Matt, F. Cooking, Vegetarian Cooking, Pizza & Pasta, Cakes & Cookies. (p. 362)
—Pasta & Pizza for Beginners. (p. 1327)
Matt, Phelan, illus. see Spinelli, Eileen.
Matta, Gabriella, illus. see Jordan, Apple.
Matta, Gabriella, illus. see Posner-Sanchez, Andrea.
Matta, Gabriella, illus. see Random House Disney Staff & Redbank, Tennant.
Matta, Gabriella, illus. see RH Disney Staff.
Matta, Gabriella, illus. see Weinberg, Jennifer Liberts.
Mattaino, J. F. Cotton Candy Circus & Other Performances. (p. 369)
Mattar, Philip. Encyclopedia of the Palestinians. (p. 525)
Mattassi, Ezio. Pepito the Penguin Mattassi, Ezio, illus. (p. 1340)
Matte, Johane, et al. Flight Explorer Kibuishi, Kazu, ed. (p. 604)
Mattei, Francesca. Caraselle. (p. 265)
Mattel. Ever after High - Sleepover Spellebration Party Planner. (p. 541)
—Monster High: the Skultimate Sticker Book. (p. 1167)
Mattel, illus. see Fontes, Justine.
Mattel, illus. see Lombardi, Kristine.
Mattel Barbie Staff, illus. see Fontes, Justine.
Mattel, creator. Barbie Box - the Enchanted Collection. (p. 138)
Mattel Inc. Staff. Barbie Always in Style. (p. 138)
Mattel Inc. Staff, illus. see Lombardi, Kristine.
Matter, Joanne. Recipe & Craft Guide to China. (p. 1451)
Matter, Sandy. Great Sea Chase. (p. 718)
Matteren, Joanne. Old Lion & the Fox. (p. 1284)
Mattern, Carrie. Papa, Why Does the Wind Blow? (p. 1322)
—Welcome Little Leo. (p. 1873)
Mattern, David B., jt. auth. see Shulman, Holly Cowan.
Mattern, Joanne. Abyssinian Cats (p. 7)
—After School. (p. 28)
—After School (Después de la Escuela) (p. 28)
—Air Force One: The President's Plane. (p. 31)
—Alamo. (p. 33)
—Alaska: Past & Present. (p. 33)
—Albert Pujols: Baseball Superstar (p. 34)
—Albert Pujols. (p. 34)
—All about Cats (p. 42)
—All about Cats. (p. 42)
—Allosaurus. Magniat, Jeffrey, illus. (p. 47)
—Allosaurus. Mangiat, Jeffrey, illus. (p. 47)
—Allosaurus; Alosaurio. (p. 47)
—American Shorthair Cats (p. 63)
—America's Gold Rush: John Sutter & the Discovery of Gold in California. (p. 64)
—Anacondas (p. 66)
—Anexion de Texas /The Annexation of Texas. (p. 73)
—Angel Falls: World's Highest Waterfall. (p. 73)
—Animals of the Savannah. (p. 83)
—Animals of the Tropical Rain Forest. (p. 83)
—Ankylosaurus. Magniat, Jeffrey, illus. (p. 84)
—Ankylosaurus. Mangiat, Jeffrey, illus. (p. 84)
—Ankylosaurus; Anquilosaurio. (p. 84)
—Annexation of Texas: From Republic to Statehood. (p. 86)
—Antarctica: World's Biggest Glacier. (p. 88)
—Antartida: El glaciar más grande del mundo (Antarctica: World's Biggest Glacier) (p. 89)
—Antartida. (p. 89)
—Apatosaurus. Magniat, Jeffrey, illus. (p. 91)
—Apatosaurus/Apatosaurio. Magniat, Jeffrey, illus. (p. 91)
—Ashley Tisdale. (p. 106)
—Asia: World's Largest Continent. (p. 106)
—Asia: El Continente Mas Grande del Mundo. (p. 106)
—Asia: El continente más grande del mundo (Asia: World's Largest Continent) (p. 106)
—Astronautas. (p. 109)
—Astronautas (Astronauts) (p. 109)
—Astronauts. (p. 109)
—At the Football Game: Learning the Symbols , And = (p. 111)
—At the Football Game. (p. 111)
—Attorney General. (p. 114)
—Barack Obama. (p. 137)
—Bats Are Night Animals: Los Murciélagos Son Animales Nocturnos. (p. 145)
—Bats Are Night Animals. (p. 145)
—Bats Are Night Animals/Los Murcielagos Son Animales Nocturnos. (p. 145)
—Batter Up! (p. 145)
—Ben & Jerry: Ice Cream Manufacturers. (p. 163)
—Benny Goodman. (p. 165)
—Bernie Mac. (p. 167)
—Birman Cats (p. 192)
—Birth of the Locomotive (1780-1820) (p. 192)
—Blake Lively. (p. 198)

—Boa Constrictors (p. 205)
—Brian Mcbride. (p. 226)
—Brigadas Aereas Contraincendios. (p. 228)
—Brigadas aéreas contraincendios (Smoke Jumpers) (p. 228)
—Búhos Son Animales Nocturnos. (p. 237)
—Built to Last. (p. 240)
—Bullying (p. 241)
—Careers in Finance. (p. 267)
—Carrie Underwood. (p. 271)
—Cataratas Ángel: Las cataratas más altas del mundo (Angel Falls: World's Highest Waterfall) (p. 278)
—Cataratas Ángel. (p. 278)
—Cats Are Night Animals. (p. 281)
—Cats Are Night Animals (Los Felinos Son Animales Nocturnos) (p. 281)
—Celebrate Christmas. (p. 283)
—Celebrate Cinco de Mayo. (p. 283)
—Celebrate Columbus Day. (p. 283)
—Chefs. (p. 297)
—Clarence Birdseye: Frozen Food Innovator. (p. 327)
—Cocineros. (p. 337)
—Cocineros (Chefs) (p. 337)
—Cómo crecen los Manzanos. (p. 350)
—Computer: Passport to the Digital Age. (p. 354)
—Copperheads (p. 366)
—Coretta Scott King: Civil Rights Activist. (p. 367)
—Cost of Freedom: Crispus Attucks & the Boston Massacre. (p. 368)
—Count Basie. (p. 369)
—Coyotes (p. 375)
—Coyotes Are Night Animals. (p. 375)
—Coyotes Are Night Animals (Los Coyotes Son Animales Nocturnos) (p. 375)
—Coyotes Are Night Animals/Los Coyotes Son Animales Nocturnos. (p. 375)
—Dakota Fanning. (p. 401)
—David Ortiz. (p. 411)
—Day by Day with Adam Jones. (p. 412)
—Derek Jeter: Baseball Superstar (p. 427)
—Despues de la Escuela (After School) (p. 430)
—Dino Disaster! Spaziante, Patrick & Giles, Mike, illus. (p. 441)
—Dinosaur Claws & Crests. (p. 441)
—Dinosaur Skeletons & Skulls. (p. 442)
—Dinosaur Spikes & Necks. (p. 443)
—Dinosaur Tails & Armor. (p. 443)
—Dinosaur Teeth & Beaks. (p. 443)
—Dinosaur Wings & Fins. (p. 443)
—Dinosaurios: Alas y Aletas. (p. 443)
—Dinosaurios: Colas y Corazas. (p. 443)
—Dinosaurios: Garras y Crestas. (p. 443)
—Dinosaurios: Espinas Oseas y Cuellos. (p. 443)
—Dinosaurios, Dientes y Picos. (p. 443)
—Diplodocus. Magniat, Jeffrey, illus. (p. 445)
—Diplodocus; Diplodocus. (p. 445)
—Do You Help Others? (p. 457)
—Do You Listen? (p. 458)
—Do You Listen?/Escuchas? (p. 458)
—Do You Share? (p. 458)
—Do You Share?/Compartes? (p. 458)
—Do You Take Turns? (p. 458)
—Do You Take Turns?/Te Turnas con Otros? (p. 458)
—Do You Take Turns?/¿Te Turnas con Otros? (p. 458)
—Donovan Mcnabb. (p. 466)
—Drake Bell & Josh Peck. (p. 480)
—Dwight Howard: Basketball Superstar (p. 491)
—Eating Lunch at School. (p. 501)
—Eating Lunch at School (El Almuerzo en la Escuela) (p. 501)
—Eleanor Roosevelt: More Than a First Lady. (p. 508)
—Elizabeth Cady Stanton & Susan B. Anthony: Fighting Together for Women's Rights. (p. 513)
—Eminem. (p. 519)
—Emt. (p. 521)
—Eva Peron. (p. 540)
—Even or Odd? (p. 541)
—Exotic Cats (p. 548)
—Famous Mystics & Psychics. (p. 569)
—Fire Trucks. (p. 591)
—Floods. (p. 605)
—Floods, Dams, & Levees. (p. 605)
—Food Dudes Set 1. (p. 613)
—Food Pyramid Disaster. (p. 614)
—Fort Sumter. (p. 623)
—Freedom Trail. (p. 635)
—Geckos (p. 659)
—Geoffrey Chaucer: Medieval Writer. (p. 661)
—George Eastman & Photographic Film. (p. 663)
—Gertrude Elion & the Development of Revolutionary Medications. (p. 667)
—Getting Ready for School. (p. 669)
—Getting Ready for School (Me Preparo para Ir a la Escuela) (p. 669)
—Giganotosaurus. Magniat, Jeffrey, illus. (p. 676)
—Giganotosaurus/Gigantosaurio. Magniat, Jeffrey, illus. (p. 676)
—Gila Monsters (p. 676)
—Gladiators. (p. 682)
—Going to School. (p. 693)
—Going to School/de camino a la Escuela. (p. 693)
—Grace Hopper: Computer Pioneer. (p. 704)
—Greenland: World's Largest Island. (p. 723)
—Groenlandia: La isla más grande del mundo (Greenland: World's Largest Island) (p. 725)
—Groenlandia. (p. 725)
—Hawaii: Past & Present. (p. 755)
—Helen Keller. (p. 762)
—Hillary Rodham Clinton. (p. 779)
—Hippos & Rhinos. (p. 781)
—Horses on the Farm. (p. 800)
—How Apple Trees Grow. (p. 805)
—How Corn Grows. (p. 806)
—How Corn Grows (Cómo Crece el Maíz) (p. 806)
—How Grass Grows. (p. 809)
—How Grass Grows (Como Crece La Hierba) (p. 809)
—How Grass Grows (Cómo crece la Hierba) (p. 809)
—How Peas Grow. (p. 811)
—How Peas Grow(Cómo Crecen los Guisantes) (p. 811)
—How Pine Trees Grow. (p. 812)
—How Pine Trees Grow (Cómo crecen los Pinos) Cómo Crecen los Pinos. (p. 812)
—How Pine Trees Grow/Cómo crecen los Pinos. (p. 812)
—How Tulips Grow. (p. 823)
—How Tulips Grow (Cómo crecen los Tulipanes) (p. 823)
—Hurricanes. (p. 830)
—I Have Cuts & Scrapes. (p. 839)
—I Have the Hiccups. (p. 839)
—I Know Baseball. (p. 840)
—I Know Football. (p. 840)
—I Know Hockey. (p. 840)
—I Know Soccer. (p. 840)
—I Use Math at the Doctor's. (p. 847)
—I Use Math at the Game. (p. 847)
—I Use Math at the Store. (p. 847)
—I Use Math in the Kitchen. (p. 847)
—I Use Math in the Workshop. (p. 847)
—I Use Math on a Trip. (p. 847)
—Igneous Rocks & the Rock Cycle. (p. 856)
—Illinois: Past & Present. (p. 857)
—In the Classroom. (p. 865)
—In the Classroom (en el salón de Clases) (p. 865)
—It's a Good Thing There Are Bats. (p. 895)
—It's a Good Thing There Are Ladybugs. (p. 895)
—Jaden Smith. (p. 905)
—Japanese Americans. (p. 909)
—Jason Derulo. (p. 910)
—Jennifer Hudson. (p. 912)
—Jonas Brothers. (p. 925)
—Jumping Spiders (p. 934)
—Katharine Graham & 20th Century American Journalism. (p. 944)
—Katherine Graham & 20th Century American Journalism. (p. 944)
—Keke Palmer. (p. 948)
—Kellogg Family: Breakfast Cereal Pioneers. (p. 948)
—Kickboxing. (p. 951)
—Kim Kardashian: Reality TV Star. (p. 956)
—King Cobras (p. 958)
—Kiteboarding. (p. 962)
—Knights. (p. 964)
—Komodo Dragons (p. 966)
—Lady Bird Johnson. (p. 970)
—LeBron James: Basketball Superstar (p. 987)
—Leif Eriksson: Viking Explorer. (p. 991)
—Let's Visit Canada: The Metric System. (p. 1001)
—Lightbulbs. (p. 1015)
—Ludacris. (p. 1063)
—Maine Coon Cats (p. 1077)
—Make It 100! (p. 1079)
—Manx Cats (p. 1089)
—Mars Family: M & M Mars Candy Makers. (p. 1096)
—Mary Todd Lincoln. (p. 1101)
—Maryland: Past & Present. (p. 1101)
—Mauna Loa: World's Largest Active Volcano. (p. 1110)
—Mauna Loa: El volcan en actividad más grande del mundo (Mauna Loa: World's Largest Active Volcano) (p. 1110)
—Mauna Loa. (p. 1110)
—Me Preparo para IR a la Escuela (Getting Ready for School) (p. 1116)
—Medieval Times: England in the Middle Ages. (p. 1119)
—Metamorphic Rocks & the Rock Cycle. (p. 1130)
—Mid-Atlantic Recipes. (p. 1137)
—Miguel Tejada. (p. 1141)
—Milton Hershey: Hershey's Chocolate Creator. (p. 1144)
—Minerals & the Rock Cycle. (p. 1146)
—More Than, Less Than. (p. 1175)
—Mount Rushmore. (p. 1180)
—Mounted Police. (p. 1181)
—Mystics & Psychics. (p. 1226)
—National Mall. (p. 1233)
—New Hampshire: The Granite State. (p. 1245)
—Nicki Minaj. (p. 1251)
—Obesity: Causes & Consequences. (p. 1275)
—Ocicats (p. 1277)
—One Direction. (p. 1294)
—Orangutans (p. 1302)
—Oriental Cats (p. 1303)
—Orlando Bloom. (p. 1304)
—Our Earth (p. 1308)
—Our Moon (p. 1309)
—Oviraptor. Magniat, Jeffrey, illus. (p. 1314)
—Oviraptor; Oviraptor. (p. 1314)
—Owls Are Night Animals. (p. 1315)
—Owls Are Night Animals/Los Buhos Son Animales Nocturnos. (p. 1315)
—Paintball. (p. 1318)
—Pebble First Guide to Nocturnal Animals (p. 1333)
—Pebble First Guide to the Solar System (p. 1333)
—Perfect Predators. (p. 1342)
—Persian Cats (p. 1344)
—Peyton Manning: Indianapolis Colts Star Quarterback. (p. 1349)
—Pilotos. (p. 1359)
—Pilotos (Pilots) (p. 1359)
—Pilots. (p. 1359)
—Pirates. (p. 1363)
—Playing at School: Juego en la Escuela. (p. 1372)
—Playing at School. (p. 1372)
—Playing at School (Juego en la Escuela) (p. 1372)
—Pocahontas. (p. 1375)
—Policia Montada. (p. 1380)
—Policía montada (Mounted Police) (p. 1380)
—Printing Press: An Information Revolution. (p. 1407)
—Que Comen los Animales del Bosque?/What Forest Animals Eat. (p. 1423)
—Queen Christina of Sweden (p. 1424)
—Raccoons Are Night Animals. (p. 1430)
—Raccoons Are Night Animals/Los Mapaches Son Animales Nocturnos. (p. 1430)
—Raccoons (Los Mapaches) (p. 1430)
—Radio: The World Tunes In. (p. 1432)
—Ragdoll Cats (p. 1433)
—Ralph Lauren. (p. 1437)
—Rattlesnakes (p. 1440)
—Ray Kroc: McDonald's Restaurants Builder. (p. 1441)
—Remote Control Planes. (p. 1460)
—Reptiles & Amphibians. (p. 1461)
—Reptiles y anfibios (Reptiles & Amphibians) (p. 1462)
—Rhinoceroses (p. 1467)
—Rhode Island: The Ocean State. (p. 1468)
—Robert Cade: Gatorade Inventor. (p. 1478)
—Sally Ride: Astronaut. (p. 1505)
—Sam Houston: Un Estadista Audaz. (p. 1506)
—Sam Houston: A Fearless Statesman. (p. 1506)
—Sand, Silt, & Mud & the Rock Cycle. (p. 1510)
—Sedimentary Rocks & the Rock Cycle. (p. 1546)
—Selena. (p. 1549)
—Sequence It! (p. 1552)
—Sheep on the Farm. (p. 1564)
—Siamese Cats (p. 1572)
—Skunks Are Night Animals. (p. 1586)
—Skunks Are Night Animals (Los Zorrillos Son Animales Nocturnos) (p. 1586)
—Smoke Jumpers. (p. 1594)
—So, You Want to Work in Sports? The Ultimate Guide to Exploring the Sports Industry. (p. 1602)
—Sojourner Truth: Early Abolitionist. (p. 1606)
—Sphynx Cats (p. 1626)
—Staying Safe at Home. (p. 1645)
—Staying Safe at Home (la Seguridad en Casa) (p. 1645)
—Staying Safe at School/la Seguridad en la Escuela. (p. 1645)
—Staying Safe in the Car. (p. 1645)
—Staying Safe in the Car (la Seguridad en el Auto) (p. 1645)
—Staying Safe on My Bike. (p. 1645)
—Staying Safe on My Bike/La Seguridad en Mi Bicicleta. (p. 1645)
—Staying Safe on the School Bus. (p. 1645)
—Staying Safe on the School Bus/La Seguridad en el Autobús Escol Ar. (p. 1645)
—Staying Safe on the Street. (p. 1645)
—Staying Safe on the Street (la Seguridad en la Calle) (p. 1645)
—Steam Engine: Fueling the Industrial Revolution. (p. 1646)
—Stegosaurus. (p. 1646)
—Stegosaurus. Magniat, Jeffrey, illus. (p. 1646)
—Stegosaurus (Estegosaurio) (p. 1646)
—Stegosaurus/Estegosaurio. Magniat, Jeffrey, illus. (p. 1646)
—Steve Jobs. (p. 1649)
—Submarines. (p. 1671)
—Super Pets: True Tales of Animal Heroes. (p. 1680)
—Swimming. Hardman, Lizabeth, ed. (p. 1691)
—Tecnicos en Emergencias Medicas. (p. 1712)
—Técnicos en emergencias Médicas (EMT) (p. 1712)
—Telescope: Looking into Space. (p. 1716)
—Television: Window to the World. (p. 1716)
—Tiki Barber: Star NY Giants Running Back. (p. 1749)
—Toilets. (p. 1762)
—Triceratops. Magniat, Jeffrey, illus. (p. 1785)
—Triceratops/Triceratops. Magniat, Jeffrey, illus. (p. 1786)
—Tricky Garden. (p. 1786)
—True Tales of Courageous Dogs. (p. 1793)
—Tyler Perry. (p. 1805)
—Tyrannosaurus Rex. (p. 1805)
—Tyrannosaurus Rex. Magniat, Jeffrey, illus. (p. 1805)
—Tyrannosaurus Rex/Tiranosaurio Rex. Magniat, Jeffrey, illus. (p. 1805)
—Velociraptor. (p. 1835)
—Velociraptor. Magniat, Jeffrey, illus. (p. 1835)
—Velociraptor/Velociraptor. Magniat, Jeffrey, illus. (p. 1835)
—Volga River. (p. 1849)
—Walt Disney. (p. 1855)
—Washington, D. C. (p. 1860)
—Water Spiders (p. 1863)
—Weathering & Erosion & the Rock Cycle. (p. 1870)
—What Are Weather & Climate? (p. 1880)
—What Desert Animals Eat. (p. 1881)
—What Desert Animals Eat (¿Qué comen los animales del Desierto?) (p. 1881)
—What Desert Animals Eat/Que Comen los Animales Del Desierto? Qué Comen los Animales Del Desierto? (p. 1881)
—What Forest Animals Eat. (p. 1884)
—What Forest Animals Eat/¿Qué Comen los Animales del Bosque? (p. 1884)
—What Grassland Animals Eat: Qué Comen los Animales de Las Praderas? (p. 1885)
—What Grassland Animals Eat. (p. 1885)
—What Grassland Animals Eat (¿Qué Comen Los Animales de Las Praderas?) (p. 1885)
—What Polar Animals Eat: Qué Comen los Animales de los Polos? (p. 1892)
—What Polar Animals Eat. (p. 1892)
—What Polar Animals Eat/¿Qué Comen los Animales de los Polos? (p. 1892)
—What River Animals Eat. (p. 1893)
—What River Animals Eat (¿Qué comen los animales de los Ríos?) (p. 1893)
—What Sea Animals Eat: Qué Comen los Animales del Mar? (p. 1893)
—What Sea Animals Eat. (p. 1893)
—What Sea Animals Eat/¿Qué Comen los Animales del Mar? (p. 1893)
—What's So Great about Michelle Obama. (p. 1899)
—Will Steger. (p. 1932)
—William Penn. (p. 1933)
—William Wrigley Jr. Wrigley's Chewing Gum Founder. (p. 1933)
—Wolf Spiders (p. 1944)
—Wrestling. (p. 1962)
—X-Ray Machines. (p. 1967)
Mattern, Joanne, jt. auth. see Brandt, Keith.
Mattern, Joanne, jt. auth. see Roome, Anne Ross.
Mattern, Joanne, jt. auth. see Sabin, Francene.
Mattern, Joanne, jt. auth. see Santrey, Laurence.
Mattern, Joanne & Artell, Mike. Superstar Athletes. (p. 1684)
Mattern, Joanne & Brandt, Keith. Marie Curie, Brave Scientist. Dugan, Karen, illus. (p. 1093)
Mattern, Joanne & Dorling Kindersley Publishing Staff. Princess Diana. (p. 1403)
Mattern, Joanne & Herndon, Ryan, compiled by. Guinness World Records: Extraordinary Records of Unusual Facts & Feats. (p. 731)
—Guinness World Records. (p. 731)
Mattern, Joanne & Rainsford, Blair. Hot Air Balloons. (p. 801)
Mattern, Joanne & Santrey, Laurence. Albert Einstein, Creative Genius. Beier, Ellen, illus. (p. 34)
Mattern, Joanne & Sirota, Lyn A. Chameleons (p. 289)
Mattern, Joanne & Toohey, Cathy. My Little Pony Phonics Fun/[stories by Joanne Mattern] ; [phonics Scope & Sequence by Cathy Toohey ; Pictures by Carlo Lo Rosa ... [et Al.] Lo Raso, Carlo et al, illus. (p. 1213)
Mattern, Joanne, et al. I Use Math at the Store (USO las Matematicas en la Tienda) (p. 847)
—I Use Math in the Kitchen (USO las Matematicas en la Cocina) (p. 847)
—North American Animals. (p. 1264)
—Superstar Athletes. (p. 1684)
Mattern, Scott, illus. see Holbrook, Sara.
Matters, Print. Advertising, Sales, & Marketing. (p. 25)
Matters, Print, jt. auth. see Dice, Elizabeth A.
Matters, Print, jt. auth. see Hackney Blackwell, Amy.
Matters, Print, jt. auth. see Morrill, Ann.
Matters, Print, jt. auth. see Shafto, Daniel.
Matters, Print & Blackwell, Amy Hackney. Independence Days. (p. 870)
—Lent, Yom Kippur, & Other Atonement Days. (p. 991)
Matters, Print & Kirk, Amanda. Education. (p. 505)
—Information Technology. (p. 874)
—Internet & Media. (p. 880)
—Nonprofits & Government. (p. 1263)
—Outdoor Careers. (p. 1312)
Matters, Print & Mondschein, Kenneth C. Advertising, Sales, & Marketing. (p. 25)
—Food & Culinary Arts. (p. 613)
Matters, Print & Montillo, Roseanne. Halloween & Commemorations of the Dead. (p. 737)
Matters, Print & Morrill, Ann. Easter, Passover, & Other Spring Festivals. (p. 499)
—Thanksgiving & Other Harvest Festivals. (p. 1725)
Matters, Print & Stratford, S. J. Health Care. (p. 757)
Matteson, Adrienne. Find Your Way with Atlases. (p. 587)
—Using Digital Maps. Petelinsek, Kathleen, illus. (p. 1828)
Matteson, George & Ursone, Adele. Christmas Tugboat: How the Rockefeller Center Christmas Tree Came to New York City. Ransome, James E., illus. (p. 316)
Mattes-Ruggiero, Lynn, illus. see Scanlon, Cara.
Mattews, Basil. Livingstone: The Pathfinder. (p. 1042)
Matthe, John, jt. auth. see Matthews, John.
Mattheis, Philipp. How to Lose Everything: A Mostly True Story. Malczyk, Kathryn, tr. from GER. (p. 820)
Matthes, Justice, illus. see Frazier, Kelly.
Mattheson, Jenny, illus. see Brust, Beth Wagner.
Mattheson, Jenny, illus. see Duke, Shirley Smith.
Mattheson, Jenny, illus. see Wallach, Michelle.
Matthew, Anna. Goal! Heyworth, Heather, illus. (p. 687)
—Hide & Seek. Heyworth, Heather, illus. (p. 776)
—Hopscotch. Heyworth, Heather, illus. (p. 797)
—Jumping Rope! Heyworth, Heather, illus. (p. 934)
Matthew, John. Foods of Italy. (p. 614)
Matthew, Kathryn I., jt. auth. see Lowe, Joy L.
Matthew, Kathryn I. & Lowe, Joy L. Neal-Schuman Guide to Celebrations & Holidays Around the World: The Best Books, Media, & Multicultural Learning Activities. (p. 1238)
Matthew, Michael, Jr. Wonderful Words. (p. 1948)
Matthew, Patricia D. THG-Mystery... Treehouse Gargoyle. (p. 1732)
Matthew-Barnes, David. Wonderland. (p. 1948)
Matthews. Death in the Desert. (p. 420)
Matthews, Alex. Penguins of Madagascar Fereyra, Lucas, illus. (p. 1337)
Matthews, Andrew. Breakfast Museum. (p. 225)
—Gulliver's Travels. Horrocks, Steve, illus. (p. 731)
—Ladron y la Bailarina. Rubio, Esther, tr. (p. 970)
Matthews, Annette. Mischievous Molly. (p. 1150)
Matthews, Aria A. Emily Ann in Ucanotland. (p. 518)
Matthews, Ashley, illus. see Bucki, Jo Dee & O'Malley, John.
Matthews, Bonnie, illus. see DePino, Catherine S.
Matthews, Bonnie, illus. see Earle, Sylvia A.
Matthews, Bonnie, illus. see Huebner, Dawn.
Matthews, Brett, illus. see Edlund, Ben, et al.
Matthews, Brett & Marvel Comics Staff. Spider-Man & Wolverine Mavlian, Vatche, illus. (p. 1626)
Matthews, C. M., et al. Pageant of Kings & Queens. Brooke, Iris, illus. (p. 1318)
Matthews, Caitlín. Barefoot Book of Princesses. Whelan, Olwyn, illus. (p. 139)
—Celtic Memories. Whelan, Olwyn, illus. (p. 286)
—How to Be a Princess. Willey, Bee, illus. (p. 814)
—How to Be the Perfect Princess. Willey, Bee, illus. (p. 815)
Matthews, Caitlín, illus. see Matthews, John.
Matthews, Caitlín, jt. auth. see Matthews, John.
Matthews, Caitlín & Matthews, John. Fairy Magic: Create-a-Story Kit. (p. 563)
—Legends of the Sea: Create-A-Story Kit. (p. 990)
Matthews, Caitlín & Williams, Sophy. Secret Bride, Runaway Princess: Two Stories from Rwanda. (p. 1540)
Matthews, Caitlín, et al. Barefoot Book of Princesses. Whelan, Olwyn, illus. (p. 139)
—Fireside Stories: Tales for a Winter's Eve. (p. 592)
—Tales from Celtic Lands. Whelan, Olwyn, illus. (p. 1701)
Matthews, Camille. Quincy Finds a New Home. Black, Michelle, illus. (p. 1428)
Matthews, Caroline. Uncle Orange. (p. 1812)
Matthews, Carolyn. True Stories of Rescue & Survival: Canada's Unknown Heroes. (p. 1792)
Matthews, Cerys. Gelert - A Man's Best Friend. Evans, Fran, illus. (p. 659)
Matthews Culp, Dawn. What's up Willie? the Birthday Puppy! (p. 1900)

M

Matthews, Curtis. Boots Meets the Grizzly Bears. (p. 213)
Matthews, Derek. Animales de la Granja. (p. 80)
—Animales de la Selva. (p. 80)
—Escucha y Aprende - Mascotas. (p. 535)
—Tráfico: Con Graciosos Sonidos de vehículos. (p. 1776)
Matthews, Derek, illus. see Steer, Dugald A.
Matthews, Derek, illus. see Taylor, Jane & Macleod, Una.
Matthews, Douglas L., ed. see Bingaman, Jay.
Matthews, Douglas L., ed. see Blount, Diana.
Matthews, Douglas L., ed. see Festante, Dom.
Matthews, Douglas L., ed. see Kautza, Jeremy.
Matthews, Douglas L., ed. see Kokino, Olga.
Matthews, Douglas L., ed. see Lovell, David.
Matthews, Douglas L., ed. see Reeves, Brian & Robinson, Craig.
Matthews, Douglas L., ed. see Starno, Nancy.
Matthews, Douglas L., ed. see Taylor, Lacy.
Matthews, Douglas L., ed. see Turrell, Linda.
Matthews, Douglas L., ed. see Zebrowski, Debra.
Matthews, Elizabeth. Different Like Coco. Matthews, Elizabeth, illus. (p. 438)
Matthews, Elli. Everyday Easter Dress. Matthews, John, illus. (p. 543)
—Surprising Katie on Halloween. Written by Elli Matthews; Illustrated by, illus. (p. 1686)
Matthews, Frederick. American Merchant Ships, 1850-1900 (p. 62)
Matthews, Gail. Our Forever Family (p. 1308)
Matthews, Helen. In a Pocket of Time. (p. 863)
Matthews, Ian. Albert the Big Eyed Squirrel. (p. 34)
Matthews, Jackie. Grand Adventure: Journey from the Castle of Safe. (p. 707)
Matthews, Jacqueline M., illus. see Blanchet, M. Wylie.
Matthews, Jean, et al. Formula One Maths. (p. 620)
—Formula One Maths Practice Book Series Book A1 (p. 620)
Matthews, Jennifer V. For A Ghetto Child: An Anthology of Poems & Art. (p. 615)
Matthews, Jenny. Children Growing up with War. Matthews, Jenny, photos by. (p. 302)
Matthews, Jenny, photos by see Thomson, Ruth.
Matthews, John. Barefoot Book of Giants, Ghosts, & Goblins. Manna, Giovanni, illus. (p. 139)
—Barefoot Book of Knights. Manna, Giovanni, illus. (p. 139)
—Chronicles of Arthur: Sword of Fire & Ice. Collins, Mike, illus. (p. 317)
—DVDs. (p. 491)
—Interactive Whiteboards. (p. 879)
—Knights. Manna, Giovanni, illus. (p. 964)
—StoryWorld: Quests & Adventures: Create-A-Story. Matthews, Caitlin, illus. (p. 1664)
Matthews, John, illus. see Matthews, Elli.
Matthews, John, jt. auth. see Matthews, Caitlin.
Matthews, John and Caitlin. StoryWorld: Christmas Tales: Create-A-Story Kit. (p. 1664)
—StoryWorld: Tales from the Haunted House: Create-A-Story Kit. (p. 1664)
Matthews, John & Matthe, John. Arthur of Albion. Tatamikau, Pavel, illus. (p. 104)
Matthews, John & Matthews, Caitlin. Storyworld: Create a Story Kit. (p. 1664)
Matthews, John R. Light Bulb. (p. 1015)
—Railroad. (p. 1433)
Matthews, Kay. Anasazi Welcome. Belknap, Barbara, illus. (p. 67)
Matthews, Kendall J. Mommy I Want to Be a Cop. (p. 1162)
Matthews, L. S. Fish. (p. 598)
—Lexi. (p. 1004)
Matthews, Leeana. Dimetriuses. (p. 440)
Matthews, Melanie, illus. see Park, Louise.
Matthews, Miriam, illus. see Blanchet, M. Wylie.
Matthews, Morgan & Sinden, David. Yuck's Robotic Butt Blast. Baines, Nigel, illus. (p. 1983)
Matthews, Owen. How to Win at High School. (p. 822)
Matthews, Patrick. Dragon Run. (p. 478)
Matthews, Penny. Pudding & Chips. Dawson, Janine, illus. (p. 1414)
Matthews, Rachael. Flowers. (p. 608)
—Fruit. (p. 645)
Matthews, Rebecca L. Little Birch Finds Peace. (p. 1024)
Matthews, Regina Stone. Elizabeth Marie Hutchinson - When I Dream. (p. 513)
Matthews, Richard P. Good Soldiers: The History of the 353rd Infantry Regiment, 89th Infantry Division (p. 700)
Matthews, Rodney. Greek & Norse Legends. (p. 720)
—Tales of King Arthur. (p. 1702)
Matthews, Rodney, illus. see Evans, Cheryl & Millard, Anne.
Matthews, Rupert. Ancient Mysteries. (p. 70)
—Arms & Armor. (p. 100)
—Assyrian Soldier! An Ancient Army You'd Rather Not Join. Antram, David, illus. (p. 107)
—Battle at the Castle. (p. 145)
—Be a Mayan Soothsayer! Fortunes You'd Rather Not Tell. Antram, David, illus. (p. 148)
—Dinosaur Families: Unearth the Secrets Behind Dinosaur Fossils. (p. 442)
—Dinosaur Food: Unearth the Secrets Behind Dinosaur Fossils. (p. 442)
—Dinosaurs. (p. 443)
—Disappearances. (p. 446)
—Explorer. (p. 551)
—Fun Kits Let's Learn Dinosaurs. (p. 648)
—Ghosts & Spirits. (p. 672)
—Gladiators. (p. 682)
—Hide-And-Ghost Seek... Le Ray, Marina, illus. (p. 776)
—Illustrated Encyclopedia of Mammals. (p. 857)
—Know How Know Why Dinosaurs. Head-Weston, Alex et al, illus. (p. 965)
—Mayan Soothsayer! Fortunes You'D Rather Not Tell. Antram, David, illus. (p. 1113)
—Mongols. (p. 1164)
—Ninjas. (p. 1256)
—Prehistoric Life. (p. 1395)
—Rain Forest Explorer. (p. 1434)
—Samurai. (p. 1509)
—Spartans. (p. 1622)
—Strange Animals. (p. 1664)
—Weapons & Armor. (p. 1869)
—World Wars. (p. 1959)
—World's Biggest Dinosaurs (p. 1960)
—World's Dumbest Dinosaurs (p. 1960)
—World's Fastest Dinosaurs (p. 1960)
—World's Scariest Dinosaurs (p. 1961)
—World's Smallest Dinosaurs (p. 1961)
—World's Weirdest Dinosaurs (p. 1961)
—You Wouldn't Want to Be a Chicago Gangster! Some Dangerous Characters You'd Better Avoid. Bergin, Mark, illus. (p. 1976)
Matthews, Rupert, jt. auth. see Dorling Kindersley Publishing Staff.
Matthews, Rupert, jt. auth. see Murphy, Lauren.
Matthews, Rupert, jt. auth. see Ripley's Believe It or Not Editors.
Matthews, Rupert & Dorling Kindersley Publishing Staff. Battle at the Castle. (p. 145)
Matthews, Rupert & Salariya, David. You Wouldn't Want to Be a Chicago Gangster! Some Dangerous Characters You'd Better Avoid. Bergin, Mark, illus. (p. 1976)
Matthews, Rupert & Van Pelt, Todd. Ancient Chinese Civilization. D'Ottavi, Francesca, illus. (p. 68)
Matthews, Sandra D. Boomer & Friends: Adventure Number One. (p. 213)
Matthews, Sheelagh. Beijing National Stadium. (p. 160)
—Bono. (p. 209)
—Canadian Shield. (p. 260)
—Gordon Korman. (p. 702)
—Pyramids of Giza. (p. 1421)
—South Africa. (p. 1616)
—Steve Irwin. (p. 1649)
—Sydney Opera House. (p. 1692)
—Trade & Global Impact. (p. 1776)
Matthews, Sheelagh & Kissock, Heather. Sydney Opera House. (p. 1692)
Matthews, Steve. CIC for Older Youth & Young Adults: Traveling Companions on the Pilgrimage. (p. 318)
Matthews, T. J. Canoeing Safari. Rheburg, Judy, illus. (p. 261)
—Hunting Safari. Rheberg, Judy, illus. (p. 829)
—Village Safari. Rheburg, Judy, illus. (p. 1842)
Matthews, Tom L. Always Inventing: A Photobiography of Alexander Graham Bell. (p. 51)
Matthews, Trisha. I Smell Pancakes! (p. 845)
Matthews-Dodd, Melissa. Chase Coming Home. (p. 294)
Matthewson, Emma, ed. see Blight, Peter.
Matthewson, Sarah. On the Lookout: Lives of Naturalists. (p. 1290)
Matthias, Catherine. Too Many Balloons. Sharp, Gene, illus. (p. 1766)
Matthias, Catherine & Sharp, Gene. Demasiados Globos. Sharp, Gene, illus. (p. 425)
Matthias, John. New Selected Poems. (p. 1247)
—Working Progress, Working Title: Automystifstical Plaice. (p. 1953)
Matthies, Don-Oliver. Detective Mazes. (p. 431)
—Magician's Castle. (p. 1075)
Matthies, Don-Oliver & Arena Verlag Staff. Castle Mazes. (p. 277)
—Explorer Mazes. (p. 551)
—Mummy Mazes. (p. 1191)
—Pirate Mazes. (p. 1362)
—Spooky Mazes. (p. 1631)
Matthies, Jana. Goodbye Cancer Garden Valiant, Kristi, illus. (p. 700)
Matthies, Janna. Monster Trucks. Barretta, Gene, illus. (p. 1168)
Matthiessen, F. O. Worlds Apart: An Anthology of Russian Science Fiction & Fantasy. Levitsky, Alexander, ed. (p. 1960)
Matthiessen, F. O., jt. auth. see Levitsky, Alexander.
Matti, Truus. Departure Time. (p. 427)
—Departure Time. Forest-Flier, Nancy, tr. from DUT. (p. 427)
—Mister Orange. (p. 1155)
Mattie, Dugan, ed. see Sommers, Audrey.
Mattingley, Christobel. Asmir No Quiere Pistolas. Balseiro, Maria Luisa, tr. (p. 106)
—Battle Order 204: A Bomber Pilot's Story. (p. 147)
—Chelonia Green: Champion of Turtles. (p. 297)
Mattingley, Christobel, jt. auth. see Yalata and Oak Valley Communities.
Mattingly Jr., Joseph C. Logan's Big Surprise. (p. 1045)
Mattingly, Robin. Chicken Church. Swope, Brenda, illus. (p. 300)
Mattison, Booker T. Unsigned Hype. (p. 1822)
Mattison, Christopher. Reptiles & Amphibians. (p. 1461)
Mattison, Mary Lee. You be the Artist. (p. 1973)
Mattix, Tracy. Begging for Marshmallows. (p. 159)
Mattocks, Kikki. In His Hands. (p. 863)
Mattoon, Cathleen Piilani. Lei Pipipi. (p. 991)
—What's for Lunch? (p. 1897)
Mattotti, Lorenzo, illus. see Gaiman, Neil.
Mattox, Brenda Sneathen. Favorite Ballets Coloring Book. (p. 578)
—Ladies in Red Paper Dolls: Famous Fashions from Great Designers. (p. 970)
—Naughty Girls Paper Dolls. (p. 1237)
—Nutcracker Ballet Coloring Book. (p. 1274)
—Wedding Traditions from Around the World Coloring Book. (p. 1871)
Mattox, Brenda Sneathen, et al. Fashion Fads Paper Dolls. (p. 575)
Mattox, Wendy A., jt. auth. see Mattox, Wendy Ann.
Mattox, Wendy Ann & Mattox, Wendy A. Babysitting Activities: Fun with Kids of All Ages. (p. 129)
Mattox-Primacio, M. Nalani. Mahalo e ke Akua. (p. 1076)
Mattozzi, Patricia, illus. see Andes, Mary Lou.
Mattozzi, Patricia, illus. see Will, Julianne M.
Mattozzi, Patricia R., illus. see Bosco, Antoinette.
Mattozzi, Patricia R., illus. see Muldoon, Kathleen M.
Mattozzi, Patricia R., illus. see Muldoon, Kathleen M. & Wallace, Susan Helen.
Mattson, James Iver, jt. auth. see Brauner, Barbara.
Mattsson, Jude. Angus Emu & Sara Mare. (p. 75)
Mattucci, Sandra. Levi the Lightning Bug's Amazing Discovery. Mattucci, Sandra, illus. (p. 1004)
Matulay, Laszlo, illus. see Sutton, Felix & Loening, Grover.
Matulay, Laszlo, illus. see Sutton, Felix.
Matulewicz, Elisabeth Ann. Benny & Marshmallow. Sponaugle, Kim, illus. (p. 165)
—Gift of Love. (p. 675)
Maturi, Richard J. Triple Crown Winner: Tragedy to Triumph: The Earl Sande Saga. (p. 1787)
Matuszak, Dagmara, illus. see Rebscher, Susanne.
Matuszak, Pat. Angela's Answer (p. 74)
—Simone's Secret (p. 1577)
Matute, Ana María. Polizón del Ulises. (p. 1381)
—Saltamontes Verde. (p. 1505)
Matuz, Roger & Baker, Lawrence W. Reconstruction Era: Biographies. (p. 1452)
Matyas, Diane. Terrible Captain Jack Visits the Museum: Or A Guide of Museum Manners for Incorrigible Pirates & the Like. (p. 1721)
Matyschenko, Tanya, illus. see Bollen, Christine.
Matysiak, Janek, illus. see O'Donnell, Liam.
Matyuschenko, Tanya, illus. see Bollen, Christina.
Matyuschenko, Tanya, illus. see Bollen, Christine.
Matz, Carol. 4 Pop Hits Issue 2: Everything Is Awesome * Best Day of My Life * Everything I Didn't Say * Clouds. (p. 1992)
—Learn to Play Piano with Strawberry Shortcake: Early Elementary. (p. 984)
Matz, Carol, contrib. by. Best of Strawberry Shortcake: Early Elementary. (p. 170)
—Strawberry Shortcake; Berry Merry Christmas: Early Elementary. (p. 1666)
Matz, Rita T. What Can I Do Today? (p. 1880)
Matzen, Deon C., illus. see Martin, Martha M.
Matzigkeit, Philip, jt. auth. see Marsden, Carolyn.
Matzke, Ann. Plus 0, Minus 0. (p. 1374)
—Plus 2, Minus 2. (p. 1374)
—Who's Right, Addition or Multiplication? (p. 1921)
Matzke, Ann H. Can You Guess? (p. 259)
—My Life As a Native American. (p. 1212)
—My Life As a Pioneer. (p. 1212)
—Plus 1, Minus 1. (p. 1374)
—What Are the Branches of Democracy? (p. 1879)
Matzke, Jenny & Perry, Jerry, II. Eric & the Christmas Card. (p. 533)
Mau, Carol Demma. Wisdom from the Pearl Necklace. (p. 1939)
Mau, Connie. Catch me if you Can. Lemus, Kristina, illus. (p. 279)
Mauch, Jason, jt. auth. see Books, D. W. J.
Mauchline, Sarah, illus. see Hill, Sarah.
Maude Spelman, Cornelia & Spelman, Cornelia Maude. When I Feel Worried. Parkinson, Kathy, illus. (p. 1902)
Maude, Tony. Without Surprise. Monica, Brufton, illus. (p. 1942)
Maudet, Y., tr. see Bondoux, Anne-Laure.
Maudet, Y., tr. see Perro, Bryan.
Mauerman, John, ed. see Mauerman, Nancy.
Mauerman, Nancy. Bearos. Mauerman, John & Anderson, Amy, eds. (p. 151)
Maugham, W. Somerset. Siamese Fairy Tale. (p. 1572)
Maughan, Jennifer, jt. auth. see Kinsel, Kate.
Maughan, William, illus. see Bridges, Shirin Yim & Yim Bridges, Shirin.
Maughan, William L., illus. see Bruchac, Marge.
Mauk, Susan & Stettler, Linda. Taxonomy Trail. (p. 1707)
Mauldin, Mary. What a Carrot-Astrophy! (p. 1878)
Maule, David. Are You Listening? the Sense of Hearing High Beginning Book with Online Access. (p. 97)
—Genius Beginning Book with Online Access. (p. 661)
—Romans. (p. 1486)
—Stealing High Beginning Book with Online Access. (p. 1646)
—What Makes a Place Special? (p. 1892)
Maunder, Brian. Polly's Little Kite. Maunder, Brian, illus. (p. 1381)
Maunder, Roger. Mundy Pond. (p. 1191)
Maunsell, Simonne. Fluffy Clouds. (p. 608)
Maupin, Melissa. Calvin Coolidge. (p. 255)
—Franklin D. Roosevelt. (p. 630)
Maureen, Roffey. B C Animals Teach Me! (p. 122)
Maurer, Amy J. Purple Hippopotamus Pillow & Pink Penguin Sheets. Smith, Rachel, illus. (p. 1419)
Maurer, Christine. Autumn Splendor. (p. 118)
Maurer, Eileen. Bear Who Needs Your Help. (p. 151)
Maurer, Gretchen. Call Me Isis: Egyptian Goddess of Magic. (p. 254)
—Mary Tudor: "Bloody Mary" Malone, Peter, illus. (p. 1101)
Maurer, Jayne. Grandpa Goes to Horse Camp. (p. 709)
Maurer, Norman. Best of the Three Stooges (p. 171)
—Best of the Three Stooges. (p. 171)
Maurer, Shari. Change of Heart. (p. 290)
Maurer, Toby, jt. auth. see Wilson, Kris E.
Maurer, Tracy. Aaron Rodgers. (p. 2)
—Cactus. (p. 250)
—Cave. (p. 282)
—Cupcakes, Cookies, & Cakes. (p. 392)
—Fabulous Fashion Crafts. (p. 560)
—Hole. (p. 788)
—Jonathan Toews. (p. 925)
—Land Rover. (p. 973)
—LeBron James. (p. 987)
—Log. (p. 1045)
—Mike Trout. (p. 1141)
—NASCAR Racers. (p. 1230)
—Outrageous Car Racing Rivalries. (p. 1313)
—Paper Crafts with Pizzazz. (p. 1322)
—Playground Games. (p. 1372)
—Rock Your Room with Crafts. (p. 1482)
—Scrapbook Starters. (p. 1532)
—Shell. (p. 1564)
—Storm Codes. Rodriguez, Christina, illus. (p. 1656)
—Tree. (p. 1783)
—What's in A... ? (p. 1897)
Maurer, Tracy, jt. auth. see Maurer, Tracy N.
Maurer, Tracy N. & Maurer, Tracy. Basketball. (p. 143)
—Bicycle Riding. (p. 177)
—Swimming. (p. 1691)
Maurer, Tracy Nelson. Atoms & Molecules. (p. 113)
—ATV Racing (p. 114)
—Changing Matter: Understanding Physical & Chemical Changes. (p. 290)
—Cheerleaders. (p. 296)
—Competitive Cheerleading. (p. 352)
—Famous Athletes. (p. 569)
—Ford Thunderbird. (p. 617)
—Go-Kart Racing (p. 686)
—Lamborghini. (p. 972)
—Maserati. (p. 1102)
—Mix It up! Solution or Mixture? (p. 1156)
—Scoop about Measuring Matter. (p. 1529)
—Stock Car Racing (p. 1651)
—Truck Racing (p. 1791)
Maurer, Tracy Nelson, jt. auth. see Polydoros, Lori.
Maurice, creator. Spanish Question Game. (p. 1621)
Mauricet, illus. see Rodi, Rob.
Mauricet, illus. see Vanholme, Virginie.
Mauro, Paul & Melton, H. Keith. Collecting & Handling Evidence. (p. 339)
—Crime Scene & Surveillance Photography. (p. 382)
—Crime Scene Investigation. (p. 382)
—Detective Mastery. (p. 431)
—Interviews & Interrogations. (p. 881)
—Tracking & Surveillance. (p. 1775)
—Undercover Operations. Aycock, Daniel et al, illus. (p. 1814)
Mauro, Tony. Illustrated Great Decisions of the Supreme Court (p. 857)
Mauro, Tony, illus. see Leonard, Julia Platt.
Maury, Rob. Citizenship: Rights & Responsibilities. (p. 323)
—Immigration from the Middle East. (p. 861)
Maus, Derek C., ed. Living under the Threat of Nuclear War. (p. 1042)
Mauser McCord, Pat. Bundle of Sticks. (p. 242)
Mauss, Doug, ed. see Herrera, Erik, et al.
Mauss, Doug, ed. Action Bible: God's Redemptive Story. Cariello, Sergio, illus. (p. 10)
—Biblia en Acción: La Historia Redentora de Dios. Cariello, Sergio, illus. (p. 176)
Maust, Misty. Daily Bread. (p. 399)
Mauter, Jennifer. Illumination Station. (p. 857)
Mauterer, Erin Marie, illus. see McKay, Sindy.
Mauthe, Deb. Bishop's Christmas Tree. (p. 193)
Mauzy, Barbara. Don't Be a Schwoe: Embracing Differences (p. 466)
Mauzy, Barbara E. Don't Be a Schwoe: Fitness. Stuhmer, Bob, illus. (p. 466)
—Don't Be a Schwoe: Manners Mauzy, Barbara E., illus. (p. 466)
Maval Publishing Inc. Staff, illus. see Hernandez, Mary L.
Maverick, Peter. Old Man & the Peach. (p. 1284)
Maves, Paul D. Finding Your Way Through the Bible. (p. 588)
Mavlian, Vatche, illus. see Matthews, Brett & Marvel Comics Staff.
Mavor, Salley. Pocketful of Posies: A Treasury of Nursery Rhymes. (p. 1375)
Mavreas, Billy. Inside Outside Overlap: A Boy Priest & Lifeform the Cat Adventure. (p. 877)
Mavrikis, Peter. Battleships & Aircraft Carriers. (p. 147)
—Classic Warships. (p. 328)
—Tanks. (p. 1705)
Mavronis, Michelle, illus. see Gesser, Bernadette.
Mavrophilipos, Carol. Clovis the Seahorse. (p. 335)
Mawhinney, Art. Diego's Arctic Rescue. (p. 437)
—Diego's Wolf Pup Rescue. (p. 437)
—Dora & Diego Help the Dinosaur. (p. 470)
—Dora & Diego to the Rescue! (p. 470)
—Look & Find Disney Princess Worlds of Wonder. (p. 1048)
—Look & Find Open Season. (p. 1048)
—Olivia the Magnificent: A Lift-the-Flap Story. (p. 1287)
Mawhinney, Art, illus. see Bergen, Lara.
Mawhinney, Art, illus. see Bryant, Megan E.
Mawhinney, Art, illus. see Burroughs, Caleb.
Mawhinney, Art, illus. see Kunkel, Mike.
Mawhinney, Art, illus. see Lagonegro, Melissa & RH Disney Staff.
Mawhinney, Art, illus. see Lindner, Brooke.
Mawhinney, Art, illus. see Romay, Alexis.
Mawhinney, Art, illus. see Sollinger, Emily.
Mawhinney, Art, jt. illus. see DiCicco, Sue.
Mawhinney, Art, jt. illus. see Johnson, Shane L.
Mawhinney, Art & Disney Storybook Artists Staff. Fairies. (p. 562)
Mawhinney, Art & Johnson, Shane L. OLIVIA Meets Olivia. (p. 1287)
Mawson, illus. see Adams, Keith.
Mawson, Alan, illus. see Adams, Keith.
Mawter, J. A. Launched! (p. 980)
—So Festy! Gordon, Gus, illus. (p. 1602)
—So Grotty! Gordon, Gus, illus. (p. 1602)
—So Sick! Gordon, Gus, illus. (p. 1602)
—So Stinky! Gordon, Gus, illus. (p. 1602)
—Unleashed. (p. 1821)
Max, illus. see Bailer, Darice, et al.
Max, illus. see Cosmic Debris Etc., Inc. Staff & Chronicle Books Staff.
Max and Sid Staff, illus. see Little Bee Books Staff & Brook-Piper, Holly.
Max And Steven Oscherwitz. Gilbert's Adventure. (p. 676)
Max, Iman, illus. see Titan Comics Staff & Furman, Simon.
Max, Jill. Strangers in Black: A Young Boy's Struggle to Survive in Khmer Rouge Cambodia. (p. 1665)
Max, Jill, compiled by. Spider Spins a Story: Fourteen Legends from Native America. (p. 1626)
Max, Querido, jt. auth. see Grindley, Sally.
Maxey. Keeko & the Beastie Three. (p. 946)
Maxey, Ann. Country Style Oklahoma. (p. 372)
Maxey, David, illus. see Auerbach, Annie.
Maxfield, Deanna. Maggie Mae Moose. Landry, Douglas, illus. (p. 1071)

Maxim, Bailey. 100 Most Influential Technology Leaders. (p. 1998)
Maximilian Press Publishers staff, ed. see Hichs, Donald E. & Demers, Aimee.
Maximilian Press Publishers Staff, ed. see McCoy, M. M.
Maximilian Press staff, ed. see Ashley, Jane, IV.
Maximilian Press Staff, ed. see Liddle, Sharon.
Maximilian Staff, ed. see van Gosen, Ryan O'Dell, IV.
Maximus, jt. auth. see Majewski, Anthony M. T.
Maximus, Sofia. Badgers in the Dark. (p. 132)
Maxner, Pearl, illus. see Coste, Marion.
Maxson, H. A. & Young, Claudia H. Along the Chesapeake & Delaware Canal. Yarnall, Karen Sturdy, illus. (p. 48)
—Tea Party at Chestertown. Kosits, Andrew, illus. (p. 1708)
Maxwell, Amanda L., jt. auth. see Maxwell, Andre L.
Maxwell, Andre L. & Maxwell, Amanda L. Great Chicken Caper. Carter, Jill, illus. (p. 714)
Maxwell, Calvin. American Pool Player. (p. 62)
Maxwell, Cassandre. Fur, Fins, & Feathers: Abraham Dee Bartlett & the Invention of the Modern Zoo. (p. 650)
Maxwell, Cassandre, illus. see McCullough, L. E.
Maxwell, Glenn, jt. auth. see Loughlin, Patrick.
Maxwell, Glyn. Merlin & the Woods of Time. (p. 1128)
Maxwell, James Clerk. Theory of Heat. (p. 1729)
Maxwell, Jeremy, illus. see Robinson, Zan D.
Maxwell, John C. There's No Such Thing as Business Ethics: There's Only One Rule for Making Decisions. (p. 1731)
Maxwell, Katie. Taming of the Dru. (p. 1704)
Maxwell, Lisa. Sweet Unrest. (p. 1690)
Maxwell, Noel. Kid's Alaska; Workbook of Alaska & its History. (p. 952)
Maxwell, Robert. Life's Work, the Kids Are Home: Better Take Care of Them. (p. 1013)
Maxwell, Robert W. Weeb Book. Maxwell, Robert W., illus. (p. 1871)
Maxwell, Ruth H. Eighteen Roses Red: A Young Girl's Heroic Mission in the Revolutionary War. (p. 507)
Maxwell, Sarah. I Can Cook: Recipes for Kids Shown Step by Step. (p. 835)
Maxwell, Scott & Chambers, Catherine. Mars Rover Driver. (p. 1096)
Maxwell, Scott, et al. Coolest Jobs on the Planet. (p. 364)
Maxwell, Shannon. Our Daddy Is Invincible! Biggers, Liza, illus. (p. 1308)
Maxwell, Stuart "Son". Starting Blues Harmonica: The Number One Method for Young Blues Harp Players. (p. 1644)
Maxwell, Wayne F., Jr. Miracle of Sandy Duck: A True Story. McCabe, Jane M., illus. (p. 1148)
Maxwell, William. William Maxwell - Later Novels & Stories. Carduff, Christopher, ed. (p. 1933)
Maxwell, William, creator. Inventive Quotient, I. Q. (p. 884)
Maxwell, Yolanda. Famous Bridges of the World: Measuring Length, Weight, & Volume. (p. 569)
Maxwell-Hyslop, Miranda. Fish Go Woof! (p. 598)
—Princess Lola's Wobbly Week. (p. 1404)
MaxwellJr, Calvin. American Pool Player. (p. 62)
Maxwell-Snyder, Hope. Lullaby for George. (p. 1064)
May, Ashley, illus. see Jeffords, Stephanie & Branum, Anita.
May, Bob. Snowmen, elves & Nutcrackers. (p. 1601)
May, Bonnie. Tale of a Rabbit's Tail. (p. 1699)
May, Carrie L. Ruth Lovell or Holidays at Home. (p. 1498)
May, Chris. Cricketing Dream. (p. 382)
May, Cynthia. Ryan's Vitiligo. Nelson, Shannon, illus. (p. 1499)
May, Dan, illus. see Romeyn, Debra.
May, Dan, tr. see Romeyn, Debra.
May, Darcy. Fairies to Paint or Color. (p. 563)
—Fairy of the Seasons Sticker Paper Doll. (p. 563)
—Garden Fairies GemGlow Stained Glass Coloring Book. (p. 656)
—Glitter Christmas Fairy Sticker Paper Doll. (p. 683)
—Glitter Fairies Stickers. (p. 684)
—Glow-in-the-Dark Tattoos Fairies. (p. 685)
—Heirloom Christmas Ornaments Stickers. (p. 762)
May Doan, Catriona Le, see Le May Doan, Catriona.
May, E. J. Louis' School Days: A Story for Boys. (p. 1058)
May, Eleanor. Albert Adds Up! Melmon, Deborah, illus. (p. 34)
—Albert Is Not Scared. (p. 34)
—Albert Is Not Scared. Melmon, Deborah, illus. (p. 34)
—Albert Starts School. Melmon, Deborah, illus. (p. 34)
—Albert the Muffin-Maker. Melmon, Deborah, illus. (p. 35)
—Albert's Amazing Snail. Melmon, Deborah, illus. (p. 35)
—Albert's Bigger Than Big Idea. Melmon, Deborah, illus. (p. 35)
—Bay School Blogger. (p. 147)
—Beach for Albert. Melmon, Deborah, illus. (p. 149)
—Best Mother's Day Ever. Pilz, M. H., illus. (p. 170)
—Great Shape-up. (p. 718)
—Great Shape-up. Gott, Barry, illus. (p. 718)
—Keesha's Bright Idea. Wummer, Amy, illus. (p. 948)
—Lost in the Mouseum. Melmon, Deborah, illus. (p. 1055)
—Mac & Cheese, Pleeeeeeze! (p. 1067)
—Mac & Cheese, Pleeeeze! Palmisciano, Diane, illus. (p. 1067)
—Mice on Ice. Melmon, Deborah, illus. (p. 1134)
—Mousier the Merrier. Melmon, Deborah, illus. (p. 1182)
—Real Me. Gott, Barry, illus. (p. 1448)
—Ty's Triple Trouble. Wummer, Amy, illus. (p. 1805)
—Who Needs It? Sims, Blanche, illus. (p. 1917)
May, Erica. Emerson Learns about Surgery. Millward, Hayley, illus. (p. 518)
May, Gary L. Wilkins Family Farm Monks, Christian, illus. (p. 1932)
May, Gillie, illus. see Schieber, Jennifer.
May, Gin, illus. see Maher, Liam.
May, Gin, jt. auth. see Maher, Liam.
May, J. E. Louis' School Days. (p. 1058)
May, Jason J., illus. see McCarthy, Rebecca.
May, Jim. Farm on Nippersink Creek: Stories from a Midwestern Childhood. (p. 574)
May, Judy. Blue Lavender Girl. (p. 203)
—Copper Girl. (p. 365)
May, Karen. Shy Saelig. (p. 1572)
—Thelma the Tiny Sea Turtle. (p. 1728)
—Walk in the Woods. (p. 1853)
May, Karl F. Oriental Odyssey IV: The Caravan of the Dead. (p. 1303)
—Winnetou. (p. 1937)
May, Kate. Dog Wit: Quips & Quotes for the Canine-Obsessed. (p. 462)
May, Kate, illus. see Hay, Sam.
May, Kyla. Coco: My Delicious Life. (p. 337)
—Introducing Kyla May Miss. Behaves. May, Kyla, illus. (p. 882)
—Kiki: My Stylish Life. (p. 955)
—Kiki: My Stylish Life. Bk. 1 (p. 955)
—Kyla Miss. Behaves Around the World. May, Kyla, illus. (p. 969)
—Live Onstage. (p. 1040)
—Lulu: My Glamorous Life. (p. 1064)
—Lulu My Glamorous Life. (p. 1065)
—Mika: My New Life. (p. 1141)
—My Glamorous Life. (p. 1210)
May, Kyla, illus. see La Rue, Coco.
May, Kyla, illus. see Park, Louise.
May, Kyla, jt. auth. see Horsfall, Kyla May.
May, Leslie, jt. auth. see Mitchell, Ronnie.
May, Maggie. Pilot, Swaydy & Friends. Larade, April, illus. (p. 1359)
—Times Three. L, Joe, illus. (p. 1754)
May, Marcie & Zerhusen, Margaret. Adventures of Penny & Tubs: The City on the Sea. Chamberlin, Maggie, illus. (p. 21)
May, Martin M. Great Art Glass Lamps: Tiffany, Duffner & Kimberly, Pairpoint, & Handel (p. 713)
May, Matthew. Industrial Revolution Reference Library Cumulative Index. (p. 872)
May, Melba L. Old Swinging Bridge. (p. 1284)
May, Paul. Dinosaurs. (p. 443)
—Elephants. (p. 511)
May, Pete. Players. (p. 1372)
—Teams. (p. 1710)
May, R. B. Charlie Finds a Friend. (p. 293)
May, Robert L. Rudolph Shines Again. Caparo, Antonio Javier, illus. (p. 1494)
May, Ruthie. Count My Kisses, Little One. Ainslie, Tamsin, illus. (p. 369)
—Stew a Cockatoo: My Aussie Cookbook. Hobbs, Leigh, illus. (p. 1649)
May, Sandy, illus. see Mitchell, Gwendolyn.
May, Sophie. Dotty Dimple at Play. (p. 472)
—Dotty Dimple Out West. (p. 472)
May, Stephan. Leo the Entrepreneurial Hippo. (p. 992)
May, Suellen. Invasive Aquatic & Wetland Animals. (p. 883)
—Invasive Microbes. (p. 883)
—Invasive Terrestrial Animals. (p. 883)
—Invasive Terrestrial Plants. (p. 883)
—Ritalin & Related Drugs. (p. 1475)
May, Suellen & Triggle, David J. Steroids & Other Performance-Enhancing Drugs. (p. 1649)
May, Susie. Colour. (p. 346)
May, Susie & Whitely, Heather. Shape. (p. 1560)
May, Tessa. Bella Wishes. Rodriguez, Dave, illus. (p. 162)
Maya, Valorie & Sharma, Neal. Ivan Idea Has a Big Ide. (p. 900)
Maya Z And Nadajia R. Hall. New-Fangled Adventures of Alexia & Z: The Case of Grams' Missing Teeth. (p. 1244)
Mayabb, Darrell, ed. see Garrelts, Christopher.
Mayall, Beth. Mermaid Park. (p. 1128)
Mayall, David. Gypsies Identities, 1500-2000: From Egyptians & Moonmen to Ethnic Romany. (p. 734)
Mayaprua, Alejandro Taish. Nantu & Auju: How the Moon & the Potoo Bird Came to Be. Youth of the Achuar Tribe of Ecuador, illus. (p. 1229)
Maybank, Roger. Sun Boat: A Fairytale. (p. 1676)
Maybarduk, Linda. James the Dancing Dog. Johnson, Gillian, illus. (p. 907)
Mayberry, Becky. Always Listen to Your Mom, Even If She Is a Duck: Even If She Is A Duck. (p. 51)
Mayberry, Maranda, illus. see Feldman, Thea.
Mayberry, Michael. Kid Donut: How to Handle Strangers. (p. 951)
Maybury, Ged. Into the Storm's Domain. (p. 881)
Maybury, Richard J. Ancient Rome: How It Affects You Today. Williams, Jane A., ed. (p. 70)
—Are You Liberal? Conservative? or Confused? Williams, Jane A., ed. (p. 97)
—Clipper Ship Strategy: For Success in Your Career, Business, & Investments. Williams, Jane A., ed. (p. 333)
—Evaluating Books - What Would Thomas Jefferson Think about This? Guidelines for Selecting Books Consistent with the Principles of America's Founders. Williams, Jane A. & Daniels, Kathryn, eds. (p. 540)
—Money Mystery: The Hidden Force Affecting Your Career, Business, & Investments. Williams, Jane A., ed. (p. 1164)
—Uncle Eric Talks about Personal, Career, & Financial Security. Williams, Jane A. & Daniels, Kathryn, eds. (p. 1811)
—Whatever Happened to Justice? Williams, Jane A., ed. (p. 1896)
—World War I: The Rest of the Story & How It Affects You Today, 1870 To 1935. Williams, Jane A., ed. (p. 1958)
—World War II: The Rest of the Story & How It Affects You Today, 1930 to September 11 2001. Williams, Jane A., ed. (p. 1959)
Maycock, Dianne. Lucky's Mountain (p. 1063)
Maydak, Michael, illus. see Schur, Maxine Rose.
Maydak, Michael S. Wild Stickers - Sharks & Rays. (p. 1930)
Maydak, Michael S., illus. see Ellis, Brian.
Maydak, Michael S., illus. see Field, Nancy H.
Maydak, Michael S., illus. see Reed-jones, Carol.
Maydak, Michael S., illus. see Rice, David L.
Maydak, Michael S., illus. see Roop, Connie & Roop, Peter.
Maydak, Michael S., illus. see Schur, Maxine Rose.
Maydak, Mike, illus. see Parker, Katie.
Maydell, Natalie & Riahi, Sep. Extraordinary Women from the Muslim World. Amin, Heba, illus. (p. 555)
Mayeaux, Alicia, illus. see Leleux, Skip.
Mayer, Allie, jt. auth. see Mayer, Mindy.
Mayer, Bill, illus. see Beaty, Andrea.
Mayer, Bill, illus. see Kessler, Brad & Harris, Joel Chandler.
Mayer, Bill, illus. see Meadows, Michelle.
Mayer, Bill, illus. see Schnitzlein, Danny.
Mayer, Bill, illus. see Stiles, Norman.
Mayer, Bill, jt. auth. see Demarest, Chris L.
Mayer, Bill, jt. auth. see Hallowell, Edward M.
Mayer, Cassie. Abigail Adams (p. 5)
—Abraham Lincoln (p. 6)
—Agricultura (p. 30)
—Agua (p. 30)
—Automóvil. (p. 117)
—Being a Leader (p. 160)
—Being Fair (p. 161)
—Being Helpful (p. 161)
—Being Honest (p. 161)
—Being Responsible (p. 161)
—Benjamin Franklin (p. 164)
—Bosque Tropical (p. 215)
—By Bicycle (p. 249)
—By Boat (p. 249)
—By Car (p. 249)
—By Plane (p. 249)
—By Train (p. 249)
—Canales (p. 260)
—Caucho (p. 281)
—Caves (p. 282)
—Citizenship (p. 323)
—Civismo (Citizenship) (p. 326)
—Clouds (p. 335)
—Comparing Materials. (p. 352)
—Cuevas (p. 390)
—Desert (p. 428)
—Desierto (p. 429)
—En Avión (p. 522)
—En Barco (p. 522)
—En Bicicleta (p. 522)
—En Tren (p. 523)
—Farming (p. 574)
—Feathers (p. 579)
—Following Rules (p. 612)
—Frederick Douglass (p. 633)
—Fur (p. 650)
—George Washington (p. 664)
—Glass (p. 682)
—Hacer Amigos. (p. 735)
—Harriet Tubman (p. 749)
—Hogares (p. 787)
—Homes (p. 793)
—Islands (p. 892)
—Islas (p. 892)
—Lagos y Estanques (p. 971)
—Lluvia (p. 1043)
—Madera (p. 1070)
—Making Friends (p. 1081)
—Markets (p. 1095)
—Mercados (p. 1127)
—Metal (p. 1130)
—Montañas (p. 1170)
—Mountains (p. 1181)
—Música (p. 1193)
—Nieve (p. 1252)
—Nubes (p. 1269)
—Ocean (p. 1276)
—Océano (p. 1277)
—Océanos y Mares (p. 1277)
—Oceans & Seas (p. 1277)
—On Foot (p. 1288)
—Pie (p. 1356)
—Piedra (p. 1357)
—Plastic (p. 1370)
—Plástico (p. 1370)
—Polar Region (p. 1379)
—Pradera (p. 1392)
—Prairie (p. 1392)
—Rain (p. 1434)
—Rain Forest (p. 1434)
—Región Polar (p. 1457)
—Ríos y Arroyos (p. 1473)
—Rock (p. 1481)
—Ropa (p. 1488)
—Rubber (p. 1493)
—Scales (p. 1519)
—Seguir las Reglas. (p. 1548)
—Ser Honesto (p. 1552)
—Ser Responsable (p. 1552)
—Ser Servicial (p. 1552)
—Ser un Líder (p. 1552)
—Shells (p. 1565)
—Snow (p. 1598)
—Soil (p. 1606)
—Sol (p. 1606)
—Sunshine (p. 1677)
—Tecumseh (p. 1712)
—Thomas Jefferson (p. 1739)
—Thunder & Lightning (p. 1746)
—Tierra (p. 1748)
—Truenos y Relámpagos (p. 1793)
—Valles (p. 1830)
—Valleys (p. 1831)
—Vidrio (p. 1841)
—Viento (p. 1841)
—Volcanoes (p. 1849)
—Water (p. 1862)
—Wind (p. 1935)
—Wood (p. 1949)
Mayer, Cassie, jt. auth. see Easterling, Lisa.
Mayer, Cassie & Resl, Brigitte. Al Iltizam Bil Qawaed. Mahmoud, Ghada Mohamed, tr. (p. 32)
—Takouna Adelan. Mahmoud, Ghada Mohamed, tr. (p. 1698)
—Takouna Masoulan. Mahmoud, Ghada Mohamed, tr. (p. 1698)
—Takouna Sadeqan. Mahmoud, Ghada Mohamed, tr. (p. 1698)
—Takween Sadaqat. Mahmoud, Ghada Mohamed, tr. (p. 1699)
—Tosaed. Mahmoud, Ghada Mohamed, tr. (p. 1771)
Mayer, Danuta, illus. see Soros, Barbara.
Mayer, Gina, jt. auth. see Mayer, Mercer.
Mayer, Helena. Lost Riolu: Pokémon Academy. (p. 1056)
Mayer, Jason, jt. auth. see Mayer, Linda.
Mayer, Jeffrey J. Il y a Cauchemar dans Mon Placard. (p. 856)
—Si Javais Gorille. (p. 1572)
Mayer, Jeni. Mystery of the Missing Will. (p. 1225)
—Mystery of the Turtle Lake Monster. (p. 1226)
Mayer, Jeremy. Shubha & Shanti: Dallas to Delhi. (p. 1571)
Mayer, Jonathan, illus. see Doeden, Matt.
Mayer, Julia. Eyes in the Mirror. (p. 558)
Mayer, Kathy, jt. auth. see Birke, Szfra.
Mayer, Kirsten. Alvin & the Chipmunks: Alvin Gets an A. Rogers, Jacqueline, illus. (p. 51)
—Alvin Gets an A. (p. 51)
—Attack of the Evil Minions! Miller, Ed, illus. (p. 113)
—Big Dude-L Book. Ostrom, Bob, illus. (p. 181)
—Chipmunk Valentine. (p. 308)
—Danger at Sea. (p. 403)
—Despicable Me 2 - Undercover Super Spies. (p. 430)
—Did Scrat Do That? (p. 436)
—Disney Fairies: the Pirate Fairy: Adventure at Skull Rock. (p. 451)
—Disney Fairies: the Pirate Fairy: Reusable Sticker Book. (p. 451)
—Disney Fairies: the Pirate Fairy: Wake up, Croc! (p. 451)
—Dude-It-Yourself Adventure Journal. Spaziante, Patrick, illus. (p. 489)
—I Am Aquaman. Smith, Andy & Vancata, Brad, illus. (p. 832)
—Justice League Classic: I Am Aquaman. (p. 940)
—Make a Minion. (p. 1078)
—Marmaduke: Meet Marmaduke. (p. 1096)
—Meet Team Prime. (p. 1122)
—Meet the Ghouls Character Guidebook. (p. 1122)
—Monster High. (p. 1167)
—Monster High: Create-A-Monster Design Lab Sticker Book. (p. 1167)
—Monster High: Ghoul Spirit: A Monster High Doodle Book. GONZALES, Chuck, illus. (p. 1167)
—Pack Is Back! (p. 1317)
—Transformers Prime: Meet Team Prime. (p. 1778)
Mayer, Kirsten, jt. auth. see Marvel Comics Staff.
Mayer, Kirsten, jt. ed. see Taylor, Julie.
Mayer, Kirsten & Auerbach, Annie, texts. Hop: The Chapter Book. (p. 796)
Mayer, Kirsten & Kelly, Michael, texts. Transformers Dark of the Moon the Junior Novel. (p. 1778)
Mayer, Kirsten & Turner, Katharine, texts. More Than Meets the Eye. (p. 1175)
—Transformers Dark of the Moon - Bumblebee's Best Friend. (p. 1778)
—Transformers Dark of the Moon - The Lost Autobot. (p. 1778)
Mayer, Kirsten & Yu, Melissa. Ever after High: the Hat-Tastic Tea Party Planner. (p. 541)
Mayer, Kirsten, et al, texts. Meet the Easter Bunny. (p. 1122)
Mayer, Kirsten, text. Chicks Versus Bunnies. (p. 301)
—World's Greatest Villain. (p. 1960)
Mayer, Kristen. Autobots Versus Decepticons. (p. 117)
Mayer, Kristin. Alvin & the Chipmunks: Joke Book. (p. 51)
Mayer, Kristin, ed. see Carvin, Rose-Mae.
Mayer, Linda & Mayer, Jason. Frankie: The World's Greatest Hot Dog. (p. 629)
Mayer, Lynne. Newton & Me. Rogers, Sherry, illus. (p. 1249)
Mayer, Marianna. Adventures of Tom Thumb. Craft, Kinuko Y., illus. (p. 24)
Mayer, Marianna, jt. auth. see Mayer, Mercer.
Mayer, Marvin. Day X Ran Away. (p. 415)
—Ferdinand Frog's Flight. Macquignon, Stephen, illus. (p. 581)
Mayer, Marvin S. Sammy Squirrel & the Sunflower Seeds. Johns, Dick, illus. (p. 1508)
Mayer, Matthew J., et al, eds. Cognitive-Behavioral Interventions for Emotional & Behavioral Disorders: School-Based Practice. (p. 338)
Mayer, Melody, illus. see Greiner, Ruth B.
Mayer, Mercer. All by Myself. (p. 44)
—Bedtime Stories - Little Critter. Mayer, Mercer, illus. (p. 157)
—Best Teacher Ever No. 6. Mayer, Mercer, illus. (p. 171)
—Best Yard Sale. Mayer, Mercer, illus. (p. 171)
—Boy, a Dog, & a Frog. Mayer, Mercer, illus. (p. 217)
—Bravest Knight. Mayer, Mercer, illus. (p. 223)
—Bubble Bubble. (p. 233)
—Bye-Bye, Mom & Dad. Mayer, Mercer, illus. (p. 249)
—Fair Play. (p. 562)
—Fall Festival. (p. 566)
—Fall Festival. Mayer, Mercer, illus. (p. 566)
—First Day of School No. 3. Mayer, Mercer, illus. (p. 594)
—Frog Goes to Dinner. Mayer, Mercer, illus. (p. 640)
—Frog on His Own. Mayer, Mercer, illus. (p. 640)
—Frog, Where Are You? Mayer, Mercer, illus. (p. 640)
—Going to the Firehouse. Mayer, Mercer, illus. (p. 693)
—Going to the Sea Park. Mayer, Mercer, illus. (p. 693)
—Good for Me & You. Mayer, Mercer, illus. (p. 698)
—Grandma, Grandpa, & Me. (p. 708)
—Grandma, Grandpa, & Me. Mayer, Mercer, illus. (p. 708)
—Green, Green Garden. Mayer, Mercer, illus. (p. 722)
—Hansel & Gretel: A Lift-the-Flap Book. (p. 743)
—Happy Halloween, Little Critter! Mayer, Mercer, illus. (p. 745)
—Happy Mother's Day! Mayer, Mercer, illus. (p. 746)
—Happy Valentine's Day, Little Critter! Mayer, Mercer, illus. (p. 747)
—Helping Mom. (p. 766)
—Helping Out. (p. 766)
—I Was So Mad. (p. 848)
—It's Earth Day! Mayer, Mercer, illus. (p. 896)
—It's Easter, Little Critter! Mayer, Mercer, illus. (p. 896)
—It's True (p. 899)
—It's True! (p. 899)
—Just a Big Storm. (p. 937)
—Just a Big Storm. Mayer, Mercer, illus. (p. 937)
—Just a Day at the Pond. Mayer, Mercer, illus. (p. 937)
—Just a Kite. (p. 937)

—Just a Kite. Mayer, Mercer, illus. (p. 937)
—Just a Little Critter Collection. Mayer, Mercer, illus. (p. 937)
—Just a Little Love. (p. 937)
—Just a Little Love. Mayer, Mercer, illus. (p. 937)
—Just a Little Luck. Mayer, Mercer, illus. (p. 937)
—Just a Little Music. (p. 937)
—Just a Little Music. Mayer, Mercer, illus. (p. 937)
—Just a Little Sick. (p. 937)
—Just a Little Sick. Mayer, Mercer, illus. (p. 937)
—Just a Little Too Little. (p. 937)
—Just a Little Too Little. Mayer, Mercer, illus. (p. 937)
—Just a School Project. Mayer, Mercer, illus. (p. 937)
—Just a Special Day. (p. 937)
—Just a Storybook Collection: Bye-Bye, Mom & Dad; Just a School Project; Just a Snowman; Good for Me & You; Just Big Enough; My Trip to the Hospital. Mayer, Mercer, illus. (p. 937)
—Just a Teacher's Pet. Mayer, Mercer, illus. (p. 937)
—Just Big Enough. (p. 938)
—Just Big Enough. Mayer, Mercer, illus. (p. 938)
—Just Critters Who Care. Mayer, Mercer, illus. (p. 938)
—Just Helping My Dad. Mayer, Mercer, illus. (p. 938)
—Just Me & My Mom/Just Me & My Dad. (p. 939)
—Just Me & My Mom/Just Me & My Dad (Mercer Mayer's Little Critter) Mayer, Mercer, illus. (p. 939)
—Just My Lost Treasure. Mayer, Mercer, illus. (p. 939)
—Just One More Pet. (p. 939)
—Just One More Pet. Mayer, Mercer, illus. (p. 939)
—Just Saving My Money. Mayer, Mercer, illus. (p. 939)
—Little Critter: Just Helping My Dad. (p. 1026)
—Little Critter: Going to the Sea Park. (p. 1026)
—Little Critter: We Are Moving. Mayer, Mercer, illus. (p. 1026)
—Little Critter: Just a Snowman. Mayer, Mercer, illus. (p. 1026)
—Little Critter Collection. Mayer, Mercer, illus. (p. 1026)
—Little Critter Fall Storybook Collection. Mayer, Mercer, illus. (p. 1026)
—Little Critter Jack & the Beanstalk: A Lift-the-Flap Book. (p. 1026)
—Little Critter: Just a Kite. Mayer, Mercer, illus. (p. 1026)
—Little Critter: Just a Kite 6c Clip Strip. (p. 1026)
—Little Critter - Just a Little Love. Mayer, Mercer, illus. (p. 1026)
—Little Critter Storybook Collection. Mayer, Mercer, illus. (p. 1026)
—Little Critter(r) ABCs. (p. 1026)
—Little Critter(r) Colors. (p. 1026)
—Little Critter(r) - I Am Helping. (p. 1026)
—Little Critter(r) I Am Sharing. (p. 1026)
—Little Critter(r) Numbers. (p. 1026)
—Little Critter(r) Shapes. (p. 1026)
—Little Critters. (p. 1026)
—Little Critter's Bedtime Storybook. (p. 1026)
—Little Red Riding Hood. (p. 1035)
—Lost Dinosaur Bone. Mayer, Mercer, illus. (p. 1055)
—Mercer Mayer's Little Critter's Series. (p. 1127)
—Mercer Mayer's Little Monster Fun & Learn Book. (p. 1127)
—Mercer Mayer's Little Monster Home School & Work Book. (p. 1127)
—Mercer Mayer's Little Monster Word Book with Mother Goose. (p. 1127)
—Merry Christmas, Little Critter! Mayer, Mercer, illus. (p. 1128)
—My Family: A Big Little Critter Book. (p. 1202)
—My Trip to the Hospital Mayer, Mercer, illus. (p. 1220)
—Octopus Soup Mayer, Mercer, illus. (p. 1278)
—On the Go. (p. 1290)
—Pesadilla en Mi Armario. (p. 1345)
—Phonics Fun. Mayer, Mercer, illus. (p. 1352)
—Play It Safe. (p. 1371)
—Professor Wormbog in Search for the Zipperump-a-Zoo. (p. 1409)
—Scholastic Success with Writing. (p. 1522)
—Shibumi & the Kitemaker (p. 1566)
—Sleeps Over. Mayer, Mercer, illus. (p. 1589)
—Snowball Soup. Mayer, Mercer, illus. (p. 1600)
—Staying Well. (p. 1645)
—There Are Monsters Everywhere. (p. 1729)
—This Is My Town. (p. 1736)
—This Is My Town. Mayer, Mercer, illus. (p. 1736)
—To the Rescue! Mayer, Mercer, illus. (p. 1759)
—Too Many Dinosaurs. Mayer, Mercer, illus. (p. 1766)
—We All Need Forgiveness (p. 1865)
—We Are Moving. (p. 1865)
—What a Good Kitty! (p. 1878)
—What a Good Kitty. Mayer, Mercer, illus. (p. 1878)
—What Do You Do with a Kangaroo? Mayer, Mercer, illus. (p. 1883)
—When I Get Bigger. (p. 1902)
—When I Grow Up. (p. 1902)
—When I Grow Up. (p. 1903)
—Where's Kitty? (p. 1910)
—You Go First (p. 1975)
Mayer, Mercer, illus. see Fitzgerald, John D.
Mayer, Mercer, illus. see Konigsburg, E. L. & Haley, Gail E.
Mayer, Mercer, illus. see Skorpen, Liesel Moak.
Mayer, Mercer & Mayer, Gina. Just Fishing with Grandma. (p. 938)
—Just Fishing with Grandma. Mayer, Mercer, illus. (p. 938)
—New Potty. (p. 1246)
Mayer, Mercer & Mayer, Marianna. Boy, a Dog, a Frog & a Friend. Mayer, Mercer & Mayer, Marianna, illus. (p. 217)
—One Frog Too Many. Mayer, Mercer & Mayer, Marianna, illus. (p. 1295)
Mayer, Mercer & Moore, Clement C. Little Critter's the Night Before Christmas. (p. 1026)
Mayer, Meyer. y a un cauchemar dans Mon. (p. 1968)
Mayer, Mindy & Mayer, Allie. Sheltered Friends. (p. 1565)
Mayer, Nicole & Mayer, Ryan. Hannah's Homework. Simmons, Russell, illus. (p. 743)
Mayer, Pamela. Don't Sneeze at the Wedding. Aviles, Martha, illus. (p. 468)
—Don't Sneeze at the Wedding. Avilés, Martha, illus. (p. 468)
Mayer, Robert H. When the Children Marched: The Birmingham Civil Rights Movement. (p. 1904)
Mayer, Robert H., ed. Civil Rights Act of 1964. (p. 324)
Mayer, Ryan, jt. auth. see Mayer, Nicole.
Mayer, Sheldon, ed. see Fox, Gardner.
Mayer, Uwe, illus. see Daynes, Katie.
Mayer, Uwe, illus. see Dickins, Rosie.
Mayer, Uwe, illus. see Helbrough, Emma.
Mayer, Uwe, illus. see Turnbull, Stephanie.
Mayer, Uwe, illus. see Wheatley, Abigail.
Mayerhofer, Felix. Horace the Great Harmonica King. MacFarlane, John, illus. (p. 797)
Mayer-Johnson, illus. see McIlquham, Mary Caroline.
Mayers, Annette Courtenay, tr. see Erguner, Kudsi.
Mayers, Shareen. Spelling & Phonics Age 5-6. (p. 1625)
Mayes, David G., et al. Adjusting to EMU. (p. 13)
Mayes, Joanne. I'm Isaac: My Brain Is Green. (p. 859)
Mayes, Rosey. Introducing... Max Mayes, Steven, illus. (p. 882)
Mayes, Stanley. Great Belzoni: The Circus Strongman Who Discovered Egypt's Treasures. (p. 714)
Mayes, Steven, illus. see Mayes, Rosey.
Mayes, Susan. Starting Point Science: What Makes It Rain? / What Makes a Flower Grow? / Where Does Electricity Come from? / What's under the Ground? Amery, Heather, ed. (p. 1644)
—Usborne Book of Dinosaurs. Rey, Luis & Trotter, Stuart, illus. (p. 1827)
—Where Does Electricity Come From? Shackell, John, illus. (p. 1907)
—Where Does Electricity Come From? Shackell, John & Scorey, John, illus. (p. 1907)
Mayesky & Kalz, Jill. My First German Phrases Translations.com Staff, tr. (p. 1206)
Mayeux, Gertie. Jesse the Oil Patch Kid. (p. 914)
Mayfield, Christine & Quinn, Kristine M. Hammurabi: Babylonian Ruler (p. 739)
—Mesopotamia. (p. 1129)
Mayfield, Dan. Jasper & the Magpie: Enjoying Special Interests Together. Merry, Alex, illus. (p. 910)
Mayfield, Helen. Enchanted Deer. (p. 523)
Mayfield, Helen, illus. see Robbins, Neal.
Mayfield, Holly. Melvin: A True Story with a Happy Ending. Gilman, Sara, illus. (p. 1125)
Mayfield, Jacqueline V. Step over into Wealth: A Step-By-Step System to Help You Manage Your Current Income. (p. 1648)
Mayfield, Jamie. Choices. (p. 309)
—Choices [Library Edition]. (p. 309)
—Destiny. (p. 430)
—Determination. (p. 431)
Mayfield, Marilee Joy. Chef Etouffee & the Great Gumbo Day. (p. 297)
—Golden Cricket: A Story of Luck & Prosperity. (p. 694)
—Tiny Adventures of Big Sister & Little Sister: A Hearts-Beared Book. (p. 1756)
Mayfield, Mary. Snowbank, the Great Texas Cow. (p. 1600)
Mayfield, Sue. Four Franks. (p. 625)
—Four Franks. Parsons, Garry, illus. (p. 625)
—I Can, You Can, Toucan! (p. 837)
—Under the Sea. Hendra, Sue, illus. (p. 1814)
Mayfield-Ingram, Karen. Journey Through Middle School Math. Humphrey Williams, Ann, illus. (p. 928)
Mayglothling, Rosie & Mayglothling, Tristan. Rowing & Sculling: Skills - Training - Techniques. (p. 1492)
Mayglothling, Tristan, jt. auth. see Mayglothling, Rosie.
Mayhall, Robin. He Loves Me, He Loves Me Not. Cella, Kristen et al, illus. (p. 756)
—He Loves Me, He Loves Me Not. Cella, Kristen & Tiede, Dirk, illus. (p. 756)
—Quest for Dragon Mountain. Martinez, Alitha, illus. (p. 1426)
—Quest for Dragon Mountain. Martinez, Alitha E., illus. (p. 1426)
Mayhar, Ardath. Medicine Walk. (p. 1119)
Mayher, Lauren. Legend of Darien: A Hero Rises: Book 1. (p. 988)
Mayhew, James. Boy. Mayhew, James, illus. (p. 217)
—Bubble & Squeak. Vulliamy, Clara, illus. (p. 233)
—Can You See a Little Bear? Morris, Jackie, illus. (p. 259)
—Ella Bella Ballerina & Cinderella. (p. 513)
—Ella Bella Ballerina & Swan Lake. (p. 513)
—Ella Bella Ballerina & the Midsummer Night's Dream. (p. 513)
—Ella Bella Ballerina & the Nutcracker. (p. 513)
—Ella Bella Ballerina & the Sleeping Beauty. (p. 513)
—Katie & the Dinosaurs. Mayhew, James, illus. (p. 944)
—Katie & the Spanish Princess. Mayhew, James, illus. (p. 944)
—Katie & the Starry Night. Mayhew, James, illus. (p. 944)
—Katie Meets the Impressionists. (p. 945)
—Katie's London Christmas. Mayhew, James, illus. (p. 945)
—Katie's Picture Show. Mayhew, James, illus. (p. 945)
—Starlight Sailor. Morris, Jackie, illus. (p. 1642)
Mayhew, James, illus. see Berry, James.
Mayhew, James, illus. see Ryan, Patrick.
Mayhew, James, jt. auth. see Husain, Shahrukh.
MAYHEW, JAMES, jt. auth. see Mayhew, James.
Mayhew, James & MAYHEW, JAMES. Carlota Visita Londres. (p. 270)
—Miranda Da la Vuelta Al Mundo. (p. 1149)
Mayhew, James & Ryan, Patrick. Shakespeare's Storybook. (p. 1559)
Mayhew, Jon. Blood Cave. Bacchin, Giorgio, illus. (p. 200)
Mayhew, Sara E., illus. see Low, Vicki.
Mayhoe, Kimberly. Miles & Zoey: Family Tree. (p. 1142)
Mayle, Peter. Amazing Adventures of Chilly Billy. Robins, Arthur, illus. (p. 52)
Mayled, Jon & Ahluwalia, Libby. Discovery: Philosophy & Ethics for OCR GCSE Religious Studies. (p. 450)
—Philosophy & Ethics. (p. 1351)
Maylin, Grace B. There Will Come Another: A Lesson from the Trees. Maylin, Grace B., photos by. (p. 1730)
Maymin, Zak. Truth: Ethics for Your Child (Black & White Edition) (p. 1794)
Maynard, Adam G. Adventures of Dynamo Dog & the Case of the Missing Jewelery. (p. 17)
Maynard, Charles W. Alps. (p. 50)
—Andes. (p. 72)
—Appalachians. (p. 92)
—Castillo de San Marcos. (p. 276)
—Fort Clatsop. (p. 623)
—Fort Laramie. (p. 623)
—Fort McHenry. (p. 623)
—Fort Sumter. (p. 623)
—Fort Ticonderoga. (p. 623)
—Going to the Great Smoky Mountains National Park. (p. 693)
—Himalayas. (p. 780)
—Jedediah Smith: Mountain Man of the American West. (p. 911)
—Jim Bridger: Frontiersman & Mountain Guide. (p. 917)
—John Charles Fremont: The Pathfinder. (p. 921)
—John Muir: Naturalist & Explorer. (p. 922)
—John Wesley Powell: Soldier, Scientist, & Explorer. (p. 923)
—Rocky Mountains. (p. 1484)
—Technology of Ancient Greece. (p. 1711)
—Technology of Ancient Rome. (p. 1711)
—Ural Mountains. (p. 1825)
—Zebulon Pike: Soldier Explorer of the American Southwest. (p. 1985)
—Zebulon Pike: Soldier-Explorer of the American Southwest. (p. 1985)
Maynard, Christopher. I Wonder Why Planes Have Wings: And Other Questions about Transportation. (p. 849)
—Why Do Sunflowers Face the Sun? Questions Children Ask about Nature. (p. 1924)
Maynard, Christopher & Christopher, Maynard. Aviones Tienen Alas. (p. 120)
Maynard, Christopher & Martin, Terry. Why Do We Laugh? Questions Children Ask about the Human Body. (p. 1924)
—Why Does Lightning Strike? Questions Children Ask about Weather. (p. 1924)
Maynard, Christopher & White, Terry. Why Are Zebras Black & White? Questions Children Ask about Colour. (p. 1922)
Maynard, Christopher, et al. How Your Body Works. (p. 823)
Maynard, Deanne. Whisper on Your Pillow. (p. 1912)
Maynard, Joyce. Cloud Chamber. (p. 334)
Maynard, Marc, illus. see Litchfield, Jo.
Mayne, Andrew. Handbook of Super Powers: Magic Tricks that Make It Look Like You Possess Super-human Abilities. (p. 740)
Mayne, Brian. Sam, el Genio Magico: Piensa lo Que Quieres, No lo Que Temes. (p. 1506)
Mayne, Michael, illus. see Biggs, Pauline.
Mayne, Ruth, ed. see Drahos, Peter.
Mayne, William. Earthfasts. (p. 497)
Maynor, Megan. Ella & Penguin Stick Together. Bonnet, Rosalinde, illus. (p. 513)
Mayo, C. M., ed. Reconquest/Reconquista: Bi-Lingual Writing from North America. (p. 1452)
Mayo Clinic Center for Social Media Staff. Mayo Clinic Kids' Cookbook: 50 Favorite Recipes for Fun & Healthy Eating. (p. 1113)
Mayo Clinic Staff. Mayo Clinic Plan: 10 Essential Steps to a Better Body & Healthier Life. (p. 1113)
Mayo Clinic Staff & Mayo Foundation for Medical Education and Research Staff, contrib. by. Heart Healthy Eating Guide for Women. (p. 759)
Mayo Clinic Staff, contrib. by. 10 Tips for Better Hearing. (p. 1994)
—20 Tasty Recipes for People with Diabetes. (p. 1995)
—8 Ways to Lower Your Risk of Heart Attack or Stroke. (p. 1993)
—Alternative Medicine & Your Health. (p. 50)
—Eating Out: Your Pocket Guide to Healthy Dining. (p. 501)
—Everyday Fitness: Look Good, Feel Good. (p. 543)
—Getting the Most from Your Medications. (p. 669)
—Healthy Meals for Hurried Lives. (p. 758)
—Healthy Traveler: Answers on Staying Well While Away from Home. (p. 759)
—Healthy Weight for Life. (p. 759)
—Live Longer, Live Better: Personal Advice from Mayo Clinic Experts. (p. 1040)
—Living Disease-Free: Strategies for Reducing Your Risk of Disease. (p. 1040)
—Medical Tests Every Man Needs. (p. 1119)
—Your Guide to Vitamin & Mineral Supplements. (p. 1980)
—Your Healthy Back. (p. 1980)
Mayo, Diana. House That Jack Built. (p. 804)
—Isis & Osiris. (p. 891)
Mayo, Diana, illus. see Barkow, Henriette.
Mayo, Diana, illus. see Casey, Dawn.
Mayo, Diana, illus. see Dorling Kindersley Publishing Staff.
Mayo, Diana, illus. see Lister, Mary.
Mayo, Diana, illus. see Lupton, Hugh.
Mayo, Diana, illus. see Peters, Andrew Fusek.
Mayo, Diana, illus. see Peters, Andrew.
Mayo, Diana, jt. auth. see Williams, Brenda.
Mayo, Edith P., ed. Smithsonian Book of the First Ladies. (p. 1594)
Mayo Foundation for Medical Education and Research Staff, jt. contrib. by see Mayo Clinic Staff.
Mayo, Frank. King Midas & the Golden Touch: A Tale about Greed. (p. 958)
Mayo, Frank, illus. see Wilsdon, Christina.
Mayo, Gretchen Will. Applesauce. (p. 93)
—Cereal. (p. 287)
—Frank Lloyd Wright. (p. 628)
—Milk. (p. 1143)
—Where Does Our Food Come From? (p. 1907)
Mayo, Gretchen Will & O'Hern, Kerri. Hermanos Wright. Isaacs, Rebekah & Timmons, Jonathan, illus. (p. 771)
—Wright Brothers. Isaacs, Rebekah & Timmons, Jonathan, illus. (p. 1963)
Mayo, Gretchen Will, et al. Wright Brothers. (p. 1963)
Mayo, Jason. Do Witches Make Fishes? (p. 457)
Mayo, Jeanne. Uncensored: Dating, Friendship, & Sex. (p. 1811)
Mayo, Margaret. Choo Choo Clickety-Clack! Ayliffe, Alex, illus. (p. 310)
—Dig Dig Digging. Ayliffe, Alex, illus. (p. 438)
—Polly of the Circus. (p. 1381)
—Zoom, Rocket, Zoom! Ayliffe, Alex, illus. (p. 1989)
Mayo, Simon. Itch: The Explosive Adventures of an Element Hunter. (p. 895)
—Itch Rocks: It's Time to Save the World Again. (p. 895)
Mayor, Adrienne, jt. auth. see Aronson, Marc.
Mayor, Archer. Second Mouse. (p. 1539)
—Sniper's Wife. (p. 1598)
Mayor, Virgil & Apostol, Virgil Mayor. Way of the Ancient Healer: Sacred Teachings from the Philippine Ancestral Traditions. (p. 1864)
Mayowa-Harrison, Lady Paula Merry. Buckaroos. (p. 234)
Mayr, Amy. I Can Cut! (p. 835)
—I Can Trace! (p. 836)
Mayr, Diane. North Carolina. (p. 1264)
—Run, Turkey, Run! Rader, Laura, illus. (p. 1496)
Mayr, Diane & Sisters, Write. Women of the Constitution State: 25 Connecticut Women You Should Know. Greenleaf, Lisa, illus. (p. 1946)
Mayrl, Damon. Potawatamie of Wisconsin. (p. 1388)
—Potawatomi of Wisconsin. (p. 1388)
Mayrock, Aija. Survival Guide to Bullying: Written by a Teen. (p. 1686)
Mays, Blanche, ed. My Book about God's World. Magagna, Anna Marie, illus. (p. 1198)
Mays, Charli. Lifetime from Before (p. 1014)
Mays, Lydia, jt. auth. see Meyers, Barbara.
Mays, Stan. Wicked Little Camp Story. (p. 1927)
Mays, Victor, illus. see Campion, Nardi Reeder.
Mays, Victor, illus. see Moody, Ralph.
Mayse, Arthur. Handliner's Island. (p. 740)
Maysonet, Melody. Work of Art. (p. 1952)
Mazali, Gustavo, illus. see Brooks, Felicity & Durber, Matt.
Mazali, Gustavo, illus. see Flor Ada, Alma.
Mazali, Gustavo, illus. see Gikow, Louise.
Mazali, Gustavo, illus. see Moore-Mallinos, Jennifer.
Mazali, Gustavo, illus. see Munoz, Isabel.
Mazali, Gustavo, illus. see Munoz, Isabel.
Mazali, Gustavo, illus. see Muñoz, Isabel.
Mazali, Gustavo, illus. see Muñoz, Isabel.
Mazali, Gustavo, illus. see Olesen, Cecilie.
Mazdra, Marian. Austria. (p. 116)
Maze, Aubrie. Cutting up Laughing & Crafting: Ideas That Helped One Teenager Through Cancer Treatments. (p. 396)
Maze, Deborah, illus. see Collins, Carolyn Strom & Eriksson, Christina Wyss.
Maze, Ellen, illus. see Ridley, K. F.
Maze, Stephanie. Momentos Tiernos en el Reino Animal: Los Animales y Sus Bebes. (p. 1161)
Maze, Stephanie, ed. Amusing Moments in the Wild: Animals & Their Friends. (p. 66)
—Beautiful Moments in the Wild: Animals & Their Colors. (p. 153)
—Healthy Foods from A to Z: Comida Sana de la a a la Z. Comet, Renee, photos by. (p. 758)
—Momentos de Paz en el Reino Animal: Los Animales y Sus Hogares. (p. 1161)
—Momentos Divertidos en el Reino Animal: Los Animales y Sus Amigos. (p. 1161)
—Momentos Hermosos en el Reino Animal: Los Animales y Sus Colores. (p. 1161)
—Momentos Tiernos en el Reino Animal: Los Animales y Sus Bebes. (p. 1162)
—Peaceful Moments in the Wild: Animals & Their Homes. (p. 1332)
—Tender Moments in the Wild: Animals & Their Babies. (p. 1719)
Mazeikas, Joy. Egg Song. (p. 506)
Mazellan, Ron. We Will Walk. (p. 1868)
Mazellan, Ron, illus. see Dungy, Tony & Dungy, Lauren.
Mazellan, Ron, illus. see Fawcett, Cheryl & Newman, Robert C.
Mazellan, Ron, illus. see Harper, Jo & Harper, Josephine.
Mazellan, Ron, illus. see Michelson, Richard.
Mazellan, Ron, illus. see Vaughan, Marcia.
Mazellan, Ron, jt. auth. see Johnston, Tony.
Mazer, Anne. Best Is Yet to Come. (p. 170)
—Everything New under the Sun. (p. 545)
—Good Things Come in Small Packages. (p. 700)
—It's Music to My Ears. (p. 897)
—Now You See It, Now You Don't. (p. 1269)
—Some Things Never Change. (p. 1609)
—That's the Way the Cookie Crumbles. (p. 1727)
—Violet Makes a Splash. Brown, Bill, illus. (p. 1843)
Mazer, Anne, jt. auth. see Danziger, Paula.
Mazer, Anne, jt. auth. see Potter, Ellen.
Mazer, Harry. Boy at War: A Novel of Pearl Harbor. (p. 217)
—Boy No More. (p. 218)
—Heroes Don't Run. (p. 772)
—Last Mission. (p. 978)
—My Brother Abe: Sally Lincoln's Story. (p. 1199)
—Snow Bound. (p. 1598)
Mazer, Harry & Lerangis, Peter. Somebody, Please Tell Me Who I Am. (p. 1609)
Mazer, Norma Fox. Babyface. (p. 128)
—Crazy Fish. (p. 377)
—Good Night, Maman. (p. 699)
—Missing Girl. (p. 1152)
—Missing Pieces. (p. 1152)
—Ten Ways to Make My Sister Disappear. (p. 1719)
—What I Believe. (p. 1886)
—When We First Met. (p. 1905)
Mazer, Norma Fox, jt. auth. see Metzger, Lois.
Mazerac, Joseph. ANDY, Book 1: The Rise of David. Mazerac, Joseph, illus. (p. 73)
—Andy, Book 2: The Rise of David. (p. 73)
Mazeroski, Kelly. Maz, You're Up! Lauso, Judith, illus. (p. 1113)
Mazibuko, Luthando, illus. see Garrott, Dawn E.
Mazibuko, Luthando, illus. see Jaskwhich, Cynthia Shepard.
Mazille, Capucine, illus. see Davidson, Alice Joyce.
Mazille, Capucine, illus. see Harcourt, Lalie & Wortzman, Rickie.
Mazo, Chaim, ed. see Karlin, Ann Bell.
Mazo, Chaim, ed. see Karlin, Ann.
Mazula, Derek. Drifen's Tale. (p. 485)
Mazumdar, Sintu, illus. see Thorp, Michael C.
Mazur, Allan. Implausible Beliefs: In the Bible, Astrology, & UFOs. (p. 862)

Mazur, Barry. Imagining Numbers: (Particularly the Square Root of Minus Fifteen) (p. 861)
Mazur, Cathy. Stanley Seagull. Gedrich, Colleen, illus. (p. 1640)
Mazur, Cathy May. Pizza Heart. Tyler, Tim, illus. (p. 1365)
Mazur, Danielle, ed. see Emerson, Kim & Antebi, Marcus.
Mazur, Gabrielle. Boppy & Me. Collins, Linda, illus. (p. 213)
—Boppy & Me. Colllins, Linda, illus. (p. 213)
Mazur, Glen A. Digital Multimeter Principles. (p. 439)
—Electrical Motor Controls for Integrated Systems Resource Guide: Resource Guide. (p. 509)
—Electrical Motor Controls for Integrated Systems Applications Manual: Manual. (p. 509)
—Electrical Motor Controls for Integrated Systems Applications Manual: Instructor's Guide. (p. 509)
—Electrical/Electronic Fundamentals Video Series. (p. 509)
—Instructor's Guide. (p. 878)
—Principios del Multimetro Digital. (p. 1406)
—Workbook. (p. 1952)
Mazur, Glen A., jt. auth. see Rockis, Gary.
Mazur, Glen A. & Proctor, Thomas E. Electrical/Electronic Symbol Transparencies: Transparencies. (p. 509)
—Electrical/Electronic Systems: Transparencies. (p. 509)
—Troubleshooting Electrical/Electronic Systems: Transparencies. (p. 1790)
—Troubleshooting Electrical/Electronic Systems: Answer Key (for Text) (p. 1790)
—Troubleshooting Electrical/Electronic Systems: Answer Key (for Workbook) (p. 1790)
—Troubleshooting Electrical/Electronic Systems. (p. 1790)
Mazur, Glen A. & Weindorf, William J. Electric Motor Drive Installation & Troubleshooting: Text. (p. 508)
—Electric Motor Drive Installation & Troubleshooting: Answer Key. (p. 508)
Mazur, Glen A. & Zurlis, Peter A. Electrical Principles & Practices: Text. (p. 509)
—Electrical Principles & Practices: Answer Key. (p. 509)
—Electrical Principles & Practices: Resource Guide. (p. 509)
—Electrical Principles & Practices. (p. 509)
Mazur, Joseph. Euclid in the Rainforest: Discovering Universal Truth in Logic & Math. (p. 540)
Mazur, Kathy. It's Springtime in My Backyard. (p. 899)
—My Story... I'd like to Tell. (p. 1219)
Mazurak, Tena. Harley Hits a Homer. (p. 749)
Mazurick, Shannon K. Gemm: The Search for the Gem. (p. 660)
—Gemm: The Treasure Hunt with Griffin. (p. 660)
Mazurke, Rachel. Mr. & Mrs. Duck: Busy Day, The Accident, New Home or the Brook, Dirty Water Again. (p. 1184)
Mazurkiewicz, Jessica. 3-D Coloring Book—Abstractions. (p. 1991)
—3-D Coloring Book—Butterflies. (p. 1991)
—3-D Coloring Book—Crazy Christmas. (p. 1991)
—3-D Coloring Book—Happy Halloween. (p. 1991)
—3-D Coloring Book—Mosaic Madness. (p. 1991)
—Abstractions. (p. 7)
—Alphascapes. (p. 50)
—Animals Mosaics Coloring Book. (p. 83)
—Butterfly Fun Activity Book. (p. 247)
—ChristmasScapes. (p. 316)
—COLORTWIST — Blue Coloring Book. (p. 346)
—COLORTWIST — Green Coloring Book. (p. 346)
—COLORTWIST — Pink Coloring Book. (p. 346)
—COLORTWIST — Purple Coloring Book. (p. 346)
—Coral Reef Stained Glass Coloring Book. (p. 366)
—Creative Haven Beautiful Butterfly Designs Coloring Book. (p. 379)
—Creative Haven Magnificent Mosaics Stained Glass Coloring Book. (p. 379)
—Creative Haven Simply Abstract Stained Glass Coloring Book. (p. 379)
—Creatures of the Night Stained Glass Coloring Book. (p. 380)
—Dragons Activity Book. (p. 478)
—Eco-Mania Mazes. (p. 502)
—Glitter Fantasy Butterflies Stickers. (p. 684)
—HalloweenScapes. (p. 739)
—Haunted House Activity Book. (p. 753)
—How to Create Mehndi Designs. (p. 816)
—How to Draw Mandalas. (p. 818)
—Magnificent Mosaics. (p. 1076)
—Out of This World Circular Designs Stained Glass Coloring Book. (p. 1311)
—Psalms Stained Glass Coloring Book. (p. 1413)
—Santa's Busy Workshop Stained Glass Jr. Coloring Book. (p. 1513)
—Santa's Workshop Stained Glass Coloring Book. (p. 1513)
—Seashell Patterns Coloring Book. (p. 1538)
—SPARK - Mandalas Coloring Book. (p. 1622)
—Treasure Hunt. (p. 1781)
—Winter Fun Activity Book. (p. 1938)
—Wonder Wings Butterfly Coloring Book. (p. 1947)
Mazurkiewicz, Jessica & Coloring Books Staff. Creatures of the Deep Stained Glass Coloring Book. (p. 380)
—Organic Designs Coloring Book. (p. 1303)
Mazurkiewicz, Jessica & Dahlen, Noelle. 3-D Coloring Book—Here Comes Santa Claus! (p. 1991)
Mazurkiewicz, Jessica & Noble, Marty. 3-D Coloring Book - Christmas Designs. (p. 1991)
Mazurkiewicz, Jessica, et al. Floral Designs. (p. 606)
—Skyscapes. (p. 1587)
Mazxzeo, J. L. Xavia's X Book (BL) el libro X de Xavia (PB) (p. 1967)
Mazza, Barbara. How the Short Vowels Got Their Sound. (p. 813)
Mazzafro, Howard. No Room for George. (p. 1260)
Mazzara, Mauro, illus. see Breed, Simon & Butterfield, Moira.
Mazzara, Mauro, illus. see Ticktock & Pipe, Jim.
Mazzei, Miriam, illus. see Pinto, Marie Parks.
Mazzeo, J. L. Aimee's A Book. (p. 30)
—Aimee's A Book (BL) el libro A de Aimée (p. 30)
—Aimee's A Book (PB) (p. 30)
—Bebe's B Book. (p. 155)
—Bebe's B Book/ el libro B de Bebé (p. 155)
—Cassie's C Book. (p. 276)
—Cassie's C Book (BL) el libro C de Cassie: S (p. 276)
—Cassie's C Book (BL) el libro C de Cassie (PB) (p. 276)
—Cassie's C Book (PB) (p. 276)
—Delia's D Book. (p. 425)
—Delia's D Book /el libro D de Delia (p. 425)
—Emma's E Book. (p. 520)
—Emma's E Book (PB) (p. 520)
—Emma's E-Book / El Libro E de Emma (p. 520)
—Faye's F Book. (p. 578)
—Faye's F Book (BL) el libro F de Faye (PB) (p. 578)
—Faye's F Book (PB) (p. 578)
—George's G Book. (p. 665)
—George's G Book (BL) el libro G de George (p. 665)
—George's G Book (BL) el libro G de George (PB) (p. 665)
—George's G Book (PB) (p. 665)
—Henry's H Book. (p. 769)
—Henry's H Book (BL) el libro H de Henry (p. 769)
—Henry's H Book (BL) el libro H de Henry (PB) (p. 769)
—Henry's H Book (PB) (p. 769)
—Izzy's I Book. (p. 901)
—Izzy's I Book (BL) el libro I de Izzy (p. 901)
—Izzy's I Book (BL) el libro I de Izzy (PB) (p. 901)
—Izzy's I Book (PB) (p. 901)
—Jade's J Book. (p. 905)
—Jade's J Book (BL) el libro J de Jade (p. 905)
—Jade's J Book (BL) el libro J de Jade (PB) (p. 905)
—Jade's J Book (PB) (p. 905)
—Kelsey's K Book. (p. 948)
—Kelsey's K Book (BL) el libro K de Kelsey (p. 948)
—Kelsey's K Book (BL) el libro K de Kelsey (PB) (p. 948)
—Kelsey's K Book (PB) (p. 948)
—Libro F de Faye (p. 1006)
—Logan's L Book. (p. 1045)
—Logan's L Book (BL) el libro L de Logan (p. 1045)
—Logan's L Book (BL) el libro L de Logan (PB) (p. 1045)
—Logan's L Book (PB) (p. 1045)
—Mia's M Book. (p. 1134)
—Mia's M Book (BL) el libro M de Mia (p. 1134)
—Mia's M Book (BL) el libro M de Mia (PB) (p. 1134)
—Mia's M Book (PB) (p. 1134)
—Nate's N Book. (p. 1231)
—Nate's N Book (BL) el libro N de Nate (p. 1231)
—Nate's N Book (BL) el libro N de Nate (PB) (p. 1231)
—Nate's N Book (PB) (p. 1231)
—Owen's O Book. (p. 1314)
—Owen's O Book (BL) el libro O de Owen (p. 1314)
—Owen's O Book (BL) el libro O de Owen (PB) (p. 1314)
—Owen's O Book (PB) (p. 1314)
—Perer's P Book (p. 1341)
—Peter's P Book (BL) el libro P de Peter (p. 1347)
—Peter's P Book (BL) el libro P de Peter (PB) (p. 1347)
—Peter's P Book (PB) (p. 1347)
—Quinn's Q Book. (p. 1428)
—Quinn's Q Book (BL) el libro Q de Quinn (p. 1428)
—Quinn's Q Book (BL) el libro Q de Quinn (PB) (p. 1428)
—Quinn's Q Book (PB) (p. 1428)
—Rosie's R Book. (p. 1490)
—Rosie's R Book (BL) el libro R de Rosie (p. 1490)
—Rosie's R Book (BL) el libro R de Rosie (PB) (p. 1490)
—Rosie's R Book (PB) (p. 1490)
—Sofie's S Book. (p. 1605)
—Sofie's S Book (BL) el libro S de Sofie (p. 1605)
—Sofie's S Book (BL) el libro S de Sofie (PB) (p. 1605)
—Sofie's S Book (PB) (p. 1605)
—Tad's T Book. (p. 1695)
—Tad's T Book (BL) el libro T de Tad (p. 1695)
—Tad's T Book (BL) el libro T de Tad (PB) (p. 1695)
—Tad's T Book (PB) (p. 1695)
—Uri's U Book. (p. 1825)
—Uri's U Book (BL) el libro U de Uri (p. 1825)
—Uri's U Book (BL) el libro U de Uri (PB) (p. 1825)
—Uri's U Book (PB) (p. 1825)
—Vera's V Book. (p. 1836)
—Vera's V Book (BL) el libro V de Vera (p. 1836)
—Vera's V Book (BL) el libro V de Vera (PB) (p. 1836)
—Vera's V Book (PB) (p. 1836)
—Will's W Book. (p. 1934)
—Will's W Book (BL) el libro W de Will (p. 1934)
—Will's W Book (BL) el libro W de Will (PB) (p. 1934)
—Will's W Book (PB) (p. 1934)
—Xavia's X Book. (p. 1967)
—Xavia's X Book (BL) el libro X de Xavia (p. 1967)
—Xavia's X Book (PB) (p. 1967)
—Yola's Y Book. (p. 1972)
—Yola's Y Book (BL) el libro Y de Yola (p. 1972)
—Yola's Y Book (BL) el libro Y de Yola (PB) (p. 1972)
—Yola's Y Book (PB) (p. 1972)
—Zach's Z Book. (p. 1984)
—Zach's Z Book (BL) el libro Z de Zach (p. 1984)
—Zach's Z Book (BL) el libro Z de Zach (PB) (p. 1984)
—Zach's Z Book (PB) (p. 1984)
Mazzino, Christopher, jt. auth. see High School, West Scranton.
Mazzio, Joann. Leaving Eldorado. (p. 986)
—One Who Came Back. (p. 1297)
Mazzola, Frank, Jr., illus. see Pallotta, Jerry.
Mazzola, Lori. Tales of the Tree People to Tree... or. (p. 1703)
Mazzola, Lori E. Forbidden Forest: Tales of the Tree People (p. 616)
Mazzon, Michelle, illus. see Castellan, Andrea
Mazzucchelli, David, illus. see Various Authors.
Mazzucco, Jennifer, illus. see Davis, Donald.
Mazzucco, Jennifer, illus. see Wahl, Jan.
Mba, Ogochukwu. Roaches (p. 1476)
Mbairamadji, Koffi. African Savannah Stories: Volume 2 Of 2. (p. 28)
—African Savannah Stories, Volume 1. Mbairamadji, Koffi, illus. (p. 28)
Mbanze, Dinah M. & Daly, Niki. Berry Basket: Three African Folktales. (p. 167)
Mbonu, Ngozi Elizabeth. Tatiana. Taylor, Kristen Michelle, illus. (p. 1707)
Mboya, Sharif. Heart Fealt Doses of Reality. Mboya, Sharif, illus. (p. 759)
Mbuthia, Waithira. My Sister's Wedding: A Story of Kenya. Karanja, Geoffrey Gacheru, illus. (p. 1218)
Mbuyazi, Phiwayinkosi G. Wiby Kids - How It All Began. (p. 1927)
MC, ed. see Inkpen, Mick.
Mc Collin, Alethea. Cloud Catcher. (p. 334)
Mc Daniel, Jessica & Morgan, Amanda. Goodnight Tigers. (p. 701)
Mc Kelvey, Shawn, illus. see Hurwitz, Kathleen A.
Mc Shane, Mary. Karena the Fairy. (p. 943)
—Karena the Fairy & the Bat Colony. (p. 943)
McAdam, Claudia Cangilla. Christmas Tree Cried: The Story of the White House Christmas Tree. Crum, Anna-Maria, illus. (p. 316)
—Do You See What I See? Texas. (p. 458)
McAdam, Fraser, jt. auth. see Prins, Piet.
McAdam, Jessica & Aitchison, Kathleen. Symbols of Freedom. (p. 1693)
McAdams, Caleb, illus. see McAdams, Susan.
Mcadams, Kate. Flynn the Post Office Mouse. (p. 610)
McAdams, Marisa. Mouse Adventures. (p. 1181)
McAdams Moore, Carol. Phonics Comics: Cave Dave - Level 1. Dammer, Mike, illus. (p. 1352)
McAdams, Susan. Shubert. McAdams, Caleb, illus. (p. 1571)
McAdoo, Grami, illus. see Kaulen, Diane Bouman.
McAdoo, O'Pa, illus. see Kaulen, Diane Bouman.
McAfee, Joan K. Road to el Dorado. (p. 1477)
McAleer, Kathleen, jt. auth. see Mcaleer, Sarah.
Mcaleer, Sarah & McAleer, Kathleen. Don't Tee Tee in Your Tutu: A Potty Training Book for Young Ballerinas. (p. 468)
Mcaleney, Kimberly. Mouse & the Music Box: A Bedtime Story. (p. 1182)
McAlley, Susan, illus. see Hirsch, Jennifer & Jones, Michelle.
McAlley, Susan, illus. see McDonald, Megan.
McAlley, Susan, illus. see Tripp, Valerie.
McAlister, Bobbie. Prancing Deer: An Alegory, for Kids, for Parents, for Lovers...for Life. McAlister, Bobbie, illus. (p. 1393)
McAlister, Caroline. Holy Mole! A Folktale from Mexico. Czerneckí, Stefan, illus. (p. 791)
McAlister, Hugh. Flight of the Silver Ship: Around the World Aboard a Giant Dirigible. (p. 604)
McAlister, Kerrie, jt. auth. see Kirkman, Steve.
McAllan, Kate. Arctic & Antarctic Habitats. (p. 96)
—Urban Habitats. (p. 1825)
—Water Is Precious. (p. 1863)
McAllan, Marina, illus. see Egan, Cecilia.
McAllen, Bob. Dirtiest Hair in the World. (p. 446)
McAllister, Angela. Dyna Lle'r Wyt Ti! Williams, Dylan & Jones, Gwen Angharad, trs. from ENG. (p. 491)
—Jasmine's Lion. Fitzpatrick, Marie-Louise, illus. (p. 910)
—My Mom Has X-Ray Vision. Smith, Alex T., illus. (p. 1214)
—Runaway. (p. 1496)
—Żółw I Zajac: Bajka Ezopa. Heale, Jonathan, illus. (p. 1987)
McAllister, Angela, jt. auth. see Churchill, Vicki.
McAllister, Angela & Hooper, Mary. Take a Kiss to School. Hellard, Sue, illus. (p. 1696)
McAllister, Angela & Scholastic, Inc. Staff. Santa's Little Helper. Howarth, Daniel, illus. (p. 1513)
McAllister, Ava. Honor Tree. (p. 795)
Mcallister, Bruce. Village Sang to the Sea. (p. 1842)
McAllister, Chris, illus. see Walton, Rick.
McAllister, Heather. Who You Are Is What You Do: Making Choices about Life after School. (p. 1919)
Mcallister, Herb West. Doo West to Toadstool. (p. 469)
McAllister, Ian. Attitude Matters: Public Opinion in Australia Towards Defence & Security. (p. 114)
—Great Bear Sea: Exploring the Marine Life of a Pacific Paradise (p. 714)
—Salmon Bears: Giants of the Great Bear Rainforest (p. 1505)
—Sea Wolves: Living Wild in the Great Bear Rainforest (p. 1536)
McAllister, Margaret. Emily & the Lamb. Vince, Dawn, illus. (p. 518)
—High Crag Linn. (p. 777)
—Life Shop. (p. 1013)
—Octave of Angels. (p. 1277)
—Stories of the Saints. Massari, Alida, illus. (p. 1655)
—Women of the Bible. Massari, Alida, illus. (p. 1946)
McAllister, Melanie. Rain Music. (p. 1435)
McAllister O'Connell, Andrea. Jackson, Josie, & the (almost) Free Lunch. (p. 904)
McAlpin, Autumn. Real Life, Here I Come! A Personal Guide to Making It on Your Own. (p. 1448)
McAlpine, Gordon. Mystery Box: A Novel about the Creators of Nancy Drew & the Hardy Boys. (p. 1224)
—Once upon a Midnight Eerie: Book #2. Zuppardi, Sam, illus. (p. 1293)
—Once upon a Midnight Eerie. Zuppardi, Sam, illus. (p. 1293)
—Pet & the Pendulum. Zuppardi, Sam, illus. (p. 1345)
—Tell-Tale Start. Zuppardi, Sam, illus. (p. 1717)
McAlpine, Margaret. Working in Banking & Finance. (p. 1953)
—Working in Film & Television. (p. 1953)
—Working in Health Care. (p. 1953)
—Working in Music & Dance. (p. 1953)
—Working in the Fashion Industry. (p. 1953)
—Working in the Food Industry. (p. 1953)
—Working in Travel & Tourism. (p. 1953)
—Working with Animals. (p. 1953)
—Working with Children. (p. 1953)
—Working with Computers. (p. 1953)
McAlpine, Stacy. To Be with You (p. 1758)
McAndrew, Kelly, jt. auth. see Fluharty, Jeff.
Mcandrew, Maria. Invasion of the Evil Chocolate Chips. (p. 883)
McAneney, Caitie. 20 Fun Facts about Native American Women. (p. 1995)
—Bottlenose Dolphins. (p. 215)
—Freaky Stories from Beneath the Sea. (p. 632)
Mcaneney, Caitie. Let's Talk about It (p. 1001)
McAneney, Caitie. Life of Sacagawea. (p. 1012)
—Look Out for the Raccoon! (p. 1050)
—Mujeres en la Exploracion Del Espacio (Women in Space) (p. 1189)
—Scorpion vs. Black Widow. (p. 1530)
—Standing in the Secretary of State's Shoes. (p. 1639)
Mcaneney, Caitie. Topaz. (p. 1769)
McAneney, Caitlin. Becoming Texas: Early Statehood. (p. 156)
—Compass Rose & Cardinal Directions. (p. 352)
—First Flight Across the Atlantic. (p. 595)
—Graphing the Weather. (p. 711)
—How Elephants & Other Animals Hear the Earth. (p. 809)
—I Have Been Cyberbullied. Now What? (p. 839)
—Life Cycle of a Butterfly. (p. 1008)
—Locusts. (p. 1045)
—Lost Colony of Roanoke. (p. 1055)
—Moving (p. 1183)
—North American Birds: Represent & Solve Problems Involving Multiplication. (p. 1264)
—Peanut & Other Food Allergies (p. 1332)
—Quadrilaterals in Art: Reason with Shapes & Their Attributes. (p. 1422)
—Women in Space. (p. 1946)
McAneney, Robert. America's Natural Resources. (p. 64)
McAnlis-McMurdie, Jean. Land of the Morning. (p. 973)
McAnulty, Stacy. Dear Santasaurus. Kaminsky, Jef, illus. (p. 419)
McArdle, Donald. Santa's Newest Friend. (p. 1513)
McArdle, Paula, illus. see Shelby, Anne.
McArdle, Thaneeya. Draw Groovy: Groovy Girls Do-It-Yourself Drawing & Coloring Book. (p. 480)
—Everything Girls Ultimate Body Art Book: 50+ Cool Doodle Tattoos to Create & Wear! (p. 544)
McArthur, Amanda, jt. auth. see Stuart.
McArthur, Cathy E. Adventures of Elvis the Groundhog: The Golden Glow. (p. 17)
—Adventures of Elvis the Groundhog: Mulberry's Field. (p. 17)
—Story of Chris Moose Stutz, Chris, illus. (p. 1657)
McArthur, Debra. Desert Storm—the First Persian Gulf War in American History. (p. 429)
—John Steinbeck: The Grapes of Wrath & of Mice & Men. (p. 922)
—Kansas-Nebraska Act & Bleeding Kansas in American History. (p. 943)
—Mark Twain. (p. 1095)
—Raoul Wallenberg: Rescuing Thousands from the Nazis' Grasp. (p. 1438)
—Student's Guide to Edgar Allan Poe. (p. 1669)
—Student's Guide to William Faulkner. (p. 1669)
—Voice for Kanzas. (p. 1847)
McArthur, Meher. ABC of What Art Can Be. Watson, Esther Pearl, illus. (p. 3)
McArthur, Nancy. Mystery of the Plant That Ate Dirty Socks. (p. 1226)
—Plant That Ate Dirty Socks. (p. 1369)
McArthur, Shallee. Unhappening of Genesis Lee. (p. 1817)
McArtor, Mike. Dragons Revisited. (p. 479)
McAskin, Denice, illus. see Hemminger, Marcia.
McAtee, Rick. Alphabetland the Beginning. Hammons, Barbara, illus. (p. 50)
—Alphabetland the Story of R. Hammons, Barbara, illus. (p. 50)
McAteer, Thomas, illus. see Vetter Squires, Diane.
McAulay, Alex. Oblivion Road. (p. 1275)
McAulay, Mary. Prudence's Progress: A Battered Woman Gets Revenge— Non-Violently. (p. 1413)
McAuley, Amy. Violins of Autumn. (p. 1843)
McAuley, Kelly & Kalman, Bobbie. Living in Shelters. (p. 1041)
—Preparing for Disasters. (p. 1396)
McAuley, Mary & Bloomsbury Publishing Staff. Children in Custody: Anglo-Russian Perspectives. (p. 302)
McAuley, Rowan. Best Christmas Ever. (p. 168)
—Big Split. (p. 184)
—Class Captain. (p. 327)
—Holiday. (p. 788)
—Music Mad. (p. 1193)
—New Girl. Oswald, Ash, illus. (p. 1244)
—Sleepover! Oswald, Ash, illus. (p. 1589)
McAuley, Rowan, jt. auth. see Badger, Meredith.
McAuliffe, Bill. Alzheimer's Disease. (p. 51)
—Cancer. (p. 260)
—Clouds. (p. 335)
—Colorado - Avalanche. (p. 343)
—Diabetes. (p. 433)
—Forecasting. (p. 617)
—Galaxies. (p. 653)
—Hurricanes. (p. 830)
—Mysteries of the Universe: Galaxies. (p. 1222)
—NHL - History & Heroes: The\Story of the Toronto Maple Leafs. (p. 1250)
—Snow. (p. 1598)
—Story of the Colorado Avalanche. (p. 1660)
—Thunderstorms. (p. 1746)
—Tornadoes. (p. 1770)
—Toronto - Maple Leafs. (p. 1770)
McAuliffe, Carolyn. Assassination of John F. Kennedy. (p. 107)
McAuliffe, Carolyn, ed. Assassination of John F. Kennedy. (p. 107)
McAuliffe, Emily. Alabama Facts & Symbols. (p. 33)
—Arizona Facts & Symbols. (p. 98)
—California Facts & Symbols. (p. 253)
—Colorado Facts & Symbols. (p. 343)
—Connecticut Facts & Symbols. (p. 358)
—Florida Facts & Symbols. (p. 607)
—Illinois Facts & Symbols. (p. 857)
—Maine Facts & Symbols. (p. 1077)
—New York Facts & Symbols. (p. 1248)
—Ohio Facts & Symbols. (p. 1281)
—Oregon Facts & Symbols. (p. 1303)
McAuliffe, John Jobin, jt. auth. see Mcauliffe, Timothy.
McAuliffe, Nichola. Attila, Loolagax & the Eagle. Collins, Ross, tr. (p. 114)
Mcauliffe, Timothy & McAuliffe, John Jobin. Snappy the Fox & Other Sleep Time Stories. (p. 1597)
McAuslan, Fiona & Nicholson, Peter. Resolving Anger Book. (p. 1463)

—Resolving Bereavement. (p. 1463)
—Resolving Bullying Book. (p. 1463)
—Resolving Sibling Rivalry Book. (p. 1463)
McAvinn, Douglas, illus. see Opie, Brenda.
McAvinn, Douglas, jt. auth. see Opie, Brenda.
McBain, Ed, ed. see Farris, John & King, Stephen.
McBain, Madelaine (Maddie). Day with Non. (p. 415)
McBay, Bruce. Angels Inc. LaFave, Kim, illus. (p. 75)
—Waiting for Sarah. (p. 1853)
McBay, Bruce, jt. auth. see Heneghan, James.
McBay, Bruce & Heneghan, James. Waiting for Sarah. (p. 1853)
McBee, Scott, illus. see Koeppel, Ruth.
McBee, Travis. Little Holiday Thrill. (p. 1029)
McBratney, Sam. Adventures of Little Nutbrown Hare. (p. 19)
—Colors Everywhere. Jeram, Anita, illus. (p. 345)
—Guess How Much I Love You. Jeram, Anita, illus. (p. 728)
—Guess How Much I Love You. Jeram, Anita, illus. (p. 729)
—Guess How Much I Love You 20th Anniversary Edition. Jeram, Anita, illus. (p. 729)
—Guess How Much I Love You All Year Round. Jeram, Anita, illus. (p. 729)
—Guess How Much I Love You: Baby Book. Jeram, Anita, illus. (p. 729)
—Guess How Much I Love You: Colors. Jeram, Anita, illus. (p. 729)
—Guess How Much I Love You Lap-Size Board Book. Jeram, Anita, illus. (p. 729)
—Guess How Much I Love You: Look What I Can Do: A First Concepts Book. Jeram, Anita, illus. (p. 729)
—Guess How Much I Love You Sweetheart Edition. Jeram, Anita, illus. (p. 729)
—Henry Seamouse. (p. 768)
—I Love It When You Smile. Fuge, Charles, illus. (p. 842)
—I'll Always Be Your Friend. (p. 856)
—I'll Always Be Your Friend. Lewis, Kim, illus. (p. 856)
—I'm Sorry. Eachus, Jennifer, illus. (p. 860)
—Let's Play in the Snow. Jeram, Anita, illus. (p. 1000)
—Nutbrown Hare Storybook Pair. Jeram, Anita, illus. (p. 1273)
—Surprise for the Nutbrown Hares: A Guess How Much I Love You Storybook. Jeram, Anita, illus. (p. 1686)
—Surprise for the Nutbrown Hares. Jeram, Anita, illus. (p. 1686)
—There, There. Bates, Ivan, illus. (p. 1730)
—Todos Son Mis Favoritos. Jeram, Anita, illus. (p. 1761)
—Tomhais Méid Mo Ghrá Duit (Guess How Much I Love You in Irish) Jeram, Anita, illus. (p. 1764)
—You're All My Favorites. Jeram, Anita, illus. (p. 1982)
—You're All My Favorites with Audio. Jeram, Anita, illus. (p. 1982)
McBrayer, Cassidy. You Can, Toucan! You Can. (p. 1974)
McBride, Alisha. No Way! (p. 1261)
McBride, Anthony. Fish That Was Afraid to Swim. (p. 598)
—Willie the Whiskers. (p. 1934)
McBride, Anthony & McBride, Autumn. Lost Cat. (p. 1055)
McBride, Autumn, jt. auth. see McBride, Anthony.
McBride, Carol. Making Magnificent Machines: Fun with Math, Science, & Engineering. (p. 1081)
McBride, Earvin, Jr. Adventurous Cyborg. McBride, Earvin, Jr., illus. (p. 25)
—Blockheads from Planet Ecto. (p. 200)
—Bowdery Rodeo Cowboys of Texas. McBride, Earvin, Jr., illus. (p. 216)
—Earvin MacBride's Amazing Sci-Fi & Adventure Heroes McBride, Earvin, Jr., illus. (p. 498)
—Eerie Adventures of Detective Omar Mendez. McBride, Earvin, Jr., illus. (p. 505)
—Space - M. D. 3001. McBride, Earvin, Jr., illus. (p. 1618)
McBride, Eve. Dandelions Help. (p. 403)
McBride, Heddrick, jt. auth. see World Peace, Metta.
McBride, Helen, et al. Kimono (p. 957)
McBride, James. Miracle at St. Anna. (p. 1148)
McBride, Jim, et al. History for CCEA GCSE. (p. 783)
McBride, Judith, jt. auth. see McBride, Peter.
McBride, Kate, et al. Tales of Two Worlds: Arnie & Soot Navigate Florence. (p. 1703)
McBride, Linda Ray. Mema Has Cancer DeNault, Shirl, illus. (p. 1125)
McBride, Lish. Firebug. (p. 591)
—Hold Me Closer, Necromancer. (p. 787)
—Necromancing the Stone. (p. 1239)
McBride M. D., Mark A., et al. Chickens & the Ice Cream. (p. 300)
McBride, Marc, illus. see Rodda, Emily.
McBride, Martha J. And You Love Me. (p. 71)
—Avery Finds Five Dollars. (p. 119)
McBride, Mary. Ms. Simon Says. (p. 1188)
McBride, Maurice & Wallace, Jessica K. Oliver Vance Pull up Your Pants! Jackson, Anthony B., illus. (p. 1286)
McBride, P. K. Career Award Information & Communication Technology: Foundation Level. (p. 266)
—Skills Award Information Technology: Standard Level. (p. 1585)
McBride, Peter & McBride, Judith. Bug & Budgie. (p. 236)
—Bug & Budgie Fly Away. (p. 236)
McBride, Regina. Fire Opal. (p. 590)
McBride, Roxie. Caroline's Crinolines. (p. 270)
McBride, Roxie, ed. see Davis, Marilyn.
McBride, Shaylah. All the Stars in the Sky. (p. 46)
McBride, Susan. Debs: Gloves Off. (p. 421)
—Very Bad Things. (p. 1837)
McBride, Susan Carro. Katrina & the Magic Skates. (p. 945)
McBride-Smith, Barbara. Greek Myths, Western Style: Toga Tales with an Attitude. (p. 721)
—Tell It Together: Foolproof Scripts for Story Theatre. (p. 1716)
McBrier, Page. Abracadabra Tut. (p. 6)
—Beatrice's Goast. (p. 153)
—Beatrice's Goat. Lohstoeter, Lori, illus. (p. 153)
—Chicken & the Worm. Peterson, Rick, illus. (p. 300)
McBroom, Christopher Erik & Grissom, Michael Andrew. Southern Book of Quotes. (p. 1617)
McBroom, Danielle Loiselle. Painted Dream. (p. 1318)
McBroom, Jill D. Here Comes Bobtyblob! (p. 770)
McBroom, Linda Perry. Lord of the Action Figures. (p. 1052)
McC, Meg. Goodnap, Brewer (p. 701)
McCabb, Jamie, illus. see Martin, Anne E.
McCabe, Chris. Hutton Inquiry. (p. 830)
McCabe, Dennis. Haunted Halloween: Color & Create with Spooky Stickers. (p. 753)
McCabe, Ginny, jt. auth. see Hubbard, Jill.
McCabe, Ginny, jt. auth. see Tracy, Mary Lee.
McCabe, Gusty. Most Important Critter in the Whole Wide World: Why the Coyote Howls at Night. (p. 1177)
McCabe, James Dabney, Jr. Planting the Wilderness or, the Pioneer Boys: a Story of Frontier Life. (p. 1369)
McCabe, Jane. Remarkable Story of the Very First Flower: And How She Changed the World. (p. 1459)
McCabe, Jane M., illus. see Maxwell, Wayne F., Jr.
McCabe, Joyce. Flugel Mcdougel (p. 608)
McCabe, Larry. Easiest Country Guitar for Children: In Standard Notation & Tablature (p. 498)
—Easiest Fiddle Tunes for Children (p. 498)
—Easiest Fingerpicking Guitar for Children: In Standard Notation & Tablature (p. 498)
—Easiest Mandolin Tunes for Children (p. 498)
McCabe, Lauren A. How Many Spots Have I Got? Foulke, Nancy, illus. (p. 811)
McCabe, Patrick, ed. American Postal Portrait: A Photographic Legacy. (p. 62)
McCabe, Steve, illus. see MacDonald, George.
McCabe, Timothy Lee, jt. auth. see Rittner, Don.
McCafferty, Catherine. Gingerbread Man (El Hombre de Pan de Jengibre), Grades PK - 3. Bowles, Doug, illus. (p. 677)
—Rapunzel. Spong, Clive, illus. (p. 1439)
McCafferty, Catherine, et al. Forever After. Disney Storybook Artists Staff, illus. (p. 619)
McCafferty, Jan, illus. see Bailey, Jacqui.
McCafferty, Jan, illus. see Coe, Catherine.
McCafferty, Jan, illus. see Cox, Phil Roxbee.
McCafferty, Jan, illus. see Gilpin, Rebecca.
McCafferty, Jan, illus. see Goodhart, Pippa.
McCafferty, Jan, illus. see McQuinn, Anna.
McCafferty, Jan, illus. see Milbourne, Anna.
McCafferty, Jan, illus. see Roxbee Cox, Phil.
McCafferty, Jan, illus. see Shipton, Paul.
McCafferty, Jan, jt. auth. see Dickins, Rosie.
McCafferty, Megan. Bumped. (p. 241)
—Jessica Darling's It List 2: The (Totally Not) Guaranteed Guide to Friends, Foes & Faux Friends. (p. 914)
—Thumped. (p. 1746)
—(Totally Not) Guaranteed Guide to Popularity, Prettiness & Perfection. (p. 1771)
—(Totally Not) Guaranteed Guide to Stressing, Obsessing & Second-Guessing. (p. 1771)
McCaffery, William. Flea Circus. (p. 603)
McCaffrey, Anne. Búsqueda del Dragón. Aroca, José María, tr. (p. 245)
—Dragondrums. (p. 478)
—If Wishes Were Horses. (p. 854)
—No One Noticed the Cat. (p. 1259)
McCaffrey, Anne & Call, Greg. Dragondrums. (p. 478)
—Dragonsinger. (p. 479)
—Dragonsong. (p. 479)
McCaffrey, Brendan, illus. see Hames, Annette & McCaffrey, Monica, eds.
McCaffrey, Debra. Fly...Ball: Illustrated by 2nd Grade Students of Mrs. Young's 2KY at Mohansic Elementary School. (p. 609)
McCaffrey, Kate. Crashing Down. (p. 376)
—Destroying Avalon. (p. 431)
—In Ecstasy. (p. 863)
McCaffrey, Monica, jt. ed. see Hames, Annette.
McCaffrey, Paul. Michelle Obama. (p. 1135)
—Zora Neale Hurston: Author. (p. 1990)
McCaffrey, Susie, illus. see Chandler, Fiona.
McCaffrey, Susie, jt. auth. see Chandler, Fiona.
McCaffrey- Fassler, Ruth. Safe Place. (p. 1502)
McCage, Crystal D. Hallucinogens: Drugs. (p. 739)
—Inhalants. (p. 874)
McCage, Crystal D., ed. see Metcalf, Tom.
McCage, Crystal D. & Amend, Allison. Asian-American Writers. (p. 106)
McCage, Crystal D., ed. Prejudice. (p. 1395)
McCahan, Erin. I Now Pronounce You Someone Else. (p. 844)
—Love & Other Foreign Words. (p. 1059)
McCaig, Dave, illus. see Aaron, Jason.
McCain, Becky Ray. Grandmother's Dreamcatcher Schuett, Stacey, illus. (p. 709)
McCain, Diana. To All on Equal Terms: The Life & Legacy of Prudence Crandall. (p. 1758)
McCain, Kevin, illus. see Arquette, Kerry.
McCain, Malinda, ed. see Dharkar, Anuja & Tapley, Scott.
McCain, Malinda, ed. see Underwood, Dale & Aho, Kirsti.
McCain, Margaret. My Star of the East. (p. 1219)
McCain, Murray. Books! Alcorn, John, illus. (p. 212)
Mccain-Buzzelli, Vic. Adventures of Milly & Mikey: Womb Mates Book #1. (p. 20)
McCall, Anthony, illus. see Cox, Roy.
McCall, Edith. Heroes of American Explorations: Frontiers of America Series. Borja, Robert, illus. (p. 773)
—Stories of American Steamboats. Borja, Robert, illus. (p. 1654)
McCall, Edith S. Adventures of the American Colonies. Rogers, Carol, illus. (p. 23)
McCall, Gerrie. Fierce Water Creatures. (p. 584)
—Weird & Wonderful Fish. (p. 1872)
McCall, Gerrie & McNab, Chris. Movie Monsters. (p. 1183)
McCall, Gerrie & Regan, Lisa. Ancient Legends. (p. 69)
—Classical Myths. (p. 328)
—Dragons & Serpents. (p. 479)
—Ferocious Giants. (p. 582)
—Half-Man, Half-Monster. (p. 736)
McCall, Guadalupe Garcia. Summer of the Mariposas. (p. 1674)
—Under the Mesquite. (p. 1813)
McCall, Jack. Fireflies in Winter: Lessons for Living an Extraordinary Life. (p. 592)
Mccall, Philip, 2nd. Adaxxis Nightshade. (p. 11)
McCall, R. Allan. Double Exposure. (p. 472)
—Perilous Odyssey. (p. 1343)
McCall Smith, Alexander. Akimbo & the Snakes. Pham, LeUyen, illus. (p. 32)
—Arbol del Chicle Hinchable. (p. 94)
—Cowgirl Aunt of Harriet Bean. Rankin, Laura, illus. (p. 374)
—Great Cake Mystery: Precious Ramotswe's Very First Case. (p. 714)
—Harriet Bean & the League of Cheats. (p. 749)
—Max & Maddy & the Bursting Balloons Mystery. Pamintuan, Macky, illus. (p. 1110)
—Mystery of Meerkat Hill: A Precious Ramotswe Mystery for Young Readers. McIntosh, Iain, illus. (p. 1224)
—Mystery of Meerkat Hill. McIntosh, Iain, illus. (p. 1224)
—Mystery of the Missing Lion: A Precious Ramotswe Mystery for Young Readers. (p. 1225)
—Precious & the Puggies: Precious Ramotswe's Very First Case. Robertson, James, tr. from ENG. (p. 1394)
McCall, Val. Twelve Rabbits & a Turtle: Bilingual English French. (p. 1800)
McCall, William L., illus. see Hill, Genita.
McCalla, Darrell, illus. see Mollel, Tololwa.
McCalla Njee, Lena. Ivan Consigue la Casa de Sus Suenos. Urruela, Maria Cristina, tr. (p. 900)
—Ivan Gets a Dream House. (p. 900)
McCalla, Priscilla R. & McGraw-Hill Staff. Retailing. (p. 1464)
McCallen, A. J. Praise! Songs & Poems from the Bible Retold for Children. (p. 1393)
McCallister, Colleen. Boaz the Ginger Cat & the Mysterious Mishap of the Kitchen Sponge. (p. 205)
McCallister, Wendy. Shapes: 4 Friends Lost. (p. 1560)
McCallum, Andrew, tr. see Carroll, Lewis, pseud.
McCallum, Ann. Beanstalk: The Measure of a Giant. Balkovek, James, illus. (p. 150)
—Eat Your Math Homework: Recipes for Hungry Minds. Hernandez, Leeza, illus. (p. 501)
—Eat Your Science Homework: Recipes for Inquiring Minds. Hernandez, Leeza, illus. (p. 501)
—Kid's Multicultural Math Adventure: Amazing Activities to Explore Math's Global Roots! Norton, Carolyn, illus. (p. 954)
—Rabbits Rabbits Everywhere: A Fibonacci Tale. Kendall, Gideon, illus. (p. 1430)
—Secret Life of Math: Discover How (and Why) Numbers Have Survived from the Cave Dwellers to Us! Norton, Carolyn McIntyre, illus. (p. 1541)
McCallum, Jodie, illus. see Navillus, Nell.
McCalment, Diana, jt. auth. see McCalment, Ray.
McCalment, Ray & McCalment, Diana. Route 66 Fun Coloring Book. (p. 1491)
McCament, Janice Marjorie. 'Ole Paint Rocks. (p. 1285)
McCampbell, Darlene Z., jt. ed. see Rochman, Hazel.
McCandless, Helen. Kyle Walks a Mile. (p. 969)
McCandless Iii, Bruce. Beatrice & the Basilisk. (p. 153)
McCann, Carol. 12 Apple Trees. (p. 1994)
McCann, David. Garda Gaby: The Danger of Playing Truant. Brundige, Britt, ed. (p. 656)
McCann, Eliza, jt. auth. see Gwynne, Phillip.
McCann, Emily. Animal Doodles. McCann, Emily, illus. (p. 77)
McCann, Emma, illus. see Norton, Liss.
McCann, Gerald, illus. see Meadowcroft, Enid Lamonte & Vigilante, Sylvester.
McCann, Jesse L., et al. Bad Moon Rising (p. 132)
—Crisis of Infinite Kryptos (p. 383)
—Here Comes Krypto (p. 770)
—Houndin' the Mail Carrier! (p. 802)
—Krypto the Superdog (p. 968)
—Purr-Fect Crime (p. 1419)
—Three Naughty Doggies! (p. 1743)
McCann, Jesse Leon. Cat in the Hat. (p. 278)
—Creepy Chef. Davis, Dan, illus. (p. 381)
—Museum Madness. (p. 1192)
—Rock 'n' Roll Zombie. Duendes Del Sur Staff, illus. (p. 1482)
—Science Project. Fruchter, Jason, illus. (p. 1527)
—Scooby-Doo! (p. 1529)
—Scooby-Doo & Museum Madness. Duendes Del Sur Staff, illus. (p. 1529)
—Scooby-Doo & the Creepy Chef. Davis, Dan, illus. (p. 1529)
—Scooby-Doo & the Fishy Phantom. Duendes Del Sur Staff, illus. (p. 1529)
—Scooby-Doo & the Mummy's Curse. Duendes del Sur, illus. (p. 1529)
—Scooby-Doo & the Rock 'n' Roll Zombie. Duendes del Sur, illus. (p. 1529)
—Scooby-Doo & the Samurai Ghost. Davis, Dan, illus. (p. 1529)
—Scooby-Doo & the Tiki's Curse. Duendes del Sur, illus. (p. 1529)
—Scooby-Doo & the Werewolf. Duendes del Sur, illus. (p. 1529)
—Super Spooky Double Storybook. Duendes Del Sur Staff, illus. (p. 1682)
McCann, John & Brothers Grimm, Becky. Loom Magic! 25 Awesome, Never-Before-Seen Designs for an Amazing Rainbow of Projects. (p. 1051)
McCann, John, et al. Loom Magic Xtreme! 25 Spectacular, Never-Before-Seen Designs for Rainbows of Fun. (p. 1052)
McCann, Judith. Things My Momma Said. (p. 1733)
McCann, Liam. Battle of Boxhill. (p. 146)
McCann, M. L. Search for Black January: Third Mystery in the Longjohners' Series. (p. 1537)
McCann, Margaret, jt. auth. see Mills, Nathan.
McCann, Martin, illus. see Rudd, Brandon Kyle.
McCann, Michelle, ed. see Alaska Boys and Girls Clubs Staff.
McCann, Michelle, ed. see Boys and Girls Club of Greater Fort Worth.
McCann, Michelle, ed. see Boys and Girls Club of Oklahoma County.
McCann, Michelle, ed. see Spooner, Joe.
Mccann, Michelle Roehm. Boys Who Rocked the World: Heroes from King Tut to Shaun White. (p. 220)
McCann, Michelle Roehm. Boys Who Rocked the World: Heroes from King Tut to Bruce Lee. Hahn, David, illus. (p. 220)
Mccann, Michelle Roehm & Welden, Amelie. Girls Who Rocked the World: From Anne Frank to Natalie Portman. (p. 681)
McCann, Michelle Roehm & Welden, Amelie. Girls Who Rocked the World: Heroines from Joan of Arc to Mother Teresa. Hahn, Daniel & Hahn, David, illus. (p. 681)
McCann, Shawn. Catch the Wind. (p. 279)
—Why the Owl Has Big Ears. (p. 1926)
McCann, Thomas P. "Tom". Tree Nobody Wanted: A Christmas Story. (p. 1783)
McCanna, Tim. Bitty Bot. Carpenter, Tad, illus. (p. 194)
Mccants, Bruce C. Legend of the White Cockroach. (p. 989)
McCardell, KennethW. Bible Rhymes' Christmas Story. Chirco, Antonella, illus. (p. 176)
—Bible Rhymes' Creation. Chirco, Antonella, illus. (p. 176)
—Bible Rhymes' Noah & the Ark. Chirco, Antonella, illus. (p. 176)
McCarnes, Kayla, et al. Bully-Proofing in Early Childhood: Building a Caring Community. (p. 241)
—Making a Happy Heart: A Storybook to Accompany Bully-Proofing in Early Childhood: Building a Caring Community. (p. 1080)
McCarney, Rosemary. Because I Am a Girl: I Can Change the World (p. 155)
—Dear Malala, We Stand with You. (p. 419)
—Every Day Is Malala Day (p. 542)
—Tilt Your Head Rosie the Red Cathcart, Yvonne, illus. (p. 1750)
McCarrier, Andrea, et al. Fact & Fiction 1: Reece to the Rescue; Here Comes a Thunderstorm; Garden Giant; A Sunflower Life Cycle; Mugs Indoors & Outdoors; Cats Are Hunters; Beach Days; Oceans All Around Us Morley, Amanda et al, illus. (p. 561)
McCarroll, Barbara. There's Always Two Sides to Every Story. (p. 1731)
—Tongue Turning Tales for the Classroom. Godfrey, Arthur Dwayne, illus. (p. 1765)
McCarroll, Tolbert. Winter Walk. Beebee, Dorothy, illus. (p. 1938)
McCarry, Charles. Christopher's Ghosts. (p. 317)
McCarry, Sarah. All Our Pretty Songs. (p. 45)
—Dirty Wings. (p. 446)
McCarter, Zack, illus. see Randall, MarilynMae.
McCarthy, Arica G., jt. auth. see McCarthy, Sally J.
McCarthy, Cecilia Pinto. Baboons (p. 124)
—Betta Fish (p. 172)
—Capuchin Monkeys (p. 265)
—Flamingos. (p. 602)
—Green Tree Pythons. (p. 722)
—Hawks (p. 755)
—Macaws (p. 1067)
—Mandrill Monkeys (p. 1087)
—Monkeys. (p. 1165)
—Poison Dart Frogs (p. 1377)
—Vultures (p. 1851)
McCarthy, Cecilia Pinto & Marx, Mandy R. Colorful World of Animals. (p. 344)
McCarthy, Christina. Forbidden Magic: A Druid Born. (p. 616)
McCarthy, Colin. DK Eyewitness Books: Reptile: Reptile. (p. 456)
—Reptile. (p. 1461)
McCarthy, Conor Clarke, jt. auth. see McMahon, Patricia.
McCarthy, Cori. Breaking Sky. (p. 225)
McCarthy, Dan, illus. see Orenstein, Denise Gosliner.
McCarthy, Dan & Rosen, Anne. Good Night Oregon. Veno, Joe, illus. (p. 700)
McCarthy, Diana. Big Old House & the Scary Storm. (p. 183)
McCarthy, Diane Marie. Arlington's Dream. (p. 99)
McCarthy, Elizabeth. Patrick's Home Run. (p. 1329)
McCarthy, Erin. High Stakes: A Tale of Vegas Vampires. (p. 778)
—Sucker Bet (p. 1672)
McCarthy, Jane, compiled by. Living in San Miguel. (p. 1041)
McCarthy, Jenna. Lola Knows a Lot. Palacios, Sara, illus. (p. 1045)
McCarthy, Jenna & Evans, Carolyn. Maggie Malone Makes a Splash. (p. 1071)
McCarthy, Jenna, et al. Maggie Malone & the Mostly Magical Boots. (p. 1071)
McCarthy, John. Childrens Guitar Method: The Road to Stardom Begins Here! Gorenburg, Steve, ed. (p. 303)
—Clap, Tap, Sing & Swing: Rockin' Kids Motor Skills. Gorenburg, Steve, ed. (p. 326)
—Ireland: A Reference Guide from the Renaissance to the Present. (p. 887)
McCarthy, Jon-Paul. Eddie the Egg. (p. 503)
McCarthy, Kai. Unpredictable Prophecies. (p. 1822)
McCarthy, Kate, illus. see McCarthy, Terry.
McCarthy, Kevin, illus. see Smith, Robert W.
McCarthy, Laura. My Daddy Can Too!!! (p. 1201)
McCarthy, Margaret. Cat Did Not Know. Molloy, Sophie, illus. (p. 277)
McCarthy, Maria S. 101 Indoor Activities for Toddlers & Preschoolers - Triple Tested! Recycling Friendly Boredom Busters, Creative Learning, & Physical Activities. (p. 1999)
McCarthy, Mary. Closer Look. (p. 334)
—Closer Look. McCarthy, Mary, illus. (p. 334)
McCarthy, Mary Tola, illus. see Kaspee.
McCarthy, Maureen. When You Wish upon a Rat. (p. 1905)
McCarthy, Meghan. Aliens Are Coming! The True Account of the 1938 War of the Worlds Radio Broadcast. (p. 41)
—Astronaut Handbook. (p. 109)
—City Hawk: The Story of Pale Male. McCarthy, Meghan, illus. (p. 323)
—Daredevil: The Daring Life of Betty Skelton. McCarthy, Meghan, illus. (p. 406)
—Earmuffs for Everyone! How Chester Greenwood Became Known As the Inventor of Earmuffs. McCarthy, Meghan, illus. (p. 494)
—Incredible Life of Balto. (p. 869)
—Pop! The Invention of Bubble Gum. McCarthy, Meghan, illus. (p. 1384)
—Seabiscuit: The Wonder Horse. McCarthy, Meghan, illus. (p. 1536)

—Strong Man: The Story of Charles Atlas. (p. 1668)
McCarthy, Michael. Man Who Made It Rain: A True Story Based on the Experiences of J. Dietrich Stroeh. (p. 1086)
—Story of Daniel in the Lions' Den. Ferri, Giuliano, illus. (p. 1658)
McCarthy, Michael, et al. Touchstone (p. 1772)
McCarthy, Pat. Canada: A MyReportLinks. com Book. (p. 260)
—Dominican Republic: A MyReportLinks. com Book. (p. 465)
—Famous Confederate Generals & Leaders of the South: A Myreportlinks. com Book. (p. 569)
—Famous Union Generals & Leaders of the North: A MyReportLinks. com Book. (p. 570)
—Friends of the Earth: A History of American Environmentalism with 21 Activities. (p. 638)
—Heading West: Life with the Pioneers, 21 Activities. (p. 756)
—Henry David Thoreau: Writer, Thinker, Naturalist. (p. 768)
—Thirteen Colonies from Founding to Revolution in American History. (p. 1735)
McCarthy, Pat, illus. see James, Yolanda, et al.
McCarthy, Peggy & Rivers, Julia. Not for the Meek. (p. 1267)
—Tough Break: The Barn Girls. (p. 1772)
McCarthy, Ralph, tr. see Murakami, Ryu.
McCarthy, Ralph F. Adventure of Momotaro, the Peach Boy Saito, loe, illus. (p. 14)
—Moon Princess Oda, Kancho, illus. (p. 1172)
McCarthy, Rebecca. Hanukkah Mad Libs. (p. 744)
—Kate & Humphrey's Big Adventure: All about Wolves. (p. 944)
—Laugh Your Rabbids Off! A Rabbids Joke Book. Ruiz, Fernando, illus. (p. 980)
—Mr. Men, Little Miss, & Me. (p. 1185)
—Save This Christmas! May, Jason J., illus. (p. 1517)
Mccarthy, Rebecca L. Save This Christmas! (p. 1517)
McCarthy, Rose. Dictatorship: A Primary Source Analysis. (p. 436)
—Food Labels: Using Nutrition Information to Create a Healthy Diet. (p. 613)
—Food Labels: Using Nutritional Information to Create a Healthy Diet. (p. 613)
—Paul Revere: Freedom Rider. (p. 1330)
—Paul Revere: Jinete de la guerra de Independencia. (p. 1330)
—Paul Revere: Freedom Rider / Jinete de la causa Revolucionaria. (p. 1330)
—Paul Revere: Jinete de la causa revolucionaria (Paul Revere: Freedom Rider) (p. 1330)
McCarthy, Rose, jt. auth. see Link, Theodore.
McCarthy, Ruth. Princess Sofia & the Invitation. (p. 1405)
McCarthy, Sally J. & McCarthy, Arica G. Hope & Wishie. (p. 796)
McCarthy, Steve, illus. see Webb, Sarah & Ranson, Claire.
McCarthy, Steven, illus. see Webb, Sarah & Ranson, Claire.
McCarthy, Tara, jt. auth. see Staton, Hilarie N.
McCarthy, Terry. Little Girl with a Loud Voice. McCarthy, Kate, illus. (p. 1028)
McCartin, Brain. Thomas Paine: "Common Sense" & Revolutionary Pamphleteering. (p. 1739)
McCartin, Brian. Thomas Paine: Common Sense, & Revolutionary Pamphleteering. (p. 1739)
McCartney, Jen, illus. see Sheridan, Luke.
McCartney Lewis, Pat. Colors of the Coloni: Los Colores de la Colonia. (p. 345)
McCartney, Michael David, illus. see Alderton, Sylvia.
McCartney, Tania. Peas in a Pod. Snerling, Tina, illus. (p. 1333)
—Tottie & Dot. Snerling, Tina, illus. (p. 1772)
McCartney, Tania Maree. Riley & the Sleeping Dragon: A Journey Around Beijing. Qovaizi, Mo, illus. (p. 1472)
McCarty, Bill. Turn to the Right. (p. 1798)
McCarty, Bryan. Devyn's Gold. (p. 432)
McCarty, Diane Bischoff. Copywork for Children: For Grades 1-3. (p. 366)
—My First Holy Communion: A non-Denominational Program for Preparing young Children to receive Communion for the first Time. (p. 1206)
McCarty, Jerry. Dog to Treasure. (p. 461)
McCarty, Marty. Hard Girl Goes to a Scary Movie. (p. 748)
McCarty, Michael. Welcome to Michael's: Great Food, Great People, Great Party! Pool, Steve, photos by. (p. 1873)
McCarty, Nick. Marco Polo: The Boy Who Traveled the Medieval World. (p. 1092)
—Marco Polo: El Joven Que Viajo Por el Mundo Medieval. (p. 1092)
—Troy: The Myth & Reality Behind the Epic Legend. (p. 1790)
—World History Biographies: Marco Polo: The Boy Who Traveled the Medieval World. (p. 1955)
McCarty, Peter. Chloe. McCarty, Peter, illus. (p. 308)
—Fabian Escapes. McCarty, Peter, illus. (p. 559)
—Fall Ball. McCarty, Peter, illus. (p. 566)
—First Snow. McCarty, Peter, illus. (p. 596)
—Henry in Love. McCarty, Peter, illus. (p. 768)
—Hondo & Fabian. (p. 794)
—Hondo & Fabian. McCarty, Peter, illus. (p. 794)
—Jeremy Draws a Monster. McCarty, Peter, illus. (p. 913)
—Little Bunny on the Move. McCarty, Peter, illus. (p. 1025)
—Monster Returns. McCarty, Peter, illus. (p. 1168)
—Moon Plane. McCarty, Peter, illus. (p. 1172)
—T Is for Terrible. McCarty, Peter, illus. (p. 1694)
McCarty, Peter, illus. see Seidler, Tor & Tor, Seidler.
McCarty, Willard. Humanities Computing. (p. 826)
McCarville, Mary Michele. Merry Hairy. (p. 1129)
McCaslin, Anna, illus. see Ferer, Whitney H.
McCaslin, Donna B. My Medical Assistant. (p. 1214)
McCaslin, Nellie. Angel of the Battlefield. (p. 74)
—Bailiff's Wonderful Coat. (p. 133)
—Bluebonnets. (p. 204)
—Brave New Banner. (p. 223)
—Broken Rehearsal. (p. 230)
—Children & Drama. Landes, William Alan, ed. (p. 302)
—Christmas Fiesta. (p. 314)
—Christmas Lamb. (p. 314)
—Clever Marya & the Czar. (p. 331)
—Coins of Lin Foo. (p. 338)
—Cold Face - Warm Heart. (p. 338)
—Johnny Appleseed. (p. 923)
—Leading Lady: Playscript. (p. 982)
—Legend of Minna Lamourrie. (p. 988)
—Legends in Action: Ten Plays of Ten Lands. (p. 990)
—Little Squire of Flanders. (p. 1036)
—Mercy in Moccasins: Playscript. (p. 1127)
—Miracle in the Christmas City: Playscript. (p. 1148)
—Paul Bunyan: Lumberjack. (p. 1330)
—Prelude to Fame. (p. 1395)
—Straight Shooter (Playscript) (p. 1664)
—Theatre for Children in the United States: A History. Landes, William-Alan, ed. (p. 1728)
—Three Meals a Day. (p. 1743)
—Tinker of Toledo. (p. 1756)
—Too Many Cooks. (p. 1766)
—Who Laughs Last? (p. 1916)
McCathern, Gerald. Palo Duro Gold. (p. 1320)
McCaughan, Timothy. Crimson Soul. (p. 383)
McCaughrean, Geraldine. Aventuras de Ulises. Barroso, Paz, tr. (p. 119)
—Caballo de Madera. Barroso, Paz, tr. (p. 250)
—Casting the Gods Adrift: A Tale of Ancient Egypt. Ludlow, Patricia D., illus. (p. 276)
—Death-Defying Pepper Roux. (p. 420)
—Dédalo e Ícaro: El Rey Midas. Barroso, Paz, tr. (p. 422)
—Doce Trabajos de Hércules: Eco y Narciso. Barroso, Paz, tr. (p. 459)
—Fig's Giant. (p. 586)
—Ghosts, Rogues & Highwaymen: 20 Stories from British History. Brassey, Richard, illus. (p. 673)
—Gilgamesh the Hero. Parkins, David, illus. (p. 676)
—Glorious Adventures of the Sunshine Queen. (p. 685)
—Jason y el Vellocino de Oro: Aracne, la Tejedora. Barroso, Paz, tr. (p. 910)
—Jesse Tree. Willey, Bee, illus. (p. 914)
—Kite Rider. (p. 962)
—Monacello: The Little Monk. Diemberger, Jana, illus. (p. 1163)
—Not the End of the World. (p. 1267)
—Perseo y la Gorgona Medisa. Barroso, Paz, tr. (p. 1344)
—Perseus. (p. 1344)
—Peter Pan de Rojo Escarlata. Gonzalez-Gallarza, Isabel, tr. (p. 1347)
—Peter Pan in Scarlet. Fischer, Scott M., illus. (p. 1347)
—Pilgrim's Progress. Cockcroft, Jason, illus. (p. 1359)
—Rebels & Royals: 20 Stories from British History. Brassey, Richard, illus. (p. 1451)
—Sky Ship & Other Stories. (p. 1587)
—Stones Are Hatching. (p. 1653)
—Stop the Train! (p. 1654)
—Wenceslas. Birmingham, Christian, illus. (p. 1875)
—White Darkness. (p. 1912)
—Wish-Bringer. Diemberger, Jana, illus. (p. 1940)
McCaughrean, Geraldine, jt. auth. see Sánchez, Haroldo.
McCaughrean, Geraldine & Dubravka, Kolanovic. Nativity Story. Williams, Sophy, illus. (p. 1235)
McCaughrean, Geraldine & Hoffmann, E. T. A. Nutcracker: A Magic Theater Book. Swarner, Kristina, illus. (p. 1274)
McCaughrean, Geraldine & Willey, Bee. Collins Big Cat - Think Again! (p. 340)
McCaughrean, Geraldine, retold by. Hercules. (p. 769)
—Odysseus. (p. 1278)
—Theseus. (p. 1732)
McCaughren, Tom. Children of the Forge. (p. 302)
—Legend of the Corrib King. (p. 989)
—Legend of the Golden Key. (p. 989)
—Legend of the Phantom Highwayman. (p. 989)
McCaughtry, Keith. All about Street Signs & Laws. (p. 43)
McCaughtry, Michele L. Literary Elements: Reproducible, Skill-Building Packs-One for Each Literary Element-That Engage Students in Meaningful & Structured Reading Response Activities. Kit (p. 1022)
McCaulay, Philip Martin. Nursery Rhymes. (p. 1273)
McCauley, Adam, illus. see Cotler, Steve.
McCauley, Adam, illus. see Duval, Kathy.
McCauley, Adam, illus. see Hicks, Betty.
McCauley, Adam, illus. see Sachar, Louis.
McCauley, Adam, illus. see Scieszka, Jon.
McCauley, Adam, illus. see Shulman, Mark.
McCauley, Adam, illus. see Walsh, Vivian.
McCauley, Adam, jt. auth. see Hicks, Betty.
McCauley, Adam & Shulman, Mark. Mom & Dad Are Palindromes. (p. 1161)
McCauley, Marlene. Song of Kateri: Princess of the Eucharist. McCauley, R. Allan, ed. (p. 1611)
Mccauley, Plum. It All Started with A Bicycle. (p. 893)
McCauley, R. Allan, ed. see McCauley, Marlene.
McCaw, Neil. My Dad the Crab. (p. 1201)
McCaw, Robert, jt. auth. see Earley, Chris G.
McCay, William. After the Earthquake & Después del Terremoto: 6 English, 6 Spanish Adaptations (p. 28)
—Después del Terremoto: Set Of 6. (p. 430)
—Matemáticas en el Jardín. Hanner, Albert, illus. (p. 1104)
—Math in the Garden & Matemáticas en el Jardín: 6 English, 6 Spanish Adaptations Hanner, Albert, illus. (p. 1106)
—Native Peoples & Pueblos del Mundo: 6 English, 6 Spanish Adaptations (p. 1235)
—Pueblos del Mundo. (p. 1414)
McChesney, Ruth Lozano, ed. see McChesney, Terry.
McChesney, Terry. Dog Tacos. McChesney, Ruth Lozano & Brannon, Brian, eds. (p. 461)
McChiller, BBH. Monster Moon: Curse of Zala Manor. (p. 1168)
McClafferty, Carla Killough. Fourth down & Inches: Concussions & Football's Make-or-Break Moment. (p. 625)
—In Defiance of Hitler: The Secret Mission of Varian Fry. (p. 863)
—Many Faces of George Washington: Remaking a Presidential Icon. (p. 1089)
McClafferty, Lisa. Is the Sky Really Falling? A Matilda Private Eye Book. (p. 890)
—Matilda Private Eye: The Case of the Missing Socks. Aines, Diane, illus. (p. 1109)
McClain, Charles. Big Jake Plants a Garden: Big Jake Adventures. Southern Lion Books, ed. (p. 182)
McClain, Jennie. Monday I Was a Monkey: A "Tale" of Reverence. Eichelberger, Jennifer, illus. (p. 1163)
McClain M.Ed. Ncc, Ashley. Not So Perfect Polly. (p. 1267)
McClain, Tania, illus. see McClain, Charles.
McClaine, Jamie. Have You Ever Seen a Moose Brushing His Teeth? Willy, April, illus. (p. 754)
—Have You Ever Seen a Moose Taking a Bath? Willy, April, illus. (p. 754)
McClaine, Les, illus. see Grillo-Marxuach, Javier.
McClaine, Les, illus. see Wilson, Daniel H. & Trippe, Dean.
McClanahan, Barbara. Train to Perry. (p. 1777)
McClanahan, Teel, 3rd. Dragons' Truth. (p. 479)
McClarnon, Marciann. Painless Junior: Grammar. Oliverio, Donna Christina, ed. (p. 1318)
McClarrin Vaupel, Lynn. Queen of Hearts. (p. 1425)
McClatchy, J. D. Poets of the Civil War. (p. 1376)
McClatchy, Lisa. Dear Tyrannosaurus Rex. Manders, John, illus. (p. 419)
—Eloise Skates! Lyon, Tammie, illus. (p. 516)
—Eloise's Mother's Day Surprise. Lyon, Tammie, illus. (p. 516)
—Eloise's Pirate Adventure. Lyon, Tammie Speer & Lyon, Tammie, illus. (p. 516)
McClatchy, Lisa, jt. auth. see Thompson, Kay.
McClatchy, Lisa & Knight, Hilary. Eloise Decorates for Christmas. Lyon, Tammie Speer & Lyon, Tammie, illus. (p. 516)
McClatchy, Lisa & Thompson, Kay. Eloise & the Big Parade. Lyon, Tammie, illus. (p. 516)
—Eloise & the Dinosaurs. Lyon, Tammie Speer & Lyon, Tammie, illus. (p. 516)
—Eloise & the Snowman. Lyon, Tammie Speer, illus. (p. 516)
—Eloise's New Bonnet. Lyon, Tammie Speer & Lyon, Tammie, illus. (p. 516)
—Eloise's Summer Vacation. Lyon, Tammie Speer, illus. (p. 516)
McClaurin, Irma & Schomp, Virginia. Civil Rights Movement. (p. 325)
—Facing the Future. (p. 561)
McClean, Shorty, jt. auth. see Butler, Berwyn.
McClean, Will. Go, Bluey Go! Turnmyre, Dustin, illus. (p. 686)
McClear, Preston. Frannie & Pickles. Dollak, Nicholas, illus. (p. 631)
McCleary, Stacey. Here Comes a Kiss. Cornish, David, illus. (p. 770)
McCleary, Twila, illus. see Juckes, Deborah Sioux.
McCleery, William. Wolf Story. Chappell, Warren, illus. (p. 1944)
McCleese, Don. Insects. (p. 875)
—Spiders. (p. 1627)
McClellan, Adam & Schifini, Alfredo. Southwest: Its History & People. (p. 1617)
McClellan, Adam & Wilson, Martin. Uniquely North Carolina (p. 1818)
McClellan, Brian. Love Letter to Black People: Audaciously Hopeful Thoughts on Race & Success. (p. 1060)
McClellan, Cheryl. Bunny Flu Flu Gets Well. (p. 242)
McClellan, David, illus. see Alvarez, Jennifer Lynn.
McClellan, David, illus. see Epstein, Adam Jay & Jacobson, Andrew.
McClellan, David, illus. see Salerni, Dianne K.
McClellan, Maddy, illus. see Gates, Susan.
McClellan, Maddy, illus. see McMahon, Kara.
McClellan, Mae. Just Friends. (p. 938)
McClellan, Marilyn. Big Deal about Alcohol: What Teens Need to Know about Drinking. (p. 181)
—Madeleine L'Engle: Banned, Challenged, & Censored. (p. 1070)
—Organ & Tissue Transplants: Medical Miracles & Challenges. (p. 1303)
McClellan, Rachel. Fractured Truth. (p. 627)
McClellan, Ray. Alien Abductions. (p. 40)
—Backhoes. (p. 130)
—Baseball. (p. 140)
—Basketball. (p. 143)
—Bermuda Triangle. (p. 167)
—Bigfoot. (p. 184)
—BMX Freestyle. (p. 204)
—Chris Jericho. (p. 311)
—Concrete Mixers. (p. 355)
—Downhill BMX. (p. 474)
—Dump Trucks. (p. 489)
—Football. (p. 615)
—Golf. (p. 696)
—Hockey. (p. 786)
—Hot Rods. (p. 802)
—Hydroplanes. (p. 831)
—Kane. (p. 942)
—Loch Ness Monster. (p. 1044)
—Maori Warriors. (p. 1089)
—Rally Cars. (p. 1437)
—Skateboarding. (p. 1583)
—Snocross. (p. 1598)
—Snowboarding. (p. 1600)
—SuperMoto. (p. 1684)
—Surfing. (p. 1685)
—Undertaker. (p. 1816)
—Volleyball. (p. 1849)
McClellan, Ray & Von Finn, Denny. Dragsters. (p. 479)
McClellan, Sara, ed. see Davis, Daniel M. & Davis, Dawna Jo.
McClellan, Sara, ed. After Halloween. Davis, Daniel M., illus. (p. 28)
Mcclelland, Grace. Gift of Grace. (p. 675)
McClelland, Katherine. Second Chances. (p. 1539)
McClelland, Maddy, illus. see Graves, Sue.
McClelland, Pam. Turn It Around, Sadie! DePaulo, Dorothy, illus. (p. 1797)
McClelland, Rosie, jt. auth. see Brownlee, Sophia Grace.
McClements, George. Dinosaur Woods: Can Seven Clever Critters Save Their Forest Home? McClements, George, illus. (p. 443)
—Night of the Veggie Monster. McClements, George, illus. (p. 1254)
Mcclements, George. Super Secret Adventure Club. (p. 1681)
Mcclendon, John. How to Sunday School Guide Curriculum Workshop for Adult Leaders. (p. 821)
McClendon, Kimberli A. Have You Heard? Jesus Walks on Water. (p. 754)
McClenney, Earl H., Jr. Mamma, Is the Maid Goin' Teach? Portraits of Black Women Who Integrated the Public Schools in Richmond, VA. (p. 1084)
McCliggott, Timothy M. Report on Quibnoida. McCliggott, Timothy M., illus. (p. 1461)
McClintic, Ben, jt. illus. see Woods, Christopher.
McClintock. Little Princess Picture Book. (p. 1034)
McClintock, Barbara. Adèle & Simon. McClintock, Barbara, illus. (p. 12)
—Adèle & Simon in America. McClintock, Barbara, illus. (p. 12)
Mcclintock, Barbara, illus. see Aesop.
McClintock, Barbara, illus. see Aylesworth, Jim.
McClintock, Barbara, illus. see Block, Francesca Lia.
McClintock, Barbara, illus. see Donofrio, Beverly.
McClintock, Barbara, illus. see Obed, Ellen Bryan.
Mcclintock, Barbara, illus. see Potter, Beatrix.
McClintock, Barbara, illus. see Stevenson, Robert Louis.
McClintock, Mike. Fly Went By. Siebel, Fritz, illus. (p. 609)
McClintock, Norah. About That Night (p. 6)
—At the Edge. (p. 111)
—Back (p. 130)
—Bang (p. 136)
—Break & Enter (p. 224)
—Change of Heart. (p. 290)
—Close to the Heel (p. 334)
—Dead & Gone. (p. 416)
—Dead Silence. (p. 417)
—Dooley Takes the Fall (p. 470)
—Double Cross. (p. 472)
—Down (p. 474)
—Falsa Identidad. (p. 567)
—Guilty (p. 730)
—Hit & Run. (p. 785)
—Homicide Related (p. 794)
—I, Witness Deas, Mike, illus. (p. 849)
—In Too Deep. (p. 868)
—Last Chance. (p. 977)
—Marked (p. 1095)
—Marqué (p. 1096)
—Masked (p. 1102)
—My Side (p. 1218)
—Nothing to Lose. (p. 1268)
—Nowhere to Turn. (p. 1269)
—Out of the Cold. (p. 1311)
—Picture This (p. 1356)
—Regreso (p. 1457)
—Scared to Death. (p. 1519)
—Seeing & Believing. (p. 1548)
—Shadow of Doubt. (p. 1557)
—Snitch (p. 1598)
—Soplón (p. 1614)
—Taken (p. 1697)
—Tell (p. 1716)
—Tell. (p. 1716)
—Tru Detective Hughes, Steven, illus. (p. 1791)
—Truth & Lies. (p. 1794)
—Victim Rights (p. 1840)
—Watch Me (p. 1861)
—You Can Run. (p. 1974)
McClinton, Theresa. Stone Guardian. (p. 1652)
McClinton-Temple, Jennifer & Velie, Alan. Encyclopedia of American Indian Literature. (p. 524)
McClish, Bruce. Southeast Asia, Australia, & the Pacific Realm. (p. 1617)
McCloskey, Erin, ed. see Francia, Giada.
McCloskey, John J. Warrior Ching. (p. 1858)
McCloskey, Kevin. We Dig Worms! (p. 1867)
McCloskey, Kevin, illus. see Campbell, Howard.
McCloskey, Larry. Murder Fit for a King. (p. 1192)
McCloskey, Leigh J. Tarot Revisioned - Linen. (p. 1706)
McCloskey, Robert. Abran Paso a los Patitos. Blanco, Osvaldo, tr. from ENG. (p. 7)
—Blueberries for Sal (p. 203)
—Blueberries for Sal. (p. 203)
—Homer Price. (p. 793)
—Homer Price. McCloskey, Robert, illus. (p. 793)
—Make Way for Ducklings (p. 1079)
—Make Way for McCloskey. (p. 1079)
McCloskey, Robert, illus. see Bishop, Claire Huchet.
McCloskey, Robert, illus. see Robertson, Keith.
McCloud, Carol. As-Tu Rempli un Seau Aujourd'hui? Un Guide du Bonheur Quotidien Pour Enfants. Messing, David, illus. (p. 105)
—Growing up with a Bucket Full of Happiness: Three Rules for a Happier Life. Weber, Penny, illus. (p. 727)
—Has Llenado una Cubeta Hoy? Una Guia Diaria de Felicidades para Nios. Messing, David, illus. (p. 752)
—Have You Filled a Bucket Today? A Guide to Daily Happiness for Kids. Messing, David, illus. (p. 754)
McCloud, Carol & Martin, Katherine. Fill a Bucket: A Guide to Daily Happiness for the Young Children. David, Messing, illus. (p. 586)
McCloud, Carol & Wells, Karen. Will You Fill My Bucket? Daily Acts of Love Around the World. Weber, Penny, illus. (p. 1932)
McCloud, Carol, et al. Fill a Bucket: A Guide to Daily Happiness for Young Children. Messing, David, illus. (p. 586)
McCloud, Lady Alice. Dark Mischief. (p. 407)
—Imperial Lace. (p. 862)
Mccloud, Sadie. Winter Chores: Commas in A Series. (p. 1938)
McCloud, Scott. Balance of Power Austin, Terry & Blevins, Bret, illus. (p. 133)
—Be Careful What You Wish For... Burchett, Rick & Austin, Terry, illus. (p. 148)
—Big Problem! Austin, Terry & Burchett, Rick, illus. (p. 183)
—Distant Thunder Burchett, Rick & Austin, Terry, illus. (p. 453)
—Eye to Eye Burchett, Rick & Austin, Terry, illus. (p. 558)

—Seonimod Austin, Terry & Burchett, Rick, illus. (p. 1551)
—Superman Adventures. (p. 1683)
—Tiny Problems! Austin, Terry & Burchett, Rick, illus. (p. 1756)
McCloy, Helen. Pleasant Assassin & Other Cases for Dr. Basil Willing. (p. 1373)
McCloy, James F. & Miller, Ray, Jr. Phantom of the Pines: More Tales of the Jersey Devil. (p. 1349)
McCloy, James F., et al. Jersey Devil. (p. 914)
McClue-Tate, Brucetta. Jolly the Computer. (p. 924)
McCluire, Brian D. Sun & the Moon. (p. 1676)
McClung, Gavin Kent. Hyperion Series Astrological Degree Symbols. (p. 831)
McClure, Beverly Stowe. Frankie's Perfect Home. Morris, Alexander, illus. (p. 630)
McCLure, Beverly Stowe. Listen to the Ghost. (p. 1022)
McClure, Beverly Stowe. Tumbleweed Christmas. McKenna, Bridgett, illus. (p. 1796)
McClure, Brian D. Ants. Plumlee, Buddy, illus. (p. 90)
—Birds & the Frogs. Plumlee, Buddy, illus. (p. 191)
—Bubble. (p. 233)
—Meal. Plumlee, Buddy, illus. (p. 1116)
—Raindrop. (p. 1436)
—Up down Day. Plumlee, Buddy, illus. (p. 1824)
—Who Am I? (p. 1914)
McClure, C. R. Legend of Papa Balloon Kemen, Steven, illus. (p. 988)
McClure, Denise, jt. auth. see Smith, Dana C.
McClure, Derrick, tr. see Carroll, Lewis, pseud.
Mcclure, Gillian. My First Prayers. Fournier, Laure, illus. (p. 1207)
McClure, Holly. Secrets & Ghost Horses. (p. 1544)
McClure, Jessica, illus. see Hanh, Thich Nhat.
McClure, Kim. Edgar the Seagull who was Afraid to Fly. (p. 504)
McClure, Nancy. If You'd Made the World. (p. 855)
McClure, Nikki. Apple. (p. 92)
—Awake to Nap. (p. 120)
—How to Be a Cat. (p. 814)
—In. (p. 862)
—Mama, Is It Summer Yet? (p. 1084)
—To Market, to Market. (p. 1759)
McClure, Nikki, illus. see Chatelain, Jeremy.
McClure, Nikki, illus. see Rylant, Cynthia.
McClure, Rhys. Wylee: Whitesquirrel of Arden. (p. 1966)
McClure, Wendy. Escape to the World's Fair. (p. 535)
—On Track for Treasure. (p. 1292)
—Princess & the Peanut Allergy Lyon, Tammie, illus. (p. 1403)
—Princess & the Peanut Allergy. Lyon, Tammie, illus. (p. 1403)
—Wanderville. (p. 1856)
McClurkan, Rob. Aw, Nuts! McClurkan, Rob, illus. (p. 120)
—What to Doodle? Jr. —On the Farm & in the Wild. (p. 1894)
—What to Doodle? on the Farm. (p. 1894)
McClurkan, Rob, illus. see Cunningham, Anna.
McClurkan, Rob, illus. see Higginson, Sheila Sweeny.
McClurkan, Rob, jt. auth. see Cunningham, Anna.
McCluskey, Cindy, illus. see Chandler, Murray & Milligan, Helen.
McCluskey, J. E. Adventures of Peter the Pleasant Platypus & Friends: First Adventure, Tidy Time. (p. 21)
—Platypus Tales. (p. 1370)
McCluskey, John A., ed. see Johnston, Brenda A. & Pruitt, Pamela.
McClymer, Kelly. Competition's a Witch. (p. 352)
—Getting to Third Date. (p. 670)
—Must Love Black. (p. 1194)
—Salem Witch Tryouts. (p. 1504)
—She's a Witch Girl. (p. 1566)
McCold, Uldine. Little Girls Play Dress Up. (p. 1028)
McColl, R. W. Encyclopedia of World Geography. (p. 525)
McColley, Poetess Victoria L. Patty Poet: Forever Friends. (p. 1330)
McCollon, Donell. Tell Me about God Please. (p. 1716)
—When Fear Knocks at the Door. (p. 1902)
McCollough, Aaron. Double Venus. (p. 473)
McCollum, Betty, intro. Women in the Arts. (p. 1946)
McCollum, Bobby. Must I Go to Church. (p. 1194)
McCollum, Kimberly. Gloves in a Hat. (p. 685)
McCollum, Lynn Tragesser. Green School Caper: The Adventures of the Five Amigos. (p. 722)
McCollum, Nicole, jt. auth. see King-Cason, Jermaine.
McCollum, Rick, et al. Teenage Mutant Ninja Turtles Classics Volume 5. (p. 1714)
McCollum, Sean. Anatomy of a Shipwreck (p. 67)
—Australia. (p. 116)
—Bill Clinton. (p. 186)
—Chairman: Mao Unleashes Chaos in China. (p. 288)
—CIA: The Missions. (p. 318)
—Custom Cars: The Ins & Outs of Tuners, Hot Rods, & Other Muscle Cars. (p. 395)
—Deadly Despot: Idi Amin Rains Terror on Uganda. (p. 417)
—Dragsters (p. 479)
—Fascinating, Fantastic Unusual History of Robots (p. 575)
—Indy Cars (p. 873)
—Joseph Stalin. (p. 926)
—Poland. (p. 1378)
—Racecars: The Ins & Outs of Stock Cars, Dragsters, & Open-Wheelers (p. 1431)
—Segmented Worms: Earthworms, Leeches, & Their Relatives. (p. 1548)
—Sports Cars (p. 1632)
—Vikings: A Guide to the Terrifying Conquerors (p. 1842)
—Volcanic Eruptions, Earthquakes, & Tsunamis. (p. 1848)
—Werewolves: The Truth Behind History's Scariest Shape-Shifters. (p. 1875)
McCollum, Sean & Banas, Sharon L. Managing Conflict Resolution. (p. 1086)
McCollum, Sean & Yomtov, Nel. Unusual Histories. (p. 1823)
McCollum, Sean, et al. Eyewitness to Titanic. (p. 558)
—Monster Handbooks. (p. 1167)
McComb, Marianne. Emancipation Proclamation. (p. 517)
McCombie, Karen. Candy Girl. (p. 261)
—My Big (Strange) Happy Family. Monks, Lydia, illus. (p. 1197)
McCombs, A. Lisa. Abby. (p. 2)
McCombs, C. A. Daddy's Going Away... (p. 399)
—Daddy's Going Away... Heart-Kisses Keep Us Close. (p. 399)
McCombs, Lisa A. Abby. (p. 2)
McCombs, Margi. Dios es Bueno Todo el Tiempo. Ivanov, Aleksey & Ivanov, Olga, illus. (p. 445)
—God Is Good... All the Time. Ivanov, Aleksey & Ivanov, Olga, illus. (p. 689)
—Noah's Ark. Fox, Lisa, illus. (p. 1261)
McConaghy, Lorraine & Bentley, Judy. Free Boy: A True Story of Slave & Master. (p. 634)
Mcconaghy, Taylor. Too Good to Be True: Book One of the Beholder Trilogy. (p. 1766)
McConchie, Lyn. Autumn of the Wild Poney. (p. 118)
—Winter of Waiting. (p. 1938)
McConduit, Denise & Harrington, David. Boy Who Wouldn't Read Harrington, David, illus. (p. 219)
McConduit, Denise Walter. D. J. & the Debutante Ball Henriquez, Emile F., illus. (p. 397)
McCone, Sandra. Magical Tea Party: Book Two in the Three Little Lasses Series. (p. 1075)
—Midsummer's Magic: Book Three of the Three Little Lasses Series. (p. 1139)
—Woods Keep Secrets: The Fourth Book in the Three Little Lasses Series. (p. 1950)
McConkey, Barbara, illus. see Trowbridge, Terri.
McConnaughhay, JoDee H. Tell the Truth, Tyler. (p. 1717)
McConnell, Bill, et al, eds. Watergate. (p. 1863)
McConnell, Bryan. Donny the Donkey: The First Christmas. (p. 466)
McConnell, Cara. We Can Recycle: Represent & Solve Addition Problems. (p. 1866)
McConnell, Clem. I Speak to Myself: Encouraging Words for Children. McConnell, Clem, illus. (p. 846)
McConnell, Craig, ed. Theo Tams: Inside the Music. (p. 1729)
McConnell, Edith J. Their Times. (p. 1728)
McConnell, J. Bradfield. What a Blind Dog Sees. (p. 1878)
McConnell, James, illus. see Hawthorne, Nathaniel.
McConnell, James, illus. see Poe, Edgar Allen.
McConnell, James, illus. see Wharton, Edith.
McConnell, Karen, et al. Health for Life with Web Resources - Cloth. (p. 758)
McConnell, Kathleen & Flatau, Susie Kelly. Reaching Out to Today's Kids: 15 Helpful Ways to Bridge the Gap Between Parents, Teachers & Kids. (p. 1442)
McConnell, L'Rain. What If the Rainbow Is a Place: A Magic Rainbow Story. (p. 1887)
McConnell, Lynn. Grandma's Tree. (p. 709)
McConnell, Mac. Hadad: The Innkeeper's Journey Vol. 1 Kulp, Jodee, ed. (p. 735)
McConnell, Nancy, jt. auth. see LoGiudice, Carolyn.
McConnell, Robert L., jt. contrib. by. see Baxter, Kathleen.
McConnell, Robert L. & Baxter, Kathleen, contrib. by. Split History of the Women's Suffrage Movement: A Perspectives Flip Book (p. 1630)
McConnell, Robert L., contrib. by. Assassination & Its Aftermath: How a Photograph Reassured a Shocked Nation (p. 107)
—Civil War Witness: Mathew Brady's Photos Reveal the Horrors of War (p. 326)
—Split History of the Women's Suffrage Movement: A Perspectives Flip Book (p. 1630)
McConnell, S. Let's Bring Mom Breakfast: Learning the BR Sound. (p. 994)
—What a Baker Makes: Learning the Long A Sound. (p. 1878)
McConnell, Sarah, illus. see Clarke, Jane.
McConnell, Sarah, illus. see Courtenay, Lucy.
McConnell, Sarah, illus. see Gilman, Grace.
McConnell, Sarah, illus. see Molitoris, Cathy.
McConnell, Sarah & Courtenay, Lucy. Loony Doubloon. McConnell, Sarah, illus. (p. 1052)
McConnell, Steve. Software Estimation: Demystifying the Black Art. (p. 1606)
Mcconnell, Steve, jt. auth. see McConnell, Steve.
McConnell, Steve & Mcconnell, Steve. Code Complete. (p. 338)
McConnell, William. Crystals & Gems. (p. 387)
—Rocks & Fossils. (p. 1483)
—What Makes Clocks Tick? (p. 1892)
McConnell, William, jt. auth. see Reid, Struan.
McConnell, William S., ed. Living Through the Space Race. (p. 1042)
McConney, Aldith Olive. Stargazing in Autumn. (p. 1642)
McConnie Zapater, Beatriz. Fiesta. Ortega, Jose, illus. (p. 584)
McConochie, Jennifer. Shape & Say. (p. 1560)
McConville, Alexandra. Adventures of Sass-O-Frask: A Tale of Kindness. (p. 22)
McConville, Brendan, jt. auth. see Doak, Robin S.
McCooey, David. Blister Pack. (p. 199)
McCook, Eileen, illus. see Cavins, Emily.
McCook, William. Windmills of the World. Harris, Coy F., ed. (p. 1936)
McCooke, Valerie J. Grandfather's Chest. (p. 707)
McCool, Arlene, illus. see Lawless, Mary Ann.
McCool, Barry, jt. auth. see Carlson, Nancy.
McCool, Ben. Souljacker: #2. Rousseau, Craig, illus. (p. 1614)
—Star Lord: #4. Rousseau, Craig, illus. (p. 1640)
—Strange Days: #1. Rousseau, Craig, illus. (p. 1665)
—Traveler: #3. Rousseau, Craig, illus. (p. 1780)
McCoola, Marika. Baba Yaga's Assistant. (p. 123)
McCord, David, illus. see Reeder, Larry.
McCord, Joseph Lennon. Where Do Socks Go? Eller, Sydney, illus. (p. 1907)
McCord, Kathi, illus. see Wilkinson, Lisa.
McCord, Marianne. Gilbert! Front & Center! Maginn, Traci, illus. (p. 676)
McCorev, LuVara P. Purity - It's a Teen Thing. (p. 1419)
McCorkindale, Bruce, illus. see Oguneye, Kunle.
McCorkle, Barbara. Bandit Raccoon. Taylor, David A., illus. (p. 136)
—Brutis' New Friend. (p. 233)
—Brutis' New Friend. Taylor, David A., illus. (p. 233)
McCorkle, Brent & Parker, Amy. Firebird: He Lived for the Sunsine. Corley, Rob & Vollmer, Chuck, illus. (p. 591)
McCorkle, Denise. On Angels Wings - Softball. (p. 1288)
McCorkle, Mark, illus. see Schooley, Bob.
McCorkle, Mark, jt. auth. see Schooley, Bob.
McCorkle, Mark & Schooley, Bob. Grudge Match. (p. 727)
McCorkle, Michelle M. Voices from Beyond. (p. 1848)
McCormack, Caren McNelly. Fiesta Dress: A Quinceanera Tale Aviles, Martha, illus. (p. 584)
McCormack, Chris. Fight Before Christmas. Lunn, Naomi, illus. (p. 585)
McCormack, Jim, et al. Birds of Ohio. (p. 191)
McCormack, Patrick, jt. auth. see Cooke, C. W.
McCormack, Rachel L., jt. ed. see Paratore, Jeanne R.
McCormack, Shaun. Inside Britain's MI6: Military Intelligence 6. (p. 876)
—Ted Williams. (p. 1712)
McCormack, Staci. Mingled Blessings. (p. 1146)
McCormic, Maxine Griffith. Casey's Hoof Prints. Christensen, D. J., illus. (p. 275)
McCormick, Anita Louise. Industrial Revolution in United States History. (p. 872)
—Invention of the Telegraph & Telephone in American History. (p. 884)
—Native American Struggle in United States History. (p. 1234)
McCormick, Deborah J., jt. auth. see Robinson, James.
McCormick, Kimberly A. Hey, Girlfriend: Seventy-five monologues for Girls (p. 774)
McCormick, Lacey. Sea Turtle's Journey. (p. 1536)
—Signing Together: Sign Language. (p. 1574)
McCormick, Lisa Wade. Alien Abductions: The Unsolved Mystery. (p. 40)
—Bigfoot: The Unsolved Mystery (p. 184)
—Biographies (p. 188)
—Christopher Columbus. (p. 316)
—Christopher Paolini. (p. 317)
—Financial Aid Smarts: Getting Money for School. (p. 587)
—Frequently Asked Questions about Growing up As an Undocumented Immigrant. (p. 636)
—Ghosts: The Unsolved Mystery (p. 672)
—Haunted Houses: The Unsolved Mystery. (p. 753)
—Mothman: The Unsolved Mystery. (p. 1179)
—Near-Death Experiences: The Unsolved Mystery (p. 1239)
—Pie Grande/Bigfoot: El Misterio Sin Resolver/the Unsolved Mystery Strictly Spanish, LLC., tr. from ENG. (p. 1356)
—Psychic Powers: The Unsolved Mystery. (p. 1413)
—Wright Brothers. (p. 1963)
McCormick, Lisa Wade & Miller, Connie Colwell. Misterios de la Ciencia/Mysteries of Science. Strictly Spanish, LLC., tr. (p. 1155)
McCormick, Michelle. Priscilla Willa, Party Planner: Night at the Haunted Hotel. (p. 1407)
—Priscilla Willa, Party Planner. (p. 1407)
McCormick, Patricia. Cut. (p. 395)
—Just Add One Chinese Sister (p) (p. 937)
—Never Fall Down: A Novel. (p. 1242)
—Never Fall Down. (p. 1242)
—Purple Heart. (p. 1419)
—Sold. (p. 1607)
McCormick, Rhea. Road to Home. (p. 1477)
McCormick, Rosie. Homes. (p. 793)
McCormick, Scott. It's Go Time! Lazzell, R. H., illus. (p. 897)
Mccormick, Scott. Mr. Pants: It's Go Time! Lazzell, R. H., illus. (p. 1186)
—Mr. Pants: Slacks, Camera, Action! Lazzell, R. H., illus. (p. 1186)
McCormick, Scott. Slacks, Camera, Action! Lazzell, R. H., illus. (p. 1587)
—Trick or Feet! Lazzell, R. H., illus. (p. 1786)
McCormick, Shawn R. Zoey & the Zones: A Story for Children with Asthma. (p. 1987)
McCormick, Wendy. Daniel & His Walking Stick Bergum, Constance R., illus. (p. 404)
McCormick, Wilfred. Bases Loaded: A Bronc Burnett Story. (p. 141)
—Eagle Scout: A Bronc Burnett Story. (p. 492)
—Fielder's Choice: A Bronc Burnett Story. (p. 584)
—Flying Tackle: A Bronc Burnett Story. (p. 610)
—Quick Kick: A Bronc Burnett Story. (p. 1427)
—Three-Two Pitch: A Bronc Burnett Story. (p. 1744)
McCorquodale, Elizabeth. Kids in the Wild Garden. (p. 954)
McCorvie, D. Lawrence. Timothy Hunt: The Great Candy Caper. (p. 1755)
McCoshan, Duncan, jt. auth. see & Packer, Knife.
McCourt, Lisa. Deadly Snakes. Eitzen, Allan, illus. (p. 418)
—Happy Halloween, Stinky Face. Moore, Cyd, illus. (p. 745)
—I Love You, Stinky Face. Moore, Cyd, illus. (p. 844)
—I Miss You, Stinky Face. Moore, Cyd, illus. (p. 844)
—I Miss You, Stinky Face Board Book. Moore, Cyd, illus. (p. 844)
—Merry Christmas, Stinky Face. Moore, Cyd, illus. (p. 1129)
—Te Quiero, Carita Sucia. (p. 1708)
McCourt, Mariah, jt. auth. see Rice, Anne.
McCourt, Nicola Stott. Tiger in a Pink Hat. (p. 1748)
McCourt, Richard & Wood, Dominic. Dick & Dom's Big Fat & Very Silly Joke Book. (p. 435)
—Dick & Dom's Slightly Naughty but Very Silly Words. (p. 435)
McCowan, Linda. Cancer Rhymes with Dancer. (p. 260)
McCowan Nevills, Jennifer. Have You Ever? Part 2. (p. 754)
McCowan, Patricia. Honeycomb (p. 795)
McCoy, Allen. Cat That Was Elected President. (p. 278)
McCoy, Angie. Starchild's Adventures on Earth. McCoy, Derrick, illus. (p. 1642)
McCoy, Chris. Prom Goer's Interstellar Excursion. (p. 1411)
McCoy, Dave, illus. see Polack, Peter J.
McCoy, Derrick, illus. see McCoy, Angie.
McCoy, Emily. Storey Finds a Baby Racoon: And Other Puppy Tales. (p. 1654)
McCoy, Glenn, illus. see Colfer, Eoin.
McCoy, Heather. French Crossword Puzzles for Practice & Fun. (p. 635)
McCoy, Isabelle, jt. auth. see Graham, Leland.
McCoy, Jacquelyn. Heavenly Hen. (p. 761)
McCoy, Jody, illus. see Beck, Timothy P.
McCoy, John, illus. see Shemin, Craig.
McCoy, Lisa. Bahrain. (p. 132)
—Cheerleading. (p. 296)
—Middle East: Facts & Figures. (p. 1137)
—Qatar. (p. 1422)
—United Arab Emirates. (p. 1818)
—Video Games. (p. 1841)
McCoy, Lisa, jt. auth. see Oppedisano, Robert.
McCoy, M. M. Where Is Cecil? Maximilian Press Publishers Staff, ed. (p. 1908)
McCoy, Mary. Dead to Me. (p. 417)
McCoy, Mimi, pseud. Dead End. (p. 416)
McCoy, Robbi. Waltzing at Midnight. (p. 1856)
McCoy, Sharon. What If? (p. 1887)
McCoy, Tanya. If My Best Friend was an Elephant (p. 853)
McCoy, Virginia, illus. see Delaronde, Deborah L.
McCoy-Waller, Courtney. Seasons Come: A Collection of Poetry. (p. 1538)
McCracken, Connie. Indigo Boy & Crystalline Girl. Craig, Chris, illus. (p. 872)
McCracken, Craig, et al. Power Party (p. 1390)
McCracken, Harold. Pirate of the North. Tonk, Ernest, illus. (p. 1362)
Mccracken, Heather. That's What's Different about Me! Helping Children Understand Autism Spectrum Disorders - Story & Coloring BK. Robbins, Kathryn, illus. (p. 1727)
McCracken, Jaime, photos by see Pugh, Tracey D.
McCracken, Janet, ed. see De Long, Ron, et al.
McCranie, Stephen. Belly Flop! Book 3. McCranie, Stephen, illus. (p. 163)
—Mal & Chad - Food Fight! McCranie, Stephen, illus. (p. 1083)
—Mal & Chad - The Biggest, Bestest Time Ever! McCranie, Stephen, illus. (p. 1083)
McCrary, G. D. Guerrillas in the Midst. (p. 728)
McCrary, Greta. Kidz in the Kitchen. (p. 955)
McCraughrean, Geraldine, tr. see Ikeda, Daisaku.
McCraw, S. L. Love Life & Liberation. (p. 1060)
McCray, Bennie. Benito's Ninjabot 1 Of 2. (p. 164)
—Dragon Cookies Anniversary Edition: The Complete Story. (p. 476)
McCray, Bennie, 3rd. Servant the Complete Story (UNCUT EDITION) (p. 1552)
McCray, Ed. Jill Chill & the Baron of Glacier Mountain: Wonder Tales from the Book of Ed. Brewer, Tammy & Harms, Cathy, eds. (p. 917)
McCray, Kathy. Journey to the Junior Honor Society. (p. 929)
McCray, Thomas R. Uzbekistan. (p. 1829)
McCrea, John, illus. see Limke, Jeff.
McCreadie, Sandi. Thistle Fables. (p. 1737)
McCready, Philip, ed. see Minev, Nikolay.
McCreary, Candace. Meki & the Three Cockers. (p. 1125)
McCreary, Jane, illus. see Wilsdon, Christina.
McCreedy, J. L. Orphan of Torundi. (p. 1304)
McCreery, Conor. Kill Shakespeare Volume 2 (p. 956)
McCreight, Barbara. Promises for: Boys. (p. 1411)
McCrie, Thomas. Life of John Knox. (p. 1012)
McCrimmon, Linda. Can You Please tie My Shoes? (p. 259)
McCrite, K. D. In Front of God & Everybody (p. 863)
Mccroary, Greg. Mia. (p. 1133)
McCrory, Anik, jt. auth. see Hurwitz, Johanna.
McCroskey, Christine, illus. see Furbush, Helen.
McCroskey, Mona Lange, ed. Summer Sojourn to the Grand Canyon: The 1898 Diary of Zella Dysart. (p. 1675)
McCue, Gil. Buzzy the Honey Bee. (p. 249)
McCue, Kerin, jt. auth. see Bath, K. P.
McCue, Lisa. Animals' Advent. (p. 82)
—Busy Bunnies. (p. 246)
—Corduroy's Thanksgiving. (p. 367)
—Corduroy's Valentine's Day. McCue, Lisa, illus. (p. 367)
—HideAway Hedgehog & the Magical Rainbow. (p. 777)
—Little Bunny. (p. 1025)
—My First Mother Goose. (p. 1207)
—Quiet Bunny. (p. 1428)
—Quiet Bunny & Noisy Puppy. (p. 1428)
—Quiet Bunny's Many Colors. (p. 1428)
McCue, Lisa, illus. see Berlin, Irving.
McCue, Lisa, illus. see Chaconas, Dori.
McCue, Lisa, illus. see Freeman, Don.
McCue, Lisa, illus. see Hennessy, B. G.
McCue, Lisa, illus. see Kimmelman, Leslie.
McCue, Lisa, illus. see Namm, Diane.
McCue, Lisa, illus. see Packard, Mary.
McCue, Lisa, illus. see Potter, Beatrix.
McCue, Lisa, illus. see Reader's Digest Staff.
McCue, Lisa, illus. see Thayer, Jane.
McCue, Lisa, illus. see Wallace, Bill.
McCue, Lisa, jt. auth. see Freeman, Don.
McCue, Lisa, jt. auth. see Schaefer, Lola M.
McCue, Lisa & Falken, L. C. Snuggle Bunnies. McCue, Lisa, illus. (p. 1601)
McCue, Patrick, illus. see Knapp-Grosz, Tamara & Loyd, Elizabeth.
McCuin, Sam. Story of Camo Kitty. (p. 1657)
McCullagh, Sheila K. & Myers, Lois. Galapagos. (p. 653)
McCullen, Sam, illus. see Whybrow, Ian.
McCulley, Johnston. Zorro! (p. 1990)
—Zorro. (p. 1990)
McCulloch, Amy. Oathbreaker's Shadow. (p. 1275)
McCulloch, Derek. Stagger Lee. (p. 1638)
McCulloch, Julie. Caribbean (p. 268)
—China (p. 306)
—India (p. 870)
—Italy (p. 895)
—Japan (p. 909)
—Mexico (p. 1131)
McCulloch, Susan. Uniquely Pennsylvania (p. 1818)
McCullough, Ana L. Zoo at the End of My Book. (p. 1988)
McCullough, Angela. Night Nite. (p. 1253)
McCullough, Dicy. Tired of Being Different. (p. 1757)
—Tired of School. (p. 1757)
McCullough, Jerletha. Fairies of the Lilies. (p. 563)
McCullough, Joseph A. Dragonslayers (p. 479)
McCullough, Karen. Wizard's Bridge. (p. 1943)
McCullough, Kathy. Who Needs Magic? (p. 1917)
McCullough, Kelly. School for Sidekicks: The Totally Secret Origin of Foxman Jr. (p. 1523)
McCullough, L. E. Classroom Plays for Social Studies America in the 1800s Mason, Mark, illus. (p. 329)
—Classroom Plays for Social Studies Ancient Civilizations Mason, Mark, illus. (p. 329)

—Classroom Plays for Social Studies Early America Mason, Mark, illus. (p. 329)
—Silent Night: A Christmas Story. Maxwell, Cassandre, illus. (p. 1575)
—We Three Kings: A Christmas Story. Maxwell, Cassandre, illus. (p. 1868)
McCullough, Lesa. Jonathan Bear Plays Baseball. (p. 925)
McCullough, Marilyn, illus. see Kilpatrick, Leanne.
McCullough, Myrina D. Feet. Schafrath, Ty, illus. (p. 580)
Mcullough, Noah, jt. auth. see McCullough, Noah.
McCullough, Noah & Mcullough, Noah. First Kids: The True Stories of All the Presidents' Children. (p. 595)
McCullough, Sharon Pierce. Bunbun. (p. 241)
McCullough, Victoria. Charlotte's Hummock: a Young Adult Woman's Mystery Detective Novel. (p. 293)
McCully, Emily Arnold. 3, 2, 1, Go! McCully, Emily Arnold, illus. (p. 1991)
—Escape of Oney Judge: Martha Washington's Slave Finds Freedom. McCully, Emily Arnold, illus. (p. 535)
—First Snow. McCully, Emily Arnold, illus. (p. 596)
—Ida M. Tarbell: The Woman Who Challenged Big Business-and Won! (p. 851)
—Late Nate in a Race. (p. 979)
—Late Nate in a Race. McCully, Emily Arnold, illus. (p. 979)
—Little Ducks Go. McCully, Emily Arnold, illus. (p. 1027)
—Marvelous Mattie: How Margaret E. Knight Became an Inventor. (p. 1099)
—Mirette on the High Wire. (p. 1149)
—My Heart Glow: Alice Cogswell, Thomas Gallaudet, & the Birth of American Sign Language. McCully, Emily Arnold, illus. (p. 1211)
—Pete Makes a Mistake. (p. 1346)
—Pete Won't Eat. (p. 1346)
—Pete Won't Eat. McCully, Emily Arnold, illus. (p. 1346)
—Picnic. McCully, Emily Arnold, illus. (p. 1355)
—Queen of the Diamond: The Lizzie Murphy Story. (p. 1425)
—Sam & the Big Kids. McCully, Emily Arnold, illus. (p. 1506)
—School. McCully, Emily Arnold, illus. (p. 1522)
—Secret Cave: Discovering Lascaux. McCully, Emily Arnold, illus. (p. 1540)
—Strongheart: The World's First Movie Star Dog. McCully, Emily Arnold, illus. (p. 1668)
—Wonder Horse: The True Story of the World's Smartest Horse. McCully, Emily Arnold, illus. (p. 1947)
McCully, Emily Arnold, illus. see Adoff, Arnold.
McCully, Emily Arnold, illus. see Bauer, Marion Dane.
McCully, Emily Arnold, illus. see Bunting, Eve.
McCully, Emily Arnold, illus. see Fern, Tracey E.
McCully, Emily Arnold, illus. see Kent, Allegra.
McCully, Emily Arnold, illus. see Kinsey-Warnock, Natalie.
McCully, Emily Arnold, illus. see Rockwell, Thomas.
McCully, Emily Arnold, illus. see Van Rynbach, Iris & Shea, Pegi Deitz.
McCully, Emily Arnold, illus. see Zarins, Kim.
McCully, Emily Arnold & Schertle, Alice. 1, 2, I Love You. (p. 1990)
McCumbee, Stephie. Garden in My Mind: Growing Through Positive Choices. Griffin, Lisa M., illus. (p. 656)
—Garden in My Mind Activity Guide: Lessons for Social Skill & Common Core Development. Griffin, Lisa M., illus. (p. 656)
—Priscilla & the Perfect Storm. DeWeerd, Kelsey, illus. (p. 1407)
—Spacing Out: Discovering the Importance of Completing Tasks. Griffin, Lisa M., illus. (p. 1620)
McCumbers, Jaime. Don't Step on the Flowers! (p. 468)
McCune, Jamie. First Look at Ocean Animals. (p. 596)
—Lion Cub Roars: Baby Animals. (p. 1020)
McCune, Jamie, jt. auth. see Galvin, Laura.
McCune, Joshua. Invisible Monsters. (p. 885)
—Talker 25. (p. 1703)
McCune, Mark, illus. see Gibbons, Ted & Wilcox, S. Michael.
McCurdy, Brenda. Adam's Midnight Flight to Heaven. (p. 11)
McCurdy, Michael. So Said Ben. (p. 1602)
—Walden Then & Now: An Alphabetical Tour of Henry Thoreau's Pond. McCurdy, Michael, illus. (p. 1853)
McCurdy, Michael, illus. see Forbes, Esther.
McCurdy, Michael, illus. see Fradin, Dennis Brindell.
McCurdy, Michael, illus. see Goodman, Steve.
McCurdy, Michael, illus. see Hall, Donald.
McCurdy, Michael, illus. see Hayford, James.
McCurdy, Michael, illus. see San Souci, Robert D. & Burroughs, Edgar Rice.
McCurdy, Steve. Keeper at the Inn. Lohmann, Stephanie, illus. (p. 947)
McCurdy, Michael, illus. see Philip, Neil, ed.
McCurrach, Moriah. Kids Without Limits: You can be anything you want to Be! (p. 955)
McCurry, Janice. Grandma's Wish: A Keepsake Book for All Grandchildren. (p. 709)
McCurry, Kristen. Alike or Not Alike? A Photo Sorting Game (p. 41)
—City Babies. (p. 323)
—Counting. Banks, Timothy, illus. (p. 370)
—Desert Babies. (p. 428)
—Eye-Look Picture Games. (p. 557)
—How to Draw Amazing Airplanes & Spacecraft Edwards, Mat, illus. (p. 816)
—How to Draw Amazing Animals Meschini, Leonardo, illus. (p. 816)
—How to Draw Incredible Dinosaurs Calle, Juan, illus. (p. 817)
—How to Draw Incredible Ocean Animals Osterhold, Jared, illus. (p. 817)
—Little Scribe. (p. 1036)
—Look & Compare: A Photo Analogy Game (p. 1048)
—Look & Remember: A Photo Memory Game (p. 1048)
—Pick a Picture, Write a Poem! (p. 1354)
—Pick a Picture, Write a Report! (p. 1354)
—Pick a Picture, Write a Story! (p. 1354)
—Pick a Picture, Write an Opinion! (p. 1354)
—Smithsonian Drawing Books. (p. 1594)
—Smithsonian Drawing Books. Edwards, Mat, illus. (p. 1594)
—Smithsonian Drawing Books. Edwards, Mat et al, illus. (p. 1594)

—Smithsonian Drawing Books. Meschini, Leonardo & Osterhold, Jared, illus. (p. 1594)
—Smithsonian Drawing Books. Osterhold, Jared & Meschini, Leonardo, illus. (p. 1594)
—Up-Close Mysteries: Zoomed-In Photo Puzzles (p. 1824)
McCurry, Kristen & Jackson, Aimee. Ocean Babies. NorthWord Books for Young Readers Staff, ed. (p. 1276)
McCurry, Kristin. Farm Babies. (p. 573)
—Mountain Babies. (p. 1180)
McCurry, Meryl. Monto. (p. 1170)
McCurry, Miya. Foods Return. (p. 614)
McCurry, Steve. Looking East. McCurry, Steve, photos by. (p. 1051)
—Path to Buddha: A Tibetan Pilgrimage. (p. 1328)
—Sanctuary: The Temples of Angkor. (p. 1510)
McCurry, Steve, jt. auth. see Bannon, Anthony.
McCurtin, Arlene. Manual of Paediatric Feeding Practice. (p. 1089)
McCusker, Paul. Danger Lies Ahead! (p. 404)
—Memory's Gate (p. 1126)
—Out of Time (p. 1311)
—Point of No Return. (p. 1377)
—Strange Journey Back. (p. 1665)
McCusker, Paul & Elmer, Robert. Ripple Effect (p. 1474)
McCusker, Paul & Hering, Marianne. Attack at the Arena. (p. 113)
—Peril in the Palace. (p. 1343)
—Revenge of the Red Knight. (p. 1466)
—Voyage with the Vikings. (p. 1850)
McCusker, Tammy. Move over! Princess Coming Through! Greve, Hannah K., illus. (p. 1183)
McCutcheon, Bobbi, jt. auth. see McCutcheon, Scott.
McCutcheon, Chuck. What Are Global Warming & Climate Change? Answers for Young Readers. (p. 1879)
Mccutcheon, George B. Purple Parasol. (p. 1419)
McCutcheon, George Barr. Purple Parasol. (p. 1419)
McCutcheon, Janette. RMS Queen Elizabeth 2: The Last Great Liner. (p. 1476)
McCutcheon, John. Christmas in the Trenches Sorensen, Henri, illus. (p. 314)
McCutcheon, Marc. Student's Thesaurus. (p. 1669)
McCutcheon, Randall, et al. Glencoe Speech. (p. 683)
McCutcheon, Scott & McCutcheon, Bobbi. Facts on File Marine Science Handbook. (p. 561)
—Space & Astronomy: The People Behind the Science. (p. 1618)
McDade Jr, Bert M. Why Santa Claus Comes at Christmas. Swope, Brenda, illus. (p. 1925)
McDade, Melissa C., jt. auth. see Grzimek, Bernhard.
McDaid, Mark. Billy the Bus. (p. 187)
McDaniel, Becky Bring. Katie Did It. Hoit, Richard, illus. (p. 945)
McDaniel, Carren. Fresh Air Friends: The Dangers of Secondhand Smoke. (p. 1539)
McDaniel, Catherine A. My First Pet. (p. 1207)
Mcdaniel, Chris M. Adventures of Dusty Popsallot. (p. 17)
McDaniel, Faux. I Picked up a Book & Became a Millionaire. (p. 844)
McDaniel Hailey. Amazing Angelina: And Her Hula Hoop. (p. 52)
McDaniel, J. T., ed. U. S. S. Wahoo (SS-238) American Submarine War Patrol Reports. (p. 1807)
McDaniel, Jan. Food of Mexico. (p. 613)
—Indian Immigration. (p. 871)
Mcdaniel, Jan. Lebanon. (p. 986)
McDaniel, Jan. Lebanon. (p. 986)
—Zesty & Colorful Cuisine: The Food of Mexico. (p. 1986)
McDaniel, Jequita Potts. Mardy Murie Did! Grandmother of Conservation. Van Zyle, Jon, illus. (p. 1092)
McDaniel, Jequita Po & Van Zyle, Jon. Mardi Murie Did! Grandmother of Conservation. (p. 1092)
McDaniel, Lurlene. Always & Forever. (p. 51)
—As Long as We Both Shall Live. (p. 105)
—Breathless. (p. 226)
—Briana's Gift. (p. 226)
—End of Forever. (p. 526)
—Garden of Angels. (p. 656)
—Heart to Heart. (p. 760)
—Hit & Run. (p. 785)
—Holly's Story. (p. 789)
—I Want to Live. (p. 848)
—If I Should Die Before I Wake. (p. 853)
—Kathleen's Story. (p. 944)
—Keep Me in Your Heart: Three Novels. (p. 947)
—Last Dance. (p. 977)
—Letting Go of Lisa. (p. 1003)
—Mother, Please Don't Die. (p. 1178)
—My Secret Boyfriend. (p. 1218)
—No Time to Cry. (p. 1260)
—Prey. (p. 1398)
—Raina's Story. (p. 1435)
—Red Heart Tattoo. (p. 1454)
—Six Months to Live. (p. 1582)
—So Much to Live For. (p. 1602)
—Sometimes Love Isn't Enough. (p. 1610)
—Starry, Starry Night: Three Holiday Stories. (p. 1642)
—True Love. (p. 1792)
—Why Did She Have to Die? (p. 1923)
—Year of Chasing Dreams. (p. 1969)
—Year of Luminous Love. (p. 1969)
McDaniel, Melissa. Declaration of Independence. (p. 422)
—Disaster Search Dogs. (p. 446)
—Earth Slow Changes: Set Of 6. (p. 497)
—Earth: Slow Changes: Text Pairs. (p. 497)
—Ellis Island. (p. 515)
—Great Basin Indians (p. 714)
—Great Depression. (p. 715)
—Guide Dogs. (p. 730)
—Industrial Revolution. (p. 872)
—Monkeys. (p. 1165)
—Mysterious Nature: A Chapter Book. (p. 1223)
—Pushing the Limits: A Chapter Book. (p. 1420)
—South Dakota. (p. 1617)
—Southwest Indians (p. 1618)

McDaniel, Melissa & Kras, Sara Louise. North Dakota. (p. 1265)
McDaniel, Melissa & Mead, Wendy. Arizona. (p. 98)
McDaniel, Melissa, et al. New Mexico. (p. 1246)
McDaniel, Paula. Grandpa's Woods. Austin, Tereesa, illus. (p. 710)
McDaniel, Richard. Little Tree. (p. 1037)
McDaniel, Rick, illus. see Murcray, Rod.
McDaniel Rockstad, Jean. Eric Jay, Eric Jay, What Are You Gonna Do All Day? (p. 533)
McDaniel, Scott, jt. auth. see Defalco, Tom.
McDaniel, Scott, illus. see Daredevil & Elektra: Fall from Grace. (p. 406)
McDaniel, Sean. Ninja. (p. 1256)
—Stonehenge. (p. 1653)
McDaniel, Thomas, illus. see Goodwin, Carol.
McDaniels, Preston. Lord Is My Shepherd: Psalm 23 for Children. (p. 1052)
—Perfect Snowman. McDaniels, Preston, illus. (p. 1342)
—Phineas L. MacGuire ... Gets Cooking! (p. 1351)
—Prince of Ireland & the Three Magic Stallions. (p. 1401)
—Squire & the Scroll: A Tale of the Rewards of a Pure Heart. (p. 1637)
McDaniels, Preston, illus. see Bishop, Jennie.
McDaniels, Preston, illus. see Dowell, Frances O'Roark.
McDaniels, Preston, illus. see Rylant, Cynthia.
McDaniels, Preston, illus. see Webber, Christopher L.
McDaniels, Skeeter. Brewed in Rochester: A Photographic History of Beer in Rochester, New York 1885-1975. (p. 226)
McDaniel-Sanderson, Lynne. Mattie Tells Her Secret. (p. 1110)
McDaris, Terry. Black Fox Tribe: The Beginning. (p. 196)
McDavid, Richard, jt. auth. see Echaore-McDavid, Susan.
McDavid, Richard A. & Echaore-McDavid, Susan. Career Opportunities in Engineering. (p. 267)
McDavid-Jones, Elizabeth. Ghost Light on Graveyard Shoal. (p. 671)
—Mystery on Skull Island. (p. 1226)
—Night Flyers. (p. 1253)
—Secrets on 26th Street. (p. 1546)
—Watcher in the Piney Woods. (p. 1861)
McDee, Katie, illus. see Hansen, Amy S. & Olien, Rebecca.
McDee, Katie, illus. see Olien, Rebecca.
McDee, Katie, illus. see St. John, Amanda.
McDermid, Val. My Granny Is a Pirate. Robins, Arthur, illus. (p. 1210)
Mcdermot, Jessie, illus. see Coolidge, Susan.
McDermott, Gerald. Arrow to the Sun: A Pueblo Indian Tale. McDermott, Gerald, illus. (p. 101)
—Fox & the Stork. (p. 626)
—Jabuti the Tortoise: A Trickster Tale from the Amazon. (p. 902)
—Light of the World. McDermott, Gerald, illus. (p. 1015)
—Monkey: A Trickster Tale from India. (p. 1164)
—Pig-Boy: A Trickster Tale from Hawai'i. (p. 1357)
McDermott, Gerald, illus. see Stott, Jon C.
McDermott, Jesse. Rhode Island, 1636-1776. (p. 1468)
McDermott, Jesse John. Rhode Island, 1636-1776. (p. 1468)
McDermott, John Francis. Adventures of Izzy & Bitty Bee. (p. 19)
McDermott, Kristen, jt. auth. see Berk, Ari.
McDermott, Mary. Special Women We Call Grandmom Braun, Lisa, illus. (p. 1623)
McDermott, Mustafa Yusuf. Muslim Nursery Rhymes (p. 1194)
—Muslim Nursery Rhymes. Norridge, Terry, illus. (p. 1194)
McDermott, Nancie. Quick & Easy Thai: 70 Everyday Recipes. Miksch, Alison, photos by. (p. 1427)
—Southern Cakes: Sweet & Irresistible Recipes for Everyday Celebrations. Luigart-Stayner, Becky & Luigart-Staynes, Becky, photos by. (p. 1617)
McDermott, Robert, illus. see Wood, Francis Eusene.
McDermott, Robert, jt. auth. see Wood, Francis Eugene.
McDermott, Robert W. illus. see Wood, Francis Eugene.
McDermott, Tom. Ghouls Come Haunting One by One McGrath, Liz, illus. (p. 673)
—Otis Steele & the Taileebone: A Southern Tall Tale Crosby, Jeff, illus. (p. 1307)
McDevitt, Bradley. Oddly Adorable Coloring Book 1. Leon, Richard, ed. (p. 1278)
McDevitt, Brian. Ode to General George Washington. (p. 1278)
McDiarmid, Gail S. & McGee, Marilyn S. Running for Home. Coffey, Durwood, illus. (p. 1497)
McDiarmid, Karen, ed. see Sams, Carl R., II & Stoick, Jean.
McDine, Donna M. Hockey Agony. Hammond, Julie, illus. (p. 786)
—Powder Monkey. Snider, Kc, illus. (p. 1389)
McDivitt, Barry. Youngest Spy. (p. 1979)
McDivitt, Zach. See Feinman, Anthony & Hall, Andrew.
McDonagh, Christelle, et al. Mission Magic Bubble. (p. 1153)
McDonagh, Joe. Opening Night. (p. 1300)
McDonald, Abby. Anti-Prom. (p. 89)
—Boys, Bears, & a Serious Pair of Hiking Boots. (p. 220)
—Getting over Garrett Delaney. (p. 669)
—Jane Austen Goes to Hollywood. (p. 908)
—Sophomore Switch. (p. 1614)
McDonald, Amanda, illus. see McDonald, Regina.
McDonald, Andrew. Greatest Blogger in the World. (p. 719)
McDonald, Ann-Eve. Bad Day. (p. 131)
—Dragon's Lair, a Counterpane Story. (p. 479)
—I Can't Go to School Today, My Horses Might Escape. (p. 837)
—MaGook. (p. 1076)
—Tale of the Black Square. (p. 1700)
—There are No Such Thing as Monsters. (p. 1729)
McDonald, Archie R. Primary Source Accounts of the Civil War. (p. 1399)
McDonald, Arthur. Ye Must Be Born Again. (p. 1969)
McDonald, Bernadette & Jehl, Douglas, eds. Whose Water Is It? The Unquenchable Thirst of a Water-Hungry World. (p. 1922)
McDonald, Brenda. How Do You Love A Big Dog? (p. 808)

McDonald, Candice Hartsough, illus. see Shreeve, Elizabeth.
McDonald, Caryl. On the Team: Count to Tell the Number of Objects. (p. 1291)
—Rural Life, Urban Life. (p. 1497)
—Who Was Helen Keller? (p. 1918)
McDonald, Catherine. Challenging Social Work: The Institutional Context of Practice. (p. 289)
McDonald, Cecil. Charley's Rumbly Tummy. (p. 292)
McDonald, Charles. Speech Family. McDonald, Trevy, illus. (p. 1624)
McDonald, Cheryl, jt. auth. see Taylor, Kristen Fitz.
McDonald, Danielle. Fun Bums. (p. 647)
McDonald, Danielle, jt. auth. see Phelan, Cathy.
McDonald, Dawn M. Kiki Koala Wanders Away. (p. 955)
McDonald, Diane O. Adventures of Tweed. (p. 24)
McDonald, Eleanor, illus. see Hassler, Jill K.
McDonald, Ellie. Danger after Dark. (p. 403)
McDonald, Fiona. Everyday Clothes Through History. (p. 543)
—Ghost Doll & Jasper. (p. 670)
—Jewelry & Makeup Through History. (p. 917)
—Shoes & Boots Through History. (p. 1568)
—Uniforms Through History. (p. 1818)
McDonald, Ian. Planesrunner. (p. 1367)
McDonald, J. Donnelly. I Gazed in Amazement: (Ordinary Creatures Do Extraordinary Things) (p. 838)
McDonald, Janet. Chill Wind. (p. 305)
McDonald, Jill. Ghoulish Gang. (p. 673)
—Opposites: A Play-with-Me BK. (p. 1300)
—Over in the Meadow. (p. 1313)
—Over in the Meadow. McDonald, Jill & Reed, Susan, illus. (p. 1313)
—Shapes: A Play-with-Me BK. McDonald, Jill, illus. (p. 1560)
McDonald, Jill, illus. see Gershator, Phillis.
McDonald, Jill, illus. see Gershator, Phyllis.
McDonald, Jill, illus. see Karr, Lily.
McDonald, Jill, illus. see Law, Jessica.
McDonald, Jill, illus. see Perlman, Willa.
McDonald, Jill, illus. see Scholastic, Inc. Staff & Karr, Lily.
Mcdonald, Jill & Fatus, Sophie. Over in the Meadow Puzzle. Modonald, Jill, illus. (p. 1313)
McDonald, Jody. Who Is in the Egg? (p. 1916)
McDonald, Joe, photos by see Markle, Sandra.
McDonald, John. Tempest: The Graphic Novel. Gale Editor, ed. (p. 1717)
McDonald, John, jt. auth. see Shakespeare, William.
McDonald, Joyce. Shades of Simon Gray. (p. 1557)
—Swallowing Stones. (p. 1688)
McDonald, Kim, illus. see Martin, Brian.
McDonald, Lisa. Adventures of Penelope the Tea Cup Pig. (p. 21)
McDonald, Marc, et al. Practical Guide to Defect Prevention. (p. 1392)
McDonald, Marion. Missing Mom. McDonald, Marion & Brown, Marion, illus. (p. 1152)
McDonald, Mary Ann. Boas. (p. 205)
—Toucans. (p. 1772)
McDonald, Mary-Kate. Carving My Name (p. 273)
McDonald, Megan. Amy Namey in Ace Reporter. Madrid, Erwin, illus. (p. 66)
—Ant & Honey Bee: A Pair of Friends in Winter. Karas, G. Brian, illus. (p. 88)
—Ant & Honey Bee: A Pair of Friends at Halloween. Karas, G. Brian, illus. (p. 88)
—Around the World in 8 1/2 Days Reynolds, Peter H., illus. (p. 100)
—Around the World in 8 1/2 Days. (p. 100)
—Around the World in 8 1/2 Days. Reynolds, Peter H., illus. (p. 100)
—Baya, Baya, Lulla-By-a. Rosenberry, Vera, illus. (p. 147)
—Beetle Mcgrady Eats Bugs! Manning, Jane K., illus. (p. 158)
—Big Bad Blackout. (p. 177)
—Cloudy with a Chance of Boys. (p. 335)
—Doctor Is In! (p. 459)
—Doctor Is In! Reynolds, Peter H., illus. (p. 459)
—Doctora Judy Moody. Reynolds, Peter H., illus. (p. 459)
—Frank Pearl in the Awful Waffle Kerfuffle. Madrid, Erwin, illus. (p. 629)
—Girl Detective. Reynolds, Peter H., illus. (p. 678)
—Happy New Year, Julie McAliley, Susan & Hunt, Robert, illus. (p. 746)
—Hen Hears Gossip. Kim, Joung Un, illus. (p. 767)
—Holly Joliday. Reynolds, Peter H., illus. (p. 789)
—Incredible Shrinking Kid. Reynolds, Peter H., illus. (p. 869)
—It's Picture Day Today! Tillotson, Katherine, illus. (p. 898)
—Jessica Finch in Pig Trouble. (p. 914)
—Jessica Finch in Pig Trouble. Madrid, Erwin, illus. (p. 914)
—Judy Moody. (p. 931)
—Judy Moody. Reynolds, Peter H., illus. (p. 931)
—Judy Moody Advina el Futuro. Reynolds, Peter H., illus. (p. 931)
—Judy Moody & Stink: The Mad, Mad, Mad, Mad Treasure Hunt. (p. 931)
—Judy Moody & Stink: La Loca, Loca Busqueda del Tesoro. Reynolds, Peter, illus. (p. 931)
—Judy Moody & Stink: The Mad, Mad, Mad, Mad Treasure Hunt. Reynolds, Peter H., illus. (p. 931)
—Judy Moody & Stink: the Big Bad Blackout. Reynolds, Peter H., illus. (p. 931)
—Judy Moody & Stink: the Wishbone Wish. Reynolds, Peter H., illus. (p. 931)
—Judy Moody & the Bad Luck Charm. (p. 931)
—Judy Moody & the Bad Luck Charm. Reynolds, Peter H., illus. (p. 931)
—Judy Moody & the Bad Luck Charm (Book #11) Reynolds, Peter H., illus. (p. 931)
—Judy Moody & the Not Bummer Summer. (p. 931)
—Judy Moody & the Not Bummer Summer. Reynolds, Peter H., illus. (p. 931)
—Judy Moody Declares Independence. (p. 931)
—Judy Moody Declares Independence. Reynolds, Peter H., illus. (p. 931)
—Judy Moody Esta de Mal Humor, de Muy Mal Humor. Mendoza Garcia, Isabel, tr. (p. 931)
—Judy Moody Gets Famous! (p. 931)

For book reviews, descriptive annotations, tables of contents, cover images, author biographies & additional information, updated daily, subscribe to www.booksinprint2.com

2495

—Judy Moody Gets Famous! Reynolds, Peter H., illus. (p. 931)
—Judy Moody Goes to College Reynolds, Peter H., illus. (p. 931)
—Judy Moody Goes to College. (p. 931)
—Judy Moody Goes to Hollywood: Behind the Scenes with Judy Moody & Friends. Reynolds, Peter H. & Candlewick Press Staff, illus. (p. 931)
—Judy Moody Mood Journal. Reynolds, Peter H., illus. (p. 931)
—Judy Moody, Mood Martian. (p. 931)
—Judy Moody, Mood Martian. Reynolds, Peter H., illus. (p. 931)
—Judy Moody Predicts the Future. (p. 931)
—Judy Moody Predicts the Future. Reynolds, Peter H., illus. (p. 931)
—Judy Moody Salva el Planeta. Reynolds, Peter H., illus. (p. 931)
—Judy Moody Saves the World! (p. 931)
—Judy Moody Saves the World! Reynolds, Peter H., illus. (p. 931)
—Judy Moody se Vuelve Famosa! Mendoza Garcia, Isabel, tr. (p. 931)
—Judy Moody - Uber Awesome Collection Reynolds, Peter H., illus. (p. 931)
—Judy Moody va a la Universidad. Rozarena, P., tr. (p. 931)
—Judy Moody - Was in a Mood. Reynolds, Peter H., illus. (p. 931)
—Judy Moody y Stink: ¡Felices Fiestas! Rozarena, P., tr. (p. 931)
—Judy Moody's Best Mood Ever Coloring & Activity Book. Reynolds, Peter H., illus. (p. 931)
—Judy Moody's Double-Rare Way-Not-Boring Book of Fun Stuff to Do. Reynolds, Peter H., illus. (p. 931)
—Judy Moody's Mini-Mysteries & Other Sneaky Stuff for Super-Sleuths. Reynolds, Peter H., illus. (p. 931)
—Judy Moody's Way Wacky Uber Awesome Book of More Fun Stuff to Do. Reynolds, Peter H., illus. (p. 931)
—Julie Story Collection. Hunt, Robert, illus. (p. 932)
—Mad, Mad, Mad, Mad Treasure Hunt. Reynolds, Peter H., illus. (p. 1069)
—Mood Martian. Reynolds, Peter H., illus. (p. 1171)
—More Super-Stinky Stuff from A to Z. Reynolds, Peter H., illus. (p. 1175)
—Pair of Friends in Winter. Karas, G. Brian, illus. (p. 1318)
—Rocky Zang in the Amazing Mr. Magic. (p. 1484)
—Saving the Liberty Bell. Carrington, Marsha Gray, illus. (p. 1517)
—Shark Sleepover Reynolds, Peter H., illus. (p. 1562)
—Shoe Dog. Tillotson, Katherine, illus. (p. 1568)
—Sisters Club. (p. 1581)
—Solar System Superhero. (p. 1607)
—Solar System Superhero. Reynolds, Peter H., illus. (p. 1607)
—Stink. (p. 1651)
—Stink & the Freaky Frog Freakout. (p. 1651)
—Stink & the Freaky Frog Freakout. Reynolds, Peter H., illus. (p. 1651)
—Stink & the Great Guinea Pig Express Reynolds, Peter H., illus. (p. 1651)
—Stink & the Great Guinea Pig Express. (p. 1651)
—Stink & the Incredible Super-Galactic Jawbreaker. (p. 1651)
—Stink & the Incredible Super-Galactic Jawbreaker. Reynolds, Peter H., illus. (p. 1651)
—Stink & the Midnight Zombie Walk. (p. 1651)
—Stink & the Midnight Zombie Walk. Reynolds, Peter H., illus. (p. 1651)
—Stink & the Shark Sleepover. (p. 1651)
—Stink & the Shark Sleepover. Reynolds, Peter H., illus. (p. 1651)
—Stink & the Ultimate Thumb-Wrestling Smackdown. Reynolds, Peter H., illus. (p. 1651)
—Stink & the World's Worst Super-Stinky Sneakers Reynolds, Peter H., illus. (p. 1651)
—Stink & the World's Worst Super-Stinky Sneakers. (p. 1651)
—Stink, el Increíble Niño Menguante. (p. 1651)
—Stink It Up! A Guide to the Gross, the Bad, & the Smelly. (p. 1651)
—Stink It Up! A Guide to the Gross, the Bad, & the Smelly. Reynolds, Peter H., illus. (p. 1651)
—Stink Moody in Master of Disaster. Madrid, Erwin, illus. (p. 1651)
—Stink: the Absolutely Astronomical Collection: Books 4-6. Reynolds, Peter H., illus. (p. 1651)
—Stink - The Super-Incredible Collection Reynolds, Peter H., illus. (p. 1651)
—Stink y el Gran Expreso del Cobaya. Rozarena, P., tr. (p. 1651)
—Stink y el Increíble Rompemuelas Supergaláctico. (p. 1651)
—Stink y los Tenis Más Apestosos del Mundo. (p. 1651)
—Stink-O-Pedia: Super Stink-Y Stuff from A to Zzzzz. Vol. 2 Reynolds, Peter H., illus. (p. 1651)
—Stink-O-Pedia. (p. 1651)
—Triple Pet Trouble. Madrid, Erwin, illus. (p. 1787)
—Twice as Moody. Reynolds, Peter H., illus. (p. 1801)
—Was in a Mood. Reynolds, Peter H., illus. (p. 1859)
—When the Library Lights Go Out. Tillotson, Katherine, tr. (p. 1904)
—When the Library Lights Go Out. Tillotson, Katherine, illus. (p. 1904)
McDonald, Megan, jt. auth. see Christopher, Garrett.
McDonald, Megan & Michalak, Jamie. Poop Picnic. Reynolds, Peter H. & Candlewick Press Staff, illus. (p. 1383)
McDonald, Meinir & Evans, Anthony. Bant I Batagonia. (p. 137)
McDonald, Mercedes, illus. see Costales, Amy.
McDonald, Mercedes, illus. see Harjo, Joy.
McDonald, Michelle. My Day. (p. 1201)
McDonald, Muriel. Muriel Remembers. (p. 1192)
Mcdonald, P. J. Cry for Help No One Heard. (p. 387)
McDonald, Patrick, illus. see Borer, Christopher.
McDonald, Paulette N. Crimson Blade. (p. 382)
McDonald, Rae A. Fishing Surprise. Kemly, Kathleen, illus. (p. 599)
McDonald, Regina. Friday Night at the Zoo McDonald, Amanda, illus. (p. 637)
McDonald, Robert, jt. auth. see Bergquist, Kathie.
McDonald, Stacy. Raising Maidens of Virtue: A Study of Feminine Loveliness for Mothers & Daughters. (p. 1437)
McDonald, Steve. Fantastic Cities: A Coloring Book of Amazing Places Real & Imagined. (p. 571)
McDonald, Susan. I Like Different Books with Different Looks. (p. 841)
—Only Just One Mushroom. (p. 1298)
McDonald, Suzi, illus. see Hart, Janice.
McDonald, Trevy. Brandi Surfs the Web. (p. 222)
McDonald, Trevy, illus. see McDonald, Charles.
McDonald-Mitchell, Carolyn. Secret Hiding Place. (p. 1541)
McDonial, R. Sport Shortz(r) Move, Run, Jump(tm) Book. (p. 1631)
McDoniel, Estelle. Registered Nurse to Rear Admiral: A First for Navy Women. (p. 1457)
McDonnell, Chris & Cartoon Network Staff. Adventure Time: the Art of Ooo. (p. 14)
McDonnell, David, ed. Fantasy Worlds (p. 572)
—Spiderman & Other Amazing Heroes. (p. 1626)
McDonnell, Flora. Splash! (p. 1629)
—Splash. (p. 1629)
McDonnell, Flora & Habashi, Azza. Splash. (p. 1629)
McDonnell, Flora & Jones, Gordon. Rwy'n Hoffi Anifeiliaid. (p. 1499)
McDonnell, Ginger. Next Stop: Mexico. (p. 1249)
—Next Stop: The Caribbean. (p. 1249)
—Next Stop: The Caribbean. (p. 1249)
—Next Stop - Canada. (p. 1249)
—Next Stop - Mexico. (p. 1249)
McDonnell, Janet, illus. see Dellinger, Annetta.
McDonnell, Janet, illus. see Freeland, Claire A.B. & Toner, Jacqueline B.
McDonnell, Janet, illus. see Wittenback, Janet.
McDonnell, John. Christmas Gift. (p. 314)
McDonnell, Julia . Being a Sloth. (p. 160)
McDonnell, Julia. Coast Guard. (p. 336)
—Gophers. (p. 702)
—Legend of Robin Hood. (p. 988)
—Sitting Bull in His Own Words. (p. 1582)
McDonnell, Kathleen. 1212: Year of the Journey (p. 2002)
—Putting on a Show: Theater for Young People (p. 1420)
—Shining World (p. 1567)
—Songweavers (p. 1612)
McDonnell, Kevin, illus. see Jones, Shelley V. & Sprick, Marilyn.
McDonnell, Margot. Torn to Pieces. (p. 1770)
McDonnell, Mary Ann, ed. see Bauchner, Elizabeth.
McDonnell, Mary Ann, ed. see Bonnice, Sherry & Hoard, Carolyn.
McDonnell, Mary Ann, ed. see Bonnice, Sherry.
McDonnell, Mary Ann, ed. see Brinkerhoff, Shirley.
McDonnell, Mary Ann, ed. see Esherick, Joan.
McDonnell, Mary Ann, ed. see Hovius, Christopher.
McDonnell, Mary Ann, ed. see Hunter, Miranda & Hunter, William.
McDonnell, Mary Ann, ed. see Lange, Donna.
McDonnell, Mary Ann, ed. see Libal, Autumn.
McDonnell, Mary Ann, ed. see Libal, Joyce.
McDonnell, Mary Ann, ed. see Simons, Rae.
McDonnell, Mary Ann, ed. see Vitale, Ann.
McDonnell, Mary Rose. Sorting with Snakes. (p. 1614)
McDonnell, Melissa. Tell Time with Turtles. (p. 1717)
McDonnell, Patrick. Art. (p. 101)
—Gift of Nothing. (p. 675)
—Hug Time. (p. 824)
—I Want to Be the Kitty (p. 848)
—Just Like Heaven. (p. 939)
—Me... Jane. (p. 1116)
—Monsters' Monster. (p. 1169)
—Mutts: Tiere sind auch nur Menschen. Dickerhof-Kranz, Susanne, tr. from ENG. (p. 1195)
—Mutts Diaries. (p. 1195)
—Perfectly Messed-Up Story. (p. 1342)
—Wag! (p. 1852)
McDonnell, Patrick, illus. see Barnett, Mac.
McDonnell, Patrick & Mystery Writers of America Staff. South. (p. 1616)
McDonnell, Peter. Helping Others: The Story of Fanny Jackson Coppin. (p. 766)
—Last Princess. (p. 978)
—Soldier in Disguise. Tormey, Carlotta, illus. (p. 1607)
McDonnell, Peter, illus. see Englar, Mary.
McDonnell, Peter, illus. see Glaser, Jason.
McDonnell, Peter, illus. see Lassieur, Allison.
McDonnell, Vincent. Can Timmy Save Toyland? (p. 258)
—Catalpa Adventure: Escape to Freedom. (p. 278)
—Children of Stone. (p. 302)
—Chill Factor. (p. 305)
—Ireland Our Island Story. (p. 887)
—Knock Airport Mystery. (p. 965)
—Michael Collins: Most Wanted Man. (p. 1134)
—Race Against Time. (p. 1430)
—Story of the GAA. (p. 1661)
—Titanic Tragedy. (p. 1758)
McDonough, Judy. Online Privacy & Hacking. (p. 1298)
McDonough, Kelly. Things I Don't Like. (p. 1733)
McDonough, Yona Zeldis. Cats in the Doll Shop. Maione, Heather, illus. (p. 281)
—Doll Shop Downstairs. Maione, Heather, illus. (p. 463)
—Little Author in the Big Woods: A Biography of Laura Ingalls Wilder. Thermes, Jennifer, illus. (p. 1023)
—Louisa: The Life of Louisa May Alcott. Andersen, Bethanne, illus. (p. 1058)
—Louisa. Andersen, Bethanne, illus. (p. 1058)
—What Was the Underground Railroad? (p. 1895)
—What Was the Underground Railroad? Mortimer, Lauren & Bennett, James, illus. (p. 1895)
—Who Was Harriet Tubman? Harrison, Nancy, illus. (p. 1918)
—Who Was John F. Kennedy? Weber, Jill & Harrison, Nancy, illus. (p. 1918)
—Who Was Louis Armstrong? O'Brien, John A. & Harrison, Nancy, illus. (p. 1918)
—Who Was Rosa Parks? Harrison, Nancy & Marchesi, Stephen, illus. (p. 1919)
—Who Was Wolfgang Amadeus Mozart? (p. 1919)
—Who Was Wolfgang Amadeus Mozart? Robbins, Carrie, illus. (p. 1919)
—¿Quién Fue Harriet Tubman? (Who Was Harriet Tubman?) Harrison, Nancy, illus. (p. 1427)
McDoogle, Farrah. Mike & the Dragons. (p. 1141)
—Mystery in Gabba Land. Scanlon, Michael, illus. (p. 1224)
—OLIVIA & the Sea Lions. Spaziante, Patrick, illus. (p. 1286)
—OLIVIA Makes a Charm Bracelet. Osterhold, Jared, illus. (p. 1287)
—OLIVIA Talks Turkey. Osterhold, Jared, illus. (p. 1287)
—Olivia the Ballerina. Spaziante, Patrick, illus. (p. 1287)
—Party for Brobee! (p. 1326)
Mcdoogle, Farrah. Sweet Surprise for Mom. (p. 1690)
—Thank You Day. (p. 1725)
McDoogle, Farrah & Pulliam, Gabe. OLIVIA Says Good Night. Spaziante, Patrick, illus. (p. 1287)
McDougall, Carol, jt. auth. see LaRamee-Jones, Shanda.
McDougall, Carol & LaRamee-Jones, Shanda. Baby Look. (p. 127)
—Baby Play (p. 127)
McDougall, Chros. Arthur Ashe: Tennis Great & Civil Rights Leader. (p. 103)
—Best Soccer Players of All Time. (p. 171)
—Girls Play to Win Figure Skating. (p. 680)
—Girls Play to Win Track & Field. (p. 680)
—Girls Play to Win Volleyball. (p. 680)
—Jesse Owens: Trailblazing Sprinter. (p. 914)
—Kurt Cobain: Alternative Rock Innovator. (p. 968)
—San Francisco Earthquake & Fire. (p. 1510)
—Soccer. (p. 1603)
McDougall, Chrs. San Francisco Earthquake & Fire Paperback. (p. 1510)
McDougall, Jill. Anna the Goanna: And Other Poems. Taylor, Jenny, illus. (p. 85)
—Jinxed! (p. 919)
McDougall, Nancy. Ultimate Step-By-Step Kid's First Cookbook: Delicious Recipe Ideas for 5-12 Year Olds, from Lunch Boxes & Picnics to Quick & Easy Meals, Sweet Treats, Desserts, Drinks & Party Food. (p. 1810)
—We Can Cook! Kids in the Kitchen. (p. 1866)
McDougall, Nancy & Hendy, Jenny. 300 Step-By-Step Cooking & Gardening Projects for Kids: The Ultimate Book for Budding Gardeners & Super Chefs with Amazing Things to Grow & Cook Yourself, Shown in over 2300 Photographs. (p. 2001)
—300 Step-By-Step Cooking & Gardening Projects for Kids: The Ultimate Book for Budding Gardeners & Super Chefs, with Amazing Things to Grow & Cook Yourself, Shown in over 2300 Photographs. (p. 2001)
—Ultimate Book of Step-By-Step Cooking & Gardening Projects for Kids: The Best-Ever Book for Budding Gardeners & Super Chefs with 300 Things to Grow & Cook Yourself, Shown in over 2300 Photographs. (p. 1809)
McDougall, Sophia. Mars Evacuees. (p. 1096)
McDougal-Littell Publishing Staff. Changing Earth. (p. 290)
—Chemical Interactions. (p. 297)
—Diversity of Living Things. (p. 454)
—Dragonwings. (p. 479)
—Earth Science. (p. 496)
—Earth's Surface. (p. 498)
—Earth's Surface 2005. (p. 498)
—Electricity & Magnetism 2005. (p. 509)
—Geometry: Concepts & Skills: Notetaking Guide. (p. 662)
—Integrated Course. (p. 879)
—Integrated Course 3. (p. 879)
—Language Network. (p. 975)
—Life over Time, Grade 6-8. (p. 1012)
—Literature Connections English: Dogsong. (p. 1023)
—Literature Connections English: Homecoming. (p. 1023)
—Literature Connections English: Trouble River. (p. 1023)
—Literature Connections English: Tuck Everlasting. (p. 1023)
—Literature Connections English: I, Juan de Pareja. (p. 1023)
—Literature Connections English: Across Five Aprils. (p. 1023)
—Literature Connections English: The Call of the Wild. (p. 1023)
—Literature Connections English: When Rain Clouds Gather. (p. 1023)
—Literature Connections English: Where the Red Fern Grows. (p. 1023)
—Literature Connections English: Roll of Thunder, Hear My Cry. (p. 1023)
—Literature Connections English: A Place Where the Sea Remembers. (p. 1023)
—Literature Connections Spanish: Yo, Juan de Pareja (I, Juan de Pareja) (p. 1023)
—Literature Connections Spanish. (p. 1023)
—Matter & Energy. (p. 1109)
—McDougal Littell Middle School Math: Notetaking Guide. (p. 1114)
—Middle School Math: Practice Workbook. (p. 1137)
—Middle School Math. (p. 1137)
—Middle School Math, Course 1: Notetaking Guide. (p. 1138)
—Middle School Math, Course 1: Practice Workbook, PE. (p. 1138)
—Modern World History: Patterns of Interaction. (p. 1159)
—Modern World History: Patterns of Interaction - Reading Study Guide. (p. 1159)
—Modules: Physical Science. (p. 1159)
—Modules: Life Science; Human Biology. (p. 1159)
—Modules: Physical Science; Ecology Unit. (p. 1159)
—Modules: Physical Science - Space Science. (p. 1159)
—Modules: Earth Science - Earth's Waters PE. (p. 1159)
—Modules: Physical Science, Matter & Energy. (p. 1159)
—Modules: Physical Science - Earth's Atmosphere. (p. 1159)
—Modules: Physical Science; Cells & Heredity Unit. (p. 1159)
—Modules: Physical Science - Chemical Interactions. (p. 1159)
—Modules: Physical Science - Diversity of Living Things. (p. 1159)
—Notetaking Guide: Pre-Algebra. (p. 1268)
—Physical Science. (p. 1353)
—Pre-Algebra: Exercises in Spanish. (p. 1393)
—Pre-Algebra: Chapter Reviews & Tests. (p. 1393)
—Pre-Algebra. (p. 1393)
—Science: Integrated Course 1. (p. 1524)
—Space Science. (p. 1619)
—True Confessions of Charlotte Doyle. (p. 1792)
—Waves, Sound, & Light. (p. 1864)
—Waves, Sound, & Light. (p. 1864)
—World History: Patterns of Interaction. (p. 1955)
—World History - Patterns of Interaction: Reading Study Guide. (p. 1955)
—World History - Patterns of Interaction. (p. 1955)
McDougal-Littell Publishing Staff & Nextext Staff, contrib. by. Stories in History. (p. 1654)
McDougal-Littell Publishing Staff, contrib. by. Nation Dividing 1800-1860. (p. 1231)
McDougal-Littell Publishing Staff, creator. 1984: And Related Readings. (p. 2002)
—Algebra 1: Concepts & Skills. (p. 38)
—American Literature. (p. 62)
—Creating America Workbook: A History of the United States. (p. 378)
—Geometry. (p. 662)
—Grammar, Usage, & Mechanics Book: Teaching, More Practice, Application. (p. 706)
—Grammar, Usage, & Mechanics Book Grade 8: Teaching More Practice Application. (p. 706)
—Language Network. (p. 975)
—Language of Literature. (p. 975)
—Latin America. (p. 979)
—McDougal Littell Pre-Algebra Special Activities Book. (p. 1114)
—Motion & Forces. (p. 1179)
—Picture Bride & Related Readings. (p. 1355)
—Writing Research Reports. (p. 1965)
McDowell, Andrew. Beyond the Forest. (p. 174)
McDowell, Barbara. Animals. (p. 81)
McDowell, Beck. This Is Not a Drill. (p. 1736)
McDowell, Josh. Is Christ Really God? Grades 1-3. (p. 889)
—Is Christ Really God? Grades 3-6. (p. 889)
McDowell, Josh, jt. auth. see Stewart, Ed.
McDowell, Josh & Bellis, Dave. Is Christ Really God? Children's Workbook. (p. 889)
—Is the Bible Personally from God? The Real Truth about Living Like Jesus. (p. 890)
McDowell, Josh & Hostetler, Bob. Truth Twisters. (p. 1794)
McDowell, Josh & Johnson, Kevin. Great Treasure Quest. Jones, Buck, illus. (p. 719)
McDowell, Josh & Stewart, Ed. Divorce of Parents. (p. 455)
—My Friend Is Struggling with Unplanned Pregnancy. (p. 1209)
—Past Sexual Abuse. (p. 1327)
—Youth Devotions (p. 1982)
McDowell, Julie. Metals. (p. 1130)
—Nervous System & Sense Organs (p. 1241)
McDowell, Julie & Windelspecht, Michael. Lymphatic System (p. 1066)
McDowell, Marilyn Taylor. Carolina Harmony. (p. 270)
McDowell, Pamela. Adele. (p. 12)
—Águilas de Cabeza Blanca. (p. 30)
—Anne Frank. (p. 85)
—Bald Eagle. (p. 133)
—Benjamin Franklin. (p. 164)
—Birds. (p. 191)
—Black Bear. (p. 195)
—Clownfish. (p. 335)
—Farm. (p. 573)
—Fishing Town. (p. 599)
—Flight. (p. 604)
—Gorillas. (p. 703)
—Hibernation. (p. 775)
—Japan. (p. 909)
—Landslides. (p. 974)
—Liebres. (p. 1007)
—Lobos. (p. 1044)
—Manta Rays. (p. 1088)
—Maryland: The Old Line State. (p. 1101)
—Massachusetts: The Bay Btate. (p. 1102)
—Michael Phelps. (p. 1134)
—Michigan: The Wolverine State. (p. 1135)
—Minnesota: The North Star State. (p. 1147)
—Mississippi: The Magnolia State. (p. 1154)
—Missouri: The Show Me State. (p. 1154)
—Osos Negros. (p. 1306)
—Ospreys in Danger Charko, Kasia, illus. (p. 1306)
—Rabbits. (p. 1430)
—Sea Dragons. (p. 1534)
—Selena Gomez. (p. 1549)
—Small Town. (p. 1592)
—Teen Pregnancy. (p. 1713)
—Tennessee: The Volunteer State. (p. 1720)
—Wolves. (p. 1945)
McDowell, Pamela, jt. auth. see Rose, Simon.
McDowell, Pamela & Rose, Simon. Sea Dragons. (p. 1534)
McDowell, Sean. Ethix: Being Bold in a Whatever World. (p. 539)
—Eti-k: En un Mundo Donde Todo Cuenta. (p. 539)
McDowell, Tina. At Home Around the World. (p. 110)
Mcduffee, William. Story Time with Grandpa Bill Collection. (p. 1663)
McDuffie, Daryl L. ABC's to Unlimited Success: How to Turn All Your Dreams into Reality. (p. 4)
McDuffie, Linda. Underwater Adventures of Little Ki. (p. 1817)
McDuke, Doc. Emily, the Brave. Morse, Michelle, illus. (p. 519)
McDunn, Linda L. Color of Me. Knutson, Barbara, illus. (p. 343)
McDunn, Rosemary. When Kids Dream & Trucks Fly. (p. 1903)
Mceldowney, Connie. Josiah's Journey. (p. 927)
Mcelfresh, Lynn. Strong Deaf. (p. 1668)
McElhinney, Glenn, illus. see Graves, Annie.
McElligott, Matthew. Absolutely Not. McElligott, Matthew, illus. (p. 7)
—Backbeard: Pirate for Hire. McElligott, Matthew, illus. (p. 130)
—Backbeard & the Birthday Suit: The Hairiest Pirate Who Ever Lived. (p. 130)
—Backbeard - Pirate for Hire. McElligott, Matthew, illus. (p. 130)
—Bean Thirteen. McElligott, Matthew, illus. (p. 150)
—Even Aliens Need Snacks. (p. 541)

Mcelligott, Matthew. Even Aliens Need Snacks. (p. 541)
McElligott, Matthew. Even Aliens Need Snacks. McElligott, Matthew, illus. (p. 541)
—Even Monsters Need Haircuts. (p. 541)
—Even Monsters Need Haircuts. McElligott, Matthew, illus. (p. 541)
—Lion's Share: A Tale of Halving Cake & Eating It, Too. McElligott, Matthew, illus. (p. 1021)
—Lion's Share. (p. 1021)
—Lion's Share. McElligott, Matthew, illus. (p. 1021)
—Mad Scientist Academy: the Dinosaur Disaster. (p. 1069)
McElligott, Matthew, illus. see Patschke, Steve.
McElligott, Matthew & Tuxbury, Larry. Benjamin Franklinstein Meets the Fright Brothers. (p. 165)
Mcelligott, Matthew & Tuxbury, Larry. Benjamin Franklinstein Meets the Fright Brothers. (p. 165)
McElligott, Matthew & Tuxbury, Larry David. Benjamin Franklinstein Lives! McElligott, Matthew, illus. (p. 165)
—Benjamin Franklinstein Meets Thomas Deadison. McElligott, Matthew, illus. (p. 165)
McElligott, Walter Lee. Blessed Bethlehem Birth: As told by Abraham & Anna Mousenstem. Collier, Kevin Scott, illus. (p. 199)
McElmeel, Sharon L. Best Teen Reads. (p. 171)
McElmeel, Sharron L. Children's Authors & Illustrators Too Good to Miss: Biographical Sketches & Bibliographies (p. 303)
McElmurry, Jill. Mario Makes a Move. McElmurry, Jill, illus. (p. 1094)
McElmurry, Jill, illus. see Appelt, Kathi.
McElmurry, Jill, illus. see Bardhan-Quallen, Sudipta.
McElmurry, Jill, illus. see Hopkins, H. Joseph.
McElmurry, Jill, illus. see Knapp, Ruthie.
McElmurry, Jill, illus. see Miller, Pat Zietlow.
McElmurry, Jill, illus. see Schertle, Alice.
McElmurry, Jill, illus. see Spinner, Stephanie.
McElmurry, Jill, jt. auth. see Schertle, Alice.
McElrath-Eslick, Lori, illus. see Carlstrom, Nancy White.
McElrath-Eslick, Lori, illus. see Hoppey, Tim.
McElrath-Eslick, Lori, illus. see Thomas, Joan G.
McElrath-Eslick, Lori, illus. see Weisburd, Stefi.
McElreath, Kim. Mikey the Schoolhouse Mouse. (p. 1141)
—Pouring in Love. (p. 1389)
McElroy, Bonnie. Jagannath Coloring Book. McElroy, Bonnie, illus. (p. 905)
McElroy, Bonnie & Mandala Publishing Staff. Gopal Coloring Book. (p. 702)
—Nimai Coloring Book. (p. 1255)
McElroy, Bonnie, et al. Damodara Coloring Book. (p. 401)
—Jagannatha Coloring Book. (p. 905)
McElroy, Jean. Baby's Colorful World. (p. 128)
—It's Harvest Time! A Book with Foldout Pages. Tilde, photos by. (p. 897)
—Let's Get Cleany-Clean! Zdanowicz, Paul, illus. (p. 996)
McElroy, Jean & Childrens Books Staff. Let's Count 1 2 3! (p. 995)
McElroy, Kim, illus. see Van Zant, Dawn.
McElroy, Laurie. Teenick: Drake & Josh Scrapbook/Episode Guide. (p. 1714)
McElroy, Laurie, adapted by. Super Sneak. (p. 1682)
McElroy, Lisa Tucker. John G. Roberts, Jr: Chief Justice. (p. 921)
—Love, Lizzie: Letters to a Military Mom. Paterson, Diane, illus. (p. 1060)
—Nancy Pelosi: First Woman Speaker of the House. (p. 1229)
—Nancy Pelosi. (p. 1229)
—Sonia Sotomayor: First Hispanic U. S. Supreme Court Justice. (p. 1612)
—Ted Kennedy: A Remarkable Life in the Senate. (p. 1712)
McElroy, Roland. Jibicle & Cokie: Friends at Last. (p. 917)
McElvaine, Robert S. Depression & New Deal: A History in Documents. (p. 427)
McElvane, Catherine, illus. see Patterson, Irania.
McElvane, Catherine, jt. auth. see Patterson, Irania.
McElvany, Katherine. God's World through the Eyes of Baxter: Baxter the Bug & the Bright Red Boots. (p. 692)
McElwain, Kelly A., jt. auth. see Baker, Robin J.
McElwain, Sarah & O'Neal, John H. Saying Grace: Blessings for the Family Table. McElwain, Sarah, ed. (p. 1519)
McElwee, Renee. Goddesses Paper Dolls. (p. 690)
McEnroe, Jim. Rabbit King: Kingdom Leporidae. (p. 1429)
McEntee, Bill, jt. auth. see O'Kane, George.
McEntee, Joe, jt. auth. see McNicholas, Jim.
McEntee, Sean & Breen, Michael, eds. Columba Lectionary for Masses with Children Year C. (p. 346)
McEntire, K. D. Lightbringer. (p. 1015)
—Never. (p. 1242)
—Reaper. (p. 1450)
Mceowen, Mari R. Maggie Braves the Waves with Asthma. (p. 1071)
McEvenue, Tim, illus. see Walsh, Brendan & Benchmark Education Co., LLC.
McEvey, Shane F. & Australian Museum Archives Staff. Insects & Spiders Series (p. 876)
McEvoy, Anne. Fashions of a Decade: The 1990s. (p. 576)
McEvoy, Anne, jt. auth. see Bailey Publishing Staff.
Mcevoy, Ariane. Little Monkey Learns to Share. (p. 1032)
McEvoy, Grace. Tiniest Tepee. (p. 1755)
McEvoy, Paul. Alien Files. (p. 40)
—Plants. (p. 1369)
McEwan, Elaine K., et al. Word Analysis,Grades 4-8. (p. 1950)
McEwan, Ian. Daydreamer (p. 415)
—Daydreamer. (p. 415)
McEwan, Jamie. Scrubs Forever! Margeson, John, illus. (p. 1533)
—Whitewater Scrubs. Margeson, John, illus. (p. 1914)
—Willy the Scrub. Kennedy, Victor, illus. (p. 1934)
McEwan, Joseph, illus. see Faulkner, Keith.
McEwan, Rebecca. Lost Cities & Ciudades Perdidas: 6 English, 6 Spanish Adaptations. (p. 1055)
—Telling Time Through the Ages & Comó medir el tiempo desde la antiguedad hasta nuestros Días: 6 English, 6 Spanish Adaptations. (p. 1717)
McEwen, Alastair, tr. see Hornby, Simonetta Agnello.
McEwen, John. Paula Rego. (p. 1331)
McEwen, Katharine. Bear Hug. McEwen, Katharine, illus. (p. 150)
McEwen, Katharine, illus. see Ahlberg, Allan.
McEwen, Katharine, illus. see Davies, Nicola.
McEwen, Katharine, illus. see Durant, Alan.
McEwen, Katharine, illus. see Kelly, Mij.
McEwen, Katharine, illus. see Rosen, Michael.
McEwen, Katharine, illus. see Webb, Steve.
McEwen, Priscilla, jt. auth. see Bredin, Henrietta.
McEwen, Sarah, jt. auth. see Scace, Orsolya Lorincz.
McFadden, Brenda. Destanie's Journey. McFadden, Brenda, illus. (p. 430)
McFadden, Deanna. Cinderella. Sokolava, Valerie, illus. (p. 320)
—Elves & the Shoemaker. Calo, Marcos, illus. (p. 517)
—Hansel & Gretel. Graegin, Stephanie, illus. (p. 743)
—Little Red Riding Hood. Wakefield, Scott J., illus. (p. 1035)
—Rapunzel. Mims, Ashley, illus. (p. 1439)
—Robin Hood. Calo, Marcos, illus. (p. 1479)
—Rumpelstiltskin. Quarello, Maurizio A. C., illus. (p. 1495)
—Snow White & the Seven Dwarfs. Woo Kim, Jin, illus. (p. 1600)
McFadden, Deanna & Andersen, Hans Christian. Little Mermaid. Mims, Ashley, illus. (p. 1031)
McFadden, Deanna, et al. Sleeping Beauty. Graegin, Stephanie, illus. (p. 1589)
McFadden, Jennifer. Rusty My Playful Cat. (p. 1498)
McFadden, Jesse. Construction Worker's Tools. (p. 360)
—Franklin's Farm Stand: Understand Place Value. (p. 631)
McFadden, Joline, illus. see Cheng, Andrea.
McFadden, Kevin, see Pike, Christopher, pseud.
McFadden, Patricia. Oh No, Woolly Bear! Coxon, Michele, illus. (p. 1281)
McFadden, Stephen, jt. auth. see Berman, Ron.
McFadden, Tara. Kael. (p. 941)
McFadzean, Lesley. Birds: Flying High. (p. 191)
—Creating & Cracking Codes. (p. 378)
—Earth in Peril. (p. 496)
—Forest Habitats. (p. 618)
—Insects. (p. 875)
—Ocean Habitats. (p. 1276)
—Technology & Treatments. (p. 1711)
McFall, Christie. America Underground. McFall, Christie, illus. (p. 59)
McFall, Ernest, jt. auth. see McFall, Jessica.
McFall, Jessica & McFall, Ernest. Unselfish Love. (p. 1822)
McFall, Sally, ed. Pro/Con 2 (p. 1408)
—Pro/Con 3 (p. 1408)
McFarlan, Donald, ed. see Stevenson, Robert Louis & Stevenson, Robert Louis.
McFarland, Bill, jt. auth. see Deffenbaugh, David.
McFarland, Cynthia. Foaling Primer: A Step-By-Step Guide to Raising a Healthy Foal. Langrish, Bob, photos by. (p. 610)
Mcfarland, Jewel. Zach & His Frog. (p. 1984)
McFarland, Jim, illus. see McFarland, Lyn Rossiter.
McFarland, John S. Annette a Big, Hairy Mom. (p. 86)
McFarland, Kim. Refugee in Oz. (p. 1456)
McFarland, Lyn Rossiter. Widget. McFarland, Jim, illus. (p. 1927)
McFarland, Myndie. Squigley the Squirrel. (p. 1637)
McFarland, Richard, illus. see England, Kathryn.
McFarland, Shea, illus. see Carmichael, Heather.
McFarland, Sheryl. Smell of Paint (p. 1593)
McFarland, Wysotski, jt. auth. see McFarlane, Sheryl.
McFarlane, Marilyn. Sacred Stories: Wisdom from World Religions. Berg, Caroline O., illus. (p. 1500)
Mcfarlane, Seth, creator. Family Guy (p. 568)
McFarlane, Sheryl. At the Circus LaFave, Kim, illus. (p. 111)
—Island Santa Lott, Sheena, illus. (p. 892)
—Pod of Orcas Wakelin, Kirsti Anne, illus. (p. 1375)
—This is the Dog Wysotski, Chrissie, illus. (p. 1736)
McFarlane, Sheryl & McFarland, Wysotski. This Is the Dog (p. 1736)
McFarren, Kathleen. Marco Polo (p. 1092)
—Vasco Da Gama (p. 1833)
McFarren, Kathleen, jt. auth. see Evan-Moor.
McFarren, Kathleen & Graf, Mike. Science Fair Projects & Activities: Creative Ideas Using Easy-to-Find Materials. Valko, Diane & Corbin, Hillam, illus. (p. 1526)
Mcfaul, Jason & Macdonald, Eric. What A Trip. (p. 1878)
McFay, Edgar. Angelina Jolie: Angel in Disguise. (p. 74)
—Cast of the O. C. The Stories Behind the Faces. (p. 276)
McFay, Edgar & Thay, Edrick. Hilary Duff: Her Story & Her Rise to Fame. Vol. 1 (p. 779)
McFee, Shane. Bungee Jumping. (p. 242)
—Deadly Fish. (p. 417)
—Deadly Lizards. (p. 417)
—Deadly Spiders. (p. 418)
—Jellyfish. (p. 912)
—Let's Learn Martial Arts. (p. 998)
—Let's Play Baseball. (p. 1000)
—Let's Play Basketball. (p. 1000)
—Let's Play Football. (p. 1000)
—Let's Play Ice Hockey. (p. 1000)
—Let's Play Soccer. (p. 1000)
—Rock Climbing. (p. 1482)
—Scorpions. (p. 1530)
—Scuba Diving. (p. 1533)
—Skydiving. (p. 1587)
—Stingrays. (p. 1651)
—Surfing. (p. 1685)
—Whitewater Rafting. (p. 1914)
McFeeley, Dan, illus. see Levy, Elizabeth & Havlan, J. R.
McFeeley, Daniel, illus. see Schlessinger, Laura.
McG, Shane. Tennis, Anyone? McG, Shane, illus. (p. 1720)
McG, Shane, illus. see Fox, Lee.
McGaa, Ed. Spirit Horse: An Adventure in Crazy Horse Country. (p. 1628)
McGaa, Ed, jt. auth. see McGaa Tonemah, Paula.
McGaa Tonemah, Paula & McGaa, Ed. Animals Talk. (p. 84)
McGaffey, Kenneth. Sorrows of A Show Girl. (p. 1614)
Mcgaffey, Kenneth. Sorrows of a Show Girl. (p. 1614)
McGaffey, Leta & Spilling, Michael. Honduras. (p. 794)
McGahey, Suzanne. Winter Guard. (p. 1938)
McGairy, James, jt. illus. see Aldous, Kate.
McGalliard, Julie. Waking Up Naked in Strange Places. (p. 1853)
—Waking up Naked in Strange Places. (p. 1853)
McGann, Amber Ann. Windrush the Crooked Llama. (p. 1936)
McGann, Erika. Broken Spell. (p. 230)
—Demon Notebook. (p. 426)
McGann, James, illus. see Feierabend, John M.
McGann, Oisín. Evil Hairdo. (p. 546)
—Mad Grandad & the Kleptoes. (p. 1069)
—Mad Grandad & the Mutant River. (p. 1069)
—Mad Grandad's Flying Saucer. McGann, Oisín, illus. (p. 1069)
—Mad Grandad's Robot Garden. (p. 1069)
—Mad Grandad's Wicked Pictures. (p. 1069)
—Poison Factory. (p. 1377)
—Under Fragile Stone (p. 1813)
McGann, Oisín, illus. see O'Brien, Joe.
McGarrahan, Sean, jt. auth. see Gay, Kathlyn.
McGarry, Katie. Dare You To. (p. 406)
—Pushing the Limits. (p. 1420)
—Take Me On. (p. 1696)
McGarvey, A. J. Loyalty Unbroken: A Mustang's Tale. (p. 1061)
McGary, Norman, illus. see O'Nan, Gerald D.
McGary, Norman, illus. see O'Nan, Lawrence W. & O'Nan, Gerald D.
McGaughrean, Geraldine, et al. Sonrie! Clement, Edgar, illus. (p. 1612)
McGavin, George. Bugs: A Stunning Pop-Up Look at Insects, Spiders, & Other Creepy-Crawlies. Kay, Jim, illus. (p. 237)
McGavin, George C. Amazing Insects & Spiders. (p. 54)
—Bugs & Spiders. (p. 237)
McGaw, Laurie, illus. see Bierman, Carol.
McGaw, Laurie, illus. see Blumberg, Margie.
McGaw, Laurie, illus. see Bosak, Susan V.
McGeachy, Andrew. Flight of Louis Blaireau. (p. 604)
McGearhart, Susea, jt. auth. see Ashcraft, Tami Oldham.
McGee. Logger's Return: The Continuing Adventures of our White-Tailed Deer Friend. (p. 1045)
McGee, Anne Loader. Anni's Attic. (p. 87)
McGee, Anne Loader, jt. auth. see Vendera, Jaime.
Mcgee, B., jt. auth. see Smith, L.
McGee, Barbi. Jumping Game. (p. 934)
McGee, Brenda Holt & Keiser, Debbie Triska. High-Interest Nonfiction: Survivors 3-5. Hoelscher, Wolfgang, ed. (p. 777)
Mcgee, Cotton. Bookman's Adventures: The Valley of the Frogs. (p. 212)
McGee, E. Alan, photos by see Pierce, Paul.
McGee, Helen. Ikky Dikky Dak: Magical Adventures with Googler! Book Two. Kaltenborn, Karl, illus. (p. 856)
McGee, Holly, illus. see Moritz, Dianne.
McGee, Joe. Peanut Butter & Brains. Santoso, Charles, illus. (p. 1332)
McGee, John F., illus. see Dennard, Deborah.
McGee, Kathleen M. & Buddenberg, Laura J. Unmasking Sexual Con Games: Helping Teens Avoid Emotional Grooming & Dating Violence. (p. 1821)
—Unmasking Sexual Con Games Teen's Guide: A Teen's Guide to Avoiding Emotional Grooming & Dating Violence. (p. 1821)
Mcgee, Ken. Forever. (p. 619)
McGee, Krista. Revolutionary (p. 1466)
McGee, Marilyn S., jt. auth. see McDiarmid, Gail S.
McGee, Marni. Ancient Greece: Archaeology Unlocks the Secrets of Greece's Past. (p. 69)
—Hallowed Be. (p. 737)
—National Geographic Investigates: Ancient Greece: Archaeology Unlocks the Secrets of Ancient Greece. (p. 1231)
—Song in Bethlehem. Cockcroft, Jason, illus. (p. 1611)
—Winston the Book Wolf. Beck, Ian, illus. (p. 1937)
McGee, Marni, jt. auth. see Mellor, Ronald J.
McGee, Marni, jt. auth. see Podany, Amanda H.
Mcgee, Mike, et al. Aspects of Mel's Hole: Artists Respond to a Paranormal land Event Occurring in Radiospace. (p. 107)
McGee, Mo, illus. see Parent, Lauren A.
McGee, Pamela M. Keri: Dandelions. Miller, Dawn Ellen, illus. (p. 949)
—Keri: The Wedding. Miller, Dawn Ellen, illus. (p. 949)
—Keri. Miller, Dawn Ellen, illus. (p. 949)
McGee, Patty, ed. see Gregorich, Barbara.
McGee, Randel. Celebrate Chinese New Year with Paper Crafts. (p. 283)
—Celebrate Christmas with Paper Crafts. (p. 283)
—Celebrate Day of the Dead with Paper Crafts. (p. 283)
—Celebrate Halloween with Paper Crafts. (p. 283)
—Celebrate Kwanzaa with Paper Crafts. (p. 284)
—Celebrate Valentine's Day with Paper Crafts. (p. 284)
—Fun & Festive Fall Crafts: Leaf Rubbings, Dancing Scarecrows, & Pinecone Turkeys. (p. 647)
—Fun & Festive Spring Crafts: Flower Puppets, Bunny Masks, & Mother's Day Pop-Up Cards. (p. 647)
—Fun & Festive Summer Crafts: Tie-Dyed Shirts, Bug Cages, & Sand Castles. (p. 647)
—Fun & Festive Winter Crafts: Snow Globes, Groundhog Puppets, & Fairy Masks. (p. 647)
—Paper Crafts for Chinese New Year. (p. 1322)
—Paper Crafts for Christmas. (p. 1322)
—Paper Crafts for Day of the Dead. (p. 1322)
—Paper Crafts for Easter. (p. 1322)
—Paper Crafts for Halloween. (p. 1322)
—Paper Crafts for Kwanzaa. (p. 1322)
—Paper Crafts for Mardi Gras. (p. 1322)
—Paper Crafts for Presidents' Day. (p. 1322)
—Paper Crafts for St. Patrick's Day. (p. 1322)
—Paper Crafts for Thanksgiving. (p. 1322)
—Paper Crafts for the 4th of July. (p. 1322)
—Paper Crafts for Valentine's Day. (p. 1322)
McGee, Rick. Eleven Chickens in a Boat: A Story of Faith, Fear, & Feathers! (p. 512)
McGee, Robert. Father Hunger. (p. 577)
McGee, Robert S. & Flippin, Ian. Search: A Student Workbook Based on the Search for Significance. (p. 1537)
McGee, Sandy. Golden Easter Hen. (p. 694)
McGee, Thomas, illus. see Osborne, Amy, ed.
McGee, W. J. Prehistoric North America. (p. 1395)
McGee, Warner. Ariel's Song. (p. 98)
—Diego Saves a Butterfly. (p. 437)
—Diego's Egyptian Expedition. (p. 437)
—Mission to Mars. (p. 1153)
—Monster Halloween Party. (p. 1167)
—Run, Run, Koala! (p. 1496)
McGee, Warner, illus. see David, Erica.
McGee, Warner, illus. see Fernandez, Rafael.
Mcgee, Warner, illus. see Golden Books Staff.
Mcgee, Warner, illus. see Golden Books.
McGee, Warner, illus. see Higginson, Sheila Sweeny.
McGee, Warner, illus. see Rao, Lisa.
McGee, Warner, illus. see Ricci, Christine.
Mcgee, Warner, illus. see Rosebrough, Ellen.
McGee, Warner, illus. see Sander, Sonia.
McGee, Warner, illus. see Spelvin, Justin.
McGee-Childs, Maisha. Writing My Story: A Journaling Guide for Kids. (p. 1965)
McGeehan, Dan, illus. see Bernard, Jan.
McGeehan, Dan, illus. see Heinrichs, Ann.
McGeehan, Dan, illus. see Jacobson, Ryan.
McGeehan, Dan, illus. see Lindeen, Mary & Kesselring, Susan.
McGeehan, Dan, illus. see Lynette, Rachel.
McGeehan, Dan, illus. see Owens, L. L.
McGeehan, Dan, illus. see Ringstad, Arnold.
McGeehan, Dan, illus. see Rosa-Mendoza, Gladys.
McGeehan, Dan, illus. see Shaffer, Jody Jensen.
McGehee, Claudia. My Wilderness: An Alaskan Adventure. (p. 1221)
—Tallgrass Prairie Alphabet. McGehee, Claudia, illus. (p. 1704)
—Where Do Birds Live? (p. 1906)
—Woodland Counting Book. (p. 1949)
McGehee, Claudia, illus. see Bissonette, Aimee M.
McGeorge, Constance W. Chestnut Whyte, Mary, illus. (p. 298)
McGeorge, Darby Q. Trickster Tre. (p. 1786)
McGeorge Endres. Boomer's Halloween. (p. 213)
McGeveran, William, jt. auth. see Burgan, Michael.
McGeveran, William, jt. auth. see Hess, Debra.
McGeveran, William, jt. auth. see King, David C.
McGeveran, William, jt. auth. see Petreycik, Rick.
McGhee, Alison. All Rivers Flow to the Sea. (p. 45)
—Always. Lemaitre, Pascal, illus. (p. 51)
—Bye-Bye, Crib. MacDonald, Ross, illus. (p. 249)
—Case of the Missing Donut. Roxas, Isabel, illus. (p. 274)
—Countdown to Kindergarten. Bliss, Harry, illus. (p. 370)
—Firefly Hollow. Denise, Christopher, illus. (p. 592)
—Julia Gillian - And the Art of Knowing. Kozjan, Drazen, illus. (p. 932)
—Julia Gillian (and the Dream of the Dog) Kozjan, Drazen, illus. (p. 932)
—Julia Gillian (and the Quest for Joy) Kozjan, Drazen, illus. (p. 932)
—Little Boy. Reynolds, Peter H., illus. (p. 1025)
—Making a Friend. Rosenthal, Marc, illus. (p. 1080)
—Mrs. Watson Wants Your Teeth. Bliss, Harry, illus. (p. 1188)
—Only a Witch Can Fly. (p. 1298)
—Only a Witch Can Fly. Yoo, Taeeun, illus. (p. 1298)
—So Many Days. Yoo, Taeeun, illus. (p. 1602)
—Someday. (p. 1609)
—Someday. Reynolds, Peter H., illus. (p. 1609)
—Song of Middle C. Menchin, Scott, illus. (p. 1611)
—Sweetest Witch Around. Bliss, Harry, illus. (p. 1690)
—Very Brave Witch. (p. 1837)
—Very Brave Witch. Bliss, Harry, illus. (p. 1837)
McGhee, Alison, jt. auth. see DiCamillo, Kate.
McGhee, Allison. Julia Gillian 3. (p. 932)
McGhee, Chelsea, illus. see Matalonis, Anne.
McGhee, Heather. Wild Adventures of a Curious Princess. Myers, Shari, illus. (p. 1928)
McGhee, J. Jewel of Ithesda. (p. 917)
McGhee, Karen, jt. auth. see McKay, George.
McGhee, Katie Mariah. Case of the Missing Chimpanzee from Classroom C2. McGhee, Katie Mariah & Herrera, Aaron Jeremiah, illus. (p. 274)
McGhee, Kerry, illus. see Bernhardt, William.
McGhee, Neil. Unbroken Circle: A Cross-Generational Historical Novel of the McGhee Family Pilgrimage from Tennessee to Missouri 1802 - 1941. (p. 1811)
McGhee, Patti Gray. Ducky Bill's Great Race. Vermillion, Danny, illus. (p. 488)
McGhee, Sally. Take Back Your Life! Using Microsoft Outlook(r) to Get Organized & Stay Organized. (p. 1696)
McGhee, Sally & Wittry, John. Take Back Your Life! Using Microsoft(r) Office Outlook(r) 2007 to Get Organized & Stay Organized. (p. 1696)
McGhee, Stuart, illus. see Perree, Leyland.
McGill, Debora J. Faith Journeys with Hope & Love: Short Stories of Inspiration. (p. 565)
McGill, Imo Von. Carry Patch. (p. 271)
McGill, Jordan. Amazing Animals. (p. 53)
—Ardillas. (p. 96)
—Backyard Animals. (p. 130)
—Coyotes. (p. 375)
—Deer. (p. 423)
—Dinosaurs. (p. 443)
—Earth Science Fair Projects. (p. 496)
—Edificios. (p. 504)
—Farm Life: Pioneers of Canada. (p. 574)
—Life Science Fair Projects. (p. 1013)
—Machines. (p. 1068)
—Mapaches. (p. 1090)
—Medios de Transporte. (p. 1120)
—Opossums. (p. 1300)
—Raccoons. (p. 1430)
—Skunks. (p. 1586)
—Space. (p. 1618)
—Space Science Fair Projects. (p. 1619)

—Squirrels. (p. 1637)
—Transportation. (p. 1779)
—Venados. (p. 1835)
—Water Science Fair Projects. (p. 1863)
—Zarigüeyas. (p. 1985)
—Zorrillos. (p. 1990)
McGill, Jordan, jt. auth. see Kissock, Heather.
McGill, Jordan, ed. Amazing Animals. (p. 53)
—Backyard Animals. (p. 130)
—Christmas. (p. 312)
—Cinco de Mayo. (p. 319)
—Dinosaurs. (p. 443)
—Machines. (p. 1068)
—Pets. (p. 1348)
—Space. (p. 1618)
—Thanksgiving. (p. 1725)
McGill, Joshua, illus. see Simone, Val Edward.
McGill, Justin. Friends Forever, Signed Jeremy E. (p. 638)
McGill, Kerry Lance. Bear's Flower. (p. 152)
Mcgill, Leslie. Fighter. (p. 585)
—Hacker. (p. 735)
—Running Scared. (p. 1497)
McGill, Mick. Tommy & His Time Machine. (p. 1764)
McGill-Franzen, Anne. Kindergarten Literacy: Matching Assessment & Instruction in Kindergarten. (p. 957)
McGillian, Jamie Kyle. Kids' Money Book: Earning * Saving * Spending * Investing * Donating. (p. 954)
—Kids' Money Book. Phillips, Ian, illus. (p. 954)
—Sidewalk Chalk: Outdoor Fun & Games. Sims, Blanche, illus. (p. 1573)
McGillicuddy, Barbara. Adventures in the Kingdom of Mim: Buddie Saves the Day. (p. 15)
McGillivray, Alice V., et al. America at the Polls, 1920-1956: A Handbook of American Presidential Election Statistics Set (p. 59)
—America at the Polls, 1960-2004: A Handbook of American Presidential Election Statistics (p. 59)
McGillivray, Kim, illus. see Hesse, Karen.
McGinley, M. D. Highliner: The Nature, Philosophy & Science of Automobile Driving. (p. 779)
McGinley, Phyllis, et al. Little Golden Book Farm Favorites. Rojankovsky, Feodor & Gergely, Tibor, illus. (p. 1028)
McGinley-Nally, Sharon, illus. see Axelrod, Amy.
McGinley-Nally, Sharon, jt. auth. see Axelrod, Amy.
McGinn, William. Blacktop Brothers. (p. 198)
McGinness, Suzanne, illus. see Quarto Generic Staff.
McGinnis, Ben, illus. see Goodboby, Slim & Burstein, John.
McGinnis, Ben, illus. see Goodboby, Slim.
McGinnis, Bsn. Call My Mom!! (p. 254)
McGinnis, Chelsea. Mk Frogg & the Lily Pad Adventures (p. 1157)
McGinnis, Mark W. Buddhist Animal Wisdom Stories. (p. 234)
McGinnis, Mary Lane. Ten Commandments for Children. (p. 1718)
McGinnis, Maura. Greece: A Primary Source Cultural Guide. (p. 720)
McGinnis, Maxine. It's in Your Genes - the What of Who We Are. (p. 897)
McGinnis, Megan, ed. see Kuffner, Trish.
McGinnis, Mindy. In a Handful of Dust. (p. 863)
—Madness So Discreet. (p. 1070)
—Not a Drop to Drink. (p. 1266)
McGinnis, Scott, jt. auth. see Yao, Tao-chung.
McGinnis, Steve, illus. see Campbell, Cheryl.
Mcginniss, Jim. Jimmy's Other Glove. (p. 918)
McGintry, Alice B. Cynthia Rylant. (p. 397)
McGinty, Alice B. Cynthia Rylant. (p. 397)
—Eliza's Kindergarten Pet Speir, Nancy, illus. (p. 513)
—Eliza's Kindergarten Surprise Speir, Nancy, illus. (p. 513)
—Gandhi: The March to the Sea Gonzalez, Thomas, illus. (p. 655)
—Jumping Spider. (p. 934)
—Katherine Paterson. (p. 944)
—Meet Daniel Pinkwater. (p. 1120)
—Meet Eve Bunting. (p. 1121)
—Meet Jane Yolen. (p. 1121)
—Meet Laurence Yep. (p. 1121)
—Mission San Gabriel Arcangel. (p. 1153)
—Rabbi Benjamin's Buttons. Reinhardt, Jennifer Black, illus. (p. 1429)
—Sharon Creech. (p. 1563)
—Software Designer. (p. 1606)
—Tarantula. (p. 1706)
—Wolf Spider. (p. 1944)
McGinty, Alice B. & Stevens, Madeline. Discovering Mission San Gabriel Arcángel. (p. 449)
McGinty, Brian. Strong Wine: The Life & Legend of Agoston Haraszthy. (p. 1668)
Mcginty, Ian. Hello Kitty: Surprise! (p. 764)
McGinty, Ian, illus. see Chabot, Jacob.
McGinty, Ian, illus. see Nichols, Travis.
McGinty, Ian, illus. see West, Tracey.
Mcginty, Ian, jt. auth. see Chabot, Jacob.
McGinty, Mick, illus. see Rosenthal, Sue.
McGinty, Patrick, jt. auth. see Brown, Cynthia Light.
McGirr, Randel W. Bible Camp. (p. 175)
McGlame, Jack. Majik: The Beginning. (p. 1078)
McGlaun, Steven, ed. Teaching Activities Manual for the Catholic Faith Handbook for Youth. (p. 1709)
McGlone, Catherine. New York Times V. Sullivan & the Freedom of the Press Debate. (p. 1248)
—Visitando Volcanes con una Cientifica/Visiting Volcanoes with a Scientist. (p. 1845)
—Visiting Volcanoes with a Scientist. (p. 1845)
McGlotham, L. R. E. I Didn't Do Nuthin' Bailin, Jill, ed. (p. 837)
—Special Place. (p. 1623)
McGohon, Doris. Paintings of the Imagination. (p. 1318)
McGoldrick, Bernita. Pretty Pretty Picky Penelope. McGoldrick, Bernita, illus. (p. 1398)
McGoldrick, Megan. All about Armor. (p. 42)
McGonagle, Joanne L. Tiniest Tiger. (p. 1755)
McGonagle, Riona. Crystal Tower of Light. (p. 387)
McGoogan, Ken, jt. auth. see Le May Doan, Catriona.
McGougan, Kathy. Buddy on the Farm. (p. 235)
—Buddy Plays Ball. (p. 235)
—Buddy's Christmas Joy. (p. 235)
—Buddy's Toys. (p. 235)
—Fixin' Buddy's Little Red Wagon. Hale, Sally, illus. (p. 601)
—NO, Buddy! (p. 1257)
McGough, Michael R. Lincoln Inn. (p. 1018)
McGough, Roger. Daniel & the Beast of Babylon. Newton, Jill, illus. (p. 404)
—Sensational! Poems Inspired by the Five Senses. (p. 1550)
—Until I Met Dudley: How Everyday Things Really Work. Riddell, Chris, illus. (p. 1823)
—Wicked Poems. Layton, Neal, illus. (p. 1927)
McGough, Roger, et al. You Tell Me! Paul, Korky, illus. (p. 1976)
McGough, Wallace D. Adventures of Walter Ant: The Unknown. Bk. I (p. 24)
McGovan, Michael. Bobby Dazzlers. (p. 206)
McGovern, Ann. Aesop's Fables. Tercio, Ricardo, illus. (p. 25)
—Little Wolf. (p. 1038)
—Native American Heroes: Osceola, Tecumseh & Cochise. (p. 1234)
—Too Much Noise. (p. 1767)
—Who Has a Secret? (p. 1915)
—Why it's a Holiday. (p. 1925)
McGovern, Cammie. Say What You Will. (p. 1519)
McGovern, DeeDee. Zachary, the Adventure Boy! (p. 1984)
McGovern, DeeDee Jean. Heartland of Home: Tight Quarters in the City. (p. 760)
McGovern, Matt. Currents: Every Life Leaves an Imprint. McGovern, Matt, ed. (p. 394)
McGovern, Sheila. Entire World of S & Z Book of Stories: 58 Targeted S & Z Pure Stories to Remediate Frontal & Lateral Lisps. (p. 531)
McGovern, Suzanne. Gator & Pete - More Alike Than It Seems. Bizjak, Donna, illus. (p. 658)
McGowan, Angel. Stomp Out the Bullying! (p. 1652)
McGowan, Anthony. Bare Bum Gang & the Holy Grail. (p. 138)
—Bare Bum Gang & the Valley of Doom. (p. 138)
—Bare Bum Gang Battles the Dogsnatchers. (p. 138)
—Fall. (p. 566)
—Knife That Killed Me. (p. 964)
McGowan, Chris. Abacus. (p. 2)
—Dinosaur Discovery: Everything You Need to Be a Paleontologist. Schmidt, Erica Lyn, illus. (p. 442)
McGowan, Cynthia C. On Defoe's Robinson Crusoe. (p. 1288)
McGowan, Gary, jt. auth. see Hansen, Joyce.
McGowan, Jayme. One Bear Extraordinaire. (p. 1293)
McGowan, Jennifer. Maid of Secrets. (p. 1076)
—Maid of Wonder. (p. 1076)
McGowan, Joby. Bossy Bianc. (p. 215)
McGowan, Joe. Al Gore. (p. 32)
McGowan, Joseph. Al Gore. (p. 32)
—Will Smith. (p. 1932)
McGowan, Keith. Witch's Curse. Tanaka, Yoko, illus. (p. 1941)
—Witch's Guide to Cooking with Children. Tanaka, Yoko, illus. (p. 1941)
McGowan, Kim. Fish Tale. (p. 598)
McGowan, Kristan Harrell. Weirdy Cat. (p. 1873)
McGowan, Maureen. Cinderella: Ninja Warrior. (p. 320)
—Compliance (p. 354)
—Deviants (p. 432)
—Glory (p. 685)
—Sleeping Beauty: Vampire Slayer. (p. 1589)
McGowan, Patricia. House of Friends. (p. 803)
McGowan, Shane, illus. see Costain, Meredith.
McGowan, Sharlene. Macaroni Monday. (p. 1067)
McGowan, Steve. Adventures of Keke & the Golden Coconut. (p. 19)
McGowan, Timothy. Plants Around the World. (p. 1370)
McGowan-Lowe, Jake. Jake's Bones. (p. 906)
McGowen, Julie. Virginia's Voyage. (p. 1844)
McGowen, Tom. 1968 Democratic Convention. (p. 2002)
—Alexander the Great: Conqueror of the Ancient World. (p. 36)
—Jesse Bowman: A Union Boy's War Story. (p. 914)
—Revolutionary War & George Washington's Army in American History. (p. 1466)
—Space Race: The Mission, the Men, the Moon. (p. 1619)
—Spanish-American War & Teddy Roosevelt in American History. (p. 1620)
—William the Conqueror: Last Invader of England. (p. 1933)
Mcgowen, Tom, jt. auth. see McGowen, Tom.
McGowen, Tom & Mcgowen, Tom. D-Day. (p. 397)
McGrade, Francis & Juliana, M., Sr. I Believe: The Creed, Confession & the Ten Commandments for Children. (p. 834)
McGrady, Mike, jt. auth. see Floherty, John Joseph.
McGrail-Gamble, Vicki. Kindergarten Colors. (p. 957)
McGranaghan, John. Conoce Los Planetas Klein, Laurie Allen, illus. (p. 358)
—Meet the Planets Klein, Laurie Allen, illus. (p. 1123)
—Saturn for My Birthday Edelson, Wendy, illus. (p. 1515)
Mcgranahan, Patrick D. Imaginary Jerry: And the Tale of His Daring Escape from Imaginaria. (p. 860)
McGrath, Alister. Chosen Ones (p. 311)
—Flight of the Outcasts Nowakowski, Voytek, illus. (p. 604)
McGrath Avery, Pat. 15 Dogs & a Cat Speak Out: Interviews by Luke the Detective Dog. (p. 1995)
—Famous Dogs & a Cat. (p. 569)
McGrath, Barbara Barbieri. Halloween Colors. (p. 737)
—Little Gray Bunny. Kim, Violet, illus. (p. 1028)
—Little Green Witch. Alexander, Martha, illus. (p. 1028)
—Little Red Elf. Bonnet, Rosalinde, illus. (p. 1034)
—M & M's(r) Brand Addition Book. (p. 1067)
—M & M's(r) Brand All-American Parade Book. Tagel, Peggy, illus. (p. 1067)
—M & M's(r) Brand Birthday Book. Tagel, Peggy, illus. (p. 1067)
—M & M's(r) Brand Color Pattern Book. Glass, Roger, illus. (p. 1067)
—M & M's(r) Brand Count Around the Circle. (p. 1067)
—M & M's(r) Brand Count to One Hundred Book. (p. 1067)
—M & M's(r) Brand Counting Book. Glass, Roger, illus. (p. 1067)
—M & M's(r) Brand Easter Egg Hunt. Tagel, Peggy, illus. (p. 1067)
—M & M's(r) Brand Halloween Treat Book. (p. 1067)
—M & M's(r) Brand Valentine Book. Tagel, Peggy, illus. (p. 1067)
—M&M's(r) Brand Subtraction Book. (p. 1087)
—Mas Matematicas con los Chocolates de M & M's Brand. Mlawer, Teresa, tr. (p. 1101)
—Storm: Students of Biloxi, Mississippi, Remember Hurricane Katrina. (p. 1655)
—Teddy Bear Addition. Nihoff, Tim, illus. (p. 1712)
—Teddy Bear Counting. Nihoff, Tim, illus. (p. 1712)
—Teddy Bear Math. Nihoff, Tim, illus. (p. 1712)
—Teddy Bear Patterns. Nihoff, Tim, illus. (p. 1712)
—Teddy Bear Subtraction. Nihoff, Tim, illus. (p. 1712)
—Teddy Bear, Teddy Bear, School Day Math. Nihoff, Tim, illus. (p. 1712)
—Time for Thanksgiving! (p. 1752)
McGrath, Barbara Barbieri & Alderman, Peter. Soccer Counts! Estrada, Pau, illus. (p. 1603)
—Soccer Counts! (El Futbol Cuenta!) Estrada, Pau, illus. (p. 1603)
McGrath, Barbara Barbieri & Shaw, Brian. Cuenta con el Beisbol. Canetti, Yanitzia, tr. from SPA. (p. 389)
McGrath, Barbara Barbieri & Togel, Peggy. M & M's(r) Brand Christmas Gift Book. (p. 1067)
McGrath, Brenda. Ding Bat Audio Book. (p. 440)
McGrath, Carmelita. Boston Box. Baker, Rochelle, illus. (p. 215)
McGrath, Carolann C. Five Angels. (p. 599)
McGrath, Chris, jt. auth. see McGrath, Milo.
McGrath, Craig. Chocolate Cake Goes to the Gas Station. (p. 309)
McGrath, Linda L. Most Unusual Day at Gemini Springs. (p. 1177)
—Our Amazing Little Cally: A Novel. (p. 1307)
McGrath, Liz, illus. see McDermott, Tom.
McGrath, Liz & Quick, Barbara. Even More/Todavía Más. de la Vega, Eida, tr. from ENG. (p. 541)
McGrath, Marci, jt. auth. see Smith, Chris.
McGrath, Maureen. Spunky's Special Friend. (p. 1635)
McGrath, Maureen Julie. Tale of the Cat with the Crooked Tail. (p. 1700)
McGrath, Michael, illus. see White.
McGrath, Michael O'Neill. Patrons & Protectors: In Times of Need. (p. 1329)
McGrath, Milo & McGrath, Chris. South Pole Santa. (p. 1617)
McGrath, Noelle. Dupes & How Not to Be Them: A Primer on the Perils of Political Correctness. (p. 490)
McGrath, Raymond. Moon: Individual Title Six-Packs. (p. 1171)
—My Alien: Individual Title Six-Packs. (p. 1195)
McGrath, Raymond, illus. see Eggleton, Jill.
McGrath, Renee Vaillancourt, ed. Excellence in Library Services to Young Adults. (p. 547)
McGrath, Robin. Livyers World. (p. 1042)
McGrath, Ryan, illus. see Joachimowski, Paula L.
McGrath, Sheelagh. Magick It Up: A Children's Story for Grown Ups Too. (p. 1075)
McGrath, Tom, illus. see Sautter, A. J.
Mcgraw, Caroline. Litsemamba! Litsemba! (p. 1023)
McGraw, Earl. Electing Our Leaders. (p. 508)
McGraw, Earl, jt. auth. see Mills, Nathan.
McGraw, Eloise. Moorchild. (p. 1173)
McGraw, Eloise Jarvis. Golden Goblet. (p. 694)
McGraw, Eloise Jarvis & McGraw, Lauren Lynn. Forbidden Fountain of Oz. (p. 616)
McGraw, Jason. Beating the Odds. (p. 152)
McGraw, Jay & Björkman, Manns. Life Strategies for Dealing with Bullies. Björkman, Steve, illus. (p. 1013)
McGraw, Lauren Lynn, jt. auth. see McGraw, Eloise Jarvis.
McGraw, Mike. Doodle Land. (p. 469)
McGraw, Penny Underwood. Jay's Vacation (p. 910)
McGraw, Sheila, illus. see Ward, Heather P.
McGraw, Sheila, jt. auth. see Munsch, Robert.
McGraw-Hill Book Company Staff, jt. auth. see Fisher, Douglas.
McGraw-Hill Companies Staff, jt. contrib. by see LiveABC (Firm) Staff.
McGraw-Hill Editors. Economics: Principles & Practices. (p. 502)
—Math, Grade 5. (p. 1106)
—McGraw-Hill Math Grade 2. (p. 1114)
McGraw-Hill Editors, jt. auth. see Spielvogel, Jackson J.
McGraw-Hill Editors & McGraw-Hill Education Staff. McGraw-Hill Math Grade 1. (p. 1114)
McGraw-Hill Education. Human Heritage: A World History. (p. 826)
—World Geography & Cultures, Spanish Reading Essentials & Note-Taking Guide. (p. 1955)
McGraw-Hill Education (Firm) Staff. Buyer Beware: Rates, Ratios, Percents, & Proportions. (p. 248)
—Exploring Our World: People, Places, & Cultures - Eastern Hemisphere. (p. 553)
—Getting down to Business: Functions & Spreasheets. (p. 669)
—Glencoe Accounting: Real-World Applications & Connections. (p. 683)
—Glencoe Accounting: First Year Course, Electronic Learning Center Student Package. (p. 683)
—Impact Mathematics Course 1: Algebra & More. (p. 862)
—Roads & Ramps: Slopes, Angles, & Ratios. (p. 1477)
—What Does the Data Say? Graphs & Averages. (p. 1884)
—World & Its People: Western Hemisphere, Europe & Russia. (p. 1954)
McGraw-Hill Education (Firm) Staff, jt. auth. see Glencoe McGraw-Hill Staff.
McGraw-Hill Education Staff. American Journey. (p. 62)
—American Journey, Active Reading Note-Taking Guide, Student Edition. (p. 62)
—American Journey, Interactive Tutor Self Assessment CD-ROM. (p. 62)
—American Journey Modern Times. (p. 62)
—American Journey Spanish Reading Essentials & Note-Taking Guide. (p. 62)
—American Journey to World War 1, Reading Essentials. (p. 62)
—American Journey to World War 1, StudentWorks Plus! (p. 62)
—American Republic to 1877 StudentWorks Plus. (p. 63)
—American Vision: Modern Times, StudentWorks Plus. (p. 63)
—American Vision: Modern Times, Interactive Tutor Self-Assessment. (p. 63)
—American Vision, Interactive Tutor. (p. 63)
—American Vision, Spanish Reading Essentials & Study Guide, Student Edition. (p. 64)
—American Vision, StudentWorks Plus CD-ROM. (p. 64)
—Beside the Point: Operating with Decimals, Percents, & Integers. (p. 168)
—Biology: The Dynamics of Life. (p. 189)
—Civics Today: Citizenship, Economics & You, Interactive Tutor Self-Assessment. (p. 324)
—Designing Spaces: Visualizing, Planning, & Building. (p. 430)
—Economics: Principles & Practices. (p. 502)
—Economics: Principles & Practices, Interactive Tutor. (p. 502)
—Economics: Today & Tomorrow, StudentWorks with Audio. (p. 502)
—Economics: Today & Tomorrow, Interactive Tutor: Self Assessment. (p. 502)
—Economics: Principles & Practices: Reading Essentials & Study Guide. (p. 503)
—Economics Spanish Reading Essentials & Note-Taking Guide Student Workbook: Principles & Practices. (p. 503)
—Electricity & Magnetism. (p. 509)
—ESL Math Overhead Manipulatives. (p. 536)
—Exploring Our World: People, Places, & Culture. (p. 553)
—Exploring Our World Standardized Test Practice: People, Places, & Cultures. (p. 553)
—Exploring the Unknown: Writing & Solving Equations. (p. 554)
—Family Portraits: Comparing Function Families. (p. 568)
—Geometry: Concepts & Applications. (p. 662)
—Geometry Reading to Learn Mathematics Workbook. (p. 663)
—Glencoe Keyboarding Connections: Projects & Applications Home Version. (p. 683)
—Glencoe World Geography. (p. 683)
—Glencoe World History: Modern Times. (p. 683)
—Glencoe World History. (p. 683)
—Gulliver's Words: Measuring & Scaling. (p. 731)
—Introduction to Physical Science. (p. 882)
—Journey Across Time, Early Ages. (p. 927)
—Looking Behind the Numbers: Correlations, Rankings, & Permutations. (p. 1051)
—Macmillan/McGraw-Hill Math: Pupil Edition. (p. 1068)
—Macmillan/McGraw-Hill Math. (p. 1068)
—Matematicas: Aplicaciones y Conceptos: Libro de Ejercicios de la Guia de Estudio para Padres y Alumnos, Curso 2. (p. 1104)
—Matematicas - Guia de Estudio y Libro de Ejercicios de Intervencion: Aplicaciones y Conceptos, Curso 3. (p. 1104)
—Matematicas: Guia de Estudio y Libro de Ejercicios de Intervencion: Aplicaciones y Conceptos, Curso 1. (p. 1104)
—Matematicas Practica: Ejercicios para Desarrollar Destrezas: Aplicaciones y Conceptos, Curso 3. (p. 1104)
—Matematicas Practica: Ejercicios para Resolve Problemas: Aplicaciones y Conceptos, Curso 3. (p. 1104)
—Math: Power up Your Math Skills. Grd. 7 (p. 1105)
—Math Skills Maintenance Workbook: Course 3. (p. 1107)
—Math Skills Maintenance Workbook, Course 1. (p. 1107)
—Mathematicas: Aplicaciones y Conceptos: Curso 2: Guia de Estudio y Libro de Ejercicios de Intervencion. (p. 1107)
—Mathematics: Applications & Concepts. (p. 1107)
—Mathematics: Applications & Concepts. (p. 1108)
—Mathematics: Applications & Concepts, Course 2. (p. 1108)
—Mathematics Reading to Learn Mathematics Workbook: Applications & Concepts, Course 1. (p. 1108)
—McGraw-Hill Math, Grade 1. (p. 1114)
—McGraw-Hill Math Grade 3. (p. 1114)
—McGraw-Hill's Math, Grade 6. (p. 1114)
—McGraw-Hill's Spanish Picture Dictionary. (p. 1114)
—Michigan 2009 Gr 3 Practice & Activity Workbook. (p. 1135)
—Michigan Studies. (p. 1135)
—Nutrition & Wellness. (p. 1274)
—Our World Today Reading Essentials & Study Guide Student Workbook: People, Places, & Issues. (p. 1310)
—Repaso Breve - Manual de Mathematicas. (p. 1460)
—Reprise: A Review Workbook for Grammar, Communication, & Culture. (p. 1461)
—Shapes & Space: Thinking Three-Dimensionally. (p. 1560)
—Timelinks, Grade 5, Leveled Reader, Approaching Level, Leveled Places & Events. (p. 1754)
—Understanding Psychology Reading Essentials & Study Guide Student Workbook. (p. 1816)
—United States Government: Democracy in Action. (p. 1819)
—United States Government: Democracy in Action: Spanish Reading Essentials & Study Guide. (p. 1819)
—United States Government: Democracy in Action, Spanish Reading Essentials & Study Guide: Student Workbook. (p. 1819)
—What Comes Next? Modeling & Predicting. (p. 1881)
—World & Its People: Eastern Hemisphere. (p. 1953)
—World & Its People. (p. 1953)
—World & Its People: Western Hemisphere, Europe & Russia. (p. 1954)
—World & Its People: Western Hemisphere, Europe & Russia: Spanish Reading Essentials. (p. 1954)
—World & Its People, Reading Essentials & Study Guide Student Workbook: Western Hemisphere, Europe & Russia. (p. 1954)
—World & Its People, StudentWorks Plus CD-ROM. (p. 1954)
—World & Its People, Western Hemisphere, Europe, & Russia, StudentWorks Plus CD-ROM. (p. 1954)
—World Geography: Spanish Reading Essentials. (p. 1955)
—World History: Spanish Reading Essentials & Note-Taking Guide. (p. 1955)

—World History: Modern Times: Spanish Reading Essentials & Note-Taking Guide. (p. 1955)
—Writer's Choice, Grade 9: Grammar & Composition. (p. 1964)
McGraw-Hill Education Staff, jt. auth. see Bailey, Annette Gentry.
McGraw-Hill Education Staff, jt. auth. see Glencoe McGraw-Hill Staff.
McGraw-Hill Education Staff, jt. auth. see Hunkins, Boehm Armstrong.
McGraw-Hill Education Staff, jt. auth. see McGraw-Hill Editors.
McGraw-Hill Education Staff, jt. auth. see McGraw-Hill Staff.
McGraw-Hill Education Staff, jt. auth. see McGraw-Hill-Glencoe Staff.
McGraw-Hill Education Staff, jt. auth. see Sasse, Connie R.
McGraw-Hill Education Staff, jt. auth. see Schmitt, Conrad J.
McGraw-Hill Education Staff, jt. auth. see Spielvogel, Jackson J.
McGraw-Hill Education Staff, jt. auth. see Zike, Dinah.
McGraw-Hill - Jamestown Education Staff. American History Ink: The Underground Railroad. Bk. 4 (p. 61)
—American History Ink: Taming Horses on the Great Plains. (p. 61)
—Impact Mathematics: Algebra & More. (p. 862)
—Timed Readings Plus in Mathematics: Book 1 (p. 1753)
—Timed Readings Plus in Mathematics: Book 2 (p. 1753)
—Timed Readings Plus in Mathematics: Book 3 (p. 1753)
—Timed Readings Plus in Mathematics: Book 4 (p. 1753)
—Timed Readings Plus in Mathematics: Book 5 (p. 1754)
—Timed Readings Plus in Social Studies (p. 1754)
—Timed Readings Plus in Social Studies Bk. 3. (p. 1754)
McGraw-Hill - Jamestown Education Staff, jt. auth. see Fisher, Douglas.
McGraw-Hill - Jamestown Education Staff, creator. Reading Science: Strategies for English Language Learners. (p. 1446)
McGraw-Hill Staff. Advanced Mathematical Concepts: Precalculus with Applications. (p. 13)
—Algebra: Concepts & Applications. (p. 38)
—American Journey. (p. 62)
—American Journey, Student Edition. (p. 62)
—American Republic since 1877: StudentWorks. (p. 63)
—American Republic since 1877, Reading Essentials & Study Guide, Student Edition. (p. 63)
—American Republic to 1877, Teacher. (p. 63)
—Applications & Concepts: Parent & Student Study Guide Workbook, Course 1. (p. 93)
—Biology: The Dynamics of Life. (p. 189)
—Biology: The Dynamics of Life Online: MHLN Stand Alone Version. (p. 189)
—Bon Voyage, Level 1. (p. 208)
—Chemistry: Concepts & Applications. (p. 297)
—Clinical Applications Manual to Accompany Anatomy & Physiology. (p. 333)
—Contemporary Mathematics in Context: A Unified Approach. Pt. A (p. 360)
—Economics: Principles & Practices. (p. 502)
—Economics Today & Tomorrow: Reading Essentials & Study Guide. (p. 503)
—Experiencing Choral Music: Treble. (p. 548)
—Experiencing Choral Music. (p. 548)
—Experiencing Choral Music, Proficient Mixed Voices. (p. 548)
—Experiencing Choral Music, Proficient Tenor Bass Voices. (p. 548)
—Exploring Art. (p. 551)
—Exploring Our World, Eastern Hemisphere, Interactive Tutor Self Assessment. (p. 553)
—Exploring Our World, Western Hemisphere with Europe & Russia. (p. 553)
—Geometry: Concepts & Applications. (p. 662)
—Geometry. (p. 662)
—Glencoe Accounting: Real-World Applications & Connections. (p. 683)
—Glencoe Accounting Advanced Course. (p. 683)
—Glencoe Geometry: Concepts & Applications. (p. 683)
—Glencoe Keyboarding Connections: Projects & Applications with Office 2000. (p. 683)
—Glencoe Science: Ecology Standardized Test Practice. (p. 683)
—Grade: Gr 4-8 Sound Perc. Video Share Music 2000. (p. 705)
—Grade: Gr 6 Playing Guitar Share Music 2000. (p. 705)
—Grade: Gr K CDs Share the Music 2000. (p. 705)
—Grade: Gr1 Cd(8) Share the Music. (p. 705)
—Human Heritage, Spanish Reading Essentials & Study Guide, Student Edition. (p. 826)
—Jo Tries: And Other Selections (p. 919)
—Journey Across Time: Early Ages. (p. 927)
—Journey Across Time, Early Ages. (p. 927)
—Journey Across Time, Early Ages, Active Reading Note-Taking Strategies. (p. 927)
—Journey Across Time - The Early Ages: Standardized Test Skills Practice Workbook. (p. 927)
—Jumbo Pocket Dice Grade Pre K. (p. 933)
—Kaleidoscope. (p. 941)
—Life Science Animations. (p. 1013)
—Listening Library. (p. 1022)
—Listen!Listen!Letter Sounds in Rhymes Complt Set. (p. 1022)
—Mathematics: Applications & Concepts. (p. 1107)
—Mathematics: Applications & Concepts. (p. 1108)
—Mathematics: Applications & Concepts, Course 2. (p. 1108)
—Mathematics: Applications & Concepts, Course 2, StudentWorks. (p. 1108)
—Mathematics: Applications & Concepts, Course 1, StudentWorks CD-ROM. (p. 1108)
—Mathematics with Business Applications. (p. 1108)
—MathScape: Seeing & Thinking Mathematically. Pack (p. 1108)
—MathScape: Seeing & Thinking Mathematically. Bk. 3 (p. 1108)
—MathScape: Seeing & Thinking Mathematically, Course 2, StudentWorks. (p. 1108)
—MathScape: Seeing & Thinking Mathematically, Course 3, Student Modular Package. (p. 1108)
—Mythology & You, Student Edition. (p. 1227)
—Quick Review Math Handbook: Hot Words, Hot Topics. Bk. 1 (p. 1427)
—Skills Intervention for Pre-Algebra: Diagnosis & Remediation. (p. 1585)
—Song Box Sets & Resources:Save the Tree for Me Cass. (p. 1611)
—United States Government, Democracy in Action, StudentWorks CD-ROM. (p. 1819)
—Videocassette: Video Gr 3-6 Signing Share Music 2000. (p. 1841)
—World Geography & Cultures, StudentWorks Plus. (p. 1955)
—¡Buen Viaje! (p. 235)
McGraw-Hill Staff, jt. auth. see Boehm, Richard G.
McGraw-Hill Staff, jt. auth. see Booth.
McGraw-Hill Staff, jt. auth. see Fisher, Douglas.
McGraw-Hill Staff, jt. auth. see McCalla, Priscilla R.
McGraw-Hill Staff, jt. auth. see Miller, Roger LeRoy.
McGraw-Hill Staff, jt. auth. see Rosenberg, Donna.
McGraw-Hill Staff, jt. auth. see Schmitt.
McGraw-Hill Staff, jt. auth. see Spielvogel, Jackson J.
McGraw-Hill Staff & Glencoe McGraw-Hill Staff. Journey Across Time, Early Ages, Interactive Tutor. (p. 927)
McGraw-Hill Staff & McGraw-Hill Education Staff. Experiencing Choral Music, Intermediate Mixed Voices. (p. 548)
—MathScape: Seeing & Thinking Mathematically, Course 1, StudentWorks. (p. 1108)
—Skills Intervention for Middle School Mathematics: Diagnosis & Remediation. (p. 1585)
McGraw-Hill Staff & WrightGroup/McGraw-Hill Staff. Open Court Reading Pre-K: Pre-Decodable Takehome 4 Color. (p. 1299)
—Third Grade Mathematics. (p. 1734)
—VHS Lesson Models - Level K. (p. 1839)
McGraw-Hill Staff, creator. American Vision: Modern Times, Reading Essentials & Study Guide: Student Workbook. (p. 64)
—Chance Encounters: Probability in Games & Simulations. (p. 289)
—Civics Today: Citizenship, Economics, & You. (p. 324)
—Experiencing Choral Music: Unison. Pt. 2 & 3 (p. 548)
—Forsenics & Biotechnology Lab Manual. (p. 623)
—From the Ground Up: Modeling, Measuring, & Constructing Homes. (p. 644)
—From Wholes to Parts: Operating with Factors, Multiples, & Fractions. (p. 644)
—Galeria de Arte y Vida, Nivel Avanzado: Writing Activities Workbook & Audio Activites. (p. 653)
—Geometry. (p. 662)
—Geometry, Prerequisite Skills Workbook: Remediation & Intervention. (p. 663)
—Glencoe Science Probeware for Biology Lab Manual. (p. 683)
—Glencoe Science Study Guide & Reinforcement: Motion, Forces, & Energy/Electricity & Magnetism/The Nature of Matter/Waves, Sound, & Light/Chemistry. (p. 683)
—Glencoe Writer's Choice: Grammar & Composition, Grade 8. (p. 683)
—Intervención para Mejorar Destrezas para Pre-Algebra: Diagnóstico y Remediación - Libro de Ejercicios para el Alumno. (p. 881)
—Language of Algebra: Equations, Tables, & Graphs. (p. 975)
—Language of Numbers: Inventing & Comparing Number Systems. (p. 975)
—Making Mathematical Arguments: Generalizing about Numbers. (p. 1081)
—Mas Fascinantes del Mundo Latino. (p. 1101)
—Matematicas, Practica: Ejercicios para Desarrollar Destrezas: Aplicaciones y Conceptos: Curso 2. (p. 1104)
—Matematicas Practica - Ejercicios para Resolve Problemas: Aplicaciones y Conceptos, Curso 1. (p. 1104)
—Math Skills Maintenance. (p. 1107)
—Mathematics: Applications & Concepts. (p. 1107)
—Mathematics: Applications & Concepts. (p. 1108)
—Mathematics, Parent & Student Study Guide Workbook: Applications & Concepts, Course 3. (p. 1108)
—Mathematics Practice: Word Problems Workbook: Applications & Concepts, Course 1. (p. 1108)
—Mathematics Reading to Learn Mathematics Workbook: Applications & Concepts, Course 2. (p. 1108)
—McGraw-Hill's Hospital Billing. (p. 1114)
—Patterns in Numbers & Shapes: Using Algebraic Thinking. (p. 1329)
—Physical Science. (p. 1353)
—Repaso Breve Manual de Matematicas, Libro 2. (p. 1461)
—Science. (p. 1524)
—Science Level Red, Mastering Standardized Tests. (p. 1526)
—Waves, Sound, & Light Laboratory Activities Manual. (p. 1864)
—World & Its People: Standardized Test Skills Practice. (p. 1953)
—World & Its People. (p. 1953)
—World & Its People - Eastern Hemisphere. (p. 1954)
—World History: Modern Times. (p. 1955)
—World History. (p. 1955)
—World History - Journey Across Time, the Early Ages. (p. 1955)
McGraw-Hill, Wright. Amazing Plants (p. 55)
—Purl & the Bird (p. 1419)
—Treacherous Ice (p. 1781)
McGraw-Hill-Glencoe Staff. Air Around You. (p. 31)
—American Journey Early Years Graphic Novel (Set Of 30) (p. 62)
—American Journey Full Survey Graphic Novel (Set Of 30) (p. 62)
—Animal Diversity - Glencoe Science. (p. 77)
—Civics Graphic Novel (Set Of 30) (p. 324)
—Experiencing Choral Music. (p. 548)
—Exploring Our World. (p. 553)
—Exploring Our World East Graphic Novel (Set Of 30) (p. 553)
—Geography in Graphic Novel (Set Of 30) (p. 662)
—Glencoe Science: Earth Science Modules. (p. 683)
—Glencoe Science. (p. 683)
—Glencoe Science - Study Guide & Reinforcement: Human Body Systems; Ecology; from Bacteria to Plants; Life's Structure & Function; Animal Diversity. (p. 683)
—Journey Across Time Full Survey Graphic Novel (Set Of 30) (p. 927)
—Latin for Americans (p. 979)
—World History in Graphic Novel (Set Of 30) (p. 1955)
McGraw-Hill-Glencoe Staff, jt. auth. see Fisher, Douglas.
McGraw-Hill-Glencoe Staff, jt. auth. see Zike, Dinah.
McGraw-Hill-Glencoe Staff & McGraw-Hill Education Staff. Exploring Our World, Western Hemisphere with Europe & Russia, Student Edition. (p. 553)
McGraw-Hill-Glencoe Staff, creator. American Journey, Early Years: Reading Essentials & Note-Taking Guide. (p. 62)
—Automotive Excellence (p. 117)
—Glencoe Automotive Excellence, Volume 2 (p. 683)
—World & Its People: Spanish Reading Essentials & Study Guide: Student Workbook. (p. 1954)
McGreal, Carol, jt. auth. see McGreal, Pat.
McGreal, Pat & McGreal, Carol. Uncle Scrooge #385. (p. 1812)
McGreal, Pat, et al. Uncle Scrooge Clark, John, ed. (p. 1812)
—Uncle Scrooge #390. (p. 1812)
—Walt Disney's Comics Clark, John, ed. (p. 1855)
—Walt Disney's Comics & Stories #701. (p. 1855)
McGreal, Sue. Jimmy Fox's Great Pet Adventure. (p. 918)
McGregor, Barbara, illus. see Bryan, Sarah Jane & Bellenson, Suzanne.
McGregor, Barbara, illus. see Paratore, Coleen Murtagh.
McGregor, Don. Flights. Lima, Sidney, illus. (p. 604)
McGregor, Don & Lima, Sidney. Flights. (p. 604)
McGregor, Harriet. Electricity. (p. 509)
—Globalization. (p. 685)
—Magnets & Springs. (p. 1076)
—Sound. (p. 1615)
Mcgregor, Harriet. Ultimate Book of Science. (p. 1809)
McGregor, Janet C. Happy for a Honk & a Wave. Craft, Donna, illus. (p. 745)
McGregor, John. Daisy & Her Autumn & Winter Adventures. (p. 400)
McGregor, Kristen. Danny & Jacob Case #081548 Savanco Inc (p. 405)
McGregor, Malcolm, illus. see Clarke, Phillip & Khan, Sarah.
McGregor, Malcolm, illus. see Clarke, Phillip, ed.
McGregor, Melissa Lee. Ainsley & Owen: An Unexpected Friendship. (p. 30)
McGregor, Susan. Amazing Adventures of Mystica: Book 1: the Magic House. (p. 52)
McGregor, Suzy. Garden Fairy & Mrs. Mouse. (p. 656)
—Moon Leopard. (p. 1172)
McGregor, Tony L., illus. see Kelley, Walter P.
McGregor, Wynn. Way of the Child: Helping Children Experience God. (p. 1864)
—Way of the Child: Helping Children Experience God Family Booklet. (p. 1864)
McGrellis, Barbara. Love Never Fails. (p. 1060)
McGrellis, Cynthia, illus. see Ayder, Earl.
McGrew, Michael. Saint Brendan & the Voyage Before Columbus. Litz, Marnie Saebz, illus. (p. 1503)
McGriff, Aaron, ed. see Walsh, Patrick M., Jr.
McGriff, Aaron C., ed. see Walsh, Patrick M., Jr.
McGriff, Shawna A. Princess Pink: Princess Pink Saves the Girls of Lahappyville. (p. 1405)
—Princess Pink: Sam Loses Her Mother, but She Gains Her Mother's Heart. (p. 1405)
—Princess Pink: Princess Pink Helps Zion, Melinda, & Jasmine Learn to Communicate about Their Parents' Divorces. (p. 1405)
McGroary, Mary Beth. My Teacher Hates Me. (p. 1220)
McGrory, Anek, illus. see Hurwitz, Johanna.
McGrory, Anik, illus. see Downs, Mike.
McGrory, Anik, illus. see Goldin, Barbara Diamond.
McGrory, Anik, illus. see Hurwitz, Johanna & McCrory, Anik.
McGrory, Anik, illus. see Hurwitz, Johanna.
McGrory, Paul, illus. see Price, Robin.
McGuckie, Cierra Jade, illus. see Stanglin, Jackie A.
McGuckin, Mitchelle. Bullfrog Henry. (p. 240)
McGuffey, William H. New Mcguffey Fourth Reader. (p. 1246)
McGugan, Jim. Bridge 6. (p. 227)
McGuigan, Mary Ann. Crossing into Brooklyn. (p. 385)
—Morning in a Different Place. (p. 1175)
McGuiness, Elle J. & Brown, Heather. Bee & Me: A Mini-Motion Book. (p. 157)
McGuinness, Aûine, illus. see Boland, Gerry.
McGuinness, Bill, photos by see Bryan, Ashley.
McGuinness, Daniel. Cool Careers Without College for People Who Are Really Good at Science & Math. (p. 362)
McGuinness, Denis E. & Spencer, Lauren. Writing to Describe. (p. 1965)
McGuinness, Denis E. & Thomson, Sarah L. Gary Paulsen. (p. 657)
McGuinness, Ed. Amazing X-Men (p. 56)
McGuinness, Elle J. Baby Turtle's Tale. Caron, Romi, illus. (p. 128)
—Bee & Me. (p. 157)
—Bee & Me. Brown, Heather, illus. (p. 157)
McGuinness, Elle J. & Caron, Romi. Baby Turtle's Tale: A Mini Animotion Book. (p. 128)
McGuinness, Jeff. Paddy the Penguin's Adventure. Starr, Lisa, illus. (p. 1317)
McGuinness, Nanette, jt. auth. see Baccalario, Pierdomenico.
McGuinness, Nanette, tr. see Adler, Irene.
McGuinness, Nanette, tr. see Baccalario, Pierdomenico.
McGuinness, Tracey, illus. see Raymer, Dottie.
McGuinness, Tracy, illus. see Falligant, Erin, ed.
McGuinness, Tracy, illus. see Long, Lynette.
McGuinness, Tracy, illus. see Raymer, Dottie.
McGuinness, Tracy, illus. see Tenah, Ann.
McGuinness-Kelly, Tracy-Lee. Bad Cat. McGuinness-Kelly, Tracy-Lee, illus. (p. 131)
McGuire, jt. auth. see Campbell, J.
McGuire, Andy. Lulu on the Loose: A Bible Memory Buddy Book about Self-Control. Harrington, David, illus. (p. 1065)
McGuire, Barry. Elephant in the Room. (p. 511)
McGuire, Bill, illus. see Meister, Cari.
McGuire, Bryan, illus. see Menix, Cinda.
McGuire, Colin, photos by see Butler, Amy.
McGuire, Erin, illus. see Freymann-Weyr, Garret.
McGuire, Erin, illus. see Littlewood, Kathryn.
McGuire, Erin, illus. see Lord, Cynthia.
McGuire, Erin, illus. see Patron, Susan.
McGuire, Erin, illus. see Rylant, Cynthia.
McGuire, Erin, illus. see Ursu, Anne.
McGuire, Erin K. Careers in Database Design. (p. 267)
McGuire, Erin K., illus. see Patron, Susan.
McGuire, George. God & Me. (p. 688)
McGuire, Heather Ridgway. Vegetable Garden. (p. 1834)
McGuire, Jeremy. O'shaughnessey: Boy & His Leprechaun. (p. 1305)
McGuire, Kara. All about the Green: The Teens' Guide to Finding Work & Making Money (p. 43)
—Cover Your Assets: The Teens' Guide to Protecting Their Money, Their Stuff, & Themselves (p. 373)
—Financial Literacy for Teens (p. 587)
—Making Money Work: A Teen's Guide to Saving, Investing, & Building Wealth (p. 1081)
—Smart Spending: The Teens' Guide to Cash, Credit, & Life's Costs (p. 1593)
—Teen Money Manual: A Guide to Cash, Credit, Spending, Saving, Work, Wealth, & More (p. 1713)
McGuire, Kevin. All-New Woodworking for Kids. (p. 45)
McGuire, Leslie. We Read Phonics-If I Had a Snake. Johnson, Meredith, illus. (p. 1868)
McGuire, Michael, jt. auth. see Keylor, William R.
McGuire, Molly. Barbie in a Mermaid Tale Golden Books Staff, illus. (p. 138)
McGuire, Robert, illus. see Fleischman, Sid.
McGuire, Robert, illus. see Hubbard, Crystal.
McGuire, Robert, illus. see Mortensen, Lori.
McGuire, Robert, illus. see Slade, Suzanne & Picture Window Books Staff.
McGuire, Robert, jt. auth. see Hubbard, Crystal.
McGuire, Roberta Libby. Adventures of the Cape Cod Bear. (p. 23)
McGuire, Stryker, et al. Vertigo: First Taste. (p. 1837)
McGuire, Tom. Poison in Your Teeth: Mercury Amalgam (Silver) Fillings ... Hazardous to Your Health! (p. 1377)
McGuire Woods, Molly. Barbie in Princess Power. (p. 138)
—Barbie in Rock 'n Royals. (p. 138)
—Pearl Princess. (p. 1333)
McGuirk, Leslie. Gobble, Gobble, Tucker! McGuirk, Leslie, illus. (p. 688)
—Ho, Ho, Ho, Tucker! McGuirk, Leslie, illus. (p. 786)
—If Rocks Could Sing: A Discovered Alphabet. (p. 854)
—Lucky Tucker. (p. 1063)
—Lucky Tucker. McGuirk, Leslie, illus. (p. 1063)
—Moogees Move House. McGuirk, Leslie, illus. (p. 1171)
—Tucker's Spooky Halloween. (p. 1796)
—Tucker's Spooky Halloween. McGuirk, Leslie, illus. (p. 1796)
—Tucker's Valentine. McGuirk, Leslie, illus. (p. 1796)
McGuirk, Leslie & Von Bidder, Alex. Wiggens Learns His Manners at the Four Seasons Restaurant. McGuirk, Leslie, illus. (p. 1927)
McHaffie, Natalie. C-Growl: The Daring Little Airplane. McHaffie, Natalie, illus. (p. 249)
McHale, Conor. Ancient Ireland Colouring Book: From Newgrange to the Vikings. McHale, Conor, illus. (p. 69)
McHale, Remme. No Place for Niappy. (p. 1259)
McHale, Scarlett. Brady Makes a Weather Graph. (p. 221)
McHaney, Eric & McHaney, Mandy. Rich the Itch. Smith, Jordyn, illus. (p. 1469)
McHaney, Mandy, jt. auth. see McHaney, Eric.
McHargue, D., illus. see Anderson, Dale & O'Hern, Kerri.
McHargue, D., illus. see Brown, Jonatha A. & Goff, Elizabeth Hudson.
McHargue, D., illus. see Brown, Jonatha A., et al.
McHargue, D., illus. see Holland, Gini & O'Hern, Kerri.
McHargue, D., illus. see Riehecky, Janet & O'Hern, Kerri.
McHargue, D., illus. see Walsh, Frank & O'Hern, Kerri.
McHargue, Dove, illus. see Kneece, Mark & Serling, Rod.
McHatton, Todd. Grass Stained Twilight. (p. 711)
McHay, Micki. Ugly Snowflake (children's hard cover book with musical C. D.) (p. 1808)
McHeffey, Adam. Asiago McHeffey, Adam, illus. (p. 106)
McHeffey, Adam, illus. see Bonnett-Rampersaud, Louise.
McHenry, Colin, jt. auth. see Brochu, Christopher.
McHenry, E. B. Poodlena. (p. 1383)
—Poodlena. McHenry, E. B., illus. (p. 1383)
McHenry, Eric. Mommy Daddy Evan Sage. Garland, Nicholas, illus. (p. 1162)
McHenry, Irene & Moog, Carol. Autism Playbook for Teens: Imagination-Based Mindfulness Activities to Calm Yourself, Build Independence, & Connect with Others. (p. 117)
McHone, Greg. Great Day Trips to Discover the Geology of Connecticut. (p. 715)
McHose, Jean, illus. see Smith, Maggie Caldwell.
McHugh, Erin. Arizona. Schrier, Alfred, illus. (p. 98)
—National Parks: A Kid's Guide to America's Parks, Monuments & Landmarks. Aspinall, Neal, illus. (p. 1233)
—New Jersey. Schrier, Alfred, illus. (p. 1245)
—Ohio. Schrier, Alfred, illus. (p. 1281)
—Pennsylvania. Schrier, Alfred, illus. (p. 1337)
McHugh, Fiona. Anne of Green Gables Story Book: Based on the Kevin Sullivan Film of Lucy Maud Montgomery's Classic Novel. (p. 86)
Mchugh, Gelolo. Baby's House. (p. 129)
—Baby's House. Blair, Mary, illus. (p. 129)
McHugh, Janet. Great Chicago Fire. (p. 714)
McHugh, Jeff. Maintaining a Positive Digital Footprint. (p. 1077)
McHugh, Maura. Twisted Fairy Tales. Laurie, Jane, illus. (p. 1802)
—Twisted Myths: 20 Classic Stories with a Dark & Dangerous Heart. (p. 1802)

M

McHugh, Michael. Giant of the Western Trail: Father Peter de Smet. Dougherty, Charles L., illus. (p. 673)
—Writing with Prayer (p. 1965)
McHugh, Michael J., ed. see Bond, Douglas.
McHugh, Michael J., ed. see Haggard, H. Rider.
McHugh, Michael J., ed. see Latham, Frank.
McHugh, Michael J. & Bachman, Frank P. Story of Inventions. (p. 1658)
McHugh Parker, Katie, jt. auth. see McHugh, Sean.
McHugh, Patricia, ed. see Lavin, Christine & Franco-Feeney, Betsy.
McHugh, Rosetta. Poodiky Oglethorpe. (p. 1383)
—Poodiky Oglethorpe's First Christmas (p. 1383)
McHugh, Sean & McHugh Parker, Katie. Broomsticks the Halloween Spirit. (p. 231)
McIlhany, illus. see Prus, Jennifer.
McIlquham, Mary Caroline. Full Schedule: A Picture Symbol Activity Book. Mayer-Johnson, illus. (p. 646)
McIlroy, Michelle, jt. auth. see Louise, Cristina.
McIlvain, Terry. Vital Skills: How to Resolve Conflict. (p. 1846)
McIlwain, Harris H. & Bruce, Debra Fulghum. Pain-Free Arthritis: A 7-Step Plan for Feeling Better Again. (p. 1318)
McIlwain, Harris H., et al. Fibromyalgia Handbook: A 7-Step Program to Halt & Even Reverse Fibromyalgia. (p. 583)
McInerney, Kathleen, jt. auth. see Ryan, Pam Muñoz.
McInerney, Kunyi June-Anne, illus. see Kartinyeri, Doris.
McInerney, Kunyi June-Anne, jt. auth. see Randall, Bob.
McInnes, Dawn Daniels. I Want off This Stinkin' Plane Daniels, Greg, illus. (p. 847)
McInnes, Lisa. Evelyn's Special Eggs. Duersch, Gretchen, ed. (p. 541)
McInnes, Nicole. Brianna on the Brink. (p. 227)
McInnes, Rob, jt. auth. see McInnes, Robert.
McInnes, Robert & McInnes, Rob. Action/Adventure Films. (p. 10)
McIntee, David. Wizards: From Merlin to Faust. Stacey, Mark, illus. (p. 1943)
McIntee, David A. & McIntee, Lesley. Wizards. (p. 1943)
McIntee, Lesley, jt. auth. see McIntee, David A.
McIntee, Ross. WAY of Salvation. (p. 1864)
McIntosh, Anne. Montana Love Affair: Letting Go & Being Free. Campbell-Quillen, Virginia, illus. (p. 1170)
McIntosh, Cherie, jt. auth. see Cook, Deena.
McIntosh, Edgar, jt. auth. see Peck, Marilu.
McIntosh, Fiona. Goddess. (p. 690)
—Whisperer. (p. 1912)
McIntosh, G. B., jt. auth. see Nussbaum, Ben.
McIntosh, Gabe, illus. see Bailey, Gerry.
McIntosh, Gabe, illus. see Bentley, Dawn.
McIntosh, Gabe, illus. see Nussbaum, Ben.
McIntosh, Gavin. Hausaland Tales from the Nigerian Market Place. (p. 754)
McIntosh, Helen B. Eric, Jose, & the Peace Rug. (p. 533)
—Eric, Jose & the Peace Rug(r). (p. 533)
McIntosh High School Sophomores. High School 101: Freshman Survival Guide (p. 778)
McIntosh, Iain, illus. see McCall Smith, Alexander.
McIntosh, J. S. Elite Forces Selection. (p. 513)
—Football. (p. 615)
—Gymnastics. (p. 733)
—Martial Arts. (p. 1097)
—Soccer. (p. 1603)
—Wrestling. (p. 1962)
McIntosh, Jane R. Handbook to Life in Prehistoric Europe. (p. 740)
McIntosh, Jonathan S. & McIntosh, Kenneth R. Growth of North American Religious Beliefs: Spiritual Diversity. (p. 727)
McIntosh, Kenneth. Apache. (p. 91)
—Buggies, Bicycles & Iron Horses: Transportation in the 1800s. (p. 236)
—Clergy. (p. 331)
—Close-Up: Forensic Photography. (p. 334)
—Close-Up: Forensic Photography Sanborn, Casey, illus. (p. 334)
—Controversial World of Biblical Archaeology: Tomb Raiders, Fakes, & Scholars. (p. 361)
—Crime Scene Club: Facts & Fiction (p. 382)
—Devil's Canyon: Forensic Geography. (p. 432)
—Devil's Canyon: Forensic Geography. Miller, Justin, illus. (p. 432)
—Earth Cries Out: Forensic Chemistry & Environmental Science. (p. 495)
—Earth Cries Out: Forensic Chemistry & Environmental Science Miller, Justin, illus. (p. 495)
—Face from the Past: Skull Reconstruction. (p. 560)
—Grail, the Shroud, & Other Religious Relics: Secrets & Ancient Mysteries. (p. 705)
—Grateful Dead. (p. 712)
—History of Depression: the Mind-Body Connection. (p. 784)
—If the Shoe Fits: Footwear Analysis. (p. 854)
—If the Shoe Fits: Footwear Analysis Miller, Justin, illus. (p. 854)
—Latino Religious Experience: People of Faith & Vision. (p. 979)
—Latinos Today: Facts & Figures. (p. 979)
—Monsoon Murder: Forensic Meteorology. (p. 1166)
—Monsoon Murder: Forensic Meteorology Holland, Joe, illus. (p. 1166)
—Natural Alternatives to Antidepressants: St. John's Wort, Kava Kava, & Others. (p. 1235)
—Navajo. (p. 1237)
—Numbering the Crime: Forensic Mathematics Golden, John Ashton, illus. (p. 1271)
—Outlaws & Lawmen: Crime & Punishment in the 1800s. (p. 1312)
—Over the Edge: Forensic Accident Reconstruction. (p. 1314)
—Over the Edge: Forensic Accident Reconstruction Sanborn, Casey, illus. (p. 1314)
—Poison & Peril: Forensic Toxicology. (p. 1377)
—Poison & Peril: Forensic Toxicology Miller, Justin, illus. (p. 1377)
—Prophecies & End-Time Speculations: The Shape of Things to Come. (p. 1411)
—Pueblo. (p. 1414)
—Reviving the Spirit, Reforming Society: Religion in The 1800s. (p. 1466)
—Reviving the Spirit, Reforming Society: Religion in the 1800s. (p. 1466)
—Saloons, Shootouts, & Spurs: The Wild West in The 1800's. (p. 1505)
—Stranger's Voice: Forensic Speech. (p. 1665)
—Stranger's Voice: Forensic Speech Identification Golden, John Ashton, illus. (p. 1665)
—Things Fall Apart: Forensic Engineering. (p. 1733)
—Things Fall Apart: Forensic Engineering Golden, John Ashton, illus. (p. 1733)
—Trickster's Image: Forensic Art. (p. 1786)
—Trickster's Image: Forensic Art Miller, Justin, illus. (p. 1786)
—U2. (p. 1807)
—Women in North America's Religious World. (p. 1946)
McIntosh, Kenneth, jt. auth. see Intosh, Kenneth Mc.
McIntosh, Kenneth & Kleiman, Andrew. Natural Alternatives to Antidepressants: St. John's Wort, Kava Kava, & Others. (p. 1235)
McIntosh, Kenneth & Livingston, Phyllis. Youth with Alcohol & Drug Addiction: Escape from Bondage. (p. 1982)
—Youth with Conduct Disorder: In Trouble with the World. (p. 1982)
—Youth with Impulse-Control Disorders: On the Spur of the Moment. (p. 1982)
—Youth with Juvenile Schizophrenia: The Search for Reality. (p. 1982)
—Youth with Juvenile Schizophrenia: the Search for Reality. (p. 1982)
McIntosh, Kenneth & McIntosh, Marsha. Cheyenne. (p. 299)
—Flight from Turmoil. (p. 604)
—Issues of Church, State, & Religious Liberties: Whose Freedom, Whose Faith? (p. 893)
—Seminoles (p. 1550)
McIntosh, Kenneth & Walker, Ida. Interpreting an Alien World: Youth with Cultural/Language Differences. (p. 880)
—Youth with Cultural/Language Differences: Interpreting an Alien World. (p. 1982)
—Youth with HIV/AIDS: Living with the Diagnosis. (p. 1982)
—Youth with HIV/AIDS: Living with the Diagnosis. (p. 1982)
McIntosh, Kenneth R. Following Aslan: A Book of Devotions for Children Based on the Chronicles of Narnia by C. S. Lewis. (p. 612)
—Women & Religion: Reinterpreting Scriptures to Find the Sacred Feminine. (p. 1945)
McIntosh, Kenneth R., jt. auth. see McIntosh, Jonathan S.
McIntosh, Maria J. Evenings at Donaldson Manor: Or- the Christmas Guest. (p. 541)
—Florence Arnott; or, Is She Generous? by M J McIntosh. (p. 606)
McIntosh, Marsha. Teen Life on Reservations & in First Nation Communities: Growing up Native. (p. 1713)
McIntosh, Marsha, jt. auth. see McIntosh, Kenneth.
McIntosh, Marsha & Smith, jt. auth. see Smith, Roger.
McIntosh, Roswita. Live, Laugh & Learn. (p. 1040)
McIntosh, Sharon. Grandma S Donut Hat. (p. 708)
McIntosh Williams, Samantha. Last Bear on Brandywine Crick. (p. 977)
McInturff, Linda, illus. see Cunningham, Edie.
McInturff, Linda & Pope, Patricia. I Love to Tell the Story: A Visualized Gospel Song. (p. 843)
McInturff, Linda & Tweed, Sean. Light of the World Is Jesus. (p. 1015)
McIntyre, Abigael. Insider's Guide to Field Hockey (p. 878)
McIntyre, Abigael & Giddens, Sandra. Insider's Guide to Volleyball. (p. 878)
McIntyre, Abigael & Wesley, Ann. Fastpitch Softball: Girls Rocking It. (p. 576)
McIntyre Brister, Mary. Ollie the Orange Octopus. (p. 1287)
McIntyre, Coleen, illus. see Davis, Sharon & Patton, Charlene.
McIntyre, Connie. Flowers for Grandpa Dan: A Gentle Story to Help Children Understand Alzheimer's Disease. McIntyre, Louise, illus. (p. 608)
McIntyre, Connie, jt. auth. see Gage, Amy Glaser.
McIntyre, Gary P. Jake Fall & Winter. (p. 906)
—Little People up Jump. (p. 1033)
McIntyre, Georgina, illus. see Elliott, Odette.
McIntyre, John T. Fighting King George. (p. 585)
McIntyre, Laura. Everything Girls Ultimate Sleepover Party Book: 100+ Ideas for Sleepover Games, Goodies, Makeovers, & More! (p. 544)
McIntyre, Louise, illus. see McIntyre, Connie.
McIntyre, Mel. Flutter Bunnies. Grady, Kit, illus. (p. 609)
—Legend of Lumpus & Ogols. McQuillan, David, illus. (p. 988)
McIntyre, Mel, jt. auth. see McIntyre, Mel.
McIntyre, Mel & McIntyre, Mel. Flutter Bunnies Fossil of Fortune. Grady, Kit, illus. (p. 609)
McIntyre, Pat. It's about Time. (p. 896)
McIntyre, Sandra. Canoes: Canadian Icons. (p. 261)
—Canots: Les Emblèmes Canadiens. McMann, Julie, tr. from ENG. (p. 261)
—Carcajous: Les Animaux du Canada. Karvonen, Tanjah, tr. from ENG. (p. 265)
—Wolverines. (p. 1944)
McIntyre, Sarah, illus. see Andreae, Giles.
McIntyre, Sarah, illus. see Lumry, Amanda & Hurwitz, Laura.
McIntyre, Sarah, illus. see Reeve, Philip.
McIntyre, Sarah & O'Connell, David. Jampires. (p. 907)
McIntyre, Sasha, illus. see Jennings, Sharon.
McIntyre, Sasha & Ghione, Yvette. Franklin's Easter: A Sticker Activity Book. (p. 631)
McIntyre, Sasha & Sinkner, Alice, adapted by. Franklin's Easter: A Sticker Activity Book. (p. 631)
McIntyre, Sharyn. Christmas Tea with the Angels. (p. 316)
McIntyre, Sheila Adam. Cave in the Forest. (p. 282)
McIntyre, Sterlynett. Closing Argument. (p. 334)
McIntyre, Thomas. Survival Guide for Kids with Behavior Challenges: How to Make Good Choices & Stay Out of Trouble. (p. 1686)
McInvale, Rebecca. Emmy the Bug-Gulping Dog. (p. 520)
McIsaac, Gerald. Bird from Hell: Third Edition. (p. 190)
McIsaac, Meaghan. Boys of Fire & Ash. (p. 220)
McJarrow, Shandy. Adventures of Papilio the Butterfly. (p. 21)
McKain, Kelly. Haunted Shipwreck. Johansson, Cecilia, illus. (p. 753)
—Megan & Mischief. (p. 1124)
—Poppy & Prince. (p. 1385)
McKain, Susan, jt. auth. see Swann, Sandy.
McKain, Susan & Swann, Sandy. Tugger & Mini-Mew. (p. 1796)
McKain, W. J. Morris Hollett - & St Vernon's Ward for Strange & Unusual Diseases. (p. 1176)
McKann, Anna. Chavos: The Kids of Distrito Federal. (p. 295)
McKay, Amanda S. New Night Sky. (p. 1246)
McKay, Ann Marie, illus. see McLaughlin, Julie.
McKay, Chelsea. Tangram ABC: Shaping the Alphabet from an Ancient Chinese Puzzle. Firos, Daphne, illus. (p. 1705)
McKay, Donald, illus. see Howard, Joan.
McKay, George & McGhee, Karen. Encyclopedia of Animals. (p. 524)
—National Geographic Encyclopedia of Animals. (p. 1231)
McKay, Graham. Hymn a Day. (p. 831)
McKay, Hilary. Binny for Short. Player, Micah, illus. (p. 188)
—Caddy Ever After. (p. 250)
—Caddy's World. (p. 250)
—Cold Enough for Snow. Melling, David, tr. (p. 338)
—Exiles at Home. (p. 548)
—Exiles in Love. (p. 548)
—Forever Rose. (p. 619)
—Indigo's Star. (p. 872)
—Lulu & the Cat in the Bag. Lamont, Priscilla, illus. (p. 1064)
—Lulu & the Dog from the Sea. Lamont, Priscilla, illus. (p. 1064)
—Lulu & the Duck in the Park. Lamont, Priscilla, illus. (p. 1064)
—Lulu & the Hamster in the Night. Lamont, Priscilla, illus. (p. 1064)
—Lulu & the Hedgehog in the Rain. Lamont, Priscilla, illus. (p. 1064)
—Permanent Rose. (p. 1343)
—Saffy's Angel. (p. 1502)
—Terrible Time Without Tilly. Scott, Kimberley, illus. (p. 1721)
—Tilly & the Dragon: Red Banana. Shaw, Mick & Scott, Kimberley G., illus. (p. 1750)
—Wishing for Tomorrow: The Sequel to a Little Princess. Maland, Nick, illus. (p. 1940)
McKay, Hilary, jt. auth. see McKay, Hilary.
McKay, Hilary & McKay, Hilary. Perro Viernes. (p. 1344)
McKay, James, jt. auth. see Millidge, Gary Spencer.
McKay, James C. Spike! The Journey of a Boy & His Dog during the Great Depression. (p. 1627)
McKay, Jane. Tess & the Star Traveller. (p. 1722)
McKay, Jeffrey, jt. auth. see Kavanagh, Shannon.
McKay, Jenny. Children of the Holocaust. (p. 302)
McKay, John. History of Western Society: Advanced Placement with Database Questions. (p. 785)
McKay, Karen J. Amazing Grace. (p. 54)
Mckay, Kim & Bonnin, Jenny. True Green Kids: 100 Things You Can Do to Save the Planet. (p. 1792)
McKay, Kirsty. Undead. (p. 1813)
—Unfed. (p. 1817)
McKay, Laura Lee. Write Fantasy Fiction in 5 Simple Steps. (p. 1963)
McKay, Laurie. Villain Keeper. (p. 1842)
McKay, Lise Y. Mysterious Well. (p. 1223)
McKay, Lucia & Guscott, Maggie. Budgeting & Banking Math. (p. 235)
—Budgeting & Banking Math Answer Key: Teacher's Notes. (p. 235)
—Everyday Life, Book 1. (p. 543)
—Everyday Life Math Answer Key. (p. 544)
—Home & School, Book 2. (p. 791)
—Home & School Math Answer Key. (p. 792)
—On the Job Answer Key: Teacher's Notes. (p. 1290)
—Smart Shopping Math. (p. 1593)
—Smart Shopping Math Answer Key. (p. 1593)
—Sports & Hobbies Math. (p. 1632)
—Sports & Hobbies Math Answer Key. (p. 1632)
McKay, Malcolm. Thistown. (p. 1737)
McKay, Nellie Y., ed. see Gates, J.
McKay, Sharon E. End of the Line. (p. 526)
—Enemy Territory. (p. 527)
—Esther. (p. 538)
—Thunder over Kandahar. Gerszak, Rafal, photos by. (p. 1746)
McKay, Sharon E. & Lafrance, Daniel. War Brothers: The Graphic Novel. Lafrance, Daniel, illus. (p. 1857)
McKay, Sindy. Animals under Our Feet. Hunt, Judith, illus. (p. 84)
—Los dos leemos-Fiebre de Beisbol: Nivel 1-2. Johnson, Meredith, illus. (p. 1053)
—Los dos leemos-la Cama Colorada: Nivel 1. Mauterer, Erin Marie, illus. (p. 1053)
—Los dos leemos-Mi Dia: Nivel K. Johnson, Meredith, illus. (p. 1054)
—Los dos leemos-Mi Dia. Canetti, Yanitzia James, tr. (p. 1054)
—Too Many Cats: Demasiados Gatos. (p. 1766)
—We Both Read Bilingual Edition-About Bats/Acerca de Los Murcielagos. Canetti, Yanitzia, tr. (p. 1866)
—We Both Read Bilingual Edition-About Dinosaurs/Acerca de Los Dinosaurios. Walters, Robert, illus. (p. 1866)
—We Both Read Bilingual Edition-Too Many Cats/Demasiados Gatos. Johnson, Meredith, illus. (p. 1866)
—We Both Read-A Pony Named Peanut. Johnson, Meredith, illus. (p. 1866)
—We Both Read-About Dinosaurs. Walters, Robert, illus. (p. 1866)
—We Both Read-about Dinosaurs. Walters, Robert, illus. (p. 1866)
—We Both Read-Animals under Our Feet. Hunt, Judith, illus. (p. 1866)
—We Both Read-Being Safe. Photodisc-Getty Staff, Images, photos by. (p. 1866)
—We Both Read-Being Safe Big Book: Being Safe Big Book Edition. (p. 1866)
—We Both Read-Big Cats, Little Cats. (p. 1866)
—We Both Read-Happy & Healthy. (p. 1866)
—We Both Read-Jack & the Toddler. Zivoin, Jennifer, illus. (p. 1866)
—We Both Read-My Car Trip. Johnson, Meredith, illus. (p. 1866)
—We Both Read-My Day Big Book. Johnson, Meredith, illus. (p. 1866)
—We Both Read-My Day (Picture Book) Johnson, Meredith, illus. (p. 1866)
—We Both Read-My Town. Johnson, Meredith, illus. (p. 1866)
—We Both Read-President Theodore Roosevelt. Gampert, John, illus. (p. 1866)
—We Both Read-Sharks! Hunt, Judith & Smith, Wendy, illus. (p. 1866)
—We Both Read-the Oprah Winfrey Story. Scott, Marc, illus. (p. 1866)
—We Both Read-The Ruby Rose Show. Johnson, Meredith, illus. (p. 1866)
—We Both Read-Too Many Cats. Johnson, Meredith, illus. (p. 1866)
—We Read Phonics-I Want to Be a Cowboy! Raglin, Tim, illus. (p. 1868)
—We Read Phonics-Magic Tricks. Johnson, Meredith, illus. (p. 1868)
—We Read Phonics-Matt & Sid. Reinhart, Larry, illus. (p. 1868)
—We Read Phonics-Pat, Cat, & Rat. Johnson, Meredith, illus. (p. 1868)
—We Read Phonics-the Garden Crew. Johnson, Meredith, illus. (p. 1868)
McKay, Sindy, jt. auth. see Johnson, Bruce.
McKay, Sindy & Johnson, Meredith. We Both Read-Baseball Fever. (p. 1866)
McKay, Siobhan, illus. see Alsop, Bonnie.
McKay, Susan. France. (p. 627)
—Japan. (p. 909)
McKay, Susan, jt. auth. see North, Peter.
McKay, Traci, illus. see Langdown, Leanne Shea.
McKayhan, Monica. Jaded. (p. 905)
—Pact. (p. 1317)
—Step Up. (p. 1648)
—Trouble Follows. (p. 1789)
McKayhan, Norma J. Mighty King & the Small Creature. (p. 1140)
McKay-Lawton, Toni. Family Favourites. Manning, Eddie, illus. (p. 568)
—In Bloom. Manning, Eddie, illus. (p. 863)
—Under the Sea. Manning, Eddie, illus. (p. 1814)
McKeague. Ssm Elementary Algebra. (p. 1637)
—Ssm Intermediate Algebra. (p. 1637)
McKean, Dave. Mirrormask. McKean, Dave, illus. (p. 1149)
McKean, Dave, illus. see Almond, David.
McKean, Dave, illus. see Gaiman, Neil, et al.
McKean, Dave, illus. see Gaiman, Neil.
McKean, Dave, illus. see King, Stephen.
McKean, Dave, illus. see Said, S. F.
McKechnie, Edward. Sweet Dreams for Scotty. Blanding, Allison, illus. (p. 1689)
McKee. Two Monsters. (p. 1804)
McKee, Brett. Monsters Don't Cry! Burfoot, Ella, illus. (p. 1169)
—Tickle Ghost. McKee, David, illus. (p. 1747)
McKee, Brett & McKee, David. George's Invisible Watch. McKee, David, illus. (p. 665)
McKee, Darren, illus. see Fertig, Michael P.
McKee, Darren, illus. see Mulcahy, William.
McKee, Darren, illus. see Neusner, Dena Wallenstein.
McKee, David. Big-Top Benn. (p. 184)
—Charlotte's Piggy Bank. McKee, David, illus. (p. 294)
—Conquerors. (p. 358)
—Denver. McKee, David, illus. (p. 427)
—Elmer McKee, David, illus. (p. 515)
—Elmer. (p. 515)
—Elmer. McKee, David, illus. (p. 515)
—Elmer & Butterfly. (p. 515)
—Elmer & Rose. McKee, David, illus. (p. 515)
—Elmer & Snake. McKee, David, illus. (p. 515)
Mckee, David. Elmer & Super El. McKee, David, illus. (p. 515)
McKee, David. Elmer & the Big Bird. McKee, David, illus. (p. 515)
—Elmer & the Birthday Quake. (p. 515)
—Elmer & the Butterfly. (p. 515)
—Elmer & the Flood. McKee, David, illus. (p. 515)
—Elmer & the Hippos. McKee, David, illus. (p. 515)
—Elmer & the Lost Teddy. McKee, David, illus. (p. 515)
—Elmer & the Monster. McKee, David, illus. (p. 515)
—Elmer & the Rainbow. McKee, David, illus. (p. 515)
—Elmer & the Whales. McKee, David, illus. (p. 515)
—Elmer & Wilbur. McKee, David, illus. (p. 515)
—Elmer Board Book. McKee, David, illus. (p. 515)
—Elmer in the Snow. McKee, David, illus. (p. 515)
—Elmer Sobre Zancos. (p. 515)
—Elmer's Baby Record Book. McKee, David, illus. (p. 515)
—Elmer's Christmas. (p. 515)
—Elmer's Colours. Al-Hamdi, Ahmed, tr. (p. 515)
—Elmer's Colours. Mo'Allim, Nur M., tr. (p. 515)
—Elmer's Colours. Umicini, Roberta, tr. (p. 515)
—Elmer's Colours (English-Polish) (p. 515)
—Elmer's Day. (p. 515)
—Elmer's Day. Al-Hamdi, Ahmed, tr. (p. 515)
—Elmer's Day. McKee, David, illus. (p. 515)
—Elmer's Day. Mo'Allim, Nur M., tr. (p. 515)
—Elmer's Day. Umicini, Roberta, tr. (p. 515)
—Elmer's Friends. (p. 515)
—Elmer's Friends. Al-Hamdi, Ahmed, tr. (p. 515)
—Elmer's Friends. Mo'Allim, Nur M., tr. (p. 515)
—Elmer's Friends. Umicini, Roberta, tr. (p. 515)
—Elmer's New Friend. (p. 515)
—Elmer's Special Day. McKee, David, illus. (p. 515)
—Elmer's Weather. (p. 515)
—Elmer's Weather. Al-Hamdi, Ahmed, tr. (p. 515)
—Elmer's Weather. McKee, David, illus. (p. 515)
—Elmer's Weather. Mo'Allim, Nur M., tr. (p. 515)
—Elmer's Weather (Il Tempo di Elmer) Umicini, Roberta, tr. (p. 515)
—Gladiator. McKee, David, illus. (p. 682)
—Hill & the Rock. McKee, David, illus. (p. 779)
—Isabel's Noisy Tummy. McKee, David, illus. (p. 891)

—Melric: The Magician Who Lost His Magic. McKee, David, illus. (p. 1125)
—Melric & the Petnapping. (p. 1125)
—Melric & the Sorcerer. (p. 1125)
—Melric the Magician Who Lost His Magic. McKee, David, illus. (p. 1125)
—Mr Benn - Red Knight. (p. 1184)
—Principe Pedro y el oso de Peluche. (p. 1406)
—Sad Story of Veronica: Who Played the Violin. McKee, David, illus. (p. 1501)
—Six Men. (p. 1582)
—Three Monsters. (p. 1743)
—Tusk Tusk. McKee, David, illus. (p. 1799)
—Zebra's Hiccups. McKee, David, illus. (p. 1985)
McKee, David, illus. see McKee, Brett.
McKee, David, illus. see Mckee, David.
McKee, David, illus. see Snell, Gordon.
McKee, David, jt. auth. see Birchall, Mark.
McKee, David, jt. auth. see McKee, Brett.
McKee, David, jt. auth. see Mckee, David.
Mckee, David, jt. auth. see McKee, David.
Mckee, David, jt. auth. see Mckee, David.
McKee, David & L'Ecole des loisirs/LeapFrog. Elmer. (p. 515)
Mckee, David & McKee, David. Elmer's First Counting Book. McKee, David, illus. (p. 515)
—Elmer's Opposites. McKee, David, illus. (p. 515)
McKee, David & Mckee, David. Tres Monstruos. (p. 1784)
McKee, Jenn. Jack Kerouac. (p. 903)
Mckee, Jessica. Piddle Diddie Stuck in the Middle. (p. 1356)
McKee, Jonathan. Guy's Guide to God, Girls, & the Phone in Your Pocket: 101 Real-World Tips for Teenaged Guys. (p. 733)
—Sex Matters. (p. 1556)
McKee, Karen & Griffin, Georgene. Hot Wings. (p. 802)
McKee, Mabel A. Heart of the Rose. (p. 759)
McKee, Ruby. Land of Phonicia: An Enchanted Tale to Learn Phonics. Allen, Timothy, illus. (p. 973)
Mckee-Kastl, Patricia. Old Witch & the Boy. (p. 1285)
McKeever, Sean. Gravity: Big-City Super Hero. (p. 712)
—Inhumans: Lunar Clark, Matthew, illus. (p. 874)
—Inhumans. (p. 874)
—Sentinel: Salvage (p. 1551)
McKeever, Sean, et al. Frontline: Oneshots. Vol. 4 Love, Jeremy et al, illus. (p. 644)
McKell, Theresa Kane. Algebra: Middle/High School. (p. 38)
—Pre-Algebra. (p. 1393)
McKellar, Danica. Math Doesn't Suck: How to Survive Middle School Math Without Losing Your Mind or Breaking a Nail. (p. 1105)
McKellar, Irma V. My Furry Critters. (p. 1209)
McKellop, Holly R. To the Moon. (p. 1759)
McKelvain, Dana, jt. auth. see Woods, Denise M.
McKelvain Kite, Karen. I Had a Dream. (p. 838)
McKelvey, Lonnie. Benny the Brave. Wooten, Neal, illus. (p. 165)
—Ralph & His New Friends. (p. 1437)
McKelvey, Pat. Fuzzy Lie. (p. 651)
—Game. (p. 654)
McKelvie, Melissa, told to. Serena & the Turtle Eggs. (p. 1552)
McKendall, Kerry. My Imagination Book. (p. 1211)
McKendrick, Scot & O'Sullivan, Orlaith, eds. Bible As Book: The Transmission of the Greek Text (p. 175)
McKendry, Joe. Beneath the Streets of Boston: Building America's First Subway. (p. 164)
—One Times Square: A Century of Change at the Crossroads of the World. McKendry, Joe, illus. (p. 1297)
McKendry, Sam. Are You Ticklish? Mitchell, Melanie, illus. (p. 97)
—Are You Ticklish? A Touch & Tickle Book. Mitchell, Melanie, illus. (p. 97)
—Are You Ticklish?/Tienes Cosquillas? Mitchell, Melanie, illus. (p. 97)
—Bless Everyone. (p. 199)
—Curious Kitties: A Color Book. Mitchell, Melanie, illus. (p. 394)
—Curious Kitties: A Colors Book. Mitchell, Melanie, illus. (p. 394)
—Imagine That! Samuel, Janet, illus. (p. 861)
—Little Whale Tale. Castillon, Carly, illus. (p. 1037)
—To the Rescue! (p. 1759)
McKendry, Sam, jt. auth. see DePrisco, Dorothea.
McKenna, Alexandra, jt. auth. see Kovalkova-McKenna, Svetlana.
McKenna, Allen, jt. auth. see Box, Marty.
McKenna, Amy. Britannica Guide to Africa (p. 229)
—History of Northern Africa. (p. 784)
—History of Southern Africa. (p. 784)
—History of Western Africa. (p. 785)
McKenna, Amy, jt. auth. see Morkes, Andrew.
McKenna, Amy, ed. 100 Most Influential World Leaders of All Time. (p. 1998)
—Denmark, Finland, & Sweden. (p. 426)
—Estonia, Latvia, Lithuania, & Poland. (p. 538)
McKenna, Brenton, illus. see Wingfield, Eileen Wani & Austin, Emily Munyungka.
McKenna, Bridgett, illus. see McClure, Beverly Stowe.
McKenna, Donna, jt. ed. see O'Loughlin, Declan.
McKenna, Gwen, ed. see Bennett, Cynthia L.
McKenna, Gwen, ed. see Haaglund, Lois F.
McKenna, Gwen, ed. see James, Will.
McKenna, Jacqueline & Manarino-Leggett, Priscilla. Sourpuss Sue. Manarino, Mark, illus. (p. 1616)
McKenna, James. Mind Traveller. (p. 1145)
McKenna, K. J. Take Three Girls. (p. 1697)
McKenna, Kerin Elaine. I Like Shoes. (p. 841)
McKenna, Konstantin, jt. auth. see Kovalkova-McKenna, Svetlana.
McKenna, Lou, illus. see Wright, Joe.
McKenna, Lou, illus. see Wright, Joseph B.
McKenna, Mark. Banana Tail's Colorful Adventure. (p. 136)
McKenna, Mark, illus. see Bedard, Tony.
McKenna, Mark, creator. Banana Tail's Tales & Activities. (p. 136)
McKenna, Mark, et al. Banana Tail. (p. 136)
McKenna, Marla. Mom's Big Catch. (p. 1163)
McKenna, Martin. Octopuppy. (p. 1278)
McKenna, Michael C., jt. ed. see Stahl, Katherine A. Dougherty.
McKenna, Michael C. & Walpole, Sharon. Literacy Coaching Challenge: Models & Methods for Grades K-8. (p. 1022)
McKenna, Molly, jt. auth. see Gowen, L. Kris.
McKenna, Nancy Durrell, photos by see Stoppard, Miriam.
McKenna, Paul. Golden Rule Poster. (p. 695)
McKenna, Sharon Michelle. Good Morning, Sunshine: A Grandpa Story. (p. 698)
McKenna, Susan. Feelings Only I Know: Mom & Dad Are Getting Divorced. Johannes, Shelley, illus. (p. 580)
—More Feelings Only I Know: Divorce & Fighting Are Hurting My Heart. Johannes, Shelley, illus. (p. 1174)
McKenna, Terry, illus. see Clarke, Catriona.
McKenna, Terry, illus. see Pratt, Leonie.
McKenney, J. David, illus. see Petroff, Shani.
McKenney, M. W. Roosevelt Junior High. (p. 1488)
McKennon, Tony. You're Moving Where?! (p. 1982)
McKenny, Stephanie L. Pearls of My Own. (p. 1333)
McKenny, Stewart, illus. see Fisch, Sholly.
McKenzie, Ann Marie. Four-Eyed Boy. (p. 624)
McKenzie, C. Lee. Alligators Overhead. (p. 47)
—Princess of Las Pulgas. (p. 1404)
McKenzie, C. Lee, jt. auth. see Binns, B. A.
McKenzie, Heath. My Rules for Being a Pretty Princess. (p. 1218)
McKenzie, Heath, illus. see Clark, Sherryl.
McKenzie, Heath, illus. see Cordina, Annette.
McKenzie, Heath, illus. see Hathorn, Libby.
McKenzie, Heath, illus. see Metz, Melinda.
McKenzie, Heath, illus. see Mewburn, Kyle.
McKenzie, Heath, illus. see Morrison, Yvonne.
McKenzie, Heath, illus. see Reynolds, Alison.
McKenzie, Heath, illus. see Stills, Caroline.
McKenzie, Heath, illus. see Wallace, Adam.
McKenzie, Heath, illus. see Whamhower, Shogun.
McKenzie, Heather, jt. auth. see Mitchell, Julie.
McKenzie, Heather, jt. auth. see Wall, Julia.
McKenzie, J. Lee. Vampires Don't Believe in Mermaids. (p. 1832)
McKenzie, Janet. Graced Encounters with Mary Fabyan Windeatt's Saints: 344 Ways to Imitate the Holy Habits of the Saints. (p. 705)
McKenzie, Janet P. RACE for Heaven's Catholic Study Guides for Mary Fabyan Windeatt's Saint Biographies Grade 6: Saint Dominic, the Children of Fatima, Saint John Masias, & Saint Benedict. (p. 1430)
—RACE for Heaven's Catholic Study Guides for Mary Fabyan Windeatt's Saint Biographies Grade 5: Saint Rose of Lima, Saint Martin de Porres, King David & His Songs, & Blessed Marie of New France. (p. 1430)
—RACE for Heaven's Catholic Study Guides for Mary Fabyan Windeatt's Saint Biographies Grade 8: Saint Margaret Mary, Saint Francis Solano, Pauline Jaricot, & Saint Paul the Apostle. (p. 1431)
—RACE for Heaven's Catholic Study Guides for Mary Fabyan Windeatt's Saint Biographies Grade 7: The Curé of Ars (St. John Vianney), the Little Flower (St. Therese of the Child Jesus), Saint Hyacinth of Poland, & Saint Louis de Montfort. (p. 1431)
—RACE for Heaven's Catholic Study Guides for Mary Fabyan Windeatt's Saint Biographies Grades 3 And 4: Saint Thomas Aquinas, the Patron Saint of First Communicants, Saint Catherine of Siena, & the Miraculous Medal. (p. 1431)
—Reading the Saints: Lists of Catholic Books for Children Plus Book Collecting Tips for the Home & School Library. (p. 1446)
McKenzie, Josie, illus. see Abbott, D. K.
McKenzie, Larry. Leonardo the Lopsided Lion. (p. 992)
McKenzie, Lisa-Dawn. Golden Acorn Project: A Not-Just-for-Children Story. (p. 694)
McKenzie, Lyn. Betsy, Girl Scout of Woodward Center 1935. (p. 172)
—Lavinia's Shoes. (p. 981)
McKenzie, Marni Shideler & Bridges, Nancy S. Quest - Faith at Work: Romans, Galatians, & James. Murtha, Dee, ed. (p. 1426)
McKenzie, Michelle. Jellyfish Inside Out. (p. 912)
McKenzie, Michelle A. B. Beavers' Big Discovery. (p. 155)
—Beavers' Big Problem. (p. 155)
McKenzie, Nancy. Guinevere's Gamble. (p. 731)
—Guinevere's Gift. (p. 731)
Mckenzie, Natalie. Children of New York City: Straight from the Heart 2009. (p. 302)
McKenzie, Paige. Haunting of Sunshine Girl. (p. 754)
Mckenzie, Precioius. At Bat. Byrne, Mike, illus. (p. 110)
—Bus Troubles. Anglicas, Louise, illus. (p. 244)
—Condoleezza Rice: Little World Biographies. (p. 356)
—Condoleezza Rice. (p. 356)
—Duck Doctor. Byrne, Mike, illus. (p. 488)
—Fish Mission. Mones, Marc, illus. (p. 598)
—Get the Prize. Allen, Marie, illus. (p. 668)
—Lake Mistake. Mones, Marc, illus. (p. 972)
—Lost in the Corn Maze. Allen, Marie, illus. (p. 1055)
—Off to the Yogurt Factory. Allen, Marie, illus. (p. 1279)
—Pitch the Tent. Byrne, Mike, illus. (p. 1364)
—Surfing Safari. Mones, Marc, illus. (p. 1685)
Mckenzie, Precious. Buff Ducks. Reasoner, John, illus. (p. 235)
McKenzie, Precious. Cleaning up the Earth. (p. 330)
—Coral Reefs. (p. 366)
Mckenzie, Precious. Disaster Day. Mones, Marc, illus. (p. 446)
McKenzie, Precious. Eye to Eye with Endangered Habitats (p. 558)
—Fishing for Danger. (p. 599)
—Glaciers. (p. 682)
—Group Projects. (p. 725)
—Isle of Enchantment. (p. 893)
—Library Skills & Internet Research. (p. 1006)
Mckenzie, Precious. Now or Later Alligator. Snape, Jenny, illus. (p. 1269)
McKenzie, Precious. Oceans. (p. 1277)
—Our Organic Garden. (p. 1309)
—People Who Care for Animals. (p. 1340)
Mckenzie, Precious. Presidents Yearbook 2013: Rourke's Complete History of Our Presidents Encyclopedia. (p. 1397)
McKenzie, Precious. Rainforests. (p. 1436)
—Savannahs. (p. 1516)
—Search & Rescue Animals. (p. 1537)
—Water World. (p. 1863)
Mckenzie, Precious. Who Stole the Veggies from the Veggie Patch? Snape, Jenny, illus. (p. 1917)
McKenzie, Precious. Writing an Informational Essay. (p. 1964)
McKenzie, Richard. Poems from the Playground & Other Places. Gervasi, Christine, illus. (p. 1376)
Mckenzie, Riford. Witches of Dredmoore Hollow (p. 1941)
McKenzie, Riford. Witches of Dredmoore Hollow Ferguson, Peter, illus. (p. 1941)
McKenzie, Roger. How Awesome Will It Be? A Teenager's Guide to Understanding & Preparing for the Second Coming. (p. 805)
McKenzie, Rosemarie. Cupcakes for Penny. (p. 392)
McKenzie, Sophie. Every Second Counts. (p. 543)
—In a Split Second. (p. 863)
McKenzie, Tiffany M. Adventures of Alan & the Man-Eating Rabbits. (p. 16)
McKenzie, Tim A. Baxter Barret Brown's Bass Fiddle. Shaw, Charles, illus. (p. 147)
—Baxter Barret Brown's Cowboy Band. Atkinson, Elaine, illus. (p. 147)
McKenzie, Walter, ed. see Archibald, Donna, et al.
Mckeon, Kathryn, jt. auth. see Stilton, Geronimo.
McKeon, Tess. Carried in Our Hearts. (p. 271)
McKeown, Christian, illus. see Anglen, Becca.
McKeown, David, illus. see Fant, Donna.
McKeown, Theresa. ABCs of Being Me. (p. 4)
Mckerley, Jennifer. Amazing Armadillos. Mirocha, Paul, illus. (p. 53)
Mckerley, Jennifer Guess. Hydra. (p. 831)
McKerley, Jennifer Guess. Kraken. (p. 967)
—Rules of the Net Duverne, Evelyne, illus. (p. 1495)
Mckerley, Jennifer Guess, ed. see Greenhaven Press Editors.
McKernan, Victoria. Devil's Paintbox. (p. 432)
—Shackleton's Stowaway. (p. 1556)
McKernan, Wendy. Thing I Say I Saw Last Night: A Christmas Story. Bzymek, Izabela, illus. (p. 1732)
McKibben, Marion A. Pearl the Rodeo Queen. (p. 1333)
McKie, Roy, illus. see Low, Alice.
McKie, Roy, illus. see Seuss, Dr.
McKig, Susan, illus. see Advance Cal-Tech Inc. Staff.
McKillip, Patricia A. Changeling Sea. (p. 290)
—Forgotten Beasts of Eld. (p. 619)
McKillip Thornburgh, Rebecca, illus. see Davis Jones, Melanie, et al.
McKim, Brian, illus. see Trahan, Kendra.
McKimmie, Chris. Maisie Moo & Invisible Lucy. McKimmie, Chris, illus. (p. 1077)
—Scarlett & the Scratchy Moon. McKimmie, Chris, illus. (p. 1520)
—Special Kev. McKimmie, Chris, illus. (p. 1623)
—Two Peas in a Pod. McKimmie, Chris, illus. (p. 1804)
McKinlay, Helen. Grandma Joins the All Blacks. Smith, Craig, illus. (p. 708)
McKinlay, Meg. Below. (p. 163)
—Duck for a Day. Rudge, Leila, illus. (p. 488)
—No Bears. Rudge, Leila, illus. (p. 1257)
—Ten Tiny Things. Hughes-Odgers, Kyle, illus. (p. 1719)
McKinlay, Penny. Bumposaurus. Teckentrup, Britta, illus. (p. 241)
—Flabby Tabby. Teckentrup, Britta, illus. (p. 601)
McKinley, Blake. Happy Tooth & Sad Tooth. (p. 747)
McKinley, Fred B. Chinqua Where? The Spirit of Rural America, 1947-1955. Blassingame, Calvin, illus. (p. 308)
McKinley, Herald. Myths of the Native Americans. (p. 1227)
—Persia, the Rise of Islam, & the Holy Roman Empire. (p. 1344)
—Turning Wax into Crayons. (p. 1798)
—Vikings: Raiders & Explorers. (p. 1842)
McKinley, Herald P. Turning Beans into Chocolate. (p. 1798)
McKinley, John, illus. see Klein, Abby.
Mckinley, John, jt. auth. see Klein, Abby.
McKinley, Kay, photos by see Freese, Joan.
McKinley, Kay, photos by see Marrewa, Jennifer.
McKinley, Kay, photos by see Rauen, Amy & Ayers, Amy.
McKinley, Kay, photos by see Rauen, Amy.
McKinley, Mary. Beau, Lee, the Bomb & Me. (p. 153)
—Rusty Summer. (p. 1498)
McKinley, Michael. Ice Time: The Story of Hockey. (p. 851)
—Temps de Glace: L'histoire du Hockey. (p. 1718)
McKinley, Robin. Beauty: A Retelling of the Story of Beauty & the Beast. (p. 154)
—Chalice. (p. 288)
—Door in the Hedge. (p. 470)
—Dragonhaven. (p. 478)
—Pegasus. (p. 1335)
—Shadows. (p. 1558)
—Spindle's End. (p. 1628)
McKinley, Robin & Dickinson, Peter. Fire: Tales of Elemental Spirits. (p. 590)
—Water: Tales of Elemental Spirits. (p. 1862)
McKinley, Ryan. Lost Crew. (p. 1055)
—Pirate Bride. (p. 1362)
McKinley, Teri, jt. auth. see Bowman, Crystal.
McKinna, Caelaach. Lion in the Living Room. Stone, A. R., illus. (p. 1020)
McKinnell, Robert G. Prevention of Cancer. (p. 1398)
McKinney, Ann. Loneliest Little Heart. (p. 1046)
McKinney, Barbara Shaw. Pass the Energy, Please! Wallace, Chad, illus. (p. 1326)
—Water Words Rhymed & Defined. Stich, Carolyn R., illus. (p. 1863)
McKinney, Dan, jt. auth. see Lammers, Elizabeth A.
McKinney, Devon. Firefighter's Tools. (p. 592)
—Monuments of Washington, D. C. Use Place Value Understanding & Properties of Operations to Add & Subtract. (p. 1171)
McKinney, Donna & Herrmann, Angela. Undercover Heroes of the Bible: Ages 2 & 3. (p. 1814)
—Undercover Heroes of the Bible: Ages 4 & 5. (p. 1814)
—Undercover Heroes of the Bible: Grades 1 & 2. (p. 1814)
—Undercover Heroes of the Bible: Grades 3 & 4. (p. 1814)
—Undercover Heroes of the Bible: Grades 5 & 6. (p. 1814)
McKinney, Doris, jt. auth. see Louise, Verna.
McKinney, Frank & Mason, Kate. Dead Fred, Flying Lunchboxes & the Good Luck Circle. (p. 416)
McKinney, Jason. Sheriff Teddy & the Plutonian Invaders. (p. 1565)
McKinney, John, jt. auth. see Cheri, Rae.
McKinney, John, jt. auth. see Rae, Cheri.
McKinney, Leslie. They're Nuts: Another Homophone Book. (p. 1732)
—Too Much! (p. 1767)
McKinney, Malachy, illus. see Harper, Helena.
McKinney, Nancy Kruschke, compiled by. Bible Story Collection: For Kids, by Kids. (p. 176)
McKinney-Whitaker, Courtney. Last Sister: A Novel. (p. 978)
McKinnon, Elaine. Life Cycle of a Beetle. (p. 1008)
—Magnets Are Fun! (p. 1076)
McKinnon, Gay, illus. see Morgan, Anne.
McKinnon, Hannah Roberts. Properties of Water. (p. 1411)
McKinnon, James, illus. see Dennard, Deborah.
McKinnon, Joy, illus. see Mancil, Arlene.
McKinnon, Margie. Repair for Teens: A Program for Recovery from Incest & Childhood Sexual Abuse. Spiho, Michal, illus. (p. 1460)
McKinnon, Margie & McKinnon, Tom W. Repair for Kids: A Children's Program for Recovery from Incest & Childhood Sexual Abuse. McKinnon, Margie & McKinnon, Tom W., illus. (p. 1460)
McKinnon, Robert Scott. Tooth Fairy Came to Gopher Gulch. (p. 1768)
McKinnon, Tom W., jt. auth. see McKinnon, Margie.
McKinnon, Yolanda Amos. Why Is the Moon Following Me? (p. 1925)
Mckinsey, Michelle. Weird O. (p. 1872)
McKinstry, J. A. Adventures of the 31st Street Saints: BOOK 2 Escape for Answers. (p. 23)
McKinty, Adrian. Deviant. (p. 432)
—Lighthouse Keepers. (p. 1015)
—Lighthouse Land. (p. 1015)
—Lighthouse War. (p. 1015)
McKirdy, Mark. Garden Party. (p. 656)
McKissack, Fredrick L. Shooting Star. (p. 1568)
—This Generation of Americans. (p. 1735)
McKissack, Fredrick L., jt. auth. see McKissack, Patricia C.
McKissack, Fredrick L. & McKissack, Lisa Beringer. Chinese New Year-Count & Celebrate! (p. 307)
—Christmas. (p. 312)
—Cinco de Mayo-Count & Celebrate! (p. 319)
—Counting in the Desert. (p. 371)
—Counting in the Grasslands. (p. 371)
—Counting in the Oceans. (p. 371)
—Counting in the Rain Forest. (p. 371)
—Counting in the Taiga. (p. 371)
—Counting in the Temperate Forest. (p. 371)
—Counting in the Tundra. (p. 371)
—Counting in the Wetlands. (p. 371)
—Kwanzaa-Count & Celebrate! (p. 969)
—Martin Luther King, Jr. Count & Celebrate! (p. 1098)
—Ramadan-Count & Celebrate! (p. 1437)
McKissack, Fredrick L. & McKissack, Patricia C. Hard Labor: The First African Americans 1619. Fiedler, Joseph Daniel, illus. (p. 748)
McKissack, Fredrick L., et al. Cyborg. (p. 396)
McKissack, Lisa Beringer, jt. auth. see McKissack, Fredrick L.
McKissack, Lisa Beringer & Compass Point Books Staff. Women of the Harlem Renaissance (p. 1946)
McKissack, Patricia C. Abby Takes a Stand. James, Gordon C., illus. (p. 2)
—Abby Takes a Stand. James, Gordon C. et al, illus. (p. 2)
—All-I'll-Ever-Want Christmas Doll. Pinkney, Jerry, illus. (p. 44)
—Amistad: The Story of a Slave Ship. Stanley, Sanna, illus. (p. 65)
—Away West. James, Gordon C. & James, Gordon, illus. (p. 120)
—Dark-Thirty: Southern Tales of the Supernatural. Pinkney, Brian, illus. (p. 408)
—Friendship for Today. (p. 639)
—Goin' Someplace Special. Pinkney, Jerry, illus. (p. 692)
—Home-Run King. (p. 792)
—Loved Best. Marshall, Felicia, illus. (p. 1061)
—Never Forgotten. Dillon, Leo & Dillon, Diane, illus. (p. 1242)
—Ol' Clip-Clop: A Ghost Story. Velasquez, Eric, illus. (p. 1283)
—Picture of Freedom: The Diary of Clotee, a Slave Girl, Belmont Plantation, Virginia 1859. (p. 1355)
—Porch Lies: Tales of Slicksters, Tricksters, & Other Wily Characters. Carrilho, Andre, illus. (p. 1386)
—Song for Harlem. (p. 1611)
—Tippy Lemmey. Keeter, Susan, illus. (p. 1757)
—Where Crocodiles Have Wings. Barner, Bob, illus. (p. 1906)
McKissack, Patricia C., jt. auth. see McKissack, Fredrick L.
McKissack, Patricia C. & McKissack, Fredrick L. Booker T. Washington: African-American Leader. (p. 212)
—Carter G. Woodson: Black History Pioneer. (p. 272)
—Closet de Bessey, la Desordenada. Regan, Dana, illus. (p. 334)
—Frederick Douglass: Fighter Against Slavery. (p. 633)
—George Washington Carver: Scientist & Inventor. (p. 664)
—Ida B. Wells-Barnett: Fighter for Justice. (p. 851)
—Jesse Owens: Legendary Track Star. (p. 914)
—Louis Armstrong: King of Jazz. (p. 1058)
—Madam C. J. Walker: Inventor & Millionaire. (p. 1069)
—Marian Anderson: Amazing Opera Singer. (p. 1093)
—Martin Luther King, Jr: Civil Rights Leader. (p. 1098)
—Mary Mcleod Bethune: Woman of Courage. (p. 1101)

M

—Messy Bessey: Messy Bessey's Closet - Messy Bessey's Family Reunion - Messy Bessey's Garden. Vol. 2 Regan, Dana, illus. (p. 1130)
—Paul Robeson: A Voice for Change. (p. 1330)
McKissack, Patricia C. & Moss, Onawumi Jean. Precious & the Boo Hag. Brooker, Kyrsten, illus. (p. 1394)
McKissack, Patricia C. & Potter, Giselle. Honest-to-Goodness Truth. Potter, Giselle, illus. (p. 794)
McKissack, Patricia C., et al. Best Shot in the West: The Adventures of Nat Love. DuBurke, Randy & Duburke, Randy, illus. (p. 171)
—Visitors. (p. 1845)
Mckissack, Robert. Try Your Best. (p. 1795)
McKissack, Robert L. Try Your Best. Cepeda, Joe, illus. (p. 1795)
McKissick, Angela Lorraine (Dame). Jonathan & Elizabeth Meet Jesus of Nazareth. (p. 925)
McKissock, Charmaine, illus. see Williams, Jan.
McKitterick, David, ed. Trinity Apocalypse. (p. 1786)
McKitterick, David, et al. Trinity Apocalypse. (p. 1786)
Mckneally, Ranida T., jt. auth. see Lin, Grace.
McKnight, Alex. Waiting for Ding. Tellekamp, Lynda, illus. (p. 1852)
McKnight Barringer, Laura, jt. auth. see McKnight, Scot.
McKnight Barringer, Laura, jt. auth. see Mcknight, Scot.
McKnight D'Andrea, Gina. Blackberry Patch. (p. 197)
McKnight, Diane. Lost Seal. Emerling, Dorothy, illus. (p. 1056)
McKnight, Gillian. To Catch a Prince: To Catch a Prince; the Frog Prince. (p. 1758)
—To Catch a Prince. (p. 1758)
McKnight, Marty. Jim Nasium Is a Basket Case. Jones, Chris B., illus. (p. 918)
—Jim Nasium Is a Football Fumbler. Jones, Chris B., illus. (p. 918)
—Jim Nasium Is a Hockey Hazard. Jones, Chris B., illus. (p. 918)
—Jim Nasium Is a Soccer Goofball. Jones, Chris B., illus. (p. 918)
McKnight, Penny. Nix. (p. 1257)
McKnight, Robin. Change Your Reality, Change Your Life. (p. 290)
McKnight, Scot & McKnight Barringer, Laura. Sharing God's Love: The Jesus Creed for Children. Hill, David, illus. (p. 1561)
Mcknight, Scot & McKnight Barringer, Laura. Sharing God's Love: the Jesus Creed for Children: Teacher Lesson & Activity Guide. (p. 1561)
McKnight-Trontz, Jennifer. How to Be Popular: Everything You Need to Know, & More. (p. 815)
McKoin, Cathy Taylor. Little Pup Finds a Home! (p. 1034)
McKone, Mike. Avengers Academy: Will We Use This in the Real World? Vol. 2 (p. 118)
McKone, Mike, illus. see Gage, Christos.
McKowen, Scott, illus. see Alcott, Louisa May.
McKowen, Scott, illus. see Barrie, J. M.
McKowen, Scott, illus. see Baum, L. Frank.
McKowen, Scott, illus. see Burnett, Frances Hodgson.
McKowen, Scott, illus. see Carroll, Lewis, pseud.
McKowen, Scott, illus. see Collodi, Carlo.
McKowen, Scott, illus. see Defoe, Daniel.
McKowen, Scott, illus. see Dickens, Charles.
McKowen, Scott, illus. see Doyle, Arthur.
McKowen, Scott, illus. see Grahame, Kenneth.
McKowen, Scott, illus. see Grimm, Jacob & Grimm, Wilhelm.
McKowen, Scott, illus. see Irving, Washington.
McKowen, Scott, illus. see Kipling, Rudyard.
McKowen, Scott, illus. see Lofting, Hugh.
McKowen, Scott, illus. see London, Jack.
McKowen, Scott, illus. see Montgomery, L. M.
McKowen, Scott, illus. see Poe, Edgar Allen.
McKowen, Scott, illus. see Porter, Eleanor H.
McKowen, Scott, illus. see Pyle, Howard.
McKowen, Scott, illus. see Sewell, Anna.
McKowen, Scott, illus. see Stevenson, Robert Louis.
McKowen, Scott, illus. see Stoker, Bram.
McKowen, Scott, illus. see Twain, Mark, pseud.
McKowen, Scott, illus. see Verne, Jules.
McKowen, Scott, illus. see Wyss, Johann David.
McKown, Hunter. Meet Jack Truck! Shannon, David et al, illus. (p. 1121)
—Sand Castle Bash: Counting from 1 To 10. Shannon, David et al, illus. (p. 1510)
McKown, Martha. Adventures of Zingway, the Monster. (p. 24)
—Elephant Story for Alex. Pfisterer Clark, Pem, illus. (p. 511)
McKown, Robin. Marie Curie. Rethi, Lili, illus. (p. 1093)
—Roosevelt's Americ. (p. 1488)
McKracken, Heather. That's What's Different about Me: Helping Children Understand Autism Spectrum Disorders. Robbins, Kathryn, illus. (p. 1727)
McKy, Katie. It All Began with a Bean: The True Story of the World's Biggest Fart. Hill, Tracy, illus. (p. 893)
Mcky, Katie. It All Began with a Bean. Hill, Tracy, illus. (p. 893)
McKy, Katie. Pumpkin Town! or, Nothing Is Better & Worse Than Pumpkins. Bernasconi, Pablo, illus. (p. 1416)
—Wolf Camp. Leick, Bonnie, illus. (p. 1943)
McLachlan, Brian & Owlkids Books Inc. Staff. Draw Out the Story: Ten Secrets to Creating Your Own Comics. (p. 481)
McLachlan, Hollis. 101 Monologues for Kids! (p. 1999)
McLachlan, J. P., illus. see McLachlan, Joni.
McLachlan, Jenny. Flirty Dancing (p. 605)
McLachlan, Joni. Twilla & the Fuzzy Finger. McLachlan, J. P., illus. (p. 1801)
Mclanson, Matt, illus. see Brown, Liz.
McLaren, Chesley, illus. see Cabot, Meg.
McLaren, Clemence. Aphrodite's Blessing. (p. 91)
—Dance for the Aina. (p. 402)
—Inside the Walls of Troy: A Novel of the Women Who Lived the Trojan War. (p. 878)
—Waiting for Odysseus. (p. 1853)
McLaren, Duncan, illus. see Mackenzie, Carine & Ross, Neil M.
McLaren, Duncan, illus. see MacKenzie, Carine.
McLaren, Duncan, illus. see Mackenzie, Carine.
McLaren, Duncan, illus. see MacKenzie, Carine.
McLaren, Duncan, illus. see Mackenzie, Carine.
McLaren, Duncan, illus. see MacKenzie, Carine.
McLaren, Duncan, illus. see Mackenzie, Carine.
McLaren, Keir. Henry Meets a Three-Legged Dog. Demarie, Teresa, ed. (p. 768)
McLaren, Maria. Seven with One Blow. (p. 1555)
McLaren, Thando. My Day, My Way. Villet, Olivia, illus. (p. 1201)
McLaren-Tishler, Sylvia. Finn the Fireman. (p. 589)
McLauchlan, Shirley. Girls Get Stitching! (p. 680)
McLaughlin, B. G. Reuben Rides the Rails. (p. 1465)
McLaughlin, David. Unfolding History of the Berkshires. McLaughlin, David & Rocheleau, Paul, photos by. (p. 1817)
McLaughlin, Dawn L. Two Tickets to Heaven, Please! (p. 1804)
McLaughlin, Dennis R., jt. auth. see Anthony, Michelle.
McLaughlin, Diane & Tully, Lisa. WhizAnt Who Isn't Coloring & Activity Book. (p. 1914)
McLaughlin, Emma & Kraus, Nicola. Over You. (p. 1314)
—Real Real. (p. 1448)
McLaughlin, Harry. Ribeye the Bullbarian & the Jewel of Baloni. (p. 1469)
McLaughlin, Jerry & Krohn, Katherine E. Dealing with Your Parents' Divorce. (p. 418)
McLaughlin, Julie. Hungry Mr. Gator. McKay, Ann Marie, illus. (p. 828)
—Mr. Gator Hits the Beach. McKay, Ann Marie, illus. (p. 1185)
—Mr. Gator's up the Creek. McKay, Ann Marie, illus. (p. 1185)
McLaughlin, Julie, illus. see Keenan, Edward.
McLaughlin, Julie, illus. see Rohmer, Harriet.
McLaughlin, Julie, illus. see Vermond, Kira.
McLaughlin, Karl Massie. Get Your Muster in a Cluster. (p. 668)
—Get Your Troop in a Group! (p. 668)
—My Adventure in Ancient Egypt. (p. 1195)
—My Adventure with Dragonflies. (p. 1195)
—My Adventure with Flamingos. (p. 1195)
—My Adventure with Ladybugs. (p. 1195)
—My Adventure with Penguins. (p. 1195)
—My Adventure with the Cherokee. (p. 1195)
—My Adventure with the Wright Brothers. (p. 1195)
—My Adventure with Thomas Edison. (p. 1195)
McLaughlin, Lauren. Mitzi Tulane, Preschool Detective, in What's That Smell? Ohi, Debbie Ridpath, illus. (p. 1156)
—Scored. (p. 1530)
McLaughlin, Marc, et al. How Cells Send, Receive, & Process Information (p. 805)
McLaughlin, Maureen & DeVoogd, Glenn. Critical Literacy - Enhancing Students' Comprehension of Text. (p. 383)
McLaughlin, Mendy. Katie the Drama Queen. (p. 945)
McLaughlin, Pat, ed. see Flaherty, Patrick.
McLaughlin, Patrick, ed. see Flaherty, Patrick F. & Harper, Steven.
McLaughlin, Richard. Skunk with the Stinky Attitude. Wilson, Mark, illus. (p. 1586)
McLaughlin, Sako, tr. see Shimizu, Michio.
McLaughlin, Sherry Lynn. Lessons from the Couch. (p. 993)
McLaughlin, Tom. Story Machine. (p. 1657)
McLaughlin, Tom, illus. see Hart, Caryl.
McLaughlin, Tom, illus. see Jobling, Curtis.
McLaughlin, Vicki. Dancer of Her Dreams. (p. 402)
McLaughlin, Zack, illus. see Amstutz, Lisa J.
McLaughlin, Zack, illus. see Slade, Suzanne.
McLaurin, Corey F. Larry, Lisa & the Missing Kite Dixon, Corey, illus. (p. 976)
McLaurin, Eric. Sneaker Kings. (p. 1597)
McLean, Adam. What Is Atomic Theory? (p. 1889)
McLean, Alan C. Ghost of the Glen. (p. 671)
McLean, Alice L. Cooking in America, 1840-1945 (p. 362)
McLean, Allan Campbell. Hill of the Red Fox. (p. 779)
McLean, Andrew, illus. see Milne, Rosemary.
McLean, Beresford. Providence Pond. (p. 1413)
McLean, Claire. Bo & the Ghosts of the White House Pets. (p. 204)
McLean, Gill, illus. see Doyle, Malachy.
McLean, Gill, illus. see Harker, Jillian.
McLean, Hope. Battle of the Brightest. (p. 146)
Mclean, Hope. Battle of the Brightest. (p. 146)
—Catch Us If You Can. (p. 279)
McLean, Hope. Diamonds Are a Thief's Best Friend. (p. 434)
Mclean, Hope. Diamonds Are a Thief's Best Friend. (p. 434)
McLean, Hope. Jewel Society #3: Keep Friends Close, Emeralds Closer. (p. 917)
—Jewel Society #4: Battle of the Brightest. (p. 917)
Mclean, Hope. Keep Friends Close, Emeralds Closer. (p. 946)
McLean, Jacqueline. Victoria Woodhull: First Woman Presidential Candidate. (p. 1840)
—Women of Adventure. (p. 1946)
McLean, Linda. Adventures of Simba the Frisky Feline. Faschi, Silvia, illus. (p. 23)
—Heidelberg Project: A Street of Dreams. (p. 762)
McLean, Linda & Duncan, Caroline. National 4 & 5 Physical Education. (p. 1231)
McLean, Matthew. Bewitching Summer (p. 173)
—Invisible War: Book One of the Disciple Trilogy. (p. 886)
McLean, Michael & McLean, Scott. Fairy Tale Christmas. (p. 564)
McLean, P. J. Bears & the Baby. Jenkins, C. S., illus. (p. 151)
McLean, Polly, tr. see Molla, Jean.
McLean, Sandra. Monkey Business. (p. 1165)
McLean, Scott, jt. auth. see McLean, Michael.
McLean, Wendy. Whizz! (p. 1914)
McLean, Wendy & Book Company Staff. Follow an Elf. Worthington, Leonie, illus. (p. 612)
Mcleay, Rob. Monsters Handbook: With Notes! (p. 1169)
McLechlinno, Adam Edward. Star Current. (p. 1640)
McLees, David, jt. auth. see Tickoo, Sham.
McLeese, Don. Albert Einstein. (p. 34)
—Alexander Hamilton. (p. 36)
—Benjamin Franklin. (p. 164)
—Cell Phones. (p. 286)
—Crispus Attucks. (p. 383)
—Gorillas. (p. 703)
—Gray Wolves. (p. 713)
—Internet & Email. (p. 880)
—Jonas Salk. (p. 925)
—Knights. (p. 964)
—Phillis Wheatley. (p. 1350)
—Pirates. (p. 1363)
—Robert Fulton. (p. 1479)
—Samurai. (p. 1509)
—Sharks. (p. 1562)
—Sitting Bull. (p. 1582)
—Spartans. (p. 1622)
—Stonewall Jackson. (p. 1653)
—Thomas Jefferson. (p. 1739)
—Vikings. (p. 1842)
Mcleese, Don, jt. auth. see McLeese, Don.
McLeese, Don & Mcleese, Don. Frogs. (p. 641)
—Sharks. (p. 1562)
McLeese, Peggy Anne. Magic. (p. 1071)
McLeese, Tex. Carrera de Barril. Palacios, Argentina, tr. (p. 271)
—Enlace en el Rodeo. Palacios, Argentina, tr. (p. 530)
—Lucha con Novillos. Palacios, Argentina, tr. (p. 1062)
—Monta deToro y Toreo. Palacios, Argentina, tr. (p. 1170)
—Monta en Silla y a Pelo. Palacios, Argentina, tr. (p. 1170)
McLeish, Ewan. Challenges to Our Energy Supply. (p. 289)
—Earthquakes in Action. (p. 498)
—Overcrowded World. (p. 1314)
—Pros & Cons of Nuclear Power. (p. 1412)
—Rain Forest Destruction. (p. 1434)
—Sports Industry. (p. 1632)
McLeish, Ewan & Whitecap Books Staff. South America (p. 1616)
McLeish, Kenneth. Shakespeare's Characters: A Players Press Guide. (p. 1559)
McLeish, Mary & Rogers, Sally. Cambridge Checkpoints VCE Health & Human Development 2005. (p. 255)
McLellan, Cortney. Woodoodyots. (p. 1949)
McLellan, Dora. Stevie Star... the Star That Was Afraid to Shine. (p. 1649)
McLellan, Richard A. Land of Truth & Phantasy: Life & Painting at Ring Farm USA. Wyeth, Andrew N. & Kuerner, Karl J., illus. (p. 973)
McLellan, Sean. Red Booted Chicken. (p. 1453)
McLellan, Stephanie Simpson. Leon's Song. Bonder, Dianna, illus. (p. 992)
McLellan, Vernon. Billy Graham: A Tribute from Friends. (p. 187)
McLelland, Michael J. Beating the Bully. Kirk, Andrea Cope, illus. (p. 152)
McLellen, Christoph Elizabeth, jt. auth. see Abbrederis, Christoph.
McLemore, Glenda. Adventures of Max the Poodle: Finding a New Home. (p. 20)
McLendon, Jacquelyn. Phillis Wheatley: A Revolutionary Poet. (p. 1350)
Mclendon, Jacquelyn & Roza, Greg. Katie's Candy. (p. 945)
McLendon, Jacquelyn Y. Phillis Wheatley: A Revolutionary Poet. (p. 1350)
McLennan, Connie. Domitila: A Cinderella Tale from the Mexican Tradition. (p. 465)
McLennan, Connie, illus. see Karwoski, Gail Langer.
McLennan, Connie, illus. see Mitchell, Susan K.
McLennan, Connie, illus. see Pittman, Rickey.
McLennan, Connie, illus. see Rathmell, Donna & Rathmell, Doreen.
McLennan, Connie, illus. see Roemer, Heidi Bee.
McLennan, Connie, illus. see Thong, Roseanne.
McLennan, Connie, illus. see Zelch, Patti R.
McLennan, Terri. Prescription to Destiny. (p. 1396)
McLeod, Bob. New Mutants (p. 1246)
—SuperHero ABC. McLeod, Bob, illus. (p. 1683)
—Superhero ABC. McLeod, Bob, illus. (p. 1683)
McLeod, Chum, illus. see Nanji, Shenaaz.
McLeod, Chum, illus. see Rovetch, L. Bob.
McLeod, David, illus. see Hastings, Leon.
McLeod, Elaine. Lessons from Mother Earth Wood, Colleen, illus. (p. 993)
McLeod, Heather. Kiss Me! (I'M a Prince) Kerrigan, Brooke, illus. (p. 961)
McLeod, Herbert, illus. see McLeod, Rona.
McLeod, Kimberly. Cooking Is for Girls! (p. 362)
—Little Mitchell Tried to Be Good, but Most of the Time He Was Misunderstood. (p. 1032)
McLeod, Kris Aro. Hush-a-Bye Counting: A Bedtime Book. Allyn, Virginia, illus. (p. 830)
McLeod, Kris Aro, illus. see Noble, Trinka Hakes.
McLeod, Laura. George the Squirrel. (p. 663)
McLeod, Len & Martens, Elisabeth. Faery Flag of Dunvegan. (p. 562)
Mcleod, Rebecca, illus. see Walford, Rod.
McLeod, Rona. Big Daddy Chinaberry: Love Given - Love Returned. McLeod, Herbert, illus. (p. 180)
McLeod, Tom & Willett, Mindy. Delta Is My Home Macintosh, Tessa, photos by. (p. 425)
Mcleod-Stecy, Tracey. Stone Guardian. (p. 1652)
Mclerran, Alice, jt. auth. see McLerran, Alice.
McLerran, Alice & Mclerran, Alice. Roxaboxen. Cooney, Barbara, illus. (p. 1492)
McLewn, Sandra. Cuisine D'art. (p. 390)
McLimans, David. Big Turtle. (p. 184)
—Gone Fishing: Ocean Life by the Numbers. McLimans, David, illus. (p. 697)
Mclwain, John, et al. Collins Primary Literacy (p. 341)
McLoon, Linda Snow. Crown Prince. (p. 386)
—Crown Prince Challenged. (p. 386)
McLoone, Margo. Girlwonder: Every Girl's Guide to the Fantastic Feats, Cool Qualities, & Remarkable Abilities of Women & Girls. Hartman, Holly, ed. (p. 681)
McLoughlin Brothers, creator. Snowflake Stories. (p. 1600)
Mcloughlin, Jane. At Yellow Lake. (p. 111)
McLoughlin, Nancy. Color Me Orange. (p. 343)
McLoughlin, Wayne. Warriors - Tales from the Clans. (p. 1859)
McLoughlin, Wayne, illus. see Dunphy, Madeleine.
McLoughlin, Wayne, illus. see Hunter, Erin.
McLuskey, Krista. Colorado. (p. 343)
—Montana. (p. 1170)
—Nevada. (p. 1242)
—Red Cross. (p. 1453)
McMachan, Susan K. Forest of the Leprechauns. Skiadas, Melissa & Skiadas, Stephanie, illus. (p. 618)
McMackin, Mary C. & Witherell, Nancy L. Teaching Writing Through Differentiated Instruction with Leveled Graphic Organizers: 50+ Reproducible, Leveled Organizers That Help You Teach Writing to All Students & Manage Their Different Learning Needs Easily & Effectively. (p. 1710)
McMahan, Gregg. Christmas Honey. (p. 314)
McMahan, Stephanie K. Mystery of the Golden Rings. (p. 1225)
McMahan, Virginia, told to. Mushgnome Legend of the African Spear. (p. 1193)
McMahen, Chris. Box of Shocks (p. 216)
—Klutzhood (p. 964)
—Tabloidology (p. 1694)
Mcmahon, Barbara. Cita con el Jefe. (p. 322)
McMahon, Bea Prior. Queen & I. Green, Jackie Fourcade, illus. (p. 1424)
McMahon, Bea Prior & Green, Jackie Fourcade. Queen & I. (p. 1424)
McMahon, Bob, illus. see Fertig, Dennis.
McMahon, Bob, illus. see Robinson, Elizabeth Keeler & Keeler Robinson, Elizabeth.
McMahon, Bob, illus. see Soffer, Allison Sarnoff.
McMahon, Bob, illus. see Soffer, Allison.
McMahon, Bob, tr. see Fertig, Dennis.
McMahon, Brad, illus. see Auerbach, Annie.
Mcmahon, Brett, jt. auth. see McMahon, Brett.
McMahon, Brett & Mcmahon, Brett. Baby Read Patterns: For Fun & Play. (p. 127)
McMahon, Dave. Alex Ovechkin: NHL Superstar. (p. 36)
—Atlanta Falcons. (p. 112)
—Baseball Skills: How to Play Like a Pro. (p. 141)
—Girls Play to Win Hockey. (p. 680)
—Miami Dolphins. (p. 1133)
—Sidney Crosby: Hockey's Golden Boy. (p. 1573)
McMahon, David H. Peril in the Powder Mills: Gunpowder & Its Men. (p. 1343)
McMahon, James P., illus. see McMahon, Kathleen A.
McMahon, James P. & Ryan, Nancy. Buttonbush. (p. 248)
McMahon, Jean. Rex Finally Finds a Friend. (p. 1467)
McMahon, Jeff. Running to the Sun: Another Collection of Rhymes Without Reason. Warrick, Jessica, illus. (p. 1497)
—Swimming to the Moon: A Collection of Rhymes Without Reason. Warrick, Jessica, illus. (p. 1691)
McMahon, Kara. Dress up Dora! Aikins, Dave, illus. (p. 485)
—Elmo's World: Love! Nelson, Mary Beth, illus. (p. 516)
—Everyone Is Different. Giles, Mike & Style Guide Staff, illus. (p. 544)
—Friday the Scaredy Cat. McClellan, Maddy, illus. (p. 637)
—Playdates Are Not Scary! McClellan, Maddy, illus. (p. 1372)
—Scariest Day Ever... So Far. McClellan, Maddy, illus. (p. 1520)
—Scariest Day Ever ... So Far. McClellan, Maddy, illus. (p. 1520)
McMahon, Kara & Jordan, Apple. My Growing-Up Library. (p. 1210)
McMahon, Kara & Random House Disney Staff. Animal Alphabet: From Ape to Zebra. Moroney, Christopher, illus. (p. 76)
McMahon, Kate. That Touch of Magic. (p. 1726)
McMahon, Kathleen A. Mister Pudge. McMahon, James P., illus. (p. 1155)
—Mister Pudge Meets Baby Beth. (p. 1155)
Mcmahon, Kelly. Mazes, Grade K-1. (p. 1113)
—More Mazes, Grade K-1. (p. 1174)
McMahon, Kelly, illus. see Crane, Kathy Dickerson.
McMahon, Kelly, illus. see Shiotsu, Vicky.
McMahon, Kim. Curious Prince. (p. 394)
—My Dog, Buddy (p. 1202)
McMahon, Maureen, jt. auth. see O'Hara, Susan.
McMahon, Michael. Patrick & Paloma. (p. 1329)
—Space Ace. (p. 1618)
—Why Do Magnets Attract? Level 4 Factbook. (p. 1923)
—Why Do Stars Twinkle? (p. 1924)
—Why Do the Stars Shine? Level 4 Factbook. (p. 1924)
—Why Does Thunder Clap? (p. 1924)
—Zoo & You: A Guidebook (p. 1988)
—Zoo & You: A Guidebook. (p. 1988)
McMahon, Michele. Butterfly Promise. (p. 248)
McMahon, P. J. Case of the Psychic Hamster. Manders, John, illus. (p. 275)
—Case of the Singing Sea Dragons. Manders, John, illus. (p. 275)
—Case of the Smiling Shark. Manders, John, illus. (p. 275)
—Mystery of the Morphing Hockey Stick. Manders, John, illus. (p. 1225)
—Mystery of the Swimming Gorilla. Manders, John, illus. (p. 1226)
McMahon, Patricia. Mystery of the Morphing Hockey Stick. Manders, John, illus. (p. 1225)
McMahon, Patricia & McCarthy, Conor Clarke. Just Add One Chinese Sister: An Adoption Story. Jerome, Karen A., illus. (p. 937)
McMahon, Peter. Space Tourism. Mora, Andy, illus. (p. 1620)
—Ultimate Trains. Mora, Andy, illus. (p. 1810)
McMahon, Susan. Billy Mcgee. (p. 187)
—Sean O'Grady. (p. 1537)
—Wee Mary from Derry. (p. 1871)
—Wouldn't It Be Funny. (p. 1962)
McMahon, V. Karen. I Saw a White Horse Today. Bailey, Loretta Dovell, illus. (p. 845)
McMahon, William. Pine Barrens Legends & Lore. (p. 1359)
McMahon, Wm. Franklin, photos by see Stanek, Muriel.
McMahon-Dumas, Carmen E. Grammie Award (p. 706)
McMakin, Jordan. Prince Ezrick & the Morpheus Curse (p. 1401)
McManama, Kerry, jt. auth. see Mehra, Heather.
McManaman, Yelena & Droujkova, Maria. Moebius Noodles: Adventurous Math for the Playground Crowd. (p. 1160)
McManis, Margaret. Olé! Cinco de Mayo! Harrington, David, illus. (p. 1285)

—Wild Texas Stampede! Dupree, Bruce, illus. (p. 1930)
McMann, Julie, tr. see Bekkering, Annalise.
McMann, Julie, tr. see Diemer, Lauren.
McMann, Julie, tr. see Howse, Jennifer.
McMann, Julie, tr. see McIntyre, Sandra.
McMann, Julie, tr. see Rose, Simon.
McMann, Laney. Tied. (p. 1747)
McMann, Lisa. Bang. (p. 136)
—Crash. (p. 376)
—Cryer's Cross. (p. 387)
—Dead to You. (p. 417)
—Don't Close Your Eyes: Wake; Fade; Gone. (p. 467)
—Fade. (p. 561)
—Fade. (p. 562)
—Gasp. (p. 657)
—Gone. (p. 697)
—Island of Fire. (p. 892)
—Island of Graves. (p. 892)
—Island of Legends. (p. 892)
—Island of Silence. (p. 892)
—Trap Door. (p. 1779)
—Unwanteds. (p. 1823)
—Unwanteds. (p. 1823)
—Unwanteds Set: The Unwanteds; Island of Silence; Island of Fire. (p. 1823)
—Wake. (p. 1853)
—Wake Trilogy: Wake; Fade; Gone. (p. 1853)
McManus, Donald. Emmett Kelly: The Greatest Clown on Earth. (p. 520)
McManus, James. Physical: An American Checkup. (p. 1353)
McManus, John C. Alamo in the Ardennes: The Untold Story of the American Soldiers Who Made the Defense of Bastogne Possible. (p. 33)
McManus, Lori. Algeria (p. 38)
—Cell Systems (p. 286)
—Gorillas (p. 703)
—Key People of the Civil War (p. 950)
—Meet Our New Student from Japan. (p. 1122)
—Mexican Culture (p. 1131)
—Money Through History (p. 1164)
—Producing Fruits (p. 1409)
McManus, Madelyn. Britney Makes a Budget. (p. 230)
McManus, Patrick F. Bear in the Attic. (p. 151)
McManus, Sean, et al. Raspberry Pi for Kids for Dummies. (p. 1439)
McManus, Shawn, illus. see Bright, J. E.
McManus, Shawn, illus. see Bright, J. E. & Loughridge, Lee.
McManus, Shawn, illus. see Buckhingham, Mark & Willingham, Bill.
McManus, Shawn, illus. see Fein, Eric, et al.
McManus, Shawn, illus. see Kupperberg, Paul & Loughridge, Lee.
McManus, Shawn, illus. see Manning, Matthew K., et al.
McManus, Shawn, illus. see Sonneborn, Scott & Loughridge, Lee.
McManus, Shawn, illus. see Sonneborn, Scott.
McManus, Shawn, illus. see Sutton, Laurie S.
McManus, Shawn, illus. see Sutton, Laurie S. & Loughridge, Lee.
McManus, Valerie Rainon. Look in the Mirror: Freeing Yourself from the Body Image Blues. (p. 1049)
McMaster, Alex. Giant George & Little Leo. (p. 673)
McMasters, Anne. Anne's Stories for Children of All Ages. (p. 86)
McMasters, Gretchen. Aesock's Travels & Los Viajes de Aesock: Lights, Camera, Edison! & Luz, Cámara, Edison. (p. 25)
McMath, David. Happiest Christmas Tree. (p. 744)
McMaugh, Kimberly, illus. see Baird, Noah.
McMeans, Bonnie. Vampires. (p. 1832)
McMenemy, Sarah. London: A 3D Keepsake Cityscape. (p. 1046)
—New York - A 3D Keepsake Cityscape. (p. 1247)
—Paris: A 3D Keepsake Cityscape. McMenemy, Sarah, illus. (p. 1324)
—Washington D. C. A 3D Keepsake Cityscape. McMenemy, Sarah, illus. (p. 1860)
McMenemy, Sarah, illus. see Candlewick Press, Candlewick.
McMenemy, Sarah, illus. see Candlewick Press.
McMenemy, Sarah, illus. see Davis, Jill.
McMenemy, Sarah, illus. see Kimmelman, Leslie.
McMenemy, Sarah, illus. see Stauffacher, Sue.
McMickle, Marvin Andrew. Profiles in Black: Phat Facts for Teens. Elster, Jean Alicia, ed. (p. 1409)
McMilin, Jack. Dodger the Dragon. (p. 460)
—Dodger the Dragon Nevarez, Lisa, illus. (p. 460)
McMilin, Jack D. Water Dog. Nevarez, Lisa D., illus. (p. 1862)
McMillan, Angelo. Adventures of W D: The Dreamers Series Vol. 1. (p. 24)
McMillan, Beverly & Musick, John A. Oceans. (p. 1277)
—Sharks. (p. 1562)
McMillan, Bruce. Mouse Views. (p. 1182)
—Problem with Chickens. Gunnella & Gunnella, illus. (p. 1408)
McMillan, Dawn. Awake in the Dark! Fino, Roberto, illus. (p. 120)
—Catch of the Day! Vignolo, Enrique, illus. (p. 279)
—Estimating with the Newspaper (p. 538)
—Learning about Percentages at the Mall (p. 984)
—Learning Algebra with Pizza (p. 985)
—Understanding Animal Graphs (p. 1815)
—Woolly Wally. Kinnaird, Ross, illus. (p. 1950)
McMillan, Dawn & Kinnaird, Ross. I Need a New Butt! (p. 844)
McMillan, Ernest. Psalms of Passion. (p. 1413)
McMillan, Frank. Cezanne Is Missing. (p. 288)
McMillan, Gregory K. & Cameron, Robert A. Models Unleashed: Virtual Plant & Model Predictive Control Applications. (p. 1158)
McMillan, J. Ann. Billy Bob Bear's Six Wishes. (p. 187)
McMillan, Jenna. East Tennessee from a to Z. Patients from East Tennessee Children's Hospital, illus. (p. 498)
McMillan, Kathleen. Very Blueberry Christmas - a Show-And-Tell Book. (p. 1837)
McMillan, Melody DeFields. Addison Addley & the Things That Aren't There (p. 12)
—Addison Addley & the Trick of the Eye (p. 12)
McMillan, Stephanie, illus. see Jensen, Derrick.
McMillan, Sue, jt. auth. see Green, Dan.
McMillan, Sue & Wainwright, Jen. Justin Bieber: 100% Unauthorized. (p. 940)
McMillan, Tracy. Model Behaviour. (p. 1157)
—Where Lily Goes... (p. 1909)
McMillan, Charlotte Palmer. Little Sea Rock & His Friend Arena. (p. 1036)
Mcmillen, Michelle. Brothers in the Storm. (p. 231)
McMiller, Theresa R. Bessie Goes All over the World. (p. 168)
McMillian, Gordon. Scout. (p. 1532)
McMillion, Gloria. Whirlwinds Whirl Around. (p. 1912)
McMillion, Lindsey, illus. see Cooper, Heather, et al.
McMonigle, Orin. Complete Guide to Rearing the Elephant Stag Beetle: And Other Stags. (p. 353)
McMonigle, Orin A. Giant Millipedes: The Enthusiast's Handbook. (p. 673)
McMorrine, David. Tim, Sherri & Formula One. (p. 1750)
McMorris, Kelley, illus. see Johnson, Allen, Jr.
McMorris, Kelley, illus. see Messner, Kate.
McMorrow-Hernandez, Joshua. Valley of Curiosity. (p. 1831)
McMullan, Akilah. Best Me I Can Be. (p. 170)
McMullan, James. Leaving China: An Artist Paints His World War II Childhood. (p. 986)
McMullan, Jim, illus. see Andrews, Julie & Hamilton, Emma Walton.
McMullan, Jim, illus. see McMullan, Kate.
McMullan, Jim, illus. see Wilson, Karma.
McMullan, Jim, jt. auth. see McMullan, Kate.
McMullan, Kate. 97 Ways to Train a Dragon. Basso, Bill, illus. (p. 1998)
—Amazing Adventures of Supercat! Making the World Safe for Blankies. LeMaitre, Pascal, illus. (p. 52)
—Beware! It's Friday the 13th. Basso, Bill, illus. (p. 173)
—Bulldog's Big Day. Lemaitre, Pascal, illus. (p. 240)
—Class Trip to the Cave of Doom Basso, Bill, illus. (p. 327)
—Class Trip to the Cave of Doom. Basso, Bill, illus. (p. 327)
—Countdown to the Year 1000. Basso, Bill, illus. (p. 370)
—Danger! Wizard at Work Basso, Bill, illus. (p. 404)
—Dinosaur Hunters. Jones, John R., illus. (p. 442)
—Double Dragon Trouble. Basso, Bill, illus. (p. 472)
—Dragon Slayers' Academy Set 2. Basso, Bill, illus. (p. 478)
—Fine Start: Meg's Prairie Diary. Bk. 3 (p. 589)
—Five Days till Summer. Alley, R. W., illus. (p. 600)
—Fluffy's Happy Halloween. Smith, Mavis, illus. (p. 608)
—For This Land: Meg's Prairie Diary. Bk. 2 (p. 616)
—Four Eyes. Alley, R. W., illus. (p. 624)
—Get Lost, Odysseus! (p. 667)
—Get to Work, Hercules! (p. 668)
—Get to Work, Hercules! Zilber, Denis, illus. (p. 668)
—Ghost of Sir Herbert Dungeonstone Basso, Bill, illus. (p. 671)
—Ghost of Sir Herbert Dungeonstone. Basso, Bill, illus. (p. 671)
—Go for the Gold, Atalanta! (p. 686)
—Go for the Gold, Atalanta! Zilber, Denis, illus. (p. 686)
—Hail! Hail! Camp Dragononka! Basso, Bill, illus. (p. 735)
—Have a Hot Time, Hades! Zilber, Denis, illus. (p. 754)
—Help! It's Parent's Day at DSA. Basso, Bill, illus. (p. 765)
—Hit the Road, Helen! (p. 786)
—I Stink! McMullan, Jim, illus. (p. 846)
—I'm Bad! McMullan, Jim, illus. (p. 858)
—I'm Big! McMullan, Jim, illus. (p. 858)
—I'm Brave! McMullan, Jim, illus. (p. 858)
—I'm Cool! McMullan, Jim, illus. (p. 858)
—I'm Dirty! (p. 858)
—I'm Dirty! McMullan, Jim, illus. (p. 858)
—I'm Dirty! Board Book. McMullan, Jim, illus. (p. 858)
—I'm Fast! McMullan, Jim, illus. (p. 858)
—I'm Mighty! McMullan, Jim, illus. (p. 859)
—Keep a Lid on It, Pandora! (p. 946)
—Keep a Lid on It, Pandora! Zilber, Denis, illus. (p. 946)
—Knight for a Day. Basso, Bill, illus. (p. 964)
—Little Giant-Big Trouble Basso, Bill, illus. (p. 1028)
—Myth-O-Mania. (p. 1227)
—Never Trust a Troll! Basso, Bill, illus. (p. 1243)
—New Kid at School. (p. 1245)
—New Kid at School. Basso, Bill, illus. (p. 1245)
—New Kid at School. Basso, Bill & Gilpin, Stephen, illus. (p. 1245)
—Nice Shot, Cupid! Zilber, Denis, illus. (p. 1250)
—One Funny Day. (p. 1295)
—One Funny Day. Alley, R. W., illus. (p. 1295)
—Pearl & Wagner: Three Secrets. (p. 1333)
—Pearl & Wagner: Five Days till Summer. (p. 1333)
—Pearl & Wagner: Two Good Friends. Alley, R. W., illus. (p. 1333)
—Phone Home, Persephone! Zilber, Denis, illus. (p. 1351)
—Pig Latin - Not Just for Pigs! Basso, Bill, illus. (p. 1357)
—Pig Latin—Not Just for Pigs! Basso, Bill, illus. (p. 1357)
—Revenge of the Dragon Lady Basso, Bill, illus. (p. 1466)
—Revenge of the Dragon Lady. (p. 1466)
—Revenge of the Dragon Lady. Basso, Bill, illus. (p. 1466)
—Say Cheese, Medusa! Zilber, Denis, illus. (p. 1518)
—School! Adventures at the Harvey N. Trouble Elementary School. (p. 1522)
—School! Adventures at the Harvey N. Trouble Elementary School. Booth, George, illus. (p. 1522)
—School's Out... Forever! Basso, Bill & Gilpin, Stephen, illus. (p. 1524)
—Sir Lancelot, Where Are You? Basso, Bill, illus. (p. 1580)
—Stop That Bull, Theseus! Zilber, Denis, illus. (p. 1653)
—Stop That Bull, Theseus! LaFleur, David, illus. (p. 1653)
—Three Secrets. Alley, R. W., illus. (p. 1743)
—Wedding for Wiglaf? Basso, Bill, illus. (p. 1871)
—Wheel of Misfortune. Basso, Bill, illus. (p. 1900)
—World's Oldest Living Dragon Basso, Bill, illus. (p. 1961)
McMullan, Kate, jt. auth. see Maddox, Jake.
McMullan, Kate, see Hall, Katy, pseud.
McMullan, Kate & McMullan, Jim. I'm Dirty! (p. 858)
McMullan, Margaret. How I Found the Strong: A Civil War Story. (p. 810)
—In My Mother's House. (p. 864)
—When I Crossed No-Bob. (p. 1902)
McMullan, Tigre. Collectible Girlie Glasses (p. 339)
McMullen, Anne, illus. see Bayrock, Fiona.
McMullen, Anne, illus. see Graf, Mike & Snedden, Robert.
McMullen, Anne, illus. see Jackson, Kay.
McMullen, Anne, illus. see Niz, Xavier & Niz, Xavier W.
McMullen, Anne, illus. see Webster, Christine.
McMullen, Brad, illus. see Bruno, Susan.
McMullen, Brian & Jägel, Jason. Hang Glider & Mud Mask. (p. 742)
McMullen, Chris. Practice Adding, Subtracting, Multiplying, & Dividing Mixed Fractions Workbook: Improve Your Math Fluency Series (Volume 14) (p. 1392)
McMullen, David. Somewhere on A Railroad Platform. (p. 1610)
McMullen, Jill. Toby & Friends: Therapy Dogs. (p. 1760)
McMullen, Judy. Stephanie & the Excellent E's. (p. 1648)
McMullen, Judy Benson, ed. Ghost in the Gazebo. (p. 670)
McMullen, M. J. Leo & Gracie: Cat Detectives in the Ghost of Mr. Doodles (case 4) (p. 992)
—Leo & Gracie: Cat Detectives in Where's Ricky? (case 3) A Missing Cat Case. (p. 992)
McMullen, Nigel. Let's Dance, Grandma! McMullen, Nigel, illus. (p. 995)
McMullen, Nigel, illus. see Morton, Christine.
McMullen, Nigel, illus. see Tyrrell, Melissa.
McMullen, Sean. Before the Storm. (p. 158)
McMullen, T. C., illus. see Ruble, Kam.
McMullin, Jordan, ed. Marijuana. (p. 1094)
McMullin, Marcus, illus. see Kimball, Allan.
McMullin, Perry. Boy Who Could Fly. (p. 219)
—Fireflies. (p. 592)
McMurchie, Susan. Understanding My Learning Differences. (p. 1816)
McMurchy-Barber, Gina. Bone Deep. (p. 208)
—Reading the Bones. (p. 1446)
—When Children Play: The Story of Right to Play (p. 1901)
McMurchy-Barber, Gina & Zweig, Eric. Free as a Bird. (p. 634)
McMurry Edwards, Linda. George Washington Carver: The Life of the Great American Agriculturist. (p. 664)
McMurry, Marena, illus. see Booth, Chrissie.
McMurry, Rebecca. Tell Your Secret. (p. 1717)
—Very Special Cat. (p. 1838)
McMurtrey, Martin. Loose to the Wilds. (p. 1052)
McMurtrie, Kevin. Day I Was Invisible. (p. 413)
—Have You Seen My Duck? (p. 754)
—Prince That Always Wore His Top Hat. (p. 1401)
—Succotash Pudding. (p. 1672)
—Very Thoughtful Turtle. (p. 1839)
McMurtry, Ken. Zombie Penpal. (p. 1988)
McMurtry, Larry. By Sorrow's River. (p. 249)
McMurtry, Robby, tr. Song of Moon Pony. (p. 1611)
McNab, Chris. Endangered Reptiles. (p. 527)
—Escape & Evasion. (p. 534)
—Everyday Dress. (p. 543)
—Extreme Sports. (p. 557)
—Frogs, Toads, & Salamanders. (p. 641)
—Hostage Rescue with the SAS. (p. 801)
—How to Pass Elite Forces Selection. (p. 821)
—Learning Mental Endurance for Survival. Carney, John, ed. (p. 985)
—Learning Mental Endurance with the U. S. Marines. (p. 985)
—Martial Arts for People with Disabilities. (p. 1097)
—Mythical Monsters: The Scariest Creatures from Legends, Books, & Movies. (p. 1227)
—Protecting the Nation with the U. S. Air Force. (p. 1412)
—Protecting the Nation with the U. S. Army. (p. 1412)
—Survival at Sea. Carney, John, ed. (p. 1686)
—Survival in the Wilderness. (p. 1686)
—Survival in the Wilderness. Carney, John, ed. (p. 1686)
—Survive in the Arctic with the Royal Marine Commandos. (p. 1687)
—Survive in the Desert with the French Foreign Legion. (p. 1687)
—Survive in the Mountains with the U. S. Rangers & Army Mountain Division. (p. 1687)
—Survive in the Wilderness with the Canadian & Australian Special Forces. (p. 1687)
—Surviving Captivity. Carney, John, ed. (p. 1687)
—Surviving Captivity with the U. S. A. F. (p. 1687)
—Surviving Hostage Rescue Missions. Carney, John, ed. (p. 1687)
—Surviving the World's Extreme Regions: Desert, Arctic, Mountains, & Jungle. Carney, John, ed. (p. 1687)
—Training to Fight with the Parachute Regiment. (p. 1777)
—World's Best Soldiers. (p. 1960)
—World's Worst Historical Disasters. (p. 1961)
—Wrestling. (p. 1962)
McNab, Chris, jt. auth. see McCall, Gerrie.
McNab, Chris, jt. auth. see Regan, Lisa.
McNab, Chris, jt. auth. see Sutherland, Jonathan.
McNab, Chris & Sutherland, Jonathan. Dangerous Insects & Spiders. (p. 404)
—Giant Spiders & Insects. (p. 674)
McNab, Laura. Glitter Art. (p. 683)
McNab, Nan, jt. ed. see Carmody, Isobelle.
McNab, Rosi. French Club (p. 635)
McNabb, Linda. Dragons' Bane. (p. 479)
—Seventh Son. (p. 1555)
—Shadow Hunters. (p. 1557)
—Stone Keeper's Daughter. (p. 1652)
—Valley of Silver Test. (p. 1831)
McNabb, Vincent. Children's Hour of Heaven on Earth. Symington, Lindsay, illus. (p. 303)
McNair, Barbara. Tea Parties with Grandm. Hogan, Eric, illus. (p. 1708)
McNair, Don J. Who Wants to Play? (p. 1918)
McNair, Randall. To the North. Morris, Katherine, ed. (p. 1759)
McNally, Amber. Henry & the World of the Missing Socks. (p. 767)
McNally, Bruce, illus. see Clarke, Jacqueline A.
McNally, Jeanne. Girl Who Wore Many Hats. (p. 679)
McNally, Timothy J. Kringle's Ring. (p. 967)
McNally, Tom, illus. see Waldman, Stuart.
McNamara, Amy. Lovely, Dark & Deep. (p. 1061)
McNamara, Andrew. Being a Good Citizen. (p. 160)
McNamara, Brian. Bottled up Secret. (p. 215)
McNamara, Catherine & Provencal, Francis. Nii Kwei's Day: From Dawn to Dusk in a Ghanaian City. (p. 1255)
McNamara, Connie. My First Florida State Words. (p. 1206)
—My First IU Words Go Hoosiers. (p. 1207)
—My First Kansas Words Go Jayhawks. (p. 1207)
—My First Michigan State Words Go State. (p. 1207)
—My First Michigan Words. (p. 1207)
—My First Nebraska Words. (p. 1207)
—My First Notre Dame Words GO IRISH. (p. 1207)
—My First Ohio State Words Go Buckeyes. (p. 1207)
—My First Pittsburgh Words Go Pitt. (p. 1207)
—My First Purdue University Words. (p. 1207)
—My First U of I Words Go Illini. (p. 1208)
—My First University of Florida Words. (p. 1208)
—My First University of Florida Words Go Gators. (p. 1208)
—My First University of Pittsburgh Words. (p. 1208)
—My First University of Tennessee Words. (p. 1208)
—My First Wisconsin Words Go Badgers. (p. 1208)
McNamara, Joan. Borya & the Burps: An Eastern European Adoption Story. Majewski, Dawn, illus. (p. 214)
McNamara, Josephine. Mork the Dancing Moose. (p. 1175)
McNamara, Ken. It's True! We Came from Slime. Plant, Andrew, illus. (p. 899)
McNamara, Lisa, illus. see Taylor, Eileen.
McNamara, Margaret. Apple ABC. Parker, Jake, illus. (p. 92)
—Apple Orchard Riddle. Karas, G. Brian, illus. (p. 92)
—Apples A to Z. Parker, Jake, illus. (p. 92)
—Battle of Gettysburg. (p. 146)
—Brazil. (p. 224)
Mcnamara, Margaret. Butterfly Garden. (p. 247)
McNamara, Margaret. Butterfly Garden. Gordon, Mike, illus. (p. 247)
—Canada. (p. 260)
Mcnamara, Margaret. Clara & the Magical Charms. (p. 326)
McNamara, Margaret. Clara & the Magical Charms. Denos, Julia, illus. (p. 326)
—Class Mom. Gordon, Mike, illus. (p. 327)
—Class Picture Day. Gordon, Mike, illus. (p. 327)
—Counting Race. Gordon, Mike, illus. (p. 371)
—Dad Goes to School. Gordon, Mike, illus. (p. 398)
—Discover Brazil. (p. 447)
—Discover Canada. (p. 447)
—Discover Mexico. (p. 447)
—Discover the Battle of Gettysburg. (p. 448)
—Discover the Iroquois. (p. 448)
—Discover the Lakota. (p. 448)
—Discover the Navajo. (p. 448)
—Discover the North & the South. (p. 448)
—Discover the Underground Railroad. (p. 448)
—Earth Day. Gordon, Mike, illus. (p. 495)
—Election Day. Gordon, Mike, illus. (p. 508)
—Fairy Bell Sisters: Sylva & the Lost Treasure. Vol. 5 Denos, Julia, illus. (p. 563)
—Fairy Bell Sisters: Golden at the Fancy-Dress Party. No. 3 Denos, Julia, illus. (p. 563)
—Fairy Bell Sisters #3: Golden at the Fancy-Dress Party. Denos, Julia, illus. (p. 563)
—Fairy Bell Sisters - Christmas Fairy Magic. (p. 563)
—Fall Leaf Project. Gordon, Mike, illus. (p. 566)
—First Day of School. Gordon, Mike, illus. (p. 594)
—First-Grade Bunny. Gordon, Mike, illus. (p. 595)
—Garden Project. Gordon, Mike, illus. (p. 656)
—George Washington's Birthday: A Mostly True Tale. Blitt, Barry, illus. (p. 665)
Mcnamara, Margaret. Golden at the Fancy - Dress Party. (p. 694)
McNamara, Margaret. Groundhog Day. Gordon, Mike, illus. (p. 725)
—Halloween Fun. Gordon, Mike, illus. (p. 737)
—Happy Graduation! Gordon, Mike, illus. (p. 745)
—Happy Thanksgiving. Gordon, Mike, illus. (p. 746)
—How Many Seeds in a Pumpkin? Karas, G. Brian, illus. (p. 811)
—Martin Luther King Jr. Day. Gordon, Mike, illus. (p. 1098)
—Mexico. (p. 1131)
—Native Americans of the Eastern Woodlands: The Iroquois. (p. 1234)
—Native Americans of the Plains: The Lakota. (p. 1234)
—Native Americans of the Southwest: The Navajo. (p. 1234)
—North & the South. (p. 1264)
—One Hundred Days. (p. 1295)
—One Hundred Days (Plus One) Gordon, Mike, illus. (p. 1295)
—Picking Apples. Gordon, Mike, illus. (p. 1354)
—Playground Problem. Gordon, Mike, illus. (p. 1372)
—Poem in Your Pocket. Karas, G. Brian, illus. (p. 1375)
—Presidents' Day. Gordon, Mike, illus. (p. 1397)
—Pumpkin Patch. Gordon, Mike, illus. (p. 1416)
Mcnamara, Margaret. Rosy & the Secret Friend. (p. 1490)
McNamara, Margaret. Rosy & the Secret Friend. Denos, Julia, illus. (p. 1490)
—Secret Santa. Gordon, Mike, illus. (p. 1543)
—Snow Day. Gordon, Mike, illus. (p. 1598)
Mcnamara, Margaret. Summer Treasure. (p. 1675)
McNamara, Margaret. Summer Treasure. Gordon, Mike, illus. (p. 1675)
Mcnamara, Margaret. Sylva & the Fairy Ball. (p. 1692)
McNamara, Margaret. Sylva & the Fairy Ball. Denos, Julia, illus. (p. 1692)
Mcnamara, Margaret. Sylva & the Lost Treasure. (p. 1692)
McNamara, Margaret. Sylva & the Lost Treasure. Denos, Julia, illus. (p. 1692)
—Three Little Aliens & the Big Bad Robot. Fearing, Mark, illus. (p. 1742)
—Too Many Valentines. Gordon, Mike, illus. (p. 1767)
—Tooth Story. Gordon, Mike, illus. (p. 1768)
—Underground Railroad. (p. 1814)
—Wash Your Hands! Gordon, Mike, illus. (p. 1859)
McNamara, Margaret & Gordon, Mike. Luck of the Irish. (p. 1062)
—Pumpkin Patch. (p. 1416)
McNamara, Margaret & Thompson, Kay. Eloise Breaks Some Eggs. Lyon, Tammie, illus. (p. 516)

—Eloise Has a Lesson. Mitter, Kathryn, illus. (p. 516)
McNamara, Pat & Turner, Gary. Last Realm Dragonscarpe. Dutkiewicz, Michal, illus. (p. 978)
McNamee, Barbara Oakley. Kelsey & Seattle. (p. 948)
McNamee, Eoin. Frost Child. (p. 644)
—Ghost Roads. (p. 671)
—Ring of Five. (p. 1473)
—Unknown Spy. (p. 1821)
McNamee, Graham. Acceleration. (p. 8)
—Acelercion. (p. 8)
—Beyond: A Ghost Story. (p. 173)
—Bonechiller. (p. 209)
McNamee, Gregory. North Wind & the Sun: And Other Fables of Aesop. (p. 1265)
McNamee, Kevin. If I Could Be Anything. Movshina, Marina, illus. (p. 852)
—Just for Today. Movshina, Marina, illus. (p. 938)
—My Brother the Frog. Morris, Alexander, illus. (p. 1199)
—Soggy Town of Hilltop. Ruble, Eugene, illus. (p. 1606)
—What Is That Thing? Snider, K. C., illus. (p. 1890)
McNaney, Jeanne. Miracle in Sumatra: The Story of Gutsy Gus. Cochard, David, illus. (p. 1148)
McNaney, Lowell & Lambert, Andy. Fuel for the Journey. (p. 646)
McNatt, Martha. Grandmother's Face in the Mirror. (p. 709)
McNaught, Harry, illus. see Kean, Edward.
McNaught, Maria. Grandma's Ashanti Cloth. (p. 708)
McNaughton, Colin. Cushie Butterfield. (p. 395)
—Dracula's Tomb. McNaughton, Colin, illus. (p. 476)
—Gô! Williams, Dylan, tr. from ENG. (p. 693)
—Lemmy Was a Diver. (p. 991)
—M. W. S. G. Williams, Dylan, tr. (p. 1067)
McNaughton, Colin, et al. Wps! (p. 1962)
McNaughton, Janet. Brave Jack & the Unicorn. Tooke, Susan, illus. (p. 223)
McNaughton, Karen. What Makes the Thunder? (p. 1892)
Mcnaughton, Phoebe, jt. auth. see Lundy, Miranda.
McNaughton, Tina, illus. see Chiew, Suzanne.
McNaughton, Jonathan, illus. see Hartnett, Sonya.
McNeal, Carl. What Would I Do If I Had a Zoo? Balogh, Jared, illus. (p. 1895)
McNeal, Drema & Teets, Ashley. Jake Learns All 8 Parts of Speech. (p. 906)
McNeal, Laura. Dark Water. (p. 408)
McNeal, Laura & McNeal, Tom. Crooked. (p. 384)
McNeal, Mallori. down Chic. (p. 474)
McNeal, Tom. Far Far Away. (p. 572)
McNeal, Tom, jt. auth. see McNeal, Laura.
McNease, Mitzy. Chester's Presents. Cox, Kim, illus. (p. 298)
McNee, I. Knights - Internet Referenced. (p. 964)
McNee, Ian. Treasure Island. (p. 1781)
McNee, Ian, illus. see Brook, Henry.
McNee, Ian, illus. see Claybourne, Anna & Daynes, Katie.
McNee, Ian, illus. see Claybourne, Anna.
McNee, Ian, illus. see Harvey, Gill.
McNee, Ian, illus. see Sims, Lesley & Stowell, Louie.
McNee, Ian, illus. see Sims, Lesley.
McNee, Ian, illus. see Taplin, Sam.
McNee, Ian, illus. see Wheatley, Abigail.
McNeece, Alexander. Sam Iver: Imminent Threat. (p. 1506)
McNeely, Marian Hurd. Jumping-off Place. Siegel, William, illus. (p. 934)
McNeely, Tom. Isis & the Seven Scorpions (p. 891)
McNeely, William, illus. see Ross, Margaret Clark.
McNeese, Tim. Alexander Hamilton: Framer of the Constitution. (p. 36)
—Attack on Pearl Harbor: America Enters World War II. (p. 114)
—Battle of the Bulge. (p. 146)
—Brown V. Board of Education: Integrating America's Schools. (p. 232)
—Christopher Columbus & the Discovery of the Americas, Explorers of New Lands. Goetzmann, William H., ed. (p. 317)
—Civil Rights Movement: Striving for Justice. (p. 325)
—Civil War: A Nation Divided Set, 8-Volumes. (p. 325)
—Civil War Battles. (p. 325)
—Civil War Era, 1851-1865. (p. 325)
—Civil War Leaders. (p. 325)
—Cold War & Postwar America 1946-1963. (p. 339)
—Colonial America, 1543-1763. (p. 341)
—Colorado River. (p. 343)
—Disability Rights Movement. (p. 446)
—Donner Party: A Doomed Journey. (p. 466)
—Dred Scott V. Sandford: The Pursuit of Freedom. (p. 484)
—Early National America ,1790-1850. (p. 494)
—Fascinating History of American Indians: The Age Before Columbus. (p. 575)
—Francisco Goya. (p. 628)
—George W. Bush: First President of the New Century. (p. 664)
—Gilded Age & Progressivism, 1891-1913. (p. 676)
—Great Depression 1929-1938. (p. 715)
—Industrial Revolution. (p. 872)
—Jamestown. (p. 907)
—John Smith. (p. 922)
—Labor Movement: Unionizing America. (p. 969)
—Louisiana Purchase. (p. 1058)
—Marco Polo & the Realm of Kublai Khan. Goetzmann, William H., ed. (p. 1092)
—Michelangelo: Painter, Sculptor & Architect. (p. 1135)
—Mississippi River. (p. 1154)
—Missouri River. (p. 1154)
—Modern America 1964-present. (p. 1158)
—New Amsterdam. (p. 1243)
—New South & the Old West, 1866-1890. (p. 1247)
—New World: Prehistory To 1542. (p. 1247)
—Ohio River. (p. 1281)
—Oregon Trail. (p. 1303)
—Panama Canal: Connecting the Atlantic with the Pacific. (p. 1320)
—Perry Expedition & the Opening of Japan. (p. 1344)
—Plessy V. Ferguson: Separate but Equal. (p. 1374)
—Plymouth. (p. 1374)
—Political Revolutions of the 18th, 19th, & 20 Centuries. (p. 1380)
—Pony Express: Bringing Mail to the American West. (p. 1382)
—Progressive Movement: Advocating Social Change. (p. 1410)
—Reconstruction. (p. 1452)
—Reform Movements in American History Set, 8-Volumes. (p. 1456)
—Regents of the University of California V. Bakke: American Education & Affirmative Action. (p. 1457)
—Remember the Maine! The Spanish-American War Begins. (p. 1459)
—Revolutionary America, 1783-1799. (p. 1466)
—Rio Grande. (p. 1473)
—Rise & Fall of American Slavery: Freedom Denied, Freedom Gained. (p. 1474)
—Robert E. Lee. (p. 1479)
—Salvador Dali. (p. 1506)
—Santa Fe. (p. 1511)
—St. Lawrence River. (p. 1638)
—Tito Puente. (p. 1758)
—Transcontinental Railroad & Westward Expansion: Chasing the American Frontier. (p. 1778)
—Volga River. McNeese, Tim, ed. (p. 1849)
—Williamsburg. (p. 1934)
—World War I & the Roaring Twenties, 1914-1928. (p. 1959)
—World War II 1939-1945. (p. 1959)
—Yukon River. McNeese, Tim, ed. (p. 1983)
McNeese, Tim, ed. see Mountjoy, Shane.
McNeese, Tim, jt. auth. see Mountjoy, Shane.
McNeese, Tim, ed. Rivers in American Life & Times. (p. 1476)
—Rivers in World History. (p. 1476)
McNeice, Connie-Lee. Big Game. (p. 181)
McNeil, Daniel J. Tri-Star Conspiracy. (p. 1785)
McNeil, Gretchen. Get Dirty. (p. 667)
—Possess. (p. 1387)
—Ten. (p. 1718)
Mcneil, I. M. J. F. MAM & J. JASON, His Dog: All the Months of the Year Made Easy! (p. 901)
McNeil, Natalie. Wylli Nilly's Amazing Adventures. (p. 1966)
McNeil, Niki, et al. Africa. (p. 26)
—Ancient China. (p. 68)
—Antarctica. (p. 88)
—Asia. (p. 106)
—Australia: Project Pack Continent Study Series, Multi-Grade Level. (p. 116)
—Botany. (p. 215)
—Connecticut. (p. 357)
—Desert Habitats. (p. 429)
—Egyptian Mummies. (p. 506)
—Forest Habitats. (p. 618)
—Foundations for Chemistry. (p. 624)
—Grassland Habitats. (p. 712)
—HOCPP 1033 Valentine's Day. (p. 787)
—HOCPP 1053 Narnia. (p. 787)
—HOCPP 1054 Middle Ages. (p. 787)
—HOCPP 1055 Martin Luther King Jr. (p. 787)
—HOCPP 1058 Benjamin Franklin. (p. 787)
—HOCPP 1059 Isaac Newton. (p. 787)
—HOCPP 1060 the French Revolution. (p. 787)
—HOCPP 1061 American Revolution. (p. 787)
—HOCPP 1062 Saint Patrick's Day. (p. 787)
—HOCPP 1066 Human Body. (p. 787)
—HOCPP 1067 the Five Senses. (p. 787)
—HOCPP 1069 Curious George Rides a Bike. (p. 787)
—HOCPP 1070 Mike & Mary Anne the Steam Shovel. (p. 787)
—HOCPP 1072 Katy's Big Snow Day. (p. 787)
—HOCPP 1073 Charlotte & Wilbur. (p. 787)
—HOCPP 1075 Florida. (p. 787)
—HOCPP 1077 Predators of the Deep. (p. 787)
—HOCPP 1078 Gladiators. (p. 787)
—HOCPP 1079 All about Ping. (p. 787)
—HOCPP 1080 North Carolina. (p. 787)
—HOCPP 1081 Galaxies. (p. 787)
—HOCPP 1082 Vikings. (p. 787)
—HOCPP 1084 California. (p. 787)
—HOCPP 1085 Sharks. (p. 787)
—HOCPP 1086 World War I. (p. 787)
—HOCPP 1087 Electricity. (p. 787)
—HOCPP 1088 Advanced Astronomy. (p. 787)
—HOCPP 1089 World War II. (p. 787)
—HOCPP 1090 Native Americans of California. (p. 787)
—HOCPP 1091 Forces. (p. 787)
—HOCPP 1092 Romans in Britain. (p. 787)
—HOCPP 1094 Red Clogs. (p. 787)
—HOCPP 1096 Missionaries to Know. (p. 787)
—HOCPP 1097 Anglo-Saxons. (p. 787)
—HOCPP 1098 Disneyland. (p. 787)
—HOCPP 1102 Roald Amundsen. (p. 787)
—HOCPP 1103 Mollusks. (p. 787)
—HOCPP 1105 September 11th 2001. (p. 787)
—HOCPP 1106 the United States Navy. (p. 787)
—HOCPP 1107 Steve Irwin. (p. 787)
—HOCPP 1108 Harvest Festival. (p. 787)
—HOCPP 1110 Five Little Pumpkins. (p. 787)
—HOCPP 1114 Ancient India. (p. 787)
—HOCPP 1115 Multiplication Party. (p. 787)
—HOCPP 1117 Turkey Time. (p. 787)
—HOCPP 1118 Beginning Reading. (p. 787)
—HOCPP 1120 Texas. (p. 787)
—HOCPP 1121 Kangaroos. (p. 787)
—HOCPP 1122 Healthy Bodies. (p. 787)
—HOCPP 1123 Penguins. (p. 787)
—HOCPP 1124 the Sun. (p. 787)
—HOCPP 1125 Pigs. (p. 787)
—HOCPP 1126 the Pilgrims. (p. 787)
—HOCPP 1127 Bees. (p. 787)
—HOCPP 1128 the History of Sports. (p. 787)
—HOCPP 1129 Birds. (p. 787)
—HOCPP 1130 Christmas Cheer. (p. 787)
—HOCPP 1131 Invertebrates. (p. 787)
—HOCPP 1132 Robert Falcon Scott. (p. 787)
—HOCPP 1133 Vertebrates. (p. 787)
—HOCPP 1134 10 Commandments. (p. 787)
—HOCPP 1136 Let it Snow. (p. 787)
—HOCPP 1139 Pirates. (p. 787)
—HOCPP 1140 Germs. (p. 787)
—HOCPP 1143 Winter Sports. (p. 787)
—HOCPP 1145 Be My Valentine. (p. 787)
—HOCPP 1146 Mr. Groundhog. (p. 787)
—HOCPP 1147 King of the Apes: The Gorilla: the Gorilla. (p. 787)
—HOCPP1021 Symbols of Christmas. (p. 787)
—HOCPP1022 New Years. (p. 787)
—HOCPP1029 the Iditarod. (p. 787)
—HOCPP1032 American Government. (p. 787)
—HOCPP1036 Horses. (p. 787)
—Labor Day. (p. 969)
—Moon. (p. 1171)
—North America. (p. 1264)
—Polar Habitats. (p. 1379)
—Pyramids of Egypt. (p. 1421)
—Rainforest Habitats. (p. 1436)
McNeil, Tom & Benchmark Education Co. Staff. Take-Off: A Pilot's Memoir. (p. 1697)
McNeil, W. K., ed. Ghost Stories from the American South. Taylor, Byron, illus. (p. 671)
McNeill, Allison, jt. auth. see Hanes, Sharon M.
McNeill, Allison & Hanes, Richard Clay. American Home Front in World War II Reference Library Cumulative Index. (p. 61)
McNeill, Audrey. From the Desk of a Three-Year-Old. Grondel, April, illus. (p. 644)
McNeill, Jim, illus. see Geiger Stephens, Pamela.
McNeill, Jim, illus. see Stephens, Pamela Geiger.
McNeill, Jim, illus. see Stephens, Pamela Greiger.
McNeill, Jim, illus. see Stephens, Pamela.
McNeill, Michele Babineau. Whales. (p. 1878)
McNeill, Suzanne, et al. Wire Art for Kids. (p. 1939)
McNeill, William H., et al, eds. Berkshire Encyclopedia of World History (p. 167)
McNevin, Dale, illus. see MacDonald, Hugh.
McNevin, Dale, illus. see Stretch, Ian.
McNevin, Dale, illus. see Weale, David.
McNichol, John. Tripods Attack! (p. 1787)
McNicholas, Anne. Sequel of Thank You Jesus. (p. 1552)
McNicholas, Dick. Amusement Machines: Your Route to Success. (p. 66)
—Bulk Vending Machines: Your Route to Success. (p. 240)
McNicholas, Jim & McEntee, Joe. Games to Improve Reading Levels. (p. 655)
McNicholas, June. Ferrets (p. 582)
—Rats (p. 1440)
McNicholas, Shelagh. This Little Light of Mine. (p. 1737)
McNicholas, Shelagh, illus. see Allison, Catherine.
McNicholas, Shelagh, illus. see Anderson, Rachael.
McNicholas, Shelagh, illus. see Balsley, Tilda.
McNicholas, Shelagh, illus. see Bradley, Kimberly Brubaker.
McNicholas, Shelagh, illus. see Brownlee, Sophia Grace & McClelland, Rosie.
McNicholas, Shelagh, illus. see Davidson, Susanna & Daynes, Katie.
McNicholas, Shelagh, illus. see Dombey, Elizabeth.
McNicholas, Shelagh, illus. see Geras, Adèle.
McNicholas, Shelagh, illus. see Holub, Joan.
McNicholas, Shelagh, illus. see Watt, Fiona.
McNicholas, Shelagh, jt. auth. see Geras, Adèle.
McNicholas, Shelagh, jt. illus. see Guicciardini, Desideria.
McNickle, D'Arcy. They Came Here First; The Epic of the American Indian. (p. 1732)
McNicol, Alison. My First Learn to Sew Book. (p. 1207)
—My First Sewing Machine Book: Learn to Sew Kids. (p. 1207)
McNicolas, Shelagh, illus. see Aspley, Brenda.
McNicoll, Sylvia. Beauty Returns (p. 154)
—Best Friends Through Eternity. (p. 169)
—Crush. Candy. Corpse (p. 386)
—Different Kind of Beauty (p. 438)
—Dying to Go Viral (p. 491)
—Last Chance for Paris (p. 977)
McNiff, Dawn. Mommy's Little Monster. Willis-Crowley, Kate, illus. (p. 1163)
McNish, Cliff. Angel. (p. 73)
—Breathe: A Ghost Story. (p. 226)
—Savannah Grey. (p. 1516)
—Silver Child. (p. 1576)
—Silver City. (p. 1576)
—Silver World. (p. 1577)
McNiven, Kelly. Carly Rae Jepsen. (p. 270)
McNiven, Steve. Sentry (p. 1551)
McNiven, Steve, illus. see Kesel, Barbara.
McNulty, Faith. If You Decide to Go to the Moon. Kellogg, Steven, illus. (p. 854)
McNulty, Faith & Shiffman, Lena. Chant des Baleines. (p. 290)
McNulty, Janet. Are You the Monster under My Bed? (p. 97)
—Mrs. Duck & the Dragon. (p. 1187)
—Rhymes-A-lot. (p. 1468)
McNulty John. I Am Your Emotions. Gilmour, Karen, illus. (p. 834)
—I Am Your Health. (p. 834)
—I Am Your Imagination. Gilmour, Karen, illus. (p. 834)
—I Am Your Self-Esteem. Gilmour, Karen, illus. (p. 834)
McNulty, Mark. Karate. (p. 943)
McNutt, Dave. Safety Dave & Daisy Take on the Bullies. (p. 1502)
McNutt, Nan. Spindle Whorl. Fernandes, Roger & Point, Susan, illus. (p. 1628)
—Twined Basket. Youso, Justin & Kaino, Kim, illus. (p. 1802)
McNutt, William Slavens. Poor Little Eddie. (p. 1383)
McO-Campbell, Adrian. Wildness Within & the Tree of Eyes. (p. 1931)
McOmber, Rachel B., ed. Bags... Bags (Animals) (p. 132)
—Bags... Bags (Holidays) (p. 132)
—McOmber Phonics Storybooks: Bug. (p. 1114)
—McOmber Phonics Storybooks: Kim. (p. 1114)
—McOmber Phonics Storybooks: Max. (p. 1114)
—McOmber Phonics Storybooks: Razz. (p. 1114)
—McOmber Phonics Storybooks: A Box. (p. 1114)
—McOmber Phonics Storybooks: On TV. (p. 1114)
—McOmber Phonics Storybooks: Hen Pox. (p. 1114)
—McOmber Phonics Storybooks: Max Ran. (p. 1114)
—McOmber Phonics Storybooks: Fizz Mix. (p. 1114)
—McOmber Phonics Storybooks: Fizz Mud. (p. 1114)
—McOmber Phonics Storybooks: Miss Vie. (p. 1114)
—McOmber Phonics Storybooks: A Hum-Bug. (p. 1114)
—McOmber Phonics Storybooks: A Red Hen. (p. 1114)
—McOmber Phonics Storybooks: Ben in Bed. (p. 1114)
—McOmber Phonics Storybooks: Chatsworth. (p. 1114)
—McOmber Phonics Storybooks: Jud & Nell. (p. 1114)
—McOmber Phonics Storybooks: Max Is Six. (p. 1114)
—McOmber Phonics Storybooks: Number Fun. (p. 1114)
—McOmber Phonics Storybooks: At the Fair. (p. 1114)
—McOmber Phonics Storybooks: Boe E. Toad. (p. 1114)
—McOmber Phonics Storybooks: Hello Again. (p. 1114)
—McOmber Phonics Storybooks: In the Dell. (p. 1114)
—McOmber Phonics Storybooks: Me & the Bee. (p. 1114)
—McOmber Phonics Storybooks: Ben Has a Pet. (p. 1114)
—McOmber Phonics Storybooks: Humps & Lumps. (p. 1114)
—McOmber Phonics Storybooks: Max the Grand. (p. 1114)
—McOmber Phonics Storybooks: A Trip to China. (p. 1114)
—McOmber Phonics Storybooks: Fizz in the Pit. (p. 1114)
—McOmber Phonics Storybooks: Pete's Bike Ride. (p. 1114)
—McOmber Phonics Storybooks: Ben Will Get Well. (p. 1114)
—McOmber Phonics Storybooks: Boyer's Toy Store. (p. 1114)
—McOmber Phonics Storybooks: Mom & Dad Hop-Jig. (p. 1114)
—McOmber Phonics Storybooks: A Game for Champions. (p. 1114)
—McOmber Phonics Storybooks: A Night to Celebrate. (p. 1114)
—McOmber Phonics Storybooks: Choose Which One - 1. (p. 1114)
—McOmber Phonics Storybooks: A Nifty Ball of String. (p. 1114)
—McOmber Phonics Storybooks: A Package from Hong Kong. (p. 1114)
—McOmber Phonics Storybooks: Everyone Knows a Pitcher. (p. 1114)
—McOmber Phonics Storybooks. (p. 1114)
—McOmber Phonics Storybooks: The Bag. (p. 1115)
—McOmber Phonics Storybooks: The Kit. (p. 1115)
—McOmber Phonics Storybooks: The Map. (p. 1115)
—McOmber Phonics Storybooks: The Sub. (p. 1115)
—McOmber Phonics Storybooks: The Tub. (p. 1115)
—McOmber Phonics Storybooks: The Cake. (p. 1115)
—McOmber Phonics Storybooks: The Rope. (p. 1115)
—McOmber Phonics Storybooks: Tid Bits. (p. 1115)
—McOmber Phonics Storybooks: The Fumes. (p. 1115)
—McOmber Phonics Storybooks: The Prize. (p. 1115)
—McOmber Phonics Storybooks: The TV Box. (p. 1115)
—McOmber Phonics Storybooks: The Box Mix. (p. 1115)
—McOmber Phonics Storybooks: The Haircut. (p. 1115)
—McOmber Phonics Storybooks: The Pit Kit. (p. 1115)
—McOmber Phonics Storybooks: The Tan Cab. (p. 1115)
—McOmber Phonics Storybooks: The Tin Lid. (p. 1115)
—McOmber Phonics Storybooks: The Big Deal. (p. 1115)
—McOmber Phonics Storybooks: The Big Hole. (p. 1115)
—McOmber Phonics Storybooks: The Gal Pals. (p. 1115)
—McOmber Phonics Storybooks: The Magic "E" (p. 1115)
—McOmber Phonics Storybooks: The Time Box. (p. 1115)
—McOmber Phonics Storybooks: The Wizz Kid. (p. 1115)
—McOmber Phonics Storybooks: Snores & More. (p. 1115)
—McOmber Phonics Storybooks: Ten in the Hut. (p. 1115)
—McOmber Phonics Storybooks: The Neat Trick. (p. 1115)
—McOmber Phonics Storybooks: The Quiz Is (1) (p. 1115)
—McOmber Phonics Storybooks: The Quiz Is (2) (p. 1115)
—McOmber Phonics Storybooks: The Video Show. (p. 1115)
—McOmber Phonics Storybooks: The Bon-Bon Box. (p. 1115)
—McOmber Phonics Storybooks: The Hum-Bug Hop. (p. 1115)
—McOmber Phonics Storybooks: You Can Make It. (p. 1115)
—McOmber Phonics Storybooks: Yellow Crocodile. (p. 1115)
—McOmber Phonics Storybooks: Robin Hood's Cook. (p. 1115)
—McOmber Phonics Storybooks: The Cove of Gloom. (p. 1115)
—McOmber Phonics Storybooks: The Lemonade Sale. (p. 1115)
—McOmber Phonics Storybooks: Under the Rainbow. (p. 1115)
—McOmber Phonics Storybooks: The Land of Morning. (p. 1115)
—McOmber Phonics Storybooks: Writing Book. Vol. 1 (p. 1115)
—McOmber Phonics Storybooks: Writing Book. Vol. 2 (p. 1115)
—McOmber Phonics Storybooks: The Prime Time Trick. (p. 1115)
—McOmber Phonics Storybooks: Tale of the Green Glob. (p. 1115)
—McOmber Phonics Storybooks: The Invisible Crocodiles. (p. 1115)
—McOmber Phonics Storybooks: Razz Visits Raz in Israel. (p. 1115)
—McOmber Phonics Storybooks: The Confection Connection. (p. 1115)
—String Art: For All Seasons. Vol. 1 (p. 1667)
—String Art: For All Seasons. Vol. 2 (p. 1667)
MCP Staff. Baby Bear's Ride (p. 125)
—Baby Who Got All the Blame. (p. 128)
—Bags, Cans, & Pots (p. 132)
—Ben's Pets (p. 165)
—Big Cat (p. 180)
—Busy World R. Scarry Big Book Collection (p. 246)
—By the Tree (p. 249)
—Can a Cow Hop? (p. 258)
—Cat Came Back (Consonant c) (p. 277)
—Cat Chat (p. 277)
—Cat's Trip (p. 281)
—Dive In! (p. 454)
—Dragon's Lunch (p. 479)
—Eight Friends in All (p. 507)
—Fast As a Fox (p. 576)
—Good Girl! (Consonant g) (p. 698)
—Good Night Little Bug (p. 699)
—Goose Chase (p. 702)
—How to Make a Hen House (Consonant h) (p. 820)

—Humpback Whales (p. 827)
—I Like to Count (p. 841)
—Jan Can Juggle (Consonant j) (p. 907)
—Keys (Consonant k) (p. 950)
—Let's Move! (p. 999)
—Little Bunny's Lunch: Short u; Consonants b, h; Blends br, cr; Digraphs ch, sh, th. (p. 1025)
—Look Closer (Consonant l) (p. 1049)
—Lost in the Fog (p. 1055)
—Mess (p. 1129)
—My Cat (p. 1200)
—My Monster & Me (p. 1214)
—Name Is the Same (p. 1228)
—Nanny Goat's Nap (p. 1229)
—Night Animals (p. 1252)
—Nut Pie for Judy (p. 1273)
—One Bee Got on the Bus (p. 1294)
—Party (p. 1325)
—Ready Reader S1. (p. 1447)
—Safety Outside Your Home Big Book. (p. 1502)
—Sandy (p. 1511)
—Shell Shopping (p. 1564)
—Six Go By (p. 1582)
—Small Baby Raccoon (p. 1591)
—Socks: Consonant N (p. 1605)
—Stage Two - Early. (p. 1638)
—Stop That! (p. 1653)
—Story Time (Consonant d) (p. 1663)
—Ted's Red Sled (p. 1713)
—Terrific Shoes (p. 1721)
—That Fly (p. 1726)
—That Pig Can't Do a Anything (p. 1726)
—Too High! (p. 1766)
—True or False? (p. 1792)
—Two Turtles (Consonant t) (p. 1804)
—Very Big (p. 1837)
—Vulture on Vacation (p. 1851)
—We Are Singing (p. 1865)
—Whale Watch (Consonant w) (p. 1877)
—What Rhymes with Cat? (p. 1893)
—When Bob Woke up Late (p. 1901)
—Where Can a Hippo Hide? (p. 1906)
—Where Do They Live? (p. 1907)
—Who Made That? (p. 1916)
—Who Said Boo? Long u; Consonants d, m; Blend dr. (p. 1917)
—Wilma's Wagon (p. 1934)
—Yes I Can! Consonants j, f, g, l, d (p. 1970)
—Zebra's Yellow Van (Consonant v) (p. 1985)
—Zelda's Zipper. (p. 1986)
McPartland, Dorothy. Wishing Stars. McPartland, Dorothy, illus. (p. 1940)
McPartland, Randall. E. Coli. (p. 492)
—Tay-Sachs Disease. (p. 1707)
—Tuberculosis. (p. 1795)
—Understanding Quantum Physics. (p. 1816)
—Understanding the Laws of Thermodynamics. (p. 1816)
—Understanding Waves & Wave Motion. (p. 1816)
McPartland, Randall, jt. auth. see Cefrey, Holly.
McPhail, jt. auth. see McPhail, David.
McPhail, David. Andrew Draws. McPhail, David, illus. (p. 72)
—Baby Pig Pig Talks. McPhail, David, illus. (p. 127)
—Baby Pig Pig Walks. McPhail, David, illus. (p. 127)
—Bad Dog. (p. 131)
—Bella Loves Bunny. Brukoff, Barry, photos by. (p. 162)
—Ben Loves Bear. (p. 163)
—Ben Over Night. Ellis, Sarah, ed. (p. 163)
—Big Brown Bear. (p. 180)
—Big Brown Bear/El Gran Oso Pardo. Flor Ada, Alma & Campoy, F. Isabel, trs. (p. 180)
—Big Brown Bear's up & down Day. McPhail, David, illus. (p. 180)
—Big Pig & Little Pig. (p. 183)
—Big Pig & Little Pig(Cerdo y Cerdito) (p. 183)
—Boy, Bird, & Dog. McPhail, David, illus. (p. 217)
—Brothers. (p. 231)
—Budgie & Boo. (p. 235)
—Cerdo y Cerdito. Flor Ada, Alma & Campoy, F. Isabel, trs. from ENG. (p. 287)
—Dot & Bob. (p. 472)
—Family Tree. McPhail, David, illus. (p. 569)
—I Get Dressed. (p. 838)
—I Play. (p. 844)
—Jack & Rick. (p. 902)
—My Mother Goose: A Collection of Favorite Rhymes, Songs, & Concepts. McPhail, David, illus. (p. 1214)
—No! McPhail, David, illus. (p. 1257)
—Peter Loves Penguin. (p. 1346)
—Pig Pig Meets the Lion. McPhail, David, illus. (p. 1357)
—Pig Pig Returns. McPhail, David, illus. (p. 1357)
—Rick Is Sick. (p. 1470)
—Searcher & Old Tree. McPhail, David, illus. (p. 1537)
—Sick Day. (p. 1572)
—Sisters. (p. 1581)
—Sisters. McPhail, David, illus. (p. 1581)
—Teddy Bear. McPhail, David, illus. (p. 1712)
—Truffle Man. (p. 1793)
—Waddles. (p. 1852)
—Water Boy. (p. 1862)
—Weezer Changes the World. (p. 1872)
—Weezer Changes the World. McPhail, David, illus. (p. 1872)
McPhail, David, illus. see Ashman, Linda.
McPhail, David, illus. see Avery, Kristin.
McPhail, David, illus. see Baker, Liza.
McPhail, David, illus. see Belle, Jennifer.
McPhail, David, illus. see Dragonwagon, Crescent.
McPhail, David, illus. see Floyd, Lucy.
McPhail, David, illus. see Freeman, Martha.
McPhail, David, illus. see Lamb, Albert.
McPhail, David, illus. see Lloyd-Jones, Sally.
McPhail, David, illus. see Maccarone, Grace.
McPhail, David, illus. see MacDonald, Steven.
McPhail, David, illus. see Spinelli, Eileen.
McPhail, David, jt. auth. see McPhail, David.
McPhail, David & McPhail. Blue Door O'Connor, John, illus. (p. 202)
McPhail, David & McPhail, David. Bad Dog. (p. 131)
McPhail, J. A. Dawn of Day. Battis, Gwen, illus. (p. 411)
McPhate, Paul. Puggles: The Adventures of Carly & Vinigin. (p. 1415)
McPhate, Paul J. Puggle King. (p. 1415)
McPhee, Peter. Every Move (p. 543)
—New Blood (p. 1243)
—Out of Time (p. 1311)
McPherrin, Bob. Murder at the Applegate Hotel. (p. 1192)
—Mysterious Tale of Culpepper Mansion: Stingray Cole & the Elm Street Daredevils. (p. 1223)
McPherson, Barbara J., ed. Lost Soles: A Collection of Stories about Shoes. (p. 1056)
McPherson, Christopher. Mama Cat. (p. 1084)
McPherson, Dottie. Kizzi's Special Friends. (p. 963)
McPherson, Heath, illus. see B&H Editorial Staff, ed.
McPherson, Heath, illus. see Chin, Oliver.
McPherson, Heather L. A. Sonja's Wish. Cartwright, Christina, illus. (p. 1612)
McPherson, Melinda, illus. see DeGrasse, Samantha.
McPherson, Miriam. I Call Myself Me. (p. 834)
McPherson, Missie, jt. auth. see O'Neill, Elizabeth.
Mcpherson, Missie & O'Neill, Elizabeth. Alfred Visits Alaska. (p. 37)
McPherson, Missie & O'Neill, Elizabeth. Alfred Visits Indiana. (p. 37)
—Alfred Visits Washington, D. C. (p. 37)
McPherson, Stephanie. My Dear Husband: Important Letters of Abigail Adams. (p. 1201)
McPherson, Stephanie Sammartino. Alexander Graham Bell. Butler, Tad, illus. (p. 36)
—Arctic Thaw: Climate Change & the Global Race for Energy Resources. (p. 96)
—Are You Stressed Out in School? (p. 97)
—Bakke Case & the Affirmative Action Debate: Debating Supreme Court Decisions. (p. 133)
—Bill Clinton. (p. 186)
—Biography Coretta Scott King. (p. 189)
—Doping in Sports: Winning at Any Cost? (p. 470)
—First Men on the Moon. (p. 596)
—Iceberg, Right Ahead! The Tragedy of the Titanic. (p. 851)
—Liberty or Death: A Story about Patrick Henry. Debon, Nicolas, illus. (p. 1005)
—Martha Washington: Legendary First Lady of the United States. (p. 1097)
—Political Parties: From Nominations to Victory Celebrations. (p. 1380)
—Sonia Sotomayor: Supreme Court Justice. (p. 1612)
—Stressed Out in School? Learning to Deal with Academic Pressure. (p. 1667)
—Tim Berners-Lee: Inventor of the World Wide Web. (p. 1750)
—War of the Currents: Thomas Edison vs. Nikola Tesla. (p. 1857)
McPhillips, Robert, illus. see Quinn, Jordan.
McPhillips, Robert, jt. illus. see Bently, Peter.
McPike, Elizabeth. Little Sleepyhead. Barton, Patrice, illus. (p. 1036)
McQuaid, John & Schleifstein, Mark. Path of Destruction: The Devastation of New Orleans & the Coming Age of Superstorms. (p. 1328)
McQuaid, Matilda & Otto, Frei. Shigeru Ban. (p. 1566)
McQuane, Antonia, illus. see Joe, Saqamaw Mi'sel.
McQuarrie, Ralph, illus. see Disney Book Group Staff & DiTerlizzi, Tony.
McQueen, Amelia. Penny for Your Thoughts. (p. 1338)
McQueen, Lucinda. Little Red Hen. (p. 1034)
—Little Red Hen. McQueen, Lucinda, illus. (p. 1034)
McQueen, Lucinda, illus. see Fontes, Justine.
McQueen, Lucinda, illus. see Katz, Julie & Merberg, Julie.
McQueen, Lucinda, illus. see Korman, Justine.
McQueen, Lucinda, illus. see Merberg, Julie.
McQueen, Stacey Dressen, illus. see Heller, Linda.
McQueen, Todd. Bob & Rob & Corn on the Cob. McQueen, Todd, illus. (p. 205)
McQuein, Josin L. Premeditated. (p. 1395)
McQuerry, Maureen Doyle. Peculiars. (p. 1334)
—Time Out of Time: Beyond the Door. Bk. 1 (p. 1752)
—Time Out of Time: Book One: Beyond the Door. (p. 1752)
—Time Out of Time. (p. 1752)
McQuestion, Karen. Celia & the Fairies (p. 286)
—Favorite (p. 577)
—Life on Hold (p. 1012)
—Secrets of the Magic Ring (p. 1545)
McQuilkin, John A., jt. auth. see Young, Martha.
McQuillan, David, illus. see Mcintyre, Mel.
McQuillan, Mary, illus. see Gray, Kes.
McQuillan, Mary, illus. see Harper, Anita.
McQuillan, Mary, illus. see Kelly, Mij.
McQuillan, Mary, illus. see Moss, Miriam.
McQuillan, Mary, tr. see Gray, Kes.
McQuillan, Susan, jt. auth. see Sesame Workshop, Sesame.
McQuillan, Susan & Sesame Workshop Staff. Sesame Street C Es de Cocinar: Recetas de Nuestra Comunidad. (p. 1553)
McQuinn, Anna. Colm's Lambs. Young, Paul, illus. (p. 341)
—If You're Happy & You Know It. Fatus, Sophie, illus. (p. 855)
—Ireland. (p. 887)
—Leo Loves Baby Time. Hearson, Ruth, illus. (p. 992)
—Lola at the Library. Beardshaw, Rosalind, illus. (p. 1045)
—Lola le Lee Al Pequeño Leo. Beardshaw, Rosalind, illus. (p. 1045)
—Lola Loves Stories. Beardshaw, Rosalind, illus. (p. 1045)
—Lola Plants a Garden. Beardshaw, Rosalind, illus. (p. 1045)
—Lola Reads to Leo. (p. 1045)
—Lola Reads to Leo. Beardshaw, Rosalind, illus. (p. 1045)
—My Friend Jamal. Frey, Ben, illus. (p. 1209)
—My Friend Mei Jing. Frey, Ben, illus. (p. 1209)
—Rosette for Maeve? Young, Paul, illus. (p. 1490)
—Wanda's Washing Machine. McCafferty, Jan, illus. (p. 1856)
McQuinn, Anna & Beardshaw, Rosalind. Lola le Encantan Los Cuentos. Canetti, Yanitzia, tr. from ENG. (p. 1045)
McQuinn, Anna & Fatus, Sophie. If You're Happy & You Know It. (p. 855)
—If You're Happy & You Know It! Fatus, Sophie, illus. (p. 855)
McQuinn, Anna, et al. Leo le Gusta Bebelandia. Hearson, Ruth, illus. (p. 992)
McQuiston, Liz. Graphic Agitation: Social & Political Graphics in the Digital Age. Vol. 2 (p. 710)
McQuitty, LaVonia Corbin, illus. see Oliver, Sheila.
McQuitty, LaVonia Corbin, illus. see Ralls, Ken.
McQuitty, LaVonia Corbin, illus. see Ware, Richard.
McQuitty, LaVonia Corbin, illus. see White, Susan K.
McRae, Angel, illus. see Sperounis, Kathy.
McRae, Anne. Animal Atlas. De Luca, Daniela, illus. (p. 76)
McRae, Anne, ed. see Davies, Gill.
McRae, Anne, jt. auth. see Cooper, Alison.
McRae, Anne & Agosta, Loredana. Mammals. Dogi, Fiammetta, illus. (p. 1085)
—Vikings. Cecchi, Lorenzo et al, illus. (p. 1842)
McRae Books Staff, ed. see Morris, Neil & Morris, Ting.
McRae, David. Blood of the Donnellys. (p. 200)
McRae, G. c. Pretty Ballerina. Anderson, David, illus. (p. 1398)
—Tooth. Anderson, David, illus. (p. 1768)
McRae, J. R. Cats' Eyes. Grivas, Vasilis, illus. (p. 281)
—Free Passage. Hand, Terry, illus. (p. 634)
—Tatter Wings. Shamshirsaz, Shahab, illus. (p. 1707)
McRae, Patrick, illus. see Castaldo, Nancy F.
McRae, Sloan. Atlanta Braves. (p. 112)
McRae, Suzanne. Pick-a-WooWoo - KC the Conscious Camel: A furry jaunt to peace & Contentment. Mortimer, Alexander, illus. (p. 1354)
McRae, W. David. Calculus Student Activity Book. (p. 252)
McRary, Janie. Rock That Became a Friend. (p. 1482)
McRedmond, Sarah, jt. auth. see Duffy, Kate.
McRee Turner, Amber. Sway. (p. 1689)
McReynolds, Linda. Eight Days Gone. O'Rourke, Ryan, illus. (p. 507)
McReynolds, Stacy. San Antonio Zoo. (p. 1510)
McRitchie, Mike. Best Friends. (p. 169)
McRobb, Will & Viscardi, Chris. Battle of the Bands. (p. 146)
McRobbie, David. Strandee. (p. 1664)
—Vinnie's War. (p. 1843)
—Whole Lot of Wayne. (p. 1920)
McRobbie, Narelle. Bip the Snapping Bungaroo. Fielding, Grace, illus. (p. 190)
McRobert, Megan & Skindzier, Jon. Smith College College Prowler off the Record. (p. 1594)
McRoberts, Eddison. Sneaking Treats: A Halloween Hunt. Gadra, Jessica, illus. (p. 1597)
—Sneaking Treats. Gadra, Jessica, illus. (p. 1597)
McRoberts, Richard. Curious Incident of the Dog in the Night Time. (p. 394)
McShane, Pol. Button That Should Never, Ever, Ever Be Pushed! (p. 248)
Mcshane, Pol. Magic Elevator: The Adventures of Johnny & Joey. (p. 1072)
McShane, Pol. Return to Animal Land: The Adventures of Johnny & Joey. (p. 1465)
McSorley, Paul J. & Bearss, Patricia. Adventures of Forealdo: Finding Millie. (p. 18)
Mcspadden, Elizabeth. My Daddy Twinkles from Above. (p. 1201)
McSpadden, J. Walker. Famous Dogs in Fiction. (p. 569)
—Robin Hood. (p. 1480)
McSpadden, Judy. Heart for Thunder. (p. 759)
McSpadden, Kay. Child's Book of Virtues. (p. 304)
McSpadden, Warren W., jt. auth. see Wyler, Rose.
McStay, Moriah. Everything That Makes You. (p. 545)
McSwain, Ray, illus. see Blondin, John & Blondin, George.
McSween, Michele. Gordon & Li Li Count in Mandarin. Nam, Doan, illus. (p. 702)
—Gordon & Li Li Learn Animals in Mandarin. Nam, Doan, illus. (p. 702)
McSweeney, Ben, illus. see Sanderson, Brandon.
McSweeney's. Goods: Volume 1. (p. 701)
McSweeney's Books Staff. Noisy Outlaws, Unfriendly Blobs, & Some Other Things... Thompson, Ted & Horowitz, Eli, eds. (p. 1263)
McSweeney's Editors, creator. Author-Illustrator Starter Kit. (p. 117)
McSweeny, Catherine, jt. auth. see Hanrahan, Abigail.
McSwigan, Marie. Snow Treasure. (p. 1599)
—Snow Treasure. Reardon, Mary, illus. (p. 1599)
McTaggart, Debra, jt. auth. see McTaggart, Stephen.
McTaggart, Stephen & McTaggart, Debra. ABC Talking Book Adventures. Nord, Mary, illus. (p. 3)
—Bookee Presents 1, 2, 3 Count with Me. Nord, Mary, illus. (p. 212)
—Bookee's Sounds Around. Nord, Mary, illus. (p. 212)
McTague, Charles. Bernard Overall: The Russian Tom Sawyer. (p. 167)
McTavish, Sandra. Life Skills: 225 Ready-to-Use Health Activities for Success & Well-Being (Grades 6-12) (p. 1013)
McTeer, Rhonda, ed. see Page, Julie & Adams, Sabrina.
McTeigue, Jane, jt. illus. see Miralles, Jose.
McTiernan, Deborah. Lilly Noble & Actual Magic. (p. 1017)
McTighe, Carolyn. How to Ruin Your Life; And Other Lessons School Doesn't Teach You (p. 821)
—Sakura Tree Brownlee, Karen, illus. (p. 1504)
McTrustry, Chris. Cleopatra's Report. (p. 331)
—Red Goes Green. (p. 1454)
McTyre, Robert E., ed. see Eubanks, Jacquelyn R.
McVaugh, Julia A., ed. see Swalin, Benjamin.
McVay, Chrissy. Souls of the North Wind. (p. 1614)
McVay, Elizabeth. Baby Bun & the Littlest Tree. (p. 125)
McVay, Kinsy. Just Live Around. (p. 939)
McVeagh, John, jt. auth. see Defoe, Daniel.
McVeigh, Kevin, illus. see Demuth, Patricia Brennan.
McVeigh, Kevin, illus. see Holub, Joan.
McVeigh, Kevin, illus. see Koontz, Robin.
McVeigh, Kevin, illus. see Pascal, Janet.
McVeigh, Kevin, illus. see Pollack, Pamela D. & Belviso, Meg.
McVeigh, Mark. Hello Kitty: Superterrific Sleepover! (p. 764)
—Julio & Enrique Iglesias. (p. 932)
McVeigh, Mark, et al. Clifford for President. LaPadula, Tom, illus. (p. 332)
McVeigh, Mark W. Lizard's Legacy. Sazaklis, John, illus. (p. 1043)
McVey, James. Martha Maxwell: Natural History Pioneer. (p. 1097)
McVey, Randall, et al. Mesmerizing Mandalas. (p. 1129)
McVicar, William E. Turtle Tries. (p. 1798)
McVicker, Mary. Secret of Belle Meadow Ramsey, Marcy Dunn, illus. (p. 1542)
McVicker, Maryellen. Joseph Kinney: Steamboat Captain. Hare, John, illus. (p. 926)
McVoy, Terra Elan. After the Kiss. (p. 28)
—Being Friends with Boys. (p. 161)
—Criminal. (p. 382)
—Drive Me Crazy. (p. 485)
—In Deep. (p. 863)
—Pure. (p. 1419)
—Summer of Firsts & Lasts. (p. 1674)
McWade, Michael. Reindeer Chronicles: The Green Scarf. (p. 1457)
McWatt, Irene. Pongo-Peter: The Life & Thoughts of an Extraordinary Mongrel. (p. 1382)
McWeeney, Tom, illus. see Bowyer, Clifford B.
Mcwethy, Betty. That Fat White Cat & the Missing Socks. (p. 1726)
Mcwherter, Barbara. I Should Have Been a Bear. McWherter, Seth, illus. (p. 845)
—Little Pumpkin & Sally: It's O. K. to Be Different. (p. 1034)
—Oliver & His Mountain Climbing Adventures. McWherter, Shelley, illus. (p. 1285)
—Wren & the Groundhog. Brandon, Vicky, illus. (p. 1962)
McWherter, Seth, illus. see Mcwherter, Barbara.
McWherter, Shelley, illus. see Mcwherter, Barbara.
McWherter, Susie. Search for the Tiny Princess. (p. 1537)
McWhirt, Brad, jt. auth. see Mcwhirt, Debbie.
Mcwhirt, Debbie & McWhirt, Brad. Pork Chop & Friends. (p. 1386)
McWhorter, Diane. Dream of Freedom: The Civil Rights Movement from 1954 to 1968. (p. 483)
McWhorter Sember, Brette. Money Book: Earn It, Save It, & Watch It Grow! (p. 1164)
McWilliam, Howard, illus. see Enderle, Dotti.
McWilliam, Howard, illus. see Markle, Sandra.
McWilliam, Howard, illus. see Moore, Jodi.
McWilliam, Howard, illus. see Noll, Amanda.
McWilliam, Howard, illus. see Pallotta, Jerry.
McWilliams, Amanda & Moore, Clement C. Ozark Night Before Christmas Rice, James, illus. (p. 1316)
McWilliams, Brady & McWilliams, Brandi. Just a Handful. (p. 937)
McWilliams, Brandi, jt. auth. see McWilliams, Brady.
McWilliams, Eileen. Pioneers of Electricity. (p. 1361)
McWilliams, Joan. PeaceFinder: Riley Mcfee's Quest for World Peace. (p. 1332)
McWilliams, Pamela Marie. Naval Navel Academy/ the Naval Navel Cadets. (p. 1237)
McWilliams Pittard, Irene. Goose Dreams. Kiplinger Pandy, Lori, illus. (p. 702)
Mcwilliams, Ronnie. Leaf People: Philip & the Wolf. (p. 982)
Meacham, Jon. Thomas Jefferson: President & Philosopher. (p. 1739)
Meacham, Liz. Three Wise Women: A Christmas Story / A Christmas Play. (p. 1744)
Meacham, Margaret. Fairy's Guide to Understanding Humans. (p. 565)
—Mid-Semester Night's Dream. (p. 1137)
Meachen Rau, Dana. Adivina Quién (p. 12)
—Adivina Quién Brinca. (p. 12)
—Adivina Quién Caza. (p. 12)
—Adivina Quién Gruñe. (p. 12)
—Adivina Quién Nada. (p. 12)
—Adivina Quién Pica. (p. 12)
—Adivina Quién Ronronea. (p. 12)
—Air. (p. 31)
—Airé. (p. 31)
—Albert Einstein (p. 34)
—Andrew Carnegie: Captain of Industry (p. 72)
—Applesauce. (p. 93)
—Arco Iris. (p. 95)
—Arrecifes de Coral. (p. 101)
—Artists. (p. 104)
—Artists/Las Artistas. (p. 104)
—At a Fair. (p. 110)
—At a Picnic. (p. 110)
—At the Beach. (p. 110)
—At the Park. (p. 111)
—At the Zoo. (p. 111)
—Baker. (p. 133)
—Ballena en el Oceano. (p. 134)
—Blow Out. (p. 202)
—Bombero. (p. 208)
—Bookworms: Verbs in Action (p. 213)
—Bookworms: The Inside Story (p. 213)
—Bookworms: The Shape of the World (p. 213)
—Bread. (p. 224)
—Brilla Luciernaga, Brilla! (p. 228)
—Builders. (p. 238)
—Builders/Los Contructores. (p. 238)
—Butterfly in the Sky. (p. 248)
—Buzz, Bee, Buzz! (p. 248)
—Buzz, Bee, Buzz!/Zumba Abeja, Zumba! (p. 248)
—Cake. (p. 252)
—Cansada de Esperar Ruiz, Carlos, tr. (p. 261)
—Carry On. (p. 271)
—Cartero. (p. 272)
—Castle. (p. 276)
—Caves. (p. 282)
—Caves/Las Cuevas. (p. 282)
—Cerebro: Que Hay Dentro de Mi? (p. 287)
—Chefs. (p. 297)
—Chefs/Los Chefs. (p. 297)
—Chile. (p. 305)
—Cinco. (p. 319)
—Circles. (p. 321)

—Climbing. (p. 333)
—Clothing in American History. (p. 334)
—Coins. (p. 338)
—Comida y la Cocina: en la historia de América. (p. 348)
—Comida y la Cocina en la Historia de América. (p. 348)
—Conejo en el Huerto. (p. 356)
—Constellations (p. 359)
—Cookies. (p. 361)
—Coral Reefs. (p. 366)
—Coral Reefs/Los Arrecifes de Coral. (p. 366)
—Corazon y la Sangre. (p. 366)
—Count on It! (p. 369)
—Count on It! ¡Cuenta con Ello! (p. 369)
—Crawl, Ladybug, Crawl! (p. 377)
—Crawl, Ladybug, Crawl!/Trepa Mariquita, Trepa! (p. 377)
—Cuatro. (p. 388)
—Deserts. (p. 429)
—Deserts/Los Desiertos. (p. 429)
—Desiertos. (p. 429)
—Diez. (p. 437)
—Dig In. (p. 438)
—Doctors. (p. 459)
—Doctors/Los Doctores. (p. 459)
—Dos. (p. 472)
—Driving. (p. 485)
—Earth Matters (p. 496)
—Earth Matters/El Planeta Es Importante (p. 496)
—EMTs. (p. 521)
—EMTs/Los Paramedicos. (p. 521)
—En el Parque. (p. 522)
—En el Parque de Atracciones. (p. 522)
—En el Picnic. (p. 522)
—En el Trabajo (p. 522)
—En el Zoologico. (p. 522)
—En la Granja. (p. 522)
—En la Playa. (p. 522)
—Escuela en la Historia de América. (p. 535)
—Estomago: Que Hay Dentro de Mi? (p. 538)
—Fall Down. (p. 566)
—Firefighter. (p. 591)
—Fitness for Fun! (p. 599)
—Five. (p. 599)
—Five/Cinco. (p. 601)
—Flash, Firefly, Flash! (p. 602)
—Flash, Firefly, Flash!/Brilla Luciernaga, Brilla! (p. 602)
—Floating. (p. 605)
—Flotar. (p. 607)
—Fly, Butterfly, Fly! (p. 609)
—Fly, Butterfly, Fly!/Vuela Mariposa, Vuela! (p. 609)
—Food & Cooking in American History. (p. 613)
—Four. (p. 624)
—Four/Cuatro. (p. 625)
—Frog in the Pond. (p. 640)
—Fun Time (p. 648)
—Galletas. (p. 653)
—Gastando el dinero (Spending Money) (p. 657)
—George Washington Carver. (p. 664)
—Go, Critter, Go! (p. 686)
—Go, Critter, Go!/¡Vamos Criaturita, Vamos! (p. 686)
—Going to School in American History. (p. 693)
—Great Women of the Suffrage Movement (p. 719)
—Grocer. (p. 725)
—Grow Up. (p. 726)
—Harlem Renaissance. (p. 749)
—Helado. (p. 762)
—History of Money. (p. 784)
—Holiday Time. (p. 788)
—Huesos y Musculos: Que Hay Dentro de Mi? (p. 824)
—Ice Cream. (p. 850)
—Igloo. (p. 856)
—Instrumentos de Trabajo (p. 879)
—Jobs in Town (p. 919)
—Juegos y Diversiones en la Historia de América. (p. 931)
—Juegos y diversiones en la historia de America (Toys, Games, & Fun in American History) (p. 931)
—Land. (p. 973)
—Land/La Tierra. (p. 974)
—Las Cataratas. (p. 976)
—Las Cuevas. (p. 976)
—Las Monedas (Coins) (p. 977)
—Leon en la Hierba. (p. 992)
—Let's Share. (p. 1000)
—Librarian. (p. 1005)
—Librarians. (p. 1005)
—Librarians/Los Bibliotecarios. (p. 1005)
—Life. (p. 1007)
—Lion in the Grass. (p. 1020)
—Log Cabin. (p. 1045)
—Look! A Book about Sight Peterson, Rick, illus. (p. 1047)
—Look! [Scholastic]: A Book about Sight. Peterson, Rick, illus. (p. 1050)
—Los Artistas. (p. 1053)
—Los Bibliotecarios. (p. 1053)
—Los billetes (Paper Money) (p. 1053)
—Los Chefs. (p. 1053)
—Los Constructores. (p. 1053)
—Los Doctores. (p. 1053)
—Los Paramedicos. (p. 1054)
—Los Volcanes. (p. 1054)
—Mail Carrier. (p. 1077)
—Many-Sided Shapes. (p. 1089)
—Mapas. (p. 1090)
—Maps. (p. 1090)
—Maps/Los Mapas. (p. 1090)
—Maravillas de la Naturaleza (p. 1091)
—Mariposa en el Aire. (p. 1094)
—Mi Lugar Preferido: My Special Space. Kim, Julie J., illus. (p. 1132)
—Montar! (p. 1170)
—Move Along. (p. 1183)
—My Bones & Muscles. (p. 1198)
—My Bones & Muscles/Huesos y Musculos. (p. 1198)
—My Brain/el Cerebro. (p. 1199)
—My Heart & Blood/el Corazon y la Sangre. (p. 1210)
—My Lungs/Los Pulmones. (p. 1213)
—My Skin/la Piel. (p. 1219)
—My Special Space. Kim, Julie J., illus. (p. 1219)
—My Stomach/el Estomago. (p. 1219)
—Naturaleza (p. 1236)
—Nature (p. 1236)
—Neil Armstrong. (p. 1240)
—Night Light: A Book about the Moon Shea, Denise, illus. (p. 1253)
—Océanos. (p. 1277)
—Oceans. (p. 1277)
—Oceans/Los Oceanos. (p. 1277)
—Oficial de Policia. (p. 1280)
—On a Farm. (p. 1288)
—On the Run. (p. 1291)
—One. (p. 1293)
—One/Uno. (p. 1298)
—Ovals. (p. 1313)
—Pan. (p. 1320)
—Panadero. (p. 1320)
—Paper Money. (p. 1322)
—Pasteles. (p. 1327)
—Piel: Que Hay Dentro de Mi? (p. 1357)
—Pizza. (p. 1365)
—Planeta Es Importante (p. 1368)
—Play Ball. (p. 1371)
—Police Officer. (p. 1380)
—Pulmones. (p. 1416)
—Puré de Manzana. (p. 1419)
—Purrs: Ronronea. (p. 1419)
—Pyramid. (p. 1421)
—Rabbit in the Garden. (p. 1429)
—Rainbows. (p. 1436)
—Rainbows/el Arco Iris. (p. 1436)
—Rana en el Estanque. Vargus, Nanci R., ed. (p. 1438)
—Rectangles: The Shape of the World. (p. 1452)
—Riding. (p. 1471)
—Robin en el Arbol. Vargus, Nanci R., ed. (p. 1479)
—Robin in the Tree. (p. 1480)
—Rodar! (p. 1484)
—Rolling. (p. 1485)
—Ropa en la Historia de América. (p. 1488)
—Safety on the Go. (p. 1502)
—Saving Money. (p. 1517)
—Serpentea Lombriz, Serpentea! (p. 1552)
—Shhhh... A Book about Hearing. Peterson, Rick, illus. (p. 1566)
—Shhhh... [Scholastic]: A Book about Hearing. Peterson, Rick, illus. (p. 1566)
—Skyscraper. (p. 1587)
—Sniff, Sniff [Scholastic]: A Book about Smell. Peterson, Rick, illus. (p. 1597)
—Soft & Smooth, Rough & Bumpy: A Book about Touch. Peterson, Rick, illus. (p. 1606)
—Soft & Smooth, Rough & Bumpy [Scholastic]: A Book about Touch. Peterson, Rick, illus. (p. 1606)
—Space & Time. (p. 1618)
—Space & Time/El Tiempo y Espacio. (p. 1618)
—Space Leftovers: A Book about Comets, Asteroids, & Meteoroids Shea, Denise, illus. (p. 1619)
—Spending Money. (p. 1625)
—Spin Around. (p. 1627)
—Spin, Spider, Spin! (p. 1627)
—Spin, Spider, Spin!/Teje Arana, Teje! (p. 1627)
—Spots of Light: A Book about Stars Shea, Denise, illus. (p. 1634)
—Spring Out. (p. 1635)
—Squares. (p. 1636)
—Squirm, Earthworm, Squirm! (p. 1637)
—Squirm, Earthworm, Squirm!/Serpentea Lombriz, Serpentea! (p. 1637)
—Stickers, Shells, & Snowglobes. (p. 1650)
—Sweet Pea: Escape in the Garden. Hannon, Holly, illus. (p. 1690)
—Teje Arana, Teje! (p. 1715)
—Ten. (p. 1718)
—Ten/Diez. (p. 1719)
—Tendero. (p. 1719)
—Tepee. (p. 1721)
—Thailand. (p. 1724)
—Three. (p. 1741)
—Three/Tres. (p. 1744)
—Tiempo y el Espacio. (p. 1748)
—Tierra. (p. 1748)
—Tired of Waiting. (p. 1757)
—Tools We Use (p. 1767)
—Tools We Use/Instrumentos de Trabajo (p. 1767)
—Top 10 Cats for Kids. (p. 1768)
—Top 10 Fish for Kids. (p. 1768)
—Toys, Games, & Fun in American History. (p. 1774)
—Travel in American History. (p. 1780)
—Trepa Mariquita, Trepa! (p. 1784)
—Trepar! (p. 1784)
—Tres. (p. 1784)
—Triangles. (p. 1785)
—Turn Into. (p. 1797)
—Two. (p. 1803)
—Two/Dos. (p. 1804)
—Undersea City: A Story of a Caribbean Coral Reef. (p. 1815)
—Uno. (p. 1822)
—Verbs in Action Group 2 (p. 1836)
—Verbs in Action: Make a Face. (p. 1836)
—Veterinaria. (p. 1839)
—Veterinarian. (p. 1839)
—Viajes en la Historia de América. (p. 1839)
—Vida. (p. 1840)
—Volcanoes. (p. 1849)
—Volcanoes/Los Volcanes. (p. 1849)
—Vuela Mariposa, Vuela! (p. 1851)
—Waterfalls. (p. 1863)
—Whale in the Water. (p. 1877)
—What Is a Bank? (p. 1888)
—What's Cooking? (p. 1896)
—What's Inside Me? (¿Qué Hay Dentro de Mi?) (p. 1898)
—When Crocodiles Attack! (p. 1901)
—Wonders of Nature (p. 1948)
—Wonders of Nature/Maravillas de la Naturaleza. (p. 1948)
—Yum! A Book about Taste. Peterson, Rick, illus. (p. 1983)
—Yum! [Scholastic]: A Book about Taste. Peterson, Rick, illus. (p. 1983)
—Zumba Abeja, Zumba! (p. 1990)
—¡A Divertimos! (p. 1)
—¡Cuenta con Ello! (p. 389)
—¡Mira! Un Libro Sobre la Vista. Abello, Patricia, tr. from ENG. (p. 1148)
—¡Oye! Un Libro Sobre el Oído. Abello, Patricia, tr. from ENG. (p. 1316)
—¡Vamos, Criaturita, Vamos! (p. 1831)
—¿A Qué Huele? Un Libro Sobre el Olfato. Abello, Patricia, tr. from ENG. (p. 1)
—¿Qué es un banco? (What Is a Bank?) (p. 1423)
—¿Qué Hay Dentro de Mí? (p. 1423)
—¿Qué Preparamos Hoy? (p. 1424)
Meachen Rau, Dana, jt. auth. see Meachen Rau, Dana.
Meachen Rau, Dana, jt. auth. see Rau, Dana Meachen.
Meachen Rau, Dana & Brown, Jonatha A. Pennsylvania. (p. 1337)
Meachen Rau, Dana & Franco-Feeney, Betsy. All about Me: My Book by Me - My Pinkie Finger - My Special Space. Meachen Rau, Dana et al, illus. (p. 43)
Meachen Rau, Dana & Meachen Rau, Dana. Clothing in American History. (p. 334)
Meachen Rau, Dana & Picture Window Books. Puntos de Luz: Un Libro Sobre las Estrellas. Robledo, Sol, tr. (p. 1417)
Meachen Rau, Dana & Picture Window Books Staff. Altas y Bajas, Blancas y Grises: Un Libro Sobre las Nubes. Robledo, Sol, tr. from ENG. (p. 50)
—Caliente y Brillante: Un Libro Sobre el Sol Robledo, Sol, tr. (p. 253)
—Giran en el Espacio: Un Libro Sobre Los Planetas. Robledo, Sol, tr. from ENG. (p. 678)
—Luz de Noche: Un Libro Sobre la Luna Robledo, Sol, tr. from ENG. (p. 1066)
Meachen Rau, Dana, ed. Conducir! (p. 356)
Meachen-Rau, Dana. Midwest. (p. 1139)
—Neil Armstrong. (p. 1240)
—Rookie Biographies: Dr. Seuss. (p. 1487)
—Rookie Biographies: Dr. Seuss. (p. 1487)
—Southeast. (p. 1617)
—West. (p. 1876)
Mead, Alice. Crossing the Starlight Bridge. (p. 385)
—Junebug. (p. 934)
—Junebug in Trouble. (p. 934)
—Year of No Rain. (p. 1969)
Mead, Andy. Fly Away Home: And Other Caribbean Stories. (p. 609)
Mead, Brian. Creatures of the Deep Coloring Book. (p. 380)
—Monsters of the Ice Age Coloring Book. (p. 1169)
—Spooky Halloween Cut & Color Activity Book. (p. 1631)
Mead, David. Forgetful Little Leprechaun. Sharp, Chris, illus. (p. 619)
—Joy to the World. Sharp, Chris, illus. (p. 930)
—Little Abe Lincoln Learns a Lesson in Honesty: Honesty. Sharp, Chris, illus. (p. 1023)
—Little Ben Franklin Learns a Lesson in Generosity: Generosity. Sharp, Chris, illus. (p. 1024)
—Little George Washington Learns about Responsibility: Responsibility. Sharp, Chris, illus. (p. 1028)
—Little Teddy Roosevelt Learns a Lesson in Courage: Courage. Sharp, Chris, illus. (p. 1037)
—Noah's Babies Colors & Caring. Byers, Brian, illus. (p. 1261)
—Noah's Babies Shapes & Sharing. Byers, Brian, illus. (p. 1261)
—Silent Night. Sharp, Chris, illus. (p. 1575)
Mead, David, jt. auth. see Berry, Ron.
Mead, David & Berry, Ron. Can You Make the Monster Giggle? A Halloween Self-Scare Book! Sharp, Chris, illus. (p. 259)
—Who's at the Door? (p. 1920)
Mead, Emi. Ryan Is Moving Away. (p. 1499)
Mead, Jay. Little Farm Story. (p. 1027)
Mead, Jay H., et al. Slim, Sane, & Sexy: Pocket Guide to Natural, Bioidentical Hormone Balancing. (p. 1590)
Mead, Jean. What religions are in our Neighbourhood? (p. 1893)
Mead, Maggie. Exploring the West: Tales of Courage on the Lewis & Clark Expedition. Jacobsen, Laura, illus. (p. 554)
—Suffrage Sisters: The Fight for Liberty. Feeney, Siri, illus. (p. 1672)
Mead, Margaret R. Christina Aguilera. (p. 312)
Mead, Matthew. Monster Book of Halloween: Hundreds of Spooky Treats & Clever Crfts for the Best Holiday Ever! (p. 1166)
Mead, Purnima. Bibia Meets Gripper. (p. 175)
—Bibia Tells Her Story! (p. 175)
Mead, Purnima & Kerber, Kathy. Bibia, the Butterfly. (p. 175)
Mead, Richelle. Blood Promise. (p. 200)
—Bloodlines. (p. 201)
—Fiery Heart. (p. 584)
—Frostbite. (p. 644)
—Frostbite. Vieceli, Emma, illus. (p. 644)
—Golden Lily. (p. 695)
—Indigo Spell. (p. 872)
—Last Sacrifice. (p. 978)
—Ruby Circle. (p. 1493)
—Shadow Kiss. (p. 1557)
—Shadow Kiss. Vieceli, Emma, illus. (p. 1557)
—Silver Shadows. (p. 1577)
—Spirit Bound. (p. 1628)
—Vampire Academy. (p. 1831)
—Vampire Academy. Vieceli, Emma, illus. (p. 1831)
—Vampire Academy Box Set 1-3 (p. 1831)
Mead, Richelle, jt. auth. see Rowen, Michelle.
Mead, Sue. Monster Trucks & Tractors. (p. 1168)
—Off Road Racing. (p. 1279)
Mead, Tom, illus. see Johnson, Hal.
Mead, Wendy. Alternative Rock Scene: The Stars, the Fans, the Music. (p. 50)
—Judy Blume. (p. 931)
—Kids Top 10 Pet Birds. (p. 955)
—Maurice Sendak. (p. 1110)
—Merchant. (p. 1127)
—Sharon Creech. (p. 1563)
—Top 10 Birds for Kids. (p. 1768)
—William H. Taft. (p. 1933)
Mead, Wendy, jt. auth. see Bennett, Clayton.
Mead, Wendy, jt. auth. see McDaniel, Melissa.
Mead, Wendy, jt. auth. see Stefoff, Rebecca.
Meade, Deborah & National Geographic Learning Staff. Africa. (p. 26)
Meade, Gregory S., illus. see E.C., Nanci.
Meade, Holly. If I Never Forever Endeavor. Meade, Holly, illus. (p. 853)
—John Willy & Freddy Mcgee (p. 923)
Meade, Holly, illus. see Bartoletti, Susan Campbell.
Meade, Holly, illus. see Brenner, Tom.
Meade, Holly, illus. see Chaconas, Dori.
Meade, Holly, illus. see Elliott, David.
Meade, Holly, illus. see Gershator, Phillis.
Meade, Holly, illus. see Heide, Florence Parry & Clief, Sylvia Van.
Meade, Holly, illus. see Heide, Florence Parry.
Meade, Holly, illus. see Ho, Mingfong.
Meade, Holly, illus. see Root, Phyllis.
Meade, Jean McCurdy. Tale of Rebekah Rabbit. Clark, Barbara Hoseman, illus. (p. 1700)
Meade, L. Little Mother to the Others. (p. 1032)
Meade, L. T. Children's Pilgrimage. (p. 304)
—Little Mother to the Others. (p. 1032)
—Modern Tomboy. (p. 1159)
—Palace Beautiful: A Story for Girls. (p. 1319)
—Rebel of the School. (p. 1451)
—Red Rose & Tiger Lily or in a Wider Wo. (p. 1455)
—Sue A Little Heroine. (p. 1672)
Meade, L. T., jt. auth. see Eustace, Robert.
Meade, Marion. Free Woman: The Life & Times of Victoria Woodhull. (p. 634)
Meade, Saci & Nonino, Lila. ABCs for Little Yogis. Meade, Sarah, illus. (p. 4)
Meade, Sarah, illus. see Meade, Saci & Nonino, Lila.
Meade, Starr. Grandpa's Box: Retelling the Biblical Story of Redemption. Van Patter, Bruce, illus. (p. 709)
—Mighty Acts of God: A Family Bible Story Book. O'Connor, Tim, illus. (p. 1139)
—Most Important Thing You'll Ever Study: A Survey of the Bible. (p. 1177)
Meade, Starr, et al. Keeping Holiday. Gerard, Justin, illus. (p. 947)
Meador, Karen. Tiered Activities for Learning Centers. (p. 1748)
Meadow, Amy, illus. see Whimsy.
Meadowbrook Press. Meadowbrook Kids Three Book Back to School Set. (p. 1116)
Meadowbrook Press Staff. I Hope I Don't Strike Out! And Other Funny Sports Poems. Carpenter, Stephen, illus. (p. 839)
—If Kids Ruled the School. Carpenter, Stephen, illus. (p. 853)
Meadowbrook Press Staff, jt. auth. see Lansky, Bruce.
Meadowcroft, Enid Lamonte, ed. see Howard, Joan.
Meadowcroft, Enid Lamonte, ed. see Kaufmann, Helen L.
Meadowcroft, Enid Lamonte, ed. see Kjelgaard, Jim.
Meadowcroft, Enid Lamonte, ed. see Malkus, Alida Sims.
Meadowcroft, Enid Lamonte & Vigilante, Sylvester. We Were There at the Opening of the Erie Canal. McCann, Gerald, illus. (p. 1868)
Meadown, Daisy. Ellie the Guitar Fairy #2. (p. 514)
Meadows, Amy. Emma's American Chinese New Year. (p. 520)
Meadows, Amy Parsons. Elizabeth Grace Quadrapuss Goes to Kindergarten. (p. 513)
—Freddy Meets His Goliath: Book 1 in the Sweet Frog Bible Story Series. (p. 633)
Meadows, Ashten. Heroes Never Die (p. 773)
Meadows, Daisy. Abigail the Breeze Fairy. Ripper, Georgie, illus. (p. 5)
—Addison the April Fool's Day Fairy. (p. 12)
—Adele the Voice Fairy. (p. 12)
—Alexa the Fashion Editor Fairy. (p. 36)
—Alice the Tennis Fairy. (p. 39)
—Ally the Dolphin Fairy. (p. 48)
—Alyssa the Star-Spotter Fairy. (p. 51)
—Amber the Orange Fairy. Ripper, Georgie, illus. (p. 57)
—Amelie the Seal Fairy. (p. 58)
—Amy the Amethyst Fairy. (p. 66)
—Amy the Amethyst Fairy. Ripper, Georgie, illus. (p. 66)
—Annabelle the Drawing Fairy. (p. 85)
—Anya the Cuddly Creatures Fairy. (p. 90)
—Anya the Cuddly Creatures Fairy. (p. 90)
—Ashley the Dragon Fairy. (p. 106)
—Autumn the Falling Leaves Fairy. (p. 118)
—Ava the Sunset Fairy. (p. 118)
—Azafran, el Hada Amarilla. (p. 121)
—Bella Tabbypaw I Trouble. (p. 162)
—Bella Tabbypaw in Trouble. (p. 162)
—Bella the Bunny Fairy. Ripper, Georgie, illus. (p. 162)
—Belle the Birthday Fairy. (p. 163)
—Best Friends in Fairyland. (p. 169)
—Bethany the Ballet Fairy. (p. 171)
—Brianna the Tooth Fairy. (p. 227)
—Brittany the Basketball Fairy. (p. 230)
—Brooke the Photographer Fairy. (p. 230)
—Caitlin the Ice Bear Fairy. (p. 252)
—Cara the Camp Fairy. (p. 265)
—Carrie the Snow Cap Fairy. (p. 271)
—Cassidy the Costume Fairy. (p. 276)
—Cassie the Concert Fairy. (p. 276)
—Chelsea the Congratulations Fairy. (p. 297)
—Cherry the Cake Fairy. (p. 298)
—Cheryl the Christmas Tree Fairy. (p. 298)
—Chloe the Topaz Fairy. (p. 308)
—Chloe the Topaz Fairy. Ripper, Georgie, illus. (p. 308)
—Clara the Chocolate Fairy. (p. 326)
—Claudia the Accessories Fairy: A Rainbow Magic Book. (p. 329)
—Claudia the Accessories Fairy. (p. 329)

—Coco the Cupcake Fairy. (p. 337)
—Complete Book of Fairies. (p. 352)
—Coral the Reef Fairy. (p. 366)
—Courtney the Clownfish Fairy. (p. 373)
—Crystal the Snow Fairy. Ripper, Georgie, illus. (p. 387)
—Danni the Drum Fairy #4. (p. 405)
—Destiny the Rock Star Fairy. (p. 431)
—Earth Fairies #1: Nicole the Beach Fairy. (p. 496)
—Earth Fairies #2: Isabella the Air Fairy. (p. 496)
—Earth Fairies #5: Lily the Rain Forest Fairy. (p. 496)
—Earth Fairies #6: Milly the River Fairy. (p. 496)
—Earth Fairies #7: Carrie the Snow Cap Fairy. (p. 496)
—Edie the Garden Fairy. (p. 504)
—Elisa the Royal Adventure Fairy. (p. 513)
—Ella the Rose Fairy. (p. 514)
—Ellie Featherbill All Alone. (p. 514)
—Ellie the Guitar Fairy. (p. 514)
—Emily the Emerald Fairy. Ripper, Georgie, illus. (p. 519)
—Emily, the Emerald Fairy. Ripper, Georgie, illus. (p. 519)
—Emma the Easter Fairy. (p. 520)
—Erin the Phoenix Fairy. (p. 533)
—Esme the Ice Cream Fairy. (p. 536)
—Eva the Enchanted Ball Fairy. (p. 540)
—Evie the Mist Fairy. Ripper, Georgie, illus. (p. 546)
—Fairies' Birthday Surprise. (p. 563)
—Fairy Ballet. (p. 563)
—Fairy Treasure Hunt. (p. 564)
—Fairyland Costume Ball. (p. 564)
—Fashion Fairies #1: Miranda the Beauty Fairy: A Rainbow Magic Book. (p. 575)
—Fashion Fairies #5: Jennifer the Hairstylist Fairy: A Rainbow Magic Book. (p. 575)
—Fashion Fairies #6: Brooke the Photographer Fairy: A Rainbow Magic Book. (p. 575)
—Fern the Green Fairy. Ripper, Georgie, illus. (p. 582)
—Fiona the Flute Fairy. (p. 589)
—Fiona the Flute Fairy #3. (p. 589)
—Flora the Dress-Up Fairy. (p. 606)
—Florence the Friendship Fairy. (p. 606)
—Frankie the Makeup Fairy. (p. 630)
—Gabriella the Snow Kingdom Fairy. (p. 652)
—Gemma the Gymnastics Fairy. (p. 660)
—Georgia the Guinea Pig Fairy. Ripper, Georgie, illus. (p. 665)
—Goldie the Sunshine Fairy. (p. 696)
—Goldie the Sunshine Fairy. Ripper, Georgie, illus. (p. 696)
—Harriet the Hamster Fairy. Ripper, Georgie, illus. (p. 749)
—Hayley the Rain Fairy. (p. 755)
—Hayley the Rain Fairy. Ripper, Georgie, illus. (p. 755)
—Heather the Violet Fairy. (p. 760)
—Heather the Violet Fairy. Ripper, Georgie, illus. (p. 760)
—Helena the Horse-Riding Fairy. (p. 763)
—Holly the Christmas Fairy. Ripper, Georgie, illus. (p. 789)
—Honey the Candy Fairy. (p. 794)
—Hope the Happiness Fairy. (p. 796)
—India the Moonstone Fairy. (p. 871)
—India the Moonstone Fairy. Ripper, Georgie, illus. (p. 871)
—Inky the Indigo Fairy. Ripper, Georgie, illus. (p. 874)
—Isabella the Air Fairy. (p. 891)
—Isabelle the Ice Dance Fairy. (p. 891)
—Jade the Disco Fairy. (p. 905)
—Jennifer the Hairstylist Fairy. (p. 913)
—Jessica the Jazz Fairy. (p. 914)
—Jessie the Lyrics Fairy. (p. 914)
—Josie the Jewelry Fairy. (p. 927)
—Joy the Summer Vacation Fairy. Ripper, Georgie, illus. (p. 930)
—Juliet the Valentine Fairy. (p. 932)
—Katie the Kitten Fairy. Ripper, Georgie, illus. (p. 945)
—Kayla the Pottery Fairy. (p. 946)
—Keira the Movie Star Fairy. (p. 948)
—Kimberly the Koala Fairy: A Rainbow Magic Book. (p. 957)
—Kimberly the Koala Fairy. (p. 957)
—Kitty the Tiger Fairy: A Rainbow Magic Book. (p. 963)
—Kitty the Tiger Fairy. (p. 963)
—Kylie the Carnival Fairy. Ripper, Georgie, illus. (p. 969)
—Lara the Black Cat Fairy. (p. 975)
—Lauren the Puppy Fairy. Ripper, Georgie, illus. (p. 980)
—Layla the Cotton Candy Fairy. (p. 981)
—Leona the Unicorn Fairy. (p. 992)
—Lexi the Firefly Fairy. (p. 1004)
—Libby the Writing Fairy. (p. 1005)
—Lila & Myla, the Twins Fairies. (p. 1017)
—Lily the Rain Forest Fairy. (p. 1018)
—Lindsay the Luck Fairy. (p. 1019)
—Lisa the Lollipop Fairy. (p. 1022)
—Lizzie the Sweet Treats Fairy. (p. 1043)
—Lola the Fashion Show Fairy. (p. 1045)
—Louise the Lily Fairy. (p. 1058)
—Lucy Longwhiskers Gets Lost. (p. 1063)
—Lucy the Diamond Fairy. Ripper, Georgie, illus. (p. 1063)
—Maddie the Fun & Games Fairy. (p. 1069)
—Madeline the Cookie Fairy. (p. 1070)
—Mae the Panda Fairy: A Rainbow Magic Book. (p. 1070)
—Mae the Panda Fairy. (p. 1070)
—Mara the Meerkat Fairy: A Rainbow Magic Book. (p. 1091)
—Mara the Meerkat Fairy. (p. 1091)
—Maya the Harp Fairy. (p. 1112)
—Maya the Harp Fairy. (p. 1113)
—Maya the Harp Fairy #5. (p. 1113)
—Melodie the Music Fairy. (p. 1125)
—Mia the Bridesmaid Fairy. (p. 1133)
—Miley the Stylist Fairy. (p. 1142)
—Milly the River Fairy. (p. 1144)
—Miranda the Beauty Fairy. (p. 1149)
—Molly the Goldfish Fairy. Ripper, Georgie, illus. (p. 1161)
—Molly Twinkletail Runs Away. (p. 1161)
—Morgan the Midnight Fairy. (p. 1175)
—My Rainbow Magic Birthday Secrets. (p. 1217)
—My Rainbow Magic Friendship Secrets. (p. 1217)
—Natalie the Christmas Stocking Fairy. (p. 1230)
—Nicole the Beach Fairy. (p. 1251)
—Nina the Birthday Cake Fairy. (p. 1256)
—Nora the Arctic Fox Fairy: A Rainbow Magic Book. (p. 1264)
—Nora the Arctic Fox Fairy. (p. 1264)
—Olympia the Games Fairy. (p. 1287)
—Paige the Christmas Play Fairy. (p. 1318)
—Pearl the Cloud Fairy. Ripper, Georgie, illus. (p. 1333)
—Penny the Pony Fairy. (p. 1338)
—Pet Fairies to the Rescue! (p. 1345)
—Pet Parade. (p. 1345)
—Phoebe the Fashion Fairy. (p. 1351)
—Pia the Penguin Fairy. (p. 1354)
—Polly the Party Fun Fairy. (p. 1381)
—Poppy the Piano Fairy #1. (p. 1385)
—Rainbow Fairies. (p. 1435)
—Rainbow Magic Special Edition: Addison the April Fool's Day Fairy. (p. 1435)
—Rainbow Magic Special Edition: Autumn the Falling Leaves Fairy. (p. 1435)
—Rainbow Magic Special Edition: Bailey the Babysitter Fairy. (p. 1435)
—Rainbow Magic Special Edition: Brianna the Tooth Fairy. (p. 1435)
—Rainbow Magic Special Edition: Chelsea the Congratulations Fairy. (p. 1435)
—Rainbow Magic Special Edition: Keira the Movie Star Fairy. (p. 1435)
—Rainbow Magic Special Edition: Lila & Myla the Twins Fairies. (p. 1435)
—Rainbow Magic Special Edition: Lindsay the Luck Fairy. Dynamo Limited Staff, illus. (p. 1435)
—Rainbow Magic Special Edition: Natalie the Christmas Stocking Fairy. (p. 1435)
—Rebecca the Rock 'N Roll Fairy. (p. 1450)
—Rebecca the Rock 'n Roll Fairy. (p. 1450)
—Rihanna the Seahorse Fairy. (p. 1472)
—Rosie the Honey Bear Fairy: A Rainbow Magic Book. (p. 1490)
—Rosie the Honey Bear Fairy. (p. 1490)
—Roxie the Baking Fairy. (p. 1492)
—Ruby the Red Fairy. Ripper, Georgie, illus. (p. 1493)
—Sabrina the Sweet Dreams Fairy. (p. 1500)
—Sadie the Saxophone Fairy. (p. 1501)
—Sadie the Saxophone Fairy #7. (p. 1501)
—Saffron the Yellow Fairy. Ripper, Georgie, illus. (p. 1502)
—Samantha the Swimming Fairy. (p. 1507)
—Savannah the Zebra Fairy: A Rainbow Magic Book. (p. 1516)
—Savannah the Zebra Fairy. (p. 1516)
—Scarlett the Garnet Fairy. (p. 1520)
—Scarlett the Garnet Fairy. Ripper, Georgie, illus. (p. 1520)
—Scholastic Reader Level 2: Rainbow Magic: Pet Fairies to the Rescue! Artful Doodlers Ltd Staff, illus. (p. 1522)
—Scholastic Reader Level 2: Rainbow Magic: Pet Parade. (p. 1522)
—Selena the Sleepover Fairy. (p. 1549)
—Serena the Salsa Fairy. (p. 1552)
—Shannon the Ocean Fairy. (p. 1559)
—Sky the Blue Fairy. Ripper, Georgie, illus. (p. 1587)
—Sophia the Snow Swan Fairy. (p. 1613)
—Sophie the Sapphire Fairy. (p. 1613)
—Stacey the Soccer Fairy. (p. 1638)
—Stella the Star Fairy. Ripper, Georgie, illus. (p. 1647)
—Stephanie the Starfish Fairy. (p. 1648)
—Storm the Lightning Fairy. (p. 1656)
—Storm the Lightning Fairy. Ripper, Georgie, illus. (p. 1656)
—Sunny the Yellow Fairy. Ripper, Georgie, illus. (p. 1677)
—Tasha the Tap Dance Fairy. (p. 1706)
—Tess the Sea Turtle Fairy. (p. 1722)
—Trixie the Halloween Fairy. (p. 1788)
—Tyra the Designer Fairy (p. 1805)
—Tyra the Designer Fairy. (p. 1805)
—Vanessa the Choreography Fairy. (p. 1833)
—Victoria the Violin Fairy #6. (p. 1840)
—Violet the Painting Fairy. (p. 1843)
—Whitney the Whale Fairy. (p. 1914)
—Zadie the Sewing Fairy. (p. 1984)
—Zara the Starlight Fairy. (p. 1985)
—Zoe the Skating Fairy. (p. 1987)
Meadows, Daisy & Scholastic, Inc. Staff. Fairy Friends. Ripper, Georgie, illus. (p. 563)
—Jewel Fairies Collection (p. 917)
Meadows, Foz. Solace & Grief. (p. 1606)
Meadows, James. Slavery: The Struggle for Freedom. (p. 1588)
Meadows, James L. God Speaks to Today's Teenagers. (p. 690)
Meadows, Jodi. Asunder. (p. 109)
—Incarnate. (p. 868)
—Infinite. (p. 873)
—Orphan Queen. (p. 1304)
Meadows, Kelly. Dating Game: Comedy Monologue. (p. 409)
—Dumping Ground: A Ten-Minute Comedy Duet. (p. 490)
—Ghost of a Chance: A One-Act Comedy Play. (p. 671)
—How the West Was Wed: A Full-Length Comedy. (p. 813)
—Not Ready! A Ten-Minute Comedy Monologue. (p. 1267)
—Teen Comedy Playlets: A Collection of Six Skits: Third Time's a Charm (p. 1713)
—Ten Easy Steps to Humiliation: A Ten-Minute Comedy Duet. (p. 1718)
Meadows, Laura LyAn. Adventures with Scruffy: A New Purpose. (p. 25)
—Scruffy's Big Search. (p. 1533)
Meadows, Melissa. What's the Word, Thunderbird? (p. 1900)
—What's the Word, Thunderbird? Book A: the Alamo. (p. 1900)
Meadows, Michelle. Hibernation Station. Cyrus, Kurt, illus. (p. 775)
—Itsy-Bitsy Baby Mouse. Cordell, Matthew, illus. (p. 900)
—Piggies in Pajamas. Hoyt, Ard, illus. (p. 1358)
—Piggies in the Kitchen. Hoyt, Ard, illus. (p. 1358)
—Pilot Pups. Andreasen, Dan, illus. (p. 1359)
—Super Bugs. Mayer, Bill, illus. (p. 1679)
—Traffic Pups. Andreasen, Dan, illus. (p. 1776)
Meadows, Sarah, illus. see Aryal, Aimee Sutter.
Meadows, Thomas. Tales of Tommy Tucker: Pizza Pie Patty! (p. 1703)
—Tales of Tommy Tucker: My Private Parts Are Private! (p. 1703)
—Tales of Tommy Tucker: The Thought That Out Thunk the Thinker! (p. 1703)
Meagher, Ed. D. Zach & His Dog: A Story of Bonding, Love, & Loss for Children & Adults to Share Together. (p. 1984)
Meagher, Susan X. Lies That Bind. (p. 1007)
Meaker, Dennis. Extraordinary New Testament People. (p. 555)
—Following Jesus. (p. 612)
—Jesus, the Christ. (p. 916)
—Radical Jesus. (p. 1432)
Meaker, Marijane, see Kerr, M. E., pseud.
Meaker, Mary. Quinton, Brewster & Chaley. (p. 1428)
Mealer, Bryan, jt. auth. see Kamkwamba, William.
Mealer, Bryan & Kamkwamba, William. Boy Who Harnessed the Wind. Hymas, Anna, illus. (p. 219)
Mealing, Ronald. Adventures in the Lost Kingdom of Radish: A Fantasy for Children & Others. (p. 15)
Mealue, Monique. Johnny Goes Camping. (p. 923)
—Johnny Goes Shopping. (p. 923)
Meaney, Flynn. Bloodthirsty. (p. 201)
—Boy Recession. (p. 218)
Meaney, Roisin. Don't Even Think about It. (p. 467)
Meaney, Roisin, jt. auth. see Curtin, Judi.
Means, A. L. Student's Guide to George Orwell. (p. 1669)
Means, Arloa L. Read-Rhyme-Remember: A Poetic Overview of the Book of Genesis. (p. 1443)
Means, J. D. Millie & Honey: The Incredible, Instantaneous, Interplanetary Adventure - Volume Ii - Appleopolis. (p. 1144)
Means, J. P. Tales from Mean County Morgue. (p. 1701)
Means-Dallas, Anastasia. Fourth Street. (p. 625)
Meany, John. Has the Civil Rights Movement Been Successful? (p. 752)
Meany, John & Shuster, Kate. Speak Out: A Guide to Middle School Debate. (p. 1622)
Mear, Shirley A. Feathers from Heaven. (p. 579)
Mearns, Martha, jt. auth. see Haar, Jaap Ter.
Mearns, Martha, tr. see Ter Haar, Jaap.
Mears, Henrietta C. What Jesus Is All About: Meet the Man Whose Life - & Death - Changed the Course of History. (p. 1891)
Mears, Ray. Northern Wilderness: Bushcraft of the Far North. (p. 1266)
Mears, Richard Chase. Saint Nick & the Space Nicks. Westerfield, William Stephen, illus. (p. 1504)
Measday, Stephen. Send Simon Savage. (p. 1550)
—Send Simon Savage: Return of the Black Death. Sheehan, Peter, illus. (p. 1550)
Mebane, Jeanie. Animal Hibernation (p. 78)
—Animal Migration (p. 78)
—Ice Fishing (p. 850)
—Pheasant Hunting (p. 1350)
Mebane, Jeanie, jt. auth. see Jenson-Elliott, Cindy.
Mebane, Jeanie, et al. Learn about Animal Behavior. (p. 982)
Mebane, Robert C., jt. auth. see Rybolt, Thomas R.
Mebane-Walker, Vinita. Shareeka's Life. (p. 1561)
Mebberson, Amy, illus. see Benjamin, Paul & Rosa, Don.
Mebberson, Amy, illus. see Benjamin, Paul.
Mebberson, Amy, illus. see Langridge, Roger.
Mebberson, Amy, illus. see Randolph, Grace & Barks, Carl.
Mebberson, Amy, illus. see Randolph, Grace.
Mebberson, Amy, illus. see Storck, Patrick.
Mebus, Scott. Gods of Manhattan (p. 691)
—Sorcerer's Secret (p. 1614)
—Spirits in the Park. (p. 1629)
Mecca, Judy T. Plays for Reading Success. (p. 1373)
—Red, White, & You: Patriotic Plays to Develop Reading & Language Skills. (p. 1455)
Meccia, Marc. Wendell Starling: The Story of a Bird Who Was Afraid to Fly. (p. 1875)
Mecham, Janeal A. Christmas Gifts. Mecham, Janeal A., illus. (p. 314)
Mechanech Publications Staff. Writing Better with Every Letter: My Handwriting Practice Book. (p. 1964)
Mechling, Lauren & Moser, Laura. All Q, No A: More Tales of a 10th-Grade Social Climber. (p. 45)
—Foreign Exposure: The Social Climber Abroad. (p. 617)
Mechling, Lauren, et al. Rise & Fall of a 10th Grade Social Climber. (p. 1474)
Meckel, Jamie. Down at the Beach. (p. 474)
Meckenstock, Shay, jt. auth. see Jamison, Heather.
Meckler, Linda. Ghost Kids Trilogy. (p. 671)
Meckley, Phyllis. Free Puppies. (p. 634)
Meconis, Dylan, illus. see Fontes, Justine & Fontes, Ron.
Meconni, Beppe, illus. see Brignole, Giancarla, tr.
Mecozzi, Maureen. Uncanny Can. (p. 1811)
Mecum, Shelly & Chun, Peggy. Watercolor Cat. (p. 1863)
Medcalf, Carol & Hempstock, Becky. Letts Monster Practice e Counting Age 3-5. (p. 1003)
—Letts Monster Practice e Numbers Age 3-5. (p. 1003)
—Letts Monster Practice e Starting School Age 4-5. (p. 1003)
—Letts Monster Skills Practice e Alphabet Age 3-5. (p. 1003)
—Letts Monster Skills Practice e Writing Age 3-5. (p. 1003)
Meddaugh, Susan. Campfire Stories. (p. 257)
—Canine Comics: Six Daring Doggie Adventures. (p. 261)
—Detective Dog. (p. 431)
—Farm Dog Martha. (p. 574)
—Fireworks for All. (p. 592)
—Fireworks for All/Fuegos Artificiales para Todos. (p. 592)
—Football Fumble. (p. 615)
—Funny Bone Jokes & Riddles. (p. 649)
—Good Luck, Martha. (p. 698)
—Haunted House. (p. 753)
—Leader of the Pack. (p. 981)
—Martha & Skits. (p. 1097)
—Martha & Skits Out West. (p. 1097)
—Martha Bakes a Cake. (p. 1097)
—Martha Bakes a Cake (Martha Hornea un Pastel) (p. 1097)
—Martha Camps Out. (p. 1097)
—Martha Camps Out (Martha Va de Campamento) (p. 1097)
—Martha Go, Go, Goes Green! (p. 1097)
—Martha on the Case. (p. 1097)
—Martha Says It with Flowers. (p. 1097)
—Martha Speaks: Campfire Stories (Chapter Book) (p. 1097)
—Martha Speaks: Detective Dog (Chapter Book) (p. 1097)
—Martha Speaks: Football Fumble (Reader) (p. 1097)
—Martha Speaks: Funny Bone Jokes & Riddles. (p. 1097)
—Martha Speaks: Good Luck, Martha! (Reader) (p. 1097)
—Martha Speaks: Martha Go, Go, Goes Green! (Reader) (p. 1097)
—Martha Speaks: Martha Stinks! (Reader) (p. 1097)
—Martha Speaks: Martha's Nose for News (chapter Book) (p. 1097)
—Martha Speaks: Secret Agent Dog (Chapter Book) (p. 1097)
—Martha Speaks: So You Want to Be a Dog? (Chapter Book) (p. 1097)
—Martha Speaks Story Time Collection: Special 20th Anniversary Edition. (p. 1097)
—Martha Speaks: Thanksgiving Reunion (Chapter Book) (p. 1097)
—Martha Stinks! (p. 1097)
—Martha Walks the Dog. (p. 1097)
—Meet Martha. (p. 1121)
—Nose for News. (p. 1266)
—Perfectly Martha. (p. 1342)
—Perritos en Invierno. (p. 1343)
—Play Ball! (p. 1371)
—Pool Party. (p. 1383)
—Puppy Dog Tales Collection. (p. 1418)
—Pup's Tale. (p. 1418)
—Purrfect Friends. (p. 1419)
—Secret Agent Dog. (p. 1540)
—Shelter Dog Blues. (p. 1565)
—Show Must Go On. (p. 1570)
—Sniffing for Clues Collection. (p. 1597)
—So You Want to Be a Dog? (p. 1602)
—Space Dogs. (p. 1619)
—Summer Fun (p. 1674)
—Teacher's Pet. (p. 1709)
—Thanksgiving Reunion. (p. 1726)
—Thief of Hearts. (p. 1732)
—Toy Trouble. (p. 1774)
—White House Dog. (p. 1913)
—Winter's Tail. (p. 1938)
—Witches' Supermarket. (p. 1941)
Meddaugh, Susan, illus. see Bunting, Eve.
Meddaugh, Susan, illus. see Wojciechowski, Susan.
Meddemmen, John, tr. see Milne, A. A.
Medders, James. Tooth Fairy's Quest. Hardin, Teresa, illus. (p. 1768)
Meddour, Wendy. Black Cat Detectives. (p. 195)
—Hen in the Wardrobe. (p. 767)
Medearis, Angela Shelf. Best Friends Forever? Papp, Robert, illus. (p. 169)
—Coretta Scott King: Dare to Dream. Rich, Anna, illus. (p. 367)
—Ethnic Vegetarian: Traditional & Modern Recipes from Africa, America, & the Caribbean. (p. 539)
—Lucy's Quiet Book. Ernst, Lisa Campbell, illus. (p. 1063)
—Singing for Dr. King. Hu, Ying-Hwa & Van Wright, Cornelius, illus. (p. 1579)
Medearis, Angela Shelf, jt. auth. see Medearis, Michael.
Medearis, Angela Shelf, jt. auth. see Scholastic, Inc. Staff.
Medearis, Mary. Big Doc's Girl. (p. 181)
Medearis, Michael & Medearis, Angela Shelf. Daisy & the Doll. Johnson, Larry, illus. (p. 400)
Medeiros, Giovana, illus. see Chronicle Books Staff.
Medeiros, J. de. Touch. (p. 1772)
Medeiros, Jamie. Perfect Patty. (p. 1342)
Medeiros, Jennifer, illus. see Greber, Barbara.
Medendorp, Donna & Medendorp, Nick. Keeping CHRIST in Christmas for Kids. (p. 947)
—Keeping CHRIST in Easter for Kids. (p. 947)
Medendorp, Nick, jt. auth. see Medendorp, Donna.
Medernach, T. K. On the High Seas. (p. 1290)
Mederos, Miriam. Vidas Desesperadas. Hernández, René Mario, illus. (p. 1841)
Media Books Staff. Bible Experience Companion Bible (p. 175)
Media, Cont. Animal Kingdom: The World of Mammals. (p. 78)
—Cosmos. (p. 368)
—Dinosaurs. (p. 443)
—Earth. (p. 495)
—Greatest Inventions. (p. 720)
—Human Body. (p. 825)
—Inventions. (p. 884)
—Knights & Castles. (p. 964)
—Our Body. (p. 1308)
—Our Earth. (p. 1308)
—Sun Moon Stars. (p. 1676)
Media Projects, Inc., Staff. Almanac of Asian American History (p. 48)
—Life & Times in Twentieth Century America: Promise & Change, 1981-2000 (p. 1007)
—Student Almanac of Hispanic American History (p. 1669)
—Student Almanac of Native American History (p. 1669)
Media Projects, Inc., Staff, contrib. by. Student Almanac of African American History (p. 1669)
Media Staff, jt. auth. see Jungle Factor Staff.
Media Write, ed. see Avista Products.
Median, Jane, jt. auth. see Medina, Jane.
Medina, Candace, tr. see Holaves, Chris.
Medina, Conni. Haz Papel Picado. (p. 756)
—Haz un Dragón del Año Nuevo Chino. (p. 756)
—Haz un Muñequito de Jengibre. (p. 756)
—Make a Chinese New Year Dragon. (p. 1078)
—Make a Gingerbread Man. (p. 1078)
—Make Papel Picado. (p. 1079)
Medina, Conni, ed. see Bradley, Timothy.
Medina, Cuauhtemoc, et al, contrib. by. Francis Alÿs. (p. 627)
Medina, F. Xavier. Food Culture in Spain (p. 613)
Medina, Hector, illus. see Rendon, Gilberto.
Medina, Jamie B. Juan Carlos & the Hairy-Chested Chili Pepper. (p. 930)
Medina, Jane. Tomás Rivera. Martinez, Edward, illus. (p. 1764)
Medina, Jane & Median, Jane. Dream on Blanca's Wall: Poems in English & Spanish. Casilla, Robert, illus. (p. 483)

M

Medina, Joe. Toberman Street: A Hypothetic Statistic Tale: Based on True Events. (p. 1760)
Medina, Juana, illus. see Cronin, Doreen.
Medina, Kathleen. Born into Greyworld. (p. 214)
Medina, Lan, et al. Minimum Carnage. (p. 1147)
Medina, Larry. Adventures of Peek a Boo the Sea Lion. (p. 21)
Medina, Loreta M., ed. Euthanasia. (p. 540)
Medina, Mariana & Wooten, Sara McIntosh. Frida Kahlo: Self-Portrait Artist. (p. 637)
Medina, Meg. Girl Who Could Silence the Wind. (p. 679)
—Mango, Abuela, & Me. Dominguez, Angela, illus. (p. 1087)
—Mango, Abuela y Yo. Dominguez, Angela, illus. (p. 1087)
—Tía Isa Quiere un Carro. (p. 1746)
—Tía Isa Quiere un Carro. Munoz, Claudio, illus. (p. 1746)
—Tía Isa Quiere un Carro. Munzo, Claudio, illus. (p. 1746)
—Tía Isa Wants a Car. Muñoz, Claudio, illus. (p. 1746)
—Yaqui Delgado Wants to Kick Your Ass. (p. 1968)
Medina, Myra M., jt. auth. see Benz, Cheryl.
Medina, Nico. Fat Hoochie Prom Queen. (p. 577)
—Straight Road to Kylie. (p. 1664)
—Where Is Mount Everest? (p. 1908)
—Where Is Mount Everest? Hinderliter, John & Groff, David, illus. (p. 1908)
—Who Was Genghis Khan? (p. 1918)
—Who Was Genghis Khan? Thomson, Andrew & Harrison, Nancy, illus. (p. 1918)
—Who Was Julius Caesar? (p. 1918)
—Who Was Julius Caesar? Foley, Tim, illus. (p. 1918)
Medina, Nico & Merrell, Billy. Go Ahead, Ask Me. (p. 686)
Medina, Nico & Putra, Dede. Who Was Jacques Cousteau? (p. 1918)
—Who Was Jacques Cousteau? Harrison, Nancy, illus. (p. 1918)
Medina, Paco. X-Men: First to Last. (p. 1967)
Medina, Paco, illus. see Gischler, Victor.
Medina, Paco, jt. auth. see Way, Daniel.
Medina, Paco & Barberi, Carlo. Nova - Rookie Season (p. 1268)
Medina, Phil. Homework Helpers: Earth Science. (p. 794)
Medina, Sarah. Angry Brooker, Jo, illus. (p. 75)
—Brave Brooker, Jo, illus. (p. 223)
—Day to Remember. Brecknell, Annie, illus. (p. 414)
—Graphing Habitats. (p. 711)
—Graphing Water. (p. 711)
—Having Fun with Collage. (p. 755)
—Having Fun with Paint. (p. 755)
—Having Fun with Paper. (p. 755)
—Having Fun with Printing. (p. 755)
—Having Fun with Sculpture. (p. 755)
—Having Fun with Textiles. (p. 755)
—Jealous (Al Gheera) Mohamed Mahmoud, Ghada, tr. (p. 911)
—Know the Facts about Drugs. (p. 965)
—Know the Facts about Relationships. (p. 965)
—Lonely Brooker, Jo, illus. (p. 1046)
—Proud Brooker, Jo, illus. (p. 1412)
—Proud (Fakhr) Mohamed Mahmoud, Ghada, tr. (p. 1412)
—Sad (Al Hozn) Mahmoud, Ghada Mohamed, tr. (p. 1501)
—Worried Brooker, Jo, illus. (p. 1961)
Medina, Sarah & Brooker, Jo. Bondad Brooker, Jo, illus. (p. 208)
—Celos Brooker, Jo, illus. (p. 286)
—Enojo Brooker, Jo, illus. (p. 530)
—Felicidad Brooker, Jo, illus. (p. 581)
—Impaciencia Brooker, Jo, illus. (p. 862)
—Preocupación. Brooker, Jo, illus. (p. 1395)
—Soledad Brooker, Jo, illus. (p. 1607)
—Timidez Brooker, Jo, illus. (p. 1754)
—Tristeza Brooker, Jo, illus. (p. 1787)
—Valentía Brooker, Jo, illus. (p. 1830)
—Vergüenza (p. 1837)
Medina, Sylvia M., jt. auth. see Ballock-Dixon, Saige J.
Medina, Sylvia M. & B alloxk-Dixon, Saige J. Gorilla's Roar. Eagle, Joy, illus. (p. 703)
Medina, Sylvia M. & Ballock-Dixon, Saige J. Desert Mirage. Eagle, Joy, illus. (p. 429)
—Green Springs Junior. Eagle, Joy, illus. (p. 722)
—Jade Elephant. Eagle, Joy, illus. (p. 905)
Medina, Tony. I & I: Bob Marley. Watson, Jesse Joshua, illus. (p. 834)
—Just Us. (p. 940)
—Love to Langston Christie, R., illus. (p. 1060)
—Love to Langston. Christie, R. Gregory, illus. (p. 1060)
Medina, Tony & Watson, Jesse Joshua. I & I Bob Marley (p. 834)
Medina, Zenaides A., Jr., jt. auth. see Marchesani, Laura.
Medlen, Donnie. Spirit Eyes. (p. 1628)
Medlen, Ellen. Voice for Joey. (p. 1847)
Medler, John, Jr. Mommy Mole. Wagoner, Kim, illus. (p. 1162)
Medley, Shari. Adventure of a Lifetime! LaGrange, Tiffany, illus. (p. 14)
Medlicott, Mary. Open Secret. (p. 1299)
Medlock-Adams, Michelle. Counting Cows. Meyers, Mark, illus. (p. 371)
Medlyn, Lynda Lee & Staudenmier, Kelley Anne. Best Belcher. Parish, Shannon, illus. (p. 168)
Medoff, Francine. Mouse in the Matzah Factory. Bosch, Nicole in den, illus. (p. 1182)
Medolla, Adele. Sex, Obsession & Murder. (p. 1556)
Medoza, Chris, jt. auth. see Lucas, Ian.
Medsker, Lynne. Zendala Coloring Book. (p. 1986)
Medvic, Stephen K., ed. see Herrnson, Paul S., et al.
Medway, Geri. Watercolor (p. 1863)
MEE (Minoru Tachikawa). Hyper Police MEE (Minoru Tachikawa), illus. (p. 831)
Meed, Douglas V. Comanche 1800-74. Smith, Jonathan, illus. (p. 346)
Meegan, Britta. Farming Then & Now. (p. 574)
Meehan, Kelly. Star Named Symphony. (p. 1640)
Meehan, Laura, ed. March in Line, Please. (p. 1091)
Meehan, Patricia, illus. see Emerick, Yahiya.
Meehan, Patrick, jt. auth. see Spratt, Niall.
Meehan, Patrick & Spratt, Niall. Shamrogues: Second Challenge. (p. 1559)
Meehan, Thomas. Annie. (p. 86)
—Annie. Kath, Katie, illus. (p. 86)
Meehan, William. Amulets of Acacia. (p. 66)
—Fife. (p. 584)
Meehl, Brian. Suck It Up. (p. 1672)
Meehl, Debra & Meehl, Mark. Family & Friends Bipolar Sussival Guide: Survive Today, Thrive Tomorrow. (p. 568)
Meehl, Mark, jt. auth. see Meehl, Debra.
Meek, Carol. Believer Boy's Power. (p. 162)
Meek, Elin. Creu Brawddegau. Howells, Graham, illus. (p. 382)
Meek, H. A. Synagogue. Weinreb, Matthew, photos by. (p. 1693)
Meek, Janis P. & Kopan, Alice Orphanos. Food for Today Student Workbook. (p. 613)
Meek, Jeffrey/K. Nimble the Thimble Mouse Dungey, Thomas, illus. (p. 1255)
Meek, Nora. Sniffing for Democracy. (p. 1597)
Meek, S. P. Pagan: A Border Patrol Horse. (p. 1317)
—Surfman: The Adventures of A Coast Guard Dog. (p. 1685)
Meekins, Evan. Black Banner. (p. 195)
Meeks, Arone Raymond. Enora & the Black Crane. Meeks, Arone Raymond, illus. (p. 530)
Meeks, Connor. Sports! Have Fun & Stay Healthy. (p. 1632)
Meeks, Elizbiff. Without Millard's Wings. (p. 1942)
Meeks, Jane. Finding Home. (p. 588)
Meeks, John R. Dugan's Magical Island. (p. 489)
Meeks, Linda, et al. Health & Wellness. (p. 757)
Meens, Estelle. Boss No More. (p. 215)
Meer, Pippa Lee. Matilda's Marvellous Monday. (p. 1109)
Meerbott, Otto. My Six Years at St. Al's. (p. 1218)
Meers, Whitney & Nash, Kevin. University of South Florida College Prowler off the Record. (p. 1821)
Meese, Ruth Lyn. Family Matters: Adoption & Foster Care in Children's Literature (p. 568)
Meeter, Brian. Golden Mullet. (p. 695)
Meeuwissen, Tony. Remarkable Animals: 1000 Amazing Amalgamations. (p. 1458)
Mefford, David. How to Make A Friend in Three Days or Less. (p. 820)
Meg. Adventures of Meg: Wiggles Learns about Making Good Choices. (p. 20)
Meg Belviso, jt. auth. see Pollack, Pam.
Meg, Magic. Fairyspotters Guide. Loveheart, Lucy & Clibbon, Lucy, illus. (p. 565)
Meg, Meg, jt. auth. see Alcott, Louisa May.
Meg, Merry, jt. auth. see Clibbon, Meg.
Meg, Mighty, jt. auth. see Clibbon, Meg.
Megahan, John, illus. see Smith, Marie & Smith, Roland.
Megale, Marina, illus. see Boelts, Maribeth & Boelts, Darwin.
Megan, Lappi. Mount Everest: The Highest Mountain in the World. (p. 1180)
Meganck, Glenn. After the Fall. (p. 28)
Meganck, Robert, illus. see Shaskan, Trisha Speed.
Megarry, Tim, jt. auth. see Levine, Ellen.
Megenhardt, Bill, illus. see Bigalow, Stephen W.
Megenhardt, Bill, illus. see Wright, Mary H.
Megerdichian, Janet. Pine Needle Pedro. Adams, Allysa, illus. (p. 1359)
Megill, Colin & Davis, Cristine. University of Connecticut College Prowler off the Record. (p. 1820)
Mehing, Carl. Before the Dinosaurs. (p. 158)
—Giant Meat-Eating Dinosaurs. (p. 673)
—Prehistoric Creatures of the Sea & Skies. (p. 1395)
—Prehistoric Mammals. (p. 1395)
—Small & Deadly Dinosaurs. (p. 1591)
Mehl, Ron, et al. Who Did It? Taylor, Jeannie St. John & St. John Taylor, Jeannie, illus. (p. 1915)
Mehler, Ed. Scrawny Little Tree. Pollard, Susie, illus. (p. 1532)
Mehlhaff, Christine. Don't Talk to Strangers. Ember, Kathi, illus. (p. 468)
Mehling, Carl. Armored Dinosaurs. (p. 100)
—Giant Plant-Eating Dinosaurs. (p. 674)
—Horned, Spiked, & Crested Dinosaurs. (p. 798)
Mehling, Carl, ed. Armored Dinosaurs. (p. 100)
—Giant Plant-Eating Dinosaurs. (p. 674)
—Horned, Spiked, & Crested Dinosaurs. (p. 798)
Mehling, Randi. Great Extinctions of the Past. (p. 715)
—Hallucinogens. (p. 739)
—Weather, & How It Works. (p. 1869)
Mehlman, Barbara. Safety: Preventing Accidents & Injuries. (p. 1502)
Mehnert, Robert. Spelunkers. (p. 1625)
Mehr, Bethany. Adventures of Reggie Elder & the Sourc. (p. 22)
Mehra, Heather & McManama, Kerry. Peanut-Free Tea for Three. Kline, Michael, illus. (p. 1332)
Mehrlich, Cynthia, illus. see Mehrlich III, Ferdinand Paul.
Mehrlich III, Ferdinand Paul. Splugworth Saves the Day Mehrlich, Cynthia, illus. (p. 1630)
Mehta, Anurag & Prajapati, Rajesh. India after Independence: For Children. (p. 871)
Mehta, Baldev. I Like Spiders. (p. 841)
Mehta, Lila. Anklet for a Princess: A Cinderella Story from India. Tang, Youshan, illus. (p. 84)
Mehta, Poonam V. A-B-C in Action. Kurup, Prakash, illus. (p. 1)
Mehta, Sangeeta, ed. see Sanchez, Alex.
Mehta, Shyam. Stories for Children. (p. 1654)
Mehta, Sonia, jt. auth. see Fox, Tim.
Mehta, Sonia, jt. auth. see Powell, Michael.
Mehta, Sonia, jt. auth. see Roberts, Jane.
Mehta, Sonia, jt. auth. see Stanbury, Sarah.
Mehta-Jones, Shilpa. Earthquake Alert! (p. 497)
—Life in Ancient Mesopotamia. (p. 1010)
—Life in Ancient Rome. (p. 1010)
Mei, Michael. Goofy Gourmet: Let's Cook Today! (p. 702)
Meidav, Edie. Crawl Space. (p. 377)
Meidell, Sherry, illus. see Gibbons, Faye.
Meier, Joanne. Airplane Daydream. Ostrom, Bob, illus. (p. 31)
—Best Mates on the Boat. Ostrom, Bob, illus. (p. 170)
—Carrie's Surprise: The Sound of Hard C. Ostrom, Bob, illus. (p. 271)
—Dan's Darn Dog: The Sound of D. Ostrom, Bob, illus. (p. 406)
—Fire Truck Adventure. Ostrom, Bob, illus. (p. 591)
—Fran & Fay Find a Bird: The Sound of F. Ostrom, Bob, illus. (p. 627)
—Gary Gets a Gift: The Sound of Hard G. Ostrom, Bob, illus. (p. 657)
—Gina & the Magic Bear: The Sound of Soft G. Ostrom, Bob, illus. (p. 676)
—Holly & Hank's Snow Holiday: The Sound of H. Ostrom, Bob, illus. (p. 789)
—Home Run. Ostrom, Bob, illus. (p. 792)
—It's Time to Listen. Ostrom, Bob, illus. (p. 899)
—Lilly's Lost Lunch: The Sound of L. Ostrom, Bob, illus. (p. 1017)
—Max & the Mail: The Sound of M. Ostrom, Bob, illus. (p. 1110)
—Pam's Trip to the Park: The Sound of P. Ostrom, Bob, illus. (p. 1320)
—Purple Paint Everywhere! Ostrom, Bob, illus. (p. 1419)
—Soccer Game. Ostrom, Bob, illus. (p. 1603)
—Taking Turns. Ostrom, Bob, illus. (p. 1698)
—Wendy & the Dog Wash: The Sound of W. Ostrom, Bob, illus. (p. 1875)
Meier, Joanne D., jt. auth. see Minden, Cecilia.
Meier, Joanne D. & Minden, Cecilia. Aquarium Adventure. Ostrom, Bob, illus. (p. 94)
—Energy Expert at Home. Ostrom, Bob, illus. (p. 528)
—Every Drop Helps! Ostrom, Bob, illus. (p. 542)
—Hospital Helper. Ostrom, Bob, illus. (p. 801)
—Make-Believe Store. Ostrom, Bob, illus. (p. 1079)
—Nice Clean Park. Ostrom, Bob, illus. (p. 1250)
—Prepare for Blastoff! Ostrom, Bob, illus. (p. 1396)
—Teamwork at Lotsaluck Camp: A Storytime Book. Ostrom, Bob, illus. (p. 1711)
Meier, Kerry L., illus. see Howard-Parinam, Pam.
Meier, Kerry L., illus. see Jarrell, Pamela R.
Meier, Kerry L., illus. see Muench-Williams, Heather.
Meier, Kerry L., illus. see Vonthron, Satanta C.
Meier, Paul, illus. see Alsbrooks, Stephanie.
Meier, Paul, illus. see Hansen, Eric.
Meier, Paul, illus. see Parra, Jen.
Meier, Paul, illus. see Pope, Amy.
Meier, Ty, illus. see Ruby, Anne.
Meierhenry, Mark & Volk, David. Mystery of the Pheasants. Turnbull, Susan, illus. (p. 1226)
Meierhenry, Mark V. & Volk, David. Mystery of the Maize. Two Bulls, Marty Grant, illus. (p. 1225)
—Mystery of the Round Rocks. Folkerts, Jason, illus. (p. 1226)
—Mystery of the Tree Rings. Folkerts, Jason, illus. (p. 1226)
Meierhofer, Brian, illus. see Knoch, Frank.
Meiers, Drew. Fearful Little Flag. (p. 579)
Meighan, Julie. Drama Start Two Drama Activities & Plays for Children. (p. 480)
—Stage Start 20 Plays for Children. (p. 1638)
Meigs, Cornelia. Invincible Louisa. (p. 885)
Meigs, Cornelia & Holm, Jennifer L. Swift Rivers. Orr, Forrest W., illus. (p. 1690)
Meigs, Elizabeth Bleecker. White Winter: A Story of Scarlet Hill. Chapman, Frederick T., illus. (p. 1913)
Meijer, Fik. Gladiators: History's Most Deadly Sport. Waters, Liz, tr. (p. 682)
Meijer, Marja, illus. see De Smet, Marian.
Meijer, Marja, jt. auth. see De Smet, Marian.
Meil, Gabriel & Rylander, Emily. Goodbye Earth Hello Moon. (p. 700)
Meilichson, Alex, illus. see Bloom, Daniel Halevi.
Meiliken, Jeffrey. Genesis Prayer: The Ancient Secret That Can Grant You Miracles. (p. 660)
Meinderts, Koos. In Our Street. Fienieg, Annette, illus. (p. 864)
—Man in the Clouds. Fienieg, Annette, illus. (p. 1085)
Meiners, Cheri J. Accept & Value Each Person. Johnson, Meredith, illus. (p. 8)
—Be Careful & Stay Safe. Johnson, Meredith, illus. (p. 148)
—Be Honest & Tell the Truth. Johnson, Meredith, illus. (p. 148)
—Be Polite & Kind. (p. 149)
—Be Positive! Allen, Elizabeth, illus. (p. 149)
—Bounce Back! Allen, Elizabeth, illus. (p. 216)
—Cool down & Work Through Anger. (p. 363)
—Cool down & Work Through Anger/Cálmate y Supera la Ira. (p. 363)
—Feel Confident! Allen, Elizabeth, illus. (p. 580)
—Forgive & Let Go! A Book about Forgiveness. Allen, Elizabeth, illus. (p. 619)
—Join in & Play. (p. 924)
—Know & Follow Rules. Johnson, Meredith, illus. (p. 965)
—Learning to Get along Series Interactive Software. Johnson, Meredith, illus. (p. 986)
—Listen & Learn. (p. 1022)
—Reach Out & Give. Johnson, Meredith, illus. (p. 1442)
—Respect & Take Care of Things. (p. 1463)
—Respect & Take Care of Things. Johnson, Meredith, illus. (p. 1463)
—Share & Take Turns. (p. 1561)
—Share & Take Turns. Johnson, Meredith, illus. (p. 1561)
—Share & Take Turns/Comparte y Turna. (p. 1561)
—Stand Tall! A Book about Integrity. Allen, Elizabeth, illus. (p. 1639)
—Talk & Work It Out. Johnson, Meredith, illus. (p. 1703)
—Talk & Work It Out / Hablar y Resolver. Johnson, Meredith, illus. (p. 1703)
—Try & Stick with It. Johnson, Meredith, illus. (p. 1794)
—Understand & Care. (p. 1815)
—When I Feel Afraid. (p. 1902)
Meiners, Cheri J. & Allen, Elizabeth. Have Courage! (p. 754)
Meinke, Amanda & Stegmann, Lisa. Lewis & Clark Famous Faces. Adams Marks, Elizabeth, illus. (p. 1004)
Meinking, Mary. Cash Crop to Cash Cow: The History of Tobacco & Smoking in America. (p. 276)
—Crocodile vs. Wildebeest (p. 384)
—Demi Lovato. (p. 425)
—Development of U. S. Industry. (p. 432)
—Development of U.S. Industry. (p. 432)
—Dingoes. (p. 440)
—Dolphin vs. Fish (p. 464)
—Easy Origami (p. 500)
—Gray Wolves. (p. 713)
—Lion vs. Gazelle (p. 1020)
—Machu Picchu. (p. 1068)
—Not-Quite-So-Easy Origami (p. 1267)
—Owl vs. Mouse (p. 1315)
—Polar Bear vs. Seal (p. 1379)
—Predator vs. Prey (p. 1394)
—Shark vs. Penguin (p. 1562)
—Stylish Shoes for the Crafty Fashionista (p. 1670)
—Tarantula vs. Bird (p. 1706)
—What's Great about Colorado? (p. 1897)
—What's Great about Florida? (p. 1897)
—What's Great about Hawaii? (p. 1897)
—What's Great about New Jersey? (p. 1897)
—What's Great about South Dakota? (p. 1897)
—What's Great about Washington? (p. 1897)
—Wolf vs. Elk (p. 1944)
Meinking, Mary, jt. auth. see Chambers, Mary.
Meinking, Mary, jt. auth. see Schwartz, Heather E.
Meinking, Mary & Alexander, Chris. Easy Origami: A Step-by-Step Guide for Kids. (p. 500)
Meinking, Mary & Peschke, Marci. Kylie Jean Pirate Craft Queen Mourning, Tuesday, illus. (p. 969)
—Kylie Jean Rodeo Craft Queen Mourning, Tuesday, illus. (p. 969)
Meintjes, Chris. Angel's Flight. (p. 75)
Meirink, Tineke, illus. see Winters, Pierre.
Meirion, Dafydd, et al. Anturio ar Ynys Mon: Sawl Taith Stori i Ti ac i'r Teulu. (p. 90)
Meirose, James. Marcia. (p. 1092)
Meisel, Abigail. Depression & Bipolar Disorder: Examining Chemical Imbalances & Mood Disorders. (p. 427)
—Investigating Depression & Bipolar Disorder: Real Facts for Real Lives. (p. 884)
Meisel, Abigail, et al. Investigating Eating Disorders (Anorexia, Bulimia, & Binge Eating) Real Facts for Real Lives. (p. 884)
Meisel, James H. Counterrevolution: How Revolutions Die. (p. 370)
Meisel, Paul. See Me Dig. Meisel, Paul, illus. (p. 1546)
—See Me Run. Meisel, Paul, illus. (p. 1546)
Meisel, Paul, illus. see Bateman, Teresa.
Meisel, Paul, illus. see Bell, Karen Magnuson.
Meisel, Paul, illus. see Bennett, Kelly.
Meisel, Paul, illus. see Bradley, Kimberly Brubaker.
Meisel, Paul, illus. see Brunelle, Lynn.
Meisel, Paul, illus. see Capucilli, Alyssa Satin.
Meisel, Paul, illus. see Cox, Judy.
Meisel, Paul, illus. see Cushman, Jean, et al.
Meisel, Paul, illus. see Duval, Kathy.
Meisel, Paul, illus. see Elliott, David.
Meisel, Paul, illus. see George, Jean Craighead.
Meisel, Paul, illus. see Guest, Elissa Haden.
Meisel, Paul, illus. see Hennessy, B. G.
Meisel, Paul, illus. see Keenan, Sheila.
Meisel, Paul, illus. see Kimmelman, Leslie.
Meisel, Paul, illus. see Martin, Bill, Jr. & Sampson, Michael.
Meisel, Paul, illus. see Miller, J. Philip & Greene, Sheppard M.
Meisel, Paul, illus. see Nodset, Joan L.
Meisel, Paul, illus. see Pfeffer, Wendy.
Meisel, Paul, illus. see Regan, Dian Curtis.
Meisel, Paul, illus. see Rockwell, Anne F.
Meisel, Paul, illus. see Rockwell, Anne F. & Rockwell.
Meisel, Paul, illus. see Rosenberg, Madelyn.
Meisel, Paul, illus. see Ross, Michael Elsohn.
Meisel, Paul, illus. see Schaefer, Lola M.
Meisel, Paul, illus. see Shields, Carol Diggory.
Meisel, Paul, illus. see Sullivan, Sarah.
Meisel, Paul, illus. see Thomas, Shelley Moore.
Meisel, Paul, illus. see Ward, D. J.
Meisel, Paul, illus. see Zoehfeld, Kathleen Weidner.
Meisel, Paul, tr. see Bell, Karen Magnuson.
Meisels, Dovid. Bar Mitzvah & Tefillin Secrets: The Mysteries Revealed. (p. 137)
—Shabbos Secrets: The Mysteries Revealed. (p. 1556)
Meisgeier, Charles H., jt. auth. see Coombs-Richardson, Rita.
Meislin, Barbara. No One Can Ever Steal Your Rainbow. Webber, Helen, illus. (p. 1259)
Meissner, Amy, illus. see Cassidy, Sara.
Meissner, Amy, illus. see Citra, Becky.
Meissner, Amy, illus. see Gaetz, Dayle Campbell.
Meissner, Amy, illus. see Gilmore, Rachna.
Meissner, Amy, illus. see Peterson, Lois.
Meissner, Amy, illus. see Springer, Susan Woodward.
Meissner, Amy, illus. see Walters, Eric.
Meissner, David. Habitat Rescue: Set Of 6. (p. 734)
—Habitat Rescue & Rescate del Hábitat: 6 English, 6 Spanish Adaptations. (p. 734)
—Lost City of the Inca. Leon, Karen, illus. (p. 1055)
—Missing Parrot: Set Of 6. (p. 1152)
—My Neighborhood: Set Of 6. (p. 1216)
—My Neighborhood. (p. 1216)
—Race to Recycle: Set Of 6. (p. 1431)
—Where Does Your Garbage Go? (p. 1907)
—Where Does Your Garbage Go? Set Of 6. (p. 1907)
Meissner, David & Richardson, Kim. Call of the Klondike: A True Gold Rush Adventure. (p. 254)
Meissner, Jacqueline. I Am a Doctor: A Child's View of Adoption (p. 832)
—Why Am I Brown? A Child's View of Multi-cultural Adoption Stabile, Nicolette, illus. (p. 1922)
Meiste, Kimberly. Song of Joy: An Easy-to-Sing, Easy-to-Stage Christmas Musical for Children. (p. 1611)
Meister, Carl. Airplane Adventure Janovitz, Marilyn, illus. (p. 31)
—Brave Puffer Fish Harpster, Steve, illus. (p. 223)
—Brown Bears. (p. 231)
—Bus Ride Bully Simard, Remy, illus. (p. 244)
—Buzz Beaker & the Cave Creatures. McGuire, Bill, illus. (p. 248)
—Buzz Beaker & the Cool Caps McGuire, Bill, illus. (p. 248)
—Buzz Beaker & the Growing Goo McGuire, Bill, illus. (p. 248)

—Buzz Beaker & the Outer Space Trip. McGuire, Bill, illus. (p. 248)
—Buzz Beaker & the Putt-Putt Contest. McGuire, Bill, illus. (p. 248)
—Buzz Beaker & the Race to School McGuire, Bill, illus. (p. 248)
—Buzz Beaker & the Speed Secret. McGuire, Bill, illus. (p. 248)
—Buzz Beaker & the Super Fast Car McGuire, Bill, illus. (p. 248)
—Buzz Beaker Books. (p. 248)
—Chameleons. (p. 289)
—Chefs. (p. 297)
—Chickens. (p. 300)
—Cinderella Stories Around the World: 4 Beloved Tales Belloni, Valentina et al, illus. (p. 320)
—Clever Dolphin Harpster, Steve, illus. (p. 331)
—Clownfish. (p. 335)
—Clues in the Attic Simard, Remy, illus. (p. 336)
—Construction Workers. (p. 360)
—Corals. (p. 366)
—Cows. (p. 374)
—Crabs. (p. 375)
—Crocodiles. (p. 384)
—Davy Crockett & the Great Mississippi Snag George, Peter, illus. (p. 411)
—Do You Really Want to Meet a Cape Buffalo? Fabbri, Daniele, illus. (p. 458)
—Do You Really Want to Meet a Crocodile? Fabbri, Daniele, illus. (p. 458)
—Do You Really Want to Meet a Kangaroo? Fabbri, Daniele, illus. (p. 458)
—Do You Really Want to Meet a Lion? Fabbri, Daniele, illus. (p. 458)
—Do You Really Want to Meet a Monkey? Fabbri, Daniele, illus. (p. 458)
—Do You Really Want to Meet a Moose? Fabbri, Daniele, illus. (p. 458)
—Dolphins. (p. 464)
—Dump Truck Day Emmerson, Michael, illus. (p. 489)
—Eels. (p. 505)
—Everyone Feels Angry Sometimes Ward, Damian, illus. (p. 544)
—Everyone Feels Happy Sometimes Ward, Damian, illus. (p. 544)
—Fall Is Fun Lingenfelter, Jim, illus. (p. 566)
—Fancy Octopus Harpster, Steve, illus. (p. 570)
—Farmers. (p. 574)
—First Graphics - Seasons Lingenfelter, Jim, illus. (p. 595)
—Flash Forward Fairy Tales: Cinderella in the City. (p. 602)
—Garbage Trucks. (p. 655)
—Goalkeeper Goof Doerrfeld, Cori, illus. (p. 687)
—Goats. (p. 687)
—Groundhogs. (p. 725)
—Grumpy Lobster Harpster, Steve, illus. (p. 727)
—Hiding Eel Harpster, Steve, illus. (p. 777)
—Hi-Ho, Tiny. Davis, Rich, illus. (p. 775)
—Horned Lizards. (p. 798)
—Horses. (p. 800)
—I Love Trees. Sirrell, Terry, illus. (p. 843)
—Jellyfish. (p. 912)
—John Henry vs. the Mighty Steam Drill Rivas, Victor, illus. (p. 922)
—Kickball Kids Olson, Julie, illus. (p. 951)
—King Arthur & the Sword in the Stone Erkocak, Sahin, illus. (p. 958)
—Kit & Mateo Journey into the Clouds: Learning about Clouds Record, Adam, illus. (p. 962)
—Komodo Dragons. (p. 966)
—Librarians. (p. 1005)
—Lily's Lucky Leotard Ho, Jannie, illus. (p. 1018)
—Lobsters. (p. 1044)
—Lost Treasure of Larry Longfoot: Learning to Use a Map. Record, Adam, illus. (p. 1057)
—Lucky Manatee Harpster, Steve, illus. (p. 1063)
—Mechanics. (p. 1118)
—Moopy el Monstruo Subterráneo/Moopy the Underground Monster. Heck, Claudia M., tr. from ENG. (p. 1173)
—Moopy on the Beach Messner, Dennis, illus. (p. 1173)
—Moopy the Underground Monster Messner, Dennis, illus. (p. 1173)
—Nurses. (p. 1273)
—Ocean Tales. Harpster, Steve, illus. (p. 1277)
—Octopuses. (p. 1278)
—Ora at the Monster Contest Messner, Dennis, illus. (p. 1301)
—Ora - El Monstruo Marino. Heck, Claudia M., tr. from ENG. (p. 1301)
—Ora the Sea Monster. Messner, Dennis, illus. (p. 1301)
—Ora - The Sea Monster. Messner, Dennis, illus. (p. 1301)
—Peacocks. (p. 1332)
—Plumbers. (p. 1374)
—Police Officers. (p. 1380)
—Pythons. (p. 1422)
—Rapunzel Stories Around the World: 3 Beloved Tales Belloni, Valentina et al, illus. (p. 1439)
—Rio 2: Off & Flying. (p. 1473)
—Rio 2: Untamed Talent. (p. 1473)
—Rio 2 - Off & Flying. (p. 1473)
—Sasha Sings: Understanding Parts of a Sentence. Whitehouse, Ben, illus. (p. 1515)
—Scholastic Reader Level 2: Flash Forward Fairy Tales: Cinderella in the City. Waters, Erica-Jane, illus. (p. 1522)
—Scholastic Reader Level 2: Flash Forward Fairy Tales: Snow White & the Seven Dogs. Waters, Erica-Jane, illus. (p. 1522)
—Sea Horses. (p. 1534)
—Sea Stars. (p. 1535)
—Sea Turtles. (p. 1536)
—Seals. (p. 1536)
—Shark in the Library! Simard, Remy, illus. (p. 1562)
—Sharks. (p. 1562)
—Ships. (p. 1567)
—Shivery Shark Harpster, Steve, illus. (p. 1567)
—Snapping Turtles. (p. 1597)
—Snorp: The City Monster. Messner, Dennis, illus. (p. 1598)
—Snorp el Monstruo de la Ciudad/Snorp the City Monster Heck, Claudia M., tr. from ENG. (p. 1598)
—Snorp on the Slopes Messner, Dennis, illus. (p. 1598)
—Snow White & the Seven Dogs. (p. 1599)
—Spring Is Special Lingenfelter, Jim, illus. (p. 1635)
—Stranded Orca Harpster, Steve, illus. (p. 1664)
—Summer Is Super Lingenfelter, Jim, illus. (p. 1674)
—T-Ball Trouble Ho, Jannie, illus. (p. 1693)
—They're up to Something in There: Understanding There, Their, & They're. Jagucki, Marek, illus. (p. 1732)
—Three Claws in the City Messner, Dennis, illus. (p. 1741)
—Three Claws the Mountain Monster. Messner, Dennis, illus. (p. 1741)
—Tigers. (p. 1749)
—Tiny Goes Back to School. Davis, Rich, illus. (p. 1756)
—Tiny Goes Camping. Davis, Rich, illus. (p. 1756)
—Tiny on the Farm. Davis, Rich, illus. (p. 1756)
—Tiny the Birthday Dog. (p. 1757)
—Tiny the Birthday Dog. Davis, Rich, illus. (p. 1757)
—Totally Wacky Facts about Animals. (p. 1771)
—Totally Wacky Facts about Land Animals. (p. 1771)
—Totally Wacky Facts about Sea Animals. (p. 1771)
—Tow Trucks. (p. 1773)
—Train Trip Janovitz, Marilyn, illus. (p. 1777)
—Untamed Talent. (p. 1823)
—Veterinarians. (p. 1839)
—Walruses. (p. 1855)
—Whales. (p. 1878)
—What Can I Be? (p. 1880)
—What Can I Be? Phillips, Matt, illus. (p. 1880)
—When & Why Did the Horse Fly? Knowing & Using Question Words Jagucki, Marek, illus. (p. 1901)
—Winter Is Wonderful Lingenfelter, Jim, illus. (p. 1938)
—Wolves. (p. 1945)
—Zebras. (p. 1985)
Meister, Cari, jt. auth. see Braun, Eric.
Meister, Cari, jt. auth. see Dybvik, Tina.
Meister, Cari, jt. auth. see Gunderson, Jessica.
Meister, Cari & Loewen, Nancy. Language on the Loose Jagucki, Marek, illus. (p. 975)
Meister, Cari & Ritchey, Kate. Happy Doodling! (p. 745)
Meister, Cari & Sirrell, Terry. Me Fascinan Los Árboles. Sirrell, Terry, illus. (p. 1115)
—Me Fascinan Los árboles. Sirrell, Terry, illus. (p. 1115)
—Me Fascinan Los Arboles. Sirrell, Terry, illus. (p. 1115)
Meister, Cari & Stone Arch Books Staff. Train Trip Janovitz, Marilyn, illus. (p. 1777)
Meister, Charles, illus. see Stein, Evaleen.
Meister, Charles E., illus. see Stein, Evaleen.
Meister, Christine, ed. see Freedman, Anne.
Meister, Christine, ed. see Woodson, J. L.
Meister, Deborah. What Catholic Teens Should Know about Capital Punishment. Larkin, Jean, ed. (p. 1881)
—What Catholics Teens Should Know If Pregnant & Panicked. Larkin, Jean K., ed. (p. 1881)
Meister, Solzick, illus. see Lee, Ingrid.
Meister, Solzick & George, Kallie. Mr. M: The Exploring Dreamer. (p. 1185)
Meister, Victoria Buhlig. Our Playtime Friend. (p. 1309)
Meistle, Jarrod. Victor the Vampire. (p. 1840)
—Victor the Vampire & the Bully. (p. 1840)
Meithrin, Mudiad Ysgolion. Llyfr Lliwio Dydd a Nos. (p. 1044)
Mejia, Estella, illus. see Balletta, Janet.
Mejia Soto, Guillermina. Higiene de la Pubertad. (p. 779)
Mejias, John, jt. illus. see Mejias, John.
Mejias, John & Mejias, John. Hungry Brothers. (p. 828)
Mejías, Mónica. Aprendiendo a Leer con Mili y Molo: Learn How to Read in Spanish. Mejías, Mónica, illus. (p. 93)
Mejuto, Eva. Run Pumpkin, Run. Letría, Andre, illus. (p. 1496)
Mejuto, Eva, tr. see Bansch, Helga.
Mekis, Pete, illus. see Brown, Mark.
Mekonnen, Tsion. I Will Do It! (p. 848)
Melady, John. Maple Leaf in Space: Canada's Astronauts. (p. 1090)
Melancon, Lenell Levy. Tootles the Turtle Tells the Truth: An Interactive Tale about Secrets. (p. 1768)
Melania, Mother. Baby Moses. Gillis, Bonnie, illus. (p. 127)
—Jonah's Journey to the Deep. (p. 925)
Melanie Z. Kato the True Story of a Siamese Cat. (p. 945)
Melanson, Caroline. Two Old Shoes. (p. 1804)
Melanson, Luc, illus. see Dube, Pierrette.
Melanson, Luc, illus. see Fagan, Cary.
Melanson, Luc, illus. see Luttrel, Bill.
Melanson, Luc, illus. see Wahl, Charis.
Melanson, Matt, illus. see Kropp, Paul.
Melanson, Matt, illus. see Paton, Doug.
Melanson, Tina. Operation: Ice Maker: Tales of the Super Sib Squad. (p. 1300)
—Operation: SOS: Tales of the Super Sib Squad: Book 2. (p. 1300)
Melaranci, Elisabetta, illus. see Gianatti, Silvia, et al.
Melaranci, Elisabetta, illus. see Machetto, Augusto, et al.
Melbo, Irving Robert. Our Americ: A Textbook for Elementary School History & Social Studies. (p. 1307)
Melcher, Mary. Puppies Count. (p. 1418)
Melcher, Michele, illus. see Collins, Terry.
Melcher, Rich. Work in Progress. (p. 1952)
Melchionno, Marion. Patty & the Little Ponies That Could: Hunt for the Collar of Sparkle. (p. 1329)
—Patty & the Little Pony That Could. (p. 1329)
Melchiore, Dondino, jt. auth. see Gummelt, Donna.
Melchisedech Olson, Kay, jt. auth. see Olson, Kay Melchisedech.
Melchishua, Tewodross, illus. see Winmilawe.
Meldrum, Christina. Madapple. (p. 1069)
Meldrum, Margaret. Peter Panda & His Friends. (p. 1347)
Meldrum, Ned, photos by see Dale, Jay.
Meldrum, Ned, photos by see Giulieri, Anne.
Mele, Leo. Closet Creeps: A Bedtime Mystery. Demmers, Justina, illus. (p. 334)
Melean, Mary & Lascaris, Alexia. Adventures of Don Quixote of la Mancha. (p. 17)
Melendez, Alicia & Benchmark Education Co. Staff. Behind the Microscope: Solving Scientific Mysteries. (p. 160)
Melendez-Shafe, Yvette. Adventures of Mudpie. (p. 21)
Meler, Kerry L., illus. see Jarrell, Pamela R.
Meler, Kerry L., illus. see Mullican, Judy.
Meler, Kerry L., illus. see Williams, Heather L.
Melfa, Frank. Pharmaceutical Landing: How to Land the Pharmaceutical Sales Job You Want & Succeed in It! (p. 1350)
Melhuish, Clare. Modern House (p. 1158)
Melhuish, Eva, illus. see Stainton, Sue.
Melia, John. Casebook of Mysterious Morris. (p. 275)
Melillo, Joe. Parker Helps Hubert the Hippopotamus. (p. 1324)
—Parker the Platypus. (p. 1324)
Melin, Jen. Examining Volcanic Eruptions. (p. 547)
Melinda, Braun. Luella. (p. 1064)
Melinda, Luke. perro verde (the Green Dog) (p. 1344)
Melinda, Sheffler, illus. see Edmond, Wally.
Melinda, Shoals. Spritelees: A Christmas Tale about Kindness. (p. 1634)
Melis, Luisanna Fodde. Noah Webster & the First American Dictionary. (p. 1261)
Melish, John. Harmony In 1811: From Travels in the United States of America. (p. 749)
Melissa Bank Staff. Girls' Guide to Hunting & Fishing: A Novel. (p. 680)
Melissa, Boyd. Christmas Wish. (p. 316)
Melissa, De La Cruz, et al. 21 Proms. Levithan, David & Ehrenhaft, Daniel, eds. (p. 1996)
Melissa Strangway. Abigail's Mirror. (p. 5)
Melki-Wegner, Skye. Chasing the Valley. (p. 294)
Melkonian, Sheyda Mia. Nika Goes to Camp. OConner, Kim, illus. (p. 1255)
Mellado, Carisa. Mythic Oracle: Wisdom of the Ancient Greek Pantheon. Phelan, Michele-lee, illus. (p. 1227)
Mellanby, Alex. Tregarthur's Promise. (p. 1784)
Mellark, Kat. Louis Armstrong: American Musician. (p. 1058)
—Our Zoo Adventure: Compare Numbers. (p. 1310)
Mellema, Valerie. Professional Bartender's Handbook: A Recipe for Every Drink Known - Including Tricks & Games to Impress Your Guests. (p. 1409)
Mellen, Wynette. What Do You See? Rasmussen, Jennifer, illus. (p. 1883)
Mellet, Peter. Find Out about Trees: With 18 Projects & More Than 250 Pictures. (p. 587)
Mellet, Peter, et al, trs. Cars. (p. 272)
Mellett, Peter. Find Out about Flight: With 18 Projects & More Than 240 Pictures. (p. 587)
—Find Out about Pyramids. (p. 587)
Mellett, Peter, et al. Exploring Science: What Is Flight? Birds Planes Kites Balloons. (p. 553)
Mellgren, Jöns. Elsa & the Night. (p. 516)
Melling, jt. auth. see French, Vivian.
Melling, David. Dont Worry Douglas. Melling, David, illus. (p. 469)
—First Italian Words. (p. 595)
—First Polish Words. (p. 596)
—First Russian Words. (p. 596)
—Good Knight Sleep Tight. Melling, David, illus. (p. 698)
—Hugless Douglas & the Big Sleepover. (p. 825)
—Hugless Dougless. Melling, David, illus. (p. 825)
—Scallywags Blow Their Top! (p. 1519)
—Splish, Splash, Sploshl Melling, David, illus. (p. 1630)
—Three Wishes. Melling, David, illus. (p. 1744)
—Two by Two & a Half. Melling, David, illus. (p. 1803)
Melling, David, illus. see Boswall, Nigel.
Melling, David, illus. see McKay, Hilary.
Melling, David, illus. see Morris, Neil.
Melling, David, tr. see McKay, Hilary.
Melling, David & Mellingdavid. En Busca Del Beso. (p. 522)
Melling, David & Whybrow, Ian. Flying Diggers. (p. 609)
Melling, O. R. Book of Dreams. (p. 211)
—Chronicles of Faerie: The Book of Dreams. (p. 317)
—Hunter's Moon. (p. 828)
—Light-Bearer's Daughter. (p. 1015)
—Summer King. (p. 1674)
Mellingdavid, jt. auth. see Melling, David.
Mello, Alondra. Alanora's Magic Tree: Alanora's Spirit Journey. (p. 33)
Mello, Craig. Difference: the Rainbow Zebra: An African Tale of Diversity. (p. 437)
Mello, Mary. Johnny Makes a Friend. (p. 923)
Mello, Tara Baukus. Danica Patrick. (p. 404)
—Mark Martin. (p. 1095)
—Need for Speed. (p. 1239)
—Pit Crew. (p. 1364)
—Rusty Wallace. (p. 1498)
—Stunt Driving. (p. 1670)
—Tony Stewart. (p. 1766)
Mellom, Robin. Classroom: When Nature Calls, Hang Up! (p. 328)
—Classroom Trick Out My School! Gilpin, Stephen, illus. (p. 329)
—Ditched: A Love Story. (p. 454)
—Student Council Smackdown! Gilpin, Stephen, illus. (p. 1669)
Mellon, Gray. Weird Worlds of Willoughby Wren Wren & the Pigeons. (p. 1873)
Mellon, Nancy. Knottles. Lieberherr, Ruth, illus. (p. 965)
Mellor, C. Michael. Louis Braille: A Touch of Genius. (p. 1058)
Mellor, Christie. You Look Fine, Really. (p. 1976)
Mellor, Christie S. Three-Martini Play Date: A Practical Guide to Happy Parenting. (p. 1743)
Mellor, Colleen Kelly. Grandpa & the Truck Book 2. Irwin, Dana M., illus. (p. 709)
—Grandpa & the Truck Book One. Irwin, Dana, illus. (p. 709)
Mellor, Corinne & Ericksson, Ashe. Snowlies Find a Letter. (p. 1600)
Mellor, Jodie. Missing! Dann, Penny, illus. (p. 1152)
Mellor, Robin, jt. auth. see Foster, John.
Mellor, Robin, jt. selected by see Foster, John.
Mellor, Ronald & Podany, Amanda H. World in Ancient Times: Primary Sources & Reference Volume. (p. 1956)
Mellor, Ronald J. & McGee, Marni. Ancient Roman World. (p. 70)
Mellors, Julie. U-X-L American Decades 2000-09 Cumulative Index. (p. 1807)
Melman, Anna. Islam, Law & Human Rights. (p. 891)
—Muslims in America. (p. 1194)
Melman, Peter, jt. auth. see Melman, Peter Charles.
Melman, Peter Charles & Melman, Peter. Uniquely New Hampshire (p. 1818)
Melmed, Laura Krauss. Before We Met. Tsong, Jing Jing, illus. (p. 159)
—Capital! Washington D. C. from A to Z. Lessac, Frané, illus. (p. 262)
—I Love You As Much... Board Book & Picture Frame. (p. 843)
—Moishe's Miracle: A Hanukkah Story. Slonim, David, illus. (p. 1160)
—My Love Will Be with You. Sorensen, Henri, illus. (p. 1213)
—New York, New York! The Big Apple from A to Z. Lessac, Frané, illus. (p. 1248)
—New York, New York City: The Big Apple from A to Z. Lessac, Frané, illus. (p. 1248)
—Rainbabies. LaMarche, Jim, illus. (p. 1435)
—This First Thanksgiving Day: A Counting Story. Buehner, Mark, illus. (p. 1735)
Melmon, Deborah, illus. see Abramson, Jill & O'Connor, Jane.
Melmon, Deborah, illus. see Dembar Greene, Jacqueline.
Melmon, Deborah, illus. see Driscoll, Laura.
Melmon, Deborah, illus. see Fields, Terri.
Melmon, Deborah, illus. see Gorey, Jill & Haller, Nancy.
Melmon, Deborah, illus. see Greene, Jacqueline Dembar.
Melmon, Deborah, illus. see Houran, Lori Haskins.
Melmon, Deborah, illus. see Hunt, Connie.
Melmon, Deborah, illus. see Jules, Jacqueline & Hechtkopf, Jacqueline.
Melmon, Deborah, illus. see Jules, Jacqueline.
Melmon, Deborah, illus. see Loewen, Nancy.
Melmon, Deborah, illus. see MacDonald, Margaret Read.
Melmon, Deborah, illus. see May, Eleanor.
Melmon, Deborah, illus. see Ring, Susan.
Melmon, Deborah, illus. see Sateren, Shelley Swanson.
Melmon, Deborah, illus. see Skinner, Daphne.
Melmon, Deborah, illus. see Swanson Sateren, Shelley.
Melmon, Deborah H., illus. see Bullard, Lisa.
Melnychuk, Monika, illus. see Birmingham, Maria.
Melnychuk, Monika, illus. see Katz, Anne.
Melnychuk, Monika, illus. see Roderick, Stacey & Warwick, Ellen.
Melnyczuk, Peter, illus. see Hill, Douglas.
Melo, Esperanca, illus. see Barclay, Jane.
Melo, Esperanca, illus. see Blakley Kinsler, Gwen & Young, Jackie.
Melo, Esperanca, illus. see Jackson, Ellen B.
Melo, Esperanca, illus. see Kulling, Monica.
Melo, Esperança, illus. see Musgrave, Susan.
Melo, Esperanca, jt. auth. see Slavin, Bill.
Melo, Filipe. Incredible Adventures of Dog Mendonca & Pizzaboy II - Apocalypse. Simon, Philip, ed. (p. 869)
Meloan, Becky, jt. auth. see Bryant, Kim.
Meloch, Renee. Heroes for Young Readers Activity Guide Package Books 1-4: Includes: Activity Guide, Audio CD, & Books 1-4. Pollard, Bryan, illus. (p. 773)
Meloche, Renee. Heroes for Young Readers - Cameron Townsend: Planting God's Word. Pollard, Bryan, illus. (p. 772)
—Heroes for Young Readers - Hudson Taylor: Friend of China. Pollard, Bryan, illus. (p. 772)
—Heroes for Young Readers - Jim Elliot: A Light for God. Pollard, Bryan, illus. (p. 772)
—Heroes for Young Readers - Jonathan Goforth: Never Give Up. Pollard, Bryan, illus. (p. 773)
—Heroes for Young Readers - Lottie Moon: A Generous Offering. Pollard, Bryan, illus. (p. 773)
Meloche, Renee Taft. Daniel Boone: Bravery on the Frontier. Pollard, Bryan, illus. (p. 405)
—Heroes for Young Readers Activity Guide for Books 1-4: Educational & Character-Building Lessons for Children. (p. 773)
—Heroes for Young Readers Activity Guide for Books 13-16: Educational & Character-Building Lessons for Children. (p. 773)
—Heroes for Young Readers Activity Guide Package Books 5-8: Includes: Activity Guide, Audio CD, & Books 5-8. Pollard, Bryan, illus. (p. 773)
—Heroes for Young Readers Activity Guide Package Books 9-12: Includes: Activity Guide, Audio CD, & Books 9-12. Pollard, Bryan, illus. (p. 773)
—Heroes for Young Readers Activity Guide Package Books 13-16: Includes: Activity Guide, Audio CD, & Books 13-16. Pollard, Bryan, illus. (p. 773)
—Heroes of History for Young Readers - Clara Barton: Courage to Serve. Pollard, Bryan, illus. (p. 773)
—Heroes of History for Young Readers - George Washington: America's Patriot. Pollard, Brian, illus. (p. 773)
—Heroes of History for Young Readers - George Washington Carver: America's Scientist. Pollard, Bryan, illus. (p. 773)
—Heroes of History for Young Readers - Meriwether Lewis: Journey Aross America. Pollard, Brian, illus. (p. 773)
Melodie. Arabian Nights Collective Work Staff, illus. (p. 94)
Melon, Zach. Rocky's Rock Collection. (p. 1484)
Meloy, Alice McFeely. As the Crow Flies: Preface to Gettysburg: the Enemy Is Here! (p. 105)
Meloy, Colin. Under Wildwood. Ellis, Carson, illus. (p. 1814)
—Wildwood. Ellis, Carson, illus. (p. 1931)
—Wildwood. Ellis, Carson, illus. (p. 1932)
—Wildwood Imperium: The Wildwood Chronicles, Book III. Ellis, Carson, illus. (p. 1932)
—Wildwood Imperium. Ellis, Carson, illus. (p. 1932)
Meloy, Maile. Apothecary. (p. 92)
—Apothecary. Schoenherr, Ian, illus. (p. 92)
—Apprentices. (p. 93)
—Apprentices. Schoenherr, Ian, illus. (p. 93)
Melrose, Laurie. Willow Wood. (p. 1934)
Melson, William G. Geology Explained: Virginia's Fort Valley & Massanutten Mountains. (p. 662)
Melton, Buckner F. Aaron Burr: The Rise & Fall of an American Politician. (p. 2)
—Law. (p. 981)
Melton, Cheri. Baby Wild Horses of the Comstock. (p. 128)
Melton, David. Wonder Years of Oscar the Raccoon. (p. 1947)
Melton, Eric, illus. see Tuck, Helen.

Melton, H. Keith, jt. auth. see Mauro, Paul.
Melton, H. Keith, jt. auth. see Vale, A. M.
Melton, H. Keith, jt. auth. see Wiese, Jim.
Melton, Henry. Lighter Than Air. (p. 1015)
Melton, J. Gordon. Encyclopedia of Protestantism. (p. 525)
Melton, J. Gordon, ed. see Jones, Constance & Ryan, James Daniel.
Melton, J. Gordon, ed. Faith in America (p. 565)
Melton, Jelina Guffey. Carson the Cowboy: A Little Boy Waiting to Be a Cowboy. (p. 272)
Melton, Jo Lynn, illus. see Blake-Brekke, Carri.
Melton, Jodi, illus. see Blake-Brekke, Carri.
Melton, John Gordon. Protestant Faith in America. (p. 1412)
Melton, Lexi. Buck Toothed Charlie & Other Stories. (p. 234)
—Max the Superdog. (p. 1111)
Melton, Marcia. Boarding House. Doran, Fran, illus. (p. 205)
Meltzer, Amy. Shabbat Princess. Avilés, Martha, illus. (p. 1556)
Meltzer, Brad. Heroes for My Daughter. (p. 772)
—I Am Abraham Lincoln. Eliopoulos, Christopher, illus. (p. 832)
—I Am Albert Einstein. Eliopoulos, Christopher, illus. (p. 832)
—I Am Amelia Earhart. Eliopoulos, Christopher, illus. (p. 832)
—I Am Helen Keller. Eliopoulos, Christopher, illus. (p. 833)
—I Am Jackie Robinson. Eliopoulos, Christopher, illus. (p. 833)
—I Am Lucille Ball. Eliopoulos, Christopher, illus. (p. 833)
—I Am Rosa Parks. Eliopoulos, Christopher, illus. (p. 833)
—Identity Crisis. (p. 852)
—Identity Crisis. Bair, Michael, illus. (p. 852)
Meltzer Kleinhenz, Sydnie. Bats in My Attic. Stromoski, Rick, illus. (p. 145)
—Coral Reefs. (p. 366)
—Work & Play. Reasor, Mick, illus. (p. 1952)
Meltzer Kleinhenz, Sydnie & Kleinhenz, Sydnie M. Elephants Saunders-Smith, Gail, ed. (p. 511)
Meltzer, Lynn. Construction Crew. Eko-Burgess, Carrie, illus. (p. 359)
Meltzer, Mark, jt. auth. see Howard, Clark.
Meltzer, Milton. Albert Einstein: A Biography. (p. 34)
—Edgar Allan Poe: A Biography. (p. 504)
—Emily Dickinson: A Biography. (p. 518)
—Francisco Pizarro: The Conquest of Peru. (p. 628)
—Henry David Thoreau: A Biography. (p. 767)
—Herman Melville: A Biography. (p. 771)
—Underground Man. (p. 1814)
—Willa Cather: A Biography. (p. 1933)
Meltzer, Mirta. My Hands Mis Manos. (p. 1210)
Melville, Herman. Apple-Tree Table & Other Sketches. (p. 92)
—Battle-Pieces & Aspects of the War: Civil War Poems. (p. 147)
—Billy Budd, Sailor. (p. 187)
—Cities of the Fantastic: Brusel. Eisner, Will, illus. (p. 322)
—Herman Melville/Moby Dick. Niño, Alex, illus. (p. 771)
—Moby Dick: Or, the Whale. (p. 1157)
—Moby Dick: With a Discussion of Determination. (p. 1157)
—Moby Dick. (p. 1157)
—Moby Dick. Needle, Jan, ed. (p. 1157)
—Moby Dick. Eisner, Will, illus. (p. 1157)
—Moby Dick. Espinosa, Rod, illus. (p. 1157)
—Moby Dick. Félix, José María, tr. (p. 1157)
—Moby Dick. Elphinstone, Katy, illus. (p. 1157)
—Moby Dick, Grades 5-12. (p. 1157)
—Moby Dick, or the Whale. (p. 1157)
—Moby-Dick. Freeberg, Eric, illus. (p. 1157)
—Moby-Dick. Benson, Patrick, illus. (p. 1157)
Melville, Herman, jt. auth. see Eisner, Will.
Melville, Herman & Huth, Michael. Moby Dick. (p. 1157)
Melville, Herman, et al. Moby Dick. (p. 1157)
Melville, Jacqui, photos by see Parrini, Sabrina.
Melville, Johnathan, et al. Investigating Biology through Inquiry. (p. 884)
Melville, V. H. Livia the Scientist. (p. 1040)
Melvin, Alice. A to Z Treasure Hunt. Melvin, Alice, illus. (p. 2)
—High Street. (p. 778)
Melvin, Anita. What to do with Boogers. Melvin, Anita, illus. (p. 1894)
Melvin, Anita, illus. see Salyers, Rita.
Melvin, Anita Flannery, illus. see Fuzy, Jim.
Melvin E., Meggan & Williams, Cornelius. Learn to Read with M. C. Ant Tanna. (p. 984)
Melvin, J. C. I Think I Smell Garlic: A Recipe for Life. Johnston, Annabelle, ed. (p. 846)
Melvin, Jackie. Bartholomew Bear Gets His Badge. (p. 140)
—Bartholomew Bear Is on the Case! (p. 140)
Melvin, James, illus. see Tate, Suzanne.
Melvin, Treva. Mr. Samuel's Penny. (p. 1186)
Melwani, Mona, jt. auth. see Scholastic, Inc. Staff.
Melzer, Richard. When We Were Young in the West: True Histories of Childhood. (p. 1905)
Memarzadeh, Sudabeh, illus. see Valderrama, Linda N.
Membrino, Anna. I Want to Be a Ballerina. Coh, Smiljana, illus. (p. 847)
Meminger, Neesha. Shine, Coconut Moon. (p. 1566)
Memling, Carl. Our Flag. (p. 1308)
—Sword in the Stone (Disney) RH Disney Staff, illus. (p. 1692)
Memmott, JanaLe. Monkey for Sale. (p. 1165)
Mena Cco-Sip, Gretchen. I Won't Bite. (p. 849)
Menapace, John. With Hidden Noise: Photographs by John Menapace. (p. 1942)
Menard, Adrienne, illus. see Menard, Michele Rose.
Menard, James. Bees & the Bears. Menard, John C., illus. (p. 158)
Menard, Jean-François, tr. see Rowling, J. K.
Menard, John C., illus. see Menard, James.
Menard, Lucille. Top of the Bottom: Inky to the Rescue, Volume 1. (p. 1769)
Menard, Lucille & Menard, Michele R. Inky's Missing Bow. (p. 874)
Menard, Lucille R. & Menard, Michele R. Inky the Talent Scout. (p. 874)
Menard, Menard & Menard, Michele. Wood, You Be Real! (p. 1949)
Menard, Michele. Invisible Giant's Whisper. (p. 885)
Menard, Michele, jt. auth. see Menard, Menard.
Menard, Michele R. Canopy House - Lost among the Stars. (p. 261)
—Canopy House - Vol 2- Gus & Ester Meet the Neighbors. (p. 261)
—Canopy House - Volume 1. (p. 261)
—Cardinal Christmas. (p. 266)
—Cherub in the Lily Field. (p. 298)
—Moon Means Business. (p. 1172)
—Thanksgiving Ring. (p. 1726)
—Who Do I Think You Are? (p. 1915)
Menard, Michele R., jt. auth. see Menard, Lucille R.
Menard, Michele R., jt. auth. see Menard, Lucille.
Menard, Michele Rose. Ghoul in Our School. Menard, Adrienne, illus. (p. 673)
Menard, Valerie. Jennifer Lopez. (p. 913)
Menary, Richard. Cognitive Integration: Mind & Cognition Unbounded. (p. 338)
Menase Debora. Purple Butterflies. Wanha lidih, illus. (p. 1419)
Menase, Debra. I Am Beautiful. Arin, Dilara, illus. (p. 832)
Menchen, Antonio Martinez. Fosco. (p. 623)
Menchin, Scott. Grandma in Blue with Red Hat. Bliss, Harry, illus. (p. 708)
—Harry Goes to Dog School. Menchin, Scott, illus. (p. 750)
—Taking a Bath with the Dog & Other Things That Make Me Happy. Menchin, Scott, illus. (p. 1697)
—What If Everything Had Legs? Menchin, Scott, illus. (p. 1887)
Menchin, Scott, illus. see Cronin, Doreen.
Menchin, Scott, illus. see McGhee, Alison.
Menchin, Scott, illus. see Skye, Ione.
Menchú, Rigoberta & Liano, Dante. Girl from Chimel Unger, David, tr. from SPA. (p. 678)
—Secret Legacy. Unger, David, tr. from SPA. (p. 1541)
—Vaso de Miel. Tebalan, Helman, illus. (p. 1833)
Mencio, Anna. Day the Wind Changed. (p. 414)
Mencius. Mencius. Lau, D. C., ed. (p. 1126)
Menck, Kevin, illus. see Elkins, Stephen.
Menconi, Al. But It Doesn't Affect Me. (p. 246)
—Full Tilt Media Challenge: 30 Day Devotional Guide. (p. 646)
Menconi, James Pasqual. Queen Mariella & the Fable of the Peony. (p. 1425)
Mendell, David & Thomson, Sarah L. Obama: A Promise of Change. (p. 1275)
Mendelsohn, Jeffrey. Grumpalina. (p. 727)
Mendelson, Aaron. Gospel Grooves, Funky Drummers, & Soul Power. (p. 703)
Mendelson, Abby. Paradise Boys. (p. 1323)
Mendelson, Edward, ed. Lewis Carroll. Copeland, Eric, illus. (p. 1004)
—Poetry for Young People: Edward Lear. Huliska-Beith, Laura, illus. (p. 1376)
Mendelson, Harvey, photos by see Routenburg, Rise' & Wasser, Barbara.
Mendelson, Lee, jt. auth. see Schulz, Charles M.
Mendenhall, Cheryl. Joseph & His Coat of Many Colors. (p. 926)
—Moses Baby in the Bulrushes. (p. 1176)
—Moses Parting the Red Sea. (p. 1176)
Mendenhall, Cheryl, illus. see Dalmatian Press Staff.
Mendenhall, Cheryl, illus. see Mara, Wil.
Mendenhall, Emily & Koon, Adam, eds. Environmental Health Narratives: A Reader for Youth. Burque, Hannah Adams, illus. (p. 532)
Mendenhall, Gaylee. My Teacher Is Bald! (p. 1220)
Mendenhall, Sandra. Frizzle & Grizzle. (p. 639)
Mendes, Barbara, illus. see Lipner, Joseph & Yasgur, Abigail.
Mendes, Melissa, illus. see Greenwald, Tommy.
Mendes, Valerie. Drowning. (p. 486)
—Lost & Found. (p. 1054)
Mendex, Leticia. Pinata. (p. 1359)
Mendez, Antonio J. & Mendez, Jonna. Gathering Info: Getting the Scoop by Using Your Wits. (p. 658)
—Going Undercover: Disguise & Secret Identities. (p. 693)
Mendez, Horatio. Understanding Sound. (p. 1816)
Mendez, Jonna, jt. auth. see Mendez, Antonio J.
Mendez, Raquel & Manero, Elia. Hombrecito de Mazapan. (p. 791)
Mendez, Simon, illus. see Butterfield, Moira.
Mendez, Simon, illus. see Diaz, Joanne Ruelos.
Mendez, Simon, illus. see Edwards, Katie.
Mendez, Simon, illus. see Freedman, Claire, et al.
Mendez, Simon, illus. see Freedman, Claire.
Mendez, Simon, illus. see Landa, Norbert.
Mendez, Simon, illus. see Lewellyn, Claire.
Mendez, Simon, illus. see Llewellyn, Claire.
Mendez, Simon, illus. see Rake, Matthew.
Mendez, Simon, illus. see Ticktock Media, Ltd. Staff & Parker, Steve.
Mendez, Simon, illus. see Wilson, Karma.
Mendez, Simon, jt. auth. see Allen, Judy.
Mendez, Simon, jt. auth. see Wilson, Hannah.
Mendez, Simon, tr. see Llewellyn, Claire.
Mendicino, Ellen, et al. Zuko the Zany Dog. (p. 1990)
Mendle, Jane. My Ultimate Sister Disaster: A Novel. (p. 1220)
Mendo, Miguel A., tr. see Byrd, Robert.
Mendo, Miguel Angel, tr. see Child, Lauren.
Mendon Center Elementary School (Pittsford, N.Y.) Staff, contrib. by. Rejoice! Poetry Celebrating Life in the Amazon Rainforest. (p. 1457)
Mendonca, Angela. Nursery Rhymes Island Style. Mendonca, Angela, illus. (p. 1273)
Mendonsa, Mark. Semi for a Sleigh. (p. 1550)
Mendoza, Amanda. Karlyndria (p. 944)
Mendoza, Carlos, illus. see Hulin, Pamela.
Mendoza Garcia, Isabel, tr. see McDonald, Megan.
Mendoza, George, illus. see Powers, J. L.
Mendoza, Isabel C., ed. see Molina, Maria I.
Mendoza, Javier, et al. Mundo. (p. 1191)
Mendoza, Madeleine. Simply & the Shiny Quarter. Abasta, Mary, illus. (p. 1578)
Mendoza, Megan Elizabeth, illus. see Riddle, Sharon Kay & Sanders, Nancy/Ida.
Mendoza, Melissa. My Mommy & Daddy Are in Heaven. (p. 1214)
Mendoza, Patrick M. Between Midnight & Morning: Historic Hauntings from the Frontier, Hispanic, & Native American Traditions. (p. 172)
Mendoza, S. J. How about Me. (p. 804)
Mendralla, Valerie & Grosshandler, Janet. Drinking & Driving, Now What? (p. 485)
Menear, Linda. Little Groundhog Discovers the True Meaning of Christmas. (p. 1028)
Meneely, Starr. What a Lovely Sound! (p. 1878)
Menefee, Angelo K. Billy's First Summer Vacation. (p. 187)
Meneley, Anne, jt. auth. see Kulick, Don.
Menéndez González, Elvira, et al. máquina maravillosa. (p. 1091)
Menéndez, Margarita, illus. see Fuertes, Gloria.
Menéndez, Margarita, tr. see Fuertes, Gloria.
Menendez, Shirley. B Is for Blue Crab: A Maryland Alphabet. Stutzman, Laura, illus. (p. 122)
Menéndez-Aponte, Emily. My Family Is Changing: A Book about Divorce. Fitzgerald, Anne, illus. (p. 1203)
Meng, Cece. Bedtime Is Canceled. Neyret, Aurélie, illus. (p. 157)
—I Will Not Read This Book. Ang, Joy, illus. (p. 848)
Meng, Cece & Suber, Melissa. Tough Chicks. Suber, Melissa, illus. (p. 1772)
Menge, Dawn. Queen Vernita Visits the Blue Ice Mountains. (p. 1425)
—Queen Vernita Visits the Islands of Enchantment. (p. 1425)
—Queen Vernita's Visitors. Switzer, Bobbi, illus. (p. 1425)
Menge, Dawn & Rhoades, Heath. Queen Vernita Meets Sir HeathyBean the Astronomer. (p. 1425)
Mengert, Hollie E., illus. see Penrod, Kathy Webb.
Menges, Jeff A. Glow-in-the-Dark Night Sky. (p. 685)
—Glow-in-the-Dark Tattoos Haunted Pirates. (p. 685)
—Glow-in-the-Dark Tattoos Pirate Skulls & Crossbones. (p. 685)
—Greek Gods Tattoos. (p. 720)
—Haunted Pirates Tattoos. (p. 753)
—House of Horror Stained Glass Coloring Book. (p. 803)
—Mythological Creatures Stained Glass Coloring Book. (p. 1227)
—Norse Gods & Goddesses. (p. 1264)
—Shiny War of the Worlds Stickers. (p. 1567)
Menges, Jeff A., ed. Dulac's Fairy Tale Illustrations in Full Color. Dulac, Edmund, illus. (p. 489)
Menges, Thais D. Granny & the Tractor. King, Joseph, illus. (p. 710)
Mengham, Rod. Vanishing Points: New Modernist Poems. Kinsella, John, ed. (p. 1833)
Mengham, Rod, ed. Salt Companion to John Tranter. (p. 1505)
Mengis, Heidi A. Lily Pad & the Dragonfly: A Story of Spiritual Enlightenment as told by Arden L. Johnson. (p. 1018)
Menhard, Francha Roffe & Salas, Laura Purdie. Facts about Inhalants. (p. 561)
Menifield, Gloria. What's the Matter, Mr. Giraffe? (p. 1899)
Menix, Cinda. Tenbrook Farms. Menix, Cinda & McGuire, Bryan, illus. (p. 1719)
Menken, John. Hands-on English with Linking Blocks Program Handbook. (p. 741)
Menking, Amanda, jt. auth. see Bucher, Heatherly.
Menna, Lynn Maddalena. Piece of My Heart. (p. 1356)
Mennen, Esther Thieme. Letters from Tim & Granma. (p. 1002)
Menocal, Maria Rosa. Ornament of the World: How Muslims, Jews, & Christians Created a Culture of Tolerance in Medieval Spain. (p. 1304)
Menon, Geeta. Classic Collection: 22 Short Stories. Suman, Surendra, illus. (p. 328)
Menon, Radhika. Line & Circle. Marudu, Trotsky, illus. (p. 1019)
Menon, Sujatha. Celebrating Holi: A Hindu Celebration of Spring. (p. 285)
—Discover Snakes. (p. 448)
—Fire & Flood. (p. 590)
—Fire & Floods. (p. 590)
—Mountain Creatures. (p. 1180)
—Safari Creatures. (p. 1502)
Menotti, Andrea. How Many Jelly Beans? A Giant Book of Giant Numbers! Labat, Yancey, illus. (p. 811)
—How to Tackle Puzzles, Unravel Riddles, Crack Codes, & Other Ways to Bend Your Brain. (p. 822)
—Operation Fowl Play. Kennedy, Kelly, illus. (p. 1300)
—Operation Master Mole. Kennedy, Kelly, illus. (p. 1300)
Menotti, Gian Carlo. Amahal y Los Tres Reyes. (p. 52)
Menotti, Gian Carlo, jt. auth. see Combel Editorial Staff.
Menozzi, Maria M. Poet Who Wouldn't Be King. (p. 1376)
Men's Health Staff, ed. see Schisgal, Zachary.
Menten, Ted. Evil Queens & Wicked Witches Paper Dolls. (p. 546)
—Little Goth Girl Sticker Paper Doll. (p. 1028)
—Paper Doll Design Studio. (p. 1322)
—Steampunk Vixens Paper Dolls. (p. 1646)
—Victorian Vixens Paper Dolls. (p. 1840)
—Wizard of Oz Paper Dolls. (p. 1943)
Menten, Ted, illus. see Baum, L. Frank.
Mentis, Anastassios, photos by see Palomino, Rafael.
Menton, Seymour, jt. auth. see Muñiz-Huberman, Angelina.
Menzel, Jö, et al. Verfassungsrechtsprechung: Ausgewählte Entscheidungen des Bundesverfassungsgerichts in Retrospektive. (p. 1836)
Menzel, Peter, jt. auth. see D'Aluisio, Faith.
Menzie, Morgan. Diary of an Anorexic Girl (p. 435)
Menzies, Britt. StinkyKids Have a Heart. Trent, John, illus. (p. 1651)
Menzin, Marit. Song for Papa Crow (p. 1611)
Meomi (Firm) Staff. Meomi Journal. (p. 1127)
—Octonauts & the Frown Fish. (p. 1278)
—Octonauts & the Great Ghost Reef. (p. 1278)
—Octonauts & the Sea of Shade. (p. 1278)
Meomi (Firm) Staff, contrib. by. Octonauts & the Only Lonely Monster. (p. 1278)
Meppem, William, photos by see Longbotham, Lori.
Meppem, William, photos by see Marchetti, Domenica.
Meppem, William, photos by see Mitchell, Paulette.
Merali, Alim. Talk the Talk: Speech & Debate Made Easy. (p. 1703)
Merasty, Maria Paul. Chuck the Different Vampire. (p. 318)
Merberg, Julie. My Favorite Shoes: A Touch-and-Feel Shoe-Stravaganza! Bove, Neysa & Rucker, Georgia, illus. (p. 1203)
—Turn the Key: Around Town: Look & See! McQueen, Lucinda, illus. (p. 1797)
Merberg, Julie, illus. see Bober, Suzanne.
Merberg, Julie, jt. auth. see Katz, Julie.
Merberg, Julie & Bober, Suzanne. Animals in Art: Art from the Start. (p. 83)
—Dancing with Degas. (p. 403)
—Dreaming with Rousseau. (p. 484)
—Green Squares & More Colors & Shapes: Art from the Start. (p. 722)
—Mini Masters: 4 Board Books Inside! Degas, Matisse, Monet, Van Gogh (p. 1146)
—On an Island with Gauguin. (p. 1288)
—Painting with Picasso. (p. 1318)
—Picnic with Monet. (p. 1355)
—Quiet Time with Cassatt. (p. 1428)
—Sharing with Renoir. (p. 1561)
—Sunday with Seurat. (p. 1676)
Merboth, Natalie. Blessing the Cat: A Newfound Family. (p. 199)
Mercadante, Frank. Positively Dangerous: Live Loud, Be Real, Change the World. (p. 1387)
Mercado, Ariano. Soccer Shoes from Americ. (p. 1603)
Mercado, Ashley K. Brother for Christmas. (p. 231)
Mercado, Jorge, illus. see Sommer, Carl & Aesop.
Mercado, Jorge, illus. see Sommer, Carl.
Mercado, Mary M., tr. see Morelllon, Judi.
Mercado, Nancy, jt. ed. see Mercado, Nancy E.
Mercado, Nancy E. Boredom Busters! Activities to Do for Kids Like You! (p. 214)
Mercado, Nancy E. & Mercado, Nancy, eds. Every Man for Himself: Ten Short Stories about Being a Guy. (p. 543)
Mercado, Nancy, ed. Baseball Crazy: Ten Stories That Cover All the Bases. (p. 141)
Mercado, Yehudi. Pantalones, TX: Don't Chicken Out. Mercado, Yehudi, illus. (p. 1321)
Mercafi, Cindy. Faces of Freedom. (p. 561)
Mercaldo, David. Little Boy Boo: The Adventures of A Yorkshire Terrier Who Thought He Was a Boy. (p. 1025)
Mercardante-Byrtus, Renee. Daniel the Dolphin Makes Friends. (p. 405)
Merce Company Staff. Charlot. (p. 293)
—Don Gil y el Paraguas Magico. (p. 465)
Merced, Eric, illus. see Rogers, Bud & Avery, Ben.
Merced, Zuleika. Mujer de Medio Siglo... Atesorndo Vivencias. Merced, Zuleika, ed. (p. 1189)
mercedes cecilia. Kusikiy A Child from Taquile, Peru. mercedes cecilia & mercedes cecilia, illus. (p. 968)
Mercedes, Neuschäfer Carlón, jt. auth. see Equipo Staff.
Mercer, Abbie. Chickens on a Farm. (p. 300)
—Cows on a Farm. (p. 374)
—Goats on a Farm. (p. 688)
—Happy 4th of July. (p. 744)
—Happy Halloween. (p. 745)
—Happy New Year. (p. 746)
—Happy St. Patrick's Day. (p. 746)
—Happy Thanksgiving. (p. 746)
—Happy Valentine's Day. (p. 747)
—Horses on a Farm. (p. 800)
—Pigs on a Farm. (p. 1358)
—Sheep on a Farm. (p. 1564)
Mercer, Bobby. Junk Drawer Chemistry: 50 Awesome Experiments That Don't Cost a Thing. (p. 936)
—Junk Drawer Physics: 50 Awesome Experiments That Don't Cost a Thing. (p. 936)
—Racecar Book: Build & Race Mousetrap Cars, Dragsters, Tri-Can Haulers & More. (p. 1431)
—Robot Book: Build & Control 20 Electric Gizmos, Moving Machines, & Hacked Toys. (p. 1480)
Mercer, Bonnie Kyllo, jt. auth. see Zannes, Addie Mercer.
Mercer, Christa Blum. German War Child: Growing Up in World War II. (p. 666)
Mercer, Christina. Arrow of the Mist. (p. 101)
Mercer, Erin. How Do You Count To 10? (p. 808)
Mercer, Gabrielle. Prayers for Boys. (p. 1393)
—Prayers for Girls. (p. 1393)
Mercer, Gerald. What's Going on at the Time Tonight? DeWolf, Holly, illus. (p. 1897)
Mercer, Graham. Secret Cave. (p. 1540)
Mercer, Henry C., et al. Color Me Pennsylvania: Our Heritage. (p. 343)
Mercer, Lynn, illus. see Allan, Jayne.
Mercer, M. J. O'No It's Henry. (p. 1298)
Mercer, Matthew, illus. see Butterworth, MyLinda.
Mercer, Rita C. Earl the Squatchem. (p. 492)
Mercer, Sienna. Date with Destiny. (p. 409)
—Fangtastic! (p. 571)
—Fashion Frightmare! (p. 575)
—Flipping Out ! (p. 605)
—Howl-Oween! (p. 823)
—Love Bites. (p. 1059)
—Lucky Break. (p. 1062)
—My Brother the Werewolf - Cry Wolf! (p. 1199)
—My Brother the Werewolf - Tail Spin Vol. 4. (p. 1199)
—My Sister the Vampire: Twin Spins! (p. 1218)
—Puppy Love! (p. 1418)
—Re-Vamped! (p. 1442)
—Secrets & Spies. (p. 1544)
—Star Style. (p. 1641)
—Switched. (p. 1691)
—Take Two. (p. 1697)
—Vampalicious! (p. 1831)
Mercer, Sienna & Miller, Sienna. Flying Solo. (p. 610)
—My Sister the Vampire: Double Disaster! (p. 1218)
—Stake Out! (p. 1638)
Mercer, Steven A. Florence the Fir Tree: (and the Angels of the Forest) (p. 606)
Mercer, Susan. Pathway to Pre-Algebra Proficiency. (p. 1328)
Merchant, Brenda C. Huga Huga Hippo. (p. 824)

M

Merchant, Damon. CCNA Examlet + Router Simulator. (p. 283)
Merchant, Donna, illus. see Donnell, Frances.
Merchant, Eryn. My Little Bumblebee. (p. 1212)
Merchant, Peter. Eleanor Roosevelt & the Scary Basement. DiVito, Anna, illus. (p. 508)
—Sojourner Truth: Path to Glory. Denos, Julia, illus. (p. 1606)
Merchant, Raina G. Engineering. (p. 529)
Merchant, Raina G. & Favor, Lesli J. How Eukaryotic & Prokaryotic Cells Differ (p. 809)
Merchant, Richard. Anise Seed. (p. 84)
Mercier, Deborah. Captain's Hat. Mills, Faythe, illus. (p. 264)
Mercier, Deirdre McLaughlin. Yesterday We Had a Hurricane. (p. 1971)
—Yesterday We Had a Hurricane/Ayer Tuvimos un Huracan. (p. 1971)
Mercier, Jean. Imagine Society: A Poema a Day. Vol. 5 (p. 861)
Mercier, Johanne. Caillou - Merry Christmas! Brignaud, Pierre, illus. (p. 251)
Mercurio, Jodi. Life in an Aquarium. (p. 1010)
Meredith, Amberley. Bessie Bump Gets a New Family. Lee, Nikita, illus. (p. 168)
Meredith Books Staff. Batman Activity Kit. (p. 144)
—Batman Sticker Story Adventure. (p. 144)
—Foodfight! Curry, Don, ed. (p. 614)
—Foodfight! Deluxe Sound Storybook. Curry, Don, ed. (p. 614)
Meredith Books Staff, ed. see DC Comics Staff.
Meredith Books Staff, jt. auth. see Black, Jake.
Meredith Books Staff, jt. auth. see Evento, Susan.
Meredith Books Staff, jt. auth. see Segovia, Patty.
Meredith Books Staff, jt. auth. see Shulman, Mark.
Meredith Books Staff, jt. auth. see Sudduth, Brent.
Meredith Books Staff, creator. Kung Fu Panda. (p. 968)
Meredith Books Staff, ed. Cooking for Kids. (p. 361)
—Fantastic Four Classic Color & Activity Book with Poster. (p. 571)
—Madagascar Activity Book & Floor Puzzle. (p. 1069)
—Madagascar Stencil Activity Book with Stickers. (p. 1069)
—Spider-Man Color & Activity Book with Poster. (p. 1626)
Meredith, Christina. Kiss Crush Collide. (p. 961)
Meredith, Christopher. King & Queen of Slop. (p. 958)
Meredith, Randy. Marvel Heros: Mix & Match Storybook. Barberi, Carlo, illus. (p. 1098)
—Marvel Puzzle Peril! (p. 1099)
Meredith, S. Night Animals. (p. 1252)
Meredith, Samantha, illus. see Clarke, Catriona.
Meredith, Samantha & Wyk, Hanri van. Weddings Sticker Color Book. (p. 1871)
Meredith, Sue. GRAN LIBRO DELAWARE LOS GENES y el ADN - INTERNET LINKED. (p. 706)
—Night Animals: Level 1. Donaera, Patrizia & Larkum, Adam, illus. (p. 1252)
—Why Should I Bother about the Planet? - Internet Referenced. (p. 1926)
Meredith, Sue, jt. auth. see Hickman, Clare.
Meredith, Susan. Cells. (p. 286)
—Cows on the Farm. (p. 374)
—Flowers to Color. Cooper, Jenny, illus. (p. 608)
—Genes & Dna - Internet Linked. (p. 660)
—Going Green. (p. 692)
—Growing Up. (p. 726)
—Half or Whole? (p. 736)
—Hamsters. (p. 740)
—Las Rocas, los Minerales y el Suelo. (p. 977)
—Rocks, Minerals, & Soil. (p. 1484)
—Undersea Life to Color. Cooper, Jenny, illus. (p. 1815)
—Usborne Book of World Religions. Evans, Cheryl, ed. (p. 1827)
—Using Scientific Tools. (p. 1828)
—Uso de Instrumentos Cientificos. (p. 1829)
—What's Happening to Me? (Girls Edition) Leschnikoff, Nancy, illus. (p. 1897)
—What's Inside You? (p. 1898)
—Why Should I Recycle? (p. 1926)
Meredith, Susan, ed. see Firth, Alex.
Meredith, Susan, ed. see Unwin, Mike & Woodward, Kate.
Meredith, Susan & Cullis, Megan. Nature to Color. Cooper, Jenny, illus. (p. 1236)
Meredith, Susan & Hickman, Claire. Encyclopedia of World Religions. (p. 526)
Meredith, Susan & Merideth, Susan. Left or Right ? (p. 987)
Meredith, Susan, et al. Hamsters. Fox, Christyan, illus. (p. 740)
Meredith, Susan Markowitz. All Work, No Play: Set Of 6. (p. 46)
—Bitsy the Beaver. (p. 194)
—Environmentally Friendly World. (p. 532)
—Finding Fossils: Set Of 6. (p. 588)
—Frances the Fairy Dressmaker. (p. 627)
—Fruit Salad. (p. 645)
—Happy Summer Day: Set Of 6. (p. 746)
—Hiding in the Sea: Set Of 6. (p. 777)
—Hiding in the Sea. (p. 777)
—Inupiaq Live Here: Set Of 6. (p. 883)
—Inupiaq Live Here. (p. 883)
—Maggie Makes Macaroni. (p. 1071)
—New Friend: Set Of 6. (p. 1244)
—New Friend. (p. 1244)
—Patterns at the Beach. (p. 1329)
—Royal Zookeeper. (p. 1492)
—States of Matter: Set Of 6. (p. 1644)
—Stump Hill. (p. 1670)
Meredith, Susan Markowitz, jt. auth. see Schafer, Susan.
Meredith, Susan Markowitz, et al. How Do Aircraft Fly? (p. 806)
Meredith-Markowitz, Susan. Bitsy the Beaver: Set Of 6. (p. 194)
—Charlie's Museum Adventure: Set Of 6. (p. 293)
—Maggie Makes Macaroni: Set Of 6. (p. 1071)
Merello, Gwyn. Piccola Pooch. (p. 1354)
Merer, Laura. Fuzzy Ducky's Birthday: A Touch-and-Feel Pop-up Book. (p. 651)
—My Five Senses. (p. 1208)
Merer, Laura, illus. see Rosa-Mendoza, Gladys.
Merer, Laura Blanken. My Five Senses. (p. 1208)
Meres, Jonathan. May Contain Nuts. (p. 1112)
—May Require Batteries. (p. 1112)
—Xmas Factor. (p. 1967)
Meret, Sasha, illus. see Feiler, Bruce.
Meret, Sasha, tr. see Feiler, Bruce.
Meriaido, Lee K. Kidnapped. (p. 952)
Merical, Nancy. Someday. (p. 1609)
Mericle Harper, Charise, jt. auth. see Harper, Charise Mericle.
Mericle, Melodye, ed. see Steele, Samantha.
Merideth, Susan. Left or Right. (p. 987)
Merideth, Susan, jt. auth. see Meredith, Susan.
Meridith, Brenda C. High Tide at Hopewell Rocks. (p. 778)
—She's Funny That Way. Meridith, Brenda C., ed. (p. 1566)
Merilatt, James & Frainier, Tamara. Miles Grand Adventures: The Denver Broncos Mascot's A-to-Z Journey Around Colorado. Malone, Kyle, illus. (p. 1142)
Merimee, Prosper. Carmen. (p. 270)
Merino, Gemma. Crocodile Who Didn't Like Water. (p. 384)
Merino, Jesus, illus. see Loeb, Jeph.
Merino, Jose Luis, illus. see Perrault, Charles.
Merino, Noel. Abortion. Greenhaven Press Editors, ed. (p. 5)
Merino, Noël. Abortion. Greenhaven Press Editors & Gale Editors, eds. (p. 5)
—AIDS in Developing Countries. (p. 30)
Merino, Noel. Birth Control. Greenhaven Press Editors, ed. (p. 192)
Merino, Noël. Capitalism. (p. 262)
—Censorship. (p. 287)
Merino, Noel. Civil Liberties. (p. 324)
—Criminal Justice. (p. 382)
—Drug Legalization. Greenhaven Press Editors, ed. (p. 486)
—Drugs. Greenhaven Press Staff, ed. (p. 487)
—Education. Greenhaven Press Editors & Gale Editors, eds. (p. 505)
Merino, Noël. Election Process. (p. 508)
Merino, Noel. Emancipation. Greenhaven Press Staff, ed. (p. 517)
Merino, Noël. Ethics. Greenhaven Press Staff, ed. (p. 539)
—European Union. (p. 540)
—Extremism. (p. 557)
—Gateway Drugs. (p. 658)
—Gender. (p. 660)
Merino, Noel. Genetic Engineering. (p. 660)
Merino, Noël. Globalization. (p. 685)
—Hate Crimes. (p. 752)
—Health Care. Gale Editors, ed. (p. 757)
Merino, Noel. Health Care. Greenhaven Press Staff, ed. (p. 758)
Merino, Noël. Human Genetics. (p. 826)
—Illegal Immigration. Greenhaven Press Staff, ed. (p. 856)
Merino, Noel. Media Ethics. (p. 1118)
Merino, Noël. Medical Testing. Greenhaven Press Editors, ed. (p. 1119)
—Medical Testing. Greenhaven Press Editors & Gale Editors, eds. (p. 1119)
—Poverty & Homelessness. Greenhaven Press Staff, ed. (p. 1389)
—Poverty & Homelessness. Greenhaven Press Editors & Gale Editors, eds. (p. 1389)
—Prison. (p. 1407)
Merino, Noel. Privacy. Greenhaven Press Staff, ed. (p. 1407)
Merino, Noël. Privacy. Greenhaven Press Editors, ed. (p. 1407)
—Rap Music. (p. 1439)
Merino, Noel. Selfincrimination. Gale, ed. (p. 1549)
Merino, Noël. Sex Discrimination. (p. 1556)
—Should Character Be Taught in School? (p. 1569)
—Tax Reform. (p. 1707)
—Teens & Privacy. (p. 1714)
—Teens & Privacy. Gale Editor, ed. (p. 1714)
—Unemployment. Greenhaven Press Editors, ed. (p. 1817)
—Unemployment. Greenhaven Press Editors & Gale Editors, eds. (p. 1817)
—Vaccines. (p. 1830)
Merino, Noel. Vaccines. Greenhaven Press Staff, ed. (p. 1830)
Merino, Noël. What Rights Should Illegal Immigrants Have? (p. 1893)
—World Economy. (p. 1955)
Merino, Noël, jt. auth. see Gale Editors.
Merino, Noël, jt. auth. see Tuyl, Christine Van.
Merino, Noël & Williams, Heidi. Juvenile Crime. (p. 941)
Merino, Noël, ed. Capitalism. (p. 262)
—Drug Legalization. (p. 486)
—Underage Drinking. (p. 1814)
Merino, No'l, ed. Abortion. (p. 5)
—Civil Liberties. (p. 324)
—Criminal Justice. (p. 382)
—Genetic Engineering. (p. 660)
—Government Spending. (p. 704)
—Gun Control. (p. 732)
—Media Ethics. (p. 1118)
Merioux, Paulie. Grandma, Can I Have a Pet? (p. 708)
Merivale, Jane, jt. auth. see Page, Jack.
Merkaz le-Inyene hinukh (Brooklyn, New York, N.Y.) Staff, contrib. by. Hagadah Shel Pesah: Haggadah Shel Pesach for Youth: With Explanatory English Translation & Selected Insights from the Rebbe's Haggadah. (p. 735)
Merkel, Jenna. Troubles of a Snowball Kid. (p. 1790)
Merkel, Joe F., illus. see Egan, Kate.
Merkel, Joe F., illus. see Rao, Lisa.
Merkel, Joe F., jt. auth. see Sazaklis, John.
Merkel, Ruth Vitrano. Ann: 1833-1897. (p. 84)
—Grace: 1890-1973 (p. 704)
—Hannah's Girls: Elaine. (p. 743)
—Hannah's Girls: Erin (Born 1988) (p. 743)
—Marilla 1851-1916 (p. 1094)
—Ruthie: Born 1931. (p. 1499)
Merkel, Tara & Monahan, Ryan. Thunderstorm. (p. 1746)
Merker, Gerold, photos by see Mulks, Mitchell.
Merker, Patricia D. Love Has Many Faces. Wilhelm, Lauren, illus. (p. 1059)
—Sink or Swim. Wilhelm, Lauren, illus. (p. 1579)
Merki, Mary Bronson & Glencoe McGraw-Hill Staff. Human Sexuality. (p. 826)
Merkin, Richard, illus. see Ritter, Lawrence S.
Merkle, Blair Geise, jt. auth. see Geise, Brenda.
Merkos L'Inyonei Chinuch. Shaloh (p. 1559)
Merlin. Wizardology: The Book of the Secrets of Merlin. Steer, Dugald A., ed. (p. 1943)
—Wizardology Code-Writing Kit. Steer, Dugald A., ed. (p. 1943)
Merlin, Christophe. Under the Hood. (p. 1813)
Merlin, Hope & Green, Naima. Insider's Guide to Surfing (p. 878)
Merlin, Isabelle. Bright Angel. (p. 228)
—Cupid's Arrow. (p. 392)
—Pop Princess. (p. 1384)
—Three Wishes. (p. 1744)
Merlin, Master. Wizardology: A Guide to Wizards of the World. Steer, Dugald A., ed. (p. 1943)
Merline, Sharlene. Sharlene & Her Animal Friends. Rongner, Bridget, ed. (p. 1563)
Merlino, Kim. Insects & Spiders: Grades 2 & 3. (p. 876)
—Ocean Life: Grades 2 Through 4. (p. 1276)
Merlo, Maria. Leon Ruge. Keeter, Susan, illus. (p. 992)
Mermelstein, Yael. Car That Goes Far. Rosenfeld, Dina, ed. (p. 265)
—Face in the Mirror: A Fantasy. (p. 560)
—Izzy the Whiz & Passover McClean. Hartman, Carrie, illus. (p. 901)
—Stupendous Adventures of Shragi & Shia. Katz, Avi, illus. (p. 1670)
Merola, Caroline. Toni Biscotti's Magic Trick. Cummins, Sarah, tr. from FRE. (p. 1765)
—Trahison de Laurent Lareau. Merola, Caroline, illus. (p. 1776)
Merola, Caroline, illus. see Dumont, C. & Lacoursiere, Suzanne.
Merola, Caroline, illus. see Machado, Ana Maria.
Merola, Caroline, tr. see Dumont, C. & Lacoursiere, Suzanne.
Merola, Marcelo, illus. see Leiter, Andrew S.
Meron, Renato Mas. Why Corn Kernels Pop Up. (p. 1923)
—Why Mangrove Roots Float. (p. 1925)
Meroto, Tina. Tooth Gnashing Witch. Quarello, Maurizio A. C., illus. (p. 1768)
Merrell, Billy, jt. auth. see Levithan, David.
Merrell, Billy, jt. auth. see Medina, Nico.
Merrell, David, illus. see Abbott, Tony.
Merrell, David, illus. see Cooper, Ilene.
Merrell, Judith. New Ideas for Creative Prayer: 101 Ideas for Praying with 3-11 Year Olds. (p. 1245)
Merrell, Mar'ce. Wicked Sweet. (p. 1927)
Merrell, Patrick. iFlush - Plunging into Mystery Bathroom Reader for Kids Only! (p. 855)
—iFlush Swimming in Science. (p. 855)
—iFlush- Hunting for Heroes. (p. 855)
—Uncle John's iFlush - Hurtling Thru History Bathroom Reader for Kids Only! (p. 1811)
Merrell, Patrick, illus. see Bathroom Readers' Institute Staff.
Merrell, Patrick, jt. auth. see Hovanec, Helene.
Merrell, Patrick & Bathroom Readers' Institute Staff. Flapjacks from Space - 36 Tear-Off Placemats: Puzzles, Mazes, Brainteasers, Weird Facts, Jokes, & More! (p. 602)
Merrell, Patrick & Hovanec, Helene. Pony Play Games & Puzzles. (p. 1382)
Merrell, Vernon R., illus. see Hilderbrandt, Sandra June.
Merriam, Charles. History of American Political Theories. (p. 783)
Merriam-Webster, Inc. Staff. Merriam-Webster's Collegiate Dictionary. Mish, Frederick C., ed. (p. 1128)
—Merriam-Webster's First Dictionary. Heller, Ruth, illus. (p. 1128)
—Merriam-Webster's Illustrated Spanish-English Student Dictionary. (p. 1128)
—Merriam-Webster's School Dictionary. (p. 1128)
Merriam-Webster, Inc. Staff, ed. Merriam-Webster's Dictionary for Children. (p. 1128)
—Merriam-Webster's Elementary Dictionary. (p. 1128)
—Merriam-Webster's Notebook Atlas. (p. 1128)
—Merriam-Webster's Notebook Spanish-English Dictionary. (p. 1128)
—Merriam-Webster's Notebook Thesaurus. (p. 1128)
—Merriam-Webster's School Dictionary. (p. 1128)
Merrick, Caitlin & Houghton, Gillian. Primary Source Investigation of Ellis Island. (p. 1400)
Merrick, Daniel. Sir up & Sir Down: The Story of Cakes Made in Pans with Syrup. Robinson, Tanya, illus. (p. 1580)
Merrick, Laurie K. Mama, Don't! Eremeyev, Margarita, illus. (p. 1084)
Merrick, M.R. Endure. (p. 527)
Merrick, Patrick. Avalanches. (p. 118)
—Droughts. (p. 486)
—Easter Bunnies. (p. 499)
—Forest Fires. (p. 618)
—Fourth of July Fireworks. (p. 625)
—Thanksgiving Turkeys. (p. 1726)
Merrick, Rebecca. Rain Harbor. (p. 1435)
Merrick, Sylvia Bach. Me & My Flea Steed, Clyde, at Home on Ralph. Cerda, Edward, illus. (p. 1115)
Merrifield, Monarca, illus. see Kayaalp, Suzan.
Merrill, Amy French. Day in the Life of a Colonial Cabinetmaker. (p. 413)
—Day in the Life of a Colonial Dressmaker. (p. 413)
—Day in the Life of a Colonial Surveyor. (p. 413)
—Everyday Physical Science Experiments with Gases. (p. 544)
—Everyday Physical Science Experiments with Gravity. (p. 544)
—Everyday Physical Science Experiments with Light & Sound. (p. 544)
—Everyday Physical Science Experiments with Solids. (p. 544)
Merrill, Bob. How Much Is That Doggie in the Window? Trapani, Iza, illus. (p. 811)
Merrill, Dennis & Paterson, Thomas. Major Problems in American Foreign Relations: Documents & Essays, Concise Edition. (p. 1078)
Merrill, Eugene H. Kingdom of Priests: A History of Old Testament Israel. (p. 960)
Merrill, Frank T., illus. see Eaton, Walter Prichard.
Merrill, Jean. Elephant Who Liked to Smash Small Cars. Solbert, Ronni, illus. (p. 511)
—Pushcart War. (p. 1420)
—Pushcart War. Solbert, Ronni, illus. (p. 1420)
—Toothpaste Millionaire. (p. 1768)
Merrill, Jennifer. Briar Hill Brats. (p. 227)
Merrill, John. Submarines, Technology, & History. (p. 1671)
Merrill, Karen Grill. Oh, What a State I'm In: The USA in Rhyme & Riddle Grill, Gerald, illus. (p. 1281)
—Rhyme Time. (p. 1468)
Merrill, Libby, ed. see Waters, Tony.
Merrill, Mike, jt. auth. see Pearson, Iris.
Merrill, Yvonne Y. America: Art Activities about Colonial America, African-Americans, & Southeast Indians. Vol. 2 (p. 58)
—America: Art Activities about Lewis & Clark, Pioneers, & Plains Indians. Vol. 3 Simpson, Mary, illus. (p. 58)
—Ancient People: Art Activities about Mesopotamia, Egypt, & Islam. Simpson, Mary, illus. (p. 70)
—Ancient People: Art Activities about Minoans, Mycenaeans, Trojans, Ancient Greeks, Etruscans, & Romans. Vol. 2 Simpson, Mary, illus. (p. 70)
Merrill-Maker, Andrea. Montana: People & Their Stories. (p. 1170)
Merriman, Christi, illus. see Bernal, Sandra Marie.
Merriman, Lisa P., illus. see Moran, Katherine J.
Merriman, Rachel. Story of Me: A Girl's Journal. (p. 1659)
Merrison, Stacy, illus. see LeGrand, Hank, 3rd.
Merritt, Ginny. Window in the Wall. (p. 1936)
Merritt, Kate. Indestructibles: Baby Babble. (p. 870)
—Indestructibles: Baby Faces. (p. 870)
Merritt, Kate, illus. see Pixton, Amy.
Merritt, Michael. Tack & Mame Book. (p. 1694)
Merritt, Richard. Where Are Santa's Pants? (p. 1906)
Merritt, Robin. Life Cycle of a Butterfly. (p. 1008)
—Life Cycle of a Chicken. (p. 1009)
—Life Cycle of a Frog. (p. 1009)
—Life Cycle of a Human. (p. 1009)
—Life Cycle of a Polar Bear. (p. 1009)
—Life Cycle of a Snake. (p. 1009)
Merritt, Virginia. Ram for Isaac. (p. 1437)
Merriweather-Beech, Myrtle. Unfroggettable Fiona Fayetta Froggee: A Green Pond Memoir. Sanda-Ebosh, Mary, illus. (p. 1817)
Merrow, John, jt. auth. see Hersh, Richard H.
Merry, Alex, illus. see Mayfield, Dan.
Merry, Lindsay R. Dackshew Dragonfly. (p. 398)
Merry, Margaret. Adventures of Princess the Pony. (p. 22)
—Lonely Digger. (p. 1046)
—Wise Old Boar. (p. 1940)
Merryman, Mary Alice. Mothers at the Manger. (p. 1178)
Merryweather, Jack, illus. see Beals, Frank Lee.
Mersey, Daniel. King Arthur (p. 958)
Mersky, Roy M., et al. Landmark Supreme Court Cases (p. 974)
Mertins, Lisa, illus. see Doti, James.
Mertz, Alyssa. Lucky Farm Boy Crum, A. M., illus. (p. 1062)
Mertz, Leslie. Dinosaurs: Walk in the Footsteps of the World's Largest Lizards. (p. 444)
—Extreme Bugs. (p. 556)
Mertz, Leslie A. Circulatory System (p. 321)
Mertz, Leslie A., et al. Amphibians (p. 65)
—Grzimeks Student Animal Life Resource (p. 728)
—Grzimek's Student Animal Life Resource (p. 728)
Merveille, David. Hello Mr. Hulot. (p. 764)
—Juke Box. Merveille, David, illus. (p. 932)
Mervine, M. A. How Katie Got a Voice: (and a Cool New Nickname) (p. 810)
Mervis (Pantoja), Judith. Yuyl y la Rama: Yuyl y la Rama. (p. 1983)
Mervyn, Catherine Antolino. Call Me Nona. (p. 254)
—Lesson from a Tree. Carr, Tabatha, illus. (p. 993)
Merwin, Decie, illus. see Caudill, Rebecca.
Merworth, Carol. I Am Somebody. (p. 834)
Merz, Bruno, illus. see Smallman, Steve.
Merz, Caroline & Lee-Browne, Patrick, trs. Post-War Literature: 1945 to the Present Day. Vol. 5 (p. 1387)
Merz, Jennifer. Playground Day. (p. 1372)
Merz, Kathleen, jt. auth. see Weulersse, Odile.
Merz, Robert L. Quips, Quotes & Oats: Smarty Jones Talks. (p. 1428)
Mesak, Olga, illus. see Chase, Anita, et al.
Mesalles, Monica, tr. see Reddy, Prerana & Strauss, David, eds.
Mescall, Ron. Adventures of Goo Goo Malou: A Parent's Guide for Teaching Values. (p. 18)
Mesch, Kate, ed. see Yeager, Allison Blair.
Meschenmoser, Sebastian. 3 Wishes for Pugman. Meschenmoser, Sebastian, illus. (p. 1991)
—Learning to Fly. Meschenmoser, Sebastian, illus. (p. 985)
—Mr. Squirrel & the Moon. (p. 1186)
—Waiting for Winter. Meschenmoser, Sebastian, illus. (p. 1853)
Meschini, Leonardo. Prince & the Sphinx (p. 1401)
Meschini, Leonardo, illus. see McCurry, Kristen.
Meschke, Nimi Srivastava. Meeting Aldo Ant: Learning to Appreciate Mexican Culture. (p. 1123)
—Meeting Geeta Grasshopper. (p. 1123)
Mese, John R. & Kelsey, Dawn M. On the Flippy Side. Holden, Chanler, illus. (p. 1290)
Meserve, Adria. Cleopatra Silverwing. (p. 331)
Meserve, Jessica. Bedtime Without Arthur. Meserve, Jessica, illus. (p. 157)
Meserve, Jessica, illus. see Carris, Joan Davenport.
Meserve, Jessica, illus. see Dencer, Christine.
Meserve, Jessica, illus. see Schaefer, Lola M.
Meserve, Jessica, illus. see Schaefer, Lola.
Meserve, Jessica, illus. see Thebo, Mimi.
Meserve, Jessica, illus. see Voake, Steve.
Meshach, Joanna. Land of the Magical Mirrors. (p. 973)
Meshbesher, Wendy, jt. auth. see Hartman, Eve.
Meshon, Aaron. Take Me Out to the Yakyu. Meshon, Aaron, illus. (p. 1696)

—Tools Rule! Meshon, Aaron, illus. (p. 1767)
Mesibere, Ellen. Curse of the Laulau Tree. Manasau, Amos, illus. (p. 395)
—Magic Log. Naime, Sophie, ed. (p. 1072)
Meskar, Sara, jt. auth. see Ghounem, Mohamed.
Mesker, Erma Medrano. Bullies on the Prowl on a Hallow's Eve. (p. 240)
Meskill, Elizia. Heart Pendant: A Princess' Search for True Love Resplendent. (p. 760)
Meskunas, Brenda. Very Strange Medley. (p. 1839)
Mesmer, Heidi Anne E. Tools for Matching Readers to Texts: Research-Based Practices. (p. 1767)
Mesplay, Gail G. Sally Sue & the Hospice of Saint John. Corrette, Keith F., photos by. (p. 1505)
Mesquita, Camila, illus. see Camossa, Silvia.
Mesquita, Camila, illus. see Lenero, Carmen.
Mesrobian, Carrie. Cut Both Ways. (p. 396)
—Perfectly Good White Boy. (p. 1342)
—Sex & Violence. (p. 1556)
Messenger, Lois. Fairy Magic & the Healing Rainbow Colours. (p. 563)
Messenger, Norman. Imagine. Messenger, Norman, illus. (p. 860)
—Land of Neverbelieve. Messenger, Norman, illus. (p. 973)
Messenger, Norman, jt. auth. see Equipo Staff.
Messenger, Shannon. Exile. (p. 548)
—Keeper of the Lost Cities. (p. 947)
—Let the Sky Fall. (p. 994)
—Let the Storm Break. (p. 994)
Messenger, Stephanie. Melanie's Marvelous Measles. (p. 1125)
Messer, Celeste M. Andi's Choice. Hoeffner, Deb, illus. (p. 72)
—Angel Experiment J134 Bk #1. (p. 73)
—Boy Who Cried Wolf. Hoeffner, Deb, illus. (p. 219)
—Broken Wing: The Adventures of Andi O'Malley. Hoeffner, Deb, illus. (p. 230)
—Circle of Light. (p. 321)
—Forever & Always. Hoeffner, Deb, illus. (p. 619)
—Ghost of Piper's Landing. Hoeffner, Deb, illus. (p. 671)
—Gift. (p. 674)
—Message from Teddy. Hoeffner, Deb, illus. (p. 1129)
—Three Miracles. (p. 1743)
—When Eagles Fly. Hoeffner, Deb, illus. (p. 1902)
Messer, Celia, illus. see Gray, Susan.
Messer, Corey, illus. see Wolf, Clarissa.
Messer, Jennifer K., illus. see Messer, Luke.
Messer, Jon, illus. see Facklam, Margery & Thomas, Peggy.
Messer, Kimberly. Patriotic Program Builder: Creative Resources for Program Directors. (p. 1329)
Messer, Luke. Hoosier Heart. Messer, Jennifer K., illus. (p. 796)
Messer, Neil. Christian Ethics. (p. 311)
Messer, Stephen. Death of Yorik Mortwell. Grimly, Gris, illus. (p. 420)
—Windblowne. (p. 1935)
Messerly, Svetlana. Once I Was an Angel. (p. 1292)
Messersmith, Heather. Seasons. (p. 1538)
Messersmith, Patrick, illus. see Alter, Judy.
Messersmith, Patrick, jt. auth. see Stumpff, April D.
Messervy-Norman, J. Philos. (p. 1351)
Messick, Joshua Robert. Elves & the Secret Society. (p. 517)
Messick, Maxine. Use Your Noodle! The Adventures of a Hollywood Poodle Named Doodle. Hodsdon-Carr, Sandra, ed. (p. 1827)
Messier, Mireille. Competition: From Start to Finish Murray, Steven, illus. (p. 352)
Messier, Solange, tr. see Quintin, Michel & Bergeron, Alain.
Messier, Solange, tr. see Quintin, Michel, et al.
Messimer, Wanda Fay. Tiny Teacup & Pot Belly Pig Go to Africa to Meet the 'Great Lion' (p. 1756)
Messina, Lawrence, et al. Secret Undercover Bodyguards: The Hidden Passage. (p. 1544)
Messina, Leslie-Ann. Adventures of Dolly the Dollar Bill: Dolly Meets Matilda. (p. 17)
Messina, Lilli, illus. see Law, Felicia.
Messina, Linda, illus. see Lightner, Laura.
Messina, Lynn. Savvy Girl. (p. 1518)
Messina, Lynn, jt. auth. see Alcott, Louisa May.
Messina, Noreen E. Now Hiring: A Story of Four Teens Finding Their First Jobs. (p. 1269)
—Teenwork: Four Teens Tell All: A Guide for Finding Jobs. (p. 1715)
Messing, Dave, illus. see Baum, Lonna.
Messing, Dave, illus. see Sicks, Linda.
Messing, David, illus. see Dillon-Butler, Marybeth.
Messing, David, illus. see McCloud, Carol, et al.
Messing, David, illus. see McCloud, Carol.
Messing, Debra, jt. auth. see Finch, Mary.
Messinger, Laura M., jt. auth. see Messinger, Robert M.
Messinger, Midge. Freddie Q. Freckle. Messinger, Robert, ed. (p. 632)
Messinger, Robert. I've Got Mail! Salerno, John, illus. (p. 901)
Messinger, Robert, ed. see Messinger, Midge.
Messinger, Robert M. & Messinger, Laura M. Why Me? Why Did I Have to Get Diabetes? (p. 1925)
Messner, Dennis, illus. see Meister, Cari.
Messner, Kate. All the Answers. (p. 45)
—Brilliant Fall of Gianna Z. (p. 228)
—Capture the Flag. (p. 265)
—Champlain & the Silent One. Gulley, Martha, illus. (p. 289)
—Danger in Ancient Rome. McMorris, Kelley, illus. (p. 403)
—Eye of the Storm. (p. 557)
—Hide & Seek. (p. 776)
—How to Read a Story. Siegel, Mark, illus. (p. 821)
—Manhunt. (p. 1087)
—Marty McGuire. Floca, Brian, illus. (p. 1098)
—Marty McGuire Digs Worms! (p. 1098)
—Marty McGuire Digs Worms! Floca, Brian, illus. (p. 1098)
—Marty Mcguire Has Too Many Pets! (p. 1098)
—Marty McGuire Has Too Many Pets! Floca, Brian, illus. (p. 1098)
—Over & under the Snow. Neal, Christopher Silas, illus. (p. 1313)
—Rescue on the Oregon Trail. McMorris, Kelley, illus. (p. 1462)
—Sea Monster & the Bossy Fish. Rash, Andy, illus. (p. 1535)
—Sea Monster's First Day. Rash, Andy, illus. (p. 1535)
—Spitfire. (p. 1629)
—Sugar & Ice. (p. 1672)
—Tree of Wonder. Mulazzani, Simona, illus. (p. 1783)
—Up in the Garden & down in the Dirt. (p. 1824)
—Wake up Missing. (p. 1853)
Mestas. Nolan & the Magic Bridge. (p. 1263)
Mesturini, C., illus. see Caviezel, Giovanni.
Mesturini, Cristina, illus. see Caviezel, Giovanni.
Mesturini, Cristina, jt. auth. see Caviezel, Giovanni.
Metal, Liana. Storytime. (p. 1664)
Metaxas, Eric. Amazing Grace: William Wilberforce & the Heroic Campaign to End Slavery. (p. 54)
—Fool & the Flying Ship. Drescher, Henrick, illus. (p. 614)
—Jack & the Beanstalk. Sorel, Edward, illus. (p. 902)
—King Midas & the Golden Touch. Prato, Rodica, illus. (p. 958)
—Monkey People. Bryan, Diana, illus. (p. 1165)
—Mose the Fireman. Peck, Everett, illus. (p. 1176)
—Peachboy. Smith, Jeffrey, illus. (p. 1332)
—Princess Scargo & the Birthday Pumpkin. Barbour, Karen, illus. (p. 1405)
—Puss in Boots. Le-Tan, Pierre, illus. (p. 1420)
—Squanto & the First Thanksgiving: The Legendary American Tale. Donato, Michael A., illus. (p. 1636)
—Stormalong. Vanderbeek, Don, illus. (p. 1656)
Metaxas, Eric, jt. auth. see Tillman, Nancy.
Metaxas, Eric, ed. Khalil & the Big Gulp. (p. 951)
Metayer, Michel. Erwin Blumenfeld. (p. 534)
Metcalf, Calvin John. Literary World Seventh Reader. (p. 1023)
Metcalf, Dawn. Indelible. (p. 870)
—Insidious. (p. 878)
—Invisible. (p. 885)
Metcalf, Gena, ed. see Metcalf, Tom.
Metcalf, Gena, jt. ed. see Metcalf, Tom.
Metcalf, Gena, ed. Cancer. (p. 260)
Metcalf, Kristin, illus. see Zelaya, Carol.
Metcalf, Maggie, illus. see Obray, C. J.
Metcalf, Paula. Guide to Sisters. Barton, Suzanne, illus. (p. 730)
—Mouse's Sock Tree. Mitchell, Susan, illus. (p. 1182)
Metcalf, Paula, illus. see Phillips, Sarah.
Metcalf, Tania, illus. see Robinson, Ann.
Metcalf, Tom. Oil. Des Chenes, Elizabeth & McCage, Crystal D., eds. (p. 1282)
—Phobias. Metcalf, Gena, ed. (p. 1351)
Metcalf, Tom & Metcalf, Gena, eds. Nuclear Power. (p. 1270)
Metcalfe, Jack & Apps, John. Marquetry Course. (p. 1096)
Metebole, Mattie. Lunar Cycle: Phases of the Moon. (p. 1065)
Meter, Pete, jt. auth. see Meter, Pete O.
Meter, Pete O. & Meter, Pete. Walk the Walk: The Kid's Book of Pedometer Challenges. (p. 1854)
Methold, Graham, photos by see Day, Martin.
Metikosh, Anne. Terra Incognita. (p. 1721)
Metivier, Gary. Saluting Grandpa: Celebrating Veterans & Honor Flight Rath, Robert, illus. (p. 1506)
—Until Daddy Comes Home Rath, Robert, illus. (p. 1823)
Metlen, Ryan, jt. auth. see Metlen, Ryan W.
Metlen, Ryan W. & Metlen, Ryan. Ewe. (p. 547)
Metola, Patricia, illus. see Maestro, Pepe.
Metropolitan Museum of Art Staff. Christmas Story. (p. 315)
—Nyc ABC. (p. 1274)
Metropolitan Museum of Art Staff, jt. auth. see Falken, Linda.
Metropolitan Museum of Art Staff & Roehrig, Catharine. Fun with Hieroglyphs. (p. 648)
Metropolitan Museum of Art Staff, compiled by. My First ABC. (p. 1204)
Metropolitan Museum of Art Staff, contrib. by. Color Magic Sticker Play Book. (p. 342)
—Museum Colors: The Metropolitan Museum of Art. (p. 1192)
—Museum Shapes. (p. 1193)
Mets, Marilyn, illus. see Hatkoff, Craig & Hatkoff, Juliana Lee.
Mets, Marilyn, illus. see Ledwon, Peter.
Mets, Marilyn, illus. see Lohans, Alison.
Metselaar, Menno & van der Rol, Ruud. Anne Frank: Her Life in Words & Pictures from the Archives of the Anne Frank House. Pomerans, Arnold J., tr. from DUT. (p. 85)
Metter, Bert & Metter, Bertram. Bar Mitzvah, Bat Mitzvah: The Ceremony, the Party, & How the Day Came to Be. Reilly, Joan & Katz, Avi, illus. (p. 137)
Metter, Bertram, jt. auth. see Metter, Bert.
Mettler, Joe, illus. see Morris, Lynn.
Mettler, René. Birds. Mettler, René, illus. (p. 191)
Mettler, René. Jungle. (p. 934)
Mettler, René. Pinguin. (p. 1359)
Mettler, René, illus. see Harvey, Bev, et al.
Mettler, Réne, jt. auth. see Delafosse, Claude.
Mettler, René, jt. auth. see First Discovery Staff.
Mettler, René, jt. auth. see Mathews, Sarah.
Mettler, René, jt. auth. see Mettler, Ren'e.
Mettler, René & Jeunesse, Gallimard. Selva. Mettler, René & Barroso, Paz, trs. (p. 1550)
Mettler, Ren'e & Mettler, René. Flor. (p. 606)
Mettler, Ren'e, et al. Huevo. (p. 824)
—Pajaro. (p. 1319)
Mettler-Eells, Kimberly. Does God Have an Airplane? A Candid Journey of Bereavement Through the Eyes of a Child. (p. 460)
Metts, Wallis C., et al. Children's Book of the Bible. (p. 303)
Metu, jt. illus. see Lakes, Lofton.
Metz, Diana. Brinn & the Dragons of Pallan Cliffs. (p. 229)
Metz, Gabriele. Get to Know Cat Breeds: Over 40 Best-Known Breeds. (p. 668)
Metz, L. Every Egg: Learning the Short E Sound. (p. 542)
—On the Job: Learning the O Sound. (p. 1290)
Metz, Lauren. Prom Book: The Only Guide You'll Ever Need. (p. 1411)
Metz, Leon C. Roadside History of Texas. Greer, Daniel, ed. (p. 1477)
Metz, Lorijo. Arabian Horses. (p. 94)
—Cattle: Cows, Bulls, & Calves. (p. 281)
—Chickens: Hens, Roosters, & Chicks. (p. 300)
—Clydesdales. (p. 336)
—Discovering Clams. (p. 449)
—Discovering Crabs. (p. 449)
—Discovering Jellyfish. (p. 449)
—Discovering Sea Lions. (p. 449)
—Discovering Seagulls. (p. 449)
—Discovering Starfish. (p. 449)
—Donkeys: Jennies, Jacks, & Foals. (p. 466)
—Friesians. (p. 639)
—Geese: Geese, Ganders, & Goslings. (p. 659)
—Goats: Nannies, Billies, & Kids. (p. 687)
—Lipizzans. (p. 1021)
—Lusitanos. (p. 1066)
—Sheep: Ewes, Rams, & Lambs. (p. 1564)
—Thoroughbreds. (p. 1740)
—Using Beakers & Graduated Cylinders. (p. 1828)
—Using Clocks & Stopwatches. (p. 1828)
—Using Hand Lenses & Microscopes. (p. 1828)
—Using Rulers & Tape Measures. (p. 1828)
—Using Scales & Balances. (p. 1828)
—Using Thermometers. (p. 1828)
—What Can We Do about Global Warming? (p. 1880)
—What Can We Do about Invasive Species? (p. 1880)
—What Can We Do about Trash & Recycling? (p. 1881)
Metz, Melinda. Echoes. (p. 502)
—Raven's Point. (p. 1441)
—S. M. A. R. T. S. & the 3-D Danger. McKenzie, Heath, illus. (p. 1499)
—S. M. A. R. T. S. & the Invisible Robot. McKenzie, Heath, illus. (p. 1499)
—S. M. A. R. T. S. & the Missing UFO. McKenzie, Heath, illus. (p. 1499)
—S. M. A. R. T. S. & the Poison Plates. McKenzie, Heath, illus. (p. 1499)
Metz, Melinda, jt. auth. see Burns, Laura J.
Metz, Melinda & Burns, Laura J. Crave (p. 376)
Metz, Teresa L. Friends for Phoebe. (p. 638)
Metzenthen, David. Bay Boys: Big Wave Day, Adrian over the Top, Adrian Goes Out There! (p. 147)
—One Minute's Silence. Camilleri, Michael, illus. (p. 1296)
—Tiff & the Trout. (p. 1748)
Metzger, Clancy, jt. auth. see Cosby, Sam.
Metzger, Haley & Banks, Rayelynn. I Am Not Weird (p. 833)
Metzger, Jan, illus. see Lambert, Joyce.
Metzger, Joanna. Space Program. Elizalde, Marcelo, illus. (p. 1619)
Metzger, Julie & Lehman, Robert. Will Puberty Last My Whole Life? Real Answers to Real Questions from Preteens about Body Changes, Sex, & Other Growing-Up Stuff. (p. 1932)
Metzger, Lois. Be Careful What You Wish For: Ten Stories about Wishes. (p. 148)
—Can You Keep a Secret? Ten Stories about Secrets. (p. 259)
—Trick of the Light. (p. 1786)
Metzger, Lois & Mazer, Norma Fox. Year We Missed My Birthday: Eleven Birthday Stories. (p. 1969)
Metzger, Martina, jt. ed. see Fritz, Barbara.
Metzger, Steve. Big Shark's Valentine Surprise. Hohnstadt, Cedric, illus. (p. 183)
—Biggest Leaf Pile. Dubin, Jill, illus. (p. 185)
—Dancing Clock. Nez, John Abbott, illus. (p. 402)
—Easter Bunny Is Missing! Spurll, Barbara, illus. (p. 499)
—Five Little Bunnies Hopping on a Hill. (p. 600)
—Five Little Penguins Slipping on the Ice. Bryant, Laura, illus. (p. 600)
—Five Little Penguins Slipping on the Ice. Bryant, Laura J., illus. (p. 600)
—Five Little Sharks Swimming in the Sea. Bryant, Laura, illus. (p. 601)
—Five Spooky Ghosts Playing Tricks at School. Harrald-Pilz, Marilee, illus. (p. 601)
—Great Turkey Race. Paillot, Jim, illus. (p. 719)
—I Love You All Year Long. Keay, Claire, illus. (p. 843)
—Ice Cream King. Downing, Julie, illus. (p. 850)
—Leaves Are Falling One by One. Sagasti, Miriam, illus. (p. 986)
—Little Snowflake. Wellington, Monica, illus. (p. 1036)
—Little Snowflake's Big Adventure. (p. 1036)
—Mixed-Up Alphabet. Ho, Jannie, illus. (p. 1156)
—Pluto Visits Earth! Lee, Jared, illus. (p. 1374)
—Princess Kitty. Okstad, Ella K., illus. (p. 1404)
—Skeleton Meets the Mummy. Zenz, Aaron, illus. (p. 1584)
—This Is the House That Monsters Built. Lee, Jared D., illus. (p. 1736)
—Tooth Fairy Loses a Tooth! Busby, Ailie, illus. (p. 1768)
—Turkey Train. Paillot, Jim, illus. (p. 1797)
—Under the Apple Tree. Girasole, Alessia, illus. (p. 1813)
—Way I Act. Cain, Janan, illus. (p. 1864)
—We're Going on a Leaf Hunt. Sakamoto, Miki, illus. (p. 1875)
—Will Princess Isabel Ever Say Please? Haley, Amanda, illus. (p. 1932)
Metzger, Steve & Antonini, Gabriele. Huggapotamus. (p. 825)
Metzger, Steve & Hohnstadt, Cedric. Big Shark's Halloween Mystery. (p. 183)
Metzger, Steve & Kronheimer, Ann. Lincoln & Grace: Why Abraham Lincoln Grew a Beard. (p. 1018)
Metzger, Wolfgang, illus. see Caballero, D.
Metzl, Jordan D. & Shookhoff, Carol. Young Athlete: A Sports Doctor's Complete Guide for Parents. (p. 1978)
Metzler, Chris & Kim, Sunyoung. Me & 10 Babies. (p. 1115)
Metzner, Ralph. Know Your Type. (p. 965)
Metzroth, Rupert A. Think for Yourself. (p. 1734)
Meucci, Sandra. Antonio & the Electric Scream: The Man Who Invented the Telephone. (p. 90)
Meunier, Sylvain. Ma Premiere de Classe. Eudes-Pascal, Elisabeth, tr. (p. 1067)
—Raffi's Animal Rescue Cummins, Sarah, tr. from FRE. (p. 1433)
—Raffi's Animal Rescue. Cummins, Sarah, tr. from FRE. (p. 1433)
—Raffi's Island Adventure Cummins, Sarah, tr. from FRE. (p. 1433)
—Raffi's New Friend Cummins, Sarah, tr. from FRE. (p. 1433)
Meunier, Sylvain & Lapierre, Steeve. Graindsel et Bretel. Fil et, Julie, illus. (p. 705)
Meurer, Caleb, illus. see Golden Books Staff & Smith, Geof.
Meurer, Caleb, illus. see Golden Books Staff.
Meurer, Caleb, illus. see Golden Books.
Meurer, Caleb, illus. see Miglis, Jenny.
Meurer, Caleb, illus. see Posner-Sanchez, Andrea.
Meurer, Caleb, illus. see Random House Staff.
Meurer, Caleb, illus. see Smith, Geof.
Meuse, Theresa. Sharing Circle: Stories about First Nations Culture Stevens, arthur, illus. (p. 1561)
Mewburn, Kyle. Bog Frog Hop. Cool, Rebecca, illus. (p. 207)
—Funny Little Dog. McKenzie, Heath, illus. (p. 650)
—Kiss! Kiss! Yuck! Yuck! Teo, Ali & O'Reilly, John, illus. (p. 961)
—Scruffy Old Cat. McKenzie, Heath, illus. (p. 1533)
—Slowcoach Turtle. McKenzie, Heath, illus. (p. 1591)
Mey, illus. see Schuff, Nicolás & Fraticelli, Damin.
Meyell, Lenaise. Stiletto 101: Don't Let the Stilettos Fool You. Smith, Joanie, ed. (p. 1650)
Meyer, Alison, illus. see Ragan, Lyn.
Meyer, Ashley M., illus. see Lynn, Elizabeth B.
Meyer, Brad. Matchless Age. (p. 1104)
Meyer, Brian E. What You Mean to Me. (p. 1896)
Meyer, Brigit. Christmas Surprise. Mussenbrock, Anne, illus. (p. 315)
—Merry Christmas, Little Bear. Mussenbrock, Anne, illus. (p. 1128)
Meyer, Bryce. Anna's Antarctica: A Combat-Fishing Book. (p. 85)
Meyer, Bryce L. Dolphin & Manatee Friends End to End: Formerly Grant's Book of Manatees & Dolphins. (p. 464)
Meyer, C. Very First Unicorn. (p. 1838)
Meyer, Carolyn. Anastasia & Her Sisters. (p. 67)
—Anastasia: the Last Grand Duchess, Russia 1914. (p. 67)
—Bad Queen: Rules & Instructions for Marie-Antoinette. (p. 132)
—Beauty's Daughter: The Story of Hermione & Helen of Troy. (p. 154)
—Cleopatra Confesses. (p. 331)
—Diary of a Waitress: The Not-So-Glamorous Life of a Harvey Girl. (p. 435)
—Doomed Queen Anne. (p. 470)
—Duchessina: A Novel of Catherine de' Medici. (p. 488)
—Jubilee Journey. (p. 930)
—Loving Will Shakespeare. (p. 1061)
—Marie, Dancing. (p. 1093)
—Miss Patch's Learn-To-Sew Book. Suzuki, Mary, illus. (p. 1151)
—Patience, Princess Catherine: A Young Royals Book. (p. 1328)
—Rio Grande Stories. (p. 1473)
—True Adventures of Charley Darwin. (p. 1791)
—Victoria Rebels. (p. 1840)
—White Lilacs. (p. 1913)
—Wild Queen: The Days & Nights of Mary, Queen of Scots. (p. 1930)
Meyer, Carolyn & Gallenkamp, Charles. Mystery of the Ancient Maya: Revised Edition. (p. 1225)
Meyer, Chloe, illus. see Hurth, Barbi.
Meyer, D J. Sibling Slam Book. (p. 1572)
Meyer, Dana. Allen & Alley: The Perfect House. (p. 46)
—Gift for Prince Eli. (p. 675)
Meyer, Deanna. Buffalo on the Ridge. (p. 235)
Meyer, Diana. Samson's Great Adventure. (p. 1509)
Meyer, Diana Lambdin. Kid's Guide to Kansas City. (p. 953)
Meyer, Donald J. & Vadasy, Patricia. Living with a Brother or Sister with Special Needs: A Book for Sibs. (p. 1042)
Meyer, Edith Patterson. Friendly Frontier: The Story of the Canadian-American Border. Mars, W. T., illus. (p. 638)
Meyer, Edwin, 3rd. KillerSports.com NBA Annual. (p. 956)
Meyer, Eileen R. Sweet Dreams, Wild Animals! A Story of Sleep. Caple, Laurie A., illus. (p. 1689)
—Who's Faster? Animals on the Move. Bergum, Constance Rummel, illus. (p. 1920)
Meyer, Emily, ed. see Rey, H. A.
Meyer, Eric Christopher. Art in the Renaissance: Set Of 6. (p. 102)
Meyer, Franklyn. More Me & Caleb Again. (p. 1174)
Meyer, Franklyn E. Me & Caleb. Smith, Lawrence Beall, illus. (p. 1115)
—Me & Caleb Again. Liese, Charles, illus. (p. 1115)
Meyer, Henye. Fall of the Sun God. (p. 566)
Meyer, James. Minimalism. (p. 1146)
Meyer, Jan. Brain Quest Grade 3: A Whole Year of Curriculum-Based Exercises & Activities in One Fun Book! Shults, Anna, ed. (p. 222)
Meyer, Jan & Brain Quest Editors. Brain Quest Grade 3 Math. (p. 222)
Meyer, Jane G. Man & the Vine. Gannon, Ned, illus. (p. 1085)
Meyer, Jane G. & Gannon, Ned. Woman & the Wheat. Meyer, Jane G. & Gannon, Ned, illus. (p. 1945)
Meyer, Jared. Frequently Asked Questions about Being an Immigrant Teen. (p. 636)
—Homeland Security Officers. (p. 793)
—Making Friends: The Art of Social Networking in Life & Online. (p. 1081)
—Working in a War Zone: Military Contractors. (p. 1952)
Meyer, Jared, jt. auth. see Bergin, Rory M.
Meyer, Jared & Jolis, Annie. University of Maryland College Prowler off the Record. (p. 1820)
Meyer, Jean, illus. see Sabin, Francene & Mattern, Joanne.
Meyer, Jeff, illus. see Eareckson Tada, Joni.
Meyer, Jeffrey. If Trees Could Talk: At the Alamo. (p. 854)
Meyer, Jeffrey G. If Trees Could Talk: At Mount Vernon. (p. 854)
Meyer, John, jt. auth. see Meyer, Stephanie H.
Meyer, John H. Wilmington Today: A Guide to Cape Fear Leisure. (p. 1934)
Meyer, Joyce. 21 Ways to Finding Peace & Happiness: Overcoming Anxiety, Fear, & Discontentment Every Day. (p. 1996)
—Be Healed in Jesus' Name. (p. 148)
—Beauty for Ashes: Receiving Emotional Healing. (p. 154)
—Campo de Batalla de la Mente para Ninos. (p. 258)

—Disfrute Donde Esta Camino a Donde Va. (p. 450)
—Eight Ways to Keep the Devil under Your Feet. (p. 507)
—Every Which Way to Pray Sullivan, Mary, illus. (p. 543)
—Healing the Brokenhearted: Experience Restoration Through the Power of God's Word. (p. 757)
—How to Hear from God: Learn to Know His Voice & Make Right Decisions. (p. 820)
—Knowing God Intimately: Being as Close to Him as You Want to Be. (p. 965)
—Most Important Decision You Will Ever Make: A Complete & Thorough Understanding of What It Means to Be Born Again. (p. 1177)
—Peace: Cast All Your Cares upon Him. (p. 1331)
—Power of Being Positive: Enjoying God Forever. (p. 1389)
—Power of Determination: Looking to Jesus. (p. 1389)
—Power of Forgiveness: Keep Your Heart Free. (p. 1389)
—Seven Things That Steal Your Joy: Overcoming the Obstacles to Your Happiness. (p. 1555)
—Starting Your Day Right: Devotions for Each Morning of the Year. (p. 1644)
—Straight Talk on Depression: Overcoming Emotional Battles with the Power of God's Word! (p. 1664)
—Straight Talk on Discouragement: Overcoming Emotional Battles with the Power of God's Word! (p. 1664)
—Straight Talk on Fear: Overcoming Emotional Battles with the Power of God's Word! (p. 1664)
—Straight Talk on Insecurity: Overcoming Emotional Battles with the Power of God's Word! (p. 1664)
—Straight Talk on Loneliness: Overcoming Emotional Battles with the Power of God's Word! (p. 1664)
—Straight Talk on Stress: Overcoming Emotional Battles with the Power of God's Word! (p. 1664)
—Straight Talk on Worry: Overcoming Emotional Battles with the Power of God's Word! (p. 1664)
—Tell Them I Love Them: Receiving a Revelation of God's Love for You. (p. 1717)
—When, God, When? Learning to Trust in God's Timing. (p. 1902)
—Why, God, Why? How to Be Delivered from Confusion. (p. 1925)
—Word, the Name, the Blood. (p. 1951)
Meyer, Joyce & Hafer, Todd. Battlefield of the Mind - For Teens: Winning the Battle in Your Mind. (p. 147)
Meyer, Joyce & Moore, Karen. Battlefield of the Mind for Kids. (p. 147)
Meyer, Julia & Tabler, Marie. One Pea. Tabler, Marie, illus. (p. 1296)
Meyer, Kai. Arcadia Awakens. (p. 95)
—Arcadia Burns. (p. 95)
—Arcadia Falls. (p. 95)
—Dark Reflections: The Water Mirror - The Stone Light; the Glass Word. Crawford, Elizabeth D., tr. from GER. (p. 408)
—Glass Word. Crawford, Elizabeth D., tr. from GER. (p. 682)
—Palabra de Cristal. Serra Huerta, Luis, tr. (p. 1319)
—Pirate Wars. Crawford, Elizabeth D., tr. (p. 1363)
—Stone Light. Crawford, Elizabeth D., tr. (p. 1652)
Meyer, Karen. Conflict at Chillicothe. (p. 357)
Meyer, Karen, illus. see Christopher, Matt.
Meyer, Karl. Dog Heroes: A Poster Book. (p. 461)
Meyer, Kathy. Daisy & Digger. (p. 400)
—Gymnastics. (p. 733)
Meyer, Kay L. Adventures of Billie & Annie—Baby Bison. Kirchoff, Arthur, illus. (p. 16)
Meyer, Ken, Jr. Lucky Lionel. (p. 1062)
Meyer, Kerry, illus. see Watt, Fiona.
Meyer, Kerstin, illus. see Funke, Cornelia.
Meyer, Kerstin, illus. see Steinhöfel, Andreas.
Meyer, Kim Shapiro. Journey of the Coconut. Shapiro, Pepper, illus. (p. 928)
Meyer, Koston. Where Does the Mail Go? (p. 1907)
Meyer, L. A. Bloody Jack: Being an Account of the Curious Adventures of Mary "Jacky" Faber, Ship's Boy. (p. 201)
—Boston Jacky: Being an Account of the Further Adventures of Jacky Faber, Taking Care of Business. (p. 215)
—Curse of the Blue Tattoo: Being an Account of the Misadventures of Jacky Faber, Midshipman & Fine Lady. (p. 394)
—In the Belly of the Bloodhound: Being an Account of a Particularly Peculiar Adventure in the Life of Jacky Faber. (p. 865)
—Mark of the Golden Dragon: Being an Account of the Further Adventures of Jacky Faber, Jewel of the East, Vexation of the West & Pearl of the South China Sea. (p. 1095)
—Mississippi Jack: Being an Account of the Further Waterborne Adventures of Jacky Faber, Midshipman, Fine Lady, & the Lily of the West. (p. 1154)
—My Bonny Light Horseman: Being an Account of the Further Adventures of Jacky Faber, in Love & War. (p. 1198)
—Rapture of the Deep: Being an Account of the Further Adventures of Jacky Faber, Soldier, Sailor, Mermaid, Spy. (p. 1439)
—Under the Jolly Roger: Being an Account of the Further Nautical Adventures of Jacky Faber. (p. 1813)
—Viva Jacquelina! Being an Account of the Further Adventures of Jacky Faber, over the Hills & Far Away. (p. 1846)
—Wake of the Lorelei Lee: Being an Account of the Further Adventures of Jacky Faber, on Her Way to Botany Bay. (p. 1853)
—Wild Rover No More: Being the Last Recorded Account of the Life & Times of Jacky Faber. (p. 1930)
Meyer, Linda. Jones & the Great Act. (p. 925)
—Kid in My Closet. Roberts, Miranda, illus. (p. 951)
Meyer, Linda Ross. Recipe Box. (p. 1451)
Meyer, Lisa O. Sheep & the Chicken. Winward, Makenzie, illus. (p. 1564)
Meyer, Maggie. Big Foot Adventures down Under: Book One in the Series 'Spirits Alive' (p. 181)
Meyer, Marissa. Cinder. (p. 319)
—Cress. (p. 381)
—Fairest: Levana's Story. (p. 562)
—Fairest: The Lunar Chronicles: Levana's Story. (p. 562)
—Scarlet. (p. 1520)
Meyer, Marissa & Meyermarissa. Cinder. (p. 319)
—Scarlet. (p. 1520)
Meyer, Matthew. Raising Hare: Welcome to Sherwood Acores. (p. 1437)
Meyer, Megan. Flicker Finds His Flame. (p. 603)
—Great Adventures of Larriot the Liger. Meyer, Megan, ed. (p. 713)
Meyer, Michael, jt. auth. see Plaut, W. Gunther.
Meyer, Molly. Never Alone a Girl of Hope. (p. 1242)
Meyer, Naama. Siddurchik: Prayer Book for Young Children. (p. 1573)
Meyer, Nancy, illus. see Cerulean, Susan I., et al, eds.
Meyer, Richard. This Faith Is Mine. (p. 1735)
Meyer, Ronald. Casey Cougar. (p. 275)
—Freddy Fox. (p. 633)
Meyer, Sarah, illus. see Rader, Josh.
Meyer, Shawna Rae. When the Baby-Sitter Comes. (p. 1904)
Meyer, Sheldon, ed. see Fox, Gardner, et al.
Meyer, Stan. I Remember Christmas. (p. 844)
Meyer, Stephanie H. & Meyer, John. Teen Ink: Written in the Dirt: A Collection of Short Stories, Poetry, Art & Photography. (p. 1713)
Meyer, Stephanie H., et al. Teen Ink: What Matters. (p. 1713)
Meyer, Stephenie. Amanecer. Pallarés, José Miguel & Sánchez, María Jesús, trs. (p. 52)
—Breaking Dawn (p. 225)
—Breaking Dawn. (p. 225)
—Crepúsculo Kim, Young, illus. (p. 381)
—Eclipse. (p. 502)
—Eclipse. Pallarés, José Miguel & Sánchez, María Jesús, trs. (p. 502)
—Luna Nueva. (p. 1065)
—Luna Nueva. Pallares, Jose Miguel, tr. from ENG. (p. 1065)
—Luna Nueva. Pallarés, José Miguel & Sánchez, María Jesús, trs. from ENG. (p. 1065)
—New Moon. (p. 1246)
—Segunda Vida de Bree Tanner. Oliveras, Julio Hermoso, tr. (p. 1548)
—Short Second Life of Bree Tanner. (p. 1569)
—Twilight. (p. 1801)
—Twilight Saga: The Official Illustrated Guide. (p. 1801)
Meyer, Susan. Branding: Creating an Identity on the Web. (p. 222)
—Career As a Chef. (p. 266)
—Careers As a Bookkeeper & Auditor. (p. 267)
—Gases & Their Properties. (p. 657)
—Gayle Forman. (p. 659)
—Getting a Job in Sanitation. (p. 668)
—How Buying & Selling Futures Work. (p. 805)
—Hunting Dogs: Different Breeds & Special Purposes. (p. 829)
—Jimmy Wales & Wikipedia. (p. 918)
—Matthew & Tall Rabbit Go Camping. Huntington, Amy, illus. (p. 1109)
—Nazi Concentration Camps: A Policy of Genocide. (p. 1238)
—Performing & Creating Speeches, Demonstrations, & Collaborative Learning Experiences with Cool New Digital Tools. (p. 1343)
—Totally Gross History of Ancient Greece. (p. 1771)
—Understanding Digital Piracy. (p. 1815)
Meyer, Susan Lynn. Black Radishes. (p. 196)
—New Shoes. Velasquez, Eric, illus. (p. 1247)
Meyer, Terry. Navigating a New School. (p. 1238)
Meyer, Terry Teague. Careers in Computer Forensics. (p. 267)
—Female Genital Cutting. (p. 581)
—I Have an Alcoholic Parent. Now What? (p. 839)
—Juvenile Detention Centers: Your Legal Rights. (p. 941)
—Know Your Rights: Set 2. (p. 965)
—Navigating a New School. (p. 1238)
—Social Entrepreneurship: Doing Well While Doing Good. (p. 1604)
Meyer, Therese. Little Ballerina & Her Friends the Swans. (p. 1023)
—Petite Ballerine et Ses Amis les Cygnes (The Little Ballerina & Her Friends the Swans) Meyer, Therese, illus. (p. 1348)
Meyer, Victoria. Dream Catcher (p. 483)
Meyer, Zachary. Book Buddies' Adventures the Dragon Story. (p. 210)
Meyerhoff, Jenny. Barftastic Life of Louie Burger. Week, Jason, illus. (p. 139)
—Class B. U. R. P. Week, Jason, illus. (p. 327)
—Green Thumbs-Up! Chatelain, Éva, illus. (p. 722)
Meyerhoff, Jill, illus. see Goldish, Meish.
Meyer-Hullmann, Kerstin. Grundschulwoerterbuch. (p. 727)
—Rechtschreibtraining fuer die 3. Klasse. (p. 1451)
—Rechtschreibtraining fuer die 3. und 4. Klasse. (p. 1451)
Meyermarissa, jt. auth. see Meyer, Marissa.
Meyerowitz, Rick, illus. see Gleeson, Brian.
Meyers. Playground Opposites. (p. 1372)
Meyers, Ann Marie. Up in the Air. (p. 1824)
Meyers, Barbara & Mays, Lydia. Long & the Short of It: A Tale about Hair. Bersani, Shennen, illus. (p. 1047)
Meyers, Barbara Frances & Rahman, Peggy Jane. Caring Congregation Handbook & Training Manual: Resources for Welcoming & Supporting Those with Mental Disorders & their Families into Our Congregations (p. 269)
Meyers, Carly J. J. Michael's Superheroes. Bruner, Garth, illus. (p. 1135)
Meyers, David. Illustrated Life of Jesus: Through the Gospels, Arranged Chronologically. (p. 857)
—Poisoned Kool-Aid. (p. 1377)
Meyers, Dolores. Herbie's New Home. (p. 769)
Meyers Editors. Bauernhof. (p. 147)
—Schiff. (p. 1521)
Meyers, Haily & Meyers, Kevin. All Aboard California Meyers, Haily, illus. (p. 42)
—All Aboard NYC Meyers, Haily, illus. (p. 42)
—All Aboard Paris Meyers, Haily, illus. (p. 42)
Meyers, Jeff, illus. see Busic, Valerie.
Meyers, John. Now What? Time Machine Project Master Disc. (p. 1269)
Meyers, Kevin, jt. auth. see Meyers, Haily.
Meyers, Mark, illus. see Clickard, Carrie.
Meyers, Mark, illus. see Kelly, David A.
Meyers, Mark, illus. see Medlock-Adams, Michelle.
Meyers, Mark, illus. see Norworth, Jack.
Meyers, Mark, illus. see Roozen, John.
Meyers, Mark, illus. see Spetzler, Carl.
Meyers, Nancy. Doodles 123. Meyers, Nancy, illus. (p. 469)
—Doodles ABC: Alphabet Fun with Dots to Join & Doodles to Do. Meyers, Nancy, illus. (p. 469)
—Doodles Shapes. Meyers, Nancy, illus. (p. 469)
—Doodles Time. Meyers, Nancy, illus. (p. 469)
Meyers, Nancy, illus. see Bankert, Lisa.
Meyers, Nancy, illus. see Lorbiecki, Marybeth.
Meyers, Phyllis. Animals! Animals! Animals! (p. 82)
Meyers, Sarah, illus. see Rader, Jared.
Meyers, Susan. Bear in the Air. Bates, Amy, illus. (p. 151)
—Everywhere Babies. Frazee, Marla, illus. (p. 546)
—Rock-A-Bye Room. Bates, Amy June, illus. (p. 1481)
—This Is the Way a Baby Rides. Nakata, Hiroe, illus. (p. 1736)
Meyers, Susan A. Callie & the Stepmother. Gauss, Rose, illus. (p. 254)
Meyers, Susan & Fox, Mem. Sweet Stories for Baby Gift Set. Frazee, Marla et al, illus. (p. 1690)
Meyers, Ted (E.C.). Totem Tales: Legends of the Rainforest. Miller, Nancy, ed. (p. 1772)
Meyers, Terri. Shih Tzu Achoo!! (p. 1566)
Meyers, Tim. Let's Call Him Lau-Wiliwili-Humuhumu-Nukunuku-Nukunuku-Apua'a-Oi'oi. (p. 994)
Meylani, Rusen. SAT Math Subject Test with Ti 83-84 Family: With 10 Fully Solved Sample Tests. (p. 1515)
Meyler, Gladstone. Voices from the Forest. (p. 1848)
Meyn, Eric. Why Is the Grass Green? (p. 1925)
Meynell, Louis, illus. see Johnston, Annie Fellows.
Meyrand, Estelle, illus. see Dickens, Charles.
Meyrick, Caroline & Dwamena, Kwame. Mathematical Studies Standard Level for the IB Diploma Coursebook. (p. 1107)
Meyrick, Judith. Gracie: The Public Gardens Duck Rudnicki, Richard, illus. (p. 705)
Meyrick, Kathryn. Lost Music. (p. 1056)
Meza, Erika, illus. see Ransom, Candice F.
Meza, Martin. Martin Meza's Color Me in Coloring Book. (p. 1098)
—Martin Mezas Story Time Three Short Stories (p. 1098)
—Martin Meza's story time Volume 5. (p. 1098)
Meza-Riedewald, Leticia, jt. auth. see Blackstone, Stella.
Mezetovic, Aftaba. Refugee: The Ugliest Word. (p. 1456)
Mezieres, Jean-Claude, jt. auth. see Christin, Pierre.
Mezrich, Ben. Bringing down the Mouse. (p. 229)
Mezzanotte, Jim. Camiones Basculantes. (p. 256)
—Cargadores. (p. 268)
—Cómo Cambia el Agua. (p. 350)
—Cómo Funcionan Las Palancas. (p. 351)
—Cómo Funcionan las Palancas. (p. 351)
—Como Funcionan las Rampas, las Cunas y los Tornillos. (p. 351)
—Cómo Funcionan las Rampas, las Cuñas y los Tornillos. (p. 351)
—Cómo Funcionan Las Ruedas y Los Ejes. (p. 351)
—Cómo Funcionan las Ruedas y los Ejes. (p. 351)
—Connecticut. (p. 357)
—Dust Storms. (p. 490)
—Excavadoras. Acosta, Tatiana & Gutierrez, Guillermo, trs. (p. 547)
—Flat Track. (p. 603)
—Gases. (p. 657)
—Giant Bulldozers. (p. 673)
—Giant Diggers. (p. 673)
—Giant Dump Trucks. (p. 673)
—Giant Loaders. (p. 673)
—Giant Scrapers. (p. 674)
—Giant Tractors. (p. 674)
—Granizadas. (p. 710)
—Granizadas (Hailstorms) (p. 710)
—Hailstorms. (p. 735)
—Hillclimb. (p. 780)
—How Levers Work. (p. 810)
—How Pulleys Work. (p. 812)
—How Ramps, Wedges, & Screws Work. (p. 812)
—How Water Changes. (p. 823)
—How Wheels & Axles Work. (p. 823)
—Huracanes. (p. 829)
—Huracanes (Hurricanes) (p. 829)
—Hurricanes. (p. 830)
—Liquidos. (p. 1021)
—Líquidos. (p. 1021)
—Liquids. (p. 1021)
—Motocross. (p. 1179)
—Niveladoras. Acosta, Tatiana & Gutierrez, Guillermo, trs. (p. 1257)
—Police. (p. 1379)
—Raspadores. (p. 1439)
—Snowstorms. (p. 1601)
—Sólidos. (p. 1607)
—Solids. (p. 1607)
—Story of Jaguar. (p. 1658)
—Story of the Cadillac Eldorado. (p. 1660)
—Story of the Ford Mustang. (p. 1661)
—Story of the Jeep. (p. 1661)
—Superbike. (p. 1682)
—Supercross. (p. 1683)
—Supermoto. (p. 1684)
—Thunderstorms. (p. 1746)
—Tormentas de Nieve. (p. 1770)
—Tormentas de Nieve (Snowstorms) (p. 1770)
—Tormentas de Polvo. (p. 1770)
—Tormentas de polvo (Dust Storms) (p. 1770)
—Tormentas Eléctricas. (p. 1770)
—Tormentas Eléctricas (Thunderstorms) (p. 1770)
—Tornadoes. (p. 1770)
—Tornados. (p. 1770)
—Tornados (Tornadoes) (p. 1770)
—Tractores (Giant Tractors) (p. 1775)
Mezzanotte, Jim, jt. auth. see Ryback, Carol.
Mezzanotte, Jim & Orr, Tamra B. New York. (p. 1247)
MGH. Sra Spelling. (p. 1637)
Mhasane, Ruchi, illus. see Joslin, Mary.
Mhlophe, Gcina. African Tales. Griffin, Rachel, illus. (p. 28)
—Our Story Magic. (p. 1310)
—Stories of Africa. (p. 1654)
M.H.Prultt. Adventures of Rexie the Bear. (p. 22)
Mi. Mi's Pets. (p. 1150)
Mia, Tjalaminu & Lister, Jessica. Yippee! Summer Holidays. (p. 1971)
Miah, Esmail. I Once Knew... (p. 844)
Mian, Matthew K., jt. ed. see Hwang, William Liang.
Mian, Mian. Candy. Lingenfelter, Andrea, tr. from CHI. (p. 261)
Miao, Huai-Kuang, illus. see Shaw, Luci.
Micale, Albert, illus. see Kolars, Frank.
Micci, Ronald. Night & the Proofreader: A One-Act Comedy Play. (p. 1252)
Micco, Trudy. Discover Abyssinian Cats. (p. 447)
—Discover Maine Coon Cats. (p. 447)
—Discover Mixed-Breed Cats. (p. 447)
—Discover Oriental Shorthair Cats. (p. 447)
—Discover Persian Cats. (p. 448)
—Discover Ragdoll Cats. (p. 448)
—I See Blue. (p. 845)
—I See Green. (p. 845)
—I See Orange. (p. 845)
—I See Purple. (p. 845)
—I See Red. (p. 845)
—I See Yellow. (p. 845)
Miceli, Mary Anne. Boston North Shore's. (p. 215)
—Boston North Shore's Car Wash Squid. (p. 215)
—Boston North Shore's ... Salem's Golden Broomstick. (p. 215)
—Confessor's Animal Wartime Blues. (p. 356)
—How 'Pilly-Pine', the Alpaca, Lost His Quills. Terry, Roger, illus. (p. 812)
Miceli, Monica, illus. see Aldovini, Giulia.
Miceli, Monica, illus. see Mostacchi, Massimo.
Miceli, Robert L. Adventures of Twilight. (p. 24)
Michaan, Steven. American Fish Decoy Note Cards Set 1: Beautiful American Folk Art Blank Note Cards, 4x6 printed on museum-grade stock, packed in heavy, reusable gift Boxes. (p. 60)
—American Fish Decoy Note Cards Set 2. the Master Carver Series: Beautiful American Folk Art Blank Note Cards, 4x6 printed on museum-grade stock, packed in heavy, reusable gift Boxes. (p. 60)
—American Fish Decoy Note Cards, Set 4, the Master Carver Series: Beautiful American Folk Art Blank Note Cards, 4x6 printed on museum-grade stock, packed in heavy, reusable gift Boxes. (p. 60)
Michael. Bedwin David, Amanda, illus. (p. 157)
Michael A. Cicchetti, illus. see Sherri L. Berner.
Michael, Alexander. Until Wishes Are Fulfilled. (p. 1823)
Michael, Allaby. Planeta Tierra. (p. 1368)
Michael, Batdorf. Pair of Jacks: A Novel. (p. 1318)
Michael, Cavallaro, illus. see Baum, L. Frank.
Michael, Chinery, jt. auth. see Chinery, Michael.
Michael, David. Serene Morning & Other Tales of a Little Girl. (p. 1552)
Michael, Davidson William. Dragon Who Tamed Her Temper: The Everwynn Chronicles. (p. 478)
Michael, Ende, jt. auth. see Ende, Michael.
Michael, Fitterling, illus. see Newcomer, Mary Jane, et al.
Michael, Folloni, ed. see Folloni, Larry.
Michael Hemphill, jt. auth. see Riddleburger, Sam.
Michael Horn, Geoffrey, jt. auth. see Lantier, Patricia.
Michael J. Larson, jt. auth. see Michael J. Larson, J. Larson.
Michael J. Larson, J. Larson & Michael J. Larson. Easter Sparrows. (p. 499)
Michael, Jan. Just Joshua. (p. 938)
Michael, Joan. Five Senses/Opposites & Position Words Larsen, Eric, illus. (p. 601)
Michael, Joan, illus. see Behrens, Janice.
Michael, Joan, illus. see Falk, Laine.
Michael, Joan, illus. see Miller, Amanda.
Michael, Judah Israel. New Music. (p. 1246)
Michael, Melanie. Nerfnerd. Alderton, John, illus. (p. 1241)
Michael O'Mara Books UK Staff. Gift for Boys. (p. 675)
Michael, Pamela, ed. River of Words: Young Poets & Artists on the Nature of Things. (p. 1476)
Michael R. Zomber. Sweet Betsy That's Me: A child of the Civil War. (p. 1689)
Michael Ray Knauff. Roubidoux: A Story for 12-Year Olds & Those Who Wish They Still Were. (p. 1491)
Michael, Sally. God's Names. Apps, Fred, illus. (p. 691)
—God's Providence. (p. 691)
—Jesus Is Most Special. Apps, Fred, illus. (p. 915)
Michael, Ted. So You Wanna Be a Superstar? The Ultimate Audition Guide. (p. 1602)
Michael, Ted & Pultz, Josh. Starry-Eyed: 16 Stories That Steal the Spotlight. (p. 1642)
Michael, Todd. Evolution Angel: An Emergency Physician's Lessons with Death & the Divine. (p. 546)
—Hidden Parables: Activating the Secret of the Gospels. (p. 776)
—Texas State Bird Pageant. Randall, Lee Brandt, illus. (p. 1724)
—Twelve Conditions of a Miracle: The Miracle Worker's Handbook. (p. 1800)
Michaelides, M. Rainbow Angel. (p. 1435)
Michaelides, Marina. Renegade Women of Canada: The Wild, Outrageous, Daring & Bold. (p. 1460)
Michaelides, Marina, jt. auth. see Aadland, Dan.
Michaelis, Antonia. Dragons of Darkness. Bell, Anthea, tr. (p. 479)
—Dragons of Darkness. Bell, Anthea, tr. from GER. (p. 479)
—Secret of the Twelfth Continent. Hosmer-Dillard, Mollie, tr. from GER. (p. 1543)
—Secret Room. (p. 1543)
—Storyteller. (p. 1663)
—Tiger Moon. (p. 1748)
—Tiger Moon. Bell, Anthea, tr. from GER. (p. 1748)
Michaels, Alexandra. Kids' Multicultural Art Book: Art & Craft Experiences from Around the World. (p. 954)
Michaels, Anna. Best Friends. Karas, G. Brian, illus. (p. 169)
Michaels, Chris. Animal Babies. (p. 76)
—Finding Stripes. (p. 588)

—On My Desk. (p. 1289)
—Our Tag Sale. (p. 1310)
—Playtime at Home. (p. 1373)
Michaels, Chrissie. In Lonnie's Shadow. (p. 864)
Michaels, Craig. Blackbeard's Treasure. (p. 197)
Michaels, David. Bye-Bye, Katy Platt, Pierre, illus. (p. 249)
Michaels, Doad. Tennyshoe Adventures: the Doghead Whistle. (p. 1720)
—Tennyshoe Adventures: Treasure Hunters. (p. 1720)
Michaels, Eric. Flowers (p. 608)
—Fossils (p. 624)
—Women of Courage (p. 1946)
Michaels, Eric & Capstone Press Editors. Women of Courage (p. 1946)
Michaels, Evan. Tressa & Dan's Picnic at the Zoo. (p. 1785)
Michaels, Fern. Paint Me Rainbows. (p. 1318)
Michaels, Fern, et al. Silver Bells. (p. 1576)
Michaels, Gregory. Our Families Help. (p. 1308)
Michaels, J. Preston's Prickly Adventure. (p. 1397)
Michaels, J. C. Firebelly: A Journey into the Heart of Thinking. (p. 591)
Michaels, Joanna. Call Me Charly. Specht, Jessica, illus. (p. 254)
Michaels, Julie, jt. auth. see Rubin, Bruce Joel.
Michaels, Kasey. Kissing Game. (p. 962)
Michaels, Kat. Gentle Is the Night. (p. 661)
—Willow's Bend. (p. 1934)
Michaels, Kay. Golden Tassel's Graduation. (p. 695)
Michaels, Kim. Jesus Koans. (p. 915)
Michaels, Kitty. Ballet Friends #1 Toe-tally Fabulous. (p. 134)
—Ballet Friends #10 the Nutcracker Ballet Club. (p. 134)
—Ballet Friends #2 Join the Club. (p. 134)
—Ballet Friends #3 Birthday at the Ballet. (p. 134)
—Ballet Friends #4 Nowhere to Turn. (p. 134)
—Ballet Friends #5 Waiting in the Wings. (p. 134)
—Ballet Friends #9 the Triple Threats. (p. 134)
Michaels, Laura. Shanny Gets Her License. (p. 1559)
Michaels, Lisa J., illus. see Porada, Henry.
Michaels, Marion. Dana's Dreams. (p. 402)
—September's Song. (p. 1551)
Michaels, Melissa. Look Within. (p. 1050)
Michaels, Mishon. Big Adventures of Little Again Sam. (p. 177)
Michaels, Pat. W Is for Wind: A Weather Alphabet. Rose, Melanie, illus. (p. 1851)
Michaels, Robbie. Star Is Born. (p. 1640)
Michaels, Rune. Fix Me. (p. 601)
—Genesis Alpha. (p. 660)
—Nobel Genes. (p. 1262)
Michaels, Sarah, et al. Extra Ring Bling Rings: Rb67. (p. 555)
—Ring Bling Extra Hands: Rb69. (p. 1473)
Michaels, Vanessa Lynn & Harrow, Jeremy. Frequently Asked Questions about Family Violence. (p. 636)
Michaelson Entertainment Staff, ed. see Epstein, Brad M.
Michaelson, Peter. Freedom from Self-Sabotage: The Intelligent Reader's Guide to Success & Self Fulfillment. (p. 634)
—Phantom of the Psyche: Freeing Ourselves from Inner Passivity. (p. 1349)
Michaelson, Sandra. Is Anyone Listening? Repairing Broken Lines of Communication. (p. 889)
—Love Smart: Transforming the Emotional Patterns that Sabotage Our Relationships. (p. 1060)
Michalak, Jamie. Coziest Place. Davis, Jon, illus. (p. 375)
—Fairy Goodnight Kisses. Watanabe, Kaori, illus. (p. 563)
—Fairy Tea Party. Watanabe, Kaori, illus. (p. 564)
—Joe & Sparky Get New Wheels. Remkiewicz, Frank, illus. (p. 920)
—Joe & Sparky Go to School. Remkiewicz, Frank, illus. (p. 920)
—Joe & Sparky, Superstars! Remkiewicz, Frank, illus. (p. 920)
—Judy Moody & the Thrill Points Race. Candlewick Press Staff, illus. (p. 931)
—Larry & Rita. Newton, Jill, illus. (p. 976)
Michalak, Jamie, jt. auth. see McDonald, Megan.
Michalak, Michael. Voice from the Ashes. (p. 1848)
Michalak, Michael, tr. from GER. Oriental Odyssey III. (p. 1303)
Michalczewski, Raime. Monsters of a Different Color: Being Different Is Beautiful. (p. 1169)
Michalek, Erin. Fun Food Trivia. (p. 647)
Michalenko, Seraphim & Flynn, Vinny, eds. Divine Mercy - Message & Devotion: With Selected Prayers from the Diary of Saint Maria Faustina. (p. 454)
Michalopulos, Anastasios, ed. see Adel, Kaveh N.
Michalski, C J. Bound by Time. (p. 216)
Michaud, Christopher. Gonorrhea. (p. 697)
Michaud, Monique, illus. see Michaud, Sylvie.
Michaud, Nancy, illus. see Monnar, Ana.
Michaud, Sylvie. Book of Dreams - the Ringtail Family. Michaud, Monique, illus. (p. 211)
—Book of Love - the Ringtail Family. Michaud, Monique, illus. (p. 211)
—Book of Wishes - the Ringtail Family. Michaud, Monique, illus. (p. 212)
Miché, Mary. Nature's Patchwork Quilt: Understanding Habitats. Powell, Consie, illus. (p. 1237)
Michel, Barbara. Awake to Victory. (p. 120)
Michel, Becky. Miles of Smiles. (p. 1142)
Michel, Gay, jt. auth. see Gay, Michel.
Michel, June. Going Places: True Tales from Young Travelers. (p. 693)
Michel, Pauline. Haunted Childhoods. (p. 753)
—Haunted Childhoods. Spencer, Nigel, tr. from FRE. (p. 753)
Michelangelo. Sistine Chapel Coloring Book. (p. 1581)
Michelangelo Buonarroti, jt. auth. see Bingham, Jane.
Michelangelo Buonarroti, jt. auth. see Connolly, Sean.
Michele, Angela. Books at the Library: Understanding Addition. (p. 212)
Michele, Tracey. African Art. (p. 27)
—Big Cats, Little Cats. (p. 180)
—Big Machines. (p. 182)
—Bugs & Beetles. (p. 237)
—Clocks. (p. 333)
—Earth's Land & Water. (p. 498)
—Follow the Road Map. (p. 612)
—From Plan to House. (p. 643)
—Games Around the World. (p. 654)
—Gas & Air. (p. 657)
—Getting Around the City. (p. 669)
—Having Fun with Matter. (p. 755)
—How Can You Group Animals? (p. 805)
—Life Cycle of a Frog. (p. 1009)
—Life of a River. (p. 1011)
—Make a Color. (p. 1078)
—Make a String Phone. (p. 1079)
—Make a Treasure Map. (p. 1079)
—Map the School. (p. 1090)
—Measure the Weather. (p. 1117)
—Moon. (p. 1171)
—Musical Instruments. (p. 1194)
—My School, Your School. (p. 1218)
—Old Buildings, New Buildings. (p. 1283)
—People Who Help at Car Accidents. (p. 1340)
—People Who Work for the City. (p. 1340)
—Pumpkin Time. (p. 1416)
—Riding a Bike. (p. 1471)
—What Can You Buy at the Mall? (p. 1881)
—What Do Firefighters Do? (p. 1882)
—What Do Police Officers Do? (p. 1882)
—What Is a Mammal? (p. 1888)
—What Is A Natural Resource? (p. 1888)
—When Can A Flood Happen? (p. 1901)
—When Can I Help in the Classroom? (p. 1901)
—Where Does the Garbage Go? (p. 1907)
—Why Is it Expensive? (p. 1925)
Micheletti, Judy. Snibbles: Really Creative Problem Solving Lessons & Mind-Stimulating Exercises for Gifted Students & Their Teachers, Ages 5 through Really Old! (p. 1597)
Michelinie, David, jt. auth. see Defalco, Tom.
Michelinie, David, et al. Freemind - The Origin. (p. 635)
Michelle, Alyssa. Be Careful What You Wish For: A Fairy Tale ... of Sorts. (p. 148)
Michelle, Jean. Naba II: A Journey. Michelle, Jean & D'Ariggo, Jay, illus. (p. 1227)
Michelle, Michelle. Letters to Mom (p. 1002)
Michelle, Nelson-Schmidt. Jonathan James & Whatif Monster. Michelle, Nelson-Schmidt, illus. (p. 925)
Michelle, Sara. Beginning: Book 5 (p. 159)
Michelle, Tanya. President Looks Like Me Fall, Brandon, illus. (p. 1397)
Michelle Washington. Home & School Communication Journal: For Parents, Teachers & Students. (p. 791)
Michelon, Laura. Lari, Layne, & the Cat Colony. (p. 975)
Michelotti, Graciela, ed. see Fernandez de Lizardi, Jose Joaquin.
Michels, Dia. Look What I See! Where Can I Be? With My Animal Friends. Bowles, Michael J. N. & Bowles, Michael J. N., photos by. (p. 1050)
Michels, Dia & Levy, Nathan. 101 Things Everyone Should Know about Science TEST BOOKLET. (p. 2000)
Michels, Dia L. If My Mom Were a Platypus: Mammal Babies & Their Mothers. Barthelmes, Andrew, illus. (p. 853)
—If My Mom Were A Platypus- Hebrew Language Edition. Barthelmes, Andrew, illus. (p. 853)
—If My Mom Were a Platypus- Hebrew Language Edition. Barthelmes, Andrew, illus. (p. 853)
—Look What I See! Where Can I Be? At Home. Bowles, Michael J. N., photos by. (p. 1050)
—Look What I See! Where Can I Be? Visiting China. Bowles, Michael J. N., photos by. (p. 1050)
—Look What I See! Where Can I Be? In the Neighborhood. Bowles, Michael J. N., illus. (p. 1050)
—Look What I See! Where Can I Be? At the Synagogue. Bowles, Michael J. N., photos by. (p. 1050)
—Look What I See! Where Can I Be? With My Animal Friends. Bowles, Michael J. N., photos by. (p. 1050)
—Look What I See! Where Can I Be? 5 Book Set Bowles, Michael J. N., photos by. (p. 1050)
—Zack in the Middle. Bell, Fred, illus. (p. 1984)
Michels, Dia L., et al. Breastfeeding at a Glance: Facts, Figures, & Trivia about Lactation. (p. 225)
Michels, Elizabeth. Desperately Seeking Suzanna. (p. 430)
Michels, Michael, et al. Cooperative Learning & Science High School Activities. (p. 365)
Michels, Troy. Atlantis. (p. 112)
Michels-Boyce, Steven. When Jesus Was A Kid Like Me: A Counting Song about Jesus When He Was a Kid Like You & Me. (p. 1903)
Michels-Gualtieri, Akaela S. I Was Born to Be a Sister. Ramsey, Marcy Dunn, illus. (p. 848)
Michels-Gualtieri, Akaela S., jt. auth. see Michels-Gualtieri, Zaydek G.
Michels-Gualtieri, Zaydek G. I was Born to Be a Brother. Liegey, Daniel, illus. (p. 848)
Michels-Gualtieri, Zaydek G. & Michels-Gualtieri, Akaela S. I Was Born to be a Brother/I Was Born to be a Sister. Ramsey, Marcy Dunn & Liegey, Daniel, illus. (p. 848)
Michelson, Grant & Ryan, Shaun. Just Work: Narratives of Employment in the 21st Century. (p. 940)
Michelson, Herbert J. Consciousness: The Infinite Journey. (p. 358)
Michelson, Richard. Across the Alley. Lewis, E. B., illus. (p. 9)
—Animals Anonymous. Fischer, Scott M., illus. (p. 82)
—Animals That Ought to Be: Poems about Imaginary Pets. Baskin, Leonard, illus. (p. 84)
—As Good as Anybody: Martin Luther King Jr. & Abraham Joshua Heschel's Amazing March Toward Freedom. Colón, Raúl, illus. (p. 105)
—As Good As Anybody. Colón, Raúl, illus. (p. 105)
—Busing Brewster. Roth, R. G., illus. (p. 245)
—Is for Abraham: A Jewish Family Alphabet. Mazellan, Ron, illus. (p. 889)
—Language of Angels: A Story about the Reinvention of Hebrew. Gudeon, Karla, illus. (p. 975)
—Lipman Pike: America's First Home Run King. Pullen, Zachary, illus. (p. 1021)
—S Is for Sea Glass: A Beach Alphabet. Ettlinger, Doris, illus. (p. 1499)
—Twice as Good: The story of William Powell & Clearview, the only golf course designed, built, & owned by an African-American. (p. 1801)
Michener, Tara. 100% Real: A Who I Am Book. (p. 1998)
—No Longer Besties: And Other Assorted Teenage Drama. (p. 1258)
—Summer Camp Survival. (p. 1674)
Michie, Brandon J. Andie the Ant: Animal Lessons. (p. 72)
—Caleb the Porcupine: Animal Lessons. (p. 252)
—Eddie the Elephant: Animal Lessons. (p. 503)
—Ollie the Octopus: Animal Lessons. (p. 1287)
Michie, Melissa. Camera Shop Kid: A Tale of the Discovery of Oklahoma's 1889 Territorial Schoolhouse. (p. 256)
Michie, Sue. Possie & Neggie. (p. 1387)
Michiels, Cedric, jt. auth. see Davis, Jim.
Michno, Gregory. Encyclopedia of Indian Wars: Western Battles & Skirmishes, 1850-1890. Vol. 1 (p. 525)
Michno, Gregory F. Lakota Noon: The Indian Narrative of Custer's Defeat. (p. 972)
—Mystery of E Troop: Custer's Gray Horse Company at the Little Bighorn. (p. 1224)
Michot, Fabienne. Maki, I Am Happy. (p. 1080)
—Maki, I Love to Kiss You. (p. 1080)
Micich, Paul, illus. see Tazewell, Charles.
Micinilio, Leanne Plein. Tia's Troubles: The First in a series of Tia's Adventures. (p. 1747)
Mickel, Sharon. Uniquely Me, Nicci B. (p. 1818)
Mickelson, Marcia. Huaca. (p. 824)
Mickelson, Richard. Frog Who Jumped over the Moon. (p. 640)
—Richie & the Baby Boy. (p. 1470)
—Richie & the Baby Girl. (p. 1470)
—Richie the Teddy Bear Gets a Puppy. (p. 1470)
—Richie the Teddy Bear Who Saved Christmas. (p. 1470)
—Richie the Teddy Bear's Amazing Halloween Adventure. (p. 1470)
—Richie's Glorious Valentine Adventure. (p. 1470)
Mickelson, Scott. Artichoke Boy. (p. 104)
Mickem, Mandy. Puffy, Squiggy, & the Chance of a Flu Shot. (p. 1415)
Mickey, Thomas, jt. auth. see Beck, Alison.
Mickiewicz, Ricky. Adventure of Wormee the Worm. (p. 14)
Mickle, Jed, illus. see Beckham, Robert.
Mickle, Jed, illus. see Clark, Connie.
Mickle, Jed, illus. see Lambert, Lorene.
Mickle, Shelley Fraser. Barbaro: America's Horse. (p. 137)
—Turning Hour. (p. 1798)
Mickles Sr., Robert T. S. Blood Kin, a Savannah Story. (p. 200)
Micklethwait, Lucy. Colours: A First Art Book. (p. 346)
—I Spy Colors in Art. (p. 846)
—I Spy Shapes in Art. (p. 846)
—In the Picture: Get Looking! Get Thinking! (p. 867)
Micklethwait, Lucy & Quarto Generic Staff. Children: A First Art Book. (p. 302)
Micklos, John. African Americans & American Indians Fighting in the Revolutionary War. (p. 27)
—American Indians & African Americans of the American Revolution—Through Primary Sources. (p. 62)
—American Indians & African Americans of the American Revolution—Through Primary Sources. (p. 62)
—Brave Women & Children of the American Revolution. (p. 223)
—Courageous Children & Women of the American Revolution: Through Primary Sources. (p. 372)
—Courageous Children & Women of the American Revolution—Through Primary Sources. (p. 373)
—Crossing the Delaware & Valley Forge: Two Wild Winters with Washington. (p. 385)
—Elvis Presley: "I Want to Entertain People" (p. 517)
—How the Revolutionary War Was Won. (p. 813)
—Jennifer Hudson: A Biography of an American Music Idol. (p. 912)
—Making of the United States from Thirteen Colonies—Through Primary Sources. (p. 1082)
—Making of the United States from Thirteen Colonies—Through Primary Sources. (p. 1082)
—Muhammad Ali: "I Am the Greatest" (p. 1189)
—Overview of the American Revolution—Through Primary Sources. (p. 1314)
—Overview of the American Revolution-Through Primary Sources. (p. 1314)
—Washington's Crossing the Delaware & the Winter at Valley Forge: Through Primary Sources. (p. 1860)
—Washington's Crossing the Delaware & the Winter at Valley Forge—Through Primary Sources. (p. 1860)
—Why We Won the American Revolution—Through Primary Sources. (p. 1926)
—Why We Won the American Revolution—Through Primary Sources. (p. 1926)
Micklos, John & Micklos, John, Jr. From Thirteen Colonies to One Nation. (p. 644)
—Unsolved: What Really Happened to Amelia Earhart? (p. 1822)
—What Was the Revolutionary War All About? (p. 1895)
Micklos, John, Jr. 1918 Flu Pandemic: Core Events of a Worldwide Outbreak. (p. 2002)
—Bold Riders: The Story of the Pony Express. (p. 208)
—Challenger Explosion: Core Events of a Space Tragedy. (p. 289)
—Discovering the West: The Expedition of Lewis & Clark (p. 450)
—Jerry Spinelli: Master Teller of Teen Tales. (p. 913)
—To the Last Man: The Battle of the Alamo. (p. 1759)
—What Went Wrong? (p. 1895)
Micklos, John, Jr., jt. auth. see Micklos, John.
Micklos, John, Jr., et al. Adventures on the American Frontier. (p. 24)
Micucci, Charles. Life & Times of Corn. Micucci, Charles, illus. (p. 1008)
—Life & Times of the Ant. (p. 1008)
—Life & Times of the Peanut. (p. 1008)
Midda, Sara. How to Build an A. (p. 815)
Middaugh, Dallas, jt. auth. see Duprau, Jeanne.
Middeldyk, R. A. Van, see Van Middeldyk, R. A.
Midden, Maribeth Grubb. Rosie: The Patchwork Bunny. Techau, Ashlyn, illus. (p. 1490)
Middendorf, Gay. Little Girl Who Lived on the Countertop. (p. 1028)
Middle, Myra. Rabi's Halloween Adventure. (p. 1430)
Middlebrook, Amy. Meet My Cat. (p. 1121)
Middleditch, Susan. Monty the Mountain Duck. (p. 1170)
Middleman, Amy B., ed. see Pfeffer, Kate Gruenwald & American Medical Association Staff.
Middleman, Amy B., ed. see Pfeffer, Kate Gruenwald, et al.
Middlemiss, David. Great Hamstini. Middlemiss, Laura B., illus. (p. 716)
Middlemiss, Laura B., illus. see Middlemiss, David.
Middlestadt, Donna. Little Miss No Name. (p. 1032)
Middleton, Alasdair & Dove, Jonathon. Enchanted Pig. (p. 523)
Middleton, Casey Olsson. Flying the Imaginarium: Book One, Coconut. (p. 610)
Middleton, Charlotte, illus. see Franco, Betsy.
Middleton, Don. Polar Bears. (p. 1379)
—Polar Bears with Code. (p. 1379)
Middleton, Gayle, illus. see Bak, Jenny.
Middleton, Gayle, illus. see Benjamin, Ruth.
Middleton, Gayle, illus. see Frantz, Jennifer.
Middleton Gray, Family Np. Maddie Goes to the Nurse Practitioner. (p. 1069)
Middleton, Greg E. Pearls of Wisdom: A Collection of Spiritual Essays. (p. 1333)
Middleton, Haydn. Shakespeare. (p. 1559)
Middleton, Josh & Winick, Judd. First Thunder. (p. 597)
Middleton, Joshua, illus. see Kesel, Barbara.
Middleton, Julian. Joanna Beyond the Veil. (p. 919)
—Rebecca's Book of Dreams. (p. 1450)
Middleton, Julie. Are the Dinosaurs Dead, Dad? Ayto, Russell, illus. (p. 96)
Middleton, Leeanne. Sweetest Joy Boyer, Christine M., illus. (p. 1690)
Middleton, Mikell, illus. see Hensley, Sarah M.
Middleton, Mikell, illus. see Jarrell, Pamela R.
Middleton, Nancy. Zookeeper's Christmas Eve. (p. 1989)
Middleton, Patricia T. Given Strength. (p. 681)
Middleton, Patrick. Healing Our Imprisoned Minds. (p. 757)
Middleton, Peter. Aftermath. (p. 28)
Middleton, Shawn. Sam & the Peanut Butter Crackers. (p. 1506)
Middleton, Sydney Elise. Green Dog & Red Cat. (p. 721)
Middleton, Taquon, illus. see Owens, Carmen.
Middleton, Theresa. Little Town in Faraway USA. (p. 1037)
Middleton, William. Chipmunk Jamboree. (p. 308)
Middlewood, G. & Debenham, A. 43 Team-Building Activities. (p. 1997)
Middy Chilman, Thomas, illus. see Lowry, Lois.
Midence, Dominica. Mary's Fairy Learns to Exercise. (p. 1101)
Midgley, Elizabeth Cole. Daily Discoveries for August. Mitchell, Judith, ed. (p. 399)
—Daily Discoveries for October. Mitchell, Judith, ed. (p. 399)
—Daily Discoveries for September. Mitchess, Judith, ed. (p. 399)
Midgley, Ralph, tr. see Carroll, Lewis, pseud.
Midgorden, Barry, illus. see Sage-Midgorden, Lucinda.
Midland, C. J. Found Guilty. (p. 624)
Midland, Greg & Allen, Dave. Better by Saturday - Driving: Featuring Tips by Golf Magazine's Top 100 Teachers. (p. 172)
Midorikawa, Yuki. Natsume's Book of Friends. Midorikawa, Yuki, illus. (p. 1235)
Midthun, Joseph. Addition. Hiti, Samuel, illus. (p. 12)
—Division. Hiti, Samuel, illus. (p. 455)
—Fractions. Hiti, Samuel, illus. (p. 626)
—Multiplication. Hiti, Samuel, illus. (p. 1190)
—Plant Life Cycles. (p. 1369)
—Plant Structure & Classification. (p. 1369)
Midthun, Joseph & Hiti, Samuel. Addition. (p. 12)
—Division. (p. 455)
—Endocrine & Reproductive Systems. (p. 527)
—Gravity. (p. 712)
Midthun, Joseph & Samuel, Hiti. Multiplication. (p. 1190)
Miedzybrodzka, Wiktoria. Farm. Fretczak-Rodak, Monika, illus. (p. 573)
—Jungle. Fretczak-Rodak, Monika, illus. (p. 934)
Mielcarek, David. Time for your Mind. Mielcarek, David, ed. (p. 1752)
Miele, Brianna, illus. see Sexton, Jessa Rose.
Mier, Colin, illus. see Blackman, Malorie.
Mier, Colin, illus. see Cross, Gillian.
Mier, Vanessa, illus. see Pomerance, Diane.
Mier-Jedrzejowicz, Wlodek. Guide to HP Handheld Calculators & Computers. (p. 730)
Mierka, Gregg A. Nathanael Greene: The General Who Saved the Revolution. (p. 1231)
Miers, Doug, jt. auth. see Sherrill, Rusty.
Miers, Doug, compiled by. Prophecy Anthology (p. 1411)
Mierzwik, Nancy Diane. Quick & Easy Ways to Connect with Students & Their Parents, Grades K-8: Improving Student Achievement Through Parent Involvement. (p. 1427)
Miesen, Christina, illus. see Novick, Mary & Peterson, Jenna.
Miesen, Christina, illus. see Novick, Mary.
Miesen, Christina, jt. auth. see Novick, Mary.
Miesen, Christina, jt. auth. see Reilly, Carmel.
Miesen, Christina & Novick, Mary. Colours & Shapes: With Flip the Flap Pages. (p. 346)
Miether, Jeannette, ed. Horse Specialist's Guide to Educational Opportunities: A comprehensive guide to trade schools, degree programs, & certificate programs covering activities & careers with Horses. (p. 800)
Miéville, China. Lun Dun. (p. 1065)
—Railsea. (p. 1434)
Miéville, China, jt. auth. see Cook, Hugh.
Miffleton, Jack. Sing a Song of Joy. (p. 1578)
Migachyov, Dina & Migachyov, Larisa. Equations in Geometry: How to Make Your Child Successful in Math. Migachyov, Larisa, ed. (p. 533)
Migachyov, Larisa, jt. auth. see Migachyov, Dina.

Migdale, Lawrence, illus. see Hoyt-Goldsmith, Diane.
Migdale, Lawrence, photos by see Hoyt-Goldsmith, Diane.
Migdalias, Maria, et al. Tiny Immense Thoughts. (p. 1756)
Might Be Giants Staff, et al. Bed, Bed, Bed. Ozama, Marcel & Dzama, Marcel, illus. (p. 156)
Mighton, John. Jump at Home: Math Worksheets for the Elementary Curriculum. (p. 934)
—JUMP at Home— Grade 4: Math Worksheets for the Elementary Curriculum. (p. 934)
—Myth of Ability: Nurturing Mathematical Talent in Every Child. (p. 1227)
Migits, Anna, ed. see AZ Books Staff.
Migiz, Anna, ed. see AZ Books Staff.
Migliaccio, Eric, ed. see Reynolds, Laureen.
Migliari, Paola, illus. see Page, Josephine.
Miglio, Paige. Bear's Baby. Miglio, Paige, illus. (p. 151)
Miglio, Paige, illus. see Walton, Rick.
Migliore, R. Elizabeth. Stanley (p. 1639)
Miglis, Jenny. And the Winner Is... Meurer, Caleb, illus. (p. 71)
—My Talking Clock: Hannah's Busy Day. (p. 1219)
—New Student Starfish. Martinez, Heather, illus. (p. 1247)
Mignano, Daniel, illus. see Wingate, Barbara.
Mignano, Regina. Autism - A Holistic View, 2nd Edition. (p. 117)
Mignerey, Mary Buhs. If Dogs Could Talk: & Dogs Can Talk Two. (p. 852)
Mignola, Mike. Batman/Hellboy/Starman (En Español) Riera, Ernest, tr. from ENG. (p. 144)
—Chained Coffin & Others (p. 288)
—Conqueror Worm. Allie, Scott, ed. (p. 358)
—Hellboy: La Caja del Mal Abuli, Enrique Sanchez, tr. from ENG. (p. 763)
—Hellboy: El gusano Vencedor Abuli, Enrique Sanchez, tr. from ENG. (p. 763)
—Hellboy: Despierta al Demonio Abuli, Enrique Sanchez, tr. from ENG. (p. 763)
—Hellboy: Semilla de Destrucción Abuli, Enrique Sanchez, tr. from ENG. (p. 763)
—Hellboy: Baba Yaga y Otros Relatos Abuli, Enrique Sanchez, tr. from ENG. (p. 763)
—Hellboy: La Mano Derecha del Destino Abuli, Enrique Sanchez, tr. from ENG. (p. 763)
—Right Hand of Doom. (p. 1472)
—Wake the Devil. (p. 1853)
Mignola, Mike, illus. see Golden, Christopher.
Mignola, Mike, illus. see Starlin, Jim.
Mignola, Mike & Byrne, John. Seed of Destruction. (p. 1547)
Mignola, Mike, et al. Dark Horse Book of Hauntings. (p. 407)
Migron, Hagit, jt. auth. see Epstein, Sylvia.
Miguel, Angela. Harold the Duck. (p. 749)
Miguel Carbonell. King Tut's Tomb Robbers. (p. 959)
Miguel, Isabel de, tr. see Pullman, Philip.
Miguel, Medina Vicario, jt. auth. see Vicario, Miguel Medina.
Miguens, Silvia. Cuento el Aleph: Jorge Luis Borges. (p. 389)
—Estudio Literario: Ficciones. (p. 538)
Migy. And Away We Go! Migy, illus. (p. 71)
Mihai, Adriana. Inner of the Diamond Shoes. (p. 875)
Mihailescu, Maureen. Fruits & Veggies Are Really Great! (p. 645)
Mihalek, Alex, et al. Adventures of Captain Fishhook Waterflea: the Invasion of Lake Champlain. (p. 17)
Mihaley, James. You Can't Have My Planet: But Take My Brother, Please. (p. 1974)
Mihalko, Ross & Swift, Donna. Ant & the Grasshopper (Play) (p. 88)
—Beanstalk! the Play! (p. 150)
Mihalko, Ross, et al. Ant & the Grasshopper (Musical) (p. 88)
Mihaltchev, Atanas. Kid-Agami — Dinosaurs: Kiragami for Kids: Easy-To-Make Paper Toys. (p. 951)
—Kid-Agami — Jungle Animals: Kirigami for Kids: Easy-To-Make Paper Toys. (p. 951)
—Kid-Agami — Sea Life: Kiragami for Kids: Easy-To-Make Paper Toys. (p. 951)
Mihaly, Mary E. Getting Your Own Way: A Guide to Growing up Assertively. (p. 670)
Mihara, Mitsukazu. Beautiful People (p. 154)
—Doll (p. 463)
—Embalmer (p. 517)
—Mitsukazu Mihara - Haunted House. Mihara, Mitsukazu, illus. (p. 1156)
Mihara, Mitsukazu, creator. Doll (p. 463)
Mihran, Turley Joyce, illus. see Love, Donna.
Mihura, Miguel. Tres Sombreros de Copa. (p. 1784)
Miiller, Van Haaften Jane Elizabeth. CHUCK- the Only Ducken. (p. 318)
Mika, Christina & Benchmark Education Co., LLC. My Trip to Greece. (p. 1220)
Mika, Sharon Ann. Penny's Big Day. Wilson, Kay, illus. (p. 1338)
Mikaelian, Allen & Wallace, Mike. Medal of Honor: Profiles of America's Military Heroes from the Civil War to the Present. (p. 1118)
Mikaelsen, Ben. Ghost of Spirit Bear. (p. 671)
—Jungle of Bones. (p. 935)
—Petey. (p. 1348)
—Red Midnight. (p. 1454)
—Sparrow Hawk Red. (p. 1622)
—Stranded. (p. 1664)
—Touching Spirit Bear. (p. 1772)
—Tree Girl. (p. 1783)
Mikayla. Our Friend Mikayla. Resh, Kimberly, ed. (p. 1308)
Mike. Lemon Drop Rain: Poems & Drawings by Mr. Mike. Mike, illus. (p. 991)
—New Pet. Mike, illus. (p. 1246)
Mike, Grandpa. Hoppy the Happy Frog: A Grandpa Mike Tale. (p. 797)
Mike, Marion. Abagail Goes to Camp. (p. 2)
Mike, Norton, jt. auth. see Auerbach, Annie.
Mikec, Larry, illus. see Pfeffer, Wendy.
Mikelsons, Emily Samantha Ruth. Snowflakes Aren't Scared Because... (p. 1600)
MikeMotz.com, illus. see Grimes, Craig & Washington, Aimee.
Mikhail, Jess, illus. see Katzler, Eva.
Mikhail, Jess, illus. see Morgan, Michaela.
Mikhail, Jess, illus. see Morgan, Ruth.
Mikhail, Jessica, illus. see Gassman, Julie A.
Miki, Roy & Miki, Slavia. Dolphin Sos Flett, Julie, illus. (p. 464)
Miki, Slavia, jt. auth. see Miki, Roy.
Mikimoto, Haruhiku. Ecole du Ciel (p. 502)
Mikkelsen, Jon. Empty Room. Lueth, Nathan, illus. (p. 521)
—Green Team. Lueth, Nathan, illus. (p. 722)
—Kids Against Hunger. Lueth, Nathan, illus. (p. 952)
—Race for Home. Lueth, Nathan, illus. (p. 1431)
—Skateboard Buddy. Lueth, Nathan, illus. (p. 1583)
—Storm Shelter. Lueth, Nathan, illus. (p. 1656)
Mikkelsen, Nina. Powerful Magic: Learning from Children's Responses to Fantasy Literature. (p. 1390)
Mikki, illus. see Abrams, Penny.
Mikle, Toby, illus. see Chaudhary, Shahida.
Mikle, Toby, illus. see Freund, William C.
Mikle, Toby, illus. see Glass, Timothy.
Mikle, Toby, illus. see Hull, Claudia.
Mikle, Toby, illus. see Jones, Linda.
Mikle, Toby, illus. see Palumbo, Mary Lou.
Mikle, Toby, illus. see Voiles, Alison.
Mikler, Lisa M., illus. see Smith, Ruth J.
Miklowitz, Gloria. Anne Frank. (p. 85)
—Camouflage. (p. 257)
—Cesar Chavez. (p. 288)
Miklowitz, Gloria D. Enemy Has a Face. (p. 527)
—Masada: The Last Fortress. (p. 1102)
—Secrets in the House of Delgado. (p. 1544)
Miko-Ray, Yours Truly. June's Scrapbook. (p. 934)
Mikowski, Tracy L. Squirt the Otter: The True Story of an Orphaned Otter who Finds Friendship & Happiness. Richard, P. M., illus. (p. 1637)
Miksch, Alison, photos by see McDermott, Nancie.
Miksch, Alison, photos by see Schloss, Andrew & Joachim, David.
Mikulski, Keri & Shepherd, Nicole Leigh. Stealing Bases (p. 1646)
Mikus, Paul. Wow, I've Changed! (p. 1962)
Mi-Kyung, Kim. 11th Cat. (p. 1994)
Mila, R. L., tr. see Aristophanes.
Miladovich, Dragana, illus. see Brott, Ardyth.
Milagrito, El, illus. see Rendon, Gilberto.
Milah, Nick. Trip to the Aquarium: Add Within 20. (p. 1787)
Milam, C. J., illus. see Parrish, Kat.
Milam, Mary Kay. Zooming Star Babies. (p. 1989)
Milan, D. S. Year of Starless Nights. (p. 1969)
Milanese, Celestine Marie & Peck, Carolyn. Math 8 X-treme Review: Concise Training for NYS Math Intermediate Assessment. Stich, Paul, ed. (p. 1105)
Milani, Joan. Secret Society of the Palos Verdes Lizards. Schartup, Adam, illus. (p. 1544)
Milani, Mino. Ultimo Lobo. (p. 1810)
Milano, Brett. Vinyl Junkies: Adventures in Record Collecting. (p. 1843)
Milano, Jacque. Stay-at-Home Hank: The Little Hummingbird That Couldn't Fly. Milano, Jacque, illus. (p. 1645)
Milanowski, Lorraine. Holly the Lucky Little Kitten. (p. 789)
Milbourne, A. Baby Animals Jigsaw Book. (p. 124)
—Drawing Cartoons. (p. 481)
—Tadpoles & Frogs. (p. 1695)
Milbourne, A. & Wells, R. Mouse on the Moon. (p. 1182)
—Panda in the Park. (p. 1320)
Milbourne, Anna. 1001 Things to Spot in the Town. (p. 2002)
—Butterfly. (p. 247)
—Cats. Donaera, Patrizia, illus. (p. 280)
—Cats. Donaera, Patrizia & Fox, Christyan, illus. (p. 280)
—Christmas Activities. Cartwright, Stephen, illus. (p. 312)
—Dinosaur. (p. 441)
—Drawing Animals. (p. 481)
—Drawing Cartoons: Internet-Linked. McCafferty, Jan, illus. (p. 481)
—Familias de Animales Libro Con Paginas Puzzle. Butler, John, illus. (p. 567)
—Farmyard Tales Things to Make & Do. (p. 575)
—Horses & Ponies. Gaudenzi, Giacinto & Haggerty, Tim, illus. (p. 800)
—How Big Is a Million? Doherty, Gillian, ed. (p. 805)
—How Big Is a Million? Riglietti, Serena, illus. (p. 805)
—How Big Was a Dinosaur? (p. 805)
—How Deep Is the Sea? Riglietti, Serena, illus. (p. 806)
—How High Is the Sky? Riglietti, Serena, illus. (p. 809)
—Illustrated Hans Christian Andersen's Fairy Tales IR. (p. 857)
—In the Castle. Davies, Benji, illus. (p. 865)
—In the Nest. (p. 866)
—In the Pond. (p. 867)
—Little Pony. Roberti, Alessandra, illus. (p. 1033)
—On the Farm. Roberti, Alessandra, illus. (p. 1290)
—On the Moon. (p. 1291)
—On the Seashore. Waters, Erica-Jane, illus. (p. 1291)
—Peek Inside Animal Homes. Dimitri, Simona, illus. (p. 1335)
—Snowy Day. Temporin, Elena, illus. (p. 1601)
—Stories of Knights & Castles. Doherty, Gillian, ed. (p. 1655)
—Sunny Day (Picture Book) (p. 1677)
—Tadpoles & Frogs. Donaera, Patrizia & Wray, Zoe, illus. (p. 1695)
—Under the Ground. Riglietti, Serena, illus. (p. 1813)
—Under the Sea. Shimmen, Cathy, illus. (p. 1814)
—Very First Christmas. (p. 1838)
—Viaje a la Luna. (p. 1839)
—Where Do Baby Animals Come From? (p. 1906)
—Windy Day. Temporin, Elena, illus. (p. 1936)
Milbourne, Anna, ed. see Doherty, Gillian.
Milbourne, Anna, ed. see Helbrough, Emma.
Milbourne, Anna, ed. see Pearcey, Alice.
Milbourne, Anna & Field, Mandy. Dinosaur. (p. 441)
Milbourne, Anna & Roberti, Alessandra. Story of the Nativity. (p. 1661)
Milbourne, Anna & Stowell, Louie. Usborne Book of Greek Myths. Brocklehurst, Ruth, ed. (p. 1827)
Milbourne, Anna, et al. Myths & Legends. (p. 1227)
Milburn, Trish. White Witch. (p. 1914)
Milde, Jeanette. Once upon a Wedding. Sandin, Joan, tr. from SWE. (p. 1293)
Mildenstein, Tammy. Philippines. (p. 1350)
Mileham, Rebecca. Global Pollution. (p. 684)
Mi-Leing. Chrystal's Castle. (p. 317)
Milelli, Pascal, illus. see Spalding, Andrea.
Milelli, Pascal, illus. see Whelan, Gloria.
Miles, Bernard. Robin Hood: His Life & Legend. Ambrus, Victor G., illus. (p. 1480)
Miles, Bill, jt. auth. see Myers, Walter Dean.
Miles, Brenda. Stickley Sticks to It! A Frog's Guide to Getting Things Done. Mack, Steve, illus. (p. 1650)
Miles, Brenda, jt. auth. see Lane, Sandra.
Miles, Brenda, jt. auth. see Patterson, Colleen A.
Miles, Brenda, jt. auth. see Sweet, Susan D.
Miles, Brenda & Patterson, Colleen A. How I Learn: A Kid's Guide to Learning Disability. Heinrichs, Jane, illus. (p. 810)
—Moo, Moo, Move Your Mood! A Guide for Kids about Mind-Body Connection. Clifton-Brown, Holly, illus. (p. 1171)
Miles, Bryan. Faithful the Fire Truck. (p. 565)
Miles, Celia H. On a Slant: A Collection of Stories. (p. 1288)
Miles, Cindy. Forevermore. (p. 619)
Miles, Colin. Naughty Nicky & the Good Ship Oggy. Miles, Gail, illus. (p. 1237)
Miles, David. Brave Queen Esther (p. 223)
Miles, David, illus. see Declercq, Al, et al.
Miles, David, illus. see Harrison, Michael.
Miles, David, illus. see Zondervan Bibles Staff.
Miles, David, illus. see Zondervan.
Miles, Elizabeth. Envy. (p. 532)
—Eternity. (p. 539)
—Fog & Mist (p. 611)
—Forecasting the Weather (p. 617)
—Fury (p. 650)
—Fury. (p. 650)
—Rain. (p. 1434)
—Snow (p. 1598)
—Sunshine. (p. 1677)
—Thunder & Lightning. (p. 1746)
—Wind (p. 1935)
Miles, Elizabeth, illus. see Williams, Margery.
Miles, Ellen. Bandit. (p. 136)
—Bear. (p. 150)
—Buddy. (p. 234)
—Chewy & Chica. (p. 299)
—Cocoa. (p. 337)
—Cooper. (p. 364)
—Domino. (p. 465)
—Flash. (p. 602)
—Gizmo. (p. 681)
—Goldie. (p. 695)
—Guide to Puppies. (p. 730)
—Gus. (p. 732)
—Honey. (p. 794)
—Jack. (p. 902)
—Kitty Corner: Guide to Kittens. (p. 963)
—Kitty Corner: Guide to Kittens. (p. 963)
—Liberty. (p. 1005)
—Lucky. (p. 1062)
—Maggie & Max. (p. 1071)
—Mocha. (p. 1157)
—Molly. (p. 1160)
—Noodle. (p. 1263)
—Oscar. (p. 1305)
—Patches. (p. 1328)
—Princess. (p. 1402)
—Pugsley. (p. 1415)
—Puppy Place #31: Molly. (p. 1418)
—Puppy Place #34: Zipper. (p. 1418)
—Puppy Place #35: Cooper. (p. 1418)
—Puppy Place #36: Stella. (p. 1418)
—Puppy Place #39: Gus. (p. 1418)
—Rascal. (p. 1439)
—Rocky. (p. 1484)
—Scout. (p. 1532)
—Shadow. (p. 1557)
—Snowball. (p. 1600)
—Stella. (p. 1646)
—Teddy. (p. 1712)
—Ziggy. (p. 1986)
—Zipper. (p. 1987)
Miles, Gail, illus. see Miles, Colin.
Miles, Justin. Ultimate Explorer Guide for Kids. (p. 1809)
Miles Kelly Publishing, creator. Children's Classic Stories: Fairytales, Fables & Folktales. (p. 303)
—Stories for Girls. (p. 1654)
Miles Kelly Staff. Animals: Flip Quiz. (p. 81)
—Animals: Family Flip Quiz. (p. 81)
—Animals. (p. 81)
—Bible: Family Flip Quiz. (p. 175)
—Geography. (p. 662)
—Geography Age 10-11: Flip Quiz. (p. 662)
—Geography Age 11-12: Flip Quiz. (p. 662)
—Geography Age 7-9: Flip Quiz. (p. 662)
—Geography Age 9-10: Flip Quiz. (p. 662)
—History: Family Flip Quiz. (p. 783)
—History. (p. 783)
—History Age. (p. 783)
—How Things Work. (p. 814)
—Larger Than Life: Gigantic Views of the Microscopic. (p. 975)
—Mix-Ups. (p. 1156)
—Nature. (p. 1236)
—Noises: Let's Learn. Nilsen, Anna, ed. (p. 1262)
—Opposites: Let's Learn. Nilsen, Anna, ed. (p. 1300)
—Our Planet. (p. 1309)
—People & Places. (p. 1339)
—Rock & Pop. (p. 1481)
—Science: Family Flip Quiz. (p. 1524)
—Science. (p. 1524)
—Science & Maths. (p. 1525)
—Sizes: Let's Learn. Nilsen, Anna, ed. (p. 1583)
Miles Kelly Staff & Nilsen, Anna. Actions: Let's Learn. (p. 10)
—Numbers: Let's Learn. (p. 1272)
—Shapes: Let's Learn. (p. 1560)
Miles, Kiwuan D. Guardians of Earth: A Hero's Life & Death. (p. 728)
Miles, L. Empiezo a Contar. (p. 521)
—Hair Braiding Kid Kit. (p. 736)
Miles, Linda, et al. Amanda Salamander & the Secret of Happily Ever After. (p. 52)
Miles, Lisa. Astronomy & Space. (p. 109)
—Ballet Spectacular: A Young Ballet Lover's Guide & an Insight into a Magical World. (p. 134)
—Best Friends: Over 1000 Reusable Stickers! (p. 169)
—Book of Girls' Activity Fun: Join Milly & Her Friends for Hours of Puzzle Fun! (p. 211)
—Fairy Tale Creativity Book: Games, Cut-Outs, Art Paper, Stickers, & Stencils! (p. 564)
—Flags Sticker Book. (p. 602)
—Girls' Super Activity Book. (p. 681)
—Let's Be Friends! Follow the Reader Level 2. (p. 994)
—Libro de Pegatinas Banderas Todos los Paises del Mundo. (p. 1006)
—Origami Birds & Butterflies. (p. 1304)
—Origami Dinosaurs. (p. 1304)
—Origami Farm Animals. (p. 1304)
—Origami Pets. (p. 1304)
—Origami Sea Creatures. (p. 1304)
—Origami Wild Animals. (p. 1304)
—Rocks & Minerals. (p. 1483)
—Starting to Read. (p. 1644)
—Usborne Rocks & Minerals Sticker Book. Khan, Sarah & Armstrong, Carrie, eds. (p. 1827)
Miles, Lisa, ed. see Tatchell, Judy.
Miles, Lisa, jt. auth. see Cook, Trevor.
Miles, Lisa & Chown, Xanna Eve. Backyardigans Gang: Follow the Reader Level 1. (p. 131)
—How to Survive Being Dumped. (p. 821)
—How to Survive Dating. (p. 821)
—How to Survive Having a Crush. (p. 821)
—How to Survive Mean Girls. (p. 822)
—How to Survive Online Embarrassment. (p. 822)
—How to Survive Zits & Bad Hair Days. (p. 822)
Miles, Lisa & Smith, Alastair. Astronomy & Space. (p. 109)
Miles, Lisa, et al. Usborne Encyclopedia of Ancient Greece: Internet Linked. (p. 1827)
Miles, Liz. Clothes: From Fur to Fair Trade. (p. 334)
—Coping with Domestic Violence (p. 365)
—Dino Safari: Go Wild on a Prehistoric Adventure! (p. 441)
—Dinosaurs & the Prehistoric World. (p. 444)
—Flying Monsters. (p. 610)
—Games: From Dice to Gaming. (p. 654)
—Giant Dinosaurs. (p. 673)
—Humorous & Nonsensical Poems (p. 827)
—Killer Dinosaurs. (p. 956)
—Louis Pasteur (p. 1058)
—Meet the Ancient Greeks. (p. 1122)
—Meet the Medievals. (p. 1123)
—Meet the Pirates. (p. 1123)
—Orchestra (p. 1302)
—Playing the Spoons & Other Curious Instruments (p. 1372)
—Sea Monsters. (p. 1535)
—Sports: From Ancient Olympics to the Super Bowl. (p. 1632)
—Structure of Words: Understanding Roots & Smaller Parts of Words. (p. 1668)
—Terrifying Tales: Ghosts, Ghouls, & Other Things That Go Bump in the Night. (p. 1722)
—Will Smith (p. 1932)
—Writing a Screenplay (p. 1964)
Miles, Liz, jt. auth. see Vickers, Rebecca.
Miles, Liz & Heinemann Library Staff. Writing a Screenplay (p. 1964)
Miles, Lucinda (Cindy). Old-Time Fiddling Gospel Favorites. (p. 1285)
Miles, Patricia. Gods in Winter. (p. 691)
Miles, Peregrine B., illus. see Smithrud, Norma.
Miles, Robert. Jane Austen. (p. 908)
Miles, Robin, reader. Mufaro's Beautiful Daughters: An African Tale. (p. 1189)
Miles, Ryan. Picnic Nightmare. (p. 1355)
Miles, Sandy. Birthday: Words by John Lennon & Paul Mccartney. (p. 192)
Miles, Talaythea L. Fly, My Lupus Butterfly, Fly. (p. 609)
Miles, Victoria. Magnifico (p. 1076)
—Mimi Power & the I-Don't-Know-What Mongeau, Marc, illus. (p. 1145)
—Sea Otter Pup Gatt, Elizabeth, illus. (p. 1535)
Miles, Victoria, et al. Henry Chow & Other Stories Juhasz, George, illus. (p. 767)
Milet Limited Publishing Staff & Swain, Gwenyth. Eating. (p. 501)
Milet Publishing Staff. Animals. (p. 81)
—Animals - My First Bilingual Book. (p. 82)
—Bilingual Visual Dictionary. (p. 186)
—Bilingual Visual Dictionary CD-ROM (English-Korean) (p. 186)
—Clothes. (p. 334)
—Clothes - My First Bilingual Book. (p. 334)
—Colors. (p. 344)
—Colors. (p. 345)
—Colors - My First Bilingual Book. (p. 345)
—Colours. (p. 346)
—Colours - My First Bilingual Book. (p. 346)
—Fruit. (p. 645)
—Fruit (English-French) (p. 645)
—Fruit - My First Bilingual Book. (p. 645)
—Home. (p. 791)
—Home (English-Arabic) (p. 792)
—Home (English-French) (p. 792)
—Home (English-Polish) (p. 792)
—Home (English-Portuguese) (p. 792)
—Home - My First Bilingual Book. (p. 791)
—Jobs. (p. 919)
—Jobs - Berufe. (p. 919)
—Jobs Empregos. (p. 919)
—Jobs - My First Bilingual Book. (p. 919)
—Jobs Profesiones. (p. 919)
—Milet Bilingual Visual Dictionary. (p. 1142)
—Milet Bilingual Visual Dictionary (English-Bengali) (p. 1142)
—Milet Bilingual Visual Dictionary (English-Farsi) (p. 1142)
—Milet Bilingual Visual Dictionary (English-French) (p. 1142)

—Milet Bilingual Visual Dictionary (English-Portuguese) (p. 1142)
—Milet Bilingual Visual Dictionary (English-Urdu) (p. 1142)
—Milet Interactive for Kids - Chinese for English Speakers. (p. 1142)
—Milet Interactive for Kids - English for French Speakers. (p. 1142)
—Music. (p. 1193)
—Music - English-Spanish. (p. 1193)
—Music - My First Bilingual Book. (p. 1193)
—Musique. (p. 1194)
—My Bilingual Book - Sight. (p. 1197)
—My Bilingual Book-Hearing. (p. 1197)
—My Bilingual Book-Hearing (English-Arabic) (p. 1197)
—My Bilingual Book-Hearing (English-Bengali) (p. 1197)
—My Bilingual Book-Hearing (English-Farsi) (p. 1197)
—My Bilingual Book-Hearing (English-Portuguese) (p. 1197)
—My Bilingual Book-Hearing (English-Urdu) (p. 1197)
—My Bilingual Book-Sight. (p. 1197)
—My Bilingual Book-Sight (English-Bengali) (p. 1197)
—My Bilingual Book-Sight (English-Farsi) (p. 1197)
—My Bilingual Book-Sight (English-French) (p. 1197)
—My Bilingual Book-Sight (English-German) (p. 1198)
—My Bilingual Book-Sight (English-Italian) (p. 1198)
—My Bilingual Book-Sight (English-Portuguese) (p. 1198)
—My Bilingual Book-Sight (English-Urdu) (p. 1198)
—My Bilingual Book-Smell. (p. 1198)
—My Bilingual Book-Smell (English-Arabic) (p. 1198)
—My Bilingual Book-Smell (English-Bengali) (p. 1198)
—My Bilingual Book-Smell (English-Farsi) (p. 1198)
—My Bilingual Book-Smell (English-Urdu) (p. 1198)
—My Bilingual Book-Smell (English-Vietnamese) (p. 1198)
—My Bilingual Book-Taste (English-Arabic) (p. 1198)
—My Bilingual Book-Taste (English-Bengali) (p. 1198)
—My Bilingual Book-Taste (English-Farsi) (p. 1198)
—My Bilingual Book-Taste (English-Portuguese) (p. 1198)
—My Bilingual Book-Taste (English-Urdu) (p. 1198)
—My Bilingual Book-Touch. (p. 1198)
—My Bilingual Book-Touch (English-Arabic) (p. 1198)
—My Bilingual Book-Touch (English-Bengali) (p. 1198)
—My Bilingual Book-Touch (English-Farsi) (p. 1198)
—My Bilingual Book-Touch (English-Portuguese) (p. 1198)
—My Bilingual Book-Touch (English-Urdu) (p. 1198)
—My First Bilingual Book - Animals. (p. 1204)
—My First Bilingual Book - Animals (English-Somali) (p. 1204)
—My First Bilingual Book - Colors. (p. 1204)
—My First Bilingual Book - Colors (English-Urdu) (p. 1204)
—My First Bilingual Book - Fruit. (p. 1204)
—My First Bilingual Book - Home. (p. 1204)
—My First Bilingual Book - Opposites. (p. 1204)
—My First Bilingual Book - Plants (English-Farsi) (p. 1204)
—My First Bilingual Book - Plants (English-Korean) (p. 1204)
—My First Bilingual Book - Tools - English. (p. 1204)
—My First Bilingual Book - Vegetables. (p. 1204)
—My First Bilingual Book - Vehicles. (p. 1204)
—My First Bilingual Book - Vehicles (English-Russian) (p. 1204)
—My First Bilingual Book-Fruit (English-Somali) (p. 1204)
—My First Bilingual Book-Fruit (English-Urdu) (p. 1204)
—My First Bilingual Book-Home (English-Somali) (p. 1204)
—My First Bilingual Book-Jobs. (p. 1204)
—My First Bilingual Book-Jobs (English-Urdu) (p. 1204)
—My First Bilingual Book-Music. (p. 1204)
—My First Bilingual Book-Opposites (English-Bengali) (p. 1204)
—My First Bilingual Book-Opposites (English-Vietnamese) (p. 1204)
—My First Bilingual Book-Sports (English-Spanish) (p. 1205)
—My First Bilingual Book-Sports (English-Urdu) (p. 1205)
—My First Bilingual Book-Sports (English-Vietnamese) (p. 1205)
—My First Bilingual Book-Vegetables. (p. 1205)
—My First Bilingual Book-Vegetables (English-Farsi) (p. 1205)
—My First Bilingual Book-Vegetables (English-Spanish) (p. 1205)
—My First Bilingual Book-Vegetables (English-Urdu) (p. 1205)
—My First Bilingual Book-Vegetables (English-Vietnamese) (p. 1205)
—Numbers. (p. 1272)
—Numbers - My First Bilingual Book. (p. 1272)
—Opposites. (p. 1300)
—Opposites - My First Bilingual Book. (p. 1300)
—Plants - My First Bilingual Book. (p. 1369)
—School. (p. 1522)
—School - My First Bilingual Book. (p. 1522)
—Sight - English-Arabic. (p. 1574)
—Smell / Das Riechen. (p. 1593)
—Smell (English-French) (p. 1593)
—Smell O olfato. (p. 1593)
—Sports. (p. 1632)
—Sports (English-Italian) (p. 1632)
—Sports - My First Bilingual Book. (p. 1632)
—Taste. (p. 1707)
—Taste / Das Schmecken. (p. 1707)
—Taste - My Bilingual Book. (p. 1707)
—Tools. (p. 1767)
—Tools - My First Bilingual Book. (p. 1767)
—Touch - My Bilingual Book. (p. 1772)
—Vegetables. (p. 1834)
—Vegetables (Le Verdure) (p. 1834)
—Vegetables - My First Bilingual Book. (p. 1834)
—Vehicles. (p. 1834)
—Vehicles (English-German) (p. 1834)
—Vehicles - My First Bilingual Book. (p. 1834)
Mileto, Richard. Superbird. (p. 1682)
Miley, Berry. Christmas Village Chronicles & Other Short Stories. (p. 316)
Miley, Dan. 50 Word Bible. (p. 1997)
Milford, Diana Viola. Fuzzum & Wuzzum (p. 651)
Milford, Kate. Boneshaker. Offermann, Andrea, illus. (p. 209)
—Broken Lands. Offermann, Andrea, illus. (p. 230)
—Greenglass House. Zollars, Jaime, illus. (p. 723)
Milgram, Al, illus. see Krohn, Katherine.
Milgram, Al, illus. see Lemke, Donald B.
Milgrim, David. Eddie Gets Ready for School. Milgrim, David, illus. (p. 503)
—My Friend Lucky: A Love Story. Milgrim, David, illus. (p. 1209)
—Santa Duck. Milgrim, David, illus. (p. 1511)
—Some Monsters Are Different. Milgrim, David, illus. (p. 1609)
—Swing Otto Swing! Milgrim, David, illus. (p. 1691)
—Wild Feelings. (p. 1929)
Milgrim, Sally-Anne. Plays to Play with in Class. Vercesi, Anthony, illus. (p. 1373)
Milgrom, Al. Avengers: West Coast Avengers: Sins of the Past. (p. 119)
—Secret Wars II. (p. 1544)
Milgrom, Al, illus. see Adamson, Heather.
Milgrom, Al, illus. see Glaser, Jason.
Milgrom, Al, illus. see Krohn, Katherine E.
Milgrom, Al, illus. see Lemke, Donald B.
Milgrom, Al, jt. auth. see Fandel, Jennifer.
Milgrom, Al, jt. auth. see Krohn, Katherine.
Milgrom, Al & Howell, Richard. Avengers - West Coast Avengers: Family Ties. (p. 118)
Milgrom, Al, et al. Spider-Man: Deadly Foes of Spider-Man. (p. 1626)
Milham, Mary W. Hamilton Lake Bird Population. (p. 739)
Milhander, Laura Aron. Not for All the Hamantaschen in Town. Chernyak, Inna, illus. (p. 1267)
Milian, Tomaso, illus. see Joosse, Barbara M.
Milicevic, Adam, illus. see Delittle, Cathy.
Milich, Zoran. City 123 (p. 323)
—City ABC Book. (p. 323)
—City Colors. (p. 323)
—City Signs. (p. 324)
Miline, Bill, photos by see Shulman, Mark.
Milios, Rita. Bears, Bears, Everywhere. Motoyama, Keiko, illus. (p. 151)
—Democratic Republic of the Congo. (p. 426)
—Democratic Republic of the Congo. Rotberg, Robert I., ed. (p. 426)
—Sound in the Real World. (p. 1615)
Miliotis, Patti Rae, jt. auth. see Altson, John.
Milisic, Roman. Apes A-Go-Go! Allen, A. Richard, illus. (p. 91)
Militello, Joy, illus. see Hodkin, Faith.
Militello, Vincent. Nicholas the Naked Sicilian, & Other Stories. (p. 1251)
Militzer, Jill. Kizzy's Castle. (p. 963)
Milivojevic, JoAnn. Czech Republic. (p. 397)
—Iran. (p. 886)
—Puerto Rico. (p. 1415)
Milivojevic, JoAnn & Milivojevic, Jovanka J. Afghanistan (p. 26)
Milivojevic, Jovanka J. Afghanistan (p. 26)
Milivojevic, Jovanka J., jt. auth. see Milivojevic, JoAnn.
Milkau, Liz, illus. see Gray, Jane.
Milken-Noah, Joni, ed. see Noah, Ian & Logan, Stephanie.
Milkweed Editions Staff. California Coast: A Literary Field Guide. St. Antoine, Sara, ed. (p. 253)
—South Atlantic Coast & Piedmont: A Literary Field Guide. St. Antoine, Sara, ed. (p. 1616)
Milkweed Editions Staff, jt. auth. see Douglas, Marjory Stoneman.
Milkweed Editions Staff, jt. auth. see St. Antoine, Sara.
Milky, D. J. Treasure Chess. (p. 1781)
Milky, D. J., jt. auth. see Seidenberg, Mark.
Milky, D. J. & Kujiradov, Misaho. Princess Ai: Lumination Fujikawa, Kimiko & Johnson, Yuki N., trs. from JPN. (p. 1402)
Milky, D. J., et al. Princess Ai: Destitution Fujikawa, Kimiko & Johnson, Yuki N., trs. from JPN. (p. 1402)
Mill, Fran. Harriet's Hunt for the Sun. (p. 750)
Mill, Lynda. Let's Climb the Apple Tree. (p. 995)
—Let's Meet Harry, Ted & Mike. (p. 999)
Millán, John Henry. Los Hijos del Dolor: ¿Gestado por Amor? (p. 1054)
Millar, Goldie & Berger, Lisa. F Is for Feelings. Mitchell, Hazel, illus. (p. 559)
Millar, Goldie, et al. F Is for Feelings. (p. 559)
Millar, H., illus. see Nesbit, E.
Millar, H. R., illus. see Nesbit, E.
Millar, Louise, jt. auth. see Bruzzone, Catherine.
Millar, Louise, jt. auth. see Tran, Kim-Lan.
Millar, Mark. Ultimate X-Men (p. 1810)
Millar, Mark & Austen, Chuck. Ultimate X-Men Kubert, Adam et al, illus. (p. 1810)
Millar, Mark & Santoro, Frank. Spider-Man by Mark Millar Ultimate Collection. Dodson, Terry & Cho, Frank, illus. (p. 1626)
Millar, Martin. Curse of the Wolf Girl. (p. 395)
—Lonely Werewolf Girl. (p. 1046)
Millar, Robert McColl. Language, Nation & Power: An Introduction. (p. 975)
Millar, Ruth. Saskatchewan Heroes & Rogues. (p. 1515)
Millard, A. World History. (p. 1955)
Millard, A., jt. auth. see Evans, C.
Millard, A. & Sims, L. Visitor's Guide to the Ancient World. (p. 1846)
Millard, Adam. Peter Crombie, Teenage Zombie. (p. 1346)
Millard, Anne. Great Pyramid of Giza. (p. 718)
—Misterios de las Piramides. (p. 1155)
—Street Through Time. Noon, Steve, illus. (p. 1667)
Millard, Anne, jt. auth. see Evans, Cheryl.
Millard, Anne, jt. auth. see MacDonald, Fiona.
Millard, Anne, jt. auth. see Millard, Anne.
Millard, Anne, jt. auth. see Peach, Susan.
Millard, Anne, jt. auth. see Wingate, Philippa.
Millard, Anne & Millard, Anne. Misterios de las Civilizaciones Perdidas. (p. 1155)
Millard, Glenda. Isabella's Garden. Cool, Rebecca, illus. (p. 891)
—Once a Shepherd. Lesnie, Phil, illus. (p. 1292)
—Small Free Kiss in the Dark. (p. 1592)
Millard, Kerry, illus. see Hilton, Nette.
Millard, Kerry, illus. see Orr, Wendy.
Millard, Mary Weeks. Live Wires & Lobster Pots. (p. 1040)
Millay, Edna St. Vincent. Renascence & Other Poems. (p. 1460)
Millbourne, Anna, jt. auth. see Brooks, Felicity.
Mille Lacs Indian Museum, jt. auth. see Minnesota Historical Society.
Millen, C. M. Ink Garden of Brother Theophane. Wisnewski, Andrea, illus. (p. 874)
Millender, Gwyn. Essie's Birthday Surprise. (p. 537)
—Morning Glory. (p. 1175)
Miller, Adam. Finding a Music Style (p. 587)
—Front-Page Lives (p. 644)
—Mastering Media (p. 1103)
—Research It! (p. 1462)
—Sci-Hi: Earth & Space Science Set (p. 1524)
—U. S. Air Force True Stories: Tales of Bravery. (p. 1806)
—U. S. Marines True Stories: Tales of Bravery. (p. 1806)
Miller, Adam, et al. Courage under Fire: Tales of Bravery (p. 372)
—Courage under Fire: True Stories of Bravery from the U. S. Army, Navy, Air Force, & Marines (p. 372)
Miller, Al. Patricia the Duck. (p. 1329)
Miller, Albert G. Fury & the White Mare. (p. 650)
Miller, Alex. Beyond the River Miller, Caroline, illus. (p. 174)
Miller, Alexandra, illus. see Grigsby, Susan.
Miller, Alexandra, illus. see Harter, Penny.
Miller, Allan, jt. auth. see Miller, Chris.
Miller, Allan, jt. auth. see Miller, Christopher.
Miller, Allen R. Living with Anxiety Disorders. (p. 1042)
—Living with Depression. (p. 1042)
Miller, Amanda. Let's Be Friends. (p. 994)
—Let's Play a Five Senses Guessing Game. Michael, Joan, illus. (p. 999)
—Let's Talk Soccer. (p. 1001)
—Library's Secret: A Hidden Adventure. (p. 1006)
—Pat the Enormous Brat! (p. 1327)
—This Is the Way We Help at Home. (p. 1736)
—This Is the Way We Play. (p. 1736)
—We Help Out at School. (p. 1867)
—What Does the President Do? (p. 1884)
—What Is Air Force One? (p. 1888)
Miller, Amanda & Falk, Laine. What Is Air Force One? (p. 1888)
Miller, Amanda E. Pete the Pencil. (p. 1346)
Miller, Amanda, et al. Sprout Your Own Sweet Scents. (p. 1635)
Miller, Amanda K. Lily's Grand Adventures. (p. 1018)
Miller, Amy. Colorado. (p. 343)
—Delaware. (p. 424)
—Idaho. (p. 851)
Miller, Andrew. Alcohol & Your Liver: The Incredibly Disgusting Story. (p. 35)
—Arthur Dudley Dunstan. (p. 103)
Miller, Andy, jt. auth. see Mills, Nathan.
Miller, Ann. Proverbs, Prayers, Poems for Children & Teens. (p. 1413)
Miller, Anna Carew & Carew-Miller, Anna. Confucius: Great Chinese Philosopher. (p. 357)
Miller, Anne Meeker. Baby Sing & Sign: A Play-filled Language Development Program for Hearing Infants & Toddlers. (p. 128)
Miller, Antonia, illus. see Watt, Fiona.
Miller, Arthur. Jane's Blanket. Al, Parker, illus. (p. 908)
Miller, Arthur, jt. auth. see Crow, Anne.
Miller, Ashley Edward & Stentz, Zack. Colin Fischer. (p. 339)
Miller, Austin. Let's Look at the Dinosaurs: Set Of 6. (p. 999)
—Sam Is Special: Set Of 6. (p. 1506)
—Sam Is Special. (p. 1506)
Miller, Barbara Anne. Adventures of Emily-Faith. (p. 18)
Miller, Barbara Kiely. Anne Hutchinson. (p. 86)
—Chief Joseph. (p. 301)
—Frederick Douglass. (p. 633)
—George Washington Carver. (p. 664)
—Grandes Personajes (Great Americans) (p. 707)
—Great Americans (p. 713)
—Jefe Joseph. (p. 911)
—Jefe Joseph (Chief Joseph) (p. 911)
—John Muir. (p. 922)
—Sam Houston. (p. 1506)
Miller, Barnabas. Rock God: The Legend of BJ Levine. (p. 1482)
Miller, Bernice J. Bernice's Childrens Stories. (p. 167)
Miller, Bernice Joyce. Nicholas' Christmas Eve Journey! (p. 1250)
Miller, Bob, illus. see Paul, Sherry.
Miller, Bobbi. Big River's Daughter. (p. 183)
—Girls of Gettysburg. (p. 680)
—Miss Sally Ann & the Panther. Lloyd, Megan, illus. (p. 1152)
—One Fine Trade. Hillenbrand, Will, illus. (p. 1295)
Miller, Bondell, ed. see Campodonica, Carol A.
Miller, Brandon Marie. Benjamin Franklin, American Genius: His Life & Ideas with 21 Activities. (p. 165)
—Declaring Independence: Life During the American Revolution. (p. 422)
—George Washington for Kids: His Life & Times - 21 Activities. (p. 664)
—Thomas Jefferson for Kids: His Life & Times with 21 Activities. (p. 1739)
—Women of the Frontier: 16 Tales of Trailblazing Homesteaders, Entrepreneurs, & Rabble-Rousers. (p. 1946)
Miller, Brandy. My First Abc Poem (p. 1204)
Miller, Brian Cole. Quick Meeting Openers for Busy Managers: More Than 50 Icebreakers, Energizers, & Other Creative Activities That Get Results (p. 1427)
Miller, Britt Ekland, jt. auth. see Bradley, Jeffery.
Miller, Bruce R. Wizard of the Wall. (p. 1943)
Miller, Bryan. Dinosaur Fun: With Letters. (p. 442)
Miller, Bryan, illus. see Rundstrom, Teressa.
Miller, Bryan Q. Guardian Perez, Pere, illus. (p. 728)
—Space Mountain: A Graphic Novel. (p. 1619)
Miller, Bryan Q., jt. auth. see Disney Book Group Staff.
Miller, Callie, ed. see Balmer, Fred.
Miller, Calvin. Hunger for the Holy: Nurturing Intimacy with Christ Member. (p. 827)
Miller, Calvin Craig. A. Philip Randolph & the African American Labor Movement. (p. 1)
—Che Guevara: In Search of Revolution. (p. 295)
—David Beckham. (p. 410)
—Mary Wollstonecraft: And the Rights of Women. (p. 1101)
—Reggae Poet: The Story of Bob Marley. (p. 1457)
—Roy Wilkins: Leader of the NAACP. (p. 1492)
—Spirit Like a Storm: The Story of Mary Shelley. (p. 1628)
—Tom Brady. (p. 1762)
Miller, Carol. Maurice the Mole: Can You Guess Series. (p. 1110)
Miller, Carol Rawlings. Powerful Paragraphs: Standards-Based Mini-Lessons - Overheads - Reproducibles. (p. 1390)
Miller, Carol Rawlings & Glasscock, Sarah. Strong Sentences: Standards-Based Mini-Lessons * Overheads * Reproducibles. (p. 1668)
Miller, Caroline, illus. see Miller, Alex.
Miller, Carolyn. Teaching Little Fingers to Play More Broadway Songs: 10 Mid to Later Elementary Show Tunes for Piano. (p. 1710)
Miller, Char, ed. Atlas of U. S. & Canadian Environmental History. (p. 113)
Miller, Chris. Real Animal House: The Awesomely Depraved Saga of the Fraternity That Inspired the Movie. (p. 1448)
Miller, Chris & Miller, Allan. Hunter Brown & the Consuming Fire (p. 828)
Miller, Christian. Champagne Sandwich. (p. 289)
Miller, Christopher & Miller, Allan. Hunter Brown & the Eye of Ends (p. 828)
—Hunter Brown & the Secret of the Shadow (p. 828)
—Legend of Gid the Kid & the Black Bean Bandits Miller, Christopher & Miller, Allan, illus. (p. 988)
—Legend of Ten-Gallon Sam & the Perilous Mine Miller, Christopher & Miller, Allan, illus. (p. 988)
Miller, Chuck. Alexander Hamilton. (p. 36)
—Benjamin Franklin. (p. 164)
—George Washington. (p. 664)
—John Adams. (p. 921)
—John Jay. (p. 922)
Miller, Cindy M. Little Green Truck: The Adventures of a 1998 Ford Ranger & Its Owner. (p. 1028)
Miller, Claire. Christmas Message. Dorenkamp, Michelle, illus. (p. 314)
—Easter Surprise. (p. 499)
—hijo pródigo (The Prodigal Son) - Bilingual. (p. 779)
—Parable of the Lost Sheep. van der Sterre, Johanna, illus. (p. 1323)
—parabola de la oveja perdida (The Parable of the Lost Sheep) (p. 1323)
—Ten Commandments. Miyake, Yoshi, illus. (p. 1718)
Miller, Cliff, illus. see DiMare, Loren Spiotta, et al.
Miller, Connie Colwell. Agencia Central de Inteligencia: Detienen a los Terroristas. Strictly Spanish LLC. Staff, tr. from ENG. (p. 29)
—Angry Is... (p. 75)
—Basset Hounds Saunders-Smith, Gail, ed. (p. 143)
—Birman Cats. (p. 192)
—BMX Park (p. 204)
—Carl Edwards. (p. 269)
—Central Intelligence Agency: Stopping Terrorists (p. 287)
—Chihuahuas. (p. 301)
—Creepiest Animals (p. 381)
—Crime Scene Investigators: Uncovering the Truth (p. 382)
—Dale Earnhardt, Jr. (p. 401)
—Danica Patrick. (p. 404)
—Deadliest Jobs on Earth. (p. 417)
—Deadliest Places on Earth. (p. 417)
—Deadliest Plants on Earth. (p. 417)
—Deadliest Weather on Earth. (p. 417)
—Disgusting Foods [Scholastic]. (p. 450)
—Dolphins Rasch, Patricia, illus. (p. 464)
—El/Servicio Secreto de EE. UU. Protege a Nuestros Líderes. Strictly Spanish LLC. Staff, tr. from ENG. (p. 516)
—Enojo Es... Strictly Spanish LLC. Staff, tr. from ENG. (p. 530)
—Equipos SWAT: Armados y Listos. Strictly Spanish LLC. Staff, tr. (p. 533)
—Exotic Cats. (p. 548)
—Federal Bureau of Investigation: Hunting Criminals (p. 580)
—Fireflies (p. 592)
—Garbage, Waste, Dumps, & You: The Disgusting Story Behind What We Leave Behind (p. 656)
—German Shepherds (p. 666)
—Getting to Know Your Toilet: The Disgusting Story Behind Your Home's Strangest Feature. (p. 670)
—Great Danes Saunders-Smith, Gail, ed. (p. 715)
—Happy Is... (p. 746)
—Happy Is ... (p. 746)
—Happy Is... (Felicidad Es...) Strictly Spanish LLC. Staff, tr. (p. 746)
—Investigadores de Escenas de Crímenes: Descubren la Verdad. Strictly Spanish LLC. Staff, tr. from ENG. (p. 884)
—Jimmie Johnson. (p. 918)
—Labradores. (p. 970)
—Loch Ness Monster: The Unsolved Mystery (p. 1044)
—Manatees Rasch, Patricia, illus. (p. 1086)
—Marie Curie & Radioactivity Larson, Scott & Heike, Mark, illus. (p. 1093)
—Matt Kenseth. (p. 1109)
—Monster Knows Excuse Me Chiodi, Maira, illus. (p. 1167)
—Monster Knows I'm Sorry. Chiodi, Maira, illus. (p. 1167)
—Monster Knows Manners Chiodi, Maira, illus. (p. 1167)
—Monster Knows Please & Thank You Chiodi, Maira, illus. (p. 1167)
—Monster Knows Table Manners Chiodi, Maira, illus. (p. 1167)
—Monstruo Del Lago Ness/the Loch Ness Monster: El Misterio Sin Resolver/the Unsolved Mystery. Strictly Spanish, LLC., tr. (p. 1169)
—Mosquitoes (p. 1176)
—Most Dangerous Animals (p. 1177)
—Mother Jones: Labor Leader Erwin, Steve & Barnett, Charles, III, illus. (p. 1178)
—Mother Jones: Labor Leader. Erwin, Steve & Barnett, Charles, III, illus. (p. 1178)
—Moto X Best Trick (p. 1179)
—Moto X Freestyle [Scholastic]. (p. 1179)
—Movie Animals. (p. 1183)
—National Security Agency: Cracking Secret Codes (p. 1233)

M

—Ovnis/UFOs: El Misterio Sin Resolver/the Unsolved Mystery Strictly Spanish, LLC., tr. from ENG. (p. 1314)
—Ragdoll Cats. (p. 1433)
—Rosa Parks & the Montgomery Bus Boycott Kalal, Dan, illus. (p. 1489)
—Scottish Fold Cats. (p. 1532)
—Search & Rescue Dogs. (p. 1537)
—Skateboarding Big Air (p. 1583)
—Skateboarding Vert (p. 1583)
—Slimy Book of Spit (p. 1590)
—Snotty Book of Snot (p. 1598)
—Snowboard Superpipe (p. 1600)
—Snowboarder X (p. 1600)
—Stinkiest Animals (p. 1651)
—SWAT Teams: Armed & Ready (p. 1689)
—Therapy Animals. (p. 1729)
—This Book Might Make You Gag: A Collection of Crazy Gross Trivia (p. 1735)
—U. S. Border Patrol: Guarding the Nation (p. 1806)
—U. S. Marshals Service: Catching Fugitives (p. 1806)
—U. S. Secret Service: Protecting Our Leaders (p. 1807)
Miller, Connie Colwell, jt. auth. see Fandel, Jennifer.
Miller, Connie Colwell, jt. auth. see McCormick, Lisa Wade.
Miller, Connie Colwell, jt. auth. see Nichols, Cheyenne.
Miller, Connie Colwell & Capstone Press Editors. Labradors Saunders-Smith, Gail, ed. (p. 970)
Miller, Connie Colwell & Capstone Press Staff. Bichons Frises (p. 177)
—Bloodhounds (p. 201)
—Cocker Spaniels Saunders-Smith, Gail, ed. (p. 337)
—Disgusting Animals (p. 450)
—Disgusting Bugs (p. 450)
—Disgusting Foods (p. 450)
—Disgusting Jobs (p. 450)
—Disgusting Places (p. 450)
—Disgusting Plants (p. 450)
Miller, Connie Colwell & Nichols, Cheyenne. Know Your Emotions. (p. 965)
Miller, Connie Colwell, et al. Reconoce Tus Emociones/Know Your Emotions. Strictly Spanish, LLC., tr. (p. 1452)
—Tickles, Pickles, & Floofing Persnickles: Reading & Writing Nonsense Poems Smith, Simon et al, illus. (p. 1747)
Miller, Connie R. Apache. (p. 91)
—Cherokee. (p. 298)
—Chumash. (p. 318)
—Inuit. (p. 883)
—Iroquois. (p. 888)
—Lakota. (p. 972)
—Nez Perce. (p. 1249)
Miller, Constances. Mommy Always Comes Back. (p. 1162)
Miller Cormier, Susan. Life on the Farm. (p. 1012)
Miller, D. C. Hurricane Hunters: A Craig Hancock Adventure. (p. 829)
Miller, Dalton, jt. auth. see Friend, Gaythel Boggs.
Miller, Dalton, jt. auth. see Friend, Gaythel.
Miller, Dani. Paxton & Mali Find Their Boat. (p. 1331)
Miller, Daniel, et al. Miller Cousin Mystery. (p. 1143)
Miller, Danny & National Geographic Learning Staff. African Journeys, 1850-1900. (p. 27)
Miller, Dave. Birds, Bugs, & Bees. (p. 191)
—Dogs, Frogs, & Hogs. (p. 463)
—Draw with the Cartoon Dude. (p. 481)
Miller, David. Big & Me. (p. 177)
—Heat 16. (p. 760)
—Refugees. (p. 1456)
Miller, David, illus. see Willoughby, Robert.
Miller, David Humphreys, illus. see Heiderstadt, Dorothy.
Miller, Davis Worth, jt. auth. see Brevard, Katherine McLean.
Miller, Davis Worth & Brevard, Katherine M. Political Elections Barnett, Charles, III, illus. (p. 1380)
Miller, Davis Worth & Brevard, Katherine McLean. Story of Guns: How They Changed the World (p. 1658)
Miller, Dawn. Prophecy (p. 1411)
Miller, Dawn Ellen, illus. see McGee, Pamela M.
Miller, Dean. Becoming a Pro Auto Racer. (p. 156)
Miller, Dean & Talbot, Jeffrey. Annie Oakley. (p. 87)
—Johnny Appleseed. (p. 923)
Miller, Deanna. Sky Bounce. (p. 1586)
Miller, Debbie S. Arctic Lights, Arctic Nights. Van Zyle, Jon, illus. (p. 96)
—Are Trees Alive? Schuett, Stacey, illus. (p. 96)
—Big Alaska: Journey Across America's Most Amazing State. Van Zyle, Jon, illus. (p. 177)
—Caribou Journey. (p. 269)
—Flight of the Golden Plover: The Amazing Migration Between Hawaii & Alaska. Van Zyle, Daniel, illus. (p. 604)
—Great Serum Race: Blazing the Iditarod Trail. Van Zyle, Jon, illus. (p. 718)
—Grizzly Bears of Alaska: Explore the Wild World of Bears. Endres, Patrick J., photos by. (p. 724)
—Polar Bear Journey. Van Zyle, Jon, illus. (p. 1378)
—Survival at 120 Above. Van Zyle, Jon, illus. (p. 1686)
—Survival at 40 Below. Van Zyle, Jon, illus. (p. 1686)
—Woolly Mammoth Journey. Van Zyle, Jon, illus. (p. 1950)
—Wooly Mammoth Journey. (p. 1950)
Miller, Debbie S. & Eiler, John H. King Salmon Journey. Van Zyle, Jon, illus. (p. 959)
Miller, Deborah J. Careers with an Internet Service Provider. (p. 268)
—Careers with Internet Service Providers. (p. 268)
Miller, Debra A. Alternative Therapies. (p. 50)
—Belize. (p. 162)
—Biodiversity. (p. 188)
—Civil Liberties. (p. 324)
—Confronting Global Warming (p. 357)
—Conserving the Environment. (p. 359)
—Developing Nations. (p. 431)
—Dolores Huerta: Labor Leader. (p. 464)
—Energy Production & Alternative Energy. (p. 528)
—Factory Farming. Greenhaven Press Editors, ed. (p. 561)
—Fair Trade. (p. 562)
—Farming & the Food Supply. (p. 574)
—Gasoline. (p. 657)
—Global Warming. (p. 684)
—Homeland Security. (p. 793)
—Illegal Immigration. (p. 857)
—Iran. Gale Editors, ed. (p. 886)
—Medicare. (p. 1119)
—Middle East. (p. 1137)
—Nuclear Energy. Gale Editors, ed. (p. 1269)
—Oil. Gale Editors, ed. (p. 1282)
—Organic Foods. (p. 1303)
—Pandemics. (p. 1321)
—Patriot Act. (p. 1329)
—Political Corruption. (p. 1380)
—Politics & Religion. Greenhaven Press Editors, ed. (p. 1381)
—Postpartum Depression. (p. 1388)
—Rights of Animals. (p. 1472)
—Social Security. Greenhaven Press Editors, ed. (p. 1604)
—Terrorism. (p. 1722)
—U. S. Economy. (p. 1806)
—Vegetarianism. Gale Editors, ed. (p. 1834)
—War Against Iraq. (p. 1857)
—Women in Politics. (p. 1946)
Miller, Debra A., jt. auth. see Gale Editors.
Miller, Debra A., ed. Biodiversity. (p. 188)
—Illegal Immigration. (p. 856)
—Will the World Run Out of Fresh Water? (p. 1932)
Miller, Debra J. Pony Tale: The Truth about Timberlin. (p. 1383)
Miller, Debra Warren. Grandpa Popsicle. (p. 709)
Miller, Denise. Annie's Shoes. (p. 87)
Miller, Dennis. ABCs of Character. Wallace, Sam Amber, illus. (p. 4)
Miller, Diane D., jt. auth. see Miller, Diane Disney.
Miller, Diane Disney & Miller, Diane D. Walt Disney: His Life in Pictures. (p. 1855)
Miller, Donna C. Me & Mister Squirrel. (p. 1115)
Miller, Dorcas S. Constellation Finder: A Guide to Patterns in the Night Sky with Star Stories from Around the World. Miller, Dorcas S., illus. (p. 359)
Miller, Dorothy North. How Mr Foxy Fox Was Outfoxed. (p. 811)
Miller, Ed, illus. see Mayer, Kirsten.
Miller, Ed, illus. see Rosen, Lucy.
Miller, Ed. L. & Jensen, Jon. Questions That Matter: An Invitation to Philosophy. (p. 1426)
Miller, Edward. Fireboy to the Rescue: A Fire Safety Book. Miller, Edward, illus. (p. 591)
—Monster Health Book: A Guide to Eating Healthy, Being Active & Feeling Great for Monsters & Kids! (p. 1167)
—Recycling Day. Miller, Edward, illus. (p. 1453)
—Tooth Book: A Guide to Healthy Teeth & Gums. Miller, Edward, illus. (p. 1768)
Miller, Edward, illus. see Adler, David A.
Miller, Edward, illus. see Adler, David.
Miller, Edward, illus. see Bardhan-Quallen, Sudipta.
Miller, Edward, illus. see Branley, Franklyn M.
Miller, Edward, illus. see Branley, Franklyn Mansfield.
Miller, Edward, illus. see Murphy, Stuart J.
Miller, Edward, illus. see Pearson, Debora.
Miller, Edward, illus. see Showers, Paul.
Miller, Eileen Rudisill. Ballet Dancers Paper Dolls. (p. 134)
—Fairy Paper Doll. (p. 563)
—Fairy Tale Princesses Paper Dolls. (p. 564)
—Fashion Models Paper Dolls. (p. 576)
—Glitter Princess Stickers. (p. 684)
—Glitter Rapunzel Sticker Paper Doll. (p. 684)
—Glitter Sleeping Beauty Sticker Paper Doll. (p. 684)
—Glitter Snow Princess Sticker Paper Doll. (p. 684)
—Glitter Snow Queen Sticker Paper Doll. (p. 684)
—Glitter Snow White Sticker Paper Doll. (p. 684)
—Happy Easter Stained Glass Coloring Book. (p. 745)
—Jane Austen Paper Dolls: Four Classic Characters. (p. 908)
—KATE: the Duchess of Cambridge Paper Dolls. (p. 944)
—Mermaids Stained Glass Coloring Book. (p. 1128)
—Nutcracker Ballet Paper Dolls with Glitter! (p. 1274)
—Princess Coloring Book. (p. 1403)
—Princess Leonora Stained Glass Coloring Book. (p. 1404)
—Princess Stained Glass Jr. Coloring Book. (p. 1405)
—Princess Super Sticker Book. (p. 1405)
—Teen Pop Stars Paper Dolls. (p. 1713)
—True Love Stained Glass Coloring Book. (p. 1792)
Miller, Elaine Hobson. Nat King Cole: Unforgettable Musician. (p. 1230)
Miller, Elizabeth D. Read It! Draw It! Solve It! (p. 1443)
—Read It! Draw It! Solve It! Animal Book. (p. 1443)
Miller, Elizabeth I. Just Like Home: Como en Mi Tierra. Mlawer, Teresa, tr. (p. 939)
Miller, Erin L., illus. see Handelsman, Valerie.
Miller, Ev. Here's to the Winner. (p. 771)
Miller, Francis Trevel. Thomas A Edison an Inspiring Story for B. (p. 1737)
Miller, Frank. Alcohol, Chicas y Balas. (p. 35)
—Hard Boiled. Prosser, Jerry, ed. (p. 748)
—Ida y Vuelta al Infierno. Navarro, Francisco Perez, tr. from ENG. (p. 851)
—Sin City: Valores Familiares (p. 1578)
Miller, Frank, jt. auth. see Eisner, Will.
Miller, Frank & Klein, Todd. Batman - The Dark Knight Strikes Again. (p. 144)
Miller, Frank, et al. Autobiographix. Schutz, Diana, ed. (p. 117)
Miller, Frank L. Newtown's Trees. (p. 1249)
Miller, Frank, text. Born Again. (p. 214)
Miller, Frederic P., et al, eds. Carnivorous Carnival. (p. 270)
—Five Go off to Camp. (p. 600)
Miller, Fujiko, illus. see Brin, Susannah.
Miller, Fujiko, illus. see Epstein, Dwayne.
Miller, Fujiko, illus. see Schraff, Anne.
Miller, Fujiko, illus. see West, Casey.
Miller, Gabriella, jt. auth. see Chambers, Cindy.
Miller, Gary. Auto Mania. (p. 117)
—Bible Stories for Faith Kids. (p. 176)
—Outer Limits: The Future of Space Exploration. (p. 1312)
—Rhine: Europe's River Highway. (p. 1467)
—Staying Alive. (p. 1645)
Miller, Gary, jt. auth. see Miller, Gary G.
Miller, Gary & Miller, Lynda. Adventures of Bob & Betty. (p. 16)
Miller, Gary G. & Miller, Gary. Rhine: Europe's River Highway. (p. 1467)
—Tigris & Euphrates: Rivers of the Fertile Crescent. (p. 1749)
Miller, George, tr. see de Vigan, Delphine.
Miller, Gina, illus. see Tingle, Tim & Moore, James W.
Miller Goode, Dixie. Duffy Barkley: Seek Well: Tales of Uhrlin Book 2. (p. 489)
Miller, H. James. Willy the Worm Gets Lost. (p. 1934)
Miller, Heather. 10 Most Outstanding American Symbols. (p. 1994)
—10 Most Provocative 20th Century Artworks. (p. 1994)
—AC/DC: Hard Rock Band. (p. 8)
—Artista. (p. 104)
—Bigfoot. (p. 184)
—Celebrate St. Patrick's Day. (p. 284)
—Changing Earth. (p. 290)
—Daddy Longlegs (Bugs) (p. 398)
—Lo Que Hacen los Trabajadores Sanitarios. (p. 1044)
—Matter. (p. 1109)
—Nifty Thrifty Art Crafts. Ponte, June, illus. (p. 1252)
—Panama Canal. (p. 1320)
—Rolling Stones: The Greatest Rock Band. (p. 1485)
—Smoking. (p. 1595)
—What Does a Dentist Do? (p. 1883)
—What Does a Sanitation Worker Do? (p. 1884)
Miller, Heather Lynn. Subway Ride. Rama, Sue, illus. (p. 1671)
Miller, Heather Lynn, jt. auth. see Schaefer, Lola M.
Miller, Heidi, illus. see Catanzarite, Lisa.
Miller, Helen Markley. Thunder Rolling: The Story of Chief Joseph. Orbaan, Albert, illus. (p. 1746)
Miller, Henley. Meet Giganotosaurus. (p. 1121)
Miller, Holly & Schwartzkopf, Jere. Horse Named Princess: Hola Princess Adios Thistle. (p. 799)
Miller, House Joy. Nesting Place: A Bird's Eye View of Easter. (p. 1242)
Miller, J. Tiburones. (p. 1747)
Miller, J. Cris. Stories to Read to Children: The Pony & the Unicorn & 3 other Stories (p. 1655)
Miller, J. P. No Greater Love: The History of the African American Nurse (p. 1258)
Miller, J. P., illus. see Golden Books Staff.
Miller, J. P., illus. see Golden Books.
Miller, J. P., illus. see Scarry, Patricia M.
Miller, J. Philip & Greene, Sheppard M. We All Sing with the Same Voice. Meisel, Paul, illus. (p. 1865)
Miller, Jack E., jt. auth. see Bernstein, Robert.
Miller, Jade S. Sybil's Ride of Courage. (p. 1692)
Miller, Jake. 1963 March on Washington: Speeches & Songs for Civil Rights. (p. 2002)
—Bearded Dragon. (p. 151)
—Chameleon. (p. 289)
—Cobweb Weavers. (p. 337)
—Colony of Connecticut: A Primary Source History. (p. 342)
—Colony of Delaware: A Primary Source History. (p. 342)
—Colony of Massachusetts: A Primary Source History. (p. 342)
—Colony of New Jersey: A Primary Source History. (p. 342)
—Colony of Rhode Island: A Primary Source History. (p. 342)
—Colony of Virginia: A Primary Source History. (p. 342)
—Community Needs: Meeting Needs & Wants in Communities. (p. 350)
—Community Needs: Meeting Needs & Wants in the Communities. (p. 350)
—Fishing Spiders. (p. 599)
—Funnel Weavers. (p. 649)
—Gila Monster. (p. 676)
—Green Iguana. (p. 722)
—Komodo Dragon. (p. 966)
—Leopard Gecko. (p. 992)
—Lost Colony of Roanoke: A Primary Source History. (p. 1055)
—March from Selma to Montgomery: African Americans Demand the Vote. (p. 1091)
—Montgomery Bus Boycott: Integrating Public Buses. (p. 1170)
—Sit-Ins & Freedom Rides: The Power of Nonviolent Resistance. (p. 1581)
—Trap Door Spiders. (p. 1779)
—Trap-Door Spiders. (p. 1779)
—Who's Who in a Neighborhood. (p. 1921)
—Who's Who in a Public Housing Community. (p. 1921)
—Who's Who in a Rural Community. (p. 1921)
—Who's Who in a School Community. (p. 1921)
—Who's Who in an Urban Community. (p. 1921)
—Who's Who in School Community. (p. 1921)
Miller, James K. Albie the Albatross: An Adventurous Tale of Life. (p. 35)
—Leviathon the Dragon. (p. 1004)
Miller, Jane. Statistics 3 & 4 for OCR. (p. 1644)
Miller, Jane, jt. auth. see Dobbs, Steve.
Miller, Janet. Cut, Color & Paste: Bible Workers. (p. 396)
—Cut, Color & Paste: God's Creatures. (p. 396)
—DuckDumB. (p. 488)
—Fox Tail Farms. (p. 626)
—Little House on the Highway - a Story of a Homeless Family & School Bullying. (p. 1029)
Miller, Janie Evans. How Randy the Moose Turned His Frown Upside Down. (p. 812)
Miller, Jay. American Indian Families. (p. 62)
—American Indian Foods. (p. 62)
—American Indian Games. (p. 62)
—Bingo the Banjo Picking Bear. (p. 188)
—Opal, Herby, & Squeaky. (p. 1299)
—Sal & Sally. (p. 1504)
Miller, Jayna. Too Much Trick or Treat. Thatch, Nancy, ed. (p. 1767)
Miller, Jean. Curious Chucky. (p. 392)
Miller, Jeanne. Food Science. (p. 614)
—Grandpa Has Shark Teeth. (p. 709)
—My Eyelids Are Drooping. (p. 1202)
Miller, Jeff. Close Encounters of the Nerd Kind. (p. 333)
—Nerdy Dozen. (p. 1241)
—Nerdy Dozen #1. (p. 1241)
Miller, Jeffrey D. Home for Bella. (p. 792)
Miller, Jenifer. Chicken Noodle Soup Train. (p. 300)
Miller, Jennifer. Best Friends for Life. Choi Sung Hwan, Aragon Noel, illus. (p. 169)
—Christmas Tails. Knight, Vanessa, illus. (p. 316)
—Jennifer Miller's Run, Rasputin Run! Rasputin's Redemption (Book 3) (p. 913)
—Run, Rasputin, Run! Trials & Friendships (Book 2) (p. 1496)
—South Korea. (p. 1617)
—Two Snowflakes. (p. 1804)
Miller, Jennifer A. Chile. (p. 305)
—Iceland. (p. 851)
—South Korea. (p. 1617)
Miller, Jerry. Screws. (p. 1533)
Miller, Jo, illus. see Hall, Margaret C.
Miller, Jo, illus. see Hall, Margaret C. & Hall, Margaret.
Miller, Jo, illus. see Olson, Gillia M.
Miller, Joanna, illus. see Kimmel, Eric A.
Miller, Jocelyn. My Carry-Along Noah: Activity Book with Stickers. Hughes, Cathy, illus. (p. 1200)
—My Carry-Along Santa Activity Book: Christmas Fun with Stickers. Hughes, Cathy, illus. (p. 1200)
Miller, John. Simple Studies for Beginner Brass. (p. 1578)
—Winston & George. Cucco, Giuliano, illus. (p. 1937)
Miller, John Jackson, et al. Star Wars - Knights of the Old Republic (p. 1641)
Miller, Jonathan. Kim's Introductions. (p. 957)
—Sharks. (p. 1562)
—When I Grow Up. (p. 1902)
—Winter, Spring, Summer, Fall. (p. 1938)
Miller, Josh, illus. see Penn, Audrey.
Miller, Joshua. Extraterrestrial Compendium. (p. 555)
Miller, Joshua, illus. see Penn, Audrey.
Miller, Joshua, jt. auth. see Penn, Audrey.
Miller, Judith J. Hidden Treasure. Beers, Robert Lee, illus. (p. 776)
—Just Too Little. Panse, Sonal, illus. (p. 940)
Miller, Jules. Ellie & the Truth about the Tooth Fairy. Miller, Jules, illus. (p. 514)
—When Night Became Day. (p. 1904)
Miller, Julia Love, illus. see Feierabend, John M.
Miller, Justin, illus. see McIntosh, Kenneth.
Miller, Kane. Oh Baby! (p. 1280)
Miller, Karen. Achievement Gap. (p. 9)
—Children & the Entertainment Industry. (p. 302)
—Family. (p. 568)
—Girls & Sports. (p. 679)
—Japan. (p. 909)
—Outside Play & Learning Book: Activities for Young Children. Charner, Kathleen, ed. (p. 1313)
—Race Relations. (p. 1431)
—Resurgent Diseases. (p. 1464)
—Student Life. (p. 1669)
Miller, Kari. Mud Monster. (p. 1188)
Miller, Karl. Bongo Boy's Magical Drums. (p. 209)
Miller, Kat. I Love Daniel Radcliffe. (p. 842)
—I Love Kristen Stewart. (p. 842)
—I Love Miley Cyrus. (p. 842)
—I Love Robert Pattinson. (p. 843)
—I Love Taylor Swift. (p. 843)
—I Love the Jonas Brothers. (p. 843)
Miller, Kat & Manley, Claudia B. Volleyball: Girls Rocking It. (p. 1849)
Miller, Kate. Poems in Black & White. (p. 1376)
Miller, Katherine A., jt. auth. see Palika, Liz.
Miller, Kathleen. Fair Share Divorce for Women: The Definitive Guide to Creating a Winning Solution. (p. 562)
Miller, Kathryn L. Abc's with Sadie: Sadie Goes to the Zoo. (p. 4)
Miller, Kathy Collard. un-Devotional for Teens. (p. 1810)
Miller, Kathy M. Chippy Chipmunk Parties in the Garden. Miller, Kathy M., photos by. (p. 308)
Miller, Keith Ruskin. Indonesian Street Food Secrets: A Culinary Travel Odyssey. (p. 872)
Miller, Kelley. Funny Fill-In: Inside the Earth Adventure. (p. 649)
Miller, Kelli, jt. auth. see Watson, Stephanie.
Miller, Kelly Hufnagle. Monster in the Washer. (p. 1167)
Miller, Kerri. My Twin & Me - Fun with Twin Brothers & Sisters. (p. 1220)
Miller, Kevin M. My Effort Unaccepted My Pain Redundant: A Poetry Book. (p. 1202)
Miller, Kirsten. All You Desire. (p. 46)
—Darkness Dwellers. (p. 408)
—Empress's Tomb. (p. 521)
—Eternal Ones: What If Love Refused to Die? (p. 539)
—Inside the Shadow City. (p. 877)
Miller, Kirsten, jt. auth. see Segel, Jason.
Miller, Kirystan & Burns, Adam. Iowa State University College Prowler off the Record. (p. 886)
Miller, Kris Taft, illus. see Peters, Dylan.
Miller, Kristine Elizabeth. Albert's Lunch Box. (p. 35)
Miller, Kyle Linda. Dillo - A Baby Armadillo's Adventure on Sanibel Island. Eddy, Randon T., illus. (p. 440)
Miller, Kymberly. My Mommy's Having a Baby. (p. 1214)
—There's a Secret at My House. (p. 1731)
Miller, Larry, Jr. Long Live the Queen. (p. 1047)
Miller, Larry W., Jr. Droptroopers: Gauntlet of Fear. (p. 486)
Miller, Lauren. Free to Fall. (p. 634)
—Parallel. (p. 1323)
Miller, Leah, jt. auth. see Jacobs, Karen.
Miller, Leah Rae. Summer I Became a Nerd. (p. 1674)
Miller, Lee. Ete: (Extraterrestrial Elements) (p. 539)
Miller, Lester, jt. contrib. by see Hobbs, Ruth.
Miller, Linda K. Ronald the Church Mouse. (p. 1487)
Miller, Lindsey Michael. Circus. Griswold, Phillip, illus. (p. 322)
Miller, Linzi, illus. see Harris, Tumeka.
Miller, Liza. BusyBugz Adventures: Izzi Goes Missing. Bolton, Bill, illus. (p. 246)
Miller, Lois. Last Three Tall Tales. (p. 979)
Miller, Lois J. Three More Tall Tales. (p. 1743)
Miller, Loma. Jumper the Pony: Thomas Learns a Lesson. (p. 934)
Miller, Lorraine T., jt. auth. see Heuvel, Eric.
Miller, Lorraine T., tr. see Heuvel, Eric, et al.
Miller, Lynda, jt. auth. see Miller, Gary.

Miller, M. Terry Trackhoe Goes Missing. Monti, Carmelo, illus. (p. 1722)
Miller, M. F., jt. auth. see Miller, W. R.
Miller, Madison. Pulleys. (p. 1416)
—What Happens When I Sneeze? (p. 1886)
Miller, Maia. Drugs & Mental Illness. (p. 487)
Miller, Malinda. Ecstasy: Dangerous Euphoria. Henningfield, Jack E., ed. (p. 503)
—Green Construction: Creating Energy-Efficient, Low-Impact Buildings. (p. 721)
—Modern Mechanics: Maintaining Tomorrow's Green Vehicles. (p. 1158)
—Pharmaceutical Industry: Better Medicine for the 21st Century. (p. 1350)
—Tomorrow's Teachers: Urban Leadership, Empowering Students & Improving Lives. (p. 1765)
—Tomorrow's Teachers: Urban Leadership, Empowering Students, & Improving Lives. (p. 1765)
—Tomorrow's Transportation: Green Solutions for Air, Land & Sea. (p. 1765)
—Tomorrow's Transportation: Green Solutions for Air, Land, & Sea. (p. 1765)
Miller, Mara. Hurricane Katrina Strikes the Gulf Coast: Disaster & Survival. (p. 830)
—Iraq War: A Controversial War in Perspective. (p. 887)
—Remembering September 11, 2001: What We Know Now. (p. 1460)
—School Desegregation & the Story of the Little Rock Nine. (p. 1522)
—Terrorist Attacks: Disaster & Survival. (p. 1722)
Miller, Mara, jt. auth. see Taylor, Charlotte.
Miller, Marcia, jt. auth. see Frances, Ethel.
Miller, Marcia, et al. Tunes That Teach Multiplication Facts: 12 Lively Tunes & Hands-On Activities That Teach the Times Table. (p. 1797)
Miller, Margaret. Baby Faces. Miller, Margaret, photos by. (p. 126)
—Baby Food. Miller, Margaret, photos by. (p. 126)
—I Love Colors. Miller, Margaret, photos by. (p. 842)
—Now I'm Big. (p. 1269)
—What's on My Head? Miller, Margaret, photos by. (p. 1899)
Miller, Margaret, photos by see Bardley, Kimberly Brubaker.
Miller, Marie. Great Complaint: Oh! What a Day! (p. 714)
—Party Time. (p. 1326)
Miller, Marie-Therese. Distinguished Dogs. (p. 454)
—Helping Dogs. (p. 766)
—Hunting & Herding Dogs. (p. 829)
—Police Dogs. (p. 1380)
—Rachel Carson. (p. 1431)
—Search & Rescue Dogs. (p. 1537)
Miller, Marie-Therese & Banas, Sharon L. Managing Responsibilities. (p. 1086)
Miller, Marina, jt. auth. see Dorsey, Angela.
Miller, Marisa, tr. see Schneider, Antonie.
Miller, Mark. Meerkats Don't Fly. Butterfield, Cathy, illus. (p. 1120)
Miller, Mark, illus. see German, Lana.
Miller, Mark A. & Zelman, Laurie. Bethlehem's Best: A Children's Musical Based on the Story from Luke 2:1-20; Matthew 2:1-2, 8-11. (p. 171)
Miller, Marlene. I Know Where the Freighters Go. Miller, Marlene, illus. (p. 840)
Miller, Marlowe A. Masterpieces of British Modernism (p. 1103)
Miller, Martin. Antiques Source Book: The Definitive Guide to Retail Prices for Antiques & Collectables. (p. 89)
Miller, Marvin. Did You Know Did You: A Children's Book of Motivation & Inspiration. (p. 437)
—You Be the Jury: Courtroom Collection. Roper, Bob, illus. (p. 1973)
Miller, Mary, jt. auth. see Zeinert, Karen.
Miller, Mary Beth. Aimee. (p. 30)
Miller, Matthias. Zepho's Box. (p. 1986)
Miller, Mechele. My Friends the Stars. (p. 1209)
Miller, Megan. Hacks for Minecrafters: The Unofficial Guide to Tips & Tricks That Other Guides Won't Teach You. (p. 735)
—Hacks for Minecrafters: The Unofficial Guide to Tips & Tricks the Official Guides Won't Teach You. (p. 735)
—Hacks for Minecrafters - Master Builder: The Unofficial Guide to Tips & Tricks That Other Guides Won't Teach You. (p. 735)
—Hacks for Minecrafters: Redstone: The Unofficial Guide to Tips & Tricks That Other Guides Won't Teach You. (p. 735)
Miller, Meghan. Goose Named Lily. (p. 702)
Miller, Michael. Complete Idiot's Guide to Music History. (p. 353)
—Hilde und Günter Level Two Reader (p. 779)
Miller, Michael John. Harry Hamster Adventures. (p. 750)
Miller, Michael Paul. Kid Tales. (p. 951)
Miller, Michaela. Surviving Gangs & Bullying. (p. 1687)
Miller, Mike. Woodland Girls: Quest for the Rings. (p. 1949)
Miller, Mike, illus. see Bishop, Debbie.
Miller, Mike, illus. see Brandreth, Gyles.
Miller, Mike S. Confession Ninaltowski, Eric, illus. (p. 356)
Miller, Millie & Nelson, Cyndi. United States of America: A State-by-State Guide. (p. 1820)
Miller, Mirella S. Compost Center Operator. (p. 354)
—Life in Freshwater Lakes. (p. 1010)
—Life in Freshwater Marshes. (p. 1010)
—Life in Rivers. (p. 1011)
—Ocean Habitats. (p. 1276)
—Oil Worker. (p. 1282)
—Prairie Habitats. (p. 1392)
Miller, Mitzi, jt. auth. see Millner, Denene.
Miller, Mona. Call of the Wild! Golden Books Staff & Fruchter, Jason, illus. (p. 254)
—Hey, Buddy! Fruchter, Jason, illus. (p. 774)
—Very Busy Coloring Book. Golden Books, illus. (p. 1837)
Miller, Moses. Barack in Me: An Inspirational Novel for Young African American Males. (p. 137)
Miller, Nancy, ed. see Meyers, Ted (E.C.).
Miller, Nancy, illus. see Tietz, Heather.
Miller, Nate. Sam's Soccer Game: Work with Addition & Subtraction Equations. (p. 1509)
Miller, Nathan. Official Librarian: Bessy's Back! (p. 1280)
Miller, Nelson. Little Lake Saga. Bedard, Kathy, illus. (p. 1030)
Miller, Nick, illus. see Smelcer, John E., et al.
Miller, Olive Beaupr. Magic Garden of My Book House. (p. 1072)
Miller, Olive Beaupre & Baum, Harry Neal. Picturesque Tale of Progress. (p. 1356)
Miller, Olive Beaupre, ed. My Book House—In the Nursery. (p. 1198)
—My Book House—Story Time. (p. 1198)
Miller, Pam. Wrinkles. Ostrom, Bob, illus. (p. 1963)
Miller, Pam, et al. Beach Box: Going to the Beach/Sand/Shells. Warren, Shari et al, illus. (p. 149)
Miller, Pat. Collaborative Bridges: Me, Myself & You. (p. 339)
—More Library Skills. (p. 1174)
—Pet for Every Person. (p. 1345)
—Squirrel's New Year's Resolution. Ember, Kathi, illus. (p. 1637)
—Substitute Groundhog Ember, Kathi, illus. (p. 1671)
—Substitute Groundhog. Ember, Kathi, illus. (p. 1671)
—We're Going on a Book Hunt. Bernard Westcott, Nadine, illus. (p. 1875)
—Whole Story of the Doughnut. Kirsch, Vincent X., illus. (p. 1920)
Miller, Pat Zietlow. Sharing the Bread: An Old-Fashioned Thanksgiving Story. McElmurry, Jill, illus. (p. 1561)
—Sophie's Seeds. (p. 1613)
—Sophie's Squash. Wilsdorf, Anne, illus. (p. 1613)
—Wherever You Go. (p. 1911)
Miller, Paton, illus. see Margolis, Alysia.
Miller, Patricia. Tale of Polly Puffin. (p. 1700)
Miller, Patti. Mother Earth Has Seven Kids! (p. 1177)
Miller, Patty. Bridge Between Two Worlds. (p. 227)
Miller, Paula. One-Eyed Jack. Forrest, Chris, illus. (p. 1294)
Miller, Paula K. Amy, Louise & Me. (p. 66)
Miller, Peggy Reiff. Seagoing Cowboy. Ewart, Claire, illus. (p. 1536)
Miller, Penelope. Farbedrook. (p. 573)
Miller, Peter. Vermont People. Miller, Peter, photos by. (p. 1837)
Miller, Petra. Earthquakes. (p. 497)
—Ebola. (p. 501)
—Floods. (p. 605)
—Hepatitis. (p. 769)
—Hurricanes. (p. 830)
Miller, Phil, illus. see Burgan, Michael & Hoena, Blake A.
Miller, Phil, illus. see Doeden, Matt.
Miller, Phil, illus. see Gianopoulos, Andrea & Barnett III, Charles.
Miller, Phil, illus. see Gianopoulos, Andrea & Barnett, Charles, III.
Miller, Phil, illus. see Gianopoulos, Andrea & Capstone Press Editors.
Miller, Phil, illus. see Gunderson, Jessica Sarah & Gunderson, Jessica.
Miller, Phil, illus. see Hoena, Blake A. & Hoena, B. A.
Miller, Phil, illus. see O'Hearn, Michael.
Miller, Phil, illus. see Olson, Kay Melchisedech.
Miller, Phil, illus. see Welvaert, Scott R.
Miller, R. L. Birthentine's Day Present. (p. 193)
—Tale of Little Fanny Flip-Flop. Brooks, Katie, illus. (p. 1699)
Miller, R. T. Printreading Based on the 2005 NEC: Text. (p. 1407)
—Printreading Based on the 2005 NEC: Answer Key. (p. 1407)
Miller, R. T., jt. auth. see Moniz, B. J.
Miller, R. T., jt. auth. see Moniz.
Miller, R. T., contrib. by. ABCs of DMM Safety Videotape. (p. 4)
Miller, Randy. Fiddler's Throne: A Selection of 375 Tunes for Contra Dances, Sessions, & House Parties (p. 583)
Miller, Randy & Perron, Jack. New England Fiddler's Repertoire: A Source Book of Established Contra Dance Music Bley-Vroman, Robert, ed. (p. 1244)
Miller, Ray. Shaquille O'Neal. (p. 1561)
Miller, Ray, jt. auth. see Miller, Ray JR.
Miller, Ray, et al. Beat the Clock Sports. Thorp, Cameron, illus. (p. 152)
Miller, Ray, Jr., jt. auth. see McCloy, James F.
Miller, Ray JR. & Miller, Ray. How Kris Became Claus. (p. 810)
Miller, Raymond H. Jaromir Jagr. (p. 909)
—Jhalak Man Tamang: Slave Labor Whistleblower. (p. 917)
—Kobe Bryant. (p. 966)
—Matt Groening. (p. 1109)
—Michelle Kwan. (p. 1135)
—Milton Bradley. (p. 1144)
—Stan Lee: Creator of Spider-Man. (p. 1639)
—Tony Hawk. (p. 1766)
—Vampires. (p. 1832)
—War in Afghanistan. (p. 1857)
Miller, Reagan. 100th Day of School. (p. 1999)
—Engineering in Our Everyday Lives. (p. 529)
—Engineers Build Models. (p. 529)
—Engineers Solve Problems. (p. 529)
—High-Flying Airplanes. (p. 777)
—Martin Luther King, Jr. Day. (p. 1098)
—Moon. (p. 1171)
—Mother's Day & Other Family Days. (p. 1178)
—Sukkot. (p. 1673)
—Sun. (p. 1675)
—Valentine's Day. (p. 1830)
—What Is a Democracy? Crabtree Publishing Staff, ed. (p. 1888)
—What Is a Monarchy? Crabtree Publishing Staff, ed. (p. 1888)
—What Is a Theocracy? Crabtree Publishing Staff, ed. (p. 1888)
Miller, Reagan, jt. auth. see Crabtree Editor.
Miller, Reagan, jt. auth. see Crabtree Editors.
Miller, Reagan, jt. auth. see Kalman, Bobbie.
Miller, Reagan & Alexander, Carol. How to Tell a Folktale. (p. 822)
—How to Tell a Folktale. Crabtree Publishing Staff, ed. (p. 822)
Miller, Reagan & Aloian, Molly. Ferrari. (p. 582)
Miller, Reagan & Arthur, Martin. Great Leaders of the Civil War. (p. 717)
Miller, Reagan & Berry, Minta. Beginner Word Problems. (p. 159)
—Beginner Word Problems. Crabtree Publishing Co. Staff, ed. (p. 159)
—Building Sets of Ten. (p. 239)
—Comparing Fractions. (p. 352)
—Comparing Fractions. Crabtree Publishing Staff, ed. (p. 352)
—Patterning. (p. 1329)
—Patterning. Crabtree Publishing Staff, ed. (p. 1329)
—Perimeter. (p. 1343)
—What Comes in Sets? (p. 1881)
—What Comes in Sets? Crabtree Publishing Staff, ed. (p. 1881)
Miller, Reagan & Bow, James. Lamborghini. (p. 972)
Miller, Reagan & Boyle, Sarah B. What Is a Dictatorship? Crabtree Publishing Staff, ed. (p. 1888)
—What Is a Theocracy? (p. 1888)
Miller, Reagan & Brennan, Joseph K. What Is an Oligarchy? (p. 1889)
Miller, Reagan & Claus, J. Matteson. Life on a Civil War Battlefield. (p. 1012)
Miller, Reagan & Cocca, Lisa Colozza. Reconstruction & the Aftermath of the Civil War. (p. 1452)
Miller, Reagan & Doak, Melissa J. Life on the Homefront During the Civil War. (p. 1012)
Miller, Reagan & Gould, Jane H. Civil War Begins. (p. 325)
Miller, Reagan & Hiller, Sandi J. Turning Point Battles of the Civil War. (p. 1798)
Miller, Reagan & Hyde, Natalie. What's in the Southeast? (p. 1898)
Miller, Reagan & Johnson, Robin. How Engineers Find Solutions. (p. 809)
—Jaguar. (p. 905)
—What's in the Midwest? (p. 1898)
—What's in the Midwest? Crabtree Publishing Staff, ed. (p. 1898)
Miller, Reagan & Margaret, R. Mead. What Is a Monarchy? (p. 1888)
Miller, Reagan & Peppas, Lynn. Corvette. (p. 368)
—Mustang. (p. 1194)
—What's in the Southwest? (p. 1898)
—What's in the Southwest? Crabtree Publishing Staff, ed. (p. 1898)
Miller, Reagan & Putnam, Jeff. Nation Divided: Causes of the Civil War. (p. 1231)
Miller, Reagan & Richardson, Hazel. Arts & Culture in the Ancient World. (p. 105)
—Arts & Culture in the Ancient World. Crabtree Publishing Co. Staff, ed. (p. 105)
—Communication in the Ancient World. (p. 349)
—Communication in the Ancient World. Crabtree Publishing Staff, ed. (p. 349)
—Government in the Ancient World. (p. 704)
—Government in the Ancient World. Crabtree Publishing Co. Staff, ed. (p. 704)
—Religion in the Ancient World. (p. 1458)
—Technology in the Ancient World. (p. 1711)
—Technology in the Ancient World. Crabtree Publishing Co. Staff, ed. (p. 1711)
—Trade & Commerce in the Ancient World. (p. 1776)
Miller, Reagan & Rosen, Suri. How to Tell a Fable. (p. 822)
—How to Tell a Fable. Crabtree Publishing Staff, ed. (p. 822)
Miller, Reagan & Stone, Janet. How to Tell a Legend. (p. 822)
—How to Tell a Legend. Crabtree Publishing Staff, ed. (p. 822)
Miller, Reagan & Stowell, Cinci. Final Campaigns of the Civil War. (p. 586)
Miller, Reagan & Sue, Bright-Moore. What Is a Democracy? (p. 1888)
Miller, Reagan & Walker, Robert. How to Tell a Myth. (p. 822)
—How to Tell a Myth. Crabtree Publishing Staff, ed. (p. 822)
—Porsche. (p. 1386)
—What's in the the West? Crabtree Publishing Staff, ed. (p. 1898)
—What's in the West? (p. 1898)
Miller, Rebecca, illus. see Hammari, Kimiko.
Miller, Rebecca, illus. see Olsen, Bevan Lloyd.
Miller, Richard, illus. see Clown, Pogo the.
Miller, Richard, illus. see Pogo the Clown.
Miller, Richard D., illus. see Pogo the Clown.
Miller, Robert, illus. see Haile, Carol J.
Miller, Robert H. Reflections of a Black Cowboy: Cowboys. (p. 1456)
—Reflections of a Black Cowboy: Buffalo Soldiers. (p. 1456)
Miller, Robin Spanier. Biblical Journey of ABC's. (p. 177)
Miller, Roger, photos by see Foster, Linda.
Miller, Roger Carlton. Ant & the Grasshopper (p. 88)
Miller, Roger G. Billy Mitchell: Evangelist of Airpower. (p. 187)
Miller, Roger LeRoy & McGraw-Hill Staff. Economics Today & Tomorrow. (p. 503)
Miller, Ron. Chasing the Storm: Tornadoes, Meteorology, & Weather Watching. (p. 294)
—Curiosity's Mission on Mars: Exploring the Red Planet. (p. 392)
—Digital Art: Painting with Pixels. (p. 439)
—Elements: What You Really Want to Know. (p. 510)
—Recentering the Universe: The Radical Theories of Copernicus, Kepler, & Galileo. (p. 1451)
—Recentering the Universe: The Radical Theories of Copernicus, Kepler, Galileo, & Newton. (p. 1451)
—Robot Explorers. (p. 1480)
—Rockets. (p. 1483)
—Satellites. (p. 1515)
—Seven Wonders Beyond the Solar System. (p. 1555)
—Seven Wonders of Asteroids, Comets, & Meteors. (p. 1555)
—Seven Wonders of Engineering. (p. 1555)
—Seven Wonders of the Gas Giants & Their Moons. (p. 1555)
—Seven Wonders of the Rocky Planets & Their Moons. (p. 1555)
—Space Exploration. (p. 1619)
—Space Innovations (p. 1619)
—Special Effects: An Introduction to Movie Magic. Miller, Ron, illus. (p. 1623)
Miller, Ron, illus. see Carson, Mary Kay.
Miller, Ron & Browning, Sommer. Cleopatra. (p. 331)
Miller, Ron Jay. Medallion. (p. 1118)
Miller, Ross, ed. see Roth, Philip.
Miller, Russell, illus. see King, Bart.
Miller, Ruth L. Power of Self Ralph Waldo Emerson's Wonder Filled Life. Shonkwiler, Martha, illus. (p. 1389)
Miller, S. L. Yellow Kitty, Life in the Garden. (p. 1970)
Miller, Sabine. Renoir (p. 1460)
Miller, Samantha A. Princess & Her Servant. (p. 1402)
Miller, Sara. My Pod: Libro de Cuentos y Reproductor Personal de Musica. Peterson, Stacy & Maberry, Maranda, illus. (p. 1217)
Miller, Sara, jt. auth. see Reader's Digest Editors.
Miller, Sara, jt. auth. see Reader's Digest Staff.
Miller, Sara F. Gift for Pooh. (p. 675)
—Pooh's Honey Trouble. (p. 1383)
Miller, Sara Swan. All Kinds Of (p. 44)
—All Kinds of Eyes. (p. 44)
—All Kinds of Feet. (p. 44)
—All Kinds of Noses. (p. 45)
—All Kinds of Skin. (p. 45)
—Caribou of the Arctic. (p. 269)
—Eagles. (p. 492)
—Emperor Penguins of the Antarctic. (p. 521)
—Otters. (p. 1307)
—Owls. (p. 1315)
—Polar Bears of the Arctic. (p. 1379)
—Red Pandas. (p. 1454)
—Seals of the Antarctic. (p. 1536)
—Secret Lives of Burrowing Beasts. (p. 1541)
—Secret Lives of Cave Creatures. (p. 1541)
—Secret Lives of Deep Sea Creatures. (p. 1541)
—Secret Lives of Seashell Dwellers. (p. 1541)
—Secret Lives of Soil Creatures. (p. 1541)
—Sloths. (p. 1591)
—Walruses of the Arctic. (p. 1855)
—Whales of the Arctic. (p. 1878)
—Wolves. (p. 1945)
Miller, Sarah. Inside the Mind of Gideon Rayburn. (p. 877)
—Lost Crown. (p. 1055)
—Miss Spitfire: Reaching Helen Keller. (p. 1152)
—Other Girl. (p. 1306)
Miller, Scott. Prairie Whispers. (p. 1392)
Miller, Scott E. Prairie Sunsets. (p. 1392)
Miller, Shakeera. Little One Did You Know. (p. 1032)
Miller, Shane. Riddles, Riddles, Riddles: Enigmas & Anagrams, Puns & Puzzles, Quizzes & Conundrums! (p. 1471)
Miller, Shane, illus. see Green, Robert James.
Miller, Shannon. Be Nice Online. (p. 148)
—Don't Share Your Address Online. (p. 468)
—Don't Share Your Phone Number Online. (p. 468)
—Don't Share Your Plans Online. (p. 468)
—Don't Talk to Strangers Online. (p. 468)
—Keep Your Passwords Secret. (p. 947)
Miller, Sharon Schwab. Good Morning Otis. (p. 698)
Miller, Shauna, creator. Penny Chic: How to Be Stylish on a Real Girl's Budget. (p. 1338)
Miller, Sibley. Heads Up, Horses! (p. 757)
—Horse Magic - Or Not? Chang, Tara Larsen & Gershman, Jo, illus. (p. 799)
—Horse, of Course! Chang, Tara Larsen & Gershman, Jo, illus. (p. 799)
—Horse's Best Friend. Chang, Tara Larsen & Gershman, Jo, illus. (p. 800)
—Horses Her Way. Chang, Tara Larsen & Gershman, Jo, illus. (p. 800)
—Horsey Trails. Chang, Tara Larsen & Gershman, Jo, illus. (p. 800)
—Hungry as a Horse. (p. 828)
—Merry-Go-Horses. Chang, Tara Larsen & Gershman, Jo, illus. (p. 1129)
Miller, Sibley & Lenhard, Elizabeth. Horse Happy. Chang, Tara Larsen & Gershman, Jo, illus. (p. 799)
—Horses' Night Out. Chang, Tara Larsen & Gershman, Jo, illus. (p. 800)
—If Wishes Were Horses. Chang, Tara Larsen & Gershman, Jo, illus. (p. 854)
Miller, Sienna, jt. auth. see Mercer, Sienna.
Miller, Stan. Night Before Easter. (p. 1253)
Miller, Stanley W. Wishing Willow: A Young People's Story for All Ages. (p. 1941)
Miller, Steve, illus. see Nash, Damien K. H. & Nash, Kathy.
Miller, Steven. Samantha's Christmas Kitten. (p. 1507)
Miller, Sue. I'm Thinking... My Brain Is a Pain: But Then, Maybe I Should Think Again! Broome, Shannon, illus. (p. 860)
Miller, Sue F. Targeting Pronunciation: Communicating Clearly in English. (p. 1706)
Miller, Susan, illus. see Taylor-Butler, Christine.
Miller, Susan A. My First 1000 Words. (p. 1203)
—My First Dictionary. Williams, Ted, illus. (p. 1206)
Miller, Susan B. When Parents Have Problems: A Book for Teens & Older Children Who Have a Disturbed or Difficult Parent. (p. 1904)
Miller, Susan Hoskins. Canada. (p. 260)
—Germany. (p. 666)
Miller, Susan Martins. Elijah. (p. 512)
Miller, Susan Martins, jt. auth. see Blackwood, Gary L.
Miller, Suzanne. Pirates! That Is Who We Be! (p. 1364)
—You Can Be... (p. 1973)
Miller, Sy, jt. auth. see Jackson, Jill.
Miller, Terry. D-Day at Omaha Beach: Turning the Tide of World War II. (p. 397)
Miller, Tim. Vroom! Motoring into the Wild World of Racing. (p. 1851)
Miller, Tiwana Mutch. Positive Outweighs Negative. (p. 1387)
—Praying Time. (p. 1393)
—You Can Learn from Any Level. (p. 1974)
Miller, Toby. 7 Things Christians Don't Do: And What to Do Instead. (p. 1993)
—Audio Cassette: Used with ... Miller-Targeting Pronunciation: Communicating Clearly in English. (p. 114)

—Audio Cd: Used with ... Miller-Targeting Pronunciation: Communicating Clearly in English. (p. 114)
—Handbook for College Teaching. (p. 740)
—Magic Word. (p. 1074)
—Rockin' Rainstricks: And Other Music Activities. (p. 1483)
Miller, Tom, illus. see Hernandez, Regina.
Miller, Tori. Eels. (p. 505)
—Manta Rays. (p. 1088)
—Octopuses & Squid. (p. 1278)
—Pufferfish. (p. 1415)
—Scorpion Fish. (p. 1530)
—Sea Urchins. (p. 1536)
Miller, Tori & Lynette, Rachel. Who Lives in a Colorful Coral Reef? (p. 1916)
—Who Lives in the Dry, Hot Desert? (p. 1916)
Miller, Ura. 101 Favorite Stories from the Bible. (p. 1999)
Miller, Vern. Gypsy the Goat. Cotes Stanley, Marsha, illus. (p. 734)
Miller, Victoria. Dora & the Unicorn King. (p. 470)
—Flowers for Mami Unicorn! (p. 608)
—Super Babies! (p. 1679)
Miller, Victoria, illus. see Banks, Steven.
Miller, Victoria, illus. see Bergen, Lara Rice & Bergen, Lara.
Miller, Victoria, illus. see Burroughs, Caleb.
Miller, Victoria, illus. see Depken, Kristen L.
Miller, Victoria, illus. see Driscoll, Laura.
Miller, Victoria, illus. see Golden Books Staff.
Miller, Victoria, illus. see Golden Books.
Miller, Victoria, illus. see Inches, Alison.
Miller, Victoria, illus. see Larsen, Kirsten.
Miller, Victoria, illus. see Random House Staff.
Miller, Victoria, illus. see Random House.
Miller, Victoria, illus. see Rao, Lisa.
Miller, Victoria, illus. see Ricci, Christine.
Miller, Victoria, illus. see Tillworth, Mary.
Miller, Violet. Why Does the Sun Set? (p. 1924)
Miller, Vivian. Grandma's Mercedes. (p. 709)
Miller, W. R. & Miller, M. F. American Tech's Hints for the Highly Effective Instructor: Survival Skills for the Technical Trainer: Text. (p. 63)
Miller, Walton. Rise of the Dirtlings (p. 1474)
Miller, Warner Etta. Max's Wish. (p. 1112)
Miller, Whitney A. Crimson Gate. (p. 383)
—Violet Hour. (p. 1843)
Miller, William. Bus Ride. Ward, John, illus. (p. 244)
—Joe Louis, My Champion Pate, Rodney, tr. (p. 920)
—Joe Louis, My Champion. Pate, Rodney S., illus. (p. 920)
—Rent Party Jazz. Riley-Webb, Charlotte, illus. (p. 1460)
—Richard Wright y el Carne de Biblioteca. Christie, Gregory R., illus. (p. 1470)
—Tales of Persia: Missionary Stories from Islamic Iran. Van Patten, Bruce, illus. (p. 1702)
—Zora Hurston & the Chinaberry Tree. (p. 1990)
Miller, William & Lucas, Cedric. Frederick Douglass: The Last Day of Slavery. (p. 633)
Miller, Wilma H. Improving Early Literacy: Strategies & Activities for Struggling Students (K-3) (p. 862)
Miller, Woody. Adventures of the Wee People. (p. 24)
—Tefilat Haderech: The Traveler's Prayer. (p. 1715)
Miller, Woody, illus. see Rubinstein, Robert E.
Miller, Woody, illus. see Rubinstein, Robert.
Miller, Woody, illus. see Sayre, April Pulley.
Miller, Wray. Cerulean Blue. (p. 287)
Miller, Zachary N., ed. see Bankler, William.
Miller, Zachary N., ed. see Bricker, Sandra D.
Miller, Zachary N., ed. see Schreiber, Sophia.
Miller, Zachary N., ed. see Skip Press Staff.
Miller, Zoe, jt. auth. see Goodman, David.
Miller-Burke, Jude. Snowball, Come Home! (p. 1600)
Miller-Gill, Angela. There Are No Blankets on the Moon. Kellem-Kellner, Blynda, illus. (p. 1729)
Miller-Johnston, Renee. Courtney Logan Kennedy Presents Zoe. (p. 373)
—Double Trouble for Courtney Logan Kennedy (p. 473)
Miller-Lachmann, Lyn. Gringolandia. (p. 724)
—Once upon a Cuento. (p. 1292)
—Rogue. (p. 1484)
—Surviving Santiago. (p. 1687)
Millerm, April. Holy Book. (p. 791)
Miller-Ray, Pamela. Tiddels's Journey to Hoot Owl Canyon. (p. 1747)
Miller-Schroeder, Patricia. ASPCA. (p. 107)
—Blue Whales. (p. 203)
—Blue Whales, with Code. (p. 203)
—Boreal Forests. (p. 214)
—Gorillas. (p. 703)
—Gorillas with Code. (p. 703)
—Minerals. (p. 1146)
—Science of the Environment. (p. 1527)
—Senses. (p. 1551)
—Underwater Life. (p. 1817)
Miller-Stehr, Felicia. Are You Chanukah or Christmas? (p. 97)
Milles, Harriet. Japanese (p. 909)
Millet, Claude, illus. see Marchon, Blandine.
Millet, Claude, jt. auth. see First Discovery Staff.
Millet, Claude, et al. Castillo. Millet, Claude et al, trs. (p. 276)
—Raton y Otros Roedores. Jeunesse, Gallimard et al, trs. (p. 1440)
Millet, Denise, illus. see Marchon, Blandine.
Millet, Denise, tr. see Millet, Claude, et al.
Millet, Esao, illus. see Lecreux, Michele & Gallais, Celia.
Millet, Fred B., ed. see Webster, John & Webster, John.
Millet, Jason. War with the Evil Power Master. (p. 1858)
Millet, Jason, illus. see Capstone Press Staff.
Millet, Jason, illus. see Rieber, John Ney.
Millet, Jason, illus. see Robbins, Trina.
Millet, Jason, et al. Beyond Escape! (p. 174)
—Escape. (p. 534)
Millet, Jocelyn, illus. see Lecreux, Michele & Gallais, Celia.
Millet, Lydia. Fires Beneath the Sea. (p. 592)
—Pills & Starships. (p. 1359)
—Shimmers in the Night. (p. 1566)
Millett, Melanie. CTR Boy. (p. 387)
—Teeny Tiny Talks: Junior Primary: I Will Follow God's Plan for Me Millett, Melanie, illus. (p. 1715)
Millett, Peter. Jump! (p. 933)
—Mercury & the Woodcutter (p. 1127)
Millett, Peter & Chambers, Mal. Goal! (p. 687)
Millett, Peter & Morden, Richard. It's a Jungle Out There. (p. 895)
Millett, Peter & Scales, Simon. Game. (p. 654)
Millett, Peter & Texidor, Dee. On the Team. (p. 1291)
Millett, Peter & Wallace-Mitchell, Jane. Lions! (p. 1021)
Millhoff, Brian L. Micronesian Coloring Book. (p. 1136)
Millhouse, Charles F. In Memory Alone. (p. 864)
Millhouse, Jackie. Tiger & the General. Girouard, Patrick, illus. (p. 1748)
Millican, Jacob. Ballad of Koko-Ma. Millican, JoAnn, illus. (p. 134)
Millican, JoAnn, illus. see Millican, Jacob.
Millidge, Gary Spencer & McKay, James. Draw Fantasy Figures: Basic Drawing Techniques - Develop Characters from Elves to Dragons - Create Fantasy Worlds. (p. 480)
Milligan, Bryce. Brigid's Cloak: An Ancient Irish Story. Cann, Helen, illus. (p. 228)
—Comanche Captive. (p. 346)
Milligan, Chris & Smith, David. Check Mate! Two Boys Experience the Life & Death Fight for Control of the Hudson Bay Fur Trade. (p. 295)
Milligan, Domino. Sandman. Spiller, Michael, illus. (p. 1511)
Milligan, Helen, jt. auth. see Chandler, Murray.
Milligan, Jean F. Inferences for Young Audiences. Kennedy, Allan, illus. (p. 873)
Milligan, Lynda & Smith, Nancy. Best of Sewing Machine Fun for Kids. (p. 170)
Milligan, Peter. Good Omens Allred, Mike, illus. (p. 700)
—Shade Changing: The American Scream. Pennington, Mark, illus. (p. 1556)
—X-Force: Famous, Mutant & Mortal. Allred, Mike, illus. (p. 1967)
Millikan, Desiree, photos by see Baker, Georgette.
Millikan, Jeff, photos by see Baker, Georgette.
Millin, Christopher. King of Arugula. (p. 958)
Milliner, Donna L. Kingdom of Wish & Why. Snyder, Ronda, illus. (p. 960)
Millington, Jon. Mathematical Snacks: A Collection of Interesting Ideas to Fill Those Spare Moments. (p. 1107)
—Tables Cubes: Make These Two Sets of Special Cubes & Use Them for Tables Practice. (p. 1694)
Million, Liz, illus. see Cox, Michael.
Million, Liz, illus. see Gurney, Stella.
Million, Liz, illus. see Harrison, Paul.
Millionaire, Tony. That Darn Yarn. (p. 1726)
—Uncle Gabby. (p. 1811)
Millis, Lokken, illus. see Conway, Jill Ker, et al.
Millis, Lokken, illus. see Conway, Jill Ker.
Millman, Calanitte. Adventures of the Gimmel Gang III: The Cave. (p. 23)
—Adventures of the Gimmel Gang IV: Triple Trouble (p. 23)
Millman, Christian. Absolutely Crazy Knowledge: The World's Funniest Collection of Amazing Facts. (p. 7)
Millman, Dan. Secreto Del Guerrero Pacifico. (p. 1544)
Millman, Isaac & Leslie, Jennifer. Arbeit Macht Frei: Work Sets You Free. (p. 94)
Millman, Jason, jt. auth. see Ennis, Robert.
Millman, Lawrence. Kayak Full of Ghosts. White, Timothy, illus. (p. 946)
Millman, M. C. Always Something Else: The whimsical adventures of Elisheva Raskin. (p. 51)
—Always Something Else 2. (p. 51)
—CLASS-ified Information: Suri. (p. 327)
—CLASS-ified Information: Baila. (p. 327)
—CLASS-ified Information: Tziporah. (p. 327)
—Juggling Act. (p. 932)
—One Step Ahead. (p. 1297)
—Time Will Tell. (p. 1753)
Millman, Selena. Anyone Can Make A Difference. (p. 91)
—Ever Notice. (p. 541)
—More Than a Hero. (p. 1175)
—Our Dream Project. (p. 1308)
—Prince & Me. (p. 1401)
Millmann, Anita Sutherland. Zitta & Nelli. (p. 1987)
Millner, Denene. Miss You, Mina. (p. 1152)
Millner, Denene & Miller, Mitzi. What Goes Around. (p. 1884)
Millner, Robert W. Chicken Coop Gang. (p. 300)
Millonzi, Kara A., jt. auth. see Lawrence, David M.
Mills, illus. see Osborn.
Mills, Ami Chen. How to Be Happy: A.K.A. Don't Trip, Just Kick It! (p. 815)
Mills, Andy & Osborn, Becky. Shapesville. Neitz, Erica, tr. (p. 1561)
—Shapesville. Neitz, Erica, illus. (p. 1561)
Mills, Arthur. Crawl Space. Mills, Arthur & Tichelaar, Tyler, eds. (p. 377)
Mills, Barbara, jt. auth. see Stiles, Mary.
Mills, Bronwyn. U. S. -Mexican War. (p. 1805)
Mills, Charles. Bandit of Benson Park. (p. 136)
—Great Sleepy-Time Stew Rescue. (p. 718)
—Secret of Scarlett Cove. (p. 1542)
—Storm on Shadow Mountain. (p. 1656)
—Wings over Oshkosh. (p. 1936)
Mills, Christopher, illus. see Gershenson, Harold P.
Mills, Cindy. Cass Railroad Fun Book. (p. 276)
Mills, Claudia. 7 X 9 = Trouble! Karas, G. Brian, illus. (p. 1993)
—Annika Riz, Math Whiz. Shepperson, Rob, illus. (p. 87)
—Basketball Disasters. Francis, Guy, illus. (p. 143)
—Being Teddy Roosevelt. Alley, R. W., illus. (p. 161)
—Fractions = Trouble! Karas, G. Brian, illus. (p. 626)
—How Oliver Olson Changed the World. Maione, Heather, illus. (p. 811)
—How Oliver Olson Changed the World. Maione, Heather Harms, illus. (p. 811)
—Izzy Barr, Running Star. Shepperson, Rob, illus. (p. 901)
—Kelsey Green, Reading Queen Shepperson, Rob, illus. (p. 948)
—Kelsey Green, Reading Queen. Shepperson, Rob, illus. (p. 948)
—Mason Dixon: Fourth-Grade Disasters. Francis, Guy, illus. (p. 1102)
—Pet Disasters. Francis, Guy, illus. (p. 1345)
—Trouble with Ants. Kath, Katie, illus. (p. 1790)
—Zero Tolerance. (p. 1986)
Mills, Cliff. Clayton Kershaw. (p. 330)
—Virginia Woolf. (p. 1844)
Mills, Clifford W. Adrian Peterson. (p. 13)
—Ang Lee. (p. 73)
—Angela Merkel. (p. 74)
—Bernie Williams. (p. 167)
—Curt Schilling. (p. 395)
—Derek Jeter. (p. 427)
—Hannibal. (p. 743)
—Isaac Mizrahi. (p. 890)
—Justin Timberlake. (p. 940)
—Lord Baltimore. (p. 1052)
—Tony Romo. (p. 1766)
—Tupac Shakur. (p. 1797)
Mills, Craylon. Missing Pant Leg. (p. 1152)
Mills, Dan, photos by see Luebbermann, Mimi.
Mills, David. Lima's Red Hot Chilli. Brazell, Derek, illus. (p. 1018)
—Mei Ling's Hiccups: Higgadi Mil Ling. Brazell, Derek, illus. (p. 1124)
—Mei Ling's Hiccups. Brazell, Derek, illus. (p. 1124)
—Sam's First Day. Finlay, Lizzie, illus. (p. 1509)
—Wibble Wobble. Crouth, Julia, illus. (p. 1927)
—Wibbly Wobbly Tooth. Crouth, Julia, illus. (p. 1927)
Mills, David & Finlay, Lizzie. Sam's First Day. (p. 1509)
Mills, DiAnn. Kaleidoscope: Love in Pursuit, Perspective Changes in a Suspense-Filled Romance. Bk. 3 (p. 941)
Mills, Donald, illus. see Moore, Clement C.
Mills, Elizabeth. Ken Griffey Sr. & Ken Griffey Jr. Baseball Heroes. (p. 948)
Mills, Enos A. Cricket, A Mountain Pony (p. 382)
—Stories of Scotch. (p. 1655)
Mills, Faythe, illus. see Mercier, Deborah.
Mills, G. Riley. Son of the Sea. (p. 1611)
Mills, G. Riley, jt. auth. see Covert, Ralph.
Mills, Gordon. Introduction to Linear Algebra: A Primer for Social Scientists. (p. 882)
Mills Inc. Letters to Antonio Andrew Anderson from His Mother. Steinhardt, Marge, illus. (p. 1002)
Mills, J. Goodfellow Chronicles: The Messengers. (p. 701)
—Goodfellow Chronicles: The Sacred Seal. (p. 701)
—Goodfellow Chronicles: The Book of the Sage. (p. 701)
Mills, J. Elizabeth. Creating Content: Maximizing Wikis, Widgets, Blogs, & More. (p. 378)
—Creation of Caves. (p. 379)
—Expectations for Women: Confronting Stereotypes. (p. 548)
—Horns, Tails, Spikes, & Claws. Czekaj, Jef, illus. (p. 798)
—Ken Griffey Sr. & Ken Griffey Jr: Baseball Heroes. (p. 948)
—Ken Griffey Sr. & Ken Griffey Jr. Baseball Heroes. (p. 948)
—New York: Past & Present. (p. 1247)
—Spooky Wheels on the Bus. Mantle, Ben, illus. (p. 1631)
—Witches in America. (p. 1941)
Mills, Joyce C. Gentle Willow: A Story for Children about Dying. Pillo, Cary, illus. (p. 661)
—Little Tree: A Story for Children with Serious Medical Illness. Sebern, Brian, illus. (p. 1037)
Mills, Joyce C. & Crowley, Richard J. Sammy the Elephant & Mr. Camel: A Story to Help Children Overcome Bedwetting. Pillo, Cary, illus. (p. 1508)
Mills, Judith. Painted Chest. (p. 1318)
Mills, Lamonte. Franklin Basketball (p. 630)
Mills, Linda Sue. Meet Toado & Friends. Mills, Lori, illus. (p. 1123)
Mills, Liz, ed. see Scholastic, Inc. Staff.
Mills, Lois. Saddles & Sails. (p. 1501)
—Three Together: Story of the Wright Brothers & Their Sister. Moyers, William, illus. (p. 1744)
Mills, Lori, illus. see Brooks, Linda Sue.
Mills, Lori, illus. see Mills, Linda Sue.
Mills, Nancy Libbey. And Dance with the Orange Cow. Wells, Shan, illus. (p. 71)
—Never Eat Cabbage on Thursday. Wells, Shan, illus. (p. 1242)
Mills, Nathan. Living or Nonliving? (p. 1041)
Mills, Nathan & Abbott, Henry. How Plants Live & Grow. (p. 812)
Mills, Nathan & Allyn, Daisy. Around My Neighborhood. (p. 100)
Mills, Nathan & Anderson, Joanna. Many People of America. (p. 1089)
Mills, Nathan & Baker, Rick. More or Less? (p. 1174)
Mills, Nathan & Beckett, David. My Family. (p. 1202)
Mills, Nathan & Biehn, Mike. Alexander Graham Bell: Famous Inventor. (p. 36)
—Things I Need, Things I Want. (p. 1733)
Mills, Nathan & Block, Dakota. Exploring the Solar System. (p. 554)
Mills, Nathan & Charleston, Janice. Our Country's Holidays. (p. 1308)
Mills, Nathan & Christopher, Nick. Time for a Field Trip. (p. 1751)
Mills, Nathan & Coleridge, Margaret. Who Was Benjamin Franklin? (p. 1918)
Mills, Nathan & Cortland, Riley. I'm from Kenya. (p. 859)
Mills, Nathan & Davidson, Amy. My Busy Week. (p. 1200)
Mills, Nathan & Diggory, Nikki. Our Five Senses. (p. 1308)
Mills, Nathan & Englund, Frederick. Celebrating Our Holidays. (p. 285)
Mills, Nathan & Ericson, Emma. Up or Down? (p. 1824)
Mills, Nathan & Faraday, Daniel. Walk, Run, Skip, & Jump! (p. 1854)
Mills, Nathan & Flynn, Wesley. Big or Small? (p. 183)
Mills, Nathan & Frampton, Callie. Tools Tell the Weather. (p. 1767)
Mills, Nathan & Francis, Bill. Hannah's Four Seasons. (p. 743)
Mills, Nathan & Fudoli, Melissa. I Have One More. (p. 839)
Mills, Nathan & Golightly, Anne. Amelia Earhart: Female Aviator. (p. 58)
Mills, Nathan & Goodwin, Josh. How Do I Get There? (p. 807)
Mills, Nathan & Granger, Ronald. Exploring Earth's Surface. (p. 552)
Mills, Nathan & Herman, Alley. Plants Live Everywhere. (p. 1370)
Mills, Nathan & Hicks, Dwayne. Paul Revere: American Patriot. (p. 1330)
Mills, Nathan & Hill, Laura. George Washington Leads the Country. (p. 664)
Mills, Nathan & Holtz, Mary Elizabeth. Sabrina's School. (p. 1500)
Mills, Nathan & Honders, Jamie. I Can Count My Blocks. (p. 835)
Mills, Nathan & Hudson, Rachel. Objects in the Sky. (p. 1275)
Mills, Nathan & Hume, Desmond. Earth's Water. (p. 498)
Mills, Nathan & Jamison, Linc. Caring for My Pet. (p. 269)
—Getting Around Our City. (p. 669)
Mills, Nathan & Jefferson, Dave. Let's Do Math at the Store. (p. 995)
Mills, Nathan & Kawa, Katie. Barack Obama: First African American President. (p. 137)
Mills, Nathan & Kurkowiak, Anne. Tyler's New Friend. (p. 1805)
Mills, Nathan & Lewis, Charlotte. Plant Parts. (p. 1369)
Mills, Nathan & Li, John. I'm from China. (p. 859)
Mills, Nathan & Ludlow, Susan. From Ice to Steam. (p. 643)
Mills, Nathan & Machajewski, Sarah. Nurses Are There to Help. (p. 1273)
—Symbols of the United States. (p. 1693)
Mills, Nathan & McCann, Margaret. How We Use Water. (p. 823)
Mills, Nathan & McGraw, Earl. Electing Our Leaders. (p. 508)
Mills, Nathan & Miller, Andy. Is It Cloth, Clay, or Paper? (p. 889)
Mills, Nathan & Morrison, Chloe. Animals & Their Babies. (p. 82)
Mills, Nathan & Nolan, Mary. Mike's Busy Neighborhood. (p. 1141)
Mills, Nathan & Okon, Jodi. Ava Goes Shopping. (p. 118)
Mills, Nathan & Peck, Audrey. Helen Keller: Miracle Child. (p. 763)
Mills, Nathan & Pickman, Richard. Let's Volunteer! (p. 1001)
Mills, Nathan & Rau, Heather. I Can Count To 50! (p. 835)
Mills, Nathan & Ridolfi, Isabella. Sue Goes to the Store. (p. 1672)
Mills, Nathan & Ripley, Ellen. What Are Rules & Laws? (p. 1879)
Mills, Nathan & Rodgers, Katherine. What Season Is It? (p. 1893)
Mills, Nathan & Rose, Craig. Carlos Reads a Map. (p. 270)
—We Help at School. (p. 1867)
Mills, Nathan & Roza, Greg. Exploring Rocks & Minerals. (p. 553)
—Firefighters Help Us. (p. 591)
Mills, Nathan & Sotherden, Nora. Our Classroom Rules. (p. 1308)
Mills, Nathan & Star, Pat. Describe It: Size, Shape, & Color. (p. 428)
Mills, Nathan & Stern, Robin. Sara's Seeds. (p. 1514)
Mills, Nathan & Stevens, Alex. Who Works at the Hospital? (p. 1919)
Mills, Nathan & Stiegler, Lorraine. Space Probes. (p. 1619)
Mills, Nathan & Swan, Henry. How Animals Live & Grow. (p. 804)
Mills, Nathan & Vasquez, Gloria. Animal Homes. (p. 78)
Mills, Nathan & Waters, Grace. Changing Weather. (p. 290)
Mills, Nathan & Weir, William. Wright Brothers: The First to Fly. (p. 1963)
Mills, Nathan & Wesolowski, Harriet. Songs We Sing: Honoring Our Country. (p. 1612)
Mills, Nathan & White, Ella. Months of the Year. (p. 1170)
Mills, Nathan & Wilson, Emily. Good Night, Bears: Learning about Hibernation. (p. 699)
Mills, Nathan & Worthy, Shanya. Ana's Community Helpers. (p. 67)
—Shapes. (p. 1560)
Mills, Nikki Holder, jt. auth. see Schneithorst, Penny Pohrer.
Mills, Patricia Anne. Oswald Daydreams. (p. 1306)
—Stevie's First Christmas. (p. 1649)
Mills, Paul A. Chipper & Fluffy's Big Adventure. (p. 308)
Mills, Rachel. Wraiths. (p. 1962)
Mills, Rob. Charlie's Key (p. 293)
Mills, Robert. Lump of Gump. (p. 1065)
Mills, Samuel. Demon Slayer. (p. 426)
—Fire Bringer. (p. 590)
Mills, Shella A. Until Infinity. (p. 1823)
Mills, Stacey. Awesome Adventures of Catherine Cow: Billy the Bully Goat. (p. 120)
—Awesome Adventures of Catherine Cow. (p. 120)
Mills, Steve & Koll, Hilary. Fast Forward Maths. (p. 576)
—Quick Revision KS3 Maths. (p. 1427)
Mills, Susan & Shara, Diana. Frankie & Her Little Pals - Save the Watermelons. (p. 629)
—Frankie & Her Little Pals - Stir It Up. (p. 629)
Mills, Terence C., jt. ed. see Patterson, Kerry.
Mills, Tessa L. Adventures of Avery & Cali. (p. 16)
Mills, Timothy. Mystery Kids: the Mystery of Ghost Lake. (p. 1224)
—Mystery Kids: the Phantom Camper. (p. 1224)
Mills, Tom, illus. see Lewis, Anne Margaret.
Mills, Tricia. Heartbreak River. (p. 760)
Mills, Wendy. Positively Beautiful. (p. 1387)
Mills, Wynette. Backyard Explorer: The Nana & Me Series. (p. 131)
—Nana's Backyard Alphabet. (p. 1228)
Millsap, Cindy. Callie the Cow & the Great State Fair Adventure. (p. 254)
—Little Scotty Doggy. (p. 1036)
Millsap, Ella. Portrait of a Church in Stone: The Keeper of the Honeybees. (p. 1386)
Millsap, Lonnie, illus. see Butler, James L.
Millsaps, Grace & Murphy, Ryan. You Wouldn't Like Me Without My Coffee. Marin, Danny, illus. (p. 1976)
Mills-Darlow, Beryl C. My Beach Granny. (p. 1196)
Mills-Naim, Ami Chen. Spark Inside: A Special Book for Youth. (p. 1622)

Millward, Andras & Bevan, Sara. Parti Tom. (p. 1325)
Millward, Carol. Star in the Middle. (p. 1640)
Millward, Gwen, illus. see Doyle, Malachy.
Millward, Gwen, illus. see Isop, Laurie.
Millward, Gwen, illus. see Knapman, Timothy.
Millward, Gwen, illus. see Nimmo, Jenny.
Millward, Gwen, illus. see Willis, Jeanne.
Millward, Hayley, illus. see May, Erica.
Millward, S. L. Mission - Mongolia. (p. 1153)
Millward, Sharon L. Tropical Twins. (p. 1789)
Milne, A. A. ABC. Shepard, Ernest H., illus. (p. 3)
—Gallery of Children. Le Mair, Henriette Willebeek, illus. (p. 653)
—Giant. Shepard, Ernest H., illus. (p. 673)
—House at Pooh Corner Shepard, Ernest H., illus. (p. 803)
—House at Pooh Corner. Shepard, Ernest H., illus. (p. 803)
—In Which a House Is Built at Pooh Corner for Eeyore. Shepard, Ernest H., illus. (p. 868)
—In Which Christopher Robin Gives Pooh a Party. Shepard, Ernest H., illus. (p. 868)
—In Which Everyone Has a Birthday & Gets Two Presents. Shepard, Ernest H., illus. (p. 868)
—In Which It Is Shown That Tiggers Don't Climb Trees. Shepard, Ernest H., illus. (p. 868)
—In Which Piglet Meets a Heffalump. Shepard, Ernest H., illus. (p. 868)
—In Which Pooh Goes Visiting & Gets into a Tight Place & in Which Pooh & Piglet Go Hunting & Nearly Catch a Woozle. Shepard, Ernest H., illus. (p. 868)
—In Which Tigger Is Unbounced. Shepard, Ernest H., illus. (p. 868)
—In Which We Are Introduced to Winnie the Pooh & Some Bees, & the Stories Begin. Shepard, Ernest H., illus. (p. 868)
—Now We Are Six. Shepard, Ernest H., illus. (p. 1269)
—Positively Pooh: Timeless Wisdom from Pooh. Shepard, Ernest H., illus. (p. 1387)
—Pu Baut ein Haus. (p. 1414)
—Smackerel of Pooh: Ten Favorite Stories & Poems. Shepard, Ernest H., illus. (p. 1591)
—Tigger Tales. Shepard, Ernest H., illus. (p. 1749)
—When We Were Very Young. Shepard, Ernest H., illus. (p. 1905)
—Winnie Puh. Meddemmen, John, tr. (p. 1937)
—Winnie the Pooh & When We Were Young. Shepard, Ernest H., illus. (p. 1937)
—Winnie the Pooh Tells Time. Shepard, Ernest H., illus. (p. 1937)
—Winnie the Pooh's 1,2,3. Shepard, Ernest H., illus. (p. 1937)
—Winnie the Pooh's Colors. Shepard, Ernest H., illus. (p. 1937)
—Winnie-the-Pooh. Shepard, Ernest H., illus. (p. 1937)
—World of Pooh: The Complete Winnie-the-Pooh & the House at Pooh Corner. Shepard, Ernest H., illus. (p. 1957)
Milne, A. A., jt. auth. see Gaines, Isabel.
Milne, A. A. & Soman, David. Winnie Ille Pu: A Latin Edition of Winnie-the-Pooh Lenard, Alexander, tr. (p. 1937)
Milne, Alex, illus. see Roe, David & Reader's Digest Editors.
Milne, Barbara L. W. Opposites Are Fun. Munoz, Olga M., illus. (p. 1301)
Milne, Bill, photos by see Sarvady, Andrea, et al.
Milne, Christopher. Bravest Kid I've Ever Known: And Other Naughty Stories for Good Boys & Girls. (p. 223)
—Crazy Dentist. (p. 377)
—Day Our Teacher Went Mad. (p. 414)
—Girl Who Blew up Her Brother. (p. 679)
—Girl with Death Breath. (p. 679)
—That Dirty Dog & Other Naughty Stories for Good Boys & Girls. (p. 1726)
—Upside down Boy. (p. 1825)
Milne, David, illus. see Herzog, Brad.
Milne, David, photos by see Napier, Matt.
Milne, Drew. Go Figure. (p. 686)
Milne, J. E. Adventures of Haole the Penguin: The Inner Game of Surfing. (p. 18)
Milne, Jessica, illus. see Citra, Becky.
Milne, Marywinn, jt. ed. see Hearn, Emily.
Milne, Rg. Quibble Tales: Davey Sprocket & the Alamo Alamode Pie Factory. (p. 1427)
—Quibble Tales: The Adventures of Bobin Hood of Sherworm Forest. (p. 1427)
Milne, Rosemary. There's a Goat in My Coat. McLean, Andrew, illus. (p. 1730)
Milne, Terry, illus. see Mahy, Margaret.
Milner, Claudette. Children of Plaines Estates. (p. 302)
—Silent Tears: Children of Plains Estates. (p. 1575)
Milner, Elizabeth B., illus. see Beasley, David R.
Milner, Fran, illus. see Pluto Project Staff & Semkiw, Walter.
Milner Halls, Kelly. National Geographic Kids Chapters: Courageous Canine: And More True Stories of Amazing Animal Heroes. (p. 1232)
Milner, Isaac, ed. see Marquitz, Tim.
Milner-Gulland, Robin, tr. see Yevtushenko, Yevgeny.
Milo, Margaret D. Matthew Pet Adventure. (p. 1109)
Milord, Susan. Ghost on the Hearth. Dabcovich, Lydia, illus. (p. 671)
—If I Could. Denise, Christopher, illus. (p. 852)
—Pebble: A Story about Belonging. Milord, Susan, illus. (p. 1333)
—Tales Alive! Donato, Michael A., illus. (p. 1701)
Milosevic, Tamara, illus. see Knight, Deidre Denise.
Milot, Carryanne. Austin & the Bully. Proulx, Denis, illus. (p. 116)
Milroy, Gladys. Emu & the Water Tree. (p. 522)
Milson, Matthew R. Young Arcan & the Garden of Loc. (p. 1978)
Milstein, Janet. Winners Competition Series: Award-Winning, Custom-Made, 90-Second Comic Monologues Ages 13-18 (p. 1937)
—Winners Competition Series Volume I: Award-winning, Custom-made, 60-Second Comic Monologues Ages 4-12. (p. 1937)
Milstein, Karen Kaufman. Hot Spots for Teens: Cold Readings for Commercial Audition Success. (p. 802)
Milstein, Larry. Spring's Bright Colors. (p. 1635)
Milstein, Seymour W. Elements of Yiedish. (p. 511)
Milstrey, Dawn Bourdeau, illus. see Mahr, Frank J.
Miltenberg, Robert. Thank God: Thoughts on an Eternally Grateful Gathering. (p. 1725)
Miltenberger, Dave, illus. see Johnson, Gerald J. J.
Miltenberger, Dave, illus. see Johnson, Gerald Jj.
Miltenberger, Dave & Jeri, illus. see Johnson, Gerald J. J.
Miltenberger, Jeri, illus. see Johnson, Gerald J. J.
Miltenberger, Jeri, illus. see Johnson, Gerald Jj.
Miltenberger, Jeri and Dave, illus. see Johnson, Gerald J. J.
Miltner, Robert. Rock the Boat. (p. 1482)
Milton, Alexandra, illus. see Milton, Giles.
Milton, Bess. Language Development Writing Process. (p. 975)
Milton, Cathlene. Wonders of Billy Sniggles: Billy Sniggles Sees a Frog. (p. 1948)
—Wonders of Billy Sniggles: Billy Sniggles & the Dead Fish. (p. 1948)
—Wonders of Billy Sniggles. (p. 1948)
Milton, Freddy, illus. see Erickson, Byron, et al.
Milton, Giles. Good Luck Baby Owls. Milton, Alexandra, illus. (p. 698)
Milton, John. Complete Poetry & Essential Prose of John Milton. Kerrigan, William et al, eds. (p. 353)
—John Milton - Selected Poems. Ricks, Christopher, ed. (p. 922)
Milton, Joyce. Bears Are Curious. Santoro, Christopher, illus. (p. 151)
—Dinosaur Days. Tempesta, Franco, illus. (p. 442)
—Honeybees. Mueller, Peter R. & Mueller, Pete, illus. (p. 794)
—Who Was Ronald Reagan? Wolf, Elizabeth & Harrison, Nancy, illus. (p. 1919)
Milton, Nancy. Giraffe That Walked to Paris. Roth, Roger, illus. (p. 677)
Milton, Nina. Tough Luck. (p. 1772)
Milton, Paul R., tr. see Salten, Felix.
Milton, Stephanie. Minecraft: Combat Handbook (Updated Edition) An Official Mojang Book. (p. 1146)
Milton, Stephanie, et al. Minecraft: Essential Handbook (Updated Edition) An Official Mojang Book. (p. 1146)
Milway, Alex. Alien Moon. Milway, Alex, illus. (p. 41)
—Curse of Mousebeard. (p. 394)
—Magma Conspiracy: Armed, Dangerous & Covered in Fur! Milway, Alex, illus. (p. 1075)
—Operation Robot Storm: The Mythical 9th Division. Milway, Alex, illus. (p. 1300)
—Pigsticks & Harold & the Incredible Journey. Milway, Alex, illus. (p. 1358)
—Pigsticks & Harold & the Tuptown Thief. Milway, Alex, illus. (p. 1358)
—Terror of the Deep: Armed, Dangerous & Covered in Fur! Milway, Alex, illus. (p. 1722)
Milway, Katie Smith. Good Garden: How One Family Went from Hunger to Having Enough. Daigneault, Sylvie, illus. (p. 698)
—Mimi's Village & How Basic Health Care Transformed It. Fernandes, Eugenie, illus. (p. 1145)
—One Hen: How One Small Loan Made a Big Difference. Fernandes, Eugenie, illus. (p. 1295)
Milz, Cynthia A. Waiting for the Last Leaf to Fall. (p. 1853)
Mimi, Vance, jt. auth. see White, Andrea.
Mimms, Cory Wheeler. Trailing Tennessee. (p. 1776)
Mims, Ashley, illus. see Alcott, Louisa May & Naxos of America Staff.
Mims, Ashley, illus. see McFadden, Deanna & Andersen, Hans Christian.
Mims, Ashley, illus. see McFadden, Deanna.
Mims, Ashley, illus. see Namm, Diane.
Mims, Lisa Cuomo. Sleepy Town. (p. 1590)
Mims, Melanie. Neeko's Angel: A Story about Kindness. Floyd, John, Jr., illus. (p. 1240)
—Not All Angels Have Wings. Floyd, John, Jr., illus. (p. 1267)
Mims-Word, Marsha. Great Vacation. (p. 719)
Min, Ellen. Midnight Ride of Paul Revere: One If by Land, Two If by Sea. (p. 1139)
Min, Fang. Giant Panda. Daggers, Ben, tr. (p. 673)
Min, Grace, tr. see So-Young, Lee.
Min, Ken, illus. see Zia, F.
Min, Laura. Gallinas de la Senora Sato Flor Ada, Alma, tr. (p. 653)
Min, SooHyeon. Drummer Boy. Nille, Peggy, illus. (p. 487)
Minagawa, Ryoji, illus. see Nanatsuki, Kyoichi.
Minagawa, Ryoji, jt. auth. see Nanatsuki, Kyoichi.
Minagawa, Ryoji & Nanatsuki, Kyoichi. Project Arms (p. 1410)
Minahan, James. Former Soviet Union's Diverse Peoples: A Reference Sourcebook Barkan, Elliott Robert, ed. (p. 620)
Minaki, Christina. Zoe's Extraordinary Holiday Adventures (p. 1987)
Minako, Chiba. Somebody for Me. (p. 1609)
MinaLima, illus. see Lewis, J. Patrick & Nesbitt, Kenn.
Minami, Maki. S. A. Minami, Maki, illus. (p. 1499)
Minamide, Elaine. How Should One Cope with Death? (p. 812)
Minamide, Elaine, jt. auth. see Kiesbye, Stefan.
Minari, Endoh. Dazzle (p. 415)
Minarik, Else Holmelund. Amigos de Osito. Benavides, Rosa, tr. (p. 65)
—Beso para Osito. (p. 168)
—Beso para Osito. Benavides, Rosa, tr. (p. 168)
—Beso para Osito. Sendak, Maurice, tr. (p. 168)
—Cat & Dog. Langdo, Bryan, illus. (p. 277)
—Little Bear. Sendak, Maurice, illus. (p. 1023)
—Little Bear & the Marco Polo. Doubleday, Dorothy, illus. (p. 1023)
—Little Bear's Visit. Sendak, Maurice, illus. (p. 1024)
—No Fighting, No Biting! Sendak, Maurice, illus. (p. 1258)
—Osito. Aguilar, Joaquina, tr. (p. 1305)
—Papa Oso Vuelve a Casa. Benavides, Rosa, tr. (p. 1322)
—Visita de Osito. Puncel, María, tr. (p. 1845)
Minarik, Else Holmelund & Tashlin, Frank. Oso Que No lo Era. Sendak, Maurice, illus. (p. 1305)
Minase, Masara. Empty Heart. (p. 521)
Minazuki, Suu. Gou-Dere Sora Nagihara. (p. 704)
Minch, Edwin, illus. see Minch, John, et al.
Minch, Jason, ed. see Minch, John, et al.
Minch, John, et al. Caminos de Baja California: Geologia y Biologica Para Su Viaje. Minch, Jason, ed. (p. 256)
Mincher, Scott. Blanket. (p. 198)
Minchin, Adele. Beat Goes On. (p. 152)
—Caravan Club. (p. 265)
Minciell, Rose Laura & Ross, Rose Laura. Tales Merry & Wise. Werth, Kurt, illus. (p. 1702)
Mincin, Sabrina. Catching a Shooting Star. (p. 279)
Minckler, Kathleen L., illus. see Lauture, Mireille B.
Mind Candy Ltd. Staff, illus. see Reader's Digest Editors & Bell, Megan.
Mind Wave Inc. MoshiMoshiKawaii: Strawberry Princess Moshi's Activity Book. Mind Wave Inc., illus. (p. 1176)
—Strawberry Moshi's Activity Book. Mind Wave Inc., illus. (p. 1666)
Mind Wave Staff, contrib. by. Where Is Strawberry Mermaid Moshi? (p. 1909)
—Where Is Strawberry Princess Moshi? (p. 1909)
Mindel, Nissan. Eight Chanukah Tales. Toron, Eli & Graybar, Shmuel, illus. (p. 507)
—Maharal to the Rescue. Ayache, Avraham, illus. (p. 1076)
Mindel, Nissan, tr. see Lehman, Marcus.
Minden, Cecilia. Alex & the Box Shop: The Sound of X. Ostrom, Bob, illus. (p. 35)
—Baseball. (p. 140)
—Basketball. (p. 143)
—Big Race. Ostrom, Bob, illus. (p. 183)
—Breakfast by the Numbers. (p. 224)
—Cindy, Cedric, & the Circus: The Sound of Soft C. Ostrom, Bob, illus. (p. 321)
—Cooking by the Numbers. (p. 361)
—Dinner by the Numbers. (p. 441)
—Earthquakes! (p. 497)
—Electricians. (p. 509)
—Exercise by the Numbers. (p. 548)
—Farm Animals: Cows. (p. 573)
—Farm Animals: Dogs. (p. 573)
—Farm Animals: Pigs. (p. 573)
—Farm Animals: Ducks. (p. 573)
—Farm Animals: Goats. (p. 573)
—Farm Animals: Sheep. (p. 573)
—Farm Animals: Horses. (p. 573)
—Farm Animals: Chickens. (p. 573)
—Firefighters. (p. 591)
—Floods! (p. 605)
—Foals Grow up to Be Horses. (p. 610)
—Forests. (p. 618)
—Gardening by the Numbers. (p. 656)
—Germ Free. (p. 666)
—Giving Back. (p. 681)
—Grocery Shopping by the Numbers. (p. 725)
—How Tall? How Wide? (p. 812)
—Investing: Making Your Money Work for You. (p. 885)
—It Is about Time! (p. 894)
—Jeff's Job: The Sound of J. Ostrom, Bob, illus. (p. 912)
—Keep It Clean: Achoo! (p. 946)
—Keep It Clean: Get Well Soon. (p. 946)
—Kids Can Clean up Trash. (p. 953)
—Kids Can Keep Air Clean. (p. 953)
—Kids Can Keep Water Clean. (p. 953)
—Kids Can Recycle. (p. 953)
—Kids Can Reuse. (p. 953)
—Kids Can Use Less. (p. 953)
—Kits Grow up to Be Rabbits. (p. 962)
—Kittens Grow up to Be Cats. (p. 963)
—Lakes. (p. 972)
—Letter Carriers. (p. 1002)
—Living on a Budget. (p. 1041)
—Lunch by the Numbers. (p. 1065)
—Most Unbelievable First Day of School: A Storytime Book. Ostrom, Bob, illus. (p. 1177)
—Mountains. (p. 1181)
—Nick & Ned: The Sound of N. Ostrom, Bob, illus. (p. 1251)
—Payday! (p. 1331)
—Puppies Grow up to Be Dogs. (p. 1418)
—Raising Your Hand. Ostrom, Bob, illus. (p. 1437)
—Real World Math: Personal Finance (p. 1449)
—Real World Math: Health & Wellness (p. 1449)
—Restaurants by the Numbers. (p. 1464)
—Rivers. (p. 1476)
—Roy on the Ranch: The Sound of R. Ostrom, Bob, illus. (p. 1492)
—Runaway Train. Ostrom, Bob, illus. (p. 1496)
—Sara at the Store: The Sound of S. Ostrom, Bob, illus. (p. 1514)
—Save the Planet: Reduce, Reuse, & Recycle. (p. 1516)
—Saving for the Future. (p. 1517)
—Saying "Thank You" Ostrom, Bob, illus. (p. 1519)
—Shapes Everywhere. (p. 1560)
—Sharing the Green Ball. Ostrom, Bob, illus. (p. 1561)
—Skateboarding Friends. Ostrom, Bob, illus. (p. 1583)
—Smart Shopping. (p. 1593)
—Soccer. (p. 1603)
—Starting Your Own Business. (p. 1644)
—Swimming. (p. 1691)
—Teachers. (p. 1709)
—Ted & Tim: The Sound of T. Ostrom, Bob, illus. (p. 1712)
—Time to Wash Up. (p. 1753)
—Tornadoes! (p. 1770)
—Tractor Saves the Day. Ostrom, Bob, illus. (p. 1775)
—Understanding Taxes. (p. 1816)
—Using Credit Wisely. (p. 1828)
—Veterinarians. (p. 1839)
—What Does It Weigh? (p. 1884)
—What Is Money? (p. 1890)
—Wildfires! (p. 1931)
—Winning Basket. Ostrom, Bob, illus. (p. 1937)
—Wishing for a Red Balloon. Ostrom, Bob, illus. (p. 1940)
Minden, Cecilia, jt. auth. see Cupp, Dave.
Minden, Cecilia, jt. auth. see Meier, Joanne D.
Minden, Cecilia & Armantrout, Linda M. Dentists. (p. 427)
—Nurses. (p. 1273)
Minden, Cecilia & Cupp, Dave. TV-Station Secrets. (p. 1799)
Minden, Cecilia & Meier, Joanne D. Best Cookies of All. Ostrom, Bob, illus. (p. 168)
—Drawing Lesson. Ostrom, Bob, illus. (p. 482)
—Halloween Costume Contest. Ostrom, Bob, illus. (p. 737)
—Mom's Birthday Surprise. Ostrom, Bob, illus. (p. 1163)
—Postcards from All Over. Ostrom, Bob, illus. (p. 1388)
—Smile for the Dentist. Ostrom, Bob, illus. (p. 1594)
—Thanksgiving Play. Ostrom, Bob, illus. (p. 1726)
—Tree for the City. Ostrom, Bob, illus. (p. 1783)
—Valentines for Everyone. Ostrom, Bob, illus. (p. 1830)
—Walk Across Town. Ostrom, Bob, illus. (p. 1853)
Minden, Cecilia & Minden-Zins, Mary. Auto Mechanics. (p. 117)
—Pilots. (p. 1359)
Minden, Cecilia & Roth, Kate. How to Write a Biography. (p. 822)
—How to Write a Business Letter. (p. 822)
—How to Write a Fairy Tale. (p. 822)
—How to Write a How To. (p. 822)
—How to Write a Journal. (p. 822)
—How to Write a Letter. (p. 822)
—How to Write a Mystery. (p. 822)
—How to Write a News Article. (p. 822)
—How to Write a Play. (p. 822)
—How to Write a Poem. (p. 822)
—How to Write a Report. (p. 822)
—How to Write a Review. (p. 822)
—How to Write a Thank-You Letter. (p. 822)
—How to Write about Your Adventure. (p. 822)
—How to Write an Ad. (p. 822)
—How to Write an E-Mail. (p. 822)
—How to Write an Essay. (p. 822)
—How to Write an Interview. (p. 823)
—How to Write & Give a Speech. (p. 823)
—Language Arts Explorer Junior (p. 974)
Minden, Cecilia, et al. How to Write a Fairy Tale. (p. 822)
—How to Write a How To. (p. 822)
—How to Write a News Article. (p. 822)
—How to Write a Review. (p. 822)
Minden-Zins, Mary, jt. auth. see Minden, Cecilia.
Mindes, Erin. Missy Moo, Where Are You off to? Surfing Adventure. Harston, David, illus. (p. 1154)
Mindler, Jason. Giralon. (p. 678)
Mindlin, Helen Mather-Smith, jt. auth. see Arnov Jr., Boris.
Mindorff, David, jt. auth. see Allott, Andrew.
Mindy, Miss. Artist Sisters: Princess la la & the Little Bee - Teenie Weenie Tales. Vol. 2 (p. 104)
—Miss Mindy's Sassy Paper Doll Bonanza. (p. 1151)
Mine, Valerie. To Bee... or Not to Be a Bee. (p. 1758)
Minear, Jason. Jr & the Carrot Coaster. (p. 930)
Minekura, Kazuya. Saiyuki (p. 1504)
—Saiyuki Nibley, Alethea & Nibley, Athena, trs. from JPN. (p. 1504)
Minekura, Kazuya, creator. Saiyuki (p. 1504)
Mineo, Ella. Sea Otters in Danger. (p. 1535)
Mineo, Kate. Compare with Bears. (p. 351)
Mineo, Tyrone. Near & Far with Birds. (p. 1238)
Miner, Ann. Polly Possum's Wandering Path. Farmer, Libby, illus. (p. 1381)
Miner, Audrey. Rebbie. (p. 1450)
Miner, Deb. I get Around. Miner, Deb, illus. (p. 838)
Miner, Jerry, jt. auth. see Burkhead, Jesse.
Miner, Julia, illus. see Hunter, Sara Hoagland.
Miner, Sharon. Beloved School Horses. (p. 163)
—Octavia's Quest. (p. 1277)
Miner, Valerie. Winter's Edge. (p. 1938)
Miner, W. Lawrence, Jr. Journey into the Fourth Dimension: The Lasting Legacy of Derek Saul. Dailey, Christopher, ed. (p. 928)
Minert, Roger P. Pomerania Place Name Indexes: Identifying Place Names Using Alphabetical & Reverse Alphabetical Indexes. (p. 1382)
Mines, Cynthia J. Cubism. (p. 389)
Mineuittie, Abike. Nandi & Masani. Jacques Huiswood, illus. (p. 1229)
Minev, Nikolay. Rudolf Spielmann: Fifty Great Short Games. McCready, Philip, ed. (p. 1494)
Ming, Choo Hill, illus. see Cowley, Joy.
Ming, Markay. Bear's Great Adventure (p. 152)
Minger, Janet. How Do Strawberries & Green Beans Sleep at Night? (p. 807)
Minger, Nancy, illus. see Key, Francis Scott.
Minges, Barbara. Bible Our Book of Faith: Faith for Life2 Course Seven Teacher Guide. Janssen, Patricia E., ed. (p. 175)
—Investigator's Notebook: Faith for Life2 Course Seven Student Book. Janssen, Patricia E., ed. (p. 885)
Mingle, Pamela. Kissing Shakespeare. (p. 962)
Mingming. Neon Genesis Evangelion: Campus Apocalypse Vol. 2 Mingming, illus. (p. 1241)
Mingo, Norman. Alice Faye Paper Dolls: Glamorous Movie Star Paper Dolls & Costumes. Mingo, Norman & Ernst, Clara, illus. (p. 39)
—Bette Davis Paper Dolls. Taliadoros, Jenny, ed. (p. 172)
—Deanna Durbin Paper Dolls. Mingo, Norman & Ernt, Clara, illus. (p. 418)
—Navy Scouts Paper Dolls. Taliadoros, Jenny, ed. (p. 1238)
—Rita Hayworth Paper Dolls. Taliadoros, Jenny, ed. (p. 1475)
Mingolello, Terrie. Peep's Day Out. (p. 1335)
Minguet, Anne, tr. see Burke, Christina.
Mingus, Cathi, illus. see Holyoke, Nancy.
Mingus, Cathi, illus. see Kimmel, Elizabeth Cody.
Minh Quoc. Tam & Cam/Tam Cam: The Ancient Vietnamese Cinderella Story. Smith, William, tr. from VIE. (p. 1704)
Minhós Martins, Isabel. At Our House. Matoso, Madalena, illus. (p. 110)
—World in a Second. Carvalho, Bernardo, illus. (p. 1956)
Mini Pois Etc, illus. see Bakker, Merel.
Minich, Eric. Digger & the Search for Home. (p. 438)
Minick, Jim. Finding a Clear Path. (p. 587)
MiniKim, illus. see Mariolle, Mathieu.
Mininni, Darlene. Emotional Toolkit: Seven Power-Skills to Nail Your Bad Feelings. (p. 520)
Mininsky, Janina. Mischief in Trouble. (p. 1150)

Minister, Peter, illus. see Rake, Matthew.
Ministry of Education Staff, creator. Te Kete Kupu: 300 Essential Words in Maori. (p. 1708)
Minix, Holly. What Does Mommy Do at Night? (p. 1884)
MINJA, ADVELINE J. Clean Kid Is A Healthier Kid. (p. 330)
Minjung's Editorial Staff. Essence English-Korean Dictionary. (p. 536)
—Minjung's Pocket English-Korean & Korean-English Dictionary. (p. 1147)
Minjung's Editorial Staff, ed. Essence Korean-English Dictionary (p. 536)
Minke, Shari. Airplane Story: A Blended Family's Journey. (p. 32)
Minkema, Douglas D. System 35. (p. 1693)
Minkova, Milena & Tunberg, Terence O. Lingua Latina Perennis: An Introductory Course to the Language of the Ages. (p. 1019)
Minks, Joshua. Humania & the Legend of Commander Pancreator. (p. 826)
Minne, Brigitte. Best Bottom. Pottie, Marjolein, illus. (p. 168)
Minnema, Cheryl. Hungry Johnny. Ballinger, Wesley, illus. (p. 828)
Minner, Ray. Disciple Diaries. (p. 447)
Minnerly, Denise Bennett. Molly Meets Mona & Friends: A Magical Day in the Museum. (p. 1160)
—Painting the Town. (p. 1318)
Minnerly-Figueroa, Maria, illus. see Basso, Michael.
Minnesota Association for Children's Mental Health. Educator's Guide to Children's Mental Health. (p. 505)
Minnesota Historical Society & Mille Lacs Indian Museum. Ojibwe Shoulder Bag Kit. (p. 1282)
Minneus, Steve. Nukes: The Spread of Nuclear Weapons. (p. 1270)
Minnich, Matt, illus. see Prokopchak, Ann.
Minnick, Chris & Holland, Eva. JavaScript for Kids for Dummies. (p. 910)
Minnie, jt. auth. see Minnie.
Minnie & Minnie. Science Playground: Fun with Science Concepts & Nature. (p. 1527)
Minnis, Ivan. You Are in Ancient China. (p. 1973)
—You Are in Ancient Rome. (p. 1973)
Minns, Karen M. C., illus. see Glenn, Suki & Carpenter, Susan.
Minns, Karen Marie Christa, illus. see Glenn, Suki & Carpenter, Susan.
Minoglou, Ioanna & Cassis, Youssef, eds. Country Studies in Entrepeneurship: A Historical Perspective. (p. 372)
Minolli Skupinski, Teresa. Courtship of Leonora: A Fable about Gentle Hearts & Timeless Values. (p. 373)
Minond, Edgardo. Drac, Tell Us about Modernism. (p. 476)
Minor, Florence F. If You Were a Panda Bear. Minor, Wendell, illus. (p. 855)
—If You Were a Penguin. Minor, Wendell, illus. (p. 855)
Minor, Florence F., jt. auth. see Minor, Wendell.
Minor, Florence F. & Minor, Wendell. Christmas Tree! Minor, Wendell, illus. (p. 316)
Minor, Pamela, jt. auth. see Rupprecht, Karen.
Minor, Sarah. Pillow Talk: Loving affirmations to encourage & guide your Children. (p. 1359)
Minor, Wendell. Daylight Starlight Wildlife. Minor, Wendell, illus. (p. 415)
—How Big Could Your Pumpkin Grow? Minor, Wendell, illus. (p. 805)
—My Farm Friends. Bodett, Tom, illus. (p. 1203)
—My Farm Friends. Minor, Wendell, illus. (p. 1203)
—Sitting Bull Remembers. (p. 1582)
—Yankee Doodle America: The Spirit of 1776 from A to Z. (p. 1968)
Minor, Wendell, illus. see Aldrin, Buzz.
Minor, Wendell, illus. see Bates, Katharine Lee & Bates, Katharine.
Minor, Wendell, illus. see Bates, Katherine Lee.
Minor, Wendell, illus. see Brown, Margaret Wise.
Minor, Wendell, illus. see Burleigh, Robert.
Minor, Wendell, illus. see Calvert, Patricia.
Minor, Wendell, illus. see Cimarusti, Marie Torres & George, Jean Craighead.
Minor, Wendell, illus. see Clark, Mary Higgins.
Minor, Wendell, illus. see Ehrlich, Amy.
Minor, Wendell, illus. see George, Jean Craighead.
Minor, Wendell, illus. see Johnston, Tony.
Minor, Wendell, illus. see Minor, Florence F.
Minor, Wendell, illus. see Schertle, Alice.
Minor, Wendell, illus. see Silvey, Anita.
Minor, Wendell, illus. see Titcomb, Gordon.
Minor, Wendell, illus. see Turner, Ann Warren & Turner, Ann.
Minor, Wendell, illus. see Turner, Ann Warren.
Minor, Wendell, illus. see Turner, Ann.
Minor, Wendell, illus. see Zolotow, Charlotte.
Minor, Wendell, jt. auth. see Minor, Florence F.
Minor, Wendell & Minor, Florence F. If You Were a Penguin. Minor, Wendell, illus. (p. 855)
Minquini, Lourdes, jt. auth. see Robles, D.
Minshall, Caleigh. Blue: Voyage to the Sky. (p. 202)
Minsky, Hyman P. Can It Happen Again? Essays on Instability & Finance. (p. 258)
Minsky, Michael. Greenwood Word Lists: One-Syllable Words. (p. 723)
Minsky, Terri. All over It! (p. 45)
—Gordo & the Girl & You're a Good Man. (p. 702)
—Mom's Best Friend & Movin' on Up (p. 1163)
Minsky, Terri, jt. auth. see Banim, Lisa.
Minsky, Terri, jt. auth. see Papademetriou, Lisa.
Minsky, Terri, creator. Lizzie McGuire: Pool Party; Picture Day (p. 1043)
—Lizzie McGuire Cine-Manga: Rumors & I've Got Rhythmic Vol. 2 (p. 1043)
—Lizzie McGuire Cine-Manga: I Do, I Don't & Come Fly with Me Vol. 4 (p. 1043)
—Lizzie McGuire Cine-Manga: When Moms Attack & Misadventures in Babysitting Vol. 3 (p. 1043)
Minter, Daniel, illus. see Lyons, Kelly Starling.
Minter, J. Insiders. (p. 878)
Minter, Margee. Ollie's Unlucky Day. (p. 1287)
Minter, Peter. Blue Grass. (p. 203)
Minton, Eric. Powering up a Career in Biotechnology. (p. 1391)
Minton, Ross. Baseball, from the Street to the Diamond (p. 141)
Minton, Sessily. Fred's Family Farm: Derek the Donkey Makes New Friends/ Cindy the Chick Learns to Share. (p. 633)
Minty, Dennis, et al. Resources for Tomorrow: Science, Technology & Society. (p. 1463)
Mintz, Leon. Memoir of the Masses: A Tale of Smoking Mirrors. (p. 1125)
Mintzer, Rich. Coping with Random Acts of Violence. (p. 365)
—Meth & Speed = Busted! (p. 1130)
—Steroids = Busted! (p. 1649)
Mintzer, Richard. Alcohol = Busted! (p. 35)
—Latino Americans in Sports, Film, Music & Government: Trailblazers. (p. 979)
—Story of So So Def Records. (p. 1660)
Mintzi, Vali, illus. see Jahanforuz, Rita.
Minuto, Kristin. My First Day of Kindergarten. (p. 1206)
Minz-Kammer, Koda. Pinpot Tiger & the Lost Monkey. (p. 1361)
Miocevich, Grant. Investigating Japan: Prehistory to Postwar. Cheng & Tsui, ed. (p. 884)
Mioduchowska, Anna. In Between Season. (p. 863)
Mioroney, Tracy, illus. see Froeb, Lori.
Miot, Ray. Alexis the Wizard Rabbit: Pascale & Alain Adventures. (p. 37)
Miotto, Enrico. Universo. (p. 1821)
Miquel, Isabel de, tr. see Pullman, Philip.
Mirabella, Erin. Shawn Sheep the Soccer Star. Davis, Sarah, illus. (p. 1563)
Mirabelli, Eugene. Queen of the Rain Was in Love with the Prince of the Sky. (p. 1425)
Mirabile, Michele. Choir of Angels. (p. 309)
Miracle, Joan. Tia's Shoes. (p. 1747)
Miracle, Julia Ann. Plastic Crowns & Muddy Feet. (p. 1370)
Miracles, Max & Brigitte, Smadja. Milagros de Max. Rubio, Gabriela, illus. (p. 1142)
Miracola, Jeff, illus. see Chin, Oliver.
Miraglia, Matthew. Maria & the Carrot Patch. (p. 1093)
Miralles, Ana, illus. see Ruiz, Emilio.
Miralles, Charles, tr. see Hart, Christopher.
Miralles, Jose, illus. see Golden Books Staff.
Miralles, Jose & McTeigue, Jane. Christmas Star: A Light-up Shadow-Box Book. (p. 315)
Miralles, Joseph, illus. see Austen, Jane.
Miramontes, Arthur J., jt. auth. see Miramontes, Arturo J.
Miramontes, Arturo J. & Miramontes, Arthur J. There's an Elephant in My Bathtub. (p. 1731)
Miranda, Anne. Best Place. (p. 171)
—Looking at Lizards (p. 1051)
—Peach Tree Street Lodge, Katherine, illus. (p. 1332)
—Pignic: An Alphabet Book in Rhyme. Hoffman, Rosekrans, illus. (p. 1358)
—Weather Wise (p. 1870)
Miranda, Conchita. Yago's Heartbeat. (p. 1968)
Miranda, Conchita & Miranda Ros, Conchita. Los Latidos de Yago. Carretero, Monica, illus. (p. 1054)
Miranda, Deborah A. Zen of la Llorona. (p. 1986)
Miranda, Edward. Ribbon for Diego. Bohart, Lisa, illus. (p. 1469)
—Truth about Dragons & Dinosaurs. Cassetta, Andrea, illus. (p. 1794)
Miranda, et al. Alejandro Magno en unos Años Levante un Colosal Imperio. (p. 35)
Miranda, Francisco, illus. see Linn, Dennis, et al.
Miranda, Inaki, illus. see Kittredge, Caitlin.
Miranda, Justo, jt. auth. see Nomura, Ted.
Miranda, K. Fifth Sun. (p. 584)
Miranda, Megan. Fracture. (p. 627)
—Hysteria. (p. 831)
—Soulprint. (p. 1614)
—Vengeance. (p. 1835)
Miranda, Patti. Sonny's Flower Garden. (p. 1612)
Miranda, Pedro, illus. see Eckdahl, Judith & Eckdahl, Kathryn.
Miranda Ros, Conchita, jt. auth. see Miranda, Conchita.
Miranda, Twyla. Longfeather Ponds: A Chipmunk's Tale. (p. 1047)
Miranda, Twyla T. Beagles' Tale: A Longfeather Ponds Adventure (p. 150)
Mirande, Jaqueline. Arturo y los Caballeros de la Tabla Redonda. (p. 105)
Mirarchi, Anthony J. King's Challenge. (p. 960)
Miras, Christie. First Christmas Day. (p. 593)
Mire, Sahra. Too Many Sweets. (p. 1767)
Mire - Umm Mariam, Sahra. Boy with One Ear. (p. 219)
Mireles, Debbie. Map & the Pirate Ship. (p. 1089)
Mirhady, Irandought. Thorn-Bush Boy: Pesare Tigh. Mirhady, Irandought, illus. (p. 1740)
Mirman, Heather Moehn. Issues in Drug Abuse. (p. 893)
Miro. Watermelon Story. Brown, Nick, illus. (p. 1864)
Mirocha, Paul, illus. see Batten, Mary.
Mirocha, Paul, illus. see Clarke, Ginjer L.
Mirocha, Paul, illus. see Cohn, Diana & Buchmann, Stephen.
Mirocha, Paul, illus. see Cohn, Diana.
Mirocha, Paul, illus. see Mckerley, Jennifer.
Mirocha, Paul, illus. see Milkweed Editions Staff.
Mirocha, Paul, illus. see St. Antoine, Sara, ed.
Mirocha, Stephanie, illus. see Marston, Hope Irvin.
Miroglio, Brian, illus. see Stoker, Bram.
Mirpuri, Gouri, et al. Indonesia. (p. 872)
Mirriam-Goldberg, Caryn. Write Where You Are: How to Use Writing to Make Sense of Your Life: A Guide for Teens. (p. 1964)
Miryam. Happy Man & His Dump Truck. Gergely, Tibor, illus. (p. 746)
Miryam, jt. auth. see Golden Books Staff.
Miryam, jt. auth. see Shealy, Dennis.
Mis, M. S. How to Draw New Jersey's Sights & Symbols. (p. 818)
—How to Draw North Dakota's Sights & Symbols. (p. 818)
—How to Draw Pennsylvania's Sights & Symbols. (p. 818)
—How to Draw Tennessee's Sights & Symbols. (p. 818)
—How to Draw the Life & Times of Franklin Delano Roosevelt. (p. 818)
—How to Draw the Life & Times of Lyndon B. Johnson. (p. 819)
—How to Draw the Life & Times of Ronald Reagan. (p. 819)
—How to Draw the Life & Times of Woodrow Wilson. (p. 819)
—How to Draw Virginia's Sights & Symbols. (p. 819)
—How to Draw Wyoming's Sights & Symbols. (p. 819)
Mis, Melody S. Civil Rights Leaders (p. 324)
—Colony of Georgia: A Primary Source History. (p. 342)
—Colony of Maryland: A Primary Source History. (p. 342)
—Colony of New Hampshire: A Primary Source History. (p. 342)
—Colony of New York: A Primary Source History. (p. 342)
—Colony of North Carolina: A Primary Source History. (p. 342)
—Colony of Pennsylvania: A Primary Source History. (p. 342)
—Colony of South Carolina: A Primary Source History. (p. 342)
—Edgar Degas. (p. 504)
—Edouard Manet. (p. 504)
—Exploring Canyons. (p. 551)
—Exploring Caves. (p. 551)
—Exploring Glaciers. (p. 552)
—Exploring Islands. (p. 552)
—Exploring Mountains. (p. 552)
—Exploring Peninsulas. (p. 553)
—Greco. (p. 720)
—How to Draw Australia's Sights & Symbols. (p. 816)
—How to Draw Brazil's Sights & Symbols. (p. 817)
—How to Draw China's Sights & Symbols. (p. 817)
—How to Draw India's Sights & Symbols. (p. 817)
—How to Draw Kenya's Sights & Symbols. (p. 817)
—How to Draw Norway's Sights & Symbols. (p. 818)
—How to Draw Poland's Sights & Symbols. (p. 818)
—How to Draw Portugal's Sights & Symbols. (p. 818)
—How to Draw Russia's Sights & Symbols. (p. 818)
—How to Draw South Africa's Sights & Symbols. (p. 818)
—How to Draw South Korea's Sights & Symbols. (p. 818)
—How to Draw the Life & Times of Andrew Jackson. (p. 818)
—How to Draw the Life & Times of Benjamin Harrison. (p. 818)
—How to Draw the Life & Times of Franklin Delano Roosevelt. (p. 818)
—How to Draw the Life & Times of James Buchanan. (p. 819)
—How to Draw the Life & Times of James K. Polk. (p. 819)
—How to Draw the Life & Times of Lyndon B. Johnson. (p. 819)
—How to Draw the Life & Times of Rutherford B. Hayes. (p. 819)
—How to Draw the Life & Times of Thomas Jefferson. (p. 819)
—Kid's Guide to Drawing the Countries of the World: Set 2 (p. 953)
—Meet Al Sharpton. (p. 1120)
—Meet Coretta Scott King. (p. 1120)
—Meet Jesse Jackson. (p. 1121)
—Meet Malcolm X. (p. 1121)
—Meet Martin Luther King Jr. (p. 1121)
—Meet Rosa Parks. (p. 1122)
—Paul Cezanne. (p. 1330)
—Rembrandt. (p. 1459)
—Vermeer. (p. 1837)
Misakonis, Amy. Best Place for Me. (p. 171)
Mischel, Jenny Ann. Animal Alphabet. Bell-Myers, Darcy, illus. (p. 76)
Miserius, Felicitatus. Terrible Tales: A the Absolutely, Positively, 100 Percent True Stories of Cinderella, Little Red Riding Hood, Those Three Greedy Pigs, Hairy Rapunzel. (p. 1721)
Mish. Softly Comes the Rain. Mish, illus. (p. 1606)
Mish, Frederick C., ed. see Merriam-Webster, Inc. Staff.
Mishica, C. Twins. (p. 1802)
Mishica, Claire. Superstar Charlie. (p. 1684)
Mishica, Clare. Here Comes the Parade. Richard, Ilene, illus. (p. 770)
—Samantha Stays Safe. Dubin, Jill, illus. (p. 1507)
—Vamos al Desfile. (p. 1831)
Mishkin, Dan. Warren Commission Report: A Graphic Investigation into the Kennedy Assassination. Colón, Ernie & Drozd, Jerzy, illus. (p. 1858)
Mishler, Ashley. Anya Tap. (p. 90)
—One Fairy Night. (p. 1294)
Mishler, Clark James, photos by see Randall, Jack.
Mishra, Ajay R., ed. Advanced Cellular Network Planning & Optimisation: 2G/2.5G/3G... Evolution To 4G. (p. 13)
Mishra, Samina, jt. auth. see Husain, Zakir.
Misiroglu, Gina. Handy Answer Book for Kids (and Parents) (p. 741)
Miskimen, Cora. Mrs. Hunny Bunny's New Spring Hat. (p. 1187)
Miskimins, Jason, illus. see Cleary, Brian P.
Miskimins, Jason, illus. see Cleary, Brian P. & Maday, Alice M.
Mismas, L. J., Jr. Write on! Printing: Tutor Kit (English) (p. 1963)
Misra, M. J. Sky High! (p. 1586)
Misra, Michelle. Angel Wings: New Friends. (p. 74)
—Angel Wings: Secrets & Sapphires. (p. 74)
—Angel Wings - Rainbows & Halos. (p. 74)
—Birthday Surprise. (p. 193)
Miss Cheryl, jt. auth. see Cargile, Phillip.
Miss Conner'S Class. Look How We've Grown! A Collection of First Grade Writing. (p. 1049)
Miss Gomez's Third Grade Class Staff. Wacky Stories from Wisdom Academy for Young Scientists. (p. 1852)
Miss Karen. Precious Gets a Surprise. (p. 1394)
Miss Linda. Stanzas of Biblical Giants. (p. 1640)
"Miss Nancy" Sorensen. President Barack Obam. (p. 1396)
Miss Riedel. Superheroes Breathe Cancer Away: (a Little Book for Children Living with Cancer in Their Lives.) (p. 1683)
Misseijer, Tamra K. Bailey Bathes in the Potty. (p. 133)
Misseijer, Tamra K. & A. Pryor, Scott. Going Green Gang Helps Save the Nature Preserve. (p. 692)
Mission City Press Inc. Staff, jt. auth. see Pulley, Kelly.
Mission City Press Inc. Staff & Zondervan Publishing Staff. Animal Adventures Collection (p. 76)
Mississippi Staff. Best of Mississippi Childrens. (p. 170)
Misstigri, illus. see Goyer, Katell.
Mist, Rosalind. Asteroids, Comets, & Meteors. Taylor, Lauren, ed. (p. 108)
—Earth & Mars. Taylor, Lauren, ed. (p. 495)
—Jupiter & Saturn. Taylor, Lauren, ed. (p. 937)
—Mercury & Venus. Taylor, Lauren, ed. (p. 1127)
—Sun & Moon. Taylor, Lauren, ed. (p. 1676)
—Uranus & Neptune. Taylor, Lauren, ed. (p. 1825)
Mister, Marita. Who's That Kid? (p. 1921)
Mistral, Gabriela. Poesia Infantil. (p. 1376)
—Ronda de Astros. (p. 1487)
Mistretta, Jay. Joe E Gallet, Karl, illus. (p. 920)
Mistretta, Jay Francis. Parkour Code. Lulu.com, ed. (p. 1325)
Mistretta, T. P. C. Jay Francis. Parkour Code. (p. 1325)
Mistry, Kamlesh. Humorous Hunt. (p. 827)
Mistry, Nilesh, illus. see Casey, Dawn.
Mistry, Nilesh, illus. see Daynes, Katie.
Mistry, Nilesh, illus. see Gilchrist, Cherry & Cann, Helen.
Mistry, Nilesh, illus. see Gilchrist, Cherry.
Mistry, Nilesh, illus. see Pitcher, Caroline.
Mistry, Nilesh, illus. see Robert, Na'ima Bint, tr.
Mistry, Nilesh, illus. see Robert, Na'ima Bint.
Mistry, Nilesh, illus. see Robert, Na'ima bint.
Mistry, Nilesh, illus. see Robert, Naima Bint, tr.
Mistry, Nilesh, illus. see Verma, Jatinder.
Misty. Tristan, the Youngest Blue Jay. (p. 1787)
Misu, Max, jt. auth. see Chima, Ahiru.
Misuraca, Thomas J., jt. auth. see Davis, Darren G.
Misztal, Fred. What I See in the Sky. (p. 1887)
Misztal, Maggie. Be Creative with Beads! Use Place Value Understanding & Properties of Operations to Add & Subtract (p. 148)
—Colony of New Jersey. (p. 342)
Misztal, Yvonne. How Bugs & Plants Live Together. (p. 805)
Mitakidou, Christodoula, jt. auth. see Manna, Anthony L.
Mitakidou, Christodoula, jt. auth. see Manna, Anthony.
Mitaro, S. Clara. Good Eggs. (p. 698)
Mitch, Karlie. Green Stone House (p. 722)
Mitcham Davis, Zipporah. Fox & Emily's Long Migration. (p. 626)
Mitchard, Jacquelyn. All We Know of Heaven. (p. 46)
—Baby Bat's Lullaby. Noonan, Julia, illus. (p. 125)
—Look Both Ways. (p. 1049)
—Now You See Her. (p. 1269)
—Starring Prima! The Mouse of the Ballet Jolie. Tusa, Tricia, illus. (p. 1642)
—What We Lost in the Dark. (p. 1895)
—What We Saw at Night. (p. 1895)
Mitchard, Jacquelyn, ed. see Askew, Kim & Helmes, Amy.
Mitchard, Jacquelyn, ed. see Benedis-Grab, Daphne.
Mitchard, Jacquelyn, ed. see Plissner, Laurie.
Mitchard, Jacquelyn & Lewis, Michael S. Eagle Eyes. (p. 492)
Mitchelhill, Barbara. Livewire Chillers Hit & Run. (p. 1040)
—Livewire Plays Mobile Phoney. (p. 1040)
—Twist of Fortune. (p. 1802)
Mitchell, Ainslie. Collecting Seashells. Walker, Anna, illus. (p. 339)
Mitchell, Alison. Check It Out: Bible Discovery for Children. (p. 295)
—Christmas Unpacked: Bible Discovery for Children & Families. (p. 316)
—Easter Unscrambled: Bible Discovery for Children & Families. (p. 499)
—End to End: Bible Discovery for Children. (p. 526)
Mitchell, Alison, jt. auth. see Boddam-Whetham, Jo.
Mitchell, Alycen. France. (p. 627)
—Performing Arts. (p. 1343)
Mitchell, Andrew. Young Naturalist. Jacquemier, Sue & Bramwell, Martyn, eds. (p. 1979)
Mitchell, Andrew, jt. auth. see Ames, Lee J.
Mitchell, Andrew B. Bubbles, Bubbles & More Bubbles. (p. 233)
Mitchell, Anna B., jt. auth. see Riachi, Ghassan Diab.
Mitchell, Anne, illus. see Schantz, Becky.
Mitchell, Anthony W., illus. see Terrell, Andrea M.
Mitchell, Arnold. Arnold's Dream. (p. 100)
Mitchell, Barbara. Father of the Constitution: A Story about James Madison. Tavoularis, Alex, illus. (p. 577)
—Maker of Machines: A Story about Eli Whitney. Jones, Jan Naimo, tr. (p. 1080)
—Raggin' A Story about Scott Joplin. Mitchell, Hetty, illus. (p. 1433)
Mitchell, Barbara A. Boomerang Age: Transitions to Adulthood in Families. (p. 213)
Mitchell, Billy. Mitchls Elementary Arithmetic: Memorized Multiplication Tables Replaced. (p. 1155)
Mitchell, Breanne. Love You from the Tippy Tippy Top to Your Teeny Tiny Toes! (p. 1060)
Mitchell, Brooks, narrated by. Kipling's Error III: They Were Good Americans. (p. 961)
Mitchell, Bryan. NWQ Blackjack. (p. 1274)
—Top Producer: A Ten Step Plan to Successful Selling. (p. 1769)
Mitchell, Carol. Another Day. Ward, Cherise, illus. (p. 87)
Mitchell, Carolann. Song of the Snow. (p. 1611)
Mitchell, Carolyn. Tale of the Pumpkin Seed Squad. (p. 1700)
Mitchell, Charlie. Great M & M Caper. (p. 717)
Mitchell, Christine. Family Day: Celebrating Ethan's Adoption Anniversary. (p. 568)
Mitchell, Cindi. Connect-the-Dot Math: 35 Reproducible Dot-to-Dot Activities That Help Kids Practice Multi-Digit Addition & Subtraction & Basic Multiplication & Division Facts. (p. 357)
—Dazzling Math Line Designs: Dozens of Reproducible Activities That Help Build Addition, Subtraction. (p. 415)
—Math Line Designs from Around the World: Dozens of Engaging Practice Pages That Build Skills in Addition, Subtraction, Multiplication Facts, & More. (p. 1106)
—Math Line Designs from Around the World: Dozens of Engaging Practice Pages That Build Skills in

Multiplication, Division, Fractions, Decimals, & More. (p. 1106)
—Math Skills Made Fun: Dazzling Math Line Designs; Dozens of Reproducible Activities That Build Skills & Working Fractions, Decimals, Percents, Integers & Prime Numbers. (p. 1107)
—Quilt Math: 100 Reproducible Activities That Motivate Kids to Practice Multi-Digit Addition & Subtraction, Multiplication & Division, Fractions, Decimals, & More. (p. 1428)
Mitchell, Cindi, jt. auth. see Kiernan, Denise.
Mitchell, Colleen. Dinosaur under My Bed. Daly, Karen Anne, illus. (p. 443)
Mitchell, Cynthia. Big & Beastly Alphabet. (p. 177)
Mitchell, David. Wonders of Waldorf Chemistry: Notes from a Teacher's Notebook. Odermatt, Brian, illus. (p. 1949)
Mitchell, David, ed. see Adams, David.
Mitchell, David, ed. see Streit, Jakob.
Mitchell, David, illus. see Ashley, Bernard.
Mitchell, David S., ed. see Betteridge, Barbara Dawson.
Mitchell, David S., ed. see Pittis, Arthur M.
Mitchell, David S., ed. see Streit, Jakob.
Mitchell, David S., ed. see von Mackensen, Manfred, et al.
Mitchell, Dawn. Bird in a Bathing Suit. (p. 190)
Mitchell, Deborah, jt. auth. see Edelson, Stephen B.
Mitchell, Denise K. Starbyte the Computer Fairy Collection. (p. 1642)
Mitchell, Dennis. First Day of School: A Day in the Life of Noah. (p. 594)
Mitchell, Derrick Lee & Howard, Assuanta. Miyah & Koala's First Day. Mitchell, Derrick Lee, illus. (p. 1156)
Mitchell, Devon L. Candy Dragon: Torchy's Adventures of Starting School. (p. 261)
Mitchell, Don. Driven: A Photobiography of Henry Ford. (p. 485)
—Freedom Summer Murders. (p. 635)
—Liftoff: A Photobiography of John Glenn. (p. 1014)
Mitchell, Donald Grant. About Old Story Tellers. (p. 6)
—American Lands & Letters. (p. 62)
—English Land, Letters, & Kings. (p. 530)
Mitchell, E. Siobhan. Anti-Depressants. (p. 89)
Mitchell, Ed. You Never Can Tell What's Least Expected Most. (p. 1976)
mitchell, Ed. You never can tell what's least expected Most. (p. 1976)
Mitchell, Edgar & Mahoney, Ellen. Earthrise: My Adventures As an Apollo 14 Astronaut. (p. 498)
Mitchell, Elyne. Silver Brumby: Including Elyne Mitchell's Ast Brumby Story, 'Wild Echoes Ringing' Power, Margaret, illus. (p. 1576)
Mitchell, Francis G., jt. auth. see Roach-Langille, Nancy.
Mitchell, G., jt. auth. see Mitchell, G. Duncan.
Mitchell, G. Duncan & Mitchell, G. Hundred Years of Sociology. (p. 827)
Mitchell, Gail A. Learning English the Cultural Way. Mitchell, Gail A., photos by. (p. 985)
Mitchell, Ged, illus. see Naylor, Brenda & Naylor, Stuart.
Mitchell, George. Marmots of Lenk & the Long Sleep. (p. 1096)
—My handwriting & colouring Book. (p. 1210)
Mitchell, Gloria. Mouse That Went to Find Christmas. Johnson, Jerome A., illus. (p. 1182)
Mitchell, Grace. Across the Desert: Chosen. (p. 9)
Mitchell, Gwendolyn. For the Love of Sapphire: The Promise. May, Sandy, illus. (p. 616)
Mitchell, Hazel, illus. see Barth, Linda J.
Mitchell, Hazel, illus. see Gomez, Sally.
Mitchell, Hazel, illus. see Groeneweg, Nicole.
Mitchell, Hazel, illus. see Kelly, Matthew.
Mitchell, Hazel, illus. see Marek, Catherine.
Mitchell, Hazel, illus. see Millar, Goldie & Berger, Lisa.
Mitchell, Hazel, illus. see Pighin, Marcel.
Mitchell, Hazel, illus. see Powell, Glenda.
Mitchell, Hazel, illus. see Suen, Anastasia.
Mitchell, Hazel, illus. see Wallace, Rich.
Mitchell, Hazel, jt. auth. see Moritz, S. Dianne.
Mitchell, Hazel, jt. auth. see Suen, Anastasia.
Mitchell, Hazell, illus. see Brown-Wood, Janay.
Mitchell, Hazle, illus. see Bradley, Judy.
Mitchell, Hetty, illus. see Lowery, Linda.
Mitchell, Hetty, illus. see Mitchell, Barbara.
Mitchell, J. Barton. Midnight City. (p. 1138)
—Valley of Fires. (p. 1831)
Mitchell, Jack. Ancient Ocean Blues. (p. 70)
—Roman Conspiracy. (p. 1485)
Mitchell, James. Kids' Cookbook. (p. 953)
Mitchell, James O. Her Black Sparkles! (p. 769)
Mitchell, Jana Christy, illus. see MacDonald, Maryann.
Mitchell, Janet Lynn. Family Fun. (p. 568)
—Family Nights. (p. 568)
Mitchell, Jeff. Young, Innocent & in Prison: The Story of Robert Baltovich (p. 1979)
Mitchell, Joan & Schreiber, Angela. Together in Jesus: First Eucharist TG. (p. 1762)
—Together in Jesus: First Reconciliation TG. (p. 1762)
—Together in Jesus: Spanish First Eucharist TG. (p. 1762)
—Together in Jesus: Spanish First Reconciliation TG. (p. 1762)
Mitchell, Joanne, illus. see Virr, Paul.
Mitchell, Joyce. Button. (p. 248)
—Selfish Little Bob, Selfish No More! (p. 1549)
Mitchell Jr., Leonard, illus. see Alexander, Troas James.
Mitchell, Judith, ed. see Gould, Judith S. & Burke, Mary F.
Mitchell, Judith, ed. see Midgley, Elizabeth Cole.
Mitchell, Judith, ed. see Myers, R. E.
Mitchell, Judith, ed. see Rife, Douglas M. & Capaldi, Gina.
Mitchell, Judy, ed. see Cecchini, Marie E.
Mitchell, Judy, ed. see Connolly, Debbie & Danley, Laurie.
Mitchell, Judy, ed. see Enderle, Dotti.
Mitchell, Judy, ed. see Etringer, Kathy.
Mitchell, Judy, ed. see Fisher, Ann Richmond.
Mitchell, Judy, ed. see Gould, Judith S. & Gould, Evan Jay.
Mitchell, Judy, ed. see Moen, Christine Boardman.
Mitchell, Judy, ed. see Storey, Melinda.
Mitchell, Judy, ed. see Tucker, Mary.
Mitchell, Judy, ed. see Tuszynski, Kathy & Yarber, Angela.
Mitchell, Julie, jt. auth. see Holt, Sharon.
Mitchell, Julie & Chambers, Mal. Bertha. (p. 168)
—Vega Bay. (p. 1834)
Mitchell, Julie & Konye, Paul. Bully. (p. 241)
Mitchell, Julie & McKenzie, Heather. Metal Mouth. (p. 1130)
Mitchell, Julie & Rinkel, Ken. Slow down, Mrs. Brown! (p. 1591)
Mitchell, Katherine. Another Day & Lots to Do. (p. 87)
Mitchell, Kathy. Daddy Got His Orders. Hergenroeder, Ernie, illus. (p. 398)
—Story of the Statue of Liberty. (p. 1662)
Mitchell, Kirstin. Madame Anopheles. (p. 1069)
Mitchell, Kyra & Varacalli, Lauren. Baylor University College Prowler off the Record. (p. 147)
Mitchell, Lakeya Geneene. Devon Iscariot. (p. 432)
—King of Mud! (p. 959)
Mitchell, Lance B. Penguin Adventures of Ping & Pong. (p. 1336)
Mitchell Lane Publishers Inc. Staff. Art Profiles for Kids (p. 103)
—Blue Banner Biographies (p. 202)
—Blue Banner Biographies: Pop Entertainers II (p. 202)
—Blue Banner Biographies-Child Stars. (p. 202)
—Gardening for Kids (p. 656)
—How to Convince Your Parents You Can... (p. 816)
—Latinos in American History: The Hispanic Influence in the United States (p. 979)
—Masters of Music: The World's Greatest Composers (p. 1103)
—Natural Disasters (p. 1235)
—On the Verge of Extinction: Crisis in the Environment (p. 1291)
—Profiles in American History. (p. 1409)
—Profiles in Greek & Roman Mythology (p. 1409)
—Robbie Reader-Contemporary Biographies (p. 1478)
—Robbie Reader-Extreme Sports (p. 1478)
—Robbie Reader-No Hands Allowed (p. 1478)
—Robbie Reader-Science Biography (p. 1478)
Mitchell Lane Publishers Inc. Staff, creator. My Guide to the Constitution Set. (p. 1210)
Mitchell, Laurence. Fish with Feet: From the Travels of Guppy Flynn, Book # 3. (p. 598)
—Friends & Forgiving! Character Tales. (p. 638)
—Mean Root of Crowteal Pond: Inside a Hollow Oak Tree, Book #4. (p. 1116)
—Parents Don't Always Do the Right Things: Character Tales. (p. 1324)
—Patty Liz & Kindness: Character Tales. (p. 1330)
Mitchell, Lebbeus. Circus Comes to Town. (p. 322)
Mitchell, Lee Ann. Milo the Mighty Protector. (p. 1144)
Mitchell, Lindy. Pick-a-WooWoo - the Elf That Flew: Love & Joy give you wings to Fly. Gray, Karen, illus. (p. 1354)
Mitchell, Loretta. One, Two, Three... Echo Me! Ready-to-Use Songs, Games & Activities to Help Children Sing in Tune. (p. 1297)
—Ready-to-Use Music Reading Activities Kit: A Complete Sequential Program for Use with Mallet & Keyboard Instruments. (p. 1448)
Mitchell, Lori. Marfan Syndrome A-Z. (p. 1092)
Mitchell, Lori, illus. see Ashman, Sarah & Parent, Nancy.
Mitchell, Lucinda Orr. Ladon's Lapse: The Story of Draco. (p. 970)
Mitchell, Lucy Sprague. Here & Now Story Book. Van Loon, Hendrik & Price, Christine, illus. (p. 769)
Mitchell, Malinda. Spencer the Spring Chicken & Other Stories. Schandy, Rosita & Wooten, Neal, illus. (p. 1625)
Mitchell, Margaree King. Uncle Jed's Barbershop. Ransome, James, illus. (p. 1811)
—When Grandmama Sings. Ransome, James E., illus. (p. 1902)
Mitchell, Mari Rutz. Creating Clever Castles & Cars (from Boxes & Other Stuff) Kids Ages 3-8 Make Their Own Pretend Play Spaces. Kline, Michael, illus. (p. 378)
Mitchell, Marianne. Finding Zola. (p. 588)
—Firebug. (p. 591)
Mitchell, Marie & Smith, Mason. Squatch Watch & Other Stories. (p. 1636)
Mitchell, Mark. Raising la Belle. Mitchell, Mark, illus. (p. 1437)
Mitchell, Mark, illus. see Reichart, George.
Mitchell, Mark & Evans, Allan, eds. Moriz Rosenthal in Word & Music: A Legacy of the Nineteenth Century. (p. 1175)
Mitchell, Marva, frwd. Hallelujah Anyhow the Best is yet to Come. (p. 737)
Mitchell, Marvin. Calvin's Giant Jumps. Mitchell, Suzanne, illus. (p. 255)
Mitchell, Marvin T. Bully Me No More: How Everyone Can Be Bullied! (p. 241)
Mitchell, Mary Esther. Adventures of Timmy Gills. (p. 24)
Mitchell, Melanie. Deep in the Jungle. (p. 423)
—From Maple Tree to Syrup. (p. 643)
—Good Morning. (p. 698)
—Good Morning, Good Night! (p. 698)
—Good Morning, Good Night! A Touch & Feel Bedtime Book. (p. 698)
—Good Morning, Good Night Bilingual: Buenos Dias! Buenas Noches! (p. 698)
—Good Night. (p. 699)
—Killing Germs. (p. 956)
—Matar los Gérmenes. Aguirre, Barbara & Fitzpatrick, Julia, trs. (p. 1104)
—School Bus Drivers. (p. 1522)
—Sun. (p. 1675)
—Teachers. (p. 1709)
—Wake up Little Ones. (p. 1853)
—Who Do You Love? (p. 1915)
Mitchell, Melanie, illus. see Gibbs, Lynne.
Mitchell, Melanie, illus. see Goodings, Christina.
Mitchell, Melanie, illus. see Imperato, Teresa.
Mitchell, Melanie, illus. see McKendry, Sam.
Mitchell, Melanie, illus. see Nolan, Allia Zobel.
Mitchell, Melanie, illus. see Prasadam, Smriti.
Mitchell, Melanie, illus. see Price, Olivia.
Mitchell, Melanie, illus. see Senior, Suzy.
Mitchell, Melanie, illus. see Steven, Kenneth C.
Mitchell, Melanie, illus. see Tebbs, Victoria.
Mitchell, Melanie, illus. see Wang, Margaret.
Mitchell, Melanie, illus. see Zondervan & Lyons, P. J.
Mitchell, Melanie S. Beans. (p. 150)
—Black. (p. 194)
—Blue. (p. 202)
—Brown. (p. 231)
—Butterflies. (p. 247)
—Cloth. (p. 334)
—Ears. (p. 494)
—Eyes. (p. 558)
—Feet. (p. 580)
—Flowers. (p. 608)
—Frogs. (p. 641)
—Green. (p. 721)
—Leaves. (p. 986)
—Metal. (p. 1130)
—Moon. (p. 1171)
—Mouths. (p. 1183)
—Orange. (p. 1301)
—Plastic. (p. 1370)
—Purple. (p. 1419)
—Red. (p. 1453)
—Roots. (p. 1488)
—Seeds. (p. 1547)
—Stars. (p. 1643)
—Stems. (p. 1647)
—Wood. (p. 1949)
—Yellow. (p. 1969)
Mitchell, Michael D. Cinnamon Von Strudel Story: The Little Dachshund Who Tried to Become A City Mascot. (p. 321)
Mitchell, Mike, ed. see Holden-Rowley, Tim & Blewitt, John.
Mitchell, Mike, et al. Citizenship Studies for AQA GCSE Short Course. (p. 323)
Mitchell, Missy. Ballet: Pointe by Pointe. (p. 134)
Mitchell, N. J. W. Saraly & the Dragons. (p. 1514)
—Search. (p. 1537)
Mitchell, Nanci, illus. see Champion, Gina.
Mitchell, P. S. I Don't Wanna Be Me. (p. 838)
Mitchell, Patricia. Saints Tell Their Stories. Casco, Maria Cristina Lo, illus. (p. 1504)
Mitchell, Paulette. Beautiful Bowl of Soup: The Best Vegetarian Recipes. Meppem, William, photos by. (p. 153)
Mitchell, Peter. Ancient Maya & Aztec Civilization. (p. 70)
Mitchell, Peter, illus. see Scowen, Kate, ed.
Mitchell, Peter, illus. see Wells, Polly.
Mitchell, Peter, ed. Peoples & Cultures of Africa (p. 1340)
Mitchell, Polly, illus. see Renfrew, Catherine.
Mitchell, Pratima. Raju's Ride. Waterhouse, Stephen, illus. (p. 1437)
Mitchell, Racquel L. Penny Pincher Teaches: Tithing. (p. 1338)
Mitchell, Rae. Anna's Wish. (p. 85)
Mitchell, Randall. Teenership: Leadership for Teens. (p. 1714)
Mitchell, Rhonda, illus. see Johnson, Angela.
Mitchell, Rita Phillips. Hue Boy. Binch, Caroline, illus. (p. 824)
Mitchell, Robin. Snowy & Chinook. Steedman, Judith, illus. (p. 1601)
Mitchell, Ronnie & May, Leslie. Catching the Wind: Beanie's First Flight. (p. 279)
Mitchell, Sandra. Butterfly Buddies. (p. 247)
Mitchell, Saundra. Elementals. (p. 510)
—Mistwalker. (p. 1155)
—Springsweet. (p. 1635)
—Vespertine. (p. 1839)
Mitchell, Saundra, et al. Defy the Dark. (p. 424)
Mitchell, Sharon Kay, VIII. What Great Thing Can Patches Do? (p. 1885)
Mitchell, Sheena. Out of the Ark. (p. 1311)
Mitchell, Sherry. Fernando the Veterinarian. (p. 582)
—Growing up on the Lake: Sherry Mitchell. (p. 727)
—Snowy Days. (p. 1601)
Mitchell, Shirley Lipscomb. Legend of the Sweet Potato Pie. Tombers, Monica, ed. (p. 989)
Mitchell, Stan R. Oskar & Myer at the Lake. (p. 1305)
—Oskar Wins the Race. (p. 1305)
Mitchell, Stanley, ed. see Pushkin, Alexander.
Mitchell, Stanley, tr. see Pushkin, Alexander.
Mitchell, Stephen. Wishing Bone, & Other Poems. Pohrt, Tom, illus. (p. 1940)
Mitchell, Steven, illus. see Farenhorst, Christine.
Mitchell, Susan. Amusement Park Rides. (p. 66)
—Will Ferrell. (p. 1932)
Mitchell, Susan, illus. see Baillie, Marilyn.
Mitchell, Susan, illus. see Bauer, Marion Dane.
Mitchell, Susan, illus. see Capucilli, Alyssa Satin.
Mitchell, Susan, illus. see Deen, Paula.
Mitchell, Susan, illus. see Hennessy, B. G.
Mitchell, Susan, illus. see MacDonald, Margaret Read.
Mitchell, Susan, illus. see Metcalf, Paula.
Mitchell, Susan, illus. see Simpson, Roberta.
Mitchell, Susan, illus. see Smith, Nikki Shannon.
Mitchell, Susan, illus. see Zobel-Nolan, Allia.
Mitchell, Susan K. Animal Body-Part Regenerators: Growing New Heads, Tails, & Legs. (p. 76)
—Animal Chemical Combat: Poisons, Smells, & Slime. (p. 77)
—Animal Mimics: Look-Alikes & Copycats. (p. 78)
—Animals with Awesome Armor: Shells, Scales, & Exoskeletons. (p. 84)
—Animals with Crafty Camouflage: Hiding in Plain Sight. (p. 84)
—Animals with Wicked Weapons: Stingers, Barbs, & Quills. (p. 84)
—Biggest Thrill Rides. (p. 185)
—Biggest vs. Smallest Amazing Mammals. (p. 185)
—Biggest vs. Smallest Creepy, Crawly Creatures. (p. 185)
—Biggest vs. Smallest Incredible Insects. (p. 185)
—Biggest vs. Smallest Sea Creatures. (p. 185)
—Biggest vs. Smallest Slimy, Scaly Creatures. (p. 185)
—Biggest vs. Smallest Things with Wings. (p. 185)
—Humorous Small Critter Jokes to Tickle Your Funny Bone. (p. 827)
—Jack Black. (p. 902)
—Jessica Simpson. (p. 914)
—Kersplatypus Rogers, Sherry, illus. (p. 949)
—Largest Stadiums. (p. 975)
—Longest Bridges. (p. 1047)
—Longest Tunnels. (p. 1047)
—Rainforest Grew All Around McLennan, Connie, illus. (p. 1436)
—Secret World of Spy Agencies. (p. 1544)
—Spies & Lies: Famous & Infamous Spies. (p. 1627)
—Spies & Lies-Famous & Infamous Spies. (p. 1627)
—Spies, Double Agents, & Traitors. (p. 1627)
—Spy Codes & Ciphers. (p. 1636)
—Spy Gizmos & Gadgets. (p. 1636)
—Spy Tech-Digital Dangers. (p. 1636)
—Spy Tech—Digital Dangers. (p. 1636)
—Tallest Buildings. (p. 1704)
—Tyra Banks. (p. 1805)
Mitchell, Suzanne, illus. see Mitchell, Marvin.
Mitchell, Tammy. Rachel & the Magical Butterfly. (p. 1431)
Mitchell, Taylor. Blue Bell. (p. 202)
Mitchell, Tina, illus. see Lovell, Brandy.
Mitchell, Todd. Backwards. (p. 130)
—Secret to Lying. (p. 1544)
Mitchell, Toni, jt. auth. see Popek, Penelope.
Mitchell, Tracy, illus. see Dodds, Dayle Ann.
Mitchell, Trish. Noah Pals: Journey to the Apple Tree. (p. 1261)
—Noah Pals: Noah & Friends Awesome Adventure. (p. 1261)
—Noah Pals No Bullies No Way: Second Edition. (p. 1261)
Mitchell, W. A. Larry & Yuki Go into Business. (p. 976)
Mitchell-Cranfield, Robin, jt. auth. see Steedman, Judith.
Mitchell-George, Joanne. John Bunyan: Prisoner for Christ. (p. 921)
Mitchell-Hughes, Kimberley. 10 Most Extreme Sports. (p. 1994)
Mitchells, Brett. Dixie Chicks. (p. 455)
Mitchell-Tulloss, Delores. ABCs of Character for People Around the World. Hardison, Brian, illus. (p. 4)
Mitcheltree, Frani B. Liberty Blue. (p. 1005)
Mitchem, Gary, ed. see Claudy, C. H.
Mitchem, James. Big Book of Things to Make. (p. 179)
Mitchen, Scott. Will of the Pirates. (p. 1932)
Mitchess, Judith, ed. see Midgley, Elizabeth Cole.
Mitchison, Naomi. Travel Light. (p. 1780)
Mitchum, Lynn Tyner. Happy Being Me. Mitchum, Lynn Tyner, illus. (p. 744)
Mitchusson, Eva. Precious Is a Pretty Bird. (p. 1394)
Miteff, Deb & Falk, Cathy. un-Halloween Book: A Complete Fall Festival for Children's Ministry. (p. 1811)
Mithrandir, Astre, jt. auth. see Waters, Galadriel.
Mithuna, R. Michael, illus. see Hernandez, Jewel.
Mithuna, R. Michael, jt. auth. see Hernandez, Jewel.
Mitra, Ananda. Digital Research. (p. 440)
—Digital World (p. 440)
Mitsui Brown, Janet. Oshogatsu with Obaachan. (p. 1305)
Mitsui, Eiichi, illus. see Yasuda, Yuri & Yasuda, Yuri Old tales of Japan.
Mitsui-Kids. Duel on the Dark Side Shogakukan, ed. (p. 489)
Mitsui-Kids, jt. illus. see Shogakukan.
Mitsuko, Kimiko -, jt. auth. see Kimiko, Mitsuko.
Mittal, Amitabh. Heir Apparent. (p. 762)
Mittal, Anjali. Convent Rules. (p. 361)
Mittal, Shiekha, illus. see Karla, Roopal.
Mittan, J. Barry, photos by see Dzidrums, Christine & Rendon, Leah.
Mittelstaedt, Walt. Student's Guide to William Shakespeare. (p. 1669)
Mitten, Ellen. Aguas Navegables (Waterways) (p. 30)
—Appalachian Region. (p. 92)
—Consumers & Producers. (p. 360)
—Counting the Continents. (p. 371)
—Goods or Services? (p. 701)
—Looking at Landforms. (p. 1050)
—Moving People, Moving Stuff. (p. 1184)
—My Flag. (p. 1208)
—My Money. (p. 1214)
—Waterways. (p. 1864)
Mitten, Ellen K. My Country. (p. 1200)
Mitten, Luana. Farm 123. (p. 573)
—How Do Animals Use... ? (Board Book) (p. 806)
—Jungle ABC. (p. 935)
—Numbers (Board Book) (p. 1272)
—Ocean Colors. (p. 1276)
—Opposites (Board Book) (p. 1301)
—Shapes (Board Book) (p. 1560)
—Sizes (Board Book) (p. 1583)
—Squeak, Squeal, Squawk. (p. 1636)
—What Do You See in the Sea? (Board Book) (p. 1883)
—Zoom to the Zoo. Anglicas, Louise, illus. (p. 1989)
Mitten, Luana & Freeman, Marcia S. Descubre el Mundo de Las Ciencias Enciclopedia (p. 428)
Mitten, Luana & Mitten, Luana K. Bunches of Lunches. (p. 242)
—Squeak, Squeal, Squawk. (p. 1636)
Mitten, Luana K. Arriba y abajo (under & Over) (p. 101)
—?Cómo Usan Los Animales... ? How Do Animals Use... ? (p. 351)
—Dentro y fuera (in & Out) (p. 427)
—Good Night, Sleep Tight. (p. 700)
—Mi Calendario: Los Meses Del Año/My Calendar: Months of the Year. (p. 1132)
—My Calendar: Days of the Week. (p. 1200)
—Peek-a-Boo, Baby. (p. 1334)
—Tamaños: Sizes. (p. 1704)
—Three Dimensional Shapes: Cones. (p. 1742)
Mitten, Luana K., jt. auth. see Mitten, Luana.
Mittendorf, Adam And Alex. Beth the Tracker. (p. 171)
Mitter, Kathryn, illus. see Bergt, Carolyn.
Mitter, Kathryn, illus. see Hamilton, Laura.
Mitter, Kathryn, illus. see Jules, Jacqueline.
Mitter, Kathryn, illus. see McNamara, Margaret & Thompson, Kay.
Mitter, Kathryn, illus. see Peters, Stephanie.
Mitter, Kathryn, illus. see Stiegemeyer, Julie.
Mitter, Kathy, illus. see Hartman, Sara.
Mitter, Kathy, illus. see Stiegemeyer, Julie.
Mitter, Kathy, illus. see Stohs, Anita.

M

Mitter, Kathy, jt. auth. see Stiegemeyer, Julie.
Mitter, Matt. Elmo's Christmas Hugs. Brannon, Tom, illus. (p. 515)
—Fisher Price Little People Curious Little Chicks. S. I. Artists Staff, illus. (p. 598)
—Guess Who Noah's Boat Jarzabek, Ela, illus. (p. 729)
—Hippos on Holiday. Gevry, Claudine, illus. (p. 781)
—Hungry Monsters: A Book of Colors. Brown, Jo, illus. (p. 828)
—Little People on the Farm. (p. 1033)
—Penny Penguin. Brown, Jo, illus. (p. 1338)
—Sesame Street Grouchy Hugs! Brannon, Tom, illus. (p. 1553)
—Sesame Street Guess Who, Easter Elmo! Guess Who Easter Elmo! Mathieu, Joe, illus. (p. 1553)
Mitter, Matt, jt. auth. see Reader's Digest Editors.
Mitter, Matt, jt. auth. see Reader's Digest Staff.
Mitter, Matt & Peyo. I Smurf You! Peyo, illus. (p. 845)
Mitter, Matt & Reader's Digest Editors. Worlds of Adventure. SI Artists Staff, illus. (p. 1960)
Mitter, Matt & Rudko, Che. Ready, Set, Brush! Brannon, Tom, illus. (p. 1447)
Mittler, et al. Introducing Art. (p. 882)
—Understanding Art. (p. 1815)
Mittmann, Gerald & Mittmann, Laura. Rockie Rock-A-Teller on Preparing for the Loudy-Cloudy-Typhooner-Kaboomer. Cannone, Gregory, illus. (p. 1483)
Mittmann, Laura, jt. auth. see Mittmann, Gerald.
Mitton, David, photos by see Random House Staff.
Mitton, Jacqueline. Once upon a Starry Night: A Book of Constellations. Balit, Christina, illus. (p. 1293)
—Planet Gods: Myths & Facts about the Solar System. Balit, Christina, illus. (p. 1367)
—Zoo in the Sky: A Book of Animal Constellations. Balit, Christina, illus. (p. 1989)
—Zoo in the Sky. (p. 1989)
Mitton, Jacqueline, jt. auth. see Dorling Kindersley Publishing Staff.
Mitton, Jacqueline & Balit, Christina. Once upon a Starry Night: A Book of Constellations. (p. 1293)
Mitton, Jacqueline & Quarto Generic Staff. I See the Moon. Pal, Erika, illus. (p. 845)
Mitton, Tony. African Adventure. (p. 26)
—Amazing Machines - Truckload of Fun Parker, Ant, illus. (p. 55)
—Dinosaurumpus! Parker-Rees, Guy, illus. (p. 445)
—Forest Adventure. Parker, Ant, illus. (p. 618)
—Ocean Adventure. (p. 1276)
—Playful Little Penguins. Parker-Rees, Guy, illus. (p. 1372)
—Plum. GrandPré, Mary, illus. (p. 1374)
—Rainforest Adventure. (p. 1436)
—Snowy Bear. Brown, Alison, illus. (p. 1601)
—Somethingosaur. Ayto, Russell, illus. (p. 1610)
Mitton, Tony & Parker, Ant. Amazing Airplanes. (p. 52)
—Amazing Machines. (p. 55)
—Busy Boats. (p. 245)
—Cool Cars. (p. 363)
—Rainforest Romp. (p. 1436)
—Super Submarines. (p. 1682)
—Tough Trucks. (p. 1773)
—Tremendous Tractors. (p. 1784)
Miucha. Boom Boom Went the Thunder. (p. 213)
Miura, Taro. Big Princess. Miura, Taro, illus. (p. 183)
—Crazy Days. (p. 377)
—Tiny King. Miura, Taro, illus. (p. 1756)
Mixter, Helen, tr. see Akbarpour, Ahmad.
Mixter, Helen, tr. see Bouchard, Hervé.
Mixter, Helen, tr. see Serres, Alain.
Miyabe, Miyuki. Book of Heroes. Miyabe, Miyuki, illus. (p. 211)
—Brave Story. Smith, Alexander O., tr. from JPN. (p. 223)
Miyabi, Haruka, illus. see Wilson, Sean Michael.
Miyake, Okiko, ed. Miyake: Japan in English Books for Boys & Girls, 1819-1935. (p. 1156)
Miyake, Yoshi, illus. see Hillert, Margaret.
Miyake, Yoshi, illus. see Kain, Kathleen.
Miyake, Yoshi, illus. see Maas, Alice E.
Miyake, Yoshi, illus. see Miller, Claire.
Miyake, Yoshi, illus. see Sabin, Francene & Macken, JoAnn Early.
Miyake, Yoshi, illus. see Schkade, Jonathan.
Miyake, Yoski, illus. see Rottmann, Erik.
Miyakoshi, Akiko. Tea Party in the Woods. (p. 1708)
Miyakoshi, Junko, tr. see Komiya, Teruyuki.
Miyakoshi, Junko, tr. see Lazoo Publishing Staff & ZOO, La.
Miyakoshi, Junko, tr. see Lazoo Publishing Staff.
Miyakoshi, Junko, tr. see ZOO, La.
Miyakoshi, Wason, illus. see Morioka, Hiroyuki.
Miyamoto, Kano. Lovers & Souls. (p. 1061)
Miyamoto, Yuki. Cafe Kichijouji De (p. 251)
—Cafe Kichijouji de Volume 2 (p. 251)
Miyamoto, Yuki, jt. auth. see Negishi, Kyoko.
Miyanishi, Tatsuya. Mr. Reaper. (p. 1186)
Miyares, Daniel. Float. Miyares, Daniel, illus. (p. 605)
—Pardon Me! Miyares, Daniel, illus. (p. 1324)
Miyares, Daniel, illus. see Chambers, Veronica & Clampet, Jason.
Miyares, Daniel, illus. see Maltbie, P. I.
Miyares, Daniel, illus. see Sedaka, Neil, et al.
Miyares, Ines M., et al. World Cultures & Geography: Western Hemisphere & Europe. (p. 1954)
Miyasaka, Kaho. Kare First Love (p. 943)
—Kare First Love Miyasaka, Kaho, illus. (p. 943)
—Kare First Love Watanabe, Akira, tr. from JPN. (p. 943)
Miyazaki, Hayao. Art of Howl's Moving Castle. Miyazaki, Hayao, illus. (p. 102)
—Art of Kiki's Delivery Service. (p. 102)
—Art of Porco Rosso. Searleman, Eric, ed. (p. 102)
—Castle in the Sky. Miyazaki, Hayao, illus. (p. 276)
—Howl's Moving Castle (p. 824)
—Howl's Moving Castle Jones, Diana Wynne & Miyazaki, Hayao, illus. (p. 824)
—Howl's Moving Castle. Jones, Diana Wynne & Miyazaki, Hayao, illus. (p. 824)
—Howl's Moving Castle Film Comic Miyazaki, Hayao, illus. (p. 824)
—Howl's Moving Castle Picture Book. Miyazaki, Hayao, illus. (p. 824)
—Kiki's Delivery Service (p. 955)
—Kiki's Delivery Service Picture Book (p. 955)
—My Neighbor Totoro. Miyazaki, Hayao, illus. (p. 1215)
—My Neighbor Totoro Picture Book (New Edition) New Edition. (p. 1215)
—Nausicaä of the Valley of the Wind Lewis, David & Smith, Toren, trs. from JPN. (p. 1237)
—Nausicaä of the Valley of the Wind. Miyazaki, Hayao, illus. (p. 1237)
—Ponyo. Miyazaki, Hayao, illus. (p. 1383)
—Ponyo Film Comic. Miyazaki, Hayao, illus. (p. 1383)
—Ponyo Picture Book. Miyazaki, Hayao, illus. (p. 1383)
—Princess Mononoke (p. 1404)
—Spirited Away. Miyazaki, Hayao, illus. (p. 1629)
Miyazaki, Hayao, jt. auth. see Kadono, Eiko.
Miyazaki, Hayao, jt. auth. see Yonebayashi, Hiromasa.
Miyazaki, Hayao & Watsuki, Nobuhiro. Art of My Neighbor Totoro. Miyazaki, Hayao & Watsuki, Nobuhiro, illus. (p. 102)
Miyazawa, Kenji. Restaurant of Many Colors. Sato, Kunio, illus. (p. 1464)
Miyazawa, Takeshi, jt. illus. see Alphona, Adrian.
Miyazoe, Ikuo, illus. see Saguchi, Kensaku.
Mizell, Sandra. Biggest & Best Trip Ever: A Trip to Heaven. (p. 185)
Mizer, Lindsay, ed. see King, J. Eric & Graham, Greg.
Mizielinska, Aleksandra & Mizielinski, Daniel. Maps. (p. 1090)
—Maps Activity Book. (p. 1090)
—Welcome to Mamoko. (p. 1873)
—World of Mamoko in the Time of Dragons. (p. 1957)
—World of Mamoko in the Year 3000. (p. 1957)
Mizielinski, Daniel, jt. auth. see Mizielinska, Aleksandra.
Mizobuchi, Makoto, jt. auth. see Viz Media Staff.
Mizsenko, Ingrid, illus. see Härtling, Peter.
Mizuki, Hakase. Demon Ororon (p. 426)
Mizuki, Shigeru. Showa 1944-1953: A History of Japan. Davisson, Zack, tr. from JPN. (p. 1571)
Mizuna, Tomomi. Big Adventures of Majoko Volume 5 (p. 177)
Mizuna, Tomomi, jt. auth. see Udon Kids Staff.
Mizuno, Eita, jt. auth. see Shirodaira, Kyo.
Mizuno, Junko. Junko Mizuno's Hansel & Gretel. Mizuno, Junko, illus. (p. 936)
—Junko Mizuno's Princess Mermaid. Mizuno, Junko, illus. (p. 936)
Mizuno, Junko & Anzai, Yuko. Yu's Cutie Dolls Vol. 3. Mizuno, Junko & Ishibash, Toshiharu, illus. (p. 1983)
Mizushiro, S. X-Day (p. 1967)
Mizushiro, Seton. X-Day. (p. 1967)
Mizutani, Yuzu. Magical X Miracle. (p. 1075)
Mizuto, Aqua, jt. auth. see Mizuto, Aqua.
Mizuto, Aqua & Mizuto, Aqua. Yume Kira Dream Shoppe Mizuto, Aqua & Mizuto, Aqua, illus. (p. 1983)
Mizzoni, Chris. Sterling Seven, Hockey's First Team Ever. (p. 1649)
MJ Illustrations, illus. see Brooke, Samantha, et al.
MJ Illustrations, illus. see Random House.
MJ Illustrations, illus. see Tillworth, Mary.
MJ Illustrations Staff. Berry Little Princesses. (p. 167)
—Have a Sweet Easter! (p. 754)
MJ Illustrations Staff, illus. see Ackelsberg, Amy.
MJ Illustrations Staff, illus. see Cecil, Lauren.
MJ Illustrations Staff, illus. see Golden Books Staff.
MJ Illustrations Staff, illus. see Inches, Alison.
MJ Illustrations Staff, illus. see Jacobs, Lana.
MJ Illustrations Staff, illus. see Rosebrough, Ellen.
MJ Illustrations Staff, illus. see Tillworth, Mary & Random House Children's Books Staff.
MJ Illustrations Staff, illus. see Tillworth, Mary.
M.J.Higgy. Bombay Bear. (p. 208)
Mjolhus, Joy. Squirrel Babies & Friends. (p. 1637)
Mlawer, Teresa. If I Had a Dragon/Si Yo Tuviera un Dragon. Ellery, Tom & Ellery, Amanda, illus. (p. 853)
Mlawer, Teresa, jt. auth. see Murphy, Stuart J.
Mlawer, Teresa, tr. see Brown, Margaret Wise & Brown, Wise M.
Mlawer, Teresa, tr. see Brown, Margaret Wise.
Mlawer, Teresa, tr. see Carle, Eric.
Mlawer, Teresa, tr. see Carlson, Nancy.
Mlawer, Teresa, tr. see Danneberg, Julie.
Mlawer, Teresa, tr. see Eastman, P. D.
Mlawer, Teresa, tr. see Falconer, Ian.
Mlawer, Teresa, tr. see Henkes, Kevin.
Mlawer, Teresa, tr. see Jeram, Anita.
Mlawer, Teresa, tr. see Kranz, Linda.
Mlawer, Teresa, tr. see Kraus, Robert.
Mlawer, Teresa, tr. see Lionni, Leo.
Mlawer, Teresa, tr. see Martin, Bill, Jr.
Mlawer, Teresa, tr. see McGrath, Barbara Barbieri.
Mlawer, Teresa, tr. see Miller, Elizabeth I.
Mlawer, Teresa, tr. see Montijo, Rhode.
Mlawer, Teresa, tr. see Most, Bernard.
Mlawer, Teresa, tr. see Murphy, Stuart J.
Mlawer, Teresa, tr. see Numeroff, Laura Joffe.
Mlawer, Teresa, tr. see Quezada, Juan.
Mlawer, Teresa, tr. see Segal, John.
Mlawer, Teresa, tr. see Waber, Bernard.
Mlawer, Teresa, tr. What Do I Feel? / ¿Qué Siento? Kubler, Annie, illus. (p. 1882)
—What Do I Hear? / ¿Qué Oigo? Kubler, Annie, illus. (p. 1882)
—What Do I See? / ¿Qué Veo? Kubler, Annie, illus. (p. 1882)
—What Do I Smell? / ¿Qué Huelo? Kubler, Annie, illus. (p. 1882)
—What Do I Taste? / ¿Qué Saboreo? Kubler, Annie, illus. (p. 1882)
Mlawer, Teresa, tr. from ENG. Olivia Se Prepara para la Navidad. Falconer, Ian, illus. (p. 1287)
Mlynowski, Sarah. Bad Hair Day. (p. 131)
—Beauty Queen. (p. 154)
—Bras & Broomsticks. (p. 222)
—Cold as Ice. (p. 338)
—Don't Even Think about It. (p. 467)
—Dream On. (p. 483)
—Fairest of All. (p. 562)
—Frogs & French Kisses. (p. 641)
—Gimme a Call. (p. 676)
—If the Shoe Fits. (p. 854)
—Magic in Manhattan: Bras & Broomsticks Frogs; French Kisses. (p. 1072)
—Parties & Potions. (p. 1325)
—Sink or Swim. (p. 1579)
—Spells & Sleeping Bags. (p. 1625)
—Ten Things We Did (and Probably Shouldn't Have) (p. 1719)
mmediajohn. Daytraders. (p. 415)
MMStudios, photos by see Brooks, Felicity.
MMStudios, photos by see Durber, Matt & Jones, Stephanie, illus.
MMStudios, photos by see Durber, Matt, illus.
MMStudios, photos by see Helbrough, Emma & Brooks, Felicity.
MMStudios, photos by see Litchfield, Jo & Allen, Francesca, illus.
MMStudios, photos by see Litchfield, Jo & Sanchez Gallego, Maria Isabel.
MMStudios & Allman, Howard, photos by. Big & Little: A Book about Opposites. (p. 177)
Mo, Grandma. Liberty the Lion Hearted. (p. 1005)
Mo, Xiangyi, illus. see Glascodine, Carolyn, ed.
Moad, Judy. Willie the Chow Chow. (p. 1934)
Moak, Allan. Big City Alphabet. (p. 180)
Mo'Allim, Nur M., tr. see McKee, David.
Moates, Carol Meetze, illus. see Silcox, Diane.
Moats, Louisa. LETRS (Language Esssentials for Teachers of Reading & Spelling): Presenter's Edition. Bk. 1 (p. 994)
—LETRS:Book One: Language Essentials for Teachers of Reading & Spelling: Participant's Edition. (p. 994)
Moats, Louisa C. Language Essentials for Teachers of Reading & Spelling: Modules 4, 5, 6 Presenter's Edition. (p. 975)
—LETRS (Language Essentials for Teachers of Reading & Spelling) Module 10 Reading Big Words: Syllabication & Advanced Decoding. (p. 994)
Moberg, Julia. Historical Animals. Jeff Albrecht Studios Staff, illus. (p. 782)
—Presidential Pets: The Weird, Wacky, Little, Big, Scary, Strange Animals That Have Lived in the White House. (p. 1397)
—Presidential Pets: The Weird, Wacky, Little, Big, Scary, Strange Animals That Have Lived in the White House. Albrecht, Jeff & Jeff Albrecht Studios Staff, illus. (p. 1397)
—Skies over Sweetwater. (p. 1584)
Mobielle, Grant. Changing Lanes: An Automotive Mystery. (p. 290)
Mobielle, Grant U. Changing Times: Transform your life in 4 easy steps using the Triangle of Change. (p. 290)
Mobin-Uddin, Asma. Best Eid Ever. Jacobsen, Laura, illus. (p. 169)
—My Name Is Bilal. Kiwak, Barbara, illus. (p. 1215)
—Party in Ramadan. Jacobsen, Laura, illus. (p. 1326)
Mobley, Clint & Mobley, Michelle. I'd Rather Be Grilling! A Golfer's Cookbook. (p. 851)
Mobley, Cyn. Very Airey Christmas. (p. 1837)
Mobley, Jeannie. Katerina's Wish. (p. 944)
Mobley, Michelle, jt. auth. see Mobley, Clint.
Mobley, Monica W. Moving Out. (p. 1183)
Mobley, W. Lenore. Enjoy the Journey: Of Women & Their Horses along the Snake River Plain. (p. 530)
Mobley- Williams, Equinta Charee. Reach One Teach Juan: It's All about One. (p. 1442)
Moceanu, Dominique & Thompson, Alicia. Reaching High. (p. 1442)
—Winning Team (p. 1937)
Mocerino, P. A. Invisibull. (p. 886)
Mochizuki, Chiemi. Promise. Randle, Walt R., ed. (p. 1411)
Mochizuki, Ken. Baseball Saved Us. (p. 141)
—Baseball Saved Us. Lee, Dom, illus. (p. 141)
—Beacon Hill Boys. (p. 149)
—Beisbol Nos Salvo. (p. 161)
—Pasajea la Libertad. (p. 1326)
—Passage to Freedom: The Sugihara Story. (p. 1326)
Mochizuki, Ken & Lee, Dom. Be Water, My Friend: The Early Years of Bruce Lee (p. 149)
Mock, Chara. Cajun Nutcracker Cassels, Jean, illus. (p. 252)
Mock, Darci. I Can Be Anything. (p. 835)
Mock, Jarret C. Aeneas. (p. 25)
Mock, Jean. Amazing Animal ABC Book. Martin, Joyce, illus. (p. 52)
—Amazing Animal ABC Book (big Format) (p. 52)
—Amazing Animal ABC Book the Study Guide. Martin, Joyce, illus. (p. 53)
Mock, Katelyn Marie. Lost Herd: Callie's Adventure. (p. 1055)
Mockaitis, Thomas R. Osama Bin Laden: A Biography (p. 1305)
Mockford, Caroline. Cleo the Cat. (p. 331)
—What's This? (p. 1900)
—What's This? A Seed's Story. Mockford, Caroline, illus. (p. 1900)
Mockford, Caroline, illus. see Blackstone, Stella.
Mockford, Caroline, illus. see Chamber, Catherine.
Mockford, Caroline, jt. auth. see Blackstone, Stella.
Mockford, Caroline & Blackstone, Stella. Cleo's Alphabet Book. (p. 331)
—Cleo's Color Book. Mockford, Caroline, illus. (p. 331)
Mockford, Patricia, ed. see Byrne, Andrew.
Mockler, Sean, illus. see Johnson Mockler, Nicole.
Mocombe, Paul C. Mocombe's Reading Room Series. (p. 1157)
—Mocombe's Reading Room Series Advance 1: Advance 1. (p. 1157)
Modak, Tejas, tr. see Bhagwat, B. R.
Modan, Rutu. Maya Makes a Mess. (p. 1112)
Modarressi, Mitra. Owlet's First Flight. Modarressi, Mitra, illus. (p. 1315)
—Taking Care of Mama. Modarressi, Mitra, illus. (p. 1698)
Modéré, Armelle. My First English/Norwegian Dictionary of Sentences. (p. 1206)
Modéré, Armelle, illus. see Dufresne, Didier, et al.
Modéré, Armelle & Hokenson, Linda. My First English/Swedish Dictionary of Sentences. (p. 1206)
Modern Curriculum Press Staff. MCP Spelling Workout. (p. 1115)
—McP Spelling Workout Student B (p. 1115)
—Phonics Practice Readers. (p. 1352)
Modern Painters Staff & Quarto Generic Staff. Colour It! Various Artists, illus. (p. 346)
Modern Publishing, creator. Friends, Silliness & Fun! (p. 639)
—Once upon a Zoo! (p. 1293)
—Sew Much Fun! (p. 1555)
—Smurfs & Smiles! Giant Coloring & Activity Book. (p. 1595)
—Smurfs Super Coloring & Activity Bk. (p. 1595)
—Smurfy Day! Giant Coloring & Activity Book. (p. 1595)
—Traintastic Crew! (p. 1777)
—Way to Go, Wildcats! (p. 1864)
—Wheels to the Rails! (p. 1901)
—Wildlife Adventures! (p. 1931)
Modern Publishing Staff. ABCs! (p. 4)
—Angry Birds Giant Coloring & Activity Book-Big Surprise! (p. 75)
—Ariel's World! (p. 98)
—Batman: The Caped Crusader. (p. 144)
—Batman the Brave & the Bold. (p. 144)
—Colors! (p. 344)
—Counting! (p. 370)
—Feelings! (p. 580)
—Fisher Price Little People Kindergarten (p. 598)
—Fisher-Price Laugh, Smile & Learn. (p. 598)
—Fisher-Price Precious Planet. (p. 599)
—Fisher-Price Spike. (p. 599)
—Fisher-Price Spike the Ultra Dinosaur. (p. 599)
—I Love You... Big Book of Stickers. (p. 843)
—Lisa Frank Super Coloring & Activity Book with Handle: A Colorful World! (p. 1022)
—Look at Me! (p. 1048)
—Opposites! (p. 1300)
—Toys! (p. 1774)
—When I Grow Up: Giant Wall Art Flash Cards. (p. 1903)
—Zhu Zhu Pets Giant Coloring & Activity Book: Furry Friends! (p. 1986)
—Zhu Zhu Pets Giant Coloring & Activity Book: Happy Hamsters! (p. 1986)
Modern Publishing Staff & Disney Staff, contrib. by. Day in the Life. (p. 413)
Modern Publishing Staff, ed. First to the Finish Line. (p. 597)
—Here Comes Tonka. (p. 770)
—Lean Mean Screamin Machines. (p. 982)
—Lots of Fun in Care a Lot. (p. 1057)
—Make Way for Tonka. (p. 1079)
—No Place Like Celesteville. (p. 1260)
—Record Breaking Racers. (p. 1452)
—Sun & Fun in Care a Lot. (p. 1676)
—Tuned up Challengers. (p. 1796)
—Welcome to the Kingdom. (p. 1874)
Modern Staff. Apple Tree. (p. 92)
—Bean & Plant. (p. 150)
—Best Friends: Short e; Consonants f, y; Blends fr, fl (p. 169)
—City Rhythms: Short i; Consonants k, s; Blends str, sw, sp, spl, sk, squ; Digraphs ck, qu. (p. 324)
—Comparing World Communites-Cll (p. 352)
—Day at Our Dairy Farm. (p. 412)
—Discovery Phonics I: Lively Tales Unlock the Mystery of Long & Short Vowels. (p. 450)
—Feather for Her Hair Big Book. (p. 579)
—Kites in Flight & Mosquito Bites. (p. 962)
—Marcos is Magnificent Big Book (p. 1092)
—Paco's Pockets: Consonants p, s. (p. 1317)
—Positively Me! (p. 1387)
—Positively Me! Big Book Collection (p. 1387)
Modesitt, Jeanne & Spowart, Robin. Oh, What a Beautiful Day! A Counting Book. Spowart, Robin, illus. (p. 1281)
Modesitt, L. E., Jr. Ghosts of Columbia. (p. 672)
Modiano, Patrick. Catherine Certitude. (p. 280)
Modica, Cathy & Van Eyck, Laura. Niik & Bling: The Friendship Begins. Modica, Cathy, photos by. (p. 1255)
Modifica, Lisa. Goldie Hawn & Kate Hudson. (p. 695)
—Timeline of Congress. (p. 1754)
—Timeline of the White House. (p. 1754)
Modoc Press Editors. Directory of Distance Learning Opportunities: K-12 (p. 445)
Modotti, Tina, photos by see Hooks, Margaret.
Modugno, Maria. Santa Claus & the Three Bears. Dyer, Jane & Dyer, Brooke, illus. (p. 1511)
Modugno, Tina, illus. see Lambert, Susan Dodd.
Mody, Maria & Silliman, Elaine R., eds. Brain, Behavior, & Learning in Language & Reading Disorders. (p. 221)
Moe, Al W. Stealing from Bandits: In Nevada's Casinos Just Staying Alive Is a Gamble. (p. 1646)
Moe, Barbara. Coping with Mental Illness. (p. 365)
—Coping with PMS (Premenstrual Syndrome) (p. 365)
—Coping with Rejection. (p. 365)
—Coping with Tourette's Syndrome & Other Tic Disorders. (p. 365)
—Drug Abuse Relapse: Helping Teens to Get Clean Again. (p. 486)
—Everything You Need to Know about Migraines & Other Headaches. (p. 545)
—Revolution in Medical Imaging. (p. 1466)
—Search for Weapons of Mass Destruction in Iraq. (p. 1537)
—Understanding Negative Body Image. (p. 1816)
Moe, Barbara A. Charter of the Massachusetts Bay Colony: A Primary Source Investigation of the 1629 Charter. (p. 294)
—Coping with Tourette's & Tics. (p. 365)
—Search for Weapons of Mass Destruction in Iraq. (p. 1537)
Moe, Barbara A., jt. auth. see Wolfe, James.
Moeckel, Christine. Dick the Duck. Moeckel, Christine, illus. (p. 436)
Moehlenpah, Arlo. Creation Versus Evolution: Scientific & Religious Considerations. (p. 379)
Moehn, Heather. Coping with Social Anxiety. (p. 365)
—Everything You Need to Know about Cliques. (p. 545)
—Everything You Need to Know When Someone You Know Has Leukemia. (p. 546)
—Understanding Eating Disorder Support Groups. (p. 1815)

Moeling, Nell. Secret Adventures of Prince Justin & the Dragon. (p. 1540)
Moeller, Bill & Moeller, Jan. Chief Joseph & the Nez Perces: A Photographic History. Greer, Dan, ed. (p. 301)
Moeller, Bill, et al. Crazy Horse: A Photographic Biography. Moeller, Bill, photos by. (p. 377)
Moeller, Jack, et al. Deutsch Heute: Introductory German. (p. 431)
—World Languages. (p. 1956)
Moeller, Jan, jt. auth. see Moeller, Bill.
Moeller mé illuminé, Jo. Hormiguita ¿ A Folktale about the Perseverant Little Ant. (p. 798)
Moeller, Richard, illus. see García, Nasario.
Moeller, Richard, photos by see García, Nasario.
Moen, Ashley. Fantastic Journey: A Trip on a Raindrop. (p. 571)
Moen Cabanting, Ruth. 1-2-3 Waikiki Trolley. (p. 1990)
Moen Cabanting Ruth, illus. see Arita Vera.
Moen Cabanting, Ruth & Jensen, Natalie Mahina. Happy Honu Makes a Friend. (p. 746)
Moen, Christine Boardman. 25 Reproducible Literature Circle Role Sheets for Fiction & Nonfiction Books, Grades 4-6 Revised & Updated. Mitchell, Judy, ed. (p. 1996)
Moen, Ruth, illus. see Gillespie, Jane.
Moen, Ruth, illus. see Wing, Carol.
Moen, Tyler, illus. see Seelen, Christopher.
Moench, Doug. Hong Kong. (p. 795)
—Shang-Chi - Master of Kung Fu: The Hellfire Apocalypse. Vol. 1 Gulacy, Paul, illus. (p. 1559)
Moerbe, Mary. How Can I Help? God's Calling for Kids - Mini Book. (p. 805)
Moerbeck, Kees. Cinderella. (p. 320)
—Goldilocks. (p. 696)
—Three Little Pigs. (p. 1742)
Moerbeek, Kees. Cinderella. (p. 320)
—Jack's & the Beanstalk. (p. 904)
—Jungle Explorers. (p. 935)
—Little Red Riding Hood. (p. 1035)
—Ocean Explorers. (p. 1276)
—Puss in Boots. (p. 1420)
—Snow Explorers. (p. 1599)
—Space Explorers. (p. 1619)
—Three Little Pigs. (p. 1743)
—Ugly Duckling. (p. 1808)
Moerbeek, Kees, illus. see Golding, Elizabeth.
Moerbeek, Kees, illus. see Gruelle, Johnny.
Moerder, Lynne. Things That Go Burp! in the Night. Moerder, Lynne, illus. (p. 1733)
Moeri, Louise. Devil in Ol' Rosie. (p. 432)
—Star Mother's Youngest Child. Hyman, Trina Schart, illus. (p. 1640)
Moerner, John, illus. see Rock, Brian.
Moers, Walter. City of Dreaming Books. (p. 323)
—Wild Ride Through the Night. Brown, John, tr. from GER. (p. 1930)
Moesta, Rebecca & Anderson, Kevin J. Space Station Crisis. (p. 1620)
Moesta, Rebecca, et al. Star Challengers Trilogy. (p. 1640)
Moeyaert, Bart. Brothers: The Oldest, the Quietest, the Realest, the Farthest, the Nicest, the Fastest, & I. Boeke, Wanda, tr. from DUT. (p. 231)
—Dani Bennoni: Long May He Live. Boeke, Wanda, tr. (p. 404)
Mofett, Patricia, illus. see Dahl, Michael.
Moffat, Nichola. High Voltage Smile. (p. 778)
Moffat, Ross, illus. see Arkangel, Brian.
Moffatt, Frances. My Fashion Doodles & Designs: 200 Activities to Sketch, Color & Create. (p. 1203)
Moffatt, J., jt. auth. see Nolan, J.
Moffatt, Judith. Slide & Discover: It's Time! (p. 1590)
—Slide & Discover: What's My Job? (p. 1590)
Moffet, Patricia, illus. see O'Hearn, Michael.
Moffett, Elzater. Tenan & Colleen: Who Is Harry? (p. 1719)
—Tenan & Colleen: I Don't Want to Go to Bed. Thibodeaux, Rebecca, illus. (p. 1719)
Moffett, Mark W. Face to Face with Frogs. (p. 560)
Moffett, Rodney. Eighth Crest. (p. 507)
Moffett, Slyvia. Missionary Kids Adventure Series: Bo. (p. 1153)
Moffett, Sonja. Epiphany. (p. 532)
Moffit, Linda L. Magic Mirror. (p. 1072)
Moffitt, Debra. Best Kept Secret. (p. 170)
—Girls in Charge. (p. 680)
Moffitt, Sara. Merlin & the Frog Meet Chatty & Noble. (p. 1128)
Mofford, Juliet. Raphael. (p. 1439)
—Recipe & Craft Guide to Japan. (p. 1451)
—Recipe & Craft Guide to the Caribbean. (p. 1451)
Mogavera, Cyndie Lepori & Richards, Courtland William. Bubbles & Billy Sandwalker. Murrish, Layne Keeton, illus. (p. 233)
Mogensen, Jan. Go to Sleep, Little Bear. (p. 687)
Mogensen, Jan, illus. see Kipling, Rudyard.
Mogford, Thomas. Sleeping Dogs: A Spike Sanguinetti Novel. (p. 1589)
Moggie, Felix. Living with the Mach Factor: Four Paws. (p. 1042)
Moghimi, Salmeh. Adventures of Anoo & Pashmack. (p. 16)
Mogil, H. Michael & Levine, Barbara G. Extreme Weather. (p. 557)
Mogk, Matt. That's Not Your Mommy Anymore: A Zombie Tale. Wells, Aja, illus. (p. 1727)
Moglia, Amy. Alfalfa Kitty. (p. 37)
Mogollon, Abby. Do You See What I See? SW Nature Walk. (p. 458)
Mogonye, Marjorie. Judah's Shepherd King: The Incredible Story of David. (p. 930)
Mogorrón, Guillermo, illus. see Beauregard, Lynda.
Mogyorosi, Nicole, illus. see Post, Grace.
Moh Ana. Kookaburra Tales # 4: Lighten My Path, Brighten My Heart. (p. 967)
Mohamed, Abdullahi. Forbidden Cake. (p. 616)
Mohamed Mahmoud, Ghada, tr. see Medina, Sarah.
Mohamed, Paloma. Caribbean Mythology & Modern Life: 5 Plays for Young People. Braithwaithe, Barry, illus. (p. 268)
—Man Called Garvey: The Life & Times of the Great Leader Marcus Garvey. Braithwaithe, Barrington, illus. (p. 1085)
Mohamed, Sultan, tr. Story of Coffee. (p. 1657)
Mohammad, Khadra, jt. auth. see Williams, Karen Lynn.
Mohammed, Khadra & Williams, Karen Lynn. My Name Is Sangoel. Stock, Catherine, illus. (p. 1215)
Mohamoud, Ashlee. Brown Is Beautiful (p. 232)
Mohan, Claire Jordan. Joseph from Germany: The Life of Pope Benedict XVI for Children. Craig, Charlie, illus. (p. 926)
Mohan, et al. Parties with Pizzazz: A Complete Resource for Holiday Classroom Parties. (p. 1325)
Mohanraj, Amirthi. Poet's Journey. (p. 1376)
Mohd Salleh, Muhammad Ashraf. Tubby the Tabby. (p. 1795)
Mohiuddin, Yasmeen Niaz. Pakistan: A Global Studies Handbook (p. 1319)
Mohler, Diana, jt. auth. see Turner, Deborah.
Mohler, Marie. Habit of Rabbits. (p. 734)
—Hearts of Trees. (p. 760)
—Knight & His Armored Heart. (p. 964)
—Leonard's Song. (p. 992)
—Little Bird's Earth Nest. (p. 1024)
—Swallow the Sun. (p. 1688)
Mohn, Eric A. Ocean Encounter. (p. 1276)
Mohr, Angie. Bookkeepers' Boot Camp: Get a Grip on Accounting Basics. (p. 212)
Mohr, Janet. Flight of Change. (p. 604)
Mohr, Janet & Howard, Adeline. Backyard Bird Book for Kids. (p. 131)
Mohr, Jay. Gasping for Airtime: Two Years in the Trenches of Saturday Night Live. (p. 657)
Mohr, Joseph. Silent Night, Holy Night Book & Advent Calendar. Dusikova, Maja, illus. (p. 1575)
Mohr, Kathryn. Real Beauty. Aryan, Kiana, illus. (p. 1448)
Mohr, L. C. Krumbuckets. Musheno, Erica, illus. (p. 968)
Mohr, Rowena. My Life & Other Catastrophes. (p. 1211)
Mohr, Tim, tr. see Herrndorf, Wolfgang.
Mohrbacher, Peter, illus. see Kingsley, Kaza.
Mohsenian, Javad. 9/11 Children. (p. 1993)
Moignot, Daniel. Animals Underground. (p. 84)
—Atlas of the Earth. (p. 113)
Moignot, Daniel, tr. see Bour-Chollet, Céline, et al.
Moignot, Daniel, et al. Atlas de la Tierra. Moignot, Daniel & Barroso, Paz, trs. (p. 112)
Moise, Nahomie, illus. see Fichthorn, Ashley.
Moiser, Liam. Moore Field School & the Mystery. (p. 1173)
Moisher, Phil. Long Before I Knew Better. (p. 1047)
Moix, Ana M. Miguelon. (p. 1141)
Moiz, Azra & Wu, Janice. Taiwan. (p. 1696)
Mojica, Barbara Ann. Little Miss History Travels to Mount Rushmore. Mojica, Victor Ramon, illus. (p. 1031)
Mojica, Victor Ramon, illus. see Mojica, Barbara Ann.
Mok, Kathy, tr. see Lei, Xu.
Mok, Kathy, tr. see Xu, Lei.
Mokhemar, Mary Ann. Just for Kids Interactive Auditory Processing Pictures Manual. (p. 938)
Mokhtari, Sophie. China Girl: A Daughter's Journey. (p. 306)
Mokona & Clamp Staff. Okimono Kimono. Mokona, illus. (p. 1282)
Mokosso, Henry Efesoa. Triplex Volume: Stories, Poems & Songs for Children. (p. 1787)
Mola, Astrid & Khakdan, Wahed. Good-Night Kiss. (p. 699)
Mola, Maria, illus. see Gellman, Ellie.
Molare, Syndey. Grandmama's Mojo Still Working. (p. 708)
Moldaw, Carol. Lightning Field. (p. 1016)
Moldovo, Eustacia. Baby Elephants at the Zoo. (p. 126)
—Baby Giraffes at the Zoo. (p. 126)
—Baby Lions at the Zoo. (p. 127)
—Baby Monkeys at the Zoo. (p. 127)
—Baby Pandas at the Zoo. (p. 127)
—Baby Zebras at the Zoo. (p. 128)
Mole, Gavin. Sing It & Say - Ancient Greece. (p. 1579)
Mole, Gavin, jt. auth. see Ridgley, Sara.
Molen, Ron. Bishop. (p. 193)
Molengraf, Jonathan Eric. Take Me to Your Leader. (p. 1696)
Molesworth. Cuckoo Clock. (p. 389)
—Rectory Children. (p. 1452)
—Tapestry Room: A Child's Romance. (p. 1705)
Molesworth, jt. auth. see Molesworth, Mary Louisa S.
Molesworth & Molesworth, Mary Louisa S. Cuckoo Clock. (p. 389)
—Grandmother Dear. (p. 709)
—Peterkin. (p. 1347)
—Rectory Children. (p. 1452)
—Robin Redbreast. (p. 1480)
—Rosy. (p. 1490)
—Tapestry Room. (p. 1705)
—Us. (p. 1826)
Molesworth, Mary Louisa. Carrots, Just a Little Boy. Oldham, Marion, illus. (p. 271)
—Cuckoo Clock. (p. 389)
—Rosy. (p. 1490)
Molesworth, Mary Louisa S. Us: An Old Fashioned Story. (p. 1826)
Molesworth, Mary Louisa S., jt. auth. see Molesworth.
Molesworth, Mary Louisa S., jt. auth. see Mrs Molesworth.
Molesworth, Mary Louisa S. & Molesworth. Grandmother Dear. (p. 709)
—Palace in the Garden. (p. 1319)
—Peterkin. (p. 1347)
—Rosy. (p. 1490)
Molière. Doctor in Spite of Himself. Landes, William-Alan, ed. (p. 459)
—Misanthrope. Wall, Charles H., tr. from FRE. (p. 1150)
—School for Wives. Landes, William-Alan, ed. (p. 1523)
Moliken, Paul, ed. see Hawthorne, Nathaniel.
Moliken, Paul, ed. see Shakespeare, William.
Moliken, Paul, ed. see Shelley, Mary & Shelley, Mary.
Moliken, Paul, ed. Adventures of Huckleberry Finn. (p. 18)
Molina, Adrian H., illus. see RH Disney Staff & Auerbach, Annie.
Molina, Angeles. Principe Que No Queria Ser Principe. (p. 1406)
—Sopa de Hortalizas. Ortiz, Nivea, illus. (p. 1613)
Molina, Jorge, illus. see Parker, Jeff, ed.
Molina, Jorge, illus. see Waid, Mark.
Molina Llorente, Pilar. Miguel Angel, El terrible florentino. (p. 1141)
Molina Llorente, Pilar, jt. auth. see Llorente, Pilar Molina.
Molina, M. Isabel. Arco Iris (The Rainbow) (p. 95)
Molina, Maria I. Conoce a Cristobal Colon: Get to Know Christopher Columbus. Mendoza, Isabel C., ed. (p. 358)
Molina, Maria Isabel. De Victoria para Alejandro. (p. 416)
—Senor del Cero. Sole, Francisco, illus. (p. 1550)
Molina, Ruben, jt. auth. see Molina, Violet S.
Molina, Silvia & Silvia, Molina. Comieron la Lengua los Ratones. Rodriguez, Mari, illus. (p. 348)
Molina Temboury, Pedro. No Encontrarás el Tibet en un Mapa. (p. 1258)
Molina, Violet S. & Molina, Ruben. Animals Can Do Nothing. (p. 82)
Molinari, Carlo, illus. see Harness, Cheryl.
Molinari, Carlo, illus. see Hughes, Langston.
Molinari, Carlo, illus. see Osborne, Mary Pope & Boyce, Natalie Pope.
Molinari, Carlo, illus. see Yomtov, Nel.
Molinari, Carlo, illus. see Yomtov, Nelson.
Molinari, Fernando, illus. see Benatar, Raquel.
Molinari, Fernando, illus. see Dahl, Michael.
Molinari, Fernando, illus. see Villacis, Alexandra.
Molinari, Fernando, illus. see Villacís, Alexandra.
Molinari, Laurice Elehwany. Ether: Vero Rising (p. 539)
—Pillars of Fire. (p. 1359)
Molinaro, Fernando, jt. auth. see Malam, John.
Moline, Karl, illus. see Allie, Scott, et al.
Moline, Karl, illus. see Bedard, Tony.
Molinet, Kelly, jt. auth. see Molinet, Michael.
Molinet, Michael & Molinet, Kelly. Before You Were Born. Molinet, Michael, illus. (p. 159)
—Just Like You. Molinet, Michael, illus. (p. 939)
Molino & AWAN, SHEILA. Mi Primer Libro Del Cuerpo Humano. (p. 1133)
Molins, Liliana. Bringing Baby Blue Bird Home. (p. 229)
Molinsky, Steven J. & Bliss, Bill. Word by Word Primary. (p. 1950)
Molitor, Sherrie, illus. see DoNascimento, Nicole.
Molitoris, Cathy. I've Got Music! McConnell, Sarah, illus. (p. 901)
Molk, Laurel. Eeny, Meeny, Miney, Mo, & Flo. Molk, Laurel, illus. (p. 505)
Molk, Laurel, illus. see Heiman, Diane & Suneby, Liz.
Molk, Laurel, illus. see Suneby, Liz & Heiman, Diane.
Moll, Amanda. Liam's Lost It. (p. 1004)
Molla, Jean. Sobibor. (p. 1603)
—Sobibor. McLean, Polly, tr. from FRE. (p. 1603)
Mollel, Tololwa. From the Lands of the Night McCalla, Darrell, illus. (p. 644)
Mollel, Tololwa M. Orphan Boy Morin, Paul, illus. (p. 1304)
Moller, Jonathan R. Bath Time: Picture Book. (p. 144)
Moller, Ray, photos by see Caudron, Chris & Childs, Caro.
Moller, Sharon Chickering. Jeep: The Coyote Who Flew in World War II. Cranford, Darren, illus. (p. 911)
Mollett, Irene, illus. see Williamson, Linda.
Mollis Lindquist, Melody Rose. Oak Tree. (p. 1274)
Molloy, Anne Stearns Baker. Captain Waymouth's Indians. Gorsline, Douglas, illus. (p. 264)
Molloy, Bonnie. Ms Flitter-Flutter. (p. 1188)
Molloy, Bonnie G. When the Rock Rocked... (p. 1905)
Molloy, J., illus. see Folliard, Kevin.
Molloy, Michael. Secreto de los Brujos. Alonso Blanco, Victoria, tr. (p. 1544)
Molloy, Michael, illus. see Molloy, Sheila.
Molloy, Sheila. Jack - King of the Dogs. Steed, Tobias, ed. (p. 902)
Molloy, Sophie, illus. see McCarthy, Margaret.
Molnar, Albert, illus. see Davis Jones, Melanie, et al.
Molnar, Albert, illus. see Jones, Melanie Davis.
Molnar, Cheri Eplin. Dee Diddly Dragon Is Not a Wimp. Gutwein, Gwendolyn, illus. (p. 422)
Molnar, Ferenc. Liliom. (p. 1017)
Molnár, Ferenc, jt. auth. see Molnar, Ferenc.
Molnar, Ferenc & Molnár, Ferenc. Muchachos de la Calle Pal. (p. 1188)
Molnar, Gwen. Hate Cell: A Casey Templeton Mystery. (p. 752)
—Old Bones: A Casey Templeton Mystery. (p. 1283)
Molnar, Haya Leah. Under a Red Sky: Memoir of a Childhood in Communist Romania. (p. 1813)
Molnar, Michael, jt. auth. see Green, Jen.
Molnar, Michael, jt. auth. see Morgan, Sally.
Molock, Anthony. Adventures of Cocoa Pelou: Cocoa Pelou Meets Alabama Black. (p. 17)
Molokie, Tom. Introducing Willy Mcspry. (p. 882)
Moloney, James. Black Taxi. (p. 197)
—Book of Lies. (p. 211)
—Doomsday. (p. 470)
—In the Lair of the Mountain Beast. (p. 866)
—Malig Tumora. (p. 1083)
—Tunnels of Ferdinand. (p. 1797)
Moloney, Kate, ed. see Laouénan, Christine.
Moloney, Kate, ed. see Pouilloux, David.
Moloney, Maria. Changeling Quest: Children of the Fae. (p. 290)
Molski, Carol. Bible Puzzlers. Koehler, Ed, illus. (p. 176)
—Bible Word Suduko. Koehler, Ed, illus. (p. 176)
—Life of Christ. (p. 1011)
—Swimming Sal. DePalma, Mary Newell, illus. (p. 1691)
Molter, Carey. -Ain As in Train. (p. 30)
—Ake As in Cake. (p. 32)
—Dime = 10 Cents. (p. 440)
—Dollar = $1.00. (p. 463)
—Eam As in Ice Cream. (p. 492)
—En As in Pen. (p. 522)
—Half-Dollar = 50 Cents. (p. 736)
—How Much Is $10. 00? (p. 811)
—How Much Is $1.00? (p. 811)
—How Much Is $100. 00? (p. 811)
—How Much Is $20. 00? (p. 811)
—How Much Is $5. 00? (p. 811)
—How Much Is $50.00? (p. 811)
—Ide As in Tide. (p. 852)
—Nickel = 5 Cents. (p. 1251)
—One As in Stone. (p. 1293)
—Oon As in Spoon. (p. 1298)
—Penny = 1 Cent. (p. 1338)
—Quarter= 25 cents. (p. 1422)
—Silent B As in Lamb. (p. 1575)
—Silent Gh As in Light. (p. 1575)
—Silent H As in Ghost. (p. 1575)
—Silent K As in Knot. (p. 1575)
—Silent L As in Chalk. (p. 1575)
—Silent W As in Wreath. (p. 1575)
Molter, Carey, jt. auth. see ABDO Publishing Company Staff.
Molter, Carey & ABDO Publishing Company Staff. Silent Letters. (p. 1575)
Moltgen, Ulrike, jt. auth. see Fanger, Rolf.
Molyneux, Caroline. 1940 Christmas. (p. 2002)
—Red for Stop. Green for Go. Yellow for Be Careful. (p. 1454)
Molzahn, Arlene Bourgeois. Airplanes. (p. 32)
—Christopher Columbus: Famous Explorer. (p. 316)
—Ferdinand Magellan: First Explorer Around the World. (p. 582)
—Henry Hudson: Explorer of the Hudson River. (p. 768)
—Hernan Cortes: Conquistador & Explorer. (p. 771)
—Lewis & Clark: American Explorers. (p. 1004)
—Ponce de Leon: Explorer of Florida. (p. 1382)
—Salle: Explorer of the Mississippi. (p. 1505)
—Ships & Boats. (p. 1567)
—Trucks & Big Rigs. (p. 1791)
—Vasco Nunez de Balboa: Explorer to the Pacific Ocean. (p. 1833)
Molzan, Janet & Lloyd, Sue. Manuel Phonique. (p. 1089)
Mom, jt. auth. see Spenser.
Mom, jt. auth. see Uncle, J.
Momaday, N. Scott. Four Arrows & Magpie: A Kiowa Story. Momaday, N. Scott, illus. (p. 624)
Momaday, N. Scott, illus. see Andrews, Lynn V.
Momatiuk, Yva. Face to Face with Penguins. Eastcott, John, photos by. (p. 560)
—Face to Face with Wild Horses. Eastcott, John, photos by. (p. 560)
Mombourquette, Paul, illus. see Lawson, Julie.
Mommaerts, Robb, illus. see Crane Johnson, Amy.
Mommaerts, Robb, illus. see Johnson, Amy Crane.
Momochi, Nozomi. Brigadoon (p. 228)
momodu, oshiomowe. Tales by Moonlight. (p. 1701)
Momokawa, Haruhiko, illus. see Ogiwara, Noriko & Noriko, Ogiwara.
Momose, Takeaki, illus. see Izubuchi, Yutaka.
Momperousse, Anthony. Ballon de mes Rêves. (p. 135)
Mon, Aunty. Braxton the Bull. (p. 224)
Mon, S. Aka - the Wonder Girl. (p. 32)
Mona, Erik, ed. see Cook, Hugh & Miéville, China.
Mona, Erik, ed. see Wilson, F. Paul & Brackett, Leigh.
Mona, Erik, jt. auth. see Gygax, Gary.
Mona, Larkins. Pablo's Art Adventures: Exploring the Studio. Mona, Larkins, illus. (p. 1317)
Monachino, Teresa. Words Fail Me. (p. 1951)
Monaco, Octavia, illus. see Capatti, Bérénice.
Monaco, Octavia, illus. see Lossani, Chiara & van Gogh, Vincent.
Monaco, Octavia, illus. see Lossani, Chiara.
Monaghan, Annabel. Double Digit. (p. 472)
—Girl Named Digit: Under Cover, under Pressure, under Estimated. (p. 678)
—Girl Named Digit: Undercover, under Pressure, & Underestimated. (p. 678)
Monaghan, Annabel & Wolfe, Elisabeth. Click! The Girl's Guide to Knowing What You Want & Making It Happen. (p. 331)
Monaghan, Jennifer. Illustrated Phonics Booklet. (p. 857)
Monaghan, Joseph. Boy Who Loved Trees. (p. 219)
Monaghan, Kimberly. Organic Crafts: 75 Earth-Friendly Art Activities. (p. 1303)
Monaghan, Patricia & Managhan, Patricia. Wild Girls: The Path of the Young Goddess. Forrester, Anne Marie, illus. (p. 1929)
Monaghan, Stephen, jt. auth. see Blackwood, Melissa.
Monahan, Erin. Arabian Horses (Caballos Árabes) Strictly Spanish Translation Services Staff, tr. from ENG. (p. 94)
—Palomino Horses (p. 1320)
—Ponis Shetland (Shetland Ponies) Strictly Spanish Translation Services Staff, tr. from ENG. (p. 1382)
—Shetland Ponies (p. 1566)
Monahan, Erin & O'Brien, Kim. Caballos/Horses. Strictly Spanish, LLC., tr. (p. 250)
Monahan, Hillary. Bloody Mary, Book 2 Mary: Unleashed. (p. 201)
—Mary: The Summoning. (p. 1100)
—Summoning. (p. 1675)
Monahan, Holly. Flip Wanders Off (p. 605)
Monahan, Jerome, ed. see Shakespeare, William.
Monahan, Joan. St. Therese of Lisieux: Missionary of Love. (p. 1638)
Monahan, Leo. Twelve Days of Christmas. Monahan, Leo, illus. (p. 1800)
Monahan, Ryan, jt. auth. see Merkel, Tara.
Monalisa, DeGross. Donavan's Word Jar. (p. 466)
Monari, Manuela. Zero Kisses for Me. Soumagnac, Virginie, illus. (p. 1986)
Monceaux, Morgan & Katcher, Ruth. My Heroes, My People: African Americans & Native Americans in Thewest. Monceaux, Morgan, illus. (p. 1211)
Monchamp, Genny. God Made Wonderful Me! Kaminski, Karol, illus. (p. 690)
—Historias de la Biblia para Los Pequenitos. Stott, Apryll, illus. (p. 782)
—Shine: Choices to Make God Smile. Kaminski, Karol, illus. (p. 1566)
Monckeberg, Paulina. Artilugia 2006 - Diary for Crushes & Craziness: Of Aldanza Della Calabrezza. (p. 104)
—Artilugia 2006 Portuguese. (p. 104)
—Artilugia 2007 English. (p. 104)
—Artilugia Agenda: Diario de Amores y Locuras. (p. 104)
—Artilugia English 2008. (p. 104)

—Artilugia Spanish 2008. (p. 104)
—Pascualina 2005 Portuguese. (p. 1326)
—Pascualina 2006. (p. 1326)
—Pascualina 2006 Portuguese. (p. 1326)
—Pascualina English 2008. (p. 1326)
—Rosamunda Della Calabazza 2006: The Youngest & Most Dangerous Sister of Pascualina. Agenda & Stationary 2006 (p. 1489)
Monckeberg, Paulina, jt. auth. see Calabazza, Della.
Moncomble, Gerard & Arinouchkine, Andrei. Nine Lives of the Cat. (p. 1256)
Moncomble, Gerard & Van den Dries, Sidonie. Half & Half-A Doctor for the Animals. Fortier, Natali & Brenier, Claire, illus. (p. 736)
Moncue, Steve. Fish Police Volume 1. (p. 598)
Moncure, Jane Belk. Apes Find Shapes: A Book about Recognizing Shapes. Ronney, Ronnie, illus. (p. 91)
—Away Went the Farmer's Hat: A Book about an Adventure. Regan, Dana, illus. (p. 120)
—Bears Upstairs: A Book of Creative Dramatics. Girouard, Patrick, illus. (p. 152)
—Biggest Snowball of All: A Book about Sizes. Rooney, Ronnie, illus. (p. 185)
—Butterfly Express: A Book about Life Cycles. Billin-Frye, Paige, illus. (p. 247)
—Color Clown Comes to Town: A Book about Recognizing Colors. Girouard, Patrick, illus. (p. 342)
—Dragon in a Wagon: A Book about Ways to Travel. Regan, Dana, illus. (p. 477)
—Here We Go 'Round the Year: A Book about the Months. Billin-Frye, Paige, illus. (p. 771)
—Hop-Skip-Jump-a-Roo Zoo: A Book about Imitating. Girouard, Patrick, illus. (p. 796)
—How Many Ways Can You Cut a Pie? A Book about Math. Rooney, Ronnie, illus. (p. 811)
—Ice Cream Cows & Mitten Sheep: A Book about Farm Animals. Billin-Frye, Paige, illus. (p. 850)
—Little Too-Tall: A Book about Friendship. DeSantis, Susan, illus. (p. 1037)
—Magic Moon Machine: A Counting Adventure. Rooney, Ronnie, illus. (p. 1072)
—Mousekin's Special Day: A Book about Special Days. Gallagher-Cole, Mernie, illus. (p. 1182)
—Mr. Doodle Had a Poodle: A Book about Fun Activities. Regan, Dana, illus. (p. 1184)
—My "a" Sound Box. Thornburgh, Rebecca, illus. (p. 1195)
—My "b" Sound Box. Thornburgh, Rebecca, illus. (p. 1196)
—My "c" Sound Box. Thornburgh, Rebecca, illus. (p. 1200)
—My "d" Sound Box. Thornburgh, Rebecca, illus. (p. 1200)
—My 'e' Sound Box. Thornburgh, Rebecca, illus. (p. 1202)
—My "f" Sound Box. Thornburgh, Rebecca, illus. (p. 1202)
—My 'g' Sound Box. Thornburgh, Rebecca, illus. (p. 1209)
—My 'h' Sound Box. Thornburgh, Rebecca, illus. (p. 1210)
—My "i" Sound Box. Thornburgh, Rebecca, illus. (p. 1211)
—My 'j' Sound Box. Thornburgh, Rebecca, illus. (p. 1211)
—My "k" Sound Box. Thornburgh, Rebecca, illus. (p. 1211)
—My "l" Sound Box. Thornburgh, Rebecca, illus. (p. 1211)
—My 'm' Sound Box. Thornburgh, Rebecca, illus. (p. 1213)
—My "n" Sound Box. Thornburgh, Rebecca, illus. (p. 1215)
—My 'o' Sound Box. Thornburgh, Rebecca, illus. (p. 1216)
—My 'p' Sound Box. Thornburgh, Rebecca, illus. (p. 1216)
—My 'q' Sound Box. Thornburgh, Rebecca, illus. (p. 1217)
—My "r" Sound Box. Thornburgh, Rebecca, illus. (p. 1217)
—My 's' Sound Box. Thornburgh, Rebecca, illus. (p. 1218)
—My 't' Sound Box. Thornburgh, Rebecca, illus. (p. 1219)
—My "u" Sound Box. Thornburgh, Rebecca, illus. (p. 1220)
—My 'v' Sound Box. Thornburgh, Rebecca, illus. (p. 1220)
—My "w" Sound Box. Thornburgh, Rebecca, illus. (p. 1221)
—My "xyz" Sound Box. Thornburgh, Rebecca, illus. (p. 1222)
—Nanny Goat's Boat: A Book of Rhyming. Girouard, Patrick, illus. (p. 1229)
—One Tricky Monkey up on Top: A Counting Adventure. Rooney, Ronnie, illus. (p. 1297)
—Pocketful of Pets: A Search-and-Count Adventure. Billin-Frye, Paige, illus. (p. 1375)
—Polka-Dot Puppy: A Just-for-Fun Book. Regan, Dana, illus. (p. 1381)
—Rabbits' Habits: A Book about Good Habits. DeSantis, Susan, illus. (p. 1430)
—'Smile,' Says Little Crocodile: A Book about Good Habits. DeSantis, Susan, illus. (p. 1594)
—What Can We Play Today? A Book about Community Helpers. Gallagher-Cole, Mernie, illus. (p. 1881)
—What Do You Do with a Grumpy Kangaroo? A Book about Feelings. Gallagher-Cole, Mernie, illus. (p. 1883)
—What Do You Say When a Monkey Acts This Way? A Book about Manners. Gallagher-Cole, Mernie, illus. (p. 1883)
—Where Is Baby Bear? A Book about Animal Homes. Billin-Frye, Paige, illus. (p. 1908)
—Wish-For Dinosaur: A Just-for-Fun Book. Regan, Dana, illus. (p. 1940)
—Yes, No, Little Hippo: A Book about Safety. DeSantis, Susan, illus. (p. 1970)
Monda, Joseph, creator. Unnaturals. (p. 1822)
Mondalto, Diane. Have You Ever Wished. (p. 754)
Monde, Mathew. Integrated Science for Zambia Basic Education Grade 1 Pupil's Book. (p. 879)
Monde, Mathews. Integrated Science for Zambia Basic Education Grade 2 Pupil's Book. (p. 879)
Mondesir-Prescott, Sherley. If Your Shoes Could Speak. (p. 855)
Mondor, Lyne, tr. see Walker, Niki & Kalman, Bobbie.
Mondragon, Manny, illus. see Chinn, Jacqueline.
Mondragon, Philip. Going Beyond. (p. 692)
Monds, Pirkko. Thanks Series Edition: Therapeutic Healing & Nurturing Kid's Stories. (p. 1725)
Mondschein, Kenneth C. Communications, the Arts, & Computers. (p. 349)
—Construction & Trades. (p. 359)
Mondschein, Kenneth C., jt. auth. see Matters, Print.
Mondzac, Myra. Rheingold. (p. 1467)
Mone, Gregory. Dangerous Waters: An Adventure on Titanic. (p. 404)
—Fish. (p. 598)
Moneer, Simi. Once upon a Time: Part (1) (p. 1293)
Monelli, Marta, illus. see Axe-Bronk, Susan.
Mones, Isidre, illus. see Barrett, Judi.
Mones, Isidre, illus. see Disney Staff & Posner-Sanchez, Andrea.
Mones, Isidre, illus. see Gerber, Carole.
Mones, Isidre, illus. see RH Disney Staff & Posner-Sanchez, Andrea.
Mones, Isidre, illus. see Rylant, Cynthia.
Mones, Isidre, jt. auth. see Rylant, Cynthia.
Mones, Marc, illus. see Daniel, Claire.
Mones, Marc, illus. see Garcia, Ellen.
Mones, Marc, illus. see Giachetti, Julia.
Mones, Marc, illus. see Greve, Meg.
Mones, Marc, illus. see Linde, Barbara M.
Mones, Marc, illus. see Mckenzie, Precioius.
Mones, Marc, illus. see Mckenzie, Precious.
Mones, Marc, illus. see Reed, Jennifer.
Mones, Marc, illus. see Robertson, J. Jean.
Mones, Marc, illus. see Robertson, Jean.
Mones, Marc, illus. see Williams, Dinah.
Monescillo, Maria, illus. see Bridges, Shirin Yim.
Monescillo, Maria, illus. see Lucado, Max.
Monescillo, Maria, illus. see Manushkin, Fran.
Monescillo, Maria, jt. auth. see Wolfe, Myra.
Monet, Claude, jt. auth. see Connolly, Sean.
Monet, Claude, jt. auth. see Danneberg, Julie.
Monet, Claude, jt. auth. see Rodriguez, Susan.
Monet, Claude & Noble, Marty. Colorier Vos Propres Tableaux de Monet. (p. 344)
Monet, Rae, et al. Secrets Volume 24 Surrender to Seduction - the Secrets Collection: The Best in Women's Erotic Romance: Surrender to Seduction (p. 1546)
Moneta. Journey to the Money Tree. (p. 929)
Monette, Roz. Alex & the Enderson Brothers: Book One Andressen, Mark, illus. (p. 35)
Money, Greg, illus. see Morrissey, Lynda I.
Money, Mo. Little Sister. (p. 1036)
Moneymaker, Janet, illus. see Keller, Rebecca W.
Moneysmith, David, illus. see Repkin, Mark.
Monge, Marlyn & Wolfe, Jaymie Stuart. Jorge de Argentina: Historia Del Papa Francisco para Ninos. (p. 925)
—Jorge from Argentina: The Story of Pope Francis for Children. Kizlauskas, Diana, illus. (p. 926)
Monge, Nieves. Adventures of Three Raccoons Raised by a Human Mother. (p. 24)
Mongeau, Marc, illus. see Barcelo, François.
Mongeau, Marc, illus. see Brenna, Beverley.
Mongeau, Marc, illus. see Cotter, Charis.
Mongeau, Marc, illus. see Heidbreder, Robert.
Mongeau, Marc, illus. see Miles, Victoria.
Monger, J. W. H (Jim), jt. auth. see Mathews, Bill.
Mongillo, John F. & Mongillo, Peter A. Teen Guides to Environmental Science (p. 1713)
Mongillo, Michael. Philistine: Anthology/Chronology Zittel, Michael, illus. (p. 1350)
Mongillo, Peter A., jt. auth. see Mongillo, John F.
Mongiovi, Jorge, illus. see Orme, David.
Mongiovi, Jorge, illus. see Orme, Helen.
Mongredien, Sue. Be My Valentine. (p. 148)
—Harry & the Monster. East, Nick, illus. (p. 750)
—Oliver Moon & the Broomstick Battle. (p. 1285)
—Oliver Moon & the Dragon Disaster. (p. 1285)
—Oliver Moon & the Monster Mystery. (p. 1285)
—Oliver Moon & the Nipperbat Nightmare. (p. 1285)
—Oliver Moon & the Spell Off. (p. 1285)
—Oliver Moon's Fangtastic Sleepover. (p. 1285)
—Star Girls. (p. 1640)
—Tigers Love to Say Goodnight. Braun, Sebastien, illus. (p. 1749)
Mongredien, Sue, see Moss, Alexandra, pseud.
Mongtomery Gibson, Jane. Don't Renege! It's Just an Egg! Mongtomery Gibson, Jane, illus. (p. 468)
—In Olden Days. Mongtomery Gibson, Jane, illus. (p. 864)
—Jesus' Bread. Mongtomery Gibson, Jane, illus. (p. 915)
—My Heart Goes with You. Mongtomery Gibson, Jane, illus. (p. 1211)
Mongtomgery Gibson, Jane. Angels Long. Mongtomgery Gibson, Jane, illus. (p. 75)
Monhollon, Lake Pylant. Eagle Rock: The Memoirs of a Little Girl, 1941-1945. Brock, George Ann, illus. (p. 492)
Monica, Brufton, illus. see Maude, Tony.
Monica, Carol. Elmo's Easy as 1 2 3. (p. 515)
Monica, Carol & Mathieu, Joe. Elmo's Favorite Places. (p. 515)
Monica, Monica L. Freckles Goes to Grand Cayman Island. (p. 632)
Monical, Olivia R. Forest of Thinks. Monical, Olivia R., illus. (p. 618)
Monick, Susie, illus. see Fite, Ramona.
Monier, Eric M., ed. How Life on Earth Is Affected by Earth's Unique Placement & Orientation in Our Solar System: An Anthology of Current Thought. (p. 810)
Monigold, Jason, jt. auth. see Plantain Press.
Monin, Luke & Family. Bow Wow Bones: How I Got My Dogs. (p. 216)
Moniot, Janet. Silbatos de Arcilla: ... la Voz del Barro. (p. 1575)
Monir, Alexandra. Timekeeper. (p. 1754)
—Timeless. (p. 1754)
Moniz & Miller, R. T. Welding Skills. (p. 1874)
Moniz, B. J. Metallurgy: Answer Key. (p. 1130)
—Metallurgy. (p. 1130)
Moniz, B. J. & Miller, R. T. Welding Skills: Answer Key. (p. 1874)
—Welding Skills: Resource Guide. (p. 1874)
Moniz, Michael. Boy & the Whale. (p. 217)
—Cardinal & the Crow. Moniz, Michael, illus. (p. 266)
—My Little Superhero. (p. 1213)
—Tristan: The Changeling Prince (Book 2) (p. 1787)
—Wazzyjump. (p. 1865)
—Whalemaster. (p. 1877)
Moniz, Teresa, jt. auth. see Stockwell-Moniz, Marc.
Monk, Carol & O'Connor, Ruth. Walking Adventures of Ruthie & Coco. (p. 1854)
Monk, Geraldine. Selected Poems. (p. 1549)
Monk, Isabell. Family. Porter, Janice Lee, illus. (p. 568)
Monk, L. Scott. Choose Health. (p. 310)
Monk, Linda R. Words We Live By: Your Annotated Guide to the Constitution. (p. 1952)
Monk, Scott. Crush. (p. 386)
—Raw. (p. 1441)
Monkey Girl Staff. Jay Travels to the U S A. (p. 910)
Monkey, Micah, illus. see Schroeder, Abraham.
Monkeys, J. Dixie & Taco: Dixie & Taco go to the Zoo: Enfield CT Version. Vol. 2 Muzak, Warren, illus. (p. 455)
—Dixie & Taco Go to Grandmother's House. Muzak, Warren, illus. (p. 455)
—Dixie & Taco Go to the Zoo. Muzak, Warren, illus. (p. 455)
Monkman, Olga. Dos Perros y una Abuela. Calderon, Marcela, illus. (p. 472)
—Lo Que Cuentan los Inuit. (p. 1044)
—Rey sin Corona. Sanchez, Javier G., illus. (p. 1467)
Monkman, William Kent, illus. see King, Thomas.
Monks, Barbara. Thank You Weasel Abbs! (p. 1725)
Monks, Christian, illus. see May, Gary L.
Monks, Julie. Let's Read! Marcello Mouse & the Masked Ball (p. 1000)
—Marcello Mouse & the Masked Ball Monks, Julie, illus. (p. 1091)
Monks, Lydia. Aaaarrgghh! Spider! (p. 2)
—Aaaarrgghh, Spider! (p. 2)
—Mungo Monkey Has a Birthday Party. (p. 1191)
Monks, Lydia, illus. see Agnew, Kate.
Monks, Lydia, illus. see Bergman, Mara.
Monks, Lydia, illus. see Donaldson, Julia.
Monks, Lydia, illus. see Duffy, Carol Ann.
Monks, Lydia, illus. see McCombie, Karen.
Monks, Lydia, illus. see Rees, Gwyneth.
Monks, Lydia, illus. see Turner, James.
Monks, Lydia, illus. see Wilcox, Leah.
Monlongo, Jorge, illus. see Kimmelman, Leslie.
Monlongo, Jorge, illus. see Turner, James.
Monlongo, Jorge, jt. auth. see Chabot, Jacob.
Monlongo, Jorge & Chabot, Jacob. Hello Kitty: Just Imagine. Monlongo, Jorge, illus. (p. 764)
Monn, Margaret A. Cause I Live Here. Monn, Margaret A., illus. (p. 282)
Monnar, Alberto. Girl & the Mirror. Weiner, Linda, ed. (p. 678)
Monnar, Alexander. Annoying Alex. Pileggi, Steven, illus. (p. 87)
Monnar, Ana. Heart of Stone. Michaud, Nancy, illus. (p. 759)
Monnette, Kayla, illus. see Monnette, Kimberly.
Monnette, Kimberly. I Wish, I Wish. Monnette, Kimberly & Monnette, Kayla, illus. (p. 849)
Monnig, Alex. Aikido. (p. 30)
—Albert Pujols: Groundbreaking Slugger. (p. 34)
—Arizona Cardinals. (p. 98)
—Arkansas Razorbacks. (p. 99)
—Atlanta Falcons. (p. 112)
—Carolina Panthers. (p. 270)
—Drag Racing. (p. 476)
—Eli Manning: Super Bowl Hero. (p. 512)
—Florida State Seminoles. (p. 607)
—Girls' Soccer. (p. 680)
—Motocross Racing. (p. 1179)
—Nebraska Cornhuskers. (p. 1239)
—New Orleans Saints. (p. 1246)
—North Carolina Tar Heels. (p. 1265)
—Oklahoma Sooners. (p. 1283)
—Roy Halladay: Superstar Pitcher. (p. 1492)
—San Francisco 49ers. (p. 1510)
—San Francisco Giants. (p. 1510)
—Seattle Seahawks. (p. 1539)
—St. Louis Rams. (p. 1638)
—Tampa Bay Buccaneers. (p. 1704)
—Texas Rangers. (p. 1724)
—Tim Tebow: Quarterback Sensation. (p. 1750)
—World Cup. (p. 1954)
Monnin, Sheena. Discover Your Destiny. (p. 448)
Monninger, Joseph. Breakdown. (p. 224)
—Cave-In. (p. 282)
—Crash. (p. 376)
—Finding Somewhere. (p. 588)
—Flood. (p. 605)
—Stay Alive #1: Crash. (p. 1645)
—Stay Alive #3: Breakdown. (p. 1645)
—Stay Alive #4: Flood. (p. 1645)
—Whippoorwill. (p. 1912)
—Wish. (p. 1940)
Monopoly Media Marketing, des. Not for women only! My life in Poem. (p. 1267)
Monrad, Ditlev, et al. Statistics: Concepts & Methods. (p. 1644)
Monreal, Jeannie. What Will I Be? Asked Little Miss Christina Magee. (p. 1895)
Monreal, Violeta, illus. see Osorio, Marta.
Monreal, Violeta & Violeta, Monreal. Mio, Mio! el Huevo Es Mio. (p. 1148)
Monro, Rona, jt. auth. see O'Donnell, Mabel.
Monroe, Andrea. Science of Tools. (p. 1527)
Monroe, Ayshia. Kiki: Doin' It (p. 955)
—Mamyke: The Fake Date. (p. 1096)
—Mamyke - The Fake Date. (p. 1096)
—Nishell: Tempted. (p. 1257)
—Nishell; Tempted (p. 1257)
—Sherise: Stalked (p. 1565)
—Tia: Diva. (p. 1746)
—Tia; Diva (p. 1746)
Monroe, Caleb. Ice Age Paroline, Shelli & Lamb, Branden, illus. (p. 850)
Monroe, Caleb & Lamb, Branden. Ice Age: Past, Presents, & Future! Paroline, Shelli, illus. (p. 850)
Monroe, Caleb & Paroline, Shelli. Hidden Treasure Paroline, Shelli & Lamb, Branden, illus. (p. 776)
Monroe, Chris. Bug on a Bike. Monroe, Chris, illus. (p. 236)
—Cookie, the Walker. (p. 361)
—Monkey with a Tool Belt. Monroe, Chris, illus. (p. 1165)
—Monkey with a Tool Belt & the Noisy Problem. Monroe, Chris, illus. (p. 1165)
—Monkey with a Tool Belt & the Seaside Shenanigans. Monroe, Chris, illus. (p. 1165)
—Sneaky Sheep. Monroe, Chris, illus. (p. 1597)
Monroe, Chris, illus. see Kling, Kevin.
Monroe, Chris, illus. see Yolen, Jane.
Monroe, Colleen. Is for Ark: Noah's Journey. Monroe, Michael Glenn, illus. (p. 889)
—Wish to Be a Christmas Tree. Monroe, Michael Glenn, illus. (p. 1940)
—Wonders of Nature Sketchbook: Learn about Nature & How to Draw It. Monroe, Michael Glenn, illus. (p. 1948)
Monroe, Dan, illus. see Burwick, Josh.
Monroe, Daniel, illus. see Eleniak, Erika.
Monroe, Darrell. Sammy Sunflower. (p. 1508)
Monroe Donovan, Jane. Winter's Gift. Monroe Donovan, Jane, illus. (p. 1938)
Monroe Donovan, Jane, illus. see Brennan-Nelson, Denise.
Monroe Donovan, Jane, illus. see Crane, Carol.
Monroe, Ella. Secrets & Lies: A Capital Girls Novel. (p. 1544)
—Truth or Dare. (p. 1794)
Monroe, George. Secret Cave on the Hill. (p. 1540)
Monroe, Gregory. It's Chili & I Don't Like It! (p. 896)
Monroe, Guy. Bird's Day at Yaquina Head. Monroe, Karol, ed. (p. 191)
Monroe, Jean Guard, jt. auth. see Williamson, Ray A.
Monroe, Joan Kiddell, illus. see Patchett, Mary Elwyn.
Monroe, Judith W. Gypsy Chickens Alphabet. Montague, Ruth, illus. (p. 734)
Monroe, Judy. Coping with Ulcers, Heartburn & Stress-Related Stomach Disorders. (p. 365)
—Day in the Life of a Librarian (p. 413)
—Duke Ellington: Jazz Composer (p. 489)
—Northwest Indians: Daily Life in The 1700s (p. 1266)
—Steroids, Sports, & Body Image: The Risks of Performance-Enhancing Drugs. (p. 1649)
—Thurgood Marshall: Civil Rights Champion. (p. 1746)
Monroe, Judy, jt. auth. see Way, Jennifer L.
Monroe, Karol, ed. see Monroe, Guy.
Monroe, Mary. Milagro en la Escuela Monty. (p. 1142)
Monroe, Mary A. Tagger: Graffiti Was His Life - & Soul. (p. 1695)
Monroe, Mary Alice. Butterfly Called Hope Bergwerf, Barbara J., illus. (p. 247)
—Turtle Summer: A Journal for My Daughter Bergwerf, Barbara J., illus. (p. 1798)
Monroe, Michael Glenn, illus. see Brennan, Martin.
Monroe, Michael Glenn, illus. see Brennan-Nelson, Denise & Brennan-Nelson, Dense.
Monroe, Michael Glenn, illus. see Brennan-Nelson, Denise.
Monroe, Michael Glenn, illus. see Crane, Carol.
Monroe, Michael Glenn, illus. see Hershenhorn, Esther.
Monroe, Michael Glenn, illus. see Monroe, Colleen.
Monroe, Michael Glenn, illus. see Schonberg, Marcia.
Monroe, Michael Glenn, illus. see Wargin, Kathy-jo.
Monroe Peterson, Judy. Sickle Cell Anemia. (p. 1572)
—Smart Strategies for Investing Wisely & Successfully. (p. 1593)
—Trout Fishing. (p. 1790)
—Truth about Barbiturates. (p. 1794)
—Walleye Fishing. (p. 1855)
Monroe, Ron. What Are Electrical Circuits? (p. 1879)
—What Is Electricity? (p. 1889)
Monroe, Sue & Sif, Birgitta. Magnificent Moon Hare & the Foul Treasure. (p. 1076)
Monroe, Tilda. What Do You Know about Atoms & Molecules? (p. 1883)
—What Do You Know about Electricity? (p. 1883)
—What Do You Know about Forces & Motion? (p. 1883)
—What Do You Know about Light? (p. 1883)
—What Do You Know about States of Matter? (p. 1883)
Monroe, Tyler. American Flag. (p. 60)
—Bald Eagle. (p. 133)
—Pledge of Allegiance. (p. 1373)
—Star-Spangled Banner. (p. 1641)
—Statue of Liberty. (p. 1645)
—U. S. Symbols. (p. 1807)
—Uncle Sam (p. 1812)
Monroy, B. Cristo Pobre y Crucificado de Francisco de Asis. (p. 383)
Monroy, Eva. Little Mountain. (p. 1032)
Monroy, Manuel, illus. see Amado, Elisa.
Monroy, Manuel, illus. see Chacek, Karen.
Monroy, Manuel, illus. see Delano, Poli.
Monroy, Manuel, illus. see Luján, Jorge Elias.
Monroy, Manuel, illus. see Luján, Jorge.
Monsell, Mary Elise. Fish Named Yum: MR. PIN. Vol. IV (p. 598)
—Mr Pin: The Chocolate Files. (p. 1186)
—Mysterious Cases of Mr. Pin (p. 1223)
—Spy Who Came North from the Pole. (p. 1636)
—Underwear! Munsinger, Lynn, illus. (p. 1817)
Monserud, Gary L. Law of Liquidated Damages in Massachusetts. (p. 981)
Monsho, Seikaino & Yoshinaga, Aya. Seikai Trilogy - Crest of the Stars (p. 1548)
Monsivais, Maria Estela, tr. see Lachtman, Ofelia Dumas.
Monson, Christy & Nawyn, Lori. Love, Hugs, & Hope: When Scary Things Happen. (p. 1059)
Monson, Lois. God Is for Every Day(r) - Horse Dreams: Teach-a-Child Companion Book/DVD Set. Monson, Lois, photos by. (p. 689)
—God Is for Every Day(r) - Horse Dreams: Teach-A-Child Companion Book with VCD JoySoul Corporation, illus. (p. 689)
Monson, Marianne. Enchanted Tunnel: Journey to Jerusalem. Vol. 3 Burr, Dan, illus. (p. 523)
—Enchanted Tunnel: Wandering in the Wilderness. Vol. 4 Burr, Dan, illus. (p. 523)
—Escape from Egypt. (p. 535)
—Pioneer Puzzle. (p. 1361)
Monson, Thomas S. One Little Match. Burr, Dan, illus. (p. 1295)
Monstrata, Nessi. Monster High Diaries: Draculaura & the New Stepmonster. (p. 1167)
Mont, Eve Marie. Phantom Enchantment. (p. 1349)
Montag, Aileen. All I Ever Wanted to Be. (p. 44)
Montag, Emily. Coral Reefs. (p. 366)

Montagna, Frank, illus. see Harrison, Emma.
Montague, Brad, jt. auth. see Novak, Robby.
Montague, Chester. Timmy's Vacation. (p. 1755)
Montague, Christine, illus. see Sithole, Thelma.
Montague, Gay & Wise, Erin. Peace Is a Bright Delight. (p. 1331)
Montague, Marjorie & Jitendra, Asha K., eds. Teaching Mathematics to Middle School Students with Learning Difficulties. (p. 1710)
Montague, Ruth, illus. see Monroe, Judith W.
Montague-Smith, Ann. Adding (p. 11)
—Adding & Subtracting Book Two (p. 11)
—Counting Book 1. (p. 370)
—Dividing (p. 454)
—Measuring. (p. 1117)
—Multiplying (p. 1190)
—Numbers. (p. 1272)
—Sizes & Shapes. (p. 1583)
—Subtracting (p. 1671)
—Using Numbers. (p. 1828)
—Using Numbers Book One (p. 1828)
Montague-Smith, Ann, jt. auth. see Harrison, Paul.
Montague-Smith, Ann & Harrison, Paul. Extension for All Through Problem Solving. (p. 555)
Montaie, Vanskie. From Crackhouse to Churchhouse. (p. 642)
—Speak the Word. (p. 1622)
Montaini-Klovdahl, Luisa, illus. see Leventhal-Belfer, Laurie.
Montalbano, Andrea. Breakaway. (p. 224)
—Lily Out of Bounds. (p. 1018)
Montalbano, Julie Williams. Smart Girl's Guide: Middle School. (p. 1592)
Montaldo, Stuart. Cogno: The Alien Adventure Game. (p. 338)
—Cogno: the Alien Legends: Synapse. (p. 338)
Montaldo, Stuart, creator. Cogno: Deep Worlds. (p. 338)
Montale, Eugenio. Selected Poems. Young, David et al, trs. from ITA. (p. 1549)
Montalto, Luisa, illus. see Jakubowski, Michele.
Montalvo, Daniel, et al. Cultura política de la democracia en Ecuador 2008: El impacto de la Gobernabilidad. (p. 390)
Montalvo, Rodolfo, illus. see DeWitt, Fowler.
Montalvo-Lagos, Tomas, illus. see Ballantine Books Staff & Cartoon Network Staff.
Montana, Brenda. Jamie & Lacy & the Adventures of the White Chihuahuas Book. (p. 907)
Montana, Francisco, tr. see Tolstoy, Leo.
Montana, Hannah. Live from London. (p. 1040)
Montana, Jack. Marines. (p. 1094)
—Navy SEALs. (p. 1238)
—Parachute Regiment. (p. 1323)
—Urban Warfare. (p. 1825)
Montañá, Marta, illus. see Bailer, Darice & Dominguez, Madelca.
Montana, Scarlett. Lunch with a Blue Kitty. Montana, Scarlett, illus. (p. 1065)
Montanari, Donata. Children Around the World. Montanari, Donata, illus. (p. 302)
Montanari, Eva. Chasing Degas. (p. 294)
—Go-Cart Number 1. (p. 686)
—Princess Matilda. (p. 1404)
Montanari, Eva, illus. see Griffith, Victoria.
Montanari, Eva, illus. see Nobisso, Josephine.
Montaner, Carlos Alberto. Latinoamericanos y la Cultura Occidental. (p. 979)
Montanha. Brazilian Jiu-Jitsu Mind Set: To Submit Your Opponent from Any Position ! (p. 224)
—Techniques of Brazilian Jiu-Jitsu. (p. 1711)
Montano, Josie. Chicken Pox. . . Yuck! (p. 300)
—Pop Starlets. (p. 1384)
Montardre, Hélène. Cat & the Dog. (p. 277)
—Little Cats. (p. 1026)
—Little Wolves. Castle, Muriel, tr. from FRE. (p. 1038)
—Night & Day. (p. 1252)
Monte, Diane E. Coming Home: Welcome Home at Last. (p. 348)
Montecalvo, Jane. Sammy C-Gull. (p. 1507)
—Sammy C-Gull: Second Adventure. (p. 1508)
Montecalvo, Janet, illus. see De Anda, Diane.
Montecalvo, Janet, illus. see Grant, Karima.
Montefiore, Jan. Feminism & Poetry: Language, Experience, Identity in Women's Writing. (p. 581)
Montefiore, Jan, ed. see Kipling, Rudyard.
Monteiro, Francelina. Star That Couldn't Shine. (p. 1641)
Montejo, Andrea, tr. see De La Hoya, Oscar.
Montejo, Eugenio. Trees: Selected Poems, 1967-2004. Boyle, Peter, tr. from SPA. (p. 1784)
Montejo, Victor. Blanca Flor: Una Princessa Maya Yockteng, Rafael, illus. (p. 198)
—Popol Vuh: A Sacred Book of the Maya Unger, David, tr. from SPA. (p. 1384)
Montejo, Victor, tr. see Ortiz, Simon J. & Lacapa, Michael.
montell, alicia. Our Friend Oso. (p. 1308)
Montelongo, Monica. Adventures of Roxy & Mozart. (p. 22)
Montemayor, Jerry & Montemayor, Sherry. From Sin to Serenity: My Father's Story. (p. 643)
Montemayor, Sherry, jt. auth. see Montemayor, Jerry.
Montero Galan, Daniel, illus. see Gil, Carmen & Gil Martinez, Carmen.
Montero, Jose Perez. Seek & Find in the Bible. (p. 1548)
Montero, Jose Perez, illus. see De Graaf, Anne.
Montero, Jose Perez, illus. see Dickens, Charles & De Graaf, Anne.
Montero, Jose Perez, illus. see Mortensen, Carl Anker.
Montero, Mayra. Viaje a Isla de Mona. Torres, Walter, illus. (p. 1839)
Montero, Miguel, illus. see Ronnholm, Ursula O.
Monterroso, Augusto. Obras Completas y Otros Cuentos. (p. 1275)
Montes de Oca, Gonzalo, illus. see Roque-Velasco, Ismael.
Montes, Gerardo David. My Grandmother's Tortillas. (p. 1210)
Montes Gonzalo, Juan Mari, jt. auth. see Montes, Juan Mari.
Montes, Graciela. Cuentos del Sapo. (p. 390)
—Federico Dice No. (p. 580)
—Federico Se Hizo Pis. (p. 580)
—Habia una Vez una Casa. Rojas, Saul Oscar, illus. (p. 734)
—Habia una Vez una Llave. Isol, illus. (p. 734)
—Habia una Vez una Nube. Legnazzi, Claudia, illus. (p. 734)
—Habia una Vez una Princesa. Torres, Elena, illus. (p. 734)
Montes, Graciela, jt. auth. see Montes, Graciela.
Montes, Graciela & Montes, Graciela. Valentin Se Parece A... Gusti, illus. (p. 1830)
Montes, Hugo & Montes, Michelle. Young Eagles Armor Academy: Fear of Flying, V01. (p. 1978)
—Young Eagles Armor Academy: Caught in the Storm, V02. (p. 1978)
—Young Eagles Armor Academy: The Whispering Cave, V03. (p. 1978)
—Young Eagles Armor Academy Box Set: Volumes 1 - 3. (p. 1978)
Montes, Juan Mari & Montes Gonzalo, Juan Mari. Diario del Autobus a de la Linea 3. Fra, Irene, illus. (p. 434)
Montes, Keoni, illus. see Germain, Kerry.
Montes, Marisa. Crazy Mixed-Up Spanglish Day. Cepeda, Joe, illus. (p. 377)
—Gatos Black on Halloween. (p. 658)
—Gatos Black on Halloween. Morales, Yuyi, illus. (p. 658)
—Get Ready for Gabi: All in the Familia. No. 5 Cepeda, Joe, illus. (p. 668)
—Juan Bobo Busca Trabajo. Cepeda, Joe, illus. (p. 930)
Montes, Michelle, jt. auth. see Montes, Hugo.
Montesinos Anzures, Luis. Tecolote. (p. 1712)
Montessori ADvantage, des. Addition Wokbook. (p. 12)
Monteverde, Matt. Baseball in the American League East Division. (p. 141)
—Frequently Asked Questions about Budgeting & Money Management. (p. 636)
Monteverde, Matthew. American Presence in Iraq: Winning the Peace. (p. 62)
—America's Presence in Iraq: Winning the Peace. (p. 64)
—Baseball in the American League East Division. (p. 141)
—Frequently Asked Questions about Budgeting & Money Management. (p. 636)
—Giants vs. Cowboys. (p. 674)
—Michigan vs. Ohio State. (p. 1135)
—Notre Dame vs. USC. (p. 1268)
Montez, Michele, illus. see Javna, John, et al.
Montgomary, Beverly. Mommy where Is Heaven. (p. 1162)
—Mommy Why Don't I Look Good in the Mirror. (p. 1162)
Montgomerie, Adrienne. Ghost Ships. (p. 671)
Montgomerie, Adrienne, jt. auth. see Crabtree Publishing Company Staff.
Montgomerie, Claire. Knitters Yarn Palette. (p. 965)
Montgomerie, Genevieve, illus. see Vagner, Bohdanka.
Montgomery, Alesia K., jt. auth. see Buddenberg, Laura J.
Montgomery, Anne. I Spy. (p. 846)
—Nature Made. (p. 1236)
—Solid or Liquid? (p. 1607)
—Tell Me about It. (p. 1716)
Montgomery, Anson. Dragon Day. (p. 477)
—Escape from the Haunted Warehouse. (p. 535)
—Golden Path: Into the Hollow Earth (p. 695)
—Moon Quest. Semionov, Vladimir, illus. (p. 1172)
—Paying the Ferryman. (p. 1331)
—Search for the Dragon Queen. (p. 1537)
—Your Grandparents Are Spies. (p. 1980)
Montgomery, Arch. Hank. (p. 742)
—Jake. (p. 905)
Montgomery, Benjamin. Who Is God? (p. 1915)
Montgomery, Claire & Montgomery, Monte. Hubert Invents the Wheel. Shelly, Jeff, illus. (p. 824)
Montgomery, Corey. Ask Grandma Pearl. (p. 106)
Montgomery, E. J. Hailey Walker & the Mystery of the Absent Professor. (p. 735)
Montgomery Gibson, Jane. Claire, Claire! Wash Your Hair! Montgomery Gibson, Jane, illus. (p. 326)
—Daddy's Valentine. Montgomery Gibson, Jane, illus. (p. 399)
—Go Find Christmas. Montgomery Gibson, Jane, illus. (p. 686)
—God's Little Boy. Montgomery Gibson, Jane, illus. (p. 691)
—God's Little Girl. Montgomery Gibson, Jane, illus. (p. 691)
—Gracie Got Glasses. Montgomery Gibson, Jane, illus. (p. 705)
—Hey, You Birds! Montgomery Gibson, Jane, illus. (p. 775)
—How Do You Clean a Ballerina? Montgomery Gibson, Jane, illus. (p. 808)
—I Touched Jesus Today. Montgomery Gibson, Jane, illus. (p. 847)
—I'll Tell You in Heaven. Montgomery Gibson, Jane, illus. (p. 856)
—Inner Soul. Montgomery Gibson, Jane, illus. (p. 875)
—Jake the Fake Snake. Montgomery Gibson, Jane, illus. (p. 906)
—Jesus Is! Montgomery Gibson, Jane, illus. (p. 915)
—Jesus Loves Me. Montgomery Gibson, Jane, illus. (p. 915)
—Jesus Smith or Jones. Montgomery Gibson, Jane, illus. (p. 916)
—Keeper of Lost & Found. Montgomery Gibson, Jane, illus. (p. 947)
—Little Bit Gone. Montgomery Gibson, Jane, illus. (p. 1024)
—Mabel at the Table. Montgomery Gibson, Jane, illus. (p. 1067)
—Maggie Makeup. Montgomery Gibson, Jane, illus. (p. 1071)
—Maker of Prayer. Montgomery Gibson, Jane, illus. (p. 1080)
—Mama's Wings. Montgomery Gibson, Jane, illus. (p. 1084)
—Measure My Heart. Montgomery Gibson, Jane, illus. (p. 1117)
—My Christmas Friend. Montgomery Gibson, Jane, illus. (p. 1200)
—Oh Forsooth! I've Lost a Tooth! Montgomery Gibson, Jane, illus. (p. 1280)
—Pink Potatoes. Montgomery Gibson, Jane, illus. (p. 1360)
—Shiny Pants. Montgomery Gibson, Jane, illus. (p. 1567)
—Sit down, Clown! Montgomery Gibson, Jane, illus. (p. 1581)
—Through Jesus Eyes. Montgomery Gibson, Jane, illus. (p. 1745)
Montgomery, Heather. Wild Discoveries: Wacky New Animals. (p. 1929)
Montgomery, Heather L. Case of the Missing Arctic Fox & Other True Animal Mysteries for You to Solve (p. 274)
—Garter Snakes (p. 657)
—How Is Soil Made? (p. 810)
—How to Survive an Earthquake (p. 821)
—Kingsnakes (p. 961)
—Mummies: Truth & Rumors. Doty, Eldon, illus. (p. 1190)
—Rattlesnakes (p. 1440)
—Unsolved Mysteries of Nature. (p. 1822)
—Why Do My Teeth Fall Out? And Other Questions Kids Have about the Human Body Davis, Jon, illus. (p. 1924)
Montgomery, Janice. Inside Stories: Study Guides for Children's Literature. Bk. 1 (p. 877)
—Inside Stories: Study Guides for Children's Literature. Bk. 2 (p. 877)
—Inside Stories: Study Guides for Children's Literature. Bk. 4 (p. 877)
—Inside Stories: Study Guides for Children's Literature. Vol. 5 (p. 877)
Montgomery, Jason, illus. see Wilkes, Irene.
Montgomery, Karen & Ollerhead, Sue. English for Zambia Basic Education Grade 6 Pupil's Book. (p. 530)
Montgomery, Karen, et al. English Matters Grade 4 Learner's Pack. (p. 530)
Montgomery, Kate' A. End Your Carpal Tunnel Pain Without Surgery. (p. 526)
—Hand Health: The Artistic Ritual for the Artist & Musician. (p. 740)
Montgomery, Kelly. Go Wild! Wildlife Designs to Color. (p. 687)
Montgomery, Kelly & Creative Haven Staff. Sea Life Designs Coloring Book. (p. 1534)
Montgomery, L. M. Akin to Anne: Tales of Other Orphans. (p. 32)
—Along the Shore: Tales by the Sea. (p. 48)
—Ana la de Alamos Ventosos. Fantín de Bellocq, Constanza, tr. (p. 66)
—Ana la de Avonlea. García Díaz, José, tr. (p. 66)
—Ana la de Ingleside. (p. 66)
—Ana la de Isla. (p. 66)
—Ana la de Tejas Verdes. García Díaz, José, tr. (p. 66)
—Ana y la Casa de Sus Sueños. (p. 66)
—Anne of Avonlea. (p. 86)
—Anne of Avonlea. Andreasen, Dan, illus. (p. 86)
—Anne of Avonlea. McKowen, Scott, illus. (p. 86)
—Anne of Green Gables. (p. 86)
—Anne of Green Gables. Fiona Fox Staff, ed. (p. 86)
—Anne of Green Gables. Corvino, Lucy, illus. (p. 86)
—Anne of Green Gables. Devereux, Cecily, ed. (p. 86)
—Anne of Green Gables. McKowen, Scott, illus. (p. 86)
—Anne of Green Gables. Rubio, Mary Henley & Waterston, Elizabeth, eds. (p. 86)
—Anne of Green Gables Collection: Six Complete & Unabridged Novels in One Volume. (p. 86)
—Anne of Green Gables Cookbook. (p. 86)
—Anne of Green Gables Diary. (p. 86)
—Anne of the Green Gables. (p. 86)
—Anne of the Island. (p. 86)
—Anne's House of Dreams. (p. 86)
—Blue Castle. (p. 202)
—Doctor's Sweetheart. (p. 459)
—Emily Climbs: Emily of New Moon Series. (p. 518)
—Emily Climbs. (p. 518)
—Emily of New Moon. (p. 519)
—Emily's Quest: Emily of New Moon Series. (p. 519)
—Emily's Quest. (p. 519)
—Further Chronicles of Avonlea. (p. 650)
—Golden Road. (p. 695)
—Jane of Lantern Hill. (p. 908)
—Kilmeny of the Orchard. (p. 956)
—Magic for Marigold. (p. 1072)
—Mistress Pat: From the Author of Anne of Green Gables. (p. 1155)
—Pat of Silver Bush. (p. 1327)
—Rainbow Valley. (p. 1436)
—Rilla of Ingleside. (p. 1472)
—Rilla of Ingleside. (p. 1473)
—Story Girl. (p. 1657)
—Tangled Web. (p. 1705)
Montgomery, L. M., jt. auth. see Kessler, Deirdre.
Montgomery, L. M. & Pearson Education Staff. Anne of Green Gables. (p. 86)
Montgomery, Lee, illus. see Davidson, Susanna & Unwin, Mike.
Montgomery, Lee, illus. see Firth, Rachel.
Montgomery, Lee, illus. see Hawcock, David.
Montgomery, Lee, jt. auth. see Hawcock, David.
Montgomery, Lewis B. #7 the Case of the Purple Pool. Wummer, Amy, illus. (p. 1993)
—Case of the Amazing Zelda. Wummer, Amy, illus. (p. 273)
—Case of the Buried Bones. Wummer, Amy, illus. (p. 273)
—Case of the Crooked Campaign. Wummer, Amy, illus. (p. 274)
—Case of the Diamonds in the Desk. Wummer, Amy, illus. (p. 274)
—Case of the Haunted Haunted House Wummer, Amy, illus. (p. 274)
—Case of the Haunted Haunted House. Wummer, Amy, illus. (p. 274)
—Case of the July 4th Jinx. (p. 274)
—Case of the July 4th Jinx. Wummer, Amy, illus. (p. 274)
—Case of the Locked Box. Wummer, Amy, illus. (p. 274)
—Case of the Missing Moose. Wummer, Amy, illus. (p. 274)
—Case of the Poisoned Pig. Wummer, Amy, illus. (p. 275)
—Case of the Poisoned Pig. Montgomery, Lewis B., illus. (p. 275)
—Case of the Purple Pool. Wummer, Amy, illus. (p. 275)
—Case of the Stinky Socks. Wummer, Amy, illus. (p. 275)
—Case of the Superstar Scam. Wummer, Amy, illus. (p. 275)
Montgomery, Margaret. Adventures of Anna Banana Shoeshine: Anna Banana Takes a Bath. (p. 16)
Montgomery, Martha, jt. auth. see Howell, Mark.
Montgomery, Mary Sue. Cloud Is a Cloud Is a What? You've got to be Kidding (p. 334)
Montgomery, Michael, illus. see Ashby, Ruth.
Montgomery, Michael, illus. see Posey, Lee.
Montgomery, Michael G., illus. see Hart, Alison.
Montgomery, Michael G., illus. see Reiss, Mike.
Montgomery, Michael G., illus. see Van Steenwyk, Elizabeth.
Montgomery, Monte. Kid Confidential: An Insider's Guide to Grown-Ups. Storms, Patricia, illus. (p. 951)
Montgomery, Monte, jt. auth. see Montgomery, Claire.
Montgomery, Mykah. Little Girl Who Wanted a Tail. (p. 1028)
Montgomery, R. A. Abominable Snowman Peguy, Laurence, illus. (p. 5)
—Abominable Snowman. (p. 5)
—Always Picked Last. (p. 51)
—Behind the Wheel. (p. 160)
—Beyond Escape. (p. 174)
—Blood on the Handle. (p. 200)
—Brilliant Dr. Wogan. (p. 228)
—Chinese Dragons. Semionov, Vladimir, illus. (p. 307)
—Choose Your Own Adventure 4 Book Boxed Set #3: Lost on the Amazon; Prisoner of the Ant People; Trouble on Planet Earth; War with the Evil Power Master. (p. 310)
—Choose Your Own Adventure 6 Book Boxed Set #2: Race Forever; Escape, Lost on the Amazon; Prisoner of the Ant People; Trouble on Planet Earth; War with the Evil Power Master (p. 310)
—Dragonlark Bind Up-#02. (p. 478)
—Escape. (p. 534)
—Fire! (p. 590)
—House of Danger. (p. 803)
—Island of Time. Louie, Wes & Cannella, Marco, illus. (p. 892)
—Journey under the Sea. (p. 929)
—Journey under the Sea. Montgomery, R. A. & Thongmoon, Kriangsak, illus. (p. 929)
—Lost Dog! (p. 1055)
—Lost Jewels of Nabooti. (p. 1056)
—Lost on the Amazon. (p. 1056)
—Monsters of the Deep. (p. 1169)
—Owl Tree. (p. 1315)
—Prisoner of the Ant People. (p. 1407)
—Project UFO. Semionov, Vladimir & Cannella, Marco, illus. (p. 1410)
—Punishment: Earth. (p. 1417)
—Race Forever. (p. 1431)
—Return to Atlantis. (p. 1465)
—Return to Haunted House. (p. 1465)
—Sand Castle. Newton, Keith, illus. (p. 1510)
—Smoke Jumpers. Peguy, Laurence, illus. (p. 1594)
—Track Star! (p. 1775)
—Trail of Lost Time. (p. 1776)
—Trouble on Planet Earth. (p. 1790)
—War with the Evil Power Master. (p. 1858)
—Your Grandparents Are Zombies! (p. 1980)
—Your Very Own Robot Goes Cuckoo Bananas. (p. 1981)
Montgomery, Ramsey. U. N. Adventure: Mission to Molowa. (p. 1805)
Montgomery, Richard. Pechuck. (p. 1334)
Montgomery, Robert. Gary Carter's Iron Mask: Home Run! (p. 657)
Montgomery, Robert, ed. see Harrison, Winston E.
Montgomery, Rutherford G. Capture of the Golden Stallion. (p. 265)
—Golden Stallion's Victory. (p. 695)
Montgomery, Samantha, illus. see Lujan Ed.D., Nan.
Montgomery, Sharon, text. Your Invisible Bodies: A Reference Book for Children & Adults about Human Energy Fields. (p. 1980)
Montgomery, Sy. Chasing Cheetahs: The Race to Save Africa's Fastest Cats. Bishop, Nic, illus. (p. 294)
—Great White Shark Scientist. (p. 719)
—Kakapo Rescue: Saving the World's Strangest Parrot. Bishop, Nic, illus. (p. 941)
—Man-Eating Tigers of Sundarbans. Briggs, Eleanor, photos by. (p. 1085)
—Octopus Scientists. Ellenbogen, Keith, illus. (p. 1278)
—Quest for the Tree Kangaroo: An Expedition to the Cloud Forest of New Guinea. Bishop, Nic, photos by. (p. 1426)
—Saving the Ghost of the Mountain: An Expedition among Snow Leopards in Mongolia. Bishop, Nic, illus. (p. 1517)
—Snowball: The Dancing Cockatoo. Oksner, Judith, illus. (p. 1600)
—Tarantula Scientist. Bishop, Nic, photos by. (p. 1706)
—Temple Grandin: How the Girl Who Loved Cows Embraced Autism & Changed the World (p. 1718)
Montgomery, Sy & Bishop, Nic. Saving the Ghost of the Mountain: An Expedition among Snow Leopards in Mongolia. (p. 1517)
—Tapir Scientist: Saving South America's Largest Mammal. (p. 1705)
Montgomery, Sy & Grandin, Temple. Temple Grandin: How the Girl Who Loved Cows Embraced Autism & Changed the World. (p. 1718)
Montgomery, Tamara, jt. auth. see Belknap, Jodi P.
Montgomery, Tamara & Belknap, Jodi. TiQri the Little Snow Fox. (p. 1757)
Montgomery, Violet, illus. see Murphy, Eileen.
Montgomery-Higham, Amanda. Max & the Doglins. (p. 1110)
Montgomery-Higham, Amanda, illus. see Peters, Andrew.
Montgomery-Higham, Amanda, tr. see Peters, Andrew.
Montgomery-Ilori, Iris. Little Iris's First Day of School. (p. 1029)
Montgormary, Beverly. In Deep Thought. (p. 863)
Monthel, Betty. Looking for Normal. (p. 1051)
Monti, Carmelo, illus. see Miller, M.
Monti, Joe, ed. see Le Guin, Ursula K., et al.
Monti, Joe, jt. ed. see Buckell, Tobias S.
Monticone, Ann, jt. auth. see Sleator, William.
Montiel, Joaquin Londaiz, et al. Hormigosaurios/The Antosaurus. (p. 798)
Montijo, Rhode. Chews Your Destiny. (p. 299)
—Cloud Boy. Montijo, Rhode, illus. (p. 334)
—Cloud Boy/Nino Nube. Mlawer, Teresa, tr. from ENG. (p. 334)
—Halloween Kid. Montijo, Rhode, illus. (p. 738)
Montijo, Rhode, illus. see Preciado, Tony.
Montijo, Rhode, illus. see Trine, Greg.
Montileaux, Donald F., illus. see Baum, L. Frank.

Montillo, Roseanne, jt. auth. see Matters, Print.
Montinar, Roldimy. Succeed Financially & Be Debt Free. (p. 1671)
Montmeat, Jack, illus. see Neff, Fred.
Montoya, Carina Monica. Let's Cook Adobo! Silva, Eliseo Art, illus. (p. 995)
Montoya, Jeremy, illus. see Garcia, Nasario.
Montoya, Jerry, jt. illus. see Randles, Slim.
Montoya, Louis R. Camilla. (p. 256)
Montoya, Martha, creator. Cenando con el Monstruo: Take-Home. (p. 286)
—Huevos o Pollitos: Take-Home. (p. 824)
—Mi heroe Favorito: Take-Home. (p. 1132)
—No, no a la Biblioteca! Take-Home. (p. 1259)
Montoya, Robin Michelle, illus. see Weller, Sadie Bedoka.
Montoya-Read, Rosalee, jt. auth. see Martinez, Demetria.
Montparker, Carol. Polly & the Piano. (p. 1381)
Montpellier, Paul, illus. see Barber-Starkey, Joe.
Montreuil, Gaetane. Leelo. Goodway, Simon, illus. (p. 987)
Montroll, John. Batman Origami: Amazing Folding Projects for the Dark Knight. Ku, Min Sung, illus. (p. 144)
—DC Origami. Ku, Min Sung, illus. (p. 415)
—DC Super Heroes Origami: 46 Folding Projects for Batman, Superman, Wonder Woman, & More! Ku, Min Sung, illus. (p. 416)
—Dollar Bill Origami. (p. 463)
—Justice League Origami: Amazing Folding Projects for the JLA. Ku, Min Sung, illus. (p. 940)
—Superman Origami: Amazing Folding Projects for the Man of Steel. Ku, Min Sung, illus. (p. 1683)
—Wonder Woman Origami: Amazing Folding Projects for the Warrior Princess. Ku, Min Sung, illus. (p. 1947)
Montross, Doug, illus. see Schroedel, Jenny.
Montserrat, Del Amo. Mao Tiang Pelos Tiesos. (p. 1089)
Montserrat, Pep. Aladdin & the Magic Lamp/(Aladino y la Lampara Maravillosa) (p. 33)
Montserrat, Pep, illus. see Chronicle Books Staff.
Montserrat, Pep, illus. see Kimmel, Eric A.
Montserrat, Pep, illus. see Ros, Roser.
Montserratt, Pep, illus. see Sierra i Fabra, Jordi.
Monvel, Maurice Boutet De, see Boutet de Monvel, Maurice.
Moodey, Mary. Christopher Counts the Constellation Shingle, Jude, illus. (p. 317)
Moodie, Fiona. Noko's Surprise Party. (p. 1263)
Moodie, Fiona, jt. auth. see Rode, Linda.
Moodley, Ermila. Path to My African Eyes. (p. 1328)
Moody, Cynthia. Dream, the Big Elephant. (p. 484)
Moody, D. L. Children's Stories. (p. 304)
—President Lincoln Listened: A Story of Compassion. Bond, Bob, illus. (p. 1397)
Moody, Gloria. Two Beautiful Butterflies. Doering, Kimber, illus. (p. 1803)
Moody, Jason, illus. see Powers, Emily.
Moody, Julie, illus. see Hansen, Eric.
Moody, Julie, illus. see Henson, Andora.
Moody, Julie, illus. see Sama, Kent.
Moody Publishing Staff, jt. auth. see Moore, Stephanie Perry.
Moody Publishing Staff & Lawton, Wendy G. Freedom's Pen: A Story Based on the Life of Freed Slave & Author Phillis Wheatley (p. 635)
Moody, Ralph. American Horses. O'Keeffe, Neil, illus. (p. 61)
—Geronimo: Wolf of the Warpath. (p. 667)
—Kit Carson & the Wild Frontier. Galli, Stanley W., illus. (p. 962)
—Riders of the Pony Express. Riger, Bob, illus. (p. 1471)
—Wells Fargo. Mays, Victor, illus. (p. 1874)
Moody, Rick. Black Veil: A Memoir with Digressions. (p. 197)
Moody, Rick, jt. ed. see Norman, Howard.
Moody, Sylvia. Dyslexia. (p. 491)
Moody, William B. Eureka Math Moments. (p. 540)
Moody-Luther, Jacqueline. Panda Bear Cub. Nelson, Will, illus. (p. 1320)
Moody-Luther, Jacqui. Word World Cow. (p. 1951)
—Word World Dog. (p. 1951)
—Word World Frog. (p. 1951)
Moog, Bob. Do I Bug You? A Who Am I? Book. San Francisco School, illus. (p. 457)
—Do You Sudoku? Spicy: Over 200 Puzzles for Experienced Sudoku Solvers. (p. 458)
—I-Ballers: Little Books for Big Minds. (p. 834)
—Made You Laugh for Kids: Truth or Dare! (p. 1070)
—More 30 Second Mysteries. (p. 1173)
—Spinner Books: Two-Book Set. (p. 1628)
—Spinner Books for Kids 20-Copy Counter Display. (p. 1628)
—Spinner Books: the Grateful Dead. (p. 1628)
Moog, Bob, jt. auth. see Griffiths-Jones, Sam.
Moog, Carol, jt. auth. see McHenry, Irene.
Moog, Richard S., et al. Physical Chemistry: A Guided Inquiry - Atoms, Molecules & Spectroscopy. (p. 1353)
Moog, Richard Samuel, et al. Complete Solutions Manual: Used with ... Moog-Physical Chemistry: A Guided Inquiry: Atoms, Molecules, & Spectroscopy. (p. 353)
Moog, Robert. Spinner Books Junior: Totally Gross. (p. 1628)
—Spinner Books Junior: 20 Questions for Kids. (p. 1628)
—Spinner Books Junior: Kids Battle the Grown-Ups. (p. 1628)
—Spinner Books Junior: 30 Second Mysteries for Kids. (p. 1628)
Mookeeo. Dolphin's View: Transformation. Bk. 1 (p. 465)
—Dolphin's View: The Impossible Dream. Bk. 2 (p. 465)
—Dolphin's View: Hannibal Invades Washington. Bk. 3 (p. 465)
Moolenaar Bernier, Ashley-Ruth. Sand, Sea & Poetry. Fundora, Yolanda V., illus. (p. 1510)
Moolenschot, Catherine. Rough Road. (p. 1491)
Moon, Adam. Fuzzle. (p. 651)
Moon, Alan R. & Borg, Richard. Dragon Hordes: Warrior's Expansion 1. (p. 477)
—Warriors: It's Monsters, Myth, & Mayhem! (p. 1859)
Moon, Alice. Lucky's Special Thanksgiving. (p. 1063)
Moon, Catherine R. & Everette, Maureen C. Adventures of NanaCat & Her Children: Moving In. Richardson, Kara, illus. (p. 21)
—Adventures of NanaCat & Her Children: Someone New. Richardson, Kara, illus. (p. 21)
Moon, Cliff, ed. see Bishop, Nic & Hughes, Jon.
Moon, Cliff, ed. see Carter, James.
Moon, Cliff, ed. see Clarke, Jane.
Moon, Cliff, ed. see Collins Educational Staff & Hughes, Monica.
Moon, Cliff, ed. see Collins Educational Staff, et al.
Moon, Cliff, ed. see Cooling, Wendy.
Moon, Cliff, ed. see Freeman, Maggie & Murray, Pat.
Moon, Cliff, ed. see Hughes, Mónica.
Moon, Cliff, ed. see Newman, Lee.
Moon, Cliff, ed. see Owen, Anna.
Moon, Cliff, ed. see Rayner, Shoo.
Moon, Cliff, ed. see Scott, Johnathan & Scott, Angela.
Moon, Cliff, ed. see Shipton, Paul.
Moon, Cliff, ed. Collins Big Cat - Slumbery Stumble in the Jungle: Orange/Band 06. (p. 340)
Moon, Emily Kate. Joone. (p. 925)
Moon, Fabio. Ursula. Pinto, Joan De Sola & Pinto, Guilherme, trs. (p. 1826)
Moon, Harold K. Ghost Coach. (p. 670)
Moon, Jo. Buggy Buddies. (p. 236)
—Counting. (p. 370)
—In the Pond. (p. 867)
—Making Letters. (p. 1081)
—Making Numbers. (p. 1082)
—My First Buggy Buddy - Noises. (p. 1206)
—Noises. (p. 1262)
—Under the Sea. (p. 1814)
Moon, Jo, illus. see Butler, Roberta.
Moon, Jo, illus. see Munro, Fiona & Phillipson, Fiona.
Moon, Jonny. Beach Buoy. (p. 149)
—Dog's Dinner. (p. 462)
—Elephant's Trump. (p. 512)
—Nit Picker. (p. 1257)
—Sewers Crisis. (p. 1555)
—Verruca Bazooka. (p. 1837)
Moon, Josephine. Tale of the Lucky Cat. Seki, Sunny, illus. (p. 1700)
Moon, Jung Who, illus. see Ryu, Ki Woon.
Moon, Keri & Fischer, Rita. Balduin. (p. 134)
Moon, Nicola. Margarine & Marbles. (p. 1092)
Moon, Paul, illus. see King, Carrie.
Moon, Poppy. Kicky's Friendship Card Game. (p. 951)
Moon, Poppy, illus. see Nass, Marcia.
Moon, Susan, jt. auth. see Worthington, Lisa.
Moon, Tabitha. Hoppin' Snake. (p. 797)
Moon, Young Sook. Across the Tumen: A North Korean Kkotjebi Boy's Quest. (p. 9)
Moonah, Karen. Spring into Summer! - Fall into Winter! (p. 1635)
Moonbot & Joyce, William. Mischievians. Moonbot & Joyce, William, illus. (p. 1150)
Moonchild, Karen Davies. Moon Dreams. (p. 1172)
Moone, Colin. Wonderful Adventures of the Magicians: The One Bad Apple. (p. 1948)
Mooney, Alyssa, illus. see Velasquez, Maria.
Mooney, Annabelle. Rhetoric of Religious Cults: Terms of Use & Abuse. (p. 1467)
Mooney, Bel. Mr. Tubs Is Lost. (p. 1186)
—Mr. Tubs Is Lost! Chamberlain, Margaret, illus. (p. 1186)
—Who Loves Mr Tubs? Hellard, Susan, illus. (p. 1916)
Mooney, Belinda. Itty-Bitty Book: New Testament. (p. 900)
—Itty-Bitty Book: Old Testament. (p. 900)
Mooney, Bill, jt. auth. see Holt, David.
Mooney, Bill, jt. ed. see Holt, David.
Mooney, Brian. Great Leaders. (p. 717)
Mooney, Carla. Amazing Africa Projects. Stems, Megan, illus. (p. 52)
—Asante Samuel. (p. 105)
—Awesome Military Robots. (p. 121)
—Becoming Invisible: From Camouflage to Cloaks. (p. 156)
—Biodiversity. (p. 188)
—Bomb Disposal: Diffusing Danger. (p. 208)
—Brain: Journey Through the Universe Inside Your Head. Casteel, Tom, illus. (p. 221)
—Bullying. (p. 241)
—Climate & Weather. (p. 332)
—Cool Careers Without College for People Who Love Music. (p. 363)
—Creators & Cast of Glee. (p. 380)
—Dragons. (p. 478)
—Duke Basketball. (p. 489)
—Earthquakes. (p. 497)
—Explore Rivers & Ponds! With 25 Great Projects. Stone, Bryan, illus. (p. 550)
—Explorers of the New World: Discover the Golden Age of Exploration with 22 Projects. Casteel, Tom, illus. (p. 551)
—Fema: Prepare, Respond, & Recover. (p. 581)
—Forensics: Uncover the Science & Technology of Crime Scene Investigation. Carbaugh, Samuel, illus. (p. 617)
—Forest Surprise Harpster, Steve, illus. (p. 618)
—Genetics: Breaking the Code of Your DNA. Carbaugh, Samuel, illus. (p. 661)
—George Washington: 25 Great Projects You Can Build Yourself. Carbaugh, Samuel, illus. (p. 664)
—Get All Tied Up: Tying Knots. (p. 667)
—Healthy Weight Loss for Teens. (p. 759)
—How the Internet Is Changing Society. (p. 813)
—Industrial Revolution: Investigate How Science & Technology Changed the World with 25 Projects. Vaughn, Jenn, illus. (p. 872)
—Isaac Newton: Genius Mathematician & Physicist. (p. 890)
—It's Electric! Currents. (p. 896)
—Junk Food Junkies. (p. 936)
—Light Your Way: Make a Candle. (p. 1015)
—Medical Technology & Engineering. (p. 1119)
mooney, carla. Mental Illness Research. (p. 1126)
Mooney, Carla. More Than the Blues: Understanding Depression (p. 1175)
—Music & Video Streaming. (p. 1193)
—Nebraska Football. (p. 1239)
—Ninjas. (p. 1256)
—Oil Spills & Offshore Drilling. (p. 1282)
mooney, carla. Online Predators. (p. 1298)
Mooney, Carla. Online Privacy & Business. (p. 1298)
—Online Privacy & Social Media. (p. 1298)
mooney, carla. Online Security. (p. 1298)
Mooney, Carla. Online Social Networking. (p. 1298)
—Pilotless Planes. (p. 1359)
—Recycling. (p. 1453)
—Remarkable Military Animals. (p. 1459)
—Rocketry: Investigate the Science & Technology of Rockets & Ballistics. Denham, Caitlin, illus. (p. 1483)
—Skydiving. (p. 1587)
—Standardized Testing. (p. 1639)
—Starting a Business: Have Fun & Make Money. (p. 1644)
—STEM Jobs in Fashion & Beauty. (p. 1647)
—STEM Jobs in Movies. (p. 1647)
—Stephen Hillenburg SpongeBob SquarePants: SpongeBob SquarePants. (p. 1648)
—Sun Screen for Plants. (p. 1676)
—Surviving in Cold Places. (p. 1687)
—Surviving in Wild Waters. (p. 1687)
mooney, carla. Teen Violence. (p. 1714)
Mooney, Carla. Tennis. (p. 1720)
—Thinking Critically: Distracted Driving. (p. 1734)
—Understanding Credit. (p. 1815)
—Vanessa Hudgens. (p. 1833)
—Vanessa Hudgens/Carla Mooney. (p. 1833)
—What Are Minerals? (p. 1879)
—What Is Anxiety Disorder? (p. 1889)
—What Is Panic Disorder? (p. 1890)
mooney, carla. What Is the Future of Biofuels? (p. 1890)
—What Is the Future of Hydrogen Power? (p. 1890)
Mooney, Carla. Your Legal Rights Regarding Misdemeanor Prosecution (p. 1981)
Mooney, Carla & Currie-McGhee, Leanne K. Bioethics. (p. 188)
Mooney, Carla & Gale Editors. Jonas Brothers. (p. 925)
Mooney, Carla & Stearns, Megan. Amazing Africa Projects. (p. 52)
Mooney, Carla, ed. African Americans in Sports. (p. 27)
Mooney, Dean J. M., jt. auth. see Shortle, Stacy.
Mooney, Ginger. Grandmother Rabbit's Old Red Hat. (p. 709)
—Spirit Elk. (p. 1628)
Mooney, Jim, illus. see Conway, Gerry & Lee, Stan.
Mooney, Jim, illus. see David, Peter.
Mooney, Maggie, jt. auth. see Benjamin, Michelle.
Mooney, Melissa Duke & Print Mafia Staff. ABCs of Rock. (p. 4)
Mooney, Ms Olive. Chronicles of Cadaver College: Book of Omis. (p. 317)
Mooney, Silk Waters. Puka the Moose. (p. 1415)
Mooney, Sinead. Samuel Beckett. (p. 1509)
Mooney, Sinead, jt. auth. see Elam, Keir.
Mooney, Stephen. Half Past Danger. (p. 736)
MOONEY, Tara. Big Blue Bus. (p. 178)
Mooney, Tara. Tot Island. (p. 1771)
Moonjar, ed. Conversations to Go - Money. (p. 361)
—Moonjar Moneybox Classic. (p. 1172)
—Noom & Raj Start Business. (p. 1264)
Moonlight Publishing Ltd Staff & Allaire, Caroline. Let's Look at the Garden. (p. 999)
Moonlight Publishing Ltd Staff, et al. Let's Look at the Pond. Sautai, Raoul, illus. (p. 999)
MoonRattles. Heritage Holiday Activity Guide: Mid Autumn Festival. (p. 771)
—Heritage Holiday Activity Guide: Seventh Lunar Month. (p. 771)
—Heritage Holiday Activity Guide: Chinese New Year 2007 (p. 771)
MoonRattles, compiled by. Heritage Holiday Activity Guide: Dragon Boat Festival. (p. 771)
Moonshower, Candie. Legend of Zoey. (p. 989)
—Vivian Vande Velde: Author of Fantasy Fiction. (p. 1846)
Moor, Becka, illus. see MacLaine, James.
Moor, Evan. Daily Reading Comprenesion, Grade 8. (p. 400)
Moorash, Marc. Romanti-Goth A to Z Coloring Book. (p. 1486)
Moorby, Tony. Ollie the Alien. (p. 1287)
Moorcroft, Christine, jt. auth. see Barker, Ray.
Moor-Doucette, Saba. Dinosaurs & Donuts. Noon, Connie & Zraick, Robert, illus. (p. 444)
Moore, A. C. Always Room for Dessert. (p. 51)
Moore, Aisha. Daughter of the Game II. (p. 409)
Moore, Alan. Another Suburban Romance. (p. 88)
—Promethea Gray, M., illus. (p. 1411)
—Stories of Alan Moore. (p. 1654)
—Voice of the Fire. (p. 1848)
—Watchmen. (p. 1862)
Moore, Alan & Baker, Bill. Alan Moore on His Work & Career. (p. 33)
Moore, Alan & Gray, Mick. Promethea. (p. 1411)
Moore, Alan & Moore, Steve. Tom Strong's Terrific Tales (p. 1763)
Moore, Alan & Tavner, Gill. Jesus of Nazareth. Donnelly, Karen, illus. (p. 916)
—Judas Iscariot. Donnelly, Karen, illus. (p. 930)
—Mary Magdalene. Donnelly, Karen, illus. (p. 1100)
—Mary of Galilee. Donnelly, Karen, illus. (p. 1101)
—Paul of Tarsus. Donnelly, Karen, illus. (p. 1330)
—Simon Peter. Donnelly, Karen, illus. (p. 1577)
Moore, Alan, et al. Reunion. Yeates, Tom et al, illus. (p. 1465)
—Tom Strong (p. 1763)
Moore, Alan, Intro. Brickman Begins! (p. 227)
Moore, Alice. Surrounded by Darkness. (p. 1686)
—Touched by Darkness. (p. 1772)
Moore, Alison. What the Pond Frog Said. (p. 1893)
Moore, Andrew. Meditation. (p. 1120)
—New York City's Industries: Jobs for People. (p. 1248)
—Traveling in New York City. (p. 1780)
Moore, Angel. Squinky the Squid (p. 1637)
Moore, Angela. Rebecca's Ducks Keating, Nancy, illus. (p. 1450)
Moore, Angela Hays. Maggie Seeks the Kingdom of God. Kiel, Casey Kizer, illus. (p. 1071)
Moore, Ann & Culpin, Christopher. Holocaust. (p. 789)
Moore, Ann C. Colors Join Hands for A Surprise. (p. 345)
—Looking for a Place to Take a Long Winter Nap. (p. 1051)
Moore, Ann Peeples. Isn't the World Beautiful? (p. 893)
Moore, Arden. Obesity. Jones, Buck, illus. (p. 1275)
Moore, Armando. Clare of Assisi. (p. 326)
Moore, Ashley L. Story of Princess K. (p. 1659)
Moore, B. Clay. Battle Hymn. (p. 145)
—Byrd of Paradise. (p. 249)
Moore, B. Clay, jt. auth. see Smith, Brian.
Moore, B. Clay, et al. Put the Book Back on the Shelf: A Belle & Sebastian Anthology. (p. 1420)
Moore, Baba Evans. While the Village Sleeps. (p. 1911)
Moore, Barbara R. Sojourner Truth. (p. 1606)
Moore, Basil John. Shaking the Invisible Hand: Complexity, Choices & Critiques. (p. 1559)
Moore, Beth. Believing God Leader Guide. (p. 162)
—Believing God Member. (p. 162)
—Believing God Vhs. (p. 162)
—Christ Through the Ages. (p. 311)
—Discipulo Amado: Libro Para el Discipulo. (p. 447)
—Fundamentals: Beloved Disciple Child's Cards. (p. 649)
—Fundamentals: Beloved Disciple Child's Card Part 2. (p. 649)
—Jesus el Unico Y Suficiente, Libro Para el Discipulo. (p. 915)
—John the Beloved Disciple. (p. 923)
—Living Beyond Yourself: Exploring the Fruit of the Spirit Member. (p. 1040)
—Living Beyond Yourself Leader Guide. (p. 1040)
—My Child, My Princess: A Parable about the King. Warren, Beverly, illus. (p. 1200)
—When Godly People Do Ungodly Things: Arming Yourself Member. (p. 1902)
—When Godly People Do Ungodly Things Leader. (p. 1902)
—When Godly People Do Ungodly Things Vhs. (p. 1902)
Moore, Beth, ed. Heart for Jesus. (p. 759)
Moore, Bette Dale. My Best-est Friend: A Simple Christmas Music Program for Preschoolers. (p. 1196)
Moore, Billy Loran. Little Brother Real Snake. (p. 1025)
Moore, Bob, ed. see Schelvis, Jules.
Moore, Bonnie S. Honey Bear & the Honey Horde: Bear Tales. (p. 794)
Moore, Bradley. Introducing Serina K. , Ph. D. & Future Famous Person. (p. 882)
Moore, Brenna L. Out of Place in Outer Space. (p. 1311)
—Under the Halloween Moon. (p. 1813)
Moore, Brian L. Story Behind Santa Sacks. Mulligan, Todd, illus. (p. 1656)
Moore, Bud. Lochsa Story: Land Ethics in the Bitterroot Mountains. (p. 1045)
Moore, Carol H. Marvin the Magnificent Nubian Goat. Harrell, Micheael, illus. (p. 1100)
Moore, Carol Hair. Busy Bumble Bee Rides the Waves. Harrell, Michael, illus. (p. 246)
—Marvin the Magnificent Nubian Goat. (p. 1100)
—Marvin the Magnificent Nubian Goat. Harrell, Michael, illus. (p. 1100)
Moore, Carol Lynn. Dare U 2 Open This Book: 90 Ways to Rock Your Faith (p. 406)
Moore, Carol-Lynne. Movement & Making Decision: The Body-Mind Connection in the Workplace. (p. 1183)
Moore, Cassandra. Shape/Color Master. (p. 1560)
Moore, Cathy. Ellen Craft's Escape from Slavery. (p. 514)
—Ellen Craft's Escape from Slavery. Braught, Mark, illus. (p. 514)
Moore, Christopher. Champlain. Back, Francis, illus. (p. 289)
—From Then to Now: A Short History of the World. Krystoforski, Andrej, illus. (p. 644)
—Lamb: The Gospel According to Biff, Christ's Childhood Pal. (p. 972)
Moore, Clarence Bloomfield. Additional Mounds of Duval & of Clay Counties, Florida. Mound Investigation on the East Coast of Florida: Certain Florida Coast Mounds North of the St. Johns River. (p. 12)
—Antiquities of the Ouachita Valley, by Clarence B. Moore Report on an Additional Collection of Skeletal Remains, from Arkansas & Louisiana: Made & Presented to the National Museum, in 1909, by Mr. Clarence B. Moore. (p. 89)
—Antiquities of the St. Francis, White, & Black Rivers, Arkansas: Part I. St. Francis River; Part II. White, & Black Rivers. (p. 89)
—Certain Aboriginal Mounds of the Apalachicola River (p. 287)
—Certain Aboriginal Mounds of the Florida Central West-Coast. (p. 287)
—Certain Aboriginal Remains of the Black Warrior River: Certain Aboriginal Remains of the Lower Tombigbee River Certain Aboriginal Remains of Mobile Bay & Mississippi Sound Miscellaneous Investigation in Florida. (p. 287)
—Certain Aboriginal Remains of the Northwest Florida Coast. (p. 287)
—Certain Antiquities of the Florida West-Coast. (p. 287)
—Certain Mounds of Arkansas & of Mississippi: Part I. Mounds & Cemeteries of the Lower Arkansas River, Part II. Mounds of the Lower Yazoo & Lower Sunflower Rivers, Mississippi, Part III. The Blum Mounds, Mississippi. (p. 287)
—Certain Shell Heaps of the St. John's River, Florida, Hitherto Unexplored (p. 287)
—Moundville Revisited. Crystal River Revisited Mounds of the Lower Chattahoochee & Lower Flint Rivers. Notes on the Ten Thousand Islands, Florida. (p. 1180)
—Northwestern Florida Coast Revisited. (p. 1266)
—Sheet-Copper from the Mounds Is Not Necessarily of European Origin. (p. 1564)
—Some Aboriginal Sites in Louisiana & in Arkansas Atchafalaya River, Lake Larto, Tensas River, Bayou Macon, Bayou D'Arbonne, in Louisiana Saline River, in Arkansas by Clarence B. Moore. (p. 1608)
—Some Aboriginal Sites of Green River, Kentucky; Certain Aboriginal Sites on Lower Ohio River; Additional Investigation on Mississippi River. (p. 1608)
—Some Aboriginal Sites on Mississippi River. (p. 1609)
—Some Aboriginal Sites on Red River. (p. 1609)
Moore, Clement C. C'Etait la Veille de Noel. Santore, Charles, illus. (p. 288)
—Christmas Carol. (p. 313)
—Cuento de Nochebuena. Santore, Charles, illus. (p. 389)
—Era la Vispera de Navidad. (p. 533)

—Grumpy Santa. Spiridellis, Gregg & Spiridellis, Evan, illus. (p. 727)
—Magie de Noel. (p. 1075)
—My First Night Before Christmas. Newsom, Tom, illus. (p. 1207)
—Night Before Christmas (p. 1252)
—Night Before Christmas: A Christmas Treasury. (p. 1252)
—Night Before Christmas: A Bedtime Shadow Book. (p. 1252)
—Night Before Christmas Santore, Charles, illus. (p. 1252)
—Night Before Christmas: A Visit from St. Nicholas. (p. 1252)
—Night Before Christmas: A Brick Story. Brack, Amanda, illus. (p. 1252)
—Night Before Christmas: Peek Inside the 3D Windows. Alderson, Lisa, illus. (p. 1252)
—Night Before Christmas: A Magical Cut-Paper Edition. Puttapipat, Niroot, illus. (p. 1252)
—Night Before Christmas: Or, a Visit from St. Nicholas. Santore, Charles, illus. (p. 1252)
—Night Before Christmas. (p. 1252)
—Night Before Christmas. Rand, Ted, illus. (p. 1252)
—Night Before Christmas. Bell, Bill, illus. (p. 1252)
—Night Before Christmas. Newsom, Tom, illus. (p. 1252)
—Night Before Christmas. Kesler, Matt, illus. (p. 1252)
—Night Before Christmas. Tudor, Tasha, illus. (p. 1252)
—Night Before Christmas. Cone, William, illus. (p. 1252)
—Night Before Christmas. Fisher, Henry, illus. (p. 1252)
—Night Before Christmas. Fujikawa, Gyo, illus. (p. 1252)
—Night Before Christmas. Mills, Donald, illus. (p. 1252)
—Night Before Christmas. Reid, Barbara, illus. (p. 1252)
—Night Before Christmas. Samuel, Janet, illus. (p. 1252)
—Night Before Christmas. Puybaret, Eric, illus. (p. 1252)
—Night Before Christmas. Whatley, Bruce, illus. (p. 1252)
—Night Before Christmas. dePaola, Tomie, illus. (p. 1252)
—Night Before Christmas. Adolphe, Joseph, illus. (p. 1252)
—Night Before Christmas. Barrett, Angela, illus. (p. 1252)
—Night Before Christmas. Eldredge, Larry, illus. (p. 1252)
—Night Before Christmas. Rackham, Arthur, illus. (p. 1252)
—Night Before Christmas. Engelbreit, Mary, illus. (p. 1252)
—Night Before Christmas. Malvern, Corinne, illus. (p. 1252)
—Night Before Christmas. Zwerger, Lisbeth, illus. (p. 1252)
—Night Before Christmas. Gurney, John Steven, illus. (p. 1252)
—Night Before Christmas. Birmingham, Christian, illus. (p. 1252)
—Night Before Christmas. Price, Margaret Evans, illus. (p. 1252)
—Night Before Christmas. Watson, Richard Jesse, illus. (p. 1252)
—Night Before Christmas. Thomas, Tina & Witter, Rahad, illus. (p. 1252)
—Night Before Christmas / by Clement C Moore; Illustrated by Arthur Rackham. (p. 1252)
—Night Before Christmas Board Book: The Classic Edition. Santore, Charles, illus. (p. 1252)
—Night Before Christmas Mini Edition. Santore, Charles, illus. (p. 1253)
—Nochebuena Alvarez, Lourdes, tr. (p. 1262)
—Twas the Night Before Christmas: A Visit from St. Nicholas. Smith, Jessie Willcox, illus. (p. 1799)
—Twas the Night Before Christmas: Edited by Santa Claus for the Benefit of Children of the 21st Century. (p. 1799)
—Twas the Night Before Christmas. (p. 1799)
—Twas the Night Before Christmas. Goodell, Jon, illus. (p. 1799)
—'Twas the Night Before Christmas. Whelan, Kat, illus. (p. 1799)
—'Twas the Night Before Christmas. Wormell, Christopher, illus. (p. 1799)
—Visit from St. Nicholas. Nast, Thomas, illus. (p. 1845)
Moore, Clement C., jt. auth. see Andrews McMeel Publishing Staff.
Moore, Clement C., jt. auth. see Birmingham, Christian.
Moore, Clement C., jt. auth. see Browning, Tom.
Moore, Clement C., jt. auth. see Duvoisin, Roger.
Moore, Clement C., jt. auth. see Goodrich, Carter.
Moore, Clement C., jt. auth. see Lawler, Janet.
Moore, Clement C., jt. auth. see Mayer, Mercer.
Moore, Clement C., jt. auth. see McWilliams, Amanda.
Moore, Clement C., jt. auth. see Muecke, Anne.
Moore, Clement C., jt. auth. see Rand, Ted.
Moore, Clement C., jt. auth. see Smith, Jessie Willcox.
Moore, Clement C., jt. auth. see Sullivan, Ellen.
Moore, Clement C. & Curto Family, The. Night Before Christmas. Creative Illustrations Studio & Good Times At Home LLC, illus. (p. 1252)
Moore, Clement C. & Denslow, W. w. Denslow's Night Before Christmas. (p. 426)
Moore, Clement C. & Linz, Peter. Night Before Christmas. Gurney, John Steven, illus. (p. 1252)
Moore, Clement C., ed. Night Before Christmas. Porfirio, Guy, illus. (p. 1252)
—Night Before Christmas. Winget, Susan, illus. (p. 1252)
—Night Before Christmas. Gorsline, Douglas, illus. (p. 1252)
—Night Before Christmas. Price, Margaret Evans, illus. (p. 1252)
Moore, Clement C., et al. C'etait la Veille de Noel. (p. 288)
Moore, Colin. Modern Nursery Rhymes: For Grown-Ups. (p. 1158)
Moore, Colista. Student's Dictionary. (p. 1669)
—Student's Dictionary & Gazetteer. (p. 1669)
—Student's English Dictionary. (p. 1669)
Moore, Crystal. Moon Dust. (p. 1172)
Moore, Cyd. Diary of a Michigan Kid. (p. 434)
—Diary of a Minnesota Kid. (p. 434)
—Diary of a Ohio Kid. (p. 434)
Moore, Cyd, illus. see Brennan-Nelson, Denise & Brennan, Rosemarie.
Moore, Cyd, illus. see Brennan-Nelson, Denise.
Moore, Cyd, illus. see Galbraith, Kathryn Osebold.
Moore, Cyd, illus. see Marx, Pamela.
Moore, Cyd, illus. see McCourt, Lisa.
Moore, Cyd, illus. see Nelson, Joanne.
Moore, Cyd, illus. see Oppenheim, Shulamith.
Moore, Cyd, illus. see Raffi.
Moore, Cyd, illus. see Ransom, Jeanie Franz.
Moore, Cyd, illus. see Sleeping Bear Press.
Moore, Cyd, illus. see Spinelli, Eileen.
Moore, D., illus. see Aryal, Aimee.
Moore, Daniel. Abdallah Jones & the DisappearingDust. (p. 4)
Moore, Danny, illus. see Aryal, Aimee.
Moore, Danny, illus. see Berra, Yogi.
Moore, Danny, illus. see Remy, Jerry.
Moore, Danny, illus. see Staub, Rusty.
Moore, Darryl, illus. see Loftis, Chris & Lowenthal, Gary T.
Moore, Dave, compiled by. Free People: Tracing Our Hmong Roots. (p. 634)
Moore, David. Amazing Adventures of Fizzlegrits Books 1 2 3 the Fizzlegrits Trilogy. Moore, Sarah, illus. (p. 52)
Moore, David, illus. see Heinrichs, Ann.
Moore, David, illus. see Lindeen, Mary & Kesselring, Susan.
Moore, Dawnyelle, jt. auth. see Yarbray Brucke, Candice.
Moore, Debbie. Penelope, the Peculiar Purple Porpoise. (p. 1336)
Moore, Deborah K. & Mulbah-Bondo, Gbolu. Girl Like Me. (p. 678)
Moore, Debra, illus. see Joyce, Samantha & Joyce, Caroline.
Moore, Denetra. Little Soldier. (p. 1036)
Moore, Derrick, jt. auth. see Moore, Stephanie Perry.
Moore, Diane. Aniville Tales Presents: O. C.'s Big Lesson. (p. 84)
Moore, Dorothy. Tooth Fairy & the Princess. (p. 1768)
Moore, Dwain, illus. see Jones, Brenda.
Moore Ed. S., Maria A. If a Kid Ruled the World. (p. 852)
Moore, Eileen. Arizona Trails for Children: 135 Trails Across Arizona for Children & Adults. Moore, Eileen, photos by. (p. 99)
Moore, Eileen, jt. auth. see Moore, James W.
Moore, Elizabeth. All Kinds of Signs. (p. 45)
—Clothes Around the World. (p. 334)
—Farms (p. 575)
—Keeping Us Safe. (p. 948)
—Let's Communicate. (p. 995)
—Looking at Rocks (p. 1051)
—Making Maple Syrup. (p. 1081)
—Matter Is Everything! (p. 1109)
—Oceans (p. 1277)
—Sports Rules (p. 1633)
—Taking Care of a Pet (p. 1698)
—Toys from the Past. (p. 1774)
—Toys in the Past (p. 1774)
—Wants or Needs (p. 1857)
—Watch Out! (p. 1861)
Moore, Elizabeth, jt. auth. see Couvillon, Alice.
Moore, Elizabeth, jt. auth. see Gregory, Helen.
Moore, Elizabeth & Couvillon, Alice. How the Gods Created the Finger People Lopez, Luz-Maria, illus. (p. 813)
Moore, Elizabeth & Gregory, Helen. Where Do People Work? (p. 1907)
Moore, Elyse, illus. see Cayce, Jw & Guy, K. T.
Moore, Emma V. Manu's Ark: India's Tale of the Great Flood. (p. 1089)
Moore, Emma V., illus. see Greene, Joshua M.
Moore, Eva. Lucky Ducklings. Carpenter, Nancy, illus. (p. 1062)
Moore, Felicia. Children, Sing along & Learn with Me in Support of Antibullying Awareness! (p. 303)
Moore, Frances, illus. see Aboff, Marcie.
Moore, Frances, illus. see Mortensen, Lori.
Moore, Gareth. Brain Games for Clever Kids. Dickason, Chris, illus. (p. 221)
—Kids' Book of Mazes. Moore, Gareth, illus. (p. 952)
—Not So Ordinary. (p. 1267)
—Seeing Is Believing. (p. 1548)
—Think Outside the Box. (p. 1734)
Moore, Gary W. Becoming a Master Student: Keys to Student Success. (p. 156)
Moore, Genevieve. Catherine's Story. Littlewood, Karin, illus. (p. 280)
Moore, Gigi, jt. auth. see Hopkins, Lee Bennett.
Moore, Ginny. Fast. (p. 576)
Moore, Graeme. Ruin. (p. 1494)
Moore, Gustav, illus. see Mason, Cherie.
Moore, Gustav, illus. see Ross, Michael Elsohn.
Moore, Gustav, illus. see Thorson, Kristine, et al.
Moore, Gustav, illus. see Thorson, Robert & Thorson, Kristine.
Moore, H G, III, photos by see Wicker, Jan L.
Moore, H G, III, photos by see Wicker, Jan Lee.
Moore, H G, III, photos by see Wyatt, Laura.
Moore, Harker. Cruel Season for Dying. (p. 386)
Moore, Harry, illus. see Banks, Steven.
Moore, Harry, illus. see Random House & Pohlmeyer, Krista.
Moore, Harry, illus. see Random House Staff.
Moore, Harry, illus. see Random House.
Moore, Harry, illus. see Willson, Sarah.
Moore, Harry, Jr., illus. see Lewman, David.
Moore, Heidi. Chimpanzees (p. 306)
—Dian Fossey (p. 434)
—Giant Isopod: And Other Crafty Crustaceans. (p. 673)
—Giant Isopods & Other Crafty Crustaceans (p. 673)
—Giant Tube Worms & Other Interesting Invertebrates (p. 674)
—Joseph Banks (p. 926)
—Ocean Food Chains (p. 1276)
—Rain Forest Food Chains (p. 1434)
—Story Behind Cotton (p. 1656)
—Story Behind Oil (p. 1656)
—Story Behind Salt (p. 1656)
Moore, Heidi, et al. Creatures of the Deep. (p. 380)
Moore, Helen H. Nobody Else's Grannie. (p. 1262)
—Secret of Willow Ridge: Gabe's Dad Finds Recovery. Blackford, John, illus. (p. 1543)
Moore, Hugh. Bug Jokes. (p. 236)
—Food Jokes. (p. 613)
—School Jokes. (p. 1523)
—Sports Jokes. (p. 1632)
Moore, Inga. Captain Cat. Moore, Inga, illus. (p. 263)
—Horse Tales. (p. 800)
—House in the Woods. (p. 803)
—Raising Readers House in the Woods. (p. 1437)
—Six Dinner Sid. Moore, Inga, illus. (p. 1582)
Moore, Inga, illus. see Burnett, Frances Hodgson.
Moore, Inga, illus. see Grahame, Kenneth.
Moore, J. S. Outside Kitty. Warder, Aaron, illus. (p. 1313)
Moore, James A. Subject Seven (p. 1671)
Moore, James W., jt. auth. see Tingle, Tim.
Moore, James W. & Moore, Eileen. Dark at the Foot of the Stairs. (p. 407)
Moore, Jason Colin. Walk with God for Teens: Brief Meditations & Prayers for Teenagers. (p. 1854)
Moore, Jennifer. Reading Bridge Enriching Classroom Skills: 5th Grade. Willie, Kirsten et al, eds. (p. 1445)
—Seven Days. (p. 1554)
Moore, Jennifer, et al. Math Bridge Enriching Classroom Skills: 4th Grade. Willie, Kirsten et al, eds. (p. 1105)
—Math Bridge Enriching Classroom Skills: 5th Grade. Willie, Kirsten et al, eds. (p. 1105)
—Powerpuff Girls Classics Volume 2: Power Up: Power Up. (p. 1391)
Moore, Jess. Economy of Texas. (p. 503)
—Texas During the Great Depression. (p. 1724)
Moore, Jim. All Animal Band. Hall, Norris, illus. (p. 43)
Moore, Jo, illus. see Petty, Kate.
Moore, Jo, illus. see Watt, Fiona.
Moore, Jodi. When a Dragon Moves In. McWilliam, Howard, illus. (p. 1901)
Moore, John Travers, jt. auth. see Moore, Margaret.
Moore, Johnny Ray. But Still, We Dream: (a novel in Verse) (p. 246)
Moore, Jonathan, illus. see Pollack, Pamela D. & Belviso, Meg.
Moore, Jordan. Marshmallow Man. (p. 1096)
—Mystery of the Grand Bazaar. (p. 1225)
—Queen Serena. (p. 1425)
—Sinbad the Sailor. (p. 1578)
Moore, Joseph. I Have Chosen You. (p. 839)
—I Have Chosen You - Candidate's Journal. (p. 839)
Moore, Judith. Jessica the Furry Baroo. Brown, Karen, illus. (p. 914)
Moore, Julianne. Best Friends Forever. Pham, LeUyen, illus. (p. 169)
—Freckleface Strawberry: Best Friends Forever. Pham, LeUyen, illus. (p. 632)
—Freckleface Strawberry. Pham, LeUyen, illus. (p. 632)
—Freckleface Strawberry & the Dodgeball Bully. Pham, LeUyen, illus. (p. 632)
—Freckleface Strawberry: Backpacks! Pham, LeUyen, illus. (p. 632)
—Freckleface Strawberry: Lunch, or What's That? Pham, LeUyen, illus. (p. 632)
—My Mom Is a Foreigner, but Not to Me. So, Meilo, illus. (p. 1214)
Moore, June Hines. Manners Made Easy. Osborn, Jim, illus. (p. 1088)
—Social Skills Survival Guide: A Handbook for Interpersonal & Business Etiquette. (p. 1604)
Moore, Karen. Daddy Loves Me. Stanley, Mandy, illus. (p. 398)
—Dear God, Let's Talk about YOU. Wummer, Amy, illus. (p. 419)
—Everybody Counts. Reed, Lisa, illus. (p. 543)
—Hi God, Let's Talk about My Life. Wummer, Amy, illus. (p. 775)
—Latin for Children: A History Reader. (p. 979)
—Mommy Loves Me. Stanley, Mandy, illus. (p. 1162)
Moore, Karen, jt. auth. see Meyer, Joyce.
Moore, Karen & Davis, Erin. Latin for Children, Primer B History Reader. (p. 979)
—Latin for Children, Primer C History Reader: Libellus de Historia. (p. 979)
Moore, Katharine & Sonne, Lisa T. E., texts. Zoo Animals. (p. 1988)
Moore, Katherine Roberts. Is God Behind the Big Blue Sky? Moore, Kristen L., illus. (p. 889)
Moore, Katrina. So Long Gnop-Jiye: A Memoir. (p. 1602)
Moore, Kelly, et al. Amber House. (p. 57)
—Amber House: Neverwas. (p. 57)
—Neverwas. (p. 1243)
Moore, Kevin. Road Maker. (p. 1476)
Moore, Kevin M. What You Need to Know about the Law & Cyberspace (p. 1896)
Moore, Kim, ed. see Lee, Brittany.
Moore, Kimberly. Arithmetic Village Presents King David Divide. Moore, Kimberly, illus. (p. 98)
—Arithmetic Village Presents Linus Minus. Moore, Kimberly, illus. (p. 98)
—Arithmetic Village Presents Tina Times. Moore, Kimberly, illus. (p. 98)
Moore, Kimberly, jt. auth. see Moore, Kimberly.
Moore, Kimberly & Moore, Kimberly. Arithmetic Village Presents Arithmetic Village. (p. 98)
Moore, Kimberly Ann. Arithmetic Village Presents Polly Plus. Moore, Kimberly Ann, illus. (p. 98)
Moore, Kristen L., illus. see Moore, Katherine Roberts.
Moore, Lace Rosalia. Scrabble King. (p. 1532)
Moore, Leslie. Day in the Life of Whiskers. (p. 413)
—Guess What Ryan Saw at the Farm. (p. 729)
—Hey Dude, Know Your Scripture-Oye Chico, Conoce Tu Biblia: Find the Hidden Crosses-Encuentra Las Cruces Escondidas. (p. 774)
—Right Left: A Boy Named Grey. (p. 1472)
Moore, Lilian. Mural on Second Avenue & Other City Poems. (p. 1191)
—Mural on Second Avenue & Other City Poems. Karas, Roma, illus. (p. 1191)
—My First Counting Book. Williams, Garth, illus. (p. 1206)
Moore, Lisa. Elie Wiesel: Surviving the Holocaust, Speaking Out Against Genocide. (p. 512)
Moore, Lishia, illus. see Warner, Penny.
Moore, Lishia, photos by see Warner, Penny.
Moore, Lonnette. Misplaced Splatter. (p. 1151)
Moore, Lori A. Grady the Gray Cat. (p. 705)
—Hannah the Hedgehog Goes to Heaven & Lily Loses Her Best Friend. (p. 742)
Moore, Lorraine. Lidoo Woodo's Goes to Daycare. (p. 1007)
Moore, Lorraine O., jt. auth. see Henrikson, Peggy.
Moore, M. Meet My Mom: Learning the M Sound. (p. 1121)
Moore, Margaret. Complete Charleston: A Guide to the Architecture, History & Gardens of Charleston & the Low Country. Moore, Truman, photos by. (p. 352)
Moore, Margaret & Moore, John Travers. Three Tripps. Funk, Clotilde Embree, illus. (p. 1744)
Moore, Margie, illus. see Carlstrom, Nancy White.
Moore, Margie, illus. see Chaconas, Dori.
Moore, Margie, illus. see Hill, Susan.
Moore, Margie, illus. see Lubner, Susan.
Moore, Margie, illus. see Raisner Glass, Beth.
Moore, Margie, illus. see Ryder, Joanne.
Moore, Margie, illus. see Tolan, Stephanie S.
Moore, Margie, illus. see Williams, Rozanne Lanczak.
Moore, Marian & Kensington, Mary Jane. Dear Cinderella. Olson, Julie, illus. (p. 418)
Moore, Mark, jt. auth. see Dahl, Michael.
Moore, Mark & Moore, Sheila. Swankyswigs (p. 1688)
Moore, Mary. Blacks in Ohio II Caesor, Ebraska, ed. (p. 197)
Moore, Mel. Mother's Little Helper. (p. 1179)
—Mr P's Tale or Two. (p. 1186)
—Way Cool Book of Poetry. (p. 1864)
Moore, Meredith. I Am Her Revenge. (p. 833)
Moore, Michael, illus. see Kenney, Cindy & Peterson, Doug.
Moore, Michael, illus. see Kenney, Cindy, et al.
Moore, Michael, illus. see Kenney, Cindy.
Moore, Michael, illus. see Peterson, Doug.
Moore, Mike. Importance of Being Ernest: A Jewish Life Spent in Christian Mission. (p. 862)
Moore, Moira J. Heroes Adrift. (p. 772)
Moore, Monica A. Everyday Heroes. (p. 543)
Moore, Mykela. Meet the Super Sisters. Garrett, Myers, illus. (p. 1123)
Moore, Nancy Delano. Kiernan's Jam. Peck, Bill, illus. (p. 955)
Moore, Natascha. Circus der Zirkus. (p. 322)
—Little Bear Kleiner Bär. (p. 1024)
—Lost Verloren. (p. 1057)
Moore, Nathan. Little Princess & the Backyard Mystery: A Children's Story. (p. 1034)
Moore, Nicholas & Murton, Gareth. Princess Lydia & the wailing Monster. (p. 1404)
Moore, Nicolette, illus. see Germain, Kerry.
Moore Niver, Heather. 20 Fun Facts about Rocky Planets. (p. 1995)
—Chimps & Monkeys Are Not Pets! (p. 306)
—Cool Careers Without College for People Who Can Build Things. (p. 362)
—Executions & Sacrifices. (p. 548)
—Getting to Know Arduino. (p. 669)
—Getting to Know Ruby. (p. 669)
—Trip Through a Coral Reef. (p. 1787)
—Viaje Dentro de un Arrecife de Coral (a Trip Through a Coral Reef) (p. 1839)
Moore Niver, Heather, jt. auth. see Niver, Heather Moore.
Moore, Noreen. Reaching Tidewater: Life on the Delaware Canal. (p. 1442)
Moore, P. B. Day the Buffalo Ran. (p. 414)
Moore, P. M., illus. see Lewis, Regina N.
Moore, Patrick. First Book of Stars. (p. 593)
Moore, Paul, photos by see Goldstein, Sidney.
Moore, Paula & Lyon, Anna. New Essentials for Teaching Reading in Prek-2: Comprehension, Vocabulary, Fluency. (p. 1244)
Moore, P.D. About Harry Potter: What Every Kid Should Know... Moore, Rema Harracksingh- & Delande, J., eds. (p. 5)
Moore, Perry. B Is for Beatle. (p. 122)
—Hero. (p. 772)
Moore, Pete. Stem Cell Research. (p. 1647)
Moore, Peter. Red Moon Rising. (p. 1454)
—V Is for Villain. (p. 1829)
Moore, Peter D. Agricultural & Urban Areas. Garratt, Richard, illus. (p. 30)
—Tundra. Garratt, Richard, illus. (p. 1796)
—Wetlands. Garratt, Richard, illus. (p. 1877)
Moore, Peter D. & Garratt, Richard. Tropical Forests. (p. 1789)
Moore, Philip. How Can You Use A Computer? (p. 805)
—What Is Weather? (p. 1891)
—When Did American Astronauts Explore Space? (p. 1901)
—When Is This A Home? (p. 1903)
Moore, Phillip. How Many Parts Do Dandelions Have? (p. 811)
—When Did People Start to Count? (p. 1902)
—Where Does Used Paper Go? (p. 1907)
Moore, Phoebe, jt. auth. see Moore, Phoebe V.
Moore, Phoebe V. & Moore, Phoebe. Globalisation & Labour Struggle in Asia: A Neo-Gramscian Critique of South Korea's Political Economy. (p. 685)
Moore, Phyllis M., illus. see Lewis, Regina N.
Moore, Raina. Charming Princess. (p. 294)
—How Do You Say Good Night? Luebs, Robin, illus. (p. 808)
Moore, Ralph. Thoughts of Roses: A Collection of Poems by Ralph S. Moore (p. 1740)
Moore, Rema Harracksingh-, ed. see Moore, P.D.
Moore, Rita A. & Gilles, Carol J. Reading Conversations: Retrospective Miscue Analysis with Struggling Readers, Grades 4-12. (p. 1445)
Moore, Rita M. Big Bell Goes Shopping. (p. 178)
Moore, Rob. Why Do Airplanes Fly? (p. 1923)
—Why Do Airplanes Fly? All about Flight. (p. 1923)
—Why Do Balls Bounce? (p. 1923)
—Why Does Electricity Flow? (p. 1924)
—Why Does Electricity Flow? Level 6 Factbook. (p. 1924)
—Why Does Water Evaporate? (p. 1924)
—Why Does Water Evaporate? All about Heat & Temperature. (p. 1924)
Moore, Robert. Oil 1: Learn the Basics of Oil Painting. (p. 1282)
Moore, Roland D. Bugging in the City. (p. 236)
Moore, Rosey. Dreams. (p. 484)
Moore, Russell, illus. see Najimy, Norman.

Moore, Ruth Nulton. Christmas Surprise. Eitzen, Allan, illus. (p. 315)
Moore, S. Tiger Talk: Learning the T Sound. (p. 1748)
Moore, S. D. Adventures of Pj & Split Pea. Switzer, Bobbi, illus. (p. 21)
—Adventures of PJ & Split Pea Vol. II: Nothing but the Tooth. (p. 21)
Moore S., et al. If a Kid Ruled the World. (p. 852)
Moore, Sally, jt. auth. see Walking Bull, Gilbert.
Moore, Sandra. Peace Tree from Hiroshima: A Little Japanese Bonsai with a Big Story. Wilds, Kazumi, illus. (p. 1331)
Moore, Sarah, illus. see Moore, David.
Moore, Sarah W. Rap Scene: The Stars, the Fans, the Music. (p. 1439)
Moore, Sasha, illus. see Elliott, Sherria L.
Moore, Saxton, illus. see Flasterstein, Ran.
Moore, Saxton, illus. see Sander, Sonia.
Moore, Scott, illus. see Hama, Larry.
Moore, Sean L., illus. see Wishinsky, Frieda.
Moore, Shahari. It's Good Sunday. Waddington, Nicole, illus. (p. 897)
Moore, Shannon Baker. History of Music. (p. 784)
—King Tut's Tomb. (p. 959)
—Korean War. (p. 967)
Moore, Sharon. Food Fractions: Learning How Fractional Parts Equal a Whole. (p. 613)
—Native American Foods & Recipes. (p. 1234)
—Runaway Kite. (p. 1496)
—Starry Sky. (p. 1642)
Moore, Sharon Arthur. Conversations in a Four-Blocks Classrooms: Encouraging Literacy Interactions with Students. (p. 361)
Moore, Shawn. Sam & the Tale of the Dragon Prints. Baker, David, illus. (p. 1506)
Moore, Sheila. Abadaba Alphabet: Learning Letter Sounds. Holsinger, Carol, illus. (p. 2)
Moore, Sheila, jt. auth. see Moore, Mark.
Moore, Shekina. Shoeing the Fat: Real Women, Real Challenges, Real Talk. (p. 1568)
Moore, Shelbie. Words Scribbled in My Notebook. (p. 1952)
Moore, Sherry. Crab Is Back in Town. (p. 375)
—Dude; You're a Crab! (p. 489)
—Jason's #16 Dream. (p. 910)
Moore, Sonja E. Santa & His Special Christmas Gift. (p. 1511)
Moore, Sonya. Kitchen Talk. (p. 962)
Moore, Stephanie. Better Than Picture Perfect. (p. 172)
—Icing on the Cake. (p. 851)
—Make Something of It. (p. 1079)
—Truth & Nothing But. (p. 1794)
—Turn up for Real. (p. 1798)
Moore, Stephanie, jt. auth. see Moore, Stephanie Perry.
Moore, Stephanie Perry. Absolutely Worthy (p. 7)
—Always Upbeat/All That. (p. 51)
—Back That Thing. (p. 130)
—Better Than Picture Perfect. (p. 172)
—Enjoying True Peace (p. 530)
—Equally Yoked (p. 533)
—Experiencing the Joy (p. 549)
—Finally Sure (p. 587)
—Forever Hot/Truly Fine. (p. 619)
—Get What You Give. (p. 668)
—Give It Up. (p. 681)
—Golden Spirit. (p. 695)
—Got It Going On. (p. 703)
—Happy Princess. (p. 746)
—Icing on the Cake. (p. 851)
—Keep Jumping/No Hating. (p. 947)
—Make Something of It. (p. 1079)
—On Your Knees. (p. 1292)
—Perfect Joy. (p. 1342)
—Prayed Up (p. 1393)
—Problem Solved (p. 1408)
—Settle down/Be Real. (p. 1554)
—Shake It/Got Pride. (p. 1558)
—Sit on Top. (p. 1581)
—Sweet Honesty. (p. 1689)
—True Friends. (p. 1792)
—Truth & Nothing But. (p. 1794)
—Turn up for Real. (p. 1798)
—Yell Out/Do You. (p. 1969)
Moore, Stephanie Perry & Moody Publishing Staff. Believing in Hope. (p. 162)
—Finding Your Faith (p. 588)
Moore, Stephanie Perry & Moore, Derrick. All in/Stand Firm. (p. 44)
—Forever Hot/Truly Fine (p. 619)
—Golden Heart - Deep Soul (p. 694)
—Golden Heart/Deep Soul. (p. 694)
—Real Diva/Man Up. (p. 1448)
—Scream Loud/Quiet Strength. (p. 1532)
Moore, Stephanie Perry & Moore, Stephanie. Way We Roll. (p. 1864)
Moore, Stephen. Dancing in the Arms of Orion. (p. 403)
—Skin & Bone. (p. 1585)
Moore, Steve, jt. auth. see Moore, Alan.
Moore, Stuart. Giant Robot Warriors. (p. 674)
Moore, Stuart, jt. auth. see Lee, Stan.
Moore, Suse. Ella Power & the Sun Puppies: A Power Families Adventure. Elkerton, Andy, illus. (p. 514)
Moore, Suzanne & Henry, Lucia Kemp. Toss & Learn Games Science: 10 Learning-Packed Games Young Children Can Play All by Themselves. (p. 1771)
Moore, Suzi. Lexiland. (p. 1004)
Moore, Ted. Eagle Eye & the Fall of Creek Canyon. (p. 492)
Moore, Tessa. Dad & the Mad Cow Roundabout. (p. 398)
Moore, Thomas. Memoirs, Journal, & Correspondence of Thomas Moore. (p. 1125)
—Tom Moore's Diary: A Selection. (p. 1763)
—Zoe & the Back Yard Boys: The Magic Garden Haunted House Adventure. (p. 1987)
Moore Thomas, Shelley & Thomas, Shelley Moore. Seven Tales of Trinket (p. 1555)
Moore, Tijon Adamson. Pigeon Toed. Baker, David, illus. (p. 1357)
Moore, Tim. Must Be Santa. Whitehead, Pete, illus. (p. 1194)
Moore, Trudy E., jt. auth. see Kinderman, Robert W.
Moore, Truman, photos by see Moore, Margaret.
Moore, Victor L. Pentacle of Northumbria. (p. 1338)
Moore, Wendy Leptien. Eaglet & the River. (p. 492)
Moore, Willamarie, jt. auth. see Broderick, Setsu.
Moore, Willamarie & Wilds, Kazumi. All about Japan: Stories, Songs, Crafts & More. (p. 42)
Moore, Yvette, illus. see Bannatyne-Cugnet, Jo.
Moore, Yvonne. Listening Gift. (p. 1022)
Moore-Berggren, Monique. Pick of the Litter. (p. 1354)
Moore-Chambers, Robin. Dark Skin, Light Skin, Straight or Nappy... It's All Good! An Educational Coloring Book about the Beauty & Diversity of African-American Features. (p. 408)
Moorehead, Warren. Stone Ornaments Used by Indians in the United States & Canada: Being a Description of Certain Charm Stones, Gorgets, Tubes, Bird Stones & Problematical Forms. (p. 1652)
Moorehead, Warren King. Cahokia Mounds: With 16 plates; A Preliminary Paper. (p. 251)
—Field Diary of an Archaeological Collector. (p. 583)
—Stone Age in North America: An Archaeological Encyclopedia of the Implements, Ornaments, Weapons, Utensils, Etc. of the Prehistoric Tribes of North America. (p. 1652)
Moore-Malinos, Jennifer. It's Ok to Be Me! Just Like You, I Can Do Almost Anything! Fabrega, Marta, illus. (p. 898)
Moore-Malinos, Jennifer & Fabrega, Marta. When My Parents Forgot How to Be Friends. (p. 1904)
Moore-Malinos, Jennifer & Moore-Mallinos, Jennifer. I Have Asthma. Curto, Rosa M. & Curto, Rosa Maria, illus. (p. 839)
Moore-Mallinos, Jennifer. Colors of the Rainbow. Fabrega, Marta, illus. (p. 345)
—Daddy Lost His Job. Mazali, Gustavo, illus. (p. 398)
—Do You Have a Secret? Fabrega, Marta, illus. (p. 457)
—I Am Deaf. Fabrega, Marta, illus. (p. 832)
—Money Doesn't Grow on Trees! (p. 1164)
—Studying Is Hard. Mazali, Gustavo, illus. (p. 1670)
Moore-Mallinos, Jennifer, jt. auth. see Moore-Malinos, Jennifer.
Moore-Mallinos, Jennifer & Roca, Nuria. Mi Hermano Tiene Autismo. Fabrega, Marta, illus. (p. 1132)
—Mom Has Cancer! Fabrega, Marta, illus. (p. 1161)
—My Brother Is Autistic. Fabrega, Marta, illus. (p. 1199)
—My Friend Has down Syndrome. Fabrega, Marta, illus. (p. 1209)
Moore-Mallinos, Jennifer, et al. It's Called Dyslexia. Fabrega, Marta, illus. (p. 896)
Moorenson, D. Wayne. Dream Sprites: Alisha's Nightmare. (p. 484)
Moorer, Lela Stephenson. Impossible Journey. (p. 862)
Moores, Ian, illus. see Richards, Jon.
Moores, Jeff, illus. see Kramer, Jennifer E.
Moores, Katie. Land of Havala. Foote, Dan, illus. (p. 973)
Moores, Susanna. It's Not Yours, It's Mine! Moores, Susanna, illus. (p. 898)
Moorey, Teresa. Fortune Telling: What Does the Future Hold for You? (p. 623)
—Graphology: What Does Your Handwriting Reveal about You? (p. 711)
—Spells: Unleash Your Magic Powers! (p. 1625)
Mooring, John L. Cricket's Chronicles: The Third Grade Science Fair. (p. 382)
Moors, Paul C. Legal Guide for Elders: An Easy to Understand Explanation of Solutions to Legal Issues Encountered by Our Elders & their Families. (p. 987)
Moorthy, Anita. Monkey's Drum. Sarkar, Soumitro, illus. (p. 1166)
Moosa, Tracey J., jt. auth. see Edelfield, Bruce.
Moose, David, illus. see Gill, Jim.
Mooser, Stephen. Class Clown Academy. Reese, Rick, illus. (p. 327)
—Young Marian's Adventures in Sherwood Forest. Lansky, Bruce, ed. (p. 1979)
Moosmann, Heidi. Winter Games with Woodland Will. (p. 1938)
Mora, Andy, illus. see McMahon, Peter.
Mora, Ebie. Kai: The Honu Didn't Know He Was Brave. Tackett, Mike, illus. (p. 941)
Mora, Elsa, illus. see Ormsbee, K. E.
Mora, Francisco X., illus. see Mora, Pat.
Mora, Giovanni, illus. see García, Nasario.
Mora, Giovanni, illus. see Saldana, Rene.
Mora, Janet, jt. auth. see Kashman, Nancy.
Mora, Julissa, illus. see Loewen, Nancy & Skelley, Paula.
Mora, Julissa, illus. see Loewen, Nancy.
Mora, Mauricio, illus. see Drew, Alejandrina.
Mora, Pat. Agua Agua Agua Flor Ada, Alma, tr. (p. 30)
—Book Fiesta! Celebrate Children's Day. López, Rafael, illus. (p. 210)
—Carrera del Sapo y el Venado. Domi, illus. (p. 271)
—Cesta de Cumpleanos para Tia Abuela. Lang, Cecily, illus. (p. 288)
—Confeti: Poemas para Ninos Mora, Pat & Fernandez, Queta, trs. (p. 356)
—Delicious Hullabaloo (Pachanga Deliciosa) Mora, Francisco X., illus. (p. 425)
—Desert is My Mother/El Desierto Es Mi Madre: CD & Book Set. Lechon, Daniel, illus. (p. 429)
—Desert Is My Mother/el Desierto Es Mi Madre. Lechon, Daniel, illus. (p. 429)
—Doña Flor: Un Cuento de una Mujer Gigante con un Gran Corazon. Colón, Raúl, illus. (p. 465)
—Doña Flor: A Tall Tale about a Giant Woman with a Great Big Heart. Colón, Raúl, illus. (p. 465)
—Here, Kitty, Kitty! (Ven, Gatita, Ven!) Suarez, Maribel, illus. (p. 770)
—Here Kitty Kitty!/Ven Gatita Ven! Suarez, Maribel, illus. (p. 770)
—Join Hands! The Ways We Celebrate Life. Ancona, George, photos by. (p. 924)
—Let's Eat! - ¡A Comer! Suarez, Maribel, illus. (p. 996)
—Night the Moon Fell: A Maya Myth Domi, Carlos, illus. (p. 1254)
—Noche Que Se Cayó la Luna. Domi, illus. (p. 1262)
—Piñata in a Pine Tree: A Latino Twelve Days of Christmas. Morales, Magaly, illus. (p. 1359)
—Rainbow Tulip. (p. 1436)
—Rainbow Tulip. Sayles, Elizabeth, illus. (p. 1436)
—Song of Francis & the Animals. Frampton, David, illus. (p. 1611)
—Sweet Dreams/Dulces Suenos. Suarez, Maribel, illus. (p. 1689)
—Tomas & the Library Lady. Colón, Raúl, illus. (p. 1764)
—Tomas y la Senora de la Biblioteca. (p. 1764)
—Wiggling Pockets (Los Bolsillos Saltarines) Suarez, Maribel, illus. (p. 1928)
—Yum! Mmmm! Que Rico! America's Sproutings López, Rafael, illus. (p. 1983)
—Yum! ¡Mmmm! ¡Qué Rico! Americas' Sproutings. López, Rafael, illus. (p. 1983)
—Yum! ¡MmMm! ¡Qué Rico! Brotes de las Américas. López, Rafael, illus. (p. 1983)
Mora, Pat & Carling, Amelia Lau. Abuelos (p. 7)
Mora, Pat & Dominguez, Adriana. Agua Rueda, el Agua Sube. So, Meilo, illus. (p. 30)
Mora, Pat & López, Rafael. Yum! Mmmm! Que Rico! America's Sproutings. Mora, Pat & López, Rafael, illus. (p. 1983)
Mora, Pat & Martinez, Libby. Bravo, Chico Canta! Bravo! Carling, Amelia Lau, illus. (p. 224)
—Bravo, Chico Canta! Bravo! Iribarren, Elena, tr. from ENG. (p. 224)
—I Pledge Allegiance. Barton, Patrice, illus. (p. 844)
Mora, Pat & Parra, John. Gracias/Thanks. (p. 705)
Mora, Pat & Sanchez, Enrique O. Confetti: Poems for Children. (p. 356)
Mora, Pat & Ventura, Gabriela Baeza. Remembering Day / El Día de los Muertos. Casilla, Robert, illus. (p. 1459)
Mora, Pat, et al. Hermosa Señora: Nuestra Señora de Guadalupe. Johnson, Steve & Fancher, Lou, illus. (p. 771)
—Water Rolls, Water Rises So, Meilo, illus. (p. 1863)
—Yum! Mmmm! Qué Rico! Brotes de las Américas. López, Rafael & Ada, Alma Flor, illus. (p. 1983)
Morábito, Fabio. Gerardo y la Cama. Cardemil, Carmen, illus. (p. 666)
Morable, Linda, jt. auth. see Griffin, Ricky W.
Moracho, Cristina. Althea & Oliver. (p. 50)
Morado, Leah. What's on My Plate? Develop Understanding of Fractions & Numbers (p. 1899)
Moraghan, Stephanie. Harry's Magic Tables: Learn Your Times Tables in as Little as a Week! (p. 751)
Moragne, Wendy. Allergies. (p. 46)
—Depression. (p. 427)
Moragne, Wendy & Orr, Tamra. New Jersey. (p. 1245)
Morah, Chizoba. Anderson Twins. (p. 72)
Morahan, Nancy. Kind Keepers. (p. 957)
Morais, Flavio, illus. see Carlson, Lori M., ed.
Morais, Joan. Time to Celebrate: A Celebration of a Girl's First Menstrual Period. (p. 1753)
Morait, Tracey. Goalden Girl. (p. 687)
Moraja, Melissa Perry. Jake & the Fly. (p. 905)
—Jake's Adventures - the Secret of the Shark Tooth Crab Claw. Moraja, Melissa Perry, illus. (p. 906)
—Madison & G. A. - a Tale of the Slimy Spitball. Moraja, Melissa Perry, illus. (p. 1070)
—Madison & Ga: Tale of the Messed up Talent Show. (p. 1070)
—Stranger Danger! Play & Stay Safe, Splatter & Friends. (p. 1665)
Moral, Samantha Caballero Del. 100 Cuentos Clasicos. (p. 1998)
Morales, Alejandro. Little Nation & Other Stories. (p. 1032)
Morales, Amparo, ed. Diccionario Didáctico Básico del Español. (p. 435)
Morales, Andrea, tr. see Butcher, A. J. & Butcher, Andrew J.
Morales, Andrea, tr. see Butcher, Andrew & Butcher, Andrew J.
Morales, Andrew, illus. see Mutrie, Matthew.
Morales, Carlos, illus. see Fenne, Edwin & Poehlmann, Jeffrey.
Morales, Carlos, illus. see Poehlmann, Jeffrey & Fenne, Edwin.
Morales, Fifi, illus. see Nohemi, Esther.
Morales, Gilbert, ed. Critical Perspectives on the Vietnam War. (p. 383)
Morales, Jose, illus. see Willow, Bim.
Morales, Judith, illus. see Heiguera, Luis Ignacio.
Morales, Leslie. Esther Dyson: Internet Visionary. (p. 538)
Morales, Magaly, illus. see Brown, Monica.
Morales, Magaly, illus. see Mora, Pat.
Morales, Magaly, illus. see Tafolla, Carmen.
Morales, Melita. Jam & Honey. Bryant, Laura J., illus. (p. 906)
Morales, Robert. Truth: Red, White & Black. Baker, Kyle, illus. (p. 1794)
Morales, Rose. Mary's Egg (p. 1101)
Morales, Yuyi. Just a Minute: A Trickster Tale & Counting Book. (p. 937)
—Just in Case: A Trickster Tale & Spanish Alphabet Book. Morales, Yuyi, illus. (p. 938)
—Niño: Wrestles the World. Morales, Yuyi, illus. (p. 1257)
—Nino Wrestles the World. (p. 1257)
—Viva Frida. O'Meara, Tim, photos by. (p. 1846)
Morales, Yuyi, illus. see Johnston, Tony.
Morales, Yuyi, illus. see Krull, Kathleen.
Morales, Yuyi, illus. see Lacámara, Laura.
Morales, Yuyi, illus. see Montes, Marisa.
Morales, Yuyi, illus. see Soetoro-Ng, Maya.
Morales, Yuyi, illus. see White, Amanda.
Morales, Yuyi, jt. auth. see Novesky, Amy.
Moran, Alex. Boots for Beth. (p. 213)
—Boots for Beth. Ernst, Lisa Campbell, illus. (p. 213)
—Come Here, Tiger! (p. 347)
—Come Here, Tiger! Ernst, Lisa Campbell, illus. (p. 347)
—Popcorn. (p. 1384)
—Popcorn. Everitt, Betsy, illus. (p. 1384)
—Sam & Jack: Three Stories. Bowers, Tim, illus. (p. 1506)
—Six Silly Foxes. Baker, Keith, illus. (p. 1582)
—What Day Is It? (¿Qué Día es Hoy?) Campoy, F. Isabel & Flor Ada, Alma, trs. (p. 1881)
Moran, Alex, jt. auth. see Trimble, Patti.
Moran, Alex & Sullivan, Paula. Todd's Box. (p. 1761)
—Todd's Box. Westcott, Nadine Bernard, illus. (p. 1761)
Moran, Alex & Trimble, Patti. What Day Is It? Moreton, Daniel, illus. (p. 1881)
Moran, C. Bobindy Twins & the Angel Abode. (p. 206)
Moran, Camille. Little Mountain. (p. 1032)
—Scarecrow Pie. (p. 1519)
Moran, Chris, jt. auth. see Barr, Matt.
Moran Cruz, Jo Ann Hoeppner, jt. auth. see Gerberding, Richard.
Moran, Edna, illus. see Schlegel, William.
Moran, Edna Cabcabin. Sleeping Giant: A Tale from Kauai. (p. 1589)
Moran, Edna Cabcabin, illus. see Arita, Vera.
Moran, Erin. Colorful Spring. Pickett, Danny, illus. (p. 344)
Morán, Esteban, tr. see Kinney, Jeff.
Moran, Jeffrey B., jt. auth. see Kantrowitz, Joseph.
Moran, Katherine J. Diabetes: The Ultimate Teen Guide. (p. 433)
—Diabetes: The Ultimate Teen Guide. Merriman, Lisa P., illus. (p. 433)
Moran, Katy. Bloodline. (p. 201)
—Bloodline Rising. (p. 201)
Moran, Kelly. Tiny Caterpillar & the Great Big Tree. (p. 1756)
Moran, Lisa. Making a Difference SB1 the Gift of Time. (p. 1080)
Moran, Lisa & Hawley, Mary. Making a Difference Let the Evidence Decide. (p. 1080)
—Making a Difference SB2 to the Rescue. (p. 1080)
Moran, Lyn, illus. see Claus, Rimana.
Moran, Maggie A. Someone Took Vanessa's Bike. Sasaki, Chie, illus. (p. 1609)
Moran, Margaret. Coming to America Immigration from 1840 To 1930: Set Of 6. (p. 348)
—Cowhands & Cattle Trails: Set Of 6. (p. 374)
—Cowhands & Cattle Trails & Los vaqueros y el arreo de Ganado: 6 English, 6 Spanish Adaptations. (p. 374)
—Lewis & Clark: Set Of 6. (p. 1004)
—Lewis & Clark & Lewis y Clark: 6 English, 6 Spanish Adaptations. (p. 1004)
Moran, Margaret Edward, tr. see Giraldo, Maria Loretta.
Moran, Martin, V, ed. Town Turtles of Sandy Springs: The Stories Behind the Turtles by the Children Who Saw Them. (p. 1773)
Moran, Mary C. Digby's Rescue. (p. 438)
Moran, Mary Y. & Flanagan, Anne J. Jesus Comes to Us: Activity Book. (p. 915)
—Jesus Loves Us: Activity Book. (p. 916)
Moran, Mary Y. & Myers, Theresa F. Jesus Teaches Us. (p. 916)
Moran, Michael, illus. see Allison, Jennifer.
Moran, Michael, illus. see Bullard, Lisa.
Moran, Michael, illus. see Weakland, Mark.
Moran, Michele. Inside Dog & the Outside Dog. (p. 876)
Moran, Michelle. Nana's Secret Christmas Room. (p. 1228)
Moran, Mike, illus. see Bennett, Artie.
Moran, Mike, illus. see Bullard, Lisa.
Moran, Mike, illus. see Finn, Perdita.
Moran, Mike, illus. see Heos, Bridget.
Moran, Mike, illus. see Weakland, Mark.
Moran, Paul. Where's the Meerkat? (p. 1911)
—Where's the Meerkat? Journey Through Time. (p. 1911)
—Where's the Meerkat? - Journey Through Time. (p. 1911)
—World's Greatest Who What Where When Quiz Book for Kids. (p. 1960)
Moran, Paul, illus. see Campbell, Guy.
Moran, Paul, illus. see Taylor, Marianne.
Moran, Raphael. Flee. Hendrix, Amanda, ed. (p. 603)
Moran, Rita. Library Kids Cry of the Banshee. (p. 1006)
—Library Kids Talking Stones. (p. 1006)
—Library Kids the Serpent of Rock Lake. (p. 1006)
Moran, Rod. Paradoxes of Water: Selected & New Poems 1970-2005. (p. 1323)
Moran, Rosslyn, illus. see Rowlands, Avril.
Moran, Sarah. Alien Art: Extraterrestrial Expressions on Earth. (p. 40)
Moran, Theresa & Malone, Dan. Crocodilians in Captivity. Gurley, Russ, ed. (p. 384)
Morandi, Andrea, illus. see Parker, Steve.
Morandi, Andrea, illus. see Wildwood, Gretchen.
Morandin, Mike, illus. see Rustad, Martha E. H.
Morano, John. Makoona. (p. 1083)
—Wing & a Prayer. (p. 1936)
Moratis, Judy Catherine. Angel: And Love Came Down. (p. 73)
Morby, Connie Stradling, tr. see Rylance, Ulrike.
Morcan, Dorina, prod. StarDial Planisphere. (p. 1642)
Mörchen, Roland. Wir Gehen in Die Bibliothek - A Visit to the Library: Deutsch-Englische Ausgabe. Kiefer, Katja, illus. (p. 1939)
—Wir Gehen Ins Fernsehstudio. Kiefer, Katja, illus. (p. 1939)
Morchiladze, Manana, illus. see Baghdasaryan, Rouzanna.
Morchiladze, Manana, illus. see Kruk, Halya.
Morck, Irene. Between Brothers (p. 172)
—Old Bird Wood, Muriel, illus. (p. 1283)
—Tiger's New Cowboy Boots Graham, Georgia, illus. (p. 1749)
—Tough Trails (p. 1773)
Mordan, C., illus. see Boring, Mel & Dendy, Leslie.
Mordan, C. B., illus. see Avi.
Mordan, C. B., illus. see Boring, Mel & Dendy, Leslie.
Mordan, C. B., illus. see Marrin, Albert.
Mordecai & Gordon Staff. Sunsong. (p. 1679)
Mordecai, Martin. Blue Mountain Trouble. (p. 203)
Morden, Daniel. Dark Tales from the Woods. Breckon, Brett, illus. (p. 408)
—So Hungry. Carpenter, Suzanne, illus. (p. 1602)
—Weird Tales from the Storyteller. Jones, Jac, tr. (p. 1872)
Morden, Daniel, jt. auth. see Lupton, Hugh.
Morden, Richard. Ziggy & Zrk & the Meteor of Doom. (p. 1986)
Morden, Richard, illus. see Dallimore, Jan.
Morden, Richard, jt. auth. see Graf, Mike.

Morden, Richard, jt. auth. see Millett, Peter.
Mordenga, Michael P. Spirit Box. (p. 1628)
Mordhorst, Heidi. Pumpkin Butterfly: Poems from the Other Side of Nature. Reynish, Jenny, illus. (p. 1416)
—Squeeze: Poems from a Juicy Universe. Torrey, Jesse, photos by. (p. 1636)
Mordi, Nicku. Know Before You Grow. (p. 965)
More, Frances Mary, creator. Listen to Your Fingers: Fingerithmatic. (p. 1022)
—Multi-Sensory Touch Typing in Minutes: Qwertyqwik. (p. 1189)
—Telling the Time on Your Hands: Quick Time. (p. 1717)
More, Francisco J., Sr. Carousel de Fantasias (p. 271)
More Gordon, Domenica. Archie. More Gordon, Domenica, illus. (p. 95)
Moreau, Chris. Professor's Telescope. Marek, Jane, illus. (p. 1409)
Moreau, Hélène, illus. see Machado, Ana Maria.
Moreau, Kim. Louisiana State University College Prowler off the Record. (p. 1059)
Moreau, Maryellen Rooney & Welch, Brian Scott. Talk to Write, Write to Learn Manual: A Teachers' Manual for Differentiated Instruction & Tiered Intervention. (p. 1703)
Moreau, Nancy. Physics: Physical Setting STAReview. (p. 1353)
Moreau, Nancy & Moreau, Wayne. Math A STAReview: Math Grade 9-10 Test Preparation. Stich, Paul, ed. (p. 1105)
Moreau, Roger. Dragon Mazes: An A-Maze-Ing Colorful Adventure! (p. 477)
Moreau, Wayne, jt. auth. see Moreau, Nancy.
Moreci, Michael & Seeley, Steve. Murder, Death, & the Devil. (p. 1192)
Morecroft, Judith. Malu Kangaroo. Bancroft, Bronwyn, illus. (p. 1084)
Morecroft, Richard & MacKay, Alison. Zoo Album. Lloyd-Diviny, Karen, illus. (p. 1988)
Morecroft, Richard, et al. Zoo Album. Lloyd-Diviny, Karen, illus. (p. 1988)
Moredun, P. R. World of Eldaterra: The Dragon Conspiracy. Vol. 1 (p. 1956)
Moredun, P.R. World of Eldaterra: The Dragon Conspiracy (p. 1956)
Moree, Katie. Jesse's Peekaboo Safari. (p. 914)
Moree, Ronda. Story of Squeaks: Princess Baby Meets Squeaks. (p. 1660)
Moreel, Yvette. Whirly's Autumn Surprise. (p. 1912)
Morehouse, Toni B. Junie's Unicorn Horn. (p. 936)
Moreillon, Judi. Read to Me Teis, Kyra, illus. (p. 1443)
—Ready & Waiting for You. Stock, Catherine, illus. (p. 1447)
—Vamos a Leer. Mercado, Mary M., tr. from ENG. (p. 1831)
Moreira, Carol. Charged (p. 291)
—Membrane. (p. 1125)
Moreira, Carol, jt. auth. see Diersch, Sandra.
Moreira, Joe & Beneville, Ed. Strategic Guard: Brazilian Jiu-Jitsu Details & Techniques: Volume 3. (p. 1666)
Moreiro, Enrique S., illus. see Perera, Hilda & Hilda, Perera.
Moreiro, Enrique S., illus. see Romeu, Emma.
Moreiro, Enrique S., jt. auth. see Lázaro, Georgina.
Morejon, Tom, illus. see Ladd, Debbie.
Morel, Alicia. Cuentos Araucanos: La Gente de la Tierra. (p. 389)
Morel, Diane, jt. auth. see Loisillier, Maud.
Morel, John Henry. Is It True. (p. 889)
—Little Button Annie. (p. 1025)
—Mary Winkle Umperdinck. (p. 1101)
—Odd Events Happen All Around Me. (p. 1278)
—Who Is Me? (p. 1916)
Moreland, Janet & Webb, Shirley G. Dance in the Rain. (p. 402)
Moreland, Karla Carter. Fishing with Daddy. (p. 599)
Moreland Krass, Melanie, illus. see Trudgian, Sherri.
Moreland, Melanie. Psalm 148: Let all Heaven & Earth Praise the Lord! (p. 1413)
—Psalm 23: The Lord Is my Shepherd. I am His Lamb. (p. 1413)
Morell, Ivonne Bonsfill, tr. see Nilsen, Anna.
Morell, Ivonne Bonsfill, tr. see Parr, Todd.
Morelli, Christelle, tr. see Britt, Fanny & Ouriou, Susan.
Morelli, Dave. Journey to Remember. (p. 929)
Morelli, Jack. Heroes of the Negro Leagues. (p. 773)
Morelli, Rolando, ed. Cuentos orientales y otra Narrativa. (p. 390)
Morelli, Yamile, tr. Me Robaron a Mi Mejor Amig. (p. 1116)
Morello, Charles, ed. see Lishinski, Ann King.
Morello, Jill. Lily Goes to School. (p. 1018)
Morem, Susan. How to Gain the Professional Edge: Achieve the Personal & Professional Image You Want. (p. 819)
—How to Gain the Professional Edge. (p. 819)
Morena - di Palma, Alicia. One Damp Dawn. (p. 1294)
Morency, Scott P. What a CEO Can Learn from a 4th Grader. (p. 1878)
Moreno, Barry. African Americans. (p. 27)
—Arab Americans. (p. 94)
—Chinese Americans. (p. 307)
—Cuban Americans. (p. 388)
—German Americans. (p. 666)
—History of American Immigration. (p. 783)
—Irish Americans. (p. 887)
—Italian Americans. (p. 894)
—Japanese Americans. (p. 909)
—Jewish Americans. (p. 917)
—Korean Americans. (p. 967)
—Mexican Americans. (p. 1131)
—Native Americans. (p. 1234)
—Polish Americans. (p. 1380)
—Russian Americans. (p. 1498)
Moreno, Barry, ed. see Ferry, Joseph.
Moreno, Barry, ed. see Hahn, Laura.
Moreno, Barry, ed. see Kozleski, Lisa.
Moreno, Barry, ed. see Marcovitz, Hal.
Moreno, Barry & Ashbrock, Peg. German Americans. (p. 666)
Moreno, Barry & Bowen, Richard A. Italian Americans. (p. 894)
Moreno, Barry & Haugen, Brenda. Irish Americans. (p. 887)
Moreno, Barry & Lingen, Marissa. Chinese Americans. (p. 307)
Moreno, Barry & Temple, Bob. Arab Americans. (p. 94)
Moreno, Barry, ed. We Came to America. (p. 1866)
Moreno, Chris, illus. see Beranek, Adam & Beranek, Christian.
Moreno, Chris, illus. see Jolley, Dan.
Moreno, Daniel, et al. Cultura política de la democracia en Bolivia 2008: El impacto de la Gobernabilidad. (p. 390)
Moreno Lcsw, Melissa. My Feelings Are Mine to Have: Love, Happy, Sad, Afraid, Anger. (p. 1203)
Moreno, Rene King, illus. see Fine, Edith Hope.
Moreno, Rene King, illus. see Goldman, Judy.
Moreno, Rene King, illus. see Guy, Ginger Foglesong & Guy, Ginger F.
Moreno, Rene King, illus. see Guy, Ginger Foglesong.
Moreno, Rene King, illus. see Stanton, Karen.
Moreno, Sergio, illus. see Anaya, Hector.
Moreno Winner, Ramona. Wooden Bowl/El Bol de Madera. Garay, Nicole, illus. (p. 1949)
Moreno-Hinojosa, Hernan. Ghostly Rider & Other Chilling Tales. (p. 672)
Moreno-Velazquez, Juan A. Desmitificacion de una Diva: La Verdad Sobre la Lupe. Restrepo, Carlos Jose, tr. (p. 430)
Morenton, Alice, illus. see Amholt, Laurence.
Morenz, Justin, creator. Cardlings. (p. 266)
Moresby, J. Anderson. My Father's House: A Novel of Suspense Greed & Power. (p. 1203)
Moresco, Jamie, ed. see Larichev, Andrei Borisovich.
Moreta, Gladys, jt. auth. see Karapetkova, Holly.
Moreta, Gladys, jt. auth. see Picou, Lin.
Moreta, Gladys, jt. auth. see Steinkraus, Kyla.
Moreta, Gladys & Picou, Lin. Puppy Trouble. Reese, Bob, illus. (p. 1418)
Moreton, Charles. Green Christmas: An Environmental Musical. (p. 721)
Moreton, Clara. Frank & Fanny: A Rural Story. (p. 628)
Moreton, Daniel, illus. see Barrett, Judi.
Moreton, Daniel, illus. see Moran, Alex & Trimble, Patti.
Moreton, Daniel, illus. see Moran, Alex.
Moreton, Daniel, illus. see Trimble, Patti & Moran, Alex.
Moreton, Daniel, illus. see Trimble, Patti.
Moreton, Daniel, jt. auth. see Katz, Alan.
Moretti, Danilo, illus. see Hammock, Lee & Jacobson, Justin.
Morey, Allan. Basketball. (p. 143)
—Birds. (p. 191)
—Camels Are Awesome! (p. 256)
—Desert Food Chains. (p. 429)
—Gymnastics. (p. 734)
—Insects. (p. 875)
—Jacques Cartier. (p. 905)
—John Cabot. (p. 921)
—Ocean Food Chains. (p. 1276)
—Orangutans Are Awesome! (p. 1302)
—Rain Forest Food Chains. (p. 1434)
—Rhinoceroses Are Awesome! (p. 1467)
—Swimming & Diving. (p. 1691)
—Timeline History of the Declaration of Independence. (p. 1754)
—Timeline History of the Early American Republic. (p. 1754)
—Vasco Da Gama. (p. 1833)
Morey, Allan, jt. auth. see Rustad, Martha E. H.
Morey, Walt. Gentle Ben. Schoenherr, John, illus. (p. 661)
—Year of the Black Pony. (p. 1969)
Morfonios, Nia, jt. auth. see Kamateros, Litsa.
Morgan, Aishling. Conceit & Consequence. (p. 355)
—Natural Desire, Strange Design. (p. 1235)
—Sin's Apprentice. (p. 1580)
Morgan, Alex. Breakaway. (p. 224)
—Hat Trick. (p. 752)
—Sabotage Season. (p. 1500)
—Saving the Team. (p. 1517)
—Saving the Team. Franco, Paula, illus. (p. 1517)
—Win or Lose. (p. 1935)
Morgan, Allen. Matthew & the Midnight Firefighter Martchenko, Michael, tr. (p. 1109)
—Matthew & the Midnight Firefighters. (p. 1109)
—Matthew & the Midnight Hospital. (p. 1109)
—Matthew & the Midnight Movie Martchenko, Michael, illus. (p. 1109)
—Matthew & the Midnight Pirates Martchenko, Michael, illus. (p. 1109)
—Matthew & the Midnight Wrecker. (p. 1109)
—Matthew & the Midnight Wrestlers Martchenko, Michael, illus. (p. 1109)
Morgan, Amanda, jt. auth. see Mc Daniel, Jessica.
Morgan, Andre, jt. auth. see Smith, Jennifer.
Morgan, Anna. Daughters of the Ark (p. 410)
Morgan, Anna & Turkienicz, Rachael. My (Worst) Best Sleepover Party (p. 1222)
Morgan, Anne. Captain Clawbeak & the Ghostly Galleon. Harris, Wayne, illus. (p. 263)
—Captain Clawbeak & the Red Herring. Harris, Wayne, illus. (p. 263)
—Sky Dreamer / Le Bateau de Reves. Eimann, Céline, tr. from ENG. (p. 1586)
—Smallest Carbon Footprint in the Land & Other Eco-Tales. McKinnon, Gay, illus. (p. 1592)
Morgan, Anne & Harris, Wayne. One & Only. (p. 1293)
Morgan, Ben. Tropical Grasslands (p. 1789)
Morgan, Ben & Palmer, Douglas. Rock & Fossil Hunter. (p. 1481)
Morgan, Bernard. Beekeeper. Emecz, Steve, ed. (p. 157)
Morgan, Bernard P. Pszczelarz. Juraszek, Barbara, tr. (p. 1413)
Morgan, Beth. Earth's Treasure Green Pearl. (p. 498)
Morgan, Beverly. Gregory & the Stars: A Little Story about Independence. Joyful Noise, ed. (p. 723)
—Gregory Likes Saturdays: A Little Story about Being Lost in Wal-Mart. Brady, Jeannette, ed. (p. 723)
Morgan, C. M. Silver Doorway #1: A Gnome Away from Home. (p. 1576)
—Silver Doorway #2: Dwarves in the Dark. (p. 1576)
—Silver Doorway #3: An Elf's Adventure. (p. 1576)
MOrgan, C. M. Silver Doorway #4: Dragon on the Loose. (p. 1576)
Morgan, C. M. Silver Doorway #5: Orcs Ahoy! (p. 1576)
—Silver Doorway #6: The Alchemist's Girl. (p. 1576)
Morgan, Charles. Flight of the Solar Ducks. (p. 604)
Morgan, Charlie. Classic American Cars (p. 327)
Morgan, Chris. Grandma's Big Blue Apron. (p. 708)
Morgan, Christopher, illus. see Everett, Melissa.
Morgan, Cindy. Dance Me, Daddy O'Neill, Philomena, illus. (p. 402)
Morgan, Clay. Boy Who Returned from the Sea. (p. 219)
—Boy Who Spoke Dog. (p. 219)
Morgan, Cliff. Like You, Like Me Taylor, Stephen, illus. (p. 1017)
Morgan, Connie & Morgan, Connie Collins. Runaway Beignet. Leonhard, Herb, illus. (p. 1496)
Morgan, Connie Collins, jt. auth. see Morgan, Connie.
Morgan, Cythia. Day I Met You & You Met Me! Cable, Annette, illus. (p. 413)
Morgan, David Lee, Jr. LeBron James: The Rise of a Star. (p. 987)
Morgan, Denise N., et al. Independent Reading: Practical Strategies for Grades K-3. (p. 870)
Morgan, Dennis W. Stubby the Giraffe Who Wouldn't Take Chances. (p. 1668)
Morgan, Dennis W., jt. auth. see Morgan, Dennis W.
Morgan, Dennis W. & Morgan, Dennis W. Pumpkin Head Harvey. (p. 1416)
Morgan, Derek T. Cats Tails. (p. 281)
Morgan, Diane. Delicious Dips. Pool, Joyce Oudkerk, photos by. (p. 425)
—Grill Every Day: 125 Fast-Track Recipes for Weeknights at the Grill. Armstrong, E. J., photos by. (p. 724)
Morgan, Diane & Gemignani, Tony. Pizza: More Than 60 Recipes for Delicious Homemade Pizza. Peterson, Scott, photos by. (p. 1365)
Morgan, Elizabeth. Around My Town: Describe & Compare Measurable Attributes. (p. 100)
—Gemini. (p. 659)
—My Shopping Trip. (p. 1218)
—Nickels! (p. 1251)
—What Is Energy? (p. 1889)
Morgan, Elizabeth, jt. auth. see Sullivan, Kevin.
Morgan, Ellen. Who Was Jesus? (p. 1918)
—Who Was Jesus? Marchesi, Stephen & Harrison, Nancy, illus. (p. 1918)
Morgan, Emily. Lucy & the Halloween Miracle. Prince, Andrea, illus. (p. 1063)
Morgan, Emily R. Next Time You See a Firefly. (p. 1249)
—Next Time You See a Maple Seed. (p. 1249)
—Next Time You See a Seashell. (p. 1249)
—Next Time You See the Moon. (p. 1249)
Morgan, G. A. Chantarelle (p. 291)
Morgan, Gaby. Christmas Poems. Scheffler, Axel, illus. (p. 315)
—I Love My Mum. (p. 842)
—My Christmas. (p. 1200)
—Poems from the First World War: Published in Association with Imperial War Museums. (p. 1376)
Morgan, Gil, et al. Cleared for Takeoff: Have You Got What It Takes to Be an Airline Pilot? (p. 330)
Morgan, Gloria. Dream Me Home. (p. 483)
—Ducking Stool. (p. 488)
Morgan, Gwyn & Owen, Dai. Babi Ben. (p. 123)
Morgan, Helen L. Liberty Maid: The Story of Abigail Adams. (p. 1005)
Morgan, J. Tom. Ignorance Is No Defense: A Teenager's Guide to Georgia Law. (p. 856)
Morgan, Jack. True Story of How Lacy Gasper Solved the Crime Spree. (p. 1793)
Morgan, Jana & Espinal, Rosario. Cultura política de la democracia en República Dominicana 2008: El impacto de la Gobernabilidad. (p. 390)
Morgan, Jeanette, ed. Activate!: Music, Movement & More: The Music Magazine for Grades K-6. (p. 10)
Morgan, Jennifer. Born with a Bang: The Universe Tells Our Cosmic Story. Andersen, Dana Lynne, illus. (p. 214)
—From Lava to Life: The Universe Tells Our Earth Story. Andersen, Dana Lynne, illus. (p. 643)
—Mammals Who Morph: The Universe Tells Our Evolution Story: Book 3. Andersen, Dana Lynne, illus. (p. 1085)
—Wind from the Sea. (p. 1935)
Morgan, Jessica, jt. auth. see Cocks, Heather.
Morgan, Jill, tr. see Lindgren, Astrid.
Morgan, Jody. Elephant Rescue: Changing the Future for Endangered Wildlife. (p. 511)
Morgan, John C. Little Wisdom for Growing Up: From Father to Son. (p. 1038)
Morgan, Julian. Cleopatra: Ruling in the Shadow of Rome. (p. 331)
—Constantine: Ruler of Christian Rome. (p. 359)
—Hadrian: Consolidating the Empire. (p. 735)
—Nero: Destroyer of Rome. (p. 1241)
Morgan, Kass. 100. (p. 1998)
—Day 21. (p. 412)
—Homecoming. (p. 793)
Morgan, Kathryn. Zombies. (p. 1988)
Morgan, Kayla. Barnes & Noble: Groundbreaking Entrepreneurs. (p. 139)
—Cold War. (p. 339)
—Kanye West: Soul-Fired Hip-Hop. (p. 943)
—Legalizing Marijuana. (p. 988)
Morgan, Kerry. Lickety Lick. (p. 1007)
—Smile Rhymes. (p. 1594)
Morgan, Kris, jt. auth. see Morgan, Retta.
Morgan, Kristy. Adventures of Rocky & Skeeter: Rocky Goes to Jail. (p. 22)
Morgan, Leon. Tom: The Fighting Cowboy. Arbo, Hal, illus. (p. 1762)
Morgan, Lori. Healing the Bruises Kaulbach, Kathy R., illus. (p. 757)
Morgan, Lynne. Crackers. (p. 375)
Morgan, M. I. Llên, Llun, Llwyfan. (p. 1043)
Morgan, Margaret. Wuffy the Wonder Dog. Knight, Vanessa, illus. (p. 1966)
Morgan, Marilyn. Alaska Alphabet CD-ROM. (p. 34)
Morgan, Mark, illus. see Underwood, Dale & Aho, Kirsti.
Morgan, Marlee. Soujon's Journey. (p. 1614)
Morgan, Marlo. Making the Message Mine. Grimme, Jeannette, ed. (p. 1082)
Morgan, Mary. Hear Me Squeak! (p. 759)
—Sleep Tight, Little Mouse. Morgan, Mary, illus. (p. 1588)
Morgan, Mary, illus. see Engle, Margarita.
Morgan, Mary, illus. see Winter, Jonah.
Morgan, Mary Sue. Swifty. (p. 1690)
Morgan, Matthew, et al. Yuck's Fart Club. Baines, Nigel, illus. (p. 1983)
Morgan, Melanie J. Goodbye Forever. Breyfogle, Norm, illus. (p. 700)
Morgan, Melissa. Tip Trip. (p. 1757)
Morgan, Melissa, jt. auth. see Morgan, Melissa J.
Morgan, Melissa J. Alex's Challenge. (p. 37)
—And the Winner Is... (p. 71)
—Best (Boy) Friend Forever. (p. 168)
—Camp Confidential - Complete First Summer. (p. 257)
—Charmed Forces. (p. 294)
—Fair to Remember (p. 562)
—Falling in Like (p. 567)
—Freaky Tuesday (p. 632)
—Golden Girls. (p. 694)
—Grace's Twist. (p. 705)
—In It to Win It (p. 863)
—Jenna's Dilemma (p. 912)
—Natalie's Secret (p. 1230)
—Over & Out. (p. 1313)
—Politically Incorrect. (p. 1380)
—Reality Bites (p. 1449)
—RSVP (p. 1493)
—Second Time's the Charm. (p. 1539)
—Sunrise. (p. 1677)
—Sunset. (p. 1677)
—Super Special. (p. 1682)
—Topsy-Turvy (p. 1769)
—TTYL. (p. 1795)
—Twilight. (p. 1801)
—Winter Games. (p. 1938)
—Wish You Weren't Here. (p. 1940)
Morgan, Melissa J. & Morgan, Melissa. Super Special No. 21 (p. 1682)
Morgan, Michaela. Band of Friends. Price, Nick, illus. (p. 136)
—Collins Big Cat - Tiger's Tales: Band 10/White. Boon, Debbie, illus. (p. 340)
—Mouse with No Name. Mikhail, Jess, illus. (p. 1182)
—Never Shake a Rattlesnake Sharratt, Nick, illus. (p. 1243)
—Shy Shark. Gomez, Elena, illus. (p. 1572)
—Silly Sausage & the Little Visitor Shulman, Dee, illus. (p. 1576)
—Silly Sausage & the Spooks Shulman, Dee, illus. (p. 1576)
—Silly Sausage in Trouble Shulman, Dee, illus. (p. 1576)
—Walter Tull's Scrapbook. (p. 1856)
Morgan, Michaela & Hinnant, Skip. Dear Bunny: A Bunny Love Story. Church, Caroline Jayne, illus. (p. 418)
Morgan, Michaela & Phillips, Mike. Tig in the Dumps: Lime. (p. 1748)
Morgan, Michelle. Colorsaurus. (p. 345)
—Colorsaurus ABC. (p. 345)
Morgan, Molly. Skinny Rules: The 101 Secrets Every Skinny Girl Knows. (p. 1585)
—Skinny-Size It: 101 Recipes That Will Fill You up & Slim You Down. (p. 1585)
Morgan, Niclas, jt. auth. see Morgan, Randolph.
Morgan, Nicola. Blame My Brain. (p. 198)
—Highwayman's Curse. (p. 779)
—Passion Flower Massacre. (p. 1327)
—Two-Can First Dictionary. (p. 1803)
—Two-Can First Encyclopedia. (p. 1803)
Morgan, Nicolette. All about Me: Briana's Neighborhood. (p. 43)
Morgan, Nikki. Mithendrove: Escaping Callendae. (p. 1156)
Morgan, Page. Beautiful & the Cursed. (p. 153)
—Lovely & the Lost. (p. 1061)
Morgan, Palo. Crocodile Cake. Nixon, Chris, illus. (p. 384)
Morgan, Pamela. Great Game of Angels. (p. 716)
Morgan, Pau, jt. auth. see Young, Karen Romano.
Morgan, Paul & Drewett, Jim. Toughest Test. (p. 1773)
Morgan, Philip. Fighting Diseases. (p. 585)
—Getting Energy. (p. 669)
—Moving Your Body. (p. 1184)
—Sending Messages. (p. 1550)
—Sensing the World. (p. 1551)
Morgan, Philip & Martineau, Susan. Fighting Diseases. (p. 585)
—Moving Your Body. (p. 1184)
—Sending Messages. (p. 1550)
Morgan, Philip & Turnbull, Stephanie. Generating Energy. (p. 660)
—Sending Messages. (p. 1550)
Morgan, Phillip. Abused, Alone & Forsaken: Mommy, Don't Leave Me. (p. 7)
Morgan, Pierr, illus. see Schaefer, Carole Lexa, et al.
Morgan, Randolph & Morgan, Niclas. Search for Young Niclas: Young Niclas Disappears & His Magical Friends Witch Hilga & Jackie the Ghost Help to Find Him. Stanley, Amanda, illus. (p. 1537)
Morgan, Retta & Morgan, Kris. Love Hates. (p. 1059)
Morgan, Richard. Fox & the Stork. (p. 626)
—Wheels on the Bus; The Boat on the Waves. (p. 1901)
—Wheels on the Bus - The Boat on the Waves. (p. 1901)
—Zoo Poo: A First Toilet Training Book. (p. 1989)
Morgan, Richard, illus. see Dickens, Charles.
Morgan, Richard, illus. see Gowar, Mick.
Morgan, Richela Fabian. Tape It & Wear It: 60 Duct-Tape Activities to Make & Wear. (p. 1705)
Morgan, Rick, illus. see Pruett, Scott, et al.
Morgan, Rick, illus. see Spengler, Kremena T.
Morgan, Rick, illus. see Wooster, Patricia.
Morgan, Robert. Bob Tales. Banton, Amy Renee, illus. (p. 205)
Morgan, Robert F. Partners: A Three Act Play. (p. 1325)

Morgan, Rosemarie. Student Companion to Thomas Hardy (p. 1669)
Morgan, Rowland. Brain Bafflers. (p. 221)
Morgan, Roxy. Melvin the Moose & Mr. Bluefish. (p. 1125)
Morgan, Ruth. Batter Splatter! Mikhail, Jess, illus. (p. 145)
—Behind You! Glyn, Chris, tr. (p. 160)
—Big Liam, Little Liam. Archbold, Tim, illus. (p. 182)
—Funny Easter Bunny. (p. 649)
—Happy Christmas Sglod. Carpenter, Suzanne, illus. (p. 745)
—Jess & the Bean Root. Vagnozzi, Barbara, illus. (p. 914)
Morgan, Sally. Alligators & Crocodiles. (p. 47)
—Amazing A-Z Thing. Bancroft, Bronwyn, illus. (p. 52)
—Ants: Animal Lives Series. (p. 90)
—Baby Bilby's Question. Jaunn, Adele, illus. (p. 125)
—Bats: Animal Lives Series. (p. 145)
—Bears. (p. 151)
—Bees. (p. 157)
—Bees. (p. 158)
—Bees & Wasps. (p. 158)
—Birds. (p. 191)
—Body Doubles: Cloning Plants & Animals. (p. 207)
—Bush Bash. Kwaymullina, Ambelin, illus. (p. 244)
—Butterflies (p. 247)
—Changing Planet: What Is the Environmental Impact of Human Migration & Settlement? (p. 290)
—Cheetahs: Animal Lives Series. (p. 296)
—Cheetahs. (p. 296)
—Children's Animal Encyclopedia. (p. 303)
—Dogs. (p. 462)
—Dolphins & Porpoises: Animal Lives Series. (p. 465)
—Ducks. (p. 488)
—Eagles. (p. 492)
—Earth's Energy Sources. (p. 498)
—Earth's Water Cycle. (p. 498)
—Elephants. (p. 511)
—Encyclopedia of Ocean Life. (p. 525)
—Fish. (p. 598)
—Flowers, Fruits & Seeds. (p. 608)
—Focus on Indonesia. (p. 610)
—Focus on Pakistan. (p. 611)
—Food Cycle. (p. 613)
—Frogs & Toads: Animal Lives Series. (p. 641)
—Gerbils & Hamsters. (p. 666)
—Germ Killers: Fighting Disease (p. 666)
—Giraffes. (p. 677)
—Global Warming (p. 684)
—Goats. (p. 687)
—Horses. (p. 800)
—How Do We Move? (p. 808)
—How Hearing Works. (p. 809)
—How Hearing Works (Our Senses) (p. 809)
—How Sight Works. (p. 812)
—How Smell Works. (p. 812)
—How Taste Works. (p. 812)
—How Touch Works. (p. 823)
—How We Use Plants: For Food. (p. 823)
—How We Use Plants for Making Everyday Things. (p. 823)
—How We Use Plants for Medicine & Health. (p. 823)
—How We Use Plants for Shelter. (p. 823)
—How We Use Plants to Make Everyday Things. (p. 823)
—In the Ground & Other Landscapes. (p. 866)
—Insect Eaters. (p. 875)
—Inside Your Mouth & Other Body Parts. (p. 878)
—Last Dance. Morgan, Sally, illus. (p. 977)
—Lizards & Snakes. (p. 1043)
—Magic Fair. Gibbs, Tracy, illus. (p. 1072)
—Marsupials. (p. 1097)
—Natural Resources. (p. 1235)
—Old Clothes. (p. 1283)
—Orangutans. (p. 1302)
—Our Senses (p. 1310)
—Penguins. (p. 1337)
—Plant Cycle. (p. 1369)
—Plant Life Cycles. (p. 1369)
—Rabbits. (p. 1430)
—Rats & Mice. (p. 1440)
—Remembered by Heart: An Anthology of Indigenous Writing. (p. 1459)
—Rock Cycle. (p. 1482)
—Rocks. (p. 1483)
—Rodents. (p. 1484)
—Seasons. (p. 1538)
—Sharks. (p. 1562)
—Small Cats. (p. 1592)
—Small Primates. (p. 1592)
—Spiders. (p. 1627)
—Superfoods: Genetic Modification of Food. (p. 1683)
—Tigers. (p. 1749)
—Turtles. (p. 1799)
—Under a Leaf in Forests & Jungles. (p. 1813)
—Under a Stone & Other Rocky Places. (p. 1813)
—Waste & Recycling. (p. 1860)
—Water Cycle. (p. 1862)
—Weasel Family. (p. 1869)
—Whales. (p. 1878)
—Wild Horses: Animal Lives Series. (p. 1929)
Morgan, Sally, jt. auth. see Connolly, Sean.
Morgan, Sally & Martineau, Susan. Tigers. (p. 1749)
Morgan, Sally & Molnar, Michael. Alligators & Crocodiles. (p. 47)
—Eagles. (p. 492)
—Spiders. (p. 1627)
Morgan, Sally & Teacher Created Resources Staff. Alligators & Crocodiles. (p. 47)
—Bees & Wasps. (p. 158)
—Gorillas. (p. 703)
—Penguins. (p. 1337)
—Sharks. (p. 1562)
—Tortoises & Turtles. (p. 1771)
—Whales. (p. 1878)
Morgan, Sally, et al. Charlie Burr & the Great Shed Invasion. Sheehan, Peter, illus. (p. 292)
—Charlie Burr & the Three Stolen Dollars. Ottley, Matt & Sheehan, Peter, illus. (p. 292)
Morgan, Sarah. Addition & Subtraction. (p. 12)
—Multiplication & Division. (p. 1190)
—Place Value. (p. 1366)
Morgan, Tesni. Always the Bridegroom. (p. 51)
Morgan, Todd. Why the Long Face: A Book about Thumb Sucking. (p. 1926)
Morgan, Tom, illus. see Cerasini, Marc.
Morgan, Trish, illus. see Malpass, Suzanne M.
Morgan, Vicky S. Jim & Me & Theo T. (p. 917)
Morgan, Vincent, illus. see Banks, Robin Washington.
Morgan, William, tr. see Crowder, Jack L., et al.
Morgan, Winter. Endermen Invasion: A Minecraft Gamer's Adventure, Book Three. (p. 527)
—Mystery of the Griefer's Mark: A Minecraft Gamer's Adventure, Book Two. (p. 1225)
—Quest for the Diamond Sword: An Awesome Minecraft Adventure. (p. 1426)
—Skeletons Strike Back: An Unofficial Gamer's Adventure, Book Five. (p. 1584)
—Treasure Hunters in Trouble: A Minecraft Gamer's Adventure (p. 1781)
Morgan-Cole, Trudy J. Esther: Courage to Stand. (p. 538)
Morganelli, Adrianna. Biography of Chocolate. (p. 189)
—Biography of Coffee. (p. 189)
—Biography of Tomatoes. (p. 189)
—Bruno Mars. (p. 232)
—Christopher Columbus: Sailing to a New World. (p. 316)
—Formula One. (p. 620)
—Lorde. (p. 1052)
—Samuel de Champlain: From New France to Cape Cod. (p. 1509)
—Trucks: Pickups to Big Rigs. (p. 1791)
Morganelli, Adrianna, jt. auth. see Dunlop, Jenna.
Morganelli-Sacco, Adrianna. Liam Hemsworth. (p. 1004)
Morgan-Jones, Tom, illus. see Geography Collective Staff.
Morgan-Jones, Tom, illus. see Hench, Larry.
Morgan-Jones, Tom, illus. see Humphreys, Alastair.
Morgan-Magee, Mary, ed. see Evans, Andy.
Morgan-McCray, Sheila. Untied Shoes. (p. 1823)
Morgante, Roxanne & Callies, Pat. Justin & Travis: Games They Play (p. 940)
Morganti, Jerre. World of Priscilla Gingold. (p. 1957)
Morgaut, Philippe, tr. Cheval et Son Ecuyer. Baynes, Pauline, illus. (p. 298)
Morgenroth, Connie. In the Beginning. (p. 865)
Morgenroth, Kate. Echo. (p. 502)
—Jude. (p. 930)
Morgenstern, Constance. Waking Day. (p. 1853)
Morgenstern, Gretchen L. Privilege of Colorado Citizenship: Rights & Responsibilities. (p. 1408)
Morgenstern, Susie, jt. auth. see Morgenstern, Susie Hoch.
Morgenstern, Susie Hoch & Morgenstern, Susie. I Will Make Miracles. Chen, Jiang Hong, illus. (p. 848)
Morgin, W. J., illus. see Leslie, Emma.
Mori, Kotaro. Stray Little Devil. (p. 1666)
Mori, Midori, illus. see Shah, Idries.
Moriarty, Aleta. Australia in Our World. (p. 116)
Moriarty, Chris. Inquisitor's Apprentice. Geyer, Mark Edward, illus. (p. 875)
—Watcher in the Shadows. Geyer, Mark Edward, illus. (p. 1861)
Moriarty, J. T. Birth of American Capitalism: The Growth of American Banks. (p. 192)
—Davy Crockett: Frontier Hero. (p. 411)
—Davy Crockett: Defensor de la Frontera. (p. 411)
—Manifest Destiny: A Primary Source History of America's Territorial Expansion in the 19th Century. (p. 1087)
—Phillis Wheatley: African American Poet. (p. 1351)
—Rise of American Capitalism: The Growth of American Banks. (p. 1474)
Moriarty, Jaclyn. Corner of White: "A Corner of White Slips Through a Previously Unnoticed Crack in the Reader's Heart & Changes Everything." Bk. 1 (p. 367)
—Cracks in the Kingdom. (p. 375)
—Ghosts of Ashbury High. (p. 672)
—Murder of Bindy MacKenzie. (p. 1192)
—Spell Book of Listen Taylor. (p. 1625)
Moriarty, Kathleen M. Will Waal: A Somali Folktale. Adam, Jamal, tr. (p. 1928)
Moriarty, Ros. Splosh for the Billabong. Balarinji, illus. (p. 1630)
Moriarty, Siobhan. Visit the Statue of Liberty. (p. 1845)
Moriarty, Susie. Mmmmmm My Blankie. (p. 1157)
Morice, Dave. Visit from St. Alphabet. Morice, Dave, illus. (p. 1845)
Moricuchi, Mique, illus. see Hughes, Mónica.
Moricz-Goodwin, Jennifer. Keys. (p. 950)
Morillo Caballero, Manuel, notes. Romancero. (p. 1486)
Morimoto, Diana. Max, He Likes it that Way (p. 1111)
—Max Makes a Visit. Wright, Sara Ann, illus. (p. 1111)
Morimoto, Mari, tr. see Donbo, Koge.
Morimoto, Mari, tr. see Toriyama, Akira.
Morimoto, Masaharu & Dorling Kindersley Publishing Staff. Morimoto: The New Art of Japanese Cooking. (p. 1175)
Morimoto, Sango. Taro & the Carnival of Doom. Morimoto, Sango, illus. (p. 1706)
—Taro & the Magic Pencil. Morimoto, Sango, illus. (p. 1706)
—Taro & the Terror of Eats Street. Morimoto, Sango, illus. (p. 1706)
Morin, Amanda. Learning Activities Book: 145 Entertaining Activities & Learning Games for Kids. (p. 985)
Morin, James F. Rothshield Chasing Shadows. (p. 1490)
Morin, Kimberly. Pup Is Born (p. 1417)
Morin, Leane, illus. see Broyles, Anne.
Morin, Leane, illus. see Shea, Pegi Deitz & Deitz Shea, Pegi.
Morin, Mauricio Gomez, illus. see Hendry, Diana.
Morin, Paul, illus. see Grimes, Nikki.
Morin, Paul, illus. see Kessler, Tim.
Morin, Paul, illus. see Mollel, Tololwa M.
Morin, Paul, illus. see Trottier, Maxine.
Morin, Paul, illus. see Whetung, James.
Morin, Paul, tr. see Schwartz, Virginia Frances.
Morin, Tara. There's an Iguana in My Bed. (p. 1731)
Morin, William J., jt. auth. see Ellig, Janice Reals.
Morina, Barbara, concept. Films, a Movie Lover's Journal: Journals Unlimited. (p. 586)
Morinaga, Ai. Duck Prince: Transformation Pannone, Frank, ed. (p. 488)
—Your & My Secret (p. 1979)
Morin-Neilson, Leona, tr. see Nicholson, Caitlin Dale.
Morino, Brandon, illus. see Skies, Apryl.
Morino, Sakana. Becoming a Dragon. Morino, Sakana, illus. (p. 156)
Morioka, Hiroyuki. Seikai Trilogy: Banner of the Stars II Vol. 3 Miyakoshi, Wasoh, illus. (p. 1548)
—Seikai Trilogy: Banner of the Stars: The Shape of Bonds Ono, Toshihiro, illus. (p. 1548)
Morison, Murray C. Time Sphere. (p. 1752)
Morita, Hiroyuki. Cat Returns Picture Book. Searleman, Eric, ed. (p. 278)
Morita, Kotaro G., jt. auth. see Ariga, Minatsu.
Moritsu, Wakako, illus. see Yamamoto, Makoto.
Moritz, Albert, jt. auth. see Moritz, Theresa.
Moritz, Dianne. Hush Little Beachcomber. McGee, Holly, illus. (p. 830)
Moritz, Dianne, adapted by. Santa Lives! The Night Before Christmas. (p. 1513)
Moritz, Patricia M. Indonesia. (p. 872)
Moritz, S. Dianne & Mitchell, Hazel. 1, 2, 3 ... by the Sea. (p. 1990)
Moritz, Theresa & Moritz, Albert. Stephen Leacock (p. 1648)
Moritzky, Kayla. Great I Don't Know. (p. 716)
Moritzky, Sager. Super Bad Slime Ball from Outer Space. (p. 1679)
Moriuchi, Mique. Mix & Match Animals: Over 20 Different Animal Combinations! (p. 1156)
—My Village: Rhymes from Around the World. (p. 1221)
Moriuchi, Mique, illus. see Jolley, Mike.
Moriuchi, Mique, illus. see Kim, YeShil.
Moriuchi, Mique, illus. see Piper, Sophie.
Moriuchi, Mique, illus. see Puttock, Simon.
Moriuchi, Mique, illus. see Williams, Sam.
Moriyama, Daisuke. Chrono Crusade. (p. 317)
Morkane, Sue. Original Writing. (p. 1304)
Morkes, Andrew & McKenna, Amy. College Exploration on the Internet: A Student & Counselor's Guide to More Than 685 Websites. (p. 340)
—Nontraditional Careers for Women & Men: More Than 30 Great Jobs for Women & Men with Apprenticeships Through Phds. (p. 1263)
Morley, Amanda, illus. see McCarrier, Andrea, et al.
Morley, Ben. Silence Seeker. Pearce, Carl, illus. (p. 1575)
Morley, Catherine Weyerhaeuser. James. (p. 906)
—Where Do Mountains Come from, Momma? (p. 1907)
Morley, Christine. Freaky Facts about Spiders. (p. 632)
Morley, David. Healing Our World: Inside Doctors Without Borders (p. 757)
Morley, Diane, jt. auth. see Job, Barbara.
Morley, Elizabeth. Let Sleeping Hedgehogs Spy. (p. 994)
Morley, Farah. Spider & the Doves: The Story of the Hijra. (p. 1626)
Morley, Jacqueline. Ancient Greek Athlete. (p. 69)
—Be a Sumerian Slave! A Life of Hard Labor You'd Rather Avoid. Antram, David, illus. (p. 148)
—Be in the Forbidden City! A Sheltered Life You'd Rather Avoid. Antram, David, illus. (p. 148)
—How to Be an Ancient Greek Athlete. Antram, David, illus. (p. 815)
—How to Be an Egyptian Princess. Hewetson, Nicholas J., illus. (p. 815)
—Inside the Tomb of Tutankhamun. James, John, illus. (p. 878)
—Live in a Medieval Castle! A Home You'D Rather Not Inhabit. Antram, David, illus. (p. 1040)
—World of Gods & Goddesses. Stewart, David, illus. (p. 1956)
—You Wouldn't Want to Be a Pyramid Builder! A Hazardous Job You'd Rather Not Have. (p. 1976)
—You Wouldn't Want to Be a Pyramid Builder! A Hazardous Job You'd Rather Not Have. Antram, David, illus. (p. 1976)
—You Wouldn't Want to Be a Shakespearean Actor! Some Roles You Might Not Want to Play. Antram, David, illus. (p. 1977)
—You Wouldn't Want to Be an American Colonist! A Settlement You'd Rather Not Start. (p. 1977)
—You Wouldn't Want to Be an American Colonist! A Settlement You'd Rather Not Start. Antram, David, illus. (p. 1977)
—You Wouldn't Want to... Be an American Pioneer! Antram, David, illus. (p. 1977)
—You Wouldn't Want to Be Cursed by King Tut! Antram, David, illus. (p. 1977)
—You Wouldn't Want to Be Cursed by King Tut! A Mysterious Death You'd Rather Avoid. Antram, David, illus. (p. 1977)
—You Wouldn't Want to Be in Alexander the Great's Army! Miles You'd Rather Not March. Antram, David, illus. (p. 1977)
—You Wouldn't Want to Explore with Lewis & Clark! An Epic Journey You'd Rather Not Make. (p. 1977)
—You Wouldn't Want to Explore with Lewis & Clark! An Epic Journey You'd Rather Not Make. Bergin, Mark, illus. (p. 1977)
—You Wouldn't Want to Explore with Marco Polo! A Really Long Trip You'd Rather Not Take. Antram, David, illus. (p. 1977)
—You Wouldn't Want to Meet Typhoid Mary! A Deadly Cook You'D Rather Not Know. (p. 1977)
—You Wouldn't Want to Meet Typhoid Mary! A Deadly Cook You'd Rather Not Know. Antram, David, illus. (p. 1977)
—You Wouldn't Want to Work on the Great Wall of China! Defenses You'd Rather Not Build. Antram, David, illus. (p. 1977)
Morley, Jacqueline & Salariya, David. You Wouldn't Want to Be a Shakespearean Actor! Some Roles You Might Not Want to Play. Antram, David, illus. (p. 1977)
Morley, Margaret W. Little Wanderers. (p. 1037)
—Seed-Babies. (p. 1547)
Morley, Margaret Warner. Song of Life 1922. Forsyth, Robert, illus. (p. 1611)
Morley, P. Kevin. Stinky Pirate & the Princess. (p. 1651)
Morley, Taia, illus. see Bunting, Eve.
Morley, Taia, illus. see DeCristofano, Carolyn Cinami.
Morley, Taia, illus. see Hubbell, Patricia.
Morley, Taia, illus. see Hurley, Jo.
Morley, Taia, illus. see Stewart, Melissa.
Morling, Donovan, illus. see Carter, Grant Matthew.
Morlock, Lisa. Track that Scat! (p. 1775)
Morn, September. Golden Retriever. (p. 695)
Mornard, Germaine & Farish, Catherine. Fille Orange. (p. 586)
Morneau, J. Gator Pit. (p. 658)
Morneau, Ronald E. Moondancer's Adventures. Rodstrom, Terri, illus. (p. 1172)
Morningforest, Chris & Raymond, Rebecca. Adventures of Nate & Naomi. (p. 21)
—Mooseman Reindeer & Uncle Utley. (p. 1173)
—Princess Underdrawers & the Dragon. (p. 1406)
—Taking Care of Funny Pets. (p. 1698)
Morningstar, Jeremy. My Own Special Angel. (p. 1216)
—Penalty Kick. (p. 1336)
Morningstar, Sally. Sabiduria de la Luna. (p. 1500)
Mornu, Nathalie & Lark Crafts Staff, eds. Craft Camp. (p. 375)
Moro, Robin, et al. Read Aloud Spooky Stories. (p. 1442)
Morog, Joyce Jo. Boots A Fireside Critter: A Fireside Critter. (p. 213)
Moroney, Christopher, illus. see Albee, Sarah.
Moroney, Christopher, illus. see Golden Books.
Moroney, Christopher, illus. see Hays, Anna Jane.
Moroney, Christopher, illus. see Kleinberg, Naomi.
Moroney, Christopher, illus. see McMahon, Kara & Random House Disney Staff.
Moroney, Christopher, illus. see Rabe, Tish.
Moroney, Christopher, illus. see Random House.
Moroney, Christopher, illus. see Sawyer, Parker K.
Moroney, Christopher, illus. see Shepherd, Jodie.
Moroney, Christopher, illus. see Tillworth, Mary.
Moroney, Christopher, illus. see Webster, Christy.
Moroney, Christopher, illus. see Worth, Bonnie.
Moroney, Trace. Bathtime: Baxter Bear Chubby. Moroney, Trace, illus. (p. 144)
—Bedtime: The Baxter Bear Collection. Moroney, Trace, illus. (p. 156)
—Dinnertime: Baxter Bear Chubby. Moroney, Trace, illus. (p. 441)
—My First Book of Nursery Rhymes: Jigsaw Book. (p. 1205)
—My First Book of Nursery Songs: Jigsaw Book. (p. 1205)
—Playtime. Moroney, Trace, illus. (p. 1373)
—Things I Love about Bedtime. Moroney, Trace, illus. (p. 1733)
Moroney, Trace, illus. see Littleton, Mark.
Moroney, Trace, illus. see Nolan, Allia Zobel.
Moroney, Trace, creator. Baa, Baa, Black Sheep. (p. 123)
—Owl & the Pussy Cat. (p. 1314)
Moroney, Tracey. Classic Treasury of Nursery Songs & Rhymes. (p. 328)
Moroney, Tracey, illus. see Jones, Sally Lloyd.
Moroney, Tracey, illus. see Tuck, Mildred.
Moroni, Lisa. Watch Out for the Crocodile. (p. 1861)
Morozova, Anastasia, illus. see Sexton, Jessa Rose.
Morozumi, Atsuko. Elves' First Christmas. (p. 517)
Morphew, Chris. Phoenix Files, Arrival. (p. 1351)
—Phoenix Files, Mutation. (p. 1351)
Morpurgo, Clare, jt. auth. see Morpurgo, Michael.
Morpurgo, Michael. Animal Tales (p. 80)
—Beowulf. Foreman, Michael, illus. (p. 166)
—Best Christmas Present in the World. Foreman, Michael, illus. (p. 168)
—Billy the Kid. Foreman, Michael, illus. (p. 187)
—Conker. Brown, Petra, illus. (p. 357)
—Dear Olly. Birmingham, Christian, illus. (p. 419)
—Dolphin Boy. Foreman, Michael, illus. (p. 464)
—Elephant in the Garden. (p. 511)
—Farm Boy. Foreman, Michael, illus. (p. 573)
—Gentle Giant. Foreman, Michael, illus. (p. 661)
—Half a Man. O'Callaghan, Gemma, illus. (p. 736)
—It's a Dog's Life. Allibone, Judith & Benson, Patrick, illus. (p. 895)
—Jo-Jo the Melon Donkey. Stephens, Helen, illus. (p. 919)
—Kaspar the Titanic Cat. Foreman, Michael, illus. (p. 944)
—Kensuke's Kingdom. (p. 949)
—Kingfisher Book of Great Boy Stories: A Treasury of Classics from Children's Literature. (p. 960)
—Little Albatross. Foreman, Michael, illus. (p. 1023)
—Little Foxes. (p. 1028)
—Mairi's Mermaid. (p. 1077)
—Mairi's Mermaid. Richards, Lucy, illus. (p. 1077)
—Medal for Leroy. (p. 1118)
—Meeting Cezanne. Place, Francois, illus. (p. 1123)
—Michael Morpurgo Christmas Stories. (p. 1134)
—Mimi & the Mountain Dragon. Stephens, Helen, illus. (p. 1145)
—Mozart Question. Foreman, Michael, illus. (p. 1184)
—Nine Lives of Montezuma. (p. 1256)
—On Angel Wings. Blake, Quentin, illus. (p. 1288)
—Out of the Ashes (p. 1311)
—Pied Piper of Hamelin. Chichester Clark, Emma, illus. (p. 1356)
—Private Peaceful. (p. 1407)
—Private Peaceful. (p. 1408)
—Reino de Kensuke. Aguilar, Carmen, tr. (p. 1457)
—Shadow. (p. 1557)
—Snakes & Ladders. Wilson, Anne, illus. (p. 1596)
—Toro! Toro! Foreman, Michael, illus. (p. 1770)
—Twist of Gold. (p. 1802)
—War Horse. (p. 1857)
—White Horse of Zennor. (p. 1913)
—White Horse of Zennor & Other Stories. Foreman, Michael, illus. (p. 1913)
Morpurgo, Michael & Aesop. McElderry Book of Aesop's Fables. Chichester Clark, Emma, illus. (p. 1114)
Morpurgo, Michael & Foreman. Delfin de Luis. Foreman, Michael, illus. (p. 424)
Morpurgo, Michael & Morpurgo, Clare. Where My Wellies Take Me. Lomenech Gill, Olivia, illus. (p. 1909)
Morrall, Heather. Echo Glass. (p. 502)

Morreale, Marie. 5 Seconds of Summer. (p. 1992)
—Ansel Elgort. (p. 88)
—Ariana Grande. (p. 98)
—Austin Mahone. (p. 116)
—Cast of Girl Meets World. (p. 276)
—Ed Sheeran. (p. 503)
—Guys You Love! (p. 733)
—Jennifer Lawrence. (p. 912)
—Lionel Messi. (p. 1021)
—One Direction. (p. 1294)
—Pharrell Williams. (p. 1350)
—Ross Lynch. (p. 1490)
—Selena Gomez. (p. 1549)
—Taylor Swift. (p. 1708)
—What's in the Stars? (p. 1896)
Morreale, Marie & Johns, Michael-Anne. Zac Efron Scrapbook. (p. 1984)
Morreale, Vin, Jr. Day the Woods Were One. (p. 414)
—Nicky's Secret. (p. 1251)
Morrel Disbrow, Corlyss. Ran's Upside-Down Day. (p. 1438)
Morrell, Chris, jt. auth. see BradyGames Staff.
Morrell, Cris, illus. see Pittar, Gill & Gill, Pittar.
Morrell, Cris, illus. see Pittar, Gill.
Morrell, David. Inspector of the Dead. (p. 878)
Morrell, Marcia. Mister Meister. (p. 1155)
Morrett, John J. Saints I Have Known & Known About. (p. 1504)
—Soldier Priest: An Adventure in Faith. (p. 1607)
Morretta, Alison. Frederick Douglass & William Garrison. (p. 633)
—How to Buy & Share Files Safely Online. (p. 815)
—How to Maintain Your Privacy Online. (p. 820)
Morrice, Polly Alison & Hart, Joyce. Iowa. (p. 886)
Morrill, Amos. Augusta & Elliott. (p. 115)
Morrill, Ann, jt. auth. see Matters, Print.
Morrill, Ann & Matters, Print. Religious New Year's Celebrations. (p. 1458)
Morrill, Lauren. Being Sloane Jacobs. (p. 161)
—Meant to Be. (p. 1117)
Morrill, Leslie, illus. see Howe, James.
Morrill, Leslie, illus. see Wallace, Bill.
Morrill, Leslie H., illus. see Howe, James.
Morrill, Madge Haines. Angel Stories of the Bible. (p. 74)
Morrill, Rania. How Many Carbs Is a Booger: Make Carb Counting Fun. (p. 811)
Morrill, Scott, jt. auth. see Pickering, Sean.
Morrill, Stephanie. Me, Just Different. (p. 1116)
Morrill, Stephanie & Baker Publishing Group Staff. Out with the in Crowd (p. 1312)
Morris. Doc Doxey's Elixir. (p. 459)
—Lucky Luke Vol. 40: Phil Wire. (p. 1062)
—Lucky Luke Vol. 43 the Bluefeet Are Coming! (p. 1062)
—Lucky Luke Vol. 44: Lucky Luke Versus Pat Poker. (p. 1063)
Morris, illus. see Goscinny, Rene.
Morris, illus. see Goscinny, René.
Morris, illus. see Léturgie, Jean & Fauche, Xavier.
Morris, Adrienne, ed. see Russell, Ann.
Morris, Alana. Vocabulary Unplugged: 30 Lessons That Will Revolutionize How You Teach Vocabulary K-12. (p. 1847)
Morris, Alex, et al. Eyes for Evidence: Have You Got What It Takes to Be a Forensic Scientist? (p. 558)
Morris, Alexander, illus. see Abramovitz, Melissa.
Morris, Alexander, illus. see Calvani, Mayra.
Morris, Alexander, illus. see Esparza-Vela, Mary.
Morris, Alexander, illus. see Kennedy, J. Aday.
Morris, Alexander, illus. see McClure, Beverly Stowe.
Morris, Alexander, illus. see McNamee, Kevin.
Morris, Alfred. Judge. (p. 930)
Morris, Alfred, illus. see Goscinny, Rene.
Morris, Alfred, illus. see Goscinny, René.
Morris, Alison. I Love My Family. (p. 842)
—I Love to Learn. (p. 843)
Morris & Goscinny, Rene. Dalton City. (p. 401)
Morris, Andrea. Caterpillar. (p. 279)
Morris, Ann. Dancing to America. Kolnik, Paul, photos by. (p. 403)
—Grandma Hekmat Remembers: An Arab-American Family Story. Linenthal, Peter, photos by. (p. 708)
—On the Go. Heyman, Ken, photos by. (p. 1290)
—Surprise in Auntie's Garden! Varkarotas, Heather, illus. (p. 1686)
—That's Our Custodian! Linenthal, Peter, illus. (p. 1727)
—That's Our Gym Teacher! Linenthal, Peter, illus. (p. 1727)
—That's Our Librarian! Linenthal, Peter, illus. (p. 1727)
—That's Our Nurse! Linenthal, Peter, illus. (p. 1727)
—Tools. Heyman, Ken, photos by. (p. 1767)
Morris, April. Eldon the Elephant. (p. 508)
Morris, Ashara. Let's Find Lucy! (p. 996)
Morris, Bill & Lynch, David. Math Primer with Emphasis on Fractions & Primes. (p. 1107)
Morris, Bob. Tommy Tott's Raft Adventure. (p. 1765)
Morris, Brian. Insects & Human Life. (p. 876)
Morris, Brian, ed. see Shurin, Masha.
Morris, Brian Lee & Ramirez, Sharon. Teen Heart Speaks: 16 Short Plays for Christian Youth. (p. 1713)
Morris, Brian Lee, compiled by. Little Town: Anthology of Sierra Foothill Poets. (p. 1037)
Morris, Bridgette. I Wish I Was All Grown-up. (p. 849)
Morris, C. J. Stone Children. (p. 1652)
Morris, Carla. Boy Who Was Raised by Librarians Sneed, Brad, illus. (p. 219)
Morris, Cathy. I'm a Perfectly Normal Kid Who Happens to Have Diabetes! Grunden, Kimberly, illus. (p. 858)
Morris, Chad. Cragbridge Hall, Book 1: The Inventor's Secret. (p. 376)
—Cragbridge Hall, Book 2: The Avatar Battle. (p. 376)
—Cragbridge Hall, Book 3: The Impossible Race. (p. 376)
Morris, Charles. Historic Tales the Romance of Reality Spanish America. (p. 782)
Morris, Charlie. Avery's Art Supplies: Compare Numbers. (p. 119)
Morris, Christopher G., ed. see Simon and Schuster Staff.
Morris, Claire. Basic Language Arts: Sentences (p. 142)
—Basic Language Arts, Grades 1-2: Parts of Speech (p. 142)
Morris, Claire, ed. Basic Language Arts, Grades 1-2: Capitalization & Punctuation (p. 142)
—Step by Step Math: Time & Money (p. 1647)
Morris, Daphne. Trevor Romain's How to Do Homework Without Throwing up DVD Educator Kit. (p. 1785)
—Trevor Romain's Tips, Strategies & Activities for Dealing with Bullies Resource Guide. (p. 1785)
Morris, Dave. Crypt of the Vampire. Hartas, Leo, illus. (p. 387)
—Kingdom of Dream. (p. 959)
Morris, David. My Twins First Christmas. (p. 1220)
Morris, Dawn. Concorde the Beautiful Flying Collie. (p. 355)
Morris, Deborah & Morris, Larry. American History: Presidents: Grade 4-5. Carlson, Andy, illus. (p. 61)
Morris, Deborah K. Here I Am Look at Me! Morris, Douglas, illus. (p. 770)
Morris, Deborah K. & Morris, Douglas. How Are You? (p. 805)
Morris, Dick, et al. Dubs Goes to Washington: Dubs Discovers America. (p. 487)
—Dubs Goes to Washington: And Discovers the Greatness of America. Liotta, Clayton, illus. (p. 487)
—Dubs Runs for President. (p. 487)
Morris, Don, illus. see Day, Shirley.
Morris, Douglas, illus. see Morris, Deborah K.
Morris, Douglas, jt. auth. see Morris, Deborah K.
Morris, Dudley. Mike the Monk. (p. 1141)
Morris, Eamonn, jt. auth. see Finn, Cheryl.
Morris, Edmund. Ten Acres Enough: A Practical Experience, Showing How A Very Small Farm May Be Made to Keep A Very Large Family. with Extensive & Profitable Experie. (p. 1718)
Morris, Edwin, ed. see Nohemi, Esther.
Morris, Eileen. Original "Shnoozies" Starring in "and Next Came a Roar" (p. 1304)
Morris, Elizabeth. Quest for the Tellings. Troy, Michael, illus. (p. 1426)
Morris, Elli. Cooling the South: The Block Ice Era, 1875-1975. (p. 364)
Morris, Garvin. Dump Dog. Morris, Garvin, illus. (p. 489)
Morris, Gerald. Adventures of Sir Balin the Ill-Fated. Renier, Aaron, illus. (p. 23)
—Adventures of Sir Gawain the True. Renier, Aaron, illus. (p. 23)
—Adventures of Sir Givret the Short. Renier, Aaron, illus. (p. 23)
—Ballad of Sir Dinadan. (p. 134)
—Lioness & Her Knight. (p. 1021)
—Parsifal's Page. (p. 1325)
—Princess, the Crone, & the Dung-Cart Knight. (p. 1405)
—Quest of the Fair Unknown. (p. 1426)
—Savage Damsel & the Dwarf. (p. 1516)
—Squire, His Knight, & His Lady. (p. 1637)
—Squire's Tale. (p. 1637)
Morris, Gilbert. Drummer Boy at Bull Run. (p. 487)
Morris, Gilbert & Morris, Lynn, told to. Exiles (p. 548)
Morris, Hannah, illus. see Bloch, Carole.
Morris, Ian Macgregor. Leonidas: Hero of Thermopylae. (p. 992)
—Themistocles: Defender of Greece. (p. 1729)
Morris, J. & J. Little Black Pearl. (p. 1024)
Morris, J. C. End of Arrogance. (p. 526)
Morris, J. M. Adventures of the Nickerbocker: The Dark Castle. Morris, Jerry L., ed. (p. 23)
Morris, J. S. Jewel. (p. 916)
Morris, Jackie. Barefoot Book of Classic Poems. (p. 139)
—Cat & the Fiddle: A Treasury of Nursery Rhymes. (p. 277)
—East of the Sun, West of the Moon. (p. 498)
—I Am Cat. (p. 832)
—Ice Bear. (p. 850)
—Jackie Morris Notebooks (p. 903)
—Little Evie in the Wild Wood. Hyde, Catherine, illus. (p. 1027)
—Snow Leopard. (p. 1599)
—Song of the Golden Hare. (p. 1611)
—Tell Me a Dragon. (p. 1716)
—Y Tu Dragón, ¿Cómo Es? Morris, Jackie, illus. (p. 1968)
Morris, Jackie, illus. see French, Vivian.
Morris, Jackie, illus. see Hughes, Ted & Quarto Generic Staff.
Morris, Jackie, illus. see Mayhew, James.
Morris, Jackie, illus. see Pitcher, Caroline.
Morris, Jackie, illus. see Quarto Generic Staff.
Morris, Jackie, illus. see Summers, Susan.
Morris, Jackie, des. Jackie Morris Notecards in a Wallet. (p. 903)
Morris, James. Diamond in the Rough. (p. 434)
Morris, James R., illus. see Yanuchi, Lori & Yanuchi, Jeff.
Morris, Janel. Disaster Planning. (p. 446)
Morris, Janet, jt. auth. see Mort, Linda.
Morris, Jean, illus. see Goscinny, René.
Morris, Jeanne L., illus. see Arrathoon, Leigh A. & Davio, John.
Morris, Jen. Granddaddy's Hands. (p. 707)
Morris, Jennifer, illus. see Cochran, Jean M.
Morris, Jennifer, illus. see Fliess, Sue.
Morris, Jennifer E. Ice Cream Shop. (p. 850)
—Ice Cream Shop. Morris, Jennifer E., illus. (p. 850)
—May I Please Have a Cookie? Morris, Jennifer E., illus. (p. 1112)
—Please Write Back! (p. 1373)
—Please Write Back! Morris, Jennifer E., illus. (p. 1373)
—Scholastic Reader Level 1: the Sea Monster: A Steve & Wessley Reader. (p. 1522)
—Sea Monster. (p. 1535)
Morris, Jennifer E., illus. see Cochran, Jean M.
Morris, Jennifer E., illus. see O'Connell, Jennifer Barrett.
Morris, Jerry L., ed. see Morris, J. M.
Morris, Jessica, illus. see Lynn, Deidre.
Morris, John D. Geology Book. (p. 662)
Morris, Joseph. Nuclear Proliferation. (p. 1270)
Morris, Juddi. Route 66: Main Street of America. (p. 1491)
Morris, Julie, jt. auth. see Nieto-Phillips, John M.
Morris, Katherine, ed. see McNair, Randall.
Morris, Kathleen. Lost & Found - a Children's Christmas Play. (p. 1054)
Morris, Keith E. J., jt. auth. see Dowson, Anthony.
Morris, Kerry Nicole. Baby Who Just... WON't Sleep! Parker's Story. (p. 128)
Morris, Kerry-Ann. Jamaica. (p. 906)
Morris, Kerry-Ann & Ismail, Nafisah. Dominican Republic. (p. 465)
Morris, Kim. Tinker Bell & the Great Fairy Rescue. (p. 1755)
Morris, Kim Ely. Through the Eyes of Love. (p. 1745)
Morris, Kimberly & Burke, Kathleen. Just for Now: Kids & the People of the Court. Sansevero, Tony, illus. (p. 938)
Morris, Kiran, illus. see O'Neil, Dave.
Morris, Kirkland. Alley that Wanted to be a Street: Kirkland Morris. Kinra, Richa, illus. (p. 47)
Morris, Larry, jt. auth. see Morris, Deborah.
Morris, Lee. Marshmellow Little Cloud Discovers an Island. (p. 1096)
—Marshmellow Little Cloud Discovers England. (p. 1096)
Morris, Lillie, illus. see Riner, Sherry.
Morris, Linda Loper. No Yellow Horse, If You Please. (p. 1261)
Morris, Lolita. Mike & Me-Sh. (p. 1141)
Morris, Lynn. Belinda the Butterfly's Beautiful Colors. (p. 162)
—Don't eat your Broccoli! Mettler, Joe, illus. (p. 467)
Morris, Lynn, jt. told to see Morris, Gilbert.
Morris, M. R. Midnight's Court. (p. 1139)
Morris, Margery, ed. see Weatherby, W. J.
Morris, Mark, jt. auth. see Mahase, Compton.
Morris, Mary Ann. My Sunshine-A Mind of Her Own: Lessons My Dog Taught Me. (p. 1219)
Morris, Matthew W., et al. Identite, Modernite, Texte. (p. 852)
Morris, Michael. Puzzle Cards Letters. (p. 1420)
—Puzzle Cards Numbers. (p. 1420)
Morris, Michael, illus. see Quest, Stacy.
Morris, Neil. African Myths. Kennedy, Graham, illus. (p. 27)
—African Myths. Sansom, Fiona & Kennedy, Graham, illus. (p. 27)
—Air Pioneers. (p. 31)
—Ancient Egypt. (p. 68)
—Ancient World. (p. 71)
—Astronomers. (p. 109)
—Atlas of Ancient Civilizations. De Luca, Daniela, illus. (p. 112)
—Biomass Power: Now & in the Future. (p. 189)
—Biomass Power. (p. 189)
—Cars. (p. 272)
—Children's Picture Atlas: A First Introduction to the Countries of the World. (p. 304)
—Communities (p. 349)
—Do You Know Where Your Food Comes From? (p. 458)
—Energy Mix. (p. 528)
—Everyday Life in Ancient Egypt. (p. 543)
—Everyday Life in Ancient Greece. (p. 543)
—Everyday Life in Ancient Rome. (p. 543)
—Everyday Life in Medieval Europe. (p. 543)
—Everyday Life in Prehistory. (p. 543)
—Everyday Life in the Renaissance. (p. 543)
—First Arabic Words. Melling, David, illus. (p. 593)
—First Chinese Words. Melling, David, illus. (p. 593)
—Food Technology (p. 614)
—Fossil Fuels: Now & in the Future. (p. 623)
—Fossil Fuels. (p. 623)
—Gadgets & Inventions (p. 652)
—Geothermal Power. (p. 665)
—Geothermal Power: Now & in the Future. (p. 666)
—Glass. (p. 682)
—Global Warming. (p. 684)
—Industrial Revolution (p. 872)
—Junior Atlas. (p. 936)
—Living & Growing. (p. 1040)
—Living in the Arctic (p. 1041)
—Lost Cities. (p. 1055)
—Metals. (p. 1130)
—Minibeasts. (p. 1146)
—Modern World Leaders. (p. 1159)
—North & East Asia (p. 1264)
—Nuclear Power. (p. 1270)
—Our Wonderful World: Fun Finding Out. (p. 1310)
—Paper. (p. 1322)
—Pirates. (p. 1363)
—Plastics. (p. 1370)
—Settlements & Cities (p. 1554)
—Ships. (p. 1567)
—Should Substance-Using Athletes Be Banned for Life? (p. 1570)
—Solar Power: Now & in the Future. (p. 1606)
—Solar Power. (p. 1606)
—Textiles. (p. 1724)
—Trains. (p. 1777)
—Transportation (p. 1779)
—Water Power: Now & in the Future. (p. 1863)
—Water Power. (p. 1863)
—Weather. (p. 1869)
—What Does Space Exploration Do for Us? (p. 1884)
—Who Traveled to the Moon? (p. 1918)
—Wind Power. (p. 1935)
—Wood. (p. 1949)
—World Cultures (p. 1954)
Morris, Neil, jt. auth. see Davies, Gill.
Morris, Neil, jt. auth. see Gibbs, Lynne.
Morris, Neil, jt. auth. see Graham, Ian.
Morris, Neil, jt. auth. see Morris, Ting.
Morris, Neil, jt. auth. see Springer, Lisa.
Morris, Neil, jt. auth. see Steele, Philip.
Morris, Neil & Heinemann Library Staff. Communities (p. 349)
—Settlements & Cities (p. 1554)
Morris, Neil & Johnson, Jinny. Metals. (p. 1130)
Morris, Neil & Morris, Ting. Ant. (p. 88)
—Butterfly. (p. 247)
—Dragonfly. (p. 478)
—Grasshopper. (p. 711)
—Illustrated Bible. McRae Books Staff, ed. (p. 857)
Morris, Neil & Steele, Philip. Inside Earthquakes. (p. 876)
—Inside Hurricanes & Tornadoes. (p. 876)
Morris, Olivia. Twelve Days of Christmas Candy: A Counting Book. (p. 1800)
Morris, Paris. My Twins First Halloween. (p. 1220)
Morris, Paris & Florzak, Douglas. My Twins Are Coming Home. (p. 1220)
—My Twins First Birthday. (p. 1220)
Morris, Paris & Singer, Thom. I'm Having Twins (p. 859)
Morris, Paul. 101 Language Activities. (p. 1999)
Morris, Paula. Dark Souls. (p. 408)
—Eternal City. (p. 539)
—Ruined. (p. 1494)
—Unbroken. (p. 1811)
Morris Publishing Company Staff, illus. see Banda, Lo Hartog Van.
Morris Publishing Company Staff, illus. see Goscinny, R.
Morris Publishing Company Staff, illus. see Goscinny, René.
Morris Publishing Company Staff, jt. auth. see de Groot, Bob.
Morris Publishing Company Staff, jt. auth. see Goscinny, R.
Morris Publishing Company Staff, jt. auth. see Goscinny, René.
Morris Publishing Company Staff & Goscinny, René. Daltons' Escape (p. 401)
Morris, Rene. Sonshine Girls: Summer Secret. Casale, Paul, illus. (p. 1613)
—Sonshine Girls: Operation Salvation. Casale, Paul, illus. (p. 1613)
Morris, Richard & Morris, Winifred. What If the Shark Wears Tennis Shoes? (p. 1887)
Morris, Richard B. First Book of the Indian Wars. Fisher, Leonard Everett & Waltrip, Mildred, illus. (p. 593)
Morris, Richard T. Bye-Bye, Baby! Day, Larry, illus. (p. 249)
—This Is a Moose. (p. 1735)
Morris, Rick A. & Sember, Brette McWhorter. Project Management That Works: Real-World Advice on Communicating, Problem-Solving, & Everything Else You Need to Know to Get the Job Done (p. 1410)
Morris, Rob & Marcello, Paul. Civil War Close Up. (p. 325)
Morris, Rob, et al. Battle of Gettysburg Close Up. (p. 146)
Morris, Robert. Grandma Ursu, Think Blue. (p. 708)
Morris, Robin C., illus. see Huebner, Dawn.
Morris, Rooster. Gate of No Return. Cummins, Scott, illus. (p. 658)
Morris, Roz. Nelle Harper Lee: Master Storyteller. (p. 1240)
—Rosa Parks: Mother of the Civil Rights Movement. (p. 1489)
Morris, Samuel L., illus. see Diggs, Linda.
Morris, Sandra. Willow & Her Grandm. (p. 1934)
Morris, Sandra, illus. see Holden, Pam.
Morris, Sheila L. Sweet Baby's Fun Months of the Year. (p. 1689)
Morris, Siôn, jt. auth. see Myrddin ap Dafydd.
Morris, Susan. Fritha's Summer. (p. 639)
—Practical Guide to Dragon Magic. (p. 1392)
Morris, Susan, illus. see Dede, Vivian Hughes.
Morris, Susan, illus. see Dreyer, Nicole E.
Morris, Susan, illus. see Thoreson-Snipes, Nanette.
Morris, Taylor. BFF Breakup. (p. 174)
—Blowout Higgins, Anne Keenan, illus. (p. 202)
—Class Favorite. (p. 327)
—Foiled #2. Higgins, Anne Keenan, illus. (p. 611)
Morris, Tim. Wallace Stevens: Poetry & Criticism. (p. 1855)
Morris, Ting. Arts & Crafts of Ancient China. Young, Emma, illus. (p. 104)
—Arts & Crafts of Ancient Greece. Young, Emma, illus. (p. 104)
—Arts & Crafts of Ancient Rome. Young, Emma, illus. (p. 104)
—Arts & Crafts of the Aztecs & Maya. Young, Emma, illus. (p. 104)
—Arts & Crafts of the Native Americans. Young, Emma, illus. (p. 105)
Morris, Ting, illus. see Goscinny, Rene & Spear, Luke.
Morris, Ting, illus. see Goscinny, René.
Morris, Ting, jt. auth. see Morris, Neil.
Morris, Ting & Morris, Neil. Animals. Levy, Ruth, illus. (p. 81)
—Dinosaurs. Levy, Ruth & Cowne, Joanne, illus. (p. 443)
—Masks. (p. 1102)
—Rainforest. Hulse, Gillian, illus. (p. 1436)
—Space. Turvey, Raymond, illus. (p. 1618)
Morris, Tony, illus. see Frank, Penny.
Morris, Tony, illus. see Robinson, Sue.
Morris, Tony, illus. see Willoughby, Robert.
Morris, William. House of the Wolfings: A Book That Inspired J. R. R. Tolkien. (p. 803)
—House of the Wolfings: A Book That Influenced J. R. R. Tolkien. (p. 803)
—More to William Morris: Two Books That Inspired J. R. R. Tolkien-the House of the Wolfing & the Roots of the Mountains. (p. 1175)
—On the Lines of Morris' Romances: Two Books That Inspired J. R. R. Tolkien-the Wood Beyond the World & the Well at the World's End. (p. 1290)
—Roots of the Mountains: A Book That Inspired J. R. R. Tolkien. (p. 1488)
Morris, Winifred, jt. auth. see Morris, Richard.
Morrisette, Sharon. Toads & Tessellations. O'Neill, Philomena, illus. (p. 1760)
Morris-Lipsman, Arlene. Presidential Races: Campaigning for the White House. (p. 1397)
—Presidential Races: The Battle for Power in the United States. (p. 1397)
Morrison, Alastair. Government & Society. (p. 704)
Morrison, Anna C. & Movshina, Marina. Silly Moments. (p. 1576)
Morrison, Ben. Digestive System. (p. 438)
Morrison, Blake. Yellow House. Craig, Helen, illus. (p. 1970)
Morrison, Britta. Zara by the Se. (p. 1985)
Morrison, Cameron, illus. see Morrison, Maria.
Morrison, Cathy. I Want a Pet. (p. 847)
Morrison, Cathy, illus. see Berkes, Marianne Collins, et al.
Morrison, Cathy, illus. see Berkes, Marianne Collins.
Morrison, Cathy, illus. see Berkes, Marianne.
Morrison, Cathy, illus. see Borland, Kathryn Kilby & Speicher, Helen Ross.
Morrison, Cathy, illus. see Ciocchi, Catherine.
Morrison, Cathy, illus. see Diehl, Jean Heilprin.
Morrison, Cathy, illus. see Donald, Rhonda Lucas.
Morrison, Cathy, illus. see Dunham, Montrew.

Morrison, Cathy, illus. see Higgins, Helen Boyd.
Morrison, Cathy, illus. see Lord, Michelle.
Morrison, Cathy, illus. see Mason, Miriam E.
Morrison, Cathy, illus. see Myers, Elisabeth P.
Morrison, Cathy, illus. see Rhonda Lucas Donald, Rhonda Lucas.
Morrison, Cathy, illus. see Sisson, Kathryn Cleven.
Morrison, Cathy, illus. see Speicher, Helen Ross & Borland, Kathryn Kilby.
Morrison, Cathy, illus. see Sullivan, Martha.
Morrison, Cathy, illus. see Trouvé, Marianne Lorraine.
Morrison, Cathy, illus. see Wilkie, Katharine E.
Morrison, Cathy, illus. see Zimelman, Nathan.
Morrison, Cathy, jt. auth. see Ciocchi, Catherine.
Morrison, Chloe. Laura's Lemonade Stand: Represent & Interpret Data. (p. 980)
Morrison, Chloe, jt. auth. see Mills, Nathan.
Morrison, Connor, illus. see Morrison, Maria.
Morrison, Craig. Rock & Roll. (p. 1481)
Morrison, D. F. Lapis Key Adventures of Ernie & Daisy. (p. 975)
Morrison, Daequan T. What's the Spook? (p. 1899)
Morrison, Danette W. & Johnson, Dana A. My Eyebrows Are Hiding. (p. 1202)
Morrison, Denis. Gumball. (p. 731)
Morrison, Dorothy. Whimsical Tarot: A Deck for Children & the Young at Heart. (p. 1911)
Morrison, Frank, illus. see Abrahams, Peter.
Morrison, Frank, illus. see Barrett, Mary Brigid.
Morrison, Frank, illus. see DePrince, Michaela & DePrince, Elaine.
Morrison, Frank, illus. see Paul, Chris.
Morrison, Frank, illus. see Queen Latifah.
Morrison, Frank, illus. see Rodriguez, Alex.
Morrison, Frank, illus. see Russell-Brown, Katheryn.
Morrison, Frank, illus. see Schofield-Morrison, Connie.
Morrison, Frank, illus. see Smith, Charles R., Jr.
Morrison, Frank, illus. see Taylor, Debbie A.
Morrison, Frank, illus. see Taylor, Gaylia.
Morrison, Frank, illus. see Thomson, Melissa.
Morrison, Frank, illus. see Weinstein, Muriel Harris.
Morrison, Frank, jt. auth. see Taylor, Debbie.
Morrison, Frank, jt. auth. see Taylor, Gaylia.
Morrison, Gertrude W. Girls of Central High Aiding the Red Cross. (p. 680)
Morrison, Glenda. Lilly Beans. (p. 1017)
Morrison, Gordon. Bald Eagle. (p. 133)
—Nature in the Neighborhood. (p. 1236)
Morrison, Gordon, illus. see Kricher, John C.
Morrison, Grant. American Dreams (p. 60)
—Animal Man. (p. 78)
—Animal Man. Hill, Michael, ed. (p. 78)
—Bloody Hell in America Kahan, Bob, ed. (p. 201)
—Counting to None Weston, Chris, illus. (p. 371)
—Doom Patrol: Down Paradise. Vol. 3 (p. 470)
—Doom Patrol: Crawling from the Wreckage. Vol. 1 Kahan, Bob, ed. (p. 470)
—Doom Patrol - The Painting That Ate Paris. (p. 470)
—Earth (p. 495)
—Filth. Erskine, Gary, illus. (p. 586)
—Invisible Kingdom. (p. 885)
—Kissing Mister Quimper. Weston, Chris, illus. (p. 962)
—Origin of the Species Truog, Chas, illus. (p. 1304)
—Seven Soldiers of Victory Williams, J. H., III & Bianchi, Simone, illus. (p. 1555)
Morrison, Grant & DeMatteis, J. M. World War III Dell, John, illus. (p. 1959)
Morrison, Grant, et al. Apocalipstick (p. 91)
—Doom Patrol - Magic Bus Bolland, Brian, illus. (p. 470)
—Entropy in the U. K. (p. 531)
—Seven Soldiers of Victory (p. 1555)
—Strength in Numbers. (p. 1667)
Morrison, Harry Steele. Adventures of A Boy Reporter. (p. 16)
Morrison, Heather S. Inventors of Communications Technology. (p. 884)
—Inventors of Everyday Technology. (p. 884)
—Inventors of Food & Agriculture Technology. (p. 884)
—Inventors of Health & Medical Technology. (p. 884)
—Inventors of Industrial Technology. (p. 884)
—Inventors of Transportation Technology. (p. 884)
Morrison, Ian. Skiing in the Desert: Asian Innovation. (p. 1584)
Morrison, Ian A. Deserts of the World. (p. 429)
Morrison, J. A. & Goldsworthy, Steve. English-French Relations. (p. 530)
Morrison, James. Companion to Homer's Odyssey (p. 351)
Morrison, Janet Love. Radar the Rescue Dog. (p. 1432)
Morrison, Jaydene & Peterson, Russell. I Hate You, Miss Bliss. (p. 839)
Morrison, Jeff, illus. see Carney, Larry.
Morrison, Jennifer. Beware of the Bull: Stories for the Young & the Incurably Eccentric. (p. 173)
—White House. (p. 1913)
Morrison, Jessica. Christmas. (p. 312)
—Cordillera. (p. 366)
—Easter. (p. 499)
—Eclipses. (p. 502)
—Fête du Travail: Les Célébrations Canadiennes. Karvonen, Tanjah, tr. from ENG. (p. 583)
—Hank Aaron: Home Run Hero. (p. 742)
—Investing. (p. 885)
—Jour de la SaintJeanBaptiste: Les Célébrations Canadiennes. Karvonen, Tanjah, tr. from ENG. (p. 927)
—Jour de L'Action de Grâce: Les Célébrations Canadiennes. Karvonen, Tanjah, tr. from ENG. (p. 927)
—Labour Day. (p. 970)
—Maritimes. (p. 1094)
—Military. (p. 1142)
—Saint-Jean-Baptiste Day. (p. 1503)
—Saving. (p. 1517)
—Thanksgiving. (p. 1725)
—Wayne Gretzky: Greatness on Ice. (p. 1865)
—Women's Issues. (p. 1946)
Morrison, Jessica & Kissock, Heather. White House. (p. 1913)
Morrison, John. Frida Kahlo. (p. 637)
—Mathilde Krim. (p. 1108)
—Sammy Sosa. (p. 1508)
Morrison, Julia. Wishes. Fabian, Gabriella, illus. (p. 1940)
Morrison, Karen. International Science Coursebook 3. (p. 880)
—Nelson International Mathematics. (p. 1240)
Morrison, Karen, jt. auth. see Page, Claire.
Morrison, Karen & Press, Karen. Study & Master Mathematical Literacy Grade 11 Learner's Book. (p. 1670)
—Study & Master Mathematical Literacy Grade 11 Learner's Book Afrikaans Translation. (p. 1670)
Morrison, Karen, et al. Collins Primary Science - Student's Book Stage 6. (p. 341)
Morrison, Kathryn, jt. auth. see Dittrich, Tina.
Morrison, Kathy & Dittrich, Tina. Literature-Based Workshops for Language Arts: Ideas for Active Learning. (p. 1023)
Morrison, Kenny. Sevenlives & the Woof Pack. (p. 1555)
Morrison, Kevin. Frank Is a Chihuahua. De La Cruz, Erin Harris, illus. (p. 628)
—God's Garden: A story about What Happens When We Die. Bachoc, Patricia, illus. (p. 691)
—I Can Speak Bully. Kemble, Mai S., illus. (p. 836)
—Stitches. Nixon, John, illus. (p. 1651)
Morrison, Lillian. Guess Again! Riddle Poems. Hale, Christy, illus. (p. 728)
—I Scream, You Scream: A Feast of Food Rhymes. Dunaway, Nancy, illus. (p. 845)
Morrison, Maria. Why Bears Don't Live in Humble Morrison, Cameron & Morrison, Connor, illus. (p. 1922)
Morrison, Marianne. Mysteries of the Sea: How Divers Explore the Ocean Depths. (p. 1222)
—Saddleshoe Quackers Present Lucky's Adventure. (p. 1501)
Morrison, Marion. Brazil. (p. 224)
—Brazil. (p. 224)
—Chile (p. 305)
—Guatemala. (p. 728)
—Guyana. (p. 733)
—Mexico City. (p. 1131)
—Rio de Janeiro. (p. 1473)
Morrison, Matthew. Big Questions: Incredible Adventures in Thinking. Chalk, Gary, illus. (p. 183)
Morrison, Megan. Grounded: The Tale of Rapunzel. (p. 725)
Morrison, Michele. Comet's Tale. (p. 348)
Morrison, Nancy. Tock the Clock (p. 1760)
Morrison, Nancy, illus. see Sylvester, Sr.
Morrison, Patricia. Shadow Girl. (p. 1557)
Morrison, Robbie. Wildcats: Nemesis. Caldwell, Talent, illus. (p. 1931)
Morrison, Slade, jt. auth. see Morrison, Toni.
Morrison, Susan. Kamehameha: The Warrior King of Hawai'i. Kiefer, Karen, tr. (p. 942)
Morrison, Taylor. Buffalo Nickel. Morrison, Taylor, illus. (p. 235)
—Civil War Artist. (p. 325)
—Wildfire. (p. 1931)
Morrison, Toni. Little Brother. (p. 1025)
—Remember: The Journey to School Integration. (p. 1459)
Morrison, Toni & Morrison, Slade. Lion or the Mouse? Lemaitre, Pascal, illus. (p. 1020)
—Little Cloud & Lady Wind. Qualls, Sean, illus. (p. 1026)
—Peeny Butter Fudge. Cepeda, Joe, illus. (p. 1335)
—Please, Louise. Strickland, Shadra, illus. (p. 1373)
—Tortoise or the Hare. Cepeda, Joe, illus. (p. 1771)
Morrison, Tyler, illus. see Wilson, Murray.
Morrison Walton, Jeannie. Little Lemur, a Fable of Pride. (p. 1030)
Morrison, William. Robert Fulton: American Inventor. (p. 1479)
Morrison, Yvonne. Carved in Stone: Clues about Cultures. (p. 273)
—Cocky Who Cried Dingo. McKenzie, Heath, illus. (p. 337)
—Earth Matters. (p. 496)
—Earth Partners: Saving the Planet. (p. 496)
—Emu That Laid the Golden Egg. McKenzie, Heath, illus. (p. 522)
—Stuck on Cactus: American Desert Life. (p. 1669)
—Three Wallabies Gruff. McKenzie, Heath, illus. (p. 1744)
—Town Possum, Outback Possum. McKenzie, Heath, illus. (p. 1773)
Morrison-Smyth, Anne, tr. see Carroll, Lewis, pseud.
Morriss, Deborah, illus. see Andersen, Hans Christian & Stevenson, Robert Louis.
Morriss, Roger. Captain Cook & His Exploration of the Pacific. (p. 264)
Morrissette, Cora. Adventures in the Land of Make Believe. (p. 15)
—Life Stories in the World of Fiction. (p. 1013)
Morrissey, Bridgette, illus. see Morrissey, Donna.
Morrissey, Dean & Krensky, Stephen. Crimson Comet. Morrissey, Dean, illus. (p. 382)
—Monster Trap. Morrissey, Dean, illus. (p. 1168)
—Wizard Mouse. Morrissey, Dean, illus. (p. 1943)
Morrissey, Donna. Cross Katie Kross. Morrissey, Bridgette, illus. (p. 385)
—What Beautiful Mistake Did You Make Today? (p. 1880)
Morrissey, Jean. Agapegrams. (p. 29)
Morrissey, Kay, photos by see Kassandra, ed.
Morrissey, Lynda I. Monsters in My Class. (p. 1169)
—Princesses Don't Hit. Money, Greg, illus. (p. 1406)
Morrissey, Paul. Casper's Scare School TP. (p. 276)
Morrissey, Paul, ed. see Hester, Phil.
Morrissey, Paul, ed. see Labbe, Jesse & Coffey, Anthony.
Morrissey, Simon. Richard Wilson. (p. 1470)
Morrissey, Tricia. Everyday Life: Through Chinese Peasant Art. Mak, Ding Sang, illus. (p. 543)
—H Is for Hong Kong: A Primer in Pictures. Briel, Elizabeth, illus. (p. 734)
—Hiss! Pop! Boom! Celebrating Chinese New Year. Lee, Kong, illus. (p. 781)
—My Mom Is a Dragon: And My Dad Is a Boar. (p. 1214)
Morro, Scott. Danni's Gift. (p. 405)
Morrone, Marc & Fernandez, Amy. Ask the Dog Keeper. (p. 106)
Morrone Pedowitz, Laura. Elephant Who Couldn't Eat Peanuts. (p. 511)
Morrow. Lima Bean Dream. (p. 1018)
—Make Things Without Needles. (p. 1079)
Morrow & Cash, T. Getting Ahead in Science. (p. 669)
Morrow, Ann. Gilded Age. (p. 676)
Morrow, Barbara Olenyik. Good Night for Freedom. Jenkins, Leonard, illus. (p. 699)
—Mr. Mosquito Put on His Tuxedo. Goembel, Ponder, illus. (p. 1185)
Morrow, Carol. Forgiveness Is Smart for the Heart. Alley, R. W., illus. (p. 619)
Morrow, Daniel & Strobel Morrow, Alison. That's Where God Is Godbey, Cory, illus. (p. 1727)
Morrow, David C. How Women Manipulate. (p. 823)
Morrow, Dj. Charlie & Joe. (p. 292)
—Good Ol' Boys. (p. 700)
—Two Bears Short. (p. 1803)
Morrow, E., illus. see Petersen, Jean.
Morrow, George, illus. see Wyke-Smith, E. A.
Morrow, Glenn, illus. see Fleischman, Paul.
Morrow, Glenn, illus. see Frankfeldt, Gwen & Fleischman, Paul.
Morrow, Gray, illus. see Lee, Stan.
Morrow, Gray, illus. see Myers, Hortense & Burnett, Ruth.
Morrow, J. T., illus. see Bailer, Darice.
Morrow, J. T., illus. see Cernak, Linda.
Morrow, J. T., illus. see Doyle, Arthur.
Morrow, J. T., illus. see Higgins, Nadia.
Morrow, J. T., illus. see Krieg, Katherine.
Morrow, J. T., illus. see Owings, Lisa.
Morrow, J. T., illus. see Ringstad, Arnold.
Morrow, J. T., illus. see York, J.
Morrow, J. T., illus. see Zee, Amy Van.
Morrow, James. Algeria. (p. 38)
—Djibouti. (p. 455)
Morrow, Jason, illus. see Lashley, Beverly.
Morrow, Jennifer Cameron. Baby Doll Jenny. (p. 126)
Morrow, John. Lilly Lightbug. (p. 1017)
—Ostrich Egg Omelets. (p. 1306)
Morrow, Jt, illus. see Doyle, Arthur.
Morrow, Mark. Dangerous Children. (p. 404)
Morrow, Paula. Mo Willems (p. 1157)
—My Parents Are Divorcing. Now What? (p. 1216)
Morrow, Sherry. Woman of the Mountains. (p. 1945)
Morrow, Tara Jaye. Just Mommy & Me. Bratun, Katy, illus. (p. 939)
Mors, Peter D. & Mors, Terry M. L D the Littlest Dragster. Weiss, Tracy, illus. (p. 969)
Mors, Terry M., jt. auth. see Mors, Peter D.
Morse, Dorothy Bayley, illus. see Jones, Ruth Fosdick.
Morse, ed. ABC's For Your Health. (p. 4)
Morse, Jenifer Corr. Scholastic Book of World Records. (p. 1521)
—Scholastic Book of World Records, 2008. (p. 1521)
—Scholastic Book of World Records 2014. (p. 1521)
Morse, Joe, illus. see Coy, John.
Morse, Joe, illus. see Krensky, Stephen.
Morse, Joe, illus. see Thayer, Ernest L.
Morse, Letitia M. Yellow Roses on Her Feet. (p. 1970)
Morse, Michelle, illus. see Marshall, Stacey A.
Morse, Michelle, illus. see McDuke, Doc.
Morse, Nessa Neilson, illus. see St. James, Leah.
Morse, Patti, illus. see MacVicar, Andrea.
Morse, Philip C. Kick Out Stress - Teen Stress Reduction Program: Improving Self-Esteem, Optimizing Performance in School & Sports & Improving Physical & Emotional Health. (p. 951)
Morse, Rose. Everlasting Evergreen. (p. 542)
Morse, Scott. Magic Pickle. Morse, Scott, illus. (p. 1073)
—Visitations. (p. 1845)
Morse, Scott, jt. auth. see Ruijters, Marcel.
Morse, Tony, illus. see Honigsberg, Peter Jan.
Morse, Virginia, jt. auth. see Nottage, Cindy.
Morse, Virginia & Nottage, Cindy. Iim: Independent Investigation Method Teacher Manual with Companion CD. (p. 856)
Morse, William A. Bip & the Bulb. (p. 190)
—Kurkle Kids: Pirate Lostman's Great Adventure. (p. 968)
Morse, William A. and & Morse, William A. And Dana Jo. Kurkle Kids: Spirit of America. (p. 968)
Morse, William A. And Dana Jo, jt. auth. see Morse, William A. and.
Morshead, E. D., tr. see Aeschylus.
Morss, Ben. Cinderella's Mice. (p. 320)
Morss, Martha. Advantage Reading Grade 3 Hamaguchi, Carla, ed. (p. 14)
Morss, Martha, jt. auth. see Crabtree Publishing Company Staff.
Morstad, Julie. How To. Morstad, Julie, illus. (p. 814)
—Julia, Child. (p. 932)
—T Is for Tumbling. (p. 1694)
Morstad, Julie, illus. see Andersen, Hans Christian & Stevenson, Robert Louis.
Morstad, Julie, illus. see Cuevas, Michelle.
Morstad, Julie, illus. see Lawson, JonArno.
Morstad, Julie, illus. see O'Leary, Sara & Opal, Paola.
Morstad, Julie, illus. see O'Leary, Sara.
Morstad, Julie, illus. see Snyder, Laurel.
Morstad, Julie, illus. see Woodward, Caroline.
Morstad, Julie, jt. auth. see Porter, Matthew.
Mort, Linda & Morris, Janet. Families. (p. 567)
Mort, Norm, jt. auth. see Morton, Norman.
Mortensen, Carl. Flea & Gang & the Tube Dogs. Mortensen, Carl, illus. (p. 603)
Mortensen, Carl Anker. Gruff Ar Antur Yn y Beibl. Davies, Aled, tr. from ENG. (p. 727)
Mortensen, Denise Dowling. Bug Patrol. Bell, Cece, illus. (p. 236)
Mortensen, Erik. Sir Cook, the Knight? Harrison, Laura, illus. (p. 1580)
Mortensen, Lori. Amelia Earhart: Female Pioneer in Flight. McGuire, Robert, illus. (p. 58)
—Boston Tea Party Griffith, Gershom, illus. (p. 215)
—Bree's Bike Jump Sullivan, Mary, illus. (p. 226)
—Cat That Disappeared Simard, Remy, illus. (p. 278)
—Cindy Moo. Mack, Jeff, illus. (p. 321)
—Cowpoke Clyde & Dirty Dawg. Austin, Michael Allen, illus. (p. 374)
—Day at the Fire Station. Thompson, Jeffrey, illus. (p. 412)
—Declaration of Independence Skeens, Matthew, illus. (p. 422)
—Dirty Gertie Perry, Gina Marie, illus. (p. 446)
—Ellis Island Skeens, Matthew, illus. (p. 515)
—End Zone Sullivan, Mary, illus. (p. 526)
—First Day, No Way! Simard, Remy, illus. (p. 594)
—George Washington Carver: Teacher, Scientist, & Inventor. O'Connor, Niamh, illus. (p. 664)
—Going to the Dentist Thompson, Jeffrey, illus. (p. 693)
—Harriet Tubman: Hero of the Underground Railroad Moore, Frances, illus. (p. 750)
—In the Trees, Honey Bees. Arbo, Cris, illus. (p. 867)
—Killer Sharks. (p. 956)
—Leprechauns. (p. 993)
—Lost Lunch Simard, Remy, illus. (p. 1056)
—Manners Matter in the Classroom Hunt, Lisa, illus. (p. 1088)
—Manners Matter in the Library Hunt, Lisa, illus. (p. 1088)
—Manners Matter on a Field Trip Hunt, Lisa, illus. (p. 1088)
—Manners Matter on the Playground Hunt, Lisa, illus. (p. 1088)
—Marie Curie: Prize-Winning Scientist Jaekel, Susan, illus. (p. 1093)
—Missing Monster Card Simard, Remy, illus. (p. 1152)
—Paul Revere's Ride Orback, Craig, illus. (p. 1330)
—Satoshi Tajiri: Pokemon Creator. (p. 1515)
—Sphinx. (p. 1626)
—Thomas Jefferson: A Founding Father of the United States of America Ebert, Len, illus. (p. 1739)
—Visit to the Police Station Set. Thompson, Jeffrey, illus. (p. 1845)
—Visit to the Vet Thompson, Jeffrey, illus. (p. 1845)
—Voices of the Civil Rights Movement. (p. 1848)
—Working on the Farm Thompson, Jeffrey, illus. (p. 1953)
—Writing the U. S. Constitution Feeney, Siri Weber, illus. (p. 1965)
Mortensen, Lori, jt. auth. see Schwabacher, Martin.
Mortensen, Lori & Kimmel, Allison Crotzer. We Shall Overcome. (p. 1868)
Mortensen, Lori & Picture Window Books Staff. Thomas Edison: Inventor, Scientist, & Genius Thompson, Jeffrey, illus. (p. 1738)
Mortensen, Lyn. Effie May & Her Outrageous Hats. Mortensen, Lyn, illus. (p. 505)
—My Favorite Flower Is the Daisy... & other Silly Poems. Mortensen, Lyn, illus. (p. 1203)
Mortenson, jt. auth. see Johnson, Anne.
Mortenson, Greg. Stones into Schools: Promoting Peace, One School at a Time. (p. 1653)
Mortenson, Greg & Husain, Farzana. Listen to the Children: The Story of Dr. Greg & Stones into Schools. Roth, Susan L., illus. (p. 1022)
Mortenson, Greg & Relin, David Oliver. Three Cups of Tea: One Man's Journey to Change the World... One Child at a Time. (p. 1741)
—Three Cups of Tea: One Man's Journey to Change the World... One Child at a Time. (p. 1742)
Mortenson, Greg & Roth, Susan L. Listen to the Wind: The Story of Dr. Greg & Three Cups of Tea. Roth, Susan L., illus. (p. 1022)
Mortenson, Greg, et al. Three Cups of Tea: One Man's Journey to Change the World... One Child at a Time. (p. 1742)
Morter, Peter. Atlas Visual de los Descubrimientos. (p. 113)
Morthland, John. Texas Music: Legends from the Lone Star State (p. 1724)
Mortillaro, Nicole. Connor Mcdavid. (p. 358)
—Jarome Iginla: How the NHL's First Black Captain Gives Back (p. 909)
—Something to Prove: The Story of Hockey Tough Guy Bobby Clarke (p. 1610)
—Willie O'Ree: The Story of the First Black Player in the NHL (p. 1934)
Mortimer, jt. auth. see Lear, Edward.
Mortimer, Alexander, illus. see McRae, Suzanne.
Mortimer, Anne. Bunny's Easter Egg. Mortimer, Anne, illus. (p. 242)
—Christmas Mouse. Mortimer, Anne, illus. (p. 314)
—Pumpkin Cat. Mortimer, Anne, illus. (p. 1416)
Mortimer, Anne, illus. see Brown, Margaret Wise.
Mortimer, Anne, illus. see Lear, Edward & Mortimer.
Mortimer, Anne, illus. see Stainton, Sue.
Mortimer, F. L. Lines Left Out. (p. 1019)
—More about Jesus. (p. 1173)
—Precept upon Precept. (p. 1394)
Mortimer, J. R. This or That? 2: More Wacky Choices to Reveal the Hidden You. (p. 1737)
Mortimer, John. Rumpole & the Reign of Terror. (p. 1495)
Mortimer, Lauren, illus. see Krull, Kathleen.
Mortimer, Lauren, illus. see McDonough, Yona Zeldis.
Mortimer, Mitch, illus. see Spiegel, Al.
Mortimer, Rachael. Red Riding Hood & the Sweet Little Wolf. Pichon, Liz, illus. (p. 1454)
—Three Billy Goats Fluff. Pichon, Liz, illus. (p. 1741)
Mortimer, Sean, jt. auth. see Mullen, Rodney.
Mortimer, Sheila. St. Patrick & the Shamrock. Catchpole, Diana, illus. (p. 1638)
Mortimer, Susan. Alphabet Island Phonics 2B. (p. 49)
Morton, Alan. Einstein's Theories of Relativity. (p. 507)
Morton, Aretha E. Heap See But Few Know: The Autobiography of Aretha Morton. (p. 759)
Morton, Carlene. Alpha Betti. Lucas, Margeaux, illus. (p. 48)
—Library Pages. Docampo, Valeria, illus. (p. 1006)
Morton, Carlos. At Risk. (p. 110)
—Drop-Out. Landes, William-Alan, ed. (p. 486)
—Drug-O. Landes, William-Alan, ed. (p. 486)
—Fatherless. Landes, William-Alan, ed. (p. 577)
—Johnny Tenorio. (p. 923)
—Johnny Tenorio & Other Plays. (p. 923)
—Miser of Mexico. (p. 1150)
—Rancho Hollywood. (p. 1438)
Morton, Christine. No Te Preocupes, Guille. McMullen, Nigel, illus. (p. 1260)

Morton Cuthrell, Kimberly. Splinters of My Soul. Malone, Susan Mary & Woodson, Lissa, eds. (p. 1630)
Morton, David L. & Gabriel, Joseph. Electronics: The Life Story of a Technology (p. 510)
Morton, Debra & Stover, Elizabeth. Math Tub Topics: Math Instruction Through Discovery. Jennett, Pamela, ed. (p. 1107)
—Science Tub Topics: Approaching Science Through Discovery. Jennett, Pamela, ed. (p. 1528)
Morton, E. D. Frasier: Help Me! I Just Do Not Understand! (p. 631)
Morton, Emma. 18: Starting the Great Journey of Life on Your Eighteenth Birthday. (p. 1995)
Morton, Jane & Dreier, Ted. Moozie's Cow Wisdom for Loving to the "Uddermost" Royse, Jane, illus. (p. 1173)
Morton, Jim. Let's Make Memories ... (p. 999)
Morton, Ken. Cinderella. (p. 320)
—Goldilocks & the Three Bears. (p. 696)
—Three Billy Goats Gruff: My First Reading Book. (p. 1741)
Morton, Ken, illus. see Baxter, Nicola.
Morton, Ken, illus. see Brown, Janet.
Morton, Ken, jt. auth. see Baxter, Nicola.
Morton, Lisa, illus. see Monnar, Alberto.
Morton, Machel. Tales of Shimmerlee: The MuriMuri. Galloway, Amy, illus. (p. 1702)
Morton, Michelle, ed. Karen Hewitt Hagan: An American Impressionist. (p. 943)
Morton, Norman & Mort, Norm. Classic Cars, 1931-1980. (p. 327)
Morton, Rick. Vital Skills: How to Respond to Culture. (p. 1846)
Morton, Robert, illus. see Unwin, Mike.
Morton, Sasha. Good Samaritan. Belli, Alfredo, illus. (p. 700)
—Huckleberry Finn. Belli, Alfredo, illus. (p. 824)
—Jonah & the Whale. Belli, Alfredo, illus. (p. 925)
—Joseph & His Coat of Many Colors. Belli, Alfredo, illus. (p. 926)
—Moses. Belli, Alfredo, illus. (p. 1176)
Morton, Sasha, jt. auth. see Tick Tock Musical Staff.
Morton, Scott. Encyclopedia for My Son (p. 524)
Morton, Vivian, illus. see Cole, Bob.
Morton, William A. From Plowboy to Mormon Prophet Being a Short History of Joseph Smith for Children. Ramsey, L. A., illus. (p. 643)
Morton-Shaw, Christine. Hunt for the Seventh. (p. 828)
—Riddles of Epsilon. (p. 1471)
Morty, Ducktor. Can Do & Friends to the Rescue! A Story about Getting along & Working Together. (p. 258)
—Can Do & the Mall: A Story for Us All. (p. 258)
Morvan, Jean-David, jt. auth. see Poe, Edgar Allen.
Morwood, James. Oxford Grammar of Classical Greek. (p. 1315)
Morwood, James, ed. Pocket Oxford Latin Dictionary. (p. 1375)
Mosatche, Harriet S. & Lawner, Elizabeth K. Ask Dr. M & Liz. (p. 106)
Mosby, Pamela. I'm So Angry. Brever, Amy, illus. (p. 860)
Mosby, Sandy. How Much Do You Know about It? Rev. Martin Luther King, Jr. (p. 811)
Mosby, Tia. Extraordinary Annie. (p. 555)
Mosca, Isabelle. Adventure to Autism Planet. (p. 15)
Moscal, Manuela, illus. see Panaitescu, Simona.
Moscatello, Ramona, et al. Aerola's Big Trip. (p. 25)
Moscattini, Alexander. Classroom Chair: A True Story. (p. 328)
Moscoso, Edgar. Doll Repairman. (p. 463)
Moscovich, Rotem, et al. Curious George Snowy Day. (p. 393)
Moscovitch, Arlene. Egypt: The Culture. (p. 506)
—Egypt - The Culture. (p. 506)
—Egypt - The Land. (p. 506)
—Egypt - The People. (p. 506)
Moscowitz, Moshe & Resnick, Yael. Queen of Persia. Sokoloff, David, illus. (p. 1425)
Mosdi, Thomas, et al. Bit of Madness. Civiello, Emmanuel, illus. (p. 194)
Mosedale, Julian, illus. see Donbavand, Tommy & Harpercollins Staff.
Mosedale, Julian, illus. see Strong, Jeremy.
Mosedale, Julian, illus. see Taylor, Sean.
Mosedale, Julian, jt. auth. see Bailey, Ellen.
Mosel, Arlene. Tikki Tikki Tembo. Lent, Blair, illus. (p. 1749)
—Tikki Tikki Tembo. Lent, Blair, illus. (p. 1750)
—Tikki Tikki Tembo Book & CD Storytime Set. Lent, Blair, illus. (p. 1750)
Moseley, Charles. J. R. R. Tolkien. (p. 902)
Moseley, Cherri & Rees, Janet. Cambridge Primary Mathematics Stage 1 Learner's Book. (p. 255)
Moseley, Christopher & Campbell, George L. Routeldge Handbook of Scripts & Alphabets. (p. 1491)
Moseley, Dudley, illus. see Dowley, Tim.
Moseley, Keith. Where's the Fairy? (p. 1911)
—Where's the Knight? (p. 1911)
Moseley, Rachel, illus. see Goldman, Karen.
Moseley, Rachel, jt. ed. see Hollows, Joanne.
Moseley, Sophia. Adventures of Charlie. Delderfield, Angela, illus. (p. 17)
Moseley, Steven. Trailer Park King. (p. 1776)
Moseley, Tabitha. Pearl's Tales a Collection of Children's Stories. (p. 1333)
Mosely, Winifred. Did You See the Moon Go By. (p. 437)
Moseng, Elisabeth, illus. see Brug, Sandra Gilbert.
Mosenson, Cecil. Work Hard-Never Give Up. (p. 1952)
Mosenthal, Basil, et al. Getting Afloat: All You Need to Know about Sailing Small Boats. (p. 669)
Moser, Barry, illus. see Deedy, Carmen Agra & Wright, Randall.
Moser, Barry, illus. see Doyen, Denise.
Moser, Barry, illus. see Edelman, Marian Wright & Edelman, Marian W.
Moser, Barry, illus. see Harper, Dan.
Moser, Barry, illus. see Kumin, Maxine.
Moser, Barry, illus. see London, Jack.
Moser, Barry, illus. see MacLachlan, Patricia & Charest, Emily MacLachlan.
Moser, Barry, illus. see MacLachlan, Patricia.
Moser, Barry, illus. see Nichol, Barbara.
Moser, Barry, illus. see Palatini, Margie.
Moser, Barry, illus. see Pochocki, Ethel & Helms, Hal M.
Moser, Barry, illus. see Pochocki, Ethel.
Moser, Barry, illus. see Schmidt, Gary D.
Moser, Barry, illus. see Wales, Dirk.
Moser, Barry, illus. see Winters, Kay.
Moser, Barry, illus. see Wood, Douglas.
Moser, Barry & Maser, Barry. Scary Stories. (p. 1520)
Moser, Cara, illus. see Harper, Dan.
Moser, Chris & Moser, Liz. Discoveries of Shuggs, A Curious Cat. Moser, Chris & Moser, Liz, illus. (p. 448)
Moser, Diane, jt. auth. see Spangenburg, Ray.
Moser, Diane Kit, jt. auth. see Spangenburg, Ray.
Moser, Elise. Lily & Taylor. (p. 1018)
Moser, Erwin. Sapitio Solitario (The Lonely Toad) (p. 1514)
—Vicente, el Elefantito. (p. 1840)
Moser, Erwin, et al. Manuel y Didi y el Sombrero Volador. (p. 1089)
—Manuel y Didi y el Coche de Maiz. (p. 1089)
—Manuel y Didi y el Gato de Nieve. (p. 1089)
—Manuel y Didi y el Hombre de las Nieves. (p. 1089)
Moser, Franz, jt. auth. see Tompkins, Robyn.
Moser, Jason. Ellium. (p. 515)
Moser, Kit, jt. auth. see Spangenburg, Ray.
Moser, Laura, jt. auth. see Mechling, Lauren.
Moser, Linda M. Over the Fence. (p. 1314)
Moser, Lisa. Cowboy Boyd & Mighty Calliope. Doninck, Sebastiaan Van, illus. (p. 373)
—Kisses on the Wind. Brown, Kathryn, illus. (p. 962)
—Monster in the Backpack. Jones, Noah Z., illus. (p. 1167)
—Squirrel's Fun Day. Gorbachev, Valeri, illus. (p. 1637)
—Squirrel's World. Gorbachev, Valeri, illus. (p. 1637)
Moser, Liz, jt. auth. see Moser, Chris.
Moser, Manuel, et al. Manuel y Did y la Seta Gigante. (p. 1089)
Moser, Richard. Examined Universe. (p. 547)
Moser, Summer. Adventures of Mackenzie the Pug. (p. 20)
Moser, Victoria. Zigzag & the Pet Swap. (p. 1986)
Moses, Albert. Hawk & the Turtles. Roberts, Pam, illus. (p. 755)
Moses, Anne E. Gatos Musikos: A Secret Told by the Moon. (p. 658)
Moses, Antoinette. Girl at the Window. (p. 678)
Moses, Brian. Animal Pants! Boretzki, Anja, illus. (p. 79)
—Anna Angrysaurus. (p. 85)
—Brian Moses' School Report: Very Funny Poems about School! (p. 226)
—Cookie Crumbs (p. 361)
—Don't Look at Me with That Tone of Voice. (p. 468)
—Favourite Classic Poets. (p. 578)
—Hey Diddle Diddle & Hey Diddle Doodle. (p. 774)
—Humpty Dumpty & Humpty Dumpty at Sea. (p. 827)
—I'm Telling on You! Poems about Brothers & Sisters. Maddison, Lucy, illus. (p. 860)
—Jayden Jealousaurus. (p. 910)
—Samuel Scaredosaurus. (p. 1509)
—Sophie Shyosaurus. (p. 1613)
—Taking Out the Tigers. Garbutt, Chris, illus. (p. 1698)
—There's a Hamster in the Fast Lane (p. 1731)
—William Worrydactyl. (p. 1933)
Moses, Brian, jt. auth. see Stevens, Roger.
Moses, Brian & Stevens, Roger. Olympic Poems - 100% Unofficial! (p. 1288)
Moses, Brian, ed. Performance Poems. Pascoe, Jed, illus. (p. 1343)
Moses, Donald A., jt. auth. see Moss, Wendy L.
Moses, Grandma. Night Before Christmas. (p. 1252)
—Prayer in Spring. (p. 1393)
Moses, Grandma, illus. see Frost, Robert.
Moses, Jennifer Anne. Tales from My Closet. (p. 1701)
Moses, Melissa. Parts of Me: A Story for Children Who Have Experienced Scary Things. (p. 1325)
Moses, Shelia P. Baptism. (p. 137)
—Joseph. (p. 926)
—Joseph's Grace. (p. 926)
—Legend of Buddy Bush (p. 988)
—Legend of Buddy Bush. (p. 988)
—Return of Buddy Bush. (p. 1464)
—Sittin' Up. (p. 1582)
Moses, Tammy. Prophecy. (p. 1411)
Moses, Will. Fairy Tales for Little Folks. (p. 564)
—Hansel & Gretel. Moses, Will, illus. (p. 743)
—Mary & Her Little Lamb: The True Story of Famous Nursery Rhyme. Moses, Will, illus. (p. 1100)
—Raining Cats & Dogs: A Collection of Irresistible Idioms & Illustrations to Tickle the Funny Bones. Moses, Will, illus. (p. 1436)
—Will Moses' Mother Goose. Moses, Will, illus. (p. 1932)
Mosesson, Connie. Lovey Dovey & the Makeover Mistake. (p. 1061)
Mosha, Mirriam. Polina! (p. 1380)
Moshay, G. J. O. Who Is This Allah? (p. 1916)
Moshel, Eluzer. Learn to Write. (p. 984)
—My Number Book (p. 1216)
Mosher, Barry, illus. see Pochocki, Ethel.
Mosher, Geraldine. Madcap Mother Goose. Rocque, Rose, illus. (p. 1069)
Mosher, Jennifer. Who Caught the Yawn? & Where Did the Sneeze Go? Sharp, Todd, illus. (p. 1915)
Mosher, Kim, jt. auth. see Froeber, Sarah.
Mosher, Nancy, jt. ed. see Campbell, Diana.
Mosher, Nancy & Turney, Maria. Fancy's Playground. (p. 570)
Mosher, Richard. Zazoo. (p. 1985)
Mosher, Scott, illus. see Gelber, Peter Frost.
Mosher, Steven, jt. auth. see Mosher, Steven W.
Mosher, Steven W. & Mosher, Steven. Population Control: Real Costs, Illusory Benefits. (p. 1385)
Moshi Monsters Staff. Moshi Monsters Poppet's Crazy Day. (p. 1176)
Moshier, Joe & Sonnenburg, Chris. Go, Pea, Go! (p. 687)
Mosier, Pamela. Elizabeth, the Eastern Gray Squirrel. (p. 513)
Mosier, Scott & Son, Eugene. Marvel Universe Ultimate Spider-Man Volume 6. (p. 1099)
Moskal, G. Family Fun: Learning the F Sound. (p. 568)
—I Like Winter: Learning the ER Sound. (p. 841)
Moskal, Greg. Apache Indian Community. (p. 91)
—Give the Band a Hand. (p. 681)
—History of Space Exploration: Sequencing Events Chronologically on a Timeline. (p. 784)
—Meet Officer Jerry. (p. 1121)
—Modern Buildings: Identifying Bilateral & Rotational Symmetry & Transformations. (p. 1158)
—Our Sun. (p. 1310)
—pueblo apache (an Apache Indian Community) (p. 1414)
Moskof, Martin, jt. auth. see Chwast, Seymour.
Moskovitz, Rick. Carousel Music. (p. 271)
Moskowitz, Cheryl. Can It Be about Me? Asquith, Ros, illus. (p. 258)
Moskowitz, Hannah. Break. (p. 224)
—Gone, Gone, Gone. (p. 697)
—History of Glitter & Blood. (p. 784)
—Invincible Summer. (p. 885)
—Marco Impossible. (p. 1092)
—Not Otherwise Specified. (p. 1267)
—Teeth. (p. 1715)
—Zombie Tag. (p. 1988)
Moskowitz, Nachama Skolnik. Bridge to Our Tradition: Pirkei Avot. Lewy, Faye Tillis, ed. (p. 227)
—Bridge to Our Tradition. Lewy, Faye Tillis, ed. (p. 227)
Moskowitz, Tobias J., jt. auth. see Wertheim, L. Jon.
Mosley, Anthony D. & Romaine, Deborah S. A to Z of Parkinson's Disease. (p. 2)
Mosley, Candyce. Buddy the Bucking Ballerina. (p. 235)
Mosley, Kenneth. We're Getting a Divorce. (p. 1875)
Mosley, Kim, text. Workbook for Black & White Photography (p. 1952)
Mosley, Nina Simone. Studying & Test Taking. (p. 1670)
Mosley, Shelley & Charles, John. Suffragists in Literature for Youth: The Fight for the Vote. (p. 1672)
Mosley, Walter. 47. (p. 1997)
—Cinnamon Kiss. (p. 321)
—Fear of the Dark. (p. 579)
—Fortunate Son. (p. 623)
—Wave. (p. 1864)
—When the Thrill Is Gone (p. 1905)
Mosqueda, Olga, illus. see Disney Book Group Staff & Hicks, Barbara Jean.
Mosqueda, Olga, illus. see Disney Book Group Staff & Lewis, Kevin.
Mosqueda, Olga T. & Tucker, Marianne. Learn to Draw Plus Disney Winnie the Pooh. (p. 983)
Mosquito, Angel, illus. see Slingerland, Janet.
Moss, Alexandra. Lara's Leap of Faith. (p. 975)
Moss, Alexandra, pseud. Boys or Ballet? (p. 220)
—Ellie's Chance to Dance. (p. 514)
—Grace's Show of Strength. (p. 705)
—Isabelle's Perfect Performance. (p. 891)
—Kate's Special Secret (p. 944)
—Lara's Leap of Faith. (p. 975)
Moss, Anne H. Amazing, True-To-Life Tale of Me Do It. (p. 56)
Moss, Barbara E. Adventures of Sir Goblin, the Feline Knight. Houx, Emily Marie Cornell du, illus. (p. 23)
Moss, Christopher Hawthorne. Beloved Pilgrim. (p. 163)
Moss, Deborah. Shelley, the Hyperactive Turtle. Schwartz, Carol, illus. (p. 1564)
Moss, J. P. Kind Fairy Adventures: 3 Loving Fairy Tales from the Land of the Faye. (p. 957)
Moss, Jennifer, et al. One-in-a-Million Baby Name Book: The Babynames.com Guide to Choosing the Best Name for Your New Arrival. (p. 1295)
Moss, Jenny. How Robots Work. (p. 812)
—Look Inside a Castle. (p. 1049)
—Look Inside a Pueblo. (p. 1049)
—Shadow. (p. 1557)
—Taking Off. (p. 1698)
Moss, Joanne, jt. auth. see Mangan, Anne.
Moss, Lloyd. Zin! Zin! Zin! A Violin. Priceman, Marjorie, illus. (p. 1986)
—Zin! Zin! Zin! A Violin. (p. 1987)
Moss, Lucille. Gift Within. Uhouse, Debra, illus. (p. 675)
Moss, Marissa. Alien Eraser Reveals the Secret of Evolution. Moss, Marissa, illus. (p. 40)
—Alien Eraser to the Rescue. Moss, Marissa, illus. (p. 40)
—All-New Amelia. Moss, Marissa, illus. (p. 45)
—Amelia Tells All. Moss, Marissa, illus. (p. 58)
—Amelia Writes Again. Moss, Marissa, illus. (p. 58)
—Amelia's 5th-Grade Notebook. Moss, Marissa, illus. (p. 58)
—Amelia's 6th-Grade Notebook. Moss, Marissa, illus. (p. 58)
—Amelia's 7th-Grade Notebook. Moss, Marissa, illus. (p. 58)
—Amelia's Are-We-There-Yet Longest Ever Car Trip. Moss, Marissa, illus. (p. 58)
—Amelia's Back-to-School Survival Guide: Vote 4 Amelia - Amelia's Guide to Babysitting. Moss, Marissa, illus. (p. 58)
—Amelia's BFF. Moss, Marissa, illus. (p. 58)
—Amelia's Book of Notes & Note Passing. Moss, Marissa, illus. (p. 58)
—Amelia's Boredom Survival Guide. Moss, Marissa, illus. (p. 58)
—Amelia's Boy Survival Guide. Moss, Marissa, illus. (p. 58)
—Amelia's Bully Survival Guide. Moss, Marissa, illus. (p. 58)
—Amelia's Cross-My-Heart, Hope-to-Die Guide to the Real, True You! Moss, Marissa, illus. (p. 58)
—Amelia's Family Ties. Moss, Marissa, illus. (p. 58)
—Amelia's Guide to Babysitting. Moss, Marissa, illus. (p. 58)
—Amelia's Guide to Gossip: The Good, the Bad, & the Ugly. Moss, Marissa, illus. (p. 58)
—Amelia's Itchy-Twitchy, Lovey-Dovey Summer at Camp Mosquito. Moss, Marissa, illus. (p. 58)
—Amelia's Longest, Biggest, Most-Fights-Ever Family Reunion. Moss, Marissa, illus. (p. 58)
—Amelia's Middle School Survival Guide: Amelia's Most Unforgettable Embarrassing Moments, Amelia's Guide to Gossip. Moss, Marissa, illus. (p. 58)
—Amelia's Middle-School Graduation Yearbook. (p. 58)
—Amelia's Most Unforgettable Embarrassing Moments. Moss, Marissa, illus. (p. 58)
—Amelia's Must-Keep Resolutions for the Best Year Ever! Moss, Marissa, illus. (p. 58)
—Amelia's Notebook. Moss, Marissa, illus. (p. 58)
—Amelia's School Survival Guide. Moss, Marissa, illus. (p. 58)
—Amelia's Science Fair Disaster. Moss, Marissa, illus. (p. 58)
—Amelia's Summer Survival Guide: Amelia's Longest, Biggest, Most-Fights-Ever Family Reunion; Amelia's Itchy-Twitchy, Lovey-Dovey Summer at Camp Mosquito. Moss, Marissa, illus. (p. 58)
—Barbed Wire Baseball. Shimizu, Yuko, illus. (p. 137)
—Blood Diaries: Tales of a 6th-Grade Vampire. Moss, Marissa, illus. (p. 200)
—Brave Harriet. Payne, C. F., illus. (p. 223)
—Bravest Woman in America. U'Ren, Andrea, illus. (p. 223)
—Emma's Journal. (p. 520)
—Fake Friend! Moss, Marissa, illus. (p. 565)
—Friendship Survival Guide: And Trying to Be the Best BFF Amelia. Moss, Marissa, illus. (p. 639)
—Home Sweet Rome. (p. 793)
—Max Disaster: Alien Eraser Unravels the Mystery of the Pyramids. Bk. 2 Moss, Marissa, illus. (p. 1111)
—Mighty Jackie: The Strike-Out Queen. Payne, C. F., tr. (p. 1140)
—Mira's Diary: Lost in Paris. (p. 1149)
—Mira's Diary: Bombs over London. (p. 1149)
—Name Game! Moss, Marissa, illus. (p. 1228)
—Nurse, Soldier, Spy: The Story of Sarah Edmonds, a Civil War Hero. Hendrix, John, illus. (p. 1273)
—Pharaoh's Secret. (p. 1350)
—Rose's Journal: The Story of a Girl in the Great Depression. (p. 1490)
—Vampire Dare! Moss, Marissa, illus. (p. 1832)
—Vote 4 Amelia. Moss, Marissa, illus. (p. 1850)
Moss, Maureen. God's Promise. Purnell, Gerald, illus. (p. 691)
Moss, Miriam. Bare Bear. McQuillan, Mary, illus. (p. 138)
—Matty in a Mess! Simmons, Jane, illus. (p. 1110)
—Matty Takes Off! Simmons, Jane, illus. (p. 1110)
—This Is the Oasis. Kennaway, Adrienne, illus. (p. 1736)
—This Is the Tree. Kennaway, Adrienne, illus. (p. 1736)
—Wiley & Jasper. Bucker, Jutta, tr. (p. 1932)
Moss, Olivia. Joy's Close Call. Turner, Helen, illus. (p. 930)
Moss, Onawumi Jean, jt. auth. see McKissack, Patricia C.
Moss, Patricia Crocker. Dillie & the Baby Deer. (p. 440)
—Dillie & the Dragonfly: Second Edition. (p. 440)
—Dillie & the Dragonfly. (p. 440)
—Dillie & the Lesson of the Special Golden Fish. (p. 440)
—Dillie's Encounter with the Bucket Man. (p. 440)
—Dillie's Ride to the Sea: A Visit to Savannah. (p. 440)
—Dillie's Summer with Aunt Juliette. (p. 440)
Moss, Peggy. One of Us Weber, Penny, illus. (p. 1296)
—Say Something Lyon, Lea, illus. (p. 1518)
—Say Something: 10TH Anniversary Edition. Lyon, Lea, illus. (p. 1518)
Moss, Peggy & Lyon, Lea. Say Something (p. 1518)
Moss, Peggy, et al. Our Friendship Rules Geis, Alissa Imre, illus. (p. 1308)
Moss, Ronald. Wizard Next Door. (p. 1943)
Moss, Samantha. Where's My Stuff? The Ultimate Teen Organizing Guide. Wertz, Michael, illus. (p. 1910)
Moss, Samantha & Schwartz, Lesley. Where's My Stuff? The Ultimate Teen Organizing Guide. (p. 1910)
Moss, Ted. Puppeteers. (p. 1417)
Moss, Wendy. Being Me: A Kid's Guide to Boosting Confidence & Self-Esteem. (p. 161)
—Bounce Back: How to Be a Resilient Kid. (p. 216)
—School Made Easier: A Kids Guide to Study Strategies & Anxiety-Busting Tools. (p. 1523)
Moss, Wendy L. & DeLuca-Acconi, Robin. School Made Easier: A Kid's Guide to Study Strategies & Anxiety-Busting Tools. (p. 1523)
Moss, Wendy L. & Moses, Donald A. Tween Book: A Growing-Up Guide for the Changing You. (p. 1799)
Moss, Wendy L & Taddonio, Susan A. Survival Guide for Kids with Physical Disabilities & Challenges. (p. 1686)
Moss, Yvonne. Butterfly Princess. (p. 248)
—Green Eyed Chick. (p. 721)
—Seasons Through the Eyes of A Child: The Snow, the Spring, the Summer, the Fall. (p. 1539)
Mossiano, Lilly. My New Mommy. Mossiano, Sage, illus. (p. 1216)
Mossiano, Sage, illus. see Mossiano, Lilly.
Mosso, Tyfanny. Mud Puddle Gang. (p. 1188)
Most, Andee, illus. see Plum, Joan Ensor & Plum, Paul S.
Most, Bernard. ABC T-Rex. (p. 3)
—Catch Me If You Can! (p. 279)
—Catch Me If You Can! (¡A Que No Me Alcanzas!) Flor Ada, Alma & Campoy, F. Isabel, trs. from ENG. (p. 279)
—Cow That Went OINK. (p. 373)
—Dinosaur Questions. (p. 442)
—How Big Were the Dinosaurs? (p. 805)
—Vaca Que Decia Oink. Mlawer, Teresa, tr. from ENG. (p. 1829)
—Very Boastful Kangaroo. (p. 1837)
Mostacchi, Massimo. Rey Perezoso. Brignole, Giancarla, tr. (p. 1467)
Moster, Jamey S. Fly, Fly Away. (p. 609)
Mostofizadeh, Hoornaz. MMA Coloring Book: Mixed Martial Arts Coloring Book. (p. 1157)
Mostoller, Marcia. Emma's Dilemm. (p. 520)
—Emma's Summer Camp Dilemm. (p. 520)
—Poor William Dill. (p. 1384)
Mostow, Sarah, illus. see Talmadge, Joyce.
Mostue, Trude. Wild about Animals: A Book of Beastly Behaviour. (p. 1928)
Mostyn, David. Amazing Magic Tricks. (p. 55)
—Super Doodles: Complete the Crazy Pictures! (p. 1679)
Mostyn, David, illus. see Atkins, Jill.
Mostyn, David, illus. see Clarke, Jane.
Mostyn, David, illus. see Hooper, Ruth.
Mostyn, David, illus. see Lane, Mike.
Mostyn, David, illus. see Law, Felicia & Way, Steve.
Mostyn, David, illus. see Owen, Christopher.
Mostyn, David, illus. see Pullman, Philip.
Mostyn, David, jt. auth. see Turner, Steve.
Mosz, Gosia, illus. see Da Costa, Deborah.

Motalebi, Majede. Wise Animals 2. (p. 1939)
Mother Goose. Three Little Kittens. Winter, Milo, illus. (p. 1742)
Mother Goose, ed. Nursery Rhyme Classics. (p. 1273)
—Nursery Rhyme Songs. (p. 1273)
Mother Goose Programs, prod. What's the BIG Idea? Shapes & Spaces Librarian Manual. (p. 1899)
Mother Goose Staff & Studio Mouse Staff. Let's Learn. (p. 998)
—Sugar & Spice (p. 1672)
Mother Goose Staff & Studiomouse Staff. Let's Laugh. (p. 998)
Mother's Bridge of Love Staff, jt. auth. see Xinran, Xinran.
Mothershead, Martha Fulford. Petoskey Stone Soup. Clarkson, Janet M., illus. (p. 1348)
Motley, Chris and Jim Young, illus. see Hardy, Ed & Young, Jim.
Motley, T., illus. see Usher, M. D.
Moto, Mikki, ed. see Takahashi, Peter X.
Motomi, Kyousuke. Dengeki Daisy , Vol. 16. (p. 426)
Moton, Veronica. Beauty & the Firefly: A Book about Self Esteem. Moton, Veronica, illus. (p. 154)
Mototsune, Kat. Cliques: Using What You Have Inside Shannon, Ben, illus. (p. 333)
—Image: Deal with It from the Inside Out Shannon, Ben, illus. (p. 860)
—Money: Deal with It or Pay the Price Geoffroi, Remie, illus. (p. 1163)
Motoyama, Keiko, illus. see Burch, Regina G. & Donovan Guntly, Jenette.
Motoyama, Keiko, illus. see Dreyer, Nicole E.
Motoyama, Keiko, illus. see Lewison, Wendy Cheyette.
Motoyama, Keiko, illus. see Milios, Rita.
Motoyama, Keiko, illus. see Williams, Rozanne Lanczak.
Mott, A. S. Fireside Ghost Stories (p. 592)
—Ghost Stories of Missouri: True Tales of Ghostly Hauntings. (p. 671)
—Ghost Stories of New Jersey. (p. 671)
—Ghost Stories of Tennessee (p. 671)
—Ghost Stories of Wisconsin. (p. 671)
—Haunting Fireside Stories Vol. 1. (p. 754)
—Scary Movies: Behind the Scenes Stories, Reviews, Biographies, Anecdotes, History & Lists. Vol. 1 (p. 1520)
—Urban Legends: Strange Stories Behind Modern Myths Norell, Aaron, illus. (p. 1825)
Mott, A. S., jt. auth. see Teel, Gina.
Mott, A. S., jt. auth. see Warwick, Andrew.
Mott, A. S. & Dean, Jessica Casey. Gothic Ghost Stories: Tales of Intrigue & Fantasy from Beyond the Grave. Vol. 1 (p. 704)
Mott, Allan. Haunted Schools: Ghost Stories & Strange Tales Vol. 1 (p. 753)
Mott, Brian. Monsters Do Not Know Tae Kwon Do. (p. 1169)
Mott, Chuck. Hannukah Moose. (p. 743)
Mott, Julian & Rendell, Ian. Database Projects in Access for Advanced Level. (p. 409)
—Spreadsheet Projects in Excel for Advanced Level. (p. 1634)
Mott, Lorenzo, jt. auth. see Werther, Mark.
Mott, Professor. Flight: First Vehicles. Lenehan, Mary & Weber, Rich, illus. (p. 604)
Mottashed, Susie. Who Lives in Your Backyard? Creating a journal that opens your eyes & heart to nature's nearby Wonders. Mottashed, Susie, illus. (p. 1916)
Motter, Dean, ed. see Coleridge, Samuel Taylor.
Motter, Dean, et al. Mister X: The Definitive Collection (p. 1155)
Mottershead, Lorraine. Metamorphosis. (p. 1130)
Mottley, William W. Narrow Strip of World War II: D-Day to the Rhine River. (p. 1229)
Motto, Bernadine. Adventures of Fluff the Bunny. (p. 18)
Mottola, Burt. Operation Zenith. (p. 1300)
Motz, Mike, illus. see Crosson, Denise D.
Motz, Mike, illus. see Esparza- Vela, Mary.
Motz, Mike, illus. see Esparza-Vela, Mary.
Motz, Mike, illus. see Haitz, Rochelle.
Motz, Mike, illus. see Little, Celeste.
Motz, Mike, illus. see Page, Julie & Adams, Sabrina.
Motz, Mike, illus. see Snow, Susie.
Motz, Mike, illus. see Tennsiwood, Mark.
Motzko, Mary. New England Patriots. (p. 1244)
Moua, Mayhoua, et al. Mayhoua Moua: A Real-Life Story from a Hmong Story Cloth. (p. 1113)
Mouazen, Deema, jt. auth. see Khalifé, Fatima.
Mouchet, Klutt, jt. illus. see Schmitz, Cecile.
Mould, Chris. Dust 'n' Bones: Ten Ghost Stories. (p. 490)
—Fangs 'n' Fire: Ten Dragon Tales. (p. 571)
—Fangs 'n' Fire. (p. 571)
—Icy Hand. Mould, Chris, illus. (p. 851)
—Pip & the Wood Witch Curse: A Spindlewood Tale (p. 1361)
—Pirates 'n' Pistols. (p. 1363)
—Treasure Keepers. Mould, Chris, illus. (p. 1782)
Mould, Chris, illus. see Coats, Lucy.
Mould, Chris, illus. see Graham, Elspeth.
Mould, Chris, illus. see Hawes, Alison.
Mould, Chris, jt. auth. see Campbell, James.
Mould, Chris, jt. auth. see Redmond, Diane.
Mould, Paul. Mould's Movie Careers - Directors (p. 1180)
Mould, Paul, ed. see Bennett, Ron.
Mould, Paul, ed. Magnificent Six. (p. 1076)
Moulder, Bob, illus. see Hardcastle, Michael.
Moulder, Bob, illus. see Jeffrey, Gary.
Moulder, Bob, illus. see Tango Books Staff.
Moulder, Holly. Eyes of the Calusa. (p. 558)
Moulding, Lynne, illus. see Rivers-Moore, Debbie.
Moult, Sarah. Classworks - Literacy Year 2. (p. 329)
Moulton, Bob. Rosey & Josey Meet Big Feet. (p. 1490)
Moulton, Candy. Roadside History of Nebraska. (p. 1477)
—Roadside History of Wyoming. Greer, Dan, ed. (p. 1477)
Moulton, Courtney Allison. Angelfire. (p. 74)
—My Soul to Reap. (p. 1219)
—Shadows in the Silence. (p. 1558)
—Wings of the Wicked. (p. 1936)
Moulton, Erin E. Chasing the Milky Way. (p. 294)
—Flutter: The Story of Four Sisters & an Incredible Journey. (p. 608)
—Keepers of the Labyrinth. (p. 947)
—Tracing Stars. (p. 1775)
Moulton, Eugena. Age of Merrik: The Anointing. (p. 29)
Moulton, Kathy. Six Small Rabbits. Moulton, Kathy, illus. (p. 1582)
—View from You. Moulton, Kathy, illus. (p. 1842)
Moulton, Mark. Miss Fiona's Stupendous Pumpkin Pies. Good, Karen Hillard, illus. (p. 1151)
—Mr Sparrows Merry Fairy Circus. Good, Karen, illus. (p. 1186)
Moulton, Mark K. Royal Wedding. Good, Karen H., illus. (p. 1492)
—Visit. Winget, Susan, illus. (p. 1845)
Moulton, Mark Kimball. Annual Snowman's Ball. Good, Karen Hillard, illus. (p. 87)
—Cricket's Carol. Blowers, Lisa, illus. (p. 382)
—Everyday Angels. Winget, Susan, illus. (p. 543)
—Miss Fiona's Stupendous Pumpkin Pies. Crouch, Karen Hillard, illus. (p. 1151)
—Miss Sadie Mogee Who Lived in a Tree. Good, Karen H., illus. (p. 1152)
—One Enchanted Evening. Crouch, Karen Hillard, illus. (p. 1294)
—Reindeer Christmas. Good, Karen Hillard, illus. (p. 1457)
—Scarecrow Pete & His Suitcase of Dreams. Crouch, Karen Hillard, illus. (p. 1519)
—Snowgirl Named Just Sue. Good, Karen Hillard, illus. (p. 1600)
—Snowman Named Just Bob. Hillard Good, Karen, illus. (p. 1601)
—Snowman Named Just Bob. Crouch, Karen Hillard, illus. (p. 1601)
—Twisted Sistahs. (p. 1802)
—Twisted Sistahs. Good, Karen H., illus. (p. 1802)
—Very Best Pumpkin. Good, Karen Hillard, illus. (p. 1837)
—Visit: The Origin of the Night Before Christmas Winget, Susan, illus. (p. 1845)
—Visit. Winget, Susan, tr. (p. 1845)
Moulton, Mark Kimball & Chalmers, Josh. Change the World Before Bedtime Good, Karen, illus. (p. 290)
Moulton, Mark Kimball & Good, Karen Hillard. Snowman Named Just Bob. Good, Karen Hillard, illus. (p. 1601)
Moulton, Mike. Tina Talinka's Travels: Tina Talinka & the Knights of Sacrifice & Tina Talinka & the Echo of the Allohom. Vol. 1 (p. 1755)
Mouly, Francoise, ed. see Hayes, Geoffrey.
Mouly, Francoise, ed. see Lynch, Jay.
Mouly, Francoise, ed. see Rosenstiehl, Agnes.
Mouly, Francoise, ed. see Spiegelman, Nadja.
Mouly, Françoise, jt. auth. see Close, Chuck.
Mouly, Françoise, jt. auth. see Spiegelman, Art.
Mouly, Françoise, jt. ed. see Spiegelman, Art.
Mound, Laurence & Dorling Kindersley Publishing Staff. Insect. (p. 875)
Moundlic, Charlotte. Bathing Costume. Tallec, Olivier, illus. (p. 144)
—Scar. Tallec, Olivier, illus. (p. 1519)
Mounfield, Jenny. Ice-Cream Man. (p. 850)
Mount, Arthur, illus. see Brunelle, Lynn.
Mount, Arthur, illus. see Hellmich, Mittie.
Mount, Arthur, illus. see Icanberry, Mark.
Mount, Arthur, jt. auth. see Icanberry, Mark.
Mount, Jane. 26 Animals! (p. 1996)
Mount, Jill. Mystery of the Dirty Bike. (p. 1225)
Mountbatten-Windsor, Sarah & York, Sarah. Tea for Ruby. (p. 1708)
Mounteer, J. B. Franky Frankinstain. (p. 631)
—I Think My Brother Is a Werewolf. (p. 846)
Mounter, Paddy. Aladdin & His Magical Lamp. (p. 33)
—Ali Baba & the Forty Thieves. (p. 39)
Mounter, Paddy, illus. see Daynes, Katie.
Mounter, Paddy, illus. see Sims, Lesley.
Mounter, Paddy, retold by. Ali Baba & the Forty Thieves. (p. 39)
Mountford, Katie, illus. see Lenhart, Kristin & Passamani, Julia.
Mountford, Peter, et al. Cambridge Checkpoints VCE Legal Studies 2004. (p. 255)
Mountjoy, Shane. Alamo: The Battle for Texas. (p. 33)
—Causes of the Civil War: The Differences Between the North & South. McNeese, Tim, ed. (p. 282)
—Engel V. Vitale: School Prayer & the Establishment Clause. (p. 529)
—Francisco Coronado & the Seven Cities of Gold. Goetzmann, William H., ed. (p. 628)
—Francisco Pizarro & the Conquest of the Inca. Goetzmann, William H., ed. (p. 628)
—Indus River. (p. 872)
—Manifest Destiny: Westward Expansion. (p. 1087)
—Philadelphia. (p. 1350)
—St. Augustine. (p. 1637)
—Technology & the Civil War. McNeese, Tim, ed. (p. 1711)
—Tigris & Euphrates Rivers. (p. 1749)
—Women's Rights Movement: Moving Toward Equality. (p. 1947)
Mountjoy, Shane & McNeese, Tim. Marbury V. Madison. (p. 1091)
Mounts, Paul, illus. see Cerasini, Marc.
Mounts, Samia. Frunk the Skunk. Matricardi, Luca, illus. (p. 646)
Mour, Stanley I. Innovators of American Jazz. (p. 875)
Mourabiti, Hassan & Rosen, Lynn. Once upon a Time in Hunger Land. (p. 1293)
Mouraviova, Yulia, illus. see Haupt, Wolfgang & Bland, Janice.
Moure, Gonzalo & Moure Trenor, Gonzalo. Caballos de Mit Tio. (p. 250)
Moure Trenor, Gonzalo, jt. auth. see Moure, Gonzalo.
Moureau, Yves & Reboul, Elyan. French Enameled Ware for the Collector (p. 635)
Mourlevat, Jean-Claude. Winter's End. Bell, Anthea, tr. from FRE. (p. 1938)
Mourning, Tuesday, illus. see Feldman, Eve B.
Mourning, Tuesday, illus. see Hurwitz, Johanna.
Mourning, Tuesday, illus. see Maddox, Jake & Berne, Emma Carlson.
Mourning, Tuesday, illus. see Maddox, Jake.
Mourning, Tuesday, illus. see Meinking, Mary & Peschke, Marci.
Mourning, Tuesday, illus. see Peschke, Marci.
Mourning, Tuesday, illus. see Schkade, Jonathan.
Mourning, Tuesday, illus. see Ventura, Marne & Peschke, Marci.
Mourning, Tuesday, illus. see Ventura, Marne, et al.
Mourusund, Gry, illus. see Sande, Hans.
Mouse Works Staff. Snow White Classic. (p. 1600)
—Winnie the Pooh's Touch & Feel Book. (p. 1937)
Mouser, Barbara K., jt. auth. see Mouser, William E.
Mouser, Mary. Chigger: A Prairie Dog Tale. (p. 301)
Mouser, William E. & Mouser, Barbara K. Five Aspects of Masculinity for Young Men: A Biblical Theology of Manhood (p. 600)
Moussa, Karen M., illus. see Valeska, John & Fripp, Jean.
Moutafis, Greg, illus. see Becker, Jason Earl.
Moutarde, illus. see Kemoun, Hubert Ben & Grenier, Christian.
Moverley, Richard. Reluctant Rajput. Dean, David, illus. (p. 1458)
Movsessian, Shushann. Puberty Girl. (p. 1414)
Movshina, Marina, illus. see Clineff, Jeff.
Movshina, Marina, illus. see Cox, Tracey M.
Movshina, Marina, illus. see Kennedy, J. Aday.
Movshina, Marina, illus. see Kirk, Bill.
Movshina, Marina, illus. see Maher, Liam.
Movshina, Marina, illus. see McNamee, Kevin.
Movshina, Marina, illus. see Reed, Emma & Reed, Jennifer.
Movshina, Marina, illus. see Reeg, Cynthia.
Movshina, Marina, jt. auth. see Morrison, Anna C.
Mowat, Diane. Pair of Ghostly Hands & Other Stories. Oxford University Press Staff & Bassett, Jennifer, eds. (p. 1318)
Mowat, Farley. Black Joke. (p. 196)
—Dog Who Wouldn't Be. (p. 462)
—Owls in the Family. Frankenberg, Robert, illus. (p. 1315)
Mowatt, Ken N., illus. see Smith, M. Jane.
Mowery, Julia M. Chester the Cat. (p. 298)
Mowery, Linda Williams, illus. see Gunderson, Vivian D.
Mowery, Peg K. Once upon A Princess. (p. 1293)
Mowll, Joshua. Operation Storm City (p. 1300)
—Operation Typhoon Shore. Mowll, Joshua et al, illus. (p. 1300)
Mowry, Chris. Godzilla: Rulers of Earth Volume 2: Rulers of Earth Volume 2. (p. 692)
Mowry, Jess. Skeleton Key. (p. 1584)
—Tyger Tales. (p. 1805)
—Voodu Dawgz. (p. 1850)
Mowry, Tamera, jt. auth. see Mowry, Tia.
Mowry, Tia & Mowry, Tamera. Twintuition - Double Vision. (p. 1802)
Moxham, Rose. Teeth Marks. (p. 1715)
Moxilada, J. L. Jonty Jones Takes Guard. (p. 925)
Moxley, Jennifer. Imagination Verses. (p. 860)
Moxley, Sheila, illus. see Anholt, Laurence.
Moxley, Sheila, illus. see Cooling, Wendy, ed.
Moxley, Sheila, illus. see Fry, Stella.
Moxley, Sheila, illus. see Heine, Teresa & Heine, Theresa.
Moxley, Sheila, illus. see Heine, Theresa.
Moxley, Sheila, illus. see Maisner, Heather.
Moxley, Sheila, jt. auth. see Fry, Stella.
Moxley, Sheila, tr. see Cooling, Wendy, ed.
Moxley, Susan, jt. auth. see Bawden, Juliet.
Moxon, Kay & Magee, Eric. A2 US Government & Politics: Representation in the USA. (p. 2)
Moy, Phil, illus. see Fisch, Sholly.
Moy, Philip, illus. see Fisch, Sholly.
Moy, Philip, illus. see Wayne, Matt.
Moya, Patricia, illus. see Sharpe, Gerald.
Moyal-Sharrock, Danièle & Brenner, William H., eds. Readings of Wittgenstein's on Certainty. (p. 1447)
Moyer, Anna B. Her Name Is Sophi. (p. 769)
Moyer, Bess. Gypsies of the Air. (p. 734)
Moyer, Brett, illus. see Stauffer, Lori & Deblinger, Esther.
Moyer, J., illus. see Page, J. & Rainier, S. T.
Moyer, Tom, illus. see Noland, Charles.
Moyers, William, illus. see Mills, Lois.
Moyers, William, illus. see Murphy, Bud.
Moylan, Holly Handler, jt. auth. see Ames, Lee J.
Moyle, Philippa, jt. auth. see Watson, Carol.
Moyler, Alan, illus. see Rubin, Elizabeth.
Moynahan, Jamie. Ben at the Seaside. (p. 163)
—Fly with Ben. (p. 609)
—Tiger Bunnies. (p. 1748)
Moynihan, Dan. Hiding Dinosaurs. (p. 777)
Moynihan, Daniel Patrick, intro. Immigrants in America. (p. 861)
Moynihan, Lindsay. Waiting Tree (p. 1853)
Moyoco, Anno & Higuchi, Daisuke. Whistle! Higuchi, Daisuke, illus. (p. 1912)
Moyston, Connaelia. God's Faith Is Real. (p. 691)
Mozelle, Shirley. Zack's Alligator & the First Snow. Watts, James, illus. (p. 1984)
Mozer, Mindy. Big Data & You. (p. 180)
—Careers As a Commissioned Sales Representative. (p. 267)
—Getting a Job in Automotive Care & Service. (p. 668)
—Pier Fishing. (p. 1357)
Mozi, Jennifer, illus. see Bidelman, Jeff.
Moziak, Rose Mary Casciano, jt. illus. see Casciano, Christie.
Mozley, Peggy, illus. see Wimbrey, Crystal M.
Mozz. In Search of the Holey Whale: The Top Secret Riddles & Left-Handed Scribbles of Mozz. Mozz, illus. (p. 864)
—Pearls of Wisdumb: The Electric Light Verse & Shocking Scribbles of Mozz. (p. 1333)
mpMann, illus. see Lewis, A. David.
MpMann, illus. see Vollmar, Rob.
Mqp, creator. Sisters Make the Best Friends. (p. 1581)
Mr. Blue. From Underdog to Wonderdog: Top Ten Tricks to Lead Your Pack. (p. 644)
Mracek, Ann. Friendship Flies the Sun: The Ancient Egyptian Legend of Scarab Beetle. (p. 639)
Mravetz, Pete. Sammy's Big Adventure: Sammy's Super Safari. Gantt, Amy, illus. (p. 1508)
Mraz, Maryann, jt. auth. see Wood, Karen D.
Mrazovic, Ivan. Phobias - Crash Course. (p. 1351)
Mrowczynska, Agnieszka. P Is for Poland. Das, Prodeepta, photos by. (p. 1316)
Mrowiec, Katia. Most Beautiful Images from the Bible: Sharing the Stories with Children. Pillot, édéric, illus. (p. 1177)
Mrowiec, Katia, et al. God, Yahweh, Allah. (p. 690)
Mrozek, Elizabeth. Fifth Chair. Mrozek, Elizabeth, illus. (p. 584)
Mrs Molesworth & Molesworth, Mary Louisa S. Thirteen Little Black Pigs & Other Stories. (p. 1735)
Mrs Molesworth, et al. Thirteen Little Black Pigs & Other Stories. (p. 1735)
Ms. G. Mommy, Why Can't I Be Rich? Dade, Raheem, illus. (p. 1162)
MS K. Goal Journal. (p. 687)
Ms. Sue. Where Is Your Name? Ducy, George, illus. (p. 1909)
Ms. T. Chincoteague Pony Finds a Friend. (p. 307)
Mshindu, illus. see Taylor, Maxwell.
Msmh. Learning to Count, Alphabets a-J & Colours. (p. 985)
Mubarak, Enoch, jt. auth. see Brown, Celease N.
Mubiru, Bertha, ed. Kabaka,Kulabako & Kakookolo. (p. 941)
Mubiru, Betha. Muzinge the Bird. (p. 1195)
Mucha Aydlott, Julie A. My Favorite Time of Year. Mucha-Sullivan, Kalie A. & Mucha-Sullivan, Emily V., illus. (p. 1203)
Mucha, Corinne. Freshman: Tales of 9th Grade Obsessions, Revelations, & Other Nonsense. (p. 636)
Mucha, Mark. Adventures with Edison & His Friends: "Crab in a Bucket" Vol. 1 (p. 25)
Mucha, Peter, ed. Kids Have All the Answers: And All the Drawings, Too! (p. 954)
Mucha, Susan Polonus. Deadly Deception. (p. 417)
Muchamore, Robert. Dealer. (p. 418)
—Eagle Day. (p. 492)
—Escape. (p. 534)
—Grey Wolves. (p. 723)
—Killing. (p. 956)
—Maximum Security. (p. 1112)
—Recruit. (p. 1452)
—Secret Army. (p. 1540)
Mucha-Sullivan, Emily V., illus. see Mucha Aydlott, Julie A.
Mucha-Sullivan, Kalie A., illus. see Mucha Aydlott, Julie A.
Muckle, Christine, illus. see Saunders, Vivien.
Mucklow, Hope. Rojo the Baby Red Panda at the Zoo: An Allegory about Self-Worth Through a Red Panda & Giant Panda Comparison. (p. 1485)
Mucklow, Nancy. Sensory Team Handbook: A Hands-on Tool to Help Young People Make Sense of Their Senses & Take Charge of Their Sensory Processing. (p. 1551)
Mudaly, Jessica. And That's Just the Trouble with Cats! (p. 71)
—Cats Can Be So Cattish! (p. 281)
Mudd, Barbra, illus. see Benhardt, Will.
Mudd, Missy. Candy Bar Caper. (p. 261)
Mudd Ruth, M., jt. auth. see Mudd-Ruth, Maria.
Mudd-Ruth, Maria. Owls. (p. 1315)
Mudd-Ruth, Maria & Mudd Ruth, M. Insectos. (p. 875)
Mudenda, Duly & Nagunga, Kansi. Syankombo. (p. 1692)
Mudgal, Nishant, illus. see Singh, Asavari.
Mudge, Michael. Spiritual Warfare Basic Training. (p. 1629)
Mudpuppy Press Staff. Alligator Alligator Floor Puzzle. (p. 47)
—Dinosaur Block Puzzle. (p. 441)
—Magic Horses 100-piece Puzzle. (p. 1072)
—Magic Horses Seal & Send Stationery. (p. 1072)
—My Travel Journal. Corr, Christopher, illus. (p. 1220)
Mudrovich, Jane. Exorcising the Google. (p. 548)
Muecke, Anne & Moore, Clement C. Dinosaurs' Night Before Christmas. Hale, Nathan, illus. (p. 445)
Muehlenhardt, Amy Bailey. Beginner's Guide to Drawing: Animals, Bugs, Dinosaurs, & Other Cool Stuff!! Muehlenhardt, Amy Bailey, illus. (p. 159)
—Drawing & Learning about Bugs: Using Shapes & Lines Muehlenhardt, Amy Bailey, illus. (p. 481)
—Drawing & Learning about Faces: Using Shapes & Lines. Muehlenhardt, Amy Bailey, illus. (p. 481)
—Drawing & Learning about Fashion: Using Shapes & Lines Muehlenhardt, Amy Bailey, illus. (p. 481)
—Sketch It! Set of 6 Muehlenhardt, Amy Bailey, illus. (p. 1584)
—Thanksgiving Crafts Takvorian, Nadine, illus. (p. 1726)
Muehlenhardt, Amy Bailey, illus. see Blackaby, Susan.
Muehlenhardt, Amy Bailey, illus. see Blair, Eric.
Muehlenhardt, Amy Bailey, illus. see Bridges, Sarah.
Muehlenhardt, Amy Bailey, illus. see Cooper, Sharon Katz.
Muehlenhardt, Amy Bailey, illus. see Finn, Carrie.
Muehlenhardt, Amy Bailey, illus. see Jones, Christianne C.
Muehlenhardt, Amy Bailey, illus. see Nettleton, Pamela Hill.
Muehlenhardt, Amy Bailey, illus. see Salas, Laura Purdie.
Mueller, Cynthia Jean. Dorfuss Bubblebutt. (p. 471)
Mueller, Dagmar H. David's World: A Picture Book about Living with Autism. Ballhaus, Verena, illus. (p. 411)
Mueller, Dagmar H., jt. auth. see Fahy, Davene.
Mueller, Doris. Small One's Adventure. Guevara, Linda L., ed. (p. 1592)
Mueller, George Levy, et al. Lucie's Hope: George Levy Muellers of the Holocaust. (p. 1062)
Mueller, Janet. Star from Grandma. Mueller, Janet, illus. (p. 1640)
Müeller, Jörg, illus. see Steiner, Jörg.
Mueller, Kirk Jay. Harriet Can Carry It Vonthron-Laver, Sarah, illus. (p. 749)
Mueller, Laurie A. Eva's Day with Daddy. (p. 541)
Mueller, Marilyn J. Thank You God for Everything! Gracias a Dios por Todo. (p. 1725)
Mueller, Mary. Stargazer: The Story of Mary Mother of God. (p. 1642)
Mueller, Mike, photos by see Zuehlke, Jeffrey.
Mueller, Miranda. Mishka: An Adoption Tale. (p. 1150)
Mueller, Miranda, illus. see Brunsvold, Eric.
Mueller, Pamela Bauer. Aloha Crossing. (p. 48)
—Hello, Goodbye, I Love You: The Story of Aloha, a Guide Dog for the Blind. (p. 764)
Mueller, Paul G. Abigail & Blueboy. (p. 5)

Mueller, Pete, illus. see Clarke, Ginjer L.
Mueller, Pete, illus. see Milton, Joyce.
Mueller, Peter, illus. see Walter Foster Creative Team.
Mueller, Peter, jt. auth. see Farrell, Russell.
Mueller, Peter R., illus. see Milton, Joyce.
Mueller, Richard. Naval Warfare of the Future. (p. 1237)
—Zoonauts: The Secret of Animalville. Gosline, Sheldon, ed. (p. 1989)
Mueller, Ross. Boy Who Built the Boat. Smith, Craig, illus. (p. 219)
Mueller, Ruth Ann. Bumpy Bear's Escape. (p. 241)
Mueller, Stephen R. Hermie & Bernie (p. 771)
Mueller, Steve. First Eucharist & Beyond: Ongoing Initiation into Communion with Christ. Vol. 2 (p. 594)
Mueller, Steve, ed. see Living the Good News Staff.
Mueller, Sylvia Price. Barnyard Stories. (p. 140)
Mueller, Todd & Boland, Hank. Soup du Jour (mus) (p. 1615)
Mueller, Virginia. What Is Faith? Kolding, Richard Max, illus. (p. 1889)
Muellner, Nancy, illus. see Berggren, Joyce D.
Muench, Cinda. Would You Love Me Always. (p. 1962)
Muench-Williams, Heather. Adam's Grouchy Day. Meier, Kerry L., illus. (p. 11)
—Amy Washes Her Hands. Teeple, Jackie, illus. (p. 66)
—At the Circus. Storch, Ellen N., illus. (p. 111)
—Cold Winter Day. Crowell, Knox, illus. (p. 339)
—I Want a Pet. Teeple, Jackie, illus. (p. 847)
Muench-Williams, Heather, jt. auth. see Williams, Heather L.
Muench-Williams, Heather & Jarrell, Pamela R. Caillou's Hiking Adventure. Storch, Ellen N., illus. (p. 251)
Mugambi, Christina Nkirote, illus. see Powell Zalewski, Amy.
Mugford, Simon. Essential BMX. (p. 536)
—Mi Gran Libro de la Ciencia. (p. 1132)
—My Big Dinosaur World. Francis, John, illus. (p. 1197)
—Shark. (p. 1561)
Mugford, Simon & Priddy, Roger. Reptiles & Other Scaly Friends. (p. 1461)
—Sharks: And Other Dangers of the Deep. (p. 1562)
Muggenthaler, Eva, creator. Fish on a Walk. (p. 598)
Mugisa, Richard. Curse of the Bachweizi. (p. 394)
Mugnaini, Joe, illus. see Bradbury, Ray.
Mugnaini, Joseph, illus. see Bradbury, Ray.
Muha, Christina. Porchville. (p. 1386)
Muhaiyaddeen, M. R. Bawa. Golden Words of a Sufi Sheikh: Revised Edition. (p. 695)
Muhall, Jill K. & Alarcon, Jill. Causes of the Revolution. (p. 282)
Muhammad, Khaleel. Helping the Polonskys. (p. 766)
Muhammad, Professor Kelmer. Legendary Secret about the Letter Q. (p. 989)
Muhammad, Raychelle. Fit Boys Like You. Muhammad, Raychelle, illus. (p. 599)
—Fit Girls Like You. Muhammad, Raychelle, illus. (p. 599)
—Little Boys Like You. (p. 1025)
—Little Girls Like You. (p. 1028)
Muhammad, Renay. Daddy Why Do We Have Rain. (p. 399)
—Dreams Do Come True. (p. 484)
—I Am an American. (p. 832)
—People Shackled Through Time. (p. 1340)
Muhammad, Shahid. Adventures of the Math Doctor: Book One: King Jafiz & the Evil Farmer Nimra. (p. 23)
—How to Teach Math to Black Students. (p. 822)
Mühlberger, Detlef. Social Bases of Nazism, 1919-1933. (p. 1604)
Mühle, Jörg, illus. see Hub, Ulrich & Ragg-Kirkby, Helena.
Mühle, Jörg, illus. see Hub, Ulrich.
Muhle, Jorg, illus. see Jones, Rob Lloyd.
Muhmood, Laith, jt. auth. see Hassig, Susan M.
Muhn, Gu-seon, illus. see Kim, Tae-yeon.
Muir, Duncan. Optical Illusions. (p. 1301)
Muir, Frances Wilcox. Mommy, Daddy, Can I Get a Horse? A Getting Started Guide for Parents of Horse-Crazy Children. (p. 1162)
Muir, Hamish, jt. auth. see Holt, Mark.
Muir, John. Stickeen. Buell, Carl Dennis, illus. (p. 1650)
Muir, John & Cornell, Joseph Bharat. John Muir: My Life with Nature. (p. 922)
Muir, Kerry. Childsplay: A Collection of Scenes & Monologues for Children Johnson, Kris, photos by. (p. 305)
—Three New Plays for Young Actors: From the Young Actor's Studio. (p. 1743)
Muir, Leslie. C. R. Mudgeon. Hector, Julian, illus. (p. 250)
Muir, Nicola. Baba Didi & the Godwits Fly. Hayward, Annie, illus. (p. 123)
Muir, Roberto, jt. auth. see Hilgenberg, Bob.
Muir, Sabine. Meeting Wolfie: A Story about Mozart. (p. 1124)
Muir, Suzanne. Animal Homes. (p. 78)
—Magic Tile. (p. 1074)
Muir-Chase, Marlene. Miranda the Mallard from Moose Jaw (p. 1149)
Muirden, James. Enciclopedia Visual (p. 524)
Muire, Penny, jt. auth. see Clarke, Nancy.
Muirhead, Deborah, illus. see Nelson, Marilyn.
Muirhead, Maria. My Asthma Book. (p. 1196)
Mukbaniani, O. V., et al. Modification Reactions of Oligomethylhydridesiloxanes. (p. 1159)
Mukherjee, Aiswarya & S., Bijan. My Family! ABCs with Keesha. (p. 1202)
Mukherjee, Aniruddha, illus. see Seth, Shantum.
Mukhid, Abdul, tr. see Crouch, Adele.
Mukhida, Zul, illus. see Ganeri, Anita.
Mukthavaram, Vasantha. Aesop's Fables: Eternal Leaf Art. Mukthavaram, Vasantha, illus. (p. 26)
Mula, Tom. Hackers of Oz. (p. 735)
Mulabdic, Sonja, illus. see Quednau, Marion.
Mulanax, Carol. How to Make a Towel Monkey & other Cruise Ship Favorites. (p. 820)
Mulazzani, Simona, illus. see Messner, Kate.
Mulazzani, Simona, illus. see Zoboli, Giovanna & Mathews, Leslie.
Mulazzani, Simona, illus. see Zoboli, Giovanna & Watkinson, Laura.
Mulazzani, Simona, illus. see Zoboli, Giovanna.
Mulazzi, Paola & Machetto, Augusto. Tinker Bell & Her Stories for a Rainy Day. (p. 1755)
Mulazzi, Paola, et al. Disney Fairies Graphic Novel #4: Tinker Bell to the Rescue. Urbano, Emilio et al, illus. (p. 451)
—Disney Fairies Graphic Novel #8: Tinker Bell & Her Stories for a Rainy Day. (p. 451)
—Tinker Bell & the Pirate Adventure Urbano, Emilio et al, illus. (p. 1755)
—Tinker Bell the Perfect Fairy. Urbano, Emilio et al, illus. (p. 1755)
Mulbah-Bondo, Gbolu, jt. auth. see Moore, Deborah K.
Mulcahy, Lisa, et al. Bye Bye Boredom! The Girl's Life Big Book of Fun. (p. 249)
Mulcahy, Lucille. Magic Fingers. Lambo, Don, illus. (p. 1072)
Mulcahy, William. Zach Apologizes. McKee, Darren, illus. (p. 1984)
Mulder, Michelle. Brilliant! Shining a Light on Sustainable Energy (p. 228)
—Every Last Drop: Bringing Clean Water Home (p. 542)
—Maggie & the Chocolate War (p. 1071)
—Not a Chance (p. 1266)
—Out of the Box (p. 1311)
—Out of the Box. (p. 1311)
—Pedal It! How Bicycles Are Changing the World (p. 1334)
—Trash Talk: Moving Toward a Zero-Waste World (p. 1780)
—Yeny & the Children for Peace (p. 1970)
Mulder, Nancy. Caring for Your Hedgehog. (p. 269)
Muldoon, Kathleen M. Forces & Motion in the Real World. (p. 617)
—Jim Crow Era. (p. 917)
—Little Book of Saints Mattozzi, Patricia R., illus. (p. 1025)
—Runaway Skeleton. Hilliker, Phillip, illus. (p. 1496)
Muldoon, Kathleen M. & Wallace, Susan Helen. My First Book of Saints. Mattozzi, Patricia R. & Kinarney, Tom, illus. (p. 1205)
Muldoon Zappa, Shana, jt. auth. see Zappa, Ahmet.
Muldrow, Diane. Boiling Point. Pollack, Barbara, illus. (p. 208)
—Chocolate Cakes & Cookie Bakes! Swanson, Maggie, illus. (p. 309)
—Deep Freeze. Pollack, Barbara, illus. (p. 423)
—Everything I Need to Know about Love I Learned from a Little Golden Book. (p. 545)
—Frosty the Snowman. Golden Books, illus. (p. 645)
—How Do Lions Say I Love You? Walker, David, illus. (p. 807)
—Into the Mix. Pollak, Barbara, illus. (p. 881)
—Measure of Thanks. Pollak, Barbara & Pollack, Barbara, illus. (p. 1117)
—On the Back Burner. Pollak, Barbara, illus. (p. 1289)
—Stirring It Up. Pollak, Barbara, illus. (p. 1651)
—Sweet-and-Sour Summer. Pollack, Barbara, illus. (p. 1689)
—Turning up the Heat Pollak, Barbara, illus. (p. 1798)
—We Planted a Tree. Staake, Bob, illus. (p. 1868)
Muldrow, Diane, jt. auth. see Dombey, Elizabeth.
Muldrow, Diane & Golden Books Staff. Where Do Giggles Come From? Kennedy, Anne, illus. (p. 1907)
Mulfinger, George, jt. auth. see Orozco, Julia.
Mulford, Carolyn. Feedsack Dress. (p. 580)
Mulford, Marcy. Molly in the Classroom: A Child's Perspective of Bullying. (p. 1160)
Mulford, Prentice. Life by Land & Sea. (p. 1008)
Mulhall, Jill K. Abigail Adams. (p. 5)
—Declaration of Independence. (p. 422)
—Expanding the Nation. (p. 548)
—James Madison. (p. 907)
—Lewis & Clark. (p. 1004)
—Thomas Jefferson. (p. 1739)
—War of 1812. (p. 1857)
Mulhall, MB. Heavyweight. (p. 761)
Mulherin, Jennifer & Frost, Abigail. Othello. Heap, Jonathon, illus. (p. 1306)
Mulholland, Bailey, illus. see Durben, Toni.
Mulholland, Clara. Naughty Miss Bunny. (p. 1237)
Mulholland, Jane. Ribeye, the Vegetarian Dragon. (p. 1469)
Mulholland, Marie. Study Guide for the Necklace of Terrersylvanous. (p. 1670)
mulholland, robin. Bolivia & the sunshine King. (p. 208)
Mulkey Young, Kim, illus. see Hoessle, Maureen.
Mulks, Mitchell. Zonata: The California Mountain Kingsnake. Merker, Gerold, photos by. (p. 1988)
Mull, Brandon. Arcade Catastrophe. (p. 95)
—Candy Shop War. (p. 261)
—Chasing the Prophecy. (p. 294)
—Crystal Keepers. (p. 387)
—Fablehaven: The Complete Series Boxed Set. Vol. 5 (p. 559)
—Fablehaven: Las Llaves de la Prision de los Demonios. (p. 559)
—Fablehaven. (p. 559)
—Fablehaven. Belaustegui, Inés, tr. (p. 559)
—Fablehaven. Dorman, Brandon, illus. (p. 559)
—Fablehaven Collection Set. Dorman, Brandon, illus. (p. 559)
—Grip of the Shadow Plague. Dorman, Brandon, illus. (p. 724)
—Keys to the Demon Prison. (p. 951)
—Keys to the Demon Prison. Dorman, Brandon, illus. (p. 951)
—Pingo. Dorman, Brandon, illus. (p. 1359)
—Pingo & the Playground Bully. Dorman, Brandon, illus. (p. 1359)
—Rise of the Evening Star. Dorman, Brandon, illus. (p. 1474)
—Rise of the Evening Star. Dorman, Brandon, illus. (p. 1475)
—Rogue Knight. (p. 1485)
—Secrets of the Dragon Sanctuary. (p. 1545)
—Secrets of the Dragon Sanctuary. Dorman, Brandon, illus. (p. 1545)
—Seeds of Rebellion. (p. 1548)
—Sky Raiders. (p. 1587)
—Wild Born. (p. 1929)
—World Without Heroes. (p. 1959)
—World Without Heroes; Seeds of Rebellion; Chasing the Prophecy (p. 1959)
Mull, Brandon, et al. Tales of the Great Beasts. (p. 1702)
Mull, David Kenneth. His Date for the Dance was His Science Project. (p. 781)
Mullaly, Glen, illus. see Jacobson, Ryan.
Mullaly, Glen, illus. see Swanson, Jennifer.
Mullan, G. E., illus. see Shea, John.
Mullan, Michael, illus. see Donovan, Sandy.
Mullaney, Patricia E. Documentary of an Airman' Tour with the Eighth 1944-1945. (p. 459)
Mullaney, Polly. Three Kids Gripped by Evil. (p. 1742)
Mullarkey, John, jt. auth. see Mullarkey, Lisa.
Mullarkey, John & Mullarkey, Lisa. Johnstown Flood: An Up2U Historical Fiction Adventure. Martin, Dana, illus. (p. 924)
Mullarkey, Lisa. Campfire Capers. (p. 257)
—Carly. Franco, Paula, illus. (p. 270)
—Cheerleading Basics. (p. 296)
—Cheerleading Spirit. (p. 296)
—Cheerleading Stunts & Tumbling. (p. 296)
—Cheerleading Tryouts & Competitions. (p. 296)
—Daniela. Franco, Paula, illus. (p. 405)
—Gabriela. Franco, Paula, illus. (p. 652)
—Gold Medal Glitch. (p. 693)
—Horsenapped! (p. 800)
—Kianna. Franco, Paula, illus. (p. 951)
—Splashing by the Shore: Beach Activities for Kids Dixon, Debra Spina, illus. (p. 1629)
—Thinking Kids' Math, Grade 2. Stith, Jennifer & Hoople, Barrie, eds. (p. 1734)
—TJ Zaps a Nightmare: Stopping Blackmail Bullying #5. LaCoste, Gary, illus. (p. 1758)
—TJ Zaps the Freeze Out: Stopping the Silent Treatment #3. LaCoste, Gary, illus. (p. 1758)
—TJ Zaps the New Kid: Stopping a Social Bully #1. LaCoste, Gary, illus. (p. 1758)
—TJ Zaps the One-Upper: Stopping One-Upping & Cell Phone Bullying #2. LaCoste, Gary, illus. (p. 1758)
—TJ Zaps the Rumor Mill: Stopping Gossip #4. LaCoste, Gary, illus. (p. 1758)
—TJ Zaps the Smackdown: Stopping a Physical Bully #6. LaCoste, Gary, illus. (p. 1758)
—Trail Ride Troubles. (p. 1776)
Mullarkey, Lisa, jt. auth. see Mullarkey, John.
Mullarkey, Lisa & Library. Cheerleading Stunts & Tumbling. (p. 296)
Mullarkey, Lisa & Mullarkey, John. Get Ella to the Apollo. Bernard, Courtney, illus. (p. 667)
—Mary Molds a Monster. Bernard, Courtney, illus. (p. 1101)
—Monet Changes Mediums. Bernard, Courtney, illus. (p. 1163)
—Shakespeare Saves the Globe. Bernard, Courtney, illus. (p. 1559)
Mullarky, Eric, ed. see Strunk, Crisman.
Mullen, Jodi Ann. Naughty No More: A Workbook for Children Who Want to Make Good Decisions. (p. 1237)
Mullen, Lana, illus. see Ewing, Susan.
Mullen, Michael & Stockdale, Patricia Ann. over Land: A Magical Kingdom. (p. 1313)
Mullen, Paul Michael. Day I Hit a Home Run at Great American Ball Park. (p. 413)
—Swinging for the Fences at Citizens Bank Park. (p. 1691)
Mullen, Robert. Where Do Your Animals Live. (p. 1907)
Mullen, Rodney & Mortimer, Sean. Mutt: How to Skateboard & Not Kill Yourself. (p. 1194)
Mullenbach, Cheryl. Great Depression for Kids: Hardship & Hope in 1930s America, with 21 Activities. (p. 715)
—Industrial Revolution for Kids: The People & Technology That Changed the World, with 21 Activities. (p. 872)
Mullendore, Bryan L. Scott's Many Adventures. (p. 1532)
Mullenix, Craig Steven. Standing Ground. (p. 1639)
Muller, Birte, jt. auth. see Hachler, Bruno.
Muller, Carrie & Halsey, Jacqueline. Terrible, Horrible, Smelly Pirate Orchard, Eric, illus. (p. 1721)
Müller, Chris, illus. see Aronson, Marc & Mayor, Adrienne.
Muller, Cristina, illus. see Strepponi, Blanca.
Muller, Daniel, illus. see Linke, Uwe.
Muller, Daniel, illus. see Thorup, Bryce.
Muller, Daniella L. Rumble, Rumble, Boom! (p. 1495)
Muller, Gerda. Autumn (p. 118)
—Spring (p. 1634)
—Summer (p. 1673)
—Winter (p. 1937)
Müller, Gerhard Ludwig, et al. Hope of the Family: A Dialogue with Gerhard Cardinal Müller. (p. 796)
Muller, Gilbert H. Many Americas: Reading & Writing Across the Cultural Divides. (p. 1089)
Müller, Hildegard. Cowboy. Müller, Hildegard, illus. (p. 373)
Müller, Hildegard, illus. see Maccarone, Grace.
Müller, Isabel. Green Sea Turtle. (p. 722)
Müller, Jan-Werner. German Ideologies Since 1945: Studies in the Political Thought & Culture of the Bonn Republic. Müller, Jan-Werner, ed. (p. 666)
Muller, Jean Powers. Rudolph's Sniffalator. (p. 1494)
—Santa's New Reindeer, RUBIN. (p. 1513)
Müller, Jörg. Changing Countryside. (p. 290)
Muller, Lisa M. Master smokey & mr. Duck. (p. 1103)
Muller, Marcia. Dead Midnight. (p. 417)
Muller, Marie. 'Twas the Night Before Winter. (p. 1799)
Muller, Max. Memories: A Story of German Love. Upton, George, tr. (p. 1126)
Muller, Michael. Mirabelle & the Bouncy Red Ball. (p. 1148)
—Mirabelle & the Butterfly. (p. 1148)
—Mirabelle Goes for a Walk. (p. 1148)
Muller, Rachel. Ten Thumb Sam (p. 1719)
—When the Curtain Rises (p. 1904)
Muller, Rachel Dunstan. Solstice Cup (p. 1608)
—Squeeze (p. 1636)
Muller, Ruth, illus. see Thorup, Bryce.
Muller, Seth. Keepers of the WindClaw Chronicles: The Day of Storms Dubay, Tayloe, ed. (p. 947)
—Keepers of the WindClaw Chronicles: The Mockingbird's Manual. Tayloe, McConnell Dubay, ed. (p. 947)
Müller-Brockmann, Josef, et al. History of the Poster. (p. 785)
Mullerova, Lucie, illus. see Bruno, Pep.
Mullery Jr., Matthew W. Hanging Out with Happy Crackers, Fingers Baloo & Stinky Magoo: One Sunny Morning. (p. 742)
Mullett, Viv, illus. see Emerson, Scott.
Mullican, Jody. What Can It Be? Gray, Stacy A., illus. (p. 1880)
Mullican, Judy. Big Mess. Gray, Stacy A., illus. (p. 182)
—Caillou & the Storyteller. Storch, Ellen N., illus. (p. 251)
—Caillou Is Healthy. Gray, Stacy A., illus. (p. 251)
—Fall on the Farm. Gray, Stacy A., illus. (p. 566)
—Jonah Starts School. Cress, Michelle H., illus. (p. 925)
—Let's Take a Ride. Gillen, Lisa P., illus. (p. 1001)
—Mary & Marsha Make Cookies. Storch, Ellen N., illus. (p. 1100)
—May We Go to the Zoo? Gray, Stacy A., illus. (p. 1112)
—My Toys. Bicking, Judith, illus. (p. 1220)
—Pretend. Meier, Kerry L., illus. (p. 1398)
—Someone New in the Neighborhood. Storch, Ellen N. & Gillen, Lisa P., illus. (p. 1609)
—Taking Care of Pets. Ruminski, Jeff, illus. (p. 1698)
Mullican, Judy, jt. auth. see Black, Jessica L.
Mullican, Judy & Crowell, Knox. Caillou Finds Shapes. Gillen, Lisa P., illus. (p. 251)
Mullican, Judy & Williams, Heather L. Building a Sand Castle. Storch, Ellen N., illus. (p. 238)
Mullican, Norma Waldon & Zivney, Missy Mullican. Collection of Squirrel Tales: Something to Crow About. (p. 340)
Mulligan, Andy. Ribblestrop. (p. 1469)
—Trash. (p. 1779)
Mulligan, Frank. Cookie & Curley. Myler, Terry, illus. (p. 361)
Mulligan, Kelly. Monster Who Learnt to Fly. (p. 1168)
Mulligan, Lenz, jt. auth. see ImageBooks Staff.
Mulligan, Richard. Marvin's Mysteries. (p. 1100)
Mulligan, Simon. Porsche. (p. 1386)
Mulligan, Todd, illus. see Moore, Brian L.
Mullin, Caryl Cude. Rough Magic (p. 1491)
Mullin, Chris. Jovenes Jugadores de Baloncesto. (p. 929)
Mullin, James V., ed. Irish Americans. (p. 887)
Mullin, Michael, illus. see Skewes, John & Schwartz, Robert.
Mullin, Michael, jt. auth. see Skewes, John.
Mullin, Michael & Skewes, John. Larry Gets Lost in the Twin Cities. Skewes, John, illus. (p. 976)
Mullin, Mike. Ashen Winter. (p. 105)
—Ashfall. (p. 106)
—Sunrise. (p. 1677)
Mullin, Rene. Aibitr. (p. 30)
Mullin, Rita Thievon. Anne Frank: Hidden Hope. (p. 85)
—Harry Houdini: Death-Defying Showman. (p. 750)
—Sterling Biographies - Thomas Jefferson: Architect of Freedom. (p. 1649)
Mullinax, Jerry. Enoree. (p. 530)
Mullings, Leith, jt. auth. see Marable, Manning.
Mullins, Allene. Katie's Wish. (p. 945)
Mullins, Amy. I'm Reverent When- Bagley, Val Chadwick, illus. (p. 860)
Mullins, Amy, jt. auth. see Bagley, Val Chadwick.
Mullins, Dari, jt. auth. see Pettit, Loree.
Mullins, George. What Christmas Means to Me. (p. 1881)
Mullins, Julie. School Play Stars. Maddock, Monika, illus. (p. 1523)
—Sleepover. Foye, Lloyd, illus. (p. 1589)
Mullins, Lisa. Inventing the Electric Light. (p. 883)
—Inventing the Printing Press. (p. 883)
Mullins, Lisa & Smith, Elizabeth. Science in the Renaissance. (p. 1526)
Mullins, Matt. Electricity. (p. 509)
—Elements. (p. 510)
—Energy. (p. 528)
—Experiment with Liquids. (p. 549)
—Friction: Phosphorus Matches Were Invented in 1831. (p. 637)
—Geoscientist. (p. 665)
—Gravity. (p. 712)
—Homeland Security. (p. 793)
—How Did They Build That? Airport. (p. 806)
—How Did They Build That? Dam. (p. 806)
—How Did They Build That? School. (p. 806)
—How Does It Fly? Bomber Plane. (p. 808)
—How Does It Fly? Fighter Plane. (p. 808)
—How Does It Fly? Helicopter. (p. 808)
—How Does It Fly? Jet Plane. (p. 808)
—Meteorologist. (p. 1130)
—Multimedia Artist & Animator. (p. 1190)
—Remote Systems Control Engineer. (p. 1460)
—Scriptwriter. (p. 1533)
—Special Effects Technician. (p. 1623)
—Super Cool Science Experiments: Cells. (p. 1679)
—Super Cool Science Experiments: Ecosystems. (p. 1679)
—Surgical Technologist. (p. 1685)
—Think Like a Scientist in the Backyard. (p. 1734)
—Think Like a Scientist in the Car. (p. 1734)
—Think Like a Scientist in the Garden. (p. 1734)
—Think Like a Scientist in the Kitchen. (p. 1734)
—Trucks. (p. 1791)
Mullins, Matt & Plummer, Todd. Super Cool Science Experiments: Planet Earth. (p. 1679)
—Super Cool Science Experiments: States of Matter. (p. 1679)
Mullins, Matthew. Matt Mullins' Basic Tricks Book & DVD: The 1st Step by Step Book on Acrobatics for Martial Artists. (p. 1109)
Mullins, Norman D. Mountain Boy: The Adventures of Orion Saddler. (p. 1180)
Mullins, Patty Rutland. All about Sports with Inspector McQ. Ebert, Len, illus. (p. 43)
—All about You with Inspector McQ. Holub, Joan, illus. (p. 43)
Mullins, Rebecca. Tristan (p. 1787)
Mullins, Tammy. Preston Falls Up. (p. 1397)
—Preston's Biggest Summer: A Book about Growing. (p. 1397)
Mullins, Terry. Melungeons Out of the Dungeon. (p. 1125)
Mullins, Tinnesha, jt. auth. see Trufant, Robert.
Mullins, Tom, ed. Irish Stories for Children. (p. 888)
Mullins, V. K. Case of the Missing Crown: A Gloria Jean Mystery. (p. 274)
Mulneix, Kimberly. No, Piper, No! (p. 1259)
Muloch, Miss. Little Lame Prince & Other Tales. (p. 1030)
Mulock, Dinah Maria. Fairy Book: The Best Popular Stories Selected & Rendered Anew. (p. 563)
—Little Lame Prince & His Traveling Cloak. (p. 1030)
—Little Lame Prince & the Adventures of a Brownie. (p. 1030)
Mulock, Julian, illus. see Froman, Nan.
Mulock, Julian, illus. see Hodge, Deborah.
Mulrain, Sabrina. Prince's Happy Ever After. (p. 1402)

—Ultimate Dreamer. (p. 1809)
Mulrine, Jennifer. Breaking Free. Doherty, Catherine, illus. (p. 225)
Mulroy, Tanya. Mozambique. (p. 1184)
—Senegal. (p. 1550)
—Senegal. Rotberg, Robert I., ed. (p. 1550)
Mulstay, Linda Muratore. Autism & PDD Answering Questions, Level 1. (p. 117)
Multicultural Staff. Ravi's Diwali Surprise Story P. (p. 1441)
Mulubah, Sr. Denise's Pet Dove. (p. 426)
Muluka, B. Kandu & the Lake. (p. 942)
Mulvany, Christine, jt. auth. see Stoyles, Pennie.
Mulvihill, Tina. Ollie's Geometry Adventure. (p. 1287)
Mumaugh, Lene. Touch of Christmas. Skrbic, Melissa, illus. (p. 1772)
Mumby, Hazel. Hazel Mumby's Hairy Tails: Atcea to Zeea. (p. 756)
Mumford, Carole. Caribbean Cruise Summer Vacation: A Magnificent Six Adventure (p. 268)
—Christmas Vacation in Colorado: A Magnificent Six Adventure (p. 316)
—Magnificent: Their Yellowstone Adventure (p. 1076)
Mumford, Jeanette, et al. Busy Ant Maths Clarke, Peter, ed. (p. 245)
—Busy Ant Maths Evans, Steve et al, illus. (p. 245)
—Busy Ant Maths. Clarke, Peter, ed. (p. 245)
—Busy Ant Maths - Year 3 Clarke, Peter, ed. (p. 245)
—Busy Ant Maths - Year 6 Pupil Clarke, Peter, ed. (p. 245)
—Busy Ant Maths - Year 6 Pupil Evans, Steve et al, illus. (p. 245)
—Pupil Book Clarke, Peter, ed. (p. 1417)
Mumford, Nana. In the Wake of the Quake. (p. 867)
Mummakay. Flying Free: Meditations for Kids in Star Language. (p. 610)
Mumme, Sarah. Guess Who's at the Zoo. Samuel, Janet, illus. (p. 729)
—Guess Who's My Pet. Samuel, Janet, illus. (p. 729)
—Guess Who's on the Farm. Samuel, Janet, illus. (p. 729)
—Guess Who's under the Sea. Samuel, Janet, illus. (p. 729)
Mumper-Drumm, Heidrun, illus. see Hillings, Phyllis & Hillings, Pamela.
Munaka, Marie, et al. This Country Anytime Anywhere: An Anthology of New Indigenous Writing from the Northern Territory. Thatcher, Allison, ed. (p. 1735)
Munamarty, Lasya. Fun Days at School. (p. 647)
Munan, Heidi, et al. Malaysia. (p. 1083)
Munari, Bruno. Bruno Munari's ABC: Semplice Lezione Di Inglese. (p. 232)
—Bruno Munari's ABC. (p. 232)
—Bruno Munari's Zoo. (p. 232)
—Speak Italian: The Fine Art of the Gesture. (p. 1622)
Munari, Bruno & Agostinelli, Enrica. Caperucita Roja, Verde, Amarilla, Azul, y Blanca. (p. 262)
Munárriz Guezala, Mercedes, jt. auth. see Munrriz, Mercedes.
Muncaster, Harriet. Happy Halloween, Witch's Cat! Muncaster, Harriet, illus. (p. 745)
—I Am a Witch's Cat. (p. 832)
Munch, Donna. Dark Tales of the Tower. (p. 408)
Munday, Dj. Secret Dummy of Joshua Bean. (p. 1540)
Munday, Evan. Dead Kid Detective Agency. (p. 417)
—Dial M for Morna. (p. 433)
Mundera, Kristina. Day in Pueblo Nuevo. (p. 413)
Mundie, Ken, illus. see Jepperson, Richard.
Mundt, A. S. Letter. (p. 1001)
Mundt, Anja, jt. auth. see Stille, Ljuba.
Mundy, Charlene & Chapline, Jo. David's Donkey Tales. (p. 411)
Mundy, Dawn. Gift: A Woodsong Story. Tigue, Terry & Turner, Diane, illus. (p. 675)
Mundy, Jen, illus. see Adhikary, Anita.
Mundy, Jen, illus. see Coniglio, Rebecca Perlman.
Mundy, Jen, illus. see Connolly, Megan B.
Mundy, Linus. Being Sad When Someone Dies: A Book about Grief... Just for Me! Fitzgerald, Anne, illus. (p. 161)
Mundy, Michaelene. Book of Prayers for All Your Cares. Alley, R. W., illus. (p. 211)
—It's Great to Be Grateful! A Kid's Guide to Being Thankful. Alley, R. W., illus. (p. 897)
—One Caring Kid: A Book about You-and What Your Kindness Can Do! (p. 1294)
—Saying Good-Bye, Saying Hello... When Your Family Is Moving. Alley, R. W., illus. (p. 1519)
—Sometimes I'm Afraid: A Book about Fear... Just for Me! Fitzgerald, Anne, illus. (p. 1610)
—What Happens When Someone Dies? A Child's Guide to Death & Funerals. (p. 1886)
Mundy, Talbot. For the Salt He Had Eaten. (p. 616)
Muneefa. My Tales for Children. (p. 1219)
Mun-Ensor, Michelle. Aloh. (p. 48)
—Angel's Garden. (p. 75)
—Faithful Christmas. (p. 565)
—Ten Bridesmaids. (p. 1718)
Munerlyn, Lorraine. John's Obedient Ants. (p. 924)
Munford, Rebecca, jt. auth. see Soderberg, Erin.
Munger, Mark. Pigs, a Trial Lawyer's Story. (p. 1358)
Munger, Nancy, illus. see Adams, Michelle Medlock.
Munger, Nancy, illus. see Higgs, Liz Curtis.
Munger, Nancy, illus. see Hoffman, Patricia.
Munger, Nancy, illus. see Holder, Jennifer.
Munger, Nancy, illus. see Olive, Teresa, et al.
Munger, Nancy, illus. see Pingry, Patricia A.
Munger, Nancy, illus. see Simon, Mary Manz.
Munger, Nancy, jt. auth. see Flegal, Daphna.
Mungin, Shanyece. Entwined (p. 531)
Muniz, Jim, illus. see Aguirre-Sacasa, Roberto.
Muñiz-Huberman, Angelina & Menton, Seymour. Dreaming of Safed. (p. 484)
Munnerlyn, Cindy, ed. Investigating Science - Animals. (p. 885)
Munns, Skye. Who's at the Zoo. (p. 1920)
Munoz, Adolfo, tr. see Gordon, Roderick & Williams, Brian.
MuÑoz, Alejandra DáVila. I Want to Paint Heaven. (p. 848)
Muñoz, Claudio, illus. see Ashman, Linda.
Muñoz, Claudio, illus. see Laurence, Daniel.
Munoz, Claudio, illus. see Medina, Meg.
Muñoz, Claudio, illus. see Thomas, Maria Jose & Thomas, María José.
Munoz de Coronado, Martha, ed. Subidos de Tono: Cuentos de Amor. (p. 1671)
Munoz, Elizabeth Cummins, tr. see Villasenor, Victor.
Munoz, Isabel. Como Mamá. Mazali, Gustavo, illus. (p. 351)
Muñoz, Isabel. Desastre en la Cocina. Mazali, Gustavo, illus. (p. 428)
Munoz, Isabel. En el Museo. Mazali, Gustavo, illus. (p. 522)
—It's Mine (Es Mío) Mazali, Gustavo, illus. (p. 897)
Muñoz, Isabel. Just Like Mom. Mazali, Gustavo, illus. (p. 939)
Munoz, Isabel. Where Is Eric? (¿Donde Está Eric?) Mazali, Gustavo, illus. (p. 1908)
Munoz, Martin J. Pirata Garrapata (The Garrapata Pirate) (p. 1362)
Muñoz, Mercedes. Boogie the Booger. (p. 210)
—Is Poverty a Serious Threat? (p. 889)
Munoz, Mercedes C. Nalu the Dinosaur. (p. 1228)
Munoz, Miguel. Diccionario Juvenil de Musica. (p. 435)
—Sonodiccionario: Asi Suenan los Instrumentos. (p. 1612)
Munoz, Norma. Cuentos de la Casa del Arbol. Olson, John & Olson, Johan, illus. (p. 390)
Munoz, Olga M., illus. see Milne, Barbara L. W.
Muñoz Puelles, Vicente. Laura y el Raton. (p. 980)
Muñoz Puelles, Vicente, jt. auth. see Puelles, Vicente Munoz.
Munoz, R. C. In Honor of the Oak Tree. (p. 863)
Munoz, Rie, illus. see Rogers, Jean.
Munoz, Ruby. Tomorrow I Am a Big Sister, but Today I Am Me. Maes, Ame, illus. (p. 1765)
Muñoz, William, illus. see Patent, Dorothy Hinshaw.
Muñoz, William, photos by see Patent, Dorothy Hinshaw.
Muñoz, Yenny, tr. see Bunnett, Rochelle.
Munro, Alice. Dance of the Happy Shades. (p. 402)
—Eye Spy. (p. 558)
—Friend of My Youth. (p. 637)
—Open Secrets. (p. 1299)
—Runaway. (p. 1496)
—Selected Stories. (p. 1549)
Munro, Alice, jt. auth. see Smith, Kathie Billingslea.
Munro, David. Lyrical Poetry for Boys & Girls 1891. (p. 1067)
Munro, Fiona. Princesses: With 200 Stickers, Puzzles & Games, Fold-Out Pages, & Creative Play. (p. 1406)
—Under the Sea. (p. 1814)
—Vacation: Creative Play, Fold-Out Pages, Puzzles & Games, over 200 Stickers! (p. 1829)
—Whose Ears? Garden, Jo, illus. (p. 1921)
—Whose Spots? Garden, Jo, illus. (p. 1922)
Munro, Fiona & Phillipson, Fiona. Whose Nose? Moon, Jo, illus. (p. 1922)
—Whose Stripes? Garden, Jo, illus. (p. 1922)
Munro, George, tr. see Verne, Jules.
Munro, Guillermo, illus. see Pintozzi, Nick.
Munro, Ken. Cross Keys Caper. (p. 385)
—Fireball. (p. 591)
—Grandfather's Secret: Sammy & Brian Mystery Series #16. (p. 707)
—Mysterious Baseball Scorecard: Sammy & Brian Mystery Series #17. (p. 1222)
Munro, Maisie. Shoes. Hale, Jenny, illus. (p. 1568)
—Slippers. Hale, Jenny, illus. (p. 1590)
—What Day Is It, Missie Mouse? Broekstra, Lorette, illus. (p. 1881)
—Whose Knickers? Worthington, Leonie, illus. (p. 1921)
—Whose Pyjamas? A Flip the Flap Book. Worthington, Leonie, illus. (p. 1922)
Munro, Marija. Mardi Loves Lipstick. (p. 1092)
Munro, Moira. Mermaid Who Came to School. (p. 1128)
Munro, Roxie. Busy Builders (p. 246)
—Christmastime in New York City. (p. 316)
—Desert Days, Desert Nights. (p. 429)
—Go! Go! Go! More Than 70 Flaps to Uncover & Discover! (p. 686)
—Hatch! Munro, Roxie, illus. (p. 752)
—Inside-Outside Book of London. (p. 877)
—Inside-Outside Book of New York City. Munro, Roxie, illus. (p. 877)
—Inside-Outside Dinosaurs (p. 877)
—Market Maze. (p. 1095)
—Market Maze. Munro, Roxie, illus. (p. 1095)
—Rodeo. (p. 1484)
—Slithery Snakes (p. 1591)
—Wild West Trail Ride Maze. (p. 1930)
Munro, Roxie, illus. see Spradlin, Michael P.
Munro, Roxie, illus. see Zaunders, Bo.
Munro, Sandie. Harriet Lane: First Lady of the White House. (p. 749)
—Karlee's Other Family. (p. 943)
Munroe, C. K. Attack of the Mutant Squirrels. (p. 114)
Munroe, Jeff. Six Unsolved Mysteries: Signs & Wonders in the Gospel of John. (p. 1583)
Munroe, Kevin. Zombo Fantasma. (p. 1988)
Munroe, Kirk. Flamingo Feather. (p. 602)
—'Forward, March' (p. 623)
Munroe, Myles. Purpose & Power of God's Glory. Sherman, Jan, ed. (p. 1419)
Munroe, Terri, et al. Rachel's Challenge: A Columbine Legacy Student Workbook. (p. 1432)
Munrriz, Mercedes & Munárriz Guezala, Mercedes. Por Qué? Martinez, Rocio, illus. (p. 1385)
—Qué Es? Martinez, Rocio, illus. (p. 1423)
Munsch, Audrey. Tale of the Red Ribbon. (p. 1700)
Munsch, Robert. 50 below Zero. Martchenko, Michael, illus. (p. 1997)
—Alligator Baby. (p. 47)
—Andrew's Loose Tooth. (p. 72)
—Anniversaire. Martchenko, Michael, illus. (p. 87)
—Bébé Alligator? (p. 155)
—Bola de Mugre. Lopez, Jose M., tr. from ENG. (p. 208)
—Dodo. Martchenko, Michael, illus. (p. 460)
—Espera y Verás. Aguirre, Rigo, tr. from ENG. (p. 536)
—Get Out of Bed! (p. 667)
—I Have to Go! (p. 839)
—I'm So Embarrassed! (p. 860)
—Kiss Me, I'm Perfect! Martchenko, Michael, illus. (p. 961)
—Love You Forever. (p. 1060)
—Makeup Mess. (p. 1080)
—Makeup Mess. Martchenko, Michael, illus. (p. 1080)
—Marilou Casse-Cou. (p. 1094)
—MMM, Cookies. (p. 1157)
—More Pies! (p. 1174)
—More Pies. Martchenko, Michael, illus. (p. 1174)
—Mortimer. Martchenko, Michael, illus. (p. 1176)
—Mortimer. Canetti, Yanitzia, tr. from ENG. (p. 1176)
—Mud Puddle. Petricic, Dusan, illus. (p. 1188)
—Munsch Mini-Treasury One. (p. 1191)
—Murmel, Murmel, Murmel. (p. 1192)
—On Partage Tout! (p. 1289)
—Paper Bag Princess: The Story Behind the Story. Martchenko, Michael, illus. (p. 1322)
—Paper Bag Princess. Martchenko, Michael, illus. (p. 1322)
—Purple, Green & Yellow. Desputeaux, Helene, illus. (p. 1419)
—Ribbon Rescue. (p. 1469)
—Sandcastle Contest. (p. 1511)
—Sandcastle Contest. Martchenko, Michael, illus. (p. 1511)
—Siempre Te Querre. (p. 1573)
—Smelly Socks. (p. 1593)
—Smelly Socks. Martchenko, Michael, illus. (p. 1593)
—Stephanie's Ponytail. (p. 1648)
—Stephanie's Ponytail. Martchenko, Michael, illus. (p. 1648)
—Thomas' Snowsuit. Martchenko, Michael, illus. (p. 1739)
—Tonne de Tartes! (p. 1765)
—Traje de Nieve de Tomas. (p. 1777)
—Up, up, Down. (p. 1824)
—We Share Everything! (p. 1868)
Munsch, Robert & Kusugak, Michael. Munschworks Grand Treasury. Desputeaux, Helene et al, illus. (p. 1191)
Munsch, Robert & Martchenko, Michael. Fire Station. Martchenko, Michael, illus. (p. 591)
Munsch, Robert & McGraw, Sheila. Love You Forever. (p. 1060)
Munsell, Jill. What a Day for a Parade. (p. 1878)
Munsell, Mary E. Let's Dance in the Rain, Josh. (p. 995)
Munshey, Sana. We're Off to Make 'Umrah. (p. 1875)
Munsinger, Lynn. Untitled Lynn Munsinger. (p. 1823)
Munsinger, Lynn, illus. see Brenner, Barbara, et al.
Munsinger, Lynn, illus. see Crimi, Carolyn.
Munsinger, Lynn, illus. see Elliott, Laura Malone.
Munsinger, Lynn, illus. see Howe, James.
Munsinger, Lynn, illus. see Katz, Susan B.
Munsinger, Lynn, illus. see Koller, Jackie French.
Munsinger, Lynn, illus. see Lester, Helen.
Munsinger, Lynn, illus. see Lewis, J. Patrick.
Munsinger, Lynn, illus. see Monsell, Mary Elise.
Munsinger, Lynn, illus. see Numeroff, Laura Joffe & Evans, Nate.
Munsinger, Lynn, illus. see Numeroff, Laura Joffe.
Munsinger, Lynn, illus. see Sauer, Tammi.
Munsinger, Lynn, illus. see Strauss, Linda Leopold.
Munsinger, Lynn, illus. see Winters, Kay.
Munsinger, Lynn, illus. see Wise, William.
Munsinger, Lynn, jt. auth. see Lester, Helen.
Munsinger, Lynn, jt. auth. see Numeroff, Laura Joffe.
Munson, Derek. Pastel para Enemigos. King, Tara Calahan, illus. (p. 1327)
Munson, Jared. Courageous Witness: A Teenager Shares Jesus. (p. 373)
Munson, Kyle Lloyd. King They Call Dumm. (p. 959)
Munson Scullin, Wendy. Young Person's Guide to the Prairie. (p. 1979)
Munson, Weegie. Tales of Weegie Munson. (p. 1703)
Münsterberg, Hugo. Americans. Holt, Edwin B., tr. from GER. (p. 64)
Muntadas, Antoni. Antoni Muntadas: On Translation. (p. 90)
Munte, Marta, et al. Kuku & Mwewe: A Swahili Folktale. (p. 968)
Muntean, Michael. Brain Quest Grade 3 Reading. (p. 222)
Muntean, Michaela. Do Not Open This Book. Lemaitre, Pascal, illus. (p. 457)
—Elmo Can... Taste! Touch! Smell! See! Hear! (Sesame Street) Swanson, Maggie, illus. (p. 515)
—True Story of Ten Dogs - Stay. Bailey, K. C., illus. (p. 1793)
—Zip! Pop! Hop! And Other Fun Words to Say. Prebenna, David, illus. (p. 1987)
Munter, June. Noah's Ark: The Animals Story. (p. 1261)
Munton, Gill. Who Ate All the Lettuce? Top That Publishing Staff, ed. (p. 1914)
Munves, James. We Were There with Lewis & Clark. (p. 1868)
Munz, Casey "Naanaage Binesik". Sshtaa taa Haa! Oh No! (p. 1637)
Munz, Michael. Shadow in the Flames. (p. 1557)
Munzel, Alexander. Allí Donde Florece el Cardo Sagrado/Where the Holy Thistle Blooms. (p. 47)
—Where the Holy Thistle Blooms. (p. 1909)
Munzo, Claudio, illus. see Medina, Meg.
Muphry, Lorna, jt. auth. see Murphy, Glenn.
Muqoz, Mercedes, ed. What Causes Addiction? (p. 1881)
Mur, Cindy. Does the Internet Benefit Society? (p. 460)
—Drug Testing. (p. 486)
Mur, Cindy, jt. auth. see Espejo, Roman.
Murad, Khurram, ed. see Tarantino, Mardijah Aldrich.
Muradov, Roman, illus. see Lloyd-Jones, Sally.
Muraida, Thelma, illus. see Bertrand, Diane Gonzales.
Muraida, Thelma, illus. see Brown, Monica & Ventura, Gabriela Baeza.
Muraida, Thelma, illus. see Caraballo, Samuel.
Muraida, Thelma, illus. see Luna, James, et al.
Murail, Elvire, jt. auth. see Murail, Marie-aude.
Murail, Marie-aude. Sin Azúcar, Gracias. (p. 1578)
Murail, Marie-aude & Murail, Elvire. Santa's Last Present. Blake, Quentin, illus. (p. 1513)
Murakami, Jon. Geckos Go to Bed. (p. 659)
—Geckos Make a Rainbow. (p. 659)
—Geckos Surf. (p. 659)
—Geckos Trick or Treat. (p. 659)
—Geckos Up Geckos Down. (p. 659)
Murakami, Jon, jt. auth. see Cowing, Sue.
Murakami, Jon & Yeh, Phil. Winged Tiger & the Dragons of Hawaii. (p. 1936)
Murakami, Jon J., jt. auth. see Suzuki, Genevieve A.
Murakami, Maki. Gravitation. (p. 712)
—Gravitation Murakami, Maki, illus. (p. 712)
—Gravitation Yoshimoto, Ray, tr. from JPN. (p. 712)
—Gravitation. Murakami, Maki, illus. (p. 712)
—Kanpai! (p. 942)
Murakami, Maki, illus. see Yoshimoto, Ray, tr.
Murakami, Maki, creator. Gravitation. (p. 712)
Murakami, Ryu. In the Miso Soup. McCarthy, Ralph, tr. from JPN. (p. 866)
Murakami, Yasunari & Kimura, ken. 999 Frogs & a Little Brother. (p. 2001)
Murakami, Yasunari, jt. auth. see Kimura, ken.
Murakami, Yoshiko, illus. see Kumon Staff.
Murariu, Lorraine, illus. see Gulino, ViTina Corso.
Murase, Sho, illus. see Conway, Gerry.
Murase, Sho, illus. see Petrucha, Stefan & Kinney, Sarah.
Murase, Sho, illus. see Petrucha, Stefan.
Murase, Sho, jt. auth. see Petrucha, Stefan.
Murata, Yusuke, illus. see Inagaki, Riichird & Inagaki, Riichiro.
Murata, Yusuke, illus. see Inagaki, Riichiro.
Muratore, Linda Mulstay. Autism & PDD Answering Questions, Level 2. (p. 117)
—Reinforcers to Go. (p. 1457)
Murawski, Darlyne. Face to Face with Butterflies. (p. 560)
—Face to Face with Caterpillars. (p. 560)
Murawski, Darlyne A. Face to Face with Caterpillars. Murawski, Darlyne A., illus. (p. 560)
—Spiders & Their Webs. (p. 1627)
—Spiders & Their Webs. Murawski, Darlyne A., photos by. (p. 1627)
Murawski, Darlyne & Honovich, Nancy. Ultimate Bugopedia: The Most Complete Bug Reference Ever. (p. 1809)
Murawski, Kevin, illus. see Marsoli, Lisa Ann.
Murayama, Kei. Centaur's Life (p. 287)
Murberger, Lori. Justin's First Crush. (p. 940)
Murch, Frank, illus. see Latham, Frank.
Murchison, Leon, illus. see Johnston, Brenda A. & Pruitt, Pamela.
Murcia, Rebecca Thatcher. Carl Sandburg. (p. 269)
—Civil Rights Movement. (p. 325)
—E. B. White. (p. 491)
—Legislative Branch. (p. 990)
—Meet Our New Student from Colombia. (p. 1121)
—Ronaldinho. (p. 1487)
—Shakira. (p. 1559)
—Threat to the Monarch Butterfly. (p. 1741)
—What It's Like to Be Kaka. de la Vega, Eida, tr. (p. 1891)
Murciano, Carlos. Bufanda Amarilla y Don Abecedario. (p. 235)
—Gigante Que Perdio una Bota. (p. 676)
—Mar Sigue Esperando. (p. 1091)
Murcott, Toby. Whole Story: Alternative Medicine on Trial? (p. 1920)
Murcray, Rod. Tuttle Stories. McDaniel, Rick, illus. (p. 1799)
Murdico, Suzanne. Earthquakes: A Practical Survival Guide. (p. 497)
Murdico, Suzanne J. Bomb Squad Experts: Life Defusing Explosive Devices. (p. 208)
—Earthquakes: A Practical Survival Guide. (p. 497)
—Gulf War. (p. 731)
—In-Line Skating: Techniques & Tricks. (p. 864)
—Meet the Blob. (p. 1122)
—Osama Bin Laden. (p. 1305)
—Osama bin Laden. (p. 1305)
—Possibilities & Problems in America's New Urban Centers: The Rise of Cities. (p. 1387)
—Railroads & Steamships: Important Developments in American Transportation. (p. 1434)
—Russia: A Primary Source Cultural Guide. (p. 1498)
—Snowboarding: Techniques & Tricks. (p. 1600)
—Snowboarding. (p. 1600)
—Street Luge & Dirtboarding. (p. 1666)
Murdin, Lesley. Understanding Transference: The Power of Patterns in the Therapeutic Relationship. Scott, Ann, ed. (p. 1816)
Murdocca, Sal, illus. see Boyce, Natalie Pope & Osborne, Mary Pope.
Murdocca, Sal, illus. see Osborne, Mary Pope & Boyce, Natalie Pope.
Murdocca, Sal, illus. see Osborne, Mary Pope & Osborne, Magic Tree.
Murdocca, Sal, illus. see Osborne, Mary Pope & PLC Editors Staff.
Murdocca, Sal, illus. see Osborne, Mary Pope, et al.
Murdocca, Sal, illus. see Osborne, Mary Pope.
Murdocca, Sal, illus. see Osborne, Will & Osborne, Mary Pope.
Murdocca, Sal, illus. see Stanley, George E.
Murdocca, Sal, illus. see Stanley, George Edward.
Murdocca, Sal, illus. see Winthrop, Elizabeth & Winthrop.
Murdocca, Sal, jt. auth. see Osborne, Mary Pope.
Murdocca, Sal, tr. see Osborne, Mary Pope & Boyce, Natalie Pope.
Murdocca, Sal, tr. see Osborne, Mary Pope.
Murdocca, Salvatore, illus. see Stanley, George E.
Murdoch, Brian, tr. see Pressler, Mirjam.
Murdoch, Brian & Salem Press Staff. All Quiet on the Western Front, by Erich Maria Remarque. (p. 45)
Murdoch, David & Dorling Kindersley Publishing Staff. Eyewitness - North American Indian. (p. 558)
Murdoch, David S., jt. auth. see Dorling Kindersley Publishing Staff.
Murdoch, Emily. If You Find Me. (p. 854)
Murdoch, J. D. African Wild Dog. (p. 28)
Murdoch, Patricia. Exposure (p. 554)
—Revelación (p. 1465)
Murdock, Bob E. Come on Down. Woodard, Sorah Junkin, illus. (p. 347)
Murdock, Catherine Gilbert. Dairy Queen. (p. 400)
—Front & Center. (p. 644)
—Heaven Is Paved with Oreos. (p. 761)

—off Season. (p. 1279)
—Princess Ben. (p. 1403)
—Wisdom's Kiss: A Thrilling & Romantic Adventure, Incorporating Magic, Villany, & a Cat. (p. 1939)
—Wisdom's Kiss. (p. 1939)
Murdock Elementary Student Council. Gallop to Glory: Mustangs Write Like the Wind: Volume 2. (p. 653)
Murdock, Hy. Daniel. (p. 404)
—David. (p. 410)
—Joseph. (p. 926)
Murdock, Kita Helmetag & Helmetag, Patricia. Cecily Cicada. (p. 283)
Mureddu, R. Laundromat. (p. 980)
Murfield, Anna, illus. see Goebel, Kelly.
Murfield, Anna, illus. see Gray, Shannon.
Murfield, Anna, illus. see Marquardt, Michelle.
Murfield, Anna, illus. see Merline, Sharlene.
Murfin, Teresa, illus. see Bonwill, Ann.
Murfin, Teresa, illus. see Friedman, Laurie B.
Murfin, Teresa, illus. see Friedman, Laurie.
Murfin, Teresa, illus. see Ryan, Margaret.
Murfree, Mary N. Mystery of Witch-Face Mountain & Other Stories. (p. 1226)
Murfree, Mary Noailles. Amulet. (p. 66)
—Champion. (p. 289)
—Fair Mississippian. (p. 562)
—Frontiersmen. (p. 644)
—Ordeal. (p. 1302)
—Raid of the Guerilla & Other Stories. (p. 1433)
—Storm Centre. (p. 1655)
—Story of Duciehurst. (p. 1658)
Murgia, Jennifer. Forest of Whispers. (p. 618)
Murguia, Bethanie. Buglette, the Messy Sleeper. Murguia, Bethanie, illus. (p. 237)
—Snippet the Early Riser. Murguia, Bethanie, illus. (p. 1598)
—Zoe's Jungle. (p. 1987)
Murguia, Bethanie Deeney. Best Parts of Christmas. Murguia, Bethanie Deeney, illus. (p. 171)
—I Feel Five! Murguia, Bethanie Deeney, illus. (p. 838)
—Princess Fairy Ballerina. (p. 1403)
—Zoe Gets Ready. (p. 1987)
—Zoe's Room (No Sisters Allowed) Murguia, Bethanie Deeney, illus. (p. 1987)
Murguia, Bethanie Deeney, illus. see Kuipers, Alice.
Murguia, Jose J., illus. see Andrade, Mary J.
Murguía, Verónica. Lo Que Sí y lo Que No. Quintero, José, illus. (p. 1044)
Muria, Anna. Maravilloso Viaje. (p. 1091)
Murica, Rebecca Thatcher, jt. auth. see Sherman, Patrice.
Murillo, Alan, jt. auth. see Balagura, Saul.
Murillo, Vinicio. Roderick Roach. (p. 1484)
Murkoff, Heidi. What to Expect at Preschool. Rader, Laura, illus. (p. 1894)
—What to Expect When Mommy's Having a Baby. Rader, Laura, illus. (p. 1894)
Murley, Karen O., illus. see Hutton, Linda.
Murley, Leon & Wilson, Antoine. Distribution of Goods & Services. (p. 454)
Muro, Claudia Burr. Yo Miro, Miro Todo el Tiempo: Basada en Pinturas y Textos de Rufino Tamayo. (p. 1971)
Muro, Claudia Burr, jt. auth. see Orozco, Rebeca.
Muro, Jenny, illus. see Waterbury, Matthew.
Muronaka, Michael, illus. see Peterson, Hiromi & Omizo, Naomi.
Murov. Instructor's Manual to Accompany Experiments & Exercises in Basic Chemistry, 6 Edition. (p. 878)
Murozumi, Hikaru & Inokuma, Shinobu. School of Water Business. (p. 1523)
Murphey, Cecil, jt. auth. see Piper, Don.
Murphy, jt. auth. see Murphy, Stuart J.
Murphy, Aileen, illus. see Gaynor, Kate.
Murphy, Alexa Gordon. Chico Mendes. (p. 301)
Murphy, Allyson, jt. auth. see Weaver, Kimberley.
Murphy & Pimlott. Certain Island. (p. 287)
Murphy, Andrea. Georgia. (p. 665)
Murphy, Andrea, illus. see Wilkinson, Richard Fergus.
Murphy, Andrea & Ray, Joyce. Women of the Pine Tree State: 25 Maine Women You Should Know. Greenleaf, Lisa, illus. (p. 1946)
Murphy, Angela. Canadian Crimes & Capers: A Rogue's Gallery of Notorious Escapades. (p. 260)
—Great Canadians: Twelve Profiles of Extraordinary People. (p. 714)
—Tricks & Treats of Halloween! Wake, Rich, illus. (p. 1786)
Murphy, Angela C. Bathroom Book of Canadian Trivia. (p. 144)
Murphy, Anne. Animal Island. (p. 78)
Murphy, Antoinette S. Does It Hurt When You Die? (p. 460)
Murphy, Austin. Scientific Investment Analysis Bloomquist, Don/Lee, Jr., ed. (p. 1528)
Murphy, B. B. My Spanish Treasure. (p. 1219)
Murphy, Barbara & Murphy, Barbara Beasley. Life! How I Love You! Baca, Elena, illus. (p. 1010)
Murphy, Barbara Beasley. Ace Flies Like an Eagle. (p. 8)
Murphy, Barbara Beasley, jt. auth. see Murphy, Barbara.
Murphy, Barbara Beasley & Wolkoff, Judie. Ace Hits Rock Bottom. (p. 8)
—Ace Hits the Big Time. (p. 8)
Murphy, Bernadette & Surridge, Gerry. Sport Readiness. (p. 1631)
Murphy, Betsy, illus. see Yaun, Ellen R.
Murphy, Bob, illus. see Paul, Sherry.
Murphy, Bobby. Ted the Turtle's Trip to the Moon. (p. 1712)
Murphy, Bonnie S. Puzzle Piece Thief. (p. 1421)
Murphy, Breena. Fairy Seekers - the Sand Fairy Wald, Sara J. & Wald, Antoinette M., illus. (p. 564)
—Fairy Seekers - the Sand Fairy. Wald, Sara Joyce & Wald, Antoinette M., illus. (p. 564)
Murphy, Brendán. Ready for School, Murphy? Murphy, Brendán, illus. (p. 1447)
Murphy, Brian. Movement. (p. 1183)
—San Francisco Giants: 50 Years. (p. 1510)
Murphy, Brian, et al. Chemistry 2014. (p. 297)
Murphy, Bud. Wild Stallion. Moyers, William, illus. (p. 1930)
Murphy, Buelina. Boke. (p. 208)
Murphy, Charles R. Waking Hour: A Collection of Illustrated Verse. (p. 1853)
Murphy, Charles R., illus. see Smith, Bill O.
Murphy, Chris, illus. see Logue, Stephanie.
Murphy, Christine Faye. Nature Doesn't Scare Me Bees. (p. 1236)
Murphy, Chuck. Animal Babies A to Z. (p. 76)
Murphy, Claire Rudolf. Child's Alaska. Mason, Charles, photos by. (p. 304)
—Marching with Aunt Susan: Susan B. Anthony & the Fight for Women's Suffrage Schuett, Stacey, illus. (p. 1092)
—My Country, 'Tis of Thee: How One Song Reveals the History of Civil Rights. Collier, Bryan, illus. (p. 1200)
Murphy, Claire Rudolf & Haigh, Jane G. Children of the Gold Rush. (p. 302)
—Gold Rush Dogs: And Other Favorite Dogs of the Last Frontier. (p. 694)
—Gold Rush Dogs. (p. 694)
—Gold Rush Women. (p. 694)
Murphy, D. Cathy. Animals, Animals Everywhere. Burbridge, William J., illus. (p. 82)
Murphy, Daniel. Bug Dance. (p. 236)
—Captain Invincible: Teacher's Guide. (p. 264)
—Dinosaur Deals. (p. 442)
—Racing Around: Teacher's Guide. (p. 1432)
—Safari Park. (p. 1502)
—Seaweed Soup. (p. 1539)
Murphy, David, illus. see Black, Robyn Hood.
Murphy, Dennis, illus. see Triplett, Annette.
Murphy, Derrick. United States 1918-1941. (p. 1819)
Murphy, Derrick, et al. Britain 1783-1918. (p. 229)
Murphy, Diane. Magnificent Pet. (p. 1076)
Murphy, Donald J. America's Entry into World War I. (p. 64)
Murphy, Ed. Wogs. (p. 1943)
Murphy, Ed, jt. auth. see Lewers, Rob.
Murphy, Eileen. 3 Big Steps. Montgomery, Violet, illus. (p. 1991)
Murphy, Elspeth Campbell. God Makes It Right: Three Stories for Children Based on Favorite Bible Verses. Nelson, Jane E., illus. (p. 690)
Murphy, Emily. Princess of Booray. Smith, Richard G., illus. (p. 1404)
Murphy, Emmy Lou, illus. see Gunderson, Vivian D.
Murphy, Frank. Babe Ruth Saves Baseball! Walz, Richard, illus. (p. 123)
—George Washington & the General's Dog. (p. 664)
—George Washington & the General's Dog. Walz, Richard, illus. (p. 664)
—Thomas Jefferson's Feast. Walz, Richard, illus. (p. 1739)
Murphy, Frank & Brenner, Martha. George, Thomas, & Abe! Walz, Richard & Cook, Donald, illus. (p. 663)
Murphy, Fredrick, illus. see Poole, Catherine Cheyenne.
Murphy, Glenn. Bodies: The Whole Blood-Pumping Story. (p. 206)
—Disgusting Science: A Revolting Look at What Makes Gross Things Gross. (p. 451)
—Evolution: The Whole Life on Earth Story. (p. 546)
—How Loud Can You Burp? More Extremely Important Questions (and Answers) (p. 810)
—Inventions. (p. 884)
—Space: The Whole Whizz-Bang Story. (p. 1618)
—Stuff That Scares Your Pants Off! The Science Scoop on More Than 30 Terrifying Phenomena! Phillips, Mike, illus. (p. 1670)
—Supergeek: Robots, Space & Furry Animals. Vol. 1 (p. 1683)
—Supergeek: Dinosaurs, Brains & Supertrains. Vol. 1 (p. 1683)
—Why Is Snot Green? And Other Extremely Important Questions (And Answers) Phillips, Mike, illus. (p. 1925)
Murphy, Glenn & Muprhy, Lorna. Poo! What Is That Smell? Everything You Ever Needed to Know about the Five Senses. (p. 1383)
Murphy, Harriet. Diego in Action! Follow the Reader Level 2. (p. 437)
Murphy, Hugh. T-Rex Trying. (p. 1694)
Murphy, Indera. No Stress Tech Guide to Business Objects Crystal Reports 2008 for Beginners. (p. 1260)
—No Stress Tech Guide to Crystal Reports Basic for Visual Studio 2008 for Beginners. (p. 1260)
—No Stress Tech Guide to Crystal Reports for Visual Studio 2005 for Beginners. (p. 1260)
—No Stress Tech Guide to Microsoft Works 9. (p. 1260)
—No Stress Tech Guide to What's New in Crystal Reports 2008: (Also includes What's New in Crystal Reports XI) (p. 1260)
Murphy, Ivan, illus. see Kent, Jennifer McGrath.
Murphy, Jason Robert, jt. auth. see Purcell, Mark.
Murphy, Jennifer. Storm. (p. 1655)
Murphy, Jill. All for One. (p. 44)
—Bad Spell for the Worst Witch. Murphy, Jill, illus. (p. 132)
—Dear Hound. (p. 419)
—Five Minutes' Peace. Murphy, Jill, illus. (p. 601)
—Lista para Salir. (p. 1022)
—Mr. Large in Charge. Murphy, Jill, illus. (p. 1185)
—On the Way Home. Murphy, Jill, illus. (p. 1291)
—Worst Witch & the Wishing Star. Murphy, Jill, illus. (p. 1961)
—Worst Witch Saves the Day. Murphy, Jill, illus. (p. 1961)
—Worst Witch to the Rescue. Murphy, Jill, illus. (p. 1961)
Murphy, Jim. Across America on an Emigrant Train. (p. 9)
—American Plague: The True & Terrifying Story of the Yellow Fever Epidemic Of 1793. (p. 62)
—Baffling & Bizarre Inventions. (p. 132)
—Blizzard! The Storm That Changed America. (p. 199)
—Crossing: How George Washington Saved the American Revolution. (p. 385)
—Giant & How He Humbugged America. (p. 673)
—Great Fire. (p. 716)
—Journal of James Edmond Pease, a Civil War Union Soldier. (p. 927)
—On Enemy Soil: The Journal of James Edmond Pease, a Civil War Union Soldier. (p. 1288)
—Savage Thunder: Antietam & the Bloody Road to Freedom. (p. 1516)
—Truce. (p. 1791)
—Weird & Wacky Inventions. (p. 1872)
Murphy, Jim & Blank, Alison. Invincible Microbe: Tuberculosis & the Never-Ending Search for a Cure. (p. 885)
Murphy, Jobi, illus. see Abela, Deborah.
Murphy, Jobi, illus. see Dumbleton, Mike.
Murphy, John. Essentials of Teaching Academic Oral Communication. (p. 537)
Murphy, John A. Ali Khamenei. (p. 39)
—Impeachment Process. (p. 862)
Murphy, John Cullen, jt. auth. see Foster, Hal.
Murphy, John, ed. Gods & Goddesses of the Inca, Maya, & Aztec Civilizations. (p. 690)
—Physics: Understanding the Properties of Matter & Energy. (p. 1353)
—Socialism & Communism. (p. 1605)
Murphy, John Paul. Watt's Special Purpose. (p. 1864)
Murphy, Joseph. Power of Your Subconscious Mind. (p. 1390)
Murphy, Joseph, et al. Putting the Power of Your Subconscious Mind to Work: Reach New Levels of Career Success Using the Power of Your Subconscious Mind. (p. 1420)
Murphy, Julie. Anglerfish. (p. 75)
—Arachnids. (p. 94)
—Desert Animal Adaptations (p. 428)
—Dumplin' (p. 490)
—Ocean Animal Adaptations (p. 1276)
—Seabirds. (p. 1536)
—Side Effects May Vary. (p. 1573)
—Whale Sharks. (p. 1877)
—Whose Baby Is This? (p. 1921)
—Whose Home Is This? (p. 1921)
Murphy, Julie & Amstutz, Lisa J. Amazing Animal Adaptations. (p. 53)
—Nature Starts. (p. 1236)
Murphy, Julie R. What If We Were All Gray? (p. 1887)
Murphy, Kelly. Historical Heartthrobs: 50 Timeless Crushes-from Cleopatra to Camus. (p. 783)
Murphy, Kelly, illus. see Appelt, Kathi.
Murphy, Kelly, illus. see Ashburn, Boni.
Murphy, Kelly, illus. see Aston, Dianna Hutts.
Murphy, Kelly, illus. see Bateman, Teresa.
Murphy, Kelly, illus. see Broach, Elise.
Murphy, Kelly, illus. see Brodien-Jones, Christine.
Murphy, Kelly, illus. see Cohen, Rich.
Murphy, Kelly, illus. see LaFevers, R. L.
Murphy, Kelly, illus. see Lewis, J. Patrick.
Murphy, Kelly, illus. see Martin, Lisa & Martin, Valerie.
Murphy, Kelly, illus. see Peck, Richard.
Murphy, Kelly, illus. see San Souci, Robert D.
Murphy, Kelly, illus. see Steensland, Mark.
Murphy, Kelly, illus. see Stratford, Jordan.
Murphy, Kelly, illus. see Yolen, Jane.
Murphy, Kevin. Water for Hartford: The Story of the Hartford Water Works & the Metropolitan District Commission. (p. 1862)
Murphy, Laura Blake. Mi Pequeño Mensajero / My Little Messenger. (p. 1133)
—My Little Messenger. (p. 1212)
Murphy, Lauren. Art & Culture of the Renaissance World. (p. 101)
Murphy, Lauren & Matthews, Rupert. Art & Culture of the Renaissance World. (p. 101)
Murphy, Linda, tr. see deLeon Diaz, Rosa, et al.
Murphy, Lisa. Even More Fizzle Bubble Pop & Wow! Simple Science for Young Children. (p. 541)
—Little Vampire. (p. 1037)
—Secret Smile. (p. 1544)
Murphy, Liz. Dictionary of Dance. (p. 436)
Murphy, Liz, illus. see Peters, Bernadette & Blue Apple Staff.
Murphy, Liz, illus. see Peters, Bernadette.
Murphy, Liz, illus. see Rizzuto, Katherine.
Murphy, Liz, illus. see Ziefert, Harriet.
Murphy, Liz & Ziefert, Harriet. Dictionary of Dance. Murphy, Liz, illus. (p. 436)
Murphy, Lorna. Maisie's Mountain. (p. 1077)
Murphy, Maggie. High-Tech DIY Projects with Electronics, Sensors, & LEDs. (p. 778)
—High-Tech DIY Projects with Flying Objects. (p. 778)
—High-Tech DIY Projects with Musical Instruments. (p. 778)
—High-Tech DIY Projects with Robotics. (p. 778)
—Johnny Depp. (p. 923)
—Jonas Brothers: Rock Stars. (p. 925)
—Kristen Stewart: Twilight Star. (p. 967)
—Megan Fox. (p. 1124)
—Miley Cyrus: Rock Star. (p. 1142)
—Movie Superstars (p. 1183)
—Reese Witherspoon. (p. 1456)
—Shia Labeouf. (p. 1566)
—Taylor Lautner: Twilight Star. (p. 1708)
—Taylor Lautner. (p. 1708)
—Taylor Swift: Country Music Star. (p. 1708)
—Zac Efron: Movie Star. (p. 1984)
—Zoe Saldana. (p. 1987)
Murphy, Mary. Are You My Mommy? Murphy, Mary, illus. (p. 97)
—Christmas Is the Best Bit. (p. 314)
—How Kind! Murphy, Mary, illus. (p. 810)
—I Like It When... (p. 841)
—I Like It When... Campoy, F. Isabel & Flor Ada, Alma, trs. from ENG. (p. 841)
—Kiss Like This. Murphy, Mary, illus. (p. 961)
—Let's Go! (p. 997)
—Panda Foo & the New Friend. Murphy, Mary, illus. (p. 1320)
—Quick Duck! Murphy, Mary, illus. (p. 1427)
—Say Hello Like This. Murphy, Mary, illus. (p. 1518)
—Slow Snail. (p. 1591)
—Utterly Lovely One. (p. 1829)
Murphy, Mary Elizabeth. I Kissed the Baby! Murphy, Mary Elizabeth, illus. (p. 840)
Murphy, Matt, illus. see Newman, Paul S.
Murphy, Megan. Breakfast Book. (p. 224)
Murphy, Mel. Barnyard Bully. (p. 139)
Murphy, Michael. Demons of Chaos. (p. 426)
Murphy, Michael E. Candy Cane Christmas. (p. 261)
Murphy, Nancy K. Rv Adventures by Sweetie, Miss Bell, Pierce & Sadie: By Sweetie Miss Bell, Pierce & Sad. (p. 1499)
Murphy, Nick V., jt. auth. see O'Dowd, Chris.
Murphy, Pat. Air Power: Rocket Science Made Simple. (p. 31)
—Wild Girls. (p. 1929)
Murphy, Pat, jt. auth. see Chorba, April.
Murphy, Pat, jt. auth. see Johnson, Anne Akers.
Murphy, Pat & Klutz Editors. Guide to the Galaxy. (p. 730)
Murphy, Pat & Klutz Labs Scientists Staff. Lego: Chain Reactions. (p. 990)
Murphy, Pat J. J., jt. auth. see Murphy, Shirley Rousseau.
Murphy, Patricia. Everything You Need to Know about Staying in the Hospital. (p. 546)
Murphy, Patricia J. Adding Puppies & Kittens. (p. 11)
—Avoiding Drugs. (p. 120)
—Counting Puppies & Kittens. (p. 371)
—Counting with an Abacus: Learning the Place Values of Ones, Tens, & Hundreds. (p. 371)
—Creative Minds. (p. 379)
—Day (p. 412)
—Discovering Underwater Secrets with a Nature Photographer. (p. 450)
—Explorando el Espacio con una Astronauta/Exploring Space with an Astronaut. (p. 550)
—Exploring Space with an Astronaut. (p. 553)
—First Day at Soccer, Level 1. (p. 594)
—Frog's Life: Learning Sequential Order Using a Timeline. (p. 641)
—Garrett Morgan: Inventor of the Traffic Light & Gas Mask. (p. 657)
—Grace Hopper: Computer Pioneer. (p. 704)
—Hearing: Your Ears are the Key to Your Sense of Hearing. (p. 759)
—Horse Club. (p. 799)
—How Does the Wind Blow? (p. 809)
—Huerta de Manzanas. (p. 824)
—I Need You. Bryant, Laura J., illus. (p. 844)
—Investigating Insects with a Scientist. (p. 884)
—Journey of a Pioneer. (p. 928)
—Measuring Puppies & Kittens. (p. 1117)
—Mirando a las Plantas con un Científico. (p. 1149)
—Months (p. 1170)
—Never Eat Soggy Waffles: Fun Mnemonic Memory Tricks. LaBaff, Tom, illus. (p. 1242)
—Peeking at Plants with a Scientist. (p. 1335)
—Sight. (p. 1574)
—Simple Machines. (p. 1577)
—Smell. (p. 1593)
—Staying Happy. (p. 1645)
—Subtracting Puppies & Kittens. (p. 1671)
—Taste. (p. 1707)
—Telling Time with Puppies & Kittens. (p. 1717)
—Touch. (p. 1772)
—Week (p. 1871)
—Why Are the North & South Poles So Cold? (p. 1922)
—Why Do Some Animals Shed. (p. 1924)
—Why Do Some Animals Shed Their Skin? (p. 1924)
—Why Is Earth Round? (p. 1925)
—Why Is the Sun So Hot? (p. 1925)
—Year (p. 1969)
Murphy, Patricia J., jt. auth. see Dorling Kindersley Publishing Staff.
Murphy, Patricia J. & Coughlan Publishing Staff. Huerta de Manzanas (p. 92)
Murphy, Patrick, jt. auth. see Crisfield, Deborah.
Murphy, Patrick J., illus. see Reiter, David P.
Murphy, Patty. I Wonder Who? (p. 849)
—When I Grow Up. (p. 1902)
Murphy, Paul. 13th Apostle. (p. 1995)
Murphy, Peg. I Can Do Anything. (p. 835)
Murphy, Pete. Five Short Blasts: A New Economic Theory Exposes the Fatal Flaw in Globalization & Its Consequences for America. (p. 601)
Murphy, Robert. Pond. (p. 1382)
Murphy, Rose. Monster Mayhem. Arthur, Jenny, illus. (p. 1167)
Murphy, Ryan, jt. auth. see Millsaps, Grace.
Murphy, Ryan & Varacalli, Lauren. Drexel University College Prowler off the Record. (p. 485)
Murphy, Sage. Sally Ride: Female Astronaut. (p. 1505)
Murphy, Sally. Meet Mary MacKillop. Martinez, Sonia, illus. (p. 1121)
—Pearl Verses the World. Potter, Heather, illus. (p. 1333)
—Toppling. James, Rhian Nest, illus. (p. 1769)
Murphy, Sally, jt. auth. see UC Publishing Staff.
Murphy, Scott, illus. see Brezenoff, Steve.
Murphy, Sean M. Common. (p. 349)
Murphy, Shirley Rousseau. Silver Woven in My Hair. (p. 1577)
Murphy, Shirley Rousseau & Murphy, Pat J. J. Cat, the Devil, the Last Escape: A Novel. (p. 278)
Murphy, Sonia, jt. auth. see Murphy, Steve.
Murphy, Steve & Murphy, Sonia. Secret. Ostrom, Bob, illus. (p. 1540)
Murphy, Stuart J. 100 Days of Cool. Bendall-Brunello, John, illus. (p. 1998)
—3 Little Firefighters. (p. 1991)
—3 Little Firefighters. Lum, Bernice, illus. (p. 1991)
—Camille y Su Equipo. (p. 256)
—Camille's Team. (p. 256)
—Coyotes All Around. Bjorkman, Steve, illus. (p. 375)
—Double the Ducks. (p. 473)
—Double the Ducks. Petrone, Valeria, illus. (p. 473)
—Earth Day - Hooray! Andriani, Renee, illus. (p. 495)
—Earth Day—Hooray! Andriani, Renee, illus. (p. 495)
—Emma Hace Amigos. (p. 519)
—Emma's Friendwich. (p. 520)
—En Busca de Freda. Mlawer, Teresa, tr. from ENG. (p. 522)
—Freda Is Found. (p. 632)
—Freda Organiza una Merienda. (p. 632)
—Freda Plans a Picnic. (p. 632)
—Freda Says Please. Jones, Tim, illus. (p. 632)
—Freda Stops a Bully. Jones, Tim, illus. (p. 632)

—Good Job, Ajay! (p. 698)
—Great Choice, Camille! (p. 714)
—Grizzly Gazette. (p. 724)
—Hamster Champs. Martin, Pedro, illus. (p. 739)
—Happy, Healthy Ajay! (p. 746)
—House for Birdie. Miller, Edward, illus. (p. 803)
—It's about Time! Speirs, John, illus. (p. 896)
—Jack the Builder. Rex, Michael, illus. (p. 903)
—Leaping Lizards. Adinolfi, JoAnn, illus. (p. 982)
—Left, Right, Emma! (p. 987)
—Less Than Zero. (p. 993)
—Less Than Zero. Remkiewicz, Frank, illus. (p. 993)
—Mall Mania. Andriani, Renee W., illus. (p. 1083)
—Mighty Maddie. Lum, Bernice, illus. (p. 1140)
—More or Less. Wenzel, David T., illus. (p. 1174)
—Percy Gets Upset. (p. 1341)
—Percy Juega con Cuidado. (p. 1341)
—Percy Listens Up. (p. 1341)
—Percy Plays It Safe. (p. 1341)
—Percy Se Enoja. (p. 1341)
—Percy's Neighborhood. (p. 1341)
—Polly's Pen Pal. Simard, Remy, illus. (p. 1381)
—Rodeo Time. Wenzel, David T., illus. (p. 1484)
—Same Old Horse. Björkman, Steve, illus. (p. 1507)
—Scrubba Dub, Carlos. Jones, Tim, illus. (p. 1533)
—Seaweed Soup. Remkiewicz, Frank, illus. (p. 1539)
—Tally O'Malley. Jabar, Cynthia, illus. (p. 1704)
—Write on, Carlos! Jones, Tim, illus. (p. 1963)
—¡Bien Hecho, Ajay! (p. 177)
Murphy, Stuart J. & Andriani, Renee. Mall Mania. (p. 1083)
Murphy, Stuart J. & Mlawer, Teresa. Carlos Escribe Su Nombre! Jones, Tim, illus. (p. 270)
Murphy, Stuart J. & Murphy. Treasure Map. Tusa, Tricia, illus. (p. 1782)
Murphy, Stuart J. & Rex, Michael. Jack the Builder. (p. 903)
Murphy, Susan White. D. J. 's Special Tree. (p. 398)
Murphy, T. M. Saving Santa's Seals. Taylor, Adam, illus. (p. 1517)
Murphy, Terri. My School. (p. 1218)
Murphy, Terri, illus. see Bennett, Kelly.
Murphy, Terri, illus. see Bohnet, Eric C.
Murphy, Terri, illus. see Hartman, Sara.
Murphy, Terri, illus. see Rosa-Mendoza, Gladys.
Murphy, Thomas. Island Boy. (p. 892)
Murphy, Timothy. Sugarbowl. (p. 1673)
Murphy, Todd. Go Fast, Goo. (p. 686)
Murphy, Tom, illus. see Bryan, Sean & Thomas, Evan.
Murphy, Tom, illus. see Bryan, Sean.
Murphy, Tracy. Everyday Adventures with Mickey & Seed. (p. 543)
Murphy, Troy, jt. auth. see DeVries, Mike.
Murphy, W. Ten Commandments for Children. (p. 1718)
Murphy, Wendy. Asthma. (p. 108)
Murphy, Wendy B. Weight & Health. (p. 1872)
Murphy, Yannick. Signed, Mata Hari: A Novel. (p. 1574)
Murr, Bob, illus. see Cardie, John P.
Murray, Aaron R. Aircraft of World War II. (p. 31)
—Counting in the Desert 1-2-3. (p. 371)
—Counting in the Forest 1-2-3. (p. 371)
—Counting in the Grasslands 1-2-3. (p. 371)
—Counting in the Oceans 1-2-3. (p. 371)
—Counting in the Rain Forest 1-2-3. (p. 371)
—Counting in the Tundra 1-2-3. (p. 371)
—Dentists Help Us. (p. 427)
—EMTs Help Us. (p. 521)
—Firefighters Help Us. (p. 591)
—Modern Military Aircraft/[author, Aaron R. Murray]. (p. 1158)
—Nurses Help Us. (p. 1273)
—Police Officers Help Us. (p. 1380)
—Sanitation Workers Help Us. (p. 1511)
—Teachers Help Us. (p. 1709)
—Veterinarians Help Us. (p. 1839)
Murray, Alison. Hickory Dickory Dog. Murray, Alison, illus. (p. 775)
—One Two That's My Shoe! Murray, Alison, illus. (p. 1297)
Murray, Alison, illus. see Nosy Crow Staff.
Murray, Amy. Character & Career Connection. (p. 291)
Murray, Amy, jt. auth. see Bender, Janet.
Murray, Andrew. Lord's Table: A Help to the Right Observance of the Holy Supper. Greater Truth Publishers, ed. (p. 1053)
—On a Tall, Tall Cliff. Snow, Alan, illus. (p. 1288)
—Very Sleepy Sloth. Tickle, Jack, tr. (p. 1838)
Murray, Barbara. Seasons of Life. Corbin, Marissa, illus. (p. 1538)
Murray, Barbara, ed. John Paul II, We Love You! World Youth Day Reflections, 1984-2005. (p. 922)
Murray, Bill, illus. see Barksdale-Hall, Roland.
Murray, Brendan. Tev on Home Turf. (p. 1723)
Murray, Brian Robert. Belle Curve: In Lemonade into Lemons. (p. 162)
Murray, C. J. Shayna Gladstone: In Search of the Scientist. (p. 1563)
Murray, Carol. ABC Art Riddles. Levin, Freddie, illus. (p. 3)
—Hurry Up! Garbot, Dave, illus. (p. 830)
—Sharks at Sea. LaCoste, Gary, illus. (p. 1563)
Murray, Carol, illus. see Keenan, Penny.
Murray, Caryn Eve. Philomena's Homecoming: The (mostly) true story of a New York prairie dog's search for a Family. (p. 1351)
Murray, Cassie. Olivia, the Olive Bug. (p. 1287)
Murray, Cecile. Fairies at Play:Tell a Story book About... (p. 562)
Murray, Colleen O., jt. auth. see Murray, Fisher C.
Murray, D., illus. see Marshall, Jo.
Murray, D. W., illus. see Marshall, Jo.
Murray, Diana. City Shapes. Collier, Bryan, illus. (p. 324)
Murray, Donna. Mottsie, Wolf of Great Price. (p. 1180)
Murray, Doug. D-Day. (p. 397)
Murray, Elizabeth A. Death: Corpses, Cadavers, & Other Grave Matters. (p. 420)
—Forensic Identification: Putting a Name & Face on Death. (p. 617)
—Overturning Wrongful Convictions: Science Serving Justice. (p. 1314)
Murray, Ev. Young Child's Totem. (p. 1978)
Murray, Fisher C & Murray, Colleen O. One & Only Bernadette P. McMull. (p. 1293)
Murray, George. Tales of Molly Brand & MacNessie. (p. 1702)
Murray, Glen L. Dumbing down of America. (p. 489)
Murray, Glenn, jt. auth. see Kotzwinkle, William.
Murray, Guillermo. Internet para Nino. (p. 880)
—Te Dije Que No Miraras. (p. 1708)
Murray, Guillermo, jt. auth. see Prisant, Guillermo Murray.
Murray, Helen. Awesome Adventures. (p. 120)
—Calling All Master Builders! (p. 254)
—Calling All Master Builders!, Level 1. (p. 254)
—Lego Movie. (p. 990)
Murray, Jacqui. Fifth grade Technology: 32 lessons every fifth grader should Know (p. 584)
Murray, James, illus. see Shelton, Angela.
Murray, Jaye. Bottled Up. (p. 215)
Murray, Jennifer. Flight & Fancy: The Airline Industry. (p. 604)
—'Twas a Dark & Stormy Night- Why Writers Write. (p. 1799)
—Twas a Dark & Stormy Night... Why Writers Write. (p. 1799)
Murray, Joan. Lawren Harris: An Introduction to His Life & Art. (p. 981)
Murray, Jocelyn. Africa. (p. 26)
Murray, John A. American Nature Writing 2003: Celebrating Emerging Women Nature Writers. Vol. 1 Murray, John A., ed. (p. 62)
Murray, Julie. Acting Animals. (p. 9)
—Afghanistan. (p. 26)
—Alabama. (p. 33)
—Alaska. (p. 33)
—Alligators. (p. 47)
—American Curl Cats. (p. 60)
—Ants. (p. 90)
—Apples. (p. 92)
—Arabian Horses. (p. 94)
—Arctic Foxes. (p. 96)
—Argentina. (p. 97)
—Arizona. (p. 98)
—Arkansas. (p. 99)
—Baboons. (p. 124)
—Backyard. (p. 130)
—Barcos. (p. 138)
—Beagles. (p. 150)
—Beans. (p. 150)
—Bees. (p. 158)
—Beluga Whales. (p. 163)
—Biggest Animals. (p. 185)
—Black Bears. (p. 195)
—Black Widow Spiders. (p. 197)
—Blue Whales. (p. 203)
—Boats. (p. 205)
—Body. (p. 207)
—Bottle-Nosed Dolphins. (p. 215)
—Bus Drivers. (p. 244)
—Butterflies. (p. 247)
—California. (p. 253)
—Canada. (p. 260)
—Cane to Sugar. (p. 261)
—Cardinals. (p. 266)
—Carros. (p. 271)
—Cars. (p. 272)
—Cheetahs. (p. 296)
—Chickens. (p. 300)
—Chimpanzees. (p. 306)
—China. (p. 306)
—Chinese New Year. (p. 307)
—Christmas. (p. 312)
—Cinco de Mayo. (p. 319)
—Clydesdale Horses. (p. 336)
—Cocker Spaniels. (p. 337)
—Cocoa Bean to Chocolate. (p. 337)
—Colombia. (p. 341)
—Color. (p. 342)
—Colorado. (p. 343)
—Columbus Day. (p. 346)
—Common Dolphins. (p. 349)
—Connecticut. (p. 357)
—Copperheads. (p. 366)
—Corn. (p. 367)
—Counselors. (p. 369)
—Cows. (p. 374)
—Crime-Fighting Animals. (p. 382)
—Crocodiles. (p. 384)
—Cuba. (p. 388)
—Dalmatians. (p. 401)
—Deer. (p. 423)
—Delaware. (p. 424)
—Disgusting Animals. (p. 450)
—Dragonflies. (p. 478)
—Eagles. (p. 492)
—Easter. (p. 499)
—Egypt. (p. 506)
—Electricity. (p. 509)
—Elephants. (p. 511)
—Emus. (p. 522)
—Erie Canal. (p. 533)
—Fastest Animals. (p. 576)
—Fireflies. (p. 592)
—Floating & Sinking. (p. 605)
—Florida. (p. 606)
—Flower to Honey. (p. 607)
—Frogs. (p. 641)
—Gateway Arch. (p. 658)
—Georgia. (p. 665)
—Giant Pandas. (p. 674)
—Gibbons. (p. 674)
—Giraffes. (p. 677)
—Goats. (p. 687)
—Golden Gate Bridge. (p. 694)
—Golden Retrievers. (p. 695)
—Gorillas. (p. 703)
—Grand Canyon. (p. 707)
—Grass to Milk. (p. 711)
—Grasshoppers. (p. 711)
—Gravity. (p. 712)
—Gray Whales. (p. 713)
—Great White Sharks. (p. 719)
—Greece. (p. 720)
—Grizzly Bears. (p. 724)
—Halloween. (p. 737)
—Hammerhead Sharks. (p. 739)
—Hamsters. (p. 740)
—Hanukkah. (p. 743)
—Hawaii. (p. 755)
—Hippopotamuses. (p. 781)
—Home. (p. 791)
—Hoover Dam. (p. 796)
—Hospital. (p. 801)
—Hot & Cold. (p. 801)
—Hummingbirds. (p. 826)
—Humpback Whales. (p. 827)
—Idaho. (p. 851)
—Iguanas. (p. 856)
—Illinois. (p. 857)
—Independence Day. (p. 870)
—India. (p. 870)
—Indiana. (p. 871)
—Iowa. (p. 886)
—Iran. (p. 886)
—Iraq. (p. 887)
—Ireland. (p. 887)
—Israel. (p. 893)
—Jack Russell Terriers. (p. 903)
—Jaguars. (p. 905)
—Japan. (p. 909)
—Jumping Spiders. (p. 934)
—Juneteenth. (p. 934)
—Kangaroos. (p. 942)
—Kansas. (p. 942)
—Kentucky. (p. 949)
—King Cobras. (p. 958)
—Koalas. (p. 966)
—Komodo Dragons. (p. 966)
—Kwanzaa. (p. 968)
—Labrador Retrievers. (p. 970)
—Ladybugs. (p. 971)
—Liberty Bell. (p. 1005)
—Librarians. (p. 1005)
—Light & Dark. (p. 1014)
—Lincoln Memorial. (p. 1018)
—Lions. (p. 1021)
—Lizards. (p. 1043)
—Llamas. (p. 1043)
—Louisiana. (p. 1058)
—Magnets. (p. 1076)
—Maine. (p. 1077)
—Martin Luther King, Jr. Day. (p. 1098)
—Maryland. (p. 1101)
—Massachusetts. (p. 1102)
—Matter. (p. 1109)
—Michigan. (p. 1135)
—Military Animals. (p. 1142)
—Milk to Ice Cream. (p. 1143)
—Minnesota. (p. 1147)
—Mississippi. (p. 1154)
—Missouri. (p. 1154)
—Monarch Butterflies. (p. 1163)
—Monkeys. (p. 1165)
—Montana. (p. 1170)
—Mosquitos. (p. 1177)
—Motion. (p. 1179)
—Mount Rushmore. (p. 1180)
—Mutts. (p. 1195)
—Navy SEALs. (p. 1238)
—Nebraska. (p. 1239)
—Nevada. (p. 1242)
—New Hampshire. (p. 1244)
—New Jersey. (p. 1245)
—New Mexico. (p. 1246)
—New York. (p. 1247)
—New Zealand. (p. 1249)
—North Carolina. (p. 1264)
—North Dakota. (p. 1265)
—North Korea. (p. 1265)
—Norway. (p. 1266)
—Nurses. (p. 1273)
—Ohio. (p. 1281)
—Oil to Gas. (p. 1282)
—Oklahoma. (p. 1282)
—Orangutans. (p. 1302)
—Oregon. (p. 1302)
—Owls. (p. 1315)
—Pakistan. (p. 1319)
—Pandas. (p. 1321)
—Parrots. (p. 1325)
—Passover. (p. 1327)
—Penguins. (p. 1337)
—Pennsylvania. (p. 1337)
—Persian Cats. (p. 1344)
—Pigs. (p. 1358)
—Pinto Horses. (p. 1361)
—Planes. (p. 1367)
—Platypuses. (p. 1370)
—Polar Bears. (p. 1379)
—President's Day. (p. 1397)
—Principals. (p. 1406)
—Puffins. (p. 1415)
—Pythons. (p. 1422)
—Ramadan. (p. 1437)
—Rattlesnakes. (p. 1440)
—Rhode Island. (p. 1468)
—Russia. (p. 1498)
—Saint Patrick's Day. (p. 1504)
—Salamanders. (p. 1504)
—Salmon. (p. 1505)
—School. (p. 1522)
—Sea Turtles. (p. 1536)
—Search-and-Rescue Animals. (p. 1537)
—Sears Tower. (p. 1538)
—Service Animals. (p. 1553)
—Sheep. (p. 1564)
—Sheep to Sweater. (p. 1564)
—Siamese Cats. (p. 1572)
—Sloth Bears. (p. 1591)
—Slowest Animals. (p. 1591)
—Smallest Animals. (p. 1592)
—Solids, Liquids, & Gasses. (p. 1608)
—Sound & Hearing. (p. 1615)
—South Carolina. (p. 1616)
—South Dakota. (p. 1617)
—South Korea. (p. 1617)
—Spaceships. (p. 1620)
—Spotted Dolphins. (p. 1634)
—Statue of Liberty. (p. 1645)
—Strongest Animals. (p. 1668)
—Sweden. (p. 1689)
—Tabby Cats. (p. 1694)
—Tarantula Spiders. (p. 1706)
—Tasmanian Devils. (p. 1707)
—Teachers. (p. 1709)
—Tennessee. (p. 1720)
—Termites. (p. 1721)
—Texas. (p. 1723)
—Thanksgiving. (p. 1725)
—That's Wild! A Look at Animals (p. 1727)
—Therapy Animals. (p. 1729)
—Tiger Sharks. (p. 1748)
—Tigers. (p. 1749)
—Toads. (p. 1760)
—Trains. (p. 1777)
—Trucks. (p. 1791)
—Turkey. (p. 1797)
—Turkeys. (p. 1797)
—Turtles. (p. 1799)
—Underwater. (p. 1817)
—United States. (p. 1819)
—United States Air Force. (p. 1819)
—United States Army. (p. 1819)
—United States Coast Guard. (p. 1819)
—United States Marine Corps. (p. 1819)
—United States Navy. (p. 1819)
—Utah. (p. 1829)
—Valentine's Day. (p. 1830)
—Vampire Bats. (p. 1831)
—Vermont. (p. 1837)
—Veterans Day. (p. 1839)
—Virginia. (p. 1844)
—Walruses. (p. 1855)
—Washington. (p. 1859)
—Washington Monument. (p. 1860)
—Water. (p. 1862)
—Watermelon. (p. 1863)
—Wax to Crayon. (p. 1864)
—West Virginia. (p. 1876)
—White House. (p. 1913)
—Wisconsin. (p. 1939)
—Wolf Spiders. (p. 1944)
—Wombats. (p. 1945)
—Woodpeckers. (p. 1949)
—Wrinkle-Faced Bats. (p. 1963)
—Wyoming. (p. 1966)
—Zebras. (p. 1985)
Murray, Julie, jt. auth. see ABDO Publishing Company Staff.
Murray, Julie, et al. Aviones. (p. 120)
—Camiones. (p. 256)
—Naves Espaciales. (p. 1237)
—Trenes. (p. 1784)
Murray, Kara. Adjectives & Adverbs. (p. 13)
—Capitalization & Punctuation. (p. 262)
—Contractions & Possessives. (p. 361)
—Nouns & Pronouns. (p. 1268)
—Simple & Compound Sentences. (p. 1577)
—Verbs. (p. 1836)
Murray, Karessa M. Campbell. High Class: {Friendship, Love, Sex, Relationships & Money} (p. 777)
Murray, Kiel. Mater Saves Christmas. (p. 1104)
Murray, Kiel & Disney Book Group Staff. Mater Saves Christmas. Disney Storybook Artists Staff, illus. (p. 1104)
Murray, Kirsty. Bridie's Fire. (p. 227)
—Four Seasons of Lucy McKenzie. (p. 625)
—Red Camel. Culkin-Lawrence, Teresa, illus. (p. 1453)
—Secret Life of Maeve Lee Kwong. (p. 1541)
—Vulture's Wake. (p. 1851)
Murray, Laura. Gingerbread Man Loose at the Zoo. Lowery, Mike, illus. (p. 677)
—Gingerbread Man Loose in the School. Lowery, Mike, illus. (p. 677)
—Gingerbread Man Loose on the Fire Truck. Lowery, Mike, illus. (p. 677)
Murray, Laura K. Ants. (p. 90)
—Ariana Grande. (p. 98)
—ATandT. (p. 111)
—Bean. (p. 150)
—Corn. (p. 367)
—Crickets. (p. 382)
—Fighter Jets. (p. 585)
—Iggy Azalea. (p. 855)
—Koala. (p. 966)
—Lululemon Athletica. (p. 1065)
—Penguin. (p. 1336)
—Retrievers. (p. 1464)
—Southwest Airlines. (p. 1617)
—Spiders. (p. 1627)
—Spies in the CIA. (p. 1627)
—Spies in the KGB. (p. 1627)
—Spies in the Mossad. (p. 1627)
—Spies in the SIS. (p. 1627)
—Story of Berkshire Hathaway. (p. 1657)
—Tanks. (p. 1705)
—Terriers. (p. 1721)
—Worms. (p. 1961)
Murray, Leinster. Space Tug. (p. 1620)
Murray, Libby. BeBe's Merry Christmas... to You. Hedrick, David, photos by. (p. 155)

Murray, Lisa A. Portend Learns That We Need Each Other. (p. 1386)
Murray, Lorraine, ed. Austria, Croatia, & Slovenia. (p. 117)
—Italy. (p. 894)
Murray, Lyn. Little Book of Memories: Volume 1. (p. 1025)
—Little Book of Memories. (p. 1025)
Murray, M. A., tr. Pinocchio, As First Translated into English by M a Murray & Illustrated by Charles Folkard. Folkard, Charles, illus. (p. 1360)
Murray, Marjorie D., jt. auth. see Murray, Marjorie Dennis.
Murray, Marjorie Dennis. Don't Wake up the Bear! Wittman, Patricia, illus. (p. 469)
—Halloween Night. Dorman, Brandon, illus. (p. 738)
Murray, Marjorie Dennis & Murray, Marjorie D. Halloween Night. Dorman, Brandon, illus. (p. 738)
Murray, Martine. Henrietta: There's No One Better. (p. 767)
—Henrietta the Great Go-Getter. Murray, Martine, illus. (p. 767)
—How to Make a Bird. (p. 820)
—Mannie & the Long Brave Day. Rippin, Sally, illus. (p. 1088)
Murray, Mary. Larry Lights the Way (p. 976)
Murray, Mary, et al. Bob Lends a Helping ... Hand? (p. 205)
Murray, Maturin. Circassian Slave. (p. 321)
Murray, Melanie & Varacalli, Lauren. College of Charleston College Prowler off the Record. (p. 340)
Murray, Millie. Kiesha. (p. 955)
Murray, Molly. Everyone Just Yell No at the Bullies! That Should Help to Stop Them! (p. 544)
Murray, P. D. Cat & Caboodle. (p. 277)
Murray, Pamela. Pirates of Texas. (p. 1364)
Murray, Pat, jt. auth. see Freeman, Maggie.
Murray, Patricia. Make It & Pray It: The Rosary Kit for Young People Murray, Patricia, illus. (p. 1079)
—Make It & Pray It. Murray, Patricia, illus. (p. 1079)
Murray, Patricia Lei. Let's Learn the Hawaiian Alphabet. Carter, Sharon, illus. (p. 998)
Murray, Paula, illus. see Keylock, Joanna Murray.
Murray, Penny, jt. auth. see Kelly, Frances.
Murray, Peter. Chameleons. (p. 289)
—Earthquakes. (p. 497)
—Floods. (p. 605)
—Hurricanes. (p. 830)
—Tornadoes. (p. 1770)
—Volcanoes. (p. 1849)
Murray Prisant, Guillermo. Mas Que Oscuro. (p. 1102)
Murray, Raymond C. Evidence from the Earth: Forensic Geology & Criminal Investigation. (p. 546)
Murray, Regina Waldron. Very Exciting Train Ride: An Adventure. (p. 1837)
Murray, Rhett E., illus. see Daybell, Chad.
Murray, Robb. Daredevil's Guide to Car Racing (p. 406)
—Washington Monument: Myths, Legends, & Facts (p. 1860)
Murray, Robb & Leavitt, Amie Jane. Daredevil's Guide. (p. 406)
Murray, Rosalie. Bobby & Bun Bun's Afternoon Adventure. Swope, Brenda, illus. (p. 206)
—Breakfast for Two. Balogh, Jared, illus. (p. 225)
—Yum Yum & Her Christmas Mouse. (p. 1983)
Murray, Scott. Granny's Christmas Blunder. (p. 710)
Murray, Sean, illus. see del Toro, Guillermo & Kraus, Daniel.
Murray, Shannon & Groenendyk, Doretta. Bounce & Beans & Bum (p. 216)
Murray, Steve. Reiki the Ultimate Guide: Past Lives & Soul Retrieval, Remove Psychic Debris & Heal Your Life. Vol. 4 (p. 1457)
Murray, Steven, illus. see Alkins, Anne Marie.
Murray, Steven, illus. see Messier, Mireille.
Murray, Steven, illus. see Peters, Diane.
Murray, Steven, illus. see Pitt, Steve.
Murray, Steven, illus. see Slavens, Elaine & James Lorimer and Company Ltd. Staff.
Murray, Steven, illus. see Slavens, Elaine.
Murray, Stuart. Submarines. (p. 1671)
—World War II. (p. 1959)
Murray, Stuart A. P. John Trumbull: Painter of the Revolutionary War. (p. 923)
—Mathew Brady: Photographer of Our Nation. (p. 1108)
—Matty in the Goal. (p. 1110)
—Score with Baseball Math. (p. 1530)
—Score with Basketball Math. (p. 1530)
—Score with Football Math. (p. 1530)
—Score with Race Car Math. (p. 1530)
—Score with Soccer Math. (p. 1530)
—Score with Track & Field Math. (p. 1530)
—Todd Goes for the Goal. (p. 1761)
—World War II: Step into the Action & Behind Enemy Lines from Hitler's Rise to Japan's Surrender. (p. 1959)
Murray, Stuart & Dorling Kindersley Publishing Staff. Eyewitness - Vietnam War. (p. 558)
—Vietnam War. (p. 1841)
Murray, Tamsyn. Snug as a Bug. Abbot, Judi, illus. (p. 1601)
—Snug As a Bug. Abbot, Judi & Gaviraghi, Giuditta, illus. (p. 1601)
Murray, Victoria Christopher. Aaliyah. (p. 2)
—Diamond. (p. 434)
—India. (p. 870)
—Joy. (p. 929)
—Veronique. (p. 1837)
Murray, W. On the Beach. (p. 1289)
—We Have Fun. (p. 1867)
—Workbook 1: For Use with Books 1a/1b/1c. (p. 1952)
—Workbook 3: To Be Used with Books 3a, 3b, 3c. (p. 1952)
—Workbook 4: To Be Used with Books 4a, 4b, 4c. (p. 1952)
—Workbook 6: To Be Used with Books 6A, 6B, 6C) (p. 1952)
Murray, Yxta Maya. Good Girl's Guide to Getting Kidnapped. (p. 698)
Murray-Gibson, Lynnette A. Clara & Mr. Twiddles: The Magical Adventures of Clara the Cleaning Lady. Scheibe, Nancy, illus. (p. 326)
Murrell, Belinda. Forgotten Pearl. (p. 620)
—Ivory Rose. (p. 901)
—Locket of Dreams. (p. 1045)
—Lulu Bell & the Birthday Unicorn. Geddes, Serena, illus. (p. 1064)
—Lulu Bell & the Christmas Elf. Geddes, Serena, illus. (p. 1064)
—Lulu Bell & the Circus Pup. Geddes, Serena, illus. (p. 1064)
—Lulu Bell & the Cubby Fort. Geddes, Serena, illus. (p. 1064)
—Lulu Bell & the Fairy Penguin. Geddes, Serena, illus. (p. 1064)
—Lulu Bell & the Moon Dragon. Geddes, Serena, illus. (p. 1064)
—Lulu Bell & the Pyjama Party. Geddes, Serena, illus. (p. 1064)
—Lulu Bell & the Sea Turtle. Geddes, Serena, illus. (p. 1064)
—Lulu Bell & the Tiger Cub. Geddes, Serena, illus. (p. 1065)
—Quest for the Sun Gem. (p. 1426)
—River Charm. (p. 1475)
—Ruby Talisman. (p. 1493)
—Sequin Star. (p. 1552)
—Snowy Tower. (p. 1601)
—Voyage of the Owl. (p. 1850)
Murrell, Deborah. Gladiator. (p. 682)
—Knight. (p. 964)
—Lift & Explore: Animals. Bull, Peter, illus. (p. 1014)
—Lift & Explore: Rainforests. Bull, Peter, illus. (p. 1014)
—Samurai. (p. 1509)
—Things That Go. Lewis, Anthony, illus. (p. 1733)
Murrell, Deborah, ed. see Gunzi, Christane.
Murrell, Deborah, jt. auth. see Kingfisher Editors.
Murrell, Deborah & Brooks, Susie. Human Body Lift-The-Flap. Lewis, Anthony, illus. (p. 825)
Murrell, Deborah Jane. Castles. (p. 277)
—Fighting a Battle. (p. 585)
—Knights & Armor. (p. 964)
—Weapons. (p. 1869)
Murrell, Deborah Jane & Dennis, Peter. Gladiator. (p. 682)
—Greek Warrior. (p. 721)
—Knight. (p. 964)
—Samurai. (p. 1509)
Murrell, Diane. Friends Learn about Tobin. Murrell, Diane, illus. (p. 638)
—Oliver Onion: The Onion Who Learns to Accept & Be Himself. Murrell, Diane, illus. (p. 1285)
Murrell, Susan. Worship ASAP: 40+ pick-up-and-use collective worship ideas for children with special Needs. (p. 1961)
Murrie, Matthew, jt. auth. see Murrie, Steve.
Murrie, Steve & Murrie, Matthew. While You Were Sleeping. (p. 1911)
Murrish, Layne Keeton, illus. see Mogavera, Cyndie Lepori & Richards, Courtland William.
Murrow, Marjorie. Surprise in Grandma's Eyes. (p. 1686)
Murtagh, Ciaran. Blackbeard & the Monster of the Deep. Aardvark, Nathan, illus. (p. 197)
Murtha, Dee, ed. see McKenzie, Marni Shideler & Bridges, Nancy S.
Murtha, Dee M., ed. see Russell, Patricia Constance.
Murthy, Amishi & Chou, Vivian. Joey Panda & His Food Allergies Save the Day. Cannon, Joseph, illus. (p. 920)
Murton, Gareth, jt. auth. see Moore, Nicholas.
Murty, Sudha. How I Taught My Grandmother to Read & Other Stories. (p. 810)
Murugarren, Miguel. Animalario Universal. Saez, Javier, illus. (p. 80)
Musacchia, Sofia Rose. Dog's Tail Will Not Wag. (p. 463)
Musacchia, Vince. Scooby-Doo! The Case of the Disappearing Scooby Snacks. (p. 1529)
Musariri, Blessing. Going Home: A Tree's Story. (p. 692)
Muscarello, James, illus. see Drachman, Eric.
Musch, Donald. Rise of Arnold Schwarzenegger & the Fall of Gray Davis: Recall Elections in the United States. (p. 1474)
Muschal, Frank. Bio-fuels. (p. 188)
—Energy from Wind, Sun, & Tides. (p. 528)
—Local Action. (p. 1044)
Muschal, Frank, jt. auth. see Lippman, David.
Muschal, Frank, jt. auth. see Orr, Tamra.
Muschell, David. Invisible Princess: A Full-Length Comedy-Dramatic Play. (p. 886)
Muschinske, Emily. Fingerprint Critters: Turning Your Prints into Fun Art. (p. 589)
Muschinske, Emily, illus. see Campbell, Kathy Kuhtz.
Muschinske, Emily, illus. see Randolph, Joanne.
Muschinske, Emily, tr. see Campbell, Kathy Kuhtz.
Muschinske, Emily, tr. see Randolph, Joanne.
Muschinske, Victoria. Honey Pie Pony's Book: A Fun with Fillies Adventure. (p. 794)
Muschla, Erin. Fractions & Decimals. (p. 626)
—Practice Makes Perfect Pre-Algebra. (p. 1392)
Muschla, Gary Robert. Crusader. (p. 386)
—Crusaders. (p. 386)
—Exploring Grammar. (p. 552)
—Exploring Vocabulary, Grades 4-5. (p. 554)
—Mastering Grammar. (p. 1103)
—Practice Makes Perfect Exploring Writing. (p. 1392)
—Practice Makes Perfect Multiplication & Division. (p. 1392)
—Ready-to-Use Reading Proficiency Lessons & Activities. (p. 1448)
—Sword & the Cross. (p. 1692)
Muschla, Gary Robert, jt. auth. see Muschla, Judith A.
Muschla, Gary Robert, jt. auth. see Muschla, Judith.
Muschla, Gary Robert & Muschla, Judith A. Math Games: 180 Reproducible Activities to Motivate, Excite, & Challenge Students, Grades 6-12. (p. 1106)
Muschla, Judith, jt. auth. see Hood, Christine.
Muschla, Judith A., jt. auth. see Muschla, Gary Robert.
Muschla, Judith A. & Muschla, Gary Robert. Algebra Readiness: 50 Independent Practice Pages That Help Kids Master Essential Math Skills-And Meet the NCTM Standards. (p. 38)
Muschla, Judith & Muschla, Gary Robert. Fractions & Decimals: 50 Independent Practice Pages That Help Kids Master Essential Math Skills-And Meet the Nctm Standards. (p. 626)
—Word Problems: 50 Independent Practice Pages That Help Kids Master Essential Math Skills-And Meet the NCTM Standards. (p. 1951)
Muscia, Marilena Carrubba. Misses Cowy to the Rescue. (p. 1152)
Musco, Rance. Hunt: Adventures of Austin & Rance. (p. 828)
Musco, Rance K. Legend of Sabor. (p. 988)
Muse, Elizabeth St. Cloud. Child's Garden: Introducing Your Child to the Joys of the Garden. Saull, Eve, illus. (p. 305)
Muse, Ludi. My Day at the Park. (p. 1201)
Museum of Modern Art (New York, N.Y.) Staff, jt. auth. see Chronicle Books Staff.
Museum of Modern Art (New York, N.Y.) Staff & Chronicle Books Staff. Lacing Shapes. (p. 970)
Museum of Modern Art Staff, jt. auth. see Gaumont Cinémathèque Muse Staff.
Museum of Science. Reminder for Emily: An Electrical Engineering Story. (p. 1460)
Musgrave, Al. Happy Harry Hoptoe. (p. 745)
Musgrave, Hilary, jt. auth. see Brown, Monica.
Musgrave, Machiko Yamane, jt. auth. see Musgrave, Paul Christopher.
Musgrave, Paul Christopher & Musgrave, Machiko Yamane. Doctor Mozart Music Theory Workbook Level 3 - in-Depth Piano Theory Fun for Children's Music Lessons & Home Schooling - Highly Effective for Beginn. (p. 459)
Musgrave, Ruth. Funny Fill-In: My Animal Adventure. Tharp, Jason, illus. (p. 649)
—Funny Fill-In - My Pets Adventure. (p. 649)
—Sharks: All the Shark Facts, Photos, & Fun That You Can Sink Your Teeth Into! (p. 1562)
Musgrave, Ruth A., jt. auth. see National Geographic Kids Staff.
Musgrave, Sugin. Butterfly in the Sky: Daddy's Little Girl. (p. 248)
Musgrave, Susan. Dreams Are More Real Than Bathtubs. (p. 484)
—Kiss, Tickle, Cuddle, Hug (p. 961)
—Love You More Melo, Esperança, illus. (p. 1060)
Musgrave, Susan, ed. Certain Things About My Mother: Daughters Speak. (p. 287)
—Perfectly Secret: The Hidden Lives of Seven Teen Girls. (p. 1342)
Musgrove, Margaret. Ashanti to Zulu: African Traditions. Dillon, Leo & Dillon, Diane, illus. (p. 105)
Musgrove, Marianne. Beginner's Guide to Revenge. (p. 159)
—Forget-Me-Not Fairy Treasury. MacCarthy, Patricia, illus. (p. 619)
Musheno, Erica, illus. see Mohr, L. C.
Mushet, Cindy, jt. auth. see Sur La Table Staff.
Mushko, Becky. Girl Who Raced Mules & Other Stories. (p. 679)
Music. ABCs & Much More Activity & Coloring Book. (p. 4)
—Gr 1 Share the Music Pe. (p. 704)
—Gr 6 Share the Music Pe. (p. 704)
—Gr 6 Stm Te/Piano Accomp. (p. 704)
—Gr K-3 Stm Instrument Sou. (p. 704)
—Gr K-3 Stm Music & Moveme. (p. 704)
—Instrmnts of the Orch(Cd- (p. 878)
—Instrmnts of the World(Cd. (p. 878)
—Instrumental Sounds. (p. 879)
—Share the Music Big Book Grade 1. (p. 1561)
Music for Little People, contrib. by. Let's Go Chipper! into the Great Outdoors. (p. 997)
Music Sales. Animal Songbook. (p. 79)
—Nursery Rhyme Songbook. (p. 1273)
Music Sales Corporation Staff, jt. auth. see Balmer, Paul.
Musick, David. Jeremy Daniels with the Bambles: The Adventure in the Mountains. (p. 913)
Musick, John A., jt. auth. see McMillan, Beverly.
Musick, Stacy. Waiting for Wings, Angel's Journey from Shelter Dog to Therapy Dog. Cotton, Sue Lynn, illus. (p. 1853)
Musilli Whitesell, Marjorie. I Have Four Parents. (p. 839)
Muskat, Carrie, jt. auth. see Wood, Kerry.
Musleah, Rahel & Jarrett, Judy. Apples & Pomegranates: A Family Seder for Rosh Hashanah. (p. 92)
Musmanno, Albert J. Little Poems about Big Ideas in Science. (p. 1033)
Musmon, Margaret. Latin & Caribbean Dance. (p. 979)
Musolf, Nell. Built for Success: The\Story of Microsoft. (p. 240)
—Jessica James. (p. 914)
—Split History of Westward Expansion in the United States: A Perspectives Flip Book (p. 1630)
—Story of Ford. (p. 1658)
—Story of Microsoft. (p. 1659)
—Story of Microsoft - Built for Success. (p. 1659)
—Teens in Greece (p. 1715)
Muss, Angela. Frog & Me. (p. 640)
—Monkey & Me. (p. 1165)
—Panda & Me. (p. 1320)
—Penguin & Me. (p. 1336)
Muss, Angela, illus. see Goodings, Christina.
Muss, Angela, illus. see Stone, Julia.
MUSS, Anon E. Time Portal. (p. 1752)
Mussari, Mark. Amy Tan. (p. 66)
—Haruki Murakami. (p. 751)
—Othello. (p. 1306)
—Poetry. (p. 1376)
—Sonnets. (p. 1612)
Musselman, Barbara. My Mad Book: I Get Mad & Granny Says It's Ok. (p. 1213)
Musselman, Christian, illus. see Golden Books.
Musselwhite, Harry. Martin - The Guitar. (p. 1097)
Mussenbrock, Anne. Easter Notes. (p. 499)
Mussenbrock, Anne, illus. see Meyer, Brigit.
Musser, George. Complete Idiot's Guide to String Theory. (p. 353)
Musser, Michele H. SleepyDo. (p. 1590)
Musser, Susan. Religion in America. Haugen, David M., ed. (p. 1458)
Musser, Susan, jt. auth. see Haugen, David M.
Musser, Susan, jt. ed. see Haugen, David M.
Musser, Susan, ed. America's Global Influence. (p. 64)
Mussi, Sarah. Door of No Return. (p. 470)
Mussler-Wright, Richard, jt. auth. see Baran, Laura.
Mussler-Wright, Richard & Baran, Laura. PCS Edventures! Bricklab Grade 3. (p. 1331)
Musson, Matt. Batboy on the Worst Team Ever! (p. 143)
Mustaine Hettinger, Cynthia. Boomerang, the Farm Cat. Ramsey, Jayne, illus. (p. 213)
—Casey the Confused Cow. Ramsey, Jayne, illus. (p. 275)
—Doc the Pygmy Goat. Ramsey, Jayne, illus. (p. 459)
—More Than You'll Ever Know. Gutwein, Gwendolyn, illus. (p. 1175)
—Penelope, the Busy Hen. Ramsey, Jayne, illus. (p. 1336)
—Travis, the Shetland Sheep. Ramsey, Jayne, illus. (p. 1781)
Mustard Seed Comics, Benito. NinjaBot Volume # 2 (p. 1256)
—Samurai Nightfall Vol # 1 Of 2 (p. 1510)
Mustazza, Leonard & Salem Press Staff. Slaughterhouse-Five, by Kurt Vonnegut. (p. 1588)
Musteen, Jason R., ed. see Corrigan, Jim.
Musteen, Jason R., ed. see Crompton, Samuel W.
Musteen, Jason R., ed. see Gallagher, Jim.
Musteen, Jason R., ed. see Galliker, Leslie.
Musteen, Jason R., ed. see Kavanaugh, Dorothy.
Musteen, Jason R., ed. see Rice, Earle.
Musteen, Jason R., ed. see Toler, Pamela.
Musteen, Jason R., ed. see Ziff, John.
Mustill, Caroline, tr. see Gombrich, E. H.
Mustoo, Terence. Sherlock Holmes in the Deerstalker: Chameleons' Dramascripts. (p. 1565)
Muszynski, Eva, illus. see Stowell, Louie.
Muszynski, Jim. Nothing Good Comes Easy. (p. 1268)
Muszynski, Julie. Henley in Hollywood. (p. 767)
—Henley on Safari. (p. 767)
Mutch Miller, Tiwana. Be Encouraging. (p. 148)
Mutcherson, Toni. Adventures of Jett Antoinette: Where Does Time Go? (p. 19)
Mutchnick, Brenda & Casden, Ron. Noteworthy Tale. Penney, Ian, illus. (p. 1268)
Muten, Burleigh. Goddesses: A World of Myth & Magic. Guay, Rebecca, illus. (p. 690)
—Grandfather Mountain: Stories of Gods & Heroes from Many Cultures. Bailey, Sian, illus. (p. 707)
—Miss Emily. Phelan, Matt, illus. (p. 1151)
Muth, Jon J. Hi, Koo! A Year of Seasons. (p. 775)
—Stone Soup. (p. 1652)
—Stone Soup. Muth, Jon J., illus. (p. 1652)
—Zen Ghosts. (p. 1986)
—Zen Ghosts. Muth, Jon J., illus. (p. 1986)
—Zen Shorts. (p. 1986)
—Zen Shorts. Muth, Jon J., illus. (p. 1986)
—Zen Ties. Muth, Jon J., illus. (p. 1986)
Muth, Jon J., illus. see Dylan, Bob.
Muth, Jon J., illus. see Hest, Amy.
Muth, Jon J., illus. see Kennedy, Caroline & Sampson, Ana.
Muth, Jon J., illus. see Kennedy, Caroline.
Muth, Jon J., illus. see Manzano, Sonia.
Muth, Jon J., illus. see Thompson, Lauren.
Muth, Jon J., illus. see Willems, Mo.
Muth, Jon J., illus. see Wood, Douglas.
Muth, Jon J., illus. see Zuckerman, Linda.
Muth, Jon J., jt. auth. see Manzano, Sonia.
Muth, Jon J. & Buscema, John. Galactus the Devourer. (p. 652)
Muther, Connie. My Monarch Journal. Bibeau, Anita, photos by. (p. 1214)
Muths, Tohn, illus. see Dzidrums, Christine.
Muths, Tohn Fayette, illus. see Dzidrums, Christine.
Muthu, Antony M. Athim. (p. 112)
Mutis, Alvaro. Mansión de Araucaíma: Diario de Lecumberri. (p. 1088)
Mutrie, Matthew. Brady O'Brian Saves the Day. Morales, Andrew, illus. (p. 221)
Mutton, Craig. Rearing Faithful Children: Handbook for Biblical Discipline. (p. 1450)
Mutuku, E. M. When the Sun Challenged the Moon. (p. 1905)
Mutyala, Sita. What Is Vemana Saying? (p. 1891)
Muzak, Warren, illus. see Monkeys, J.
Mwalimu. Mixed Medicine Bag: Original Black Wampanoag Folklore. Nurse, Shirley et al, eds. (p. 1156)
Mwanamwalye, Crebby Ilishebo. Story Time. (p. 1663)
Mwangi, Meja. Mzungu Boy (p. 1227)
Mwangi, Nyarual. Argwings & the Lamplighters. (p. 98)
Mwangi, Simmon, tr. see Ferrin, Wendy Wakefield.
My Children Publishing, prod. I am the Judge. (p. 834)
My Little Pony, My Little. My Little Pony Equestria Girls: Rainbow Rocks! (p. 1213)
My Little Pony Staff. I Love to Draw! Design & Draw Your Favorite Ponies with Stickers, Stencils, & More! (p. 843)
My Wolf Dog, illus. see Avignone, June.
Myagmardorj, Enkhtungalag, illus. see Batkhuu, Kh.
Myall, Julia. Cook It in a Cup! Quick Meals & Treats Kids Can Cook in Silicone Cups. Lowe, Greg, photos by. (p. 361)
Mycek-Wodecki, Anna. Bilingual Dog. (p. 186)
—Bilingual Dog. Abt, Diana, tr. (p. 186)
—Bilingual Dog. Sheng, Y. Karen, tr. (p. 186)
—Bilingual Dog/Iki Dilli Kopek. Erdogan, Fatih, tr. (p. 186)
—Cagnetta Bilingue (The Bilingual Dog) Umicini, Roberta, tr. (p. 251)
—Minutka: The Bilingual Dog & Friends. Mycek-Wodecki, Anna, illus. (p. 1148)
—Minutka: The Bilingual Dog/La Petite Chienne Bilingue. Sommer, Patricia, tr. (p. 1148)
Mycek-Wodecki, Anna, illus. see Goddard, Mary Beth.
Mydin, Liza. Three Village Boys of Al Haidar: The First Adventure. (p. 1744)
Myer, Andy. Delia's Dull Day: An Incredibly Boring Story. (p. 425)
—Henry Hubble's Book of Troubles. (p. 768)
—Pickles, Please! A Dilly of a Book. (p. 1354)
Myer, Ed, illus. see Bellisario, Gina.
Myer, Ed, illus. see Greve, Meg.
Myer, Ed, illus. see Robertson, J. Jean.
Myer, Ed, illus. see Robertson, Jean J.
Myer, Ed, illus. see Selleck, Richelle.
Myer, Ed, illus. see Steinkraus, Kyla.
Myer, Ed, illus. see Suen, Anastasia.
Myers. Holt Chemistry: Premier Online Edition. (p. 789)

Myers, Albert Cook, ed. William Penn's Own Account of the Lenni Lenape or Delaware Indians. (p. 1933)
Myers, Alishea, illus. see Wafer, C. K.
Myers, Alishea, illus. see Wafer, C. K. & Wafer, C. K.
Myers, Anna. Assassin. (p. 107)
—Grave Robber's Secret. (p. 712)
—Hoggee. (p. 787)
—Spy! (p. 1635)
—Time of the Witches. (p. 1752)
—Tulsa Burning. (p. 1796)
—Tumbleweed Baby. Vess, Charles, illus. (p. 1796)
—Wart. (p. 1859)
Myers, Barbara, jt. auth. see Hamilton, Lily.
Myers, Benjamin J. Blood Alchemy. (p. 200)
Myers, Bernice, illus. see Ives, Burl.
Myers, Bill. Aaaargh!!! (p. 2)
—Baseball for Breakfast: The Story of a Boy Who Hated to Wait. Riccio, Frank, illus. (p. 141)
—Chamber of Lies (p. 289)
—Choices: A Truth Seekers Novel. (p. 309)
—Enemy Closes In (p. 527)
—My Life as a Haunted Hamburger, Hold the Pickles (p. 1212)
—My Life As a Prickly Porcupine from the Planet Pluto (p. 1212)
—My Life as a Stupendously Stomped Soccer Star (p. 1212)
—My Life as a Supersized Superhero... with Slobber (p. 1212)
—My Life As a Tarantula Toe Tickler (p. 1212)
—New Kid Catastrophes. (p. 1245)
—Trapped by Shadows (p. 1779)
Myers, Bill, jt. auth. see Johnson, Ken.
Myers, Bill & Riordan, James. On the Run (p. 1291)
Myers, Bob. Trinity Goes to Soccer Camp. Bunker, Tom, illus. (p. 1787)
Myers, Byrona. Turn Here for Strawberry Roam. Jauss, Anne Marie, illus. (p. 1797)
—Yo Ho for Strawberry Roam! Jauss, Anne Marie, illus. (p. 1971)
Myers, Caron. Captain Steven: The Little Pirate who fought the Big C to Rule the Big Sea. (p. 264)
Myers, Carrie Mieko. What If You'd Met Beethoven? (p. 1887)
Myers, Christopher. My Pen. Myers, Christopher, illus. (p. 1216)
Myers, Christopher, illus. see Copeland, Misty.
Myers, Christopher, illus. see Hurston, Zora Neale & Thomas, Joyce Carol.
Myers, Christopher, illus. see Myers, Walter Dean.
Myers, Christopher, jt. auth. see Myers, Walter Dean.
Myers, Christopher, jt. auth. see Timbaland.
Myers, Christopher A., illus. see Myers, Walter Dean.
Myers, Connie Ellis. Words to Say out Loud: A Safety Book for Children. (p. 1952)
Myers, Dean. School. (p. 1522)
Myers, Dennis, jt. auth. see O'Connor, Rebecca.
Myers, Don. My Life with Roger. (p. 1212)
Myers, Doug, illus. see Schaaf, Fred.
Myers, Douglas E. Pivot-Point: The Beginning of Your Financial Journey. (p. 1365)
Myers, Edward. Duck & Cover. (p. 488)
—Ice. (p. 850)
—Let's Build a Playground. (p. 994)
Myers, Elaine. Adventures of Lizzy Beth. (p. 20)
—Adventures of Lizzy Beth at Grandma's Ranch. (p. 20)
Myers, Elisabeth P. Frederick Douglass: Young Defender of Human Rights. Morrison, Cathy, illus. (p. 633)
Myers, Glenice, jt. auth. see Lee, Josie D.
Myers, Glenn. Solomon Builds the Temple: 1 Kings 5:1-8:66. (p. 1608)
Myers, Glenn, illus. see Stiegemeyer, Julie.
Myers, Grandpa Don. Adventures of Willie Wonder. (p. 24)
Myers, Hortense & Burnett, Ruth. Carl Ben Eielson: Young Alaskan Pilot. Morrow, Gray, illus. (p. 269)
Myers, Jack. How Dogs Came from Wolves: And Other Explorations of Science in Action. Rice, John, illus. (p. 809)
—On Top of Mount Everest: And Other Explortions of Science in Action. Rice, John, illus. (p. 1292)
—Puzzle of the Platypus: And Other Explorations of Science in Action. Rice, John, illus. (p. 1421)
Myers, Jack & Jack Myers Ministries. Flowing in the Anointing: Understanding the Anointing of God. (p. 608)
Myers, Janet Nuzum. Critter Jokes & Riddles. Clegg, Dave, illus. (p. 384)
—Water Wonders of the World: From Killer Waves to Monsters of the Deep. (p. 1863)
Myers, Janice Limb. Carolee Sings in the Christmas Choir: A Christmas Story for Children of All Ages. Velica, Teodora, illus. (p. 270)
Myers, Jason. Blazed. (p. 199)
—Dead End. (p. 416)
—Exit Here. (p. 548)
—Mission. (p. 1153)
—Run the Game: Play or Be Played. (p. 1496)
Myers, Jeff. Secrets of Everyday Leaders Student Text: Create Positive Change & Inspire Extraordinary Results. (p. 1545)
—Secrets of Great Communicators Student Text: Simple, Powerful Strategies for Reaching the Heart of Your Audience, Student Textbook. (p. 1545)
—Secrets of World Changers Student Text: How to Achieve Lasting Influence as a Leader. (p. 1546)
Myers, Jenna. Australia. (p. 116)
—J. Paul Getty Museum. (p. 901)
Myers, Kate Kae. Inherit Midnight. (p. 874)
—Vanishing Game. (p. 1833)
Myers, Kristen, illus. see Lowry, Mark & Bolton, Martha.
Myers, Laurie. Easy Street. (p. 500)
—Escape by Night: A Civil War Adventure. Bates, Amy June, illus. (p. 534)
Myers, Lawrence E., illus. see Dakota, Heather.
Myers, Lawrence E., illus. see Hall, Kirsten.
Myers, Lawrence E., illus. see Salzano, Tammi J.
Myers, Lawrence Eddie, jt. auth. see Stieg, Megan.
Myers, Linda. Stoney the Pony's Most Inspiring Year: Teaching Children about Addiction Through Metaphor. (p. 1653)
Myers, Lois, jt. auth. see McCullagh, Sheila K.
Myers, Lou, illus. see Ives, Burl.
Myers, Madeleine M. Pocketful of Feathers. (p. 1375)
Myers, Marie Honre, illus. see Barrows, Marjorie.
Myers, Marion P. Never That! Whatever... Duh, get with the program & follow the Rules! (p. 1243)
Myers, Martha. Nibbles, the Mostly Mischievous Monkey. (p. 1250)
Myers, Mary Jo. Inner Workbook. (p. 875)
Myers, Matt, illus. see Masessa, Ed.
Myers, Matt, illus. see Rosenberg, Liz.
Myers, Matthew, illus. see Barnett, Mac.
Myers, Matthew, illus. see Cabatingan, Erin.
Myers, Matthew, illus. see DiPucchio, Kelly.
Myers, Matthew, illus. see Rosenberg, Liz.
Myers, Matthew, illus. see Ross, Gary.
Myers, Matthew, illus. see Scieszka, Jon & Barnett, Mac.
Myers, Micheline, jt. auth. see Coursaget, Catherine.
Myers, Nancy. Super Ben. (p. 1679)
—Tad's Story. (p. 1695)
Myers, Nancy & Charles, Rodney. Where's My Brother Joshua? (p. 1910)
Myers, R. E. Language Fundamentals. Mitchell, Judith, ed. (p. 975)
Myers, Rashida D. There's a Tear in Angel's Eye(A Mama Drama) (p. 1731)
Myers, Robert. 365 Knock-Knock Jokes. Toohey, Eileen N., illus. (p. 2001)
Myers, Robert E. Respect Matters: Real Life Scenarios Provide Powerful Discussion Starters for All Aspects of Respect. (p. 1463)
Myers, Robin. Pinky Rabbit Learns to Share. (p. 1360)
Myers, Roger. Oh, What a Joy It Is! An Adventure. (p. 1281)
Myers, Sarah, jt. auth. see Spitzer, Linda.
Myers, Shari, illus. see DeFrancesco, B. J.
Myers, Shari, illus. see McGhee, Heather.
Myers, Sharon A. Slumber Party. (p. 1591)
Myers, Sondra & Barber, Benjamin R., eds. Interdependence Handbook: Looking Back, Living the Present, Choosing the Future. (p. 879)
Myers, Stacy Erin. Lil Bug. (p. 1017)
Myers, Stephanie L. Bedtime Lullaby for Baby. (p. 157)
Myers, Suzanne. Stone Cove Island. (p. 1652)
Myers, Tamar. Angels, Angels Everywhere. (p. 75)
Myers, Theresa F., jt. auth. see Moran, Mary Y.
Myers, Theresa F., jt. text see Tschanz, Mary K.
Myers, Tim. Basho & the Fox Han, Oki S., illus. (p. 141)
—If You Give a T-Rex a Bone. Hovemann, Anisa Claire, illus. (p. 854)
—Looking for Luna Reed, Mike, illus. (p. 1051)
Myers, Tim & Pamintuan, Macky. Down at the Dino Wash Deluxe. (p. 474)
Myers, Tim J. Basho & the River Stones Han, Oki, illus. (p. 141)
—Christmas Stick: A Children's Story. Yilmaz, Necdet, illus. (p. 315)
—Furry-Legged Teapot (p. 650)
—Outfoxed Fox: Based on a Japanese Kyogen (p. 1312)
—Thunder Egg. Coleman, Winfield, illus. (p. 1746)
Myers, V. G., illus. see Gardner, Martin.
Myers, Walter Dean. 145th Street: Short Stories. (p. 2000)
—All the Right Stuff. (p. 46)
—Autobiography of My Dead Brother. (p. 117)
—Autobiography of My Dead Brother. (p. 117)
—Autobiography of My Dead Brother. Myers, Christopher, illus. (p. 117)
—Beast. (p. 152)
—Blues Journey. Myers, Christopher A. & Myers, Christopher, illus. (p. 204)
—Blues of Flats Brown. Laden, Nina, illus. (p. 204)
—Checkmate. (p. 295)
—Cruisers. (p. 386)
—Crystal. (p. 387)
—Darius & Twig. (p. 407)
—Dope Sick. (p. 470)
—Dream Bearer. (p. 483)
—Escorpiones. (p. 535)
—Fallen Angels. (p. 566)
—Frederick Douglass: The Lion Who Wrote History. Cooper, Floyd, illus. (p. 633)
—Game. (p. 654)
—Gifts We Bring. (p. 676)
—Glory Field. (p. 685)
—Handbook for Boys. (p. 740)
—Harlem Summer. (p. 749)
—Here in Harlem: Poems in Many Voices. (p. 770)
—Hoops. (p. 795)
—Ida B. Wells: Let the Truth Be Told. Christensen, Bonnie, illus. (p. 851)
—Invasion. (p. 883)
—It Ain't All for Nothin' (p. 893)
—I've Seen the Promised Land: The Life of Dr. Martin Luther King, Jr. Jenkins, Leonard, tr. (p. 901)
—I've Seen the Promised Land: The Life of Dr. Martin Luther King, Jr. Jenkins, Leonard, illus. (p. 901)
—Jazz. Myers, Christopher, illus. (p. 910)
—Juba! (p. 930)
—Just Write: Here's How! (p. 940)
—Lockdown. (p. 1045)
—Looking for the Easy Life. Harper, Lee, illus. (p. 1051)
—Malcolm X: A Fire Burning Brightly. (p. 1083)
—Malcolm X: A Fire Burning Brightly. Jenkins, Leonard, illus. (p. 1083)
—Monster. (p. 1166)
—Monster. Myers, Christopher, illus. (p. 1166)
—Mouse Rap. (p. 1182)
—Muhammad Ali: The People's Champion. Delinois, Alix, illus. (p. 1189)
—Oh, Snap! (p. 1281)
—On a Clear Day. (p. 1288)
—Patrol: An American Soldier in Vietnam. (p. 1329)
—Patrol: An American Soldier in Vietnam. Grifalconi, Ann, illus. (p. 1329)
—Righteous Revenge of Artemis Bonner. (p. 1472)
—Scorpions. (p. 1530)
—Shooter. (p. 1568)
—Slam! (p. 1587)
—Somewhere in the Darkness. (p. 1610)
—Star Is Born. (p. 1640)
—Street Love. (p. 1666)
—Sunrise over Fallujah. (p. 1677)
—USS Constellation: Pride of the American Navy. (p. 1829)
—We Are America: A Tribute from the Heart. Myers, Christopher, illus. (p. 1865)
—We Are America. (p. 1865)
—We Were Heroes: The Journal of Scott Pendleton Collins, a World War II Soldier, Normandy, France 1944. (p. 1868)
—What They Found: Love on 145th Street. (p. 1894)
Myers, Walter Dean, jt. auth. see Sims, Guy A.
Myers, Walter Dean & Miles, Bill. Harlem Hellfighters: When Pride Met Courage. (p. 748)
Myers, Walter Dean & Myers, Christopher. We Are America: A Tribute from the Heart. (p. 1865)
Myers, Walter Dean & William Miles. Harlem Hellfighters: When Pride Met Courage. (p. 748)
Myers, Walter Dean & Workman, Ross. Kick. (p. 951)
Myers-Bachmann, Jaycinth. Virtual Baby Nurse Feeding Guidelines with Records for Daily Feeds Health & Development in the First Year of Life. (p. 1844)
Myerson, Joel, ed. see Cranch, Christopher Pearse.
Myerson, Jonathan. Your Father. (p. 1980)
Myhan, Esther. Boy & His Dog. (p. 217)
Myklusch, Matt. Accidental Hero. (p. 8)
—End of Infinity. (p. 526)
—Jack Blank & the Imagine Nation. (p. 902)
—Jack Blank Collection: The Accidental Hero; The Secret War; The End of Infinity. (p. 902)
—Secret War. (p. 1544)
Myler, Terry, illus. see Farrell, Liam.
Myler, Terry, illus. see Harrison, Cora.
Myler, Terry, illus. see Hickey, Tony.
Myler, Terry, illus. see Keilty, Derek.
Myler, Terry, illus. see Mulligan, Frank.
Myler, Terry, illus. see Regan, Peter.
Mylin, Janet, jt. auth. see Gresh, Dannah.
Myott, Lanita. RJ Saves the Day. (p. 1476)
Myracle, Lauren. Awesome Blossom: A Flower Power Book. (p. 121)
—Bff: A Girlfriend Book You Write Together. (p. 174)
—Bliss. (p. 199)
—Eleven. (p. 512)
—Fashion Disaster That Changed My Life. (p. 575)
—Friends of a Feather. Henry, Jed, illus. (p. 638)
—Infinite Moment of Us. (p. 873)
—Kissing Kate. (p. 962)
—L8r, G8r. (p. 969)
—Life of Ty: Penguin Problems. Henry, Jed, illus. (p. 1012)
—Life of Ty - Non-Random Acts of Kindness. Henry, Jed, illus. (p. 1012)
—Luv Ya Bunches (p. 1066)
—Luv Ya Bunches: A Flower Power Book. (p. 1066)
—Non-Random Acts of Kindness. Henry, Jed, illus. (p. 1263)
—Oopsy Daisy: A Flower Power Book. (p. 1299)
—Oopsy Daisy. (p. 1299)
—Peace, Love, & Baby Ducks. (p. 1331)
—Penguin Problems. (p. 1337)
—Rhymes with Witches. (p. 1468)
—Rodney's SsssSolution - Big Book. Renooy, "Cosmic" Ray, illus. (p. 1484)
—Shine. (p. 1566)
—Ten. (p. 1718)
—Thirteen. (p. 1734)
—Thirteen Plus One. (p. 1735)
—Ttfn. (p. 1795)
—TTFN (Ta-Ta for Now) (p. 1795)
—Ttyl (Talk to You Later) (p. 1795)
—Twelve. (p. 1800)
—Violet in Bloom: A Flower Power Book. (p. 1843)
—Violet in Bloom. (p. 1843)
—Winnie's Journal. Yoskowitz, Lisa, ed. (p. 1937)
—Yolo. (p. 1972)
Myracle, Lauren, et al. How to Be Bad. (p. 815)
Myrddin ap Dafydd. Briwsion Yn y Clustiau: Cyfrol o Farddoniaeth I Blant. (p. 230)
—Mul Bach Ar Gefn Ei Geffyl: Cerddi Am Greaduriaid. (p. 1189)
Myrddin ap Dafydd & Morris, Siôn. Armadilo Ar Fy Mhen. (p. 99)
—Chwarae Plant. (p. 318)
—Sach Gysgu Yn Llawn o Greision. (p. 1500)
—Tabledi-Gwneud-'chi-Wenu: Dôs Arbennig o Farddoniaeth Loerig Am Salwch Ac Afiechydon. (p. 1694)
—Y Llew Go Lew. (p. 1968)
Myrddin ap Dafydd, et al. Caneuon y Coridorau: Barddoniaeth Ar Gyfer Pobl Ifanc. (p. 261)
Myrick, Gladys, jt. ed. see de Niles, Anita.
Myrick, Gladys, jt. ed. see Niles de Martin, Anita.
Myrieckes, Eric. Street Games. (p. 1666)
Myrl, Melanie. Why Some Birds Don't Eat Worms. (p. 1926)
Myron, Vicki & Witter, Bret. Dewey: There's a Cat in the Library! James, Steve, illus. (p. 432)
—Dewey the Library Cat. (p. 432)
Myrus, Donald. Keeping up with the Astronauts: The Story of Man's Greatest Adventures in Outer Space Including the John Glenn & Scott Carpenter Flights. (p. 948)
Mysak, Mary. Little Train! Stickley, Kelly, illus. (p. 1037)
Mysko, Claire. You're Amazing! A No-Pressure Guide to Being Your Best Self. (p. 1982)
!Myster?Ous M! & Courageous $Oul. Lonely Flower. Courageous $oul, illus. (p. 1046)
Mystery Staff, et al. Mystery Method: How to Get Beautiful Women into Bed. (p. 1224)
Mystery Writers of America Staff, jt. auth. see McDonnell, Patrick.
Mystic. Talon Hawke: A Journey Through Darkness. (p. 1704)
Mzjica, Elisa. Cuentos para Ninos de la Candelaria. Franco, Mauricio, illus. (p. 390)

N

N. Skills Handbook Using Science: Teacher's Guide. (p. 1585)
—Skills Handbook Using Science: Skills Workbook Package Pack (p. 1585)
—Skills Handbook Using Science: Skills Workbook Package (Pkg. Of 10) (p. 1585)
N. E. Thing Enterprises Staff. Garfield's Magic Eye. (p. 657)
—Magic Eye III. (p. 1072)
N Gallerie Studios. Island Hunters Book II: Trail of the Tomb Robbers (p. 892)
—Island Hunters Book III: The Legend of Brown Eyed James (p. 892)
N Gallerie Studios, illus. see Walford, N. E.
Na, An. Step from Heaven. (p. 1648)
Na, Il Sung. Book of Sleep. (p. 211)
—Hide & Seek. (p. 776)
—Snow Rabbit, Spring Rabbit: A Book of Changing Seasons. (p. 1599)
—Thingamabob. (p. 1733)
—Welcome Home, Bear: A Book of Animal Habitats. (p. 1873)
Na, In-Soo. King of Hell Jae-Hwan, Kim, illus. (p. 958)
Na, Lauren, tr. see Hee, Lee Yun.
Na, Lauren, tr. see Hwa, Kim Dong.
Na, Lauren, tr. see Jae-Hwan, Kim.
Na, Lauren, tr. see Kang Won, Kim.
Na, Lauren, tr. see So-Yong, Lee.
Na, Lauren, tr. see Won, Kim Kang.
Na, Yeri. Do Whatever You Want. (p. 457)
Naasel, Kenrya R. & Rankin, Kenrya. Start It Up: The Complete Teen Business Guide to Turning Your Passions into Pay. Takada, Eriko, illus. (p. 1643)
Naba, Dajana, illus. see Jones, Angela & Jones, Sourou.
Nabb, Magdalen. Marshal & the Murderer. (p. 1096)
Naber, Therese. Native Nations of California. (p. 1235)
—Native Nations of the Southeast. (p. 1235)
Nabil, Dina E. L. Eleanor Roosevelt First Lady of the World. (p. 508)
Nabokov, Vladimir, tr. see Carroll, Lewis, pseud.
Nabors, Murray. Romantic Christmas Stories of the Old West. (p. 1486)
Nabors, V. L. Mad Craze Middle School; the Case of the Crumpled Balls. (p. 1069)
Nacerous, Roman P. Jay-Z. (p. 910)
Nachbar, Patricia Depoyster. Love Doesn't Die. (p. 1059)
Nachtwey, James. Inferno. (p. 873)
Nadakavukaren Schefer, Krista. Social Regulation in the WTO: Trade Policy & International Legal Development. (p. 1604)
Nadal, Gloria. No No Foca Loca. (p. 1259)
Nadaskay, Lori, illus. see Johnson, Sandi.
Nadeau, Isaac. Canyons. (p. 262)
—Caves. (p. 282)
—Glaciers. (p. 682)
—Interdependence of Organisms & Environments. (p. 879)
—Interdependence of Organisms & the Environment. (p. 879)
—Islands. (p. 892)
—Learing about the Water Cycle with Graphic Organizers. (p. 982)
—Learning about Earth's Cycles with Graphic Organizers. (p. 984)
—Learning about the Movement of the Sun & Other Stars with Graphic Organizers. (p. 985)
—Learning about the Water Cycle with Graphic Organizers. (p. 985)
—Mountains. (p. 1181)
—Peninsulas. (p. 1337)
—Plant Development & Growth. (p. 1369)
—Water in Glaciers. (p. 1862)
—Water in Oceans. (p. 1862)
—Water in Plants & Animals. (p. 1863)
—Water in Rivers & Lakes. (p. 1863)
—Water in the Atmosphere. (p. 1863)
—Water under Ground. (p. 1863)
Nadeau, Janice, illus. see Bouchard, Hervé.
Nadeau, Janice, illus. see Hood, Susan.
Nadeau, Janice, illus. see Schotter, Roni.
Nadeau, Janice, illus. see Winstanley, Nicola.
Nadeau, Kathleen G. & Dixon, Ellen B. Learning to Slow Down & Pay Attention: A Book for Kids about ADHD. Beyl, Charles, illus. (p. 986)
Nadeau, Nicole. Caillou: I'm Not Hungry! Brignaud, Pierre, illus. (p. 251)
—Caillou - The Shopping Trip. Brignaud, Pierre, illus. (p. 251)
Nadel, Carolina. Daddy's Home. Nadel, Carolina, illus. (p. 399)
Nadelstern, Paula. Fantastical Designs Coloring Book. (p. 572)
Naden, Corinne J. Abortion. (p. 5)
—Ancient Chinese & the Great Wall of China. (p. 68)
—As You Like It. (p. 105)
—Benazir Bhutto. (p. 163)
—Facts about the A-Z of Drugs. (p. 561)
—Health Care: A Right or a Privilege? (p. 758)
—Mao Zedong & the Chinese Revolution. (p. 1089)
—Patients' Rights. (p. 1328)
—Political Campaigns. (p. 1380)
—Taming of the Shrew. (p. 1704)
Naden, Corinne J., jt. auth. see Blue, Rose.
Naden, Corinne J., jt. auth. see Gillespie, John T.
Naden, Corinne J. & Blue, Rose. Ancient Egyptians & the Pyramids. (p. 69)
—Ancient Greeks & the Parthenon. (p. 69)
—Ancient Maya & Tikal. (p. 70)
—Ancient Romans & the Colosseum. (p. 70)
—Aztecs & Tenochtitlan. (p. 122)
—Fidel Castro & the Cuban Revolution. (p. 583)
—James Monroe. (p. 907)
—Massachusetts: A MyReportLinks.com Book. (p. 1102)
—Mississippi: A MyReportLinks.com Book. (p. 1154)
—Mormonism. (p. 1175)
Naderi, Babak. Adventures of Captain Zero. (p. 17)

N

—King of the Universe. (p. 959)
Nadimi, Suzan. Hungry Cat Downie, Christopher, illus. (p. 828)
Nadin, Joanna. Paradise. (p. 1323)
—Penny Dreadful Causes a Kerfuffle. (p. 1338)
—Penny Dreadful Is a Complete Catastrophe. (p. 1338)
—Penny Dreadful Is a Magnet for Disaster. (p. 1338)
—Wonderland. (p. 1948)
Nadin, Mihai, ed. see Loesch, Uwe.
Naditch, Beth, jt. ed. see Bardack, Amy.
Nadja. Cinco Deditos. (p. 319)
—Perro Azul. (p. 1343)
Nadler, Beth. Magic School Bus Inside Ralphie. Duchesne, Lucie, tr. (p. 1073)
Nadler, Ellis, illus. see Lawrence, Michael.
Nadler, Ellis, jt. auth. see Lawrence, Michael.
Nadler, Holly Mascott. Vineyard Supernatural: True Ghost Stories from America's Most Haunted Island. (p. 1843)
Nadol, Jen. Mark. (p. 1095)
Naegele, K. Z. Chatty Hat. (p. 295)
Naenix, Robin, illus. see Brewer, Dottie A.
Naff, Clay Farris. Conflict in the Middle East. (p. 357)
—Do Cell Phones Cause Cancer? Greenhaven Press Editors, ed. (p. 456)
—Evolution. (p. 546)
—Gene Therapy. (p. 660)
—Medical Imaging. (p. 1118)
—Nicotine & Tobacco. (p. 1251)
—Solar Power. (p. 1606)
—Why Is Autism on Rise? Gale, ed. (p. 1925)
Naff, Clay Farris, ed. Wind. (p. 1935)
Naff, Clayton Farris. Allergies. (p. 46)
—Asthma. (p. 108)
—Deafness & Hearing Impairment. (p. 418)
—Designer Babies. (p. 430)
—Heart Disease. (p. 759)
—Influenza. (p. 873)
Naff, Clayton Farris, jt. auth. see Dziedzic, Nancy.
Naff, Clayton Farris, ed. Huntington's Disease. (p. 829)
—Multiple Sclerosis. (p. 1190)
—Muscular Dystrophy. (p. 1192)
—Sexually Transmitted Diseases. (p. 1556)
Naftali, Joel, jt. auth. see Pryce, Trevor.
Nafts, Sara. Happily Five. (p. 744)
Naga, Ann Whitehead. World above the Clouds: A Story of a Himalayan Ecosystem. (p. 1953)
Naga, Karun, jt. auth. see Garcia, Tom.
Nagai, Tomohiro. Full Metal Panic! Vol. 2. (p. 646)
Nagai, Tomohiro, illus. see Gatou, Shouji.
Nagami, Pamela. Bitten: True Medical Stories of Bites & Stings. (p. 194)
Nagar, Sachin, illus. see Foley, Ryan.
Nagar, Sachin, illus. see Helfand, Lewis.
Nagar, Sachin, illus. see Tulsidas.
Nagara, Innosanto. A de Activista. (p. 1)
—A Is for Activist. (p. 1)
—A Is for Activist. Nagara, Innosanto, illus. (p. 1)
Nagaraj, Geetha, jt. auth. see Cholij, Mark.
Nagaraj, Josephine. Big Magic Show! (Bubble Guppies) Jackson, Mike, illus. (p. 182)
—Giddy-Up, Guppies! (p. 674)
—Giddy-Up, Guppies! (Bubble Guppies) Huxtable, John, illus. (p. 674)
Nagaraja, Dharmachari. Buddha at Bedtime: Tales of Love & Wisdom for You to Read with Your Child to Enchant, Enlighten & Inspire. Tancredi, Sharon, illus. (p. 234)
—Buddha's Apprentice at Bedtime: Tales of Compassion & Kindness for You to Read with Your Child - To Delight & Inspire. (p. 234)
Nagaraju, Harsha, illus. see Yelagalawadi, Jyoti.
Nagast, Kebra. Queen of Sheba. (p. 1425)
Nagata, Noriko. Robo-Sensei: Personal Japanese Tutor. (p. 1480)
Nagda, Ann Whitehead. Cheetah Math: Learning about Division from Baby Cheetahs. (p. 296)
—Home for Panda. Effler, Jim, illus. (p. 792)
—Kevin Keeps Up. (p. 950)
—Perfect Cat-Sitter. Roth, Stephanie, illus. (p. 1341)
—Tarantula Power! (p. 1706)
—Tiger Tale. Kratter, Paul, illus. (p. 1748)
—Time to Eat, Panda! (p. 1753)
—Valentine Cat. Roth, Stephanie, illus. (p. 1830)
—World above the Clouds: A Story of a Himalayan Ecosystem. Kratter, Paul, illus. (p. 1953)
Nagda, Ann Whitehead & Bickel, Cindy. Polar Bear Math: Learning about Fractions from Klondike & Snow. (p. 1378)
Nagda, Ann Whitehead, text. Time to Eat, Panda! (p. 1753)
Nagel, Jeanne. Living Green. (p. 1041)
Nagel, Karen. Shapes That Roll. Wilson, Steve, illus. (p. 1561)
Nagel, Karen, jt. auth. see Ziefert, Harriet.
Nagel, Rob. Space Exploration - Almanac (p. 1619)
—UXL Encyclopedia of Landforms & Other Geologic Features (p. 1829)
Nagel, Thomas. Qué Significa Todo Esto? Una Brevísima Introducción a la Filosofía. (p. 1424)
Nagelhout, Ryan. 20 Fun Facts about Auto Racing. (p. 1995)
—20 Fun Facts about Baseball. (p. 1995)
—20 Fun Facts about the Moon. (p. 1995)
—20 Fun Facts about the White House. (p. 1995)
—Awesome Ostriches. (p. 121)
—Awesome Ostriches / Avestruces Increbles. (p. 121)
—Basketball's Greatest Records (p. 143)
—Be a Geologist. (p. 148)
—Becoming a Pro Football Player. (p. 156)
—Becoming a Pro Hockey Player. (p. 156)
—Beth Phoenix. (p. 171)
—Big Bison. (p. 178)
—Big Bison / Grandes Bisontes. (p. 178)
—Big Show. (p. 183)
—Christian. (p. 311)
—Clownfish. (p. 335)
—Clownfish / Peces Payaso. (p. 335)
—CM Punk. (p. 336)
—Crabs: Cangrejos. (p. 375)
—Crabs. (p. 375)
—David Ortiz: World Series Champion. (p. 411)
—Discovering STEM at the Baseball Game. (p. 449)
—Diving with Sharks. (p. 455)
—Drones. (p. 485)
—Enormous Elephants. (p. 531)
—First Moon Walk. (p. 596)
—Football's Greatest Records (p. 615)
—Fracking. (p. 626)
—Giant Giraffes. (p. 673)
—Giant Giraffes / Jirafas Gigantes. (p. 673)
—Great Big Grizzlies. (p. 714)
—Great Big Grizzlies / Enormes Osos Pardos. (p. 714)
—Haunted! Alcatraz. (p. 753)
—Haunted! Edinburgh Castle. (p. 753)
—Heart & Blood in Your Body (p. 759)
—Henry Ford in His Own Words. (p. 768)
—Hindenburg Disaster. (p. 780)
—How Pigeons & Other Animals Sense Magnetic Fields. (p. 812)
—Huge Hippos. (p. 824)
—Huge Hippos / Grandes Hipopótamos. (p. 824)
—I Love Baseball. (p. 841)
—I Love Basketball. (p. 841)
—I Love Gymnastics. (p. 842)
—I Love Hockey. (p. 842)
—I Love Soccer. (p. 843)
—I See a Squirrel. (p. 845)
—John Cena. (p. 921)
—Martin Luther King Jr. (p. 1098)
—Me Encanta el Baloncesto / I Love Basketball. (p. 1115)
—Me Encanta el Béisbol / I Love Baseball. (p. 1115)
—Me Encanta el Fútbol / I Love Soccer. (p. 1115)
—Me Encanta el Fútbol Americano / I Love Football. (p. 1115)
—Me Encanta el Hockey / I Love Hockey. (p. 1115)
—Me Encanta la Gimnasia / I Love Gymnastics. (p. 1115)
—People of the Great Lakes. (p. 1339)
—Preserving the Dead. (p. 1396)
—Problem with Early Cameras. (p. 1408)
—Problem with Early Cars. (p. 1408)
—Problem with Early Clocks. (p. 1408)
—Problem with Early Computers. (p. 1408)
—Problem with Early Flying Machines. (p. 1408)
—Randy Orton. (p. 1438)
—Saving the Chesapeake Bay. (p. 1517)
—Science of Football. (p. 1527)
—Science of Hockey. (p. 1527)
—Sea Stars: Estrellas de Mar. (p. 1535)
—Sea Stars. (p. 1535)
—Sharks. (p. 1562)
—Sharks: Tiburones. (p. 1563)
—Smart Machines & the Internet of Things. (p. 1593)
—Standing in a Governor's Shoes. (p. 1639)
—Standing in a Senator's Shoes. (p. 1639)
—Tanks. (p. 1705)
—Thomas Paine's Common Sense. (p. 1739)
—Time Zones. (p. 1753)
—Turtles: Tortugas. (p. 1799)
—Turtles. (p. 1799)
—We Need Honeybees. (p. 1867)
—Whales: Ballenas. (p. 1878)
—Whales. (p. 1878)
—What Is a Moon? (p. 1888)
—When Lightning Strikes. (p. 1903)
Nagelhout, Ryan & Appleby, Alex. I See a Squirrel: Puedo Ver una Ardilla. (p. 845)
—I See a Squirrel. (p. 845)
Nagelhout, Ryan, ed. Awesome Ostriches. (p. 121)
—Enormous Elephants / Elefantes Enormes. (p. 531)
—Problem with Early Navigation Tools. (p. 1408)
Nagelkerke, Bill, tr. see Kromhout, Rindert.
Nagelkerke, Bill, tr. see Timmers, Leo.
Nagelkerke, Bill, tr. see Vanden Heede, Sylvia.
Nagia, Jyoti. Smile: It's a Curved Line That Sets Everything Straight & Fine! (p. 1594)
Nagle, Barbara. Duck & Spider (p. 488)
Nagle, Cristen. Your Legal Rights As a Juvenile Being Tried As an Adult (p. 1981)
Nagle, Frances. Zombie Ants. (p. 1988)
—Zombie Caterpillars. (p. 1988)
Nagle, Garrett. Access to Geography - Development. (p. 8)
—North America. (p. 1264)
—Rivers & Water Management. (p. 1476)
Nagle, Garrett, jt. auth. see Guinness, Paul.
Nagle, Jeanne. Archie, Peyton, & Eli Manning: Football's Royal Family. (p. 95)
—Careers in Internet Advertising & Marketing. (p. 268)
—Coniferous Forests: An Evergreen World. (p. 357)
—Dalai Lama. (p. 401)
—Deciduous Forests: Seasons of Survival. (p. 421)
—Delta Force. (p. 425)
—Endangered Wildlife: Habitats in Peril. (p. 527)
—Extreme Biking. (p. 556)
—Frequently Asked Questions about Avian Flu. (p. 636)
—Frequently Asked Questions about Wii & Video Game Fitness & Injuries. (p. 636)
—Getting to Know Alice. (p. 669)
—Getting to Know Scratch. (p. 669)
—GLBT Teens & Society. (p. 682)
—Great Lifelong Learning Skills. (p. 717)
—How Do Animals Hunt & Feed? (p. 806)
—Investigating the Abominable Snowman & Other Legendary Beasts (p. 885)
—Jennifer Hudson. (p. 912)
—Kite Surfing & Kite Skiing. (p. 962)
—Making Good Choices about Renewable Resources. (p. 1081)
—Navy. (p. 1238)
—Reducing Your Carbon Footprint at School. (p. 1456)
—Same-Sex Marriage: The Debate. (p. 1507)
—Saving the Endangered American Alligator. (p. 1517)
—Sidney Crosby: The NHL's Top Scorer. (p. 1573)
—Sidney Crosby: One of the NHL's Top Scorers. (p. 1573)
—Smart Shopping: Shopping Green. (p. 1593)
—Top 5 Reasons Why People Get Tattoos & Other Body Art. (p. 1768)
—What Happens to Your Body When You Swim. (p. 1886)
—What Is Nonfiction? (p. 1890)
—Working Horses. (p. 1952)
Nagle, Jeanne, ed. Feudalism, Monarchies, & Nobility. (p. 583)
—Great Authors of Children's Books. (p. 713)
—Great Authors of Classic Literature. (p. 713)
—Great Authors of Mystery, Horror & Thrillers. (p. 713)
—Great Authors of Nonfiction. (p. 713)
—Great Authors of Science Fiction & Fantasy. (p. 713)
—Great Poets & Playwrights. (p. 718)
—Native American Spirit Beings. (p. 1234)
Nagle, Jeanne M. Careers in Coaching. (p. 267)
—Careers in Television. (p. 268)
—Choosing a Career as a Coach. (p. 310)
—Coniferous Forests: An Evergreen World. (p. 357)
—Endangered Wildlife: Habitats in Peril. (p. 527)
—Great Lifelong Learning Skills. (p. 717)
—How a Recession Works. (p. 804)
—Polysubstance Abuse. (p. 1381)
—Texas: Past & Present. (p. 1724)
Nagle, Kerry. Crabs. (p. 375)
—Marine Creatures. (p. 1094)
—Marine Minibeasts. (p. 1094)
Nagle, Paul, illus. see Oswalt, Kay.
Nagle, Shane, illus. see Davis, Tony.
Nagourney, Eric, jt. auth. see Hanson, Paul.
Nagpal, Saraswati. Draupadi: The Fire-Born Princess. Chandu & Manu, illus. (p. 480)
Nagulakonda, Rajesh, illus. see Taneja, Sweta.
Nagunga, Kansi, jt. auth. see Mudenda, Duly.
Nagus, Karl. Congratulations Q & U. (p. 357)
Nagy, Frances. Science with Water. (p. 1528)
Nagy, Ian, illus. see Fletcher, Ralph.
Nagy, Jennifer. Goats in Coats. Broughton, Ilona & Szijgyarto, Cynthia, illus. (p. 687)
Nagy, Jim. Daniel the Spaniel- Let's Go Home! (p. 405)
Nagy, Krisztina, illus. see Bentley, Dawn.
Nagy, Krisztina, illus. see Ross, Mandy.
Nagy, Krisztina, tr. see Ross, Mandy.
Nagy, Krisztina Kállai, illus. see Hartman, Bob.
Nagy, Krisztina Kallai, jt. auth. see Hartman, Bob.
Nagy, Robert, illus. see Norris, Christine.
Naha, Ed. Ten Commandments Movie Storybook. (p. 1718)
Nahabedian, Dallas, illus. see Gemstone, Rose.
Nahal, Denise Abda. Hello Birdie! Tale of a Classroom Pet Based on a True Story. (p. 763)
Nahall Nikoo Fells. Drowning in the Mainstream: Confessions of a Sister. (p. 486)
Nahm, Andrew C. I Love Korea! Jones, B. J. & Lee, Gi-eun, eds. (p. 842)
Nahum, Andrew, jt. auth. see Dorling Kindersley Publishing Staff.
Naian, Shi. Water Margin. Chiang, Shirley, illus. (p. 1863)
Naiara, Alvarez, jt. auth. see Alvariz, Naiara.
Naiditch, Dov, jt. auth. see Burston, Chaim.
Naidoo, Beverley. Aesop's Fables. Grobler, Piet, illus. (p. 25)
—Aesop's Fables. Grobler, Piet, illus. (p. 26)
—Burn My Heart. (p. 243)
—Making It Home: Real-Life Stories from Children Forced to Flee. (p. 1081)
—Other Side of Truth. (p. 1306)
—Out of Bounds: Seven Stories of Conflict & Hope. (p. 1311)
—S Is for South Africa. Das, Prodeepta, illus. (p. 1499)
—Who Is King? Grobler, Piet, illus. (p. 1916)
Naidoo, Beverley, intro. Making It Home: Real-Life Stories from Children Forced to Flee. (p. 1081)
Naidoo, Jamie Campbell. Rainbow Family Collections: Selecting & Using Children's Books with Lesbian, Gay, Bisexual, Transgender, & Queer Content (p. 1435)
Naidoo, Mathevan & Lague, Peter. Study & Master English Grade 11 Learner's Book. (p. 1670)
Naidoo, Vahini. Fall to Pieces (p. 566)
Naifeh, Ted. Courtney Crumrin: The Coven of Mystics. (p. 373)
—Courtney Crumrin & the Coven of Mystics (p. 373)
—Courtney Crumrin & the Coven of Mystics, Volume 2. Nozemack, Joe & Jones, James Lucas, eds. (p. 373)
—Courtney Crumrin & the Fire Thief's Tale. (p. 373)
—Courtney Crumrin & the Night Things Jones, James Lucas, ed. (p. 373)
—Courtney Crumrin & the Prince of Nowhere. Nozemack, Joe & Beaton, Jill, eds. (p. 373)
—Courtney Crumrin Volume 1: The Night Things Special Edition. (p. 373)
—Courtney Crumrin Volume 3: the Twilight Kingdom: The Twilight Kingdom. (p. 373)
—Courtney Crumrin Volume 4: Monstrous Holiday Special Edition: Monstrous Holiday Special Edition. (p. 373)
—Courtney Crumrin Volume 5: the Witch Next Door: The Witch Next Door. (p. 373)
—Courtney Crumrin's Monstrous Holiday (p. 373)
—League of Ordinary Gentleman. (p. 982)
Naifeh, Ted, illus. see Black, Holly.
Naik, Anita. Bras, Boys & Bad Hair Days: A Girl's Guide to Living with Style. (p. 222)
—Coping with Loss: The Life Changes Handbook. (p. 365)
—My Body, Myself: The Ultimate Health Book for Girls. (p. 1198)
—Think Yourself Gorgeous: How to Feel Good - Inside & Out. (p. 1734)
—Wise Guides - Fit. (p. 1940)
Naik, Anita, jt. auth. see Croke, Liam.
Naik, Anita, jt. auth. see Sayer, Melissa.
Naik, Anita & Croke, Liam. Beat Stress! The Exam Handbook. (p. 152)
Naik, Anita & Cronin, Ali. Coping with Loss: The Life Changes Handbook. (p. 365)
—Read the Signals: The Body Language Handbook. (p. 1443)
Nail, Eric. Wave Wranglers & the New Order of the Pyramid. (p. 1864)
Naim, Deborah, prod. SCUBA 2005, Datebook & Logbook. (p. 1533)
Naiman, Gary. Revolution! (p. 1466)
Naime, Sophie, ed. see Mesibere, Ellen.
Nair, Anita. Adventures of Nonu, the Skating Squirrel. (p. 21)
Nair, Charissa M., jt. auth. see Seah, Audrey.
Naish, Darren. Build the T. Rex. Bernstein, Galia & Ruffle, Mark, illus. (p. 238)
—Dinosaur Record Breakers: Awesome Dinosaur Facts. (p. 442)
Naish, Darren, contrib. by. IDinosaur. (p. 852)
Najafi, Imran. Dreams. (p. 484)
Najar, Teresa. Wanted: One Comfy, Cozy, Clean, Fluffy, Soft Pillow. (p. 1856)
Naji, Jamila. Musical Storyland: A Sing-A-Long Book with Musical Disc. (p. 1194)
Najimy, Norman. Phonics Readers - Big Books: Grade 1 Moore, Russell, illus. (p. 1352)
Najman, Alexander. Assassin GN. O'Reilly, Sean Patrick, ed. (p. 107)
Nakagawa, Chihiro. Who Made This Cake? Koyose, Junji, illus. (p. 1917)
Nakagawa, Masafumi. Dr. Mouse's Mission. Perry, Mia Lynn, tr. (p. 475)
Nakahara, Aya. Love. Com, Volume 1. Nakahara, Aya, illus. (p. 1059)
—Love.com Rolf, Pookie, tr. from JPN. (p. 1061)
Nakahira, Masahiko. Alpha (p. 48)
—Sakura Ganbaru! (p. 1504)
—Street Fighter Alpha (p. 1666)
Nakai, Marekatsu. Blue Blue Glass Moon, under the Crimson Air (p. 202)
Nakai, Ryan, illus. see Marbury, Stephon & Dean, Marshall.
Nakajo, Hisaya. For You in Full Blossom Vol. 2. Nakajo, Hisaya, illus. (p. 616)
—Hana-Kimi. Nakajo, Hisaya, illus. (p. 740)
—Sugar Princess: Skating to Win. Nakajo, Hisaya, illus. (p. 1673)
—Sugar Princess - Skating to Win. Nakajo, Hisaya, illus. (p. 1673)
Nakakuma, Chie. Whazzup, Wolly Ayaka? (p. 1900)
Nakamura, Yuki, tr. see Kuga, Cain.
Nakamura, Yuki, tr. see Ohkami, Mineko.
Nakasone, Devin. Lucky Ducky. (p. 1062)
Nakasone, Shaun, illus. see Ladd, Debbie.
Nakata, Hiroe, illus. see Adler, Victoria.
Nakata, Hiroe, illus. see Berry, Lynne.
Nakata, Hiroe, illus. see Colman, Michelle Sinclair.
Nakata, Hiroe, illus. see Hubbell, Patricia.
Nakata, Hiroe, illus. see Lester, J. D.
Nakata, Hiroe, illus. see Lewison, Wendy Cheyette.
Nakata, Hiroe, illus. see Lund, Deborah S.
Nakata, Hiroe, illus. see Meyers, Susan.
Nakata, Hiroe, illus. see Rose, Deborah Lee.
Nakata, Hiroe, illus. see Simon, Mary Manz, et al.
Nakata, Hiroe, illus. see Slater, Dashka.
Nakata, Ritsuko & Hanson, Anders. Let's Go. (p. 997)
Nakatani, Andy, ed. see Aoyama, Gôshô.
Nakatani, Andy, jt. auth. see Aoyama, Gôshô.
Nakawaki, Hatsue. Wait! Wait! Sakai, Komako, illus. (p. 1852)
nakaya, andrea. Biomedical Ethics. (p. 189)
Nakaya, Andrea C. Adhd. (p. 12)
—Alcohol. (p. 35)
—Censorship: Opposing Viewpoints. (p. 287)
—Civil Rights in Wartime. (p. 324)
—Energy Alternatives. (p. 528)
—Juvenile Crime: Opposing Viewpoints. (p. 941)
—Marijuana. (p. 1094)
—Reed Hastings & Nexflix. (p. 1456)
—Steve Jobs & Apple. (p. 1649)
—Teens & Sex. (p. 1715)
—Thinking Critically Mass Shootings. (p. 1734)
—Video Games & Youth. (p. 1841)
—What Is Bipolar Disorder? (p. 1889)
Nakaya, Andrea C., ed. Censorship. (p. 287)
—Is Air Pollution a Serious Threat to Health? (p. 889)
—Obesity. (p. 1275)
—Terminal Illness. (p. 1721)
Nakayama, Bunjuro. Mahoromatic: Automatic Maiden Ditama, Bow, illus. (p. 1076)
—Mahoromatic: Automatic Maiden: The Misato Residence's Maid Ditama, Bow, illus. (p. 1076)
Nakell, Eugenie, ed. see Thorpe, Rochelle O'Neal.
Nakhat, Shamim. Story of Yaqub & Yusuf: Based on Qur'anic Facts. (p. 1663)
Nalbandian, Paisely Lineyeia. Treasure Seekers. (p. 1782)
Nalbantsky, Danail. Bludnia Sin (the Prodigal Son) Guetov, Dimitar, ed. (p. 202)
Naliboff, Jane. Only One Club. Hopkins, Jeff, illus. (p. 1298)
Nall, Gail. Breaking the Ice. (p. 225)
Nall, Gail, jt. auth. see Malone, Jen.
Nallam, Stu. Freddie, the Unhappy Firecracker (p. 633)
Nalls, Charles. Prayer: A field Guide. (p. 1393)
Nam, Doan, illus. see McSween, Michele.
Nam, Elain, et al. Organic Chemistry with Vernier. (p. 1303)
Nam, Jongpil. Fish. (p. 598)
Nama, Michael D., et al. Stay Tuned for 5 Éme. (p. 1645)
—Stay Tuned for 6 Éme. (p. 1645)
—Stay Tuned Student's Book For 3 éme. (p. 1645)
—Stay Tuned Student's Book For 5 éme. Tamla, Berthe Kamga & Nijbamum, John Suh, eds. (p. 1645)
—Stay Tuned Workbook 3 éme. (p. 1645)
—Stay Tuned Workbook For 5 éme. (p. 1645)
Namblar, Vinesh. Adventures in Human Values - Series 1: Courage, Kindness, Forgiveness, Teamwork, Compassion, Listening, Caring, Self-Confidence, Sharing. (p. 15)
—Adventures in Human Values - Series 4: Strength, Bravery, Gratitude, Acceptance, Discipline, Happiness, Cooperation, Hope, Self-Control. Ralte, Albert Lalmuanpuia, illus. (p. 15)
Namioka, Lensey. April & the Dragon Lady. (p. 93)
—Half & Half. (p. 736)
—Valley of the Broken Cherry Trees. (p. 1831)
Namjoshi, Suniti & Jain, Shefalee. Aditi & the Marine Sage. (p. 12)
Namm, Diane. Emperor's New Clothes. Mims, Ashley, illus. (p. 521)
—Frog Prince. Quarello, Maurizio A. C., illus. (p. 640)
—Gingerbread Boy. Wakefield, Scott J., illus. (p. 677)

—Goldilocks & the Three Bears. Graegin, Stephanie, illus. (p. 696)
—Guess Who? Sheldon, David, illus. (p. 729)
—Jack & the Beanstalk. Quarello, Maurizio A. C., illus. (p. 902)
—King Arthur & His Knights. Calo, Marcos, illus. (p. 958)
—Laugh Out Loud Jokes. Becker, Wayne, illus. (p. 980)
—Little Bear. McCue, Lisa, illus. (p. 1023)
—Monsters! (p. 1168)
—Monsters! Chambliss, Maxie, illus. (p. 1168)
—My Best Friend. Gordon, Mike, tr. (p. 1196)
—My Best Friend. Gordon, Mike, illus. (p. 1196)
—Pick a Pet. Suarez, Maribel, tr. (p. 1354)
—Puss in Boots. Zilber, Denis, illus. (p. 1420)
—Roman Myths. Freeberg, Eric, illus. (p. 1486)
—Slithery Squirmy Jokes. Becker, Wayne, illus. (p. 1591)
—Three Little Pigs. Wakefield, Scott, illus. (p. 1743)
—Ugly Duckling. Brannen, Sarah, illus. (p. 1808)
Namm, Diane & Andersen, Hans Christian. Princess & the Pea. Zilber, Denis & Olafsdottir, Linda, illus. (p. 1402)
Namowitz, jt. auth. see Spaulding.
Namukasa, Glaydah. Voice of a Dream. (p. 1848)
Nan, Carol. Nana the Baby Pine Tree. (p. 1228)
Nana, Auntie. I Can't Go to School Today. (p. 837)
—I Can't Go to School Today with CD. (p. 837)
Nana B. & Brittany. Forest Friends of Maine: The Chipmunks Have an Argument. (p. 618)
Nana, Old. Girl Who Converses with Butterflies. (p. 679)
—Just Right. (p. 939)
Nanatsuki, Kyoichi. Project Arms (p. 1410)
—Project Arms Minagawa, Ryoji, illus. (p. 1410)
—Project Arms Nanatsuki, Kyoichi, illus. (p. 1410)
Nanatsuki, Kyoichi, jt. auth. see Minagawa, Ryoji.
Nanatsuki, Kyoichi & Minagawa, Ryoji. First Revelation: Jabberwock. Vol. 3 (p. 596)
—Gallows Bell. Nanatsuki, Kyoichi, illus. (p. 653)
—Project Arms (p. 1410)
—White Rabbit (p. 1913)
Nanatsuki, Kyoichi & Nanatsuki, Nyoichi. Project Arms: The First Revelation: Egrigori. Vol. 2 (p. 1410)
Nanatsuki, Kyoichi, et al. First Revelation - The Awakening. (p. 596)
—Second Revelation: The X-Army. Vol. 5 (p. 1539)
Nanatsuki, Nyoichi, jt. auth. see Nanatsuki, Kyoichi.
Nanavati, Daniel. Midrak Earthshaker. Pryor, John-Thomas, illus. (p. 1139)
Nance, Andrew. Return to Daemon Hall: Evil Roots. Polhemus, Coleman, illus. (p. 1465)
Nance, Christopher. Choices. (p. 309)
Nance, Dan, illus. see Hawk, Frank.
Nance, James B. Intermediate Logic - Student (2nd Edition) (p. 880)
Nance, James B. & Wilson, Douglas J. Introductory Logic - Student (4th Edition) (p. 883)
Nance, Kimberly A. & Rivera, Isidro J. Aprendizaje: Tecnicas de Composicion. (p. 93)
Nancee Jean. Boomerang Babies Club. (p. 213)
Nancy Elizabeth Bateman. Jason the Brat. (p. 910)
Nancy, Farmer. House of the Scorpion. (p. 803)
Nancy Giorgio-Kupiec. Nanje's Imagination or Is It ? (p. 1229)
Nancy Mann Israel. Juggler & His Wife. (p. 932)
Nancy Raj, illus. see Jeeva Raghunath & Nayar, Deeya.
Nancy, Scheibe, illus. see Dickens, Sara Jo.
Nancy St. Paul-Martin. Go to the Nurse: Peanut Puffs & Snicker-Doodles. (p. 687)
Nanette. Black Alligator. (p. 194)
—Blue the Frog. (p. 203)
—Buddy & Muddy: The Twin Brown Skunks. (p. 234)
—Little Red. (p. 1034)
—Oinky the Yellow Pig. (p. 1282)
—Pancake the Purple Pony. (p. 1320)
—Sunny the Orange Puppy. (p. 1677)
—Tootie the Green Kitten. (p. 1768)
Nanevich, Julia, tr. see Downie, David.
Nanevych, Julia, tr. see Downie, David.
Nani. Special Time with Grandm: Grandma & the Camping Trip. (p. 1623)
Nanji, Shenaaz. Alien in My House McLeod, Chum, illus. (p. 40)
—Child of Dandelions. (p. 301)
—Notre Dame. (p. 1268)
—Vatican City. (p. 1833)
Nanji, Shenaaz & Corr, Christopher. Indian Tales: A Barefoot Collection. Corr, Christopher, illus. (p. 871)
Nannas, Anastasia. Let Us Learn Greek Book I (p. 994)
Nannetti, Jorge Cardenas, tr. see Senge, Peter, et al.
Nanni, Lyn, jt. auth. see Hemperly, Ilona K.
Nannini, Randi. My Brother's A Pirate Clark, Wendy, illus. (p. 1199)
Nanny, B. Spider who Lived in our Grandads Car. (p. 1626)
Nanny Fanny, illus. see Fanny, Nanny.
Nanten, Yutaka. Cowboy Bebop VI. (p. 373)
Nantus, Sheryl. Mexico's Pacific South States. (p. 1131)
—Pacific South States of Mexico. (p. 1317)
Nanus, Susan & Juster, Norton. Phantom Tollbooth: A Children's Play in Two Acts. (p. 1349)
Naohman, jt. auth. see Philip, Neil.
Naomi, Aunt. Jewish Fairy Tales & Legends. (p. 917)
Naomi, Aunt & Landa, Gertrude. Jewish Fairy Tales & Legends. Thomas, Tom, ed. (p. 917)
Naoura, Salah. Auf dem Bauernhof. (p. 115)
—Im Eis. (p. 858)
—Im Regenwald. (p. 860)
—In der Savanne. (p. 863)
Nap, Dug, illus. see Rupp, Rebecca.
Naphot, John A. God Culture for Kids: Why Do People Die. (p. 688)
Napier, Angi. Bible Baby: Shapes. (p. 175)
Napier, H. Albert, et al. Learning with Computers I. (p. 986)
—Learning with Computers II. (p. 986)
Napier, Louise S., illus. see Ballard, Elizabeth Silance.
Napier, Matt. Hat Tricks Count: A Hockey Number Book. Rose, Melanie, illus. (p. 752)
—Hockey Numbers. Rose, Melanie, illus. (p. 786)
—I Spy with My Little Eye - Hockey. Milne, David, photos by. (p. 846)
—Little Canada. (p. 1025)
—Little Hockey. (p. 1029)
—Z Is for Zamboni: A Hockey Alphabet. Rose, Melanie, illus. (p. 1984)
Napier, Matt & Rose, Melanie. Z Is for Zamboni: A Hockey Alphabet. Rose, Melanie, illus. (p. 1984)
Napier, Rodney W. & Gershenfeld, Matti K. Groups: Theory & Experience. (p. 725)
Naples, Thomas R., ed. see Fletcher, Robert A.
Napoles, Ann & Duke, Sharon. Tres Partes de Dios/Three-Part God. Napoles, Martin, tr. (p. 1784)
Napoles, Martin, tr. see Napoles, Ann & Duke, Sharon.
Napoli, Donna Jo. Albert. LaMarche, Jim, illus. (p. 34)
—Alligator Bayou. (p. 47)
—Beast. (p. 152)
—Bound. (p. 216)
—Crossing. Madsen, Jim, illus. (p. 385)
—Dark Shimmer. (p. 408)
—Daughter of Venice. (p. 409)
—Fire in the Hills. (p. 590)
—Hands & Hearts: With 15 Words in American Sign Language. Bates, Amy, illus. (p. 741)
—Hush: An Irish Princess' Tale. (p. 830)
—King of Mulberry Street. (p. 959)
—Lights on the Nile. (p. 1016)
—Mama Miti: Wangari Maathai & the Trees of Kenya. Nelson, Kadir, illus. (p. 1084)
—perla única. (p. 1343)
—Skin (p. 1585)
—Smile. (p. 1593)
—Song of the Magdalene. (p. 1611)
—Storm. (p. 1655)
—Three Days. (p. 1742)
—Treasury of Egyptian Mythology: Classic Stories of Gods, Goddesses, Monsters & Mortals. Balit, Christina, illus. (p. 1782)
—Treasury of Greek Mythology: Classic Stories of Gods, Goddesses, Heroes & Monsters. Balit, Christina, illus. (p. 1783)
—Treasury of Norse Mythology: Stories of Intrigue, Trickery, Love, & Revenge. Balit, Christina, illus. (p. 1783)
—Wager. (p. 1852)
—Wishing Club: A Story about Fractions. Currey, Anna, illus. (p. 1940)
—Zel. (p. 1986)
Napoli, Donna Jo & DeLuca, Doreen. Handy Stories to Read & Sign. Klusza, Maureen, illus. (p. 742)
Napoli, Donna Jo & Furrow, Elena. Ready to Dream. Bancroft, Bronwyn, illus. (p. 1447)
Napoli, Donna Jo & Johnston, Shelagh. Hotel Jungle. Spengler, Kenneth, tr. (p. 802)
Napoli, Linda. Sailing Away on a Windy Day. (p. 1503)
Napoli, Tony. Justin Timberlake: Breakout Music Superstar. (p. 940)
—Vasco Da Gama: Discovering the Sea Route to India. (p. 1833)
Napolitano, Gretchen. Christopher Lee & Bozzie Bear's First Day of School. (p. 317)
Napora, Tabetha. Great Forest: Twigtown Tales: One. (p. 716)
Nappa, Jon. God's Got an Answer for That: Using Your Bible to Solve Everyday Problems. (p. 691)
—My First Message Bible Search: Discovering Answers in God's Word. (p. 1207)
Nappa, Jon & Gosselin, Suzanne Hadley. Exploring the Great Bible Mysteries: A Devotional Adventure. (p. 553)
—God's Got an Answer for That Activity Book. (p. 691)
—God's Got an Answer for That Devotional. (p. 691)
Nappa, Mike. Pogo's Prank-A-Paloosa: A Bible Memory Buddy Book about Respecting Others. Harrington, David, illus. (p. 1376)
—When Pigs Fly: A Bible Memory Buddy Book. Harrington, David, illus. (p. 1904)
Nappa, Mike, et al. Zachary's Zoo Boyer, Lyn, illus. (p. 1984)
Nappi, Frank. Legend of Mickey Tussler. (p. 988)
—Sophomore Campaign: A Mickey Tussler Novel. (p. 1614)
Napthine, Margaret. Kittens Thomas & Tut. Lovejoy, Brenda, illus. (p. 963)
Napton, Robert Place. Son of Merlin Volume 1 TP. (p. 1611)
—Tokyo Knights. (p. 1762)
Napue, Gene A., Jr. Little Ant & the Giant Castle: (An Elementary Adventure in Cross Curriculum) (p. 1023)
Naquin, Roy. Tales of Little Bear & Little Buffalo. (p. 1702)
Naquvi, Syed-mohsin. Defending the shia faith without being Defensive. (p. 423)
—house of Love: The verse of mawaddata fil Qurba. (p. 803)
—Understanding Karbala. (p. 1815)
Nara. Yoshitomo Nara. (p. 1972)
Nara, Yoshitomo. Lonesome Puppy. (p. 1046)
Naraghi, Dara, jt. auth. see Patterson, James.
Naraghi, Dara & Patterson, James. Battle for Shadowland (p. 145)
Naranjo, K. L. Adventures of Ariel & Eden & the Lost Treasures of Zion. (p. 16)
Narayan, Natasha. Black Death & Other Putrid Plagues of London. (p. 195)
—Bloody Kings & Killer Queens of London. (p. 201)
—Shaman's Secret: A Kit Salter Adventure. (p. 1559)
—Spies, Secret Agents & Spooks of London. (p. 1627)
—Time Traveler's Guide to Victorian London. (p. 1753)
—Tudor London. (p. 1796)
—Witches, Wizards & Warlocks of London. (p. 1941)
Narayan, R. K. Ramayana: A Shortened Modern Prose Version of the Indian Epic. (p. 1437)
Narayanamoorthy, Maanasa R. Queen Bee. (p. 1424)
Naraynan, Manjula. Green Green Pear. (p. 722)
—Grey Grey Cloud. (p. 723)
—Red Red Car. (p. 1454)
Nardandrea, Swannee, illus. see Stroud, David Wayne.
Nardi, Dorianne, jt. auth. see Arvoy, Marsha.
Nardi, James. In Mouse's Backyard (p. 864)
Nardi, Tisa, illus. see Carmen, Indigo.
Nardo, Don. Age of Colonialism. (p. 29)
—Alamo. (p. 33)
—Alexander the Great: Conqueror of the Known World. (p. 36)
—American Revolution. (p. 63)
—Ancient Egypt. (p. 68)
—Ancient Greece (p. 69)
—Ancient Roman Art & Architecture. (p. 70)
—Architecture. (p. 95)
—Arts & Literature in Ancient Mesopotamia. (p. 105)
—Arts, Leisure, & Sport in Ancient Egypt. (p. 105)
—Asteroids & Comets. (p. 108)
—Atlantic Slave Trade. (p. 112)
—Aztec Civilization. (p. 122)
—Aztec Mythology. Currie, Stephen, ed. (p. 122)
—Barack Obama (p. 137)
—Bernie Madoff. (p. 167)
—Biological Warfare. (p. 189)
—Biomedical Ethics. (p. 189)
—Birth of Christianity. (p. 192)
—Birth of Islam. (p. 192)
—Buddhism (p. 234)
—Bull Run to Gettysburg: Early Battles of the Civil War (p. 240)
—Catholicism. (p. 280)
—Cause & Effect the Fall of Rome: The Fall of Rome. (p. 282)
—Christianity (p. 312)
—Civil War. (p. 325)
—Clara Barton: Face Danger, but Never Fear It. (p. 326)
—Classical Civilization: Rome. (p. 328)
—Classical Civilization: Medieval Europe. (p. 328)
—Cleopatra: Egypt's Last Pharoah. (p. 331)
—Climate Change. (p. 332)
—Climate Crisis: The Science of Global Warming (p. 332)
—Cloning. (p. 333)
—Cure Quest: The Science of Stem Cell Research (p. 392)
—Daily Life in Ancient Civilizations. (p. 399)
—Daily Life in Ancient Egypt. (p. 399)
—Daily Life in Ancient Greece. (p. 400)
—Daily Life in Ancient Rome. (p. 400)
—Daily Life in Colonial America. (p. 400)
—Daily Life in the Islamic Golden Age. (p. 400)
—Declaration of Independence. (p. 422)
—Destined for Space: Our Story of Exploration (p. 430)
—DNA Evidence. (p. 456)
—Early Native North Americans. (p. 494)
—Early River Civilizations. (p. 494)
—Eating Disorders. (p. 501)
—Establishment of the Thirteen Colonies. (p. 538)
—European Colonization of Africa. (p. 540)
—European Exploration of America. (p. 540)
—Founders of Faiths. (p. 624)
—Freedom Fighter: William Wallace & Scotland's Battle for Independence (p. 634)
—French Revolution. (p. 636)
—Frogmen & Commandos. (p. 641)
—Genghis Khan & the Mongol Empire. (p. 661)
—Golden Spike: How a Photograph Celebrated a Connected Continent. (p. 695)
—History of Television. (p. 784)
—History of Terrorism (p. 784)
—Human Papillomavirus (HPV) (p. 826)
—In the Water: Torpedoes, Missiles, & Dive-Bombs. (p. 867)
—India. (p. 870)
—Industrial Revolution in Britain. (p. 872)
—Industrial Revolution in the United States. (p. 872)
—Industrial Revolution's Workers & Their Lives. (p. 872)
—Influential Figures of Ancient Rome. (p. 873)
—Invisible Weapons: The Science of Biological & Chemical Warfare (p. 886)
—Islamic Empire. (p. 891)
—Kinetic Energy: The Energy of Motion Hossain, Farhana & Schultz, Ashlee, illus. (p. 958)
—Life & Worship in Ancient Mesopotamia. (p. 1008)
—Life in Ancient Greece. (p. 1010)
—Malnutrition. (p. 1084)
—Martians. (p. 1097)
—Mathew Brady: The Camera Is the Eye of History. (p. 1108)
—Maya Angelou: Poet, Performer, Activist (p. 1112)
—Medusa. (p. 1120)
—Mesopotamia. (p. 1129)
—Migrant Mother: How a Photograph Defined the Great Depression (p. 1140)
—Mummies, Myth, & Magic: Religion in Ancient Egypt. (p. 1191)
—Mythology of the Egyptians. (p. 1227)
—Nation Divided: The Long Road to the Civil War (p. 1231)
—Nazi War Criminals. (p. 1238)
—Oil Spills. (p. 1282)
—Orbiting Eyes: The Science of Artificial Satellites (p. 1302)
—Painting. Parks, Peggy, ed. (p. 1318)
—Peoples & Empires of Ancient Mesopotamia. (p. 1340)
—Pericles: Great Leader of Ancient Athens. (p. 1343)
—Presidency of Abraham Lincoln: The Triumph of Freedom & Unity (p. 1396)
—Presidency of Franklin D. Roosevelt: Confronting the Great Depression & World War II. (p. 1396)
—Ramesses II: Ruler of Ancient Egypt. (p. 1438)
—Religious Beliefs in Colonial America. (p. 1458)
—Roman Empire. (p. 1485)
—Roman Gladiator. (p. 1485)
—Roman Roads & Aqueducts. (p. 1486)
—Rwanda Genocide. (p. 1499)
—Science, Technology, & Warfare of Ancient Mesopotamia. (p. 1528)
—Scientific Revolution. (p. 1528)
—Sculpture. (p. 1533)
—Slavery Through the Ages. Greenhaven Press Editors, ed. (p. 1588)
—Spanish Conquistadors. (p. 1621)
—Special Operations: Search & Rescue. (p. 1623)
—Storm Surge: The Science of Hurricanes (p. 1656)
—Strategies & Tactics. (p. 1666)
—Submarines. (p. 1671)
—Surfing. Gale, ed. (p. 1685)
—Theory of Evolution: A History of Life on Earth (p. 1729)
—Today's U. S. Navy (p. 1761)
—United in Cause: The Sons of Liberty (p. 1818)
—Vegan Diets. Greenhaven Press Editors, ed. (p. 1834)
—Vikings. (p. 1842)
—World War II. (p. 1959)
Nardo, Don, ed. see Yancey, Diane.
Nardo, Don, jt. auth. see Cerullo, Mary M.
Nardo, Don, ed. Creation of the U. S. Constitution. (p. 379)
—Frank Lloyd Wright. (p. 628)
—Frida Kahlo. (p. 637)
—Greek Mythology. (p. 720)
—Hugh Jackman. (p. 825)
—Leonardo da Vinci. (p. 992)
—Medieval European Art & Architecture. (p. 1119)
—Persian Mythology. (p. 1344)
—Roman Mythology. (p. 1486)
—Rulers of Ancient Egypt. (p. 1495)
Nardo, Don, et al. Julius Caesar: Roman General & Statesman. (p. 933)
Nardone, Frank. Something's Brewing in Salem. (p. 1610)
Nargi, Lela. Honeybee Man. Brooker, Kyrsten, illus. (p. 794)
Narimattom, Joseph. Valley of the Mountain Goddess. (p. 1831)
Narine, Vidya D. Kari. (p. 943)
Narr, Rachel. Fuzzy Wishey Dandelion. (p. 651)
Narr, Rachel K. You're the Same As Me. Baker, David, illus. (p. 1982)
Narsimhan, Mahtab. Deadly Conch: Tara Trilogy. (p. 417)
—Silver Anklet. (p. 1576)
—Third Eye. (p. 1734)
Narukami, Yutta. Pretty Poison. (p. 1398)
Narváez, Concha López. Amigo Oculto y los Espíritus de la Tarde. (p. 65)
—Aventuras de Picofino. (p. 119)
Narvaez, Concha Lopez. Colina de Edeta. (p. 339)
Narváez, Concha López. Endrina y el Secreto del Peregrino. (p. 527)
—Fuego de los Pastores. (p. 646)
—Tiempo y la Promesa. (p. 1748)
Narváez, Concha López & Concha, López Narváez. Cemicalo Porque. Salmeron, Rafael, illus. (p. 287)
Narváez, Concha López & Salmeron, Carmelo. Tomas Es Distinto a los Demas. (p. 1764)
Narváez, Concha López, et al. Horas Largas. (p. 797)
—Memorias de una Gallina. Alonso Díaz-Toledo, Juan Ramón, illus. (p. 1126)
Narvarro, jt. auth. see Lance, John.
Nasario, Garcia, tr. see Anaya, Rudolfo A.
Nasaw, David. Andrew Carnegie. (p. 72)
Nascimbene, Yan, illus. see Chronicle Staff.
Nascimbene, Yan, illus. see Coleman, Janet Wyman.
Nascimbene, Yan, illus. see Compestine, Ying Chang.
Nascimbene, Yan, illus. see Hunter, Ryan Ann, et al.
Nascimbene, Yan, illus. see Quackenbush, Robert.
Nascimbene, Yan, illus. see Whelan, Gloria.
Nascimbene, Yan, illus. see Wilbur, Helen L.
Nascimbeni, Barbara. Animals & Their Families. Zimic, Lesley, tr. from FRE. (p. 82)
—Little Miss Muffet. (p. 1031)
Nascimbeni, Barbara, illus. see Delval, Marie-Hélène.
Nascimbeni, Barbara, illus. see Harrison, Paul.
Nascimbeni, Barbara, illus. see Piumini, Roberto & Aesop.
Nascimbeni, Barbara, jt illus. see Kubler, Annie.
Nash, Alice & Strobel, Christoph. Daily Life of Native Americans from Post-Columbian Through Nineteenth-Century America (p. 400)
Nash, Andy. Marcus & His Monkey: For Kids Blessed with Popularity. (p. 1092)
—Melinda & Her Mule: For Kids Blessed with a Strong Will. (p. 1125)
—Tatum & Her Tiger: For Kids Blessed with Passion. (p. 1707)
Nash, Arizona. Red Rooster, Green Rooster. (p. 1455)
Nash, C. Clackers: Penguin. Rinaldo, Luana, illus. (p. 326)
—Clackers: Santa. (p. 326)
Nash, Carol Rust. Women Winning the Right to Vote in United States History. (p. 1946)
Nash, Claire. Food Safety Management Principles: Costco Edition 2004. (p. 614)
Nash, Damien K. H. & Nash, Kathy. Big Box, Little Box: The Forecast Calls for Potential Rain! Miller, Steve, illus. (p. 179)
Nash, Damien Kheri Harris. How to Load Your Truck: One Box at a Time. (p. 820)
Nash, David. Pete & Charley Adventure: The Sheri. (p. 1346)
Nash, Doug, jt. auth. see Griffiths, Neil.
Nash, Dylan M. Dinosaurs. Barnard, Bryn, illus. (p. 443)
Nash, Gary B. Encyclopedia of American History (p. 524)
Nash, Gary B. & Smith, Carter, eds. Atlas of American History. (p. 112)
Nash, Gisele, illus. see Alexander, Marilee.
Nash, Ilana. American Sweethearts: Teenage Girls in Twentieth-Century Popular Culture. (p. 63)
Nash, J. Madeleine. Nino: Unlocking the Secrets of the Master Weather-Maker. (p. 1257)
Nash, J. Q. Fishin' Hole. (p. 599)
Nash, Josh, jt. auth. see Jonath, Leslie.
Nash, Joshua, illus. see Loggins, Kenny.
Nash, Kathy, jt. auth. see Nash, Damien K. H.
Nash, Kelli, illus. see Allen, Elaine Ann.
Nash, Kelli, illus. see Allen, Elaine.
Nash, Kelli, illus. see Glick, Susan.
Nash, Kevin. Suny Stony Brook College Prowler off the Record: Inside State University of New York. (p. 1679)
—Valparaiso University College Prowler off the Record. (p. 1831)
Nash, Kevin, jt. auth. see Ayala, Anikka.
Nash, Kevin, jt. auth. see Chadderdon, Andrea.
Nash, Kevin, jt. auth. see Cloud, Megan.
Nash, Kevin, jt. auth. see Connell, Sarah.
Nash, Kevin, jt. auth. see Cook, Peter.
Nash, Kevin, jt. auth. see Eske, Aaron.
Nash, Kevin, jt. auth. see Gilbert, Heather.
Nash, Kevin, jt. auth. see Goldsmith, Emily.
Nash, Kevin, jt. auth. see Gordon, Lily.
Nash, Kevin, jt. auth. see Gossett, Kelley.
Nash, Kevin, jt. auth. see Hayes, Matt.
Nash, Kevin, jt. auth. see Hondorp, Michael.
Nash, Kevin, jt. auth. see Huang, Christine.
Nash, Kevin, jt. auth. see Killeen, Jared.
Nash, Kevin, jt. auth. see L. Wright, Sean.

Nash, Kevin, jt. auth. see Langston, Mandy.
Nash, Kevin, jt. auth. see Leanoard, James.
Nash, Kevin, jt. auth. see Low, Jessica.
Nash, Kevin, jt. auth. see Maehl, Sarah.
Nash, Kevin, jt. auth. see Meers, Whitney.
Nash, Kevin, jt. auth. see Pouliot, Seth.
Nash, Kevin, jt. auth. see R., Ben.
Nash, Kevin, jt. auth. see Rossi, Regine.
Nash, Kevin, jt. auth. see Shaw, Katie.
Nash, Kevin, jt. auth. see Steinman, Joshua.
Nash, Kevin, jt. auth. see Stewart, Nicolette.
Nash, Kevin, jt. auth. see Tafoya, Nathan.
Nash, Kevin, jt. auth. see Tran, Christine.
Nash, Kevin, jt. auth. see Wild, Cynthia.
Nash, Kimberley. Book Reports: A one-year writing Course. (p. 212)
—Creative Writing Textbook: A one-year Course. (p. 380)
—Essays & Research Reports - Level A: A one year writing Course. Level A (p. 536)
—Essays & Research Reports - Level B: A one year writing Course. (p. 536)
—Lab Reports: 10 Experiments. (p. 969)
Nash, Leonard. You Can't Get There from Here & Other Stories. (p. 1974)
Nash, Linda. Legend of the Lilies. (p. 989)
Nash, Margaret. Dad's Cake. (p. 399)
—Dog's New Coat. (p. 463)
—Hetty's New Hat. Impey, Martin, illus. (p. 774)
—My Big, New Bed. Blake, Beccy, illus. (p. 1197)
—Sammy's Secret. Axworthy, Anni, illus. (p. 1508)
Nash, Mike, et al. Drawing. (p. 481)
—How to Draw the Coolest, Most Creative Tattoo Art (p. 818)
—How to Draw the Meanest, Most Terrifying Monsters (p. 819)
Nash, Myrna Lee. Spinman, Katydid & Bump: A Spider Vane Collection. Johnson, Sharon, illus. (p. 1628)
Nash, Nancy. Mama's Books: An Oregon Trail Story. Burke, Ruth Anne, illus. (p. 1084)
Nash, Ogden. Lineup for Yesterday. Payne, C. F., illus. (p. 1019)
—Lineup for Yesterday ABC Baseball Cards. Payne, C. F., illus. (p. 1019)
Nash, Ronza R. Chocolate Wonders: The Adventures of Lila & Lester. (p. 309)
Nash, Sarah. Scaredy Bear. Everitt-Stewart, Andy, illus. (p. 1519)
—Smelly Blanket. Everitt-Stewart, Andy, illus. (p. 1593)
Nash, Scott. High-Skies Adventures of Blue Jay the Pirate. Nash, Scott, illus. (p. 778)
—Tuff Fluff: The Case of Duckie's Missing Brain. Nash, Scott, illus. (p. 1796)
Nash, Scott, illus. see Brown, Jeff.
Nash, Scott, illus. see Cash, John Carter.
Nash, Scott, illus. see Coffelt, Nancy.
Nash, Scott, illus. see Leuck, Laura.
Nash, Scott, illus. see Levine, Gail Carson.
Nash, Scott, illus. see Seuss, Dr.
Nash, Scott, illus. see Shields, Carol Diggory.
Nash, Scott, illus. see Umansky, Kaye.
Nash, Susan Smith. Good Deeds Society: Family Plot. (p. 697)
Nash, Tim. Club. (p. 335)
Na'Shae. Magic Chronicles: Ice. (p. 1072)
Nashton, Nashon, illus. see Kelin, Daniel.
Nasiatska, Maryanne, jt. auth. see Ruschmann, Paul.
Nasir, Safia. Princess Neelam & Other Stories. (p. 1404)
Nasium, James. African Americans in Sports. (p. 27)
—African Americans in Sports. Hill, Marc Lamont, ed. (p. 27)
Naslund, Gorel Kristina & Digman, Kristina. Our Apple Tree. Digman, Kristina, illus. (p. 1307)
Nasman, Leonard & Smith, Michael. DataCad 11 Project Book. (p. 409)
Nasmith, Ted, illus. see Findon, Joanne.
Nason, Ruth. Celebrating Harvest. (p. 284)
—Jewish Faith. (p. 917)
—Visiting a Mosque. (p. 1845)
Nass, Marcia. How to be a Bully... NOT! Moon, Poppy, illus. (p. 814)
Nass, Marcia & Campisi, Stephanie. Mini Mysteries & Kooky Spookies. Innes, Calvin, illus. (p. 1146)
Nass, Marcia Shoshana. Rabbit Who Lost His Hop: A Story about Self-Control. Gilgannon-Collins, Denise, illus. (p. 1429)
Nasser, Sarah. Busy Ben Gets Dressed. (p. 245)
—Busy Ben Make Stir Fry. (p. 245)
Nassief, Adel, illus. see Macdonald, Alastair.
Nassner, Alyssa. Lullaby & Kisses Sweet: Poems to Love with Your Baby. (p. 1064)
Nassner, Alyssa, illus. see Brown, Carron.
Nassner, Alyssa, illus. see George, Bobby & George, June.
Nassner, Alyssa, illus. see Golden, Erin Lee.
Nasso, Christine, ed. see Friedman, Lauri S.
Nast, Thomas. Fat Boy. (p. 576)
Nast, Thomas, illus. see Moore, Clement C.
Nastanlieva, Vanya. Mo & Beau. (p. 1157)
—New Arrival. Nastanlieva, Vanya, illus. (p. 1243)
Nastari, Nadine. Mr. TLC (Three-Legged Cat) (p. 1186)
Nasu, Yukie. Here Is Greenwood. (p. 770)
—Here Is Greenwood. Nasu, Yukie, illus. (p. 770)
Nasu, Yukie & Smith, Joe. Here Is Greenwood Nasu, Yukie, illus. (p. 770)
Natale, Christine. Fairy Tales. (p. 564)
Natale, Noel. Adventures of Nicholas: The Boy Who Grew up to Become Santa Claus. (p. 21)
Natale, Vince, illus. see Del Negro, Janice M.
Natali, Andrew. Delta One West. (p. 425)
Natalini, Sandro, jt. auth. see Baruzzi, Agnese.
Natalini, Sandro & Baruzzi, Agnese. True Story of Goldilocks. Natalini, Sandro & Baruzzi, Agnese, illus. (p. 1793)
Natarajan, Srividya, illus. see Whitaker, Zai.
Natasha & David Breen. Feisty Cats. (p. 581)
Natashya, Wilson, jt. auth. see Wilson, Natashya.
Natchev, Alexi, illus. see Hamm, Diane Johnston.
Natchev, Alexi, illus. see Strauss, Linda Leopold.
Natelli, Kenny, illus. see Welch, Eric.
Natelson, Robyn. My First 100 Words: Where Learning & Creativity Take Shape. (p. 1203)
—Play-Doh: My First 100 Words - On the Move! (p. 1371)
—PLAY-DOH: My First 100 Words: Animals. (p. 1371)
Natera, Jasmin A. & Hollis Iv, John H. Medellin: The City of Eternal Spring. (p. 1118)
Natera, Jasmin A., ed. Battle armor Iraq: A Pictorial of Hard Armor in the Iraq War on Terrorism (p. 145)
—Birds of prey in Iraq: A Pictorial of Helicopters in Iraqi Airspace (p. 192)
—children of Iraq: A Pictorial of Children Living in Iraq's War Zone (p. 302)
—Enter Iraq: A Pictorial of U. S. Marine Force Recon on the Syrian Border (p. 531)
—funny place called Iraq: The Boyz in Iraq Just Wanna Have Fun (p. 650)
—Iraq without Words: A Pictorial of Insurgent Ambushes in Iraq (p. 887)
—Iraq's hidden Beauty: A Pictorial of Iraq's Regional Beauty (p. 887)
—rebuilding of Iraq: A Pictorial of Iraq's Reconstruction (p. 1451)
—To live & die in Iraq: The Gripping True Story of Iraq's Secret Soldiers (p. 1759)
Nath, D. Smith. She, the Tale of a Sail. (p. 1564)
Nath, Vann, illus. see pierSath, Chath.
Nathan. Decouvre les Temps Qu'il. (p. 422)
Nathan, Adele Gutman. Lincoln's Americ. (p. 1019)
Nathan, Amy. Count on Us: American Women in the Military. (p. 370)
—Round & Round Together: Taking a Merry-Go-Round Ride into the Civil Rights Movement. (p. 1491)
Nathan, Cheryl. Wildlife Hidden Pictures. (p. 1931)
Nathan, Cheryl, illus. see Deak, Gloria.
Nathan, Cheryl, illus. see Groner, Judye & Wikler, Madeline.
Nathan, Cheryl, illus. see Harrison, David L.
Nathan, Cheryl, illus. see Newman, Vivian.
Nathan, Cheryl, illus. see Weston, Anne.
Nathan, Debbie. Pornography (p. 1386)
Nathan, Helen. Flossie Crums & the Enchanted Cookie Tree: A Flossie Crums Baking Adventure. Stevenson, Daryl, illus. (p. 607)
—Flossie Crums & the Fairies' Cupcake Ball. Stevenson, Daryl, illus. (p. 607)
—Flossie Crums & the Royal Spotty Dotty Cake. Stevenson, Daryl, illus. (p. 607)
Nathan, Jacintha & Oleksy, Walter G. Head & Neck in 3D. (p. 756)
Nathan, James, illus. see Doeden, Matt.
Nathan, James, illus. see Hoena, Blake & Doeden, Matt.
Nathan, James, illus. see Wacholtz, Anthony.
Nathan, Jared. All the Beautiful Butterflies: Wendell's Adventures Are Just Beginning. Nathan, Jared, illus. (p. 45)
Nathan, Jeff. Calling All Animals: The First Book of PunOETRY. Ball, Liz, illus. (p. 254)
Nathan, Kris. Kris's Key - Math & Pre-Algebra Concepts. (p. 967)
Nathan, Krivitzky, jt. auth. see Krivitzky, Nathan.
Nathan, Nadine Rubin. Adventures of Coco le Chat: The World's Most Fashionable Feline. Cascino, Jennifer, illus. (p. 17)
Nathan, Paul, photos by see Nathan, Nadine Rubin.
Nathan, Sandy. Tecolote: The Little Horse That Could. (p. 1712)
Nathan, Sarah. Jasmine: The Missing Coin. Studio IBOIX, illus. (p. 909)
—Sofia the First: Blue Ribbon Bunny. (p. 1605)
—Sofia's Magic Lesson. (p. 1605)
Nathan, Sarah & Disney Book Group Staff. Blue Ribbon Bunny, Level 1. Disney Storybook Art Team, illus. (p. 203)
—Sofia the First Sofia's Magic Lesson. (p. 1605)
Nathanael, Ardella. Butterfly Dance: Peter Deunov's PanEuRhythmy. (p. 247)
Nathanson, Amy, ed. see Wallace, Daniel.
Nathanson, Laura. Problema de los Miercoles. (p. 1408)
Nathan-Wlodarski, Anne, jt. auth. see Wlodarski, Robert James.
Nathar, Marisa, jt. auth. see Irwin, Bindi.
Nathoo, Aalaynah. World above Us!!! (p. 1953)
Nation, Kaleb. Bran Hambric: The Farfield Curse. (p. 222)
—Specter Key. (p. 1624)
Nation, Kay. Jamie Learns to Love. (p. 907)
Nation, Richard D., jt. auth. see Aufmann, Richard N.
Nation, Tate, illus. see Cleveland, Will & Alvarez, Mark.
Nation, Tate, illus. see Hahn, Blair.
National Children's Book and Literacy Alliance Staff. Our White House: Looking in, Looking Out. (p. 1310)
National Concrete Masonry Association Staff, jt. auth. see Skinner, Tina.
National Consultants for Education, creator. Treasure of My Catholic Faith: 1st Grade. (p. 1782)
—Treasure of My Catholic Faith: 2nd Grade. (p. 1782)
—Treasure of My Catholic Faith: 3rd Grade. (p. 1782)
—Treasure of My Catholic Faith: 4th Grade. (p. 1782)
—Treasure of My Catholic Faith: 5th Grade. (p. 1782)
—Treasure of My Catholic Faith: 6th Grade. (p. 1782)
National Crime Prevention Council (U.S.) Staff, contrib. by. McGruff & Scruff(r)'s Stories & Activities for Children of Promise. (p. 1114)
National Curriculum Development Centre Staff. Ateso Pupil. (p. 112)
—Luganda. (p. 1064)
—Luganda Pupil (p. 1064)
—Luo. (p. 1066)
—Runyankore-Rukiga. (p. 1497)
—Uganda Mother Tongue: Primary 1. (p. 1808)
—Uganda Mother Tongue: Primary 2. (p. 1808)
—Uganda Mother Tongue: Primary 3. (p. 1808)
—Uganda Mother Tongue: Primary 4. (p. 1808)
National Foundation for Educational Research in England and Wales Staff, contrib. by. Testun Trafod. (p. 1723)
National Gallery of Art. Eye for Art: Focusing on Great Artists & Their Work. (p. 557)
National Gallery of Art Staff. Hark! The Herald Angels Sing: The National Gallery, London. (p. 748)
—Jesus of Nazareth: The National Gallery of Art, Washington. (p. 916)
National Gallery of Australia Staff. Looking at Art 123: How Many Do You See? (p. 1050)
—Looking at Art ABC: Alphabet (p. 1050)
—Looking at Art Colours: What Colour Is That? (p. 1050)
—Parole Grande per Persone Piccole: Big Words for Little People. (p. 1325)
—Raining Cats & Dogs. (p. 1436)
National Gallery Staff. First Christmas. (p. 593)
National Geographic. 125 Cool Inventions. (p. 2000)
—125 Cute Animals. (p. 2000)
—National Geographic Kids: 125 True Stories of Amazing Pets. (p. 1231)
—National Geographic Kids Almanac 2015. (p. 1231)
—National Geographic Kids: Animal Creativity Book: Cut-Outs, Games, Stencils, Stickers. (p. 1231)
—National Geographic Kids Quiz Whiz 2: 1,000 Super Fun Mind-Bending Totally Awesome Trivia Questions. (p. 1232)
—National Geographic Kids Ultimate Weird but True 2: 1,000 Wild & Wacky Facts & Photos! (p. 1232)
—National Geographic Kids Weird but True! (p. 1232)
—National Geographic Kids Weird but True! Ripped from the Headlines 2. (p. 1232)
—National Geographic Kids World Atlas. (p. 1232)
—NG Kids Ultimate Weird but True 2: 1,000 Wild & Wacky Facts & Photos! (p. 1250)
—Predators Collection: Readers That Grow with You. (p. 1395)
—Things That Go! Collection. (p. 1733)
—Xtreme Illusions 2. (p. 1967)
National Geographic Book Service Staff, jt. auth. see Baines, Becky.
National Geographic Editors. 1001 Inventions & Awesome Facts from Muslim Civilization. (p. 2002)
—Creepy Crawly Collection. (p. 381)
—Every Human Has Rights: A Photographic Declaration for Kids. (p. 542)
—Every Human Has Rights: What You Need to Know about Your Human Rights. (p. 542)
—Favorite Animals Collection. (p. 578)
—National Geographic Readers: Creepy Crawly Collection. (p. 1233)
National Geographic Editors & Esbaum, Jill. Angry Birds Playground - Dinosaurs. Tempesta, Franco, illus. (p. 75)
—Angry Birds Playground: Rain Forest: A Forest Floor to Treetop Adventure. (p. 75)
—Dinosaurs: A Prehistoric Adventure! Tempesta, Franco, illus. (p. 444)
National Geographic Editors & Pattison, Rosie Gowsell. Just Joking 4: 300 Hilarious Jokes about Everything, Including Tongue Twisters, Riddles, & More! (p. 938)
National Geographic Editors & Rizzo, Johnna. Oceans: Dolphins, Sharks, Penguins, & More! (p. 1277)
National Geographic, et al. Living on the Plains. (p. 1041)
National Geographic Kids. 125 Cool Inventions: Super Smart Machines & Wacky Gadgets You Never Knew You Wanted. (p. 2000)
—125 Cute Animals: Meet the Cutest Critters on the Planet, Including Animals You Never Knew Existed, & Some So Ugly They're Cute. (p. 2000)
—Boredom-Busting Fun Stuff. (p. 214)
—National Geographic Kids Adorable Animals Super Sticker Activity Book: 2,000 Stickers! (p. 1231)
—National Geographic Kids Almanac 2016. (p. 1231)
—National Geographic Kids Amazing Animals Super Sticker Activity Book: 2,000 Stickers! (p. 1231)
—National Geographic Kids Ferocious Animals Super Sticker Activity Book: 2,000 Stickers! (p. 1232)
—National Geographic Kids Funny Fill-In: My Amazing Earth Adventures. (p. 1232)
—National Geographic Kids Funny Fill-In: My Far-Out Adventures. (p. 1232)
—National Geographic Kids Funny Fill-In: My Flying Adventure. (p. 1232)
—National Geographic Kids Funny Fill-In: My Haunted House Adventure. (p. 1232)
—National Geographic Kids Funny Fill-In: My Rain Forest Adventure. (p. 1232)
—National Geographic Kids Funny Fill-In: My Wild West Adventure. (p. 1232)
—National Geographic Kids Look & Learn: Dig! (p. 1232)
—National Geographic Kids Look & Learn: Ocean Creatures. (p. 1232)
—National Geographic Kids on the Farm Sticker Activity Book: Over 1,000 Stickers! (p. 1232)
—National Geographic Kids Quiz Whiz 5: 1,000 Super Fun Mind-Bending Totally Awesome Trivia Questions. (p. 1232)
—National Geographic Kids Ultimate Weird but True 3. (p. 1232)
—National Geographic Kids Weird but True!: Ripped from the Headlines 2: Real-Life Stories You Have to Read to Believe. (p. 1232)
—National Geographic Readers: Ocean Animals Collection. (p. 1233)
—United States Encyclopedia: America's People, Places, & Events. (p. 1819)
National Geographic Kids Staff. 1,000 Facts about the Bible. (p. 2001)
—125 True Stories of Amazing Animals. (p. 2000)
—5,000 Awesome Facts. (p. 2003)
—5,000 Awesome Facts (About Everything!) (p. 2003)
—5,000 Awesome Facts (about Everything!) 2. (p. 2003)
—Angry Birds Explore the World. (p. 75)
—Animal Friendship! Collection: Amazing Stories of Animal Friends & the Humans That Love Them. (p. 78)
—Bears - National Geographic Little Kids. (p. 151)
—Dinos! (p. 441)
—Fierce Animals. (p. 584)
—Funny Animals! Collection: Amazing Stories of Hilarious Animals & Surprising Talents. (p. 649)
—Just Joking Collector's Set (Boxed Set) 900 Hilarious Jokes about Everything. (p. 938)
—Little Kids First Big Book Collector's Set. (p. 1030)
—Match! (p. 1104)
—National Geographic Kids 125 True Stories of Amazing Pets: Inspiring Tales of Animal Friendship & Four-Legged Heroes, Plus Crazy Animal Antics. (p. 1231)
—National Geographic Kids 125 True Stories of Amazing Animals: Inspiring Tales of Animal Friendship & Four-Legged Heroes, Plus Crazy Animal Antics. (p. 1231)
—National Geographic Kids Almanac 2012. (p. 1231)
—National Geographic Kids Amazing Pets Sticker Activity Book: Over 1,000 Stickers! (p. 1231)
—National Geographic Kids Cool Animals Sticker Activity Book: Over 1,000 Stickers! (p. 1232)
—National Geographic Kids Cutest Animals Sticker Activity Book: Over 1,000 Stickers! (p. 1232)
—National Geographic Kids Just Joking: 300 Hilarious Jokes, Tricky Tongue Twisters, & Ridiculous Riddles. (p. 1232)
—National Geographic Kids Just Joking 2: 300 Hilarious Jokes about Everything, Including Tongue Twisters, Riddles, & More! (p. 1232)
—National Geographic Kids Just Joking 6. (p. 1232)
—National Geographic Kids Look & Learn: All about Me. (p. 1232)
—National Geographic Kids Quiz Whiz: 1,000 Super Fun, Mind-Bending, Totally Awesome Trivia Questions. (p. 1232)
—National Geographic Kids Quiz Whiz 3: 1,000 Super Fun Mind-Bending Totally Awesome Trivia Questions. (p. 1232)
—National Geographic Kids Super Space Sticker Activity Book: Over 1,000 Stickers! (p. 1232)
—National Geographic Kids Ultimate Globetrotting World Atlas. (p. 1232)
—National Geographic Kids Weird but True! 6: 300 Outrageous Facts. (p. 1232)
—National Geographic Kids - Weird but True!: Ripped from the Headlines: Real-Life Stories You Have to Read to Believe. (p. 1231)
—National Geographic Little Kids Look & Learn Bugs. (p. 1232)
—National Geographic Little Kids Look & Learn: Colors. (p. 1233)
—National Geographic Little Kids Look & Learn: Dogs. (p. 1233)
—National Geographic Little Kids Look & Learn: Patterns! (p. 1233)
—National Geographic Little Kids Look & Learn: Same & Different. (p. 1233)
—National Geographic Little Kids Look & Learn: Things That Go. (p. 1233)
—National Geographic Readers: Planet Earth Collection: Readers That Grow with You. (p. 1233)
—National Geographic Student World Atlas. (p. 1233)
—National Parks Guide U. S. A. The Most Amazing Sights, Scenes, & Cool Activities from Coast to Coast! (p. 1233)
—Opposites! (p. 1300)
—Ponies & Horses. (p. 1382)
—Shapes! (p. 1560)
—Sharks! (p. 1562)
—To the Rescue! Collection: Amazing Stories of Courageous Animals & Animal Rescues. (p. 1759)
—Weird but True: 900 Outrageous Facts. Set (p. 1872)
—Weird but True! (p. 1872)
—Weird but True! 2: 300 Outrageous Facts. Halling, Jonathan, illus. (p. 1872)
—Weird but True! 4: 300 Outrageous Facts. (p. 1872)
—Weird but True! 5: 300 Outrageous Facts. (p. 1872)
—What in the World? (p. 1887)
National Geographic Kids Staff, jt. auth. see U. S. National Geographic Society Staff.
National Geographic Kids Staff & Beer, Julie. Weird but True Food: 300 Bite-Size Facts about Incredible Edibles. (p. 1872)
—Weird but True! Food: 300 Bite-Size Facts about Incredible Edibles! (p. 1872)
National Geographic Kids Staff & Donohue, Moira Rose. Kangaroo to the Rescue! And More True Stories of Amazing Animal Heroes. (p. 942)
—National Geographic Kids Chapters - Kangaroo to the Rescue! And More True Stories of Amazing Animal Heroes. (p. 1232)
—Parrot Genius: And More True Stories of Amazing Animal Talents. (p. 1325)
—Parrot Genius! And More True Stories of Amazing Animal Talents. (p. 1325)
National Geographic Kids Staff & Esbaum, Jill. National Geographic Little Kids First Big Book of Who. (p. 1232)
National Geographic Kids Staff & Gerry, Lisa. 100 Things to Do Before You Grow Up. (p. 1999)
National Geographic Kids Staff & Gilpin, Caroline Crosson. National Geographic Readers: Barack Obama. (p. 1233)
—National Geographic Readers: George Washington. (p. 1233)
National Geographic Kids Staff & Gleason, Carrie. National Geographic Kids Everything Insects: All the Facts, Photos, & Fun to Make You Buzz. (p. 1232)
National Geographic Kids Staff & Hoena, Blake. National Geographic Kids Everything Birds of Prey: Swoop in for Seriously Fierce Photos & Amazing Info. (p. 1232)
National Geographic Kids Staff & Kramer, Barbara. National Geographic Readers: Thomas Edison. (p. 1233)
National Geographic Kids Staff & Musgrave, Ruth A. National Geographic Kids Just Joking 3: 300 Hilarious Jokes about Everything, Including Tongue Twisters, Riddles, & More! (p. 1232)
National Geographic Kids Staff & Neuman, Susan B. Hop Bunny. (p. 796)
—National Geographic Readers: Hang on Monkey! (p. 1233)
—National Geographic Readers - Hop Bunny. (p. 1233)
National Geographic Learning. National Geographic Explore: Endangered Species. (p. 1231)
—South America - People & Places. (p. 1616)

National Geographic Learning (Firm) Staff, jt. auth. see Geiger, Beth.
National Geographic Learning, National Geographic Learning & Rossi, Ann. Reading Expeditions - The Anti-Slavery Movement. (p. 1445)
National Geographic Learning Staff. Famous Landmarks, Level 3. (p. 569)
National Geographic Learning Staff, jt. auth. see Ashcroft, Minnie.
National Geographic Learning Staff, jt. auth. see Buckley, Susan Washburn.
National Geographic Learning Staff, jt. auth. see Byers, Helen.
National Geographic Learning Staff, jt. auth. see Chanek, Sherilin.
National Geographic Learning Staff, jt. auth. see Connell, Kate.
National Geographic Learning Staff, jt. auth. see Currie, Stephen.
National Geographic Learning Staff, jt. auth. see Garey, Marita.
National Geographic Learning Staff, jt. auth. see Goodman, Susan E.
National Geographic Learning Staff, jt. auth. see Halpern, Monica.
National Geographic Learning Staff, jt. auth. see Jerome, Kate Boehm.
National Geographic Learning Staff, jt. auth. see Johnson, Rebecca L.
National Geographic Learning Staff, jt. auth. see Meade, Deborah.
National Geographic Learning Staff, jt. auth. see Miller, Danny.
National Geographic Learning Staff, jt. auth. see Phelan, Glen.
National Geographic Learning Staff, jt. auth. see Proujan, Carl.
National Geographic Learning Staff, jt. auth. see Rosen, Daniel.
National Geographic Learning Staff, jt. auth. see Rossi, Ann.
National Geographic Learning Staff, jt. auth. see Sarver, Amy.
National Geographic Learning Staff, jt. auth. see Sheinkin, Steve.
National Geographic Learning Staff, jt. auth. see Stephens, Catherine.
National Geographic Learning Staff, jt. auth. see Street, Sharon.
National Geographic Learning Staff, jt. auth. see Supples, Kevin.
National Geographic Learning Staff, jt. auth. see Thompson, Gare.
National Geographic Learning Staff, jt. auth. see Tull, Mary.
National Geographic Learning Staff, jt. auth. see Tunkin, David.
National Geographic Learning Staff, jt. auth. see Winkler, Peter.
National Geographic Learning Staff, jt. auth. see Yero, Judith Lloyd.
National Geographic Society (U.S.) Staff, contrib. by. Just Joking: 300 Hilarious Jokes, Tricky Tongue Twisters, & Ridiculous Riddles. (p. 938)
—National Parks Guide U. S. A: The Most Amazing Sights, Scenes, & Cool Activities from Coast to Coast! (p. 1233)
National Geographic Staff. Things That Go Collection: Readers That Grow With You. (p. 1733)
National Indonesian Curriculum Project Staff. Suara Siswa: Indonesian Language (p. 1670)
National Japanese Curriculum Project Staff. Pera Pera. (p. 1341)
National Marine Fisheries Service (U.S.), jt. compiled by see National Oceanic and Atmospheric Administration (U.S.).
National Marine Fisheries Service (U.S.), ed. Understanding Marine Debris: Games & Activities for Kids of All Ages. (p. 1815)
National Maritime Museum (Great Britain) Staff, contrib. by. Alphabet of Ships. (p. 49)
National Museum of the American Indian (U.S.) Staff, contrib. by. When the Rain Sings: Poems by Young Native Americans. (p. 1905)
National Oceanic and Atmospheric Administration (U.S.) & National Marine Fisheries Service (U.S.), compiled by. Chesapeake Bay Activity Book. (p. 298)
National Parents Council - Primary Staff. Whiz Quiz Book: For Children & Grown-Up Children. (p. 1914)
National Parents Council - Primary Staff, ed. More Whiz Quiz: For Children & Grown-up Children. (p. 1175)
National Park Service (U.S.), ed. see Romero, Kyle & Padron, Maria Lorena.
National Park Service (U.S.), ed. Discovering the Underground Railroad: Junior Ranger Activity Book. (p. 450)
—Junior Paleontologist Activity Book: Ages 5 to 12: Explore, Learn, Protect. (p. 936)
National Science Resources Center, creator. Science & Technology for Children Books: Animal Studies. (p. 1525)
National Science Teachers Association. Safety in the Elementary Science Classroom. (p. 1502)
National Society of American Staff, ed. American Indian: Culture, Spirit, Tradition. (p. 61)
National System Of Public Lands, et al. Jurassic Explorer: Cleveland-Lloyd Dinosaur Quarry. (p. 937)
National Taiwan Normal University Staff. Practical Audio-Visual Chinese: B. Vol. 3 (p. 1392)
National Taiwan Normal University Staff, compiled by. Practical Audio-Visual Chinese: A. (p. 1391)
—Practical Audio-Visual Chinese: B. Vol. 3 (p. 1392)
National Thai Language Curriculum Project Staff. Sanuk Sanuk: Thai Language (p. 1513)
National, Walt. I Am Responsible. (p. 833)
—I Am Responsible / Soy Responsable. (p. 833)
National Wildlife Federation Staff. My First Book of Baby Animals (National Wildlife Federation) (p. 1205)
—My First Book of Funny Animals. (p. 1205)
—My First Book of Wild Animals (National Wildlife Federation) (p. 1205)
National Wildlife Federation Staff, jt. auth. see Cusick, Dawn.
National Wildlife Federation Staff, jt. auth. see Kurki, Kim.
National Youth Department Staff. Guia Practica para Lideres de Jovenes. Rdm, tr. from ENG. (p. 730)
Nations, Susan. Hace Sol. (p. 735)
—I Know Big & Small. (p. 840)
—Let's Read about Sun. (p. 1000)
—Things at Home. (p. 1733)
—Things at School. (p. 1733)
Nations, Susan, jt. auth. see Brode, Robyn.
Nations, Susan, jt. auth. see Gorman, Jacqueline Laks.
Nations, Susan, jt. auth. see Guidone, Lisa M.
Nations, Susan, jt. auth. see Hudson, Amanda.
Nations, Susan, jt. auth. see Hutchings, Amy.
Nations, Susan, jt. auth. see Pohl, Kathleen.
Nations, Susan, jt. auth. see Ranchetti, Sebastiano.
Nations, Susan, jt. auth. see Thomas, William David.
Nations, Susan & Alonso, Melissa. Primary Literacy Responses: Core Tasks for Readers & Writers. (p. 1399)
Nations, Susan & Boyett, Suzi. Hace Sol. (p. 735)
Nations, Susan & Weekly Reader Editorial Staff. I Know Big & Small/Grande y Pequeño. (p. 840)
—I Know Same & Different (Igual y Diferente) (p. 840)
Natl Children's Book & Literacy Alliance. Exquisite Corpse Adventure. (p. 555)
Natlie, Jeffrey Michael. Emily Gets Angry. (p. 519)
Nato, creator. Mikoyan-Gurevich MiG-21 Pilot's Flight Operating Instructions. (p. 1142)
Natori. Josie & the Dragon. (p. 927)
Natsukawa, Maiko. Rachel, Grace, & Pony Club. (p. 1432)
Natsumoto, Masato. Lost War Chronicles (p. 1057)
Natsumoto, Masato, illus. see Chiba, Tomohiro & Games, Incbandai.
Natterson, Cara. Care & Keeping of You 2: The Body Book for Older Girls. Masse, Josée, illus. (p. 266)
Natterson, Cara Familian. Your Newborn: Head to Toe - Everything You Want to Know about Your Baby's Health Through the First Year. (p. 1981)
Natti, S., illus. see Adler, David A.
Natti, Susanna, illus. see Adler, David A.
Natti, Susanna, illus. see Watson, Clyde.
Natti, Susanna, illus. see Wojciechowski, Susan.
Natural History Museum. Ocean Sticker Book. (p. 1276)
Natural History Museum Collection Staff. Rocks & Minerals Sticker Book. (p. 1483)
Natural History Museum Staff. Sensational Butterflies Sticker Book. (p. 1550)
Natural History Museum Staff, jt. auth. see Sterling Publishing Company Staff.
Natural Resources Conservation Service (U.S.), ed. see Kauble, Christa.
Natural Resources Defense Council Staff, et al. Simple Steps Toward a Healthier Earth. Carpenter, Tad, illus. (p. 1578)
Nauck, Todd. Wildguard: Casting Call. (p. 1931)
Nauck, Todd, jt. illus. see Frenz, Ron.
Nauck, Todd, et al. Deadpool/Amazing Spider-Man/Hulk: Identity Wars. (p. 418)
Naughton, Bill. Goalkeeper's Revenge. (p. 687)
—Pony Boy. (p. 1382)
Naughton, Christine, ed. see Kurtz, Barbara.
Naughton, Colin Charles. Not So Spooky Book Series: Book One. (p. 1267)
Naughton, Diane. Bones: And the Stories They Tell. (p. 209)
—Our Green Future. (p. 1309)
—Rescued. (p. 1462)
—True Colors Intermediate Book with Online Access. (p. 1792)
—Venice: The Floating City. (p. 1835)
—What Are You Afraid of? Fears & Phobias Intermediate Book with Online Access. (p. 1880)
Naughton, Diane, jt. auth. see Harris, Nic.
Naughton, Geraldine. Owl's Birthday. (p. 1315)
Naughton, Michael P., ed. see Madsen, Michael.
Naughton, Patrick. Colonel Tiger on the Raft. (p. 341)
Naughton, Paul. Welcome to Ziklag. (p. 1874)
Naughton, Sarah. Blood List. (p. 200)
—Hanged Man Rises. (p. 742)
Naughton, Terry, illus. see Cesak, Jerry.
Naujokaitis, Pranas T. Dinosaurs in Space. (p. 444)
—Radically Awesome Adventures of the Animal Princess. (p. 1432)
—Totally Awesome Epic Quest of the Brave Boy Knight. (p. 1771)
Naujokaitis, Pranas T., illus. see Bennett, Artie.
Nault, Jennifer. Earthquakes. (p. 497)
—Georgia. (p. 665)
—Judy Blume. (p. 931)
—Kansas. (p. 942)
—Michelle Obama. (p. 1135)
—New Jersey. (p. 1245)
—Project Polar Bear. Kissock, Heather & Marshall, Diana, eds. (p. 1410)
—Save the Children. (p. 1516)
—Volcanoes. (p. 1849)
Nault, Jennifer, ed. see Craats, Rennay.
Nault, Jennifer, ed. see Foran, Jill.
Nault, Jennifer, ed. see Hamilton, Lynn A.
Nault, Jennifer, ed. see Ring, Susan.
Nault, Jennifer, ed. see Weigl Publishers Staff & Craats, Rennay.
Nault, Jennifer, jt. auth. see Ashmore, Wayne.
Nault, Jennifer & Riley, Joelle. Volcanoes. (p. 1849)
Nault, S. &R, illus. see Nault, Susan.
Nault, Susan. Mr Scruffpot's Pony. Nault, S. &R, illus. (p. 1186)
Naumann, jt. auth. see Naumann-Villemin, Christine.
Naumann, Jen. Cheating Death. (p. 295)
Naumann-Villemin, Christine & Naumann. Chupete de Gina. Barcilon, Marianne, illus. (p. 318)
Naumovets, Elena, ed. see AZ Books Staff.
Naurighi, John, jt. auth. see Parrish, Charles.
Nausley, Kathy, illus. see Sheets, Judy.
Nautilus Studio Staff, illus. see Bruneau, Clotilde, et al.
Naux-McVicker, S. Petit Guide Pour Ados Avant d'Aller en Amérique! For Teenagers. (p. 1348)
Nava, Francisco, illus. see Lujan, Jorge Elias.
Navar, Nora Cecilia. Catire Valentin. (p. 280)
Navarra, Nino. How to Draw Nickelodeon Teenage Mutant Ninja Turtles: /step-By-Step Illustrations by Niño Navarra. (p. 818)
Navarra, Nino, illus. see Random House Staff.
Navarra, Tova. Encyclopedia of Vitamins, Minerals, & Supplements. (p. 525)
Navarre, Gabrielle. Cool Careers Without College for People Who Love Nature. (p. 363)
Navarre, Sam. Masculinity, Bullying, & Aggression: A Guy's Guide. (p. 1102)
—Vampires in America. (p. 1832)
Navarrete, Federico. Invencion de Los Canibales. Rendon, Joel, illus. (p. 883)
Navarrete, Vinny, jt. auth. see Williamson, Joshua.
Navarro, Carlos. Supermusicos. Tobella, Montse, illus. (p. 1684)
Navarro, Cece P. My Cherry Tree House. (p. 1200)
Navarro, Dominique & Baha El Din, Sherif. Wildlife of the Holy Land: An AUC Press Nature Foldout. (p. 1931)
Navarro, Francisco Perez, tr. see Miller, Frank.
Navarro, Jose, et al. Enorme Pequenoz de la Abuela Tierra. (p. 530)
Navarro, Larry. Story of Jack Frost. (p. 1658)
Navarro, Paula & Jimenez, Angels. Amazing Experiments with Electricity & Magnetism. Cuxart, Bernadette, illus. (p. 54)
—Incredible Experiments with Chemical Reactions & Mixtures. Cuxart, Bernadette, illus. (p. 869)
—Magical Experiments with Light & Color. Cuxart, Bernadette, illus. (p. 1074)
—Surprising Experiments with Sound. Cuxart, Bernadette, illus. (p. 1686)
Navarro-Talavera, Carmen. Ant Lucy & the Hurricane. (p. 88)
—Hormiguita Lucy y el Huracán. (p. 798)
Navasky, Victor S. Matter of Opinion. (p. 1109)
Nave, Jeff. Obama's Pajamas. (p. 1275)
Navía, Miguel, illus. see Cerdá, Alfredo Gómez.
Navigators Staff, The, jt. auth. see Student Life Staff.
Navillus, Nell. God's Christmas Gift. McCallum, Jodie, illus. (p. 691)
—Happy Birthday, Jesus. McCallum, Jodie, illus. (p. 744)
—Verdadero Cuento de Navidad. Alvarez, Lourdes, tr. (p. 1836)
Nawashani. Stepping Stones to the Sun. Wiles, Pat, illus. (p. 1648)
Nawyn, Lori, jt. auth. see Monson, Christy.
Naxos of America Staff, jt. auth. see Alcott, Louisa May.
Naxos of America Staff, jt. auth. see Burnett, Frances Hodgson.
Nayak, Anoop. Race, Place & Globalization: Youth Cultures in a Changing World. (p. 1431)
Nayar, Deeya, jt. auth. see Jeeva Raghunath.
Nayar, Nandini. What Could It Be? Manetti, Francesco, illus. (p. 1881)
Nayberg, Yevgenia, illus. see Lewis, J. Patrick.
Nayer, Judy. 25 Easy Bilingual Nonfiction Mini-Books: Easy-to-Read Reproducible Mini-Books in English & Spanish That Build Vocabulary & Fluency-And Support the Social Studies & Science Topics You Teach. (p. 1996)
—Androcles & the Lion: An Aesop's Fable. (p. 72)
—Best Wishes for Eddie. Franson, Leanne, illus. (p. 171)
—John James Audubon. (p. 922)
Nayeri, Daniel. How to Tell a Story: Read the Book, Roll the Blocks, Build Adventures! Won, Brian, illus. (p. 822)
—Straw House, Wood House, Brick House, Blow: Four Novellas by Daniel Nayeri. Weinberg, James, illus. (p. 1666)
Nayeri, Daniel and Dina. Another Faust. (p. 87)
—Another Jekyll, Another Hyde. (p. 88)
—Another Pan. (p. 88)
Nayeri, Daniel & Nayeri, Dina. Another Jekyll, Another Hyde. (p. 88)
—Another Pan. (p. 88)
Nayeri, Dina, jt. auth. see Nayeri, Daniel.
Nayler, Sarah, illus. see Gray, Kes, et al.
Nayler, Sarah, illus. see Kebbe, Jonathan.
Nayler, Sarah, illus. see Wallace, Karen.
Naylor, Amy. Whoosh! Easy Paper Airplanes for Kids! Color, Fold & Fly! (p. 1920)
Naylor, Beth, jt. auth. see Seifert, Sheila.
Naylor, Beth & Seifert, Sheila. Where Is God? (p. 1908)
Naylor, Brenda & Naylor, Stuart. Snowman's Coat & Other Science Questions Mitchell, Ged, illus. (p. 1601)
Naylor, Clare, jt. auth. see Hare, Mimi.
Naylor, Phyllis Reynolds. Achingly Alice. (p. 9)
—Agony of Alice. (p. 30)
—Alice in April. (p. 39)
—Alice in Blunderland. (p. 39)
—Alice in Charge. (p. 39)
—Alice in Lace. (p. 39)
—Alice in Rapture, Sort Of. (p. 39)
—Alice In-Between. (p. 39)
—Alice on Board. (p. 39)
—Alice on Her Way. (p. 39)
—Alice on the Outside. (p. 39)
—Alice the Brave. (p. 39)
—All but Alice. (p. 44)
—Almost Alice. (p. 48)
—Anyone Can Eat Squid! Ramsey, Marcy, illus. (p. 91)
—Bernie Magruder & the Bats in the Belfry. (p. 167)
—Boys in Control. (p. 220)
—Boys Return. (p. 220)
—Boys Rock! (p. 220)
—Cricket Man. (p. 382)
—Cuckoo Feathers Ramsey, Marcy, illus. (p. 389)
—Dangerously Alice. (p. 404)
—Eating Enchiladas Ramsey, Marcy, illus. (p. 501)
—Emily & Jackson Hiding Out. (p. 518)
—Emily's Fortune. (p. 519)
—Faith, Hope, & Ivy June. (p. 565)
—Girls Rule! (p. 680)
—Girls Take Over. (p. 681)
—Grand Escape. Daniel, Alan, illus. (p. 707)
—Grooming of Alice. (p. 725)
—Healing of Texas Jake. Daniel, Alan, illus. (p. 757)
—I Like Him, He Likes Her: Alice Alone; Simply Alice; Patiently Alice. (p. 841)
—Including Alice. (p. 869)
—Incredibly Alice. (p. 870)
—Intensely Alice. (p. 879)
—It's Not Like I Planned It This Way: Including Alice; Alice on Her Way; Alice in the Know. (p. 898)
—Lovingly Alice. (p. 1061)
—Now I'll Tell You Everything. (p. 1269)
—Outrageously Alice. (p. 1313)
—Patches & Scratches Ramsey, Marcy, illus. (p. 1328)
—Please Do Feed the Bears. Escriva, Ana Lopez, illus. (p. 1373)
—Please Don't Be True: Dangerously Alice; Almost Alice; Intensely Alice. (p. 1373)
—Polo's Mother. Daniel, Alan, illus. (p. 1381)
—Reluctantly Alice. (p. 1458)
—Roxie & the Hooligans. Boiger, Alexandra, illus. (p. 1492)
—Sang Spell. (p. 1511)
—Saving Shiloh. (p. 1517)
—Shiloh. (p. 1566)
—Shiloh Christmas. (p. 1566)
—Shiloh Season. (p. 1566)
—Simply Alice. (p. 1578)
—Starting with Alice. (p. 1644)
—Walker's Crossing. (p. 1854)
—Who Won the War? (p. 1919)
—Witch Returns. (p. 1941)
—Witch Weed. (p. 1941)
—You & Me & the Space in Between: Alice in Charge; Incredibly Alice; Alice on Board. (p. 1973)
Naylor, Sean. Not a Good Day to Die: The Untold Story of Operation Anaconda. (p. 1266)
Naylor, Stuart, jt. auth. see Naylor, Brenda.
Naythons, Will, tr. see Anh, Nguyen Nhat.
Nazar, Alexandria, illus. see Riggs, Jon & Evanoff, Corrine R.
Nazarchyk, Elizabeth M. Town of Mclee. (p. 1773)
Nazareth, Carla, illus. see Carvalho, et al.
Nazareth, Melanie. Can I Have Some Cake Too? Lehner-Rhoades, Shirley, illus. (p. 258)
Nazarian, George, jt. auth. see Nazarian, Leslie.
Nazarian, Leslie. Orelda & Corelda's Ocean Voyage. (p. 1303)
Nazarian, Leslie & Nazarian, George. Orelda & Corelda on Wall Street. (p. 1303)
Nazario, Rafael, illus. see Kennedy, Kirk.
Nazario, Sonia. Enrique's Journey: The True Story of a Boy Determined to Reunite with His Mother. (p. 531)
—Enrique's Journey: The True Story of a Boys Determined to Reunite with His Mother. (p. 531)
—Travesía de Enrique. (p. 1781)
Nazeer, Tasnim & Publishing, Greenbirdbooks Childrens. Allah's Gifts. Frongia, Daniela, illus. (p. 46)
Nazemi, Mary. Kaveh, Jolly & the Super Giant. (p. 946)
Nazif, Iwan, illus. see Titan Comics Staff & Furman, Simon.
Nazoa, Aquiles. Retablillo de Navidad. Oliver, Maria Fernanda, illus. (p. 1464)
Nazran, Govinder. Aladdin. (p. 33)
Nazzaro, Robin M. Wind Power: Impacts on Wildlife & Government Responsibilities for Regulating Development & Protecting Wildlife. (p. 1935)
N.C.B.L.A. Our White House: Looking in, Looking Out. (p. 1310)
NCPTA Staff, et al. Better Maths. (p. 172)
—Home Learning 11 SATs Practical Science. (p. 792)
—Home Learning 5-7 English. (p. 792)
—Maths for the Brighter Child. (p. 1108)
N'Deeo Beauty Staff, creator. Our Little Girls: The African-American Female Pre-Teen Guide to Health & Beauty. (p. 1309)
—Our Teenagers: The African-American Female Teen Guide to Health & Beauty. (p. 1310)
Ndegwa, Catherine. A to Z Through Africa, Swahili & English. (p. 2)
Ndu, Matt. Playreview Science: Science Word Search Puzzles. (p. 1373)
Ne, Harriet, jt. auth. see Davies, Ann.
Neal, Albert, ed. see Perry, Melanie Denise.
Neal, Allyson. Ava Lillian's Blessing. Bynum, Saran, illus. (p. 118)
Neal, Angie. Pirate Who Couldn't Say Arrr! (p. 1363)
Neal, Angie & Kjesbo, Rynette. Simply Social 7 at School. Bristol, Mark, illus. (p. 1578)
Neal, Bethany. My Last Kiss. (p. 1211)
Neal, Bill, illus. see Laird, Elizabeth.
Neal, Christopher Silas, illus. see Messner, Kate.
Neal, Christopher Silas, illus. see Ray, Mary Lyn.
Neal, Christopher Silas, illus. see Schaefer, Lola M.
Neal, Chuck. Grizzlies in the Mist. (p. 724)
Neal, David, jt. auth. see Powell, Marc.
Neal, Dick. Introduction to Population Biology. (p. 882)
Neal, Isla, jt. auth. see Leicht, Martin.
Neal, Jill Faith, illus. see Dudley, Linda S.
Neal, Kathleen A. Sun Begins Its Daily Flight. (p. 1676)
Neal, Michael. Bonnie's Rescue: A Courageous Critters« Series Book. (p. 209)
—Rex's Secret: A Courageous CrittersTM Book. (p. 1467)
Neal, Nate & Sim, Dave. Sanctuary. (p. 1510)
Neal, Penelope, illus. see Cowan, Charlotte.
Neal, Sharon, ed. see Carvin, Rose-Mae.
Neal, Sharon, ed. see Greiner, Ruth.
Neal, Sharon, ed. see Piepgrass, Arlene S.
Neal, Sharon, ed. Great Is Thy Faithfulness. (p. 716)
—Who Is He in Yonder Stall? Jarrett, Sandra, illus. (p. 1915)
Neal, Terry L. Find It Club. (p. 587)
—Find It Club & the Prankster. (p. 587)
Neal, Vonda & Herbold, Marvin, compiled by. British Sign Language American Sign Language Translator. (p. 230)
Neal-Bailey, Ashley L. I Don't Want To. (p. 838)

N

Neale, Cynthia. Hope in New York City: The Continuing Story of the Irish Dresser. (p. 796)
Neale, Cynthia G. Irish Dresser: A Story of Hope During the Great Hunger (an Gorta Mor, 1845-1850) (p. 887)
Neale, J. B. In the Shadow of the Guillotine. (p. 867)
Neale, J. M. Good King Wenceslas. Ladwig, Tim, illus. (p. 698)
Neale, Jonathan. Himalaya. (p. 780)
—Lost at Sea. (p. 1055)
Neale, Karen. Boy Who Burped Butterflies. (p. 219)
Neale, Melanie. Boat Kid: How I Survived Swimming with Sharks, Being Homeschooled, & Growing up on a Sailboat. (p. 205)
Neale, R. W. Harry the Rally Car: The Beginning. (p. 751)
Neale, Vivienne. Keep Your Options Open. (p. 947)
Nealeigh, Thomas. See You in the Backlot. (p. 1547)
Nealon, Eve, illus. see Webb, Mack H., Jr.
Neary, Paul. Nick Fury vs. S. H. I. E. L. D. (p. 1251)
—S. H. I. E. L. D. Nick Fury vs. S. H. I. E. L. D. (p. 1499)
Neasi, Barbara J. Como Yo. Hantel, Johanna, illus. (p. 351)
—Just Like Me. Hantel, Johanna, illus. (p. 939)
—So Many Me's. (p. 1602)
—So Many Me's. Ochoa, Ana, illus. (p. 1602)
Neasi, Barbara J. & Ochoa, Ana. Muchas Veces Yo. Ochoa, Ana, illus. (p. 1188)
Neate, Andy, illus. see Deveze, Winky.
Nebelsieck, Ashley. Axis: Dark Shaman. (p. 121)
Nebens, Amy M. Gracious Welcome: Etiquette & Ideas for Welcoming Houseguests. An, Sang, photos by. (p. 705)
Nebesky, Donna Martin. Beatrice the Bear Cub. (p. 153)
Necas, Daniel C., tr. see Culen, Konstantin.
Nechkash, Peg Hutson. Word Catchers for Articulation. (p. 1950)
Necochea, Kristi Landry. First Day of Forever. (p. 594)
Nedelcu, Ovi. Just Like Daddy. (p. 939)
Nee, Chris, jt. auth. see Scollon, Bill.
Neeck, Alessa. Bella Bunhead. (p. 162)
Needham B.Ed, Louise. Flossie's Escape to Freedom. (p. 607)
Needham, James M., illus. see Collard, Sneed B., III.
Needham, Kate. Pony Guide. (p. 1382)
—Usborne the Great Undersea Search. Brooks, Felicity, ed. (p. 1827)
—Why Do People Eat? Spenceley, Annabel & Chen, Kuo Kang, illus. (p. 1924)
Needham, Kate, jt. auth. see O'Brien, Eileen.
Needham, Kate, jt. auth. see Young, Caroline.
Needham, Louise. Adventure with Katy the Pony. (p. 15)
Needham, Peter, tr. see Rowling, J. K.
Needham, T. L. Kitty Claus. (p. 963)
Needham, Tom. Albert Pujols: MVP on & off the Field. (p. 34)
—Tiki Barber: All-Pro on & off the Field. (p. 1749)
Needle, Jan, ed. see Melville, Herman.
Needler, Matthew & Southam, Phil. Minecraft: Construction Handbook (Updated Edition) An Official Mojang Book. (p. 1146)
Needles, Belverd E. Principles of Accounting & Principles of Financial Accounting. (p. 1406)
Neel, Julien. Down in the Dumps. Neel, Julien, illus. (p. 474)
—Lou! Neel, Julien, illus. (p. 1057)
—Lou! 6Pack Set. Neel, Julien, illus. (p. 1057)
—Lou! Single Copy Set. Neel, Julien, illus. (p. 1057)
—Perfect Summer. Neel, Julien, illus. (p. 1342)
—Secret Diary. Neel, Julien, illus. (p. 1540)
—Summertime Blues. Neel, Julien, illus. (p. 1675)
Neel, Julien, illus. see Burrell, Carol Klio.
Neel, Julien & Burrell, Carol Klio. Down in the Dumps. Neel, Julien, illus. (p. 474)
—Perfect Summer. Neel, Julien, illus. (p. 1342)
Neel, Preston, illus. see Appleton-Smith, Laura.
Neeld, Elizabeth Harper. Seven Choices: Finding Daylight after Loss Shatters Your World. (p. 1554)
Neeley, Deta Petersen & Neeley, Nathan Glen. Paul of Tarsus, V2: A Child's Story of the New Testament. (p. 1330)
Neeley, Nathan Glen, jt. auth. see Neeley, Deta Petersen.
Neelly, Linda Page. Musical ConverSings with Children. (p. 1194)
Neelon, Caleb. Lilman Makes a Name for Himself. (p. 1017)
Neely, Anisa. My Ten Little Toes. (p. 1220)
Neely, Daniel, jt. auth. see Manuel, Peter.
Neely, J. Crucifixion - Countdown to a Promise. (p. 386)
—Daily Bible Study Charts & Graphs. (p. 399)
Neely, Judith. And Even More. (p. 71)
—Goodnight Honey Bear. (p. 701)
—Never Too Big for Monkey Hugs. Joslin, Irene, illus. (p. 1243)
Neely, Keith. Illustrated Bible: Joshua / Judges / Ruth. (p. 857)
Neely, Keith, illus. see Aquilina, Michael, III.
Neely, Keith, illus. see Krasner, Steven.
Neely, Keith R., illus. see Davis, Diane.
Neely, Kirk H. Santa Almost Got Caught: Stories for Thanksgiving, Christmas, & the New Year. Cash, Emory, illus. (p. 1511)
Neely, M. W. Saving the Kilda Street Zoo. (p. 1517)
Neely, Scott, illus. see Bright, J. E.
Neely, Scott, illus. see Sazaklis, John.
Neely, Scott, illus. see Sutton, Laurie S.
Neely, Wilma F. Aaron & Abbey Go to School: Trevor Tutors His Friends. (p. 2)
Neeman, Sylvie. Something Big. Godon, Ingrid, illus. (p. 1609)
Neenan, Colin. Idiot! A Love Story with Drama, Betrayal & E-mail. (p. 852)
—Thick. (p. 1732)
Neer, P. J. Cats Can't Fly: Teaching Children to Value New Friendships. Gazsi, Benjamin, illus. (p. 281)
—Home for Ruby: Helping Children Adjust to New Families. Blankenship, Robert, illus. (p. 792)
Nees, Diane L. As Constant As the Stars. Elsen, Janis A., illus. (p. 105)
—Bunny Tail. Lueer, Carmen A., illus. (p. 242)
Nees, Susan. Class Pets. (p. 327)
—Field Trip. (p. 584)
—Picture Day. (p. 1355)
—School Play. (p. 1523)
Neff, C. M. Glue Volcano. (p. 685)
Neff, Ethel Maxine. Packy: The Runaway Elephant. (p. 1317)
—Pokey, the Runaway Bear. (p. 1378)
—Sally: The Runaway Monkey. (p. 1505)
Neff, Fred. Memory Tree. Montmeat, Jack, illus. (p. 1126)
Neff, Henry H. Fiend & the Forge. (p. 584)
—Fiend & the Forge. Neff, Henry H., illus. (p. 584)
—Hound of Rowan. (p. 802)
—Maelstrom: Book Four of the Tapestry. Neff, Henry H., illus. (p. 1070)
—Second Siege. (p. 1539)
Neff, Larry M. Ha Nacido Jesus (Vida de Cristo) (p. 734)
Neff, LaVonne. Jesus Book: 40 Bible Stories. Goffe, Toni, illus. (p. 915)
Neff, Merlin L. Conquering Heroes. (p. 358)
—Mighty Prince. (p. 1140)
Nefflen, Marjorie E. Bashful the Brown-Eyed Dog Gets a Home. (p. 141)
—My Big Sister Knows... (p. 1197)
Neft, David S., et al. Boston Red Sox Fan Book: 100 Years of Red Sox History. (p. 215)
Neftzger, Amy. All That the Dog Ever Wanted. (p. 45)
Negishi, Kyoko & Miyamoto, Yuki. Cafe Kichijouji De (p. 251)
Negley, Sam, jt. auth. see Scholastic, Inc. Staff.
Negri, Paul, jt. auth. see Green, John.
Negrin, Fabian. Princess & the Rainbow Coat. Waters, Fiona, illus. (p. 1403)
—Wizard Tales. (p. 1943)
Negrin, Fabian, illus. see Darwin, Charles.
Negrin, Fabian, illus. see Du Bouchet, Paule.
Negrin, Fabian, illus. see Gousseff, Catherine.
Negrin, Fabian, illus. see Oppenheim, Joanne F.
Negrin, Fabian, tr. see Du Bouchet, Paule.
Negrin, Fabian, tr. see Gousseff, Catherine.
Negron, Eunice. Timothy's Special Weather Report. (p. 1755)
Negroni, Jay. Emerald's Flight (p. 518)
Neher, Anna-Luise. Tale from the Trunk: No. 4 called Yum! Yum! (p. 1699)
—Tale from the Trunk No. 2: With Words! Words! Words! (p. 1699)
Nehme, Marina, jt. auth. see Adams, Michael A.
Nei, Molly, illus. see Bayrock, Fiona.
Nei, Molly, illus. see Niz, Ellen.
Nei, Molly, illus. see Ollen, Rebecca.
Nei, Molly, illus. see Richardson, Adele D.
Neibert, Alissa, illus. see Haskins, Jim & Benson, Kathleen.
Neidich, Warren. Warren Neidich's Blow Up: Photography, Cinema & the Brain (p. 1858)
Neidigh, Sherry, illus. see Donald, Rhonda Lucas.
Neidigh, Sherry, illus. see Hawk, Fran.
Neidigh, Sherry, illus. see Helt Schwaeber, Barbie.
Neidigh, Sherry, illus. see Lynch, Wayne.
Neidigh, Sherry, illus. see Warrick, Karen Clemens.
Neidigh, Sherry, tr. see Warrick, Karen Clemens.
Neighbor, Douglas, illus. see Godell, Rick.
Neighbors, Jared. Rivals (p. 1475)
Neighbors, Jolene. Nobody's Dog. (p. 1262)
Neighbors, Judy. Learn with BunnBunn: Hopping Through Months, Seasons & Holidays. (p. 984)
Neighbour, Leona. Fairly Ballerina Princess. (p. 563)
Neighly, Patrick. Black-Eyed Susan. (p. 196)
—Supernaturalists. (p. 1684)
Neil Armstrong Elementary Students. Neil a Armstrong Student Anthology. (p. 1240)
Neil, Deanna. Land of Curiosities (Book 2)) Lost in Yellowstone, 1872-1873. (p. 973)
—Lost in Yellowstone: The Land of Curiosities, 1872-1873 (p. 1056)
Neil Wallace, Sandra. Muckers. (p. 1188)
Neilan, Eujin Kim, illus. see Pringle, Laurence.
Neilan, Eujin Kim, illus. see San Souci, Daniel.
Neilan, Eujin Kim, illus. see Thong, Roseanne.
Neilan, Eujin Kim, illus. see Williams, Laura E.
Neilands, Lynda. 50 Bible Dramas for Children: For Use in Church, Clubs, & School. (p. 1997)
Neild, Robyn, illus. see Ward, Wendy.
Neill, Chloe. Charmfall. (p. 294)
—Firespell: A Novel of the Dark Elite. (p. 592)
Neill, Grace. Luke & His Motorbike. (p. 1064)
Neill, Hugh, jt. auth. see Quadling, Douglas.
Neill, Jane, jt. auth. see Gilliam, Thomas.
Neill, Joan Walmer. Amazing Tale of Bub the Trier. (p. 56)
Neill, John R., illus. see Baum, L. Frank.
Neill, John R., illus. see Thompson, Ruth Plumly & Baum, L. Frank.
Neill, Patricia S. Christmas Is a Gift from God. (p. 314)
Neilly, Lori Ann. Oracle & the Mirror. (p. 1301)
Neils, Jenifer & Tracy, Stephen V. Games at Athens. (p. 654)
Neilsen, L. Michelle, jt. auth. see Nielsen, L. Michelle.
Neilson, G. E. F. Cosmic Aviators - Book 1 - Flight Edition. (p. 368)
—Cosmic Aviators - Nathaniel's 1st Adventure. (p. 368)
Neilson, G. G. Beogall's Choice - How a Boy & a Bird Rescue Nature. (p. 166)
Neilson, Ginger. Gunter the Underwater Elephant. Neilson, Ginger, illus. (p. 732)
Neilson, Heidi, illus. see Lewis, Richard.
Neilson, Joseph T. War & Pieces: Damn You Vietnam. (p. 1857)
Neiman, Jahcolyn Russell. Kekula. (p. 948)
Neiman, Tommy & Reynolds, Sue. Sirens for the Cross for the Rookie Rescuer. Reynolds, Sue & Hygh, Angela, eds. (p. 1581)
Neimark, Anne E. Johnny Cash: A Twentieth-Century Life. (p. 923)
—Johnny Cash. (p. 923)
—Mythmaker: The Life of J. R. R. Tolkien, Creator of the Hobbit & the Lord of the Rings. Weinman, Brad, illus. (p. 1227)
Neimark, Gillian. Golden Rectangle. (p. 695)
—Secret Spiral. (p. 1544)
Neimark, Jill. Hugging Tree: A Story about Resilience. Wong, Nicole, illus. (p. 825)
Neimark, Jill, jt. auth. see Weiner, Marcella Bakur.
Neimark, Jill & Weiner, Marcella Bakur. Toodles & Teeny: A Story about Friendship. (p. 1767)
Neimark, Susie. Adventures of Sunny & the Chocolate Dog: Sunny Meets Her Baby Sister. Hammerstrom, Kent, illus. (p. 23)
—Adventures of Sunny & the Chocolate Dog: Sunny & the Chocolate Dog Go to the Beach. Hammerstrom, Kent, illus. (p. 23)
—Adventures of Sunny & the Chocolate Dog: Sunny & the Chocolate Dog Go to the Doctor. Hammerstrom, Kent, illus. (p. 23)
Neipris, Janet. Jeremy & the Thinking Machine: A Musical for Young Audiences. (p. 913)
Neira, Elsy. Kid That Flew to the Moon: El niño que volo a la Luna. (p. 951)
Neira, Maria Lia. Accesorios Con Chaquiras - Transformer Muebles Con Pintura. (p. 8)
—Accesorios Con Semillas - Juguetes de Madera. (p. 8)
—Arte Ruso Sobre Laminas de Aluminio: El Teatro y los Titeres. Panamericana Editorial, ed. (p. 103)
—Articulos en Cuero: Articulos con Madera. Panamericana Staff, ed. (p. 104)
—Bordados de la Abuela - Origami. (p. 213)
—Con Flores y Esencias: Simbolos de Tradicion. (p. 355)
—Decoracion con Sellos. (p. 422)
—Decorando al Estilo Country: Papel Hecho A Mano. (p. 422)
—Decorar con Chocolate: Recetas de la Abuela. (p. 422)
—Flores Frescas para el Matrimonio: Decorando Utensilios para la Casa. Panamericana Editorial, ed. (p. 606)
—Frutas para Ocasiones Especiales: Con Carton y Papel Articulos para el Escritorio. Panamericana Editorial, ed. (p. 646)
—Marcos para Todo USO/Vistiendo la Cocina. Panamericana Staff, ed. (p. 1092)
—Munecos de Trapo: A la Luz de las Velas. (p. 1191)
—Papier Mache - Entre Espumas y Fragancias. (p. 1323)
—Para Uso Personal: Decoracion con Frutas Verduras. (p. 1323)
—Pintar Paredes: Maquillaje de Fantasia. Panamericana Staff, ed. (p. 1361)
—Preparando la Primera Comunion: Para Decorar su Hogar A Traves de los Cristales. (p. 1395)
—Utensilios en Madera para su Mesa: Ideas para Modernizar Sus Prendas. Panamericana Editorial, ed. (p. 1829)
Neira, Muyi, illus. see Escobar, Melba.
Neis, Izzy. I Want to Potty. Shakir, Susie, illus. (p. 848)
Neis, Therese. Extraordinary African-American Poets. (p. 555)
Neissany, Ebrahim. Muchos Errores Muchas Vidas: Kabbalah, la Reencarnacion, Y el Proposito de la Vida. (p. 1188)
Neitz, Erica, illus. see Mills, Andy & Osborn, Becky.
Neitz, Erica, tr. see Mills, Andy & Osborn, Becky.
Neitzel, Shirley. Who Will I Be? A Halloween Rebus Story. Parker, Nancy Winslow, illus. (p. 1919)
Nejime, Shoichi. Bit by Bit. Castles, Heather, illus. (p. 193)
Nekounam, Hannah. My New Baby Brother. (p. 1216)
Nekrasov, Andrei. Adventures of Captain Vrungel. Kay, Nicole, tr. from ENG. (p. 17)
Nell, William C. Black Patriots of the American Revolution, with Sketches of Several Distinguished Black Persons to Which Is Added a Brief Survey of the Condition & Prospects of Black Americans. (p. 196)
Nelligan, Kevin, illus. see Nelligan, Patty.
Nelligan, Patty. Peppy Up: Eat Your Best, Be Your Best! Ocello, Salvatore & Nelligan, Kevin, illus. (p. 1340)
Nellis, Philip, illus. see Persons, Marjorie Kiel.
Nellist, Glenys. Love Letters from God: Bible Stories Allsopp, Sophie, illus. (p. 1060)
Nelly. Nelly Music Manga. (p. 1240)
Nelms, Davis Kenyon. Inner-Fire Kindling: Simple Exercises for the Permanent Establishment of Fulfilling Thoughts. (p. 875)
Nelms, Kate, illus. see Butterworth, Chris.
Nelms, Kate, illus. see Butterworth, Christine.
Nelsen, Marjorie R. Child's Book of Responsibilities: Developing Self-reliance Through Guided Tasks Ages 3 - 8 Years. (p. 304)
—Gently into Sleep, A Bedtime Ritual: A Child's Delightful Bedtime Routine with a Definite Beginning & a Definite, No Tears Ending Ages 2-6 Years. (p. 661)
Nelsen, Sissy. Wiggy & Giggly. (p. 1928)
Nelson. Finding Places: American Readers. (p. 588)
—Looking Out, Climbing Up, Going Far: American Readers. (p. 1051)
—Marching Along: American Readers. (p. 1091)
—Moving On: American Readers. (p. 1183)
—Turning Corners: American Readers. (p. 1798)
Nelson, Adam K. Night with St. Nick. (p. 1254)
Nelson, Alan E., jt. auth. see Nelson, Linda S.
Nelson, Alexis Andria. Sing Mommie Sing: Lullabies from the Heart. (p. 1579)
Nelson, Amanda. Buttermilk Biscuit Boy Klein, Laurie, illus. (p. 248)
Nelson, Andy. Carl Larsson Coloring Book. (p. 269)
—Impressionists Coloring Book. Nelson, Andy, illus. (p. 862)
—Renaissance Painters Coloring Book: Donatello, Raphael, Leonardo & Michelangelo. (p. 1460)
Nelson, Angela, ed. see Rodriguez, David.
Nelson, Annabelle. Angelica's Hope: A Story for Young People & Their Parents about the Need to Talk about Things That No One Talks About. Palomares, Franz, illus. (p. 74)
—Ricardo's Pain: A Story for Young People & Their Parents about Staying Strong, Finding Courage & Overcoming Adversity. Palomares, Franz, illus. (p. 1469)
Nelson, Anndria, illus. see Williams, Shannon.
Nelson, Annika, illus. see Soto, Gary.
Nelson, Annika, illus. see Yonikus, Sandi.
Nelson, Annika M., illus. see Barnes, Brynne.
Nelson, Ashley Howard, jt. auth. see Robertson, Si.
Nelson, Beth. Science Spectacular Physics: Enhanced Online Edition. (p. 1528)
Nelson Bibles Staff, jt. auth. see Thomas Nelson Publishing Staff.
Nelson, Birgitta. Sacking of Visby. (p. 1500)
Nelson, Blake. Destroy All Cars. (p. 431)
—Girl. (p. 678)
—New Rules of High School. (p. 1247)
—Paranoid Park. (p. 1324)
—Prom Anonymous. (p. 1411)
Nelson, Brett Alan. Magical Forest. Ueda, Kumiko, illus. (p. 1074)
Nelson, Bruce. Captain Black Licorice. (p. 263)
Nelson, Bruce M. Magician's Hat. (p. 1075)
Nelson, Carmen R. Jacob & Katie in Japan: The Adventures of Tcks in a New Home. (p. 904)
Nelson, Casey, illus. see Buck, Deanna Draper.
Nelson, Casey, illus. see Jones, Nathan Smith.
Nelson, Charlie. Circus Life. (p. 322)
Nelson, Christine, illus. see Collisin, Shauna.
Nelson, Christine, illus. see Collison, Shauna.
Nelson, Connie. Lizard's Secret Door. Waller, Joyce, illus. (p. 1043)
Nelson, Craig, illus. see Eareckson Tada, Joni.
Nelson, Cyndi. Rocky Mountain Mushrooms: Edible & Poisonous. (p. 1484)
Nelson, Cyndi, jt. auth. see Miller, Millie.
Nelson, D. J. One-Eyed Spotogon. (p. 1294)
Nelson, David. Teen Drug Abuse. (p. 1713)
Nelson, David E. Chile. Greenhaven Press Editors, ed. (p. 305)
Nelson, David, ed. Penguin Dictionary of Mathematics. (p. 1336)
—Race in John Howard Griffinrsquo's Black Like Me. (p. 1431)
Nelson, David Erik. Soldering. (p. 1607)
Nelson, David K. Trucking with Noah: North Dakota to Arizona. (p. 1791)
Nelson, Deanna. Amazing Stevie B. (p. 56)
Nelson, Dianne, ed. see Webster, Jeanne.
Nelson, Dianne Elizabeth. By Here. (p. 249)
Nelson, Don, illus. see Heal, Edith.
Nelson, Douglas, jt. auth. see Nelson, Ray.
Nelson, Drew. Armored Vehicles. (p. 100)
—Dealing with Cyberbullies. (p. 418)
—Green Berets. (p. 721)
—Haunted! the Tower of London. (p. 754)
—Life on an Oil Rig. (p. 1012)
—Meet the Supreme Court. (p. 1123)
—Navy SEALs. (p. 1238)
—Submarines & Submersibles. (p. 1671)
Nelson, Drew, jt. auth. see Nelson, Vaunda Micheaux.
Nelson, Dwayne. Merlin's Book of Poems. (p. 1128)
Nelson, Edward William, jt. auth. see Du Puy, William Atherton.
Nelson, Elizabeth Stowe. Night Before the First Christmas. (p. 1253)
Nelson, Ernist, illus. see Flying Eagle & Whispering Wind.
Nelson, Esther. Movement Games for Children of All Ages. (p. 1183)
Nelson, Esther & Hirsch, Davida. Riggeldy Jiggeldy Joggeldy Jam: Can You Guess Who I Am? Ellis, Libby, illus. (p. 1472)
—Riggeldy Jiggeldy Joggeldy Roo: Can You Guess What I Do? Ellis, Libby, illus. (p. 1472)
Nelson, Esther L. Everybody Sing & Dance. (p. 543)
Nelson, Esther Whitt, ed. see Carter, Aubrey Smith.
Nelson, G. Lynn. Writing & Being: Embracing Your Life Through Creative Journaling. (p. 1964)
Nelson, Gail M. & Nelson, Katie M. Go Eat, Pete. Nelson, Gail M., illus. (p. 686)
Nelson, Gayle, et al. Do As I Say: Operations, Procedures, & Rituals for Language Acquisition. (p. 456)
Nelson, H. Erin. Bibletoons: Book One: Adventure with Noah. (p. 176)
Nelson, Heather L. Daisy the Protector Dog. (p. 401)
Nelson, Holly. Ig's Apples. (p. 856)
Nelson, Holly, illus. see Johnson, Alice W. & Warner, Allison H.
Nelson, J. Ron & Marchland-Martella, Nancy. Multiple Meaning Vocabulary Program: Level I. (p. 1190)
—Multiple Meaning Vocabulary Program: Level II. (p. 1190)
—Multiple Meaning Vocabulary Program Instructor's Manual: Level I & Level II. (p. 1190)
Nelson, J. Ron, et al. Instructional Practices for Students with Behavioral Disorders: Strategies for Reading, Writing, & Math. (p. 878)
Nelson, Jacob. And Then There Was Jake. (p. 71)
Nelson, James Gary. Dientecito y la Placa Peligros. Bumstead, Debbie, illus. (p. 437)
—Smileytooth & Bushwack Plaque. Bumstead, Debbie, illus. (p. 1594)
—Smileytooth & the Castle Hassle. Bumstead, Debbie, illus. (p. 1594)
—Smileytooth & the Plaque Attack. Bumstead, Debbie, illus. (p. 1594)
Nelson, Jan. Signs of Love. Bohart, Lisa, illus. (p. 1574)
Nelson, Jandy. I'll Give You the Sun. (p. 856)
—Sky Is Everywhere. (p. 1586)
Nelson, Jane E., illus. see Murphy, Elspeth Campbell.
Nelson, Jennifer K., jt. auth. see Cleary, Brian P.
Nelson, Jim. Bear Encounters: Tales from the Wild. (p. 150)
—Crosstown Crush. (p. 385)
Nelson, Jim, illus. see Worth, Bonnie.
Nelson, Jim, illus. see Zoehfeld, Kathleen Weidner.
Nelson, Jo. Welcome to the Museum: Historium. Wilkinson, Richard, illus. (p. 1874)
Nelson, Jo & Bustamente, Martin. Copernicus, Galileo & Newton. (p. 365)
Nelson, Joanne. When It Snows. Moore, Cyd, illus. (p. 1903)
Nelson, John. Collision Course: Asteroids & Earth. (p. 341)
—Polar Ice Caps in Danger: Expedition to Antarctica. (p. 1379)
—Trayectoría de Choque: Los Asteroides y la Tierra. (p. 1781)
Nelson, John & Obregón, José María. Casquetes Polares en Riesgo: Expedición a la Antártida. (p. 276)
Nelson, Jon. Story of Snow: The Science of Winter's Wonder. Cassino, Mark, photos by. (p. 1660)
Nelson, Judy, illus. see Kenna, Kara.
Nelson, Judy, illus. see Reasoner, Charles.
Nelson, Judy A., illus. see Kenna, Kara.
Nelson, Julie. Families Change: A Book for Children Experiencing Termination of Parental Rights. Gallagher, Mary, illus. (p. 567)

—Kids Are Important: A Book for Young Children in Foster Care. (p. 952)
—Kids Need to Be Safe: A Book for Children in Foster Care. Gallagher, Mary, illus. (p. 954)
Nelson, Kadir. Baby Bear. Nelson, Kadir, illus. (p. 125)
—Heart & Soul: The Story of America & African Americans. (p. 759)
—Heart & Soul: The Story of America & African Americans. Nelson, Kadir, illus. (p. 759)
—He's Got the Whole World in His Hands. (p. 774)
—He's Got the Whole World in His Hands. Nelson, Kadir, illus. (p. 774)
—If You Plant a Seed. Nelson, Kadir, illus. (p. 854)
—Nelson Mandela. (p. 1240)
—Nelson Mandela. Nelson, Kadir, illus. (p. 1240)
—We Are the Ship: The Story of Negro League Baseball. (p. 1866)
—We Are the Ship: The Story of Negro League Baseball. Nelson, Kadir, illus. (p. 1866)
Nelson, Kadir, illus. see Allen, Debbie.
Nelson, Kadir, illus. see De la Peña, Matt.
Nelson, Kadir, illus. see Green, Michelle Y.
Nelson, Kadir, illus. see Grifalconi, Ann.
Nelson, Kadir, illus. see Jordan, Deloris & Jordan, Roslyn M.
Nelson, Kadir, illus. see Jordan, Deloris.
Nelson, Kadir, illus. see King, Martin Luther, Jr.
Nelson, Kadir, illus. see Lee, Spike & Lee, Tonya Lewis.
Nelson, Kadir, illus. see Lee, Tonya Lewis & Lee, Spike.
Nelson, Kadir, illus. see Levine, Ellen.
Nelson, Kadir, illus. see Napoli, Donna Jo.
Nelson, Kadir, illus. see Nolen, Jerdine.
Nelson, Kadir, illus. see Rappaport, Doreen.
Nelson, Kadir, illus. see Richardson, Charisse K.
Nelson, Kadir, illus. see Robinson, Sharon.
Nelson, Kadir, illus. see Shange, Ntozake.
Nelson, Kadir, illus. see Staines, Bill.
Nelson, Kadir, illus. see Weatherford, Carole Boston.
Nelson, Kadir, jt. auth. see Obama, Barack.
Nelson, Karen, creator. Crystal Brave: Literature Theme Unit. (p. 387)
Nelson, Kathy Harvey. Ev: The Perfect Little Puppy. (p. 540)
Nelson, Katie M., jt. auth. see Nelson, Gail M.
Nelson, Kristin. King Josiah & God's Book. (p. 958)
—Tractores Agricolas. Translations.com Staff, tr. from ENG. (p. 1775)
Nelson, Kristin L. African Rhinos. (p. 28)
—Alamo. (p. 33)
—Camionetas Gigantes. Translations.com Staff, tr. from ENG. (p. 256)
—Dentists. (p. 427)
—EMTs. (p. 521)
—Farm Tractors on the Move. (p. 574)
—Let's Look at Sharks. (p. 999)
—Lincoln Memorial. (p. 1018)
—Monster Trucks on the Move. (p. 1168)
—Tractores Agricolas. Translations.com Staff, tr. from ENG. (p. 1775)
—Washington Monument. (p. 1860)
Nelson, Linda. Friends of Choice. (p. 638)
Nelson, Linda & Logie, Daniel. Writing Sourcebook: Foundations for Writing. (p. 1965)
Nelson, Linda S. & Nelson, Alan E. Child Care Administration: Planning Quality Programs for Young Children. (p. 301)
—Child Care Administration Planning Quality Programs for Young Children. (p. 301)
Nelson, Lisa W. Mammoth Site: A Treasure of Clues to the Past. (p. 1085)
Nelson, Lori. Hillary's BIG Business Adventure. (p. 780)
Nelson, M. R. Zebra Said Shhh. Sheldon, Tamia, illus. (p. 1985)
Nelson, M. Rae & Krapp, Kristine M. Experiment Central: Understanding Scientific Principles Through Projects. (p. 549)
Nelson, Maria. 20 Fun Facts about Dragonflies. (p. 1995)
—20 Fun Facts about the US Flag. (p. 1995)
—Bald Eagle. (p. 133)
—Cells up Close. (p. 286)
—Coretta Scott King. (p. 367)
—Earth's Minerals. (p. 498)
—Gross Things about Your Food. (p. 725)
—Gross Things in Your House. (p. 725)
—Heroes of the US Marines. (p. 773)
—I Am a Good Friend. (p. 832)
—I Am a Good Neighbor. (p. 832)
—I Am Polite. (p. 833)
—I Can Listen. (p. 836)
—I Can Share. (p. 836)
—I Can Volunteer. (p. 837)
—Igneous Rocks. (p. 856)
—I'm Allergic to Milk. (p. 858)
—I'm Allergic to Peanuts. (p. 858)
—I'm Allergic to Pets. (p. 858)
—I'm Allergic to Strawberries. (p. 858)
—I'm Allergic to Wheat. (p. 858)
—Jokes & More about Bees. (p. 924)
—Jokes & More about Dogs. (p. 924)
—Jokes & More about Fish. (p. 924)
—Jokes & More about Horses. (p. 924)
—Jokes & More about Monkeys & Apes. (p. 924)
—Jokes & More about Snakes. (p. 924)
—Labrador Retrievers. (p. 970)
—Liberty Bell. (p. 1005)
—Life of Abigail Adams. (p. 1011)
—Life of Abigail Adams / la Vida de Abigail Adams. (p. 1011)
—Life of Abraham Lincoln. (p. 1011)
—Life of Abraham Lincoln / la Vida de Abraham Lincoln. (p. 1011)
—Life of Ben Franklin. (p. 1011)
—Life of Ben Franklin / la Vida de BenjamiN Franklin. (p. 1011)
—Life of George Washington. (p. 1012)
—Life of George Washington / la Vida de George Washington. (p. 1012)
—Life of Paul Revere. (p. 1012)
—Life of Paul Revere / la Vida de Paul Revere. (p. 1012)
—Life of Sacagawea. (p. 1012)
—Life on the International Space Station. (p. 1012)
—Mastiffs. (p. 1103)
—Metamorphic Rocks. (p. 1130)
—National Anthem. (p. 1231)
—Red Cloud. (p. 1453)
—Red Jacket. (p. 1454)
—Robert Pattinson. (p. 1479)
—Rock Cycle. (p. 1482)
—Saint Bernards. (p. 1503)
—Saying Please & Thank You. (p. 1519)
—Sedimentary Rocks. (p. 1546)
—Selena Gomez. (p. 1549)
—Taylor Lautner. (p. 1708)
—Weathering & Erosion. (p. 1870)
Nelson, Marian, jt. auth. see Yankee, Kris.
Nelson, Marietjie, jt. auth. see Penning, L.
Nelson, Marilyn. Fortune's Bones: The Manumission Requiem. (p. 623)
—Freedom Business: Including a Narrative of the Life & Adventures of Venture, a Native of Africa. Dancy, Deborah & Muirhead, Deborah, illus. (p. 634)
—How I Discovered Poetry. Hooper, Hadley, illus. (p. 810)
—Ostrich & Lark. Artists of the Kuru Art Project in Botswana, San, illus. (p. 1306)
—Pemba's Song. (p. 1336)
—Snook Alone. Ering, Timothy Basil, illus. (p. 1598)
—Wreath for Emmett Till. Lardy, Philippe, illus. (p. 1962)
Nelson, Marilyn, jt. auth. see Alexander, Elizabeth.
Nelson, Marilyn, tr. see Rasmussen, Halfdan.
Nelson, Mary. Catla & the Vikings (p. 280)
Nelson, Mary Beth, illus. see McMahon, Kara.
Nelson, Mary Beth, illus. see RH Disney Staff, et al.
Nelson, Mary Beth & Linn, Laurent. Elmo's Big Word Book/el Libro Grande de Palabras de Elmo. Barrett, John E., photos by. (p. 515)
Nelson, Marybeth, jt. auth. see Weiss, Ellen.
Nelson, Megan, illus. see Freedman, Sharon.
Nelson, Michael. Queen Victoria & the Discovery of the Riviera. (p. 1425)
Nelson, Michael Alan. Hexed: The Sisters of Witchdown. (p. 774)
—Second Wave. Chee, illus. (p. 1540)
Nelson, Michael Alan, jt. auth. see Cosby, Andrew.
Nelson, Michiyo, illus. see Scholastic Book Editors.
Nelson, Michiyo, illus. see Scholastic, Inc. Staff.
Nelson, N. A. Bringing the Boy Home. (p. 229)
Nelson, Nancy. Grandma's Drip Castles. (p. 708)
Nelson, O. T. Girl Who Owned a City: Graphic Novel. Delk, Chrissy, illus. (p. 679)
—Girl Who Owned a City. (p. 679)
Nelson, O. T., jt. auth. see Jolley, Dan.
Nelson, Peter. Creature Keepers & the Hijacked Hydro-Hide. Rao, Rohitash, illus. (p. 380)
—Herbert's Wormhole: The Rise & Fall of el Solo Libre. (p. 769)
—Herbert's Wormhole: AeroStar & the 3 1/2-Point Plan of Vengeance. (p. 769)
—Herbert's Wormhole: The Rise & Fall of el Solo Libre. Rao, Rohitash, illus. (p. 769)
—Herbert's Wormhole: AeroStar & the 3 1/2-Point Plan of Vengeance. Rao, Rohitash, illus. (p. 769)
—Herbert's Wormhole. Rao, Rohitash, illus. (p. 769)
—Herbert's Wormhole: AeroStar & the 3 1/2-Point Plan of Vengeance. Rao, Rohitash, illus. (p. 769)
—Left for Dead. (p. 987)
—Rise & Fall of el Solo Libre. Rao, Rohitash, illus. (p. 1474)
Nelson, R. Sammy the Spider Likes to Bite: Moral of the Story - Just Because You Can Bite, Does Not Mean You Should Bite. (p. 1508)
Nelson, R. A. Breathe My Name. (p. 226)
—Teach Me. (p. 1708)
—Throat. (p. 1744)
Nelson, Ray & Nelson, Douglas. Greetings from America: Postcards from Donovan Willoughby. Tronslin, Andrea, ed. (p. 723)
Nelson, Rhonda. Life Adventures of Robbie Dog Volume 1: A Children's Book to Help with Understanding Hard Life Events. (p. 1007)
Nelson, Richard E., jt. auth. see Galas, Judith C.
Nelson, Robert Lyn. Ocean Friends. (p. 1276)
Nelson, Robin. Am I a Good Friend? A Book about Trustworthiness. (p. 51)
—Apple Trees. (p. 92)
—Baseball Is Fun! (p. 141)
—Basketball Is Fun! (p. 143)
—Being a Leader. (p. 160)
—Being Fair. (p. 161)
—Being Responsible. (p. 161)
—Can People Count on Me? A Book about Responsibility. (p. 258)
—Carnes y las Proteinas. Castañer, Mercedes P. & Fitzpatrick, Julia, trs. (p. 270)
—Chickens. (p. 300)
—Ciclo Del Agua (Earth's Water Cycle) (p. 319)
—Cielo de Noche (the Night Sky) (p. 319)
—Circle. (p. 321)
—Clothing. (p. 334)
—Cloudy. (p. 335)
—Cómo Se Mueven Las Cosas. Translations.com Staff, tr. from ENG. (p. 351)
—Como Se Mueven Las Cosas; Way Things Move. (p. 351)
—Constitution Day. (p. 359)
—Cows. (p. 374)
—Dairy. (p. 400)
—Dance Is Fun! (p. 402)
—Dandelions. (p. 403)
—Day & Night. (p. 412)
—De la Cera Al Crayon. Translations.com Staff, tr. from ENG. (p. 416)
—Deer. (p. 423)
—Del Cemento Al Puente. Translations.com Staff, tr. from ENG. (p. 424)
—Día Con Viento. Translations.com Staff, tr. from ENG. (p. 433)
—Día Lluvioso. Translations.com Staff, tr. from ENG. (p. 433)
—Día Nevado. Translations.com Staff, tr. from ENG. (p. 433)
—Día Nublado. Translations.com Staff, tr. from ENG. (p. 433)
—Día Soleado. Translations.com Staff, tr. from ENG. (p. 433)
—Día y Noche (Day & Night) (p. 433)
—Dragonflies. (p. 478)
—Earth's Water Cycle. (p. 498)
—Empujar y Jalar. Translations.com Staff, tr. from ENG. (p. 521)
—Empujar Y Jalar; Push & Pull. (p. 521)
—Estaciones (Seasons) (p. 538)
—Exercising. (p. 548)
—Fats, Oils, & Sweets. (p. 577)
—First Step Nonfiction: Discovering Nature's Cycles (p. 597)
—Flag Day. (p. 602)
—Flotar y Hundirse. Translations.com Staff, tr. from ENG. (p. 607)
—Flotar Y Hundirse; Float & Sink. (p. 607)
—Following Rules. (p. 612)
—Food. (p. 612)
—Football Is Fun! (p. 615)
—Freezing & Melting. (p. 635)
—From Cocoa Bean to Chocolate. (p. 642)
—From Cotton to T-Shirt. (p. 642)
—From Egg to Chicken. (p. 642)
—From Flower to Honey. (p. 642)
—From Foal to Horse. (p. 642)
—From Kernel to Corn. (p. 643)
—From Leather to Basketball Shoes. (p. 643)
—From Leather to Football. (p. 643)
—From Peanut to Peanut Butter. (p. 643)
—From Plastic to Soccer Ball. (p. 643)
—From Sea to Salt. (p. 643)
—From Sheep to Sweater. (p. 643)
—From Steel to Bicycle. (p. 643)
—From Wax to Crayon. (p. 644)
—From Wood to Baseball Bat. (p. 644)
—Fuerzas Y Movimiento; Forces & Motion: Classroom Set. (p. 646)
—Fuerzas Y Movimiento (Forces & Motion) Complete Set. (p. 646)
—George Washington Carver: A Life of Devotion. (p. 664)
—Germany. (p. 666)
—Getting Rest. (p. 669)
—Globes. (p. 685)
—Goats. (p. 687)
—Grains. (p. 706)
—Grasshoppers. (p. 711)
—Gravedad. Translations.com Staff, tr. from ENG. (p. 712)
—Gravedad; Gravity. (p. 712)
—Gravity. (p. 712)
—Gusto. Translations.com Staff, tr. from ENG. (p. 733)
—Hibernación. (p. 775)
—Hibernation. (p. 775)
—Homes. (p. 793)
—Horses. (p. 800)
—How Can I Help? A Book about Caring. (p. 805)
—How I Clean My Room. (p. 810)
—How I Reduce, Reuse, & Recycle. (p. 810)
—How We Clean up a Park. (p. 823)
—Jobs. (p. 919)
—Jugar Sin Peligro. Aguirre, Barbara & Fitzpatrick, Julia, trs. (p. 931)
—Juneteenth. (p. 934)
—Land. (p. 973)
—Las Frutas. Castañer, Mercedes & Fitzpatrick, Julia, trs. (p. 976)
—Las Grasas, los Aceites, y los Dulces. Castañer, Mercedes P. & Fitzpatrick, Julia, trs. (p. 976)
—Las Verduras. Castañer, Mercedes & Fitzpatrick, Julia, trs. (p. 977)
—Let's Make a Bar Graph. (p. 999)
—Let's Make a Circle Graph. (p. 999)
—Let's Make a Picture Graph. (p. 999)
—Let's Make a Tally Chart. (p. 999)
—Los Cereales. Castañer, Mercedes & Fitzpatrick, Julia, trs. (p. 1053)
—Los Imanes. Translations.com Staff, tr. from ENG. (p. 1054)
—Los Imanes; Magnets. (p. 1054)
—Los Productos Lacteos. Castañer, Mercedes & Fitzpatrick, Julia, trs. (p. 1054)
—Maps. (p. 1090)
—Meats & Proteins. (p. 1118)
—Mi Primer Paso al Mundo Real - Fuerzas y Movimiento (First Step Nonfiction - Forces & Motion) Translations.com Staff, tr. (p. 1133)
—Migración. (p. 1140)
—Migration. (p. 1141)
—Morocco. (p. 1176)
—Mother Teresa: A Life of Caring. (p. 1178)
—Night Sky. (p. 1254)
—Obedecer Las Reglas. Translations.com Staff, tr. from ENG. (p. 1275)
—Olfato. Translations.com Staff, tr. from ENG. (p. 1285)
—Pigs. (p. 1358)
—Playing Safely. (p. 1372)
—Pumpkins. (p. 1416)
—Push & Pull. (p. 1420)
—Que Es el Agua? Castañer, Mercedes & Fitzpatrick, Julia, trs. (p. 1423)
—Rainy. (p. 1436)
—Rectangle. (p. 1452)
—Respecting Others. (p. 1463)
—Respetar a los Demás. Translations.com Staff, tr. from ENG. (p. 1463)
—Robins. (p. 1480)
—Salamanders. (p. 1504)
—Se Congela y Se Derrite. Castañer, Mercedes & Fitzpatrick, Julia, trs. (p. 1534)
—Seasons. (p. 1538)
—Selena Gomez: Pop Star & Actress. (p. 1549)
—Ser Justo. Translations.com Staff, tr. (p. 1552)
—Ser un Lider. Translations.com Staff, tr. (p. 1552)
—Sheep. (p. 1564)
—Snowy. (p. 1601)
—Soccer Is Fun! (p. 1603)
—Squares. (p. 1636)
—Staying Clean. (p. 1645)
—Staying Safe in Emergencies. (p. 1645)
—Strawberries. (p. 1666)
—Sunflowers. (p. 1676)
—Sunny. (p. 1677)
—Swimming Is Fun! (p. 1691)
—Tacto. Translations.com Staff, tr. from ENG. (p. 1695)
—Tally Charts. (p. 1704)
—Taylor Swift: Country Pop Hit Maker. (p. 1708)
—Thanksgiving. (p. 1725)
—Tomatoes. (p. 1764)
—Triangle. (p. 1785)
—Usamos el Agua. Castañer, Mercedes & Fitzpatrick, Julia, trs. from ENG. (p. 1826)
—Vegetables. (p. 1834)
—Veterans Day. (p. 1839)
—Vista. Translations.com Staff, tr. from ENG. (p. 1846)
—Water. (p. 1862)
—We Use Water. (p. 1868)
—What Do Pliers Do? (p. 1882)
—What Do We Buy? A Look at Goods & Services. (p. 1882)
—What Does a Hammer Do? (p. 1883)
—What Does a Level Do? (p. 1883)
—What Does a Saw Do? (p. 1884)
—What Does a Screwdriver Do? (p. 1884)
—What Does a Wrench Do? (p. 1884)
—What Is Water? (p. 1891)
—Windy. (p. 1936)
—Working Then & Now. (p. 1953)
—Worms. (p. 1961)
—¿Dónde Hay Agua? Castañer, Mercedes P. & Fitzpatrick, Julia, trs. (p. 466)
Nelson, Robin, jt. auth. see Lanier, Wendy.
Nelson, Robin, jt. auth. see Owings, Lisa.
Nelson, Robin & Donovan, Sandra. Congress: A Look at the Legislative Branch. (p. 357)
—Getting Elected: A Look at Running for Office. (p. 669)
Nelson, Robin & Donovan, Sandy. Congress: A Look at the Legislative Branch. (p. 357)
—Getting Elected: A Look at Running for Office. (p. 669)
Nelson, Roger. Does God Watch the Super Bowl? Christians & Sports. (p. 460)
Nelson, S. D. Black Elk's Vision: A Lakota Story. (p. 196)
—Buffalo Bird Girl: A Hidatsa Story. (p. 235)
—Coyote Christmas: A Lakota Story. (p. 374)
—Greet the Dawn: The Lakota Way. (p. 723)
—Quiet Hero: The Ira Hayes Story. (p. 1428)
—Star People: A Lakota Story. (p. 1641)
Nelson, S. D., illus. see Bruchac, Joseph.
Nelson, S. D., illus. see Zitkala-Sa.
Nelson, S. D., tr. see Bruchac, Joseph.
Nelson, Sam. Addict. (p. 11)
Nelson, Sandi. Fly on the Wall Street. Beckstrand, Jared, illus. (p. 609)
Nelson, Sara. Butterflies. (p. 247)
—Stay Safe! How You Can Keep Out of Harm's Way. (p. 1645)
Nelson, Sara E., jt. auth. see Nelson, Sara Elizabeth.
Nelson, Sara Elizabeth & Nelson, Sara E. Let's Reduce Garbage! (p. 1000)
—Let's Reuse! (p. 1000)
—Let's Save Energy! (p. 1000)
—Let's Save Water! (p. 1000)
Nelson, Sara Kirsten. Stay Safe! How You Can Keep Out of Harm's Way. Desrocher, Jack, illus. (p. 1645)
Nelson, Sarah. Just for You. (p. 938)
Nelson, Sarah, illus. see Werner, Sharon, et al.
Nelson, Scott. Mulch the Lawnmower. (p. 1189)
—My Tummy Disaster. (p. 1220)
—Patch the Porcupine & the Bike Shop Job. Nelson, Scott, illus. (p. 1328)
Nelson, Scott, photos by see Teitelbaum, Michael.
Nelson, Scott Reynolds & Aronson, Marc. Ain't Nothing but a Man: My Quest to Find the Real John Henry. (p. 30)
Nelson, Sean. Bungles Does the Bunny Op. (p. 242)
—Bungles Loses His Marbles. (p. 242)
Nelson, Seth. We Love Art Class! Analyze, Compare, Create, & Compose Shapes. (p. 1867)
Nelson, Shannon, illus. see May, Cynthia.
Nelson, Shareese. Me Inside. (p. 1116)
Nelson, Sharlene P., jt. auth. see Nelson, Ted W.
Nelson, Sheila. Americans Divided: The Civil War. (p. 64)
—Birth of the un, Decolonization & Building Strong Nations Russett, Bruce, ed. (p. 192)
—Britain's Canada, 1613-1770. (p. 229)
—Canada's Changing Society, 1984-the Present. (p. 260)
—Cultural Globalization & Celebrating Diversity Russett, Bruce, ed. (p. 391)
—Decolonization: Dismantling Empires & Building Independence. (p. 422)
—From Sea to Shining Sea: Americans Move West (p. 643)
—From the Atlantic to the Pacific: Canadian Expansion, 1867-1909. (p. 644)
—Hallucinogens: Unreal Visions. (p. 739)
—Hallucinogens: Unreal Visions. Henningfield, Jack E., ed. (p. 739)
—International Law & Playing by the Rules Russett, Bruce, ed. (p. 880)
—Nation Is Born: World War I & Independence, 1910-1929. (p. 1231)
—Never Again: Survivors of the Holocaust. (p. 1242)
—Original United States of America. (p. 1304)
—Redefining Canada: A Developing Identity, 1960-1984. (p. 1455)
—Southern Colonies: The Quest for Prosperity. (p. 1617)
—Thomas Jefferson's America: The Louisiana Purchase (1800-1811) (p. 1739)
—What the Land Means to Americans: Alaska & Other Wilderness Areas (1865-1890) (p. 1893)
Nelson, Sheila & Livingston, Phyllis. Youth Who Are Gifted: Integrating Talents & Intelligence. (p. 1982)
Nelson, Sheila & Walker, Ida. Youth with Cancer: Facing the Shadows. (p. 1982)

N

Nelson, Sheila & Zoldak, Joyce. In Defense of Our Country: Survivors of Military Conflict. (p. 863)
Nelson, Sheila, et al. In Defense of Our Country: Survivors of Military Conflict. (p. 863)
Nelson, Sheila K. Backpack Bears' Adventure: Friendship. (p. 130)
—Backpack Bears' Adventure: No Bullies Allowed. Kerber, Kathy, illus. (p. 130)
Nelson, Steve, jt. auth. see Rollins, Jack.
Nelson, Steve, jt. auth. see Rollins, Walter.
Nelson, Steve & Rollins, Jack. Here Comes Peter Cottontail Levy, Pamela R., illus. (p. 770)
—Here Comes Peter Cottontail! (p. 770)
—Here Comes Peter Cottontail! Levy, Pamela R., illus. (p. 770)
—Here Comes Peter Cottontail. Rasmussen, Wendy, illus. (p. 770)
Nelson, Su. I'm No Dummy! (p. 859)
Nelson, Sue Ellen. Missing Easter Bunny. (p. 1152)
Nelson, Suzanne. Heart & Salsa. (p. 759)
—Horseshoe. Nowak, Cheri, illus. (p. 800)
Nelson, Suzanne Marie. Cake Pop Crush. (p. 252)
—Dead in the Water. (p. 416)
—Ghoul Next Door. (p. 673)
—You're Bacon Me Crazy. (p. 1982)
Nelson, Sybil. Priscilla the Great: The Kiss of Life. (p. 1407)
—Priscilla the Great the Kiss of Life. (p. 1407)
—Priscilla the Great Too Little Too Late. (p. 1407)
Nelson, Tamieka Lewis -. Step Friend. (p. 1647)
Nelson, Ted W. & Nelson, Sharlene P. Nez Perce. (p. 1249)
Nelson, Thea. Swute's Stories: The Circle Must Grow. Smith, Nina & Nelson, Thea, illus. (p. 1692)
Nelson, Theresa. Ruby Electric. (p. 1493)
Nelson, Valerie. I Can Do It Myself! (p. 835)
Nelson, Vaunda Micheaux. Almost to Freedom. Bootman, Colin, illus. (p. 48)
—Bad News for Outlaws: The Remarkable Life of Bass Reeves, Deputy U. S. Marshall. Christie, R. Gregory, illus. (p. 132)
—Book Itch: Freedom, Truth & Harlem's Greatest Bookstore. Christie, R. Gregory, illus. (p. 210)
—Grandma Nell. Zunon, Elizabeth, illus. (p. 708)
—No Crystal Stair: A Documentary Novel of the Life & Work of Lewis Michaux, Harlem Bookseller. Christie, R. Gregory, illus. (p. 1258)
Nelson, Vaunda Micheaux & Nelson, Drew. Juneteenth. Schroder, Mark, illus. (p. 934)
Nelson, Walter Henry. Buddha: His Life & His Teaching. (p. 234)
Nelson, Wendy Watson. Not Even Once Club: My Promise to Heavenly Father. Dorman, Brandon, illus. (p. 1267)
Nelson, Will, illus. see Galvin, Laura Gates.
Nelson, Will, illus. see Moody-Luther, Jacqueline.
Nelson, Will, illus. see Schwaeber, Barbie Heit.
Nelson, William, illus. see Stonesifer, Gertrude.
Nelson-Anderson, Joanna. Dragonfly Ceremony. (p. 478)
Nelson-Anderson, Joanna "J. O. ". I Spy a Dragonfly. (p. 846)
Nelson-Schmidt, Michelle. Bob Is a Unicorn. Nelson-Schmidt, Michelle, illus. (p. 205)
—Cats, Cats! (p. 281)
—Cats, Cats! Nelson-Schmidt, Michelle, illus. (p. 281)
—Dogs, Dogs! Nelson-Schmidt, Michelle, illus. (p. 462)
—Jonathan James & the Whatif Monster. (p. 925)
—Jonathan James & the Whatif Monster. Nelson-Schmidt, Michelle, illus. (p. 925)
Neme, Laurel. Orangutan Houdini. Kelleher, Kathie, illus. (p. 1302)
Nemec, Gale. Great Elephant Rescue. (p. 715)
Nemec, Gale & Guy, Big. Little Stockey & the Miracle of Christmas. (p. 1037)
Nemec, Nina. Play with Scissors & Little Miss Scribble. (p. 1372)
Nemec, Thomas F., creator. Owenopolis: A New Childrens Book, Created by Thomas Nemec-N. Y. C. (p. 1314)
Nemerdy, Edward. Another Place in Space. (p. 88)
Nemerson, Roy. Daniel Boone. (p. 405)
Nemet, Andrea, illus. see Schmidt, Hans-Christian.
Nemet, Andreas, illus. see Schmidt, Hans-Christian & Schmid, A, HC;Nemet.
Nemeth, Jason D. Atmosphere. (p. 113)
—Climate Change. (p. 332)
—Earth's Layers. (p. 498)
—Ice Ages. (p. 850)
—Matt Hardy (p. 1109)
—Plate Tectonics. (p. 1370)
—Randy Orton (p. 1438)
—Rivers, Lakes, & Oceans. (p. 1476)
—Voices of the Civil War: Stories from the Battlefields (p. 1848)
—Voices of the Civil War. (p. 1848)
Nemeth, Jason D., jt. auth. see Brown, Louann Mattes.
Nemeth, Jason D. & Skog, Jason. Kurt Angle (p. 968)
Nemett, Barry, illus. see Leopold, Nikia Speliakos Clark.
Nemett, Laini, illus. see Leopold, Nikia Speliakos Clark.
Nemiroff, Marc, jt. auth. see Annunziata, Jane.
Nemiroff, Marc A. & Annunziata, Jane. All about Adoption: How Families Are Made & How Kids Feel about It. Koeller, Carol, tr. (p. 42)
—Shy Spaghetti & Excited Eggs: A Kid's Menu of Feelings. Battuz, Christine, illus. (p. 1572)
Nemmers, Lee. Monsters: An Art Activity Book for Creative Kids of All Ages. Zschock, Martha Day, illus. (p. 1168)
—No Monsters Here! A Bedtime Shadow Book. Zschock, Martha Day, illus. (p. 1259)
—Scratch & Sketch Trace-Along Constellations: An Art Activity Book for Artistic Stargazers of All Ages. Zschock, Martha Day, illus. (p. 1532)
—Scratch & Sketch Trace-Along Robots: An Art Activity Book for Artistic Inventors of All Ages. Wheeler, David Cole, illus. (p. 1532)
Nemmers, Tom. Knights Scratch & Sketch: For Brave Artists & Loyal Subjects of All Ages. Barbas Steckler, Kerren, illus. (p. 964)
—Pirates Scratch & Sketch: For Adventurous Artists & Explorers of All Ages. Zschock, Martha Day, illus. (p. 1364)
Nemukula, Zandile. I Am No Better Than You. (p. 833)
Nemzer, Marilyn, ed. Energy for Keeps: An Illustrated Guide for Everyone Who Uses Electricity (p. 528)
Nena L. Kircher & Julie A. Kircher. Laid Back Legend of the Three Billy Goats Gruff. (p. 971)
Neno, Michael. Children's Magical Adventure: 1 the Rescue. (p. 303)
Neogi, Joyeeta, illus. see Williams, Vivienne.
NeonSeon. Life of Shouty: Good Habits NeonSeon, illus. (p. 1012)
—Life of Shouty: Food & Fitness NeonSeon, illus. (p. 1012)
Nèostlinger, Christine. Abuelo Misterioso. Pastor, Luis, tr. (p. 7)
—Konrad. Ampudia, María Jesús & Wittkamp, Frantz, trs. (p. 967)
Nepomniachi, Leonid, illus. see Dayan, Linda Marcos.
Nepomniatchi, Leonid, illus. see Barrera, Norma Anabel.
Neradova, Maria, illus. see Ruzicka, Oldrich & Kolcavova, Klara.
Neri, G. Chess Rumble. Watson, Jesse Joshua, illus. (p. 298)
—Ghetto Cowboy. Watson, Jesse Joshua, illus. (p. 670)
—Hello, I'm Johnny Cash. Ford, A. G., illus. (p. 764)
—Knockout Games. (p. 965)
Neri, G. & DuBurke, Randy. Yummy: The Last Days of a Southside Shorty. (p. 1983)
Neri, Greg. Surf Mules. (p. 1685)
—Tru & Nelle. (p. 1790)
Neri, P. J. Hawaii. (p. 755)
Nerlove, Miriam, illus. see Olswanger, Anna.
Nero, Molly. Smarty Pig & the Test Taking Terror. Turchan, Monique, illus. (p. 1593)
Neru, Enna. African Tale. (p. 28)
Neruda, Pablo. Veinte Poemas de Amor y una Canción Desesperada. (p. 1834)
Nerve.com Editors. Naughty Crosswords. (p. 1237)
—Position of the Day Playbook: Sex Every Day in Every Way. (p. 1387)
—Positions of the Day: Sex Every Day in Every Way. (p. 1387)
Nervelle, Rosemarie. Witch of Beaver Creek Mine. (p. 1941)
Nesbet, Anne. Box of Gargoyles. (p. 216)
—Cabinet of Earths. (p. 250)
—Wrinkled Crown. (p. 1963)
Nesbit, E. 7 Books in 1 - "The Railway Children", "Five Children & It", "The Phoenix & the Carpet", "The Story of the Amulet", "The Story of the Treasure-Seekers", "The Would-Be-Goods" & "The Enchanted Castle" (p. 1992)
—Beautiful Stories from Shakespeare. (p. 154)
—Beautiful Stories from Shakespeare (Yesterday's Classics) (p. 154)
—Book of Dragons. (p. 211)
—Book of Dragons. Fell, H. Granville & Millar, H. R., illus. (p. 211)
—Butterfly Alphabet Counter. (p. 247)
—Enchanted Castle. (p. 523)
—Five Children & It. (p. 600)
—Five Children & It. Millar, H. R., illus. (p. 600)
—Five Children & It. Hische, Jessica, illus. (p. 600)
—Five Children & It. Nesbit, E. & Millar, H. R., illus. (p. 600)
—Five Children & It. Oxford University Press Staff & Bassett, Jennifer, eds. (p. 600)
—Harding's Luck. (p. 748)
—House of Arden. (p. 803)
—In Homespun. (p. 863)
—Jack & the Beanstalk. Tavares, Matt, illus. (p. 902)
—Magic City. (p. 1072)
—Magic World. (p. 1074)
—New Treasure Seekers. (p. 1247)
—Oswald Bastable & Others. (p. 1306)
—Phoenix & the Carpet. (p. 1351)
—Phoenix & the Carpet. Millar, H., illus. (p. 1351)
—Railway Children. (p. 1434)
—Railway Children. Brock, C. E., illus. (p. 1434)
—Railway Children. Dryhurst, Dinah, tr. (p. 1434)
—Railway Children. Hartmetz, Richard, ed. (p. 1434)
—Railway Children. Brock, Charles Edmund, illus. (p. 1434)
—Rainbow & the Rose. (p. 1435)
—Red House. (p. 1454)
—Seven Dragons & Other Stories. (p. 1554)
—Shakespeare's Stories for Young Readers. (p. 1559)
—Story of the Amulet. (p. 1660)
—Story of the Treasure Seekers: Being the Adventures of the Bastable Children in Search of a Fortune. (p. 1662)
—Story of the Treasure Seekers. (p. 1662)
—These Little Ones. (p. 1732)
—Wet Magic. (p. 1877)
—Wouldbegoods. (p. 1962)
Nesbit, E. & Edith, Nesbit. Salvadores del Pais. Zwerger, Lisbeth, illus. (p. 1506)
Nesbit, Edith. Flehes an Hens Horn. Williams, Nicholas, tr. from ENG. (p. 603)
—Phoenix & the Carpet. (p. 1351)
—Pussy & Doggy Tales. (p. 1420)
Nesbit, Sara E. Mary Wants to Be an Artist. (p. 1101)
Nesbit, Troy. Diamond Cave Mystery. (p. 434)
—Forest Fire Mystery. (p. 618)
—Indian Mummy Mystery. (p. 871)
—Jinx of Payrock Canyon. (p. 919)
—Mystery at Rustlers Fort. (p. 1223)
—Sand Dune Pony. (p. 1510)
Nesbitt, Ken. When the Teacher Isn't Looking: And Other Funny School Poems. Gordon, Mike, illus. (p. 1905)
Nesbitt, Kenn. Aliens Have Landed at Our School! Lucas, Margeaux, illus. (p. 41)
—Believe It or Not, My Brother Has a Monster! Slonim, David, illus. (p. 161)
—Kiss, Kiss Good Night. Elliott, Rebecca, illus. (p. 961)
—More Bears! Cummings, Troy, illus. (p. 1174)
—Revenge of the Lunch Ladies: The Hilarious Book of School Poetry. Gordon, Mike & Gordon, Carl, illus. (p. 1466)
—Ultimate Top Secret Guide to Taking over the World. Long, Ethan, illus. (p. 1810)
—When the Teacher Isn't Looking: And Other Funny School Poems. Gordon, Mike, illus. (p. 1905)
Nesbitt, Kenn, jt. auth. see Lewis, J. Patrick.
Nesbitt, Kris, jt. auth. see Lau, Barbara.
Nesbitt, M. L. Grammar-Land. Waddy, F., illus. (p. 706)
Nesbitt, Mark R., ed. Living in Renaissance Italy. (p. 1041)
Nesbitt, Shawntelle. Kids' Power Series Teacher Resource (p. 955)
Nesbo, Jo. Bubble in the Bathtub. Chace, Tara F., tr. (p. 233)
—Bubble in the Bathtub. Chace, Tara, tr. from NOR. (p. 233)
—Doctor Proctor's Fart Powder. (p. 459)
—Doctor Proctor's Fart Powder. Chace, Tara F., tr. (p. 459)
—Doctor Proctor's Fart Powder. Chace, Tara, tr. from GER. (p. 459)
—Magical Fruit. (p. 1074)
—Magical Fruit. Chace, Tara F., tr. from NOR. (p. 1074)
—Who Cut the Cheese? (p. 1915)
—Who Cut the Cheese? Chace, Tara F., tr. (p. 1915)
—Who Cut the Cheese? Chace, Tara, tr. from NOR. (p. 1915)
Nesci, Andrea Lynn & Nesci, Jim. Bubba: A True Story about an Amazing Alligator. Kostelyk, Jason, illus. (p. 233)
Nesci, Jim, jt. auth. see Nesci, Andrea Lynn.
NeSmith, R. Keao, tr. see Carroll, Lewis, pseud.
Nesquens, Daniel & Martos Sánchez, José Daniel. Kangu Va de Excursión. Arguilé, Elisa, illus. (p. 942)
Nesquens, Daniel & Schimel, Lawrence. Mister H. Lozano, Luciano, illus. (p. 1155)
Ness, Berthetta. Originals: Short Stories for Children. (p. 1304)
Ness, Howard, jt. auth. see Broyles, Duane.
Ness, Immanuel & Ciment, James. Encyclopedia of Third Parties in America (p. 525)
Ness, Patrick. Ask & the Answer (p. 106)
—Ask & the Answer. (p. 106)
—Monster Calls: Inspired by an Idea from Siobhan Dowd. (p. 1166)
—Monster Calls: Inspired by an Idea from Siobhan Dowd. Kay, Jim, illus. (p. 1166)
—Monsters of Men (p. 1169)
—More Than This. (p. 1175)
—Rest of Us Just Live Here. (p. 1464)
Ness, Shirley Fillmore. Mom's New Testament Bible Stories: Heroes & Scoundrels. (p. 1163)
Nessa, J. B. Princess Gracie's Journey to Heaven. (p. 1404)
Nesselrode, Sandra. Princess Kelsie & Her Special Gifts. (p. 1404)
Nestell, Mark. Gordon & the Magic Fishbowl Daley-Prado, M. J., illus. (p. 702)
Nester, Tony. Desert Survival Tips, Tricks, & Skills. (p. 429)
Nester, William. Arikara War: The First Plains Indian War, 1823 (p. 98)
Nesterova, Natalia, illus. see Powers, David M. F.
Nestler, Dave. Dave Nestler Sketchbook Volume 2 (p. 410)
Nestler, David. Art of Dave Nestler. (p. 102)
Nestor, James. Role of Fiction: How Our Own Imaginations Enrich Our Lives. (p. 1485)
Nestor, John. Rivers. (p. 1476)
—Volcanoes. (p. 1849)
Nestorowich, Sherry. Wisdom of the Golden Goose. (p. 1939)
Netelkos, Jason, jt. auth. see Jovinelly, Joann.
Nethaway, Misty. I Know My Mommy Loves Me. (p. 840)
Nethery, Mary, jt. auth. see Larson, Kirby.
Nethery, Susan, illus. see Shulman, Mark.
NETS Project Staff, et al. NETS*S Curriculum Series: Multidisciplinary Units for Prekindergarten Through Grade 2. (p. 1242)
Nettis, Donna, illus. see Grier, Kerry.
Nettles, Granny Sarah A. I Baked Cookies at Granny's House. (p. 834)
Nettles Jr, J. H. Hit Em' with Words Jones, Jeff, illus. (p. 785)
Nettles, Sarah A. Benjamin, the Bully & the Butterfly. (p. 165)
Nettleton, Pamela Hill. Amazing Body Shipe, Becky, illus. (p. 54)
—Bend & Stretch: Learning about Your Bones & Muscles. Shipe, Becky, illus. (p. 164)
—Benjamin Franklin: Writer, Inventor, Statesman. Yesh, Jeff, illus. (p. 165)
—Biographies Yesh, Jeff, illus. (p. 188)
—Breathe in, Breathe Out: Learning about Your Lungs. Shipe, Becky, illus. (p. 226)
—George Washington: Farmer, Soldier, President. Yesh, Jeff, illus. (p. 664)
—Gurgles & Growls: Learning about Your Stomach. Shipe, Becky, illus. (p. 732)
—Look, Listen, Taste, Touch, & Smell: Learning about Your Five Senses. Shipe, Becky, illus. (p. 1049)
—Martin Luther King Jr. Preacher, Freedom Fighter, Peacemaker. Yesh, Jeff & Nichols, Garry, illus. (p. 1098)
—Pitch In! Kids Talk about Cooperation. Muehlenhardt, Amy Bailey, illus. (p. 1364)
—Pocahontas: Peacemaker & Friend to the Colonists. Yesh, Jeff, illus. (p. 1375)
—Sally Ride: Astronaut, Scientist, Teacher. Yesh, Jeff & Nichols, Garry, illus. (p. 1505)
—Think, Think, Think: Learning about Your Brain. Shipe, Becky, illus. (p. 1734)
Netto, Lydia, tr. see Cleary, Beverly.
Nettrour, Autumn, illus. see Nettrour, Nelani.
Nettrour, Heather, illus. see Nettrour, Nelani A.
Nettrour, Heather, illus. see Nettrour, Nelani.
Nettrour, Nelani. Angels in Training. (p. 75)
—Banshees: Dragon Lands. Bk. 2 Nettrour, Heather, illus. (p. 136)
—Dragon Lands: The Ripple. Bk. 1 Nettrour, Heather, illus. (p. 477)
—Dragonfly Flight. Lesnick, Tina, illus. (p. 478)
—Dragonlands: The Village. Bk. 3 (p. 478)
—Imagynairs of Jemmidar (p. 861)
—Imagynairs of Jemmidar. Nettrour, Autumn, illus. (p. 861)
—Jodi & the Seasons. Nettrour, Heather, illus. (p. 919)
—Jodi's Bugs. Nettrour, Heather, illus. (p. 919)
—Jodi's Garden. (p. 919)
—Meeshu's Keep: Dragon Guardians. Bk. 1 Nettrour, Heather, illus. (p. 1120)
—Nunkey's Adventures: Birth of Reekey. Bk. 2 (p. 1273)
—Nunkey's Adventures Nettrour, Autumn, illus. (p. 1273)
—Sun Griffins: Dragonlands, Book 4. (p. 1676)
Nettrour, Nelani A. All about Krammer: Dogtails 2. Nettrour, Heather, illus. (p. 42)
Netzel, Carmen, tr. see Pullman, Philip.
Netzley, Patricia. Cell Phones: Threats to Privacy & Security. (p. 286)
—How Do Video Games Affect Society? (p. 807)
netzley, patricia. Paranormal Activity. (p. 1324)
Netzley, Patricia D. Alien Encounters. (p. 40)
—Do Vampires Exist? (p. 457)
—Do Witches Exist? (p. 457)
—How Do Cell Phones Affect Health? (p. 806)
netzley, patricia D. How Does Cell Phone Use Impact Teenagers? (p. 808)
Netzley, Patricia D. How Does Video Game Violence Affect Society? (p. 809)
netzley, patricia D. How Serious a Threat Are Online Predators? (p. 812)
Netzley, Patricia D. Is Legalized Marijuana Good for Society? (p. 889)
—Teens & Sexting. (p. 1715)
—Video Games, Violence & Crime. (p. 1841)
—What Impact Does Mental Illness Have on Crime? (p. 1887)
Neu, Debra, illus. see Lohnes, Marilyn.
Neu, Kerrian. Picture Book Writing & Creation: A Companion to Picture Book Writing & Creation. (p. 1355)
—Picture Book Writing & Creation. (p. 1355)
Neu, Laronia. Nicole's New Book. (p. 1251)
Neubauer, Bonnie. Emblem3: Test Your Super-Fan Status: Packed with Puzzles, Quizzes, Crosswords, & More! (p. 517)
Neubauer, Jeffrey. Fuck You Book. (p. 646)
Neubauer, Joan & Steve, ed. Noble Generation (p. 1262)
Neubauer, Julie. Ten Little Freckles. (p. 1719)
Neubeck, Jon. Quest. (p. 1426)
Neubecker, Robert. Days of the Knights. (p. 415)
—Linus the Vegetarian T. Rex. Neubecker, Robert, illus. (p. 1019)
—Racing the Waves. (p. 1432)
—Scholastic Reader Level 2: Tales of the Time Dragon #2: Racing the Waves. (p. 1522)
—Scholastic Reader Level 2: Tales of the Time Dragon #1: Days of the Knights. (p. 1522)
—Too Many Monsters! A Halloween Counting Book. Neubecker, Robert, illus. (p. 1766)
—What Little Boys Are Made Of. Neubecker, Robert, illus. (p. 1891)
—Winter Is for Snow. Neubecker, Robert, illus. (p. 1938)
Neubecker, Robert, illus. see Bagert, Brod.
Neubecker, Robert, illus. see Braeuner, Shellie.
Neubecker, Robert, illus. see Cuyler, Margery.
Neubecker, Robert, illus. see Florian, Douglas.
Neubecker, Robert, illus. see Katz, Susan.
Neubecker, Robert, illus. see Lithgow, John.
Neubecker, Robert, illus. see Regan, Dian Curtis.
Neubecker, Robert, illus. see Richards, Dan.
Neubecker, Robert, illus. see Weeks, Sarah.
Neuberger, Anne E. Blessed Kateria & the Cross in the Forest. (p. 199)
Neubert, Oliver. Chantel's Quest for the Enchanted Medallion. (p. 291)
—Chantel's Quest for the Golden Sword. (p. 291)
—Chantel's Quest for the Silver Leaf. (p. 291)
Neuborne, Ellen & Sade, Orly. How Ella Grew an Electric Guitar. (p. 809)
Neuburger, Emily K. Show Me a Story: 40 Craft Projects & Activities to Spark Children's Storytelling. (p. 1570)
Neuburger, Jenny, illus. see Danner, Pamela.
Neuburger, Jenny, illus. see Goss, Leon.
Neuburger, Kimberly. Take the Fear Out of Basic Algebra. (p. 1697)
—Take the Fear out of Basic Algebra & Take the Fear Out of Intermediate Algebra (p. 1697)
—Take the Fear Out of Basic Math. (p. 1697)
Neuendorf, Abedi -, jt. auth. see Abedi, Isabel.
Neuendorf, Silvio, illus. see Abedi, Isabel & Neuendorf, Abedi -.
Neuenschwander, B. L. That's Not a Unicorn. (p. 1727)
Neufeld, John. Edgar Allan. (p. 504)
—Lisa, Bright & Dark: A Novel. (p. 1022)
Neufeld, Josh. Few Perfect Hours & Other Stories from Southeast Asia & Central Europe. (p. 583)
Neufeld, Juliana, illus. see Patterson, James & Grabenstein, Chris.
Neufeld, Juliana, illus. see Patterson, James, et al.
Neufeld, Juliana, illus. see Shraya, Vivek.
Neugroschel, Joachim, jt. auth. see Hoffmann, E. T. A.
Neuharth, Dan. Secrets You Keep from Yourself: How to Stop Sabotaging Your Happiness. (p. 1546)
Neuhaus, David. His Finest Hour. (p. 781)
Neuhaus, Julia, illus. see Gouichoux, René.
Neuhaus, Richard A. Science Projects: Book 1. Project Ideas in the Life Sciences Gormley, Julia Ann, illus. (p. 1527)
—Science Projects: How to Collect, Analyze, & Present Your Data. Gormley, Julia Ann, illus. (p. 1527)
—Science Projects: Book 2. Project ideas in Chemistry & Biochemistry Gormley, Julia Ann, illus. (p. 1527)
Neuhauser, Sandra. Celebrating Life: One Page at a Time. (p. 285)
Neuhofer, Sheri L. Courageous Warrior. Amory, Deanna & O'Hara, Cynthia, illus. (p. 373)
Neuls, Lillian. It's Okay to Talk to God. L'Eplattenier, Michelle, illus. (p. 898)
Neuman, Carolyn. Adventures with the Winglets. (p. 25)
Neuman, M. Robert. Clawing & Scratching & Thumping About. (p. 330)
Neuman, Maria & Dorling Kindersley Publishing Staff. Fabulous Hair. Coppola, Angela, photos by. (p. 560)
Neuman, Pearl. Bloodsucking Leeches. (p. 201)
Neuman, Richard, illus. see Gabel, Stacey.
Neuman, Susan. National Geographic Readers: Jump Pup! (p. 1233)
—Swim Fish! (p. 1690)
Neuman, Susan B. National Geographic Readers: Go Cub! (p. 1233)
—Swing Sloth! Explore the Rain Forest. (p. 1691)

Neuman, Susan B., jt. auth. see National Geographic Kids Staff.
Neumann, A. C. Drawer's Gift. (p. 481)
Neumann, Dietrich. Joe & the Skyscraper: The Empire State Building in New York City. Heritage, Anne, tr. (p. 920)
Neumann, Jeanne L. Wendell the Weasel. (p. 1875)
Neumann, Jeff. How Do You Do? (p. 808)
Neumann, Marty G. Adventures of Woodmouth & Moxy the Monkey: A Merry Christmas. (p. 24)
Neumeier, Rachel. Black Dog. (p. 195)
—Floating Islands. (p. 605)
Neumeyer, P. & Gorey, E. Donald Boxed Set. (p. 465)
Neumeyer, Peter F. & Gorey, Edward. Why We Have Day & Night. (p. 1926)
Neundorf, Alyse. Navajo/English Bilingual Dictionary: Alchini Bi Naaltsoostsoh. (p. 1237)
Neusca, Guy, Jr., illus. see Beasley, Jonathan & Porter, Rosanna I.
Neuschwander, Angel & Johnston, Becky. Gretchen Asks, How Do Cars Work? (p. 723)
Neuschwander, Cindy. Mummy Math: An Adventure in Geometry. Langdo, Bryan, illus. (p. 1191)
—Pastry School in Paris: An Adventure in Capacity. Langdo, Bryan, illus. (p. 1327)
—Sir Cumference & All the King's Tens. Geehan, Wayne, illus. (p. 1580)
—Sir Cumference & the Isle of Immeter. Geehan, Wayne, illus. (p. 1580)
—Sir Cumference & the off-The-Charts Dessert. (p. 1580)
—Sir Cumference & the Roundabout Battle. Geehan, Wayne, illus. (p. 1580)
—Sir Cumference & the Viking's Map. Geehan, Wayne, illus. (p. 1580)
Neuschwander, Cindy & Geehan, Wayne. Sir Cumference & the off-The-Charts Dessert. (p. 1580)
Neusner, Dena. Fun at the County Fair. Carbajal, Richard & Stubbs, Tommy, illus. (p. 647)
Neusner, Dena & Running Press Staff. Johnny Tractor's Fun Farm Day. Fuller, Steve, illus. (p. 923)
Neusner, Dena, et al. Danny Dozer Hits a Home Run. (p. 405)
—Danny Dozer's Perfect Christmas Tree. (p. 405)
Neusner, Dena Wallenstein. Colors of Spring. McKee, Darren, illus. (p. 345)
Neusner, Sam. Bounce Bounce Bounce. (p. 216)
Neusom, Sherman. Big Fat Hunka Cheese's Quest Restored Svelte. (p. 181)
Neuville, Loyal de, illus. see Cohen, Lee.
Nevarez, Lisa, illus. see McMilin, Jack.
Nevarez, Lisa D., illus. see McMilin, Jack D.
Nevels, Lourene. Dog's Life. (p. 463)
Nevers, Merri B. Lonely Lucille. (p. 1046)
Neves, Diogenes, illus. see Kirkman, Robert.
Neves, Vanessa Leonor. Tommy's Big Race. (p. 1765)
Neveu, Fred, illus. see Howard-Parham, Pam.
Neveu, Fred, illus. see Vonthron, Satanta C.
Nevid, Jeffrey S. Psychology: Concepts & Applications. (p. 1413)
—Psychology Premium Blackboard: Used with ... Nevid-Psychology: Concepts & Applications. (p. 1413)
Neville, Bill, illus. see Pyne, Lynette & Pressnall, Debra Olson.
Nevins, Daniel, illus. see Ehrlich, Amy.
Nevins, Debbie, jt. auth. see DuBois, Jill.
Nevins, Debbie, jt. auth. see Dubois, Jill.
Nevins, Debbie, jt. auth. see Esbenshade, Richard S.
Nevins, Debbie, jt. auth. see Fuller, Barbara.
Nevins, Debbie, jt. auth. see Levy, Patricia.
Nevins, Debbie, jt. auth. see Sheehan, Sean.
Nevins, Mary. Adventures of Molly. (p. 20)
Nevins, Paul. Dante's War. (p. 406)
Nevis, Lance. Animal Rain. Laible MBA, Steve William, ed. (p. 79)
—Pollywog Prince. Laible MBA, Steve William, ed. (p. 1381)
—Silly Stew. Laible MBA, Steve William, ed. (p. 1576)
Nevius, Carol. Baseball Hour Thomson, Bill, illus. (p. 141)
—Building with Dad Thomson, Bill, illus. (p. 239)
—Karate Hour Thomson, Bill, illus. (p. 943)
—Soccer Hour Thomson, Bill, illus. (p. 1603)
Nevius, Carol & Nevius, Thomson. Karate Hour Thomson, Bill, illus. (p. 943)
Nevius, Kate. Cuento de Penguina Antes de Dormir / Penguina's Bedtime Story. (p. 389)
—Penguina's Bedtime Story. (p. 1337)
Nevius, Thomson, jt. auth. see Nevius, Carol.
New Burlington Books, creator. Great Big Book of Bedtime Stories & Rhyme. (p. 714)
New, David W. Constitution for Beginners. (p. 359)
—Religious Freedom in America for Beginners. (p. 1458)
—Ten Commandments for Beginners. (p. 1718)
New Frontiers Group. There's Nobody Like You! The World of Howie & Friends. (p. 1731)
New Holland Staff. My Diary. (p. 1201)
New Life Publishing House. down to Earth God: Devotionals for the Nature Lover. (p. 474)
New Mexico School for the Deaf Staff, 2nd Grade. Too Many Hands??? (p. 1766)
New Players Club LLC Staff, New Players Club L. L. C. Coco Boom Boom. (p. 337)
New Strategist Publications, Incorporated Staff. Who's Buying Entertainment. (p. 1920)
New, William. Dream Helmet. Bevis, Vivian, illus. (p. 483)
—Llamas in the Laundry. Bevis, Vivian, illus. (p. 1043)
—Sam Swallow & the Riddleworld League Yayo, illus. (p. 1507)
New, William H. Year I Was Grounded (p. 1969)
New York City High School Staff, ed. Sonny Paine. (p. 1612)
New York City Students Staff. 82NYC Review. Seeley, Scott & Potts, Sam, illus. (p. 1998)
New York Hall of Science Staff. Charlie & Kiwi: An Evolutionary Adventure. Reynolds, Peter H. & Fable Vision Studios Staff, illus. (p. 292)
New York Public Library Staff. Folk Music of the Western Hemisphere: A List of References in the New York Public Library, Compiled by Julius Mattfield, Music Division. (p. 611)
New York Times Staff. Cup of Tea & Crosswords: 75 Light & Easy Puzzles. Shortz, Will, ed. (p. 392)
—New York Times after Dinner Crosswords: 75 Refreshing Puzzles. Shortz, Will, ed. (p. 1248)
—New York Times Biggest Beach Crossword Omnibus: 200 Super, Sunny Puzzles. Maleska, Eugene T., ed. (p. 1248)
—New York Times Crosswords for a Relaxing Vacation: 200 Light & Easy Puzzles. Shortz, Will, ed. (p. 1248)
—New York Times Crosswords for Stress Relief: Light & Easy Puzzles. Shortz, Will, ed. (p. 1248)
—New York Times Expand Your Mind Crosswords: 75 Brain-Boosting Puzzles. Shortz, Will, ed. (p. 1248)
—New York Times Jewish Cookbook: More Than 825 Traditional & Contemporary Recipes from Around the World. Amster, Linda, ed. (p. 1248)
—New York Times Sunday Brunch Crosswords: From the Pages of the New York Times. Shortz, Will, ed. (p. 1248)
—New York Times Tough Crossword Puzzle Omnibus: 200 Challenging Puzzles from the New York Times. Vol. 1 Shortz, Will, ed. (p. 1248)
—New York Times Ultimate Crossword Omnibus: 1,001 Puzzles from the New York Times. Shortz, Will, ed. (p. 1248)
—New York Times Will Shortz Presents Crosswords to Go: Fun, Portable Puzzles. Shortz, Will, ed. (p. 1248)
—Sunday Crossword Omnibus: 200 World-Famous Sunday Puzzles from the Pages of the New York Times. Vol. 7 Shortz, Will, ed. (p. 1676)
—Sunday Crossword Puzzles: 50 Sunday Puzzles from the Pages of the New York Times. Vol. 31 Shortz, Will, ed. (p. 1676)
New York Times Staff, jt. auth. see Shortz, Will.
New York Times Staff, et al. Best DVDs You've Never Seen, Just Missed or Almost Forgotten: A Guide for the Curious Film Lover. Nichols, Peter M., ed. (p. 169)
New York Transit Museum Staff. New York City Subway Trains: 12 Classic Punch-and-Build Trains. (p. 1248)
Newark, Tim. In Heroes' Footsteps: A Walker's Guide to the Battlefields of the World. (p. 863)
Newberry, Clare Turlay. Marshmallow. Newberry, Clare Turlay, illus. (p. 1096)
Newberry, Gabriel S. Elli & Gabe's Big Christmas Adventure. (p. 514)
Newberry, Geoffrey C. Cape Don Adventure. (p. 262)
Newberry, Loretta, illus. see Marlow, Herb.
Newberry, Peggy. Margie & the Goat. (p. 1092)
Newbery, Elizabeth. First Elizabeth. (p. 594)
Newbery, L. Azul, el Gato de Humo. (p. 122)
—Poni de Mermelada. (p. 1382)
Newbery, Linda. Andie's Moon. (p. 72)
—Dog Called Whatnot. (p. 461)
—Polly's March. (p. 1381)
—Posy. Rayner, Catherine, illus. (p. 1388)
Newbigging, Martha, illus. see Bourgeois, Paulette.
Newbigging, Martha, illus. see Butcher, Kristin.
Newbigging, Martha, illus. see Coulter, Laurie.
Newbigging, Martha, illus. see Galloway, Priscilla.
Newbigging, Martha, illus. see Kyi, Tanya Lloyd.
Newbigging, Martha, illus. see Shulman, Mark & Krog, Hazlitt.
Newbigging, Martha, illus. see Toronto Public Library & Toronto Public Library.
Newbigging, Martha, illus. see Toronto Public Library.
Newbigging, Martha, illus. see Tsiang, Sarah.
Newbigging, Mary, illus. see Coulter, Laurie.
Newbigging, Robert Delford. Robert Rat Has A Problem: A Tale of Broccoli. (p. 1479)
Newbigin, Lesslie. Unfinished Agenda. (p. 1817)
Newbold, Dale L. Funny Facts & Fun Facts! (p. 649)
Newbold, Keva N. Family's Sorrow. (p. 569)
Newborne, David / F., illus. see Chidebelu-Eze / Dove Publishing, Chibueze Obi.
Newborne, David / F., illus. see Chidebelu-Eze/Dove Publishing, Chibueze / Obi.
Newbound, Andrew. Ghoul Strike! (p. 673)
Newby, Jae. Dimensions of a Woman. (p. 440)
Newby, John. Heart of the Game. (p. 759)
—Summer Dreams. (p. 1674)
Newby, Rick. Rocky Mountains Region (p. 1484)
Newby-Tynes, Claudia. His Love Flows. (p. 781)
Newcomb, Ambrose. Eagles of the Sky or with Jack Ralston along the Air Lanes. (p. 492)
—Flying the Coast Skyways or Jack Ralston. (p. 610)
Newcomb, Harvey. Young Lady's Guide: To the Harmonious Development of Christian Character. (p. 1979)
Newcomb, Kristene. Molly Q's Trash Travels Through the Water Cycle. Paschall, Patricia A., ed. (p. 1161)
Newcomb, Kristene, illus. see Balmer, Fred.
Newcomb, Simon. Astronomy for Everybody. (p. 109)
—Elements of Astronomy. (p. 510)
—His Wisdom: The Defender. (p. 781)
—Reminiscences of an Astronomer. (p. 1460)
—Side Lights of Astronomy. (p. 1573)
—Sperical Astronomy. (p. 1625)
—Stars. (p. 1643)
Newcomb, Tim. FBI Agent (p. 578)
—Search & Rescue Team (p. 1537)
—Secret Service Agent (p. 1543)
—STEM in Sports: Engineering. (p. 1647)
Newcomb, Victoria. Gathering Grace. (p. 658)
Newcome, Zita. This Royal Baby. Newcome, Zita, illus. (p. 1737)
Newcomer, Carolyn. Barf's First Flight. Raschke, Andrea, illus. (p. 139)
Newcomer, Mary Jane, et al. Elson Readers Fitterling, Michael, illus. (p. 516)
—Elson Readers Teacher's Guide Michael, Fitterling, illus. (p. 516)
Newcomer, Ruth. Silly Songs for Little People. (p. 1576)
Newell, Brian, illus. see Jones, Angela.
Newell, Carol Donsky. Blue Lewis & Sasha the Great. Grisham, Betty, illus. (p. 203)
Newell, Cheri Cameron. Angel Just Like You. (p. 73)
Newell, Claudia, illus. see Arato, Rona.
Newell, Ella. Energy. (p. 528)
—Hidden Story of Alcoholism. (p. 776)
Newell, Jeff. Skimper-Scamper. Hranilovich, Barbara, illus. (p. 1585)
Newell, Karmel H. Come Follow Me: A Child's Guide to Faith, Hope, & Charity. Smith, Mary Ann Free, illus. (p. 347)
Newell, Keith. Models. (p. 1158)
Newell, Keith, illus. see Brooks, Felicity.
Newell, Keith, illus. see Helbrough, Emma & Brooks, Felicity.
Newell, Lennette, illus. see Wyatt, Valerie.
Newell, Peter. Slant Book. (p. 1587)
Newell, Riki. Angel Presence Angel Presents A Most Holy Book: Two Disc CD. (p. 74)
Newell, Robert Henry. Orpheus C. Kerr Papers. (p. 1305)
Newell, Stephanie Jordy. Nite, Nite Farm. (p. 1257)
Newell, William Wells, ed. Games & Songs of American Children. (p. 654)
Newey, Gail. Faerie Stickers. (p. 562)
Newey, Gail, illus. see Batt, Tanya Robyn.
Newey, Gail, illus. see Katz, Susan B.
Newgarden, Mark, illus. see Cash, Megan Montague.
Newgarden, Mark & Cash, Megan Montague. Bow-Wow Bugs a Bug. (p. 216)
Newhall, Mary & Campbell, Joanna. Bridal Dreams. (p. 227)
—Samantha's Irish Luck. (p. 1507)
Newhouse, Debbie. Magic Seed. (p. 1073)
Newhouse Jr., Quentin. Hope, the Big Headed Cat: Not Just Another Animal Story. (p. 796)
Newhouse, Judy, illus. see Justesen, Kim Williams.
Newhouse, Mark. Rockhound Science Mysteries: Tenth Anniversary Special Edition. Gilgannon, Denise, illus. (p. 1483)
Newhouse, Maxwell. Counting on Snow. (p. 371)
—House That Max Built. (p. 804)
—RCMP Musical Ride. (p. 1441)
—Weber Street Wonder Work Crew. (p. 1870)
Newhouse, Maxwell, illus. see Bogart, Jo Ellen.
Newhouse, Maxwell, illus. see Lunn, Janet.
Newirth, Richard, jt. auth. see Aguado, Bill.
Newkey-Burden, Chas. One Way Street: One Direction: The Story of Britain's Biggest Boy Band. (p. 1297)
Newkirk, Errol Q., illus. see Edison-Clark, Gina.
Newkirk, Ingrid. 50 Awesome Ways Kids Can Help Animals: Fun & Easy Ways to Be a Kind Kid. (p. 1997)
Newkirk, Jacqualine. Collective Thoughts from God's Table to Yours. (p. 340)
Newkirk, Stephanie. I'm So Madd!!! (p. 860)
Newkirk, Thomas, frwd. Reviving the Essay w/forword by Thomas Newkirk: How to Teach Structure without Formula. (p. 1466)
Newland, g. f., illus. see Enik, Ted.
Newland, Gillian, illus. see Bogart, Jo Ellen.
Newland, Gillian, illus. see Jennings, Sharon.
Newland, Gillian, illus. see Kacer, Kathy.
Newland, James P. Smile Says It All. (p. 1594)
Newland, Laura. Nicky Boy, I Love You. (p. 1251)
Newland, Sonya. Desert Animals. (p. 428)
—Doodle Yourself Smart... Geometry. (p. 469)
—Doodle Yourself Smart... Physics. (p. 469)
—Grassland Animals. (p. 712)
—Mountain Animals. (p. 1180)
—Ocean Animals. (p. 1276)
—Polar Animals. (p. 1378)
—Rain Forest Animals. (p. 1434)
—Wetland Animals. (p. 1877)
—Woodland & Forest Animals. (p. 1949)
Newland, Sonya, jt. auth. see Pipe, Jim.
Newland, Trevor. Scallywag Solution (p. 1519)
Newlands, Anne. Clarence Gagnon: An Introduction to His Life & Art. (p. 327)
Newlands, Anne & Thomson, Tom. Group of Seven & Tom Thomson: An Introduction. (p. 725)
Newlin, D. S. Smiley's Happy Dolphin Day—the Artist in You: Workbook Edition. (p. 1594)
—Smiley's Happy Dolphin Day—In Living Color. (p. 1594)
Newlin, Keith & Salem Press Staff. Sun Also Rises, by Ernest Hemingway. (p. 1675)
Newlin, Kris. I Saw God Today. (p. 845)
—Silly Sweet Dreams. (p. 1576)
Newlin, Nick, ed. see Shakespeare, William.
Newlin-Chase, Edith. Ternero Recien Nacido. Reid, Barbara, illus. (p. 1721)
Newlon, Stephanie, jt. auth. see Fowler, Jane.
Newlun, Shawn, illus. see Peterson, Janie & Peterson, Macy.
Newman, Aline Alexander. Animal Superstars: And More True Stories of Amazing Animal Talents. (p. 80)
—Ape Escapes! And More True Stories of Animals Behaving Badly. (p. 91)
—Lucky Leopards! (p. 1062)
—Lucky Leopards! And More True Stories of Amazing Animal Rescues! (p. 1062)
—National Geographic Kids Chapters - Ape Escapes! And More Stories of Animals Behaving Badly. (p. 1232)
Newman, Aline Alexander & Weitzman, Gary. How to Speak Cat: A Guide to Decoding Cat Language. (p. 821)
—How to Speak Dog: A Guide to Decoding Dog Language. (p. 821)
Newman, Barbara, illus. see Adler, David A.
Newman, Barbara Johansen. Glamorous Garbage. (p. 682)
—Glamorous Glasses. (p. 682)
Newman, Barbara Johansen, illus. see Adler, David A.
Newman, Barbara Johansen, illus. see Grambling, Lois G. & Grambling.
Newman, Barbara Johansen, illus. see Terwilliger, Kelly.
Newman, Barbara Johansen, illus. see Torrey, Michele.
Newman, Barbara Johansen, illus. see Wing, Natasha.
Newman, Ben, illus. see Walliman, Dominic.
Newman, C. Edward. Enchanted Bat. (p. 523)
—Little Leaguer Wore #7. (p. 1030)
Newman, Claire M. Exploring Probability. (p. 553)
Newman, Dawn A., et al. Bully Busters, Grades 6-8 (Book & CD) A Teacher's Manual for Helping Bullies, Victims, & Bystanders. (p. 241)
Newman, Diana Marie. Gramps' Tales: Pig Ride (p. 706)
—Gramps' Tales: Pig Ride. (p. 706)
Newman, Elizabeth. Instant Replay. Goehner, Amy Lennard, ed. (p. 878)
Newman, Ernest, tr. see Schweitzer, Albert.
Newman, Gary, jt. auth. see James, Martin.
Newman, Gerald & Layfield, Eleanor Newman. Student's Guide to John Steinbeck. (p. 1669)
Newman, Gerry. Nellie, the Scarecrow: A Dorset Fable. (p. 1240)
Newman, Gwill York. Bingo Bear Was Here: A Toy Bear's Climb to the Top of Africa's Highest Mountain. Babcock, Jeff, illus. (p. 188)
Newman, Heather. Creating Digital Brochures. Petelinsek, Kathleen, illus. (p. 378)
Newman, Heather, illus. see Schultz, Leslie & Braulick, J. J. M.
Newman, J. Heidi, ed. see Randall, Barbara.
Newman, J. Heidi, ed. see Roman Saint-Pierre, Erika.
Newman, Jacqueline M. Food Culture in China (p. 613)
Newman, Jeff. Boys. Newman, Jeff, illus. (p. 220)
—Greedy Worm. (p. 720)
—Hand Book. Newman, Jeff, illus. (p. 740)
Newman, Jeff, illus. see Reynolds, Aaron.
Newman, Jeff, illus. see Richards, Dan.
Newman, Jeff, illus. see Springstubb, Tricia.
Newman, John. Mimi. (p. 1145)
Newman, John, jt. auth. see Halligan, Jim.
Newman, Joye, jt. auth. see Kranowitz, Carol.
Newman, Judy, jt. auth. see Stickler, LeeDell.
Newman, Langley, illus. see Holt, Deloris L.
Newman, Lee. How Many Animals? Moon, Cliff, ed. (p. 810)
Newman, Lesléa. Best Cat in the World. Himler, Ronald, illus. (p. 168)
—Boy Who Cried Fabulous. Ferguson, Peter, illus. (p. 219)
—Cats, Cats, Cats! Oller, Erika, illus. (p. 281)
—Dogs, Dogs, Dogs! Oller, Erika, illus. (p. 462)
—Donovan's Big Day. Dutton, Mike, illus. (p. 466)
—Felicia's Favorite Story. Romo, Adriana, illus. (p. 581)
—Hachiko Waits. Kodaira, Machiyo, illus. (p. 735)
—Heather Has Two Mommies. Cornell, Laura, illus. (p. 760)
—Here Is the World: A Year of Jewish Holidays. Gal, Susan, illus. (p. 770)
—Just Like Mama. Gorton, Julia, illus. (p. 939)
—Kiss on the Keppie Blackmore, Katherine & Wiltse, Kris, illus. (p. 961)
—Miss Tutu's Star. Armstrong-Ellis, Carey, illus. (p. 1152)
—My Name Is Aviva. Jatkowska, Ag, illus. (p. 1215)
—Sweet Passover. Slonim, David, illus. (p. 1690)
—Where Is Bear? Gorbachev, Valeri, illus. (p. 1908)
Newman, Lesléa, jt. auth. see Thompson, Carol.
Newman, Lori M. What Rights Should Illegal Immigrants Have? (p. 1893)
Newman, Marjorie. Yo Ho Ho! Sheppard, Kate, illus. (p. 1971)
Newman, Mark. Polar Bears. (p. 1379)
—Polar Bears. Newman, Mark, illus. (p. 1379)
—Sooper Yooper: Environmental Defender. Heckman, Mark, illus. (p. 1613)
Newman, Marlene. Myron's Magic Cow. (p. 1222)
Newman, Matthew. You Have Mail: True Stories of Cybercrime. (p. 1975)
Newman, Michael E. Soft Tissue Sarcomas. (p. 1606)
Newman, Nanette. Ben's Book. Birkett, Georgie, illus. (p. 165)
—What Will You Be, Grandma? Chichester Clark, Emma, illus. (p. 1895)
Newman, Nanette & Cook, Beryl. My Granny. (p. 1210)
Newman, Pamela Lillie. Lissie at Lincoln Lake: Book 2 of Lissie's Series. (p. 1022)
Newman, Patrice Tomasetti. Beautiful Colors. (p. 153)
—Where Oh Where? It's in My Hair! (p. 1909)
Newman, Patricia. Army Special Forces: Elite Operations. (p. 100)
—Biofuels. (p. 188)
—Ebola: Fears & Facts. (p. 501)
—Navy Seals: Elite Operations. (p. 1238)
—Nugget on the Flight Deck. Zenz, Aaron, illus. (p. 1270)
—Plastic, Ahoy! Investigating the Great Pacific Garbage Patch. Crawley, Annie, illus. (p. 1370)
—Surviving Animal Attacks. (p. 1687)
—Water Power. (p. 1863)
Newman, Paul. Ambrose the Whale: A Novel for Children & Adults. (p. 57)
Newman, Paul S. Man of the Atom Murphy, Matt, illus. (p. 1085)
—Man of the Atom. (p. 1085)
Newman, Robert C., jt. auth. see Fawcett, Cheryl.
Newman, Robin. Wilcox & Griswold Mystery: the Case of the Missing Carrot Cake. Zemke, Deborah, illus. (p. 1928)
Newman, Samantha. Sammy Skizzors & the Rainbow Knight. (p. 1508)
Newman, Sandra. Ancient Greece. (p. 69)
—Europe. (p. 540)
—Inca Empire. (p. 868)
Newman, Timothy, ed. see Justus, Barbara & Starbird, Caroline.
Newman, Tracy. Passover Is Coming! Garófoli, Viviana, illus. (p. 1327)
—Shabbat Is Coming! Garofoli, Viviana, illus. (p. 1556)
—Uncle Eli's Wedding. Isik, Semur, illus. (p. 1811)
Newman, Vivian. Ella's Trip to Israel. Nathan, Cheryl & Gutierrez, Akemia, illus. (p. 514)
—Tikkun Olam Ted. Mack, Steve, illus. (p. 1750)
Newman, Winifred Barnum, illus. see Barnum-Newman, Winifred.
Newman, Yvette. Missy's Day with Butterflies. (p. 1155)
Newman-D'Amico, Fran. ABC Crosswords. (p. 3)
—All about America: Facts & Fun. (p. 42)
—Alphabet Mazes. (p. 49)
—Animal Friends Mazes. (p. 77)
—Animal Spot-the-Differences. (p. 79)
—Birthday Activity Book. (p. 192)
—BOOST Favorite Fairy Tales Coloring Book. (p. 213)
—BOOST My First Book of Puzzle Fun. (p. 213)
—Bugs Activity & Coloring Book. (p. 237)
—Busy Backyard Coloring & Activity Book. (p. 245)
—Christmas Fun Activity Book. (p. 314)

N

—Design Your Own Ugly Christmas Sweater Sticker Activity Book. (p. 430)
—Favorite Fairy Tales Coloring Book. (p. 578)
—Fun Farm Animal Mazes. (p. 647)
—Fun on the Go. (p. 648)
—Funny Animal Faces Sticker Activity Book. (p. 649)
—Girlfriends Activity Book. (p. 679)
—Glitter Decorate a Christmas Tree Sticker Activity Book. (p. 683)
—Halloween Fun. (p. 737)
—Little Gardener's. (p. 1028)
—Make Your Own Ice Cream Sundae with 54 Stickers. (p. 1080)
—Make Your Own Pizza Sticker. (p. 1080)
—My First Book of Number Fun. (p. 1205)
—My First Book of Puzzle Fun. (p. 1205)
—My Vacation Activity Book. (p. 1220)
—Spot the Differences Picture Puzzles. (p. 1633)
—Spot the Differences Puzzle Fun. (p. 1633)
—Story of the Pilgrims. (p. 1662)
—Travel Fun. (p. 1780)
—Vacation Fun Activity Book. (p. 1830)
—Zoo Animal Mazes. (p. 1988)
Newman-D'Amico, Fran, jt. auth. see Pomaska, Anna.
Newmann, Ed. Marvin Monster's Big Date. (p. 1099)
—Marvin Monster's Teacher Jitters. (p. 1099)
Newmark, Ann & Dorling Kindersley Publishing Staff. Chemistry. (p. 297)
Newmark, Assaf, jt. adapted by see Newmark, Deborah.
Newmark, Assaf, jt. auth. see Newmark, Deborah.
Newmark, Deborah & Newmark, Assaf. Mis Manitas. (p. 1150)
Newmark, Deborah & Newmark, Assaf, adapted by. Blanca Nieves y Los Siete Enanos. (p. 198)
—Rana Principe. (p. 1438)
Newmark Learning. Famous Inventors Grades 1-2 CD-ROM: Reader's Theater Theme Collections. (p. 569)
—How & Why Tales Grades 1-2 CD-ROM: Reader's Theater Theme Collections. (p. 804)
Newmark Learning, compiled by. Complete Fluency Instruction & Practice Set Grades 1-3 with Audio CDs. (p. 352)
—Fluency Mini-Lessons Grade 2 with Audio CD: Independent Fluency Practice Passages. (p. 608)
—Rising Readers Set A Sets Of 6. (p. 1475)
—Sight Word Readers 12 copy set with Rack Set A. (p. 1574)
Newmark, Rachel J. Fearless Faith: And the New School. Specialty Publishing Company, illus. (p. 579)
Newmarket Press Staff. Junior Su Doku. (p. 936)
Newmyer, R. Kent. Supreme Court under Marshall & Taney. Eisenstadt, Abraham S. & Franklin, John Hope, eds. (p. 1685)
Newnham, Jack, jt. auth. see Handy, Libby.
Newport, Chelsea. Visiting the White House. (p. 1845)
Newport, Kate, jt. auth. see Jeffrey, Gary.
Newquist, H. P. Book of Blood: From Legends & Leeches to Vampires & Veins. (p. 211)
—Here There Be Monsters: The Legendary Kraken & the Giant Squid. (p. 770)
Newquist, H. P., jt. auth. see Aronson, Marc.
Newroad, Adele. Carrie Underwood. (p. 271)
Newry, Patricia. Like Jesus Did. (p. 1017)
Newsham, Gavin. London 2012 Games Fact File. (p. 1046)
Newsom, Carol, illus. see Cohan, George M. & Schwaeber, Barbie.
Newsom, Carol, illus. see Gill, Vince.
Newsom, Mary T. & Jones, Joy. Homework Survival Kit. (p. 794)
Newsom, Tom. First Noel. (p. 596)
—Our Family Christmas Album: A Book about Us! (p. 1308)
—Our Night Before Christmas: Memory Book - A Book about Us! (p. 1309)
Newsom, Tom, illus. see Banks, Lynne Reid.
Newsom, Tom, illus. see Moore, Clement C.
Newsom, Tony. High School Student Safety Tips. (p. 778)
—Middle School Student Safety Tips. (p. 1138)
—Student Safety Tips: 40 that Every 1st - 2nd Grader Must Know! (p. 1669)
—Student Safety Tips: 45 that Every 3rd - 5th Grader Must Know! (p. 1669)
Newsom, William Chad. Polycarp: The Crown of Fire. (p. 1381)
Newsome, Andy, illus. see Bauld, Jane S.
Newsome, Eric. Adventures of Eric: Starry Beginnings. (p. 18)
Newsome, Richard. Billionaire's Curse. Duddle, Jonny, illus. (p. 187)
—Crystal Code Claffaglione, Sebastian, illus. (p. 387)
—Emerald Casket. Duddle, Jonny, illus. (p. 517)
—Mask of Destiny. Duddle, Jonny, illus. (p. 1102)
Newsome, Tandy. Mr. Miyataki's Marvelous Machine. Robinson, Don, illus. (p. 1185)
Newson, Lesley & Wadsworth, Pamela. Defnyddiau. (p. 424)
—Rhagor Am Ddefnyddiau. (p. 1467)
—Rhagor Am Greigiau, Pridd a Thywydd. (p. 1467)
—Trydan a Magnetedd. (p. 1795)
Newswanger, Rebecca. God Gave Us Fathers & Mothers. Steiner, Maria, illus. (p. 688)
Newth, Rebecca. Tinkum's Dog. Primm, Thomas, illus. (p. 1756)
Newton, Afton Lisette. Mystery of the Sabotaged Dig. (p. 1226)
Newton, Barbara. Sammie. (p. 1507)
Newton, Chelle. Butterfly Princess. Padovano, Chris, illus. (p. 248)
Newton, Dan. Wildcat. (p. 1931)
Newton, David E. Chemistry of Drugs. (p. 297)
—Chemistry of New Materials. (p. 297)
—Chemistry of Space. (p. 297)
—Chemistry of the Environment. (p. 297)
—Food Chemistry. (p. 613)
—Forensic Chemistry. (p. 617)
—Latinos in Science, Math, & Professions. (p. 979)
—New Chemistry Set. (p. 1244)
—Nuclear Power. (p. 1270)
Newton, Derek & Smith, David. Practice in the Basic Skills Maths (p. 1392)
Newton, Diane J., et al. Secrets, Fact or Fiction? Which Is Which. Newton, Diane J., ed. (p. 1544)
Newton Driscoll, Ell. Dragons of Candlewood. (p. 479)
Newton Driscoll, Ellen. Legend of the Dragon Sword. (p. 989)
Newton, Eve. Tea Party in Muffinville. (p. 1708)
Newton, H. L., jt. auth. see Flannagan, J. S.
Newton, Jennifer, photos by see Barrette, Melanie.
Newton, Jill. Crash Bang Donkey! (p. 376)
—Don't Wake Mr Bear! Newton, Jill, illus. (p. 469)
Newton, Jill, illus. see Camp, Lindsay.
Newton, Jill, illus. see Kuenzler, Lou & Powell, Jillian.
Newton, Jill, illus. see Lloyd-Jones, Sally.
Newton, Jill, illus. see McGough, Roger.
Newton, Jill, illus. see Michalak, Jamie.
Newton, Jill, illus. see Ziefert, Harriet.
Newton, Joan. Gravity in Action: Roller Coasters! (p. 712)
Newton, June. Kingdom of the Doberman. (p. 960)
Newton, Keith, illus. see Gilligan, Shannon.
Newton, Keith, illus. see Montgomery, R. A.
Newton, Kimberly, illus. see Haidar, Hanna.
Newton, Lesley. Ralphie's Christmas Story (p. 1437)
Newton, Maria. Sol the Sun. (p. 1606)
Newton, Michael. Bank Robbery. (p. 136)
—Drug Enforcement Administration. (p. 486)
—Encyclopedia of Serial Killers. (p. 525)
—Gangs & Gang Crimes. (p. 655)
—Serial Killers. (p. 1552)
—SWAT Teams. (p. 1689)
—Texas Rangers. (p. 1724)
—Unsolved Crimes. (p. 1822)
Newton, Pilar, illus. see Arruzza, Rick.
Newton, R. H. Oceannis. (p. 1277)
Newton, Renae. Having Fun with Granny. (p. 755)
Newton, Rhonda. Little Folks Book of Rhymes. (p. 1027)
Newton, Richard. Bible Promises: Sermons for Children on. (p. 176)
—Bible Warnings: Sermons to Children. (p. 176)
—Leaves from the Tree of Life: Sermons for Children. (p. 986)
—Life of Jesus Christ for the Young. (p. 1012)
—Pebbles from the Brook: Sermons for Children Fighting the Good Fight of Faith. (p. 1333)
—Safe Compass & How It Points. (p. 1502)
Newton, Richard V., Sr. One Bat, 2 Bats. (p. 1293)
Newton, Robert. Punjabi Pappadum. (p. 1417)
—Saturday Morning, Mozart & Burnt Toast. (p. 1515)
Newton, Robyn & Barber, Nicola, eds. Dinosaurs: Uncover the Prehistoric World! Horas, Elena, tr. (p. 444)
Newton, Samantha. Being Nine Isn't So Bad. (p. 161)
Newton, Sydney, jt. auth. see Gerrits, Julie.
Newton, Sydney, jt. auth. see Peppas, Lynn.
Newton, Teddy & Pixar Firm Staff. Day & Night. (p. 412)
Newton, Vanessa. Let Freedom Sing. Newton, Vanessa, illus. (p. 994)
Newton, Vanessa, illus. see Marley, Cedella & Marley, Bob.
Newton, Vanessa, illus. see Scanlon, Liz Garton.
Newton, Vanessa Brantley, illus. see Barnes, Derrick D.
Newton, Vanessa Brantley, illus. see Barnes, Derrick.
Newton, Vanessa Brantley, illus. see Dungy, Tony & Dungy, Lauren.
Newton, Vanessa Brantley, illus. see Harris, Marie.
Newton, Vanessa Brantley, illus. see Holland, Trish.
Newton, Vanessa Brantley, illus. see Humphrey, Anna.
Newton, Vanessa Brantley, illus. see Johnston, Teresa.
Newton, Vanessa Brantley, illus. see Loehr, Mallory.
Newton, Vanessa Brantley, illus. see Novesky, Amy.
Newton-Gamble, Ivy. Read to Me Neny: Beyond Baby Talk Teaching Simple African Words to the 21st Century Child. (p. 1443)
Newton-Kowalsky, Jacqueline. Itsy Bitsy Stories for Itsy Bitsy Tigers. (p. 900)
Newton-Perry, Linda. Eye of the Beast. (p. 557)
—Little Red Car & Bigfoot. (p. 1034)
—Lock Your Doors Country Folk. (p. 1045)
Nex, Anthony, photos by. Little Feet Love. (p. 1027)
—Little Hands Love. (p. 1029)
Nextext. American Short Stories. (p. 63)
Nextext, creator. Ana Maria Matute. (p. 66)
—Ancient Greece. (p. 69)
—Civil War: 1860-1865. (p. 325)
—Latin American Writers. (p. 979)
—Latino Writers in the U.S. (p. 979)
—Major World Dramas. (p. 1078)
—Tales of O. Henry. (p. 1702)
Nextext Staff, jt. contrib. by see McDougal-Littell Publishing Staff.
Nextext Staff, contrib. by. Ancient Americas: 30,000 B.C.-A.D.1600. (p. 67)
—Middle Ages. (p. 1137)
Nextoy Staff, et al. I Can Kenken!: 75 Puzzles for Having Fun with Math. Vol. 1 (p. 836)
—I Can Kenken!: 75 Puzzles for Having Fun with Math. Vol. 2 (p. 836)
—I Can Kenken!: 75 Puzzles for Having Fun with Math. Vol. 3 (p. 836)
Nexus Staff & Ashton, Lisette. Fairground Attractions. (p. 562)
Nexus Staff, et al. Torment, Incorporated. (p. 1769)
Neyer, Daniel. Bulkington. Wilmot, Anita, illus. (p. 240)
Neylon, Robbie. Real Me. (p. 1448)
Neyret, Aurélie, illus. see Meng, Cece.
Neysters, Silvia & Soll-Tauchert, Sabine. Andy Warhol: Paintings for Children. (p. 73)
Nez, John. Dragon Painter. (p. 477)
—My Vacation Diary. (p. 1220)
—One Smart Cookie. Nez, John, illus. (p. 1297)
Nez, John, illus. see Cronin, Doreen.
Nez, John, illus. see Dussling, Jennifer.
Nez, John, illus. see Gabriel, Nat.
Nez, John, illus. see Herman, Gail.
Nez, John, illus. see Skinner, Daphne.
Nez, John, tr. see Gabriel, Nat.
Nez, John A., illus. see Harkrader, Lisa.
Nez, John A., illus. see Haskins, Lori.
Nez, John A., illus. see Wilson, Sarah.
Nez, John Abbott. Twelve Days of Christmas in Washington. Nez, John Abbott, illus. (p. 1800)
Nez, John Abbott, illus. see Metzger, Steve.
Nez, Jon, illus. see Bennett, Artie.
Nez, Jon, illus. see Thomas, Patricia.
Neznansky, Friedrich. Night Wolves. (p. 1254)
Ng, Cindy. Girligami: Fun & Fashionable Origami! (p. 679)
Ng, Drew, illus. see Boyd, David.
Ng, Drew, illus. see Cutting, Robert.
Ng, James, illus. see Kingsley, Kaza.
Ng, Leandro, illus. see Roman, Annette.
Ng, Neiko, illus. see Schwartz, Betty Ann & Seresin, Lynn.
Ng, Neiko, illus. see Seresin, Lynn & Schwartz, Betty Ann.
Ng, Neiko, illus. see Yeretskaya, Yevgeniya.
Ng, Robyn, illus. see Ashburn, Boni.
Ng, Simon, illus. see Yee, Paul.
Ng, Yumi. Welcome to Liberia. (p. 1873)
—Welcome to Venezuela. (p. 1874)
Ngarimu-Cameron, Roka. Toku Haerenga: A Transformation of Maori Cloaks. (p. 1762)
Ng-Benitez, Shirley, illus. see Foley, James.
NgCheong-Lum, Roseline. Eritrea. (p. 533)
—Fiji. (p. 586)
—Tahiti. (p. 1695)
NgCheong-Lum, Roseline, jt. auth. see Cheong-Lum, Roseline Ng.
NgCheong-Lum, Roseline, jt. auth. see Conboy, Fiona.
Ngcheong-Lum, Roseline & Jermyn, Leslie. Haiti. (p. 736)
Ngo, illus. see Ngo, Lap.
Ngo, Lap. Teaser Monster. Ngo, illus. (p. 1711)
N'Guessan, Marc & Gibelin, Christophe. Quest of Aberzen: To the Death. Bk. 1 (p. 1426)
Ngui, Marc, illus. see Dyer, Hadley.
Ngui, Marc, illus. see Niedzviecki, Hal.
Nguy, Hoa X. Bamboo Girl. (p. 135)
Nguyen, Albert, illus. see Bridges, Shirin Yim & Yim Bridges, Shirin.
Nguyen, Albert, illus. see Bridges, Shirin Yim.
Nguyen, Albert, illus. see Yim, Natasha.
Nguyen, An Mai. Let's Learn Animals in Vietnamese. (p. 998)
—Let's Learn Colors in Vietnamese. (p. 998)
—Let's Learn How to Count in Vietnamese. (p. 998)
—Let's Learn the Vietnamese Alphabet. (p. 998)
Nguyen, Anthony. Santa with His Reindeer. (p. 1513)
Nguyen, Bich, illus. see Tran, Quoc.
Nguyen, Cindy, illus. see Capozzola, Christine.
Nguyen, Duke, ed. see Lavette, Lavaille.
Nguyen, Duke, illus. see Epner, Paul.
Nguyen, Dustin, illus. see Kane, Bob.
Nguyen, Dustin, illus. see Stone Arch Books.
Nguyen, Dustin Tri, illus. see Stone Arch Books.
Nguyen, Duy. Zombigami: Paper Folding for the Living Dead. (p. 1988)
Nguyen, Hoang & Gardner, Paul. Carbon Grey Volume 2: Daughters of Stone TP: Daughters of Stone TP. (p. 265)
Nguyen, Hy Thi. Challenges. (p. 289)
Nguyen, Kien. Tapestries: A Novel. (p. 1705)
Nguyen, Llustrated By Luan. Story of an Ant: Ant & an Elephant. (p. 1657)
Nguyen, My-Trang, tr. see Crepeau, Pierre & Hamilton, Garry.
Nguyen, Peter, jt. auth. see Aguirre-Sacasa, Roberto.
Nguyen, Tao. Mighty Mite: A New Beginning. Nguyen, Tao, illus. (p. 1140)
Nguyen, Taohuu. Mighty Mite 2: Zoo Gone Wild. Nguyen, Taohuu, illus. (p. 1140)
—Mighty Mite 3: Good Mites, Bad Mites. Nguyen, Taohuu, illus. (p. 1140)
Nguyen, Thanh-Trieu, jt. auth. see Khuc, Mimi.
Nguyen, Thao. Consequences: A Chance for Hope. (p. 358)
Nguyen, Vincent. Crabfish. (p. 375)
Nguyen, Vincent, illus. see Bergen, Lara.
Nguyen, Vincent, illus. see Kroll, Steven.
Nguyen, Vincent, illus. see Macomber, Debbie & Carney, Mary Lou.
Nguyen, Vincent, illus. see Paul, Donita K. & Denmark, Evangeline.
Nguyen, Vincent, illus. see Rostoker-Gruber, Karen.
Nguyen, Vincent, illus. see Shulman, Mark.
Nguyen, Vincent, illus. see Spinelli, Eileen.
Nguyen-Tuong, Karine. Arnold the Smiling Horse. (p. 100)
Nhem, Sopaul, illus. see Smith, Icy.
NHLPA. We Are the Goal Scorers: The Top Point Leaders of the NHL. (p. 1865)
—We Are the Goalies: The Top Netminders of the NHL. (p. 1865)
NHR Staff, ed. National Honor Roll PhotoDisc Staff, photos by. (p. 1233)
Ni Dheirg, Iosold. Story of Michael Collins. (p. 1659)
Ni, Maoshing. Secrets of Longevity: Hundreds of Ways to Live to Be 100. (p. 1545)
Ni Mhurchú, Caitríona & Feeney, Tatyana. Run Mor. (p. 1496)
Nia, jt. auth. see Glenn, Lexi.
Nia, Nikki. Mommy's Love. (p. 1163)
Niball, Ellen Cook. Secret of St. Nicholas. (p. 1542)
Nibley, Alethea, tr. see Capcom Japan Staff.
Nibley, Alethea, tr. see Fumizuki, Kou.
Nibley, Alethea, tr. see Minekura, Kazuya.
Nibley, Alethea, tr. see Sugisaki, Yukiru.
Nibley, Alethea, tr. see Takaya, Natsuki.
Nibley, Athena, tr. see Fumizuki, Kou.
Nibley, Athena, tr. see Minekura, Kazuya.
Nibley, Athena, tr. see Sugisaki, Yukiru.
Nibley, Athena, tr. see Takaya, Natsuki.
Nibley, Lydia, jt. auth. see Martin, Russell.
Nice, Jason. Sacred History & National Identity: Comparisons Between Early Modern Wales & Brittany (p. 1500)
Niceley, Hank. Pockets Full of Babies. (p. 1375)
Nicely, Adam. Bedtime for Tad. (p. 157)
Nicely, Darthy, illus. see Lampkin, Laveta M.
Nicewander, Carol, jt. auth. see Daniels, Cheri.
Nichele, Neika. Tayance, a Young Sioux Indian. Bright, Phyllis, illus. (p. 1708)
Nichills, Dee. Visit the Rainforest. (p. 1845)
Nichol, Barbara. Beethoven Vive Arriba. (p. 158)
—One Small Garden. Moser, Barry, illus. (p. 1297)
Nicholai, Mary K., illus. see Slim, Lillian, et al.
Nicholai, Rachel, et al. Bird Adventures. Nicholai, Rachel et al, illus. (p. 190)
Nicholas, Christopher. Toy Story 2 Butcher, Ben, illus. (p. 1774)
Nicholas, Corasue, illus. see Malokas, Ann.
Nicholas, Frank, illus. see Clark, Electa.
Nicholas, J. B. Waving Girl Waites, Joan C., illus. (p. 1864)
Nicholas, Jacob, illus. see Rogala, Jennifer.
Nicholas, Jeff D. Sequoia & Kings Canyon. (p. 1552)
Nicholas, Kristin. Amazing Stitching Handbook for Kids: 17 Embroidery Stitches * 15 Fun & Easy Projects. (p. 56)
Nicholas, Kristin, illus. see Falick, Melanie.
Nicholas, Melissa. Pumpkin Days (p. 1416)
—Stop by a Pond. Gram, Patrick, illus. (p. 1653)
—Who Is My Mom? Cassels, Jean, illus. (p. 1916)
Nicholas, Mother Andrea, compiled by. My Little Orthodox Christian Feast Days Activity Book. (p. 1212)
Nicholas, Nicki. Peter & Lil on a Winter's Day. (p. 1346)
—Peter & Lil's Amazing Autumn Day. (p. 1346)
—Peter & Lil's Summer Day Adventure. (p. 1346)
—Spring Has Sprung for Peter & Lil. (p. 1635)
Nicholasa, Mohr. Bronx Remembered. (p. 230)
Nicholaus, Bret & Lowrie, Paul. KidChat: 222 Creative Questions to Spark Conversations. (p. 952)
—KidChat Too! All-New Questions to Fuel Young Minds & Mouths. (p. 952)
Nicholl, Jacqueline. Pick-a-WooWoo - Born to Love Frogs: All children have a Gift! Evans, Gabriel, illus. (p. 1354)
Nicholls, Calvin, illus. see Martin, Rafe.
Nicholls, Claire. In it to win It. (p. 863)
Nicholls, Dee. Hurricane Day. (p. 829)
Nicholls, Emma, illus. see Twist, Clint & Fitzgibbon, Monty.
Nicholls, Judith. Sun in Me: Poems about the Planet. Krommes, Beth, illus. (p. 1676)
Nicholls, Judith, ed. Sun in Me: Poems about the Planet. Krommes, Beth, illus. (p. 1676)
Nicholls, Mark. Scorsese's Men: Melancholia & the Mob. (p. 1530)
Nicholls, Maureen. Sylvester. (p. 1692)
Nicholls, Paul. I Want to Be A... Pirate. (p. 847)
—Wind-up Race Cars. (p. 1935)
Nicholls, Paul, illus. see Dowley, Tim & David, Juliet.
Nicholls, Paul, illus. see Holub, Joan.
Nicholls, Paul, illus. see Wang, Adria.
Nicholls, Sally. Season of Secrets. (p. 1538)
Nicholls, Shawn. Sports Gamer: The Best Games, Gear, & Tips. (p. 1632)
Nicholls, Shawn, jt. auth. see Carter, André.
Nichols, Alan, jt. auth. see Hendtlass, Jane.
Nichols, Amie. Journey to Saturn (p. 929)
Nichols, Amy K. Now That You're Here. (p. 1269)
—While You Were Gone (Duplexity, Part II) (p. 1911)
Nichols, C. D. Kids Courageous. (p. 953)
Nichols, Catherine. Barack Obama. (p. 137)
—Claude Monet. (p. 329)
—Color Yourself Smart: Masterpieces of Art. Bright, Joe, illus. (p. 343)
—Emerald Boas: Rain Forest Undercover. (p. 517)
—Leonardo Da Vinci. (p. 992)
—Leonardo da Vinci. (p. 992)
—Madam C.J. Walker. (p. 1069)
—Michelangelo Buonarroti. (p. 1135)
—Mysterious Creatures: A Chapter Book. (p. 1223)
—Pablo Picasso. (p. 1316)
—Pierre-Auguste Renoir. (p. 1357)
—Polar Adventures. (p. 1378)
—Prickly Porcupines. (p. 1398)
—Record Breakers: A Chapter Book. (p. 1452)
—Smelly Skunks. (p. 1593)
—Tricky Opossums. (p. 1786)
—Vincent Van Gogh. (p. 1842)
—Vincent van Gogh. (p. 1843)
Nichols, Catherine, jt. auth. see Gleason, Katherine.
Nichols, Cherrie L. Curtiz Says: I'm Not Blue! (p. 395)
—Curtiz Says: I Hate My Shoestrings. (p. 395)
Nichols, Cheyenne. Miedo Es... Strictly Spanish Translation Services Staff, tr. from ENG. (p. 1139)
—Sad Is... (p. 1501)
—Tristeza Es... Strictly Spanish LLC. Staff, tr. from ENG. (p. 1787)
Nichols, Cheyenne, jt. auth. see Miller, Connie Colwell.
Nichols, Cheyenne, jt. auth. see Salas, Laura Purdie.
Nichols, Cheyenne & Miller, Connie Colwell. Know Your Emotions. (p. 965)
Nichols, Chris, illus. see Goss, Leon.
Nichols, Clayton, illus. see Showell, Isaiah, Sr.
Nichols, Clive & Bussing-Burks, Marie. Taxes & Government Spending. (p. 1707)
Nichols, Dave, illus. see Claire, Elizabeth.
Nichols, David, et al. Brands & Gaming: The Computer Gaming Phenomenon & Its Impact on Brands & Businesses. (p. 222)
Nichols, Donna. Mikey's Big Adventure. (p. 1141)
Nichols, Earline. Through the Eyes of Casey. (p. 1745)
Nichols, Garry, illus. see Dahl, Michael.
Nichols, Garry, illus. see Nettleton, Pamela Hill.
Nichols, Grace. Whoa, Baby, Whoa! Taylor, Eleanor, illus. (p. 1919)
Nichols, Gregory G., ed. see Trummel, D. Pauline.
Nichols, Joan K. Matter of Conscience: The Trial of Anne Hutchinson. Krovatin, Dan, illus. (p. 1109)
Nichols, Joan Kane. Civil War Heroines. (p. 325)
—Civil War Sisterhood: Women Who Made a Difference. (p. 325)
—Women of the Civil War. (p. 1946)
Nichols, John. Green Bay Packers, the History. (p. 721)
—History of the Baltimore Ravens. (p. 784)
—NHL - History & Heroes: The Story of the Boston Bruins. (p. 1250)
—Philadelphia Flyers. (p. 1350)
—Story of the Charlotte Bobcats. (p. 1660)

—Story of the Los Angeles Dodgers. (p. 1661)
—Story of the Pittsburgh Steelers. (p. 1662)
—Story of the Toronto Raptors. (p. 1662)
Nichols, Jon, jt. illus. see Nichols, Tucker.
Nichols, Judy Davis. Or-Ange Juice Fight: Adventure in the Big Kitchen. (p. 1301)
Nichols, Kaitlyn. Davey Crockett. (p. 410)
—Draw the DC Universe: Learn to Draw the Heroes & the Villains. (p. 481)
—Felted Friends: Create Your Own Soft, Fuzzy Animals. (p. 581)
—Make Clay Charms. (p. 1079)
—Martin Luther King. (p. 1097)
—Safety Pin Bracelets: Turn Ordinary Safety Pins into Extraordinary Bracelets. (p. 1502)
—Toolbox Jewelry. (p. 1767)
Nichols, Kathleen. My Five Senses. (p. 1208)
Nichols, Lee. Deception. (p. 421)
—Surrender. (p. 1686)
Nichols, Lee & Nicholson, Emma. Betrayal. (p. 171)
Nichols, Leigh, pseud & Koontz, Dean. Shadowfires. (p. 1558)
Nichols, Lori. Maple. Nichols, Lori, illus. (p. 1090)
—Maple & Willow Together. Nichols, Lori, illus. (p. 1090)
Nichols, Lori, illus. see Elliott, David.
Nichols, Lori, illus. see Thomas, Shelley Moore.
Nichols, Melva. Spinning the Beginning. (p. 1628)
Nichols, Michael. Beating the Air. (p. 152)
Nichols, Michael & Carney, Elizabeth. Face to Face with Gorillas. (p. 560)
Nichols, Niki. Your Karma, DeeDee. (p. 1981)
Nichols, Paul, illus. see Watt, Fiona.
Nichols, Peter M., ed. see New York Times Staff, et al.
Nichols, Rod & Johnson, Tim. God's Prosperity Plan. (p. 691)
Nichols, Rosemary, jt. auth. see MacColl, Michaela.
Nichols, Roy & Corley, Monte. Bible Discovery: Ideas. (p. 175)
—Bible Puzzles: Match-It. (p. 176)
—Bible Puzzles: Crosswords. (p. 176)
—Bible Puzzles: Word Search. (p. 176)
—Bible Puzzles: Pencil Games. (p. 176)
Nichols, Stephen J. & Bustard, Ned. Church History ABCs: Augustine & 25 Other Heroes of the Faith. (p. 318)
Nichols, Susan. James Patterson. (p. 907)
Nichols, Travis. Fowl Play. (p. 625)
—Matthew Meets the Man. (p. 1109)
—Monstrous Fun: A Doodle & Activity Book. Nichols, Travis, illus. (p. 1169)
—Uglydoll - Eat Dat! McGinty, Ian, illus. (p. 1808)
Nichols, Travis & Horvath, David. Goin' Places! (p. 692)
—Shhhhhhhh! (p. 1566)
Nichols, Tucker & Nichols, Jon. Crabtree. (p. 375)
Nichols, V. Incredible Dionsaur. M. J. Studios Staff, illus. (p. 869)
Nichols, Vivian. Telluride! (p. 1717)
Nichols, Walter H. Measure of a Boy. (p. 1117)
Nichols, Willie Charles. Adventures of Bo & His Pal Boboy. (p. 16)
Nichols-Lee, Hattie Marie. Angel Bell: The crown of Glory. (p. 73)
Nicholson, Caitlin Dale. Niwechihaw / I Help Morin-Neilson, Leona, tr. (p. 1257)
Nicholson, David L. Little Johnny's First Day of School (p. 1029)
Nicholson, Devon, et al. Fundi the Snail. (p. 649)
Nicholson, Dorinda. Remember World War II: Kids Who Survived Tell Their Stories. (p. 1459)
Nicholson, Dorinda Makanaonalani Stagner. Remember World War II: Kids Who Survived Tell Their Stories. (p. 1459)
Nicholson, Doris. Day with Grandma. (p. 415)
—Michael & His Animals. (p. 1134)
Nicholson, Emma, jt. auth. see Nichols, Lee.
Nicholson, Karen. Birthday Fun. (p. 192)
Nicholson, Kat, illus. see Shakespeare, William.
Nicholson, Kat, illus. see Shelley, Mary & Shelley, Mary.
Nicholson, Lorna Schultz. Delaying the Game (p. 424)
—Holding (p. 788)
—Interference (p. 879)
—Pink Power: The First Women's Hockey World Champions. (p. 1360)
—Puckster Goes to the Olympics. Findley, Kelly, illus. (p. 1414)
—Puckster's First Hockey Tournament. Findley, Kelly, illus. (p. 1414)
—Puckster's First Hockey Tryout. Findley, Kelly, illus. (p. 1414)
—Too Many Men (p. 1766)
—Winning Gold: Canada's Incredible 2002 Olympic Victory in Women's Hockey (p. 1937)
Nicholson, Lorna Schultz & Schultz Nicholson, Lorna. Against the Boards (p. 29)
—Holding (p. 788)
Nicholson, Mike. Catscape (p. 281)
Nicholson, Nancy. Devotional Stories for Little Folks Too. (p. 432)
Nicholson, Peter, jt. auth. see McAuslan, Fiona.
Nicholson, Simon. Demon Curse. (p. 426)
—Magician's Fire. (p. 1075)
Nicholson, Sue. All about Me. (p. 42)
—Animal Babies in Deserts. (p. 76)
—Drawing (p. 481)
—Painting (p. 1318)
—Printing (p. 1407)
—Sculpture (p. 1534)
—Sleepover. (p. 1589)
—World Art (p. 1954)
—World Art: Unique Projects from Cultures Around the Globe. (p. 1954)
—World Art. (p. 1954)
Nicholson, Sue & Robins, Deri. Great Big Art Activity Book. (p. 714)
Nicholson, Trudy, illus. see Douglas, Marjory Stoneman & Milkweed Editions Staff.
Nicholson, Trudy, illus. see Milkweed Editions Staff.
Nicholson, Trudy, illus. see St. Antoine, Sara, ed.
Nicholson, Wanda. Mr Henry's Grass. Webb, Shamore, illus. (p. 1185)
Nicholson, William. Jango: Book Two of the Noble Warriors. (p. 908)
—Jango. (p. 908)
—Noman: Book Three of the Noble Warriors. (p. 1263)
—Noman: La Orden de los Guerreros Misticos. (p. 1263)
—Seeker: Book One of the Noble Warriors. (p. 1548)
—Silbador del Viento. Manero, Laura, tr. (p. 1575)
—Viento en Llamas: Son del Fuego. Manero Jimenez, Laura, tr. (p. 1841)
—Viento en Llamas: Siervos del Maestro. Manero Jimenez, Laura, tr. (p. 1841)
Nicholson, William, illus. see Bianco, Margery Williams.
Nicholson, William, illus. see Williams, Margery & Raiten-D'Antonio, Toni.
Nicholson, William, illus. see Williams, Margery.
Nichx, illus. see Leiter, Andrew S.
Nicieza, Fabián. One Step Forward (p. 1297)
—X-Force: Big Guns. Liefeld, Rob, illus. (p. 1967)
Nicieza, Mariano. Phazer: A Man Lost in Alternative Universes. Olivetti, Ariel, illus. (p. 1350)
Nick, Barbara. Bella the Dragon. Steckler, Elaine, illus. (p. 162)
Nick Barry. Revenge of Poseidon's Trident: An Ethan Sparks Adventure. (p. 1465)
Nick, Charles. Sir Francis Drake: Slave Trader & Pirate. (p. 1580)
Nick, Papa. Never Ending Stories: Part Four. (p. 1242)
—Never Ending Stories: Part Three. (p. 1242)
—Never Ending Stories. (p. 1242)
Nickel. Pinocchio. (p. 1360)
Nickel, Adam, jt. auth. see Brasch, Nicolas.
Nickel, Adam, jt. auth. see Ellis, Julie.
Nickel, Adam, jt. auth. see Wall, Julia.
Nickel, Barbara. Hannah Waters & the Daughter of Johann Sebastian Bach. (p. 742)
Nickel, Barbara Kathleen. Secret Wish of Nannerl Mozart: Sumach Classic Edition (p. 1544)
Nickel, Bonnie. Those Kooky Kangaroos. (p. 1740)
—Those Mischievous Monkeys. (p. 1740)
—Those Mischievous Monkeys. Weaver, Steve, illus. (p. 1740)
Nickel, Laura. Alexander's Hospital Stay. (p. 37)
Nickel, Scott. Attack of the Mutant Lunch Lady: A Buzz Beaker Brainstorm Smith, Andy J., illus. (p. 113)
—Attack of the Mutant Lunch Lady. Smith, Andy J., illus. (p. 113)
—Back to the Ice Age. Corts, Enrique, illus. (p. 130)
—Backyard Bug Battle: A Buzz Beaker Brainstorm Smith, Andy J., illus. (p. 131)
—Billions of Bats. Smith, Andy J., illus. (p. 187)
—Blast to the Past. Harpster, Steve, illus. (p. 198)
—Blastoff to the Secret Side of the Moon! Bradley, Jessica, illus. (p. 198)
—Boy Who Burped Too Much Harpster, Steve, illus. (p. 219)
—Buzz Beaker vs Dracula: A Buzz Beaker Brainstorm Smith, Andy J., illus. (p. 248)
—Curse of the Red Scorpion Harpster, Steve, illus. (p. 395)
—Day of the Field Trip Zombies Hohnstadt, Cedric, illus. (p. 414)
—Dognapped! Harpster, Steve, illus. (p. 462)
—Dognapped! Jimmy Sniffles. Harpster, Steve, illus. (p. 462)
—Double Trouble Harpster, Steve, illus. (p. 473)
—Egg Hunt. Fentz, Mike & Barker, Lori, illus. (p. 506)
—Garfield & Friends. Flowerpot Press, ed. (p. 656)
—I Could Be a One-Man Relay Santillan, Jorge H., illus. (p. 837)
—Incredible Rockhead Jennings, C. S., illus. (p. 869)
—Incredible Rockhead vs Papercut! Jennings, C. S., illus. (p. 869)
—Invasion of the Gym Class Zombies. Luxich, Matt, illus. (p. 883)
—It's a Wrestling Mat, Not a Dance Floor Santillan, Jorge H., illus. (p. 896)
—Jimmy Sniffles Dognapped! (p. 918)
—Jimmy Sniffles vs the Mummy Harpster, Steve, illus. (p. 918)
—Monster Trouble. Fentz, Mike, illus. (p. 1168)
—Race on the River Harpster, Steve, illus. (p. 1431)
—Robot Rampage: A Buzz Beaker Brainstorm. Smith, Andy J., illus. (p. 1480)
—Rock, Paper, Scissorlegz. Jennings, C. S., illus. (p. 1482)
—Secret of the Summer School Zombies Luxich, Matt, illus. (p. 1543)
—Skiing Has Its Ups & Downs Santillan, Jorge H., illus. (p. 1584)
—Super-Powered Sneeze. Harpster, Steve, illus. (p. 1680)
—T. Rex vs Robo-Dog 3000 Corts, Enrique, illus. (p. 1694)
—Up the President's Nose Harpster, Steve, illus. (p. 1824)
—Wind Power Whiz Kid: A Buzz Beaker Brainstorm Smith, Andy J., illus. (p. 1935)
Nickel, Scott, jt. auth. see Dahl, Michael.
Nickel, Scott & Dahl, Michael. Evil Echo Crowther, Jeff, illus. (p. 546)
Nickel, Scott, et al. Incredible Rockhead & the Spectacular Scissorlegz Jennings, C. S., illus. (p. 869)
Nickell, Judy. New Mexico Dictionary for Young People. (p. 1246)
Nickelodeon. SpongeBob SquarePants: Goodnight Lagoon. (p. 1630)
—Surf's Up, SpongeBob! (p. 1685)
—Swim, Boots, Swim! (p. 1690)
Nickelodeon / LeapFrog, jt. auth. see Nickelodeon Staff.
Nickelodeon Dora the Explorer Staff. Dora the Explorer Movie Theater Storybook & Movie Projector(r). (p. 471)
—Say Boo! (p. 1518)
Nickelodeon SpongeBob SquarePants Staff. SpongeBobSquarePants Ocean Close-Up. (p. 1631)
Nickelodeon Staff. All Grown up: Coup Deville Rau, Zachary, ed. (p. 44)
—Dora. (p. 470)
—Hooray for School: Going to School With Nick. (p. 796)
—Party Time! (p. 1326)
—Teenage Mutant Ninja Turtles Mix & Match. (p. 1714)
Nickelodeon Staff, illus. see Reader's Digest Staff.
Nickelodeon Staff & LeapForg Staff/Nickelodeon. Dora the Explorer: Dora Goes to School. (p. 471)
Nickelodeon Staff & Nickelodeon / LeapFrog. Go Diego Go! Underwater Mystery. (p. 686)
—SpongeBob SquarePants: The Tour de Bikini Bottom. (p. 1630)
Nickelodeon Staff, creator. All Grown Up. (p. 44)
—Amanda Show. (p. 52)
Nickelodeon Staff, ed. 1-2-3 - Go Diego Go! (p. 1990)
—ABC, Dora the Explorer. (p. 3)
—Phonics - Spongebob Squarepants. (p. 1351)
—Words - Dora the Explorer. (p. 1951)
Nickelodeon Teenage Mutant Ninja Turtles Staff. Masked Heroes. (p. 1102)
Nickels, Greg, jt. auth. see Nickles, Greg.
Nickelsen, Leann. Memorizing Strategies & Other Brain-Based Activities: That Help Kids Learn, Review, & Recall. (p. 1126)
Nickelsen, LeAnn & Glasscock, Sarah. Inference & Cause & Effect. (p. 873)
Nickelsen, Leann & Glasscock, Sarah. Point of View & Fact & Opinion. (p. 1377)
—Sequencing & Context Clues: Mini-Lessons Activities Warm-Up Prjects Graphic Organizers Evaluation Ideas. (p. 1552)
Nickens, Ramona. Grandma's Brown Cookies: Made with the Good Stuff. (p. 708)
Nickens, T. Eward. Field & Stream's Guide to Camping. (p. 583)
—Field & Stream's Guide to Outdoor Survival. (p. 583)
Nickerson, Jane. Mirk & Midnight Hour. (p. 1149)
—Strands of Bronze & Gold. (p. 1664)
Nickerson, Sara, tr. see Rosen, Maureen.
Nickerson, Sara. How to Disappear Completely & Never Be Found. Comport, Sally Wern, illus. (p. 816)
—Secrets of Blueberries, Brothers, Moose & Me. (p. 1545)
Nicklas, James. Study Hall Story. (p. 1670)
Nicklas, Rita. B-Liminator & I Fight Cancer. (p. 123)
Nicklaus, Carol, illus. see Carlson, Dale Bick & Carlson, Hannah.
Nicklaus, Carol, illus. see Carlson, Dale Bick.
Nicklaus, Carol, illus. see Carlson, Dale.
Nicklaus, Carol, illus. see Linn, Margot.
Nicklaus, Carol, illus. see November, Deborah.
Nicklaus, Terry. Schweppe. (p. 1524)
Nickle, John, illus. see Barrett, Judi.
Nickle, John, illus. see DeKeyser, Stacy.
Nickle, John, illus. see Grimm, Jacob & Grimm, Wilhelm K.
Nickle, John, illus. see Levinthal, David.
Nickle, John, jt. auth. see Katschke, Judy.
Nickles, Clay & Ayres, Ella. Ali's Treasure. (p. 41)
Nickle's, Greg. Hispanics: We Came to North America. (p. 781)
Nickles, Greg. Irish: We Came to North America. (p. 887)
—Italians: We Came to North America. (p. 894)
—Japanese: We Came to North America. (p. 909)
—Poles: We Came to North America. (p. 1379)
—Russia: The Culture. (p. 1498)
—Russia - The Land. (p. 1498)
—Russia - The People. (p. 1498)
Nickles, Greg & Kalman, Bobbie. Russia - The Culture. (p. 1498)
Nickles, Greg & Nickels, Greg. Russia: The People. (p. 1498)
Nicklin, Flip, jt. auth. see Nicklin, Linda.
Nicklin, Flip & Nicklin, Linda. Face to Face with Dolphins. (p. 560)
—Face to Face with Whales. (p. 560)
Nicklin, Linda, jt. auth. see Nicklin, Flip.
Nicklin, Linda & Nicklin, Flip. Face to Face with Dolphins. (p. 560)
Nicklin, Miriam & Pecsenye, Jessica. University of Virginia College Prowler off the Record. (p. 1821)
nicklin, philip. Belly Button Fluff Pixie. (p. 163)
Nicko. Tiki Junior: And the Secret Book. (p. 1749)
Nickoloff, Michael, jt. ed. see Smith, Dan.
Nickson, Marilyn. Teaching & Learning Mathematics: A Teacher's Guide to Recent Research & Its Application. (p. 1710)
Nicodemus, Laura Konger. Growing up on the Farm in The 1930s' (p. 727)
Nicol, Brock, illus. see Walters III, Harry C.
Nicol, C. W. Raven's Tale. Amaktauyok, Germaine, illus. (p. 1441)
Nicol, Scott Thomas. Dr. Jim & the Special Stethoscope. Youngblood, David W., illus. (p. 475)
Nicola. Lost Boomerang. (p. 1055)
Nicola A Green. Pumpkin: The easter Bunny. (p. 1416)
Nicola Baxter Staff. Fairy Palace Pop up. (p. 563)
Nicola, Christos, jt. auth. see Taylor, Peter Lane.
Nicola, Robbin. Fighter Joe: The Fish of Which Dreams Are Made. Wolf, Claudia, illus. (p. 585)
Nicola, Tuxworth. Learn-A-Word Book: Bodies. (p. 982)
—Learn-A-Word Book: Animals. (p. 982)
Nicolas, Otero, illus. see Anaya, Rudolfo A.
Nicolas, Ron. Northern Lights: A Wilderness Adventure. (p. 1266)
Nicolas, Stephanie. Forged Report Card. (p. 619)
Nicolay, Helen. Boys Life of Abraham Lincoln. (p. 220)
—Boys' Life of Abraham Lincoln. (p. 220)
Nicole, Bridget & Gray, Kevan. University of Illinois College Prowler off the Record. (p. 1820)
Nicole Davis, Jodie. Elva Jean Prays for Her Green Beans! (p. 516)
Nicole, Heather. What Is a Food Chain? (p. 1888)
Nicole, Natorya. EJ & Sis: Time Out... Learning Tool. (p. 507)
Nicoll, Allison. Sew It! Make 17 Projects with Yummy Precut Fabric - Jelly Rolls, Layer Cakes, Charm Packs & Fat Quarters. (p. 1555)
Nicoll, David. Bean at the Beach. (p. 150)
—Bean at the Fair. (p. 150)
—Bean on the Farm. (p. 150)
Nicoll, Helen & Pienkowski, Jan. Meg y Mog Juegan Al Escondite. (p. 1124)
Nicoll, Jacqueline. Pick-a-WooWoo - Oceans Calling: An enlightening journey to the lost city of Atlantis. Evans, Gabriel, illus. (p. 1354)
Nicolle, Ethan. Kill the Devil. (p. 956)
Nicolle, Malachai. Axe Cop (p. 121)
—Axe Cop Volume 3. (p. 121)
—Bad Guy Earth (p. 131)
—President of the World. Edidin, Rachel, ed. (p. 1397)
Nicolotti, Muriel. Madhi: A Child of Egypt. (p. 1070)
Nicolson, Cynthia. Discover Space. Slavin, Bill, illus. (p. 448)
—Discover Space Rocks. Slavin, Bill, illus. (p. 448)
—Discover the Planets. Slavin, Bill, illus. (p. 448)
—Discover the Stars. Slavin, Bill, illus. (p. 448)
Nicolson, Cynthia, jt. auth. see Nicolson, Cynthia Pratt.
Nicolson, Cynthia Pratt. Discover Space. Slavin, Bill, illus. (p. 448)
—Totally Human: Why We Look & Act the Way We Do. Eastman, Dianne, illus. (p. 1771)
Nicolson, Cynthia Pratt & Nicolson, Cynthia. Discover Space Rocks. Slavin, Bill, illus. (p. 448)
Nicolson, Cynthia Pratt & Slavin, Bill. Starting with Space: The Earth. (p. 1644)
Nicolson, Cynthia Pratt, et al. Jumbo Book of Space. Nicolson, Cynthia Pratt & Slavin, Bill, illus. (p. 933)
Nicolson, Paula. Love Book Healing Poems for Broken Hearts. (p. 1059)
Nicori, Sandi, illus. see Wassillie, Eliza, et al.
Niddrie, June. E. B. & the Bees. (p. 491)
—Fly Ladybird, Fly. (p. 609)
—Great Scott & Otis. (p. 718)
—Pom, the Pomegranate Pixie. (p. 1382)
—Quiet Queenie. (p. 1428)
—Sweetpea & His Friends. (p. 1690)
Nidenoff, Michele, illus. see Fitch, Sheree.
Nidey, Kelli. When Autumn Falls. Swan, Susan, illus. (p. 1901)
Nidiffer, Nina J. Un-Natural Disaster: Stories of Survival after Graniteville Tragedy. (p. 1811)
Niebergall, Jane Sutherland. Bears to Barely Bears. (p. 152)
Niebisch, Jackie. Escuela de los Vampiritos. (p. 535)
—Escuela de los Vampiritos - Examen. (p. 535)
Niedda, Jeshica. Bird Name Baby Blue. (p. 190)
Niedergall, Jane. Primary Alaska. (p. 1399)
Niederhofer, Renate, jt. auth. see Rathore, Jazz Kopecek.
Niederman, Derrick. Mind-Stretching Math Puzzles. (p. 1145)
Niednagel, David, illus. see Niednagel, Jonathan P.
Niednagel, Jonathan P. Your Key to Sports Success: Using Your Unique Brain Type to Maximize Athletic Performance. Niednagel, David & Marco, Harvey, illus. (p. 1981)
Niedworok, Claudio O. Seafarers: Chronicles of the Suspense & Romance of the Sea. Knight, Tori, ed. (p. 1536)
Niedzviecki, Hal. Big Book of Pop Culture: A How-To Guide for Young Artists. Ngui, Marc, illus. (p. 179)
Nieh, Camellia, tr. see Kitoh, Moiro.
Niehaus, Rebecca. Birth of a Kitten. (p. 192)
Niekerk, Katie & Seaman, Jim. University of Denver College Prowler off the Record. (p. 1820)
Nielander, Amy. Ladybug Race. Nielander, Amy, illus. (p. 971)
Nieländer, Peter, illus. see Preller, James.
Nielandt, Dirk. Qui?! Sarfati, Sonia, tr. from DUT. (p. 1427)
—Qui Est-Ce Qui... Sarfati, Sonia, tr. from DUT. (p. 1427)
Nield, Joan. Children's Story Book. (p. 304)
Nield, Maureen. How Different from Us. (p. 806)
Nield, Sue. Raps & Rhymes about Primary School Times: A Children's Poetry Anthology. (p. 1439)
—Raps & Rhymes about Tudor Times: A Poetic Interpretation of History. (p. 1439)
Nielsen, Amy. Victor & the Sun Orb. (p. 1840)
Nielsen, Aubrie. After School. (p. 28)
—At School. (p. 110)
Nielsen, Emily, tr. see Romano, Elaine.
Nielsen, Gwyn English. Serendipity & the Dream Catcher. Nielsen, Gwyn English, ed. (p. 1552)
—Torey the Turkey Goes Skiing. (p. 1769)
Nielsen, Janet Marie, illus. see Abdelsalam, Lisa.
Nielsen, Jennifer A. Behind Enemy Lines. (p. 160)
—Elliot & the Last Underworld War. Kendall, Gideon, illus. (p. 514)
—Elliot & the Pixie Plot. Kendall, Gideon, illus. (p. 514)
—False Prince. (p. 567)
—Mark of the Thief. (p. 1095)
—Runaway King. (p. 1496)
—Shadow Throne. (p. 1558)
Nielsen, Jon. Laney Gets Her Ridge. (p. 974)
Nielsen, Julia L., illus. see Clay, Kathryn.
Nielsen, Kay, illus. see Quiller-Couch, Sir Arthur.
Nielsen, Kelli & Benham, Kelly. You Will Always Be My Son. (p. 1976)
Nielsen, L. Michelle & Neilsen, L. Michelle. Vintage Cars. (p. 1843)
—Vintage Cars, 1919-1930. (p. 1843)
Nielsen, L. Michelle & Nielson, L. Michelle. Biography of Corn. (p. 189)
Nielsen, Laura, jt. auth. see Nielsen, Laura F.
Nielsen, Laura F. & Nielsen, Laura. Mrs. Muddle's Holidays. Yezerski, Thomas F., illus. (p. 1187)
Nielsen, Pamela & Luhmann, Edward Q. Behold the Lamb: An Introduction to the Signs & Symbols of the Church. Kirchhoff, Art, illus. (p. 160)
Nielsen, Ric, illus. see Madaras, Diana.
Nielsen, Ron. Little Green Handbook: Seven Trends Shaping the Future of Our Planet. (p. 1028)
Nielsen, Shaw, illus. see Friedman, Caitlin.
Nielsen, Susin. Dear George Clooney: Please Marry My Mom. (p. 419)
—Reluctant Journal of Henry K. Larsen. (p. 1458)
—Snake (p. 1596)
—We Are All Made of Molecules. (p. 1865)
—Word Nerd. (p. 1950)
Nielsen-Fernlund, Susin. Magic Beads. Cote, Genevieve, illus. (p. 1071)
Nielson, Ane O. Lone Star G Brand on My Behind. (p. 1046)
Nielson, Cliff, illus. see Pearson, Ridley.
Nielson, Doug, illus. see Carlson, Glenn E.

N

Nielson, Ginger. Willow, an Elephant's Tale. Nielson, Ginger, illus. (p. 1934)
Nielson, Ginger, illus. see Arnold, Connie.
Nielson, Ginger, illus. see Dubreuil, Robert.
Nielson, Ginger, illus. see Jones, Rena.
Nielson, Ginger, illus. see Jones, Rene'.
Nielson, Ginger, illus. see Lallouz, Michele.
Nielson, Ginger, illus. see Reinke, Beth Bence.
Nielson, Ginger, illus. see Zabel, Vivian.
Nielson, Kelli S. Stone Mage Wars, Book 1: Journey to the Fringe. (p. 1652)
Nielson, L. Michelle, jt. auth. see Nielsen, L. Michelle.
Nielson, Mark S. I Believe in Jesus Too. Stapley, Craig, illus. (p. 834)
Nielson, Sam, illus. see Gale, Eric Kahn.
Nielson, Sam, illus. see Wolverton, Barry.
Nielson, Sheila A. Forbidden Sea. (p. 616)
Nielson, Wendy. Is for Asking: A Spiritual Frolic through the Alphabet. (p. 889)
Niem, Thay, jt. auth. see Marsden, Carolyn.
Niem, Thay Phap, jt. auth. see Marsden, Carolyn.
Niemann, Christoph. Pet Dragon: A Story about Adventure, Friendship, & Chinese Characters. Niemann, Christoph, illus. (p. 1345)
—Potato King. (p. 1388)
—Subway. Niemann, Christoph, illus. (p. 1671)
—That's How! Niemann, Christoph, illus. (p. 1726)
Niemann, Christoph, illus. see Dubner, Stephen J.
Niemela, JoAnn Huston. Crows of Hidden Creek. Bradley, Sandy, illus. (p. 386)
Niemi, Renee. Because Gage Believed. (p. 155)
—Riia's Dream Diary. (p. 1472)
Nieminen, Lotta, illus. see Broom, Jenny.
Nienstedt, L. a. Phineas T Pudgepot & the Mysterious Flying Fish. (p. 1351)
Niepold, Mil & Verdu, Jeanyves. Oooh! Picasso. Niepold, Mil & Verdu, Jeanyves, illus. (p. 1298)
Niethammer, Carolyn J. Keeping the Rope Straight: Annie Dodge Wauneka's Life of Service to the Navajo. (p. 948)
Nieting, Sherry. Adventures in Hope Forest: Isabelle's Search for God. (p. 15)
Nieto, Gina L., illus. see Nieto, Nancy.
Nieto, Laura. Patrulla Del Castillo Volador/ the Flying Castle Patrol. Nieto, Laura, illus. (p. 1329)
Nieto, Nancy. My Angel & Me. Nieto, Gina L., illus. (p. 1196)
Nieto, Terry. Sun Go Away. (p. 1676)
Nieto-Phillips, John M. & Morris, Julie. Telma, la Hormiguita. Nieto-Phillips, John M. & Morris, Julie, illus. (p. 1717)
Nietzsche, Friedrich. Birth of Tragedy. Ian, Johnston, tr. (p. 192)
Nieuwenhuizen, John, jt. auth. see Kuijer, Guus.
Nieuwenhuizen, John, tr. see van Rijckeghem, Jean-Claude & van Beirs, Pat.
Nievelstein, Ralf, illus. see Michaelis, Antonia.
Nigg, Joe. How to Raise & Keep a Dragon. (p. 821)
Nigg, Jospeh, ed. see Topsell, John.
Nigh, Linda. Emily's Christmas Tree. (p. 519)
Night & Day Studios. Peekaboo Presents. Lunn, Corey, illus. (p. 1335)
Night, P. J. Best Friends Forever. (p. 169)
—Don't Drink the Punch! (p. 467)
—Home, Sweet Haunt. (p. 793)
—House Next Door. (p. 803)
—Is She for Real? (p. 890)
—It's All Downhill from Here. (p. 896)
—No Trick-Or-Treating! (p. 1260)
—No Trick-or-Treating! Superscary Superspecial. (p. 1260)
—Off the Wall. (p. 1279)
—Read It & Weep! (p. 1443)
—Ready for a Scare? (p. 1447)
—Ride of Your Life. (p. 1471)
—Show Must Go On! (p. 1570)
—Show Must Go On! (p. 1571)
—Terror Behind the Mask. (p. 1722)
—There's Something Out There. (p. 1731)
—Together Forever. (p. 1762)
—Truth or Dare... (p. 1794)
—Truth or Dare ... (p. 1794)
—What a Doll! (p. 1878)
—Will You Be My Friend? (p. 1932)
—You Can't Come in Here! (p. 1974)
—Your Worst Nightmare. (p. 1981)
—You're Invited to a Creepover Collection: Truth or Dare...; You Can't Come in Here!; Ready for a Scare?; the Show Must Go On! (p. 1982)
Nighthawk, Tori. Don't Judge a Bird by Its Feathers. Nighthawk, Tori, illus. (p. 467)
Nightingale, Clare Theresa. Adventures of Fishkins & Pepperjacket. (p. 18)
Nightingale, Jenny, illus. see Getz, Jeanine Behr.
Nightow, Yasuhiro. Break Out Nightow, Yasuhiro, illus. (p. 224)
—Gunslinger (p. 732)
—Happy Days (p. 745)
—Silent Ruin (p. 1575)
—Trigun Maximum - Bottom of the Dark Vol. 4 (p. 1786)
Nigro, D. M. Wolfman, the Shrink & the Eighth-Grade Election. (p. 1944)
Nigro Heroux, Regina. Grandma's Butterfly Garden. (p. 708)
Nigrosh, Millicent. Camilla Makes a Choice. (p. 256)
—Huh' Is Not a Word. (p. 825)
Nihart, Gene. Fox Island Cup. (p. 626)
Nihei, Tsutomu. Biomega Nihei, Tsutomu, illus. (p. 190)
—Wolverine Legends: Snikt! Vol. 5 Nihei, Tsutomu, illus. (p. 1944)
Nihoff, Tim, illus. see Hurwitz, Johanna, ed.
Nihoff, Tim, illus. see McGrath, Barbara Barbieri.
Nihoff, Tim, illus. see Webster, Christine.
Nihon Falcom. Legend of Heroes: the Characters: The Characters. (p. 988)
—Legend of Heroes: the Illustrations: The Illustrations. (p. 988)
Niida, Jack, tr. see Tsuda, Masami.
Niimi, Ryu, et al. Tokujin Yoshioka Design. (p. 1762)
Nijbamum, John Suh, ed. see Nama, Michael D., et al.
Nijland, Stern, jt. auth. see Haan, Linda de.
Nijs, Erika de. Carpenter's Job. (p. 271)
Nijssen, Elfi. Laurie. van Lindehuizen, Eline, illus. (p. 980)
Nijyo, Rin. Tales of the Abyss: Asch the Bloody Volume 1: Asch the Bloody Volume 1 (p. 1702)
Nikakhtar, Manijeh. Love & Joy. (p. 1059)
Nikiel, Laura Gibbons, illus. see Egermeier, Elsie E.
Nikiel, Laura Gibbons, illus. see Egermeier, Elsie.
Nikiel, Laura Gibbons, illus. see Lewis, Beverly.
Nikki, Grimes. Bronx Masquerade. (p. 230)
Niklas, JoAda Marie. Curious Little Ladybug. (p. 394)
Nikola-Lisa, W. Alegriade Ser Tu Yo. (p. 35)
—America: A Book of Opposites/Un Libro de Contrarios. 14 Outstanding American Artists Staff, illus. (p. 58)
—Bein' with You This Way. Bryant, Michael, illus. (p. 160)
—My Teacher Can Teach... Anyone! Galindo, Felipe, illus. (p. 1219)
Nikola-lisa, W. Till Year's Good End. Manson, Christopher, illus. (p. 1750)
Nikola-lisa, W., jt. auth. see Nikola-lisa, W.
Nikola-lisa, W. & Nikola-lisa, W. Hallelujah! A Christmas Celebration. Saint James, Synthia, illus. (p. 737)
Nikolet, C. T. From Bullies to Friends. Howe, Cindy T., illus. (p. 642)
Nikolo, Martin. Physics for the Rest of Us. (p. 1353)
Nikolov, Stefan V., tr. see Ashley, Elana.
Nikovics, Anne. Adventures of Katie Ladybug. (p. 19)
Niland, Deborah. Annie's Chair. Niland, Deborah, illus. (p. 87)
—When Coco Was a Kitten. Niland, Deborah, illus. (p. 1901)
Niland, Deborah, illus. see Wild, Margaret.
Niland, Kilmeny. Gingerbread Man. (p. 677)
—Two Bad Teddies. Niland, Kilmeny, illus. (p. 1803)
—Two Tough Teddies. Niland, Kilmeny, illus. (p. 1804)
—Two Tough Teddies Boxed Set. (p. 1804)
Niland, Kurt, Sr. Gwinnett: Success Lives Here. (p. 733)
Niles de Martin, Anita & Myrick, Gladys, eds. Manual de Estrellas se Honor-Alumna: Alumna (p. 1088)
Niles, Kim. Muggles' New Home. (p. 1189)
Niles, Kim, illus. see Anjou, Colette.
Niles, Steve. War of the Worlds. Ryall, Chris, ed. (p. 1857)
Niles, Steve & Santoro, Matt. Breath of Bones: a Tale of the Golem: A Tale of the Golem. Allie, Scott, ed. (p. 225)
Niles, Steve & Villarrubia, Jose. Gotham County Line. (p. 704)
Nilesh, Misty, illus. see Tarnowska, Wafa'.
Nille, Peggy, illus. see Min, SooHyeon.
Nille, Peggy, jt. auth. see Elschner, Geraldine.
Nilsen, Anna. Amazeing Voyage of Charles Darwin. Nilsen, Anna, illus. (p. 52)
—Bella's Butterfly Ball. Partis, Joanne, illus. (p. 162)
—Bella's Midsummer Secret. Partis, Joanne, illus. (p. 162)
—My Mum's Best. Dodd, Emma, illus. (p. 1215)
—Pirates: All Aboard for Hours of Puzzling Fun! (p. 1363)
—Robotics: Maths, Games & Puzzles. Nilsen, Anna, illus. (p. 1481)
—¿Baño o Cama? Morell, Ivonne Bonsfill, tr. (p. 136)
—¿Osito o Tren? Morell, Ivonne Bonsfill, tr. (p. 1305)
—¿Viento o Lluvia? Morell, Ivonne Bonsfill, tr. (p. 1841)
—¿Zanahorias o Guisantes? Morell, Ivonne Bonsfill, tr. (p. 1984)
Nilsen, Anna, ed. see Miles Kelly Staff.
Nilsen, Anna, jt. auth. see Miles Kelly Staff.
Nilsen, Anna & Bentley, Jonathan. Swim, Duck, Swim! (p. 1690)
—Tip, Truck, Tip! (p. 1757)
—Wave, Baby, Wave! (p. 1864)
Nilsen, Erika. Blessing of Feelings. Nilsen, Mary Ylvisaker, photos by. (p. 199)
Nilsen, Lenie. Elephant & the Dove. (p. 511)
Nilsen, Mary Ylvisaker, photos by see Nilsen, Erika.
Nilsen, Morten. Snyder: The Pig's Tale. Osenchakov, Yuri, illus. (p. 1601)
Nilsen, Richard J., ed. see Carothers, Nina.
Nilson, Anna. Art Shark: Collect Great Art, Auction It, Hide It, Steal It! (p. 103)
Nilsson, Al. Tennessee Tater. Nilsson, Al, illus. (p. 1720)
Nilsson, Bo Sigvard. Come on, Brian! A Young Boy's Struggle to Play in an All-Star Hockey Tournament. (p. 347)
Nilsson, Janet Busbey, ed. see Saldivar, Jose A.
Nilsson, Lennart, contrib. by. Wonder of Life (p. 1947)
Nilsson, Oscar. Lowrider Coloring Book. (p. 1061)
Nilsson, Per. Heart's Delight. Chace, Tara, tr. from SWE. (p. 760)
—Seventeen. Chace, Tara, tr. from SWE. (p. 1555)
—You & You & You. Chace, Tara, tr. from SWE. (p. 1973)
Nilsson, Troy, 2nd. Hiroshima Stones: The Shadow Stones of Hiroshima. Nilsson, Troy, 2nd, illus. (p. 781)
—Hiroshima Stones: The Shadow Stones of Hiroshima - a Story of Love & War. Nilsson, Troy, 2nd, illus. (p. 781)
Nilsson, Ulf. Detective Gordon - The First Case. Spee, Gitte, illus. (p. 431)
Nimble, Jacque. Prank Wars. (p. 1393)
Nimmo, Jenny. Beasties. Millward, Gwen, illus. (p. 152)
—Box Boys & the Magic Shell. (p. 216)
—Charlie Bone & the Beast. (p. 292)
—Charlie Bone & the Time Twister. (p. 292)
—Chestnut Soldier. (p. 298)
—Dragon's Child. (p. 479)
—Emlyn's Moon. (p. 519)
—Leopards' Gold. (p. 993)
—Matty Mouse. (p. 1110)
—Midnight for Charlie Bone. (p. 1138)
—Pig on a Swing. Uff, Caroline, illus. (p. 1357)
—Secret Kingdom. (p. 1541)
—Stones of Ravenglass. (p. 1653)
Nimmo, Paul. Will Shakespeare Save Us! Will Shakespeare Save the King! (p. 1932)
Nimmons, David. Soul Beneath the Skin: The Unseen Hearts & Habits of Gay Men. (p. 1614)
Nimoy, Leonard. Leonard Nimoy's Primortals: Origins. Vol. 1, No. 1 Chambers, James et al, eds. (p. 992)
Ninaltowski, Eric, illus. see Miller, Mike S.
Ninan, A. Chemistry: Chemistry Calculations Explained. (p. 297)
—Chemistry - AS Level Chemistry Explained. (p. 297)
Niner, Holly L. Mr. Worry: A Story about OCD. Swearingen, Greg, illus. (p. 1187)
Ninnes, Jay. Smelly Footed Toad. (p. 1593)
Niño, Alex, illus. see Melville, Herman.
Niño, Hugo. Primitivos Relatos Contados Otra Vez: Heroes y Mitos Amazonicos. Gonzalez, Henry, illus. (p. 1401)
Nino, Jairo Anibal. Alegria de Querer: Poemas de Amor para Ninos. Acosta, Patricia, illus. (p. 35)
—Aviador Santiago. Gonzalez, Henry, illus. (p. 119)
—Estrella de Papel. (p. 538)
—Monte Calvo y la Madriguera. (p. 1170)
—Musico Del Aire. (p. 1194)
—Nido Mas Bello del Mundo. (p. 1251)
—Papeles de Miguela. Rincon, Fernando, illus. (p. 1322)
—Quinto Viaje y Otras Historias del Nuevo Mundo. Isaza, Juanita, illus. (p. 1428)
—Razzgo, Indo y Zaz. Sierra, Juan Ramon, illus. (p. 1441)
—Senora Contraria. (p. 1550)
—Zoro. (p. 1990)
Ninos Aprenden Ingles Corp. Children Learning English. (p. 302)
—Children Learning French. (p. 302)
—Children Learning Spanish. (p. 302)
Ninteau, Sherrie. Rick's Story-the Story of Rick Hoyt. (p. 1470)
Nipp, Susan Hagen, jt. auth. see Beall, Pamela Conn.
Nippert, Brenda & Nippert, George. Alphabet of Catholic Saints Nippert, Brenda & Nippert, George, illus. (p. 49)
—Alphabet of Mary Nippert, Brenda & Nippert, George, illus. (p. 49)
Nippert, George, jt. auth. see Nippert, Brenda.
Nirattisai, Preston, illus. see DeGaetano, Steve.
Nirgad, Lia. Kiss for Lily. Abulafia, Yossi, illus. (p. 961)
Nirgiotis, Nicholas. Killer Ants. Stevenson, Emma, illus. (p. 956)
Nishat-Botero, Hannah. Hannah Banana's Book of Poems. (p. 742)
Nishi, Dennis, ed. Korean War. (p. 967)
Nishi, Yoshiyuki. Muhyo & Roji's Bureau of Supernatural Investigation. Nishi, Yoshiyuki, illus. (p. 1189)
—Muhyo & Roji's Bureau of Supernatural Investigation, Vol. 18. Nishi, Yoshiyuki, illus. (p. 1189)
Nishida, Masaki. Drawing Manga Animals. (p. 482)
—Drawing Manga Dinosaurs. (p. 482)
—Drawing Manga Insects. (p. 482)
—Drawing Manga Martial Arts Figures. (p. 482)
—Drawing Manga Medieval Castles & Knights. (p. 482)
—Drawing Manga Vehicles. (p. 482)
Nishii, illus. see Johnsen, Erin L.
Nishimori, Hiroyuki. Cheeky Angel (p. 295)
—Cheeky Angel Nishimori, Hiroyuki, illus. (p. 295)
—Cheeky Angel. Nishimori, Hiroyuki, illus. (p. 295)
—Cheeky Angel. Yamazaki, Joe, tr. from JPN. (p. 295)
Nishimura, Kae. Dinah! (p. 440)
Nishiyama, Akira & Komatsu, Eiko. Wonderful Houses Around the World. Komatsu, Yoshio, photos by. (p. 1948)
Nishizuka, Koko. Beckoning Cat: Based on a Japanese Folktale. Litzinger, Rosanne, illus. (p. 156)
Nislick, June Levitt. Zayda Was a Cowboy. (p. 1985)
Nissen Samuels, Linda. Draw Water & Other Things. Malvezi, Irene, illus. (p. 481)
Nissenberg, Sandra K. Kids' Cookbook: From Mac 'n Cheese to Double Chocolate Chip Cookies-90 Recipes to Have Some Finger-Lickin' Fun. (p. 953)
Nister, Ernest. Merry Magic-Go-Round: An Antique Book of Changing Pictures. (p. 1129)
Nite, Aluta. Folk Tales for Children's Enjoyment Book: Why & How Fables Number Two. (p. 611)
—Why & How Fables Number Three: Folk Tales for Children's Enjoyment Book 3. (p. 1922)
Nithyananda, Paramahamsa. Who You Truly Are... The Lion & Cub Story. (p. 1919)
Nittinger, Sharon. How Did They Build That? Road. (p. 806)
—How Does It Fly? Blimp. (p. 808)
Nitto, Tomio. Red Rock: A Graphic Fable (p. 1455)
Nitz, Kristin Wolden. Defending Irene (p. 423)
—Saving the Griffin Jaeggi, Yoshiko, illus. (p. 1517)
—Suspect (p. 1688)
Nitzberg, Chuck, illus. see Backer, Miles.
Nitzberg, Chuck, illus. see Bhagat-Clark, Duryan & Backer, Miles.
Nitzsche, Shane, illus. see Ellis, Paula.
Nitzsche, Shane, illus. see Jacobson, Ryan.
Nitzsche, Shane, illus. see Temple, Bob.
Niven, Bill, ed. Germans As Victims: Remembering the Past in Contemporary Germany. (p. 666)
Niven, David. Los 100 Secretos de la Gente Feliz: Lo que los Cientificos han Descubierto y como Puede Aplicarlo a su Vida. (p. 1053)
Niven, Felicia Lowenstein. Brainless Birthday Jokes to Tickle Your Funny Bone. (p. 222)
—Fabulous Fashions of The 1920s. (p. 560)
—Ha-Ha Holiday Jokes to Tickle Your Funny Bone. (p. 734)
—Hilarious Huge Animal Jokes to Tickle Your Funny Bone. (p. 779)
—Hysterical Dog Jokes to Tickle Your Funny Bone. (p. 831)
—Learning to Care for a Bird. (p. 985)
—Learning to Care for a Cat. (p. 985)
—Learning to Care for Fish. (p. 985)
—Learning to Care for Small Mammals. (p. 985)
—Lo Que Hacen los Doctores. (p. 1044)
—Lo Que Hacen los Oficiales de Policia. (p. 1044)
—Nifty Thrifty Music Crafts. Ponte, June, illus. (p. 1252)
—Weird Science Jokes to Tickle Your Funny Bone. (p. 1872)
Niven, Felicia Lowenstein & Library Association Staff. Learning to Care for a Dog. (p. 985)
—Learning to Care for a Horse. (p. 985)
—Learning to Care for Reptiles & Amphibians. (p. 985)
Niven, Jennifer. Ada Blackjack: A True Story of Survival in the Arctic. (p. 10)
—All the Bright Places. (p. 45)
Niven, Larry. Draco Tavern. (p. 476)
Nivens, Karen. Benjamin P. Blizzard: Welcome to Christmastown. Grisham, Jason, illus. (p. 165)
Niver, Heather. Midget Cars. (p. 1138)
—Porsches. (p. 1386)
Niver, Heather Moore. 20 Fun Facts about Anglerfish. (p. 1995)
—20 Fun Facts about Barracudas. (p. 1995)
—20 Fun Facts about Bats. (p. 1995)
—20 Fun Facts about Crocodiles. (p. 1995)
—20 Fun Facts about Dolphins. (p. 1995)
—20 Fun Facts about Lionfish. (p. 1995)
—20 Fun Facts about Moray Eels. (p. 1995)
—20 Fun Facts about Penguins. (p. 1995)
—20 Fun Facts about Sharks. (p. 1995)
—20 Fun Facts about Stick Bugs. (p. 1995)
—20 Fun Facts about Stingrays. (p. 1995)
—20 Fun Facts about the Declaration of Independence. (p. 1995)
—20 Fun Facts about US Monuments. (p. 1995)
—Archaeology: Excavating Our Past. (p. 95)
—Aziz Ansari. (p. 122)
—Breaking the Sound Barrier. (p. 225)
—Camaros. (p. 255)
—Careers for Tech Girls in Computer Science. (p. 267)
—Careers in Construction. (p. 267)
—Corvettes. (p. 368)
—Dracula & Other Vampires. (p. 476)
—Foxes after Dark. (p. 626)
—GTOs. (p. 728)
—Life on an Aircraft Carrier. (p. 1012)
—Malala Yousafzai. (p. 1083)
—Nervous System. (p. 1241)
—Ostriches Are Not Pets! (p. 1306)
—Racing's Greatest Records (p. 1432)
—Skydiving. (p. 1587)
—Sojourner Truth. (p. 1606)
—Tributaries of the Chesapeake Bay. (p. 1785)
—Veronica Roth (p. 1837)
—We Need Bats. (p. 1867)
Niver, Heather Moore & Moore Niver, Heather. 20 Fun Facts about the Declaration of Independence. (p. 1995)
—20 Fun Facts about US Monuments. (p. 1995)
—Ostriches Are Not Pets! (p. 1306)
Nivola, Claire A. Life in the Ocean: The Story of Oceanographer Sylvia Earle. (p. 1011)
—Life in the Ocean: The Story of Oceanographer Sylvia Earle Nivola, Claire A., illus. (p. 1011)
—Orani: My Father's Village. Nivola, Claire A., illus. (p. 1302)
—Planting the Trees of Kenya: The Story of Wangari Maathai. Nivola, Claire A., illus. (p. 1369)
—Star Child. Nivola, Claire A., illus. (p. 1640)
Nivola, Claire A., illus. see Bartoletti, Susan Campbell.
Nivola, Claire A., illus. see Friedman, Robin.
Nivola, Claire A., illus. see Glaser, Linda.
Niwano, Makoto, illus. see Rodda, Emily.
Nix, Garth. Abhorsen. (p. 5)
—Abhorsen. Filipetto, Celia, tr. (p. 5)
—Abhorsen Chronicles. (p. 5)
—Abhorsen Trilogy: Sabriel - Lirael - Abhorsen. Set (p. 5)
—Across the Wall: A Tale of the Abhorsen & Other Stories. (p. 9)
—Aenir. (p. 25)
—Clariel: The Lost Abhorsen. (p. 327)
—Confusion of Princes. (p. 357)
—Drowned Wednesday. (p. 486)
—Fall. (p. 566)
—Into Battle. (p. 881)
—Lirael. (p. 1021)
—Lirael, Daughter of the Clayr. (p. 1021)
—Lord Sunday. (p. 1052)
—Newt's Emerald. (p. 1249)
—One Beastly Beast: Two Aliens, Three Inventors, Four Fantastic Tales. Biggs, Brian, illus. (p. 1294)
—Ragwitch. (p. 1433)
—Sabriel. (p. 1500)
—Shade's Children. (p. 1556)
—Sir Thursday. (p. 1580)
—Superior Saturday. (p. 1683)
—To Hold the Bridge. (p. 1759)
—Violet Keystone. (p. 1843)
Nix, Garth & Williams, Sean. Blood Ties. (p. 200)
—Magic (p. 1071)
—Missing. (p. 1152)
—Monster. (p. 1166)
—Mystery. (p. 1223)
—Troubletwisters (p. 1790)
Nix, Harvey. How to Ride a Bike: My Very First Learn-To Book. (p. 821)
—Learning to Ride with the Bits. (p. 986)
Nix, Jonathan J. Egghead: The Story of One Small Trout. (p. 506)
Nix, Josef. My Mama's War. (p. 1214)
Nix, Mario. Rayne the Raindrop. (p. 1441)
Nix, Pamela. Tummel the Tumbleweed. Barnes, Trisha, ed. (p. 1796)
Nixon & Brush. Champagne with a Corpse. (p. 289)
Nixon, Audrey. Jennifer's Body. (p. 913)
Nixon, C. Song of the Painted Obelisk. (p. 1611)
Nixon, Caroline. Kid's Box Level 3 Activity Book with Online Resources. (p. 952)
—Kid's Box Level 3 Pupil's Book. (p. 953)
Nixon, Caroline & Tomlinson, Michael. Kid's Box American English Level 1 Student's Book. (p. 952)
—Kid's Box Level 1 Flashcards (Pack Of 96) (p. 952)
—Kid's Box Level 1 Pupil's Book. (p. 952)
—Kid's Box Level 2 Pupil's Book. (p. 952)
—Kid's Box Starter Flashcards. (p. 953)
Nixon, Chris, illus. see Morgan, Palo.
Nixon, James. Cars. (p. 272)
—Defending & Goaltending. (p. 423)
—Motorcycles. (p. 1179)
—Passing & Dribbling. (p. 1326)
—Rules of the Game. Humphrey, Bobby, photos by. (p. 1495)
—Tractors. (p. 1775)
—Trucks. (p. 1791)
Nixon, James, jt. auth. see Corporate Contributor Staff.
Nixon, James, jt. auth. see Loveless, Antony.
Nixon, Joan Lowery. Ann's Story, 1747. (p. 87)
—Before You Were Born. Heaston, Rebecca J., illus. (p. 159)

—Caesar's Story, 1759. (p. 250)
—Deadly Game of Magic. (p. 417)
—If You Were a Writer. Degen, Bruce, illus. (p. 855)
—John's Story, 1775. (p. 924)
—Kidnapping of Christina Lattimore. (p. 952)
—Maria's Story, 1773. (p. 1093)
—Nancy's Story, 1765. (p. 1229)
—Nightmare. (p. 1255)
—Spirit Seeker (p. 1628)
—Will's Story, 1771. (p. 1934)
Nixon, Joan Lowery & Harwood, John. Séance. (p. 1537)
Nixon, John, illus. see Morrison, Kevin.
Nixon, Kareh. Little Woman in My House. (p. 1038)
Nixon, Mallory. Color Cats. (p. 342)
Nixon, Sidney. Chikka the Kangaroo. (p. 301)
Nixon, Tom. Sled Dog Wisdom: Humorous & Heartwarming Tales from Alaska's Mushers. (p. 1588)
Nixon-Roulet, Mary F. Kalitan Our Little Alaskan Cousin. (p. 942)
Niz, Ellen. Color Nei, Molly, illus. (p. 342)
Niz, Ellen S. Floating & Sinking Sturm, Ellen, illus. (p. 605)
—Friction Thoms, Scott, illus. (p. 637)
Niz, Ellen Sturm. Philo Farnsworth & the Television Tucker, Keith, illus. (p. 1351)
Niz, Xavier. Spotlight on Australia (p. 1634)
Niz, Xavier & Niz, Xavier W. Elephants. (p. 511)
—Kangaroos (p. 942)
—Kentucky. (p. 949)
—Mystery of the Roanoke Colony Denton, Shannon & Denton, Shannon E., illus. (p. 1226)
—Paul Revere's Ride. Bascle, Brian, illus. (p. 1330)
—Story of the Statue of Liberty Martin, Cynthia & Schoonover, Brent, illus. (p. 1662)
—Volcanoes. McMullen, Anne, illus. (p. 1849)
Niz, Xavier, et al. Medusa (p. 1120)
—Wright Brothers & the Airplane Erwin, Steve et al, illus. (p. 1963)
Niz, Xavier W. Animals Communicating. (p. 82)
—Animals Staying Safe. (p. 84)
Niz, Xavier W., jt. auth. see Englar, Xavier.
Niz, Xavier W., jt. auth. see Niz, Xavier.
Niz, Xavier W., et al. Wright Brothers & the Airplane Erwin, Steve, illus. (p. 1963)
Njeleshi, Chansa. Integrated Science for Zambia Basic Education Grade 5 Pupil's Book. (p. 879)
Njenga, Wamoro P. Goodnight Kuu~Kuu: My Cozy All Day Village Safari. O'Brien, Anne, illus. (p. 701)
—Wow, What a Mama!! Webber, Penny, illus. (p. 1962)
Njike, Jacinda. World of Shapes. (p. 1957)
Nkemayang, Chelsea. Split Ville. (p. 1630)
N'Leh, Anne-Claire. Planet of Trainiacs. Elyum Studio, illus. (p. 1368)
Nnabuchi, Afam. Emeka Transforms in the Pit. (p. 517)
Nnamoko, Johanan U. Greatest Mom (p. 720)
Nnodim, Paul. Tortoise & the Birds. Pierotti, Yvonne, illus. (p. 1771)
No New Art Needed, illus. see Disney Book Group Staff.
No, Yee-Jung. Visitor. (p. 1845)
No, Yi-Jung. Visitor. (p. 1845)
Noad, Jordan, illus. see Pachek, Mary C.
Noad, Sarah, tr. see Huancai, Yang, et al.
Noah, Ian & Logan, Stephanie. Mike's Math Club Presents the Monstrously Fun Fraction Book. Noah, Ian et al, eds. (p. 1141)
Noah, Jennifer. Nala's Magical Mitsiaq: A Story of Inuit Adoption Leng, Qin, illus. (p. 1228)
Noah, Jennifer & Giroux, Chris. Our First Caribou Hunt Lim, Hwei, illus. (p. 1308)
Noah, Michal Y. A-Z the Universe in Me. (p. 2)
Nobacon, Danbert. 3 Dead Princes: An Anarchist Fairy Tale. Cox, Alex, illus. (p. 1991)
Nobati, Eugenia, illus. see Aesop.
Nobati, Eugenia, illus. see Flor Ada, Alma.
Nobati, Eugenia, illus. see MacDonald, Margaret Read.
Nobati, Eugenia, illus. see White, Amy.
Nobel, DeAnna, jt. auth. see Watts, Jane.
Nobel, Zack. Twisted Teenage Mysteries. (p. 1802)
Nobens, C. A., illus. see Doudna, Kelly.
Nobens, C. A., illus. see Hanson, Anders.
Nobens, C. A., illus. see Holder, Jennifer.
Nobens, C. A., illus. see Kompelien, Tracy.
Nobens, C. A., illus. see Kuskowski, Alex.
Nobens, C. A., illus. see Salzmann, Mary Elizabeth.
Nobens, C. A., illus. see Scheunemann, Pam.
Nobens, C. A., illus. see Stortz, Diane & Holder, Jennifer.
Nobens, C. A., illus. see Tangvald, Christine Harder.
Nobens, C. A., illus. see Tuminelly, Nancy.
Nobens, C. A., illus. see Williams, Rozanne Lanczak.
Nobens, Cheryl. Colores - Colors. (p. 344)
Nobens, Cheryl, illus. see Williams, Rozanne Lanczak.
Nobens, Cheryl A., illus. see Doudna, Kelly.
Nobens, Cheryl A., illus. see Hanson, Anders.
Nobens, Cheryl A., illus. see Kompelien, Tracy.
Nobens, Cheryl A., illus. see Salzmann, Mary Elizabeth.
Nobens, Cheryl A., illus. see Scheunemann, Pam.
Nobens, Cheryl A., illus. see Tuminelly, Nancy.
Nobisso, Josephine. En Ingles, por Supuesto. Ziborova, Dasha, illus. (p. 522)
—En ingles, por Supuesto. Ziborova, Dasha, illus. (p. 522)
—Francis Woke up Early. Hyde, Maureen, illus. (p. 628)
—Hot Cha-Cha! Holub, Joan, illus. (p. 801)
—In English, of Course. Ziborova, Dasha, illus. (p. 863)
—Numbers Dance: A Counting Comedy. Ziborova, Dasha, illus. (p. 1272)
—Peso de Una Misa: Un Relato de Fe. Szegedi, Katalin, illus. (p. 1345)
—Peso de Una Misa: Un Relato de fe. Szegedi, Katalin, Illus. (p. 1345)
—Show; Don't Tell! Secrets of Writing. Montanari, Eva, illus. (p. 1570)
—Take It to the Queen: A Tale of Hope. Szegedi, Katalin, illus. (p. 1696)
—Take It to the Queen. (p. 1696)
—Weight of a Mass: A Tale of Faith. Szegedi, Katalin, illus. (p. 1872)
Noble, Alan R. Foundations of the Christian Faith. (p. 624)
Noble, Amy, illus. see Bielski, Ursula.
Noble, David Grant. Santa Fe: History of an Ancient City. (p. 1511)
Noble, Dennis L. U. S. Coast Guard. (p. 1806)
Noble, Edwin, illus. see Talbot, Ethel.
Noble, Jonathan & Owen, Ruth. Pole Position! (p. 1379)
Noble, Kate. Pamela's Plan. Bass, Rachel, illus. (p. 1320)
Noble, Mariagorretti. Animal Kingdom in Confusion. (p. 78)
Noble, Marty. 3-D Coloring Book—Horses. (p. 1991)
—3-D Coloring Book—Mystic Mandalas. (p. 1991)
—3-D Coloring Book—Paisley Designs. (p. 1991)
—Ancient Mexican Art Tattoos. (p. 70)
—Angels. (p. 75)
—Artful Eggs from Around the World Stained Glass Coloring Book. (p. 103)
—Body Art: Tattoo Designs Coloring Book. (p. 207)
—Chinese Kites Stained Glass Coloring Book. (p. 307)
—Christmas. (p. 312)
—Christmas Mandalas Coloring Book. (p. 314)
—Color Your Own Angels in Art Masterpieces. (p. 343)
—Color Your Own Classic Movie Posters. (p. 343)
—Color Your Own Great Fairy Tale Illustrations. (p. 343)
—Color Your Own Great Flower Paintings. (p. 343)
—Color Your Own Great Horse Paintings. (p. 343)
—Color Your Own Great Paintings by Women Artists. (p. 343)
—Color Your Own Japanese Woodblock Prints. (p. 343)
—Color Your Own Poster Masterpieces. (p. 343)
—Color Your Own Still Life Paintings. (p. 343)
—Creative Haven Incredible Insect Designs Coloring Book. (p. 379)
—Creative Haven Mandalas Stained Glass Coloring Book. (p. 379)
—Creative Haven Mexican Folk Art Coloring Book. (p. 379)
—Creative Haven Paisley Designs Stained Glass Coloring Book. (p. 379)
—Creative Haven Tibetan Designs Coloring Book. (p. 379)
—Creative Haven Wild Horses Stained Glass Coloring Book. (p. 379)
—Decorative Tile Designs. (p. 422)
—Dover Masterworks: Color Your Own American Folk Art Paintings. (p. 473)
—Dover Masterworks: Color Your Own Famous American Paintings. (p. 473)
—Dover Masterworks: Color Your Own Impressionist Paintings. (p. 473)
—Dover Masterworks: Color Your Own Monet Paintings. (p. 473)
—Dover Masterworks: Color Your Own Renoir Paintings. (p. 473)
—Dover Masterworks: Color Your Own Van Gogh Paintings. (p. 473)
—Fairy Babies Stained Glass Coloring Book. (p. 563)
—Fairy Princesses Stained Glass Coloring Book. (p. 564)
—Famous Fairy Tales Coloring Book. (p. 569)
—Fanciful Butterflies Stained Glass Coloring Book. (p. 570)
—Floral Mandalas Stained Glass Coloring Book. (p. 606)
—Fun with Christmas Ornaments Stencils. (p. 648)
—Fun with Emergency Vehicles Stencils. (p. 648)
—Fun with Fire Trucks Stencils. (p. 648)
—Fun with Good Luck Symbols Stencils. (p. 648)
—Fun with Mother Goose Stencils. (p. 648)
—Fun with Native American Masks Stencils. (p. 648)
—Fun with Noah's Ark Stencils. (p. 648)
—Fun with Wedding Stencils. (p. 649)
—Garden Flowers Stained Glass Coloring Book. (p. 656)
—Glitter Angels Stickers. (p. 683)
—Glitter Wizards & Dragons Stickers. (p. 684)
—Goddesses Coloring Book. (p. 690)
—Heart Mandalas Coloring Book. (p. 759)
—Impressionist Art. (p. 862)
—Japanese Designs Stained Glass Coloring Book. (p. 909)
—Little Dancers. (p. 1026)
—Mandala Mazes. (p. 1087)
—Mandalas GemGlow Stained Glass Coloring Book. (p. 1087)
—Medieval Tapestries Coloring Book. (p. 1119)
—Mexican Designs Stained Glass Coloring Book. (p. 1131)
—Mexican Folk Art Tattoos. (p. 1131)
—Mike Piazza: Mike & the Mets. Rains, Rob, ed. (p. 1141)
—Mini Angels Tattoos. (p. 1146)
—Nativity Stained Glass Coloring Book. (p. 1235)
—Paisley Designs Coloring Book. (p. 1319)
—Shiny Christmas Ornaments Stickers. (p. 1567)
—Shiny Tiffany Windows Stickers. (p. 1567)
—Thai Decorative Designs. (p. 1724)
—Twelve Wizards & Dragons Bookmarks. (p. 1800)
—Vampires Coloring Book. (p. 1832)
—Wild Cards Stained Glass Coloring Book. (p. 1929)
Noble, Marty, ed. see Erte.
Noble, Marty, jt. auth. see Constable, John.
Noble, Marty, jt. auth. see Doyle, Richard.
Noble, Marty, jt. auth. see Mazurkiewicz, Jessica.
Noble, Marty, jt. auth. see Monet, Claude.
Noble, Marty, jt. auth. see van Gogh, Vincent.
Noble, Marty & Coloring Books for Adults. Ancient Mexican Designs. (p. 70)
Noble, Marty & Coloring Books Staff. Day of the Dead (Dia de los Muertos) (p. 414)
Noble, Marty & Creative Haven. Creative Haven African Designs Coloring Book. (p. 379)
Noble, Marty & Creative Haven Staff. Creative Haven Day of the Dead Coloring Book. (p. 379)
—Steampunk Designs. (p. 1646)
Noble, Marty & Da Vinci, Leonardo. Leonardo Da Vinci Stained Glass. (p. 992)
Noble, Marty & Denslow, W. W. Land of Oz Stained Glass Coloring Book. (p. 973)
Noble, Marty & Dover, A. T. Impressionist Art Masterpieces to Color: 60 Great Paintings from Renoir to Gauguin. (p. 862)
Noble, Marty & Smith, A. G. Chinese Designs Stained Glass Coloring Book. (p. 307)
Noble, Marty, et al. Mosaic Masterpieces. (p. 1176)
—Nature Mandalas. (p. 1236)
—Wild Horses Stained Glass Coloring Book. (p. 1929)
Noble, Midge. Ice Cube Award: Learning to Be Cool under Pressure. (p. 850)
Noble, Penny, illus. see Brown, Linda Kayse.
Noble, Roger, illus. see Baker, Jaime.
Noble, Ron. Letter Beasties. (p. 1002)
Noble, Sarah. Hannah & Horatio Pea. (p. 742)
Noble, Sheilagh, illus. see Sideri, Simona.
Noble, Stuart, illus. see Donald, Margaret.
Noble, Trinka Hakes. Apple Tree Christmas. Noble, Trinka Hakes, illus. (p. 92)
—Christmas Spider's Miracle. Costanza, Stephen, illus. (p. 315)
—Jimmy's Boa & the Bungee Jump Slam Dunk. Kellogg, Steven, illus. (p. 918)
—Last Brother: A Civil War Tale. Papp, Robert, illus. (p. 977)
—Legend of Michigan. Van Frankenhuyzen, Gijsbert, illus. (p. 988)
—Legend of the Cape May Diamond. Lewis, E. B., illus. (p. 989)
—Little New Jersey. Brett, Jeannie, illus. (p. 1032)
—Little Pennsylvania Board Book. Brett, Jeannie, illus. (p. 1033)
—Lizzie & the Last Day of School. McLeod, Kris Aro, illus. (p. 1043)
—New Jersey Reader. Darnell, K. L., illus. (p. 1245)
—One for All: A Pennsylvania Number Book. Papp, Lisa, illus. (p. 1295)
—Orange Shoes. Ettlinger, Doris, illus. (p. 1302)
—Pennsylvania Reader. Darnell, K. L., illus. (p. 1338)
—People of Ten Thousand Winters. (p. 1339)
—Scarlet Stockings Spy. Papp, Robert, illus. (p. 1520)
Noble, Trinka Hakes, jt. auth. see Papp, Lisa.
Noble, Val. Elsie the Sheep & the Kings of the Castle. (p. 516)
Noble, William. Aztec Empire. (p. 122)
—Presidential Power on Trial: From Watergate to All the President's Men. (p. 1397)
Noble-Goodman, Katherine. Zebras. (p. 1985)
Nobleman, Marc Tyler. Bill the Boy Wonder: The Secret Co-Creator of Batman. Templeton, Ty, illus. (p. 186)
—Boys of Steel: Creators of Superman. (p. 220)
—Boys of Steel: The Creators of Superman. MacDonald, Ross, illus. (p. 220)
—Contortionists & Cannons: An Acrobatic Look at the Circus. (p. 361)
—Countries & Cultures (p. 372)
—Cowboy (p. 373)
—Eagles. (p. 492)
—Foxes. (p. 626)
—Green Berets in Action. (p. 721)
—Klondike Gold Rush (p. 963)
—Math Puzzles: Grades 3 & 4. (p. 1107)
—Pakistan (p. 1319)
—Sharks. (p. 1562)
—Sinking of the USS Indianapolis. (p. 1580)
—Telephone (p. 1716)
—Tigers. (p. 1749)
—Triangle Shirtwaist Factory Fire (p. 1785)
—Vocabulary Cartoon of the Day: 180 Reproducible Cartoons That Help Kids Build a Robust & Prodigious Vocabulary. (p. 1847)
—Vocabulary Cartoon of the Day: 180 Reproducible Cartoons That Expand Students' Vocabularies to Help Them Become Better Readers & Writers. (p. 1847)
Nobleman, Marc Tyler & Besel, Jennifer M. Captivating, Creative, Unusual History of Comic Books (p. 264)
Nobleman, Marc Tyler & Compass Point Books Staff. San Francisco Earthquake of 1906. (p. 1510)
Nobleman, Marc Tyler & Yanuck, Debbie L. Star-Spangled Banner. (p. 1641)
Nobleman, Marc Tyler, et al. Rescue in the Bermuda Triangle: An Isabel Soto Investigation (p. 1462)
Nobles, Scott, photos by see Bruder, Mikyla.
Noblet, Jean-François & Levesque, Catherine, texts. Keeping It Green! (p. 947)
Nobumoto, Keiko. Wolf's Rain. Iida, Toshitsugu, illus. (p. 1944)
Nobumoto, Keiko, jt. auth. see Bones.
Nobuyuki, Anzai, et al. Flame of Recca Anzai, Nobuyuki, illus. (p. 602)
Nocenti, Ann. Someplace Strange. Jefferson, Jemiah, ed. (p. 1609)
—Typhoid Mary Romita, John, Jr., illus. (p. 1805)
Nocenti, Ann, text. X-Men: Longshot. (p. 1967)
Noda, Takayo. Dear World. (p. 419)
Nodel, Norman, illus. see Rosenfeld, Dina.
Nodelman, Perry, jt. auth. see Matas, Carol.
Nodset, Joan L. Come Back, Cat. Kellogg, Steven, illus. (p. 347)
—Go Away, Dog. Meisel, Paul, illus. (p. 686)
Noé, illus. see Reif, Cheryl.
Noé, illus. see Sommer, Carl.
Noe, Amy, ed. see Salter, Kay.
Noe, Carol. Farewell, My Free Bird: A Mother's Story of Her Daughter's Life in the Dark World of Drugs & Prostitution... & the Phone Call That Changed Their Family Forever. (p. 573)
Noe, David C. Tres Mures Caeci. Thoburn, Michelle, illus. (p. 1784)
Noe, Ignacio, illus. see Sommer, Carl.
Noe, Katherine Schlick. Something to Hold. (p. 1610)
Noël, Alyson. Art Geeks & Prom Queens. (p. 102)
—Beginning: Evermore + Blue Moon. (p. 159)
—Blue Moon: The Immortals. (p. 203)
—Blue Moon. (p. 203)
Noel, Alyson. Cazadora de Almas. (p. 283)
Noël, Alyson. Cruel Summer. (p. 386)
—Dark Flame. (p. 407)
—Desafio: Quinto Libro de la Serie de Los Inmortales. (p. 428)
—Dreamland. (p. 484)
—Echo. (p. 502)
—Eternidad: Libro Primero de la Serie de Los Inmortales. (p. 539)
Noel, Alyson. Everlasting. (p. 542)
Noël, Alyson. Everlasting. (p. 542)
—Evermore: The Immortals. (p. 542)
—Evermore. (p. 542)
—Fated. (p. 577)
—Fly Me to the Moon. (p. 609)
—Forever Summer. (p. 619)
—Horizon. (p. 797)
—Keeping Secrets. (p. 947)
—Kiss & Blog. (p. 961)
—Laguna Cove. (p. 971)
—Luna Azul. (p. 1065)
—Mystic. (p. 1226)
Noel, Alyson. Night Star. (p. 1254)
Noël, Alyson. Night Star. (p. 1254)
—Radiance. (p. 1432)
—Saving Zoe. (p. 1518)
—Shadowland: The Immortals. (p. 1558)
—Shadowland. (p. 1558)
—Shimmer. (p. 1566)
—Whisper (p. 1912)
—Whisper. (p. 1912)
Noel, Genevieve. Que Amor de Cocodrilo!/Al Agua, Leo. (p. 1423)
Noel, Green, illus. see Beth, Robinson.
Noel III, jt. auth. see Rio, Adam del.
Noel, Michel. Good for Nothing Tanaka, Shelley, tr. from FRE. (p. 698)
Noel, Pamela. Same Ol' Moon: The little things of life & Love. (p. 1507)
Noel Paul, Chrisana B. Crescent Street Crew: A novel teens & young adults can identify With. (p. 381)
Noel, Thomas J. & Smith, Duane A. Colorado: The Highest State. (p. 343)
Noelia. Sagebrush Woolies. (p. 1502)
—Sagebrush Woolies up up & Away. (p. 1502)
—Tale of the Sagebrush Woolies Lexy's Lex First Birthday. (p. 1700)
—Until Cow Comes Home. (p. 1823)
—Woolies Artemisa. (p. 1950)
Noensie, Pamela & Lamore, Garretta. Tari: the Little Balinese Dancer. (p. 1706)
Noeth, Chris, illus. see Bilgrey, Marc, et al.
Nogarr, Ilona. Lola & the Apple. (p. 1045)
Nogelmeier, Puakea, ed. Keiki's First Word Book. (p. 948)
Noguchi, Rick & Jenks, Deneen. Flowers from Mariko. Kumata, Michelle Reiko, illus. (p. 608)
Noguchi, Tomoko. Object of Desire. (p. 1275)
Nogueras, Paola. ABC de Puerto Rico. (p. 3)
Noh, Mi Young. Threads of Time (p. 1741)
—Threads of Time Shin, Hwan, illus. (p. 1741)
—Threads of Time Noh, Mi Young, illus. (p. 1741)
Noh, Mi Young, creator. Threads of Time (p. 1741)
Noh, Seong-bin, illus. see Choi, Eun-Mi.
Nohemi, Esther. Welcome to the USA. Morris, Edwin, ed. (p. 1874)
Nohl, Frederick. Martin Luther: Hero of Faith. Hook, Richard, illus. (p. 1097)
Nohrden, Patrick. Crystal Monkey. (p. 387)
Noiset, Michele, illus. see Orshoski, Paul.
Noiset, Michele, illus. see Rosa-Mendoza, Gladys.
Noj, Nahta, illus. see Broom, Jenny.
Noj, Nahta, illus. see Ritchie, Alison.
Nojiri, Housuke. Rocket Girls - The Last Planet. Nojiri, Housuke, illus. (p. 1482)
Nol, Sally. Watch Where You Go! (p. 1861)
Nolan, jt. auth. see Nolan, Lucy.
Nolan, Alan. Destination: Homicide! (p. 430)
—Fintan's Fifteen: Ireland's Worst Hurling Team Wants You! (p. 589)
Nolan, Allia Zobel. Animal Parade. Maddocks, Maria, illus. (p. 79)
—Bible Adventures. Moroney, Trace, illus. (p. 175)
—Easter Story. Moroney, Trace, illus. (p. 499)
—Fair & Squaresville: A Lesson in Playing Fair. Carter, Tod et al, illus. (p. 562)
—God's Light, Shining Bright. Bryant, Laura J., illus. (p. 691)
—God's Oak Tree. Chung, Chi, illus. (p. 691)
—God's Rainbow. Chung, Chi, illus. (p. 691)
—God's Winter Wonderland. Mitchell, Melanie, illus. (p. 692)
—Moses' Big Adventure. Cox, Steve, illus. (p. 1176)
—My Bible Story Collection. Moroney, Trace, illus. (p. 1197)
—Psalms & Prayers for Little Ones. Lyon, Tammie, illus. (p. 1413)
—Story of Noah's Ark. Moroney, Trace, illus. (p. 1659)
—Ten Commandments for Little Ones. Samuel, Janet, illus. (p. 1718)
—Touch & Feel Bible Animal Friends. Steele-Morgan, Alex, illus. (p. 1772)
—Whatever (p. 1896)
—When God Tucks in the Day. Chung, Chi, illus. (p. 1902)
Nolan, Amanda M., illus. see Symington, Martha M.
Nolan, Arthea. Whitey Ford. (p. 1914)
Nolan, Carla. Someone I Love Is in the Air Force. (p. 1609)
Nolan, Carrie Stewart. My Little Miracle. (p. 1212)
Nolan, Cathal J. Concise Encyclopedia of World War II (p. 355)
Nolan, Chris & Spencer, Lauren. Writing to Persuade. (p. 1965)
Nolan, Dennis. Hunters of the Great Forest. Nolan, Dennis, illus. (p. 829)
—Sea of Dreams. Nolan, Dennis, illus. (p. 1535)
—William Shakespeare's a Midsummer Night's Dream. (p. 1933)
Nolan, Dennis, illus. see Coville, Bruce.
Nolan, Dennis, illus. see Kennedy, Robert F., Jr.
Nolan, Dennis, illus. see Leighton, Maxinne Rhea.
Nolan, Douglas. Cider House Bears. (p. 319)
Nolan, Ernie. Snow White & the Seven Dwarfs as Performed by Professor TJ Barker's Troupe of Theatricals. (p. 1600)
Nolan, Frederick. Trailblazing the Way West. (p. 1776)
Nolan, Frederick W. Gunslingers & Cowboys. (p. 732)
—Native Peoples. (p. 1235)
—Outlaws & Rebels. (p. 1312)
Nolan, Han. Born Blue. (p. 214)
—Dancing on the Edge. (p. 403)
—Face in Every Window. (p. 560)
—If I Should Die Before I Wake. (p. 853)

N

—Pregnant Pause. (p. 1395)
—Send Me down a Miracle. (p. 1550)
—Summer of Kings. (p. 1674)
—When We Were Saints. (p. 1905)
Nolan, Henry. Sophia Sows Seeds: Work with 11-19 to Gain Foundations for Place Value. (p. 1613)
Nolan, J. & Moffatt, J. Floaties: Five Little Ducks. (p. 605)
—Floaties: Teddy Bear Teddy Bear. (p. 605)
Nolan, Janet. Father's Day Thank You Ember, Kathi, illus. (p. 577)
—Firehouse Light. Lafrance, Marie, illus. (p. 592)
—PB&J Hooray! Your Sandwich's Amazing Journey from Farm to Table. Patton, Julia, illus. (p. 1331)
—PBandJ Hooray! (p. 1331)
Nolan, Jenny, jt. auth. see Whelan, Gloria.
Nolan, Joy. Animals of North America: Set Of 6. (p. 83)
—Animals of North America: Text Pairs. (p. 83)
Nolan, Lea. Allure. (p. 48)
—Conjure. (p. 357)
Nolan, Lindsey & Varacalli, Lauren. Auburn University College Prowler off the Record. (p. 114)
Nolan, Lucy. Bad to the Bone Reed, Mike, illus. (p. 132)
—Fairy in a Dairy Bryant, Laura J., illus. (p. 563)
—Home on the Range Reed, Mike, illus. (p. 792)
—Lizard Man of Crabtree County Kastner, Jill, illus. (p. 1042)
—On the Road Reed, Mike, illus. (p. 1291)
—Smarter Than Squirrels Reed, Mike, illus. (p. 1593)
Nolan, Lucy & Nolan. Jack Quack Wesson, Andrea, illus. (p. 903)
Nolan, M. L. Hello Dollie. (p. 763)
Nolan, Mary. Totem Poles & Masks: Art of Northwest Coast Tribes. (p. 1771)
Nolan, Mary, jt. auth. see Mills, Nathan.
Nolan, Nancy. Mr. Munson's Itvice on Bullying. Scadden, Kathryn, illus. (p. 1185)
Nolan, Nina. Mahalia Jackson: Walking with Kings & Queens. Holyfield, John, illus. (p. 1076)
Nolan, Tammy. Smiles: It's Really Amazing What They Can Do. (p. 1594)
Nolan, Tina. Charlie, the Home-Alone Kitten. Rentta, Sharon, illus. (p. 293)
—Honey the Unwanted Puppy. Rentta, Sharon, illus. (p. 794)
Noland, Charles. Adventures of Drew & Ellie: The Daring Rescue. Moyer, Tom, illus. (p. 17)
—Adventures of Drew & Ellie: The Magical Dress. Baker, Sherri, illus. (p. 17)
Noland, Karen L. Friends of the Menehune. (p. 638)
Noland, Monica. My Nana Looks Like a Telephone (p. 1215)
—Slide. (p. 1590)
Noland, Thelma. Annie Sweet Annie. (p. 87)
Nolen, Gale. Johnny, My Favorite Mouse. Cain, Doreyl Ammons, illus. (p. 923)
Nolen, Jerdine. Big Jabe. Nelson, Kadir, illus. (p. 182)
—Bradford Street Buddies: Block Party Surprise. Henninger, Michelle, illus. (p. 221)
—Eliza's Freedom Road: An Underground Railroad Diary. Strickland, Shadra, illus. (p. 513)
—Hewitt Anderson's Great Big Life. Nelson, Kadir, illus. (p. 774)
—Max & Jax Plant a Garden. Schmidt, Katen, illus. (p. 1110)
—Pitching in for Eubie. Lewis, E. B., illus. (p. 1364)
—Plantzilla Goes to Camp. Catrow, David, illus. (p. 1370)
—Thunder Rose. Nelson, Kadir, illus. (p. 1746)
Nolen, Jerdine & Kellher, Brian. Plantzilla. Catrow, David, illus. (p. 1370)
Nolen, Jerdine, et al. Bradford Street Buddies: Backyard Camp-Out. Henninger, Michelle, illus. (p. 221)
Nolen, T. K. Magical Fantastical Big Red Balloon. (p. 1074)
Nolen-Hoeksema, Susan. Eating, Drinking, Overthinking: The Toxic Triangle of Food, Alcohol, & Depression—And How Women Can Break Free. (p. 501)
Noll, Amanda. I Need My Monster. McWilliam, Howard, illus. (p. 844)
Noll, Cheryl, illus. see Krensky, Stephen.
Noll, Cheryl Kirk, illus. see Brennan, Linda.
Noll, Cheryl Kirk, illus. see Krensky, Stephen.
Noll, Katherine. Animal Jam: Official Insider's Guide. (p. 78)
Noll, Katherine, jt. auth. see West, Tracey.
Noll, Katherine & West, Tracey. Pokémon: Kanto Handbook. (p. 1377)
—Sinnoh. (p. 1580)
Noll, Kathy. Encounters with Every-Day Angels (Workbook) Can You See the Angels (A Workbook on Bullying & Character Development) (p. 524)
Noll, Rhyn. Skateboarding: Past—Present—Future (p. 1583)
Noll, Tom. Bicycle Fence. Fall, Brandon, illus. (p. 177)
Nolls, Katherine, jt. auth. see West, Tracey.
Nolt, Debbie. Love for Lyndon. (p. 1059)
Nolte, Larry, illus. see Greene, Inez.
Nolte, Larry, illus. see Gunn, Barbara & Dunn, Richard.
Nolte, Larry, illus. see Sprick, Marilyn.
Nolte, Lysne. Big Sister Babysitter: Im Going to Be a What? Vol 1 Second Edition. (p. 183)
Nolte, Nancy. Gingerbread Man. Scarry, Richard, illus. (p. 677)
—Richard Scarry's the Gingerbread Man. Scarry, Richard, illus. (p. 1469)
Nolting, Anne Carse. Pythagoras Eagle & the Music of the Spheres. (p. 1421)
Nomansen, Kerra. On My Silly Trip to the Zoo. (p. 1289)
Nomura, Mizuki. Book Girl & the Captive Fool. (p. 210)
—Book Girl & the Corrupted Angel. (p. 210)
—Book Girl & the Scribe Who Faced God (p. 210)
—Book Girl & the Suicidal Mime. (p. 210)
—Book Girl & the Undine Who Bore a Moonflower. (p. 210)
—Book Girl & the Wayfarer's Lamentation (p. 210)
Nomura, Tatsutoshi. Merry on the Move (p. 1129)
—Poe at Play (p. 1375)
—Stray Sheep (p. 1666)
Nomura, Ted. Luftwaffe 1946. (p. 1064)
Nomura, Ted & Miranda, Justo. Luftwaffe: 1946 Technical Manual. (p. 1064)
Nona Theresa Perez - Bayanin. Birth of Nadia Mei. (p. 192)
—Nadia Mei's First Spring: A Season of Growth. (p. 1227)
—Nadia Mei's First Winter in the Forest & Meeting with First Friends. (p. 1227)
Nonaka, Eiji. Cromartie High School (p. 384)
Nonemaker, Laura Allen. Benny's Angel: A God's Secret Garden Adventure. (p. 165)
—Fred d's Amazing Escape. (p. 632)
Nonenmacher, Dawn Marie. Piccolo's Personal Case: The Talented Trio Series Story #2 (p. 1354)
Nonino, Lila, jt. auth. see Meade, Saci.
Nonnen, Emily, jt. auth. see Carroll, Lewis, pseud.
Nono, Auntie. Solar System Song. Shirasu, Nori, illus. (p. 1607)
Nonsensibus, P. Porkknuckle Book* Or, the Curious End of the Morg-Rain War. (p. 1386)
Nooger & Neville, jt. auth. see Valkenburgh, Van.
Nooks, Nanny. Nina in the Forest of Faces. (p. 1256)
Nooks, Simone. Mommy's Best Helper. (p. 1162)
Noon, Connie, illus. see Moor-Doucette, Saba.
Noon, Steve, illus. see Dorling Kindersley Publishing Staff.
Noon, Steve, illus. see Millard, Anne.
Noon, Steve, illus. see Steele, Philip & Dorling Kindersley Publishing Staff.
Noonan, Diana. Collecting Data in Animal Investigations (p. 339)
—Old Things (Paperback) Copyright 2016. (p. 1285)
—On the Move (p. 1291)
Noonan, Helen. Mom Let Me Be Me. (p. 1161)
Noonan, John. Bunny Thing Happened Today! (p. 242)
Noonan, Joseph. What Is My Vocation? Student Edition. (p. 1890)
Noonan, Julia. My Pumpkin. Lawson, Peter, illus. (p. 1217)
Noonan, Julia, illus. see Harburg, E. Y.
Noonan, Julia, illus. see Harburg, E. Y. & Arlen, Harold.
Noonan, Julia, illus. see Mitchard, Jacquelyn.
Noonan, Julia, illus. see Yep, Laurence.
Noonan, Loretta. My Gramma Doesn't Knit. (p. 1210)
Noonan, Robert, et al. Three Weavers Plus Companion: A Father's Guide to Guarding His Daughter's Purity. (p. 1744)
Noonan, Rosalind, et al. Love Factor. (p. 1059)
Noonan, Sean. First Christmas; Friends & Festivity: Book two of the Everlasting & Fantastical Adventures of Elannah & Sam. (p. 593)
—Of Lights in the Night; Friends & Adventure: The Everlasting & Fantastical Adventures of Elannah & Sam. (p. 1279)
Noonan, Sheila Smith. Korean Immigration. (p. 967)
—South Africa. (p. 1616)
—South Africa. Rotberg, Robert I., ed. (p. 1616)
Noonan, Shelley & Sangster, Margret Elizabeth. Winsome Womanhood - Daybreak: Journal Edition. (p. 1937)
Noone, Cathleen L., illus. see Kelly, Elaine A. & Carl, Jean R.
Noordeman, Jelmer, illus. see Hearst, Michael.
Noppe-Brandon, Gail. Tilly Takes A Try. (p. 1750)
Nora, David, Jr. Happy Balloon to You. (p. 744)
Noraas, Margaret. Math Activities for Preschool. (p. 1105)
Norac, Carl. Isla de los Mimos. (p. 891)
—Me Quieres O No Me Quieres? DuBois, Claude K., illus. (p. 1116)
—My Daddy Is a Giant: For Everyone Who Has the Best Daddy in the World. (p. 1201)
—My Daddy Is a Giant: For Everyone Who Has the Best Daddy in the World. Godon, Ingrid, illus. (p. 1201)
—My Daddy Is a Giant. (p. 1201)
—My Mummy Is Magic. Godon, Ingrid, illus. (p. 1215)
—Palabras Dulces. (p. 1319)
—Swing Café. Dautremer, Rébecca, illus. (p. 1691)
Norac, Carl & Dubois, Claude K. Fuera El Panal! (p. 646)
—Las Palabras Dulces. (p. 977)
Norac, Carl & Gordon, Ingrid. My Daddy Is a Giant: For Everyone Who Has the Best Daddy in the World. (p. 1201)
Norac, Carl, et al. Quiero un Beso! (p. 1428)
—Soy un Cielo. (p. 1618)
Norberg, A. Tell Me about Our Christmas Tree. Barton, Deborah, illus. (p. 1716)
Norberg, Ken, illus. see Lynn, Debbie.
Norbu, Tenzing, illus. see Townshend, Dominique.
Norby, Lisa. Animals of Africa: Set Of 6. (p. 83)
—Animals of Africa: Text Pairs. (p. 83)
Norcia, James R. Jim's Journey: A Saga of One of the First RV's to Cross America. (p. 918)
Norcross, David, illus. see Almarode, John.
Norcross, Harry, illus. see Call, Charlene C.
Norcross, Matthew E. Grayface. (p. 713)
Nord, Kristin Magnuson. Moosh & Grizzle. (p. 1173)
Nord, Mary, illus. see Kidd, Ron.
Nord, Mary, illus. see McTaggart, Stephen & McTaggart, Debra.
Nordahl, Carolyn. Braxton & Fluff. (p. 224)
Norden, Barbara. Meteorite. (p. 1130)
Nordenson, Guy, et al. Seven Structural Engineers: The Felix Candela Lectures (p. 1555)
Nordenstrom, Michael. Hina & the Sea of Stars. (p. 780)
Nordhagen, Ted, illus. see Burrows, Roger & Gilligan, Jeff.
Nordhoff, Charles & Hall, James Norman. Pitcairn's Island. (p. 1364)
Nordin, Hans. Ice Fishing. (p. 850)
Nordin, Ruth Ann. Witness to a Murder. (p. 1942)
Nordli, Ernest, illus. see Beecher, Elizabeth.
Nordling, Lee. BirdCatDog. (p. 190)
—BirdCatDog. Bosch, Meritxell, illus. (p. 190)
—Bramble. Zick, Bruce, illus. (p. 222)
—FishFishFish. Bosch, Meritxell, illus. (p. 599)
—Fishfishfish. Bosch, Meritxell, illus. (p. 599)
—SheHeWe. Bosch, Meritxell, illus. (p. 1564)
Nordmann, Lutz, jt. auth. see Barth, Katrin.
Nordquist, Donna M. Petey the Pigasaurus. Fortune, Leslie, illus. (p. 1348)
Nordqvist, Sven. Birthday Cake: The Adventures of Pettson & Findus. (p. 192)
—Findus Disappears! (p. 588)
—Findus Plants Meatballs. Large, Nathan, tr. from SWE. (p. 588)
—Pancakes for Findus. Nordqvist, Sven, illus. (p. 1320)
Nordstrom, Brian, jt. auth. see Halka, Monica.
Nordstrom, Ursula. Secret Language. (p. 1541)
Noreika, Robert, illus. see Berkes, Marianne Collins.
Noreika, Robert, illus. see Berkes, Marianne.
Norell, Aaron, illus. see Mott, A. S.
Norell, Aaron, illus. see Smitten, Susan.
Norell, Aaron, illus. see Zenko, Darren.
Norfleet, Celeste O. Download Drama. (p. 474)
—Fast Forward. (p. 576)
Norfleet, Celeste O., jt. auth. see Cavanagh, Helen.
Norfleet, Celeste O. & Norfleet, Jennifer. She Said, She Said. (p. 1564)
Norfleet, Jennifer, jt. auth. see Norfleet, Celeste O.
Norfleet, Mary Crockett. Hand Me down House. Mallory, Edgar, illus. (p. 740)
Norfleet, Rickey. Three More Wishes. (p. 1743)
Norfolk, Bobby, jt. auth. see Norfolk, Sherry.
Norfolk, Bobby & Norfolk, Sherry. Anansi & the Pot of Beans. Hoffmire, Baird, illus. (p. 67)
—Anansi & the Sky Kingdom. Hoffmire, Baird, illus. (p. 67)
—Anansi & Turtle Go to Dinner. Hoffmire, Baird, illus. (p. 67)
—Anansi Goes to Lunch. Hoffmire, Baird, illus. (p. 67)
—Billy Brown & the Belly Button Beastie. Hoffmire, Baird, illus. (p. 187)
Norfolk, Sherry, jt. auth. see Norfolk, Bobby.
Norfolk, Sherry & Norfolk, Bobby. Virginia Giant: The True Story of Peter Francisco. Brennan, Cait, illus. (p. 1844)
Norgaard, Martin. Jazz Cello/Bass Wizard Junior, Book 2 (p. 911)
—Jazz Fiddle Wizard Junior, Book 2 (p. 911)
—Jazz Viola Wizard Junior, Book 2 (p. 911)
Norgren, Jill. Belva Lockwood: Equal Rights Pioneer. (p. 163)
—Belva Lockwood: The Woman Who Would Be President. (p. 163)
Norheim, Karen, illus. see Theis, Patricia & Theis, Matthew.
Norie, Rooney, illus. see Knights, Nancy.
Noriega, Fernando, illus. see Torices, Jose Gonzalez, et al.
Noriko, Ogiwara, jt. auth. see Ogiwara, Noriko.
Norlander, Britt. I've Discovered Electricity! (p. 900)
Norling, Beth. Las Hermanitas Son... Norling, Beth, illus. (p. 976)
—Little Sisters Are... (p. 1036)
—Los Hermanitos Son... Norling, Beth, illus. (p. 1054)
—Stone Baby. Norling, Beth, illus. (p. 1652)
Norling, Beth, illus. see Condon, Bill.
Norling, Beth, illus. see Herrick, Steven.
Norling, Beth, illus. see Hunt, Julie.
Norma Staff. Mi Primer Vocabulario (My First Vocabulary Dict.) (p. 1133)
Norma Staff, ed. Animales Bebe. (p. 80)
—Colores. (p. 344)
—Formas. (p. 620)
—Numeros. (p. 1273)
Norman. Worship Feast Prayer Stations: Creating Unforgettable Experiences. (p. 1961)
Norman, Andrew, et al. Diesel Technology. (p. 437)
Norman, Andrew P. Theseus Learning System: A Practical Guide to Mastering Essential Thinking Skills (with Software) (p. 1732)
—Theseus Learning System: A Practical Guide to Mastering Essential Thinking Skills - Lesson Book (with Software) (p. 1732)
Norman, C. S. Lockview Logans: Fire One. (p. 1045)
Norman, Claire. At the End of the Lane. (p. 111)
Norman, Cook. Sam & the Glass Palace. (p. 1506)
Norman, D. Dinosaurs Sticker & Puzzle Kid Kit (Bag) (p. 445)
Norman, Dave. Loves Company. (p. 1061)
Norman, David. Artists' Questions Answered - Drawing. (p. 104)
—Dinosaurs Sticker Book. Clarke, Phillip, ed. (p. 445)
Norman, Dayle. Tre's Surprise the Move. (p. 1784)
Norman, Dean, illus. see Watson, Richard A.
Norman, Donna Marie. Just a Swim? Widowati, Marini, illus. (p. 937)
Norman, Geoffrey. Stars above Us. Lewis, E. B., illus. (p. 1643)
Norman, Howard & Moody, Rick, eds. Two Kingdoms (p. 1803)
Norman, Jonathon, et al. CIC for Older Youth & Young Adults: Way of Pilgrimage Leader's Guide. (p. 318)
Norman, Justin, illus. see Seagle, Steven T.
Norman, Kim. I Know a Wee Piggy. Cole, Henry, illus. (p. 840)
—Puddle Pug. Yamaguchi, Keika, illus. (p. 1414)
—Still a Gorilla. Geran, Chad, illus. (p. 1650)
—Ten on the Sled. Woodruff, Liza, illus. (p. 1719)
—This Old Van. Conahan, Carolyn Digby, illus. (p. 1737)
Norman, Kim & American Museum of Natural History Staff. Dinosaurs: And Other Prehistoric Animals. Csotonyi, Julius & Marshall, Todd, illus. (p. 444)
—Whales. Schwartz, Carol, illus. (p. 1878)
Norman, Kim & Ogden, Betina. Storytime Stickers: All Kinds of Kittens. (p. 1664)
Norman, Kimberly. If It's Snowy & You Know It, Clap Your Paws! Woodruff, Liza, illus. (p. 853)
—Ten on the Sled. Woodruff, Liza, illus. (p. 1719)
Norman, Matthew. Domestic Violets. (p. 465)
Norman, Penny. Science One Two Three Chemistry. Einstein, Ann, ed. (p. 1527)
—Science One Two Three Electricity. Einstein, Ann, ed. (p. 1527)
—Science One Two Three Inventions. Einstein, Ann, ed. (p. 1527)
Norman, Rick. Fielder's Choice. (p. 584)
Norman, Taylor, jt. auth. see Parot, Annelore.
Norman, Thelma G. Wife Called Tommie. (p. 1927)
Norman, Tony. Auto Racing. (p. 117)
—Diving. (p. 454)
—Motorbike Racing. (p. 1179)
—Skydiving. (p. 1587)
Norman, Travis D. Christmas Island. Baker, David, illus. (p. 314)
Norman, Tyler & Perez, Jose S. Banjoman/El Hombre del Banjo. Perez, Jose S., illus. (p. 136)
Norman, Vera Stone, illus. see Parkman, Mary Rosetta.
Norman-Bellamy, Kendra. Fifteen Years (p. 584)
Normand, Bridgid, jt. auth. see Bramwell, Wendie.
Normand, Hal, illus. see Alter, Judy.
Normand, James G. My Funny Little Zoo. (p. 1209)
Normand, Jean-Pierre, illus. see Czerneda, Julie E., ed.
Normandin, Jeri. Nicole's Adventures in Her Wheelchair. (p. 1251)
Normark, Don. Chávez Ravine 1949: A Los Angeles Story. (p. 295)
Norona, Bill, illus. see Gerstler, J. C.
Norquist, Lara & Spalding, Frank. Truth about Methamphetamine & Crystal Meth. (p. 1794)
Norridge, Terry, illus. see Kayani, M. S.
Norridge, Terry, illus. see McDermott, Mustafa Yusuf.
Norrie, Louise Rosalyn. Adventures of Flat Cat. (p. 18)
Norrington, Leonie. Brigid Lucy & the Princess Tower. Ainslie, Tamsin, illus. (p. 228)
—Brigid Lucy Needs a Friend. Ainslie, Tamsin, illus. (p. 228)
—Brigid Lucy Wants a Pet. Ainslie, Tamsin, illus. (p. 228)
—Look See, Look at Me! Huxley, Dee, illus. (p. 1050)
Norrington, Leonie, illus. see Bedford, David & Worthington, Leonie.
Norrington, Leonie & Camelleri, Michael. Devil You Know. (p. 432)
Norris, A. Smokey the Kitten - A True Story. (p. 1594)
Norris, Aaron, jt. illus. see Jones, Penny.
Norris, Ashley P. Watson. Falcons (p. 566)
—How to Canoe & Kayak Like a Pro. (p. 815)
—How to Hike Like a Pro. (p. 820)
Norris, Chad, jt. auth. see Rhodes, David.
Norris, Christine. Crown of Zeus. (p. 386)
—Sword of Danu. (p. 1692)
—Talisman of Zandria Nagy, Robert, illus. (p. 1703)
—Talisman of Zandria. (p. 1703)
Norris, David A. CBARCs of Cannon Bay: Storm Clouds over Cannon Bay Norris, Judy-Jo Harris, illus. (p. 283)
—Lasting Success: Quality Decisions, Relationships & Untamed Emotions. (p. 979)
Norris, Elizabeth. Unbreakable. (p. 1811)
—Unraveling. (p. 1822)
Norris, Frank. Pit: A Story of Chicago. (p. 1364)
Norris, Gayle A. Bed Bug (p. 156)
Norris II, Charles H. Fat Little Ugly Friend. (p. 577)
Norris, Jeannine Q. Tonight You Are My Baby: Mary's Christmas Gift. Ladwig, Tim, illus. (p. 1765)
Norris, Jill, ed. see Forte, Imogene.
Norris, Jill, ed. see Hunt-Ullock, Kathy, et al.
Norris, Jill, ed. see Katz, Nevin.
Norris, Jill, ed. see Pino, Santo & Hook, Dena.
Norris, Jill, jt. auth. see Frank, Marjorie.
Norris, Johanna. Day Prince Snot Nose Made Friends. (p. 414)
Norris, Judy-Jo Harris, illus. see Norris, David A.
Norris, L. Wayne. Adventures of Ricky Raccoon & Jodi the Cat with Boomer. (p. 22)
Norris, Leslie. Albert, Lucille & the Two Williams. (p. 34)
Norris, Lew. Growing the Spirit. (p. 726)
Norris, Pamela. Visit to Grandma's. (p. 1845)
Norris, Robert. Made in the Wild: Animal Builders. (p. 1070)
—On the Move: Animal Migration. (p. 1291)
Norris, Roger & Ryan, Lawrie. Essential Chemistry for Cambridge Secondary 1. Ryan Books Ltd. Staff & Ryan, Lawrie, eds. (p. 536)
Norris, Sandy. Run Away to Danger. (p. 1496)
Norris, Shana. Something to Blog About. (p. 1610)
—Troy High. (p. 1790)
Norris, Siân. Greta & Boris: A Daring Rescue. (p. 723)
Norris, Valderia D. Skoldier Poet. (p. 1586)
Norris, Zack. Danger on Shadow Mountain. (p. 404)
—Monkey Howled at Midnight. (p. 1165)
—Secret of Skull Island. (p. 1542)
—Tunnel of Bones. (p. 1797)
Norris-Gooding, S. M. Legend of Kerloup. (p. 988)
Norsgaard, E. Jaediker. How Krokken & Poppen Made Peace. (p. 810)
Norsic, Donald. To Save Russia. Charles, Rodney & Pasco, Elizabeth, eds. (p. 1759)
Norsigian Rowles, Helen. Armenian History: A Journey for Children. (p. 99)
Norstrand, Torstein, illus. see Lerangis, Peter.
North American Bear Center & Lackner, Michelle Myers. Finding Hope (p. 588)
North American Cambridge Classics Project Staff. Cambridge Latin Course Unit 4. (p. 255)
North, B. C. What Small Vertical Line Learned. (p. 1893)
North Bedford, Annie. Jolly Barnyard. Gergely, Tibor, illus. (p. 924)
North, Charles & Caes, Charles J. Stock Market. (p. 1651)
North, Cindy. Joy Moves to Gathering Glen. (p. 929)
North, Dan. Explorers. (p. 551)
North, Dawn. Pull-Alongs: Digger. (p. 1415)
North, Laura. Big Bad Wolf & the Robot Pig. (p. 178)
—Boy with the Pudding Touch. Chapman, Neil, illus. (p. 220)
—Cinderella: The Terrible Truth. Dreidemy, Joëlle, illus. (p. 320)
—Cinderella's Big Foot. (p. 320)
—Hansel & Gretel & the Green Witch. Jevons, Chris, illus. (p. 743)
—Jack & the Bean Pie. (p. 902)
—Pied Piper & the Wrong Song. Anderson, Scoular, illus. (p. 1356)
—Princess & the Frozen Peas. (p. 1402)
—Sleeping Beauty—100 Years Later. (p. 1589)
North, Lucy, jt. auth. see Kimura.
North, Lynne. Gerties Gets It Right. (p. 667)
North, Merry. All Gone. Woolf, Julia, illus. (p. 44)
—My Christmas: Picture, Play & Tote Book. (p. 1200)
—My Family. (p. 1202)
—My Grandma & Me: A Picture, Play & Tote Book. (p. 1210)
—My Vacation: Picture, Play, & Tote. (p. 1220)
—Squeaky Clean. (p. 1636)
North, Pearl. Book of the Night. (p. 212)
—Libyrinth. (p. 1007)
North, Peter & McKay, Susan. Australia. (p. 116)
—England. (p. 529)
North, Phoebe. Starbreak. (p. 1642)
—Starglass. (p. 1642)
North, Poppy. Ruby Stone. (p. 1493)

North, Ryan. Adventure Time Paroline, Shelli & Lamb, Braden, illus. (p. 14)
—Adventure Time Vol. 2. Paroline, Shelli & Lamb, Braden, illus. (p. 15)
—Adventure Time Volume 2. (p. 15)
—Dinosaur Comics. North, Ryan, illus. (p. 441)
North, Ryan & Lamb, Branden. Adventure Time Paroline, Shelli, illus. (p. 14)
—Adventure Time. (p. 14)
North, Ryan & Paroline, Shelli. Adventure Time Vol.4 - Mathematical Edition. (p. 15)
North, Sharon Rae. My Brand New Leg. (p. 1199)
North, Sherry. Because I Am Your Daddy. Hall, Marcellus, illus. (p. 155)
—Because You Are My Baby. Hall, Marcellus, illus. (p. 155)
—Champ's Story: Dogs Get Cancer Too! Rietz, Kathleen, illus. (p. 289)
—Historia de Campeona: ¡a Los Perros También les Da Cáncer! Rietz, Kathleen, illus. (p. 782)
North, Sterling. Mark Twain & the River. (p. 1095)
—Racal. (p. 1430)
—Rascal. (p. 1439)
—Young Thomas Edison. (p. 1979)
North, Tiana & Holliday, Taliba. Go - Cook Something! A Cooking Survival Guide for Active Independent Children. (p. 686)
Northcott, Ed, illus. see Torres, J.
Northcott, Richard. In the Mountains. Geatches, Hazel, ed. (p. 866)
—Meet Molly. Wright, Craig, ed. (p. 1121)
—Where People Live, Level 4. Wright, Craig, ed. (p. 1909)
Northcraft, Gregory B., jt. auth. see Pinkley, Robin L.
Northcutt, Allen. Legend of Chris Moose: The Most Beautiful Moose in the World. (p. 988)
Northcutt, Leslie L., illus. see Redmond, Stephanie L.
Northcutt, Mark. I Want My Daddy: Why Do Most Black Men Grow up Without A Father. (p. 847)
Northcutt, Wendy & Kelly, Christopher M. Intelligent Design. (p. 879)
Northeast Editing, Inc Staff, contrib. by. Gerbils. (p. 666)
—Turtles. (p. 1799)
Northfield, Gary. Derek the Sheep. Northfield, Gary, illus. (p. 427)
Northland Editors. Great Yellowstone Grand Teton Glacier Activity Book. (p. 719)
Northrop, Michael. Amulet Keepers. (p. 66)
—Book of the Dead. (p. 212)
—Gentlemen. (p. 661)
—Plunked. (p. 1374)
—Rotten. (p. 1490)
—Surrounded by Sharks. (p. 1686)
—Trapped. (p. 1779)
Northrop, Michael, jt. auth. see Scholastic, Inc. Staff.
Northrop, Nancy. Momma - Where Has Grandpa Gone? (p. 1162)
Northrup, Christiane. Beautiful Girl: Celebrating the Wonders of Your Body. (p. 153)
Northrup, Mary. Pioneering American Computer Geniuses. (p. 1361)
NorthSouth Editors. Doodletastic! You Complete the Pictures! (p. 470)
Northway, Jennifer. That's Mine! (p. 1727)
Northway, Jennifer & Quarto Generic Staff. See You Later, Mom! (p. 1547)
NorthWord Books for Young Readers Editors. Ocean Babies. (p. 1276)
NorthWord Books for Young Readers Editors, contrib. by. Desert Babies. (p. 428)
—Polar Babies. (p. 1378)
—Prairie Babies. (p. 1392)
NorthWord Books for Young Readers Editors, ed. Forest Babies. (p. 618)
NorthWord Books for Young Readers Staff, ed. see McCurry, Kristen & Jackson, Aimee.
Norton, Andre. Key Out of Time. (p. 950)
—Ralestone Luck. (p. 1437)
—Time Traders. (p. 1753)
Norton, C. L. Alibi for The Wicked. (p. 39)
Norton, Carolyn, illus. see McCallum, Ann.
Norton, Carolyn McIntyre, illus. see McCallum, Ann.
Norton, Charles. Perfect Plan & the Four Brother's Pact. (p. 1342)
Norton, Curtis, et al. Financial Reporting: Student Text. (p. 587)
Norton, Dorothy S., illus. see Lange, Ian.
Norton, Dorothy S., illus. see Norton, O. Richard.
Norton, Dr J. Renae & Norton, J. Renae. Maji & Mongo Book. (p. 1078)
Norton, Frances Maree. Victorian Tea Spirit: A Girl's Guide to Her Secret Self (p. 1840)
Norton, George. Papa Golley's Journey Home. Hutcherson, Darren, illus. (p. 1322)
—Ten Buttermilk Pancakes. Hutcherson, Darren, illus. (p. 1718)
Norton, Grace R. Count Us in Too. (p. 370)
Norton, J. Renae. How Maji Gets Mongo off the Couch! Reed, Cleone, ed. (p. 810)
Norton, J. Renae, jt. auth. see Norton, Dr J. Renae.
Norton, Jack, Jr., as told by. Brave from Thunders. (p. 223)
Norton, James. Holocaust: Jews, Germany, & the National Socialists. (p. 789)
Norton, James R. Haydn's World. (p. 755)
—Holocaust: Jews, Germany, & the National Socialists. (p. 789)
—Looking at the Mechanisms & Patterns of Evolution with Graphic Organizers. (p. 1051)
—Russell Simmons. (p. 1498)
Norton Kreider, Barbara. Mr Squealy Goes to Town. Dimbylow, Jube, illus. (p. 1186)
—Mr Squealy Makes a Friend. Dimbylow, Jube, illus. (p. 1186)
—Mr Squealy Meets Scarecrow. Dimbylow, Jube, illus. (p. 1186)
—Surprise Party. Dimbylow, Jube, illus. (p. 1686)
Norton, Liss. Crocodile! McCann, Emma, illus. (p. 384)
Norton, Mary. Borrowers. (p. 214)
—Borrowers. Krush, Beth & Krush, Joe, illus. (p. 214)
—Borrowers Afield. Krush, Beth & Krush, Joe, illus. (p. 214)
—Borrowers Afloat. Krush, Beth & Krush, Joe, illus. (p. 214)
—Borrowers Aloft: Plus the Short Tale Poor Stainless. Krush, Beth & Krush, Joe, illus. (p. 214)
—Borrowers Aloft. (p. 214)
—Borrowers Avenged. Krush, Joe et al, illus. (p. 214)
Norton, Mike, illus. see Baltazar, Art & Aureliani, Franco.
Norton, Mike, illus. see Flynn, Ian.
Norton, Mike, jt. auth. see Torres, J.
Norton, Mike, jt. illus. see Alphona, Adrian.
Norton, Mike & Hopeless, Dennis. Answer! Thorpe, Patrick, ed. (p. 88)
Norton, Miriam. Kitten Who Thought He Was a Mouse. Williams, Garth, illus. (p. 962)
Norton, O. Richard. Rocks from Space: Meteorites & Meteorite Hunters. Ort, Kathleen & Carey, Jennifer, eds. (p. 1483)
Norton, Sally, jt. auth. see Scholastic, Inc. Staff.
Norton, Tamra. Bearubs & Flutterberries. (p. 152)
—Bearubs Clydes New Job. (p. 152)
—Comfortable in My Own Genes: A Novel. (p. 348)
—Make Me a Home. (p. 1079)
—Meet Bearubs. (p. 1120)
—Molly Married? (p. 1160)
—Molly Mormon? Myth or Me? (p. 1161)
—Shayla Witherwood: A Half-Faerie Tale. (p. 1563)
Noruzi, Charlotte, illus. see Cart, Michael.
Noruziaan, Bahman. Lonely Snake: Stories of Inspector Rabbit. (p. 1046)
Norvell, Candyce & Gregg, Paula. Reading Comprehension Saddleback Educational Publishing Staff, ed. (p. 1445)
Norvell, Walter. Fundamentals: Web Wise:-) (p. 649)
Norville, Alison G. Kart Racers. (p. 944)
Norville, Rod. Moonshine Express: Revised Edition with a History of Moonshine Today & Yesterday. (p. 1173)
Norwich, Grace. Albert Einstein. Simon, Ute, illus. (p. 34)
—Daniel Radcliffe: No Ordinary Wizard. (p. 405)
—I Am #10: Cleopatra. (p. 831)
—I Am #11: Walt Disney. (p. 831)
—I Am #12: Lebron James. (p. 831)
—I Am #5: George Washington. (p. 831)
—I Am #6: Harriet Tubman. (p. 831)
—I Am #9: John F. Kennedy. (p. 831)
—I Am Harriet Tubman. Simon, Ute, illus. (p. 833)
—I Am Helen Keller. Elliot, Mark, illus. (p. 833)
—Martin Luther King, Jr. Alba, Elisabeth, illus. (p. 1098)
—Sacajawea. Vanarsdale, Anthony, illus. (p. 1500)
Norwich, Grace & Pinkney, Andrea Davis. Meet the Obamas: America's First Family. (p. 1123)
Norwood, Mandi. Hitched Chick's Guide to Modern Marriage: Essential Advice for Staying Single-Minded & Happily Married. (p. 786)
Norwood, R. Edward. Kids under$Tanding Money. (p. 955)
Norworth, Jack. Take Me Out to the Ball Game. Meyers, Mark, illus. (p. 1696)
—Take Me Out to the Ball Game. Huntington, Amy, illus. (p. 1696)
Norworth, Jack & Simon, Carly. Take Me Out to the Ball Game. Hirao, Amiko, illus. (p. 1696)
Nosaka, Akiyuki. Whale That Fell in Love with a Submarine. Takemori, Ginny Tapley, tr. from JPN. (p. 1877)
Nosek, Jude. Homeowner's Handbook: A Guide to Getting Your Act Together & Keeping It That Way. Grabas, Peter & Parts, Art, illus. (p. 793)
Nosov, Nikolai. Adventures of Dunno & His Friends. Kay, Nicole, tr. from ENG. (p. 17)
Nöstlinger, Christine. De Por Que a Franz le Dolio el Estomago. (p. 416)
—Enfermedades de Franz. (p. 529)
—Franz Se Mete en Problemas de Amor. (p. 631)
Nostlinger, Christine. Good Dragon, Bad Dragon. Rassmuss, Jens, illus. (p. 697)
Nöstlinger, Christine. Juan, Julia y Jerico. (p. 930)
—Juanito Habichuela y Otros Cuentos. (p. 930)
—Lobo y los Siete Cabritos. (p. 1044)
—Marido para Mama. (p. 1093)
—Mas Historias de Franz. (p. 1101)
—Nuevas Historias de Franz en la Escuela. (p. 1270)
—Piruleta. Kaufman, Angelika, illus. (p. 1364)
—Piruleta. Kaufmann, Angelika, illus. (p. 1364)
—Por Favor, Vuelve a Casa (Please, Come Back Home) (p. 1385)
—Rosalinde Tiene Ideas en la Cabeza. Balzola, Sofia, illus. (p. 1489)
—Vacaciones de Franz. (p. 1829)
Nöstlinger, Christine & Christine, Nöstlinger. Querido Senor Diablo. (p. 1426)
Nosy Crow. Bizzy Bear: Dinosaur Safari. Davies, Benji, illus. (p. 194)
—Bizzy Bear: Fun on the Farm. Davies, Benji, illus. (p. 194)
—Bizzy Bear: Knights' Castle. Davies, Benji, illus. (p. 194)
—Bizzy Bear: Let's Get to Work! Davies, Benji, illus. (p. 194)
—Bizzy Bear: Let's Go & Play. Davies, Benji, illus. (p. 194)
—Bizzy Bear: off We Go! Davies, Benji, illus. (p. 194)
—Bizzy Bear: Spacebear. Davies, Benji, illus. (p. 194)
—Bizzy Bear's Big Building Book. Davies, Benji, illus. (p. 194)
—Can You Say It, Too? Arf! Arf! Braun, Sebastien, illus. (p. 259)
—Can You Say It, Too? Growl! Growl! Braun, Sebastien, illus. (p. 259)
—Can You Say It, Too? Hoot! Hoot! Braun, Sebastien, illus. (p. 259)
—Cutie Pie Looks for the Easter Bunny: A Tiny Tab Book. Ho, Jannie, illus. (p. 396)
—Fire Rescue! Davies, Benji, illus. (p. 590)
—Flip Flap Safari. Scheffler, Axel, illus. (p. 604)
—Get Out of My Bath! Teckentrup, Britta, illus. (p. 667)
—Little Bubba Looks for His Elephant. Ho, Jannie, illus. (p. 1025)
—Noodle Loves Bedtime. Billet, Marion, illus. (p. 1263)
—Noodle Loves the Beach. Billet, Marion, illus. (p. 1263)
—Noodle Loves the Park. Billet, Marion, illus. (p. 1264)
—Noodle Loves to Cuddle. Billet, Marion, illus. (p. 1264)
—Noodle Loves to Drive. Billet, Marion, illus. (p. 1264)
—Noodle Loves to Eat. Billet, Marion, illus. (p. 1264)
—Pip & Posy: the Little Puddle. Scheffler, Axel, illus. (p. 1361)
—Pip & Posy: the Scary Monster. Scheffler, Axel, illus. (p. 1361)
—Pip & Posy: the Super Scooter. Scheffler, Axel, illus. (p. 1361)
—Pirate Adventure. Davies, Benji, illus. (p. 1362)
—Pookie Pop Plays Hide-And-Seek: A Tiny Tab Book. Ho, Jannie, illus. (p. 1383)
—Wickle Woo Has a Halloween Party. Ho, Jannie, illus. (p. 1927)
Nosy Crow Staff. Princess Penelope & the Runaway Kitten. Murray, Alison, illus. (p. 1405)
Nosy Crow Staff, jt. auth. see Dodd, Emma.
Nosy Crow Staff, jt. auth. see Lodge, Jo.
Nosy Crow Staff, jt. auth. see Scheffler, Axel.
Not Home Yet Publishing, Patty Ross, prod. Rocky Mountain Sweet Shoppe Cookbook: Culinary Sensations for the Sweet Tooth. (p. 1484)
Notarfrancesco, Lisa Christiano & Padovano, Chris. Catherine the Caterpillar & Friends Coloring Book: A Children's Guide to Autism. (p. 280)
Notgrass, Ray. Exploring World History. (p. 554)
Nothdruft, Dennis, jt. auth. see Joicey, Celia.
Nothof, Anne, et al. Ethnicities: Plays from the New West. Vol. 16 (p. 539)
Nothomb, Amélie. Character of Rain: A Novel. Bent, Timothy, ed. (p. 291)
Notkin, Jerome J., jt. auth. see Gulkin, Sidney.
Notley, Alice, ed. see Oliver, Douglas.
Noto, Larissa, jt. auth. see Noto, Nick.
Noto, Nick & Noto, Larissa. Adventures of Pyrgos: Volume 1. (p. 22)
Noto, Phil. Wolverine & Jubilee: Curse of the Mutants. (p. 1944)
Noto, Phil, illus. see Immonen, Kathryn.
Nottage, Cindy, jt. auth. see Morse, Virginia.
Nottage, Cindy & Morse, Virginia. Iim: Teaching Research Skills - Grades K-12. (p. 856)
—Parent Guide to Raising Researchers. (p. 1324)
Nottingham, Andrea. Woman's Worth ... (p. 1945)
Notto, E. T. Light of God Bible Books: Bible Book 2. (p. 1015)
—Light of God Bible Books: Book 1 (Creation, God's Commandments, Faith) (p. 1015)
Nouf, Feras, illus. see Butcher, Tami.
Noufer, M. M. Adventures of Millie & May: Millie & Maya Discover the New World. (p. 20)
Noughton, Barbara. Adventures of Feefeen & Friends. Considine, Declan, illus. (p. 18)
Noullet, Georgette. Bed Hog Slonim, David, illus. (p. 156)
Nourigat, Natalie, illus. see Jolley, Dan.
Nourigat, Natalie, illus. see Nourigat, Paul.
Nourigat, Paul. Debt Dangers: A Book in the Series Marvels of Money ... for Kids. Nourigat, Natalie, illus. (p. 421)
—Earning Excitement: A Book in the Series Marvels of Money ... for Kids. Nourigat, Natalie, illus. (p. 494)
—Earning Excitement: a book in the series Marvels of Money ... for Kids. Nourigat, Natalie, illus. (p. 494)
—Giving Greatness: A Book in the Series Marvels of Money ... for Kids. (p. 681)
—Giving Greatness: A Book in the Series Marvels of Money ... for Kids. Nourigat, Natalie, illus. (p. 681)
—Spending Success: A Book in the Series Marvels of Money for Kids. (p. 1625)
—Spending Success: A Book in the Series Marvels of Money ... for Kids. Nourigat, Natalie, illus. (p. 1625)
—Terrific Tools for Money: A Book in the Series Marvels of Money ... for Kids. (p. 1721)
—Terrific Tools for Money: A Book in the Series Marvels of Money ... for Kids. Nourigat, Natalie, illus. (p. 1721)
—Why Is There Money? A Facinating Journey Through the Evolution of Money. Schofield, Angela, illus. (p. 1925)
Nourse, Audrey S. & Shelton, Giulia M. Timothy Tree Frog. (p. 1755)
Nova Blue, jt. auth. see Lynn, Richard.
Nova, Jacy & Nova, Nick. City of the Lost Souls. (p. 324)
Nova, Nick, jt. auth. see Nova, Jacy.
Novack, Danielle. My Two Holidays - A Hanukkah & Christmas Story. Harris, Phyllis, illus. (p. 1220)
Novak, Ali. Heartbreakers. (p. 760)
—My Life with the Walter Boys. (p. 1212)
Novak, David. String Figure Jack! (p. 1667)
Novak, Donna, ed. see Madsen, Michael.
Novak, Marisol, jt. auth. see Bianchi, Mike.
Novak, Matt. Jazzbo (p. 911)
—No Zombies Allowed. Novak, Matt, illus. (p. 1261)
—Wish for You. Novak, Matt, illus. (p. 1940)
Novak, Robby & Montague, Brad. Kid President's Guide to Being Awesome. (p. 951)
Novak, Steven. Snow Man Is My Friend. Novak, Steven, illus. (p. 1599)
Novak, Steven, illus. see Widgen, Susan.
Novalis Staff, jt. auth. see Wood Lake Books Staff.
Novara, Joe. Road Wrangler: Cowboys on Wheels. Lawson, Robert & Spatrisano, Kimberly, illus. (p. 1477)
—Wa-Tonka! Camp Cowboys Lawson, Robert & Spatrisano, Kimberly, illus. (p. 1851)
Novaskshonoff, Varlaam. Creation of the World: For Young People. (p. 379)
Noveck, Ira A. & Sperber, Dan, eds. Experimental Pragmatics. (p. 549)
Novel Units, Inc. Staff. I, Houdini Teacher Guide. (p. 839)
—Tenth Good Thing about Barney Teacher Guide. (p. 1720)
Novel Units, Inc. Staff, creator. 20,000 Leagues under the Sea Student Packet. (p. 2003)
—20,000 Leagues under the Sea Teacher Guide. (p. 2003)
—Adam of the Road Student Packet. (p. 11)
—Adam of the Road Teacher Guide. (p. 11)
—Alice in Wonderland/Through the Looking Glass Student Packet. (p. 39)
—Alice in Wonderland/Through the Looking Glass Teacher Guide. (p. 39)
—Amos Fortune Free Man Teacher Guide. (p. 65)
—Arthur's Nose/Arthur's Eyes Teacher Guide. (p. 104)
—Before We Were Free Student Packet. (p. 159)
—Before We Were Free Teacher Guide. (p. 159)
—Beowulf Student Packet. (p. 166)
—Beowulf Teacher Guide. (p. 166)
—Black Beauty Student Packet. (p. 195)
—Black Beauty Teacher Guide. (p. 195)
—Black Like Me Student Packet. (p. 196)
—Black Like Me Teacher Guide. (p. 196)
—Book of Three Student Packet. (p. 212)
—Book of Three Teacher Guide. (p. 212)
—Bread & Jam for Francis Teacher Guide. (p. 224)
—Cage Student Packet. (p. 251)
—Cage Teacher Guide. (p. 251)
—Chinese Cinderella Student Packet. (p. 307)
—Chinese Cinderella Teacher Guide. (p. 307)
—Clay Marble Student Packet. (p. 330)
—Clay Marble Teacher Guide. (p. 330)
—Crime & Punishment Student Packet. (p. 382)
—Crime & Punishment Teacher Guide. (p. 382)
—Crispin, the Cross of Lead Student Packet. (p. 383)
—Crispin, the Cross of Lead Teacher Guide. (p. 383)
—Danger in Quicksand Swamp Student Packet. (p. 403)
—Danger in Quicksand Swamp Teacher Guide. (p. 403)
—Daniel's Story Student Packet. (p. 405)
—Daniel's Story Teacher Guide. (p. 405)
—Danny the Champion of the World Student Packet. (p. 406)
—Danny the Champion of the World Teacher Guide. (p. 406)
—Fellowship of the Ring Student Packet. (p. 581)
—Fever 1793 Student Packet. (p. 583)
—Fever 1793 Teacher Guide. (p. 583)
—Five People You Meet in Heaven Student Packet. (p. 601)
—Forged by Fire Student Packet. (p. 619)
—Forged by Fire Teacher Guide. (p. 619)
—Gathering Blue Student Packet. (p. 658)
—Gathering Blue Teacher Guide. (p. 658)
—Gift of the Magi & Other Stories Student Packet. (p. 675)
—Gift of the Magi & Other Stories Teacher Guide. (p. 675)
—Grendel Student Packet. (p. 723)
—Harold & the Purple Crayon Teacher Guide. (p. 749)
—Homeless Bird Student Packet. (p. 793)
—Homeless Bird Teacher Guide. (p. 793)
—Hoot Student Packet. (p. 796)
—Hoot Teacher Guide. (p. 796)
—Hound of the Baskervilles Student Packet. (p. 802)
—Hound of the Baskervilles Teacher Guide. (p. 802)
—House of the Seven Gables Student Packet. (p. 803)
—House of the Seven Gables Teacher Guide. (p. 803)
—Hunchback of Notre Dame Student Packet. (p. 827)
—Hunchback of Notre Dame Teacher Guide. (p. 827)
—Janitor's Boy Student Packet. (p. 908)
—Janitor's Boy Teacher Guide. (p. 908)
—Journey to Jo'Burg Student Packet. (p. 928)
—Journey to Jo'Burg Teacher Guide. (p. 928)
—Jungle Student Packet. (p. 935)
—Jungle Teacher Guide. (p. 935)
—Kira-Kira Student Packet. (p. 961)
—Kira-Kira Teacher Guide. (p. 961)
—Landry News Student Packet. (p. 974)
—Landry News Teacher Guide. (p. 974)
—Lupita Manana Student Packet. (p. 1066)
—Lupita Manana Teacher Guide. (p. 1066)
—Magician's Nephew Student Packet. (p. 1075)
—Magician's Nephew Teacher Guide. (p. 1075)
—Make Lemonade Student Packet. (p. 1079)
—Malcolm X by Any Means Necessary Student Packet. (p. 1083)
—Malcolm X by Any Means Necessary Teacher Guide. (p. 1083)
—Misty of Chincoteague. (p. 1155)
—Misty of Chincoteague Student Packet. (p. 1155)
—October Sky Teacher Guide. (p. 1277)
—Oliver Twist Student Packet. (p. 1286)
—Oliver Twist Teacher Guide. (p. 1286)
—Olive's Ocean Student Packet. (p. 1286)
—Olive's Ocean Teacher Guide. (p. 1286)
—One Flew over the Cuckoo's Nest Student Packet. (p. 1295)
—One Flew over the Cuckoo's Nest Teacher Guide. (p. 1295)
—Parrot in the Oven Student Packet. (p. 1325)
—Parrot in the Oven Teacher Guide. (p. 1325)
—Pedro's Journal Student Packet. (p. 1334)
—Pedro's Journal Teacher Guide. (p. 1334)
—Phoenix Rising Student Packet. (p. 1351)
—Phoenix Rising Teacher Guide. (p. 1351)
—Pictures of Hollis Woods Student Packet. (p. 1356)
—Red Scarf Girl Student Packet. (p. 1455)
—Red Scarf Girl Teacher Guide. (p. 1455)
—Riding Freedom Student Packet. (p. 1471)
—Riding Freedom Teacher Guide. (p. 1471)
—Rosencrantz & Guildenstern are Dead Student Packet. (p. 1489)
—Rosencrantz & Guildenstern are Dead Teacher Guide. (p. 1489)
—Sideways Stories from Wayside School Student Packet. (p. 1573)
—Sideways Stories from Wayside School Teacher Guide. (p. 1573)
—Stargirl Student Packet. (p. 1642)
—Stargirl Teacher Guide. (p. 1642)
—Streetcar Named Desire Student Packet. (p. 1667)
—Sun Also Rises Student Packet. (p. 1676)
—Sun Also Rises Teacher Guide. (p. 1676)
—Surviving the Applewhites Student Packet. (p. 1687)
—Surviving the Applewhites Teacher Guide. (p. 1687)
—Things They Carried Student Packet. (p. 1733)
—Things They Carried Teacher Guide. (p. 1733)
—Thunder Cave Student Packet. (p. 1746)
—Thunder Cave Teacher Guide. (p. 1746)
—Tiger Rising Student Packet. (p. 1748)
—Tiger Rising Teacher Guide. (p. 1748)
—Tuesdays with Morrie Student Packet. (p. 1796)
—Tuesdays with Morrie Teacher Guide. (p. 1796)
—Tunes for Bears to Dance to Student Packet. (p. 1797)
—Tunes for Bears to Dance to Teacher Guide. (p. 1797)
—Uncle Tom's Cabin Student Packet. (p. 1812)
—Uncle Tom's Cabin Teacher Guide. (p. 1812)
—Wanderer Student Packet. (p. 1856)

—Wanderer Teacher Guide. (p. 1856)
—Warriors Don't Cry Student Packet. (p. 1859)
—Warriors Don't Cry Teacher Guide. (p. 1859)
—When My Name Was Keoko Student Packet. (p. 1904)
—When My Name Was Keoko Teacher Guide. (p. 1904)
—Winterdance Student Packet. (p. 1938)
—Winterdance Teacher Guide. (p. 1938)
—Witness Student Packet. (p. 1942)
—Witness Teacher Guide. (p. 1942)
—Yearling Student Packet. (p. 1969)
—Yearling Teacher Guide. (p. 1969)
Novella, Nicholas. My Robot Named Spot. (p. 1217)
Novelli, Joan. Phonics: 30 Instant Centers with Reproducible Templates & Activities That Help Kids Practice Important Literacy Skills-Independently! (p. 1351)
—Shoe Box Learning Centers: Phonics: 30 Instant Centers with Reproducible Templates & Activities That Help Kids Practice Important Literacy Skills-Independently! (p. 1568)
Novelli, Joan, jt. auth. see Krech, Bob.
Novelli, Joan & Grundon, Holly. Instant Content Area Vocabulary Packets: 25 Independent Practice Packets That Help Boost Reading Comprehension in Science, Social Studies, & Math - Grades 2-3. (p. 878)
Novello, John. Song That Never Ended: A Jazz Musician's Journey to a Love Beyond Life. (p. 1611)
November, Deborah. Elmo's ABC Book. Nicklaus, Carol, illus. (p. 515)
November, Deborah, et al. Let's Visit Sesame Street. Mathieu, Joe, illus. (p. 1001)
November, Deena & Rosenberg, Liz, eds. I Just Hope It's Lethal: Poems of Sadness, Madness, & Joy. (p. 840)
November, S., ed. see Cashore, Kristin.
November, S., ed. see Fisher, Catherine.
Novesky, Amy. Cat's Not-So-Perfect Sandcastle. Wakiyama, Hanako, illus. (p. 281)
—Elephant Prince: The Story of Ganesh. Wedman, Belgin K., illus. (p. 511)
—Me, Frida. Diaz, David, illus. (p. 1116)
—Mister & Lady Day: Billie Holiday & the Dog Who Loved Her. Newton, Vanessa Brantley, illus. (p. 1155)
Novesky, Amy & Morales, Yuyi. Georgia in Hawaii: When Georgia O'Keeffe Painted What She Pleased. Morales, Yuyi, illus. (p. 665)
Novesky, Amy & Wedman, Belgin K. Elephant Prince: The Story of Ganesh. (p. 511)
Novick, Mary. Baby Animals: With Flip the Flap Pages. Miesen, Christina, illus. (p. 124)
—Big Book of Alphabet & Numbers. Harlin, Sybel, illus. (p. 178)
—Big Book of Animals & Bugs. Hale, Jenny, illus. (p. 178)
—Big Book of Nursery Rhymes & Songs. Hale, Jenny, illus. (p. 179)
—Bugs. Hale, Jenny, illus. (p. 237)
—Double Delight - Nursery Rhymes. Hale, Jenny, illus. (p. 472)
—Farm. Hale, Jenny, illus. (p. 573)
—Little Bugs: With Flip the Flap Pages. Miesen, Christina, illus. (p. 1025)
—Nursery Songs. Hale, Jenny, illus. (p. 1273)
—Opposites. Harlin, Sybel, illus. (p. 1300)
—Zoo. Hale, Jenny, illus. (p. 1988)
Novick, Mary, jt. auth. see Miesen, Christina.
Novick, Mary & Hale, Jenny. Farm & Zoo. (p. 573)
—Farm Animals Jigsaw Book. (p. 573)
—Numbers. Harlin, Sybel, illus. (p. 1271)
—Zoo Animals Jigsaw Book. (p. 1988)
Novick, Mary & Miesen, Christina. Alphabet. (p. 49)
Novick, Mary & Peterson, Jenna. Numbers. Miesen, Christina, illus. (p. 1271)
Novick, Mary, et al. Alphabet. (p. 49)
Novik, Naomi. Will Supervillains Be on the Final? Liberty Vocational. Li, Yishan, illus. (p. 1932)
Novis, Jovita. Tiny Ballerina in the Garden. (p. 1756)
Novit, Renee Z. Alphabet Aa to Zz. R. Z. Novit Graphic Design Staff, illus. (p. 49)
—Counting by Tens & Fives. (p. 371)
—Counting One to Twenty. (p. 371)
Novoa, Teresa. Azul. (p. 122)
—Rojo. (p. 1485)
Novoa, Teresa, illus. see Garralón, Ana, et al.
Novoa, Teresa, illus. see Paloma, David & Paloma Sanllehí, David.
Novoa, Teresa, tr. see Garralón, Ana, et al.
Novosel, Scott. Creactivate! ATextbook for Heroes. (p. 378)
Nowak, Cheri, illus. see Nelson, Suzanne.
Nowak, Jeffrey, jt. auth. see Dumit, Sharon.
Nowak, Linda Y. Cinnamon: A Teen's Survival & Romance on the Appalachian Trail. (p. 321)
Nowak, Pat, jt. auth. see Carolina Canines for Service.
Nowakowski, Voytek, illus. see McGrath, Alister.
Nowark, Jennifer. At the Flower Shop: Learning Simple Division by Forming Equal Groups. (p. 111)
Nowell, Daphne A. Juana Meets Gabriel, the Small Business Angel: What if you Don't Want to Wait Around for a Prince Charming? (p. 930)
Nowers, William S. In the Beginning... & the Six Day Creation. (p. 865)
Nowicki, Colin J. Lamia High: Moon of Destiny (p. 972)
Nowiki, Boszenna. Why Some Cats Are Rascals: Book 3 (p. 1926)
—Why Some Cats Are Rascals: Book 1. (p. 1926)
—Why Some Cats Are Rascals: Book 2 (p. 1926)
Nowlan, Philip Francis, jt. auth. see Dille, John F.
Nowlin, Laura. If He Had Been with Me. (p. 852)
Nowra, Louis. Into That Forest (p. 881)
Noyce, Pendred. Lost in Lexicon: An Adventure in Words & Numbers. Charles, Joan, illus. (p. 1055)
Noyed, Bob, jt. auth. see Amoroso, Cynthia.
Noyed, Bob & Amoroso, Cynthia. Cute! The Sound of Long U. (p. 396)
—Smiles: The Sound of Long I. (p. 1594)
Noyed, Robert B., jt. auth. see Amoroso, Cynthia.
Noyed, Robert B., jt. auth. see Klingel, Cynthia.
Noyes, Alfred. Highwayman. Kimber, Murray, illus. (p. 779)
—Highwayman. Keeping, Charles, illus. (p. 779)
Noyes, Deborah. Angel & Apostle. (p. 73)
—Ghosts of Kerfol. (p. 672)
—Plague in the Mirror. (p. 1366)
Noyes, Deborah, illus. see Harley, Avis.
Noyes, Deborah, photos by see Harley, Avis.
Noyes, Deborah, ed. Gothic! (p. 704)
—Restless Dead: Ten Original Stories of the Supernatural. (p. 1464)
—Sideshow: Ten Original Tales of Freaks, Illusionists, & Other Matters Odd & Magical. (p. 1573)
Noyes, Diana. Tickle Bug. Noyes, Diana, illus. (p. 1747)
Noyes, Eli, illus. see Harding, James.
Noyes, Kristie Spangler. Mr. Daisy. (p. 1184)
Noyes, Leighton, illus. see Bailey, Gerry & Foster, Karen.
Noyes, Leighton, illus. see Ganeri, Anita.
Noyes, Leighton, illus. see Martineau, Susan.
Noyes, Nancy, ed. see Libal, Autumn.
Noyes, William H., Jr. Mittens. (p. 1156)
Nozemack, Joe, ed. see Naifeh, Ted.
Noziere, Jean P. Aventuras de Dos Amigos en las Filipinas (The Adventures of Two Friends in the Philippines) (p. 119)
Noziglia, Carla Miller, ed. see Bauchner, Elizabeth.
Noziglia, Carla Miller, ed. see Esherick, Joan.
Noziglia, Carla Miller, ed. see Ford, Jean.
Noziglia, Carla Miller, ed. see Hunter, William.
Noziglia, Carla Miller, ed. see Libal, Angela.
Noziglia, Carla Miller, ed. see Walker, Maryalice.
NS. It's My State 5. (p. 897)
—Leading Women 2. (p. 982)
—Today's Writers & Their Works. (p. 1761)
Nsrc. Science & Technology for Children Books: Ecosystems. (p. 1525)
—Science & Technology for Children Books: Microworlds. (p. 1525)
—Science & Technology for Children Books: Land & Water. (p. 1525)
—Science & Technology for Children Books: Food Chemistry. (p. 1525)
—Science & Technology for Children Books: Measuring Time. (p. 1525)
—Science & Technology for Children Books: Motion & Design. (p. 1525)
—Science & Technology for Children Books: Magnets & Motors. (p. 1525)
—Science & Technology for Children Books: Electric Circuits. (p. 1525)
—Science & Technology for Children Books: Floating & Sinking. (p. 1525)
—Science & Technology for Children Books: Technology of Paper. (p. 1525)
—Science & Technology for Children Books: Experiments with Plants. (p. 1525)
—Science & Technology for Children BOOKS: Plant Growth & Development. (p. 1525)
Nsrc, prod. Science & Technology for Children BOOKS: Sound. (p. 1525)
—Science & Technology for Children BOOKS: Chemical Tests. (p. 1525)
—Science & Technology for Children BOOKS: Rocks & Minerals. (p. 1525)
NTC Publishing Group Staff. De Tous Cotes (p. 416)
—Por Todos Lados 1. (p. 1386)
Ntihemuka, Patty Froese. Hyacinth Doesn't Go to Jail: And, Hyacinth Doesn't Miss Christmas. (p. 831)
—Hyacinth Doesn't Grow Up: And Hyacinth Doesn't Drown. (p. 831)
Nuchols, Galand A. Dragon Hatchling. (p. 477)
Nuckles, Glynn McMichael. Young & Old Alike!? The Nut Doesn't Fall Far from the Tree. (p. 1978)
Nuckolls, Les. Chester the Chimpanzee. (p. 298)
Nudelman, Edwar, ed. Halloween Reader. (p. 738)
Nudelman, Edward, ed. see Young, Claiborne.
Nuez, Marisa & Caetano, Joao. Lucinda y el Inspector Vinagre. (p. 1062)
Nuff, E. Why Aren't U Married? The Inconclusive, but Thought Provoking, Answers of a Suspected Confirmed Bachelor. (p. 1922)
Nuffer, Bruce, ed. see Schrader, Missy Wolgemuth & Schrader, Missy W.
Nuffield, Edward W. With the West in Her Eyes. (p. 1942)
Nugent, Cynthia. Francesca & the Magic Bike. (p. 627)
—Fred & Pete at the Beach (p. 632)
Nugent, Cynthia, illus. see Richardson, Bill.
Nugent, Cynthia, illus. see Rose, Simon.
Nugent, Cynthia, illus. see Saunders, Tom.
Nugent, Cynthia, illus. see Simmie, Lois.
Nugent, Cynthia, illus. see Stuchner, Joan Betty.
Nugent, Matthew. Nightmares on Goose Rocks Beach in Kennebunkport, Maine: Book 4 of the Goose Rocks Tales. (p. 1255)
Nugent, Penn. Come down & Play. (p. 347)
Nugent, Suzanne, illus. see Gilligan, Shannon.
Nugent, Suzanne, illus. see Leibold, Jay.
Nugent, Suzanne, illus. see Wallace, Jim.
Nugent Williams, Linda. God Is Beauty. (p. 689)
Nuhfer, Heather. Hopes & Screams. (p. 797)
—I Only Have Eye for You. Riley, Kellee, illus. (p. 844)
—My Little Pony: Friendship Is Magic. Vol. 2 (p. 1213)
Null, David. Introduction to Mennonite Doctrine & Practice. (p. 882)
Null Petersen, Casey. Games Around the World. (p. 654)
—Markets Around the World. (p. 1095)
Null Petersen, Kathleen C. Theater Actors Then & Now. (p. 1728)
—Writers Then & Now. (p. 1964)
Numan, Aisha. Chameleon Pet. (p. 289)
Numberman, Neil. Do Not Build a Frankenstein! Weaver, Brian M., illus. (p. 457)
Numberman, Neil, illus. see Gill, Timothy.
Numberman, Neil, illus. see Reynolds, Aaron.
Numeroff, Laura. If You Give a Cat a Cupcake. Bond, Felicia, illus. (p. 854)
—If You Give a Dog a Donut. Bond, Felicia, illus. (p. 854)
—If You Give a Pig a Party. Bond, Felicia, illus. (p. 854)
—Mouse Cookies & More: A Treasury. Bond, Felicia, illus. (p. 1182)
Numeroff, Laura Joffe. Bear a Brownie. (p. 150)
—Beatrice Doesn't Want To. Munsinger, Lynn, illus. (p. 153)
—Best Mouse Cookie. Bond, Felicia, illus. (p. 170)
—Chicken Sisters. Collicott, Sharleen, illus. (p. 300)
—Dogs Don't Wear Sneakers. Mathieu, Joe, illus. (p. 462)
—Easter Egg Designs. (p. 499)
—Happy Birthday, Mouse! Bond, Felicia, illus. (p. 745)
—Happy Easter, Mouse! Bond, Felicia, illus. (p. 745)
—Happy Valentine's Day, Mouse! Bond, Felicia, illus. (p. 747)
—If You Give a Bear a Brownie: Book & Doll. Bond, Felicia, illus. (p. 854)
—If You Give a Bear a Brownie Recipes. Bond, Felicia, illus. (p. 854)
—If You Give a Cat a Cupcake: Book & Doll. Bond, Felicia, illus. (p. 854)
—If You Give a Cat a Cupcake. Bond, Felicia, illus. (p. 854)
—If You Give a Cat a Cupcake Recipes. Bond, Felicia, illus. (p. 854)
—If You Give a Dog a Donut. Bond, Felicia, illus. (p. 854)
—If You Give a Moose a Matzoh. (p. 854)
—If You Give a Moose a Muffin: Book & Doll. Bond, Felicia, illus. (p. 854)
—If You Give a Moose a Muffin. Bond, Felicia, illus. (p. 854)
—If You Give a Moose a Muffin Recipe Book. Bond, Felicia, illus. (p. 854)
—If You Give a Mouse a Cookie. (p. 854)
—If You Give a Mouse a Cookie. Bond, Felicia, illus. (p. 854)
—If You Give a Pig a Pancake. Bond, Felicia, illus. (p. 854)
—If You Give a Pig a Pancake Big Book. (p. 854)
—If You Give a Pig a Party. Bond, Felicia, illus. (p. 854)
—If You Give a Pig a Pumpkin: Book & Doll. Bond, Felicia, illus. (p. 854)
—If You Take a Mouse to School. (p. 854)
—If You Take a Mouse to the Movies. (p. 854)
—If You Take a Mouse to the Movies. Bond, Felicia, illus. (p. 854)
—It's Pumpkin Day, Mouse! Bond, Felicia, illus. (p. 898)
—Lots of Lambs. Munsinger, Lynn, illus. (p. 1057)
—Merry Christmas, Mouse! Bond, Felicia, illus. (p. 1129)
—Moose Stroller Songs. Bond, Felicia, illus. (p. 1173)
—Mouse Cookie First Library: If You Give a Mouse a Cookie; If You Take a Mouse to School. Bond, Felicia, illus. (p. 1182)
—Mouse Stroller Songs. (p. 1182)
—Mouse's Family Album. (p. 1182)
—Otis & Sydney & the Best Birthday Ever. Andreasen, Dan, illus. (p. 1307)
—Pig Pancakes. Bond, Felicia, illus. (p. 1357)
—Pig Stroller Songs. Bond, Felicia, illus. (p. 1357)
—Si le das un Pastelito a un Gato. Bond, Felicia, illus. (p. 1572)
—Si le Haces una Fiesta a una Cerdita. Mlawer, Teresa, tr. from ENG. (p. 1572)
—Si Llevas un Ratón a la Escuela. Bond, Felicia, illus. (p. 1572)
—Time for School, Mouse! Bond, Felicia, illus. (p. 1751)
—What Aunts Do Best / What Uncles Do Best. Munsinger, Lynn, illus. (p. 1880)
—What Brothers Do Best. Munsinger, Lynn, illus. (p. 1880)
—What Puppies Do Best. Munsinger, Lynn, illus. (p. 1893)
—What Sisters Do Best. Munsinger, Lynn, illus. (p. 1893)
—Would I Trade My Parents? Bernardin, James, illus. (p. 1962)
Numeroff, Laura Joffe & Evans, Nate. Jellybeans & the Big Art Adventure. Munsinger, Lynn, illus. (p. 912)
—Jellybeans & the Big Book Bonanza. Munsinger, Lynn, illus. (p. 912)
—Jellybeans & the Big Dance. Munsinger, Lynn, illus. (p. 912)
—Jellybeans Love to Dance. Munsinger, Lynn, illus. (p. 912)
—Jellybeans Love to Read. Munsinger, Lynn, illus. (p. 912)
—Ponyella. Munsinger, Lynn, illus. (p. 1383)
Numeroff, Laura Joffe & Munsinger, Lynn. Nighty-Night, Cooper. Munsinger, Lynn, illus. (p. 1255)
Numeroff, Laura Joffe, et al. Jellybeans & the Big Camp Kickoff. (p. 912)
Numminen, Mark. Rain Forest Plants. (p. 1434)
Nunally, Richard, jt. auth. see Peters, Laura.
Nunally, Tina, tr. see Lindgren, Astrid.
Nunamaker, Eric, et al. Game Design for Teens. (p. 654)
Nunes, Bill. 284 Things a Bright Midwest Boy Should Know How to Do. (p. 2001)
—301 Things a Bright St Louis Southern Illinois Girl Can Do. (p. 2001)
Nunes, Ernest. Oh! How I Wish I Could Play Soccer with Ernie & the Dreamers. (p. 1280)
Nunes, Ligia B. Angelica. (p. 74)
Nunes, Lygia Bojunga. Bolsa Amarilla. (p. 208)
—Cuerda Floja. (p. 390)
—Seis Veces Lucas. (p. 1548)
—Sofa Estampado. (p. 1605)
Nunes, Rachel & Lindsley, David. Daughter of a King Board Book. (p. 409)
Nunes, Rachel Ann. Daughter of a King. (p. 409)
—Secret of the King. Ward, Jay Bryant, illus. (p. 1542)
Nunes, Shiho S. & Tay-Audouard, Lak-Khee. Chinese Fables: The Dragon Slayer & Other Timeless Tales of Wisdom. (p. 307)
Nuñes, Sofia. Discovering Mission Santa Inés. (p. 449)
Nuñes, Sofia, jt. auth. see Margaret, Amy.
Nuñes, Sofia, jt. auth. see Ostrow, Kim.
Nunes, Terezinha, ed. see Hancock, Nicky & Sunderland, Margot.
Nunez, Alonso. Invencible y Malvado Dragon Curiambro. (p. 883)
Núñez Cabeza de Vaca, Alvar, jt. auth. see Johnston, Lissa J.
Nunez, Jose Luis, illus. see Elkus, Julie.
Nunez, Kent Hamilton. Mish: The Desert. (p. 1150)
Nunez, Marisa. Camilla the Zebra. Villan, Oscar, illus. (p. 256)
—Cebra Camila. Villan, Oscar, illus. (p. 283)
Núñez, Marisa. Chocolate. Bansch, Helga, illus. (p. 309)
Nunez, Marisa. Featherless Chicken. Thomassen, Hellen, illus. (p. 579)
Núñez, Pablo, illus. see Sierra i Fabra, Jordi.
Núñez, Pablo, tr. see Sierra i Fabra, Jordi.
Nunez, Ralph da Costa & Ellison, Jesse Andrews. Voyage to Shelter Cove. Simon, Madeline Gerstein, illus. (p. 1850)
Nuñez, Rebecca. Tail about Spike, the Best Doggie Ever: Spike Meets His Mommy. (p. 1695)
Nuñez, Ruddy, illus. see Alvarez, Julia.
Nuñez, Ruddy, illus. see Alvarez, Julia.
Nunez, Sigrid. Last of Her Kind. (p. 978)
Nuñez, Veronica, illus. see Fitzsimons, Morgan.
Nunn, Daniel. ABCs at Home (p. 4)
—ABCs in Nature (p. 4)
—Air (p. 31)
—All about Dinosaurs (p. 42)
—Animals Big & Small (p. 82)
—Brachiosaurus (p. 221)
—Braquiosaurio (p. 222)
—Brass (p. 222)
—Brown (p. 231)
—Buttons & Beads (p. 248)
—Cardboard (p. 265)
—Colors (p. 344)
—Colors. (p. 344)
—Colors in English (p. 345)
—Colors in French: Les Couleurs (p. 345)
—Colors in German: Die Farben (p. 345)
—Colors in Italian: I Colori (p. 345)
—Colors in Polish: Kolory (p. 345)
—Colors in Spanish: Los Colores (p. 345)
—Colors - True or False? (p. 345)
—Counting 1 To 10 (p. 370)
—Diplodoco (p. 445)
—Diplodocus (p. 445)
—Eddie & Ellie's Opposites. (p. 503)
—Eddie & Ellie's Opposites at the Circus (p. 503)
—Eddie & Ellie's Opposites at the Zoo (p. 503)
—Eyes (p. 558)
—Families in English (p. 567)
—Families in French: Les Familles. (p. 567)
—Families in French - Les Familles. (p. 567)
—Families in German: Die Familien (p. 567)
—Families in Italian: le Famiglie (p. 567)
—Families in Polish - Rodziny. (p. 567)
—Families in Spanish: Las Familias (p. 567)
—Farm Animals (p. 573)
—Farm Animals. (p. 573)
—Farm Animals - True or False? (p. 573)
—Food (p. 612)
—Green (p. 721)
—Homes (p. 793)
—How Do We Use Light? (p. 808)
—I Can Be a Friend. (p. 835)
—I Can Listen (p. 836)
—I Can Take Turns (p. 836)
—In Front of or Behind: Where's Eddie? (p. 863)
—Inside or Outside: Where's Eddie? (p. 877)
—Instruments & Music (p. 879)
—Jars & Pots (p. 909)
—Keyboards (p. 950)
—Left or Right: Where's Eddie? (p. 987)
—Light (p. 1014)
—Light & Dark (p. 1014)
—Me & My Friends (p. 1115)
—Mouths (p. 1183)
—Narices (p. 1229)
—Near or Far: Where's Eddie? (p. 1239)
—Noses (p. 1266)
—Numbers in English: One, Two, Three... (p. 1272)
—Numbers in English. (p. 1272)
—Numbers in French: Les Chiffres - 1 2 3. (p. 1272)
—Numbers in French - Les Chiffres: Un, Deux, Trois... (p. 1272)
—Numbers in German: Die Zahlen - 1 2 3. (p. 1272)
—Numbers in German (Die Zahlen) Eins, Zwei, Drei... (p. 1272)
—Numbers in Italian: I Numeri - 1 2 3. (p. 1272)
—Numbers in Italian. (p. 1272)
—Numbers in Polish: Liczby - 1 2 3. (p. 1272)
—Numbers in Polish - Liczby: Jeden, Dwa, Trzy... (p. 1272)
—Numbers in Spanish: Los Números (p. 1272)
—Old Clothes (p. 1283)
—On or Under: Where's Eddie? (p. 1289)
—Opposites with Eddie & Ellie Walker, Steve, illus. (p. 1301)
—Orejas (p. 1303)
—Paper (p. 1322)
—Patterns Outside (p. 1329)
—Percussion (p. 1341)
—Plastic (p. 1370)
—Pterodáctilo (p. 1413)
—Pterodactyl (p. 1413)
—Red (p. 1453)
—Seasons. (p. 1538)
—Seasons - True or False? (p. 1538)
—Shadows & Reflections (p. 1558)
—Shapes Around Us (p. 1560)
—Sources of Light (p. 1616)
—Strings (p. 1667)
—Tiranosaurio Rex (p. 1757)
—Transportation. (p. 1779)
—Triceratops (p. 1785)
—True or False? (p. 1792)
—Tyrannosaurus Rex (p. 1805)
—Velociraptor (p. 1835)
—Voices (p. 1848)
—Water (p. 1862)
—Weather. (p. 1869)
—Weather - True or False? (p. 1869)
—Where's Eddie? (p. 1910)
—White (p. 1912)
—Woodwind (p. 1950)
—World Languages - Families. (p. 1956)
—Yellow (p. 1969)
Nunn, Daniel, jt. auth. see Rissman, Rebecca.
Nunn, Daniel & Rissman, Rebecca. Counting 1 To 10 (p. 370)
—Patterns Outside (p. 1329)
—Pink (p. 1359)
—Shapes Around Us (p. 1560)
Nunn, Daniel & Smith, Sian. Manners at Home (p. 1088)

—Manners at School (p. 1088)
—Manners at the Table (p. 1088)
—Manners in the Community (p. 1088)
Nunn, Kem. Chance: A Novel. (p. 289)
Nunn, Laura Silverstein, jt. auth. see Silverstein, Virginia B.
Nunn, Laura Silverstein, jt. auth. see Silverstein, Virginia.
Nunn, Paul, illus. see Random House Staff.
Nunn, Paul, illus. see Tillworth, Mary.
Nunn, Paul E., illus. see Forrester, Emma.
Nunnally, Carson, illus. see Wellings, Chris R.
Nunnally, Tiina, tr. see Lindgren, Astrid & Nyman, Ingrid.
Nunnally, Tiina, tr. see Lindgren, Astrid & Vang Nyman, Ingrid.
Nunnally, Tiina, tr. see Lindgren, Astrid.
Nunnery, Donna. Leaf That Was Afraid to Fall Scardina, Tom, illus. (p. 982)
Nuño, Fran. Fairground Lights. (p. 562)
—Great Magician of the World. (p. 717)
Nuño, Fran, jt. auth. see Nuno, Fran.
Nuno, Fran & Nuño, Fran. Poebromario. (p. 1375)
Nunokawa, Jeff. Oscar Wilde. (p. 1305)
Nunzio, Mario R. Di, see Di Nunzio, Mario R.
Nuo, Johnny. Dinh Van Binh: Vietnamese Village Boy. (p. 440)
Nuri, Alya, jt. auth. see Nuri, Alya.
Nuri, Alya & Nuri, Alya. Amr's Adventure in Europe. (p. 66)
Nuri, Amanda. Emerald Butterfly. (p. 517)
Nurk, Enn & Telgmaa, Aksel. Mathematics 6. Harte, Will, tr. from RUS. (p. 1108)
Nurney, David, jt. auth. see Couzens, Dominic.
Nurse, B. A. Outrageously Cool Nurses. (p. 1313)
Nurse, Holly. Meridian Brown Goes to School. (p. 1127)
Nurse Leeda. Healthy Beginnings: Five Ways You Can Stay Healthy! (p. 758)
Nurse, Lesley D. Tale of Greedy Reeby. (p. 1699)
Nurse, Shirley, ed. see Mwalimu.
Nurston, Nicholas. Adventures of Smoky: (It's a Cat's Life) (p. 23)
Nurullah, Seitu, illus. see Fogerty, Ramona.
Nury, Fabian, jt. auth. see Dorison, Xavier.
Nury, Fabien, jt. auth. see Dorison, Xavier.
Nury, Fabien & Cassady, John. I am Legion. (p. 833)
Nusach Hari B'nai Zion Congregation. Let My People Go! (p. 994)
Nusbaum, J. C. Mystic Travelogues. (p. 1226)
Nusom, Jacqueline. My Little Sister & Me. (p. 1213)
Nussbaum, Ben. All about Planets: Stitch Explores the Solar System. (p. 43)
—First Words Playtime. (p. 597)
—Friends Treasury. (p. 639)
—Grand Old Flag. Pamintuan, Macky, illus. (p. 707)
—Home on Range Pack. (p. 792)
—Is Apatosaurus Okay? Reavely, Trevor, illus. (p. 889)
—Is Apatosaurus Okay? Reaveley, Trevor, illus. (p. 889)
—Lilo & Stitch Todo Sobre los Planetas: Stitch Explora el Sistema Solar. Giblin, Brian E. & Luther, Jacqueline, eds. (p. 1017)
—Loli the Leopard. Wenzel, Gregory, illus. (p. 1046)
—Monsters Inc Things That Go. (p. 1169)
—Monsters Inc Transportation Pack. (p. 1169)
—Nemo's Birthday. (p. 1241)
—Nemos Busy Day. (p. 1241)
—PEEP Measuring. (p. 1335)
—PEEP Shadows. (p. 1335)
—Spinosaurus in the Storm. Scalf, Chris, illus. (p. 1628)
—Spinosaurus in the Storm. Scalf, Christopher, illus. (p. 1628)
—Spinosaurus in the Storm. Scalf, Christopher & McIntosh, Gabe, illus. (p. 1628)
—Take Me Out to the Ballgame. Studio Mouse Staff, ed. (p. 1696)
—Toko the Hippo. Wenzel, Gregory, illus. (p. 1762)
—Tracing Shapes. (p. 1775)
Nussbaum, Ben, ed. see Schwaeber, Barbie H.
Nussbaum, Ben, ed. see Schwaeber, Barbie.
Nussbaum, Ben & McIntosh, G. B. Spinosaurus in the Storm. Scalf, Chris, illus. (p. 1628)
Nussbaum, Ben & Studio Mouse Editorial. Snow White: A New Beginning. (p. 1599)
Nussbaum, Ben & Wenzell, Gregory. Loli Leopard. (p. 1046)
Nussbaum, Dori. Hungry Potty. (p. 828)
Nusz, Janean. Littlest Cowboy. (p. 1039)
Nutkis, Phyllis. When the World Was Quiet. Argoff, Patti, illus. (p. 1905)
Nutt, Don, illus. see Hammer, Larry.
Nutt, Robert. Amy's Light. Nutt, Robert, illus. (p. 66)
Nutt, Robert Van, see Van Nutt, Robert.
Nuttall, Chris, jt. auth. see Chappell, Mike.
Nuttall, Darcie. Yipper & His Quest for Mindfulness. (p. 1971)
Nuttall, Darcie, Lmhc. Yipper & His Quest for Mindfulness. (p. 1971)
Nuttall, Gabriella. College Writing (p. 340)
Nuttall, Gina. Is Lion Sick? (p. 889)
—Puppets Around the World. (p. 1417)
—Volcanoes & Earthquakes. (p. 1849)
Nuttall, Jeff. Selected Poems. (p. 1549)
Nuttall, Lesley. Ollie the Ogre. (p. 1287)
Nuttall, Neil & Hawkins, Andy, eds. Second Thoughts. Fell, Jenny, illus. (p. 1539)
Nuttbucket, Oliver S., III. Boy Scout's Handbook of Madcap Tales. Glover, Robert, illus. (p. 218)
Nuttle, Marc. Moment of Truth: How Our Government's Addiction to Spending & Power Will Destroy Everything That Makes America Great. (p. 1161)
Nuzum, K. A. Leanin' Dog. (p. 982)
—Small White Scar. (p. 1592)
Nuzzolo, Deborah. Bull Shark. (p. 240)
—Bull Shark [Scholastic]. (p. 240)
—Cheetahs (p. 296)
—Cheetahs Saunders-Smith, Gail, ed. (p. 296)
—Cheetahs [Scholastic]. (p. 296)
—Commerson's Dolphin Story. (p. 349)
—Dolphin Discovery: Bottlenose Dolphin Training & Interaction. (p. 464)
—Goblin Shark (p. 688)
—Gran Tiburón Blanco. (p. 707)
—Great White Shark. (p. 719)
—Great White Shark [Scholastic]. (p. 719)
—Hammerhead Shark. (p. 739)
—Hammerhead Shark [Scholastic]. (p. 739)
—Journey to Atlantis Funbook. (p. 928)
—Leopards (p. 993)
—Leopards Saunders-Smith, Gail, ed. (p. 993)
—Mako Shark. (p. 1082)
—Megamouth Shark (p. 1124)
—Nurse Shark (p. 1273)
—Shrimp (p. 1571)
—Tiger Shark (p. 1748)
—Tiger Shark [Scholastic]. (p. 1748)
—Whale Shark (p. 1877)
—Zebra Shark (p. 1985)
Nuzzolo, Deborah & Parham, Donna. Whales K-3 (p. 1878)
Nwapa-Ibuaka, Njideka. Tales from Animal Kingdom. (p. 1701)
Nwokolo, Nwanneka. Zara: The Girl Traveller. (p. 1985)
—Zara: Daughter of the Kings. (p. 1985)
NY Boys and Girls Clubs Rochester Staff & Boys & Girls Clubs Rochester, Ny. N Is for New York. (p. 1227)
NY CE Staff. Biyografi. (p. 194)
Nyamnjoh, Francis B. Stories from Abakwa. (p. 1654)
Nyamor, Eric, illus. see Jackson, Sharinese.
Nyamor, Eric, illus. see Pope, Cheryl Lynn.
Nyaradi, J. A. Catching Santa. (p. 279)
Nyberg, Judy. Just Pretend. (p. 939)
Nybo, B. J. Elmo Jackson Great Yellow Ball. (p. 515)
Nydam, Anne. Bad Advice of Grandma Hasenfuss. (p. 131)
Nye, Alex. Chill (p. 305)
Nye, Barry. Hannah & the Magic Blanket - Land of the Dinosaurs. (p. 742)
—Hannah & the Magic Blanket - Land of the Robots. (p. 742)
Nye, Christopher. Old Shepherd's Tale. (p. 1284)
Nye, Donna Kight. Sammi & the Tree. (p. 1507)
Nye, Julie, jt. auth. see Nye, Julie.
Nye, Julie & Nye, Julie. Scout: The Secret at les Cheneaux. (p. 1532)
Nye, Ken. Searching for the Spring: Poetic Reflections of Maine. (p. 1538)
Nye, Mark Aaron. Scriptureabble Game Book - Bible King James Version. (p. 1533)
—Scriptureabble Game Book - LDS Version. (p. 1533)
Nye, Naomi Shihab. 19 Varieties of Gazelle: Poems of the Middle East. (p. 1995)
—Baby Radar. Carpenter, Nancy, illus. (p. 127)
—Going Going. (p. 692)
—Honeybee: Poems & Short Prose. (p. 794)
—I'll Ask You Three Times, Are You Ok? Tales of Driving & Being Driven. (p. 856)
—Is This Forever, or What? Poems & Paintings from Texas. (p. 890)
—Maze Me: Poems for Girls. Maher, Terre, illus. (p. 1113)
—There Is No Long Distance Now: Very Short Stories. (p. 1730)
—Time You Let Me In: 25 Poets under 25. (p. 1753)
—Turtle of Oman. (p. 1798)
Nye, Penny. My Kindergarten Year. (p. 1211)
Nye, Robert. Beowulf. (p. 166)
Nye, Russel B., jt. auth. see Gardner, Martin.
Nyeu, Tao. Bunny Days. Nyeu, Tao, illus. (p. 242)
—Squid & Octopus: Friends for Always. (p. 1637)
—Wonder Bear. (p. 1947)
Nygaard, Orla & Lonvig, Asbjorn. Biggi Verdens Bedste Hund. (p. 185)
Nygard, Bonnie K., et al. Cody Investigates the World of Wellness. (p. 338)
—Health Education. (p. 758)
—Ruby Explores the World of Wellness. (p. 1493)
—Ruby Learns about the World of Wellness. (p. 1493)
—T. J.'s Adventures in the World of Wellness. (p. 1694)
—Wow! Health Education. (p. 1962)
—WOW! Sydney Travels Through the World of Wellness. (p. 1962)
Nygren, Kelsie. Line Between. (p. 1019)
Nyhus, Svein, illus. see Louise, Märtha.
Nyhus, Svein, illus. see Märtha Louise, Princess.
Nyhus, Svein, illus. see Ylvis & Lochstoer, Christian.
Nyika, Tendayi R. Disappearance of the Any Flavor Cake. (p. 446)
Nyikos, Stacy. Dizzy. Lee, Kary, illus. (p. 455)
—Dragon Wishes. (p. 478)
—Rope 'Em! Conover, Bret, illus. (p. 1488)
—Shelby. Sisneros, Shawn, illus. (p. 1564)
—Waggers. Anegon, Tamara, illus. (p. 1852)
Nyikos, Stacy Ann. Squirt. Sisneros, Shawn, illus. (p. 1637)
Nyirenda, Vukani G. Wise Old Tortoise & the Monkey. (p. 1940)
Nykiel, Connie. After the Loss of Your Baby: For Teen Mothers. (p. 28)
Nykko. Book One: The Shadow Door. Bannister, A., illus. (p. 212)
—Book Six: The Tower of Shadows. Bannister, illus. (p. 212)
—Book Three: The Master of Shadows. Bannister, A., illus. (p. 212)
—Calling. Bannister, illus. (p. 254)
—Elsewhere Chronicles. (p. 516)
—Master of Shadows Bannister, illus. (p. 1103)
—Parting Bannister, illus. (p. 1325)
—Parting. Bannister, illus. (p. 1325)
—Shadow Door. Bannister, illus. (p. 1557)
—Shadow Spies. Bannister, illus. (p. 1558)
Nyland, Richard. Jesus. (p. 914)
Nylund, Eric. Resisters. (p. 1463)
—Resisters #1: the Resisters. (p. 1463)
—Resisters #2: Sterling Squadron. (p. 1463)
—Resisters #3: Titan Base. (p. 1463)
—Resisters #4: Operation Inferno. (p. 1463)
Nylund, Eric S. Sterling Squadron. (p. 1649)
Nyman, Debbie, jt. auth. see Katz, Ben.
Nyman, Debbie & Wortzman, Ricki. 10 Best Plays. (p. 1993)
—10 Most Notable Elected Female Leaders. (p. 1994)
—10 Most Outstanding Women. (p. 1994)
Nyman, Ingrid, illus. see Lindgren, Astrid.
Nyman, Ingrid, jt. auth. see Lindgren, Astrid.
Nyman, Mary. High School Stories: Short Takes from the Writers' Club. (p. 778)
Nysewander, Mark & Bickle, Mike. Fasting Key. (p. 576)
Nystrom, Carolyn. Before I Was Born. Speidel, Sandra, illus. (p. 158)
—Preach, Paul! (p. 1394)
—Sing, Mary! (p. 1579)
—Will I Live Forever? Shilliam, Jo-Anne, illus. (p. 1932)
Nystrom, Carolyn, et al. 5 Languages of Appreciation in the Workplace: Empowering Organizations by Encouraging People Walles, Dwight, illus. (p. 1992)
Nystrom, Gregg. Golden Age of Hollywood Paper Dolls with Glitter! (p. 694)
Nystrom, Jennifer. Favorite Bible Children: Grades 1 & 2. (p. 578)
—Favorite Bible Children: Grades 3 & 4. (p. 578)
Nystrom, Kim, jt. auth. see Kola, Sari.
Nystrom Paine, Valerie. Amazing Little Seed: An Aunt Valsy Story. (p. 55)
Nytra, David. Secret of the Stone Frog. (p. 1543)
—Windmill Dragons: A Leah & Alan Adventure - A Toon Graphic. (p. 1936)
Nyznyk, Darryl. Mary's Son: A Tale of Christmas. (p. 1101)

O

O' Byrne, Lorraine. Hippity Dippity Witch. Martin, Laura & Kennedy, Seamus, illus. (p. 780)
O' Donoghue, Rachel. Please Don't Call Me Fatty! (p. 1373)
O Donovan, Christina, illus. see Ziefert, Harriet.
O Flatharta, Antoine. Hurry & the Monarch. So, Meilo, illus. (p. 830)
O., Lila. Lulabelle's Jewels: The Christmas Wish of Mrs. Claus. (p. 1064)
O., Lila, jt. auth. see O, Lila.
O, Lila & O., Lila. Lula Belle's Jewels: The Christmas Wish of Mrs. Claus. (p. 1064)
O' Murchadha, Niall, tr. see Priddy, Roger.
O. Shelley Dunn. Brown Like You. (p. 232)
Oachs, Emily Rose. Thomas Jefferson's Presidency. (p. 1739)
Oakes, Cory Putman. Dinosaur Boy. (p. 441)
Oakes, Elizabeth H. American Writers. (p. 64)
—Encyclopedia of Sports Medicine. (p. 525)
Oakes, John. Kitchener's Lost Boys: From the Playing Fields to the Killing Fields. (p. 962)
Oakes, Kim. Aurelia's Journey Home. (p. 116)
Oakes, Krista Ralston. Jake the Puppy & Emma the Cat. Fuhriman, Raphael Scott, illus. (p. 906)
Oakes, Loretta. Peek-a-Boo Christmas! Hall, Mary, illus. (p. 1334)
—Peek-a-Boo Jesus! Hall, Mary, illus. (p. 1334)
Oakes, Lorna. Hands-On History! Mesopotamia. (p. 741)
—Mesopotamia. (p. 1129)
Oakes, Shirley. No Bed for Mommy. (p. 1257)
Oakes, Stephanie. Sacred Lies of Minnow Bly. (p. 1500)
Oakes, Terry, jt. auth. see Delalandre, Benoit.
Oakhill, Jane, jt. ed. see Cain, Kate.
Oaklee, Mammy. Mailbox Kitten. (p. 1077)
—My Keyboard Was Hi~Jacked! (p. 1211)
Oakley, Darlene, ed. see Radford, Heather.
Oakley, Graham. Church Mice Take a Break. (p. 318)
—Church Mouse. Oakley, Graham, illus. (p. 318)
Oakley, Jacqui, illus. see Austen, Jane.
Oakley, Jacqui, illus. see Rondina, Catherine.
Oakley, Lisa. Cognitive Development. (p. 338)
Oaks, J. Adams. Why I Fight. (p. 1925)
Oaks, Kristen M. & Phillips, JoAnn. Testimony Glove. Burr, Dan, illus. (p. 1723)
Oaks, Robert C. Believe! Helping Youth Learn to Trust in the Lord. (p. 161)
Oaks, Tina. Sister Trap (p. 1581)
Oapos, Jem, jt. illus. see Bronte, Jules.
Oard, Beverly & Oard, Michael. What Ever Happened to the Wooly Mammoth: Life at the End of the Great Ice Age. Looney, Bill, illus. (p. 1884)
Oard, Michael, jt. auth. see Oard, Beverly.
Oarr, Chris, ed. Edge. (p. 504)
—Forge. (p. 619)
Oates, Betsy. Journey to Earth (p. 928)
Oates, Gary. Open My Eyes, Lord: A Practical Guide to Angelic Visitations & Heavenly Experiences. (p. 1299)
Oates, Joyce Carol. After the Wreck, I Picked Myself Up, Spread My Wings, & Flew Away. (p. 28)
—Big Mouth & Ugly Girl. (p. 182)
—Freaky Green Eyes. (p. 632)
—Naughty Cherie! Graham, Mark, illus. (p. 1237)
—Sexy. (p. 1556)
—Small Avalanches & Other Stories. (p. 1591)
—Two or Three Things I Forgot to Tell You. (p. 1804)
—Where Is Little Reynard? Graham, Mark, illus. (p. 1908)
Oatman, Eric. Amending the Constitution: Set Of 6. (p. 58)
—Amending the Constitution: Text Pairs. (p. 58)
—Cowboys & Cattle Drives: Life on the Western Trail. (p. 374)
Oatman, M. Scott, illus. see Lynch, Kelly Ann.
Oatman, Michael, jt. auth. see Bailey, Mark.
Obadina, Elizabeth. Ethnic Groups in Africa. Ojakorotu, Victor & Rotberg, Robert I., eds. (p. 539)
Obadina, Tunde. Making of Modern Africa. Ojakorotu, Victor & Rotberg, Robert I., eds. (p. 1082)
—Population & Overcrowding. (p. 1385)
—Population & Overcrowding. Ojakorotu, Victor & Rotberg, Robert I., eds. (p. 1385)
Obama, Barack. Of Thee I Sing: A Letter to My Daughters. Long, Loren, illus. (p. 1279)
—Our Enduring Spirit: President Barack Obama's First Words to America. Ruth, Greg, illus. (p. 1308)
—Yes We Can! A Salute to Children from President Obama's Victory Speech. (p. 1971)
Obama, Barack & Nelson, Kadir. Change Has Come: An Artist Celebrates Our American Spirit. Nelson, Kadir, illus. (p. 290)
Obasi, Lucy. My Short Story of Jesus on Earth. (p. 1218)
Obata, Claudia, illus. see Gregory, Steven.
Obata, Kazuko, et al. Ngaanyatjarra Picture Dictionary. (p. 1250)
Obata, Takeshi, illus. see Hotta, Yumi & Shindo, Hikaru.
Obata, Takeshi, illus. see Hotta, Yumi.
Obata, Takeshi, illus. see Ohba, Tsugumi.
Obata, Takeshi, jt. auth. see Ohba, Tsugumi.
Obata, Takeshi, jt. auth. see Takano, Tsuneo.
Obed, Ellen Bryan. Twelve Kinds of Ice. McClintock, Barbara, illus. (p. 1800)
—Who Would Like a Christmas Tree? A Tree for All Seasons. Hunter, Anne, illus. (p. 1919)
O'Beirne, Mike. Wine Tasting Guide to California's Central Coast. (p. 1936)
Obejas, Ofra, tr. see Burke, David.
Ober, Jillian, jt. auth. see Fish, Thomas R.
Ober, Jonathan, illus. see Weitzel, Karen E.
Ober, Jonathan, jt. illus. see Hertzler, Frances B.
Oberbillig, Deborah Richie. Bug Feats of Montana. Rath, Robert, illus. (p. 236)
Oberdieck, Bernhard. Princess & the Pea. (p. 1402)
Oberdieck, Bernhard, illus. see Peters, Stephanie True.
Oberg, Brent C. Interpersonal Communication: An Introduction to Interpersonal Communication. (p. 880)
Oberhauser, Karen, ed. Monarchs & More: 3-6 Curriculum Guide. (p. 1163)
—Monarchs & More: K-2 Curriculum Guide. (p. 1163)
—Monarchs & More: Middle School Curriculum Guide. (p. 1163)
Oberle, Kori, jt. auth. see Malone, Bobbie.
Oberle, Mark William. Puerto Rico's Birds in Photographs: A Complete Guide & CD-ROM Including the Virgin Islands. (p. 1415)
Oberlin, Linda. Eco in the Garden. Oberlin, Linda, illus. (p. 502)
Oberman, Sheldon. Always Prayer Shawl. Lewin, Ted, illus. (p. 51)
—Island of the Minotaur: The Greek Myths of Ancient Crete. Drawson, Blair, illus. (p. 892)
—Wind That Wanted to Rest. Waldman, Neil, illus. (p. 1935)
Oberman, Sheldon, illus. see Fischman, Sheila, tr.
Oberne, Sharon. Kelsey. (p. 948)
Oberon, Daphne. Ghost Tree: Tonantzin's Blessing. (p. 672)
O'Berry, Jan. Journey Home. (p. 928)
Oberst M. D., Faap Byron. Brownie Bill & the Health Pirates. (p. 232)
Obert, Lois. Help! Willie's Choking! (p. 766)
Obi Shaaim Maa. Kheru Nefer (Beautiful Night) A Khamitic (Ancient Egyptian) Lullaby. (p. 951)
Obie, Christopher R. Dumisai & the Enchanted Journey. (p. 489)
Obioha, Natalie O. Emotions. (p. 520)
Obiols, Anna. Pequeño Dali y el Camino Hacia Los Sueños. (p. 1341)
—Stegosaurus: the Friendliest Dinosaur. Subi, illus. (p. 1646)
—Triceratops: the Strongest Dinosaur. Subi, illus. (p. 1786)
—Tyrannosaurus Rex: the King of the Dinosaurs. Subi, illus. (p. 1805)
Oblich, Kathleen. Jake & the Scarecrow. (p. 906)
Oboh, Rolic. Treasure Hunt. (p. 1781)
O'Boyle, Laurel. Froggy & Bug (p. 640)
O'Brady, Terry, et al. Count the Animals. (p. 370)
—Watermelons. (p. 1864)
Obray, C. J. Franny & Mirus. Metcalf, Maggie, illus. (p. 631)
Obregon, Jose M. David Beckham. Benson, Megan, tr. (p. 410)
Obregon, Jose Maria. Alaska. (p. 33)
Obregón, José María. Alaska. (p. 33)
—Argentina. (p. 97)
—Argentina. Benson, Megan, tr. from SPA. (p. 97)
—Brazil: Brasil. (p. 224)
Obregon, Jose Maria. California. (p. 253)
Obregón, José María. California. (p. 253)
Obregon, Jose Maria. Colorado. (p. 343)
Obregón, José María. Colorado. (p. 343)
—Cuauhtémoc Blanco. (p. 388)
Obregon, Jose Maria. David Beckham. (p. 410)
Obregón, José María. Didier Drogba. (p. 437)
—England: Inglaterra. (p. 529)
—England: Inglaterra. Benson, Megan, tr. (p. 529)
Obregon, Jose Maria. Florida. (p. 606)
Obregón, José María. Florida. (p. 606)
—Freddy Adu. (p. 633)
—Germany: Alemania. (p. 666)
—Germany: Alemania. Benson, Megan, tr. (p. 666)
—Hawaii. (p. 755)
Obregon, Jose Maria. Hawaii/Hawai. (p. 755)
Obregón, José María. Italy: Italia. (p. 895)
—Italy: Italia. Benson, Megan, tr. (p. 895)
—Juan Pablo Ángel. (p. 930)
—Kaká. (p. 941)
Obregon, Jose Maria. Kansas. (p. 942)
Obregón, José María. Kansas. (p. 942)
—Lionel Messi. (p. 1021)
—Maine. (p. 1077)
Obregon, Jose Maria. Maine. Brusca, Maria Cristina, tr. (p. 1077)
Obregón, José María. Massachusetts. (p. 1102)
Obregon, Jose Maria. Massachusetts. Brusca, Maria Cristina, tr. (p. 1102)
Obregón, José María. Mexico/México. (p. 1131)
—Mexico/México. Benson, Megan, tr. (p. 1131)
—Michigan. (p. 1135)
Obregon, Jose Maria. Michigan. Brusca, Maria Cristina, tr. (p. 1135)
Obregón, José María. Missouri. (p. 1154)
Obregon, Jose Maria. Missouri. Brusca, Maria Cristina, tr. (p. 1154)
Obregón, José María. Nevada. (p. 1242)
Obregon, Jose Maria. Nevada. Brusca, Maria Cristina, tr. from ENG. (p. 1242)

O

Obregón, José María. New Mexico. (p. 1246)
Obregon, Jose Maria. New Mexico/Nuevo Mexico. Brusca, Maria Cristina, tr. (p. 1246)
Obregón, José María. New York / Nueva York. (p. 1247)
Obregon, Jose Maria. Nueva York/New York. Brusca, Maria Cristina, tr. (p. 1270)
Obregón, José María. Puerto Rico. (p. 1415)
Obregon, Jose Maria. Puerto Rico. Brusca, Maria Cristina, tr. from ENG. (p. 1415)
—Ronaldhino. (p. 1487)
—Ronaldinho. Benson, Megan, tr. (p. 1487)
Obregón, José María. Texas. (p. 1723)
Obregon, Jose Maria. Texas. De Leon, Mauricio Velzaquez, tr. (p. 1723)
Obregón, José María. Utah. (p. 1829)
Obregon, Jose Maria. Utah. Brusca, Maria Cristina, tr. from ENG. (p. 1829)
Obregón, José María. Wisconsin. (p. 1939)
Obregón, José María, illus. see Daning, Tom.
Obregón, José María, illus. see Faust, Daniel R.
Obregon, Jose Maria, illus. see Herdling, Glenn.
Obregón, José María, jt. auth. see Daning, Tom.
Obregón, José María, jt. auth. see Faust, Daniel R.
Obregón, José María, jt. auth. see Herdling, Glenn.
Obregón, José María, jt. auth. see Nelson, John.
Obregon, Jose Maria, tr. see Daning, Tom.
Obregón, José María, tr. see DeMolay, Jack.
Obregon, Jose Maria, tr. see Roth, Carol.
Obregon, Jose Maria, tr. see Twine, Alice.
Obrero, Rudy, illus. see Anderson, R. P.
O'Brian, Fitz-James. Collected Stories. (p. 339)
O'Brian, Pliny. Empires, Crusaders, & Invasions Through the Middle Ages. (p. 521)
—Feudalism in Medieval Europe. (p. 583)
—Knights: Warriors of the Middle Ages. (p. 964)
O'Brian, Virginia. Librarian's Job. (p. 1005)
O'Brien, Andrew & O'Brien, Emma. Little Bubishi: A History of Karate for Children. (p. 1025)
O'Brien, Anne. Patches in Her Dreams: An Alaskan Children's Story. (p. 1328)
O'Brien, Anne, illus. see Njenga, Wamoro P.
O'Brien, Anne Sibley. I'm New Here. O'Brien, Anne Sibley, illus. (p. 859)
—Legend of Hong Kil Dong: The Robin Hood of Korea. O'Brien, Anne Sibley, illus. (p. 988)
—Path of Stars. O'Brien, Anne Sibley, illus. (p. 1328)
O'Brien, Anne Sibley, illus. see Avraham, Kate Aver.
O'Brien, Anne Sibley, illus. see Burns Knight, Margy, et al.
O'Brien, Anne Sibley, illus. see Burns Knight, Margy.
O'Brien, Anne Sibley, illus. see Coburn, Jewell Reinhart & Lee, Tzexa Cherta.
O'Brien, Anne Sibley, illus. see Havill, Juanita.
O'Brien, Anne Sibley, illus. see Jalali, Reza.
O'Brien, Anne Sibley, illus. see Knight, Margy Burns.
O'Brien, Anne Sibley & O'Brien, Perry Edmond. After Gandhi: One Hundred Years of Nonviolent Resistance. O'Brien, Anne Sibley & O'Brien, Perry Edmond, illus. (p. 28)
O'Brien, Annemarie. Lara's Gift. (p. 975)
O'Brien, Bridget. Alligators: Level 1. (p. 47)
—Alligators Eat & Grow: Level 2. (p. 47)
—Alligators in the Swamp: Level 3. (p. 47)
—Deer: Level 1. Keimig, Candice, illus. (p. 423)
—Deer Eat & Grow: Level 2. Keimig, Candice, illus. (p. 423)
—Deer in the Woods: Level 3. Keimig, Candice, illus. (p. 423)
O'Brien, Caragh M. Birthmarked. (p. 193)
—Prized. (p. 1408)
—Promised. (p. 1411)
—Vault of Dreamers. (p. 1833)
O'Brien, Carola. Bobby Dazzler & the Three Rubies of Ishmalan. (p. 206)
O'Brien, Claudia Moore. My Mom's Apron. Friar, Joanne, illus. (p. 1214)
O'Brien, Cormac. Secret Lives of the Civil War: What Your Teachers Never Told You about the War Between the States. Suteski, Monika, illus. (p. 1541)
O'Brien, Cynthia. Amazing Brain Mysteries. (p. 54)
—Explore with Christopher Columbus. (p. 550)
—Explore with Francisco Pizarro. (p. 550)
—Explore with John Franklin. (p. 550)
—Explore with Ponce de León. (p. 551)
—Explore with Samuel de Champlain. (p. 551)
—Explore with Sieur de la Salle. (p. 551)
—Lost Treasures. (p. 1057)
—Myths & Legends of North America: Canada & the Northern United States. (p. 1227)
O'Brien, Cynthia, jt. auth. see Cole, Joanna.
O'Brien, Cynthia, jt. auth. see Corporate Contributor Staff.
O'Brien, David M. Supreme Court Watch 2003. (p. 1685)
O'Brien, Duncan. Matson the Mouse. Drage, Robyn, illus. (p. 1109)
O'Brien, Eileen. Introduction to Music. Alaverdy, Melissa, illus. (p. 882)
—Space. (p. 1618)
—This Little Piggy. Tyler, Jenny, ed. (p. 1737)
—Usborne Story of Music. Danes, Emma, ed. (p. 1827)
—Usborne Story of Music. Danes, Emma & Hooper, Caroline, eds. (p. 1827)
O'Brien, Eileen & Denne, Ben. Space. (p. 1618)
O'Brien, Eileen & Needham, Kate. Origami Pack. (p. 1304)
Obrien, Elaine F. Anita of Rancho del Mar. (p. 84)
O'Brien, Emma, jt. auth. see O'Brien, Andrew.
O'Brien, Fitz James. Wondersmith. (p. 1949)
O'Brien, Frances. Sheer Bliss: Confessions of a (Reluctant) Celebrity Spawn. (p. 1564)
O'Brien, Geoffrey. Red Sky Café. (p. 1455)
O'Brien, Geoffrey & Collins, Billy. Bartlett's Poems for Occasions. (p. 140)
O'Brien, Gerry. Bubba Begonia, You'll Be Sorry. Jones, Brenda, illus. (p. 233)
O'Brien, Gregory. Back & Beyond: New Zealand in Painting for the Young & Curious. (p. 130)
—Welcome to the South Seas: Contemporary New Zealand Art for Young People. (p. 1874)
O'Brien, Jack. Return of Silver Chief. (p. 1464)
—Silver Chief's Revenge. Wiese, Kurt, illus. (p. 1576)
O'Brien, Jeanne. Finding Shapes in Nature: Parks, Forests & Backyards. (p. 588)
O'Brien, Jerry. Giretsu. (p. 678)
O'Brien, Joan. Christmas Around the World Coloring Book. (p. 312)
—Fashion Accessories Stickers. (p. 575)
—Halloween Picture Sticker Activity Book. (p. 738)
—Holidays Around the World. (p. 788)
—Hot Air Balloons Stickers. (p. 801)
—Littlest Angels Stickers. (p. 1038)
—Lucky Ladybug Stickers. (p. 1062)
O'Brien, Joe. Alfie Green & the Bee-Bottle Gang. Texier, Jean, illus. (p. 37)
—Alfie Green & the Conker King. Texier, Jean, illus. (p. 37)
—Beyond the Cherry Tree. McGann, Oisin, illus. (p. 174)
O'Brien, John. Look ... Look Again! (p. 1048)
O'Brien, John, illus. see Bader, Bonnie.
O'Brien, John, illus. see Buckley, James, Jr.
O'Brien, John, illus. see D'Agnese, Joseph.
O'Brien, John, illus. see Demuth, Patricia Brennan.
O'Brien, John, illus. see Edgers, Geoff.
O'Brien, John, illus. see Edwards, Roberta.
O'Brien, John, illus. see Ekeland, Ivar.
O'Brien, John, illus. see Fradin, Dennis Brindell.
O'Brien, John, illus. see Frith, Margaret.
O'Brien, John, illus. see Garriel, Barbara S.
O'Brien, John, illus. see Garriel, Barbara.
O'Brien, John, illus. see Herman, Gail.
O'Brien, John, illus. see Holub, Joan.
O'Brien, John, illus. see Kelley, True.
O'Brien, John, illus. see Magaziner, Henry Jonas.
O'Brien, John, illus. see Mannis, Celeste Davidson & Davidson, Mannis.
O'Brien, John, illus. see Mannis, Celeste Davidson & Kramer, Sydelle.
O'Brien, John, illus. see O'Connor, Jim.
O'Brien, John, illus. see Pascal, Janet.
O'Brien, John, illus. see Prince, April Jones.
O'Brien, John, illus. see Reed, Avery.
O'Brien, John, illus. see Rosenstock, Barb.
O'Brien, John, illus. see Schroeder, Alan.
O'Brien, John, illus. see Stine, Megan.
O'Brien, John A. Elves, Gnomes, & Other Little People Coloring Book. (p. 517)
—Twelve Days of Christmas. (p. 1800)
—Who Was Helen Keller? Harrison, Nancy, illus. (p. 1918)
O'Brien, John A., illus. see Branley, Franklyn M.
O'Brien, John A., illus. see Estes, Eleanor.
O'Brien, John A., illus. see Frith, Margaret.
O'Brien, John A., illus. see Low, Alice.
O'Brien, John A., illus. see Magaziner, Henry Jonas.
O'Brien, John A., illus. see McDonough, Yona Zeldis.
O'Brien, John A., illus. see Prince, April Jones.
O'Brien, John A., illus. see Swain, Ruth Freeman.
O'Brien, John A., illus. see Thompson, Gare.
O'Brien, John A. & Thompson, Gare. Who Was Helen Keller? Harrison, Nancy, illus. (p. 1918)
O'Brien, Johnny. Day of Deliverance. Hardcastle, Nick, illus. (p. 414)
—Day of the Assassins: A Jack Christie Novel. Hardcastle, Nick, illus. (p. 414)
—Day of the Assassins. Hardcastle, Nick, illus. (p. 414)
O'Brien, Kathryn. I'd Be Your Princess: A Royal Tale of Godly Character. Garland, Michael, illus. (p. 851)
O'Brien, Kevin J. My Macaroni Whales. (p. 1213)
O'Brien, Kim. American Paint Horses (p. 62)
—American Quarter Horses (p. 63)
—Appaloosa Horses (p. 92)
—Caballos Cuarto de Milla. Strictly Spanish LLC. Staff, tr. from ENG. (p. 250)
—Caballos Paint. Strictly Spanish Translation Services Staff, tr. from ENG. (p. 250)
—Caballos Pura Sangre. Strictly Spanish Translation Services Staff, tr. from ENG. (p. 250)
—Friesian Horses (p. 639)
—Lipizzan Horses (p. 1021)
—Thoroughbred Horses (p. 1740)
O'Brien, Kim, jt. auth. see Monahan, Erin.
O'Brien, Kristen. Little Red Riding Hood Story in a Box. Winter, Janet, illus. (p. 1035)
O'Brien, Lara. Chesca & the Spirit of Grace. (p. 298)
O'Brien, Laurel, illus. see Riley, Christine.
O'Brien, Lindsy. Communication Long Ago & Today (p. 349)
—World's Weirdest Animals. (p. 1961)
O'Brien, Mandie. Molly's Christmas Gift. (p. 1161)
O'Brien, May L. Legend of the Seven Sisters: A Traditional Aboriginal Story from Western Australia. Wyatt, Sue, illus. (p. 989)
—Wunambi the Water Snake. Wyatt, Sue, illus. (p. 1966)
O'Brien, Melanie. My Belly Button. (p. 1196)
—No More Diapers. (p. 1259)
—No More Pacifiers! With Disappearing Pacifiers! Enright, Amanda, illus. (p. 1259)
—Pat Them Gently. Runnells, Treesha, illus. (p. 1327)
O'Brien Novak, Patty. Engineering the ABCs. (p. 529)
O'Brien, Patricia. Glory Cloak: A Novel of Louisa May Alcott & Clara Barton. (p. 685)
O'Brien, Patrick. Duel of the Ironclads: The Monitor vs. the Virginia. (p. 489)
—Fantastic Flights: One Hundred Years of Flying on the Edge. (p. 571)
—Hindenburg. (p. 780)
—Mutiny on the Bounty. O'Brien, Patrick, illus. (p. 1194)
—Untitled O'brien 2/2 (p. 1823)
—You Are the First Kid on Mars. O'Brien, Patrick, illus. (p. 1973)
O'Brien, Patrick, illus. see O'Malley, Kevin.
O'Brien, Perry Edmond, jt. auth. see O'Brien, Anne Sibley.
O'Brien, Phil T. Cullinan Foible. (p. 390)
O'Brien, Renee McMullen. Amazing Mocha & His Courageous Journey. O'Brien, Renee McMullen, illus. (p. 55)
O'Brien, Richard. Christopher & Joshua Go Fishing. (p. 316)
O'Brien, Robert C. Senora Frisby y las Ratas de NIMH. (p. 1550)
—Z for Zachariah. (p. 1984)
O'Brien, Sarah. Whack-a-Zombie: You Can't Keep a Good Zombie Down! (p. 1877)
O'Brien, Susan. Child Abduction & Kidnapping. (p. 301)
O'Brien, Thomas C. Off the Path Math with Tobbs Reynolds, Peter H., illus. (p. 1279)
O'Brien, Thomas E. Magic of Finbar. (p. 1073)
O'Brien, Tim. Billy-Goats Tough. Mancini, Robert, illus. (p. 187)
O'Brien, Tim, illus. see Collins, Suzanne.
O'Brien, Tim, illus. see Reeder, Carolyn.
O'Brien, Timothy J. Rheemer the Rhymer Rhinoceros. (p. 1467)
O'Brien, Timothy L. TrumpNation: The Art of Being the Donald. (p. 1793)
O'Brien, Tony & Sullivan, Michael P. Afghan Dreams: Young Voices of Afghanistan. (p. 26)
O'Brien-Palmer, Michelle. Beyond Book Reports. (p. 173)
Obrist, Jürg. Case Closed?! 40 Mini-Mysteries for You to Solve. (p. 273)
—Complex Cases: Three Major Mysteries for You to Solve. Obrist, Jürg, illus. (p. 353)
Obrist, Jurg. Open & Shut Cases: 40 More Mini-Mysteries for You to Solve. (p. 1299)
Obrist, Jürg. Open & Shut Cases: 40 More Mini - Mysteries for You to Solve. (p. 1299)
Obrist, Paul A., et al, eds. Cardiovascular Psychophysiology: Current Issues in Response Mechanisms, Biofeedback & Methodology. (p. 266)
Obrochta, Dale. Faces, Faces, Balloon Faces. (p. 561)
Obstfeld, Raymond, jt. auth. see Abdul-Jabbar, Kareem.
Obunge, Adesola. Conversations with God for 5 to 10 Year Olds: Hidden Treasure for Little Minds(r). (p. 361)
Oburkova, Eva. Toby's Travels Through Time: Puzzle Adventures in Dinosaur Days. Oburkova, Eva, illus. (p. 1760)
O'Byrne, John, ed. Space. (p. 1618)
O'Byrne, Nicola. Count & Color - Swim. O'Byrne, Nicola, illus. (p. 369)
—Fly. O'Byrne, Nicola, illus. (p. 609)
—Use Your Imagination. O'Byrne, Nicola, illus. (p. 1827)
O'Byrne, Nicola, illus. see Bromley, Nick.
O'Byrne, Nicola, illus. see Halfmann, Janet.
O'Byrne, Tim. Cowboys & Dog Tales. (p. 374)
Ocala National Forest Staff, prod. Exploring Ocala National Forest & Central Florida's Parks. (p. 553)
O'Callaghan, Elena. Color de la Arena. Santos, Ma Jesus, illus. (p. 342)
—What's Going On? Fanlo, Africa, illus. (p. 1897)
O'Callaghan, G. Eternals. (p. 539)
—Slave Prince. (p. 1588)
—Sorcerers Apprentice. (p. 1614)
—Tektite. (p. 1716)
O'Callaghan, Gemma, illus. see Morpurgo, Michael.
O'Callahan, Jay. Herman & Marguerite: An Earth Story O'Callahan, Laura, illus. (p. 771)
O'Callahan, Laura, illus. see O'Callahan, Jay.
O'Campo, Allicia. Tinky Goes to North Americ. (p. 1756)
Ocampo, L. A. Cardboard Sisters Save the World: An Activity Storybook. (p. 265)
Ocampo Ruiz, Jose Alfonso, illus. see Fuentes, Benny & Stoker, Bram.
Ocanas, Alicia Urista. Cuaderno de Telpochcalli: The Most Practical & User Friendly Spanish Grammar & Workbook. (p. 387)
Ocean, Davy. Boy Who Cried Shark. Blecha, Aaron, illus. (p. 219)
—Deep-Sea Disaster. Blecha, Aaron, illus. (p. 423)
—Deep-Sea Treasury: Deep-Sea Disaster; Lights! Camera! Hammerhead!; Squid-Napped; the Boy Who Cried Shark. Blecha, Aaron, illus. (p. 423)
—Lights! Camera! Hammerhead! Blecha, Aaron, illus. (p. 1016)
Ocean Front Books. Coloring Book. (p. 344)
Oceanak, Karla. All Me, All the Time: The Authorized Art-O-Biography Of... Spanjer, Kendra, illus. (p. 45)
—Cahoots. Spanjer, Kendra, illus. (p. 251)
—Dumbstruck. Spanjer, Kendra, illus. (p. 489)
—Egghead. Spanjer, Kendra, illus. (p. 506)
—Finicky. Spanjer, Kendra, illus. (p. 589)
—Glitch. Spanjer, Kendra, illus. (p. 683)
—Hotdogger. Spanjer, Kendra, illus. (p. 802)
—Ignoramus. Spanjer, Kendra, illus. (p. 856)
Oceano Editorial Staff, ed. see Tullet, Hervé.
Ocello, Salvatore, illus. see Nelligan, Patty.
Ocelot, Michel. Kirikou et la Sorciere. (p. 961)
—Kirikou et la Sorciere. (p. 961)
Ochester, Betsy, ed. see Boyds Mills Press Staff.
Ochi, Chifumi. Honey Senior, Darling Junior (p. 794)
Ochiai, Midori & Oyama, Shigeki. Different Croaks for Different Folks: All about Children with Special Learning Needs. Sanders, Esther, tr. from JPN. (p. 438)
Ochiltree, Dianne. It's a Seashell Day. Kreloff, Elliot, illus. (p. 896)
—Molly, by Golly! The Legend of Molly Williams, America's First Female Firefighter. Kemly, Kathleen, illus. (p. 1160)
—Sunflowers Measure Up! (p. 1677)
Ochoa, Ana, illus. see Antillano, Laura.
Ochoa, Ana, illus. see Neasi, Barbara J.
Ochoa, Ana, illus. see Rosa-Mendoza, Gladys.
Ochoa, Ana, jt. auth. see Neasi, Barbara J.
Ochoa, Edna, tr. see Valdez, Luis.
Ochoa, Edna, tr. see Villaseñor, Victor.
Ochoa, Francisco, illus. see Deltoro, Antonio.
Ochoa, George. America in The 1990s. (p. 59)
Ochoa, George & Smith, Carter. Atlas of Hispanic-American History. (p. 112)
Ochoa, Louisa & Benchmark Education Co., LLC Staff. Know about Storms. (p. 965)
Ochoa, Mary Lou. Andy's Arctic Party. (p. 73)
Ochoa, Minerva. De la Vez Que Tino Perdio Su Par. Garcia, Victor Manuel Gut, illus. (p. 416)
Ochs, Bill. Clarke Learn-to-Play Tin Whistle Set: Includes Clarke Original D Tin Whistle on Blister Card: Book, Whistle & Compact Disc. (p. 327)
—Clarke Tin Whistle. (p. 327)
Ochs, Carol. Reaching Godward: Voices from Jewish Spiritual Guidance. Kofsky, Ann, illus. (p. 1442)
Ochs, Susan A., jt. auth. see Trembley, Skip.
Ochs, Tom. Day on the Farm Playing Along Dindar, Kubra, illus. (p. 414)
Ochse, Bobbie Colliton. Nana's Magic Closet. (p. 1228)
Ocker, Christ Holder. Mouse Without a House. (p. 1182)
Ocker, Christa Holder. Crow Named Robin. (p. 386)
—Rooster Named Lorenz. (p. 1488)
—Smitten the Kitten. (p. 1594)
Ockler, Sarah. Bittersweet. (p. 194)
—Book of Broken Hearts. (p. 211)
—Fixing Delilah. (p. 601)
—#scandal. (p. 1519)
—Summer of Chasing Mermaids. (p. 1674)
—Twenty Boy Summer. (p. 1801)
Ockun, Lisa C. Sammy the Tin Man. (p. 1508)
O'Clair, Robert, et al, eds. Norton Anthology of Modern & Contemporary Poetry (p. 1266)
O'Connell, Bailey. Earth's Rainiest Places. (p. 498)
O'Connell, Caitlin. Baby Elephant in the Wild. O'Connell, Caitlin & Rodwell, Timothy, illus. (p. 126)
O'Connell, Caitlin & Jackson, Donna M. Elephant Scientist. Rodwell, Timothy, illus. (p. 511)
O'Connell, Carol. Winter House. (p. 1938)
O'Connell, Dave, illus. see Krivitzky, Nathan & Nathan, Krivitzky.
O'Connell, David, jt. auth. see McIntyre, Sarah.
O'Connell, Diane. People Person: The Story of Sociologist Marta Tienda. (p. 1339)
—Strong Force: The Story of Physicist Shirley Ann Jackson. (p. 1668)
O'Connell, Emma. We Love Blue! (p. 1867)
—We Love Green! (p. 1867)
—We Love Orange! (p. 1867)
O'Connell, Isabel. Gypsy. Scott, Susan, illus. (p. 734)
O'Connell, Jack. Derek Jeter: The Yankee Kid. Rains, Rob, ed. (p. 427)
O'Connell, Janet. When They Died, Where Did They Go? (p. 1905)
O'Connell, Jeff, jt. auth. see Kleiner, Susan M.
O'Connell, Jennifer. Eye of the Whale: A Rescue Story O'Connell, Jennifer, illus. (p. 558)
O'Connell, Jennifer Barrett. It's Halloween Night! (p. 897)
—It's Halloween Night! Morris, Jennifer E., illus. (p. 897)
O'Connell, Jennifer Barrett, illus. see Davis, Maggie Steincrohn.
O'Connell, Jenny. Book of Luke. (p. 211)
—Local Girls: An Island Summer Novel. (p. 1044)
—Plan B. (p. 1366)
—Rich Boys: An Island Summer Novel. (p. 1469)
O'Connell, Kim A. Ancient Greece: A MyReportLinks. com Book. (p. 69)
—China: A MyReportLinks. com Book. (p. 306)
—Civil War: A MyReportLinks. Com Book. (p. 325)
—Discover Ancient Greece. (p. 447)
—Galapagos Penguin: A MyReportLinks. com Book. (p. 653)
—Major Battles of the Civil War: A MyReportLinks. com Book. (p. 1078)
—Mercury: A Myreportlinks. com Book. (p. 1127)
—Mexican-American War: A MyReportLinks.com Book. (p. 1131)
—Pennsylvania: A MyReportLinks. Com Book. (p. 1338)
—Pluto: A Myreportlinks. com Book. (p. 1374)
—Primary Source Accounts of the Vietnam War. (p. 1399)
—Slavery, Emancipation, & the Civil War: A MyReportLinks. com Book. (p. 1588)
—Virginia: A MyReportLinks.com Book. (p. 1844)
—Wallaby: A MyReportLinks. com Book. (p. 1855)
—William Howard Taft: A MyReportLinks.com Book. (p. 1933)
O'Connell, Lorraine, illus. see Random House Staff.
O'Connell, Matthew J. Adventures of Rick Cliff: The Almost Great Penguin Race. (p. 22)
O'Connell, Rebecca. Baby Goes Beep. Wilson-Max, Ken, illus. (p. 126)
—Baby Parade. Poole, Susie, illus. (p. 127)
—Baby Party. Poole, Susie, illus. (p. 127)
—Penina Levine Is a Hard-boiled Egg. Lue Sue, Majella, illus. (p. 1337)
O'Connell, S. L. Short Stories to Tickle the Imagination. (p. 1569)
O'connell, Tyne. Royal Match. (p. 1492)
O'Connell, Tyne. Royal Mess. (p. 1492)
OConner, Kim, illus. see Melkonian, Sheyda Mia.
O'Conner, Patricia T. Woe Is I Jr. The Younger Grammarphobe's Guide to Better English in Plain English. Stiglich, Tom, illus. (p. 1943)
O'Connor, Bailey, illus. see Ceballos, Jacalyn Martin.
O'Connor, Barbara. Fame & Glory in Freedom, Georgia. (p. 567)
—Fantastic Secret of Owen Jester. (p. 572)
—Greetings from Nowhere. (p. 723)
—How to Steal a Dog. (p. 821)
—On the Road to Mr. Mineo's. (p. 1291)
—On the Road to Mr. Mineo's. (p. 1291)
—Small Adventure of Popeye & Elvis. (p. 1591)
O'Connor, Crystal Ball. Gift/ Book Combo. Hollinger, Valerie Bunch, illus. (p. 675)
—Jake & the Migration of the Monarch. Hollinger, Valerie Bunch, illus. (p. 905)
—Jake & the Migration of the Monarch with CD. Hollinger, Valerie Bunch, illus. (p. 905)
—Jake y la Migracion de la Monarca. Brenes-Sotela, Guillermo J. & Quave, Gloria Martinez, trs. from ENG. (p. 906)
—Katherine's Quilt. (p. 944)
O'Connor, Dagmar. How to Make Love to the Same Person for the Rest of Your Life & Still Love It! (p. 820)
O'Connor, Daniel & Barrie, J. M. Peter Pan Picture Book. Woodward, Alice B., illus. (p. 1347)

O'Connor, Eddie, et al. Donald Duck Adventures Clark, John, ed. (p. 465)
O'Connor, Edward. G Man's Son. (p. 651)
O'Connor, Edwin. Benjy: A Ferocious Fairy Tale. O'Neill, Catharine, illus. (p. 165)
O'Connor, Finbar. Wolfgran Returns. Fagan, Martin, illus. (p. 1944)
O'Connor, Frances. Frequently Asked Questions about Academic Anxiety. (p. 636)
—Frequently Asked Questions about Stuttering. (p. 636)
—History of Islam. (p. 784)
—Understanding Islam: History of Islam. (p. 1815)
O'Connor, Frankie. Ants Go Marching One by One. Groot, Nicole, illus. (p. 90)
O'Connor, George. Aphrodite: Goddess of Love. O'Connor, George, illus. (p. 91)
—Ares. O'Connor, George, illus. (p. 97)
—Athena: Grey-Eyed Goddess. Bk. 2 O'Connor, George, illus. (p. 112)
—Hades: Lord of the Dead. O'Connor, George, illus. (p. 735)
—Hera: The Goddess & Her Glory. O'Connor, George, illus. (p. 769)
—If I Had a Raptor. O'Connor, George, illus. (p. 853)
—If I Had a Triceratops. O'Connor, George, illus. (p. 853)
—Kapow! O'Connor, George, illus. (p. 943)
—Ker-Splash! O'Connor, George, illus. (p. 949)
—Poseidon: Earth Shaker. O'Connor, George, illus. (p. 1387)
—Zeus: King of the Gods. O'Connor, George, illus. (p. 1986)
O'Connor, George, illus. see Abela, Deborah.
O'Connor, George, illus. see Kirby, Stan.
O'Connor, George, illus. see Simmons, Michael.
O'Connor, George, jt. auth. see Bogaert, Harmen Meyndertsz van den.
O'Connor, Grandma. Rodney the Robot: Why Rodney Rebels. (p. 1484)
O'Connor, Jane. 100th Day of School. Glasser, Robin Preiss & Enik, Ted, illus. (p. 1999)
—Apples Galore! Glasser, Robin Preiss, illus. (p. 93)
—Aspiring Artist. Glasser, Robin Preiss, illus. (p. 107)
—Bonjour, Butterfly. Glasser, Robin Preiss, illus. (p. 209)
—Budding Ballerina. (p. 234)
—Dazzling Book Report. Glasser, Robin Preiss & Enik, Ted, illus. (p. 415)
—Every Day Is Earth Day. Ivanov, Aleksey et al, illus. (p. 542)
—Explorer Extraordinaire! Glasser, Robin Preiss, illus. (p. 551)
—Express Yourself! A Doodle & Draw Book. Glasser, Robin Preiss, illus. (p. 554)
—Fanciest Doll in the Universe. Glasser, Robin Preiss, illus. (p. 570)
—Fancy Day in Room 1-A. (p. 570)
—Fancy Day in Room 1-A. Glasser, Robin Preiss, illus. (p. 570)
—Fancy Nancy: Just My Luck! (p. 570)
—Fancy Nancy: Apples Galore! (p. 570)
—Fancy Nancy: Too Many Tutus. (p. 570)
—Fancy Nancy: Every Day Is Earth Day. (p. 570)
—Fancy Nancy: Nancy Clancy, Super Sleuth. (p. 570)
—Fancy Nancy: Pajama Day. Drainville, Beth et al, illus. (p. 570)
—Fancy Nancy: Tea for Two. Glasser, Robin Preiss, illus. (p. 570)
—Fancy Nancy: Too Many Tutus. Glasser, Robin Preiss, illus. (p. 570)
—Fancy Nancy: Bonjour, Butterfly. Glasser, Robin Preiss, illus. (p. 570)
—Fancy Nancy: Hair Dos & Hair Don'ts. Glasser, Robin Preiss, illus. (p. 570)
—Fancy Nancy: My Family History. Glasser, Robin Preiss et al, illus. (p. 570)
—Fancy Nancy: Our Thanksgiving Banquet. Glasser, Robin Preiss, illus. (p. 570)
—Fancy Nancy: Poison Ivy Expert. Glasser, Robin Preiss & Enik, Ted, illus. (p. 570)
—Fancy Nancy: The Show Must Go On. Glasser, Robin Preiss & Enik, Ted, illus. (p. 570)
—Fancy Nancy: The Dazzling Book Report. Glasser, Robin Preiss & Enik, Ted, illus. (p. 570)
—Fancy Nancy. Glasser, Robin Preiss, illus. (p. 570)
—Fancy Nancy 10th Anniversary Edition. Glasser, Robin Preiss, illus. (p. 570)
—Fancy Nancy & the Boy from Paris. Enik, Ted & Glasser, Robin Preiss, illus. (p. 570)
—Fancy Nancy & the Delectable Cupcakes. Glasser, Robin Preiss & Enik, Ted, illus. (p. 570)
—Fancy Nancy & the Fabulous Fashion Boutique. Glasser, Robin Preiss, illus. (p. 570)
—Fancy Nancy & the Fall Foliage. Glasser, Robin Preiss, illus. (p. 570)
—Fancy Nancy & the Late, Late, Late Night. (p. 570)
—Fancy Nancy & the Late, Late, Late Night. Glasser, Robin Preiss, illus. (p. 570)
—Fancy Nancy & the Mean Girl. Glasser, Robin Preiss, illus. (p. 570)
—Fancy Nancy & the Mermaid Ballet. Glasser, Robin Preiss, illus. (p. 570)
—Fancy Nancy & the Mermaid Ballet. Glasser, Robin Preiss & Bracken, Carolyn, illus. (p. 570)
—Fancy Nancy & the Posh Puppy. Glasser, Robin Preiss, illus. (p. 570)
—Fancy Nancy & the Posh Puppy (Nancy la Elegante y la Perrita Popoff) Glasser, Robin Preiss, illus. (p. 570)
—Fancy Nancy & the Sensational Babysitter. (p. 570)
—Fancy Nancy & the Sensational Babysitter. Glasser, Robin Preiss et al, illus. (p. 570)
—Fancy Nancy & the Too-Loose Tooth. (p. 570)
—Fancy Nancy & the Too-Loose Tooth. Glasser, Robin Preiss & Enik, Ted, illus. (p. 570)
—Fancy Nancy & the Wedding of the Century. Glasser, Robin Preiss, illus. (p. 570)
—Fancy Nancy - Apples Galore! Glasser, Robin Preiss, illus. (p. 570)
—Fancy Nancy at the Museum. Enik, Ted & Glasser, Robin Preiss, illus. (p. 570)
—Fancy Nancy - Budding Ballerina. Glasser, Robin Preiss, illus. (p. 570)
—Fancy Nancy: Candy Bonanza. Glasser, Robin Preiss, illus. (p. 570)
—Fancy Nancy Collector's Quintet. Glasser, Robin Preiss, illus. (p. 570)
—Fancy Nancy - Just My Luck! Glasser, Robin Preiss, illus. (p. 570)
—Fancy Nancy Loves! Loves!! Loves!!! Glasser, Robin Preiss & Bracken, Carolyn, illus. (p. 570)
—Fancy Nancy: Nancy Clancy Sees the Future Glasser, Robin Preiss, illus. (p. 570)
—Fancy Nancy - Nancy Clancy Sees the Future. Glasser, Robin Preiss, illus. (p. 570)
—Fancy Nancy: Nancy Clancy, Soccer Mania. Glasser, Robin Preiss, illus. (p. 570)
—Fancy Nancy - Nancy Clancy's Ultimate Chapter Book Quartet. Glasser, Robin Preiss, illus. (p. 570)
—Fancy Nancy - Peanut Butter & Jellyfish. Glasser, Robin Preiss, illus. (p. 570)
—Fancy Nancy Petite Library. Glasser, Robin Preiss, illus. (p. 570)
—Fancy Nancy Sees Stars. Glasser, Robin Preiss & Enik, Ted, illus. (p. 570)
—Fancy Nancy Storybook Treasury. Glasser, Robin Preiss, illus. (p. 570)
—Fancy Nancy - Super Secret Surprise Party. Glasser, Robin Preiss, illus. (p. 570)
—Fancy Nancy - There's No Day Like a Snow Day. (p. 570)
—Fancy Nancy's Absolutely Stupendous Sticker Book. Glasser, Robin Preiss, illus. (p. 570)
—Fancy Nancy's Elegant Easter. Bracken, Carolyn & Glasser, Robin Preiss, illus. (p. 570)
—Fancy Nancy's Fabulous Fall Storybook Collection. Glasser, Robin Preiss, illus. (p. 570)
—Fancy Nancy's Fabulously Fancy Treasury. Glasser, Robin Preiss, illus. (p. 570)
—Fancy Nancy's Fantastic Phonics Glasser, Robin Preiss, illus. (p. 570)
—Fancy Nancy's Fashion Parade! Reusable Sticker Book. Glasser, Robin Preiss & Bracken, Carolyn, illus. (p. 570)
—Fancy Nancy's Favorite Fancy Words: From Accessories to Zany. Glasser, Robin Preiss, illus. (p. 570)
—Fancy Nancy's Gloriously Gigantic Sticker-Tivity Book. Glasser, Robin Preiss & Levin, Kate, illus. (p. 570)
—Fancy Nancy's Marvelous Mother's Day Brunch. Glasser, Robin Preiss, illus. (p. 570)
—Fancy Nancy's Perfectly Pink Playtime Purse. Glasser, Robin Preiss, illus. (p. 570)
—Fancy Nancy's Perfectly Posh Paper Doll Book. Glasser, Robin Preiss & Bracken, Carolyn, illus. (p. 570)
—Fashionista. Glasser, Robin Preiss, illus. (p. 576)
—Flutter of Butterflies. Glasser, Robin Preiss & Bracken, Carolyn, illus. (p. 609)
—Girl on the Go: A Doodle & Draw Book. Glasser, Robin Preiss et al, illus. (p. 678)
—Hair Dos & Hair Don'ts. Glasser, Robin Preiss, illus. (p. 736)
—Halloween... or Bust! Glasser, Robin Preiss & Bracken, Carolyn, illus. (p. 738)
—Haunted Mansion: A Reusable Sticker Book for Halloween. Glasser, Robin Preiss, illus. (p. 753)
—Heart to Heart. Glasser, Robin Preiss & Bracken, Carolyn, illus. (p. 760)
—Hidden Army: Clay Soldiers of Ancient China. (p. 775)
—If the Walls Could Talk: Family Life at the White House. Hovland, Gary, illus. (p. 854)
—Just My Luck! Glasser, Robin Preiss, illus. (p. 939)
—Lulu & the Witch Baby. Sinclair, Bella, illus. (p. 1064)
—Lulu Goes to Witch School. Sinclair, Bella, illus. (p. 1065)
—Mary Cassatt: Family Pictures. Kalis, Jennifer, illus. (p. 1100)
—My Family History. Glasser, Robin Preiss et al, illus. (p. 1202)
—My Family History. (p. 1203)
—Nancy Clancy: My Secret Diary. Glasser, Robin Preiss, illus. (p. 1228)
—Nancy Clancy, Secret Admirer. (p. 1228)
—Nancy Clancy, Secret Admirer. Glasser, Robin Preiss, illus. (p. 1228)
—Nancy Clancy, Secret of the Silver Key. (p. 1228)
—Nancy Clancy - Secret of the Silver Key. Glasser, Robin Preiss, illus. (p. 1228)
—Nancy Clancy Sees the Future. (p. 1228)
—Nancy Clancy Sees the Future. Glasser, Robin Preiss, illus. (p. 1228)
—Nancy Clancy, Star of Stage & Screen. Glasser, Robin Preiss, illus. (p. 1228)
—Nancy Clancy, Super Sleuth Glasser, Robin Preiss, illus. (p. 1228)
—Nancy Clancy - Super Sleuth. Glasser, Robin Preiss, illus. (p. 1228)
—Nancy Clancy's Tres Charming Glasser, Robin Preiss, illus. (p. 1228)
—Nancy la Elegante. Valenzuela, Liliana, tr. from ENG. (p. 1229)
—Ooh La La! It's Beauty Day. Glasser, Robin Preiss, illus. (p. 1298)
—Pajama Day. Drainville, Beth et al, illus. (p. 1319)
—Peanut Butter & Jellyfish. (p. 1332)
—Peanut Butter & Jellyfish. Glasser, Robin Preiss, illus. (p. 1332)
—Poet Extraordinaire! Glasser, Robin Preiss, illus. (p. 1376)
—Puppy Party. (p. 1418)
—Puppy Party. Glasser, Robin Preiss, illus. (p. 1418)
—Puzzle-Palooza. Glasser, Robin Preiss, illus. (p. 1421)
—Sand Castles & Sand Palaces. (p. 1510)
—Sand Castles & Sand Palaces. Glasser, Robin Preiss, illus. (p. 1510)
—Secret Admirer Glasser, Robin Preiss, illus. (p. 1540)
—Secret of the Silver Key. Glasser, Robin Preiss, illus. (p. 1543)
—Show Must Go On. Enik, Ted & Glasser, Robin Preiss, illus. (p. 1570)
—Snow Globe Family. Schindler, S. D., illus. (p. 1599)
—Spectacular Spectacles. Glasser, Robin Preiss & Enik, Ted, illus. (p. 1624)
—Spectacular Spectacles, Level 1. Glasser, Robin Preiss & Enik, Ted, illus. (p. 1624)
—Splendid Speller. Glasser, Robin Preiss, illus. (p. 1630)
—Splendiferous Christmas. Glasser, Robin Preiss, illus. (p. 1630)
—Spring Fashion Fling. (p. 1635)
—Spring Fashion Fling. Glasser, Robin Preiss, illus. (p. 1635)
—Stellar Stargazer! Glasser, Robin Preiss, illus. (p. 1647)
—Super Secret Surprise Party. (p. 1681)
—Super Secret Surprise Party. Glasser, Robin Preiss, illus. (p. 1681)
—Super Sleuth. Glasser, Robin Preiss, illus. (p. 1681)
—Tea for Two. Glasser, Robin Preiss, illus. (p. 1708)
—Tea Parties. Glasser, Robin Preiss, illus. (p. 1708)
—There's No Day Like a Snow Day. Glasser, Robin Preiss, illus. (p. 1731)
—Too Many Tutus. Glasser, Robin Preiss, illus. (p. 1767)
—Yours till Niagara Falls, Abby. Apple, Margot, illus. (p. 1982)
O'Connor, Jane, jt. auth. see Abramson, Jill.
O'Connor, Jane & Harper Collins / LeapFrog. Fancy Nancy at the Museum. Glasser, Robin Preiss, illus. (p. 570)
O'Connor, Jeff, illus. see Mackall, Dandi Daley.
O'Connor, Jim. What Was Pompeii? (p. 1895)
—What Was Pompeii? Harper, Fred & Hinderliter, John, illus. (p. 1895)
—What Was the Battle of Gettysburg? (p. 1895)
—What Was the Battle of Gettysburg? Mantha, John & Bennett, James, illus. (p. 1895)
O'connor, Jim. Where Is the Grand Canyon? (p. 1909)
O'connor, Jim. Where Is the Grand Canyon? Groff, David & Colón, Daniel, illus. (p. 1909)
—Who Is Bob Dylan? (p. 1915)
—Who Is Bob Dylan? Harrison, Nancy & O'Brien, John, illus. (p. 1915)
O'Connor, John. Literacy in Context for AQA A. (p. 1022)
O'Connor, John, illus. see McPhail, David & McPhail.
O'Connor, John, illus. see McPhail, David.
O'Connor, Karen. Animals on the Verge of Extinction. (p. 83)
—Threat of Invasive Species. (p. 1741)
O'Connor, Marcy, illus. see Ceballos, Jacalyn Martin.
O'Connor, Martha. Bitch Posse. (p. 194)
O'Connor, Maureen. Equal Rights. (p. 533)
O'Connor, Melisa Bass. Master's Brick: A Story about Purpose. (p. 1103)
O'Connor, Miles. Tree That Moved. (p. 1783)
O'Connor, Mimi. City of Bones: The Official Illustrated Movie Companion. (p. 323)
—City of Bones. (p. 323)
—Reel Culture: 50 Classic Movies You Should Know about (So You Can Impress Your Friends) (p. 1456)
O'Connor, Niamh, illus. see Mortensen, Lori.
O'Connor, Niamh, illus. see Peschke, Marci & Townson, H.
O'Connor, Niamh, illus. see Peschke, Marci.
O'Connor, Peggy. Little Boy Who Was Born Purple (p. 1025)
O'Connor, Rachel. Construction Worker. (p. 360)
—Halloween / Halloween. (p. 737)
O'Connor, Rebecca & Myers, Dennis. Uniquely Nevada (p. 1818)
O'Connor, Rebecca K. Frogs & Toads. (p. 641)
O'Connor, Rebecca K., ed. Is There Life after Death? (p. 890)
O'Connor, Ruth, jt. auth. see Monk, Carol.
O'Connor, Sandra Day. Finding Susie. Pohrt, Tom, illus. (p. 588)
O'Connor, Shannon, illus. see Jackson, Ann.
O'Connor, Sheila. Keeping Safe the Stars. (p. 947)
—Sparrow Road. (p. 1622)
O'Connor, Tim, illus. see Cogar, Tubal U., et al.
O'Connor, Tim, illus. see Elkins, Stephen.
O'Connor, Tim, illus. see Holmes, Andy.
O'Connor, Tim, illus. see Meade, Starr.
O'Coyne, James. Gravelle's Land of Horror. Whispering Pine Press International, Inc. Staff, ed. (p. 712)
Oczkus, Lori. Close Reading with Paired Texts. (p. 333)
—Close Reading with Paired Texts, Level 5. (p. 334)
—Disappearing Rainforests. (p. 446)
—Turtles. (p. 1799)
Oda, Eiichiro. Buggy the Clown Oda, Eiichiro, illus. (p. 236)
—For Whom the Bell Tolls. Oda, Eiichiro, illus. (p. 616)
—Oath Oda, Eiichiro, illus. (p. 1275)
—One Piece (p. 1296)
—One Piece Oda, Eiichiro, illus. (p. 1296)
—One Piece. Oda, Eiichiro, illus. (p. 1296)
—One Piece: East Blue 10-11-12. Oda, Eiichiro, illus. (p. 1296)
—One Piece: East Blue 4-5-6. Oda, Eiichiro, illus. (p. 1296)
—One Piece - East Blue & Baroque Works. (p. 1296)
—Recipe for Disaster. (p. 1451)
Oda, Eiichiro, jt. auth. see Steele, Michael Anthony.
Oda, Eiichiro & Caselman, Lance. One Piece (p. 1296)
—One Piece Oda, Eiichiro, illus. (p. 1296)
—One Piece. (p. 1296)
Oda, Eiichiro & Kawasaki, Beth. One Piece. (p. 1296)
Oda, Kancho, illus. see McCarthy, Ralph F.
Oda, Matthew K. Time MacHine: Mario's Box A Journey into Creativity. (p. 1752)
Oda, Takashi, illus. see Grooms, Molly.
O'Daly, Anne, ed. Encyclopedia of Life Sciences (p. 525)
Odanaka, Barbara. Crazy Day at the Critter Café. White, Lee, illus. (p. 377)
—Smash! Mash! Crash! There Goes the Trash! Hillenbrand, Will, illus. (p. 1593)
O'Day, John. Reggie Bush: Superstar on Offense. (p. 1457)
O'Day, Joseph E. I Like Sunshine! Foster, Ron, illus. (p. 841)
Oddey, Alison. Performing Women: Stand-Ups, Strumpets & Itinerants. (p. 1343)
Oddo, Jennifer M. Asim the Awesome Possum: Asim Gets His Awesome. Lamb, T. S., illus. (p. 106)
Oddo, Joanne. Strawberry Moon. (p. 1666)
Ode, Eric. Boy & the Dragon Harris, Jim, illus. (p. 217)
—Busy Trucks on the Go. (p. 246)
—Busy Trucks on the Go. Culotta, Kent, illus. (p. 246)
—Dan, the Taxi Man. Culotta, Kent, illus. (p. 402)
—Sea Star Wishes: Poems from the Coast. Brooks, Erik, illus. (p. 1535)
—Tall Tales of the Wild West: A Humorous Collection of Cowboy Poems & Songs. Crane, Ben, illus. (p. 1704)
—When You're a Pirate Dog & Other Pirate Poems Harris, Jim, illus. (p. 1906)
Ode, Eric, jt. auth. see Skewes, John.
O'Dea, Colleen. Tajikistan. (p. 1696)
O'Dea, Kendra J. Polar Bear Pond. (p. 1379)
O'Dea, Michael, Rory and Cavanaugh & Benchmark Education Co. Staff. Wall. (p. 1854)
O'Dea, Rory & Benchmark Education Co. Staff. Books That Changed My Life. (p. 212)
—Opinions about Art - a Study of Paintings from the Romantic Era. (p. 1300)
O'Dea, Tierney, jt. auth. see Gendell, Megan.
Odegaard, Sarah. Don Hummer Visits Nana Jane. (p. 465)
Odell. Elementos del Lenguaje: Grade 6. (p. 510)
O'Dell. Elements of Language. (p. 510)
Odell, Carol. Once upon a Time in the Kitchen. Pignataro, Anna, illus. (p. 1293)
O'Dell, Kathleen. Agnes Parker... Girl in Progress. (p. 29)
—Agnes Parker... Happy Camper? (p. 30)
—Agnes Parker... Keeping Cool in Middle School. (p. 30)
—Aviary. (p. 119)
O'Dell, Kathryn. Bright Lights on Broadway. (p. 228)
—Life Online: the Digital Age Low Intermediate Book with Online Access. (p. 1012)
—Science of Darkness Low Intermediate Book with Online Access. (p. 1527)
—Science of Light Low Intermediate Book with Online Access. (p. 1527)
—Shark Attack Low Intermediate Book with Online Access. (p. 1562)
—Shoot to Kill: Why We Hunt. (p. 1568)
—Survival Guide: Lost in the Mountains Low Intermediate Book with Online Access. (p. 1686)
O'Dell, Nicole. Girl Talk: a Journal: ... for Life's Ups, Downs, & In-Betweens. (p. 679)
O'Dell, Patrick Timothy Wayne. Elvin. (p. 517)
O'Dell, Scott. 290. (p. 2001)
—Black Pearl. (p. 196)
—Black Star, Bright Dawn. (p. 197)
—Isla de los Delfines Azules. (p. 891)
—Island of the Blue Dolphins: And Related Readings. (p. 892)
—Island of the Blue Dolphins. (p. 892)
—Island of the Blue Dolphins. Lewin, Ted, illus. (p. 892)
—King's Fifth. (p. 960)
—My Name Is Not Angelica. (p. 1215)
—Road to Damietta. (p. 1477)
—Seven Serpents Trilogy. (p. 1554)
—Sing Down the Moon. (p. 1579)
—Sing down the Moon. (p. 1579)
—Streams to the River, River to the Sea. (p. 1666)
—Thunder Rolling in the Mountains. (p. 1746)
—Zia. (p. 1986)
O'Dell, Scott & Berg, Rea. Cruise of the Arctic Star: A Voyage from San Diego to the Columbia River. (p. 386)
Odems, Carlee. Thin Line. (p. 1732)
Oden, Annette. Born to Worship: A Contemporary Kids Musical for Every Season: Unison/2-Part Book. (p. 214)
Odendahl, Jodi. Praying Hands. (p. 1393)
Odenthal, Ingrid. Warm Heart. (p. 1858)
Odentz, Howard. Dead. (p. 416)
Odermatt, Brian, illus. see Mitchell, David.
Odezi, Jesse. Little Sunny & the Giants: The World's Greatest. (p. 1037)
Odgers, Darrel, jt. auth. see Odgers, Sally.
Odgers, Darrel & Odgers, Sally. Awful Pawful. (p. 121)
—Awful Pawful. Dawson, Janine, illus. (p. 121)
—Blue Stealer. Dawson, Janine, illus. (p. 203)
—Cranky Paws. Dawson, Janine, illus. (p. 376)
—Ham Heist. Dawson, Janine, illus. (p. 739)
—Inspector Jacques. Dawson, Janine, illus. (p. 878)
—Kitnapped Creature. (p. 962)
—Kitnapped Creature. Dawson, Janine, illus. (p. 962)
—Kitten's Tale. Dawson, Janine, illus. (p. 963)
—Lying Postman. (p. 1066)
—Mare's Tale. Dawson, Janine, illus. (p. 1092)
—Mugged Pug. Dawson, Janine, illus. (p. 1189)
—Python Problem. Dawson, Janine, illus. (p. 1422)
—Sausage Situation. (p. 1516)
—Sausage Situation. Dawson, Janine, illus. (p. 1516)
Odgers, Darrel & Sally. Pup's Tale: Pet Vet Book 6. Dawson, Janine, illus. (p. 1418)
Odgers, Sally. Felix & His Flying Machine. (p. 581)
—Glory Gate: Level Q (p. 685)
—Journey to the Center of the Earth. (p. 929)
—Untold Story of Ms. Mirabella. (p. 1823)
—Where Did the Dinosaurs Go? (p. 1906)
Odgers, Sally, ed. see Winter, Isobelle.
Odgers, Sally, jt. auth. see Odgers, Darrel.
Odgers, Sally & Odgers, Darrel. Buried Biscuits. Dawson, Janine, illus. (p. 243)
—Dog Den Mystery. Dawson, Janine, illus. (p. 461)
—Lying Postman. Dawson, Janine, illus. (p. 1066)
—Mugged Pug. Dawson, Janine, illus. (p. 1189)
—Phantom Mudder. Dawson, Janine, illus. (p. 1349)
Odhiambo, Tori. Close to Home: The African Savannah. (p. 334)
Odierno, Lisa. Bunny Hide-and-Seek. (p. 242)
—Kitten & Her Sister. (p. 962)
Odierno, Lisa, jt. auth. see Galvin, Laura Gates.
Odierno, Lisa & Soundprints Staff. Bunny Hide-and-Seek. (p. 242)
Odin, Jey. Chicken Fighter. (p. 300)
Odjick, Jay & Tenascon, Patrick. Kagagi: the Raven: The Raven. O'Reilly, Sean Patrick, ed. (p. 941)
Odle, Ingrid. Case of the Missing Abacus. (p. 274)
Odogbo, Fidelis C. Principles for Living: Inspiring & Motivating Stories for Overcoming Life's Storms. (p. 1406)
O'Doherty, Orla. That's Odi! (p. 1727)
Odom, Douglas. Freddy the Hummingbird. (p. 633)
Odom, Kelly, illus. see Parrish, Edith E.
Odom, Kelly, illus. see Parrish, Edith.
Odom, Mel. Conspiracy Revealed. (p. 359)
—His Legacy Avenged. (p. 781)
—Mystery Unravels. (p. 1226)
—Secret Explodes. (p. 1540)
—Unlock the Secrets of Oddworld: Official Strategy Guide. (p. 1821)

O

Odom, Rebecca. Grandpa & the Raccoon. Tebbit, Jake, illus. (p. 709)
Odom, Sara S. Absolutely Adorable! (p. 7)
—Lost in New York City. (p. 1055)
—My Lucky Irish Ear. (p. 1213)
—Precious Puddin' (p. 1394)
Odone, Jamison. Alice's Adventures in Wonderland. Odone, Jamison, illus. (p. 40)
—Honey Badgers. (p. 794)
—Mole Had Everything. (p. 1160)
Odone, Jamison, illus. see Cowley, Joy.
O'Donnel, Liam. Scout Hits the Trail. Huerta, Catherine, illus. (p. 1532)
O'Donnell, Barbara. Mrs Mumble, Bumble, Grumble. (p. 1187)
O'Donnell, Candy. Where Is God, Grandfather. Gillen, Rosemarie, illus. (p. 1908)
O'Donnell, E. E. Father Browne's Galway. Browne, Frank, photos by. (p. 577)
O'Donnell, Elizabeth. Maggie Does Not Want to Move. (p. 1071)
O'Donnell, Jane. Hey! There's a Donkey in the Boro. (p. 774)
O'Donnell, Jessica. Egyptian Cobra. (p. 506)
—Egyptian Cobra / Cobra Egipcia. (p. 506)
—Leontyne Price: First Lady of Opera. (p. 992)
O'Donnell, John. Doggy Poo (Picture Book) (p. 462)
O'Donnell, Judith A., et al. Pelvic Inflammatory Disease. Alcamo, I. Edward, ed. (p. 1336)
O'Donnell, K. So Many Seeds: Learning the S Sound. (p. 1602)
O'Donnell, Kathleen Marie. Suddenly a Light Shines: Poems Celebrating Nature, the Ties that Bind, & Moments of Inspiration. (p. 1672)
O'Donnell, Kayla. What Do Carpenters Do? Relate Addition & Subtraction to Length (p. 1882)
O'Donnell, Kerri. Ancient Civilizations of Greece & Rome: Solving Algebraic Equations. (p. 68)
—Ancient Civilizations of Greece & Rome: Solving Algebraic Equations Big Book. (p. 68)
—Ancient Civilizations of Greece & Rome: Solving Algebraic Equations (Big Book) (p. 68)
—Aves: Dinosaurios de nuestros días (Birds: Modern-Day Dinosaurs) (p. 119)
—Bats. (p. 144)
—Birds: Modern-Day Dinosaurs. (p. 191)
—California Gold Rush: Multiplying & Dividing Using Three- & Four-Digit Numbers. (p. 253)
—Careers in Modeling. (p. 268)
—Denali National Park: An Alaskan Ecosystem: Creating Graphical Representations of Data. (p. 426)
—Denali National Park, an Alaskan Ecosystem: Creating Graphical Representations of Data. (p. 426)
—Denali State Park - An Alaskan Ecosystem: Creating Graphical Representation of Data. (p. 426)
—Explorers in North America: Solving Addition & Subtraction Problems Using Timelines. (p. 551)
—Galileo: Man of Science. (p. 653)
—Ghosts & Poltergeists. (p. 672)
—Giraffe Can Laugh. (p. 677)
—Great Wall of China. (p. 719)
—How Chocolate Is Made: From Natural Resource to Finished Product. (p. 805)
—King of the Swamp. (p. 959)
—Komodo Dragons. (p. 966)
—Moons of Our Solar System. (p. 1173)
—Natural Wonders of the World: Converting Measurements to Metric Units. (p. 1236)
—Natural Wonders of the World: Converting Distance Measurements to Metric Units. (p. 1236)
—Natural Wonders of the World: Understanding & Representing Numbers in the Billions. (p. 1236)
—Primary Source Guide to Mexico. (p. 1399)
—Primary Source Guide to Pakistan. (p. 1399)
—Pyramids of Egypt. (p. 1421)
—Sir Isaac Newton: Using the Laws of Motion to Solve Problems. (p. 1580)
—Snakes of the World: Learning to Use Inches & Feet to Measure an Object. (p. 1597)
—Space Circles: Learning about Radius & Diameter. (p. 1618)
—Sue Helps Out. (p. 1672)
—Timeline of the California Gold Rush. (p. 1754)
—Trip Around the World: Using Expanded Notation to Represent Numbers. (p. 1787)
—Ugly Bugs. (p. 1808)
—Ugly Sea Creatures. (p. 1808)
—Vultures. (p. 1851)
—When Sue Is Sad. (p. 1904)
—Whose Hat Is That? (p. 1921)
O'Donnell, Kerri, jt. auth. see Gildenstein, Melanie.
O'Donnell, Kerri, jt. auth. see Humphrey, Jeff.
O'Donnell, Kevin & Gon, Zang Sung. Stone Age Santa. Kim, Boo Young et al, illus. (p. 1652)
O'Donnell, Laura, jt. auth. see O'Donnell, Liam.
O'Donnell, Liam. Baxter Needs a Home. Hynes, Robert, illus. (p. 147)
—Blackbeard's Sword: The Pirate King of the Carolinas. Spoor, Mike, illus. (p. 197)
—Daisy on the Farm. (p. 400)
—Daisy on the Farm. Hatala, Dan, illus. (p. 400)
—Daisy the Farm Pony. Hatala, Dan, illus. (p. 400)
—Duncan: A Brave Rescue. Hynes, Robert, illus. (p. 490)
—Food Fight Deas, Mike, illus. (p. 613)
—Ganked: Geeked Out Mysteries #1. (p. 655)
—Ginger Leads the Way. Diefendorf, Cathy, illus. (p. 677)
—Lucy & the Busy Boat. Hynes, Robert, illus. (p. 1063)
—Max Finder Mystery Cho, Michael & Owlkids Books Inc. Staff, illus. (p. 1111)
—Max Finder Mystery Collected Casebook Cho, Michael & Owlkids Books Inc. Staff, illus. (p. 1111)
—Max Finder Mystery Collected Casebook Vol. 3 Cho, Michael & Owlkids Books Inc. Staff, illus. (p. 1111)
—Media Meltdown: A Graphic Guide Adventure Deas, Mike, illus. (p. 1118)
—Pepper: A Snowy Search. Diefendorf, Cathy, illus. (p. 1340)
—Pepper, a Snowy Search. Diefendorf, Cathy, illus. (p. 1340)
—Pirate Gear: Cannons, Swords, & the Jolly Roger Knudson, Jason, illus. (p. 1362)
—Pirate Ships: Sailing the High Seas Alvarado, Tom, illus. (p. 1363)
—Pirate Treasure: Stolen Riches Alvarado, Tom, illus. (p. 1363)
—Power Play Deas, Mike, illus. (p. 1390)
—Ramp Rats: A Graphic Guide Adventure Deas, Mike, illus. (p. 1438)
—Scout Hits the Trail. Huerta, Catherine, illus. (p. 1532)
—Soccer Sabotage: A Graphic Guide Adventure Deas, Mike, illus. (p. 1603)
—System Shock Matysiak, Janek, illus. (p. 1693)
—Tank & Fizz: the Case of the Slime Stampede Deas, Mike, illus. (p. 1705)
—Tracker on the Job. Hynes, Robert, illus. (p. 1775)
—U. S. Immigration. Barnett, Charles, illus. (p. 1806)
—Understanding Photosynthesis with Max Axiom, Super Scientist Dominguez, Richard & Barnett, Charles, III, illus. (p. 1816)
—United Force. Rooth, Mike, illus. (p. 1818)
—Wild Ride: A Graphic Guide Adventure Deas, Mike, illus. (p. 1930)
—Winston in the City. (p. 1937)
—Winston in the City. Hatala, Dan, illus. (p. 1937)
O'Donnell, Liam, jt. auth. see Anderson, Bill.
O'Donnell, Liam & Anderson, Bill. World of Food Chains with Max Axiom, Super Scientist Martin, Cynthia, illus. (p. 1956)
O'Donnell, Liam & Barnett, Charles, III. Cómo Comprender la Fotosíntesis con Max Axiom, Supercientífico. Dominguez, Richard, illus. (p. 350)
O'Donnell, Liam & Barnett III, Charles. Shocking World of Electricity with Max Axiom, Super Scientist Dominguez, Richard, illus. (p. 1568)
—Shocking World of Electricity with Max Axiom, Super Scientist Barnett, Charles, III & Dominguez, Richard, illus. (p. 1568)
—Understanding Photosynthesis with Max Axiom, Super Scientist Dominguez, Richard et al, illus. (p. 1816)
O'Donnell, Liam & Battle, Craig. Max Finder Mystery Collected Casebook Pérez, Ramón & Owlkids Books Inc. Staff, illus. (p. 1111)
O'Donnell, Liam & Dorling Kindersley Publishing Staff. Amazing Animal Journeys, Level 3. (p. 53)
O'Donnell, Liam & O'Donnell, Laura. Duncan: A Brave Rescue. Hynes, Robert, illus. (p. 490)
O'Donnell, Linda. Just Like Him. (p. 939)
O'Donnell, Mabel & Monro, Rona. Janet & John: Off to Play. (p. 908)
O'Donnell, Peter. Puppet Master. Romero, Enric Badia, illus. (p. 1417)
O'Donnell, Sallie. Animals, Vegetables & Minerals from A to Z. Plumley, Alea, illus. (p. 84)
O'Donnell, Shannon. Lion's Son. (p. 1021)
O'donnell, Tamara J. Grand Mommy's Dress up Box. (p. 707)
O'Donnell, Tom. For the Love of Gelo! (p. 616)
O'Donoghue, Chris. Charlie's Reading Rescue: Improve an Older Child's Reading. (p. 293)
O'Donoghue, Michael. Rocks & Minerals of the World. (p. 1483)
O'Donoghue, Sean. Create a Quilt: Understand Concepts of Area. (p. 378)
—Disaster of the Irish Potato Famine: Irish Immigrants Arrive in America (1845-1850) (p. 446)
Odor, Ruth Shannon. Child's Book of Manners. (p. 304)
O'Dowd, Chris & Murphy, Nick V. Moone Boy: The Blunder Years. (p. 1172)
O'Dowd, Elizabeth, jt. auth. see Mahnke, M. Kathleen.
O'Dowd, Katy. Lady Astronomer. (p. 970)
Odriozola, Elena, illus. see Baranda, María.
Odriozola, Elena, illus. see Chandler, Susan.
Odriozola, Elena, illus. see MacRae, Tom.
Odriozola, Elena, illus. see Wolff, Ferida & Savitz, Harriet May.
O'Driscoll, Nina & Scott-Barrett, Fiona. BEC Vantage Masterclass. (p. 155)
Odu, Nkemakolam. My Horrible Trip to New York. (p. 1211)
Oduka, Dorris. Nyamgondo & the Lucky Charm: An African Folk Tale. (p. 1274)
Oduwole, Ben. Flying Tortoise. (p. 610)
O'Dwyer, Bridget. Celtic Night: A Fifteen-Year-Old Girl's Modern Retelling of Shakespeare's a Midsummer Night's Dream. (p. 286)
O'Dwyer, Edward. Rain on Cruise's Street. (p. 1435)
Oe, Patricia Daly. Blue Mouse, Yellow Mouse. Oe, Patricia Daly, illus. (p. 203)
—Where Are My Stripes? Oe, Patricia Daly, illus. (p. 1906)
Oechsli, Helen. Fly Away. (p. 609)
—In My Garden. (p. 864)
Oechsli, Kelly, illus. see Hillert, Margaret.
Oechsli, Kelly, illus. see Rose, Dorothy.
Oehler, David A. Cincinnati Zoo & Botanical Garden. (p. 319)
Oehlers, Adam. Babble of Words. (p. 123)
Oehlers, Adam, illus. see Atkinson, Joelie & Dinkles.
Oehlers, Adam, illus. see Badaoui, Chad.
Oehm, Kent, illus. see Hall, Francie.
Oehmichen, Ariel. Chosen Last. Du Pont, Brittany, illus. (p. 310)
Oehrle, Richard T., jt. ed. see Kruijff, Geert-Jan M.
Oelofsen, Vian, illus. see Hay, Sam.
Oelofsen, Vian, illus. see Stinson, Kathy.
Oelrich, Deborah, photos by. Amazing Creatures. (p. 54)
Oelrich, Ryan. Grand Adventures of Carson the Balloonatic! A Peculiar Hero Story for Children & Adults Who Are Brave Enough to Believe in the Unbelievable. (p. 707)
Oelschlager, Van. My Grampy Can't Walk. (p. 1210)
Oelschlager, Vanita. Ariel Bradley, Spy for General Washington. (p. 98)
—Birds of a Feather: A Book of Idioms & Silly Pictures. Hegan, Robin, illus. (p. 191)
—Birds of a Feather. Hegan, Robin, illus. (p. 191)
—Bonyo Bonyo. Blackwood, Kristin & Blanc, Mike, illus. (p. 209)
—Carrot. Blackwood, Kristin, illus. (p. 271)
—Elefante. Blackwood, Kristin, illus. (p. 510)
—Farfalla: A Story of Loss & Hope. Blackwood, Kristin, illus. (p. 573)
—Francesca. Blanc, Mike, illus. (p. 627)
—I Came from the Water: One Haitian Boy's Incredible Tale of Survival. Blanc, Mike, illus. (p. 834)
—Ivan's Great Fall: Poetry for Summer & Autumn from Great Poets & Writers of the Past. Blackwood, Kristin, illus. (p. 900)
—Ivy in Bloom: The Poetry of Spring from Great Poets & Writers from the Past. Blackwood, Kristin, illus. (p. 901)
—Knees: The Mixed up World of a Boy with Dyslexia. Rossi, Joe, illus. (p. 964)
—Let Me Bee. Blackwood, Kristin, illus. (p. 994)
—Life Is a Bowl Full of Cherries. (p. 1011)
—Made in China: A Story of Adoption. Blackwood, Kristin, illus. (p. 1070)
—Magic Words: From the Ancient Oral Tradition of the Inuit. Blanc, Mike, illus. (p. 1074)
—Mother Goose/Other Goose. Hegan, Robin, illus. (p. 1178)
—My Grampy Can't Walk. Hegan, Robin & Blackwood, Kristin, illus. (p. 1210)
—Out of the Blue: A book of color idioms & silly Pictures. Hegan, Robin, illus. (p. 1311)
—Porcupette Finds a Family. Blanc, Mike, illus. (p. 1386)
—Postcards from a War. Blanc, Mike & Bauknight, Wilfred, illus. (p. 1388)
—Tale of Two Daddies. Blackwood, Kristin, illus. (p. 1700)
—Tale of Two Mommies. Blanc, Mike, illus. (p. 1700)
—What Pet Will I Get? Blackwood, Kristin, illus. (p. 1892)
Oelschlager, Vanita & Blackwood, Kristin. Farfalla: A Story of Loss & Hope. (p. 573)
Oelschlager, Vanita & Blanc, Mike. I Came from the Water: One Haitian Boy's Incredible Tale of Survival. (p. 834)
Oelschlager, Vanita & Durrant, Lynda. Ariel Bradley, Spy for General Washington. Rossi, Joe, illus. (p. 98)
Oeltjenbruns, Joni. Where Is God. (p. 1908)
Oeltjenbruns, Joni, illus. see Bullard, Lisa.
Oeltjenbruns, Joni, illus. see Clairmont, Patsy.
Oeltjenbruns, Joni, illus. see Gold-Vukson, Marji E.
Oeltjenbruns, Joni, illus. see Kelley, Emily.
Oeming, Michael. Who Killed Retro Girl? (p. 1916)
Oeming, Michael Avon. Powers: Roleplay. (p. 1391)
—Powers: The Definitive Collection. (p. 1391)
—Takio 2. (p. 1698)
Oeming, Michael Avon, illus. see Bendis, Brian Michael.
Oeming, Michael Avon & Glass, Bryan J. L. Mice Templar (p. 1134)
—Mice Templar Volume 4. 1 HC. (p. 1134)
—Mice Templar Volume 4. 1: Legend Part 1 TP: Legend Part 1 TP. (p. 1134)
—Quixote Novel. (p. 1429)
Oeming, Michael, et al. Fear Itself: The Home Front. (p. 579)
Oeppen, Ceri. Hopes, Needs, Rights, & Laws: How Do Governments & Citizens Manage Migration & Settlement? (p. 797)
Oesch, Brian, illus. see Turner, Juliette.
Oeslchager, Vanita. Big Blue. Blackwood, Kristin, illus. (p. 178)
Oester, Dave. My Adventure in a Haunted House. (p. 1195)
Oestreicher, David M. Algonquian of New York. (p. 38)
—Algonquin of New York. (p. 38)
Oestreicher, Mark, jt. auth. see Rubin, Scott.
Oestreicher, Mark & Lindsey, Brooklyn. 99 Thoughts for Junior Highers: Biblical Truths in Bite-Size Pieces. (p. 1998)
Oestreicher, Mark, et al. My Faith (p. 1202)
—My Family (p. 1202)
Oetting, Judy. Germs. Herr, Tad, illus. (p. 667)
Ofanansky, Allison. Cheesecake for Shavuot. Alpern, Eliyahu, illus. (p. 296)
—Cheesecake for Shavuot. Alpern, Eliyahu, photos by. (p. 296)
—Harvest of Light. Alpern, Eliyahu, photos by. (p. 751)
—New Month, New Moon. Alpern, Eliyahu, photos by. (p. 1246)
—Patchwork Torah. Oriol, Elsa, illus. (p. 1328)
—Sukkot Treasure Hunt. Alpern, Eliyahu, illus. (p. 1673)
—What's the Buzz? Honey for a Sweet New Year. Alpern, Eliyahu, photos by. (p. 1899)
O'Farrell, Suma. Rangoli: An Indian Art Activity Book. (p. 1438)
Ofelia, Dumas Lachtman. Big Enough Bastante Grande. Enrique, Sanchez, illus. (p. 181)
Offen, Hilda. There Might Be Giants. (p. 1730)
Offen, Hilda, illus. see Proysen, Alf.
Offermann, Andrea, illus. see Appelbaum, Susannah.
Offermann, Andrea, illus. see Hartnett, Sonya.
Offermann, Andrea, illus. see Milford, Kate.
Offermann, Andrea, illus. see White, J. A.
Office, Go, jt. auth. see Hayashi, Hikaru.
Officer, Robyn, illus. see Setzer, Lee Ann.
Offill, Jenny. 11 Experiments That Failed. Carpenter, Nancy, illus. (p. 1994)
—17 Things I'm Not Allowed to Do Anymore. Carpenter, Nancy, illus. (p. 1995)
—Sparky! Appelhans, Chris, illus. (p. 1622)
—While You Were Napping. Blitt, Barry, illus. (p. 1911)
Offner, Naomi, illus. see Faith, Susan.
Offodile, Buchi. Orphan Girl & Other Stories: West African Folk Tales. (p. 1304)
Offord, Alexander. Causes of World War II. (p. 282)
—Communication Inventions: The Talk of the Town. (p. 349)
Offredi, James, illus. see Dickens, Charles.
Offutt, Jason. Helen Stephens: The Fulton Flash. Hare, John, illus. (p. 763)
Offutt, William. Winner. (p. 1937)
Oflesh, Nicole, jt. auth. see Watson, Philip.
O'Flahertie Wills Wilde, Oscar Fingal, jt. auth. see Wilde, Oscar.
Ofoche, Uzo. Monte & Me. (p. 1170)
Ofori-Mankata. Dede Akai. (p. 422)
Ofrane, Avi & Harte, Lawrence. Introduction to Wireless Billing: Usage Recording, Charge Processing, System Setup, & Real Time Billing. (p. 882)
O'Garden, Irene. Forest, What Would You Like? Schories, Pat, illus. (p. 618)
—Scrubbly-Bubbly Car Wash. Jabar, Cynthia, illus. (p. 1533)
Ogasawara, Tomofumi, illus. see Goto, Liu & Yatate, Hajime.
Ogata, Michael. New Friend for Nai'a. (p. 1244)
Ogawa, Evan, jt. auth. see Ogawa, Grace.
Ogawa, Grace. Angeldevil V: Tales, Tools, Pawns & Fools. Ogawa, Grace, illus. (p. 74)
Ogawa, Grace, illus. see Herman, R. A.
Ogawa, Grace & Ogawa, Evan. Iron Wizard II: Only Fear What You Do Not Know. (p. 888)
Ogawa, Yayoi. Tramps Like Us (p. 1778)
—Tramps Like Us. Ogawa, Yayoi, illus. (p. 1778)
Ogburn, Jacqueline. Little Treasures: Endearments from Around the World. Raschka, Chris, illus. (p. 1037)
Ogburn, Jacqueline K. Bake Shop Ghost. Priceman, Marjorie, illus. (p. 133)
—Dignity of Dragons. Ceccoli, Nicoletta, illus. (p. 440)
Ogden, Betina, illus. see Arruda, Suzanne M.
Ogden, Betina, illus. see Baillie, Allan.
Ogden, Betina, illus. see Herman, R. A.
Ogden, Betina, jt. auth. see Norman, Kim.
Ogden, Charles. Frost Bites. Carton, Rick, illus. (p. 644)
—High Wire. Carton, Rick, illus. (p. 778)
—Hot Air. Carton, Rick, illus. (p. 801)
—Nod's Limbs. Carton, Rick, illus. (p. 1262)
—Pet's Revenge. Carton, Rick, illus. (p. 1348)
—Rare Beasts. Carton, Rick, illus. (p. 1439)
—Tourist Trap. Carton, Rick, illus. (p. 1773)
—Under Town. Carton, Rick, illus. (p. 1814)
Ogden, Charles, ed. Edgar & Ellen Graphic Novelty: A Comics Collection. (p. 504)
Ogden, Denise T., jt. auth. see Ogden, James R.
Ogden, James R. & Ogden, Denise T. Retailing: Integrated Retail Management. (p. 1464)
Ogden, Lesley Evans. Canada's Flag. (p. 260)
Ogdon, Dennis. Conflict on Last Chance. (p. 357)
Ogene, Chuma C., illus. see Perkins, Nicole D.
Oghenekaro, Elsie Ovhe. Speaking Donkey & other Bible Stories. (p. 1623)
Oghojafor, Kingsley. Uganda. (p. 1808)
Ogilvie, Elizabeth. Masquerade at Sea House. (p. 1102)
—Pigeon Pair. (p. 1357)
Ogilvie, Heather, jt. auth. see Sewell, Amy.
Ogilvie, Isabel. Luchair Stones. (p. 1062)
Ogilvie, J. G., tr. see Verne, Jules.
Ogilvie, Marilyn Bailey. Marie Curie: A Biography (p. 1093)
Ogilvie, Sara, illus. see Bently, Peter.
Ogilvie, Sara, illus. see Kemp, Anna.
Ogilvie, Yolanda. Nana: A Portrait of Inspiration. (p. 1228)
Ogilvy, Ian. Measle & the Dragodon. (p. 1117)
—Measle & the Wrathmonk. (p. 1117)
Ogilvy, Shell. Alphabet Bird Collection. (p. 49)
Oginga, Effua. Little Red Apple. (p. 1034)
—Morgan Erika Pearl. (p. 1175)
Oginga, Odinga. Wake up Blackman & Women. (p. 1853)
Ogintz, Eileen. Kid's Guide to Chicago. (p. 953)
—Kid's Guide to Denver, Boulder & Colorado's Ski Country. (p. 953)
—Kid's Guide to San Diego. (p. 953)
—Kid's Guide to Washington, DC. (p. 954)
—Los Angeles County - Kid's Guide. (p. 1053)
Ogiwara, Noriko. Good Witch of the West, the (Novel) Volume 2. (p. 700)
—Mirror Sword & Shadow Prince. Ogiwara, Noriko, illus. (p. 1149)
Ogiwara, Noriko & Noriko, Ogiwara. Good Witch of the West Momokawa, Haruhiko, illus. (p. 700)
Ogle, Bonnie. Arthur the Arthropod. (p. 104)
Ogle, David B., jt. ed. see Little, Thomas Hamilton.
Ogle, Donna, jt. auth. see Blachowicz, Camille.
Ogle, Jennifer & Darcy, James. Alberta Seasonal Cookbook: History, Folklore & Recipes with a Twist. (p. 35)
Ogle, Jennifer & Kennedy, Gregory. Canadian Cookbook: Classics with a Twist. (p. 260)
Ogle, Jennifer, et al. British Columbia Seasonal Cookbook: History, Folklore & Recipes with a Twist. Samol, Nanette & Prosofsky, Merle, photos by. (p. 229)
—Ontario Seasonal Cookbook: History, Folklore & Recipes with a Twist. (p. 1298)
Ogle, Nancy, illus. see Mason, Adrienne.
Ogle, Nancy Gray, illus. see Hodge, Deborah.
Ogle, Nancy Gray, illus. see Mason, Adrienne.
Ogle, Steve. Chyouga Kids: Snow Treasure. (p. 318)
Ogle-Graham, Laura. No-No Nona & No-No Nit. (p. 1259)
Oglesby, Tamsin. Mouse & His Child. (p. 1181)
Ogo, Luis S., illus. see Sanchez, John Joseph P.
Ogorek, Keith. Eli the Stable Boy. (p. 512)
O'Gorman, Neil. Plants & Their Environments. (p. 1370)
O'Gorman, Sarah, ed. see Hill, Sarah.
O'Grady, Patricia. Naughty Ones. (p. 1237)
O'Grady, Standish Hayes. Pursuit of the Gilla Decair & His Horse. (p. 1419)
Oguneye, Kunle. Sikulu & Harambe by the Zambezi River: An African Vversion of the Good Samaritan Story. McCorkindale, Bruce & Youtsey, Scott, illus. (p. 1575)
Ogunkoya, Olukayode. Godly Children, Praying Children. (p. 690)
Ogunnaike, Anna M. Meet Our New Student from Nigeria. (p. 1122)
Ogunnaike, Oludamini. Meet Our New Student from Mali. (p. 1122)
Ogunsuyi, Melissa. Grumpy Caterpillar. (p. 727)
Ogwang, Evelynn. My Alphabet Safari. (p. 1196)
Oh, Charlotte, illus. see Gates Galvin, Laura.
Oh, Cirro. Greek & Roman Mythology. Chun, C. S., illus. (p. 720)
Oh, Daniella. 3 Trees. (p. 1991)
Oh, DaYun. We Are Brothers. Godeassi, Anna, illus. (p. 1865)
Oh, Ellen. Prophecy. (p. 1411)
—Warrior. (p. 1858)
Oh, H. Too. Super Duper Water Balloon Launcher Kit: Ready! Aim! Splash! (p. 1679)
Oh, Jina, reader. Step from Heaven. (p. 1648)
Oh, Jiwon. Mr. Monkey's Classroom. Oh, Jiwon, illus. (p. 1185)

Oh, Lee, illus. see Joo, Mi-hwa.
Oh, Mo, illus. see Robbins, Trina.
Oh Rhe Bar Ghun. Peigenz Park, Sung-Woo, illus. (p. 1335)
—Peigenz Oh Rhe Bar Ghun, illus. (p. 1335)
Oh, Seung-min, illus. see Jang, Ki-hwa & Kim, In-sook.
Oh, Soo & Yoon, Seok. Journey into the Human Body (p. 928)
Oh! Suzannah. Prayers for Children: Sunshine Meadows. Dunnahoe, Hugh, illus. (p. 1393)
O'Hagan, William. Anything Else but Me. (p. 91)
O'Hair, Margaret. My Kitten Lyon, Tammie, illus. (p. 1211)
—My Pup Lyon, Tammie, illus. (p. 1217)
—Sweet Baby Feet Dockray, Tracy, illus. (p. 1689)
—Twin to Twin. Courtin, Thierry, illus. (p. 1802)
O'Haire, Daniel, jt. auth. see Connor, Cathy.
Ohanesian, Diane. ABCs of Thanks & Please. Chamberlain, Margaret, illus. (p. 4)
—Rocks, Rocks, Rocks. (p. 1484)
Ohanesian, Diane, jt. auth. see Daronco, Mickey.
Ohanesian, Diane C. Seeds & Plants: Grades 2 & 3. (p. 1547)
Ohanian, Armineh. Talking Animals Part 2: Magic. Reeves, Louise, illus. (p. 1703)
O'Hanlon, Nancy, jt. auth. see Diaz, Karen R.
O'Hanlon, Toni. Cappy the Caterpillar. (p. 263)
—Cappy's Playground Adventure. Payne, Stephanie, illus. (p. 263)
—KiddiCards. Payne, Stephanie, illus. (p. 952)
—KiddiVersity KiddiCards Rhyming Edition - Modules Three & Four. Payne, Stephanie, illus. (p. 952)
—KiddiVersity KiddiCards Rhyming Edition Modules Five & Six. Payne, Stephanie, illus. (p. 952)
—KiddiVersity's KiddiCards Rhyming Edition Modules Eleven & Twelve. Payne, Stephanie, illus. (p. 952)
O'Hanlon-Lincoln, Ceane. County Chronicles Volume III: A Vivid Collection of Pennsylvania Histories (p. 372)
O'Hara, Cynthia, illus. see Neuhofer, Sheri L.
O'Hara, Diarmuid H. Pool. (p. 1383)
O'Hara, Ellen, jt. auth. see RH Disney Staff.
O'Hara, James. Managing Your Business to its Maximum Sales Potential. (p. 1086)
Ohara, Maricarmen. Amiguitos. (p. 65)
—Capullitos. (p. 265)
—Tesoro de Poesia Juvenil. (p. 1722)
O'Hara, Mary. My Friend Flicka Book. (p. 1209)
O'Hara, Megan. Plains Communities Past & Present (p. 1366)
O'Hara, Mo. Fins of Fury. Jagucki, Marek, illus. (p. 589)
—My Big Fat Zombie Goldfish. (p. 1197)
—My Big Fat Zombie Goldfish. Jagucki, Marek, illus. (p. 1197)
—Sea-Quel. Jagucki, Marek, illus. (p. 1535)
O'Hara, Nicholas. Sonidos / Sort It by Sound. de la Vega, Eida, tr. (p. 1612)
—Sort It by Sound. (p. 1614)
—Sort It by Texture. (p. 1614)
—Sort It by Weight. (p. 1614)
—Textura / Sort It by Texture. de la Vega, Eida, tr. (p. 1724)
O'Hara, Scarlett, jt. auth. see Dorling Kindersley Publishing Staff.
O'Hara, Shelley. ICan IPod. (p. 850)
—Improving Your Study Skills: Study Smart, Study Less. (p. 862)
O'Hara, Susan. Christie Plays Softball. Barrett, Rebecca, illus. (p. 312)
—Tim's First Soccer Game. Barrett, Rebecca, illus. (p. 1755)
O'Hara, Susan & McMahon, Maureen. NETS*S Curriculum Series: Multidisciplinary Units for Grades 6-8. (p. 1242)
O'Hare, Greg, et al. Weather, Climate & Climate Change: Human Perspectives. (p. 1870)
O'Hare, J. Dragonball Z: Book of Heroes (and Villains) (p. 478)
—Highlights Big Book of Fun: An Amazing Collection of Jokes, Riddles, Puzzles, & More! (p. 779)
O'Hare, J., ed. Big Book of Mazes. (p. 179)
O'Hare, Mark. Ciudadano Can. Falcó, Roberto, tr. from ENG. (p. 324)
O'Hare, Ted. Amazing Rain Forest. (p. 55)
—Amphibians. (p. 65)
—Animals of the Rain Forest. (p. 83)
—Birds. (p. 191)
Ohare, Ted. Boas. Rourke Publishing Staff, ed. (p. 205)
O'Hare, Ted. Boas. (p. 205)
Ohare, Ted. Cobras. Rourke Publishing Staff, ed. (p. 337)
O'Hare, Ted. Cobras. (p. 337)
—Copperheads. (p. 366)
—Coral Snakes. (p. 366)
—Fish. (p. 598)
—Invertebrates. (p. 884)
—Mambas. (p. 1084)
—Mammals. (p. 1085)
—Plants of the Rain Forest. (p. 1370)
—Pythons. (p. 1422)
Ohare, Ted. Rattlesnakes. Rourke Publishing Staff, ed. (p. 1440)
O'Hare, Ted. Vanishing Rain Forests. (p. 1833)
—Vertebrates. (p. 1837)
Ohashi, Kaoru. Sengoku Nights Kusunoki, Kei, illus. (p. 1550)
Ohashi, Kaoru, jt. auth. see Kusunoki, Kei.
Ohashi, Kaoru & Kusunoki, Kei. Diabolo (p. 433)
Ohba, Tsugumi. Death Note Obata, Takeshi, illus. (p. 420)
Ohba, Tsugumi & Takeshi, Obata. Death Note (p. 420)
O'Hearn, Audrey. Me & Luke (p. 1115)
O'Hearn, Kate. Flame of Olympus. (p. 602)
—New Olympians. (p. 1246)
—Olympus at War. (p. 1288)
—Shadow of the Dragon: Elspeth. (p. 1557)
O'Hearn, Michael. Allosaurus vs. Brachiosaurus: Might Against Height. Renne, Philip K., illus. (p. 47)
—Awesome Space Robots. (p. 121)
—Deinonychus vs. Styracosaurus: When Claws & Spikes Collide Renne, Philip K., illus. (p. 424)
—Dilophosaurus vs. Ankylosaurus: Weapons Against Armor Renne, Philip K., illus. (p. 440)
—el Dorado Map. (p. 507)
—Ghosts vs. Witches: Tussle of the Tricksters. Moffet, Patricia, illus. (p. 673)
—Henry Ford & the Model T Miller, Phil et al, illus. (p. 768)
—History Debate: A Rip-Roaring Game of Either-Or Questions. (p. 783)
—Jake Burton Carpenter & the Snowboard Barnett, Charles, III et al, illus. (p. 906)
—Kids' Guide to Monster Trucks (p. 953)
—Monster Wars. Moffet, Patricia et al, illus. (p. 1168)
—Sea Monsters vs. Dragons: Showdown of the Legends Altmann, Scott, illus. (p. 1535)
—Spinosaurus vs. Giganotosaurus: Battle of the Giants Renne, Philip K., illus. (p. 1628)
—Story of the Chicago White Sox. (p. 1660)
—Story of the New England Patriots. (p. 1661)
—Story of the St. Louis Cardinals. (p. 1662)
—This or That History Debate: A Rip-Roaring Game of Either/or Questions. (p. 1737)
—Triceratops vs. Stegosaurus: When Horns & Plates Collide. Renne, Philip K., illus. (p. 1786)
—Tyrannosaurus Rex vs. Velociraptor: Power Against Speed. Renne, Philip K., illus. (p. 1805)
—Vampires vs. Werewolves: Battle of the Bloodthirsty Beasts. Kendree, McLean, illus. (p. 1832)
—Zombies vs. Mummies: Clash of the Living Dead. Moffet, Patricia, illus. (p. 1988)
O'Hearn, Michael, et al. This or That? (p. 1737)
Ohebsion, Rodney. Collection of Wisdom. (p. 340)
O'Hegarty, Kate. Mieradome. (p. 1139)
O'hehir, Trisha. Toothpaste Secret. O'hehir, Trisha, illus. (p. 1768)
O'Hely, Eileen. P. E. P. Squad. (p. 1316)
—Penny in Space. Phelan, Nicky, illus. (p. 1338)
—Penny on Safari. Phelan, Nicky, illus. (p. 1338)
—Penny the Pencil. Phelan, Nicky, illus. (p. 1338)
O'Hern, Kerri, jt. auth. see Anderson, Dale.
O'Hern, Kerri, jt. auth. see Holland, Gini.
O'Hern, Kerri, jt. auth. see Mayo, Gretchen Will.
O'Hern, Kerri, jt. auth. see Raatma, Lucia.
O'Hern, Kerri, jt. auth. see Riehecky, Janet.
O'Hern, Kerri, jt. auth. see Walsh, Frank.
O'Hern, Kerri & Anderson, Dale. Battle of Gettysburg. (p. 146)
O'Hern, Kerri & Holland, Gini. Louis Armstrong. Spay, Anthony & Campbell, Alex, illus. (p. 1058)
O'Hern, Kerri & Raatma, Lucia. Jackie Robinson. (p. 903)
O'Hern, Kerri & Riehecky, Janet. Battle of the Alamo. (p. 146)
O'Hern, Kerri & Walsh, Frank. Montgomery Bus Boycott. (p. 1170)
O'Hern, Kerri & Will Mayo, Gretchen. Hermanos Wright. (p. 771)
O'Hern, Kerri, et al. Batalla de el Álamo. (p. 143)
—Batalla de Gettysburg. (p. 143)
—Boicot a los Autobuses de Montgomery. (p. 207)
O'Herron, Mary. Letter from Marty: Grandma & Grandpa's Cat. O'Herron, Mary, illus. (p. 1002)
Ohi, Debbie Ridpath. Where Are My Books? Ohi, Debbie Ridpath, illus. (p. 1906)
Ohi, Debbie Ridpath, illus. see Black, Michael Ian.
Ohi, Debbie Ridpath, illus. see Blume, Judy.
Ohi, Debbie Ridpath, illus. see McLaughlin, Lauren.
Ohi, Debbie Ridpath, illus. see Sanders, Rob.
Ohi, Ruth. Chicken, Pig, Cow. Ohi, Ruth, illus. (p. 300)
—Chicken, Pig, Cow, & the Purple Problem. Ohi, Ruth, illus. (p. 300)
—Chicken, Pig, Cow Horse Around. (p. 300)
—Chicken, Pig, Cow Horse Around. Ohi, Ruth, illus. (p. 300)
—Chicken, Pig, Cow on the Move. Ohi, Ruth, illus. (p. 300)
—Clara & the Bossy. Ohi, Ruth, illus. (p. 326)
—Couch Was a Castle. Ohi, Ruth, illus. (p. 369)
—Fox & Squirrel. Ohi, Ruth, illus. (p. 626)
—Me & My Brother. Ohi, Ruth, illus. (p. 1115)
—Me & My Sister. Ohi, Ruth, illus. (p. 1115)
—Trip with Grandma. Ohi, Ruth, illus. (p. 1787)
Ohi, Ruth, illus. see Hutchins, Hazel J. & Hutchins, Hazel.
Ohi, Ruth, illus. see Jennings, Sharon.
Ohi, Ruth, illus. see Kogawa, Joy.
Ohi, Ruth, illus. see Page, P. K. & Ellis, Sarah.
Ohio Historical Society Staff. Ohio, A Sentimental Journey Study Guide (p. 1281)
Ohizep, Zoiea. Rainbow's Ring. (p. 1436)
Ohkami, Mineko. Dragon Knights (p. 477)
—Dragon Knights Ohkami, Mineko, illus. (p. 477)
—Dragon Knights Johnson, Yuki, tr. from JPN. (p. 477)
—Dragon Knights Nakamura, Yuki, tr. from JPN. (p. 477)
—Dragon Knights Yoshida, Agnes, tr. from JPN. (p. 477)
—Dragon Knights: Volume 12 Ohkami, Mineko, illus. (p. 477)
—Dragon Knights: Volume 14 Ohkami, Mineko, illus. (p. 477)
—Dragon Knights: Volume 16 Ohkami, Mineko, illus. (p. 477)
—Dragon Knights: Volume 18 Ohkami, Mineko, illus. (p. 477)
—Dragon Knights. Ohkami, Mineko, illus. (p. 477)
Ohkubo, Atsushi. Soul Eater. (p. 1614)
—Soul Eater. (p. 1614)
Ohlenroth, Patricia. Up from the Ashes: Rebuilding Japan after World War II. (p. 1824)
Ohlenroth, Patricia, jt. auth. see Sohn, Emily.
Ohlig, Rudolf & Hogen, Hildegard. Kunst und Kultur (p. 968)
Ohlin, Nancy. Always, Forever. (p. 51)
—Beauty. (p. 154)
—Thorn Abbey. (p. 1740)
Ohmura, Tomoko. Long, Long Line. (p. 1047)
Ohnogi, Hiroshi. Rahxephon (p. 1433)
Ohnogi, Hiroshi, jt. auth. see Izubuchi, Yutaka.
OHora, Zachariah. My Cousin Momo. (p. 1200)
—No Fits, Nilson! OHora, Zachariah, illus. (p. 1258)
—Stop Snoring, Bernard! OHora, Zachariah, illus. (p. 1653)
OHora, Zachariah, illus. see Bardhan-Quallen, Sudipta.
OHora, Zachariah, illus. see Dyckman, Ame.
OHora, Zachariah, illus. see Wheeler, Lisa.
Ohrt, Kate. Dancing Dreams. Valiant, Kristi, illus. (p. 402)
—Rainbow Book. (p. 1435)
Ohrt, Kate, jt. auth. see Accord Publishing Staff.
Ohta, Akiyoshi. Kaze No Hana Ishikawa, Elina, tr. from JPN. (p. 946)
Ohtaka, Shinobu. Strongest Bride on Earth (p. 1668)
Ohtsuka, Tommy. 15-Love. (p. 1995)
Ohtsuka, Tommy, illus. see Komada, Yoshihiro, et al.
O'Hurley, John. It's Okay to Miss the Bed on the First Jump: And Other Life Lessons I Learned from Dogs. (p. 898)
—Perfect Dog. (p. 1341)
OI Foundation, ed. see Busic, Valerie.
Oickle, Vernon. Disasters of Atlantic Canada: Stories of Courage & Chaos. (p. 447)
Oien, Jennifer, illus. see Grandma Poo Poo.
Oiler, Terry W. Lucky Gets Adopted. (p. 1062)
Oirechman, Chana, jt. auth. see Verzov, Ella.
Oirich, Alan. Amnesia Countdown. Randall, Ron, illus. (p. 65)
Oja, L. G. Little Miss Izzy's Adventures - Miss Izzy & the Monsters. (p. 1031)
Ojakorotu, Victor, ed. see Baughan, Brian.
Ojakorotu, Victor, ed. see Friedenthal, Lora & Kavanaugh, Dorothy.
Ojakorotu, Victor, ed. see Gelletly, LeeAnne.
Ojakorotu, Victor, ed. see Habeeb, William Mark.
Ojakorotu, Victor, ed. see Lewis, Susan Grant.
Ojakorotu, Victor, ed. see Marcovitz, Hal.
Ojakorotu, Victor, ed. see Obadina, Elizabeth.
Ojakorotu, Victor, ed. see Obadina, Tunde.
Ojakorotu, Victor, ed. see Rotberg, Robert I.
Ojakorotu, Victor, ed. see Shah, Anup.
Ojala, Sara. Little Sparrow: A Story of God's Provision. (p. 1036)
Ojeda, Auriana. Turbulent 60s - 1969. (p. 1797)
Ojha, Siva Gopal. Twilight Days. (p. 1801)
Ok, SeoJeong, illus. see Kim, JeongHo.
Oka, Joseph J. Rosary Reflections for Kids. (p. 1489)
Okada, Toshihiko. Balloon. (p. 135)
Okami, Mineko. Dragon Knights (p. 477)
Okamoto, Alan, illus. see Bennett, Jeffrey.
Okamoto, Alan, illus. see Okamoto, Rod.
Okamoto, Rod. Kingdom of Nu - TJ's Tale: TJ's Tale. Okamoto, Alan, illus. (p. 960)
Okamura, Tensai, jt. auth. see Bones Brigade Staff.
O'Kane, George & McEntee, Bill. Hook Em's Colorful Campus Tour - University of Texas A-Z: Forty Acres (A-Z) (p. 795)
O'Kane, George & Weikert, Dana. Baldwin's Colorful Campus Tour - Boston College A-Z. (p. 134)
Okaty, Nicole. Custard & Pupcake's Book: A Pet Pals Adventure. (p. 395)
—Orange Blossom's Fruity Fun Book: A Juicy Orange Adventure. (p. 1301)
Okawa, Junko & Uonca Staff. Carefree Clothes for Girls: 20 Patterns for Outdoor Frocks, Playdate Dresses, & More. (p. 268)
Oke, Janette. Bluebird & the Sparrow. (p. 204)
—Drums of Change: The Story of Running Fawn. (p. 487)
—I Wonder... Did Jesus Have a Pet Lamb? Gauthier, Corbert, illus. (p. 849)
Oke, Rachel, illus. see Guess, Catherine Ritch.
O'Keefe, Allan, jt. auth. see Hemmings, Lisa.
O'Keefe, Cynthia A. Exploring the Real World: Secondary Edition. (p. 554)
—Exploring the Real World: Middle School Edition. (p. 554)
—Exploring the Real World: Primary School Edition. (p. 554)
O'Keefe, Deborah. Readers in Wonderland: The Liberating Worlds of Fantasy Fiction. (p. 1444)
O'Keefe, Emily. Crop Circles. (p. 385)
—UFOs. (p. 1807)
O'Keefe, Karin, ed. see Zaikine, Zak.
O'Keefe, Kathy Della Torre. Child's Guide to the Beatitudes. (p. 305)
—Child's Guide to the Holy Days. (p. 305)
O'Keefe, Lauren. Raindrop Flies a Kite. (p. 1436)
O'Keefe, Laurie, illus. see Jennings, Terry Catasús.
OKeefe, Raven, illus. see Lofficier, Randy.
O'Keefe, Ruth A. Starter One Hundred One AEVAC, Inc. Staff, ed. (p. 1643)
O'Keefe, Sean, ed. STS 107 Memories: Forever in Our Hearts. (p. 1668)
O'Keefe, Sherry. Champion of Freedom: Aung San Suu Kyi. (p. 289)
—From China to America: The Story of Amy Tan. (p. 642)
—Spin: The Story of Michael Jackson. (p. 1627)
O'Keefe, Susan Heyboer. Baby Day. Spowart, Robin, illus. (p. 125)
—Be the Star That You Are: A Book for Kids Who Feel Different. Alley, R. W., illus. (p. 149)
—Christmas Gifts. Emery, Jennifer, illus. (p. 314)
—Esperpento Hambriento: Un Libro Rimado Para Contar. (p. 536)
—My Life & Death by Alexandra Canarsie (p. 1211)
O'Keefe, Vivien. Short & Sweet. (p. 1569)
O'Keefe-Moore, Jeanmarie. Very Special Zoo. (p. 1838)
O'Keeffe, Frank. Harry Flammable: A Novel (Large Print 16pt) (p. 750)
—Harry Flammable. (p. 750)
O'Keeffe, Neil, illus. see Moody, Ralph.
O'Keeffe, Stuart. Quick Six Fix: 100 No-Fuss, Full Flavor Recipes - 6 Ingredients, 6 Minutes Prep, 6 Minutes Clean-Up. (p. 1427)
Okeke, Paulicap Okechukwu. Biribamba the Lonely Elephant. (p. 192)
Okeke-Ibezim, Felicia. African Folk Tales: Obiageli & Other Stories. (p. 27)
O'Kelley, Jeff. Mapping the Way. (p. 1090)
—Sam Finds the Way. (p. 1506)
—Sharing Our Stories. (p. 1561)
—Visit to the United Nations. (p. 1845)
O'Kelly, James. Mambi-land, or Adventures of a Herald Correspondent in Cuba (p. 1084)
Okereke, Laurence. Barry & Big Joe. (p. 140)
—Barry & the Gombeys. (p. 140)
—Barry Plays with Fire. (p. 140)
Oketani, Shogo. J-Boys: Kazuo's World, Tokyo 1965. Udagawa, Avery Fischer, tr. from JPN. (p. 901)
Oketani, Shogo, jt. auth. see Lowitz, Leza.
Oketch, Alphonce Omondi, illus. see Carlson, Martin D.
Oki, Blessed Edewor & Olaolu, Akinola Mishael. Tribute to the Child. Oki, Blessed Edewor, ed. (p. 1785)
Okibedi, Agnes Ada-Nwaneri. Happy Times with Grandm. (p. 747)
Okido. Head to Toe: My Body & How It Works. (p. 756)
Okido Staff. Color Me In! An Activity Book. (p. 343)
—How Things Work: Facts & Fun, Questions & Answers, Things to Make & Do. (p. 814)
—My Animal Book: Facts & Fun, Questions & Answers, Things to Make & Do. (p. 1196)
—My Big World: Facts & Fun Questions & Answers Things to Make & Do. (p. 1197)
—What's Inside? See-Through Pages & Magic Surprises! (p. 1898)
Okido Staff, creator. Let's Play a Game: All You Need to Play Six Board Games. (p. 1000)
O'Kif. No Somos Irrompibles (12 Cuentos de Chicos Enamorados) (p. 1260)
O'Kif, illus. see Adeney, Anne.
O'Kif, illus. see Benjamin, A. H.
O'Kif, illus. see Foxley, Janet.
O'Kif, illus. see Pescetti, Luis Mariá.
Okimoto, Jean Davies. Dear Ichiro. Keith, Doug, illus. (p. 419)
Okin, J. R. Information Revolution: The Not-for-Dummies Guide to the History, Technology, & Use of the World Wide Web (p. 874)
—Internet Revolution: The Not-for-Dummies Guide to the History, Technology, & Use of the Internet (p. 880)
—Technology Revolution: The Not-for-Dummies Guide to the Impact, Perils, & Promise of the Internet (p. 1712)
Oklahoma Energy Resoures Board, creator. Road to Petroville: Petro Pete's Adventure. (p. 1477)
Okon, Jodi, jt. auth. see Mills, Nathan.
Okonji, Azuka, illus. see Chukwumerije, Dikeogu.
Okonkwo, Chidi, creator. Destiny, Neo Genesis (p. 431)
Okorafor, Nnedi. Akata Witch. (p. 32)
Okorafor-Mbachu, Nnedi. Zahrah the Windseeker. (p. 1984)
Okoronkwo, Stella. Communication with Children & Youth: A Guide for Parents, Social & Youth Workers, (p. 349)
Okrant, Mark. Judson's Island. (p. 931)
Oksanen, Sue & Zeisler, Riley. Isn't It Great? DeRungs, Tina, illus. (p. 893)
Oksner, Judith, illus. see Montgomery, Sy.
Okstad, Ella, illus. see Rees, Gwyneth.
Okstad, Ella K., illus. see Metzger, Steve.
Oku, Makiko, tr. see Lazoo Publishing Staff & ZOO, La.
Oku, Makiko, tr. see Lazoo Publishing Staff.
Okubo, Margaret. Story of Angelo. (p. 1657)
Okugas, Juanaiga. tales of Mew the Cat. (p. 1702)
Okum, David. Manga Madness. (p. 1087)
—Manga Monster Madness. (p. 1087)
Okum, David, illus. see Boyd, David.
Okum, David, illus. see Downey, Glen.
Okun, Milton, ed. All My Life - Karla Bonoff (Piano - Vocal) (p. 45)
—Christmas Carols for Piano Duet. (p. 313)
—Cliff Eberhardt Songbook. (p. 332)
—From a Distance & Twenty-Four Other Easy Listening Favorites for Easy Piano. (p. 641)
—From the Heart - 30 Love Songs. (p. 644)
—Great Rock Ballads. (p. 718)
—Just for Kids. (p. 938)
—Leslie Bricusse Theatre Book. (p. 993)
—Shawn Colvin - Cover Girl. (p. 1563)
Okwelume, O. Charles, ed. Drumbeats of Black Africa. (p. 487)
Okwu, Bernadette. Unbeatable Brothers: The Adventures of Three Brothers. (p. 1811)
Olabi, Adriana. Fine Motor Activities. (p. 589)
Oladimeji, Solomon, illus. see Edwards-Tomdio, Stacy.
Oladokun, Alexander. Acrux Manor: The Prodigal's Curse (Hardcover) (p. 9)
Olafsdottir, Linda, illus. see Namm, Diane & Andersen, Hans Christian.
Olafsdottir, Linda, illus. see Olmstead, Kathleen.
Olafsdottir, Linda, jt. auth. see Olmstead, Kathleen.
Olaizola, José Luis. Cazador Urbano. (p. 283)
—Mi Hermana Gabriela. Alonso Díaz-Toledo, Juan Ramón, illus. (p. 1132)
—Secreto de Gabriela. Alonso, Juan Ramón, tr. (p. 1544)
Olan, Agnieszka, illus. see Lenington, Paula.
Olan, Menetta. Huggin' Jesus. (p. 825)
Olander, Johan. Field Guide to Aliens: Intergalactic Worrywarts, Bubblonauts, Silver-Slurpers, & Other Extraterrestrials (p. 583)
—Field Guide to Monsters: Googly-Eyed Wart Floppers, Shadow-Casters, Toe-Eaters, & Other Creatures (p. 583)
—My Robots: The Robotic Genius of Lady Regina Bonquers III (p. 1217)
Olaogbebikan, Michael Olumide. Playmate. (p. 1373)
Olaolu, Akinola Mishael, jt. auth. see Oki, Blessed Edewor.
Olasky, Susan. Annie Henry: Adventures in the American Revolution. (p. 86)
—Annie Henry & the Birth of Liberty. (p. 86)
—Annie Henry & the Mysterious Stranger. (p. 87)
—Annie Henry & the Redcoats. (p. 87)
—Annie Henry & the Secret Mission. (p. 87)
O'Laughlin, Ann. Amazing Bi-Ski Rescue. Foster-Fell, Jeremy, ed. (p. 54)
O'Laughlin, Michael C. By Mac & 'O' You'll Always Know, Mac, Mc, & 'O' Names in Ireland, Scotland & America: With Census Records from the 17th to 20th Century. (p. 249)
O'Laughlin, Michael C., intro. Birth Index of Ireland: Showing the locations of Surnames in Ireland. (p. 192)
Olazagasti-Segovia, Elena, tr. see Cofer, Judith Ortiz.
Olberg, Henry. Magical Tooth Fairies: A Surprise in Mexico. (p. 1075)
—Magical Tooth Fairies: The Secret of the Magic Dust. (p. 1075)
Olbrys, Brooks. Adventures of Blue Ocean Bob: Blue Ocean Bob Discovers His Purpose. Hamilton, Emma Walton, ed. (p. 16)
Olcott, Frances Jenkins. Good Stories for Great Holidays. (p. 700)
—Good Stories for Holidays. (p. 700)
Old Farmer's Almanac Staff. Old Farmer's Almanac for Kids (p. 1283)

O

Old Farmer's Almanac Staff, ed. Old Farmer's Almanac for Kids (p. 1283)
Old, Kenneth G., jt. auth. see Old, Patty West.
Old, Kenneth G., jt. auth. see West, Patty Old.
Old, Kenneth G. & West, Patty Old. Circus in Sellindge: The Twith Logue Chronicles: Adventures with the Little People, Volume Nine. (p. 322)
—Magician's Twitch: The Twith Logue Chronicles: Adventures with the Little People, Volume Ten. (p. 1075)
—Secret Quest. (p. 1543)
—Snugglewump Roars: The Twith Logue Chronicles: Adventures with the Little People. (p. 1601)
Old, Kennth G. & West, Patty Old. Beyonders in Gyminge: The Twith Logue Chronicles: Adventures with the Little People. (p. 174)
Old, Patty West & Old, Kenneth G. Wizard of Wozzle: Second Edition. (p. 1943)
Old, Richard. 1,000 Weeds of North America: An Identification Guide. (p. 2001)
Old, Wendie C. Life of Duke Ellington: Giant of Jazz. (p. 1012)
—Life of Louis Armstrong: King of Jazz. (p. 1012)
—Wright Brothers: Aviation Pioneers & Inventors. (p. 1963)
Old West, Patty. Wizard Strikes Twice: The Twith Logue Chronicles: Adventures with the Little People. (p. 1943)
Oldaker, Vivian. Killer's Daughter. (p. 956)
Oldaugh, Charles. Frog Knight. (p. 640)
Oldcorne, Michelle. Landy Saves the Day. (p. 974)
Oldenburg, Richard. How the Quail Earned His Topknot. (p. 813)
—Three Little Green Pigs, Llc: A Recycling Pig Tale. Samantha May Cerney, illus. (p. 1742)
—Three Little Green Pigs, Llc: A Recycling Pig Tale. Cerney, Samantha May, illus. (p. 1742)
Oldendorf, Sandra Brenneman, jt. auth. see Green, Connie R.
Older, Daniel José. Shadowshaper. (p. 1558)
Older, Jules. Pig. Severance, Lyn, illus. (p. 1357)
—Snowmobile: Bombardier's Dream Machine. Lauritano, Michael, illus. (p. 1601)
Older, Jules, et al. Pig. Severance, Lyn, illus. (p. 1357)
Oldfather, William Abbott, tr. see Pufendorf, Samuel.
Oldfield, Dawn Bluemel. Abyssinians: Egyptian Royalty? (p. 7)
—English Mastiff: The World's Heaviest Dog. (p. 530)
—Killer Whale: Water Bullet! (p. 956)
—Leaping Ground Frogs. (p. 982)
—Newfoundland: Water Rescuer. (p. 1249)
—Venus: Super Hot. (p. 1836)
—Venus: Supercaliente. (p. 1836)
—Water Frog Polliwogs. (p. 1862)
Oldfield, Jenny. Crash. (p. 376)
—Crazy Horse. (p. 377)
—Danny Boy. (p. 405)
—Don't Make Me Laugh, Liam. Layton, Neal, illus. (p. 468)
—Drop Dead, Danielle. Layton, Neal, illus. (p. 485)
—Get Lost, Lola. Layton, Neal, illus. (p. 667)
—Golden Dawn. (p. 694)
—Gunsmoke. (p. 732)
—Half Moon Ranch: Johnny Mohawk. (p. 736)
—Hollywood Princess. (p. 789)
—Home Farm Twins Christmas Mystery. (p. 792)
—Horses of Half-Moon Ranch: Jethro Junior. (p. 800)
—I'd Like a Little Word, Leonie! Child, Lauren, illus. (p. 851)
—Johnny Mohawk. (p. 923)
—Lady Roseanne. (p. 971)
—Midnight Lady. (p. 1139)
—Not Now, Nathan! Child, Lauren, illus. (p. 1267)
—Rodeo Rocky. (p. 1484)
—Skin & Bone (p. 1585)
—Skye - The Champion (p. 1587)
—Sophie Show Off (p. 1613)
—Sorrel Substitute (p. 1614)
—Speckled & Sinbad (p. 1624)
—Stanley the Troublemaker. (p. 1640)
—Stevie the Rebel. (p. 1649)
—Sugar & Spice (p. 1672)
—Sultan Patient (p. 1673)
—Sunny the Hero. (p. 1677)
—Third-Time Lucky. (p. 1734)
—What's the Matter, Maya? Child, Lauren, illus. (p. 1899)
—When Scott Got Lost No. 2. (p. 1904)
—Wild Horses. (p. 1929)
Oldfield, Jenny, jt. auth. see Pennington, Kate.
Oldfield, Rachel. Up up Up. Reed, Susan, illus. (p. 1824)
Oldfield, Rachel, illus. see Reed, Susan.
Oldfield, Rachel, illus. see Williams, Brenda.
Oldham, Cindi, illus. see Williams, Annie Morris.
Oldham, John. Sashi Goes to the Doctor. (p. 1515)
Oldham, June. In the Blood. (p. 865)
Oldham, Lacy. Dog Named Timmy (p. 461)
Oldham, Marion, illus. see Molesworth, Mary Louisa.
Oldham, Todd. All about Collage. (p. 42)
—All about Dye. (p. 42)
—Kid Made Modern. (p. 951)
Olding, Lori. Origami Nun. (p. 1304)
Oldland, Nicholas. Big Bear Hug. (p. 178)
—Big Bear Hug. Oldland, Nicholas, illus. (p. 178)
—Busy Beaver. Oldland, Nicholas, illus. (p. 245)
—Dinosaur Countdown. Oldland, Nicholas, illus. (p. 441)
—Making the Moose Out of Life. Oldland, Nicholas, illus. (p. 1082)
Oldman, James. Superhighway. Ingram, Chris, illus. (p. 1683)
Oldroyd, Brittany. Segolia: Daughter of Prophecy. (p. 1548)
Oldroyd, Mark, illus. see Jarman, Julia.
Oldroyd, Mark, illus. see Jones, Carrie.
Oldroyd, Mark, illus. see Knudsen, Shannon.
Oldroyd, Mark, illus. see Krensky, Stephen.
Olds, Barbara Anne. Haven House. Amatrula, Michele, illus. (p. 754)
Olds, Helen Diehl. Fisherman Jody. Gotlieb, Jules, illus. (p. 599)
Olds, Irene, illus. see Denis, Toni.
Olds, Laurie. Cars on Vacation. (p. 272)
Olearczyk, Erin A. Bats, Bats, Bats. (p. 145)
O'Leary Brown, Erin, illus. see Curry, Don L.
O'Leary Brown, Erin, illus. see Hoffmann, Catherine E. & Hoffmann, Dana Marie.
O'Leary Brown, Erin, illus. see Hoffmann, Dana Marie.
O'Leary Brown, Erin, illus. see Hoffmann, Dana.
O'Leary Brown, Erin, jt. auth. see Curry, Don L.
O'Leary, Denyse. What Are Newton's Laws of Motion? (p. 1879)
O'Leary, Edward J. Murder in the I. R. S. (p. 1192)
O'Leary, John. Goldilocks: A Pop-Up Book. O'Leary, John, illus. (p. 696)
—¡En Busca del Tesoro del Pirata! O'Leary, John, illus. (p. 522)
O'Leary, Sara. This Is Sadie. Morstad, Julie, illus. (p. 1736)
—When I Was Small. Morstad, Julie, illus. (p. 1903)
—When You Were Small. Morstad, Julie, illus. (p. 1905)
—Where You Came From. Morstad, Julie, illus. (p. 1910)
O'Leary, Sara & Opal, Paola. Zingy. Morstad, Julie, illus. (p. 1987)
O'Leary, Terence. More than a Game. (p. 1175)
O'Leary, Timothy F., ed. see Theresine, Mary.
O'Leary, Timothy J., et al. Computing Essentials 2004. (p. 355)
O'Leary-Coggins, Annette. Rescueteers' Christmas Mission: Book 2. (p. 1462)
Oleck, Joan. Graphic Design & Desktop Publishing. (p. 710)
Olek, Lisa B. Naked Cat With The Velvet Paws. Gruenfelder, Robin, illus. (p. 1228)
—Yoshka's Journey to Christmas. Gruenfelder, Robin, illus. (p. 1972)
Oleksy, Walter. Choosing a Career in Agriculture. (p. 310)
—Circulatory System. (p. 321)
—Mapping the Skies. (p. 1090)
—Mapping the World. (p. 1090)
—Maps in History. (p. 1090)
Oleksy, Walter G. Careers in Web Design. (p. 268)
Oleksy, Walter G., jt. auth. see Nathan, Jacintha.
Olena Rudge. Adventures of Sophie & Katia in the Enchanted Forest. (p. 23)
Oler, Robyn. My Friend the Dentist. (p. 1209)
Olesen, Andrew. George Washington: The First President of the United States. (p. 664)
Olesen, Cecilie. My First Handy Bible. Mazali, Gustavo, illus. (p. 1206)
Olesen, Demetria Vassiliou. Lambyro. Forcada, Adiela & Giron, Elizabeth, illus. (p. 972)
Olesha, Yuri. Three Fat Men. Kay, Nicole, tr. from RUS. (p. 1742)
Olesky, Walter. Choosing a Career in Agriculture. (p. 310)
Oleson, Susan. Sammy Tails: Finding a Home (p. 1508)
Oleynikov, Igor. King with Horse's Ears & Other Irish Folktales. (p. 959)
Oleynikov, Igor, illus. see Andersen, Hans Christian.
Oleynikov, Igor, illus. see Dargaw, Kate.
Oleynikov, Igor, illus. see Lithgow, John.
Oleynikov, Igor, illus. see Lloyd-Jones, Sally.
Olfet, Omid. In the Dark: Parts 3 And 4. (p. 865)
Olien, Becky. Erosion (p. 534)
—Fossils (p. 624)
Olien, Becky, jt. auth. see Olien, Rebecca.
Olien, Jessica. Shark Detective! Olien, Jessica, illus. (p. 1562)
Olien, Rebecca. Arkansas. (p. 99)
—Circulatory System (p. 321)
—Digestive System (p. 438)
—Endocrine System (p. 527)
—Exploring Earth. (p. 552)
—Exploring Meteors. (p. 552)
—Exploring the Moon. (p. 554)
—Exploring the Planets in Our Solar System. (p. 554)
—Exploring the Sun. (p. 554)
—Hearing Nei, Molly, illus. (p. 759)
—How Do We Know about Dinosaurs? A Fossil Mystery McDee, Katie, illus. (p. 807)
—Kansas. (p. 942)
—Kids Care! 75 Ways to Make a Difference for People, Animals & the Environment. Kline, Michael, illus. (p. 953)
—Kids Write: Fantasy & Sci Fi, Mystery, Autobiography, Adventure & More! Kline, Michael, illus. (p. 955)
—Longitude & Latitude. (p. 1047)
—Looking at Maps & Globes. (p. 1051)
—Magnets (p. 1076)
—Making Water Clean Williams, Ted, illus. (p. 1082)
—Map Keys. (p. 1089)
—Nervous System (p. 1241)
—Patience (p. 1328)
—Respiratory System (p. 1463)
—Tasting Nei, Molly, illus. (p. 1707)
—Temperature (p. 1717)
—Water Cycle Williams, Ted, illus. (p. 1862)
—What Happened to the Dinosaurs? A Book about Extinction (p. 1885)
—Where Do the Birds Go? A Migration Mystery McDee, Katie, illus. (p. 1907)
Olien, Rebecca, jt. auth. see Hansen, Amy S.
Olien, Rebecca & Olien, Becky. Police Cars in Action (p. 1380)
—Rescue Helicopters in Action (p. 1462)
Oliffe, Pat, illus. see Marvel Press Group Staff, et al.
Olin, Marilyn. Mom, Mac & Cheese, Please! Pantic, Dunja, illus. (p. 1161)
Olin, Nicki. God Made Me Special, Just Like You! (p. 689)
Olin, Rita & Olin, Spencer. Trouble in Soccertown: A Lazer Mcnulty Adventure. (p. 1790)
Olin, Sean. Killing Britney. (p. 956)
—Reckless Hearts. (p. 1451)
—Wicked Games. (p. 1927)
Olin, Spencer, jt. auth. see Olin, Rita.
Oliphant, Manelle, illus. see Earl, Cheri Pray & Williams, Carol Lynch.
Oliphant, Manelle, illus. see Spurr, Elizabeth.
Oliphant, Manelle, illus. see Williams, Carol Lynch & Earl, Cheri Pray.
Oliva, Octavio, illus. see Smith, Michael & Wang, Emily.
Oliva, Octavio, illus. see Smith, Michael.
Oliva, Octavio, jt. auth. see Smith, Michael.
Olivares, Katie Lydon. ABC Book of Shadows. (p. 3)
Olivas, Daniel. Benjamin & the Word: Benjamin y la Palabra. Baeza Ventura, Gabriela, tr. (p. 164)
—Benjamin & Word Benjamin Y la Palabra. (p. 164)
Olivas, John D. Endeavour's Long Journey: Celebrating 19 Years of Space Exploration. Roski, Gayle Garner, illus. (p. 527)
—Endeavour's Long Journey. Roski, Gayle Garner, illus. (p. 527)
Olivas, Nancy Gilson. Christmas on K Street: The Ornament Divine. (p. 315)
Olive and Moss Staff, jt. auth. see Govan, Nina.
Olive Branch Publishing, ed. Boogaloo Meets Ranger Bob. (p. 210)
Olive, Gloria D. My Hat! My Hat! Where Is My Hat? Barge III, John, illus. (p. 1210)
Olive, Guillaume & He, Zihong. My First Book of Chinese Calligraphy. (p. 1205)
Olive, M. Foster. Morphine. (p. 1176)
—Prescription Pain Relievers. Triggle, David J., ed. (p. 1396)
—Sleep AIDS. Triggle, David J., ed. (p. 1588)
—Understanding Drugs: Ecstasy. (p. 1815)
Olive, Phyllis Carol. Gift of the Holy Ghost. Olive, Phyllis Carol, illus. (p. 675)
Olive, Teresa, et al. Best-Loved Christmas Stories. Munger, Nancy et al, illus. (p. 170)
Oliveira, Jô de. Kuarup, a Festa DOS Mortos: Lendas DOS Povos Indigenas Do Xingu. (p. 968)
Oliveira, Luis. Children of Hope 2. (p. 302)
—Children of Hope 3. (p. 302)
—DogMan 2. (p. 462)
Oliver, A. J. Tizzy Blenkinsop. Kinsella, Sophie, illus. (p. 1758)
Oliver, Alison. Addition & Subtraction Age 5-6. (p. 12)
Oliver, Alison, illus. see Adams, Jennifer.
Oliver, Alison, illus. see Gibbs Smith & Adams, Jennifer.
Oliver, Alison & HarperCollins Publishers Ltd. Staff. Addition & Subtraction Age 6-7. (p. 12)
Oliver, Amanda Eaddy. Cheyenne the Cat. (p. 299)
Oliver, Andrew. Haunted Hill. (p. 753)
—If Photos Could Talk. (p. 854)
—Scrambled. (p. 1532)
Oliver, Angel, illus. see Rowland, Dawn.
Oliver, Archie. First Picture Dictionary. (p. 596)
Oliver, Butterworth. Enormous Egg. (p. 531)
Oliver, Chad. Far from This Earth & Other Stories. Olson, Priscilla, ed. (p. 572)
—Star Above It & Other Stories. Olson, Priscilla, ed. (p. 1640)
Oliver, Charlene. Life & Tails of Herman the Worm. (p. 1007)
Oliver, Charles Folkes. Little Willy & the Party Animals. (p. 1037)
Oliver, Charles M. Critical Companion to Ernest Hemingway: A Literary Reference to His Life & Work. (p. 383)
Oliver, Claire. Marvellous Magic. (p. 1099)
—Mind-Boggling Science. (p. 1145)
—Terror under the Sea. (p. 1722)
Oliver, Clare. Great Britain. (p. 714)
—Natural Disasters: Atlas in the Round. (p. 1235)
—Tell Me Who Lives in Space? And More about Space. (p. 1717)
OLIVER, Clare. Weather. (p. 1869)
Oliver, Clare, jt. auth. see Fecher, Sarah.
Oliver, Douglas. Arrondissements. Notley, Alice, ed. (p. 101)
Oliver, Gary J. & Wright, H. Norman. Good Women Get Angry. (p. 700)
Oliver, Gloria. Cross-eyed Dragon Troubles. (p. 385)
Oliver, Helen. Ellen's First Swim. (p. 514)
Oliver, Ilanit. Are You My Daddy? Parker-Rees, Guy, illus. (p. 97)
—Olivia & the Best Teacher Ever. (p. 1286)
—OLIVIA & the Best Teacher Ever. Johnson, Shane L., illus. (p. 1286)
—Ten Flying Brooms. Poling, Kyle, illus. (p. 1718)
Oliver, Jamie. Jamie's Italy. Loftus, David & Terry, Chris, photos by. (p. 907)
Oliver, Jan. Heart of Fire. (p. 759)
Oliver, Jana. Briar Rose (p. 227)
—Demon Trapper's Daughter. (p. 426)
—Foretold. (p. 618)
—Forgiven. (p. 619)
Oliver, Jane. Birthday Surprise. Raga, Silvia, illus. (p. 193)
Oliver, Jasmine. Prada Princesses. (p. 1392)
Oliver, Jenni, illus. see Lowry, Lois.
Oliver, Julia, illus. see Darens, Cat.
Oliver, K. Wade. Ringneck Doves: A Handbook of Care & Breeding. (p. 1473)
Oliver, Kara Lassen. Stepping into the World. (p. 1648)
Oliver, Kimberly, ed. see Trumbauer, Lisa.
Oliver, Lauren. Before I Fall. (p. 158)
—Delirium. (p. 425)
—Delirium Stories: Hana, Annabel, & Raven. (p. 425)
—Delirium Stories. (p. 425)
—Liesl & Po. (p. 1007)
—Liesl & Po. Acedera, Kei, illus. (p. 1007)
—Pandemonium. (p. 1321)
—Panic. (p. 1321)
—Requiem. (p. 1462)
—Spindlers. (p. 1628)
—Spindlers. Bruno, Iacopo, illus. (p. 1628)
—Vanishing Girls. (p. 1833)
Oliver, Lauren & Chester, H. C. Shrunken Head. Lacombe, Benjamin, illus. (p. 1571)
Oliver, Liana, illus. see Adams, Paul Robert.
Oliver, Lin. Almost Identical. (p. 48)
—Attack of the Growling Eyeballs. Gilpin, Stephen, illus. (p. 113)
—Double-Crossed #3. (p. 472)
—Escape of the Mini-Mummy. Gilpin, Stephen, illus. (p. 535)
—Little Poems for Tiny Ears. dePaola, Tomie, illus. (p. 1033)
—Revenge of the Itty-Bitty Brothers. Gilpin, Stephen, illus. (p. 1466)
—Secret of the Super-Small Superstar. Gilpin, Stephen, illus. (p. 1543)
—Twice As Nice. (p. 1801)
—Twice as Nice. (p. 1801)
—Two-Faced (p. 1803)
Oliver, Lin, jt. auth. see Winkler, Henry.
Oliver, Lin & Baker, Theo. Shadow Mask (p. 1557)
—Sound Bender. (p. 1615)
Oliver, Lin & Winkler, Henry. My Book of Pickles... Oops, I Mean Lists. Heitz, Tim, illus. (p. 1199)
—There's a Zombie in My Bathtub. (p. 1731)
—There's a Zombie in My Bathtub #5. Garrett, Scott, illus. (p. 1731)
Oliver, Maria Fernanda, illus. see Nazoa, Aquiles.
Oliver, Marilyn Tower. Infamous Alcatraz Prison in United States History. (p. 873)
Oliver, Mark. Robot Dog Oliver, Mark, illus. (p. 1480)
Oliver, Mark, illus. see Emmett, Jonathan.
Oliver, Mark, illus. see Ewart, Franzeska G.
Oliver, Mark, illus. see Fuerst, Jeffrey B.
Oliver, Mark, illus. see Harris, Brooke.
Oliver, Mark, illus. see Harvey, Damian.
Oliver, Martin. Boys Only: How to Survive Anything! Ecob, Simon, illus. (p. 220)
—Esas Geniales Peliculas. Reeve, Tony, tr. (p. 534)
—Esos Extintos Dinosaurios. Postgate, Daniel, tr. (p. 536)
—Off with Their Heads! All the Cool Bits in British History. Pinder, Andrew, illus. (p. 1279)
Oliver, Martin, jt. auth. see Scholastic, Inc. Staff.
Oliver, Martin, jt. auth. see Stride, Lottie.
Oliver, Martin & Johnson, Alexandra. How-To Handbook: Shortcuts & Solutions for the Problems of Everyday Life. (p. 820)
Oliver, Martin & Pinder, Andrew. Off with Their Heads! All the Cool Bits in British History. (p. 1279)
Oliver, Max. Little Boy. (p. 1025)
—Little Dancer Learns. (p. 1026)
Oliver, Merlin. John Laughinghouse. (p. 922)
Oliver, Narelle. Best Beak in Boonaroo Bay. Oliver, Narelle, illus. (p. 168)
—Sand Swimmers: The Secret Life of Australia's Desert Wilderness. Oliver, Narelle, illus. (p. 1510)
—Twilight Hunt Oliver, Narelle, illus. (p. 1801)
Oliver Optic. Across India: Or - Live Boys in the Far East. (p. 9)
—Poor & Proud: Or the Fortunes of Katy Redburn: a Story for Young. (p. 1383)
Oliver, Patricia. Double Deception: A Regency Romance Novel. (p. 472)
Oliver, Patrick M., ed. Turn the Page & You Don't Stop: Sharing Successful Chapters in Our Lives with Youth. (p. 1797)
Oliver, Sarah. Be the Best. (p. 149)
Oliver, Sheila. Tinky Turtle Finds the Word. McQuitty, LaVonia Corbin, illus. (p. 1756)
Oliver, Simon. Exterminators - Bug Brothers (p. 555)
Oliver, Simon, et al. Exterminators - Insurgency (p. 555)
Oliver, Stephen, photos by. Tamanos. (p. 1704)
Oliver, Tony, illus. see Winer, Yvonne.
Oliver, Veronica A. Rainbow Colors: Learning Primary & Secondary Colors. (p. 1435)
Olivera, Martin Bonfil. Barriga Llena. Estrada, Ixchel, illus. (p. 140)
Olivera, Ramon. ABCs on Wings. Olivera, Ramon, illus. (p. 4)
Oliveras, Julio Hermoso, tr. see Meyer, Stephenie.
Oliveri, Lisa L. Last Pacifier. Fisher, Marianne, illus. (p. 978)
Oliverio, Daniel, tr. see Ruiz, Emilio.
Oliverio, Donna Christina, ed. see McClarnon, Marciann.
Oliver-Miles, Zelda. Amelia Gayle Gorgas: First Woman of Position. (p. 58)
Oliveto, Michelle. My Dog the Faker. (p. 1202)
Olivetti, Ariel, illus. see Nicieza, Mariano.
Olivetti, Ariel, illus. see Spencer, Nick.
Olivetti, Ariel, et al. Thor: Heaven & Earth. (p. 1739)
Olivia, Cynthia. In January & June (p. 864)
Olivieri, Laura. Where Are You: A Child's Book about Loss. (p. 1906)
Oliviero, Jamie. Som See & the Magic Elephant. Kelly, Jo'Anne, illus. (p. 1608)
Olivo, Andy. Brothers. (p. 231)
Olizon-Chikiamco, Norma, et al. Pan de Sal Saves the Day: A Filipino Children's Story. Salvatus, Mark & Salvatus III, Mark Ramsel N., illus. (p. 1320)
Olker, Constance. Punctuation Pals Go Snow Skiing. (p. 1417)
—Punctuation Pals Go Snow Skiing. Guzman, Minerva, illus. (p. 1417)
—Punctuation Pals Go to the Baseball Park. (p. 1417)
—Punctuation Pals Go to the Baseball Park. Guzman, Minerva, illus. (p. 1417)
—Punctuation Pals Go to the Beach. (p. 1417)
—Punctuation Pals Go to the Beach. Guzman, Minerva, illus. (p. 1417)
—Punctuation Pals Meet at School. (p. 1417)
—Punctuation Pals Meet at School. Guzman, Minerva, illus. (p. 1417)
Olla, Debbie. Confirmation Certificate. (p. 357)
—Retreats for Teens: Planning Strategies & Teen-Tested Models. Cannizzo, Karen A., ed. (p. 1464)
Ollendorff, Valli. Fate Did Not Let Me Go: A Mother's Farewell Letter Pervan, Ivo & Bemporad, Alex, photos by. (p. 577)
Oller, Erika, illus. see Newman, Lesléa.
Ollerenshaw, Jenny. Practical Guide to Teaching Reading Skills at All Levels: With Examples in French, German & Spanish. Ollerenshaw, Sue, illus. (p. 1392)
Ollerenshaw, Rod, ed. see Yoe, Craig, et al.
Ollerenshaw, Sue, illus. see Ollerenshaw, Jenny.
Ollerhead, Sue, jt. auth. see Montgomery, Karen.
Ollhoff, Jim. African Mythology. (p. 27)
—African-American History (p. 27)
—Alaska. (p. 33)
—Arizona. (p. 98)
—Beginning Genealogy. (p. 159)
—Black Death. (p. 195)
—Brain. (p. 221)
—Captain Cook. (p. 264)
—Chinese Mythology. (p. 307)
—Christopher Columbus. (p. 316)
—Civil Rights Movement. (p. 325)
—Civil War: Slavery. (p. 325)
—Civil War: Weapons. (p. 325)

—Civil War: Early Battles. (p. 325)
—Civil War: Turning Points. (p. 325)
—Civil War: The Final Years. (p. 325)
—Civil War: Leaders & Generals. (p. 325)
—Civil War. (p. 325)
—Collecting Primary Records. (p. 339)
—Colorado. (p. 343)
—Conflicts & Independence. (p. 357)
—Connecticut. (p. 357)
—Conquistadors. (p. 358)
—Courage & Growth. (p. 372)
—Delaware. (p. 424)
—Digestive System. (p. 438)
—DNA: Window to the Past. (p. 456)
—Ear, Nose, & Throat. (p. 492)
—Egyptian Mythology. (p. 507)
—EMT. (p. 521)
—European Mythology. (p. 540)
—Exploring Immigration. (p. 552)
—Ferdinand Magellan. (p. 581)
—Filling the Family Tree. (p. 586)
—Firefighter. (p. 591)
—Florida. (p. 606)
—Flu. (p. 608)
—Fossil Fuels. (p. 623)
—Freedom & the Future. (p. 634)
—Future Energy (p. 651)
—Geothermal, Biomass, & Hydrogen. (p. 665)
—Germ Detectives. (p. 666)
—Grappling. (p. 711)
—Greek Mythology. (p. 720)
—Hawaii. (p. 755)
—Hazmat. (p. 756)
—Heart. (p. 759)
—Idaho. (p. 851)
—Identity & Civil Rights. (p. 852)
—Jacques Cousteau. (p. 905)
—Japanese Mythology. (p. 909)
—Karate. (p. 943)
—Kung Fu. (p. 968)
—Living in a Warmer World. (p. 1041)
—Malaria. (p. 1083)
—Marco Polo. (p. 1092)
—Martial Arts Around the Globe. (p. 1097)
—Masters & Heroes. (p. 1103)
—Mayan & Aztec Mythology. (p. 1113)
—Middle Eastern Mythology. (p. 1137)
—Missouri. (p. 1154)
—Montana. (p. 1170)
—Mummies. (p. 1190)
—Muscles & Bones. (p. 1192)
—Myths & Controversies. (p. 1227)
—Native American Mythology. (p. 1234)
—Nebraska. (p. 1239)
—Neil Armstrong. (p. 1240)
—Nevada. (p. 1242)
—Ninja. (p. 1256)
—Norse Mythology. (p. 1264)
—North Dakota. (p. 1265)
—Nuclear Energy. (p. 1269)
—Pioneers of Equality. (p. 1361)
—Police. (p. 1379)
—Puerto Rico. (p. 1415)
—Roots of Humanity. (p. 1488)
—Samurai. (p. 1509)
—Science. (p. 1524)
—Search & Rescue. (p. 1537)
—Skin. (p. 1585)
—Smallpox. (p. 1592)
—Social Solutions. (p. 1604)
—Solar Power. (p. 1606)
—South Carolina. (p. 1616)
—South Dakota. (p. 1617)
—Sport Karate. (p. 1631)
—Swat. (p. 1689)
—Technological Solutions. (p. 1711)
—Tennessee. (p. 1720)
—Texas. (p. 1724)
—Using Your Research. (p. 1829)
—Utah. (p. 1829)
—Washington. (p. 1859)
—Washington, D. C. (p. 1860)
—Water & Ice. (p. 1862)
—Weapons. (p. 1869)
—Werewolves. (p. 1875)
—West Virginia. (p. 1876)
—What Are Germs? (p. 1879)
—Wind & Water. (p. 1935)
—Wisconsin. (p. 1939)
—World in Crisis. (p. 1956)
—World of Mythology. (p. 1957)
—Wyoming. (p. 1966)
—Years of Slavery. (p. 1969)
—Your Family Tree (p. 1980)
Olliffe, Pat, illus. see Macri, Thomas.
Olliffe, Pat, illus. see Thomas, Rich, Jr.
Olliffe, Pat, illus. see Thomas, Rich.
Olliffe, Pat, jt. illus. see Marvel Artists Staff.
Olliffe, Patrick, illus. see Powell, Martin.
Olliges, Rob. Que Viene Primero/What Comes First. Mallick, David, tr. (p. 1424)
Ollivant, Alfred, jt. auth. see Davis, Lydia.
Ollivier, Stephane. Piotr Ilyich Tchaikovski. Voake, Charlotte, illus. (p. 1361)
Ollweiler, Angela Messina. Strange Wish. Ollweiler, D. R., illus. (p. 1665)
Ollweiler, D. R., illus. see Ollweiler, Angela Messina.
Olmedillas, Cathy, jt. compiled by see Anorak Press Staff.
Olmedillas, Cathy, compiled by. Anorak. (p. 87)
Olmos, Edward J., et al. Latins Anonymous. (p. 979)
Olmos, Edward James, intro. 2004 Hispanic Scholarship Directory: Over 1,000 Ways to Finance Your Education. (p. 2003)
Olmos, Gabriela. I Dreamt... A Book about Hope Amado, Elisa, tr. from SPA. (p. 838)
Olmos, Roger, illus. see Bruno, Pepe & Bruno, Pep.
Olmos, Roger, illus. see Figueras, Nuria.
Olmos, Roger, illus. see Liván, Paco.
Olmstead. Hispanic-American Biographies Series (p. 781)
Olmstead, Kathleen. Enormous Turnip. Olafsdottir, Linda, illus. (p. 531)
—Fox & the Grapes. Brannen, Sarah S., illus. (p. 626)
—King Midas. Quarello, Maurizio A. C., illus. (p. 958)
—Lion & the Mouse. Wakefield, Scott, illus. (p. 1020)
—Matthew Henson: The Quest for the North Pole. (p. 1109)
—Pied Piper of Hamelin. Brannen, Sarah S., illus. (p. 1356)
Olmstead, Kathleen & Andersen, Hans Christian. Little Match Girl. Kim, Jin-Woo, illus. (p. 1031)
—Steadfast Tin Soldier. Calo, Marcos, illus. (p. 1645)
Olmstead, Kathleen & Olafsdottir, Linda. Beauty & the Beast. (p. 154)
Olmstead, Kathleen & Porter, Eleanor H. Pollyanna. Akib, Jamel, illus. (p. 1381)
Olmstead, Kathleen, et al. Thumbelina. Sokolava, Valerie, illus. (p. 1745)
Olmstead, Lucinda. But Not on My Ice Cream, Please. (p. 246)
Olmstead, Mary. César Chávez Pomenta, Allison, tr. from ENG. (p. 288)
—Judy Baca Pomenta, Allison, tr. (p. 931)
—Roberto Clemente Lopez, Jose Miguel, tr. (p. 1479)
—Tito Puente Lopez, Jose Miguel, tr. from ENG. (p. 1758)
Olmsted, Frederick Law. Frederick Law Olmsted, Professional Papers. (p. 633)
Olmsted, Frederick Law, jt. auth. see Dunlap, Julie.
Olmsted, Jennifer. Art of the Middle Ages (p. 102)
Olney, Ross R. Time Dial (p. 1751)
Olney, Timothy Michael. Life Positive. (p. 1012)
Olofsdotter, Marie, illus. see Adler, David A.
Olofson, Darrell. Yarns of Ballpoint. (p. 1968)
—Yarns of Ballpoint II. Taylor, Sue, illus. (p. 1968)
O'Loughlin, Chloe & Borrowman, Mary. Rescue of Nanoose Wang, Jacqueline, illus. (p. 1462)
O'Loughlin, Cindy & O'Loughlin, Dennis. Debbie Duck & the Cranky Blankie Day. (p. 421)
O'Loughlin, Declan & McKenna, Donna, eds. Fone a Friend: A Prayer Book by Children for Children. (p. 612)
O'Loughlin, Dennis, jt. auth. see O'Loughlin, Cindy.
O'Loughlin, Diane, ed. see Hackenberg, Richard.
O'Loughlin, Diane, ed. see Russ, Tony.
O'Loughlin, Erin. Bluebird Dance. (p. 204)
Olowoyeye, Ola. Critters! II: Mary Moth. (p. 384)
—Rhythm & Motion: Volume 2. (p. 1468)
—Rhythm & Motion. (p. 1468)
Olrun, Prudy, jt. auth. see Amos, Muriel.
Ols, Angela M. What Is a Vote? (p. 1888)
Olsen, Alana. Look Out for the Blue-Ringed Octopus! (p. 1049)
—What Do You Know about Bugs? Understand Place Value. (p. 1883)
Olsen, Ashley, jt. auth. see Olsen, Mary-Kate.
Olsen, Bevan. Bethlehem's Star. (p. 171)
—Innkeeper's Christmas. (p. 875)
—Magi. (p. 1071)
Olsen, Bevan Lloyd. Littlest Nephite in Nephi & the Brass Plates. Miller, Rebecca, illus. (p. 1039)
Olsen, Beverly J. Vi's Pie. (p. 1844)
Olsen, Christian, illus. see Flikkema, Elizabeth.
Olsen, Debi W. My Very Own Book about God. (p. 1221)
—My Very Own Book about Religious Science. (p. 1221)
Olsen EdS, Marci. Lessons to Live by: Character Building Books for School-Age Children. (p. 994)
Olsen, Elizabeth. - Z Kids. (p. 1984)
Olsen, Erik. Cobble Cavern. (p. 336)
—Garden of the Lost Souls. (p. 656)
—Quest & Honor (Flin's Destiny 4) (p. 1426)
Olsen, Gail. Home at Last. (p. 792)
Olsen, Gina Ann. I Can't, Even Though I Should (p. 837)
Olsen, Grant Orrin. Rhino Trouble. Carpenter, Mike, illus. (p. 1467)
Olsen, Greg. Beautiful Savior. (p. 154)
—I Am a Child of God. (p. 832)
Olsen, J. J. Mystic Kingdom: A Jenny Dewberry Series. (p. 1226)
Olsen, Jan Z. Mat Man Hats. Delaney, Molly, illus. (p. 1104)
—Mat Man on the Go. Delaney, Molly, illus. (p. 1104)
—Mat Man Opposites. Delaney, Molly, illus. (p. 1104)
—Mat Man Shapes. Delaney, Molly, illus. (p. 1104)
Olsen, Jan Z., creator. Color Print & Number Wall Cards. (p. 343)
Olsen, Judith K. I Can Hardly Wait. (p. 835)
Olsen, Kent L. Tales of Kalindia. (p. 1702)
Olsen, La Verne C. If A Peacock Follows You Home: Children's Stories by Grandma. (p. 852)
Olsen, Lauri. Pacific Bound: The Adventures of Lewis & Clark. (p. 1317)
—Pacific Bound: The Adventures of Lewis & Clark. Toonz Animation, ed. (p. 1317)
Olsen, Leigh, jt. auth. see Ostby, Kristin.
Olsen, Leigh & S. I. International. What Do You Say? A Book about Manners. (p. 1883)
Olsen, Lillian, tr. see Kishimoto, Masashi, et al.
Olsen, Lillian, tr. see Takei, Hiroyuki, et al.
Olsen, Lillian, tr. see Tamura, Yumi.
Olsen, Lillian, tr. see Togashi, Yoshihiro.
Olsen, Lillian, tr. see Toriyama, Akira & Jones, Gerard.
Olsen, Lillian, tr. see Watase, Yuu.
Olsen, Lillian, tr. see Watase, Yû.
Olsen, Mary. I'm Made of Mama's Milk. (p. 859)
Olsen, Mary-Kate & Olsen, Ashley. Beach Collection (p. 149)
—Best Friends Forever (p. 169)
—Calling All Boys. (p. 254)
—Camp Rock 'N' Roll. (p. 257)
—Closer Than Ever. (p. 334)
—Cool Club. (p. 363)
—Dare to Scare. (p. 406)
—Dating Game (p. 409)
—Facts about Flirting. (p. 561)
—Girl's Guide to Guys. (p. 680)
—Heart to Heart. (p. 760)
—Hocus Pocus. (p. 787)
—Influence. (p. 873)
—Let's Party (p. 999)
—Love, Set, Match. (p. 1060)
—Making a Splash. (p. 1080)
—Mary-Kate & Ashley: Our Story. (p. 1100)
—Mary-Kate & Ashley Style Secrets. (p. 1100)
—Mary-Kate & Ashley Yearbook. (p. 1100)
—MKA Two of a Kind 2003 Boxed Set. (p. 1157)
—New Adventures (p. 1243)
—P. S Wish You Were Here. (p. 1316)
—Santa Girls (p. 1512)
—Secret Crush. (p. 1540)
—Sleepover Party Mini Box. (p. 1589)
—Spring Breakup. (p. 1635)
—Surf, Sand & Secrets. (p. 1685)
—Tell Me about It. (p. 1716)
—Twist & Shout. (p. 1802)
—Two of a Kind Diaries: Winner Take All. (p. 1804)
—Ultimate Guide to Mary-Kate & Ashley. (p. 1809)
Olsen, Mary-Kate, et al. Secret of Jane's Success. (p. 1542)
—There's Something about Roxy. (p. 1731)
Olsen, Nora. Frenemy of the People. (p. 636)
—Maxine Wore Black. (p. 1112)
—Swans & Klons. (p. 1689)
Olsen, Rodger. Empire of Texas: And the Star of India. (p. 521)
Olsen, Rodger, jt. auth. see Frankowski, Leo.
Olsen, S. R. When Dogs Dream. Showalter, Kristin, illus. (p. 1902)
Olsen, Sven. Oh for smart book One: The Northern Minnesota Pretty Good Way to Lose Weight & Get in Shape (p. 1280)
Olsen, Sylvia. Catching Spring (p. 279)
—Counting on Hope (p. 371)
—Different Game (p. 438)
—Girl with a Baby (p. 679)
—Middle Row (p. 1137)
—Molly's Promise (p. 1161)
—White Girl (p. 1913)
—Yellow Line (p. 1970)
—Yetsa's Sweater Larson, Joan, illus. (p. 1971)
Olsen, Sylvia & Charko, Kasia. Sebastian Sasquatch (p. 1539)
Olsen, Sylvia & Martin, Ron. Which Way Should I Go? Charko, Kasia, illus. (p. 1911)
Olsen, Ted. Christianity & the Celts. (p. 312)
Olshan, Matthew. Flown Sky (p. 608)
—Mighty Lalouche. Blackall, Sophie, illus. (p. 1140)
Olshine, David. Revelation Epic: Preparing Youth Groups for the Earth's Final Days. Vol. 2 (p. 1465)
Olson, Amy. What's Bugging Camo the Chameleon. (p. 1896)
Olson, Arielle North & Schwartz, Howard. More Bones: Scary Stories from Around the World. Gist, E. M., illus. (p. 1174)
Olson, Barbara. Christmas in Gondar: Five Ethiopian Stories. (p. 314)
Olson, Bethany. Baby Cats. (p. 125)
—Baby Deer. (p. 125)
—Baby Horses. (p. 126)
—Baby Pandas. (p. 127)
—Baby Rabbits. (p. 127)
—Baby Wolves. (p. 128)
Olson, Branden. Tuke the Noozle in... Just in Case... (p. 1796)
Olson, Carl. 50 Common Insects of the Southwest. (p. 1997)
Olson, Carole, jt. auth. see Schneider, Cheryl.
Olson, Christine. Moving? Nope, Not Me! (p. 1183)
Olson, Cindy, illus. see Hoffman, Peter.
Olson, Cynthia. Cherise's Christmas Wish. (p. 297)
Olson, Cynthia J. Kiera's Cry (p. 955)
Olson, D. A. Treasure Map. (p. 1782)
Olson, Dan, jt. auth. see Baum, Diane Ganzer.
Olson, Denise. Geoff the Green Hippo: A Children's Book about Adoption. (p. 661)
—P Is for Picky. (p. 1316)
Olson, Ed, illus. see Carvin, Rose-Mae.
Olson, Ed, illus. see Greiner, Ruth B.
Olson, Ed, illus. see Greiner, Ruth B., et al.
Olson, Ed, illus. see King, Emily.
Olson, Ed, illus. see Lyster, R. Iona, et al.
Olson, Ed, illus. see Martonyi, E. Andrew.
Olson, Gillia & Olson, Gillia M. Siberian Huskies (p. 1572)
Olson, Gillia M. Afghanistan: A Question & Answer Book (p. 26)
—Fases de la Luna. (p. 575)
—Monsters Can Mosey: Understanding Shades of Meaning Stevanovic, Ivica, illus. (p. 1169)
—MyPlate & You (p. 1222)
—Needs & Wants. (p. 1239)
—Pakistan: A Question & Answer Book (p. 1319)
—Pet Cats up Close. (p. 1345)
—Phases of the Moon Miller, Jo, illus. (p. 1350)
—Phases of the Moon Saunders-Smith, Gail, ed. (p. 1350)
—Polar Bears' Search for Ice: A Cause & Effect Investigation (p. 1379)
—Stickler on Stilts. (p. 1650)
Olson, Gillia M., jt. auth. see Olson, Gillia.
Olson, Greg. Great Walker: Ioway Leader. Hare, John, illus. (p. 719)
Olson, Gretchen. Call Me Hope. (p. 254)
Olson, Jennifer Gray. Ninja Bunny. (p. 1256)
Olson, Jennifer Lynn. Chef Charlie & the Great Escape (p. 297)
Olson, Johan, illus. see Munoz, Norma.
Olson, John, illus. see Munoz, Norma.
Olson, John J. Wild Child & Annie. (p. 1929)
Olson, Julie. Already Asleep. (p. 50)
—Discover America: From Sea to Shining Sea. Olson, Julie, illus. (p. 447)
—Fairy Garden: A Magnifying Mystery. (p. 563)
—Tickle, Tickle! Itch, Twitch! (p. 1747)
Olson, Julie, illus. see Dion, L. M.
Olson, Julie, illus. see Hickman, Kirt.
Olson, Julie, illus. see London, Jonathan.
Olson, Julie, illus. see Meister, Carl.
Olson, Julie, illus. see Moore, Marian & Kensington, Mary Jane.
Olson, Julie, illus. see Walton, Rick.
Olson, K. C. Construction Countdown. Gordon, David, illus. (p. 359)
Olson, Karen. Cooper Gets a Cast. Pritchett and Hull Associates, Inc., illus. (p. 365)
—Cooper Has Diabetes. Pritchett and Hull Associates, illus. (p. 365)
—Eat, Run & Live Healthy. Hamelin, Marie-Micheline, illus. (p. 501)
Olson, Karen W. Eyes, Ears, Nose & Mouth. George, Leonard, Jr., illus. (p. 558)
—Healthy Choices, Healthy Lives. Hamelin, Marie-Micheline, illus. (p. 758)
—Living Safe, Playing Safe. George, Leonard, Jr., illus. (p. 1041)
—Living Safe, Playing Safe. Hamelin, Marie-Micheline, illus. (p. 1041)
Olson, Kay Melchisedech. Assassination of Abraham Lincoln Lohse, Otha Zackariah Edward, illus. (p. 107)
—Benjamin Franklin: An American Genius Purcell, Gordon & Schulz, Barbara, illus. (p. 164)
—Benjamin Franklin: Un Genio Norteamericano. Purcell, Gordon et al, illus. (p. 165)
—Betsy Ross & the American Flag Cool, Anna Maria et al, illus. (p. 172)
—D. B. Cooper Hijacking: Vanishing Act (p. 397)
—Frank Zamboni & the Ice-Resurfacing Machine Dominguez, Richard & Barnett, Charles, III, illus. (p. 629)
—Gettysburg Address in Translation: What It Really Means. (p. 670)
—Great Chicago Fire Of 1871 Miller, Phil et al, illus. (p. 714)
—Johann Gutenberg & the Printing Press Smith, Tod G., illus. (p. 920)
—Murderers & Serial Killers: Stories of Violent Criminals (p. 1192)
—Terrible, Awful Civil War: The Disgusting Details about Life During America's. (p. 1721)
—Terrible, Awful Civil War: The Disgusting Details about Life During America's Bloodiest War. (p. 1721)
Olson, Kay Melchisedech, jt. auth. see Schuh, Mari C.
Olson, Kay Melchisedech & Boonyadhistarn, Thiranut. Beginning Knitting: Stitches with Style Opseth, Katie, illus. (p. 159)
Olson, Kay Melchisedech & Melchisedech Olson, Kay. Assassination of Abraham Lincoln Lohse, Otha Zackariah Edward, illus. (p. 107)
—China (p. 306)
—England (p. 529)
Olson, Kevin Noel. Eerey Tocsin in the Cryptoid Zoo. Hammack, Debi, illus. (p. 505)
Olson, Kris C. Shepherd & the Wolf. (p. 1565)
Olson, Lute. Hello, Wilbur! De Angel, M., illus. (p. 765)
Olson, Marie. Tlingit Coloring Book. (p. 1758)
Olson, Mark K., ed. see Wesley, John.
Olson, Mark L., ed. see de Camp, L. Sprague.
Olson, Martin. Adventure Time Encyclopaedia: Inhabitants, Lore, Spells, & Ancient Crypt Warnings of the Land of Ooo Circa 19. 56 B. G. E. - 501 A. G. E. French, Renee et al, illus. (p. 14)
Olson, Mary W. Nice Try, Tooth Fairy. Tillotson, Katherine, illus. (p. 1250)
Olson, Meagan, illus. see Johnson, Alaya Dawn.
Olson, Mildred Thompson. Diamondola: A Little Diamond. (p. 434)
Olson, Nancy. Thanksgiving at Grandma's. Marino, Michael F., illus. (p. 1725)
Olson, Nathan. Animal Patterns (p. 79)
—Australia in Colors (p. 116)
—Building of the Transcontinental Railroad Dominguez, Richard et al, illus. (p. 239)
—Canada: A Question & Answer Book (p. 260)
—China: A Question & Answer Book (p. 306)
—City Patterns (p. 324)
—Cubes (p. 389)
—Cubos/Cubes Strictly Spanish, LLC., tr. (p. 389)
—Cylinders (p. 397)
—Esferas/Spheres Strictly Spanish, LLC., tr. (p. 535)
—Farm Patterns (p. 574)
—Figuras en 3-D/3-d Shapes. Strictly Spanish, LLC., tr. (p. 586)
—Finding Patterns. (p. 588)
—Food Patterns (p. 613)
—George Washington Carver: Ingenious Inventor Tucker, Keith, illus. (p. 664)
—Heavy & Light: An Animal Opposites Book (p. 761)
—High & Low: An Animal Opposites Book (p. 777)
—India: A Question & Answer Book (p. 870)
—India in Colors (p. 871)
—Italy. (p. 894)
—John F. Kennedy: American Visionary Bascle, Brian, illus. (p. 921)
—Levi Strauss & Blue Jeans Hoover, Dave et al, illus. (p. 1004)
—Levi Strauss & Blue Jeans Barnett, Charles, III et al, illus. (p. 1004)
—Nathan Hale: Revolutionary Spy. Martin, Cynthia & Schoonover, Brent, illus. (p. 1231)
—People Patterns (p. 1339)
—Pesados y Ligeros: Un Libro de Animales Opuestos. Ferrer, Martin Luis Guzman, tr. (p. 1345)
—Pirámides - Pyramids. Strictly Spanish, LLC., tr. (p. 1362)
—Plant Patterns (p. 1369)
—Pyramids (p. 1421)
—Spheres (p. 1626)
Olson, Nathan & Capstone Press Editors. Food Patterns (p. 613)
Olson, Nathan & Capstone Press Staff. Farm Patterns (p. 574)
—John F. Kennedy: American Visionary Bascle, Brian, illus. (p. 921)
—People Patterns (p. 1339)
Olson, Nathan & Glaser, Jason. Nathan Hale: Revolutionary Spy Martin, Cynthia & Schoonover, Brent, illus. (p. 1231)

O

Olson, Nathan, et al. Theodore Roosevelt: Bear of a President Martin, Cynthia et al, illus. (p. 1729)
Olson, Norah. Twisted Fate: A Novel. (p. 1802)
Olson, Olivia L. Eva's Gift. (p. 541)
Olson, Priscilla, ed. see Oliver, Chad.
Olson, Regan. Penny Penelope & the Beep Factory. (p. 1338)
Olson, Remy & Mason, Chris. Case Western Reserve University College Prowler off the Record. (p. 275)
Olson, Robert. Alaska - Hints of Paradise: Photographs & Essays by Robert Olson. Olson, Robert, photos by. (p. 34)
Olson, Ryan, illus. see Jakary, Lin.
Olson, Stan, illus. see Kunstler, James Howard.
Olson, Steve. Lincoln's Gettysburg Address: A Primary Source Investigation. (p. 1019)
—My Grandpa & Me: The Grandpa Steve Series. (p. 1210)
Olson, Steven. Oregon Trail: A Primary Source History of the Route to the American West. (p. 1303)
Olson, Steven P. Attack on U. S. Marines in Lebanon on October 23, 1983. (p. 114)
—Henry David Thoreau: American Naturalist, Writer, & Transcendentalist. (p. 767)
—International Atomic Energy Agency. (p. 880)
—Lincoln's Gettysburg Address: A Primary Source Investigation. (p. 1019)
—Oregon Trail. (p. 1303)
—Sir Walter Raleigh: Explorer for the Court of Queen Elizabeth. (p. 1580)
—Trial of John T. Scopes: A Primary Source Account. (p. 1785)
Olson, Tod. How to Get Rich in the California Gold Rush: An Adventurer's Guide to the Fabulous Riches Discovered In 1848. Allred, Scott, illus. (p. 820)
—How to Get Rich on a Texas Cattle Drive: In Which I Tell the Honest Truth about Rampaging Rustlers, Stampeding Steers & Other Fateful Hazards on the Wild Chisolm Trail. Allred, Scott & Proch, Gregory, illus. (p. 820)
—How to Get Rich on the Oregon Trail. Allred, Scott & Proch, Gregory, illus. (p. 820)
—How to Get Rich on the Oregon Trail. Proch, Gregory & Allred, Scott, illus. (p. 820)
—Leopold II: Butcher of the Congo. (p. 993)
Olson, Tod, jt. auth. see Hess, Debra.
Olson, Tom, illus. see Cruikshank, Fran.
Olsson, Elizabeth. Tiny Pink House. (p. 1756)
Olsson, Jan. Trolling. (p. 1788)
Olsson, Liselott Mariett, jt. auth. see Borgnon, Liselotte.
Olswanger, Anna. Greenhorn. Nerlove, Miriam, illus. (p. 723)
—Shlemiel Crooks. Goodman Koz, Paula, illus. (p. 1567)
—Shlemiel Crooks. Koz, Paula Goodman, illus. (p. 1568)
Olszewski, Raymond VanCe. Chucky the Car: A Children's Story & Coloring Book. (p. 318)
Oltchick, Peter. Clean Clara. Jasuna, Aija, illus. (p. 330)
Olten, Manuela, illus. see James, J. Alison, tr.
Olten, Manuela, illus. see Raab, Brigitte.
OLTEN, MANUELA, jt. auth. see Olten, Manuela.
Olten, Manuela & OLTEN, MANUELA. Ninos Valientes. (p. 1257)
Oluogbagbemi, Funke. Touch & Count. (p. 1772)
Oluonye, Mary. South Africa. (p. 1616)
Oluonye, Mary N. Madagascar. (p. 1069)
—South Africa. (p. 1616)
Olvera, Jillann. Christian's Lullaby. (p. 312)
O'Mahony, John. Elton John. (p. 516)
O'Maley, Elizabeth. Bones on the Ground. (p. 209)
—By Freedom's Light. (p. 249)
O'Malley, Bryan Lee. Precious Little Life. (p. 1394)
—Scott Pilgrim Color Hardcover Volume 2: Vs. the World. (p. 1531)
—Scott Pilgrim Color Hardcover Volume 4: Scott Pilgrim Gets It Together: Scott Pilgrim Gets It Together. (p. 1531)
O'Malley Cerra, Kerry. Just a Drop of Water. (p. 937)
O'Malley, Jason, illus. see White, George.
O'Malley, John, jt. auth. see Bucki, Jo Dee.
O'Malley, Judy, ed. see Achor, Shawn & Blankson, Amy.
O'Malley, Judy, ed. see Deak, JoAnn.
O'Malley, Judy, ed. see Paratore, Coleen.
O'Malley, Judy, ed. see Ward, Helen.
O'Malley, Judy, ed. see Wilson, Land.
O'Malley, Kathleen, illus. see Smith, Stan.
O'Malley, Kathleen, illus. see Zimelman, Nathan.
O'Malley, Kathy, illus. see Gilman, Jan Levinson.
O'Malley, Kathy, illus. see Hamilton, Martha & Weiss, Mitch.
O'Malley, Kathy, illus. see Wargin, Kathy-jo.
O'Malley, Kathy, illus. see Young, Judy.
O'Malley, Kevin. Animal Crackers Fly the Coop. O'Malley, Kevin, illus. (p. 77)
—Backpack Stories. O'Malley, Kevin, illus. (p. 130)
—Bruno, You're Late for School! (p. 232)
—Captain Raptor & the Moon Mystery. O'Brien, Patrick, illus. (p. 264)
—Captain Raptor & the Space Pirates. O'Brien, Patrick, illus. (p. 264)
—Gimme Cracked Corn & I Will Share. O'Malley, Kevin, illus. (p. 676)
—Great Race. (p. 718)
—Herbert Fieldmouse, Secret Agent. (p. 769)
—Lucky Leaf. O'Malley, Kevin, illus. (p. 1062)
—Mount Olympus Basketball. (p. 1180)
—Mount Olympus Basketball. O'Malley, Kevin, illus. (p. 1180)
—Once upon a Cool Motorcycle Dude. O'Malley, Kevin et al, illus. (p. 1292)
—Once upon a Royal Superbaby. O'Malley, Kevin et al, illus. (p. 1293)
—Straight to the Pole. (p. 1664)
O'Malley, Kevin, illus. see Bragg, Georgia.
O'Malley, Kevin, illus. see Branley, Franklyn M.
O'Malley, Kevin, illus. see Brennan-Nelson, Denise.
O'Malley, Kevin, illus. see Finchler, Judy.
O'Malley, Kevin, illus. see Javernick, Ellen.
O'Malley, Kevin, illus. see Ketteman, Helen.
O'Malley, Kevin, illus. see Pearson, Susan.
O'Malley, Kevin, illus. see Snell, Gordon.
O'Malley, Kevin, jt. auth. see Bragg, Georgia.
O'Malley, Kevin, jt. auth. see Finchler, Judy.
O'Malley, Mary. Gift of Our Compulsions: A Revolutionary Approach to Self-Acceptance & Healing. (p. 675)
O'Malley, Michael. Big Bad Word Monster. (p. 178)
—Fairy Godmother Who Lost Her Touch (hardback) (p. 563)
—Most Beautiful Kite. (p. 1177)
—Raccoon Family That Lived in the Tree, Beside the Garden, in the Backyard. (p. 1430)
O'Malley, Michael, jt. auth. see Baker, William F.
O'Malley, Tom. Top Trumps Marvel Heroes. (p. 1769)
Omar, Abdul. Dictionary of the Holy Quran: Arabic - English. (p. 436)
Omar, Abdul Mannan. Dictionary of the Holy Quran: Arabic - English. (p. 436)
O'Mara, Blanche. Year with Carmen. (p. 1969)
O'Mara Books, Michael & Allan, Stewart. 5 Seconds of Summer: Test Your Super-Fan Status. (p. 1992)
Omara, Charlotte. My Scary First Day of School. (p. 1218)
O'Mara, Genevieve. Lunar Cycle: Phases of the Moon. (p. 1065)
O'Mara, Jack. How Railroads Shaped America. (p. 812)
O'Mara, Jean Claude. Raccoons in the Dark. (p. 1430)
O'Mara, Kennon. Camouflage: Survival in the Wild. (p. 257)
—Hunting with Hyenas (p. 829)
O'Mara, Mary. Monsoon! An Extreme Weather Season. (p. 1166)
—Monsoon! an Extreme Weather Season. (p. 1166)
—Visit Mount Rushmore. (p. 1845)
O'Mara, Robert J. Friends Are Special (p. 638)
Omari Jr. Jungle Save. (p. 935)
Omartian, Stormie. I Talk to God about How I Feel: Learning to Pray, Knowing He Cares. Warren, Shari, illus. (p. 846)
—Little Prayers for Little Kids. Warren, Shari, illus. (p. 1033)
—Power of a Praying Kid. (p. 1389)
—Prayer That Makes God Smile. Warren, Shari, illus. (p. 1393)
—What Happens When I Talk to God? The Power of Prayer for Boys & Girls. Warren, Shari, illus. (p. 1886)
Omary, Rachel. Animals in Dari. (p. 83)
—Animals in Farsi. (p. 83)
—Animals in Pashto. (p. 83)
—Shapes & Colors in Dari. (p. 1560)
—Shapes & Colors in Farsi. (p. 1560)
—Shapes & Colors in Pashto. (p. 1560)
Omawumi Kola-Lawal, Constance. We Learn about Preserving the Environment. (p. 1867)
—We Learn about Road Safety. (p. 1867)
Omaya, Tam. Passion & Pain. (p. 1326)
O'Meara, David. Modular Maths for Edexcel Mechanics 2 (p. 1159)
O'Meara, Donna. Into the Volcano: A Volcano Researcher at Work. O'Meara, Stephen, photos by. (p. 881)
O'Meara, Gerald B. Papa's Message. (p. 1322)
O'Meara, Sandra F. Charli's First Christmas. (p. 293)
O'Meara, Stephen, photos by see O'Meara, Donna.
O'Meara, Stephen James. Are You Afraid Yet? The Science Behind Scary Stuff. Kaposy, Jeremy, illus. (p. 97)
O'Meara, Tim, photos by see Morales, Yuyi.
O'Meara, Walter. Guns at the Forks. (p. 732)
óMeta, CéSar. Blue Dragonflies. (p. 202)
Omishi, Ray. Sorcerer Hunters: Authentic Relaunch. Vol. 2 (p. 1614)
—Sorcerer Hunters Authentic Relaunch. (p. 1614)
Omizo, Emiko, jt. auth. see Peterson, Hiromi.
Omizo, Naomi, jt. auth. see Peterson, Hiromi.
Omnigraphics, creator. Biography Today: Profiles of People of Interest to Young Readers. (p. 189)
Omololu, C. J. Dirty Little Secrets. (p. 446)
—Intuition. (p. 883)
—Third Twin. (p. 1734)
—Transcendence. (p. 1778)
Omololu, Cynthia Jaynes. When It's Six O'Clock in San Francisco: A Trip Through Time Zones. DuBurke, Randy, illus. (p. 1903)
Omoth, Tyler. Bizarre Things We've Done for Sport. (p. 194)
—Building a Motorcycle (p. 238)
—Building a Spacecraft (p. 238)
—Duck Hunting for Kids (p. 488)
—Fly Fishing for Kids (p. 609)
—Incredible Car Stunts. (p. 869)
—Six Degrees of David Ortiz: Connecting Baseball Stars. (p. 1582)
—Story of the Atlanta Hawks. (p. 1660)
—Story of the Baltimore Orioles. (p. 1660)
—Story of the Chicago Cubs. (p. 1660)
—Story of the Colorado Rockies. (p. 1660)
—Story of the Dallas Mavericks. (p. 1660)
—Story of the Denver Broncos. (p. 1660)
—Story of the Golden State Warriors. (p. 1661)
—Story of the Indianapolis Colts. (p. 1661)
—Story of the New Orleans Hornets. (p. 1661)
—Story of the Philadelphia Eagles. (p. 1662)
—Story of the San Diego Chargers. (p. 1662)
—Stunning Motorcycle Stunts. (p. 1670)
—Turkey Hunting for Kids (p. 1797)
—Ultimate Collection of Pro Basketball Records. (p. 1809)
—Who's Who of Pro Basketball: A Guide to the Game's Greatest Players. (p. 1921)
Omoth, Tyler, jt. auth. see Hammelef, Danielle S.
Omoth, Tyler & Bihrle, Craig. Ice Fishing for Kids (p. 850)
Omoth, Tyler Dean. Duck Hunting for Kids (p. 488)
—Ultimate Collection of Pro Basketball Records (p. 1809)
Omoth, Tyler, et al. Six Degrees of Sports. (p. 1582)
Omoto, Gail. Kai the 'Opihi Gets the Point. Omoto, Garrett, illus. (p. 941)
Omoto, Garrett. Ke Kino - The Body. (p. 946)
—Na Waihooluu. (p. 1227)
—Pili the 'Iwa Bird Shares the Letter P: Book #2 in the Gift of Reading Series. (p. 1359)
—Tutu Books Preschool Library (p. 1799)
—'Umi Keiki Li'i Li'i - Ten Little Children. (p. 1810)
Omoto, Garrett, illus. see Hu, Lorna.
Omoto, Garrett, illus. see Omoto, Gail.
O'Muhr, G. Causes & Effects of the American Civil War. (p. 282)
Ona, Mel A. Changing Bodies, Transforming Lives: Your Ultimate Guide to FAD-FREE Fat Loss. (p. 290)
Onajin, Alaba. Adventures of Atioro: the Rainmaker of Aramada (Colour Edition) (p. 16)
O'Nan, Denny. My Local Government. (p. 1213)
O'Nan, Gerald D. Adventures of Andy Ant: Lawn Mower on the Loose. McGary, Norman, illus. (p. 16)
O'Nan, Gerald D., jt. auth. see O'Nan, Lawrence W.
O'Nan, Lawrence W. & O'Nan, Gerald D. Adventures of Andy Ant: The Swimming Hole Disaster. McGary, Norman, illus. (p. 16)
Ondaatje, Griffin. Camel in the Sun Wolfsgruber, Linda, illus. (p. 256)
Ondrey, James H. Physician-Assisted Suicide. (p. 1353)
Ondrias, Rachel. Cindy Lou Ella: A Country Fairy Tale. Scarborough, Casey, illus. (p. 321)
—Kolby, the Skating Bear: A Kalamazoo Christmas. Scarborough, Casey, illus. (p. 966)
—Kolby, the Skating Bear from Kalamazoo! (p. 966)
—There's a Pig in My Fridge. Scarborough, Casey, illus. (p. 1731)
One Direction. Dare to Dream: Life As One Direction. (p. 406)
—One Direction: Behind the Scenes. (p. 1294)
—One Direction: A Year with One Direction. (p. 1294)
—One Direction: Where We Are - Our Band, Our Story - 100% Official. (p. 1294)
—One Direction - A Year with Us. (p. 1294)
—One Direction - Dare to Dream: Life as One Direction. (p. 1294)
—One Direction: Meet One Direction. (p. 1294)
—One Direction: Where We Are: Our Band, Our Story: 100% Official. (p. 1294)
—Who We Are: One Direction: Our Autobiography. (p. 1919)
One Direction Staff. One Direction: Dare to Dream; Life as One Direction. (p. 1294)
O'Neal, Bill. Great Gunfighters of the Wild West: Twenty Courageous Westerners Who Struggled with Right & Wrong, Good & Evil, Law & Order. (p. 716)
O'Neal, Claire. Andrew Luck. (p. 72)
—Artemis. (p. 103)
—Care for a Pet Horse. (p. 266)
—Chicago. (p. 299)
—Cole Hamels. (p. 339)
—Extreme Snowboarding with Lindsey Jacobelis. (p. 557)
—How to Use Wind Power to Light & Heat Your Home. (p. 822)
—Influenza Pandemic of 1918. (p. 873)
—Mississippi River. (p. 1154)
—Mount Olympus. (p. 1180)
—Project Guide to Earthquakes. (p. 1410)
—Project Guide to Matter. (p. 1410)
—Project Guide to Rocks & Minerals. (p. 1410)
—Project Guide to Volcanoes. (p. 1410)
—Projects in Genetics. (p. 1411)
—T. I. (p. 1693)
—Teen Guide to Buying Stocks. (p. 1713)
—Threat to the Bengal Tiger. (p. 1741)
—Volunteering in School: A Guide to Giving Back. (p. 1850)
—Washington, D. C. (p. 1860)
—Ways to Help in Your Community: A Guide to Giving Back. (p. 1865)
—We Visit Cambodia. (p. 1868)
—We Visit Iraq. (p. 1868)
—We Visit Libya. (p. 1868)
—We Visit Yemen. (p. 1868)
—What's So Great about Barack Obama. (p. 1899)
O'Neal, Debbie Trafton. Advent Wreath: A Light in the Darkness. (p. 14)
—J Is for Jesus: An Easter Alphabet & Activity Book. Bryan-Hunt, Jan, illus. (p. 901)
O'Neal, Gena L. I'mpossible. (p. 862)
O'Neal, Jayce. Crazy Circus World. (p. 377)
O'Neal, John H., jt. auth. see McElwain, Sarah.
O'neal, Katherine Pebley. Fume in the Tomb. Collins, Daryl, illus. (p. 647)
O'Neal, Kerry. I Wish I Could Fly/I Can Fly! The Lonely Caterpillar BOOK I & the Lonely Butterfly BOOK II. O'Neal, Kerry, illus. (p. 848)
O'Neal, Michael J. America in The 1920s. (p. 59)
O'Neal, Michael J., et al. Crusades Almanac. (p. 386)
O'neal, Mike. Beaver Book of Family Finances. (p. 154)
O'Neal, Rajah. U Draw Faces. (p. 1805)
O'Neal, Shereka N. Ask for Help! (p. 106)
O'Neal, Ted. When Bad Things Happen: A Guide to Help Kids Cope. Alley, R. W., illus. (p. 1901)
O'Neal-Thorpe, Rochelle. Adventures of Captain Remarkable: Companion chapter book to Captain Remarkable. Tamang, Mayan, illus. (p. 17)
—Doll at the Christmas Bazaar: Christmas Miracles. Penn, Karen V., illus. (p. 463)
—Gabe & the Bike: Riding the Minuteman Trail. O'Neal-Thorpe, Rochelle, illus. (p. 652)
—Gabe & the Park & his Big Toy Box: The Adventures of Gabe Series. O'Neal-Thorpe, Rochelle, illus. (p. 652)
O'Neil, Daryl. And to the Unmarried I Say: Things to Consider Before Saying I Do. (p. 71)
O'Neil, Dave. Lies Your Parents Tell You. Morris, Kiran, illus. (p. 1007)
O'Neil, Dennis, ed. see Starlin, Jim, et al.
O'Neil, Dennis, ed. see Starlin, Jim.
O'Neil, Dennis, jt. auth. see Fox, Gardner.
O'Neil, Denny & Fleisher, Michael. Spider-Man Romita, John, Jr. et al, illus. (p. 1626)
O'Neil, Kevin. How to Recall Your Past & Future Lives. (p. 821)
O'Neil, Patrick. Washington Farm-Toons Coloring & Activity Book. Pastars, Chris, illus. (p. 1860)
O'Neil, Paula. Valley of the Moon. (p. 1831)
O'Neil, Sharron, illus. see Rosa-Mendoza, Gladys.
O'Neil, Shirley, jt. auth. see Derrick, Patricia.
O'Neil, W. J. Adventures of Ernie I Saw: I Saw It in the Jungle / I Saw It Underwater. (p. 18)
O'Neil-Andrews, Milly. Bandolines & Bubbles. (p. 136)
O'Neill, Alexis. Estela en el Mercado de Pulgas. de la Vega, Eida, tr. from ENG. (p. 538)
O'Neill, Alexis & Sanchez, Enrique O. Estela's Swap (p. 538)
O'Neill, Amanda. I Wonder Why Snakes Shed Their Skin. (p. 849)
—I Wonder Why Spiders Spin Webs: And Other Questions about Creepy Crawlies. (p. 849)
O'Neill, Catharine. Annie & Simon: The Sneeze & Other Stories. O'Neill, Catharine, illus. (p. 86)
—Annie & Simon. O'Neill, Catharine, illus. (p. 86)
O'Neill, Catharine, illus. see O'Connor, Edwin.
O'Neill, Catharine, illus. see Sathre, Vivian.
O'Neill, Dave, illus. see Shankman, Ed.
O'Neill, David & Sullivan, Janet O'Neill. Collecting Rose O'Neill's Kewpies (p. 339)
O'Neill, Dennis. Justice League of America Archives (p. 940)
O'Neill, Elizabeth. Alfred Visits Arizona. (p. 37)
—Alfred Visits California. (p. 37)
—Alfred Visits Colorado. (p. 37)
—Alfred Visits Connecticut. (p. 37)
—Alfred Visits Georgia. (p. 37)
—Alfred Visits Hawaii. (p. 37)
—Alfred Visits Idaho. (p. 37)
—Alfred Visits Louisiana. (p. 37)
—Alfred Visits Maine. (p. 37)
Oneill, Elizabeth. Alfred Visits Maryland. (p. 37)
O'Neill, Elizabeth. Alfred Visits Massachusetts. (p. 37)
—Alfred Visits Michigan. (p. 37)
—Alfred Visits Minnesota. (p. 37)
—Alfred Visits Missouri. (p. 37)
—Alfred Visits Montana. (p. 37)
—Alfred Visits Nevada. (p. 37)
—Alfred Visits New Jersey. (p. 37)
—Alfred Visits New Mexico. (p. 37)
Oneill, Elizabeth. Alfred Visits Ohio. (p. 37)
—Alfred Visits Oregon. (p. 37)
O'Neill, Elizabeth. Alfred Visits Rhode Island. (p. 37)
—Alfred Visits South Carolina. (p. 37)
—Alfred Visits Tennessee. (p. 37)
—Alfred Visits Texas. (p. 37)
—Alfred Visits Utah. (p. 37)
Oneill, Elizabeth. Alfred Visits Vermont. (p. 37)
O'Neill, Elizabeth. Alfred Visits Virginia. (p. 37)
—Alfred Visits Washington State. (p. 37)
Oneill, Elizabeth. Alfred Visits West Virginia. (p. 37)
O'Neill, Elizabeth. Alfred Visits Wisconsin. (p. 37)
Oneill, Elizabeth. Alfred Visits Wyoming. (p. 37)
O'Neill, Elizabeth. World's Story. (p. 1961)
O'Neill, Elizabeth, jt. auth. see McPherson, Missie.
O'Neill, Elizabeth, jt. auth. see Mcpherson, Missie.
O'Neill, Elizabeth & McPherson, Missie. Alfred Visits Florida. (p. 37)
—Alfred Visits New York City. (p. 37)
O'Neill, Eugene. Emperor Jones. (p. 520)
O'Neill, Gemma. Monty's Magnificent Mane. O'Neill, Gemma, illus. (p. 1170)
—Oh Dear, Geoffrey! O'Neill, Gemma, illus. (p. 1280)
O'Neill Grace, Catherine. Forces of Nature: The Awesome Power of Volcanoes, Earthquakes, & Tornadoes. (p. 617)
O'Neill, Ian. Jimmy First & Destiny's Watch. (p. 918)
O'Neill, Jacquie. Figure Skating. (p. 586)
O'Neill, Joan. Daisy Chain Dream. (p. 400)
—Dream Chaser. (p. 483)
—Rainbow's End. (p. 1436)
O'Neill, Joe. Legends of the Rif Addicott, Sara & Walton, Bedelia C., eds. (p. 990)
O'Neill, John R. Mahatma Gandhi, Nelson Mandela. (p. 1076)
O'Neill, Joseph. Movie Director. (p. 1183)
O'Neill, Joseph R. Bolshevik Revolution. (p. 208)
—Great Wall of China. (p. 719)
—Irish Potato Famine. (p. 888)
O'Neill, Josh, et al, eds. Little Nemo's Big Dreams: A Toon Graphic. (p. 1032)
O'Neill, Joy. Why Do We Have to Move? (p. 1924)
O'Neill, Kaney. Dream & Reach. (p. 483)
O'Neill, Karl. Most Beautiful Letter in the World. Byrne, Emma, illus. (p. 1177)
O'Neill, Katrina. Key of the Mayan Kingdom. (p. 950)
—Protecting the Sunken City. (p. 1412)
—Red Rain of Easter Island. (p. 1454)
O'Neill, Katrina & Thompson, Lisa. Hunting down the Grail. (p. 829)
—Missing among the Pyramids. (p. 1152)
O'Neill, Mary. Pick Your Brains about Ireland. Williams, Caspar, illus. (p. 1354)
O'Neill, Mary, et al. Primary Dictionary. (p. 1399)
—Primary Thesaurus. (p. 1400)
O'Neill, Michael Patrick. Fishy Friends: A Journey Through the Coral Kingdom. O'Neill, Michael Patrick, photos by. (p. 599)
—Let's Explore Coral Reefs. O'Neill, Michael Patrick, photos by. (p. 996)
—Let's Explore Sea Turtles. O'Neill, Michael Patrick, photos by. (p. 996)
—Let's Explore Sharks. O'Neill, Michael Patrick, photos by. (p. 996)
—Wild Waters: Photo Journal. (p. 1930)
O'Neill, Michael Patrick, photos by. Ocean Magic. (p. 1276)
—Shark Encounters. (p. 1562)
O'Neill, Philomena, illus. see Kroll, Virginia.
O'Neill, Philomena, illus. see Morgan, Cindy.
O'Neill, Philomena, illus. see Morrisette, Sharon.
O'Neill, Philomena, illus. see Stolberg, Tina.
O'Neill, Rachael. Baby! (p. 124)
—Do You Want a Hug, Honey Bunny? O'Neill, Rachael, illus. (p. 458)
—My First Library: With Nine Colorful Books. (p. 1207)
O'Neill, Rachael, illus. see Davies, Gill.
O'Neill, Rachael, illus. see Repchuk, Caroline.
O'Neill, Rachael, illus. see Wallace, Karen.
O'Neill, Robert, ed. see Engle, Stephen Douglas.
O'Neill, Robert John. World War II: Essential Histories (p. 1959)
O'Neill, Robert John, jt. auth. see Collier, Paul H.
O'Neill, Robert John, jt. auth. see Havers, R. P. W.
O'Neill, Robert John, jt. auth. see Horner, D. M.
O'Neill, Robert John, jt. auth. see Jukes, Geoffrey.
O'Neill, Robert John, jt. auth. see Marston, Daniel.

O'Neill, Robert John & Gallagher, Gary W. Civil War: Bull Run & Other Eastern Battles, 1861-May 1863. (p. 325)
O'Neill, Robert John & Glatthaar, Joseph T. Civil War: Sherman's Capture of Atlanta & Other Western Battles, 1863-1865. (p. 325)
O'Neill, Robert John, et al. World War II: Northwest Europe, 1944-1945. (p. 1959)
O'Neill, Sean, illus. see Bailer, Darice.
O'Neill, Sean, illus. see Yomtov, Nel, et al.
O'Neill, Sean, illus. see Yomtov, Nel.
O'Neill, Sean, illus. see Yomtov, Nelson.
O'Neill, Susan, jt. auth. see Cullen, Murray.
O'Neill, Terence & Williams, Josh. 3D Printing. (p. 1992)
—Arduino. (p. 96)
O'Neill, Teresa. Dear Jesus. (p. 419)
O'Neill, Terry, ed. UFOs. (p. 1807)
O'Neill, Todd, illus. see Cohen, Mary.
O'Neill, Tom. Old Friends. (p. 1283)
O'Neill, Tony, jt. auth. see Currie, Cherie.
O'Neill-McGrath, Michael. Jesus A to Z. O'Neill-McGrath, Michael, illus. (p. 914)
Oneka, Angelo O. Mary & Jackie Discovered Jupiter. (p. 1100)
Oneones. Happy Birthday Coco. Oneones, illus. (p. 744)
Oneones (Firm) Staff, contrib. by. Happy Birthday Coco. (p. 744)
Oness, Elizabeth. Twelve Rivers of the Body. (p. 1800)
Oneto, Maria Teresa. Liliana, la Iguan. (p. 1017)
Onetti, Juan Carlos. Los Adioses. (p. 1053)
Oney, Yannick. Abe Lincoln: President for the People. (p. 4)
—First American Colonies. (p. 593)
Ong, Alvin & Ong, Cheri. Being Different Is a Good Thing. Ong, Cheri, illus. (p. 161)
Ong, Cheri. Tomato Potato Strips Issue #1. (p. 1764)
Ong, Cheri, jt. auth. see Ong, Alvin.
Ong, Cristina, illus. see Dorfman, Craig.
Ong, Cristina, illus. see Parker, David.
Ong, Gelyn. Forest Fable. (p. 618)
Ong, Jacqueline, jt. auth. see Sheehan, Patricia.
Ong, Wilson, illus. see James, Helen Foster & Loh, Virginia Shin-Mui.
Ong, Wilson, illus. see Rodriguez, Sonia & Browning, Kurt.
Ong, Wilson, illus. see Steigemeyer, Julie.
Onghai, Mike, jt. auth. see Ching, Jerry Yu.
Ongman, Gudrun. Sleep Pony Dreams. (p. 1588)
Onieva Morales, Juan Luis. Como Dominar la Ortografia: Ortografia Moderna. (p. 350)
Oniki, Yuji, tr. see Yamada, Masaki.
Onish, Liane. Brain Quest: A Whole Year of Curriculum-Based Exercises & Activities in One Fun Book! Swann, Jill, ed. (p. 221)
—Brain Quest Workbook, Pre-K: A Whole Year of Curriculum-Based Exercises & Activities in One Fun Book! Fung, Jane, ed. (p. 222)
—Solve-the-Riddle Math Practice - Fractions & Decimals: 50+ Reproducible Activity Sheets That Help Students Master Fraction & Decimal Skills. (p. 1608)
Onish, Liane B. Mr. Potato Head: the Busy Day. Durk, Jim, illus. (p. 1186)
—Solve-the-Riddle Math Practice: 50+ Reproducible Activity Sheets That Help Students Master Key Math Skills - And Solve Rib - Tickling Riddles. (p. 1608)
Onishi, Mika, tr. see Clamp Staff.
Onishi, Satoru. Quien Se Esconde? Onishi, Satoru, illus. (p. 1427)
Onley, Sandra. Halley the Sheepdog. (p. 737)
Ono, Fuyumi. Sea of Shadow. (p. 1535)
—Twelve Kingdoms (p. 1800)
Ono, Mari & Ono, Roshin. Origami for Children (p. 1304)
—Origami for Children: 35 Easy-to-Follow Step-by-Step Projects. (p. 1304)
Ono, Roshin, jt. auth. see Ono, Mari.
Ono, Toshihiro, illus. see Morioka, Hiroyuki.
Onoda, Yuta, illus. see Lewis, Gill.
Onque, Sulaiman. It's in the Book: Good Ol' Friends (p. 897)
Onsgard, Bethany. Asia. (p. 106)
—Life During the California Gold Rush. (p. 1010)
—Life on the Frontier. (p. 1012)
Ontario, Canada, Elementary Students from, Elementary Students from. Trouble Triplets. (p. 1790)
Ontario Science Centre Staff. Ciencia Divertida. (p. 319)
—Ciencia y Tú: Selección de Los Mejores Experimentos Del Ontario Science Center. (p. 319)
Onuoha-Ezemma, Glory. Don't Make Fun of My Name: My Name Is Special to My Parents & Me. (p. 468)
Onur, Rina, jt. auth. see Kunze, Lauren.
Onus, Katie. Island of the Wolves. (p. 892)
Onwusilikam, Ify Chinedum. Drama Queen. (p. 480)
Onyefulu, Ifeoma. African Christmas. (p. 27)
—de Africa. (p. 416)
—Deron Goes to Nursery School. Onyefulu, Ifeoma, photos by. (p. 427)
—Girl Who Married a Ghost: And Other Tales from Nigeria. (p. 679)
—Grandma Comes to Stay. Onyefulu, Ifeoma, photos by. (p. 708)
—Home. (p. 791)
—Look at This! - Play. (p. 1049)
—My Grandfather Is a Magician: Work & Wisdom in an African Village. (p. 1210)
—New Shoes for Helen. (p. 1247)
—Triangle for Adaora: An African Book of Shapes. (p. 1785)
—Welcome Dede! An African Naming Ceremony. (p. 1873)
—Your Name Is Dede: An African Baby's Naming Ceremony. (p. 1981)
Onyefulu, Ifeoma & Quarto Generic Staff. Chidi Only Likes Blue: An African Book of Colours. (p. 301)
—Clothes. (p. 334)
—Girl Who Married a Ghost: And Other Tales from Nigeria. (p. 679)
—Here Comes Our Bride! An African Wedding Story. (p. 770)
—Ife's First Haircut. (p. 855)
—Look at This! - Food. (p. 1049)
—Omer's Favorite Place. (p. 1288)
—Vicky Goes to the Doctor. (p. 1840)
Onyett, Nicola & Williams, Tennessee. Streetcar Named Desire. (p. 1667)
Onyumbe, Jacob. Kevin the Wild Boy: The Diaries of a Survivor (p. 950)
Oobayashi, Kaoru, illus. see Imamura, Keiko & Imamura, Keiko.
Oobayashi, Kaoru, illus. see Imamura, Keiko.
Oosthuizen, Sarah & Groenewald, Catherine. Nosipho Comes to Stay. (p. 1266)
Ooten, Tara Broeckel. Female Force: Ruth Handler, Creator of Barbie. (p. 581)
—Justin Bieber - Fame. (p. 940)
Ooten, Tara Broeckel & Cooke, C. W. Fame: Justin Bieber. (p. 567)
—Fame: The Cast of Glee. (p. 567)
Opal, Paola. Bitsy. (p. 194)
—Dotty. (p. 472)
—Emma. (p. 519)
—Ollie. (p. 1287)
—Perry. (p. 1344)
—Pippy. (p. 1362)
—Rokko. (p. 1485)
—Saffy. (p. 1502)
—Saffy & Ollie. (p. 1502)
—Saffy Looks for Rain. (p. 1502)
—Totty. (p. 1772)
Opal, Paola, illus. see Winters, Kari-Lynn & Van Turennout, Paola.
Opal, Paola, jt. auth. see O'Leary, Sara.
Opalinska, Wanda. Animal Farm (p. 77)
Oparin, Alexandr Ivanovich. Origen de la Vida. (p. 1304)
Opatz, Shane, illus. see Holtz, Monica Stauber.
Opatz, Shane, photos by see Holtz, Monica Stauber.
Opdyke, Irene Gut. In My Hands: Memories of a Holocaust Rescuer. (p. 864)
Opdyke, Irene Gut & Armstrong, Jennifer. In My Hands: Memories of a Holocaust Rescuer. (p. 864)
Open Churches Trust Staff, jt. auth. see Frewins, Clive.
Open Court Staff. Breaking Code Cursive Alphabet. (p. 225)
—Breaking Code Manuscript Alphabet. (p. 225)
—Breaking Code Sentence Strips. (p. 225)
—Fire Fire. (p. 590)
—Intermediate Think Storybook: Level 4. (p. 880)
—Real Math: Level 8. (p. 1448)
—We Feed Deer. (p. 1867)
Opheim, Sandra. Whose Hat Is That? Horton, Lori, illus. (p. 1921)
Opie, Brenda. Masterminds Riddlemath for Elementary: Whole Numbers, Addition, Subtraction, Multiplication, & Division. McAvinn, Douglas, illus. (p. 1103)
Opie, Brenda & McAvinn, Douglas. Masterminds Riddlemath for Elementary: Measurement, Fractions, Probability, & Logical Thinking. (p. 1103)
Opie, David. Monkey & the Engineer. (p. 1165)
Opie, David, illus. see Levy, Debbie & Panza, Rosana.
Opie, David, illus. see Smith, Molly.
Opie, Ian, ed. My Very First Mother Goose. Wells, Rosemary, illus. (p. 1221)
Opie, Iona. Mother Goose's Little Treasures. Wells, Rosemary, illus. (p. 1178)
—Very Best Mother Goose Book Tower. Wells, Rosemary, illus. (p. 1837)
Opie, Iona & Opie, Peter. I Saw Esau: The Schoolchild's Pocket Book. (p. 845)
Opie, Iona, ed. Snuggle up with Mother Goose. Wells, Rosemary, illus. (p. 1601)
Opie, Peter, jt. auth. see Opie, Iona.
Opini, Bathseba & Lee, Richard B. Africans Thought of It: Amazing Innovations. (p. 28)
Opio, Leoncio. Adventures of Mr. Nimbus & the School House Bullies. (p. 21)
Opitz, Todd. Football & the Fly. (p. 615)
Opler, Paul. Butterflies of North America: An Activity & Coloring Book. (p. 247)
Oplinger, Jon & Cooke, Elizabeth. Wicked Small People of Whiskey Bridge. (p. 1927)
O'Porter, Dawn. Goose. (p. 702)
—Paper Airplanes. (p. 1322)
Oppatt, Karen, jt. auth. see Gabolinscy, Jack.
Oppedisano, Robert & McCoy, Lisa. Internet. (p. 880)
Oppel, Kenneth. Airborn. (p. 31)
—Boundless. Tierney, Jim, illus. (p. 216)
—Darkwing. Thompson, Keith, illus. (p. 409)
—Firewing. (p. 592)
—Half Brother. (p. 736)
—King's Taster. Johnson, Steve & Fancher, Lou, illus. (p. 961)
—Peg & the Whale. (p. 1335)
—Silverwing. (p. 1577)
—Skybreaker. (p. 1587)
—Starclimber. (p. 1642)
—Such Wicked Intent. (p. 1672)
—Sunwing. (p. 1679)
—This Dark Endeavor: The Apprenticeship of Victor Frankenstein. (p. 1735)
Oppen, Mark van & Marvano. Berlin: The Seven Dwarves. (p. 167)
Oppenheim, Joanne F. Dear Miss Breed: True Stories of the Japanese American Incarceration During World War II & a Librarian Who Made a Difference. (p. 419)
—Milagro de la Primera Flora de Nochebuena: Un Cuento Mexicano Sobre la Navidad. Negrin, Fabian, illus. (p. 1142)
—Miracle of the First Poinsettia. Negrin, Fabian, illus. (p. 1148)
—Prince's Bedtime. Latimer, Miriam, illus. (p. 1401)
Oppenheim, Joanne F. & Barefoot Books. Desayuno Del Principe. Latimer, Miriam, illus. (p. 428)
Oppenheim, Joanne F. & Barefoot Books Staff. Prince's Breakfast. Latimer, Miriam, illus. (p. 1401)
—Principe No Duerme. Latimer, Miriam, illus. (p. 1406)
Oppenheim, Joanne F. & Latimer, Miriam. Prince's Bedtime. Latimer, Miriam, illus. (p. 1401)
Oppenheim, Joanne F. & Oppenheim, Stephanie. Leer y Jugar! con Bebés y Niños Pequeños. Auclair, Joan, illus. (p. 987)
—Read It! Play It! Auclair, Joan, illus. (p. 1443)
—Read It! Play It! with Babies & Toddlers. (p. 1443)
Oppenheim, Shulamith. I Blis: An Islamic Tale. Young, Ed, illus. (p. 834)
—I Love You, Bunny Rabbit. Moore, Cyd, illus. (p. 843)
—Rescuing Einstein's Compass. Juhasz, George, illus. (p. 1462)
—Where Do I End & You Begin? Felix, Monique, illus. (p. 1907)
Oppenheim, Stephanie, jt. auth. see Oppenheim, Joanne F.
Oppenheimer, Nancy, illus. see Rouss, Sylvia A.
Oppenlander, Annette. Escape from the Past: The Duke's Wrath. (p. 535)
Oppenlander, Meredith. How to Make Snack Mix: Math B. Harston, Jerry, illus. (p. 820)
—Howard the Hippo & the Great Mountain Adventure. Chacon, Pam & Chacon, Rick, illus. (p. 823)
—Howard the Hippo, Meets a New Friend. (p. 823)
—In the Hen House. Gedeon, Gloria, illus. (p. 866)
Oppong, Esther D., jt. auth. see Oppong, Joseph R.
Oppong, Joseph R. Rwanda. (p. 1499)
—Sudan. (p. 1672)
Oppong, Joseph R. & Oppong, Esther D. Kenya. (p. 949)
Oppong, Joseph R. & Woodruff, Tania. Democratic Republic of the Congo. (p. 426)
Oprea, Tiberiu. Romania. (p. 1486)
Oprisko, Kris. Clive Barker - The Thief of Always. Ryall, Chris & Garner, Alex, eds. (p. 333)
Oprisko, Kris, jt. auth. see Kurtz, Rob.
Opsahl, Gail Kohler, illus. see Van Dernoot, Peter R. & van Dernoot, Peter R.
Opseth, Katie, illus. see Olson, Kay Melchisedech & Boonyadhistarn, Thiranut.
Optic, Oliver, pseud. Fighting for the Right. (p. 585)
—Fighting for the Right. Shute, A. B. & Fitterling, Michael A., illus. (p. 585)
—Haste & Waste; or, the Young Pilot of Lake Champlain. (p. 752)
—Haste & Waste or the Young Pilot of Lake Champlain A Story for Young People. (p. 752)
—Little by Little or the Cruise of the Fl. (p. 1025)
—Northern Lands: Or, Young America in Russia & Prussia; A Story of Travel & Adventure / by William T. Adams (Oliver Optic). (p. 1265)
—Northern Lands; or, Young America in Russia & Prussia a Story of Travel & Adventure. (p. 1265)
—Now or Never: The Adventures of Bobby Bright. (p. 1269)
—Now or Never; or, the Adventures of Bobby Bright. (p. 1269)
—Outward Bound: Or Young America Afloat. (p. 1313)
—Outward Bound. (p. 1313)
—Poor & Proud; or, the Fortunes of Katy Redburn a Story for Young Folks by Oliver Optic [Pseud]. (p. 1383)
—Soldier Boy; or, Tom Somers in the Army. (p. 1607)
—Stand by the Union. (p. 1639)
—Sunny Shores; or, Young America in Italy & Austria a Story of Travel & Adventure by William T Adams. (p. 1677)
—Taken by the Enemy. (p. 1697)
—[the Boat Club; or, the Bunkers of Rippleton a Tale for Boys by Oliver Optic, Pseud. (p. 1728)
—Victorious Union: The Blue & the Gray-Afloat Book 6. (p. 1840)
—Victorious Union. Burgess, H. & Fitterling, Michael A., illus. (p. 1840)
—Watch & Wait; or, the Young Fugitives a Story for Young People by Oliver Optic [Pseud]. (p. 1860)
—Within the Enemy's Lines: SERIES: the Blue & the Gray—Afloat. (p. 1942)
—Within the Enemy's Lines. (p. 1942)
Oquendo, Lisa. Abecedario. (p. 4)
—Números - Numbers. (p. 1273)
O'quinn, Louise & Bensinger, Marilyn. 25 Read & Write Mini-Books That Teach Sight Words. (p. 1996)
Oral, Osman. I Believe in Allah. (p. 834)
—I Believe in the Angels. (p. 834)
—I Believe in the Books. (p. 834)
—I Believe in the Divine Destiny & Decree. (p. 834)
—I Believe in the Hereafter. (p. 834)
—I Believe in the Prophets. (p. 834)
Oram, Hiawyn. Beetle & Bug & the Grissel Hunt. Kitamura, Satoshi, illus. (p. 158)
—Counting Leopard's Spots & other Stories. Warnes, Tim, illus. (p. 371)
—Filbert, the Good Little Fiend. Liao, Jimmy, illus. (p. 586)
—Giant Surprise: A Narnia Story. Humphries, Tudor, illus. (p. 674)
—Heffalump Grump. Gardiner, Lindsey, illus. (p. 762)
—In the Attic. Kitamura, Satoshi, illus. (p. 865)
—Little Brother & the Cough. Rees, Mary, illus. (p. 1025)
—Mr Strongmouse & the Baby. Chapman, Lynne, illus. (p. 1186)
—My Friend Fred. Reeve, Rosie, illus. (p. 1209)
—My Unwilling Witch Gets a Makeover. Warburton, Sarah, illus. (p. 1220)
—My Unwilling Witch Goes to Ballet School. Warburton, Sarah, illus. (p. 1220)
—My Unwilling Witch Sleeps Over. Warburton, Sarah, illus. (p. 1220)
—My Unwilling Witch Starts a Girl Band. Warburton, Sarah, illus. (p. 1220)
—Ned & the Joybaloo. Kitamura, Satoshi, illus. (p. 1239)
—Rubbaduck & Ruby Roo. Lucas, David, illus. (p. 1493)
—What's Naughty? Reynolds, Adrian, illus. (p. 1898)
Oramas, Jennifer. Peter's Purpose. Huseman, Ryan, illus. (p. 1347)
Oramasionwu, Angela. Sammy the Cell & the Healthy 1s: Let's Learn about Nutrition. (p. 1508)
Orange County Association Staff, jt. auth. see Field, Shelly.
Oransky Wittenstein, Vicki. For the Good of Mankind? The Shameful History of Human Medical Experimentation. (p. 616)
Orante, Ann-Jeanette P. Best Sisters for Life... (p. 171)
Orbaan, Albert, illus. see Miller, Helen Markley.
Orbach, Ruth. Acorns & Stew, Too. Orbach, Ruth, illus. (p. 9)
Orback, Craig. Paul Bunyan. (p. 1330)
Orback, Craig, illus. see Brill, Marlene Targ.
Orback, Craig, illus. see Deutsch, Stacia & Cohon, Rhody.
Orback, Craig, illus. see Dokey, Cameron.
Orback, Craig, illus. see Figley, Marthy Rhodes.
Orback, Craig, illus. see Figley, Marty Rhodes.
Orback, Craig, illus. see Hopkinson, Deborah.
Orback, Craig, illus. see Jazynka, Kitson & Tripp, Valerie.
Orback, Craig, illus. see Jazynka, Kitson.
Orback, Craig, illus. see Lehman-Wilzig, Tami.
Orback, Craig, illus. see Ludwig, Trudy.
Orback, Craig, illus. see Mortensen, Lori.
Orback, Craig, illus. see Slade, Suzanne & Picture Window Books Staff.
Orback, Craig, illus. see Thomas, Patricia.
Orback, Craig, illus. see Wadsworth, Ginger.
Orback, Craig, illus. see Waxman, Laura Hamilton.
Orback, Craig, jt. auth. see Williams, Laura E.
Orban, Paul, illus. see Anderson, Floyd.
Orbeck, R. My Beautiful Feathers. (p. 1196)
Orbeck-Nilssen, Constance. I'm Right Here. Düzakin, Akin, illus. (p. 860)
Orchard, Eric, illus. see Halsey, Jacqueline.
Orchard, Eric, illus. see Muller, Carrie & Halsey, Jacqueline.
Orchard, Eric, illus. see Wells, Zachariah, et al.
Orchid Publishing, prod. Sleeping Beauty Ballet by Aleksandra. (p. 1589)
Orcutt, Cherie. Beautiful Husky Needs a Home. Frongia, Daniela, illus. (p. 153)
Orcutt, Georgia, jt. auth. see Margolies, John.
Orczy, Emmuska. Castles in the Air. (p. 277)
—Gallant Pimpernel - Unabridged - Lord Tony's Wife, the Way of the Scarlet Pimpernel, Sir Percy Leads the Band, the Triumph of the Scarlet Pimperne. (p. 653)
—I Will Repay. (p. 848)
—League of the Scarlet Pimpernel. (p. 982)
—Nest of the Sparrowhawk. (p. 1242)
—Old Man in the Corner. (p. 1284)
—Scarlet Pimpernel. (p. 1520)
—Unto Caesar. (p. 1823)
Ord, G. W., illus. see Selous, Edmund.
Ord, Mandy. Sensitive Creatures. Ord, Mandy, illus. (p. 1551)
Ord, Michael. Weather Book. (p. 1870)
Ordal, Stina Langlo. Princess Aasta Event Kit. (p. 1402)
Ordas, Emi, illus. see Gillespie, L.
Ordas, Emi, illus. see Gillespie, Lisa Jane.
Ordaz, Francisco, illus. see Maier, Paul L.
Ordaz, Frank, illus. see Doherty, Patrick.
Ordaz, Frank, illus. see Langeland, Deirdre.
Ordaz, Frank, illus. see Warner, Michael N.
Ordiway, Clipper Zane. There's a Bear on the Porch & There's a Bear on the Hill! (p. 1730)
Ordóñez, María Antonia, illus. see Landrón, Rafael & Landrón, José Rafael.
Ordóñez, Miguel, illus. see Fallon, Jimmy.
Ordonez, Paulino. Otra Vez Ese Tal Principito! Torres, Raul Vazquez, illus. (p. 1307)
Orea, Lucia, tr. see Zak, Monica.
O'Regan, Lucy, ed. see Eckdahl, Judith & Eckdahl, Kathryn.
Oregon Center for Applied Science, creator. Bike Smart. (p. 185)
—Walk Smart: Children's Pedestrian Safety Program. (p. 1854)
Orehovec, Barbara & Alley, Marybeth. Revisiting the Writing Workshop: Management, Assessment, & Mini-Lessons. (p. 1466)
Orehovec, Barbara, et al. Revisiting the Reading Workshop: Management, Mini-Lessons, & Strategies. (p. 1466)
O'Reilly, Avril. Fairy in the Family. (p. 563)
O'Reilly, Basha. Count Pompeii - Stallion of the Steppes. (p. 370)
O'Reilly, Bill. Hitler's Last Days: The Death of the Nazi Regime & the World's Most Notorious Dictator. (p. 786)
—Kennedy's Last Days: The Assassination That Defined a Generation. (p. 948)
—Kennedy's Last Days: The Assassination That Defined a Generation. (p. 949)
—Last Days of Jesus: His Life & Times. Low, William & Cobalt Illustrations Studio Staff, illus. (p. 977)
—Últimos Días de Jesús. Uxó, Carlos, tr. from ENG. (p. 1810)
O'Reilly, Bill & Zimmerman, Dwight Jon. Lincoln's Last Days: The Shocking Assassination That Changed America Forever. (p. 1019)
—Lincoln's Last Days. (p. 1019)
O'Reilly, Elaine & Pearson Education Staff. Another World (p. 88)
O'Reilly, Gillian. Slangalicious: Where We Got That Crazy Lingo. Johnson, Krista M., illus. (p. 1587)
O'Reilly, Gillian, jt. auth. see Lee, Cora.
O'Reilly, John, illus. see Mewburn, Kyle.
O'Reilly, Sally. Henry Moore. (p. 768)
O'Reilly, Sean. Abominable Snow Kid (p. 5)
—Abominable Snow Kid. (p. 5)
—Ezra: Egyptian Exchange. (p. 559)
—Gremlin's Curse (p. 723)
—Gremlin's Curse. (p. 723)
—Hide & Shriek! (p. 777)
—Hide & Shriek! Arcana Studio Staff, illus. (p. 777)
—Homesick Witch (p. 793)
—Kade: Identity (p. 941)
—King of Halloween Castle (p. 958)
—King of Halloween Castle Arcana Studio Staff, illus. (p. 958)
—Lost in Spooky Forest (p. 1055)
—Lost in Spooky Forest Arcana Studio Staff, illus. (p. 1055)
—Mighty Mighty Monsters (p. 1140)
—Mighty Mighty Monsters. (p. 1140)
—Missing Mummy (p. 1152)
—Missing Mummy Arcana Studio Staff, illus. (p. 1152)
—Monster Beach (p. 1166)
—Monster Beach Arcana Studio Staff, illus. (p. 1166)
—Monster Crooks (p. 1167)
—Monster Crooks Arcana Studio Staff, illus. (p. 1167)
—Monster Mansion (p. 1167)
—My Missing Monster (p. 1214)
—New Monster in School Arcana Studio, Arcana, illus. (p. 1246)
—Scare Fair (p. 1519)

O

—Scare Fair Arcana Studio Staff, illus. (p. 1519)
—Science Fair Nightmare (p. 1526)
—Toy Snatcher (p. 1774)
—Toy Snatcher Arcana Studio Staff, illus. (p. 1774)
—Wolfboy's Wish (p. 1944)
—Wolfboy's Wish Arcana Studio Staff, illus. (p. 1944)
O'Reilly, Sean Patrick. Gwaii. Chastain, Grant, ed. (p. 733)
—Kade: Sun of Perdition. (p. 941)
O'Reilly, Sean Patrick, ed. see Adams, Matthew R.
O'Reilly, Sean Patrick, ed. see Blaylock, Josh.
O'Reilly, Sean Patrick, ed. see Brown, Bruce.
O'Reilly, Sean Patrick, ed. see Kinney, Scott.
O'Reilly, Sean Patrick, ed. see Kirkham, Tyler & Kirkham, Rian.
O'Reilly, Sean Patrick, ed. see MacPherson, Dwight L.
O'Reilly, Sean Patrick, ed. see Mangels, Andy, et al.
O'Reilly, Sean Patrick, ed. see Marz, Ron & Poulton, Mark.
O'Reilly, Sean Patrick, ed. see Najman, Alexander.
O'Reilly, Sean Patrick, ed. see Odjick, Jay & Tenascon, Patrick.
O'Reilly, Sean Patrick, ed. see Patterson, Michael.
O'Reilly, Sean Patrick, ed. see Pell, Jason.
O'Reilly, Sean Patrick, ed. see Raymond, Roger & Savoy, Darryl.
O'Reilly, Sean Patrick, ed. see Rodriguez, Alfredo.
O'Reilly, Sean Patrick, ed. see Sherman, M. Zachary & Martinek, Tom.
O'Reilly, Sean Patrick, ed. see Tra, Frank.
O'Reilly, Wenda. Amazing places natl Parks. (p. 55)
—American Art Ditto. (p. 59)
—Art Ditto. (p. 102)
—Go Fish for Art. (p. 686)
—Go fish wildlife Mammals. (p. 686)
—GO FISH WILDLIFE REPTILES & AMPHIBIANS. (p. 686)
—Go fish wildlife sea Creatures. (p. 686)
—Wild Cards. (p. 1929)
Orellana, Nery, illus. see Gillooly, Jessica B.
Orem, Hiawyn, jt. auth. see Lewis, C. S.
Oremland, Jason, jt. auth. see Erb, Greg.
Oren, Miriam & Schram, Peninnah. Tree in the Garden: A New Vision. Whyte, Alice, illus. (p. 1783)
Oren, Rony. Animaged Haggadah. (p. 76)
Oren, Rony, illus. see Sidon, Ephraim.
Oren, Sue. God Book: A Necessarily Incomplete Look at the Essence of God Teacher's Guide. (p. 688)
Orenstein, Denise G., jt. auth. see Orenstein, Denise Gosliner.
Orenstein, Denise Gosliner. Secret Twin. McCarthy, Dan, illus. (p. 1544)
—Unseen Companion. (p. 1822)
Orenstein, Denise Gosliner & Orenstein, Denise G. Unseen Companion. (p. 1822)
Orero, Maria Jesus. Nico y Las Estaciones. (p. 1251)
—Nico y los Colores. (p. 1251)
—Nico y Sus Cosas. (p. 1251)
—Nico y Sus Trajes. (p. 1251)
Orfeo, Christine Virginia. My First Book about Mary. Darrenkamp, Julia Mary, illus. (p. 1205)
Orfirer, Julie, ed. see Markey, Robert.
Orford, Margie. Little Red Hen. Lilje, Karen, illus. (p. 1034)
—Magic Fish. Littlewort, Lizza, illus. (p. 1072)
Orgad, Dorit. Boy from Seville. Silverston, Sondra, tr. from HEB. (p. 218)
Organ, Beryl E. Tiggy's World. (p. 1749)
Organ, Betty. Peter's Christmas Eve Adventure Martin, Shawn, illus. (p. 1347)
Organization of African Unity Staff. Best American History Essays 2006. Appleby, Joyce & Organization of American Historians Staff, eds. (p. 168)
Organization of American Historians Staff, ed. see Organization of African Unity Staff.
Orgel, Doris. Devil in Vienna. (p. 432)
—Sarah's Room. Sendak, Maurice, illus. (p. 1514)
Orgel, Doris, jt. auth. see Chotjewitz, David.
Orgel, Doris, tr. see Chotjewitz, David.
Orgill, jt. auth. see Orgill, Roxane.
Orgill, Rosanne Buhler. Mama Knows about Fences. (p. 1084)
Orgill, Roxane. Footwork: The Story of Fred & Adele Astaire. Jorisch, Stéphane, illus. (p. 615)
—Shout, Sister, Shout! Ten Girl Singers Who Shaped a Century. (p. 1570)
—Skit-Scat Raggedy Cat: Ella Fitzgerald. Qualls, Sean, illus. (p. 1586)
Orgill, Roxane & Orgill. Go-Go Baby! Salerno, Steven, tr. (p. 686)
Ori, Anthony. Snow Makes a Snowman. (p. 1599)
Oriah Mountain Dreamer Staff. Opening the Invitation: The Poem That Has Touched Lives Around the World. (p. 1300)
Orietta, Susan. Day Tyson Became a Hero. (p. 414)
Oriev, Uri & Orlev, Uri. Lidia, Reina de Palestina. (p. 1007)
Origami, jt. auth. see Maekawa, Jun.
Origami, jt. auth. see Robinson, Nick.
Origin Communications. Princess Amara & the Magic Fruit. (p. 1402)
Origlio, Peter. Charlie & Albert. (p. 292)
Orihuela, Luz, et al. Tres Cerditos. Rius, Maria, illus. (p. 1784)
Oriol, Elsa, illus. see Ofanansky, Allison.
Orion, Cody. Do You Believe? (p. 457)
O'Riordan, Aileen & Triggs, Pat. Following in Darwin's Footsteps. (p. 612)
O'Riordan, Ryan. Overcast. (p. 1314)
Ortiz, Orlando, jt. auth. see Ortiz, Orlando.
Orkrania, Alexia, illus. see Graham, Oakley.
Orkrania, Alexia, illus. see Reasoner, Charles.
Orkrania, Alexia, illus. see Rose, Eilidh.
Orlan, Pierre Mac & B., David. Littlest Pirate King. (p. 1039)
Orlandi, Lorenzo, illus. see Rock, Lois.
Orlando, jt. auth. see Gribel, Christiane.
Orlando, Linda M. Island Boy. (p. 892)
Orlando, Mardi. Wishall. (p. 1940)
Orlando, Martha Jane. Trip, a Tryst & a Terror. (p. 1787)
Orlando, Nancy. Good Grief! It's Winter! (p. 698)

Orlean, Susan & Bradford, Chris. Young Samurai the Way of the Warrior. (p. 1979)
Orlev, Uri. Pequena Nina Grande. Gleich, Jacky, illus. (p. 1341)
—Run, Boy, Run. Halkin, Hillel, tr. (p. 1496)
Orlev, Uri, jt. auth. see Oriev, Uri.
Orliac, Catherine. Te Tumu o Rapa Nui: El Arbolito de Rapa Nui. the Little Tree of Rapa Nui. le Petit Arbre de Rapa Nui. Haoa Cardinali, Viki et al, trs. (p. 1708)
Orliczky P. T., Kristina. Mona's Mitten: A Story to Move To. (p. 1163)
Orlin, Lena Cowen. Othello. Orlin, Lena Cowen, ed. (p. 1306)
Orloff, Erica. In Dreams. (p. 863)
Orloff, Karen Kaufman. I Wanna Go Home. Catrow, David, illus. (p. 847)
—I Wanna Iguana. Catrow, David, illus. (p. 847)
—I Wanna New Room. Catrow, David, III, illus. (p. 847)
—Mystery at the Aquarium (a Nightlight Detective Book) Smith, Jamie, illus. (p. 1224)
—Nightlight Detective: Mystery at the Museum. Smith, Jamie, illus. (p. 1255)
—Nightlight Detective: Big Top Circus Mystery. Smith, Jamie, illus. (p. 1255)
Orman, Roscoe. Ricky & Mobo. (p. 1470)
Ormand, Kate & Louise, Kate. Dark Days. (p. 407)
—Pierre the French Bulldog Recycles. Straker, Bethany, illus. (p. 1357)
Orme, David. Amazing Gadgets. (p. 54)
—Ancient Mysteries. (p. 70)
—Blitz. (p. 199)
—Bugs & Spiders. (p. 237)
—Bugs & Spiders. Mongiovi, Jorge, illus. (p. 237)
—Comets. (p. 348)
—Crime. (p. 382)
—Deadly Virus. (p. 418)
—Death. (p. 420)
—Dinosaur! (p. 441)
—Dinosaurs! (p. 444)
—Donkey That Went Too Fast. Rivers, Ruth, illus. (p. 466)
—Don't Try This at Home. (p. 469)
—Endangered Animals. (p. 526)
—Extreme Science. (p. 556)
—Extreme Sports. (p. 557)
—Fashion. (p. 575)
—Fear. (p. 579)
—Football. (p. 615)
—Formula One. (p. 620)
—Galactic Shopping Mall. (p. 652)
—Great Disasters. (p. 715)
—Great Journeys. (p. 716)
—How to Be a Pop Star. (p. 814)
—Jungle Planet. (p. 935)
—Lost Animals. Mongiovi, Jorge, illus. (p. 1055)
—Lost Explorers. (p. 1055)
—Manga. (p. 1087)
—Mummies. (p. 1190)
—Plague. (p. 1366)
—Plagues. (p. 1366)
—Planet of the Vampires. (p. 1368)
—Sea Killers. (p. 1534)
—Space Explorers. (p. 1619)
—Speed. (p. 1624)
—Spies. (p. 1627)
—Spies. Martin, Jan, illus. (p. 1627)
—Strange Creatures. (p. 1665)
—Strange Creatures. Lindblad, Stefan, illus. (p. 1665)
—UFOs - Are They Real? (p. 1808)
—Ultimate Secret. (p. 1810)
—Vampires. (p. 1832)
—Vampires. Hovland, Oivind, illus. (p. 1832)
—Weird Places. (p. 1872)
Orme, David, jt. auth. see Orme, David.
Orme, David, jt. auth. see Orme, Helen.
Orme, David, jt. auth. see Ruffell, Ann.
Orme, David & Baines, Menna. Llanast Llyr. (p. 1043)
Orme, David & Banks, J. Gateway to Hell. (p. 658)
Orme, David & Orme, David. Endangered Animals. (p. 526)
—Great Disasters. (p. 715)
—Science Fiction. (p. 1526)
—Vampires. (p. 1832)
Orme, David & Orme, Helen. Up for It? (p. 1824)
Orme, Harinani, illus. see Crowl, Janice.
Orme, Helen. 800 Words. (p. 2001)
—Body Art. (p. 207)
—Boys! Brett, Cathy, illus. (p. 220)
—Brother Bother. (p. 231)
—Climate Change. (p. 332)
—Don't Even Think It. (p. 467)
—Elephants in Danger. (p. 512)
—Energy for the Future. (p. 528)
—Garbage & Recycling. (p. 655)
—Gorillas in Danger. (p. 703)
—Habitat Destruction. (p. 734)
—Healthy Eating. (p. 758)
—Horsing Around. (p. 801)
—Leave Her Alone. (p. 986)
—Life in Space. Mongiovi, Jorge, illus. (p. 1011)
—Lions in Danger. (p. 1021)
—Living Green. (p. 1041)
—Lost! Brett, Cathy, illus. (p. 1054)
—Magic. (p. 1071)
—Moving. (p. 1183)
—New Boy. (p. 1243)
—New Man. (p. 1246)
—No More School. (p. 1259)
—Odd One Out. Brett, Cathy, illus. (p. 1278)
—Orangutans in Danger. (p. 1302)
—Out to Work. (p. 1312)
—Party Time. (p. 1326)
—Polar Bears in Danger. (p. 1379)
—Pollution. (p. 1381)
—Rats! (p. 1440)
—Rhinos in Danger. (p. 1467)
—Secrets. (p. 1544)

—Seeds, Bulbs, Plants & Flowers: The Best Start in Science. (p. 1547)
—Seeds, Bulbs, Plants & Flowers. (p. 1547)
—Sharks. (p. 1562)
—She's My Friend Now. (p. 1566)
—Sleepover. (p. 1589)
—Solar System: The Best Start in Science. (p. 1607)
—Solar System. (p. 1607)
—Stalker. Brett, Cathy, illus. (p. 1639)
—Taken for a Ride. Brett, Cathy, illus. (p. 1697)
—Trouble with Teachers. Brett, Cathy, illus. (p. 1790)
—Weather: The Best Start in Science. (p. 1869)
—Weather. (p. 1869)
—Wet! (p. 1877)
—What Things Are Made Of. (p. 1894)
—Who Can I Tell? (p. 1914)
—Who Cares? (p. 1914)
—Who's Who? (p. 1921)
—Won't Talk, Can't Talk. (p. 1949)
Orme, Helen, jt. auth. see Orme, David.
Orme, Helen, jt. auth. see Randall, Ronne.
Orme, Helen, jt. auth. see Twist, Clint.
Orme, Helen & Orme, David. Let's Explore Comets & Asteroids. (p. 996)
—Let's Explore Earth. (p. 996)
—Let's Explore Jupiter. (p. 996)
—Let's Explore Mars. (p. 996)
—Let's Explore Mercury. (p. 996)
—Let's Explore Neptune. (p. 996)
—Let's Explore Pluto & Beyond. (p. 996)
—Let's Explore Saturn. (p. 996)
—Let's Explore the Moon. (p. 996)
—Let's Explore the Sun. (p. 996)
—Let's Explore Uranus. (p. 996)
—Let's Explore Venus. (p. 996)
Orme, Nicholas. Fleas, Flies, & Friars: Children's Poetry from the Middle Ages. (p. 603)
Ormerod, Jan. Animal Bop Won't Stop! Gardiner, Lindsey, illus. (p. 77)
—Baby Swap. Joyner, Andrew, illus. (p. 128)
—Doing the Animal Bop. (p. 463)
—If You're Happy & You Know It! Gardiner, Lindsey, illus. (p. 855)
—Lizzie Nonsense. (p. 1043)
—Lizzie Nonsense. Ormerod, Jan, illus. (p. 1043)
—Lizzie Nonsense Book & DVD Pack. (p. 1043)
—Molly & Her Dad. Thompson, Carol, illus. (p. 1160)
—Over in the Clover. Gardiner, Lindsey, illus. (p. 1313)
—Water Witcher. Ormerod, Jan, illus. (p. 1863)
—When an Elephant Comes to School. (p. 1901)
Ormerod, Jan, illus. see Applegate, Katherine.
Ormerod, Jan, illus. see Ashman, Linda.
Ormerod, Jan, illus. see Calmenson, Stephanie.
Ormerod, Jan, illus. see Harris, Robie H.
Ormerod, Jan, illus. see Hooper, Meredith & Quarto Generic Staff.
Ormerod, Jan, illus. see Wild, Margaret.
Ormerod, Jan & Gardiner, Lindsey. Doing the Animal Bop. (p. 463)
Ormerod, Jan, et al. Doing the Animal Bop. (p. 463)
Ormerod, Nicola. Roxy May, Help My Boyfriend Is a Fairy. (p. 1492)
Ormiston, Rickey. My Dog Wiggles. (p. 1202)
Ormond, Jennifer. DJ's Allergies. Walstead, Curt, illus. (p. 455)
Ormond Writers League Staff. Peanut Butter & Jellyfish. (p. 1332)
Ormondroyd, Edward. Castaways on Long Ago. (p. 276)
—David & the Phoenix. (p. 410)
—David & the Phoenix. Raysor, Joan, illus. (p. 410)
—Time at the Top. Ericksen, Barbara, illus. (p. 1751)
—Time at the Top & All in Good Time: Two Novels. Ericksen, Barb et al, illus. (p. 1751)
Ormsbee, K. E. Water & the Wild. Mora, Elsa, illus. (p. 1862)
Ormsby, Nathaniel Hosea. Timeless Tales of Anansi: Ancestral Realm of Africa. (p. 1754)
Orndorff, Richard L., et al. Geology Underfoot in Central Nevada. (p. 662)
Ornelas, Lourdes. So Can I. (p. 1602)
Orner, Peter. Second Coming of Mavala Shikongo. (p. 1539)
Ornes, Stephen. Sophie Germain. (p. 1613)
Ornia-Blanco, Miguel, illus. see Dahl, Michael.
Ornoff, Theresa, illus. see Heath, Kathy & Martin, Karla.
Ornstein, Allan C. & Levine, Daniel U. Educator's Guide to Student Motivation. (p. 505)
Ornstein, Esther. Middos Man Book & CD. Judowitz, Yoel, illus. (p. 1138)
Ornstein, Robert E. Multimind. (p. 1190)
Orobosa-Ogbeide, Kathryn. Adam's Magic Pebble. (p. 11)
—Boy & the Moon. (p. 217)
—Owl That Couldn't Fly. (p. 1315)
Oroge, Sabinah. Oluwatofarati & Friends. (p. 1287)
Oroma Alikor-Adele. Bugerfly Finds Friends. (p. 236)
—Lonely Bugerfly. (p. 1046)
Oron, Judie. Cry of the Giraffe. (p. 387)
Orona-Ramirez, Kristy. Kiki's Journey. Warm Day, Jonathan, illus. (p. 956)
O'Rourke, Erica. Dissonance. (p. 453)
—Resonance. (p. 1463)
—Tangled. (p. 1705)
—Torn. (p. 1770)
O'Rourke, Molly. Adventures of Gleeson & Cormac: Why Do People Cry? (p. 18)
O'Rourke, Page Eastburn, illus. see Driscoll, Laura.
O'Rourke, Page Eastburn, illus. see Felton, Carol & Felton, Amanda.
O'Rourke, Page Eastburn, illus. see Kassirer, Sue.
O'Rourke, Page Eastburn, illus. see Skinner, Daphne.
O'Rourke, Ryan. Bella Lost & Found. O'Rourke, Ryan, illus. (p. 162)
—Bella, Up, Up & Away. O'Rourke, Ryan, illus. (p. 162)
—One Big Rain: Poems for Every Season. (p. 1294)
O'Rourke, Ryan, illus. see Loeb, Lisa.
O'Rourke, Ryan, illus. see McReynolds, Linda.
O'Rourke, Ryan, illus. see Vamos, Samantha R.

O'Rourke, Ryan, jt. auth. see Loeb, Lisa.
Orozco, Jose-Luis. Diez Deditos. (p. 437)
—Rin, Rin, Rin - Do, Re, Mi. Diaz, David, illus. (p. 1473)
Orozco, Julia & Mulfinger, George. Christian Men of Science. (p. 312)
Orozco, Kristy Marie. Izzy's Pancake Surprise. (p. 901)
Orozco, Maria. Lizards on 41st Street. (p. 1043)
Orozco, Mike. War-Time Paragons. (p. 1858)
Orozco, Rebeca. It's Our Nature. Cottin, Menena, illus. (p. 898)
Orozco, Rebeca, jt. auth. see Urrutia, Maria Cristina.
Orozco, Rebeca & Muro, Claudia Burr. Dona Josefa y sus Conspiraciones. (p. 465)
Orpinas, Jean-Paul, illus. see Kidd, Rob.
Orpinas, Jean-Paul, illus. see RH Disney Staff & Peymani, Christine.
Orpinas, Jean-Paul, illus. see Saxon, Victoria & RH Disney Staff.
Orpinas, Jean-Paul, illus. see Vick-E & RH Disney Staff.
Orpinas, Jean-Paul & Tilley, Scott. Cars. (p. 272)
Orr, Andy. Jett Smith & the Alien Grave. Erwin, J. L., illus. (p. 916)
Orr, Forrest W., illus. see Meigs, Cornelia & Holm, Jennifer L.
Orr, Fran E. When Mommy Was a Soldier (p. 1903)
Orr, Joel N. Structure Is Destiny: The Dandelion Paradox. (p. 1668)
Orr, Judith. Fairy Walk. (p. 564)
Orr, Katherine, illus. see Cook, Mauliola.
Orr, Katherine, jt. auth. see Cook, Mauliola.
Orr, Leah. Messy Tessy. (p. 1130)
Orr, Peter. Now I Get It - Angry & Sharing: Social Stories for children with Autism. (p. 1269)
Orr, Richard. Richard Orr's Nature Cross-Sections. (p. 1469)
Orr, Ryan. Jeremy Ruhl Africa. (p. 913)
—Jeremy Ruhl Savannah Wars (p. 913)
Orr, Tamara. Emily Osment. (p. 519)
Orr, Tamara B. Extreme Skysurfing. (p. 557)
—Extreme Wakeboarding. (p. 557)
Orr, Tamra. Achilles. (p. 9)
—Alan Shepard: The First American in Space. (p. 33)
—Amenorrhea: Why Your Period Stops. (p. 58)
—Amy Tan: Author Extraordinaire. (p. 66)
—Ancient Egypt. (p. 68)
—AnnaSophia Robb. (p. 85)
—Apollo. (p. 91)
—Atom Bomb: Creating & Exploding the First Nuclear Weapon. (p. 113)
—Avian Flu. (p. 119)
—Aztecs. (p. 122)
—Bangladesh. (p. 136)
—Barbados Henderson, James D., ed. (p. 137)
—Barbados. (p. 137)
—Beautiful Me: Finding Personal Strength & Self Acceptance. (p. 153)
—Bermuda. (p. 167)
—Brenda Song. (p. 226)
—Brunei. (p. 232)
—Budgeting Tips for Kids. (p. 235)
—Camouflage & Mimicry in the Wild. (p. 257)
—Care for a Pet Ferret. (p. 266)
—Care for a Potbellied Pig. (p. 266)
—Career as an Auto Mechanic. (p. 266)
—Careers in Glasswork. (p. 268)
—Careers in Sheet Metal & Ironwork. (p. 268)
—Careers in the Courts. (p. 268)
—Charles Dickens. (p. 292)
—Chris Johnson. (p. 311)
—Coins & Other Currency. (p. 338)
—Crime Scene Investigator. (p. 382)
—Day by Day with Dwayne the Rock Johnson. (p. 412)
—Day by Day with Selena Gomez. (p. 412)
—Day by Day with Willow Smith. (p. 412)
—Department of Transportation. (p. 427)
—Ecstasy. (p. 503)
—Egyptian Islamic Jihad. (p. 506)
—Electing Leaders. (p. 508)
—Environmentalist. (p. 532)
—Experiment with Weather. (p. 549)
—Extreme In-Line Skating. (p. 556)
—Extreme Street Luge. (p. 557)
—Food of China. (p. 613)
—Food of Greece. (p. 613)
—Forensic Science Investigator. (p. 617)
—Frequently Asked Questions about Bone Cancer. (p. 636)
—Frequently Asked Questions about Date Rape. (p. 636)
—Gary Soto. (p. 657)
—George Clooney & the Crisis in Darfur. (p. 663)
—Geothermal Energy. (p. 665)
—Government at Work. (p. 704)
—History of Voting Rights. (p. 785)
—Home & Family Relationships. (p. 791)
—How Did They Build That? Zoo. (p. 806)
—How to Research Your Ancestry. (p. 821)
—Hydroelectric Energy. (p. 831)
—Hydrogen Bomb: Unleashing the Nuclear & Arms Race. (p. 831)
—Hydrogen Bomb: Unleashing the Nuclear Age & Arms Race. (p. 831)
—I Spy in the Sky the Clouds. (p. 846)
—I Spy in the Sky the Moon. (p. 846)
—I Spy in the Sky the Stars. (p. 846)
—I Spy in the Sky the Sun. (p. 846)
—Indonesia. (p. 872)
—Iran & Nuclear Weapons. (p. 886)
—Jennifer Lawrence. (p. 912)
—Jonas Brothers. (p. 925)
—Jordin Sparks. (p. 925)
—Kid's Guide to Earning Money. (p. 953)
—Kid's Guide to Perennial Gardens. (p. 953)
—Kid's Guide to Stock Market Investing. (p. 954)
—Kid's Guide to the Economy. (p. 954)
—Kristen Stewart. (p. 967)
—Lewis & Clark Expedition: A Primary Source History of the Journey of the Corps of Discovery. (p. 1004)

—Liver Cancer: Current & Emerging Trends in Detection & Treatment. (p. 1040)
—Liver Cancer. (p. 1040)
—Louis Armstrong. (p. 1058)
—Manga Artists. (p. 1087)
—Marcus Brutus. (p. 1092)
—Marie Curie. (p. 1093)
—Meet Our New Student from China. (p. 1121)
—Meet Our New Student from Great Britain. (p. 1121)
—Meet Our New Student from Mexico. (p. 1122)
—Memorial Day/Dia de los Caidos. de la Vega, Eida, tr. from ENG. (p. 1126)
—Miles Davis. (p. 1142)
—Money Matters: A Kid's Guide to Money (p. 1164)
—Monsters of Hercules. (p. 1169)
—Motion & Forces. (p. 1179)
—Murder. (p. 1192)
—Native American Medicine. (p. 1234)
—Native American Medicine. Johnson, Troy, ed. (p. 1234)
—Nigeria. (p. 1252)
—No Hands Allowed, Plus Robbie & Ryan Play Indoor Soccer (p. 1258)
—Organic Farmer. (p. 1303)
—Ovarian Tumors & Cysts. (p. 1313)
—Piranhas. (p. 1362)
—Playing Safe, Eating Right: Making Healthy Choices. (p. 1372)
—Primary Source History of the Colony of New Jersey. (p. 1400)
—Public Health Microbiologist. (p. 1414)
—Qatar. (p. 1422)
—Racial Profiling. (p. 1432)
—Railroad & the Civil War (1860s) (p. 1433)
—Robert Pattison. (p. 1479)
—Ronald Reagan. (p. 1486)
—Savings Tips for Kids. (p. 1518)
—Shia Labeouf. (p. 1566)
—Sirens. (p. 1580)
—Southwest. (p. 1617)
—St. Lucia. (p. 1638)
—Stephanie Meyer. (p. 1648)
—Story of the Constitution. (p. 1660)
—Super Cool Science Experiments: Circulation. (p. 1679)
—Telescope. (p. 1716)
—Tenth Amendment: Limiting Federal Powers. (p. 1720)
—Truth about Cocaine. (p. 1794)
—Understanding Economic Systems. (p. 1815)
—Violence in Our Schools: Halls of Hope, Halls of Fear. (p. 1843)
—Ways to Help the Elderly: A Guide to Giving Back. (p. 1865)
—We Visit Afghanistan. (p. 1868)
—We Visit Chile. (p. 1868)
—What Degree Do I Need to Pursue a Career in Business? (p. 1881)
—What's So Great about the Buffalo Soldiers. (p. 1899)
—What's So Great about the Tuskegee Airmen. (p. 1899)
—Windward Islands Henderson, James D., ed. (p. 1936)
—Windward Islands. (p. 1936)
—Working at the Zoo. (p. 1952)
—Your Career in the Coast Guard. (p. 1980)
—Your Career in the Navy. (p. 1980)
—Zest. (p. 1986)
Orr, Tamra, jt. auth. see Brown, Jonatha A.
Orr, Tamra, jt. auth. see Campbell, Carol P.
Orr, Tamra, jt. auth. see Daniels, Leonard.
Orr, Tamra, jt. auth. see LeVert, Suzanne.
Orr, Tamra, jt. auth. see Moragne, Wendy.
Orr, Tamra & Greenblatt, Miriam. Indonesia. (p. 872)
Orr, Tamra & Muschal, Frank. Beyond Government. (p. 174)
Orr, Tamra & Orr, Tamra B. California. (p. 253)
Orr, Tamra & Sommers, Michael A. Avi. (p. 119)
Orr, Tamra B. Abby Wambach. (p. 2)
—Alaska (Revised Edition) (p. 34)
—Amelia Earhart. (p. 58)
—Animals Helping to Keep the Peace. (p. 82)
—Avian Flu. (p. 119)
—Battling Extinction. (p. 147)
—California. (p. 253)
—Creating Multimedia Presentations. (p. 378)
—Dawn of Aviation: The Story of the Wright Brothers. (p. 411)
—Department of Transportation. (p. 427)
—Extraordinary Debates. (p. 555)
—Extreme Skysurfing. (p. 557)
—Extreme Wakeboarding. (p. 557)
—Florida. (p. 606)
—Forecasting a Flood. (p. 617)
—Frequently Asked Questions about Bone Cancer. (p. 636)
—How Did They Build That? Lighthouse. (p. 806)
—Ice Cube. (p. 850)
—Investigating a Crime Scene. (p. 884)
—It's Cool to Learn about the United States Midwest. (p. 896)
—It's Cool to Learn about the United States Southwest. (p. 896)
—Jamie Foxx. (p. 907)
—Jay-Jay Okocha. (p. 910)
—Jojo. (p. 924)
—Life & Times of Susan B. Anthony. (p. 1008)
—Manga Artists. (p. 1087)
—Michael Owen. (p. 1134)
—Midwest. (p. 1139)
—Money-Making Opportunities for Teens Who Like Working Outside. (p. 1164)
—Oklahoma. (p. 1282)
—Orlando Bloom. (p. 1304)
—Polar Bears. (p. 1379)
—Pondering Pollution. (p. 1382)
—Primary Source History of the Colony of New Jersey. (p. 1400)
—Ronaldo. (p. 1487)
—Searching the Sky. (p. 1538)
—Steam Engine. (p. 1646)
—Super Cool Science Experiments: Weather. (p. 1679)
—Super Cool Science Experiments: Digestion. (p. 1679)
—Super Cool Science Experiments: Respiration. (p. 1679)
—Telescope. (p. 1716)
—Tornadoes. (p. 1770)
—Tracking an Epidemic. (p. 1775)
—Tsunamis. (p. 1795)
—Turkey. (p. 1797)
—Understanding Insects. (p. 1815)
—Unearthing Fossils. (p. 1817)
—USMC Special Reaction Teams. (p. 1829)
—Vo-Tech Track to Success in Law, Public Safety, Corrections, & Security. (p. 1847)
—Walt Disney: The Man Behind the Magic. (p. 1855)
—Walt Disney. (p. 1855)
—Wildfires. (p. 1931)
—Zest. (p. 1986)
Orr, Tamra B., jt. auth. see Brown, Jonatha A.
Orr, Tamra B., jt. auth. see King, David C.
Orr, Tamra B., jt. auth. see Mezzanotte, Jim.
Orr, Tamra B., jt. auth. see Orr, Tamra.
Orr, Tina. Misfits & the Magical Pond. (p. 1150)
Orr, Wendy. Abandoned! - A Lion Called Kiki. Castelao, Patricia, illus. (p. 2)
—Across the Dark Sea. Rawlins, Donna, illus. (p. 9)
—Ark in the Park. (p. 99)
—Discovered! A Beagle Called Bella. (p. 448)
—Discovered! A Beagle Called Bella. Castelao, Patricia, illus. (p. 448)
—Lost! - A Dog Called Bear. Boase, Susan, illus. (p. 1054)
—Missing! - A Cat Called Buster. Boase, Susan, illus. (p. 1152)
—Mokie & Bik Go to Sea. Bean, Jonathan, illus. (p. 1160)
—Nim's Island. (p. 1256)
—Nim's Island. Millard, Kerry, illus. (p. 1256)
—Princess & Her Panther. Stringer, Lauren, illus. (p. 1402)
—Raven's Mountain. (p. 1441)
—Stolen! - A Pony Called Pebbles. (p. 1652)
—Stolen! - A Pony Called Pebbles. Castelao, Patricia, illus. (p. 1652)
—Wanted! - A Guinea Pig Called Henry. Castelao, Patricia, illus. (p. 1856)
Orrell, Brenda M. Eliza Blackbird. (p. 513)
Orrell, Julie. Classworks Fiction & Poetry Year 1. (p. 329)
Orris, Cornelius F. Curious Adventures of Nigel & Viol. (p. 392)
Orsak, Lane Rockford. Keiko the Fairy, the Kujiki. (p. 948)
Orser-Mokelky, Jacqueline. If I Had ... (p. 853)
Orshoski, Paul. We Both Read-My Sitter Is a T-Rex! (Level 1-2) Ebbeler, Jeffrey, illus. (p. 1866)
—We Both Read-The Mouse in My House. Ebbeler, Jeffrey, illus. (p. 1866)
—We Read Phonics-Ant in Her Pants. Ebbeler, Jeffrey, illus. (p. 1868)
—We Read Phonics-Ants in Her Pants. Ebbeler, Jeffrey, illus. (p. 1868)
—We Read Phonics-Bugs on the Bus. Noiset, Michele, illus. (p. 1868)
—We Read Phonics-Dad Does It All. Ebbeler, Jeffrey, illus. (p. 1868)
—We Read Phonics-I Do Not Like Greens! Ebbeler, Jeffrey, illus. (p. 1868)
—We Read Phonics-Robot Man. Ebbeler, Jeffrey, illus. (p. 1868)
—We Read Phonics-Sports Dream. Ebbeler, Jeffrey, illus. (p. 1868)
—We Read Phonics-Talent Night. Kulka, Joe, illus. (p. 1868)
—We Read Phonics-Who Took the Cookbook? Light, Kelly, illus. (p. 1868)
Orsi, Leo N., Jr. Striper Chronicles: East Coast Surf Fishing Legends & Adventures (p. 1667)
Orsi, Tea. Tinker Bell & the Legend of the NeverBeast. (p. 1755)
—Tinker Bell & the Pirate Fairy. (p. 1755)
—Tinker Bell & the Secret of the Wings. (p. 1755)
Orsi, Tea & Panaro, Carlo. Disney Fairies Graphic Novel #13: Tinker Bell & the Pixie Hollow Games. Razzi, Manuela et al, illus. (p. 451)
—Tinker Bell & Blaze. (p. 1755)
—Tinker Bell & the Lost Treasure. Razzi, Manuela et al, illus. (p. 1755)
Orsini, Cheryl, jt. auth. see Reilly, Carmel.
Orsini, Cheryl, jt. auth. see Vasiliu, Michelle.
Orsolini, Laura, illus. see Jeong, SoYun.
Orson, Claire M. My Name Is Misty: This Is My Book. (p. 1215)
Ort, Kathleen, ed. see Caldwell, D. W.
Ort, Kathleen, ed. see Clarke, Herbert.
Ort, Kathleen, ed. see Horn, Elizabeth L.
Ort, Kathleen, ed. see Ippisch, Hanneke.
Ort, Kathleen, ed. see Norton, O. Richard.
Ort, Kathleen, ed. see Rutter, Michael.
Ort, Kathleen, ed. see Taylor, Ronald J.
Ort, Kathleen, ed. see Taylor, Ronald J. & Douglas, George.
Ortac, Arda. Sharp Kids Activity. Ortac, Feride, illus. (p. 1563)
Ortac, Feride, illus. see Ortac, Arda.
Ortakales, Denise. Legend of the Old Man of the Mountain. Crawford, Robert, illus. (p. 989)
Ortakales, Denise, illus. see Brenner, Barbara.
Ortas, Rachel. Messy Monster Book. (p. 1130)
Ortberg, John. Life You've Always Wanted: Spiritual Disciplines for Ordinary People. (p. 1013)
Ortega, Cristina. Eyes of the Weaver: Los Ojos Del Tejedor. Garcia, Patricio, illus. (p. 558)
Ortega, Damian, illus. see French, Vivian.
Ortega, David, illus. see Lisi, Charlotte.
Ortega, Esperanza, ed. see varios & Varios.
Ortega, Esperanza, tr. see varios & Varios.
Ortega, Gemma Rovira, tr. see Rowling, J. K.
Ortega, Ingrid. Cuentos Golosos. Welin, Raquel, illus. (p. 390)
Ortega, James, illus. see Ortiz, Andrea.
Ortega, Jose, illus. see McConnie Zapater, Beatriz.
Ortega, Jose, illus. see Mora, Pat.
Ortega, Julian G. Warrior Inspiration. (p. 1858)
Ortega, Macarena, illus. see Campos, Paula.
Ortegon, Sharon A. Cookie Planet. (p. 361)
—Return to Cookie Planet. (p. 1465)
—You. (p. 1972)
Ortelli, Barbara, illus. see Winters, Pierre.
Ortells, Estela. En Africa. (p. 522)
—En el Aire. (p. 522)
—En el Bosque. (p. 522)
—En el Colegio. (p. 522)
—En el Rio. (p. 522)
—En Japon. (p. 522)
—En la India. (p. 522)
—En la Montana. (p. 522)
—En la Nieve. (p. 522)
—En la Playa. (p. 522)
—Pequeno Castor. (p. 1341)
—Y los Chihuhuas. (p. 1968)
Orth, Jack. Happy Days: Book 1. Sunshine, Mary Lou, illus. (p. 745)
—Happy Days: Book 2. Sunshine, Mary Lou, illus. (p. 745)
—Happy Days: Book 3. Sunshine, Mary Lou, illus. (p. 745)
Ortiz, Ada, illus. see Whaley, Michelle Marie.
Ortiz, Andrea. Snowflakes in June. Ortega, James, illus. (p. 1600)
Ortiz, Associate Professor Enrique. Ten Elephants & a Spider's Web: A Traditional Latin American Counting Rhyme & Other Activities: Spanish/English. (p. 1718)
Ortiz Cofer, Judith. Animal Jamboree: Latino Folktales / la Fiesta de los Animales: Leyendas Latinas. Rosales-Yeomans, Natalia, tr. from ENG. (p. 78)
—Poeta Del Piso de Arriba. Baeza Ventura, Gabriela, tr. from ENG. (p. 1376)
Ortiz Cofer, Judith, ed. Riding Low Through Streets of Gold: Latino Literature for Young Adults. (p. 1471)
Ortiz de Zárate, Marisol, jt. auth. see Ortiz de Zarate, Marisol.
Ortiz de Zarate, Marisol & Ortiz de Zárate, Marisol. Canción de Shao Li. (p. 261)
Ortiz, Gaye Williams & Joseph, Clara A. B., eds. Theology & Literature: Rethinking Reader Responsibility. (p. 1729)
Ortiz, Gilberto Rendon. Tuiiiii el Murcielago. (p. 1796)
Ortiz, Gilberto Rendon & Rendon, Gilberto. En la Ultima Frontera. Broeck, Fabricio Vanden, illus. (p. 522)
Ortiz, Joan. Letting Grow: A Fairy Tale. (p. 1003)
Ortiz, Michael J. Swan Town: The Secret Journal of Susanna Shakespeare. (p. 1688)
Ortiz Montanez, Nivea, illus. see Iturrondo, Angeles Molina & Iguina, Adriana.
Ortiz Montanez, Nivea, illus. see Quinones, Juan Carlos.
Ortiz, Nivea, illus. see Molina, Angeles.
Ortiz, Orlando & Ortiz, Orlando. Que Te Pasa, Calabaza! Pacheco, Alma Rosa & Pacheco, Guadalupe, illus. (p. 1424)
Ortiz, Oscar, illus. see Cofer, Judith Ortiz.
Ortiz, Oscar, illus. see Ortiz Cofer, Judith.
Ortiz, Raquel M. & Ventura, Gabriela Baeza. Sofi & the Magic, Musical Mural. Dominguez, Maria, illus. (p. 1605)
Ortiz, Simon J. Good Rainbow Road. Lacapa, Michael, illus. (p. 700)
Ortiz, Simon J. & Lacapa, Michael. Good Rainbow Road. Montejo, Victor, tr. (p. 700)
Ortiz, Teresa, et al. Under What Bandera? Anti-War Ofrendas from Minnesota y Califas. Garcia Echeverria, Olga Angelina et al, eds. (p. 1814)
Ortiz, Tracy. As Dreamtime Unfolds. (p. 105)
Ortiz, Victoria, tr. see Christelow, Eileen.
Ortiz, Zirzeria. Queen in Me & My Bumblebee. (p. 1424)
Ortiz-Griffin, Julia & Griffin, William D. Spain & Portugal: A Reference Guide from the Renaissance to the Present. (p. 1620)
Ortman, Don. 4th of July. (p. 1992)
Orton, Greg, ed. Rock Climbing Western Oregon : Willamette: Compiled by Oregon Climbers (p. 1482)
Orton, J. R. Trial Trip of the Flying Cloud. (p. 1785)
Orton, W. George. Bob Hunt in Canada. (p. 205)
Orttenburger, Rhonda Shew, jt. auth. see Shew, David.
Oru, Gideon. Walking Garden. (p. 1854)
Orwell, George. 1984: Bloom's Guide. Orwell, George & Bloom, Harold, eds. (p. 2002)
Orwick, Penny, et al. Developing Drivers with the Windows(r) Driver Foundation. (p. 431)
Orwin, Joanna. Guardian of the Land. (p. 728)
O'Ryan, Ellie. Belle: The Charming Gift. (p. 162)
O'ryan, Ellie. Boogie Down. (p. 210)
O'Ryan, Ellie. Case of the Digital Deception. (p. 274)
—Jasmine: The Jewel Orchard. (p. 909)
—Journey to Mars (p. 929)
—Journey to Mars. (p. 929)
—Phineas & Ferb: Lights, Camera, Perry? Jeff, Marsh & Povenmire, Dan, illus. (p. 1351)
O'Ryan, Ellie, jt. auth. see Bryant, Megan E.
O'Ryan, Ellie, jt. auth. see Disney Book Group Staff.
O'Ryan, Ellie, adapted by. Ice Age 2: The Meltdown: Geyser Blast! (p. 850)
—Ice Age 2: The Meltdown: Join the Pack! (p. 850)
O'Ryan, Ellie & Disney Book Group Staff. Jasmine: The Jewel Orchard. Disney Storybook Artists Staff, illus. (p. 909)
—Planes Read-Along Storybook & CD. Disney Storybook Artists Staff, illus. (p. 1367)
O'Ryan, Ellie & Lewman, David. Case of the Disappearing Dogs. (p. 274)
O'ryan, Ray. Annoying Crush. (p. 87)
O'Ryan, Ray. Drake Makes a Splash! Jack, Colin, illus. (p. 480)
O'ryan, Ray. Galactic Easter! (p. 652)
O'Ryan, Ray. Galactic Easter! Jack, Colin, illus. (p. 652)
—Galaxy Zack 3-Pack: Hello, Nebulon!; Journey to Juno; the Prehistoric Planet. Jack, Colin, illus. (p. 653)
O'ryan, Ray. Green Christmas! (p. 721)
O'Ryan, Ray. Green Christmas! Jack, Colin, illus. (p. 721)
—Haunted Halloween. Kraft, Jason, illus. (p. 753)
O'ryan, Ray. Hello, Nebulon! (p. 764)
O'Ryan, Ray. Hello, Nebulon! Jack, Colin, illus. (p. 764)
O'ryan, Ray. Journey to Juno. (p. 928)
O'Ryan, Ray. Journey to Juno. Jack, Colin, illus. (p. 928)
O'ryan, Ray. Monsters in Space! (p. 1169)
O'Ryan, Ray. Monsters in Space! Jack, Colin, illus. (p. 1169)
—Operation Twin Trouble. Kraft, Jason, illus. (p. 1300)
O'ryan, Ray. Prehistoric Planet. (p. 1395)
O'Ryan, Ray. Prehistoric Planet. Jack, Colin, illus. (p. 1395)
—Return to Earth! Kraft, Jason, illus. (p. 1465)
O'Ryan, Ray. Three's a Crowd! (p. 1744)
O'Ryan, Ray. Three's a Crowd! Jack, Colin, illus. (p. 1744)
Orzechowski, Shawneen. Midnight Journey: Running for Freedom on the Underground Railroad. (p. 1139)
—Sarah's Secret: Civil War Deserter at Fredericksburg. (p. 1514)
Osa, Nancy. Cuba 15. (p. 388)
Osada, Ryuta, illus. see Shakespeare, William.
Osadchuk, Keit, illus. see Kaplan, Debbie.
Osakawa. Hiking in the Wilds: Level Q. Group 1. (p. 779)
Osban, Rodger, illus. see Jepson-Gilbert, Anita.
Osborn. Born to Fly. (p. 214)
—Understanding Jason. Mills, illus. (p. 1815)
Osborn & Andrews. Videolab: Used with ... Engleberg-Presentations in Everyday Life: Strategies for Effective Speaking; Andrews-Public Speaking: Connecting You & Your Audience, Multimedia Edition. (p. 1841)
Osborn, Anna. Cambridge English - Flyers: Three Practice Tests for Cambridge English. (p. 255)
—Movers: Three Practice Tests for Cambridge English. (p. 1183)
Osborn, Becky, jt. auth. see Mills, Andy.
Osborn, Carolyn. Where We Are Now. (p. 1910)
Osborn, D. W. Why Can't I Ribbit? (p. 1923)
Osborn, Jacob, jt. auth. see Belasen, Amy.
Osborn, Jim, illus. see Moore, June Hines.
Osborn, Kathy, illus. see Ablow, Gail.
Osborn, Kelly. Green Knight. (p. 722)
Osborn, Linda. Giant Mike & the Four Fairies. Friesen, Ray, illus. (p. 673)
Osborn School Students. Paw-Sing for Positive Daily Affirmations: Lion Pride. Rosa, M. Nina & Perrien, Vicki, eds. (p. 1331)
Osborn, Sonnie. Silly Ole Spilly Lilly. (p. 1576)
Osborn, Susan, ed. see Marshall, John A.
Osborn, Susan Titus. Parables in Action Set (p. 1323)
Osborn, Tonia Bennington, illus. see Kyrja.
Osborne, Amber & Osborne, Dwight. Puffy Buffy Jones Jones Osborne Dadoot Da Do. Osborne, Amber, illus. (p. 1415)
Osborne, Amy, ed. Multables, Inc. McGee, Thomas, illus. (p. 1189)
Osborne, Corinne. Picture Book Learning (p. 1355)
Osborne, Dwight, jt. auth. see Osborne, Amber.
Osborne, Erin. Spy Recruit Simmons, Bethany, illus. (p. 1636)
Osborne, Graham, illus. see Farrington, Karen & Constable, Nick.
Osborne Hale, Jennifer. Danny Blue! What Did You Do? (p. 405)
Osborne, J. E. Inventions. (p. 884)
Osborne, Jill. Riley Mae & the Sole Fire Safari (p. 1472)
—Sam Feels Better Now! An Interactive Story for Children. Collier, Kevin Scott, illus. (p. 1506)
Osborne, Joey N. Boxes, Boxes, Everywhere Boxes (p. 217)
Osborne, Jolinda. Touch All the Bases: The Culture & Idioms of America's Pastime. (p. 1772)
Osborne, Kent. Adventure Time: Banana Guard Academy. (p. 14)
Osborne, Linda Barrett. Miles to Go for Freedom: Segregation & Civil Rights in the Jim Crow Years. (p. 1142)
—Traveling the Freedom Road: From Slavery & the Civil War Through Reconstruction. (p. 1780)
Osborne, M. D. Rescue of Mr. Goldsmith. (p. 1462)
Osborne, Magic Tree, jt. auth. see Osborne, Mary Pope.
Osborne, Mary A. Last of the Magicians. (p. 978)
—Nonna's Book of Mysteries. (p. 1263)
Osborne, Mary Pope. Abe Lincoln at Last! (p. 4)
—Abe Lincoln at Last! Murdocca, Sal, illus. (p. 4)
—Adaline Falling Star. (p. 10)
—Afternoon on the Amazon. (p. 29)
—Barcos Vikingos al Amanecer. Brovelli, Marcela, tr. from ENG. (p. 138)
—Blizzard of the Blue Moon. Murdocca, Sal, illus. (p. 200)
—Brave Little Seamstress. Potter, Giselle, illus. (p. 223)
—Buffalo Before Breakfast. (p. 235)
—Caballero del Alba. (p. 250)
—Carnival at Candlelight. Murdocca, Sal, illus. (p. 270)
—Christmas in Camelot Murdocca, Sal, illus. (p. 314)
—Christmas in Camelot. (p. 314)
—Civil War on Sunday. (p. 325)
—Crazy Day with Cobras. (p. 377)
—Crazy Day with Cobras. Murdocca, Sal, illus. (p. 377)
—Danger in the Darkest Hour. Murdocca, Sal, illus. (p. 403)
—Dark Day in the Deep Sea. (p. 407)
—Dark Day in the Deep Sea. Murdocca, Sal, illus. (p. 407)
—Das magische Baumhaus 09. Der Ruf der Delfine. (p. 409)
—Day of the Dragon King. (p. 414)
—Dingoes at Dinnertime. (p. 440)
—Dinosaurios al Atardecer. (p. 443)
—Dinosaurs Before Dark Murdocca, Sal, illus. (p. 444)
—Dinosaurs Before Dark. (p. 444)
—Dinosaurs Before Dark. Murdocca, Sal, illus. (p. 444)
—Dogs in the Dead of Night. (p. 463)
—Dogs in the Dead of Night. Murdocca, Sal, illus. (p. 463)
—Dolphins at Daybreak. (p. 465)
—Dolphins at Daybreak; Ghost Town at Sundown; Lions at Lunchtime; Polar Bears Past Bedtime Murdocca, Sal, illus. (p. 465)
—Dragon of the Red Dawn. Murdocca, Sal, illus. (p. 477)
—Earthquake in the Early Morning. (p. 497)
—Eve of the Emperor Penguin. Murdocca, Sal, illus. (p. 541)
—Ghost Tale for Christmas Time. Murdocca, Sal, illus. (p. 671)
—Ghost Tale for Christmas Time. (p. 672)
—Ghost Town at Sundown. (p. 672)
—Good Night for Ghosts. (p. 699)
—Good Night for Ghosts. Murdocca, Sal, illus. (p. 699)
—Happy Birthday, America. Catalanotto, Peter, illus. (p. 744)
—Haunted Castle on Hallows Eve. (p. 753)
—Haunted Castle on Hallows Eve. Murdocca, Sal, illus. (p. 753)
—Haunted Waters. (p. 754)

—High Tide in Hawaii. (p. 778)
—High Tide in Hawaii. Murdocca, Sal, illus. (p. 778)
—High Time for Heroes. Murdocca, Sal, illus. (p. 778)
—Hora de los Juegos Olimpicos. Brovelli, Marcela, tr. (p. 797)
—Hour of the Olympics. (p. 802)
—Hurry Up, Houdini! Murdocca, Sal, illus. (p. 830)
—Kate & the Beanstalk. Potter, Giselle, illus. (p. 944)
—Knight at Dawn Murdocca, Sal, illus. (p. 964)
—Knight at Dawn. (p. 964)
—Knight at Dawn. Murdocca, Sal, illus. (p. 964)
—Leprechaun in Late Winter. (p. 993)
—Leprechaun in Late Winter. Murdocca, Sal, illus. (p. 993)
—Lions at Lunchtime. (p. 1021)
—Magic Tree House: Vacation under the Volcano; Day of the Dragon King; Viking Ships at Sunrise; Hour of the Olympics Murdocca, Sal, illus. (p. 1074)
—Magic Tree House #3: Mummies in the Morning. Murdocca, Sal, illus. (p. 1074)
—Magic Tree House #47: Abe Lincoln at Last! Murdocca, Sal, illus. (p. 1074)
—Magic Tree House #50: Hurry up, Houdini! Murdocca, Sal, illus. (p. 1074)
—Magic Tree House #53: Shadow of the Shark. Murdocca, Sal, illus. (p. 1074)
—Magic Tree House Volumes 21-24 Boxed Set: American History Quartet Murdocca, Sal, illus. (p. 1074)
—Medianoche en la Luna. (p. 1118)
—Midnight on the Moon. (p. 1139)
—Mitos Griegos. (p. 1156)
—Momia en la Manana. (p. 1162)
—Monday with a Mad Genius. (p. 1163)
—Monday with a Mad Genius. Murdocca, Sal, illus. (p. 1163)
—Moonlight on the Magic Flute. Murdocca, Sal, illus. (p. 1172)
—Mummies in the Morning. (p. 1191)
—My Secret War: The World War II Diary of Madeline Beck, Long Island, New York 1941. (p. 1218)
—Mysteries of Spider Kane. (p. 1222)
—Mystery of the Enchanted Dog Murdocca, Sal, illus. (p. 1225)
—New York's Bravest. Johnson, Steve & Fancher, Lou, illus. (p. 1248)
—Night of the New Magicians. (p. 1254)
—Night of the New Magicians. Murdocca, Sal, illus. (p. 1254)
—Night of the Ninjas. (p. 1254)
—Noche de los Ninjas. (p. 1262)
—Osos Polares Despues de la Medianoche. (p. 1306)
—Perfect Time for Pandas. (p. 1342)
—Perfect Time for Pandas. Murdocca, Sal, illus. (p. 1342)
—Piratas Despues del Mediodia. (p. 1362)
—Pirates Past Noon. (p. 1364)
—Polar Bears Past Bedtime. (p. 1379)
—Pompeii: Lost & Found. Christensen, Bonnie, illus. (p. 1382)
—Rain Forests: A Nonfiction Companion to Afternoon on the Amazon. Osborne, Will & Murdocca, Sal, illus. (p. 1434)
—Revolutionary War on Wednesday. (p. 1466)
—Season of the Sandstorms. (p. 1538)
—Season of the Sandstorms. Murdocca, Sal, illus. (p. 1538)
—Soccer on Sunday. Murdocca, Sal, illus. (p. 1603)
—Stallion by Starlight. (p. 1639)
—Stallion by Starlight. Murdocca, Sal, illus. (p. 1639)
—Standing in the Light: The Diary of Catharine Carey Logan, Delaware Valley, Pennsylvania, 1763. (p. 1639)
—Summer of the Sea Serpent. Murdocca, Sal, tr. (p. 1674)
—Summer of the Sea Serpent. Murdocca, Sal, illus. (p. 1674)
—Sunset of the Sabertooth. (p. 1677)
—Tales from the Odyssey (p. 1702)
—Tarde en el Amazonas. (p. 1706)
—Tigers at Twilight. (p. 1749)
—Tigre Dientes de Sable en el Ocaso. (p. 1749)
—Tonight on the Titanic. (p. 1765)
—Twister on Tuesday. (p. 1803)
—Twisters & Other Terrible Storms: A Nonfiction Companion to Twister on Tuesday. Osborne, Will & Murdocca, Sal, illus. (p. 1803)
—Vacaciones Al Pie de un Volcan. Brovelli, Marcela, tr. from ENG. (p. 1829)
—Vacation under the Volcano. (p. 1830)
—Viking Ships at Sunrise. (p. 1842)
—Winter of the Ice Wizard. Murdocca, Sal, illus. (p. 1938)
Osborne, Mary Pope, jt. auth. see Boyce, Natalie Pope.
Osborne, Mary Pope, jt. auth. see Osborne, Will.
Osborne, Mary Pope & Boyce, Natalie Pope. Abraham Lincoln: Abe Lincoln at Last! Murdocca, Sal, illus. (p. 6)
—American Revolution: A Nonfiction Companion to Revolutionary War on Wednesday. Murdocca, Sal, illus. (p. 63)
—Ancient Greece & the Olympics: A Nonfiction Companion to Hour of the Olympics. Murdocca, Sal, tr. (p. 69)
—Ancient Rome & Pompeii: A Nonfiction Companion to Vacation under the Volcano. Murdocca, Sal, illus. (p. 70)
—China: Land of the Emperor's Great Wall. Murdocca, Sal, illus. (p. 306)
—China: Land of the Emperor's Great Wall: a Nonfiction Companion to Magic Tree House #14: Day of the Dragon King. (p. 306)
—Dog Heroes: A Nonfiction Companion to Magic Tree House No. 46 Dogs in the Dead of Night. Murdocca, Sal, illus. (p. 461)
—Dolphins & Sharks: Dolphins at Daybreak. Murdocca, Sal, illus. (p. 465)
—Games & Puzzles from the Tree House. Murdocca, Sal, illus. (p. 654)
—Ghosts: A Nonfiction Companion to a Good Night for Ghosts. (p. 672)
—Ghosts: A Nonfiction Companion to a Good Night for Ghosts. Murdocca, Sal, illus. (p. 672)
—Heroes for All Times: A Nonfiction Companion High Time for Heroes. Murdocca, Sal, illus. (p. 772)
—Heroes for All Times. (p. 772)
—Horse Heroes: Stallion by Starlight. Murdocca, Sal, illus. (p. 799)
—Leonardo Da Vinci: A Nonfiction Companion to Monday with a Mad Genius. (p. 992)
—Leonardo Da Vinci: A Nonfiction Companion to Monday with a Mad Genius. Murdocca, Sal, illus. (p. 992)
—Leprechauns & Irish Folklore: A Nonfiction Companion to Leprechaun in Late Winter. (p. 993)
—Leprechauns & Irish Folklore: A Nonfiction Companion to Leprechaun in Late Winter. Murdocca, Sal, illus. (p. 993)
—Magic Tree House: Animal Games & Puzzles. Murdocca, Sal, illus. (p. 1074)
—Magic Tree House Fact Tracker #30: Ninjas & Samurai: A Nonfiction Companion to Magic Tree House #5: Night of the Ninjas. Murdocca, Sal, illus. (p. 1074)
—Magic Tree House Fact Tracker #33: Vikings: A Nonfiction Companion to Magic Tree House #15: Viking Ships at Sunrise. Molinari, Carlo, illus. (p. 1074)
—Magic Tree House Survival Guide. Murdocca, Sal, illus. (p. 1074)
—Magic Tricks from the Tree House: A Fun Companion to Magic Tree House 50: Hurry up, Houdini! (p. 1074)
—Magic Tricks from the Tree House. Murdocca, Sal & Vilela, Luiz, illus. (p. 1074)
—Ninjas & Samurai: A Nonfiction Companion to Magic Tree House #5: Night of the Ninjas. (p. 1256)
—Pandas & Other Endangered Species: A Perfect Time for Pandas. (p. 1321)
—Pandas & Other Endangered Species: A Perfect Time for Pandas. Murdocca, Sal, illus. (p. 1321)
—Penguins & Antarctica: A Nonfiction Companion to Eve of the Emperor Penguin. Murdocca, Sal, illus. (p. 1337)
—Pilgrims: A Nonfiction Companion to Thanksgiving on Thursday. Murdocca, Sal, illus. (p. 1358)
—Polar Bears & the Arctic: A Nonfiction Companion to Polar Bears Past Bedtime. Murdocca, Sal, illus. (p. 1379)
—Random House Book of Bible Stories. Welply, Michael, illus. (p. 1438)
—Sabertooths & the Ice Age: A Nonfiction Companion to Sunset of the Sabertooth. Murdocca, Sal, illus. (p. 1499)
—Sea Monsters: A Nonfiction Companion to Dark Day in the Deep Sea. Murdocca, Sal, illus. (p. 1535)
—Sharks & Other Predators. Molinari, Carlo, illus. (p. 1563)
—Snakes & Other Reptiles: A Nonfiction Companion to a Crazy Day with Cobras. Murdocca, Sal, illus. (p. 1596)
—Soccer: Soccer on Sunday. Murdocca, Sal, illus. (p. 1603)
—Soccer: A Nonfiction Companion to Magic Tree House #52: Soccer on Sunday. Murdocca, Sal, illus. (p. 1603)
—Soccer. (p. 1603)
—Tsunamis & Other Natural Disasters: A Nonfiction Companion to High Tide in Hawaii. Murdocca, Sal, illus. (p. 1795)
Osborne, Mary Pope & Murdocca, Sal. Esta Noche en el Titanic. Murdocca, Sal, illus. (p. 538)
Osborne, Mary Pope & Osborne, Magic Tree. Dark Day in the Deep Sea. Murdocca, Sal, illus. (p. 407)
Osborne, Mary Pope & Osborne, Will. Sleeping Bobby. Potter, Giselle, illus. (p. 1589)
Osborne, Mary Pope & PLC Editors Staff. Carnival at Candlelight. Murdocca, Sal, illus. (p. 270)
Osborne, Mary Pope, et al. Buenos Días, Gorilas. Murdocca, Sal, illus. (p. 235)
—Búfalos Antes del Desayuno. Murdocca, Sal, illus. (p. 235)
—Favorite Series Starters Boxed Set: A Collection of First Books from Five Favorite Series for Early Chapter Book Readers (p. 578)
—Horse Heroes. (p. 799)
—Jueves de Acción de Gracias. Murdocca, Sal, illus. (p. 931)
—Maremoto en Hawái. Murdocca, Sal, illus. (p. 1092)
—Miedo Escénico en una Noche de Verano. Murdocca, Sal, illus. (p. 1139)
—Perros Salvajes a la Hora de la Cena. Murdocca, Sal, illus. (p. 1344)
—Tigres Al Anochecer. Murdocca, Sal, illus. (p. 1749)
—Time to Dance: Virginia's Civil War Diary. (p. 1753)
Osborne, Mike, jt. auth. see Edom, Helen.
Osborne, Nancy. Rhyming Words: Cut & Paste. (p. 1468)
Osborne, Richard, illus. see Carter, Russell Gordon.
Osborne, Richard, illus. see Thomas, David, ed.
Osborne, Rick. Amazing & Unexplainable Things in the Bible. (p. 52)
—Legend of the Christmas Stocking: An Inspirational Story of a Wish Come True Griffin, Jim, illus. (p. 989)
Osborne, Rick, jt. auth. see Blackaby, Tom.
Osborne, Rick & Strauss, Ed. Angels & Demons (p. 75)
Osborne, Rick, et al. Creepy Creatures & Bizarre Beasts from the Bible Carpenter, Anthony, illus. (p. 381)
—Weird & Gross Bible Stuff Carpenter, Anthony, illus. (p. 1872)
Osborne, Robin. Boy who Loved to Shim-sham Shimmy. (p. 219)
Osborne, Will, illus. see Osborne, Mary Pope.
Osborne, Will, jt. auth. see Osborne, Mary Pope.
Osborne, Will & Osborne, Mary Pope. Dinosaurs: A Nonfiction Companion to Dinosaurs Before Dark. Murdocca, Sal, illus. (p. 444)
Osborne, William. Hitler's Secret. (p. 786)
Osbourne, David. World of Waters or A Peaceful Progress O'er the Unpathed Sea. (p. 1957)
Osbourne, John, see Osbourne, Ozzy, pseud.
Osbourne, Ozzy, pseud & Zink, Michelle. Guardian of the Gate. (p. 728)
Osburn, Jacquelyn. Willy, the Worried Worm. (p. 1934)
Osburn, LeaAnn. Latin Verbs Rock! Exercise Book. (p. 979)
Oscar, Erica. Heart to Love. (p. 760)
Oscar, Hijuelos, jt. auth. see Hijuelos, Oscar.
Oscar Wilde. Happy Prince & Other Tales. Charles Robinson, illus. (p. 746)
Oscar, Wilde, jt. auth. see Wilde, Oscar.
Osei, Leah. Boy Who Cried Wolf & Other Aesop Fables. (p. 219)
—Bremen Town Musicians: A Retelling of the Story by the Brothers Grimm. (p. 226)
—Bremen Town Musicians: A Retelling of the Story by the Brother's Grimm. (p. 226)
—Why Anansi Has Eight Thin Legs: A Tale from West Africa (p. 1922)
Osei, Nana. Young & Debt Free: Practical Advice for the Financially Challenged. (p. 1978)
Osei-Agyemang, Andrew Nana. Before the Lion Became King. (p. 158)
Osei-Bonsu, Patrick. Run to Win: Releasing the Champion Within You. (p. 1496)
Oseid, Kelsey, illus. see Adams, B.
Oseid, Kelsey, illus. see Atwood, Megan.
Oseid, Kelsey, illus. see Baller, Darice.
Oseman, Alice. Solitaire. (p. 1608)
Osenchakov, Yuri, illus. see Nilsen, Morten.
Oser, Bodhi. Fuck This Book. (p. 646)
O'Shaughnessy, Brendan, jt. auth. see Guibert, Susan Mullen.
O'Shaughnessy, Darren, see Shan, Darren, pseud.
O'Shaughnessy McKenna, Colleen. Third Grade Wedding Bells? Roth, Stephanie, illus. (p. 1734)
O'Shaughnessy, Nancy, illus. see Macaluso, Jennifer.
O'Shaughnessy, Ruth. Bats after Dark. (p. 145)
—Big Cats after Dark. (p. 180)
—Crocodiles & Alligators after Dark. (p. 384)
—Owls after Dark. (p. 1315)
—Raccoons after Dark. (p. 1430)
—Snakes after Dark. (p. 1596)
O'Shaughnessy, Tam, jt. auth. see Ride, Sally.
O'Shaughnessy, Tam E. Inside Story of Earth. (p. 877)
—Totally Amazing Careers in Earth Science. (p. 1771)
O'Shaughnessy, Tam E., jt. auth. see Ride, Sally.
O'Shay, Alex. Ten Acts of Kindess: An Alex Story. (p. 1718)
O'Shea, Bonnie, illus. see Winter, Christopher.
O'Shea, Clare, jt. auth. see Llewellyn, Claire.
O'Shea, Clare, jt. auth. see Powell, Jillian.
O'Shea, Maria & Spilling, Michael. Kuwait. (p. 968)
O'Shea, Mark. Exploring Nature: Incredible Lizards - Discover the Astonishing World of Chameleons, Geckos, Iguanas & More, with over 190 Pictures. (p. 552)
O'Shea, Mark, jt. auth. see Taylor, Barbara.
O'Shea, Mick. One Direction: No Limits. (p. 1294)
O'Shea, Mick, jt. auth. see Shields, Clarissa.
O'Shea, Miranda, illus. see Weinstein, Grit.
O'Shea, M.J. Blood Moon [Library Edition]. (p. 200)
—Catch My Breath. (p. 279)
—Cold Moon [Library Edition]. (p. 338)
O'Shea, Pauleen. Buddy's Bedtime. Dohanish, Jason, illus. (p. 235)
O'Shei, Tim. Alone in the Wilderness! Brennan Hawkins' Story of Survival (p. 48)
—Batista (p. 144)
—Bill Clinton: A MyReportLinks. Com Book. (p. 186)
—Bone-Chilling Myths (p. 208)
—Civil War Spies (p. 325)
—Creepy Urban Legends (p. 381)
—Diana, Princess of Wales (p. 434)
—Gerald R. Ford: A MyReportLinks.com Book. (p. 666)
—How to Survive in the Wilderness (p. 822)
—How to Survive on a Deserted Island (p. 822)
—John Cena (p. 921)
—Karate (p. 943)
—Kendo [Scholastic]. (p. 948)
—Left for Dead! Lincoln Hall's Story of Survival (p. 987)
—Marconi & Tesla: Pioneers of Radio Communication. (p. 1092)
—Muay Thai (p. 1188)
—Philo T. Farnsworth: Visionary Inventor of Television. (p. 1351)
—Princess Kiko of Japan (p. 1404)
—Secrets of Pompeii: Buried City of Ancient Rome (p. 1545)
—Shawn Michaels (p. 1563)
—Shipwreck! Debbie Kiley's Story of Survival (p. 1567)
—Spy Basics (p. 1636)
—Stranded! Amy Racina's Story of Survival (p. 1664)
—Tae Kwon Do (p. 1695)
—Undertaker (p. 1816)
—World War II Spies (p. 1959)
—World's Most Dangerous Jobs (p. 1960)
—World's Zaniest Sports. (p. 1961)
O'Shei, Tim & Capstone Press Editors. Shark Attack! Bethany Hamilton's Story of Survival (p. 1562)
O'Shei, Tim & Capstone Press Staff. Disaster in the Mountains! Colby Coombs' Story of Survival (p. 446)
—Stranded in the Snow! Eric Lemarque's Story of Survival (p. 1664)
O'Shei, Tim & Marren, Joe. George H. W. Bush: A MyReportLinks. Com Book. (p. 663)
—George W. Bush: A MyReportLinks. Com Book. (p. 664)
O'Shei, Tim, et al. Archaeological Mysteries (p. 95)
Osher, David, et al. Safe, Supportive, Successful Schools Step by Step. (p. 1502)
Oshida, Tim. Society's Traitor. (p. 1605)
Oshii, Mamoru, jt. auth. see Katsura, Masakazu.
Oshima, Ken Tadashi, jt. auth. see Isozaki, Arata.
Oshima, Towa. High School Girls. (p. 778)
—High School Girls Volume 1-6 Set. (p. 778)
Oshiro, Beverly & Sachs, Ruth. Adolf Eichmann. (p. 13)
Oshiro, Kim Teresa. B C in Harmony. (p. 122)
Oshiro, Kimberley. Saga of Simon the Skinny Pig: Simon Saves the Day. Yee, Jeanne, illus. (p. 1502)
Osho International Foundation Staff. Sex Matters: From Sex to Superconsciousness. (p. 1556)
Osho Staff, et al. Compassion: The Ultimate Flowering of Love. (p. 352)
Osier, Dan. Basketball's MVPs (p. 143)
—Dirk Nowitzki. (p. 445)
—Kevin Garnett. (p. 950)
—Kobe Bryant. (p. 966)
—LeBron James. (p. 987)
—Steve Nash. (p. 1649)
—Tim Duncan. (p. 1750)
Osier, Peter. History of Western Sculpture. (p. 785)
Osier, Peter, ed. History of Western Sculpture. (p. 785)
Osilaja, Peter Deji. My Body Is Mine! Phillips, Gary, illus. (p. 1198)
Osiyemi, Linda Omonike. Pot & the Necklace. (p. 1388)
Oskarsson, Bardur. Flat Rabbit. (p. 603)
Osker, Denise, illus. see Davis, Dayna.
Osle, Janessa. Animals Around the World. Legendre, Philippe, illus. (p. 82)
—Favorite Pets. Legendre, Philippe, illus. (p. 578)
—Planes, Trains & Moving Machines. Legendre, Philippe, illus. (p. 1367)
—Princesses, Fairies & Fairy Tales. Legendre, Philippe, illus. (p. 1406)
—Sea Creatures & Other Favorite Animals. Legendre, Philippe, illus. (p. 1534)
Osleeb, Rebecca, jt. auth. see London, S. Keith.
Osman, Haslinah. Asmaullahil Husnaa Book 1: Hayya Naqraak Bismillah Reading Series. (p. 106)
Osment, Philip. Duck! (p. 488)
—Palace of Fear. (p. 1319)
—Plays for Young People: Who's Breaking - Listen - Sleeping Dogs - Wise Guys. (p. 1373)
Osment, Philip, et al. Class Acts. (p. 327)
Osmer, Janice. Timmy & the Captain. (p. 1754)
Osmond, Claudia. Smudge's Mark. (p. 1595)
Osmond, Claudia, jt. auth. see Lloyd, Jennifer.
Osmond, Jack, illus. see Osmond, Joanne H.
Osmond, Jimmy. Awesome Possum Family Band. (p. 121)
Osmond, Joanne H. Fishy Adventure. Osmond, Jack, illus. (p. 599)
Osmundson, Linda. How the West Was Drawn: Women's Art (p. 813)
—How the West Was Drawn: Cowboy Charlie's Art (p. 813)
Osmundson, Linda L. Frederic Remington's Art (p. 633)
Osnaya, Ricardo, illus. see Manning, Matthew K.
Osofsky, Randy & Charlesbridge Publishing Staff. Art in Early America. (p. 102)
Osorio, Marta. Caballito Que Queria Volar. (p. 250)
—Manuela. Monreal, Violeta, illus. (p. 1089)
—Manuela en el Campo. (p. 1089)
—Manuela y el Mar. Monreal, Violeta, illus. (p. 1089)
Osorio, Marta & Marta, Osorio. Caballito Que Queria Volar. (p. 250)
—Lagarto Sonador. (p. 971)
Osorio, Rick. Great Adventure of Sally Rock & el Lobo. (p. 713)
—Great Adventure of Sally Rock & the Cretaceous Chicken. (p. 713)
—Great Adventure of Sally Rock & the Secret of Man (p. 713)
Osorio, Sergio, illus. see Fernandez, Francisco.
Osorio, Sergio, illus. see Kidder, Harvey.
Osornio, Catherine L. Declaration of Independence from A to Z Johnson, Layne, illus. (p. 422)
Osorno, Laura, illus. see Baena, Gloria.
O'Sorus, Roman. Eminem. (p. 519)
O'sorus, Roman, jt. auth. see O'Sorus, Roman.
O'Sorus, Roman & O'sorus, Roman. Eminem. (p. 519)
Ospital, Geneveive, illus. see Kamke, Bridget.
Osseo-Asare, Fran. Good Soup Attracts Chairs Haynes, Joyce, illus. (p. 700)
Ossipova, Irina, tr. see King, Dedie.
Ost, Nina. Gingerbread Man & the Dinosaurs. (p. 677)
Ostby, Kristin. Baby Panda Is Born. Washburn, Lucia, illus. (p. 127)
Ostby, Kristin & Olsen, Leigh. Doodle All Around the World with Hello Kitty. (p. 469)
—Hello Kitty's Super Sweet Journal. (p. 764)
Osteen, Joel. Lecturas Diarias de Su Mejor Vida Ahora. (p. 987)
—Scriptures & Meditations for Your Best Life Now. (p. 1533)
—Your Best Life Now for Moms. (p. 1980)
Osteen, Victoria. Gifts from the Heart. Palmisciano, Diane, illus. (p. 675)
—My Happy Heart Books Day, Betsy, illus. (p. 1210)
—Unexpected Treasures. Palmisciano, Diane, illus. (p. 1817)
Ostendorf, Jenifer Wirth & Bisbee, Richard J. Worthwhile Family Tales. (p. 1962)
Oster, Kalab J. Lacivious. Oster, Kalab J. et al, eds. (p. 970)
Osterbach, Batya. Pini the Pitcher: A Story for Hanukkah. Eisby, Lizzy, illus. (p. 1359)
Osterbach, Batya Kirshenbaum. Pini the Pitcher: A Story for Hanukkah. Eisby, Lizzy, illus. (p. 1359)
Osterhold, Jared. Cooks up a Surprise. (p. 362)
—Olivia & the Babies. (p. 1286)
—OLIVIA & the Pet Project. (p. 1286)
—OLIVIA Becomes a Vet. (p. 1286)
—Olivia Claus. (p. 1286)
—OLIVIA Goes Camping. (p. 1286)
—OLIVIA Goes to the Library. (p. 1286)
—OLIVIA Helps Mother Nature. (p. 1286)
—OLIVIA Measures Up. (p. 1287)
—Olivia Opens a Lemonade Stand. (p. 1287)
—OLIVIA Plants a Garden. (p. 1287)
—OLIVIA Plays Soccer. (p. 1287)
—OLIVIA Takes a Trip. (p. 1287)
—OLIVIA Wishes on a Star. (p. 1287)
—Search for the Book of Thoth (p. 1537)
Osterhold, Jared, illus. see Banks, Steven, et al.
Osterhold, Jared, illus. see Barton, Elizabeth & Shaw, Natalie.
Osterhold, Jared, illus. see Falconer, Ian, et al.
Osterhold, Jared, illus. see Gallo, Tina.
Osterhold, Jared, illus. see McCurry, Kristen.
Osterhold, Jared, illus. see McDoogle, Farrah.
Osterhold, Jared, illus. see Shaw, Natalie.
Osterhold, Jared, illus. see Sollinger, Emily.
Osterhold, Jared, illus. see Testa, Maggie.
Osterkamp, Ole. Sharefish Tale: A Story about Learning to Share. Scott, Korey, illus. (p. 1561)
Osterlund, Anne. Academy 7. (p. 7)
—Aurelia. (p. 116)
Ostermann, Riley. So Big. (p. 1601)
Ostermann, Ruby. Willie Tucker & His Gramma: The Life of a Dog. (p. 1934)
Ostermeyer Photography. Frosty & Snowy's Arctic Adventures. (p. 645)
Ostermeyer, Tim. Snowball's Antarctic Adventures. (p. 1600)
Ostermeyer, Tim, photos by. Titus & Tiana: Lesson for Baby Tigers. (p. 1758)
Osterwell, Adam. Amulet of Komondor. Thorpe, Peter, illus. (p. 66)
—Cooper & the Enchanted Metal Detector. (p. 365)
—Lost Treasure of Talus Scree. Thorpe, Peter, illus. (p. 1057)

 Full bibliographic information is available on the Title Index page number referenced in parentheses at the end of each entry

Osterweil, Adam & Smith, Craig. Baseball Card Kid. Smith, Craig, illus. (p. 141)
Ostin, Joyce, photos by. Hollywood Moms: Photographs by Joyce Ostin. (p. 789)
Ostler, Heather. Siren's Secret. (p. 1581)
Ostlere, Cathy. Karma. (p. 944)
Ostopowich, Melanie. Oceans, Lakes, & Rivers. (p. 1277)
—Oceans, Rivers, & Lakes. (p. 1277)
—Rock Cycle. (p. 1482)
—Rocks. (p. 1483)
—Waste. (p. 1860)
—Water Pollution. (p. 1863)
Ostow, David, jt. auth. see Ostow, Micol.
Ostow, Micol. 30 Guys in 30 Days. (p. 1996)
—Emily Goldberg Learns to Salsa. (p. 519)
—Gettin' Lucky. (p. 668)
—GoldenGirl. (p. 695)
—House of Shards. (p. 803)
—Louise Trapeze Is Totally 100% Fearless. Barrager, Brigette, illus. (p. 1058)
—Popular Vote. (p. 1385)
—What Would My Cell Phone Do? (p. 1895)
Ostow, Micol & Harlan, Noah. Up over Under. (p. 1824)
Ostow, Micol & Ostow, David. So Punk Rock: And Other Ways to Disappoint Your Mother. (p. 1602)
Ostrander, John. GrimJack: the Manx Cat: The Manx Cat. (p. 724)
Ostrander, P. Martin. P Martin Ostrander's Dangerous Four Series: Book #1. (p. 1316)
Ostroff, Neil. Tim Madison, Galactic Warrior. (p. 1750)
Ostrom, Bob. Friends till the End! (p. 639)
Ostrom, Bob, illus. see Duke, Shirley.
Ostrom, Bob, illus. see Hagler, Gina.
Ostrom, Bob, illus. see Hall, Pamela.
Ostrom, Bob, illus. see Jacobson, Ryan.
Ostrom, Bob, illus. see Kelley, C.
Ostrom, Bob, illus. see Marsico, Katie.
Ostrom, Bob, illus. see Mayer, Kirsten.
Ostrom, Bob, illus. see Meier, Joanne D. & Minden, Cecilia.
Ostrom, Bob, illus. see Meier, Joanne.
Ostrom, Bob, illus. see Miller, Pam.
Ostrom, Bob, illus. see Minden, Cecilia & Meier, Joanne D.
Ostrom, Bob, illus. see Minden, Cecilia.
Ostrom, Bob, illus. see Murphy, Steve & Murphy, Sonia.
Ostrom, Bob, illus. see Random House.
Ostrom, Bob, illus. see Rosenberg, Pam.
Ostrom, Bob, illus. see Scelsa, Greg.
Ostrom, Bob, illus. see Shulman, Mark.
Ostrom, Bob, illus. see StJohn, Amanda.
Ostrom, Gladys. Leggys in Number-land. Suits, Rosella, illus. (p. 990)
Ostrove, Karen. Rise & Shine: A Challah-Day Tale. Scott, Kimberley, illus. (p. 1474)
Ostrovski, Emil. Paradox of Vertical Flight. (p. 1323)
Ostrovsky, Alexsandr. Birthday: Companies-Products-Services. Ostrovsky, Alexsandr, illus. (p. 192)
—Clouds: Companies-Products-Services. Ostrovsky, Alexsandr, illus. (p. 335)
—Paper Kite. Ostrovsky, Alexsandr, illus. (p. 1322)
Ostrow, Kim. Bear in the Big Blue House. (p. 151)
—Great Snail Race. Bond, Clint & Clark, Andy, illus. (p. 718)
—Mission Nuestra Senora de la Soledad. (p. 1153)
—Mission Santa Cruz. (p. 1153)
Ostrow, Kim, jt. auth. see Reisner, Molly.
Ostrow, Kim & Nuñes, Sofia. Discovering Mission Santa Cruz. (p. 449)
Ostrowski, Jesse Feathers. God's Little Princess Warrior. (p. 691)
Ostrowski, Justin, illus. see Vezeau, Sheila.
Ostrowski, Thaddeus & Smith, Robert J. Primary Source Readings in Christian Morality. (p. 1400)
Ostrowski-Young, Lori. Aboo & Sidekick: Adventures of Two Cats in a People World. (p. 5)
O'Such, Holly. Aunt Ruby, Do I Look Like God? (p. 115)
O'Sullivan, Darren. Sleep Taker. (p. 1588)
O'Sullivan, Deirdre. Cousin Caleigh's Cartoons: And Other Stories (p. 373)
O'Sullivan, Elizabeth. Sugar Gliders. (p. 1673)
O'Sullivan, Helen. Magic Piano. Busuttil, Conor, illus. (p. 1073)
O'Sullivan, Jill Korey. Heinle Picture Dictionary for Children. (p. 762)
—Picture Dictionary for Children. (p. 1355)
O'Sullivan, Jill Korey & Makishi, Cynthia. Heinle Picture Dictionary for Children. (p. 762)
O'Sullivan, Joanne. Migration Nation: Animals on the Go from Coast to Coast. (p. 1141)
O'Sullivan, Joanne, jt. auth. see Cusick, Dawn.
OSullivan, Michaeleen, tr. Monarch Universe: Children's Picture Book. (p. 1163)
O'Sullivan, Mike, ed. see Blaylock, Josh.
O'Sullivan, Orlaith, jt. ed. see McKendrick, Scot.
O'Sullivan, Robyn. Jackie Robinson Plays Ball. (p. 904)
—More Than Man's Best Friend: The Story of Working Dogs. (p. 1175)
—Weedy Sea Dragons, Spitting Cobras: And Other Wild & Amazing Animals. (p. 1871)
—Wright Brothers Fly. (p. 1963)
—Your 206 Bones, 32 Teeth, & Other Body Math. (p. 1979)
O'Sullivan, Tom & Bacon, Paul. Shirley Temple's Fairyland: The Wild Swans; Beauty & the Beast; Rumpelstiltskin; the Sleeping Beauty. (p. 1567)
Osuna, Rosa. No es Facil, Pequena Ardilla. (p. 1258)
Osundare, Niyi. Early Birds: Poems for Junior Secondary Schools. (p. 493)
Oswald, Ali Rose. Maylee & the Crazy Crush. (p. 1113)
Oswald, Ash, illus. see Badger, Meredith.
Oswald, Ash, illus. see Kalkipsakis, Thalia.
Oswald, Ash, illus. see Larry, H. I.
Oswald, Ash, illus. see McAuley, Rowan.
Oswald, Ash, illus. see Perry, Chrissie.
Oswald, Ash, illus. see Steggall, Vicki.
Oswald, Bonnie, illus. see Brady, Janeen.
Oswald, Debra. Blue Noise. (p. 203)
—Getting Air. (p. 669)
Oswald, Michael J. 3 Years Apart. (p. 1992)
Oswald, Mike. Ghostly Terrors: A Haunted Houseful of Ghostly Tales. (p. 672)
Oswald, Nina. Saving Endangered Animals: Develop Understanding of Fractions & Numbers (p. 1517)
Oswald, Pete, illus. see DiSiena, Laura Lyn & Eliot, Hannah.
Oswalt, Janice. Sammie's Rock. (p. 1507)
Oswalt, Kay. Fred Threads: Book One: the Interview. Nagle, Paul, illus. (p. 632)
Oszajca, Linda, jt. auth. see Collins, Malia.
Oszkay, Zulay, tr. see Rinder, Lenore.
Osztian, Phillip J. Come off the Couch Daddy. (p. 347)
Ot, Eli, jt. auth. see Ot, Elli.
Ot, Elli. Iris y el Gato Negro. Brignole, Giancarla, tr. (p. 887)
Ot, Elli & Ot, Eli. Docto y los Jazmines. Brignole, Giancarla, tr. (p. 459)
Ota, Yuko, illus. see Johnson, Alaya Dawn.
Ota, Yuko, illus. see Robbins, Trina.
Ota, Yuko, illus. see Thielbar, Melinda.
Ota, Yuko & Panagariya, Ananth. Adventure Time: Candy Capers. (p. 14)
Otak, Leah, tr. see Awa, Simon, et al.
Otaka, Shinobu. Magi (p. 1071)
Otenbaker, Audrey Lee. God's Jewel. (p. 691)
Otero, Armando Leiero. En un Martes Trece... Pelaez, Ricardo, illus. (p. 523)
Otero, Armando Lenero. Arbol del Tiempo: Para Que Sirven las Genealogias. Estrada, Ixchel, illus. (p. 94)
Otero, Eduardo A. Alfabeto Cubano. Ganz, Cristina Milián, illus. (p. 37)
Otero, Hanna & Callery, Sean. Scholastic Discover More Reader Level 2: Branches of the Military. (p. 1521)
Otero, Nicolas, illus. see Anaya, Rudolfo.
Otero, Rodolfo. Estrella Peregrina. (p. 538)
Otero, Sole, illus. see Atwood, Megan.
Otero, Sole, illus. see Bolte, Mari.
Otero, Sole, illus. see Malaspina, Ann.
Otero, Sole, illus. see Troupe, Thomas Kingsley.
Otey Little, Mimi. Yoshiko & the Foreigner. Otey Little, Mimi, illus. (p. 1972)
Otfinoski, Steve. All in the Family: A Look-It-Up Guide to the In-Laws, Outlaws, & Offspring of Mythology. (p. 44)
—Coin Collecting for Kids. Graham, Jack, illus. (p. 338)
—Drake: Actor & Hip-Hop Artist. (p. 479)
—Television: From Concept to Consumer. (p. 1716)
Otfinoski, Steve, jt. auth. see Otfinoski, Steven.
Otfinoski, Steven. 1990-2010. (p. 2002)
—Afghanistan. (p. 26)
—Air Travel: Science Technology Engineering. (p. 31)
—Alligators. (p. 47)
—Building the Transcontinental Railroad: An Interactive Engineering Adventure (p. 239)
—Calvin Coolidge. (p. 255)
—Child Labor Reform Movement: An Interactive History Adventure. (p. 301)
—Classic Books. (p. 327)
—Coming-of-Age Fiction. (p. 348)
—Computers. (p. 355)
—Crows. (p. 386)
—David Livingstone: Deep in the Heart of Africa. (p. 411)
—Day of Infamy: The Story of the Attack on Pearl Harbor. (p. 414)
—Dogs. (p. 462)
—Extraordinary Short Story Writing. (p. 555)
—Extreme Paintball. (p. 556)
—Extreme Skateboarding. (p. 556)
—Extreme Surfing. (p. 557)
—F. W. Prep (p. 559)
—Fireflies. (p. 592)
—Georgia. (p. 665)
—Grover Cleveland. (p. 725)
—Gun Control. (p. 732)
—Henry Hudson: In Search of the Northwest Passage. (p. 768)
—Here We Go! (p. 771)
—High-Speed Trains: From Concept to Consumer. (p. 778)
—Hindenburg Explosion: Core Events of a Disaster in the Air (p. 780)
—Horses. (p. 800)
—Hummingbirds. (p. 826)
—Jaguars. (p. 905)
—Juan Ponce de Leon: Discoverer of Florida. (p. 930)
—Koalas. (p. 966)
—Latinos in the Arts. (p. 979)
—Major Disasters in U.S. History. (p. 1078)
—Manatees. (p. 1086)
—Native American Writers. (p. 1234)
—Native Americans at the Time of the Explorers: Set Of 6. (p. 1234)
—Native Americans at the Time of the Explorers: Text Pairs. (p. 1234)
—New Hampshire. (p. 1245)
—New Republic. (p. 1247)
—Outsider Fiction. (p. 1313)
—Patriots & Redcoats: Stories of American Revolutionary War Leaders. (p. 1329)
—People of the American Revolution: Set Of 6. (p. 1339)
—People of the American Revolution: Text Pairs. (p. 1339)
—Pigs & Hogs. (p. 1358)
—Primary Source History of Westward Expansion. (p. 1400)
—Quicksand. (p. 1427)
—Raccoons. (p. 1430)
—Rockets. (p. 1483)
—Roman Catholicism. (p. 1485)
—Science Fiction & Fantasy. (p. 1526)
—Scorpions. (p. 1530)
—Seahorses. (p. 1536)
—Sinking of the Lusitania: An Interactive History Adventure (p. 1580)
—Skunks. (p. 1586)
—Spartans. (p. 1622)
—Squirrels. (p. 1637)
—Storks & Cranes. (p. 1655)
—Story of Juneteenth: An Interactive History Adventure. (p. 1658)
—Television. (p. 1716)
—Tornadoes. (p. 1770)
—Triangle Shirtwaist Factory Fire: Core Events of an Industrial Disaster (p. 1785)
—U. S. Constitution, Bill of Rights, & a New Nation. (p. 1806)
—Ukraine. (p. 1808)
—Voyages of Christopher Columbus: Set Of 6. (p. 1851)
—Voyages of Christopher Columbus: Text Pairs. (p. 1851)
—Wind, Solar, & Geothermal Power: From Concept to Consumer. (p. 1935)
—World War II Infantrymen: An Interactive History Adventure. (p. 1959)
—Yankees & Rebels: Stories of U.S. Civil War Leaders. (p. 1968)
—Zachary Taylor. (p. 1984)
Otfinoski, Steven, jt. auth. see Lassieur, Allison.
Otfinoski, Steven, jt. auth. see Schwabacher, Martin.
Otfinoski, Steven & Benduhn, Tea. Washington. (p. 1859)
Otfinoski, Steven & Burgan, Michael. You Choose: History: An Interactive History Adventure. (p. 1975)
Otfinoski, Steven & Gofen, Ethel. France. (p. 627)
Otfinoski, Steven & Otfinoski, Steve. Rutherford B. Hayes. (p. 1499)
Otfinoski, Steven & Steinitz, Andy. Maryland. (p. 1101)
Otfinoski, Steven Anthony. U. S. Constitution, Bill of Rights, & a New Nation (p. 1806)
Otfinoski, Steven, et al. Civil War. (p. 325)
—Hawaii. (p. 755)
—Revolutionary War. (p. 1466)
—Vermont. (p. 1837)
Others, et al. Avatar - The Last Airbender - The Lost Adventures. (p. 118)
Othitis, Anna. My First Travel Book: Angelic Airline Adventures. (p. 1208)
Otis, James. Calvert of Maryland: A Story of Lord Baltimore's Colony. (p. 255)
—Calvert of Maryland A Story of Lord Baltimore's Colony. (p. 255)
—Dick in the Desert. (p. 435)
—District Messenger Boy & a Necktie Party. (p. 454)
—Minute Boys of Mohawk Valley. (p. 1148)
—Neal, the Miller: A Son of Liberty. (p. 1238)
—Peter of New Amsterdam: A story of Old New York. (p. 1346)
—Raising the Pearl. (p. 1437)
—Richard of Jamestown: A story of the Virginia Colony. (p. 1469)
—Ruth of Boston: A story of the Massachusetts Bay Colony. (p. 1498)
—Stephen of Philadelphia: A Story of Penn's Colony. (p. 1648)
—Toby Tyler: Or Ten Weeks with a Circus. (p. 1760)
—Toby Tyler, or Ten Weeks with a Circus. (p. 1760)
—True Indian Tales from American History: In the Stirring Days of the Early Colonists. (p. 1792)
—Under the Liberty Tree, a Story of the Boston Massacre. (p. 1813)
Otis, Michelle, ed. see Owens, Carmen.
Otitoloju/Blazing Ideas Ltd, Ololade/Adewunmi, retold by. Kunkuru Da Kare: The Tortoise & the Dog. (p. 968)
Otitoloju/Blazing Ideas ltd, Ololade/Adewunmi, retold by. Kunkuru, Jaba Da Kurege: The Tortoise, the Rat & the Squirrel. (p. 968)
—Mbe, Nkapi na Osa. (p. 1114)
Otomo, Katsuhiro. Akira (p. 32)
O'Toole, Detra. Ty-Ty Quackers & the Hidden Treasure: Biblical Lessons with Barnyard Fun. (p. 1804)
O'Toole, Janet. On the Farm. Adams, Ben, illus. (p. 1290)
O'Toole, Janet & Anness Publishing Staff. Animals. Adams, Ben, illus. (p. 81)
—First Words. Adams, Ben, illus. (p. 597)
—Lift-the-Flap Learning: Lift the flaps to find out about vehicles! Adams, Ben, illus. (p. 1014)
O'Toole, Jeanette, illus. see Filipek, Nina & Andersen, Hans Christian.
O'Toole, Jeanette, illus. see Filipek, Nina.
O'Toole, Jeanette, illus. see Massey, Kay.
O'Toole, Julianne, illus. see Giangregorio, Kimberly A.
O'Toole, Mary. Little Bite - & Other Stories. (p. 1024)
O'Toole, Patrick. Alphabetimals — in the Wild! (p. 50)
—Alphabetimals Picture Dictionary. (p. 50)
O'Toole, Patrick & Coloring Books Staff. Alphabetimals Coloring Book. (p. 50)
O'Toole, Shaun. Transforming Texts. (p. 1778)
O'Toole-Freel, Judy. Aardvark, Aardvark, How Do You Do! (p. 2)
—Zigzag the Rocking Roadrunner. Freel, Mirle, illus. (p. 1986)
Otoshi, Kathryn. One. (p. 1293)
—Simon & the Sock Monster. (p. 1577)
—Two. (p. 1803)
—What Emily Saw. Otoshi, Kathryn, illus. (p. 1884)
—Zero. (p. 1986)
Otoshi, Kathryn, illus. see Friden, Chris.
Otoshi, Kathryn, illus. see Gage, Brian.
Otoshi, Kathryn, illus. see Hockinson, Liz.
Otoshi, Kathryn, illus. see Lendroth, Susan.
Otoshi, Kathryn, tr. see Gage, Brian.
Otowa, Rebecca. My Awesome Japan Adventure: A Diary about the Best 4 Months Ever! (p. 1196)
Ott, Jamie. Nando the Brave Traveler. (p. 1229)
Ott, John. Let's Draw Manga: Using Color. (p. 996)
Ott, Karen. Foolish Dandelion. (p. 614)
Ott, Margot Janet, illus. see Romansky, Sally Rosenberg.
Ott, Thomas, illus. see Jackson, Shirley.
Ottaiano, Mela. 240 Vocabulary Words Kids Need to Know - Grade 2: 24 Ready-to-Reproduce Packets That Make Vocabulary Building Fun & Effective. (p. 2001)
Ottaviani, Jim. Dignifying Science: Stories about Women Scientists. Gladden, Stephanie et al, illus. (p. 440)
—Primates: The Fearless Science of Jane Goodall, Dian Fossey, & Biruté Galdikas. Wicks, Maris, illus. (p. 1400)
—T-Minus: The Race to the Moon. Cannon, Kevin & Cannon, Zander, illus. (p. 1694)
—T-Minus: The Race to the Moon. Cannon, Zander & Cannon, Kevin, illus. (p. 1694)
—Two-Fisted Science: Stories about Scientists. (p. 1803)
Ottaviani, Jim, ed. see Knight, Charles R.
Ottaviano, Patricia. Girl World: How to Ditch the Drama & Find Your Inner Amazing. (p. 679)
Ottaway, Jacqueline. Riddle of the Seaplanes (Level S) (p. 1470)
Otte, John W. Failstate: Legends. (p. 562)
—Failstate. (p. 562)
Otten, Charlotte. Flying Mouse. Crawford, Greg, illus. (p. 610)
Otten, Charlotte F. Home in a Wilderness Fort: Copper Harbor 1844. (p. 792)
Otten, Jack. Atletismo. (p. 113)
—Baloncesto. (p. 135)
—Baloncesto (Basketball) (p. 135)
—Beisbol. (p. 161)
—Béisbol (Baseball) (p. 161)
—Futbol. (p. 650)
—Fútbol (Soccer) (p. 651)
—Hockey Sobre Hielo. (p. 787)
—Hockey sobre hielo (Ice Hockey) (p. 787)
—Ice Hockey. (p. 850)
—Soccer. (p. 1603)
—Tenis. (p. 1720)
—Tenis (Tennis) (p. 1720)
—Tennis. (p. 1720)
—Track. (p. 1775)
Ottenbreit, Sharon. Only One Toy Allowed. (p. 1298)
Otter Tail County Historical Society Staff, compiled by. Places. (p. 1366)
Ottersley, Martha T. Dora & the Winter Games (Dora the Explorer) Hall, Susan, illus. (p. 470)
Otterstätter, Sara, illus. see Pelletier, Mia.
Ottina, Laura. In the Arctic. Ranchetti, Sebastiano, illus. (p. 865)
—In the Forest. Ranchetti, Sebastiano, illus. (p. 866)
—In the Jungle. Ranchetti, Sebastiano, illus. (p. 866)
—In the Sea. Ranchetti, Sebastiano, illus. (p. 867)
—On the Farm. Ranchetti, Sebastiano, illus. (p. 1290)
—On the Savanna. Ranchetti, Sebastiano, illus. (p. 1291)
Ottinger, Jon, illus. see Pugliano-Martin, Carol.
Ottley, Matt, illus. see Morgan, Sally, et al.
Ottley, Matt, illus. see Parker, Danny.
Ottley, Reginald. By the Sandhills of Yamboorah. (p. 249)
Ottley, Ryan, jt. auth. see Kirkman, Robert.
Ottman, Frank. Not Wanted: The Memories of Cain Mann. (p. 1267)
Ottman, Margaret B. Lonely Loon. (p. 1046)
Otto, Carolyn. Celebrate Chinese New Year: With Fireworks, Dragons, & Lanterns. (p. 283)
—Celebrate Cinco de Mayo: With Fiestas, Music, & Dance. (p. 283)
—Celebrate Valentine's Day: With Love, Cards, & Candy. (p. 284)
—Celebremos el Cinco de Mayo: Con Fiestas, Musica y Baile. (p. 285)
Otto, Carolyn B. Celebrate Kwanzaa: With Candles, Community, & the Fruits of the Harvest. (p. 284)
—Holidays Around the World: Celebrate Kwanzaa: With Candles, Community, & the Fruits of the Harvest. (p. 788)
—Raccoon at Clear Creek Road. Trachok, Cathy, illus. (p. 1430)
Otto, Denise A. You Decide. (p. 1975)
Otto, Frei, jt. auth. see McQuaid, Matilda.
Otto, Gina. Cassandra's Angel Joost, Trudy, illus. (p. 276)
Otto, Joanne. You-Song. (p. 1976)
Otto, Nancy J. My New Home. (p. 1216)
Otto, Patricia. Play Fair with Peas Please Musical Play (p. 1371)
Ottolenghi, Carol. Bella Durmiente. (p. 162)
—Juan y los Frijoles Magicos (Jack & the Beanstalk), Grades PK-3. Porfirio, Guy, illus. (p. 930)
—Little Red Hen (La Gallinita Roja), Grades PK - 3. Holladay, Reggie, illus. (p. 1035)
—Princess & the Pea. (p. 1402)
—Princess & the Pea (La Princesa y el Guisante) (p. 1402)
—Puss in Boots. (p. 1420)
—Puss in Boots (El Gato con Botas) (p. 1420)
—Sleeping Beauty. (p. 1589)
—Three Billy Goats Gruff. (p. 1741)
—Three Billy Goats Gruff (Los Tres Chivitos) (p. 1741)
Ottolini, Horacio, jt. auth. see Fisch, Sholly.
Otukile, Mpho. Lion's Deceit. Dow, S. B., illus. (p. 1021)
Otway, Helen. 1001 Unbelievable Facts: Mind-Boggling, Impossible, Weird! (p. 2002)
—Christmas Drawing & Activity Book. (p. 313)
Oubre, Glenn. Twelve Days of a Berry Christmas. (p. 1800)
Ouchley, Amy Griffin. Swamper: Letters from a Louisiana Swamp Rabbit. (p. 1688)
Oud, Pauline. Big Sister Sarah. Oud, Pauline, illus. (p. 183)
—Christmas with Lily & Milo. (p. 316)
—Eating with Lily & Milo. Oud, Pauline, illus. (p. 501)
—Getting Dressed with Lily & Milo. Oud, Pauline, illus. (p. 669)
—Going to the Beach with Lily & Milo. Oud, Pauline, illus. (p. 693)
—Going to the Zoo with Lily & Milo. Oud, Pauline, illus. (p. 693)
—Having a Party with Lily & Milo. Oud, Pauline, illus. (p. 754)
—Ian's New Potty. (p. 849)
Oudinot, Wanda, photos by see Sedlacek, Jan Gill.
Ouellet, Debbie. Hero's Worth. Hnatiuk, Charlie, illus. (p. 774)
Ouellet, Joanne, illus. see MacDonald, Anne Louise.
Ouellette, Jeannine. Day Without Immigrants: Rallying Behind America's Newcomers (p. 415)
—Hurricane Katrina. (p. 830)
Oughton, Taylor, illus. see Galvin, Laura Gates.
Oughton, Taylor, illus. see Pfeffer, Wendy.
Oughton, Taylor, illus. see Ring, Elizabeth.
Ougi, Yuzuha. Brother (p. 231)
Ouida. Dog of Flanders. (p. 461)
Ouida, jt. auth. see De La Ramee, Louise.
Ouida [Louise de la Ramee]. Bebee. (p. 155)
Ouilette, K. T. Valliere-Denis. Two Birds in a Box. Du Houx, E. M. Cornell, illus. (p. 1803)
Oulmet, David, illus. see San Souci, Robert D.
Oulton, Harry. Pig Called Heather. (p. 1357)
Ouren, Todd. Patriotic Songs (p. 1329)
—Star-Spangled Banner: America's National Anthem & Its History (p. 1641)

—You're a Grand Old Flag: A Jubilant Song about Old Glory (p. 1982)
Ouren, Todd, illus. see Blair, Eric, et al.
Ouren, Todd, illus. see Blair, Eric.
Ouren, Todd, illus. see Dahl, Michael.
Ouren, Todd, illus. see Doering Tourville, Amanda.
Ouren, Todd, illus. see Hall, M. C.
Ouren, Todd, illus. see Haugen, Brenda.
Ouren, Todd, illus. see Jones, Christianne C.
Ouren, Todd, illus. see Loewen, Nancy.
Ouren, Todd, illus. see Salas, Laura Purdie.
Ouren, Todd, illus. see Shaskan, Trisha Speed.
Ouren, Todd, illus. see Stille, Darlene R.
Ouren, Todd, illus. see Stockland, Patricia M.
Ouren, Todd, illus. see Tourville, Amanda Doering.
Ouriou, Susan, jt. auth. see Britt, Fanny.
Ouriou, Susan, tr. see Chartrand, Lili.
Ouriou, Susan, tr. see Frechette, Carole.
Ouriou, Susan, tr. see Gingras, Charlotte.
Ouriou, Susan, tr. see Hébert, Marie-Francine.
Ouriou, Susan, tr. see Luján, Jorge.
Ouriou, Susan, tr. see Marineau, Michele.
Ouriou, Susan, tr. see Serrano, Francisco.
Ousley, Clayton Gerard, photos by see Duchene-Marshall, Michele A.
Ousley, Pamala. Amy & the Pacifier. (p. 66)
Outcalt, Todd. Holidays, Holy Days, & Other Big Days for Youth. (p. 788)
—Show Me the Way: 50 Bible Study Methods for Youth. (p. 1570)
Outcault, R. F. My Resolutions, by Buster Brown. (p. 1217)
Outhwaite, Ida Rentoul, jt. auth. see Ediciones B (Firm) Staff.
Outman, James L. & Baker, Lawrence W. U. S. Immigration & Migration: Primary Sources. (p. 1806)
Outman, James L., et al. U. S. Immigration & Migration: Biographies (p. 1806)
—U.S. Immigration & Migration (p. 1826)
Outohak, Diana, illus. see Golden, Pam.
Outram, Evelyn. Sav & Josh O Lucky's Christmas Adventure & Magic Street. (p. 1516)
Outram, Richard. Adventures of Exokid: Growing Financial Wings. (p. 18)
—Adventures of Exokid & the Teachings of Money. Kapatos, Elizabeth, illus. (p. 18)
Ovadia, Ron. Hank. (p. 742)
Ovadia, Ron, jt. auth. see Grant, Ron.
Ovakimyan, Liza, illus. see Perry, Melanie Denise.
Ovalles, Misty Haney. Picture the Place. (p. 1356)
Ovani, Germano. Monkey King. (p. 1165)
Ovenden, Mark. Transit Maps of the World. Ashworth, Mike, ed. (p. 1778)
Overbeeke-Rippen, Francina van. Abraham & Ibrahim: The Bible & the Qur'an Told to Children. (p. 6)
Overbey, Theresa. Michael Jackson. (p. 1134)
Overdeck, Laura. Fun Excuse to Stay up Late. Paillot, Jim, illus. (p. 647)
—This Time It's Personal. Paillot, Jim, illus. (p. 1737)
—Truth Comes Out. Paillot, Jim, illus. (p. 1794)
Overend, Jenni. Stride's Summer. (p. 1667)
Overholser, Wayne D. Twin Rocks: A Western Duo. (p. 1802)
Overholt, Rod. I'm Lost: Which Is the Right Path? (p. 859)
Overington, Marcus. Lost on Bodmin Moor. (p. 1056)
Overland, Sarah. Pamela la Impaciente y los Microbios. Arroyo Seppa, Carmen, tr. (p. 1320)
Overly, Kristen V., illus. see Manwiller, S. A.
Overmyer-Velazquez, Mark, ed. see Doak, Robin Santos.
Overmyer-Velazquez, Mark, ed. see Katchur, Matthew & Sterngass, Jon.
Overmyer-Velazquez, Mark, ed. see Seidman, David.
Overstreet, Betty. Lord Still Speaks - Are You Listening? (p. 1052)
Overstreet, Betty Alawine. Mistletoe Memories & Sugarplum Dreams: Christmas Poetry to Make Your Heart Sing! (p. 1155)
Overstreet, Edward. From the Lion's Mouth: A Story of Daniel the Prophet. (p. 644)
Overstreet, Tommy & Vest, Dale G. Graham Cracker Kid & the Calico Girl. Anderson, Jesse, illus. (p. 705)
Overton, Carrie. Was Ist das? Animals. (p. 1859)
Overton, Lou Ann. Thank You, Moon. (p. 1725)
Overton, Pat. Mallory & Her Day Dream Adventure. (p. 1083)
—McTavish & His Bagpipe. (p. 1115)
Overwater, Georgien. Three Little Pigs. (p. 1743)
Overwater, Georgien, illus. see Daynes, Katie.
Ovresat, Laura, illus. see Gerver, Jane E.
Ovresat, Laura, illus. see Reader's Digest Staff & Shepherd, Jodie.
Ovresat, Laura, illus. see Shepherd, Jodie.
Ovresat, Laura, illus. see Williams, David K.
Ovresat, Laura, illus. see Williams, David K. & Williams, David.
Ovresat, Laura, illus. see Yee, Wong Herbert.
Ovstedal, Barbara, see Laker, Rosalind, pseud.
Owen, jt. auth. see Giddens, Sandra.
Owen, Ann. Delivering Your Mail: A Book about Mail Carriers Thomas, Eric, illus. (p. 425)
—Keeping You Healthy: A Book about Doctors. Thomas, Eric, illus. (p. 948)
—Keeping You Safe: A Book about Police Officers Thomas, Eric, illus. (p. 948)
—Protecting Your Home: A Book about Firefighters Thomas, Eric, illus. (p. 1412)
—Taking You Places: A Book about Bus Drivers Thomas, Eric, illus. (p. 1698)
Owen, Ann, ed. see D'Antonio, Sandra.
Owen, Ann & Picture Window Books Staff. Keeping You Healthy: A Book about Doctors Thomas, Eric, illus. (p. 948)
Owen, Anna. Day Out. Moon, Cliff, ed. (p. 414)
Owen, Bob. Billy. (p. 187)
Owen, Carys Eurwen, jt. auth. see Gruffudd, Elena.
Owen, Carys Eurwen, jt. auth. see Roberts, Esyllt Nest.
Owen, Carys Eurwen, jt. auth. see Roberts, Margiad.
Owen, Cheryl. Gifts for Kids to Make. (p. 675)
Owen, Chris. Hairy Mole & the Precious Islands. (p. 736)
—Hairy Mole the Pirate 1. (p. 736)
—My Superhero. Court, Moira, illus. (p. 1219)
Owen, Christopher. Hairy Mole's Adventures on the High Seas. Mostyn, David, illus. (p. 736)
Owen, Dai, jt. auth. see Morgan, Gwyn.
Owen, Dan. Ellen. (p. 514)
Owen, David. Final Frontier: Voyages into Outer Space. (p. 586)
—Spies: The Undercover World of Secrets, Gadgets & Lies. (p. 1627)
Owen, Elizabeth, illus. see Bellingham, Brenda.
Owen, Elizabeth & Daintith, Eve, eds. Facts on File Dictionary of Evolutionary Biology. (p. 561)
Owen, Erich, illus. see Batterson, Jason.
Owen, Erich, illus. see Seidenberg, Mark & Milky, D. J.
Owen, Frank, ed. Teenage Winter Sports Stories. Ricketts, William, illus. (p. 1714)
Owen, Gary. Mrs Reynolds & the Ruffian. (p. 1187)
Owen, Hywel Wyn. Place-Names of Wales. (p. 1365)
Owen, James A. Dawn of the Dragons: Here, There Be Dragons; the Search for the Red Dragon. (p. 412)
—Dragon's Apprentice. Owen, James A., illus. (p. 479)
—Dragons of Winter. Owen, James A., illus. (p. 479)
—First Dragon. Owen, James A., illus. (p. 594)
—Here, There Be Dragons. (p. 770)
—Here, There Be Dragons. Owen, James A., illus. (p. 770)
—Indigo King. Owen, James A., illus. (p. 872)
—Search for the Red Dragon. Owen, James A., illus. (p. 1537)
—Shadow Dragons. Owen, James A., illus. (p. 1557)
Owen, James A. & Owen, Jeremy. Lost Treasures of the Pirates of the Caribbean. Owen, James A., illus. (p. 1057)
Owen, James A., ed. Secrets of the Dragon Riders: Your Favorite Authors on Christopher Paolini's Inheritance Cycle: Completely Unauthorized. (p. 1545)
Owen, Jeremy, jt. auth. see Owen, James A.
Owen, Joanne. Alchemist & the Angel. (p. 35)
Owen, Karen. I Could Be- Barroux, illus. (p. 837)
—I Could Be, You Could Be. Barroux, illus. (p. 837)
Owen, Karen & Barroux. I Could Be, You Could Be. (p. 837)
Owen, Karone. Song of Alpharetta. (p. 1611)
Owen, Ken, illus. see Wadsworth, Pamela.
Owen, Leslie E. Pacific Tree Frogs Juhasz, George, illus. (p. 1317)
Owen, Linda. Robin's Song (p. 1480)
Owen, Michael. Soccer Skills: How to Become the Complete Footballer. (p. 1603)
Owen, Nick. More Magic of Metaphor: Stories for Leaders, Influencers & Motivators & Spiral Dynamics Wizards. (p. 1174)
Owen, R. Emmett, illus. see Kay, Ross.
Owen, Ramon, illus. see Cyr, Joe.
Owen, Rob. Spy Boy, Cheyenne, & Ninety-Six Crayons: A "Mardi Gras" Indian's Story Owen, Rob, illus. (p. 1636)
Owen, Ruth. 100 Words. (p. 1999)
—Aliens & Other Visitors. (p. 41)
—Amazing Apes. (p. 53)
—American Longhairs. (p. 62)
—Arctic Fox Pups. (p. 96)
—Arctic Foxes. (p. 96)
—Asteroid Hunters. (p. 108)
—Asteroids & the Asteroid Belt. (p. 108)
—Astronomers. (p. 109)
—Beaver Kits. (p. 155)
—Beluga Whales. (p. 163)
—Blast Off. (p. 198)
—Brawny Bears. (p. 224)
—Bread! Life on a Wheat Farm. (p. 224)
—Building Green Places: Careers in Planning, Designing, & Building. (p. 239)
—Carnivorous Big Cats. (p. 270)
—Cavachons. (p. 282)
—Chimpanzees. (p. 306)
—Christmas & Hanukkah Origami. (p. 312)
—Christmas Sweets & Treats. (p. 315)
—Chugs. (p. 318)
—Climatologists & Meteorologists. (p. 332)
—Cockapoos. (p. 337)
—Creepy Backyard Invaders. (p. 381)
—Crows. (p. 386)
—Desert Animals. (p. 428)
—Desert Survival Guide. (p. 429)
—Disgusting Food Invaders. (p. 450)
—Dolphins. (p. 464)
—Earth. (p. 495)
—Easter Origami. (p. 499)
—Easter Sweets & Treats. (p. 499)
—Eggs! Life on a Chicken Farm. (p. 506)
—Elephants. (p. 511)
—Energy from Atoms: Nuclear Power. (p. 528)
—Energy from Inside Our Planet: Geothermal Power. (p. 528)
—Energy from Oceans & Moving Water: Hydroelectric, Wave, & Tidal Power. (p. 528)
—Energy from Plants & Trash: Biofuels & Biomass Power. (p. 528)
—Energy from the Sun: Solar Power. (p. 528)
—Energy from the Wind: Generating Power with Wind Turbines. (p. 528)
—Exploring Distant Worlds As a Space Robot Engineer. (p. 552)
—Fruit! Life on an Apple Farm. (p. 645)
—Fun at the Beach. (p. 647)
—Fun at the Farm. (p. 647)
—Fun at the Park. (p. 647)
—Fun at the Zoo. (p. 647)
—Fun Fabrics. (p. 647)
—Galaxies. (p. 653)
—Ghosts & Other Spirits of the Dead. (p. 672)
—Gifts. (p. 675)
—Giraffes. (p. 677)
—Goldadors. (p. 694)
—Goldendoodles. (p. 695)
—Grassland Animals. (p. 712)
—Grizzly Bears. (p. 724)
—Gross Body Invaders. (p. 725)
—Half-Human Monsters & Other Fiends. (p. 736)
—Halloween Origami. (p. 738)
—Halloween Sweets & Treats. (p. 739)
—Holiday Crafts. (p. 788)
—Horses. (p. 800)
—How Do Animals Help Plants Reproduce? (p. 806)
—How Do Meat-Eating Plants Catch Their Food? (p. 807)
—How Do Plants Defend Themselves? (p. 807)
—How Do Plants Make & Spread Their Seeds? (p. 807)
—How Do Plants Make Their Own Food? (p. 807)
—How Do You Know It's Fall? (p. 808)
—How Do You Know It's Spring? (p. 808)
—How to Make an Egyptian Mummy. (p. 820)
—Hungry Bugs. (p. 828)
—Icky House Invaders. (p. 851)
—Independence Day Origami. (p. 870)
—Jewelry. (p. 917)
—Jungle Animals. (p. 935)
—Jungle Survival Guide. (p. 935)
—Jupiter. (p. 937)
—Labradoodles. (p. 970)
—Life of a Caribbean Pirate. (p. 1011)
—Life of a Gladiator. (p. 1011)
—Lion Cubs. (p. 1020)
—Lions. (p. 1021)
—Malshis. (p. 1084)
—Manatee Calves. (p. 1086)
—Marine Biologists. (p. 1094)
—Mars. (p. 1096)
—Marvelous Marine Mammals. (p. 1099)
—Meat! Life on a Sheep Farm. (p. 1117)
—Mercury. (p. 1127)
—Milk! Life on a Dairy Farm. (p. 1143)
—Mischievous Monkeys. (p. 1150)
—Moon. (p. 1171)
—More Christmas Origami (p. 1174)
—More Halloween Origami (p. 1174)
—More Hanukkah Origami (p. 1174)
—More Thanksgiving Origami (p. 1175)
—More Valentine's Day Origami (p. 1175)
—Mountain Animals. (p. 1180)
—Musk Oxen. (p. 1194)
—Nature Crafts. (p. 1236)
—Nebulae. (p. 1239)
—Neptune. (p. 1241)
—Objects in Space (p. 1275)
—Ocean Animals. (p. 1276)
—Octopuses. (p. 1278)
—Orangutans. (p. 1302)
—Orca Calves. (p. 1302)
—Paleontologists & Archaeologists. (p. 1319)
—Paper Crafts. (p. 1322)
—Parrots. (p. 1325)
—Peekapoos. (p. 1335)
—Penguin Chicks. (p. 1336)
—Persians. (p. 1344)
—Pluto & Other Dwarf Planets. (p. 1374)
—Polar Animals. (p. 1378)
—Polar Bear Cubs. (p. 1378)
—Polar Bears. (p. 1379)
—Probes (p. 1408)
—Puffins. (p. 1415)
—Puggles. (p. 1415)
—Quasars. (p. 1423)
—Raccoon Cubs. (p. 1430)
—Ragdolls. (p. 1433)
—Rhinoceroses. (p. 1467)
—Satellites (p. 1515)
—Saturn. (p. 1515)
—Schnoodles. (p. 1521)
—Science & Craft Projects with Insects, Spiders, & Other Minibeasts. (p. 1524)
—Science & Craft Projects with Plants & Seeds. (p. 1524)
—Science & Craft Projects with Rocks & Soil. (p. 1524)
—Science & Craft Projects with Weather. (p. 1524)
—Science & Craft Projects with Wildlife. (p. 1525)
—Sea Otter Pups. (p. 1535)
—Sea Turtle Hatchlings. (p. 1535)
—Seahorse Fry. (p. 1536)
—Seal Pups. (p. 1536)
—Siamese. (p. 1572)
—Skunk Kits. (p. 1586)
—Snappy Sharkes. (p. 1597)
—Snowy Owls. (p. 1601)
—Solar & Lunar Eclipses. (p. 1606)
—Space Garbage (p. 1619)
—Space Stations (p. 1620)
—Space Survival Guide. (p. 1620)
—Spacecraft (p. 1620)
—Sphynx. (p. 1626)
—Squirrel Kits. (p. 1637)
—St. Patrick's Day Origami (p. 1638)
—Stealthy Sharks. (p. 1646)
—Sun. (p. 1675)
—Supernovas. (p. 1684)
—Thanksgiving Origami. (p. 1726)
—Tiger Cubs. (p. 1748)
—Top 10 Fastest. (p. 1768)
—Top 10 Slowest. (p. 1768)
—Top 10 Tallest. (p. 1768)
—Under the Sea. (p. 1814)
—Up Close & Gross: Microscopic Creatures (p. 1824)
—Uranus. (p. 1825)
—Valentine's Day Origami. (p. 1830)
—Valentine's Day Sweets & Treats. (p. 1830)
—Vampires & Other Bloodsuckers. (p. 1832)
—Vegetables! Life on a Produce Farm. (p. 1834)
—Venus. (p. 1836)
—Volcanologists & Seismologists. (p. 1849)
—Walruses. (p. 1855)
—Werewolves & Other Shape-Shifters. (p. 1875)
—What Do Roots, Stems, Leaves, & Flowers Do? (p. 1882)
—What Happens When I Eat? (p. 1886)
—What Happens When I Grow? (p. 1886)
—What Happens When I Sleep? (p. 1886)
—Wild Baby Animals (p. 1929)
—Wild World of a Zoo Vet. (p. 1931)
—Wolves. (p. 1945)
—Wonderful Worlds of a Video Game Designer. (p. 1948)
—World of a Viking Warrior. (p. 1956)
—Yochons. (p. 1972)
—Yorkipoos. (p. 1972)
—Your Cat's Superhero Skills. (p. 1980)
—Your Dog's Superhero Skills. (p. 1980)
—Zombies & Other Walking Dead. (p. 1988)
—Zoologists & Ecologists. (p. 1989)
Owen, Ruth, illus. see Woods, Mark.
Owen, Ruth, jt. auth. see Gazlay, Suzy.
Owen, Ruth, jt. auth. see Noble, Jonathan.
Owen, Ruth, jt. auth. see Woods, Mark.
Owen, Ruth & Gazlay, Suzy. Learning Green: Careers in Education. (p. 985)
Owen, Sarah. Adventures of Molly & Polly. (p. 20)
—Enchanted Tales. (p. 523)
—Sarah the Fairy Princess's Birthday Party. (p. 1514)
Owen, Siân, illus. see Wadsworth, Pamela.
Owen, Steve & Hoeben, Peter. Chemistry for the IB Diploma. (p. 297)
Owenby, Ina, jt. auth. see Gunn, Joni.
Owens, Andy, jt. auth. see Winick, Judd.
Owens, Ann-Maureen & Yealland, Jane. Canadian Exploration. Mantha, John, illus. (p. 260)
Owens, Bettina. Athena, Never A Bite. (p. 112)
Owens, C. Denise. Help! I Can't Find My Shoes. (p. 765)
Owens, Carmen. Katy, the Cooking Kangaroo. Otis, Michelle, ed. (p. 946)
Owens, Carol, jt. auth. see Owens, Jimmy.
Owens, Chef David. Brocklee & the Little Chef. (p. 230)
Owens, Connie S. Aunt Lucy Has Cancer. (p. 115)
—I know I am Special! (p. 840)
—Missing Maggie: The Death of a Pet. (p. 1152)
Owens, David W. Overview of Zoning Districts & Design Standards in North Carolina Zoning Ordinances. (p. 1314)
Owens, Donna. NIBBLES: Volume 2, Nibbles Adventures. (p. 1250)
—NIBBLES:VOLUME 3, Nibbles enjoys the Holidays. (p. 1250)
—NIBBLES:Volume one, Nibbles finds a Home. (p. 1250)
Owens, Donna, jt. auth. see Owens, Robert.
Owens, Emily, illus. see Peysin, Shainy.
Owens, Greg. Rupert the Wrong-Word Pirate. Beaky, Suzanne, illus. (p. 1497)
Owens, Janis. Schooling of Claybird Catts: A Novel. (p. 1524)
Owens, Jeanette. Adventures of Raj: The Snow Tiger. (p. 22)
—Nature Spirits. (p. 1236)
Owens, Jim. New Allegory. (p. 1243)
—Survivorship Net: A Parable for the Family, Friends, & Caregivers of People with Cancer. Cass, Bill, illus. (p. 1687)
Owens, Jimmy & Owens, Carol. Restoring A Nations Foundations Leader's Manual: Prayer Strategies & Action Plans. (p. 1464)
Owens, Joann. I Have a Dream: A child's view of Martin Luther King Day. (p. 839)
Owens, Katherine. Tree Seasons Ball (p. 1783)
Owens, L. L. Benjamin Franklin. (p. 164)
—Christmas. Conger, Holli, illus. (p. 312)
—Cinco de Mayo. Conger, Holli, illus. (p. 319)
—Earth. McGeehan, Dan, illus. (p. 495)
—Family Gatherings. Davidson, Chris, illus. (p. 568)
—Frenemies: Dealing with Friend Drama. (p. 636)
—Go to School. Davidson, Chris, illus. (p. 687)
—Go Worship. Davidson, Chris, illus. (p. 687)
—Great Chicago Fire. (p. 714)
—Hanukkah. Conger, Holli, illus. (p. 743)
—If You Want My Advice- Tolson, Scott, illus. (p. 854)
—Join a Team. Davidson, Chris, illus. (p. 924)
—Jupiter. McGeehan, Dan, illus. (p. 937)
—Kendra's Big Decision. (p. 948)
—Life Cycle of a Clown Fish. (p. 1009)
—Life Cycle of a Daisy. (p. 1009)
—Life Cycle of a Fern. (p. 1009)
—Life Cycle of a Ladybug. (p. 1009)
—Life Cycle of an Earthworm. (p. 1009)
—Longest Car Ride Ever. Tolson, Scott, illus. (p. 1047)
—Make Friends. Davidson, Chris, illus. (p. 1079)
—Mars. McGeehan, Dan, illus. (p. 1096)
—Meet Your Neighborhood. Davidson, Chris, illus. (p. 1123)
—Mercury. McGeehan, Dan, illus. (p. 1127)
—Neptune. McGeehan, Dan, illus. (p. 1241)
—New Girl. Tolson, Scott, illus. (p. 1244)
—Pilgrims in America. (p. 1358)
—Pluto & Other Dwarf Planets. McGeehan, Dan, illus. (p. 1374)
—Saturn. McGeehan, Dan, illus. (p. 1515)
—Snail. (p. 1595)
—Sun. McGeehan, Dan, illus. (p. 1675)
—Uranus. McGeehan, Dan, illus. (p. 1825)
—Venus. McGeehan, Dan, illus. (p. 1836)
Owens, Laurella, jt. auth. see Brown, Virginia Pounds.
Owens, Laurella, jt. ed. see Brown, Virginia Pounds.
Owens, Leanne. Horses of the Sun. (p. 800)
Owens, Lisa. Southern Region. (p. 1617)
—Southwestern Region. (p. 1618)
—Uniquely Missouri (p. 1818)
Owens, Lucy. My Lime Green Butterfly. (p. 1212)
Owens, Mary Beth, illus. see Dodd, Anne Westcott.
Owens, Mary Beth, illus. see Plourde, Lynn.
Owens, Mary Beth, illus. see Pochocki, Ethel.
Owens, Melissa, jt. auth. see Diaz, Natalia.
Owens, Michael & Gelman, Amy. I'm Depressed, Now What? (p. 858)
Owens, Michael Edward. Wisdom Book: A Search for Truth, Through Simple Logical Argument. (p. 1939)
Owens, Michael T. Pick-Up Lines: A Novel. Cadet, Guichard, ed. (p. 1354)
Owens, Peter. Teens Health & Obesity. (p. 1715)
—Teens, Health & Obesity. Developed in Association with the Gallup Organization Staff, ed. (p. 1715)
Owens, Robert. Butterfly Love. (p. 248)

—Indian Ways. (p. 871)
—Littlest Warrior. (p. 1039)
Owens, Robert & Owens, Donna. Misadventures of Our Son Henry. Bollinger, Carol, illus. (p. 1150)
Owens, Robin D. Heart Thief. (p. 760)
Owens, Sharon. Immigration & Migration in Texas. (p. 861)
Owens, Steve & Peters, Laura. Best Garden Plants for Oklahoma. (p. 169)
Owens, Thomas. Muhammad Ali: Boxing Champ & Role Model. (p. 1189)
Owens, Tom. Immigrants & Neighbors. (p. 861)
—Star-Spangled Banner: The Flag & Its Anthem. (p. 1641)
—Traveling on the Freedom Machines of the Transportation Age. (p. 1780)
—Washington, D.C. (p. 1860)
Owens, Wanda. Sammie the Lil' Dog on the Porch. Hill, Shannon, illus. (p. 1507)
Owensby, Legertha. Revealing Truth. (p. 1465)
Owens-Kristenson, Jodi, jt. auth. see Ross, Patricia G.
Owenson, Meg, illus. see Roy, Jennifer.
Owens-Waters, Zelda, ed. see Goodridge, Walt F. J.
Owenz, Roger. Mr Owenz Goes to School. (p. 1186)
Owhonda, John. Congo. (p. 357)
Owings, Jeff. Tiny Todd: Swooped Away. (p. 1757)
—Tiny Todd: Tiny Todd's First Pet. (p. 1757)
Owings, Keith, jt. auth. see Owings, Kristi.
Owings, Kristi & Owings, Keith. Time Travel Adventures of the Rainier Twins: the Journey Begins. (p. 1753)
Owings, Lisa. Adele: Grammy-Winning Singer & Songwriter. (p. 12)
—Afghanistan. (p. 26)
—African Lion. (p. 27)
—Atlantis. (p. 112)
—Austria. (p. 116)
—Bear Attack. (p. 150)
—Belgium. (p. 161)
—Black Mamba. (p. 196)
—Bolivia. (p. 208)
—Bull Shark Attack. (p. 240)
—Cape Buffalo. (p. 262)
—Chile. (p. 305)
—Constellation Cassiopeia: The Story of the Queen. Morrow, J. T., illus. (p. 359)
—Constellation Ursa Major: The Story of the Big Bear. Morrow, J. T., illus. (p. 359)
—Constellation Ursa Minor: The Story of the Little Bear. Morrow, J. T., illus. (p. 359)
—Deathstalker Scorpion. (p. 420)
—Diana: The People's Princess. (p. 434)
—Do Your Research. (p. 458)
—Ecuador. (p. 503)
—Esp. (p. 536)
—From Bulb to Tulip. (p. 642)
—From Goat to Cheese. (p. 642)
—From Pumpkin to Pie. (p. 643)
—From Strawberry to Jam. (p. 643)
—From Sugar Beet to Sugar. (p. 643)
—Ghost Ships. (p. 671)
—Great White Shark. (p. 719)
—Grizzly Bear. (p. 724)
—Hippopotamus. (p. 781)
—Hungary. (p. 827)
—Iceland. (p. 851)
—Igneous Rocks. (p. 856)
—Indonesia. (p. 872)
—Iraq. (p. 887)
—Israel. (p. 893)
—Katy Perry: Chart-Topping Superstar. (p. 946)
—Killer Bees. (p. 956)
—King Cobra. (p. 958)
—Komodo Dragon. (p. 966)
—Learn about Authors & Illustrators. (p. 982)
—Learning about Australia. (p. 984)
—Lebanon. (p. 986)
—Marilyn Monroe: Hollywood Icon. (p. 1094)
—Meet a Baby Hippo. (p. 1120)
—Meet a Baby Zebra. (p. 1120)
—Moose Attack. (p. 1173)
—Mountain Lion Attack. (p. 1181)
—Mummy's Curse. (p. 1191)
—Netherlands. (p. 1242)
—Nicaragua. (p. 1250)
—Nigeria. (p. 1252)
—Peru. (p. 1345)
—Poison Dart Frogs. (p. 1377)
—Polar Bear. (p. 1378)
—Punishing Bullies: Zero Tolerance vs. Working Together. (p. 1417)
—Rat Attack. (p. 1440)
—Rev up Your Writing in Blogs. Gallagher-Cole, Mernie, illus. (p. 1465)
—Saudi Arabia. (p. 1516)
—Share Your Book Report. (p. 1561)
—Singapore. (p. 1579)
—Snake Attack. (p. 1596)
—Somalia. (p. 1608)
—South Africa. (p. 1616)
—South Sudan. (p. 1617)
—Stay Safe Online. (p. 1645)
—Stonehenge. (p. 1653)
—Tiger Attack. (p. 1748)
—Turkey. (p. 1797)
—West Virginia. (p. 1876)
—What Are Legends, Folktales, & Other Classic Stories? (p. 1879)
—What Are Plays? (p. 1879)
—What Protects Us During Natural Disasters? (p. 1893)
—Wheels. Butler, Reginald, illus. (p. 1900)
—Wild Dog Attack. (p. 1929)
Owings, Lisa & Nelson, Robin. From Sea to Salt. (p. 643)
Owings, Rae, illus. see Surman, Susan.
Owl, Grey. Adventures of Sajo & Her Beaver People. (p. 22)
—Adventures of Sajo & Her Beaver People - with Original Bw Illustrations & a Glossary of Ojibway Indian Words. (p. 22)
Owl, William, illus. see Kimmelman, Leslie.
Owlkids Books Inc. Staff. Picture My World. (p. 1355)
Owlkids Books Inc. Staff, illus. see Baillie, Marilyn.
Owlkids Books Inc. Staff, illus. see Battle, Craig.
Owlkids Books Inc. Staff, illus. see Becker, Helaine.
Owlkids Books Inc. Staff, illus. see Birmingham, Maria.
Owlkids Books Inc. Staff, illus. see chickaDEE Magazine Staff.
Owlkids Books Inc. Staff, illus. see Chirp Magazine Editors.
Owlkids Books Inc. Staff, illus. see Crossingham, John.
Owlkids Books Inc. Staff, illus. see deCarufel, Laura.
Owlkids Books Inc. Staff, illus. see Elton, Sarah.
Owlkids Books Inc. Staff, illus. see Flatt, Lizann.
Owlkids Books Inc. Staff, illus. see Glassbourg, Michael.
Owlkids Books Inc. Staff, illus. see Hyde, Natalie.
Owlkids Books Inc. Staff, illus. see Hédelin, Pascale.
Owlkids Books Inc. Staff, illus. see Kain, Bob & Becker, Helaine.
Owlkids Books Inc. Staff, illus. see Kain, Bob.
Owlkids Books Inc. Staff, illus. see Kelsey, Elin.
Owlkids Books Inc. Staff, illus. see O'Donnell, Liam & Battle, Craig.
Owlkids Books Inc. Staff, illus. see O'Donnell, Liam.
Owlkids Books Inc. Staff, illus. see Ripley, Catherine.
Owlkids Books Inc. Staff, illus. see Rivard, Émilie & Quinn, Sarah.
Owlkids Books Inc. Staff, illus. see Schwartz, Roslyn.
Owlkids Books Inc. Staff, illus. see Storms, Patricia.
Owlkids Books Inc. Staff, illus. see Szpirglas, Jeff.
Owlkids Books Inc. Staff, illus. see Thomas, Keltie.
Owlkids Books Inc. Staff, illus. see Thomas, Lyn.
Owlkids Books Inc. Staff, illus. see Thornhill, Jan.
Owlkids Books Inc. Staff, illus. see Vermond, Kira.
Owlkids Books Inc. Staff, illus. see Wallace, Mary.
Owlkids Books Inc. Staff, illus. see Whamond, Dave.
Owlkids Books Inc. Staff, illus. see Williams, Ann-Marie.
Owlkids Books Inc. Staff, illus. see Wishinsky, Frieda & Griffiths, Dean.
Owlkids Books Inc. Staff, illus. see Wishinsky, Frieda.
Owlkids Books Inc. Staff, jt. auth. see Arato, Rona.
Owlkids Books Inc. Staff, jt. auth. see Boudgourd, Vincent.
Owlkids Books Inc. Staff, jt. auth. see Gutiérrez, Elisa.
Owlkids Books Inc. Staff, jt. auth. see Helm, Charles.
Owlkids Books Inc. Staff, jt. auth. see Hughes, Susan.
Owlkids Books Inc. Staff, jt. auth. see Kelsey, Elin.
Owlkids Books Inc. Staff, jt. auth. see McLachlan, Brian.
Owlkids Books Inc. Staff, jt. auth. see Thornhill, Jan.
Owlkids Books Inc. Staff, jt. auth. see Walker, Niki.
Owlkids Books Inc. Staff, jt. auth. see Wallace, Mary.
Owlkids Books Inc. Staff, jt. auth. see Whamond, Dave.
Owlkids Books Inc. Staff, tr. see Cohen, Laurie.
Owlkids Books Inc. Staff, tr. see Manceau, Édouard.
Owlkids Books Inc. Staff & Arato, Rona. Last Train: A Holocaust Story. (p. 979)
Owsley, Anthony, illus. see Brown, Jordan D.
Owsley, Anthony, illus. see Press, Applesauce & Rhatigan, Joe.
Owsley, Anthony, illus. see Rhatigan, Joe.
Owsley, Anthony, illus. jt. auth. see Rhatigan, Joe.
Owsley, Anthony, et al. Biggest Trivia Book Ever: And That's a Fact! Burke, Theresa, illus. (p. 185)
Oxenbury, Helen. Amigos. (p. 65)
—Animales. (p. 80)
—Aprendiendo. (p. 93)
—Ayudando. (p. 121)
—Baby Love: All Fall down - Clap Hands - Say Goodnight - Tickle, Tickle. Set Oxenbury, Helen, illus. (p. 127)
—Clase de Baile (Dance Class) (p. 327)
—Comprando. (p. 354)
—Con el Medico (At the Doctor's) (p. 355)
—El Auto. (p. 507)
—El Restaurante de Mis Tios. (p. 507)
—En Casa de los Abuelos (At Grandparents' House) (p. 522)
—Fiesta de Cumpleanos. (p. 584)
—Helen Oxenbury Nursery Collection. Oxenbury, Helen, illus. (p. 763)
—It's My Birthday. Oxenbury, Helen, illus. (p. 897)
—Pig Tale. Oxenbury, Helen, illus. (p. 1357)
—Primer Dia de Escuela (First Day of School) (p. 1400)
—Vista (The Visit) (p. 1846)
—We're Going on a Bear Hunt. (p. 1875)
Oxenbury, Helen, illus. see Bently, Peter.
Oxenbury, Helen, illus. see Burningham, John.
Oxenbury, Helen, illus. see Carroll, Lewis, pseud.
Oxenbury, Helen, illus. see Cooke, Trish.
Oxenbury, Helen, illus. see Cutler, Ivor.
Oxenbury, Helen, illus. see Fox, Mem.
Oxenbury, Helen, illus. see Hest, Amy.
Oxenbury, Helen, illus. see Krauss, Ruth.
Oxenbury, Helen, illus. see Root, Phyllis.
Oxenbury, Helen, illus. see Rosen, Michael.
Oxenbury, Helen, illus. see Trivizas, Eugene.
Oxenbury, Helen, illus. see Waddell, Martin.
Oxenbury, Helen, jt. illus. see Rosen, Michael.
Oxfam (Afghanistan) Staff, photos by see Petty, Kate.
Oxfam Staff, illus. see Cave, Kathryn.
Oxford Analytica Staff & Langley, Andrew, eds. Oxford First Encyclopedia. (p. 1315)
Oxford Bible Staff, illus. see Fay, Gail.
Oxford Bible Staff, illus. see Gallagher, Brigid.
Oxford Bible Staff, illus. see Rand, Casey.
Oxford Bible Staff, illus. see Raum, Elizabeth.
Oxford Bible Staff, illus. see Weil, Ann.
Oxford Dictionaries Staff, ed. Oxford Illustrated Children's Dictionary: The Perfect Family Dictionary. (p. 1315)
—Oxford School Dictionary 2011. (p. 1315)
Oxford, ed. Dictionnaire Oxford Pocket Pour Apprendre l'Anglais. (p. 436)
—Graphic Library - Science Complete Program. (p. 711)
—Oxford Illustrated Social Studies Dictionary. (p. 1315)
—Oxford Picture Dictionary for Kids (p. 1315)
—Oxford Picture Dictionary for Kids 2e Ebook Pack. (p. 1315)
Oxford, Isabel M. Phantom of the Factory. (p. 1349)
Oxford University Press. Children's Visual Dictionary, French-English. (p. 304)
—Children's Visual Dictionary, Spanish-English. (p. 304)
Oxford University Press Staff, ed. see Akinyemi, Rowena.
Oxford University Press Staff, ed. see Bassett, Arthur R., et al.
Oxford University Press Staff, ed. see Bassett, Jennifer & Stewart, Sue.
Oxford University Press Staff, ed. see Duckworth, Michael.
Oxford University Press Staff, ed. see Escott, John & Henry, O.
Oxford University Press Staff, ed. see Gilbert, Harry.
Oxford University Press Staff, ed. see Grahame, Kenneth & Grahame, Kenneth.
Oxford University Press Staff, ed. see Mowat, Diane.
Oxford University Press Staff, ed. see Nesbit, E.
Oxford University Press Staff, ed. see Shipton, Paul & Henry, O.
Oxford University Press Staff, ed. see Vicary, Tim.
Oxford University Press Staff & Bassett, Jennifer, eds. Omega Files. (p. 1288)
Oxford University Press Staff & Lindop, Christine, eds. Australia & New Zealand, Level 3. (p. 116)
Oxford University Press Staff, ed. Times Compact Atlas of the World. (p. 1754)
Oxford-White, Bly. Mr. Woo's Zoo. (p. 1187)
Oxlade, C. & Stockley, C. Micro Kit (Box) (p. 1136)
Oxlade, Chris. 150 Amazing Science Experiments: Fascinating Projects Using Everyday Materials, Demonstrated. (p. 2000)
—150 Amazing Science Experiments: Fascinating Projects Using Everyday Materials, Demonstrated Step by Step in 1300 Photographs! (p. 2000)
—Airplanes Inside & Out. (p. 32)
—Ambulance. (p. 57)
—Animal Infographics (p. 78)
—Be a Survivor. Sassin, Eva, illus. (p. 148)
—Be a Tracker. Sassin, Eva, illus. (p. 148)
—Be an Adventurer. Sassin, Eva, illus. (p. 148)
—Calendar (p. 252)
—Cambiar la Forma (p. 255)
—Cars Inside & Out. (p. 272)
—Changing Materials. (p. 290)
—Circulatory System: Where Do I Get My Energy? (p. 322)
—Climate Change. (p. 332)
—Conductors & Insulators (p. 356)
—Cooling (p. 364)
—Design Line - Planes, Trains, & Automobiles. Lemanski, Mike, illus. (p. 430)
—Earth: Find Out about the Planet, Earthquakes, Volcanoes & Weather with 50 Great Experiments & Projects. (p. 495)
—Earth & Its Moon. (p. 495)
—Electricity (p. 509)
—Energy Technology. (p. 528)
—Enfriar (p. 529)
—Environment Infographics (p. 532)
—Excellent Science Experiments (p. 547)
—Experiments with Air & Water (p. 549)
—Experiments with Electricity & Magnets (p. 549)
—Experiments with Matter & Materials (p. 549)
—Experiments with Sound: Explaining Sound (p. 549)
—Experiments with Sound & Light (p. 549)
—Experiments with Water: Water & Buoyancy (p. 549)
—Explorers: Robots. Bull, Peter, illus. (p. 551)
—Exploring Science - Ships & Boats: Sail Navigation Radar Anchor Keel. (p. 553)
—Find Out about Machines. (p. 587)
—Fire Disaster. (p. 590)
—Fire Truck. (p. 591)
—Floods in Action. (p. 606)
—Forces & Motion: An Investigation. (p. 617)
—Friction & Resistance (p. 637)
—Gadgets & Games (p. 652)
—Gaming Technology. (p. 655)
—Garbage & Recycling (p. 655)
—Global Warming. (p. 684)
—Graphing Weather & Climate (p. 711)
—Gravity (p. 712)
—Growth (p. 727)
—Gunpowder (p. 732)
—Hands-on Science Projects: Nature. (p. 741)
—Hands-on Science Projects: Physics. (p. 741)
—Hands-on Science Projects: Transport. (p. 741)
—Heating (p. 761)
—Helicopters. (p. 763)
—Homes (p. 793)
—How Things Work. (p. 814)
—Hurricanes. (p. 830)
—Igneous Rocks (p. 856)
—Illustrated Dictionary of Science. (p. 857)
—Infographics (p. 873)
—Introducing Africa (p. 882)
—Introducing Europe (p. 882)
—Introducing North America (p. 882)
—Inventions. (p. 884)
—Inventors' Secret Scrapbook. (p. 884)
—Jet Planes. (p. 916)
—Joining Materials. (p. 924)
—Jupiter, Neptune, & Other Outer Planets. (p. 937)
—Kingfisher Readers L5: Explorers. (p. 960)
—Levers. (p. 1003)
—Light Bulb (p. 1015)
—Making a Circuit (p. 1080)
—Making Machines with Levers. (p. 1081)
—Making Machines with Pulleys. (p. 1081)
—Making Machines with Ramps & Wedges. (p. 1081)
—Mars (p. 1096)
—Mercury, Mars, & Other Inner Planets. (p. 1127)
—Metamorphic Rocks (p. 1130)
—Mezclar y Separar (p. 1131)
—Mighty Machines (p. 1140)
—Military Machines - Tanks. (p. 1143)
—Mixing & Separating (p. 1156)
—Mixing & Separating. (p. 1156)
—Moon (p. 1171)
—Moon Edwards, Jeff, illus. (p. 1171)
—Moon. (p. 1171)
—Motorcycles. (p. 1179)
—Motorcycles Inside & Out. (p. 1180)
—Mountain Rescue (p. 1181)
—Mountains (p. 1181)
—Mystery of Life on Other Planets (p. 1224)
—Mystery of the Bermuda Triangle (p. 1225)
—Mystery of Vampires & Werewolves (p. 1226)
—Nuclear Energy (p. 1269)
—Nuclear Power. (p. 1270)
—Paper. (p. 1322)
—Plane. (p. 1366)
—Police Car. (p. 1379)
—Population Infographics (p. 1385)
—Pulleys. (p. 1416)
—Ramps & Wedges. (p. 1438)
—Rescue at Sea (p. 1462)
—Rescue Boat. (p. 1462)
—Rocas Igneas. (p. 1481)
—Rocas Metamórficas. (p. 1481)
—Rocas Sedimentarias. (p. 1481)
—Rock Climbing. (p. 1482)
—Rocks & Minerals (p. 1483)
—Science Museum Book Constructions. (p. 1526)
—Screws. (p. 1533)
—Sedimentary Rocks (p. 1546)
—Shaping Materials. (p. 1561)
—Simple Experiments with Inclined Planes. (p. 1577)
—Simple Experiments with Levers. (p. 1577)
—Simple Experiments with Pulleys. (p. 1577)
—Simple Experiments with Wheels & Axles. (p. 1577)
—Simple Machine Projects. (p. 1577)
—Solar Power (p. 1606)
—Solids: An Investigation. (p. 1608)
—Space Watch: The Sun. (p. 1620)
—Sports (p. 1632)
—Sports Cars 6-Pack. (p. 1632)
—Storm Warning: Tornadoes (p. 1656)
—Submarines. (p. 1671)
—This Is My Digger. Lalla, Christine, photos by. (p. 1736)
—This Is My Dump Truck. Crawford, Andy, photos by. (p. 1736)
—This Is My Tractor. Lalla, Christine, photos by. (p. 1736)
—Top Ten Battles That Changed the World. (p. 1769)
—Top Ten Inventions That Changed the World. (p. 1769)
—Top Ten Scientific Discoveries That Changed the World. (p. 1769)
—Toys Through Time: How Toys Were Designed, Developed, & Made. (p. 1774)
—Trains. (p. 1777)
—Transportation Around the World: How Do We Get Where We're Going? (p. 1779)
—Trucks. (p. 1791)
—Trucks Inside & Out. (p. 1791)
—Using Batteries (p. 1828)
—Using Electricity (p. 1828)
—Violent Skies: Hurricanes (p. 1843)
—Volcanoes (p. 1849)
—Volcanoes. (p. 1849)
—Water (p. 1862)
—Way Things Work: The Complete Illustrated Guide to the Amazing World of Technology. (p. 1864)
—Weather Infographics (p. 1870)
—Wedges & Ramps. (p. 1871)
—Wheels. (p. 1900)
—Why Why Why... Do Astronauts Float in Space? (p. 1926)
—Why Why Why... Do Magnets Push & Pull? (p. 1926)
—Why Why Why Do Tornadoes Spin. (p. 1926)
—Why Why Why... Do Tornadoes Spin? (p. 1926)
—Why Why Why Does My Heart Begin to Race? (p. 1926)
—Why Why Why... Does My Heart Begin to Race? (p. 1926)
—Wild Weather. (p. 1930)
—World War I. (p. 1958)
Oxlade, Chris, jt. auth. see Feldman, Thea.
Oxlade, Chris, jt. auth. see Ganeri, Anita.
Oxlade, Chris, jt. auth. see Labrecque, Ellen.
Oxlade, Chris, jt. auth. see Loveless, Antony.
Oxlade, Chris, jt. auth. see Parker, Steve.
Oxlade, Chris & Baraclough, Sue. Electricity (p. 509)
—Sound (p. 1615)
Oxlade, Chris & Feldman, Thea. Kingfisher Readers L3: Firefighters. (p. 960)
Oxlade, Chris & Ganeri, Anita. Camera (p. 256)
—Car (p. 265)
—Computer (p. 354)
Oxlade, Chris & Heinemann Library Staff. Changing Shape (p. 290)
—Mixing & Separating (p. 1156)
Oxlade, Chris & Jennings, Terry. Energy. (p. 528)
Oxlade, Chris & Jennings, Terry J. Energy. (p. 528)
Oxlade, Chris & Stockley, Corinne. World of the Microscope. Chen, Kuo Kang et al, illus. (p. 1957)
Oxlade, Chris & West, David. Apollo Missions & Other Adventures in Space. (p. 92)
Oxlade, Chris, et al. Big Illustrated Book of Transport: All about Ships, Trains, Cars & Flight with Photographs, Artworks & 40 Step-by-Step Projects & Experiments! (p. 182)
—Energy Essentials (p. 528)
—Renewable Energy. (p. 1460)
—Science & History Project Book: 300 Step-By-Step Fun Science Experiments & History Craft Projects for Home Learning & School Study. (p. 1525)
—Science Book Box: Practical Projects in 8 Incredible Volumes (p. 1525)
Oxlade, Chris, et al, eds. Usborne Illustrated Dictionary of Chemistry. (p. 1827)
—Usborne Illustrated Dictionary of Physics. (p. 1827)
Oxlade, Edwin. Plant Physiology: The structure of plants Explained. (p. 1369)
Oxley, J. Mcdonald. Young Woodsman: Life in the Forests of Canada. (p. 1979)
Oxley, Jennifer, jt. auth. see Aronson, Billy.
Oxley, Jennifer & Aronson, Billy. Peg + Cat: the Race Car Problem. (p. 1335)
Oxmoor House Staff, jt. auth. see Spieler, Marlena.
Oxridge, Panama. Thyme Running Out. (p. 1746)

O

Oyaga, Irene, tr. see Agin, Élodie, et al.
Oyama, Misuzu. Rue de la Nuit: Labyrinth. (p. 1494)
Oyama, Shigeki, jt. auth. see Ochiai, Midori.
Oyebade, Adebayo O. Culture & Customs of Angola (p. 391)
Oyola, Milta, jt. ed. see Tobar, Malena.
Oyola, Milta, tr. see Jingling, Kathy, ed.
Oz, Amos. Suddenly in the Depths of the Forest. (p. 1672)
Oz, Avraham, ed. Marlowe. (p. 1096)
Oz, Mehmet C., jt. auth. see Roizen, Michael F.
Ozaki, Kaori. Immortal Rain (p. 861)
—Immortal Rain Wert, Michael, tr. from JPN. (p. 861)
—Immortal Rain. (p. 861)
Ozaki, Kaori, creator. Immortal Rain. (p. 861)
Ozaki, Yei. Warriors of Old Japan. (p. 1859)
Ozaki, Yei Theodora. Japanese Fairy Tales. (p. 909)
Ozaki, Yei Theodora, compiled by. Japanese Fairy Tales. (p. 909)
Ozaki, Yei Theodora, ed. Japanese Fairy Tales. (p. 909)
Ozama, Marcel, illus. see Might Be Giants Staff, et al.
Ozaniec, Naomi, et al. Meditation: Break down the Subject into 101 Easy-to-Grasp Tips. (p. 1120)
Ozawa, Tadashi. Bodies & Emotions. (p. 206)
—Cómo Dibujar Anime: Chicas en Acción. Vol. 5 Ferrer, María, tr. (p. 350)
—Cómo Dibujar Anime: Escenas de Combate y Acción. Vol. 4 Ferrer, María, tr. (p. 350)
—Cómo Dibujar Anime: Acciones Cotidianas. Vol. 3 Ferrer, María, tr. from JPN. (p. 350)
—Cómo Dibujar Anime: El Diseño de Personajes. Vol. 1 Ferrer, María, tr. from JPN. (p. 350)
—Cómo Dibujar Anime: Emociones y Sentimientos. Vol. 2 Ferrer, María, tr. from JPN. (p. 350)
—How to Draw Anime & Game Characters: Mastering Battle & Action Moves. Vol. 4 (p. 816)
—How to Draw Manga - Colorful Costumes. (p. 818)
Öze, Özkan. I Wonder about Allah Ayduz, Selma, tr. from TUR. (p. 849)
Ozgur, Lynne Emily. Darryl & the Mountain. Abay, Ismail, illus. (p. 409)
Ozick, Cynthia. Bear Boy. (p. 150)
Ozimkowski, Edward, jt. auth. see Sammartino, Joseph.
Ozment, Jones. Tree. (p. 1783)
Ozmun, Lori. Monster in Lulu's Head: The Tale of Two Spoons. (p. 1167)
Ozten the NonDogmatic Artist, Ozten. Understanding Terror: A Fun-Filled Coloring & Activity Book. (p. 1816)
Ozumba, Aghaegbuna & Ozumba, Chineme. Uche & Uzo Say It in Igbo Workbook (p. 1807)
Ozumba, Chineme, jt. auth. see Ozumba, Aghaegbuna.
Ozzy, illus. see Smyth, Jimmy.

P

P. Cats & Cows & Moos & Meows. (p. 281)
—Cotton & Clyde & the Chameleons. (p. 369)
P., Angie. Sneakers. (p. 1597)
P. López, Wendy, tr. see Malam, John.
P, Michael. Daniel's Ride/el Paseo de Daniel. Ballard, Lee, illus. (p. 405)
P, N. Alphabet Country: A Read-Together ABC Game. P, N., illus. (p. 49)
—Down on the Ranch: A Counting Book (p. 474)
PA Illustrator, illus. see Gittens, Sandra L.
PA Illustrator, illus. see Hauf, Kyle.
PA%rez-revertearturo. Sol de Breda. (p. 1606)
Paarmann, Al. Please Let Me Help: I Need Validation. Paarmann, Lesley, photos by. (p. 1373)
Paarmann, Lesley, photos by see Paarmann, Al.
Pabbaraju, S. Adventures of Andreux: Book One - Aranya. (p. 16)
Pablo, Norma. Albi the Pink Carabao. David, Richard, illus. (p. 35)
Pacchini, Fiorenzo. Day with Homo Habilis: Life 2,000,000 Years Ago. (p. 415)
Paccia, Abbey, illus. see Dickey, Eric Wayne.
Pace, Anne Marie. Never Ever Talk to Strangers. Francis, Guy, illus. (p. 1242)
—Teacher for Bear. Wohnoutka, Mike, illus. (p. 1709)
—Vampirina Ballerina. Pham, LeUyen, illus. (p. 1832)
—Vampirina Ballerina Hosts a Sleepover. Pham, LeUyen, illus. (p. 1832)
Pace, Betty. Abraham Lincoln. Walker, Bobbie H., illus. (p. 6)
—Donald's Dump Truck. (p. 466)
Pace, Brittany Lee Ann, illus. see Collier, Kathy Lynn.
Pace, Christine, illus. see Guess, Catherine Ritch.
Pace, Dianne. Odel's Diner. (p. 1278)
Pace, Eugenia Ann. I Am Curious. (p. 832)
Pace, Jessica. Truth Finally Comes Out. (p. 1794)
Pace, Lorenzo. Frederick Douglass & the North Star (p. 633)
—Harriet Tubman & My Grandmother's Quilts (p. 750)
—Jalani & the Lock (p. 906)
—Marching with Martin (p. 1092)
Pace, Paul. Dawn of Our Soul. (p. 411)
Pace, R. Wayne & Stephan, Eric G. Easy Leadership. (p. 500)
Pace, Renee. Forsaken. (p. 623)
—Off Leash: Bonus Content: Nitty Gritty Series. (p. 1279)
Pace, Terri L. Christmas Dream (p. 313)
Pace, Teruko, tr. Shiki O Wataru Kaze. Saito, Kazu, photos by. (p. 1566)
Pace, Yolantha. Wing-Plucked Butterfly: A Survivor Speaks One Woman's War on Hate Crimes Against Women & Children. (p. 1936)
Paceho, Carlos, jt. auth. see Johns, Geoff.
Pacemaker. Passage to Basic Math (p. 1326)
Pach, Chester. Johnson Years. (p. 924)
Pacheco, Alma Rosa, illus. see Ortiz, Orlando & Ortiz, Orlando.
Pacheco, Alma Rosa, illus. see Palacios, Maria Eugenia Blanco & Blanco, Maria.
Pacheco, Alma Rosa, jt. illus. see Pacheco, Luis Gabriel.
Pacheco, Amanda J. Designer Genes. (p. 430)
Pacheco, Carlos, illus. see Buscema, John.
Pacheco, Carlos & Klein, Nic. Captain America (p. 263)
Pacheco, Carlos, et al. Fantastic Four - Resurrection of Galactus. (p. 571)
Pacheco, Gabriel, illus. see Olmos, Gabriela.
Pacheco, Gabriel, illus. see Petterson, Aline.
Pacheco, Gabriel, illus. see Rubio, Antonio.
Pacheco, Guadalupe, illus. see Ortiz, Orlando & Ortiz, Orlando.
Pacheco, Guadalupe, illus. see Palacios, Maria Eugenia Blanco & Blanco, Maria.
Pacheco, Jorge M., illus. see Herrington, Chris.
Pacheco, Laura Emilia, tr. see De Smet, Marian & Meijer, Marja.
Pacheco, Luis Gabriel, illus. see Romero, Alfonso Suárez.
Pacheco, Luis Gabriel & Pacheco, Alma Rosa. Juegos Recreativos para Niños. (p. 931)
Pacheco, Maria & Garcia-Martinez, Julia. Hamburger Tree. Hergenroeder, Ernie, illus. (p. 739)
Pacheco, Miguel Angel. Familia de Mic. Escriva, Ana Lopez, illus. (p. 567)
Pacheco, Robert. Trade on the Taos Mountain Trail. (p. 1776)
Pachek, Mary C. Isabella & the Merry Mouse House: A Christmas Story Coloring Book. Noad, Jordan, illus. (p. 891)
Pacheva, Svetla & Cholakova, Maiia. Kushtichka S Gatanki. (p. 968)
Pacholski, Robert, creator. Aperturas a Lectura. (p. 91)
—Aperturas a Lectura—Libro de Lectura. (p. 91)
Pacileo, Cindy, creator. Virtues Activity & Coloring Book, Ages 5-7. (p. 1844)
—Virtues Activity & Coloring Book, Ages 8-10. (p. 1844)
Pacilleo, Janis. Shrimp Called Pee Wee. (p. 1571)
Paciullo, Ursula. Max's Tale: Max Makes New Friends. (p. 1112)
Pack, Linda Hager. Appalachian Toys & Games from a to Z. Banks, Pat, illus. (p. 92)
—Is for Appalachia: The Alphabet Book of Appalachian Heritage. Banks, Pat, illus. (p. 889)
Pack, Mary Fisk. Cleopatra: "Serpent of the Nile" Malone, Peter, illus. (p. 331)
Pack, Sherri. Little Cat (p. 1025)
Packard, Albert. Cavern of Babel. Boyles, Shawn, illus. (p. 282)
Packard, Chris. Queer Cowboys: And Other Erotic Male Friendships in Nineteenth-Century American Literature. (p. 1425)
Packard, Debbie. Smokey's Silly Christmas Adventures (p. 1594)
Packard, Diane. Batina & Croakus. (p. 144)
Packard, Edward. Forbidden Castle. Willis, Drew, illus. (p. 616)
—Return to the Cave of Time. Willis, Drew, illus. (p. 1465)
—Through the Black Hole. Willis, Drew, illus. (p. 1745)
Packard, Mary. Beating the Odds: A Chapter Book. (p. 152)
—Goliath Beetle: One of the World's Heaviest Insects. (p. 696)
—I Am King! Gore, Leonid, illus. (p. 833)
—Kite. (p. 962)
—Kite. Huang, Benrei, illus. (p. 962)
—Little Raccoon Learns to Share. McCue, Lisa, illus. (p. 1034)
—New Baby. Haley, Amanda, illus. (p. 1243)
—Real Thing! Stinkbugs: And Other Bugs. (p. 1449)
—Ripley's Believe It or Not! Bizarre Collection. Franson, Leanne, illus. (p. 1474)
—Storyteller. Land Eagle, illus. (p. 1663)
—Surprise! Huang, Benrei, illus. (p. 1685)
—Talented Animals. (p. 1701)
—To the Rescue. SI Artists Staff, illus. (p. 1759)
—Totally Gross. Franson, Leanne, illus. (p. 1771)
—Where Is Jake? Allen, Joy, illus. (p. 1908)
—Working Horses. (p. 1952)
Packard, Mary, jt. auth. see Casterline, L. C.
Packard, Mary, ed. Ripley's Believe It or Not! Awesome Collection. Franson, Leanne, illus. (p. 1474)
Packard, Robbi Anne. Two Daddies & Me. (p. 1803)
Packer, Alex J. How Rude! The Teen Guide to Good Manners, Proper Behavior, & Not Grossing People Out. (p. 812)
Packer, Emily, illus. see Thistle, Louise.
Packer, Evelyn. Adventures of Jarv & Trudie: Angel. (p. 19)
Packer, Kyle. Stare If You Dare. (p. 1642)
Packer, Natalie, ed. see Donbavand, Tommy.
Packer, Natalie, ed. see MacPhail, Catherine.
Packer, Natalie, ed. see Rai, Bali.
Packer, Neil, illus. see Cross, Gillian.
Packer, Z. Z. Drinking Coffee Elsewhere. (p. 485)
Pacovská, Kveta. Alphabet. (p. 49)
Pacovskà, Kveta. Flying. Pacovskà, Kveta, illus. (p. 609)
Pacovská, Kveta. Sun Is Yellow. (p. 1676)
Padak, Nancy, jt. auth. see Rasinski, Timothy V.
Padale, Jacinto. Federico García Lorca. (p. 580)
—Marco Polo. (p. 1092)
Padavick, Nate, illus. see Hansen Moench, Megan.
Paddington, Whit. Behind the Scenes at a Newscast. (p. 160)
—Behind the Scenes at an Animated TV Show. (p. 160)
Paddison, Valda. Gardener's Encyclopaedia of New Zealand Native Plants. Cave, Yvonne, photos by. (p. 656)
Paddock, Briana, jt. auth. see Brueggemann, Karen.
Paddock, Susan Star. I Want to Be a Christian: The Story of Blessed Kateri Tekakwitha. Jaurequi, Leticia & Gomez, Elisa, trs. (p. 847)
Paden, Cheryl A. Daniel. (p. 404)
—Life of Daniel. (p. 1011)
Padgett, Anthony. Divinityland. (p. 455)
Padgett, Dave, illus. see Harding, Jennie.
Padgett, Tammy. Meet Me at the Stump. (p. 1121)
Padgitt, J. Durrell. Eli the Elephant. (p. 512)
Padian, Maria. Brett McCarthy: Work in Progress. (p. 226)
—Jersey Tomatoes Are the Best. (p. 914)
—Out of Nowhere. (p. 1311)
Padilla, Ariel, illus. see Kreuger, Jim & Averdonz, N. R.
Padilla, Ariel, illus. see Krueger, Jim & Rogers, Bud.
Padilla, Ariel, illus. see Krueger, Jim & Zondervan Publishing Staff.
Padilla, Ariel, illus. see Rogers, Bud & Krueger, Jim.
Padilla, Ariel, illus. see Rogers, Bud, et al.
Padilla, Ariel, illus. see Simmons, Andrew & Averdonz, N. R.
Padilla, Claudia. Aventuras de Ceci y Azul. (p. 119)
Padilla, Eren Star, illus. see Padilla, Felix M.
Padilla, Felix M. Smiling at the Rain. Padilla, Eren Star, illus. (p. 1594)
Padilla, Gerane & Sky. Penelope Potts & the Christmas Pup. (p. 1336)
Padilla, Mara & Benchmark Education Co., LLC Staff. High in the Sky. (p. 777)
—Sled Club. (p. 1588)
Padilla, Michael J., et al. Adventures in Life, Earth, & Physical Science (p. 15)
—Discoveries in Life, Earth, & Physical Science (p. 448)
—Investigations in Life, Earth, & Physical Science (p. 885)
Padilla-Gamino, Jacqueline L. Kupe & the Corals. Leggitt, Marjorie, illus. (p. 968)
—Kupe & the Corals (Kupe y los Corales) (p. 968)
Padilla-Gamino, Jacqueline L., jt. auth. see Leggitt, Marjorie.
Padley, Steve, jt. auth. see Peck, John.
Padma, T. V. Albertosaurus Mystery: Philip Currie's Hunt in the Badlands. (p. 35)
—Cleverest Thief. (p. 331)
—Forbidden Temple: Stories from the Past. Vyas, Bhavana, illus. (p. 616)
Padma, T. V. & Wrenn, Tom. Growing Gold. (p. 726)
Padmanabhan, Anil. Kalpana Chawla: A Life. (p. 942)
Padmanabhan, Manjula. I Am Different. (p. 832)
Padmasambhava. Dzogchen Essentials: The Path That Clarifies Confusion. Schmidt, Marcia Binder, ed. (p. 491)
Padovano, Chris, illus. see Carothers, Nina.
Padovano, Chris, illus. see Newton, Chelle.
Padovano, Chris, jt. auth. see Notarfrancesco, Lisa Christiano.
Padraic & Colum, Padraic. Children of Odin: Nordic Gods & Heroes. (p. 302)
Padrick, Kendell, ed. see Le Compte, David & Rolland, Carol.
Padrick, Kendell, jt. auth. see LeCompte, David.
Padrino, Mercedes. Feudalism & Village Life in the Middle Ages. (p. 583)
Padrino, Mercedes, jt. auth. see Anderson, Mercedes Padrino.
Padron, Alicia, illus. see Huven, Kim.
Padron, Alicia, illus. see Katz, Susan B.
Padron, Alicia, illus. see Shubuck, Sheila.
Padrón, Angela, illus. see Starishevsky, Jill.
Padron, Aya, illus. see Brown, Michelle Haney.
Padron, Aya, illus. see Park, Kyubyong & Amen, Henry J.
Padron, Aya, illus. see Wu, Faye-Lynn.
Padron, Francisco Morales. Spanish Jamaica. (p. 1621)
Padron, Maria Lorena, jt. auth. see Romero, Kyle.
Padua, Grace. Travels of Chikippo. Baker, David, illus. (p. 1780)
Padula, Stacy A. Aftermath. (p. 28)
—Montgomery Lake High #2-When Darkness Tries to Hide. (p. 1170)
Padur, Simone. Things That Go Bump in the Night. (p. 1733)
Padur, Simone, illus. see Sandilands, Joyce.
Paek, Min, tr. see Shin, Sun Yung.
Paes, Rob. Mighty Machines. (p. 1140)
Paetro, Maxine, jt. auth. see Patterson, James.
Paéz, Enrique. Devuelveme el Anillo, Pelo Cepillo. (p. 432)
Pafford, John M. On the Solid Rock: Christianity & Public Policy. (p. 1291)
Pafford, Nancy McIntosh. Oscar: Legendary Alligator of the Okefenokee Swamp. (p. 1305)
—White Feather. Garza, Amy Ammons, ed. (p. 1913)
Pagan, John. Fury in the Garden. (p. 650)
Pagan, Joseph. Collection of Short Stories for Children & Young Adults. (p. 340)
Pagano, Guy A. What's That? (p. 1899)
Pagano, Mark, illus. see Cheha, Jacob.
Pagay, Jeff, illus. see Geshell, Carmen.
Page, illus. see Caban, Connie.
Page, Anna Laura & Shafferman, Jean Anne. My First Bible Songs: 12 Traditional Fun Songs with New Sacred Lyrics & Activities for Young Children. (p. 1204)
—My First Spirituals. (p. 1208)
Page, Brenda. In the Hands of the Potter: Shaped for Purpose. Elum, Deborah, ed. (p. 866)
Page, Cecelia Frances. Adventures on Ancient Continents. (p. 24)
—Phenomenal Experiences. (p. 1350)
Page, Chris. Veneficus - Stones of the Chosen. (p. 1835)
Page, Claire. Carry-Me Pets. (p. 271)
—Fashion Show Sticker Book. (p. 576)
—Five Noisy Ducks: An Action-Packed Counting Book. (p. 601)
—Hide & Seek Vehicles. (p. 777)
—I Really Like Trucks. (p. 844)
Page, Claire, jt. auth. see Bicknell, Joanna.
Page, Claire, jt. auth. see Horne, Jane.
Page, Claire, jt. auth. see Page, Nick.
Page, Claire & Make Believe Ideas Staff. Carry-Me Baby Animals. (p. 271)
Page, Claire & Morrison, Karen. Pull along Kittens. (p. 1415)
—Pull along Puppies. (p. 1415)
Page, Debbie, illus. see Keaster, Diane W.
Page, Debbie, illus. see Keaster, Diane.
Page, Frank. Sometimes a Squirrel Is Just a Squirrel. (p. 1610)
Page, Gail. How to Be a Good Cat. (p. 814)
—How to Be a Good Dog. Page, Gail, illus. (p. 814)
Page, J. & Rainier, S. T. Ben & Elvis: The Miracle of a Stormy Christmas. Moyer, J., illus. (p. 163)
—Curiosity Strikes: Ben & Elvis Adventures. Rainier, S. T., illus. (p. 392)
Page, J. & Rainier, S.T. Bullfrog Story. (p. 240)
Page, Jack & Merivale, Jane. Checkpoints: Developing College English Skills. (p. 295)
Page, Jan. Chocolate Monster. Ross, Tony, illus. (p. 309)
Page, Jason. Basketball, Soccer, & Other Ball Games. (p. 143)
—Castles & Dungeons. (p. 277)
—Cycling, Shooting, & Show Jumping: Archery, Weightlifting, & a Whole Lot More. (p. 397)
—Decathlon, High Jump, & Other Field Events. (p. 421)
—Futbol. (p. 650)
—Ghosts & Monsters. (p. 672)
—Gymnastics Events. (p. 734)
—Martial Arts, Boxing, & Other Combat Sports: Fencing, Judo, Wrestling, Taekwondo, & a Whole Lot More. (p. 1097)
—Rowing, Sailing, & Other Sports on the Water. (p. 1492)
—Sprints, Hurdles, & Other Track Events. (p. 1635)
—Swimming, Diving, & Other Water Sports. (p. 1691)
Page, Josephine. I Am a Dump Truck. Migliari, Paola, illus. (p. 832)
—I Am a Fire Truck. Migliari, Paola, illus. (p. 832)
—Thank You Prayer. Church, Caroline Jayne, illus. (p. 1725)
Page, Julie & Adams, Sabrina. Treasure of Trust: The Hidden Treasures of My Kingdom Pals McTeer, Rhonda, ed. (p. 1782)
Page, Lawana. Weeping Willow Tree. Amaya, Laura, tr. (p. 1872)
Page, Linda. Quiet Moments for Teachers. (p. 1428)
Page, Liza & Innovative Kids Staff. Colors - E-Z Page Turners. Larrañaga, Ana Martin, illus. (p. 345)
—Mommies & Babies. Larrañaga, Ana Martin, illus. (p. 1162)
—Opposites. Larrañaga, Ana Martin, illus. (p. 1300)
Page, Louise. Furballs' Fables. (p. 650)
Page, Lynda. Caley's Secret Garden. (p. 252)
Page, Mark, illus. see Hudson, Wade.
Page, Mark, illus. see Scholastic, Inc. Staff & Taylor-Butler, Christine.
Page, Nick. Amazing Academy Survival. (p. 52)
—Do You Do a Didgeridoo. Baker, Sara, illus. (p. 457)
—Read with Me Three Little Pigs. (p. 1444)
—Touch & Feel Noisy Dinosaurs. (p. 1772)
Page, Nick, jt. auth. see Bicknell, Joanna.
Page, Nick & Claire. Autumn Princess. (p. 118)
—Elves & the Shoemaker. (p. 517)
Page, Nick And Claire. Giant Sticker Activity Bible Stories. (p. 674)
Page, Nick & Claire. Jonah the Moaner. (p. 925)
—Noah & the Ark. (p. 1261)
—Snow White. (p. 1599)
Page, Nick & Page, Claire. David & Goliath. Loy, Nikki, illus. (p. 410)
—Finger Puppet Books Christmas Story. (p. 589)
—Funny Faces: Baby Animals. (p. 649)
—Funny Faces Farm Animals. (p. 649)
—Giant Sticker Activity Story Book. Baker, Sara, illus. (p. 674)
—Good Samaritan. Loy, Nikki, illus. (p. 700)
—King of Spring. Robert, Yannick, illus. (p. 959)
—Loaves & Fishes. Shimmen, Cathy, illus. (p. 1044)
—Quick Smarts Dangerous Animals. (p. 1427)
—Quick Smarts Dinosaurs. (p. 1427)
—Read W/Me 6v. (p. 1444)
—Read with Me Gingerbread Fred: Sticker Activity Book. Baker, Sara, illus. (p. 1444)
—Read with Me Jack & the Beanstalk: Sticker Activity Book. Goodberry, Jo, illus. (p. 1444)
—Read with Me Jonah the Moaner: Sticker Activity Book. Loy, Nikki, illus. (p. 1444)
—Read with Me Rumpelstiltskin: Sticker Activity Book. Baker, Sara, illus. (p. 1444)
—Read with Me Snow White: Sticker Activity Book. Willey, Bee, illus. (p. 1444)
—Read with Me the Elves & the Shoemaker: Sticker Activity Book. Baker, Sara, illus. (p. 1444)
—Read with Me Three Billy Goats Gruff: Sticker Activity Book. Saunders, Katie, illus. (p. 1444)
—Ready to Read Jack & the Beanstalk Sticker Activity Workbook. Goodberry, Jo, illus. (p. 1448)
—Runaway Son. Baker, Sara, illus. (p. 1496)
—Three Billy Goats Gruff. (p. 1741)
—Winter Prince. Shimmen, Cathy, illus. (p. 1938)
Page, Norvell. Spider #5: Empire of Doom. (p. 1626)
Page, P. K. Brazilian Alphabet for the Younger Reader. (p. 224)
—Grain of Sand Krykorka, Vladyana, illus. (p. 705)
—Jake, the Baker, Makes a Cake. Campbell, Ruth, illus. (p. 906)
—Old Woman & the Hen. Westergard, Jim, illus. (p. 1285)
—Sky Tree. Bridgeman, Kristi, illus. (p. 1587)
—Uirapurú: Based on a Brazilian Legend. Bridgeman, Kristi, illus. (p. 1808)
Page, P. K. & Ellis, Sarah. Next Stop! Krykorka, Vladyana & Ohi, Ruth, illus. (p. 1249)
Page, Phil. Hodder Graphics: Heroes. (p. 787)
Page, Phil & Blackmore, Ruth Benton. Hodder Graphics: A Kestrel for a Knave. (p. 787)
Page, Philip & Petit, Marilyn, eds. Macbeth: Livewire Shakespeare. Page, Philip, illus. (p. 1068)
—Midsummer Night's Dream. (p. 1139)
—Romeo & Juliet. Page, Philip, illus. (p. 1486)
Page, Philip & Pettit, Marilyn. Livewire Shakespeare A Midsummer Night's Dream Teacher's Resource Book. (p. 1040)
—Livewire Shakespeare Much Ado about Nothing. (p. 1040)
—Richard III. (p. 1469)
Page, Philip, et al. Great Expectations. (p. 715)
Page, Rhonda G. Most Important Thing to Have. (p. 1177)
Page, Robin. Chicken Followed Me Home! Questions & Answers about a Familiar Fowl. Page, Robin, illus. (p. 300)
—Move! Jenkins, Steve, illus. (p. 1183)
—Move! Jenkins, Steven, illus. (p. 1183)
—Sisters & Brothers: Sibling Relationships in the Animal World. (p. 1581)
—What Do You Do with a Tail Like This? Jenkins, Steve, illus. (p. 1883)
Page, Robin, jt. auth. see Jenkins, Steve.
Page, Robin & Jenkins, Steve. Animals in Flight. Jenkins, Steve, illus. (p. 83)

—Egg: Nature's Perfect Package. (p. 506)
—How to Clean a Hippopotamus: A Look at Unusual Animal Partnerships. Jenkins, Steve, illus. (p. 816)
—Sisters & Brothers: Sibling Relationships in the Animal World. Jenkins, Steve, illus. (p. 1581)
—What Do You Do with a Tail Like This? (p. 1883)
Page, Sam. Clearwell Copse: Farlie Fox Has an Invisible Friend. (p. 330)
Page, Shari. Little Master of Tall Tales. (p. 1031)
Page, Stefan. ABC Farmers' Market Flash Cards. (p. 3)
—We're Going to the Farmers' Market. (p. 1875)
Page, Terry. Fathers of the Friendly Forest. Page, Terry, illus. (p. 577)
—Fathers of the Friendly Forest Coloring Book. Page, Terry, illus. (p. 577)
—Saddest Centaur. Page, Terry, illus. (p. 1501)
—Saddest Centaur Coloring Book. Page, Terry, illus. (p. 1501)
Page, Thomas Nelson. Bred in the Bone. (p. 226)
—Burial of the Guns. (p. 243)
—Captured Santa Claus. (p. 265)
—Dante & His Influence. (p. 406)
—Gordon Keith. (p. 702)
—In Ole Virginia: Or, Marse Chan & Other Stories. (p. 864)
—Italy & the World War. (p. 895)
—John Marvel, Assistant. (p. 922)
—Land of the Sprirt. (p. 973)
—Negro: The Southerner's Problem. (p. 1240)
—Old Dominion: Her Making & Her Manners. (p. 1283)
—Old Gentleman of the Black Stock. (p. 1283)
—On Newfound River. (p. 1289)
—Pastime Stories. (p. 1327)
—Red Riders (Completed by Rosewell Page) (p. 1454)
—Red Rock: A Chronicle of Reconstruction. (p. 1455)
—Robert E. Lee: Man & Solder. (p. 1479)
—Robert E. Lee: The Southerner. (p. 1479)
—Santa Claus's Partner. (p. 1511)
—Two Little Confederates: Among the Camps. (p. 1804)
—Two Little Confederates. (p. 1804)
—Under the Crust. (p. 1813)
Page, Tyler, illus. see Robbins, Trina.
Page, Willie F. & Davis, R. Hunt. Encyclopedia of African History & Culture (p. 524)
Page, Winter. Breaking Free. (p. 225)
Pagel, Beth. What's Wrong with Grandma? (p. 1900)
Pagel, Stace. Fletcher the Fly. (p. 603)
Pagels, Douglas. What Every Teen Needs to Know. (p. 1884)
Page-Robertson, Andrew. BoomeRangers: Maralinga Countdown. (p. 213)
Pages, Christina. Mountain Boy. Caruth, Jeannette, illus. (p. 1180)
Paglia, Rhonda. Little Lambs & the Very Special Mission. Paglia, Rhonda & Galaska, Taylor, illus. (p. 1030)
Pagni, Gianpaolo. Gianpaolo Pagni: Double Face. (p. 673)
Pagnol, Marcel. Chateau de Ma Mere (p. 295)
—Jean de Florette (p. 911)
—Manon des Sources (p. 1088)
Pagnoni, Roberta. Humpty Dumpty's Nursery Rhymes. (p. 827)
—It's Easter Time. (p. 896)
Pagnoni, Roberta, illus. see Barron's Editorial Staff.
Pagnoni, Roberta, illus. see Caviezel, Giovanni.
Pagnoni, Roberta, illus. see Ravera, Giuseppe.
Pagnoni, Roberta, jt. illus. see Rigo, L.
Pagnoni, Roberta & Rigo, Laura. Twelve Days of Christmas. (p. 1800)
Pagona, Aurora, illus. see De Jesus, Opal.
Pagotto, Toni. Pope John Paul II. Toppi, Sergio, illus. (p. 1384)
Pagratis, Illustrator Liliane, MaggieGrenier, jt. auth. see Pagratis, Maggie.
Pagratis, Maggie. My Sister the Bee. (p. 1218)
Pagratis, Maggie & Pagratis, Illustrator Liliane, MaggieGrenier. Go Away Booboo! (p. 686)
—With Their Tiny Hands. (p. 1942)
Pahn, Latosha. Come go on a Read along Ride with Me: Read along Ride. (p. 347)
Pai, Chris, tr. see Tanigawa, Nagaru.
Paiba, Helen, compiled by. Scary Stories for Nine Year Olds. (p. 1521)
Paige, D. M. Box-Office Smash. (p. 216)
—Chart Topper. (p. 294)
—Going to Press. (p. 693)
—Size 0. (p. 1583)
Paige, Danielle. Dorothy Must Die. (p. 472)
—Dorothy Must Die Stories: No Place Like Oz, the Witch Must Burn, the Wizard Returns. (p. 472)
—Dorothy Must Die Stories: No Place Like Oz - The Witch Must Burn; the Wizard Returns. (p. 472)
—Wicked Will Rise. (p. 1927)
Paige, Joy. Blue Whale: World's Largest Mammal. (p. 203)
—Cool Careers Without College for People Who Love to Build Things. (p. 363)
—Ellen Ochoa: The First Hispanic Woman in Space. (p. 514)
—Giraffe: World's Tallest Animal. (p. 677)
—Hummingbird: World's Smallest Bird. (p. 826)
—Record-Breaking Animals (p. 1452)
—Sloth: World's Slowest Mammal. (p. 1591)
—Sloth / el Perezoso: The World's Slowest Mammal / el mamífero más lento del Mundo. (p. 1591)
—Sloth: The World's Slowest Mammal: El Perezoso: El Mamifero Mas Lento Del Mundo. (p. 1591)
—Stick Insect: World's Longest Insect. (p. 1649)
—Stick Insect / el insecto Palo: The World's Longest Insect / el insecto más largo del Mundo. (p. 1649)
—Stick Insect: The World's Longest Insect: El Insecto Palo:El Insecto Mas Largo Del Mundo. (p. 1649)
Paige, Nancy. Myrtle the Turtle Green, Megan, illus. (p. 1222)
Paigerac, Patricia. Chimmy '5 in 1' Language Alphabet Book. Choi, Allan Jai-Ho, illus. (p. 306)
Paikai, Tammy. Too Many Mangos. Robinson, Don, illus. (p. 1766)
Paillot, Jim. My Weirder School #12: Mrs. Lane Is a Pain! (p. 1221)
Paillot, Jim, illus. see Cleary, Brian P.
Paillot, Jim, illus. see Dinardo, Jeff.
Paillot, Jim, illus. see Gutman, Dan.
Paillot, Jim, illus. see Metzger, Steve.
Paillot, Jim, illus. see Overdeck, Laura.
Paillot, Jim, illus. see Trueit, Trudi Strain.
Paillot, Jim, illus. see Trueit, Trudi.
Pain, Catherine. Alphabet for Colouring In. (p. 49)
Pain, London. Gentle Dream. (p. 661)
Painchaud, Michelle. Pretending to Be Erica. (p. 1398)
Paine, Albert Bigelow. Hollow Tree & Deep Woods Book: Being a New Edition in One Volume of the Hollow Tree & in the Deep Woods with Several New Stories & Pictures Added. (p. 789)
—Hollow Tree & Deep Woods Book, Being a New Edition in One Volume of the Hollow Tree & in the Deep Woods with Several New Stories & Pictu. Condé, J. M., illus. (p. 789)
Paine, Colin, illus. see Pringle, Eric.
Paine, Jed. Ferrari (p. 582)
—Porsche (p. 1386)
Paine, Penelope C. Gift of Flowers. Maeno, Itoko, illus. (p. 675)
—Gift of Love. Maeno, Itoko, illus. (p. 675)
—Gift of Taste. Maeno, Itoko, illus. (p. 675)
Paine, Penelope Golville. Flower Girl A to Z. (p. 607)
Paine, Ralph D. First down, Kentucky! (p. 594)
Paine, Sheila. Afghan Amulet: Travels from the Hindu Kush. (p. 26)
—Golden Horde: From the Himalaya to the Mediterranean. (p. 694)
Paine, Thomas. Crisis. (p. 383)
—Rights of Man. (p. 1472)
Paine, Walter. Cousin John: The Story of a Boy & a Small Smart Pig. Dodson, Bert, illus. (p. 373)
Painted Daisies Inc. Staff & Borgatti, Katherine. Shermit's Adventure to Sprinkle Island. Painted Daisies Inc. Staff, illus. (p. 1566)
Painter, Annie. Vincent & Jake Learn Color Mixing. (p. 1842)
Painter, Carol. Friends Helping Friends: A Handbook for Helpers. (p. 638)
—Leading a Friends Helping Friends Peer Program. (p. 981)
Painter, Grace. Harry Bear Story. Kacer, Stephen, illus. (p. 750)
Painter, Lucy. 100 Fantastic Things to Make, Do & Play: Simple, Fun Projects That Use Easy Everyday Materials - Cooking, Growing, Science, Music, Painting, Crafts & Party Games! (p. 1998)
—Outrageously Big Activity, Play & Project Book: Cookery, Painting, Crafts, Science, & Much More. (p. 1313)
—Really Big Book of Amazing Things to Make & Do. (p. 1449)
Painter, Lucy, jt. auth. see Walton, Sally.
Painter, Mark P. William Henry Harrison: President & Chief Justice. (p. 1933)
Painter, Sue Ann. William Henry Harrison: Father of the West. (p. 1933)
Pair, Karma A. Before the Sun Could Answer. (p. 158)
—On My Way to the Market. Pressey, Deborah, illus. (p. 1289)
Pair, Regether. Little Rock Island & a Little Rock Named Sam Who Doesn't Think He Fits In. (p. 1036)
Pait, Jane Thompson. BK the Red-Headed Angel & the Empty Tomb. (p. 194)
—Red-Headed Angel Discovers the Crystal Sea. (p. 1454)
—Star of David: A Space for Everyone. (p. 1640)
Paiva, Johannah Gilman. Is There a Monster in My Closet? Long, Paulette Rich, illus. (p. 890)
Paiva, Johannah Gilman, ed. see Aladdin Books.
Paiva, Johannah Gilman, ed. see Everett, Melissa.
Paiva, Johannah Gilman, ed. see Shand, Jennifer.
Paiva, Johannah Gilman, ed. Awesome Book of Duckbills & Boneheads. Various, illus. (p. 121)
—Awesome Book of Flesh-Eaters. Various, illus. (p. 121)
—Awesome Book of Monsters of the Deep. Various, illus. (p. 121)
—Awesome Book of Planets & Their Moons. Various, illus. (p. 121)
—Awesome Book of Prehistoric Animals. Various, illus. (p. 121)
—Awesome Book of the Universe. Various, illus. (p. 121)
—Awesome Book of Tornadoes & Other Storms. Various, illus. (p. 121)
—Awesome Book of Volcanoes. Various, illus. (p. 121)
—Child's Book of Prayers: Please. (p. 304)
—Child's Book of Prayers: Thank You. (p. 304)
—Child's Book of Prayers: Good Morning, Dear God. (p. 304)
—Crazy Critters. Gardiner, Lisa M., illus. (p. 377)
—Farm Find. Gardiner, Lisa M., illus. (p. 574)
—Zoo Friends. (p. 1989)
Paiva, Teresa & Pinto, Helena Rebelo. Mein Freund, der Schlaf. (p. 1124)
—My Friend, Sleep. (p. 1209)
Paizee, Daphne, et al. Collins Primary Science - Student's Book Stage 5. (p. 341)
Paizo Publishing (Pathfinder Roleplaying Game). Conflict PvP Tactics & Teams Rulebook. (p. 357)
Paizo Publishing Staff, et al. Masters of the Pit. (p. 1103)
Paj, Eduardo, illus. see Macalino, Damien.
Pajalunga, Lorena V. Yoga for Kids: Simple Animal Poses for Any Age. Forlati, Anna, illus. (p. 1972)
Pajot, Lauren, illus. see Segel, Robert G.
Pak, Amy. History Through the Ages - America's History: Historical Timeline Figures (Explorers to 21st Century) Pak, Amy, illus. (p. 785)
—History Through the Ages - Napoleon to Now: Historical Timeline Figures (1750 AD - Present) Pak, Amy, illus. (p. 785)
Pak, Boris, jt. auth. see Hauff, Wilhelm.
Pak, Greg. Chaos War. Pham, Khoi, illus. (p. 291)
—Fall of the Hulks. (p. 566)
Pak, Greg, et al. X-Men - X-Termination. Buffagni, Matteo et al, illus. (p. 1967)
Pak, Kenard, illus. see Gray, Rita.
Pak, Mi-Son. Seven Brothers & the Big Dipper/Heungbu, Nolbu & the Magic Gourds. (p. 1554)
Pak, Mi-Son & Kim, Yon-Kyong. Greedy Princess/the Rabbit & the Tiger. (p. 720)
Pakaine, Violeta. Motorcyclist Croaker Lee. (p. 1180)
Pakenham, Sarah, jt. auth. see Lacey, Josh.
Pakizer, Debi & Sears, Mary A. Vaulting: The Art of Gymnastics on Horseback. Anderson, Julia & Barnette, Jackie, eds. (p. 1833)
Pakkala, Christine. Jasmine & Maddie. (p. 909)
—Last-But-Not-Least Lola & the Wild Chicken. Hoppe, Paul, illus. (p. 977)
—Last-But-Not-Least Lola Going Green. Hoppe, Paul, illus. (p. 977)
—Last-but-Not-Least Lola Going Green. Hoppe, Paul, illus. (p. 977)
Pal, Erika, illus. see Cornwell, Nicki.
Pal, Erika, illus. see Dale, Elizabeth.
Pal, Erika, illus. see Mitton, Jacqueline & Quarto Generic Staff.
Pal Toys, creator. Bright & Beyond - Age 1 English. (p. 228)
—Bright & Beyond - Baby English. (p. 228)
—Bright & Beyond - Bebes. (p. 228)
—Bright & Beyond - Preschool English. (p. 228)
Palacio, Carla, tr. Las Aventuras de Don Quijote. Subi, illus. (p. 976)
Palacio, R. J. Auggie & Me: Three Wonder Stories. (p. 115)
—Wonder. (p. 1947)
—Wonder Journal. (p. 1947)
Palacios, Argentina. Secreto de la Llama - The Llama's Secret: Una Leyenda Peruana. (p. 1544)
Palacios, Argentina, tr. see Goring, Ruth.
Palacios, Argentina, tr. see McLeese, Tex.
Palacios, Eustaquio. Alferez Real. (p. 37)
Palacios G., Sara Helena, illus. see Segovia, Silvia.
Palacios, John. Readers' Theater: Scripts for Young Readers: How the Tiger Got Its Stripes. (p. 1444)
Palacios, John, illus. see Stewart, Kelly, ed.
Palacios, Laura. Ten Hardworking Elves. (p. 1718)
Palacios, Maria Eugenia Blanco & Blanco, Maria. Felicia y Odicia. Pacheco, Alma Rosa & Pacheco, Guadalupe, illus. (p. 581)
Palacios, Sara, illus. see Bradley, Sandra.
Palacios, Sara, illus. see Brown, Monica.
Palacios, Sara, illus. see McCarthy, Jenna.
Palacios, Sara Helena, illus. see Leon, Georgina Lazaro.
Palacios, Tomas. Amazing Spider-Man vs. Doctor Octopus. (p. 56)
—Avengers: Age of Ultron: Friends & Foes. (p. 118)
—Captain America: The Winter Soldier. (p. 263)
—Captain America - The Winter Soldier. Disney Book Group Staff, illus. (p. 263)
—Guardians of the Galaxy: The Story of the Guardians. (p. 728)
—Guardians of the Galaxy. Disney Book Group Staff, illus. (p. 728)
—These Are the Guardians of the Galaxy. (p. 1731)
—Ultimate Spider-Man: the Really Big Sticker Book! Disney Book Group Staff, illus. (p. 1810)
Palacios, Tomas, jt. auth. see Marvel Press Staff.
Palacios, Tomas, jt. auth. see Marvel Staff.
Palacios, Tomas, jt. auth. see Marvel.
Palacios, Tomas & Marvel Press Book Group. Avengers Top Agents, Most Wanted. (p. 119)
Palacios, Tomas & Wong, Clarissa S. Guardians of the Galaxy: These Are the Guardians. (p. 728)
Palacios, Tomas & Wright, Edgar. Ant-Man: I Am Ant-Man. (p. 88)
Palacios, Vicente. Origami Animals. (p. 1303)
Palacious, John. Readers' Theater Paul Bunyan: Scripts for Young Readers. (p. 1444)
Paladin, Frank. Hole in My Stocking. Amber, Holly & Lin, Melanie, illus. (p. 788)
Paladin, Frank, jt. auth. see Johnson, Rhonda.
Palagonia, Peter, illus. see Akselrad, January & Young, Jennifer.
Palahicky, Sophia. Kid's Reading Craze - a Collection of 20 Short Stories. (p. 955)
Palatini, Margie. Bad Boys. Cole, Henry, illus. (p. 131)
—Bad Boys Get Cookie! (p. 131)
—Bad Boys Get Cookie! Cole, Henry, illus. (p. 131)
—Bad Boys Get Henpecked! Cole, Henry, illus. (p. 131)
—Bedhead. (p. 156)
—Boo-Hoo Moo. Graves, Keith, illus. (p. 209)
—Cats Hanukkah. (p. 281)
—Cheese. Johnson, Steve & Fancher, Lou, illus. (p. 296)
—Earthquack! Moser, Barry, illus. (p. 497)
—Goldie & the Three Hares. Davis, Jack E., illus. (p. 695)
—Gorgonzola: A Very Stinkysaurus. Bowers, Tim, illus. (p. 702)
—Hogg, Hogg, & Hog. Palatini, Margie, illus. (p. 787)
—Isabella for Real. Pham, LeUyen, illus. (p. 891)
—Lousy Rotten Stinkin' Grapes. Moser, Barry, illus. (p. 1059)
—Moo Who? Graves, Keith, illus. (p. 1171)
—Moosestache. (p. 1173)
—No Biting, Louise. Reinhart, Matthew, illus. (p. 1257)
—No Nap! Yes Nap! Yaccarino, Dan, illus. (p. 1259)
—Oink? Cole, Henry, illus. (p. 1282)
—Perfect Pet. Whatley, Bruce, illus. (p. 1342)
—Piggie Pie! Fine, Howard, illus. (p. 1358)
—Stuff. Jones, Noah Z., illus. (p. 1670)
—Three Silly Billies. Moser, Barry, illus. (p. 1743)
—Tub-Boo-Boo. (p. 1795)
—Under a Pig Tree: A History of the Noble Fruit. Groenink, Chuck, illus. (p. 1813)
—Untitled Picture Book. (p. 1823)
—Zoey Zone. Palatini, Margie, illus. (p. 1987)
Palatini, Margie, jt. auth. see Davis, Jack E.
Palatini, Margie & Davis, Jack E. Sweet Tooth. Davis, Jack E., illus. (p. 1690)
Palazeti, Toulla. Seed Was Planted. (p. 1547)
—Seed Was Planted/Sembré una Semilla. Barcita, Pamela, illus. (p. 1547)
Palazetti, Toulla. Seed Was Planted. Barcita, Pamela, illus. (p. 1547)
Palazzo, Christine. Josephina & Her Terrific Tomato Soup. (p. 926)
Palazzo-Craig, Janet. Language Development Variety Text. (p. 975)
—Making of the American Flag: Betsy Ross & George Washington. (p. 1082)
—Ojibwe of Michigan, Wisconsin, Minnesota, & North Dakota. (p. 1282)
Palazzolo, Fran. Wise Owl's First Sounds & Sight Words. (p. 1940)
—Wise Owl's Vowels. (p. 1940)
Palazzolo, Gail M. Mommy, How Can We Catch the Moon? (p. 1162)
Palecko-Schuck, Jenna, jt. auth. see Skinner, Tina.
Paleja, S. N. Native Americans: A Visual Exploration. (p. 1234)
—Power Up! A Visual Exploration of Energy. Tse, Glenda, illus. (p. 1390)
Palen, Debbie, illus. see Dinardo, Jeff.
Palen, Debbie, illus. see Gravelle, Karen & Gravelle, Jennifer.
Palen, Debbie, illus. see Greenburg, J. C.
Palen, Debbie, illus. see Hapka, Cathy, pseud & Titlebaum, Ellen.
Palen, Debbie, illus. see Hoyt, Beth Caldwell & Ritter, Erica.
Palencia, Ramon. Uso de la Gramatica Junior Avanzado. (p. 1829)
Palenque, Stephanie Maher. Crack & Cocaine = Busted! (p. 375)
PaleoJoe. Disappearance of Dinosaur Sue. Caszatt-Allen, Wendy, illus. (p. 446)
—Mysterious Mammoths. Caszatt-Allen, Wendy, illus. (p. 1223)
—Secret Sabertooth. Caszatt-Allen, Wendy, illus. (p. 1543)
—Stolen Stegasaurus. Caszatt-Allen, Wendy, illus. (p. 1652)
PaleoJoe & Caszatt-Allen, Wendy. Raptor's Revenge. (p. 1439)
Palermo, Miguel Angel. Lo Que Cuentan los Guaranies. (p. 1044)
—Lo Que Cuentan los Onas. (p. 1044)
—Lo Que Cuentan los Tehuelches. (p. 1044)
—Lo Que Cuentan los Wichis. (p. 1044)
Palermo, Sharon G. Lie That Had to Be. (p. 1007)
Paletta, Emilio. Squire Dumpty. (p. 1637)
Paley, Allison. Sky Is Burning. (p. 1586)
Paley, Briyah. Northeastern University. Belinsky, Robin et al, eds. (p. 1265)
Paley, Caitlyn. Pros & Cons of Nuclear Power. (p. 1412)
—Slave Narratives & the Writings of Freedmen. (p. 1588)
Paley, Daniel. Luigi & the Barefoot Races Boyd, Aaron, illus. (p. 1064)
Paley, Jane. Hooper Finds a Family: A Hurricane Katrina Dog's Survival Tale. (p. 795)
Paley, Joan, illus. see Gulberson, Brenda Z.
Paley, Joan, illus. see Halfmann, Janet.
Paley, Joan, illus. see Pringle, Laurence.
Paley, Rebecca, et al. Body Book for Boys. (p. 207)
Paley, Sasha. Huge. (p. 824)
Paley, Sasha & Greenwald, Lisa. Huge. (p. 824)
Palfreman-Bunker, Claire. Can Kittens Take a Catnap? Relf, Adam, illus. (p. 258)
Palfrey, Bernard. No Match for Uncle Charlie. (p. 1259)
Palgrave Macmillan Staff. Grants Register 2007: The Complete Guide to Postgraduate Funding Worldwide. (p. 710)
Palika, Liz. Dog Obedience: Getting Your Pooch off the Couch & Other Dog Training Tips (p. 461)
—Dog Tricks: Teaching Your Doggie to Shake Hands & Other Tricks (p. 461)
Palika, Liz & Gagne, Tammy. Dog Ownership. (p. 461)
Palika, Liz & Miller, Katherine A. Animals at Work. (p. 82)
Palin, Nicki, illus. see Goldsmith, Mike.
Palin, Nicki, illus. see Wallace, Karen.
Palin, Nicki, illus. see Wilson, Hannah.
Paling, Chris. Adventures of Rumble, Tumble, & Titch: Uncertain Times. (p. 22)
Palka, Yvonne. Dragon Fire Ocean Mist. (p. 477)
Pallace, Chris. Skallywaggs Card Game: The Mix-n-match Pirate Game. (p. 1583)
Pallace, Chris, jt. auth. see Serwacki, Kevin.
Pallares, Albert. Bosque Es de Todos. (p. 215)
Pallarés, José Miguel, tr. see Meyer, Stephenie.
Pallasch, Tina. Ever Atom: One. (p. 541)
Pallas-Luke, Barbara. Cryptic Society. (p. 387)
Palleschi, Sarah. Did I Really Dream Last Night? (p. 436)
Pallister, John, jt. auth. see Bowen, Ann.
Pallister, John C. In the Steps of the Great American Entomologist. Elgin, Kathleen, illus. (p. 867)
Pallock, Ruth. Planet Mazol: Book 2 of World Adventures of Jayden. (p. 1367)
Pallone, Robert. Adventures of Main Man: A Child's View of the World. (p. 20)
Pallotta, Jerry. Addition Book. Bolster, Rob, illus. (p. 12)
—Beetle Alphabet Book. Biedrzycki, David, tr. (p. 158)
—Beetle Alphabet Book. Biedrzycki, David, illus. (p. 158)
—Butterfly Colors & Counting. Bersani, Shennen, illus. (p. 247)
—Butterfly Counting. Bersani, Shennen, illus. (p. 247)
—Construction Alphabet Book. Bolster, Rob, illus. (p. 359)
—Count by Fives. Bolster, Rob, illus. (p. 369)
—Count by Tens. Bolster, Rob, illus. (p. 369)
—Dinosaur Christmas. McWilliam, Howard, illus. (p. 441)
—Dory Story. Biedrzycki, David, illus. (p. 472)
—F Is for Fenway Park: America's Oldest Major League Ballpark. (p. 559)
—Giraffe Did One Way up High. (p. 677)
—Going Lobstering. Bolster, Rob, illus. (p. 692)
—Hammerhead vs. Bull Shark. Bolster, Rob, illus. (p. 739)
—Hershey's Weights & Measures. Bolster, Rob, illus. (p. 774)
—How to Draw Icky Bugs. Gee, Bonnie, illus. (p. 817)
—How Will I Get to School This Year? (p. 823)
—How Will I Get to School This Year? Biedrzycki, David, illus. (p. 823)
—Icky Bug Alphabet Book. Masiello, Ralph, photos by. (p. 851)
—Icky Bug Counting Book. Masiello, Ralph, illus. (p. 851)
—Lobster vs. Crab. Bolster, Rob, illus. (p. 1044)
—Multiplication. Bolster, Rob, illus. (p. 1190)
—Ocean Alphabet Board Book. Mazzola, Frank, Jr., illus. (p. 1276)
—Ocean Counting: Odd Numbers. Bersani, Shennen, illus. (p. 1276)
—Pizza Fractions. Bolster, Rob, illus. (p. 1365)
—Subtraction Book. Bolster, Rob, illus. (p. 1671)

P

—Weights & Measures. Bolster, Rob, illus. (p. 1872)
—Whale vs. Giant Squid. Bolster, Rob, illus. (p. 1877)
—What I Saw in the Teachers' Lounge. McWilliam, Howard, illus. (p. 1887)
—Who Will Be My Valentine This Year? Biedrzycki, David, illus. (p. 1919)
—Who Will Plant a Tree? Leonard, Tom, illus. (p. 1919)
—Who Will See Their Shadows This Year? Biedrzycki, David, illus. (p. 1919)
—Wolverine vs. Tasmanian Devil. Bolster, Rob, illus. (p. 1944)
Pallotta, Jerry, jt. auth. see Garnett, Sammie.
Pallotta-Chiarolli, Maria, jt. auth. see Martino, Wayne.
Palma, Adrienne. Roza Sanchez. (p. 1493)
Palma, B. Dorado: A Palo Alto Adventure. (p. 471)
Palmenter, Mark, creator. Ivy Advising's Interview Survival Kit. (p. 901)
Palmer, Alison. Simply Singing Time. (p. 1578)
—Walking the Path of Faith: More Fun Character-Building Activities for LDS Children - a Companion Volume to Planting Seeds of Faith. (p. 1854)
Palmer, Amy. In the Doghouse. (p. 865)
Palmer, Amy & Keller, Carolyn. University of Minnesota College Prowler off the Record. (p. 1820)
Palmer, Angela Elsberry. Promise Wishes. (p. 1411)
Palmer, Barbara A. Clue Book for Boo-Boo. (p. 335)
—Finding Fido the Feline: Flip Book with American Sign Language. Palmer, Barbara A., illus. (p. 588)
—Journey of Cattail. (p. 928)
—Journey of Cattail. Palmer, Barbara A., illus. (p. 928)
Palmer, Barbara E. Recoverbee Says Learn with Me. (p. 1452)
Palmer, Bernard. Danny & Ron Orlis in the Sacred Cave. (p. 405)
Palmer, Bill. And to All a Good Night: Christmas Folklore. (p. 71)
—And to All a Good Night: Christmas Folklore. Jabbour, Alan, ed. (p. 71)
—Gallup Guides for Youth Facing Persistent Prejudice. (p. 653)
—New Generation of Homosexuality: Modern Trends in Gay & Lesbian Communities. (p. 1244)
—Trailblazing Latino Americans. (p. 1776)
—Trailblazing Latino Americans. Limón, José E., ed. (p. 1776)
—What Causes Sexual Orientation? Genetics, Biology, Psychology. (p. 1881)
Palmer, Catherine. Fatal Harvest. (p. 577)
Palmer, Connie. I Will Run Free No More (p. 848)
Palmer, Deokie Savie. My Little Baby Sister & I, on a Cold Winter Day. (p. 1212)
Palmer, Dora, jt. auth. see Lee, Dora.
Palmer, Douglas. Firefly Encyclopedia of Dinosaurs & Prehistoric Animals. (p. 592)
Palmer, Douglas, jt. auth. see Morgan, Ben.
Palmer, Edward G. Book of Edward Christian Mythology (p. 211)
—Book of Edward Christian Mythology: Itching Christian Ears (p. 211)
—Book of Edward Christian Mythology: Matters of the Heart Vol. 1 (p. 211)
—Book of Edward Christian Mythology: God Does Not Change Vol. II (p. 211)
—Book of Edward Christian Mythology: Appendixes Reference Vol. IV (p. 211)
Palmer, Evan, illus. see Grossblatt, Ben & Rippley, P. U.
Palmer, Gary, illus. see Crane, Carol.
Palmer, Gary, illus. see Young, Judy.
Palmer, Gaylon. We Are Different; We Are the Same. (p. 1865)
Palmer, Hollis A. Curse of the Veiled Murderess. (p. 395)
Palmer, Iva-Marie. Summers (p. 1675)
Palmer, James, illus. see Collodi, Carlo, et al.
Palmer, James, illus. see Smith, Carrie.
Palmer, James Lynah, Jr. Going Coastal: Twelve Months & Then Some of Stumblin' Jimmy Watermelon. (p. 692)
Palmer, Jan, illus. see Gruelle, Johnny.
Palmer, Judd. Giant Killer: Preposterous Fables for Unusual Children. Vol. 5, No. 5 (p. 673)
—Sorcerer's Last Words No. 3. (p. 1614)
—Umbrella. (p. 1810)
—Wolf King: Preposterous Fables for Unusual Children. No. 3 (p. 1944)
Palmer, Judd, illus. see Davidge, James.
Palmer, Kate S., illus. see Bauer, Roger.
Palmer, Kate S., illus. see Coulton, Mia.
Palmer, Kate S., illus. see Geddes, Diana E.
Palmer, Kate S., illus. see Mader, Jan.
Palmer, Kate S., illus. see Yukish, Joseph.
Palmer, Kate Salley. Almost Invisible Blk Patriots. Palmer, Kate Salley, illus. (p. 48)
Palmer, Kate Salley, illus. see Coulton, Mia.
Palmer, Kimmy, illus. see Flatley, Paula Chorman.
Palmer, Kristen. Wild Weather Trivia. (p. 1930)
Palmer, Kristine. Eigenoids Episode 2: Momentum Sphere Coaster. (p. 507)
Palmer, Libbi. PTSD Workbook for Teens: Simple, Effective Skills for Healing Trauma. (p. 1414)
Palmer, Magdalena, tr. see Cormier, Robert.
Palmer, Martin, jt. auth. see Lugira, Aloysius M.
Palmer, Martin, et al. Religions of the World: The Illustrated Guide to Origins, Beliefs, Traditions & Festivals. (p. 1458)
Palmer, Michael Ray. Ballpark Dog. (p. 135)
Palmer, Michele. Ghosts & Golems: Haunting Tales of the Supernatural. Black, Theodor, illus. (p. 672)
Palmer, Nigel. Heart Family Adventures. (p. 759)
Palmer, Pamela. Horse of the Dawn. (p. 800)
Palmer, Pat. Liking Myself. Shondeck, Betty, illus. (p. 1017)
—Mouse, the Monster & Me: Assertiveness for Young People. Shondeck, Betty, illus. (p. 1182)
Palmer, Peggy. Bible Discovery: Games. (p. 175)
—Bible Discovery: Crafts. (p. 175)
Palmer, Rebecca & Protopapas, Athanassios. Lemon & Lime Library: An Articulation Screen & Resource Pack. Pack (p. 991)
Palmer, Robert. In Search of Honor: Not Just A Book... A Way of Life! (p. 864)
Palmer, Robin. Cindy Ella. (p. 321)
—For Better or for Worse (p. 615)
—Geek Charming. (p. 659)
—Girl vs. Superstar (p. 679)
—Little Miss Red. (p. 1032)
—Sealed with a Kiss (p. 1536)
—Take My Advice! (p. 1696)
—Vote for Me! (p. 1850)
—Wicked Jealous: A Love Story. (p. 1927)
Palmer, Rosemary G. Jim Bridger: Trapper, Trader, & Guide. (p. 917)
Palmer, Ruth, illus. see Gamble, Adam & Jasper, Mark.
Palmer, Ruth, illus. see Kelly, Mij.
Palmer, Ruth, illus. see Knudsen, Shannon.
Palmer, Ruth, illus. see Potter, Beatrix.
Palmer, Scott, illus. see Donahue, Laurie & Phillips, Paul.
Palmer, Shelly. Television Disrupted: The Transition from Network to Networked TV. (p. 1716)
Palmer, Sue & Corbett, Pie. Literacy: What Works? (p. 1022)
Palmer, Tom. Boys United. (p. 220)
—Reading the Game. (p. 1446)
—Real Thing. (p. 1449)
—Striking Out. (p. 1667)
Palmer, Tom & Scarborough, Kate. Soccer. (p. 1603)
Palmer, Viola. Man in the Green Jeep. (p. 1085)
Palmer, W. G. Awaiting Whisperland: The Calling of Galahad Green. (p. 120)
Palmerlee, B. P. Legend of Darious: The First Part of the Chronicles of Arattoss. (p. 988)
Palmer-Skok, Virginia. Southbury Revisited. (p. 1617)
Palmieri, Kathryn & Palmieri, Patricia. GYPSY McPHEE: The New Kid in Town. (p. 734)
Palmieri, Patricia, jt. auth. see Palmieri, Kathryn.
Palmiotti, Jimmy, illus. see Andreyko, Marc.
Palmiotti, Jimmy, illus. see Carey, Mike.
Palmiotti, Jimmy, jt. auth. see Gray, Justin.
Palmisciano, Diane, illus. see Conford, Ellen.
Palmisciano, Diane, illus. see Dussling, Jennifer A.
Palmisciano, Diane, illus. see Dussling, Jennifer.
Palmisciano, Diane, illus. see Giff, Patricia Reilly.
Palmisciano, Diane, illus. see Hayward, Linda.
Palmisciano, Diane, illus. see Lunney, Linda Hayward.
Palmisciano, Diane, illus. see May, Eleanor.
Palmisciano, Diane, illus. see Osteen, Victoria.
Palmisciano, Diane, illus. see Walker, Nan.
Palmisciano, Diane, tr. see Lunney, Linda Hayward.
Palmore, Iyende, jt. auth. see Breckenridge, Trula.
Palmore, Julie. Big Brothers & Big Sisters Are VIP's (Very Important Persons) A Color Me Book. Engle, Jenny, illus. (p. 179)
Palmquist, Eric, illus. see Lindgren, Astrid.
Paloma, David. Medicina para No Llorar. Aranega, Merce, illus. (p. 1119)
Paloma, David & Paloma Sanllehi, David. Buena Costumbre. Novoa, Teresa, illus. (p. 235)
Paloma Sanllehi, David, jt. auth. see Paloma, David.
Palomaki, Kurt. Floating Men & Pale Faces: The Paintings of Kurt Palomaki. (p. 605)
Palomares, Franz, illus. see Nelson, Annabelle.
Palomares, Susanna, et al. Hearts & Minds: An Afterschool Program for Developing Reading Literacy & Emotional Intelligence. (p. 760)
Palomino, Rafael. Fiesta Latina: Fabulous Food for Sizzling Parties. Mentis, Anastassios, photos by. (p. 584)
Palone, Terry, photos by see Hooke, R. Schuyler.
Palonen, Jukka & Conrad, Tim. Game Plan: A Kids' Musical about God's Master Plan for Each of Us. (p. 654)
Palos, Lilia. Acercate a la Historia 3 de las Raices Indigenas al Mexico Contemprineo Actores Sociales, Vida Cotidiana, Mentalidades y Cultura. (p. 8)
Palou, Francisco. Life & Apostolic Labors of the Venerable Father Junipero Serra, Founder of the Franciscan Missions of California. (p. 1007)
Palser, Barb. Choosing News: What Gets Reported & Why (p. 310)
—Selling Ourselves: Marketing Body Images (p. 1550)
Paltenghi, Madalena. Remus Goes to Town. Anderson, C. W., illus. (p. 1460)
Palter, Scott, ed. Metabarons Roleplaying Game Guidebook 1: Path of the Warrior. (p. 1130)
Paltro, Piera. Learning My Prayers Daughters of St. Paul Staff, tr. (p. 985)
Paltrowitz, Donna, jt. auth. see Fink, Jeri.
Paluch, Beily. Braid the Challah: A Playful Action Rhyme. Argoff, Beily, illus. (p. 221)
—Braid the Challah: A Playful Action Rhyme. Argoff, Patti, illus. (p. 221)
—I Am a Torah: A Playful Action Rhyme. Agroff, Patti, illus. (p. 832)
—I am a Torah: A Playful Action Rhyme. Argoff, Patti, illus. (p. 832)
Palumbo, Debi, illus. see Kaplan, Richard, et al.
Palumbo, Mary Lou. Skippy the Dog in the Band. Mikle, Toby, illus. (p. 1586)
Palus, Benji Alexander. Magic Pumpkin. (p. 1073)
Paluseka, Julia, illus. see Wellings, Chris.
Pam, Miss. Never Never Be a Bully. Stutz, Chris, illus. (p. 1243)
Pamer, Rosey. Para el Abuso: La palabra asociada al Abuso. (p. 1323)
Pamintuan, Macky, illus. see Ball, Nate.
Pamintuan, Macky, illus. see Brown, Jeff.
Pamintuan, Macky, illus. see Crow, Kristyn.
Pamintuan, Macky, illus. see DiPucchio, Kelly.
Pamintuan, Macky, illus. see Greenburg, Dan.
Pamintuan, Macky, illus. see Greenhut, Josh & Brown, Jeff.
Pamintuan, Macky, illus. see Houran, Lori Haskins.
Pamintuan, Macky, illus. see Keene, Carolyn.
Pamintuan, Macky, illus. see McCall Smith, Alexander.
Pamintuan, Macky, illus. see Nussbaum, Ben.
Pamintuan, Macky, illus. see Pennypacker, Sara & Brown, Jeff.
Pamintuan, Macky, illus. see Prince, Joshua.
Pamintuan, Macky, illus. see Schnell, David.
Pamintuan, Macky, illus. see Schwaeber, Barbie.
Pamintuan, Macky, illus. see Spradlin, Michael P.
Pamintuan, Macky, illus. see Williams, Rozanne Lanczak.
Pamintuan, Macky, illus. see Zondervan.
Pamintuan, Macky, jt. auth. see Myers, Tim.
Pamment, Katie, illus. see Twain, Mark, pseud.
Pammer, Victoria. Kathryn & the Crooked Tooth. (p. 944)
Pampalone, Donna. Adventures of Koco Koala & Friends: Book One: Cuisin' with Cameron. (p. 19)
Pampel, Fred C. Drugs & Sports. (p. 487)
—Racial Profiling. (p. 1432)
Pan, Hui-Mei. Cochinito en mi Bolsillo Vernescu, Maritza, tr. from ENG. (p. 337)
—Piggy in My Pocket. (p. 1358)
—Piggy in My Pocket (Spanish/English) del Risco, Eida, tr. (p. 1358)
—What's in Grandma's Grocery Bag? (p. 1897)
—What's in Grandma's Grocery Bag? (Spanish/English) del Risco, Eida, tr. (p. 1897)
—¿Qué hay en la bolsa de Abuelita? Pan, Hui-Mei, illus. (p. 1423)
Pan Macmillan Limited Staff. Bin Weevils - The Official Annual 2014. (p. 188)
Pan MacMillan, Pan, jt. auth. see Li, Amanda.
Pan, Michelle. Bella Should Have Dumped Edward: Controversial Views on the Twilight Series. (p. 162)
Panaccione, Nancy. Mine! Diary: My Ideas Need Expressing. (p. 1145)
Panaccione, Nancy, illus. see Dakota, Heather.
Panagariya, Ananth. Buzz! (p. 248)
Panagariya, Ananth, jt. auth. see Ota, Yuko.
Panagopoulos, Janie Lynn. Castle at the Straits. Evans, Laura, illus. (p. 276)
—Little Ship under Full Sail: An Adventure in History. (p. 1036)
—Mark of the Bear Claw. (p. 1095)
Panahi, H. L. Bebop Express. Johnson, Steve & Fancher, Lou, illus. (p. 155)
Panaitescu, Simona. Unseen Paths of the Forest: 13 Tales about Love & Friendship. Moscal, Manuela, illus. (p. 1822)
Panamericana Editorial, ed. see Neira, Maria Lia.
Panamericana Editorial, creator. Barbacoas. (p. 137)
—Con Fibras Naturales Decorando Galletas. (p. 355)
Panamericana Editorial, ed. Cocteles. (p. 338)
—Espanola. (p. 536)
Panamericana Staff, ed. see Neira, Maria Lia.
Panamericana Staff, ed. see Rodriguez, Claudia Rodriguez & Ardila, Carlos.
Panamericana Staff, ed. see Silva Vallejo, Fabio.
Panamericana Staff, ed. see Hernandez Vera, Rene.
Panamericana Staff, ed. Cuentos de Fantasmas. Linares, Jairo, illus. (p. 390)
—Novena Tradicional de Aguinaldos. (p. 1268)
Panamkat, Matthew. Karan Quma & the Meluha Tree. (p. 943)
Panaro, Carlo, jt. auth. see Orsi, Tea.
Panasiuk, Andrés. ¿Cómo Compro Inteligentemente? (p. 350)
—¿Cómo Salgo de Mis Deudas? (p. 351)
Panayotis. Junior & Bo's Trip to the Olympics. Theophilopoulos, Andrew, illus. (p. 936)
Pancella, Peggy. Base Militar (p. 140)
—City (p. 323)
—Ciudad (p. 324)
—Comunidad Granjera (p. 355)
—Farm Community (p. 573)
—Pueblito (p. 1414)
—Suburb (p. 1671)
—Suburbio (p. 1671)
Pancerzewski, Scarlotte. Maria's Backseat Buddy. (p. 1093)
Pancheshnaya, Dasha, illus. see Forest, Jim.
Panchyk, Richard. Charting the World: Geography & Maps from Cave Paintings to GPS with 21 Activities. (p. 294)
—Franklin Delano Roosevelt for Kids: His Life & Times with 21 Activities. (p. 630)
—Galileo for Kids: His Life & Ideas, 25 Activities. (p. 653)
—Keys to American History: Understanding Our Most Important Historic Documents. (p. 950)
—New York City History for Kids: From New Amsterdam to the Big Apple with 21 Activities. (p. 1248)
—Our Supreme Court: A History with 14 Activities. (p. 1310)
Panchyk, Richard & Ketchum, William C., Jr. American Folk Art for Kids: With 21 Activities. (p. 60)
Panckridge, Michael. Toby Jones & the Timeless Cricket Match. (p. 1760)
Panckridge, Michael, jt. auth. see Daley, Laurie.
Panckridge, Michael, jt. auth. see Harvey, Pam.
Panckridge, Michael & Lee, Brett. Toby Jones & the Clash with Father Time. (p. 1760)
—Toby Jones & the Magic Cricket Almanack. (p. 1760)
—Toby Jones & the Mystery of the Time Travel Tour. (p. 1760)
—Toby Jones & the Secret of the Missing Scorecard. (p. 1760)
Panda Publications. Prisma: Analisis critico de textos en Espanol. (p. 1407)
Pandanas, Ms L. A. Slinky Luminescence: Two Plus Who? (p. 1590)
—Zar-Zar the Russian Ladybeetle: Easter Beetle. (p. 1985)
—Zar-Zar the Russian Ladybeetle: Bull Ants, Bindies & Bees. (p. 1985)
—Zar-Zar the Russian Ladybeetle: The Land of Black & White. (p. 1985)
Pandelis, Bloomin' Harmony Judy E. Bloomin' Harmony. (p. 201)
Pandell, Karen. I Love You, Baby, from Head to Toe! Cowen-Fletcher, Jane, illus. (p. 843)
—I Love You, Sun I Love You, Moon. dePaola, Tomie, illus. (p. 844)
—Te Amo Sol, Te Amo Luna. dePaola, Tomie, illus. (p. 1708)
Pandell, Karen, et al. Good Night Book. (p. 699)
Pandey, Pooja. Little Monk's Buddha. (p. 1032)
—Little Monk's Ganesha. (p. 1032)
—Little Monk's Hanuman. (p. 1032)
—Little Monk's Krishna. (p. 1032)
Pando, Nancy J. I Don't Want to Go to School: Helping Children Cope with Separation Anxiety. Voerg, Kathy, illus. (p. 838)
Pandora. Ankh: Conquering the Seven Deadly Sins. (p. 84)
Pandozzi, Frank W. North Side Story. (p. 1265)
Pandya, Ashish. Ping the Spider: The journey Begins... (p. 1359)
Pandya, Mamata. Hare Scare: Based on the Original Gujarati Story by Gijubhai Badheka. (p. 748)
Pandya, Yamini, illus. see Kalpish Ratna.
Paner, Amy & Fisher, Stacey. Nutty Scurries to School. (p. 1274)
Paner, Amy, illustrator, jt. auth. see Fisher, Stacey.
Panes, Kerry. Knowledge of Good & Evil. (p. 965)
Panev, Aleksandar. Queen Nzinga. Stefflbauer, Thomas, illus. (p. 1425)
Paneva, Valya, illus. see Wright, Karen.
Pang, Alex, illus. see Daynes, Katie & Wray, Zoe.
Pang, Alex, illus. see Daynes, Katie.
Pang, Alex, illus. see Hansen, Ole Steen.
Pang, Alex, illus. see Parker, Steve.
Pang, Alex, jt. auth. see Gilpin, Daniel.
Pang, Eugenia LaDeaux. Katie's Kittens. (p. 945)
Pang, Evelyn & Louie, Hilary. Good Dog! Kids Teach Kids about Dog Behavior & Training. (p. 697)
Pang, Guek Cheng. Canada. (p. 260)
—Kazakhstan. (p. 946)
—Mongolia. (p. 1164)
Pang, Guek Cheng, jt. auth. see Guek Cheng, P.
Pang, YaWen Ariel, illus. see Wargin, Kathy-jo.
Pangalos, Carol B. Gabriella & the Magic Stars. (p. 652)
Pangan, Catherine Hagerman. No Peanuts for Me! Warf, Gracie, illus. (p. 1259)
Pangbourne, Daniel, illus. see Bulloch, Ivan & James, Diane.
Pangbourne, Daniel, photos by see Bulloch, Ivan & James, Diane.
Paniagua, Kelly. Bedtime for Sarah Sullivan. Warrick, Jessica, illus. (p. 157)
Panian, Angie & Panian, Tyler. Creature Clash! Card Game. (p. 380)
—Creature Clash! Mix & Match Coloring Book. (p. 380)
Panian, Tyler, jt. auth. see Panian, Angie.
Paniccia, Mark & Cosby, Nathan, eds. Iron Armory Cordeiro, James et al, illus. (p. 888)
Panik, Alison Saeger. Angel Cake's Cupcake Book. (p. 73)
—Berry Best Friends Book: A Fun with Friends Adventure. (p. 167)
Panik, Sharon, jt. auth. see Haberstroh, Marilyn.
Panini Publishing, creator. Scooby Doo! Summer Annual. (p. 1529)
Panitch, Amanda. Damage Done. (p. 401)
Pankey, Keith. Are You Ticklish Today? (p. 97)
Pankhurst, Kate. Mariella Mystery Investigates a Cupcake Conundrum. (p. 1093)
—Mariella Mystery Investigates a Kitty Calamity. (p. 1093)
—Mariella Mystery Investigates the Disappearing Dinner Lady. (p. 1093)
—Mariella Mystery Investigates the Ghostly Guinea Pig. (p. 1093)
—Mariella Mystery Investigates the Mystery of the Cursed Poodle. (p. 1093)
—Mariella Mystery Investigates the Spaghetti Yeti. (p. 1093)
—Three Billy Goats Gruff. (p. 1741)
Pankhurst, Kate, illus. see Fine, Anne.
Pankhurst, Kate, illus. see Jarman, Julia.
Pankhurst, Kate, illus. see Peters, Rosalind.
Pankiw, Dr Mary & Pankiw, Mary. Misilla Mouse. (p. 1150)
Pankiw, Mary. Ruffles Rabbit. (p. 1494)
Pankiw, Mary, jt. auth. see Pankiw, Dr Mary.
Pankova, Yuliya, ed. Numbers - Guess What? (p. 1272)
—Veggies - Guess What? (p. 1834)
Pankow, Valerie. No Bigger Than My Teddy Bear. Connelly, Gwen, illus. (p. 1257)
Pankratz, Justin. Blue Monkey. (p. 203)
Pankratz, Justin, illus. see Summers, Sherri Pankratz.
Panks, Kristin & Harpan, Gaile. Ballad of Furrio the Cat. Reddy, Sneha, illus. (p. 134)
Panman & Panman, Richard. Writing Basics: Sentence to Paragraph to Essay. Panman, ed. (p. 1964)
Panman, Richard, jt. auth. see Panman, Sandra.
Panman, Richard, jt. auth. see Panman.
Panman, Sandra & Panman, Richard. Active Reader for Writers. Panman, Sandra, ed. (p. 10)
—Short Stories. Panman, Sandra, ed. (p. 1569)
—Writing Essentials. (p. 1964)
Pannell, Lillie Clayton, jt. auth. see Waldrop, Dave.
Pannell, Lynn K. Real: Scenes & Monologues for Urban Youth. (p. 1448)
Pannell, Nick, illus. see Mann, Scott.
Panno, Joseph. Aging. (p. 29)
—Animal Cloning: The Science of Nuclear Transfer. (p. 77)
—Cell: Nature's First Life-Form. (p. 286)
—Science of Aging: Theories & Potential Therapies. (p. 1527)
Pannone, Frank, ed. see Furuyama, Kan & Taniguchi, Jiro.
Pannone, Frank, ed. see Komada, Yoshihiro, et al.
Pannone, Frank, ed. see Morinaga, Ai.
Pannone, Frank, ed. see Taniguchi, Tomoko.
Pannone, Frank, ed. see Tomizawa, Hitoshi.
Panosian, Dan, illus. see Sudduth, Brent & Meredith Books Staff.
Panosian, Dan, illus. see West, Tracey.
Panpan, Alice. Antarctic Wings. (p. 88)
Panse, Sonal, illus. see Duncan, Al.
Panse, Sonal, illus. see Miller, Judith J.
Pansini, Anthony J. Power Transmission & Distribution. (p. 1390)
Pansy. Ester Ried. (p. 538)
Pantages, Joanna. Fairytale Fitness: Holygrain. (p. 565)
—Fairytale Fitness: The Goobyland Race. (p. 565)
Pantaleon, Tamara. Magic Tree: Home of the Fairies. Pantaleon, Tamara, photos by. (p. 1074)
Pantelides, Sherry. It's Blue Like You! A Story about Loyalty. Perez, Debi, illus. (p. 896)
—It's Red Like Me! A Story about the Blood of Jesus. Perez, Debi, illus. (p. 898)
—Make A Choice to Rejoice! A Story about Being Cheerful. Perez, Debi, illus. (p. 1078)

Pantelo, Amber. Totally Meaningless Summer. (p. 1771)
Pantely, Bonnie & Pantely, Noel. Libroman: The Unknown Superhero. (p. 1007)
Pantely, Noel, jt. auth. see Pantely, Bonnie.
Pantic, Dunja, illus. see Olin, Marilyn.
Pantin, Yolanda. Caballo en la Ciudad. Suarez, Rosa Virginia Urdaneta, photos by. (p. 250)
—Splash! Faria, Rosana, illus. (p. 1629)
Pantoja, Maria Kristina, illus. see Thielbar, Melinda.
Pantoja, Stephen. Amalaganimals: Eracism Sc. (p. 52)
Pantoja, Tintin, illus. see Thielbar, Melinda.
Panton, Constance. Danielli Brambelli: The Terrible Sleeper. (p. 405)
Pantone. Pantone: Color Cards: 18 Oversized Flash Cards. Gibbs, Andrew, illus. (p. 1321)
—Pantone: Color Puzzles: 6 Color-Matching Puzzles. Carpenter, Tad, illus. (p. 1321)
—Pantone: Colors. Dardik, Helen, illus. (p. 1321)
—Pantone: Sticker Book with Posters. (p. 1321)
Pantone, Inc Staff, contrib. by. Pantone - Box of Colour: 6 Mini Board Books! (p. 1321)
Pantoya, Michelle L., jt. auth. see Hunt, Emily M.
Panza, Rosana, jt. auth. see Levy, Debbie.
Panzieri, Lucia. Kindhearted Crocodile. Ferrari, Antongionata, illus. (p. 957)
Panzieri, Lucia & Maccarone, Grace. Little Brother Pumpkin Head. Enria, Samantha, illus. (p. 1025)
Paola, Tomie de, see dePaola, Tomie.
Paolilli, Paul & Brewer, Dan. Silver Seeds. (p. 1577)
—Silver Seeds. Fancher, Lou & Johnson, Steve, illus. (p. 1577)
Paoline, Dyann. Cecilia's Fitness Adventure. (p. 283)
Paolini, Alison, illus. see Hall, Kirk.
Paolini, Christopher. Brisingr (p. 229)
—Brisingr Isern, Carol & Rizzo, Jorge, trs. (p. 229)
—Brisingr. (p. 229)
—Eldest. (p. 508)
—Eldest. de Heriz, Enrique, tr. (p. 508)
—Eragon. (p. 533)
—Eragon; Eldest. (p. 533)
—Eragon, Eldest, Brisingr (p. 533)
—Eragon's Guide to Alagaësia. (p. 533)
—Inheritance: Eragon; Eldest; Brisingr Set (p. 874)
—Inheritance. (p. 874)
—Inheritance Cycle (p. 874)
Paone, Arthur J. Hillary in Gilo. (p. 779)
Paonessa, Mary. Growth & Development: Understanding Yourself (p. 727)
—Growth & Development with Friends (p. 727)
—Growth & Development with Friends & Family (p. 727)
Paourou, Maria. Bubblebea Wants to Be a Hero. (p. 233)
Papa Rolly. Sam the Semi Goes to Chicago. (p. 1507)
Papademetriou, Lisa. Accidentally Fabulous (p. 8)
—Aventura de Rosetta. Pombo, Mauricio, tr. (p. 119)
—Confectionately Yours #1: Save the Cupcake! (p. 356)
—Confectionately Yours #2: Taking the Cake! (p. 356)
—Confectionately Yours #3: Sugar & Spice. (p. 356)
—Fury's Fire. (p. 650)
—How to Be a Girly Girl in Just Ten Days. (p. 814)
—On the Job. (p. 1290)
—Save the Cupcake! (p. 1516)
—Siren's Storm. (p. 1581)
—Taking the Cake! (p. 1698)
—Tale of Highly Unusual Magic. (p. 1699)
Papademetriou, Lisa, jt. auth. see Patterson, James.
Papademetriou, Lisa & Minsky, Terri. Very Lizzie Summer. (p. 1838)
Papademetriou, Lisa & Tebbetts, Chris. M or F? (p. 1067)
Papagno, Noella C. Desairology: The Dressing of Decedents' Hair. (p. 428)
Papaj, Dana. Blackjack's Hare Raising Adventure. Dixon, Gary, illus. (p. 197)
Papaleo, Antonio, illus. see Williams, Simon.
Papaloizos, Theodore. Level Two - the Kids of the Neighborhood. (p. 1003)
Papaloizos, Theodore C. Level One - First Grade Primer. (p. 1003)
—My Greek Reader. Frangouli, Rena, illus. (p. 1210)
—Workbook for Learning Greek. (p. 1952)
—Workbook for Ouranias Dream. (p. 1952)
Paparone, Pam, illus. see Lewison, Wendy Cheyette.
Paparone, Pam, illus. see Love, D. Anne.
Paparone, Pam, illus. see Macken, JoAnn Early.
Paparone, Pam, illus. see Sklansky, Amy E.
Paparone, Pamela. Five Little Ducks. Paparone, Pamela, illus. (p. 600)
Paparone, Pamela, illus. see Butler, Kristi T.
Paparone, Pamela, illus. see Lewison, Wendy Cheyette.
Paparone, Pamela, illus. see Lindbergh, Reeve.
Paparone, Pamela, illus. see Love, D. Anne.
Paparone, Pamela, illus. see Polette, Nancy.
Paparone, Pamela, illus. see Roth, Carol.
Paparone, Pamela, illus. see Sklansky, Amy E.
Paparone, Pamela, tr. see Lewison, Wendy Cheyette.
Papastavrou, Vassili. Whale. Dorling Kindersley Publishing Staff, ed. (p. 1877)
Papaw. Remembering A Child's Best Christmas. (p. 1459)
Papazoglu, Paula. I Plant a Garden with My Mom. Gumm, Susan Kathleen, illus. (p. 844)
Pape, Jane, illus. see Blyton, Enid.
Pape, Wendy Fehrle, illus. see LeBlanc, Ellen Lieb.
Papell, David. Harlem Awakenings. (p. 748)
—Harlem Awakenings Color Edition. (p. 748)
Papeo, Maria Eugenia, illus. see Canady, Mary Monica.
Paper Dolls, jt. auth. see Rechlin, Ted.
Paper Dolls, jt. auth. see Swanson, Maggie.
Paper Dolls for Grownups Staff, jt. auth. see Roytman, Arkady.
Papi, Liza. Carnavalia! African-Brazilian Folklore & Crafts. Papi, Liza, illus. (p. 270)
Papia, Dan, jt. auth. see Shigeno, Shuichi.
Papia, Dan, tr. see Shigeno, Suichi.
Papile, Christopher, illus. see Slade, Suzanne Buckingham.
Papillon, Margaret. Babou & the Dream Maker. Devillers, Edith, tr. (p. 124)
Papineau, Lucie. Baby Witch, Yuck! (p. 128)
—Bebe-Vampire, Gloups! (p. 155)
—Gontrand et le Croissant des Cavernes. (p. 697)
—Leonardo le Lionceau. (p. 992)
—Lulu's Pajamas. Jorisch, Stéphane, illus. (p. 1065)
—Pas de Taches Pour une Girafe. (p. 1326)
Papish, Adam, illus. see Seglie, Susan & Schiefelbein, Janis.
Papish, Ram. Little Fox: An Alaska Adventure. Papish, Ram & Papish, Ram, illus. (p. 1028)
—Little Seal: An Alaska Adventure. (p. 1036)
Paplinskie, Cecilia, illus. see Harris, Sally M.
Paplow, Paula. Hands upon the Rock. (p. 741)
Papp, Kathy, jt. illus. see Papp, Robert.
Papp, Lisa, illus. see Bunting, Eve.
Papp, Lisa, illus. see Layne, Deborah & Layne, Steven.
Papp, Lisa, illus. see Noble, Trinka Hakes.
Papp, Lisa & Noble, Trinka Hakes. Battles. Papp, Robert, illus. (p. 147)
Papp, Lisa & Papp, Robert. Town That Fooled the British: A War of 1812 Story. Papp, Lisa & Papp, Robert, illus. (p. 1773)
Papp, Robert. Amazing Mystery Show. (p. 55)
—Box That Watch Found. (p. 216)
—Clue in the Recycling Bin. (p. 335)
—Creature in Ogopogo Lake. (p. 380)
—Cupcake Caper. (p. 392)
—From Sea to Shining Sea (p. 643)
—Game Store Mystery. (p. 654)
—Ghost in the First Row (p. 670)
—Ghost of the Chattering Bones. (p. 671)
—Giant Yo-Yo Mystery. (p. 674)
—Great Detective Race. (p. 715)
—Great Turkey Heist. (p. 719)
—Horse Named Dragon. (p. 799)
—Monkey Trouble. (p. 1165)
—Mystery of the Orphan Train. (p. 1226)
—Pumpkin Head Mystery (p. 1416)
—Rock 'n' Roll Mystery. (p. 1482)
—Seattle Puzzle. (p. 1539)
—Secret of the Mask. (p. 1542)
—Spooktacular Special. (p. 1631)
—Spy Game. (p. 1636)
—Spy in the Bleachers. (p. 1636)
—Sword of the Silver Knight. (p. 1692)
—Vanishing Passenger. (p. 1833)
—Zombie Project. (p. 1988)
Papp, Robert, illus. see Crisp, Marty.
Papp, Robert, illus. see Karwoski, Gail Langer.
Papp, Robert, illus. see Kurtz, Jane.
Papp, Robert, illus. see Layne, Deborah & Layne, Steven.
Papp, Robert, illus. see Medearis, Angela Shelf.
Papp, Robert, illus. see Noble, Trinka Hakes.
Papp, Robert, illus. see Papp, Lisa & Noble, Trinka Hakes.
Papp, Robert, illus. see Shefelman, Janice Jordan.
Papp, Robert, illus. see Sobol, Donald J.
Papp, Robert, illus. see Wilbur, Helen L.
Papp, Robert, illus. see Yep, Laurence.
Papp, Robert, jt. auth. see Papp, Lisa.
Papp, Robert & Papp, Kathy. Pumpkin Head Mystery. (p. 1416)
Papp, Robert L. Dog-Gone Mystery. (p. 461)
—Spy Game. (p. 1636)
—Superstar Watch. (p. 1684)
—Vampire Mystery. (p. 1832)
Pappas, Charles. Tree That Loved the Eagle. Schlueter, Rachel, illus. (p. 1783)
Pappas, Diane H., jt. auth. see Covey, Richard D.
Pappas, Diane H. & Covey, Richard D. It's Good to Be Clean. Estrada, Ric, illus. (p. 897)
—Why I Need My Sleep. Estrada, Ric, illus. (p. 1925)
Pappas, Maria, jt. auth. see Coughlin, Denise.
Pappas, Peter. Stu the Rabbit. (p. 1668)
Pappas, Theoni. Further Adventures of Penrose the Mathematical Cat. (p. 650)
Pappert, Edward. Do You Want to Catch a Fish? (p. 458)
Paprocki, Beth. Storyland: the Marvelous Mccrittersons — Road Trip to Grandma's: A Story Coloring Book. Paprocki, Greg, illus. (p. 1663)
Paprocki, Greg. Harajuku Paper Dolls: Japanese Street Fashions! (p. 747)
Paprocki, Greg, illus. see Lord, Cynthia.
Paprocki, Greg, illus. see Paprocki, Beth.
Paprocki, Greg, illus. see Perez, Monica & Houghton Mifflin Company Editors.
Paprocki, Greg, illus. see Rey, H. A. & Rey, Margret.
Paprocki, Greg, illus. see Tang, Greg.
Paprocki, Ray. Eli Manning. (p. 512)
Paprocki, Sherry. Oprah Winfrey. (p. 1301)
Paprocki, Sherry Beck. Anita Roddick. (p. 84)
—Bob Marley: Musician. (p. 205)
—Diana, Princess of Wales. (p. 434)
—Ellen Degeneres: Entertainer. (p. 514)
—Oprah Winfrey: Talk Show Host & Media Magnate. (p. 1301)
Paquet, Cathy, jt. auth. see Heese, Susan.
Paquet, Claudine, et al. Antonio, Plumero y Manchitas. (p. 90)
Paquette, A. J. Nowhere Girl. (p. 1269)
—Rules for Ghosting. (p. 1495)
Paquette, Ammi-Joan. Ghost in the House. Record, Adam, illus. (p. 671)
—Paradox. (p. 1323)
—Petey & Pru & the Hullabaloo. Ang, Joy, illus. (p. 1348)
—Princess Juniper of the Hourglass. (p. 1404)
—Tiptoe Guide to Tracking Fairies. Unzner, Christa, illus. (p. 1757)
—Tiptoe Guide to Tracking Mermaids. LeTourneau, Marie, illus. (p. 1757)
Paquette, Ammi-Joan & Unzner, Christa. Tiptoe Guide to Tracking Fairies. (p. 1757)
Paquette, Heather. Kammy the Chameleon Goes to School. Paquette Jr., Edward D., illus. (p. 942)
Paquette, Jessica E. Sophie the Clown in Crinkle Town. (p. 1613)
Paquette Jr., Edward D., illus. see Paquette, Heather.
Paquette, Lenny & Willis, Dan. Everett the Evergreen. (p. 542)
Paquette, Penny Hutchins. Apprenticeship: The Ultimate Teen Guide. (p. 93)
—Asthma: The Ultimate Teen Guide. (p. 108)
Paquette, Penny Hutchins & Tuttle, Cheryl Gerson. Learning Disabilities: The Ultimate Teen Guide. (p. 985)
—Learning Disabilities: The Ultimate Teen Guide. Hirschfelder, Arlene, ed. (p. 985)
Paquin, Ethan. Accumulus. (p. 8)
Paquin, Pauline, illus. see Devine, Monica.
Parable Venture Partners Staff. Ethan's Parables: Ethan & the Good Samantha. (p. 539)
—Ethan's Parables: Ethan & Goliath & Ethan & His Jacket of Many Colors. (p. 539)
—Ethan's Parables: Ethan & Goliath, Ethan & His Jacket of Many Colors & Ethan & the Good Samantha (p. 539)
Parachute Press Staff. Farm 1 2 3. (p. 573)
Parachute Press Staff, jt. auth. see Dorling Kindersley Publishing Staff.
Parachute Press Staff, jt. creator see Dorling Kindersley Publishing Staff.
Paraclete Press, Paraclete. Praying with My Fingers: An Easy Way to Talk with God. (p. 1393)
Parada, Enrique. Espartaco y Yo. Garcia, Victor Manuel Gutierrez & Garcia, Victor Manuel Gut, illus. (p. 536)
Paradine, Mike. King of Toys. (p. 959)
Paradis, Anne. Caillou Around Town. Sevigny, Eric, illus. (p. 251)
—Caillou, Search & Count: Fun Adventures! Sevigny, Eric, illus. (p. 251)
—Caillou Takes a Nap. Brignaud, Pierre, illus. (p. 251)
—Caillou - The Best Day Ever! Sevigny, Eric, illus. (p. 251)
—Caillou: the Little Christmas Artist. Sevigny, Eric, illus. (p. 251)
Paradis, Linzy. Fanny's Walk. (p. 571)
Paradis, Susan. Snow Princess. (p. 1599)
Paradise, Elizabeth. Lost Dreamer. (p. 1055)
Paragon Publishing Staff, ed. Words. (p. 1951)
Parain, Nathalie. My Cut-Out Pictures. (p. 1200)
Paraire, Philippe & Collin, Marie-Marthe. Medio Ambiente Explicado a los Ninos. (p. 1120)
Parallax, Inc. Staff. A to D & D to A: Version 1.0. (p. 1)
—Basic Stamp Manual Version 1.9. (p. 142)
—Earth Measurements Version 1.0. (p. 496)
—Robotics Version 1.0. (p. 1481)
Parallax Press Staff, jt. auth. see Hanh, Thich Nhat.
Paramahamsa, Nithyananda. De la preocupacion a la Admiracion. (p. 416)
—Descubriendo el Amor. (p. 428)
—Es la Espiritualidao Relevante en Nuestra Vida? (p. 534)
—Libro para Colorear de Swamiji. (p. 1007)
—Nithya Dhyaan. (p. 1257)
—Nithya Yoga: In Spanish. (p. 1257)
—Nithya Yoga para Ninos. (p. 1257)
—Respuestas a Tus Preguntas por Nithyananda. (p. 1464)
—Respuestas Extraordinarias Preguntas Comunes. (p. 1464)
—Solucoes Garantidas. (p. 1608)
—Verdad Simple y Directamente! (p. 1836)
Paramonova, Lea, illus. see Wildsmith, Sarah.
Paraschiv, Doina, illus. see Parr, Susan Sherwood.
Parasciuc, Natalia. Beaverlini & Rodney Are Having Fun! (p. 155)
Paraskevas, Betty. Peter Pepper's Pet Spectacular. Paraskevas, Michael, illus. (p. 1347)
Paraskevas, Michael, illus. see Maizes, Sarah.
Paraskevas, Michael, illus. see Paraskevas, Betty.
Parathian, Hannah, illus. see Hevesi, Rachel.
Paratore, Coleen. Big. O'Malley, Judy, ed. (p. 177)
Paratore, Coleen Murtagh. Catching the Sun. (p. 279)
—Cupid Chronicles. (p. 392)
—Dreamsleeves. (p. 484)
—Forget Me Not - From the Life of Willa Havisham. (p. 619)
—From Willa, with Love: From the Life of Willa Havisham. (p. 644)
—Funeral Director's Son. (p. 649)
—Kip Campbell's Gift. (p. 961)
—Mack Mcginn's Big Win. (p. 1068)
—Sunny Holiday. (p. 1677)
—Sweet & Sunny. (p. 1689)
—Wedding Planner's Daughter. (p. 1871)
—Wedding Planner's Daughter. McGregor, Barbara, illus. (p. 1871)
—Willa by Heart. (p. 1932)
—Wish I Might: From the Life of Willa Havisham. (p. 1940)
—Wish I Might. (p. 1940)
Paratore, Jeanne R. & McCormack, Rachel L., eds. Classroom Literacy Assessment: Making Sense of What Students Know & Do. (p. 329)
Parbi, Eunice Efiba Asare. Yum! Yum! Yum! Trust Us! We Will Blow It! Series 1. (p. 1983)
Parchment, Howard. Wordplay. (p. 1951)
Pardes, Bronwen. Doing It Right: Making Smart, Safe, & Satisfying Choices about Sex. (p. 463)
Pardo DeLange, Alex, illus. see Lachtman, Ofelia Dumas.
Pardoe, David. Jasper Tippett's Amazing Journey to Page 42. (p. 910)
Pardoe, Mary. Formula One Interactive Oral & Mental Starters. (p. 620)
Paré, Roger. Alphabet. (p. 49)
—Chiffres. (p. 301)
—Contraires. (p. 361)
Paredes, Julio. Eugéne Delacroix. (p. 540)
Pareja, Alejandro, ed. see Doyle, Arthur.
Parekh, Bhikhu. Rethinking Multiculturalism: Cultural Diversity & Political Theory. (p. 1464)
Parekh, R. Nursery Rhymes. (p. 1273)
Parekh, Rikin, illus. see Morgan, Bernard P.
Parekh, Rikin, illus. see Morgan, Bernard.
Paren, Liz & Coxon, Caroline. Common Family Nations Pupil Bo. (p. 349)
Parent, Dan. Betty & Veronica: Best Friends Forever. (p. 172)
—Betty & Veronica's Princess Storybook. (p. 172)
—Kevin Keller: Drive Me Crazy. (p. 950)
Parent, Dan, illus. see Aguirre-Sacasa, Roberto.
Parent, David D. Drummers Forward! Marching with Angels: The Exciting Tale of a Drummer Boy Serving with the First Vermont Brigade & His Adventures During the Americ. (p. 487)
Parent, Lauren. I'm Different but I'm Special. Parent, Lauren, illus. (p. 858)
Parent, Lauren A. Alphabet Kingdom. McGee, Mo, illus. (p. 49)
Parent, Laurence, photos by see Kimball, Allan.
Parent, Nancy. Camping Fun. Chapmanworks Staff, illus. (p. 257)
—Clifford's Big Red Easter. Cuddy, Robin, illus. (p. 332)
—Surprise Garden Harchy, Atelier Philippe, illus. (p. 1686)
—Tree for Me Harchy, Atelier Philippe, illus. (p. 1783)
Parent, Nancy, jt. auth. see Ashman, Sarah.
Parent, Nancy, jt. auth. see Scollon, William.
Parente, Peter. Boomer to the Rescue. Ivanov, Aleksey, illus. (p. 213)
—Peeper Goes to Florida. (p. 1335)
—Peeper the Kinkajou. (p. 1335)
Parente, Robin W., jt. auth. see Athans, Sandra K.
Parenteau, Shirley. Bears in Beds. Walker, David, illus. (p. 152)
—Bears in the Bath. Walker, David, illus. (p. 152)
—Bears on Chairs. Walker, David, illus. (p. 152)
—Dolls of Hope. (p. 464)
—One Frog Sang. Jabar, Cynthia, illus. (p. 1295)
—Ship of Dolls. (p. 1567)
Parenting Press & Kennedy-Moore, Eileen. What about Me? 12 Ways to Get Your Parents' Attention. Katayama, Mits, illus. (p. 1878)
Parenting Press Staff & Cain, Janan. Asi Me Siento Yo. Canetti, Yanitzia, tr. from ENG. (p. 106)
Parenzini, Charity & Gassman, Nelson. Day the Sock Circus Came to Town. (p. 414)
Parett, Lisa, illus. see Lundsten, Apryl.
Parett, Lisa, illus. see White, Kelly.
Paretzky, Leah. Doda Golda Comes for Pesach. David, Racheli, illus. (p. 460)
Parfitt, Rebecca, tr. see Luján, Jorge.
Parham, Donna. Splash of Math 4-8: 4-8. (p. 1629)
—Splash of Math K-3: K-3. (p. 1629)
Parham, Donna, jt. auth. see Nuzzolo, Deborah.
Parham, Jerrill. Boundary Breakers: Remarkable People. (p. 216)
—Thrills & Spills: Fast Sports. (p. 1744)
Parham, Keelan. Let's Toon Caricatures. (p. 1001)
Parham, Pam H. When I Take a Bath. Gillen, Lisa P., illus. (p. 1903)
Parille, Anna. Teddy & His Magical Paw: A New Home for the Honeypies. (p. 1712)
Parin, D'Aulaire Edgar, jt. auth. see Ingri, D'Aulaire.
Parini, Jay, jt. auth. see Ciongoli, A. Kenneth.
Paris, Harper. Mystery Across the Secret Bridge. Calo, Marcos, illus. (p. 1223)
—Mystery at the Coral Reef. Calo, Marcos, illus. (p. 1224)
—Mystery in the Forbidden City. Calo, Marcos, illus. (p. 1224)
—Mystery of the Gold Coin. Calo, Marcos, illus. (p. 1225)
—Mystery of the Mosaic. Calo, Marcos, illus. (p. 1225)
—Mystery of the Stolen Painting. Calo, Marcos, illus. (p. 1226)
—Mystery of the Suspicious Spices. Calo, Marcos, illus. (p. 1226)
Paris, Jacqueline. Decision. (p. 421)
—Persevere. (p. 1344)
Paris, John Ayrton. Philosophy in Sport Made Science in Earnest: Being an Attempt to Illustrate the First Principles of Natural Philosophy by the Aid of the Popular Toys & Sports. Cruikshank, George, illus. (p. 1351)
Paris, Morgaine. Composition of Matter. (p. 354)
Paris, Pat, illus. see Carolyn, Berg.
Paris, Pat, illus. see Rottmann, Erik.
Paris, Patricia. Spiritual Side of Sarah. (p. 1629)
Paris, Pilar, et al. Jesus Grows Up. (p. 915)
Paris Review Staff, ed. Paris Review Book of People with Problems (p. 1324)
Paris, Stephanie. 20th Century: Race to the Moon (p. 1996)
—21st Century: Mysteries of Deep Space (p. 1996)
—Drag! Friction & Resistance. (p. 476)
—Drugs & Alcohol. (p. 487)
—Engineering Feats & Failures. (p. 529)
—Garden Invasion. (p. 656)
—Pecos Bill & Slue-Foot Sue. (p. 1334)
—Pop! Air & Water Pressure. (p. 1384)
—Straight Talk: Smoking (p. 1664)
—Straight Talk: Smoking. (p. 1664)
—Straight Talk: Drugs & Alcohol (p. 1664)
—Straight Talk: The Truth about Food. (p. 1664)
—Straight Talk - The Truth about Food (p. 1664)
—Technology Feats & Failures. (p. 1711)
—Vroom! Speed & Acceleration. (p. 1851)
Paris, Stephanie, jt. auth. see Herwick Rice, Dona.
Paris, Stephanie & Kuligowski, Stephanie. 22nd Century - Future of Space. (p. 1996)
Paris, Stephanie Herweck. Cells. (p. 286)
Paris, Susan. High Noon: Level P (p. 778)
Paris, Tom. Tom & Pearl's Udder Stand. (p. 1762)
Parise-Peterson, Amanda. American Quarter Horse (p. 62)
—Shetland Pony (p. 1566)
Parish, Alex. Peter & the Flying Sergeant. (p. 1346)
Parish, Ellen. Spanish: Level 2. (p. 1620)
Parish, Herman. Amelia Bedelia. Avril, Lynne, illus. (p. 57)
—Amelia Bedelia & the Cat. Sweat, Lynn, illus. (p. 57)
—Amelia Bedelia Bakes Off. Sweat, Lynn, illus. (p. 57)
—Amelia Bedelia, Bookworm. Sweat, Lynn, illus. (p. 57)
—Amelia Bedelia by the Yard. Avril, Lynne, illus. (p. 57)
—Amelia Bedelia Chalks It Up! Avril, Lynne, illus. (p. 57)
—Amelia Bedelia Chalks One Up. (p. 57)
—Amelia Bedelia Chalks One Up. Avril, Lynne, illus. (p. 57)
—Amelia Bedelia Chapter Book #2: Amelia Bedelia Unleashed (Special Edition) (p. 57)
—Amelia Bedelia Chapter Book #3: Amelia Bedelia Road Trip! (Special Edition) (p. 57)
—Amelia Bedelia Chapter Book #4: Amelia Bedelia Goes Wild! (Special Edition) (p. 57)
—Amelia Bedelia Chapter Book #5. Avril, Lynne, illus. (p. 57)

—Amelia Bedelia Chapter Book #6: Amelia Bedelia Cleans Up (POB) Avril, Lynne, illus. (p. 57)
—Amelia Bedelia Cleans Up. Avril, Lynne, illus. (p. 57)
—Amelia Bedelia, Cub Reporter. (p. 57)
—Amelia Bedelia, Cub Reporter. Sweat, Lynn, illus. (p. 57)
—Amelia Bedelia Goes Back to School. Sweat, Lynn, illus. (p. 57)
—Amelia Bedelia Goes Wild! (p. 57)
—Amelia Bedelia Goes Wild! Avril, Lynne, illus. (p. 57)
—Amelia Bedelia Hits the Trail. (p. 57)
—Amelia Bedelia Hits the Trail. Avril, Lynne, illus. (p. 57)
—Amelia Bedelia Is for the Birds. Avril, Lynne, illus. (p. 57)
—Amelia Bedelia Joins the Club. (p. 57)
—Amelia Bedelia Joins the Club. Avril, Lynne, illus. (p. 57)
—Amelia Bedelia Makes a Friend. Avril, Lynne, illus. (p. 57)
—Amelia Bedelia Means Business. Avril, Lynne, illus. (p. 57)
—Amelia Bedelia Road Trip! (p. 57)
—Amelia Bedelia Road Trip! Avril, Lynne, illus. (p. 57)
—Amelia Bedelia, Rocket Scientist? Sweat, Lynn, illus. (p. 57)
—Amelia Bedelia Sets Sail. Avril, Lynne, illus. (p. 57)
—Amelia Bedelia - Sets Sail. Avril, Lynne, illus. (p. 57)
—Amelia Bedelia Shapes Up! Avril, Lynne, illus. (p. 57)
—Amelia Bedelia Sleeps Over. (p. 57)
—Amelia Bedelia Sleeps Over. Avril, Lynne, illus. (p. 57)
—Amelia Bedelia Storybook Treasury: Amelia Bedelia's First Day of School; Amelia Bedelia's First Field Trip; Amelia Bedelia Makes a Friend; Amelia Bedelia Sleeps over; Amelia Bedelia Hits the Trail. Avril, Lynne, illus. (p. 57)
—Amelia Bedelia Talks Turkey. (p. 57)
—Amelia Bedelia Talks Turkey. Sweat, Lynn, illus. (p. 57)
—Amelia Bedelia Talks Turkey. Parish, Herman & Sweat, Lynn, illus. (p. 57)
—Amelia Bedelia Tries Her Luck. Avril, Lynne, illus. (p. 57)
—Amelia Bedelia Tries Her Luck. (p. 58)
—Amelia Bedelia under Construction. Sweat, Lynn, illus. (p. 58)
—Amelia Bedelia Unleashed. Avril, Lynne, illus. (p. 58)
—Amelia Bedelia's Backpack Bundle. Sweat, Lynn, illus. (p. 58)
—Amelia Bedelia's First Apple Pie. (p. 58)
—Amelia Bedelia's First Apple Pie. Avril, Lynne, illus. (p. 58)
—Amelia Bedelia's First Day of School. Avril, Lynne, illus. (p. 58)
—Amelia Bedelia's First Field Trip. (p. 58)
—Amelia Bedelia's First Field Trip. Avril, Lynne, illus. (p. 58)
—Amelia Bedelia's First Library Card. Avril, Lynne, illus. (p. 58)
—Amelia Bedelia's First Vote. Avril, Lynne, illus. (p. 58)
—Amelia Bedelia's Masterpiece. Sweat, Lynn, illus. (p. 58)
—Be My Valentine, Amelia Bedelia. Sweat, Lynn, illus. (p. 148)
—Calling Doctor Amelia Bedelia. Sweat, Lynn, illus. (p. 254)
—Go West, Amelia Bedelia! (p. 687)
—Go West, Amelia Bedelia! Sweat, Lynn, illus. (p. 687)
—Happy Haunting, Amelia Bedelia. Sweat, Lynn, illus. (p. 746)
Parish, Herman, jt. auth. see Parish, Peggy.
Parish, James Robert. Gloria Estefan Singer: Singer. (p. 685)
—Jim Henson: Puppeteer & Filmmaker. (p. 917)
—Steven Spielberg, Filmmaker. (p. 1649)
—Tom Hanks: Actor. (p. 1763)
—Twyla Tharp: Dancer & Choreographer. (p. 1804)
Parish, James Robert, jt. auth. see Taylor, Allan.
Parish, James Robert & Taylor, Allan. Career Opportunities in the Energy Industry. (p. 267)
Parish, John Lee. Cry Aloud: From Protest to Praise. (p. 387)
Parish, Peggy. Amelia Bedelia. (p. 57)
—Amelia Bedelia. Siebel, Fritz, illus. (p. 57)
—Amelia Bedelia & the Baby. Sweat, Lynn, illus. (p. 57)
—Amelia Bedelia Goes Camping. (p. 57)
—Amelia Bedelia Goes Camping. Sweat, Lynn, illus. (p. 57)
—Amelia Bedelia Helps Out. Sweat, Lynn, illus. (p. 57)
—Amelia Bedelia's Family Album. (p. 58)
—Amelia Bedelia's Family Album. Sweat, Lynn, illus. (p. 58)
—Good Work, Amelia Bedelia. (p. 700)
—Good Work, Amelia Bedelia. Sweat, Lynn, illus. (p. 700)
—Key to the Treasure. (p. 950)
—No More Monsters for Me! (p. 1259)
—Teach Us, Amelia Bedelia. Sweat, Lynn, illus. (p. 1708)
—Thank You, Amelia Bedelia. (p. 1725)
Parish, Peggy & Parish, Herman. Amelia Bedelia Celebration: Four Stories Tall. Sweat, Lynn & Siebel, Fritz, illus. (p. 57)
Parish, Scott. Tiger at the Table. (p. 1748)
—Tigre a la Mesa. (p. 1749)
Parish, Shannon, illus. see Medlyn, Lynda Lee & Staudenmier, Kelley Anne.
Parish, Shannon, illus. see Zimet, Sara Goodman.
Parish, Steve. Kangaroos' Great Escape. (p. 942)
Parish, Steve, illus. see Johnson, Rebecca.
Parisi, Anthony. Baby Harp Seal's Snowy Day. (p. 126)
Parisi, Anthony, ed. see Galvin, Laura Gates.
Parisi, Anthony, illus. see Pollock, Hal.
Parisi, Bettie. Lullabies of Love. (p. 1064)
—Quiet. (p. 1428)
Parisse, Jerome. Body Swap: The World's First Text Message Adventure Romance with the Other Side! (p. 207)
Park, Alexander. Thunderbolts & the Circle of Power. (p. 1746)
Park, Andy, illus. see Bishop, Debbie.
Park, Angeland. Wherever I Am, I Am Home. (p. 1911)
Park, Barbara. Aloha-Ha-Ha! Brunkus, Denise, illus. (p. 48)
—Boo... & I Mean It! Brunkus, Denise, illus. (p. 209)
—Boss of Lunch. (p. 215)
—Boss of Lunch. Brunkus, Denise, illus. (p. 215)
—Cheater Pants. Brunkus, Denise, tr. (p. 295)
—Cheater Pants. Brunkus, Denise, illus. (p. 295)
—Dumb Bunny. Brunkus, Denise, illus. (p. 489)
—Graduation of Jake Moon. (p. 705)
—Jingle Bells, Batman Smells! Brunkus, Denise, illus. (p. 918)
—Jingle Bells, Batman Smells! (P. S. So Does May.) Brunkus, Denise, illus. (p. 918)
—Junie B., First Grader - Aloha-Ha-Ha! (p. 935)
—Junie B., First Grader - Aloha-Ha-Ha! Brunkus, Denise, illus. (p. 935)
—Junie B., First Grader (At Last!) (p. 935)
—Junie B., First Grader - Boo...and I Mean It! Brunkus, Denise, illus. (p. 935)
—Junie B., First Grader - Boss of Lunch. (p. 935)
—Junie B., First Grader - Boss of Lunch. Brunkus, Denise, illus. (p. 935)
—Junie B., First Grader - One-Man Band. (p. 935)
—Junie B. Jones & a Little Monkey Business (p. 935)
—Junie B. Jones & Her Big Fat Mouth. (p. 935)
—Junie B. Jones & Some Sneaky Peeky Spying. (p. 935)
—Junie B. Jones & That Meanie Jim's Birthday (p. 935)
—Junie B. Jones & the Mushy Gushy Valentine. (p. 935)
—Junie B. Jones & the Stupid Smelly Bus. (p. 935)
—Junie B. Jones & the Stupid Smelly Bus. Brunkus, Denise, illus. (p. 935)
—Junie B. Jones & the Yucky Blucky Fruitcake. (p. 936)
—Junie B. Jones Books in a Bus (Books 1-28) Brunkus, Denise, illus. (p. 936)
—Junie B. Jones Complete Kindergarten Collection Brunkus, Denise, illus. (p. 936)
—Junie B. Jones Has a Monster under Her Bed. (p. 936)
—Junie B. Jones Has a Peep in Her Pocket. (p. 936)
—Junie B. Jones Is a Beauty Shop Guy. (p. 936)
—Junie B. Jones Is a Party Animal. (p. 936)
—Junie B. Jones Is (Almost) a Flower Girl. (p. 936)
—Junie B. Jones Is Captain Field Day. (p. 936)
—Junie B. Jones Is Not a Crook. (p. 936)
—Junie B. Jones Loves Handsome Warren. (p. 936)
—Junie B. Jones Smells Something Fishy. (p. 936)
—Junie B. Jones y Su Gran Bocota. Brunkus, Denise, illus. (p. 936)
—Junie B. Jones's Fifth Boxed Set Ever! Brunkus, Denise, illus. (p. 936)
—Junie B. Jones's Fourth Boxed Set Ever! Brunkus, Denise, illus. (p. 936)
—Junie B. Jones's Third Boxed Set Ever! Brunkus, Denise, illus. (p. 936)
—Junie B. My Valentime. Brunkus, Denise, illus. (p. 936)
—Junie B.'s Essential Survival Guide to School. Brunkus, Denise, illus. (p. 936)
—Junie B.'s These Puzzles Hurt My Brain! Brunkus, Denise, illus. (p. 936)
—Ma! There's Nothing to Do Here! A Word from Your Baby-in-Waiting. Garofoli, Viviana, illus. (p. 1067)
—Mick Harte Was Here. (p. 1135)
—One-Man Band. Brunkus, Denise, tr. (p. 1296)
—One-Man Band. Brunkus, Denise, illus. (p. 1296)
—Shipwrecked Brunkus, Denise, illus. (p. 1567)
—Toothless Wonder. (p. 1768)
—Toothless Wonder. Brunkus, Denise, illus. (p. 1768)
—Turkeys We Have Loved & Eaten Brunkus, Denise, illus. (p. 1797)
—Turkeys We Have Loved & Eaten (and Other Thankful Stuff) (p. 1797)
—Turkeys We Have Loved & Eaten (And Other Thankful Stuff) Brunkus, Denise, illus. (p. 1797)
Park, Barbara & Brunkus, Denise. Junie B. Jones & That Meanie Jim's Birthday. (p. 935)
Park, Barbara & Wotherspoon, John. Adventures of Lily Leaf. (p. 19)
Park, Barbara, ed. Mick Harte Was Here. (p. 1135)
Park, Charlie & Bauer, Susan Wise, eds. Modern Age: Victoria's Empire to the End of the USSR. Bk. 4 (p. 1158)
Park, Clare, photos by see Lark, Liz.
Park, Darcie, illus. see Coerr, Eleanor.
Park, Devin & Lee, Claudia. Howl Michigan. (p. 823)
Park, Frances & Park, Ginger. My Freedom Trip: A Child's Escape from North Korea. Jenkins, Debra Reid, illus. (p. 1209)
—Where on Earth Is My Bagel? Lin, Grace, illus. (p. 1909)
Park, Ginger, jt. auth. see Park, Frances.
Park, Greg. Veil of Darkness: Book One of the Earthsoul Prophecies. (p. 1834)
Park, Hye-Jin, illus. see Yuy, Beub-Ryong.
Park, Hyeondo, illus. see Croall, Marie P.
Park, Hyeondo, illus. see Teer, Samuel.
Park, Janie Jaehyun. Tiger & the Persimmon. (p. 1748)
Park, Janie Jaehyun, illus. see Haskins, Jim & Benson, Kathleen.
Park, Je-Sung. Sweety Kim, Julie, illus. (p. 1690)
—Sweety. Kim, Julie, illus. (p. 1690)
Park, JinJun, creator. Raiders (p. 1433)
Park, Julia J. Braintext Study Guide for the SAT Reasoning Test. Park, Julia J., ed. (p. 222)
Park, Julie, illus. see Kinnear, Kay.
Park, Jung-a, illus. see Subramaniam, Manasi.
Park, KangHo. Heavenly Executioner Chiwoo (p. 761)
Park, KangHo, jt. auth. see HaNa, Lee.
Park, KangHo, jt. auth. see Lee, HaNa.
Park, Kathy, illus. see Lee, Jc.
Park, Keith. Interactive Storytelling: Developing Inclusive Stories for Children & Adults. (p. 879)
Park, Ken. Americans from India & Other South Asian Countries. (p. 64)
Park, Keun, illus. see Kim, Cecil.
Park, Kyubyong & Amen, Henry J. My First Book of Korean Words: An ABC Rhyming Book. Padron, Aya, illus. (p. 1205)
Park, Laura. I Don't Want to Be the Mom Today. Ramaiah, Rajiv, illus. (p. 838)
Park, Laura, illus. see Grabenstein, Chris & Patterson, James.
Park, Laura, illus. see Grabenstein, Chris.
Park, Laura, illus. see Patterson, James & Grabenstein, Chris.
Park, Laura, illus. see Patterson, James & Tebbetts, Chris.
Park, Laura, illus. see Patterson, James & Tebbetts, Christopher.
Park, Laura, illus. see Patterson, James, et al.
Park, Linda Sue. Archer's Quest. (p. 95)
—Bee-Bim Bop! Lee, Ho Baek, illus. (p. 157)
—Firekeeper's Son. Downing, Julie, illus. (p. 592)
—Keeping Score. (p. 947)
—Kite Fighters. (p. 962)
—Long Walk to Water: Based on a True Story. (p. 1047)
—Long Walk to Water. (p. 1047)
—Project Mulberry. (p. 1410)
—Seesaw Girl. Tseng, Mou-Sien & Tseng, Jean, illus. (p. 1548)
—Single Shard. (p. 1579)
—Storm Warning. (p. 1656)
—Tap Dancing on the Roof: Sijo (Poems) Banyai, Istvan, illus. (p. 1705)
—Third Gift. Ibatoulline, Bagram, illus. (p. 1734)
—Trust No One. (p. 1793)
—What Does Bunny See? A Book of Colors & Flowers. Smith, Maggie, illus. (p. 1884)
—When My Name Was Keoko. (p. 1904)
—Xander's Panda Party. Phelan, Matt, illus. (p. 1967)
Park, Linda Sue & Durango, Julia. Yum! Yuck! A Foldout Book of People Sounds. Rama, Sue, illus. (p. 1983)
Park, Louise. Ancient Cities. (p. 68)
—Ancient Greece. (p. 69)
—Blood in the Arena: Gladiators of Ancient Rome. (p. 200)
—Extreme Fashions. (p. 556)
—Life in the Middle Ages. (p. 1011)
—New Girl. May, Kyla & Matthews, Melanie, illus. (p. 1244)
—Odd One Out. May, Kyla & Matthews, Melanie, illus. (p. 1278)
—Pharaohs' Armies. (p. 1349)
—Sinking of the Titanic. (p. 1580)
—Three's a Crowd. May, Kyla & Matthews, Melanie, illus. (p. 1744)
—Winning Moves. May, Kyla & Matthews, Melanie, illus. (p. 1937)
Park, Louise & Love, Timothy. Japanese Samurai. (p. 909)
—Medieval Knights. (p. 1119)
—Roman Gladiators. (p. 1485)
—Scandinavian Vikings. (p. 1519)
—Spartan Hoplites. (p. 1622)
Park, Louise & Smart Apple Media Staff. Droughts. (p. 486)
—Earthquakes. (p. 497)
—Hurricanes. (p. 830)
—Tornadoes. (p. 1770)
—Tsunamis. (p. 1795)
—Volcanoes. (p. 1849)
Park, Margaret. Now for My Next Number! Songs for Multiplying Fun. Esterman, Sophia, illus. (p. 1269)
Park, Meg, illus. see Rissi, Anica Mrose.
Park, Min-Seo. Blazin' Barrels (p. 199)
—Blazin' Barrels. Park, Min-Seo, illus. (p. 199)
Park, Mi-Ok, illus. see Roh, Grace S.
Park, Peggy J. Is the Death Penalty Just? (p. 890)
Park, Robert E. Treasure Hunting on a Budget (p. 1781)
Park, Sang Sung. Tarot Cafe (p. 1706)
Park, Sang-Sun. Ark Angels (p. 99)
—Tarot Cafe (p. 1706)
Park, Sang-Sun, illus. see Jo, Eun-Ha.
Park, Sang-Sun & Kim, Jung-Su. Tarot Cafe. (p. 1706)
Park, Sang-Sun, creator. Tarot Cafe (p. 1706)
Park, Sarah, illus. see Bauer, Susan Wise.
Park, Se-Jung. Sweety Kim, Julie, illus. (p. 1690)
Park, Seung-bum, illus. see Ko, Jung-wook.
Park, So Hee, creator. Goong (p. 702)
—Royal Palace. (p. 1492)
Park, Soyoo H., illus. see Shalant, Phyllis.
Park, Sung-Woo. Now (p. 1268)
—Now. Park, Sung-Woo, illus. (p. 1268)
—Zero (p. 1986)
Park, Sung-Woo, illus. see Ihm, Dar-Young.
Park, Sung-Woo, illus. see Oh Rhe Bar Ghun.
Park, Sunny. Bboonk, the Minke Whale. (p. 147)
Park, Trip, illus. see Sayre, April Pulley.
Park, Trip, illus. see Stine, R. L.
Park, Y. H. & Tok, Stephanie. Taekwondo for Kids. (p. 1695)
Park, Yeong-jin, illus. see Gam Do, Rin Bo.
Parke, Steven, illus. see Fuqua, Jonathon Scott.
Parker. Space Mysteries - Space Busters. (p. 1619)
Parker, A. J. Table of Shadows. (p. 1694)
Parker, Alan J. American Anthology. (p. 59)
Parker, Amy. Christmas Prayer (p. 315)
—Night Night Prayer Pedler, Caroline, illus. (p. 1253)
Parker, Amy, jt. auth. see Countryman, Jack.
Parker, Amy, jt. auth. see McCorkle, Brent.
Parker, Amy Christine. Astray (Gated Sequel) (p. 109)
—Gated. (p. 658)
Parker, Andy. Ciberbichos: Cyber Bugs, Spanish-Language Edition. (p. 318)
—Mekanimals: Robotic Reef, Spanish-Language Edition. (p. 1125)
—Mekanimals: Clockwork Safari, Spanish-Language Edition. (p. 1125)
—Mekanimals Clockwork Safari. (p. 1125)
—Mekanimals Cyber Bugs. (p. 1125)
Parker, Andy, illus. see Goodhart, Pippa.
Parker, Ant. Muddle Builders: A Magnetic Play Book. (p. 1188)
Parker, Ant, illus. see Clarke, Jane.
Parker, Ant, illus. see Denchfield, Nick.
Parker, Ant, illus. see Lewis, Edwina.
Parker, Ant, illus. see Mitton, Tony.
Parker, Ant, jt. auth. see Mitton, Tony.
Parker, Barbara. Suspicion of Rage. (p. 1688)
Parker, Barbara Keevil. Giraffes. (p. 677)
Parker, Barbara Keevil & Parker, Duane F. Lynxes. (p. 1066)
—Miguel de Cervantes. (p. 1141)
Parker, Ben. My First Guitar - Learn to Play: Kids. (p. 1206)
—My First Keyboard - Learn to Play: Kids. (p. 1207)
—My First Recorder - Learn to Play: Kids. (p. 1207)
Parker, Ben & Woldegiorgis, Abraham. Ethiopia. (p. 539)
Parker, Beth. Tale of Tom Turtle (p. 1700)
—Tom Turtle Visits Grandma's Farm. (p. 1764)
—Tom Turtle's Fishing Tail (p. 1764)
Parker, Buzz, illus. see Reger, Rob & Gruner, Jessica.
Parker, Buzz, illus. see Reger, Rob & Huehner, Mariah.
Parker, C. Brad. Chosen Generation. (p. 310)
Parker, Chance. Nutrition & Science. (p. 1274)
Parker, Christi. Postcards from Dr. Seuss Book 1 (p. 1388)
Parker, Christi E. Abraham Lincoln. (p. 6)
—American Revolution. (p. 63)
—Civil War Is Coming. (p. 325)
—George Washington. (p. 664)
—Laura Ingalls Wilder. (p. 980)
—Pioneer Trails. (p. 1361)
Parker, Claudia. Children's Church with a Preschool Pastor. (p. 303)
Parker, Curtis, illus. see Hyde, Margaret E.
Parker, Curtis, illus. see Hyde, Margaret, ed.
Parker, Daniel. April. (p. 93)
—August. (p. 115)
—December. (p. 421)
—February. (p. 580)
—January. (p. 908)
—July. (p. 933)
—June. (p. 934)
—March. (p. 1091)
—May. (p. 1112)
—November. (p. 1268)
—October. (p. 1277)
—September. (p. 1551)
Parker, Danny. Tree: A Little Story about Big Things. Ottley, Matt, illus. (p. 1783)
Parker, David. I Accept You As You Are! Fiammenghi, Gioia, illus. (p. 831)
—I Am a Leader! Walker, Sylvia, illus. (p. 832)
—I Am Creative! Durrell, Julie, illus. (p. 832)
—I Can Cooperate! Dubin, Jill, illus. (p. 835)
—I Can Listen. Allen, Joy, illus. (p. 836)
—I Can Share! Dubin, Jill, illus. (p. 836)
—I Show Respect! Fiammenghi, Gioia, illus. (p. 845)
—I Tell the Truth! Goodnow, Patti, illus. (p. 846)
—I Will Keep Trying! Ramsey, Marcy Dunn, illus. (p. 848)
—I'm a Good Friend! Ong, Cristina, illus. (p. 858)
—I'm in Charge of Me! Walker, Sylvia, illus. (p. 859)
—My Best Friend Is Moving. Lucas, Margeaux, illus. (p. 1196)
—Our Class Works Together. Lucas, Margeaux, illus. (p. 1308)
—Sharing My Room. Lucas, Margeaux, illus. (p. 1561)
—We Can All Play. Lucas, Margeaux, illus. (p. 1866)
Parker, David, illus. see Schulz, Karen K.
Parker, David & Lyon, Tammie. ¡Soy Optimista! Lyon, Tammie, illus. (p. 1618)
Parker, Deborah. In the Garden (Cj) (p. 866)
Parker, Don H. Developmental 2 Reading Lab: Developmental 2 Listening Skill Builder Audiocassettes. (p. 432)
—Reading Laboratory. (p. 1446)
—Reading Laboratory 2. (p. 1446)
—Reading Laboratory 2A: Teacher's Handbook. (p. 1446)
—Reading Labs 2a, 2b, 2c: Teacher's Handbook. (p. 1446)
—Reading Labs 2a, 2b, 2c: Listening Skill Builder Audiocassettes. (p. 1446)
Parker, Donald James. Reforming the Potter's Clay. (p. 1456)
Parker, Duane F., jt. auth. see Parker, Barbara Keevil.
Parker, Ed. Discover Brazil. (p. 447)
Parker, Edward. Brazil. (p. 224)
—Mexico City. Parker, Edward, photos by. (p. 1131)
Parker, Edward, photos by see Bowden, Rob.
Parker, Edward, photos by see Scoones, Simon.
Parker, Elizabeth, jt. auth. see Blackstone, Stella.
Parker, Emma. Albert & the Dragon. (p. 34)
—All Aboard! (p. 41)
—At the Circus. (p. 111)
—At the Farm. (p. 111)
—Bath Time. (p. 144)
—Bill Hides Acorns. (p. 186)
—Billy & the Deep Sea Monster. (p. 187)
—Birthday Surprise. (p. 193)
—Blah the Bacteria. (p. 198)
—Butterfly on the Subway. (p. 248)
—Can Your Dog? (p. 260)
—Captain Gold. (p. 264)
—Carousel. (p. 271)
—Cat on the High Seas. (p. 278)
—Cecil the Caterpillar. (p. 283)
—Chuck the Chilli. (p. 318)
—Dancing Class. (p. 402)
—Davey Dory. (p. 410)
—Delia Dynamite. (p. 425)
—Fluffiest Chicken. (p. 608)
—Frog That Did Not Like Water. (p. 640)
—Fruity Girls. (p. 646)
—Granny Odd Legs. (p. 710)
—Groat & the Coat. (p. 725)
—How Many Fish? (p. 811)
—How Shall I Get to School Today? (p. 812)
—Jack & the Beanstalk. (p. 902)
—Karaoke Colin. (p. 943)
—Lightning Game. (p. 1016)
—Little Red Riding Hood. (p. 1039)
—Lucky Pearl. (p. 1063)
—Lulu & the Seed. (p. 1064)
—Magic Show. (p. 1073)
—Magic Snow Globe. (p. 1073)
—Missy Hip Hoppo. (p. 1154)
—Monkey in the Tree. (p. 1165)
—Mr Grumpy Bunny. (p. 1185)
—Naughty Puppy. (p. 1237)
—Not So Scary Scarecrow. (p. 1267)
—One Leg Ned. (p. 1295)
—Pet Day. (p. 1345)
—Robot Tim. (p. 1480)
—Safari Adventure. (p. 1501)
—Sam the Traveling Snail. (p. 1507)
—Sebastian the Ant. (p. 1539)
—Skipping Sally. (p. 1586)
—Snafu & the Shoes. (p. 1595)
—Snowman Olympics. (p. 1601)
—Sooty the Stink Bomb. (p. 1613)
—Space Rocket. (p. 1619)
—Spaghetti Tree. (p. 1620)
—Splat & the Hat. (p. 1629)
—Square Sidney. (p. 1636)
—Summer Camp. (p. 1674)
—There's a Bear in My Bed. (p. 1730)
—Wedding Day. (p. 1870)
—What a Hullabaloo. (p. 1878)
—What Will JoJo Be? (p. 1895)
—What Will the Weather Be Today? (p. 1895)
—Wickedest Witch. (p. 1927)
Parker, Emma & Aesop. Lion & the Mouse. (p. 1020)

Parker, Emma & Renaud, Marguerite. Aliens from Zen. (p. 41)
—Chatterbox Caz. (p. 295)
—Dragon Bowling. (p. 476)
—Hedgehogs. (p. 762)
—Honey Bee Race. (p. 794)
—Who Took My Things? (p. 1917)
Parker, Emma Rae. Papa's Book of Mormon Christmas. (p. 1322)
Parker, Felicity. Big Machines to Spot. (p. 182)
Parker, Francis W. Uncle Robert's Geography, Uncle Robert's (p. 1812)
—Uncle Robert's Geography, Uncle Robert's Visit (p. 1812)
—Uncle Robert's Geography (Uncle Robert's Visit, V. 3) (p. 1812)
Parker, Gary & Parker, Mary. Complete Zoo Adventure: A Field Trip in a Book. (p. 353)
—Fossil Book. (p. 623)
Parker, Gary E. Life Before Birth: A Christian Family Book. (p. 1008)
Parker, Gary E. & Parker, Mary. Fossil Book. (p. 623)
Parker, Gayle B. Ultimate Everyday Kitchen Reference. (p. 1809)
Parker, Gilbert. Carnac's Folly. (p. 270)
—Michel & Angele. (p. 1135)
—Wild Youth. (p. 1931)
Parker, Gilles N. Visit to the Farm: A Vet Makes New Friends. (p. 1845)
Parker, Glenn. Shutout Girl. (p. 1572)
Parker, Graham. 1, 2, 3 the Art of Counting. (p. 1990)
Parker, Gretel, illus. see Tarlow, Ellen.
Parker, H., jt. auth. see Gordon, B.
Parker, H., jt. auth. see Phillips, S.
Parker, Harvey C. Behavior Management at Home: A Token Economy Program for Children & Teens. (p. 160)
—Listen, Look & Think: A Self-Regulation Program for Children. (p. 1022)
Parker, Harvey C., jt. auth. see Parker, Roberta N.
Parker, Helen. Busy Baby First 100 Animals. (p. 245)
—Lift Stick & Learn: Emergency. (p. 1014)
—Trace, Stick Learn Borrar Primeras Palabras/Wipe Clean First Words. (p. 1774)
—Wipe Clean Phonics. (p. 1939)
Parker, I. J., jt. auth. see Parker, Ingrid J.
Parker, Ian. Ride On: Bikes & Riders Who Rule. (p. 1471)
Parker, Ingrid J. & Parker, I. J. Island of Exiles: A Mystery of Early Japan. (p. 892)
Parker, Jack, illus. see Patterson, Horace.
Parker, Jacob. Kestrel Midnight Song. (p. 949)
Parker, Jake. Rescue on Tankium (p. 1462)
—Star Crusher. (p. 1640)
Parker, Jake, illus. see Bernheimer, Kate.
Parker, Jake, illus. see Chabon, Michael.
Parker, Jake, illus. see Coombs, Kate.
Parker, Jake, illus. see McNamara, Margaret.
Parker, James S. My College Tips: Written by a College Student, for College Students. Stone, Karen P., ed. (p. 1200)
Parker, Jane, jt. auth. see Parker, Steve.
Parker, Janice. 1980: Canadian Decades. (p. 2002)
—Alabama. (p. 33)
—Birds. (p. 191)
—California. (p. 253)
—Communication. (p. 349)
—Crime. (p. 382)
—Crime Q & A. (p. 382)
—Insects. (p. 875)
—Machines. (p. 1068)
—Machines Q & A. (p. 1068)
—Reptiles. (p. 1461)
—Science of Liquids & Solids. (p. 1527)
—Science of Structures. (p. 1527)
—South Carolina. (p. 1616)
—Texas. (p. 1724)
—Virginia. (p. 1844)
—Weather. (p. 1869)
—Weather Q & A. (p. 1870)
—Wisconsin. (p. 1939)
—Wyoming. (p. 1966)
Parker, Jean Black. Amanda's Helping Hands. (p. 52)
Parker, Jeff. Attack of 50 Foot Girl! Kirk, Leonard, illus. (p. 113)
—Avenging Seven. Kirk, Leonard, illus. (p. 119)
—Bringers of Storm. Cafu, illus. (p. 229)
—Ego: The Loving Planet. Santacruz, Juan, illus. (p. 506)
—Even a Hawkeye Can Cry. Scott, Steve, illus. (p. 541)
—High Serpent Society. Santacruz, Juan, illus. (p. 778)
—Medieval Women. Santacruz, Juan, illus. (p. 1119)
—Not-So-Beautiful Mind. Santacruz, Juan, illus. (p. 1267)
—Shadowland. (p. 1558)
Parker, Jeff, illus. see Gage, Christos.
Parker, Jeff, ed. Perfect World Molina, Jorge et al, illus. (p. 1342)
—Planet Red Hulk. (p. 1368)
Parker, Jeff, et al. Dark Avengers: The End Is the Beginning. Edwards, Neil, illus. (p. 407)
Parker, Jessie, jt. auth. see Kilgras, Heidi.
Parker, Jim. Howard the Flying Bloodhound. (p. 823)
Parker, Jo Ann. Cow That Could, & Did! (with a Little Help from Her Friends) (p. 373)
Parker, John. Chaos Mountain. (p. 291)
—Sucked In. (p. 1672)
Parker, John F. Rosezinda: Riding Rainbows. (p. 1490)
Parker, K. J. Guardian Universe Core Fuzion. (p. 728)
Parker, Kate & Parker, Zac. Nos Gusta Tocar Musica: We Like to Play Music. (p. 1266)
—We Like to Play Music. (p. 1867)
Parker, Katie. Black Holes. (p. 196)
—Gone Extinct! Maydak, Mike, illus. (p. 697)
—Splitting the Atom. (p. 1630)
—Theory of Relativity. (p. 1729)
Parker, Katrina. Living with Diabetes. (p. 1042)
Parker, Lara. Salem Branch. (p. 1504)
Parker, Laurie. for Angels: A Bible Alphabet. (p. 615)
—It Really Said Christmas. (p. 894)
—It Really Said Christmas. Parker, Laurie, illus. (p. 894)
—Mad for Maroon. (p. 1069)
Parker, Lehua. One Boy, No Water. Egbert, Corey, illus. (p. 1294)
Parker, Lew. Genetics. Krasnow, David, ed. (p. 660)
Parker, Lewis. How to Draw the Life & Times of George H. W. Bush. (p. 819)
—How to Draw the Life & Times of Harry S. Truman. (p. 819)
—How to Draw the Life & Times of Richard M. Nixon. (p. 819)
Parker, Lewis K. Andrew Carnegie & the Steel Industry. (p. 72)
—Cornelius Vanderbilt & the Railroad Industry. (p. 367)
—Dutch Colonies in the Americas. (p. 490)
—English Colonies in the Americas. (p. 529)
—French Colonies in the Americas. (p. 635)
—Henry Ford & the Automobile Industry. (p. 768)
—How to Draw the Life & Times of George H. W. Bush. (p. 819)
—How to Draw the Life & Times of Harry S. Truman. (p. 819)
—How to Draw the Life & Times of William McKinley. (p. 819)
—Inventions of Amanda Jones: The Vacuum Method of Canning & Food Preservation. (p. 884)
—J. Pierpont Morgan & Wall Street. (p. 902)
—John D. Rockefeller & the Oil Industry. (p. 921)
—John Jacob Astor & the Fur Trade. (p. 922)
—Portuguese Colonies in the Americas. (p. 1387)
—Russian Colonies in the Americas. (p. 1498)
—Spanish Colonies in the Americas. (p. 1621)
—Why German Immigrants Came to America. (p. 1925)
—Why Irish Immigrants Came to America. (p. 1925)
—Why Italian Immigrants Came to America. (p. 1925)
—Why Japanese Immigrants Came to America. (p. 1925)
—Why Mexican Immigrants Came to America. (p. 1925)
—Why Vietnamese Immigrants Came to America. (p. 1926)
Parker, Linda & Langdon, Katie. Austin & Charlie Adventures: Washington DC Adventure. (p. 116)
Parker, Lisa L. Gray. Princesses Do Not Wear Tattoos. Logan, Desiree, illus. (p. 1406)
Parker, Lucy. Acorn Meadow has a Secret. (p. 9)
Parker Ma Csac, Nacole A. Day in the Life of Ruby. (p. 413)
Parker, Madison. Play Me, I'm Yours. (p. 1371)
—Play Me, I'm Yours [Library Edition]. (p. 1371)
Parker, Marjorie Blain. I Love You near & Far. Henry, Jed, illus. (p. 844)
—Jasper's Day. Wilson, Janet, illus. (p. 910)
—Paddling of Ducks: Animals in Groups from A to Z. Kelly, Joseph, illus. (p. 1317)
—When Dads Don't Grow Up. Alley, R. W., illus. (p. 1901)
Parker, Marjorie Blain & Matisse, Henri. Colorful Dreamer: The Story of Artist Henri Matisse. Berry, Holly, illus. (p. 344)
Parker, Martha, jt. auth. see Dorris, Donna.
Parker, Mary, jt. auth. see Parker, Gary E.
Parker, Mary, jt. auth. see Parker, Gary.
Parker, Meeta. Cookie the Clown. (p. 361)
Parker, Michael & Wiedmer, Caroline. You Are a Star! Rossell, Judith, illus. (p. 1973)
Parker, Mike. Break-In. (p. 224)
Parker, Ms. Alichia R. My Aunt & Me. Brown, Chris L., illus. (p. 1196)
Parker, Nadine. Parker & the Strawberry Patch. (p. 1324)
Parker, Nancy. Adventures of Yat & Dat: What's Cookin'? (p. 24)
Parker, Nancy Winslow. Organs! How They Work, Fall Apart, & Can Be Replaced (Gasp!) (p. 1303)
Parker, Nancy Winslow, illus. see Neitzel, Shirley.
Parker, Natalie C. Beware the Wild. (p. 173)
Parker, Natasha. You - Are Special Like the World: (English/French/Spanish/German/Italian/Portugese/Chinese) (p. 1972)
Parker, Neal. Lobsterman & the U. F. O. (p. 1044)
Parker, Patti. Book of Ominook: The Journey Begins. (p. 211)
Parker, Patty J. Little Puppy Saves the Day. (p. 1034)
Parker, Paul, illus. see MacLaine, James.
Parker, Regina F. Let Freedom Ring. (p. 994)
Parker, Richard. Voyage to Tasmani. Seward, Prudence, illus. (p. 1850)
Parker, Richard Green. Parker's Second Reader: National Series of Selections for Reading Designe. (p. 1324)
Parker, Rick. Four Frogs. (p. 625)
Parker, Rick, illus. see Gerrold, David, et al.
Parker, Rick, illus. see Petrucha, Stefan & Kinney-Petrucha, Margo.
Parker, Rick, illus. see Petrucha, Stefan.
Parker, Rick, illus. see Salicrup, Jim, et al.
Parker, Rick & Petrucha, Stefan. Breaking Down. Parker, Rick, illus. (p. 225)
Parker, Robert. Cold Service. (p. 338)
—Edenville Owls. (p. 504)
—School Days. (p. 1522)
Parker, Robert A., illus. see Tompert, Ann.
Parker, Robert Andrew. Chasing the Bear. (p. 294)
Parker, Robert Andrew, illus. see Borden, Louise & Borden, Louise W.
Parker, Robert Andrew, illus. see Brallier, Jess M.
Parker, Robert Andrew, illus. see Gauch, Patricia Lee.
Parker, Robert Andrew, illus. see Greenberg, Jan & Jordan, Sandra.
Parker, Robert Andrew, illus. see Jordan, Sandra & Greenberg, Jan.
Parker, Robert Andrew, illus. see Peretz, I. L. & Goldin, Barbara Diamond.
Parker, Robert B. Boxer & the Spy. (p. 217)
Parker, Robert H. Little Crooked Christmas Tree. Long, DeWayne Lee, illus. (p. 1026)
Parker, Robert L. To Ride the Tiger. (p. 1759)
Parker, Roberta N. Slam Dunk: A Young Boy's Struggle with Attention Deficit Disorder. DiMatteo, Richard A., illus. (p. 1587)
Parker, Roberta N. & Parker, Harvey C. Making the Grade: An Adolescent's Struggle with ADD. DiMatteo, Richard A., illus. (p. 1082)
Parker, Ron. Teen Wars. (p. 1714)
Parker, Ron, illus. see Bouchard, David.
Parker, Russ. Climate Crisis. (p. 332)
—Energy Supplies in Crisis. (p. 528)
—Planet in Crisis (p. 1367)
—Pollution Crisis. (p. 1381)
—Waste Management Crisis. (p. 1860)
—Water Supplies in Crisis. (p. 1863)
—Wildlife Crisis. (p. 1931)
Parker, Sandy. What Day Is Today? Hofher, Cathy, illus. (p. 1881)
—What Month Is It? Hofher, Cathy, illus. (p. 1892)
Parker, Sara. There's a Big Ant on Me! Get It Off! (p. 1730)
Parker, Shelley, jt. auth. see Lewis, Steven.
Parker, Sherri. God's Word Ages 4-10 (p. 692)
—Let's Seek God's Word Together. (p. 1000)
Parker, Steve. 10 Things You Should Know about Big Cats. Borton, Paula, ed. (p. 1994)
—10 Things You Should Know about Crocodiles. Gallagher, Belinda & Borton, Paula, eds. (p. 1994)
—10 Things You Should Know about Dinosaurs. Gallagher, Belinda & Borton, Paula, eds. (p. 1994)
—10 Things You Should Know about Sharks. Gallagher, Belinda & Borton, Paula, eds. (p. 1994)
—10 Things You Should Know about Spiders. Gallagher, Belinda & Borton, Paula, eds. (p. 1994)
—50 Things You Should Know about Fierce Creatures. Marshall, Anne, ed. (p. 1997)
—Adaptation. (p. 11)
—Age of the Dinosaur. (p. 29)
—Aircraft. (p. 31)
—Alexander Fleming. (p. 36)
—Animal Life. (p. 78)
—Ant Lions, Wasps & Other Insects (p. 88)
—Atlas Visual del Cuerpo Humano. (p. 113)
—Baby Animals. Jackson, Ian, illus. (p. 124)
—Bats, Blue Whales, & Other Mammals (p. 145)
—Bears. Morandi, Andrea, illus. (p. 151)
—Beyond the Solar System: From Red Giants to Black Holes. (p. 174)
—Big Cats. Jackson, Ian, illus. (p. 180)
—Brain (p. 221)
—Break It Down: The Digestive System (p. 224)
—Bubbling Biology. (p. 233)
—Bugs. (p. 237)
—Bugs. Draper, Richard, illus. (p. 237)
—Cars. Sweet, Stephen, illus. (p. 272)
—Cars Trucks & Bikes. (p. 272)
—Cats & Kittens. (p. 281)
—Changes in Animal Habitats. (p. 290)
—Changes in Climate. (p. 290)
—Changes in Food & Farming. (p. 290)
—Changes In... Population. (p. 290)
—Circulatory System. (p. 322)
—Coal (p. 336)
—Coal. (p. 336)
—Cocci, Spirilla & Other Bacteria (p. 337)
—Complete Guides Our World. (p. 353)
—Control Freak: Hormones, the Brain, & the Nervous System (p. 361)
—Crackling Chemistry. (p. 375)
—Crocodiles. Roberts, Steve, illus. (p. 384)
—Digestive & Reproductive Systems. (p. 438)
—DK Eyewitness Books: Electricity: Electricity. (p. 456)
—Earsplitters! The World's Loudest Noises (p. 494)
—Emergency Vehicles. (p. 518)
—Endangered Animals. (p. 526)
—Energy & Power. (p. 528)
—Extinction. (p. 555)
—Ferns, Mosses & Other Spore-Producing Plants (p. 582)
—Fizzing Physics. (p. 601)
—Fossils. (p. 624)
—Gadgets. (p. 652)
—Giant Machines. (p. 673)
—HMMWV Humvee Pang, Alex, illus. (p. 786)
—Hormones (p. 798)
—Hormones: Injury, Illness & Health. (p. 798)
—How Do My Braces Work? Teeth (p. 807)
—How Do My Muscles Get Strong? Muscles & Exercise (p. 807)
—How It Works (p. 810)
—Human Body. (p. 825)
—Human Body Book. (p. 825)
—Ice Age Giants. (p. 850)
—In Space. (p. 865)
—In the Air. (p. 865)
—In Vitro Fertilization. (p. 868)
—In Your Genes: Genetics & Reproduction (p. 868)
—Insects & Spiders. (p. 876)
—Kingdom Classification (p. 959)
—LCAC Military Hovercraft Pang, Alex, illus. (p. 981)
—M2 Bradley Infantry Fighting Vehicle Pang, Alex, illus. (p. 1067)
—M270 Multiple Launch Rocket Pang, Alex, illus. (p. 1067)
—Mamiferos. (p. 1084)
—Mammal: Eyewitness Books. Burton, Jane & King, Dave, photos by. (p. 1084)
—Mammal. Dorling Kindersley Publishing Staff, ed. (p. 1084)
—Microlife That Helps Us (p. 1136)
—Microlife That Lives in Soil (p. 1136)
—Microlife That Rots Things (p. 1136)
—Military Machines. (p. 1143)
—Molds, Mushrooms & Other Fungi (p. 1160)
—Move Your Body: Bones & Muscles (p. 1183)
—Muscular & Skeletal Systems. (p. 1192)
—Natural Gas (p. 1235)
—Nervous System. (p. 1241)
—Nuclear Energy. (p. 1269)
—Ocean & Sea. (p. 1276)
—Oil (p. 1282)
—Oil & Gas. (p. 1282)
—On the Building Site. (p. 1290)
—On the Race Track. (p. 1291)
—On the Road. (p. 1291)
—On the Sea. (p. 1291)
—Owls. Morandi, Andrea, illus. (p. 1315)
—Peacocks, Penguins & Other Birds. (p. 1332)
—Pond & River. (p. 1382)
—Protozoans, Algae & Other Protists (p. 1412)
—Pump It Up: Respiration & Circulation (p. 1416)
—Redwoods, Hemlocks & Other Cone-Bearing Plants (p. 1456)
—Reproductive System (p. 1461)
—Robots for Work & Fun. (p. 1481)
—Robots in Dangerous Places. (p. 1481)
—Robots in Fiction & Films. (p. 1481)
—Robots in Science & Medicine. (p. 1481)
—Robots in Space. (p. 1481)
—Robots on the Move. (p. 1481)
—Science. (p. 1524)
—Science & Technology. (p. 1525)
—Seashore. (p. 1538)
—Seashore. Dorling Kindersley Publishing Staff, ed. (p. 1538)
—Sharks. (p. 1562)
—Sharks. Butler, John, illus. (p. 1562)
—Ships & Submarines. (p. 1567)
—Skeleton. Dorling Kindersley Publishing Staff, ed. (p. 1584)
—Solar Power. (p. 1606)
—Space Exploration. (p. 1619)
—Space Objects: Comets, Asteroids & Meteors. (p. 1619)
—Speed Machines. Pang, Alex, illus. (p. 1624)
—Spiders. Draper, Richard, illus. (p. 1627)
—Spinal Cord & Nerves (p. 1628)
—Sun. (p. 1675)
—Sunflowers, Magnolia Trees & Other Flowering Plants (p. 1677)
—Survival & Change. (p. 1686)
—Tabletop Scientist — the Science of Air: Projects & Experiments with Air & Flight. (p. 1694)
—Tabletop Scientist — the Science of Light: Projects & Experiments with Light & Color. (p. 1694)
—Tabletop Scientist — the Science of Sound: Projects & Experiments with Music & Sound Waves. (p. 1694)
—Tabletop Scientist — the Science of Water: Projects & Experiments with Water Science & Power. (p. 1694)
—Tell Me How Does My Body Fit Together? And More about the Human Body. (p. 1716)
—T-Rex. (p. 1694)
—Wales & Dolphins. (p. 1853)
—Water Power. (p. 1863)
—Whales & Dolphins. (p. 1878)
—What about the Human Body. (p. 1879)
—Why Does This Bug Bite Itch? Skin & Healing (p. 1924)
—Wild Animals. (p. 1928)
Parker, Steve, jt. auth. see Becklake, Sue.
Parker, Steve, jt. auth. see Dorling Kindersley Publishing Staff.
Parker, Steve, jt. auth. see Gunston, Bill Tudor.
Parker, Steve, jt. auth. see Kerrod, Robin.
Parker, Steve, jt. auth. see Malam, John.
Parker, Steve, jt. auth. see Taylor, Barbara.
Parker, Steve, jt. auth. see Ticktock Media, Ltd. Staff.
Parker, Steve, jt. auth. see West, David.
Parker, Steve & Bingham, Jane. Robots in Space. (p. 1481)
Parker, Steve & Dewan, Ted. Inside Dinosaurs & Other Prehistoric Creatures. (p. 876)
—Inside the Whale & Other Animals. (p. 878)
Parker, Steve & Dorling Kindersley Publishing Staff. Electricity. (p. 509)
Parker, Steve & Flegg, Jim. Dinosaurs: Great Little Fact Books. (p. 444)
Parker, Steve & Gilpin, Daniel. Sponges, Jellyfish, & Other Simple Animals (p. 1631)
Parker, Steve & Heinemann Library Staff. Brain (p. 221)
—Hormones (p. 798)
—Reproductive System (p. 1461)
—Spinal Cord & Nerves (p. 1628)
Parker, Steve & Kelly, Miles. 100 Facts on Horses & Ponies. (p. 1998)
Parker, Steve & Oxlade, Chris. Earth & Space. (p. 495)
Parker, Steve & Parker, Jane. Show Me How: Nature Projects. (p. 1570)
Parker, Steve & Parker, Vic. Going to the Hospital (p. 693)
—Having a Hearing Test (p. 754)
—Having an Eye Test (p. 755)
—Moving (p. 1183)
—My First Trip on an Airplane (p. 1208)
Parker, Steve & Pipe, Jim. Robots in Dangerous Places. (p. 1481)
—Robots in Fiction & Films. (p. 1481)
—Robots in Science & Medicine. (p. 1481)
Parker, Steve & Prinja, Raman. Awesome Astronomy. (p. 121)
Parker, Steve & Ticktock Media, Ltd. Staff. Body Atlas. (p. 207)
Parker, Steve & Twist, Clint. Exploring Space. (p. 553)
Parker, Steve, et al. Big Book of Science Facts. (p. 179)
Parker, Steven. By Air. (p. 249)
—On Land. (p. 1289)
—On Water. (p. 1292)
—See-Through Reptiles. (p. 1547)
Parker, Sydney. Scoop That Snow! Shannon, David et al, illus. (p. 1529)
Parker, Theron J. June Bug & the Homemade Toys. (p. 934)
Parker, Tom S., jt. auth. see Jennewein, James.
Parker, Toni Trent. Sienna's Scrapbook: Our African American Heritage Trip. Genovese, Janell, illus. (p. 1573)
Parker, Ty. Golden Lizards. (p. 695)
Parker, Tyler, jt. auth. see Lefranc, Karin.
Parker, Vic. Acting Responsibly (p. 10)
—Agua (p. 30)
—Breakfast: Healthy Food Choices (p. 224)
—Buenas Relaciones (p. 235)
—Dinner: Healthy Food Choices (p. 440)
—Healthy Food Choices (p. 758)
—How Big Is Big? Comparing Plants (p. 805)
—How Far Is Far? Comparing Geographical Distances (p. 809)
—How Full Is Full? Comparing Bodies of Water (p. 809)
—How Heavy Is Heavy? Comparing Vehicles (p. 809)
—How Long Is Long? Comparing Animals (p. 810)
—How Small Is Small? Comparing Body Parts (p. 812)
—How Tall Is Tall? Comparing Structures (p. 812)
—I Know Someone with a Hearing Impairment (p. 840)
—I Know Someone with a Visual Impairment (p. 840)

P

—I Know Someone with Allergies (p. 840)
—I Know Someone with Asthma (p. 840)
—I Know Someone with Diabetes (p. 840)
—I Know Someone with down Syndrome (p. 840)
—Inspiring Others (p. 878)
—Let's Think about Animal Rights (p. 1001)
—Let's Think about Sustainable Energy (p. 1001)
—Little Book of Growing Up. (p. 1025)
—Lunch: Healthy Food Choices (p. 1065)
—Making Choices (p. 1080)
—Measuring & Comparing (p. 1117)
—Overcoming Personal Challenges (p. 1314)
—Queen Elizabeth II (p. 1424)
—Saving the Environment (p. 1517)
—Snacks: Healthy Food Choices (p. 1595)
—Tomar Decisiones (p. 1764)
—Traditional Tales from South America. (p. 1776)
Parker, Vic, jt. auth. see Parker, Steve.
Parker, Vic, jt. auth. see Parker, Victoria.
Parker, Vic & Heinemann Library Staff. Acting Responsibly (p. 10)
—Making Choices (p. 1080)
Parker, Vic, compiled by. 50 Scary Fairy Tales. (p. 1997)
Parker, Vic, ed. Boy Who Cried Wolf & Other Fables. (p. 219)
—Demon with the Matted Hair & Other Stories. (p. 426)
—Dog in the Manger & Other Fables. (p. 461)
—Fox & the Stork & Other Fables. (p. 626)
—Frog & the Ox & Other Fables. (p. 640)
—Goblin Pony & Other Stories. (p. 688)
—Goose That Laid the Golden Egg & Other Fables. (p. 702)
—Jack the Giant Killer & Other Stories. (p. 903)
—Lion & the Bull & Other Fables. (p. 1019)
—Little Mermaid & Other Stories. (p. 1031)
—Little Red Riding Hood & Other Stories. (p. 1035)
—Mice & the Weasels & Other Fables. (p. 1134)
—Ogre of Rashomon & Other Stories. (p. 1280)
—Prince & the Dragon & Other Stories. (p. 1401)
—Rat Catcher & Other Stories. (p. 1440)
—Snow Queen & Other Stories. (p. 1599)
—Town Mouse & the Country Mouse & Other Fables. (p. 1773)
—Wicked Witch of the West & Other Stories. (p. 1927)
—Wolf & His Shadow & Other Fables. (p. 1943)
—Wolf in Sheep's Clothing & Other Fables. (p. 1944)
Parker, Vicki Sue. Get Well Soon... Balloon. Beebe, Susan, illus. (p. 668)
Parker, Victoria. Australia. (p. 116)
—Ballet. (p. 134)
—Children's Bible in Eight Classic Volumes: Stories from the Old & New Testaments, Specially Written for the Younger Reader (p. 303)
—Children's Illustrated Bible: Classic Old & New Testament Stories Retold for the Young Reader, with Context Facts, Notes & Features. (p. 303)
—Egypt. (p. 506)
—Girls Only! All about Periods & Growing-Up Stuff. (p. 680)
—Greece. (p. 720)
—Helping Animals (p. 766)
—Helping Family & Friends (p. 766)
—Helping in the Community (p. 766)
—Helping the Environment (p. 766)
—India. (p. 870)
—Japan. (p. 909)
—Mexico. (p. 1131)
—Poland (p. 1378)
Parker, Victoria & Dyson, Janet. Children's Illustrated Bible: The New Testament. (p. 303)
—Children's Illustrated Bible: The Old Testament. (p. 303)
Parker, Victoria & Parker, Vic. Air (p. 31)
—Food (p. 612)
—Homes (p. 793)
—Water (p. 1862)
Parker, Victoria, retold by. Children's Illustrated Bible Stories from the Old & New Testaments: All the Best-Loved Tales from the Bible in Two Volumes (p. 303)
Parker, Warren K. Drugs, War & the Ci. (p. 487)
Parker, Wen-Chia Tsai. Kids Can Compost. (p. 953)
Parker, Wes. For Everything A Season. (p. 615)
—Guardian Angel. (p. 728)
Parker, Wesley. Christoph the Great. (p. 316)
Parker, Zac, illus. see Young, Mary.
Parker, Zac, jt. auth. see Parker, Kate.
Parker, Zac, jt. auth. see Young, Mary.
Parker, Zachary, illus. see Young, Mary.
Parker-Pearson, Mike & Aronson, Marc. If Stones Could Speak: Unlocking the Secrets of Stonehenge. (p. 854)
Parker-Rees, Guy. Party Time with Littlebob & Plum. (p. 1326)
—Party Time with Littlebob & Plum. Parker-Rees, Guy, illus. (p. 1326)
—Tom & Millie: Whizzy Busy People. (p. 1762)
Parker-Rees, Guy, illus. see Andreae, Giles.
Parker-Rees, Guy, illus. see Bently, Peter.
Parker-Rees, Guy, illus. see Edwards, Gareth.
Parker-Rees, Guy, illus. see Jarman, Julia.
Parker-Rees, Guy, illus. see Mitton, Tony.
Parker-Rees, Guy, illus. see Oliver, Ilanit.
Parker-Rees, Guy, illus. see Wallace, Karen.
Parker-Rees, Guy, jt. auth. see Andreae, Giles.
Parker-Rees, Guy, jt. auth. see Wallace, Karen.
Parker-Rock, Michelle. Alma Flor Ada: An Author Kids Love. (p. 48)
—Bruce Coville: An Author Kids Love. (p. 232)
—Bruce Hale: An Author Kids Love. (p. 232)
—Christopher Paul Curtis: An Author Kids Love. (p. 317)
—Diwali: The Hindu Festival of Lights, Feasts, & Family. (p. 455)
—Jack Gantos: An Author Kids Love. (p. 903)
—Joseph Bruchac: An Author Kids Love. (p. 926)
—Linda Sue Park: An Author Kids Love. (p. 1019)
—Patricia & Fredrick Mckissack: Authors Kids Love. (p. 1328)
—R. L. Stine: Creator of Creepy & Spooky Stories. (p. 1429)
—Sid Fleischman: An Author Kids Love. (p. 1572)
Parkes, Lois. Paper Sport: Activities, Games & Puzzles for Sporty Kids. (p. 1323)
Parkhouse, David. Lucy's Spoons. (p. 1063)
Parkhouse, Steve, jt. auth. see Lieber, Larry.
Parkhurst, Anthony, jt. auth. see Goldish, Meish.
Parkhurst, Carolyn. Cooking with Henry & Elliebelly. Yaccarino, Dan, illus. (p. 362)
—Lost & Found. (p. 1054)
Parkhurst, Johanna. Here's to You, Zeb Pike [Library Edition]. (p. 771)
Parkhurst, Liz, ed. see August House Publishers Staff.
Parkhurst, Liz S. Under One Flag: A Year at Rohwer. Clifton, Tom, illus. (p. 1813)
Parkhurst, Robert M. Best of Times: A Life in California. (p. 171)
Parkin, Antonia, tr. see Guéry, Anne & Dussutour, Olivier.
Parkin, Gaile. When Hoopoes Go to Heaven. (p. 1902)
Parkin, Lance & Jones, Mark. Dark Matters: An Unofficial & Unauthorised Guide to Philip Pullman's Dark Materials Trilogy. (p. 407)
Parkin, Megan, jt. auth. see Jones, Tonwen.
Parkin, Michael. Microeconomics, Student Value Edition. (p. 1136)
Parkins, David. Spic-And-Span! Lillian Gilbreth's Wonder Kitchen. (p. 1626)
Parkins, David, illus. see Andrekson, Judy.
Parkins, David, illus. see Charles, Veronika Martenova.
Parkins, David, illus. see Grindley, Sally.
Parkins, David, illus. see Helmer, Marilyn.
Parkins, David, illus. see King-Smith, Dick.
Parkins, David, illus. see Krasnesky, Thad.
Parkins, David, illus. see Kulling, Monica.
Parkins, David, illus. see Kyi, Tanya Lloyd.
Parkins, David, illus. see Leuck, Laura.
Parkins, David, illus. see London, Jonathan.
Parkins, David, illus. see Markes, Julie.
Parkins, David, illus. see McCaughrean, Geraldine.
Parkins, David, illus. see Platt, Richard.
Parkins, David, illus. see Root, Phyllis.
Parkins, David, illus. see Schertle, Alice.
Parkins, David, illus. see Smith, Linda.
Parkins, David, illus. see Stevenson, Robin.
Parkins, David, illus. see Waddell, Martin.
Parkins, David, illus. see Walters, Eric.
Parkins, David, jt. auth. see Charles, Veronika Martenova.
Parkins, Joanne. Adventures of Little Bear: Little Bear & the Potty. (p. 19)
Parkins, Rebecca Katherine. Lilly the Little Lava Mouse. (p. 1017)
Parkins, Wendy, jt. auth. see Craig, Geoffrey.
Parkinson, Cheryl, illus. see MacLennan, David.
Parkinson, Cheryl, tr. see MacLennan, David.
Parkinson, Curtis. Castle on Deadman's Island. (p. 277)
—Death in Kingsport. (p. 420)
—Domenic's War: A Story of the Battle of Monte Cassino. (p. 465)
—Emily's Eighteen Aunts von Königslöw, Andrea Wayne, illus. (p. 519)
—Emily's Eighteen Aunts. (p. 519)
—Man Overboard! (p. 1085)
—Sea Chase. (p. 1534)
—Storm-Blast. (p. 1655)
Parkinson, Ethelyn. Good Old Archibald. Stevens, Mary, illus. (p. 700)
Parkinson, Helen. How Well Can Wombats Bat? (p. 823)
Parkinson, Kate. Grace. Parkinson, Kate, illus. (p. 704)
Parkinson, Kathy, illus. see Maude Spelman, Cornelia & Spelman, Cornelia Maude.
Parkinson, Kathy, illus. see Spelman, Cornelia Maude.
Parkinson, Kathy, illus. see Spelman, Cornelia.
Parkinson, Siobhan. Spellbound: Tales of Enchantment from Ancient Ireland. Whelan, Olwyn, illus. (p. 1625)
—Thirteenth Room. (p. 1735)
Parkinson, Will. Pitch. (p. 1364)
Parkison, James, Sr., des. Big Red & the Fence Post. (p. 183)
Parkkola, Seita. School of Possibilities. Silver, Annira & Gass, Marja, trs. from FIN. (p. 1523)
Parkman, Mary Rosetta. Guide Book for Language, Grade Three: Shepherd-Parkman Language Series. Norman, Vera Stone, illus. (p. 730)
Parkman, Tina. Show Me Some Love: Recipes of Survival for at Risk Teens & Young Adults. (p. 1570)
Parkmond, Latasha A. Did You Meet the Wicked Witch? (p. 437)
Parks, Amy. Basic Concepts in Motion Fun Deck: Fd58. Vaughan, Jack, illus. (p. 141)
Parks, Amy, jt. creator see Callough, Melanee.
Parks, Barbara A. C'. Mother's Garden. (p. 1178)
Parks, Carmen. Farmers Market. Martinez, Edward, illus. (p. 574)
—Farmers Market/Dia de Mercado. Flor Ada, Alma & Campoy, F. Isabel, trs. from ENG. (p. 574)
Parks, Carmen & Martinez, Edward. Farmers Market. (p. 574)
Parks, Deborah A. Nature's Machines: The Story of Biomechanist Mimi Koehl. (p. 1237)
Parks, Gordon, Jr., photos by see Parr, Ann.
Parks, Janis. House of Music. (p. 803)
Parks, M. Elizabeth. Sea Cow. (p. 1534)
Parks, Marquin. Wrinkles Wallace: Knights of Night School. (p. 1963)
Parks, Paul, illus. see Davey, Peter.
parks, peggy. Death Penalty. (p. 420)
Parks, Peggy. How Serious a Problem Is Synthetic Drug Use? (p. 812)
—Street Crime. (p. 1666)
Parks, Peggy, ed. see Nardo, Don.
Parks, Peggy J. Aliens. (p. 41)
—Alzheimer's Disease. (p. 51)
—Animal Experimentation. (p. 77)
—Anorexia. (p. 87)
—Anxiety Disorders. (p. 90)
—Aswan High Dam. (p. 109)
—Autism. (p. 117)
—Bipolar Disorder. (p. 190)
—Coal Power. (p. 336)
—Computer Animator. (p. 354)
—Computer Hacking. (p. 354)
—Cyberbullying. (p. 396)
parks, peggy j. Cyberterrorism. (p. 396)
Parks, Peggy J. DNA Evidence & Investigation. (p. 456)
—Doctor. (p. 459)
parks, peggy j. Does the Death Penalty Deter Crime? (p. 460)
Parks, Peggy J. Down Syndrome. (p. 474)
—Driving under the Influence. (p. 485)
—Drugs & Sports. (p. 487)
—Drunk Driving. (p. 487)
—Epilepsy. (p. 532)
—Fighter Pilot. (p. 585)
—Firefighter. (p. 591)
—Foods of France. (p. 614)
—Gangs. (p. 655)
—Garbage. (p. 655)
—Garbage & Recycling. (p. 655)
—Gay Rights. (p. 659)
—Genetic Disorders. (p. 660)
—Ghosts. (p. 672)
—Great Barrier Reef. (p. 714)
—Great Depression. (p. 715)
—Heroin Addiction. (p. 773)
—How Can Suicide Be Reduced? (p. 805)
—How Prevalent Is Racism in Society? (p. 812)
—Hpv. (p. 824)
—Importance of Plate Tectonic Theory. (p. 862)
—Impressionism. (p. 862)
—Influenza. (p. 873)
—Internet. (p. 880)
—Learning Disabilities. (p. 985)
—Leukemia. (p. 1003)
—Loch Ness Monster. (p. 1044)
—Musician. (p. 1194)
—Predicting Earthquakes. (p. 1395)
—Robert Fulton: Innovator with Steam Power. (p. 1479)
parks, peggy j. Schizophrenia. (p. 1521)
Parks, Peggy J. School Violence. (p. 1523)
—Self-Injury Disorder. (p. 1549)
—Smoking. (p. 1595)
—Space Research. (p. 1619)
—Sudden Infant Death Syndrome. (p. 1672)
—Teen Depression. (p. 1713)
—Teenage Eating Disorders. (p. 1714)
parks, peggy j. Teenage Sex & Pregnancy. (p. 1714)
Parks, Peggy J. Teenage Suicide. (p. 1714)
—Teens & Cheating. (p. 1714)
—Teens & Stress. (p. 1715)
—Teens & Substance Abuse. (p. 1715)
—Teens, Cutting, & Self-Injury. (p. 1715)
—Veterinarian. (p. 1839)
parks, peggy j. Video Games. (p. 1841)
Parks, Peggy J. Wind Power. (p. 1935)
—Witches. (p. 1941)
—Writer. (p. 1964)
Parks, Peter. How to Improve at Golf. (p. 820)
Parks, Phil, illus. see Halls, Kelly Milner.
Parks, Phil, illus. see Koontz, Dean.
Parks, Phil, illus. see Strange, Jason.
Parks, Sandra, jt. auth. see Black, Howard.
Parks, Sandra & Black, Howard. Dr. Funster's Visual B1: Creative Problem-Solving Fun. (p. 475)
—Organizing Thinking: Content Instruction, Critical Thinking, Graphic Organizers - Writing, Language Arts, Social Studies, Math, & Science. Bk. 1 (p. 1303)
—Organizing Thinking: Content Instruction, Critical Thinking, Graphic Organizers - Writing, Language Arts, Social Studies, Math, & Science. Bk. 2 (p. 1303)
Parks, Sheri. Fierce Angels: Living with a Legacy from the Sacred Dark Feminine to the Strong Black Woman. (p. 584)
Parks, Stewart. Beep! Beyond the Frogpond & Back. (p. 157)
Parks, Telisa. Abigail the Angel: Series. (p. 5)
—Bad Boy Brian: Series. (p. 131)
—Fred Never Did What His Parents Said: Bad Boys Gone Good: Volume 2. (p. 632)
Parks, Tim, jt. auth. see Calasso, Roberto.
Parks, Wendy. Dark Marriage. (p. 407)
Parlagreco, Aurora M., illus. see Cleary, Beverly.
Parlakian, Rebecca, jt. auth. see Lerner, Claire.
Parlato, Stephen. World That Loved Books. (p. 1958)
Parlett, David. Penguin Book of Card Games. (p. 1336)
Parlett, George, illus. see Anglo, Mick.
Parley, Peter, pseud & Chubb, Andrew. Tales about China & the Chinese. (p. 1701)
Parlin, Tim, illus. see Sutcliffe, Jane.
Parmalee, Thomas. Genetic Engineering. (p. 660)
—Legalized Gambling. (p. 988)
Parmar, Tavisha. Class Photograph. (p. 327)
Parme, Fabrice, illus. see Surget, Alain & Yeardley, Glynne.
Parme, Fabrice, jt. auth. see Trondheim, Lewis.
Parmelee, George, illus. see Berresford, J. R.
Parmenter, Wayne, illus. see Adams, Michelle Medlock.
Parmenter, Wayne, illus. see Spinelli, Eileen.
Parmer, Paul. Overcoming that "After-Camp Spiritual Dive" (p. 1314)
Parmley, Dave & Ruffing, Eric. Alternative ABCs. (p. 50)
Parnall, Peter, jt. auth. see Baylor, Byrd.
Parnell, Fran. Abominable Snowman: A Story from Nepal. Fatus, Sophie, illus. (p. 5)
—Barefoot Book of Monsters! Fatus, Sophie, illus. (p. 139)
—Feathered Ogre: A Story from Italy. Fatus, Sophie, illus. (p. 579)
—Mother of Monsters: A Story from South Africa. Fatus, Sophie, illus. (p. 1178)
Parnell, Fran & Fatus, Sophie. Grim, Grunt & Grizzle-Tail: A Story from Chile. Fatus, Sophie, illus. (p. 724)
—Rona Long-Teeth: A Story from Tahiti. Fatus, Sophie, illus. (p. 1486)
Parnell, Frances Baynor. Skills for Personal & Family Living: Teaching Package Teacher's Resource Guide. (p. 1585)
—Skills for Personal & Family Living: Teaching Package Teacher's Resource Portfolio. (p. 1585)
Parnell, Frances Baynor & Wooten, Joyce Honeycutt. Skills for Personal & Family Living. (p. 1585)
Parnell, Frances Baynor, et al. Party Bag. (p. 1326)
Parnell, Paul. Talking Rocks. (p. 1703)
Parnell, Peter, jt. auth. see Richardson, Justin.
Parnell, Robyn. Mighty Quinn. DeYoe, Katie & DeYoe, Aaron, illus. (p. 1140)
Parodi, Francesca, ed. Big Book of Solitaire. (p. 179)
Paroline, Michelle, illus. see Schweizer, Chris.
Paroline, Shelli, illus. see Lamb, Braden.
Paroline, Shelli, illus. see Lamb, Branden & Boom Studios Staff.
Paroline, Shelli, illus. see Monroe, Caleb & Lamb, Branden.
Paroline, Shelli, illus. see Monroe, Caleb.
Paroline, Shelli, illus. see North, Ryan & Lamb, Branden.
Paroline, Shelli, illus. see North, Ryan.
Paroline, Shelli, illus. see Schweizer, Chris.
Paroline, Shelli, illus. see Snider, Jesse Blaze.
Paroline, Shelli, jt. auth. see Monroe, Caleb.
Paroline, Shelli, jt. auth. see North, Ryan.
Parot, Annelore. Kimonos. (p. 957)
—Kokeshi Style: Design Your Own Kokeshi Fashions. (p. 966)
Parot, Annelore & Franceschelli, Christopher. Yumi. (p. 1983)
Parot, Annelore & Norman, Taylor. Kokeshi: Aoki. (p. 966)
Parower, Alec. So I Wrote It Down. (p. 1602)
Parpan, Justin. Gwango's Lonesome Trail. (p. 733)
Parr, Ann. Allisons. (p. 47)
—Gordon Parks: No Excuses Breidenthal, Kathryn, illus. (p. 702)
—Lowriders. (p. 1061)
Parr, Garnet A. Mosey. (p. 1176)
Parr, Jay. Door. (p. 470)
Parr, Letitia. When Sea & Sky Are Blue. Watts, John, illus. (p. 1904)
Parr, Maria. Adventures with Waffles. Forrester, Kate, illus. (p. 25)
Parr, Martin. Boring Postcards. (p. 214)
Parr, Martin, ed. see Badger, Gerry.
Parr, Martin, photos by see Williams, Val.
Parr, Martin, photos by. Think of England. (p. 1734)
Parr, Susan Sherwood. 30 Days Out of Depression. (p. 1996)
—Christopher's Adventures: A Prayer on Angel Wings. Paraschiv, Doina, illus. (p. 317)
—Christopher's Adventures: Chris Visits the Hospital Paraschiv, Doina, illus. (p. 317)
Parr, Todd. Animals in Underwear ABC. (p. 83)
—Blanco y Negro. (p. 198)
—Caritas. (p. 269)
—Daddy Book. (p. 398)
—Doggy Kisses 123. (p. 462)
—Earth Book. (p. 495)
—Esta Bien Ser Diferente. (p. 537)
—Family Book. (p. 568)
—Family Book. Parr, Todd, illus. (p. 568)
—Feel Good Book. (p. 580)
—Feelings Book. (p. 580)
—Gran Libro de la Amistad. Morell, Ivonne Bonsfill, tr. (p. 706)
—Grandma Book. (p. 708)
—Grandpa Book. (p. 709)
—I Love You Book. (p. 843)
—I Love You Book. Parr, Todd, illus. (p. 843)
—I'm Not Scared Book. (p. 859)
—It's Okay to Be Different. (p. 898)
—It's Okay to Make Mistakes. (p. 898)
—Libro de la Paz. (p. 1006)
—Mommy Book. (p. 1162)
—Mundo de Colores! Morell, Ivonne Bonsfill, tr. (p. 1191)
—Okay Book. (p. 1282)
—Otto Goes to School. (p. 1307)
—Otto Goes to the Beach. (p. 1307)
—Peace Book. (p. 1331)
—Pelos. (p. 1336)
—Reading Makes You Feel Good. (p. 1446)
—Si y No en el Zoo. (p. 1572)
—Thankful Book. (p. 1725)
—Todd Parr Create Your Own Planet. (p. 1761)
—Todd Parr Feelings Flash Cards. (p. 1761)
—Underwear Book. (p. 1817)
—We Belong Together: A Book about Adoption & Families. (p. 1866)
—¡Me Gusta Ser Como Soy! Morell, Ivonne Bonsfill, tr. (p. 1116)
Parr, Todd & Chronicle Books Staff. Save the Blue. (p. 1516)
Parr, Todd & Pickthall M.M. Staff. Do's & Don'ts. (p. 472)
Parr, Tom. Reading Makes You Feel Good. (p. 1446)
Parra, Angelo, jt. auth. see Johnson, Nerissa.
Parra, B. A. Mystery at Hidden Valley Lodge. (p. 1223)
Parra, Jaime Barrera, tr. see Sun-Tzu.
Parra, Jen. Crazy Old Lou. Meier, Paul, illus. (p. 378)
—Princess Shannon & the Yellow Moon. Meier, Paul, illus. (p. 1405)
Parra, John, illus. see Bildner, Phil.
Parra, John, illus. see Brown, Monica.
Parra, John, illus. see Johnston, Tony.
Parra, John, illus. see Thong, Roseanne Greenfield.
Parra, John, illus. see Thong, Roseanne.
Parra, John, jt. auth. see Mora, Pat.
Parra, Kelly. Graffiti Girl. (p. 705)
Parra, Rocio, illus. see Arciniegas, Triunfo.
Parra, Rocio, illus. see Reyes, Carlos Jose.
Parra, Rocio, illus. see Rodriguez, Julia.
Parragon Publishing Staff. Busy Day at the Airport. (p. 246)
—Busy Day at the Construction Site. (p. 246)
—Busy Day at the Farm. (p. 246)
—I'm a Big Sister. (p. 858)
Parragon Publishing Staff, contrib. by. Universe: The Ultimate Guided Tour of the Cosmos from the Formation of Stars to the Farthest Reaches of the Universe. (p. 1820)
Parragon Staff. Alice in Wonderland: The Magical Story. (p. 39)
—Celebrate the Year with Winnie the Pooh. (p. 284)
—Disney Princess Sparkling Dreams. (p. 453)
—Disney Toy Story 3: Toy Stars. (p. 453)
—Disney's Alice in Wonderland. (p. 453)

—Dumbo: The Magical Story. (p. 489)
—Dumbo. (p. 489)
—Lion King. (p. 1020)
—Mickey Mouse: Adventure Tales & Stories. (p. 1136)
—My Book of Winnie the Pooh. (p. 1199)
—Once upon a Time with Winnie the Pooh. (p. 1293)
—Pinocchio: The Magical Story. (p. 1360)
—Tigger's Adventure. (p. 1749)
Parragon Staff, ed. Cerdito. (p. 287)
—Corderito. (p. 366)
—Words. (p. 1951)
Parramón Editorial Team. Urban Sketching & Painting. (p. 1825)
Parramón, José María. Mi Calle. Borday, Irene, illus. (p. 1132)
—Mi Casa. Borday, Irene, illus. (p. 1132)
—Mi Escuela. Borday, Irene, illus. (p. 1132)
—Mi Jardin. Borday, Irene, illus. (p. 1132)
Parramón, José María & Bordoy, Irene. Estoy En: Mi Casa (My House) (p. 538)
—Estoy En: Mi Jardin (In My Yard) (p. 538)
—Mi Calle. (p. 1132)
—Mi Escuela. (p. 1132)
Parramon Staff & Costa-Pau, Rosa. Gorilas. (p. 702)
Parramon Staff & Gassós, Dolors. China. (p. 306)
—Mayas. (p. 1113)
Parramon's Editorial Team, jt. auth. see Parramon's Editorial Team Staff.
Parramon's Editorial Team Staff. Papier-Mâché. Parramon's Editorial Team Staff, photos by. (p. 1323)
—Recyclables. Parramon's Editorial Team Staff, photos by. (p. 1452)
—Stones & "Stuff" Parramon's Editorial Team Staff, photos by. (p. 1653)
Parramon's Editorial Team Staff, jt. auth. see Llimos Plomer, Anna.
Parramon's Editorial Team Staff & Parramon's Editorial Team. Metal. Parramon's Editorial Team Staff, photos by. (p. 1130)
Parramore, Helen. Brian's Bird Book. (p. 227)
—Fragments of Fern Valley. (p. 639)
—Maudie's Promise: A Girl on the Florida Frontier. (p. 1110)
—Where Do Babies Come From? (p. 1906)
Parramore, Thomas C. Triumph at Kitty Hawk: The Wright Brothers & Powered Flight. (p. 1787)
Parratore, Phil. 101 Hands-On Science Experiments. (p. 1999)
Parri, Celia. Cyfoeth Cudd y Capten: Llyfr Stori a Phosau. (p. 397)
Parriera Jr., Jack. What to Do When Your Brother Is Sick. (p. 1894)
Parrinder, Patric, ed. see Wells, H. G.
Parrini, Sabrina. Little Kitchen: 40 Delicious & Simple Things That Children Can Really Make. (p. 1030)
—Little Kitchen: 40 Delicious & Simple Things That Children Can Really Make. Melville, Jacqui, photos by. (p. 1030)
Parris, Kitty, illus. see Batchler, Darla.
Parrish, Amanda. Greyhound Travels: Puma Travels to Italy. (p. 723)
Parrish, Anya. Damage. (p. 401)
Parrish, Charles & Naurlght, John. Soccer Around the World: A Cultural Guide to the Worlds Favorite Sport (p. 1603)
Parrish, Edith. Sarah the Purple Goose Gets Lost. Odom, Kelly, illus. (p. 1514)
Parrish, Edith E. It's Not Easy Being a Purple Goose. Odom, Kelly, illus. (p. 898)
—Sara the Purple Goose & Susan the Black Swan. (p. 1514)
Parrish, Emma. Doodle Farm: Oodles of Mooing, Oinking, & Quacking Doodles to Complete & Create. (p. 469)
—Halloween Doodles: Spooky Designs to Complete & Create. (p. 737)
—Lou. (p. 1057)
—Spooky Doodles: Ghostly Designs to Complete & Create. (p. 1631)
Parrish, Emma, jt. auth. see Wilson, Hannah.
Parrish, Fayrene. Pancho Saves the Day: Shipmates Learning Adventures Venture. Parrish, Fayrene, illus. (p. 1320)
Parrish, Harry. Kate & Alice. (p. 944)
Parrish, Jim. Dog Gone. (p. 461)
Parrish, Kat. Micah & the Magic Helment: The Helmet & the Dragon. Milam, C. J., illus. (p. 1134)
Parrish, MariLee. God Hearts Me: 3-Minute Devotions for Girls on the Go! (p. 689)
Parrish, Maxfield, illus. see Anonymous.
Parrish, Maxfield, illus. see Saunders, Louise.
Parrish, R. M. Jillian of Peach Creek Stables. (p. 917)
Parrish, Terry. Wiffenpoof. (p. 1927)
Parrish, William E., et al. Missouri: The Heart of the Nation. (p. 1154)
Parrott, Darcie. Ladybug's Walk. (p. 971)
Parrott, Heather, illus. see von Rosenberg, Byron.
Parrott, Les, III & Parrott, Leslie. I Love You More: How Everyday Problems Can Strenghten Your Marriage (p. 843)
Parrott, Leslie, jt. auth. see Parrott, Les, III.
Parrott, Matt. Daniel & the Bear. (p. 404)
Parry, A., jt. auth. see Parry, L.
Parry, Alan. Badger's Christmas Day. Parry, Linda, illus. (p. 132)
—Badger's Easter Surprise. Parry, Linda, illus. (p. 132)
—Badger's Lovely Day. Parry, Linda, illus. (p. 132)
—Bible Made Easy: A Pop-Up, Pull-Out, Interactive Bible Adventure. Parry, Linda, illus. (p. 175)
—Discover Oaktree Woods: A Touch & Feel Book. Parry, Linda, illus. (p. 447)
—First Seven Days. Parry, Linda, illus. (p. 596)
—Goodnight Prayers. Parry, Linda, illus. (p. 701)
—Mouse Can't Sleep. Parry, Linda, illus. (p. 1182)
—Never Mind Squirrel. Parry, Linda, illus. (p. 1243)
—Rabbit Helps Out. Parry, Linda, illus. (p. 1429)
—Woodland Bible Stories. Parry, Linda, illus. (p. 1949)
Parry, Alan, illus. see Dowley, Tim.
Parry, Alan, jt. auth. see Parry, Linda.
Parry, Alan & Parry, Linda. Herald Angels. (p. 769)
—Look for the Rainbow: Look Through the Telescope, Lift the Flaps, Work the Puzzles, See the Pop-Ups, & Enjoy Hours of Fun with Noah. (p. 1049)
Parry, Ann. Amnesty International. (p. 65)
—Doctors Without Borders: Medecins Sans Frontieres. (p. 459)
—Greenpeace. (p. 723)
—Save the Children. (p. 1516)
Parry, Glyn. Last Gasp. (p. 977)
Parry, Glyn, jt. auth. see Perry, Glyn.
Parry, Jo. Blast Off! (p. 198)
—Rainbow Fairies. (p. 1435)
—Under the Rainbow. (p. 1814)
Parry, Jo, illus. see Baxter, Nicola & Francis, Jan.
Parry, Jo, illus. see Baxter, Nicola.
Parry, Jo, illus. see David, Juliet.
Parry, Jo, illus. see Depisco, Dorothea.
Parry, Jo, illus. see DePrisco, Dorothea.
Parry, Jo, illus. see Doyle, Malachy.
Parry, Jo, illus. see Freedman, Claire.
Parry, Jo, illus. see Imperato, Teresa.
Parry, Jo, illus. see Ranson, Erin.
Parry, Jo, illus. see Thomas Nelson Publishing Staff.
Parry, Jo, illus. see Top That Publishing Staff, ed.
Parry, Jo, illus. see Top That!.
Parry Jones, Terence Graham, see Fairgray, Richard & Jones, Terry.
Parry Jones, Terence Graham, see Jones, Terry.
Parry, L. Jesus Hace Amigos (Jesus Makes Friends) (p. 915)
—Jesus Llama a Sus Discipulos (Jesus Calls His Disciples) (p. 915)
Parry, L. & Parry, A. Siguiendo la Estrella Actividades. (p. 1574)
Parry, Linda. Bible Story Time with Mr. Bear (p. 176)
—Prayer Time with Mr. Bear (p. 1393)
Parry, Linda, illus. see Parry, Alan.
Parry, Linda, jt. auth. see Parry, Alan.
Parry, Linda & Parry, Alan. Baby Jesus: A Touch & Feel Book. (p. 126)
—Bear's First Bible. (p. 152)
—Christmastime with Mr. Bear. (p. 316)
—Follow the Star. (p. 612)
Parry, Michael. Nanobot. (p. 1229)
Parry, Robert W. Chemistry: Experimental Foundations. (p. 297)
Parry, Rosanne. Daddy's Home! Leonard, David, illus. (p. 399)
—Heart of a Shepherd. (p. 759)
—Second Fiddle. (p. 1539)
—Written in Stone. (p. 1965)
Parsa, Mona. And So You Were Born. Kilmer, Nidra N., illus. (p. 71)
Parsley, Elise. If You Ever Want to Bring an Alligator to School, Dont! (p. 854)
Parsloe, Alismarie, illus. see Brown, Kathy.
Parsonage, Betty. Butterfly Wings. (p. 248)
Parsons, Alexandra & Barnes, Jon. Plants. (p. 1369)
Parsons, Arielle, illus. see Stanley, Phillip Orin, 2nd.
Parsons, Ash. Still Waters. (p. 1650)
Parsons, Bruce. Siah Carter & the Ship Monitor. (p. 1572)
Parsons, Carol. Mystery at Eagle Harbor Lighthouse. (p. 1223)
Parsons, Caroline Renee. Coffins in the Basement. (p. 338)
Parsons, Colin. Wizards' Kingdom. (p. 1943)
Parsons, Corey. I Can Read. (p. 836)
Parsons, Deborah L. Djuna Barnes. (p. 455)
Parsons, Elsie Worthington Clews. American Indian Life, by Several of its Students. (p. 62)
Parsons, Garry. Krong! Parsons, Garry, illus. (p. 968)
Parsons, Garry, illus. see Bently, Peter.
Parsons, Garry, illus. see Clarke, Jane.
Parsons, Garry, illus. see Donaldson, Julia.
Parsons, Garry, illus. see Grabham, Tim, et al.
Parsons, Garry, illus. see Gray, Kes.
Parsons, Garry, illus. see Hawking, Lucy & Hawking, Stephen W.
Parsons, Garry, illus. see Hawking, Stephen W. & Hawking, Lucy.
Parsons, Garry, illus. see Jones, Gareth P.
Parsons, Garry, illus. see Mayfield, Sue.
Parsons, Garry, illus. see Waite, Judy.
Parsons, Garry, jt. auth. see Gray, Kes.
Parsons, Gary, illus. see Agnew, Kate.
Parsons, Gary, illus. see Donaldson, Julia.
Parsons, Gary, illus. see Doyle, Malachy.
Parsons, Jackie, illus. see Jugran, Jan.
Parsons, Jayne, ed. see Dorling Kindersley Publishing Staff.
Parsons, Julie. Julianne & the Jinn, the Evil Genie. (p. 932)
Parsons, Leif. Only Fish Fall from the Sky. (p. 1298)
Parsons, Marcella & Young, Steven H. Sandlot Stories. (p. 1511)
Parsons, Marcella & Young, Steven Hayes. Sandlot Stories - Japanese. (p. 1511)
Parsons, Mark Huntley. Road Rash. (p. 1477)
Parsons, Martin. Women's War. (p. 1947)
Parsons, Michelle Hyde. Fighting Disease. (p. 585)
—Forests. (p. 618)
—Heredity. (p. 771)
—Ocean Pollution. (p. 1276)
—Oil Spills. (p. 1282)
—Your Skeleton. (p. 1981)
Parsons, Pateh. Lickitysplit, the Handicapped Horse. (p. 1007)
Parsons, Rob. 60 Minute Father. (p. 1997)
Parsons, Sally, illus. see Henry, Marcia.
Parsons, Sandra J. What Could a Kid Do? (p. 1881)
Parsons, Sarah. Clearing Season: Reflections for Lent. (p. 330)
Parsons, Stella, et al. Cover Story: Have You Got What It Takes to Be a Magazine Editor? (p. 373)
Parsons, Tom. Pinky the Rat at the Brussels Sprout Museum. (p. 1360)
Parsons, William B., Jr. Tough Talk about Fat! How to Reach & Maintain Your Ideal Weight. (p. 1773)
Parsons Yazzie, Evangeline. Little Woman Warrior Who Came Home. Ruffenach, Jessie, ed. (p. 1038)
Part, Michael, ed. see Masannak, Joachim.
Partee, Andrea. Jed, the Boy, the Snake & the Window. (p. 911)
Parthen, Kelly & Selp, Shannon Payette. Bean Appétit: Hip & Healthy Ways to Have Fun with Food. (p. 150)
Particular, Nowen N. Boomtown (p. 213)
Partil, Sravan. Measuring Quilts: Understand Concepts of Area (p. 1117)
Partin, Charlotte Corry. Charlotte's Garden. Bine-Stock, Eve Heidi, ed. (p. 293)
Partin, Judith E. Songs in the Night: (A Collection of Hymns, Choruses, & Songs...) (p. 1612)
Partis, Joanne. Look at Me! Partis, Joanne, illus. (p. 1048)
Partis, Joanne, illus. see Nilsen, Anna.
Partner, Daniel. Bible Devotions for Bedtime. (p. 175)
Partnership Staff, jt. compiled by see LeapFrog Staff.
Parton, Daron. Alligator in an Anorak. (p. 47)
Parton, Daron, jt. auth. see Brasch, Nicolas.
Parton, Matthew R. My Closet Monster Ate My Homework (p. 1200)
Parton, Nigel. Safeguarding Children: Early Intervention & Surveillance in a Late Modern Society. (p. 1502)
Parton, Paua, illus. see Parton, Paula.
Parton, Paula. I Always Wondered. Parton, Paula, illus. (p. 831)
—Room 17 'Where History Comes Alive!' Book Ii, Explorers. (p. 1488)
—Room 17 Where History Comes Alive! Book I-Indians. Parton, Paua, illus. (p. 1488)
—Room 17 Where History Comes Alive Book I—Indians. Parton, Paula, illus. (p. 1488)
—Room 17 - Where History Comes Alive - Missions. Parton, Paula, illus. (p. 1488)
—We Love Christmas! Parton, Paula, illus. (p. 1867)
Parton, Sarah. Cleisthenes: Founder of Athenian Democracy. (p. 330)
Partow, Donna. Becoming a Vessel God Can Use. (p. 156)
Partridge, Elizabeth. Dogtag Summer. (p. 463)
—Marching for Freedom: Walk Together, Children, & Don't You Grow Weary. (p. 1092)
Partridge, Helen L. Blinky: The Bear Who Wouldn't Hibernate. (p. 199)
Partridge, Kenneth. Louis Armstrong. (p. 1058)
—Marian Anderson. (p. 1093)
Parts, Art, illus. see Nosek, Jude.
Parunia, Des. Quest for the Magic Funnel. (p. 1426)
Parus, M. V. Adventures of Mamma Simone, Jodie & Zed: The Mystery of the Pirate's Lost Treasure. (p. 20)
Parveen, Tahmina. Realistic Rhymes. (p. 1449)
Parvensky Barwell, Catherine A. Tommi Goes Camping Barwell, Matthew W. et al, eds. (p. 1764)
—Tommi Goes to the Beach Barwell, Matthew W. & Parvensky, Mary T., eds. (p. 1764)
—Tommi Lance Grows Up (p. 1764)
—Tommi's First Snowfall (p. 1764)
Parvensky, Mary T., ed. see Parvensky Barwell, Catherine A.
Parvis, Sarah. Creepy Castles. (p. 381)
—Ghost Towns. (p. 672)
—Haunted Hotels. (p. 753)
—Taylor Lautner. (p. 1708)
Parzit, Andy. World Class Mulligans: For Golfers with Extra Balls. (p. 1954)
Parzybok, Tye W. Extreme Weather in the West. (p. 557)
Pasachoff, Jay M. Peterson First Guide to Astronomy. (p. 1347)
Pasachoff, Naomi E. Barbara Mcclintock: Genius of Genetics. (p. 137)
—Basic Judaism for Young People: God. Vol. 3 (p. 142)
—Ernest Rutherford: Father of Nuclear Science. (p. 533)
—Linus Pauling: Advancing Science, Advocating Peace. (p. 1019)
—Niels Bohr: Physicist & Humanitarian. (p. 1251)
—Student's Guide to T. S. Eliot. (p. 1669)
—Student's Guide to the Brontë Sisters. (p. 1669)
Pasala, Jan, jt. auth. see Dusek, Jiri.
Pasca, Pamela. If I Lived in a Balloon. (p. 853)
Pascal, Francine. Ambiente Hostil. (p. 57)
—Amigacho de Pluma del Amy. (p. 65)
—Atrapada. (p. 113)
—Betrayed. (p. 172)
—Bromas de Primavera. (p. 230)
—Cambios Oportunos. (p. 255)
—Centro de Atencion. (p. 287)
—Con las Riendas Firmes. (p. 355)
—Demasiado Perfecta. (p. 425)
—Dinero Desaparecido. (p. 440)
—Esa Clase de Chica. (p. 534)
—Estrella del Rock. (p. 538)
—Falsas Apariencias. (p. 567)
—Fearless: Fearless; Sam; Run. (p. 579)
—Fearless 2: Twisted; Kiss; Payback. (p. 579)
—Fearless 3: Rebel; Heat; Blood. (p. 579)
—Flechazo. (p. 603)
—Gemelos Consiguen Cogidos. (p. 659)
—Gran Luchadora. (p. 706)
—Guerra Entre los Gemelos. (p. 728)
—Haciendo Novelas. (p. 735)
—Jessica's Secreto. (p. 914)
—Kill Game. (p. 956)
—Larga Noche. (p. 975)
—Libertad Incondicional. (p. 1005)
—Lo Que los Padres Ignoran. (p. 1044)
—Lucha por la Fama. (p. 1062)
—Lust. (p. 1066)
—Mala Idea de Jessica. (p. 1083)
—Maria Falta. (p. 1093)
—Mocosos. (p. 1157)
—My First Love & Other Disasters: My First Love & Other Disasters; Love & Betrayal & Hold the Mayo; My Mother Was Never a Kid. (p. 1207)
—My First Love & Other Disasters. (p. 1207)
—Nueva Mirada de Jessica. (p. 1270)
—Otra Oportunidad. (p. 1307)
—Peligrosa Tentacion. (p. 1336)
—Playing with Fire. (p. 1372)
—Principe para Elisabeth. (p. 1406)
—Querida Hermana. (p. 1425)
—Rebelde con Causa. (p. 1451)
—Ruling Class. (p. 1495)
—Terror de la Escuela. (p. 1722)
—Trabajo del Equipo. (p. 1774)
Pascal, Francine & Frost, Michael. Live Bait. (p. 1039)
Pascal, Francine & Suzanne, Jamie. Señorita Jessica. (p. 1550)
Pascal, Janet. What Is the Panama Canal? (p. 1890)
—What Was the Hindenburg? (p. 1895)
—What Was the Hindenburg? Groff, David & McVeigh, Kevin, illus. (p. 1895)
—Where Is the Empire State Building? (p. 1909)
—Where Is the Empire State Building? on, Daniel & Groff, David, illus. (p. 1909)
—Who Was Abraham Lincoln? Harrison, Nancy & O'Brien, John, illus. (p. 1918)
—Who Was Dr. Seuss? Harrison, Nancy, illus. (p. 1918)
—Who Was Isaac Newton? (p. 1918)
—Who Was Isaac Newton? Foley, Tim & Harrison, Nancy, illus. (p. 1918)
—Who Was Maurice Sendak? (p. 1919)
Pascal, Janet, jt. auth. see Dubowski, Cathy East.
Pascal, Janet B. What Is the Panama Canal? Foley, Tim & Harper, Fred, illus. (p. 1890)
Pascale, Louise M., ed. Children's Songs from Afghanistan. (p. 304)
Pascaretti, Vicki & Wilkie, Sara. Super Smart Information Strategies: Team Up Online. (p. 1682)
—Super Smart Information Strategies: Team up Online. (p. 1682)
Paschal Shija. Proud Kid & the Stream. (p. 1412)
Paschalis, Juli. Druan o Mam! (p. 486)
Paschall, Patricia, ed. see Newcomb, Kristene.
Paschen, Elise. Poetry Speaks to Children. Collins, Billy et al, eds. (p. 1376)
Paschen, Elise & Raccah, Dominique. Poetry Speaks Who I Am: Poems of Discovery, Inspiration, Independence, & Everything Else. (p. 1376)
Paschkis, Julie. Apple Cake: A Recipe for Love. (p. 92)
—Flutter & Hum / Aleteo y Zumbido: Animal Poems / Poemas de Animales. Paschkis, Julie, illus. (p. 608)
—Great Smelly, Slobbery, Small-Tooth Dog: A Folktale from Great Britain. (p. 718)
—Mooshka, a Quilt Story Paschkis, Julie, illus. (p. 1173)
—P. Zonka Lays an Egg Paschkis, Julie, illus. (p. 1316)
Paschkis, Julie, illus. see Brown, Monica.
Paschkis, Julie, illus. see Engle, Margarita.
Paschkis, Julie, illus. see Fleischman, Paul.
Paschkis, Julie, illus. see Khan, Hena.
Paschkis, Julie, illus. see Lord, Janet.
Paschkis, Julie, illus. see MacDonald, Margaret Read.
Paschkis, Julie, illus. see Paye, Won-Ldy & Lippert, Margaret H.
Paschkis, Julie, illus. see Rodriguez, Rachel Victoria.
Paschkis, Julie, illus. see Shannon, George.
Paschkis, Julie, illus. see Wong, Janet S.
Paschkis, Julie, jt. auth. see Wong, Janet S.
Pasco, Elizabeth, ed. see Norsic, Donald.
PASCO Scientific Staff, prod. Advanced Biology. (p. 13)
Pascoe, Bruce. Fog a Dox. (p. 611)
Pascoe, Elaine. Animals with Backbones. (p. 84)
—Animals Without Backbones. (p. 84)
—Bugs. Kuhn, Dwight, illus. (p. 237)
—Ecosystem of a Garden. (p. 503)
—Ecosystem of a Grassy Field. (p. 503)
—Ecosystem of a Milkweed Patch. (p. 503)
—Ecosystem of a Stream. (p. 503)
—Ecosystem of an Apple Tree. (p. 503)
—Flowers. (p. 608)
—History Around You: A Unique Look at the Past, People, & Places of New York. (p. 783)
—Plant Clones. (p. 1369)
Pascoe, Elaine, ed. see Corwin, Jeff.
Pascoe, Elaine, jt. auth. see Schwartz, David M.
Pascoe, Jed, illus. see Kempton, Clive & Atkin, Alan.
Pascoe, Jed, illus. see Moses, Brian, ed.
Pascoe, Jill. Arizona's Haunted History. (p. 99)
Pascoe, Matt. Chaos Island: A Daisy Albright Adventure. (p. 291)
Pascoe, Pete, illus. see Bowater, Alan.
Pascual, Dennis Mark. Adventures of Dj the Butterfly & Friends Series Presents Dj's Birthday Party. (p. 17)
Pascual, Emilio. Dias de Reyes Magos. Serrano, Javier U., illus. (p. 435)
Pascual Marquina, Cira. Newspapers: A Project by Siemon Allen. (p. 1249)
Pascual, P. V. Beautiful Witch. (p. 154)
Pascual, Vincent. Bokabok Meets Diggy. (p. 208)
Pascucci, Adele. Duck on a Dock. (p. 488)
Pascucci, Mary Ann. Adventures on Green Pasture Farm Scruff: An Orphan Lamb. (p. 24)
Pascuzzo, Margaret I. Anton Loses a Friend. Bicking, Judith, illus. (p. 90)
Pascuzzo, Philip, illus. see Marlowe, Sara.
Pasda Diedwardo, Maryann & Pasda, Patricia J. Pennsylvania Voices Book Xi: The Marvelous Nature Alphabet Book. (p. 1338)
Pasda, Patricia J., jt. auth. see Pasda Diedwardo, Maryann.
Pasha, Georgia. Jelly Bean & Key Mystery. (p. 912)
Pashilk, Meri. Pearl the Turtle. (p. 1333)
Pashley, Hilton. Gabriel's Clock. (p. 652)
Pashley, Marian. Pick Your Brains about France. (p. 1354)
Pasiadis, Vanessa. Don't Call Me Cookie. Lowenstein, Anna, illus. (p. 467)
Pasillo, Susan. Perfect Pumpkin. (p. 1342)
Pasishnychenko, Oksana, illus. see Everett, Melissa.
Paske, Stephen. Breaking Stride. (p. 225)
Paskevska, Anna. Ballet Beyond Tradition. (p. 134)
Pasko, Martin & Loughridge, Lee. Prankster of Prime Time Burchett, Rick, illus. (p. 1393)

P

Pasnak, William. Ginger Princess (p. 677)
Pasquale, Dave. Blair the Bear. (p. 198)
Pasquali, Elena. Ituku's Christmas Journey Kolanovic, Dubravka, illus. (p. 900)
—Lion Little Book of Bedtime Stories. Smee, Nicola, illus. (p. 1020)
—Lion Nursery Bible. Lamont, Priscilla, illus. (p. 1020)
—Safe This Night: A Book of Bedtime Prayers. Kolanovic, Dubravka, illus. (p. 1502)
—Safely Through the Night. Kolanovic, Dubravka, illus. (p. 1502)
—Santa's Midnight Sleighride. Vagnozzi, Barbara, illus. (p. 1513)
—Two-Minute Bible Stories. Smee, Nicola, illus. (p. 1804)
Pasquali, Elena, jt. auth. see Dickson, John.
Pasquali, Elena & Vagnozzi, Barbara. Go Hare & Tortoise Go! (p. 686)
—Run Little Chicken Run! (p. 1496)
Pasqualin, Marcia A. Good Ozzy, Bad Bella: Sight Words for First Readers. (p. 700)
Pasqualini, Rosie. Nantarctica: Twilight-Water. (p. 1229)
Pasques, Patrick. Savanna Animals. (p. 1516)
Pass, Emma. Acid. (p. 9)
Pass, Erica. Hooray for Dads! (p. 795)
—SpongeBob LovePants. Schigiel, Gregg, illus. (p. 1630)
Pass, Erica & Artifact Group Staff. Hooray for Dads! (p. 795)
Passamani, Julia, jt. auth. see Lenhart, Kristin.
Passaniti, Connie. Fairy Garden Zodiac Adventure. (p. 563)
Passantino, Claire. Itty Bitty Bytes of Space: For the TI 99-4A Computer. (p. 900)
—Matilda, the Computer Cat: For the TI 99-4A. (p. 1109)
Passarella, Jennie, illus. see Autrey, Jacquelyn & Yeager, Alice.
Passaro, John. Frederick Douglass. (p. 633)
Passel, Martha. No Bullies in Our Trees Please. (p. 1258)
Passen, Lisa. Attack of the 50-Foot Teacher. (p. 113)
—Monkey Mountain. (p. 1165)
Passero, Barbara. Energy Alternatives. (p. 528)
Passes, David. Dragon Legends. (p. 477)
—Dragons: Truth, Myth & Legend. Anderson, Wayne, illus. (p. 478)
Passey, Brent. Spaghetti for Shoestrings. (p. 1620)
Passey, Joel. Treween. (p. 1785)
Passey, Marion. My Tiny Book of Family. (p. 1220)
—My Tiny Book of Joseph Smith. (p. 1220)
—Sneezles & Wheezles. Harston, Jerry, illus. (p. 1597)
Passicot, Monique, illus. see Schwartz, Howard.
Passman, Emily, illus. see Bissex, Rachel.
Passport Books Staff, ed. German Picture Dictionary. Goodman, Marlene, illus. (p. 666)
—Italian Picture Dictionary. Goodman, Marlene, illus. (p. 894)
—Japanese Picture Dictionary: Elementary Through Junior High. Goodman, Marlene, illus. (p. 909)
—Let's Learn American English. Goodman, Marlene, illus. (p. 998)
—Let's Learn Hebrew. Goodman, Marlene, illus. (p. 998)
Passudetti, Christopher. Being Sara. (p. 161)
Pastan, Amy, et al. Gandhi: A Photographic Stroy of Life. (p. 655)
—Martin Luther King, Jr. (p. 1098)
Pastars, Chris, illus. see O'Neil, Patrick.
Pastel, Elyse, illus. see Bergen, Lara.
Pastel, JoAnne & Fitzsimmons, Kakie. Bur Bur & Friends 3 volume Set. VanDeWeghe, Lindsay & Bohnet, Christopher, illus. (p. 243)
Pasternac, Susana, tr. see Capucilli, Alyssa Satin.
Pasternack, Susan, ed. see Mahony, Mary.
Pasternack, Susan, ed. see Spray, Michelle.
Pasternak, Boris Leonidovich. Doktor Zivago. (p. 463)
Pasternak, Carol. How to Raise Monarch Butterflies: A Step-by-Step Guide for Kids. (p. 821)
Pasternak, Ceel. Cool Careers for Girls in Travel & Hospitality. (p. 362)
Pasternak, Harley. 5-Factor Diet. (p. 1992)
Pastis, Stephan. Beginning Pearls. (p. 159)
—Croc Ate My Homework. (p. 384)
—Mistakes Were Made. Pastis, Stephan, illus. (p. 1155)
—Now Look What You've Done. Pastis, Stephan, illus. (p. 1269)
—Skip School, Fly to Space: A Pearls Before Swine Collection. (p. 1586)
—Timmy Failure: Mistakes Were Made. Pastis, Stephan, illus. (p. 1754)
—Timmy Failure: Mistakes Were Made. (p. 1755)
Pastis, Stephan, jt. auth. see Schulz, Charles M.
Pastor, A. Pearl Box: Containing One Hundred Beautiful Stories for Young People. (p. 1333)
Pastor Fernández, Andrea. Contar. (p. 360)
—Vista. (p. 1846)
Pastor, Luis, tr. see Nöstlinger, Christine.
Pastor, N. Allie Mckay: And the Keepers of the Golden Cross. (p. 47)
Pastor, Norma. Young Alchemists & the Vatican's Legion of Evil. (p. 1978)
Pastor, Terry, illus. see Bone, Emily.
Pastor, Terry, illus. see Hawcock, David.
Pastor Wil. It's Good, Okay, & Alright (p. 897)
Pastore, Laurie & Allyn, Pam. Complete Year in Reading & Writing: Daily Lessons - Monthly Units - Yearlong Calendar. (p. 353)
Pastore, Vicki. Apostles' Creed. (p. 92)
Pastrovicchio, Lorenzo, illus. see Alvarez, Miguel, et al.
Pastrovicchio, Lorenzo, illus. see Ambrosio, Stefano.
Pastuchiv, Olga, illus. see Caduto, Michael J.
Pat Carlin, Carlin & Carlin, Patricia. Cow & her Car. (p. 373)
Pata, Sharae & Linzy, Jan. Poodle (Standard) Champions, 1983-2003. (p. 1383)
Patacchiola, Amy, illus. see Conner, Bobbi.
Patacrúa. Baby Whiskers. Simatoribus, Alessandra, illus. (p. 128)
Patagonia School, illus. see Chesne, Sabrina.
Patch, Lisa. Tales of the Lush Green Woods. Patch, Michael, illus. (p. 1702)
Patch, Michael, illus. see Amdahl Elco, Anita & Welkert Stelmach, Katherine.
Patch, Michael, illus. see Gerencher, Jane.
Patch, Michael, illus. see Patch, Lisa.
Patch, Sebastion, illus. see The Fairy, Thimble.
Patchett, F. Plane Fun. (p. 1367)
—Planes. (p. 1367)
Patchett, F. & King, Colin. Planes. King, Colin, illus. (p. 1367)
Patchett, Fiona. 30 Yummy Things to Bake. (p. 1996)
—Eggs & Chicks. (p. 506)
—Eggs & Chicks. Kushii, Tetsuo & Wray, Zoe, illus. (p. 506)
—Introduction to Spreadsheets: Using Microsoft Excel 2000 or Microsoft Office 2000. (p. 882)
—Ponies (First Sticker Book) Finn, Rebecca, illus. (p. 1382)
—Puss in Boots. (p. 1420)
—Rabbits. (p. 1430)
—Starting Fishing: Internet-Linked. (p. 1644)
—Starting Fishing - Internet Linked. Venus, Joanna, illus. (p. 1644)
—Under the Sea. Kushii, Tetsuo, illus. (p. 1814)
—Under the Sea. Ibrahim, Nouran, tr. from ARA. (p. 1814)
—Under the Sea. Kushii, Tetsuo & Wray, Zoe, illus. (p. 1814)
—Usborne Healthy Cookbook. Dreidemy, Joëlle, illus. (p. 1827)
Patchett, Fiona, et al. Children's Book of Baking. Allman, Howard, photos by. (p. 303)
Patchett, Kaye. Robert Goddard: Rocket Pioneer. (p. 1479)
Patchett, Mary E. Flight to the Misty Planet. (p. 604)
Patchett, Mary Elwyn. Ajax: Golden Dog of the Australian Bush. Tansley, Eric, illus. (p. 32)
—Great Barrier Reef. Monroe, Joan Kiddell, illus. (p. 714)
Patchett, Terry. Nation. (p. 1231)
Patchin, Frank Gee. Pony Rider Boys in New Mexico. (p. 1383)
—Pony Rider Boys in Texas: Or- the Veiled Riddle of the Plains. (p. 1383)
—Pony Rider Boys in the Grand Canyon: The Mystery of Bright Angel Gulch. (p. 1383)
Patchin, Justin W. & Hinduja, Sameer. Words Wound: Delete Cyberbullying & Make Kindness Go Viral. (p. 1952)
Pate, Ginger. Look Left, Look Right, Look Left Again. Pennell, Rhett / R., illus. (p. 1049)
—Would You Invite a Skunk to Your Wedding? Blanski, Maribeth, illus. (p. 1962)
Pate, Rodney, illus. see Miller, William.
Pate, Rodney, tr. see Miller, William.
Pate, Rodney S., illus. see Miller, William.
Pate, Rodney S., illus. see Patrick, Denise Lewis.
Pate, Rodney S., illus. see Walker, Sally M.
Patel, Mukul. We've Got Your Number. Sahai, Supriya, illus. (p. 1877)
Patel, Raj, jt. ed. see Holt-Giménez, Eric.
Patel, Sanjay & Haynes, Emily. Ganesha's Sweet Tooth. (p. 655)
Patel, Sanjay J. & Haynes, Emily. Ganesha's Sweet Tooth. (p. 655)
Patel, T. M. Immigrant: Stargazer. (p. 861)
Pateman, Robert. Denmark. (p. 426)
Pateman, Robert & Cramer, Marcus. Bolivia. (p. 208)
Pateman, Robert & El Hamamsy, Salwa. Egypt. (p. 506)
Pateman, Robert & Elias, Josie. Kenya. (p. 949)
Pateman, Robert & Elliott, Mark. Belgium. (p. 161)
Pateman, Robert, et al. Egypt. (p. 506)
Patenaude, Brian, illus. see Porter, Todd.
Patenaude, Jeremy & Hicks, Charlotte. Playful Puppy. (p. 1372)
Patenaude, Jeremy & Lock, Peter. Space Quest: Mission to Mars. (p. 1619)
Patenaude, Jeremy & Unstead, Sue. Little Dolphin. (p. 1027)
Patenaude, Jeremy, et al. Little Dolphin. (p. 1027)
—Playful Puppy. (p. 1372)
Patendaude, Jeremy & Dorling Kindersley Publishing Staff. Halo 4. (p. 739)
Patent, Dorothy Hinshaw. Buffalo & the Indians: A Shared Destiny. Muñoz, William, photos by. (p. 235)
—Call of the Osprey. Muñoz, William, illus. (p. 254)
—Decorated Horses. Brett, Jeannie, illus. (p. 422)
—Dogs on Duty: Soldiers' Best Friends on the Battlefield & Beyond. (p. 463)
—Dogs on Duty: Soldiers' Best Friends on the Battlefield & Beyond. Patent, Dorothy Hinshaw, illus. (p. 463)
—Flashy Fantastic Rain Forest Frogs. Jubb, Kendahl Jan, illus. (p. 602)
—Homesteading: Settling America's Heartland. Munoz, William, photos by. (p. 794)
—Horse & the Plains Indians: A Powerful Partnership. Munoz, William, photos by. (p. 799)
—Lewis & Clark Trail: Then & Now. Muñoz, William, photos by. (p. 1004)
—Life in a Desert. Muñoz, William, illus. (p. 1010)
—Right Dog for the Job: Ira's Path from Service Dog to Guide Dog. (p. 1472)
—Saving Audie: A Pit Bull Puppy Gets a Second Chance. Muñoz, William, photos by. (p. 1517)
—Slinky, Scaly, Slithery Snakes. Jubb, Kendahl Jan, illus. (p. 1590)
—Super Sniffers: Dog Detectives on the Job. (p. 1682)
—When the Wolves Returned: Restoring Nature's Balance in Yellowstone. Hartman, Dan, illus. (p. 1905)
Paterakis, Paul. Henry the Friendly Shark. (p. 768)
Paterson, Alys, illus. see Sperring, Mark.
Paterson, Andrew Barton 'Banjo'. Three Elephant Power & Other Stories. (p. 1742)
Paterson, Brian. Picnic: Board Book. (p. 1355)
—Zigby Camps Out. (p. 1986)
Paterson, Diane. Hurricane Wolf. Paterson, Diane, illus. (p. 830)
Paterson, Diane, illus. see Corey, Dorothy.
Paterson, Diane, illus. see McElroy, Lisa Tucker.
Paterson, Huntley, tr. see Salten, Felix.
Paterson, John, jt. auth. see Paterson, Katherine.
Paterson, John B., jt. auth. see Paterson, Katherine.
Paterson, John B., Jr. & Paterson, John B., Sr. Roberto's Trip to the Top. Alarcao, Renato, illus. (p. 1479)
Paterson, John B., Sr., jt. auth. see Paterson, John B., Jr.
Paterson Jr., John B. & Paterson Sr, John B. Roberto's Trip to the Top. Alarcao, Renato, illus. (p. 1479)
Paterson, Katherine. Ame a Jacob. (p. 57)
—Bread & Roses, Too. (p. 224)
—Bridge to Terabithia. Diamond, Donna, illus. (p. 227)
—Brother Sun, Sister Moon. Dalton, Pamela, illus. (p. 231)
—Busqueda de Park. (p. 245)
—Clan de los Perros. (p. 326)
—Day of the Pelican. (p. 414)
—Giving Thanks: Poems, Prayers, & Praise Songs of Thanksgiving. Dalton, Pamela, illus. (p. 681)
—Gran Gilly Hopkins. (p. 706)
—Great Gilly Hopkins. (p. 716)
—Igual Al Rey. Vagin, Vladimir, illus. (p. 856)
—Jacob Have I Loved. (p. 904)
—Jip: His Story. (p. 919)
—Life of Jesus for Children. Roca, François, illus. (p. 1012)
—Maestro de las Marionetas. (p. 1070)
—Marvin One Too Many. Brown, Jane Clark, illus. (p. 1099)
—Marvin One Too Many. Clark Brown, Jane, illus. (p. 1099)
—Master Puppeteer. (p. 1103)
—Preacher's Boy. (p. 1394)
—Puzzling Book. (p. 1421)
—Rebels of the Heavenly Kingdom. (p. 1451)
—Same Stuff as Stars. (p. 1507)
—Signo del Crisantemo. (p. 1574)
—Stubborn Sweetness & Other Stories for the Christmas Season. (p. 1668)
—Tale of the Mandarin Ducks. (p. 1700)
—Tale of the Mandarin Ducks. Dillon, Leo & Dillon, Diane, illus. (p. 1700)
—Who Am I? (p. 1914)
—Who Am I? Exploring What It Means to Be a Child of God. (p. 1914)
Paterson, Katherine & Paterson, John. Flint Heart. (p. 604)
—Flint Heart. Rocco, John, illus. (p. 604)
Paterson, Katherine & Paterson, John B. Flint Heart. Rocco, John, illus. (p. 604)
paterson, richard. Mango Chutney. (p. 1087)
—Mango Chutney & the Accidental Dog Biscuit Invention. (p. 1087)
Paterson, Samantha. Primates. (p. 1400)
—Science of Primates. (p. 1527)
Paterson Sr, John B., jt. auth. see Paterson Jr., John B.
Paterson, Thomas, jt. auth. see Merrill, Dennis.
Paterson, Thomas, et al. American Foreign Relations: A History. (p. 60)
Patete, Christine, illus. see Tucker, Mark.
Patey, Nicola. Aspireland & the story of George. (p. 107)
Pathak, Ashutosh, illus. see Rao, Chatura.
Pati, Geeta. Finny's Voyage Through the Universe: The. (p. 589)
—Finny's Voyage Through the Universe: Nebula, Supernova, Open Star Cluster. (p. 589)
Paticoff, Melanie. Sophie's Tales: Overcoming Obstacles. Vales, Chrissie, illus. (p. 1613)
Patience, Cynthia. Christmas Tree Angel. (p. 316)
Patience, John, illus. see Gikow, Louise A.
Patience, John, illus. see Gikow, Louise.
Patients from East Tennessee Children's Hospital, illus. see McMillan, Jenna.
Patilla, Peter, jt. auth. see Broadbent, Paul.
Patillo, D. L. Jessie's World: "the New Baby" (p. 914)
Patinios, Constantinos. Forest Princess: Heart Friends. (p. 618)
Patitucci, Karen. Three-Minute Dramas for Worship. (p. 1743)
Patkau, Karen. Creatures Great & Small. (p. 380)
—Creatures Yesterday & Today. Patkau, Karen, illus. (p. 380)
—Who Needs a Desert? A Desert Ecosystem. (p. 1917)
—Who Needs a Jungle? (p. 1917)
—Who Needs a Prairie? A Grassland Ecosystem. (p. 1917)
—Who Needs a Reef? A Coral Reef Ecosystem. (p. 1917)
—Who Needs a Swamp? (p. 1917)
—Who Needs an Iceberg? (p. 1917)
Patkau, Karen, illus. see Beck, Carolyn.
Patkau, Karen, illus. see Lottridge, Celia.
Patkoske, Jennifer. All about Me. (p. 42)
Patlan, Alyssa A., illus. see Banda, Rey A.
Patnaude, Jeffrey. Penny. (p. 1338)
Patneaude, David. Thin Wood Walls. (p. 1732)
Patnicroft, Robert & Cooke, Clare. NTC Language Masters for Beginning Spanish Students. (p. 1269)
Paton, Doug. Our Plane Is Down. Melanson, Matt, illus. (p. 1309)
—Terror 911. (p. 1722)
Paton, Stuart. Extraordinary Tale of an Ordinary Boy. (p. 555)
Paton Walsh, Jill. Parcel of Patterns. (p. 1324)
Patradol Kitcharoen, illus. see Alfred Sole.
Patrice, Elena, jt. auth. see Sills, Elizabeth.
Patricelli, Leslie. Baby Happy Baby Sad. Patricelli, Leslie, illus. (p. 126)
—Be Quiet, Mike! (p. 149)
—Big Little. Patricelli, Leslie, illus. (p. 182)
—Binky. Patricelli, Leslie, illus. (p. 188)
—Birthday Box. Patricelli, Leslie, illus. (p. 192)
—Blankie. Patricelli, Leslie, illus. (p. 198)
—Boo! Patricelli, Leslie, illus. (p. 209)
—Fa la La. Patricelli, Leslie, illus. (p. 559)
—Faster! Faster! Patricelli, Leslie, illus. (p. 576)
—Faster! Faster!/Mas Rapido! Mas Rapido! Patricelli, Leslie, illus. (p. 576)
—Grande Pequeño. Rozarena, P., tr. (p. 707)
—Higher! Higher! Patricelli, Leslie, illus. (p. 778)
—Hop! Hop! Patricelli, Leslie, illus. (p. 796)
—Huggy Kissy. Patricelli, Leslie, illus. (p. 825)
—No No Yes Yes. Patricelli, Leslie, illus. (p. 1259)
—Patterson Puppies & the Midnight Monster Party. Patricelli, Leslie, illus. (p. 1329)
—Patterson Puppies & the Rainy Day. Patricelli, Leslie, illus. (p. 1329)
—Potty. Patricelli, Leslie, illus. (p. 1388)
—Quiet Loud. Patricelli, Leslie, illus. (p. 1428)
—Silencio Ruido. Rozarena, P., tr. (p. 1575)
—Tickle. Patricelli, Leslie, illus. (p. 1747)
—Toot. Patricelli, Leslie, illus. (p. 1767)
—Tubby. Patricelli, Leslie, illus. (p. 1795)
—Yummy Yucky. Patricelli, Leslie, illus. (p. 1983)
Patricelli, Leslie, illus. see Holub, Joan.
Patricia Diane Craine, Ma-Lmft. Our Miracle Our Earth. (p. 1309)
Patricia J. Pasda, jt. auth. see Maryann Pasda Diedwardo.
Patricia, MacLachlan. Sarah, Plain & Tall. (p. 1514)
Patricia Pierce. Numbers in a Row: An Iowa Number Book. Rohner, Dorothia, illus. (p. 1272)
Patrick, B. Blob's Odd Jobs. Torre, Attilio, illus. (p. 200)
Patrick, B. & Schotz, Leo D. Is That Funny? Ruell, L J, illus. (p. 890)
Patrick, Bethanne. Native American Languages. Johnson, Troy, ed. (p. 1234)
Patrick, Bethanne Kelly. Abraham Lincoln. (p. 6)
—Forts of the West. (p. 623)
—Ulysses S. Grant. (p. 1810)
Patrick, Cat. Forgotten. (p. 619)
—Originals. (p. 1304)
—Revived. (p. 1466)
Patrick, Cat & Young, Suzanne. Just Like Fate. (p. 939)
Patrick, Chris. Beyoncé & Destiny's Child. (p. 173)
Patrick, David. Nero Demare & the Legend of the Vampires. (p. 1241)
Patrick, Denise Lewis. Finding Someplace. (p. 588)
—Jackie Robinson Strong Inside & Out. (p. 904)
—Lesson for Martin Luther King, Jr. Pate, Rodney S., illus. (p. 993)
—MaDear's Old Green House. Sadler, Sonia Lynn, illus. (p. 1070)
—Matter of Souls. (p. 1109)
—Ronald Reagan from Silver Screen to Oval Office. (p. 1486)
Patrick, Denise Lewis & Time for Kids Editors. Jackie Robinson - Strong Inside & Out. (p. 904)
Patrick Green, Ann. Piano Music for Little Fingers: Book 1. (p. 1354)
—Piano Music for Little Fingers: Book 2. (p. 1354)
—Piano Music for Little Fingers: Primer. (p. 1354)
Patrick, J. Nelle. Tsarina. (p. 1795)
Patrick, James. Football Madness: The Road to Super Bowl XXXVII. (p. 615)
—Legend of the Delta Blues. (p. 989)
Patrick, James A., ed. Renaissance & Reformation (p. 1460)
Patrick, Jean L. S. Baseball Adventure of Jackie Mitchell, Girl Pitcher vs. Babe Ruth. Trover, Zachary et al, illus. (p. 141)
—Baseball Adventure of Jackie Mitchell, Girl Pitcher vs. Babe Ruth. Hammond, Ted & Carbajal, Richard, illus. (p. 141)
—Face to Face with Mount Rushmore. Patrick, Jean L. S. & Faricy, Patrick, illus. (p. 560)
—Niña Que Ponchó a Babe Ruth. Translations.com Staff, tr. from ENG. (p. 1256)
—Who Carved the Mountain? The Story of Mount Rushmore. Graef, Renee, illus. (p. 1915)
Patrick, John J. Bill of Rights: A History in Documents. (p. 186)
—Supreme Court of the United States: A Student Companion. (p. 1685)
Patrick, Joseph. Our National Symbols. (p. 1309)
Patrick, Miriam. Cinderfrog. (p. 321)
Patrick, Patsy S. Willie Wonders Why. Heiser, Aline L., illus. (p. 1934)
Patrick, Roman. Caribou. (p. 269)
—Musk Oxen. (p. 1194)
—Snowy Owls. (p. 1601)
Patrick, Rudolph. Mulligan's Rainbow. (p. 1189)
Patrick, Ruthven. Prisoners under Glass. (p. 1407)
Patrick, Scot, illus. see Frances, Dee.
Patrick, Tom, illus. see Tyrell, Melissa.
Patrick, Valerie. Safari Animal Babies. (p. 1501)
Patrick, Wellman. Mr. Duz Goes to the Doctor. Sam, Kagan, illus. (p. 1185)
—Mr. Duz Trick or Treat. Sam, Kagan, illus. (p. 1185)
Patrick, Wendy. When Passion Wins. (p. 1904)
Patrick, William, jt. auth. see DiNubile, Nicholas A.
PatrickGeorge. Drove of Bullocks: A Compilation of Animal Group Names. PatrickGeorge, illus. (p. 486)
—Filth of Starlings: A Compilation of Bird & Aquatic Animal Group Names. PatrickGeorge, illus. (p. 586)
PatrickGeorge, jt. auth. see George, Patrick.
PatrickGeorge (Firm) Staff. Little Miss Muffet & Other Rhymes. (p. 1032)
PatrickGeorge Staff. I See... (p. 845)
Patrick.J.Jardine. S r b U: Sir. Robert, Belmont, Uberdon the Third. (p. 1499)
Patridge, Bennie. Reflections: Poetry. Vol. 1 (p. 1456)
Patrizzi, Barbara. O Is for Oystercatcher: A Book of Seaside ABCs. Patrizzi, Barbara, illus. (p. 1274)
Patron, Kristine Mary. Artist? That's Me! (p. 104)
Patron, Susan. Behind the Masks: The Diary of Angeline Reddy - Bodie, California 1880. (p. 160)
—Higher Power of Lucky. (p. 779)
—Higher Power of Lucky. Phelan, Matt, illus. (p. 779)
—Lucky Breaks. Phelan, Matt, illus. (p. 1062)
—Lucky for Good. (p. 1062)
—Lucky for Good. McGuire, Erin, illus. (p. 1062)
—Lucky for Good. McGuire, Erin K., illus. (p. 1062)
—Maybe Yes, Maybe No, Maybe Maybe. Halpin, Abigail, illus. (p. 1113)
Patsakos, Julienne. Angel, Angel Where are You? (p. 73)
Patschke, Steve. Spooky Book. McElligott, Matthew, illus. (p. 1631)
Pattarozzi, Joni. Green Bean Queen. (p. 721)
Patten, Brian. Big Snuggle-Up. Bayley, Nicola, illus. (p. 184)
Patten, Brian & Assorted Staff. Puffin Utterly Brilliant Book of Poetry. Patten, Brian, ed. (p. 1415)
Patten, E. J. Legend Thief. Rocco, John, illus. (p. 989)
—Return to Exile. Rocco, John, illus. (p. 1465)
Patten, Elizabeth & Lyons, Kathy. Healthy Foods from Healthy Soils: A Hands-On Resource for Teachers Stevens, Helen, illus. (p. 758)
Patten, Laurien. Left Hand of Aneryn. (p. 987)
Patten, Lewis B. Gene Autry & Arapaho War Drums. Hampton, John W., illus. (p. 660)
—Gene Autry & the Ghost Riders. Bartram, Bob & Eggers, James, illus. (p. 660)
Patten, Linda D. Princess Alese & the Kingdom of Serenity. (p. 1402)

Patten, Robert, jt. ed. see Bowen, John.
Patten, William. Animal & Nature Stories: The Junior Classics. Vol. 8 (p. 76)
Patter, Bruce Van, see Van Patter, Bruce.
Patterson, Aaron James, ed. see Gazarik, Rebecca Renee.
Patterson, Angela. Matching Numbers. (p. 1104)
Patterson, Ann Elizabeth. Rocking Chair Bear. (p. 1483)
Patterson, Annie, illus. see Arnold, Caroline.
Patterson, Annie, illus. see Edwardson, Debby Dahl.
Patterson, Annie, illus. see Sayre, April Pulley.
Patterson, Annie, illus. see Stewart, Melissa.
Patterson, Barbara A. Sweetest Angel. (p. 1690)
Patterson, Barbara L. PICU Did You Know? (p. 1356)
—Transportation Tools. (p. 1779)
Patterson, Bill, illus. see Black, Baxter A.
Patterson, Blenna Rae Sparks, jt. auth. see Sparks, Lanny L.
Patterson, C. Marie. Little Dinky's Love for Basketball. (p. 1026)
Patterson, Caroline. Fish Do WHAT in the Water? The Secret Lives of Marine Animals. Rath, Robert, illus. (p. 598)
—Who Pooped in the Zoo? Exploring the Weirdest, Wackiest, Grossest, & Most Surprising Facts about Zoo Poop. Rath, Robert, illus. (p. 1917)
—Who Pooped in the Zoo? San Diego Zoo: Exploring the Weirdest, Wackiest, Grossest & Most Surprising Facts about Zoo Poo. Rath, Robert, illus. (p. 1917)
Patterson, Christine. Calvin Crab's Magical Wish. (p. 255)
—Conversation in the Crayon Box. (p. 361)
—On the Wings of a Butterfly. (p. 1292)
Patterson, Christine D. Conversation in the Crayon Box. (p. 361)
Patterson, Claire, et al. Estas Bien Como Eres (It's O. K. to Be You) (p. 538)
Patterson, Colleen A., jt. auth. see Miles, Brenda.
Patterson, Colleen A. & Miles, Brenda. 1-2-3 a Calmer Me. Keay, Claire, illus. (p. 1990)
Patterson, Dorothy Kelley. Handbook for Parents in Ministry: Training up a Child While Answering the Call. (p. 740)
Patterson, Drake. Slowpoke the Sloth. Quinn, Savannah, illus. (p. 1591)
Patterson, Ellie. Baby Bear & the Big, Wide World. Kolanovic, Dubravka, illus. (p. 125)
—Michael Recycle & the Tree Top Cops. (p. 1134)
Patterson, Ellie, jt. auth. see Bethel, Ellie.
Patterson, Eric. Carl Nose the Truth. Wright, Christopher, illus. (p. 269)
—Fluffy, a Puppy with a Purpose. Mathis, Leslie, illus. (p. 608)
—Legend of Skylar Swift, the Fastest Boy on Earth. Chris, Wright, illus. (p. 988)
—Nature Boy. Wright, Christopher, illus. (p. 1236)
—Nature Boy Nature Strikes Back. Wright, Chris, illus. (p. 1236)
—Something Lurking in the Bell Tower. Christopher, Wright, illus. (p. 1610)
Patterson, Erik. Day Oscar Became a Robot. (p. 414)
Patterson, Geoffrey, illus. see Kipling, Rudyard.
Patterson, Haley. Fossils Around the World: Measure Lengths in Standard Units (p. 624)
Patterson, Horace. Ernie the Ermine. Parker, Jack, illus. (p. 534)
Patterson, Ian. Time to Get Here: Selected Poems 1969-2002. (p. 1753)
Patterson, Irania. Chipi Chipis, Small Shells of the Sea. McElvane, Catherine, illus. (p. 308)
Patterson, Irania & McElvane, Catherine. Wings & Dreams (Alas y Suenos) The Legend of Angel Falls (La Leyenda del Salto Angel) (p. 1936)
Patterson, James. Along Came a Spider. (p. 48)
—Angel. (p. 73)
—Angel Experiment. (p. 73)
—Armageddon. (p. 99)
—Cat & Mouse. (p. 277)
—Cross. (p. 385)
—Dangerous Days of Daniel X. (p. 404)
—Demons & Druids. (p. 426)
—Fang. (p. 571)
—Final Warning. (p. 587)
—Fire. (p. 590)
—Four Blind Mice. (p. 624)
—Gift. (p. 674)
—Jack & Jill. (p. 902)
—Manga. (p. 1087)
—Mary, Mary. (p. 1100)
—Max. (p. 1110)
—Maximum Ride: The Manga, Vol. 7. (p. 1112)
—Maximum Ride. (p. 1112)
—Maximum Ride Forever. (p. 1112)
—Nevermore: The Final Maximum Ride Adventure. (p. 1243)
—Nevermore. (p. 1243)
—Public School Superhero. (p. 1414)
—SantaKid. Garland, Michael, illus. (p. 1513)
—Saving the World: And Other Extreme Sports. (p. 1517)
—Saving the World & Other Extreme Sports. (p. 1518)
—School's Out - Forever. (p. 1524)
—Watch the Skies. (p. 1861)
—Witch & Wizard. (p. 1941)
—Worst Years of My Life. (p. 1961)
Patterson, James, ed. see Grabenstein, Chris.
Patterson, James, jt. auth. see Grabenstein, Chris.
Patterson, James, jt. auth. see Naraghi, Dara.
Patterson, James & Bergen, Julia. Ultimate Showdown. (p. 1810)
Patterson, James & Charbonnet, Gabrielle. Witch & Wizard. (p. 1941)
Patterson, James & Dembowski, Jill. Fire. (p. 590)
—Kiss. (p. 961)
Patterson, James & Friedman, Hal. Med Head: My Knock-Down, Drag-Out, Drugged-Up Battle with My Brain. (p. 1118)
Patterson, James & Gout, Leopoldo. Alien Hunter. (p. 40)
Patterson, James & Grabenstein, Chris. Armageddon. (p. 99)
—Daniel X: Lights Out. (p. 405)
—House of Robots. (p. 803)
—House of Robots. Neufeld, Juliana, illus. (p. 803)
—I Even Funnier: A Middle School Story. Park, Laura, illus. (p. 838)
—I Funny: A Middle School Story. Park, Laura, illus. (p. 838)
—I Totally Funniest: A Middle School Story. Park, Laura, illus. (p. 847)
—Treasure Hunters: Danger down the Nile. Neufeld, Juliana, illus. (p. 1781)
—Treasure Hunters: Secret of the Forbidden City. Neufeld, Juliana, illus. (p. 1781)
—Treasure Hunters. (p. 1781)
—Treasure Hunters. Neufeld, Juliana, illus. (p. 1781)
Patterson, James & Gross, Andrew. 2nd Chance. (p. 1991)
Patterson, James & Ledwidge, Michael. Dangerous Days of Daniel X. (p. 404)
Patterson, James & Naraghi, Dara. Battle for Shadowland (p. 145)
Patterson, James & Paetro, Maxine. Confessions: The Paris Mysteries. (p. 356)
—Confessions: The Private School Murders. (p. 356)
—Confessions of a Murder Suspect. (p. 356)
—Paris Mysteries. (p. 1324)
—Private School Murders. (p. 1408)
Patterson, James & Papademetriou, Lisa. Big Fat Liar. Swaab, Neil, illus. (p. 181)
—Homeroom Diaries. Keino, illus. (p. 793)
—My Brother Is a Big, Fat Liar. Swaab, Neil, illus. (p. 1199)
Patterson, James & Raymond, Emily. First Love. (p. 596)
—First Love. Illingworth, Sasha, photos by. (p. 596)
—Lost. (p. 1054)
Patterson, James & Rust, Ned. Daniel X (p. 405)
—Game Over. (p. 654)
—Gift. (p. 674)
—Gift: You're about to Read the Most Exciting Adventure Series Ever. (p. 675)
—Gift. (p. 675)
—Watch the Skies. (p. 1861)
Patterson, James & Tebbetts, Chris. Get Me Out of Here! (p. 667)
—Get Me Out of Here! Park, Laura, illus. (p. 667)
—How I Survived Bullies, Broccoli, & Snake Hill. Park, Laura, illus. (p. 810)
—Just My Rotten Luck. Park, Laura, illus. (p. 939)
—Save Rafe! Park, Laura, illus. (p. 1516)
—Worst Years of My Life. Park, Laura, illus. (p. 1961)
—Worst Years of My Life. Park, Laura, illus. (p. 1962)
Patterson, James & Tebbetts, Christopher. Save Rafe! Park, Laura, illus. (p. 1516)
Patterson, James, et al. Middle School: The Worst Years of My Life; Get Me Out of Here!; My Brother Is a Big, Fat Liar; How I Survived Bullies, Broccoli & Snake Hill. Set Park, Laura & Swaab, Neil, illus. (p. 1137)
—Public School Superhero. (p. 1414)
—Treasure Hunters. Neufeld, Juliana, illus. (p. 1781)
Patterson, James G., jt. auth. see Luecke, Richard A.
Patterson, Janis. Danny & the Dustbunnies. (p. 405)
Patterson, Jim. Lisa B's Cookie Tree. (p. 1022)
Patterson, John Henry. Man-Eaters of Tsavo. (p. 1085)
Patterson, José. No Buts, Becky! (p. 1258)
Patterson, Kerry & Mills, Terence C., eds. Palgrave Handbook of Econometrics: Econometric Theory. Vol. 1 (p. 1320)
Patterson, L. Kahili, ed. see Day, Deborah A.
Patterson, Lagene E. What a Peculiar Day. (p. 1878)
Patterson, Marie. Early American Indian Tribes. (p. 493)
—Harriet Tubman. (p. 749)
—Pocahontas. (p. 1375)
—Slavery in America. (p. 1588)
Patterson, Matt. Daylight Moonlight (p. 415)
Patterson, Matthew. Shake Them up, Mrs Nut. (p. 1558)
Patterson, Maurice. Children's Computer Learning Cartoon Coloring Book. (p. 303)
Patterson, Michael. Adventures of Spot: Cody, Boozer & Aaliyah (p. 23)
—Blam! O'Reilly, Sean Patrick, ed. (p. 198)
Patterson, Michael & Yaiza, Alicia. Genie & the Hair/el Genio y el Pelo. (p. 661)
Patterson, Nancy. May the Magnificent Lighthouse. Patterson, Nancy, illus. (p. 1112)
Patterson, Nancy Ruth. Shiniest Rock of All. (p. 1566)
—Simple Gift. (p. 1577)
Patterson, Rebecca. Gordon Star. Rees, Mary, illus. (p. 702)
—My No, No, No Day! (p. 1216)
—Nightbear. (p. 1254)
—Pirate House. (p. 1362)
Patterson, Robin, illus. see Rodomista, Kim.
Patterson, Robin, jt. auth. see Rodomista, Kim.
Patterson, Sadie. Old Pete & Dan. (p. 1284)
Patterson, Sandra Jean. Crabby Crab. (p. 375)
Patterson, Shannon. Princess & the Cheese. (p. 1402)
Patterson, Sharon L. Where Is Happy? (p. 1908)
Patterson, Sherri, et al. No-No & the Secret Touch: The Gentle Story of a Little Seal Who Learns to Stay Safe, Say "No" & Tell! Krupp, Marian N., illus. (p. 1259)
Patterson, Stacey. Fidget's Folly. Gorbatov, Vadim, illus. (p. 583)
—Sherman Graham Cracker Saves the Town of Crusted Milk. (p. 1566)
Patterson, Teri Jo. Corky & Lizzie Go to the Circus. (p. 367)
Patterson, Trina Dawkins. Tale of Two Cookies: A Message of Kindness & Acceptance. Wilson, Bonnita, illus. (p. 1700)
Patterson, Valerie O. Operation Oleander. (p. 1300)
—Other Side of Blue. (p. 1306)
Patterson, Virginia Sharpe. Dickey Downy: The Autobiography of a Bird. (p. 436)
Patteson, Nelda. Adina de Zavala: "Angel of the Alamo" Her Life Story Presented Through the Clothes She Wore. Patteson, Nelda, illus. (p. 12)
Patti, Caroline. World Spins Madly On. (p. 1958)
Patti, Sheila, illus. see Ferguson, Linda.
Patti, Thompson. Charleigh's Shoes. (p. 291)
Pattinson, Darcy. Kentucky Basketball. (p. 949)
Pattinson, Judith, tr. see Poznanski, Ursula.
Pattis, Anne-Francoise. Let's Learn French Coloring Book. (p. 998)
—Let's Learn Spanish Coloring Book. (p. 998)
Pattison, Caroline Rennie. Whole, Entire, Complete Truth. (p. 1920)
Pattison, Darcy. Desert Baths Rietz, Kathleen, illus. (p. 428)
—Journey of Oliver K. Woodman. Cepeda, Joe, illus. (p. 928)
—Kentucky Basketball. (p. 949)
—Las Duchas en el Desierto Rietz, Kathleen, illus. (p. 976)
—Prairie Storms Rietz, Kathleen, illus. (p. 1392)
—Scary Slopes Harpster, Steve, illus. (p. 1520)
Pattison, Mark, jt. auth. see Leech, Christopher.
Pattison, Ronda, jt. auth. see Lemke, Donald B.
Pattison, Rosie Gowsell, jt. auth. see National Geographic Editors.
Patton, Addison Hannah. Treasure of the Wild: A Novel. (p. 1782)
Patton, Anne. Full Steam to Canada (p. 646)
—Through Flood & Fire: A Second Barr Colony Adventure (p. 1744)
Patton, Charlene, jt. auth. see Davis, Sharon.
Patton, Chris. Scene Immortal: Part One of the Blood Scene Trilogy. (p. 1521)
—Totally True Princess Story. Wellman, Mike, ed. (p. 1771)
Patton, Christopher. Jack Pine Young, Cybèle, illus. (p. 903)
Patton, Cristina. On My Way to School. (p. 1289)
Patton, Donna Alice. Gift of Summer Snow: A Tale from the Garden of Mysteries. (p. 675)
Patton, Geoff. Giants of the Sea. (p. 674)
—Mummies. (p. 1190)
—On the Job. (p. 1290)
—Poles Apart. (p. 1379)
—Spying Game. (p. 1636)
Patton, Jack. Battle Bugs #1: the Lizard War. (p. 145)
—Battle Bugs #2: the Spider Siege. (p. 145)
—Poison Frog Assault (Battle Bugs #3) (p. 1377)
Patton, Jean. Green Book. (p. 721)
Patton, Jim & Dee. Grandmother's Heart. (p. 709)
Patton, Julia, illus. see Daniel, Claire.
Patton, Julia, illus. see Garcia, Ellen.
Patton, Julia, illus. see Linde, Barbara M.
Patton, Julia, illus. see Nolan, Janet.
Patton, Julia, illus. see Sparks, Stacey.
Patton, Julia, illus. see Williams, Dinah.
Patton, Julie. Maximizing Your Studio's Potential: the Student Log Book: Skill Assessment & Progress Management Tools for the College-Level Musician. (p. 1112)
Patton, Katherine. Bam Bam the Bandage. (p. 135)
Patton, Lucia, illus. see Friskey, Margaret.
Patton, Roni. Opossum Dilemma: Crossing the Streets at Night. (p. 1300)
Patton, Scott, illus. see Hahn, Samuel J.
Patton, Scott, tr. see Hahn, Samuel J.
Pattou, Edith. East. (p. 498)
—Fire Arrow: The Second Song of Eirren. (p. 590)
—Hero's Song: The First Song of Eirren. (p. 774)
—Mrs. Spitzer's Garden. Tusa, Tricia, illus. (p. 1187)
Pattrick, Steve. Bees & Honey: KinderFacts Individual Title Six-Packs. (p. 158)
—Building: KinderFacts Individual Title Six-Packs. (p. 238)
Patty, Catherine. Jumbo Science Yearbook: Grade 4. (p. 933)
—Jumbo Social Studies Yearbook: Grade 3. (p. 933)
—Jumbo Social Studies Yearbook: Grade 4. (p. 933)
—Jumbo Social Studies Yearbook: Grade 6. (p. 933)
Pattyn, Denny & Flecker, Katie. SRT 434 for Small Groups. (p. 1637)
—SRT 434 Leaders Guide. (p. 1637)
Pattyn, Denny & Zahorian, Ashley. 60 Day Journey. (p. 1997)
Patz, Naomi. Jewish Holiday Treasure Trail. (p. 917)
Patzelt, Kasie, illus. see Sanders, Roy E.
Patzelt, Kasie, illus. see Staton, Debbie.
Pau Pau. Bird Bandit (p. 190)
—Princess' Adventure. (p. 1402)
Pauba, Judy. Tale of Two Dogs. (p. 1700)
Pauk, Walter. Six-Way Paragraphs: Middle Level (p. 1583)
Paul. Best Friends. (p. 169)
Paul Ahrens-Gray & Ericka Grogan. Fish. (p. 598)
Paul, Aileen. Kids Cooking Without a Stove: A Cookbook for Young Children. Inouye, Carol, illus. (p. 953)
Paul & Lady Jan. Mako in My Backyard. Beeson, Jan, illus. (p. 1082)
—Wesley the Wobbly Bear. Beeson, Jan, illus. (p. 1876)
Paul, Ann Whitford. Count on Culebra: Go from 1 to 10 in Spanish. Long, Ethan, illus. (p. 369)
—Count on Culebra. Long, Ethan, illus. (p. 369)
—Fiesta Fiasco. Long, Ethan, illus. (p. 584)
—Hasta Manana, Monito. (p. 752)
—If Animals Kissed Good Night. Walker, David, illus. (p. 852)
—Manana, Iguana. Long, Ethan, tr. (p. 1086)
—Manana, Iguana. Long, Ethan, illus. (p. 1086)
—Snail's Good Night. Litzinger, Rosanne, illus. (p. 1596)
—Tortuga in Trouble. Long, Ethan, illus. (p. 1771)
—Word Builder. Cyrus, Kurt, illus. (p. 1950)
Paul, Anthea. My Girlosophy: How to Write Your Own Life. (p. 1210)
—Oracle. (p. 1301)
Paul, Anthony & Foreman, Michael. Tiger Who Lost His Stripes. (p. 1748)
Paul, Betsy. Adventures of Tiller & Turnbuckle: Adventure One Coloring Book. (p. 24)
Paul, Bette. Nurses: Nikki, Barbara & Nick. (p. 1273)
—Nurses: Katie Goes to College (Large Pri. (p. 1273)
—Nurses: Claire's Conquests & Jan's Journey. (p. 1273)
Paul, Brian. Julio & Maria Raise the Roof: English / Spanish Edition. Marrero, J., illus. (p. 932)
Paul, Cauvin. Mache Chache: Text Comprehension Exercises in Haitian Creole. Vilsaint, Fequiere, ed. (p. 1068)
Paul, Chris. Long Shot: Never Too Small to Dream Big. Morrison, Frank, illus. (p. 1047)
Paul, Christopher, et al. Other Quiet Professionals: Lessons for Future Cyber Forces from the Evolution of Special Forces (p. 1306)
Paul, Cinco & Daurio, Ken. Sleepy Kittens. Guillon, Eric, illus. (p. 1590)
Paul, Colette. Whoever You Chose to Love. (p. 1919)
Paul, Curtis Christopher. Bud, Not Buddy. (p. 234)
—Watsons Go to Birmingham 1963. (p. 1864)
Paul, Curtis Christopher, jt. auth. see Curtis, Christopher Paul.
Paul, Dominique. Possibility of Fireflies. (p. 1387)
Paul, Donita K. Dragons of Chiril: A Novel. (p. 479)
—Dragons of the Valley: A Novel. (p. 479)
—Two Renegade Realms (p. 1804)
Paul, Donita K. & Denmark, Evangeline. Dragon & the Turtle. Nguyen, Vincent, illus. (p. 476)
—Dragon & the Turtle Go on Safari. Nguyen, Vincent, illus. (p. 476)
Paul, Dwain. Fox the Hare the Wolf & the Sheep. (p. 626)
Paul, Fiona. Belladonna. (p. 162)
Paul, Fleischman. Seedfolks. (p. 1547)
Paul Frank Industries. Let's Dance with Julius & Friends. (p. 995)
—Only in Dreams. (p. 1298)
Paul Frank Industries & Gillingham, Sara. I Love Color: A Paul Frank Book. (p. 842)
Paul Frank Industries Staff. Julius! School Planner. (p. 933)
Paul Frank Industries Staff & Chronicle Books Staff. High Five with Julius! & Friends. (p. 777)
Paul, J. D. Little Lost Dog (p. 1031)
Paul J McSorley; Illustrated By Patricia. Adventures of Forealdo. Bearss, Patricia, illus. (p. 18)
Paul, Jeanne Wl & Willis, Jeanne. Rascally Cake. Paul, Korky, illus. (p. 1439)
Paul, Jeremy. Secret of Sherlock Holmes. (p. 1542)
Paul, John. Copters. Young, Bill, illus. (p. 366)
—Porcupine. (p. 1386)
Paul, Julia Marian. Song of the Teapot: Poems about Little Babies, Little Jerry, Little Susie, & Other Things. (p. 1611)
Paul, Kate. Best Ride (p. 171)
Paul, Kate, illus. see Swift, K. Marie.
Paul, Korky, illus. see Arrigan, Mary.
Paul, Korky, illus. see Bush, John.
Paul, Korky, illus. see Foster, John L.
Paul, Korky, illus. see Foster, John.
Paul, Korky, illus. see Gray, Kes.
Paul, Korky, illus. see Harvey, Damian.
Paul, Korky, illus. see McGough, Roger, et al.
Paul, Korky, illus. see Paul, Jeanne Wl & Willis, Jeanne.
Paul, Korky, illus. see Rhodes, Julie & Quarto Generic Staff.
Paul, Korky, jt. auth. see Arrigan, Mary.
Paul, Leonard, illus. see Bouchard, David & Aleekuk, Pam.
Paul, Leonard, illus. see Dumas, William.
Paul, Marcy Beller. Underneath Everything. Davis, Bill, illus. (p. 1815)
Paul, Michael. Oklahoma City & Anti-Government Terrorism. (p. 1283)
—Pan Am 103 & State-Sponsored Terrorism. (p. 1320)
Paul, Miranda. Helping Hands. (p. 766)
—One Plastic Bag: Isatou Ceesay & the Recycling Women of the Gambia. Zunon, Elizabeth, illus. (p. 1296)
—Water Is Water: A Book about the Water Cycle. Chin, Jason, illus. (p. 1863)
—Whose Hands Are These? A Community Helper Guessing Book. (p. 1921)
Paul, Naomi. Code Name Komiko. (p. 338)
Paul, Pope John, jt. auth. see Paul, Pope John, II.
Paul, Pope John, II & Paul, Pope John. Memory & Identity: Conversations at the Dawn of a Millennium. (p. 1126)
Paul Reising, illus. see Leigh-Anna Tehan.
Paul, Ruth. Bad Dog Flash. (p. 131)
—Go Home Flash. (p. 686)
—Hedgehog's Magic Tricks. Paul, Ruth, illus. (p. 762)
—Red Panda's Candy Apples. Paul, Ruth, illus. (p. 1454)
—Stomp! (p. 1652)
Paul, Ruth & Lombana, J. P. Stomp! la Marchar! (p. 1652)
Paul, Sherry. Finn the Foolish Fish: Trouble with Bubbles Miller, Bob, illus. (p. 589)
—Two-B & the Rock 'n' Roll Band Murphy, Bob, illus. (p. 1803)
Paul, Volponi. Black & White. (p. 195)
Paula, Cristina De. Sweet Pomchu. (p. 1690)
Paula Vicens, Ines Belasategui, tr. see Kronzek, Allan Zola & Kronzek, Elizabeth.
Paulding, Barbara. Circus Scratch & Sketch: An Art Activity Book. Zschock, Martha, illus. (p. 322)
—Water Magic. Steckler, Kerren Barbas, illus. (p. 1863)
Paulding, James Kirke. Westward Ho! (p. 1876)
Paulding, Steve. Wonderful Adventures of Bradley the Bat. Schmidt, Caleb & Schmidt, Carter, illus. (p. 1948)
Paulette, Bourgeois, jt. auth. see Bourgeois, Paulette.
Paulette (Pesha Razela) Fein Lieberman. Jewish Stories & Ideas for Children: A book for bonding, educational fun, & fund-raising purposes for children & Adults! (p. 917)
Pauley, Christa. Manda Panda & the Loons. (p. 1087)
Pauley, Kimberly. Cat Girl's Day Off (p. 278)
Paulhus, Jonathan. Chester, the Light Golden Retriever. (p. 298)
Pauli, Gunter. Bruja del Desierto. (p. 232)
—Can Apples Fly? (p. 258)
—Cold Feet (Pies Frios) (p. 338)
—Columbian Mushrooms/Champinones Colombianos. (p. 346)
—Oso y el Zorro. (p. 1305)
—Red Rice (Arroces Rojos) (p. 1454)
—Shiitake Love Caffeine. (p. 1566)
—Tree Candy. (p. 1783)
Pauli, Lorenz. Fox in the Library. Schärer, Kathrin, illus. (p. 626)
—Fox in the Library. Schaerer, Kathrin, illus. (p. 626)
—You Call That Brave? Schärer, Kathrin, illus. (p. 1973)
Paulin, Chrita. Let's Bake a Family. Burns, Rosalyn, ed. (p. 994)
Pauline, Christi. Hullabaloo at the Zoo. (p. 825)
Pauline Roberts & Donnie Obina. Promises! Promises! Who Can I Trust. (p. 1411)
Pauline Wall & Shelley Smith. What the Owl Saw: (a Christmas Story) (p. 1893)
Pauling, Galen T., illus. see Sanders, Stephanie.
Pauling, Galen T., jt. auth. see Sanders, Stephanie.

P

Paulits, John. Philip & the Boy Who Said Huh? (p. 1350)
—Philip & the Case of the Mistaken Identity & Philip & the Baby. (p. 1350)
—Philip Gets Even. (p. 1350)
Paulitz, Kevin. Letter from the Tooth Fairy. (p. 1002)
Paulk, Earl. Fir for a King: The Story of Obed, the Ugly Donkey. (p. 590)
Paulk, William. Creatures of Vision City: Pokie's Party, Book One. (p. 380)
Paull, Grace, illus. see Coatsworth, Elizabeth Jane.
Paull, Jason. Twin Legends (hardback) (p. 1802)
Paull, John W. Great Stampede: A Jimmy James Story. (p. 718)
Paulsen, Aimee. Mambo & the Runaway Gorill. (p. 1084)
Paulsen, Gary. Amazing Life of Birds: The Twenty-Day Puberty Journal of Duane Homer Leech. (p. 55)
—Beet Fields. (p. 158)
—Brian's Hunt. (p. 227)
—Brian's Return. (p. 227)
—Brian's Winter. (p. 227)
—Canyons. (p. 262)
—Car. (p. 265)
—Caught by the Sea: My Life on Boats. (p. 281)
—Crossing. (p. 385)
—Crush: The Theory, Practice & Destructive Properties of Love. (p. 386)
—Culpepper's Cannon: Dunc Gets Tweaked. (p. 390)
—Dancing Carl. (p. 402)
—Dogsong. (p. 463)
—Family Ties. (p. 568)
—Flat Broke: The Theory, Practice & Destructive Properties of Greed. (p. 602)
—Foxman. (p. 626)
—Gary Paulsen Collection: Dancing Carl; Dogsong; Hatchet; Woodsong. (p. 657)
—Glass Cafe or, the Stripper & the State: How My Mother Started a War with the System That Made Us Kind of Rich & a Little Bit Famous. (p. 682)
—Harris & Me. (p. 750)
—Hatchet: With Related Readings. (p. 752)
—Hatchet. (p. 752)
—Hatchet. Willis, Drew, illus. (p. 752)
—Haymeadow. (p. 755)
—How Angel Peterson Got His Name: And Other Outrageous Tales about Extreme Sports. (p. 804)
—Island. (p. 892)
—Lawn Boy. (p. 981)
—Lawn Boy Returns. (p. 981)
—Legend of Bass Reeves: Being the True & Fictional Account of the Most Valiant Marshal in the West. (p. 988)
—Liar, Liar. (p. 1005)
—Masters of Disaster. (p. 1103)
—Molly McGinty Has a Really Good Day. (p. 1160)
—Molly Mcginty Has a Really Good Day. (p. 1160)
—Mudshark. (p. 1189)
—Night the White Deer Died. (p. 1254)
—Nightjohn: El Esclavo Que Me Enseno a Leer. (p. 1255)
—Notes from the Dog. (p. 1268)
—Paintings from the Cave: Three Novellas. (p. 1318)
—Puppies, Dogs, & Blue Northers: Reflections on Being Raised by a Pack of Sled Dogs. (p. 1418)
—Quilt. (p. 1428)
—Rifle. (p. 1471)
—River. (p. 1475)
—Shelf Life: Stories by the Book. (p. 1564)
—Soldier's Heart. (p. 1607)
—Tasting the Thunder. (p. 1707)
—Tent: A Parable in One Sitting. (p. 1720)
—This Side of Wild. (p. 1737)
—Time Hackers. (p. 1752)
—Tortilleria. Andujar, Gloria Dearagon, tr. from ENG. (p. 1770)
—Tracker. (p. 1775)
—Tucket's Travels: Francis Tucket's Adventures in the West, 1847-1849. (p. 1796)
—Vote: The Theory, Practice, & Destructive Properties of Politics. (p. 1850)
—Vote. (p. 1850)
—Voyage of the Frog. (p. 1850)
—Winter Room. (p. 1938)
—Woods Runner. (p. 1950)
—Woodsong. (p. 1950)
Paulsen, Gary & Paulsen, Jim. Field Trip. (p. 584)
—Road Trip. (p. 1477)
Paulsen, Gary & Roberts, Esyllt Nest. Craig y Diafol. (p. 376)
—Plygu Amser. (p. 1374)
Paulsen, Gary, et al. Parasiwtl (p. 1324)
Paulsen, Jim, jt. auth. see Paulsen, Gary.
Paulsen, Marc, jt. auth. see Marriott, Ashley.
Paulsen, Rosalie. My Ferrets. (p. 1203)
Paulsen, Ruth Wright, illus. see Paulsen, Gary.
Paulsen, Ted. Putting the HA into Hartford: Visions of Rivitalization. (p. 1420)
Paulson, Arlie, illus. see Nix, Pamela.
Paulson, Gary. Hatchet. (p. 752)
Paulson, Ingrid. Valkyrie Rising. (p. 1830)
Paulson, Judy. Baby Tawnies. (p. 128)
—Baby Tawnies. Paulson, Judy, illus. (p. 128)
Paulson, Michael W. Baker Street Bunch: A Double Mystery Book. No. 1 (p. 133)
—Baker Street Bunch & the Missing Pig Mystery. (p. 133)
Paulson, Michael William. Baker Street Bunch & the Hidden Map Mystery. (p. 133)
—Baker Street Bunch & the Missing Bracelet Mystery. (p. 133)
—Baker Street Bunch & the Missing Pie Mystery. (p. 133)
Paulson, Timothy J. Irish Immigrants. Asher, Robert, ed. (p. 887)
Paulus, Kristin Harkison. There's a Lion on the Dance Floor. (p. 1731)
Pauly, Heather E. Kon: The Bay Painted Stallion. (p. 966)
Pauly, Natalie. Mommy Mayhem. (p. 1162)
Paun, Alexandra. Old Man Nate's Halloween Tale. Paun, Alexandra, illus. (p. 1284)
Pausacker, Jenny. Freedom Fighters: Mindfire, Starfight, Endgame. (p. 634)
—Get a Life. (p. 667)
—Perfect Princess. (p. 1342)
Pausewang, Gudrun. Traitor. (p. 1777)
Pavan, Toni. Egypt, Nubia, & Kush: Set Of 6. (p. 506)
—Egypt, Nubia, & Kush: Text Pairs. (p. 506)
Pavanello, Roberto. Chilly Mammoth Zeni, Marco, tr. from ITA. (p. 306)
—Dancing Vampire. Zeni, Marco, tr. from ITA. (p. 403)
—Ghost of Dr. Mold. Zeni, Marco, tr. from ITA. (p. 671)
—King Tut's Grandmother Zeni, Marco, tr. from ITA. (p. 959)
—Midnight Witches Zeni, Marco, tr. from ITA. (p. 1139)
—Pirate with the Golden Tooth Zeni, Marco, tr. from ITA. (p. 1363)
—Thing in the Sewers Zeni, Marco, tr. from ITA. (p. 1732)
—Treasure in the Graveyard Zeni, Marco, tr. from ITA. (p. 1781)
Pavelka, Joe. Ned: The Story of Bear Six Nine Three Huras, Lynne, illus. (p. 1239)
Pavelka, Patricia. Adventures of Victor. (p. 24)
Pavelka, Pavelka. Foodie. (p. 614)
Paver, Michelle. Burning Shadow. (p. 244)
—Eye of the Falcon. (p. 557)
—Ghost Hunter. Taylor, Geoff, illus. (p. 670)
—Gods & Warriors. (p. 690)
—Oath Breaker. Taylor, Geoff, illus. (p. 1275)
—Outcast. Taylor, Geoff, illus. (p. 1312)
—Soul Eater. (p. 1614)
—Soul Eater. Taylor, Geoff, illus. (p. 1614)
—Spirit Walker. Taylor, Geoff, illus. (p. 1629)
—Wolf Brother. (p. 1943)
—Wolf Brother. Taylor, Geoff, illus. (p. 1943)
Paver, Michelle, jt. auth. see Paver, Michelle.
Paver, Michelle & Paver, Michelle. Clan de la Foca. Anton de vez, Patricia, tr. (p. 326)
—Hermano Lobo: Cronicas de la Prehistoria. Anton de vez, Patricia, tr. (p. 771)
Pavese, Candace. Caught in the Net. Holroyd, Geraldine, illus. (p. 282)
Pavey, Peter. One Dragon's Dream. Pavey, Peter, illus. (p. 1294)
Pavey, Stephen. Free RollinApos. (p. 634)
Pavia, Audrey & Schultz, Jacque Lynn. Having Fun with Your Dog. (p. 755)
Pavia, Jerry. Rocky Mountain Wildflowers: Photos, Descriptions, & Early Explorer Insights. Vol. 1 (p. 1484)
Pavilla, Elsie, illus. see Ayagarla, Julia, et al.
Pavlicin, Karen. Perch, Mrs. Sackets, & Crow's Nest. (p. 1341)
—Summer of Courage. (p. 1674)
PAVLICK, A. N. N. M., jt. auth. see Pavlick, Leon E.
Pavlick, Leon E. & PAVLICK, A. N. N. M. Foxes on the Ridge. Calvert, Lissa, illus. (p. 626)
Pavlicko, Marie A., jt. auth. see Farr, Michael.
Pavlik, Al. Battles in the Backcourt. (p. 147)
Pavlova, Elena. Adventures at Tall Oaks: New Friends. (p. 15)
Pavlova, Vera, illus. see Henry, Sandy.
Pavlova, Vera, illus. see Johnson, Vincent L.
Pavlovic, Milan, illus. see Bowers, Vivien.
Pavlovic, Zoran. Changing Global Economy. (p. 290)
—Greece. Gritzner, Charles F., ed. (p. 720)
—Italy. (p. 894)
—Kazakhstan. (p. 946)
—One World or Many? (p. 1297)
—Poland. (p. 1378)
—Terrorism & Security. (p. 1722)
—Turkey. (p. 1797)
Pavlovic, Zoran & Crooker, Richard A. Cuba. (p. 388)
Pavlovic, Zoran, et al. Spain. (p. 1620)
Pavlovsky, Marsha. I Am Not Scared of Halloween. (p. 833)
Pavón, Mar. Clucky & the Magic Kettle. (p. 335)
—Clucky in the Garden of Mirrors. (p. 335)
—Clucky the Hen. (p. 335)
—Could It Happen to Anyone? (p. 369)
—Gallina Cocorina. (p. 653)
—I Want to Be Philberta. (p. 848)
—Very, Very Noisy Tractor. (p. 1839)
—Zaira & the Dolphins. (p. 1984)
—Zaira y los Delfines. (p. 1984)
Pavon, Maria del Mar, et al. Selena, Seleeena! (p. 1549)
P.A.W. My Summer Road Trip. (p. 1219)
Paw Patrol, Paw. Paw Patrol: Pups Save the Day - A Slide Surprise Book. (p. 1331)
Pawagi, Manjusha. Girl Who Hated Books Franson, Leanne, illus. (p. 679)
Pawelak, Lydia, photos by see Bowes, Deborah.
Pawlak, Debra Ann. Bruce Lee. (p. 232)
Pawlak, Pawel, illus. see Horn, Emily.
Pawlett, Mark. Tae Kwon Do Handbook. (p. 1695)
Pawlett, Mark & Pawlett, Ray. Tae Kwon Do Handbook. (p. 1695)
Pawlett, Ray. Karate Handbook. (p. 943)
Pawlett, Ray, jt. auth. see Pawlett, Mark.
Pawlitz, Gail E., jt. ed. see Engelbrecht, Edward A.
Pawlitz, Gail E. & Engelbrecht, Edward A., eds. Moses, Gods Chosen Leader: Drawn directly from the Bible. (p. 1176)
Pawson, John. Minimum. (p. 1147)
Pax, H. H. -, illus. see World Peace, Metta & McBride, Heddrick.
Pax, Salam. Salam Pax: The Clandestine Diary of an Ordinary Iraqi. (p. 1504)
Paxen Learning Staff. Career Pathways: Document Literacy. (p. 267)
—Decisions. (p. 421)
Paxmann, Christine. From Mud Huts to Skyscrapers. Ibelings, Anne, illus. (p. 643)
Paxson, Dean A., ed. Real R & D Options. (p. 1448)
Paxson, Jillip Naysinthe & Siegman, Greg Forbes. First Thirty. (p. 597)
Paxson, Jillip Naysinthe, told to. First Thirty. (p. 597)
Paxton, Cameron L., illus. see Cromwell, Daisy.
Paxton, Rain. Children's Joke Book. (p. 303)
Paxton, Tom. Jungle Baseball Game. Schmidt, Karenlee, illus. (p. 935)
—Marvelous Toy. Cox, Steve, illus. (p. 1099)
—Marvelous Toy (Board) Cox, Steve, illus. (p. 1099)
Payan, Gregory. Federalists & Anti-Federalists: How & Why Political Parties Were Formed in Young America. (p. 580)
Payan, Michael. In the Ring with Bret Hart. (p. 867)
—In the Ring with Diamond Dallas Page. (p. 867)
—In the Ring with Goldberg. (p. 867)
—In the Ring with Kevin Nash. (p. 867)
—In the Ring with Scott Steiner. (p. 867)
—In the Ring with Sting. (p. 867)
Paydos, Michael. Everything(r) Bible Stories Book: Timeless Favorites from the Old & New Testaments. (p. 544)
Paye, Won-Ldy & Lippert, Margaret H. Head, Body, Legs: A Story from Liberia. Paschkis, Julie, illus. (p. 756)
—Mrs. Chicken & the Hungry Crocodile. Paschkis, Julie, illus. (p. 1187)
Payer-Smith, Heather. Nameless World. Rudy, Patricia, ed. (p. 1228)
—Ryan's Bike. (p. 1499)
Payjack, Amy J. Valorean. (p. 1831)
Payment, Simone. American Women Spies of World War II. (p. 64)
—Bass Fishing. (p. 143)
—Black Ops & Other Special Missions of the U. S. Navy Seals. (p. 196)
—Buck Leonard. (p. 234)
—Career as a Plumber. (p. 266)
—Careers in Restaurants. (p. 268)
—Cool Careers Without College for People Who Love to Travel. (p. 363)
—Finding & Capturing Saddam Hussein: A Successful Military Manhunt. (p. 587)
—Friendship, Dating, & Relationships. (p. 639)
—Getting to Know Python. (p. 669)
—Greek Mythology. (p. 720)
—Kyle Busch: NASCAR Driver. (p. 969)
—Marc Andreessen & Jim Clark: The Founders of Netscape. (p. 1091)
—Michael J. Fox: Parkinson's Disease Research Advocate. (p. 1134)
—Michael J. Fox: Parkinson's Disease Research Advocate (Celebrity Activists) (p. 1134)
—Navy SEALs: Special Operations for the U. S. Navy. (p. 1238)
—Navy Seals: Special Operations for the U. S. Navy. (p. 1238)
—Nuclear, Biological, & Chemical Disasters: A Practical Survival Guide. (p. 1269)
—Pony Express: A Primary Source History of the Race to Bring Mail to the American West. (p. 1382)
—Pony Express. (p. 1382)
—Queen Latifah. (p. 1424)
—Robotics Careers: Preparing for the Future. (p. 1481)
—Ryan Newman: NASCAR Driver. (p. 1499)
—Salle: Claiming the Mississippi River for France. (p. 1505)
—Saving the Endangered Blue Whale. (p. 1517)
—Scott O'Dell. (p. 1531)
—Taking Your Band Online. (p. 1698)
—Trial of Leopold & Loeb: A Primary Source Account. (p. 1785)
—What Happens to Your Body When You Run. (p. 1886)
Payne, Alice. City Island Tales of the Clam Diggers. (p. 323)
Payne, Anna. Extra Sepcial: For When Someone You Love Dies. (p. 555)
Payne, C. C. Lula Bell on Geekdom, Freakdom, & the Challenges of Bad Hair (p. 1064)
Payne, C. F., illus. see Bildner, Phil.
Payne, C. F., illus. see Bunting, Eve.
Payne, C. F., illus. see Frederick, Heather Vogel.
Payne, C. F., illus. see Howe, James.
Payne, C. F., illus. see Kelly, Mark.
Payne, C. F., illus. see Lithgow, John.
Payne, C. F., illus. see Martin, Steve.
Payne, C. F., illus. see Moss, Marissa.
Payne, C. F., illus. see Nash, Ogden.
Payne, C. F., illus. see Rappaport, Doreen.
Payne, C. F., illus. see Shaughnessy, Dan.
Payne, C. F., illus. see Thayer, Ernest L.
Payne, C. F., jt. auth. see Lithgow, John.
Payne, C. F., tr. see Moss, Marissa.
Payne, Carleen Dacruz. Shared Reading for Today's Classroom: Lessons & Strategies for Explicit Instruction in Comprehension, Fluency, Word Study, & Genre. (p. 1561)
Payne, Catherine Clark. Something to Sing About. (p. 1610)
Payne, Christine N. Kid Places in Colorado Springs. (p. 951)
Payne, Danyelle. McKayla, a Working Dog. (p. 1114)
Payne, Donald. Little Lost Raccoons. (p. 1031)
Payne, Edward John. History of the New World Called America. (p. 785)
Payne, Elizabeth. Pharaohs of Ancient Egypt. (p. 1350)
Payne, Emerald M., illus. see Payne, Yadira V.
Payne, Gaynell. I Go Exploring. Buffinet, Jacqueline, illus. (p. 838)
Payne, Gregory. Chase to the Brazen Head. (p. 294)
Payne, Helen. Vacation Paws. Youngblood, Carol, illus. (p. 1830)
Payne, Henry, illus. see Perkins, Al.
Payne, Jackson. Stork & the Birthday Stocking. Williams, Jean, illus. (p. 1655)
Payne, James, jt. auth. see Heller, Donna.
Payne, James S. & Payne Simmons, Kimberly. My BackPack Brain. (p. 1196)
—My Notebook Brain. (p. 1216)
Payne, Jan. World's Best Book: The Spookiest, Smelliest, Wildest, Oldest, Weirdest, Brainiest, & Funniest Facts. Phillips, Mike, illus. (p. 1960)
Payne, Jan, jt. auth. see Payne, Tony.
Payne, Jan & Payne, Tony. Not Again, Annie! Reeve, Rosie, illus. (p. 1266)
Payne, Jody. Miss Spellin' Helen. Payne, Rachel & Song, Danielle, illus. (p. 1152)
Payne, John, ed. see Kingsley, Kaza.
Payne, Johnnie Denise. Lady by Choice: What Every Girl Should Know about Bridging the Gap Between Adolescence & Womanhood. (p. 970)
Payne, K. E. 365 Days. (p. 2001)
—Another 365 Days. (p. 87)
—Because of Her. (p. 155)
—Me@You.com. (p. 1131)
Payne, Kay, illus. see Strong, Frances Dinkins.
Payne, Kimberley J. Trees of the Book: Learning from God's Creation. (p. 1784)
Payne, Lauren Murphy. Just Because I Am: A Child's Book of Affirmation. Iwai, Melissa, illus. (p. 938)
—We Can Get Along: A Child's Book of Choices. Iwai, Melissa, illus. (p. 1866)
Payne, Laurie. Mush & the Big Blue Flower. Campbell, Ruth, illus. (p. 1193)
Payne, Lawrence, ed. see Samarsky, Mikhail.
Payne, Liane. Snowy Day. (p. 1601)
Payne, M. D. Boogers from Beyond #3. Dockery, Amanda, illus. (p. 210)
—Burpstronauts Dockery, Amanda & Zoo, Keith, illus. (p. 244)
—Fartsunami. Dockery, Amanda, illus. (p. 575)
—Fear the Barftron. Dockery, Amanda, illus. (p. 579)
—Sickening Secrets from Raven Hill (Books 1 And 2) Dockery, Amanda, illus. (p. 1572)
—Tomb of Brain Ooze Zoo, Keith, illus. (p. 1764)
—Zits from Python Pit #6. Zoo, Keith, illus. (p. 1987)
Payne, M. E. Buzz the Bee in Bee Smart. (p. 248)
Payne, Mark, illus. see Lebachen, Medyhne.
Payne, Martyn. Footsteps to the Feast: 12 Two-Hour Children's Programmes for Christian Festivals & Special Times of the Year. (p. 615)
Payne, Mary Jennifer. Since You've Been Gone. (p. 1578)
Payne, Matt. Secret Agent Gear: Spy Tools & Tech: Past, Present, & Future. (p. 1540)
Payne, Nichole. Going... Going... Clean. (p. 692)
Payne, Rachel. Autumn Secrets of the Equinox. (p. 118)
—Summer of Circles & Sapphires: Iggy Colvin Adventure Series. (p. 1674)
Payne, Rachel, illus. see Payne, Jody.
Payne, Raymond. Shelter from the Storm. (p. 1565)
Payne, Reina. Woman in the Yellow Hat. (p. 1945)
Payne, Richard A. Banjo & the Telescope. (p. 136)
Payne, Ruby K. Mental Models for Math: Grades 6-12. (p. 1126)
Payne, Sandy. Find Your Magic. Goodpaster, Nancy, illus. (p. 587)
Payne, Sara Hale. Old Mr. Murphy Had a Zoo. (p. 1284)
Payne Simmons, Kimberly, jt. auth. see Payne, James S.
Payne, Stephanie, illus. see O'Hanlon, Toni.
Payne, Stephen. Teenage Stories of the West. (p. 1714)
Payne, Timothy R. Payne Man. (p. 1331)
Payne, Tony. Things to Make & Doodle: Exciting Projects to Color, Cut, & Create. (p. 1733)
Payne, Tony, jt. auth. see Payne, Jan.
Payne, Tony & Payne, Jan. Oh No, Annie! (p. 1281)
Payne, Trip. Amazing Crosswords for Kids. (p. 54)
—Awesome Crosswords for Kids. (p. 121)
—Clever Crosswords for Kids. (p. 331)
—Fantastically Fun Crosswords for Kids. Garnage, Ken, illus. (p. 572)
Payne Turner, Regina. Greatest: Little Prairie Dog Makes a Big Difference. (p. 719)
Payne, Yadira V. Brown Eyes: Ojos Marrones. Payne, Yadira V., ed. (p. 232)
—!Viva los Colores! Payne, Yadira V., ed. (p. 1846)
Payne-Krzyzanowski, Anna, et al. 52 More Crafts: For the Church Year. Kyle, Margaret, illus. (p. 1997)
Payne-Sylvester, Linda. Here Comes Christmas & the Teddy Bears Get Ready. (p. 770)
Payno, Manuel. Bandidos de Rio Frio. Camacho, Ricardo, illus. (p. 136)
Paynter, Roxanne. Small Souls: Meditations for Children. (p. 1592)
Payot Karpathakis, Emmanuelle. Nova Casa Da Pixie. (p. 1268)
—Nuevo Hogar de Pixie. (p. 1270)
—Pixie Déménage. (p. 1365)
—Pixie en Vacaciones. (p. 1365)
—Pixie's Holidays. (p. 1365)
—Pixies Neue Heimat. (p. 1365)
—Pixie's New Home. (p. 1365)
Payson, Howard. Boy Scouts at the Canadian Border. (p. 218)
—Boy Scouts at the Panama Canal. (p. 218)
—Boy Scouts' Mountain Camp. (p. 218)
—Boy Scouts on the Range. (p. 219)
—Boy Scouts under Sealed Orders. (p. 219)
Payton, Belle. Even the Score. (p. 541)
—May the Best Twin Win. (p. 1112)
—Two Cool for School. (p. 1803)
—Whole New Ball Game. (p. 1920)
Payton, Nicole. Dragon Savior. (p. 478)
Payton-Wright, Kaye. Secret Wood. (p. 1544)
Paytras, C. J. Littlest Homeless Angel: Darby's Story. (p. 1039)
Payzant, Joan M. Who's a Scaredy Cat! A Story of the Halifax Explosion Simons, Marijke, tr. (p. 1920)
PAZ, AGUSTAíN FERNAüNDEZ, et al. PASTELERIA DE DONA REMEDIOS. (p. 1327)
Paz, Agustín Fernández & Fernández Paz, Agustín. Tren Cargado de Misterios. (p. 1784)
Paz, Agustine Fernandez. Cuentos por Palabras. (p. 390)
Paz, Diana. Timespell. (p. 1754)
Paz Lozano, Octavio. Rama. Kitora, Tetsuo, illus. (p. 1437)
Paz, Myrna J. De La, see De La Paz, Myrna J.
Paz, Naomi. At the Hardware Store: Understand Place Value. (p. 111)
—At the Hardware Store. (p. 111)
Paz, Noemi, jt. auth. see Hawker, Frances.
Paz, Veronica. Play Pretend with Muno. (p. 1371)
Paz, Veronica & Echeverria, Jessica. Party in My Tummy. (p. 1326)
Pazer, Lisa, jt. auth. see Biederman, Lynn.
Pazzelli, John. First Sudoku Book. Zourelias, Diana, illus. (p. 597)
—Kids' Kakuro. Zourelias, Diana, illus. (p. 954)
PC Treasures Staff, ed. see Carney, Larry.
PC Treasures Staff, ed. Barney's Giant Coloring & Activity Book. (p. 139)
—Dale Earnhardt Jr. (p. 401)
—Jeff Gordon. (p. 911)

—Jimmie Johnson (p. 918)
—Jimmie Johnson. (p. 918)
—Kyle Busch. (p. 969)
—NASCAR Drivers Coloring Book: Kyle Busch. (p. 1230)
—Tony Stewart. (p. 1766)
PC Treasures Staff, prod. Cinderella. (p. 320)
—Gingerbread Man. (p. 677)
—Goldilocks & the Three Bears. (p. 696)
—Hansel & Gretel. (p. 743)
—Little Mermaid. (p. 1031)
—Little Red Riding Hood. (p. 1035)
—Peter Rabbit. (p. 1347)
—Snow White & the Seven Dwarfs. (p. 1600)
—Three Billy Goats Gruff. (p. 1741)
—Three Little Pigs. (p. 1743)
—Ugly Duckling. (p. 1808)
Pea, M. J. adventures of Benje & Sammy: Probably the naughtiest dogs in the World. (p. 16)
Pea, Uncle & Pomerantz, Joel. Twice Just to Be Sure: A Musicky Tale for Imaginative People. Jackson, Lance, illus. (p. 1801)
Peabody, Beth Leone. Chocolate Pie Therapy. (p. 309)
Peabody, Charles. Exploration of Mounds, Coahoma County, Mississippi. (p. 550)
Peabody, Richard. Alice Redux: New Stories of Alice, Lewis, & Wonderland. (p. 39)
Peabody, Rob, illus. see Hersey, Jodi.
Peace, Bob. Wicked Witch Pop Quiz. Rasheed, M., illus. (p. 1927)
Peace, C. J. Sneavel Stranger. (p. 1597)
Peace, J. Calvin. Sweet Street Gang & the Lost Treasure Cave. (p. 1690)
Peach, Susan & Millard, Anne. Greeks. Jackson, Ian, illus. (p. 721)
Peachey, Ann. Adventures of a Greek Cat Called Mani. (p. 16)
Peachey, Ted. Adventures of Ryan & His Magic Carrot. (p. 22)
PeachMoon Publishing. Adventures of Lucky the Lizard Las aventuras del lagarto Lucky. (p. 20)
—Lizard in the Mailbox. (p. 1042)
—Lucky Goes to School. (p. 1062)
Peach-pit. DearS Peach-Pit Press Staff, illus. (p. 419)
Peach-Pit. DearS Official Fan Book. (p. 419)
—Shugo Chara! (p. 1571)
Peach-Pit Press Staff. DearS (p. 419)
—DearS Peach-Pit Press Staff, illus. (p. 419)
—DearS. (p. 419)
Peach-Pit Press Staff, illus. see Peach-pit.
Peacock, Ann & Lewis, C. S. Chronicles of Narnia. Barbera, Tony et al, illus. (p. 317)
Peacock, Ausa M., illus. see Pittis, Arthur M.
Peacock, Bessie Merle, illus. see Peacock-Williams, Carol A. & Williams, Christy Jo.
Peacock, Carol Antoinette. Death & Dying. (p. 420)
—Pilgrim Cat. Ettlinger, Doris, illus. (p. 1358)
—Red Thread Sisters. (p. 1455)
Peacock, Hilda V. Eye-Jack & Hey-Oh. (p. 557)
Peacock, John. Story of Costume. (p. 1657)
Peacock, Kathleen. Hemlock. (p. 767)
—Thornhill. (p. 1740)
—Willowgrove. (p. 1934)
Peacock, Kathy Wilson. Natural Resources & Sustainable Development. (p. 1235)
Peacock, Kathy Wilson & Hendrickson, Mary K. Food Security. (p. 614)
Peacock, L. A. Panic in Pompeii. Hale, Nathan, illus. (p. 1321)
—Terror at Troy. Hale, Nathan, illus. (p. 1722)
—Truth (and Myths) about Thanksgiving. Wigsby, Nick, illus. (p. 1794)
—Truth (and Myths) about the Presidents. Wigsby, Nick, illus. (p. 1794)
Peacock, Louise. At Ellis Island: A History in Many Voices. Krudop, Walter Lyon, illus. (p. 110)
—Crossing the Delaware: A History in Many Voices. Krudop, Walter Lyon, illus. (p. 385)
Peacock, Phyllis Hornung, illus. see Ellis, Julie.
Peacock, Ralph, illus. see Henty, G. A.
Peacock, Robert M., photos by see Gee, Denise.
Peacock, Sarah, illus. see Chissick, Michael.
Peacock, Scott. Beacham's Guide to Literature for Young Adults (p. 149)
Peacock, Shane. Becoming Holmes: The Boy Sherlock Holmes, His Final Case. (p. 156)
—Death in the Air. (p. 420)
—Double You (p. 473)
—Dragon Turn: The Boy Sherlock Holmes, His Fifth Case. (p. 478)
—Dragon Turn. (p. 478)
—Eye of the Crow: The Boy Sherlock Holmes, His 1st Case. (p. 557)
—Eye of the Crow. (p. 557)
—Last Message (p. 978)
—Secret Fiend: The Boy Sherlock Holmes, His Fourth Case. (p. 1540)
—Secret Fiend. (p. 1540)
—Vanishing Girl: The Boy Sherlock Holmes, His 3rd Case. (p. 1833)
—Vanishing Girl: The Boy Sherlock Holmes, His Third Case. (p. 1833)
Peacock, Thomas Love & Wisuri, Marlene. Good Path: Ojibwe Learning & Activity Book for Kids. (p. 700)
—To Be Free: Understanding & eliminating Racism. (p. 1758)
Peacock, Tom. Skateboarding. (p. 1583)
—Snowboarding: Extreme Stories from Canada's Best Riders. (p. 1600)
Peacock-Williams, Carol A. Adoption of Terry the Terrible Terrier. (p. 13)
Peacock-Williams, Carol A. & Williams, Christy Jo. Benny the Beetle Peacock, Bessie Merle, illus. (p. 165)
Peagler, Melissa. Lost Creek Rising Volume 2 of the Lost Creek Saga Series. (p. 1055)
Peak, Cindy. Little Star That Shines for Jesus. (p. 1036)
Peak, Danielle. Enchanted Conquest. (p. 523)
—Single Flame in Sunset. (p. 1579)
Peak, Doris-Jean. Wernher Von Braun: Alabama's Rocket Scientist. (p. 1875)
Peak, Lizabeth. Growth Disorders. (p. 727)
Peak, Lizabeth & Hardman, Lizabeth. Mood Disorders. (p. 1171)
Peake, Marilyn, ed. see Disney Book Group Staff.
Peake, Mervyn. Boy in Darkness. (p. 218)
Peake, Mervyn, illus. see Carroll, Lewis, pseud.
Peake, Mervyn, illus. see Grimm, Jacob & Grimm, Wilhelm.
Peakler, Nicole Danette. Tayno Ti & the Legend of the Coqui. (p. 1708)
Peale, Norman Vincent. Seeds of Faith: Love. (p. 1547)
—Seeds of Faith: Faith. (p. 1547)
Peale, Norman Vincent, jt. auth. see Carney, Mary Lou.
Pealock, Staci Holland. Where I Belong. (p. 1908)
Pearce, Al. Famous Tracks. (p. 570)
Pearce, Arline June. Sunrise the Barnegat Pony. (p. 1677)
Pearce, Bryony. Weight of Souls. (p. 1872)
Pearce, Carl, illus. see Collins, Terry.
Pearce, Carl, illus. see Morley, Ben.
Pearce, Carl, illus. see Quinn, Patricia O.
Pearce, Carl, illus. see Sheth, Kashmira.
Pearce, Chris. Skills Booster. (p. 1585)
Pearce, Claudia. San Diego Zoo. (p. 1510)
Pearce, Claudia & Worley, Karen E. San Diego Zoo. Bohn, Ken & Garrison, Ron, illus. (p. 1510)
Pearce, Clemency. Frangoline & the Midnight Dream. Elliott, Rebecca, illus. (p. 628)
—Three Little Words. Beardshaw, Rosalind, illus. (p. 1743)
Pearce, Emily Smith. Slowpoke. Ritchie, Scot, illus. (p. 1591)
Pearce, Gillian M., illus. see Hill, Raine.
Pearce, Jackson. As You Wish. (p. 105)
—Doublecross: (And Other Skills I Learned As a Superspy) (p. 473)
—Fathomless. (p. 577)
—Purity. (p. 1419)
—Sisters Red. (p. 1581)
—Sweetly. (p. 1690)
Pearce, Jackson, jt. auth. see Stiefvater, Maggie.
Pearce, Jacqueline. Effet Manga (p. 505)
—Emily's Dream (p. 519)
—Flood Warning Franson, Leanne, illus. (p. 605)
—Manga Touch (p. 1087)
—Reunion (p. 1465)
—Truth about Rats (and Dogs) (p. 1794)
—Weeds & Other Stories. (p. 1871)
Pearce, Jonathan. Buds: A Story about Friendship. (p. 235)
—Community Spirits: Infestations on the Spectral Plane. (p. 350)
—Far Side of the Moon: A California Story. (p. 572)
—John-Browne's Body & Sole: A Semester of Life. (p. 921)
—Little Honesty: Aches & Joys of an American Prince. (p. 1029)
—Nobody's Fault: Surprises from the Earth & the Heart. (p. 1262)
Pearce, Kevin. Being an Octopus. (p. 161)
—Foods of Mexico. (p. 614)
—I'm Special Because... (p. 860)
Pearce, Margaret. Altar of Shulaani Series Book 1: The Altar of Shulaani. (p. 50)
—Beautiful Day. van Garderen, Ilse, illus. (p. 153)
—Belinda Robinson Novel Book 1: Belinda & the Witch's Cat. (p. 162)
—Belinda Robinson Novel Book 2: Belinda & the Holidays It Rained. (p. 162)
—Belinda Robinson Novel Book 3: Belinda & the Missing Will. (p. 162)
—Jumping into Trouble Book 3: Missing! a Horse. (p. 934)
—Jumping into Trouble Series Book 1: Wanted! a Horse. (p. 934)
Pearce, Philippa. Amy's Three Best Things. Craig, Helen, illus. (p. 66)
—Finder's Magic. Craig, Helen, illus. (p. 587)
—Little Gentleman. Pohrt, Tom, illus. (p. 1028)
—Squirrel Wife. Anderson, Wayne, illus. (p. 1637)
—Wings of Courage. (p. 1936)
Pearce, Philippa & Pearl, Matthew. Little Gentleman (p. 1028)
Pearce, Q. L. Celtic Mythology. Lucent Books, ed. (p. 286)
—Furies. (p. 650)
—Ghost Hunters. (p. 670)
—Given Kachepa: Advocate for Human Trafficking Victims. (p. 681)
—Hannah Taylor: The Ladybug Foundation. (p. 742)
—James Quadrino: Wildlife Protector. (p. 907)
—Llorona. (p. 1043)
—Mothman. (p. 1179)
—Mysterious Disappearances. (p. 1223)
—Pegasus. (p. 1335)
—Reincarnation. (p. 1457)
Pearce, Q L. Using the Standards, Grade 1: Building Grammar & Writing Skills. (p. 1828)
Pearce, Q. L. Wendigo. (p. 1875)
—Zach Hunter: Modern-Day Abolitionist. (p. 1984)
Pearce, Q. L., jt. auth. see Capaldi, Gina.
Pearce, Q. L., jt. auth. see Pearce, Q L.
Pearce, Q L & Pearce, Q. L. Using the Standards: Building Grammar & Writing Skills, Grade 2. (p. 1828)
Pearce, Richard & Story, Ken. Dorkman. (p. 471)
Pearce, Sha, ed. see Perkins, Diamond Le'na.
Pearce, Sue, jt. auth. see Quin, Caroline.
Pearce, Sue & Quin, Caroline. Pets. (p. 1348)
Pearce, Suzannah, ed. Five-Mintue Stories for Boys. (p. 601)
—Five-Minute Stories for Girls. (p. 601)
Pearce, Tracy. How to Eat Fried Worms: An Instructional Guide for Literature (p. 819)
Pearce, Valarie. When Daddy Needs a Timeout. Johnson, Meredith, illus. (p. 1901)
—When Mommy Needs a Timeout. Johnson, Meredith, illus. (p. 1903)
Pearcey, Alice. Usborne Castle Jigsaw Book. Milbourne, Anna, ed. (p. 1827)
—Usborne Dinosaur Stencil Book. Kushii, Tetsuo, illus. (p. 1827)
—Usborne Tractors & Trucks Stencil Book. Milbourne, Anna, ed. (p. 1827)
Pearcey, Alice, jt. auth. see Stowell, Louie.
Pearcey, Alice, ed. Dinosaur Jigsaw Atlas. Bird, Glen, illus. (p. 442)
Pearcey, Dawn, illus. see Posesorski, Sherie.
Pearcy, Thomas L. History of Central America. (p. 783)
Peare, Catherine Owens. Albert Einstein: A Biography for Young People. (p. 34)
Pearl, Alyson J. Big Halloween Surprise. (p. 181)
Pearl, B. B. Poerava's Heaven. (p. 1376)
Pearl, Barbara. Whale of a Tale. (p. 1877)
Pearl, Beverly. Little Cat Snowshoes. (p. 1025)
—Poison Ivy. (p. 1377)
—Poison Ivy, the Pocket Book. (p. 1377)
Pearl, David R. & Pearl, Tamara R. Stop the Bully. Ahrin, Jacob, illus. (p. 1653)
Pearl, Debi. Listen to My Dream. Pearl, Debi & Pearl, Michael, illus. (p. 1022)
Pearl, Lillie, ed. Book of Lillie: The Oracles of God — Not New Words, but New Revelations. (p. 211)
Pearl, Matthew, jt. auth. see Pearce, Philippa.
Pearl, Melissa. Golden Blood. (p. 694)
Pearl, Michael. Bien y el Mal: Abraham Comic Book Bulanadi, Danny & Cearley, Clint, illus. (p. 177)
—Gap Fact. (p. 655)
—Jumping Ship: What to Do So Your Children Don't Jump Ship to the World When They Get Older. (p. 934)
Pearl, Michael, illus. see Pearl, Debi.
Pearl, Michael & Bulanadi, Danny. Bien y el Mal Parte 1 el Principio: Good & Evil Comic Part 1 in Spanish. (p. 177)
—Good & Evil: Abraham Pt. 2 (p. 697)
Pearl, Nancy. Book Crush: For Kids & Teens - Recommended Reading for Every Mood, Moment, & Interest. (p. 210)
Pearl, Norman. Alligators: Fast & Fierce. (p. 47)
—Bald Eagle Skeens, Matthew, illus. (p. 133)
—Bill of Rights Skeens, Matthew, illus. (p. 186)
—Great Seal of the United States. Skeens, Matthew, illus. (p. 718)
—Grizzly Bears: Wild & Strong. (p. 724)
—Hyenas: Fierce Hunters. (p. 831)
—Our National Anthem Skeens, Matthew, illus. (p. 1309)
—Our National Anthem. Skeens, Matthew, illus. (p. 1309)
—Pledge of Allegiance Skeens, Matthew, illus. (p. 1373)
—Polar Bears: Arctic Hunters. (p. 1379)
—Sharks: Ocean Hunters. (p. 1563)
—Tigers: Hunters of Asia. (p. 1749)
—U. S. Constitution Skeens, Matthew, illus. (p. 1806)
Pearl, Norman & Picture Window Books Staff. Bill of Rights Skeens, Matthew, illus. (p. 186)
—Pledge of Allegiance Skeens, Matthew, illus. (p. 1374)
Pearl, Norman & Yomtov, Nel. Secret American History: From Witch Trials to Internment Camps (p. 1540)
Pearl, Paige. ARTLANTICA: the Secret Kingdom Beneath Galveston Island. (p. 104)
Pearl Production, ed. Language Arts Skills & Strategies (p. 974)
Pearl Production Staff, creator. Language Arts Skills & Strategies, Level 4 (p. 974)
Pearl Production Staff, ed. English-Language Arts Skills & Strategies, Level 8 (p. 530)
—Language Arts Skills & Strategies Level 3 (p. 974)
—Language Arts Skills & Strategies - Level 7 (p. 974)
Pearl, Sydelle. Books for Children of the World: The Story of Jella Lepman Iantorno, Danlyn, illus. (p. 212)
—Elijah's Tears: Stories for the Jewish Holidays Skortcheva, Rossitza, illus. (p. 512)
Pearl, Tamara R., jt. auth. see Pearl, David R.
Pearle, Ida. Moon Is Going to Addy's House. (p. 1172)
Pearlman, Bobby. Passover Is Here! Desmoinaux, Christel, illus. (p. 1327)
Pearlman, Carly. Ana Goes Apple Picking: Count to Tell the Number of Objects. (p. 66)
Pearlman, Debra. Where Is Jasper Johns? (p. 1908)
Pearlman, Esther, jt. illus. see Pearlman, Larry.
Pearlman, Herbert, abr. Herb P. Flyboy: The Journey from World War II Pilot to German POW. (p. 769)
Pearlman, Larry & Pearlman, Esther. Cute Li'l Donkeys: (Raisin' & Grazin') (p. 396)
Pearlman, Matthew. That's Great Advice: Advice from Pro Athletes for Kids, Written by a Kid. (p. 1726)
Pearlstein, Don. Make Your Own Laptop: Color & Build Your Own Computer! Stillerman, Robbie, illus. (p. 1080)
Pearn, Kayley, illus. see Hackett, J. J.
Pearn, Victor Wayne. Point Guard. (p. 1377)
Pears, Alison. Gus & Oliver-A Family Tale. (p. 732)
Pears, Iain. Dream of Scipio. (p. 483)
Pearsall, John. Rodney's Room: Dr. Ghoul's Party Plans. (p. 1484)
Pearsall, Shelley. All of the Above. Steptoe, Javaka, illus. (p. 45)
—All Shook Up. (p. 45)
—Crooked River. (p. 384)
—Jump into the Sky. (p. 934)
—Trouble Don't Last. (p. 1789)
Pearsall, Stephanie. When God Says Yes! (p. 1902)
Pearse, Alfred, illus. see Henty, G. A.
Pearse, Asha. Wizard of Oz. (p. 1943)
Pearse, Stephen, illus. see Halter, Reese & Turner, Nancy J.
Pearse, Stephen, tr. see Halter, Reese & Turner, Nancy J.
Pearson, jt. auth. see Pearson, Susan.
Pearson, Amy M. Mud Fight. (p. 1188)
Pearson, Andrea. Ember Gods (Kilenya Series, 2) (p. 517)
Pearson, Anne. Antigua Grecia. (p. 89)
—DK Eyewitness Books: Ancient Greece: Ancient Greece. (p. 455)
Pearson, Anthony. Baby Bear Eats the Night Leick, Bonnie, illus. (p. 125)
Pearson, Betty Jean. Learn with Ladee: A Service Dog. (p. 984)
Pearson Canada Staff. MCP "Plaid" Phonics (p. 1115)
Pearson, Carey, jt. auth. see Kivestu, Patty.
Pearson, Carol Lynn. Christmas Thief: A Novel. (p. 316)
—Christmas Thief. (p. 316)
—Modern Magi. (p. 1158)
—Summer of Truth. (p. 1674)
Pearson, Carrie. Cool Summer Tail Wald, Christina, illus. (p. 364)
Pearson, Carrie A. Cool Summer Tail Wald, Christina, illus. (p. 364)
—Invierno Muy Abrigador Wald, Christina, illus. (p. 885)
—Warm Winter Tail Wald, Christina, illus. (p. 1858)
Pearson, Carrie A. & Wald, Christina. Fresco Cuento de Verano Wald, Christina, illus. (p. 636)
Pearson, Chris. Emma & Her Friends from Bluebell Wood. (p. 519)
Pearson, creator. Tug, Tug, Tug: Comprehension Power Readers, Grade 3. (p. 1796)
Pearson, Darrell, et al. Can I Really Relate? (p. 258)
Pearson, David. English Bookbinding Styles. (p. 529)
Pearson, David, illus. see Custard, P. T.
Pearson, Debora. Alphabeep: A Zipping, Zooming ABC. Miller, Edward, illus. (p. 48)
—Alphabeep! A Zipping, Zooming ABC. Miller, Edward, illus. (p. 48)
—Big City Song. Reed, Lynn Rowe, illus. (p. 180)
—Kids Do, Animals Too: A Book of Playground Opposites. Hilb, Nora, illus. (p. 953)
—Leo's Tree. Hilb, Nora, illus. (p. 993)
—Mary Anning: the Girl Who Cracked Open the World (Paperback) Copyright 2016. (p. 1100)
—Polar Bear Alert! (p. 1378)
—Sophie's Wheels. Hilb, Nora, illus. (p. 1613)
Pearson, Debora, jt. auth. see Raskin, Lawrie.
Pearson, Douglas, jt. auth. see Gesme, Carole.
Pearson Education Staff. Pirates of the Caribbean the Curse of the Black Pearl. (p. 1364)
—Room in the Tower & Other Stories. (p. 1488)
—Spin! Grammar, Vocabulary, & Writing. (p. 1627)
—Spin!, Level C: Grammar, Vocabulary, & Writing. (p. 1627)
—Spin!, Level E. (p. 1627)
Pearson Education Staff, jt. auth. see Amos, Eduardo.
Pearson Education Staff, jt. auth. see Anderson, Kris.
Pearson Education Staff, jt. auth. see Beatty, Ken.
Pearson Education Staff, jt. auth. see Burgess, Melvyn.
Pearson Education Staff, jt. auth. see Burke, Kathy.
Pearson Education Staff, jt. auth. see Collins, Anne.
Pearson Education Staff, jt. auth. see Escott, John.
Pearson Education Staff, jt. auth. see Gilchrist, Cherry.
Pearson Education Staff, jt. auth. see Harvey, Paul.
Pearson Education Staff, jt. auth. see Hood, Thomas.
Pearson Education Staff, jt. auth. see James, M. R.
Pearson Education Staff, jt. auth. see Kotzwinkle, William.
Pearson Education Staff, jt. auth. see Lawrence, D. H.
Pearson Education Staff, jt. auth. see Montgomery, L. M.
Pearson Education Staff, jt. auth. see O'Reilly, Elaine.
Pearson Education Staff, jt. auth. see Pearson Longman Staff.
Pearson Education Staff, jt. auth. see Rabley, Stephen.
Pearson Education Staff, jt. auth. see Rollason, Jane.
Pearson Education Staff, jt. auth. see Shipton, Paul.
Pearson Education Staff, jt. auth. see Smith, Bernard.
Pearson Education Staff, jt. auth. see Veness, Coleen Degnan.
Pearson Education Staff, jt. auth. see Viney, Brigit.
Pearson Education Staff, jt. auth. see Waller, Stephen.
Pearson, Edwin. Will's Galactic Adventure. (p. 1934)
Pearson, Elizabeth. My Grandma Says. (p. 1210)
Pearson, Georgene. Country Christmas. Anderson, Marjorie M., illus. (p. 372)
—Larry the Llama. Venables, Julie, illus. (p. 976)
Pearson, Gracie. Bentley's Yard: Welcome Home! (p. 166)
Pearson, Harry. Alicia. (p. 40)
Pearson, Henrik Barkley de. Secret of the Rainbow. (p. 1542)
Pearson, Iris & Merrill, Mike. Adventures of Lady: The Big Storm. Pearson, Iris, ed. (p. 19)
—Adventures of Lady: The Big Storm Coloring Book. Pearson, Iris, ed. (p. 19)
Pearson, J. J. Anita & Ing: Garden Adventure. (p. 84)
Pearson, Jane & Bryan, Philip. Creatures of the Dark. (p. 380)
Pearson, Jason. Astonishing X-Men: Monstrous. (p. 109)
Pearson, Jason, jt. illus. see Huat, Tan Eng.
Pearson, Jean W. & Dutto, Lisa M. Gravity Rocks. (p. 713)
Pearson, Joanna. Rites & Wrongs of Janice Wills. (p. 1475)
Pearson, Judith Frank. Chester the Christmas Church Mouse. (p. 298)
Pearson, Kathleen. Polka Dot Loves Her Friends a Lot! (p. 1381)
—We Love You a Lot, Little Polka Dot. (p. 1867)
Pearson, Kim. You Can Be an Author, Even If You're Not A Writer: The 1-2-3 of Creating a Book. (p. 1974)
Pearson, Kimberly Ann. Mystling Glen Book I: The Tale of A Prince. (p. 1226)
Pearson, Kit. Daring Game. (p. 407)
—Looking at the Moon. (p. 1051)
—Perfect Gentle Knight. (p. 1341)
—Sky Is Falling. (p. 1586)
Pearson, Lance. Byte of Charity. (p. 249)
Pearson, Larry Leroy, illus. see Sanner, Jennifer Jackson, ed.
Pearson Learning Staff, creator. Trees & Leaves. (p. 1784)
—Visit to the Doctor. (p. 1845)
Pearson Longman Staff, jt. auth. see Escott, John.
Pearson Longman Staff, jt. auth. see Rosenberg, Nancy Taylor.
Pearson Longman Staff, jt. auth. see Strange, Derek.
Pearson Longman Staff & Pearson Education Staff. Longman Diccionario Pocket, Ingles-Espanol, Espanol-Ingles: Para Estudiantes Mexicanos. (p. 1047)
Pearson, Luke. Hilda & the Bird Parade. (p. 779)
—Hilda & the Black Hound. (p. 779)
—Hilda & the Troll. (p. 779)
Pearson, Maggie. Alien Draw. (p. 40)
—Dark of the Moon. (p. 408)
—Rumpelstiltskin Returns. (p. 1495)
—Short & Shocking! (p. 1569)
Pearson, Maria. Animal Stencil Cards. (p. 79)
—Spooky Stencil Cards. (p. 1631)
Pearson, Maria, illus. see Doherty, Gillian, ed.

P

Pearson, Marline. Love U 2 - Baby Smarts: Through the Eyes of A Child. (p. 1060)
Pearson, Mary E. Adoration of Jenna Fox. (p. 13)
—Fast Dan. Doty, Eldon C., illus. (p. 576)
—Fox Inheritance. (p. 626)
—Generous Me. Krejca, Gary, illus. (p. 660)
—Heart of Betrayal. (p. 759)
—I Can Do It All. Shelley, Jeff, illus. (p. 835)
—Kiss of Deception. (p. 961)
—Miles Between. (p. 1142)
—Room on Lorelei Street. (p. 1488)
Pearson, Mary E. & Shelly, Jeff. Puedo Hacer de Todo. Shelly, Jeff, illus. (p. 1414)
Pearson, Mary R. Bible Learning Games: Reproducible Activities. (p. 175)
Pearson, Mary R. & Kuhn, Pamela J. Favorite Bible Heroes: Grades 3&4. Galey, Chuck, illus. (p. 578)
Pearson, Mary Rose. Bible Animal Tales: 50 Devotionals for Teen Agers. Adcock, Kerry, illus. (p. 175)
—Bible Town Detectives. (p. 176)
Pearson, Mary Rose, jt. auth. see Jeanne Grieser.
Pearson, Michael. Tracing Your Black Country Ancestors: A Guide for Family Historians. (p. 1775)
Pearson, Nicole, jt. auth. see Dorling Kindersley Publishing Staff.
Pearson, Owen. Albania in Occupation & War: From Fascism to Communism, 1940-1945. Vol. 2 (p. 34)
Pearson, Patricia. Jane Doze Series - 2nd Edition: Patricia L. Pearson. (p. 908)
Pearson, Paul M. Fun Folk & Fairy Tales. (p. 647)
Pearson, Peter. How to Eat an Airplane. Catusanu, Mircea, illus. (p. 819)
Pearson, Ridley. Challenge. Nielson, Cliff, illus. (p. 288)
—Dark Passage. (p. 408)
—Disney after Dark. (p. 451)
—Disney after Dark. Elwell, Tristan, illus. (p. 451)
—Disney at Dawn. Elwell, Tristan, illus. (p. 451)
—Disney in Shadow. Elwell, Tristan, illus. (p. 451)
—Insider. (p. 878)
—Kingdom Keepers Boxed Set. (p. 959)
—Power Play. (p. 1390)
—Power Play. Elwell, Tristan, illus. (p. 1390)
—Return Disney Lands (p. 1464)
—Shell Game. (p. 1564)
—Syndrome. (p. 1693)
Pearson, Ridley, jt. auth. see Barry, Dave.
Pearson, Ridley & Barry, Dave. Peter & the Secret of Rundoon. Call, Greg, illus. (p. 1346)
Pearson, S. Mondays Will Never Be the Same. (p. 1163)
Pearson, S. & Ellis, Sarah. Next Door Neighbours (p. 1249)
Pearson, Shirley. 50 States, Grades 3 - 5: Great Supplemental Activities to Complement Any Social Studies Curriculum. (p. 1997)
Pearson, Stacy. Number Ladders (add/subtract/multiply/divide) (p. 1271)
Pearson, Susan. Grimericks Grimly, Gris, illus. (p. 724)
—How to Teach a Slug to Read Slonim, David, illus. (p. 822)
—Mouse House Tales. Shepherd, Amanda, illus. (p. 1182)
—Slugger Slonim, David, illus. (p. 1591)
—Slugs in Love O'Malley, Kevin, illus. (p. 1591)
—We're Going on a Ghost Hunt Schindler, S. D., illus. (p. 1875)
—Who Swallowed Harold? And Other Poems about Pets Slonim, David, illus. (p. 1917)
Pearson, Susan & Pearson. Who Swallowed Harold? And Other Poems about Pets Slonim, David, illus. (p. 1917)
Pearson, Tracey Campbell. Bob. Pearson, Tracey Campbell, illus. (p. 205)
—Elephant's Story. Pearson, Tracey Campbell, illus. (p. 512)
Pearson, Tracey Campbell, illus. see Gerber, Carole.
Pearson, Tracey Campbell, jt. auth. see Cuyler, Margery.
Pearson, Victoria, photos by see Fletcher, Janet.
Pearson, Victoria, photos by see Hellmich, Mittie.
Pearson, Victoria, photos by see Strand, Jessica.
Pearson, Yvonne. Concrete Poems. Petelinsek, Kathleen, illus. (p. 355)
—Limericks. Petelinsek, Kathleen, illus. (p. 1018)
—Narrative Poems. Petelinsek, Kathleen, illus. (p. 1229)
—Prose Poems. Petelinsek, Kathleen, illus. (p. 1412)
—Rev up Your Writing in Fictional Stories. Gallagher-Cole, Memie, illus. (p. 1465)
Peart, Hendry. Red Falcons of Tremoine. Brevannes, Maurice, illus. (p. 1454)
Peart, Jane. Orphan Train West Trilogy. (p. 1304)
Pease, D. Robert. Noah Zarc: Omnibus. (p. 1261)
—Noah Zarc: Cataclysm. (p. 1261)
—Noah Zarc: Declaration. (p. 1261)
—Noah Zarc: Mammoth Trouble. (p. 1261)
Pease, Eileen. Flooby DeLoos. (p. 605)
Pease, Elaine. Tallie's Christmas Lights Surprise! Crum, Anna-Maria, illus. (p. 1704)
Pease, J. L. Barnabas the Shaggedy, Raggedy Dog. (p. 139)
Pease, Karen Bessey. Grumble Bluff. (p. 727)
Pease, Pamela. Design Dossier. (p. 429)
—Pop-up Tour de France: The World's Greatest Bike Race. (p. 1384)
Pease, Tristyn, illus. see Jelsma, Amber.
Peaslee, Jessilyn Stewart. Ella. (p. 513)
Peaslee Levine, Martha. Twelve Days of Christmas in Pennsylvania. Dougherty, Rachel, illus. (p. 1800)
Peat, Fern Bisel, illus. see Field, Eugene.
Peat, Fern Bisel, illus. see Stevenson, Robert Louis.
Peat, Fern Bisel, jt. auth. see Stevenson, Robert Louis.
Peat, Neville. Winging It! The Adventures of Tim Wallis. (p. 1936)
Peattie, Cindy & Benchmark Education Co. Staff. Secret Language of Elephants. (p. 1541)
Peattie, Gary, illus. see Luton, Mildred.
Peaty, Mary Alice. Girl Who Lived on the Moon. (p. 679)
Peavler, Amy & Peavler, Jan. King the Queen & the Princess. Peavler, Amy & Peavler, Jan, illus. (p. 959)
Peavler, Jan, jt. auth. see Peavler, Amy.
Peay Peterson, Mitzi, jt. auth. see Peterson, Mitzi.
Pebbles & Carney, Charles. Conquers Camp. (p. 358)
Pecci, Mary. Pecci Reading Series: Primer. (p. 1333)
Pechero-Loewen, Mariella. I Want to Know How You Found Me. (p. 848)
Pechter, Edward, ed. see Shakespeare, William.
Peck. Day No Pigs Would Die. (p. 413)
Peck, Amy, jt. auth. see Purkapile, Susan.
Peck, Audrey. Helen Keller: Miracle Child. (p. 763)
Peck, Audrey, jt. auth. see Mills, Nathan.
Peck, Beth, illus. see Bryant, Jen.
Peck, Beth, illus. see Johnson, Angela.
Peck, Beth, illus. see Jones, Rebecca C.
Peck, Beth, illus. see Whelan, Gloria.
Peck, Bill, illus. see Moore, Nancy Delano.
Peck, C. L. Midnight Song. (p. 1139)
Peck, Carolyn, jt. auth. see Milanese, Celestine Marie.
Peck, Dale. Drift House: The First Voyage. (p. 485)
—Sprout. (p. 1635)
Peck, Everett, illus. see Metaxas, Eric.
Peck, Garrett, jt. ed. see Gouveia, Keith.
Peck, George W. Peck's Bad Boy at the Circus. (p. 1334)
Peck, Harry Thurston. Hilda & the Wishes. (p. 779)
—Literature. (p. 1023)
—New Baedeker. (p. 1243)
—Studies in Several Literatures. (p. 1669)
—Twenty Years of the Republic. (p. 1801)
—William Hickling Prescott. (p. 1933)
Peck, J. L. Mr Crabby Pants & the Zoo. (p. 1184)
Peck, James E. Meet Mr. Chair Bear. (p. 1121)
Peck, Jamie, illus. see Mastin, Marcus.
Peck, Jan. Giant Peach Yodel Root, Barry, illus. (p. 674)
—Pirate Treasure Hunt! Tans, Adrian, illus. (p. 1363)
—Way down Deep in the Deep Blue Sea. Petrone, Valeria, illus. (p. 1864)
—Way Far Away on a Wild Safari. Petrone, Valeria, illus. (p. 1864)
—Way Out West on My Little Pony Leonhard, Herb, illus. (p. 1864)
—Way up High in a Tall Green Tree. Petrone, Valeria, illus. (p. 1864)
Peck, Jan & Davis, David. Green Mother Goose: Saving the World One Rhyme at a Time. Berger, Carin, illus. (p. 722)
Peck, John & Padley, Steve. Key Concepts in Contemporary Literature. (p. 950)
Peck, Judith. Bright Blue Button & the Button-Hole. Stasolla, Mario, illus. (p. 228)
—Runaway Piggy Bank. Eisen, Nancy, illus. (p. 1496)
Peck, Karna, illus. see Hauser, Sheri.
Peck, Lillian Hoban, illus. see Hoban, Russell.
Peck, Lisa J. Brittany to the Rescue: CTR Club - Book Two (p. 230)
—Challenge for Brittany: CTR Club - Book One (p. 289)
—CTR Club Adventure Series: (Four-book Set) (p. 387)
—Meagan's Secret: CTR Club - Book Three (p. 1116)
—Skating with Spencer: CTR Club - Book Four (p. 1584)
Peck, Marilu & McIntosh, Edgar. Multisensory Strategies: Lessons & Classroom Management Techniques to Reach & Teach All Learners. (p. 1190)
Peck, Marshall H., III, jt. auth. see Berger, Melvin.
Peck, Michael. Booger Train (p. 210)
Peck, Richard. Amanda Miranda. (p. 52)
—Fair Weather. (p. 562)
—Ghost Belonged to Me. (p. 670)
—Here Lies the Librarian. (p. 770)
—Long Way from Chicago. (p. 1047)
—Mouse with the Question Mark Tail. (p. 1182)
—Mouse with the Question Mark Tail. Murphy, Kelly, illus. (p. 1182)
—On the Wings of Heroes. (p. 1292)
—Past Perfect, Present Tense. (p. 1327)
—Remembering the Good Times. (p. 1460)
—River Between Us. (p. 1475)
—Season of Gifts. (p. 1538)
—Secrets at Sea. (p. 1544)
—Secrets at Sea. Murphy, Kelly, illus. (p. 1544)
—Teacher's Funeral. (p. 1709)
—Three Quarters Dead. (p. 1743)
—Year down Yonder. (p. 1969)
Peck, Richard & Richard, Peck. Rio Que Nos Divide. (p. 1473)
Peck, Robert Newton. Bro. (p. 230)
—Day No Pigs Would Die. (p. 413)
—Horse Thief. (p. 800)
Peck, Steven L. Rifts of Rime (Quickened Chronicles) (p. 1471)
Peckahm, Lori, ed. 60 Years of Guide: Anniversary Story Collection. (p. 1997)
Peckham, Howard Henry. William Henry Harrison, Young Tippecanoe: Childhood of Famous Americans Series. Laune, Paul, illus. (p. 1933)
Peckham, Lori. Guide's Greatest Amazing Rescue Stories. (p. 730)
—Guide's Greatest Hero Stories. (p. 730)
—Guide's Greatest Mission Stories. (p. 730)
Peckham, Lori, ed. Guide's Greatest Animal Stories. (p. 730)
—Guide's Greatest Funny Stories. (p. 730)
—Guide's Greatest Grace Stories. (p. 730)
—Guide's Greatest Mystery Stories. (p. 730)
—Guide's Greatest Narrow Escape Stories. (p. 730)
Peckover, Lyn. Sparkling Gold Dust. (p. 1622)
Peckyno, Ryan. West Point Military Academy College Prowler off the Record. (p. 1876)
Pecora, Bet Shoshannah. One Dream & Collected Stories. Harrill, Cory, illus. (p. 1294)
Pecorella, Jane. How a Quilt Is Built: Learning to Measure an Object Using Inches. (p. 804)
—Yellowstone: Our First National Park. (p. 1970)
—Yellowstone, Our First National Park. (p. 1970)
Pecos,, 4th & 5th grade Art Students, & 5th grade Art Students, illus. see Luna, Abuela.
Pecos NM After School Program Staff, illus. see Luna, Abuela.
Pecsenye, Jessica, jt. auth. see Amodeo, Jessica.
Pecsenye, Jessica, jt. auth. see Chang, Tristen.
Pecsenye, Jessica, jt. auth. see Cruttenden, Jamie.
Pecsenye, Jessica, jt. auth. see Dickson, Kristin.
Pecsenye, Jessica, jt. auth. see Evans, Moana.
Pecsenye, Jessica, jt. auth. see Flegal, Eric.
Pecsenye, Jessica, jt. auth. see Gordon, Josh.
Pecsenye, Jessica, jt. auth. see Jardy, Adam.
Pecsenye, Jessica, jt. auth. see Johnston, Cathy.
Pecsenye, Jessica, jt. auth. see Lindin, Kerri.
Pecsenye, Jessica, jt. auth. see Nicklin, Miriam.
Pecsenye, Jessica, jt. auth. see Pinkerton, Steve.
Pecsenye, Jessica, jt. auth. see Rakovic, Robert.
Pecsenye, Jessica, jt. auth. see Schubach, Alanna.
Pecsenye, Jessica, jt. auth. see Wines, Shawn.
Pecsenye, Jessice, jt. auth. see Barrish, Lily.
Pecsenye, Jessice, jt. auth. see Foster, Jessica.
peddi, radhika. Kickhide. (p. 951)
Peddicord, Jane Ann. Night Wonders. (p. 1254)
Peden, Margaret Sayers, jt. auth. see Gallego García, Laura.
Peden, Margaret Sayers, tr. see Allende, Isabel.
Pedersen, Amy B. Miracle of Me: From Conception to Birth. (p. 1148)
Pedersen, Bettina Tate. Being Feminist, Being Christian: Essays from Academia. Jule, Allyson, ed. (p. 161)
Pedersen, Elsa. Alaska Harvest. Werth, Kurt, illus. (p. 34)
Pedersen, Janet, illus. see Breznak, Irene.
Pedersen, Janet, illus. see Clements, Andrew.
Pedersen, Janet, illus. see Donovan, Gail.
Pedersen, Janet, illus. see Jackson, Alison.
Pedersen, Janet, illus. see Spinelli, Eileen & Spinelli.
Pedersen, Judy, illus. see Fleischman, Paul.
Pedersen, Laura. Unplugged: Ella Gets Her Family Back Weber, Penny, illus. (p. 1822)
Pedersen, Mary Jo, et al. More Than Meets the Eye: Finding God in the Creases & Folds of Family Life. (p. 1175)
Pedersen, Peggy A. Jasmine & the Magic Squirrel. (p. 910)
Pedersen, Robert H. Seeds of Awareness: A Journey Towards Self Realization. Pedersen, Robert H., illus. (p. 1547)
Pedersen, Sara Pedersen. Born to Organize: Everything you need to know about a career as a professional Organizer. (p. 214)
Pedersen, Vilhelm, illus. see Andersen, Hans Christian, et al.
Pedersen, Vilhelm, illus. see Andersen, Hans Christian.
Pederson, Bridget. I Can Predict, I Wont Be Tricked! (p. 836)
—Its Not Strange, I Know about Change! (p. 898)
Pederson, Bridget & Doudna, Kelly. Don't Be Hasty with Science Safety! (p. 467)
Pederson, Charles E. French & Indian War. (p. 635)
—Jamestown Colony. (p. 907)
—Racism & Intolerance. (p. 1432)
—Thomas Edison. (p. 1738)
—U. S. Constitution & Bill of Rights. (p. 1806)
Pederson, Gunda, illus. see Harris, Mary Beth.
Pederson, Judy, illus. see Kinsey-Warnock, Natalie.
Pederson, Katie. Point of No Return. (p. 1377)
Pederson, William D. FDR Years. (p. 578)
Pedigo, Kim Tran. Having Fun with Kandai the Elephant. (p. 755)
—Having Fun with Kandai the Elephant. Pedigo, Kim Tran, illus. (p. 755)
—Kandai the Elephant Goes Bananas. (p. 942)
Pedigree Books. Angry Birds Star Wars Super Interactive Annual 2014. (p. 75)
—Angry Birds Super Interactive Annual 2014. (p. 75)
—Annoying Orange Super Interactive Annual 2014. (p. 87)
—Barbie Annual 2014. (p. 138)
—Cut the Rope Super Interactive Annual 2014. (p. 396)
—Dreamworks Heroes Annual 2014. (p. 484)
—Family Guy Annual 2014. (p. 568)
—Olly Murs Special by Smash Hits Annual 2014. (p. 1287)
—One Direction Special by Smash Hits Annual 2014. (p. 1294)
—Pokemon Annual 2014. (p. 1378)
—Shoot Annual 2014. (p. 1568)
—Smurfs 2 Annual 2014. (p. 1595)
—Sonic the Hedgehog Super Interactive Annual 2014. (p. 1612)
—South Park Annual 2014. (p. 1617)
—Star Wars Annual 2014. (p. 1641)
—Star Wars: the Clone Wars Annual 2014: The Clone Wars Annual 2014. (p. 1642)
—Tatty Teddy & Blue Nose Friends Annual 2014. (p. 1707)
—Turbo Annual 2014. (p. 1797)
Pedlar, Caroline, illus. see Howie, Vicki.
Pedlar, David Stewart. Emu Who Knew He Could Fly! (p. 522)
Pedlar, Elaine, illus. see Dole, Mayra L.
Pedlar, Elaine, illus. see Gunning, Monica.
Pedler, Caroline, illus. see Baxter, Nicola.
Pedler, Caroline, illus. see Corderoy, Tracey.
Pedler, Caroline, illus. see Freedman, Claire.
Pedler, Caroline, illus. see Grieser, Jeanne K.
Pedler, Caroline, illus. see Hubery, Julia.
Pedler, Caroline, illus. see Parker, Amy.
Pedler, Caroline, illus. see Smallman, Steve.
Pedler, Caroline, illus. see Warnes, Tim, et al.
Pedley, Ethel C. Dot & the Kangaroo. (p. 472)
Pedley, Linda J. Journey of Brothers. (p. 928)
Pedraza, M. Eugenia Rueda. Nico's Voyage. (p. 1251)
Pedrick, Cherry, jt. auth. see Hyman, Bruce M.
Pedrick, Cherry, et al. Obsessive-Compulsive Disorder. (p. 1275)
Pedro, Coach & Rita, Susan Adam. Magic Soccer Ball: Trapping & My 1st Game. (p. 1073)
Pedro, Javier Martínez, illus. see Mateo, José Manual.
Pedrow, Debra A. Aunt Debra & My Favorite Things Poster. Karper, Deborah, ed. (p. 115)
Pedroza, Georgina, tr. see Byte Me! P.
Pedroza, Georgina, tr. De COLORES the Song: All the Colors. BYTE ME! ebook inc nonprofit, Georgia C., illus. (p. 416)
Pee Wee Scouts Staff, jt. auth. see Delton, Judy.
Peebles, Alice. Demons & Dragons. Chilvers, Nigel, illus. (p. 426)
—Giants & Trolls. Chilvers, Nigel, illus. (p. 674)
—Monsters of the Gods. Chilvers, Nigel, illus. (p. 1169)
Peebles, Joseph. European Smack Down. (p. 540)
—Stickman & the Crow. (p. 1650)
Peecock, Simon, illus. see Williams, Jan.
Peek, Jeannette, illus. see Beckler, Bruce.
Peek, Lisa K. That Duck. (p. 1726)
Peek, Megan. Friendly Furries: The Annual Animal County Hop-a-Thon , the un-Surprise Birthday , the New Soccer Friend , the School Play , the Cook-off Contest. (p. 638)
Peek, Merle & Giblin, James Cross. Mary Wore Her Red Dress: And Henry Wore His Green Sneakers (p. 1101)
Peek, Patsy. Reading Comprehension Practice: Grades 2-8 Practice Worksheets Featuring Story Webs, Newspaper Ads, Fliers. (p. 1445)
Peek, Renee W. Grandma's Miracles. (p. 709)
Peek, Susan. Crusader King: A Novel of Baldwin IV & the Crusades. (p. 386)
Peekhaus, Jennifer. Little Red House. (p. 1035)
Peel, Stephanie, illus. see Shoshan, Beth.
Peel, Yana. Color for Baby. (p. 342)
—Faces for Baby: An Art for Baby Book. (p. 561)
Peele, Chandra & Spears, Aubrey. Great Love (for Guys) Truth for Teens in Today's Sexy Culture. (p. 717)
Peele, Krista. Rox Chronicle. (p. 1492)
Peeler, Gail. Jackson's Magic Wishing Well. (p. 904)
Peeler, Lorraine. Anger: Spiritual Tools to overcome your anger: What Is it good For? (p. 75)
—Your Empowerment Zones Revisited: Spiritual Tools to Empower Your Walk As A Child of God. (p. 1980)
Peeler, Penny. Adventures of Spike & Sally. (p. 23)
Peer, Kate, illus. see Johnson, Kathy.
Peer, Nancy, illus. see Lasaracina, Barbara.
Peers, Jill. Rainbow Cottage. (p. 1435)
Peers, Judi. Brontosaurus Brunch: A Smorgasbord of Dinosaur Delights. Coles, Mary, illus. (p. 230)
Peerson, Marie Graham. Joseph Wheeler: The Fearless 'Fightin' Joe' (p. 926)
Peery, Douglas B., adapted by. Book of Mormon Heroes: Nephi: His Reign & Ministry (p. 211)
Peery, L. M. God's Eternal Gift of Learning for Children. (p. 691)
Peet, Bill. Caboose Who Got Loose Peet, Bill, illus. (p. 250)
—Spooky Tail of Prewitt Peacock. (p. 1631)
Peet, Inez M. Celebrating Christmas: A Collection of Poems for Children. (p. 284)
Peet, Joy. Sophia's Flutterfly. (p. 1613)
Peet, Mal. Alf Saves the Day. Hammond, Andy, illus. (p. 37)
—Exposure. (p. 554)
—Keeper. (p. 947)
—Penalty. (p. 1336)
—Tamar. (p. 1704)
Peet, Mal & Graham, Elspeth. Cloud Tea Monkeys. Wijngaard, Juan, illus. (p. 334)
—Mysterious Traveler. Lynch, P. J., illus. (p. 1223)
—Night Sky Dragons. Benson, Patrick, illus. (p. 1254)
Peet, Rosie. Amazing Battles! (p. 54)
Peet, Stephen Denison. Prehistoric America. (p. 1395)
Peete, Holly Robinson & Peete, Ryan Elizabeth. My Brother Charlie. Evans, Shane W., illus. (p. 1199)
Peete, Ryan Elizabeth, jt. auth. see Peete, Holly Robinson.
Peetoom, Laura. Mermaid in the Bathtub Fernandes, Eugenie, illus. (p. 1128)
Peetoom, Laura, ed. see Guest, Jacqueline.
Peets, Risa. It's OK to Be Different: An Amazing School Day. (p. 898)
Pef. Belle lisse poire du prince De. (p. 163)
Peffer, J. "NeonDragon". Dragonart Fantasy Characters: How to Draw Fantastic Beings & Incredible Creatures. (p. 478)
Peffer, Jessica. Dragonart: How to Draw Fantastic Dragons & Fantasy Creatures. (p. 478)
Pefferly, Lawrence. Larry Tyler & the Planet Buksdahud. (p. 976)
Pegg, Laura Wittman. Patch Quilt Pony. (p. 1328)
Peggy J. Parks. Sand Dunes. (p. 1510)
Peggy, Nille, jt. auth. see Lindeen, Mary.
Peggykauffman.com Staff, illus. see Hambleton, Anne.
Pegis, Jessica. What Are Insulators & Conductors? (p. 1879)
Pegis, Jessica, jt. auth. see Corporate Contributor Staff.
Pegis, Jessica, jt. auth. see Crabtree Publishing Company Staff.
Pegler, Robin. Having Fun Together: A Collection of Children's Stories. (p. 755)
Pegrum, Juliet. Yoga Fun for Toddlers, Children & You. (p. 1972)
Peguero, Phillip, illus. see Barrett, Anna Pearl.
Peguy, Laurence, illus. see Montgomery, R. A.
Peha, Steve & Lester, Margot Carmichael. Be a Writer (2nd Edition) Your Guide to the Writing Life! (p. 148)
Pei, I.M., jt. auth. see Rubalcaba, Jill.
Peifer, Jane Hoober. Family Song. Hess, Ingrid, illus. (p. 568)
Peifer, Meighan. Chocolate Chip Ghost. French, Phyllis, illus. (p. 309)
Peinador, Angeles, illus. see Canetti, Yanitzia James, et al.
Peine, Jan. Nothing's Too Hard for Me. Sheldrake, Missy, illus. (p. 1268)
Peine, Jan Muir. Giving Me Away. (p. 681)
Peirce, Jeremy L. Attention-Deficit/Hyperactivity Disorder. Collins, Christine, ed. (p. 114)
Peirce, Lincoln. All Work & No Play. (p. 46)
—Big Nate: From the Top. (p. 182)
—Big Nate: I Can't Take It! (p. 182)
—Big Nate: Great Minds Think Alike. (p. 182)
—Big Nate: Game On! Peirce, Lincoln, illus. (p. 182)
—Big Nate: Mr. Popularity. Peirce, Lincoln, illus. (p. 182)
—Big Nate: The Crowd Goes Wild! Peirce, Lincoln, illus. (p. 182)
—Big Nate: Fun Blaster: Cheezy Doodles, Crazy Comix, & Loads of Laughs! Peirce, Lincoln, illus. (p. 182)
—Big Nate. (p. 182)
—Big Nate & Friends. (p. 182)
—Big Nate Boredom Buster: Super Scribbles, Cool Comix, & Lots of Laughs. Peirce, Lincoln, illus. (p. 182)
—Big Nate Boredom Buster. Peirce, Lincoln, illus. (p. 182)
—Big Nate Doodlepalooza. Peirce, Lincoln, illus. (p. 182)
—Big Nate Flips Out. (p. 182)
—Big Nate Flips Out. Peirce, Lincoln, illus. (p. 182)

—Big Nate Fun Blaster. (p. 182)
—Big Nate - Fun Blaster. Peirce, Lincoln, illus. (p. 182)
—Big Nate — Genius Mode. (p. 182)
—Big Nate — Genius Mode. Peirce, Lincoln, illus. (p. 182)
—Big Nate Goes for Broke. Peirce, Lincoln, illus. (p. 182)
—Big Nate — Great Minds Think Alike. (p. 182)
—Big Nate — Here Goes Nothing. (p. 182)
—Big Nate — Here Goes Nothing. Peirce, Lincoln, illus. (p. 182)
—Big Nate - In a Class by Himself. Peirce, Lincoln, illus. (p. 182)
—Big Nate — In a Class by Himself. (p. 182)
—Big Nate — In a Class by Himself. Peirce, Lincoln, illus. (p. 182)
—Big Nate — In the Zone. Peirce, Lincoln, illus. (p. 182)
—Big Nate Laugh-O-Rama. Peirce, Lincoln, illus. (p. 182)
—Big Nate Lives It Up. Peirce, Lincoln, illus. (p. 182)
—Big Nate Makes the Grade. (p. 182)
—Big Nate — Mr. Popularity. (p. 182)
—Big Nate on a Roll. (p. 182)
—Big Nate on a Roll. Peirce, Lincoln, illus. (p. 182)
—Big Nate Out Loud. (p. 182)
—Big Nate - Say Good-Bye to Dork City. (p. 182)
—Big Nate Strikes Again. (p. 182)
—Big Nate Strikes Again. Peirce, Lincoln, illus. (p. 182)
—Big Nate Super Scribbler. Peirce, Lincoln, illus. (p. 182)
—Big Nate - The Crowd Goes Wild! (p. 182)
—Big Nate Triple Play Box Set. Peirce, Lincoln, illus. (p. 182)
—Big Nate — What Could Possibly Go Wrong? Peirce, Lincoln, illus. (p. 182)
—Big Nate's Greatest Hits. (p. 182)
—Game On! (p. 654)
—I Can't Take It! (p. 837)
—Nate el Grande: ¡Hola! (p. 1230)
—Nate el Grande Ataca de Nuevo. (p. 1230)
—What Could Possibly Go Wrong? (p. 1881)
Peirce, Lincoln, et al. Big Nate All Work & No Play: A Collection of Sundays. (p. 182)
—Big Nate Makes the Grade. Peirce, Lincoln, illus. (p. 182)
Peirce-Bale, Mary. Noah's Moon. Suarez, Nora, illus. (p. 1262)
—Twinkle, Twinkle Little Girl. Banach, Virginia, illus. (p. 1802)
—Wilma Wombat's Trek to Back of Beyond. (p. 1934)
Peirs, Adam. Hopper's Helpful Day. (p. 797)
Peiser, Andrew, jt. auth. see Serber, Michael.
Pekar, Harvey. Quitter. (p. 1429)
Pekar, Harvey & Haspiel, Dean. Quitter. (p. 1429)
Pekar, Harvey, et al. Another Day Anderson, Ho Che et al, illus. (p. 87)
Pekarsky, Mel, illus. see Hillert, Margaret.
Pelaez, Ricardo, illus. see Burks, Brian.
Pelaez, Ricardo, illus. see Otero, Armando Leiero.
Pelaez, Ricardo, illus. see Ruiz, Maria Emilia Beyer.
Pelagotti, Alessandra, jt. auth. see Scotti, Douglas.
Pelayo, Ruben, tr. see Keylock, Joanna Murray.
Peleg-Segal, Naama, jt. auth. see Keller, Elinoar.
Pelelo-Ray, Sam. Athenrei. (p. 112)
Pelfrey, Wanda B. Bible Crafts on a Shoestring Budget. (p. 175)
Pelfrey, Wanda B. & Kuhn, Pamela J. Favorite Bible Heroes: Ages 2&3. Galey, Chuck, illus. (p. 578)
Pelham, David. Here Comes Santa: A Mini Holiday Pop-Up. Pelham, David, illus. (p. 770)
—Sam's Sandwich. Pelham, David, illus. (p. 1509)
—Stuff & Nonsense: A Touch-and-Feel Book with a Pop-Up Surprise! Pelham, David, illus. (p. 1670)
—Trail: Paper Poetry. Pelham, David, illus. (p. 1776)
Pelham, P.J. Hanna Searches for "Me!" (p. 742)
Pelham, Sophie. Colors. Pelham, Sophie, illus. (p. 344)
Peli, Peli, illus. see Silvera, Elvia.
Pelicano, Christopher J., illus. see Ellis, Colette.
Pelikan, Judy. All Around the Block: An Alphabet. (p. 43)
—Books Make Me Happy: My First Reading Log. (p. 212)
Pelizzari, Nora. Crystal Princess: The Runaway Rainbow. (p. 387)
Pell, Ed. Connecticut. (p. 357)
—Indiana. (p. 871)
—Maryland. (p. 1101)
Pell, Jason. Woody & the Noble. O'Reilly, Sean Patrick, ed. (p. 1950)
Pellant, Chris. Fossils of the World. (p. 624)
Pellant, Chris & Pellant, Helen. Crystals & Gemstones. (p. 387)
—Fossils. (p. 624)
—Granite & Other Igneous Rocks. (p. 710)
—Marble & Other Metamorphic Rocks. (p. 1091)
—Minerals. (p. 1146)
—Quartz & Other Minerals. (p. 1423)
—Rocks. (p. 1483)
—Sandstone & Other Sedimentary Rocks. (p. 1511)
Pellant, Helen, jt. auth. see Pellant, Chris.
Pellant, Terry. Real Valentine's Story. (p. 1449)
Pellaton, Karen E. Official M&M's(r) Brand History of Chocolate. (p. 1280)
Pellaton, Karen E., illus. see Brimner, Larry Dane.
Pellé, Serge, illus. see Runberg, Sylvain.
Pellé, Serge, illus. see Runberg, Sylvain.
Pellechia, Thomas. Complete Idiot's Guide to Starting & Running a Winery. (p. 353)
Pelleg, Tirtsa, illus. see Krohn, Genendel.
Pellegata, Donna. Harp Mouse Chooses Her Home: The Adventure Begins. (p. 749)
Pellegrin, Leeann. Hey I'm Alex. Rolf, Heidi, illus. (p. 774)
Pellegrini, Isabelle. Eva from Stockholm. Picard, Charline, illus. (p. 540)
Pellegrini, Isabelle, jt. auth. see Sabatier-Morel, Francoise.
Pellegrini, Mary Ellen. Managing Money: Spending & Saving Wisely. (p. 1086)
Pellegrini, Nancy. Beijing. Cooper, Adrian, photos by. (p. 160)
Pellegrini, Will, illus. see Trimble, Marcia.
Pellegrino, Frank, jt. auth. see Fallon, Kathy Reilly.
Pellegrino, Marge. Journey of Dreams. (p. 928)
Pellegrino, Rich, illus. see Doeden, Matt.
Pellegrino, Richard. Battle of the Olympians & the Titans (p. 146)
Pellegrino, Richard, illus. see Brezenoff, Steve.
Pellegrino, Richard, illus. see Dahl, Michael.
Pellegrino, Victor. Uncle Kawaiolas Dream. (p. 1812)
Pellegrino, Victor C. Writer's Guide to Powerful Paragraphs. Magee, Christopher, illus. (p. 1964)
Pellegrino-Henricks, Aliceanne. Children's Book: Fun with Friends, Animals, & Growing Up. (p. 303)
Pellerin, Mona. Peetie & the Marsh Aliens (p. 1335)
—Peetie, the Thinking Dabbler Duck. (p. 1335)
Pellerito, Mike, ed. see Gallagher, Mike, et al.
Pelleschi, Andrea. China. (p. 306)
—Crop Circles. (p. 385)
—George Washington. (p. 664)
—Juan Ponce de Leon. (p. 930)
—Life of a Colonial Innkeeper. (p. 1011)
—Life of a Colonial Schoolteacher. (p. 1011)
—Neil & Nan Build Narrative Nonfiction. Han, Yu-Mei, illus. (p. 1240)
—Olivia & Oscar Build an Opinion Piece. Hu, Caroline, illus. (p. 1286)
—Russia. (p. 1498)
—Samuel de Champlain. (p. 1509)
—Thomas Jefferson. (p. 1739)
Pelletier, Cathie. Summer Experiment. (p. 1674)
Pelletier, Christine, jt. auth. see Holmes, Wayne.
Pelletier, Cynthia L. & Rabin, Shri. She Who Walks with Tigers (p. 1564)
Pelletier, Fran. Little Pine to King Spruce: A Franco-American Childhood. (p. 1033)
Pelletier, Ingrid, jt. auth. see Lindemood, Kimmer.
Pelletier, Jennifer. Wonderful Imagination of Alish. (p. 1948)
Pelletier, Marthe. Leo a la Mer. Cote, Genevieve, tr. (p. 991)
—Violette, la Reine Muette. Côté, Geneviève, illus. (p. 1843)
Pelletier, Maryse. Chasse au Plomb. Grimard, Gabrielle, illus. (p. 294)
—Chasse Aux Moules. (p. 294)
Pelletier, Mia. Avati: Discovering Arctic Ecology Otterstätter, Sara, illus. (p. 118)
—Children's Guide to Arctic Birds Christopher, Danny, illus. (p. 303)
Pelletier, Ninon, illus. see Carter, Anne Laurel.
Pelletier, Paul, illus. see Bedard, Tony.
Pelley, Gail. Celebrate God: Seeing Him in Everyday Things. (p. 283)
Pelley, Kathleen. Giant King. Manning, Maurie J., tr. (p. 673)
—Sandal Artist Sprague, Lois, illus. (p. 1510)
Pelley, Kathleen T. Magnus Maximus, a Marvelous Measurer. Schindler, S. D., illus. (p. 1076)
—Raj the Bookstore Tiger. Keiser, Paige, illus. (p. 1437)
Pelli, Tammy. Circles: Relationships with Segments & Angles. (p. 321)
—Constructions: Creating Geometric Figures. (p. 360)
—Proofs: Reasoning with Mathematics. (p. 1411)
—Triangles: Calculating Measurements & Rations. (p. 1785)
Pellicer López, Carlos. Juan y Sus Zapatos. (p. 930)
Pellicioli, Anna. Where You End. (p. 1910)
Pelling, Lenny. Summer Days. Pelling, Lenny, illus. (p. 1674)
Pellittiere II, Michael. GROW MONEY - A Kid's Guide to Saving & Investing. (p. 726)
—GROW MONEY II - A Teenager's Guide to Saving & Investing. (p. 726)
Pellowski. Story Vine. (p. 1663)
Pellowski, Anne. First Farm in the Valley: Anna's Story. Sharpe, Roseanne, illus. (p. 595)
—Stairstep Farm: Anna Rose's Story. Sharpe, Roseanne, illus. (p. 1638)
—Storytelling Handbook. (p. 1664)
Pellowski, Michael J. Charles Manson Murder Trial: A Headline Court Case. (p. 292)
—Chicago Black Sox Baseball Scandal. (p. 299)
—Joke & Riddle Bonanza. Hoffman, Sanford, illus. (p. 924)
—Lunchroom Laughs Joke Book. Davis, Tim, illus. (p. 1065)
—Monster Jokes. Sinclair, Jeff, illus. (p. 1167)
—Super Sports Star Mike Piazza. (p. 1682)
—Terrorist Trial of the 1993 Bombing of the World Trade Center: A Headline Court Case. (p. 1722)
—Wackiest Jokes in the World. Hoffman, Sanford, illus. (p. 1852)
—Wild & Wacky Pet Jokes & Riddles. Snider, Jackie, illus. (p. 1928)
Pellowski, Michael J., et al. Belly Achers: 500 Clean, Never Mean, Good for Your Bean, Funniest Jokes You've Ever Seen. (p. 163)
—Knock-Knock Madness: Over 600 Jokes & Riddles. (p. 965)
—Most Ginormous Joke Book in the Universe! More Laughs for Everyone! More Jokes for Every Occasion! More Jokes for Every Situation! More, More, More! (p. 1177)
Pells, T., jt. auth. see Sommerville, L.
Peloquin, Lili. Innocents. (p. 875)
Pelosi. Instructor's Manual to Accompany Elementary Statis Tics. (p. 878)
—Test Bank to Accompany Elementary Statistics. (p. 1723)
Pelosi, Marilyn K. & Sandifer, Theresa M. Elementary Statistics: From Discovery to Decision. (p. 510)
Pelosi, Vincent L. Magical Underwater Kingdom of Balenarium. (p. 1075)
Pelous, Donald. Dream Come True: A Story of St. Isaac Jogues. Jagodits, Carolyn Lee, illus. (p. 483)
Pelow, Lawrence. Little Larry of Lewiston Meets Bobby the Backyard Bully. (p. 1030)
Peloza, Brian. Indianapolis Colts. (p. 871)
Pels, Winslow, illus. see Fine, Edith Hope.
Pels, Winslow Pinney, illus. see Cross, Ruth Belov.
Peltak, Jennifer. Beverly Cleary. (p. 173)
—Edgar Allan Poe. (p. 504)
Peltier, Sylvia M. Nanny & I. Peltier, Sylvia M., illus. (p. 1229)
Peltola, Anne. Boing Boing. (p. 208)
Pelton, Bonnie L., illus. see Ball Sr., Frank J.
Pelton, Deena. My Turtle. (p. 1220)
Pelton, Lisa. Logos & Adoption: Remi's Journey. (p. 1045)
—Logos & Obedience: Listening to His Father's Voice. (p. 1045)
Pelton, Lou E., et al. Business Ethics: Ethical Decision Making & Cases. (p. 245)
Pelton, Robert W. Baking Recipes of Our Founding Fathers. (p. 133)
Pelton, Stephen, et al. Basic Computers for Beginners. (p. 141)
Peltz, Jason. Who Is Hanukah Heshie? (p. 1915)
Peltz, Rakhmiel. From Immigrant to Ethnic Culture: American Yiddish in South Philadelphia. (p. 643)
Pelusey, Jane, jt. auth. see Pelusey, Michael.
Pelusey, Michael. Giraffes & Zebras. (p. 678)
—Zoo Animals (p. 1988)
Pelusey, Michael & Pelusey, Jane. Apes & Monkeys. (p. 91)
—Bears. (p. 151)
—Elephants. (p. 511)
—Film & Television. (p. 586)
—Internet. (p. 880)
—Media. (p. 1118)
—Newspapers. (p. 1249)
—Photography. (p. 1353)
—Radio. (p. 1432)
—Rhinoceroses & Hippopotamuses. (p. 1467)
—Tigers & Lions. (p. 1749)
Peluso, Beth A. Charcoal Forest: How Fire Helps Animals & Plants. Peluso, Beth A., illus. (p. 291)
Peluso, Martina, illus. see Finch, Mary & Barefoot Books.
Peluso, Martina, illus. see Flanagan, Liz, et al.
Peluso, Martina, illus. see Kimmel, Eric A.
Peluso, Martina, illus. see Malaspina, Ann.
Peluso, Martina, illus. see Marion, Dominique & Shakespeare, William.
Peluso, Martina, illus. see Marks, Allison & Marks, Wayne.
Pelz, Ramona. My Name Is Mae. Trousdale, Taryn, illus. (p. 1215)
Pember, G. H. Animals: The Classic Theological Treatise on Animal Rights: Their Past & Future. Hill, David W., ed. (p. 81)
Pemberton, Bernadette. Marshall's Marvelous Shoes. (p. 1096)
Pemberton, Bert. Three for Adventure. (p. 1742)
Pemberton, Delia. Civilization of Ancient Egypt. (p. 326)
Pemberton, Teresa. Trissy's New Shoes. (p. 1787)
Pembrook, Hattie, Jr. Messages to Awaken Yourself. (p. 1129)
Pen, Chenda. Dara Learns How to Ride a Bike! An Autism Story. (p. 406)
Pena, Amado M., Jr., illus. see Goldman, Lisa Bear.
Pena, Diana R. Sweet & Shorts! Short Stories Made of 100 Important Sight Words a First Grader Should Know. Pena, Willie R., illus. (p. 1689)
—What I Like: A Fun, Basic Reading Book for Kindergarteners & First Graders. Pena, Willie R., illus. (p. 1886)
Pena, Willie R., illus. see Pena, Diana R.
Penado, Martha. Eggstinkt. (p. 506)
—Star Stuff. (p. 1641)
Peña-Solis, Marcia. Minna Vu & Her Super Special One of a Kind Fabulous Sparkly New Shoes. (p. 1147)
Penberthy, John. To Bee or Not to Bee: A Book for Beeings Who Feel there's More to Life than Just Making Honey. Barrows, Laurie, illus. (p. 1758)
Penberthy, Stephen. Adventures of Bird Dog & Friends. (p. 16)
Pence, Shari A. Games Galore for Children's Parties & More: 80 Fun Games & Activities for Parties, Classroom, Youth Groups, Carnivals, Company Picnics, Rainy Days & Special Occasions. Stearns, Debra & Kohout, Rosemary, eds. (p. 655)
Pender, Rachel, illus. see Stone, Andrew & Bryan, Jessica.
Pendergast, Brian H. Lion in the Playground. (p. 1020)
Pendergast, George. Butterfly's Life Cycle. (p. 248)
—Deep-Sea Fishing. (p. 423)
—Deer Hunting. (p. 423)
—Duck Hunting. (p. 488)
—Fly Fishing. (p. 609)
—Freshwater Fishing. (p. 637)
—Rock Cycle at Work. (p. 1482)
—Turkey Hunting. (p. 1797)
—Water Cycle at Work. (p. 1862)
—Year of Seasons. (p. 1969)
Pendergast, Sara, jt. auth. see Pendergast, Tom.
Pendergast, Tom & Pendergast, Sara. Almanac. (p. 48)
Pendergrass, D. Louis, a Blue Dragon. (p. 1058)
Pendergrass, Daphne. Fireless Dragon. (p. 592)
—Hero's Journey. Reel FX Inc. Staff et al, illus. (p. 773)
—Meet the Penguins! Style Guide, Style, illus. (p. 1123)
—On the Go in Glendragon. HIT Entertainment Staff, illus. (p. 1290)
—Riders of Berk: A Fiery Discovery. (p. 1471)
Pendergrass, Jena R. God's Love. (p. 691)
Pendergrass, Mark D., illus. see Daubenspeck, Julie & Daubenspeck, Vince.
Penders, Ken, et al. Sonic - The Hedgehog (p. 1612)
Pendleton, Claudette M. I'm Mommy's Little Helper. Scott, Christopher L., illus. (p. 859)
Pendleton, Jack. Redbeard: Bounty Hunter, Ten Tales of Shadria (p. 1455)
Pendleton, Ken. David Beckham. (p. 410)
Pendleton, Ken & Savage, Jeff. David Beckham. (p. 410)
Pendleton, Paige. Keeper & the Alabaster Chalice: Book II of the Black Ledge Series. Block, Thomas, illus. (p. 947)
Pendleton, Sherry. 'Twas the Night Before Halloween. (p. 1799)
Pendleton, Thomas, jt. auth. see Petrucha, Stefan.
Pendziwol, Jean. No Dragons for Tea. (p. 1258)
Pendziwol, Jean, jt. auth. see Pendziwol, Jean E.
Pendziwol, Jean E. Dawn Watch Debon, Nicolas, illus. (p. 412)
—Marja's Skis Marton, Jirina, illus. (p. 1094)
—Red Sash. Debon, Nicolas, illus. (p. 1455)
—Tale of Sir Dragon: Dealing with Bullies for Kids (and Dragons) Gourbault, Martine, illus. (p. 1700)
—Treasure at Sea for Dragon & Me: Water Safety for Kids (And Dragons) Gourbault, Martine, illus. (p. 1781)
Pendziwol, Jean E. & Gourbault, Martine. Tale of Sir Dragon: Dealing with Bullies for Kids (and Dragons) Gourbault, Martine, illus. (p. 1700)
Pendziwol, Jean E. & Pendziwol, Jean. Once upon a Dragon: Stranger Safety for Kids (and Dragons) Gourbault, Martine, illus. (p. 1292)
Penecale Jr., Richard P. Luckiest Frog. (p. 1062)
Penfield, James, illus. see Baltzer, Rochelle.
Penfornis, Jean-Luc. Business French: An Intermediate Course. (p. 245)
Peng, Cathy, illus. see Louie, Ai-Ling.
Peng, Chao, illus. see Chen, Wei Dong.
Peng, Chao, illus. see Dong Chen, Wei.
Peng, Chao, jt. auth. see Dong Chen, Wei.
Peng, Tan Huay. PENG's Fun with Chinese Characters for Children: Help Your Child Learn Chinese the Fun Way! (p. 1336)
Peng, Wang, illus. see Poe, Edgar Allen & Morvan, Jean-David.
Penguin / LeapFrog, jt. auth. see Piper, Watty.
Penguin Books Staff. Vehicles. (p. 1834)
—We Look. (p. 1867)
Penguin Books Staff, ed. Animals. (p. 81)
—Dinosaurs. (p. 444)
—Ecology. (p. 502)
—My Alphabet Book. (p. 1195)
—Plants. (p. 1369)
—Sea. (p. 1534)
—Space. (p. 1618)
—Things That Fly. (p. 1733)
—Three Billy Goats Gruff. (p. 1741)
—Three Little Pigs. (p. 1743)
—Your Body. (p. 1980)
Penguin Group (USA) Staff & Grosset and Dunlap Staff. Buddy's World. (p. 235)
—I Am a T. Rex! (p. 832)
Penguin Press Staff. Táin. Carson, Ciaran, tr. from CEL. (p. 1696)
Penguin Young Readers. Angelina at Ballet Camp. (p. 74)
—I Am Lily. (p. 833)
Penguin Young Readers, jt. auth. see Potter, Beatrix.
Penguin Young Readers Group, jt. auth. see Valois, Rob.
Penguin Young Readers Group Staff. Babee's Room. (p. 123)
—Dick & Jane - Go, Go, Go (p. 435)
—Fun with Dick & Jane. (p. 648)
—Guess Who (p. 729)
—I Am Peter. (p. 833)
—Jump & Run (p. 934)
—Something Funny (p. 1610)
Penguin Young Readers Group Staff, jt. auth. see Grosset and Dunlap Staff.
Penguin Young Readers Group Staff, jt. auth. see Potter, Beatrix.
Penhale, Douglas, illus. see Swanson, Diane.
Penich, Mary. Oh No! It's Thursday! (p. 1281)
Penick Phillips-Cermak, Mosetta. Wishing Flower. (p. 1940)
Penina, M. Ant & the Wheat Kernel: For Young Readers. Kaufman, Yaki, illus. (p. 88)
—Dove Builds a Nest: For Young Readers. Kaufman, Yaki, illus. (p. 473)
Penix, Sherry. San Diego Activity & Coloring Book for All Ages. Berman, Linda, illus. (p. 1510)
Penk, Kathryn, illus. see Edgren, Elizabeth.
Penley, Janet. Boo Boo Kisses from the Littlest Angel Bartlett, Alyssa Joy, illus. (p. 209)
Penlington, Nathan. Boy in the Book: One Man's Adventure in Search of a Lost Childhood. (p. 218)
Penn, Arial. S. O. L. (p. 1499)
Penn, Audrey. A. D. D. Not B. A. D. Wyrick, Monica, illus. (p. 1)
—A. D. D. Not B. A. D. Wyrick, Monica Dunsky, illus. (p. 1)
—Beso en Mi Mano. Harper, Ruth E. & Leak, Nancy M., illus. (p. 168)
—Chester Raccoon & the Acorn Full of Memories. Gibson, Barbara L., illus. (p. 298)
—Chester the Brave. Gibson, Barbara Leonard, illus. (p. 298)
—Color Game for Chester Raccoon. Gibson, Barbara Leonard, illus. (p. 342)
—Feathers & Fur. Wyrick, Monica Dunsky, illus. (p. 579)
—Kiss Goodbye. Gibson, Barbara Leonard, illus. (p. 961)
—Kissing Hand. Harper, Ruth E. & Leak, Nancy M., illus. (p. 962)
—Kissing Hand for Chester Raccoon. Gibson, Barbara Leonard, illus. (p. 962)
—Miracle Jar: A Hanukkah Story. Lyon, Lea, illus. (p. 1148)
—Mystery at Blackbeard's Cove. Howard, Philip & Miller, Josh, illus. (p. 1223)
—Mystery at Blackbeard's Cove. Howard, Philip & Miller, Joshua, illus. (p. 1223)
—Pocket Full of Kisses. Gibson, Barbara Leonard, illus. (p. 1375)
—Whistling Tree. Gibson, Barbara, illus. (p. 1912)
—Whistling Tree. Gibson, Barbara Leonard, illus. (p. 1912)
Penn, Audrey & Cosgrove, Stephen. Sassafras. Harper, Ruth E. & James, Robin, illus. (p. 1515)
Penn, Audrey & Gibson, Barbara L. Chester Raccoon & the Big Bad Bully. (p. 298)
Penn, Audrey & Miller, Joshua. Blackbeard & the Gift of Silence. (p. 197)
—Blackbeard & the Sandstone Pillar: When Lightning Strikes. (p. 197)
Penn, Audrey, et al. Kissing Hand. (p. 962)
Penn, Barbra. Susan B. Anthony: Pioneering Leader of the Women's Rights Movement. (p. 1688)
Penn, Briony. Kids Book of Canadian Geography. Penn, Briony, illus. (p. 952)
Penn, Jim, jt. auth. see Doeden, Matt.
Penn, John I. Getting Well: A Study for Children on Spiritual & Physical Healing. (p. 670)
Penn, Karen V., illus. see O'Neal-Thorpe, Rochelle.
Penn, Linda M. Clayton's Birding Adventure: A Young Boy Learns the Secret Ways of Birds. (p. 330)
—Is Kentucky in the Sky? (p. 889)
Penn, M. W. 2 Lines. Firos, Daphne, illus. (p. 1991)
—Comparing Numbers! (p. 352)
—Counting Money! (p. 371)
—It's a Pattern! (p. 896)

P

—It's a Shape! (p. 896)
—It's Addition! (p. 896)
—It's Subtraction! (p. 899)
—Pebble Math. (p. 1333)
—Sidney the Silly Who Only Eats 6. Tommer, Sarah, illus. (p. 1573)
—Square Bear Meets Round Hound: A Fairytale of Shapes. Firos, Daphne, illus. (p. 1636)
Penn, Mw. Pe'lerin of the Orb. (p. 1335)
—Sidney the Silly Who Only Eats 6. Tommer, Sarah, illus. (p. 1573)
Penn, Sarah. Nat Love: Vaquero Afroamericano. (p. 1230)
—Nat Love: African American Cowboy. (p. 1230)
—Nat Love: African American Cowboy / Vaquero Afroamericano. (p. 1230)
—Nat Love: Vaquero afroamericano (Nat Love: African American Cowboy) (p. 1230)
Penn, Shelly. Geoma Tree. (p. 662)
Penna, Christina & Shook, Rachael. Careers in Network Engineering. (p. 268)
Penna, Christine. Careers in Network Engineering. (p. 268)
Pennac, D. & Benacquista, E. Lone Riders. (p. 1046)
Pennac, Daniel. Mirada del Lobo. (p. 1149)
—Rights of the Reader. Adams, Sarah, tr. from FRE. (p. 1472)
Pennac, Daniel & Benacquista, Tonino. Lucky Luke Versus the Pinkertons. Achdé, illus. (p. 1062)
Pennart, Geoffroy De, jt. auth. see de Pennart, Geoffroy.
Pennart, Geoffroy de, see de Pennart, Geoffroy.
Pennart, Geoggroy, et al. Lobo Sentimental. Vicens, Paula, tr. (p. 1044)
Penn-Coughin, O. Kissed by a Clown Welcome to Hell: Welcome to Hell. (p. 961)
—They're Coming for You: Scary Stories that Scream to be Read. (p. 1732)
Penne, Barbra. Susan B. Anthony: Pioneering Leader of the Women's Rights Movement. (p. 1688)
Pennebaker, H. I., jt. auth. see Martin, Gary.
Pennell, Kathleen. Phantom Stallion. Pennell, Lauren, illus. (p. 1349)
—Secret Passage: Pony Investigators Series #5. (p. 1543)
Pennell, Lauren, illus. see Pennell, Kathleen.
Pennell, Rhett / R., illus. see Pate, Ginger.
Pennels, Geraldine. School Shenanigans of Amy & Nontand. (p. 1523)
Pennels, Geraldine M. School Shenanigans of Amy & Nontand: Volume Two Fifth Grade. (p. 1523)
Penner, Evelyn. Kid Who Ate Dog Food. Chullabrahm, T. M., illus. (p. 951)
Penner, Fred. Here We Go Round the Mulberry Bush. Fatus, Sophie, illus. (p. 771)
Penner, Fred, illus. see Harter, Debbie.
Penner, Fred, jt. auth. see Corr, Christopher.
Penner, Fred, jt. auth. see Fatus, Sophie.
Penner, Fred, jt. auth. see Lumley, Jemima.
Penner, Fred & Corr, Christopher. Whole World. (p. 1920)
Penner, Jim, jt. auth. see Sinclair, Scott.
Penner, Lucille Recht. Apaguen las Luces! Smath, Jerry, illus. (p. 91)
—Bears on the Brain. Adams, Lynn, illus. (p. 152)
—Dinosaur Babies. Barrett, Peter, illus. (p. 441)
—Donde esta ese Hueso? Math Matters en Espanol. Adams, Lynne, illus. (p. 466)
—Limpiar el Campamento; Clean Sweep Campers. (p. 1018)
—Osos en la Mente. Adams, Lynn, illus. (p. 1306)
—Osos en la Mente; Bears on the Brain. (p. 1306)
—Twisters! Gams, Allen, illus. (p. 1803)
Penner, Stephen. Professor Barrister's Dinosaur Mysteries #1: The Case of the Truncated Troodon. Penner, Stephen, illus. (p. 1409)
—Professor Barrister's Dinosaur Mysteries #2: The Case of the Armored Allosaurus. (p. 1409)
—Professor Barrister's Dinosaur Mysteries #4: The Case of the Colorful Caudipteryx. Penner, Stephen, illus. (p. 1409)
Penney, Betty. Tell Your Mother. (p. 1717)
Penney, Ian, illus. see Mutchnick, Brenda & Casden, Ron.
Penney, Shannon. Decodes a Mystery. (p. 422)
Penney, Sue. Buddhism. (p. 234)
—Islam. (p. 891)
Penning, L. & Nelson, Marietjie. Hero of Spionkop. (p. 772)
—Lion of Modderspruit. (p. 1020)
Pennington, Beverly A. Jonathan's Discovery. Pennington, Beverly A., illus. (p. 925)
Pennington, Bruce F. Diagnosing Learning Disorders, Second Edition: A Neuropsychological Framework. (p. 433)
Pennington, Carole, ed. see Vance, Vince.
Pennington, Craig, illus. see Grandma Janet Mary.
Pennington, Craig, illus. see Sinke, Grandma Janet Mary.
Pennington, Craig, illus. see Sinke, Janet Mary.
Pennington, Donald C., et al. Advanced Psychology AQA. (p. 13)
Pennington, J. C. D., jt. auth. see Pennington, Stacey.
Pennington, Jack, illus. see Brand, Ruth.
Pennington, Jack & Tank, Daniel. Joseph. (p. 926)
Pennington, Kate. Brief Candle. (p. 227)
—Nightingale's Song. (p. 1255)
Pennington, Kate & Oldfield, Jenny. Tread Softly. (p. 1781)
Pennington, Kelly, illus. see Wooten, Laura.
Pennington, Mark, illus. see Carey, Mike & Fern, Jim.
Pennington, Mark, illus. see Marz, Ron.
Pennington, Mark, illus. see Milligan, Peter.
Pennington, Mark, illus. see Yasuda, Anita.
Pennington, Michael. Midsummer Night's Dream: A User's Guide. (p. 1139)
Pennington, Norma C. & Schuller, Sheldon V. Unopened Gift (p. 1822)
Pennington, Stacey & Pennington, J. C. D. Let's Go Aquarium: A Magnetic Storybook. Allen, Marie, illus. (p. 997)
Pennington, Tony. Fishing with Granddaddy B. (p. 599)
Penny, Agnes M. Story of Our Lady of Victory. Penny, Agnes M., illus. (p. 1659)
Penny, Anne. Scraper. (p. 1532)
Penny, Malcolm. Grasslands. (p. 712)
Penny, Sam. Broken River: Book 2 of the 7. 9 Scenario. (p. 230)
Penny Z. Adventures of Little Brother. (p. 19)
Pennybacker, Mindy & Streep, Meryl. Do One Green Thing: Saving the Earth Through Simple, Everyday Choices. (p. 457)
Pennypacker, Mona, illus. see Hayes, Joe.
Pennypacker, Sara. Clementine. Frazee, Marla, illus. (p. 330)
—Clementine & the Family Meeting. (p. 330)
—Clementine & the Family Meeting. Frazee, Marla, illus. (p. 330)
—Clementine & the Spring Trip. (p. 330)
—Clementine & the Spring Trip. Frazee, Marla, illus. (p. 330)
—Clementine, Friend of the Week. Frazee, Marla, illus. (p. 330)
—Clementine's Letter. Frazee, Marla, illus. (p. 331)
—Completely Clementine. Frazee, Marla, illus. (p. 353)
—Meet the Dullards. Salmieri, Daniel, illus. (p. 1122)
—Sparrow Girl. Tanaka, Yoko, illus. (p. 1622)
—Stuart Goes to School. Matje, Martin, illus. (p. 1668)
—Summer of the Gypsy Moths. (p. 1674)
—Talented Clementine. Frazee, Marla, illus. (p. 1701)
Pennypacker, Sara & Brown, Jeff. Great Egyptian Grave Robbery No. 2. Pamintuan, Macky, illus. (p. 715)
—Great Egyptian Grave Robbery. Pamintuan, Macky, illus. (p. 715)
Penot, Jessica. Monster Hunter's Manual. (p. 1167)
Penovi, Celina. Alboroto a la Hora Del Desayuno / Scrambled Breakfast. (p. 35)
—Clumsy Stork - la Cigüeña Despistad. (p. 336)
—Guess It If You Can! — ¿Adivinarás Quizás? Volume I - School Time! — Volumen I - Hora de ir a la Escuela! (p. 729)
Penrod. Indiana Coloring Book. (p. 871)
—Ohio Coloring Book. (p. 1281)
Penrod, Kathy Webb. Tumptin's Sneeze. Mengert, Hollie E., illus. (p. 1796)
Penrose, Antony & Picasso, Pablo. Boy Who Bit Picasso. (p. 219)
Penrose, Jane. Landforms (p. 974)
Penrose, Jane & Heinemann Library Staff. Landforms (p. 974)
Penrose, Margaret. Dorothy Dale: A Girl of To-day. (p. 471)
—Dorothy Dale. (p. 471)
—Dorothy Dale's Camping Days. (p. 471)
—Dorothy Dale's Camping Days. (p. 471)
—Motor Girls. (p. 1179)
—Motor Girls on a Tour. (p. 1179)
—Motor Girls on Cedar Lake: Or the Hermit of Fern Island. (p. 1179)
—Motor Girls on the Coast or the Waif from the Se. (p. 1179)
—Motor Girls on Waters Blue. (p. 1179)
—Motor Girls Through New England: Or Held by the Gypsies. (p. 1179)
Penson, Mary. Billy Bardin & the Witness Tree. (p. 187)
Penson, Mary E. Martha Mary Overstreet, M. D. (p. 1097)
Penta, Mark, creator. Cape Cod Invasion! (p. 262)
Pentabu. My Girlfriend's a Geek (p. 1209)
Pentangelo, Manuela. To the Rescue: Chicco Adventures. Pentangelo, Manuela, illus. (p. 1759)
Pentangelo, Manuela, illus. see Waite, Lance.
Penthouse International Staff. Extreme Sex, Maximum Pleasure. Penthouse Magazine Staff, ed. (p. 556)
—Letters to Penthouse XXV: She's Mine, She's Yours, She's Wild! Penthouse Magazine Staff, ed. (p. 1002)
—Penthouse Uncensored VI: Ultimate Erotica. (p. 1338)
Penthouse International Staff, jt. auth. see Penthouse Magazine Staff.
Penthouse Magazine Staff. Hottest Sex Just This Side of Legal! (p. 802)
—Letters to Penthouse XXI: When Wild Meets Raunchy. (p. 1002)
—Penthouse Unleashed: Sex Tips. (p. 1338)
Penthouse Magazine Staff, ed. see Penthouse International Staff.
Penthouse Magazine Staff & Penthouse International Staff. Letters to Penthouse XIX. (p. 1002)
—Letters to Penthouse XXII: Views from the Top & Bottom. (p. 1002)
—Letters to Penthouse XXVII: The First Time Is the Hottest. (p. 1002)
—Penthouse Variations. (p. 1338)
Penthouse Magazine Staff, ed. Take a Walk on the Wild Side. (p. 1696)
Pentland, Peter, jt. auth. see Stoyles, Pennie.
Pentney, Ryan, illus. see Loewen, Nancy, et al.
Pentney, Ryan, illus. see Loewen, Nancy.
Penton. Masterpieces Set. (p. 1103)
—Sleep Little Baby Set. (p. 1588)
Penton, ed. Happy Bugs. (p. 745)
—United States Flipper. (p. 1819)
Penton Overseas, Inc. Staff. Colors, Shapes & Sizes. (p. 345)
—States & Capitals. (p. 1644)
—U. S. Presidents. (p. 1807)
Penton Overseas, Inc. Staff, ed. see Hinkler Books Staff.
Penton-Grayson, Mildred. From A Prayer Warrior's Closet. (p. 641)
Pentz, Jane A. Horatio's Magical Journeys - Horatio's New Book. (p. 797)
—Horatio's Magical Journeys - the Secret. (p. 797)
People Magazine Editors. People - Seventy-Five Years of Oscar Style. (p. 1339)
Peoples, Alan. James the Circus Boy. (p. 907)
Peot, Margaret. Crow Made a Friend. (p. 386)
—Inkblot: Drip, Splat, & Squish Your Way to Creativity. Peot, Margaret, illus. (p. 874)
Pep, Joe, illus. see Gallagher, Mike, et al.
Peper, George. Playing Partners: A Father, a Son & Their Shared Addiction to Golf. (p. 1372)
Pepin, Brenda. Cordelia Rae Is Crazy for Hats. (p. 366)
Pepin, Claudine. Kids Cook French: Les Enfants Cuisinent en Francais. Pepin, Jacques, illus. (p. 953)
Pepin, Eric J. Handbook of the Navigator. Robison, Christopher E., ed. (p. 740)
Pepin, Jacques, illus. see Pepin, Claudine.
Pepin, Rebecca. Bobby Dog & the Flying Frog. Fuller, Cari, illus. (p. 206)
Pepis, Aaron, photos by see Khan, Aisha Karen.
Peppas, Lynn. Aircraft Carriers: Runways at Sea. (p. 31)
—Alps. (p. 50)
—Arbor Day. (p. 95)
—Atacama Desert. (p. 111)
—Atvs & Off-Roaders. (p. 114)
—Bicycles: Pedal Power. (p. 177)
—Big Buses. (p. 180)
—Boats on the Water. (p. 205)
—Camaro. (p. 255)
—Corvette. Crabtree Staff, ed. (p. 368)
—Cranes. (p. 376)
—Cultural Traditions in China. (p. 391)
—Cultural Traditions in France. (p. 391)
—Cultural Traditions in Germany. (p. 391)
—Cultural Traditions in Iran. (p. 391)
—Cultural Traditions in the United Kingdom. (p. 391)
—Demi Lovato. (p. 425)
—Drake. (p. 479)
—Election Day. (p. 508)
—Fighter Jets: Defending the Skies. (p. 585)
—Forensics: The Scene of the Crime. (p. 617)
—Great Victoria Desert. (p. 719)
—Green Machines: Eco-Friendly Rides. (p. 722)
—Groundhog Day. (p. 725)
—Gulf Oil Spill. (p. 731)
—Hiroshima & Nagasaki. (p. 781)
—Holi. (p. 788)
—Holocaust. (p. 789)
—How Do Clouds Form? (p. 806)
—How Do We Measure Matter? (p. 808)
—John Cena. (p. 921)
—Juneteenth. (p. 934)
—Justin Bieber. (p. 940)
—Life in Ancient Greece. (p. 1010)
—Life in Ancient Mesoamerica. (p. 1010)
—M. I. A. (p. 1067)
—M.I.A. (p. 1133)
—Miley Cyrus. (p. 1142)
—Military Helicopters: Flying into Battle. (p. 1143)
—Monster Trucks. (p. 1168)
—New Year's Day. (p. 1247)
—Ocean, Tidal & Wave Energy: Power from the Sea. (p. 1277)
—One Direction. (p. 1294)
—Piracy. (p. 1362)
—Plague! (p. 1366)
—Powerful Armored Vehicles. (p. 1390)
—Presidents' Day. (p. 1397)
—Road Makers & Breakers. (p. 1476)
—Robotics. (p. 1480)
—Rosh Hashanah & Yom Kippur. (p. 1490)
—Severe Storm & Blizzard Alert! (p. 1555)
—St. Lawrence: River Route to the Great Lakes. (p. 1638)
—Superstorm Sandy. (p. 1684)
—Symmetry. (p. 1693)
—Taylor Swift. (p. 1708)
—Thanksgiving. (p. 1725)
—Tracteurs. (p. 1775)
—Tractors at Work. (p. 1775)
—Trail of Tears. (p. 1776)
—Vehicles on the Farm. (p. 1834)
—Victoria Day. (p. 1840)
—What Are Cirrus Clouds? (p. 1879)
—What Are Cumulus Clouds? (p. 1879)
—What Are Stratus Clouds? (p. 1879)
—What Is a Gas? (p. 1888)
—What Is a Liquid? (p. 1888)
—What Is a Solid? (p. 1888)
—What's in the Northeast? Crabtree Publishing Staff, ed. (p. 1898)
—Why Anson Jones Matters to Texas. (p. 1922)
—Why Cabeza de Vaca Matters to Texas. (p. 1923)
—Why Charles Goodnight Matters to Texas. (p. 1923)
—Why Francisco Coronado Matters to Texas. (p. 1925)
—Why José Antonio Navarro Matters to Texas. (p. 1925)
—Why Martín de Léon Matters to Texas. (p. 1925)
—Why Sam Houston Matters to Texas. (p. 1925)
—Why Sieur de La Salle Matters to Texas. (p. 1926)
—Why Stephen F. Austin Matters to Texas. (p. 1926)
—Wildfire Alert! (p. 1931)
—Women's Suffrage. (p. 1947)
—Zac Efron. (p. 1984)
Peppas, Lynn, jt. auth. see Aloian, Molly.
Peppas, Lynn, jt. auth. see Becker, Ann.
Peppas, Lynn, jt. auth. see Challen, Paul.
Peppas, Lynn, jt. auth. see Miller, Reagan.
Peppas, Lynn & Aloian, Molly. Cultural Traditions in India. (p. 391)
Peppas, Lynn & Becker, Ann. Division. (p. 455)
Peppas, Lynn & Challen, Paul. Addition. (p. 12)
Peppas, Lynn & Newton, Sydney. Terrorism Alert! (p. 1722)
Peppas, Lynne, jt. auth. see Aloian, Molly.
Peppe, Holly, jt. auth. see Irving, Barrington.
Pepper, Dennis W. Stories of Little Joe Squirrel & Bob Rabbit. (p. 1655)
Pepper, Lily. Bananas. (p. 136)
—In the Garden at Granddad's. (p. 866)
Pepper, Lorna, et al. Cambridge IGCSE English as a Second Language. (p. 255)
Pepper, Louise. Got your Back... A Story of Friendship & Caring. (p. 703)
Pepper, Sly. Dugan Peckles & the Keepers of the Crystal Flame. Germano, Nicholas, illus. (p. 489)
—Dugan Peckles Through the Manhole. (p. 489)
Peppers, F. J. That's not a Fish! (p. 1727)
Peraire del Molino, C., tr. see Martin, Ann M.
Peraire del Molino, Conchita, tr. see Martin, Ann M.
Peralas, Jorge. Oracional Bilingue Para Ninos: A Children's Prayerbook in Spanish-English. Domeier, Renee & Grisewood, Therese U., eds. (p. 1301)
Perales, Alonso M. Brujas, Lechuzas y Espantos/Witches, Owls & Spooks. Pluecker, John, tr. from SPA. (p. 232)
Peralta, Joaquin. Almost Private Eye: Mystery of the Starfighter. (p. 48)
—Emma Snow: At the Edge of the World. (p. 520)
Perantakou-Cook, Mary, jt. auth. see Zarabouka, Sofia.
Perard, Victor, illus. see Ames, Joseph B.
Peratt, Karen, jt. auth. see Thompson, Gare.
Perchyonok, Tamara. Chemistry & Fun for Kids of All Ages: Bilingual Book. (p. 297)
Perciopelo, illus. see Burke, Ellinor Rozecki.
Percival, J. M., ed. Romanian Fairy Tales. (p. 1486)
Percival, Olive. Children's Garden Book: Instructions, Plans & Stories, a Voice from a Gentle Age. (p. 303)
Percival, Simon. Practical Guide to Revision Techniques. (p. 1392)
Percival, Tom. Bubble Trouble. (p. 233)
—Herman's Letter. (p. 771)
—Jack's Amazing Shadow. Percival, Tom, illus. (p. 904)
Percival, Tom, illus. see Brezenoff, Steve.
Percival, Tom, illus. see Landy, Derek.
Percival, Tom, illus. see Marsh, Robert.
Perconte, Jack. 60,000 Hitting Lessons: A Hands on Baseball Guide fo Parents, Coaches & Players. (p. 2003)
Percy, Graham. Ant & the Grasshopper. Percy, Graham, illus. (p. 88)
—Fox & the Stork. (p. 626)
—Heron & the Fish. Percy, Graham, illus. (p. 773)
—Tales from Around the World. (p. 1701)
—Tales from the Arabian Nights. (p. 1701)
—Tortoise & the Hare. Percy, Graham, illus. (p. 1771)
Percy, J.P. Animals. (p. 81)
—At Home. (p. 110)
—In the Street. (p. 867)
—Nature. (p. 1236)
Percy Keese, Fitzhugh. Pee-Wee Harris & Roy Blakeley's Adventures in Camp. (p. 1334)
Percy, Richard & Baudet. Silver Arrow. (p. 1576)
Percy, Sally, illus. see Cain, Sheridan.
Perdew, Laura. Animal Rights Movement. (p. 79)
—Bullying. (p. 241)
—History of Art. (p. 783)
—Internet Addiction. (p. 880)
—Understanding Jordan Today. (p. 1815)
—Understanding Lebanon Today. (p. 1815)
Perdomo, Adolfo Perez, tr. see Eastman, P. D.
Perdomo, Willie. Abuela. (p. 7)
—Clemente! Collier, Bryan, illus. (p. 330)
—Double Dutch. (p. 472)
—Untitled Perdomo 3/4. (p. 1823)
—Untitled Perdomo 4/4. (p. 1823)
—Visiting Langston. Collier, Bryan, illus. (p. 1845)
Perdue, Gillian. Buachaill Bo. Connor, Michael, illus. (p. 233)
—Conor's Canvas. Connor, Michael, illus. (p. 358)
—Conor's Concert. Connor, Michael, illus. (p. 358)
Perdue, Tito. Fields of Asphodel. (p. 584)
Peredo, Roberto. Acoyani: El Nino y el Poeta. Sanchez, Andres & Arte Y Diseno, Tane, illus. (p. 9)
Perego, Jeanne. Joseph & Chico: The Life of Pope Benedict XVI as Told by a Cat. Matt, Andrew, tr. from ITA. (p. 926)
Perego, Jeanne, et al. Max & Benedict: A Bird's Eye View of the Pope's Daily Life. (p. 1110)
Peregrinos & Extranjeros. Buen Pastor (The Good Shepherd) (p. 235)
Pereira, Chritine M. Madilynn Rose Rhyming Fairy: Volume 1 (p. 1070)
Pereira, Diego Jourdan. Animal Antics Hidden Pictures. (p. 76)
—FLIP OUTS — Fairy Fun: Color Your Own Cartoon! (p. 605)
—Glow-In-the-Dark Fairy Princess Sticker Paper Doll. (p. 685)
—Glow-In-the-Dark Zombie Sticker Paper Doll. (p. 685)
—Pink Party Coloring Book. (p. 1360)
—Thumbs up! Thumbwrestler Tattoos. (p. 1745)
Pereira, Lavinia, jt. auth. see Solomon, Michelle.
Pereira, William. Adventures of LC, the Lucky Calf. Bowlsby, Tina Marie, illus. (p. 19)
Perello, jt. auth. see Alonso.
Perelman, Helen. Bubble Gum Rescue. Waters, Erica-Jane, illus. (p. 233)
—Candy Fairies Sweet Collection: Chocolate Dreams; Rainbow Swirl; Caramel Moon; Cool Mint. Waters, Erica-Jane, illus. (p. 261)
—Caramel Moon. Waters, Erica-Jane, illus. (p. 265)
—Chocolate Dreams. Waters, Erica-Jane, illus. (p. 309)
—Chocolate Rose. Waters, Erica-Jane, illus. (p. 309)
—Cool Mint. Waters, Erica-Jane, illus. (p. 364)
—Double Dip. Waters, Erica-Jane, illus. (p. 472)
—Frozen Treats. Waters, Erica-Jane, illus. (p. 645)
—Gooey Goblins: Halloween Special. Waters, Erica-Jane, illus. (p. 702)
—Heart to Heart. (p. 760)
—Jelly Bean Jumble. Waters, Erica-Jane, illus. (p. 912)
—Magic Hearts. Waters, Erica-Jane, illus. (p. 1072)
—Marshmallow Mystery. Waters, Erica-Jane, illus. (p. 1096)
—Rainbow Swirl. Waters, Erica-Jane, illus. (p. 1436)
—Rapunzel: A Day to Remember. Studio IBOIX, illus. (p. 1439)
—Royal Wedding: Super Special. Waters, Erica-Jane, illus. (p. 1492)
—Sugar Ball. Waters, Erica-Jane, illus. (p. 1672)
—Sweet Secrets. Waters, Erica-Jane, illus. (p. 1690)
—Valentine's Surprise. Waters, Erica-Jane, illus. (p. 1830)
Perelman, Yakov. Amazing Experiments for Young Physicians. Williams, Brian, tr. (p. 54)
Perelman-Bernstein, Helen. Feel the Noise! Tips & Tricks to Rockin' Camp. (p. 580)
Perelstein, Jennifer. Who Moved the Masterpieces? A Visit to the Mcnay Art Museum. (p. 1917)
Perera, Anna. Guantanamo Boy. (p. 728)
Perera, Hilda. Kike. (p. 955)
—MAI. (p. 1076)
—Mumu. (p. 1191)
Perera, Hilda & Fraga, Mana F. Pata Pita Vuelve. (p. 1327)
Perera, Hilda & Hilda, Perera. Pedrin y la Garza. Moreiro, Enrique S., illus. (p. 1334)
—Pericopln. (p. 1343)
Perera, Oleene. Timmy Tangelo Goes Green. (p. 1755)
Peretti, Frank E. Cooper Kids Adventure Series. (p. 365)

—Deadly Curse of Toco-Rey (p. 417)
—Deadly Curse of Toco-Rey. Life Publishers International Staff, tr. from ENG. (p. 417)
—Door in the Dragon's Throat. (p. 470)
—Escape from the Island of Aquarius. (p. 535)
—Hangman's Curse. (p. 742)
—Nightmare Academy. (p. 1255)
—Tombs of Anak. (p. 1764)
—Trapped at the Bottom of the Sea. (p. 1779)
Peretti, Frank E. & Thomas Nelson & Sons Staff. Legend of Annie Murphy (p. 988)
—Mayday at Two Thousand Five Hundred (p. 1113)
—Secret of the Desert Stone (p. 1542)
Peretti, Frank E., et al. Door in the Dragon's Throat. (p. 470)
Peretti, Kim. Oodle Van Boodle & the Great Cake Adventure. (p. 1298)
Peretz, I. L. Even Higher! A Rosh Hashanah Story. Weber, Jill, illus. (p. 541)
—Seven Good Years: And Other Stories of I. L. Peretz. Hautzig, Esther, tr. (p. 1554)
Peretz, I. L. & Goldin, Barbara Diamond. Magician's Visit: A Passover Tale. Parker, Robert Andrew, illus. (p. 1075)
Pereyra, Jennifer Lynn. Mommy & Daddy Work to Make Some Dough. (p. 1162)
Pérez, Alfredo. Sueno de Novela. (p. 1672)
Pérez, Amada Irma. Mi Diario de Aquí Hasta Allá. Gonzalez, Maya Christina, illus. (p. 1132)
Perez, Amada Irma. Mi Propio Cuartito. (p. 1133)
Pérez, Amada Irma. Nana's Big Surprise. Gonzalez, Maya Christina, illus. (p. 1228)
Perez, Amada Irma, jt. auth. see Gonzalez, Maya Christina.
Perez, Amada Irma & Children's Book Press Staff. Nana, Que Sorpresa! Gonzalez, Maya Christina, illus. (p. 1228)
Perez, Angela J. Zack Attack! Hazard, Andrea, illus. (p. 1984)
Perez, Angela J., ed. see Smith, Jennifer Lynne.
Perez, Annette. My Brain Won't Float Away / Mi cerebro no va a salir Flotando. Herranz Brooks, Jacqueline, tr. (p. 1199)
Pérez, Ashley Hope. Knife & the Butterfly. (p. 964)
—Out of Darkness. (p. 1311)
—What Can't Wait. (p. 1881)
Pérez, Berta Herreros, tr. see Le Guillou, Philippe.
Pérez, Carmen, illus. see Bird, Benjamin.
Perez, Claire & Fox, Mary. Peacekeepers - the New Generation: Peace Activities for Children Ages 2-5. (p. 1332)
Pérez, Claire M. & Fox, Mary. Peacemakers: The New Generation Practical Group Activities for Grades 6-8. (p. 1332)
Perez, Claudia. Love Me. Tardif, Mandy, illus. (p. 1060)
Pérez, Daniel, illus. see Carroll, Lewis, pseud.
Pérez, Daniel, illus. see Doyle, Arthur.
Pérez, Daniel, illus. see Powell, Martin.
Pérez, Daniel, illus. see Shakespeare, William.
Perez, Debi, illus. see Pantelides, Sherry.
Perez, Dorothy Thompson, illus. see Kitch, Anne E.
Perez, Elvia, ed. see Hernandez Mora, Victor.
Perez, Esther Ido, illus. see Yerushalmi, Miriam.
Perez, Federico, jt. auth. see Villoro, Carmen.
Pérez Galdós, Benito. Desheredada (The Desinherited) (p. 429)
—Marianela. (p. 1093)
Pérez Galván, Ana, tr. see Fox, Sabrina & FOX, SABRINA.
Perez, George. Destiny Calling. Adams, Art & Bolton, John, illus. (p. 431)
—Serpent Crown. (p. 1552)
Perez, George, illus. see Kesel, Barbara.
Perez, George, illus. see Shooter, Jim & Wolfman, Marv.
Perez, George, illus. see Wein, Len & Wolfman, Marv.
Perez, George, jt. auth. see Wolfman, Marv.
Perez, George & Wolfman, Marv. New Teen Titans. (p. 1247)
Perez, George, et al. Beauty & the Beast. Giordano, Dick et al, illus. (p. 154)
—Essential Fantastic Four - Volume 9. (p. 537)
Perez, Gerry, illus. see Aryal, Aimee.
Perez III, Librado. Thank You Jesus. (p. 1725)
Perez, Irene. Rain or Shine. (p. 1435)
Perez, Isabelle, jt. auth. see Lang, Margaret.
Pérez, Javier Serrano, illus. see Virgo, Seán.
Perez, Jessica. Goodnight, Little Bug. Shelly, Jeff, illus. (p. 701)
—Hello Kitty Helps Out! (p. 764)
—Spin & Spell: A Book & Game in One! Gévry, Claudine, illus. (p. 1627)
—Under Construction: A Moving Track Book. Schneider, Christine, illus. (p. 1813)
—Who's Hiding Inside? Dinosaurs. Lensch, Chris, illus. (p. 1920)
Perez, Jonathan. Sasp. (p. 1515)
Perez, Jose S., jt. auth. see Norman, Tyler.
Perez, Julio E. Serena: A Dreaming Dog. (p. 1552)
Pérez, Karen H., tr. see Lataif, Nicole.
Perez, L. King. Remember As You Pass Me By. (p. 1459)
Perez, Laura C., tr. see Vines, Connie.
Perez, Lucia Angela, illus. see Argueta, Jorge.
Pérez, María, jt. auth. see Traynor, Tracy.
Perez, Marlene. Año del Arco Iris. Forss, Ian, illus. (p. 87)
—Colores de las Estaciones. (p. 344)
—Colors of the Seasons. (p. 345)
—Colors of the Seasons (Big Book) (p. 345)
—Comeback. (p. 347)
—Dead Is a Battlefield. (p. 416)
—Dead Is a Killer Tune. (p. 417)
—Dead Is a State of Mind. (p. 417)
—Dead Is Just a Dream. (p. 417)
—Dead Is Just a Rumor. (p. 417)
—Dead Is Not an Option. (p. 417)
—Dead Is So Last Year. (p. 417)
—Dead Is the New Black. (p. 417)
—Princess Rock & the Royal Inches. (p. 1405)
—Rainbow Year. (p. 1436)
—Skateboarding. (p. 1583)
Perez, Maureen T. Friendliness. Perez, Maureen T. & Cesena, Denise, illus. (p. 637)
—Friendliness - Companion Book. Perez, Maureen T. & Cesena, Denise, illus. (p. 637)
Perez, Maureen T., illus. see Cesena, Denise.
Perez, Maureen T., jt. auth. see Cesena, Denise.
Perez, Melissa E. Adventures of Camron, Tiffany & Lydi. (p. 17)
Perez, Mercedes Dominguez, tr. see Farshtey, Greg & Bolinaga Irasuegui, Iñigo.
Perez, Mike. Lionel Messi: The Ultimate Fan Book. (p. 1021)
Perez, Monica & Houghton Mifflin Company Editors. Curious George & Me! Paprocki, Greg & Hines, Anna Grossnickle, illus. (p. 393)
Perez, Monica, et al. Curious George Builds a Home. (p. 393)
Perez, Nomar. It's Circle Time! Shapes. (p. 896)
Perez, Norah A. Slopes of War. (p. 1591)
Perez, Nuria Marti, tr. see Higgins, F. E., et al.
Perez, Olga. Sitting on Cloud 9 at the 50-Yard Line. (p. 1582)
Pérez, Orlando. Cultura política de la democracia en Nicaragua 2008: El impacto de la Gobernabilidad. (p. 390)
—Cultura política de la democracia en Panamá 2008: El impacto de la Gobernabilidad. (p. 390)
Perez, Orlando J., jt. ed. see Weisblatt, Jayne.
Perez, Pere, illus. see Miller, Bryan Q.
Perez, Peter L., jt. auth. see Tullet, Hervé.
Pérez, Ramón, illus. see Battle, Craig.
Pérez, Ramón, illus. see Christopher, Neil.
Perez, Ramon, illus. see Flaherty, Louise & Christopher, Neil.
Perez, Ramon, illus. see Henson, Jim & Juhl, Jerry.
Pérez, Ramón, illus. see O'Donnell, Liam & Battle, Craig.
Pérez, Ramón, illus. see Szpirglas, Jeff.
Perez, Ramon, et al. Captain America: Allies & Enemies. (p. 263)
Pérez, Ramón K., illus. see Robinson, Laura.
Perez, Richard Wesley. Mousehaven Discovers Democracy: Mr. Irving Mouse's - Mousehaven Series of Stories. (p. 1182)
Perez Saez, Lucrecia, et al. Besitos de Chocolate: El Valle de la Ternura. Hormeo, Marielo Gil, illus. (p. 168)
Perez, Sara, illus. see Ikids Staff & Schimel, Lawrence.
Pérez, Sara Rojo, illus. see Ikids Staff.
Pérez, Sara Rojo, illus. see White, Mark & Aesop Enterprise Inc. Staff.
Pérez, Sara Rojo, illus. see White, Mark.
Perez, Tedi J. Cody & the Snowbirds. (p. 338)
Perez, Thierry, illus. see Relota, Agatha.
Perez, Victoria, jt. auth. see Essig, Helene.
Perez, Vivian. Stolen Stories for My Nieces. (p. 1652)
Perez, Whitney Joan. Friendship. (p. 639)
Perez-Fessenden, Lourdes. Daddy & I. Perez-Fessenden, Lourdes, illus. (p. 398)
Pérez-Foncea, Juan Antonio & Caro, Stephen. Ivan of Aldenuri: The Forest of the Tauros. (p. 900)
Perez-Martinez, Irella. Suyensita & Her Adventures. (p. 1688)
Pérez-Mercado, Mary Margaret. Splat! Torrey, Rich, illus. (p. 1629)
—¡Zas! Torrey, Richard L., illus. (p. 1985)
Pérez-Mercado, Mary Margaret & Torrey, Rich. ¡Zas! Torrey, Rich, illus. (p. 1985)
Perez-Moliere, Marnie, illus. see Barsy, Kalman.
Perez-Moliere, Marnie, illus. see Leon, Georgina Lazaro.
Pérez-Reverte, Arturo. Queen of the South. (p. 1425)
—Queen of the South. Hurley, Andrew, tr. (p. 1425)
Pérez-Sauquillo , Vanesa. Cuentos Con Beso Para Las Buenas Noches. (p. 389)
Perez-Sauquillo, Vanesa, jt. auth. see Chbosky, Stephen.
Perez-Stable, Deborah, illus. see Chaconas, Dori.
Perez-Torres, Juliana, illus. see Gilbert, George.
Perfect, Kathy A. Poetry Lessons: Everything You Need - A Mentor Teacher's Lessons & Select Poems That Help You Meet the Standards Across the Curriculum-And Teach Poetry with Confidence & Joy. (p. 1376)
Perfect Score Software, creator. CLEP / AP Courseware - American Government. (p. 331)
—CLEP / AP Courseware - Biology. (p. 331)
—CLEP / AP Courseware - Social Sciences & History. (p. 331)
—CLEP / AP Courseware - Western Civilization I: Ancient near East To 1648. (p. 331)
—CLEP / AP Financial Accounting Courseware 2008. (p. 331)
—CLEP / AP Introduction to Educational Psychology Courseware 2008. (p. 331)
Perham, Molly. Customize Your Clothes: Over 50 Simple, Fun Ideas to Transform Your Wardrobe & Accessories. Perham, Molly, ed. (p. 395)
Pericoli, Matteo. London for Children. (p. 1046)
Perihar, Amar Singh, jt. auth. see Dicker, Katie.
Perilli, Marilena, illus. see Buckley, MacKenzie.
Perilli, Marilena, illus. see Tillworth, Mary.
Perin, Pauline, illus. see Smith, Clyde R.
Perine, Jorli. Tirsah's Dream. (p. 1757)
Peringer, Stephen Mercer, illus. see Spruill, Edward L. & Spruill, Sonya.
Perini, Mark & Cross, Julie. Halfway Perfect. (p. 737)
Perios, Sylvaine, et al. Mariquita. (p. 1094)
Peris, Carme, illus. see Produccions Editorials, Trèvol & Trévol, S. A.
Peris, Nuria, illus. see Gallardo, Adam.
Perish, Patrick. Animal Trainer. (p. 80)
—Disgusting Animals. (p. 450)
—Disgusting Bodily Functions. (p. 450)
—Disgusting Bugs. (p. 450)
—Disgusting Foods. (p. 450)
—Disgusting Jobs. (p. 450)
—Disgusting Plants. (p. 450)
—Maine. (p. 1077)
—Skyscraper Builder. (p. 1587)
—SWAT Team Member. (p. 1689)
—Wilderness Rescue Pilot. (p. 1931)
Perisic, Zoran. Alien Called Freddy. (p. 40)
Perissinotto, Giorgio Sabino Antonio, ed. from SPA. California Recollections of Angustias de la Guerra Ord: (Occurrences in Hispanic California) (p. 253)
Perkins, Al. Ear Book. Payne, Henry, illus. (p. 492)
Perkins, Al, jt. auth. see Dr. Seuss Enterprises Staff.
Perkins, Anne. Trailblazers in Politics (p. 1776)
Perkins, C. Gale. Pumpkin for God. (p. 1416)
Perkins, Chelsea, illus. see Yost, B. L.
Perkins, David & Dooley, Caroline. Selfish Giant: A Children's Musical. (p. 1549)
Perkins, Diamond Le'na. Kid Problems: Let's Do It Right the First Time! Pearce, Sha, ed. (p. 951)
Perkins, Diane. Marriage Bargain. (p. 1096)
Perkins, Greg. Ninito Los Guiara. Pomeroy, John, illus. (p. 1256)
Perkins, Gwyn, jt. auth. see Hornsey, Chris.
Perkins, Jill E. Cherubs Chatter: A Collection of Original Songs & Poems. (p. 298)
Perkins, John. Perceval: King Arthur's Knight of the Holy Grail Spirin, Gennady, illus. (p. 1341)
Perkins, Ken, illus. see Butt, Sheila K.
Perkins, Kenneth B., jt. auth. see Hayes, Trudie L.
Perkins, Kevin. Little Blue Gnome. (p. 1024)
Perkins, Kevin John. Circlet. (p. 321)
Perkins, Larry B. Jake the Cow Hand. (p. 906)
—Jasper Rabbit. (p. 910)
Perkins, Lori L., illus. see Perkins, Myrna.
Perkins, Lucy. American Twins of the Revolution. Perkins, Lucy, illus. (p. 63)
Perkins, Lucy Fitch. American Twins of 1812. (p. 63)
—American Twins of the Revolution. Perkins, Lucy Fitch, illus. (p. 63)
—Belgian Twins. (p. 161)
—Cave Twins. (p. 282)
—Dutch Twins. (p. 490)
—Eskimo Twins. (p. 536)
—Eskimo Twins (Yesterday's Classics) (p. 536)
—Irish Twins. (p. 888)
—Japanese Twins. (p. 909)
—Japanese Twins (Yesterday's Classics) (p. 909)
—Rhe Japanese Twins. (p. 1467)
—Scotch Twins. (p. 1530)
—Short Works of Lucy Fitch Perkins. (p. 1569)
—Swiss Twins. (p. 1691)
Perkins, Lynne R., jt. auth. see Perkins, Lynne Rae.
Perkins, Lynne Rae. All Alone in the Universe. (p. 43)
—As Easy As Falling off the Face of the Earth. (p. 105)
—Cardboard Piano. Perkins, Lynne Rae, illus. (p. 265)
—Criss Cross. (p. 383)
—Nuts to You. Perkins, Lynne Rae, illus. (p. 1274)
—Pictures from Our Vacation. Perkins, Lynne Rae, illus. (p. 1356)
—Snow Music. Perkins, Lynne Rae, illus. (p. 1599)
Perkins, Lynne Rae, illus. see Codell, Esmé Raji.
Perkins, Lynne Rae & Perkins, Lynne R. All Alone in the Universe. (p. 43)
—Pictures from Our Vacation. Perkins, Lynne Rae, illus. (p. 1356)
—Snow Music. Perkins, Lynne Rae, illus. (p. 1599)
Perkins, Mair, illus. see Hainsworth, B. R.
Perkins, Mike, illus. see Waid, Mark.
Perkins, Miss Quinn. I Know When the Rainbow Comes. Perkins, Terrell D., illus. (p. 840)
Perkins, Mitali. Bamboo People. (p. 135)
—First Daughter: White House Rules. (p. 594)
—Not-So-Star-Spangled Life of Sunita Sen. (p. 1267)
—Rickshaw Girl. Hogan, Jamie, illus. (p. 1470)
—Secret Keeper. (p. 1541)
—Tiger Boy. Hogan, Jamie, illus. (p. 1748)
Perkins, Mitali, ed. Open Mic: Riffs on Life Between Cultures in Ten Voices. (p. 1299)
Perkins, Myrna. What Makes Honey? Perkins, William C. & Perkins, Lori L., illus. (p. 1892)
Perkins, Nancy, illus. see Greenaway, Kate.
Perkins, Nicole. I Believe God Will: Book of Devotion & Prayer for Children. Perkins, Nicole & Frisk, Maria, illus. (p. 834)
Perkins, Nicole D. I Wish for Snow. Ogene, Chuma C., illus. (p. 848)
Perkins, R. Earth Whispers. (p. 497)
Perkins, Raymond. Mystery of the Silver Statue. Perkins, Stephanie, illus. (p. 1226)
Perkins, Rodney R., illus. see VanDerTuuk-Perkins, Jennifer E.
Perkins, Ruth, illus. see Young, Elizabeth L.
Perkins, Sally J. & Stoner, Mark R. Making Sense of Messages: A Critical Apprenticeship in Rhetorical Criticism. (p. 1082)
Perkins, Stephanie. Anna & the French Kiss. (p. 85)
—Isla & the Happily Ever After. (p. 891)
—Lola & the Boy Next Door. (p. 1045)
—My True Love Gave to Me: Twelve Holiday Stories. (p. 1220)
Perkins, Stephanie, illus. see Perkins, Raymond.
Perkins, T J. Art of the Ninja: Earth. Dumas, Ryan, illus. (p. 102)
Perkins, T. J. Four Little Witches Pinero, Eimi, illus. (p. 625)
Perkins, T J. Image in the Tapestry: A Kim & Kelly Mystery. (p. 860)
—In the Grand Scheme of Things: A Kim & Kelly Mystery. (p. 866)
—Mystery of the Attic. (p. 1225)
—On Forbidden Ground: Sequel to Mystery of the Attic. (p. 1288)
Perkins, T. J. Secret in Phantom Forest: A Kim & Kelly Mystery. (p. 1541)
Perkins, T J. Wound Too Tight. (p. 1962)
Perkins, Terrell D., illus. see Perkins, Miss Quinn.
Perkins, TJ. Fantasies Are Murder: A Kim & Kelly Mystery. (p. 571)
—Trade Secret: A Kim & Kelly Mystery. (p. 1776)
Perkins, Useni Eugene. Black Arts Movement. (p. 195)
Perkins, Wendy. Abyssinian Cats (p. 7)
—Animals Building Homes. (p. 82)
—Animals Finding Food. (p. 82)
—Animals Raising Offspring. (p. 83)
—Animals Sleeping. (p. 84)
—Elephant. Longhi, Katya, illus. (p. 511)
—Let's Look at Animal Ears (p. 998)
—Let's Look at Animal Teeth (p. 998)
—Maine Coon Cats (p. 1077)
—Manx Cats (p. 1089)
—Penguin. (p. 1336)
—Persian Cats (p. 1344)
—Siamese Cats (p. 1572)
—Zebras (p. 1985)
Perkins, Wendy & Capstone Press Editors. Let's Look at Animal Legs Saunders-Smith, Gail, ed. (p. 998)
Perkins, Wendy & Capstone Press Staff. Let's Look at Animal Bottoms Saunders-Smith, Gail, ed. (p. 998)
—Let's Look at Animal Tails Saunders-Smith, Gail, ed. (p. 998)
Perkins, William C., illus. see Perkins, Myrna.
Perkins-Stell, Crystal. Never Knew a Father's Love. (p. 1243)
Perkis, Andrea. Wright Brothers Make History! (p. 1963)
PERKOWSKI, Gary, jt. auth. see Pugh, Harry F.
Perks, Brad. Inspirational Harvest & Hope: Brad Perks California Vineyards. Perks, Brad, photos by. (p. 878)
Perkyns, Dorothy. Bridget's Black '47. (p. 227)
—Last Days in Africville. (p. 977)
Perl, Erica S. Aces Wild. (p. 8)
—Chicken Bedtime Is Really Early. Bates, George, illus. (p. 300)
—Chicken Butt! Cole, Henry, illus. (p. 300)
—Chicken Butt's Back! Cole, Henry, illus. (p. 300)
—Dotty. Denos, Julia, illus. (p. 472)
—Goatilocks & the Three Bears. Howard, Arthur, illus. (p. 687)
—King of the Zoo. Urbanovic, Jackie, illus. (p. 959)
—Totally Tardy Marty. Krosoczka, Jarrett J., illus. (p. 1771)
—Vintage Veronica. (p. 1843)
—When Life Gives You O. J. (p. 1903)
Perl, Lila. Ancient Egyptians. (p. 69)
—Cruzan V. Missouri: The Right to Die. (p. 387)
—Genocide: Standby or Intervene? (p. 661)
—Immigration: This Land Is Whose Land? (p. 861)
—Isabel's War. (p. 891)
—Me & Fat Glenda. (p. 1115)
—Terrorism. (p. 1722)
—Theocracy. (p. 1729)
—Torture. (p. 1771)
Perl, Shaindy. Tell the World: The Story of the Sobibor Revolt. (p. 1717)
Perl, Sheri, jt. auth. see Corporate Contributor Staff.
Perla, Brian, illus. see Spergel, Heather.
Perla, Victoria. When Santa Turned Green. (p. 1904)
Perliger, Arie. Middle Eastern Terrorism. Eubank, Bill, ed. (p. 1137)
Perlin, Don, illus. see Gruenwald, Mark & Grant, Stephen.
Perlman, Janet. Delicious Bug. Perlman, Janet, illus. (p. 425)
—Penguin & the Pea. Perlman, Janet, illus. (p. 1336)
Perlman, Rhea. Born to Drive. Santat, Dan, illus. (p. 214)
—Canyon Catastrophe. Santat, Dan, illus. (p. 262)
—Water Balloon Doom. Santat, Dan, illus. (p. 1862)
Perlman, Willa. Good Night, World. Fisher, Carolyn, illus. (p. 700)
—Pocket Kisses. McDonald, Jill, illus. (p. 1375)
Perlmutter, Richard. Beethoven's Wig. (p. 158)
—Beethoven's Wig — Sing along Piano Classics: Book & CD. (p. 158)
Perlov, Betty Rosenberg. Rifka Takes a Bow. Kawa, Cosei, illus. (p. 1471)
Perlow, Janet. Show Dog. (p. 1570)
—Show Dog Coloring Book. (p. 1570)
Perlowitz, Rebecca & Becky, Morah. In My Family. Katz, Avi, illus. (p. 864)
Perlstein, Linda. Not Much Just Chillin': The Hidden Lives of Middle Schoolers. (p. 1267)
Perlyn, Amanda, illus. see Perlyn, Marilyn.
Perlyn, Marilyn. Biggest & Brightest Light: The Magic of Helping Others. Perlyn, Amanda, illus. (p. 185)
Perman, LeAnn. My Name Was Bert. (p. 1215)
Permane, Terry, photos by see Hooke, R. Schuyler.
Perna, Maria. Meatballs, Oddballs, & Curveballs. (p. 1118)
Pernell, Pasha. Bad Dreams Are Not Allowed! Green, Steve, illus. (p. 131)
Perner, Lars, ed. Scholars with Autism Achieving Dreams. (p. 1521)
Pernice, Clare. Circus Girl. (p. 322)
Pernigotti, Chiara, tr. see Baccalario, P. D.
Pernigotti, Chiara, tr. see Baccalario, Pierdomenico & McGuinness, Nanette.
Pernigotti, Chiara, tr. see Baccalario, Pierdomenico.
Pernigotti, Chiara, tr. see Guerra, Elisa Puricelli.
Pernikoff, Doug. So What If Im a Bully. (p. 1602)
—So What If Im Adopted. (p. 1602)
—So What If My Parents Got Divorced. (p. 1602)
Pernisco, Atilio, illus. see Santillan, Suzanne.
Pero, Denis. My First Atlas: Discovery of the World. (p. 1204)
—My Little Handbook of Experiments: Sciences, Water & Light, Ecology. (p. 1212)
Pero, Denis & Auzou Publishing Staff. My Book of Animals: A Walk Through the National Parks. (p. 1199)
Perols, Sylvaine. Body. (p. 207)
—Tierra y el Cielo. (p. 1748)
Peróls, Sylvaine, jt. auth. see Perols, Sylvaine.
Perols, Sylvaine & De Bourgoing, Pascale. Ladybird. (p. 971)
Perols, Sylvaine & Peróls, Sylvaine. Cuerpo. (p. 390)
—Granja. (p. 710)
Pérols, Sylvaine, et al. Atlas de las Plantas. Pérols, Sylvaine, tr. (p. 112)
—Atlas de los Animales en Peligro. Pérols, Sylvaine & Barroso, Paz, trs. (p. 112)
Perone, S. P. Star of the Future. (p. 1640)
Peros, Tracey E. Colors Make the World a Brighter Place. (p. 345)
Perot, Richard, jt. auth. see Hughes, David Pierce.
Perras, Marielle, illus. see Chalifoux, Lisa M.
Perrault. Bella Durmiente (Caracola) (p. 162)
Perrault, Charles. Cenicienta. (p. 286)
—Cenicienta. Porras, Javier Fernando, illus. (p. 286)
—Cinderella. Innocenti, Roberto, illus. (p. 320)
—Cinderella (Cenicienta) Fransoy, Monse, illus. (p. 320)
—Cuentos de Antano. (p. 389)
—Cuentos de Perrault. (p. 390)
—Fairies. (p. 562)
—Gato con Botas. (p. 658)
—Perrault's Fairy Tales. Johnson, A. E., tr. (p. 1343)
—Puffin Book of Five Minute Stories. (p. 1415)
—Puss in Boots. Bell, Anthea, tr. (p. 1420)

P

—Puss in Boots. Arthur, Malcolm, tr. (p. 1420)
—Puss in Boots. Adams, Frank & Lawrence, C. H., illus. (p. 1420)
—Puss in Boots (El Gato Con Botas) Merino, Jose Luis, illus. (p. 1420)
—Sleeping Beauty. Cowley, Joy, ed. (p. 1589)
—Storyteller Book: Cinderella. Spenceley, Annabel, illus. (p. 1663)
—Tales of Mother Goose. (p. 1702)
Perrault, Charles, jt. auth. see Guillain, Charlotte.
Perrault, Charles, jt. auth. see Leprince de Beaumont, Marie.
Perrault, Charles, jt. auth. see Perrault, Charles.
Perrault, Charles, jt. illus. see Clarke, Harry.
Perrault, Charles & Betts, Christopher. Complete Fairy Tales. (p. 352)
Perrault, Charles & Perrault, Charles. Cuentos Completos. Eyheramonno, Jèoelle et al, trs. (p. 389)
Perrault, Charles, contrib. by. Little Mermaid. (p. 1031)
Perreault, Bruce A., compiled by. Radiant Energy Research Collection. (p. 1432)
Perreault, Diane Juttner. Breath of the Dragon. (p. 225)
Perree, Leyland. Great Reef Race. McGhee, Stuart, illus. (p. 718)
—Unpleasant Tale of the Man-Eating Christmas Pudding. McGhee, Stuart, illus. (p. 1822)
Perren, Lew, jt. auth. see Dannreuther, Charles.
Perrenot, Christine. Jackson & Julie the Twelve-Month Chefs: A Holiday Cookbook for Families & Children. Voltz, Ralph, illus. (p. 904)
Perret, Delphine. Big Bad Wolf & Me. (p. 178)
—Big Bad Wolf Goes on Vacation. (p. 178)
—Pedro & George. Perret, Delphine, illus. (p. 1334)
Perret, Delphine, illus. see Gutman, Colas & Seegmuller, Stephanie.
Perret, Gene. Clean Underwear. (p. 330)
Perrett, Lisa. Sparkling Princess ABC. (p. 1622)
—Sparkling Princess Colors. (p. 1622)
—Sparkling Princess Opposites. (p. 1622)
Perrett, Lisa, illus. see Higginson, Hadley.
Perrett, Lisa, illus. see Hunt, Sara R.
Perrett, Lisa, illus. see Innovative Kids Staff.
Perrett, Lisa, illus. see Wax, Wendy.
Perri, Anthony F., illus. see Sims, Tom.
Perricone, Mike. Big Bang. (p. 178)
Perrien, Vicki, ed. see Osborn School Students.
Perrigo, Brad. Tuffy Mcnasty: The Rogue Elf Who Terrorized Christmas! (p. 1796)
Perril, Simon. Hearing Is Itself Suddenly a Kind of Singing. (p. 759)
Perril, Simon, ed. Salt Companion to John James. (p. 1505)
Perrin. Rafi's Song & the Stones of Erebrus. (p. 1433)
Perrin, Christopher. Greek for Children, Primer A. (p. 720)
Perrin, Christopher, jt. auth. see Baddorf, Robert A.
Perrin, Christopher, jt. auth. see Baddorf, Robert.
Perrin, Christopher, jt. auth. see Larsen, Aaron.
Perrin, Clotilde. At the Same Moment, Around the World. (p. 111)
Perrin, James W. Winter Puzzlers: An Awesome Array of Puzzles & Fun. (p. 1938)
Perrin, James W., Jr. Back to School Puzzlers: An Awesome Array of Puzzles & Fun! (p. 130)
—Holiday Puzzlers: An Awesome Array of Puzzles & Fun for November & December. (p. 788)
Perrin, Kayla. We'll Never Tell. (p. 1874)
Perrin, Martine. Look Who's There! Martens, Marianne, tr. from FRE. (p. 1050)
—What Do You See? Perrin, Martine, illus. (p. 1883)
Perrin, Melinda. Goldenrods: Love Poems for the Old & Foolish. (p. 695)
Perrin, Pat. Getting Started-America's Melting Pot. (p. 669)
—Getting Started-Our 50 United States. (p. 669)
—Getting Started-Our Government. (p. 669)
—Mystery of the Deadly Duel. (p. 1225)
Perrin, Pat, ed. see Coleman, Wim.
Perrin, Pat, jt. auth. see Coleman, Wim.
Perrin, Pat & Coleman, Wim. Mystery of the Murdered Playwright. (p. 1225)
—Mystery of the Vanishing Slaves. (p. 1226)
Perrin, Pat, ed. America's Founders. (p. 64)
—Communications. (p. 349)
—Spanish Explorers. (p. 1621)
—Transportation Stories. (p. 1779)
Perrin, Randy, et al. Time Like a River. (p. 1752)
Perrin, Sandra. Organic Gardening in Cold Climates. (p. 1303)
Perrine, David L. Birdie School Days: The First Day of School. Perry, Margie, illus. (p. 191)
Perrine, Doug, illus. see Markle, Sandra.
Perrine, Doug, photos by see Markle, Sandra.
Perrins, Karen, illus. see StJohn, Amanda.
Perris, Jaime. Soulful Journeys: The Blossoming of a Jasmine Flower. (p. 1614)
Perritano, John. American MX: From Backwater to World Leaders. (p. 62)
—Amityville. (p. 65)
—Australia. (p. 116)
—Battle of the Bots. (p. 146)
—Bomb Squad Technician (p. 208)
—Border Security (p. 214)
—Brazil (p. 224)
—Bugs on Your Body: Nature's Creepiest Creatures Live on You! (p. 237)
—Bugs That Live on Us. (p. 237)
—Building Math. (p. 239)
—China (p. 306)
—Comet of Doom. Laughead, Mike, illus. (p. 348)
—Construction Machines. (p. 359)
—Copper (p. 365)
—Desert Storm. (p. 429)
—Disgusting Stuff. (p. 451)
—Egyptian Prophecy. Laughead, Mike, illus. (p. 507)
—Football Numbers: Graphing Data. (p. 615)
—Football Numbers: Graphing Numbers. (p. 615)
—Free at Last! How the Freeing of the Slaves Changed American History. (p. 634)
—Freshwater Resources (p. 637)
—Germany (p. 666)
—Ghosts of Civil War Soldiers. (p. 672)
—Gold & Silver (p. 693)
—Iron (p. 888)
—Korean War. (p. 967)
—Lewis & Clark Expedition. (p. 1004)
—Madness of Captain Cyclops. (p. 1070)
—Marine Resources (p. 1094)
—Meltdown! Global Warming Puts the World on Thin Ice. (p. 1125)
—Most Disgusting Animals on the Planet (p. 1177)
—Most Disgusting Foods on the Planet (p. 1177)
—Most Disgusting Jobs on the Planet (p. 1177)
—Most Disgusting Places on the Planet (p. 1177)
—Mummies in the Library: Divide the Pages. (p. 1191)
—Mx Bikes: Evolution from Primitive Street Machines to State of the Art Off-Road Machines. (p. 1195)
—Planes. (p. 1367)
—Radical Republicans: The Struggle for Equality. (p. 1432)
—Revolution in Communications. (p. 1466)
—Revolution in Industry: How Machines Changed America. (p. 1466)
—Revolution in Transportation. (p. 1466)
—Salt (p. 1505)
—Science Beats Crime. (p. 1525)
—Science of Emotions. (p. 1527)
—Seeing Halves: Symmetry in Our World. (p. 1548)
—Snickerblooms & the Age Bug. Laughead, Mike, illus. (p. 1597)
—Space Machines. (p. 1619)
—Spanish Missions. (p. 1621)
—Sports Science. (p. 1633)
—Start the Game: Geometry in Sports. (p. 1643)
—SWAT Team (p. 1689)
—Toy Store Summer: Finding Area. (p. 1774)
—Transcontinental Railroad. (p. 1778)
—Uranium (p. 1825)
—Warlock Stone. (p. 1858)
—World War I. (p. 1958)
Perritano, John, jt. auth. see Corporate Contibutor.
Perritano, John, jt. auth. see Crabtree Staff.
Perritano, John & Hoena, Blake. Everything Dinosaurs: Chomp on Tons of Earthshaking Facts & Fun. (p. 544)
Perritano, John & Spears, James. National Geographic Kids Everything Battles: Arm Yourself with Fierce Photos & Fascinating Facts. (p. 1232)
Perritt, Jordona, illus. see Johnson, Sandi.
Perro, Bryan. Amos Daragon #1: the Mask Wearer. Maudet, Y., tr. (p. 65)
—Amos Daragon #2: the Key of Braha. (p. 65)
Perron, Brigitte. I'm a Champ. (p. 858)
—Je suis Grand. (p. 911)
—Je Suis un Vainqueur. (p. 911)
Perron, Debra, illus. see Burlinson, J.
Perron, Jack, jt. auth. see Miller, Randy.
Perrotta, Kevin & Darring, Gerald. Acts: The Good News of the Holy Spirit. (p. 10)
—Exodus: God to the Rescue. Perrotta, Kevin, ed. (p. 548)
—God Makes a Start. Perrotta, Kevin, ed. (p. 690)
—John 1-10: I Am the Bread of Life. Perrotta, Kevin, ed. (p. 921)
—John 11-21: My Peace I Give You. Perrotta, Kevin, ed. (p. 921)
—Luke: The Good News of God's Mercy. Perrotta, Kevin, ed. (p. 1064)
—Mark: Getting to Know Jesus. Perrotta, Kevin, ed. (p. 1095)
—Revelation: God's Gift of Hope. Perrotta, Kevin, ed. (p. 1465)
Perrotta, Tom. Little Children. (p. 1026)
Perrotti, P. Joseph & the Prodigal Son. (p. 926)
Perrotti, P. J. Jason & the Enchanted Forest. (p. 910)
Perroud, Benoit, illus. see Heymelaux, Jasmin & Biggs, Harry.
Perroud, Benoît, illus. see Heymelaux, Jasmin.
Perrow, Angeli. Many Hands: A Penobscot Indian Story. Austin, Heather, illus. (p. 1089)
Perry, Adam. Mister Ray. (p. 1155)
Perry, Alma. Gently Smiling Jaws. (p. 661)
Perry, Andrea. Bicklebys' Birdbath. Angaramo, Roberta, illus. (p. 177)
—Snack Smasher: And Other Reasons Why It's Not My Fault. Snow, Alan, illus. (p. 1595)
Perry, Andrea, jt. auth. see Perry, Andrea J.
Perry, Andrea J. & Perry, Andrea. Here's What You Do When You Can't Find Your Shoe: Ingenious Inventions for Pesky Problems. Snow, Alan, illus. (p. 771)
Perry, Anne M. Just Like Always. Lyon, Tammie, illus. (p. 939)
Perry, Aumi Kauffman, illus. see Bean, Margo Cronbaugh.
Perry, Brad Lee. Clumsy Claudia & the Gentle Forest Friends Perry, Diana Torri, illus. (p. 336)
Perry, Charles. Legend of Scarface. Perry, Charles, photos by. (p. 988)
Perry, Charlotte. Sadie's Dream. (p. 1501)
Perry, Chrissie. Flower Girl. (p. 607)
—Karate Kicks. (p. 943)
—Little Lies. (p. 1030)
—Secret Club. Oswald, Ash, illus. (p. 1540)
—Secret's Out. (p. 1546)
—Surf's Up! Oswald, Ash, illus. (p. 1685)
Perry, Chrissie & Badger, Meredith. Six Girls, One Dream, One Team! (p. 1582)
Perry, Chrissie, et al. Brilliant Besties (p. 228)
Perry, Clayton. Black Profiles: The North American Experience, Vol. 1. (p. 196)
Perry, Craig Rex, illus. see Van Dyke, Tony & Van Dyke, Tracey.
Perry, Curtis, illus. see Washington, Angel D.
Perry, Dakota. Brim's Journey. (p. 228)
—Vulture Itus (p. 1851)
Perry, Daniel. Case of the Missing Shoes. (p. 274)
Perry, Dave & Perry, Jean. Thwacked! A Fractured Fable of Frogs, Folks & Falling Skies. (p. 1746)
Perry, David Earl, retold by. Joseph Smith, a Sacred Story. (p. 926)
Perry, Dennis. Yakabou Must Choose: An African Adventure for Boys & Girls. (p. 1968)
Perry, Diana Torri, illus. see Perry, Brad Lee.
Perry, Douglas M. Boomer Likes to Point. (p. 213)
Perry Drewett, Judy. 'Til the Cows Come Home. (p. 1750)
Perry, E. Eugene. It Works for Everybody Else: Playscript. (p. 894)
Perry, Frank, tr. see Brundin, Anders & Dranger, Joanna Rubin.
Perry, Fred. Diary of a Zombie Kid GN. (p. 435)
—Gold Digger. (p. 693)
—Gold Digger Platinum (p. 693)
—Gold Digger - Platinum (p. 693)
—Gold Digger Platinum Volume 1 HC. (p. 693)
—Grossery Games. (p. 725)
—Peebomanga 1. 0 Pocket Manga Volume 1. (p. 1334)
—Playing Dead. (p. 1372)
—Time Lincoln (p. 1752)
Perry, Fred, illus. see Shakespeare, William.
Perry, Fred & Dlin, Doug. Gold Digger Tech Manual. (p. 693)
Perry, Gala, illus. see Smith, Liz.
Perry, Georgia, illus. see Kelly, Deborah.
Perry, Gina Marie, illus. see Mortensen, Lori.
Perry, Glyn & Parry, Glyn. Invisible Girl. (p. 885)
Perry, Hailey. On the Move. (p. 1291)
Perry, Henry Ten Eyck, ed. see Congreve, William.
Perry, Holly Lynn. Spinner's Mystic Travels: Lost in the Black Forest. (p. 1628)
Perry, Jacquiline. Chocolate Chip: An Urban Tale. (p. 309)
Perry, Janice Kapp. I'm Trying to Be Like Jesus. Abts, Stacey, illus. (p. 860)
Perry, Jason & Keels, Steve. You Are Not Your Own: Living Loud for God. (p. 1973)
Perry, Jean, jt. auth. see Perry, Dave.
Perry, Jennifer A., illus. see Szish, Jill Henry.
Perry, Jerry, II, jt. auth. see Matzke, Jenny.
Perry, Jodi, ed. see Bledsoe, Amanda.
Perry, John. Book That Eats People. Fearing, Mark, illus. (p. 212)
Perry, John Jasiel, jt. auth. see Defoe, Daniel.
Perry, Jolene. Summer I Found You. (p. 1674)
Perry, Jolene B. Next Door Boys. (p. 1249)
—Stronger Than You Know. (p. 1668)
Perry, Laurie. Brown Bear Mackay, Hugh, illus. (p. 231)
—Hello World, This Is Me! (p. 765)
—Kaycee's New School (p. 946)
Perry, Lee Ann, illus. see Freeman, Chip.
Perry, Lisa, jt. auth. see Allison, Lauren.
Perry, Lucinda. Ninth Child: Third Edition. (p. 1257)
Perry, M. Daily Pages to Create the Life You Want: A Companion Workbook to Pictures of My Days. (p. 400)
—Pictures of My Days: An Art & Writing Workbook for Creating the Life You Want. (p. 1356)
Perry, M. LaVora. History of the Civil Rights Movement. (p. 784)
—History of the Civil Rights Movement. Hill, Marc Lamont, ed. (p. 784)
—Taneesha Never Disparaging. Cooper, Floyd, illus. (p. 1705)
—Taneesha's Treasures of the Heart. (p. 1705)
Perry, Marcia. Here on Earth: An Animal Alphabet. (p. 770)
Perry, Margie, illus. see Perrine, David L.
Perry, Marie. Gift for Sadia. Perry, Marie, illus. (p. 675)
Perry, Marie/Fritz. Cecil's New Year's Eve Tail. Perry, Marie/Fritz, illus. (p. 283)
Perry, Marilyn. Adventures of David: The Story of a Shepherd Who Became King (p. 17)
Perry, Marvin. Sources of the Western Tradition: From Ancient Times to the Enlightenment. (p. 1616)
—Sources of the Western Tradition: From the Renaissance to the Present. Vol. 2 (p. 1616)
Perry, Marvin B., et al. Humanities in the Western Tradition: Readings in Literature & Thought. Vol. 1 (p. 826)
Perry, Matt, illus. see Banks, Celia.
Perry, Melanie Denise. Johnathan & Geneva the Adventures of Zeallionaire Kid's. Neal, Albert, ed. (p. 923)
—Jonathan y Geneva Las Aventuras de Los Zeallionaire Kids. Neal, Albert, ed. (p. 925)
Perry, Mia, tr. see Tada, Hiroshi.
Perry, Mia Lynn, tr. see Mase, Naokata.
Perry, Mia Lynn, tr. see Nakagawa, Masafumi.
Perry, Michael. Scavengers. (p. 1521)
Perry, Michael W. Untangling Tolkien: A Chronology & Commentary for the Lord of the Rings. (p. 1823)
Perry, Michael W., ed. see Allen, Thomas Gaskell, Jr. & Sachtleben, William Lewis.
Perry, Mignon Marie, text. Look at Me I Had Surgery, A Child's Personalized Guide Through the Perioperative Process. (p. 1048)
Perry, Naresha. Zora's Valentine. (p. 1990)
Perry, Naresha S. Zora's Valentine. (p. 1990)
Perry, Patricia, jt. auth. see Lynch, Marietta.
Perry, Pete. Saints in Paradise: Another Crazy Story for Crazy Kids. (p. 1504)
—Secret of Bedside Manor. (p. 1542)
Perry, Phyllis. Field Guide to Ocean Animals. Hall, Roger & Hobson, Ryan, illus. (p. 583)
Perry, Phyllis Alesia. Sunday in June. (p. 1676)
Perry, Phyllis J. Buffalo. (p. 235)
—Colorado Fun: Activities for on the Road & at Home. Tarr, Lisa M., illus. (p. 343)
—Kid's Look at Colorado. (p. 954)
—Pandas' Earthquake Escape Detwiler, Susan, illus. (p. 1321)
—Secret of the Silver Key. Lipking, Ron, illus. (p. 1543)
—Secrets of the Rock. Lipking, Ron, illus. (p. 1545)
Perry, Phyllis Jean. Alien, the Giant, & Rocketman. Francis, Guy, illus. (p. 41)
—Bold Women in Colorado History. (p. 208)
—Sherlock Hounds: Our Heroic Search & Rescue Dogs. (p. 1565)
Perry, Phyllis Jean, jt. auth. see Gardner, Robert.
Perry, R. W. Kelly Mccabe in Slow Boat to Terror. (p. 948)
Perry, Rex. All Things Bright & Beautiful. (p. 46)
—Coco's Girls. Perry, Rex, illus. (p. 337)
—Over the River & Through the Woods. (p. 1314)
—'Twas the Night Before Christmas. (p. 1799)
Perry, Robert. Down at the Seaweed Cafe. Guzek, Greta, illus. (p. 474)
—My Vancouver Sketchbook. Guzek, Greta, illus. (p. 1221)
Perry, Roseann. When Mama Said Yes. (p. 1903)
—When Mama Says No. (p. 1903)
Perry, Salena Maria. Recipe for Chocolate Soup. (p. 1451)
Perry, Sarah. Clara's Road. (p. 326)
Perry, Sarah Catherine. Clara's Test. (p. 326)
Perry, Shelly. Duckling's First Adventure. Loebel, Bonnie, illus. (p. 488)
Perry, Sherry. If It Were up to Me. (p. 853)
Perry, Sondra. Most Unusual Pet Ever, Henry Our Great Blue Heron & His Adventures 2nd Edition. Byer, Janice, illus. (p. 1177)
Perry Sr., Audie. Heroic Kids of the Inner Dimension (p. 773)
Perry, Steve & Segriff, Larry. Changing of the Guard. (p. 290)
Perry, Tally. Saving Sunny Stream, a Wormie Wormald Adventure. (p. 1517)
Perry, Thomas, jt. auth. see Deuker, Carl.
Perry, Tina. Where Do Stars Come from, Nana? (p. 1907)
Perry, Tristan. Cinnamon Takes a Vacation: Furry Tails #2 (p. 321)
—Furry Tails: The Adventures of Cinnamon Persimmon. (p. 650)
Perry, Valerie. Sweetie & Coco Go to the Zoo. (p. 1690)
Perry, Valerie J. Trilby Learns a Lesson. (p. 1786)
Perry, William G., Jr. Learn to Love to Learn. (p. 984)
Perryman, Kawanis. Gabrielle's Prayer: Gabrielle's Wish. (p. 652)
Perryman, Richard, jt. auth. see Hobbs, Chris.
Perry-Shaske, Laura. Thirty-Six Colored Roses. (p. 1735)
Persaud, Sandhya S. One Day. Ahmad, Maryam & Ramotar, Alexandra, illus. (p. 1294)
Perseghetti, Jackie & Perseghetti, Jonie. Faith Factor NT: Thru-the-Bible Devotions. (p. 565)
—Faith Factor OT: Thru-the-Bible Devotions. (p. 565)
Perseghetti, Jonie, jt. auth. see Perseghetti, Jackie.
Pershbacher, Gerald. Hero of Faith - C.F.W. Walther. (p. 772)
Persiani, Tony, illus. see Barton, Chris.
Persico, Zoe, illus. see Harrington, Claudia.
Persinger, Eric. Plaid the Platypus. (p. 1366)
Persinger, Kathy. Dale Earnhardt: The Intimidator. (p. 401)
—Mark Martin: Ozark Original. (p. 1095)
Persinger, Mary. Bailey's Butterfly. (p. 133)
Persky, Stan. Short Version: An ABC Book. (p. 1569)
Person, Hara & Lewy, Faye Tillis. My Synagogue Scrapbook. Schoenberg-Lam, Dahlia, illus. (p. 1219)
Person, Jill. Early Concepts Sing-Along Flip Chart: 25 Delightful Congs Set to Favorite Tunes That Help Children Learn Colors, Shapes & Sizes. (p. 493)
Person, Naomi, et al. Sow What? Hooper, Hadley & Stryk, Suzanne, illus. (p. 1618)
Person, Stephen. Arctic Fox: Very Cool! (p. 96)
—Army Night Stalkers in Action. (p. 100)
—Bubonic Plague! The Black Death! (p. 234)
—Collared Peccary: Cactus-Eater. (p. 339)
—Coral Reef: A Giant City under the Sea. (p. 366)
—Cougar: A Cat with Many Names. (p. 369)
—Devastated by a Volcano! (p. 431)
—Ghostly Alcatraz Island. (p. 672)
—Great Dane: Gentle Giant. (p. 715)
—Malaria: Super Killer! (p. 1083)
—Navy SEAL Team Six in Action. (p. 1238)
—Polar Bear: Shrinking Ice. (p. 1378)
—Roseate Spoonbill: Pretty in Pink. (p. 1489)
—Saving Animals after Tornadoes. (p. 1517)
—Saving Animals from Hurricanes. (p. 1517)
—Sled Dog: Powerful Miracle. (p. 1588)
—Struck by Lightning! (p. 1668)
—Voodoo in New Orleans. (p. 1850)
—Walrus: Tusk, Tusk. (p. 1855)
Persons, Katelynn, jt. auth. see Colby, J. Z.
Persons, Marjorie Kiel. Antonin Dvorak from the New World with Lyrics. Nellis, Philip & Johnson, George Ann, illus. (p. 90)
—Classical Karaoke for Kids. Nellis, Philip & Johnson, George Ann, illus. (p. 328)
—Portraits of the Music Masters. Johnson, George Ann, illus. (p. 1387)
—Themes to Remember Nellis, Philip, illus. (p. 1728)
—Themes to Remember Teacher's Guide: A Theme Recognition Based Method for Teaching Music Appreciation Vol. 2 Nellis, Philip, illus. (p. 1728)
—Themes to Remember, Volume 2 Nellis, Philip & Johnson, George Ann, illus. (p. 1729)
Pertile, Paula. Gingerbread Man. (p. 677)
Pertile, Paula, illus. see Wilson, Zachary.
Pertzborn, Cindy. How Do We Get to Heaven? (p. 807)
Perucca, Nancy Call, jt. auth. see Evans, Renee Call.
Perucca, Nancy Call & Evans, Renee Call. Sea Notes on the Keyboard: The Fast & Fun Way to Learn the Notes on the Keyboard! Perucca, Nancy Call, illus. (p. 1535)
Perugini, Donna. Adventures of Amelia Airheart Butterfly. (p. 16)
—Do Angels Go Camping? (p. 456)
Perunko, Linda, illus. see Havens, Sarita.
Peruski, Steven. My Friend & Teacher Sammie. (p. 1209)
Peruzzo, Nicolas. Safari Dreams. Peruzzo, Nicolas, illus. (p. 1502)
Pervan, Ivo, photos by see Ollendorff, Valli.
Pesca, Jodi. Angels Angels Everywhere. (p. 75)
Pescatore, Faith. Bell for Justin. (p. 162)
Pesce, Carol, illus. see Stalder, Erika.
Pesce, Dom. At the Kennel: Understanding Addition. (p. 111)
Pesce, Elena. Cola de los Ingleses. (p. 338)
Pescetti, Luis Mariá. Chat Natacha chat (Edición Especial) Fernández, Pablo, illus. (p. 294)
—Padrísimo, Natacha! Fernandez, Pablo, illus. (p. 1317)
—Tarea Segun Natacha. O'Kif, illus. (p. 1706)
Peschel, Georgia, illus. see Chen, Sam.
Peschke, Marci. Blueberry Queen Mourning, Tuesday, illus. (p. 204)
—Cupcake Queen. Mourning, Tuesday, illus. (p. 392)
—Dancing Queen Mourning, Tuesday, illus. (p. 403)
—Dead Man's Map Smith, Tod G., illus. (p. 417)

—Drama Queen Mourning, Tuesday, illus. (p. 480)
—Fashion Queen. Mourning, Tuesday, illus. (p. 576)
—Football Queen Mourning, Tuesday, illus. (p. 615)
—Ghost's Revenge Garvey, Brann & O'Connor, Niamh, illus. (p. 673)
—Green Queen Mourning, Tuesday, illus. (p. 722)
—Hoop Queen Mourning, Tuesday, illus. (p. 795)
—Kylie Jean Mourning, Tuesday, illus. (p. 969)
—Party Queen Mourning, Tuesday, illus. (p. 1326)
—Pirate Queen. Mourning, Tuesday, illus. (p. 1363)
—Rodeo Queen Mourning, Tuesday, illus. (p. 1484)
—Singing Queen Mourning, Tuesday, illus. (p. 1579)
—Soccer Queen. Mourning, Tuesday, illus. (p. 1603)
—Spelling Queen Mourning, Tuesday, illus. (p. 1625)
—Summer Camp Queen Mourning, Tuesday, illus. (p. 1674)
—Valentine Queen Mourning, Tuesday, illus. (p. 1830)
Peschke, Marci, jt. auth. see Meinking, Mary.
Peschke, Marci, jt. auth. see Ventura, Marne.
Peschke, Marci & Townson, H. Ghost's Revenge Garvey, Brann & O'Connor, Niamh, illus. (p. 673)
Pescio, Claudio. Rembrandt. (p. 1459)
Pesenti, Antonia, illus. see Bell, Hilary.
Pesetski, Larry. Journey to Lake Tahoe & Beyond. (p. 929)
Peskimo, illus. see Franceschelli, Christopher.
Peskimo, jt. auth. see Franceschelli, Christopher.
Peskowitz, Miriam, jt. auth. see Buchanan, Andrea J.
Pesout, Christine. Earth, the Alphabet, & Me. Donaldson, Jennifer, illus. (p. 497)
Pesquès, Nicolas. Juliology. Cole, Swensen, tr. from FRE. (p. 932)
Pesson, Lauren. My Little Kappa Delta. (p. 1212)
Pesta, K. My Ferret Dexter. (p. 1203)
Pestrak, Debra. Playing with the Big Boys: Success Secrets of the Most Powerful Women in Business. (p. 1372)
Peszle, Brenda, et al. Cranberry Tales. (p. 376)
Petach, Heidi. Daniel & the Lions. Dickson, Bill, illus. (p. 404)
Petch, Fionn, tr. see Saint Cyr, Vanessa.
Petechuk, David. LSD. (p. 1061)
—Non-Continental: Alaska, Hawaii (p. 1263)
—Respiratory System (p. 1463)
—Undead: Vampires, Zombies, & Other Strange Monsters. (p. 1813)
Petek-Markic, Zdenka. Birds. (p. 191)
Petelinsek, Kathleen. Crafting with Tissue Paper. Petelinsek, Kathleen, illus. (p. 375)
—Learning to Sew. Petelinsek, Kathleen, illus. (p. 986)
—Little Jack Horner. Petelinsek, Kathleen, illus. (p. 1029)
—Making Clay Bead Crafts. Petelinsek, Kathleen, illus. (p. 1080)
—Making Jewelry with Rubber Bands. Petelinsek, Kathleen, illus. (p. 1081)
—Making Sock Puppets. Petelinsek, Kathleen, illus. (p. 1082)
—Modeling Clay Creations. Petelinsek, Kathleen, illus. (p. 1157)
—Pipe Cleaner Crafts. Petelinsek, Kathleen, illus. (p. 1361)
Petelinsek, Kathleen, illus. see Bailer, Darice.
Petelinsek, Kathleen, illus. see Berendes, Mary & Eick, Jean.
Petelinsek, Kathleen, illus. see Berendes, Mary.
Petelinsek, Kathleen, illus. see Coss, Lauren.
Petelinsek, Kathleen, illus. see Eick, Jean.
Petelinsek, Kathleen, illus. see Felix, Rebecca.
Petelinsek, Kathleen, illus. see Fontichiaro, Kristin & Truesdell, Ann.
Petelinsek, Kathleen, illus. see Fontichiaro, Kristin.
Petelinsek, Kathleen, illus. see Gregory, Josh.
Petelinsek, Kathleen, illus. see Harner, Jennifer L.
Petelinsek, Kathleen, illus. see Heinrichs, Ann.
Petelinsek, Kathleen, illus. see Higgins, Nadia.
Petelinsek, Kathleen, illus. see Marsico, Katie.
Petelinsek, Kathleen, illus. see Matteson, Adrienne.
Petelinsek, Kathleen, illus. see Newman, Heather.
Petelinsek, Kathleen, illus. see Pearson, Yvonne.
Petelinsek, Kathleen, illus. see Rau, Dana Meachen.
Petelinsek, Kathleen, illus. see Reinke, Beth Bence.
Petelinsek, Kathleen, illus. see Ringstad, Arnold.
Petelinsek, Kathleen, illus. see Simons, Lisa M. Bolt.
Petelinsek, Kathleen, illus. see Thornborough, Kathy.
Petelinsek, Kathleen, illus. see Truesdell, Ann & Fontichiaro, Kristin.
Petelinsek, Kathleen, illus. see Truesdell, Ann.
Petelinsek, Kathleen, illus. see Yomtov, Nel.
Petelinsek, Kathleen, illus. see Yomtov, Nelson.
Petelinsek, Kathleen, illus. see York, J.
Peten, Chantal, illus. see Ducatteau, Florence.
Peter, jt. auth. see Aleshire.
Peter, Dawn. Mark the Remarkable & Can't Say Can't. (p. 1095)
Peter, et al. I'm in Love with a Big Blue Frog. (p. 859)
Peter, Goodrich, jt. auth. see Coveleskie, Sally.
Peter, Joshua, illus. see Grinnell, Suzanne.
Peter L. Ward. Freya & the Fenris-Wolf. (p. 637)
Peter, Linda. Cera the Triceratops's First Day at School. (p. 287)
Peter Pauper Press, Inc., creator. Handwriting: Learn Cursive! (p. 741)
—Handwriting: Learn to Print! (p. 741)
—Learn to Draw... Animals! Easy Step-By-Step Drawing Guide. (p. 983)
—Learn to Draw... Christmas! Easy Step-By-Step Drawing Guide. (p. 983)
—Learn to Draw... Dinosaurs! Easy Step-By-Step Drawing Guide. (p. 983)
—Learn to Draw... Flower Garden! Easy Step-By-Step Drawing Guide. (p. 983)
—Learn to Draw... Ocean Wonders! Easy Step-By-Step Drawing Guide. (p. 983)
—Learn to Draw... Princess Kingdom! Easy Step-By-Step Drawing Guide. (p. 983)
—Learn to Draw... Things That Go! Easy Step-By-Step Drawing Guide. (p. 984)
Peter Pauper Press Staff. Scratch & Sketch Dino Dudes: An Art Activity Book for Fossil Hunters of All Ages. (p. 1532)
Peter Pauper Press Staff & Zschock, Heather. Princess Bella: An Art Activity Story Book for Princesses of All Ages. Barbas, Kerren, illus. (p. 1403)
Peter Pauper Press Staff, creator. America: An Art Activity Book for Patriotic Artists & Explorers of All Ages. (p. 58)
—Dragons & Mythical Creatures: An Art Activity Book. (p. 479)
—Garden Fairies: Scratch & Sketch: an Art Activity Book. (p. 656)
—Merry Christmas: An Art Activity Book. (p. 1128)
Peter Pauper Press Staff, et al. Vampires, Werewolves, Zombies: From the papers of Herr Doktor Max Sturm & Baron Ludwig Von Drang. Waldman, Bruce, illus. (p. 1832)
Peter, Val J. & Dowd, Tom. Boundaries: A Guide for Teens. (p. 216)
—Girls & Boys Town Book on Patriotism: Grades 7-12. (p. 679)
Peter, Val J., creator. Gifts for a Joyous Christmas: From the Kids at Boys Town. (p. 675)
—Reflections for a Happy New Year: From the Kids at Boys Town. (p. 1456)
Peterfreund, Diana. Across a Star-Swept Sea. (p. 9)
—Ascendant. (p. 105)
—For Darkness Shows the Stars. (p. 615)
—Omega City. (p. 1288)
—Rampant. (p. 1438)
Peterka, Edward S. Zoe Isabella Goes to the Zoo. (p. 1987)
Peterman, Lori. Practical Accounting Fundamentals. (p. 1391)
Peterman, Rosie L., et al. Divorce & Stepfamilies. (p. 455)
Peters, jt. auth. see Peters, Lisa Westberg.
Peters, Andrew. Ant & the Big Bad Bully Goat. Wadham, Anna, illus. (p. 88)
—Bear & Turtle & the Great Lake Race. Edgson, Alison, illus. (p. 150)
—Dingo Dog & the Billabong Storm. Wadham, Anna, illus. (p. 440)
—Monkey's Clever Tale. Montgomery-Higham, Amanda, tr. (p. 1166)
—Rabbit Cooks up a Cunning Plan! Roberts, Bruno, illus. (p. 1429)
—Ravenwood. (p. 1441)
—Tiger & the Wise Man. Mayo, Diana, illus. (p. 1748)
Peters, Andrew & Peters, Polly. Dragon Chaser. (p. 476)
Peters, Andrew, et al. Winter Olympics. (p. 1938)
Peters, Andrew Fusek. Ant & the Big Bad Bully Goat. Wadham, Anna, illus. (p. 88)
—Bear & Turtle & the Great Lake Race. Edgson, Alison, illus. (p. 150)
—Dingo Dog & the Billabong Storm. Wadham, Anna, illus. (p. 440)
—Dragon & Mousie. Wade, Gini, illus. (p. 476)
—Dragon & Mousie & the Snow Factory. Wade, Gini, illus. (p. 476)
—Free Running. (p. 634)
—Mad, Bad & Dangerously Haddock. (p. 1068)
—Rabbit Cooks up a Cunning Plan! Robert, Bruno, illus. (p. 1429)
—Tiger & the Wise Man. Mayo, Diana, illus. (p. 1748)
Peters, Andrew Fusek & Player, Stephen. Ed & the River of the Damned. (p. 503)
—Ed & the Witchblood. (p. 503)
Peters, Andrew J. Seventh Pleiade. (p. 1555)
Peters, Andy. Around the Universe in 80 Mazes. (p. 100)
—Around the World in 80 Mazes. (p. 101)
—Maze Quest: Navigate the Mazes, Complete the Search & Find, Solve the Puzzle Fun. (p. 1113)
Peters, Andy, illus. see Giles, Sophie & Davis, Kate.
Peters, Anna. Friendly Rubbish Monsters. (p. 638)
Peters, Bernadette. Broadway Barks. Murphy, Liz, illus. (p. 230)
—Stella & Charlie, Friends Forever. Murphy, Liz, illus. (p. 1646)
Peters, Bernadette & Blue Apple Staff. Stella Is a Star! Murphy, Liz, illus. (p. 1647)
Peters, Celeste. Health. (p. 757)
Peters, Celeste A. Food. (p. 612)
—Food Q & A. (p. 614)
—Health Q & A. (p. 758)
Peters, Chris. Girls' Hockey. (p. 680)
—Great Moments in Olympic Ice Hockey. (p. 717)
—Stanley Cup Finals. (p. 1640)
Peters, Craig. Bill Gates: Software Genius of Microsoft. (p. 186)
—Chants, Cheers, & Jumps. (p. 291)
—Cheerleading Stars. (p. 296)
—Competitive Cheerleading. (p. 352)
—Larry Ellison: Database Genius of Oracle. (p. 976)
—Steve Case: Internet Genius of America Online. (p. 1649)
—Techniques of Cheerleading. (p. 1711)
—Techniques of Dance for Cheerleading. (p. 1711)
Peters, Darcy, illus. see Silcox, Beth Douglass.
Peters, Diane. Gaming: Deal with It Before It Outplays You Shannon, Ben, illus. (p. 655)
—Gaming: Deal with It Before It Outplays You Shannon, Ben, illus. (p. 655)
—Girlness: Body & Soul Murray, Steven, illus. (p. 679)
—Privacy: Deal with It Like Nobody's Business Tankard, Jeremy, illus. (p. 1407)
—Procrastination: Deal with It All in Good Time Tankard, Jeremy, illus. (p. 1409)
Peters, Dylan. Tic Talk: Living with Tourette Syndrome - A 9-Year-Old Boy's Story in His Own Words. Wendland, Zachary & Miller, Kris Taft, illus. (p. 1747)
Peters, E. G. Voyage of Noah's Ark. (p. 1850)
Peters, Elisa. Earth: La Tierra. (p. 495)
—Earth. (p. 495)
—Everyday Wonders. (p. 544)
—It's a Bird! (p. 895)
—It's a Bird! Es un Ave! (p. 895)
—It's a Bird! / ¡Es un Ave! (p. 895)
—It's a Caterpillar! (p. 895)
—It's a Caterpillar! Aes una Oruga! (p. 895)
—It's a Caterpillar! / ¡Es una Oruga! (p. 895)
—It's a Dragonfly! (p. 895)
—It's a Dragonfly! Es una Libélula! (p. 895)
—It's a Dragonfly! / ¡Es una Libélula! (p. 895)
—It's a Sunflower! (p. 896)
—It's a Sunflower! Es un Girasol! (p. 896)
—It's a Sunflower! / ¡Es un Girasol! (p. 896)
—It's an Apple Tree! (p. 896)
—It's an Apple Tree! Es un Manzano! (p. 896)
—It's an Apple Tree! / ¡Es un Manzano! (p. 896)
—It's Snow! (p. 898)
—It's Snow! La Nieve! (p. 898)
—It's Snow! / ¡la Nieve! (p. 898)
—Let's Ride the City Bus! (p. 1000)
—Let's Ride the Streetcar! (p. 1000)
—Let's Ride the Subway! (p. 1000)
—Let's Take the Ferry! (p. 1001)
—Let's Take the Train! (p. 1001)
—Moon: La Luna. (p. 1171)
—Moon. (p. 1171)
—Outer Space: El Espacio Exterior. (p. 1312)
—Outer Space. (p. 1312)
—Planets: Los Planetas. (p. 1368)
—Planets. (p. 1368)
—Stars: Las Estrellas. (p. 1643)
—Stars. (p. 1643)
—Statistics & Probability (p. 1644)
—Sun: El Sol. (p. 1675)
—Sun. (p. 1675)
—What Are Igneous Rocks? (p. 1879)
—¡Vamos a Tomar el Autobús! / Let's Ride the City Bus! de la Vega, Eida, ed. (p. 1831)
—¡Vamos a Tomar el Transbordador! / Let's Take the Ferry! de la Vega, Eida, ed. (p. 1831)
—¡Vamos a Tomar el Tranvía! / Let's Ride the Streetcar! de la Vega, Eida, ed. (p. 1831)
—¡Vamos a Tomar el Tren! / Let's Take the Train! de la Vega, Eida, ed. (p. 1831)
Peters, Elisa & Eida, de la Vega. Let's Ride the Subway! (¡Vamos a Tomar el Metro!) de la Vega, Eida, ed. (p. 1000)
Peters, Elizabeth Anne. Worms Like to Wiggle. Yerbey, Lindsey Blake, illus. (p. 1961)
Peters, Gregory N. Best of College Basketball (p. 170)
—Daredevils! (p. 406)
—Looking for Lost Treasure (p. 1051)
—Muhammad Ali Boxing Legend (p. 1189)
—Negro Leagues (p. 1240)
—Real Animal Heroes (p. 1448)
—Serena & Venus Williams Tennis Stars (p. 1552)
—Trailblazers (p. 1776)
—U. S. Navy SEALs Elite Force (p. 1807)
Peters, Jackie. Mary Maybelieve. (p. 1100)
Peters, Jean Norman. I Am Her Ears: A Story with Pictures of a Three Year Old Rescued Dog Who Leads a New Life As a Certified Hearing Dog. Archer, Mary Jane, illus. (p. 833)
Peters, Jeffrey Edward. Write a Graphic Novel in 5 Simple Steps. (p. 1963)
Peters, Judy. Little Blue Curtain. (p. 1024)
Peters, Julie Anne. Between Mom & Jo. (p. 173)
—By the Time You Read This, I'll Be Dead. (p. 249)
—Define Normal. (p. 424)
—Grl2grl: Short Fictions. (p. 725)
—How Do You Spell G-e-e-K? (p. 808)
—It's Our Prom (So Deal with It) (p. 898)
—Keeping You a Secret. (p. 948)
—Luna. (p. 1065)
—Pretend You Love Me. (p. 1398)
—Rage: A Love Story. (p. 1433)
—Revenge of the Snob Squad. (p. 1466)
—She Loves You, She Loves You Not... (p. 1564)
Peters, Kara L. Adventures of the Peters Family: A Dolphin of a Time. (p. 23)
Peters, Karen Lynn. If I Only Had a Horse. (p. 853)
Peters, Kathryn. Pet for Elizabeth Rose. Peters, Kathryn, illus. (p. 1345)
Peters, L. T. Slippery Willie's Stupid, Ugly Shoes (p. 1590)
Peters, Laura. Indoor Plants for Canada (p. 872)
Peters, Laura, jt. auth. see Beck, Pam.
Peters, Laura, jt. auth. see Calovich, Annie.
Peters, Laura, jt. auth. see Dawson, Donna.
Peters, Laura, jt. auth. see Hamilton, Susan.
Peters, Laura, jt. auth. see Hanbidge, Patricia.
Peters, Laura, jt. auth. see Humenick, Muriel.
Peters, Laura, jt. auth. see Klose, Liz.
Peters, Laura, jt. auth. see Lehndorff, Betsy.
Peters, Laura, jt. auth. see Lindley, Nancy.
Peters, Laura, jt. auth. see Owens, Steve.
Peters, Laura, jt. auth. see Porto, Chuck.
Peters, Laura & Dawson, Donna. Perennials for Alberta. (p. 1341)
Peters, Laura & Didur, Dean. Gardening Month by Month in Manitoba (p. 656)
Peters, Laura & Hanbidge, Patricia. Best Garden Plants for Saskatchewan & Manitoba (p. 169)
—Gardening Month by Month in Saskatchewan (p. 656)
—Perennials for Saskatchewan & Manitoba. (p. 1341)
Peters, Laura & Jalbert, Brad. Roses for British Columbia. (p. 1490)
—Roses for Washington & Oregon. (p. 1490)
Peters, Laura & Nunally, Richard. Best Garden Plants for Virginia. (p. 169)
Peters, Lawrence J. Getting Results from Software Development Teams. (p. 669)
Peters, Li Li, tr. see Bobrick, Julie, ed.
Peters, Liam, illus. see Burns, Laura J.
Peters, Lisa Westberg. Frankie Works the Night Shift. Taylor, Jennifer, illus. (p. 630)
—Our Family Tree: An Evolution Story. Stringer, Lauren, illus. (p. 1308)
Peters, Lisa Westberg & Peters. Earthshake: Poems from the Ground Up. Felstead, Cathie, illus. (p. 498)
Peters, Lou. Owl & the Turtle. (p. 1315)
Peters, Marilee. 10 Rivers That Shaped the World. Rosen, Kim, illus. (p. 1994)
—Patient Zero: Solving the Mysteries of Deadly Epidemics. (p. 1328)
Peters, Patrick. Hail Mary Pass. (p. 735)
Peters, Polly. Ding-Dong Bag. Stockham, Jess, illus. (p. 440)
—It's Raining, It's Pouring, We're Exploring. Stockham, Jess, illus. (p. 898)
—Wim Wom from the Mustard Mill. Angeletti, Roberta, illus. (p. 1935)
Peters, Polly, jt. auth. see Fusek Peters, Andrew.
Peters, Polly, jt. auth. see Peters, Andrew.
Peters, Polly & Fusek Peters, Andrew. Roar, Bull, Roar! Weckmann, Anke, illus. (p. 1478)
Peters, Ramona, illus. see Jennings, Paulla.
Peters, Rob. Wolf & Pig Report. (p. 1943)
Peters, Rob, illus. see Davies, Donna M.
Peters, Rob, illus. see Davies, Donna.
Peters, Rob, illus. see Falk, Kristi & Falk, Daniel.
Peters, Rob, illus. see Richter, Cindy.
Peters, Rob, illus. see Taylor, Derrick & Garnett, Kaila.
Peters, Robert. Da Goodie Monsta: Chase Dem Nightmares Away. Peters, Robert, illus. (p. 398)
Peters, Rosalind. Midnight Feast Magic: Sleepover Fun & Food. Pankhurst, Kate, illus. (p. 1138)
Peters, S. True. How to Draw New Hampshire's Sights & Symbols. (p. 818)
—How to Draw North Carolina's Sights & Symbols. (p. 818)
—How to Draw Oregon's Sights & Symbols. (p. 818)
—How to Draw South Dakota's Sights & Symbols. (p. 818)
—How to Draw Vermont's Sights & Symbols. (p. 819)
—How to Draw Wisconsin's Sights & Symbols. (p. 819)
Peters, Scott. Clock Watch. (p. 333)
—How I Go. (p. 810)
—Painting Shapes. (p. 1318)
—Today. (p. 1760)
—What We Like. (p. 1895)
Peters, Stephanie. 1918 Influenza Pandemic. (p. 2002)
—Adventures of Tintin: The Chapter Book. (p. 24)
—Andromeda. (p. 72)
—Battle Against Polio. (p. 145)
—Gemini. (p. 659)
—Little Dipper. (p. 1026)
—Orion. (p. 1304)
—Pisces. (p. 1364)
—Poetry of the Ocean & Beyond. (p. 1376)
—Raggedy Ann & the Birthday Surprise. Mitter, Kathryn, illus. (p. 1433)
—Smallpox in the New World. (p. 1592)
Peters, Stephanie, jt. auth. see Christopher, Matt.
Peters, Stephanie & Christopher, Matt. Soccer Hero. (p. 1603)
Peters, Stephanie True. Andromeda. (p. 72)
—First & Final Voyage: The Sinking of the Titanic Proctor, Jon, illus. (p. 593)
—Gemini. (p. 659)
—Little Dipper. (p. 1026)
—Orion. (p. 1304)
—Pisces. (p. 1364)
—Princess Primer: A Fairy Godmother's Guide to Being a Princess. Oberdieck, Bernhard & Gordeev, Denis, illus. (p. 1405)
Peters, Stephanie True, jt. auth. see Christopher, Matt.
Peters, Stephanie True & Cano, Fernando M. Track Team Titans Aburto, Jesus et al, illus. (p. 1775)
Peters, Stephen & Hart, Joyce. Pennsylvania. (p. 1338)
Peters, Stuart. National Systems of Innovation: Creating High Technology Industries. (p. 1234)
Peters, Suzanne. Misee Mouse. (p. 1150)
Peters, Tony. Kids on a Case: The Case of the Ten Grand Kidnapping. (p. 954)
Peters, Trudy, jt. auth. see Butler, Leah.
Peters, Victoria Smith, jt. auth. see Carson, Pat.
Peters, Yvette. Tell Me about Georgia!!!! Facts about Georgia. (p. 1716)
Peterschmidt, Betsy, illus. see Kelly, Erin Entrada.
Petersell, Shlomo. Fun with My First Words: Hebrew-English - English-Hebrew Dictionary. Gordon-Lucas, Bonnie, illus. (p. 648)
Petersell, Shlomo, ed. Fun with My First Words: French-Hebrew Picture Dictionary. Gordon-Lucas, Bonnie, illus. (p. 648)
—Fun with My First Words: Russian-Hebrew Picture Dictionary. Gordon-Lucas, Bonnie, illus. (p. 648)
—Fun with My First Words: Spanish-Hebrew Picture Dictionary. Gordon-Lucas, Bonnie, illus. (p. 648)
Petersell, Tamar. Zap It! A Microwave Cookbook Just for Kids. (p. 1985)
Petersell, Yaacov. Gang of Four Kooey-Fooey to the Rescue. Yarchi, Jacky, illus. (p. 655)
—What Can You Do with a Cheshire Smile? (p. 1881)
Petersen, Alexander, illus. see Engel, Steve.
Petersen, Alicia. Out of Darkness. (p. 1311)
—Sparrow Alone. (p. 1622)
Petersen, Brooke Griffin. Santa's Sick. (p. 1513)
Petersen, Casey Null, jt. auth. see Rice, Dona Herweck.
Petersen, Casey Null, jt. auth. see Rice, Dona.
Petersen, Casey Null & Teacher Created Resources Staff. Graphic Organizers, Grades 4-8. (p. 711)
Petersen, Christine. Apothecary. (p. 92)
—Blacksmith. (p. 197)
—Controlling Earth's Pollutants. (p. 361)
—Diamonds. (p. 434)
—Does Everyone Have ADHD? A Teen's Guide to Diagnosis & Treatment. (p. 460)
—Ecstasy. (p. 503)
—Flowers. (p. 608)
—Gold. (p. 693)
—How the Judicial Branch Works. (p. 813)
—How the Legislative Branch Works. (p. 813)
—Inhalants. (p. 874)
—Jade. (p. 905)
—Learning about Antarctica. (p. 984)
—Learning about North America. (p. 984)
—Pearls. (p. 1333)
—Plants Need Sunlight. (p. 1370)
—Printer. (p. 1407)
—Project Guide to Earth's Waters. (p. 1410)
—Project Guide to Mammals. (p. 1410)
—Protecting Earth's Food Supply. (p. 1412)
—Renewing Earth's Waters. (p. 1460)

P

—Rosie the Riveter. (p. 1490)
—Silver. (p. 1576)
—Smart Kid's Guide to Divorce. Rooney, Ronnie, illus. (p. 1592)
—Smart Kid's Guide to Losing a Pet. Rooney, Ronnie, illus. (p. 1592)
—Smart Kid's Guide to Manners. Rooney, Ronnie, illus. (p. 1592)
—Smart Kid's Guide to Moving. Rooney, Ronnie, illus. (p. 1592)
—South Africa. (p. 1616)
—South Dakota: Past & Present. (p. 1617)
—Surveyor. (p. 1686)
—Tailor. (p. 1695)
—Tanner. (p. 1705)
—Trees. (p. 1784)
—Turquoise. (p. 1798)
—Vicodin & OxyContin. (p. 1840)
—Vicodin & Oxycontin. (p. 1840)
—Wheelwright. (p. 1901)
Petersen, Christine A., jt. auth. see Petersen, David.
Petersen, Darla, illus. see Aunt Darla.
Petersen, David. Mouse Guard - Winter 1152 Illidge, Joseph Phillip, ed. (p. 1182)
—Snowy Valentine. Petersen, David, illus. (p. 1601)
Petersen, David, illus. see Beedle, Tim.
Petersen, David & Petersen, Christine A. Maps & Globes. (p. 1090)
Petersen, Dennis R. Unlocking the Mysteries of Creation - Premiere Edition: The Explorer's Guide to the Awesome Works of God. Creation Staff, ed. (p. 1821)
Petersen, George & Jenkins, J. J. Crazy Campsongs. Davis, Jack, illus. (p. 377)
Petersen, Jamee. Math & Nonfiction, Grades K-2. (p. 1105)
Petersen, James R., text. Playboy - Blondes. (p. 1372)
Petersen, Jean. Moose Shoes. Morrow, E., illus. (p. 1173)
Petersen, Jeff, illus. see Gage, Brian.
Petersen, Jeffrey Lee. Boy a Dog & a Creek. (p. 217)
Petersen, Justin. Detroit Lions. (p. 431)
Petersen, Kathleen C. Null. ¿Poesía? ¡Qué Horror! (p. 1376)
Petersen, Kristen. Understanding Forces of Nature: Gravity, Electricity, & Magnetism. (p. 1815)
—Understanding Kinetic Energy. (p. 1815)
—Understanding the Laws of Motion. (p. 1816)
Petersen, Megan Cooley & Rake, Jody Sullivan. Bottlenose Dolphins (p. 215)
Petersen, P. J. Wild River. (p. 1930)
Petersen, Pat. Make the World Pink, I Think. Danilewicz, Jamie, illus. (p. 1079)
—Turtle Who Couldn't Swim. Pham, Xuan, illus. (p. 1798)
Petersen, Patricia, tr. see Benatar, Raquel & Torrecilla, Pablo.
Petersen, Patricia, tr. see Benatar, Raquel.
Petersen, Shell, illus. see Fernandez, Giselle.
Petersen, Silke. Brot, Licht und Weinstock: Intertextuelle Analysen Johanneischer Ich-Bin-Worte. (p. 231)
Petersen, Wayne, jt. auth. see Burrows, Roger.
Petersen, William, illus. see Aguinaco, Carmen F.
Petersham, Maud, illus. see Sandburg, Carl.
Petersham, Maud, illus. see Skinner, Ada & Wickes, Frances.
Petersham, Miska, illus. see Sandburg, Carl.
Petersham, Miska, illus. see Skinner, Ada & Wickes, Frances.
Peterson, Alyson. Ian Quicksilver: The Warrior's Return. (p. 849)
Peterson, Amanda. U. S. Civil War: A Chronology of a Divided Nation. (p. 1806)
—What You Need to Know about Diabetes. (p. 1896)
Peterson, Andrew. On the Edge of the Dark Sea of Darkness: Adventure. Peril. Lost Jewels. & the Fearsome Toothy Cows of Skree. (p. 1290)
Peterson, Barbara, illus. see Callella, Trisha.
Peterson, Ben, illus. see Blair, Eric.
Peterson, Ben, illus. see Jones, Christianne C.
Peterson, Ben, jt. auth. see Blair, Eric.
Peterson, Blaire & Peterson, Brent. Bike Race. (p. 185)
Peterson, Brandon. Arcanum (p. 95)
—Rite of Passage. Johnson, Dell, illus. (p. 1475)
—Ultimate X-Men - The Tempest (p. 1810)
Peterson, Brandon, illus. see Hickman, Jonathan.
Peterson, Brandon, illus. see Lobdell, Scott, et al.
Peterson, Brandon, illus. see Marz, Ron.
Peterson, Brandon & Brereton, Dan. Giant Killer. (p. 673)
Peterson, Brenda. Leopard & Silkie: One Boy's Quest to Save the Seal Pups. Lindsey, Robin, photos by. (p. 992)
—Seal Pup Rescue. (p. 1536)
—Seal Pup Rescue. Lindsey, Robin, photos by. (p. 1536)
Peterson, Brent. Bike Race: Add Within 20. (p. 185)
Peterson, Brent, jt. auth. see Peterson, Blaire.
Peterson, Brian. Popcornmaker. (p. 1384)
Peterson, Brian C. Sports Marketing: Careers off the Field Ferrer, Al, ed. (p. 1633)
Peterson, Carol. Jump into Science: Themed Science Fairs Peterson, Carol, illus. (p. 934)
Peterson, Carol A., illus. see Bennett, Kathy.
Peterson, Casey Null & Teacher Created Resources Staff. Graphic Organizers, Grades K-3. (p. 711)
Peterson, Christine. American Presidency Martin, Cynthia, illus. (p. 62)
—Extreme Surfing (p. 557)
—U. S. Constitution (p. 1806)
—Wakeboarding (p. 1853)
Peterson, Cris. Amazing Grazing. Upitis, Alvis, photos by. (p. 54)
—Birchbark Brigade: A Fur Trade History. (p. 190)
—Century Farm: One Hundred Years on a Family Farm. Upitis, Alvis, photos by. (p. 287)
—Clarabelle: Making Milk & So Much More. Lundquist, David R., photos by. (p. 326)
—Extra Cheese, Please! Mozzarella's Journey from Cow to Pizza. Upitis, Alvis, photos by. (p. 555)
—Fantastic Farm Machines. Lundquist, David R., photos by. (p. 571)
—Harvest Year. Upitis, Alvis, photos by. (p. 752)
—Seed, Soil, Sun: Earth's Recipe for Food. Lundquist, David R., photos by. (p. 1547)
—Wild Horses: Black Hills Sanctuary. Upitis, Alvis, photos by. (p. 1929)
Peterson, Cyrus Asbury. Mound Building Age in North America. (p. 1180)
Peterson, David. 10 Days Until Forever. (p. 1993)
Peterson, Dawn, illus. see Chetkowski, Emily.
Peterson, Dawn, illus. see Johnson, Dorothea, et al.
Peterson del Mar, David & Del Mar, David Peterson. Oregon's Promise: An Interpretive History. (p. 1303)
Peterson, Donna. Misadventures of Phillip Isaac Penn. (p. 1150)
—Pip Goes to Camp. (p. 1361)
Peterson, Doug. Ben Hurry: A Lesson in Patience Moore, Michael, illus. (p. 163)
—Easy As ABC Crosswords. (p. 500)
—Field of Beans: A Lesson in Faith (p. 584)
—In the Amazing Brain-Twister (p. 865)
—Larryboy & the Abominable Trashman (p. 976)
—LarryBoy Versus the Volcano (p. 976)
Peterson, Doug, jt. auth. see Kenney, Cindy.
Peterson, Doug & Kenney, Cindy. Lost in Place: A Lesson in Overcoming Fear Big Idea Productions Staff, illus. (p. 1055)
—Spoon in the Stone: A Lesson in Serving Others (p. 1631)
Peterson, Esther Allen. Coming of Age. (p. 348)
—House That Cared. (p. 803)
—Long Journey to a New Home. (p. 1047)
—Will Spring Come? (p. 1932)
Peterson, Eugene H. Christmas Troll: Sometimes God's Best Gifts Are the Most Unexpected. Terry, Will, illus. (p. 316)
Peterson, Eugene H. & Smith Management Associates Staff. Easter Story: Featuring the Message. (p. 499)
Peterson, Eugene H., tr. My First Message: A Devotional Bible for Kids. Corley, Rob & Bancroft, Tom, illus. (p. 1207)
Peterson, Franklynn, jt. auth. see Kesselman-Turkel, Judi.
Peterson, Gail Ruth. Cadin's Heavenly Father. (p. 250)
—Jacob Wins a Soccer Game. (p. 904)
Peterson, Gary, illus. see Schilling, Vincent.
Peterson, Gary, illus. see Swanson, Bruce & Swanson, Bill.
Peterson, Hiromi & Omizo, Emiko. Adventures in Japanese (p. 15)
Peterson, Hiromi & Omizo, Naomi. Adventures in Japanese: Level 2 (p. 15)
—Adventures in Japanese: Field Test Edition. (p. 15)
—Adventures in Japanese Muronaka, Michael & Kaylor, Emiko, illus. (p. 15)
—Adventures in Japanese Level 1 Muronaka, Michael & Kaylor, Emiko, illus. (p. 15)
—Adventures in Japanese. (p. 15)
Peterson, Ingela. Ellie & Pinky's Pop-Up Shapes. (p. 514)
Peterson, J. D. R. & Reimer, Diana. Priscilla Bailey: A Story of the Great Depression. (p. 1407)
Peterson, J. E. Tensions in the Gulf, 1978-1991. (p. 1720)
Peterson, Janie & Peterson, Macy. Sleep Fairy. Newlun, Shawn, illus. (p. 1588)
Peterson, Jean S., jt. auth. see Littrell, John M.
Peterson, Jeanne Whitehouse. Don't Forget Winona. Root, Kimberly Bulcken, illus. (p. 467)
Peterson, Jenna, jt. auth. see Novick, Mary.
Peterson, Jim. Kitten Tales. (p. 962)
—Kittens in the Mall. (p. 963)
—Summer House Kitten. (p. 1674)
Peterson, Joel & Rogers, Jacqueline. Littles & the Surprise Thanksgiving Guests. (p. 1038)
Peterson, John & Slater, Teddy. Littles Have a Happy Valentine's Day. Rogers, Jacqueline, illus. (p. 1038)
Peterson, John C. Adam Has No Brothers. (p. 11)
Peterson, Joyce. Three Spinners. (p. 1744)
Peterson, Judy Monroe. Big Game Hunting. (p. 181)
—Braving Volcanoes: Volcanologists. (p. 223)
—Breathe: Keeping Your Lungs Healthy. (p. 226)
—Digging up History: Archaeologists. (p. 439)
—Exploring Space: Astronauts & Astronomers. (p. 553)
—First Budget Smarts. (p. 593)
—Fishing in Lakes & Ponds. (p. 599)
—Fossil Finders: Paleontologists. (p. 623)
—Frequently Asked Questions about Antidepressants. (p. 636)
—Frequently Asked Questions about Sleep & Sleep Deprivation. (p. 636)
—I Have a Food Allergy, Now What? (p. 839)
—I'm Suicidal, Now What? (p. 860)
—Maine: Past & Present. (p. 1077)
—Making Good Choices about Biodegradability. (p. 1081)
—Small Game Hunting. (p. 1592)
—Trout Fishing. (p. 1790)
—Understanding Cholesterol. (p. 1815)
—Underwater Explorers: Marine Biologists. (p. 1817)
—Varmint Hunting. (p. 1833)
—Weather Watchers: Climate Scientists. (p. 1870)
—What Are Metamorphic Rocks? (p. 1879)
Peterson, Julianna. They Call Me Naughty Paws: A True Kitten Tale. (p. 1732)
Peterson Kaelberer, Angie, jt. auth. see Kaelberer, Angie Peterson.
Peterson, Karen. Penny Perone & the Midnight Walker. (p. 1338)
Peterson Kathleen, illus. see Collins Malia.
Peterson, Kathleen, illus. see Han, Carolyn.
Peterson, Kathleen, illus. see Krishna, McArthur & Spalding, Bethany Brady.
Peterson, Kathleen, illus. see Shapiro, Lindy.
Peterson, Kathryn. Reilly's Leap of Faith (p. 1457)
Peterson, Kay. Tillie the Turtle. (p. 1750)
Peterson, Kevan. Turtle Takes the Bus. (p. 1798)
Peterson, Kevin S., compiled by. Collected Works - Aristotle. (p. 339)
Peterson, Lennie, illus. see Mansfield, Monica.
Peterson, Lois. Ballad of Knuckles McGraw (p. 134)
—Beyond Repair (p. 174)
—Disconnect (p. 447)
—Meeting Miss 405 (p. 1123)
—Paper House (p. 1322)
—Silver Rain (p. 1576)
—Wrong Bus Meissner, Amy, illus. (p. 1965)
Peterson, Ltc Roy E. Albert: The Cat That Thought He Could Fly. (p. 34)
Peterson, Lynn Ihsen, illus. see Wales, Dirk.
Peterson, M. E. You Are My Everything: Determined Little Maghara!!! Yang, Yi, illus. (p. 1973)
Peterson, Macy, jt. auth. see Peterson, Janie.
Peterson, Marilyn A., jt. auth. see Sonandres, Thomas William.
Peterson, Mark. Korea. (p. 967)
—Tater Tot King. (p. 1707)
Peterson, Mark, ed. see Eischen, Michael.
Peterson, Marques. Who'll Win the Girl? (p. 1920)
Peterson, Mary. Irving: The Lost Llama. (p. 888)
Peterson, Mary, illus. see Arnold, Caroline.
Peterson, Mary, illus. see Liu, Cynthea.
Peterson, Mary, illus. see Madison, Mike.
Peterson, Mary, illus. see Swinburne, Stephen R.
Peterson, Mary & Rofé, Jennifer. Piggies in the Pumpkin Patch. Peterson, Mary, illus. (p. 1358)
Peterson, Mary Joseph. Basic Prayers in My Pocket. (p. 142)
—Holy Mass in My Pocket. (p. 791)
—Rosary in My Pocket. (p. 1489)
Peterson, Mary Joseph, illus. see Tebo, Mary Elizabeth.
Peterson, Mary Joseph, illus. see Trouve, Marianne Lorraine.
Peterson, Matt. Epic Tales of a Misfit Hero. (p. 532)
Peterson, Megan Cooley. Best Camouflaged Animals. (p. 168)
—Extreme Animals. (p. 556)
—Pebble First Guide to Spiders (p. 1333)
—Smallest Animals. (p. 1592)
Peterson, Megan Cooley & Rustad, Martha E. H. Bengal Tigers Are Awesome! (p. 164)
—Best Camouflaged Animals (p. 168)
—Black Cats (p. 195)
—California Sea Lions (p. 253)
—Camouflage Clues: A Photo Riddle Book. (p. 257)
—Celebrate Halloween (p. 283)
—Chimpanzees Are Awesome! (p. 306)
—Coral Reefs (p. 366)
—Elephant Seals (p. 511)
—Encountering Chupacabra & Other Cryptids: Eyewitness Accounts Stevens, Matt, illus. (p. 524)
—Extreme Animals. (p. 556)
—First Airplanes (p. 592)
—First Computers (p. 593)
—First Space Missions (p. 597)
—Giant Pandas Are Awesome! (p. 674)
—Halloween Fun. (p. 737)
—Iguanas (p. 856)
—Jack-O'-Lanterns (p. 903)
—Kid Style: Boss Backpacks for You! (p. 951)
—Kid Style: Cool Clothes for You! (p. 951)
—Kid Style: Rockin' Bedrooms for You! (p. 951)
—Kid Style: Sweet Shoes for You! (p. 951)
—King Cobras Are Awesome! (p. 958)
—Little Scientists. (p. 1036)
—Look Inside a Beaver's Lodge (p. 1049)
—Look Inside a Bee Hive (p. 1049)
—Look Inside a Robin's Nest (p. 1049)
—Look Inside an Ant Nest (p. 1049)
—Look Inside Animal Homes. (p. 1049)
—Make It Mine (p. 1079)
—Sharks (p. 1562)
—Show Me Dogs: My First Picture Encyclopedia (p. 1570)
—Show Me Reptiles: My First Picture Encyclopedia (p. 1570)
—Smallest Animals (p. 1592)
—This Book Might Bite: A Collection of Wacky Animal Trivia (p. 1735)
—Trick-Or-Treat Safety (p. 1786)
—Zebras Are Awesome! (p. 1985)
Peterson, Megan Cooley, et al. Eyewitness to the Unexplained (p. 558)
—How to Build Hair-Raising Haunted Houses (p. 815)
—My First Picture Encyclopedias. (p. 1207)
—Reptiles. (p. 1461)
—Super Trivia Collection. (p. 1682)
Peterson, Melanie, illus. see Burshek, Edward & Burshek, Tonja.
Peterson, Mike. Freehand: A Young Boy's Adventures in the War Of 1812. Baldwin, Christopher, illus. (p. 635)
Peterson, Mitzi & Peay Peterson, Mitzi. Tenkita, Jumping on One Patita. Peterson, Nancy, illus. (p. 1720)
Peterson, Nancy, illus. see Peterson, Mitzi & Peay Peterson, Mitzi.
Peterson, Nora. Jerga de Wall Street. (p. 913)
Peterson, Oscar. Oscar Peterson Playing Cards: Boxed, Custom-designed, Poker-size Playing Cards. (p. 1305)
Peterson, Paige, jt. auth. see Cerf, Christopher.
Peterson, Paul, jt. auth. see Gilmore, Jason.
Peterson, R. E. (Robert Evans). Peterson's Familiar Science; (p. 1347)
Peterson, Rachelle (Rocky) Gibbons. Big Buckaroo's Little Sister. (p. 180)
Peterson, Rick, illus. see Bruun, Erik.
Peterson, Rick, illus. see Fauchald, Nick.
Peterson, Rick, illus. see Ganeri, Anita.
Peterson, Rick, illus. see Loewen, Nancy.
Peterson, Rick, illus. see McBrier, Page.
Peterson, Rick, illus. see Meachen Rau, Dana.
Peterson, Rick, illus. see Thomas, Isabel.
Peterson, Rick, jt. auth. see Ganeri, Anita.
Peterson, Roger Tory, ed. see Douglass, John & Douglass, Jackie Leatherbury.
Peterson, Roger Tory, ed. see Hughes, Sarah Anne.
Peterson, Roger Tory, ed. see Kricher, John C.
Peterson, Roger Tory, illus. see Kricher, John C.
Peterson, Roger Tory, jt. auth. see Alden, Peter C.
Peterson, Roger Tory, jt. auth. see Pyle, Robert Michael.
Peterson, Roger Tory, jt. auth. see Tenenbaum, Frances.
Peterson, Russell, jt. auth. see Morrison, Jaydene.
Peterson, Ruth. Its Time for Bed Stephanie... but First. (p. 899)
Peterson, S. L. Adventures in Puddle Creek: The Value of Teamwork. Hajde, Jeremy, illus. (p. 15)
Peterson, Sara, illus. see Turley, Sandy.
Peterson, Sara Budinger. Journey of Perm. Kaufman, Mary Bee, illus. (p. 928)
Peterson, Scott. Blackout! Spaziante, Patrick, illus. (p. 197)
—Joker Virus Cavallaro, Mike, illus. (p. 924)
—Learn to Draw Plus Disney Phineas & Ferb. Guler, Greg & Ulene, Nancy, illus. (p. 983)
—Parasite's Feeding Frenzy Cavallaro, Mike, illus. (p. 1324)
—Ultimate Returns. (p. 1809)
Peterson, Scott, jt. auth. see Disney Book Group Staff.
Peterson, Scott, photos by see Morgan, Diane & Gemignani, Tony.
Peterson, Scott & Disney Book Group Staff. Destination - Amazon! Disney Storybook Art Team, illus. (p. 430)
Peterson, Shauna, illus. see Calder, C. J.
Peterson, Sheryl. Alaska. (p. 33)
—Best Part of a Sauna Dupre, Kelly, illus. (p. 171)
—California. (p. 253)
—Colorado. (p. 343)
—Egyptian Pyramids. (p. 507)
—Empire State Building. (p. 521)
—Great Depression & World War II. (p. 715)
—Idaho. (p. 852)
—Iowa. (p. 886)
—Machu Picchu. (p. 1068)
—Maine. (p. 1077)
—Minnesota. (p. 1147)
—Montana. (p. 1170)
—North Dakota. (p. 1265)
—Pterodactyl. (p. 1413)
—Stegosaurus. (p. 1646)
—Story of the Florida Marlins. (p. 1661)
—Story of the Seattle Mariners. (p. 1662)
—Texas. Kania, Matt, illus. (p. 1724)
—Velociraptor. (p. 1835)
—Wisconsin. (p. 1939)
Peterson, Sheryl, jt. auth. see Hutchison, Patricia.
Peterson, Stacy. Just Dad & Me: The Fill-In, Tear-out, Fold-up Book of Fun for Girls & Their Dads. Falligant, Erin, ed. (p. 938)
Peterson, Stacy, illus. see Criswell, Patti Kelley.
Peterson, Stacy, illus. see Falligant, Erin, ed.
Peterson, Stacy, illus. see Magruder, Trula & American Girl Editors, eds.
Peterson, Stacy, illus. see Magruder, Trula, ed.
Peterson, Stacy, illus. see Miller, Sara.
Peterson, Stacy, illus. see Sund, Mike.
Peterson, Stephanie, illus. see Cimarusti, Marie Torres & George, Jean Craighead.
Peterson, Susan Lynn. Legends of the Martial Arts Masters. (p. 990)
Peterson, Tara & Hogan, Joyce W. Should We Play Video Games? A Persuasive Text. (p. 1570)
Peterson, Tiffany. Sea Creatures. Westerfield, David, illus. (p. 1534)
Peterson, Tina L. Oscar & the Amazing Gravity Repellent. Bonet, Xavier, illus. (p. 1305)
Peterson, Todd. Tony Hawk, Skateboarder & Businessman. (p. 1766)
Peterson, Valerie, jt. auth. see Fryer, Janice.
Peterson, Will. Burning. (p. 244)
—Gathering. (p. 658)
—Triskellion. (p. 1787)
Peterson, Willa. It's a Mommy Day! (p. 895)
Peterson-Hilleque, Victoria. Ana & Adam Build & Acrostic. Barnum-Newman, Winifred, illus. (p. 66)
—How to Analyze the Works of J. K. Rowling. (p. 814)
—J. K. Rowling: Extraordinary Author. (p. 901)
Peterson-Hilleque, Victoria & Llanas, Sheila Griffin. How to Analyze the Works of Sylvia Plath. (p. 814)
Peterson's Guides Staff. Get Wise! Mastering Reading Comprehension Skills. (p. 668)
—Guia Para el Estudiante Hispano Entrando a la Universidad. (p. 730)
—Peterson's Internships. (p. 1347)
—SAT Success 2004. (p. 1515)
—SAT Success Prep Kit: SAT Success; In-a-Flash: Math; Get Wise! Mastering Vocabulary Skills (p. 1515)
—Summer Opportunities for Kids & Teenagers 2005. (p. 1674)
Peterson's Guides Staff, ed. see Arco Staff.
Peterson-Shea, Julie, illus. see Boeve, Eunice.
Petert. Joetakecarer. (p. 920)
Petete, Christine, illus. see Tucker, Mark.
Pethel, Stan, contrib. by. Trombone: 12 Hymn Arrangments for One or More Wind Players. (p. 1788)
Pether, Lesley. Shells. (p. 1565)
Petheram, Louise, et al. Ascent! (p. 105)
Petit, Charles E., jt. auth. see Pettifor, Bonnie.
Petit, Cheryl. Fairy Princess Melina (p. 563)
Petit, Denice. Twenty-Two Turtles. (p. 1801)
Petit, Karen. Mystery of the Screecher Creature: A Shandon's Ivy League Mystery. (p. 1226)
—Mystery of the Stolen Stallion. (p. 1226)
Petit, Marilyn, jt. ed. see Page, Philip.
Petit, William & Adamec, Christine A. Encyclopedia of Endocrine Diseases & Disorders. (p. 525)
Petkau, Karen S. If Heaven Is So Great, Why Can't I Go Now? (p. 852)
Petkovich, David. Story of Pete the Pig: A Truly Twisted Tail. (p. 1659)
Petley, Julian. Advertising. (p. 25)
—Newspapers & Magazines. (p. 1249)
Peto, Judith E. & Talwar, Robert B. Jenny & Benny: Friends (p. 913)
Petosa-Sigel, Kristi, illus. see Crowe, Ellie & Fry, Juliet.
Petracca, C. A. B. Chronicles of Petr The. (p. 317)
Petrarca, Natalie. Stinky the Cat. (p. 1651)
Petras, Emery G. Foxes Three. (p. 626)
Petras, Julie A. Draw & Tell Sacraments. (p. 480)
—Draw & Tell Saints. (p. 480)

Full bibliographic information is available on the Title Index page number referenced in parentheses at the end of each entry

Petrash, Carol. Earthways: Simple Environmental Activities for Young Children. (p. 498)
Petre, Wanda E. Watch Chicken: The Legend of Russell the Rooster & His Friend Hortense. (p. 1860)
Petrella, Angela, et al. Recipe. Althea, Erin & Bertino, Mike, illus. (p. 1451)
Petrella, Julie. Power in Times of Unncertainty: Training Your Mind to Change Your Life. (p. 1389)
Petreman, Gwen. Aesop's Fables. (p. 25)
—Caught by Rabroar. (p. 281)
—Weird Week. (p. 1873)
—Who Laid Those Eggs? (p. 1916)
—Wish for Haidan. (p. 1940)
Petretti, Silvia I. Rachel's Easter Vacation in Mexico. James, Elizabeth, ed. (p. 1432)
Petrey, Ashley. Abc's Game. (p. 4)
Petreycik, Rick. Headaches. (p. 756)
—Rhode Island. (p. 1468)
—Tennessee. (p. 1720)
—West Virginia. (p. 1876)
—Wyoming. (p. 1966)
Petreycik, Rick & Herrington, Lisa M. Rhode Island. (p. 1468)
Petreycik, Rick & McGeveran, William. Tennessee. (p. 1720)
Petreyick, Rick. Rhode Island. (p. 1468)
—Tennessee. (p. 1720)
Petri, Gail G. American Memory Collections: Primary Resource Activities Across the Curriculum (p. 62)
—American Memory Collections from A to Z: Primary Resource Guide & Reproducible Activities Across the Curriculum (p. 62)
Petri, Michelle. Fvantom: Omegapocalypse. (p. 651)
Petricć, Dusan, illus. see Larsen, Andrew.
Petricic, Dusan. Mud Puddle. (p. 1188)
Petricic, Dusan, illus. see Andrews, Jan.
Petricic, Dusan, illus. see Davis, Aubrey.
Petricic, Dusan, illus. see Ellis, Sarah.
Petricic, Dusan, illus. see Fagan, Cary.
Petricic, Dusan, illus. see Fergus, Maureen.
Petricic, Dusan, illus. see Heidbreder, Robert.
Petricic, Dusan, illus. see Hutchins, Hazel & Herbert, Gail.
Petricic, Dusan, illus. see Munsch, Robert.
Petricic, Dusan, illus. see Richler, Mordecai.
Petricic, Dusan, illus. see Shapiro, Sheryl & Shapiro, Simon.
Petricic, Dusan, illus. see Stinson, Kathy.
Petricic, Dusan, illus. see Wynne-Jones, Tim.
Petrick, Neila S. Katherine Stinson Otero: High Flyer Wallace, Daggi, illus. (p. 944)
Petrick, Neila Skinner. Jane Wilkinson Long: Texas Pioneer Haynes, Joyce, illus. (p. 908)
Petrie, Catherine. Joshua James Likes Trucks. Snyder, Joel, illus. (p. 927)
Petrie, H. D., photos by. All God's Creatures; Jesus Loves Me. (p. 44)
Petrie, Kathye Fetsko & Boyds Mills Press Staff. Flying Jack. Mahoney, Paula J., illus. (p. 610)
Petrie, Kristin. American Bobtail Cats. (p. 60)
—American Crows. (p. 60)
—Backyard Animals. (p. 130)
—Birman Cats. (p. 192)
—Cesky Terriers. (p. 288)
—Chameleons. (p. 289)
—Chartreux Cats. (p. 294)
—Cottontail Rabbits. (p. 369)
—Food Pyramid. (p. 614)
—Garter Snakes. (p. 657)
—Hummingbirds. (p. 826)
—Iguanas. (p. 856)
—Madagascar Hissing Cockroaches. (p. 1069)
—Potbellied Pigs. (p. 1388)
—Raccoons. (p. 1430)
—Selkirk Rex Cats. (p. 1550)
—Singapura Cats. (p. 1579)
—Squirrels. (p. 1637)
—Sugar Gliders. (p. 1673)
—Tarantulas. (p. 1706)
—Turkish Angora Cats. (p. 1797)
Petrie, Roy. Joseph Brant (p. 926)
Petrikowski, Nicki Peter. Getting the Most Out of Makerspaces to Create with 3-D Printers. (p. 669)
—Getting to Know the Raspberry Pi. (p. 669)
—Teen Life 411: Set 3. (p. 1713)
—Working for Tolerance & Social Change Through Service Learning (p. 1952)
Petrikowski, Nicki Peter & Edwards, Judith. Relocation of Native Peoples of North America. (p. 1458)
Petrillo, Genevieve. Keep Your Ear on the Ball. Lyon, Lea07/, illus. (p. 947)
Petrillo, Genevieve & Lyon, Lea. Keep Your Ear on the Ball Lyon, Lea, illus. (p. 947)
Petrillo, Lisa. Isaac Mizrahi. (p. 890)
—Sarah Palin. (p. 1514)
—Vera Wang. (p. 1836)
Petrillo, Valerie. Asian American History: More Than 70 Activities. (p. 106)
—Kid's Guide to Latino History: More Than 50 Activities. (p. 953)
—Sailors, Whalers, Fantastic Sea Voyages: An Activity Guide to North American Sailing Life. (p. 1503)
Petrini, Catherine & Petrini, Catherine M. Dragons. (p. 478)
Petrini, Catherine M., jt. auth. see Petrini, Catherine.
Petrini, Catherine M., tr. Cherokee. (p. 298)
Petrlik, Andrea. Hansel & Gretel. (p. 743)
—Shoo, Fly! (p. 1568)
Petrlik, Andrea, illus. see Cabral, Jeane.
Petrlik, Andrea, illus. see Ranson, Erin.
Petrlik, Andrea, illus. see Rider, Cynthia.
Petroff, Kathryn, illus. see Williams, Joyce.
Petroff, Shani. Careful What You Wish For. McKenney, J. David, illus. (p. 268)
—Daddy's Little Angel McKenney, J. David, illus. (p. 399)
—Good, the Bad, & the Ugly Dress. McKenney, J. David, illus. (p. 700)
—Love Struck. McKenney, J. David, illus. (p. 1060)
Petrone, Catherine. Moon Worms. (p. 1172)
Petrone, Epp. Anna's Teeth. Maiste, Piia, illus. (p. 85)
Petrone, Susan, jt. auth. see Sullivan, Michael John.
Petrone, Valeria. Zapatos Divertidos. (p. 1985)
Petrone, Valeria, illus. see Bannerman, Helen.
Petrone, Valeria, illus. see Hamilton, Kersten.
Petrone, Valeria, illus. see Hays, Anna Jane.
Petrone, Valeria, illus. see Holland, Trish.
Petrone, Valeria, illus. see Imperato, Teresa.
Petrone, Valeria, illus. see Knudsen, Michelle.
Petrone, Valeria, illus. see Manushkin, Fran.
Petrone, Valeria, illus. see Murphy, Stuart J.
Petrone, Valeria, illus. see Peck, Jan.
Petrone, Valeria, illus. see Serfozo, Mary.
Petrone, Valeria, illus. see Smith, Danna.
Petrone, Valeria, illus. see Vestergaard, Hope.
Petrone, Valeria, jt. auth. see Serfozo, Mary.
Petronille, Marc & Audureau, William. History of Sonic the Hedgehog. (p. 784)
Petropouleas, Niko, illus. see Cope Bowley, Tonia.
Petropoulos, John, illus. see Edwards, Hazel.
Petrosino, Tamara. No Plain Hair. (p. 1260)
Petrosino, Tamara, illus. see Crawley, Dave.
Petrosino, Tamara, illus. see Harvey, Jayne.
Petrossi, Fabrizio, illus. see Golden Books Staff.
Petrossi, Fabrizio, illus. see Golden Books.
Petrossi, Fabrizio, illus. see Random House Staff.
Petrossi, Fabrizio, illus. see Wygand, Melissa.
Petrov, Anton, illus. see Kennedy, Pamela.
Petrov, Anton, illus. see Mackall, Dandi Daley.
Petrov, Anton, illus. see Schneider, Richard H.
Petrov, Elena. One Day in the Summer Holidays: A Compic Adventure. (p. 1294)
Petrova, Valeria, illus. see Keener, Joan N.
Petrova-Browning, Nina, jt. auth. see Robert, Na'ima Bint.
Petrovic, Svetlana. Brown Bear, White Bear. Hardy, Vincent, illus. (p. 231)
Petrovskaya, Olga, ed. see AZ Books Staff.
Petrowski, Carol. Clown Who Wears Many Hats. (p. 335)
Petru, Suzin, illus. see Costanza, Francine.
Petruccelli, Jessica, jt. illus. see Fennell, Kristen.
Petrucci, Lou. Heart of the Hide. (p. 759)
Petruccio, Stephen, illus. see Halfmann, Janet.
Petruccio, Steven. At the Construction Site (en el Sitio de Construccion) Gongora, Oscar, tr. (p. 111)
Petruccio, Steven James. American Heroes Coloring Book. (p. 61)
—American Legends & Tall Tales. (p. 62)
—At the Construction Site. (p. 111)
—BOOST Trucks Coloring Book. (p. 213)
—Cars: Doodle, Design & Draw. (p. 272)
—Construction Site Sticker Picture Puzzle. (p. 360)
—Cowboy Tattoos. (p. 374)
—Create Your Own Construction Truck Sticker Activity Book. (p. 378)
—Create Your Own Dream Car Sticker Activity Book. (p. 378)
—Create Your Own Fire Truck Sticker Activity Book. (p. 378)
—Create Your Own Robot. (p. 378)
—Emergency Vehicles Stickers. (p. 518)
—Forest Animals Sticker Activity Book. (p. 618)
—History of the Civil Rights Movement Coloring Book. (p. 784)
—History of the White House Coloring Book. (p. 785)
—Rodeo Coloring Book. (p. 1484)
—Shiny Jet Planes Stickers. (p. 1567)
Petruccio, Steven James, illus. see Galvin, Laura Gates.
Petruccio, Steven James, illus. see Halfmann, Janet.
Petruccio, Steven James, illus. see Walker, Sally M.
Petruccio, Steven James, illus. see Winkelman, Barbara Gaines.
Petruccio, Steven James, illus. see Zoehfeld, Kathleen Weidner.
Petruccio, Steven James, jt. auth. see Zoehfeld, Kathleen Weidner.
Petruccio, Steven James & Coloring Books Staff. Roadside Attractions Coloring Book: Weird & Wacky Landmarks from Across the USA! (p. 1477)
Petrucha, Stefan. Breaking Down Parker, Rick, illus. (p. 225)
—Demon of River Heights. Murase, Sho, illus. (p. 426)
—Farting Dead. Parker, Rick, illus. (p. 575)
—Global Warning. Murase, Sho, illus. (p. 685)
—Going Green. (p. 692)
—Harry Potty & the Deathly Boring. Parker, Rick, illus. (p. 751)
—Haunted Dollhouse. Murase, Sho, illus. (p. 753)
—Memory Short. (p. 1126)
—Nancy Drew Diaries. Murase, Sho, illus. (p. 1229)
—Papercutz Slices #4: the Hunger Pains. Parker, Rick, illus. (p. 1323)
—Papercutz Slices #5: the Farting Dead. Parker, Rick, illus. (p. 1323)
—Power Rangers Megaforce. Henrique, Paulo, illus. (p. 1390)
—Power Rangers Megaforce - Broken World. Henrique, Paulo, illus. (p. 1390)
—Power Rangers Super Samurai. (p. 1390)
—Prilla's Talent. Magic Eye Studios Staff et al, illus. (p. 1399)
—Ripper. (p. 1474)
—Rita Repulsa's Attitude Adjustment. (p. 1475)
—Super Samurai - Terrible Toys. Henrique, Paulo, illus. (p. 1680)
—Terrible Toys. Henrique, Paulo, illus. (p. 1721)
—Writ in Stone. Murase, Sho, illus. (p. 1963)
Petrucha, Stefan, jt. auth. see Kinney, Sarah.
Petrucha, Stefan, jt. auth. see Parker, Rick.
Petrucha, Stefan & Henrique, Paulo. Panic in the Parade. (p. 1321)
—Power Rangers Megaforce - Panic in the Parade. (p. 1390)
Petrucha, Stefan & Kinney, Sarah. City under the Basement. Murase, Sho, illus. (p. 324)
—Cliffhanger. Murase, Sho, illus. (p. 332)
—Disoriented Express. Murase, Sho & Guzman, Carlos Jose, illus. (p. 453)
—Doggone Town. Murase, Sho, illus. (p. 462)
—High School Musical Mystery. Murase, Sho, illus. (p. 778)
—Lost Verse Murase, Sho, illus. (p. 1057)
—Monkey Wrench Blues Murase, Sho, illus. (p. 1165)
—Night of the Living Chatchke. Murase, Sho, illus. (p. 1254)
—Sleight of Dan. Murase, Sho, illus. (p. 1590)
—Small Volcanoes. Goldberg, Stan, illus. (p. 1592)
—Tiger Counter. Murase, Sho, illus. (p. 1748)
—Vampire Slayer. Murase, Sho, illus. (p. 1832)
—Vampire's Kiss. Murase, Sho, illus. (p. 1832)
—What Goes Up... Murase, Sho, illus. (p. 1885)
Petrucha, Stefan & Kinney-Petrucha, Margo. Percy Jackson & the Ovolactovegetarians Parker, Rick, illus. (p. 1341)
Petrucha, Stefan & Murase, Sho. Mr. Cheeters Is Missing. (p. 1184)
Petrucha, Stefan & Pendleton, Thomas. Prey. (p. 1398)
—Wicked Dead: Skin. (p. 1927)
Petrucha, Stefan & Silvani, James. Creature from Blu's Lagoon. (p. 380)
Petrucha, Stefan, et al. Fake Heir. Ross, Daniel Vaughn, illus. (p. 565)
—Mickey Mouse Adventures Clark, John, ed. (p. 1136)
—Small Volcanoes Goldberg, Stan, illus. (p. 1592)
—X-Files Adlard, Charlie, illus. (p. 1967)
Petruck, Rebecca. Steering Toward Normal. (p. 1646)
Petrulis, Sarah, illus. see Albright, Kendra S. & Gavigan, Karen W., eds.
Petrusek, Brett, illus. see Blair, Eric.
Petry, Ann. Harriet Tubman: Conductor on the Underground Railroad. (p. 750)
Petrylak, Ashley. Guinea Pigs. (p. 731)
Petrzela, Natalia Mehlman. Classroom Wars: Language, Sex, & the Making of Modern Political Culture. (p. 329)
Petsch, Maggie, photos by. Dora the A-Dora-ble Duck. (p. 471)
Pett, Mark. Boy & the Airplane. Pett, Mark, illus. (p. 217)
—Girl & the Bicycle. Pett, Mark, illus. (p. 678)
—Lizard from the Park. Pett, Mark, illus. (p. 1042)
Pett, Mark & Rubinstein, Gary. Girl Who Never Made Mistakes. Pett, Mark, illus. (p. 679)
Pettenati, Jeanne. Galileo's Journal, 1609-1610. Rui, Paolo, illus. (p. 653)
Petterson, Aline. Papalote y el Nopal. Pacheco, Gabriel, illus. (p. 1322)
Pettersson, Aline. Ontario, la Mariposa Viajera. Valderrama, Rosario, illus. (p. 1298)
Pettibone, Glady. Caterpillar That Wanted to Be a Butterfly. (p. 279)
Pettifor, Bonnie & Petit, Charles E. McCulloch V. Maryland: When State & Federal Powers Conflict. (p. 1114)
Pettiford, Rebecca. Chinese New Year. (p. 307)
—Coaches. (p. 336)
—Crossing Guards. (p. 385)
—Garbage Collectors. (p. 655)
—Halloween. (p. 737)
—Reporters. (p. 1461)
—Thanksgiving. (p. 1725)
—Valentine's Day. (p. 1830)
—Veterans Day. (p. 1839)
Pettinato, Laura. Thirteen Americas: The Declaration of Independence. Tiwari, Saral, illus. (p. 1734)
—Thirteen Americas: American Revolution & Constitution. Tiwari, Saral, illus. (p. 1734)
Pettinella, Amy. Lady Gaga. (p. 970)
—Queen Latifah: Award-Winning Actress & Hip-Hop Activist. (p. 1425)
Pettingill, Charla, illus. see Puck.
Pettit, Jenny, jt. auth. see Downey, Matthew T.
Pettit, Loree & Mullins, Dari. Galloping the Globe: The Geography Unit Study for Young Learners: Kindergarten Through 4th Grade. (p. 653)
Pettit, Marilyn, jt. auth. see Page, Philip.
Pettitt, Emily. Dream, Dream, Little Sweet Pea. Hutton, Jason, illus. (p. 483)
Pettitt, Linda & Darrow, Sharon. Yafi's Family: An Ethiopian Boy's Journey of Love, Loss, & Adoption. Gilchrist, Jan Spivey, illus. (p. 1968)
Pettus, Tiffany. Sweetness of Christmas: The Candy Cane Story. (p. 1690)
Petty, Angel Bishop & Engel, Robert. From College to Careers: Listening in the Real World. (p. 642)
Petty, Bruce. Living Behind Walls: Inside the Desert Kingdom of Saudi Arabia. (p. 1040)
Petty, Colin. Three Little Pigs: A Tale about Working Hard. (p. 1743)
Petty, Dev. I Don't Want to Be a Frog. Boldt, Mike, illus. (p. 838)
Petty, Dini. Queen, the Bear & the Bumblebee. Cowles, Rose, illus. (p. 1425)
Petty, Heather. Lock & Mori. (p. 1045)
Petty, J. T. Fairy Killer. Davis, Will, illus. (p. 563)
—Scrivener Bees. Friend, David Michael, illus. (p. 1533)
Petty, J. T., jt. auth. see Pope, Paul.
Petty, Kate. Abraham Lincoln: The Life of America's Sixteenth President. (p. 6)
—Around the World - Hair. (p. 100)
—Around the World - Playtime. Oxfam (Afghanistan) Staff, photos by. (p. 100)
—Bicycles (p. 177)
—Don't Wake Stanley (p. 469)
—Encyclopedia of Awesome Machines. Watton, Ross & Moore, Jo, illus. (p. 525)
—Ha Ha, Baby! Birkett, Georgie, illus. (p. 734)
—Hair. (p. 735)
—Homes. (p. 793)
—Nightspinners. Smith, Mary Claire, illus. (p. 1255)
—Playtime. (p. 1373)
—Summer Heat. (p. 1674)
Petty, Kate, jt. auth. see Jeffery, Gary.
Petty, Kate, jt. auth. see Jeffrey, Gary.
Petty, Kate & Ganeri, Anita. Saving the Animals. (p. 1517)
Petty, Kate & Quarto Generic Staff. Bicycles. (p. 177)
Petty, William Kevin, illus. see Bush, Emilie P.
Petway, Jessie. Child's Book of Poetry. (p. 304)
Petz, Moritz. Bad Mood! Jackowski, Amelie, illus. (p. 132)
—Bad Mood. Jackowski, Amélie, illus. (p. 132)
—Day Everything Went Wrong. Jackowski, Amélie, illus. (p. 412)
Peurifoy, Reneau Z. Anxiety, Phobias, & Panic: A Step-by-Step Guide for Regaining Control of Your Life. (p. 90)
Pevear, Linda W., jt. auth. see Pevear, Ted F.
Pevear, Richard, tr. see Dumas, Alexandre.
Pevear, Ted F. & Pevear, Linda W. Date in the Junk Yard. (p. 409)
—Finding Little Feathers a Hub-A-Son. (p. 588)
Peyer, Tom. House of M. Larroca, Salvador, illus. (p. 803)
Peymani, Christine. Chasing Mavericks. (p. 294)
—Kitai's Journal. Katzenstein, Jason A., illus. (p. 962)
—Super Starz Masquerade. (p. 1682)
Peymani, Christine, jt. auth. see RH Disney Staff.
Peymani, Christine, jt. auth. see Tokyopop and Art Impression Staff.
Peyo. Aerosmurf. (p. 25)
—All about Brainy Smurf! (p. 42)
—Astro Smurf Blasts Off! Peyo, illus. (p. 109)
—Baby Smurf. (p. 128)
—Benny Breakiron #2: Madame Adolphine. Peyo & Maltaite, Will, illus. (p. 165)
—Find the 100 Smurfs! Peyo, illus. (p. 587)
—Giant Smurf. Peyo, illus. (p. 674)
—It's a Smurfy World! Peyo, illus. (p. 896)
—Lazy Smurf Takes a Nap. (p. 981)
—Marry Me, Smurfette! (p. 1096)
—Meet Smurfette. Peyo, illus. (p. 1122)
—Off to School! Peyo, illus. (p. 1279)
—Papa Smurf's Favorite Things. Peyo, illus. (p. 1322)
—Pitufos: El Pitufo Salvaje. Vol. 2 Díaz, Lorenzo, tr. from FRE. (p. 1365)
—Pitufos: La Flauta de los Pitufos. Vol. 1 Díaz, Lorenzo, tr. from FRE. (p. 1365)
—Rain, Rain, Smurf Away. Peyo, illus. (p. 1435)
—Red Taxis. Peyo & Maltaite, Will, illus. (p. 1455)
—Return of the Smurfette. (p. 1464)
—Scaredy Smurf Makes a Friend. (p. 1519)
—Sky-High Smurf. Peyo, illus. (p. 1586)
—Smurf Cake. Peyo, illus. (p. 1595)
—Smurf Championship Games. (p. 1595)
—Smurf Championship Games. Peyo, illus. (p. 1595)
—Smurf vs. Smurf. Peyo, illus. (p. 1595)
—Smurfette & the Beast: A Smurftastic Pop-Up Book. Peyo, illus. (p. 1595)
—Smurfiness to Go! A Smurfin' Big Adventure, Meet Smurfette!, Lazy Smurf Takes a Nap, the Thankful Smurf, Rain, Rain Smurf Away, the 100th Smurf. Peyo, illus. (p. 1595)
—Smurflings. (p. 1595)
—Smurfs #10: the Return of the Smurfette. (p. 1595)
—Smurfs #14: the Baby Smurf. (p. 1595)
—Smurfs & the Magic Egg. (p. 1595)
—Smurfs & the Magic Egg. Peyo, illus. (p. 1595)
—Smurfs Anthology. (p. 1595)
—Smurfs Anthology #2. (p. 1595)
—Smurf's Apprentice. (p. 1595)
—Smurfs Christmas. (p. 1595)
—Smurfs Graphic Novels Boxed Set: Vol. #10-12. (p. 1595)
—Smurfs Mini Library: Rise & Shine; Happy Smurfdays; Fun & Games; Making Music; Whatever the Weather. Peyo, illus. (p. 1595)
—Snow Giant. Peyo, illus. (p. 1599)
—Thankful Smurf. (p. 1725)
—Welcome, Baby Smurf! Peyo, illus. (p. 1873)
—Who's That Smurf? Peyo, illus. (p. 1921)
—Why Do You Cry, Baby Smurf? (p. 1924)
—Why Do You Cry, Baby Smurf? Peyo, illus. (p. 1924)
Peyo, illus. see Delporte, Peyo, et al.
Peyo, illus. see Delporte, Yvan.
Peyo, jt. auth. see Gos.
Peyo, jt. auth. see Mitter, Matt.
Peyo, jt. auth. see Peyo.
Peyo & Delporte, Yvan. Smurf Olympics. (p. 1595)
—Smurf Soup. (p. 1595)
—Smurfette Peyo, illus. (p. 1595)
—Smurfs #13: Smurf Soup. (p. 1595)
Peyo & Peyo. Smurf Cake. (p. 1595)
Peyo, et al. Smurfs #8: the Smurf Apprentice. Peyo, illus. (p. 1595)
—Smurfs #9: Gargamel & the Smurfs. Peyo, illus. (p. 1595)
—Smurfs & the Howlibird. Peyo, illus. (p. 1595)
Peyo, Peyo, illus. see Delporte, Yvan.
Peyo, Peyo & Delporte, Yvan. Smurfs & the Egg. Peyo, Peyo, illus. (p. 1595)
Peyrols, Sylvaine. Body. Peyrols, Sylvaine, illus. (p. 207)
—Crocodile. Peyrols, Sylvaine, illus. (p. 384)
—Historia de la Vida: Los Animales. (p. 782)
Peyrols, Sylvaine, illus. see Biard, Philippe, et al.
Peyrols, Sylvaine, jt. auth. see First Discovery Staff.
Peyrols, Sylvaine, jt. auth. see Jeunesse, Gallimard.
Peyrols, Sylvaine, et al. Volcanoes. Peyrols, Sylvaine et al, illus. (p. 1849)
Peyron, Gabriela. Quien le Toca? Callo, Valeria, illus. (p. 1427)
Peysin, Shainy. Whatever the Weather. Rosenfeld, Dina & Leverton, Yossi, eds. (p. 1896)
Peyton, Denyce Porter. Learn to Harvest Your Family History. (p. 984)
Peyton, K. M. Greater Gains. (p. 719)
—Horses. (p. 800)
—Last Ditch. (p. 977)
—Minna's Quest IR. (p. 1147)
—No Turning Back IR. (p. 1260)
—Stealaway. Wyatt, David, illus. (p. 1646)
Peyton, Katherine & George, Enzo. World War II in Europe & North Africa: Preserving Democracy. (p. 1959)
—World War II in the Pacific: War with Japan. (p. 1959)
Peyton, Km. Far from Home. (p. 572)
Pez, illus. see Bornemann, Elsa.
Pez, illus. see Wolf, Ema.
Pez, Alberto. Mario Mapache Conquista el Universo. (p. 1094)
—Martes Peludo. Gleich, Jacky, illus. (p. 1097)
—Mimosaurio! Cubillas, Roberto, illus. (p. 1145)
Pez, Christine & Duggins, Shirley. Casey & the Junkyard Cats: Pudgy's New Hero. (p. 275)

P

Pezzali, Walter, illus. see Guibert, Emmanuel & Sfar, Joann.
Pezzali, Walter, illus. see Guibert, Emmanuel.
Pezzi, Bryan. Arkansas. (p. 99)
—Craig Kielburger: Ma Vie. Karvonen, Tanjah, tr. from ENG. (p. 376)
—Craig Kielburger. (p. 376)
—David Suzuki: Ma Vie. Karvonen, Tanjah, tr. from ENG. (p. 411)
—David Suzuki. (p. 411)
—Eiffel Tower. (p. 507)
—Emily Carr. (p. 518)
—J. K. Rowling. (p. 901)
—Massachusetts. (p. 1102)
—Terry Fox: Ma Vie. Karvonen, Tanjah, tr. from ENG. (p. 1722)
—Terry Fox. (p. 1722)
Pezzimenti, Grace. Busy Families: Learning to Tell Time by the Hour. (p. 246)
—Pizza Party: Learning Basic Problem-Solving Skills. (p. 1365)
Pezzino, Martha, ed. see Rowles, Charles G., 3rd.
Pfaff, Eugene E. Guns at Guilford Court House. (p. 732)
Pfanner, Louise. Little Lucies Diary. (p. 1031)
—Little Lucie's Diary. (p. 1031)
Pfeffer, jt. auth. see Pfeffer, Wendy.
Pfeffer, Irwin, jt. auth. see Abraham, Henry.
Pfeffer, Susan Beth. Dead & the Gone. (p. 416)
—Life As We Knew It. (p. 1008)
—Life As We Knew It. Howard, Arthur, illus. (p. 1008)
—Revenge of the Aztecs. (p. 1465)
—Shade of the Moon. (p. 1556)
—This World We Live In. (p. 1737)
Pfeffer, Wendy. Dolphin Talk: Whistles, Clicks, & Clapping Jaws. Davie, Helen K., illus. (p. 464)
—Firefly at Stony Brook Farm. Mikec, Larry, illus. (p. 592)
—Firefly at Stonybrook Farm. Mikec, Larry, illus. (p. 592)
—From Seed to Pumpkin. Hale, James Graham, illus. (p. 643)
—From Tadpole to Frog. Keller, Holly, illus. (p. 644)
—Life in a Coral Reef. Jenkins, Steve, illus. (p. 1010)
—Light Is All Around Us. (p. 1015)
—Light Is All Around Us. Meisel, Paul, illus. (p. 1015)
—Light So Bright. (p. 1015)
—Log's Life. Brickman, Robin, illus. (p. 1045)
—Longest Day: Celebrating the Summer Solstice. Bleck, Linda, illus. (p. 1047)
—Mallard Duck at Meadow View Pond. Oughton, Taylor, illus. (p. 1083)
—Mallard Duck at Mountain View Pond. Oughton, Taylor, illus. (p. 1083)
—Many Ways to Be a Soldier. Verstraete, Elaine, illus. (p. 1089)
—Mysterious Spinners. Kim, Julie J., illus. (p. 1223)
—Shortest Day: Celebrating the Winter Solstice. Reisch, Jesse, illus. (p. 1569)
—We Gather Together: Celebrating the Harvest Season. Bleck, Linda, illus. (p. 1867)
—What's It Like to Be a Fish? Keller, Holly, illus. (p. 1898)
—Wiggling Worms at Work. Jenkins, Steve, illus. (p. 1928)
Pfeffer, Wendy & American Museum of Natural History Staff. Wolf Pup, Level 1. (p. 1944)
—World of Sharks. (p. 1957)
Pfeffer, Wendy & Pfeffer. Dolphin Talk: Whistles, Clicks, & Clapping Jaws. Davie, Helen K., illus. (p. 464)
—Wiggling Worms at Work. Jenkins, Steve, illus. (p. 1928)
Pfeffer, Z. My Yom Tov Album. (p. 1222)
Pfeffinger, Charla R., jt. auth. see Barchers, Suzanne I.
Pfeifer, Alice Ann. Totally Lent! A Kid's Journey to Easter 2008. (p. 1771)
—Totally Lent! My Journey to Easter 2005! Larkin, Jean K., ed. (p. 1771)
Pfeifer, Hilary. Do-It-Your-Selfabet. (p. 457)
Pfeifer, Kate Gruenwald & American Medical Association Staff. American Medical Association Boy's Guide to Becoming a Teen. Middleman, Amy B., ed. (p. 62)
Pfeifer, Kate Gruenwald, et al. American Medical Association Girl's Guide to Becoming a Teen. Middleman, Amy B., ed. (p. 62)
Pfeiffer, Judith. We Didn't Know. (p. 1867)
Pfeiffer, Judith, illus. see Boland, Janice.
Pfeiffer, Kathleen. Spartacus Sprout, Please Watch Out! (p. 1622)
Pfeil, Susan. Professor Kiwi, Explorer of the Seven Seas: The Eye of Easter Island. (p. 1409)
Pferdehirt, Julia. Blue Jenkins: Working for Workers. (p. 203)
—Caroline Quarlls & the Underground Railroad. (p. 270)
—Freedom Train North: Stories of the Underground Railroad in Wisconsin. Butler, Jerry, illus. (p. 635)
—Wisconsin Forest Tales. (p. 1939)
Pfingsten, Ralph. From Rockport to West Park. (p. 643)
Pfister, Ashley. Cindy Makes A Difference. (p. 321)
Pfister, Marcus. Adventures of Rainbow Fish. (p. 22)
—Animal ABC. (p. 76)
—Arc-En-Ciel. (p. 95)
—Ava's Poppy. (p. 118)
—Bertie: Just Like Daddy. (p. 168)
—Bertie at Bedtime. (p. 168)
—Christmas Star. (p. 315)
—Christmas Star Book & Advent Calendar. (p. 315)
—Copycat Charlie. Pfister, Marcus, illus. (p. 366)
—Estrella de Navidad. Pfister, Marcus, illus. (p. 538)
—Friendly Monsters. Pfister, Marcus, illus. (p. 638)
—Good Night, Little Rainbow Fish. (p. 699)
—Happiness Is... (p. 744)
—Happy Birthday Bertie. (p. 744)
—Just Like Daddy. Pfister, Marcus, illus. (p. 939)
—Milo & the Magical Stones. Pfister, Marcus, illus. (p. 1144)
—Milo & the Mysterious Island. (p. 1144)
—Nilo, como mi Papa. (p. 1255)
—Penguin Pete. (p. 1337)
—Penguin Pete & Pat. (p. 1337)
—Play with Rainbow Fish. (p. 1371)
—Questions, Questions. (p. 1426)
—Rainbow Fish: Finger Puppet Book. (p. 1435)
—Rainbow Fish / Perz Arco Iris. (p. 1435)
—Rainbow Fish & the Big Blue Whale. (p. 1435)
—Rainbow Fish & the Sea Monsters' Cave. (p. 1435)
—Rainbow Fish & the Whale. (p. 1435)
—Rainbow Fish Colors. (p. 1435)
—Rainbow Fish Colors/Colores. Pfister, Marcus, illus. (p. 1435)
—Rainbow Fish Counting. (p. 1435)
—Rainbow Fish Deep Sea Adventure Sticker & Coloring Storybook. (p. 1435)
—Rainbow Fish Discovers the Deep Sea. Pfister, Marcus, illus. (p. 1435)
—Rainbow Fish Finds His Way. James, J. Alison, tr. from GER. (p. 1435)
—Rainbow Fish Opposites. (p. 1435)
—Rainbow Fish Puzzle Book. (p. 1435)
—Rainbow Fish to the Rescue! (p. 1435)
—Rainbow Fish to the Rescue Tuff Book. (p. 1435)
—Snow Puppy. (p. 1599)
—Yellow Cab. (p. 1970)
Pfister, Marcus, illus. see Siegenthaler, Kathrin & Sieegenthaler, Pfist.
Pfisterer Clark, Pem, illus. see McKown, Martha.
Pfitsch, Patricia Curtis. Riding the Flume. (p. 1471)
Pfitzenmaier, Audrey. Cheating Fate (p. 295)
Pflaum Publishing Group, creator. Welcome Children! A Child's Mass Book. (p. 1873)
Pfleegor, Gina, illus. see Guard, Anara.
Pfleegor, Gina, illus. see Tango-Hampton, Doreen.
Pfloog, Jan, illus. see Lowery, Lawrence F.
Pflueger, Lynda. Amelia Earhart: Legend of Flight. (p. 58)
—Stonewall Jackson: General of the Confederate Army. (p. 1653)
—Thomas Jefferson: Creating a Nation. (p. 1739)
Pflueger, Maura McArdle, illus. see Aryal, Aimee.
Pflug, Micki. Making the Grade: Everything Your 3rd Grader Needs to Know. (p. 1082)
Pflugfelder, Bob & Hockensmith, Steve. Nick & Tesla's High-Voltage Danger Lab: A Mystery with Electromagnets, Burglar Alarms, & Other Gadgets You Can Build Yourself. (p. 1251)
—Nick & Tesla's Secret Agent Gadget Battle. (p. 1251)
—Nick & Tesla's Special Effects Spectacular: A Mystery with Animatronics, Alien Makeup, Camera Gear, & Other Movie Magic You Can Make Yourself! (p. 1251)
—Nick & Tesla's Super-Cyborg Gadget Glove: A Mystery with a Blinking, Beeping, Voice-Recording Gadget Glove You Can Build Yourself. (p. 1251)
—Robot Army Rampage: A Mystery with Hoverbots, Bristle Bots, & Other Robots You Can Build Yourself. (p. 1480)
Pfoutz, Sally. Missing Person. (p. 1152)
Pfundstein, Valerie. Veterans: Heroes in Our Neighborhood. Chernesky, Felicia, ed. (p. 1839)
PH Inc. Staff. Parade of Life: Animals. (p. 1323)
—PH Science Ecology Earth. (p. 1349)
—PH Science Evolution. (p. 1349)
—Prentice Hall Literature (p. 1395)
Phagan, R. Jesse. Applied Mathematics: Teaching Package. (p. 93)
—Applied Mathematics. (p. 93)
Phaidon Editors, jt. auth. see Altshuler, Bruce.
Phaidon Press Editors. 20th Century Art Book. (p. 1996)
—ABC del Arte. (p. 3)
—ABC de la Fotografia. (p. 3)
—Annunciation. Bosch-Abele, Susanne et al, trs. (p. 87)
—Area. (p. 97)
—Art Book for Children. (p. 101)
—Last Supper. (p. 979)
—Silver Spoon for Children: Favorite Italian Recipes. Grant, Amanda, ed. (p. 1577)
Phaidon Press Editors, jt. auth. see Jeffrey, Ian.
Phaidon Press Editors, jt. auth. see Renshaw, Amanda.
Phaidon Press Editors, creator. House Book. (p. 803)
Phaidon Press Editors, ed. Art Book. (p. 101)
—Silver Spoon. Lowe, Jason, photos by. (p. 1577)
Phaidon Press Editors, et al. PressPlay: Contemporary Artists in Conversation. (p. 1397)
Pham, Khoi, illus. see Pak, Greg.
Pham, LeUyen. All the Things I Love about You. Pham, LeUyen, illus. (p. 46)
—Big Sister, Little Sister. Pham, LeUyen, illus. (p. 183)
—Piece of Cake. Pham, LeUyen, illus. (p. 1356)
—There's No Such Thing As Little. (p. 1731)
Pham, LeUyen, illus. see Abrams, Douglas Carlton & Tutu, Desmond.
Pham, LeUyen, illus. see Asim, Jabari.
Pham, LeUyen, illus. see Barrett, Mary Brigid.
Pham, LeUyen, illus. see Beaumont, Karen.
Pham, LeUyen, illus. see Bildner, Phil.
Pham, LeUyen, illus. see DiPucchio, Kelly.
Pham, LeUyen, illus. see Hale, Shannon & Hale, Dean.
Pham, LeUyen, illus. see Heiligman, Deborah.
Pham, LeUyen, illus. see Herman, Charlotte.
Pham, LeUyen, illus. see Hill, Kirkpatrick.
Pham, LeUyen, illus. see Lasky, Kathryn.
Pham, LeUyen, illus. see Look, Lenore.
Pham, LeUyen, illus. see Markel, Michelle.
Pham, LeUyen, illus. see McCall Smith, Alexander.
Pham, LeUyen, illus. see Moore, Julianne.
Pham, LeUyen, illus. see Pace, Anne Marie.
Pham, LeUyen, illus. see Palatini, Margie.
Pham, LeUyen, illus. see Rosenthal, Amy Krouse.
Pham, LeUyen, illus. see Singer, Marilyn.
Pham, LeUyen, illus. see Snyder, Laurel.
Pham, LeUyen, illus. see Tutu, Desmond & Abrams, Douglas Carlton.
Pham, LeUyen, illus. see Viau, Nancy.
Pham, LeUyen, illus. see Wood, Douglas.
Pham, LeUyen, illus. see Zolotow, Charlotte.
Pham, Thien. Sumo. Pham, Thien, illus. (p. 1675)
Pham, Thien, illus. see Yang, Gene Luen.
Pham, Xuan, illus. see Petersen, Pat.
Phan, Aimee. We Should Never Meet. (p. 1868)
Phan, Henry, illus. see Sarja, Jennifer.
Phan, Sandy. American Indians in Texas: Conflict & Survival. (p. 62)
—Caddo & Comanche: American Indians Tribes in Texas. (p. 250)
—Caddo y los Comanche. (p. 250)
—Cecil Rhodes: The Man Who Expanded an Empire. (p. 283)
—Imperialism: Expanding Empires. (p. 862)
—Indigenas Americanos de Texas (American Indians in Texas) (p. 872)
—Learn to Draw Ancient Times. Berry, Bob, illus. (p. 983)
—Learn to Draw Forest Animals & Wildlife: Learn to Draw 20 Different Woodland Animals, Step by Easy Step, Shape by Simple Shape! Cuddy, Robbin, illus. (p. 983)
—Learn to Draw Rainforest & Jungle Animals: Learn to Draw & Color 21 Different Exotic Creatures, Step by Easy Step, Shape by Simple Shape! Cuddy, Robbin, illus. (p. 983)
Phanton, Richard G. Frankie. Baker, David, illus. (p. 629)
Phanton, Rick. Boston & the Bean. (p. 215)
Phares, Walid. Future Jihad: Terrorist Strategies Against the West. (p. 651)
Pharr, Nancy Elizabeth. When Should I Pray? Rose, Heidi, illus. (p. 1904)
Phatak, Bhakti, illus. see Chadha, Radhika.
Pheather, Heather. Sweater Trouble. (p. 1689)
Phelan, Anne. Skydive to Hive. Rottinger, Amy, illus. (p. 1587)
Phelan, Cathy & McDonald, Danielle. I'm Glad You're My Friend. (p. 859)
Phelan, Connie. Little Pink Pig That Was Different. (p. 1033)
Phelan, Gary. Chemistry in the Kitchen: Set Of 6. (p. 297)
Phelan, Glen. Chemistry in the Kitchen: Text Pairs. (p. 297)
—Double Helix: The Quest to Uncover the Structure of DNA. (p. 473)
—Earth in Space. (p. 496)
—Earth, Sun, Moon. (p. 497)
—Extreme Weather. (p. 557)
—Forces & Motion in Sports: Set Of 6. (p. 617)
—Forces & Motion in Sports: Text Pairs. (p. 617)
—Forces & Motion on Earth: Set Of 6. (p. 617)
—Forces & Motion on Earth: Text Pairs. (p. 617)
—Introduction to Energy. (p. 882)
—Invisible Force: The Quest to Define the Laws of Motion. (p. 885)
—Killing Germs, Saving Lives: The Quest for the First Vaccines. (p. 956)
—Newton's Laws. (p. 1249)
—Rocks & Minerals. (p. 1483)
—What Is Matter? (p. 1889)
Phelan, Glen & National Geographic Learning Staff. Stars. (p. 1643)
Phelan, Glen, et al. Uncovering Earth's History. (p. 1812)
Phelan, J. W. Philosophy: Themes & Thinkers. (p. 1351)
Phelan, James. Chasers. (p. 294)
—Chasers (Alone #1) (p. 294)
—Quarantine. (p. 1422)
—Survivor. (p. 1687)
Phelan, Matt. Around the World. Phelan, Matt, illus. (p. 100)
—Bluffton. Phelan, Matt, illus. (p. 204)
—Druthers. Phelan, Matt, illus. (p. 487)
—Storm in the Barn. (p. 1656)
—Storm in the Barn. Phelan, Matt, illus. (p. 1656)
Phelan, Matt, illus. see Birdsall, Jeanne.
Phelan, Matt, illus. see Birney, Betty G.
Phelan, Matt, illus. see Knudsen, Michelle.
Phelan, Matt, illus. see Manzano, Sonia.
Phelan, Matt, illus. see Muten, Burleigh.
Phelan, Matt, illus. see Park, Linda Sue.
Phelan, Matt, illus. see Patron, Susan.
Phelan, Matt, illus. see Potter, Ellen & Mazer, Anne.
Phelan, Matt, illus. see Robbins, Jacqui.
Phelan, Matt, illus. see Rockwell, Anne F.
Phelan, Matt, illus. see Schertle, Alice.
Phelan, Matt, illus. see Spinelli, Eileen.
Phelan, Matt, illus. see Stott, Ann.
Phelan, Michele-lee, illus. see Mellado, Carisa.
Phelan, Nicky, illus. see Fitzmaurice, Gabriel & Macdonald, Stella.
Phelan, Nicky, illus. see Fitzmaurice, Gabriel.
Phelan, Nicky, illus. see O'Hely, Eileen.
Phelan, Richard. Colleen Colgan Chronicles, Book I: Flowers from Cannibals. (p. 340)
Phelan, Thomas W. & Lewis, Tracy M. 1-2-3 Magia para Niños: Ayudando a Sus Hijos a Entender las Nuevas Reglas. (p. 1990)
Phelan, Thomas W. & Schonour, Sarah Jane. 1-2-3 Magic for Teachers: Effective Classroom Discipline Pre-K Through Grade 8. Farrell, Dan, illus. (p. 1990)
Phelan, Tom. Lies the Mushroom Pickers Told: A Novel. (p. 1007)
Phelps, Bonnie. Life Cycle of a Sunflower. (p. 1009)
—Map Facts: North America. (p. 1089)
Phelps, Cameron, jt. auth. see Phelps, Donna.
Phelps, Dawn. Monstrous Problem. (p. 1169)
Phelps, Donna & Phelps, Cameron. Cameron & the Dinosaur Heroes. (p. 256)
Phelps, Elizabeth Stuart. Gypsy Breynton. (p. 734)
—Jack the Fisherman. Reed, C. W., illus. (p. 903)
Phelps, Elizabeth Stuart & Robert Williams Wood. Gypsy's Cousin Joy. (p. 734)
Phelps, Janice, ed. see Harris, Tumeka.
Phelps, Karen. Grass Is Always Greener & Let Sleeping Dogs Lie: Two Original Fables. (p. 711)
Phelps, Linda. Have U Seen Me? (p. 754)
Phelps, Michael & Abrahamson, Alan. How to Train with a T. Rex & Win 8 Gold Medals. Jenkins, Ward, illus. (p. 822)
Phelps, Netta Sheldon. Valiant Seven. Wilson, Helen Hughes, illus. (p. 1830)
Phelps, Thomas. Limericks for Little Ones: And Other Poems. (p. 1018)
Phelps Williams, Janice. Still Her Spirit Sings: One Dog's Love, Lessons, Life & Legacy. (p. 1650)
Phethean, Ellen. Wall. (p. 1854)
Phidal Publishing Staff, jt. contrib. by see Walt Disney Company Staff.
Phidal Publishing Staff, ed. Colors. (p. 344)
—Construction Crew (p. 359)
—Girls World: My Best Friends. (p. 681)
—Numbers. (p. 1271)
—Rescue Squad. (p. 1462)
—Senses. (p. 1551)
—Shapes. (p. 1560)
—Totally Girls: Super Sticker Book. (p. 1771)
Phifer, jt. auth. see Phifer, Larry.
Phifer, Larry & Phifer. World on a String. (p. 1958)
Phil Brannan, illus. see Sally Spencer.
Philadelphia Writers Conference Staff. Philadelphia Writer's Conference 2002 Literary Anthology. (p. 1350)
—Pwc 2003. (p. 1421)
Philbeck, Martha. Isaha & the Donkey: Visit to a Farm Rearing Mini Donkeys. (p. 891)
—White Tailed Deer: An Introductory Booklet for Children. (p. 1913)
Philbin, Joanna. Daughters. (p. 409)
—Daughters Break the Rules. (p. 410)
—Daughters Join the Party. (p. 410)
—Daughters Take the Stage. (p. 410)
—Rules of Summer. (p. 1495)
—Since Last Summer. (p. 1578)
Philbrick, Katie, illus. see Toutz-Hager, Tanya.
Philbrick, Nathaniel. Mayflower & the Pilgrims' New World. (p. 1113)
—Revenge of the Whale: The True Story of the Whaleship Essex. (p. 1466)
Philbrick, Rodman. Freak the Mighty. (p. 631)
—Last Book in the Universe. (p. 977)
—Mostly True Adventures of Homer P. Figg. (p. 1177)
—Young Man & the Sea. (p. 1979)
—Zane & the Hurricane: A Story of Katrina. (p. 1984)
Philbrick, Rodman & Harnett, Lynn. Dernier Cauchemar: The Final Nightmare. Bk. 3 (p. 427)
—Ensorcellement: The Haunting. Bk. 1 (p. 531)
—Terreur: The Horror. Bk. 2 (p. 1721)
Philbrick, Rodman & Philbrick, W. R. Young Man & the Sea. (p. 1979)
Philbrick, W. R., jt. auth. see Philbrick, Rodman.
Philip Dadd, illus. see Wodehouse, P. G.
Philip, Hilda, jt. auth. see Conkling, Neil.
Philip, Neil. Mythology. (p. 1227)
Philip, Neil & Naohman. Pirate Princess & Other Fairy Tales. Weber, Mark M., illus. (p. 1363)
Philip, Neil, ed. American Fairy Tales: From Rip Van Winkle to the Rootabaga Stories. McCurdy, Michael, illus. (p. 60)
Philip, Steele, jt. auth. see Steele, Philip.
Philipp, Cathy. On the Trail Again: Malibu to Santa Barbara Philipp, Cathy et al, photos by. (p. 1291)
Philipp, Lillie H. Piano Technique: Tone, Touch, Phrasing & Dynamics. (p. 1354)
Philippe Chabot, Jean & Sorbier, Frédéric. Impresionismo. (p. 862)
Philippe, Dupasquier, illus. see Gray, Nigel.
Philippo, Sophie. Meet the Woolly Mammoth. Dutertre, Charles, illus. (p. 1123)
Philippot, Raymond & Graves, Michael F. Fostering Comprehension in English Classes: Beyond the Basics. (p. 624)
Philippou, Stefanie. Sammy Learns to Say I Am Sorry. (p. 1508)
Philips, A. If You Believe in Mermaids Don't Tell. (p. 854)
Philips, Chad, photos by see Marzollo, Jean.
Philips, Fleur. Crumble. (p. 386)
Philips, Karen, ed. My [Not-So] Perfect Life: A Fill-in-the-Blanks Journal. (p. 1216)
Philips, Lyn D. Curiosity. Gadeselli, Natalie, illus. (p. 392)
Philips, Mike, illus. see MacPhail, Catherine.
Philips, Tracy A. Did Someone You Love Die? (p. 437)
Philipson, Sandra. Max's Rules. Campbell, Jenny, illus. (p. 1112)
Philipson, Sandra J. Forever Home. Campbell, Jenny, illus. (p. 619)
—Ollie's Monsters & Other Stories. Campbell, Jenny, illus. (p. 1287)
Phillipe, Monica. Danielle's Dance Class: Foundations for Multiplication. (p. 405)
Phillippi, Faith, illus. see Beatty, Connie.
Phillipps, J. C. Monkey Ono. (p. 1165)
—Simples Love a Picnic. (p. 1578)
—Wink: The Ninja Who Wanted to Nap. (p. 1936)
—Wink: The Ninja Who Wanted to Be Noticed. (p. 1936)
Phillips. Bubbie's Baby. (p. 233)
Phillips, A. Color My Soul. (p. 343)
Phillips, Alan, illus. see Cushing, Mims.
Phillips, Alonzo. Follow the Course! an Action Book. (p. 612)
Phillips, Andrea, illus. see Phillips, Elizabeth.
Phillips, Anne K., ed. see Alcott, Louisa May.
Phillips, Azelin. Quicksilver. (p. 1427)
Phillips, Barry. Cave Express. (p. 282)
Phillips, Beth Ann. Crystal Kingdom (p. 387)
Phillips, Beth, ed. Boyds Tracker Resin: Value Guide. (p. 220)
Phillips, Betty Lou. Emily Goes Wild. Watts, Sharon, illus. (p. 519)
Phillips, Betty Lou & Herndon, Roblyn. Night Before Christmas in New York Dickert, Sheryl, illus. (p. 1253)
—Night Before Christmas in Texas Dickert, Sheryl, illus. (p. 1253)
Phillips, Bob. All-Time Awesome Collection of Good Clean Jokes for Kids. (p. 46)
—Awesome Knock-Knock Jokes for Kids. (p. 121)
—Best Ever Knock-Knock Jokes for Kids. (p. 169)
—Flat-Out Awesome Knock-Knock Jokes for Kids. (p. 603)
—Headache Relief: All-Natural, Drugfree Solutions in Less than 60 Seconds. (p. 756)
—Slam Dunk Jokes for Kids. (p. 1587)
—Super Duper Knock-Knock Jokes for Kids. (p. 1679)
Phillips, Bob & Hawkins, Jonny. Tackle Box of Fishing Funnies. (p. 1694)
Phillips, Bob & Russo, Steve. Fabulous & Funny Clean Jokes for Kids. (p. 559)
Phillips, Calvin. God's Works: Jake's Shoes. (p. 692)
Phillips, Carey R. & Johannen, Kevin C. Physiology of the Eye. Doggett, W. Kirk, illus. (p. 1353)
Phillips, Carlene, jt. auth. see Lotz, Nancy.
Phillips, Carleton J. & Jones, Clyde. Going Afield: Lifetime Experiences in Exploration, Science, & the Biology of Mammals. (p. 692)
Phillips, Carly. Heartbreaker. (p. 760)
—Playboy. (p. 1372)

Phillips, Chad, illus. see Marzollo, Jean.
Phillips, Chad, photos by see Marzollo, Jean.
Phillips, Charles. Japan. (p. 909)
—Kings & Queens of Britain's Modern Age: From Hanover to Windsor. (p. 960)
Phillips, Charles, jt. auth. see U. S. National Geographic Society Staff.
Phillips, Charles & Axelrod, Alan. Encyclopedia of Historical Treaties & Alliances (p. 525)
—Encyclopedia of Wars (p. 525)
Phillips, Clifton. Ten Spunky Monkeys. Jung, Shirley, illus. (p. 1719)
—Waterworld Wonderways. (p. 1864)
Phillips, Clifton C. Rabbits Rule at Night School. (p. 1430)
—We Are Children of Eden. (p. 1865)
Phillips, Craig, illus. see Avasthi, Swati.
Phillips, Craig, illus. see Holub, Joan & Williams, Suzanne.
Phillips, Craig, illus. see Hurley, Tonya.
Phillips, Craig, illus. see Mason, Jane B. & Hines-Stephens, Sarah.
Phillips, Craig, illus. see Seven, John.
Phillips, Craig, illus. see Strasser, Todd.
Phillips, Craig, illus. see West, Tracey.
Phillips, Craig, illus. see Westerfeld, Scott.
Phillips, Craig, jt. auth. see Seven, John.
Phillips, Cynthia. Way to Go! Emanuel, Effie Ann, illus. (p. 1864)
Phillips, Cynthia & Priwer, Shana. Ancient Monuments. (p. 70)
—Bridges & Spans (p. 227)
—Bridges & Spans. (p. 227)
—Dams & Waterways. (p. 401)
—Modern Wonders. (p. 1159)
—Skyscrapers & High Rises. (p. 1587)
Phillips, Dave. Americana Mazes. (p. 64)
—Ancient Treasure Mazes. (p. 71)
—Big Book of Adventure Mazes. (p. 178)
—Haunted Pirates Mazes. (p. 753)
—Set Puzzles: Find Sets, Group Them, Fill the Grid. (p. 1554)
Phillips, Dave, illus. see Carlson, Caroline.
Phillips, Dave, illus. see Epstein, Adam Jay & Jacobson, Andrew.
Phillips, Dawn, illus. see Kowalski, Bernard.
Phillips, Deborah. Parable of the Princesses. (p. 1323)
Phillips, Deborah, illus. see Brady, Carolyn.
Phillips, Dee. Amphibians. (p. 65)
—Arctic Fox. (p. 96)
—Armadillo's Burrow. (p. 99)
—Atlas of My World. (p. 112)
—Baby's Day. (p. 129)
—Badger's Burrow. (p. 132)
—Big Zoo. (p. 184)
—Blast (p. 198)
—Bugs & Spiders. (p. 237)
—Burrowing Owl's Hideaway. (p. 244)
—Chipmunk's Hole. (p. 308)
—Collared Lemming. (p. 339)
—Colors. (p. 344)
—Dare (p. 406)
—Desert Tortoise's Burrow. (p. 429)
—Dream of America (p. 483)
—Dream of America: The Story of an Immigrant. (p. 483)
—Dumped (p. 489)
—Eject (p. 507)
—Fight (p. 585)
—Find It at the Beach. (p. 587)
—Find It in a Rain Forest. (p. 587)
—Find It in the Desert. (p. 587)
—Find It in the Park. (p. 587)
—Find It on a Coral Reef. (p. 587)
—Find It on the Farm. (p. 587)
—First Addition. (p. 592)
—First Words. (p. 597)
—Flying Lemur. (p. 610)
—Fox's Den. (p. 626)
—Friends? (p. 638)
—Gila Monster's Burrow. (p. 676)
—Gladiator. (p. 682)
—Goal (p. 687)
—Goodbye (p. 700)
—Green Tree Python. (p. 722)
—Grind (p. 724)
—Groundhog's Burrow. (p. 725)
—Harp Seal. (p. 749)
—Holocaust. (p. 789)
—I Want to Know about Dinosaurs. (p. 848)
—Joyride (p. 930)
—Kangaroo Rat's Burrow. (p. 942)
—Koala. (p. 966)
—Mammals. (p. 1085)
—Meerkat's Burrow. (p. 1120)
—Mirror (p. 1149)
—Numbers. (p. 1271)
—Over the Top. (p. 1314)
—Pirate (p. 1362)
—Pirate: The Story of a Buccaneer. (p. 1362)
—Polar Bear. (p. 1378)
—Prairie Dog's Hideaway. (p. 1392)
—Rachel Carson: Environmental Pioneer. (p. 1431)
—Reindeer. (p. 1457)
—Reptiles. (p. 1461)
—Reptiles & Amphibians. (p. 1461)
—Resistance Fighter (p. 1463)
—Right Now! Sample Set (1 ea of 12 titles) (p. 1472)
—Runaway. (p. 1496)
—Samurai (p. 1509)
—Samurai: The Story of a Warrior. (p. 1509)
—Scout (p. 1532)
—Snowshoe Hare. (p. 1601)
—Spider Monkey. (p. 1626)
—Spotted Owl. (p. 1634)
—Tail Gunner. (p. 1695)
—Titanic. (p. 1757)
—Tree Frog. (p. 1783)
—Tree Kangaroo. (p. 1783)
—Vietnam (p. 1841)
—Vietnam: The Story of a Marine. (p. 1841)
—Viking (p. 1842)
—Viking: The Story of a Raider. (p. 1842)
—What Can I Be? (p. 1880)
—Who Can I Be? (p. 1914)
—Wombat's Burrow. (p. 1945)
—Woodpecker. (p. 1949)
—Yesterday's Voices Sample Set (1 ea of 6 titles) (p. 1971)
Phillips, Dee, jt. auth. see Gifford, Clive.
Phillips, Dee & Ticktock Media, Ltd. Staff. What Do Cats Do? (p. 1882)
—What Do Kangaroos Do? (p. 1882)
—What Do Monkeys Do? (p. 1882)
—What Do Rabbits Do? (p. 1882)
Phillips, Dixie. Angel Eyes. Sponaugle, Kim, illus. (p. 73)
—Baby Jesus Is Missing. Snider, K. C., illus. (p. 126)
—One Noble Journey. Sponaugle, Kim, illus. (p. 1296)
—Whistling Dixie. Caponigro, Laureen, illus. (p. 1912)
Phillips, Dixie & Phillips, Sharon. Once upon an Empty Tomb. (p. 1293)
Phillips, Dixie & Sharon, et al. Bethlehem's King Size Bed. (p. 171)
—Camiles Journey Master Playbook with Musical Scores. (p. 256)
Phillips, Dixie & Snider, K. C. Stilts the Stork. (p. 1651)
Phillips, Dorian. Rachel Carson: Environmental Pioneer. (p. 1431)
Phillips, Douglas, jt. auth. see Gritzner, Charles F.
Phillips, Douglas A. America's Role in a Changing World. (p. 64)
—Bangladesh. (p. 136)
—Finland. (p. 589)
—Human Rights. (p. 826)
—Indonesia. (p. 872)
—Nigeria. (p. 1252)
—Portugal. (p. 1387)
—Southeast Asia. (p. 1617)
—Syria. (p. 1693)
—Thailand. (p. 1724)
—Vietnam. Gritzner, Charles F., ed. (p. 1841)
Phillips, Douglas A., jt. auth. see Gritzner, Charles F.
Phillips, Elizabeth. Blueberry Princess. Phillips, Elizabeth & Phillips, Andrea, illus. (p. 204)
Phillips, Ellen Blue, jt. auth. see Ruffin, Frances.
Phillips, Gary. Midnight Mover. (p. 1139)
Phillips, Gary, illus. see Osilaja, Peter Deji.
Phillips, Gary R., illus. see Blessing, Charlotte.
Phillips, Gary R., illus. see Kramer, Jennifer Evans.
Phillips, Georgina. Ouch! Extreme Feats of Human Endurance (p. 1307)
Phillips, Gin. Hidden Summer. (p. 776)
—Little Bit of Spectacular. (p. 1024)
Phillips, Gina & Cassettari, Noeline. Mighty Tugboats. (p. 1140)
Phillips, Gina & Martin, Stuart. Ants & Caterpillars. (p. 90)
—Bees & Butterflies. (p. 158)
Phillips, Glenn O., jt. auth. see Chapelle, Suzanne Ellery Greene.
Phillips, Grant R. Jay Walker & the Case of the Missing Action Figure. (p. 910)
Phillips, H. Plants of the Lewis & Clark Expedition (p. 1370)
Phillips, H. Edwards. On a Jet Ski. (p. 1288)
Phillips, Hamilton. Inside a Sprint Car. (p. 876)
—Inside a Stock Car. (p. 876)
Phillips, Heather. Habitats. Tom, Darcy et al, eds. (p. 734)
Phillips, Helen. Here Where the Sunbeams Are Green. (p. 771)
Phillips, Hope Ann. Buddy's Play Date Day... (p. 235)
—Hoover's Day Out. (p. 796)
Phillips, Hope Ann, illus. see Taylor, Myonna.
Phillips, Ian, illus. see McGillian, Jamie Kyle.
Phillips, J. D. Dreaming While You Sleep. (p. 484)
Phillips, Jade M. Mer. (p. 1127)
Phillips, Jan. Just for Today. Shapiro, Alison Bonds, illus. (p. 938)
Phillips, Jane B., illus. see Haas, Carolyn B.
Phillips, Jane E. & Ketelsen, David P. Schizophrenia. (p. 1521)
Phillips, Jean. Meaning of Christmas: A Children's Story in Picture & Verse. (p. 1117)
Phillips, Jennifer. Adorable Accessories: Paper Creations to Wear (p. 13)
—Girls Research! Amazing Tales of Female Scientists (p. 680)
—Snappy Style: Paper Decoration Creations (p. 1597)
—Tucker's Strength. (p. 1796)
Phillips, Jennifer, jt. auth. see Tougas, Shelley.
Phillips, Jillian. What to Doodle? At the Aquarium. (p. 1894)
—What to Doodle? - Jr. Animals! (p. 1894)
—World Around Us! Hearing. (p. 1954)
—World Around Us! Seeing. (p. 1954)
Phillips, Jillian, illus. see Bockol, Leslie & Ikids Staff.
Phillips, Jillian, illus. see Ikids Staff.
Phillips, Jillian & Kurtz, John. Our Five Senses Coloring Book. (p. 1308)
Phillips, JoAnn, jt. auth. see Oaks, Kristen M.
Phillips, Joanne M. Angelique & the Green Planet. (p. 74)
Phillips, John. Leonardo Da Vinci: The Genius Who Defined the Renaissance. (p. 992)
—World History Biographies: Leonardo Da Vinci: The Genius Who Defined the Renaissance. (p. 1955)
Phillips, Joy. Jesus Saved Me. (p. 916)
Phillips, Karen. Doodle Journal: My Life in Scribbles. Gravel, Elise, illus. (p. 469)
—Fashionably Me: A Journal That's Just My Style. Higgins, Anne Keenan, illus. (p. 576)
—Lettering in Crazy, Cool, Quirky Style. (p. 1002)
—Shrink Art Jewelry. (p. 1571)
—Truth about My Name: And What It Reveals about Me! (p. 1794)
—Write in White Doodle Journal: My Brilliant Scribbles. (p. 1963)
Phillips, Karen, jt. auth. see Chorba, April.
Phillips, Karen, jt. auth. see Hutnick, Theresa.
Phillips, Karen & Klutz Editors. Friendship Pixies: Charmed Little Dolls to Make & Share. (p. 639)
—My Fabulous Look Book: Fashion Drawing Made Easy. (p. 1202)
—Sticker Design Studio: Create Your Own Custom Stickers. (p. 1650)
—Straw Shooter Jets: Make Your Own Mini Air Force. (p. 1666)
Phillips, Karen, ed. It's All about Me! Personality Quizzes for You & Your Friends. (p. 896)
—My All-Time Top 5: Make the Lists of Your Life. (p. 1195)
—What about You? (p. 1879)
Phillips, Kathy. Buddy Bear. (p. 234)
—Buddy Bear Goes to Kennecott Mine. (p. 234)
Phillips, Kelly. Macs the Wonder Dog. (p. 1068)
Phillips, Kent. Red Eyed Black Dragon. (p. 1453)
Phillips, Kevin. William McKinley. Schlesinger, Arthur M., Jr., ed. (p. 1933)
Phillips, Larissa. Cochise: Apache Chief. (p. 337)
—Cochise: Jefe apache (Cochise: Apache Chief) (p. 337)
—Cochise: Jefe apache / Cochise: Apache Chief. (p. 337)
—Cochise: Jefe Apache. de la Vega, Eida, tr. from ENG. (p. 337)
—Historical Atlas of Iraq. (p. 782)
—Wild Bill Hickok: Legend of the Wild West. (p. 1929)
—Wild Bill Hickok: Leyenda del oeste Americano. (p. 1929)
—Wild Bill Hickok: Legend of the American Wild West. (p. 1929)
—Wild Bill Hickok: Legend of the American Wild West / Leyenda del oeste Americano. (p. 1929)
—Wild Bill Hickok: Leyenda del oeste americano (Wild Bill Hickok: Legend of the American Wild West) (p. 1929)
—Women Civil War Spies of the Confederacy. (p. 1945)
Phillips, Laverne, illus. see Mandelkorn, Carole.
Phillips, Leigh Hope. Birthday Wishes. Fountain, John, illus. (p. 193)
Phillips, Liam & Plumm, Gabi. Mumble & Jumble & the Great Corpsicle Conundrum. (p. 1190)
Phillips, Linda. My Bus Adventure: My Bus Ride. (p. 1199)
Phillips, Linda T., illus. see Bjornsen, Holly.
Phillips, Linda Vigen. Crazy. (p. 377)
Phillips, Lori. Carolinian Alphabet. (p. 271)
—Chamorro Alphabet. (p. 289)
—Chuukese Alphabet. (p. 318)
—English Alphabet. (p. 529)
—Hawaiian Alphabet. (p. 755)
—Kosraean Alphabet. (p. 967)
—Marshallese Alphabet. (p. 1096)
—Palauan Alphabet. (p. 1319)
—Pohnpeian Alphabet. (p. 1377)
—Samoan Alphabet. (p. 1508)
—Satawalese Alphabet. (p. 1515)
—Yapese Alphabet. (p. 1968)
Phillips, Lorri. Ragamuffin Friends. (p. 1433)
Phillips, Lorrie, jt. auth. see Landen, Cynthia.
Phillips, Louis. Late Night in the Rain Forest. Strozier, M. Stefan & Torke, Kyle, eds. (p. 979)
Phillips, Louise, illus. see MacLeod, Elizabeth.
Phillips, Lyda. Mr Touchdown. (p. 1186)
Phillips, Margaret Coull. West Virginia. (p. 1876)
Phillips, Marie. Memoirs of a Feline Heroine. (p. 1125)
Phillips, Marilyn, photos by see Ridley, Sharon, illus.
Phillips, Marilyn & Rebekah. Princess. (p. 1402)
Phillips, Mark. Pinocchio Intermediate Vocabulary Builder. (p. 1361)
—Tarzan & Jane's Guide to Grammar. (p. 1706)
Phillips, Mary. Children'S Sermons with Humor. (p. 304)
Phillips, Matt, illus. see Martin, Justin McCory.
Phillips, Matt, illus. see Marx, David F.
Phillips, Matt, illus. see Meister, Cari.
Phillips, Matthew. Ingo Flamingo (p. 874)
Phillips Mba, Nancy. Zela Wela Kid: Build a Bank. (p. 1986)
Phillips, Merrill. Tell Me Again Grampa. (p. 1716)
Phillips, Michael. Sword, the Garden, & the King. (p. 1692)
Phillips, Mike, illus. see Bailey, Gerry & Law, Felicia.
Phillips, Mike, illus. see Grindley, Sally.
Phillips, Mike, illus. see Kessler, Liz.
Phillips, Mike, illus. see Larimore, Walt, et al.
Phillips, Mike, illus. see Mahy, Margaret.
Phillips, Mike, illus. see Murphy, Glenn.
Phillips, Mike, illus. see Payne, Jan.
Phillips, Mike, illus. see Robinson, Tony.
Phillips, Mike, jt. auth. see Coleman, Michael.
Phillips, Mike, jt. auth. see Morgan, Michaela.
Phillips, Niki. Far Side of the Rainbow. (p. 572)
Phillips, Noell G. Ants That Were & Wish They Are (p. 90)
Phillips, Paul, jt. auth. see Donahue, Laurie.
Phillips, Phil. Miracle Parenting-Participant's Study Guide. (p. 1148)
Phillips, Quency, jt. auth. see Johnson, Temeka.
Phillips, Rachael, illus. see Ganeri, Anita.
Phillips, Rachelle. Dinkey the Donkey. Randolph, Carolyn, illus. (p. 440)
Phillips, Raelene. Towpath to Truth: Finding Family on the Miami & Erie Canal. (p. 1774)
Phillips, Rebecca. Faking Perfect. (p. 565)
Phillips, Robin. Who in the World Was the Acrobatic Empress? The Story of Theodora. West, Jeff, illus. (p. 1915)
Phillips, Robin & Weiss, Jim. Who in the World Was the Acrobatic Empress? The Story of Theodora. (p. 1915)
Phillips, Ruby Ann. Dream Birthday Isik, Semur, illus. (p. 483)
—Fortune Cookie Fiasco. Isik, Semur, illus. (p. 623)
—Great & Powerful Isik, Semur, illus. (p. 713)
—Krystal Ball. (p. 968)
—Pet Psychic. Isik, Semur, illus. (p. 1345)
Phillips, Ruby Ann, jt. auth. see Sazaklis, John.
Phillips, S. & Parker, H. First 100 Box of Books Words,Animals,Things That Go. (p. 592)
Phillips, Samantha. Crow: Part 1 (p. 385)
Phillips, Samantha, jt. auth. see Gray, Heather M.
Phillips, Sara & Running Press Staff. Animals. (p. 81)
Phillips, Sarah. First 100 Words. (p. 592)
—Flip, Flap, Match Noisy Farm. (p. 604)
—Lift & Learn ABC. Snaith, Andy, photos by. (p. 1014)
—Magnet Matching ABC: Match the Magnets & Learn Your Alphabet. (p. 1075)
—My Picture Encyclopedia. Metcalf, Paula, illus. (p. 1217)
—Play It! Recorder. (p. 1371)
—Touch & Learn: ABC. (p. 1772)
—Touch & Learn 123. (p. 1772)
—Touch & Learn ABC. (p. 1772)
—Wipe Clean Giant. (p. 1939)
Phillips, Sarah, jt. auth. see Bicknell, Joanna.
Phillips, Sarah & Tattam, Mark. Numbers. (p. 1271)
—Shapes. (p. 1560)
Phillips, Sarah & Wallace, Bruce. Flip Flaps Counting. (p. 604)
—Flip Flaps Opposites. (p. 604)
Phillips, Sean, illus. see Jones, Bruce.
Phillips, Shannon & Garland, Nick. Celebrating a Century: The Birth & Growth of First Baptist Church Broken Arrow. Schilling, Sarah Phillips, ed. (p. 284)
Phillips, Sharon, jt. auth. see Phillips, Dixie.
Phillips, Sherre Florence. Teen Brain. (p. 1713)
Phillips, Shirley. Best Gift. (p. 170)
Phillips, Suzanne. Burn. (p. 243)
Phillips, Terrie. Ski Trip. (p. 1584)
Phillips, Tikera M. Thanksgiving Turkey. (p. 1726)
Phillips, Tracy A. Losing Someone You Love: Dealing with Death & Dying. (p. 1054)
—Weapons of Mass Destruction: The Threat of Chemical, Biological, & Nuclear Weapons. (p. 1869)
Phillips, Valerie A. Wish upon a Star. (p. 1940)
Phillips, Victoria. Why Is There a Raisin in My Meatloaf? (p. 1925)
Phillips, Vivian A. Biblical Alphabets Book. (p. 176)
—Education: Show & Tell. (p. 505)
—Intrique Math. (p. 882)
—My Dog & His Bone. (p. 1202)
—Show & Tell: Education. (p. 1570)
—Swan. (p. 1688)
Phillips, Wanda C. Easy Grammar Grade 3 Student Test Booklet. (p. 500)
—Easy Grammar Grade 3 Student Workbook. (p. 500)
—Easy Grammar Grade 4 Student Test Booklet. (p. 500)
—Easy Grammar Grade 5 Student Test Booklet. (p. 500)
—Easy Grammar Grade 5 Student Workbook. (p. 500)
—Easy Grammar Grade 6 Student Test Booklet. (p. 500)
—Easy Grammar Grade 6 Student Workbook. (p. 500)
—Easy Grammar Plus Student Test Booklet. (p. 500)
—Easy Grammar Plus Student Workbook. (p. 500)
—Easy Grammar Plus teacher Edition. (p. 500)
Phillips, Wendy. Fishtailing (p. 599)
Phillips, Wes. Vital Skills: How to Study the Bible. (p. 1846)
—Vital Truth Church Why Do I Need Other People. (p. 1846)
Phillips, Zelmer, illus. see Burroughs, William S.
Phillips-Duke, Barbara Jean, illus. see Scholastic, Inc. Staff & Barnes, Derrick D.
Phillips-Green, Jeanette, jt. auth. see Henry, Laura.
Phillips-Hershey, Elizabeth, jt. auth. see Weierbach, Jane.
Phillipson, Andy, jt. illus. see Tucker, Marianne.
Phillipson, Fiona. Baby Animals. (p. 124)
—Fairies. (p. 562)
—Fairy Princesses: Over 1000 Reusable Stickers! (p. 563)
Phillipson, Fiona, jt. auth. see Munro, Fiona.
Phillips-Poovey, Lisa. Lucy Wants to Go to School. (p. 1063)
Phillpotts, Eden. Flint Heart; a Fairy Story. (p. 604)
Philpot, Chelsey. Even in Paradise. (p. 541)
Philpot, Graham. Emperor & the Nightingale. (p. 520)
—Fish That Talked. (p. 598)
—Hansel & Gretel. (p. 743)
Philpot, Graham, illus. see Rossendale, Helen.
Philpot, Graham, jt. auth. see Doyle, Malachy.
Philpot, Graham, jt. auth. see Philpot, Lorna.
Philpot, Heather, illus. see Boase, Wendy.
Philpot, Lorna & Philpot, Graham. Find Anthony Ant. (p. 587)
Philpott, Keith, illus. see Harvey, Tom, et al.
Phineas and Ferb. Phineas & Ferb Batter Up! (p. 1351)
Phinn, Gervase. Our Cat Cuddles. Higham, Amanda, illus. (p. 1308)
—Royston Knapper: Return of the Rogue. Fisher, Chris, illus. (p. 1492)
—What I Like! Poems for the Very Young. Eccles, Jane, illus. (p. 1886)
—Who Am I? Phinn, Gervase, illus. (p. 1914)
Phinney, Margaret Y. Reading with the Troubled Reader. (p. 1447)
Phinney, Patty McCoy. Makayla's Rainbow. (p. 1078)
Phipps, Alisha. Growing up with Allie: The Dance. (p. 727)
Phipps, Amy, jt. auth. see Culley, Claire.
Phipps, Bebe, illus. see Smith, Karen Cecil.
Phipps, Ben. I'm a Winner You're a Winner: Remembering How Great You Are. (p. 858)
Phipps, Catherine Wood, illus. see Desch, Sandra Lee.
Phipps, Dorothy. Chocolate Milk & White Milk. (p. 309)
Phipps, Michael. Hi, My Name Is Book. (p. 775)
Phipps, Michael, illus. see Dashner, James.
Phipps, Shane. Carter Journals: Time Travels in Early U.S. History. (p. 272)
Phleger, Marjorie. Pilot Down, Presumed Dead. (p. 1359)
Phoenix Books Staff. Baby's First Stories & Songs: Read, Sing, & Play. (p. 129)
—Disney(r) PIXAR Cars! Can Drive! (p. 452)
—Sofia the First Royal Picnic - Little Sound Book. (p. 1605)
—Thomas' Piano Book. (p. 1739)
Phoenix Books Staff, illus. see Publications International Ltd. Staff, ed.
Phoenix International Staff. Baby Einstein: Little Piano Book. (p. 126)
—Princess Sofia. (p. 1405)
—Sesame at the Zoo Look & Find. (p. 1553)
—Sesame Street(r) Big Fire Truck. (p. 1553)
—Thomas & Friends(r) - Thomas' Piano Book. (p. 1738)
Phoenix Learning Resources Staff, ed. Exploring Maps Volume 1. (p. 552)
—Guidebook to Better English: Level 1 Test Answer Key. (p. 730)
—Guidebook to Better English. (p. 730)
Phoenix, Three. Daughter of the Sun. (p. 409)

Phoenix, Woodrow & Price, Robin. Count Mikula. (p. 369)
Phong, Ann, illus. see Tran, Truong.
Phonics Plus Staff. Phonics Plus. (p. 1352)
PhotoDisc Staff, photos by see NHR Staff, ed.
Photodisc-Getty Staff, Images, photos by see McKay, Sindy.
Phu, Esther. Summer Troubles (p. 1675)
Phunny, U. R. Animal Jokes. (p. 78)
—Dinosaur Jokes. (p. 442)
—More Animal Jokes. (p. 1174)
Phyllarry (Rittmueller), Kathryn. Beauregart the Bear. (p. 153)
Phyllis Stella Jadosh. Well Then, You Must Be Lucky. (p. 1874)
Phypers, Lisa Marie. My Favorite Little Boy. (p. 1203)
—My Favorite Little Girl. (p. 1203)
Pi Andreu, Andrés. Danny Said Boobie. Martinez, Enrique, illus. (p. 406)
Pi Kids, creator. Mother Goose. (p. 1177)
Piaggio Foundation Staff, jt. auth. see Buford, Bill.
Pianina, Vincent, jt. auth. see Cali, Davide.
Piano, Doreen. Violence. (p. 1843)
Piano, Liwayway. Closest Star. (p. 334)
Piano, Maureen. My Adventure to the Wonders of the World. (p. 1195)
—My Adventure with Tidepools. (p. 1195)
—When Flamingos Fly: Discovering the Wonders of the World. (p. 1902)
Piano, Renzo. On Tour with Renzo Piano. (p. 1292)
Plantedosi, John J. Cat That Purred. Maglio-Macullar, Andrea, illus. (p. 278)
—Gospel for Children. Cioffi, Ben, illus. (p. 703)
Piatt, Robert, illus. see Comley, Kathlyn.
Piatti, Celestino. Celestino Piatti's Animal ABC. (p. 286)
—Happy Owls. (p. 746)
Piatti, Federico, illus. see Dahl, Michael.
Piazza, Carmelo & Buckley, James. Crazy for Science with Carmelo the Science Fellow. (p. 377)
Piazza, Gail, illus. see Robb, Diane Burton.
Piazzola, Amy & Fischer, Julie. Ten, Nineteen, & In-Between. (p. 1719)
Pica, Steve, illus. see Doering, Jennie Spray.
Picado, Gail. Magical Bandages. (p. 1074)
Picano, Felice. Looking Glass Lives. (p. 1051)
—Lure. (p. 1066)
Picano, Jaime Gianna. Mood Ring Adventure. (p. 1171)
Picanyol, illus. see Matas, Toni.
Picard, Barbara Leonie. One Is One. (p. 1295)
—Ransom for a Knight. (p. 1438)
Picard, Charline, illus. see Pellegrini, Isabelle.
Picard, Matthias. Jim Curious: A Voyage to the Heart of the Sea in 3-D Vision. (p. 917)
Picasso, P, jt. auth. see Hodge, Susie.
Picasso, Pablo, jt. auth. see Penrose, Antony.
Picayo, Mario. Caribbean Journey from A to Y: (Read & Discover What Happened to the Z) Griswold, Earleen, illus. (p. 268)
—Fun, Fun, One Crab on the Run. Byer, Stacey, illus. (p. 648)
—Very Smart Cat: Una Gata Muy Inteligente. Fundora, Yolanda V., illus. (p. 1838)
Picayo, Mario & Picayo, Pablo. Four Wishes for Robbie. (p. 625)
Picayo, Mario, et al. Shark & the Parrotfish & Other Caribbean Fables. Ward, Cherise, illus. (p. 1562)
Picayo, Pablo, jt. illus. see Picayo, Mario.
Piccione, Dana, illus. see Wreggelsworth, Irene.
Picciotto, Linda Pierce. Learning Together: A Whole Year in a Primary Classroom. (p. 986)
Piccirilli, Tom. Fuckin' Lie down Already. Caniglia, illus. (p. 646)
Piccirillo, Renee. Big Mister Little Mister Baby Sister. Gumm, Susan Kathleen, illus. (p. 182)
Pichelli, Sara, illus. see Dragotta, Nick & Hickman, Jonathan.
Pichelli, Sara, jt. illus. see Lashley, Ken.
Pichler, Tony, jt. auth. see Broslavick, Chris.
Pichon, Liz. Bored Bill. Pichon, Liz, illus. (p. 214)
—Brilliant World of Tom Gates: Read It & Go Ha! Ha! Ha! Pichon, Liz, illus. (p. 228)
—Everything's Amazing (Sort Of) Pichon, Liz, illus. (p. 546)
—Penguins. (p. 1337)
—Three Horrid Little Pigs. Pichon, Liz, illus. (p. 1742)
—Tom Gates: Festival de Genialidades (Más o Menos) (p. 1763)
—Tom Gates: Excusas Perfectas (y Otras Cosillas Geniales) (p. 1763)
—Tom Gates: Excellent Excuses (And Other Good Stuff) Pichon, Liz, illus. (p. 1763)
—Very Ugly Bug. (p. 1839)
Pichon, Liz, illus. see Donaldson, Julia.
Pichon, Liz, illus. see Ellis, Gwen.
Pichon, Liz, illus. see Hendra, Sue.
Pichon, Liz, illus. see Laird, Elizabeth.
Pichon, Liz, illus. see Mortimer, Rachael.
Pichon, Liz, jt. auth. see Pym, Tasha.
Pichon, Liz, tr. see Laird, Elizabeth.
Picini, Frank, illus. see Gifford, Clive.
Pick, Alice. Jamey's Promise (p. 907)
Pickard, Ben & Pickard, Carolyn. Fish! Don't You Wish. (p. 598)
Pickard, Carolyn, jt. auth. see Pickard, Ben.
Pickard, Chante. Adventures of Louie the Panda. (p. 20)
Pickard, Deanna. In Dreams We Kiss Ourselves Good-Bye: Poems. (p. 863)
Pickard, W. Raymond. When an Angel Cries: (but I Don't Want to Be an Angel) (p. 1901)
Pickeral, Tamsin. Encyclopedia of Horses & Ponies. (p. 525)
Pickering, Amanda. Alfred the Alien: Number Adventure. (p. 37)
Pickering, David H., ed. see Manser, Martin H.
Pickering, Fran. Illustrated Encyclopedia of Animals in Nature & Myth. (p. 857)
Pickering, Jill. Lizard Got into the Paint Pots. Wright, Petrina, illus. (p. 1042)
Pickering, Jimmy. It's Spring. (p. 899)
—Skelly & Femur. Pickering, Jimmy, illus. (p. 1584)
—Skelly the Skeleton Girl. Pickering, Jimmy, illus. (p. 1584)
Pickering, Jimmy, illus. see Fulmer, Jeffrey.
Pickering, Jimmy, illus. see Jardine, Alan.
Pickering, Jimmy, illus. see Krensky, Stephen.
Pickering, Jimmy, illus. see Prelutsky, Jack.
Pickering, Jimmy, illus. see Sage, Angie.
Pickering, Jimmy, illus. see Siddals, Mary McKenna.
Pickering, Jimmy, tr. see Fulmer, Jeffrey.
Pickering, Ken, jt. auth. see Sunderland, Margot.
Pickering, Kenneth. Drama in the Cathedral: The Twentieth Century Encounter of Church & Stage. (p. 480)
Pickering, Kenneth, jt. auth. see Herzog, Michael.
Pickering, Kenneth, jt. auth. see Sugano, Douglas.
Pickering, Lynne. James & the Naughty Seagull. Pickering, Lynne, illus. (p. 906)
Pickering, Russell, photos by see Rauen, Amy & Ayers, Amy.
Pickering, Russell, photos by see Rauen, Amy.
Pickering, Sean & Morrill, Scott. Adventures of Danny & Spike: Underground. (p. 17)
Pickering, Todd. Lagunitas Creek: Hope in Restoration Pickering, Todd, photos by. (p. 971)
Pickersgill, J. W. Louis St. Laurent (p. 1058)
Pickersgill, Peter, illus. see Rae, Lisa.
Pickett, Anola. Callahan Crossroads. (p. 254)
—Whisper Island. (p. 1912)
Pickett, Cheryl. Creation Inspirations: A New View of Your Neighborhood. (p. 379)
Pickett, Danny, illus. see Moran, Erin.
Pickett, Elizabeth, ed. see Wood, Francis Eugene.
Pickett, Justine, jt. illus. see Pickett, Robert.
Pickett, Lanaya A. Walking with Angels. (p. 1854)
Pickett, Natalie R. S e M P Ly 4 Girlz. (p. 1499)
Pickett, Rex. Sideways: The Ultimate Road Trip, the Last Hurrah. (p. 1573)
Pickett, Robert & Pickett, Justine. Cat. Pickett, Robert & Pickett, Justine, photos by. (p. 277)
—Dog. Pickett, Robert & Pickett, Justine, photos by. (p. 460)
Pickford, Sue. Bob & Rob. (p. 205)
—When Angus Met Alvin. (p. 1901)
Pickford, Susan B. Expectations: The Life of Phillis Wheatley. (p. 548)
Pickles, Jonathan & Van Ackooy, Maureen. English (ELA) 8 X-treme Review: Concise Training for NYS ELA Intermediate Assessment. Stich, Paul & Garnsey, Wayne, eds. (p. 529)
Picklesimer, Olivia. Health Care. (p. 758)
—Teen Sex. (p. 1714)
Pickman, Marian, illus. see Anbinder, Adrienne.
Pickman, Richard. Anglo-American Colonization of Texas. (p. 75)
—Let's Volunteer! (p. 1001)
Pickman, Richard, jt. auth. see Mills, Nathan.
Pickthall M.M. Staff, jt. auth. see Parr, Todd.
Pickwell, Linda. Australia. (p. 116)
—France. (p. 627)
Picone, Emma Lee. My Blended Family. Harrel, Tina, illus. (p. 1198)
Picone, Linda. My Changing Body. (p. 1200)
Picou, Lin. Best Boat Race Ever! Reasoner, John, illus. (p. 168)
—Can You Make a Pattern? (p. 259)
—Do I Have To... Reese, Bob, illus. (p. 457)
—Do I Have To ... Reese, Bob, illus. (p. 457)
—Play with Sorting! (p. 1372)
—Who's Right. Dufalla, Anita, illus. (p. 1921)
Picou, Lin, jt. auth. see Karapetkova, Holly.
Picou, Lin, jt. auth. see Moreta, Gladys.
Picou, Lin & Moreta, Gladys. Too Much Tv! Reese, Bob, illus. (p. 1767)
Picoult, Jodi & van Leer, Samantha. Between the Lines. (p. 173)
—Off the Page. Gilbert, Yvonne, illus. (p. 1279)
Picouly, Daniel. Thumbelina of Toulaba. Bedrick, Claudia Z., tr. from FRE. (p. 1745)
Picray, Michael E. Sun with Code. (p. 1676)
Picthall & Gunzi Ltd, creator. In the Jungle. (p. 866)
Picthall, Chez. Baby Animals. (p. 124)
—Baby Sees Boxed Set: Shapes. (p. 128)
—Bedtime. Hewett, Angela, illus. (p. 156)
—First Library. (p. 595)
—Flip Flaps Zoo. (p. 605)
—My Bike. Gunzi, Christiane, ed. (p. 1197)
—My Favourite Racers Sticker Book. Rayner, Katy, ed. (p. 1203)
—My Favourite Trucks Sticker Book. Rayner, Katy, ed. (p. 1203)
—On the Move. Gunzi, Christiane, ed. (p. 1291)
—Puppies. (p. 1417)
—Racers. Gunzi, Christiane, ed. (p. 1431)
—Ultimate Car Colouring Book. (p. 1809)
—Zoo Animals. (p. 1988)
Picthall, Chez, jt. auth. see Giles, Angela.
Picthall, Chez & Award, Anna. Very First Book. (p. 1838)
Picthall, Chez & Gunzi. My Favourite Cars Sticker Book. Rayner, Katy, ed. (p. 1203)
Picthall, Chez & Gunzi, Christiane. Numbers. (p. 1271)
—Words. (p. 1951)
Picthall, Chez, creator. Flip Flap Colours: A Turn-the-Flap Book! (p. 604)
—Flip Flaps Shapes. (p. 604)
Picthall, Chez, des. Flowers. (p. 608)
—Hearts & Stars. (p. 760)
—Spots & Dots. (p. 1634)
Picture Window Books, jt. auth. see Meachen Rau, Dana.
Picture Window Books Staff. Robin Hood & the Golden Arrow Yilmaz, Necdet, illus. (p. 1480)
Picture Window Books Staff, jt. auth. see Dahl, Michael.
Picture Window Books Staff, jt. auth. see Dixon, Dougal.
Picture Window Books Staff, jt. auth. see Finn, Carrie.
Picture Window Books Staff, jt. auth. see Firestone, Mary.
Picture Window Books Staff, jt. auth. see Meachen Rau, Dana.
Picture Window Books Staff, jt. auth. see Mortensen, Lori.
Picture Window Books Staff, jt. auth. see Owen, Ann.
Picture Window Books Staff, jt. auth. see Pearl, Norman.
Picture Window Books Staff, jt. auth. see Rosinsky, Natalie M.
Picture Window Books Staff, jt. auth. see Sherman, Josepha.
Picture Window Books Staff, jt. auth. see Slade, Suzanne.
Picture Window Books Staff, jt. auth. see Stille, Darlene R.
Picture Window Books Staff, jt. auth. see Thomas, Rick.
Piddock, Charles. Afghanistan. (p. 26)
—Creeps of the Deep: Explore the Ocean's Strangest Creatures. (p. 381)
—Future Tech: From Personal Robots to Motorized Monocycles. (p. 651)
—Iran. (p. 886)
—Kazakhstan. (p. 946)
—North Korea. (p. 1265)
—Outbreaks: Science Seeks Safeguards for Global Health. (p. 1312)
—Rachel Carson: A Voice for the Natural World. (p. 1431)
—Ray Bradbury: Legendary Fantasy Writer. (p. 1441)
—Republic of Georgia. (p. 1462)
—Sudan. (p. 1672)
Piddock, Claire. Decimals. (p. 421)
—Line, Bar, & Circle Graphs. (p. 1019)
—Lines, Segments, Rays, & Angles. (p. 1019)
—Position & Direction. (p. 1387)
—Regrouping. (p. 1457)
—Slides, Flips, & Turns. (p. 1590)
Pidgeon, Jean. Brush Your Teeth, Please: A Pop-Up Book. (p. 232)
Pidlubny, Donna, illus. see Ronco, Dan.
Pidutti, Nancy L. José the Donkey. (p. 926)
Pie, Corey. Birds, Bikes, & Ice Cream: A Lesson in Overcoming Adversity. AcesGraphics, illus. (p. 191)
Piece O' Cake Designs Staff. Whimsical Designs. (p. 1911)
Piehl, Janet. Capitol Building. (p. 263)
—Explore the Library. (p. 550)
—Flying Mosquitoes. (p. 610)
—Forest Fires. (p. 618)
—Formula One Race Cars. (p. 620)
—Formula One Race Cars on the Move. (p. 620)
—Great Lakes. (p. 716)
—Humvees. (p. 827)
—Indy Race Cars. (p. 873)
—Know the Parts of a Book. (p. 965)
—Let's Look at Pigeons. (p. 999)
—Let's Look at Sloths. (p. 999)
—Northern Lights. (p. 1266)
—Sanitation Workers. (p. 1511)
—Yellowstone National Park. (p. 1970)
Piehl, Janet, jt. auth. see Lerner Classroom Staff.
Piehl, Norah. Cancer. (p. 260)
—Cults. (p. 390)
—Eating Disorders. (p. 501)
—Infertility. (p. 873)
—Teenage Pregnancy. (p. 1714)
—Underage Drinking. (p. 1814)
Piehl, Norah, ed. Choosing a College. (p. 310)
—Date Rape. (p. 409)
Piemme, P. I., illus. see Holsinger, Rosemary.
Pien, Lark. Long Tail Kitty. Pien, Lark, illus. (p. 1047)
—Long Tail Kitty - Come Out & Play. (p. 1047)
—Mr. Elephanter. Pien, Lark, illus. (p. 1185)
—Rosary Comic Book. Yang, Gene Luen, illus. (p. 1489)
Pien, Lark, illus. see Yang, Gene Luen.
Pien, Lark, jt. auth. see Yang, Gene Luen.
Pienaar, Kathy, jt. auth. see Stewart, Dianne.
Pieniozek, Lillian & Family. Meet the Knucklepuppies. (p. 1122)
Pienkowski, Jan. Easter. (p. 499)
—Ferme. (p. 582)
—First Christmas. (p. 593)
—First Noel: A Christmas Carousel. Pienkowski, Jan et al, illus. (p. 596)
Pienkowski, Jan, illus. see Walser, David.
Pienkowski, Jan, jt. auth. see Nicoll, Helen.
Pienkowski, Jan & Walser, David. Glass Mountain: Tales from Poland. Pienkowski, Jan, illus. (p. 682)
Pieper, Christiane. Sin Rumbo por el Mundo. Catalina y el Oso. (p. 1578)
Pieper, Martha Heineman. Mommy, Daddy, I Had a Bad Dream! Gershman, Jo, illus. (p. 1162)
Piepgrass, Arlene. Death, the Wages of Sin: Old Testament Volume 14, Numbers Part 2. Vol. 14 Brubaker, Audrey et al, eds. (p. 420)
Piepgrass, Arlene & Hershey, Katherine. Tabernacle, Part 1 A Picture of the Lord Jesus: Old Testament Volume 9 Exodus Part 4. Vol. 09, Pt. 1 Willoughby, Yuko, illus. (p. 1694)
Piepgrass, Arlene S. Sacrifice: Old Testament Volume 11, Leviticus Part 1: the Way to God. Vol. 11 Neal, Sharon, ed. (p. 1501)
Piepmeier, Charlotte. Lucy's Journey to the Wild West: A True Story. Blakemore, Sally, illus. (p. 1063)
Pier, Daniel Wayne. Ferrous the Venus Fly Trap Meets the Cactus. (p. 582)
Pier, Stanwood. Jester of St. Timothy's. (p. 914)
Pieramico, Hedy, mem. Remembering Rick: The Music of His Life. (p. 1459)
Pierangelo, Roger & Giuliani, George A. Why Your Students Do What They Do & What to Do When They Do It (Grades K-5) A Practical Guide for Understanding Classroom Behavior. (p. 1927)
—Why Your Students Do What They Do & What to Do When They Do It (Grades 6-12) A Practical Guide for Understanding Classroom Behavior. (p. 1927)
Pierard, John, illus. see Coville, Bruce.
Pierard, John W., illus. see Doyle, Arthur, et al.
Pierce, Alan. Apollo 13. (p. 91)
—Assasination of Martin Luther King, Jr. (p. 107)
—Bombing of Pearl Harbor. (p. 208)
—Breaking the Sound Barrier. (p. 225)
—Brown vs the Board of Education. (p. 232)
—Constitution. (p. 359)
—Declaration of Independence. (p. 422)
—Industrial Revolution. (p. 872)
—Jamestown Colony. (p. 907)
—Lincoln-Douglas Debates. (p. 1018)
—Louisiana Purchase. (p. 1058)
—Montgomery Bus Boycott. (p. 1170)
—Pony Express. (p. 1382)
—Reconstruction. (p. 1452)
—September 11 2001. (p. 1551)
—Transcontinental Railroad. (p. 1778)
—Underground Railroad. (p. 1814)
Pierce, Alyssa. Caroline & Rebecca: Rebecca Gets into Trouble. (p. 270)
—Caroline & Rebecca's Day at the Beach. (p. 270)
Pierce, Angelica. Wizard in Blue Jeans. (p. 1942)
Pierce, AnneMarie. Pieces of Me. Campbell, Donna P., illus. (p. 1356)
Pierce, Barbara A. Game That Sam Plays. (p. 654)
Pierce, Brian. Little Red Present. Crowell, Helen, illus. (p. 1035)
Pierce, Charles Santiago Sanders. Collected Papers (p. 339)
Pierce, Charlotte, ed. see Briggett, Marlissa.
Pierce, Charlotte & Schoenthaler, Robin. Compleat Day Tripper-Greater Boston: Greater Boston's Best Classic & Eclectic Destinations for Kids & Grown-Ups! Pierce, Charlotte, ed. (p. 352)
Pierce, Christa. Did You Know That I Love You? (p. 437)
Pierce Clark, Donna, illus. see Snowden, Gary.
Pierce, Craig. Greyhound's Tale: Running for Glory, Walking for Home. Santiago, Tony, illus. (p. 723)
—Labrador's Tale: An Eye for Heroism. Santiago, Tony, illus. (p. 970)
—Labrador's Tale 2: The Incredible Thank You Gift Santiago, Tony, illus. (p. 970)
—Sit. Stay. Work. Play: All Dogs Have Their Day. Santiago, Tony, illus. (p. 1582)
Pierce, Daniel W. Santa's Christmas Mouse. (p. 1513)
Pierce, Darlene. Alana's Prince. Jean, S. L., illus. (p. 33)
—Bear of Another Color. Jean, S. L., illus. (p. 151)
—Drummer. Jean, S. L., illus. (p. 487)
Pierce, Dave G., illus. see Hill, Cheryl E.
Pierce, Franklin. Fiberglass Ding Repair: The Art of Polyester Resin/Fiberglas & Polyurathane Foam Surfboard Repairwork. (p. 583)
Pierce, Heather Vowell. What Does Your Daddy Do? Price, Dana, illus. (p. 1884)
Pierce, Joanne Y., illus. see Spitz, Mary Y.
Pierce, Julie A., illus. see Pirog, Kristen T.
Pierce, Karen F. Yoga Bear: Yoga for Youngsters. Brinkman, Paula, illus. (p. 1972)
Pierce, Kelly. Boy Who Would Be King. de Polonia, Nina, illus. (p. 219)
Pierce, Kim, illus. see Cornman, Sabrina.
pierce, km. Very First Christmas. (p. 1838)
Pierce, Linda, illus. see Sutton, A. Trevor.
Pierce, M. Deborah, illus. see Bremer, Terry.
Pierce, Mark & Jennings, Karen. Wright Fright: A Guide to Writing Scary Stories. (p. 1963)
Pierce, Mark R. I'm Glad You Asked! 60 Common Questions Catholics Have about the Bible. (p. 859)
Pierce, Mary E. Permilia: A Western Children's Book. Dobler, Shirley Jean, illus. (p. 1343)
Pierce, Matthew, illus. see Saunders, Sara.
Pierce, Meredith Ann. Birth of the Firebringer (p. 192)
—Dark Moon. (p. 407)
—Darkangel. (p. 408)
—Gathering of Gargoyles. (p. 658)
—Pearl of the Soul of the World. (p. 1333)
—Son of Summer Stars (p. 1611)
—Treasure at the Heart of the Tanglewood. (p. 1781)
—Waters Luminous & Deep. (p. 1864)
Pierce, Mindy, illus. see Wing, Natasha.
Pierce, Morris A. Robert Fulton & the Development of the Steamboat. (p. 1479)
Pierce, Patricia A. H Is for Hawkeye: An Iowa Alphabet. Langton, Bruce, tr. (p. 734)
Pierce, Paul. Springer Ghost Book: A Theatre Haunting in the Deep South. Dawson, Sandy & McGee, E. Alan, photos by. (p. 1635)
Pierce, Philip N. & Schuon, Karl. John H Glenn, Astronaut. (p. 922)
Pierce, Ricky. Bouncing Billy. (p. 216)
Pierce, Seth J. Camporee of Doom. (p. 258)
—Day the School Blew Up. (p. 414)
—What We Believe for Teens. (p. 1895)
Pierce, Stacey C. Kenny's Summer Fun. (p. 949)
Pierce, Tamora. Alanna: The First Adventure. (p. 33)
—Battle Magic. (p. 146)
—Bloodhound. (p. 201)
—Cold Fire. (p. 338)
—Emperor Mage. (p. 520)
—First Test. (p. 597)
—In the Hand of the Goddess. (p. 866)
—Lady Knight. (p. 971)
—Lioness Rampant. (p. 1021)
—Magic Steps. (p. 1073)
—Mastiff. (p. 1103)
—Melting Stones. (p. 1125)
—Page. (p. 1318)
—Realms of the Gods. (p. 1450)
—Shatterglass. (p. 1563)
—Squire. (p. 1637)
—Terrier. (p. 1721)
—Tortall & Other Lands: A Collection of Tales. (p. 1770)
—Tortall & Other Lands. (p. 1770)
—Trickster's Choice. (p. 1786)
—Trickster's Queen. (p. 1786)
—Wild Magic. (p. 1929)
—Will of the Empress. (p. 1932)
—Wolf-Speaker. (p. 1944)
—Woman Who Rides Like a Man. (p. 1945)
Pierce, Tamora & Sherman, Josepha. Young Warriors: Stories of Strength. (p. 1979)
Pierce, Terry. Blackberry Banquet Downey, Lisa, illus. (p. 197)

—Coral Reefs A to Z Coloring Book. Kofsky, Kristen, illus. (p. 366)
—Greatest Goofiest Jokes. Jones, Buck, illus. (p. 720)
—Surfing A to Z Coloring Book. Kofsky, Kristen, illus. (p. 1685)
—Tae Kwon Do! Bonita, Todd, illus. (p. 1695)
—Volcanoes A to Z Coloring Book. Villalobos, Ethel M., illus. (p. 1849)
Pierce, Terry, jt. auth. see Horsfall, Jacqueline.
Pierce, Terry & Kofsky, Kristen. Dangerous Sea Creatures A to Z Coloring Book. (p. 404)
Pierce, Walter. Dreams Unseen: The Dragon of Mists. (p. 484)
Piercey, Bruce. Plank. (p. 1368)
Piercy, Helen. Animation Studio. (p. 84)
Piercy, Jennifer. Ellie's Math Adventure. (p. 514)
Pierdomenico, Baccalario. Suitcase of Stars (p. 1673)
Pierfederici, Franco. Tron: Movie Adaptation. (p. 1788)
Pierfederici, Mirco, illus. see Fraction, Matt.
Pierfederici, Mirco, jt. illus. see Edwards, Neil.
Piernas-Davenport, Gail. Shante Keys & the New Year's Peas. Eldridge, Marion, illus. (p. 1559)
Piero, Ventura, jt. auth. see Ventura, Piero.
Pierola, Mabel, illus. see Sarfatti, Esther, tr.
Pierola, Mabel, jt. auth. see Andreu, Mabel.
Pierotti, Jr. Toward the Setting Sun. (p. 1773)
Pierotti, Yvonne, illus. see Nnodim, Paul.
Pierpoint, Eric. Last Ride of Caleb O'Toole. (p. 978)
—Secret Mission of William Tuck. (p. 1542)
Pierpont, James Lord. Jingle Bells: A Magical Cut-Paper Edition. Puttapipat, Niroot, illus. (p. 918)
—Jingle Bells. Samuel, Janet, illus. (p. 918)
—Jingle Bells. Siewert, Pauline, illus. (p. 918)
Pierre, Chevelin, illus. see Papillon, Margaret.
Pierre, Dana. Mousey, Mousey Finds Cheese? Illustrated by Wellon Pierre. (p. 1182)
Pierre, Eileen. It's Not Easy Being Mean. (p. 898)
—Why Is Life So Confusing? (p. 1925)
Pierre Louis, Renaud. Burning Torch. (p. 244)
Pierre, Manes. Spinning the Globe. (p. 1628)
Pierre, Roselyn. Soul of a Poet. (p. 1614)
Pierre-Louis, Jerry, jt. auth. see Guy, Pauline.
Pierre-Louis, Phillip, illus. see Ellen, Chantal.
Pierres, Marianne De. Serious Sas & Messy Magda. Bridgen, Rachel Annie, illus. (p. 1552)
Pierro, Rita. Dear God, Will You Give Me A Dog? French, David, illus. (p. 419)
—Duck Who Couldn't Swim French, David, illus. (p. 488)
—Horse in the House French, David, illus. (p. 799)
—No Veggies for Me. Iukel, Onur, illus. (p. 1261)
Piers, Helen. Long Neck & Thunder Foot. Foreman, Michael, illus. (p. 1047)
pierSath, Chath. Sinat & the Instrument of the Heart: A Story of Cambodia. Nath, Vann & Pouriseth, Phal, illus. (p. 1578)
Piersel. Photomath. (p. 1353)
Pierson, Clara Dillingham. Among the Farmyard People. Gordon, F. C., illus. (p. 65)
—Among the Forest People (Yesterday's Classics) (p. 65)
—Among the Meadow People (Yesterday's Classics) (p. 65)
—Among the Night People (Yesterday's Classics) (p. 65)
—Among the Pond People (Yesterday's Classics) (p. 65)
Pierson, D. C. Crap Kingdom. (p. 376)
Pierson, Geraldean. Young Robin Learns about Jesus. (p. 1979)
Pierson, Jan. Haunted Horse of Gold Hill. (p. 753)
Pierson, Melinda, jt. auth. see Finlfrock, Jacob E.
Pierson, Rich. Adventures of Fred the Donkey. (p. 18)
Pierson-Solis, Lennard, jt. auth. see Hawkins-Walsh, Elizabeth.
Pietila, David, illus. see Schlesinger, Gretchen.
Pietras, Jamie. Hurricane Katrina. (p. 830)
Pietras, Jamie & Breheny, Jamie. Creepy & Crawly: Incredible Invertebrates. (p. 381)
Pietras, Jamie, et al. Getaway: Expert Escape & Evasion. (p. 668)
Pietromarchi, Sophie Benini. Book Book. (p. 210)
Pietron, Barbara. Thunderstone. (p. 1746)
Pietrzyk, Leslie & Kneib, Martha. Maryland. (p. 1101)
Pietsch, Nicole. Sideshow of Merit. (p. 1573)
Pifer, Joanne. EarthWise: Environmental Learning Series (p. 498)
Pifer, Kimberly, ed. see Brightwood, Laura.
Pigford, Grady A., illus. see Sharpe, Paula A.
Pigg, Theresa. Sunshine, the Golden Unicorn. Roberts, Rebecca, illus. (p. 1679)
Piggy Toes Press. Our Ballet Recital. Maddocks, Maria, illus. (p. 1307)
Piggy Toes Press, creator. Animals: Colors & Animals. (p. 81)
—Cars 2. (p. 272)
—Color Party! (p. 343)
—Crayola Sea Life: Counting Sea Life. (p. 377)
—Dinosaurs: Guess the Dinosaur. (p. 444)
—Disney Princess Bath Book. (p. 452)
—Five Little Kisses. (p. 600)
—Giggle & Grow Baby Counts! (p. 676)
—Giggle & Grow Baby's Body! (p. 676)
—Giggles & More! with Abby & Friends. (p. 676)
—Let's Go Potty! (p. 997)
—Let's Go Potty for Boys. (p. 997)
—Let's Read Together with Elmo & Friends. (p. 1000)
—Pop & Touch Kittens. (p. 1384)
—Toy Story 3. (p. 1774)
Piggy Toes Press Staff. All the Way's I Love You Mini. Downing, Julie, illus. (p. 46)
—Dog Walk. (p. 462)
Piggy Toes Press Staff, creator. Little Feet Like: A Tiny Tootsie Touch & Feel Book. (p. 1027)
Pighin, Marcel. Tickles the Bear Pighin, Marcel & Daggett, Irma, illus. (p. 1747)
—Tickles the Bear Goes on a Cruise Mitchell, Hazel, illus. (p. 1747)
Pigman, Shari. Little Frog Finds Jesus. (p. 1028)
Pignat, Caroline. Egghead (p. 506)
—Gospel Truth (p. 703)
—Greener Grass (p. 723)
—Timber Wolf (p. 1750)
—Wild Geese (p. 1929)
Pignataro, Anna. Mama, Will I Be Yours Forever? Pignataro, Anna, illus. (p. 1084)
—Mama, Will You Hold My Hand? Pignataro, Anna, illus. (p. 1084)
Pignataro, Anna, illus. see Kwaymullina, Ezekiel.
Pignataro, Anna, illus. see Odell, Carol.
Pignataro, Anna, illus. see Prior, Natalie Jane.
Pignataro, Anna, illus. see Takac, Esther.
Pigni, Guido, illus. see Hermsen, Ronald.
Pignone, Charles. Frank Sinatra: The Family Album. (p. 629)
Pigram, John. My Dog Jack. (p. 1202)
Pihl, Marshall R. Korean Word Book. (p. 967)
Pijoan, Teresa. White Wolf Woman: And Other Native American Transformation Myths. (p. 1914)
Pijuán Aragón, Miren, tr. see Lofficier, Randy & Lofficier, Jean-Marc.
Pikachu Press, . Catch Oshawott!: A Pokémon Look & Listen Set (p. 279)
—Catch Snivy! A Pokémon Look & Listen Set. (p. 279)
—Catch Tepig!: A Pokémon Look & Listen Set. (p. 279)
—Pokémon Find 'Em All! Welcome to Unova! (p. 1378)
Pikachu, Press. Pokemon Mini-Sticker Book: Black Edition. (p. 1378)
—Pokemon Mini-Sticker Book: Victini Edition. (p. 1378)
Pikachu Press, . Pokémon Super Activity Book: Do You Know Unova? (p. 1378)
Pike, Aprilynne. Destined. (p. 430)
—Hechizos. (p. 761)
—Illusions. (p. 857)
—Life after Theft. (p. 1007)
—Sleep No More. (p. 1588)
—Spells (p. 1625)
—Spells. (p. 1625)
—Wings. (p. 1936)
Pike, Christopher, pseud. Aliens in the Sky. (p. 41)
—Black Knight. (p. 196)
—Chain Letter: Chain Letter; the Ancient Evil. (p. 288)
—Cold People. (p. 338)
—Deepest Desires, Instant Remorse No. 2 (p. 423)
—Eternal Dawn. (p. 539)
—Haunted Cave. (p. 753)
—Hollow Skull. (p. 789)
—Howling Ghost. (p. 824)
—Human Urges, Fatal Consequences. (p. 826)
—Midnight Club. (p. 1138)
—Monstre de l'Armoire. (p. 1169)
—Red Queen. (p. 1454)
—Remember Me: Her Death Will Not Go Unpunished... (p. 1459)
—Remember Me. (p. 1459)
—Road to Nowhere. (p. 1477)
—Sacred Veil. (p. 1500)
—Secret of Ka. (p. 1542)
—Secret Path. (p. 1543)
—Shadow of Death. (p. 1557)
—Thirst (p. 1734)
—To Die For. (p. 1758)
—Until the End: The Party; the Dance; the Graduation. (p. 1823)
—Witch World. (p. 1941)
—Witch's Revenge. (p. 1941)
Pike, E. Royston. Mohammed: Founder of the Religion of Islam. (p. 1160)
Pike, Jay Scott, et al. Marvel Masterworks: Atlas Era Jungle Adventures - Volume 3. (p. 1098)
Pike, Kathy, et al. 25 Totally Terrific Social Studies Activities: Step-by-Step Directions for Motivating Projects That Students Can Do Independently. (p. 1996)
Pike, Katy. Insects. (p. 875)
Pike, Kenneth & Stewart, Isaac. Jacob's Journal of Doom: Confessions of an Almost-Deacon. (p. 904)
Pike, Tabitha R. Dragon Tears: The Legacy. (p. 478)
Pikey, Mikey. Diamond Tree. (p. 434)
Pilar, Bella, illus. see Burningham, Sarah O'Leary.
Pilatowski, Boris, illus. see Cortes, Eunice & Cortes, Laura.
Pilcher, Steve. Pixar Animation Studio Artist Showcase over There. Pilcher, Steve, illus. (p. 1365)
Pilegard, Virginia. Emperor's Army Tans, Adrian, illus. (p. 521)
Pilegard, Virginia Walton. Warlord's Alarm Debon, Nicolas, illus. (p. 1858)
—Warlord's Kites Debon, Nicolas, illus. (p. 1858)
—Warlord's Messengers Debon, Nicolas, illus. (p. 1858)
—Warlord's Puppeteers Debon, Nicolas, illus. (p. 1858)
Pileggi, Joe. No Greater Love. (p. 1258)
Pileggi, Leah. Prisoner 88. (p. 1407)
Pileggi, Steve, illus. see Deubreau, Sharon.
Pileggi, Steve, illus. see Johnson, Spencer.
Pileggi, Steve, illus. see Tucker, Angel.
Pileggi, Steven, illus. see Monnar, Alexander.
Pileggi, Steven, jt. auth. see Rowe, Jodye P.
Pilger, Mary Anne. Science Experiments Index for Young People (p. 1525)
Pilger, Seamus. Fart Squad. Gilpin, Stephen, illus. (p. 575)
—Fart Squad #2: Fartasaurus Rex. Gilpin, Stephen, illus. (p. 575)
—Fartasaurus Rex. Gilpin, Stephen, illus. (p. 575)
Pilgrim, Cheryl, illus. see Vermillion, Patricia.
Pilkey, Dav. Adventures of Captain Underpants. (p. 17)
—Adventures of Captain Underpants. Pilkey, Dav, illus. (p. 17)
—Adventures of Ook & Gluk, Kung-Fu Cavemen from the Future. (p. 21)
—Adventures of Ook & Gluk, Kung-Fu Cavemen from the Future. Pilkey, Dav, illus. (p. 21)
—Adventures of Super Diaper Baby. (p. 23)
—Adventures of Super Diaper Baby. Pilkey, Dav, illus. (p. 23)
—Aventuras de Uuk y Gluk, Cavernicolas del Futuro y Maestros de Kung Fu. Pilkey, Dav, illus. (p. 119)
—Aventures du Capitaine. (p. 119)
—Big, Bad Battle of the Bionic Booger Boy: The Night of the Nasty Nostril Nuggets. (p. 177)
—Big Dog & Little Dog Going for a Walk (Reader) (p. 181)
—Big Dog & Little Dog (Reader) (p. 181)
—Capitán Calzoncillos y la Feroz Batalla Contra el Niño Mocobionico: La Noche de los Mocos Vivientes. Pilkey, Dav, illus. (p. 262)
—Capitan Calzoncillos y la Feroz Batalla Contra el Nino Mocobionico: La Venganza de los Ridiculos Mocorobots. Pt. 2 Azaola, Miguel, tr. (p. 262)
—Capitan Calzoncillos y la Furia de la Supermujer Macroelastica. (p. 262)
—Capitan Calzoncillos y la Ridicula Historia de los Seres del Inodoro Morado. (p. 262)
—Captain Underpants & the Attack of the Talking Toilets. (p. 264)
—Captain Underpants & the Attack of the Talking Toilets. Pilkey, Dav, illus. (p. 264)
—Captain Underpants & the Big, Bad Battle of the Bionic Booger Boy: The Night of the Nasty Nostril Nuggets. Part 1 (p. 264)
—Captain Underpants & the Big, Bad Battle of the Bionic Booger Boy: The Revenge of the Ridiculous Robo-Boogers. Part 2 (p. 264)
—Captain Underpants & the Big, Bad Battle of the Bionic Booger Boy: The Night of the Nasty Nostril Nuggets. Part 1 Pilkey, Dav, illus. (p. 264)
—Captain Underpants & the Big, Bad Battle of the Bionic Booger Boy: The Revenge of the Ridiculous Robo-Boogers. Part 2 Pilkey, Dav, illus. (p. 264)
—Captain Underpants & the Invasion of the Incredibly Naughty Cafeteria Ladies from Outer Space: (and the Subsequent Assault of the Equally Evil Lunchroom Zombie Nerds) (p. 264)
—Captain Underpants & the Invasion of the Incredibly Naughty Cafeteria Ladies from Outer Space: (And the Subsequent Assault of the Equally Evil Lunchroom Zombie Nerds) Pilkey, Dav, illus. (p. 264)
—Captain Underpants & the Invasion of the Incredibly Naughty Cafeteria Ladies from Outer Space: Color Edition. (p. 264)
—Captain Underpants & the Perilous Plot of Professor Poopypants. (p. 264)
—Captain Underpants & the Preposterous Plight of the Purple Potty People. Pilkey, Dav, illus. (p. 264)
—Captain Underpants & the Revolting Revenge of the Radioactive Robo-Boxers. (p. 264)
—Captain Underpants & the Revolting Revenge of the Radioactive Robo-Boxers. Pilkey, Dav, illus. (p. 264)
—Captain Underpants & the Terrifying Return of Tippy Tinkletrousers. (p. 264)
—Captain Underpants & the Terrifying Return of Tippy Tinkletrousers. Pilkey, Dav, illus. (p. 264)
—Captain Underpants & the Tyrannical Retaliation of the Turbo Toilet 2000. (p. 264)
—Captain Underpants & the Wrath of the Wicked Wedgie Woman. (p. 264)
—Cuadros. (p. 388)
—Dog Breath! The Horrible Trouble with Hally Tosis. (p. 461)
—Dog Breath! The Horrible Trouble with Hally Tosis. Pilkey, Dav, illus. (p. 461)
—Dogzilla: Starring Flash, Rabies, Dwayne, & Introducing Leia as the Monster. (p. 463)
—Dogzilla. (p. 463)
—Dogzilla. Pilkey, Dav, illus. (p. 463)
—Dragon Gets By. (p. 477)
—Dragon's Fat Cat. (p. 479)
—Dragon's Halloween. (p. 479)
—Dragon's Halloween. Pilkey, Dav, illus. (p. 479)
—Dragon's Merry Christmas. (p. 479)
—Dumb Bunnies. (p. 489)
—Dumb Bunnies' Easter. (p. 489)
—Dumb Bunnies' Easter. Pilkey, Dav, illus. (p. 489)
—Dumb Bunnies Go to the Zoo. (p. 489)
—Friend for Dragon. (p. 637)
—Hallo-Wiener. Pilkey, Dav, illus. (p. 737)
—Invasion of the Potty Snatchers. (p. 883)
—Kat Kong. (p. 944)
—Make Way for Dumb Bunnies. (p. 1079)
—Mighty Robot vs. the Mecha-Monkeys from Mars. Santat, Dan, illus. (p. 1140)
—Mighty Robot vs. the Mutant Mosquitoes from Mercury. Santat, Dan, illus. (p. 1140)
—Paperboy. (p. 1323)
—Ricky Ricotta's Mighty Robot. (p. 1470)
—Ricky Ricotta's Mighty Robot. Santat, Dan, illus. (p. 1470)
—Ricky Ricotta's Mighty Robot vs. the Jurassic Jackrabbits from Jupiter. Santat, Dan, illus. (p. 1470)
—Super-Silly Sticker Studio. Klutz Editors, ed. (p. 1681)
—Tra-la-Laa-Mendous (p. 1774)
—Tra-la-Laa-Rific Pilkey, Dav, illus. (p. 1774)
—'Twas the Night Before Thanksgiving. (p. 1799)
—Uranium Unicorns from Uranus. (p. 1825)
—Voodoo Vultures from Venus. Santat, Dan, illus. (p. 1850)
Pilkey, Dav, illus. see Johnson, Angela.
Pilkey, Dav, jt. auth. see Denim, Sue.
Pilkey, Dav & Beard, George. Adventures of Ook & Gluk, Kung-Fu Cavemen from the Future. (p. 21)
Pilkey, Dav & Scholastic Canada Ltd. Staff. Invasion of the Potty Snatchers. Pilkey, Dav, illus. (p. 883)
Pilkington, Linda Rash. Arthur Collins & the Three Wishes: Arthur the Brave! (p. 103)
Pilkons, Alyssa. Confessions of a Teenage Lima Bean. (p. 356)
Pilling, Ann. Year of the Worm. (p. 1969)
Pilling, Ann & Ann, Pilling. Mi Primera Biblia Everest. (p. 1133)
Pillion, Dean, illus. see Forbes, Charlotte & Forbes, Charlotte.
Pillion, Dean, illus. see Forbes, Charlotte.
Pillo, Cary, illus. see Braver, Vanita.
Pillo, Cary, illus. see Hanford, Juliana.
Pillo, Cary, illus. see Hudson, Wade.
Pillo, Cary, illus. see Kilgore, Mary & Kilgore, Mitchell.
Pillo, Cary, illus. see Mills, Joyce C.
Pillo, Cary, illus. see Mills, Joyce C. & Crowley, Richard J.
Pillo, Cary, illus. see Schnurbush, Barbara.
Pillo, Cary, illus. see Shuman, Carol.
Pillo, Cary, illus. see Sileo, Frank J.
Pillo, Cary, illus. see Slade, Suzanne.
Pillo, Cary, tr. see Shuman, Carol.
Pillot, édéric, illus. see Mrowiec, Katia.
Pillow, Michelle M. Fierce Competition: An Erotic Romance. (p. 584)
Pillsbury Editors, ed. Pillsbury Kids Cookbook: Food Fun for Boys & Girls. (p. 1359)
Pillsbury, Samuel H. Invasion of Planet Wampetter. Angorn, Matthew, illus. (p. 883)
—Mission to California. Kantrowitz, David, illus. (p. 1153)
Pillsworth, Anne M. Summoned. (p. 1675)
Pilney, Dovie. Charlie the Cocky Rooster: Another Adventure. (p. 293)
—Charlie the Cocky Rooster: Leader of the Pack. (p. 293)
—Charlie the Cocky Rooster. (p. 293)
Pilo, Cary, illus. see Hall, Pamela.
Pilobolus. Human Alphabet: Pilobolus. Kane, John, photos by. (p. 825)
Pilon, Cindy Jett. Joni & the Fallen Star: Helping Children Learn Teamwork. Hazard, John, illus. (p. 925)
Pilon, Laura. Just Like My Little Sister. (p. 939)
Pilorget, Bruno, illus. see Massenot, Véronique.
Pilston, Jim, illus. see Too, Lillian.
Pilsworth, Graham, illus. see Grant, Vicki.
Pilsworth, Graham, illus. see Staunton, Ted.
Pilumeli, Tanya. Dragonfly Keeper. (p. 478)
Pilutik, Anastasia D., jt. auth. see Seco, Nina S.
Pilutti, Deb. Bear & Squirrel Are Friends ... Yes, Really! Pilutti, Deb, illus. (p. 150)
—Ten Rules of Being a Superhero. Pilutti, Deb, illus. (p. 1719)
Pilutti, Deb, illus. see Thoms, Susan Collins.
Pilz, M. H., illus. see Houran, Lori Haskins.
Pilz, M. H., illus. see May, Eleanor.
Pilz, M. H., illus. see Walker, Nan.
Pimental, Ric, jt. auth. see Wall, Terry.
Pimentel, Alejandro, tr. see Rock, Lois.
Pimentel, Annette Bay. My Brain. Alberini, Teresa, illus. (p. 1199)
—My Stomach. Alberini, Teresa, illus. (p. 1219)
Pimentel, Ric, jt. auth. see Wall, Terry.
Pimentel, Sandy. Boy with Two Homes. (p. 220)
Pimlott, jt. auth. see Murphy.
Pimm, Nancy Roe. Daytona 500: The Thrill & Thunder of the Great American Race. (p. 415)
—Indy 500: The Inside Track. (p. 873)
—Indy 500: The Insider Track. (p. 873)
Pin, Isabel. Bumblebee Blues. James, J. Alison, tr. from GER. (p. 241)
Pina, Andrew. Baseball's Greatest Records (p. 141)
—Becoming a Pro Baseball Player. (p. 156)
—Career As a Border Patrol Agent. (p. 266)
Pina, Javier, jt. auth. see Andreyko, Marc.
Pinborough, Jan. Miss Moore Thought Otherwise: How Anne Carroll Moore Created Libraries for Children. Atwell, Debby, illus. (p. 1151)
Pinborough, Sarah. Into the Silence. (p. 881)
Pinchbeck, Chris, photos by see Goodbody, Slim.
Pinchbeck, Neil. Crash, Bang, Yell! (p. 376)
—Praying Man. (p. 1393)
—Rescue on the Road. (p. 1462)
—There's a Hole in My Roof! (p. 1731)
Pinchuk, Tom. Haywire Wijngaard, Jan, illus. (p. 756)
Pinckaers, Servais. Morality: The Catholic View. Sherwin, Michael, tr. from FRE. (p. 1173)
Pinckney, Jerry, illus. see Holiday, Billie & Herzog, Arthur, Jr.
Pincock, Amy. Quiet Book Patterns. (p. 1428)
Pincock, Stephen. Codebreaker: The History of Codes & Ciphers, from the Ancient Pharaohs to Quantum Cryptography. (p. 338)
Pincus, Dion. Everything You Need to Know about Cerebral Palsy. (p. 545)
Pincus, Donna & Kaplow, Julie. Samantha Jane's Missing Smile: A Story about Coping with the Loss of a Parent. Spiegel, Beth, illus. (p. 1507)
Pincus, Gregory K. 14 Fibs of Gregory K. (p. 1995)
Pincus, Steven C., jt. auth. see Pincus, Steven C. A.
Pincus, Steven C. A. & Pincus, Steven C. England's Glorious Revolution 1688-1689: A Brief History with Documents. (p. 529)
Pinczes, Elinor J. Inchworm & a Half. Enos, Randall, illus. (p. 869)
Pinder, Andrew. Boys' Doodle Book: Amazing Pictures to Complete & Create. (p. 220)
—Boys' Doodle Book. (p. 220)
—Dinosaur Doodles: Amazing Pictures to Complete & Create. (p. 442)
—Girls' Doodle Book: Amazing Pictures to Complete & Create. (p. 680)
—Girls' Doodle Book. (p. 680)
—Icky, Sticky, Slimy Doodles: Gross, Full-Color Pictures to Complete & Create. (p. 851)
—Journey Through Time Doodles. (p. 928)
Pinder, Andrew, illus. see Bailey, Ellen & Mosedale, Julian.
Pinder, Andrew, illus. see Collins, Tim.
Pinder, Andrew, illus. see Gifford, Clive.
Pinder, Andrew, illus. see Oliver, Martin.
Pinder, Andrew, jt. auth. see Oliver, Martin.
Pinder, Andrew, jt. auth. see Running Press Staff.
Pinder, Eric. Cat in the Clouds. Walsh, T. B. R., illus. (p. 278)
—I'd Rather Be Riding My Bike. Cardinal, John, illus. (p. 851)
—If All the Animals Came Inside. Brown, Marc, illus. (p. 852)
Pindroh, Paula, illus. see Galvin, Laura Gates.
Pine, Hank, illus. see Richmond, Jacob.
Pine, Margherita N., ed. see Howard, Becky L.
Pine, Marty. Olympic Kids. (p. 1287)
Pine, Roger D. Treasures from the Heart: A Tribute to America & Its People. (p. 1782)
Pineau, Severine, tr. see Ward, John.
Pineda, Jesus, illus. see Jauregui, Patricia.
Pineda, Nancy, tr. see Larson, Beverly.
Pinehurst, Bonnie. Love, Raggedy Ann. Thomas, Laura, illus. (p. 1060)
Pinelli, Amerigo, illus. see Brezenoff, Steve.
Pinelli, Amerigo, illus. see Craver, Marcella Marino.
Pinelli, Amerigo, illus. see Yomtov, Nelson.

P

Pineno. It Doesn't Grow on Trees. (p. 894)
Piner, Huston. My Life As a Myth. (p. 1212)
Pinero, Arthur Wing. Second Mrs. Tanqueray. Landes, William-Alan, ed. (p. 1539)
Pinero, Eimi, illus. see Perkins, T. J.
Pinestein Press. Abcs of Language & Literacy. Carroll, Raymond, illus. (p. 4)
—Pre-K Prep! Carroll, Raymond, illus. (p. 1394)
Pinet, Michele. Be Your Own Rock & Mineral Expert. Greenbaum, Fay, tr. from FRE. (p. 149)
Pinette, Melanie. Looking Up. (p. 1051)
Piney Grove Elementary School (Kernsville, N.C.) Staff & Scholastic, Inc. Staff, contrib. by. Kid for Jack: A True Story. (p. 951)
Pinfold, Levi. Black Dog. Pinfold, Levi, illus. (p. 196)
—Django. Pinfold, Levi, illus. (p. 455)
Pinfold, Levi, illus. see Schafer, Albert.
Ping, Chen & Guili, Z., eds. Chinese Herbs & Compatibility. (p. 307)
Pingelton, Timothy J. Student's Guide to Ernest Hemingway. (p. 1669)
Pingk, Rubin. Samurai Santa: A Very Ninja Christmas. Pingk, Rubin, illus. (p. 1510)
Pingry, Patricia A. America the Beautiful: A Patriotic Coloring Book. (p. 59)
—Baby Beluga. Rose, Drew, illus. (p. 125)
—Baby Flamingo. Sharp, Chris, illus. (p. 126)
—Baby Giraffe. (p. 126)
—Baby Hippopotamus. Sharp, Chris, illus. (p. 126)
—Baby Koala. (p. 127)
—Baby Manatee. Rose, Drew, illus. (p. 127)
—Baby Panda. Sharp, Chris, illus. (p. 127)
—Baby Sea Otter. Rose, Drew, illus. (p. 128)
—Baby Sea Turtle. Rose, Drew, illus. (p. 128)
—Baby Zebra. Sharp, Chris, illus. (p. 128)
—Bible Story Cards: The Story of Noah. (p. 176)
—Bible Story Cards: The Story of Jesus. (p. 176)
—Cheetah. San Diego Zoo Staff, photos by. (p. 296)
—Christmas Story. Edelson, Wendy, illus. (p. 315)
—David & Goliath: A Story about Trusting in God: Based on 1 Samuel 17:1/50. Munger, Nancy, illus. (p. 410)
—Dear Santa... Rasmussen, Wendy, illus. (p. 419)
—Discover Abraham Lincoln. (p. 447)
—Discover Benjamin Franklin: Printer, Scientist, Statesman. Britt, Stephanie, illus. (p. 447)
—Discover George Washington. (p. 447)
—Discover Thomas Jefferson: Architect, Inventor, President. Johnson, Meredith, illus. (p. 448)
—Easter Story. Utt, Mary Ann, illus. (p. 499)
—Ideals Treasury of Faith in America. (p. 852)
—Jesus in the Temple: Based on Luke 2:40/52. Munger, Nancy, illus. (p. 915)
—Jesus Loves Me. (p. 915)
—Jonah & the Fish: Based on Jonah 1-3:3. Venturi-Pickett, Stacy, illus. (p. 925)
—Joseph & the Dream: Based on Genesis 37/46:7. Spence, Jim, illus. (p. 926)
—Meet Abraham Lincoln. Britt, Stephanie McFetridge, illus. (p. 1120)
—Meet George Washington. Britt, Stephanie McFetridge, illus. (p. 1121)
—Meet Robert E. Lee. Johnson, Meredith, illus. (p. 1122)
—Meet Rosa Parks. Walker, Steven, illus. (p. 1122)
—Meet Thomas Jefferson. Johnson, Meredith, ed. (p. 1123)
—Noses & Toes. Rose, Drew, illus. (p. 1266)
—O Little Town of Bethlehem. (p. 1274)
—On Christmas Morning. Barretta, Gene, illus. (p. 1288)
—On Easter Sunday. Johnson, Meredith, illus. (p. 1288)
—One Baby Jesus. Edleson, Wendy, illus. (p. 1293)
—Power of Faith for Teens: True Stories. (p. 1389)
—Sounds. Rose, Drew, illus. (p. 1615)
—Story of Adam & Eve. Thornburgh, Rebecca, illus. (p. 1657)
—Story of Christmas. (p. 1657)
—Story of Christmas. Thornburgh, Rebecca, illus. (p. 1657)
—Story of Coretta Scott King. Walker, Steven, illus. (p. 1657)
—Story of David. Pulley, Kelly, illus. (p. 1658)
—Story of Easter. Wells, Lorraine, illus. (p. 1658)
—Story of Easter. Thornburgh, Rebecca McKillip & Thornburgh, Rebecca, illus. (p. 1658)
—Story of Gettysburg. Britt, Stephanie, illus. (p. 1658)
—Story of Jesus. Pulley, Kelly, illus. (p. 1658)
—Story of Jesus. Thornburgh, Rebecca, illus. (p. 1658)
—Story of Joshua. Pulley, Kelly, illus. (p. 1658)
—Story of Loaves & Fishes. Venturi-Pickett, Stacy, illus. (p. 1659)
—Story of Mary. Venturi-Pickett, Stacy, illus. (p. 1659)
—Story of Noah. Venturi-Pickett, Stacy, illus. (p. 1659)
—Story of Robert E. Lee. Johnson, Meredith, illus. (p. 1659)
—Story of Ronald Reagan. Mahan, Ben, illus. (p. 1659)
—Story of Rosa Parks. Walker, Steven, illus. (p. 1659)
—Story of the Lord's Prayer. Garvin, Elaine, illus. (p. 1661)
—Story of the Star Spangled Banner. (p. 1662)
—Story of the Star-Spangled Banner. Munger, Nancy, illus. (p. 1662)
—Story of the Ten Commandments. (p. 1662)
—Story of the Ten Commandments. Venturi-Pickett, Stacy, illus. (p. 1662)
—Story of Thomas Jefferson. Johnson, Meredith, illus. (p. 1662)
—Treasury of New Testament Heroes. (p. 1783)
—Treasury of Old Testament Heroes. (p. 1783)
Pingry, Patricia A. & Sharp, Chris. Baby Chimpanzee. (p. 125)
—Baby Tiger. (p. 128)
Pingry, Patricia A. & Urbano, Aide. One Baby Jesus/Un Nino Dios. Edelson, Wendy, illus. (p. 1293)
Pingry, Patricia A. & Venturi-Pickett, Stacy, trs. Story of Creation. Venturi-Pickett, Stacy, illus. (p. 1657)
Pinguilly, Yves. Contes et legendes d Afrique. (p. 360)
—Contes et Legendes de Bretagne. (p. 360)
Pink, A. J. Fox at Christmas. (p. 626)
Pinkard, Alquan. Barcelona Brownsville: Life in the Hood. (p. 138)
Pinkerton, Robert E. Fourth Norwood. (p. 625)
Pinkerton, Steve & Pecsenye, Jessica. Pepperdine University College Prowler off the Record. (p. 1340)
Pinkham, Mark Amaru. Love Me Later. (p. 1060)
Pinkham, Pamela, illus. see Roland-James, Patricia & James, Robert L.
Pinkley, Robin L. & Northcraft, Gregory B. Get Paid What You're Worth: The Expert Negotiators' Guide to Salary & Compensation. (p. 668)
Pinkney, Andrea Davis. Bird in a Box. Qualls, Sean, illus. (p. 190)
—Boycott Blues: How Rosa Parks Inspired a Nation. Pinkney, Brian, illus. (p. 220)
—Duke Ellington. Pinkney, Brian, illus. (p. 489)
—Ella Fitzgerald: The Tale of a Vocal Virtuosa. Pinkney, Brian, illus. (p. 514)
—Hand in Hand: Ten Black Men Who Changed America. Pinkney, Brian, illus. (p. 740)
—Martin & Mahalia: His Words, His Song. (p. 1097)
—Peace Warriors. (p. 1332)
—Raven in a Dove House. (p. 1441)
—Red Pencil. Evans, Shane W., illus. (p. 1454)
—Rhythm Ride: A Road Trip Through the Motown Sound. (p. 1468)
—Silent Thunder: A Civil War Story. (p. 1575)
—Sit-In: How Four Friends Stood Up by Sitting Down. (p. 1581)
—Sit-in: How Four Friends Stood Up by Sitting Down. (p. 1581)
—Sit-in: How Four Friends Stood Up by Sitting Down. Pinkney, Brian, illus. (p. 1581)
—Sojourner Truth's Step-Stomp Stride. Pinkney, Brian, illus. (p. 1606)
—With the Might of Angels: The Diary of Dawnie Rae Johnson, Hadley, Virginia 1954. (p. 1942)
Pinkney, Andrea Davis, jt. auth. see Norwich, Grace.
Pinkney, Brian. Max Found Two Sticks. Pinkney, Brian, illus. (p. 1111)
—On the Ball. Pinkney, Brian, illus. (p. 1289)
Pinkney, Brian, illus. see Albert, Burton.
Pinkney, Brian, illus. see Andersen, Hans Christian.
Pinkney, Brian, illus. see Harrington, Janice N.
Pinkney, Brian, illus. see LaChanze.
Pinkney, Brian, illus. see Lorbiecki, Marybeth.
Pinkney, Brian, illus. see McKissack, Patricia C.
Pinkney, Brian, illus. see Pinkney, Andrea Davis.
Pinkney, Brian, illus. see San Souci, Robert D.
Pinkney, Brian, jt. auth. see Hughes, Langston.
Pinkney, Gloria Jean. Daniel & the Lord of Lions. Casilla, Robert, illus. (p. 404)
—Music from Our Lord's Holy Heaven. Pinkney, Jerry et al, illus. (p. 1193)
Pinkney, J. Brian, illus. see Marzollo, Jean.
Pinkney, Jane, illus. see Greaves, Margaret.
Pinkney, Jeff. Soapstone Signs Gait, Darlene, illus. (p. 1603)
Pinkney, Jerry. Fabulas de Esopo. (p. 559)
—Grasshopper & the Ants. (p. 711)
—Lion & the Mouse. (p. 1020)
—Little Red Hen. Pinkney, Jerry, illus. (p. 1034)
—Little Red Riding Hood. (p. 1035)
—Noah's Ark. (p. 1261)
—Three Little Kittens. Pinkney, Jerry, illus. (p. 1742)
—Tortoise & the Hare. (p. 1771)
—Twinkle, Twinkle, Little Star. (p. 1802)
Pinkney, Jerry, illus. see Arkhurst, Joyce Cooper.
Pinkney, Jerry, illus. see Aston, Dianna Hutts.
Pinkney, Jerry, illus. see Buxton, Jane H.
Pinkney, Jerry, illus. see Holiday, Billie & Herzog, Arthur, Jr.
Pinkney, Jerry, illus. see Holiday, Billie.
Pinkney, Jerry, illus. see Lester, Julius.
Pinkney, Jerry, illus. see McKissack, Patricia C.
Pinkney, Jerry, illus. see Pinkney, Gloria Jean.
Pinkney, Jerry, illus. see Taylor, Mildred D.
Pinkney, Jerry, illus. see Willard, Nancy.
Pinkney, Jerry, jt. auth. see Kipling, Rudyard.
Pinkney, Myles C., illus. see Pinkney, Sandra L.
Pinkney, Myles C., jt. auth. see Pinkney, Sandra L.
Pinkney, Myles C., photos by see Grimes, Nikki.
Pinkney, Myles C., photos by see Pinkney, Sandra L.
Pinkney, Sandra L. I Am Latino: the Beauty in Me. Pinkney, Myles C., photos by. (p. 833)
—Shades of Black: A Celebration of Our Children. Pinkney, Myles C., illus. (p. 1556)
Pinkney, Sandra L. & Pinkney, Myles C. I Am Latino: The Beauty in Me. (p. 833)
Pinkowski, Vern V. Twisted Pig's Tale. (p. 1802)
Pinkowski, Vernon V. Twisted Pig's Tale. (p. 1802)
Pinksterboer, Hugo. Pocket-Info Gesang: (German Text) (p. 1375)
Pinkwater, Daniel M. Adventures of a Cat-Whiskered Girl. (p. 16)
—Bear in Love. Hillenbrand, Will, illus. (p. 151)
—Beautiful Yetta: The Yiddish Chicken. Pinkwater, Jill, illus. (p. 154)
—Beautiful Yetta's Hanukkah Kitten. Pinkwater, Jill, illus. (p. 154)
—Bushman Lives! (p. 244)
—Dancing Larry Pinkwater, Jill, illus. (p. 403)
—Education of Robert Nifkin. (p. 505)
—Hoboken Chicken Emergency. Auth, Tony, illus. (p. 786)
—I Am the Dog. Davis, Jack E., illus. (p. 834)
—Irving & Muktuk: Two Bad Bears. (p. 888)
—Lizard Music. (p. 1042)
—Mrs. Noodlekugel. Stower, Adam, illus. (p. 1187)
—Mrs. Noodlekugel & Drooly the Bear. Stower, Adam, illus. (p. 1187)
—Mrs. Noodlekugel & Four Blind Mice. Stower, Adam, illus. (p. 1187)
—Neddiad: How Neddie Took the Train, Went to Hollywood, & Saved Civilization. Brown, Calef, illus. (p. 1239)
—Sleepover Larry. (p. 1589)
—Sleepover Larry. (p. 1589)
—Yggyssey: How Iggy Wondered What Happened to All the Ghosts, Found Out Where They Went, & Went There. (p. 1971)
—Young Larry Pinkwater, Jill, illus. (p. 1979)
—Yo-Yo Man. Davis, Jack E., illus. (p. 1972)
Pinkwater, Daniel M. & Johnson, D. B. Bear's Picture. Johnson, D. B., illus. (p. 152)
Pinkwater, Daniel M. & Pinkwater, Jill. Bongo Larry (p. 209)
Pinkwater, Jill, illus. see Pinkwater, Daniel M.
Pinkwater, Jill, jt. auth. see Pinkwater, Daniel M.
Pinna, Lorenzo. Clima. (p. 332)
—Conquista del Espacio. (p. 358)
Pinna, Simon de, see de Pinna, Simon.
Pinnell, Gay Su, jt. auth. see Fountas, Irene C.
Pinnell, Gay Su & Fountas, Irene C. Phonics Lessons: Letters, Words, & How They Work - Grade 2. (p. 1352)
Pinnell, Gay Su & Scharer, Patricia L. Teaching for Comprehension in Reading, Grade K-2: Strategies for Helping Children Read with Ease, Confidence, & Understanding. (p. 1710)
Pinnell, Gay Su, et al. Health & Safety 2: Safety First; Don't Be a Couch Potato; Birthday Shots; Just in Case; Time Out; Home Sick; the Eye Doctor; the Big Race Simon, Sue A. et al, illus. (p. 757)
Pinnington, Andrea. Animal Babies. (p. 76)
—Christmas Creativity Book: Includes Games, Cut-Outs, Fold-Out Scenes, Textures, Stickers, & Stencils. (p. 313)
—Christmas Pocket Activity Fun & Games: Games, Puzzles, Fold-Out Scenes, Patterned Paper, Stickers! (p. 315)
—Crias de Animales. (p. 382)
—Dragon Creativity Book: Includes Stickers, Fold-Out Scene, Stencils, & Patterned Paper. (p. 476)
—Dragon Pocket Activity Fun & Games: Includes Games, Cutouts, Foldout Scenes, Textures, Stickers, & Stencils. (p. 477)
—Fashion Tween Creativity Book. (p. 576)
—Fashion Tween Pocket Activity Fun & Games: Includes Games, Cutouts, Foldout Scenes, Textures, Stickers, & Stencils. (p. 576)
—Horse & Pony Creativity Book. (p. 799)
—Horse & Pony Pocket Activity Fun & Games: Games & Puzzles, Fold-Out Scenes, Patterned Paper, Stickers! (p. 799)
—Mi Cuerpo. (p. 1132)
—My Body. (p. 1198)
—Pirate Creativity Book. (p. 1362)
—Pirate Pocket Activity Fun & Games: Includes Games, Cutouts, Foldout Scenes, Textures, Stickers, & Stencils! (p. 1363)
—Princess Creativity Book: Includes Stickers, Fold-Out Scene, Stencils, & Pretty Paper. (p. 1403)
—Princess Pocket Activity Fun & Games: Includes Games, Cutouts, Foldout Scenes, Textures, Stickers, & Stencils. (p. 1405)
—Rainy Day. (p. 1436)
Pinnington, Andrea, jt. auth. see Whittington, M.
Pinnington, Andrea & Dorling Kindersley Publishing Staff. Big Boys Use the Potty! (p. 179)
Pinnington, Andrea & Gordon-Harris, Tory. Animal Babies. (p. 76)
Pinnington, Andrea & Lamprell, Penny. My Body. (p. 1198)
Pinnington, Andrea & Potter, William. Space Creativity Book. (p. 1618)
Pinnock, Nathan, illus. see Bytheway, John.
Pino, Montana. Tessie & Tillie. (p. 1723)
Pino, Pablo, illus. see Damiron, Anya.
Pino, Santo & Hook, Dena. Success with IEPs: Lessons Learned from Implementing the Middle School Model. Norris, Jill, ed. (p. 1672)
Pins, Javier, jt. auth. see Andreyko, Marc.
Pinson, Isabel. Bubbe's Belated Bat Mitzvah. Cis, Valeria, illus. (p. 233)
Pinson, Joseph. Big Wooley's Christmas. (p. 184)
—Joey & Big Wooley's Adventures. (p. 920)
Pinson, Mignon L. My Two Best Friends Are Hamsters. (p. 1220)
Pinter, Karin. Niki Owl: Leap of Faith. (p. 1255)
Pinter, Sarah. Electra. (p. 508)
Pinto, Amy B. Sophie's Perfume. (p. 1613)
Pinto, Dan, illus. see Sutton, Benn.
Pinto, Dan & Sutton, Benn. Hedgehug: A Sharp Lesson in Love. Pinto, Dan, illus. (p. 762)
Pinto, Diana. If Stones Could Talk: Ken Kriegh's California Landscapes, a Memoir. (p. 854)
Pinto, Ferando. Little Heroes. (p. 1029)
Pinto, Guilherme, tr. see Moon, Fabio.
Pinto, Helena Rebelo, jt. auth. see Paiva, Teresa.
Pinto, Joan De Sola, tr. see Moon, Fabio.
Pinto, Marie Parks. Does It Still Hurt. Mazzei, Miriam, illus. (p. 460)
—I Am Not Broken. Mazzei, Miriam, illus. (p. 833)
—Where Is Daddy? Mazzei, Miriam, illus. (p. 1908)
Pinto, Matthew J. Did Adam & Eve Have Belly Buttons? (p. 436)
Pinto, Mindee & Cohen, Judy. Mikey. Fairbanks, Mark, illus. (p. 1141)
Pinto, Sara. Alphabet Room. Pinto, Sara, illus. (p. 50)
—Apples & Oranges: Going Bananas with Pairs. Pinto, Sara, illus. (p. 92)
Pinto, Sara, illus. see Gold, Rozanne.
Pinto, Sara, jt. auth. see Colin, Beatrice.
Pintor, Ruben, illus. see Dawson, Mike.
Pintozzi, Connie, illus. see Pintozzi, Nick.
Pintozzi, Nick. Bentley & the Cactus Rustlers. Pintozzi, Nick & Pintozzi, Connie, illus. (p. 165)
—Bentley & the Great Fire. Pintozzi, Nick et al, illus. (p. 165)
—Bentley Finds a Home. Pintozzi, Nick et al, illus. (p. 165)
Pinz, Shelley. Holly, Bear & Coty, & the Very First Angel of Christmas. (p. 789)
Piorkowski, Sue. Herman Melville. Bloom, Harold, ed. (p. 771)
Piotrowski, Robert. Gold Rush. Alward, Jeff, illus. (p. 694)
Piotti, Dania, illus. see Bookins, Daddy.
Pipal, Michele. Lines. (p. 1019)
Pipe, Jasper, illus. see Hong, Catherine Thao.
Pipe, Jim. Aliens. (p. 41)
—Be a Salem Witch! Bizarre Accusations You'd Rather Not Face. (p. 148)
—Be an Aristocrat in the French Revolution! A Horrible Time in Paris You'd Rather Avoid. Antram, David, illus. (p. 148)
—Biofuels. (p. 188)
—Castle Sticker Book: Complete Your Own Mighty, Medieval Fortress! Taylor, Maria, illus. (p. 277)
—Coal. (p. 336)
—Conservation: Animals in Danger. (p. 358)
—Doll's House Sticker Book: Decorate Your Very Own Victorian Home! Taylor, Maria, illus. (p. 464)
—Gas. (p. 657)
—Ghosts. (p. 672)
—Hoping for Peace in Iran. (p. 797)
—Hoping for Peace in Sudan. (p. 797)
—How to Survive on a Desert Island. (p. 822)
—Japan in Our World. (p. 909)
—Lift, Look & Learn Castle: Uncover the Secrets of a Medieval Fortress. Taylor, Maria, illus. (p. 1014)
—Lift, Look & Learn Doll's House: Uncover the Secrets of a Victorian Home. Taylor, Maria, illus. (p. 1014)
—Make a Movie! (p. 1078)
—Monsters. (p. 1168)
—Mysteries of the Mayan Calendar. (p. 1222)
—Nuclear Power. (p. 1270)
—Oil. (p. 1282)
—Rescue Squad: Saving Lives. (p. 1462)
—Sail on an Irish Famine Ship! A Trip Across Teh Atlantic You'd Rather Not Make. Antram, David, illus. (p. 1503)
—Scary Creatures of the Deep. Bergin, Mark et al, illus. (p. 1520)
—Solar Power. (p. 1606)
—Spies: Behind Enemy Lines. (p. 1627)
—Stunt Crews: Death-Defying Feats. (p. 1670)
—Survivors: Into the Wilderness. (p. 1687)
—Swarms. (p. 1689)
—Titanic. (p. 1757)
—Top 10 Worst Vicious Villains. Antram, David, illus. (p. 1768)
—Undead. (p. 1813)
—Water Power. (p. 1863)
—Wind Power. (p. 1935)
—Wonderful World. (p. 1948)
—You Wouldn't Want to Be a Salem Witch! (p. 1977)
—You Wouldn't Want to Be a Salem Witch! Bizarre Accusations You'd Rather Not Face. (p. 1977)
—You Wouldn't Want to Be Cleopatra! An Egyptian Ruler You'd Rather Not Be. Antram, David, illus. (p. 1977)
—You Wouldn't Want to Live Without Cell Phones! Walker, Rory, illus. (p. 1977)
—You Wouldn't Want to Sail on an Irish Famine Ship! A Trip Across the Atlanic You'd Rather Not Make. Antram, David, illus. (p. 1977)
Pipe, Jim, jt. auth. see Connolly, Sean.
Pipe, Jim, jt. auth. see Parker, Steve.
Pipe, Jim, jt. auth. see Ticktock.
Pipe, Jim & Newland, Sonya. Extinction! (p. 555)
Pipe, Sheryl L., jt. auth. see Furstinger, Nancy.
Piper, Danny W. Skinny Boy's Close Call. (p. 1585)
Piper, Deb. From A— to Zulinski. (p. 641)
Piper, Don & Murphey, Cecil. 90 Minutes in Heaven: My True Story (p. 1998)
Piper, Henry Beam. Little Fuzzy. (p. 1028)
Piper, John. Pleasures of God. (p. 1373)
—Seeing & Savoring Jesus Christ. (p. 1548)
Piper, Molly. Rosey & Amanda. Piper, Molly, illus. (p. 1490)
Piper, Noël. Do You Want a Friend? Schoonmaker, Gail, illus. (p. 458)
—Most of All, Jesus Loves You! Anderson, Debby, illus. (p. 1177)
Piper, Paul, ed. see Mark, Rebecca & Vaughan, Rob.
Piper, Ross. Death Zone: Can Humans Survive at 26,000 Feet? (p. 420)
—Extreme Lunch! Life & Death in the Food Chain (p. 556)
—Fingerprint Wizards: The Secrets of Forensic Science (p. 589)
—Survival! Staying Alive in the Wild (p. 1686)
—Surviving in the World's Most Extreme Places (p. 1687)
Piper, Sophie. Angel & the Dove: A Story for Easter. Stephenson, Kristina, illus. (p. 73)
—Angel & the Lamb: A Story for Christmas. Stephenson, Kristina, illus. (p. 73)
—Angel to Watch over Me: Prayers & Blessings. Allsopp, Sophie, illus. (p. 74)
—Arkful of Animal Prayers. Macnaughton, Tina, illus. (p. 99)
—Baby's First Bible. Maddocks, Maria, illus. (p. 129)
—Blessings for a Baby Boy. Williams, Caroline, illus. (p. 199)
—Blessings for a Baby Girl. Williams, Caroline, illus. (p. 199)
—Everyone Needs a Friend. Williams, Caroline, illus. (p. 544)
—First Prayers for Baby. Spenceley, Annabel, illus. (p. 596)
—From the Day You Were Born. Stephenson, Kristina, illus. (p. 644)
—Goodnight Prayers. Moriuchi, Mique, illus. (p. 701)
—Lion Book of Christmas Poems. (p. 1020)
—Lion Book of Nursery Fables. Kolanovic, Dubravka, illus. (p. 1020)
—Lion Book of Prayers to Read & Know. Lewis, Anthony, illus. (p. 1020)
—My Baptism Book. Kolanovic, Dubravka, illus. (p. 1196)
—My First Holy Communion. Ruta, Angelo, illus. (p. 1206)
—My Guardian Angel. Rescek, Sanja, illus. (p. 1210)
—Prayers for Each & Every Day. Wilson, Anne, illus. (p. 1393)
Piper, Sophie, jt. auth. see Rock, Lois.
Piper, Sophie, jt. auth. see Rock.
Piper, Sophie, jt. auth. see Toulmin.
Piper, Sophie & Birkett, Georgie. Ready, Steady, Growl (p. 1447)
Piper, Sophie & Rock, Lois. God Bless. Widdowson, Kay, illus. (p. 688)
Piper, Sophie, compiled by. Poems & Prayers for Easter. (p. 1376)
Piper, Tom, illus. see Nevis, Lance.
Piper, Watty. Little Engine That Could. (p. 1027)
—Little Engine That Could. Long, Loren, illus. (p. 1027)
—Little Engine That Could. Hauman, George & Hauman, Doris, illus. (p. 1027)
—Little Engine That Could. Hauman, George and Doris & Hauman, Doris, illus. (p. 1027)
Piper, Watty & Penguin / LeapFrog. Little Engine That Could. Long, Loren, illus. (p. 1027)
Piper, Watty, et al. My First Library (p. 1207)

Piper, William Bowman. Giraffe of Montana, Volume 1 (p. 677)
—Giraffe of Montana, Volume 3. (p. 677)
Pipera, Lady. Enchanted Meadow. (p. 523)
Pipkin, Evelyn Ruth. Pretty Little Red Bird. (p. 1398)
Pippenger, Jack G. Young Rebel. (p. 1979)
Pippin, Barbara, illus. see Guiffre, William A.
Pippin, Barbara, illus. see Guiffre, William.
Pippin, Kristin A., illus. see Pippin, Sheila C.
Pippin, Sheila C. Katrina: Through Mango's Eyes. Pippin, Kristin A. & Pippin, Sheila C., illus. (p. 945)
Pippin-Mathur, Courtney. Maya Was Grumpy. (p. 1113)
—Maya Was Grumpy. Pippin-Mathur, Courtney, illus. (p. 1113)
Pirandello, Luigi. Henry IV. Landes, William-Alan, ed. (p. 768)
—Right You Are, If You Think You Are. Landes, William-Alan, ed. (p. 1472)
Pirie, Lauren, jt. auth. see Appleby, Danny.
Pirie, Mark. Gallery: A Selection. (p. 653)
Piriou, Jean Pierre, jt. auth. see Walz, Joel.
Pirner, Connie White. Even Little Kids Get Diabetes. Westcott, Nadine Bernard, illus. (p. 541)
Pirnia, Daryoush, ed. see Pirnia, Mansoreh.
Pirnia, Mansoreh. Ardeshir Zahedi: Farzand Taufan, Hamzade Shah. Pirnia, Daryoush, ed. (p. 96)
Pirnot, Dr Karen Hutchins & Pirnot, Karen Hutchins. Colors of Myself. Klanot, Sameon Clay, illus. (p. 345)
Pirnot, Karen Hutchins. Blue Penguin. Klanot, Makenna Karen, illus. (p. 203)
—Colorful Day. Klanot, Taryn Lane, illus. (p. 344)
—Door in the Floor. Ross, Julie, illus. (p. 470)
—Keeper of the Lullabies, a Book for Grandmothers Who Cherish the World of Children. Pirnot, Karen Hutchins, illus. (p. 947)
—Night Traveler. Pirnot, Karen Hutchins, illus. (p. 1254)
—Rainbows Are the Best. Allen, Sandra Hutchins, illus. (p. 1436)
—Sam's Perfect Plan. Ross, Julie, illus. (p. 1509)
Pirnot, Karen Hutchins, illus. see Klanot, Khaya Dawn.
Pirnot, Karen Hutchins, jt. auth. see Pirnot, Dr Karen Hutchins.
Pirog, Kristen T. Army ABC Book. Pierce, Julie A., illus. (p. 100)
—Marine ABC Book. Pierce, Julie A., illus. (p. 1094)
Pirolo, Neal. I Think God Wants Me to be a Missionary: Issues to Deal with Long Before You Say, Good-Bye. (p. 846)
Pirotta, Saviour. Aesop's Fables. Johnson, Richard, illus. (p. 25)
—Buccaneering Book of Pirates. (p. 234)
—Children's Stories from the Bible. Gilbert, Anne Yvonne & Andrew, Ian, illus. (p. 304)
—Chinese New Year. (p. 307)
—Chocolate. (p. 309)
—Christmas. (p. 312)
—Divali. (p. 454)
—Easter. (p. 499)
—Firebird. Hyde, Catherine, illus. (p. 591)
—Id-Ul-Fitr. (p. 851)
—Passover. (p. 1327)
—Teeth. (p. 1715)
Pirouz, Dante Monique. Simply Rich: 28 Simple Ways to Bring More Richness into Your Life Everyday. (p. 1578)
Pirz, Therese S. Kids Stuff French: Easy French Phrases for You & Your Kids. (p. 955)
Pirz, Therese S. & Hobson, Mark. Kids Stuff German: Easy German Phrases to Teach Your Kids (and Yourself) (p. 955)
Pirz, Therese Slevin. Kids Stuff Angliski: Easy English Phrases for Russian Speakers. (p. 955)
—Language Helper Spanish: Helping You Speak More Spanish. (p. 975)
Pirzada, Nefes & Simeone, Angelique. Young Equestrian: Something in Common. (p. 1978)
Pisala, Jan, jt. auth. see Dusek, Jiri.
Pisani, Onofrio John. Windy, the Magical Towel. (p. 1936)
Pisano, Maryann. Decision. (p. 421)
Pisano, Sal. Measurement. (p. 1117)
Pisapia, Blasco, illus. see Pavanello, Roberto.
Pisarik, Michael E. Loonhaunt. (p. 1052)
—Ursus: A Bear's Story. (p. 1826)
Pisarski, Patti. Princess Penny Gets a Puppy: Prince Peter Gets a Bike. (p. 1405)
Piscitelli, Donna, jt. auth. see Gorler, Rosemarie.
Piscitelli, Donna, jt. auth. see Gortler, Rosemarie.
Piscitelli, Donna & Gortler, Rosemarie. Living the 10 Commandments for Children. Sternhagen, Mimi, illus. (p. 1041)
Piscopo, Jay. Undersea Adventures of Capt'n Eli (p. 1815)
Piscopo, Samantha, illus. see Cox-Sands, Angela.
Pisella, Donna. Blue Goblin. (p. 202)
Pish, Kathryn & Crider, Darcy R. Bubble Trouble. (p. 233)
Pismarov, Vivienne. Crazy Days of Sam B. (p. 377)
Pisonero, Isidoro, et al. Pasacalle 1: Curso de Espanol para Ninos. (p. 1326)
—Pasacalle 2: Curso de Espanol para Ninos. (p. 1326)
Pissanos, Paul. From Aristotle to Hawking. (p. 642)
Pistacchio, illus. see Maccarone, Grace.
Pistinier, Caroline. Noche Del Ratoncito Perez. (p. 1262)
—Théo et le Lion. (p. 1726)
pistinier, caroline. Théo & the Lion. (p. 1729)
Pistoia, Sara. Counting. (p. 370)
—Fractions. (p. 626)
—Graphs. (p. 711)
—Measurement. (p. 1117)
—Money. (p. 1163)
—Patterns. (p. 1329)
—Shapes. (p. 1560)
—Time. (p. 1750)
Pistole, Katy. Flying High. (p. 610)
Pistone, Nicholas. Art & Culture of Ancient Rome. (p. 101)
Pistone, Nicholas, et al. Art & Culture of Ancient Rome. (p. 101)
Pistorius, Anna, illus. see Friskey, Margaret.
Pita, Lorena, illus. see Ibarrola, Begonia.
Pitamic, Maja & Laidlaw, Jill. Modern Art Adventures: 36 Creative, Hands-On Projects Inspired by Artists from Monet to Banksy. (p. 1158)
Pitcairn, Ansel, illus. see Bolden, Tonya.
Pitcher, Amy B. Bible Lessons for Crafty Kids. (p. 175)
Pitcher, Annabel. Ketchup Clouds. (p. 949)
—My Sister Lives on the Mantelpiece. (p. 1218)
—Yours Truly. (p. 1982)
Pitcher, Caroline. Cloud Cat. (p. 334)
—Lord of the Forest. Morris, Jackie, illus. (p. 1052)
—Mariana & the Merchild: A Folk Tale from Chile. Morris, Jackie, illus. (p. 1093)
—Mariana & the Merchild. Morris, Jackie, illus. (p. 1093)
—Nico's Octopus. Mistry, Nilesh, illus. (p. 1251)
—Snow Whale. Morris, Jackie, illus. (p. 1599)
Pitcher, Chelsea. Last Changeling. (p. 977)
—S-Word. (p. 1499)
Pitcher, Jeff, illus. see Howlett, Bruce, et al.
Pitcher, Jeff, jt. creator see Howlett, Bruce.
Pitches, Neale & Hollingsworth, Toni. CSI Comprehensive Strategies Instruction Kit: Grade 6. (p. 387)
Pitchford, Dean. Big One-Oh. (p. 183)
—Captain Nobody. (p. 264)
—Nickel Bay Nick. (p. 1251)
Pitchford-Zhe, Nancy. Dusty & Friends: Book 1. (p. 490)
Pitcoff, Paul, jt. auth. see Krebs, Betsy.
Pite, Ralph. Thomas Hardy: The Guarded Life. (p. 1738)
Pitino, Donna Marie. Too-Tall Tina. Woodruff, Liza, illus. (p. 1767)
Pitkethly, Maggie. Graeme Goes Home. Farmer, Suzanne, illus. (p. 705)
Pitkin, Jo, jt. auth. see Darragh, Marty.
Pitman, Colin. House That Talked. (p. 804)
Pitman, Gayle E. This Day in June. Litten, Kristyna, illus. (p. 1735)
Pitman, Norman Hinsdale. Chinese Wonder Book: A Classic Collection of Chinese Tales. Tang, Li Chu, illus. (p. 308)
Pitman, Sandra. 10 Busy Bumble Bees Sizemore, Carmen, illus. (p. 1993)
Pitre, Dawn, illus. see Gano, Debra.
Pitt, Darrell. Broken Sun. (p. 230)
—Firebird Mystery. (p. 591)
Pitt, Marilyn. Cat Walk. (p. 278)
—Run Away. (p. 1496)
—Smelling Good. Bianchi, John, illus. (p. 1593)
—What Are You Thinking? (p. 1880)
Pitt, Marilyn, jt. auth. see Hileman, Jane.
Pitt, Marilyn & Hileman, Jane. Get Up. Bianchi, John, illus. (p. 668)
—I Like My Stuff. Bianchi, John, illus. (p. 841)
—Let Me In. Bianchi, John, illus. (p. 994)
—My Babies. (p. 1196)
—My Babies. Bianchi, John, illus. (p. 1196)
—Pretty Cat. (p. 1398)
—Pretty Cat. Bianchi, John, illus. (p. 1398)
—Storm. Bianchi, John, illus. (p. 1655)
—Up Here. Bianchi, John, illus. (p. 1824)
—Where Is My Boy? Bianchi, John, illus. (p. 1908)
—Where Is That Dog? Bianchi, John, illus. (p. 1909)
Pitt, Marilyn & Sánchez, Lucía M. Mis Bebés. Bianchi, John, illus. (p. 1150)
Pitt, Marilyn & Sanchez, Lucia M. Nevada: Snow Dog. Bianchi, John, illus. (p. 1242)
—Perro en Apuros: Let Me In. Bianchi, John, illus. (p. 1343)
Pitt, Marilyn & Sánchez, Lucía M. Solos en Casa. Bianchi, John, illus. (p. 1608)
Pitt, Marilyn & Sanchez, Lucia M. Tormenta: The Storm. Bianchi, John, illus. (p. 1770)
Pitt, Marilyn & Sánchez, Lucía M. ¡Arriba! Bianchi, John, illus. (p. 101)
Pitt, Marilyn, et al. Perro en Apuros: Let Me In. Bianchi, John & Taylor, Trace, illus. (p. 1344)
Pitt, Roosevelt, Jr. Day at the Four Seasons: "Finding the Ingredients" Kuumba, Mshindo, illus. (p. 412)
Pitt, Sarah. Peek a Boo! Farm. (p. 1334)
—Peek a Boo! Garden. (p. 1334)
—Peek a Boo! Ocean. (p. 1334)
—Peek a Boo! Zoo. (p. 1335)
Pitt, Sarah, illus. see David, Juliet & Dowley, Tim.
Pitt, Sarah, illus. see David, Juliet.
Pitt, Sarah, illus. see Reader's Digest Staff.
Pitt, Sarah, illus. see Reasoner, Charles.
Pitt, Steve. Guyness: Body & Soul Murray, Steven, illus. (p. 733)
—Rain Tonight: A Story of Hurricane Hazel. Collins, Heather, illus. (p. 1435)
—Teasing: Deal with It Before the Joke's on You Geoffroi, Remie, illus. (p. 1711)
—To Stand & Fight Together: Richard Pierpoint & the Coloured Corps of Upper Canada. (p. 1759)
Pitt, Steve, jt. auth. see Slavens, Elaine.
Pitt, Tamina & Terri, Janke. What Makes a Tree Smile? Francine Ngardab, Riches, illus. (p. 1892)
Pittam, Lore M. Golden Mushrooms. (p. 695)
Pittar, Gill. Milly & Molly Go Camping. (p. 1144)
—Milly & Molly Go Camping (book W/dolls) (p. 1144)
—Milly & Molly's Monday. Morrell, Cris, illus. (p. 1144)
—Milly, Molly & Alf. (p. 1144)
—Milly, Molly & Alf (book W/dolls) (p. 1144)
—Milly, Molly & Aunt Maude. (p. 1144)
—Milly, Molly & Aunt Maude (book W/dolls) (p. 1144)
—Milly, Molly & Beaky. Morrell, Cris, illus. (p. 1144)
—Milly, Molly & Beefy. (p. 1144)
—Milly, Molly & Beefy (book W/dolls) (p. 1144)
—Milly, Molly & Betelgeuse. (p. 1144)
—Milly, Molly & Betelgeuse (book W/dolls) (p. 1144)
—Milly, Molly & Different Dads. (p. 1144)
—Milly, Molly & Different Dads (book W/dolls) (p. 1144)
—Milly, Molly & Grandpa Friday. (p. 1144)
—Milly, Molly & Grandpa Friday (book W/dolls) (p. 1144)
—Milly, Molly & Henry. (p. 1144)
—Milly, Molly & Henry (book W/dolls) (p. 1144)
—Milly, Molly & I Love You. (p. 1144)
—Milly, Molly & Jimmy's Seeds. (p. 1144)
—Milly, Molly & Jimmy's Seeds (book W/dolls) (p. 1144)
—Milly, Molly & Oink. (p. 1144)
—Milly, Molly & Sock Heaven. (p. 1144)
—Milly, Molly & Sock Heaven (book W/dolls) (p. 1144)
—Milly, Molly & Special Friends. (p. 1144)
—Milly, Molly & Special Friends (book W/dolls) (p. 1144)
—Milly, Molly & Taffy Bogle. (p. 1144)
—Milly, Molly & Taffy Bogle (book W/dolls) (p. 1144)
—Milly, Molly & the Bike Ride. (p. 1144)
—Milly, Molly & the Ferryman. Morrell, Cris, illus. (p. 1144)
—Milly, Molly & the Picnic. Morrell, Cris, illus. (p. 1144)
—Milly, Molly & the Runaway Bean. Morrell, Cris, illus. (p. 1144)
—Milly, Molly & the Secret Scarves. (p. 1144)
—Milly, Molly & the Secret Scarves (book w/dolls) (p. 1144)
—Milly, Molly & the Secret Scarves/CD-ROM. (p. 1144)
—Milly, Molly & the Stowaways. (p. 1144)
—Milly, Molly & the Stowaways (book W/dolls) (p. 1144)
—Milly, Molly & the Sunhat. (p. 1144)
—Milly, Molly & the Sunhat (book W/dolls) (p. 1144)
—Milly, Molly & the Tree Hut. (p. 1144)
—Milly, Molly & the Tree Hut (book W/dolls) (p. 1144)
—Milly, Molly & What Was That? (p. 1144)
—Milly, Molly & What Was That? (book W/dolls) (p. 1144)
Pittar, Gill & Gill, Pittar. Basura No, Gracias! Rioja, Alberto Jiménez, tr. (p. 143)
—Ciruelas de Isa Bela. Rioja, Alberto Jiménez, tr. (p. 322)
—Quien es Este Sombrero? Rioja, Alberto Jiménez, tr. (p. 1427)
Pittau, et al. Nunca he Visto. (p. 1273)
Pittau, Francesco, jt. auth. see Gervais, Bernadette.
Pittau, Francesco & Gervais, Bernadette. Open Ocean. (p. 1299)
Pittis, Arthur M. As My Heart Awakes: A Waldorf Reader for Early Third Grade. Mitchell, David S., ed. (p. 105)
—Fee Fi Fo Fum: A Waldorf Reader for Late Second Grade. Mitchell, David S., ed. (p. 580)
—Sun So Hot I Froze to Death: A Waldorf Reader for Advanced Fourth Grade. Mitchell, David S., ed. (p. 1676)
—When I Hear My Heart Wonder: A Waldorf Reader for Late Third Grade. Mitchell, David S., ed. (p. 1903)
Pittman, Gail, illus. see Carter, Catherine.
Pittman, Janet. Colourful Quilts for Playful Kids. (p. 346)
Pittman, Michael. Mackey's first Adventure. (p. 1068)
Pittman, Rickey. Jim Limber Davis: A Black Orphan in the Confederate White House Hierstein, Judith, illus. (p. 917)
—Scottish Alphabet McLennan, Connie, illus. (p. 1531)
Pittman, Rickey E. Confederate Alphabet Ford, Stephanie A., illus. (p. 356)
—Irish Alphabet (p. 887)
—Stonewall Jackson's Black Sunday School Hosegood, Lynn, illus. (p. 1653)
Pittman, Robert A. Still Waters. (p. 1650)
Pittman, Ruth. Roadside History of California. Greer, Dan, ed. (p. 1477)
Pittman, Seth. Raggy's Island. (p. 1433)
Pitts, Barbara Russell & Sarao, Mary Russell. Inventing on a Shoestring Budget! Insider Tips for Bringing Your Product to Market Without Breaking the Bank! (p. 883)
Pitts, Constance. Chulita the Blind Cat. (p. 318)
Pitts, Daphne. What Makes God Laugh. (p. 1892)
Pitts, John. Recorder from the Beginning. (p. 1452)
Pitts, Wynter. For Girls Like You: A Devotional for Tweens. (p. 615)
Pitts, Zachary. Horses. (p. 800)
—Pebble First Guide to Lizards (p. 1333)
Pittsley, B. J. Very Best Christmas. (p. 1837)
Pitz, Henry, illus. see Cooper, Page.
Pitzer, Marjorie. Animal Fun for Everyone! (p. 78)
Pitzer, Marjorie W. I Can, Can You? (p. 835)
—I Like Berries, Do You? Pitzer, Marjorie W., photos by. (p. 841)
—My up & down & All Around Book. Pitzer, Marjorie W., photos by. (p. 1220)
Pitzer, Suzanne, illus. see Grollman, Earl A.
Pitzorno, Bianca & Pitzorno, Blanca. Casa del Arbol. Blake, Quentin, illus. (p. 273)
Pitzorno, Blanca, jt. auth. see Pitzorno, Bianca.
Piu, Amandine, illus. see Hanna, Virginie.
Piu, Amandine, jt. auth. see Lhomme, Sandrine.
Piumini, Roberto. 3 Little Pigs Costa, Nicoletta, illus. (p. 1991)
—Goldilocks & the Three Bears Salmaso, Valentina, illus. (p. 696)
—Hansel & Gretel Cantone, Anna Laura, illus. (p. 743)
—Matias y el Abuelo. (p. 1109)
—Puss in Boots Chessa, Francesca, illus. (p. 1420)
Piumini, Roberto & Aesop. Raven & the Fox Bolaffio, Raffaella, illus. (p. 1441)
—Tortoise & the Hare Nascimbeni, Barbara, illus. (p. 1771)
Piumini, Roberto & Wilde, Oscar. Happy Prince Cimatoribus, Alessandra, illus. (p. 746)
—Selfish Giant Costa, Nicoletta, illus. (p. 1549)
Piumini, Roberto, et al. Sleeping Beauty Costa, Nicoletta, illus. (p. 1589)
Pivard, G., jt. auth. see Lemaresquier, D.
Pivard, Gilles. Where Is Turold. (p. 1909)
Pivarnik-Nova, Denise. Mastering the SAT Writing Test: An In-Depth Writing Workout. (p. 1103)
—McGraw-Hill's 400 Essential SAT Words. (p. 1114)
Piven Borgenicht Jordan & Jordan, Sarah. Worst Case Scenario Parenting. (p. 1961)
Piven, Hanoch. Let's Make Faces. Piven, Hanoch, illus. (p. 999)
—My Best Friend Is as Sharp as a Pencil: And Other Funny Classroom Portraits. (p. 1196)
—My Dog Is As Smelly As Dirty Socks: And Other Funny Family Portraits. (p. 1202)
—My Dog Is As Smelly As Dirty Socks: And Other Funny Family Portraits. Piven, Hanoch, illus. (p. 1202)
—My Dog Is As Smelly As Dirty Socks. (p. 1202)
—What Cats Are Made of. Piven, Hanoch, illus. (p. 1881)
—What Presidents Are Made Of. (p. 1892)
—What Presidents are Made Of. (p. 1893)
Piven, Hanoch & Thomson, Sarah L. What Presidents Are Made Of. (p. 1892)
Piven, Joshua, et al. Worst-Case Scenario Survival Handbook: College. Brown, Brenda, illus. (p. 1961)
Piwowarski, Marcin, illus. see Davies, Rhona.
Piwowarski, Marcin, illus. see Godfrey, Jan.
Pixar Animation Studios Staff, jt. contrib. by see Walt Disney Company Staff.
Pixar Firm Staff, jt. auth. see Newton, Teddy.
Pixar, told to. Monsters University Look & Find. (p. 1169)
—Monsters University Play a Sound. (p. 1169)
Pixie, B. R. Just a Little Human. (p. 937)
Pixley, Marcella. Freak. (p. 631)
—Without Tess. (p. 1942)
Pixley, Pippa, illus. see Andersen, Hans Christian.
Pixton, Amy. Hey Diddle Diddle: Hey Baby Look at the Cat & His Fiddle - in New Orleans! (p. 774)
—Indestructibles: Baby Night-Night. Merritt, Kate, illus. (p. 870)
—Indestructibles: Baby Peekaboo. Merritt, Kate, illus. (p. 870)
Pixton, Amy, jt. auth. see Pixton, Kaaren.
Pixton, Amy, jt. auth. see Sickler, Jonas.
Pixton, Amy & Pixton, Kaaren. Creep! Crawl! Hey Baby! Look at These Animals on the Ground! (p. 380)
—Wiggle! March! Hey Baby! Look at Those Animals on the Farm! (p. 1927)
Pixton, Amy, creator. Creepy Crawlies. (p. 381)
—Farm Charm. (p. 573)
—Things with Wings. (p. 1734)
Pixton, Kaaren. Mama & Baby! (p. 1084)
Pixton, Kaaren, illus. see Sickler, Jonas & Pixton, Amy.
Pixton, Kaaren, jt. auth. see Pixton, Amy.
Pixton, Kaaren & Pixton, Amy. Flutter! Fly! Hey Baby! Look at These Things with Wings. (p. 609)
—Jungle, Rumble! Hey Baby! Look at These Wild Animals! (p. 935)
—Plip, Plop, Pond! Hey Baby! Look at These Animals in the Pond! (p. 1374)
Pixton, Kaaren & Sickler, Jonas. Humpty Dumpty: Hey, Bay Look at the Humpty Dumpty - On the Great Wall of China! (p. 827)
—Mary Had a Little Lamb. (p. 1100)
Pizer, Carol. Michael Jackson Saddleback Educational Publishing Staff, ed. (p. 1134)
Pizzirani, Jolinda. Soul Survivor. (p. 1614)
Pizzoli, Greg. Impossibly True Story of Tricky Vic: The Man Who Sold the Eiffel Tower. (p. 862)
—Number One Sam. Pizzoli, Greg, illus. (p. 1271)
—Templeton Gets His Wish. Pizzoli, Greg, illus. (p. 1718)
—Watermelon Seed. Pizzoli, Greg, illus. (p. 1864)
Pizzoli, Greg, illus. see Brendler, Carol.
Pizzoli, Greg, illus. see Krumwiede, Lana.
PK Books Inc, prod. Advetures of Captain Pickles. (p. 25)
Place, Francois. Fighting Heart: The Adventures of a Foundling. Rodarmor, William, tr. (p. 585)
—Old Man Mad about Drawing: A Tale of Hokusai. Rodarmor, William, tr. from FRE. (p. 1284)
Place, Francois, illus. see De Fombelle, Timothée.
Place, François, illus. see L'Homme, Erik.
Place, Francois, illus. see Morpurgo, Michael.
Place, John. Good Artist. Trimmer, Tony, illus. (p. 697)
Place, Robert M. Astrology & Divination. (p. 109)
—Magic & Alchemy. (p. 1071)
—Shamanism. (p. 1559)
Placides, Del S., illus. see Vogel-Placides, Joan Katherine.
Plafkin-Hurwitz, Marsha. Up 2 Snuff: Illustrated Book for Children. Plafkin-Hurwitz, Marsha, illus. (p. 1824)
Plagens, Frances, illus. see Froh, Joanne.
Plain, Nancy. Eleanor of Aquitaine & the High Middle Ages. (p. 508)
—Frederic Remington: Artist of the American West. (p. 633)
—Light on the Prairie: Solomon D. Butcher, Photographer of Nebraska's Pioneer Days. (p. 1015)
Plaisted, Caroline. 10 Things to Do Before You're 16. (p. 1994)
—Boy Talk. (p. 219)
—Girl Talk. (p. 679)
—Macbeth. Shimony, Yaniv, illus. (p. 1067)
—Midsummer Night's Dream. Shimony, Yaniv, illus. (p. 1139)
—Romeo & Juliet. Shimony, Yaniv, illus. (p. 1486)
—Tempest. (p. 1717)
Plaja, Luisa. Write Your Own Blog. (p. 1964)
Plaka, Christina. Yonen Buzz (p. 1972)
Planer, Geoffrey, illus. see Seymour, Jane & Keach, James.
Plank, Alex & Plank, Lisa. How Bad Could It Be? (p. 805)
Plank, Lisa, jt. auth. see Plank, Alex.
Planned Parenthood Federation of America, Inc. Staff. Condom. (p. 356)
—Sexually Transmitted Infections: The Facts. (p. 1556)
—Teensex? It's Okay to Say: No Way! (p. 1715)
—We Believe. (p. 1866)
—Young Woman's Guide to Sexuality. (p. 1979)
Planned Parenthood Toronto Staff. Hear Me Out: True Stories of Teens Educating & Confronting Homophobia Rooney, Frances, ed. (p. 759)
Plant, Andrew, illus. see Collard, Sneed B., III.
Plant, Andrew, illus. see McNamara, Ken.
Plant, Andrew, illus. see Thomson, Sarah L.
Plant, Andrew, jt. auth. see Thomson, Sarah L.
Plant, Beth, illus. see Finch, Donna.
Plant, Cherie A. Word Roots A1: Learning the Building Blocks of Better Spelling & Vocabulary. (p. 1951)
—Word Roots B1: Learning the Building Blocks of Better Spelling & Vocabulary. (p. 1951)
Plant, Cherie A., jt. auth. see Blanchard, Cherie.
Plant, David J. Hungry Roscoe. (p. 828)
Plant, Marilyn. Trinka's Magic Bracelet. (p. 1787)
—Trinka's Music Lessons. (p. 1787)
Plant, Timothy. Beyond the Wall: Throw a Little Light - Vol 1. (p. 174)
—Watch It: Throw a Little Light, Vol III. (p. 1861)
Plantain Press. ESSENTIAL Handbook for Businesses in the US Virgin Islands: The Must-Have Guide to Help You Run Your Business. (p. 537)
Plantain Press & Monigold, Jason. Starting A Business in the US Virgin Islands: The Definitive Guide to Getting Your Business off the Ground as Quickly & Easily as Possible. (p. 1644)
Plante, Beth, illus. see Finch, Donna.

P

Plante, Clare la, see La Plante, Clare.
Plante, Patty. Early Bird Baby Bible Curriculum. (p. 493)
—Fruto Del Espiritu Garcia de Ortiz, Lic. Rosalinda, tr. from ENG. (p. 646)
—Joy for Jesus: Jesus in Me. (p. 929)
—Joy for Jesus: Doing God's Word (p. 929)
—Joy for Jesus: Friends with God (p. 929)
—Joy for Jesus: Living Like Jesus (p. 929)
—Viviendo Como Jesus Garcia de Ortiz, Lic. Rosalinda, tr. from ENG. (p. 1846)
Plante, Raymond. Dromadaire Chez Marilou Polaire. Favreau, Marie-Claude, illus. (p. 485)
—Grand Role de Marilou Polaire. Favreau, Marie-Claude, illus. (p. 707)
—Marilou Forecasts the Future Cummins, Sarah, tr. from FRE. (p. 1094)
—Marilou Keeps a Camel Cummins, Sarah, tr. from FRE. (p. 1094)
—Marilou Keeps a Camel. Favreau, Marie-Claude, illus. (p. 1094)
—Monde de Xéros. Delezenne, Christine, illus. (p. 1163)
Plante, Raymond & Prud'Homme, Jules. Attention, les Murs Ont des Oreilles. (p. 114)
Plantz, Connie. Elvis Presley: Music Legend, Movie Star, the King. (p. 517)
—Life of Bessie Coleman: First African-American Woman Pilot. (p. 1011)
Plascencia, Amira, jt. auth. see Rivas, Spelile.
Plaskonos, Lauren. Golden Horn, Silver Hooves. (p. 695)
Plass, Beverly. Functional Vocabulary for Adolescents & Adults. (p. 649)
Plass, Dawn M. Oliver Axel's Adventures: Here I Am, World! (p. 1285)
Plasse, Christopher. Secret Life of Alex Stone: Episode 1. (p. 1541)
Plastow, Joan. Adventures of Joe. (p. 19)
Platkin, Charles, jt. auth. see Platkin, Charles Stuart.
Platkin, Charles Stuart & Platkin, Charles. Lighten Up: Stay Sane, Eat Great, Lose Weight. (p. 1015)
Plato. Republica. (p. 1462)
—Timaeus & Critias. Lee, Desmond, tr. from GEC. (p. 1750)
Platt, Andy, jt. auth. see Beckett, Mike.
Platt, Brian, illus. see Cushion, Hazel.
Platt, Chris. Astra (p. 109)
—Moon Shadow. (p. 1172)
—Star Gazer (p. 1640)
—Storm Chaser (p. 1655)
—Willow King (p. 1934)
—Wind Dancer (p. 1935)
Platt, Cynthia. Little Bit of Love. Whitty, Hannah, illus. (p. 1024)
—Panda-Monium! Vasylenko, Veronica, illus. (p. 1320)
Platt, D. D. & Conkling, Philip, eds. Island Journal: An Annual Publication of the Island Institute Ralston, Peter, photos by. (p. 892)
Platt, D. D., ed. Island Journal: An Annual Publication of the Island Institute Ralston, Peter, photos by. (p. 892)
Platt, Greg, illus. see Sayles, Alayne.
Platt, Jason, illus. see Hodson, Sarah E.
Platt, Kin. Big Max & the Mystery of the Missing Giraffe. Cravath, Lynne Avril, illus. (p. 182)
—Blue Man. (p. 203)
Platt, Pierre, illus. see Michaels, David.
Platt, Randall. Incommunicado. (p. 869)
Platt, Richard. Castle Diary: The Journal of Tobias Burgess. Riddell, Chris, illus. (p. 276)
—Circus Horse Could Count?! And Other Extraordinary Entertainments. (p. 322)
—Discovering Pirates (p. 449)
—DK Adventures: Galactic Mission: Galactic Mission. (p. 455)
—Egyptian Diary: The Journal of Nakht. Parkins, David, illus. (p. 506)
—Egyptians. Lawrence, David, illus. (p. 507)
—Espias. Dann, Geoff & Gorton, Steve, illus. (p. 536)
—Greeks. Lawrence, David, illus. (p. 721)
—In 1400, Reading Could Save Your Life?! And Other Academic Advantages. (p. 862)
—In the Renaissance. Lawrence, David, illus. (p. 867)
—Pirate Diary: The Journal of Jake Carpenter. Riddell, Chris, illus. (p. 1362)
—Plagues, Pox, & Pestilence. Kelly, John, illus. (p. 1366)
—Roman Diary: The Journal of Iliona, a Young Slave. Parkins, David, illus. (p. 1485)
—Roman Diary: The Journal of Iliona of Mytilini, Who Was Captured & Sold As a Slave in Rome, AD 107. Parkins, David, illus. (p. 1485)
—Spiders' Secrets. (p. 1627)
—Spy. (p. 1635)
—Stephen Biesty's Incredible Explosions: Exploded Views of Astonishing Things. Biesty, Stephen, illus. (p. 1648)
—They Played What?! The Weird History of Sports & Recreation. (p. 1732)
—They Wore What?! The Weird History of Fashion & Beauty. (p. 1732)
—Ultimate Book about Me: Discover What Makes You 'YOU!' (p. 1809)
—Vanishing Rainforest. van Wyk, Rupert, illus. (p. 1833)
—Visitor. (p. 1845)
Platt, Richard, jt. auth. see Biesty, Stephen.
Platt, Richard, jt. auth. see Dorling Kindersley Publishing Staff.
Platt, Richard, jt. auth. see Wallace, Karen.
Platt, Richard & Biesty, Stephen. Castle. (p. 276)
—Man-of-War. (p. 1085)
—Stephen Biesty's Incredible Cross-Sections Book. (p. 1648)
Platt, Richard & Dorling Kindersley Publishing Staff. Galactic Mission. (p. 652)
—Pirate. Chambers, Tina, photos by. (p. 1362)
Platt, Richard & Gifford, Clive. Spies Revealed. (p. 1627)
Platt, Richard & Lawrie, Robin. Palaces, Peasants & Plagues: England in the 14th Century. (p. 1319)
Platt, Sharai, illus. see Feuer, Bonnie.
Platten, Carl. Once upon a Dragon: A Colouring Book. (p. 1292)
Plattner, Josh. Alligator: Master of Might. (p. 47)
—Body Manners. (p. 207)
—Manners at Mealtime. (p. 1088)
—Manners Out & About. (p. 1088)
—Manners with Family. (p. 1088)
—Manners with Friends. (p. 1088)
—Mantis Shrimp: Master of Punching. (p. 1088)
—Octopus: Master of Disguise. (p. 1278)
—Peregrine Falcon: Master of Speed. (p. 1341)
—Poison Dart Frog: Master of Poison. (p. 1377)
—Salamander: Master of Regrowth. (p. 1504)
Plaut, Michael. How to Draw the Life & Times of Gerald R. Ford. (p. 819)
Plaut, Michael F. How to Draw the Life & Times of Gerald R. Ford. (p. 819)
Plaut, Thomas F. asma en un Minuto: Lo que usted necesita Saber. Velez, Stacey, ed. (p. 106)
—One Minute Asthma: What You Need to Know. Velez, Stacey, ed. (p. 1296)
Plaut, W. Gunther & Meyer, Michael. Reform Judaism Reader: North American Documents. (p. 1456)
Plautus, Titus Maccius. Amphitryon. Landes, William-Alan, ed. (p. 66)
Plawner, Michael A. Then & Now. (p. 1729)
Plaxton, Judith & Second Story Press Staff. Morning Star (p. 1175)
Play Along Fairy Tales. Little Mermaid. (p. 1031)
Play Bac, creator. Farm Animals. (p. 573)
Play Pen Books Staff. Animals: Easy Instructions Make Bringing Your Origami to Life Fun from Start to Finish! (p. 81)
Playaway, creator. Praise Songs for Kids. (p. 1393)
—Scripture Memory Songs. (p. 1533)
Playcrib, illus. see Laar-Yond C.T.
Player, Micah. Chloe, Instead. (p. 308)
—Lately Lily: The Adventures of a Travelling Girl. (p. 979)
Player, Micah, illus. see Chronicle Books Editors.
Player, Micah, illus. see Chronicle Books Staff.
Player, Micah, illus. see McKay, Hilary.
Player, Stephen, jt. auth. see Peters, Andrew Fusek.
Playmobil & Buster Books Staff. Official Playmobil Activity Book. (p. 1280)
Playmore Publishers. Blanca Nieves: Cuento Plegable. (p. 198)
—Cenicienta. (p. 286)
Playmore Publishers Staff. Sirenita. (p. 1580)
Plaza, José María. Ya Soy Mayor. (p. 1968)
Plaza, José María, jt. auth. see Plaza, Jose Maria.
Plaza, José María & María, Plaza José. Alibaru: La Ronda de las Estaciones. (p. 39)
—Pajaruli: Poemas para Seguir Andando. Villamuza, Noemi, illus. (p. 1319)
—Tungaira: Miss Primeras Poesias. Lucini, Carmen, illus. (p. 1797)
Plaza, Jose Maria & Plaza, José María. Tierra a la Vista: La Historia de Costobal Colon. Aranda, Julio C., illus. (p. 1748)
Plaza, Miren Agur Meabe, et al. COMO CORREGIR A UNA MAESTRA MALVADA. (p. 350)
PLC Editors Staff, jt. auth. see Osborne, Mary Pope.
Pleasant, Charles. Story of Rapunzelresha's First Date. (p. 1659)
Pleasant Company Staff. American Girl Permanent Floor Display. (p. 61)
Pleasant, David, jt. auth. see Pleasant, Jalal.
Pleasant, Jalal & Pleasant, David. Pleasant Signs. (p. 1373)
Pleau-Murissi, Marilyn. Caillou, Spends the Day with Daddy. CINAR Animation Staff, illus. (p. 251)
—Happy Holidays! (p. 746)
Plec, Julie. Originals: the Loss. (p. 1304)
Plecas, Jennifer. Bah! Said the Baby. Plecas, Jennifer, illus. (p. 132)
Plecas, Jennifer, illus. see Codell, Esmé Raji.
Plecas, Jennifer, illus. see Cowley, Joy.
Plecas, Jennifer, illus. see Heos, Bridget.
Plecas, Jennifer, illus. see Joosse, Barbara M.
Plecas, Jennifer, illus. see Little, Jean.
Plecas, Jennifer, illus. see Thomas, Shelley Moore.
Plechowicz, Sue. Classworks Literacy Year 4. (p. 329)
Pledger, Maurice. Animal World. (p. 80)
—Billy Bunny & the Butterflies. (p. 187)
—Bobby Bear & the Honeybees. Pledger, Maurice, illus. (p. 206)
—Bug World. (p. 236)
—Daisy Duckling's Adventure. (p. 400)
—Dinosaur World. (p. 443)
—Dinosaurs. (p. 444)
—Dinosaurs & Bugs. (p. 444)
—Dottie Dolphin Plays Hide-And-Seek. (p. 472)
—Into the Wild. (p. 881)
—Jungle. (p. 934)
—Jungle World. (p. 935)
—Jungles & Oceans. (p. 935)
—Morris Mouse. (p. 1176)
—Nature Trails: Baby Animals. (p. 1236)
—Nature Trails: Beetles & Bugs. (p. 1236)
—Nature Trails: Dinosaurs. (p. 1236)
—Nature Trails: in the Ocean. (p. 1236)
—Nighttime. (p. 1255)
—Noisy Nature: in the Ocean. (p. 1263)
—Ocean. (p. 1276)
—Olivia Owl Finds a Friend. (p. 1287)
—Oscar Otter & the Goldfish. (p. 1305)
—Ping-Ping Panda's Bamboo Journey. (p. 1359)
—Sounds of the Wild: Birds. (p. 1615)
—Sounds of the Wild: Bugs. (p. 1615)
—Sounds of the Wild: Desert. (p. 1615)
—Sounds of the Wild: Seashore. (p. 1615)
—Wildlife World. (p. 1931)
Pledger, Maurice, illus. see Davies, Valerie.
Pledger, Maurice, illus. see Martin, Ruth.
Plehal, Christopher J. Yes, Virginia: There Is a Santa Claus. Bernardin, James, illus. (p. 1970)
Plemmons, Fred Maurice. What Day Is It, Ralphie? (p. 1881)
Plenge, Pete. Elephants Can't Hide Forever. (p. 512)
Pleshakov, Constantine. Tsar's Last Armada: The Epic Voyage to the Battle of Tsushima. (p. 1795)
Pless, Vera, jt. auth. see Beissinger, Janet.
Plesscher, Marietta. When One Little Bug Gave the World a Big Hug. (p. 1904)
Plessix, Michel. Viento en los Sauces. Gasol, Anna, tr. (p. 1841)
Plessix, Michel, illus. see Grahame, Kenneth.
Plessix, Michel, jt. auth. see Grahame, Kenneth.
Pletcher, Kenneth. Britannica Guide to Explorers & Explorations That Changed the Modern World. (p. 229)
Pletcher, Kenneth, ed. Explorers in the 20th & 21st Centuries. (p. 551)
—Nineteenth-Century Explorers. (p. 1256)
Pletka, Bob, creator. My So-Called Digital Life: 2,000 Teenagers, 300 Cameras, & 30 Days to Document Their World. (p. 1219)
Plews, Sue, et al. Dylunio a Thechnoleg, Cwrs Sylfaen Bwyd. (p. 491)
Plez, Josey. My Adventures with Granny Roo - Riding Jessy. (p. 1195)
Pliego, Jane. Reforma para Ninos. (p. 1456)
Pliljnaar, Wilbert, et al. Walt Disney's Comics Clark, John, ed. (p. 1855)
Plimoth Plantation Staff, et al. Mayflower 1620: A New Look at a Pilgrim Voyage. (p. 1113)
—Mayflower 1620: A New Look at a Pilgrim Voyage. Coulson, Cotton, photos by. (p. 1113)
Plimpton, George, ed. see Burleigh, Robert.
Pliscou, Lisa. Dude: Fun with Dude & Betty. Dunne, Tom, illus. (p. 489)
Plissner, Laurie. Louder Than Words. Mitchard, Jacquelyn, ed. (p. 1057)
—Screwed. (p. 1533)
Plisson, Phillip. Mar Explicado a los ninos. (p. 1091)
Pliszka, Jodi. Bella & Gizmo's Adventures: Bella Gets A New Sweater. (p. 162)
—Bella & Gizmo's Adventures — Bella Gets A New Sweater. (p. 162)
Pliszka, Jodi A. Bella & Gizmo's Adventures: The Hairless Sphynx Cats. (p. 162)
Plitt, Kay. Why Isn't Bobby Like Me, Mom? (p. 1925)
Plomer, William. Butterfly Ball & the Grasshopper's Feast. Aldridge, Alan, illus. (p. 247)
Plonk, Michelle. Fritz, the Forgetful Frog. (p. 639)
Ploof, Douglas. Weekend at Dad's: The Campout. (p. 1871)
—Weekend at Dad's. (p. 1871)
Ploog, Michael G. L. Frank Baum's the Life & Adventures of Santa Claus. Ploog, Michael G., illus. (p. 969)
Ploog, Mike, illus. see DeMatteis, J. M.
Ploog, Mike, illus. see Dematteis, J. M.
Ploss, Skip. If Picasso Were a Fish. Ploss, Skip, illus. (p. 854)
Plotkin, Andy. Black Block Legend. (p. 195)
Plotkin, Robert. Computers in the Workplace. (p. 355)
—Privacy, Security, & Cyberspace. (p. 1407)
Plotz, John. Time & the Tapestry. Saroff, Phyllis, illus. (p. 1751)
Plotz, Judith, ed. see Kipling, Rudyard.
Plourd, Brenden. My New Brother. (p. 1216)
Plourde, Josee. Promesse des Iles. Lemelin, Linda, tr. (p. 1411)
Plourde, Josee & Barrette, Doris. Ombre au Tableau. (p. 1288)
Plourde, Lynn. Bella's Fall Coat. Gal, Susan, illus. (p. 162)
—Blizzard Wizard. Aardema, John, illus. (p. 200)
—Book Fair Day. Wickstrom, Thor, illus. (p. 210)
—Dino Pets. Kendall, Gideon, illus. (p. 441)
—Dump Man's Treasures. Owens, Mary Beth, illus. (p. 489)
—First Feud: Between the Mountain & the Sea. Sollers, Jim, illus. (p. 595)
—Mountain of Mittens. Vane, Mitch, illus. (p. 1181)
—Only Cows Allowed! Sollers, Jim & Reed, Rebecca Harrison, illus. (p. 1298)
—Pigs in the Mud in the Middle of the Rud. Schoenherr, John, illus. (p. 1358)
—Storytime Stickers: Choo Choo Trains. Cerato, Mattia, illus. (p. 1664)
—Storytime Stickers: Cowboy Dreams. Kulka, Joe, illus. (p. 1664)
—Storytime Stickers: Farm Follies. Ferraro Close, Laura, illus. (p. 1664)
—Storytime Stickers: Springtime with Bunny. Logan, Laura, illus. (p. 1664)
—Storytime Stickers: the First Christmas. Woolf, Julia, illus. (p. 1664)
—Wild Child. (p. 1929)
Plourde, Lynn, jt. auth. see Fendler, Donn.
Plourde, Lynn & Couch, Greg. Wild Child. (p. 1929)
Plourde, Paulette. I Can Fly. (p. 835)
—My Magic Pillow. (p. 1213)
—Smitty Moose, Petey & Me - Episode One, the Witch. Golen, Jessica, illus. (p. 1594)
Plucker, Sheri. Me, Hailey. Fargo, Todd, illus. (p. 1116)
Pluckrose, Henry. Air. (p. 31)
—How Many Are There? (p. 811)
—What Shape Is It? (p. 1893)
—What Size Is It? (p. 1893)
Pluecker, John, jt. auth. see Galindo, Claudia.
Pluecker, John, tr. see Galindo, Claudia.
Pluecker, John, tr. see Perales, Alonso M.
Plum, Amy. After the End. (p. 28)
—Die for Me. (p. 437)
—If I Should Die. (p. 853)
—Until I Die. (p. 1823)
—Until the Beginning. (p. 1823)
Plum, Joan. I Am Special Four Year Old Child's. (p. 834)
Plum, Joan & Plum, Paul. I Am Special 3 Year Old Ed Program. (p. 834)
—I Am Special 3 Year Old Religious Ed Program. (p. 834)
Plum, Joan Ensor & Plum, Paul S. I Am Special: Jesus Is Our Friend. Most, Andee, illus. (p. 834)
Plum, Joanensor, jt. auth. see Plum, Paul.
Plum, Paul, jt. auth. see Plum, Joan.
Plum, Paul & Plum, Joanensor. Ias 3 Year Old Religious Education Program. (p. 849)
Plum, Paul S., jt. auth. see Plum, Joan Ensor.
Plum, Paul S., et al. Teach Me About Saints. (p. 1708)
Plumb, Jennifer. Everything You Need to Know about Chicken Pox & Shingles. (p. 545)
Plumbe, Scott, illus. see Butts, Ed.
Plumberg, William. Legend of Peggy Postue: The Girl with the Upturned Nose. (p. 988)
Plume, Ilse. Farmer in the Dell. (p. 574)
—Twelve Days of Christmas. (p. 1800)
Plume, Ilse, illus. see Farrar, Sid.
Plume, Ilse, illus. see Langton, Jane P.
Plume, Ken, et al. There's a Zombie in My Treehouse! (p. 1731)
Plumeri, Arnaud. Dinosaurs: In the Beginning... Bloz, illus. (p. 444)
Plumides, Damon & Boerke, Arthur Mark. Adventures of Caterwaul the Cat: Feline Pie. (p. 17)
Plumier, Lea. Story of Rhu the Fairy. Rambo, Angela, illus. (p. 1659)
Plumlee, Buddy, illus. see McClure, Brian D.
Plumley, Alea, illus. see O'Donnell, Sallie.
Plumley, Amie & Lisle, Andria. Sewing School: 21 Sewing Projects Kids Will Love to Make. (p. 1556)
Plumley, Amie Petronis, jt. auth. see Lisle, Andria.
Plumm, Gabi, jt. auth. see Phillips, Liam.
Plummer, Barbara. Kids in the Backyard. (p. 954)
Plummer, Bill, III. Game America Plays: Celebrating 75 Years of the Amateur Softball Association (p. 654)
Plummer, David, jt. auth. see Archambault, John.
Plummer, David & Archambault, John. I Paint a Rainbow. Hollander, Sarah, illus. (p. 844)
Plummer, Deborah. Adventures of the Little Tin Tortoise: A Self-Esteem Story with Activities for Teachers, Parents & Carers. Serrurier, Jane, illus. (p. 23)
Plummer, John. Many Paths of the Independent Sacramental Movement. (p. 1089)
Plummer, Myrtes Marie, jt. auth. see Hollmann, Clide Anne.
Plummer, Todd. I've Discovered Energy! (p. 900)
—I've Discovered Force! (p. 900)
—Superhero Science: Kapow! Comic Book Crime Fighters Put Physics to the Test. (p. 1683)
Plummer, Todd, jt. auth. see Mullins, Matt.
Plummer, Todd, et al. Superhero Science: Kapow! Comic Book Crime Fighters Put Physics to the Test. (p. 1683)
Plummer, William K., jt. auth. see Shepherd, David.
Plumridge, Marianne. If Dinosaurs Lived in My Town. Eggleton, Bob, illus. (p. 852)
Plum-Ucci, Carol. Body of Christopher Creed. (p. 207)
—Celebrate Diwali. (p. 283)
—Fire Will Fall. (p. 591)
—Following Christopher Creed. (p. 612)
—Night My Sister Went Missing. (p. 1253)
—She. (p. 1564)
—What Happened to Lani Garver. (p. 1885)
Plunkett, Windyann. Fiddle Me a Riddle & Bring Me the Moon. Davidson, Mary, illus. (p. 583)
Pluta, K. There's a Yak in my Bed. Stallop, Christy, illus. (p. 1731)
Pluth, Lisa Anderson. Haunting in Little River. (p. 754)
Pluto Project Staff & Semkiw, Walter. Astrology for Regular People. Milner, Fran & Brewer, Trish, illus. (p. 109)
Pluum, Ave, illus. see Weinstein, Natalie.
Pluym, Andrea Vander, jt. auth. see Macavinta, Courtney.
Pmei. Pmei Learning & Growing. (p. 1374)
Pneuman, Angela. Lay It on My Heart. (p. 981)
Poage, Brenda. Ima Nobody Becomes Somebody! Book One in the Ima Nobody Series. (p. 860)
Poage, Melvin L., et al. Combination for Beginning Algebra: Critical Thinking Approach. (p. 346)
—Combination for Geometric & Measurement Topics: Critical Thinking Approach. (p. 346)
—Combination for Intermediate Algebra: Critical Thinking Approach. (p. 346)
—Combination for Pre-Calculus: Critical Thinking Approach. (p. 346)
—Combination of Competency Arithmetic. (p. 347)
Poblocki, Dan. Book of Bad Things. (p. 210)
—Clocks & Robbers. (p. 333)
—Ghost of Graylock: (a Hauntings Novel) (p. 671)
—Ghost of Graylock. (p. 671)
—Haunting of Gabriel Ashe. (p. 754)
—Mysterious Four #3: Monsters & Mischief. (p. 1223)
—Nightmarys. (p. 1255)
—Stone Child. (p. 1652)
Pobst, Sandra. Animals on the Edge: Science Races to Save Species Threatened with Extinction. (p. 83)
Pobst, Sandy. Camera. (p. 256)
—Life of a Comet: Set Of 6. (p. 1011)
—Life of a Comet: Text Pairs. (p. 1011)
—Newest Americans (p. 1249)
—Scientific Discovery in the Renaissance: Set Of 6. (p. 1528)
—Scientific Discovery in the Renaissance: Text Pairs. (p. 1528)
—Virginia, 1607-1776. (p. 1844)
Pobst, Sandy & Roberts, Kevin D. Virginia, 1607-1776. (p. 1844)
Pocha, Michael J. Thomas James & the Ringmaster. (p. 1738)
Pochenko. Conspiracy Prophecy II: WWIII & Rumors of WWIV in Revelation. (p. 359)
Pochocki, Ethel. Around the Year Once Upon a Time Saints. Hatke, Ben, illus. (p. 101)
—Blessing of the Beasts. Moser, Barry, illus. (p. 199)
—Maine Marmalade. Chartier, Normand, illus. (p. 1077)
—Mushroom Man. Mosher, Barry, illus. (p. 1193)
—Penny for a Hundred. (p. 1338)
—Penny for a Hundred. Owens, Mary Beth, illus. (p. 1338)
—Rosebud & Red Flannel. (p. 1489)
—Saints & Heroes. Owens, Mary Beth, illus. (p. 1504)
—Saints & Heroes for Kids. (p. 1504)
Pochocki, Ethel & Helms, Hal M. Blessing of the Beasts. Moser, Barry, illus. (p. 199)
Poclask, Stephen. Black Hole of Sacred Mountain. (p. 196)
Pockat, Alison A. Adam's Bubble. (p. 11)
Pockell, Leslie, ed. 100 Great Poems for Boys. (p. 1998)
Pockell, Leslie M. 100 Best Love Poems of All Time. Avila, Adrienne & Rapkin, Katharine, eds. (p. 1998)

Pocket Press & Brittain, Kyle, eds. Pocket Guide to Alabama Criminal Laws. (p. 1375)
Pocock, Aaron, illus. see Blake-Wilson, Pamela.
Pocock, Aaron, illus. see Larson, Robert.
Pocock, Aaron, illus. see Tyrrell, Karen.
Podany, Amanda H., jt. auth. see Mellor, Ronald.
Podany, Amanda H. & McGee, Marni. Ancient near Eastern World. (p. 70)
Podd, Gloria. Royal Runt. (p. 1492)
Podesto, Martine. Body. (p. 207)
—Dinosaurs. (p. 444)
—Inventions. (p. 884)
—Moon. (p. 1171)
Podgurski, Sharon, illus. see Rice, Beth.
Podnecky, Janet, jt. auth. see Butler, Linda.
Podojil, Catherine. Saving Endangered Species. (p. 1517)
Podos, Rebecca. Mystery of Hollow Places. (p. 1224)
Poe. Breve Ant de Ctos Policiales. (p. 226)
Poe, Edgar Allen. Best of Poe. (p. 170)
—Complete Poetry of Edgar Allan Poe. (p. 353)
—Edgar Allan Poe. McConnell, James, illus. (p. 504)
—Edgar Allan Poe Collection. Poe, Edgar Allen, illus. (p. 504)
—Edgar Allan Poe's Tales of Death & Dementia. Grimly, Gris, illus. (p. 504)
—Edgar Allan Poe's Tales of Mystery & Madness. Grimly, Gris, illus. (p. 504)
—Escarabajo de Oro. (p. 535)
—Narraciones Extraordinarias. (p. 1229)
—Raven: Includes Sound! (p. 1441)
—Raven. Price, Ryan, illus. (p. 1441)
—Raven & Other Poems. Wilson, Gahan, illus. (p. 1441)
—Raven & Other Writings. (p. 1441)
—Stories of Edgar Allan Poe. McKowen, Scott, illus. (p. 1655)
—Tales of Horror & Suspense. (p. 1702)
—Tales of Mystery & Imagination. Jones, Barry, illus. (p. 1702)
—Tales of Terror, Level 3. (p. 1702)
—Tell-Tale Heart & Other Stories. Grimly, Gris, illus. (p. 1717)
—Tell-Tale Heart Package. Calero, Dennis, illus. (p. 1717)
Poe, Edgar Allen, jt. auth. see Bowen, Carl.
Poe, Edgar Allen, jt. auth. see Brown, Dawn.
Poe, Edgar Allen, jt. auth. see Despeyroux, Denise.
Poe, Edgar Allen, jt. auth. see Harper, Benjamin.
Poe, Edgar Allen, jt. auth. see Manning, Matthew K.
Poe, Edgar Allen, jt. auth. see Tullen, Sean.
Poe, Edgar Allen & Harper, Benjamin. Tell-Tale Heart Calero, Dennis, illus. (p. 1717)
Poe, Edgar Allen & Morvan, Jean-David. Murders in the Rue Morgue, & Other Tales. Li, Yishan & Peng, Wang, illus. (p. 1192)
Poe, Edgar Allen & Thompson, G. R. Selected Writings of Edgar Allan Poe. (p. 1549)
Poe, Edgar Allen & Wilson, Gahan. Raven, the & Other Poems. (p. 1441)
Poe, Edgar Allen, et al. Fall of the House of Usher & Other Writings: Poems, Tales, Essays, & Reviews. (p. 566)
—Horror Classics. Pomplun, Tom, ed. (p. 799)
Poe, Marshall. House Divided. Lindner, Ellen & Purvis, Leland, illus. (p. 803)
—Little Rock Nine. Purvis, Leland & Lindner, Ellen, illus. (p. 1036)
—Sons of Liberty. Purvis, Leland, illus. (p. 1613)
Poe, Roderick. Ben: A Novella from the Heart. (p. 163)
Poehler, S. Applecheeks & the Pop E. Tree. (p. 92)
Poehlmann, Jeffrey, jt. auth. see Fenne, Edwin.
Poehlmann, Jeffrey & Fenne, Edwin. Those Amazing Dogs: Trail of the Viking. Morales, Carlos, illus. (p. 1740)
Poelman, Heidi. Is for Abinadi: An Alphabet Book of Scripture Heroes. (p. 889)
Poer, Karla R. Busy-Body Book of Fun-Atomy Tunes. (p. 246)
Poer, Nancy Jewel. Mia's Apple Tree. Poer, Nancy Jewel, illus. (p. 1134)
Poes, Nancy, illus. see Heller, Marcy.
Poesch, Jessie & Main, Sally. Newcomb Pottery & Crafts: An Educational Enterprise for Women, 1895-1940. (p. 1249)
Poet. Testament: The Many Writings of a Poet. (p. 1723)
Poet, J. B. Gulley: The Seagull that Walked to the Ocean. (p. 731)
—Spade Struts to the Ocean. (p. 1620)
Poet, Jonny. Waddling to the Pond. Luchsinger, Linda, illus. (p. 1852)
Poetry Society Staff. Poetry on a Plate: A Feast of Poems & Recipes. (p. 1376)
Poetry Society Staff, ed. Poetry on a Plate: A Feast of Poems & Recipes. (p. 1376)
Poets in the Schools Staff. C Is for California: Written by Kids for Kids. (p. 249)
Poettker, Jacob D. Fallen: A Novel. (p. 566)
Pofahl, Jane. Everyday Life: Middle Ages. (p. 543)
—Westward Movement: United States History. (p. 1876)
Poffenberger, Nancy. Iraq, 2003. Gottesman, Val, illus. (p. 887)
Poffo, Lanny. Limericks from the Heart (and Lungs!) (p. 1018)
Pogany, Elaine. Golden Cockerel: From the Original Russian Fairy Tale of Alexander Pushkin. Pogány, Willy, illus. (p. 694)
Pogány, Willy, illus. see Colum, Padraic.
Pogány, Willy, illus. see Edgar, M. G.
Pogány, Willy, illus. see Hawthorne, Nathaniel.
Pogány, Willy, illus. see Pogany, Elaine.
Pogány, Willy, jt. auth. see Colum, Padraic.
Pogo the Clown. Along Little Dogie: Harley's Great Adventures. Miller, Richard, illus. (p. 48)
—Brave Little Lion: Harley's Great Adventures. Miller, Richard D., illus. (p. 223)
—Great Blue Sky: Harley's Great Adventures. Miller, Richard D., illus. (p. 714)
—Little Gray Mouse: Harley's Great Adventures. Miller, Richard D., illus. (p. 1028)
—Littlest Tiger: Harley's Great Adventures. Miller, Richard, illus. (p. 1039)
—Taste of Shrimp: Harley's Great Adventures. Miller, Richard D., illus. (p. 1707)
Pogorelsky, Antony & Spirin, Gennady. Little Black Hen. (p. 1024)
Pogue, Carolyn. Gwen (p. 733)
Pogue, Carolyn, et al. After the Beginning. (p. 28)
Pogue, David & Caparo, Antonio Javier. Abby Camelia's One & Only Magical Power. (p. 2)
Poh, Jennie, illus. see Harrod-Eagles, Cynthia.
Pohl, Amelia J. Flint River. (p. 604)
—Ocmulgee River. (p. 1277)
—Savannah River. (p. 1516)
Pohl, David, illus. see Roberts, Willo Davis.
Pohl, Dora & Kremer, Kevin. Maggie's Christmas Miracle. Ely, Dave, illus. (p. 1071)
Pohl, Frederik. Platinum Pohl: The Collected Best Stories. (p. 1370)
Pohl, Kathleen. Alemania. (p. 35)
—Alligators. (p. 47)
—Alligators (Caimanes) (p. 47)
—Alligators/Caimanes. (p. 47)
—Animales I See at the Zoo (p. 81)
—Animals I See at the Zoo/Animales Que Veo en el Zoológico (p. 82)
—Animals of the Ocean. (p. 83)
—Cheetahs. (p. 296)
—Cheetahs/Guepardos. (p. 296)
—Crocodiles. (p. 384)
—Crocodiles/Cocodrilos. (p. 384)
—Descubramos Argentina. (p. 428)
—Descubramos Canada. (p. 428)
—Descubramos Canadá. (p. 428)
—Descubramos Cuba. (p. 428)
—Descubramos el Congo. (p. 428)
—Descubramos Estados Unidos. (p. 428)
—Descubramos Etiopia. (p. 428)
—Descubramos Iran. (p. 428)
—Descubramos Irán. (p. 428)
—Descubramos Irlanda. (p. 428)
—Descubramos Israel. (p. 428)
—Descubramos México. (p. 428)
—Descubramos Paises del Mundo (Looking at Countries) (p. 428)
—Dolphins. (p. 464)
—Dolphins (Delfines) (p. 465)
—Dolphins/Delfines. (p. 465)
—Gorillas. (p. 703)
—Gorillas/Gorilas. (p. 703)
—Kangaroos. (p. 942)
—Kangaroos/Canguros. (p. 942)
—Koalas. (p. 966)
—Koalas/Koalas. (p. 966)
—Looking at Afghanistan. (p. 1050)
—Looking at Argentina. (p. 1050)
—Looking at Canada. (p. 1050)
—Looking at Countries (p. 1050)
—Looking at Cuba. (p. 1050)
—Looking at Ethiopia. (p. 1050)
—Looking at Germany. (p. 1050)
—Looking at Iran. (p. 1050)
—Looking at Ireland. (p. 1050)
—Looking at Israel. (p. 1050)
—Looking at Mexico. (p. 1051)
—Looking at the Congo. (p. 1051)
—Looking at the United States. (p. 1051)
—Looking at Venezuela. (p. 1051)
—Pandas. (p. 1321)
—Pandas/Pandas. (p. 1321)
—Peacocks. (p. 1332)
—Peacocks (Pavos Reales) (p. 1332)
—Peacocks/Pavos Reales. (p. 1332)
—Pelicans. (p. 1335)
—Pelicans (Pelicanos) (p. 1336)
—Pelicans (Pelícanos) (p. 1336)
—Rhinos. (p. 1467)
—Rhinos/Rinocerontes. (p. 1467)
—Sea Turtles. (p. 1536)
—Sea Turtles/Tortugas Marinas. (p. 1536)
—What Happens at a Bakery? (p. 1885)
—What Happens at a Bakery (¿Qué pasa en una Panadería?) (p. 1885)
—What Happens at a Bakery?/¿Qué Pasa en una Panadería? (p. 1885)
—What Happens at a Bike Shop? (p. 1885)
—What Happens at a Bike Shop? (¿Qué pasa en una tienda de Bicicletas?) (p. 1885)
—What Happens at a Bike Shop?/Que Pasa en una Tienda de Bicicletas? (p. 1885)
—What Happens at a Dairy Farm? (p. 1885)
—What Happens at a Dairy Farm? (¿Qué pasa en una granja Lechera?) (p. 1885)
—What Happens at a Dairy Farm?/¿Qué Pasa en Una Granja Lechera? (p. 1885)
—What Happens at a Firehouse? (p. 1885)
—What Happens at a Firehouse? (¿Qué pasa en una estación de Bomberos?) (p. 1885)
—What Happens at a Recycling Center? (p. 1885)
—What Happens at a Recycling Center? (Que Pasa En Un Centro De Reciclaje?) (p. 1885)
—What Happens at a Recycling Center?/Qué Pasa en un Centro de Reciclaje? (p. 1885)
—What Happens at a Toy Factory?/¿Qué Pasa en una Fábrica de Juguetes? (p. 1885)
Pohl, Kathleen & Nations, Susan. Descubramos Afganistán. (p. 428)
—Descubramos Cuba. (p. 428)
—Descubramos Polonia. (p. 428)
—Descubramos Venezuela. (p. 428)
—Looking at Poland. (p. 1051)
Pohl, Kathleen, et al. Reef & Rocketfish: Includes a Parent/Teacher Guide for Using This Story to Address Issues of Self Esteem with a Young Child. (p. 1456)
Pohl, Mayumi Ishimoto. Morning Prayer. (p. 1175)
Pohl, William L. Amazing Flight of Daisy: A Runaway Kite Circles the World on the Back of the Wind. (p. 54)
Pohle & Dowley. Maqueta del Templo de Salomon. (p. 1091)
Pohle, Peter, illus. see Dowley, Tim.
Pohlemann, Terri. She Lives in the Stars. (p. 1564)
Pohlen, Jerome. Albert Einstein & Relativity for Kids: His Life & Ideas with 21 Activities & Thought Experiments. (p. 34)
—Gay & Lesbian History for Kids: The Century-Long Struggle for LGBT Rights with 21 Activities. (p. 658)
Pohlen, Jerome, jt. auth. see Puck.
Pohlen, Jerome, jt. auth. see Shea, Tess.
Pohler, Eva. Gatekeeper's Daughter. (p. 658)
Pohlman, Jennifer & Searle, Rodney. Simply Ball: With Pilates Principles. Wakeman, Peter, photos by. (p. 1578)
Pohlmann-Eden, Bernd. Secret of the Bounce-Back Mom. Hofer, Klaus C., tr. (p. 1542)
Pohlmeyer, Krista, jt. auth. see Random House.
Pohl-Weary, Emily. Not Your Ordinary Wolf Girl (p. 1267)
—Strange Times at Western High. Cowles, Rose, illus. (p. 1665)
poho, illus. see Cowart, Logan.
Pohrt, Tom, illus. see Durango, Julia.
Pohrt, Tom, illus. see Mitchell, Stephen.
Pohrt, Tom, illus. see O'Connor, Sandra Day.
Pohrt, Tom, illus. see Pearce, Philippa.
Pohrte, Juliann, illus. see Pohrte, Kathysue, et al.
Pohrte, Kathysue, et al. In the Land of Liviaann. Pohrte, Kathysue, ed. (p. 866)
Pohrte, Olivia, illus. see Pohrte, Kathysue, et al.
Poindexter, Katherine & RH Disney Staff. Mulan. Cardona, Jose & Williams, Don, illus. (p. 1189)
Poindexter, Stephanie. Octavious & His Busy Tentacles. (p. 1277)
Point Of Grace. Girls of Grace Journal. (p. 680)
Point, Susan, illus. see McNutt, Nan.
Point, Susan A., contrib. by. People of the Land: Legends of the Four Host First Nations. (p. 1339)
Pointon, Janet. Matter of Choice. (p. 1109)
Pointon, Sarah. ColorVille. (p. 346)
Poirier, Nadine, illus. see Jaramillo, Gloria.
Poisson, Barbara Aoki. Ghana. (p. 670)
—Ghana. Rotberg, Robert I., ed. (p. 670)
—Malaysia. (p. 1083)
Poitier, Anton. Colors: Match the Words & Colors. (p. 345)
—Design & Doodle: A Book of Astonishing Invention - Amazing Things to Imagine, Draw, & Discover. Running Press Staff, ed. (p. 429)
—Flippy Floppy Farm Animals. Touliatou, Sophia, illus. (p. 605)
—Flippy Floppy Jungle Animals. Touliatou, Sophia, illus. (p. 605)
—I Wonder Who? Touliatou, Sophia, illus. (p. 849)
—My Big Book of Stencil Drawing for Little Hands: Draw Through the Stencils with Crayons, Pencils or Felt Pens. (p. 1197)
—My Busy Farm. Touliatou, Sophia, illus. (p. 1199)
—My Busy Town. Touliatou, Sophia, illus. (p. 1200)
—My First Big Book Numbers. Shakir, Susie, illus. (p. 1204)
—My First Big Book Shapes & Colors. Kallanovic, Dubravka, illus. (p. 1204)
—Numbers. (p. 1271)
—Once I Was a Cardboard Box... But Now I'm a Book about Polar Bears. Evans, Melvyn, illus. (p. 1292)
—Once I Was a Comic... But Now I'm a Book about Tigers. Evans, Melvyn, illus. (p. 1292)
—Opposites: Twist & Find the Opposite. (p. 1300)
—Shapes. (p. 1560)
Poitier, Antonine & School Zone Staff. Colors Spin Wheel. (p. 345)
—Counting Spin Wheel Board Books. (p. 371)
—Opposites Spin Wheel Board Books. (p. 1301)
—Shapes Spin Wheel Board Books. (p. 1561)
Poitras, Bruno, jt. auth. see Di Luzio-Poitras, Linda.
Poitras, Jim, illus. see Bouchard, David & Willier, Shelley.
Poitras, Tara, ed. see Thompson, Sharon.
Poj, Alejandra. Colores. (p. 344)
—Numeros. (p. 1273)
Pokas, Dora. Muriel's Red Sweater. (p. 1192)
Pokeberry, P. J. Huckenpuck Papers: The Tales of a Family's Secret & a Young Girls Search for Self-Esteem. (p. 824)
Pokémon Company International Staff. Pokemon X & Pokemon Y: The Official Kalos Region Guidebook. (p. 1378)
—Pokémon X & Pokémon y: the Official Kalos Region Guidebook: The Official Pokémon Strategy Guide. (p. 1378)
Pokemon Staff & Scholastic, Inc. Staff. Pokemon. (p. 1377)
Pokiak, James, jt. auth. see Willett, Mindy.
Pokiak-Fenton, Margaret, jt. auth. see Jordan-Fenton, Christy.
Pokrovskaya, Liya, photos by see Kvatum, Lia.
Polacco, Ernest L. When Lightning Comes in a Jar. Polacco, Patricia, illus. (p. 1903)
Polacco, Patricia. Art of Miss Chew. Polacco, Patricia, illus. (p. 102)
—Because of Thursday. (p. 155)
—Betty Doll. (p. 172)
—Betty Doll. Polacco, Patricia, illus. (p. 172)
—Blessing Cup. Polacco, Patricia, illus. (p. 199)
—Bully. Polacco, Patricia, illus. (p. 241)
—Bun Bun Button. Polacco, Patricia, illus. (p. 241)
—Butterfly. (p. 247)
—Chicken Sunday. (p. 300)
—Christmas Tapestry. (p. 316)
—Clara & Davie. (p. 326)
—Emma Kate. Polacco, Patricia, illus. (p. 519)
—Fiona's Lace. Polacco, Patricia, illus. (p. 589)
—For the Love of Autumn. Polacco, Patricia, illus. (p. 616)
—G Is for Goat. Polacco, Patricia, illus. (p. 651)
—Gifts of the Heart. Polacco, Patricia, illus. (p. 675)
—Ginger & Petunia. Polacco, Patricia, illus. (p. 676)
—Gracias, Senor Falker. (p. 705)
—Graves Family. Polacco, Patricia, illus. (p. 712)
—In Our Mothers' House. Polacco, Patricia, illus. (p. 864)
—January's Sparrow. Polacco, Patricia, illus. (p. 908)
—John Philip Duck. Polacco, Patricia, illus. (p. 922)
—Junkyard Wonders. Polacco, Patricia, illus. (p. 936)
—Just in Time Abraham Lincoln. (p. 938)
—Just in Time, Abraham Lincoln. Polacco, Patricia, illus. (p. 938)
—Keeping Quilt: 25th Anniversary Edition. Polacco, Patricia, illus. (p. 947)
—Keeping Quilt. (p. 947)
—Lemonade Club. Polacco, Patricia, illus. (p. 991)
—Meteor! (p. 1130)
—Mommies Say Shhh! Polacco, Patricia, illus. (p. 1162)
—Mr. Wayne's Masterpiece. Polacco, Patricia, illus. (p. 1187)
—Mrs. Katz & Tush. (p. 1187)
—My Rotten Redheaded Older Brother. (p. 1218)
—Oh, Look! Polacco, Patricia, illus. (p. 1280)
—Orange for Frankie. Polacco, Patricia, illus. (p. 1301)
—Picnic at Mudsock Meadow. (p. 1355)
—Pink & Say. (p. 1359)
—Pollo de los Domingos. (p. 1381)
—Rotten Richie & the Ultimate Dare. Polacco, Patricia, illus. (p. 1490)
—Someone for Mr. Sussman. Polacco, Patricia, illus. (p. 1609)
—Something about Hensley's. Polacco, Patricia, illus. (p. 1609)
—Thank You, Mr. Falker. Polacco, Patricia, illus. (p. 1725)
—Thunder Cake. (p. 1746)
—Tucky Jo & Little Heart. Polacco, Patricia, illus. (p. 1796)
—When Lightning Comes in a Jar. (p. 1903)
Polacco, Patricia, illus. see Polacco, Ernest L.
Polack, Peter J. Tooth That Mixed up Christmas. McCoy, Dave, illus. (p. 1768)
Polak, Monique. 121 Express (p. 2000)
—All In (p. 44)
—Finding Elmo (p. 588)
—Flip Turn (p. 605)
—Home Invasion (p. 792)
—Home Invasion. (p. 792)
—Middle of Everywhere (p. 1137)
—No More Pranks (p. 1259)
—On the Game (p. 1290)
—Pyro (p. 1421)
—Scarred (p. 1520)
—Straight Punch (p. 1664)
—What World Is Left (p. 1895)
Polan, Jason, illus. see Tea, Michelle.
Poland, A., jt. auth. see Haaren, John H.
Poland, A. B., jt. auth. see Haaren, John H.
Poland, Inglan, jt. auth. see Poland, Pitch.
Poland, Pitch & Poland, Inglan. Lost & Found. Rose, Drew, illus. (p. 1054)
Polanin, W. Richard, jt. auth. see Walker, John R.
Polano, H. Talmud. (p. 1704)
Polano, Sergio & Vetta, Pierpaolo. ABC of 20th-Century Graphics. (p. 3)
Polansky, Daniel. Profiles #5: the Vietnam War. (p. 1409)
—Vietnam War. (p. 1841)
Polark, Kelly. Rockabet: Classic Edition. Little, Kelli Ann, illus. (p. 1482)
Polastri, Rosa Elena, illus. see Brignole, Giancarla, tr.
Polat, Ercan, illus. see Gunes, Aysenur.
Polay, Ellyn, jt. auth. see Gurewitz, Samantha.
Polchlopek, Mary Ann, illus. see Lutterbach, Johanna.
Polcovar, Jane. Rosalind Franklin & the Structure of Life. (p. 1489)
Polden, Kelly Carper. Puppy Tales: The Adventures of Adam the Australian Sheppard. (p. 1418)
Poleahla, Anita. Celebrate My Hopi Name. James, Eric, illus. (p. 284)
Poletiek, Keith. Johnny Lazarus in Wave of Courage. (p. 923)
Polette, Keith. Isabel & the Hungry Coyote. (p. 890)
—Isabel & the Hungry Coyote/Isabel y el Coyote Hambriento. Raven Tree Press Staff, ed. (p. 890)
—Moon over the Mountain. (p. 1172)
—Moon over the Mountain. Russik, Michael, illus. (p. 1172)
—Moon over the Mountain/Luna Sobre la Montana. (p. 1172)
—Paco & the Giant Chile Plant. (p. 1317)
—Paco & the Giant Chile Plant/Paco y la Planta de Chile Gigante. de la Vega, Eida, tr. (p. 1317)
Polette, Nancy. A-Z Activities for the K-2 Student. (p. 2)
—Biography, by Golly! (p. 189)
—Blunder or Brainstorm: Fact & Fiction of Famous Inventors & Inventions. Dillon, Paul, illus. (p. 204)
—Flying with Mother Goose. (p. 610)
—Gifted or Goof Off? Fact & Fiction of the Famous. (p. 675)
—Greatest Invention: The Story of Walter Hunt. Paparone, Pamela, illus. (p. 720)
—Improvisation & Theatre Games with Children's Literature. (p. 862)
—Mae Jemison. (p. 1070)
—Pocahontas. (p. 1375)
—Reading the Fifty States: Booktalks, Response Activities, & More (p. 1446)
—Rookie Biographies: Pocahontas. (p. 1487)
—School Librarian's Grab Bag. (p. 1523)
—Spy with the Wooden Leg: The Story of Virginia Hall. (p. 1636)
—What Is This Thing? (p. 1891)
Polette, Nancy & Ebbesmeyer, Joan. Math in Fables & Myths: Solving Word Problems with Readers' Theatre. (p. 1106)
Polette, Nancy J. Teaching Economic Concepts with Picture Books & Junior Novels (p. 1710)
Polglase, Pamela. Handy & Dandy. (p. 741)
Polhamus, Bruce, illus. see Adams, Jesse.
Polhemus, Coleman. Crocodile Blues. Polhemus, Coleman, illus. (p. 384)
Polhemus, Coleman, illus. see Nance, Andrew.
Police, Gerard. Herbert the Frog Goes to the Store. (p. 769)
Police, Lou, illus. see Fletcher, Betty & Harvest House Publishers Staff.
Polidoro, J. Lavatory 101-A Bathroom Book of Knowledge. (p. 981)
Polikoff, Barbara Garland. Her Mother's Secret. (p. 769)
Polin, C. J. & Dorling Kindersley Publishing Staff. The Story of Chocolate. (p. 1728)
Poling, Atarah L. Forbidden Secret: Shadows Behind Locked Doors. (p. 616)
Poling Kilough, Melissa. Titus the Turtle & the Hard Shell Story. (p. 1758)
Poling, Kyle, illus. see Aboff, Marcie & Lee, Sally.
Poling, Kyle, illus. see Aboff, Marcie.
Poling, Kyle, illus. see Barad-Cutler, Alexis.
Poling, Kyle, illus. see Boniface, William.
Poling, Kyle, illus. see Heos, Bridget.

P

Poling, Kyle, illus. see Johnson, J. Angelique.
Poling, Kyle, illus. see Karr, Lily.
Poling, Kyle, illus. see Lee, Sally.
Poling, Kyle, illus. see Oliver, Ilanit.
Poling, Kyle, illus. see Rustad, Martha.
Poling, Kyle, illus. see Tomecek, Steve.
Polinko, Les, illus. see Karevold, Alison.
Polinko, Les, jt. auth. see Donaldson, Connie.
Polinski, Jo. Minnesota Moon. Webber, Carol, illus. (p. 1147)
Polis, Gary A., illus. see Pringle, Laurence.
Polisar, Barry Louis. Curious Creatures: Animal Poems. Clark, David, illus. (p. 392)
—Noises from under the Rug: The Barry Louis Polisar Songbook. Stewart, Michael G., illus. (p. 1262)
—Something Fishy. Clark, David, illus. (p. 1609)
—Stolen Man: The Story of the Amistad Rebellion. (p. 1652)
Polisar, Barry Louis, et al. Eso No Se Hace! (p. 536)
Polisar, Patti. Inside France's DGSE: General Directorate for External Security. (p. 876)
—Inside France's DGSE: The General Directorate for External Security. (p. 876)
Polisner, Gae. Pull of Gravity. (p. 1415)
—Summer of Letting Go. (p. 1674)
Politano, Michael. Pig in the Tree. (p. 1357)
Politi, Leo. Emmet. (p. 520)
—Juanita. (p. 930)
—Pedro: The Angel of Olvera Street. (p. 1334)
—Pedro, the Angel of Olvera Street. (p. 1334)
—Song of the Swallows. (p. 1611)
Politi, Leo, jt. auth. see Stalcup, Ann.
Polito, James A. My First Book of Critters. (p. 1205)
Polito, Mike, illus. see Donald, Diana.
Polizzotto, Carolyn & Spinks, Sarah. Trumpet's Kittens. Duke, Marion, illus. (p. 1793)
Polk, Douglas. Legend of Garle Pond. (p. 988)
—Marie's Home (p. 1094)
Polk, James. God Rules. (p. 690)
—Mr. & Mrs. Love & the Neighborhood Children. (p. 1184)
Polk, James G. Gift of Love Rudkin, Shawn, ed. (p. 675)
Pollack, Barbara, illus. see Muldrow, Diane.
Pollack, Daniel, jt. auth. see Henry, Martha J.
Pollack, Gadi. Purimshpiel. (p. 1419)
Pollack, Gadi, illus. see Chait, Baruch.
Pollack, Gadi, illus. see Schreiber, Elisheva.
Pollack, Jeff & Steinberg, Lane. Totally Bitchin' Charlie Sheen Coloring Book. Champagne, Liz, illus. (p. 1771)
Pollack, Jenny. Klepto. (p. 963)
Pollack, Pam, jt. auth. see Belviso, Meg.
Pollack, Pam & Belviso, Meg. Gallinas de Aqui para Alla. Adams, Lynn, illus. (p. 653)
—Gallinas de Aqui para Alla; Chickens on the Move. (p. 653)
—I Can't Sit Still! Living with ADHD. Fabrega, Marta, illus. (p. 837)
—Ponies Bonforte, Lisa, illus. (p. 1382)
—Who Is J. K. Rowling? Marchesi, Stephen & Harrison, Nancy, illus. (p. 1916)
—¡No Puedo Estar Quieto! Mi Vida con ADHD. Fabrega, Marta, illus. (p. 1260)
Pollack, Pam & Meg Belviso. Who Is George Lucas? (p. 1915)
Pollack, Pam, et al. Who Was Steve Jobs? Harrison, Nancy et al, illus. (p. 1919)
Pollack, Pamela. Spy Cats: Revenge of the Robot Rats. (p. 1636)
Pollack, Pamela, jt. auth. see Belviso, Meg.
Pollack, Pamela & Belviso, Meg. Who Is J. K. Rowling? (p. 1916)
—Who Was Steve Jobs? (p. 1919)
Pollack, Pamela D., jt. auth. see Belviso, Meg.
Pollack, Pamela D. & Belviso, Meg. Who Is George Lucas? Hammond, Ted & McVeigh, Kevin, illus. (p. 1915)
—Who Was Alfred Hitchcock? (p. 1918)
—Who Was Alfred Hitchcock? Moore, Jonathan & Harrison, Nancy, illus. (p. 1918)
—Who Was Charles Dickens? (p. 1918)
—Who Was Charles Dickens? Geyer, Mark Edward & Harrison, Nancy, illus. (p. 1918)
—Who Was J. R. R. Tolkien? Moore, Jonathan & Harrison, Nancy, illus. (p. 1918)
—Who Was Susan B. Anthony? (p. 1919)
—Who Was Susan B. Anthony? Lacey, Mike & Harrison, Nancy, illus. (p. 1919)
Pollack-Brichto, Mira. God Around Us: A Child's Garden of Prayer. Alko, Selina, illus. (p. 688)
Pollak, Barbara. Our Community Garden. (p. 1308)
Pollak, Barbara, illus. see Friedman, Laurie.
Pollak, Barbara, illus. see Guest, Elissa Haden & Blackstone, Margaret.
Pollak, Barbara, illus. see Muldrow, Diane.
Pollak, Dale. Velocity: From the Front Line to the Bottom Line. (p. 1835)
Pollak, Monika, illus. see Amenta, Charles A.
Pollan, Michael. Omnivore's Dilemma: The Secrets Behind What You Eat. (p. 1288)
Polland, Madeleine. City of the Golden House. (p. 324)
Pollard, Brian, illus. see Meloche, Renee Taft.
Pollard, Bryan, illus. see Meloch, Renee.
Pollard, Bryan, illus. see Meloche, Renee Taft.
Pollard, Bryan, illus. see Meloche, Renee.
Pollard, Deborah Hanna, illus. see Smith, I. J.
Pollard, Josephine. Ruth a Bible Heroine & Other Stories Told in the Language of Childhood. (p. 1498)
—Winter Sports. (p. 1938)
Pollard, Keith, illus. see Stern, Roger & Defalco, Tom.
Pollard, Keith, illus. see Wein, Len & Wolfman, Marv.
Pollard, Keith, illus. see Wolfman, Marv & Mantlo, Bill.
Pollard, Keith, jt. illus. see Tuska, George.
Pollard, Mary Jean. Octrina the Octopus. (p. 1278)
Pollard, Michael. Great Rivers of Britain: The Clyde, Mersey, Severn, Tees, Thames, Trent. (p. 718)
—Rivers of Britain & Ireland: The Avon, Yorkshire Ouse, Tyne, Wye, Forth, Liffey, Lagan. (p. 1476)
Pollard, Simon, photos by see Markle, Sandra.
Pollard, Susie, illus. see Mehler, Ed.
Pollard, Tara. Season's Christmas Quest: The Dog's Story. (p. 1538)
Pollema-Cahill, Phyllis, illus. see Reagan, Jean.
Pollema-Cahill, Phyllis, jt. auth. see Hay, Jerry M.
Pollert, Annette, jt. auth. see Smith, L. J.
Pollet, Alison. When I Was a Girl. (p. 1903)
Pollett, Allan. For My Little Princess. (p. 616)
Pollett, Libby, jt. auth. see Head, Debby.
Polley, J. Patrick & Polley, JoAnn. My Trip to Gettysburg Shekerow, Mark D., ed. (p. 1220)
Polley, JoAnn. My Trip to Washington, D. C. Hanstick, Kevin, illus. (p. 1220)
Polley, JoAnn, jt. auth. see Polley, J. Patrick.
Pollinger, Gina, ed. see Shakespeare, William.
Pollins, Ira. Conscious Executive. (p. 358)
Pollitt, Gary, jt. auth. see Baker, Craig.
Pollitz, Edith Elizabeth. Carrie. (p. 271)
Pollock, A. K. I Am Joshua: Heart Matters Series. (p. 833)
Pollock, Beth. Harley's Gift (p. 749)
—Next Step (p. 1249)
—Witch of Bloor Street (p. 1941)
Pollock, Frederick & Maitland, Frederic William. History of English Law Before the Time of Edward I (p. 784)
Pollock, Hal. Meet the Brittles: In Monstermania. (p. 1122)
—Monster at the Bat. (p. 1166)
—Monster for President. Parisi, Anthony, illus. (p. 1167)
Pollock, J. A. Titus & Otis & the Arctic Adventure. (p. 1758)
Pollock, Jim. Whole Different Animal. Pollock, Mary Ellen, illus. (p. 1920)
Pollock, Mary Ellen, illus. see Pollock, Jim.
Pollock, Naomi. Modern Japanese House. (p. 1158)
Pollock, Terry. Spider Like Me. (p. 1626)
Pollock, Tom. City's Son. (p. 324)
Pollock, Valerie. Alpha's Alphabet. (p. 50)
Pollock/Shechinah Third Temple, Jerry. Divinely Inspired: Spiritual Awakening of a Soul. from Bipolar, Primal Therapy, Suicide & Science to God's Miracles. (p. 454)
—Messiah Interviews: Belonging to God. Beyond Miracles, Primal Therapy, Religion, Science, Bible History, Evolution, & Creation. (p. 1129)
Polly Jr., Jimmy Wayne, illus. see Hayes, Angela.
Polo, Eduardo. Chamario. Ballester, Arnal, illus. (p. 289)
Polon, Linda Beth. Storywriting: Grades 1-3. (p. 1664)
—Storywriting: Grades 4-6. (p. 1664)
Polonsky, Ami. Gracefully Grayson. (p. 705)
Polseno, Jo, illus. see Lomask, Milton.
Polsky, Beanie, illus. see Cohen, Penny L.
Polsky, Cheryl. Libby & Her Friends Explore Los Angeles, Californ. (p. 1005)
Polsky, Milton. Act of Will. (p. 9)
—SATisfaction. (p. 1515)
Polsky, Milton & Gilead, Jack. Improv Workshop Handbook: Creative Movement & Verbal Interaction for Students K-8: The Object Is Teamwork. Cordero, Chris, ed. (p. 862)
Polsky, Milton E., jt. auth. see Berland, Howard.
Polsky, Milton, et al. Houdini - The King of Escapes: Playscript. (p. 802)
Polsky, Sara. This Is How I Find Her. (p. 1736)
Polson, Steven, jt. auth. see Gipson, Fred.
Polston, Deborah Ehler. Eagle Child Series. (p. 492)
—Eagle Child Series 4-6 Book 2: Including the Eagle Child Ambassador Program. (p. 492)
Poltarnees, Welleran. Hooray for Babies. (p. 795)
Poltarnees, Welleran & Laughing Elephant Publishing Staff, compiled by. Laughing Elephant's Book of Christmas. (p. 980)
Poltera, Anne. Castle Magic & the Sinister Encroaching Fir Wood. (p. 277)
Poluchowicz, Krzysztof. Brooklyn ABC: A Scrapbook of Everyone's Favorite Borough. (p. 231)
Polushkin Robbins, Maria, jt. auth. see Robbins, Maria Polushkin.
Poluzzi, Alessandro, illus. see Jeffrey, Gary.
Poluzzi, Allesandro, illus. see Jeffrey, Gary.
Polyansky, Nikita, illus. see Bloncourt, Nelson & Botero, Fernando.
Polyansky, Nikita, illus. see Bloncourt, Nelson.
Polyansky, Nikita & Ebong, Ima. Sleeping Beauty: A Journey to the Ballet of the Mariinsky Theatre. Polyansky, Nikita, illus. (p. 1589)
Polydoros, Lori. Anacondas: On the Hunt (p. 66)
—Awesome Freestyle BMX Tricks & Stunts (p. 121)
—Awesome Skateboard Tricks & Stunts (p. 121)
—Awesome Snowboard Tricks & Stunts (p. 121)
—Big Air (p. 177)
—BMX Greats (p. 204)
—Crocodiles: On the Hunt (p. 384)
—Dirt Bike Racing (p. 446)
—Dirt Bikes (p. 446)
—Drag Racing (p. 476)
—Grizzly Bears: Built for the Hunt. (p. 724)
—Indy Car Racing (p. 873)
—Lions: On the Hunt (p. 1021)
—MMA Greats (p. 1157)
—Motocross Greats (p. 1179)
—Motorcycle Racing (p. 1179)
—Piranhas: On the Hunt (p. 1362)
—Skateboarding Greats (p. 1583)
—Snowboarding Greats (p. 1600)
—Strange but True Animals (p. 1665)
—Strange but True Sports (p. 1665)
—Tigers: On the Hunt (p. 1749)
—Top 10 Ancient Mysteries (p. 1768)
—Top 10 Haunted Places (p. 1768)
—Top 10 Mythical Creatures (p. 1768)
—Top 10 UFO & Alien Mysteries (p. 1768)
—Wolves: On the Hunt (p. 1945)
Polydoros, Lori, jt. auth. see Clay, Kathryn.
Polydoros, Lori, jt. auth. see Riehecky, Janet.
Polydoros, Lori & Benchmark Education Co., LLC. Storytelling on Fabrics: Quilts, Tapestries, Story Cloths, & More. (p. 1664)
Polydoros, Lori & Clay, Kathryn. Top 10 Unexplained. (p. 1768)
Polydoros, Lori & Maurer, Tracy Nelson. Super Speed. (p. 1682)
Polydoros, Lori, et al. Best of the Best. (p. 170)
—Predator Profiles. (p. 1394)
Polzer, Tim. Peyton Manning: Leader on & off the Field. (p. 1349)
—Tim Tebow: Always a Hero. (p. 1750)
Pomaska, Anna. 3-D Coloring Book—My First Animal Mandalas. (p. 1991)
—3-D Coloring Book—My First Geometric Designs. (p. 1991)
—Anna Pomaska's Big Book of Puzzle Fun. (p. 85)
—BOOST Dinosaurs Coloring Book. (p. 213)
—Dinosaurs. (p. 444)
—Dot-to-Dot. (p. 472)
—Easy Wizards Sticker Picture Puzzle. (p. 501)
—Fun with Numbers. (p. 648)
—Glitter Tattoos Henna. (p. 684)
—Glow-in-the-Dark Tattoos Magical Butterflies. (p. 685)
—Glow-in-the-Dark Tattoos Sun, Moon, Stars. (p. 685)
—Henna Butterflies Tattoos. (p. 767)
—Let's Color Together — Mandalas. (p. 995)
—Mandalas Coloring Book. (p. 1087)
—My First Geometric Designs Coloring Book. (p. 1206)
—My First Mandalas - Animals. (p. 1207)
—My First Mandalas Coloring Book. (p. 1207)
—Same & Different. (p. 1507)
—Scruffy & Muffin in the Land of Enchantment: A Dot-to-Dot Storybook. (p. 1533)
—Shiny Christmas Balls Ornaments. (p. 1567)
—Shiny Sun, Moon, Stars Stickers. (p. 1567)
—Sun, Moon & Stars Armband Tattoos. (p. 1676)
Pomaska, Anna & Coloring Books Staff. My First Mandalas - Nature. (p. 1207)
Pomaska, Anna & Newman-D'Amico, Fran. Crazy Crosswords Activity Book. (p. 377)
Pombo, Juan Manuel, tr. see Levine, Gail Carson.
Pombo, Luis, illus. see Hernandez, Claudia.
Pombo, Luis G., illus. see Hernandez, Claudia.
Pombo, Mauricio, tr. see Papademetriou, Lisa.
Pombo, Rafael. Cuentos, Pombo Rafael. Acosta, Patricia, illus. (p. 390)
—Fabulas y Verdades. (p. 559)
Pomenta, Allison, tr. see Olmstead, Mary.
Pomerance, Diane. Animal Companions: Your Friends, Teachers & Guides. Mier, Vanessa, illus. (p. 77)
—Animal Companions: In Our Hearts, Our Lives, & Our World. Mier, Vanessa, illus. (p. 77)
Pomerans, Arnold J., tr. see Metselaar, Menno & van der Rol, Ruud.
Pomerantz, Charlotte. Thunderboom! Poems for Everyone. Shepperson, Rob, illus. (p. 1746)
Pomerantz, Joel, jt. auth. see Pea, Uncle.
Pomerantz, Norman, illus. see Roop, James Q.
Pomerantz, Riva, tr. see Sternfeld, Nathan.
Pomere, Jonas. Drug Testing. (p. 486)
—Frequently Asked Questions about ADD & ADHD. (p. 636)
—Frequently Asked Questions about Self Mutilation & Cutting. (p. 636)
Pomerleau, Annie. At the Arcade: Understand Place Value. (p. 110)
Pomeroy, George, jt. auth. see Benhart, John.
Pomeroy, John. Little Child Shall Lead Them. Pomeroy, John, illus. (p. 1026)
Pomeroy, John, illus. see Perkins, Greg.
Pomeroy, Lynn Grobler. Curly, Randi & the Poultry Show. (p. 394)
Pommaux, Yvan. Fuga. (p. 646)
—Orpheus in the Underworld. Kutner, Richard, tr. from FRE. (p. 1305)
—Theseus & the Minotaur. Kutner, Richard, tr. from FRE. (p. 1732)
Pommer, Christina & Skindzier, Jon. Johns Hopkins University College Prowler off the Record. (p. 924)
Pommerat, Joël, et al. Theatre Cafe - Plays One: Invasion! - This Child - Respect. (p. 1728)
Pommier, Maurice, illus. see Le Guillou, Philippe.
Pompei, Maria Teresa, tr. see Dateno, Maria Grace.
Pomplun, Tom, ed. see Bierce, Ambrose, et al.
Pomplun, Tom, ed. see Caputo, Antonella, et al.
Pomplun, Tom, ed. see Doyle, Arthur, et al.
Pomplun, Tom, ed. see Henry, O., et al.
Pomplun, Tom, ed. see Irving, Washington, et al.
Pomplun, Tom, ed. see Lehman, John, et al.
Pomplun, Tom, ed. see London, Jack, et al.
Pomplun, Tom, ed. see Poe, Edgar Allen, et al.
Pomplun, Tom, ed. see Radcliffe, Ann, et al.
Pomplun, Tom, ed. see Rohmer, Sax, pseud, et al.
Pomplun, Tom, ed. see Sabatini, Rafael, et al.
Pomplun, Tom, ed. see Smelcer, John E., et al.
Pomplun, Tom, ed. see Wilde, Oscar, et al.
Pomranz, Craig. Made by Raffi. Chamberlain, Margaret, illus. (p. 1070)
Pon, Cindy. Silver Phoenix. (p. 1576)
Pon, Cindy, jt. auth. see Silver Phoenix Staff.
Pon, Cynthia, illus. see Ajmera, Maya & Derstine, Elise Hofer.
Ponce, José María, illus. see Unamuno, Miguel de & Unamuno, Miguel de.
Ponce, Kevin & Ponce, Paula. Fruit, Veggies & Poi. (p. 645)
Ponce, Mari Luz, tr. see Brown, Ruth.
Ponce, Paula, jt. auth. see Ponce, Kevin.
Pond, Brenda, photos by see Pond, Roy.
Pond, Melanie. Sir Keegan the Great! (p. 1580)
Pond, Roy. Egypt Tomb Machine: A Young Archaeologist... a Life or Death Quest in a Realm Before the Pharaohs. (p. 506)
—Princess Who Lost Her Scroll of the Dead: Ancient Egypt - an Underworld Adventure. Pond, Brenda, photos by. (p. 1406)
Pongetti, Freda. Why the Chimes Rang. (p. 1926)
Ponka, Katherine. Being a Toucan. (p. 161)
—Bird Watcher's Guide to Blue Jays. (p. 190)
—Carpenter Ants. (p. 271)
Ponko, Cindy. Cartwheel Katie's Christmas. (p. 273)
Ponko, Cindy A. Busy Busy Days. (p. 246)
—Gary's Forever Christmas Tree. (p. 657)
—Olive Fingers. (p. 1285)
Ponnay, Brenda. Secret Agent Josephine in Paris. Ponnay, Brenda, illus. (p. 1540)
Ponnay, Brenda, jt. auth. see Ponnay, Brenda.
Ponnay, Brenda & Ponnay, Brenda. Secret Agent Josephine in Paris. (p. 1540)
Ponomarov, Sergius, tr. see Chekhov, Anton.
Pons, Bernadette, illus. see Buller, Jon & Schade, Susan.
Pons, Bernadette, illus. see Dokas, Dara Sanders & Dokas, Dara.
Pons, Bernadette, illus. see Van Laan, Nancy.
Ponsard, Christine, jt. auth. see Kieffer, Jean-Francois.
Pont, Beattie. Grandma, Tell Me More: Fishing with Grandpa. (p. 708)
Pont, Charles E., illus. see Leeming, Joseph.
Ponte, June. Fun & Simple Great Lakes State Crafts: Michigan, Ohio, Indiana, Illinois, Wisconsin, & Minnesota. (p. 647)
—Fun & Simple Mid-Atlantic State Crafts. (p. 647)
—Fun & Simple Midwestern State Crafts: North Dakota, South Dakota, Nebraska, Iowa, Missouri, & Kansas. (p. 647)
—Fun & Simple New England State Crafts: Maine, New Hampshire, Vermont, Massachusetts, Rhode Island, & Connecticut. (p. 647)
—Fun & Simple Pacific West State Crafts: California, Oregon, Washington, Alaska, & Hawaii. (p. 647)
—Fun & Simple Southeastern State Crafts: West Virginia, Virginia, North Carolina, South Carolina, Georgia, & Florida. (p. 647)
—Fun & Simple Southern State Crafts: Kentucky, Tennessee, Alabama, Mississippi, Louisiana, & Arkansas. (p. 647)
—Fun & Simple Southwestern State Crafts: Colorado, Oklahoma, Texas, New Mexico, & Arizona. (p. 647)
—Fun & Simple Western State Crafts: Montana, Wyoming, Idaho, Utah, & Nevada. (p. 647)
Ponte, June, illus. see Boekhoff, P. M.
Ponte, June, illus. see Erlbach, Arlene & Erlbach, Herbert.
Ponte, June, illus. see Gabriel, Faith K.
Ponte, June, illus. see Hartman, Sarah.
Ponte, June, illus. see Hollow, Michele C.
Ponte, June, illus. see Miller, Heather.
Ponte, June, illus. see Niven, Felicia Lowenstein.
Ponti, jt. auth. see Ponti, Claude.
Ponti, Claude. Arbol Sin Fin. Ponti, Claude, illus. (p. 94)
—Chick & Chickie in Play All Day! (p. 299)
—Chick & Chickie Play All Day! (p. 299)
—DeZert Isle. Holliday, Mary Martin, tr. from FRE. (p. 433)
—Mi Valle. (p. 1133)
—Okilele. (p. 1282)
—Roberto Elbanco. (p. 1479)
—Tempestad. (p. 1718)
Ponti, Claude, illus. see Seyvos, Florence.
Ponti, Claude & Desarthe, Agnes. Principito Puf. (p. 1406)
Ponti, Claude & Ponti. En El Coche. (p. 522)
Ponti, James. Blue Moon. (p. 203)
—Dead City. (p. 416)
Ponti, Jamie. Animal Attraction. (p. 76)
—Sea of Love. (p. 1535)
Ponting, Susan. Revenge of BB Wolf. (p. 1465)
Ponto, Joanna. Being Honest. (p. 161)
—Being Kind. (p. 161)
—Being Respectful. (p. 161)
—Being Responsible. (p. 161)
Ponto, Kristina. Fissy. (p. 599)
PONY, compiled by. Little Horse Book. (p. 1029)
Ponzio, Jean-Michel, illus. see Marazano, Richard.
Ponzio, Richard, ed. Earthquake! Beyond Duck, Cover, & Hold. (p. 497)
Poock, Carl. Mackenzie's Gift. (p. 1068)
Pooker, J. D. Ifs. (p. 855)
Pool, Catherine. Catrina's Journey to Her Musical Friends (p. 280)
Pool, Cathy, illus. see Masrud, Judy.
Pool, David, jt. auth. see Blumenstock, Jacqueline.
Pool, Joyce Oudkerk, photos by see Morgan, Diane.
Pool, Steve, photos by see McCarty, Michael.
Poole, Amy Lowry. Pea Blossom. (p. 1331)
Poole, Amy Lowry & Andersen, Hans Christian. Pea Blossom. (p. 1331)
Poole, Annie Mae Keeling. Billy Keith & the Tooth Fairy. (p. 187)
Poole, Barbie. High School Records: Watch Me Grow: Year by Year School Records. (p. 778)
Poole, Bud. Little Miss Muffet Gets Saved: A Christian Nursery Rhyme. (p. 1032)
Poole, Catherine Cheyenne. Batboy's Crazy Day. Murphy, Fredrick, illus. (p. 143)
Poole, Cheryl J. A. Farmer & Me! Making Silage. (p. 574)
—Farmer & Me! Milking the Cows. (p. 574)
Poole, Diamond Catherine Cheyenne. Leslie the Old Hag Who Collected Souls. (p. 993)
Poole, Gabriella. Divided Souls. (p. 454)
—Secret Lives. (p. 1541)
Poole, H. W. Alzheimer's Disease Walters, Anne S., ed. (p. 51)
—Anxiety Disorders Walters, Anne S., ed. (p. 90)
—Attention Deficit Hyperactivity Disorder Walters, Anne S., ed. (p. 114)
—Autism Spectrum Disorders Walters, Anne S., ed. (p. 117)
—Bipolar Disorder Walters, Anne S., ed. (p. 190)
—Depression Walters, Anne S., ed. (p. 427)
—Disruptive Behavior Disorders Walters, Anne S., ed. (p. 453)
—Drug & Alcohol Dependence Walters, Anne S., ed. (p. 486)
—Eating Disorders Walters, Anne S., ed. (p. 501)
—Obsessive-Compulsive Disorder Walters, Anne S., ed. (p. 1275)
—Post-Traumatic Stress Disorder Walters, Anne S., ed. (p. 1387)
—Schizophrenia Walters, Anne S., ed. (p. 1521)
—Sleep Disorders Walters, Anne S., ed. (p. 1588)
Poole, Hazel. Spies & Detectives. (p. 1627)
Poole, Helen. Clara's Crazy Curls Poole, Helen, illus. (p. 326)
Poole, Helen, illus. see Balsley, Tilda.
Poole, Helen, illus. see Daniel, Claire.
Poole, Helen, illus. see David, Juliet.

Poole, Helen, illus. see Garcia, Ellen.
Poole, Helen, illus. see Giachetti, Julia.
Poole, Helen, illus. see Greve, Meg.
Poole, Helen, illus. see Hord, Colleen.
Poole, Helen, illus. see Linde, Barbara M.
Poole, Helen, illus. see Smith, Molly.
Poole, Josephine. Ana Frank. Barrett, Angela, illus. (p. 66)
—Blancanieves. Barrett, Angela, illus. (p. 198)
Poole, Josephine & Hess, Paul. Jack & the Beanstalk. (p. 902)
Poole, LaDonna. Love Bug. (p. 1059)
Poole, Marcia. Building a Dream: The Story of the Sioux City Lewis & Clark Interpretive Center. (p. 238)
Poole, Mary Jo, ed. see Thompson, Bruce E. R.
Poole, Philip. Trouble with Time. (p. 1790)
Poole, Rebecca, jt. auth. see Markel, Rita J.
Poole, Richard. Iron Angel. (p. 888)
—Jewel & Thorn. (p. 916)
Poole, Stephanie. Adopted by Wolves. (p. 13)
Poole, Steven R., illus. see Reid, Christy.
Poole, Susie. All These Things: Based on 1 Corinthians 13:4-7. (p. 46)
—Amazing Journey: Jesus, Creation, Death & Life! (p. 54)
—Christmas Journey. Poole, Susie, illus. (p. 314)
—Whatever Is Lovely: Based on Philippians 4:4-9. (p. 1896)
Poole, Susie, illus. see Box, Su.
Poole, Susie, illus. see O'Connell, Rebecca.
Poole, Susie, jt. auth. see Hartman, Bob.
Poole, Tracy, illus. see Franklin, Cathy.
Poole, Vera. Adventures of Natsoodatie: The Stolen Blankets. (p. 21)
Poole-Carter, Rosemary. Juliette Ascending. (p. 932)
Pooler, Paige, illus. see Allen, Elise & Stanford, Halle.
Pooler, Paige, illus. see DeVillers, Julia.
Pooley, Roger, ed. see Bunyan, John.
Poolos, Christine. American Flag. (p. 60)
—Deep-Sea Fishing. (p. 423)
—John Green (p. 922)
—Truth about Pcp. (p. 1794)
—What Is an Object in the Sky? (p. 1889)
Poolos, J. Army Rangers: Surveillance & Reconnaissance for the U. S. Army. (p. 100)
—Atomic Bombings of Hiroshima & Nagasaki. (p. 113)
—ATVs/Vehiculos Todo Terreno. Alaman, Eduardo, tr. from ENG. (p. 114)
—Darius the Great. (p. 407)
—Dragsters. Alaman, Eduardo, tr. from ENG. (p. 479)
—Hot Rods. Alaman, Eduardo, tr. from ENG. (p. 802)
—Jeff Gordon: NASCAR Driver. (p. 911)
—Lowriders. Alaman, Eduardo, tr. from ENG. (p. 1061)
—Mayflower: A Primary Source History of the Pilgrims' Journey to the New World. (p. 1113)
—Mayflower. (p. 1113)
—Monster Trucks/Camionetas Gigantes. Alaman, Eduardo, tr. (p. 1168)
—Muscle Cars/Autos de Poder. Alaman, Eduardo, tr. from ENG. (p. 1192)
—Nerve Gas Attack on the Tokyo Subway. (p. 1241)
—Ralph Waldo Emerson: The Father of the American Renaissance. (p. 1437)
—Wild about ATVs. (p. 1928)
—Wild about ATVs/Vehiculos todo Terreno. (p. 1928)
—Wild about Dragsters. (p. 1928)
—Wild about Hot Rods. (p. 1928)
—Wild about Lowriders. (p. 1928)
—Wild about Monster Trucks. (p. 1928)
—Wild about Monster Trucks/Camionetas Gigantes. (p. 1928)
—Wild about Muscle Cars. (p. 1928)
—Wild about Muscle Cars/Autos de Poder. (p. 1928)
Poolos, J., jt. auth. see Poolos, Jamie.
Poolos, Jamie. Designing, Building, & Maintaining Web Sites. (p. 430)
—Hostage Rescuers. (p. 801)
—Surfing & Wind Surfing. (p. 1685)
Poolos, Jamie & Poolos, J. Hank Aaron. (p. 742)
Poon, Janice. Claire & the Bakery Thief. Poon, Janice, illus. (p. 326)
—Claire & the Water Wish. Poon, Janice, illus. (p. 326)
Poor, Shawnna D. What Kind of A Name Is That? (p. 1891)
Poortvliet, Rien, illus. see Haar, Jaap Ter & Mearns, Martha.
Poortvliet, Rien, jt. auth. see Goldstone, Bruce.
Pop Art Properties Staff, illus. see Biskup, Agnieszka.
Pop Art Properties Staff, illus. see Bolte, Mari.
Pop Art Properties Staff, illus. see Enz, Tammy & Biskup, Agnieszka.
Pop Art Properties Staff, illus. see Enz, Tammy.
Pop Art Studios, illus. see Bethea, Nikole Brooks.
Pop Art Studios, illus. see Enz, Tammy.
Pop Art Studios Staff, illus. see Bethea, Nikole Brooks.
Pop Art Studios Staff, illus. see Enz, Tammy.
Popa, Tamara. Chukcha the Mountain Monkey. (p. 318)
PopCap Games Staff, jt. auth. see Auerbach, Annie.
Pope, Amy. Big Church. Meier, Paul, illus. (p. 180)
—Moving Day. George, John, 3rd, illus. (p. 1183)
Pope, Brennan & Pope, Janet. Adventures of William Walkingstick. (p. 24)
Pope, Cheryl Lynn. Adventures of Princess Zari. Nyamor, Eric, illus. (p. 22)
Pope, Cody/Louis Ray. Andy & the Dragons. (p. 72)
Pope, Dan. In the Cherry Tree: A Novel. (p. 865)
Pope, Ellen Dittman. Friends with a Difference. Dixon, Carol, illus. (p. 639)
Pope, Franklin, jt. auth. see Hill, George.
Pope, Janet, jt. auth. see Pope, Brennan.
Pope, Jerald. Madeleine Claire & the Dinosaur. (p. 1070)
Pope, Kate, illus. see Hegarty, Pat.
Pope, Kevin. Exploding Toilet: Modern Urban Legends. (p. 549)
Pope, Kevin, illus. see Hamilton, Martha & Weise, Mutch.
Pope, Kevin, illus. see Hamilton, Martha & Weiss, Mitch.
Pope, Kristen. Black Rhinos. (p. 196)
—Chimpanzees. (p. 306)
—Fennec Foxes. (p. 581)
—Salamanders. (p. 1504)
Pope, Lauren, illus. see Sugg, Nan.
Pope, Lee Green. Cinderella Diary: A Not-So-Grimm Faerie Tale. (p. 320)
Pope, Lindsey. Oliver Oyster. (p. 1285)
Pope, Liz, illus. see Hegarty, Pat.
Pope, Mildred. But I Don't Wanna Take a Bath! A Mike & Tyke Series. (p. 246)
Pope, Miller. ABC-Pirate-Coloring Book. (p. 3)
Pope, P. R. Queens of Antares: Volume 1 of the Bloodline Trilogy: Bloodline Returned: Bloodline Returned. (p. 1425)
Pope, Patricia, jt. illus. see McInturff, Linda.
Pope, Paul. Battling Boy. Pope, Paul, illus. (p. 147)
—Sugary Shorts. (p. 1673)
—Year 100. (p. 1969)
Pope, Paul & Petty, J. T. Rise of Aurora West. Rubín, David, illus. (p. 1474)
Pope, Paul & Renier, Aaron. Adventure Time Sugary Shorts Vol. 1. (p. 14)
Pope, Psborne. Vallee des Dinosaurs. (p. 1830)
Pope, Richie, illus. see Biskup, Agnieszka & Collins, Terry.
Pope, Richie, illus. see Collins, Terry.
Pope, Stephanie L. Fedo the Frog Flew the Coop. (p. 580)
Pope, T., illus. see Letcher, MaKayla.
Popek, Emily. Copyright & Digital Ethics. (p. 366)
—Understanding the World of User-Generated Content. (p. 1816)
Popek, Penelope & Mitchell, Toni. Darby Downswallow & His Bumblebee. (p. 406)
Popek-Jones, Diane. East of the Jagged Cross. (p. 498)
Popeo, Joanie, illus. see Hollenbeck, Kathleen M.
Popeo, Joanie, illus. see Winkelman, Barbara Gaines & Thomas, Peter.
Popeo, Joanie, illus. see Winkelman, Barbara Gaines.
Pope-Roush, Jordan & Skindzier, Jon. Emory University College Prowler off the Record. (p. 520)
Popescu, Anna Ildiko. Stamps & Doodles: Animals. (p. 1639)
—Stamps & Doodles for Boys. (p. 1639)
Popescu, Petru. Birth of the Pack. (p. 192)
—Footprints in Time. (p. 615)
Popeson, Pamela, illus. see Weiss, Ellen.
Popiel, Candice Bataille, jt. auth. see Jazwierska, Jennifer.
Popke, Suzanne L. Adventures of Tolei Mergen. (p. 24)
Popkin, Michael H. & Hendrickson, Peggy. Teens in Action: A Teen's Guide for Surviving & Thriving in the 21st Century. (p. 1715)
Popko, Wendy, illus. see Lewis, Anne Margaret & Campbell, Janis.
Popko, Wendy, illus. see Williamson, Greg.
Popkp, Wendy, illus. see Williamson, Greg.
Poplak, Richard, ed. see Gilmore, Jason & Peterson, Paul.
Poplau, Ronald W. Doer of Good Becomes Good: A Primer on Volunteerism. (p. 460)
Poplawska, Yolanda. Halifax Harbour 123 (BB) A Counting Book about Halifax Harbour (p. 737)
Poplin, Isaac E. A-Z's of Ancient Rome: A Rhyming Introduction to Roman History. (p. 2)
Poploff, Michelle. Where Triplets Go, Trouble Follows. Jamieson, Victoria, illus. (p. 1910)
Popov, Nikolai, illus. see Springer, Jane, tr.
Popova, Natalya. Guinea Pig Story. (p. 731)
Popovich, Richard E., ed. see Beeson, Lea Ann.
Popp, K. Wendy, illus. see Bunting, Eve.
Popp, K. Wendy, illus. see Wood, Douglas.
Poppe, Lindsey. Snow Day. (p. 1598)
Poppel, Hans, jt. auth. see Gartner, Hans.
Poppen, Alex, illus. see Bitner, Pamela.
Poppenhager, Nicole. Snow Leopards. James, J. Alison, tr. from GER. (p. 1599)
Popper, Carol. David, Mormor, Homo & the Yak: An Alphabet Mystery. (p. 411)
Popper, Garry. Ali in Egypt. Johnson, Andi, illus. (p. 39)
—Beast of Didley Dale. Forshaw, John, illus. (p. 152)
—Big World. Johnson, Andi, illus. (p. 184)
—Billy Joe in the U. S. A. Johnson, Andi, illus. (p. 187)
—High Noon in Didley Pidley. Forshaw, John, illus. (p. 778)
—James & Jemma in Great Britain. Johnson, Andi, illus. (p. 906)
—Keito in Japan. Johnson, Andi, illus. (p. 948)
—Kez in Australia. Johnson, Andi, illus. (p. 951)
—Lena & Peter in Germany. Johnson, Andi, illus. (p. 991)
—Li & Lilly May in China. Johnson, Andi, illus. (p. 1004)
—Mario in Italy. Johnson, Andi, illus. (p. 1094)
—Mina in India. Johnson, Andi, illus. (p. 1145)
—Paul in France. Johnson, Andi, illus. (p. 1330)
—Scary Monkeys: Going Ape. Forshaw, John, illus. (p. 1520)
—Winston in the Caribbean. Johnson, Andi, illus. (p. 1937)
—Worm's Eye View: A Witch's Tale. Forshaw, John, illus. (p. 1961)
Popper, Garry & Volke, Gordon. Big World Activity Sticker Book. Johnson, Andi, illus. (p. 184)
Popper, Lisa. Bop. (p. 213)
—Bunny Bop. (p. 242)
—Danny Dragon. (p. 405)
—Dot's Pot. (p. 472)
—Drip Drop. (p. 485)
—Hanna Hippo. (p. 742)
—Hit the Mit. (p. 785)
—Len & Lil. (p. 991)
—Let' Make Music. (p. 994)
—Muddy Mud. (p. 1189)
—My Pet Jet. (p. 1217)
—My Rad Dad. (p. 1217)
—Nifty Noodle. (p. 1252)
—Patty the Pink Pig. (p. 1330)
—Rat Rap. (p. 1440)
—Sammy. (p. 1507)
—Tap the Sap. (p. 1705)
—Timmy Turtle. (p. 1755)
Popsicle, Patty. Crack-a-Doodle Horse Tales: A Tale about Biting. (p. 375)
—Crack-a-doodle Horse Tales: A Tale about Pinching. (p. 375)
—Crack-A-Doodle Horse Tales: A Tale about Scratching. (p. 375)
—Crack-a-doodle Horse Tales: A Tale about Pulling Hair. (p. 375)
Popular Book Company. Complete Math Workout, Grade 1. (p. 353)
Popular Book Company, creator. Complete Math Workout, Grade 5. (p. 353)
Popular Book Company Staff. Complete Math Workout, Grade 2. (p. 353)
Popular Mechanics, ed. Boy Scientist: 160 Extraordinary Experiments & Adventures. (p. 218)
Popular Mechanics Press Editors. Boy Mechanic. (p. 218)
popular, Tradición, jt. auth. see Fuenmayor, Morella.
Populoh, Valeska M., illus. see Cunningham, Steven C.
Porada, Henry. Inner Light. Michaels, Lisa J., illus. (p. 875)
Poratto, Maria Laura. Costura para Ninos. (p. 369)
Porcelli, Gary W. Crazy Eights. (p. 377)
Porcelli-Munisteri, Nadia. Who Are You Calling a Bully? (p. 1914)
Porcellino, John. Thoreau at Walden. Porcellino, John, illus. (p. 1740)
Porcellino, John, illus. see Gilmore, Jason & Peterson, Paul.
Porcheron, Tammy, illus. see Lewis, Carolyn & DeVince, James.
Porcheron, Tammy, illus. see Lewis, Carolyn.
Porchlight Entertainment Staff, ed. You Are Special. (p. 1973)
Porell, John. Fire! (p. 590)
—When Things Go Wrong. (p. 1905)
Porfirio, Guy. Jump! (p. 933)
Porfirio, Guy, illus. see Crystal, Billy.
Porfirio, Guy, illus. see Harvey, Gwen.
Porfirio, Guy, illus. see Levitin, Sonia.
Porfirio, Guy, illus. see Loux, Lynn Crosble.
Porfirio, Guy, illus. see Moore, Clement C., ed.
Porfirio, Guy, illus. see Ottolenghi, Carol.
Porfirio, Guy, illus. see Tazewell, Charles.
Porfirio, Guy, illus. see Wallace-Lang, Maxine Lois.
Porkess, R., ed. see Hanrahan, Val.
Pornkerd, Vorrarit, illus. see Donploypetch, Jintanan.
Pornkerd, Vorrarit, illus. see Gilligan, Shannon.
Pornkerd, Vorrarit, et al. Lost Jewels of Nabooti. (p. 1056)
—Space & Beyond. (p. 1618)
Porpora, Donnamarie. Grampa's Wings. (p. 706)
Porras, Carlos, tr. see Asimov, Isaac & Hantula, Richard.
Porras, Carlos, tr. see Ball, Jacqueline A. & Behrens, Kristen.
Porras, Carlos, tr. see Barenblat, Rachel.
Porras, Carlos, tr. see Chui, Patricia.
Porras, Carlos, tr. see Feeley, Kathleen.
Porras, Carlos, tr. see Holtz, Eric Siegfried.
Porras, Javier Fernando. Historias de Amores y Desvarios en America. (p. 782)
Porras, Javier Fernando, illus. see Perrault, Charles.
Porras, Javier Fernando, illus. see Quiroga, Horacio.
Porras, Nikki Jo & Hix, Jax. New Colorful Creatures. Steever, Sarah, illus. (p. 1244)
Porras-Ballard, Patricia, tr. see Harrison, Lisi.
Porrata, Mayra. Day Kyle Met Nuf. Rice, Kaleb & Deasey, Kevin, illus. (p. 413)
Porsenna, Sandy. My first prayer Book. (p. 1207)
Port, Cynthia. Kibble Talk. Port, Cynthia, illus. (p. 951)
Port, Moni. Bravo! Waechter, Philip, illus. (p. 224)
Porta, Bill K. Adventures of Henry the Little Boat. (p. 18)
—Rusty the Rescue Horse. (p. 1498)
Portal, Alex. Applegates (p. 92)
Portales, Marco, jt. auth. see Portales, Rita.
Portales, Rita & Portales, Marco. Quality Education for Latinos & Latinas: Print & Oral Skills for All Students, K-College. (p. 1422)
Portalupi, Laura. Spies! Real People, Real Stories. (p. 1627)
—Spies!: Real People, Real Stories Set (p. 1627)
Portavoz. Libro Abo-dario. (p. 1006)
Portch, Elizabeth, tr. see Jansson, Tove.
Portch, Larry. UNION GHOSTS of MOUNTSVILLE HOLLOW (and the Four Confederate Banshees) (p. 1818)
Porte, Barbara Ann. Beauty & the Serpent: Thirteen Tales of Unnatural Animals. Covey, Rosemary Feit, illus. (p. 154)
—Harry's Birthday. Abolafia, Yossi, illus. (p. 751)
—Harry's Pony. Abolafia, Yossi, illus. (p. 751)
Porteous, Barbara. Little Cloud's Christmas Adventure. (p. 1026)
Porter, A. P. Nebraska. (p. 1239)
Porter, Alan J. Cars: The Rookie. Carreres, Albert, illus. (p. 272)
—Cars: Route 66 Dash! Gladfelter, Allen, illus. (p. 272)
—Cars: Radiator Springs. Carreres, Albert, illus. (p. 272)
—Cars: Radiator Springs. Vol. 2 Carreres, Albert, illus. (p. 272)
—Cars: the Rookie. Carreres, Albert, illus. (p. 272)
—Rally Race. Magic Eye Studios, illus. (p. 1437)
Porter, Alfred. My Belly Button Is Missing! (p. 1196)
Porter, Amber Leann. To Be a Champion. (p. 1758)
Porter, Annaliese & Bancroft, Bronwyn. Outback. (p. 1312)
Porter, C. Coping with Crohn's Disease & Ulcerative Colitis. (p. 365)
Porter, Chip, jt. auth. see Keating, Dan.
Porter, Cullen. Grandpa Grumpy Pants. (p. 709)
Porter, Darwin. Brando Unzipped: Bad Boy, Megastar, Sexual Outlaw. (p. 222)
Porter, Douglas, jt. auth. see Towns, Elmer.
Porter, Duane. Charlie & the Chess Set. (p. 292)
—Molly O'Malley & the Leprechaun. (p. 1161)
Porter, Eleanor H. Miss Billy - Married. (p. 1151)
—Miss Billy's Decision. (p. 1151)
—Pollyanna. (p. 1381)
—Pollyanna. Akib, Jamel, illus. (p. 1381)
—Pollyanna. McKowen, Scott, illus. (p. 1381)
—Pollyanna & Pollyanna Grows Up. (p. 1381)
—Pollyanna Grows Up: The Second Glad Book. (p. 1381)
—Pollyanna Grows Up. (p. 1381)
Porter, Eleanor H., jt. auth. see Olmstead, Kathleen.
Porter, Eleanor H., jt. auth. see Wardle, Sue.
Porter, Esther. Scorpions (p. 1530)
—Sun Power: A Book about Renewable Energy (p. 1676)
—Termites (p. 1721)
—What's Sprouting in My Trash? A Book about Composting. (p. 1899)
Porter, Esther, jt. auth. see Johnson, J. Angelique.
Porter, Gary. Duffy: The Tale of a Terrier. (p. 489)
Porter, Gene Stratton. Girl of the Limberlost. (p. 678)
Porter, Harry. Dylan's Tale. Hedrick, Mandy, illus. (p. 491)
—Wolf. Stites, Theresa, illus. (p. 1943)
Porter, Howard, jt. auth. see Waid, Mark.
Porter, Jane. Flirting with Forty. (p. 605)
Porter, Jane, illus. see Kohuth, Jane.
Porter, Janice, illus. see Lowery, Linda & Keep, Richard.
Porter, Janice Lee. Allen Jay & the Underground Railroad (p. 46)
Porter, Janice Lee, illus. see Brill, Marlene Targ.
Porter, Janice Lee, illus. see Lowery, Linda & Keep, Richard.
Porter, Janice Lee, illus. see Lowery, Linda.
Porter, Janice Lee, illus. see Monk, Isabell.
Porter, Janice Lee, illus. see Simpson, Lesley.
Porter, Janice Lee, illus. see Sutcliffe, Jane.
Porter, Janice Lee, illus. see Walker, Sally M.
Porter, Jodi L. Night & Day. (p. 1252)
—Noche y Dia / Night & Day. (p. 1262)
Porter, Kevin Don. Missing. (p. 1152)
Porter, Lee. Drake. (p. 479)
Porter, Lisa. Billy & Froggy. (p. 187)
Porter, Lynda C., illus. see Beasley, Jonathan & Porter, Rosanna I.
Porter, Malcolm. Cherrytree Children's Atlas. (p. 298)
Porter, Malcolm, jt. auth. see Campbell, Rusty.
Porter, Malcolm, jt. auth. see Comire, S. Joshua.
Porter, Malcolm, jt. auth. see Gareth Stevens Publishing Staff.
Porter, Malcolm, jt. auth. see Waxman, Malcolm.
Porter, Marylyn Kight. Speedy the Snail & His New Family. (p. 1625)
Porter, Matthew. Calling All Animals. (p. 254)
—Count the Birdies. (p. 370)
—Flowers. (p. 608)
—Fox on the Loose! Porter, Matthew, illus. (p. 626)
—Monkey World. (p. 1165)
—Monkey World ABC. (p. 1165)
—Monkey World: the Thunderbolt Express. (p. 1165)
—Rise & Fall of Oscar the Magician: A Monkey World Adventure. Porter, Matthew, illus. (p. 1474)
—Tails Chasing Tails. (p. 1695)
Porter, Matthew & Morstad, Julie. ABC. (p. 3)
Porter, Michael E., ed. see Sala-I-Martin, Xavier.
Porter, Pamela. Crazy Man (p. 377)
—Crazy Man. (p. 377)
—I'll Be Watching. (p. 856)
—Sky Gerber, Mary Jane, illus. (p. 1586)
—Yellow Moon, Apple Moon James, Matt, illus. (p. 1970)
Porter, Patricia, jt. auth. see vanDommelen, Deborah.
Porter, Phil. Two Plays for Young People: The Flying Machine; Smashed Eggs. (p. 1804)
Porter, Rhonda. Brody Learns about Strangers (p. 230)
—Brody Meets a Bully. (p. 230)
Porter, Rosalie Pedalino & Clark, Kevin. Language & Literacy for English Learners: Four Programs of Proven Success. (p. 974)
Porter, Rosanna I., jt. auth. see Beasley, Jonathan.
Porter, Sarah. Lost Voices. (p. 1057)
—Twice Lost. (p. 1801)
—Waking Storms. (p. 1853)
Porter, Steven. American Musical Theatre: A Complete Musical Theatre Course. (p. 62)
—New Monologues for Reader's Theater. (p. 1246)
—Prairie Man. (p. 1392)
—Schenker Made Simple. (p. 1521)
Porter, Steven, compiled by. New Works for Readers' Theatre. (p. 1247)
Porter, Sue, illus. see Edwards, Pamela Duncan.
Porter, Suzie. Sailing. (p. 1503)
Porter, Tammy, illus. see Feather, Tami Flaming.
Porter, Tiffany McLain. Day I Cried Endlessly. (p. 413)
Porter, Tim. What's in My Purse. (p. 1898)
Porter, Todd. Firefly Fred. Patenaude, Brian, illus. (p. 592)
Porter, Tracey. Billy Creekmore. (p. 187)
—Lark. (p. 975)
Porter, Tracey Nelson. Draegon Is Two: Grandma! Draegon Was Always Right, or Was He? (p. 476)
Porter Zasada, Marc. Alice Through the Looking Glass - a Children's Play. (p. 39)
Porterfield, Deborah. Great Careers with a High School Diploma: Health Care, Medicine, & Science. (p. 714)
Porterfield, Jason. Angry Birds & Rovio Entertainment (p. 75)
—Annie Oakley: Wild West Sharpshooter. (p. 87)
—Annie Oakley: Wild West Sharpshooter / Tiradora del Lejano Oeste. (p. 87)
—Annie Oakley: Tiradora del Lejano Oeste (Annie Oakley: Wild West Sharpshooter) (p. 87)
—Baseball: Rules, Tips, Strategy, & Safety. (p. 140)
—Baseball in the American League Central Division. (p. 141)
—Baseball in the National League East Division. (p. 141)
—Basketball in the ACC (Atlantic Coast Conference) (p. 143)
—Basketball in the ACC (Atlantic Coast Conference) (p. 143)
—Basketball in the Big East Conference. (p. 143)
—Bowfishing. (p. 216)
—Calvin Hill & Grant Hill: One Family's Legacy in Football & Basketball. (p. 255)
—Calvin Hill & Grant Hill: One Family's Legacy in Football & Basketball (Sports Families) (p. 255)
—Careers in Undercover Gang Investigation. (p. 268)
—Chile: A Primary Source Cultural Guide. (p. 305)
—Communism: A Primary Source Analysis. (p. 349)
—Conducting Basic & Advanced Searches. (p. 356)
—Doping: Athletes & Drugs. (p. 470)
—Downers: Depressant Abuse. (p. 474)
—Election of Barack Obama: Race & Politics in America. (p. 508)
—File Sharing: Rights & Risks. (p. 586)
—Homestead Act Of 1862: A Primary Source History of the Settlement of the American Heartland in the Late 19th Century. (p. 793)
—Homestead Act of 1862. (p. 793)
—How a Depression Works. (p. 804)

P

—How A Depression Works (Real World Economics) (p. 804)
—Julian Assange & Wikileaks. (p. 932)
—Kurt Busch: NASCAR Driver. (p. 968)
—Law & Personal Health: Your Legal Rights. (p. 981)
—Lincoln-Douglas Senatorial Debates of 1858: A Primary Source Investigation. (p. 1018)
—Looking at How Species Compete Within Environments with Graphic Organizers. (p. 1050)
—Major League Baseball: The Great Steroid Scandals. (p. 1078)
—Montana: Past & Present. (p. 1170)
—Niklas Zennstrom & Skype. (p. 1255)
—Problems & Progress in American Politics: The Growth of the Democratic Party in the Late 1800s. (p. 1408)
—Scandinavian Mythology. (p. 1519)
—Separation of Church & State: Interpreting the Constitution. (p. 1551)
—Shipwreck: True Stories of Survival. (p. 1567)
—Terrorism, Dirty Bombs, & Weapons of Mass Destruction. (p. 1722)
—Third Amendment: Upholding the Right to Privacy. (p. 1734)
—Third Amendment: The Right to Privacy in the Home. (p. 1734)
—Treasure Island & the Pirates of the Eighteenth Century. (p. 1782)
—Treaty of Guadalupe Hidalgo 1848: A Primary Source Examination of the Treaty That Ended the Mexican-American War. (p. 1783)
—USAF Special Tactics Teams. (p. 1826)
—Virginia: Past & Present. (p. 1844)
—What Is the Executive Branch? (p. 1890)
—Your Career in the Army. (p. 1980)
Porterfield, Jason, jt. auth. see Stanley, Glen F.
Porterfield, Jason, jt. auth. see Towne, Isobel.
Porterfield, Kay Marie, jt. auth. see Keoke, Emory Dean.
Porterfield, Scott, illus. see Lee, Karin.
Porter-Gaylord, Laurel. I Love My Daddy Because... Wolff, Ashley, illus. (p. 842)
—I Love My Daddy Because... (Quiero a Mi Papa Porque...) Wolff, Ashley, illus. (p. 842)
—I Love My Mommy Because... Wolff, Ashley, illus. (p. 842)
Porter-Schofield, Dawn. Itchy Nose. (p. 895)
Portes, Andrea. Anatomy of a Misfit. (p. 67)
Porthouse, Annie. Dear Bob. (p. 418)
Portillo, Athena Yvette. Sun & Moon. (p. 1676)
Portis, Antoinette. Froodle. Portis, Antoinette, illus. (p. 644)
—Kindergarten Diary. Portis, Antoinette, illus. (p. 957)
—Not a Box. Portis, Antoinette, illus. (p. 1266)
—Not a Box Board Book. Portis, Antoinette, illus. (p. 1266)
—Not a Stick. Portis, Antoinette, illus. (p. 1266)
—Penguin Story. Portis, Antoinette, illus. (p. 1337)
—Princess Super Kitty. Portis, Antoinette, illus. (p. 1405)
—Wait. (p. 1852)
Portis, Nathanial. Things in Between. (p. 1733)
Portman, Frank. Andromeda Klein. (p. 72)
—King Dork. (p. 958)
—King Dork Approximately. (p. 958)
Portman, Michael. Are There Other Earths? (p. 96)
—Are UFOs Real? (p. 96)
—Blinding Blizzards. (p. 199)
—Chargers. (p. 291)
—Chevelles. (p. 298)
—Could an Asteroid Harm Earth? (p. 369)
—Could We Live on Other Planets? (p. 369)
—Deadly Floods. (p. 417)
—Destructive Hurricanes. (p. 431)
—Drew Brees. (p. 485)
—Fighter Jets. (p. 585)
—Gorillas in Danger. (p. 703)
—Is There Life on Mars? (p. 890)
—Marine Corps. (p. 1094)
—Mustangs. (p. 1194)
—Pandas in Danger. (p. 1321)
—Sea Turtles in Danger. (p. 1536)
—Tasmanian Devils in Danger. (p. 1707)
—Tigers in Danger. (p. 1749)
—Torinos. (p. 1769)
—Whales in Danger. (p. 1878)
—What Is an Eclipse? (p. 1888)
—Where Did the Moon Come From? (p. 1906)
—Why Do Astronauts Wear Spacesuits? (p. 1923)
—Why Isn't Pluto a Planet? (p. 1925)
Portman, Michelle Eva. Compost, by Gosh! An Adventure with Vermicomposting. Portman, Michelle Eva, illus. (p. 354)
Portmann, Alan E. Jared & Joshua's Whopper. (p. 909)
Portmann, Rosemarie & Verlag, Don Bosco Medien. Emotional Strength & Self-Esteem. (p. 520)
Portmann, Rosemarie, et al. Relaxation & Concentration. (p. 1458)
Portnoi, Jeremy, illus. see Wool, Danny & Yudin, Yefim (Chaim).
Portnoy, Amy, illus. see Becker, Bonny.
Portnoy, Mindy Avra. Tale of Two Seders. Cis, Valeria, illus. (p. 1700)
—¿Adónde Van Las Personas Cuando Mueren? Translations.com Staff, tr. from ENG. (p. 13)
Porto, Chuck & Peters, Laura. Best Garden Plants for Iowa (p. 169)
Portorrico, Silvia. Viva el Miedo. Cabrera, Giovanni, illus. (p. 1846)
Portwood, Andrew, illus. see Givens, Terryl L.
Poryes, Michael. Trouble with Boys (p. 1790)
Poryes, Michael, jt. auth. see Sherman, Susan.
Posada, Jorge. Play Ball! Colón, Raúl, illus. (p. 1371)
—Sí, Puedes. Colón, Raúl, illus. (p. 1572)
Posada, Maria Candelaria, tr. see Henkes, Kevin.
Posada, Mia. Guess What Is Growing Inside This Egg. Posada, Mia, illus. (p. 729)
—Who Was Here? Discovering Wild Animal Tracks. Posada, Mia, illus. (p. 1918)
Posada, Mia, illus. see Glaser, Linda.
Posada, Mia, illus. see Markle, Sandra.
Posadas, Carmen. Dorilda. (p. 471)
Posadas Mane, Carmen De, see De Posadas Mane, Carmen.
Posamentier, Aldred. Advanced Geometric Construction. (p. 13)
Posen, Mick, illus. see Croy, Anita.
Posener, Alan. Marchenland. (p. 1091)
—Olli Aus Ossiland. (p. 1287)
Poser, Cynthia M. Hotline to Heaven. (p. 802)
—Hotline to Heaven - Color. (p. 802)
Posesorski, Sherie. Escape Plans. Pearcey, Dawn, illus. (p. 535)
Posesorski, Sherie & Second Story Press Staff. Old Photographs (p. 1284)
Posewitz, James. Rifle in Hand: How Wild America Was Saved. (p. 1471)
Posey, Lee. Night Rabbits Montgomery, Michael, illus. (p. 1254)
Posey, S. A. M. Last Station Master: A Boy, a Terroist, a Secret, & Trouble. (p. 978)
Posey, Sandra Mizumoto. Rabbits with Stars in their Eyes. (p. 1430)
Poskitt, Kjartan & Postgate, Daniel. Esa Inmensa Galaxia. Postgate, Daniel, tr. (p. 534)
—Esas Endiabladas Mates. Postgate, Daniel, tr. (p. 534)
—Esas Insignificantes Fracciones. Postgate, Daniel, tr. (p. 534)
Poskitt, Kjartan & Reeve, Philip. Esa Condenada Mala Suerte. Reeve, Philip, tr. (p. 534)
—Esas Exasperantes Medidas de Longitud, Area y Volumen. Reeve, Philip, tr. (p. 534)
—Mas Mortiferas Mates. Reeve, Philip, tr. (p. 1101)
Posner, Pat. Gods & Goddesses from Greek Myths. (p. 690)
Posner, Renee & Quinton, Sasha. Suzy Season Loves Fall. D'Argo, Laura, illus. (p. 1688)
—Suzy Season Loves Spring. D'Argo, Laura, illus. (p. 1688)
—Suzy Season Loves Summer. D'Argo, Laura, illus. (p. 1688)
—Suzy Season Loves Winter. D'Argo, Laura, illus. (p. 1688)
Posner, Richard. Goodnight Cinderella. (p. 701)
—Sparrows Flight. (p. 1622)
—Sweet Pain. (p. 1690)
Posner, Tina. Rabbit Tricks. Corbett, Liza, illus. (p. 1429)
Posner-Sanchez, Andrea. Always a Princess (Disney Princess) Disney Storybook Artists Staff, illus. (p. 51)
—Ariel's Dolphin Adventure - Snow White's New Friend. RH Disney Staff, illus. (p. 98)
—As Big As a Whale (Disney Junior: Doc Mcstuffins) RH Disney Staff, illus. (p. 105)
—Bath Time with Ariel (Disney Princess) DiCicco, Sue, illus. (p. 144)
—Bear Hugs! (Julius Jr.) Random House, illus. (p. 150)
—Bibbidi Bobbidi Books! (Disney Princess) Disney Storybook Artists Staff, illus. (p. 175)
—Boomer Gets His Bounce Back (Disney Junior: Doc Mcstuffins) RH Disney Staff, illus. (p. 213)
—Bubble-Rific! RH Disney Staff, illus. (p. 233)
—Bunny Magic! (Disney Junior: Sofia the First) RH Disney Staff, illus. (p. 242)
—Chihuahua Power! (Julius Jr.) Unten, Eren, illus. (p. 301)
—Christmas Party. RH Disney Staff, illus. (p. 315)
—Christmas Party. Random House Disney Staff, illus. (p. 315)
—Cinderella's Fairy Merry Christmas. Marrucchi, Elisa, illus. (p. 320)
—Costume Party! (Julius Jr.) Random House Staff & Song, Jennifer, illus. (p. 368)
—Cuddly Princess Pals. RH Disney Staff, illus. (p. 389)
—Dinosaurs A to Z. Golden Books Staff et al, illus. (p. 444)
—Doc Is the Best Medicine! (Disney Junior: Doc Mcstuffins) Wall, Mike, illus. (p. 459)
—Fang-Tastic! (Disney Junior: Henry Hugglemonster) Laguna, Fabio, illus. (p. 571)
—Glamorous Gowns & Terrific Tiaras (Disney Princess) Legramandi, Francesco, illus. (p. 682)
—Good Night, Princess! (Disney Princess) Legramandi, Francesco & Matta, Gabriella, illus. (p. 700)
—Hello, Olaf! (p. 764)
—Hello, Olaf! (Disney Frozen) RH Disney Staff, illus. (p. 764)
—Hooting, Tooting Dinosaurs (Dinosaur Train) Golden Books Staff, illus. (p. 796)
—Hugglefish (Disney Junior: Henry Hugglemonster) Laguna, Fabio & Gallego, James, illus. (p. 825)
—I Am a Princess. Matta, Gabriella & Legramandi, Francesco, illus. (p. 832)
—I Am Ariel (Disney Princess) Disney Storybook Artists Staff, illus. (p. 832)
—Jake & the Never Land Pirates LGB Favorites (Jake & the Never Land Pirates) RH Disney Staff, illus. (p. 905)
—Julius Jr. - Pirates & Superheroes. Golden Books Staff & Unten, Eren, illus. (p. 933)
—Knight in Sticky Armor (Disney Junior: Doc Mcstuffins) RH Disney Staff, illus. (p. 964)
—Meet the Princesses (Disney Princess) RH Disney Staff, illus. (p. 1123)
—Monster Time (Disney/Pixar Monsters, Inc.) Tilley, Scott & Becker, Ken, illus. (p. 1168)
—Monsters in a Box (Disney/Pixar Monsters University) RH Disney Staff, illus. (p. 1169)
—Palace Pets Ultimate Handbook (Disney Princess: Palace Pets) RH Disney Staff, illus. (p. 1319)
—Perfect Tea Party (Disney Junior: Sofia the First) RH Disney Staff, illus. (p. 1342)
—Pirate Games. RH Disney Staff, illus. (p. 1362)
—Pixie Puzzles, Games, & More! Christy, Jana, illus. (p. 1365)
—Princess Big Lift-And-Look Book. Legramandi, Francesco, illus. (p. 1403)
—Princess Halloween (Disney Princess) RH Disney Staff & Storino, Sara, illus. (p. 1404)
—Princess Surprises. Legramandi, Francesco, illus. (p. 1405)
—Royal Easter. (p. 1492)
—Royal Easter (Disney Princess) RH Disney Staff et al, illus. (p. 1492)
—Royal Pet Problem. RH Disney Staff, illus. (p. 1492)
—Shadow Play! RH Disney Staff, illus. (p. 1557)
—Shake Your Tail Feathers (Disney Junior: Doc Mcstuffins) RH Disney Staff, illus. (p. 1558)
—Shop with Minnie. RH Disney Staff, illus. (p. 1568)
—Skipping Day (Disney Junior: Jake & the Neverland Pirates) Random House Disney Staff, illus. (p. 1586)
—Sleepy Time with Aurora (Disney Princess) RH Disney Staff & DiCicco, Sue, illus. (p. 1590)
—Snowman Surprise (Disney Junior: Doc Mcstuffins) Golden Books, illus. (p. 1601)
—Sofia the First Little Golden Book Favorites (Disney Junior: Sofia the First) Lee, Grace & Disney Storybook Artists, illus. (p. 1605)
—Sofia the Second (Disney Junior: Sofia the First) RH Disney Staff, illus. (p. 1605)
—Sofia's Royal World (Disney Junior: Sofia the First) Lee, Grace & Disney Storybook Artists Staff, illus. (p. 1605)
—Spiky Stegosaurus (Dinosaur Train) Aikins, Dave, illus. (p. 1627)
—Teacup to the Rescue! (Disney Princess: Palace Pets) RH Disney Staff & DiCicco, Sue, illus. (p. 1710)
—Three Royal Birthdays! (Disney Princess) Legramandi, Francesco & Matta, Gabriella, illus. (p. 1743)
—Tidy-Up Time with Cinderella (Disney Princess) DiCicco, Sue, illus. (p. 1747)
—Time to Fly! (Disney Junior: Sheriff Callie's Wild West) Fruchter, Jason, illus. (p. 1753)
—Toby the Cowsitter (Disney Junior: Sheriff Callie's Wild West) RH Disney Staff & Fruchter, Jason, illus. (p. 1760)
—Two Princesses & a Baby (Disney Junior: Sofia the First) RH Disney Staff & Studio IBOIX Staff, illus. (p. 1804)
—Undersea Friends (Disney Princess) RH Disney Staff, illus. (p. 1815)
—Winter Lights (Dinosaur Train) Meurer, Caleb, illus. (p. 1938)
—Wish upon a Star (Disney Princess) RH Disney Staff, illus. (p. 1940)
Posner-Sanchez, Andrea, jt. auth. see Disney Staff.
Posner-Sanchez, Andrea, jt. auth. see Random House Editors.
Posner-Sanchez, Andrea, jt. auth. see RH Disney Staff.
Posner-Sanchez, Andrea & Julius, Jessica. Olaf's Perfect Day (Disney Frozen) RH Disney Staff & Disney Storybook Art Team Staff, illus. (p. 1283)
Posner-Sanchez, Andrea & Weinberg, Jennifer Liberts. Bow-Bot Robot (Disney Junior: Minnie's Bow Toons) RH Disney Staff, illus. (p. 216)
Posnock, Michael A. Adventures of Wilbur the Wave. (p. 24)
Possanza, D. Mark. Translating the Heavens: Aratus, Germanicus, & the Poetics of Latin Translation (p. 1778)
Post, Andrew. Fabrick. (p. 559)
Post, Bobby. Adventures of Jimmy. (p. 19)
Post, Cynthia W. Carrie Flower: Goes to Camp. (p. 271)
—Carrie Flower: Meet Carrie Flower. (p. 271)
—Carrie Flower: Goes to the Hospital. (p. 271)
Post, Emily, jt. auth. see Senning, Cindy Post.
Post, Grace. Three Dogs Go Walking. Mogyorosi, Nicole, illus. (p. 1742)
Post, Hans. Creepy Crawlies. Goede, Irene, illus. (p. 381)
Post, Hans & Heij, Kees. Sparrows. Goede, Irene, illus. (p. 1622)
Post, Jim. Frog in the Kitchen Sink. Vasconcellos, Daniel, illus. (p. 640)
Post, John R., compiled by. NPKA Book of Blotar: Catalog of Blots & Rituals of Wotanism. Bk. 1 (p. 1269)
POST, L. E. E., illus. see Post, Lee.
Post, Lee. Alaska! Big & Small: A big book of Alaskan Animals from itsy-bitsy to Gigantic. Post, Lee, illus. (p. 34)
—Texas Animals Big & Small. POST, L. E. E., illus. (p. 1724)
Post, Peggy, jt. auth. see Senning, Cindy Post.
Post, Peggy & Senning, Cindy Post. Emily's Everyday Manners. Björkman, Steve, illus. (p. 519)
—Guide to Good Manners for Kids. Björkman, Steve, illus. (p. 730)
—Teen Manners: From Malls to Meals to Messaging & Beyond. (p. 1713)
—Teen Manners: From Malls to Meals to Messaging & Beyond. Watts, Sharon, illus. (p. 1713)
Post, Peggy, et al. Emily's Magic Words: Please, Thank You, & More. Landry, Leo, illus. (p. 519)
Post, Sam. Responsibility: A Comedy Skit (p. 1463)
Postgate, Daniel. Little Red Hen. (p. 1034)
—Love Stinks. (p. 1060)
—Richest Crocodile in the World. (p. 1470)
—Rumpled Stilton Skin. (p. 1495)
—Smelly Bill Postgate, Daniel, illus. (p. 1593)
—Ugly Duckling. (p. 1808)
Postgate, Daniel, illus. see Bird, Sheila May.
Postgate, Daniel, illus. see Oliver, Martin.
Postgate, Daniel, jt. auth. see Poskitt, Kjartan.
Postgate, Daniel, tr. see Oliver, Martin.
Postier, Jim, illus. see Allen, Janet.
Postier, Jim, illus. see Arden, Carolyn.
Postma, Carryl. Tree That Could Be Green. (p. 1783)
Poston, Karen. Baby for Mabel & Frederick. (p. 126)
Poston, Valerie Williams. ArbeZ ZebrA Teaches A to Z (p. 94)
Potach, Steven G., ed. see Culen, Konstantin.
Potapenko, Olga, ed. see AZ Books Staff.
Potarazu, Sreedhar. Get off the Dime: The Secret of Changing Who Pays for Your Health Care. (p. 667)
Potash, Dorothy. Sam & Me. (p. 1506)
Potash, Mildred. Millie & Cupcake. (p. 1144)
Poteat, Bruce S. Evil Deception. (p. 546)
Potenzone Aliano, Kimberly. Chubby Is Everywhere! (p. 318)
Potey Mollina, José Luis. pergamino de Zenit y el descubrimiento de los sellos Divinos. (p. 1343)
Poth, Karen. Larryboy in Tip, Top Cape Shape! Big Idea, Inc. Staff, illus. (p. 976)
—Listen Up, Larry (p. 1022)
—Madame Blue's Easter Hullabaloo: A Veggie Tales Book. SpringSprang Studio Staff, illus. (p. 1069)
—Mess Detectives & the Case of the Lost Temper (p. 1129)
—Pirates, A Super Hero, & a Mess Detective (p. 1363)
—Sheerluck Holmes & the Case of the Missing Friend / Veggietales / I Can Read! (p. 1564)
Poth, Karen, jt. auth. see Zondervan Publishing Staff.
Poth, Karen, jt. auth. see Zondervan Staff.
Poth, Karen, jt. auth. see Zondervan.
Poth, Karen, et al. Pirates Who Don't Do Anything & Me! (p. 1364)
Potok, Chaim. Chosen: And Related Readings. (p. 310)
Potoma, Alison. Smith Family Secret: Book 1. Reul, Sarah Lynne, illus. (p. 1594)
Potratz, Wendy. Agnes Plays Soccer: A Young Cow's Lesson in Sportsmanship. (p. 30)
Pottenkulam, Pooja, illus. see Husain, Zakir & Mishra, Samina.
Potter, Alan Mitchell & Williams, Virginia. Hoo-Hoo Hooty-Hoo-Who. (p. 795)
Potter, Alicia. Miss Hazeltine's Home for Shy & Fearful Cats. Sif, Birgitta, illus. (p. 1151)
—Mrs. Harkness & the Panda. Sweet, Melissa, illus. (p. 1187)
Potter, Anne & DeNize, Anne. Recycled Window. (p. 1453)
Potter, Barbara L. Fly That Went on Vacation. (p. 609)
Potter, Beatrix. Beatrix Potter Favorite Tales: The Tales of Peter Rabbit & Jemima Puddle-Duck. (p. 153)
—Beatrix Potter Treasury. (p. 153)
—Beatrix Potter's Nursery Rhyme Book. (p. 153)
—Classic Tale of Mr. Jeremy Fisher. Santore, Charles, illus. (p. 328)
—Classic Tale of Peter Rabbit: And Other Cherished Stories. Santore, Charles, illus. (p. 328)
—Classic Tale of the Flopsy Bunnies. Santore, Charles, illus. (p. 328)
—Conejo Pedro. (p. 356)
—Conte de Pierre Lapin. (p. 360)
—Conte de Sophie Canetang. (p. 360)
—Conte de Tom Chaton. (p. 360)
—Cuento - Perico el Conejo. (p. 389)
—Easter Surprise. (p. 499)
—Friends Forever. (p. 638)
—Gato Tomas. (p. 658)
—Geschichte Von Peter Hase. (p. 667)
—Great Big Treasury of Beatrix Potter. (p. 714)
—Grumpy Owl. (p. 727)
—Hello, Jemima! (p. 764)
—Hello, Peter! (p. 764)
—I Am Peter. (p. 833)
—Jemima Puddle-Duck - A Sound Book. (p. 912)
—Jeremias el Pescador. (p. 913)
—Miniature World of Peter Rabbit (p. 1146)
—Mystery Thief! (p. 1226)
—Night, Night, Peter Rabbit. (p. 1253)
—Nursery Rhyme. (p. 1273)
—Nutkin on the Run! (p. 1274)
—Oca Carlota. (p. 1275)
—Peekaboo! (p. 1335)
—Peter & Friends Sticker Activity Book. (p. 1346)
—Peter on the Go. (p. 1346)
—Peter Rabbit. (p. 1347)
—Peter Rabbit. Britt, Stephanie McFetridge, illus. (p. 1347)
—Peter Rabbit 1 2 3. (p. 1347)
—Peter Rabbit AB C: With Giant Fold-Out Pages. (p. 1347)
—Peter Rabbit & Friends Bedtime Stories. (p. 1347)
—Peter Rabbit & Friends Treasury. Potter, Beatrix, illus. (p. 1347)
—Peter Rabbit & the Pumpkin Patch. Palmer, Ruth, illus. (p. 1347)
—Peter Rabbit Baby Book. (p. 1347)
—Peter Rabbit Book & Toy. (p. 1347)
—Peter Rabbit Finger Puppet Book. (p. 1347)
—Peter Rabbit Lift-the-Flap Words, Colors, & Numbers. (p. 1347)
—Peter Rabbit - Munch! (p. 1347)
—Peter Rabbit Rainbow Shapes & Colors. Potter, Beatrix, illus. (p. 1347)
—Peter Rabbit What's That Noise? (p. 1347)
—Selected Tales from Beatrix Potter. (p. 1549)
—Sgeulachd Bheniamin Coineanach. MacDonald, James, 1st, tr. from ENG. (p. 1556)
—Sgeulachd Pheadair Rabaid. MacDonald, James, 1st, tr. from ENG. (p. 1556)
—Show Me Your Ears. (p. 1570)
—Story of Peter Rabbit. McCue, Lisa, illus. (p. 1659)
—Tailor of Gloucester. (p. 1695)
—Tailor of Gloucester. Jorgensen, David, illus. (p. 1695)
—Tale of Benjamin Bunny. (p. 1699)
—Tale of Benjamin Bunny. Rasmussen, Wendy, illus. (p. 1699)
—Tale of Jemima Puddle-Duck: A Sound Story Book. (p. 1699)
—Tale of Jemima Puddle-Duck. (p. 1699)
—Tale of Mr. Jeremy Fisher. (p. 1699)
—Tale of Mr. Jeremy Fisher. Jorgensen, David, illus. (p. 1699)
—Tale of Mrs. Tiggy-Winkle. (p. 1699)
—Tale of Mrs. Tittlemouse. (p. 1699)
—Tale of Mrs. Tittlemouse. Rasmussen, Wendy, illus. (p. 1699)
—Tale of Peter Rabbit (p. 1700)
—Tale of Peter Rabbit: A Sound Story Book. (p. 1700)
—Tale of Peter Rabbit: Commemorative Edition. (p. 1700)
—Tale of Peter Rabbit. (p. 1700)
—Tale of Peter Rabbit. Vining, Alex, illus. (p. 1700)
—Tale of Peter Rabbit. Hague, Michael, illus. (p. 1700)
—Tale of Peter Rabbit. Jorgensen, David, illus. (p. 1700)
—Tale of Peter Rabbit. Rasmussen, Wendy, illus. (p. 1700)
—Tale of Squirrel Nutkin. (p. 1700)
—Tale of Squirrel Nutkin. (p. 1700)
—Tale of Squirrel Nutkin. Rasmussen, Wendy, illus. (p. 1700)
—Tale of the Flopsy Bunnies. (p. 1700)
—Tale of the Flopsy Bunnies. Rasmussen, Wendy, illus. (p. 1700)
—Tale of Timmy Tiptoes. (p. 1700)
—Tale of Tom Kitten. (p. 1700)
—Tale of Two Bad Mice (p. 1700)
—Tale of Two Bad Mice. Mcclintock, Barbara, illus. (p. 1700)
—Tickle, Tickle, Peter! (p. 1747)
—Touch & Feel. (p. 1772)
—Treehouse Rescue! (p. 1784)
—Two Beatrix Potter Plays. (p. 1803)
—Where's Peter? (p. 1910)
—Winter's Tale. (p. 1938)
—World of Peter Rabbit: A Box of Postcards. (p. 1957)
Potter, Beatrix, jt. auth. see Barker, Cicely Mary.
Potter, Beatrix, jt. auth. see Santore, Charles.
Potter, Beatrix, jt. auth. see Warne, Frederick.
Potter, Beatrix & Aesop. Tale of Johnny Town-Mouse. Rasmussen, Wendy, illus. (p. 1699)

Potter, Beatrix & Penguin Young Readers. Beatrix Potter's Journal. (p. 153)
Potter, Beatrix & Penguin Young Readers Group Staff. Tale of Peter Rabbit (p. 1700)
Potter, Beatrix, tr. Cuento de los Conejitos Pelusa. (p. 389)
—Cuento Del Gato Tomás. (p. 389)
—Cuento Del Señor Jeremías Peces. (p. 389)
Potter, Beatrix, tr. from ENG. Cuento Del Conejito Benjamín. (p. 389)
—Sastre de Gloucester. (p. 1515)
Potter, Becky Ann. Have You Been to Independence Hall? (p. 754)
Potter, Carl. Gift. (p. 675)
Potter, Christina. Coping with Crohn's Disease & Ulcerative Colitis. (p. 365)
Potter, Dave. Storm Clouds over Mountain View Middle School. (p. 1656)
Potter, David. iPhone That Saved George Washington. (p. 886)
Potter, Dawn. Isobel's Tree. (p. 893)
Potter, Debra. I Am the Music Man. (p. 834)
—I am the Music Man. (p. 834)
Potter, Diane, ed. see Potter, Michael.
Potter, Diane, illus. see Potter, Michael.
Potter, Ellen. Humming Room. (p. 826)
—Kneebone Boy. (p. 964)
—Olivia Kidney. Aguilar, Carmen, tr. (p. 1286)
—Olivia Kidney. Reynolds, Peter, illus. (p. 1286)
—Olivia Kidney & the Secret Beneath the City. (p. 1286)
—Olivia Kidney Stops for No One. Reynolds, Peter H., illus. (p. 1286)
—Otis Dooda: Strange but True. Heatley, David, illus. (p. 1307)
—Otis Dooda: Downright Dangerous. Heatley, David, illus. (p. 1307)
—Piper Green & the Fairy Tree. Leng, Qin, illus. (p. 1361)
—Piper Green & the Fairy Tree: Too Much Good Luck. Leng, Qin, illus. (p. 1361)
—Pish Posh. (p. 1364)
—Slob. (p. 1591)
Potter, Ellen & Mazer, Anne. Spilling Ink: A Young Writer's Handbook. Phelan, Matt, illus. (p. 1627)
Potter, G. L. Keeping Secerts. (p. 947)
Potter, George. Wisemen of Bountiful. Harmon, Glenn, illus. (p. 1940)
Potter, Giselle. C'mon an' Swing in My Tree! (p. 336)
—Tell Me What to Dream About. (p. 1717)
Potter, Giselle, illus. see Best, Cari.
Potter, Giselle, illus. see Bolt, Ranjit.
Potter, Giselle, illus. see Gershator, Phillis.
Potter, Giselle, illus. see Harvey, Matthea.
Potter, Giselle, illus. see MacDonald, Maryann & Ingalls, Ann.
Potter, Giselle, illus. see Manna, Anthony & Mitakidou, Christodoula.
Potter, Giselle, illus. see Manna, Anthony L. & Mitakidou, Christodoula.
Potter, Giselle, illus. see Osborne, Mary Pope & Osborne, Will.
Potter, Giselle, illus. see Osborne, Mary Pope.
Potter, Giselle, illus. see Schotter, Roni.
Potter, Giselle, jt. auth. see McKissack, Patricia C.
Potter, Heather, illus. see Murphy, Sally.
Potter, Ian, jt. auth. see Halliday, Marc.
Potter, Jean. Naturaleza Explicada A Los Ninos En Pocas Palabras: Mas De 100 Actividades Realizables En 10 Minutos O Menos. (p. 1236)
Potter, Jean, jt. auth. see Kohl, MaryAnn F.
Potter, Joc, jt. auth. see Hopkins, Andy.
Potter, Jon. John the Painter. (p. 923)
Potter, Jonathan. Julie. Landes, William-Alan, ed. (p. 932)
Potter, Katherine, illus. see Gershator, Phillis.
Potter, Katherine, illus. see Schulz, Kathy.
Potter, Kay. I Hate Fairies! the Adventures of Katie James. (p. 839)
Potter, Kevin. Frugal Bear's Algebra Boot Camp. (p. 645)
Potter, Lori, illus. see Stuart, Lisa Marie.
Potter, Maureen. Tommy the Theatre Cat. Ronney, David, illus. (p. 1765)
Potter, Melisande. Dick Whittington & His Cat. (p. 436)
Potter, Melisande, illus. see Bateman, Teresa.
Potter, Melisande, illus. see Castaldo, Nancy F.
Potter, Michael. Ups & Downs. Potter, Diane, ed. (p. 1825)
Potter, Noel Gyro. Adventures of Marshall & Art (p. 20)
—Adventures of Marshall & Art - 4 Titles Cannon, Joseph, illus. (p. 20)
—Dibble Can't Dribble. Cannon, Joseph, illus. (p. 435)
—Lost in the Mall. Cannon, Joseph, illus. (p. 1055)
—Plan B. Cannon, Joseph, illus. (p. 1366)
—Spoiled Sport. Cannon, Joseph, illus. (p. 1630)
—Stranger Danger. Cannon, illus. (p. 1665)
—Very Sticky Situation. Cannon, Joseph, illus. (p. 1838)
—Wheel Life Lesson. Cannon, Joseph, illus. (p. 1900)
—Writing a Wrong. Cannon, Joseph, illus. (p. 1964)
Potter, Robert. Reader's Anthology. (p. 1444)
Potter, Robert, tr. see Aeschylus.
Potter, Ryan. Perennial (p. 1341)
Potter, Sandra Dawn, jt. auth. see Kshir, Donna M.
Potter, Scott, ed. Metabarons Roleplaying Game Gamemaster's Screen. (p. 1130)
Potter, Stan. Mind Fields. (p. 1145)
Potter, T. Amos. Gift of Scruffy: The Stevie Parker Series. (p. 675)
Potter, Tina M. Horse Story. (p. 800)
Potter, Tony, jt. compiled by see Crosbie, Duncan.
Potter, Tony, des. Finn & the Magic Harp. (p. 589)
—Goodnight, Little Leprechaun. (p. 701)
Potter, Tony, prod. Plantation Home Model. (p. 1369)
Potter, Tracy. Charlie the Chimp's Day Out. (p. 293)
Potter, William, jt. auth. see Butterfield, Moira.
Potter, William, jt. auth. see Pinnington, Andrea.
Potter-Kotecki, Kerry. I'm a Doggie Detective. (p. 858)
Pottie, Marjolein, illus. see Minne, Brigitte.
Pottie, Marjolein, illus. see Nielandt, Dirk.
Pottie, Marjolein & Auzary-Luton, Sylvie. Going Batty! Special Glow-in-the-Dark Surprise Pictures. Auzary-Luton, Sylvie, illus. (p. 692)
Pottle, Robert. I'm Allergic to School: Funny Poems & Songs about School. Gordon, Mike & Gordon, Carl, illus. (p. 858)
—Maine: A Wicked Good Book of Verse: the Way Wildlife Should Be. Hardwick, Holly, illus. (p. 1077)
—Moxie Day the Prankster: Another Laugh & Learn Book of Poetry. Jonathan Siruno, illus. (p. 1184)
—Poems with Moxie: Funny Poems & Funny Songs. (p. 1376)
Pottle, Robert, jt. auth. see Lansky, Bruce.
Pottorf, Patricia D. Hebee, the Quibber. (p. 761)
Potts, Christiane Elenes. Lola & the Caterpillar. (p. 1045)
Potts Dawson, Eileen, illus. see Wagner, Jay.
Potts, Elizabeth Ayn. Oh What Fun, You're One! (p. 1281)
Potts, Ghillian. Diary Days. (p. 434)
Potts, Kimberly. Boost Your Guy-Q: Quizzes to Test Your Guy Smarts. (p. 213)
—What's Your Mood? A Good Day, Bad Day, In-Between Day Book. (p. 1900)
Potts, Kimberly, jt. auth. see Kidz Bop Kids Staff.
Potts, Lisa, jt. auth. see Potts, Stephen.
Potts, Molly. Falling Moon. (p. 567)
Potts, Percy. Richard the Hearty Lion: Volume I: with the Bingles of Topeka. (p. 1470)
Potts, Sam, illus. see New York City Students Staff.
Potts, Stephen & Potts, Lisa. Thank You, God. (p. 1725)
Potts, Steve. American Alligators. (p. 59)
—American Bison. (p. 60)
—Armadillos. (p. 99)
—Iroquois. (p. 888)
Potts, Steve, et al. North American Animals. (p. 1264)
Potts, Sue. Get Fit with Video Workouts. (p. 667)
Potts, Will & Evans, Brian. Level Product Design. (p. 1003)
Potts, William. Under My Pillow. (p. 1813)
Potvin, Amy K. I Miss Daddy. (p. 844)
Potvin, James E. Adventures of Forest the Ferret: Forest's First Snowfall & Forest's Cottage. (p. 18)
Pouilloux, David. Do You Wonder Why? How to Answer Life's Tough Questions. Moloney, Kate, ed. (p. 458)
Poulakidas, Georgene. Black Hawk's War. (p. 196)
—Civil War. (p. 325)
—Mexican-American War. (p. 1131)
—Spanish-American War. (p. 1620)
—War of 1812. (p. 1857)
Poulin, A. & Waters, Michael. Contemporary American Poetry. (p. 360)
Poulin, Andree. Best Time. Beha, Philippe, illus. (p. 171)
—Magic Clothesline. Arbona, Marion, illus. (p. 1072)
—Monkey in the Mud. Eudes-Pascal, Elisabeth, illus. (p. 1165)
Poulin, Andrée. Worst Time. Beha, Philippe, illus. (p. 1961)
Poulin, Ashley, jt. auth. see Feierabend, John M.
Poulin, Rosa, et al. Christmas Decorations & Crafts (p. 313)
Poulin, Stephane. Agarren Esa Gata (Can You Catch Josephine?) (p. 29)
—As-Tu Vu Josephine? (p. 105)
—Peux-Tu Attraper Josephine? (p. 1349)
Poulin, Stephane, illus. see Côté, Denis.
Poulin, Stephane, illus. see Hughes, Susan.
Poulin, Stéphane, illus. see Lenain, Thierry.
Poulin, Stéphane, jt. auth. see Poulin, Stephane.
Poulin, Stephane, jt. ed. see Cote, Denis.
Poulin, Stephane, tr. see Cote, Denis.
Poulin, Stephane & Poulin, Stéphane. Agarren Esa Gata! (p. 29)
Pouliot, Seth & Nash, Kevin. University of Massachusetts College Prowler off the Record. (p. 1820)
Poulsen, David A. Jeremy's Song. (p. 913)
—Numbers. (p. 1272)
—Old Man. (p. 1284)
Poulsson, Emilie. Finger Plays for Nursery & Kindergarten. Bridgman, L. T., illus. (p. 589)
Poulter, Christine. Playing the Game. (p. 1372)
Poulter, David. Morris & Mini Minor & Friends: A Day at the Seaside. (p. 1176)
Poulter, J. R. Boat to Lullaby Bay. Leonidou, Niki, illus. (p. 205)
—Bushed! All in the Woods. Gunn, Linda, illus. (p. 244)
—Cuddle Kitten & Puddle Pup! (p. 389)
—Dang, It's the Dragons. Leonidou, Niki, illus. (p. 403)
—Extreme Pets. Ulasowski, Muza, illus. (p. 556)
—How Do You Do? Barb Dragony, illus. (p. 808)
—In the Dog House. Hand, Terry, illus. (p. 865)
—Little Bitty Octopus. Emel Alp Sari, illus. (p. 1024)
—Moi, Elle & la le, Poodle Triplets Go Glam. Crevel, Helena, illus. (p. 1160)
—Rich Man, Poor Man. Magi, Jodi, illus. (p. 1469)
—Saga of Haggle Lee Ho. Ulasowski, Muza, illus. (p. 1502)
—Sea Cat Dreams. Ulasowski, Muza, illus. (p. 1534)
—Sneakermania. Slack, Alex, illus. (p. 1597)
—Watchers. Ulasowski, Muza, illus. (p. 1861)
Poulton, J. Alexander. Canadian Hockey Record Breakers: Legendary Feats by Canada's Greatest Players. (p. 260)
—Canadian Hockey Record Breakers. (p. 260)
—Canadian Hockey Trivia: The Who's Who & What's What in Canada's Game. (p. 260)
—Great Goalies of the NHL. (p. 716)
—Greatest Games of the Stanley Cup: The Battles & the Rivalries. (p. 719)
—Greatest Moments in Canadian Hockey. (p. 720)
—Montreal Canadiens: The History & Players Behind Hockey's Most Legendary Team. (p. 1170)
—Ottawa Senators. (p. 1307)
—Toronto Maple Leafs. (p. 1770)
—World's Best Soccer Player: Today's Hottest Superstars. (p. 1960)
Poulton, Mark, jt. auth. see Marz, Ron.
Pound, Blake. Deer Hunting. (p. 423)
—Duck Hunting. (p. 488)
—Fly Fishing. (p. 609)
—Pheasant Hunting. (p. 1350)
Pound, Gomer J. Great Pendulum. (p. 717)
Pounds, Sherron. Adventures of the Four Poster Pirate Ship. (p. 23)
Poundstone, William. How Would You Move Mount Fuji? Microsoft's Cult of the Puzzle - How the World's Smartest Companies Select the Most Creative Thinkers. (p. 823)
Pountney, Beth. My Books of Animal Fun Slipcase. (p. 1199)
Pountney, Beth, jt. auth. see Bicknell, Joanna.
Poupard, illus. see Beka.
Poupart, Jean-Marie. Des Crayons Qui Trichent. (p. 427)
—Des Photos Qui Parlent. (p. 428)
—Des Pianos Qui S'Envolent. (p. 428)
Poupart, Jean-Sébastien, illus. see Sulgit, Nicole.
Pouriseth, Phal, illus. see pierSath, Chath.
Poussin, Nichol. Still Spins the Spider of Rennes-le-Chateau. (p. 1650)
Pouwels, Randall L. African & Middle Eastern World, 600-1500. (p. 27)
Pouy, Jean-Bernard. Big Book of Dummies, Rebels & Other Geniuses. Bedrick, Claudia Z., tr. from FRE. (p. 179)
Pouzadoux, Claude. Cuentos y Leyendas de la Mitologia Griega. (p. 390)
Pova, Rosie. Ladybug & Caterpillar: The Way to Friendship. (p. 971)
Povandra, Shirley. My Imaginary Friend. (p. 1211)
Póveda Piérola, Mabel, illus. see Combel Editorial Staff & Samaniego, Félix María.
Povenmire, Dan, illus. see O'Ryan, Ellie.
Povey, Andrea, illus. see Kane, Gillian.
Povey, Karen D. Animal Rights. (p. 79)
—Energy Alternatives. (p. 528)
Pow, Tom & Favre, Malika. When the Rains Come. (p. 1905)
Powell, Alma. America's Promise. Winborn, Marsha, illus. (p. 64)
—Promesa de America. Winborn, Marsha, illus. (p. 1411)
Powell, Amy. Absolutely the Best. (p. 7)
—Hope Music. Farley, Katherine, illus. (p. 796)
—Me. (p. 1115)
Powell, Angela. Alicia's Blended Family. Gillen, Rosemarie, illus. (p. 40)
Powell, Anna. Don't Say That, Willy Nilly! Roberts, David, illus. (p. 468)
Powell, Anthony. Our Cat Hogan - Could He Be Part Dog? Stodden, Lindsay, illus. (p. 1308)
Powell, Anton. Ancient Greece. (p. 69)
Powell, Anton, jt. auth. see Steele, Philip.
Powell, Ben. Skateboarding. (p. 1583)
Powell, Christine. Bootsie's Underground Adventure. (p. 213)
Powell, Consie. Bold Carnivore: An Alphabet of Predators. (p. 208)
—Old Dog Cora & the Christmas Tree. Powell, Consie, illus. (p. 1283)
Powell, Consie, illus. see Bevis, Mary.
Powell, Consie, illus. see Jones, Jennifer Berry.
Powell, Consie, illus. see Kurtz, Kevin.
Powell, Consie, illus. see Miché, Mary.
Powell, Consie, illus. see Ross, Michael Elsohn.
Powell, Dana. Oma & Opa's Closet. (p. 1288)
Powell, Daniel M. King Grrr-egory & the Angel. (p. 958)
Powell, Debbie. Trucks. Powell, Debbie, illus. (p. 1791)
Powell, Eleanor. Little Cloud That Cried. (p. 1026)
Powell, Gail. Adventures of Harold J. Kat. (p. 18)
Powell, Gary Allison. In That Land There Are Giants. Johnston, Jillian S., illus. (p. 865)
Powell, GinaMarie. Ayiana & the Hurricane Katrina Classmate. Bray, Pamela, illus. (p. 121)
Powell, Glenda. Cassie & Mr. Ant. Mitchell, Hazel, illus. (p. 276)
Powell, Glenda, jt. auth. see Powell, Jay.
Powell, Gregg E. Goobadabers. Lea, Corinne, illus. (p. 697)
Powell, Huw. Spacejackers. (p. 1620)
Powell, Inez. Sparkle, My Angel. (p. 1622)
Powell, Ives June. Due West by Covered Wagon. (p. 489)
Powell, J. Frederick. Puffy & the Witch's Revenge. (p. 1415)
Powell, J. W. Contributions to North American Ethnology. (p. 361)
Powell, James, illus. see Tingwald, Jady Ann.
Powell, James, illus. see Tingwald, July Ann.
Powell, Janet. Saint Louis Zoo. (p. 1503)
—St. Louis Zoo. (p. 1638)
Powell, Jay & Powell, Glenda. In Jay's Time. (p. 864)
Powell, Jillian. Are We There Yet? Colnaghi, Stefania, illus. (p. 96)
—Art in the Nineteenth Century. (p. 102)
—Asthma. (p. 108)
—Aztecs. (p. 122)
—Caribe. (p. 269)
—Chicken Pox. Chambers, Mark A., illus. (p. 300)
—China. (p. 306)
—Chocolate. (p. 309)
—Dance Just Like Me Gulliver, Amanda, illus. (p. 402)
—Descubramos China. (p. 428)
—Descubramos Espana. (p. 428)
—Descubramos Francia. (p. 428)
—Descubramos Gran Bretaña. (p. 428)
—Descubramos India. (p. 428)
—Descubramos Italia. (p. 428)
—Descubramos Japón (Looking at Japan) (p. 428)
—Descubramos la India. (p. 428)
—Descubramos Mexico. (p. 428)
—Descubramos paises del Caribe. (p. 428)
—Descubramos Rusia. (p. 428)
—Descubramos Rusia (Looking at Russia) (p. 428)
—Egypt. (p. 506)
—Egyptians. (p. 507)
—Explaining Cystic Fibrosis. (p. 549)
—Fats for a Healthy Body (p. 577)
—First World War. (p. 597)
—Fun Run. Gulliver, Amanda, illus. (p. 648)
—Greeks. (p. 721)
—Hattie the Dancing Hippo. Dodson, Emma, illus. (p. 753)
—Henry & the Hand-Me-Downs. Worsley, Belinda, illus. (p. 767)
—Hiccup! Chambers, Mark A., illus. (p. 775)
—History of Britain Through Art. (p. 783)
—Hurry up, Pony! Colnaghi, Stefania, illus. (p. 830)
—India. (p. 870)
—Japan. (p. 909)
—Let's Say Hello. Colnaghi, Stefania, illus. (p. 1000)
—Looking at Caribbean Countries. (p. 1050)
—Looking at China. (p. 1050)
—Looking at France. (p. 1050)
—Looking at Great Britain. (p. 1050)
—Looking at India. (p. 1050)
—Looking at Italy. (p. 1050)
—Looking at Japan. (p. 1050)
—Looking at Nigeria. (p. 1051)
—Looking at Russia. (p. 1051)
—Looking at Spain. (p. 1051)
—My New Babysitter. (p. 1216)
—My New Friend. (p. 1216)
—My New Sister. (p. 1216)
—My New Stepdad. (p. 1216)
—Oh, Jet! (p. 1280)
—Oops! Gulliver, Amanda, illus. (p. 1299)
—Projects with Rainforests. (p. 1411)
—Projects with Weather & Seasons. (p. 1411)
—Puberty. (p. 1414)
—Reading Corner: My Nan. (p. 1445)
—Roller Coaster Fun! Colnaghi, Stefania, illus. (p. 1485)
—Romans. (p. 1486)
—Sam's Sunflower. Boccardo, Johanna, illus. (p. 1509)
—Self-Harm & Suicide. (p. 1549)
—Sore Throat. (p. 1614)
—Vikings. (p. 1842)
—War Art. (p. 1857)
Powell, Jillian, jt. auth. see Kuenzler, Lou.
Powell, Jillian & Buckingham, Matt. Middle Ages. (p. 1137)
Powell, Jillian & O'Shea, Clare. Cooking with Cereals & Grains. (p. 362)
—Cooking with Eggs & Dairy. (p. 362)
Powell, Jillian & Samanich, John G. Alcohol & Drug Abuse. (p. 35)
—Family Crises. (p. 568)
Powell, Jim S. Mystery of the Totem Trees: A Plumroy Pack Adventure. (p. 1226)
Powell, Jimmie. Squirrel the Worm & the Nut Trees. (p. 1637)
Powell, Jimmie L. Squirrel, the Worm, & the Nut Trees. (p. 1637)
—Squirrel, the Worm, & the Nut Trees 2. (p. 1637)
Powell, John. Encyclopedia of North American Immigration. (p. 525)
—Immigration. (p. 861)
Powell, John Wesley. On Limitations to the Use of Some Anthropologic Data. (p. 1289)
Powell, Jonathan, illus. see Attwood, Sarah.
Powell, Joyce. Greatest Marriage Ever. Schacher, Tracey, illus. (p. 720)
Powell, Kara Eckmann, ed. see Wilson, John & Wilson, Betsy.
Powell, Kathy Bingham. Save the Seeds. (p. 1517)
Powell, Kelley. Merit Birds. (p. 1127)
Powell, Kristen. Flappy & the Big Red Sky. (p. 602)
Powell, Laura. Burn Mark. (p. 243)
—Goddess. (p. 690)
—Witch Fire. (p. 1941)
Powell, Lenora Y. Ardo: The Mysterious New House. (p. 96)
Powell, Luciana Navarro. My Dad Is the Best Playground. (p. 1201)
Powell, Luciana Navarro, illus. see Bryant, Megan E.
Powell, Luciana Navarro, illus. see Rosa-Mendoza, Gladys.
Powell, Luciana Navarro, illus. see Schwartz, Betty & Seresin, Lynn.
Powell, Marc & Neal, David. How to Draw Action Manga. (p. 816)
—How to Draw Cute Manga. (p. 817)
—How to Draw Dramatic Manga. (p. 817)
—How to Draw Fantasy Manga. (p. 817)
—How to Draw Manga Mecha. (p. 818)
Powell, Marie. Explore with Ferdinand Magellan. (p. 550)
—Explore with Jacques Cartier. (p. 550)
—Meet a Baby Ostrich. (p. 1120)
—Native Nations of the Arctic & Subarctic. (p. 1235)
—Stop Right There: A Book about Periods. (p. 1653)
—Take a Pause, Paul: A Book about Commas. Lewis, Anthony, illus. (p. 1696)
—This Is Exciting! A Book about Exclamation Points. (p. 1735)
—Unsolved! (p. 1822)
—We're Going to the Smiths' House: A Book about Apostrophes. (p. 1875)
—What Good Is a U? (p. 1885)
—What Good Is a Y? (p. 1885)
—What Good Is an A? (p. 1885)
—What Good Is an E? (p. 1885)
—What Good Is an I? (p. 1885)
—What Good Is an O? (p. 1885)
—What Is That? A Book about Question Marks. Lewis, Anthony, illus. (p. 1890)
Powell, Marie, jt. auth. see Heos, Bridget.
Powell, Martin. Frankenstein: the Graphic Novel. Olliffe, Patrick, illus. (p. 629)
—Halloween Legion: The Great Goblin Invasion. Thorpe, Patrick, ed. (p. 738)
—Hound of the Baskervilles. Thorpe, Patrick, ed. (p. 802)
—Seven Voyages of Sinbad Pérez, Daniel et al, illus. (p. 1555)
—Seven Voyages of Sinbad. Pérez, Daniel et al, illus. (p. 1555)
Powell, Martin A., et al. Fog of Fear. (p. 611)
—Stolen Superpowers Burchett, Rick, illus. (p. 1652)
—Stolen Superpowers. (p. 1652)
Powell, Martin, et al. Fog of Fear (p. 611)
—Graphic Revolve: Common Core Editions (p. 711)
Powell, Michael. Do My Ears Ever Stop Growing? And 70 Other Questions That Keep You Awake at Night. (p. 457)
Powell, Michael & Mehta, Sonia. 101 Things You Should Know about Science. (p. 2000)
Powell, Nate, illus. see Castellucci, Cecil.
Powell, Nathan, illus. see Riordan, Rick & Venditti, Robert.
Powell, Opal. Two Lives for Giant Jack Pumpkin: The Story of a Boy, a Jack o'Lantern & a Pie. Durham, Lilly, illus. (p. 1804)
Powell, Pamela. Patrulla de las Tortugas. (p. 1329)
Powell, Patricia Hruby. Ch'at to Yinilo'/Frog Brings Rain. Thomas, Peter A., tr. (p. 295)

P

—Josephine: The Dazzling Life of Josephine Baker. Robinson, Christian, illus. (p. 926)
—Zinnia: How the Corn Was Saved. Ruffenach, Jessie, ed. (p. 1987)
Powell, Polly, illus. see Vaughn, Marcia.
Powell, R. This Little Bunny. Curry, Peter, illus. (p. 1737)
—This Little Doggy. Curry, Peter, illus. (p. 1737)
—This Little Lamb. Curry, Peter, illus. (p. 1737)
Powell, Randy. Three Clams & an Oyster. (p. 1741)
—Tribute to Another Dead Rock Star. (p. 1785)
—Tribute to Another Dead Rock Star. (p. 1785)
Powell, Richard. Bear. Gardner, Louise, illus. (p. 150)
—Becky Bunny. Rhodes, Katie, illus. (p. 156)
—Duck. Gardner, Louise, illus. (p. 488)
—Flap My Wings. Martin-Laranaga, Ana, illus. (p. 602)
—Frog. Gardner, Louise, illus. (p. 639)
—Kitty's Tail. Davis, Caroline, illus. (p. 963)
—Leo Lion. Rhodes, Katie, illus. (p. 992)
—Lucy Lamb. Rhodes, Katie, illus. (p. 1063)
—Mandy Monkey. Rhodes, Katie, illus. (p. 1087)
—Peter Panda. Rhodes, Katie, illus. (p. 1347)
—Puppy's Tail. Davis, Carolina A., illus. (p. 1418)
—Quiet as a Mouse: A Moving Picture Storybook. Hendra, Sue, illus. (p. 1428)
—Seal. Gardner, Louise, illus. (p. 1536)
—Timmy Tiger. Rhodes, Katie, illus. (p. 1755)
—Wag My Tail. Martin-Larranaga, Ana, illus. (p. 1852)
—What's in the Box? Martín Larrañaga, Ana, illus. (p. 1898)
—What's in the Egg? Martín Larrañaga, Ana, illus. (p. 1898)
—Who Lives Here? Martín Larrañaga, Ana, illus. (p. 1916)
—Whose Hat Is That? Martín Larrañaga, Ana, illus. (p. 1921)
—Wiggle My Ears. Larranaga, Ana, illus. (p. 1927)
Powell, Richard & Davis, Caroline. Book for Baby for Every Time of Day. (p. 210)
—Mouse's Tail. (p. 1182)
Powell, Rick, illus. see Belanger, Jeff.
Powell, Robert. Death by Association: Exposing Relationships that Cut off Your God-Given Destiny. (p. 420)
Powell, Sarah, jt. auth. see Priddy, Roger.
Powell, Saundra. Meet William the Westie. (p. 1123)
Powell, Shirley. Making Friends with Food: Honoring the Body Temple Nutritionally. (p. 1081)
Powell Smith, Brendan. Daniel in the Lions' Den: The Brick Bible for Kids. (p. 405)
—David & Goliath: The Brick Bible for Kids. (p. 410)
—Jonah & the Whale: The Brick Bible for Kids. (p. 925)
Powell Sr., Liam Patrick. 1-2-3 Under-Dog! (p. 1990)
Powell, Walter. How to Draw the Life & Times of Andrew Johnson. (p. 818)
Powell, Walter L. Benedict Arnold: Revolutionary War Hero & Traitor. (p. 164)
Powell, Walter Louis. Benedict Arnold: Revolutionary War Hero & Traitor. (p. 164)
Powell, William Campbell. Expiration Day. (p. 549)
Powell, William F. Color Mixing Recipes for Portraits: More Than 500 Color Combinations for Skin, Eyes, Lips & Hair. (p. 343)
—Drawing- Wild Animals. (p. 481)
—Perspective. (p. 1344)
Powell Zalewski, Amy. Maybe the Truth about Santa. Mugambi, Christina Nkirote, illus. (p. 1113)
—Summer School in the City. (p. 1675)
Powell-Tuck, Maudie. Pirates Aren't Afraid of the Dark! Edgson, Alison, illus. (p. 1363)
—Very Merry Christmas. Guile, Gill, illus. (p. 1838)
Powelson, Jennifer. Rachel & Sammy Learn about Trees. (p. 1431)
Power, Barry. First Ice Pigeon of London. (p. 595)
Power, Bob. Dodge Vipers. (p. 460)
—Ferraris. (p. 582)
—Lamborghinis. (p. 972)
—Maseratis. (p. 1102)
Power, Bob & Roza, Greg. Sports Tips, Techniques, & Strategies: An Insider's Guide to Paintball (p. 1633)
Power, Brenda, et al. Back to School Book. Kaback, Suzy, illus. (p. 130)
Power, Eileen, jt. auth. see Power, Rhoda.
Power, Eloise. Apple Tree Inside of Me. (p. 92)
Power, J. Tracey. Stonewall Jackson: Hero of the Confederacy. (p. 1653)
Power, Laura. Air-Born. (p. 31)
Power, Margaret, illus. see Bursztynski, Susan.
Power, Margaret, illus. see Mitchell, Elyne.
Power, Michael. Zoo. (p. 1988)
Power, Molly. Up & down with Lena Larocha. Carter, Barbara, illus. (p. 1824)
Power, Nicholas D. Paudie's Magical Adventures. (p. 1330)
Power Of The Pencil. Round. (p. 1491)
Power, Rhoda & Power, Eileen. Boys & Girls of History. (p. 220)
Power, Samantha. Chasing the Flame: One Man's Fight to Save the World. (p. 294)
Power, Suzanne. Love & the Monroes. (p. 1059)
Power, Teresa. ABCs of Yoga for Kids. (p. 4)
Power, Teresa Anne. ABECE de Yoga para Ninos. Rietz, Kathleen, illus. (p. 4)
Power, Timothy. Boy Who Howled. (p. 219)
Powerkids Press, creator. Personal Best Set. (p. 1344)
Powers, Alfred. Marooned in Crater Lake Averill, Leas, ed. (p. 1096)
Powers, Amelia. Giant Pop-Out Shapes: A Pop-Out Surprise Book. (p. 674)
Powers, Amelia, jt. auth. see Chronicle Books Staff.
Powers, Bob. Happy Cruelty Day! Daily Celebrations of Quiet Desperation. (p. 745)
Powers, David M. F. Schmetterling Ohne Flügel. Vail, Sue, tr. (p. 1521)
Powers, Don, illus. see Hartnett, Sonya.
Powers, Elizabeth. Where Are You Taking Me? (p. 1906)
Powers, Emily. Wendell Has a Cracked Shell. Moody, Jason, illus. (p. 1875)
Powers, J. L. Colors of the Wind: The Story of Blind Artist & Champion Runner George Mendoza. Mendoza, George, illus. (p. 345)
—This Thing Called the Future. (p. 1737)
Powers, John. Seymour & the Big Red Rhino. Colavecchio, Alan, illus. (p. 1556)
Powers, Leon R. Forgotten Expedition: The 1907 Baker University Expedition into Idaho & Oregon. Powers, Leon R., ed. (p. 619)
Powers, Lillian. Girl Child: (The Transition - in Poetic Form) (p. 678)
Powers, Marilia, illus. see Powers, Mark & Powers, Megan.
Powers, Mark. Drafted (p. 476)
—Rest Christy, Stephen, ed. (p. 1464)
Powers, Mark & Powers, Megan. Tara's Tiara: Paperback. Powers, Mark & Powers, Megan, illus. (p. 1706)
Powers, Martha. Amelia's Story. (p. 58)
Powers, Megan, jt. auth. see Powers, Mark.
Powers, Michael. Selfless. (p. 1549)
Powers, Mireille Xioulan, illus. see Colby, J. Z. & Persons, Katelynn.
Powers, Nelda Means & Terrell, Caitlyn. Puddle Puppy Goes to the Farm. (p. 1414)
Powers, Retha. This Is My Best: Great Writers Share Their Favorite Work. Kiernan, Kathy, ed. (p. 1736)
Powers, Richard. Time of Our Singing. (p. 1752)
Powers, Richard M., illus. see Cottrell, Leonard.
Powers, Robert C. Black Dragon. (p. 196)
Powers, Ron, jt. auth. see Bradley, James.
Powers, Tim. Expiration Date. (p. 549)
Powers, Tom. Steven Spielberg. (p. 1649)
Powers, William F. New Blue Zoo. (p. 1243)
Powers-Fish, Amy Rose. Buddy's Forever Home. (p. 235)
—Ethics 4 Every Bunny. (p. 539)
Powless, Justin, Neal and Giles & Benchmark Education Co. Staff. Lasting Legacies - America's First Game. (p. 979)
Powling, Chris. Dick King-Smith. (p. 435)
—Sharks. (p. 1562)
Poydar, Nancy. Bad-News Report Card. Poydar, Nancy, illus. (p. 132)
—Biggest Test in the Universe. Poydar, Nancy, illus. (p. 185)
—Brave Santa. (p. 223)
—Bunny Business. (p. 242)
—Bus Driver. Poydar, Nancy, illus. (p. 244)
—Busy Bea. Poydar, Nancy, illus. (p. 245)
—Cool Ali. Poydar, Nancy, illus. (p. 362)
—Fish School. (p. 598)
—No Fair Science Fair. Poydar, Nancy, illus. (p. 1258)
—Perfectly Horrible Halloween. Poydar, Nancy, illus. (p. 1342)
—Zip, Zip... Homework. Poydar, Nancy, illus. (p. 1987)
Poyer, Joe. AK-47 & AK-74 Kalashnikov Rifles & Their Variations. (p. 32)
Poyer, Margaret A. Sapphiry Rose & the Journey to the Inner Core. (p. 1514)
Poyet, Guillaume, jt. auth. see Durand, Stephane.
Poyner, James R. Toy-Maker's Apprentice. (p. 1774)
Poynor, Alice Burnett. Coming Day: A true Christmas story from China. (p. 348)
Poynter, Linda, illus. see Whitedove, Michelle.
Poynter, Margaret. Doomsday Rocks from Space. (p. 470)
—Marie Curie: Discoverer of Radium. (p. 1093)
—Marie Curie: Genius Researcher of Radioactivity. (p. 1093)
Poythress, Jean Hill, jt. auth. see Balch, Betty Neff.
Poythress, Vern & Grudem, Wayne A. Gender Neutral Bible Controversy: Is the Age of Political Correctness Altering the Meaning of God's Words? (p. 660)
Pozdol, MaryBeth. Prison to Palace. Leonard, Erskine, illus. (p. 1407)
Poznanski, Ursula. Erebos: It's a Game. It Watches You. Pattinson, Judith, tr. from GER. (p. 533)
Pozner, Neal. Should the United States Withdraw from Iraq? (p. 1570)
Pozzo, Adam Dal. Wiggles Christmas Song & Activity Book. (p. 1928)
PQ Blackwell, Ltd. Staff, jt. auth. see Elsdale, Bob.
Prado Farina, Gabriela, jt. auth. see Farina von Buchwald, Martin.
Prado, Miguelanxo. Pedro y el Lobo. (p. 1334)
—Trazo de Tiza. (p. 1781)
PRAESA & Press, Karen. Cambridge Mathematics Dictionary for Schools Afrikaans Translation. (p. 255)
Prager, Ellen. Earthquakes & Volcanoes. (p. 497)
—Sea Slime: It's Eeuwy, Gooey & under the Sea Bersani, Shennen, illus. (p. 1535)
—Sea Slime: It's Eeuwy, Gooey & under the Sea Bersani, Shennen, illus. (p. 1535)
—Shark Rider. Caparo, Antonio Javier, illus. (p. 1562)
—Shark Whisperer. Caparo, Antonio Javier, illus. (p. 1562)
Prager, Ellen J. Earthquakes. Greenstein, Susan, illus. (p. 497)
—Sand. Woodman, Nancy, illus. (p. 1510)
—Volcano! Woodman, Nancy, illus. (p. 1848)
Prahin, Andrew. Brimsby's Hats. Prahin, Andrew, illus. (p. 228)
Prajapati, Rajesh, jt. auth. see Mehta, Anurag.
Praker, Jon, illus. see Johnson, Sandi.
Pranal. Daisy & Friends. (p. 400)
Pranali. Secret Storybook. (p. 1544)
Prandy, Manuel & Aracena, Cynthia. Dog That Found His Way Back Home. (p. 461)
Prange, Beckie, illus. see Sidman, Joyce.
Pransky, Jim. Championship Expectations: Book 1. (p. 289)
—Comeback Kid: Book 3. (p. 347)
Pranty, Bill, et al. Birds of Florida. (p. 191)
Prap, Lila. Animals Speak. Prap, Lila, illus. (p. 84)
—Cat Whys. (p. 278)
—Daddies. Prap, Lila, illus. (p. 398)
—Dinosaurs!? (p. 444)
—Doggy Whys? (p. 462)
—Papas. Campy, F. Isabel & Flor Ada, Alma, trs. (p. 1322)
—Whyld Animals Kid Kit. (p. 1927)
Prap, Lila, illus. see Hicks, Barbara Jean.
Prasad, Anshuman, ed. Postcolonial Theory & Organizational Analysis: A Critical Engagement. (p. 1388)
Prasad, H.Y. Sharada. Indira Gandhi. (p. 872)
Prasad, Kamal S. Why Can't I Jump Very High? A Book about Gravity. Simonnet, Aurore, illus. (p. 1923)
Prasad, Sheela. Apocrit. (p. 91)
Prasad, Siona, jt. auth. see Kim, Isabel Joy.
Prasad, Sunayna. Alyssa Mccarthy's Magical Missions: Book 1. (p. 51)
—Alyssa's African Adventures. (p. 51)
Prasadam, Smriti. Hello, Animals! Bolam, Emily, illus. (p. 763)
—Hello, Bugs! Bolam, Emily, illus. (p. 763)
—My Fairy Glade. Finn, Rebecca, illus. (p. 1202)
—Peepo Paw Printes. Mitchell, Melanie, illus. (p. 1335)
Prasadam-Halls, Smriti. Don't Call Me Sweet! Rozelaar, Angie, illus. (p. 467)
—Doodle on! Christmas Doodles. Boretzki, Anja, illus. (p. 469)
—Have You Seen Bunny? Berg, Michelle, illus. (p. 754)
—Have You Seen Duck? Berg, Michelle, illus. (p. 754)
—Have You Seen Kitty? Berg, Michelle, illus. (p. 754)
—Have You Seen Puppy? Berg, Michelle, illus. (p. 754)
—I Love You Night & Day. Brown, Alison, illus. (p. 844)
—Noisy Farm. Scheffler, Axel, illus. (p. 1263)
—Scary Doodles. Boretzki, Anja, illus. (p. 1520)
Prasadam-Halls, Smriti, jt. auth. see Ayliffe, Alex.
Prasadam-Halls, Smriti, jt. auth. see Rinaldo, Luana.
Prasetya, Erwin, illus. see Smith, Brian & Levine, Cory.
Pratarelli, Marc. Paradigm Shift: Environmental Psychology/Ethics for Environmentalists. (p. 1323)
Pratcher, Birgit, jt. auth. see Pratcher, Roger.
Pratcher, Roger & Pratcher, Birgit. June Bear Adventures: The Missing Pies. (p. 934)
Pratchett, Rhianna & Robson, Eddie. Video Games. (p. 1841)
Pratchett, Terry. Amazing Maurice & His Educated Rodents. (p. 55)
—Bromeliad Trilogy: Truckers, Diggers, & Wings. (p. 230)
—Carpet People. (p. 271)
—Colour of Magic. (p. 346)
—Dodger. (p. 460)
—Dragons at Crumbling Castle: And Other Tales. Beech, Mark, illus. (p. 479)
—Hat Full of Sky. (p. 752)
—I Shall Wear Midnight. (p. 845)
—Johnny & the Dead. (p. 923)
—Nation. (p. 1231)
—Night Watch. (p. 1254)
—Only You Can Save Mankind. (p. 1298)
—Wee Free Men. (p. 1871)
—Where's My Cow? (p. 1910)
—Wintersmith. (p. 1938)
—Wintersmith. (p. 1939)
Pratchett, Terry, jt. auth. see Gaiman, Neil.
Prater, Cindy. Kelsie's Potty Adventure. Williams, Denny, illus. (p. 948)
Prater, John. Billy's Box, Level 2. (p. 187)
—I Love My Bed. Prater, John, illus. (p. 842)
—Nishal's Box ELT Edition. (p. 1257)
—Wayne's Box. (p. 1865)
Prater, Linda, illus. see Black, Joe.
Prater, Linda, illus. see Malaspina, Ann.
Prather, Jeffrey. Bracelet Bound Edition (p. 221)
Prati, Elisa. Mio Libro di Natale. (p. 1148)
Prati, Pablo. Enrique VIII. (p. 531)
Pratico, Ariel R. Do You Know Where Z Is? (p. 458)
Pratico, Gary D., et al. Basics of Biblical Hebrew Grammar. (p. 142)
Prato, Rodica, illus. see Buckley, Susan & Leacock, Elspeth.
Prato, Rodica, illus. see Metaxas, Eric.
Prats, Joan de Déu. Topo en un Mar de Hierba. Caruncho, Isabel, illus. (p. 1769)
Pratt, Anna Bronson Alcott. Comic Tragedies. (p. 348)
Pratt, Anna Bronson Alcott, jt. auth. see Alcott, Louisa May.
Pratt, Brendan, jt. auth. see Gill, Nancy.
Pratt, Christine Joy, illus. see Robb, Don.
Pratt, Christine Joy, illus. see Yolen, Jane.
Pratt, Drusilla. What Do I Love. (p. 1882)
Pratt, Edward J. Game on Daddy. (p. 654)
Pratt, Gary Thomas. Code of Unaris: Chat Roleplaying LePorte, Christine, ed. (p. 338)
Pratt, Jennifer. It's Easy Being Green: The User Friendly Eco-Handbook. (p. 896)
Pratt, Kevin, jt. auth. see Khan, Jahangir.
Pratt, L. Chinese Calligraphy Kit (Bag) (p. 307)
Pratt, Laura. Arctic. (p. 95)
—Boelig;ufs Musqueacute;s: Les Animaux du Canada. Karvonen, Tanjah, tr. from ENG. (p. 207)
—Danica Patrick. (p. 404)
—Famous Monsters. (p. 569)
—Fête des Mères: Les Célébrations Canadiennes. Karvonen, Tanjah, tr. from ENG. (p. 583)
—Medieval Times. (p. 1119)
—Mother's Day: Canadian Celebrations. (p. 1178)
—Mountain Goats. (p. 1180)
—Muskox. (p. 1194)
—Plains. (p. 1366)
—Texas: The Lone Star State. (p. 1724)
—Virginia: The Old Dominion State. (p. 1844)
—Washington: The Evergreen State. (p. 1859)
—West Virginia: The Mountain State. (p. 1876)
—Wisconsin: The Badger State. (p. 1939)
—Wyoming: The Cowboy State. (p. 1966)
Pratt, Leonie. Celts: Information for Young Readers - Level 2. McKenna, Terry, illus. (p. 286)
—China (Level 2) - Internet Referenced. (p. 306)
—Knights & Castles Things to Make & Do. Thompson, Josephine Et Al, illus. (p. 964)
—Mermaid things to make & Do. (p. 1128)
—Mermaid Things to Make & Do Kid Kit. (p. 1128)
—Planet Earth: Level 2. Tudor, Andy & Haggerty, Tim, illus. (p. 1367)
—Planet Earth (Kawkab Al Ard) Ibrahim, Nouran, tr. from ARA. (p. 1367)
—Remix. (p. 1460)
—Sparkly Things to Make & Do. (p. 1622)
—Sticker Dolly Dressing Ballerinas. Baggott, Stella & Leyhane, Vici, illus. (p. 1650)
—Sticker Dolly Dressing Fairies. Baggott, Stella & Leyhane, Vici, illus. (p. 1650)
Pratt, Leonie, jt. auth. see Bone, Emily.
Pratt, Leonie, jt. auth. see Dickins, Rosie.
Pratt, Leonie, jt. auth. see Gilpin, Rebecca.
Pratt, Leonie & Atkinson, Catherine. Christmas Fairy Cooking. Sage, Molly, illus. (p. 313)
Pratt, Leonie & Stowell, Louie. How to Draw Animals. Figg, Non, illus. (p. 816)
Pratt, Liz, illus. see Pynn, Susan.
Pratt, Lizz, illus. see Dalrymple, Lisa.
Pratt, Mara L. American History Stories, Volume I - with Original Illustrations. (p. 61)
—American History Stories, Volume II - with Original Illustrations. (p. 61)
—American History Stories, Volume III - with Original Illustrations. (p. 61)
Pratt, Mary. Timeline History of the Thirteen Colonies. (p. 1754)
Pratt, Mary K. Elizabeth I: English Renaissance Queen. (p. 513)
—Exploring under the Sea. (p. 554)
—How Can We Reduce Household Waste? (p. 805)
—How to Analyze the Films of Quentin Tarantino. (p. 814)
—Michael Jackson: King of Pop. (p. 1134)
—Pandemics. (p. 1321)
—Parliaments. (p. 1325)
—US Army. (p. 1826)
—What Is Computer Coding? (p. 1889)
—World War I. (p. 1958)
Pratt, Michael E. Mid-Century Modern Dinnerware: Ak-Sar-Ben to Paden City Pottery: a Pictorial Guide (p. 1137)
Pratt, Ned, photos by see Major, Kevin.
Pratt, Non. Trouble. (p. 1789)
Pratt, Pamela. Breezes Tell. (p. 226)
Pratt, Pierre. Leon Sans Son Chapeau. (p. 992)
—Marcel et Andre. (p. 1091)
Pratt, Pierre, illus. see Jenkins, Emily & Jenkins, Emily P.
Pratt, Pierre, illus. see Jenkins, Emily.
Pratt, Pierre, illus. see Rasmussen, Halfdan.
Pratt, Pierre, illus. see Weale, David.
Pratt, Pierre, illus. see Winters, Kari-Lynn.
Pratt, Pierre, illus. see Zarin, Cynthia.
Pratt, Pierre, illus. see Ziskind, Hélio & Duchesne, Christiane.
Pratt, Sabina Carlin. Range Land Animal Tales: Nature's School on the High Desert of Oregon. (p. 1438)
Pratt, Sally. Adventures of Bernie the Bee in Sally's Garden. (p. 16)
Pratt Serafini, Kristin Joy. Swim Through the Sea. (p. 1691)
Pratt, Susan, illus. see Welty, Carolyn.
Pratt, Tim, jt. ed. see Marr, Melissa.
Pratta, Barbara. Weeping Willow Tree. (p. 1872)
Pratts, Christine. Tabby Wise for School Secretary. (p. 1694)
Pratt-Serafini, Kristin Joy. Saguaro Moon: A Desert Journal. (p. 1503)
—Salamander Rain: A Lake & Pond Journal. (p. 1504)
—Walk in the Rainforest. Pratt-Serafini, Kristin Joy, illus. (p. 1853)
Pratt-Serafini, Kristin Joy & Crandell, Rachel. Forever Forest: Kids Save a Tropical Treasure. (p. 619)
—Forever Forest: Kids Save a Tropical Treasure. Pratt-Serafini, Kristin Joy, illus. (p. 619)
Pratt-Thomas, Leslie, illus. see Wentworth, Marjory.
Praveeta. Imagine Travelling to the Most Mysterious & Unusual Places! Ash, illus. (p. 861)
Praxis Press, creator. Journey: Participant Journal: Follow God. Reach Your World. (p. 928)
Pray, Linda. Characters in the Wild. (p. 291)
—Characters of Adventure. (p. 291)
—Characters of the Dark. (p. 291)
Prayaga, Jeev. Golden Search. (p. 695)
Prayor, Erika. Heavenly Angel Bugs: Do Not Fear God Is Here. (p. 761)
Prebeg, Rick. Into the Jungle. Prebeg, Rick, photos by. (p. 881)
—Looking for Lions. Prebeg, Rick, photos by. (p. 1051)
—Night Cat. Prebeg, Rick, photos by. (p. 1253)
—You've Got Cheetah Mail. Prebeg, Rick, photos by. (p. 1982)
Prebeg, Rick, photos by see Knowlton, Laurie Lazzaro.
Prebenna, David, illus. see Allen, Constance.
Prebenna, David, illus. see Muntean, Michaela.
Preble, Joy. Anastasia Forever. (p. 67)
—a-Word: a Sweet Dead Life Novel: A Sweet Dead Life Novel. (p. 2)
—Dreaming Anastasia. (p. 484)
—Finding Paris. (p. 588)
—Haunted. (p. 753)
—Sweet Dead Life. (p. 1689)
Preble, Laura. Lica's Angel. (p. 1007)
—Prom Queen Geeks. (p. 1411)
—Queen Geek Social Club. (p. 1424)
Prechtel, Jeff. Mountain Men — the History of Fur Trapping Coloring Book. (p. 1181)
Preciado, Tony. Super Grammar. Montijo, Rhode, illus. (p. 1680)
Precious. Dymond in the Rough. (p. 491)
Precious, jt. auth. see Juwell.
Precious, Precious & Williams, Kashamba. Best Kept Secret. (p. 170)
Precourt, Barbara. Waiting for Mr. Right. (p. 1852)
Preece, Bronwyn & Walton, Alex. Gulf Islands Alphabet. (p. 731)
Preece, Mary Ellen Goble. ABC Cousins & Fun from A to Z. (p. 3)
Preece, Phil. Nightmare Park. (p. 1255)
Preece, Philip. Carnival of Horrors Kendall, Bradford, illus. (p. 270)
Preeg, Ernest H. India & China: An Advanced Technology Race & How the United States Should Respond. (p. 871)
Preik, Christel D. Growing up Joyfully. (p. 727)
—Sharing the Love. (p. 1561)
Preisler, Jerome. Wild Card. (p. 1929)
Preiss, Byron, ed. see Roman, Steven A.
Preiss, Byron, jt. auth. see Irvine, Alexander C.

Preiss, Thomas. Boat under the Boat: A Story about the Golden Rule. (p. 205)
Prejean, David. Henry's Syrup: Le Sirop D'Henri. (p. 769)
Preller, James. Along Came Spider. (p. 48)
—Before You Go. (p. 159)
—Bicicleta Robada. Nieländer, Peter, illus. (p. 177)
—Bystander. (p. 249)
—Case of the Groaning Ghost. Smith, Jamie & Alley, R. W., illus. (p. 274)
—Fall. (p. 566)
—Ghost Cat & Other Spooky Tales. (p. 670)
—Good Night, Zombie. Bruno, Iacopo, illus. (p. 700)
—Hamster Desaparecido. Nieländer, Peter, illus. (p. 739)
—Home Sweet Horror. (p. 793)
—Home Sweet Horror. Bruno, Iacopo, illus. (p. 793)
—I Scream, You Scream! (p. 845)
—I Scream, You Scream! Bruno, Iacopo, illus. (p. 845)
—Justin Fisher Declares War! (p. 940)
—Nightmareland. Bruno, Iacopo, illus. (p. 1255)
—Pirate's Guide to First Grade. (p. 1363)
—Pirate's Guide to First Grade. Ruth, Greg, illus. (p. 1363)
—Pirate's Guide to Recess. Ruth, Greg, illus. (p. 1363)
—Six Innings. (p. 1582)
—Swamp Monster. Bruno, Iacopo, illus. (p. 1688)
Preller, James, jt. auth. see Barbo, Maria S.
Preller, James, jt. auth. see Kovacs, Deborah.
Preller, James, jt. auth. see Layden, Joe.
Preller, James & Bruno, Iacopo. One-Eyed Doll. (p. 1294)
Prelutsky, Jack. Awful Ogre Running Wild. Zelinsky, Paul O., illus. (p. 121)
—Awful Ogre's Awful Day. Zelinsky, Paul O., illus. (p. 121)
—Be Glad Your Nose Is on Your Face: And Other Poems - Some of the Best of Jack Prelutsky. Dorman, Brandon, illus. (p. 148)
—Behold the Bold Umbrellaphant: And Other Poems. Berger, Carin, illus. (p. 160)
—Carnival of the Animals. GrandPré, Mary, illus. (p. 270)
—Frogs Wore Red Suspenders. Mathers, Petra, illus. (p. 641)
—Good Sports: Rhymes about Running, Jumping, Throwing, & More. Raschka, Chris, illus. (p. 700)
—If Not for the Cat. Rand, Ted, illus. (p. 853)
—In Aunt Giraffe's Green Garden. Mathers, Petra, illus. (p. 863)
—It's Christmas! (p. 896)
—It's Christmas! Hafner, Marylin, illus. (p. 896)
—It's Raining Pigs & Noodles. Stevenson, James, illus. (p. 898)
—It's Snowing! It's Snowing! Abolafia, Yossi, illus. (p. 899)
—It's Snowing! It's Snowing! Winter Poems. Abolafia, Yossi, illus. (p. 899)
—It's Thanksgiving! Hafner, Marylin, illus. (p. 899)
—It's Thanksgiving. Hafner, Marylin, illus. (p. 899)
—It's Valentine's Day! (p. 899)
—It's Valentine's Day! Hafner, Marylin, illus. (p. 899)
—I've Lost My Hippopotamus. Urbanovic, Jackie, illus. (p. 901)
—Me I Am! Davenier, Christine, illus. (p. 1116)
—My Dog May Be a Genius. Stevenson, James, illus. (p. 1202)
—My Parents Think I'm Sleeping. Abolafia, Yossi, illus. (p. 1216)
—New Kid on the Block. Stevenson, James, illus. (p. 1245)
—Pizza, Pigs, & Poetry: How to Write a Poem. (p. 1365)
—Scranimals. Sís, Peter, illus. (p. 1532)
—Silver Moon: Lullabies & Cradle Songs. Ishida, Jui, illus. (p. 1576)
—Something Big Has Been Here. Stevenson, James, illus. (p. 1609)
—Stardines Swim High Across the Sky: And Other Poems. Berger, Carin, illus. (p. 1642)
—Swamps of Sleethe: Poems from Beyond the Solar System. Pickering, Jimmy, illus. (p. 1688)
—There's No Place Like School: Classroom Poems. Manning, Jane, illus. (p. 1731)
—There's No Place Like School. Manning, Jane, illus. (p. 1731)
—What a Day It Was at School! Cushman, Doug, illus. (p. 1878)
Premise Entertainment, illus. see Weeks, Kermit.
Premonville, Marie de & Volpari, Daniela. Cleopatra: Queen of the Nile. (p. 331)
Prendergast, Gabrielle. Audacious (p. 114)
—Capricious (p. 263)
Prendergast, John, jt. auth. see Cheadle, Don.
Prendergast, R. L. Baby, Please Go to Sleep. Maciborski, Charmaine, illus. (p. 127)
Prentice, Amy. Gray Goose's Story. (p. 713)
—Mouser Cats' Story. (p. 1182)
Prentice Hall Dictionary Editors. Middle Grades Math - Course 2: Tools for Success. (p. 1137)
—Prentice Hall Math Course 1 Practice Workbook 2004. (p. 1395)
Prentice Hall Dictionary Editors, jt. auth. see Boyles, Peggy Palo.
Prentice Hall Direct Education Staff. Science Explorer - Sound & Light. (p. 1526)
Prentice Hall Direct Education Staff, jt. auth. see Boyles, Peggy Palo.
Prentice Hall Directories Staff. Middle Grades Math - Course 1: Tools for Success. (p. 1137)
Prentice Hall Directories Staff, jt. auth. see Boyles, Peggy Palo.
Prentice Hall Directories Staff, jt. auth. see Charles, Randall I.
Prentice Hall Staff. Prentice Hall - Explorations & Applications: A Pre-Algebra Approach, 1999. (p. 1395)
Prentice Hall Staff, jt. auth. see Cayton, Andrew.
Prentice Hall Staff, jt. auth. see Charles, Randall I.
Prentice Hall Staff, jt. auth. see Lappan, Glenda.
Prentice Hall Staff, jt. auth. see Maggart, Kaye Wiley.
Prentice, Jeff, jt. auth. see Prentice, Justin.
Prentice, Justin & Prentice, Jeff. It Can Be Scary When You Move. (p. 893)
Prentice, Priscilla, illus. see Robertson, Rachel.
Prentice-Hall, Inc. Staff, creator. Science Explorer - Animals. (p. 1526)
Prentice-Hall Staff. Algebra I Solutions Manual. (p. 38)
—American Express. (p. 60)
—Bridge to Terabithia. (p. 227)
—British Tradition. (p. 230)
—Building Block. (p. 239)
—Exploring Planet Earth. (p. 553)
—Heat Energy. (p. 760)
—J. Tremain. (p. 902)
—Learning System Integrated Science (p. 985)
—Nature of Science. (p. 1236)
—Of Mice & Men. (p. 1279)
—Parade of Life: Animals. (p. 1323)
—PH Grammar & Composition. (p. 1349)
—Prentice Hall Literature. (p. 1395)
—Red Pony. (p. 1454)
—Science Explorer: Prentice Hall Product Testing Activities. (p. 1526)
—Sound & Light. (p. 1615)
—Things Fall Apart. (p. 1733)
—When Legend. (p. 1903)
Prentiss, Timothy. Good Pick. (p. 700)
—Miss Keen Needs Help. (p. 1151)
—Volunteer Helps. (p. 1850)
—What Is a Good Citizen? (p. 1888)
Prentzas. Democratic Republic of Congo. (p. 426)
—It's Cool to Learn about Countries: Iran. (p. 896)
—It's Cool to Learn about Countries: Democratic Republic of Congo. (p. 896)
Prentzas, G. S. Arkansas (Revised Edition) (p. 99)
—Brooklyn Bridge. (p. 231)
—Colony of Pennsylvania. (p. 342)
—Cuban Revolution. (p. 388)
—Emancipation Proclamation. (p. 517)
—Floods, Flash Floods, & Mudslides: A Practical Survival Guide. (p. 605)
—Georgia. (p. 665)
—Gideon V. Wainwright: The Right to Free Legal Counsel. (p. 674)
—Law & Your Family: Your Legal Rights (p. 981)
—Lost at Sea. (p. 1055)
—Mario Andretti. (p. 1094)
—Marshall Plan. (p. 1096)
—Primary Source History of the Colony of Pennsylvania. (p. 1400)
—Roanoke. (p. 1478)
—Smart Strategies for Paying for College. (p. 1593)
—Wyoming (Revised Edition) (p. 1966)
Prentzas, G. S., jt. text see Wilker, Josh.
Prentzas, G. S. (Scott). Truth about Inhalants. (p. 1794)
Prentzas, Scott. FBI Special Agent. (p. 578)
—Gps. (p. 704)
—Radar Guns. (p. 1432)
Prenzlau & Suttom. by Times' Kid Sisters: Three-in-One 1-3, 4-6, 7-9, 10-12 (p. 249)
Preppernau, Joan, et al. Microsoft(r) Office Publisher 2007. (p. 1136)
Preschern, Jennifer. Strategic Learning Compound & Complex Sentences. (p. 1666)
—Strategic Learning Simple & Compound Sentences. (p. 1666)
Preschool, Lollipop. Lollipop Co-Op Preschool Cookbook. Buck, Melissa, ed. (p. 1046)
Prescott, Blake. Saturnian Snake. (p. 1515)
Prescott, Brian. Chloe Knows Her Alphabet. (p. 308)
—Chloe Saves Christmas. (p. 308)
—Chloe the Campervan Goes on Holiday. (p. 308)
Prescott, Della. Day in a Colonial Home. Dana, John Cotton, ed. (p. 413)
Prescott, Folami, jt. auth. see Kunjufu, Jawanza.
Prescott, Paul. Richard III. (p. 1469)
Prescott, Sheri. How to Be a Super Model: A Guide to Inner Beauty. (p. 815)
Prescott, William H. History of the Conquest of Mexico, with a Preliminary View of the Ancient Mexican Civilization, & the Life of the Conqueror Hernando Cortes. (p. 785)
Prescott, William Hickling. Correspondence. (p. 368)
Prescott, Yolanda. Mama's Pickaninny. (p. 1084)
Preseault, N., ed. see Brewer, Heather.
Presley, Frances. Paravane: New & Selected Poems 1996-2003. (p. 1324)
Presnall, Judith Janda. Yukon: Sled Dog Elliot, Mark, illus. (p. 1983)
Press, Applesauce. 3-D Disgusting Doodles Book & Kit: Where Your Gross-Out Imagination Jumps off the Page! (p. 1991)
—Grow Your Own Flesh-Eating Plant! Everything You Need for the Care & Feeding of Your Venus Fly Trap. (p. 726)
Press, Applesauce & Entin, Cindy. My First Counting Book - Airforce: A Celebration of the United States Air Forces from 1 to 10! (p. 1206)
—My First Counting Book - Army. (p. 1206)
Press, Applesauce & Rhatigan, Joe. Super Concentrated Brain De-Clogger Book: Hundreds of Games, Puzzles & Other Fun Activites That Are Positively Guaranteed to Remove Brain Sludge, Liquidate Blocked Brain Cells, & Stomp Out Boredom! Owsley, Anthony, illus. (p. 1679)
Press, Bothwell. Naughty Madge & Other Old-Fashioned Children's Stories. (p. 1237)
Press, Cider Mill & Entin, Cindy. Navy. (p. 1238)
Press, David P. Abraham Lincoln: The Great Emancipator. (p. 6)
Press, H. J. Science Experiments. (p. 1525)
Press, J. Abra-Ca-Doodle! (p. 6)
—Doodles of Sam Dibble. (p. 469)
—Doodles of Sam Dibble. Kline, Michael, illus. (p. 469)
—Double Trouble. (p. 473)
—Double Trouble #2. Kline, Michael, illus. (p. 473)
—Robots Don't Clean Toilets. (p. 1481)
—Robots Don't Clean Toilets. Kline, Michael, illus. (p. 1481)
Press, Jenny, illus. see Barrie, J. M.
Press, Jenny, illus. see Baxter, Nicola.
Press, Jenny, illus. see Young, Lesley.
Press, Judy. Animal Habitats! Learning about North American Animals & Plants Through Art, Science & Creative Play. Day, Betsy, illus. (p. 78)
—Big Fun Christmas Crafts & Activities: Over 200 Quick & Easy Activities for Holiday Fun! Cole, Sarah, illus. (p. 181)
—Little Hands Art Book: Exploring Arts & Crafts with 2-6 Year Olds. Braren, Loretta Trezzo, illus. (p. 1029)
—Little Hands Sea Life Art & Activities: Creative Learning Experiences for 3-7-Year Olds. (p. 1029)
Press, Judy & Trezzo-Braren, Loretta. Big Fun Craft Book: Creative Fun for 2 to 6 Year Olds. Trezzo-Braren, Loretta, illus. (p. 181)
Press, Julian. Operation Yellow Dragon (p. 1300)
Press, Karen, jt. auth. see Morrison, Karen.
Press, Karen, jt. auth. see PRAESA.
Press, Karen, jt. auth. see University of Cape Town Staff.
Press, Pikachu. Catch Pikachu! DELUXE Look & Listen Set. (p. 279)
—Guide to Pokemon Legends. (p. 730)
—Pokemon Felties: How to Make 16 of Your Favorite Pokemon. (p. 1378)
—Pokemon How-To-Draw Kit: Starting with All-Stars! (p. 1378)
—Super Pokemon Pop-Up: White Kyurem. (p. 1680)
—Super Pokemon Pop-Up! Black Kyurem. (p. 1680)
Press, Running. Howzat! Cricket Kit: The Classic Desktop Dice Game. (p. 824)
Pressberg, Dava. How Leaves Work. (p. 810)
—Life of Frederick Douglass. (p. 1012)
—Teacher's Tools. (p. 1709)
Pressey, Deborah, illus. see Pair, Karma A.
Pressler, Mirjam. Let Sleeping Dogs Lie. Macki, Erik J., tr. from GER. (p. 994)
—Malka. (p. 1083)
—Malka. Murdoch, Brian, tr. (p. 1083)
Pressley, Arthur Lee. Arizona Coopersmith. (p. 98)
Pressley, Michael, et al, eds. Shaping Literacy Achievement: Research We Have, Research We Need. (p. 1561)
Pressnall, Debra Olson. Colorful File Folder Games: Skill-Building Center Activities for Language Arts & Math. (p. 344)
Pressnall, Debra Olson, jt. auth. see Pyne, Lynette.
Presson, Leslie. What in the World Is a Homophone? Bosson, Jo-Ellen, illus. (p. 1887)
Prestel, ed. see Roeder, Annette.
Prestel, creator. Salvador Dali. (p. 1506)
Prestel, ed. Coloring Book: Turner. (p. 344)
—Coloring Book: Great Artists. (p. 344)
Prestel Publishing. Colouring Book Antoni Gaudi. (p. 346)
—Roy Lichtenstein: Coloring Book. (p. 1492)
Prestel Publishing & Roeder, Annette. Fab Fashion Coloring Book: Create Your Own Style! (p. 559)
Prestel Publishing, creator. Edward Hopper Coloring Book. (p. 505)
Prestel Staff. Antoni Gaudi: Create Your Own City. (p. 90)
Presti, Lori, jt. auth. see Daronco, Mickey.
Prestofillipo, Mary Nazarene, tr. Bible for Little Ones. Flamini, Lorella, illus. (p. 175)
—Story of Creation. Flamini, Lorella, illus. (p. 1657)
Prestofilippo, Mary Nazarene, tr. Story of Noah's Ark. Flamini, Lorella, illus. (p. 1659)
Preston, Carole, illus. see Littlewood, Graham.
Preston Chushcoff, Jennifer. Snowflakes - French Edition: A Pop-Up Book. Yeretskaya, Yevgeniya, illus. (p. 1600)
Preston, Diana. Remember the Lusitania! (p. 1459)
Preston, Douglas. Jennie. (p. 912)
Preston, Elizabeth. Very Best Christmas Plays for Kids. (p. 1837)
Preston, Felicia, illus. see Van Dyke, Tony & Van Dyke, Tracey.
Preston, Frederick James. Do As I Say, Not As I Do. Taylor, Chandra Sparks, ed. (p. 456)
Preston, Graham, illus. see Clark, Paul.
Preston, Halsey, illus. see Day, Todd.
Preston, Helen M. Gra Gra's Stories. (p. 704)
Preston, James, photos by see Smith, Loretta.
Preston, John D., jt. auth. see Fast, Julie A.
Preston, L. M. Explorer X: Beta. (p. 551)
—Pack: Retribution. (p. 1317)
—Pack. (p. 1317)
Preston, Mary Lou. Do You Know What Wildcats Do at School in P. E. Class? Wildcat's First Day in Class. (p. 458)
Preston, Natasha. Awake. (p. 120)
—Cellar. (p. 286)
Preston, Penny. Controlling the Blood. (p. 361)
Preston, Rhoda. Rock-a-Bye Toddlers & Two Leader's Guide (2009 - 2010) (p. 1481)
Preston, Rhoda & Stickler, LeeDell. Abingdon's Books of the Bible Games. (p. 5)
Preston, Sarah. The, Adventures of Abby. (p. 1728)
Preston, Wendy. Sydney for Kids: The Choice Guide to over 400 Fun Activities in & Around Sydney. (p. 1692)
Preston-Gannon, Frann. Deep Deep Sea. (p. 422)
—Dinosaur Farm. (p. 442)
—Hot Dog, Cold Dog. (p. 801)
—How to Lose a Lemur. (p. 820)
—Pepper & Poe. (p. 1340)
—What a Hoot. (p. 1878)
Preston-Gannon, Frann, illus. see Schaefer, Lola M.
Preston-Mafham, Ken, jt. auth. see Preston-Mafham, Rod.
Preston-Mafham, Rod & Preston-Mafham, Ken. Insects & Other Invertebrates. (p. 876)
Prestsater, Julie. Double Threat My Bleep. (p. 473)
Prestwood, Donna. Center World. (p. 287)
Preszler, Eric. Harley-Davidson Motorcycles (p. 749)
Preszler, June. Bats Collins, Tami, illus. (p. 144)
—Caring for Your Bird (p. 269)
—Caring for Your Dog Garvin, Kelly, illus. (p. 269)
—Flesh-Eating Machines: Maggots in the Food Chain (p. 603)
—Haiti: A Question & Answer Book (p. 736)
—Juneteenth: Jubilee for Freedom (p. 934)
—Meat-Eating Plants & Other Extreme Plant Life (p. 1118)
—Walt Disney. (p. 1855)
Preto, Antonella. Mimosa Tree. (p. 1145)
Pretreger, Lidija. Pick-a-WooWoo - Angel Steps: Love You, Miss You Rose, Carolyn Maree, illus. (p. 1354)
Preus, Margi. Bamboo Sword. (p. 135)
—Celebritrees: Historic & Famous Trees of the World. Gibbon, Rebecca, illus. (p. 285)
—Enchantment Lake: A Northwoods Mystery. (p. 523)
—Heart of a Samurai (p. 759)
—Heart of a Samurai. (p. 759)
—Shadow on the Mountain. (p. 1557)
—West of the Moon. (p. 1876)
Preuss, Sarah Louise, illus. see Diggle, David Mark.
Preussler, Otfried. Krabat & the Sorcerer's Mill. Bell, Anthea, tr. from GER. (p. 967)
—Little Water Sprite. Bell, Anthea, tr. from GER. (p. 1037)
—Little Witch. Bell, Anthea, tr. from GER. (p. 1038)
Prevac, Rose Anne, illus. see Hammond, Charmaine.
Prevec, Rose Anne, illus. see Hammond, Charmaine.
Prevedel, Brenda. Nick Gets Moving. Gulley, Robin R., ed. (p. 1251)
Prévert, Jacques. Chanson des Escargotsqui Vont l'Enterrement. (p. 290)
—Contes pour enfants pas Sage. (p. 360)
—En Sortant de l'Ecole. (p. 523)
Previn, Alicia L. Strange Disappearance of Walter Tortoise. Previn, Alicia L., illus. (p. 1665)
Previn, Stacey. Find Spot! (p. 587)
Previn, Stacey, illus. see Cooper, Sharon Katz.
Previn, Stacey, illus. see Donahue, Jill Lynn & Small, Mary.
Previn, Stacey, illus. see Donahue, Jill Lynn.
Previn, Stacey, illus. see Small, Mary.
Prevost, Guillaume. Gate of Days. (p. 658)
—Gate of Days. Rodarmor, William, tr. from FRE. (p. 658)
Prévost, Guillaume & Rodarmor, William. Circle of Gold: The Book of Time III. (p. 321)
Prevost, Jeanne. It's Raining Cats & Cats! Hansen, Amelia, illus. (p. 898)
Prevost, Mikela, illus. see Hyde, Heidi Smith.
Prevost, Mikela, illus. see Ludwig, Trudy.
Prevost, Pamela Ms Ed. Adventures of Charlie: The Curious Cat & Me. (p. 17)
Prewett, Maggie, illus. see Saffioti, Trina.
Preza, Bruno Gonzalez, illus. see Lazaro, Georgina.
Preza, Jessie. Little Harper Grace & the Hummingbird. Daly, Meghan, illus. (p. 1029)
Prezant, Fran Pollock & Marshak, Laura E. Dr. Vermeij's Conch Quest. (p. 475)
Prezio, Victor, illus. see Furman, A. L., ed.
Pribichevich-Zoric, Christina, tr. see Drakulic, Slavenka.
Price, Aleksandra. What Do You See? Poems for Young Children. (p. 1883)
Price, Alfred. Battle of Britain Day: 15 September 1940. (p. 146)
Price, Allison W. A. Dragons & the Words of Knowledge. (p. 479)
Price & Wilkinson. Saga of Aslak. (p. 1502)
Price, Andy, illus. see Cook, Katie.
Price, Athena. Angel in the Tree. (p. 73)
Price, Audrey. My best Friend: Best Friend. (p. 1196)
Price, Bc. Mabel & Her Litter Of. (p. 1067)
Price, Ben Joel. Earth Space Moon Base. (p. 497)
—In the Deep Dark Deep. (p. 865)
Price, Bobby J. How to Get Smart in School Without Thinking. (p. 820)
Price, Caroline, illus. see Sadler, Judy Ann.
Price, Carolyn, illus. see Hakowski, Maryann.
Price, Charlie. Dead Connection. (p. 416)
—Dead Girl Moon (p. 416)
Price, Cheryl. Golden Aspen. (p. 694)
Price, Cheryl A. Follow the Sun. (p. 612)
Price, Christine, illus. see Maiden, Cecil.
Price, Christine, illus. see Mitchell, Lucy Sprague.
Price, Christine, illus. see Wheeler, Opal.
Price, Christine, illus. see Wheller, Opal.
Price, Crystal R. Wise Woman's Prophecy. (p. 1940)
Price, Dan. Braces Journal. (p. 221)
Price, Dana, illus. see Pierce, Heather Vowell.
Price, Dann. Wesley the Weasel Can't Stop His Sneezel. (p. 1876)
Price, David. Sly the Fox & Advice from la Princessa Roja. (p. 1591)
Price, David, illus. see Roberts, Sheena.
Price, David A. Love & Hate in Jamestown: John Smith, Pocahontas, & the Start of a New Nation. (p. 1059)
Price, David J. Tom & Emily's Incredible Adventure to the World of the Gossamerians. (p. 1762)
Price, Diane J. Tiny Story Csavas, Sally, illus. (p. 1756)
Price, Elizabeth. Divorce & Teens: When a Family Splits Apart. (p. 455)
Price, Ellen Ann. Gladly's Magic. (p. 682)
Price, Emma, ed. Portia's Incredible Journey. (p. 1386)
Price, Erika. Turnaround: Book of Poetry (p. 1798)
Price, Erika, contrib. by. Turnaround: Book of Poetry. (p. 1798)
Price, Gene. Lukas' Maiden Voyage. (p. 1064)
Price, Geoff. Puberty Boy. (p. 1414)
Price, Hattie Longstreet, illus. see Curtis, Alice.
Price, Hope Lynne. Jump at the Sun Treasury: An African American Picture Book Collection. Collier, Bryan, illus. (p. 934)
Price, Hugh. Truth at Last about the Little Red Hen. Lowe, Isabel, illus. (p. 1794)
Price, J. M. Patience Bullard, Joyce, illus. (p. 1328)
Price, Jamie Mills. Christmastime: Between the Vines (p. 316)
Price, Jane. Underworld: Exploring the Secret World Beneath Your Feet Hancock, James Gulliver, illus. (p. 1817)
Price, Jennifer L. Half Moon: Phases of the Moon: Book 2 (p. 736)
Price, Jesse. Dad. (p. 398)
Price, Joan. J. K. Rowling. (p. 901)
—J.K. Rowling. (p. 919)
Price, Joan A. Ancient & Hellenistic Thought. (p. 67)
—Contemporary Thought. (p. 360)
Price, John. Media Studies. (p. 1118)
—Quest. (p. 1426)
Price, Justine. Class Mural: Reason with Shapes & Their Attributes. (p. 327)
—Dreams of a Puppy. (p. 484)
Price, Kathryn. Mouse & the Buddha. Price, Traer, illus. (p. 1181)
Price, Kevin, ed. see The Born Storytellers.

P

Price, Kevin, ed. Fields of Wheat: And other Romance Stories. (p. 584)
—Ice Castles: A Born Storytellers Collection of Teen Fiction & Romance. (p. 850)
—Mystery of Love: A Born Storyteller Collection of Mystery Adventure & Science Fiction Stories. (p. 1224)
Price, Lissa. Enders. (p. 527)
—Starters. (p. 1643)
Price, M. J. Skin I'm In. (p. 1585)
Price, M. J. Momot. Grandma & Grandpa Are Retiring. (p. 707)
Price, Mara & Ventura, Gabriela Baeza. Grandma's Chocolate/El Chocolate de Abuelita. Fields, Lisa, illus. (p. 708)
Price, Margaret. Chillipop. (p. 306)
Price, Margaret Evans. Betty Fairy Book. (p. 172)
—Child's Book of Myths. (p. 304)
—Mother Goose: Book of Rhymes. (p. 1177)
—Visit to Santa Claus. (p. 1845)
Price, Margaret Evans, illus. see Dover, et al.
Price, Margaret Evans, illus. see Grimm, Jacob & Grimm, Wilhelm K.
Price, Margaret Evans, illus. see Moore, Clement C.
Price, Margaret Evans, illus. see Moore, Clement C., ed.
Price, Margaret Evans & Wadsworth, Wallace C. Once upon a Time Tales: With Read & Listen MP3 Download. Bates, Katharine Lee, ed. (p. 1293)
Price, Marilyn. Grandma's Cookies. (p. 708)
Price, Mary Ellizabeth. Wallbaby Bumblebees. (p. 1855)
Price, Massoume. Ancient Iran. (p. 69)
Price, Mathew. Cachorro. Goldman, Judy, tr. (p. 250)
—Este Cerdito. (p. 538)
—Gatito. Goldman, Judy, tr. (p. 658)
—Me Encanta el Futbol. (p. 1115)
—Pollito. Goldman, Judy, tr. (p. 1381)
—Polo Tiene Una Amiga. (p. 1381)
—Polo y la Rana. (p. 1381)
—Polo y Los Conejos. (p. 1381)
—Tic, Tac Toc. (p. 1747)
—Vueltas y Vueltas en Patin. (p. 1851)
Price, Matt. Mystery of the Ancient Anchor. Ettinger, Dorris, illus. (p. 1225)
—Out on a Limb. (p. 1311)
Price, Melissa. Luke & Lori's Musical Journey: Learning the Basic Elements of Music. Keren Weaver Graphics, illus. (p. 1064)
Price, Michael, illus. see Adams, Kevin.
Price, Michael H., jt. auth. see Wooley, John.
Price, Nick. Aesop's Fables. (p. 25)
—Animal Legends. (p. 78)
—Magical Animals. (p. 1074)
—Wonderful Wizard of Oz. (p. 1948)
Price, Nick, illus. see Bearn, Emily.
Price, Nick, illus. see Beresford, Elisabeth.
Price, Nick, illus. see Blane, Francisco.
Price, Nick, illus. see Jeffries, Katherine.
Price, Nick, illus. see Morgan, Michaela.
Price, Olivia. All Aboard Noah's Ark: A Touch & Feel Book. Mitchell, Melanie, illus. (p. 42)
—Bible Stories: A Touch & Feel Book. Mitchell, Melanie, illus. (p. 176)
Price, Phyllis. Adventures of Ozzie, Otto, & Sadie: Best Friends Forever. (p. 21)
Price, Rebecca. Toby & the Flood (p. 1760)
Price, Rebecca, illus. see Holliday, Bobby.
Price, Reynolds. Perfect Friend. (p. 1341)
Price, Robin. Boudicat! (p. 215)
—Catligula (p. 280)
—Cleocatra's Kushion (p. 331)
—Die Clawdius (p. 437)
—Eye of the Cyclaw Watson, Chris, illus. (p. 557)
—Father Thames. McGrory, Paul, illus. (p. 577)
—I Am Spartapuss (p. 834)
—Son of Spartapuss Watson, Chris, illus. (p. 1611)
Price, Robin, jt. auth. see Burns-Longship.
Price, Robin, jt. auth. see Longship, Burns.
Price, Robin, jt. auth. see Phoenix, Woodrow.
Price, Roger, jt. auth. see Stern, Leonard.
Price, Roger & Accord Publishing Staff. Flip & Click Memory Match. (p. 604)
Price, Roger & Stern, Leonard. Ad Lib Mad Libs. (p. 10)
—All I Want for Christmas Is Mad Libs. (p. 44)
—Angry Birds Mad Libs. (p. 75)
—Archie Loves Betty & Veronica Mad Libs. (p. 95)
—Best of Mad Libs. (p. 170)
—Dear Valentine Letters Mad Libs. (p. 419)
—Diva Girl Mad Libs. (p. 454)
—Dude, Where's My Mad Libs (p. 489)
—Easter Eggstravaganza Mad Libs. (p. 499)
—Family Guy Mad Libs. (p. 568)
—Family Tree Mad Libs. (p. 569)
—Fionna & Cake Mad Libs. (p. 589)
—Girls Just Wanna Have Mad Libs: Ultimate Box Set. (p. 680)
—Gobble Gobble Mad Libs. (p. 688)
—Grand Slam Mad Libs. (p. 707)
—Halloween Mad Libs Junior. (p. 738)
—Happily Ever Mad Libs. (p. 744)
—Happy Birthday Mad Libs. (p. 745)
—Holly, Jolly Mad Libs. (p. 789)
—Letters from Camp Mad Libs. (p. 1002)
—Mad about Animals Mad Libs. (p. 1068)
—Mad Libs Forever. (p. 1069)
—P. S. I Love Mad Libs. (p. 1316)
—Pirates Mad Libs. (p. 1363)
—Rock 'n' Roll Mad Libs. (p. 1482)
—Skylanders Universe Mad Libs. (p. 1587)
—Sleepover Party Mad Libs. (p. 1589)
—SpongeBob SquarePants Mad Libs. (p. 1630)
—Sports Star Mad Libs Junior. (p. 1633)
—Spy Mad Libs. (p. 1636)
—Star Wars Mad Libs. (p. 1641)
—Straight a Mad Libs. (p. 1664)
—Summer Fun Mad Libs Junior. (p. 1674)
—Super Silly Mad Libs Junior. (p. 1681)
—Winter Games Mad Libs. (p. 1938)
—Wizard of Oz Mad Libs. (p. 1943)
—World's Greatest Word Game. (p. 1960)
Price, Roger & Stern, Leonard, creators. Adventure Time Mad Libs. (p. 14)
—Mr. Men Little Miss Mad Libs. (p. 1185)
—Ninjas Mad Libs. (p. 1257)
—Penguin Classics Mad Libs. (p. 1336)
—Totally Pink Mad Libs. (p. 1771)
—Undead Mad Libs. (p. 1813)
—WWE Mad Libs. (p. 1966)
Price, Ronnalda, ed. see Martin, Paige.
Price, Rosalind, tr. see Serres, Alain.
Price, Roxanne M. Buckeyes Bow Ties & Sweater Vests. (p. 234)
—Troy & the Championship Trophy. (p. 1790)
Price, Roy. Gnome Guardian: Polly's Adventure. (p. 685)
Price, Ryan, illus. see Poe, Edgar Allen.
Price, Sean. Hannibal of Carthage (p. 743)
—Ivan the Terrible: Tsar of Death. (p. 900)
—Modern Spies. (p. 1159)
—Nicotine. (p. 1251)
—Unsolved Crime Mysteries. (p. 1822)
—Water Pollution. (p. 1863)
Price, Sean, jt. auth. see Price, Sean Stewart.
Price, Sean, et al, contrib. by. Passengers of the Titanic: Traveling on an Ill-Fated Ship (p. 1326)
Price, Sean Stewart. Adolf Hitler. (p. 13)
—Amazing Military Robots (p. 55)
—Amazing Military Robots. (p. 55)
—America Has Fun: The Roaring Twenties (p. 59)
—Art of War: The Posters of World War II (p. 102)
—Benazir Bhutto. (p. 163)
—Chris Jericho (p. 311)
—Climbing Out of the Great Depression: The New Deal (p. 333)
—Cloning Pets (p. 333)
—Crooks, Cowboys, & Characters: The Wild West (p. 385)
—Designing America: The Constitutional Convention (p. 430)
—Digging up Dirt: The Muckrakers (p. 439)
—Dirty Thirties: Documenting the Dust Bowl (p. 446)
—Jackie Robinson: Breaking the Color Barrier (p. 904)
—Kids' Guide to Lost Cities (p. 953)
—Kids' Guide to Pro Wrestling (p. 953)
—Kids' Guide to Titanic (p. 954)
—Modern Spies (p. 1159)
—Nation Torn Apart: The Battle of Gettysburg. (p. 1231)
—Osama Bin Laden. (p. 1305)
—Pirates: Truth & Rumors Doty, Eldon, illus. (p. 1363)
—Rosie the Riveter: Women in World War II (p. 1490)
—Route 66: America's Road (p. 1491)
—Salem Witch Trials: Colonial Life (p. 1504)
—Smokestacks & Spinning Jennys: Industrial Revolution (p. 1594)
—Sports. Doty, Eldon, illus. (p. 1632)
—Story Behind Chocolate (p. 1656)
—Story Behind Electricity (p. 1656)
—Story Behind Skyscrapers (p. 1656)
—Tenement Stories: Immigrant Life, 1835-1935. (p. 1720)
—Top Secret: Spy Equipment & the Cold War (p. 1769)
—U. S. Presidents: Truth & Rumors. Doty, Eldon, illus. (p. 1807)
—Vanished! Magic Tricks & Great Escapes (p. 1833)
—When Will I Get In? Segregation & Civil Rights (p. 1905)
—World War II Spies (p. 1959)
—Yanks in World War I: Americans in the Trenches (p. 1968)
Price, Sean Stewart, jt. auth. see Green, Gail D.
Price, Sean Stewart & DiConsiglio, John. News Never Stops (p. 1249)
Price, Sean Stewart & Price, Sean. Attila the Hun: Leader of the Barbarian Hordes. (p. 114)
—Cixi: Evil Empress of China? (p. 326)
—Henry VIII: Royal Beheader. (p. 768)
Price, Sean Stewart, et al. Kids' Guides. (p. 954)
—Unsolved Mystery Files. (p. 1822)
Price Stern Sloan. Dog Ate My Mad Libs. (p. 461)
—Get on the Mic. (p. 667)
—Give Me Liberty or Give Me Mad Libs. (p. 681)
—History of the World Mad Libs. (p. 785)
—I Love Seattle Mad Libs. (p. 843)
—Mad Libs Mania. (p. 1069)
—Meow Libs. (p. 1127)
—SEC Mad Libs. (p. 1539)
—Uncle Grandpa Mad Libs. (p. 1811)
Price Stern Sloan Staff & Marchesani, Laura. Teachers Rule! Mad Libs. (p. 1709)
Price, Susan. Bone Dog. (p. 208)
—Cân Yr Ysbrydion. (p. 260)
—Sterkarm Kiss. (p. 1648)
—Story Collector. (p. 1657)
Price, Susan D., illus. see Bosley, Judith A.
Price, Tom. Champion Sleeper. (p. 289)
Price, Traer, illus. see Price, Kathryn.
Price, W. Morris. Gnu with a Shoe. (p. 685)
Price-Groff, Claire & Kaplan, Elizabeth. Illinois. (p. 857)
Price-Groff, Claire, et al. Illinois. (p. 857)
Priceman, Marjorie. Hot Air: The (Mostly) True Story of the First Hot-Air Balloon Ride. Priceman, Marjorie, illus. (p. 801)
—How to Make a Cherry Pie & See the U. S. A. (p. 820)
—How to Make a Cherry Pie & See the U. S. A. Priceman, Marjorie, illus. (p. 820)
Priceman, Marjorie, illus. see Andrews, Julie & Hamilton, Emma Walton.
Priceman, Marjorie, illus. see Couric, Katie & Couric, Katherine.
Priceman, Marjorie, illus. see Couric, Katie.
Priceman, Marjorie, illus. see Griffin, Kitty.
Priceman, Marjorie, illus. see Manzano, Sonia.
Priceman, Marjorie, illus. see Moss, Lloyd.
Priceman, Marjorie, illus. see Ogburn, Jacqueline K.
Priceman, Marjorie, illus. see Spinelli, Eileen.
Priceman, Marjorie, illus. see Theroux, Phyllis.
Priceman, Marjorie, illus. see Winter, Jonah.
Priceman, Marjorie, illus. see Yolleck, Joan.
Prichard, Diana. Cow in Patrick o'Shanahan's Kitchen. Knopf, Heather, illus. (p. 373)
Prichard, Kathy. Tree Twitters: An Earth Dragons Tale (p. 1784)
Prickett, Darlene. Joey Roo's Outback Adventure. (p. 920)
Prida, Isabel Suarez de la. Caracol de las Mariposas. (p. 265)
Priddis, C. Michael, illus. see Daybell, Chad G.
Priddy, Anna. Bloom's How to Write about Emily Dickinson. (p. 201)
Priddy Book. In the Yard; Fuzzy Bee & Friends. (p. 868)
Priddy Books Staff. First Concepts: Colors. (p. 593)
—First Concepts: Numbers. (p. 593)
—First Concepts: Opposite. (p. 593)
—God Made Me & God Made Us (p. 689)
—I Want to Be a Builder & Firefighter (p. 847)
—I Want to Be a Princess & I Want to Be a Ballerina (p. 847)
—Kids Can Time. (p. 953)
—My Bedtime Book of Favorite Nursery Rhymes: Including Ladybug, Baa Baa Black Sheep, I Had a Nut Tree, Plus Many More... (p. 1196)
—My Sticker Book. (p. 1219)
Priddy Books Staff, jt. auth. see Priddy, Roger.
Priddy Books Staff & Priddy, Roger. ABC: Easy Learning Fun, for the Very Young. (p. 3)
—Animals. (p. 81)
—Colors. (p. 345)
—Dinosaur A-Z: For Kids Who Really Love Dinosaurs! (p. 441)
—First Words. (p. 597)
—Fuzzy Bee & Friends. (p. 651)
—My Big Animal Book. (p. 1197)
—My Little Word Book. (p. 1213)
—Things That Go: 26 Wipe-Clean Pages of Early Learning Fun. (p. 1733)
—Wipe Clean Animals. (p. 1939)
Priddy Books Staff, creator. Farm. (p. 573)
Priddy, Roger. 1000 Activities. (p. 2001)
—1000 Animal Stickers. (p. 2001)
—1000 Stickers. (p. 2001)
—123. (p. 2000)
—123 - Happy Baby. (p. 2000)
—ABC. (p. 3)
—ABC 123. (p. 3)
—Adventure Stories for Boys. (p. 14)
—Animals. (p. 80)
—Animals. (p. 81)
—Around the Town. (p. 100)
—At My House. (p. 110)
—At the Zoo. (p. 111)
—B Is for Bear. (p. 122)
—Baby Animals. (p. 124)
—Baby Basics Animals. (p. 125)
—Baby Basics My First Animals. (p. 125)
—Baby Basics My First Words. (p. 125)
—Baby Bear, Baby Bear, What Do You See? (p. 125)
—Baby Bunny. (p. 125)
—Baby Hugs Gift Set. (p. 126)
—Baby Shaker Teethers Animals. (p. 128)
—Baby Touch & Feel Baby Bunny. (p. 128)
—Baby Touch & Feel Easter Bunny. (p. 128)
—Baby Touch & Feel: Hugs. (p. 128)
—Baby Touch & Feel Meow! Meow! (p. 128)
—Baby's Treasure Hunt. (p. 129)
—Barnyard Fun! (p. 140)
—Bedtime Lullaby. (p. 157)
—Bible Stories. (p. 176)
—Big Board Books Colors, ABC, Numbers. (p. 178)
—Braid It! (p. 221)
—Bright Baby (p. 228)
—Bright Baby 4 Copy Slipcase: Colors; Trucks; First Words; Animals. (p. 228)
—Bright Baby Touch & Feel Easter. (p. 228)
—Bright Baby Touch & Feel Hanukkah. (p. 228)
—Bright Baby Touch & Feel Hugs & Kisses. (p. 228)
—Bright Baby Touch & Feel Numbers. (p. 228)
—Bright Toddler Gift Bag First Learning. (p. 228)
—Builder: Color & Activity Book. (p. 238)
—Builders Tool Kit. (p. 238)
—Busy Babies Colors. (p. 245)
—Busy Babies Farm Animals. (p. 245)
—Busy Babies Words. (p. 245)
—Busy Babies Zoo Animals. (p. 245)
—Busy Bugs Cloth Book. (p. 246)
—Busy Farm Cloth Book. (p. 246)
—Busy Zoo Cloth Book. (p. 246)
—Can You Find Me? Over 500 Hidden Pictures to Search for, Sort & Count. (p. 258)
—Chirpy Chick. (p. 308)
—Christmas Color. (p. 313)
—Christmas Treasure Hunt. (p. 316)
—Chunky Packs: Halloween. (p. 318)
—Color Attack! (p. 342)
—Colores. (p. 344)
—Colors. (p. 344)
—Colors/Colores. (p. 346)
—Coral Reef. (p. 366)
—Counting Colors. (p. 371)
—Cow - Animal Buddies. (p. 373)
—Dino Bites. (p. 441)
—Dino IQ. (p. 441)
—Dinosaur. (p. 441)
—Dinosaurs. (p. 444)
—Doll's House. (p. 464)
—Dot to Dot for Tiny Tots. (p. 472)
—Dot-to-Dot for Tiny Tots. (p. 472)
—Dot-to-Dot Puzzles & Mazes. (p. 472)
—Early Learning Workbook - ABC 1-20: Over 50 Pages of Wipe-Clean Letters & Numbers to Practice. (p. 493)
—Easter Egg Hunt. (p. 499)
—Easter Surprise. (p. 499)
—Faces: A High Contrast Board Book. (p. 561)
—Fairytale Love Boat. (p. 565)
—Fall. (p. 566)
—Farm. (p. 573)
—Farm Friends. (p. 574)
—First 100 Animals. (p. 592)
—First 100 Animals Lift-The-Flap. (p. 592)
—First 100 Board Books First 100 Numbers. (p. 592)
—First 100 Machines. (p. 592)
—First 100 Trucks. (p. 592)
—First 100 Trucks & Things That Go Lift-The-Flap. (p. 592)
—First 100 Words. (p. 592)
—First Concepts Numbers. (p. 593)
—First Songs Library. (p. 597)
—First Words. (p. 597)
—Fluffy Chick & Friends. (p. 608)
—Fluffy Chick & Friends. Priddy, Roger, illus. (p. 608)
—Funny Faces: Easter Parade. (p. 649)
—Funny Faces Halloween Jack. (p. 649)
—Funny Faces Haunted House. (p. 649)
—Funny Friends Charlie Monkey. (p. 650)
—Fuzzy Bee & Friends. (p. 651)
—Giant Sticker Activity First Words. (p. 674)
—Great Turkey Race. (p. 719)
—Happy Birthday. (p. 744)
—Hello Baby (p. 763)
—Hello Baby. (p. 763)
—Hello Baby - A High Contrast Book. (p. 763)
—Hello Baby: Bathtime Bath Book. (p. 763)
—Hello Friends. (p. 764)
—Hello Kitty - Chalk Fun. (p. 764)
—Hello Kitty: Giant Sticker Book. (p. 764)
—Hello Kitty - My Home. (p. 764)
—Hello Kitty: My Town Slide & Find. (p. 764)
—Hello Kitty: Wipe Clean Activity Fun. (p. 764)
—Hello Kitty: Wipe Clean Dot to Dot. (p. 764)
—Hide & Seek Bunnies. (p. 776)
—Home Sweet Home. (p. 793)
—Honk! Honk! (p. 795)
—I Love Ducklings. (p. 842)
—I Love Kittens. (p. 842)
—I Love Puppies. (p. 842)
—Is for Animal. (p. 889)
—It's Time to Play. (p. 899)
—It's Time to Sleep. (p. 899)
—Kittens. (p. 963)
—Kitty's Color Activity Book. Crimi-Trent, Ellen, illus. (p. 963)
—Learn to Write Your First Words - Cat. (p. 984)
—Learn to Write Your Letters ABC. (p. 984)
—Learn to Write Your - Letters ABC. (p. 984)
—Learn to Write Your Numbers. (p. 984)
—Let's Go Learning: I Love Animals. (p. 997)
—Let's Go Learning: I Love Trucks. (p. 997)
—Let's Learn Our First - Colors. (p. 998)
—Let's Pretend Race Driver Set. (p. 1000)
—Let's Say Our Colors. (p. 1000)
—Lift-the-Flap First 100 Numbers. (p. 1014)
—Lift-the-Flap Tab - Farm. (p. 1014)
—Lift-The-Flap Tab: on the Go. (p. 1014)
—Lift-The-Flap Tab: Spooky House. (p. 1014)
—Little Alphaprints: Animals. (p. 1023)
—Little Alphaprints: Colors. (p. 1023)
—Little Alphaprints: Words. (p. 1023)
—Little Friends: Big Adventure. (p. 1028)
—Little Friends - Big & Small. (p. 1028)
—Little Friends Gift Set. (p. 1028)
—Little Friends: Let's Play. (p. 1028)
—Little Friends: Little Monkey. (p. 1028)
—Little Friends Play Set. (p. 1028)
—Little Friends: Sleepy Time. (p. 1028)
—Little Friends: Splish Splash. (p. 1028)
—Little Penguin. (p. 1033)
—Lowercase Alphabet. (p. 1061)
—Match It! (p. 1104)
—Mealtime - A High Contrast High Chair Book. (p. 1116)
—Merry Christmas. (p. 1128)
—Mo Chéad Focióir. Ó Murchadha, Niall, tr. (p. 1157)
—Monkey. (p. 1164)
—My Big Activity Workbook. (p. 1197)
—My Big Animal Book. (p. 1197)
—My Big Dinosaur Book. (p. 1197)
—My Big Dinosaur World. (p. 1197)
—My Big Farm Book. (p. 1197)
—My Big Rescue Book. (p. 1197)
—My Big Train Book. (p. 1197)
—My Big Truck Book. (p. 1197)
—My Big Word Book. (p. 1197)
—My Biggest Easy to Color. (p. 1197)
—My Carry-Along Sound Book: Perfect Pets. (p. 1200)
—My Favorite Bible Stories. (p. 1203)
—My First Peekaboo: Where's My Home? (p. 1207)
—My First Peekaboo: Who Am I? (p. 1207)
—My First Peekaboo: Who Says Roar? (p. 1207)
—My First Peekaboo: Who's My Mom? (p. 1207)
—My First Words. (p. 1208)
—My Fold Out Books I Love You. (p. 1208)
—My Fun Sticker Vacation Book. (p. 1209)
—My Giant Fold-Out Book of Animals. (p. 1209)
—My Giant Sticker. (p. 1209)
—My Giant Sticker Book. (p. 1209)
—My Giant Sticker First Words. (p. 1209)
—My Little Animal Book. (p. 1212)
—My Little Colors Book. (p. 1212)
—My Little Numbers Book. (p. 1212)
—My Little Sticker Book Valentine. (p. 1213)
—My Little Word Book: Mi Libro Pequeño de Palabras. (p. 1213)
—My Little Word Book. (p. 1213)
—My Press-Out Tea Set (p. 1217)
—My Pretty Princess. (p. 1217)
—My Super Duper Coloring Activity Book. (p. 1219)
—My Super Duper Drawing. (p. 1219)
—My Super Duper Sticker Activity Book. (p. 1219)
—My World. (p. 1221)
—Nail Art! (p. 1227)
—Natural Baby Play. (p. 1235)
—Natural Baby Sleep. (p. 1235)
—Natural Baby Splash. (p. 1235)
—Neon Dinky Doodles. (p. 1241)
—Numbers. (p. 1271)
—Numbers 1 2 3. (p. 1272)

—Numbers Colors Shapes. (p. 1272)
—Numbers (Nümeros) (p. 1272)
—Nursery Rhymes. (p. 1273)
—Ocean: Amazing Photo Pop-Ups Like You've Never Seen Before! (p. 1276)
—On the Farm. (p. 1290)
—On the Farm, Baby Animals, at the Zoo & Perfect Pets. (p. 1290)
—On the Go. (p. 1290)
—Palabras Words. (p. 1319)
—Pen Control. (p. 1336)
—Perfect Pets. (p. 1342)
—Pirate. (p. 1362)
—Play & Learn 123. (p. 1371)
—Play & Learn ABC. (p. 1371)
—Play & Learn: Colors. (p. 1371)
—Play & Learn with Wallace: Giant Sticker Book. (p. 1371)
—Play & Learn with Wallace: Everyday Math. (p. 1371)
—Play & Learn with Wallace: Giant Workbook. (p. 1371)
—Playtime. (p. 1373)
—Playtown. (p. 1373)
—Playtown: Airport. (p. 1373)
—Pop-Up Little Lamb. (p. 1384)
—Pop-Up Surprise Haunted House. (p. 1384)
—Potty Time Training Pack: A Friendly Reassuring Way to Help Your Child Learn to Use a Potty. (p. 1388)
—Predators. (p. 1394)
—Preschool Sticker Activity Book. (p. 1396)
—Princess Stories. (p. 1405)
—Puppies. (p. 1417)
—Puppy. (p. 1418)
—Puzzle Fun. (p. 1421)
—Quack! Quack! These Baby Animals Can't Wait to Meet You! (p. 1422)
—Read-Along Fairy Tales. (p. 1442)
—Rudolph the Red-Nosed Reindeer Lift-the-Flap Tab. (p. 1494)
—Rudolph the Red-Nosed Reindeer Slide & Find. (p. 1494)
—Santa Claus. (p. 1511)
—Santa Express. (p. 1511)
—Schoolies: Time for Recess. Crimi-Trent, Ellen, illus. (p. 1524)
—Seaside. (p. 1538)
—Simple First Sounds Noisy Pets. (p. 1577)
—Simple First Sounds Noisy Trucks. (p. 1577)
—Simple First Sounds Noisy Zoo. (p. 1577)
—Simple First Words Let's Talk. (p. 1577)
—Slide & Find Christmas. (p. 1590)
—Slide & Find - Colors. (p. 1590)
—Slide & Find Easter. (p. 1590)
—Slide & Find Spooky. (p. 1590)
—Slide & Surprise Alphabet. (p. 1590)
—Slide & Surprise Numbers. (p. 1590)
—Smart Kids Animals A-Z. (p. 1592)
—Smart Kids: Rainforest. (p. 1593)
—Smart Kids Science. (p. 1593)
—Sneak-a-Peek Colors. (p. 1597)
—Sneak-a-Peek Words. (p. 1597)
—Songs. (p. 1611)
—Space: For Kids Who Really Love Space! (p. 1618)
—Spooky Bus. (p. 1631)
—Spring: Bright Baby Touch & Feel. (p. 1634)
—Squishy Turtle & Friends. (p. 1637)
—Squishy Turtle Cloth Book. (p. 1637)
—Sticker Activity ABC. (p. 1650)
—Sticker Doodle Boo! (p. 1650)
—Sticker Doodle Do. (p. 1650)
—Sticker Doodle I Love You! (p. 1650)
—Sticker Doodle You. (p. 1650)
—Sun. (p. 1675)
—Super Dinky Doodles. (p. 1679)
—T Is for Truck. (p. 1694)
—Talent Show. Crimi-Trent, Ellen, illus. (p. 1701)
—Tea Party Set. (p. 1708)
—Telling Time. (p. 1717)
—Ten Barnyard Babies. (p. 1718)
—Tiger - Animal Buddies. (p. 1748)
—Toddler Town - City. (p. 1761)
—Toddler Town: Farm. (p. 1761)
—Toddler Town Play Set. (p. 1761)
—Toddler Town - Zoo. (p. 1761)
—Tracing & Pen Control. (p. 1775)
—Treasure Hunt: Around the House. (p. 1781)
—Treasure Hunt: at the Zoo. (p. 1781)
—Treasure Hunt for Boys. (p. 1781)
—Treasure Hunt for Girls. (p. 1781)
—Treasure Hunt: on the Farm. (p. 1781)
—Trucks. (p. 1791)
—Tweet! Tweet! (p. 1800)
—Uppercase Alphabet. (p. 1825)
—Vampire Pets. (p. 1832)
—Who's My Mom? (p. 1920)
—Wipe Clean Activity Work Book. (p. 1939)
—Wipe Clean - Early Learning. (p. 1939)
—Wipe Clean: Picture Puzzles. (p. 1939)
—Wipe Clean: Starting School. (p. 1939)
—Wipe Clean Workbook Numbers 1-20. (p. 1939)
—Words. (p. 1951)
—Words - A High Contrast Board Book. (p. 1951)
—Words Palabras. (p. 1952)
Priddy, Roger, jt. auth. see Crimi-Trent, Ellen.
Priddy, Roger, jt. auth. see Kappely, Sarah.
Priddy, Roger, jt. auth. see Learning Fun, Early.
Priddy, Roger, jt. auth. see Martin, Bill, Jr.
Priddy, Roger, jt. auth. see Mugford, Simon.
Priddy, Roger, jt. auth. see Priddy Books Staff.
Priddy, Roger, jt. auth. see Rigg, Jo.
Priddy, Roger, jt. auth. see Rupnik, Louise.
Priddy, Roger, jt. auth. see Tainsh, Robert.
Priddy, Roger & Crimi-Trent, Ellen. Let's Get Ready for School. (p. 997)
—My First Day at School. (p. 1206)
—School House. (p. 1523)
—Schoolies - Making Friends. (p. 1524)
—Schoolies - My School Day. (p. 1524)
—Schoolies: Spencer's Sticker Activity Book. (p. 1524)
Priddy, Roger & King, Kathleen. Tate's Bake Shop Baking with Kids. (p. 1707)
Priddy, Roger & Powell, Sarah. Cardboard Box Book. Sido, Barbi, illus. (p. 265)
Priddy, Roger & Priddy Books Staff. Adam & Eve. (p. 11)
—Noah's Ark. (p. 1261)
—Preschool Color & Activity Book. (p. 1396)
—Story of Jesus. (p. 1658)
—Story of Moses. (p. 1659)
Pride, Dana L. So How Is That a Bully? (p. 1602)
Pride, Felicia. Patterson Heights. (p. 1329)
Pride, Felicia, et al. Hallway Diaries: How to Be down Double Act the Summer She Learned to Dance. (p. 739)
Pride, Matthew, illus. see Dukovich, Amanda J.
Pride, Wallace. Mighty Christmas Oak. (p. 1140)
Pride, William M. Study Guide: Used with ... Pride-Foundations of Marketing. (p. 1670)
Pridemore, Lola. Other Girls: A Young Adult Paranormal Novel About a Witch, a Ghost & a Mystery. (p. 1306)
Pridham, Caroline. Twilight & Dawn: Simple Talks on the Six Days of Creation. (p. 1801)
Priebe, Mac. EagleQuest CD-ROM + the Bald Eagle Book (p. 492)
—FalconQuest CD-ROM + the Peregrine Falcon Book. (p. 566)
Priebe, Val. Five Fouls & You're Out! Santillan, Jorge H., illus. (p. 600)
—I Don't Want to Live on the Tennis Court Santillan, Jorge H., illus. (p. 838)
—I Only Surf Online Santillan, Jorge H., illus. (p. 844)
—It's Hard to Dribble with Your Feet Santillan, Jorge H., illus. (p. 897)
Prien, Jochen & Stemmer, Gerhard. Jagdgeswader 3 Udet in WWII: Ii. /Jg 3 in Action with the Messerschmitt Bf 109. (p. 905)
Priest, A. Breakthrough. (p. 225)
Priest, A., jt. auth. see Jacobs, John Hornor.
Priest, Bonnie. Nancy & the Nutrition Tree. (p. 1228)
Priest, Cherie. I Am Princess X. Ciesemier, Kali, illus. (p. 833)
Priest, Christopher. Avengers Disassembled: Iron Man, Thor, & Captain America. Di Vito, Andrea et al, illus. (p. 119)
—Brothers & Keepers. (p. 231)
—Crew: Big Trouble in Little Mogadishu. Bennett, Joe, illus. (p. 382)
Priest, Dick, illus. see Balch, Glenn.
Priest, Jerry and Beverly. ABC Memory Verse Program. (p. 3)
Priest, Robert. Paper Sword. (p. 1323)
—Rosa Rose. Krygsman, Joan, illus. (p. 1489)
—Second Kiss: Spell Crossed. (p. 1539)
Priest, Saira, photos by. If We Were... (p. 854)
Priesti, Lori, jt. auth. see Daronco, Mickey.
Priestley, Alice, illus. see Cumming, Peter.
Priestley, Alice, illus. see Gilmore, Rachna.
Priestley, Alice, illus. see Setterington, Ken.
Priestley, Chris. Billy Wizard. Priestley, Chris, illus. (p. 187)
—Dead of Winter. (p. 417)
—Death & the Arrow: A Gripping Tale of Murder & Revenge. (p. 420)
—Redwulf's Curse. (p. 1456)
—Tales of Terror from the Black Ship. Roberts, David, illus. (p. 1702)
—Tales of Terror from the Tunnel's Mouth. Roberts, David, illus. (p. 1702)
—Through Dead Eyes. (p. 1744)
—Uncle Montague's Tales of Terror. Roberts, David, illus. (p. 1812)
Priestley, J. B. Inspector Calls. Bryant, Clive, ed. (p. 878)
Priestley, Michael. 25 High-Interest: Low Readability Fiction & Nonfiction Passages to Help Struggling Readers Build Comprehension & Test-Taking Skills. (p. 1996)
—Hi-Lo Passages to Build Comprehension: 25 High-Interest/Low Readability Fiction & Nonfiction Passages to Help Struggling Readers Build Comprehension & Test-Taking Skills. (p. 775)
—Hi-Lo Passages to Build Reading Comprehension: 25 High-Interest/Low Readability Fiction & Nonfiction Passages to Help Struggling Readers Build Comprehension & Test-Taking Skills. (p. 775)
—Standardized Test Practice - Writing: 25 Reproducible Mini-Tests That Help Students Prepare for & Succeed on Standardized Tests. (p. 1639)
—Writing: 25 Reproducible Mini-Tests That Help Students Prepare for & Succeed on Standardized Tests. (p. 1964)
Priestley, Michael Priestley. Charts, Tables & Graphs: 30 Skill-Building Reproducible Pages That Prepare Kids for Standardized Tests. (p. 294)
Prieto, Anita C. B Is for Bookworm: A Library Alphabet. Graef, Renee, illus. (p. 122)
—Little Louisiana. Knorr, Laura, illus. (p. 1031)
—P Is for Pelican: A Louisiana Alphabet. Knorr, Laura, illus. (p. 1316)
—Timothy Hubble & the King Cake Party Howard, Virginia, illus. (p. 1755)
Prieto, Antonio, illus. see Martinez, Raul.
Prieto, Iliana. Princesa del Retrato y el Dragon Rey. (p. 1402)
Prieto, Iván, illus. see Liván, Paco.
Prieto, Rafaela. Myvera's Love of Sunshine. (p. 1227)
Prigioniero, Lily. De las cuevas a los Lienzos. (p. 416)
—From Caves to Canvas & de las cuevas a los Lienzos: 6 English, 6 Spanish Adaptations Hanner, Albert, illus. (p. 642)
Prigmore, Shane, illus. see Ganz-Schmitt, Sue.
Prigmore, Shane, illus. see Scieszka, Jon.
Prignano, Barbara. Angelo: The Underappreciated Ant. (p. 74)
—How Bunnies Got Their Cottontails. (p. 805)
—Tiny Tomato & His Terrific Manners. Kalpart, illus. (p. 1757)
Prikazsky, Amy. You Are So Special, Little One. (p. 1973)
Prima Games Staff. Pokemon Activity Book. (p. 1377)
Primavera, Elise. Auntie Claus: Home for the Holidays. Primavera, Elise, illus. (p. 115)
—Auntie Claus & the Key to Christmas. (p. 115)
—Fred & Anthony Meet the Heinie Goblins from the Black Lagoon. Primavera, Elise, illus. (p. 632)
—House at the End of Ladybug Lane. Docampo, Valeria, illus. (p. 803)
—Libby of High Hopes. Primavera, Elise, illus. (p. 1005)
—Louise the Big Cheese: Divine Diva. Goode, Diane, illus. (p. 1058)
—Louise the Big Cheese. Goode, Diane, illus. (p. 1058)
—Louise the Big Cheese & the Back-To-School Smarty-Pants. Goode, Diane, illus. (p. 1058)
—Louise the Big Cheese & the La-Di-Da Shoes. Goode, Diane, illus. (p. 1058)
—Louise the Big Cheese & the Ooh-la-La Charm School. Goode, Diane, illus. (p. 1058)
—Ms. Rapscott's Girls. (p. 1188)
—Project Blue Ribbon. Primavera, Elise, illus. (p. 1410)
—Secret Order Gumm Street Girl (p. 1543)
—Secret Order of the Gumm Street Girls. Primavera, Elise, illus. (p. 1543)
Primavera, Elise, illus. see Fred, Anthony.
Primavera, Elise, jt. auth. see Arevamirp, Esile.
Primavera, Elise & Arevamirp, Esile. Fred & Anthony Escape from the Netherworld. Primavera, Elise, illus. (p. 632)
Prime, D. De Nuevo en Vacaciones. (p. 416)
—Hacen un Album de Recortes. (p. 735)
—Van al Museo. (p. 1832)
Prime, Derek. Gofors & Gumps. (p. 692)
—Sarah & Paul Go Back to School: Discover about God & the Bible. Bk. 1 (p. 1514)
—Sarah & Paul Go on Holiday Again: Discover about Being a Christian. (p. 1514)
—Sarah & Paul Go to the Museum: Discover about the Ten Commandments. (p. 1514)
—Sarah & Paul Go to the Seaside. (p. 1514)
—Sarah & Paul Have a Visitor: Discover about the Lord Jesus Christ. (p. 1514)
—Sarah & Paul Make a Scrapbook. (p. 1514)
Prime, Ranchor. Hinduism (p. 780)
—Hinduism. (p. 780)
Primeau, Chuck, illus. see King, Trey.
Primeau, Chuck, illus. see Reader's Digest Staff.
Primiano, Jay, jt. auth. see Rocco, John.
Primm, Elvin Blake. Lyrics of Love. (p. 1067)
Primm, Patricia, illus. see Dudley, Marie Luther.
Primm, Thomas, illus. see Newth, Rebecca.
Primmasone, Bruce, illus. see Hasan, K. A.
Primmer, Rachel. Pentomino Piazza (p. 1338)
Prince, Amy, tr. see Ehlert, Lois.
Prince, Andrea, illus. see Morgan, Emily.
Prince, April Jones. Dig In! Berg, Michelle, illus. (p. 438)
—Dive In! Berg, Michelle, illus. (p. 454)
—Jackie Robinson: He Led the Way. Casilla, Robert, illus. (p. 904)
—Twenty-One Elephants & Still Standing. Roca, François, illus. (p. 1801)
—What Do Wheels Do All Day? Laroche, Giles, illus. (p. 1882)
—Who Was Frederick Douglass? (p. 1918)
—Who Was Frederick Douglass? Squier, Robert & Harrison, Nancy, illus. (p. 1918)
—Who Was Mark Twain? O'Brien, John, illus. (p. 1918)
—Who Was Mark Twain? O'Brien, John A. & Harrison, Nancy, illus. (p. 1918)
—¿Qué Hacen las Ruedas Todo el Día? Laroche, Giles, illus. (p. 1423)
—¿Quién Fue Mark Twain? (Who Was Mark Twain?) O'Brien, John, illus. (p. 1427)
Prince, Audrey, ed. see Larson, Jennifer.
Prince, Brian, illus. see Jonell, Bob.
Prince, Bryan. I Came As a Stranger: The Underground Railroad. (p. 834)
Prince, Cheryl. Belle's Wild Journey. (p. 163)
Prince, Daniel. Zoe the Zookeeper. (p. 1987)
Prince, Donnie. Baseball: It's More Than A Game. (p. 140)
Prince, JanetMcKenzie. My Gluten-Free Knoxville: Miss Janet's Gluten-Free Zone. (p. 1210)
Prince, Joshua. I Saw an Ant on the Railroad Track. Pamintuan, Macky, illus. (p. 845)
Prince, Liz. Tomboy: A Graphic Memoir. (p. 1764)
Prince, Maggie. House on Hound Hill. (p. 803)
Prince, Mark E. I'm Happy When. (p. 859)
Prince, Melissa B. Red Tutu: A Ballerina Poem. (p. 1455)
Prince of Wales Publishing Co. Staff & HRH Prince of Wales Staff. Harmony: A Vision for Our Future. (p. 749)
Prince, Ricky. What Made That Noise? (p. 1892)
Prince Rupert Writers' Group Staff. North Coast Collected. Speck, Dave, ed. (p. 1265)
Prince, Savannah. Manny the Mol. (p. 1088)
Prince Wallaker, Jillayne, jt. auth. see Wallaker, Jillayne Prince.
Princenthal, Nancy. Heide Fasnacht. (p. 762)
Princess Adjepong. My First Shapes & Numbers Colouring Book. (p. 1208)
Princess Marie, illus. see Kole, Ted & Genet, John, eds.
Princess Protection Program Staff. Palace of Mystery (p. 1319)
Prince-Stokes, Cathy. Story of Peabo Edsall, Steven, illus. (p. 1659)
Princeton Review Staff. Cracking the TOEFL IBT 2016. (p. 375)
Principe, Hilda. My Red Hat Grandma & Me. (p. 1217)
Principe, Tami. Green Rabbit: Rabbits Aren't Supposed to Be Green! (p. 722)
Prindle House, creator. Mommy's Pleasures... Children's Treasures!, Volume 1. (p. 1163)
Prindle, Twyla. Can I Have Some Money Please? Hansen, Lorie Miller, illus. (p. 258)
—Where Is My Money? Jennings, Randy, illus. (p. 1908)
Prindle, Twyla D. Can I Have Some Money Please? Hansen, Lorie, illus. (p. 258)
—Deception: The Devil Hears Your Prayers Too. (p. 421)
—Teacher's Lounge. (p. 1709)
Prineas, Sarah. Ash & Bramble. (p. 105)
—Found. Caparo, Antonio Javier, illus. (p. 624)
—Lost. (p. 1054)
—Lost. Caparo, Antonio Javier, illus. (p. 1054)
—Magic Thief. Caparo, Antonio Javier, illus. (p. 1073)
—Magic Thief - Found. Caparo, Antonio Javier, illus. (p. 1073)
—Magic Thief - Home. Caparo, Antonio Javier, illus. (p. 1073)
—Magic Thief: Home. Caparo, Antonio Javier, illus. (p. 1074)
—Magic Thief - Lost. Caparo, Antonio Javier, illus. (p. 1073)
—Moonkind. (p. 1172)
—Summerkin. (p. 1675)
—Winterling (p. 1938)
—Winterling. (p. 1938)
Pringle, Betsy Henry, ed. see Gordon, David George.
Pringle, Cindy & Pringle, Kirby. Happy Tails: The Call of Nature. (p. 746)
—Happy Tails: Earl & Pearl on the Farm. (p. 746)
Pringle, Eric. Big George & the Winter King. Paine, Colin, illus. (p. 181)
Pringle, Kirby, jt. auth. see Pringle, Cindy.
Pringle, Laurence. Alligators & Crocodiles! Henderson, Meryl, illus. (p. 47)
—American Slave, American Hero: York of the Lewis & Clark Expedition. Van Wright, Cornelius & Hu, Ying-Hwa, illus. (p. 63)
—Bats! Strange & Wonderful. Henderson, Meryl, illus. (p. 145)
—Billions of Years, Amazing Changes: The Story of Evolution. Jenkins, Steve, illus. (p. 187)
—Cicadas! Strange & Wonderful. Henderson, Meryle, illus. (p. 318)
—Crows! Strange & Wonderful. Robert, Marstall & Marstall, Bob, illus. (p. 386)
—Dog of Discovery: A Newfoundland's Adventures with Lewis & Clark. (p. 461)
—Frogs! Strange & Wonderful. Henderson, Meryl, illus. (p. 641)
—Ice! The Amazing History of the Ice Business. (p. 850)
—Imagine a Dragon. Neilan, Eujin Kim, illus. (p. 860)
—Octopuses! Strange & Wonderful. Henderson, Meryl, illus. (p. 1278)
—Penguins! Strange & Wonderful. Henderson, Meryl, illus. (p. 1337)
—Scorpion Man: Exploring the World of Scorpions. Polis, Gary A., illus. (p. 1530)
—Scorpions! Strange & Wonderful. Henderson, Meryl, illus. (p. 1530)
—Secret Life of the Woolly Bear Caterpillar. Paley, Joan, illus. (p. 1541)
—Sharks! Strange & Wonderful. Henderson, Meryl, illus. (p. 1563)
—Snakes! Strange & Wonderful. Henderson, Meryl, illus. (p. 1596)
—Whales! Strange & Wonderful. Henderson, Meryl, illus. (p. 1878)
Pringle, Victoria, illus. see Garcia, Emmett Shkeme & Garcia, Emmett.
Pringle, Victoria, illus. see Garcia, Emmett Shkeme.
Prinja, Raman. Galaxies & the Runaway Universe. (p. 653)
—Spacecraft & the Journey into Space. (p. 1620)
—To the Planets & Beyond. (p. 1759)
Prinja, Raman, jt. auth. see Parker, Steve.
Prinja, Raman K. Comets, Asteroids, & Meteors (p. 348)
—Moon (p. 1171)
—Stars & Constellations (p. 1643)
—Sun (p. 1675)
Prins, Johanna, tr. see Hof, Marjolijn.
Prins, Marcel & Steenhuis, Peter Henk. Hidden Like Anne Frank: 14 True Stories of Survival. Watkinson, Laura, illus. (p. 776)
Prins, Piet. Flying Phantom. (p. 610)
—Grim Reaper. (p. 724)
—Haunted Castle. (p. 753)
—Hideout in the Swamp. (p. 777)
—Lonely Sentinel. (p. 1046)
—Mystery of the Abandoned Mill. Kramer, Jaap, illus. (p. 1225)
—Sailing Sleuths. Kramer, Jaap, illus. (p. 1503)
—Scout's Distant Journey. (p. 1532)
—Search for Sheltie. Kramer, Jaap, illus. (p. 1537)
—Stefan Derksen's Polar Adventure. (p. 1646)
—Treasure of Rodensteyn Castle. Kramer, Jaap, illus. (p. 1782)
Prins, Piet & McAdam, Fraser. Beggars Victory: The Sequel to Dispelling the Tyranny. (p. 159)
—For the Heart of Holland. (p. 616)
Print Mafia Staff, jt. auth. see Mooney, Melissa Duke.
Print Music Staff. Wiggles Party Song & Activity Book. (p. 1928)
Printers, Caxton. Rufus & Friends. (p. 1494)
Printworks KMG Staff, jt. auth. see Dover Staff.
Printworks KMG Staff, jt. auth. see Dover.
Prinz, Yvonne. All You Get Is Me. (p. 46)
—Still There, Clare. (p. 1650)
—Vinyl Princess. (p. 1843)
Prioleau, J. N. Clyde. (p. 336)
—Clyde & His Messy Room. (p. 336)
Prior, Jennifer. All Aboard! How Trains Work (p. 42)
—All Aboard! How Trains Work. (p. 42)
—America's Man-Made Landmarks. (p. 64)
—America's Natural Landmarks. (p. 64)
—Capital Resources & the Economy. (p. 262)
—Digestive System. (p. 438)
—Five Senses. (p. 601)
—Human Life Cycle. (p. 826)
—Map Skills Grade 3. (p. 1090)
—Our Natural Resources. (p. 1309)
—Take Off! All about Airplanes (p. 1697)
—Take Off! All about Airplanes. (p. 1697)
—TIME for Kids: Practicing for Today's Tests Language Arts Level 3 (p. 1751)
—Zoom! How Cars Move (p. 1989)
—Zoom! How Cars Move. (p. 1989)
Prior, Jennifer, jt. auth. see Prior, Jennifer Overend.
Prior, Jennifer Overend. Map Skills, Grade 4. (p. 1090)
Prior, Jennifer Overend & Prior, Jennifer. Addition & Subtraction: 14 Reproducible Games That Help Struggling Learners Practice & Really Master Basic Addition & Subtraction Skills. (p. 12)

P

—Time & Money: 14 Reproducible Games That Help Struggling Learners Practice & Really Master Basic Time & Money Skills. (p. 1751)
Prior, Katherine. Workers' Rights. (p. 1952)
Prior, Natalie. Lily Quench & the Dragon of Ashby Dawson, Janine, illus. (p. 1018)
Prior, Natalie, jt. auth. see Prior, Natalie Jane.
Prior, Natalie Jane. Fireworks & Darkness. (p. 592)
—Lily Quench 6 Hand of Manuelo Dawson, Janine, illus. (p. 1018)
—Lily Quench & the Hand of Manuelo. Dawson, Janine, illus. (p. 1018)
—Lily Quench & the Lighthouse of Skellig Mor (p. 1018)
—Search for King Dragon. Dawson, Janine, illus. (p. 1537)
—Star. Pignataro, Anna, illus. (p. 1640)
—Star Locket. (p. 1640)
—Sun. Pignataro, Anna, illus. (p. 1675)
Prior, Natalie Jane & Dawson, Kathy. Lily Quench & the Magician's Pyramid (p. 1018)
Prior, Natalie Jane & Prior, Natalie. Lily Quench & the Treasure of Mote Ely (p. 1018)
Prior, R. W. Great Monarch Butterfly Chase. Loven, Beth Glick, illus. (p. 717)
Priory Books Staff, jt. auth. see Swift, Jonathan.
Pripps, Robert N., jt. auth. see Publications International Ltd. Staff.
Prisant, Guillermo Murray. Que Miedo! (p. 1424)
Prisant, Guillermo Murray & Murray, Guillermo. Escalofrio. (p. 534)
—Gente de Las Sombras. (p. 661)
Prischmann, Deirdre A. Ants (p. 90)
—Beetles (p. 158)
—Poop-Eaters: Dung Beetles in the Food Chain (p. 1383)
Priscilla, Louis, illus. see Coombs, Charles.
Priscilla, Marie. Il Bitty Book. (p. 856)
Prisco & Benchmark Education Co. Staff. Interpreting Our Dreams. (p. 880)
Prisco, Pete. Mark Brunnell: Super Southpaw. (p. 1095)
Pristash, Nicole. Blue. (p. 202)
—Carl Edwards. (p. 269)
—Dale Earnhardt Jr. (p. 401)
—Green. (p. 721)
—Jeff Gordon. (p. 911)
—Jimmie Johnson. (p. 918)
—Kevin Harvick. (p. 950)
—Orange. (p. 1301)
—Purple. (p. 1419)
—Red. (p. 1453)
—Ryan Newman. (p. 1499)
—Yellow. (p. 1970)
Pritchard, Alicia Michele. Critter Pics. (p. 384)
Pritchard, David. Ghost of Spring. (p. 671)
Pritchard, Eva. Emotional Roadtrip. (p. 520)
Pritchard, G. Rosemary Sage & the Man in Black. (p. 1489)
Pritchard, Heather. Got Baseball? (p. 703)
—Got Dementia? Riffey, Rebecca, illus. (p. 703)
—Got Dyslexia? (p. 703)
Pritchard, Herman S. Nautical Road: A Straight Forward Approach to Learning the Navigation Rules. Helwig, Teresa L., ed. (p. 1237)
Pritchard, Jean. Bobcat Bootcamp in Orange City. Dakins, Todd, illus. (p. 206)
Pritchard, John. Yazoo Blues. (p. 1968)
Pritchard, Louise, illus. see Tossell, David H.
Pritchard, Mark A. Billy Christmas. (p. 187)
Pritchard, Mary. Mrs P's Poems. Gasking, Terry, ed. (p. 1187)
Pritchard, Phil. Travels with Stanley. (p. 1780)
Pritchard, Richard Huw, jt. auth. see Richards, Aled.
Pritchett and Hull Associates, illus. see Olson, Karen.
Pritchett and Hull Associates, Inc., illus. see Olson, Karen.
Pritchett, Andy. Stick! (p. 1649)
Pritchett, Bev. Tanzania in Pictures. (p. 1705)
Pritchett, Dylan. First Music. Banks, Erin, illus. (p. 596)
Pritchett, Jerald. Mr. Bird & the Fifth Day. (p. 1184)
Pritchett, Lee. Tale of Greta Gumboot & Other Stories. (p. 1699)
Pritelli, Maria Cristina, illus. see Jones, Rob Lloyd.
Pritelli, Maria Cristina, illus. see Lewis, J. Patrick.
Pritelli, Maria Cristina, illus. see Rosen, Michael J.
Pritt, Carol. Deviltry Afoot. (p. 432)
Pritzker, Barry M. & Rosier, Paul C. Hopi. (p. 797)
Privateer, Mark & Dunlap, Jennifer. Sharks Don't Eat Peanut Butter. (p. 1563)
Privateer Press, creator. Warmachine Escalation. (p. 1858)
—Warmachine: Prime: Steam Powered Miniatures Combat. (p. 1858)
Priwer, Shana, jt. auth. see Phillips, Cynthia.
Prm, Katherine & Dee, Stacy. Veil. (p. 1834)
Pro Familia, Deutsche Gesellschaft für Sexualberatung und Familienplanung Staff, jt. auth. see International Center for Assault Prevention Staff.
Probasco, Teri. Blue Jean Gum. (p. 203)
Probert Gott, Patricia. Horse Tails by Rafiji the Safari Horse: Based on a True Story. (p. 800)
Probert, Mitzi. Esther's Miracle at the Manger. (p. 538)
Probert, Tim, illus. see Baker, Kim.
Probert, Tim, illus. see Baker, Kimberly.
Probert, Tim, illus. see Bildner, Phil.
Probsdorfer, Maria-Antoinette. Elephant World. (p. 511)
Probst, Jeff. Amazing Places: Weird Trivia & Unbelievable Facts to Test Your Knowledge about the Most Extreme Places on Earth! (p. 55)
—Outrageous Animals: Weird Trivia & Unbelievable Facts to Test Your Knowledge about Mammals, Fish, Insects & More! (p. 1313)
—Sabotage. (p. 1500)
—Stranded: the Complete Adventure. (p. 1664)
Probst, Jeff & Tebbetts, Chris. Stranded. (p. 1664)
—Trial by Fire. (p. 1785)
Probst, Jeff & Tebbetts, Christopher. Forbidden Passage. (p. 616)
—Sabotage. (p. 1500)
—Survivors. (p. 1687)
—Trial by Fire. (p. 1785)
Probst, Sharon Patrice, jt. auth. see Kratzert, Barbara.
Proch, Gregory, illus. see Olson, Tod.
Prochaska, Dan J. Courage (p. 372)
Prochovnic, Dawn Babb. Best Day in Room A: Sign Language for School Activities. Bauer, Stephanie, illus. (p. 168)
—Big Blue Bowl: Sign Language for Food. Bauer, Stephanie, illus. (p. 178)
—Famous Fenton Has a Farm: Sign Language for Farm Animals. Bauer, Stephanie, illus. (p. 569)
—Four Seasons! Five Senses! Sign Language for the Seasons & Senses. Bauer, Stephanie, illus. (p. 625)
—Hip Hip Hooray! It's Family Day! Sign Language for Family. Bauer, Stephanie, illus. (p. 780)
—Nest Where I Like to Rest: Sign Language for Animals. Bauer, Stephanie, illus. (p. 1242)
—One Trick for One Treat: Sign Language for Numbers. Bauer, Stephanie, illus. (p. 1297)
—Opposites Everywhere: Sign Language for Opposites. Bauer, Stephanie, illus. (p. 1301)
—See the Colors: Sign Language for Colors. Bauer, Stephanie, illus. (p. 1547)
—Shape Detective: Sign Language for Shapes. Bauer, Stephanie, illus. (p. 1560)
—Silly Sue: Sign Language for Actions. Bauer, Stephanie, illus. (p. 1576)
—So Many Feelings: Sign Language for Feelings & Emotions. Bauer, Stephanie, illus. (p. 1602)
—Story Time with Signs & Rhymes Bauer, Stephanie, illus. (p. 1663)
—There's a Story in My Head: Sign Language for Body Parts. Bauer, Stephanie, illus. (p. 1731)
—to Z Sign with Me: Sign Language for the Alphabet. Bauer, Stephanie, illus. (p. 1759)
—Watch Me Go! Sign Language for Vehicles. Bauer, Stephanie, illus. (p. 1861)
—Wear a Silly Hat: Sign Language for Clothing. Bauer, Stephanie, illus. (p. 1869)
Prock, Lisa Albers, ed. see Etingoff, Kim.
Prock, Lisa Albers, ed. see Scott, Celicia.
Prock, Lisa Albers, ed. see Waters, Rosa.
Procter, Bill, illus. see Procter, Diann.
Procter, Diann. It Happened in the Goldfish Bowl. Procter, Bill, illus. (p. 894)
proctor, brian, illus. see Crews, G.
Proctor, Darrell. Cigarette Monster. (p. 319)
Proctor, Jon, illus. see Peters, Stephanie True.
Proctor, Jon, illus. see Yomtov, Nel.
Proctor, Jon, illus. see Yomtov, Nelson.
Proctor, Mary. Stories of Starland. (p. 1655)
Proctor, Peter, illus. see Active Spud Press & Ettinger, Steve.
Proctor, Thomas E., jt. auth. see Mazur, Glen A.
Proctor, Thomas E. & Gosse, Jonathan F. Printreading for Welders: Text. (p. 1407)
—Printreading for Welders: Answer Key. (p. 1407)
—Printreading for Welders: Resource Guide. (p. 1407)
Proctor, Thomas E. & Toenjes, Leonard P. Printreading for Residential & Light Commercial Construction: Text. (p. 1407)
—Printreading for Residential & Light Commercial Construction: Answer Key. (p. 1407)
—Printreading for Residential Construction: Text. (p. 1407)
—Printreading for Residential Construction: Answer Key. (p. 1407)
—Printreading for Residential Construction: Resource Guide. (p. 1407)
Proctor, Tina, jt. auth. see DeNomme, Donna.
Prodor, Bob, illus. see Davidge, James.
Producciones, Sunset, illus. see Cordero, Silvia Jaeger & Cordero, Silvia Jaegar.
Produccions Editorials, Trèvol, jt. auth. see Trévol, S. A.
Produccions Editorials, Trèvol & Trévol, S. A. ¡No Quiero Bañarme! Peris, Carme, illus. (p. 1260)
Productions, Donkey Ollie. Tales of Donkey Ollie. (p. 1702)
Profane Existence. Profane Existence: Making Punk a Threat Again. (p. 1409)
Proferes, Jo, illus. see Williams, Jack R.
Professor Bubbledunk. Stories from the Mugglewhuft. (p. 1654)
Proffitt, Kim. Coco the Little Red Bird: Massy Returns. (p. 337)
Profilet, Cynthia. Maggie's Golden Moment. Barron, Ann, illus. (p. 1071)
Profiri, Charline. Guess Who's in the Desert. Swan, Susan, illus. (p. 729)
—Rain, Rain, Stay Today: Southwestern Nursery Rhymes. Watson, Laura, illus. (p. 1435)
Progressive Langauge Staff, prod. Bluw Wolf & Friends (p. 204)
Proimos, James. 12 Things to Do Before You Crash & Burn. (p. 1994)
—Complete Adventures of Johnny Mutton. (p. 352)
—Knuckle & Potty Destroy Happy World. Proimos, James, illus. (p. 965)
—Todd's TV. Proimos, James, illus. (p. 1761)
Proimos, James, illus. see Collins, Suzanne.
Proimos, James, III & Proimos, James, Jr. Apocalypse Bow Wow. Proimos, James, Jr., illus. (p. 91)
Proimos, James, Jr., jt. auth. see Proimos, James, III.
Project Firefly, illus. see Weeks, Kermit.
Project Firefly Animation Studios, illus. see Pearson, Iris & Merrill, Mike.
Project Lane County Mathematics Staff. Alternate Problem Solving Mathematics. (p. 50)
Project Runway. Project Runway Fashion Paper Doll Kit - African American Girl. (p. 1410)
—Project Runway Fashion Paper Doll Kit - Asian Girl. (p. 1410)
—Project Runway Fashion Paper Doll Kit - Blonde Girl. (p. 1410)
—Project Runway Fashion Paper Doll Kit - Brunette Girl. (p. 1410)
—Project Runway Fashion Paper Doll Kit - Caucasian Girl. (p. 1410)
Prokash, Marie. Madison's Adventure. (p. 1070)
Prokofiev, Sergei. Love for Three Oranges. Gaudasinska, Elzbieta, illus. (p. 1059)
—Peter & the Wolf. Raschka, Chris, illus. (p. 1346)
Prokofiev, Sergei, jt. auth. see Malone, Peter.
Prokopchak, Ann. Sunburn: Bridging School to Home - C. Minnich, Matt, illus. (p. 1676)
Prokopowicz, Jen. Look Out for Bugs. (p. 1049)
Prokopowicz, Linda. Rocky the Reading Dog. (p. 1484)
Prokos, Anna. Earthquakes. (p. 497)
—Guilty by a Hair! Real-Life DNA Matches! (p. 730)
—Killer Wallpaper: True Cases of Deadly Poisonings. (p. 956)
—Rocks & Minerals. (p. 1483)
—Tornadoes. (p. 1770)
Prokos, Anna & Keedle, Jayne. Tsunamis & Floods. (p. 1795)
Prokos, Anna & Voege, Debra. Half-Pipe Homonyms. Angle, Scott, illus. (p. 736)
—Slap Shot Synonyms & Antonyms. (p. 1588)
—Track Star Sentences. (p. 1775)
Prole, Helen, illus. see David, Juliet & Ayliffe, Alex.
Prole, Helen, illus. see David, Juliet.
Promitzer, Rebecca. Pickle King. (p. 1354)
Pronnette, Veronica H. Ancestors Anansi & the Light: A Delightful African Proverb Retold about How Light was Created by a Spider. (p. 67)
Propaganda, Amanda. People Flavors. (p. 1339)
Propes, Chrysti Carol. I Am. Bostrom, Laura, illus. (p. 831)
—I Am. Bostrom, Laura L., illus. (p. 831)
—I Am Here. Bostrom, Laura, illus. (p. 833)
Prophet, Elizabeth Clare. AFRA: Brother of Light. (p. 26)
Prophet, John. Mystery at the Salt Marsh Winery: A Casey Miller Mystery. (p. 1224)
Prophet, John M. Body in the Salt Marsh Boatyard: A Casey Miller Mystery. (p. 207)
Propp, Vera W. When the Soldiers Were Gone: A Novel. (p. 1905)
Propst, Milam McGraw. Further Adventures of Oclee Nash. (p. 650)
Prose, Francine. After. (p. 28)
—Bullyville. (p. 241)
—Goldengrove. (p. 695)
—Rhino, Rhino, Sweet Potato. Armstrong, Matthew S., illus. (p. 1467)
—Touch. (p. 1772)
—Turning. (p. 1798)
Prosek, James. Day My Mother Left. Prosek, James, illus. (p. 413)
—Good Day's Fishing. Prosek, James, illus. (p. 697)
Prosek, James, jt. auth. see Keats, John.
Prosmitsky, Jenya, illus. see Cleary, Brian P.
Prosmitsky, Jenya, illus. see Strom, Yale.
Prosofsky, Merle, photos by see Ogle, Jennifer, et al.
Prosofsky, Merle, photos by see Walker, Lovoni.
Prosper, Tanzia. He Chose a Coat for Me! (p. 756)
Prosser, Jerry, ed. see Miller, Frank.
Prostko, Andrea. Strike One! (p. 1667)
Prostova, Elena & Shaw, Cathleen. Toe-rrific: A Simple Guide to Creating Healthy & Beautiful Feet. (p. 1761)
Protasov, Alexander. Fairy-Tales & Fantasies. (p. 564)
Prothero, Tiffany. Let's Go Green! An Earth-Friendly Coloring Book. (p. 997)
Prothero, Tiffany, illus. see Brezenoff, Steve.
Prothero, Tiffany, illus. see Dahl, Michael.
Protobunker Studio Staff & Wells, H. G. Guerra de los Mundos. Ruiz, Alfonso, illus. (p. 728)
Protopapas, Athanassios, jt. auth. see Palmer, Rebecca.
Protopopescu, Orel O. Thousand Peaks: Poems from China. Liu, Siyu, tr. from CHI. (p. 1740)
Protopopescu, Orel Odinov. Thelonious Mouse. Wilsdorf, Anne, illus. (p. 1728)
Prou, Suzanne. Amis de Monsieur Paul (p. 65)
Proudfit, Benjamin. Benjamin Franklin. (p. 164)
—Building the White House. (p. 239)
—Writing Book Reports. (p. 1964)
—Writing Letters. (p. 1965)
—Writing Opinion Papers. (p. 1965)
—Writing Poems. (p. 1965)
—Writing Research Papers. (p. 1965)
Proudfit, Isabel. Noah Webster, Father of the Dictionary. (p. 1261)
Proudfoot, Dean, jt. auth. see Holt, Sharon.
Proudfoot, Kenneth. Home Depot Manifesto! Positive Suggestions to Boost the Future of Retailing! (p. 792)
Proudfoot, Peter R., et al. Creepy Critters: A Pop-Up Book of Creatures That Jump, Crawl, & Fly. (p. 381)
Proulx, Denis, illus. see Esparza-Vela, Mary.
Proulx, Denis, illus. see Loccisano, Rina Fuda.
Proulx, Denis, illus. see Stein, Clem.
Proujan, Carl & National Geographic Learning Staff. Oceania & Antarctica. (p. 1277)
—Oceania & Antarctica - People & Places. (p. 1277)
—South America - Geography & Environments. (p. 1616)
Proulx, Denis, illus. see Averette, Sonya M.
Proulx, Denis, illus. see Gould, Terry.
Proulx, Denis, illus. see M a.
Proulx, Denis, illus. see Milot, Carryanne.
Proulx, Roxanna Darling. Princes of Pleasant Valley: A Day in the Life of Zyler & Xavier Sandon, Gina, illus. (p. 1402)
Proulx-Willis, Dana. Cinderella vs. the Stepfamily: A Fairy Tale Courtroom Event. (p. 320)
Proust, Marcel. En busca del tiempo perdido. Tomo I. (p. 522)
Prout, Louise, illus. see Bursztynski, Sue.
Prouty, Krista. George Monkeys Around (p. 663)
Provantini, Silvia. Runaway Pancake. (p. 1496)
Provata-Carlone, Mika, tr. see Seyvos, Florence.
Provencal, Francis, jt. auth. see McNamara, Catherine.
Provencher, Annemarie, illus. see Finneron, Karyn A.
Provencher, Olga J. Joey & Mup. (p. 920)
Provencher, Rose-Marie. Slithery Jake. Carter, Abby, illus. (p. 1591)
Provencio, Marta. Christmas Dragon. (p. 313)
Provensen, Alice. Buck Stops Here: The Presidents of the United States. (p. 234)
—Buck Stops Here. (p. 234)
—Day in the Life of Murphy. Provensen, Alice, illus. (p. 413)
—Glorius Flight. (p. 685)
—Master Swordsman & the Magic Doorway: Two Legends from Ancient China. Provensen, Alice, illus. (p. 1103)
Provensen, Alice, illus. see Brown, Margaret Wise.
Provensen, Alice, illus. see Watson, Jane Werner.
Provensen, Alice, illus. see Werner Watson, Jane.
Provensen, Alice & Provensen, Martin. Book of Seasons. (p. 211)
—Glorious Flight: Across the Channel with Louis Bleriot. Provensen, Alice & Provensen, Martin, illus. (p. 685)
Provensen, Martin, illus. see Brown, Margaret Wise.
Provensen, Martin, illus. see Watson, Jane Werner.
Provensen, Martin, illus. see Werner Watson, Jane.
Provensen, Martin, jt. auth. see Provensen, Alice.
Provenzale, Joseph C. Teeny, Tiny Termite. (p. 1715)
Provenzano, Jeannine, illus. see Venditti, Stacey Marie.
Provenzano, Stella Marie. How Rusty Rooster Found His Do. (p. 812)
Provenzo, Eugene F., Jr., et al. 100 Experiential Learning Activities for Social Studies, Literature, & the Arts, Grades 5-12. (p. 1998)
Provost, Gary & Stockwell, Gail Provost. David & Max. (p. 410)
Proysen, Alf. Mrs Pepperpot & the Treasure: A Classic Story with a Touch of Magic. Offen, Hilda, illus. (p. 1187)
—Mrs Pepperpot Minds the Baby: A Classic Story with a Touch of Magic. Offen, Hilda, illus. (p. 1187)
Prudence Wickham Heston. Sadie Plants Hydrangeas. (p. 1501)
Prudente, jt. auth. see Sabio.
Prud'homme, Jules, illus. see Leblanc, Louise.
Prud'homme, Jules, jt. auth. see Leblanc, Louise.
Prud'Homme, Jules, jt. auth. see Plante, Raymond.
Prud'homme, Jules, tr. see Leblanc, Louise.
Prueitt, Elisabeth M. & Robertson, Chad. Tartine. Ruffenach, France, photos by. (p. 1706)
Pruessen, Linda. Saving Eyesight: Adventures of Seva Around the World. (p. 1517)
Pruett, Candace. Visit with My Uncle Ted. (p. 1845)
Pruett, Jason. Seek & Find Book of Mormon Stories. (p. 1548)
Pruett, Mary. Color the Western Birds. (p. 343)
Pruett, Nichole Lee. My Best Friend. Rowton, Caitlin, illus. (p. 1196)
Pruett, Scott, et al. Rookie Racer. Morgan, Rick, illus. (p. 1487)
Pruissen, Catherine M. Como Iniciar y Administrar un Jardin Infantil. (p. 351)
Pruitt. BioInquiry. (p. 189)
Pruitt, Anna Seward. Day of Small Things. (p. 414)
Pruitt, Christine Lee. I'm Alright Day & Night! (p. 858)
Pruitt, Ginny, illus. see Carson, Diana Pastora.
Pruitt, Ginny, illus. see Kelly, Veronica & Goody, Wendy.
Pruitt, Gwendolyn, illus. see Ross, Jill.
Pruitt, Jason, illus. see Thigpen, Meredith.
Pruitt, Kat. Si Si the Circus Cat. Griftner, Rebecca, illus. (p. 1572)
Pruitt, Kimberly, jt. auth. see Ross, Kathryn.
Pruitt, Lisa A. Savanna & the Magic Boots. (p. 1516)
Pruitt, Nancy, et al. BioInquiry: Making Connections in Biology: Instructor s Presentation. (p. 189)
Pruitt, Pamela, jt. auth. see Johnston, Brenda A.
Pruitt, Patti B. Meeting Paddy O'Rourke: Book One. (p. 1123)
Pruitt, Vasta Z. Buttons & Babs Run Life's Race: Heavenly Pals Series. (p. 248)
Prunier, Jameâs, et al. Dinosaurio. Prunier, Jameâs et al, trs. (p. 443)
Prunier, James. Dinosaurs. Galeron, Henri, illus. (p. 444)
—Trains. Grant, Donald & Prunier, James, illus. (p. 1777)
Prunier, James, illus. see Jeunesse, Gallimard, et al.
Prus, Jennifer. Toddler's Abc of Blessings. McIlhany, illus. (p. 1761)
Prusha, Crystal. Day I Beat Mr. C. (p. 413)
Prust, Zeke A. Graphic Communications: The Printed Image. (p. 710)
—Graphic Communications. (p. 710)
Pruzansky, Binyomin. Stories for a Child's Heart. Katz, Tova, illus. (p. 1654)
Pry, Rose. Venus Vendetta. (p. 1836)
Pryce, Denise. Alexander & the Ring of Destiny. (p. 36)
Pryce, Sasha. Labby's Adventures. (p. 969)
Pryce, Trevor. Army of Frogs: A Kulipari Novel. Greene, Sanford, illus. (p. 100)
Pryce, Trevor & Naftali, Joel. Army of Frogs. Greene, Sanford, illus. (p. 100)
—Rainbow Serpent. Greene, Sanford, illus. (p. 1436)
Pryka, Aaron, ed. see Alexios, Rene.
Pryke, Gary. Adventures of Spike & Johnny: Somewhere Close to Forty. (p. 23)
Pryor, Bonnie. Captain Hannah Pritchard: The Hunt for Pirate Gold. (p. 264)
—Greenbrook Farm. (p. 722)
—Hannah Pritchard: Pirate of the Revolution. (p. 742)
—Happy Birthday, Mama. (p. 745)
—Iron Dragon: The Courageous Story of Lee Chin. (p. 888)
—Jenny's New Baby Sister. (p. 913)
—Lottie's Dream. (p. 1057)
—Mr. Munday & the Rustlers. (p. 1185)
—Mr. Munday & the Space Creatures. (p. 1185)
—Perfect Percy. (p. 1342)
—Pirate Hannah Pritchard: Captured! (p. 1362)
—Seth of the Lion People. (p. 1554)
—Simon's Escape: A Story of the Holocaust. (p. 1577)
Pryor, Jim, illus. see Robles, Tony.
Pryor, Joanne. I Spy... the Next Stop: Kids Camping the Coast from Maine to Georgia. (p. 846)
Pryor, John-Thomas, illus. see Nanavati, Daniel.
Pryor, Kimberley Jane. Amazing Armor. (p. 53)
—Ankylosaurus. (p. 84)
—Clever Camouflage. (p. 331)
—Cooperation. (p. 365)
—Courage. (p. 372)
—Doing Your Best. (p. 463)
—Fairness. (p. 563)
—Hearing. (p. 759)
—Helpfulness. (p. 766)
—Honesty. (p. 794)

—Integrity. (p. 879)
—Kindness. (p. 957)
—Mimicry & Relationships. (p. 1145)
—Muttaburrasaurus. (p. 1195)
—Protoceratops. (p. 1412)
—Respect. (p. 1463)
—Responsibility. (p. 1463)
—Seeing. (p. 1548)
—Self-Discipline. (p. 1549)
—Smelling. (p. 1593)
—Tasting. (p. 1707)
—Tolerance. (p. 1762)
—Touching. (p. 1772)
—Tricky Behavior. (p. 1786)
—Tyrannosaurus Rex. (p. 1805)
—Values (p. 1831)
—Velociraptor. (p. 1835)
—Venom, Poison, & Electricity. (p. 1836)
—Warning Colors. (p. 1858)
—Your Senses. (p. 1981)
Pryor, Kimberley Jane & Smart Apple Media Staff. Coral Reefs. (p. 366)
—Icy Seas. (p. 851)
—Mangrove Swamps. (p. 1087)
—Open Sea. (p. 1299)
—Rocky Shores. (p. 1484)
—Sea-Grass Beds. (p. 1534)
Pryor, Michael. 10 Futures. (p. 1993)
—Beneath Quentaris. (p. 164)
—Blaze of Glory. (p. 198)
—Extraordinaires. (p. 555)
—Heart of Gold. (p. 759)
—Hour of Need. (p. 802)
—Machine Wars. (p. 1068)
—Moment of Truth. (p. 1161)
—Quentaris in Flames. (p. 1425)
—Subterranean Stratagem. (p. 1671)
—Time of Trial. (p. 1752)
—Word of Honour. (p. 1951)
Pryor, Michelle L. Morgan Finds a New Home. (p. 1175)
Pryor, Sean, illus. see Stagnaro, Angelo.
Pryse-Phillips, William. Free Flight. (p. 634)
Przybylek, Leslie, illus. see Sandage, Charley.
Przybylski, Jerzy F. Sunrise of Hope (p. 1677)
Psacharopulo, Alessandra, illus. see Barash, Chris.
Psacharopulo, Alessandra, illus. see Goebel, Jenny.
Psanis, Maria. I Love My Sister but Sometimes I Don't. (p. 842)
Psilopoulou, Koralia. Magic Amulets. (p. 1071)
PSSC Staff. Secrets of the Power Ring. (p. 1545)
Publ, Griffin. Easy Olympic Sports Reader (p. 500)
Public Domain Staff. Away in a Manger. Kinkade, Thomas, illus. (p. 120)
—Deck the Halls. Rockwell, Norman, illus. (p. 421)
—Five Little Pumpkins. Yaccarino, Dan, illus. (p. 600)
—Rise & Shine! Warnes, Tim, illus. (p. 1474)
Public Domain Staff, jt. auth. see Lewis, E. B.
Public Domain Staff, jt. auth. see Rockwell, Norman.
Publicaciones Puertorriqueñas Editores, ed. Amor a Puerto Rico. (p. 65)
—Aventuras de Valorin I. (p. 119)
—Aventuras de Valorin II. (p. 119)
—Aventuras de Valorin III. (p. 119)
—Cantemos a Naturaleza. (p. 262)
—Regalos Del Corazon. (p. 1457)
—Sembremos Semillas. (p. 1550)
—Valor Del Trabajo. (p. 1831)
Publicaciones Puertorriquenas Inc, ed. Mis Lentes. (p. 1150)
Publications, Editors of, ed. Baby Einstein My First Look & Find. (p. 126)
—Baby Einstein (tm) My First Smart Pad(tm) Library: Electronic Activity Pad & 8-Book Library. (p. 126)
—Baby Einstein(r) Baby's First Stories & Songs: Look, Listen, Laugh. (p. 126)
—BABY EINSTEIN(tm) under the Sea with Me! (p. 126)
—Best Friends Forever: Play a Sound Book. (p. 169)
—Book Block(tm) Thomas & Friends (tm) 12 Board Books. (p. 210)
—Calling all Pals. (p. 254)
—Cars My First Look & Find. (p. 272)
—Day with Hello Kitty: Play-A-Sound. (p. 415)
—Disney Big Hero 6 Look & Find. (p. 451)
—Disney Jr. : Doc Mcstuffins: 12 Board Book Block Set. (p. 451)
—Disney Jr. Look & Find. (p. 451)
—Disney Jr. Sound Storybook Treasury. (p. 451)
—Disney Mickey Mouse Clubhouse Let's Sing! Play-A-Sound Book & Cuddly Mickey. (p. 451)
—Disney Minnie Let's Have a Tea Party: Play-A-Sound Book & Cuddly Minnie. (p. 452)
—Disney Pixar:Planes: 12 Board Book Block Set. (p. 452)
—Disney Princess Look & Find Magnifying Book. (p. 453)
—Disney Princess Me Reader Electronic Reader & 8-Book Library 3 Inch. (p. 453)
—Disney Princess: My Own Carriage. (p. 453)
—Disney Princess: Songs to Treasure: Little Pop-Up Song Book. (p. 453)
—Disney Princess under the Starry Sky. (p. 453)
—Disney Princess Write & Erase Look & Find. (p. 453)
—Disney(r) Doc Mcstuffins I Can Brush My Teeth! Lift-A-Flap Sound Book. (p. 451)
—Disney(r) Doc McStuffinsOh Doc, What Can the Matter Be? (p. 451)
—Disney(r) Frozen: Giant Look & Find(tm) (p. 451)
—Disney(r) Frozen Little Look & Find(tm) (p. 451)
—Disney(r) Frozen Sing-Along Songs! Features Do You Want to Build a Snowman? (p. 451)
—Disney(r) Junior Little Look & Find(tm) Fun with Friends. (p. 451)
—Disney(r) Junior Look & Find(r) Treasury: 4 Look & Find Books & 1 Big Volume. (p. 451)
—Disney(r) JuniorLots & Lots of Look & Find(r): So Much to Find! More Than 900 Find'ems! Hours & Hours of Fun! (p. 451)
—Disney(r) Little First Look & Find(tm) Minnie Best Friends. (p. 451)
—Disney(r) Mickey Mouse Clubhouse I Can Play Christmas Songs! (p. 451)
—Disney(r) Mickey Mouse Clubhouse Let's Explore: Take a Closer Look! a Magnifying Glass & Sound Book. (p. 451)
—Disney(r) Mickey Mouse Clubhouse Silly Sing-Along: Sing High! Sing Low! Sing with an Echo! (p. 452)
—Disney(r) Mickey Mouse Clubhouse Super Look & Find(r) Activity Pad: Look, Find, & Match! Search for What's Different! Use Stickers on the Play Scene- or Anywhere! (p. 452)
—Disney(r) Mickey Mouse ClubhouseCalling All Pals. (p. 452)
—Disney(r) Mickey Mouse ClubhouseIf You're Happy & You Know It. (p. 452)
—Disney(r) Minnie My First Look & Find(r) Best Friends. (p. 452)
—Disney(r) Pixar Inside Out: Play-A-Sound(r). (p. 452)
—Disney(r) Pixar Inside Out Look & Find(r). (p. 452)
—Disney(r) Princess First Look & Find(r)Palace Pets. (p. 452)
—Disney(r) Princess Little Look & Find(tm) (p. 452)
—Disney(r) Princess Palace Pets: Little Pop-Up Songbook. (p. 453)
—Disney(r) Princess Super Look & Find(r) Activity Pad. (p. 453)
—Disney(r) Sofia the First the Perfect Party: A Flashlight Adventure Sound Book. (p. 453)
—Disney(r) Sofia the FirstShow-And-Tell Surprise. (p. 453)
—Disney(r) Super Look & Find(r) Activity Pad: 100's of Find 'ems, Best-Loved Characters! Hidden Pictures! More Than 50 Stickers! (p. 453)
—Doc Mcstuffins: the Doc Is In: Dr. Kit & Sound Book. (p. 459)
—Doc to the Rescue. (p. 459)
—Dora Explorer Write & Erase Look & Find. (p. 470)
—Dora the Explorer Ballerina Songs: Play-A-Sound Book & Huggable Dora. (p. 471)
—Elmo's Rock Star Guitar. (p. 516)
—Explore with Elmo Magnifying Glass Sound Book. (p. 550)
—First Look & Find Hello Kitty. (p. 596)
—First Look & Find Little Elf. (p. 596)
—Hello Kitty: Hello Songs: Play-A-Sound Digital Music Player Book. (p. 764)
—Hello Kitty I Love to Play Piano. (p. 764)
—Hello Kitty: My Friend Hello Kitty: Play-A-Sound Book & Cuddly Hello Kitty. (p. 764)
—Hello Kitty Sweet Songs: Play-A-Sound. (p. 764)
—Hello Kitty(r); Hello Kitty's Guitar. (p. 764)
—I Can Be a Princess: Picture Book. (p. 835)
—Jake & the Neverland Pirates. (p. 906)
—Jake & the Neverland Pirates: Playful Pirates: Play-A-Sound Book. (p. 906)
—Jake & the Neverland Pirates: What Do You See? Pop up Book & Flashlight Set. (p. 906)
—Look & Find: Disney Pixar Cars. (p. 1048)
—Look & Find: Disney Princess: Winter Dreams. (p. 1048)
—Look & Find: Nickelodeon: Teenage Mutant Ninja Turtles. (p. 1048)
—Look & Find: Snoopy. (p. 1048)
—Magic Mirror: Play a Sound Book. (p. 1072)
—Marvel: Spider-Man: Spectacular Spider Powers! (p. 1099)
—Me Reader Jr(tm) Old MacDonald's Farm: Electronic Reader & 8-Book Library. (p. 1116)
—Mickey & Friends Look & Find Extreme. (p. 1136)
—Mickey Mouse Clubhouse: Mickey's Surprise! (p. 1136)
—Minnie Mouse: Pretty Piano Play-Along: Piano Book. (p. 1148)
—Minnie Mouse: Surprise, Surprise! Play-A-Sound Book. (p. 1148)
—My Little Treasury Cuddle up Stories. (p. 1213)
—My Little Treasury: First Prayers & Blessings. (p. 1213)
—My Little Treasury My First Bible Stories. (p. 1213)
—Nickelodeon Dora the Explorer: Choo, Choo, Let's Go! (p. 1251)
—Nickelodeon Dora the Explorer: Follow the Music: Piano Book. (p. 1251)
—Nickelodeon Dora the Explorer Little Piano Book. (p. 1251)
—Nickelodeon(tm) Bubble Guppies(tm) Let's Rock! (p. 1251)
—Nickelodeon(tm) Little First Look & Find(tm) Bubble Guppies. (p. 1251)
—Nickelodeon(tm) Spongebob Squarepants: Look & Find(r). (p. 1251)
—Opposite Day. (p. 1300)
—Planes 2 Look & Find. (p. 1367)
—Pub Time Sports Trivia. (p. 1414)
—Rudolph the Red-Nosed Reindeer: Little Pop-Up Song Book. (p. 1494)
—Rudolph the Red-Nosed Reindeer(r): A Flashlight Adventure Sound Book. (p. 1494)
—Scooby Doo: Spooky Shadows: Flashlight Adventure Sound Book. (p. 1529)
—Sesame St Let's Go to School First Look & Find. (p. 1553)
—Sesame Street Happy Birthday to You. (p. 1553)
—Sesame Street: Let's Go to the Doctor. (p. 1553)
—Sesame Street: Sing & Play Guitar Songs. (p. 1553)
—Sesame Street(r) Elmo's Valentine. (p. 1553)
—Sesame Street(r) Happy Easter, Elmo! (p. 1553)
—Sesame Street(r) Listen & Learn in Your Neighborhood. (p. 1553)
—Sesame Street(r) Where Is Elmo's Friend? Play-A-Sound(r) Lift-a-Flap Sound Book. (p. 1553)
—Sesame Write & Erase Board Book. (p. 1553)
—Sketch That! The Ultimate Scribble Book. (p. 1584)
—Sketch This: Hundreds of Ways to Express Yourself! (p. 1584)
—Sofia the First: Princess in Training: Play-A-Sound Book. (p. 1605)
—Spongebob Squarepants Sea Mail. (p. 1630)
—Story Reader Me Reader & Disney 8-Book Library. (p. 1663)
—Super Fun Sticker Activities: More Than 1,000 Stickers! (p. 1680)
—Teenage Mutant Ninja Turtles(tm) Dojo: A Flashlight Adventure Sound Book. (p. 1714)
—Teenage Ninja Turtles: Skateboard Heroes! (p. 1714)
—Things That Go Board Book. (p. 1733)
—Thomas & Friends(r): Telescope Book. (p. 1738)
—Thomas & Friends(tm) Super Look & Find(r) Activity Pad: Spot the Find 'ems, Find the Differences! Giant Play Scene! More Than 50 Stickers! (p. 1738)
—Thomas & Friends(tm)I Can Drive! (p. 1738)
—Thomas, Railway Race Day Little Lift & Listen. (p. 1739)
—Thomas the Tank Good Morning Engines. (p. 1739)
—What Do You See? (p. 1883)
—World of Eric Carle: Merry Christmas: Play-A-Sound Book. (p. 1956)
—World of Eric Carle(tm) Animal Stories: 8 Animal Stories, over 35 Sounds. (p. 1956)
—World of Eric Carle(tm) Baby's First Animal Treasury: Plays Music While You Read! (p. 1956)
—World of Eric Carle(tm) Hear Bear Roar. (p. 1956)
—Write-And-Erase Look & Find(r) Disney: Packed with 'find 'ems & Picture Puzzles! Look, Circle, Wipe Clean, & Play Again! (p. 1963)
—Write-And-Erase Look & Find(r) Disney Minnie: Packed with 'find 'ems & Picture Puzzles! Look, Circle, Wipe Clean, & Play Again! (p. 1963)
—Write-And-Erase Look & Find(r) Disney(r) Sofia the First: More Than 100 Find 'ems! Find & Corcle 'em. Wipe Clean & Play Again! (p. 1963)
Publications International. My Little Pony Magic Friendship Songs. (p. 1213)
Publications International, creator. Disney Princess: the Little Mermaid: Play-A-Sound Book. (p. 453)
Publications International Ltd. Editors. Mother Goose Treasury. (p. 1178)
, Publications International Ltd, Publications International Ltd, creator. Look & Find: Disney Princess: the Little Mermaid. (p. 1048)
, Publications International Ltd, Publications International Ltd. Sesame Street: Say Cheese Elmo: Play-A-Sound Camera Book. (p. 1553)
Publications International Ltd. Staff. 1St Look & Find Spiderman. (p. 1991)
—1St Look & Find What's Different Tigger & Pooh. (p. 1991)
—Baby's Day. (p. 129)
—Barbie & the Magic of Pegasus. (p. 138)
—BK & Plush Mickey Mouse Club House. (p. 194)
—Brain Games Picture Puzzle 1. (p. 221)
—Cars. (p. 272)
—Cars Of 60's. (p. 272)
—Cars of The 50's. (p. 272)
—Cars of the Fabulous 40's Landscape. (p. 272)
—Chuggington Little Lift & Listen. (p. 318)
—Disney Princess PNO BK. (p. 453)
—Disney Princess Songs. (p. 453)
—Dora Ballerina Little Music Note Sound. (p. 470)
—Dora PNO BK Follow Music. (p. 470)
—Dora the Explorer My First Look & Find. (p. 471)
—Elmo PNO BK. (p. 515)
—Enchanted Songs. (p. 523)
—First Look & Find Cars Fast Friends. (p. 596)
—First Look & Find Wonder Pets. (p. 596)
—For the Love of Hockey BK Brick. (p. 616)
—Frozen - Anna's Friends. (p. 645)
—Giant Look & Find Disney Pixar Cars. (p. 673)
—Giant Look & Find Disney Princess. (p. 673)
—Giant Look & Find Elmo. (p. 673)
—Gilded Treasury Bible Stories. (p. 676)
—Interactive Sound Pirates of the Caribbean 3. (p. 879)
—Interactive Sound Surfs Up. (p. 879)
—Interactive Sound Transformers. (p. 879)
—John Deere Classics. (p. 921)
—Lenticular 1 Button Sesame Street. (p. 991)
—Lenticular 1 Button Thomas. (p. 991)
—Lion King Look & Find. (p. 1020)
—Little English Spanish Sound Diego. (p. 1027)
—Little Lift & Listen Sound Dora Go to School. (p. 1030)
—Little Sound Barbie Fairytopia. (p. 1036)
—Little Sound Mickey Mouse Club. (p. 1036)
—Little Treasuries Best Loved Children's Stories. (p. 1037)
—Little Treasuries Mother Goose. (p. 1037)
—Look & Find Ratatouille. (p. 1048)
—Look & Find Rio. (p. 1048)
—Look & Find Smurfs. (p. 1048)
—Look & Find Transformers. (p. 1048)
Publications International Ltd Staff. Marvel Heroes Extreme Look & Find. (p. 1098)
Publications International Ltd. Staff. Mickey Mouse Club First Look & Find. (p. 1136)
—Mickey Mouse Club House Little Pop up Sd. (p. 1136)
—Mother Goose. (p. 1177)
—My 1St Libraries Baby Enstein. (p. 1195)
—My 1St Libraries Disney Baby Animals. (p. 1195)
—My 1St Libraries Disney Princess. (p. 1195)
—My 1St Libraries Winnie the Pooh. (p. 1195)
—My 1St Look & Find Disney Pixar Friends & Heroes. (p. 1195)
—My First Look & Find Early Learning. (p. 1207)
—My First Look & Findthomas. (p. 1207)
—My Firstlibrary 12 Board Books Mickey Mouse. (p. 1208)
—Nemo First Look & Find. (p. 1241)
—Once upon a Potty. (p. 1293)
—Open Season Little Sound Bk. (p. 1299)
—Phineas & Ferb (Looks & Find) (p. 1351)
—Play A Sound Video Fifi's Painting Party. (p. 1370)
—Rio Large Play As Ound. (p. 1473)
—Sound Pooh Clues. (p. 1615)
—Steering Wheel Sound Cars. (p. 1646)
—Steering Wheel Sound Elmo Away We Go. (p. 1646)
—Storybook Paperdoll Play House Disney Fairies. (p. 1663)
—Sweet Dreams Padded Treasury. (p. 1689)
—Teenage Mutant Ninja Turtles - Ninja Heroes: Flashlight Adventure Sound Book. (p. 1714)
—Wall E Large Sound BK. (p. 1854)
—Yesterday & Today Chicago. (p. 1971)
—Yesterday & Today Detroit Tigers. (p. 1971)
—Yesterday & Today Football Universary of Florida. (p. 1971)
—Yesterday & Today Ford. (p. 1971)
—Yesterday & Today Nascar. (p. 1971)
—Yesterday & Today New York. (p. 1971)
—Yesterday & Today Nfl Chicago Bears. (p. 1971)
—Yesterday & Today Nfl Greenbay Packers. (p. 1971)
—Yesterday & Today Nfl New England Patriots. (p. 1971)
—Yesterday & Today Nfl New York Giants. (p. 1971)
—Yesterday & Today Portland. (p. 1971)
—Yesterday & Today San Francisco. (p. 1971)
—Yesterday & Today Seattle. (p. 1971)
—Yesterday & Today St. Louis. (p. 1971)
—Yesterday & Today St Louis Cardinals. (p. 1971)
—Yesterday & Todayfootball Universary of Arkansas. (p. 1971)
Publications International Ltd. Staff, ed. see Frankel, Alona.
Publications International Ltd. Staff, ed. see Kirgiss, Crystal & Lyon, Christopher.
Publications International Ltd. Staff & Flamming, James A. Cars 70s. (p. 272)
—Cars of The 50s. (p. 272)
Publications International Ltd. Staff & Frankel, Alana. Once upon a Potty Girl. (p. 1293)
Publications International Ltd. Staff & Pripps, Robert N. John Deere: Yesterday & Today. (p. 921)
Publications International Ltd. Staff & Red Giraffe, Ltd Staff, eds. Big Race - Stories Come to Life (p. 183)
Publications International Ltd. Staff, creator. Baby Einstein Animal Melodies. (p. 126)
—Barbie as the Island Princess. (p. 138)
—Best-Loved Children's Stories. (p. 170)
—Christmas Stories. (p. 315)
—Disney Best Friends. (p. 451)
—Disney Enchanted. (p. 451)
—Disney Pixar Cars Tour the Town. (p. 452)
—Disney Princess Board Books & Bookend Set. (p. 452)
—Disney Princess: Musical Pop-up Treasury. (p. 453)
—Dora the Explorer Laugh-along Sing-along. (p. 471)
—Dora the Explorer Learn to Write. (p. 471)
—Fairy Tales: Keepsake Collection. (p. 564)
—Get Ready for Fun! (p. 668)
—Hello Elmo! (p. 763)
—Help along Sing a Song. (p. 765)
—High School Musical: Let's Text. (p. 778)
—Jellyfish Jam: Pop-up Songbook. (p. 912)
—Learning Songs. (p. 985)
—Let's Dance!/Vamos a Bailar! (p. 995)
—Magic Songs. (p. 1073)
—Mother Goose. (p. 1177)
—Once upon a Time: A Treasury of Fairy Tales. (p. 1293)
—Once upon a Time. (p. 1293)
—Pooh Surprise Sing-along. (p. 1383)
—Read-along Bedtime Stories. (p. 1442)
—Scooby Doo!: Spooky Scooby Songs. (p. 1529)
—Sesame Street ABCs & 123s Wipe-off Activity Kit. (p. 1553)
—Songs That Go. (p. 1612)
—Thomas & Friends Musical Pop-up Treasury. (p. 1738)
—Tonka Wipe-off Activity Kit: ABCs And 123s. (p. 1765)
—Treasury of Bedtime Stories. (p. 1782)
—Treasury of Best Loved Children's Stories. (p. 1782)
—Treasury of Fairy Tales. (p. 1782)
—We've Got a Mission! (p. 1877)
Publications International Ltd. Staff, ed. 10 Tiny Puppies: A Counting Book. (p. 1994)
—5-Minute Good Night Stories. (p. 1992)
—9 Button Record Song Dora Superstar. (p. 1993)
—9 Button Record Song Mickey'S Christmas. (p. 1993)
—9 Button Record Song Thomas Sing Along. (p. 1993)
—9 Button Record Story Elmo Silly Stories. (p. 1993)
—Abby Cadabby Fairy Tale Fun. (p. 2)
—African American Children's Stories: A Treasury of Tradition & Pride. (p. 26)
—Airplanes! (p. 32)
—All the World's Asleep. (p. 46)
—Alphabet. (p. 49)
—Alphabet Wipe off Learning Board. (p. 50)
—Animals. (p. 81)
—Aurora Returns, Ariel's Voice, Fairy-Tale Tunes (p. 116)
—Baby Animals (Listen & Learn Sound Book) (p. 124)
—Baby Einsein Play a Sound (p. 126)
—Baby Einstein: Look, Listen, & Discover. (p. 126)
—Baby Einstein. (p. 126)
—Baby Faces. (p. 126)
—Baby Faces 6 Book Pack. (p. 126)
—Baby Is Born. (p. 126)
—Baby's 123. (p. 128)
—Baby's ABC. (p. 128)
—Baby's Animals. (p. 128)
—Baby's First Year Animals Memory Keeper. (p. 129)
—Baby's Shapes. (p. 129)
—Baby's Words. (p. 129)
—Barney: I Love You Songs. (p. 139)
—Barney: Music All Around. (p. 139)
—Barney: Let's Play Together. (p. 139)
—Barney & Friends Book Box & Plush. (p. 139)
—Barney Favorite Things. (p. 139)
—Batman: The Brave & the Bold (My First Library) (p. 144)
—Bedtime Stories. (p. 157)
—Beth Logan la Cuisine. (p. 171)
—Big Fix-It Day. (p. 181)
—Biscuit Magic Cook Book. (p. 193)
—Book Box Plush Finding Nemo. (p. 210)
—Brain Games: Logic Puzzles. (p. 221)
—Brain Games Kids: Mazes. (p. 221)
—Brain Games Kids: Preschool. (p. 221)
—Brain Games Kids: First Grade. (p. 221)
—Brain Games Kids: Word Search. (p. 221)
—Brain Games Kids: Kindergarten. (p. 221)
—Brain Games Kids: Picture Puzzles. (p. 221)
—Brain Games Kids: Super Brain Builder Puzzles. (p. 221)
—Brain Games Kids: Amazing Brain Builder Puzzles. (p. 221)
—Brain Games Kids: Awesome Brain Builder Puzzles. (p. 221)
—Busy Day - Baby's First Look & Find Sesame. (p. 246)
—Busy Little Monster. (p. 246)
—Captain America Large Play a Sound. (p. 263)
—Car Tunes. (p. 265)
—Cars: Starring Mater. (p. 272)
—Cars: Fun with Friends. (p. 272)
—Cars. (p. 272)
—Cars (Musical Treasury) (p. 272)

—Cars of the Sizzling 60s. (p. 272)
—Christmas Small Saddle Stitch (p. 315)
—Chuggington Little Music Note Sound: Traintastic Tunes. (p. 318)
—Classic Animal Tales. (p. 327)
—Come along, Sing a Song! (p. 347)
—Construction: (Play-a-Sound Book) (p. 359)
—Counting. (p. 370)
—Counting Bilingual. (p. 370)
—Counting Fun. (p. 371)
—Counting Memory Game Puzzle. (p. 371)
—Custom Cool. (p. 395)
—Dance Mat Sound Book Dora Lets Dance. (p. 402)
—Days Work. (p. 415)
—Dena Designs: My Doodles. (p. 426)
—Diego What a Team. (p. 437)
—Dinosaur Train: All Aboard! (p. 443)
—Discover the Day. (p. 448)
—Disney: Cuentos de Hadas. (p. 451)
—Disney: Cuentos para Dormir. (p. 451)
—Disney: Lee un Cuento Conmigo. (p. 451)
—Disney Bunnies. (p. 451)
—Disney Bunnies My First Library Book Block. (p. 451)
—Disney Classics. (p. 451)
—Disney Classics Shaped Books. (p. 451)
—Disney Fairies: Bienvenuda Tinker Bell! (p. 451)
—Disney Fairies: Best Friends Forever Scrapbook. (p. 451)
—Disney Fairies: Tinker Bell (Little Look & Find) (p. 451)
—Disney Fairies: Wellcome Tinker Bell: (Lenticular Play-a-Sound Book) (p. 451)
—Disney Lion King - We Can Share. (p. 451)
—Disney Little First Look & Find Pack. (p. 451)
—Disney Pixar: School Memory Keeper. (p. 452)
—Disney Pixar. (p. 452)
—Disney Pixar ABC Board Books. (p. 452)
—Disney Pixar (book Block) (p. 452)
—Disney Pixar Cars: Road Trip Adventure. (p. 452)
—Disney Pixar Cars: (Stereo Play-a-Sound) (p. 452)
—Disney Pixar Cars: Radiator Springs Sings. (p. 452)
—Disney Pixar Cars: Story Reader 2. 0 3 Storybook Library. (p. 452)
—Disney Pixar Cars: First Look & Find & Shaped Puzzle Box Set. (p. 452)
—Disney Pixar Cars: Cuentos de Miedo (Little English Spanish Sound Book) (p. 452)
—Disney Pixar Cars 2 (Look & Find Soft Cover) (p. 452)
—Disney Pixar Cars 2 Play-a-Sound Book. (p. 452)
—Disney Pixar Cars 2 - World Tour. (p. 452)
—Disney Pixar Cars (book Block) (p. 452)
—Disney Pixar Cars; Cruising' Cool. (p. 452)
—Disney Pixar Cars: Mater the Greater & More Tall Tales! (Look & Find) (p. 452)
—Disney Pixar Cars - Mater's Manners (p. 452)
—Disney Pixar Cars My First Look & Find & Shaped Puzzle. (p. 452)
—Disney Pixar Cars Ride-along Songs. (p. 452)
—Disney Pixar Cars Story Reader 2. 0 Unit. (p. 452)
—Disney Pixar Little First Look & Find 4 pack in carry Case. (p. 452)
—Disney Pixar Picture Puzzle. (p. 452)
—Disney Pixar School Memories. (p. 452)
—Disney Pixar Shaped Books. (p. 452)
—Disney Princesa. (p. 452)
—Disney Princess: Cinderella. (p. 452)
—Disney Princess: Royal Recital. (p. 452)
—Disney Princess: Cupcakes & More. (p. 452)
—Disney Princess: Enchanted Dreams. (p. 452)
—Disney Princess: Stories of Virtue. (p. 452)
—Disney Princess: Follow Your Dreams. (p. 452)
—Disney Princess: Please & Thank You. (p. 452)
—Disney Princess: 26 Stories of Virtue. (p. 452)
—Disney Princess: Just Like a Princess. (p. 452)
—Disney Princess: Magical Princess Songs. (p. 452)
—Disney Princess: Canciones the Princesas. (p. 452)
—Disney Princess: Enchanted Stables (Look & Find) (p. 452)
—Disney Princess: Dreams Come True (Talking Look & Find) (p. 452)
—Disney Princess: Princess Jewels (Little First Look & Find) (p. 452)
—Disney Princess. (p. 452)
—Disney Princess Ariel. (p. 452)
—Disney Princess Aurora. (p. 452)
—Disney Princess (book Block) (p. 452)
—Disney Princess First Look & Find & Giant Puzzle. (p. 452)
—Disney Princess Jewels First Look & Find & Shaped Puzzle. (p. 452)
—Disney Princess (Musical Treasury) (p. 453)
—Disney Princess My Charming Life Deluxe Scrapbook. (p. 453)
—Disney Princess Picture Puzzles. (p. 453)
—Disney Princess Storybook & Magic Bracelet. (p. 453)
—Disney Princesses. (p. 453)
—Disney Tales of Virtue 5 Book Set. (p. 453)
—Disney Tinkerbell Book Box Plush. (p. 453)
—Disney Virtues. (p. 453)
—Doodles for Kids. (p. 469)
—Doodles to Go: Super Duper Doodles. (p. 470)
—Doodles to Go: Razzle Dazzle Doodles. (p. 470)
—Dora Digital Music Player. (p. 470)
—Dora Little Stars, Big Adventure. (p. 470)
—Dora Says Good Night. (p. 470)
—Dora the Explorer: We Did It! (p. 471)
—Dora the Explorer: Sounds All Around! (p. 471)
—Dora the Explorer: Let's Write Letters. (p. 471)
—Dora the Explorer: Little Star's Big Adventure. (p. 471)
—Dora the Explorer: Scavenger Hunt (Little Look & Find) (p. 471)
—Dora the Explorer: Island Adventure (Talking Look & Find) (p. 471)
—Dora the Explorer: Little Star's Big Adventure (Flashlight Adventure Book & Dora Plush) (p. 471)
—Dora the Explorer. (p. 471)
—Dora the Explorer, Ding Dong! It's Dora! (p. 471)
—Dora the Explorer Look & Find. (p. 471)
—Dora's Desert Friends Plush Sound Book. (p. 471)
—Dragon Boat Festival. (p. 476)
—Early Learning: My First Library. (p. 493)
—Electronic Time for Learning: Music. (p. 509)
—Electronic Time for Learning: States. (p. 509)
—Electronic Time for Learning: The Human Body. (p. 509)
—Elmo. (p. 515)
—Elmo Goes to the Doctor. (p. 515)
—Elmos Garden Little Sound Book. (p. 515)
—Elmo's Neighborhood Lights & Music Treasury. (p. 516)
—Enchanted Forest. (p. 523)
—Eric Carle Counting Write & Erase Sound. (p. 533)
—Exploring Time with Dora Clock. (p. 554)
—Fairy Tales. Goodell, Jon & Clar, David Austin, illus. (p. 564)
—Fairy Tales Red a Long Treaury. (p. 564)
—Finding Nemo: A Party for Nemo. (p. 588)
—Finding Nemo: Let's Go to School. (p. 588)
—Finding Nemo. (p. 588)
—Finding Nemo: Hide & Seek: Book & Plush. (p. 588)
—Finding Nemo - Let's Go to School. (p. 588)
—Fire Truck: (Play-a-Sound Book) (p. 591)
—First Words (Listen & Learn Sound Book) (p. 597)
—Flashlight Book Disney Pixar Cars. (p. 602)
—Friendship Songs. (p. 639)
—Full Moon Monster Madness (Look & Find) (p. 646)
—Fun to Color. (p. 648)
—Fun to Draw. (p. 648)
—Go Diego Go. (p. 686)
—Good Night, Little Bear: A Sleepy Time Tale. (p. 699)
—Goof's Adventure. (p. 702)
—Grandma Loves You: Stories to Share. (p. 708)
—Green Lantern Large Play a Sound. (p. 722)
—Gross (Look & Find) (p. 725)
—Halloween Is Coming! (p. 738)
—Handy Manny: Fiesta Fun. (p. 742)
—Handy Manny. (p. 742)
—Happy Baby. (p. 744)
—Head to Toe! Go! Go! Go! (p. 756)
—Holiday Easter Play a Song Disney Bunnies. (p. 788)
—I Can Read! (p. 836)
—I Love You. (p. 843)
—If You're Happy & You Know It! (p. 855)
—Incredibles: Look & Find. (p. 870)
—Interactive Play a Sound Thomas the Tank. (p. 879)
—It's Riddle Time! (p. 898)
—Itsy Bitsy Spider. (p. 900)
—Jello Simply Stunning Holiday Desserts. (p. 912)
—Jesus Loves Me. (p. 915)
—Kindergarten Boot Camp. (p. 957)
—Let's Have a Race, Surprises, Little Engines. (p. 998)
—Let's Learn to Read! (p. 998)
—Lights & Music. (p. 1016)
—Lights & Music Treasury. (p. 1016)
—Lights & Music Treasury 10Led Spa Disney Classics. (p. 1016)
—Lights, Music, & Me! Love Sparkles. (p. 1016)
—Little Carry Case Spa Cars 8 Bks. (p. 1025)
—Little First Look & Find Disney Best Friends. (p. 1027)
—Little Lift & Listen Sound Mickey Mouse Clubhouse. (p. 1030)
—Little Sound the Princess & the Frog. (p. 1036)
—Look & Find: Myths & Heroes. (p. 1048)
—Look & Find: Disney Princess: Magical Moments. (p. 1048)
—Look & Find Activity Pad Mickey Mouse. (p. 1048)
—Look & Find - Animals. (p. 1048)
—Look & Find - Captain America: The First Avenger. (p. 1048)
—Look & Find - Cars (p. 1048)
—Look & Find Elmo. (p. 1048)
—Look & Find Green Lantern. (p. 1048)
—Look & Find - My First Look & Find Barney. (p. 1048)
—Look & Find - Noah's Arc & Other Bible Stories. (p. 1048)
—Look & Find Pirates of the Caribbean 3. (p. 1048)
—Look & Find Surfs Up. (p. 1048)
—Look & Find Wolverine & X Men. (p. 1048)
—Marvel Heroes. (p. 1098)
—Mater Saves the Day. (p. 1104)
—Mejores Amigos. (p. 1124)
—Mi Premera Biblioteca Cuentos. (p. 1133)
—Mickey Mouse 10 Song Sound. (p. 1136)
—Mickey Mouse Clubhouse: Count To 10. (p. 1136)
—Mickey Mouse Clubhouse: Play Day Songs. (p. 1136)
—Mickey Mouse Clubhouse: Hot Dog! Sing Along! (p. 1136)
—Mickey Mouse Clubhouse: Ask a Silly Question. (p. 1136)
—Mickey Mouse Clubhouse: Lights on, Lights Off! (p. 1136)
—Mickey Mouse Clubhouse: Telling Time with Mickey. (p. 1136)
—Mickey Mouse Clubhouse: Mickey's Silly Shadow Book. (p. 1136)
—Mickey Mouse Clubhouse: Mickey & Friends (Look & Find) (p. 1136)
—Mickey Mouse Clubhouse: Doctor Kit Book & Mickey Plush. (p. 1136)
—Mickey Mouse Clubhouse: Las canciones de piano de Mickey. (p. 1136)
—Mickey Mouse Clubhouse. (p. 1136)
—Mickey Mouse Clubhouse (book Block) (p. 1136)
—Mickey Mouse Clubhouse: Colors: Sing & Learn. (p. 1136)
—Mickey Mouse Clubhouse: Sing-along Christmas Songs: Holiday Play-a-Song Book. (p. 1136)
—Mickey Mouse Clubhouse Super Look & Find Activity Pad with Stickers. (p. 1136)
—Mickey Mouse Clubhouse, What's Different? (p. 1136)
—Mickey Mouse Clubhouse - Who's Not Sleepy? (p. 1136)
—Mickey's Adventure. (p. 1136)
—Mickey's Clubhouse Drum Song Sound. (p. 1136)
—Mickey's Piano Songs Play & Learn. (p. 1136)
—Monsters Can Share. (p. 1169)
—Mother Goose. Goodell, Jon & Borgo, Deborah Colvin, illus. (p. 1177)
—Mother Goose Read a Long Treasury. (p. 1178)
—Move to the Music. (p. 1183)
—Muscle Car Classics. (p. 1192)
—Musical Disney Princesas. (p. 1194)
—Musical Pop up Disney Princess. (p. 1194)
—My 1st Libraries Disney Classics. (p. 1195)
—My Alphabet Book. (p. 1196)
—My Colors Book. (p. 1200)
—My First Book Block - First Words. (p. 1205)
—My First Book Block Set Animals. (p. 1205)
—My First Book Block Set Disey Princess. (p. 1205)
—My First Look & Find - Chuggington. (p. 1207)
—My First Look & Find Winnie The Pooh. (p. 1207)
—My First Phonics Dictionary. (p. 1207)
—My First Story Reader Dora the Explorer. (p. 1208)
—My First Story Reader Sesame Street (p. 1208)
—My First U.S. Map Puzzle. (p. 1208)
—My First Wipe-off: A to Z Animals Dictionary. (p. 1208)
—My Friends Tigger & Pooh. (p. 1209)
—My Little Prayer Book. (p. 1213)
—My Numbers Book. (p. 1216)
—My Shapes Book. (p. 1218)
—Nickelodeon Dora the Explorer: When I Grow Up. (p. 1251)
—Nickelodeon Dora the Explorer: Follow the Music. (p. 1251)
—Nickelodeon Dora the Explorer: Let's Go! (Musical Treasury) (p. 1251)
—Nickelodeon Dora the Explorer: Cook with Dora: Abuela's Birthday Fiesta. (p. 1251)
—Night Before Christmas Giant Look & Find. (p. 1253)
—Numbers Learning Board. (p. 1272)
—Numbers (Listen & Learn Sound Book) (p. 1272)
—Old MacDonald Had a Farm. (p. 1284)
—On Sesame Street. (p. 1289)
—Once upon a Potty Sound Book for Boys. (p. 1293)
—Once upon a Time. (p. 1293)
—Out & About. (p. 1310)
—Padded Treasury 160 Spa Sesame Street. (p. 1317)
—Peter Pan. (p. 1347)
—Pirate. (p. 1362)
—Pirates of the Caribbean 2. (p. 1364)
—Play a Sound 10 Stories Winnie the Pooh. (p. 1370)
—Play & Learn Piano Dora. (p. 1371)
—Play & Learn Piano Elmo. (p. 1371)
—Play-a-Puzzle Book: Halloween. (p. 1370)
—Play-a-Puzzle trade; Book: Alphabet. (p. 1370)
—Please & Thank You. (p. 1373)
—PNO BK Spa Disney Princess. (p. 1374)
—Pooh's Heffalump Movie. (p. 1383)
—Pooh's Pop-up Stories. (p. 1383)
—Pooh's Pop-up Stories 2. (p. 1383)
—Popping up on Sesame Street. (p. 1384)
—Potty Time for Monsters. (p. 1388)
—Potty Time with Big Sister Dora. (p. 1388)
—Potty Time with Elmo. (p. 1388)
—Potty Time with Tiger: Boy. (p. 1388)
—Potty Time with Tiger: Girl. (p. 1389)
—Preschool Reading & Math Activities. (p. 1396)
—Prince Elmo & the Pea. (p. 1401)
—Princess & the Frog. (p. 1402)
—Princess Magic. (p. 1404)
—Princess Songs Play & Learn. (p. 1405)
—Puppy Learning. (p. 1418)
—Quaker Oats Old Fashioned Classic Recipes. (p. 1422)
—Race Car. (p. 1430)
—Race Day. (p. 1430)
—Rainbow Kittens A Colorful Tale. (p. 1435)
—Read to Me Grandma (Keepsake Story Collection) (p. 1443)
—Really Useful Engines. (p. 1450)
—Record a Song Old Mac Donald. (p. 1452)
—Record A Story: My Grandma Is Special. (p. 1452)
—Record a Story: My Grandpa Is Special. (p. 1452)
—Record a Story: 'Twas the Night Before Christmas. (p. 1452)
—Record a Story Elmo'S Bedtime Wish. (p. 1452)
—Record a Story with Thomas & Friends: Good Night, Little Engine. (p. 1452)
—Record Story Goldilocks 3 Bears. (p. 1452)
—Record Story Little Red Riding Hood. (p. 1452)
—Record Story Three Little Pigs. (p. 1452)
—Record Story Ugly Duckling. (p. 1452)
—Record-A-Memory School Years. (p. 1452)
—Right on Time Rescues. (p. 1472)
—Ring-a-Ling! A Friend Is Here. (p. 1473)
—Ring-A-Ling Day! (p. 1473)
—Rock & Roll with Elmo. (p. 1481)
—Rockin' on the Railway. (p. 1483)
—Rudolph the Red-Nosed Reindeer: Book & Cuddly Rudolph. (p. 1494)
—Rudolph the Red- Nosed Reindeer: My First Library. (p. 1494)
—Rudolph the Red-Nosed Reindeer (Book & Plush) (p. 1494)
—Rudolph the Red-Nosed Reindeer (Look & Find) (p. 1494)
—Scooby Doo Message in a Bottle Sound Book. (p. 1529)
—Sesame I Can Do It. (p. 1553)
—Sesame Play a Sound Stero. (p. 1553)
—Sesame Street: Potty Time Songs. (p. 1553)
—Sesame Street: Good Night Stories. (p. 1553)
—Sesame Street: Merry Christmas, Elmo! (p. 1553)
—Sesame Street: The Itsy Bitsy Spider. (p. 1553)
—Sesame Street: My First Book of Firsts. (p. 1553)
—Sesame Street: Monsters in the Bathroom. (p. 1553)
—Sesame Street: Trick or Treat with Elmo. (p. 1553)
—Sesame Street: Potty Time with Elmo (Look & Find) (p. 1553)
—Sesame Street: Elmo's Potty Book (First Look & Find) (p. 1553)
—Sesame Street: Merry Christmas, Elmo! (Book & Plush) (p. 1553)
—Sesame Street: Sing with Elmo, Let's Sing! & Wake up, Elmo! (p. 1553)
—Sesame Street, Ding Dong, Elmo's Here! (p. 1553)
—Sesame Street: Find a Friend: A Busy Box Book. (p. 1553)
—Sesame Street (Musical Treasury) (p. 1553)
—Sesame Street Picture Puzzle. (p. 1553)
—Shapes Wipe off Learning Board. (p. 1561)
—Sing-Along Songs. (p. 1578)
—Sleepy Baby. (p. 1589)
—Smurfs Large Play a Sound. (p. 1595)
—Sofia the First - Sofia's Royal Day: Includes 6 Punch-Out Play Pieces. Phoenix Books Staff, illus. (p. 1605)
—Soft! Furry! Bumpy! A Touch, Hear, & Learn with Elmo Book. (p. 1606)
—Solar System Puzzle. (p. 1607)
—Spider Sense Spider-Man: Super Villain Showdown. (p. 1626)
—Spongebob Clock It's Time Sound Book. (p. 1630)
—Spongebob Squarepants. (p. 1630)
—SpongeBob Squarepants (Little Look & Find) (p. 1630)
—Spooky Stories. (p. 1631)
—Star Wars: Revenge of the Sith: Play-a-Sound. (p. 1641)
—Starry Sky Songs. (p. 1642)
—Staying Smart in Summer: Entering 1st Grade. (p. 1645)
—Staying Smart in Summer: Entering 2nd Grade. (p. 1645)
—Staying Smart in Summer: Entering Kindergarten. (p. 1645)
—Steering Wheel Spa Cars. (p. 1646)
—Stories to Grow on Spa Disney Classics. (p. 1655)
—Stories to Grow on Spa Mickey Mouse Clubhous. (p. 1655)
—Story Reader. (p. 1663)
—Sunny Sing-Along Songs. (p. 1677)
—Surprise for Belle. (p. 1685)
—Tangled (Look & Find) (p. 1705)
—Tesoro de Los Cuentos de Hadas. LoFaro, Jerry, illus. (p. 1722)
—Thomas & Friends: Sodor Snapshots. (p. 1738)
—Thomas & Friends: Engine Roll Call. (p. 1738)
—Thomas & Friends: Let's Go, Thomas! (p. 1738)
—Thomas & Friends: Sing-Along Songs. (p. 1738)
—Thomas & Friends: Lights, Music & Me! (p. 1738)
—Thomas & Friends: A Busy Day on Sodor. (p. 1738)
—Thomas & Friends: Play-a-Tune Puzzle Book. (p. 1738)
—Thomas & Friends: Ding! Dong! A Visit from Thomas. (p. 1738)
—Thomas & Friends: Super Look & Find Activity Pad with Stickers. (p. 1738)
—Thomas & Friends Super Look & Find Activity Pad. (p. 1738)
—Thomas Celebration Pop Up Sound. (p. 1738)
—Thomas Great to be Engine Little Sound. (p. 1738)
—Thomas Songs Play & Learn. (p. 1739)
—Tinker Bell: Talent Shines Through. (p. 1755)
—Tinker Bell: Songs from Pixie Hollow. (p. 1755)
—Tinker Bell. (p. 1755)
—Tinker Bell (Book & Plush) (p. 1755)
—Tinker Bell -Tink's Magical Day. (p. 1755)
—Tinkerbell. (p. 1755)
—Touch & Hear Adventure. (p. 1772)
—Toy Story 3: New Friends. (p. 1774)
—Toys to the Rescue. (p. 1774)
—Tractor. (p. 1775)
—Trains. (p. 1777)
—Treasure Hunt. (p. 1781)
—Up & down! Play-a-Sound Book & Huggable Kai-lan. (p. 1824)
—Vampires & Other Scary Creatures(Look & Find) (p. 1832)
—Very Busy Day for Sodor: (Stereo Play-a-Sound) (p. 1837)
—Video Play a Sound Dora. (p. 1841)
—What's Different. (p. 1897)
—What's Different? (p. 1897)
—What's Different Finding Nemo. (p. 1897)
—Whats That Sound? (p. 1899)
—Where in the World. (p. 1908)
—Who's Not Sleepy? (p. 1921)
—Winnie the Pooh: I Love You Winnie the Pooh. (p. 1937)
—Winnie the Pooh: Super Look & Find Activity Pad. (p. 1937)
—Winnie the Pooh: Sing along with Pooh (Little Pop-up Songbook) (p. 1937)
—Winnie the Pooh: Super Look & Find Activity Pad with Stickers. (p. 1937)
—Winnie the Pooh. (p. 1937)
—Winnie the Pooh Drum Sound. (p. 1937)
—Winnie the Pooh (Find-A-Friend Book) (p. 1937)
—Winnie the Pooh Large Look & Find Activity Pad. (p. 1937)
—Winnie The Pooh Large Play A Sound. (p. 1937)
—Wonder Pets: Save the Baby Kitten. (p. 1947)
—World of Cars, Welcome to the Pit Crew. (p. 1956)
—World of Eric Carle - Baby Animals. (p. 1956)
—Writing Skills Wipe off Leaning Board. (p. 1965)
—Xylophone Dora. (p. 1967)
—Yesterday & Today: Chevrolet. (p. 1971)
—Zoom! (p. 1989)

Publications International Ltd. Staff, et al. Yesterday & Today Nashville. (p. 1971)

Publications Intl. Disney Adventure Look & Find. (p. 451)

Publishers, Hancock House Publishers. Raptors - Birds of Prey Coloring Book. (p. 1439)
—Wildlife Coloring Book. (p. 1931)

Publishing, Autumn. I Want to Color BIG Pictures. (p. 848)

Publishing, Chouette. Caillou, My First ABC: The Alphabet Soup. Brignaud, Pierre, illus. (p. 251)

Publishing, Greenbirdbooks Childrens, jt. auth. see Nazeer, Tasnim.

Publishing Group, Carlton. Doodle & Activity Advent Placemats: With 36 Tear-Out Doodle Placemats! (p. 469)
—Doodle & Activity Placemats: With 36 Tear-Out Doodle Placemats! (p. 469)

Publishing, Sterling. Daddy & Me. (p. 398)
—Hello, Baby! (p. 763)
—Look at Me! (p. 1048)
—Woof. (p. 1950)

Puccinelli, Joanne. Naughty Nello & the Sleds. Elam, Brock, illus. (p. 1237)

Puccinelli, Marie. Catch a Fish. (p. 279)

Puccini, Giacomo. Madame Butterfly. Fucíková, Renata, illus. (p. 1069)

Puchalski, Robin. Foo Foo the Shih Poo: My First Day Home. (p. 612)

Puche, Lola Soriano, jt. auth. see Torres Moliner, Isabel.

Puchner, Willy. ABC of Fabulous Princesses. (p. 3)
—ABC of Fantastic Princes. (p. 3)

Puchta, Herbert, jt. auth. see Gerngross, Günter.

Puchta, Herbert & Gerngross, Günter. Join Us for English 3 Language Portfolio. (p. 924)

Puchta, Herbert, et al. More! (p. 1173)
—More! Level 1 (p. 1174)
—More! Level 2. (p. 1174)
—Super Minds American English Level 3 Student's Book with DVD-ROM. (p. 1680)
—Super Minds American English Level 5 Workbook. (p. 1680)
—Super Minds Flashcards Starter (p. 1680)

—Super Minds Level 1 Student's Book with DVD-ROM. (p. 1680)
—Super Minds Level 2 Student's Book with DVD-ROM. (p. 1680)
—Super Minds Level 3 Student's Book with DVD-ROM. (p. 1680)
—Super Minds Level 3 Workbook. (p. 1680)
—Super Minds Level 4 Student's Book with DVD-ROM. (p. 1680)
—Super Minds Level 4 Workbook. (p. 1680)
—Super Minds Starter Student's Book with DVD-ROM. (p. 1680)
—Super Minds Starter Workbook. (p. 1680)
Puck. 123 Baltimore: A Cool Counting Book. (p. 2000)
—123 Beach. (p. 2000)
—123 Boston. Somers, Kevin, illus. (p. 2000)
—123 California. Somers, Kevin, illus. (p. 2000)
—123 Chicago. Somers, Kevin, illus. (p. 2000)
—123 Hawaii. (p. 2000)
—123 Minnesota: A Cool Counting Book. (p. 2000)
—123 Philadelphia. Somers, Kevin, illus. (p. 2000)
—123 San Francisco. Somers, Kevin, illus. (p. 2000)
—123 Texas. Somers, Kevin, illus. (p. 2000)
—123 USA: A Cool Counting Book. Somers, Kevin, illus. (p. 2000)
—123 Washington, D. C. (p. 2000)
—123 Zoo. (p. 2000)
—Doodle New York: Create. Imagine. Draw Your Way Through the Big Apple. Lemay, Violet, illus. (p. 469)
—My Foodie ABC: A Little Gourmet's Guide. Lemay, Violet, illus. (p. 1209)
—New York Baby. Lemay, Violet, illus. (p. 1247)
—One to Ten NYC. Pettingill, Charla, illus. (p. 1297)
Puck, jt. auth. see Somers, Kevin.
Puck & Pohlen, Jerome. Doodle Texas: Create Imagine Draw Your Way Through the Lone Star State. Lemay, Violet, illus. (p. 469)
Puckett, A. J., creator. If I Had a Pet Octopus. (p. 853)
Puckett & Gutelle. K Puckett's Baseball Game. (p. 941)
Puckett, Annie Marie. Pedro Learns about Salvation. (p. 1334)
Puckett, Charles L. Kicking Rocks in Bowling Green. (p. 951)
Puckett, Craig D., anno. 2008 PostBinder Hospital: 2008 Update:the Educational Annotation of ICD-9-CM. (p. 2003)
—2008 SoftCover Hospital: 2008 Update: the Educational Annotation of ICD-9-CM. (p. 2003)
—2009 Annual Hospital. (p. 2003)
—2009 Annual Physician. (p. 2003)
Puckett, Craig D., ed. 2009 Generic Hospital ICD-9-CM. (p. 2003)
—2009 Generic Physician ICD-9-CM. (p. 2003)
—Expanded ICD-9-CM Table of Drugs & Chemicals 6th Edition. (p. 548)
Puckett, James E. Fighting Fear with Faith: Combating Fear as a Good Soldier. (p. 585)
—Seperation of Christian & Church. (p. 1551)
Puddle, Patricia. Rascals Sing at the Opera House: Adventures of Rascals, Polly & Gertie. Puddle, Patricia, illus. (p. 1439)
Pudelko, Markus, jt. ed. see Haak, René.
Pudsey. Pudsey: A Pup Star's Story. (p. 1414)
Puebla, Teo, illus. see Gómez Cerdá, Alfredo, et al.
Puebla, Teo, illus. see Machado, Antonio.
Puelles, Vicente Munoz & Muñoz Puelles, Vicente. Oscar y el Leon de Correos. Villamuza, Noemi, illus. (p. 1305)
Puentes, Christina. On the Way to Granny's House. (p. 1292)
Pueppke, M. D. Even Fuzzier Logic: Fuzzy the Cat Digs Deeper. (p. 541)
Puerta, Carlos, illus. see Kipling, Rudyard & Solari, María J.
Puerta, Carlos, tr. see Kipling, Rudyard & Solari, María J.
Puerta, Germán. Galileo Galilei - Y Sin Embargo se Mueve. (p. 653)
Puerto, Carlos. Luna en Sus Manos. (p. 1065)
—Vero y el Fantasma de Canterville. Delclos, Jordi V., illus. (p. 1837)
Puerto, Carlos, jt. auth. see Puerto, Carlos.
Puerto, Carlos & Carlos, Puerto. Mi Tigre es Lluvia. (p. 1133)
Puerto, Carlos & Puerto, Carlos. Alas de la Pantera. (p. 33)
Pueschner, Gordon. Story of the Charlotte Bobcats. (p. 1660)
—Story of the Cleveland Indians. (p. 1660)
—Story of the Houston Texans. (p. 1661)
—Story of the Jacksonville Jaguars. (p. 1661)
—Story of the Memphis Grizzlies. (p. 1661)
—Story of the Oakland Athletics. (p. 1661)
Puett, Gayle, ed. see Irwin, Esther.
Puetz, Gary Rainer. Cooking with the Seafood Steward: Taking the Mystery Out of Seafood Preparation. Schafer, Rick, photos by. (p. 362)
Pufendorf, Samuel. Introduction to the History of the Principal Kingdoms & States of Europe. (p. 882)
—Two Books of the Elements of Universal Jurisprudence. Behme, Thomas, ed. (p. 1803)
Puff, Neal. Security for People & Computers: A Little Handbook of Useful Knowledge for Today's World. (p. 1546)
Puffin Staff, jt. auth. see Bergman, Dana.
Pugh, Harry F. & PERKOWSKI, Gary. U. S. Special Forces Group Insignia (Post 1975) (p. 1807)
Pugh, Ian. Wolfstorm: The First Danny Piper Adventure. (p. 1944)
Pugh, Jonathan, illus. see Stannard, Russell.
Pugh, Tracey D. Show & Tell Lesson. McCracken, Jaime, photos by. (p. 1570)
Pugiano-Martin, Carol & Bridwell, Norman. Snow Champion. Haefele, Steve, illus. (p. 1598)
Pugin-Rodas, M. C. Eight Ball Club: Ocean of Fire. (p. 507)
Pugliano Martin, Carol. Lonely Pluto. (p. 1046)
Pugliano-Martin, Carol. Around the World with Music: Set Of 6. (p. 101)
—Being a Bug Scout: Set Of 6. (p. 160)
—Being a Bug Scout & Como ser un explorador de Animalitos: 6 English, 6 Spanish Adaptations. (p. 160)
—Blackout. DuFalla, Anita, illus. (p. 197)
—Building with Shapes: Small Book. (p. 239)
—Building with Shapes. (p. 239)
—Cape Town, South Africa. (p. 262)
—Cats of the Serengeti: Set Of 6. (p. 281)
—Cats of the Serengeti. (p. 281)
—Day I Followed the Pickle. Beckes, Shirley, illus. (p. 413)
—Discover Cape Town. (p. 447)
—Discover Mexico City. (p. 447)
—Discover Seoul. (p. 448)
—Discover the Life Cycle of Bees. (p. 448)
—Discover the Life Cycle of Oak Trees. (p. 448)
—Discover the Life Cycle of Pine Trees. (p. 448)
—Earth on Turtles Back. (p. 496)
—Earth on Turtle's Back: Set Of 6. (p. 496)
—Famous Americans: Fluency-Building Plays with Activities That Expand Vocabulary & Content Knowledge. (p. 569)
—Frog Someday. (p. 640)
—Glooscap Makes the Seasons: A Canadian Legend. (p. 685)
—Great Big Giant Turnip: Set Of 6. (p. 714)
—Greek Myth Plays: 10 Readers Theater Scripts Based on Favorite Greek Myths That Students Can Read & Reread to Develop Their Fluency. (p. 720)
—How Davy Crockett Moved the Sun: An American Tall Tale. (p. 806)
—John Henry: An American Tall Tale. (p. 922)
—Kanchil Outsmarts Crocodile: A Folktale from Malaysia & Indonesia. (p. 942)
—Life Cycle of Bees. (p. 1009)
—Life Cycle of Oak Trees. (p. 1009)
—Life Cycle of Pine Trees. (p. 1009)
—Little Cat Goes Fast. (p. 1025)
—Little Lion: Set Of 6. (p. 1030)
—Little Lion. (p. 1030)
—Making Crafts from Around the World: Set Of 6. (p. 1081)
—Making Crafts from Around the World & Artesanías del Mundo: 6 English, 6 Spanish Adaptations. (p. 1081)
—Mexico City, Mexico. (p. 1131)
—My Little Red Lunchbox Book. Ottinger, Jon, illus. (p. 1213)
—Quetzacoatl Brings Corn to His People: A Legend from Mexico. (p. 1426)
—Ready for Fall! (p. 1447)
—See You in Spring! (p. 1547)
—Seoul, Korea. (p. 1551)
—Summer to Fall. (p. 1675)
—Very Mean King: Set Of 6. (p. 1838)
—Very Mean King & el rey Malo: 6 English, 6 Spanish Adaptations. (p. 1838)
—Watch a Frog Grow. (p. 1860)
—Why Spiders Have Small Waists. (p. 1926)
Pugliano-Martin, Carol, jt. auth. see Gordh, Bill.
Puglisi, Adriana, illus. see Gallagher, Diana G.
Puglisi, Salvatore. It's best to be Me. (p. 896)
Puhalo, Lazar. Auke Lake Tales. (p. 115)
—Lives of Saints for Young People: Twelve Saints. (p. 1040)
—Twelve Great Feast Days. (p. 1800)
Publicaciones Urbanas Staff, ed. En Guardia: combates, conquistas y legado de Mayaguez 2010 (p. 522)
Puig Rosado, Fernando, illus. see Gripari, Pierre.
Pujari, M. Nathalie. 20 Umbrellas. Sananmuang, Chatree, illus. (p. 1996)
Pujol, Miquel, et al. Uncle Scrooge #388. (p. 1812)
Pukac, Michael & Stephen, Marchesi. Flights of Marceau: Week Three. (p. 604)
Pulchinski, Erin. Ethan Is Caught Blue Faced! Werrun, Anna, illus. (p. 539)
Pulchinski, Erin Elizabeth. Why, Oh, Why Does the Rain Fall from the Sky? (p. 1925)
Pulcini, Ted. Face to Face: A Guide for Orthodox Christians Encountering Muslims. (p. 560)
Pulditor, Seth H. DeSean Jackson. (p. 428)
—Drew Brees. (p. 485)
Pulford, Elizabeth. Billy Brown's Cat Brown, Daniel J., illus. (p. 187)
—Broken. Gomes, Angus, illus. (p. 230)
—Castlecliff & the Fossil Princess. Jenner, Lorelai, illus. (p. 277)
Pulido, Brian. Dark Passage Rels, Ivan et al, illus. (p. 408)
—Medieval Tale. Lee, Tae E., illus. (p. 1119)
Pulido, Rene, illus. see Helter, Celeste.
Pulis, Carroll B. Lightning Reed: A Mighty Fine Steed. (p. 1016)
Pulitzer, Virginia L. Gwendolyn Claire vs the Foxfield Four. (p. 733)
Pullan, Jack, illus. see Hillert, Margaret.
Pullan, Jack, illus. see Katz, Jill.
Pullein-Thompson, Christine. Phantom Horse. (p. 1349)
—Phantom Horse Comes Home. (p. 1349)
—Phantom Horse Disappears. (p. 1349)
—Phantom Horse in Danger. (p. 1349)
—Phantom Horse Island Mystery. (p. 1349)
—Wait for Me. (p. 1852)
Pullen, John J. Something Abides: The Story of Joshua Chamberlain. (p. 1609)
Pullen, Ken. Rescue Me. (p. 1462)
Pullen, Zachary. Friday My Radio Flyer Flew. Pullen, Zachary, illus. (p. 637)
Pullen, Zachary, illus. see Bildner, Phil.
Pullen, Zachary, illus. see Bunting, Eve.
Pullen, Zachary, illus. see Frank, John.
Pullen, Zachary, illus. see Hershenhorn, Esther.
Pullen, Zachary, illus. see Herzog, Brad.
Pullen, Zachary, illus. see Hyman, Zachary.
Pullen, Zachary, illus. see Michelson, Richard.
Pullen, Zachary, illus. see Wargin, Kathy-jo.
Pullen, Zachary, illus. see Winters, Kay.
Pullen, Zachary, jt. auth. see Frank, John.
Pullens, Evelien, jt. auth. see Rajagopal, P.
Puller, Meredyth, jt. auth. see Darraj, Susan Muaddi.
Pulles, Elizabeth, illus. see Hodson, Christopher.
Pulley, Kelly. Beginner's Bible: Timeless Children's Stories. (p. 159)
—Beginner's Bible Collector's Edition. (p. 159)
—Cycling Wangdoos. Pulley, Kelly, illus. (p. 397)
—Jesus & His Friends. (p. 915)
—Jonah & the Big Fish. (p. 925)
—Noah & the Ark. (p. 1261)
—Ten Unusual Features of Lulu McDunn. Pulley, Kelly, illus. (p. 1719)
—Very First Christmas. (p. 1838)
Pulley, Kelly, illus. see DeVries, Catherine & Zondervan Publishing Staff.
Pulley, Kelly, illus. see Pingry, Patricia A.
Pulley, Kelly, illus. see Traditional.
Pulley, Kelly, illus. see Vischer, Phil.
Pulley, Kelly, illus. see Witherow, Wendy.
Pulley, Kelly, illus. see Zondervan Bibles Staff.
Pulley, Kelly, illus. see Zondervan Publishing Staff.
Pulley, Kelly & Mission City Press Inc. Staff. Beginner's Bible for Toddlers. (p. 159)
Pulley, Kelly & Zondervan Publishing Staff. Adan y Eva en el Jardin Pulley, Kelly, illus. (p. 11)
—Daniel y los Leones Pulley, Kelly, illus. (p. 405)
—David & the Giant (David y el Gigante) Pulley, Kelly, illus. (p. 410)
—Jesus Saves the World Pulley, Kelly, illus. (p. 916)
—Jonas y el Gran Pez Pulley, Kelly, illus. (p. 925)
—Noah & the Ark Pulley, Kelly, illus. (p. 1261)
Pulliam, Gabe, jt. auth. see McDoogle, Farrah.
Pullin, Eric. Digweed, the Cat a Bridge Too Far. (p. 440)
—Digweed the Cat, Smudge. (p. 440)
Pullman, Philip. Amber Spyglass. (p. 57)
—Catalejo Lacado. (p. 278)
—Catalejo Lacado. Gallart Iglesias, Maria Dolores & Batlles, Camila, trs. (p. 278)
—Daga. (p. 399)
—Daga. Gallart, Dolors, tr. (p. 399)
—Das Magische Messer. (p. 409)
—Der goldene Kompass. (p. 427)
—Firework-Maker's Daughter. (p. 592)
—Golden Compass. (p. 694)
—His Dark Materials: The Golden Compass, the Subtle Knife, the Amber Spyglass. (p. 781)
—His Dark Materials: The Golden Compass - The Subtle Knife - The Amber Spyglass (p. 781)
—His Dark Materials: The Golden Compass - The Subtle Knife - The Amber Spyglass Set (p. 781)
—His Dark Materials. (p. 781)
—Luces del Norte. (p. 1062)
—Lyra's Oxford. Lawrence, John, illus. (p. 1066)
—Miroir d'Ambre. (p. 1149)
—Once upon a Time in the North. (p. 1293)
—Once upon a Time in the North. Lawrence, John, illus. (p. 1293)
—Reloj Mecanico. Netzel, Carmen, tr. (p. 1458)
—Royaumes du Nord. (p. 1492)
—Ruby in the Smoke. (p. 1493)
—Sally y el Tigre en el Pozo. Miquel, Isabel de, tr. (p. 1505)
—Sally y la Sombra del Norte. Miquel, Isabel de, tr. (p. 1505)
—Scarecrow & His Servant. (p. 1519)
—Scarecrow & His Servant. Bailey, Peter, illus. (p. 1519)
—Shadow in the North. (p. 1557)
—Spring-Heeled Jack. Mostyn, David, illus. (p. 1635)
—Subtle Knife. (p. 1671)
—Tiger in the Well. (p. 1748)
—Tin Princess. (p. 1755)
—Tour des Anges. (p. 1773)
—Two Crafty Criminals! And How They Were Captured by the Daring Detectives of the New Cut Gang. (p. 1803)
Pullman, Philip & Adams, Emma. Ugly. (p. 1808)
Pulman, Felicity. Rosemary for Remembrance. (p. 1489)
—Rue for Repentance. (p. 1494)
—Turning the Page. Cox, David, illus. (p. 1798)
Puls, Ruth. Activities for Teens: 77 Ways to Build Catholic Identity. Cannizzo, Karen A., ed. (p. 10)
—Confirmation: Gifted with the Spirit. Cannizzo, Karen, ed. (p. 357)
Pulsar Studios Staff, illus. see Maddox, Jake.
Pulte, Therese Marie. Laguna Beach: A Visual Souvenir. (p. 971)
Pultz, Josh, jt. auth. see Michael, Ted.
Pulver, Beth A. & Adcock, Donald C. Evaluating Information (p. 540)
Pulver, David L. BESM Dungeon. (p. 168)
Pulver, David L. & MacKinnon, Mark C. Big Eyes, Small Mouth Third Edition Core Rulebook. (p. 181)
Pulver, David L., et al. CyborGladiators. (p. 396)
Pulver, Robin. Case of the Incapacitated Capitals. Reed, Lynn Rowe, illus. (p. 274)
—Christmas Kitten, Home at Last Johnson, Layne, illus. (p. 314)
—Happy Endings: A Story about Suffixes. (p. 745)
—Happy Endings: A Story about Suffixes. Reed, Lynn Rowe, illus. (p. 745)
—Never Say Boo! Lucke, Deb, illus. (p. 1243)
—Nouns & Verbs Have a Field Day. Reed, Lynn Rowe, illus. (p. 1268)
—Persuading Miss Doover. Sisson, Stéphanie Roth, illus. (p. 1344)
—Punctuation Takes a Vacation. Reed, Lynn Rowe, illus. (p. 1417)
—Saturday Is Dadurday. Alley, R. W., illus. (p. 1515)
—Silent Letters Loud & Clear. Reed, Lynn Rowe, illus. (p. 1575)
—Thank You, Miss Doover. Sisson, Stéphanie Roth, illus. (p. 1725)
Pulver, Robin & Reed, Lynn Rowe. Nouns & Verbs Have a Field Day. (p. 1268)
—Silent Letters Loud & Clear. (p. 1575)
Pumphrey, Margaret B. Stories of the Pilgrims. (p. 1655)
—Stories of the Pilgrims (Yesterday's Classics) (p. 1655)
Pumphrey, W. Jerome. Creepy Things Are Scaring Me! (p. 381)
Puncel, María. Manana es Domingo y Otras Rimas Infantiles. Recio, Ricardo, illus. (p. 1086)
—Patio de Mi Casa y Otras Canciones Infantiles. Escrivá, Viví, illus. (p. 1328)
—Prado del Tío Pedro. (p. 1392)
—Yo Subia la Escalera y Otras Rimas Infantiles. Bayley, Nicola, illus. (p. 1971)
Puncel, María, tr. see Blegvad, Lenore.
Puncel, María, tr. see Bosse, Wendy.
Puncel, María, tr. see Minarik, Else Holmelund.
Punch, Melissa, photos by see Abrams, Pam.
Punch Monkey Staff & Donbo, Koge. Pita-Ten (p. 1364)
Punchard, Lorraine. 200 Years of Playtime Pottery & Porcelain (p. 2001)
Pundir, Annie. Gauri & the Crocodile: Smiley Crocodiley. (p. 658)
Pundit Baraiya, Gopaldasji. Primer of Jain Principles. Gosalia, Kirit, tr. (p. 1400)
Pundyk, Grace. Welcome to Jordan. (p. 1873)
—Welcome to Romania. (p. 1873)
Pundyk, Grace & Radhakrishnan, Anand. Welcome to Malaysia. (p. 1873)
Puner, R. Stories of Robots. (p. 1655)
Punk Science Staff. Do Try This at Home! (p. 457)
—Do Try This at Home - Cook It! (p. 457)
Punk Science Staff, jt. auth. see Science, Punk.
Punnett, Dick. Count the Possums: A Talk-along Book. Punnett, Yvonne, ed. (p. 370)
—Help Dress Priscila: A Talk-along Book. Dunnington, Tom, illus. (p. 765)
—Help Jumbo Escape: A Talk-along Book. Dunnington, Tom, illus. (p. 765)
—Name Lizzy's Colors: A Talk-along Book. Punnett, Yvonne, ed. (p. 1228)
—Name Patty's Pets: A Talk-along Book. Punnett, Yvonne, ed. (p. 1228)
Punnett, Yvonne, ed. see Punnett, Dick.
Punniyamurthi, Kavitha. Lucy's Purple Pullover. Punniyamurthi, Kavitha, illus. (p. 1063)
Punter, R. Pirate Adventures. (p. 1362)
—Pirates. (p. 1363)
—Stories of Pirates. (p. 1655)
Punter, Russell. Chilly Little Penguin. (p. 306)
—Cow Takes a Bow. Blunt, Fred, illus. (p. 373)
—Danny & the Dragon. (p. 405)
—Dinosaur Who Lost His Roar. Elkerton, Andy, illus. (p. 443)
—Encyclopedia of Planet Earth: Internet-Linked. Harvey, Gil, illus. (p. 525)
—Llamas in Pajamas. (p. 1043)
—Monsters, Stories Of. (p. 1169)
—Percy & the Pirates. (p. 1341)
—Pirate Adventures. Fox, Christyan, illus. (p. 1362)
—Pirate Stories for Little Children. (p. 1363)
—Pirates Kid Kit. (p. 1363)
—Robots. Hamilton, Andrew, illus. (p. 1481)
—Scaredy Cat. (p. 1519)
—Stories of Cowboys. Fiorin, Fabiano, illus. (p. 1654)
—Stories of Dinosaurs. Decker, Cynthia, illus. (p. 1654)
—Stories of Santa. Webb, Philip, illus. (p. 1655)
—There Was a Crooked Man. Semple, David, illus. (p. 1730)
—Underpants for Ants. Blunt, Fred, illus. (p. 1815)
Punter, Russell & MacKinnon, Mairi. Snail Brings the Mail. Blunt, Fred, illus. (p. 1595)
Punter, Russell, retold by. Illustrated Stories from the Greek Myths. (p. 858)
Puppel, Douglas. Hero Named Mark. Verrill, William, illus. (p. 772)
Puppet Prod. Puppet Production - Old Testament Programs (Russian) Life Publishers International Staff, tr. from ENG. (p. 1417)
Puppet Rescue, creator. Caterpillar says Eat Your Greens. (p. 279)
—Rosie & Yellowtail Share. (p. 1490)
—Yaker Goes to School. (p. 1968)
Purcell, Arthur H., jt. auth. see Davis, Mary Byrd.
Purcell, Gordon, illus. see Adamson, Heather.
Purcell, Gordon, illus. see Adamson, Thomas K.
Purcell, Gordon, illus. see Burgan, Michael & Hoena, Blake A.
Purcell, Gordon, illus. see Burgan, Michael.
Purcell, Gordon, illus. see Doeden, Matt.
Purcell, Gordon, illus. see Fandel, Jennifer & Milgrom, Al.
Purcell, Gordon, illus. see Fontes, Ron & Fontes, Justine.
Purcell, Gordon, illus. see Fontes, Ron, et al.
Purcell, Gordon, illus. see Jacobson, Ryan.
Purcell, Gordon, illus. see Olson, Kay Melchisedech.
Purcell, John M. American City Flags: 146 Flags from Akron to Yonkers. Vols. 9&10 Kaye, Edward B., ed. (p. 60)
Purcell, Kerry William. Weegee. (p. 1871)
Purcell, Kerry William & Yoshikawa, Shizuko. Josef Müller-Brockmann. (p. 926)
Purcell, Kim. Trafficked. (p. 1776)
Purcell, Larry. Ladybug & the Talking Stone. (p. 971)
—Ladybug Picnic. (p. 971)
Purcell, Larry & Purcell, Marilyn. Ladybugs Are Siblings Too. (p. 971)
Purcell, Marilyn, jt. auth. see Purcell, Larry.
Purcell, Mark & Murphy, Jason Robert. Mindfulness for Teen Anger: A Workbook to Overcome Anger & Aggression Using MBSR & DBT Skills. (p. 1145)
Purcell, Martha Sias. Pioneer Pilots & Flying Aces of World War I. (p. 1361)
—Spies of the American Revolution. (p. 1627)
Purcell, Rebecca. Super Chicken! Purcell, Rebecca, illus. (p. 1679)
Purcell, Sarah J. Early National Period. (p. 494)
Purcell, Sherry L. Teaching Self Discipline. (p. 1710)
Purchase, Brendan, illus. see Hibbitts, Mark.
Purchase, Sean. Key Concepts in Victorian Literature. (p. 950)
Purciello, Gerard. Year They Won: A Tale of the Boston Red Sox. (p. 1969)
Purday, Paul. Two Lands. (p. 1803)
Purdie, Kate. Personal Hygiene. (p. 1344)
—Sunshine & Drought. (p. 1678)
Purdie Salas, Laura, jt. auth. see Salas, Laura Purdie.
Purdy, Elizabeth, jt. auth. see Books, Golson.
Purdy, Elizabeth Rholetter. Celebrating Women in American History. (p. 285)
Purdy, Joanne, illus. see Kormos, Lawrence.
Purdy, Rebekah L. Winter People. (p. 1938)
Purfield, M. E. Jesus Freakz + Buddha Punx. (p. 915)
Puri, Devi. Seeds, Bulbs, & Sprouts. (p. 1547)
—Sydney Works at the School Store. (p. 1692)

P

Puritz, Christian. Venture Mathematics Worksheet Geometry: Helping to Stretch the More Able 11 to 16 Year Olds. (p. 1836)
—Venture Mathematics Worksheets: Algebra & Arithmetic. (p. 1836)
—Venture Mathematics Worksheets - Statistics & Extra Investigations: Helping to Stretch the More Able 11 to 16 Year Olds. (p. 1836)
Purkapile, Susan. Nosy Noodles: The Curious Cow. Ducommon, Barbara, illus. (p. 1266)
Purkapile, Susan & Peck, Amy. Mumbles the Bumble Bee: The Bee Who Couldn't Buzz. Ducommun, Barbara, illus. (p. 1190)
Purkis, Sallie, jt. auth. see Mason, James.
Purkis, Sallie & Mason, James. Birthdays. (p. 193)
—Teddy Bears. (p. 1712)
Purkiss, Cathy. Flat on Top. (p. 603)
Purkus, Christina. Peta's Pence. (p. 1346)
Purmell, Ann. Christmas Tree Farm. Weber, Jill, illus. (p. 316)
—Maple Syrup Season. Weber, Jill, illus. (p. 1090)
Purnell, Gerald, illus. see Anderson, Richard.
Purnell, Gerald, illus. see Cole, Heidi & Vogl, Nancy.
Purnell, Gerald, illus. see Moss, Maureen.
Purnell, Teresa, illus. see Lamond, Peter.
Purney, Dawn. Lost & Found (p. 1054)
Purney, Dawn, jt. auth. see Hatch, Thomas.
Purney, Dawn, jt. auth. see Hatch, Tom.
Purney, Dawn & Hatch, Thomas. Advantage Grammar Grade 5: High Interest Skill Building for Home & School. Vol. 8141 Hamaguchi, Carla, ed. (p. 14)
Purperhart, Helen. Yoga Adventure for Children: Playing, Dancing, Moving, Breathing, Relaxing. Evans, Amina Marix, tr. from DUT. (p. 1972)
—Yoga Exercises for Teens: Developing a Calmer Mind & a Stronger Body. Evans, Amina Marix, tr. from DUT. (p. 1972)
—Yoga Zoo Adventure: Animal Poses & Games for Little Kids. (p. 1972)
—Yoga Zoo Adventure: Animal Poses & Games for Little Kids. van Amelsfort, Barbara, illus. (p. 1972)
Purple Ronnie, jt. auth. see Ronnie, Purple.
Purple Ronnie & Andreae, Giles. Purple Ronnie's Love Poems. (p. 1419)
Pursglove, Sheila. Mouse Ate the House. (p. 1182)
Pursh, Eric. I Sette Pesci: The Seven Fishes. Lucot, Erica, illus. (p. 845)
Pursley, Theresa. Days of Creation. (p. 415)
Purslow, Frances. Constellations. (p. 359)
—Descriptive Paragraphs. (p. 428)
—Expository Paragraphs. (p. 554)
—For the Love of Rugby. (p. 616)
—Narrative Paragraphs. (p. 1229)
—Persuasive Paragraphs. (p. 1344)
—Precipitation. (p. 1394)
—Rugby. (p. 1494)
—Water Cycle. (p. 1862)
Purslow, Neil. Minnesota. (p. 1147)
—R. L. Stine. (p. 1429)
—Redwood National Park: Forest of Giants. (p. 1456)
—R.L. Stine. (p. 1476)
Purtill, C. Leigh. FaceSpace Face-Off! (p. 561)
—In Your Face. (p. 868)
Purtle, Louise. Potato Pie Pirate. Guiza, Victor, illus. (p. 1388)
Purton, Marie. Josh's Day at the Zoo. (p. 926)
Purton, Michael. Show Me How: I Can Make Music. (p. 1570)
Purves, Jeff, et al. Hulk Visionaries (p. 825)
Purves, William C. Fairmont Forever. (p. 563)
Purvis, Jedda Ngwarai, tr. see Kunoth, Mark.
Purvis, Joy Pitjara, tr. see Kunoth, Mark.
Purvis, Laura, ed. Falling for the Story. (p. 566)
Purvis, Leland, illus. see Jablonski, Carla.
Purvis, Leland, illus. see Poe, Marshall.
Pusca, Anca, ed. European Union: Challenges & Promises of a New Enlargement. (p. 540)
Pusch, Joseph. Jeremy & the Storm Witch. (p. 913)
Puscheck, Herbert Charles. Why be Normal? From Soup to Nuts, Mostly Nuts. Brower, William, illus. (p. 1922)
Pushee, Marisa, illus. see Hyde, Noreen.
Pushies, Fred J., jt. auth. see Aronin, Miriam.
Pushies, Fred J., jt. auth. see Lunis, Natalie.
Pushies, Fred J., jt. auth. see Markovics, Joyce L.
Pushies, Fred J., jt. auth. see Rudolph, Jessica.
Pushies, Fred J., jt. auth. see Sandler, Michael.
Pushker, Gloria Teles. Toby Belfer Visits Ellis Island Hierstein, Judith, illus. (p. 1760)
Pushker, Gloria Teles & Tarman, Mel. Toby Belfer Learns about Heroes & Martyrs Henriquez, Emile, illus. (p. 1760)
Pushkin, Alexander. Eugene Onegin. Mitchell, Stanley, ed. (p. 540)
—Skazki Pushkina - Fairy Tales. Bilibin, Ivan, illus. (p. 1584)
Pushkin, Alexander, et al. Cuentos Clásicos Juveniles: Antología. Zuluaga, Conrado, ed. (p. 389)
Put, Klaartje van der, illus. see Chronicle Books Staff & Image Books Staff.
Put, Klaartje van der, illus. see Chronicle Books Staff & ImageBooks Staff.
Put, Klaartje van der, illus. see Image Books Staff & Chronicle Books Staff.
Put, Klaartje van der, illus. see Image Books Staff.
Put, Klaartje van der, illus. see ImageBooks Staff & Chronicle Books Staff.
Put, Klaartje van der, illus. see ImageBooks Staff.
Puth, Klaus, illus. see Bartl, Allison.
Putman, Stanley, illus. see Haines, Marie.
Putnam, Caleb & Kennedy, Gregory. Montana Birds (p. 1170)
Putnam, Dave. Britain Uber Alles. (p. 229)
Putnam, Dave J. 10 Downing Street. (p. 1993)
Putnam, Frederic Ward. Archaeological & Ethnological Research in the United States: A Bried Summary for 1901 (p. 95)
Putnam, James. Pyramid. (p. 1421)
Putnam, James, jt. auth. see Dorling Kindersley Publishing Staff.
Putnam, Jeff. Advantage Test Prep Grade 7: High Interest Skill Building for Home & School. Vol. 8137 Hamaguchi, Carla, ed. (p. 14)
—Advantage Test Prep Grade 8: High Interest Skill Building for Home & School. Vol. 8138 Hamaguchi, Carla, ed. (p. 14)
—Explorers of the Land. (p. 551)
—Explorers of the Sky. (p. 551)
—National Monuments: Nature. (p. 1233)
—National Monuments: Events & Times. (p. 1233)
Putnam, Jeff, jt. auth. see Miller, Reagan.
Putnam, Marsha. Beyond the Crooked Limb. (p. 174)
Putnam, Richelle & Aycock, John. Inspiring Life of Eudora Welty. (p. 878)
Putney, Heidi C. Mara MK: The Surprise of Five. (p. 1091)
Putney, M J. Dark Destiny. (p. 407)
Putney, M. J. Dark Mirror. (p. 407)
Putra, Dede, illus. see Fabiny, Sarah.
Putra, Dede, illus. see Holub, Joan.
Putra, Dede, jt. auth. see Medina, Nico.
Putsman, Helen, photos by see Evans, Cheryl & Smith, Lucy.
Puttapipat, Niroot, illus. see Moore, Clement C.
Puttapipat, Niroot, illus. see Mowll, Joshua.
Puttapipat, Niroot, illus. see Pierpont, James Lord.
Puttock, Simon. Baby That Roared. Shireen, Nadia, illus. (p. 128)
—Butterfly Girl. Moriuchi, Mique, illus. (p. 247)
—Day the Baby Blew Away. Gale, Cathy, illus. (p. 414)
—Goat & Donkey & the Great Outdoors (p. 687)
—Goat & Donkey in Strawberry Sunglasses Julian, Russell, illus. (p. 687)
—Miss Fox. Swain, Holly, illus. (p. 1151)
—Mouse's First Night at Moonlight School. Pye, Ali, illus. (p. 1182)
—Who's the Boss Rhinoceros? Busby, Allie, illus. (p. 1921)
—You're Too Big. (p. 1982)
Puttock, Simon & Bartlett, Alison. Pig's Prize. (p. 1358)
Putumayo Kids Staff, creator. African Sticker Collection. (p. 28)
—Europe Sticker Collection. (p. 540)
—Latin America Sticker Coll. (p. 979)
Putur, Nellie. Nine Stories: A Mystery Novel. (p. 1256)
Putz, Ali F., jt. auth. see Eismann, Sheila F.
Puybaret, Eric. Islotes de Pedestal. Krahe, Elena Gallo, tr. (p. 893)
—Over the Rainbow. (p. 1314)
—Over the Rainbow (Board) (p. 1314)
Puybaret, Éric, illus. see Berne, Jennifer.
Puybaret, Eric, illus. see Harline, Leigh & Wshington, Ned.
Puybaret, Eric, illus. see Moore, Clement C.
Puybaret, Eric, illus. see Saumande, Juliette.
Puybaret, Eric, illus. see Yarrow, Peter & Lipton, Lenny.
Puybaret, Eric, illus. see Zoehfeld, Kathleen Weidner.
Puyol, Julio, tr. see Rotterdam, Erasmo de.
Puzik, Ulijana, ed. see AZ Books Staff.
Puzo, Mario. Extranas Vacaciones de Davie Shaw. (p. 555)
Puzzanghera, Marcia. Holly the Multi-Colored Girl. (p. 789)
Puzzi, Jessica. Rosy & Simon's Front Yard Adventure (p. 1490)
Puzzle Books Staff, contrib. by. Will Shortz Presents Fitness for the Mind Sudoku: 100 Wordless Crossword Puzzles. (p. 1932)
Puzzle Media Ltd Staff. Sudoku for Beginners (p. 1672)
Puzzle Society Staff. Girl Hangman: 100 Puzzles. (p. 678)
—Mom's Pocket Posh: 100 Puzzles & Games to Play with Your Kids Ages 4 to 6. (p. 1163)
—Mom's Pocket Posh: 100 Puzzles & Games to Play with Your Kids Ages 7 to 12. (p. 1163)
—Pocket Posh Girl Crosswords: 75 Puzzles. (p. 1375)
—Pocket Posh Girl Hangman: 100 Puzzles. (p. 1375)
—Pocket Posh Girl Sudoku: 100 Puzzles. (p. 1375)
—Pocket Posh Girl Sudoku 2: 100 Puzzles. Vol. 2 (p. 1375)
—Pocket Posh Girl Word Search: 100 Puzzles. (p. 1375)
—Pocket Posh Girl Word Search 2: 100 Puzzles. Vol. 2 (p. 1375)
—Pocket Posh(r) Girl Crosswords: 75 Puzzles. Vol. 2 (p. 1375)
Puzzling Sports Institute Staff, jt. auth. see Ross, Jesse Paul.
Puzzuoli, Jon. Wishing to Whistle. (p. 1940)
Pwob. Search for the Missing Ball: Norman G. Bear. Finnell-Acosta, B. C., illus. (p. 1537)
Pyatt, A. K. Old Woman's Garbage. Hill, Lynn, illus. (p. 1285)
Pyatt, K. C. Rebekah As Her Journey Begins. (p. 1450)
—Rebekah on the Farm. (p. 1450)
Pyatt, Mary. Jack Has Moves. (p. 903)
Pyatt, Sue. Call Me Madame President. Gaston, Keith A., illus. (p. 254)
Pyburn, Alice. Daughters, Fathers, & Seashells. (p. 410)
Pybus, Judith. Ladder. (p. 970)
Pye, Ali, illus. see Hardy, Edward.
Pye, Ali, illus. see Lewis, Jill.
Pye, Ali, illus. see Puttock, Simon.
Pye, Ali, jt. auth. see Lewis, Jill.
Pye, Michael, ed. see Dalley, Kirsten.
Pye, Trevor, illus. see Cowley, Joy.
Pye, Trevor, illus. see Eggleton, Jill.
Pyers. Sail Main5 Monkeys, Diverse Animals. (p. 1503)
Pyers, Greg. Biodiversity of Alpine Regions. (p. 188)
—Biodiversity of Coasts. (p. 188)
—Biodiversity of Coral Reefs. (p. 188)
—Biodiversity of Deserts. (p. 188)
—Biodiversity of Grasslands. (p. 188)
—Biodiversity of Oceans & Seas. (p. 188)
—Biodiversity of Polar Regions. (p. 188)
—Biodiversity of Rain Forests. (p. 188)
—Biodiversity of Rivers. (p. 188)
—Biodiversity of Temperate Forests. (p. 188)
—Biodiversity of Wetlands. (p. 188)
—Biodiversity of Woodlands. (p. 188)
—How to Behave in the Animal Kingdom. (p. 815)
—Wetland Wonders: Series B Unit 4: Our Fragile Environment. (p. 1877)
—Why Am I a Bird? (p. 1922)
—Why Am I a Fish? (p. 1922)
—Why Am I a Mammal? (p. 1922)
—Why Am I a Reptile? (p. 1922)
—Why Am I an Amphibian? (p. 1922)
—Why Am I an Insect? (p. 1922)
Pyers, Kelsey, illus. see Eberhart, Nancy.
Pyhala, Jonah & Merel. Adventures of Princess Dutchy. (p. 22)
Pyke, Helen Godfrey. Julia. (p. 932)
—Pinch River: Growing up Hard & Fast on the Michigan Frontier. (p. 1359)
Pyle, Charles S., illus. see Bowen, Fred.
Pyle, Chuck, illus. see Bowen, Fred.
Pyle, Chuck, illus. see Hope, Laura Lee.
Pyle, Ernie Howard. Men of Iron. (p. 1126)
Pyle, Howard. Adventures of Robin Hood. (p. 22)
—Adventures of Robin Hood. Corvino, Lucy, illus. (p. 22)
—Garden Behind the Moon: A Real Story of the Moon-Angel. (p. 656)
—Men of Iron. (p. 1126)
—Merry Adventures of Robin Hood: With a Discussion of Fellowship. Clift, Eva, tr. (p. 1128)
—Merry Adventures of Robin Hood. (p. 1128)
—Merry Adventures of Robin Hood. Dunn, Ben, illus. (p. 1128)
—Merry Adventures of Robin Hood. McKowen, Scott, illus. (p. 1128)
—Modern Aladdin: Or, the Wonderful Adventures of Oliver Munier. (p. 1158)
—Modern Aladdin: Or the Wonderful Adventures of Oliver Munier, an Extravaganza in Four Acts (1892) (p. 1158)
—Modern Aladdin, or, the Wonderful Adventures of Oliver Munier, an Extravaganza in Four Acts. (p. 1158)
—Modern Aladdin - or, the Wondferful Adventures of Oliver Munier. (p. 1158)
—Otto of the Silver Hand. (p. 1307)
—Pepper & Salt & the Wonder Clock Pyle, Howard, illus. (p. 1340)
—Pepper & Salt or Seasoning for Young Folk. (p. 1340)
—Ruby of Kishmoor. (p. 1493)
—Stolen Treasure. (p. 1652)
—Story of Jack Ballister's Fortunes (p. 1658)
—Story of King Arthur & His Knights. Pyle, Howard, illus. (p. 1658)
—Story of King Arthur & His Knights. McKowen, Scott, illus. (p. 1658)
—Story of Sir Lancelot & His Companions. (p. 1660)
—Story of the Champions of the Round Table. (p. 1660)
—Twilight Land. (p. 1801)
—Within the Capes. (p. 1942)
—Wonder Clock. (p. 1947)
—Wonder Clock or, Four & Twenty Marvelous Tales. (p. 1947)
Pyle, Kevin C. Katman. Pyle, Kevin C., illus. (p. 945)
—Take What You Can Carry. Pyle, Kevin C., illus. (p. 1697)
Pyle, Kevin C. & Cunningham, Scott. Bad for You: Exposing the War on Fun! Pyle, Kevin C., illus. (p. 131)
Pyle, Robert. Merry Adventures of Robin Hood. (p. 1128)
Pyle, Robert Michael & Peterson, Roger Tory. Butterflies. Peterson, Roger Tory, ed. (p. 247)
Pyles, Mary Kay. Rise & Shine Rosie. (p. 1474)
Pylypchuck, Anna, illus. see Calvani, Mayra.
Pylypchuk, Anna, jt. auth. see Calvani, Mayra.
Pym, T., illus. see Andersen, Hans Christian.
Pym, Tasha. Collins Big Cat - Super Sculptures: Band 05/Green. Elworthy, Antony, photos by. (p. 340)
—Have You Ever? Elworthy, Antony, illus. (p. 754)
—Monster Mess. Villet, Olivia, illus. (p. 1167)
Pym, Tasha & Pichon, Liz. Colour Bears. (p. 346)
Pynaert, Andrea, illus. see Guibert, Susan Mullen & O'Shaughnessy, Brendan.
Pynchon, Thomas. Against the Day. (p. 29)
Pyne, Erin A. Fandom of Magical Proportions: S: an Unauthorized History of the Harry Potter Phenomenon. (p. 570)
Pyne, Jane. Billy the Banger Racer. (p. 187)
—Rosie's Story - an Alpaca's Tale. (p. 1490)
—Tommy's Secret. (p. 1765)
Pyne, Lynette & Pressnall, Debra Olson. Colorful File Folder Games: Skill-Building Center Activities for Language Arts & Math. Neville, Bill, illus. (p. 344)
—File Folder Games Grade 2: Skill-Building Center Activities for Language Arts & Math. (p. 586)
Pynn, Susan. Colours of My Home: A Portrait of Newfoundland & Labrador Keating, Nancy, illus. (p. 346)
—Jelly Bean Row Pratt, Liz, illus. (p. 912)
—Puppy Story Keating, Nancy, illus. (p. 1418)
P.Young, Linda. Adventures of Anna & Andy Hummingbird: Stories 6-10. (p. 16)
Pyrnelle, Louise Clarke. Diddie Dumps & Tot: Or, Plantation Child-life. (p. 437)
Pyron, Bobbie. Dogs of Winter. (p. 463)
—Dog's Way Home. (p. 463)
—Dog's Way Home. Jessell, Tim, illus. (p. 463)
—Lucky Strike. (p. 1063)
Pyros, Andrea. My Year of Epic Rock: How to Survive 7th Grade: Make Some Noise. (p. 1222)
Pyrtle Second Graders & Writers' Circle. Poetry & a Fifth Grade Cinderell: An Anthology from Nebraska. (p. 1376)
Pytlik, Tami S. Look What Goldilocks Did! (p. 1050)
Pyykkonen, Carrie & Washington, Linda. Secrets of the Wee Free Men & Discworld: The Myths & Legends of Terry Pratchett's Multiverse. (p. 1546)

Q

Q. Dani-L's Counting Alphabet Book. (p. 404)
Q, jt. auth. see Quiller-Couch, Arthur Thomas.
Q., Bev. Diddly Duck & His Goosie Friends. (p. 437)
—When the Carnival Comes to Town. Thomas, Lillie Michelle, illus. (p. 1904)
Q, Likit, illus. see Brown, Janet.
Q2A Staff, illus. see Abnett, Dan.
Q2AMedia Services Private Ltd, Q2AMedia Services, illus. see Young, Rae.
Q2AMedia Services Private Ltd Staff, illus. see Young, Rae.
Qahhaar El-Amin, Mary M. Baby Ears: The Littlest Elephant. (p. 126)
Qaiser, Annie. China. (p. 306)
—How to Analyze the Works of George Washington. (p. 814)
—How to Analyze the Works of Thomas Jefferson. (p. 814)
—Story of the Statue of Liberty: A History Perspectives Book. (p. 1662)
Qamar, Amjed. Beneath My Mother's Feet. (p. 164)
Qamaruddin, Rizwana. Allah Gave Me a Nose to Smell. Stratford, Stevan, illus. (p. 46)
Qaunaq, Sakiasi. Orphan & the Polar Bear Widermann, Eva, illus. (p. 1304)
Qing, Zheng. Find Out about China: Learn Chinese Words & Phrases & about Life in China. Hutchinson, Tim, illus. (p. 587)
Qitsualik, Rachel A. Shadows That Rush Past: A Collection of Frightening Inuit Folktales. MacDougall, Larry & Fiegenschuh, Emily, illus. (p. 1558)
Qitsualik-Tinsley, Rachel & Qitsualik-Tinsley, Sean. How Things Came to Be: Inuit Stories of Creation Lewis-MacDougall, Patricia Ann & Fiegenschuh, Emily, illus. (p. 814)
—Skraelings: Clashes in the Old Arctic Trabbold, Andrew, illus. (p. 1586)
—Tuniit: Mysterious Folk of the Arctic Bigham, Sean, illus. (p. 1797)
Qitsualik-Tinsley, Rachel, et al. Stories of Survival & Revenge: From Inuit Folklore (p. 1655)
Qitsualik-Tinsley, Sean, jt. auth. see Qitsualik-Tinsley, Rachel.
Qovaizi, Mo, illus. see McCartney, Tania Maree.
QTA Media Staff, illus. see Foster, Karen.
QTA Media Staff, illus. see Law, Felicia.
Qu, Zhi. Little Sima & the Giant Bowl. Wang, Lin, illus. (p. 1036)
Quaal, Jean. If Roosters Crow? (p. 854)
Quach, Lam, illus. see Lebovics, Dania.
Quackenbush, Marcia, illus. see Loulan, Joann & Worthen, Bonnie.
Quackenbush, Robert. Detective Mole. (p. 431)
—First Grade Jitters. Nascimbene, Yan, illus. (p. 595)
—Henry's Awful Mistake. Quackenbush, Robert, illus. (p. 769)
—Moose's Store. (p. 1173)
—Piet Potter Returns: A Piet Potter Mystery. (p. 1357)
—Piet Potter Strikes Again: A Piet Potter Mystery. (p. 1357)
Quackenbush-Douglas, Diane. That's Just the Way it Was! (Not a Fairy Tale) (p. 1727)
Quackenworth Publishing, creator. Quigley Mccormick Math Curriculum Guide: And the Curse of the Polka Dotted Pig. Focusing on: Elementary Measurement & Geometry, Book 1 (p. 1428)
Quadflieg, Roswitha, illus. see Ende, Michael.
Quadflieg, Roswitha, tr. see Ende, Michael.
Quadling, Douglas. Mechanics 2. (p. 1118)
—Mechanics 3 & 4. (p. 1118)
Quadling, Douglas & Neill, Hugh. Core 1 & 2 for OCR. (p. 367)
—Core 3 & 4 for OCR. (p. 367)
Quadri, Habeeb & Quadri, Sa'ad. War Within Our Hearts. (p. 1858)
Quadri, Sa'ad, jt. auth. see Quadri, Habeeb.
Quaglia, Russell & Fox, Kristine M. Raising Student Aspirations Grades 6-8: Classroom Activities. (p. 1437)
—Raising Student Aspirations Grades 9-12: Classroom Activities. (p. 1437)
Quah, Chiew Kin. Translation & Technology. (p. 1778)
Quaid, Jack, jt. auth. see Mamet, Clara.
Quail, Annette. Lucy & Coco. (p. 1063)
Quail, Jane. Easter Bunny's Journey. (p. 499)
Quail, Traci. Will Santa Find Daddy for Christmas? (p. 1932)
Qualey, Marsha. Come in from the Cold. (p. 347)
—Thin Ice. (p. 1732)
Qualey, Marsha, ed. Clementine. D'Antonio, Sandra, illus. (p. 330)
—Old MacDonald Had a Farm. D'Antonio, Sandra, illus. (p. 1284)
—She'll Be Coming Around the Mountain. D'Antonio, Sandra, illus. (p. 1564)
—Traditional Songs D'Antonio, Sandra, illus. (p. 1776)
Quality Productions Staff. Lechuzas. Rountree, Monica, tr. (p. 987)
—Owls. (p. 1315)
—Tigres. Rountree, Monica, tr. (p. 1749)
Qualls, Hannah. Ghost of Hyde: A Sequel to Jack or Hyde? (p. 671)
Qualls, Millie Marie. Miss Cooney & Her New Home. (p. 1151)
Qualls, Sean, illus. see Alko, Selina.
Qualls, Sean, illus. see Derby, Sally.
Qualls, Sean, illus. see Engle, Margarita.
Qualls, Sean, illus. see Hughes, Langston.
Qualls, Sean, illus. see Lee, Spike & Lee, Tonya Lewis.
Qualls, Sean, illus. see Morrison, Toni & Morrison, Slade.
Qualls, Sean, illus. see Orgill, Roxane.
Qualls, Sean, illus. see Pinkney, Andrea Davis.
Qualls, Sean, illus. see Thompson, Laurie Ann.
Qualls, Sean, illus. see Walker, Sally M.
Qualls, Sean, illus. see Weatherford, Carole Boston.
Qualls, Sean, illus. see Winter, Jonah.
Qualls, Shirley. Marigold Duck Comes to Our School. (p. 1094)
Quan, Adalucia. Magic of Clay. (p. 1073)
—Song of the Coconut. (p. 1611)
Quan, Elizabeth. Beyond the Moongate: True Stories of 1920s China. (p. 174)
—Once upon a Full Moon. (p. 1292)
Quan-D'Eramo, Sandra. 10 Best TV Game Shows. (p. 1993)
—10 Most Amazing Animated Movies. (p. 1993)
Quansah, Carol-Ann. Garden. (p. 656)
Quanstrom, Brenda. Gramma I'm Bored. Quinn, Peter, illus. (p. 706)
Quantrell, Angie. I Can Do It! Lollar, Cathy, illus. (p. 835)

—I Can Give. (p. 835)
Quanty, Donna. Dottie's New Look. (p. 472)
Quaratiello, Arlene R. Rachel Carson: A Biography (p. 1431)
Quarello, Maurizio A. C., illus. see Albo, Pablo.
Quarello, Maurizio A. C., illus. see Cohen-Janca, Irène.
Quarello, Maurizio A. C., illus. see McFadden, Deanna.
Quarello, Maurizio A. C., illus. see Meroto, Tina.
Quarello, Maurizio A. C., illus. see Namm, Diane.
Quarello, Maurizio A. C., illus. see Olmstead, Kathleen.
Quarles, Bernadict. Chronicles of Maya & Quincy: When I Grow Up. (p. 317)
Quarles, Jean Marie. Not Quite Angels of Icicletap. (p. 1267)
Quarles, Pamela. Jake & Josh Go Camping. Denison, Susan, illus. (p. 905)
Quarles, Patrice Michelle. Get up, & Start Your Day: Give Mommy & Daddy a Break. (p. 668)
Quarmby, Katharine. Fussy Freya. Grobler, Piet, illus. (p. 650)
QUARMBY, Katharine & GROBLER, Piet. Fussy Freya. (p. 650)
Quarmby, Toby, jt. auth. see Ivanoff, George.
Quartey, Esme. Life with My Sister ChanSadiefay Thompso. (p. 1013)
Quarto Books, Quarto, ed. see Billet, Marion.
Quarto Books, Quarto, ed. Amazing Animals: A Collection of Creatures Great & Small. (p. 53)
—Beautiful Beasts. (p. 153)
Quarto Generic Staff. Arcimboldo: With More Than 70 Reusable Stickers! (p. 95)
—Charles Dickens: Scenes from an Extraordinary Life. Manning, Mick & Granström, Brita, illus. (p. 292)
—Dragon Snatcher. (p. 478)
—E Is for Ethiopia. Abate, Betelhem et al, photos by. (p. 492)
—Eye on the Wild: Sea Otter. Eszterhas, Suzi, photos by. (p. 558)
—Frank N Stan. Robertson, M. P., illus. (p. 629)
—I Am Cat. Morris, Jackie, illus. (p. 832)
—It's Not Fairy. Asquith, Ros, illus. (p. 898)
—Johnny the Clockmaker. Ardizzone, Edward, illus. (p. 923)
—My Bear Griz. McGinness, Suzanne, illus. (p. 1196)
—Nature School. Manning, Mick & Granström, Brita, illus. (p. 1236)
—No More Kisses for Bernard! Daly, Niki, illus. (p. 1259)
—Pablo Picasso. Delpech, Sylvie & Leclerc, Caroline, eds. (p. 1316)
—Paul Klee. Delpech, Sylvie & Leclerc, Caroline, eds. (p. 1330)
—Something about a Bear. Morris, Jackie, illus. (p. 1609)
—Song for Jamela. Daly, Niki, illus. (p. 1611)
—Turtle & the Island: A Folk Tale from Papua New Guinea. Lessac, Frané, illus. (p. 1798)
—Under the Weather: Stories about Climate Change. Bradman, Tony, ed. (p. 1814)
Quarto Generic Staff, jt. auth. see Adl, Shirin.
Quarto Generic Staff, jt. auth. see Agard, John.
Quarto Generic Staff, jt. auth. see Ardizzone, Edward.
Quarto Generic Staff, jt. auth. see Arrigan, Mary.
Quarto Generic Staff, jt. auth. see Barber, Antonia.
Quarto Generic Staff, jt. auth. see Billington, Rachel.
Quarto Generic Staff, jt. auth. see Boroson, Martin.
Quarto Generic Staff, jt. auth. see Bradman, Tony.
Quarto Generic Staff, jt. auth. see Cave, Kathryn.
Quarto Generic Staff, jt. auth. see Chatterjee, Debjani.
Quarto Generic Staff, jt. auth. see Cooling, Wendy.
Quarto Generic Staff, jt. auth. see Cross, Gillian.
Quarto Generic Staff, jt. auth. see Curtis, Vanessa.
Quarto Generic Staff, jt. auth. see Dunn, James.
Quarto Generic Staff, jt. auth. see Ewart, Franzeska G.
Quarto Generic Staff, jt. auth. see Garland, Sarah.
Quarto Generic Staff, jt. auth. see Gavin, Jamila.
Quarto Generic Staff, jt. auth. see Hall, S. M.
Quarto Generic Staff, jt. auth. see Henderson, Kathy.
Quarto Generic Staff, jt. auth. see Hofmeyr, Dianne.
Quarto Generic Staff, jt. auth. see Hooper, Meredith.
Quarto Generic Staff, jt. auth. see House, Catherine.
Quarto Generic Staff, jt. auth. see Hughes, Ted.
Quarto Generic Staff, jt. auth. see Jungman, Ann.
Quarto Generic Staff, jt. auth. see Kearns, Zannah.
Quarto Generic Staff, jt. auth. see Kerven, Rosalind.
Quarto Generic Staff, jt. auth. see Laird, Elizabeth.
Quarto Generic Staff, jt. auth. see Littlewood, Karin.
Quarto Generic Staff, jt. auth. see Maddern, Eric.
Quarto Generic Staff, jt. auth. see Marsh, Graham.
Quarto Generic Staff, jt. auth. see Micklethwait, Lucy.
Quarto Generic Staff, jt. auth. see Mitton, Jacqueline.
Quarto Generic Staff, jt. auth. see Modern Painters Staff.
Quarto Generic Staff, jt. auth. see Northway, Jennifer.
Quarto Generic Staff, jt. auth. see Onyefulu, Ifeoma.
Quarto Generic Staff, jt. auth. see Petty, Kate.
Quarto Generic Staff, jt. auth. see Rahman, Urmi.
Quarto Generic Staff, jt. auth. see Rhodes, Julie.
Quarto Generic Staff, jt. auth. see Robert, Na'Ima B.
Quarto Generic Staff, jt. auth. see Robertson, M. P.
Quarto Generic Staff, jt. auth. see Roddie, Shen.
Quarto Generic Staff, jt. auth. see Rosen, Michael.
Quarto Generic Staff, jt. auth. see Salvador, Ana.
Quarto Generic Staff, jt. auth. see Simpson-Enock, Sarah.
Quarto Generic Staff, jt. auth. see Smith, Frank Dabba.
Quarto Generic Staff, jt. auth. see So, Sungwan.
Quarto Generic Staff, jt. auth. see Souhami, Jessica.
Quarto Generic Staff, jt. auth. see Steggall, Susan.
Quarto Generic Staff, jt. auth. see Stevens, Roger.
Quarto Generic Staff, jt. auth. see Stewart, Dianne.
Quarto Generic Staff, jt. auth. see Tavaci, Elspeth.
Quarto Generic Staff, jt. auth. see Taylor, Sean.
Quarto Generic Staff, jt. auth. see Wilson-Max, Ken.
Quarto Generic Staff, jt. auth. see Wolfe, Gillian.
Quarto Generic Staff, jt. auth. see Wulfsohn, Gisèle.
Quartz, Jane & Quartz, Oliver. How Much Are We Alike? (p. 811)
Quartz, Oliver, jt. auth. see Quartz, Jane.
Quasar, Gian. Hell Ship. (p. 763)
Quasha, J. How to Draw Alabama's Sights & Symbols. (p. 816)
—How to Draw Alaska's Sights & Symbols. (p. 816)
Quasha, Jennifer. Birth & Growth of a Nation: Hands-on Projects about Symbols of American Liberty. (p. 192)
—Covered Wagons: Hands-on Projects about America's Westward Expansion. (p. 373)
—Gold Rush: Hands-on Projects about Mining the Riches of California. (p. 694)
—How to Draw Arizona's Sights & Symbols. (p. 816)
—How to Draw Arkansas's Sights & Symbols. (p. 816)
—How to Draw California's Sights & Symbols. (p. 817)
—How to Draw Colorado's Sights & Symbols. (p. 817)
—How to Draw Connecticut's Sights & Symbols. (p. 817)
—How to Draw Delaware's Sights & Symbols. (p. 817)
—How to Draw Florida's Sights & Symbols. (p. 817)
—How to Draw Georgia's Sights & Symbols. (p. 817)
—How to Draw Hawaii's Sights & Symbols. (p. 817)
—How to Draw Idaho's Sights & Symbols. (p. 817)
—Jamestown: Hands-on Projects about One of America's First Communities. (p. 907)
—Mission San Luis Rey de Francia. (p. 1153)
—Robert Rogers: Rogers' Rangers & the French & Indian War. (p. 1479)
—Robert Rogers: Rogers' Rangers, & the French & Indian War. (p. 1479)
Quasha, Jennifer, ed. see Dorling Kindersley Publishing Staff.
Quasha, Jennifer, ed. see Sirett, Dawn & Dorling Kindersley Publishing Staff.
Quateman, Bill & Quateman, India. Daddy Daughter Dinner Dance: A Father's Steps to a Blended Family That Really Works. Quateman, India, illus. (p. 398)
Quateman, India, jt. auth. see Quateman, Bill.
Quattlebaum, Mary. Family Reunion. Shine, Andrea, illus. (p. 568)
—Jackson Jones & the Curse of the Outlaw Rose. (p. 904)
—Jo MacDonald Had a Garden. Bryant, Laura J., illus. (p. 919)
—Jo MacDonald Hiked in the Woods. Bryant, Laura J., illus. (p. 919)
—Jo MacDonald Saw a Pond. Bryant, Laura J., illus. (p. 919)
—Mighty Mole & Super Soil. Wallace, Chad, illus. (p. 1140)
—Pirate vs. Pirate: The Terrific Tale of a Big, Blustery Maritime Match. Boiger, Alexandra, illus. (p. 1363)
Quattro, Jack. Matt Gets in Trouble! (p. 1109)
Quattro, Jacquelyn, jt. auth. see Blue, Sky.
Quattro, Jacquelyn, jt. auth. see Foster, Greg.
Quave, Gloria Martinez, tr. see O'Connor, Crystal Ball.
Quay, Emma. Good Night, Sleep Tight: A Book about Bedtime. Walker, Anna, illus. (p. 700)
—Yummy Ice Cream: A Book about Sharing. Walker, Anna, illus. (p. 1983)
Quay, Emma, illus. see Daddo, Andrew.
Quby, A. Leigh. Every Other Weekend. (p. 543)
Quebodeaux, Vernice, jt. auth. see Martin, Tamara.
Quednau, Marion. Gift of Odin. Mulabdic, Sonja, illus. (p. 675)
Queen, Cynthia. Major's Renegade. (p. 1078)
Queen, Dana, illus. see Castleton, Chaffee.
Queen Latifah. Queen of the Scene. Morrison, Frank, illus. (p. 1425)
Queen Octavia. 10 Silly Duckies: Counting Book. (p. 1994)
Queen Rania of Jordan Al Abdullah Staff, et al. Sandwich Swap. Tusa, Tricia, illus. (p. 1511)
Queen, Stephenie. Cursed. (p. 395)
Queenston, Rory. Rachel Carson: Saving the Environment. (p. 1432)
Quek, Lynette, jt. auth. see Falconer, Kieran.
Quek, Lynette, jt. auth. see Hassig, Susan M.
Quek, Lynette, jt. auth. see Sheehan, Patricia.
Quek, Lynette, jt. auth. see Stavreva, Kirilka.
Queralt, Elisenda. Salamandra. (p. 1504)
Queralt, Elisenda & Adell, Montse. Luna Contenta. (p. 1065)
Querin, Pamela, illus. see Lewis, Beverly.
Querin, Pamela, jt. auth. see Lewis, Beverly.
Quesada, Joe, jt. auth. see Bendis, Brian Michael.
Quesada, Joe & Kubert, Andy. Origin. (p. 1304)
Quesada, Joe & Tieri, Frank. Iron Man by Joe Quesada. Martinez, Alitha et al, illus. (p. 888)
Quesada, Maria Fe, illus. see Everest.
Quesinberry, Bonita M. Truth Gathering. (p. 1794)
Quest, Stacy. Sad Sam & the Magic Cookies. Wertheimer, Beverly & Ronsley, Jill, eds. (p. 1501)
Questmarc Publishing, creator. Chat Pack for Kids: Creative Questions to Ignite the Imagination. (p. 295)
Quetel, Julie. Adventures of Shayne & His Flying Grandma. (p. 22)
Quetel, Linda. Heritage Undone. Greaux, Romea, illus. (p. 771)
Quevedo, Francisco de. Historia de la Vida del Buscan: Llamado Don Pablos. (p. 782)
Quezada, Juan. Juan Quezada. Mlawer, Teresa, tr. (p. 930)
—Juan Quezada. Dale, Shelley, illus. (p. 930)
Quible, Rennie G. Upepo the Rainmaker. (p. 1824)
Quick, Barbara. Golden Web. (p. 695)
Quick, Barbara, jt. auth. see McGrath, Liz.
Quick, Jen Lee. Off*Beat (p. 1279)
Quick, Matthew. Boy21. (p. 220)
—Forgive Me, Leonard Peacock. (p. 619)
—Sorta Like a Rock Star. (p. 1614)
Quick Revision KS3 History Staff. Quick Revision KS3 History. (p. 1427)
Quie, Sarah, jt. auth. see Bell, Michael.
Quigley, Daniel. Face Full of Wind. (p. 560)
Quigley, Karen. Everyone Loves Elwood. (p. 544)
Quigley, Mary. Middle Ages. (p. 1137)
—Renaissance. (p. 1460)
Quigley, Michael. Monkey's Riddle. (p. 1166)
Quigley, Nancy. Mouse Perspectives: Holiday Series. (p. 1182)
Quigley, Sebastian, illus. see Robinson, Nick.
Quigley, Sebastian, illus. see Steele, Philip & Lavery, Brian.
Quigley, Sebastian, illus. see Terry, Nicolas.
Quigley, Sebastian, illus. see U. S. National Geographic Society Staff.
Quigley, Sebastian, illus. see Robinson, Nick.
Quihuis, Albert. Search for the Lost Art of Making Tortillas. (p. 1537)
Quijano, Jonathan. Make Your Movie. (p. 1079)
—Make Your Own Action Thriller (p. 1079)
—Make Your Own Comedy (p. 1079)
—Make Your Own Horror Movie (p. 1080)
—Make Your Own Sci-Fi Flick (p. 1080)
Quill, Charles G. History of the Blues. (p. 784)
Quill, Charlie. History of the Blues. (p. 784)
—Michelangelo: His Life & Art. (p. 1135)
Quillen, Carl. Dragon Girl Myra. (p. 477)
Quillen, Donna Mc. I Can't Wait. (p. 837)
Quiller-Couch, Arthur Thomas. Naughts & Crosses. (p. 1237)
—Splendid Spur. (p. 1630)
—True Tilda. (p. 1793)
—White Wolf & Other Fireside Tales. (p. 1914)
Quiller-Couch, Arthur Thomas & Q. Naughts & Crosses. (p. 1237)
Quiller-Couch, Mabel. Kitty Trenire. (p. 963)
Quiller-Couch, Sir Arthur. Twelve Dancing Princesses & Other Fairy Tales. Nielsen, Kay, illus. (p. 1800)
Quimby, Laura. Carnival of Lost Souls. (p. 270)
Quin, Caroline. Shopping. (p. 1569)
Quin, Caroline, jt. auth. see Pearce, Sue.
Quin, Caroline & Pearce, Sue. Gardening. (p. 656)
—Weather. (p. 1869)
Quinby, Michelle. Connecting the 21st Century to the Past: What Makes America America, 2000-The Present. (p. 358)
—Connecting the 21st Century to the Past: What Makes America America, 2000-The Present. Rakove, Jack N., ed. (p. 358)
—Wars at Home: America Forms an Identity (1812-1820) (p. 1859)
—Wars at Home: America Forms an Identity (1812-1820). Rakove, Jack N., ed. (p. 1859)
Quince, Lia. Abby & Jules. (p. 2)
Quindlen, Anna. Imagined London: A Tour of the World's Greatest Fictional City. (p. 861)
Quin-Harkin, Janet. Forever Friday. (p. 619)
—Four's a Crowd. (p. 625)
—Friday Night Fright. (p. 637)
—Secret Valentine. (p. 1544)
—Sleepover Madness. (p. 1589)
—Toe Shoe Trouble. (p. 1761)
Quin-Harkin, Janet, see Bowen, Rhys, pseud.
Quinlan, Daniel J. Legend of Kilidiablo: Kisa Cha Kilidiablo. (p. 988)
Quinlan, David. Tim Horton: Portrait of an Extraordinary Canadian (p. 1750)
Quinlan, Divya Maureen. Baggy Duck of Rainbow's End. (p. 132)
Quinlan, Don. Rick Hansen: Larger Than Life (p. 1470)
—Rick Hansen: A Larger Than Life Biography (p. 1470)
—Tim Horton (p. 1750)
Quinlan, Julia J. Alfa Romeo. (p. 37)
—Aston Martin. (p. 108)
—Audi. (p. 114)
—Corvette. (p. 368)
—Different Kinds of Maps. (p. 438)
—Dingoes. (p. 440)
—Ferrari. (p. 582)
—GPS & Computer Maps. (p. 704)
—Honey Badgers. (p. 794)
—How to Draw a Map. (p. 816)
—Hyenas. (p. 831)
—Jaguar. (p. 905)
—Keys, Legends, & Symbols in Maps. (p. 950)
—Lamborghini. (p. 972)
—Latitude, Longitude, & Direction. (p. 980)
—Lotus. (p. 1057)
—Maserati. (p. 1102)
—Mercedes. (p. 1127)
—Mustang. (p. 1194)
—Scale & Distance in Maps. (p. 1519)
—Tasmanian Devils. (p. 1707)
—Wild Boars. (p. 1929)
—Wolverines. (p. 1944)
Quinlan, Nigel. Weatherman. (p. 1870)
Quinlan, Patricia. Tiger Flowers Wilson, Janet, illus. (p. 1748)
Quinlan, Susan E. Caribou. (p. 269)
—Case of the Monkeys That Fell from the Trees: And Other Mysteries in Tropical Nature. (p. 274)
—Puffins. (p. 1415)
Quinley, Elliot & Greene, Janice. Read Reflect Respond 2 (p. 1443)
Quinley, Elliott. Persuasive Writing Saddleback Educational Publishing Staff, ed. (p. 1344)
Quinlivan, Ada. Blake the Baker: Develop Understanding of Fractions & Numbers. (p. 198)
Quinlivan, Ana. Hummingbirds: World's Fastest Wings. (p. 827)
Quinlivan, Kelly. Science Museum Time! Work with Time (p. 1527)
Quinn, jt. auth. see Weatherall, Donald M.
Quinn, Alice, et al, trs. My Town: A Little World for You to Build. (p. 1220)
Quinn, Anna, ed. see Forte, Imogene & Frank, Marjorie.
Quinn, Barbara & Isler, Claudia. Understanding Your Right to Vote. (p. 1816)
Quinn, Courtney, illus. see Dyan, Penelope.
Quinn, Cynthia J. Priceless Gifts. (p. 1398)
—Ten Reasons Why. (p. 1719)
Quinn, Daniel P. I Am Buddhist. (p. 832)
Quinn, David B. Lost Colonists: Their Fortune & Probable Fate. (p. 1055)
Quinn, Douglas. Adventures of Quinn Higgins Boy Detective: The Case of Bigfoot on the Loose. (p. 22)
—Adventures of Quinn Higgins: Boy Detective — the Case of the Haunted House. (p. 22)
—Charles of Colshire Castle — the Purple Dragon. (p. 292)
Quinn, Edward. History in Literature: A Reader's Guide to 20th Century History & the Literature It Inspired. (p. 783)
Quinn, Frances, jt. auth. see Elliott, Catherine.
Quinn, Gloria W. Lemon Water. (p. 991)
Quinn, Jordan. Let the Games Begin! McPhillips, Robert, illus. (p. 994)
—Lost Stone. (p. 1056)
—Lost Stone. McPhillips, Robert, illus. (p. 1056)
—Scarlet Dragon. (p. 1520)
—Scarlet Dragon. McPhillips, Robert, illus. (p. 1520)
—Sea Monster! McPhillips, Robert, illus. (p. 1535)
—Secret World of Mermaids. McPhillips, Robert, illus. (p. 1544)
—Witch's Curse. McPhillips, Robert, illus. (p. 1941)
Quinn, K. A. S. Queen Alone. (p. 1424)
—Queen at War. West, Maddie, ed. (p. 1424)
—Queen Must Die. (p. 1425)
Quinn, Kate Karyus. Another Little Piece. (p. 88)
—(Don't You) Forget about Me. (p. 469)
Quinn, Kitty, illus. see Schwarz, Evelyn.
Quinn, Kristine M., jt. auth. see Mayfield, Christine.
Quinn, Lin. Best Mud Pie. Rooney, Ronnie, illus. (p. 170)
Quinn, Michael A. Chop Wood, Carry Water: Listening for the Whispers. (p. 310)
Quinn, Naomi. Finding Culture in Talk: A Collection of Methods. Quinn, Naomi, ed. (p. 588)
Quinn, Paris. Shadow & Light Quinn, Paris, illus. (p. 1557)
Quinn, Pat. Starz. (p. 1644)
Quinn, Patricia O. Attention, Girls! A Guide to Learn All about Your AD/HD. Pearce, Carl, illus. (p. 114)
Quinn, Patricia O. & Maitland, Theresa E. Laurie. On Your Own: A College Readiness Guide for Teens with ADHD/LD. Ische, Bryan, illus. (p. 1292)
Quinn, Patricia O. & Stern, Judith M. Putting on the Brakes: Understanding & Taking Control of Your ADD or ADHD. (p. 1420)
—Putting on the Brakes: Understanding & Taking Control of Your ADD or ADHD. Lee, Joe, illus. (p. 1420)
—Putting on the Brakes Activity Book for Kids with ADD or ADHD. Lee, Joe, illus. (p. 1420)
Quinn, Patrick Sean. Ceramic Petrography: The Interpretation of Archaeological Pottery & Related Artefacts in Thin Section. (p. 287)
Quinn, Paul Michael. Love Flute. (p. 1059)
Quinn, Paula. Lord of Seduction. (p. 1052)
Quinn, Peter, illus. see Quanstrom, Brenda.
Quinn, Sarah, jt. auth. see Rivard, Émilie.
Quinn, Sarah, tr. see Cohen, Laurie.
Quinn, Sarah, tr. see Manceau, Édouard.
Quinn, Sarah, tr. from FRE. Day at the Farm. (p. 412)
Quinn, Savannah, illus. see Patterson, Drake.
Quinn, Shelley J., jt. auth. see Shelton, Danny.
Quinn, Spencer, pseud. Paw & Order: A Chet & Bernie Mystery. (p. 1331)
—Woof: A Bowser & Birdie Mystery. (p. 1950)
Quinn, Stephanie. Beginning Improv Workshop for Kids. (p. 159)
—Little Stars Creative Drama for Preschoolers. (p. 1036)
—Miss Medieval Beauty Pageant. (p. 1151)
Quinn, Thalamus. Our Father God. (p. 1308)
Quinn, Timothy. Marvelous Miriam's Magnificent Hawaiian Adventure. (p. 1099)
Quino. Mafalda 9. (p. 1071)
—Mafalda & Friends. (p. 1071)
Quino & *quino. Mafalda. (p. 1070)
Quinones, Jacqueline, tr. see Hooper, Nancy.
Quinones, Joe, illus. see Weisman, Greg.
Quinones, Juan Carlos. Gang & the Biggest Book in the World. Ortiz Montanez, Nivea, illus. (p. 655)
—Pandilla Bajo el Arbol. Ortiz Montanez, Nivea, illus. (p. 1321)
Quiñones, Magaly. Quiero una Noche Azul. (p. 1428)
Quinones, Nathan, ed. see Silverstein, Ruth J., et al.
Quint, M. Preschool Readiness Book. (p. 1396)
Quintana, Adrienne. Eruption. (p. 534)
Quintana, Joela, tr. see Whybrow, Ian.
Quintana, Pamela. Silly Sweet SnuggleBugzzz Dreamzzz. (p. 1576)
Quintanilla, Billie. Greatest Mousemas Ever! Barnum, Tabatha, illus. (p. 720)
—Never Again a Homeless Christmas! (p. 1242)
Quintanilla, Efren. Aventuras de Bartolillo. (p. 119)
Quintanilla Sainz, Efren. Cervantes: Relatos Ilustrados. (p. 288)
Quintart, Natalie. Mama Bear. Blanchart, Stephanie, illus. (p. 1084)
Quintero, Aramis. Todo el Cielo un Juguete Poemas para Ninos. (p. 1761)
Quintero, Carlos, ed. Sales Lexicon: A Handy Table-Top Reference of Useful Terms & Sales Practices for Sales Organizations. (p. 1504)
Quintero, Isabel. Gabi, a Girl in Pieces. (p. 652)
Quintero, Joaquin Alvarez, see Alvarez Quintero, Serafin & Alvarez Quintero, Joaquin.
Quintero, José, illus. see Murguía, Verónica.
Quintero, michelle, illus. see Reminick, Gerald.
Quintero, Serafin Alvarez, see Alvarez Quintero, Serafin.
Quintero, Sofia. Efrain's Secret. (p. 506)
—Show & Prove. (p. 1570)
Quintin, Michel, jt. auth. see Bergeron, Alain M.
Quintin, Michel & Bergeron, Alain. Do You Know Tigers? Messier, Solange, tr. from FRE. (p. 458)
Quintin, Michel, et al. Do You Know Rhinoceros? Messier, Solange, tr. from FRE. (p. 458)
Quinton, Sasha. Eek-A-Squeak: A Phonics Reader. (p. 505)
—Florabelle. Barrager, Brigette & Tcherevkoff, Michel, illus. (p. 606)
—Go-Go-Goat: A Phonics Reader. (p. 686)
—Hoppity-Hop: A Phonics Reader. (p. 797)
—I-Spy: A Phonics Reader. (p. 846)
—Peck-A-peck: A Phonics Reader. (p. 1334)
—Rat-A-Tat: A Phonics Reader. (p. 1440)
—Ring-A-Ding: A Phonics Reader. (p. 1473)
—Root-A-Toot: A Phonics Reader. (p. 1488)
—Rub-A-Dub: A Phonics Reader. (p. 1493)
—Yay-Hooray: A Phonics Reader. (p. 1968)
Quinton, Sasha, jt. auth. see Posner, Renee.
Quinton, Sasha, text. Ears. (p. 494)
—Noses. (p. 1266)
—Paws. (p. 1331)
—Tails. (p. 1695)

Q

Quirino, Raffaele & Quirino, Ralph. Ani Difranco: Righteous Babe Revisited. (p. 76)
Quirino, Ralph, jt. auth. see Quirino, Raffaele.
Quirk, Katie. Girl Called Problem. (p. 678)
Quirke, Antonia. Choking on Marlon Brando. (p. 309)
Quiroga, Horacio. Cartas de un Cazador. (p. 272)
—Cuentos de la Selva. (p. 390)
—Cuentos de la Selva. Vallejo, Esperanza, illus. (p. 390)
—Cuentos de Mis Hijos. (p. 390)
—Historias Inmorales. Isaza, Juanita, illus. (p. 782)
—Lazy Bee. Leal, Mireya Fonseca, ed. (p. 981)
Quiroga, Luis Alberto. Chiquita. (p. 308)
Quiroz-Vega, Vashti. Basement: Robbie's Rite of Passage. (p. 141)
Quisenberry, Stacey. Dinosaur George Pre-hysterical Adventures: What Color Were Dinosaurs? Browning, Suzan, illus. (p. 442)
Quitely, Frank, illus. see Carey, Mike & Fabry, Glenn.
Quitzel, Ivey. Out of Control. (p. 1311)
Quivers, Anthony S. Lil' Johnny's First Day of School. (p. 1017)
Quixley, Barbara. Island Adventures of Jacki-Jacki. (p. 892)
Quraishi, Ibrahim, illus. see Williams, Emma.

R

R., Ben & Nash, Kevin. Suny Buffalo College Prowler off the Record: Inside State University of New York. (p. 1679)
R., Charlie. Christmas Mama Santa Delivered the Toys. (p. 314)
R, Disney. Incredibles. Stein, Erin, ed. (p. 870)
R. M. Ballantyne. Coral Island. (p. 366)
R. N., Lavanya. Bookworm. Suleman, Shilo Shiv, illus. (p. 213)
R, Sarah & Seaman, Jim. Rhodes College College Prowler off the Record. (p. 1468)
R. Tatum, W. Brooks. Childrens Short Stories for the Soul. (p. 304)
R. Z. Novit Graphic Design Staff, illus. see Novit, Renee Z.
Ra, In-Soo. King of Hell Jae-Hwan, Kim, illus. (p. 959)
Ra, In-Soo, jt. auth. see In-Soo, Ra.
Raab & Kiefe, Raab. Exploring Living Systems: Life Science. (p. 552)
Raab, Ben. Phantom: Death in the Deep Woods. (p. 1349)
Raab, Ben, jt. auth. see Johns, Geoff.
Raab, Birgitte, photos by see James, J. Alison, tr.
Raab, Brigitte. I Know Something You Don't Know. Olten, Manuela, illus. (p. 840)
—Mama, I Can't Sleep. Olten, Manuela, illus. (p. 1084)
—Where Does Pepper Come From? And Other Fun Facts. Olten, Manuela, illus. (p. 1907)
Raab, Evelyn. Clueless in the Kitchen: A Cookbook for Teens. Walker, George, illus. (p. 336)
Raab, Ralph. Dewey Deception: The First Adventure from the Biblio Files. (p. 432)
Raabe, Emily. Buffalo Soldiers & the Western Frontier. (p. 236)
—Bulldog Bats. (p. 240)
—Flying Foxes. (p. 610)
—Free-Tailed Bats. (p. 634)
—Gold Rush: California or Bust! (p. 694)
—Hanukkah Holiday Cookbook. (p. 744)
—Horseshoe Bats. (p. 800)
—Kwanzaa Holiday Cookbook. (p. 969)
—Lost Children of the Far Islands. (p. 1055)
—Mexican-American War. (p. 1131)
—Pioneers: Life as a Homesteader. (p. 1361)
—Plain-Nosed Bats. (p. 1366)
—Primary Source Guide to France. (p. 1399)
—Primary Source Guide to Morocco. (p. 1399)
—Prmiary Source Guide to France. (p. 1408)
—Thomas Jefferson & the Louisiana Purchase. (p. 1739)
—U. S. Cavalry & the Indian Wars. (p. 1806)
—Vampire Bats. (p. 1831)
Raanan, Ahuva & Walder, Chaim. Stories Straight from Avi's Heart. (p. 1655)
Raasch, Peg, illus. see Courtright, Anne.
Raasch, Sara. Ice Like Fire. (p. 850)
—Snow Like Ashes. (p. 1599)
Raatma, Lucia. African-American Soldiers in the Revolutionary War. (p. 27)
—Allosaurus. (p. 47)
—Animals Helping at Home. (p. 82)
—Ankylosaurus. (p. 84)
—Apatosaurus. (p. 91)
—Barbara Jordan. (p. 137)
—Battles of Lexington & Concord. (p. 147)
—Blogs. (p. 200)
—Bullying. (p. 241)
—Caring. (p. 269)
—China. (p. 306)
—Citizenship. (p. 323)
—Curious, Captivating, Unusual History of Sports (p. 392)
—Cyberbullying. (p. 396)
—Fairness. (p. 563)
—First of First Ladies: Martha Washington (p. 596)
—Giraffes. (p. 677)
—Good Manners. (p. 698)
—Green Living: No Action Too Small (p. 722)
—How Do We Live Together? Deer. (p. 808)
—How Do We Live Together? Mountain Lions. (p. 808)
—How Do We Live Together? Raccoons. (p. 808)
—How Do We Live Together? Snakes. (p. 808)
—Iguanodon. (p. 856)
—India. (p. 870)
—Islam (p. 891)
—It's Cool to Learn about Countries: Thailand. (p. 896)
—Jacqueline Kennedy. (p. 904)
—John Cena: Rapping Wrestler with Attitude (p. 921)
—Loyalty. (p. 1061)
—Making Smart Choices. (p. 1082)
—Michelle Obama. (p. 1135)
—Michigan. (p. 1135)
—Penguins. (p. 1337)
—Plains Zebras. (p. 1366)
—Pythons. (p. 1422)
—Respect. (p. 1463)
—Responsibility. (p. 1463)
—Rey Mysterio: High-Flying Luchador (p. 1467)
—Selma's Bloody Sunday. (p. 1550)
—Shirley Chisholm. (p. 1567)
—Signer for Independence: John Hancock (p. 1574)
—Snow Leopards. (p. 1599)
—Social Networks. (p. 1604)
—Sportsmanship. (p. 1633)
—Staying Safe Around Fire (p. 1645)
—Staying Safe Around Strangers (p. 1645)
—Staying Safe on the Playground (p. 1645)
—Stegosaurus. (p. 1646)
—Stop Bullying. (p. 1653)
—Tiger Woods. (p. 1749)
—Trustworthiness. (p. 1793)
—Tyrannosaurus Rex. (p. 1805)
—Underground Railroad. (p. 1814)
—Velociraptor. (p. 1835)
—War of 1812. (p. 1857)
—Working at a TV Station. (p. 1952)
—Working at City Hall. (p. 1952)
Raatma, Lucia, jt. auth. see Brown, Jonatha A.
Raatma, Lucia, jt. auth. see Dell, Pamela.
Raatma, Lucia, jt. auth. see O'Hern, Kerri.
Raatma, Lucia & Lee, Sally. Staying Safe. (p. 1645)
Raatma, Lucia & O'Hern, Kerri. Jackie Robinson. Campbell, Alex & Spay, Anthony, illus. (p. 903)
Raatma, Lucia & Sodaro, Craig. Unusual Histories. (p. 1823)
Rabascall, Iolanda, tr. see Sweet, J. H., et al.
Rabb, Margo. Kissing in America. (p. 962)
Rabbat, Suzy. Citing Sources: Learning to Use the Copyright Page. (p. 322)
—Post It! Sharing Photos with Friends & Family. (p. 1387)
—Super Smart Information Strategies: Hit the Books. (p. 1681)
—Super Smart Information Strategies: Find Your Way Online. (p. 1681)
—Super Smart Information Strategies: Creating a Digital Portfolio. (p. 1681)
—Super Smart Information Strategies: Using Digital Images. (p. 1682)
Rabbett, Martin. Forever Buster: What a Name! What a Dog, We Exclaim! Burns, Donna, illus. (p. 619)
Rabbi Schneur Zalman of Liadi. Shulchan Aruch: Hilchot Rosh Hashana thru Lulav -New Edition. (p. 1571)
—Shulchan Aruch - Orach Chayim 46-88: Code of Jewish Law. Vol. 3 Tauger, Eliyahu & Kaploun, Uri, trs. (p. 1571)
Rabbin, Robert & Masters, Deborah. Spiritual Wisdom of Kids. (p. 1629)
Rabbi's of Boca Raton Theological Seminary Staff. How to Raise a Jewish Dog. Burnstine, Susan, photos by. (p. 821)
Rabbit. Daniel in the Lion's Den. (p. 405)
—Parables That Jesus Told. (p. 1323)
—Ruth in Canaan. (p. 1498)
Rabe, Tish. Bamboozled. Moroney, Christopher, illus. (p. 135)
—Born to Run! Moroney, Christopher, illus. (p. 214)
—Can You See a Chimpanzee? All about Primates. Ruiz, Aristides & Mathieu, Joe, illus. (p. 259)
—Cat in the Hat Knows a Lot about Christmas! (Dr. Seuss/Cat in the Hat) Mathieu, Joe, illus. (p. 278)
—Chasing Rainbows. Ruiz, Aristides & Mathieu, Joe, illus. (p. 294)
—Chocolate Voyage. Aikins, Dave, illus. (p. 309)
—Clam-I-Am! All about the Beach. Ruiz, Aristides & Mathieu, Joe, illus. (p. 326)
—Frozen. (p. 645)
—Hello, My Baby (Dr. Seuss/Cat in the Hat) Mathieu, Joe & Ruiz, Aristides, illus. (p. 764)
—Home for Christmas. (p. 792)
—Home for Christmas. Brannon, Tom, illus. (p. 792)
—Hooray for Hair! Brannon, Tom, illus. (p. 796)
—How to Help the Earth-By the Lorax. (p. 820)
—How to Help the Earth-By the Lorax. Ruiz, Aristides et al, illus. (p. 820)
—How Wet Can You Get? Cat in the Hat Knows a Lot about That! Ruiz, Aristides & Mathieu, Joe, illus. (p. 823)
—Huff & Puff. Guile, Gill, illus. (p. 824)
—Huff & Puff & the New Train. Guile, Gill, illus. (p. 824)
—Huff & Puff Have Too Much Stuff! Guile, Gill, illus. (p. 824)
—I Love the Nightlife! Ruiz, Aristides & Mathieu, Joe, illus. (p. 843)
—If I Ran the Dog Show: All about Dogs. Ruiz, Aristides & Mathieu, Joe, illus. (p. 853)
—Innovative Kids Readers: Milly's Silly Suitcase - Level 1. Janovitz, Marilyn, illus. (p. 875)
—Inside Your Outside! All about the Human Body. Ruiz, Aristides, illus. (p. 878)
—King Cecil the Sea Horse (Dr. Seuss/Cat in the Hat) Moroney, Christopher, illus. (p. 958)
—Long Winter's Nap. Ruiz, Aristides & Mathieu, Joe, illus. (p. 1047)
—Look for the Lorax. (p. 1049)
—Lots of Flocks. (p. 1057)
—Miles & Miles of Reptiles: All about Reptiles. Ruiz, Aristides & Mathieu, Joe, illus. (p. 1142)
—My, Oh My—A Butterfly! All about Butterflies. Ruiz, Aristides & Mathieu, Joe, illus. (p. 1216)
—Night Lights. (p. 1253)
—Night Lights (Dr. Seuss/Cat in the Hat) Ruiz, Aristides & Mathieu, Joe, illus. (p. 1253)
—Oh, Baby, the Places You'll Go! Seuss, Dr., illus. (p. 1280)
—Oh, Give Me a Home! Ruiz, Aristides, illus. (p. 1280)
—Oh Say Can You Say What's the Weather Today? All about Weather. Ruiz, Aristides, illus. (p. 1281)
—Oh, the Pets You Can Get! All about Our Animal Friends. Ruiz, Aristides & Mathieu, Joe, illus. (p. 1281)
—Oh, the Things You Can Do That Are Good for You! All about Staying Healthy. Ruiz, Aristides, illus. (p. 1281)
—Out of Sight till Tonight! All about Nocturnal Animals. (p. 1311)
—Planet Name Game. (p. 1367)
—Planet Name Game (Dr. Seuss/Cat in the Hat) Brannon, Tom, illus. (p. 1367)
—Reindeer's First Christmas / New Friends for Christmas. (p. 1457)
—Reindeer's First Christmas-New Friends for Christmas. Mathieu, Joe & Ruiz, Aristides, illus. (p. 1457)
—Spring into Summer! Mathieu, Joe & Ruiz, Aristides, illus. (p. 1635)
—Step This Way (Dr. Seuss/Cat in the Hat) (p. 1648)
—Step This Way (Dr. Seuss/Cat in the Hat) Brannon, Tom, illus. (p. 1648)
—Tale about Tails. (p. 1699)
—Tale about Tails (Dr. Seuss/Cat in the Hat) Brannon, Tom, illus. (p. 1699)
—Thinga-Ma-Jigger Is Coming Today! Moroney, Christopher, illus. (p. 1733)
—Thump!/The Lost Egg (Cat in the Hat/Seuss) Ruiz, Aristides & Mathieu, Joe, illus. (p. 1746)
—Tree Doctor. (p. 1783)
—Trick-or-Treat!/Aye-Aye! Ruiz, Aristides & Mathieu, Joe, illus. (p. 1786)
—Very Crabby Christmas. Aikins, Dave, illus. (p. 1837)
—What Cat Is That? All about Cats. Ruiz, Aristides & Mathieu, Joe, illus. (p. 1881)
—Why Oh Why Are Deserts Dry? All about Deserts. Ruiz, Aristides & Mathieu, Joe, illus. (p. 1925)
—Wings & Paws & Fins & Claws. Ruiz, Aristides, illus. (p. 1936)
Rabe, Tish, ed. see Galvin, Laura Gates.
Rabe, Tish, jt. auth. see RH Disney Staff.
Rabe, Tish & Seuss, Dr. Look for the Lorax. Ruiz, Aristides et al, illus. (p. 1049)
Rabel, Carolina. Crunch! Rabel, Carolina, illus. (p. 386)
Rabelo-Beacroft, Katia. Grumpy Monkey Who Only Eats Bananas. (p. 727)
Rabenau, Francesca von, illus. see Valldejuly, Frances Bragan.
Raber, Angela. Doesn't Thatâ¿ (p. 460)
Rabideau, Dianna. Den for Ben. (p. 426)
Rabideau, Lacy. Picture Book of the Mass: Illustrated by the Masters. (p. 1355)
Rabin, Shri, jt. auth. see Pelletier, Cynthia L.
Rabin, Staton. Betsy & the Emperor. (p. 172)
—Black Powder. (p. 196)
—Mr. Lincoln's Boys. Ibatoulline, Bagram, illus. (p. 1185)
Rabinowitz, Alan. Boy & a Jaguar. Chien, Catia, illus. (p. 217)
Rabinowitz, Howard N. First New South, 1865-1920. (p. 596)
Rabisa, Tabitha. I Dream of Angels... yet I Live with Demons. (p. 838)
Rabley, Stephen. Danny's Blog/Le Blog de Danny. Bougard, Marie-Therese, tr. (p. 406)
—Fireboy. (p. 591)
—Marcel & the Mona Lisa. (p. 1091)
—Red Rock/Roca Roja. Rabley, Stephen & Ursell, Martin, illus. (p. 1455)
—Twins & the Time Machine/Les Jumeaux et la Machine du Temps. Bougard, Marie-Therese, tr. (p. 1802)
Rabley, Stephen & Pearson Education Staff. Flying Home. (p. 610)
—Maisie & the Dolphin. (p. 1077)
Rabon, Elaine Hearn, illus. see Dolson, Carol Bland.
Rabon, Elaine Hearn, illus. see Thrasher, Grady.
Rabou, John, illus. see Dowley, Tim & Bewley, Robert.
Raboy, Mac. Flash Gordon. (p. 602)
Raboy, Mac, illus. see Binder, Otto & Fox, Gardner.
Rabushka, Jerry. Breaking the Silence: A Collection of Three Skits (p. 225)
—Casket & the Casserole: A Ten-Minute Comedy Duet. (p. 276)
—Frying Pan: A Dramatic Skit (p. 646)
—Funny Way of Showing It: A One-Act Dramatic Play. (p. 650)
—Matter of Life & Death: A Dramatic Monologue. (p. 1109)
—On Location: A Ten-Minute Comedy Duet. (p. 1289)
—Saucy Mamasita: A Dramatic Monologue. (p. 1516)
—Seeking Asylum: Full-Length Comedy Play. (p. 1548)
—White Elephant: Comedy Monologue. (p. 1912)
Raby, Billy. Fizzelbritches & Raspewton: Gone Fishin' (p. 601)
Racanelli, Marie. Albino Animals. (p. 35)
—Animal Mimics. (p. 78)
—Animals with Armor. (p. 84)
—Animals with Pockets. (p. 84)
—Camouflaged Creatures. (p. 257)
—Crazy Nature (p. 377)
—Underground Animals. (p. 1814)
Racaniello, P. Emilia & Emma Say Please. (p. 518)
—Emilia & Emma Say Sorry. (p. 518)
—Emilia & Emma Say Thank You. (p. 518)
—Marcella & the Magic Hat. (p. 1091)
—Stella Asks What. (p. 1646)
—Stella Asks When. (p. 1646)
—Stella Asks Where. (p. 1646)
—Stella Asks Who. (p. 1646)
—Stella Asks Why. (p. 1646)
Raccah, Dominique, jt. auth. see Paschen, Elise.
Race, Philip. How to Study: Practical Tips for Students. (p. 821)
Racek, Jennifer. Cadberry's Letters. (p. 250)
Rach, W. Dennis. Goofy Principal at Silly School. (p. 702)
Rachael, Adams. Fisk's Fishing Adventures: The Best Catch. (p. 599)
Rachel, Drapkin, illus. see Joseph, Costa & Christopher, Romero.
Rachel Henson, illus. see Carol Henson Keesee.
Rachel, T. Cole & Costello, Rita D., eds. Bend, Don't Shatter: Poets on the Beginning of Desire. (p. 164)
Racine, Jean. Phaedra. Landes, William-Alan, ed. (p. 1349)
Racine, Patrice. Quest of the Last Dodo Bird. (p. 1426)
Racine, Sheryl, jt. auth. see Wagner, Kathi.
Racine, Victoria, illus. see Lopez, Christopher P.
Rack, Charlene. Adventures of Delaware Bear & Young Abraham Lincoln. (p. 17)
—Adventures of Delaware Bear & Young George Washington. (p. 17)
Rackers, Mark, ed. Arab-Israeli Conflict. (p. 94)
Rackham, Arthur. Cinderella. (p. 320)
—Fairy Book 1923. (p. 563)
Rackham, Arthur, illus. see Aesop.
Rackham, Arthur, illus. see Andersen, Hans Christian & Andersen.
Rackham, Arthur, illus. see Andersen, Hans Christian.
Rackham, Arthur, illus. see Barrie, J. M.
Rackham, Arthur, illus. see Barrie, J. M. & Lindner, Brooke.
Rackham, Arthur, illus. see Bianco, Margery Williams.
Rackham, Arthur, illus. see Evans, C. S.
Rackham, Arthur, illus. see Grahame, Kenneth.
Rackham, Arthur, illus. see Grimm, Jacob & Grimm.
Rackham, Arthur, illus. see Jones, Vernon.
Rackham, Arthur, illus. see Moore, Clement C.
Rackham, Katelyn. Storyteller. (p. 1663)
Rackley, Beth Shaw. Girl in the Blue & White Checked Dress. (p. 678)
Racklin-Siegel, Alison. Jacob's Travels. (p. 904)
Racklin-Siegel, Carol. Lech Lecha: The Story of Abraham & Rebecca. (p. 987)
—Noah's Ark. (p. 1261)
Racknor & Morrow. Wordszart. (p. 1952)
Ractliffe, Justin. Dads: A Field Guide. Glassby, Cathie, illus. (p. 399)
Racz, Michael, illus. see Mann, Elizabeth.
Raczka, Bob. 3-D ABC: A Sculptural Alphabet. (p. 1991)
—Action Figures: Paintings of Fun, Daring, & Adventure. (p. 10)
—Art Is... (p. 102)
—Art of Freedom: How Artists See America. (p. 102)
—Artful Reading. (p. 103)
—Fall Mixed Up. Cameron, Chad, illus. (p. 566)
—Joy in Mudville. Dibley, Glin, illus. (p. 929)
—Lemonade: And Other Poems Squeezed from a Single Word. Doniger, Nancy, illus. (p. 991)
—More Than Meets the Eye: Seeing Art with All Five Senses. (p. 1175)
—Name That Style: All about Isms in Art. (p. 1228)
—Presidential Misadventures: Poems That Poke Fun at the Man in Charge. Burr, Dan E., illus. (p. 1397)
—Snowy, Blowy Winter Stead, Judy, illus. (p. 1601)
—Speaking of Art: Colorful Quotes by Famous Painters. (p. 1623)
—Summer Wonders. Stead, Judy, illus. (p. 1675)
—Unlikely Pairs: Fun with Famous Works of Art. (p. 1821)
—Vermeer Interviews: Conversations with Seven Works of Art. (p. 1837)
—Where in the World? Around the Globe in Thirteen Works of Art. (p. 1908)
Raczka, Bob & Reynolds, Peter H. Guyku: A Year of Haiku for Boys. Reynolds, Peter H., illus. (p. 733)
Raczka, Bob & Vermeer, Johannes. Vermeer Interviews: Conversations with Seven Works of Art. (p. 1837)
Rad, Charles J. Boy they called a Snowball. (p. 219)
—Bus & Below. (p. 244)
Radamaker, Kurt, et al. Arizona & New Mexico Birds. (p. 98)
Radaviciute, Diana, illus. see Blanco, Alberto.
Radcliff, R. Bruce & Roark, Dann L. Small Engines: Text. (p. 1592)
—Small Engines: Workbook. (p. 1592)
—Small Engines: Answer Key. (p. 1592)
—Small Engines: Resource Guide. (p. 1592)
Radcliffe, Ann, et al. Gothic Classics. Pomplun, Tom, ed. (p. 704)
Radclyffe. Love's Masquerade. (p. 1061)
Radclyffe, jt. auth. see Bella Books Staff.
Radclyffe, jt. ed. see Lynch, Katherine E.
Radding, Alan. Miracles: Stories for Jewish Children & Their Families. (p. 1148)
Raden, Tammy. Every Time I Want to Play, Brother & Sister Get in My Way. (p. 543)
—Lucky Dime. (p. 1062)
—My Dog Blue. (p. 1202)
—New Puppy. (p. 1247)
—Priscilla Play. (p. 1407)
Rader, Anna Katherine. Through the Eyes of Another. (p. 1745)
Rader, Jared. Sandy's Dream. Meyers, Sarah, illus. (p. 1511)
Rader, Josh. Detective Stephy Weyhe Holmes in the Missing Cake. Meyer, Sarah, illus. (p. 431)
Rader, Laura. Twelve Days of Christmas in California. Rader, Laura, illus. (p. 1800)
—When Santa Lost His Ho! Ho! Ho! Rader, Laura, illus. (p. 1904)
Rader, Laura, illus. see Linn, Margot.
Rader, Laura, illus. see Mayr, Diane.
Rader, Laura, illus. see Murkoff, Heidi.
Rader, Laura, illus. see Ziefert, Harriet.
Rader, Laura & Utt, Mary Ann. Child's Story of Thanksgiving. (p. 305)
Rader, Mark. Dinosaur. Sanborn, Casey, illus. (p. 441)
Radermacher, Elizabeth Bebe. Danny Leprechaun & the Pot of Gold. (p. 406)
Radford, Heather. Asquinn Twins: Frontier Life. Oakley, Darlene, ed. (p. 107)
Radford, Karen, illus. see Bailey, Gerry & Foster, Karen.
Radford, Karen, illus. see Bailey, Gerry.
Radford, Karen, illus. see Ganeri, Anita.
Radford, Maude L. King Arthur & His Knights. (p. 958)
Radford, Megan. Canada Doodles Cook, Peter, illus. (p. 260)
Radford, Michelle. Totally Fabulous. (p. 1771)
Radford, Ruby Lorraine. Rose Colored Glasses. White, Iris Weddell, illus. (p. 1489)
Radford, Sheri. Penelope & the Humongous Burp. (p. 1336)
Radhakrishnan, Anand, jt. auth. see Pundyk, Grace.
Radice, Teresa, et al. Tinker Bell & the Wings of Rani. Vetro, Daniela et al, illus. (p. 1755)
Radig, B., ed. Pattern Recognition & Image Understanding (p. 1329)
Raditz, JoAnne, illus. see Savageau, Tony.
Radjev, Priya, illus. see Zawel, Marc.
Radjou, Anna Nazaretz, illus. see Trooboff, Rhoda.
Radlauer. Breakfast by Molly. (p. 224)
—Molly. (p. 1160)
—Molly at the Library. (p. 1160)

—Molly Goes Hiking. (p. 1160)
Radlauer, Edward. More Readers (p. 1174)
Radley, Gail. Kyle Jeffries, Pilgrim. Burns, Taurus, illus. (p. 969)
Radmanovic, Ljubica, illus. see Radmanovic, Rada.
Radmanovic, Rada. Color Me Trendy. Radmanovic, Ljubica, illus. (p. 343)
Radney, Blair. Ruth & Esther: A Children's Bible Reader. (p. 1498)
Rado, Martha. Beaches, Brothers, & a Blueberry Patch. (p. 149)
Radomski, Kassandra. Apollo 13 Mission: Core Events of a Crisis in Space (p. 91)
—Battle for a New Nation: Causes & Effects of the Revolutionary War. (p. 145)
—Mr. Madison's War: Causes & Effects of the War of 1812. (p. 1185)
—Secrets of Mars. (p. 1545)
—Secrets of Saturn. (p. 1545)
Radomski, Kassandra, et al. What Went Wrong? (p. 1895)
Radosevich, Tina. Binky Story. (p. 188)
Radtke, Becky. At the State Fair Coloring Book. (p. 111)
—Easter Spot-the-Differences. (p. 499)
—Fairy Tales. (p. 564)
—Going Green! Activity Book. (p. 692)
—Keep the Scene Green! Earth-Friendly Activities. (p. 947)
—Little Animals Hidden Pictures. (p. 1023)
—Little Cars & Trucks. (p. 1025)
—On the Go Mazes. (p. 1290)
—People on the Go Mazes. (p. 1339)
—Pets Activity Book. (p. 1348)
—Pets Mazes. (p. 1348)
—Pirates Ahoy! Activity Book. (p. 1363)
—Trains Activity Book. (p. 1777)
Radtke, Becky, illus. see Burke, Mary F.
Radtke, Becky, illus. see Dunn, Justine.
Radtke, Becky, illus. see Lucey, Marcia T., ed.
Radtke, Becky, jt. auth. see Dover Staff.
Radtke, Becky J. All about Marvelous Me! A Draw & Write Journal. (p. 42)
—BOOST Keep the Scene Green! Earth-Friendly Activities. (p. 213)
—Christmas Color by Number. (p. 313)
—Draw It! Animals. (p. 481)
—Draw It! Dinosaurs. (p. 481)
—Draw It! Princesses, Mermaids & Fairies. (p. 481)
—Draw It! Sea Life. (p. 481)
—Four Seasons of Fun Activity Book. (p. 625)
—Princess Activity Book. (p. 1402)
—Super Rides & Water Slides Mazes. (p. 1680)
Radtke, Becky J., illus. see Gould, Judith S. & Gould, Evan Jay.
Radtke, Dax. Karoake!Karoake!Karoake! (p. 944)
Radu, Michael. Islam in Europe. (p. 891)
Radune, Richard A. Pequot Plantation: The Story of an Early Colonial Settlement. (p. 1341)
Radunsky, Vladimir. What Does Peace Feel Like? Radunsky, Vladimir, illus. (p. 1884)
Radunsky, Vladimir, illus. see Berne, Jennifer.
Radunsky, Vladimir, illus. see Raschka, Chris.
Radunsky, Vladimir, illus. see Twain, Mark, pseud.
Radunsky, Vladimir, jt. auth. see Raschka, Chris.
Radwan, Hassan. Rashid & the Missing Body. (p. 1439)
Radwan, Hassan & Stratford, Stevan. Rashid & the Haupmann Diamond. (p. 1439)
Radway, Richard. Germany, 1918-45. (p. 666)
Rady, Michael. Quest for Neveragain. (p. 1426)
Radzilowski, John. Ukrainian Americans. (p. 1808)
Radzinski, Kandy. What Cats Want for Christmas. Radzinski, Kandy, illus. (p. 1881)
—What Dogs Want for Christmas. Radzinski, Kandy, illus. (p. 1884)
—Where to Sleep. (p. 1910)
—Where to Sleep. Radzinski, Kandy, illus. (p. 1910)
Radzinski, Kandy, illus. see Schonberg, Marcia.
Rae, Alexander. Big Sister. (p. 183)
Rae, Alison. Oil, Plastics, & Power. (p. 1282)
—Trees & Timber Products. (p. 1784)
Rae, Angela. All of Us. (p. 45)
—Choices Witch Make Us. (p. 309)
Rae, Cheri & McKinney, John. Hiking. (p. 779)
Rae, Disney. Meeting the General: Tales of 9-11 Runaways [Series Title]. (p. 1124)
Rae, Jaci. Collista's Search for the True Meaning of Christmas. (p. 341)
Rae, Jennifer. Gilbert de la Frogponde: A Swamp Story. (p. 676)
Rae, John, illus. see Larned, W. T. & La Fontaine, Jean de.
Rae, John & Carroll, Lewis. New Adventures of Alice: A Sequel to Lewis Carroll's Wonderland. (p. 1243)
Rae Johnson, Carla. Teatime Tillie. (p. 1711)
Rae, Kathryn. Always with You I Am. (p. 51)
Rae, Kimberly. Buying Samir. (p. 248)
—Capturing Jasmina. (p. 265)
—Seeking Mother. (p. 1548)
Rae, Kristin. Wish You Were Italian: An If Only Novel. (p. 1940)
—Wish You Were Italian. (p. 1940)
Rae, Lisa. Distinguished Old Bentley Drove down to the Sea Pickersgill, Peter, illus. (p. 454)
Rae, Milne. Geordie's Tryst. (p. 663)
Rae, Navah. Job for Comet. (p. 919)
Rae, Philippa. Count the Sheep to Sleep. Röhr, Stéphanie, illus. (p. 370)
Rae Strawn, Evelyn. Moncho the Mule. (p. 1163)
Rae, Thelma. Pioneer Families. (p. 1361)
Rae, Tina. Emotional Survival: An Emotional Literacy Course for High School Students (p. 520)
Raether, Erin F. When Auntie Angie Left for Iraq & Remi Came to Stay. (p. 1901)
Raf, Mindy. Symptoms of My Insanity. (p. 1693)
Rafael, Cruz-Contarini, jt. auth. see Cruz-Contarini, Rafael.
Rafael, Janis. Playing It Safe with Mr. See-More Safety: Let's Learn about Bicycle Safety. Vol. 2 Walsh, Jennifer, illus. (p. 1372)
Rafail, Dyllan. Super Senses. (p. 1681)
Rafalli, Yakeen, tr. see Crouch, Adele.
Rafey, L. D. Martin Truemartin. (p. 1098)
Raff, Anna, illus. see Adler, David A.
Raff, Anna, illus. see Lewis, J. Patrick.
Raff, Courtney Granet. Giant of the Sea: The Story of a Sperm Whale. Gould, Shawn, illus. (p. 673)
Raffa, Edwina, jt. auth. see Rigsby, Annelle.
Raffa, Edwina & Rigsby, Annelle. Escape to the Everglades. (p. 535)
—Escape to the Everglades Teacher's Activity Guide. (p. 535)
—Kidnapped in Key West. (p. 952)
Raffaele, Stefano. Fragile. (p. 627)
Raffaella, Ligi, illus. see Davidson, Susanna & Stowell, Louie.
Raffaelli, Sean & Dreske, Erin. Dogs Don't Have Pockets. Konecny, John, illus. (p. 462)
Raffa-Mulligan, Teena. Mad Dad for Sale. (p. 1069)
—Who Dresses God? ... for God's house Is this world we share & God Is in it Everywhere. Rooke, Veronica, illus. (p. 1915)
Raffel, Burton, tr. Beowulf: And Related Readings. (p. 166)
Raffensperger. Eagle Tree. (p. 492)
Rafferty, John P. Biomes & Ecosystems. (p. 190)
—Britannica Guide to Predators & Prey (p. 229)
—Carnivores: Meat-Eating Mammals. (p. 270)
—Climate & Climate Change. (p. 332)
—Conservation & Ecology. (p. 358)
—Deserts & Steppes. (p. 429)
—Forests & Grasslands. (p. 618)
—Grazers. (p. 713)
—Lakes & Wetlands. (p. 972)
—Living Earth (p. 1040)
—Meat Eaters: Raptors, Sharks, & Crocodiles. (p. 1118)
—Oceans & Oceanography. (p. 1277)
—Primates. (p. 1400)
—Rats, Bats, & Xenarthrans. (p. 1440)
—Reptiles & Amphibians. (p. 1461)
—Rivers & Streams. (p. 1476)
—Rocks. (p. 1483)
Rafferty, John P., ed. Carnivores: Meat-Eating Mammals. (p. 270)
—Primates. (p. 1400)
—Rats, Bats, & Xenarthrans. (p. 1440)
Rafferty, Michael. TAB Boys Meet the Blue Boy. (p. 1694)
Rafferty, Michael, jt. auth. see Bryan, Dick.
Raffi. Everything Grows. (p. 544)
—If You're Happy & You Know It. Moore, Cyd, illus. (p. 855)
Raffin, Deborah. Mitzi's World: Seek & Discover More Than 150 Details in 15 Works of Folk Art. Scott, Jane Wooster, illus. (p. 1156)
Raffle, Diana. Moondragon. (p. 1172)
Rafi, Natasha. Jinni on the Roof: A Ramadan Story. Channa, Abdul Malik, illus. (p. 919)
Rafter, Dan. Atlas. (p. 112)
—Gearz. (p. 659)
Raga, Silvia, illus. see Gurney, Stella.
Raga, Silvia, illus. see Harrison, Paul.
Raga, Silvia, illus. see Oliver, Jane.
Raga, Silvia, illus. see Turpin, Nick.
Ragaini, R., ed. Society & Structures: Proceedings of the International Seminar on Nuclear War & Planetary Emergencies - 27th Session, Erice, Italy, 18-26 August 2002. (p. 1605)
Ragan, Jewel Coochie. Lost & Found. Ragan, Jewel Coochie, illus. (p. 1054)
Ragan, Lyn. Berc's Inner Voice. (p. 166)
—Berc's Inner Voice. Meyer, Alison, illus. (p. 166)
Ragawa, Marimo. Baby & Me Ragawa, Marimo, illus. (p. 124)
—Baby & Me. Ragawa, Marimo, illus. (p. 124)
Ragawa, Marimo & Marimo, Ragawa. Baby & Me Robertson, Ian, ed. (p. 124)
Ragel-Dial, Tasha. Say What?, a Photo Book of Inspirational Bible Verses for Kids - Featuring the Photography of Tasha Ragel-Dial. Ragel-Dial, Tasha, photos by. (p. 1518)
Ragen, Naomi. Covenant. (p. 373)
Ragg-Kirkby, Helena, jt. auth. see Hub, Ulrich.
Raghuraman, Renuka S., jt. auth. see Sundaram, Siddhartha.
Raghuraman, Savitri, illus. see Sundaram, Siddhartha & Raghuraman, Renuka S.
Ragin, M. K. Mildred Row & Improper Bounds. (p. 1142)
Ragland, Jean. I Want to Be A Snowman. (p. 847)
—Let's Do the Right Thing! (p. 995)
Ragland, Teresa, illus. see Kile, Joan.
Raglin, Tim. Curse of Catunkhamun. (p. 394)
Raglin, Tim, illus. see Brown, Marcy & Haley, Dennis.
Raglin, Tim, illus. see Brown, Marcy, et al.
Raglin, Tim, illus. see Gleeson, Brian.
Raglin, Tim, illus. see Greene, Carol.
Raglin, Tim, illus. see Hartman, Bob.
Raglin, Tim, illus. see Kipling, Rudyard.
Raglin, Tim, illus. see McKay, Sindy.
Ragnar. Got Your Nose: A True Story. (p. 704)
Ragsdale, Tyraine D. Science of Grand Hank Lab Book of Experiments. (p. 1527)
Raham, Gary. Biodiversity & Food Chains. (p. 188)
—Bugs That Kill. (p. 237)
—Mollusks: Squids, Clams, Snails, & Their Relatives. (p. 1160)
—Teaching Science Fact with Science Fiction (p. 1710)
Raham, Gary, jt. auth. see Johnson, Anne Janette.
Rahaman, Vashanti. Divali Rose. Akib, Jamel, illus. (p. 454)
Rahayu, Abigail. How Jesus Sees You ... (p. 810)
Raheb, Donna. Adventures of Henrietta Ham: Gone Fishing. (p. 18)
—Adventures of Henrietta Ham. (p. 18)
Rahill, Alex, jt. auth. see Tissot, Bob.
Rahim, Rahimah. Trunk. (p. 1793)
Rahimi, Joey, jt. auth. see G. de la Parra, John.
Rahimi, Joey, jt. auth. see Glabe, Scott.
Rahimi, Joey, jt. auth. see Lieberman, Dan.
Rahimi, Joey, jt. auth. see Tompkins, Michelle.
Rahlens, Holly-Jane. Prince William, Maximilian Minsky, & Me. (p. 1401)
Rahm, Julie. Bessie the Amazing Cow. (p. 168)
Rahman, Bessie. Daniel & the Special Treasure. (p. 404)
Rahman, Junam. Rudy the Rooster Loses His Voice. (p. 1494)
Rahman, Peggy Jane, jt. auth. see Meyers, Barbara Frances.
Rahman, Urmi & Quarto Generic Staff. B Is for Bangladesh. Das, Prodeepta, photos by. (p. 122)
Rahmandoust, Mostafa. 7 Stories about Children & the Prophet. (p. 1993)
—Friendship Is Sweet. (p. 639)
Rahme, Linda. Adventures of Judah, the Lion Dog. (p. 19)
Rahmlow, Robert C. Nature's Store. (p. 1237)
Rahn, Jess, illus. see Hollis, Randy.
Rahnama, Seyed Javad. Minty Ear. (p. 1148)
Rai, Bali. Read on - Kiss of Death. Packer, Natalie & Gibbons, Alan, eds. (p. 1443)
—Sold as Seen. (p. 1607)
Rai, Lori. Princess Sheron & the Frog. (p. 1405)
Rai, Sarbjit. Elfins in San Francisco. (p. 512)
Raible, Alton, illus. see Snyder, Zilpha Keatley.
Raibley, Coyte. Titanic Adventure: The Time Travelers' Chronicles. (p. 1757)
Raichert, Lance. Treasury of Values for Children. (p. 1783)
Raidt, Gerda, illus. see Grimm, J. & W. & Brothers Grimm.
Raidt, Gerda, illus. see Holtei, Christa & Woofter, Susi.
Raij, Emily. Ghosts of the Rich & Famous. (p. 672)
—Most Haunted Places in the United States. (p. 1177)
—Most Haunted Places in the World. (p. 1177)
—Rey Mysterio. (p. 1467)
—Spooked! (p. 1631)
—Tracking Ghosts. (p. 1775)
Raij, Emily, jt. auth. see Kaelberer, Angie Peterson.
Raiku, Makoto. Animal Land 10. (p. 78)
—Animal Land 7. (p. 78)
—Animal Land 8. (p. 78)
—Animal Land 9. (p. 78)
Raiku, Makoto, contrib. by. Zatchbell! (p. 1985)
Railton, Fanny, illus. see Lindsay, Maud.
Raimes, Ann. Universal Keys for Writers: Answer Key. (p. 1820)
—Universal Keys for Writers. (p. 1820)
Raimes, Ann, jt. auth. see Engleberg, Isa.
Raimondi, Pablo, illus. see Reilly, Matthew.
Raimondo, Joyce. Imagine That! Activities & Adventures in Surrealism. (p. 861)
—Make It Pop! Activities & Adventures in Pop Art. (p. 1079)
—What's the Big Idea? Activities & Adventures in Abstract Art. (p. 1899)
Rain, Mandy. Rock 'n' Roll. (p. 1482)
—Spring Fling. (p. 1635)
Rainbird, Becky. Taking Notes. (p. 1698)
Rainbolt, Jo Ann Sayman. Mountain Journey (p. 1181)
Rainbow Bridge Publishing Staff. Deep Space Division Fission. (p. 423)
—Division Grades 3-5. (p. 455)
—Math Connection, Grade 2. (p. 1105)
—Test Prep Connection Grade 1. (p. 1723)
—Vocabulary: Grade 4. (p. 1847)
—World Vacation Multiplication. (p. 1958)
Rainbow Bridge Publishing Staff, jt. auth. see Rawlins, Jeanne.
Rainbow Bridge Publishing Staff, jt. auth. see VanLeeuwen.
Rainbow Bridge Publishing Staff & Bosse, Nancy Rogers. Math Connection, Grade 3. (p. 1105)
—Math Connection,Grade 1. (p. 1105)
—Reading Connection(tm), Grade 1. (p. 1445)
Rainbow Buddy. Delicious Seasons. (p. 425)
Rainbow Publishers Staff. Bible Crafts: Reproducible Activity Book. (p. 175)
—Bible Explorer: 52 Week Bible Study. (p. 175)
—Bible Explorer: 52 Week Bible Study for Grades 4, 5 & 6. (p. 175)
—Bible Games: Reproducible Activities. (p. 175)
—Bible Trivia & Truths: Bible Potuzzles. (p. 176)
—Coloring Plus Activities: God's Creation. (p. 344)
—Coloring Plus Activities: God's Promises. (p. 344)
—Coloring Plus Activities: I Go to Church. (p. 344)
—Coloring Plus Activities: Heroes of the Bible. (p. 344)
—Coloring Plus Activities: Growing up God's Way. (p. 344)
—Coloring Plus Activities: The Bible Teaches Me. (p. 344)
—Coloring Plus Activities: Jesus Our Lord & Savior. (p. 344)
—Coloring Plus Activities: Living the Christian Life. (p. 344)
—Learning Adventures! Fall. (p. 985)
—Learning Adventures! Spring. (p. 985)
—Learning Adventures! Summer. (p. 985)
—Learning Adventures! Winter. (p. 985)
—More Bible Puzzles: Memory Verse. (p. 1174)
—More Bible Puzzles: Life of Jesus. (p. 1174)
—More Bible Puzzles: New Testament. (p. 1174)
—More Bible Puzzles: Old Testament. (p. 1174)
RainbowBrush, creator. RainbowBrush Alphabet. (p. 1436)
RainboWindow. Leviticus, I Love You. RainboWindow, illus. (p. 1004)
Raine, Arne. Ray of Light: Key Keepers Book #3. (p. 1441)
Raine, Amelie. Mallomar Goes to the Moon. (p. 1083)
—Misadventures of Mallomar the Horse. (p. 1150)
Raine, Bonnie. Islands. MacMenamin, John, illus. (p. 892)
Raines, Bill. Postcards from Oncology: One Man's Light-Hearted Version of Being a Cancer Patient. (p. 1388)
Raines, Christie. My Trip to the Hospital. (p. 1220)
Raines, Gary. My Brother's Blue. (p. 1199)
Raines, Jennifer. Alex & Andrew Swap Places. (p. 35)
—Laughs for Porcupine (p. 980)
Raines, Kristy. Grizzer the Goofy Wolf. Raines, Morgan, illus. (p. 724)
Raines, Morgan, illus. see Raines, Kristy.
Raines, S. C., jt. auth. see Isbell, R.
Raines, Shirley C. & Canady, Robert J. Story S-t-r-e-t-c-h-e-r-s for the Primary Grades: Activities to Expand Children's Favorite Books. (p. 1663)
Rainey. Greatest Gift. (p. 719)
—School Is Cool. Huggens, Karin, illus. (p. 1523)
Rainey, Anne & Gordon, Ray. Tasting Candy. (p. 1707)
Rainey, Barbara. What God Wants for Christmas. Walker, John, illus. (p. 1884)
Rainey, Barbara, jt. auth. see Rainey, Dennis.
Rainey, David, Jr. Hope in the Hallways. (p. 796)
Rainey, Dennis & Rainey, Barbara. Moments Together for Weathering Life's Storms: Devotions for Drawing near to God & One Another. (p. 1162)
Rainey, Dennis, et al. So You're about to Be a Teenager: Godly Advice for Preteens on Friends, Love, Sex, Faith, & Other Life Issues (p. 1602)
Rainey, Don L., et al. Foundations of Personal Fitness. (p. 624)
Rainey, L. E. Sad Sam, Glad Sam. (p. 1501)
Rainey, Merrill, illus. see Loewen, Nancy.
Rainey, Rich. Vampire Life (p. 1832)
Rainfield, C. A. Last Dragon. (p. 977)
Rainfield, Cheryl. Scars. (p. 1520)
—Stained. (p. 1638)
Rainforth, Hannah. Barnaby Bennett Teo, Ali, illus. (p. 139)
—Barnaby Bennett. Teo, Ali, illus. (p. 139)
Rainforth, Hannah, tr. see Gabel, Ngareta.
Rainge, Linda S. Why Is God Always Picking on Me. (p. 1925)
Rainier, S. T., jt. auth. see Page, J.
Rainier, S.T., jt. auth. see Page, J.
Rainis, Kenneth G. Blood & DNA Evidence: Crime-Solving Science Experiments. (p. 200)
—Cell & Microbe Science Fair Projects: Using Microscopes, Mold, & More. (p. 286)
—Cell & Microbe Science Fair Projects. (p. 286)
—Fingerprints: Crime-Solving Science Experiments. (p. 589)
—Forgery: Crime-Solving Science Experiments. (p. 619)
—Hair, Clothing, & Tire Track Evidence: Crime-Solving Science Experiments. (p. 736)
—Microscope Science Projects & Experiments: Magnifying the Hidden World. (p. 1136)
Rainmaker Entertainment, illus. see Man-Kong, Mary.
Rainmaker Entertainment Staff, illus. see Man-Kong, Mary.
Rains, Deborah. Sebastian Rae. (p. 1539)
Rains, Deborah Jane. 2011's New Year with Cuddles & Snuggles. (p. 2003)
—Cuddles & Snuggles. (p. 389)
—Racing with Randy. (p. 1432)
—Spooky Happy Halloween with Cuddles & Snuggles. (p. 1631)
—St Patrick's Day with Cuddles & Snuggles. (p. 1638)
—Thanksgiving with Cuddles & Snuggles (p. 1726)
Rains, Evyonna. Sleep, My Child. (p. 1588)
Rains, Michael. House on the Corner. (p. 803)
Rains, Rob. Marshall Faulk: Rushing to Glory. (p. 1096)
Rains, Rob, ed. see Castle, George.
Rains, Rob, ed. see Manoloff, Dennis.
Rains, Rob, ed. see Noble, Marty.
Rains, Rob, ed. see O'Connell, Jack.
Rains, Rob, ed. see Shalin, Mike.
Rains, Rob, ed. see Stone, Larry.
Rains, Rob & Smith, Ozzie. Cardinals Sports Heroes Block: City Block St. Louis: Mark Mcgwire, Ozzie Smith. (p. 266)
Rains, Valerie & Real Simple Magazine Staff. Celebrations: Easy Entertaining for Every Occasion. Schlechter, Annie, photos by. (p. 285)
Rainsford, Blair, jt. auth. see Mattern, Joanne.
Raintree. Itlp 2004 Grade 4 Science Stat. (p. 895)
—Itlp 2004 Grade 4 Soc Stud Sta. (p. 895)
—Itlp 2004 Grades 2-4 Science S. (p. 895)
—Itlp 2004 Grades 2-4 Soc Stud. (p. 895)
—Itlp 2004 Grades 3-4 Soc Stud. (p. 895)
—Itlp 2004 Grades K-1 Soc Stud. (p. 895)
—Itlp 2004 Grades K-2 Science S. (p. 895)
—Itlp 2004 Sprouts Pkg (29 Titl. (p. 895)
Raintree Steck-Vaughn Staff. Biomes Animals: Arkansas Edition (p. 190)
Rainville, Doris I., creator. Girl Who Never Let Her Mother Brush Her Hair. (p. 679)
—Power of Love. (p. 1389)
Rainwater, Crystal. Song the Slug; Book 1 (p. 1611)
Raisinghani, Jaya. I Will Always Know. (p. 848)
—Sweet Child of Mine. (p. 1689)
Raisner Glass, Beth. Blue-Ribbon Dad. Moore, Margie, illus. (p. 203)
Raisykinder Publishing. Tofu Ling. (p. 1761)
Raiten-D'Antonio, Toni, jt. auth. see Williams, Margery.
Raitman, Ira. Amanda's Bunny. (p. 52)
Raitt, Beth. Two Shoes. (p. 1804)
Raiz, James, illus. see Ruka, Greg.
Raizk, Leyla Marie, illus. see Raizk, Mary Ann.
Raizk, Mary Ann. Happy Birthday, Ohio: Celebrating Ohio's Bicentennial 1803-2003 Raizk, Leyla Marie, illus. (p. 745)
Raj, Amita. Green Pebble of China. (p. 722)
Rajadel, Fernando López. False Love, True Love/Amor Falso, Amor Verdadero: The Alfambra Woman Buried Alive & the Lovers of Teruel. (p. 567)
Rajagopal, P. & Pullens, Evelien. Aiyappan & the Magic Horse. (p. 32)
Rajagopalan, Ashok, illus. see Ramadurai, Suchitra.
Rajan, Bilaal. Making Change: Tips from an Underage Overachiever (p. 1080)
Rajan, Gayatri. Story of Santoshi Devi. (p. 1659)
Rajan, Vithal. Jungu, the Baiga Princess. Kalyan, Srivi, illus. (p. 935)
Rajcak, Hélène, illus. see Laverdunt, Damien.
Rajchel, Diana. Spellcasting Picture Book: Visual Tools for Grown-Up Magic. (p. 1625)
Rajczak, Kristen. 20 Fun Facts about Insect Adaptations. (p. 1995)
—20 Fun Facts about Pioneer Women. (p. 1995)
—20 Fun Facts about Stars. (p. 1995)
—20 Fun Facts about Women in Ancient Egypt. (p. 1995)
—20 Fun Facts about Women in Ancient Greece & Rome. (p. 1995)
—Be a Meteorologist. (p. 148)
—Climate Zones. (p. 332)
—Comets. (p. 348)
—Commas & Colons with Your Class. (p. 348)
—Complete Sentences with Your Family. (p. 353)
—Conjunctions with Your Friends. (p. 357)

—Creative Cocoa Recipes. (p. 379)
—Delicious Dairy Recipes. (p. 425)
—Demi Lovato. (p. 425)
—Donner Party. (p. 466)
—Famous Graveyards. (p. 569)
—Fantastic Fruit Recipes. (p. 571)
—Freaky Stories about Our Bodies. (p. 632)
—German Shepherds. (p. 666)
—Great Danes. (p. 715)
—Great Grain Recipes. (p. 716)
—How Snakes & Other Animals Taste the Air. (p. 812)
—I'm Allergic to Bees. (p. 858)
—Instagram & Kevin Systrom & Mike Krieger (p. 878)
—Irish Wolfhounds. (p. 888)
—Jaden Smith. (p. 905)
—Jellyfish (p. 912)
—Justin Bieber. (p. 940)
—Latitude & Longitude. (p. 979)
—Life As a Pioneer. (p. 1008)
—Life in the American Colonies. (p. 1011)
—Life on a Wagon Train. (p. 1012)
—Lightning. (p. 1016)
—Mayflower Compact. (p. 1113)
—Mujeres en Los Negocios (Women in Business) (p. 1189)
—Nelson Mandela. (p. 1240)
—Northern Lights. (p. 1266)
—Perfect Pasta Recipes. (p. 1342)
—Pulling Dogs. (p. 1416)
—Racing the Iditarod. (p. 1432)
—Rainbows. (p. 1436)
—Rescue Dogs. (p. 1462)
—Sequential Words with Your Pets. (p. 1552)
—Shooting Stars. (p. 1568)
—Skateboarding. (p. 1583)
—Subjects & Verbs with Your Neighbors. (p. 1671)
—Terrifying Tornadoes. (p. 1722)
—Thoroughbreds. (p. 1740)
—Transition Words with Your Team. (p. 1778)
—Types of Maps. (p. 1805)
—Very Tasty Vegetable Recipes. (p. 1839)
—Watch Apple Trees Grow. (p. 1860)
—Watch Corn Grow. (p. 1860)
—Watch Corn Grow / ¡Mira cómo crece el Maíz! (p. 1860)
—Watch Grass Grow. (p. 1861)
—Watch Grass Grow / ¡Mira cómo crece el Césped! (p. 1861)
—Watch Tulips Grow. (p. 1861)
—Watch Tulips Grow / ¡Mira cómo crecen los Tulipanes! (p. 1861)
—Women in Business. (p. 1945)
Rajczak, Kristin. Civil Rights Movement in Texas. (p. 325)
Rajczak, Michael. Amber. (p. 56)
—Haunted! The White House. (p. 753)
—Haunted! Gettysburg. (p. 753)
—Haunted! the White House. (p. 754)
—Meet the President. (p. 1123)
—Meet the President's Cabinet. (p. 1123)
—Sea Urchins. (p. 1536)
—Texas Geography. (p. 1724)
—Visiting the Great Lakes. (p. 1845)
Rajendra, Vijeya & Kaplan, Gisela T. Iran. (p. 886)
Rajendra, Vijeya, et al. Iran. (p. 886)
Rajic, Alex. Alefbet Illuminated. Rajic, Alex, illus. (p. 35)
Raju, P. V. Ramaswami. Indian Fables. (p. 871)
Rajvanshi, Ayush, illus. see D'souza, Nadine.
Rake, Jody. Animal Training at SeaWorld, Busch Gardens, & Discovery Cove: Behind the Scenes. (p. 80)
Rake, Jody Sullivan. Aye-Aye (p. 121)
—Beagles/Beagles. (p. 150)
—Beluga Whales up Close (p. 163)
—Beluga Whales up Close [Scholastic]. (p. 163)
—Bloodsuckers of the Animal World. (p. 201)
—Blue Whales up Close (p. 203)
—Blue Whales up Close [Scholastic]. (p. 203)
—Bottlenose Dolphin up Close (p. 215)
—Bottlenose Dolphin up Close [Scholastic]. (p. 215)
—Boxers (Bóxers) (p. 217)
—Bull Shark (p. 240)
—Cangrejos. (p. 261)
—Carcass Chewers of the Animal World. (p. 265)
—Dálmatas. (p. 401)
—Disgusting Creature Diets. (p. 450)
—Endangered Oceans: Investigating Oceans in Crisis. (p. 527)
—Estrellas de Mar. (p. 538)
—Garbage Gorgers of the Animal World. (p. 655)
—Great White Shark (p. 719)
—Gross Me Out. (p. 725)
—Grubs, Bugs, & Worms: Invertebrates of the Underground. (p. 727)
—Hammerhead Shark (p. 739)
—Hippos: In the Wild. (p. 781)
—Human Skeleton (p. 826)
—Human Skeleton. (p. 826)
—Humpback Whales up Close (p. 827)
—Hyenas: On the Hunt (p. 831)
—Killer Whales up Close [Scholastic]. (p. 956)
—Leatherback Sea Turtles (p. 986)
—Lobsters (p. 1044)
—Mako Shark (p. 1083)
—Manatees. (p. 1086)
—Meerkats (p. 1120)
—Meerkats Saunders-Smith, Gail, ed. (p. 1120)
—Meerkats, Moles, & Voles: Animals of the Underground. (p. 1120)
—Mudskippers & Other Extreme Fish Adaptations (p. 1189)
—Mystery of Whale Strandings: A Cause & Effect Investigation (p. 1226)
—Naked Mole-Rat (p. 1228)
—Orcas (p. 1302)
—Polar Bears: On the Hunt (p. 1379)
—Poop & Puke Eaters of the Animal World. (p. 1383)
—Puffer Fish (p. 1415)
—Pugs/Pugs. (p. 1415)
—Pumas: On the Hunt. (p. 1416)
—Pythons (p. 1422)
—Pythons Saunders-Smith, Gail, ed. (p. 1422)
—Rays (p. 1441)
—Roots, Bulbs, & Bacteria: Growths of the Underground. (p. 1488)
—Sea Otters Saunders-Smith, Gail, ed. (p. 1535)
—Soil, Silt, & Sand: Layers of the Underground. (p. 1606)
—Speed, Strength, & Stealth: Animal Weapons & Defenses (p. 1624)
—Spines, Horns, & Armor: Animal Weapons & Defenses. (p. 1628)
—Sponges (p. 1631)
—Squids (p. 1637)
—Star-Nosed Moles & Other Extreme Mammal Adaptations (p. 1640)
—Underground Safari. (p. 1815)
—Why Bed Bugs Bite & Other Gross Facts about Bugs (p. 1922)
—Why Feet Smell & Other Gross Facts about Your Body (p. 1924)
—Why Rabbits Eat Poop & Other Gross Facts about Pets (p. 1925)
—Why Vampire Bats Suck Blood & Other Gross Facts about Animals (p. 1926)
Rake, Jody Sullivan, jt. auth. see Capstone Press Editors.
Rake, Jody Sullivan, jt. auth. see Iyer, Rani.
Rake, Jody Sullivan, jt. auth. see Petersen, Megan Cooley.
Rake, Jody Sullivan, jt. auth. see Riehecky, Janet.
Rake, Jody Sullivan, jt. auth. see Sullivan Rake, Jody.
Rake, Jody Sullivan & Capstone Press Editors. Sea Urchins (p. 1536)
Rake, Jody Sullivan, et al. Extreme Adaptations (p. 556)
—Marine Mammals. (p. 1094)
Rake, Matthew. Creatures of the Deep. Mendez, Simon, illus. (p. 380)
—Dawn of Planet Earth. Minister, Peter, illus. (p. 411)
—Dinosaurs Rule. Minister, Peter, illus. (p. 445)
—Scaly, Slippery Creatures. Mendez, Simon, illus. (p. 1519)
Rakes, Celeste W. All American History Student Reader: The Explorers to the Jacksonians, Vol. 1 (p. 43)
Rakes, Jerry D. Becoming an Eagle Scout: A Simplified, Step by Step Guideline for the Life Scout?S Eagle Project. (p. 156)
Rakitin, Sarah, illus. see Dall, Mary Doerfler.
Rakitin, Sarah, illus. see Henry, Sandi.
Rakola, Matthew, photos by see Young, Karen Romano.
Rakos, Lynnda. Let's Color Together — Princesses, Mermaids & Fairies. (p. 995)
—Let's Color Together — Robots. (p. 995)
Rakos, Lynnda, et al. Princesses, Mermaids & Fairies Coloring Book. (p. 1406)
Rakove, Jack N., ed. see LaClair, Teresa.
Rakove, Jack N., ed. see Quinby, Michelle.
Rakove, Jack N., ed. see Sharp, Constance.
Rakove, Jack N., ed. see South, Victor.
Rakove, Jack N., ed. see Windsor, Wesley.
Rakovic, Robert & Pecsenye, Jessica. Seton Hall University College Prowler off the Record. (p. 1554)
Rakowski, Diane M. That You May Know (p. 1726)
Raku Teapot Haiku Group, creator. Raku Teapot: Haiku. (p. 1437)
Rakusin, Sudie. Dear Calla Roo... Love, Savannah Blue: A Letter about Getting Sick & Feeling Better. No. 2 Rakusin, Sudie, illus. (p. 418)
Rakusin, Sudie, illus. see Sforza, Daniella, ed.
Raleigh, Albert Sidney. Philosophia Hermetica: A Course of Ten Lessons, Being an Introduction to the Philosophy of Alchemy. (p. 1351)
Raleigh, Michael H. Ted & Jimmy (p. 1712)
Raley, Hugh W. Erin the Excellent Elf. (p. 533)
Rall, John B. Free Spirit of Texas: Freely Given Advise on Attitude & Knowledge. (p. 634)
Ralles, H. J. Darok 10. (p. 409)
—Keeper of the Empire (p. 947)
—Keeper of the Realm (p. 947)
—Looking Out My Window. (p. 1051)
Rallis, Chris, illus. see Sollinger, Emily.
Rallison, Janette. Fame, Glory, & Other Things on My to Do List. (p. 567)
—How to Take the Ex Out of Ex-Boyfriend. (p. 822)
—It's a Mall World after All. (p. 895)
—My Fair Godmother. (p. 1202)
—My Unfair Godmother. (p. 1220)
—Revenge of the Cheerleaders. (p. 1465)
Ralls, Ken. Henrietta Hippo Learns to Dance. McQuitty, LaVonia Corbin, illus. (p. 767)
Ralph, Brian. Cave In. (p. 282)
—Reggie-12. (p. 1457)
Ralph, Donna J. Critter Chronicles: Stories of Critters in a Colorado Wildlife Rehabilitator's Life. (p. 384)
Ralph, Gordon & If. Remaking the World: Pardon My Turkey. Constantin, illus. (p. 1458)
—'Remaking' the World - Hold That Hug. Cosmin, Constantin, illus. (p. 1458)
Ralph, Grampa. How Santa Knows. (p. 812)
Ralph, Karin, illus. see Ryan, Mike.
Ralphs, Matt. Collins Big Cat Progress - Non-Fiction: Lime Band 11/Diamond Band 17. (p. 340)
Ralphson, G. Harvey. Boy Scout Camera Club. (p. 218)
—Boy Scouts in a Motor Boat or Adventures. (p. 218)
—Boy Scouts in a Submarine. (p. 218)
—Boy Scouts in an Airship. (p. 218)
—Boy Scouts in Death Valley. (p. 218)
—Boy Scouts in Mexico. (p. 218)
—Boy Scouts in Mexico or on Guard with un. (p. 218)
—Boy Scouts in Mexico,Or on Guard with Uncle Sam. (p. 218)
—Boy Scouts in Southern Waters. (p. 218)
—Boy Scouts in the Philippines: Or the Key to the Treaty Box. (p. 218)
—Boy Scouts in the Philippines. (p. 218)
—Boy Scouts on Motorcycles. (p. 218)
—Boy Scouts on the Open Plain. (p. 218)
Ralston, Carole. Light in the Forest. (p. 1015)
Ralston, Peter, photos by see Platt, D. D. & Conkling, Philip, eds.
Ralston, Peter, photos by see Platt, D. D., ed.
Ralte, Albert Lalmuanpuia, illus. see Nambiar, Vinesh.
Raluca, Cristina Cirti, illus. see Hall, Tara.
Ramá, Sue, illus. see Codell, Esmé Raji.
Rama, Sue, illus. see Fabiyi, Jan Goldin.
Rama, Sue, illus. see Miller, Heather Lynn.
Rama, Sue, illus. see Park, Linda Sue & Durango, Julia.
Rama, Sue, illus. see Ries, Lori.
Rama, Sue, illus. see Wangerin, Walter, Jr., et al.
Ramadan, Abou Bakr, jt. ed. see Linkov, Igor.
Ramadier, Cédric. Help! the Wolf Is Coming! Burgess, Linda, tr. from FRE. (p. 766)
Ramadurai, Suchitra. Runaway Peppercorn. Rajagopalan, Ashok, illus. (p. 1496)
Ramage, Dawn. Cave Adventures. (p. 282)
Ramage, Rosalyn Rikel. Graveyard: N/a. (p. 712)
—Windmill. (p. 1936)
Ramaiah, Rajiv, illus. see Park, Laura.
Ramajo, Fernando, photos by. Postres 2. (p. 1388)
Ramakar, Ram. Little Crow Feather. (p. 1026)
Ramanathan, Priya. Mustache Man. Gupta, Garima, illus. (p. 1194)
Ramanathan, Rathna, jt. auth. see Wolf, Gita.
Ramani, Madhvi. Nina & the Kung-Fu Adventure. (p. 1256)
—Nina & the Magical Carnival. (p. 1256)
—Nina & the Travelling Spice Shed. (p. 1256)
Ramaswamy, Maya. U Sier Lapalang: A Khasi Tale. (p. 1807)
Ramaswamy, Maya, illus. see Datta, Aparajita & Manjrekar, Nima.
Ramazani, Jahan. Norton Anthology Modern & Contemporary Poetry (p. 1266)
Rambeau. Mystery of the Midnight Visitor. (p. 1225)
—Mystery of the Morgan Castle. (p. 1225)
Rambo, Angela, illus. see Plumier, Lea.
Rambo, Lee Elliot, jt. auth. see Larkin, Jim.
Ramdayal, Mia. Learning How to Fly. (p. 985)
Rameaka, T. Mystery of Wolf Den Cave. (p. 1226)
—Where's Dorothy? (p. 1910)
Rameaka, Thomas. Bee Haven. (p. 157)
Rameck, Hunt, et al. We Beat the Street: How a Friendship Pact Led to Success. (p. 1866)
Ramee, Louise De La, see De La Ramee, Louise.
Ramel, Charlotte, illus. see Thydell, Johanna & Martens, Helle.
Ramen, Catherine, jt. auth. see Carson, Brian.
Ramen, Fred. Albert Speer: Hitler's Architect. (p. 34)
—Albucasis (Abu al-Qasim Al-Zahrawi) Renowned Muslim Surgeon of the Tenth Century. (p. 35)
—Basketball: Rules, Tips, Strategy, & Safety. (p. 143)
—Francisco Pizarro: The Exploration of Peru & the Conquest of the Inca. (p. 628)
—Hermann Goering: Hitler's Second in Command. (p. 771)
—Hermann Goring: Hitler's Second-in-Command. (p. 771)
—Hernán Cortés: The Conquest of Mexico & the Aztec Empire. (p. 771)
—Historical Atlas of Iran. (p. 782)
—Influenza. (p. 873)
—Jerry West. (p. 914)
—Prescription Drugs. (p. 1396)
—Reinhard Heydrich: Hangman of the Third Reich. (p. 1457)
—Sleeping Sickness & Other Parasitic Tropical Diseases. (p. 1589)
—Tuberculosis. (p. 1795)
Ramen, Fred, jt. auth. see Campbell, Forest G.
Ramesh, Serita. Jason & the Ingenious Number Trick: A Story about Patterns. (p. 910)
Ramey, Cindy, illus. see Auxier, Bryan.
Ramey, Kathy. Animal Alphabet. (p. 76)
Ramin, Nathan & Burns, Adam. Loyola University Chicago College Prowler off the Record. (p. 1061)
Ramirez, Alberto, illus. see Blasing, George.
Ramirez, Alma. Viaje-Por la matematica de la escuela Secundaria. Humphrey Williams, Ann, illus. (p. 1839)
Ramirez, Alma, jt. auth. see Gabriel, Nat.
Ramirez, Alma, jt. auth. see Haskins, Lori.
Ramirez, Alma, tr. see Driscoll, Laura.
Ramirez, Alma B., tr. see Dussling, Jennifer.
Ramirez, Alma B., tr. see James, Anne.
Ramirez, Antonio. Napí Domi, illus. (p. 1229)
—Napí Funda un Pueblo. Amado, Elisa, tr. (p. 1229)
Ramirez, Antonio. Napí Goes to the Mountain. Amado, Elisa, tr. from SPA. (p. 1229)
—Napí Va a la Montaña. Domi, illus. (p. 1229)
Ramirez, Antonio, photos by see Kassandra, ed.
Ramirez, D. A., jt. auth. see Ramirez, D. a.
Ramirez, D. a. & Ramirez, D. A. Kingdom of Glass. (p. 959)
Ramirez, David. Minimonsters (En Español) (p. 1146)
Ramirez, Elizandro de los Angeles, illus. see Batres, Ethel.
Ramirez, Frank. Bee Attitudes: And 5 More Extraordinary Plays for Ordinary Days. (p. 157)
Ramirez, Gamaliel. Night We Almost Saw the Three Kings. (p. 1254)
Ramirez, Gonzalo Canal. Relatos para Muchachos. Acosta, Patricia, illus. (p. 1458)
Ramirez, Herman, illus. see Torres, Eliseo & Sawyer, Timothy L.
Ramirez, Iz. Bob the Lizard Swope, Brenda, illus. (p. 205)
Ramirez, Jeannette. Alphabet Trip to the Limerick Zoo. AIC College of Design Staff, illus. (p. 50)
—Keepsake Book of Love & Marriage: An enchanting way to say, I love You. Long, Martha, illus. (p. 948)
Ramirez, José, illus. see Cumpiano, Ina.
Ramirez, Jose, illus. see Villasenor, Victor.
Ramirez, Jose, illus. see Villaseñor, Victor.
Ramirez, Jose, jt. auth. see Cumpiano, Ina.
RAMIREZ, Joseph P., jt. auth. see Ramirez, Joseph P.
Ramirez, Joseph P. & RAMIREZ, Joseph P. Literature Guide for the Middle School Classroom. (p. 1023)
Ramirez, Juan Antonio. Arte Prehistorico y Primitivo. (p. 103)
Ramirez, Ken. Valley of the Raven. (p. 1831)
—You, Me, Naideen & a Bee. (p. 1976)
Ramirez, Luz Elena. Encyclopedia of Hispanic-American Literature. (p. 525)
Ramirez, M. My First Latino Monologue Book: A Sense of Character: 100 Monologues for Young Children. (p. 1207)
—My Third Latino Monologue Book: Finding Your Voice. (p. 1220)
Ramirez, Martha. Fabulous Adventures of Fred the Frog. (p. 559)
Ramirez, Matthew, jt. auth. see Ramirez, Paul.
Ramirez, Orlando L., illus. see Marin, Cheech.
Ramirez, Paul & Ramirez, Matthew. Adventures of Paleta Man. Galeano, Jose Daniel, illus. (p. 21)
—Adventures of Paleta Man: Secret of the Gold Medallion. Galeano, Jose Daniel, illus. (p. 21)
—Adventures of Paleta Man: Secret of the Gold Medallion Coloring Book. Galeano, Jose Daniel, illus. (p. 21)
Ramirez, Samuel, illus. see Sanchez, Juanita L.
Ramirez, Sharon, jt. auth. see Morris, Brian Lee.
Ramirez, Tami. Fun at the Beach. (p. 647)
Ramirez, Terry. Growing up with Olivi: The Beguiling Blue-Haired Beauty of Boysenberry Lane. (p. 727)
Ramirez, Trina K. Teeny Tiny Baby Bird: An Adoption Story. (p. 1715)
Ramirez, Viviana. Pink Dolphin. (p. 1359)
Ramirez, Z. Cruz. Waking & Other Stories. (p. 1853)
Ramius, Edward. Yawnywawnys. (p. 1968)
Ramljak, Marijan. Are You My Friend? (p. 97)
—Are You My Mommy? (p. 97)
—Where Do I Live? (p. 1907)
—Where Is My Daddy? (p. 1908)
Ramnath, Vianna. Daddy Loves You! (p. 398)
Ramon, Elisa. Aquello Que Tanto Queria Susana. Lavarello, Jose Maria, illus. (p. 94)
—Las Ovejas de Nico. (p. 977)
Ramone, Phil & Granata, Charles L. Making Records: The Scenes Behind the Music. (p. 1082)
Ramos, jt. auth. see Ramos, Mario.
Ramos, Amy Jones, illus. see Martin, Brenda Darnley.
Ramos, Angelica. If My Mommy Was an Octopus. (p. 853)
Ramos, Beatriz Helena, illus. see Rosenberg, Pam.
Ramos, Belen. Way to Fairyleland: Commemorative Edition. (p. 1864)
Ramos, Doreen. Brave Ant. (p. 223)
Ramos, et al. Nueva Casa. (p. 1270)
—Pastel de Chocolate. (p. 1327)
Ramos, Gloria, tr. see Ring, Susan.
Ramos, Heidy. Girl Who Wears Gumamela Flower. (p. 679)
Ramos, Humberto, illus. see Slott, Dan.
Ramos, Humberto, illus. see Waid, Mark.
Ramos, Humberto, jt. illus. see Martin, Marcos.
Ramos, Humberto, et al. Spider-Man - Trouble on the Horizon. (p. 1626)
Ramos, Jorge. I'm Just Like My Mom. Gutierrez, Akemi, illus. (p. 859)
Ramos, José, illus. see Sanderson, Jeannette & Benchmark Education Co., LLC.
Ramos, José, illus. see Swain, Cynthia & Benchmark Education Co., LLC.
Ramos, Juan Antonio. Principe de Blancanieves. (p. 1406)
Ramos, Manuel Joao, illus. see Zink, Rui.
Ramos, Maria Cristina. De Barrio Somos. (p. 416)
—Del Amor Nacen Los Rios. (p. 424)
—Mi Mano. Serrano, Pablo, illus. (p. 1132)
—Ruedamares Pirata de la Mar Bravia. (p. 1494)
Ramos, Marielly. Fast Getting Married Ugly Changing Bear. (p. 576)
Ramos, Mario. I Am So Handsome. (p. 834)
—I Am So Strong. (p. 834)
—La Cama, Monstruito! (p. 969)
Ramos, Mario & Ramos. Mama! (p. 1084)
Ramos, Odalys Q. Allow Me to Introduce Myself. Graham, Michael, illus. (p. 48)
Ramos, Peregrina. Little Clay Jar: La Vasijita de Barro. Graham, Dennis, illus. (p. 1026)
Ramos, Pilar. Invitacion. (p. 886)
Ramos, Pilar, jt. auth. see Elena, Horacio.
Ramos, Ramona J. Summer with Kaitlyn & Lexi. (p. 1675)
Ramos, Sarah, jt. auth. see Bright, Philip.
Ramos, Violet M., ed. see James, Larry W.
Ramotar, Alexandra, illus. see Persaud, Sandhya S.
Ramoutar, Christine L. Tales from the Pine Forest. (p. 1702)
Ramoutar, Tagore. Brownie the Monkey Visits the Zoo. Cline, Ian, photos by. (p. 232)
—Eric Boyle the Crocodile Chooses a New Car. (p. 533)
—I Love Birds! (p. 841)
—Trains, Engines & Locomotives: I Love Trains. (p. 1777)
Rampersad, Arnold, jt. ed. see Roessel, David.
Rampersad, Arnold & Blount, Marcellus, eds. Poetry for Young People: African American Poetry. Barbour, Karen, illus. (p. 1376)
Rampley, Leigh, illus. see Huffman, Jared.
Ram-Prasad, Chakravarthi. Exploring the Life, Myth, & Art of India. (p. 554)
Ramrath Garner, Eleanor, jt. auth. see Garner, Eleanor Ramrath.
Ramrattan Smith, Sherry & Smith, Benjamin Eric. Brothers: Best Friends Growing Up. (p. 231)
Ramsaroop, Bibi. As I Remember. (p. 105)
Ramsay, A. Turtle Soup & Tiramisu. (p. 1798)
Ramsay, Betsy. Cecil Centipede's Career. Christman, Therese, illus. (p. 283)
Ramsay, David. History of the American Revolution Cohen, Lester H., ed. (p. 784)
Ramsay, Elizabeth. Burning Light. Katz, Avi, illus. (p. 244)
Ramsay, Jana & Ramsay, Nicole. Comedy. (p. 347)
Ramsay, Kim Heaton. Will You Be My Friend? (p. 1932)
Ramsay, Mark. Good Neighbors' Cheese Feast: A Cheesy Mouse Tale of Subtraction with Regrouping. Robinson, Susan G., illus. (p. 699)
—Good Neighbors Store an Award: A Cheesy Mouse Tale of Addition with Regrouping. Robinson, Susan G., illus. (p. 699)
Ramsay, Nicole. Comedy. (p. 347)
Ramsay, Nicole, jt. auth. see Ramsay, Jana.
Ramsden, Ashley. Seven Fathers. Young, Ed, illus. (p. 1554)
Ramsden, Julie & Ramsden, Michael. Autos with Attitude. (p. 118)
—Discover the Deep. (p. 448)
—Made for Speed. (p. 1070)
—Mini Beasts. (p. 1146)
—Robots. (p. 1481)

—To the Max. (p. 1759)
Ramsden, Melvyn. Rescuing Spelling. (p. 1462)
Ramsden, Michael, jt. auth. see Ramsden, Julie.
Ramsey, Ann Louise. Me, the Tree. Ramsey, Ann Louise, illus. (p. 1116)
Ramsey, Byra L. Little Stick. (p. 1036)
Ramsey, Calvin Alexander, jt. auth. see Stroud, Bettye.
Ramsey, Charlotte. Go Global with Charlotte. (p. 686)
Ramsey, Charmaine J. Frollica & Frenzi: New York City Friends. Steinlage, Kelly, illus. (p. 641)
Ramsey, Connie M. Calvin Coyote & the Chicken Coop Caper. (p. 255)
Ramsey, Dave. Big Birthday Surprise: Junior Discovers Giving. Ramsey, Marshall, illus. (p. 178)
—Careless at the Carnival: Junior Discovers Spending. Ramsey, Marshall, illus. (p. 268)
—Dave Ramsey's 6 Kids Books Boxed Set. (p. 410)
—My Fantastic Fieldtrip: Junior Discovers Saving. Ramsey, Marshall, illus. (p. 1203)
—Super Red Racer: Junior Discovers Work. (p. 1680)
Ramsey, Grandma. Surprise Birthday Gift. (p. 1685)
Ramsey, Jayne, illus. see Mustaine Hettinger, Cynthia.
Ramsey, Jo. Jet Black. (p. 916)
—Nail Polish & Feathers. (p. 1227)
—Opening Up. (p. 1300)
—Time of Darkness. (p. 1752)
Ramsey, Kirby. Pen & Quill: A Book of Poetry. (p. 1336)
Ramsey, L. A., illus. see Morton, William A.
Ramsey, Marcy, illus. see Dietrich, Julie.
Ramsey, Marcy, illus. see Naylor, Phyllis Reynolds.
Ramsey, Marcy Dunn, illus. see Bunting, Elaine & D'Amario, Patricia.
Ramsey, Marcy Dunn, illus. see Cummings, Priscilla.
Ramsey, Marcy Dunn, illus. see Curtis, Jennifer Keats.
Ramsey, Marcy Dunn, illus. see Lonczak, Heather Suzanne.
Ramsey, Marcy Dunn, illus. see McVicker, Mary.
Ramsey, Marcy Dunn, illus. see Michels-Gualtieri, Akaela S.
Ramsey, Marcy Dunn, illus. see Michels-Gualtieri, Zaydek G. & Michels-Gualtieri, Akaela S.
Ramsey, Marcy Dunn, illus. see Parker, David.
Ramsey, Marshall, illus. see Ramsey, Dave.
Ramsey, Patricia. Mr. Quadrilateral & His Four Sided Family. (p. 1186)
Ramsey, R. M. Browser Bunch: The Browser Files Presents... the Big Lie. (p. 232)
Ramsey, Torren. Ojibwe. (p. 1282)
Ramshaw, Gail. Every Day & Sunday, Too. Jarret, Judy, illus. (p. 542)
Ramski, Mitch. Firehouse Cat: How Cinder Became a Firehouse Cat. (p. 592)
Ramsland, Marcia. Before & After: Makeovers for Your Life. (p. 158)
Ramsnips, Tunder. Hardly Boys. (p. 748)
Ramstad, Ralph L., illus. see Streissguth, Tom.
Ramstein, Anne-Margot, jt. auth. see Arégui, Matthias.
Ramthun, Bonnie. White Gates. (p. 1913)
Ran, Gila. Lemonheads, the Crown of Wisdom. (p. 991)
Rana, Tariq. Five Baby Blackbirds: Learn How to Fly. (p. 600)
Ranade, Soumitra. Tak-Tak! Suleman, Shilo Shiv, illus. (p. 1696)
Ranchetti, Sebastiano. Animal Opposites. (p. 79)
—Animal Opposites/Opuestos Animales. (p. 79)
—Animals in Color (Animales en Color) (p. 83)
—Animals in Color/Animales en Color. (p. 83)
—Counting with Animals. (p. 371)
—Counting with Animals/Cuenta con los Animales. (p. 372)
—Opuestos Animales. (p. 1301)
—Shapes in Animals. (p. 1560)
—Shapes in Animals/Figuras en los Animales. (p. 1560)
Ranchetti, Sebastiano, illus. see Ottina, Laura.
Ranchetti, Sebastiano & Nations, Susan. Animals in Color. (p. 83)
—Counting with Animals. (p. 372)
Rancic, Bill. Beyond the Lemonade Stand: Starting Small to Make It Big! (p. 174)
Ranciere, Jacques. Film Fables. Battista, Emiliano, tr. from FRE. (p. 586)
Rancourt, Cheryle. Puff Family: Volume 1. (p. 1415)
Rancourt, Heather & Gauches, Claudia. Fossibles-Bursting from Extinction to Distinction. (p. 623)
Rand, Ann. I Know a Lot of Things. Rand, Paul, illus. (p. 840)
Rand, Ann & Rand, Paul. Sparkle & Spin: A Book about Words. (p. 1622)
Rand, Betseygail & Rand, Colleen. Big Bunny. Rand, Colleen, illus. (p. 180)
Rand, Carol. Lydia Darragh: Quaker Patriot. Marshall, Dan, illus. (p. 1066)
Rand, Casey. Communication. (p. 349)
—DNA & Heredity. (p. 456)
—Food. (p. 612)
—Forces & Motion. (p. 617)
—George Washington. (p. 664)
—George Washington Oxford Bible Staff, illus. (p. 664)
—Giant Morays & Other Extraordinary Eels. (p. 673)
—Graphing Sports. (p. 711)
—Human Reproduction De Angelis, Maurizio & Escott, Ian, illus. (p. 826)
—Producing Vegetables. (p. 1409)
—Temperature. (p. 1717)
—Time. (p. 1750)
Rand, Casey & Heinemann Library Staff. Classification of Animals Escott, Ian & Joynes, Gary, illus. (p. 328)
—Human Reproduction De Angelis, Maurizio & Escott, Ian, illus. (p. 826)
Rand, Colleen, jt. auth. see Rand, Betseygail.
Rand, Edward A. Knights of the White Shield: Up-the-Ladder Club Series Round One Play. (p. 964)
—Knights of the White Shield; or, up-the-Ladder Club Series, Round One Play. (p. 964)
Rand, Emily. Dog Day. (p. 461)
Rand, Jason. Helios. (p. 763)
Rand, Johnathan. Amer Ch Double Thrillers. (p. 58)
—American Chillers #1 Michigan Mega-Monsters. (p. 60)
—American Chillers #22 Nuclear Jelly Fish of New Jersey. (p. 60)
—American Chillers #23 Wicked Velociraptors of West Virginia. (p. 60)
—American Chillers #24 Haunting in New Hampshire. (p. 60)
—American Chillers #25 Mississippi Megalodon. (p. 60)
—American Chillers #26 Oklahoma Outbreak. (p. 60)
—American Chillers #27 Kentucky Komodo Dragons. (p. 60)
—American Chillers #29 Oregon Oceanauts. (p. 60)
—Freddie Fernortner #1 the Fantastic Flying Bicycle. (p. 632)
—Freddie Fernortner #11: Tadpole Trouble. (p. 632)
—Freddie Fernortner #8: Chippers Crazy Carnival. (p. 632)
—Freddie Fernortner #9: Attack of the Dust Bunnies from Outer Space. (p. 632)
—Michigan Chillers #11 Great Lakes Ghost Ship. (p. 1135)
Rand, Jonathan. Freddie Fernortner #7: Fearless First Grader: the Magical Wading Pool. Bk 7 (p. 632)
—Michigan Chillers #14 Bionic Bats Bay City. (p. 1135)
Rand McNally. Are We There Yet? Awty. (p. 96)
—Kids' Road Atlas: Kra. (p. 955)
Rand McNally, creator. Coast-To-Coast Games. (p. 336)
—Kids' Backseat Travel Kit. (p. 952)
Rand McNally Staff. Are We There Yet? (p. 96)
—Atlas Schoolhouse Beginner's Workbook. (p. 113)
—Atlas Schoolhouse Illustrated United States Atlas. (p. 113)
—Atlas Schoolhouse Illustrated World Atlas. (p. 113)
—Atlas Schoolhouse Intermediate World Atlas. (p. 113)
—Atlas Scoolhouse Beginner's World Atlas. (p. 113)
—Kids' Road Atlas. (p. 955)
Rand McNally Staff, creator. Atlas of American History. (p. 112)
—Intermediate Geography & Map Activities. (p. 880)
Rand, Paul, illus. see Rand, Ann.
Rand, Paul, jt. auth. see Rand, Ann.
Rand, Ted, illus. see Archambault, John & Martin, Bill, Jr.
Rand, Ted, illus. see Gibbons, Faye.
Rand, Ted, illus. see Moore, Clement C.
Rand, Ted, illus. see Prelutsky, Jack.
Rand, Ted, illus. see Tunnell, Michael O.
Rand, Ted & Moore, Clement C. Night Before Christmas. (p. 1252)
Rand, Tracy, illus. see Westendorf, Sandra.
Randall, Alex. Rhyming Book. (p. 1468)
Randall, Alice. Diary of B. B. Bright, Possible Princess. (p. 435)
Randall, Alice & Williams, Caroline Randall. Diary of B. B. Bright, Possible Princess. Strickland, Shadra, illus. (p. 435)
Randall, Alison L. Wheat Doll Farnsworth, Bill, illus. (p. 1900)
Randall, Angel. Snow Angels. (p. 1598)
Randall, Barbara. Jacob Daddy. Randall, Barbara & Newman, J. Heidi, eds. (p. 904)
Randall, Bernard. Solon: The Lawmaker of Athens. (p. 1608)
Randall, Bob & McInerney, Kunyi June-Anne. Tracker Tjugingji. (p. 1775)
—Tracker Tjungingji. (p. 1775)
Randall, Chuck. Curley's Wish Comes True. (p. 394)
Randall, Daniel & Randall, Ronne. Tales of King Arthur: Ten Legendary Stories of the Knights of the Round Table. Howells, Graham, illus. (p. 1702)
Randall, David. Clovermead: In the Shadow of the Bear. (p. 335)
Randall, Dennis E. Those Darn Cats Patchie & Teddy: Having Fun & Making Friends. (p. 1740)
Randall, Emma, illus. see Jones, Christianne C.
Randall, Harold. Accounting: As Level & a Level. (p. 8)
Randall, Henry. Bobcats: Linces Rojos. (p. 206)
—Bobcats. (p. 206)
—Cheetahs: Guepardos. (p. 296)
—Cheetahs. (p. 296)
—Cougars. (p. 369)
—Cougars / Pumas. (p. 369)
—Lynxes: Linces. (p. 1066)
—Lynxes. (p. 1066)
—Ocelots: Ocelotes. (p. 1277)
—Ocelots. (p. 1277)
—Wildcats: Gatos Monteses. (p. 1931)
—Wildcats. (p. 1931)
Randall, Homer. Army Boys in the French Trenches: Or, Hand to Hand Fighting with the Enemy. (p. 100)
Randall, Jack. Old Lady of Wasilla Lake: A Story of the Red-necked Grebes of Wasilla Lake, Alaska. Randall, Jack, illus. (p. 1284)
Randall, Jesseca. Christopher Columbus: Navigated by God - A Historical Children's Novel about One of the Most Important Figures of the Age of Exploration. (p. 316)
Randall, Jory. My Day at the Beach. (p. 1201)
—My Day at the Farm. (p. 1201)
—My Day at the Park. (p. 1201)
—My Day in the City. (p. 1201)
—My Day in the Forest. (p. 1201)
—My Day in the Mountains. (p. 1201)
Randall, Kat. Yoga for Youngsters: Playful Poses for Little People. (p. 1972)
Randall, Lee Brandt, illus. see Michael, Todd.
Randall, Marilyn. Best of Best Friends. (p. 170)
—Elmer the Christmas Elf. (p. 515)
—Hard Nut to Crack. (p. 748)
—Inside Out. (p. 877)
Randall, Marilyn Mae. Three Wives of Hero the Second. Heavner, Jodi, illus. (p. 1744)
Randall, MarilynMae. Wellington's Windows. McCarter, Zack, illus. (p. 1874)
Randall, Marisa. Geographic Features of New York City. (p. 662)
Randall, Maxine. Bright Gems for His Crown. (p. 228)
Randall, Rod, jt. auth. see Buchanan, Paul.
Randall, Rommie. Mommy's Little Boy. (p. 1163)
Randall, Ron. Trekker Omnibus. Gibbons, Jim, ed. (p. 1784)
Randall, Ron, illus. see Croall, Marie P.
Randall, Ron, illus. see Jolley, Dan.
Randall, Ron, illus. see Limke, Jeff.
Randall, Ron, illus. see Olrich, Alan.
Randall, Ron, illus. see Storrie, Paul D.
Randall, Ron, illus. see Willingham, Bill.
Randall, Ronne. Before I Go to Sleep. Kerins, Tony, illus. (p. 158)
—Birth. (p. 192)
—Children's Book of Myths & Legends. Howells, Graham, illus. (p. 303)
—Hanukkah Mice. Kneep, Maggie, illus. (p. 744)
—Hanukkah Sweets & Treats. (p. 744)
—Marriage. (p. 1096)
—Snuggle up, Little Penguin! Church, Caroline Jayne, illus. (p. 1601)
—Thanksgiving Sweets & Treats. (p. 1726)
—Where Food Comes From: The Best Start in Science. (p. 1907)
—Where Food Comes From. (p. 1907)
Randall, Ronne, jt. auth. see Randall, Daniel.
Randall, Ronne & Orme, Helen. Healthy Eating: The Best Start in Science. (p. 758)
Randall, Thomas. Waking: A Winter of Ghosts. (p. 1853)
—Waking: Dreams of the Dead. (p. 1853)
Randall, Thomas & Golden, Christopher. Spirits of the Noh. (p. 1629)
Randazzo, Angela. Don't Call Me Cranberry. (p. 467)
Randazzo, Dottie. Blue Girl. (p. 202)
—Praying 101 for Kids & Teens. (p. 1393)
Randazzo, Michael. Just Do Your Homework! (p. 938)
Randazzo, Tony, illus. see Ikids Staff.
Randel, Jackie. Calendar Friends. (p. 252)
Randerath, Jeanette & Winterhager, Randerath -. ¡vuela, Yoa, Vuela! (p. 1851)
Randle, Janice W. Issues in the Spanish-Speaking World (p. 893)
Randle, Kristen D. Only Alien on the Planet. (p. 1298)
—Slumming. (p. 1591)
Randle, Leila. Home Gurl Shopping: Keeping your family afloat, when there ain't no Boat! (p. 792)
Randle, Walt R., ed. see Mochizuki, Chiemi.
Randles, Slim & Montoya, Jerry. Ol' Jimmy Dollar. (p. 1283)
Rando, Licia. Warmest Place of All. Jewett, Anne, illus. (p. 1858)
Randol, Susan. I Before e (Except after C) Easy, Cool Ways to Remember Facts. (p. 834)
Randol, Susan, et al. I Wish I Knew That: U. S. Presidents: Cool Stuff You Need to Know. Halbert, Patricia, ed. (p. 849)
Randolph, Carolyn, illus. see Phillips, Rachelle.
Randolph, Connie. Casper Joe. (p. 276)
—Casper Joe & the Eagle Feather. (p. 276)
—Emblem Brightly Shines with Casper Joe. (p. 517)
—Fur-Raising Adventure of Casper Joe. (p. 650)
—Wagging Tails of Casper Joe: Book Two. (p. 1852)
Randolph, Grace. Muppet Peter Pan. Mebberson, Amy, illus. (p. 1191)
Randolph, Grace, jt. auth. see Ghiglione, Marco.
Randolph, Grace & Barks, Carl. Muppet Peter Pan. Mebberson, Amy, illus. (p. 1191)
Randolph, Grace, et al. Fraggle Rock: Tails & Tales. Beedle, Tim, ed. (p. 627)
Randolph, Jennifer & Benchmark Education Co. Staff. Women of the Civil War. (p. 1946)
Randolph, Joane. Light in My World. (p. 1015)
Randolph, Joanne. All about a Day. (p. 42)
—All about a Day/Los Días. (p. 42)
—All about A Day/Los Días. Brusca, Maria Cristina, tr. from ENG. (p. 42)
—All about A Months/Los Meses. Brusca, Maria Cristina, tr. (p. 42)
—All about an Hour. (p. 42)
—All about an Hour/Las Horas. (p. 42)
—All about an Hour/Las Horas. Brusca, Maria Cristina, tr. from ENG. (p. 42)
—All about the Months. (p. 43)
—All about the Months/Los Meses. (p. 43)
—All about the Seasons. (p. 43)
—All about the Seasons/Las Estaciones. (p. 43)
—All about the Seasons/Las Estaciones. Brusca, Maria Cristina, tr. (p. 43)
—Ambulances. (p. 57)
—Ambulances/Ambulancias. (p. 57)
—Ambulances/Ambulancias. Alaman, Eduardo, tr. from ENG. (p. 57)
—Angel of Goliad: Francisca Alvarez & the Texas War for Independence. (p. 74)
—Bella: A Butterfly's Story. (p. 162)
—Bulldozers. (p. 240)
—Call of Liberty: Marquis de Lafayette & the American Revolution. (p. 254)
—Classroom Pets. (p. 329)
—Coast Guard Boats. (p. 336)
—Coast Guard Boats/Lanchas Guardacostas. Alaman, Eduardo, tr. from ENG. (p. 336)
—Coastguard Boats/Lanchas Guardacostas. (p. 336)
—Concrete Mixers. (p. 355)
—Dennis Tito: First Space Tourist. (p. 426)
—Dennis Tito, First Space Tourist. (p. 426)
—Earth Movers. (p. 496)
—Electricity in My World. (p. 509)
—Electricity in My World / la Electricidad en Mi Mundo. Brusca, Maria Cristina, tr. from ENG. (p. 509)
—Electricity in My World/la electricidad en mi Mundo. (p. 509)
—Emergency Helicopters. (p. 518)
—Emergency Helicopters/Helicopteros de Emergencia. (p. 518)
—Emergency Helicopters/Helicopteros de Emergencia. Alaman, Eduardo, tr. from ENG. (p. 518)
—Fire Trucks. (p. 591)
—Fire Trucks/Caminones de Bomberos. Alaman, Eduardo, tr. from ENG. (p. 591)
—Fire Trucks/Camiones de Bomberos. (p. 591)
—Fish. (p. 598)
—Frankie: A Frog's Story. (p. 629)
—Gases in My World. (p. 657)
—Gases in My World / Los Gases en Mi Mundo. Brusca, Maria Cristina, tr. from ENG. (p. 657)
—Gases in My World/Los gases en mi Mundo. (p. 657)
—Gears in My World: Engranajes en Mi Mundo. (p. 659)
—Gears in My World. (p. 659)
—Gears in My World/Engranajes en mi Mundo. (p. 659)
—Great White Shark: King of the Ocean. (p. 719)
—Greenley: A Tree's Story. (p. 723)
—Guinea Pigs. (p. 731)
—Hammerhead Shark: Coastal Killer. (p. 739)
—Home for Sue. (p. 792)
—Inclined Planes in My World: Planos Inclinados en Mi Mundo. (p. 869)
—Inclined Planes in My World. (p. 869)
—Inclined Planes in My World/Planos inclinados en mi Mundo. (p. 869)
—Iroquois League. (p. 888)
—Let's Draw a Bird with Shapes: Vamos a Dibujar un Ave Usando Figuras. Muschinske, Emily, illus. (p. 995)
—Let's Draw a Bird with Shapes. (p. 995)
—Let's Draw a Bird with Shapes. Muschinske, Emily, illus. (p. 995)
—Let's Draw a Bird with Shapes/Vamos a dibujar un ave usando Figuras. (p. 995)
—Let's Draw a Butterfly with Circles: Vamos a Dibujar una Mariposa Usando Circulos. Muschinske, Emily, illus. (p. 995)
—Let's Draw a Butterfly with Circles. (p. 995)
—Let's Draw a Butterfly with Circles. Muschinske, Emily, illus. (p. 995)
—Let's Draw a Butterfly with Circles / Vamos a dibujar una mariposa usando Círculos. (p. 995)
—Let's Draw a Dinosaur with Shapes: Vamos a Dibujar un Dinosaurio Usando Figuras. (p. 995)
—Let's Draw a Dinosaur with Shapes. (p. 995)
—Let's Draw a Dinosaur with Shapes. Muschinske, Emily, illus. (p. 995)
—Let's Draw a Dinosaur with Shapes/Vamos a dibujar un dinasaurio usando Figuras. (p. 995)
—Let's Draw a Fire Truck with Shapes: Vamos a Dibujar un Camion de Bomberos Usando Figuras. Muschinske, Emily, illus. (p. 995)
—Let's Draw a Fire Truck with Shapes. Muschinske, Emily, illus. (p. 995)
—Let's Draw a Horse with Rectangles: Vamos a Dibujar un Caballo Usando Rectangulos. (p. 996)
—Let's Draw a Horse with Rectangles. (p. 996)
—Let's Draw a Horse with Rectangles. Muschinske, Emily, tr. (p. 996)
—Let's Draw a Horse with Rectangles / Vamos a dibujar un caballo usando Rectángulos. (p. 996)
—Let's Draw a House with Shapes: Vamos a Dibujar una Casa Usando Figuras. Muschinske, Emily, illus. (p. 996)
—Let's Draw a House with Shapes. Muschinske, Emily, illus. (p. 996)
—Let's Draw a School Bus with Shapes: Vamos a Dibujar un Autobus Escolar Usando Figuras. Muschinske, Emily, illus. (p. 996)
—Let's Draw a School Bus with Shapes. Muschinske, Emily, illus. (p. 996)
—Let's Draw a Truck with Shapes: Vamos a Dibujar un Camion Usando Figuras. Muschinske, Emily, illus. (p. 996)
—Let's Draw a Truck with Shapes. (p. 996)
—Let's Draw a Truck with Shapes. Muschinske, Emily, illus. (p. 996)
—Let's Draw a Truck with Shapes/Vamos a dibujar un camión usando Figuras. (p. 996)
—Let's Draw a Turtle with Half Circles. (p. 996)
—Let's Draw a Turtle with Half Circles/ Vamos a dibujar una tortuga usando medios Círculos. (p. 996)
—Let's Draw a Turtle with Half Circles/Vamos a Dibujar una Tortuga Usando Medios Circulos. Brusca, Maria Cristina, tr. (p. 996)
—Levers in My World: Palancas en Mi Mundo. (p. 1004)
—Levers in My World. (p. 1004)
—Levers in My World/Palancas en mi Mundo. (p. 1004)
—Light in My World: La Luz en Mi Mundo. (p. 1015)
—Light in My World. (p. 1015)
—Light in My World/la luz en mi Mundo. (p. 1015)
—Liquids in My World: Los Líquidos en Mi Mundo. (p. 1021)
—Liquids in My World. (p. 1021)
—Liquids in My World/Los líquidos en mi Mundo. (p. 1021)
—Mako Shark: Built for Speed. (p. 1083)
—Math Exploration: Using Math to Learn about the Continents Set. (p. 1106)
—My Friend the Box Turtle. (p. 1209)
—My Friend the Ferret. (p. 1209)
—My Friend the Hermit Crab. (p. 1209)
—My Friend the Iguana. (p. 1209)
—My Friend the Miniature Horse. (p. 1209)
—My Friend the Potbellied Pig. (p. 1209)
—Number Crunch Your Way Around Africa. (p. 1271)
—Number Crunch Your Way Around Asia. (p. 1271)
—Number Crunch Your Way Around Australia. (p. 1271)
—Police Cars. (p. 1380)
—Police Cars/Patruallas. (p. 1380)
—Police Cars/Patrullas. Alaman, Eduardo, tr. (p. 1380)
—Pulleys in My World: Poleas en Mi Mundo. (p. 1416)
—Pulleys in My World. (p. 1416)
—Pulleys in My World/Poleas en mi Mundo. (p. 1416)
—Rabbits. (p. 1430)
—Road Machines. (p. 1476)
—Road Milling Machines. (p. 1476)
—Road Pavers. (p. 1477)
—Road Rollers. (p. 1477)
—Road Scrapers. (p. 1477)
—Rose: A Flower's Story. (p. 1489)
—Sharks: Hunters of the Deep (p. 1562)
—Snakes. (p. 1596)
—Snowplows. (p. 1601)
—Solids in My World: Los Sólidos en Mi Mundo. (p. 1608)
—Solids in My World. (p. 1608)
—Solids in My World/Los sólidos en mi Mundo. (p. 1608)
—Sounds in My World: Los Sonidos en Mi Mundo. (p. 1615)
—Sounds in My World. (p. 1615)
—Sounds in My World/Los sonidos en mi Mundo. (p. 1615)
—Stormy: A Storm Cloud's Story. (p. 1656)
—Tarantulas. (p. 1706)

R

—Tow Trucks. (p. 1773)
—Tow Trucks/Gruas. (p. 1773)
—Tow Trucks/Gruas. Alaman, Eduardo, tr. from ENG. (p. 1773)
—Turtles. (p. 1799)
—Wedges in My World: Cuñas en Mi Mundo. (p. 1871)
—Wedges in My World. (p. 1871)
—Wedges in My World/Cunas en mi Mundo. (p. 1871)
—Whale Shark: Gentle Giant. (p. 1877)
—What Are the Elements of Weather? (p. 1880)
—What I Look Like When I Am Confused. (p. 1886)
—What I Look Like When I am Confused / Cómo me veo cuando estoy Confundido. (p. 1887)
—What I Look Like When I Am Sad. (p. 1887)
—What I Look Like When I am Sad / Cómo me veo cuando estoy Triste. (p. 1887)
—What Is the US Constitution? (p. 1890)
—Wheel Loaders. (p. 1900)
—Wheels & Axels in My World/Ejes y ruedas en mi Mundo. (p. 1900)
—Wheels & Axles in My World: Ejes y Ruedas en Mi Mundo. (p. 1900)
—Wheels & Axles in My World. (p. 1900)
—Whose Back Is This? (p. 1921)
—Whose Back Is This? De Quién Es Esta Espalda? (p. 1921)
—Whose Back Is This? / ¿de quién es esta Espalda? (p. 1921)
—Whose Eyes Are These? (p. 1921)
—Whose Eyes Are These? De Quién Son Estos Ojos? (p. 1921)
—Whose Eyes Are These? / ¿de quién son estos Ojos? (p. 1921)
—Whose Nose Is This? (p. 1922)
—Whose Nose Is This? De Quién Es Esta Nariz? (p. 1922)
—Whose Nose Is This? / ¿de quién es esta Nariz? (p. 1922)
—Whose Teeth Are These? (p. 1922)
—Whose Teeth Are These? De Quién Son Estos Dientes? (p. 1922)
—Whose Teeth Are These? / ¿de quién son estos Dientes? (p. 1922)
—Whose Toes Are Those? (p. 1922)
—Whose Toes Are Those? De Quién Son Estas Patas? (p. 1922)
—Whose Toes Are Those? / ¿de quién son estas Patas? (p. 1922)
—Whose Tongue Is This? (p. 1922)
—Whose Tongue Is This? De Quién Es Esta Lengua? (p. 1922)
—Whose Tongue Is This? / ¿de quién es esta Lengua? (p. 1922)
Randolph, Robert. Ben Goes to the Farmer's Market (p. 163)
—Ben the Flying Cat Sappington, Ray, illus. (p. 163)
—Their Very Own Bike (p. 1728)
Randolph, Ryan. Alexander Hamilton's Economic Plan: Solving Problems in America's New Economy. (p. 36)
—Bank Robber's End: The Death of Jesse James. (p. 136)
—Betsy Ross: The American Flag, & Life in a Young America. (p. 172)
—How to Spend Smart. (p. 821)
—Karts. (p. 944)
—Marbury V. Madison: The New Supreme Court Gets More Powers. (p. 1091)
Randolph, Ryan P. Benjamin Franklin: Inventor, Writer & Patriot. (p. 165)
—Benjamin Franklin: Inventor, Writer, & Patriot. (p. 165)
—Betsy Ross: The American Flag & Life in Young America. (p. 172)
—Black Cowboys. (p. 195)
—Following the Great Herds: The Plains Indians & the American Buffalo. (p. 612)
—Frontier Schools & Schoolteachers. (p. 644)
—Frontier Women Who Helped Shape the American West. (p. 644)
—How to Draw the Life & Times of Andrew Johnson. (p. 818)
—How to Draw the Life & Times of Dwight D. Eisenhower. (p. 818)
—How to Draw the Life & Times of John Adams. (p. 819)
—How to Draw the Life & Times of Millard Fillmore. (p. 819)
—How to Draw the Life & Times of William Howard Taft. (p. 819)
—How to Earn Money. (p. 819)
—How to Make a Budget. (p. 820)
—How to Manage Risk. (p. 820)
—How to Save & Invest. (p. 821)
—How to Spend Smart. (p. 821)
—How to Use Credit. (p. 822)
—Marbury V. Madison: The New Supreme Court Gets More Power. (p. 1091)
—New Research Techniques: Getting the Most Out of Search Engine Tools. (p. 1247)
—Price You Pay: A Look at Supply & Demand. (p. 1398)
—Robotics. (p. 1480)
—Santa Fe Trail. (p. 1511)
—Wild West Lawmen & Outlaws. (p. 1930)
Randolph, Tammy. Cricket Hunts for the Easter Bunny. (p. 382)
—Cricket's Starry Night. (p. 382)
Random House. Big Fish, Little Fish: a Book of Opposites (Bubble Guppies) Random House, illus. (p. 181)
—Dinos & Discoveries/Emily Saves the World (p. 441)
—Dora Goes to School/Dora Va a la Escuela (Dora the Explorer) MJ Illustrations, illus. (p. 470)
—Dora's Farm Rescue! (Dora the Explorer) Random House, illus. (p. 471)
—Dora's Lift-And-Look Book (Dora the Explorer) Roper, Bob, illus. (p. 471)
—Elmo's 123. (p. 515)
—Elmo's ABC Song (Sesame Street) (p. 515)
—Epic Turtle Tales (Teenage Mutant Ninja Turtles) Random House, illus. (p. 532)
—Farm Alarm! (Team Umizoomi) Fruchter, Jason, illus. (p. 573)
—Fearsome Footprints/Thomas the Brave (Thomas & Friends) Stubbs, Tommy, illus. (p. 579)
—Five Fin-Tastic Stories (Bubble Guppies) Random House, illus. (p. 600)
—Five Playtime Tales (Nick, Jr.) Random House, illus. (p. 601)
—Five Tank Engine Tales (Thomas & Friends) Courtney, Richard, illus. (p. 601)
—Five Undersea Stories (SpongeBob SquarePants) Random House, illus. (p. 601)
—Follow That Egg! (Team Umizoomi) Aikins, David, illus. (p. 612)
—Funny-Side Up: A SpongeBob Joke Book. Random House, illus. (p. 650)
—Great Train Mystery. (p. 718)
—Haunted House Party! (Bubble Guppies) MJ Illustrations, illus. (p. 753)
—Here Comes Peter Cottontail. Random House, illus. (p. 770)
—Hide-And-Go-Swim! (Bubble Guppies) MJ Illustrations, illus. (p. 776)
—Hooray for Dads! (SpongeBob SquarePants) Random House, illus. (p. 795)
—I Am Baymax. (p. 832)
—Ice Team (Paw Patrol) Jackson, Mike, illus. (p. 851)
—Inside the Maze Runner: the Guide to the Glade. (p. 877)
—Isa's Flower Garden (Dora the Explorer) Miller, Victoria, illus. (p. 891)
—It's a SpongeBob Christmas! (SpongeBob SquarePants) Random House, illus. (p. 896)
—Let Them Eat Cake! (Mr. Peabody & Sherman) Laguna, Fabio & Gallego, James, illus. (p. 994)
—Let's Find Adventure! (Paw Patrol) Jackson, Mike, illus. (p. 996)
—Loose Tooth (Barbie) (p. 1052)
—Mutant Files (Teenage Mutant Ninja Turtles) Random House, illus. (p. 1194)
—Ninjas on Ice! (Teenage Mutant Ninja Turtles) Spaziante, Patrick, illus. (p. 1257)
—P Is for Potty! (Sesame Street) Moroney, Christopher, illus. (p. 1316)
—Patrol Pals (Paw Patrol) Random House, illus. (p. 1329)
—Pizza Party! (Teenage Mutant Ninja Turtles) Spaziante, Patrick, illus. (p. 1365)
—Plankton's Christmas Surprise! (SpongeBob SquarePants) Martinez, Heather, illus. (p. 1368)
—Pup, Pup, & Away! (Paw Patrol) Moore, Harry, illus. (p. 1417)
—Pups to the Rescue! (Paw Patrol) Random House, illus. (p. 1418)
—Ready to Race! (Blaze & the Monster Machines) Kobasic, Kevin, illus. (p. 1448)
—Red Alert! (Teenage Mutant Ninja Turtles) Spaziante, Patrick, illus. (p. 1453)
—Santa's Little Helpers (Team Umizoomi) Ostrom, Bob, illus. (p. 1513)
—Save the Kitten!/Buster's Big Day (Team Umizoomi) Ostrom, Bob, illus. (p. 1516)
—Show Your Colors! (Teenage Mutant Ninja Turtles) Spaziante, Patrick, illus. (p. 1571)
—Sisters on Safari (Barbie) Riley, Kellee, illus. (p. 1581)
—SpongeBob's Slap Shot (SpongeBob SquarePants) Random House, illus. (p. 1631)
—Strength in Numbers! (Teenage Mutant Ninja Turtles) Spaziante, Patrick, illus. (p. 1667)
—Team Colors (Paw Patrol) Random House, illus. (p. 1710)
—Teenage Mutant Ninja Turtles Collection (Teenage Mutant Ninja Turtles) Random House, illus. (p. 1714)
—Thomas & Friends Spills & Thrills/No More Mr. Nice Engine (Thomas & Friends) (p. 1738)
—Thomas & Friends: the Adventure Begins (Thomas & Friends) (p. 1738)
—Thomas & the Lost Pirate / The Sunken Treasure Stubbs, Tommy, illus. (p. 1738)
—Thomas at the Animal Park (Thomas & Friends) Lapadula, Thomas, illus. (p. 1738)
—Top Cops (Team Umizoomi) Fruchter, Jason, illus. (p. 1769)
Random House, illus. see Banks, Steven.
Random House, illus. see Carbone, Courtney.
Random House, illus. see David, Erica.
Random House, illus. see Depken, Kristen L.
Random House, illus. see Gilbert, Matthew.
Random House, illus. see Gomez, Yuliana.
Random House, illus. see Homberg, Ruth.
Random House, illus. see James, Hollis.
Random House, illus. see Kratt, Chris & Kratt, Martin.
Random House, illus. see Lewman, David & Gomez, Yuliana.
Random House, illus. see Lewman, David.
Random House, illus. see Man-Kong, Mary.
Random House, illus. see Posner-Sanchez, Andrea.
Random House, illus. see Tillworth, Mary.
Random House, jt. auth. see Man-Kong, Mary.
Random House & David, Erica. Teenage Mutant Ninja Turtles: Special Edition Movie Novelization (Teenage Mutant Ninja Turtles) Random House, illus. (p. 1714)
Random House & Golden Books Staff. To the Hall of Doors! Random House & Golden Books Staff, illus. (p. 1759)
Random House & Man-Kong, Mary. Happy Birthday, Barbie! Riley, Kellee, illus. (p. 744)
Random House & Pohlmeyer, Krista. Bug Parade! (Bubble Guppies) Moore, Harry, illus. (p. 236)
Random House & Shealy, Dennis R. Park Is Open. Random House, illus. (p. 1324)
Random House & Wilson, Sarah. Moms Are the Best! (SpongeBob SquarePants) Random House, illus. (p. 1163)
Random House Audio Publishing Group Staff, illus. see Landolf, Diane Wright.
Random House Beginners Books Staff, illus. see Inches, Alison.
Random House Beginners Books Staff, illus. see Tillworth, Mary.
Random House Children's Books Staff. Happy Love Day! Aikins, David, illus. (p. 746)
Random House Children's Books Staff, jt. auth. see Tillworth, Mary.
Random House Dictionary Staff. You're Fired! (SpongeBob SquarePants) Random House Dictionary Staff & Aikins, Dave, illus. (p. 1982)
Random House Disney Staff. Anna's Act of Love - Elsa's Icy Magic Random House Disney Staff, illus. (p. 85)
—Brave Firefighters (Disney Planes: Fire & Rescue) Random House Disney Staff, illus. (p. 223)
—Frozen Little Golden Book (Disney Frozen) Random House Disney Staff, illus. (p. 645)
—Glamour Pets! Disney Storybook Artists Staff, illus. (p. 682)
—Journey to the Ice Palace. Random House Disney Staff, illus. (p. 929)
—New Reindeer Friend. Random House Disney Staff, illus. (p. 1247)
—Planes: Fire & Rescue Paper Airplane Book (Disney Planes Fire & Rescue) Random House Disney Staff, illus. (p. 1367)
—Power of a Princess Random House Disney Staff, illus. (p. 1389)
—Princess Story Collection. (p. 1405)
—Race Team. Random House Disney Staff, illus. (p. 1431)
—Snow Place Like Home. Random House Disney Staff, illus. (p. 1599)
—Squiggles & Giggles (Disney/Pixar) Random House Disney Staff, illus. (p. 1637)
—Sweet & Spooky Halloween. Marrucchi, Elisa, illus. (p. 1689)
—Sweet & Spunky. Random House Disney Staff, illus. (p. 1689)
—Time to Shine! Random House Disney Staff, illus. (p. 1753)
—Wreck-It Ralph Little Golden Book (Disney Wreck-It Ralph) Random House Disney Staff, illus. (p. 1962)
Random House Disney Staff, illus. see Berrios, Frank.
Random House Disney Staff, illus. see Depken, Kristen L.
Random House Disney Staff, illus. see Jordan, Apple & Amerikaner, Susan.
Random House Disney Staff, illus. see Lagonegro, Melissa.
Random House Disney Staff, illus. see Posner-Sanchez, Andrea.
Random House Disney Staff, illus. see Redbank, Tennant.
Random House Disney Staff, jt. auth. see McMahon, Kara.
Random House Disney Staff & Redbank, Tennant. Teacup: Belle's Star Pup (Disney Princess: Palace Pets) Legramandi, Francesco & Matta, Gabriella, illus. (p. 1710)
Random House Editors. Disney Peter Pan. (p. 452)
—Don't Be a Jerk, It's Christmas! Random House Editors, illus. (p. 466)
—Good, the Bad, & the Krabby! Aikins, David, illus. (p. 700)
—Nickelodeon Story Time Collection (Nickelodeon) Random House Editors & Golden Books Staff, illus. (p. 1251)
—Tea Party in Wonderland. (p. 1708)
—Too Much Ooze! (Teenage Mutant Ninja Turtles) Random House Editors & Spaziante, Patrick, illus. (p. 1767)
Random House Editors, illus. see Carbone, Courtney.
Random House Editors, illus. see Gilbert, Matthew.
Random House Editors, illus. see Man-Kong, Mary & Hashimoto, Meika.
Random House Editors, illus. see Man-Kong, Mary.
Random House Editors, illus. see Shealy, Dennis.
Random House Editors, illus. see Tillworth, Mary.
Random House Editors, illus. see Webster, Christy.
Random House Editors, illus. see Wrecks, Billy.
Random House Editors, jt. auth. see Awdry, Wilbert V.
Random House Editors & Kleinberg, Naomi. Elmo & Ernie's Joke Book (Sesame Street) Brannon, Tom, illus. (p. 515)
Random House Editors & Posner-Sanchez, Andrea. Beauty of Nature. Marrucchi, Elisa, illus. (p. 154)
—I Am Cinderella. Random House Editors & Disney Storybook Artists Staff, illus. (p. 832)
Random House Editors & Random House Staff. I Can Be a Movie Star. Random House Editors & Random House Staff, illus. (p. 835)
Random House Editors & RH Disney Staff. Aurora & the Helpful Dragon - Tiana & Her Furry Friend. Disney Storybook Artists Staff & Studio Iboix Staff, illus. (p. 116)
Random House Staff. 1, 2, 3 under the Sea (SpongeBob SquarePants) Random House Staff, illus. (p. 1990)
—500 Palabras Nuevas Para Ti. Kest, Kristin, illus. (p. 2001)
—500 Words to Grow On. Kest, Kristin, illus. (p. 2001)
—Ballet Dreams. Random House Staff, illus. (p. 134)
—Barbie Fairytale Collection. (p. 138)
—Best Doghouse Ever! Random House Staff & Jackson, Mike, illus. (p. 168)
—Big Truck Show! Jackson, Mike, illus. (p. 184)
—Bikini Bottom Buddies (SpongeBob SquarePants) Random House Staff, illus. (p. 186)
—Blaze of Glory (Blaze & the Monster Machines) Foley, Niki, illus. (p. 198)
—Blue Wish (Maryoku Yummy) Conrad, Jeffrey, illus. (p. 203)
—Chase Is on the Case! (Paw Patrol) Random House Staff & Petrossi, Fabrizio, illus. (p. 294)
—Colors Everywhere! (Bubble Guppies) Random House Staff, illus. (p. 345)
—Count with Us! (Team Umizoomi) Random House Staff, illus. (p. 370)
—Dancing with the Star (SpongeBob SquarePants) Random House Staff, illus. (p. 403)
—Demolition Derby/Class Confusion (SpongeBob SquarePants) Aikins, Dave, illus. (p. 426)
—Dog Days (Team Umizoomi) Random House Staff & O'Connell, Lorraine, illus. (p. 461)
—Dora & the Unicorn King (Dora the Explorer) Random House Staff, illus. (p. 470)
—Dora Saves the Enchanted Forest/Dora Saves Crystal Kingdom (Dora the Explorer) Random House Staff, illus. (p. 470)
—Dora's Big Birthday Adventure (Dora the Explorer) Random House Staff, illus. (p. 471)
—Dora's Easter Bunny Adventure (Dora the Explorer) Random House Staff, illus. (p. 471)
—Dora's Puppy, Perrito! (Dora the Explorer) Aikins, David, illus. (p. 471)
—Egg-Stra Special Easter! (Barbie) Duarte, Pamela, illus. (p. 506)
—Five Tales from the Road. (p. 601)
—Friend at the Zoo (Bubble Guppies) Random House Staff & Nunn, Paul, illus. (p. 637)
—Get Moving with Elmo! (Sesame Street) Mathieu, Joe, illus. (p. 667)
—Good Night, Dora! (Dora the Explorer) Hall, Susan, illus. (p. 699)
—Great Train Mystery (SpongeBob SquarePants) Random House Staff, illus. (p. 718)
—Happiness to Go! (SpongeBob SquarePants) Random House Staff, illus. (p. 744)
—Haunted Houseboat (SpongeBob SquarePants) Random House Staff & Aikins, Dave, illus. (p. 753)
—Hero Story Collection (DC Super Friends) (p. 772)
—I Can Be... A Zoo Vet/I Can Be... A Cheerleader. Riley, Kellee, illus. (p. 835)
—I Can Be... Story Collection (Barbie) (p. 835)
—I Love Colors (Dora the Explorer) Random House Staff, illus. (p. 842)
—I Love My Mami! (Dora the Explorer) Random House Staff & Aikins, Dave, illus. (p. 842)
—Legend of the Blue Mermaid (Team Umizoomi) Fruchter, Jason, illus. (p. 989)
—Meet the Fresh Beats! Random House Staff, illus. (p. 1122)
—Mega-Justice Collection (SpongeBob SquarePants) Random House Staff, illus. (p. 1124)
—Monkey Business (Teenage Mutant Ninja Turtles) Random House Staff & Spaziante, Patrick, illus. (p. 1165)
—Ooze Control. Navarra, Nino, illus. (p. 1299)
—Outer-Space Chase (Team Umizoomi) Fruchter, Jason, illus. (p. 1312)
—Party Time! (SpongeBob SquarePants) Random House Staff & Moore, Harry, illus. (p. 1326)
—Pest of the West. Random House Staff & Meurer, Caleb, illus. (p. 1345)
—Railway Adventures. Random House Staff, illus. (p. 1434)
—Riddle Me This! Random House Staff, illus. (p. 1470)
—Saved by the Shell! (p. 1517)
—SpongeBob's Easter Parade (SpongeBob SquarePants) Random House Staff, illus. (p. 1631)
—Spring Chicken! (Bubble Guppies) Random House Staff & Trover, Zachary, illus. (p. 1635)
—Super Soap (Team Umizoomi) O'Connell, Lorraine, illus. (p. 1682)
—Surf's Up, Spongebob! - Runaway Roadtrip. Random House Staff, illus. (p. 1685)
—Swim, Boots, Swim! (Dora the Explorer) Random House Staff, illus. (p. 1690)
—Tea Party in Wonderland (Dora the Explorer) Miller, Victoria, illus. (p. 1708)
—Team Power! (Team Umizoomi) Random House Staff, illus. (p. 1710)
—Thomas & Friends: Percy's Chocolate Crunch & Other Thomas the Tank Engine Stories. Random House Staff, illus. (p. 1738)
—Time for School! (Bubble Guppies) Random House Staff, illus. (p. 1751)
—T-Machine Turbo Guide (Teenage Mutant Ninja Turtles) Random House Staff & Spaziante, Patrick, illus. (p. 1694)
—Traveling Tales. Random House Staff, illus. (p. 1780)
—UmiCar's Big Race (Team Umizoomi) Random House Staff & Aikins, David, illus. (p. 1810)
—Whiplash! (p. 1911)
—You're Fired! (p. 1982)
Random House Staff, illus. see Awdry, W.
Random House Staff, illus. see Awdry, W. & Berrios, Frank.
Random House Staff, illus. see Awdry, Wilbert V.
Random House Staff, illus. see Awdry, Wilbert V. & Wrecks, Billy.
Random House Staff, illus. see Bright, J. E.
Random House Staff, illus. see Depken, Kristen L.
Random House Staff, illus. see Eberly, Chelsea.
Random House Staff, illus. see Gilbert, Matthew.
Random House Staff, illus. see Harper, Ben.
Random House Staff, illus. see Homberg, Ruth.
Random House Staff, illus. see Man-Kong, Mary & Inches, Alison.
Random House Staff, illus. see Man-Kong, Mary, et al.
Random House Staff, illus. see Man-Kong, Mary.
Random House Staff, illus. see Posner-Sanchez, Andrea.
Random House Staff, illus. see Scarry, Richard.
Random House Staff, illus. see Teitelbaum, Michael.
Random House Staff, illus. see Tillworth, Mary.
Random House Staff, illus. see Trimble, Irene.
Random House Staff, illus. see Webster, Christy.
Random House Staff, illus. see Wrecks, Billy.
Random House Staff, jt. auth. see Eliopulos, Nick.
Random House Staff, jt. auth. see Golden Books Staff.
Random House Staff, jt. auth. see Holtz, Thomas R.
Random House Staff, jt. auth. see Random House Editors.
Random House Staff, jt. auth. see RH Disney Staff.
Random House Staff, jt. auth. see Seiss, Ellie.
Random House Staff, jt. auth. see Shealy, Dennis.
Random House Staff & Carbone, Courtney. Danger Dinosaurs! Random House Staff, illus. (p. 403)
Random House Staff & Cartobaleno. Happy Birthday, Bloom! (Winx Club) (p. 744)
Random House Staff & Depken, Kristen L. Dream Closet. (p. 483)
Random House Staff & Holtz, Thomas R. T. Rex: Hunter or Scavenger? (Jurassic World) Random House Staff, illus. (p. 1694)
Random House Staff & Roper, Robert. Dora Goes to the Doctor/Dora Goes to the Dentist (Dora the Explorer) Random House Staff, illus. (p. 470)
Random House Staff & Tillworth, Mary. Happy Birthday, Chelsea! (p. 744)
Random House Staff & Webster, Christy. Robot Rampage! (Teenage Mutant Ninja Turtles) Random House Staff & Spaziante, Patrick, illus. (p. 1480)
Random House Staff & Wilson, Sarah. Moms Are the Best! (SpongeBob SquarePants) Random House Staff, illus. (p. 1163)
Random House Value Publishing Staff, illus. see Golden Books Staff & Lewman, David.
Random House Value Publishing Staff, illus. see Man-Kong, Mary.
Random, Jack. Jazzman Chronicles: The War Chronicles. Vol. II (p. 911)

Random, Melanie, des. Alphabet Song Book. (p. 50)
Randoplh, Grace, illus. see Ghiglione, Marco & Randolph, Grace.
Rands, Bernard. Concerto (p. 355)
Randy. Adventures of Rico. (p. 22)
—Charlie the Fox & Mr Cricket. (p. 293)
Rane, Walter, illus. see Brown, Harriet & Witowski, Teri.
Rane, Walter, illus. see Tripp, Valerie.
Ranes, Robert. Bear with the Square Nose. (p. 151)
Raney, Barbara. Willie & the Lost Pacifier: The Marvelous & Many Adventures of Willie the Worm (series Title) (p. 1934)
Raney, Ken. It's Probably Good Dinosaurs Are Extinct. (p. 898)
Raney, Tom, illus. see Jurgens, Dan, et al.
Raney, Tom, et al. Infinity War. (p. 873)
Ranft, Patricia. Theology of Work: Peter Damian & the Medieval Religious Renewal Movement. (p. 1729)
Ranga, Katherine. Jesus Loves Me: A Bedtime Prayer. Ang, Selvi, illus. (p. 915)
Ranganathan, Babu G. Selfish Apple Tree. (p. 1549)
Ranganathan, Murali, ed. Govind Narayan's Mumbai: An Urban Biography From 1863. (p. 704)
Range, Ellen. Take Note! Taking & Organizing Notes. (p. 1696)
Range, Maureen. Perfectly Bonkers Birthday. (p. 1342)
Rangel, Fernando, illus. see Mann, Elizabeth.
Rangel, Graciela. Anthony's Christmas Journey. (p. 89)
—Anthony's Journey to God's Ark. (p. 89)
Rangel, Louis. Kids Workout Too! (p. 955)
Rangel, Mario Hugo, illus. see Rodriguez, Orlando A.
Rangel, Rawderson, illus. see Rinker, Gary W.
Rangner, Mike K., illus. see Ward, Jennifer.
Ranjalkar, Shreyans. My Sunny British Days - Stories for Children by a Child. (p. 1219)
Rankie, Barbara. Addition Unplugged (p. 12)
—Subtraction Unplugged (p. 1671)
Rankin, Bruce H., illus. see Ivanoff, George.
Rankin, Debbie. Butch the Blue Jay. (p. 246)
Rankin, H. L. Chaya & the Spider Gem. White, Siobhán, illus. (p. 295)
Rankin, Heather, jt. auth. see Rankin, Heather.
Rankin, Heather & Rankin, Heather. All It Takes Is One Friend. (p. 44)
Rankin, Joan, illus. see Capucilli, Alyssa Satin.
Rankin, Joan, illus. see Hatton, Jenny.
Rankin, Joan, illus. see Ruddell, Deborah.
Rankin, Joan, illus. see Stewart, Dianne.
Rankin, Joan, illus. see Wilson, Karma.
Rankin, Joan E. First Day. Rankin, Joan E., illus. (p. 594)
Rankin, Joan E., illus. see Capucilli, Alyssa Satin.
Rankin, Joan E., illus. see Ruddell, Deborah.
Rankin, Kenrya, jt. auth. see Naasel, Kenrya R.
Rankin, Kim, illus. see Tucker, Mary.
Rankin, Laura. Ruthie & the (Not So) Teeny Tiny Lie. Rankin, Laura, illus. (p. 1499)
—Ruthie & the (Not So) Very Busy Day. Rankin, Laura, illus. (p. 1499)
Rankin, Laura, illus. see Gibson, Ginger Foglesong.
Rankin, Laura, illus. see McCall Smith, Alexander.
Rankin, Laura, illus. see Shore, Diane Z.
Rankin, Laura, illus. see Stewart, Amber.
Rankin, Laura, illus. see Underwood, Deborah.
Rankin, Laura, jt. auth. see Stewart, Amber.
Rankin, Peter, illus. see Taylor, Joanne.
Rankin, Renee. Miss Lantz & Sadey: First in the Series of Little Sunshines Life Journey. (p. 1151)
Rankin, Robert. Chickens of Atlantis & Other Foul & Filthy Fiends. (p. 300)
Rankin, Shelly, illus. see Marino, Lia.
Rankin, Stephanie. Becoming Prince Charming. Allman, Kari, illus. (p. 156)
Rankin, Tony. Vital Skills: How to Help Friends in Crisis. (p. 1846)
Rankine-Van Wassenhoven, Jacqueline. Frog Named Waldor. Zhang, Annie, illus. (p. 640)
—Little Honey for Serge. (p. 1029)
—Sundays at Grandmother's House. (p. 1676)
—Three Pumpkin Pies for Three Good Neighbors. (p. 1743)
—Who Stole Grandpa's Teeth? (p. 1917)
Ranney, Jennifer Mozart. Birthday Star. (p. 193)
Ranola-Collier, Jean. Living Water. (p. 1042)
Ransburg, Ashley B. Evie Finds Her Family Tree. (p. 546)
Ransford, Sandy. 2001 A Joke Odyssey: The Millennium Joke Book. (p. 2003)
—At the Show. (p. 111)
—Jokes & Pranks (p. 924)
—Kingfisher Illustrated Horse & Pony Encyclopedia. (p. 960)
—Learn to Ride. (p. 984)
—Pony Care. (p. 1382)
—Pony Club. (p. 1382)
Ransom, Candice. Big Rigs on the Move. (p. 183)
—Camiones Grandes. Translations.com Staff, tr. from ENG. (p. 256)
—Camiones Grandes (Big Rigs) Translations.com Staff, tr. (p. 256)
—Daniel Boone. (p. 405)
—Endangered & Extinct Amphibians. (p. 526)
—George Washington & the Story of the U. S. Constitution. Reeves, Jeni, illus. (p. 664)
—Iva Honeysuckle Meets Her Match. Ross, Heather, illus. (p. 900)
—Key to the Griffon's Lair. Fiegenshuh, Emily, illus. (p. 950)
—Life-Saving Adventure of Sam Deal, Shipwreck Rescuer. (p. 1013)
—Life-Saving Adventure of Sam Deal, Shipwreck Rescuer. Trover, Zachary, illus. (p. 1013)
—Maggie L. Walker: Pioneering Banker & Community Leader. (p. 1071)
—Martha Washington. Ritz, Karen, illus. (p. 1097)
—Night of the Hurricane's Fury. Tong, Paul, illus. (p. 1254)
—Parts of a Flower. (p. 1325)
—Rebel Mckenzie. (p. 1450)
—Rescue Adventure of Stenny Green, Hindenburg Crash Eyewitness. Hammond, Ted & Carbajal, Richard, illus. (p. 1462)
—Sam Collier & the Founding of Jamestown. Archambault, Matthew, illus. (p. 1506)
—Tools & Treasures of Ancient China. (p. 1767)
—Twelve Days of Christmas in Washington, D. C. Hollander, Sarah, illus. (p. 1800)
—Underground Adventure of Arly Dunbar, Cave Explorer. Hammond, Ted & Carbajal, Richard, illus. (p. 1814)
—Underground Adventure of Arly Dunbar, Cave Explorer. Hammond, Ted & Carbajal, Richard Pimentel, illus. (p. 1814)
—What Was the Continental Congress? And Other Questions about the Declaration of Independence. (p. 1895)
—Who Wrote the U. S. Constitution? And Other Questions about the Constitutional Convention of 1787. (p. 1919)
—Why Did English Settlers Come to Virginia? And Other Questions about the Jamestown Settlement. (p. 1923)
—Willie McLean & the Civil War Surrender. Reeves, Jeni, illus. (p. 1934)
Ransom, Candice & Lyon, Tammie. Goldilocks & the Three Bears, Grades Pk - 3 (Ricitos de Oro y los Tres Osos) (p. 696)
—Little Red Riding Hood, Grades PK - 3: Caperucita Roja. (p. 1035)
Ransom, Candice & Walker, David. Hello, Washington, D. C.! (p. 765)
Ransom, Candice F. Apple Picking Day! Meza, Erika, illus. (p. 92)
—Cross-Pollination. (p. 385)
—Investigating the Water Cycle. (p. 885)
—Parts of a Flower. (p. 1325)
—Pumpkin Day! Meza, Erika, illus. (p. 1416)
—What's Great about Indiana? (p. 1897)
Ransom, Candice F. & Bryant, Laura J. Tractor Day. Bryant, Laura J., illus. (p. 1775)
Ransom, Candice F. & Zahares, Wade. Pony Island. (p. 1382)
Ransom, Jeanie Franz. Crown Affair. Axelsen, Stephen, illus. (p. 386)
—Don't Squeal Unless It's a Big Deal: A Tale of Tattletales. Urbanovic, Jackie, illus. (p. 468)
—What Do Parents Do? (When You're Not Home) Moore, Cyd, illus. (p. 1882)
—What Really Happened to Humpty? From the Files of a Hard-Boiled Detective. Axelsen, Stephen, illus. (p. 1893)
Ransom, Marty. Our Father, Our Soldier, Our Hero. (p. 1308)
Ransom, Nicole. Mimi: Takes a Bath. (p. 1145)
Ransom, Sharon L., ed. Cocurricular Activities: Their Values & Benefits (p. 338)
Ransome, Arthur. Aladdin & His Wonderful Lamp in Rhyme. Mackenzie, Thomas, illus. (p. 33)
—Favorite Russian Fairy Tales. Galkin, Simon, illus. (p. 578)
—Firebird & Other Russian Fairy Tales. (p. 591)
—Great Northern? (p. 717)
—Old Peter's Russian Tales. (p. 1284)
—Swallowdale. (p. 1688)
—Swallowdale. Ransome, Arthur, illus. (p. 1688)
—Swallows & Amazons. (p. 1688)
—Swallows & Amazons. Ransome, Arthur, illus. (p. 1688)
—We Didn't Mean to Go to Sea. (p. 1867)
Ransome, Galya. Russia in Our World. (p. 1498)
Ransome, Galya, jt. auth. see Bowden, Rob.
Ransome, James, illus. see Bandy, Michael S. & Stein, Eric.
Ransome, James, illus. see Cline-Ransome, Lesa.
Ransome, James, illus. see Howard, Elizabeth Fitzgerald.
Ransome, James, illus. see Mitchell, Margaree King.
Ransome, James, illus. see Turner, Ann.
Ransome, James, illus. see Woodson, Jacqueline.
Ransome, James E. Gunner, Football Hero. Ransome, James E., illus. (p. 732)
—New Red Bike! (p. 1247)
Ransome, James E., illus. see Alexander, Jessica & Shore, Diane Z.
Ransome, James E., illus. see Cline-Ransome, Lesa.
Ransome, James E., illus. see Hansen, Joyce & McGowan, Gary.
Ransome, James E., illus. see Hopkinson, Deborah.
Ransome, James E., illus. see Jordan, Deloris.
Ransome, James E., illus. see Matteson, George & Ursone, Adele.
Ransome, James E., illus. see Mitchell, Margaree King.
Ransome, James E., illus. see Shore, Diane Z. & Alexander, Jessica.
Ransome, James E., illus. see Thomson, Sarah L.
Ransome, James E., illus. see Wolff, Ferida.
Ranson, Arthur, illus. see Jenson, Jeff.
Ranson, Claire, jt. auth. see Webb, Sarah.
Ranson, Erin. Bright New Star: With Color-Changing Star Light. Crisp, Dan, illus. (p. 228)
—Magnetic Color Safari. Parry, Jo, illus. (p. 1075)
—Magnetic Playtime Shapes. Parry, Jo, illus. (p. 1075)
—Ocean Wonders. Top That! Staff, ed. (p. 1277)
—One Little Bear & Her Friends. Gévry, Claudine, illus. (p. 1295)
—Rainforest Wonders. Wood, Hannah & Mahoney, Daniel J., illus. (p. 1436)
—Story of Noah's Ark. Petrlik, Andrea, illus. (p. 1659)
—Woodland Fairies. Top That Publishing Staff, ed. (p. 1949)
Ransone Associates Inc Staff, jt. auth. see Ransone, Rob.
Ransone, Rob & Ransone Associates Inc Staff. Lit'L Drip: The Life Story of a Drop of Water. (p. 1023)
Ranucci, Claudia, illus. see Aliaga, Roberto.
Ranucci, Claudia, illus. see Escrivá, Victoria Pérez.
Ranulfo. Nirvana's Children. (p. 1257)
Rao, Chatura. Amie & the Chawl of Colour. Pathak, Ashutosh, illus. (p. 65)
Rao, Cheryl. Mixed Score: Ghost & Other Stories. (p. 1156)
Rao, Lisa. Diego & the Baby Sea Turtles. McGee, Warner, illus. (p. 437)
—Don't Bite Your Friends! (p. 467)
—Dora's Magic Watering Can. Miller, Victoria, illus. (p. 471)
—I Love to Color. Yoe! Studio Staff, illus. (p. 843)
—Iron Man: I Am Iron Man! Guidi, Guido, illus. (p. 888)
—Playtime in Trucktown. Shannon, David et al, illus. (p. 1373)
—Surf's Up. Merkel, Joe F. & Sazaklis, John, illus. (p. 1685)
—Whales. (p. 1878)
Rao, Lisa, jt. auth. see Ciminera, Siobhan.
Rao, Lisa & Gallo, Tina. It's Nice to Be Nice! Giles, Mike, illus. (p. 897)
Rao, Nikhil & Wolf, Gita. All about Indian Food. (p. 42)
Rao, Rohitash, illus. see Nelson, Peter.
Rao, Sandhya. My Mother's Sari. Sabnani, Nina, illus. (p. 1215)
Rao, Sirish. Monkey Photo. Chitrakar, Swarna, illus. (p. 1165)
—Old Animals' Forest Band. Bai, Durga, illus. (p. 1283)
Rao, Sirish, tr. see Wolf, Gita & Ramanathan, Rathna.
Raote, Komilla. Princess with the Longest Hair. Bist, Vandana, illus. (p. 1406)
Raoul, Cauvin, jt. auth. see Lambil, Willy.
Rapaport, David. Julius Deetken: Pioneer Druggist. (p. 933)
Rapaport, Giles, jt. auth. see Levy, Didier.
Raphael, jt. auth. see Talvacchia, Bette.
Raphael, Akili & Lewis, Harriet. Malik & the Malaria-Carrying Mosquito. (p. 1083)
—Malik Says, Turn off the Water! (p. 1083)
Raphael, Antoine. Young Wise Man. (p. 1979)
Raphael, Elaine, illus. see Hillert, Margaret.
Raphael, Marie. Boy from Ireland. (p. 217)
Rapier, Darren. Little Mermaid. (p. 1031)
Rapine, Dawn. Federal Forces: Careers As Federal Agents Set. (p. 580)
Rapini, Mary Jo & Sherman, Janine. Start Talking: A Girl's Guide for You & Your Mom about Health, Sex, or Whatever. (p. 1643)
Rapkin, Katharine, ed. see Pockell, Leslie M.
Rapley, Elizabeth, tr. see Dubé, Jean-Claude.
Rapoport, Cindy. Adventures of Poca & Flea Bert. (p. 21)
Raposo, Joe. Sing. Lichtenheld, Tom, illus. (p. 1578)
Raposo, Nick. PEEP Friends Travel Pack. (p. 1335)
Rapp, Adam. 33 Snowfish. Ering, Timothy Basil, illus. (p. 1996)
—Buffalo Tree. (p. 236)
—Children & the Wolves. Ering, Timothy Basil, illus. (p. 302)
—Copper Elephant. (p. 365)
—Punkzilla. (p. 1417)
—Under the Wolf, under the Dog. (p. 1814)
Rapp, Pat. Noisy Nativity. (p. 1263)
Rapp, Val. Protecting Earth's Air Quality. (p. 1412)
Rappa, Desiree & Brian. Big Red. (p. 183)
Rappa, Francesca. Melody West & the Cherry Blossom: The Adventurous Melody West Series Book Five. (p. 1125)
Rappaport, Doreen. Abe's Honest Words: The Life of Abraham Lincoln. Kelley, Gary & Nelson, Kadir, illus. (p. 5)
—Abe's Honest Words. Nelson, Kadir, illus. (p. 5)
—Beyond Courage: The Untold Story of Jewish Resistance During the Holocaust. (p. 173)
—Eleanor, Quiet No More. Kelley, Gary, illus. (p. 508)
—Free at Last! Stories & Songs of Emancipation. Evans, Shane W., illus. (p. 634)
—Helen's Big World: The Life of Helen Keller. Tavares, Matt, illus. (p. 763)
—In the Promised Land: Lives of Jewish Americans. Van Wright, Cornelius, illus. (p. 867)
—Jack's Path of Courage: The Life of John F. Kennedy. Tavares, Matt & Borgens, Matthew Todd, illus. (p. 904)
—Lady Liberty: A Biography. Tavares, Matt, illus. (p. 971)
—Martin's Big Words: The Life of Dr. Martin Luther King, Jr. Collier, Bryan, illus. (p. 1098)
—No More! Stories & Songs of Slave Resistance. Evans, Shane W., illus. (p. 1259)
—Nobody Gonna Turn Me 'Round: Stories & Songs of the Civil Rights Movement. Evans, Shane W., illus. (p. 1262)
—To Dare Mighty Things: The Life of Theodore Roosevelt. Payne, C. F., illus. (p. 1758)
Rappaport, Doreen & Verniero, Joan C. United No More! Stories of the Civil War. Reeves, Rick, illus. (p. 1819)
Rappaport, Josh, jt. auth. see Bortz, Trudy.
Rappaport, Josh & Bortz, Trudy. Play Your Way to Math Success. (p. 1372)
Rappaport, Page. Time Passes II. (p. 1752)
Rapparlie, Leslie & Wurdinger, Scott. Kayaking. (p. 946)
—Mountain Biking. (p. 1180)
—Rock Climbing. (p. 1482)
Rappe-Flowers, Hedvig, illus. see Ippisch, Hanneke.
Rappoport, Bernice. Baby Animals. Cassels, Jean, illus. (p. 124)
—Community of Washington, D. C. Set Of 6. (p. 350)
—Community of Washington, D. C. Text Pairs. (p. 350)
—Habitats of Africa: Set Of 6. (p. 735)
—Habitats of Africa: Text Pairs. (p. 735)
—Outside My Window. Johnson, Pamela G., illus. (p. 1313)
Rappoport, Ken. Alex Rodriguez: Champion Baseball Star. (p. 36)
—Baseball's Top 10 Home Run Hitters. (p. 141)
—Baseball's Top 10 Pitchers. (p. 141)
—Basketball's Top 10 Slam Dunkers. (p. 143)
—Biggest Upsets in Sports. (p. 185)
—Dale Earnhardt, Jr. A Car Racer Who Cares. (p. 401)
—David Wright: A Baseball Star Who Cares. (p. 411)
—Derek Jeter: Champion Baseball Star. (p. 427)
—Jason Kidd: Leader on the Court. (p. 910)
—Ladies First: Women Athletes Who Made a Difference (p. 970)
—LeBron James: King on & off the Court. (p. 987)
—Michigan Wolverines. (p. 1135)
—Peyton Manning: Champion Football Star. (p. 1349)
—Profiles in Sports Courage (p. 1409)
—Richard Sherman. (p. 1470)
—Russell Wilson. (p. 1498)
—Super Sports Star Alex Rodriguez. (p. 1682)
—Super Sports Star Derek Jeter. (p. 1682)
—Super Sports Star Ichiro Suzuki. (p. 1682)
—Super Sports Star Jerome Bettis. (p. 1682)
—Super Sports Star Peyton Manning. (p. 1682)
—Texas a & M Aggies. (p. 1724)
—Tim Tebow: A Football Star Who Cares. (p. 1750)
Rapson, Helen. One Lucky Goose (p. 1296)
—Reggie Did It! (p. 1457)
Raquel, Israel & Sissom, Carol. Help Mommy Clean-Up! (p. 765)
Rarick, Frances. Bubba the Cat. (p. 233)
Rarick, James A. Minnesota Military Air Disasters: Minnesota Military Air Incidents & Disasters 1940 To 1960. (p. 1147)
Ras. Oh No, the Leaves Are Moving! (p. 1281)
Ras, J. J. Ketchup Story. (p. 949)
Rasamimanana, Hantanirina, tr. see Jolly, Alison.
Rasch, Patricia, illus. see Miller, Connie Colwell.
Rasch, Patricia, illus. see Richardson, Adele & Richardson, Adele D.
Rasch, Patricia, illus. see Velthaus, Sally.
Rasche, Shelly, illus. see Anders, Isabel.
Rasche, Shelly S., illus. see Gould, Judith S. & Burke, Mary F.
Raschka, Chris. Ball for Daisy. Raschka, Chris, illus. (p. 134)
—Buggy Bug. (p. 236)
—Clammy Clam. Raschka, Christoph, illus. (p. 326)
—Cowy Cow. (p. 374)
—Crabby Crab. (p. 375)
—Daisy Gets Lost. Raschka, Chris, illus. (p. 400)
—Doggy Dog. Raschka, Christoph, illus. (p. 462)
—Everyone Can Learn to Ride a Bicycle. Raschka, Chris, illus. (p. 544)
—Farmy Farm. Raschka, Chris, illus. (p. 575)
—Five for a Little One. Raschka, Chris, illus. (p. 600)
—Foot in the Mouth: Poems to Speak, Sing, & Shout. (p. 614)
—Hip Hop Dog. Radunsky, Vladimir, illus. (p. 780)
—John Coltrane's Giant Steps. (p. 921)
—John Coltrane's Giant Steps. Raschka, Chris, illus. (p. 921)
—Kick in the Head: An Everyday Guide to Poetic Forms. (p. 951)
—Lamby Lamb. (p. 972)
—Little Black Crow. Raschka, Chris, illus. (p. 1024)
—Moosey Moose. (p. 1173)
—Mysterious Thelonious. Raschka, Chris, illus. (p. 1223)
—New York Is English, Chattanooga Is Creek. Raschka, Chris, illus. (p. 1248)
—Seriously, Norman! Raschka, Chris, illus. (p. 1552)
—Simple Gifts. Raschka, Chris, illus. (p. 1577)
—Whaley Whale. (p. 1878)
—Yo! Yes? Raschka, Chris, illus. (p. 1971)
Raschka, Chris, illus. see Bell, Marvin.
Raschka, Chris, illus. see Bitterman, Albert.
Raschka, Chris, illus. see Brown, Margaret Wise & Brown.
Raschka, Chris, illus. see Creech, Sharon.
Raschka, Chris, illus. see Harris, Robie H.
Raschka, Chris, illus. see Howe, James.
Raschka, Chris, illus. see Janeczko, Paul B.
Raschka, Chris, illus. see Janeczko, Paul B., ed.
Raschka, Chris, illus. see Juster, Norton.
Raschka, Chris, illus. see Martin, Bill, Jr. & Sampson, Michael.
Raschka, Chris, illus. see Ogburn, Jacqueline.
Raschka, Chris, illus. see Prelutsky, Jack.
Raschka, Chris, illus. see Prokofiev, Sergei.
Raschka, Chris, illus. see Swenson, Jamie A.
Raschka, Chris & Radunsky, Vladimir. Alphabetabum: An Album of Rare Photographs & Medium Verses. (p. 50)
Raschka, Christoph, illus. see Raschka, Chris.
Raschke, Andrea, illus. see Newcomer, Carolyn.
Raschke, Erik. Book of Samuel: A Novel. (p. 211)
Rasemas, Joe, illus. see Kondrchek, Jamie.
Rasemas, Joe, illus. see Sherman, Patrice & Murica, Rebecca Thatcher.
Rasemas, Joe, jt. auth. see Kondrchek, Jamie.
Rash, Andy. Agent A to Agent Z. (p. 29)
—Archie the Daredevil Penguin. Rash, Andy, illus. (p. 95)
Rash, Andy, illus. see Balaban, Bob.
Rash, Andy, illus. see Messner, Kate.
Rash, Andy, illus. see Schreiber, Joe.
Rash, Andy, jt. auth. see Reynolds, Aaron.
Rash, Ron. Saints at the River. (p. 1504)
—Shark's Tooth. Martin, Cecile L. K., illus. (p. 1563)
—World Made Straight. (p. 1956)
Rashad, Girmen. How Does God See Me? David, Amor, illus. (p. 808)
Rashad, Phylicia, reader. Baby's Lap Book. (p. 129)
Rasheed, Leila. Chips, Beans, & Limousines. (p. 308)
—Diamonds & Deceit. (p. 434)
—Doughnuts, Dreams & Drama Queens. (p. 473)
—Socks, Shocks & Secrets. (p. 1605)
Rasheed, M. Monsters 101, Book One. (p. 1169)
Rasheed, M., illus. see Peace, Bob.
Rasheed, Winnona. Itchy Scratchy Spots. (p. 895)
Rasheed, Winona. Smiles & Frowns Through Animal Town's Storybook. (p. 1594)
—Stories from Grandma's Garden. (p. 1654)
—Sugar & Spice Fairy Tales for Girls. (p. 1672)
Rashid, Abdul, illus. see Cowan, C. C.
Rashin, illus. see Rumi.
Rashkin, Rachel. Feeling Better: A Kid's Book about Therapy. Adamson, Bonnie, illus. (p. 580)
—Feeling Better: A Kid's Books about Therapy. Adamson, Bonnie, illus. (p. 580)
Rasinski, Tim. Practice with Prefixes (p. 1392)
Rasinski, Timothy. Reader's Theater Scripts: Texas History. (p. 1444)
—Starting with Prefixes & Suffixes (p. 1644)
—Understanding Word Nuances Level 5. (p. 1816)
—Understanding Word Nuances, Level 6. (p. 1816)
—Vocabulary Ladders: Understanding Word Nuances, Level 4. (p. 1847)
Rasinski, Timothy & Zutell, Jerry. Essential Strategies for Word Study: Effective Methods for Improving Decoding, Spelling, & Vocabulary. (p. 537)
Rasinski, Timothy V. 100 Reproducible Word Study Lessons That Help Kids Boost Reading, Vocabulary, Spelling & Phonics Skills—Independently! (p. 1998)
—100 Reproducible Word Study Lessons That Help Kids Boost Reading, Vocabulary, Spelling & Phonics Skills - Independently! (p. 1998)
—Daily Word Ladders: 150+ Reproducible Word Study Lessons That Help Kids Boost Reading, Vocabulary, Spelling & Phonics Skills! (p. 400)

R

—Daily Word Ladders: 80+ Word Study Activities That Target Key Phonics Skills to Boost Young Learners' Reading, Writing & Spelling Confidence. (p. 400)
—Daily Word Ladders, Grades 1-2: 150+ Word Study Activities That Help Kids Boost Reading, Vocabulary, Spelling & Phonics Skills. (p. 400)
—Daily Word Ladders - Grades 2-3: 100 Word Study Activities That Help Kids Boost Reading, Vocabulary, Spelling & Phonics Skills. (p. 400)
—Daily Word Ladders, Grades 4-6: 100 Word Study Activities That Help Kids Boost Reading, Vocabulary, Spelling & Phonics Skills. (p. 400)
—Daily Word Ladders, Grades K-1: 80+ Word Study Activities That Target Key Phonics Skills to Boost Young Learners' Reading, Writing & Spelling Confidence. (p. 400)
Rasinski, Timothy V. & Padak, Nancy. Word Recognition, Fluency, & Comprehension: Short Passages & Step-by-Step Directions to Assess Reading Performance Throughout the Year-And Quickly Identify Students Who Need Help. (p. 1951)
—Word Recognition, Fluency, & Comprehension: Short Passages & Step-by-Step Directions to Assess Reading Performance Throughout the Year-And Quickly Identify Students Who Need Help. Davis-Swing, Joanna, ed. (p. 1951)
Rasinski, Timothy V., et al. Fast Start for Early Readers: A Research-Based, Send-Home Literacy Program with 60 Reproducible Poems & Activities That Ensures Reading Success for Every Child. (p. 576)
—Fluent Reader in Action, Grades 5 & Up: A Rich Collection of Research-Based, Classroom-Tested Lessons & Strategies for Improving Fluency & Comprehension. (p. 608)
Rask Knudsen, Eva. Circle & the Spiral: A Study of Australian Aboriginal & New Zealand Maori Literature. (p. 321)
Raskauskas, Sally, illus. see Elda, Doug & Elda, Dorry.
Raskauskas, Sally, illus. see Elda, Doug & Elda, Dory.
Raskavskas, Sally, illus. see Eldon, Doug & Eldon, Dorry.
Raskin, Ellen. Disfraz Disfrazado y Otros Casos. (p. 450)
—Figgs & Phantoms. Raskin, Ellen, illus. (p. 585)
—Mysterious Disappearance of Leon (I Mean Noel) (p. 1223)
—Mysterious Disappearence of Leon. Raskin, Ellen, illus. (p. 1223)
—Tattooed Potato & Other Clues. Raskin, Ellen, illus. (p. 1707)
—Westing Game. (p. 1876)
Raskin, Ellen, illus. see Thomas, Dylan.
Raskin, Lawrie & Pearson, Debora. 52 Days by Camel: My Sahara Adventure. Raskin, Lawrie, photos by. (p. 1997)
Rasmusen, Jan. Scared Poopless: The Straight Scoop on Dog Care. (p. 1519)
Rasmussen, Alis A., see Elliott, Kate, pseud.
Rasmussen, Brent. Motorcycles Race On. (p. 1180)
Rasmussen, Dale K. Down on the Farm. (p. 474)
Rasmussen, Donald & Goldberg, Lynn. Hen in a Fox's Den. (p. 767)
Rasmussen, Gerry, illus. see Eagle, Rita.
Rasmussen, Gerry, illus. see Lesynski, Loris.
Rasmussen, Halfdan. Ladder. Nelson, Marilyn, tr. from DAN. (p. 970)
Rasmussen, Halfdan Wedel, et al. Little Bitty Man & Other Poems for the Very Young. Hawkes, Kevin, illus. (p. 1024)
Rasmussen, Jason. House of the Lord: A Pop-Up Book. (p. 803)
Rasmussen, Jennifer, illus. see Mellen, Wynette.
Rasmussen, Kenneth L., jt. auth. see Webster, Raelyn.
Rasmussen, Kitrisha. Dumb Bunny's Guide to Basic Hair Bows. (p. 489)
Rasmussen, Klayne & Rasmussen, Verena. Beyond the Spell for Teens: What Guys & Girls Wonder about Each Other. (p. 174)
Rasmussen, Knud. Eagle's Gift: Alaska Eskimo Tales. Hutchinson, Isabel, tr. (p. 492)
Rasmussen, Liz. Too Fat to Fly. (p. 1766)
Rasmussen, R. Kent. Bloom's How to Write about Mark Twain. (p. 201)
—Critical Companion to Mark Twain: The Literary Reference to His Life & Work (p. 383)
—Mark Twain for Kids: His Life & Times, 21 Activities. (p. 1095)
—World War I for Kids: A History with 21 Activities. (p. 1959)
Rasmussen, R. Kent, ed. African American Encyclopedia (p. 27)
Rasmussen, Verena, jt. auth. see Rasmussen, Klayne.
Rasmussen, Wendy, illus. see Hinkes, Enid.
Rasmussen, Wendy, illus. see Nelson, Steve & Rollins, Jack.
Rasmussen, Wendy, illus. see Pingry, Patricia A.
Rasmussen, Wendy, illus. see Potter, Beatrix & Aesop.
Rasmussen, Wendy, illus. see Potter, Beatrix.
Rasmussen, Wendy, illus. see Rowland, Patty.
Rasmussen, Wendy, tr. see Rowland, Patty.
Raspanti, Celeste. Terezin Promise. (p. 1721)
Raspe, Rudolf Erich. Surprising Adventures of Baron Munchausen. Doré, Gustave, illus. (p. 1686)
Raspe, Rudolph. Surprising Adventures of Baron Munchause. (p. 1686)
Rasphoumy, Wendy. Cory & Hailey, Finding You II (p. 368)
Rassi, Lee. Capital Heroes. (p. 262)
Rassmuss, Jens, illus. see Nostlinger, Christine.
Ratchford, Marjorie. Party in the Sky (p. 1326)
Ratcliff, Carol J. Grannie's Secret Garden: (Somewhere in England) (p. 710)
Ratcliff, Charline. Princess, the Toad & the Whale. (p. 1406)
Ratcliffe, Bob. Dawn Hee-Haw. (p. 411)
Ratcliffe, Linda. Lindylou Starts a Fire. (p. 1019)
Ratcliffe-Kitchingman, Linda. Lindylou in I Hate Porridge. (p. 1019)
Rate, Kristina. Potato Boy. Formosa, Natasha, illus. (p. 1388)
Rateau, Loy. David's Prayers: A Boy's Perseverance of Conquering the Enemy. (p. 411)
Ratey, John J. Spark: The Revolutionary New Science of Exercise & the Brain. (p. 1622)
Rath, Robert. Go Wild for Puzzles Glacier National Park. Rath, Robert, illus. (p. 687)
—Go Wild Puzzles: Great Smoky Mountains National Park. (p. 687)
Rath, Robert, illus. see Davies, Jon.
Rath, Robert, illus. see Horner, Jack.
Rath, Robert, illus. see Kemp, Steve.
Rath, Robert, illus. see Metivier, Gary.
Rath, Robert, illus. see Oberbillig, Deborah Richie.
Rath, Robert, illus. see Patterson, Caroline.
Rath, Robert, illus. see Robson, Gary D.
Rath, Robert, illus. see Solberg, Jessica L.
Rath, Robert, illus. see Solberg, Jessica.
Rath, Robert, jt. auth. see Robson, Gary D.
Rath, S. M. Jesus's Echo. (p. 916)
Rath, Tom. Kittencat Adventures for a Special Person. (p. 962)
Rath, Tom & Clifton, Donald O. How Full Is Your Bucket? (p. 809)
Rath, Tom & Reckmeyer, Mary. How Full Is Your Bucket? For Kids. Manning, Maurie J., illus. (p. 809)
Rath, Tom H. Donkey Oatie's Christmas Pageant. Townshend, Katie, illus. (p. 466)
—Donkey Oatie's Fashion Statement. MacAdam, Ian Paul, illus. (p. 466)
—Donkey Oatie's Field Trip. Gaudet, Christine, illus. (p. 466)
—Donkey Oatie's Impossible Dream. MacAdam, Reegory, illus. (p. 466)
Rathborne, St. George. Canoe Mates in Canada; or, Three Boys Afloat on the Saskatchewan. (p. 261)
—House Boat Boys. (p. 803)
—House Boat Boys; or, Drifting down to the Sunny South. (p. 803)
Rather, Sherri. Upside down Danny Rather, Sherri, illus. (p. 1825)
Rathkamp, Angela. Ruby the Roly Poly Ladybug. (p. 1493)
Rathke, Kathryn, illus. see Hautzig, Deborah.
Rathmann, Peggy. 10 Minutes to Bedtime. (p. 1993)
—10 Minutos Antes de Dormir. (p. 1993)
—Buenas Noches, Gorila. Rathmann, Peggy, illus. (p. 235)
—Day the Babies Crawled Away. Rathmann, Peggy, illus. (p. 414)
—Good Night, Gorilla. Rathmann, Peggy, illus. (p. 699)
—Ruby the Copycat. (p. 1493)
Rathmann, Rodney L., jt. auth. see Berndt, Clarence.
Rathmann, Rodney L. & Bergt, Carolyn, eds. Family Time: A Collection of 98 Bible Stories & Devotions. (p. 568)
Rathmell, Donna. Carolina's Story: Sea Turtles Get Sick Too! Bergwerf, Barbara J., illus. (p. 270)
Rathmell, Donna & Rathmell, Doreen. Octavia & Her Purple Ink Cloud McLennan, Connie, illus. (p. 1277)
Rathmell, Doreen, jt. auth. see Rathmell, Donna.
Rathore, Jazz Kopecek & Niederhofer, Renate. Adler the Eagle Boy. (p. 13)
Rathvon, Natalie. Effective School Interventions: Evidence-Based Strategies for Improving Student Outcomes. (p. 505)
Ratliff, Charles R. Bass Lake Bunch: The Hideout at the Abandoned Fish Hatchery. (p. 143)
Ratliff, Lana. Blanket Full of Blessings. (p. 198)
Ratliff, Thomas. How to Be a Revolutionary War Soldier. (p. 815)
—How to Be a Revolutionary War Soldier. James, John, illus. (p. 815)
—You Wouldn't Want to Be a Civil War Soldier! A War You'D Rather Not Fight. (p. 1976)
—You Wouldn't Want to Be a Civil War Soldier! A War You'd Rather Not Fight. Antram, David, illus. (p. 1976)
—You Wouldn't Want to Be a Pony Express Rider! A Dusty, Thankless Job You'd Rather Not Do. Bergin, Mark, illus. (p. 1976)
—You Wouldn't Want to Work on the Brooklyn Bridge! An Enormous Project That Seemed Impossible. Bergin, Mark, illus. (p. 1977)
Ratliff, Tom. You Wouldn't Want to Work on the Brooklyn Bridge! An Enormous Project That Seemed Impossible. Bergin, Mark, illus. (p. 1977)
Ratnayake, Kumari/Keiko. Monsieur Bagel's War. Ratnayake, Kumari/Keiko, illus. (p. 1166)
Ratner, Phillip, illus. see Guttman, S. Daniel.
Ratnett, Michael. Dracula Steps Out. Goulding, June & Smyth, Iain, illus. (p. 476)
Rattay, Deidra. My Best Friend the Gnome. (p. 1196)
Rattini, Kristin. National Geographic Readers: Coral Reefs. (p. 1233)
Rattini, Kristin Baird. National Geographic Readers: Seed to Plant. (p. 1233)
—National Geographic Readers: Weather. (p. 1233)
Ratto, Cinzia, illus. see Arengo, Sue.
Ratto EdM, Linda Lee, jt. auth. see Cunningham, David L.
Ratto, Linda Lee. (dis) Ability. (p. 446)
—Perfection. (p. 1342)
—We Catch Them Falling. Mari, Ian Robert, photos by. (p. 1866)
—Where Dreams Come True. (p. 1907)
—Where Dreams Come True Workbook. (p. 1907)
Ratway, Michael J. & Ratway, Virginia K. Fractured Femur Fable. (p. 627)
Ratway, Virginia K., jt. auth. see Ratway, Michael J.
Ratyna, Linda, illus. see Lamaro, Glenda.
Ratzlaff, Aaron J. Quills. (p. 1428)
Rau, Harry the Cat. (p. 751)
Rau, Dana. Moon Walk. Buchs, Thomas, illus. (p. 1172)
Rau, Dana Meachen. Ace Your Creative Writing Project. (p. 8)
—Ace Your Writing Assignment. (p. 8)
—Aliens. (p. 41)
—Animals. (p. 81)
—Animals/Los Animales. (p. 84)
—Artists. (p. 104)
—Athletic Shoes. (p. 112)
—Become an Explorer: Make & Use a Compass. (p. 156)
—Bill & Melinda Gates. (p. 186)
—Boats. (p. 205)
—Boats/En Barcos. (p. 205)
—Bookworms: Nature's Cycles (p. 213)
—Bookworms We Go! (p. 213)
—Braiding Hair. (p. 221)
—Builders. (p. 238)
—Building Sandcastles. (p. 239)
—Building Snow Forts. (p. 239)
—Buses. (p. 244)
—Buses/En Autobuses. (p. 244)
—By the Ocean. (p. 249)
—Cars. (p. 272)
—Cars/En Carros. (p. 272)
—Carving Pumpkins. (p. 273)
—Castle. (p. 276)
—Chefs. (p. 297)
—Coins. (p. 338)
—Cooking Around the World (p. 361)
—Corn Aplenty. Iwai, Melissa, illus. (p. 367)
—Crafting with Duct Tape. Petelinsek, Kathleen, illus. (p. 375)
—Crafting with Recyclables. Petelinsek, Kathleen, illus. (p. 375)
—Creating Halloween Crafts. Petelinsek, Kathleen, illus. (p. 378)
—Creating Thanksgiving Crafts. Petelinsek, Kathleen, illus. (p. 379)
—Creating Winter Crafts. Petelinsek, Kathleen, illus. (p. 379)
—Day & Night. (p. 412)
—Day & Night/El Día y la Noche. (p. 412)
—Decorating Eggs. (p. 422)
—Dessert Designer: Creations You Can Make & Eat! (p. 430)
—Dessert Designer. (p. 430)
—Doctors. (p. 459)
—Dragons. (p. 478)
—Electricity & Magnetism. (p. 509)
—EMTs. (p. 521)
—Eye Candy: Crafting Cool Candy Creations (p. 557)
—Family Photo. Gordon, Mike, illus. (p. 568)
—Fire Safety: Seguridad en Caso de Incendio. (p. 590)
—Fireworks. (p. 592)
—Folding Origami. Petelinsek, Kathleen, illus. (p. 611)
—Food Chains. (p. 613)
—Food Chains/Las Cadenas Alimentarias. (p. 613)
—Food Safety: Seguridad de Los Alimentos. (p. 614)
—Freaking Out! The Science of the Teenage Brain (p. 631)
—Gastar el Dinero. (p. 657)
—Get Connected: Make a Friendship Bracelet. (p. 667)
—Glass. (p. 682)
—Go Bot, Robot! Jung, Wook Jin, illus. (p. 686)
—Going Organic: A Healthy Guide to Making the Switch (p. 692)
—Going Vegan: A Healthy Guide to Making the Switch (p. 693)
—Going Vegetarian: A Healthy Guide to Making the Switch (p. 693)
—Guess Who Grunts/Adivina Quién Gruñe. (p. 729)
—Guess Who Hunts/Adivina Quién Caza. Victory Productions, Inc. Staff, tr. from ENG. (p. 729)
—Guess Who Jumps/Adivina Quién Brinca. (p. 729)
—Guess Who Stings/Adivina Quién Pica. (p. 729)
—Guess Who Swims/Adivina Quién Nada. (p. 729)
—History of Money. (p. 784)
—Hot Air Balloons. (p. 801)
—Igloo. (p. 856)
—In the City. (p. 865)
—In the Desert. (p. 865)
—Kids Top 10 Pet Cats. (p. 955)
—Kids Top 10 Pet Fish. (p. 955)
—Learning to Knit. (p. 986)
—Librarians. (p. 1005)
—Log Cabin. (p. 1045)
—Los Billetes. (p. 1053)
—Making a Paper Airplane & Other Paper Toys. (p. 1080)
—Making Books for Fun! (p. 1080)
—Making Butterfly Gardens. (p. 1080)
—Making Jewelry. (p. 1081)
—Mermaids. (p. 1128)
—Metal. (p. 1130)
—Midwest. (p. 1139)
—Monsters. (p. 1168)
—Moon Walk. Buchs, Thomas, illus. (p. 1172)
—Mummies. (p. 1190)
—My Bones & Muscles. (p. 1198)
—My Brain. (p. 1199)
—My Heart & Blood. (p. 1210)
—My Lungs. (p. 1213)
—My Skin. (p. 1219)
—My Stomach. (p. 1219)
—Nigeria. (p. 1252)
—Northeast. (p. 1265)
—On the Mountain. (p. 1291)
—On the Ranch. (p. 1291)
—Painting Rocks. (p. 1318)
—Paper. (p. 1322)
—Paper Money. (p. 1322)
—Piece of Cake! Decorating Awesome Cakes (p. 1356)
—Planes. (p. 1367)
—Planes/En Aviones. (p. 1367)
—Plants. (p. 1369)
—Plants/Las Plantas. (p. 1370)
—Plastic. (p. 1370)
—Pyramid. (p. 1421)
—?Que Es un Banco? (p. 1423)
—Recipes from China (p. 1451)
—Recipes from India (p. 1451)
—Recipes from Italy (p. 1451)
—Recipes from Mexico (p. 1451)
—Robot, Go Bot! (p. 1480)
—Robots. (p. 1481)
—Rocks & Minerals. (p. 1483)
—Roller Coasters. (p. 1485)
—Safety at Home: Seguridad en la Casa. (p. 1502)
—Safety on the Go: Seguridad en el Viaje. (p. 1502)
—Saving Money. (p. 1517)
—School Safety: Seguridad en la Escuela. (p. 1523)
—Seasons. (p. 1538)
—Seasons/Las Estaciones. (p. 1539)
—Simple Machines. (p. 1577)
—Skyscraper. (p. 1587)
—Smart Cookie: Designing Creative Cookies (p. 1592)
—Southeast. (p. 1617)
—Southwest. (p. 1617)
—Spending Money. (p. 1625)
—Sports Nutrition for Teen Athletes: Eat Right to Take Your Game to the Next Level (p. 1633)
—Star in My Orange: Looking for Nature's Shapes. (p. 1640)
—Super Cool Science Experiments: Light. (p. 1679)
—Super Cool Science Experiments: Levers & Pulleys. (p. 1679)
—Teen Cookbooks (p. 1713)
—Teen Guide to Breakfast on the Go (p. 1713)
—Teen Guide to Creative, Delightful Dinners (p. 1713)
—Teen Guide to Fast, Delicious Lunches (p. 1713)
—Teen Guide to Quick, Healthy Snacks (p. 1713)
—Tepee. (p. 1721)
—Think Like a Scientist at the Beach. (p. 1734)
—Think Like a Scientist on the Playground. (p. 1734)
—Trains. (p. 1777)
—Trains/En Trenes. (p. 1777)
—Trucks. (p. 1791)
—Trucks/En Camiones. (p. 1791)
—U. S. Landforms. (p. 1806)
—Unicorns. (p. 1818)
—Vietnam. (p. 1841)
—Water. (p. 1862)
—Water Safety: Seguridad en el Agua. (p. 1863)
—Water/El Agua. (p. 1863)
—West. (p. 1876)
—What Is a Bank? (p. 1888)
—What's up, Cupcake? Creating Amazing Cupcakes (p. 1900)
—Who Was Gandhi? (p. 1918)
—Who Was Gandhi? Hoare, Jerry & Harrison, Nancy, illus. (p. 1918)
—Who Was Harriet Beecher Stowe? (p. 1918)
—Who Was Harriet Beecher Stowe? Harrison, Nancy & Copeland, Gregory, illus. (p. 1918)
—Wood. (p. 1949)
Rau, Dana Meachen, jt. auth. see Jemison, Mae.
Rau, Dana Meachen, jt. auth. see Jordan, Apple.
Rau, Dana Meachen & Jemison, Mae. 100 Year Starship. (p. 1999)
Rau, Dana Meachen & Meachen Rau, Dana. Alternative Energy: Beyond Fossil Fuels (p. 50)
—Fire Safety: Seguridad en Caso de Incendio. (p. 590)
—Food Safety: Seguridad de Los Alimentos. (p. 614)
—Safety at Home: Seguridad en la Casa. (p. 1502)
—School Safety: Seguridad en la Escuela. (p. 1523)
—Water Safety: Seguridad en el Agua. (p. 1863)
Rau, Dana Meachen, et al. Sports Training Zone. (p. 1633)
Rau, Dinah M., illus. see Rau-Tobin, Joanna.
Rau, Heather. Through My Telescope. (p. 1745)
Rau, Heather, jt. auth. see Mills, Nathan.
Rau, Margaret. Belle of the West: The True Story of Belle Starr. (p. 163)
—Mail Must Go Through: The Story of the Pony Express. (p. 1077)
—Ordeal of Olive Oatman: A True Story of the American West. (p. 1302)
—Wells Fargo Book of the Gold Rush. (p. 1874)
Rau, Zachary. Autobots Versus Zombies. (p. 117)
—Superman - The Incredible Shrinking Super Hero! With Wonder Woman. Gordon, Steven E., illus. (p. 1683)
Rau, Zachary, ed. see Nickelodeon Staff.
Rau, Zachary, jt. ed. see Stein, Erin.
Rau, Zachary & Eisinger, Justin. Transformers - Animated (p. 1778)
Rauch, Earl Mac. Buckaroo Banzai TP Vol 02 No Matter Where You Go. (p. 234)
Rauch, Georg. Unlikely Warrior: A Jewish Soldier in Hitler's Army. (p. 1821)
Rauch, Katie J. Animal Rhymes. (p. 79)
Rauch, Mac & Richter, W. D. BUCKAROO BANZAI: TPB Vol. 1: Return of the Screw: TPB Vol. 1: Return of the Screw. (p. 234)
Rauch-Mannino, Ned. FingerTip Island: The Vincenzo Adventure. (p. 589)
—Fingertip Island II: The Vincenzos' Bully Problem. (p. 589)
—FingerTip Island III: The Vincenzos' Missing Sister. (p. 589)
Rauchwerger, Diane Levin. Dinosaur Goes to Israel. Wolff, Jason, illus. (p. 442)
—Dinosaur on Hanukkah. Wolff, Jason, illus. (p. 442)
—Dinosaur on Passover. Wolff, Jason, illus. (p. 442)
—Dinosaur on Shabbat. Wolff, Jason, illus. (p. 442)
Rauchwerger, Lisa. Chocolate Chip Challah: And Other Twists on the Jewish Holiday Table. Rauchwerger, Lisa, illus. (p. 309)
—Chocolate Chip Challah. Rauchwerger, Lisa, illus. (p. 309)
—P: Winter, Spring & Summer Holidays. Rauchwerger, Lisa, illus. (p. 1316)
Rauchwerger, Lisa, illus. see Halper, Sharon D.
Raude, Karina, illus. see Avi.
Raudenbush, Amy. Lucy More Needs Less. (p. 1063)
Rauen, Amy. Adding & Subtracting at the Lake. (p. 11)
—Adding & Subtracting at the Lake. Walter, Lorin, illus. (p. 11)
—Counting at the Market. Pickering, Russell, photos by. (p. 370)
—Finding Shortest & Longest. (p. 588)
—Usamos Dinero en el Puesto de Limonada. (p. 1826)
—Using Math at the Class Party. McKinley, Kay, photos by. (p. 1828)
—Using Math Outdoors. Walter, Lorin, illus. (p. 1828)
—Vamos a Contar en el Mercado. (p. 1831)
—Vamos a Contar en el Mercado. Pickering, Russell, photos by. (p. 1831)
—Vamos a Encontrar lo Más Corto y lo Más Largo. (p. 1831)
—Vamos a Sumar y Restar en el Lago. Walter, Lorin, illus. (p. 1831)
—Vamos a Usar las Matematicas al Aire Libre. Walter, Lorin, illus. (p. 1831)
Rauen, Amy & Ayers, Amy. Contando en el Zoologico. (p. 360)
—Counting at the Zoo. Andersen, Gregg, photos by. (p. 370)
—Measuring at the Dog Show. (p. 1117)
—Measuring at the Dog Show. Walter, Lorin, photos by. (p. 1117)
—Midiendo en la Exposicion de Perros. Walter, Lorin, illus. (p. 1138)
—Midiendo en la Exposicion de Perros. (p. 1138)
—Sumando y Restando en el Club de Matematicas. (p. 1673)

—Sumando y Restando en el Club de Matematicas. Andersen, Gregg, photos by. (p. 1673)
—Usamos Dinero en el Puesto de Limonada. Pickering, Russell, photos by. (p. 1826)
—Usamos Matemáticas en la Fiesta Del Salón. (p. 1826)
—Usamos Matematicas en la Fiesta del Salon. McKinley, Kay, photos by. (p. 1826)
—Using Money at the Lemonade Stand. Pickering, Russell, photos by. (p. 1828)
Rauenhorst, Linda. Frohliche Weihnachten: Learning Songs & Traditions in German. Collier, Roberta, illus. (p. 641)
Rauf, Don. Bobby Flay. (p. 206)
—Careers in Janitorial & Cleaning Services (p. 268)
—Getting the Most Out of Makerspaces to Build Unmanned Aerial Vehicles. (p. 669)
—Getting the Most Out of Makerspaces to Explore Arduino & Electronics. (p. 669)
—Getting to Know Hackety Hack. (p. 669)
—Killer Lipstick: And Other Spy Gadgets. (p. 956)
—Miguel Cabrera: Triple Crown Winner. (p. 1141)
—Powering up a Career in Internet Security. (p. 1391)
—Protecting the Environment Through Service Learning (p. 1412)
—Social Network-Powered Investing & Saving Opportunities. (p. 1604)
—Virtual Reality. (p. 1844)
—Working As a Hairstylist in Your Community. (p. 1952)
Rauf, Don & Vescia, Monique. Actor. (p. 10)
—Airline Pilot. (p. 31)
—Cartoon Animator. (p. 272)
—Computer Game Designer. (p. 354)
—Fashion Designer. (p. 575)
—Oceanographer. (p. 1277)
—Pop Musician. (p. 1384)
—Virtual Apprentice: Oceanographer. (p. 1844)
—Virtual Apprentice: Cartoon Animator. (p. 1844)
Rauf, Don & Williams, Judith. Forensic Science Specialists: Making Sense of Crime Scene Evidence. (p. 617)
Rauf, Don, et al. Are You Depressed? (p. 97)
—What You Can Do about Breast Cancer. (p. 1895)
—What You Can Do about Food Poisoning. (p. 1896)
Rauh, Anna Isabel, jt. auth. see Hobson, Mary Daniel.
Rauker, Lucy. Awesome Animal Trivia. (p. 120)
Raúl, Ill. Otto Es un Rinoceronte. (p. 1307)
Raúl, Ill, illus. see Boie, Kirsten.
Raúl, Ill, illus. see Camper, Cathy.
Raum, Elizabeth. Abraham Lincoln (p. 6)
—Abraham Lincoln Oxford Bible Staff, illus. (p. 6)
—At Battle in the Revolutionary War: An Interactive Battlefield Adventure. (p. 110)
—Aztec Empire: An Interactive History Adventure (p. 122)
—Bearded Dragons. (p. 151)
—Birth & Death of a City. (p. 192)
—Black Widow Spiders. (p. 197)
—Blue-Ringed Octopuses. (p. 203)
—Boston Massacre: An Interactive History Adventure (p. 215)
—Box Jellyfish. (p. 216)
—Bullying (p. 241)
—California Gold Rush: An Interactive History Adventure (p. 253)
—Can You Survive Storm Chasing? An Interactive Survival Adventure (p. 259)
—Cedric & the Dragon. Crittenden, Nina Victor, illus. (p. 283)
—Chameleons. (p. 289)
—Christmas Crossroads. (p. 313)
—Christmas Star. Johnson, Meredith, illus. (p. 315)
—Cold, Hard Facts about Science & Medicine in Colonial America (p. 338)
—Costa Rica (p. 368)
—Cutting a Path: Daniel Boone & the Cumberland Gap. (p. 396)
—Declaration of Independence (p. 422)
—Dreadful, Smelly Colonies: The Disgusting Details about Life in Colonial Amer. (p. 482)
—Dreadful, Smelly Colonies: The Disgusting Details about Life in Colonial America. (p. 482)
—Easter Island. (p. 499)
—Egyptian Pyramids. (p. 507)
—Expanding a Nation: Causes & Effects of the Louisiana Purchase (p. 548)
—Fossil Fuels & Biofuels (p. 623)
—Geckos. (p. 659)
—German Immigrants in America: An Interactive History Adventure (p. 666)
—Gift of Peace: The Jimmy Carter Story (p. 675)
—Gila Monsters. (p. 676)
—Great Wall of China. (p. 719)
—Green Iguanas. (p. 722)
—Guide Dogs. (p. 730)
—Gwen Stefani (p. 733)
—Haiti (p. 736)
—Helping Others (p. 766)
—History of the Computer (p. 785)
—History of the Computer. (p. 785)
—Homes: From Caves to Eco-Pods. (p. 793)
—I Know Someone with ADHD (p. 840)
—I Know Someone with HIV/AIDS (p. 840)
—Irish Immigrants in America: An Interactive History Adventure. (p. 887)
—K-9 Police Dogs. (p. 941)
—Komodo Dragons. (p. 966)
—Let's Think about the Power of Advertising (p. 1001)
—Machu Picchu. (p. 1068)
—Mayflower Compact (p. 1113)
—North Korea (p. 1265)
—Orphan Trains: An Interactive History Adventure (p. 1305)
—Pledge of Allegiance in Translation: What It Really Means. (p. 1374)
—Poetry (p. 1376)
—Poison Dart Frogs. (p. 1377)
—Potato Clocks & Solar Cars: Renewable & Nonrenewable Energy (p. 1388)
—Revolutionary War: An Interactive History Adventure (p. 1466)
—Revolutionary War Timeline (p. 1467)
—Scoop on Clothes, Homes, & Daily Life in Colonial America (p. 1529)
—Scorpions. (p. 1530)
—Song & Dance: A Journey Through Musical Theater. (p. 1611)
—South Korea (p. 1617)
—Spies of the American Revolution: An Interactive Espionage Adventure. (p. 1627)
—Star-Spangled Banner in Translation: What It Really Means. (p. 1641)
—Stealing Nazi Secrets in World War II: An Interactive Espionage Adventure. (p. 1646)
—Stingrays. (p. 1651)
—Stonefish. (p. 1653)
—Stonehenge. (p. 1653)
—Story Behind Bread (p. 1656)
—Story Behind Gold (p. 1656)
—Story Behind Time (p. 1656)
—Story Behind Toilets (p. 1656)
—Surviving Floods (p. 1687)
—Surviving Hurricanes (p. 1687)
—Surviving Tornadoes (p. 1687)
—Taipans. (p. 1696)
—Taj Mahal. (p. 1696)
—Transportation: From Walking to High Speed Rail. (p. 1779)
—True Stories of the Revolutionary War Kinsella, Pat, illus. (p. 1793)
—Twenty-First Century Shakespeare. (p. 1801)
—U. S. Marines by the Numbers (p. 1806)
—Water & Geothermal Energy (p. 1862)
—What Did the Aztecs Do for Me? (p. 1882)
—What Did the Vikings Do for Me? (p. 1882)
—What's the Attraction? Magnetism (p. 1899)
—William Clark. (p. 1933)
—Wind Energy (p. 1935)
—Work: From Plows to Robots. (p. 1952)
—World War II: An Interactive History Adventure (p. 1959)
—World War II Naval Forces (p. 1959)
—World War II Naval Forces: An Interactive History Adventure. (p. 1959)
—World War II Timeline (p. 1959)
Raum, Elizabeth, jt. auth. see Burgan, Michael.
Raum, Elizabeth, jt. auth. see Schuh, Mari C.
Raum, Elizabeth & Collins, Terry. You Choose: Historical Eras (p. 1975)
Raum, Elizabeth & Heinemann Library Staff. Poetry (p. 1376)
Raum, Elizabeth, et al. Cause & Effect (p. 282)
—Let's Think About (p. 1001)
—Life in the American Colonies. (p. 1011)
—Stories of War. (p. 1655)
—True War Stories: Personal Accounts of History's Greatest Conflicts. Kinsella, Pat et al, illus. (p. 1793)
—You Choose: Historical Eras. (p. 1975)
Raun, Robert L. Tales of the Clam Club: Turtle Soup. (p. 1702)
Rauner, Michael, photos by see Davis, Erik.
Rausch, David. Major League Baseball. (p. 1078)
—Major League Soccer. (p. 1078)
—National Basketball Association. (p. 1231)
—National Football League. (p. 1231)
—National Hockey League. (p. 1233)
—United States Tennis Association. (p. 1820)
Rausch, Kathy. King Louis: The Sun Cat! (p. 958)
Rausch, Monica. Andrew Jackson. (p. 72)
—Benjamin Franklin. (p. 164)
—Crispus Attucks. (p. 383)
—Harriet Tubman. (p. 749)
—Sacagawea. (p. 1500)
—Thomas Jefferson. (p. 1739)
Rausch, Monica & Benduhn, Tea, eds. Murder & Mystery: The Hound of the Baskervilles/Macbeth/the Legend of Sleepy Hollow. (p. 1192)
Rausch, Monica L. Andrew Jackson. (p. 72)
—Benjamin Franklin. (p. 164)
—Crispus Attucks. (p. 383)
—George Eastman & the Camera. (p. 663)
—George Eastman y la Cámara. (p. 663)
—Harriet Tubman. (p. 750)
—Henry Ford & the Model T Car. (p. 768)
—Henry Ford y el Automovil Modelo T. (p. 768)
—Hermanos Wright y el Avion. (p. 771)
—Sacagawea. (p. 1500)
—Thomas Edison & the Light Bulb. (p. 1738)
—Thomas Edison & the Lightbulb. (p. 1738)
—Thomas Edison y la Bombilla Eléctrica. (p. 1738)
—Thomas Edison y la bombilla Eléctrica. (p. 1738)
—Thomas Jefferson. (p. 1739)
—Wright Brothers & the Airplane. (p. 1963)
Rauscher, C D. Fairies of the Clouds. (p. 563)
—Matchmaking Fairies. (p. 1104)
Raushenbush, Paul. Teen Spirit: One World, Many Paths. (p. 1714)
Rausin, K. D. Elle & Buddy. Ulasowski, Muza, illus. (p. 514)
Rauss, Ron. Can I Just Take a Nap? Shepperson, Rob, illus. (p. 258)
Rautenberg, Karen Rita. Ballerina Detective & the Missing Jeweled Tiara. (p. 134)
—Lady Lucy's Gallant Knight. (p. 971)
Rau-Tobin, Joanna. Ted E. Bear the Labradoodle. Rau, Dinah M., illus. (p. 1712)
Rauzi, Kelly Emerling. Fearless John: The Legend of John Beargrease. Horak, Mila, illus. (p. 579)
Ravaglia, Paola, illus. see Davies, Gill.
Raval, Anuja, jt. auth. see Bhawnani, Henna.
Ravanelli, Terry, illus. see Gosselin, Kim.
Ravarra, Katana, jt. auth. see Seals, Loretta.
Ravasi, Gianfranco. Abraham: Father of Our Faith. (p. 6)
Rave, Friedrike. Outfoxing the Fox. (p. 1312)
Ravel, Edeet. Held. (p. 762)
—Saver (p. 1517)
Ravel, Maurice, et al. Boy & the Spell. Riglietti, Serena, illus. (p. 217)
Raven. Environment (Instructor's Resource Cd-Rom) (p. 532)
Raven, Catherine. Forestry. (p. 618)
Raven, Margot Theis. America's White Table. Ellison, Chris & Benny, Mike, illus. (p. 64)
—Challenger: America's Favorite Eagle. Frankenhuyzen, Gijsbert van, illus. (p. 289)
—Circle Unbroken. Lewis, E. B., illus. (p. 321)
—Happy Birthday to You! The Mystery Behind the Most Famous Song in the World. Soentpiet, Chris K., illus. (p. 745)
—Let Them Play. Ellison, Chris, illus. (p. 994)
—Night Boat to Freedom. Lewis, E. B., illus. (p. 1253)
—Rags Hero Dog of WWI: A True Story. Brown, Petra, illus. (p. 1433)
Raven, Paul. Story of Colours. (p. 1657)
Raven Tree Press Staff, ed. see Polette, Keith.
Raven Tree Press Staff, ed. see Rockhill, Dennis.
Raven-Ellison, Daniel, ed. see Blewett, Ashlee Brown.
Raven-Ellison, Daniel, ed. see Jazynka, Kitson.
Ravenhill, John A., illus. see Friederich, Uve.
Ravenhill, Mark. Plays for Young People: Citizenship; Scenes from Family Life; Totally over You. (p. 1373)
RavenWolf, Silver. Jóvenes y Brujas. (p. 929)
Ravenwolf, Silver. Solitary Witch: The Ultimate Book of Shadows for the New Generation. (p. 1608)
Raver, Miki. Listen to Her Voice: Women of the Hebrew Bible. (p. 1022)
Ravera, Giuseppe. Gingerbread Man House. Pagnoni, Roberta & Rigo, Laura, illus. (p. 677)
—My Ballet Bag. Pagnoni, Roberta et al, illus. (p. 1196)
—Snowflake. (p. 1600)
Raver-Lampman, Greg. Adrift: Lost in Life, Marooned at Sea. (p. 13)
Ravert, Melody. Night Wolf. (p. 1254)
Ravilious, Kate. Power: Ethical Debates about Resources & the Environment. (p. 1389)
—Power - Ethical Debates about Resources & the Environment. (p. 1389)
Ravishankar, Anushka. Catch That Crocodile! Biswas, Pulak, illus. (p. 279)
—Excuse Me, Is This India? Leutwiler, Anita, illus. (p. 548)
—Excuses Excuses. Manglou, Gabrielle, illus. (p. 548)
—Rumor. Kini, Kanyika, illus. (p. 1495)
—Today Is My Day. Grobler, Piet, illus. (p. 1760)
Rawal, Ishita, illus. see Crofoot, Nancy.
Rawat, Tania, illus. see Crofoot, Nancy.
Rawcliffe, Lee, illus. see Manci, Arlene.
Rawl, Paige, et al. Positive. (p. 1387)
Rawle, Martin. Dinasyddiaeth Weithredol. (p. 440)
Rawlett, Robert, jt. auth. see Espinosa, Chris.
Rawlings, Darren, illus. see Lieberman, A. J.
Rawlings, John S. Sometimes Boxes Make the Best Forts. Espina, Vito, illus. (p. 1610)
Rawlings, Louise, illus. see Rock, Lois.
Rawlings, Marjorie Kinnan. Secret River. Dillon, Leo & Dillon, Diane, illus. (p. 1543)
—Yearling. Wyeth, N. C., illus. (p. 1969)
Rawlings Miller, Carol & Glasscock, Sarah. Exceptional Essays. (p. 547)
Rawlins, Donna. Big & Little. Rawlins, Donna, illus. (p. 177)
Rawlins, Donna, illus. see Edwards, Hazel, et al.
Rawlins, Donna, illus. see Orr, Wendy.
Rawlins, Donna, illus. see Wild, Margaret.
Rawlins, Donna, jt. auth. see Wild, Margaret.
Rawlins, George & Rich, Jillian. Look, Listen & Trust: A Framework for Learning Through Drama. (p. 1049)
Rawlins, Jeanne & Rainbow Bridge Publishing Staff. Math Comprehension Grade 6. (p. 1105)
Rawlins, P. S. Angel's Kisses. (p. 75)
Rawlins, Trey. When Mommy Had Cancer. (p. 1903)
Rawlinson, jt. auth. see Rawlinson, Julia.
Rawlinson, Julia. Fletcher & the Falling Leaves. (p. 603)
—Fletcher & the Falling Leaves. Beeke, Tiphanie, illus. (p. 603)
—Fletcher & the Snowflake Christmas. Beeke, Tiphanie, illus. (p. 603)
—Fletcher & the Springtime Blossoms. (p. 603)
—Fletcher & the Springtime Blossoms. Beeke, Tiphanie, illus. (p. 603)
—Fred & the Little Egg. Massey, Jane, illus. (p. 632)
—Mule School Chapman, Lynne, illus. (p. 1189)
Rawlinson, Julia & Rawlinson. Fletcher & the Falling Leaves. Beeke, Tiphanie, illus. (p. 603)
Rawlinson, Julia & Warnes, Tim. Surprise for Rosie. (p. 1686)
Rawls, Anne. Oops Plays Ball. (p. 1299)
Rawls, Wilson. Where the Red Fern Grows. (p. 1909)
Rawlyk, George, jt. auth. see Downie, Mary Alice.
Rawson, C. Stories of Giants. (p. 1655)
—Stories of Witches. (p. 1655)
—Wizards. (p. 1943)
Rawson, Christopher. Dragons, Stories Of. Cartwright, Stephen, illus. (p. 479)
—Gnomes & Goblins. Cartwright, Stephen, illus. (p. 685)
—Stories of Giants. Cartwright, Stephen, illus. (p. 1655)
—Stories of Witches. Cartwright, Stephen, illus. (p. 1655)
Rawson, Christopher, jt. auth. see Dennis, Peter.
Rawson, Christopher, jt. auth. see Everett, Felicity.
Rawson, Christopher, jt. auth. see Wilkes, Angela.
Rawson, Dave, jt. auth. see Van Horn, William.
Rawson, Dave & Van Horn, William. Walt Disney's Comics & Stories Clark, John, ed. (p. 1855)
Rawson, Katherine. Abigail Breslin. (p. 5)
—Brenda Song. (p. 226)
—Daniel Radcliffe. (p. 405)
—If You Were a Parrot Rogers, Sherry, illus. (p. 855)
—Jonas Brothers. (p. 925)
—Taylor Swift. (p. 1708)
—Vanessa Hudgens. (p. 1833)
Rawson, Ken. Becoming a Young Man of God: An 8-Week Curriculum for Middle School Guys (p. 156)
Rawson, Maurice, illus. see Widdemer, Mabel Cleland.
Ray, Angela M. Herbie the Worm's Journey for Apples. (p. 769)
Ray, Ann. Just Imagine What You Can Do! (p. 938)
Ray, Anna Chapin. Half A Dozen Girls. (p. 736)
—Half a Dozen Girls. (p. 736)
Ray, Baltazar, creator. Adventures of the FancyCrazyHydrants: The Mission (p. 23)
Ray, Belinda. Unicorn. (p. 1818)
Ray Charles Lockamy, Inez Eason. Adventures of Tracks & Cookout. (p. 24)
Ray, Christie Jones, jt. auth. see Ray, Christie Jones.
Ray, Christie Jones & Ray, Christie Jones. Eliz. (p. 513)
—Eliza & a Cottage Door. (p. 513)
—Eliza Celebrates a Royal Wedding. (p. 513)
—Eliza Has a Cousin. (p. 513)
—Eliza Will Not Be Afraid. (p. 513)
—Fox Family of Franklin. (p. 626)
—Goat's Milk & Gardening. (p. 688)
—Pick-A-Pick-a-Pumpkin. (p. 1354)
Ray, Cindy & Kids Write On, creators. Stapler Caper: You Write the Story. (p. 1640)
Ray, Crystol T. Grumpy the Clown. (p. 727)
Ray, Dale Marie. Moody Mae. Ray, Dale Marie & Ray, Joli, illus. (p. 1171)
Ray, Deborah K., jt. auth. see Ray, Deborah Kogan.
Ray, Deborah Kogan. Dinosaur Mountain: Digging into the Jurassic Age. Ray, Deborah Kogan, illus. (p. 442)
—Paiute Princess: The Story of Sarah Winnemucca Ray, Deborah Kogan, illus. (p. 1319)
—Wanda Gág: The Girl Who Lived to Draw. (p. 1856)
Ray, Deborah Kogan, illus. see Bardhan-Quallen, Sudipta.
Ray, Deborah Kogan, illus. see Peretz, I. L.
Ray, Deborah Kogan & Ray, Deborah K. Down the Colorado: John Wesley Powell, the One-Armed Explorer. Ray, Deborah Kogan, illus. (p. 474)
Ray, Delia. Ghost Girl: A Blue Ridge Mountain Story. (p. 670)
—Here Lies Linc. (p. 770)
Ray, Eric, illus. see Avery, Pat McGrath.
Ray, Francis. In Another Man's Bed. (p. 863)
Ray, Frederic. Gettysburg Sketches: A Concise & Illustrated History of the Battle of Gettysburg. (p. 670)
Ray, Gracie. Falling Slowly. (p. 567)
Ray, Hannah. Chickens. (p. 300)
—Cows. (p. 374)
—Great Big Friend Hunt. (p. 714)
—Katie's Mom Is a Mermaid (p. 945)
—Pigs. (p. 1358)
—Sheep. (p. 1564)
Ray, J. Hamilton. Squirrels on Skis. Lemaitre, Pascal, illus. (p. 1637)
Ray, Jackie. Ava's Amazing Adventure: Jackie L. Ray. (p. 118)
Ray, Jane. Adam & Eve & the Garden of Eden. (p. 11)
—Adam & Eve & the Garden of Eden. Ray, Jane, illus. (p. 11)
—Adán y Eva y el Jardín Del Edén. Rodríguez, Maite, tr. (p. 11)
—Can You Catch a Mermaid? Ray, Jane, illus. (p. 258)
—Cinderella. Ray, Jane, illus. (p. 320)
—Classic Fairy Tales: Candlewick Illustrated Classic. (p. 328)
—Dollhouse Fairy. Ray, Jane, illus. (p. 464)
—Emperor's Nightingale & Other Feathery Tales. (p. 521)
—Twelve Days of Christmas. (p. 1800)
Ray, Jane, illus. see Clayton, Sally Pomme.
Ray, Jane, illus. see Hofmeyr, Dianne & Quarto Generic Staff.
Ray, Jane, illus. see Seth, Vikram.
Ray, Jane, illus. see Steven, Kenneth.
Ray, Jane, jt. auth. see Joslin, Mary.
Ray, Janet. Emily Stowe (p. 519)
Ray, Joanna Z. 'elaran! Isithan! (p. 508)
Ray, Joli, illus. see Ray, Dale Marie.
Ray, Joyce, jt. auth. see Murphy, Andrea.
Ray, Keri. Dancing in the Rain: At the Zoo. (p. 403)
—Saving Journey. (p. 1517)
Ray, Kurt. Historical Atlas of Kuwait. (p. 783)
—New Roads, Canals, & Railroads in Early 19th-Century America: The Transportation Revolution. (p. 1247)
—Typhoid Fever. (p. 1805)
Ray, Liz. Bananas: From Farm to Home (p. 136)
—Coming to the United States (p. 348)
—Famous U. S. Landmarks (p. 570)
—One Land, Many Cultures (p. 1295)
Ray, Liz & Capstone Press Staff. Bananas: From Farm to Home (p. 136)
—Coming to the United States (p. 348)
—Famous U. S. Landmarks (p. 570)
—One Land, Many Cultures (p. 1295)
Ray, Lynn. Angel's Christmas. (p. 75)
Ray, Lynn E. Hallelujah. (p. 737)
Ray, Mary Lyn. Christmas Farm. Root, Barry, illus. (p. 313)
—Deer Dancer. Stringer, Lauren, illus. (p. 423)
—Go to Sleep, Little Farm. Neal, Christopher Silas, illus. (p. 687)
—Red Rubber Boot Day. Stringer, Lauren, illus. (p. 1455)
—Violin for Elva. Tusa, Tricia, illus. (p. 1843)
Ray, Mary Lyn & Frazee, Marla. Stars. (p. 1643)
Ray, Miasyn Summer. One Lucky Petal. (p. 1296)
Ray, Michael, illus. see Faircloth, M. L.
Ray, Michael, ed. France. (p. 627)
—Germany. (p. 666)
—Portugal & Spain. (p. 1387)
Ray, Michelle. Falling for Hamlet. (p. 566)
—Huntsman Spider in My House... Ashford, Sylvie, illus. (p. 829)
Ray, Mike. Flying the 700 Series Flight Simulators (B/W) How to Do It Manual. (p. 610)
Ray, Mike, illus. see Maddox, Jake.
Ray, Mike, illus. see Wacholtz, Anthony.
Ray, Nan. Friends, Friends, Friends. (p. 638)
—Meet the People. (p. 1123)
Ray, Price V. Somebody Book. (p. 1609)
Ray, Rachael. Rachael Ray's 30-Minute Meals for Kids: Cooking Rocks! Kalb, Chris, illus. (p. 1431)
Ray, Ralph, illus. see White, Robb.
Ray, Rebecca E. Amethyst Lily. (p. 65)
Ray, Rex, illus. see Ewert, Marcus.
Ray, Rhonda. David Donkey Had a Lot of Fun. (p. 411)
Ray, Sandra. Grandma & Me Oh What Do We See When We Go to the Zoo? Bailey, Sidney, illus. (p. 708)
Ray, Satyajit. Unicorn Expedition & Other Stories: The Exploits of Professor Shonku. (p. 1818)
Ray, Satyajit, illus. see Robinson, Andrew.

R

Ray, See. Caterpillar Stickers: Be Yourself & Be Butterfly Beautiful! (p. 279)
Ray, Sukhendu, jt. auth. see Tagore, Rabindranath.
Ray, Terry. Avatar ... God, Man, or the Antichrist? (p. 118)
Rayas, Rubén, illus. see Smith, Anne & Smith, Owen.
Rayban, Chloe. Drama Queen. (p. 480)
—Models Move on to Starring Roles. (p. 1158)
—Skin Deep (p. 1585)
Raybon, Charlotte. Meet the Veggies: What Happens in Miss Mae's Kitchen? (p. 1123)
Raybon, Patricia. I Told the Mountain to Move. (p. 846)
Rayburn, Cathy & Stone, Elaine Murray. Angels in the Bible. (p. 75)
Rayburn, Scooter. Animal Friends for You! Let's Be Friends! (p. 77)
Rayburn, Tricia. Maggie Bean in Love. (p. 1071)
—Maggie Bean Stays Afloat. (p. 1071)
—Melting of Maggie Bean. (p. 1125)
—Ruby's Slippers. (p. 1494)
Raye, Daniel, jt. auth. see Raye, Marianna.
Raye, Donna. Edison the Firefly & Ford the Fly. (p. 504)
—Edison the Firefly & Sierra the Special Spider. (p. 504)
—Edison the Firefly & the Invention of the Light Bulb. Balsano, Sean, illus. (p. 504)
—Faith a Leapin' The Sign (Multilingual Edition) (p. 565)
Raye, Kimberly. Kiss Me Once, Kiss Me Twice. (p. 961)
Raye, Marianna & Raye, Daniel. Olis & the Big Outside. (p. 1285)
Raye, Rebekah. Bear-ly There Raye, Rebekah, illus. (p. 151)
Raye, Rebekah, illus. see Ridley, Kimberly.
Raye, Rebekah, illus. see Sockabasin, Allen.
Raye, Varuna. Frederick & the Scaries. (p. 633)
Rayel, Michael G. 31-Day Success Principles for Kids & Teens. (p. 1996)
Rayes, Michael. Bank Robbery! (p. 136)
Rayevsky, Kim. Antonyms, Synonyms & Homonyms. Rayevsky, Robert, illus. (p. 90)
Rayevsky, Robert, illus. see Derby, Sally & Derby.
Rayevsky, Robert, illus. see Janeczko, Paul B.
Rayevsky, Robert, illus. see Kimmel, Eric A.
Rayevsky, Robert, illus. see Rayevsky, Kim.
Rayia, Tim, illus. see Hartman, Bob.
Rayles,, Amy, Amy, et al. I Am a Nurse... A Book That Tells about Nurses. (p. 832)
Rayment, Carolynn. Buster Batey & Mops. (p. 245)
Raymer, Dottie. School Smarts Projects. McGuinness, Tracy & McGuinness, Tracey, illus. (p. 1523)
—Smart Girl's Guide: Staying Home Alone. (p. 1592)
—Smart Girl's Guide to Staying Home Alone. Scheuer, Lauren, illus. (p. 1592)
Raymer, Miles. How to Analyze the Music of Paul Mccartney. (p. 814)
Raymond, Aaron. Primary Source History of the Colony of Delaware. (p. 1400)
Raymond, Edwins. Dying Moon. (p. 491)
Raymond, Emily, jt. auth. see Patterson, James.
Raymond, Janet Y., illus. see Young, Polly G.
Raymond, Jayne. Meet Deinonychus. (p. 1120)
—Meet Velociraptor. (p. 1123)
Raymond, Jeanpaul. Kids That Could. (p. 955)
Raymond, Patrick. Daniel & Esther. (p. 404)
Raymond, Rebecca, jt. auth. see Morningforest, Chris.
Raymond, Roger & Savoy, Darryl. Ralph Filmore: Paranormal Investigator. O'Reilly, Sean Patrick, ed. (p. 1437)
Raymos, Rick. Born in the Wild: Baby Animals. (p. 214)
—Fighting for Survival: Predators & Prey. (p. 585)
—STEM Jobs in Sports. (p. 1647)
Raymundo, Peter, illus. see Bloom, C. P.
Rayner, Amanda. Going to School. (p. 693)
—What We Wear. (p. 1895)
Rayner, Amanda, ed. see Watts, Claire.
Rayner, Catherine. Abigail. Rayner, Catherine, illus. (p. 5)
—Bear Who Shared. (p. 151)
—Ernest, the Moose Who Doesn't Fit. Rayner, Catherine, illus. (p. 534)
—Solomon Crocodile. Rayner, Catherine, illus. (p. 1608)
Rayner, Catherine, illus. see Newbery, Linda.
Rayner, Catherine, illus. see Williams, Ursula Moray.
Rayner, David, et al. Geographical Enquiry (p. 662)
Rayner, Katy. Cars. (p. 272)
—Trucks. (p. 1791)
Rayner, Katy, ed. see Picthall, Chez & Gunzi.
Rayner, Katy, ed. see Picthall, Chez.
Rayner, Keith. Torvig's Gift. (p. 1771)
Rayner, Matthew. Guinea Pig. Sawyer, Darren, photos by. (p. 731)
—I Am Your Pet Sawyer, Darren, photos by. (p. 834)
—Rat. Sawyer, Darren, photos by. (p. 1440)
Rayner, Matthew & BVetMed MRCVS Staff. Cat. Burton, Jane & Greenaway, Frank, photos by. (p. 277)
—Dog. Burton, Jane & Greenaway, Frank, photos by. (p. 460)
—Hamster. Greenaway, Frank & Burton, Jane, photos by. (p. 739)
—I Am Your Pet Greenaway, Frank & Burton, Jane, photos by. (p. 834)
—Rabbit. Burton, Jane & Greenaway, Frank, photos by. (p. 1429)
Rayner, Olivia. World Book Myths & Legends Series (p. 1954)
Rayner, Olivia, illus. see Imperato, Teresa.
Rayner, Philip, et al. As Media Studies: The Essential Introduction. (p. 105)
Rayner, Robert. Falling Star (p. 567)
—Just for Kicks (p. 938)
—Libby on Strike (p. 1005)
—Libby's Got the Beat (p. 1005)
—Miss Little's Losers (p. 1151)
—Suspended (p. 1688)
Rayner, Shoo. Big, Bad City. (p. 178)
—Cat & Dog Play Hide & Seek. (p. 277)
—Cat & Dog Play Hide & Seek. Moon, Cliff, ed. (p. 277)
—Cat & Dog Play Hide & Seek. Rayner, Shoo, illus. (p. 277)
—Deadly Target. (p. 418)
—Ginger Ninja 5: World Cup Winners. (p. 677)
—Jump for Glory. (p. 934)
—Monster Joke Book. Rayner, Shoo, illus. (p. 1167)
—On the Ball. Rayner, Shoo, illus. (p. 1289)
—Race for the Stars. Rayner, Shoo, illus. (p. 1431)
—Rebel Flyer. (p. 1450)
—Sweet Disaster. (p. 1689)
—Swim for Your Life. (p. 1690)
—Throw for Gold. (p. 1745)
—Vorg World. (p. 1850)
—Wrestle to Victory. (p. 1962)
Rayner, Shoo, illus. see Rosen, Michael.
Raynes, Jody, jt. auth. see Raynes, John.
Raynes, John & Raynes, Jody. How to Draw a Human Figure. (p. 816)
Raynham, Alex. Factfiles Leonardo da Vinci. (p. 561)
Raynolds, Elaine. My Dad Was a Lynx. (p. 1201)
—Rocky & Honey: A Love Story. (p. 1484)
Raynor, Jackie, illus. see Smith, Jane.
Raynor, Maggie, illus. see Cooper, Barbara.
Raynor, Michelle. Magical World. (p. 1075)
Rayson, Ann. Hawai'i: The Pacific State. (p. 755)
—Modern History of Hawai'i. (p. 1158)
Raysor, Joan, illus. see Ormondroyd, Edward.
Rayyan, Omar. My Kitten's First Year. (p. 1211)
Rayyan, Omar, illus. see Blom, Jen K.
Rayyan, Omar, illus. see Casanova, Mary.
Rayyan, Omar, illus. see Cooper, Susan.
Rayyan, Omar, illus. see Cox, Judy.
Rayyan, Omar, illus. see Downer, Ann.
Rayyan, Omar, illus. see Duey, Kathleen.
Rayyan, Omar, illus. see Ghazi, Suhaib Hamid.
Rayyan, Omar, illus. see Howe, Peter.
Rayyan, Omar, illus. see Kimmel, Eric A.
Rayyan, Omar, illus. see Seymour, Jane.
Rayyan, Omar, illus. see Wagner, Hilary.
Rayyan, Sheila, illus. see Duey, Kathleen.
RAZ. 'Cuz That's Just My Way. Kerchner, Janet Hall, illus. (p. 396)
Raz, Rachel. ABC Israel. (p. 3)
—Colors of Israel. Raz, Rachel, photos by. (p. 345)
Razcka, Bob. Here's Looking at Me: How Artists See Themselves. (p. 771)
Razilov, Evelyn. Beautiful Fish. (p. 153)
—Little Ant & the Apple Tree. (p. 1023)
Razo, Rebecca J. Monsters under My Bed. Fisher, Diana, illus. (p. 1169)
—Watch Me Draw the Monsters under My Bed: A Step-by-Step Drawing & Story Book. Fisher, Diana, illus. (p. 1861)
Razzak, Shazia. P Is for Pakistan. Das, Prodeepta, photos by. (p. 1316)
Razzell. Night Fires. (p. 1253)
Razzell, Mary. Runaway at Sea. (p. 1496)
—White Wave. (p. 1913)
Razzi, Jim. Sherluck Bones Mystery Detective. (p. 1566)
Razzi, Manuela, illus. see Orsi, Tea & Panaro, Carlo.
Razzi, Manuela, illus. see Rodrigue, Michel.
Razzi, Manuela, jt. auth. see Rodrigue, Michel.
RBA, et al. libro del aprendiz de Brujo. (p. 1006)
Rchards, Virginia Helen, illus. see Dateno, Maria Grace.
R.D.Haire & Francis, Richard E. When Good Got Better: The Adventures of Fred the Friendly Shark. (p. 1902)
Rdm, tr. see National Youth Department Staff.
Rdm, tr. see Sanford, Timothy L.
Rdm, tr. see Triplett, Donald & Elland, Marie.
Rea, Ba. Monarch! Come Play with Me. Rea, Ba, illus. (p. 1163)
Rea, Loretta Vandivier. Eddie Builds a House: Go Home, Eddie. (p. 503)
Rea, Lynn. Tug of War. (p. 1796)
Rea, Monique. Toulouse the Moose. (p. 1773)
—Toulouse the Moose & the Mystery Guests. (p. 1773)
Rea, Monique F. Original Story of Toulouse the Moose & His Friends: Book & CD. (p. 1304)
—Toulouse the Moose Coloring Book. (p. 1773)
Rea, Thelma. I Wonder Why the Sky Is Blue. (p. 849)
—Pioneer Families. (p. 1361)
—Taking Care of Our World. (p. 1698)
Read, Abigail, jt. auth. see Fox, Kate.
Read, Christine. Grunge Boy & the First Day of Summer. (p. 727)
Read, Christopher. Lenin: A Revolutionary Life. (p. 991)
Read, Howard & Chantler, Chris. Little Howard's Big Book. (p. 1029)
Read, Kit. Alexis Ant Marooned in Afric. (p. 37)
Read, Laurie. Blacky Longlegs Meets Freddy the Fly. (p. 198)
Read, Leon. George the Knight. (p. 663)
Read, Lorna. Lies They Tell. (p. 1007)
Read, Lorna & Ladybird Books Staff. Elves & the Shoemaker. Lewis, Jan, illus. (p. 517)
Read, Marya, creator. Educated Choice Journal. (p. 505)
Read, Miss. Christmas Mouse. Goodall, John S., illus. (p. 314)
—Howards of Caxley. (p. 823)
Read, Nicholas. City Critters: Wildlife in the Urban Jungle (p. 323)
Read, Rupert, jt. ed. see Goodenough, Jerry.
Read, Ruth. Sunflower & the Swan. (p. 1676)
Read, Sara. Teenagers Guide to Self-Destruction. (p. 1714)
Read Together Books Inc Staff & Shoule, Michael. My Daddy Loves Boston College Football. (p. 1201)
Read, Tracy C. Exploring the World of Bees. (p. 554)
—Exploring the World of Cougars. (p. 554)
—Exploring the World of Eagles. (p. 554)
—Exploring the World of Foxes. (p. 554)
—Exploring the World of Raccoons. (p. 554)
—Exploring the World of Seals & Walruses. (p. 554)
Reade, Clara. Cheetahs. (p. 296)
—Hippos. (p. 781)
—Lions. (p. 1021)
—Meerkats. (p. 1120)
—Warthogs. (p. 1859)
—Zebras. (p. 1985)
Reade, O. K. Little Girl & Her Shadow. (p. 1028)
Reade, Simon. Private Peaceful. (p. 1408)
Reader, Gwendolin. Life Cycle of A Snowman. (p. 1009)
Reader, Jenny. Girl 2 Girl: The Swap Book You Share with Your Friends. Martin, Caroline & Davies, Nic, illus. (p. 678)
Readers Digest Childrens Publishing Inc. Staff, jt. auth. see Harrast, Tracy.
Reader's Digest Editors. 50 States. (p. 1997)
—Barbie Mix & Match. Duarte, Pamela, illus. (p. 138)
—Barbie Movie Theater: Storybook & Movie Projector(r). (p. 138)
—Croods: Picture Puzzles, Mazes & More. (p. 384)
—DC Super Friends Heroes Unite! DC Artists Staff, illus. (p. 415)
—Disney Mickey Mouse Clubhouse Take-Along Tunes: Book with Music Player. (p. 452)
—Disney Princess Holiday Gift Set. (p. 452)
—Fisher Price Little People Halloween Is Here! (p. 598)
—Fisher-Price Little People Valentine's Day Is Here! SI Artists Staff, illus. (p. 599)
—God Made You. (p. 690)
—Guess Who, Pooh! (p. 729)
—Mighty Avengers Holiday. (p. 1140)
—My Little Pony - Cutie Mark Quest. (p. 1213)
—Nickelodeon My Pal SpongeBob: Pose-a-Book. (p. 1251)
—Ocean 3D: Fact & 3D Pics. (p. 1276)
—Off the Beaten Path: A Travel Guide to More Than 1000 Scenic & Interesting Places Still Uncrowded & Inviting. (p. 1279)
—Ride the Holiday Train! Fruchter, Jason, illus. (p. 1471)
—Sesame Street Holiday Gift Set. Brannon, Tom, illus. (p. 1553)
—Talking Puzzles Sounds on the Farm. (p. 1703)
—Thomas & Friends (p. 1737)
—When Nature Turns Nasty. (p. 1904)
Reader's Digest Editors, jt. auth. see Mitter, Matt.
Reader's Digest Editors, jt. auth. see Roe, David.
Reader's Digest Editors & Bell, Megan. Roary Eyes His Cards: Stories, Games, & 72 Collectible Playing Cards. Mind Candy Ltd. Staff, illus. (p. 1478)
Reader's Digest Editors & Froeb, Lori C. Buddy & the Nature Trackers. DiCicco, LeeAnn, illus. (p. 234)
—Let's Go to Volcano Valley! Over 30 Fun Flaps to Lift. DiCicco, Sue & DiCicco, LeeAnn, illus. (p. 998)
Reader's Digest Editors & Goldsmith, Michael. I Wish I Knew That Math: Cool Stuff You Need Know. (p. 849)
Reader's Digest Editors & Hamilton, Tisha. Minnie's Big Bow Party. (p. 1148)
Reader's Digest Editors & Lombardi, Kristine. Fun with Barbie & Friends Storybook & Magnetic Playset. Duarte, Pamela, illus. (p. 648)
Reader's Digest Editors & Miller, Sara. Cinderella: A Royal Wish. Disney Animators Staff, illus. (p. 320)
Reader's Digest Editors & Mitter, Matt. Follow Me to the Farm. SI Artists Staff, illus. (p. 612)
—Guess Who, Mickey! Loter, John & Loter Inc. Staff, illus. (p. 729)
—School Trip. SI Artists Staff, illus. (p. 1523)
Reader's Digest Editors & Rosenblum, Jill. Barbie Dreamhouse Party. (p. 138)
Reader's Digest Editors & Zobel-Nolan, Allia. See the Sea! A Book about Colors. Terry, Michael, illus. (p. 1547)
Reader's Digest Editors, creator. Humor in Uniform: Funny True Stories about Life in the Military. (p. 827)
Reader's Digest Editors, ed. Red Ribbon: A Book about Friendship. Taylor, Thomas, illus. (p. 1454)
Reader's Digest Editors, et al. Disney Mickey Mouse Clubhouse Follow That Dog! Storybook & Sound FX Car. (p. 451)
—Elmo Loves Hugs! (p. 515)
—Music Player. Brannon, Tom, illus. (p. 1193)
—Princess Style. (p. 1405)
Reader's Digest Staff. Baby's First Bible. MacLean, Colin & MacLean, Moira, illus. (p. 129)
—Barbie in a Mermaid Tale. Ulkutay Design Group Staff, illus. (p. 138)
—Busy Day Bunnies: A Carry along Treasury. McCue, Lisa, illus. (p. 246)
—Cars Movie Theater. (p. 272)
—Christmastime Is Here! (p. 316)
—Croods. (p. 384)
—Deluxe Music Player. (p. 425)
—Discover with Dora: Books & Magnetic Playset Nickelodeon Staff, illus. (p. 448)
—Disney Minnie - Take-Along Tunes; Music Player with 20 Tunes. (p. 452)
—Disney the Lion King Movie Theater: Storybook & Movie Projector. (p. 453)
—Dora Helps Swiper. (p. 470)
—Dora Music Player. Nickelodeon Staff, illus. (p. 470)
—Dora the Explorer My Favorite Story. (p. 471)
—Dora the Explorer Take-Along Tunes. (p. 471)
—Elmo One, Two, Zoo! (p. 515)
—Fisher-Price Little People Easter Is Here! (p. 598)
—I Love Drawing Moshi Monsters. (p. 842)
—Let's Go to the Zoo! (p. 998)
—Let's Help the Earth. Brannon, Tom, illus. (p. 998)
—Mickey Mouse Clubhouse Gift Set. (p. 1136)
—Movie Theater: Storybook & Movie Projector. Vol. 2 Egan, Caroline LaVelle et al, illus. (p. 1183)
—My Little Pony Fashion & Friendship Storybook & Press Outs. (p. 1213)
—My Name Is Tiny! Fruchter, Jason, illus. (p. 1215)
—Rise of the Guardians: Worlds of Wonder. Primeau, Chuck, illus. (p. 1475)
—Safari Splash. (p. 1502)
—Sesame Street Gift Set. (p. 1553)
—Thomas & Friends Movie Theater. HIT Entertainment Staff, illus. (p. 1738)
—Tractor Trouble Drive Through Storybook. Pitt, Sarah, illus. (p. 1775)
Reader's Digest Staff, jt. auth. see Disney Storybook Artists Staff.
Reader's Digest Staff, jt. auth. see Heller, Sarah.
Reader's Digest Staff & Disney Storybook Artists Staff. Disney Princess Music Player. (p. 453)
—Rapunzel's Dream Walmart Edition Storybook with Musical Hairbrush. (p. 1439)
Reader's Digest Staff & Froeb, Lori C. Buddy's Big Bite. Fruchter, Jason, illus. (p. 235)
Reader's Digest Staff & Gold, Gina. Bunny Hugs. (p. 242)
—Night, Night, Elmo! (p. 1253)
Reader's Digest Staff & Lombardi, Kristine. Barbie Style 'n Fun. Duarte, Pamela, illus. (p. 138)
Reader's Digest Staff & London, Olivia. Barbie Project Pet Park. Duarte, Pamela, illus. (p. 138)
Reader's Digest Staff & Miller, Sara. Winnie the Pooh Take-Along Tunes: Book with Music Player. Disney Storybook Artists Staff, illus. (p. 1937)
Reader's Digest Staff & Mitter, Matt. Me Love Cookies! Brannon, Tom, illus. (p. 1116)
Reader's Digest Staff & Rhodes, Lilly. Guess Who, Minnie! Loter Inc. Staff, illus. (p. 729)
Reader's Digest Staff & Roe, David. Dora the Explorer Mix & Match Dress-Up. Fruchter, Jason, illus. (p. 471)
—How to Train Your Dragon Mix & Match. (p. 822)
Reader's Digest Staff & Shepherd, Jodie. Guess Who Baby Animals. Ovresat, Laura, illus. (p. 729)
Reader's Digest Staff & Teitelbaum, Michael. Marvel Heroes Super Origins. Udon Entertainment Corp Staff, illus. (p. 1098)
Reader's Digest Staff & Tomaselli, Doris. Fisher-Price Little People Let's Go to School. S. I. Artists Staff, illus. (p. 598)
Readett, Gerard. Roadworks. Cummins, Sandy, ed. (p. 1477)
Rea-Dickins, Pauline, jt. auth. see Kiely, Richard.
Reading Friends Staff. Benjamin. (p. 164)
—Dragon Books. (p. 476)
—McBean. (p. 1114)
—Peanut Single. (p. 1332)
—Puppies Single. (p. 1418)
—Run Single. (p. 1496)
—Witches Single. (p. 1941)
Readler, Blaine C. Under the Radar: The Spy Drone Adventure. (p. 1814)
Readman, Jo. George Saves the World by Lunchtime. Roberts, Ley Honor, illus. (p. 663)
Readman, Jo & Roberts, Ley Honor. World Came to My Place Today. (p. 1954)
Ready, Anna. Mississippi. (p. 1154)
Ready, D. M., illus. see Erickson, Sharon.
Ready, Dee. Dentists Help (p. 427)
—Doctors Help. (p. 459)
—Farmers Help (p. 574)
—Firefighters Help (p. 591)
—Librarians Help. (p. 1005)
—Nurses Help. (p. 1273)
—Our Community Helpers. (p. 1308)
—Police Officers Help (p. 1380)
—Veterinarians Help. (p. 1839)
Ready, Dee, jt. auth. see Deedrick, Tami.
Ready Reader Staff. Ant (p. 88)
—Apple Farm (p. 92)
—At the Track (p. 111)
—Best Place (p. 171)
—City Cat & the Country Cat (p. 323)
—Eyes Are Everywhere (p. 558)
—Five Little Dinosaurs (p. 600)
—Fun Place to Eat (p. 648)
—Glenda the Lion (p. 683)
—Good-Bye Zoo: Consonant Z (p. 697)
—I Got a Goldfish: Hard & Soft G (p. 838)
—Just Like Us: Short U (p. 939)
—Let's Go Marching! (p. 997)
—Little Frog's Monster Story (p. 1028)
—Lucky Duck: Short Vowels (p. 1062)
—Mr. Fins' Trip: Short I (p. 1185)
—Mr. Wink (p. 1187)
—"POP" Pops the Popcorn: Short O (p. 1384)
—River Grows (p. 1476)
—Roll Out the Red Reg (p. 1485)
—Rush Rush Rush: Digraphs (p. 1498)
—Something to Munch (p. 1610)
—Stan Packs (p. 1639)
—What Do We Have to Get? (p. 1882)
—Where Does the Rabbit Hop? (p. 1907)
Reagan, Jean. Always My Brother Pollema-Cahill, Phyllis, illus. (p. 51)
—How to Amaze a Teacher. Wildish, Lee, illus. (p. 814)
—How to Babysit a Grandma. (p. 814)
—How to Babysit a Grandpa. Wildish, Lee, illus. (p. 814)
Reagan, John, jt. auth. see Reagan, Marianne.
Reagan, Marianne & Reagan, John. It's Okay to Be Me. (p. 898)
Reagan, Mike, illus. see Lerangis, Peter.
Reagan, Naomi. Butterflies & Moths: Represent & Interpret Data. (p. 247)
Reagan, Susan. Slipper & Flipper in the Quest for Don Pinguino & the Golden Sun. Reagan, Susan, illus. (p. 1590)
Reagan, Susan, illus. see DePrisco, Dorothea.
Reagan, Susan, illus. see Elkins, Stephen.
Reagan, Susan, illus. see Hill, Karen.
Reagan, Susan Joy, illus. see Carlson, Melody.
Reagan, Susan Joy, illus. see Elkins, Stephen.
Real, F. A. Casey & the Car Wash. (p. 275)
Real Simple Magazine Staff, jt. auth. see Cronstrom, Kendell.
Real Simple Magazine Staff, jt. auth. see Rains, Valerie.
Real, Stuart. Cone Stories. (p. 356)
RealBuzz Studios Staff. Girl Overboard Frankensteins Monster: Life Camera Action Book 4. (p. 678)
—Hits & Misses. (p. 786)
—Let There Be Lighten Up! (p. 994)
—Out of the Soup. (p. 1311)
—Space Cadet vs Drama Queen Terror from the Tarantula Nebula: Life Camera Action Book 1. (p. 1618)
Really Big Coloring Books Staff. ABC 123 Learn My Letters & Numbers. (p. 3)
Really Big Coloring Books Staff, compiled by. Careers in Agriculture with Ag E. Bear (p. 267)
Ream, Jacquie. Bully Dogs. (p. 241)
Ream, Robaire, illus. see Matejovsky, Char.
Reams, Clyde. Stories by the Fire. (p. 1654)

Reamy, Donna W. & Steele, Cynthia W. Perry's Department Store: An Importing Simulation. (p. 1344)
Rearden, Cynthia Ann. Gerby the Germ: And a Trip to the Bathroom. (p. 666)
Reardon, A. C. Galish: The adventure of Isabelle & Eva. (p. 653)
Reardon, Dave. Soundtrack for a Revolution: Youth Alive. (p. 1615)
Reardon, John. South Overlook Oaks. Youngbluth, Chris, illus. (p. 1617)
Reardon, Mark & Derner, Seth. Strategies for Great Teaching: Maximize Learning Moments. (p. 1666)
Reardon, Mary, illus. see McSwigan, Marie.
Reardon, Patrick T. Starting Out: Reflections for Young People. (p. 1644)
Reardon, Will, ed. see Lawrence, Linda.
Rearick, Nancy. Life Through a Kitten's Eyes. (p. 1013)
Reason, Diane. Travis the Traveling Turtle & the Beautiful Butterfly. (p. 1781)
Reasoner, Charles. 3 Blind Mice Inside the Spooky Scary & Creepy Haunted House. Reasoner, Charles, illus. (p. 1991)
—Alphabite! (p. 50)
—Animal Friends on the Farm. Pitt, Sarah, illus. (p. 77)
—Animals in the Jungle. Pitt, Sarah, illus. (p. 83)
—Bear Hugs. (p. 150)
—Boo Bat (p. 209)
—Brrrr! (p. 232)
—Bug Babies. Devaney, Adam, illus. (p. 236)
—Charles Reasoner Halloween Books. (p. 292)
—Charles Reasoner Holiday Books. (p. 292)
—Charles Reasoner Nursery Rhymes. (p. 292)
—Charles Reasoner Peek-A-Boo Books. (p. 292)
—Charles Reasoner Peek-A-Book Books. (p. 292)
—Charles Reasoner's Little Cuddles. Llewhellin, Gareth, illus. (p. 292)
—Color Crunch! (p. 342)
—Colors in the Garden. Pitt, Sarah, illus. (p. 345)
—Day Around Town. (p. 412)
—Day at School. (p. 412)
—Day at the Farm. (p. 412)
—Desert Tails. Nelson, Judy, illus. (p. 429)
—Dinosaur Babies. Devaney, Adam, illus. (p. 441)
—Dinosaurs. (p. 444)
—Dinosaurs. Doherty, Paula, illus. (p. 444)
—Fan-Tab-U-Lus: Dinosaurs. Devaney, Adam, illus. (p. 570)
—Fan-Tab-U-Lus: Jungle Animals. Devaney, Adam, illus. (p. 570)
—Farm. (p. 573)
—Farm Animals. Doherty, Paula, illus. (p. 573)
—Farm Babies. Devaney, Adam, illus. (p. 573)
—First Words at the Park. Pitt, Sarah, illus. (p. 597)
—Haatch! (p. 734)
—Halloween Ghost (p. 737)
—Hey, Diddle, Diddle Le Ray, Marina, illus. (p. 774)
—Hickory, Dickory, Dock. Le Ray, Marina, illus. (p. 775)
—Ho! Ho! Ho! Jones, Anna, illus. (p. 786)
—Honey Bunny. (p. 794)
—Humpty Dumpty Le Ray, Marina, illus. (p. 827)
—Humpty Dumpty Jones, Anna & Le Ray, Marina, illus. (p. 827)
—I'm Just a Bird. (p. 859)
—I'm Just a Bird. Reasoner, Charles, illus. (p. 859)
—I'm Just a Crab. (p. 859)
—I'M Just a Crab! Reasoner, Charles, illus. (p. 859)
—I'm Just a Fish. (p. 859)
—I'm Just a Frog. (p. 859)
—I'm Just a Little Cow. Orkrania, Alexia, illus. (p. 859)
—Insects. Doherty, Paula, illus. (p. 875)
—Inside Jolly Rodger's Pirate Ship. (p. 876)
—Inside Jolly Roger's Pirate Ship. Reasoner, Charles, illus. (p. 876)
—Inside Old MacDonald's Barn. (p. 877)
—Inside Old Mcdonald's Barn. Reasoner, Charles, illus. (p. 877)
—Inside Santa's Toy Shop. Reasoner, Charles, illus. (p. 877)
—Itsy Bitsy Spider Le Ray, Marina, illus. (p. 900)
—Itsy Bitsy Spider Jones, Anna & Le Ray, Marina, illus. (p. 900)
—Jack & Jill Le Ray, Marina, illus. (p. 902)
—Jungle. Devaney, Adam, illus. (p. 934)
—Jungle Animals. Doherty, Paula, illus. (p. 935)
—Jungle Babies. Devaney, Adam & Doherty, Paula, illus. (p. 935)
—Let It Snow. Jones, Anna, illus. (p. 994)
—Little Bo Peep Le Ray, Marina, illus. (p. 1024)
—Magic Broom (p. 1072)
—Mr. Bones (p. 1184)
—No Peeking! (p. 1259)
—Number Munch! (p. 1271)
—Numbers under the Sea. Pitt, Sarah, illus. (p. 1272)
—Ocean Tails. Nelson, Judy, illus. (p. 1277)
—Old Woman Who Swallowed a Fly. (p. 1285)
—One Blue Fish: A Colorful Counting Book. Reasoner, Charles, illus. (p. 1294)
—Ooink! (p. 1298)
—Peek-A-Boo Dinosaurs Le Ray, Marina, illus. (p. 1334)
—Peek-a-Boo Dinosaurs. Le Ray, Marina, illus. (p. 1334)
—Peek-a-Boo Fairies Le Ray, Marina, illus. (p. 1334)
—Peek-a-Boo Fairies. Le Ray, Marina, illus. (p. 1334)
—Peek-A-Boo Ghosts. Le Ray, Marina & Jones, Anna, illus. (p. 1334)
—Peek-A-Boo Monsters Le Ray, Marina, illus. (p. 1334)
—Peek-a-Boo Monsters. Le Ray, Marina, illus. (p. 1334)
—Peek-A-Boo Pirates Le Ray, Marina, illus. (p. 1334)
—Peek-a-Boo Pirates. Le Ray, Marina, illus. (p. 1334)
—Peep! Peep! (p. 1335)
—Pumpkin Shapes. (p. 1416)
—Puppy Love. (p. 1418)
—Red Nose Go! (p. 1454)
—Red Nose Go! Jones, Anna, illus. (p. 1454)
—Reptiles. (p. 1461)
—Shapes at the Beach. Pitt, Sarah, illus. (p. 1560)
—Shapes for Lunch! (p. 1560)
—This Little Piggy Le Ray, Marina, illus. (p. 1737)
—This Little Piggy Jones, Anna & Le Ray, Marina, illus. (p. 1737)
—Twinkle, Twinkle, Little Star Le Ray, Marina, illus. (p. 1802)
—Whooo? (p. 1920)
—Winter Friends Reasoner, Charles & Jones, Anna, illus. (p. 1938)
—Winter Friends. Jones, Anna, illus. (p. 1938)
Reasoner, Charles, illus. see Beall, Pamela Conn & Nipp, Susan Hagen.
Reasoner, Charles, illus. see Cooke, Brandy.
Reasoner, Charles, illus. see Lee, Howard.
Reasoner, Charles, illus. see Thompson, Kate.
Reasoner, Charles & Taylor, Jane. Twinkle, Twinkle, Little Star Jones, Anna & Le Ray, Marina, illus. (p. 1802)
Reasoner, Charles & Wood, Hannah. Peek-A-Boo Elves Reasoner, Charles, illus. (p. 1334)
—Peek-A-Boo Reindeer Reasoner, Charles, illus. (p. 1334)
—Peek-A-Boo Santa Reasoner, Charles, illus. (p. 1334)
—Peek-A-Boo Snowman Reasoner, Charles, illus. (p. 1334)
Reasoner, Charles & Wood, Steven. Little Monster. (p. 1032)
—Owl's Halloween. (p. 1315)
—Scaredy Cat. (p. 1519)
Reasoner, Charles & Wormell, Christopher. Night Before Christmas. Wormell, Christopher, illus. (p. 1252)
Reasoner, Chuck & Reasoner, John. Humpty Dumpty. (p. 827)
Reasoner, John. Hey Diddle Diddle. (p. 774)
—Hickory Dickory Dock. (p. 775)
—Itsy Bitsy Spider. (p. 900)
—Jack & Jill. (p. 902)
—Little Tea Pot. (p. 1037)
—This Old Man! (p. 1737)
—Twinkle Twinkle Little Star. (p. 1802)
Reasoner, John, illus. see Cooke, Brandy.
Reasoner, John, illus. see Mckenzie, Precious.
Reasoner, John, illus. see Picou, Lin.
Reasoner, John, jt. auth. see Reasoner, Chuck.
Reasoner, Vic, ed. see Heer, Andy.
Reasor, Mick, illus. see Kleinhenz, Sydnie Meltzer.
Reasor, Mick, illus. see Meltzer Kleinhenz, Sydnie.
Reasor, Teresa J. Willy C. Sparks. (p. 1934)
Reaugh, Clair. Sammi & Friends - the Great Gidzit Adventure: Sammi & Friends Stories & Adventures. Reaugh, Clair, illus. (p. 1507)
Reaume, Christopher J. 10 Greatest Threats to Earth. (p. 1993)
Reaveley, Trevor, illus. see Bailey, Gerry.
Reaveley, Trevor, illus. see Nussbaum, Ben.
Reaveley, Trevor, jt. auth. see Bailey, Gerry.
Reavely, Trever, illus. see Bentley, Dawn.
Reavely, Trevor, illus. see Bentley, Dawn.
Reavely, Trevor, illus. see Nussbaum, Ben.
Reaves, Daniel, illus. see Hawes, Dorothy.
Reaves, Esther R. Gammy's Snow Queen. (p. 655)
Reaves, Janice. It's Kool to Be Smart & to Have God. (p. 897)
—Ser Inteligente y Tener a Dios en Tu Corazón Es Buena Ond. (p. 1552)
Reaves, Michael, jt. auth. see Altman, Steven-Elliot.
Reaves, Michael, jt. auth. see Gaiman, Neil.
Reaves, William P., jt. auth. see Rydberg, Viktor.
Reavis, Laura. Angel to Watch Over. (p. 74)
Reavis, Vicky 'A' Blevins. Night Before Christmas. (p. 1252)
Reay, Dave. Climate Change Begins at Home: Life on the Two-Way Street of Global Warming. (p. 332)
Rebal, Tara. Sarah Sue Smith: A Crooked Wharf Adventure. (p. 1514)
Rebbie, Kevin. Mr. Stinkas & the Little Cheese Shop. (p. 1186)
Rebboah, Julie. Magic Words: Discovering the Adventure of Reading. (p. 1074)
Rebboah, Julie A. Kindergarten Sight Word Reader. Brantz, Loryn, illus. (p. 957)
—Reproducible Kindergarten Sight Word Reader. Brantz, Loryn, illus. (p. 1461)
Rebecca, Amy. Healthy Habits: The Rainbow Food. (p. 758)
Rebecca Klemm Charitable Foundation, jt. auth. see Klemm, Rebecca.
Rebecca, Rivard, illus. see Zolty, Meredith.
Rebecca, Stead. When You Reach Me. (p. 1905)
Rebein, Alyssa Chase & Chase, Andra. Stanley's "This Is the Life!" Chase, Andra, illus. (p. 1640)
Rebello, Gleeson & Harisiades, Jamie. Darebone's Big Break. (p. 406)
—Darebone's Big Break (Hardcover) (p. 406)
Rebello, Kevin. Julia & Mckinley's Day at the Beach. (p. 932)
Rebelo, Gabriel Bastos. Let's Go To... Work!: the Let's Go! Children's Book Series. (p. 998)
Rebels Animation Team, illus. see Disney Book Group Staff & Hidalgo, Pablo.
Reber, Deborah. Chill: Stress-Reducing Techniques for a More Balanced, Peaceful You. (p. 305)
—Doable: The Girls' Guide to Accomplishing Just about Anything. (p. 458)
Reber, Deborah & Goode, Caroline. Love, Love, Love: Language of Love; Cupidity. (p. 1060)
Reber, Deborah & Taylor, Keren, eds. Bold Ink: Collected Voices of Women & Girls. (p. 208)
Reber, Jack. Ghost from the Schenectady Massacre: A Haunting from the Dutch Settlers. (p. 670)
Reber, Kelseyleigh. If I Fall: The Circle & Cross: Book One. (p. 853)
Reberg, Eveline. Redaccion (The Composition) (p. 1455)
Reberg, Evelyne. Roi des de la Tambouille. (p. 1485)
—Tom Tom et la impossible Na. (p. 1764)
—Tom Tom et les idees Explosi. (p. 1764)
—Vacances infernales Tom Tom. (p. 1829)
Rebert, Brenda. Rooster Went A' Walkin' (p. 1488)
Rebiai, Marcel. Islam, Israel, & the Church. (p. 891)
Rebik, Nan, jt. auth. see Hinkelman, Carole.
Rebis, Greg. Hunchback of Notre Dame. (p. 827)
Rebis, Greg, illus. see Hugo, Victor.
Rebis, Greg, illus. see Verne, Jules.
Rebman, Renée C. Addictions & Risky Behaviors: Cutting, Bingeing, Snorting, & Other Dangers. (p. 11)
—Anatomy of an Earthquake (p. 67)
Rebman, Renee C. Anteaters. (p. 89)
—Are You Doing Risky Things? Cutting, Bingeing, Snorting, & Other Dangers. (p. 97)
Rebman, Renée C. Articles of Confederation Rebman, Renée C., illus. (p. 104)
Rebman, Renee C. Cats. (p. 280)
—Cows. (p. 374)
—How Do Tornadoes Form? (p. 807)
—Rats. (p. 1440)
—Turtles & Tortoises. (p. 1799)
—Vultures. (p. 1851)
—Walruses. (p. 1855)
Rebmann, Charles. Christmas Stories from the Jersey Cape. (p. 315)
Rebora, Cecilia, illus. see Achor, Shawn & Blankson, Amy.
Rebora, Cecilia, illus. see Casale, Karen.
Rébora, Cecilia, illus. see Gadot, A. S.
RéBora, Cecilia, illus. see Harris, Trudy.
Reboul, Elyan, jt. auth. see Moureau, Yves.
Rebscher, Susanne. Julio César. Schleper, Frank, tr. from GER. (p. 932)
—Leonardo Da Vinci. (p. 992)
Rebus, Anna. Kangaroos. (p. 942)
—PiedsNoirs: Les Autochtones du Canada. Karvonen, Tanjah, tr. from ENG. (p. 1357)
—Victoria Falls: One of the World's Most Spectacular Waterfalls. (p. 1840)
Rebus, Anna & Kissock, Heather. Blackfoot. (p. 197)
Recasens, Elena, tr. see Vail, Rachel.
Rech, Lindsay Faith. It Started with a Dare. (p. 894)
Recheis, Käethe, et al. Lisa y el Gato Sin Nombre. Weck, Claudia de & Jiménez, Alberto, trs. (p. 1022)
Recher, Andrew, illus. see Stewart, Melissa.
Recher, Andrew, illus. see Vogel, Julia.
Rechin, Kevin. Guess Again! 1,001 Rib-Tickling Riddles from Highlights. (p. 728)
Rechin, Kevin, illus. see Coyle, Carmela Lavigna.
Rechin, Kevin, illus. see Winter, Max.
Rechlin, Ted. Build Your Own Giant Robots Super Sticker Book. (p. 238)
—Changing of the Guard: The Yellowstone Chronicles. (p. 290)
—ComicQuest TIME TRAVEL TROUBLE. (p. 348)
—Superheroes! (p. 1683)
—Superheroes Stained Glass Coloring Book. (p. 1683)
—What to Doodle? Manga! (p. 1894)
Rechlin, Ted & Coloring Books Staff. Build a Poster Coloring Book—Robots & Wreckage. (p. 238)
Rechlin, Ted & Paper Dolls. Robot Battle Paper Action Figures. (p. 1480)
Rechlin, Ted & Stickers. Mecha Robot Stickers. (p. 1118)
Rechner, Amy. In Crowd: Dealing with Peer Pressure. (p. 863)
—Massachusetts. (p. 1102)
—Wisconsin. (p. 1939)
Recio, Ricardo, illus. see Puncel, Maria.
Reckmeyer, Mary, jt. auth. see Rath, Tom.
Recob, Amy. BugaBees: Friends with Food Allergies. (p. 236)
Record, Adam, illus. see Dahl, Michael.
Record, Adam, illus. see Dybvik, Tina & Meister, Cari.
Record, Adam, illus. see Dybvik, Tina.
Record, Adam, illus. see Meister, Cari.
Record, Adam, illus. see Paquette, Ammi-Joan.
Record, Adam, illus. see Sachar, Louis.
Recorvits, H., jt. auth. see Recorvits, Helen.
Recorvits, Helen. Me Llama Yoon. Swiatkowska, Gabi, illus. (p. 1116)
—My Name Is Yoon. Swiatkowska, Gabi, illus. (p. 1215)
Recorvits, Helen & Recorvits, H. Yoon & the Jade Bracelet. Swiatkowska, Gabi, illus. (p. 1972)
Rectenbaugh, Marci, illus. see Adee, Donna & Adee, Ed.
Rector, Lori. Adventures of A. (p. 16)
Reczuch, Karen, illus. see Abley, Mark.
Reczuch, Karen, illus. see Andrews, Jan.
Reczuch, Karen, illus. see Griek, Susan Vande.
Reczuch, Karen, illus. see Hodge, Deborah.
Reczuch, Karen, illus. see LeBox, Annette.
Red Baklava, photos by see Avista Products.
Red Bird Press Staff. Amazing 3D Magic. (p. 52)
—Amazing Spaceships. (p. 55)
—Dinosaurs. (p. 444)
—Flying Machines. (p. 610)
—High Flyers. (p. 777)
—Secret Spex Dinosaurs. (p. 1544)
—Secret Spex Haunted House. (p. 1544)
—Secret Spex Treasure Hunt. (p. 1544)
—Space. (p. 1618)
Red Bird Press Staff, creator. Planets. (p. 1368)
Red Brick Learning Staff. Famous Firsts (p. 569)
Red Fox, jt. auth. see Battersea Dogs and Cats Home Staff.
Red Fox Picture Books Staff, jt. auth. see Battersea Dogs and Cats Home Staff.
Red Fox Picture Books Staff & Transworld Publishing Staff. Better Play Times. (p. 172)
Red Fox Staff, jt. auth. see Battersea Dogs and Cats Home Staff.
Red Fox Staff, jt. auth. see Battersea Dogs Home Staff.
Red Giraffe, Ltd Staff, jt. ed. see Publications International Ltd. Staff.
Reda, Jaime, illus. see Golden, Ryan.
Reda, Sheryl A. Forest Tree House. Barrett, Peter, illus. (p. 618)
Redbank, Tennant. Beauty: Aurora's Sleepy Kitty. (p. 154)
—Beauty: Aurora's Sleepy Kitten. Random House Disney Staff, illus. (p. 154)
—Beauty the Sleepiest Kitty. RH Disney Staff, illus. (p. 154)
—Blondie: Rapunzel's Royal Pony. RH Disney Staff, illus. (p. 200)
—Blondie the Royal Pony. RH Disney Staff, illus. (p. 200)
—Pumpkin: Cinderella's Dancing Pup (Disney Princess: Palace Pets) RH Disney Staff et al, illus. (p. 1416)
—Teacup: Belle's Star Pup. (p. 1710)
—Treasure: Ariel's Curious Kitten. (p. 1781)
—Treasure: Ariel's Curious Kitten (Disney Princess: Palace Pets) RH Disney Staff et al, illus. (p. 1781)
Redbank, Tennant, jt. auth. see Lagonegro, Melissa.
Redbank, Tennant, jt. auth. see Random House Disney Staff.
Redbank, Tennant, jt. auth. see RH Disney Staff.
Redbank, Tennant, et al. Disney Princess Little Golden Book Favorites: Volume 3 (Disney Princess) Tyminski, Lori & Ying, Victoria, illus. (p. 452)
Redd, Faye V. Mia & Her Kitten Sophie. (p. 1133)
Redd, Michael, ed. see Tess, Jennifer.
Redden, Vicki. Heroes in Training. (p. 773)
Redden, Vicki, et al. God's Amazing Creation. (p. 690)
Reddin, Brian. What Do Rabbits Think? And Other Fun Poems for Kids. Fox, Woody, illus. (p. 1882)
Redding, David Asbury. He Never Spoke Without a Parable: His Kingdom, Your Antagonist, It's up to You (p. 756)
Redding, Mary Lou. Power of a Focused Heart: 8 Life Lessons from the Beatitudes. (p. 1389)
Reddy, Prerana & Strauss, David, eds. Healthy Taste of Corona Cookbook. Mesalles, Monica, tr. (p. 759)
Reddy, Sneha, illus. see Harpan, Gaile.
Reddy, Sneha, illus. see Panks, Kristin & Harpan, Gaile.
Redeker, Kent. Larryboy & the Yodel Napper (p. 976)
Redeker, Kent, et al. Larryboy in the Attack of Outback Jack (p. 976)
Redel, Nicole, illus. see Session, Garry.
Redenbaugh, Vicki. Skar's Picnic ... A Bear's Tale. Redenbaugh, Vicki, illus. (p. 1583)
Redenbaugh, Vicki Jo, illus. see Lanton, Sandy.
Redenbaugh, Vicki Jo, illus. see Rouss, Sylvia A. & Lanton, Sandy.
Redenius, John. Escaping the Yard, the Little Adventure of a Puppy Named Splinter. (p. 535)
Redepenning, George. Adventures of Webster. (p. 24)
Redfern, Holly. Adventures of Remmington the Dog: An Unexpected Friend. Burton, Claudia, illus. (p. 22)
Redfern, Nicholas. Top Secret Government Archives: Missing Files & Conspiracy Paper Trails (p. 1769)
Redfern, Nick. Most Mysterious Places on Earth. (p. 1177)
—True Stories of Real-Life Monsters. (p. 1792)
—True Stories of Space Exploration Conspiracies. (p. 1792)
—True Stories of the Real Men in Black. (p. 1793)
Redfield, Robert. Social Anthropology: Robert Redfield. Wilcox, Clifford, ed. (p. 1604)
Redford, Margorie & Rice, Courtney. God's Baby Animals. Marlin, Kathryn, illus. (p. 690)
Redford, Marjorie. My Bible Says. Marlin, Kathryn, illus. (p. 1197)
Redford, Marjorie & Rice, Courtney. God's Special Rule. Burroughs, Scott, illus. (p. 692)
—I Love Church! Marlin, Kathryn, illus. (p. 842)
Redgrave, Roy. Adventures of Colonel Daffodil: Balkan Beginnings, Memorable Travels & Forgotten Conflicts. (p. 17)
Redgrave, Saoirse, jt. auth. see Delany, Shannon.
Redgrave, Saoirse & Delany, Shannon. Bargains & Betrayals: A 13 to Life Novel. (p. 139)
Redhead, Janet S. & Dale, Christine. Big Block of Chocolate. (p. 178)
Rediger, Pat. Soccer. (p. 1603)
Rediger, Pat, jt. auth. see Crats, Rennay.
Redinger, Anne. Chow Now Brown Cow: Storybook Cooking. (p. 311)
Redinger, Jacob, illus. see Butler, Amy.
Redinger, Robert. Sylvan Horn: Book One of the Sylvan Chord. (p. 1692)
Redlich, Ben. Who Flung Dung? (p. 1915)
Redlich, Ben, illus. see Sunderland, Alan.
Redlich, Ben, illus. see Thompson, Colin.
Redlin, Janice L. Saving the Natural World. (p. 1517)
Redlin, Janice L., ed. Land Abuse & Soil Erosion. (p. 973)
Redman, Beth. Soul Sister: The Truth about Being God's Girl. (p. 1614)
Redman, Charles, jt. auth. see Allen, Vivian Ogea.
Redman, Kati. Kate & the Fairy. (p. 944)
Redman, Mary. Wishing Tree. Rodriguez, Christina, illus. (p. 1940)
Redman, Matt, compiled by. Heart of Worship Files: Featuring Contributions by Some of Today's Most Experienced Lead Worshippers. (p. 760)
Redman-Waldeyer, Christine. Around the World with Rosalie. Adams, Marcella Ryan, illus. (p. 101)
Redmon, Angela M., illus. see Wyatt, Cherokee.
Redmon, Jaylyle. Gracie the Lop-Eared Burro. (p. 705)
Redmond, Caitriona. Wholesome: Feed Your Family Well for Less. (p. 1920)
Redmond, Diane. Joshua Cross. (p. 927)
—Most Beautiful Horse in the World. (p. 1177)
—Odyssey Smith, Barry, illus. (p. 1279)
—Odyssey. Smith, Barry, illus. (p. 1279)
—Peter & the Wolf: Band 09/Gold. Bendall-Brunello, John, illus. (p. 1346)
Redmond, Diane & Mould, Chris. Hercules - Superhero. (p. 769)
Redmond, Diane, contrib. by. Roley & the Rock Star. (p. 1485)
Redmond, E. S. Felicity Floo Visits the Zoo. Redmond, E. S., illus. (p. 581)
—Unruly Queen. Redmond, E. S., illus. (p. 1822)
Redmond, Ian. Gorilas. Anderson, Peter & Brighting, Geoff, illus. (p. 702)
Redmond, J. B., jt. auth. see Vaught, S. R.
Redmond, Jim. Oil Makes Gasoline Power. (p. 1282)
Redmond, Jim & Ross, D. J. Uniquely North Dakota (p. 1818)
Redmond, Lea. Connexio: A Game of Infinite Associations & Imagination. (p. 358)
Redmond, Mark L. Arty's Long Day. Ury, Laura, illus. (p. 105)
Redmond, Pamela Woods. Elf Dog. LaFrance, Debbie, illus. (p. 512)
Redmond, Shirley Raye. Blind Tom: The Horse Who Helped Build the Great Railroad. Bradley, Lois, illus. (p. 199)
—Bunyips. (p. 243)
—Cerberus. (p. 287)
—Fairies! (p. 562)
—Fairies! Hajdinjak-Krec, Marsela & Hansen, Red, illus. (p. 562)
—Hiroshima. (p. 781)
—Jersey Devil. (p. 914)

R

—Lewis & Clark: A Prairie Dog for the President. Manders, John, illus. (p. 1004)
—Mermaids. (p. 1128)
—Oak Island Treasure Pit. (p. 1274)
—Pigeon Hero! Ettinger, Doris, illus. (p. 1357)
—Princess & Her Pony Senturk, Burak, illus. (p. 1402)
—Tentacles! Tales of the Giant Squid. Barnard, Bryn, illus. (p. 1720)
—Tentacles! Tales of the Giant Squid. Barnard, Bryn, illus. (p. 1720)
Redmond, Shirley Raye, jt. auth. see Redmond, Shirley Raye.
Redmond, Shirley Raye, jt. ed. see Gale Editor.
Redmond, Shirley Raye & Ettinger, Doris. Pigeon Hero! (p. 1357)
Redmond, Shirley Raye & Redmond, Shirley Raye. Dog That Dug for Dinosaurs. Sullivan, Simon, illus. (p. 461)
Redmond, Shirley Raye, ed. Norse Mythology. (p. 1264)
Redmond, Stephanie L. Christian Kids Explore Biology. Taylor, David W., illus. (p. 312)
—Earth & Space. Taylor, David W., Jr. & Northcutt, Leslie L., illus. (p. 495)
Redmond, Valerie. Emma & the African Wishing Bead. Victoria, Kirton, illus. (p. 519)
Redmond, Zelie. Adventures of Sister Regina Marie: Sister Finds a Friend. (p. 23)
Rednose, Skiddles. Tale of the Land of Umble. (p. 1700)
Redoles, Marcela, tr. see Burke, David.
Redondo, Fernando, illus. see Reyes, Carlos Jose.
Redondo, Frank, illus. see Twain, Mark, pseud.
Redondo, Jesus, illus. see Auerbach, Annie.
Redondo, Jesus, illus. see Chanda, J-P.
Redondo, Jesus, illus. see Figueroa, Acton.
Redondo, Kurt. Treasure Map. (p. 1782)
Redondo, Nestor, illus. see Stoker, Bram.
Redpath, Dale, illus. see Hulme, Lucy V.
Redshaw, Louise, illus. see Young, Annemarie.
Redston, Chris & Cunningham, Gillie. Face2face Elementary Student's Book with CD-ROM/Audio CD & Workbook Pack Italian Edition. (p. 560)
—Face2face Pre-Intermediate Student's Book with CD-ROM/Audio CD & Workbook Pack Italian Edition. (p. 560)
Redstone Press Staff, jt. auth. see Seock Seo, Hong.
Redwine, C. J. Defiance. (p. 424)
—Deliverance. (p. 425)
Redwine, Connie. Story from Graandfather Tree. Keithline, Brian, illus. (p. 1657)
Reece, Bernadette. Nervy the Ghost. (p. 1241)
Reece, Colleen L. Last Page in the Diary. (p. 978)
—Wilderness Warriors. (p. 1931)
Reece, Colleen L. & DeMarco, Julie Reece. God Loves You Whoever You Are. Snider, K. C., illus. (p. 689)
Reece, Eva. Boinking Bubble MacHine. Davis, Shelley L. A., illus. (p. 208)
—Brownie Calf & the Barnyard Babies. Davis, Shelley La, illus. (p. 232)
Reece, Gregory L. Elvis Religion: The Cult of the King. (p. 517)
Reece, James A., illus. see Lovvorn, Ann R.
Reece, Julie. Crux. (p. 387)
Reece, Katherine E. Greeks: Leaders in Democracy. (p. 721)
—Israelites: The Lawgivers. (p. 893)
—Persians: Warriors of the Ancient World. (p. 1344)
—Phoenicians: The Mysterious Sea People. (p. 1351)
—Romans: Builders of an Empire. (p. 1486)
Reece, Maynard, illus. see Green, Ivah E.
Reece, P. J. Roxy (p. 1492)
—Smoke That Thunders. (p. 1594)
Reece, Richard. Bleeding Kansas. (p. 199)
—Korean War. (p. 967)
—Medicine. (p. 1119)
Reece, Richard, jt. auth. see Jasper, Rick.
Reece, William James. Great Hippo Migration. (p. 716)
Reed, A. W. Favourite Maori Legends. Hart, Roger, illus. (p. 578)
Reed, Adolph, ed. Ice. (p. 850)
Reed, Aleta, jt. auth. see Reed, Frank.
Reed, Amy. Beautiful. (p. 153)
—Clean. (p. 330)
—Crazy. (p. 377)
—Invincible. (p. 885)
—Over You. (p. 1314)
Reed, Amy Lynn. Beautiful. (p. 153)
Reed, Ananya Mukherjee. What Is Baptism? Learning about Baptism in the United Methodist Church. (p. 1889)
—What Is Communion? Learning about Communion in the United Methodist Church. (p. 1889)
Reed, Avery. Who Were the Brothers Grimm? O'Brien, John, illus. (p. 1919)
Reed, Bill, illus. see Epner, Paul.
Reed, Bliss & Reed, Sinclair. This Summer I Plan to Rule the World. (p. 1737)
Reed, Brian, jt. auth. see Casey, Joe.
Reed, C. & Antor, Max. SAT Exam Success in Only 6 Steps! (p. 1515)
Reed, C. W., illus. see Phelps, Elizabeth Stuart.
Reed, Christina. Earth Science: Decade by Decade. (p. 496)
Reed, Cleone, ed. see Norton, J. Renae.
Reed, Cristie. Bluetooth. (p. 204)
—Liberty Bell. (p. 1005)
—Look on the Bright Side. (p. 1049)
—Microwave Ovens. (p. 1137)
—Problem Solving. (p. 1408)
—Star Spangled Banner. (p. 1641)
Reed, David E. Culture of Service: Creating Superior Customer Service that Lasts! (p. 391)
Reed, Donn, jt. auth. see Reed, Jean.
Reed, Donna. Watchfrog Story. (p. 1861)
Reed, Emma & Reed, Jennifer. Romeo's Rescue. Movshina, Marina, illus. (p. 1486)
Reed, Eric Melvin, jt. ed. see Bloomfield, Susanne George.
Reed, Frank, illus. see Xavier, Imbeus & Sanders, Martin B.
Reed, Frank & Reed, Aleta. Caracol Llamado Slick / a Snail Named Slick. (p. 265)
—Snail Named Slick. (p. 1596)
Reed, Fred, jt. auth. see Ellis, Deborah.
Reed, G L. What Is the Lord's Prayer? Learning about the Lord's Prayer. Jeffrey, Megan, illus. (p. 1890)
Reed, Gary & Shelley, Mary. Puffin Graphics: Frankenstein. Irving, Frazer, illus. (p. 1415)
Reed, Gregory J. Dear Mrs. Parks: A Dialogue with Today's Youth. (p. 419)
Reed, Jaime. Fading Amber. (p. 562)
Reed, Janet. Animal Patterns. (p. 79)
—Brave Dave & the Dragons. Fraser, Kara-Anne, illus. (p. 223)
—Everyone Eats Bread! (p. 544)
—Parts of a Whole (p. 1325)
—Parts of a Whole. (p. 1325)
—¡Todos Comen Pan! (p. 1761)
Reed, Janet, jt. auth. see Bauer, David.
Reed, Janet, jt. auth. see Trumbauer, Lisa.
Reed, Jean & Reed, Donn. Home School Source Book. (p. 792)
Reed, Jenn, Jonathan/Hale. Animal Alphabet: Sticker Activity Book. (p. 76)
—Rainy Day Sticker Activity Book. (p. 1436)
Reed, Jennifer. AIDS Epidemic: Disaster & Survival. (p. 30)
—Armada de EE. UU. (p. 99)
—Bombarderos. (p. 208)
—Cape Hatteras National Seashore: Adventure, Explore, Discover. (p. 262)
—Daring American Heroes of Flight: Nine Brave Fliers. (p. 406)
—Earthquakes: Disaster & Survival. (p. 497)
—Elizabeth Bloomer: Child Labor Activist. (p. 513)
—Falling Flowers. Cole, Dick, illus. (p. 566)
—Hadi's Journey. (p. 735)
—Infantería de Marina de EE. UU. (p. 873)
—Kansas: A MyReportLinks. Com Book. (p. 943)
—Leonardo da Vinci: Genius of Art & Science. (p. 992)
—Louisiana: A MyReportLinks. Com Book. (p. 1058)
—Marineros de la Armada de EE. UU. (p. 1094)
—Marines de la Infantería de Marina de EE. UU. (p. 1094)
—Marines of the U. S. Marine Corps. (p. 1094)
—Marines of the U. S. Marine Corps [Scholastic]. (p. 1094)
—Sailors of the U. S. Navy (p. 1503)
—Sailors of the U. S. Navy [Scholastic]. (p. 1503)
—That's Not Fair! Dufalla, Anita, illus. (p. 1727)
—Time for a Trim. Mones, Marc, illus. (p. 1751)
—U. S. Marine Corps. (p. 1806)
—U. S. Marine Corps [Scholastic]. (p. 1806)
—U. S. Navy. (p. 1807)
—U. S. Navy [Scholastic]. (p. 1807)
—Wilbur & Orville Wright: Trailblazers of the Sky. (p. 1928)
Reed, Jennifer, jt. auth. see Reed, Emma.
Reed, Jennifer Bond. Doodle Girl. Foster, Jack, illus. (p. 469)
—Saudi Royal Family. (p. 1516)
—That's a Lot of Love. Houdeshell, Jennifer Thomas, illus. (p. 1726)
Reed, Jim, photos by see Davies, Jon.
Reed, Joel B. Grandpa's New Kitty. Reed, Joel B., illus. (p. 710)
Reed, John. All the World's a Grave: A New Play. Reed, John, ed. (p. 46)
—Coming Wrath. (p. 348)
—Ten Days That Shook the World. (p. 1718)
Reed, Jonathan. Christmas Surprise. Hale, Jenny, illus. (p. 315)
Reed, Jonathan & Hale, Jenny. Christmas Surprise. (p. 315)
Reed, Ken. Sara's Big Challenge: Who's the Real Me? A Sara Thompson Sports Book. (p. 1514)
Reed, Kevin. Dog's Guide to Surfing: Hanging Ten with Man's Best Friend. Crump, A. K., ed. (p. 463)
Reed, Kit. Dogs of Truth. (p. 463)
Reed, Kyle, illus. see Apte, Sunita.
Reed, Latonya. Charlie the Lonely Whale. (p. 293)
Reed, Len. Monsters at My Bed. (p. 1169)
Reed, Linda Davis, illus. see Snavlin, Joyce Burgess.
Reed, Lisa, illus. see Adams, Michelle Medlock.
Reed, Lisa, illus. see Fritz, Greg.
Reed, Lisa, illus. see Moore, Karen.
Reed, Lisa, illus. see Rollins, Jack & Nelson, Steve.
Reed, Lisa, illus. see Rumbaugh, Melinda.
Reed, Lisa, illus. see Schaefer, Peggy.
Reed, Lisa, illus. see Stortz, Diane.
Reed, Lisa, illus. see Traditional.
Reed, Lisa, illus. see Vischer, Phil.
Reed, Lynn. Shannon's Search for the Lost Ark. (p. 1559)
Reed, Lynn Rowe. Basil's Birds (p. 142)
—Color Chaos! Reed, Lynn Rowe, illus. (p. 342)
—Fireman Fred. Reed, Lynn Rowe, illus. (p. 592)
—Fireman Jack. (p. 592)
—Oliver, the Spaceship, & Me. (p. 1285)
—Please Don't Upset P. U. Zorilla. (p. 1373)
—Roscoe & the Pelican Rescue. Reed, Lynn Rowe, illus. (p. 1489)
—Shark Kiss, Octopus Hug. Cornell, Kevin, illus. (p. 1562)
—Swim to the Moon. (p. 1691)
Reed, Lynn Rowe, illus. see Kanninen, Barbara.
Reed, Lynn Rowe, illus. see Pearson, Debora.
Reed, Lynn Rowe, illus. see Pulver, Robin.
Reed, Lynn Rowe, jt. auth. see Pulver, Robin.
Reed, M. K. Americus. Hill, Jonathan David, illus. (p. 64)
Reed, Master Amy. Adventures of A Dragon Named Ryung: Journey to Black Belt. (p. 16)
Reed, Mike, illus. see Bollard, John K. & Bollard, John.
Reed, Mike, illus. see Clements, Andrew.
Reed, Mike, illus. see Greenburg, J. C.
Reed, Mike, illus. see Kilgras, Heidi.
Reed, Mike, illus. see MacLean, Christine.
Reed, Mike, illus. see Myers, Tim.
Reed, Mike, illus. see Nolan, Lucy.
Reed, Mike, illus. see Sauer, Tammi.
Reed, Mike, illus. see Williams-Garcia, Rita.
Reed, Mike, tr. see Greenburg, J. C.
Reed, Natasha. Mythical Creatures: Sticker Book. Kincaid, Angela, illus. (p. 1227)
Reed, Nathan. Buskers of Bremen: Big Book English Only. (p. 245)
—Buskers of Bremen. (p. 245)
Reed, Nathan, illus. see Barkow, Henriette.
Reed, Nathan, illus. see Friel, Maeve.
Reed, Nathan, illus. see Sykes, Julie.
Reed, Nathan, illus. see Weatherly, Lee.
Reed, Nathan, jt. auth. see Emmett, Jonathan.
Reed, Nathan, jt. auth. see Shields, Gillian.
Reed, Nathan, jt. illus. see Barkow, Henriette.
Reed, Nathaniel J. Benny the Amazing Bird Visits Grandma & Grandpa Green. (p. 165)
—Grandma & Grandpa Green's Mattress Ride. (p. 708)
Reed, Neil, illus. see Shone, Rob.
Reed, Neil, illus. see Twain, Mark, pseud.
Reed, Nicole. Ruining You. Giblin, Erinn, ed. (p. 1494)
Reed, Patricia. Mousetrap. (p. 1182)
Reed, Phil. Extraordinary Grace. (p. 555)
Reed, Rebecca, illus. see Spencer, Jamie.
Reed, Rebecca Harrison, illus. see Plourde, Lynn.
Reed, Robert. Greetings from Ohio: Vintage Postcards 1900-1960s (p. 723)
Reed, Rosemary. Snow Painting: Chinese Brush Painting Brekke, Robert & James, Midge, eds. (p. 1599)
Reed, Sharon. Tara: Prairie Horse Series. (p. 1706)
Reed, Sinclair, jt. auth. see Reed, Bliss.
Reed, Stephanie. Light Across the River (p. 1014)
Reed, Stephen, illus. see Brallier, Max.
Reed, Stephen, illus. see Lewman, David.
Reed, Stephen, illus. see Luper, Eric.
Reed, Stuart. Oracle Edge: How Oracle Corporation's Take-No-Prisoners Strategy Has Created an $8 Billion Software Powerhouse. (p. 1301)
Reed, Susan. Up, up, Up! Oldfield, Rachel, illus. (p. 1824)
Reed, Susan, illus. see McDonald, Jill.
Reed, Susan, illus. see Oldfield, Rachel.
Reed, T. Home for Garth. (p. 792)
Reed, T. K. Quasar & the Eye of the Serpent. (p. 1423)
Reed, Talbot Baines. Boycotted & Other Stories. (p. 220)
Reed, Tanya Jo. Daddy-O. (p. 398)
Reed, Tom. Pookus & Buckie: A Children's Book Based on a True Story. Carter, Sandy Lewis, illus. (p. 1383)
Reed, Tracey. Isaiah Has the Bedtime Blues. (p. 891)
Reed, Vernon. Children of the Hollow. (p. 302)
Reed, Wilfred. Andy & Mark & the Time Machine: Custer's Last Stand. (p. 72)
Reed, Winifred. Ladybugs of Wisteria Hollow. (p. 971)
—Razi vs Vego: An Animal's Tale of Bullying. (p. 1441)
Reeder. Animals of the Arctic & Antarctic: Level O (p. 83)
Reeder, Carolyn. Moonshiner's Son. O'Brien, Tim, illus. (p. 1173)
—Secret Project Notebook. (p. 1543)
Reeder Eubank, Patricia. Countdown to Christmas. (p. 370)
—Gifts They Gave. (p. 676)
Reeder, Kim Cooley. Runaway Tomato. Agnew, Lincoln, illus. (p. 1496)
Reeder, Larry. Great Raccoon Meets the Veterinarian. McCord, David, illus. (p. 718)
Reeder, Red. Whispering Wind: A Story of the Massacre at Sand Creek. Wilson, Charles Banks, illus. (p. 1912)
Reed-Guldin, Emily. Sarah & Sammi's Playhouse: Mermaid Adventure. (p. 1514)
Reed-Jones, C, et al. Arbol Del Viejo Bosque. (p. 94)
Reed-jones, Carol. Hildegard of Bingen: Woman of Vision. (p. 779)
—Salmon Stream. Maydak, Michael S., illus. (p. 1505)
Reedy, Trent. Burning Nation. (p. 244)
—Divided We Fall. (p. 454)
—If You're Reading This. (p. 855)
—Stealing Air. (p. 1646)
—Words in the Dust. (p. 1951)
Reef, Catherine. Brontë Sisters: The Brief Lives of Charlotte, Emily, & Anne. (p. 230)
—E. E. Cummings: A Poet's Life. (p. 492)
—Education & Learning in America. (p. 505)
—Ernest Hemingway: A Writer's Life. (p. 533)
—Frida & Diego: Art, Love, Life. (p. 637)
—George Gershwin: American Composer. (p. 663)
—Jane Austen: A Life Revealed. (p. 908)
—Leonard Bernstein & American Music. (p. 992)
—Life of Paul Laurence Dunbar: Portrait of a Poet. (p. 1012)
—Noah Webster: Man of Many Words. (p. 1261)
—Poetry Came in Search of Me: The Story of Pablo Neruda. (p. 1376)
—Poverty in America. (p. 1389)
—William Grant Still: African-American Composer. (p. 1933)
Reef, Sharon. Believe in Your Self: An Ancient Sage in a Modern World. (p. 161)
Reeg, Cynthia. Gifts from God. Roberts, MarySue, photos by. (p. 675)
—Hamster Holidays: Noun & Adjective Adventures. Grady, Kit, illus. (p. 739)
—Kitty Kerplunking: Preposition Fun. (p. 963)
—Kitty Kerplunking: Preposition Fun. Movshina, Marina, illus. (p. 963)
Reekie, Jocelyn. Week of the Horse. (p. 1871)
Reekles, Beth. Kissing Booth. (p. 962)
Reel FX Inc. Staff, illus. see Evans, Cordelia.
Reel FX Inc. Staff, illus. see Pendergrass, Daphne.
Reel FX Inc. Staff, et al. Tale of Two Friends. (p. 1700)
Reely, Mary Katharine. Blue Mittens. Wiese, Kurt, illus. (p. 203)
Rees, Amanda. Great Plains Region (p. 717)
Rees, Bob. Civil War (p. 325)
Rees, Celia. A Is for Apparition. (p. 1)
—Fool's Girl. (p. 614)
—Ghost Chamber. (p. 670)
—Haunts: H Is for Haunting. (p. 754)
—Haunts: N Is for Nightmare. Vol. 4 (p. 754)
—Pirates! (p. 1363)
—Pirates. (p. 1363)
—Pirates! The True & Remarkable Adventures of Minerva Sharpe & Nancy Kington, Female Pirates. (p. 1363)
—Sovay. (p. 1618)
—This Is Not Forgiveness. (p. 1736)
—U Is for Unbeliever. (p. 1805)
—Wish House. (p. 1940)
—Witch Child. (p. 1941)
Rees, Celia & Bacchin, Giorgio. Tear Jar. (p. 1711)
Rees, Douglas. Jeannette Claus Saves Christmas. Latyk, Olivier, illus. (p. 911)
—Uncle Pirate. Auth, Tony, illus. (p. 1812)
—Uncle Pirate to the Rescue. Auth, Tony, illus. (p. 1812)
—Vampire High. (p. 1832)
Rees, Dylan & Townson, Duncan. France in Revolution. (p. 627)
Rees, Fran. Johannes Gutenberg: Inventor of the Printing Press (p. 920)
Rees, Glyn, et al. Dolig Llawen! (p. 463)
Rees, Gwyneth. Cosmo & the Great Witch Escape Hearn, Samuel, illus. (p. 368)
—Cosmo & the Magic Sneeze Hearn, Samuel, illus. (p. 368)
—Cosmo & the Secret Spell Hearn, Samuel, illus. (p. 368)
—Fairy Dreams: A Magical Journey to Fairyland. Vol. 1 (p. 563)
—Fairy Dust (p. 563)
—Fairy Gold (p. 563)
—Fairy Rescue (p. 564)
—Fairy Treasure: A Fairy Who Needs a Friend. Vol. 1 Bannister, Emily, illus. (p. 564)
—My Mum's from Planet Pluto (p. 1215)
—My Super Sister Monks, Lydia & Okstad, Ella, illus. (p. 1219)
Rees, Janet, jt. auth. see Moseley, Cherri.
Rees, Jonathan. Drugs (p. 487)
—Drugs. (p. 487)
Rees, Lesley. How to Be a Pirate in 7 Days or Less. Lewis, Jan, illus. (p. 814)
Rees, Mary, illus. see Oram, Hiawyn.
Rees, Mary, illus. see Patterson, Rebecca.
Rees, Peter. How Does It Fly? The Science of Flight. (p. 808)
—Liberty: Blessing or Burden? (p. 1005)
—Secrets of the Space Shuttle. (p. 1546)
—Why Do Crocodiles Snap? Level 3 Factbook. (p. 1923)
—Why Do Raindrops Fall? Level 3 Factbook. (p. 1924)
—Why Do Swings Swing? Level 4 Factbook. (p. 1924)
—Why Does Water Freeze? Level 3 Factbook. (p. 1924)
Rees, Rebecca. It Is Good to Be a Part of All This: Stories of a Small Part in the Great Work. (p. 894)
Rees, Rob. Backyard Cookbook. (p. 131)
Rees, Rosemary. Ancient Egyptians (p. 69)
—Aztecs (p. 122)
Rees, Rosemary & Shephard, Colin. Crime & Punishment Investigations. (p. 382)
—OCR Medieval History: Raiders & Invaders; Power & Control. (p. 1277)
Rees, Susan. First Adventure of Baby Bee. (p. 592)
Rees, Susan A. P. Pine Cone Wishing Tree. (p. 1359)
Rees, Wilbur. Growing up Crooked. (p. 726)
Reese, Amy. Illustrated Psalms of Praise: Psalmos de Albanza Ilustrados. (p. 858)
Reese, Anita. Learn to Read with Sign Language: Letters & Sounds. (p. 984)
—Learn to Read with Sign Language: Basic Sight Words. (p. 984)
Reese, Bob, illus. see Karapetkova, Holly & Moreta, Gladys.
Reese, Bob, illus. see Karapetkova, Holly & Picou, Lin.
Reese, Bob, illus. see Karapetkova, Holly & Robins, Maureen.
Reese, Bob, illus. see Moreta, Gladys & Picou, Lin.
Reese, Bob, illus. see Picou, Lin & Moreta, Gladys.
Reese, Bob, illus. see Picou, Lin.
Reese, Bob, illus. see Robbins, Maureen & Steinkraus, Kyla.
Reese, Bob, illus. see Robbins, Maureen.
Reese, Bob, illus. see Spaht-Gill, Janie.
Reese, Bob, illus. see Steinkraus, Kyla & Moreta, Gladys.
Reese, Bob, illus. see Steinkraus, Kyla.
Reese, Brandon. Draw Me Healthy! Reese, Brandon, illus. (p. 481)
Reese, Brandon, illus. see Flash Kids Editors, ed.
Reese, Elvera. Luminar. (p. 1065)
Reese, Erica. My Almighty Daddy. (p. 1195)
Reese, Honey. Inti, the Very Helpful Llama. (p. 881)
Reese, Jacob. Copperweight. (p. 366)
Reese, Jenn. Above World. (p. 6)
—Horizon. (p. 797)
—Mirage. (p. 1149)
Reese, Jonathan, illus. see Taylor, Trace, et al.
Reese, Kevin M., adapted by. Chicken Little Henny Penny. (p. 300)
—Chicken Little Henny Penny (Non-Musical Version) (p. 300)
—Pied Piper. (p. 1356)
—Pied Piper (Non-Musical Version) (p. 1356)
—Tom Sawyer: Musical Version. (p. 1763)
—Tom Sawyer: Non-Musical Version. (p. 1763)
—True Story of the Tortoise & the Hare. (p. 1793)
—True Story of the Tortoise & the Hare (Non-Musical Version) (p. 1793)
Reese Martin, Faith. Ghost Train to Freedom: An Adventure on the Underground Railroad. Sachs, Barry, illus. (p. 672)
Reese, Mary. Bio 1023 Plants & Humans: Note-Taking Manual. (p. 188)
Reese, Michael. Christmas Party on the Farm. (p. 315)
Reese, Pam Britton & Challenner, Nena C. Autism & PDD Expanding Social Options (p. 117)
Reese, Rhonda. Praisekid Just Like Jesus. (p. 1393)
Reese, Rick, illus. see Markel, Michelle.
Reese, Rick, illus. see Mooser, Stephen.
Reese, Steven, tr. see Manzano, Roberto.
Rees-Jones, Paul. Silly Animal World! (p. 1575)
Reeve, Christine E. Functional Vocabulary for Children Ben Likes All Kinds of Sports. (p. 649)
—Functional Vocabulary for Children Dontel Learns about Transportation. (p. 649)
—Functional Vocabulary for Children Jasmine Sets the Table. (p. 649)
—Functional Vocabulary for Children Kira Likes to Go to Schools. (p. 649)
—Functional Vocabulary for Children Michelle Goes for a Walk. (p. 649)
—Functional Vocabulary for Children Sarah Goes to Bed. (p. 649)

—Functional Vocabulary for Children Tyler Gets Cleaned Up. (p. 649)
Reeve, Elizabeth. Sassy: the short stories of being a service Dog. (p. 1515)
Reeve, Elizabeth, jt. auth. see Verdick, Elizabeth.
Reeve, Penny. Back Leg of a Goat: A Tania Abbey Adventure. Apps, Fred, illus. (p. 130)
—Himalayan Adventures. (p. 780)
—Water or Goo? Apps, Fred, illus. (p. 1863)
Reeve, Philip. Cakes in Space. McIntyre, Sarah, illus. (p. 252)
—Darkling Plain. (p. 408)
—Fever Crumb. (p. 583)
—Fever Crumb: a Web of Air. (p. 583)
—Goblins. (p. 688)
—Here Lies Arthur. (p. 770)
—Infernal Devices. (p. 873)
—Larklight: A Rousing Tale of Dauntless Pluck in the Farthest Reaches of Space. Wyatt, David, illus. (p. 975)
—No Such Thing As Dragons. (p. 1260)
—No Such Thing as Dragons. (p. 1260)
—Oliver & the Seawigs. McIntyre, Sarah, illus. (p. 1285)
—Predator Cities #3: Infernal Devices. (p. 1394)
—Predator's Gold. (p. 1395)
—Scrivener's Moon. (p. 1533)
—Starcross: A Stirring Adventure of Spies, Time Travel & Curious Hats. Wyatt, David, illus. (p. 1642)
—Web of Air. (p. 1870)
Reeve, Philip, illus. see d'Lacey, Chris.
Reeve, Philip, jt. auth. see Poskitt, Kjartan.
Reeve, Rosie. Lullaby Moon. Reeve, Rosie, illus. (p. 1064)
—Rory & the Monstersitter. (p. 1488)
—Training Tallulah. (p. 1777)
Reeve, Rosie, illus. see Oram, Hiawyn.
Reeve, Rosie, illus. see Payne, Jan & Payne, Tony.
Reeve, Rosie, illus. see Symes, Ruth Louise.
Reeve, Tim. Action Robots: A Pop-up Book Showing How They Work. MacLeod, Gavin, illus. (p. 10)
Reeve, Tony, illus. see Oliver, Martin.
Reeve, Tony, tr. see Oliver, Martin.
Reevely, Lorna, jt. auth. see Bardswich, Miriam.
Reeves. Day by Day Bible Daily Devotions for Reading with Children. (p. 412)
Reeves, Amy Carol. Resurrection. (p. 1464)
—Ripper. (p. 1474)
Reeves, Barbara. Grandpa's Crooked Smile: A Story of Stroke Survival. Sinclair, Peter, illus. (p. 709)
Reeves, Bob. ICT Interact for KS3. (p. 851)
Reeves, Brian & Robinson, Craig. Pre-Calculus Student Activity Book. Matthews, Douglas L., ed. (p. 1394)
Reeves, Claire. Adventures of Boots the One Eyed Cat (p. 16)
Reeves, Dale, ed. see Burgen, Jim.
Reeves, Dia. Bleeding Violet: Niemals War Wahnsinn So Verführerisch. (p. 199)
—Bleeding Violet. (p. 199)
—Slice of Cherry. (p. 1590)
Reeves, Diane Lindsey. Career Ideas for Kids Who Like Adventure & Travel. Bond, Nancy, illus. (p. 266)
—Career Ideas for Kids Who Like Animals & Nature. Bond, Nancy, illus. (p. 266)
—Career Ideas for Kids Who Like Art. Bond, Nancy, illus. (p. 266)
—Career Ideas for Kids Who Like Math & Money. Bond, Nancy, illus. (p. 266)
—Career Ideas for Kids Who Like Music & Dance. (p. 266)
—Career Ideas for Kids Who Like Science. Bond, Nancy, illus. (p. 266)
—Career Ideas for Kids Who Like Sports. Bond, Nancy, illus. (p. 266)
—Career Ideas for Teens in Architecture & Construction. (p. 266)
—Career Ideas for Teens in Education & Training. (p. 266)
—Career Ideas for Teens in Health Science. (p. 267)
—Career Ideas for Teens in Information Technology. (p. 267)
—Career Ideas for Teens in Law & Public Safety. (p. 267)
—Career Ideas for Teens in Manufacturing. (p. 267)
—Career Ideas for Teens in Science, Technology, Engineering, & Math. (p. 267)
—Career Ideas for Teens in the Arts & Communications. (p. 267)
—Career Ideas for Teens Set. (p. 267)
—Firefighter. (p. 591)
—Glamorous Jobs. (p. 682)
—Goofy Jobs. (p. 702)
—Gross Jobs. (p. 725)
—Gutsy Jobs. (p. 733)
—Health Science. (p. 758)
—TV Journalist. (p. 1799)
—Way Out Work Set, 6-Volumes. (p. 1864)
Reeves, Diane Lindsey & Clasen, Lindsey. Career Ideas for Kids Who Like Writing. Bond, Nancy, illus. (p. 266)
Reeves, Diane Lindsey & Gunzenhauser, Kelly. Career Ideas for Teens in Marketing. (p. 267)
Reeves, Diane Lindsey & Karlitz, Gail. Author. (p. 117)
—Career Ideas for Teens in Education & Training. (p. 266)
—Information Technology. (p. 874)
Reeves, Diane Lindsey, et al. Career Ideas for Kids Who Like Computers. Bond, Nancy, illus. (p. 266)
—Career Ideas for Teens in Information Technology. (p. 267)
Reeves, Don. Can Do It. (p. 258)
Reeves, Eira. Dios Te Ama. (p. 445)
—Jesus & Me Every Day Book 1 (p. 915)
—Oraciones a la Hora de Dormir (Prayers at Bedtime) (p. 1301)
—Padre Nuestro (The Lord's Prayer) (p. 1317)
—Yo Soy Valiente. (p. 1971)
Reeves, Heather. My Big Brother, He's My Best Friend (p. 1197)
Reeves, Janet. Acorn Treasure. (p. 9)
Reeves, Jeni, illus. see Brown, Susan Taylor.
Reeves, Jeni, illus. see Douglass, Susan L.
Reeves, Jeni, illus. see Fishman, Cathy Goldberg.
Reeves, Jeni, illus. see Krensky, Stephen.
Reeves, Jeni, illus. see Patrick, Jean L. S.
Reeves, Jeni, illus. see Ransom, Candice.
Reeves, Laura. Best Friend Necklace. (p. 169)
Reeves, Louise, illus. see Ohanian, Armineh.
Reeves, Pamela. Numbers All in a Row. LaGrange, Tiffany, illus. (p. 1272)
—United We Stand, a Story about Two Bullies. LaGrange, Tiffany, illus. (p. 1820)
Reeves, Patrick, jt. auth. see Madlener, Michael.
Reeves, Rick, illus. see Rappaport, Doreen & Verniero, Joan C.
Reeves, Ruth, illus. see Cooper, Paul Fenimore.
Reeves, Sue, illus. see Goldsack, Gaby.
Reeves, Thomas. I Had a Cat. (p. 838)
Reeves, William P., jt. auth. see Rydberg, Viktor.
Reference, Brown. Exploring the World of Reptiles & Amphibians, 6-Volume Set (p. 554)
Reffett, Frances. Insectaside. Losh, Eric, illus. (p. 875)
Refrolo, C. T. Grandchild of Mine: You & I. (p. 707)
Rega, Joseph & Layton, Rebecca. Arab-American & Muslim Writers. (p. 94)
Regalado, Jojo. Angel of Christ? My Little Tom Tom Book 3. (p. 73)
Regan, Dana, illus. see Berry, Eileen M.
Regan, Dana, illus. see Berry, Joy.
Regan, Dana, illus. see Buller, Jon & Warner, Sally.
Regan, Dana, illus. see Ellis, Gwen.
Regan, Dana, illus. see English, June.
Regan, Dana, illus. see Hapka, Catherine, pseud.
Regan, Dana, illus. see Hawley, Greg.
Regan, Dana, illus. see Hoena, Blake.
Regan, Dana, illus. see Kennedy, Nancy B.
Regan, Dana, illus. see McKissack, Patricia C. & McKissack, Fredrick L.
Regan, Dana, illus. see Moncure, Jane Belk.
Regan, Dana, illus. see Rosa-Mendoza, Gladys.
Regan, Dana, illus. see Steigemeyer, Julie.
Regan, Dana, illus. see StJohn, Amanda.
Regan, Dian Curtis. Barnyard Slam. Meisel, Paul, illus. (p. 140)
—Dragon Stone Curtis, Stacy, illus. (p. 478)
—Princess Nevermore. (p. 1404)
—Snow Blew Inn. Cushman, Doug, illus. (p. 1598)
—Space Boy & His Dog. Neubecker, Robert, illus. (p. 1618)
—World According to Kaley. (p. 1953)
Regan, Gregory. Boy with the Iron Will. (p. 220)
Regan Gregson, Susan. Cyber Literacy: Evaluating the Reliability of Data. (p. 396)
Regan, Laura, illus. see Fredericks, Anthony D.
Regan, Laura, illus. see Marzollo, Jean.
Regan, Lisa. Animal Riddles. (p. 79)
—Ballet Dancer. (p. 134)
—Big Cat, Little Cat. (p. 180)
—Bloodsucking Beasts. (p. 201)
—Broadway Star. (p. 230)
—Bugs. Roberts, Steve, illus. (p. 237)
—Circus Performer. (p. 322)
—Cool Kid's Field Guide to Space. Bull, Peter, illus. (p. 363)
—Cool Kid's Field Guide to Weather. Hutchinson, Tim, illus. (p. 363)
—Dinosaur Puzzles. (p. 442)
—Farm Animals. Thompson, Kim, illus. (p. 573)
—Farmyard Riddles. (p. 575)
—Fun Kits Make Your Own Finger Puppets. (p. 648)
—Horses. Jackson, Ian, illus. (p. 800)
—How to Draw Baby Animals. Roberts, Steve, illus. (p. 817)
—How to Draw Bugs. Roberts, Steve, illus. (p. 817)
—Lunchtime Riddles. (p. 1065)
—Magician. (p. 1075)
—Micro Model Battle Bots. (p. 1136)
—Monster Puzzles. (p. 1168)
—Monsters: Over 1000 Reusable Stickers! (p. 1168)
—Movie Star. (p. 1183)
—One Direction Tattoo Activity Book: With 24 Amazing Temporary Tattoos to Wear & Share. (p. 1294)
—Pirate Puzzles. (p. 1363)
—Pop Star. (p. 1384)
—Princess Puzzles. (p. 1405)
—Totally Brilliant Puzzle & Drawing Book: Can You Be the First to Spot the Yellow Pencil? (p. 1771)
—Totally Brilliant Super Puzzle Book. (p. 1771)
—Underwater Riddles. (p. 1817)
—Watch Out Below! 3-D Battle of the Sharks. (p. 1861)
Regan, Lisa, illus. see Elliot, Rachel.
Regan, Lisa, jt. auth. see Carlton Publishing Group Staff.
Regan, Lisa, jt. auth. see Carlton Publishing Group.
Regan, Lisa, jt. auth. see Carlton.
Regan, Lisa, jt. auth. see McCall, Gerrie.
Regan, Lisa & Anniss, Matt. Being a Dj. (p. 160)
Regan, Lisa & McNab, Chris. Urban Myths & Legendary Creatures. (p. 1825)
Regan, Marti. Lazy Daisy, the Love Dog. (p. 981)
Regan, Patrick. Nutcracker. Kuricheva, Natasha, illus. (p. 1274)
Regan, Peter. Fresh Start. Myler, Terry, illus. (p. 636)
—Riverside: The Spy. (p. 1476)
—Riverside: The Movie. (p. 1476)
—Riverside: Exit Point. (p. 1476)
—Riverside: Spring Fever. (p. 1476)
—Riverside: The Curse. Myler, Terry, illus. (p. 1476)
—Shannon Harps. Myler, Terry, illus. (p. 1559)
—Something New Myler, Terry, illus. (p. 1610)
Regan, Shaun, jt. auth. see Hammond, Brean.
Regard, Jady. Born to be a Longhorn. (p. 214)
—Born to be an Aggie. (p. 214)
Regelson, Abraham. Doll's Journey to Eretz Yisrael. Tel-Oren, Sharona, tr. from HEB. (p. 464)
—Dolls' Journey to Eretz-yisrael. Sharona, Tel-Oren, tr. (p. 464)
Regenold, Theresa. Not Your Average Princess: A Real-Life Fairy Tale. (p. 1267)
Reger, Jill, photos by see Costanzo, Charlene A. & Costanzo, Charlene.
Reger, Rob. Emily the Strange: The 13th Hour. (p. 519)
—Emily the Strange: Las apariencias Engañan. Vol. 4 (p. 519)
—Emily the Strange Reger, Rob & Brooks, Brian, illus. (p. 519)
—Emily's Secret Book of Strange. (p. 519)
—Libro Secreto de las Cosas Extranas. Reger, Rob, illus. (p. 1007)
Reger, Rob & Gruner, Jessica. Dark Times. Reger, Rob & Parker, Buzz, illus. (p. 408)
—Emily the Strange: Piece of Mind. Reger, Rob & Parker, Buzz, illus. (p. 519)
—Lost Days. Reger, Rob & Parker, Buzz, illus. (p. 1055)
—Piece of Mind. Reger, Rob & Parker, Buzz, illus. (p. 1356)
—Stranger & Stranger. Reger, Rob & Parker, Buzz, illus. (p. 1665)
Reger, Rob & Huehner, Mariah. Battle of the Bands. Gibbons, Jim, ed. (p. 146)
—Breaking the Record Farris, Cat, illus. (p. 225)
Reggie, Richard J. Boogerland. (p. 210)
Reggie-Foster, Debbi. It's Cool to Be Me! Mini Stories about. (p. 896)
Regholec, C. A. T. Elephant That Forgot to Remember. (p. 511)
Regin, Andrew. Guardians: Volume 1. (p. 728)
Regina Press Staff. Old Testament for Children. (p. 1284)
Reginelli, Nina. Geraldine's Rainy Day. (p. 666)
Region 4 Education Service Center. Integrating Grade 11 TAKS Geometry Objectives into Algebra II Teacher Edition. (p. 879)
—Making Connection with Measurement, TAKS Preparation Grade 6 - Student Workbook - Spanish. (p. 1081)
—Making Connections with Measurement, TAKS Preparation Grade 5 - Student Workbook - Spanish. (p. 1081)
—Making Connections with Measurement, TAKS Preparation Grade 3 TAKS - Student Workbook - Spanish. (p. 1081)
—Reading to Learn in Social Studies for Grades 6-8. (p. 1446)
—Reading to Learn in Social Studies for Grades 9-12. (p. 1446)
—TAKS Mathematics Preparation Grade 6 - Spanish. (p. 1699)
Regis, Frankye. Voice from the Civil Rights Era (p. 1848)
Regis, Natalie. Genetically Modified Crops & Food. (p. 660)
—NASCAR & Its Greatest Drivers (p. 1230)
Regis, Natalie, jt. auth. see Chiu, David.
Regis, Natalie & Chiu, David. Insider's Guide to Wrestling (p. 878)
Regis, Tessa. Hibiscus Conspiracies: Loss of Innocence. (p. 775)
Regis-Etumnu, Anusjka. Sid the Kindest Kid: Sweets ... Sweets ... Sweets! (p. 1572)
Register, J. R., illus. see Simpon, TJ.
Register, Katherine E. & LeBlanc, Steven A. Constant Battles: Why We Fight. (p. 359)
Regnew, Tera. Christopher Cricket's Christmas. (p. 317)
Regula, Linda. Cloud Fortress of Twilight. (p. 334)
—Twilight Returns to Noah's Mountain. (p. 1801)
—Woodland Palace of Twilight. (p. 1949)
Reh, Beth Donovan. Germs. (p. 667)
Reh, Rusalka. Pizzicato: The Abduction of the Magic Violin Wilson, David Henry, tr. from GER. (p. 1365)
—Secret of the Water Knight Derbyshire, Katy, tr. (p. 1543)
Rehberg, Emily. Thunder Is Not Scary. Craig, Branden Chapin & Chapin, Jimmy, illus. (p. 1746)
Reher, Matt. Blue Whale Babies. (p. 203)
—Can You See the Beetle? (p. 259)
—Grasshoppers on the Go. (p. 711)
Rehfuss, Mary. Pottsville Chronicles: Election Day Red, White, & Blues. (p. 1388)
Rehfuss, Mary E. Pottsville Chronicles: A New Beginning. (p. 1388)
Rehm, Carolyn. Flower Pot Bunnies: Not A Good Place For A Nest. Schanck, Agnes, illus. (p. 607)
Rehman, Sharaf N. You're Not Listening. (p. 1982)
Reiach, Margaret Amy, illus. see Kalman, Bobbie.
Reiach, Margaret Amy, illus. see MacAulay, Kelley & Kalman, Bobbie.
Reibeling, Brandon, illus. see Dahl, Michael & Moore, Mark.
Reibeling, Brandon, illus. see Dahl, Michael.
Reibeling, Brandon, illus. see Korb, Rena.
Reibeling, Brandon, illus. see Loewen, Nancy.
Reibeling, Brandon, illus. see Slater, David Michael.
Reibold, Mary. Ninya's Great Adventure: A Cat's Tale. (p. 1257)
Reibstein, Mark. Wabi Sabi. (p. 1851)
—Wabi Sabi. Young, Ed, illus. (p. 1851)
Reich, Ashley. Izzy Lizzy. Reich, Ashley, illus. (p. 901)
Reich, Carin, illus. see Robinson, Alise.
Reich, J. J. Deer Dad: Kampp Tales Outdoor Adventures. Johnathan, Kuehl, illus. (p. 423)
—Snort, Wheeze, Rattle & Grunt: Kampp Tales Outdoor Adventures. Johnathan, Kuehl, illus. (p. 1598)
—Snort, Wheeze, Rattle & Grunt. Hillmann, Joe & Cox, Chad, illus. (p. 1598)
Reich, Kass. Hamsters Holding Hands (p. 740)
—Hooray for Hamsters! A Two-Book Set (p. 796)
—This Little Hamster (p. 1737)
—Up Hamster, down Hamster (p. 1824)
Reich, Robert E. Harry MacFly's the Old Mill Adventure. Reich, Robert E., illus. (p. 750)
Reich, Susanna. José! Born to Dance: The Story of Jose Limon. Colón, Raúl, illus. (p. 926)
—Minette's Feast: The Delicious Story of Julia Child & Her Cat. Bates, Amy, illus. (p. 1146)
—Painting the Wild Frontier: The Art & Adventures of George Catlin. (p. 1318)
—Penelope Bailey Takes the Stage (p. 1336)
Reichard, Susan E. Who on Earth Is Sylvia Earle? Undersea Explorer of the Ocean. (p. 1917)
Reichart, George. Bag of Lucky Rice. Mitchell, Mark, illus. (p. 132)
Reiche, Dietlof. Fredy, el Hamster. (p. 633)
Reiche, Dietlof & Brownjohn, John. Freddy in Peril: Book Two in the Golden Hamster Saga. Cepeda, Joe, illus. (p. 633)
Reichel, Tammi, tr. see Röder, Marlene.
Reichel, Tammi, tr. see Schrocke, Kathrin.
Reichel, Tammi, tr. see Voorhoeve, Anne C.
Reichelt, James. Second Rate Poems Filled with Angst. (p. 1539)
Reichert, Amy. Take Your Mama to Work Today. Boiger, Alexandra, illus. (p. 1697)
—While Mama Had a Quick Little Chat. Boiger, Alexandra, illus. (p. 1911)
Reichert, Paul. Lemonade Ripple: A Sweet Story of Kindness & Charity. (p. 991)
Reichl, Donna. People Patch. (p. 1339)
Reichman, Justin. Green. (p. 721)
Reichs, Brendan, jt. auth. see Reichs, Kathy.
Reichs, Kathy. Code. (p. 338)
—Virals. (p. 1844)
Reichs, Kathy & Reichs, Brendan. Exposure. (p. 554)
—Seizure. (p. 1548)
—Terminal. (p. 1721)
Reid, A. Elaine Holt. Who Did Mr. Stork Bring to the Zoo? (p. 1915)
Reid, Aimee. Mama's Day with Little Gray. (p. 1084)
Reid, Alastair. Balloon for a Blunderbuss. Gill, Bob, illus. (p. 135)
—Ounce, Dice, Trice. Shahn, Ben, illus. (p. 1307)
—Supposing. Gill, Bob, illus. (p. 1684)
Reid Banks, Lynne & Stephenson, Omri. Polly & Jake. (p. 1381)
—Spice Rack. (p. 1626)
Reid, Barbara. Acorn to Oak Tree. (p. 9)
—Caterpillar to Butterfly. (p. 279)
—Fox Walked Alone. Reid, Barbara, illus. (p. 626)
—Perfect Snow. Reid, Barbara, illus. (p. 1342)
—Picture a Tree. Reid, Barbara, illus. (p. 1355)
—Seed to Sunflower: A First Look Board Book. Crysler, Ian, photos by. (p. 1547)
—Subway Mouse. Reid, Barbara, illus. (p. 1671)
Reid, Barbara, illus. see Moore, Clement C.
Reid, Barbara, illus. see Newlin-Chase, Edith.
Reid, Bill, et al. Raven Steals the Light. (p. 1441)
Reid, Camilla. Lulu Loves Colours. Busby, Ailie, illus. (p. 1065)
—Lulu Loves Noises. Busby, Ailie, illus. (p. 1065)
—Lulu Loves Numbers. Busby, Ailie, illus. (p. 1065)
—Lulu Loves Shapes. Busby, Ailie, illus. (p. 1065)
Reid, Carol. Oh No, It's a Boy! (p. 1281)
—Spook-Ee Wook-Ee Halloween. (p. 1631)
Reid, Charles. Chasing the Arrow. (p. 294)
—Ghost of Heroes Past. (p. 671)
—Hurricanes over London. (p. 830)
Reid, Chris. Wounded Land. (p. 1962)
Reid, Christopher. Legends from Darkwood (p. 989)
Reid, Christy. Simon the Guide Dog. Poole, Steven R., illus. (p. 1577)
REID, D. H. Fantasies & Dreams. (p. 571)
Reid, David. Honorable Fido Lincoln, Judge Teaches Property Law. (p. 795)
—Shade Girls Were Right. (p. 1556)
Reid, Demetra. Alice's ABC's: Version 2. Deffenbaugh, Dena, illus. (p. 39)
Reid, Donalda & Second Story Press Staff. Way It Is (p. 1864)
Reid, Eleanor R. STOP My Childhood from Drowning! 39 Lessons from a Child Experiencing Divorce (p. 1653)
Reid, F. J. Midwinter Child. (p. 1139)
Reid, Fiona, illus. see Alden, Peter C.
Reid, Greg. Ecosystems. (p. 503)
—Exploration. (p. 550)
—Frozen Continent. (p. 645)
Reid, Isabelle. Serafina Moon. (p. 1552)
Reid, James. Across the Sea. (p. 9)
—Dinosaur House (p. 442)
—Edward the Explorer. (p. 505)
—Ready, Set, Go! (p. 1447)
—This Is My Story by Frederick G. Frog. (p. 1736)
—Your Guide to Superheroes. (p. 1980)
Reid, Jamie. Diana Krall. (p. 434)
Reid, Janet. Granny Rags. (p. 710)
Reid, Jim, as told by. Schultze's Stories: Celebrating Friends Through a Puppy's Eyes. (p. 1524)
Reid, John. Journey of the Holy Grail: Featuring Romancing the Chalice & Secret Crisis. (p. 928)
Reid, Joy. Raspberry & Turner. Smith, Sue Millar, illus. (p. 1439)
Reid, Joy M. Essentials of Teaching Academic Writing. (p. 537)
Reid, Julia. Could You Own a Dinosaur? (p. 369)
Reid, Karlene & Reid, Mason. Me & My Big Brother. (p. 1115)
Reid, Kate. Operation Timewarp. (p. 1300)
Reid, Katie. Blood Driven. (p. 200)
Reid, Kimberly. Creeping with the Enemy. (p. 381)
—Sweet 16 to Life. (p. 1689)
Reid, Lainey. Takan. (p. 1696)
Reid, Lori, et al. Naked at the Prom: The Secret Language of Dreams. (p. 1228)
Reid, Mamta. Student Councilor: Always Remember That We Have a Choice! (p. 1669)
Reid, Margarette S. Lots & Lots of Coins. Kelley, True, illus. (p. 1057)
Reid, Mason, jt. auth. see Reid, Karlene.
Reid, Mayne. Boy Hunters or Adventures in Search of a White Buffalo. (p. 218)
—WarTrail or the Hunt of the Wild Horse A. (p. 1859)
—Young Yagers or A Narrative of Hunting A. (p. 1979)
Reid, Michael, illus. see Childs, Rob.
Reid, Mick, illus. see Braun, Eric.
Reid, Mick, illus. see Clay, Kathryn.
Reid, Mick, illus. see Dale, Jenny & Rowe, Michael.
Reid, Mick, illus. see Dale, Jenny.
Reid, Mick, illus. see Gerver, Jane E.
Reid, Mick, illus. see Troupe, Thomas Kingsley.
Reid, Mick, illus. see Williams, Rozanne Lanczak.
Reid, Mike, illus. see Arlington, Jane.
Reid, Nakeil W. & Reid, Neil W. Adventure of Avery the Ant: Experience the Next Children?ÇOS Classic. (p. 14)
Reid, Neil W., jt. auth. see Reid, Nakeil W.
Reid, P. D. Adventures of Sam the Suitcase. (p. 22)
Reid, Pamela Carrington. Little One. Tolman, Tom, illus. (p. 1032)
reid, r. m. Our Little Blessing: A Story about Sickle Cell Disease. (p. 1309)
Reid, Raziel. When Everything Feels Like the Movies. (p. 1902)

R

Reid, Rob. Comin' down to Storytime. Bernard Westcott, Nadine, illus. (p. 348)
—Storytime Slam: 15 Lesson Plans for Preschool & Primary Story Programs. (p. 1664)
—Wave Goodbye Williams, Lorraine, illus. (p. 1864)
Reid, Robin L. Rhyming Ricky Rutherford. Lipp, Tony, illus. (p. 1468)
Reid, Roger. Longleaf. (p. 1047)
—Space. (p. 1618)
—Time. (p. 1750)
Reid, S. & Chisholm, J. Who Built the Pyramids? (p. 1914)
Reid, Scott. Great Society. Greenhaven Press Staff, ed. (p. 718)
Reid, Siuna A. Reptiles Are Cool- Understanding My Tortoise. Lodge, Vivienne E., ed. (p. 1461)
Reid, Siuna Ann. Reptiles Are Cool- Understanding My Lizard. Lodge, Vivienne E., ed. (p. 1461)
Reid, Stef & Bannister, Philip. Against the Odds. (p. 29)
Reid, Stephanie. Feelings. (p. 580)
—My Body. (p. 1198)
—My Country. (p. 1200)
—School. (p. 1522)
—Space. (p. 1618)
—Time. (p. 1750)
Reid, Stephanie, jt. auth. see Acosta, Jamey.
Reid, Stephanie, jt. auth. see Smith, Jodene Lynn.
Reid, Straun, jt. auth. see Chisholm, Jane.
Reid, Struan. 120 Great History Projects: Bring the Past into the Present with Hours of Fun Creative Activity. (p. 2000)
—Astronauts Sticker Book IR. (p. 109)
—Castle Life. (p. 277)
—Dictionary of horses & ponies - internet Linked. Khan, Aziz, illus. (p. 436)
—Hands-on History Projects: Inventions. (p. 741)
—Hands-on History Projects: Art & Craft. (p. 741)
—Pirate Jigsaw Book. Allen, Peter, illus. (p. 1362)
Reid, Struan, jt. auth. see Cox, Phil Roxbee.
Reid, Struan, jt. auth. see Everett, Felicity.
Reid, Struan, jt. auth. see Halstead, Rachel.
Reid, Struan, jt. auth. see Harvey, Gill.
Reid, Struan, jt. auth. see Wingate, Philippa.
Reid, Struan & Champion, Neil. Explorers (p. 551)
Reid, Struan & Fara, Patricia. Libro de los Cientificos: Desde Arquimedes a Einstein. (p. 1006)
Reid, Struan & Halstead, Rachel. Hands-On History Projects: Clothes. (p. 741)
Reid, Struan & McConnell, William. Rocks & Fossils. (p. 1483)
Reid, Struan & Stowell, Louie. My First Pirate Book. Allen, Peter, illus. (p. 1207)
Reid, Thomas M. Boy Hunters. (p. 218)
—Forged. (p. 619)
Reid, W. Mike. Helper: A True Story. (p. 766)
Reide, MacKenzie. Adventurers the Mask of the Troll. (p. 15)
Reid-Tulloch, Joseth. Manu's Special Day. (p. 1089)
Reidy, Hannah. All Sorts of Numbers. Dodd, Emma, illus. (p. 45)
—Crazy Creature Capers. Mackie, Clare, illus. (p. 377)
—Crazy Creature Colors. Mackie, Clare, illus. (p. 377)
—Crazy Creature Contrasts. Mackie, Clare, illus. (p. 377)
—Crazy Creatures Counting. Mackie, Clare, illus. (p. 377)
Reidy, Jean. All Through My Town. Timmers, Leo, illus. (p. 46)
—Too Pickley! Leloup, Geneviève, illus. (p. 1767)
—Too Princessy! Leloup, Geneviève, illus. (p. 1767)
—Too Purpley! Leloup, Geneviève, illus. (p. 1767)
Reiersen, Ron. Adventures of Callie & Ivan: Book I: the Baraboo Secret. (p. 17)
Reif, Cheryl. Sonics on Tour: The Respiratory System. Noé, illus. (p. 1612)
Reiff, Chris, illus. see Wallace, Daniel.
Reiff, Lauren & Geiser, Christina. Meows-Key Motel: A Great Vacation Spot for Hip Cats. (p. 1127)
Reiff, Rachel Haugrud. Sandra Cisneros. (p. 1511)
Reiff, Raychel Haugrud. Aldous Huxley: Brave New World. (p. 35)
—Charlotte Bronte. (p. 293)
—Edgar Allan Poe: Tales & Poems. (p. 504)
—Herman Melville: Moby Dick & Other Works. (p. 771)
—J. D. Salinger: The Catcher in the Rye & Other Works. (p. 901)
—Sandra Cisneros. (p. 1511)
—Sylvia Plath: The Bell Jar & Poems. (p. 1693)
—William Golding. (p. 1933)
Reiffel, J. A., et al. Once upon an Antigmule: (... or, the Day Roseanna's Dreams Came True) (p. 1293)
Reihs, Linda. Adventures of Maddy Morphis. (p. 20)
Reil-Berry, Stacie. Stop! Growing. (p. 1653)
Reill, Peter Hanns, jt. auth. see Wilson, Ellen Judy.
Reilly, Aleda. Sunshine & the Ladybug: Book 2: Sharing Christmas. (p. 1678)
Reilly, Antoinette. Mr. Lobster & the Mermaid. (p. 1185)
Reilly), Avia (Aleda Jc. Sunshine & Ladybug. (p. 1678)
Reilly, Carmel. All about Chemistry (p. 42)
—Animal Hospital. (p. 78)
—Aztec Beliefs (p. 122)
—Boy at the Park. Reynolds, Pat, illus. (p. 217)
—Comets, Asteroids, & Meteoroids. (p. 348)
—Earth's Atmosphere. (p. 498)
—Harry Helps Out. (p. 750)
—Hip-Hop (p. 780)
—Inside the Gate (p. 877)
—Jewellery Shop Robbery. (p. 917)
—Join up Now! (p. 924)
—Living in Space (p. 1041)
—Magic Tricks. (p. 1074)
—Making a Cake. (p. 1080)
—Making Headlines (p. 1081)
—Moon. (p. 1171)
—More Like Home (p. 1174)
—New Neighbours. (p. 1246)
—New Tricks. (p. 1247)
—Night Out. (p. 1254)
—Noises in the Night. (p. 1262)
—Planets. (p. 1368)
—Stars. (p. 1643)
—Sun. (p. 1675)
Reilly, Carmel & Ashforth, Kate. Jewelry Story Robbery. (p. 917)
—Night Out. (p. 1254)
Reilly, Carmel & Culic, Ned. Ben Fox Saves the Day. (p. 163)
Reilly, Carmel & Hopkinson, Courtney. Magic Tricks. (p. 1074)
—New Tricks. (p. 1247)
Reilly, Carmel & Miesen, Christina. Call of the Wolf. (p. 254)
Reilly, Carmel & Orsini, Cheryl. Everything Is Changing. (p. 545)
—Saying Goodbye. (p. 1519)
Reilly, Carmel & Stewart, Christen. More Like Home. (p. 1174)
Reilly, Carmel & Wallace-Mitchell, Jane. Harry Helps Out. (p. 750)
—Mercury & the Woodcutter. (p. 1127)
Reilly, Carmel & Young, Karen. Anna Goes to the Zoo. (p. 85)
—Buzz & Zip Get Lost. (p. 248)
—Buzz Takes Over. (p. 248)
—Taking Off. (p. 1698)
Reilly, Carmel, et al. Shipwreck. (p. 1567)
Reilly, Cherie Brooks. Feathered & Furry Friends at the Farm. (p. 579)
Reilly, Cherie Brooks, et al. Animal Tales & Tracks: The Feathered & Furry Friends at Reilly's Summer Seat Farm. (p. 80)
Reilly, Christopher P. Punch & Judy. (p. 1416)
Reilly, Giff Patricia. Pictures of Hollis Woods. (p. 1356)
Reilly, Hope. Ghost Horse at Cove House: A Book about the Strength of Friendship. (p. 670)
Reilly, Joan, illus. see Metter, Bert & Metter, Bertram.
Reilly, Kathleen M. Cities: Discover How They Work. Casteel, Tom, illus. (p. 322)
—Energy: 25 Projects Investigate Why We Need Power & How We Get It. (p. 528)
—Explore Life Cycles! 25 Great Projects, Activities, Experiments. Stone, Bryan, illus. (p. 550)
—Explore Solids & Liquids! With 25 Great Projects. Stone, Bryan, illus. (p. 550)
—Explore Weather & Climate! With 25 Great Projects. Stone, Bryan, illus. (p. 550)
—Food - 25 Amazing Projects: Investigate the History & Science of What We Eat. Carbaugh, Samuel, illus. (p. 612)
—Food - 25 Amazing Projects: Investigate the History & Science of What We Eat. Carbaugh, Samuel & Rizvi, Farah, illus. (p. 613)
—Human Body: 25 Fantastic Projects Illuminate How the Body Works. Braley, Shawn, illus. (p. 825)
—Natural Disasters: Investigate Earth's Most Destructive Forces with 25 Projects. Casteel, Tom, illus. (p. 1235)
—Planet Earth: 25 Environmental Projects You Can Build Yourself. Rizvi, Farah, illus. (p. 1367)
Reilly, Kathleen M. & Takacs-Moore, Mary. Energy: 25 Projects Investigate Why We Need Power & How We Get It. Takacs-Moore, Mary, illus. (p. 528)
Reilly, Matthew. Full Throttle. Raimondi, Pablo, illus. (p. 646)
Reilly, Meghan M., illus. see Jacques, Taryn Elise.
Reilly, Michael. Monster Sandwich. (p. 1168)
Reilly, Michelle, illus. see Larsen, Donna R.
Reilly, Nichola. Drowned. (p. 486)
Reilly, Pamela. My Day at the Zoo. (p. 1201)
Reilly, Pauline. Brolga. Rolland, Will, illus. (p. 230)
—Kangaroo. Russell, Gayle, illus. (p. 942)
Reilly, Pauline & Rolland, Will. Lyrebird. (p. 1066)
Reilly, Thomas, jt. auth. see Homan, Lynn M.
Reim, Melanie, illus. see Gottfried, Ted.
Reimann, A. J., jt. auth. see Hoyes, Amy.
Reimer, Charlotte. Problems with Pies. (p. 1408)
Reimer, Diana, jt. auth. see Peterson, J. D. R.
Reimer, Jackie. No Thanks, but I'd Love to Dance! Choosing to Live Smoke Free. Reimer, Jackie, illus. (p. 1260)
Reimiller, Diane. Brayden & Ryan's Summer Vacation. Jastrzebski, Brandy, illus. (p. 224)
Reimiller, Diane L. Duck Named Quackers Jastrzebski, Brandy, illus. (p. 488)
—Ike & Jamie. Jastrzebski, Brandy, illus. (p. 856)
Reina, Lazaro Lorenzo. Profecia Del Orisha. (p. 1409)
Reina, Mary. Earn Money. (p. 494)
—Learn about Money. (p. 982)
—Make Money Choices. (p. 1079)
—Money & You. (p. 1164)
—Save Money. (p. 1516)
—Science of a Hurricane. (p. 1527)
—Tour of Your Respiratory System Jones, Chris B., illus. (p. 1773)
Reinagel, Brady. Larry Fitzgerald: Pro Bowl Receiver. (p. 976)
Reinagle, Damon J. Draw Monsters. (p. 481)
Reinckens, Sunnhild. Making Dolls (p. 1081)
Reinders, Veronica. Adventures at Angels Rest: Maggie Feathers. (p. 15)
Reiner, Angela. You Can't Dance in Those Pants. (p. 1974)
Reiner, Carl. Tell Me A Scary Story... but Not Too Scary. (p. 1716)
—Tell Me a Silly Story. Bennett, James, illus. (p. 1716)
—Tell Me Another Scary Story... but Not Too Scary! Bennett, James & Bennett, Carl A., illus. (p. 1716)
Reiner, Carl, jt. auth. see Brooks, Mel.
Reinert, Linda M. Talking Is Hard for Me! Encouraging Communication in Children with Speech-Language Difficulties. Lynch, Emily S., illus. (p. 1703)
Reinertson, Bob. Mysterious Visitor. (p. 1223)
Reinfeld, Mark, et al. Complete Idiot's Guide to Eating Raw. (p. 353)
Reingold, Adam. Beaver's Lodge: Building with Leftovers. (p. 155)
—Leveled by an Earthquake! (p. 1003)
—Smallpox: Is It Over? (p. 1592)
Reingold, Alan, illus. see Glasthal, Jacqueline B.
Reinhard, Michel. Quien Llama - Puerta - Ivan. (p. 1427)
Reinhardt, Dana. Brief Chapter in My Impossible Life. (p. 227)
—Harmless. (p. 749)
—How to Build a House. (p. 815)
—Odessa Again. (p. 1278)
—Summer I Learned to Fly. (p. 1674)
—Things a Brother Knows. (p. 1733)
—We Are the Goldens. (p. 1866)
Reinhardt, Donald S. Donald S. Reinhardt's Graduated Studies for the Brass Player for Trumpet: Beginning, Intermediate & Advanced Brass Method. (p. 466)
—Donald S. Reinhardt's Graduated Studies for the Brass Player for Trombone: Graduated Studies for the Brass Player for Trombone. (p. 466)
Reinhardt, Jennifer Black, illus. see McGinty, Alice B.
Reinhardt, Jennifer Black, illus. see Slade, Suzanne.
Reinhardt, Jennifer Black, illus. see Vaught, Susan.
Reinhardt, Swen, jt. auth. see Sommer, Isabell.
Reinhart, Larry, illus. see Blankenship, Paula.
Reinhart, Larry, illus. see McKay, Sindy.
Reinhart, Larry, illus. see Ross, Dev & Canetti, Yanitzia.
Reinhart, Larry, illus. see Ross, Dev.
Reinhart, Matthew. Ark: A Pop-up Book. Reinhart, Matthew, illus. (p. 99)
—Cinderella: A Pop-Up Fairy Tale. Reinhart, Matthew, illus. (p. 320)
—Jungle Book: A Pop-Up Adventure. Reinhart, Matthew, illus. (p. 935)
—Marvel's the Avengers - Age of Ultron: A Pop-Up Book. Reinhart, Matthew, illus. (p. 1099)
—My Little Pony: the Castles of Equestria: An Enchanted My Little Pony Pop-Up Book. (p. 1213)
—Nursery Rhymes. Reinhart, Matthew, illus. (p. 1273)
—Princess Like Me: A Royal Pop-Up. (p. 1404)
—Transformers: The Ultimate Pop-Up Universe. (p. 1778)
Reinhart, Matthew, illus. see Palatini, Margie.
Reinhart, Matthew, jt. auth. see DC Comics Staff.
Reinhart, Matthew, jt. auth. see Sabuda, Robert.
Reinhart, Matthew & Lucas, George. Pop-Up Guide to the Galaxy. (p. 1384)
Reinhart, Matthew & Lucasfilm. Galactic Pop-Up Adventure. (p. 652)
Reinhart, Matthew & Sabuda, Robert. Dragons & Monsters. Reinhart, Matthew & Sabuda, Robert, illus. (p. 478)
—Encyclopedia Mythologica: Dragons & Monsters. Reinhart, Matthew & Sabuda, Robert, illus. (p. 524)
—Encyclopedia Prehistorica Dinosaurs. Reinhart, Matthew & Sabuda, Robert, illus. (p. 526)
—Encyclopedia Prehistorica Sharks & Other Sea Monsters. Reinhart, Matthew & Sabuda, Robert, illus. (p. 526)
—Gods & Heroes. Reinhart, Matthew & Sabuda, Robert, illus. (p. 690)
Reinhart, Robin. Fierce Freshwater Fish: Measure Lengths in Standard Units. (p. 584)
Reinheimer, Melinda. Christmas Tea. (p. 316)
Reinheimer, Melinda T. Little Blue Kite Makes A Friend: Another Adventure of the Little Blue Kite. (p. 1024)
Reiniger, Lotte, illus. see Green, Roger Lancelyn.
Reinke, Beth Bence. Carla's Cloud Catastrophe. Nielson, Ginger, illus. (p. 270)
—Grains Group. (p. 706)
—Healthy Snacks. (p. 759)
—Measuring Time with a Clock. Petelinsek, Kathleen, illus. (p. 1117)
—Measuring Volume. Petelinsek, Kathleen, illus. (p. 1117)
—Measuring Weight. Petelinsek, Kathleen, illus. (p. 1117)
—Sugars & Fats. (p. 1673)
Reinke, Missy, jt. auth. see Thompson, Becki.
Reinlein, Ann. Adventures of Mister Squirrel Acorn. (p. 20)
Reino, Jessica. Food Allergies: The Ultimate Teen Guide. (p. 613)
Reinoso, Carlos. Little Ducky Jr. & the Whirlwind Storm: A Tale of Loss, Hope,and Renewal. Reinoso, Carlos, illus. (p. 1027)
Reinoso, Marta. April's Journal: A Journal for Children. Lasley, Tony, illus. (p. 93)
Reinstedt, Randall A. Tales & Treasures of California's Missions. Greco, E. D., illus. (p. 1701)
Reintjes, Susan B. Through the Fairy Door. Sparling, Bren M., illus. (p. 1745)
Reis, Erica. Sea Princess Azuri (p. 1535)
Reis, Erica, illus. see Armand, Villavert.
Reis, Ivan, illus. see Pulido, Brian.
Reis, Jason & Hurley, Meagan. Adventures of Burt: Burt & the Big Race. (p. 17)
Reis, Ronald A. Apollo 13: Crisis in Space. (p. 91)
—Buffalo Bill Cody. (p. 235)
—Christopher Columbus & the Age of Exploration for Kids: With 21 Activities. (p. 317)
—Dust Bowl. (p. 490)
—Easter Island. (p. 499)
—Empire State Building. (p. 521)
—Eugenie Clark: Marine Biologist. (p. 540)
—Great Depression & the New Deal: America's Economy in Crisis. (p. 715)
—Jonas Salk: Microbiologist. (p. 925)
—Lou Gehrig. (p. 1057)
—Mickey Mantle. (p. 1136)
—New York City Subway System. (p. 1248)
—Simon Bolivar. (p. 1577)
—Sitting Bull. (p. 1582)
—US Congress for Kids: Over 200 Years of Lawmaking, Deal-Breaking, & Compromising, with 21 Activities. (p. 1826)
—Valentino. (p. 1830)
Reisberg, Joanne. Zachary Zormer - Shape Transformer. Hohn, David & Clark, David, illus. (p. 1984)
Reisberg, Mira, illus. see Ata, Te, et al.
Reisberg, Mira, illus. see Ata, Te.
Reisberg, Mira, illus. see Corpi, Lucha.
Reisberg, Mira, illus. see Flor Ada, Alma & Zubizarreta, Rosalma, trs.
Reisberg, Mira, illus. see Miller, Elizabeth I.
Reisberg, Mira, illus. see Rohmer, Harriet.
Reisch, Jesse, illus. see Fredericks, Anthony D.
Reisch, Jesse, illus. see Pfeffer, Wendy.
Reisch, Jesse, illus. see Stevenson, Robert Louis.
Reisch, Jesse, illus. see Todd, Traci N.
Reisch, Jessie, illus. see Elkins, Stephen.
Reischel, Rob. Green Bay Packers. (p. 721)
Reisenauer, Cynthia Mauro. Emerita. Reisenauer, Cynthia Mauro, illus. (p. 518)
Reiser, Lynn. Hardworking Puppies. Reiser, Lynn, illus. (p. 748)
—My Way(A Mi Manera) A Margaret & Margarita Story(Un Cuento de Margarita y Margaret) Reiser, Lynn, illus. (p. 1221)
—Tortillas & Lullabies. Hart, Rebecca, tr. (p. 1770)
—You & Me, Baby. Gentieu, Penny, photos by. (p. 1973)
Reisfeld, Randi. All Access. (p. 43)
—CC (Cape Cod) (p. 283)
—Everyone Who's Anyone. (p. 544)
—No Strings Attached: CC (Cape Cod); Partiers Preferred. (p. 1260)
—Partiers Preferred. (p. 1325)
—Rehab. (p. 1457)
—This Is the Sound: The Best of Alternative Rock. (p. 1736)
—Welcome to Alfea. (p. 1873)
Reisfeld, Randi & Bell, Taryn. Face Value. (p. 560)
—Skin Deep. Fiedler, Lisa, illus. (p. 1585)
—Strike a Pose. Fiedler, Lisa, illus. (p. 1667)
Reisfeld, Randi & Gilmour, H. B. What the Dog Said. (p. 1893)
Reisfeld, Randi, et al. Eye Candy. (p. 557)
Reish, Kathleen. Matthew's Box. Leonhard, Herb, illus. (p. 1110)
Reisinger, John. Duckworth Chronicles. (p. 488)
Reisinger, Manfred, jt. auth. see Eidenbuller, Bernd.
Reisman, Dave. Cows Can't Jump. Maas, Jason/A, illus. (p. 374)
Reisman, Michael. Simon Bloom, the Gravity Keeper. (p. 1577)
Reisner, Molly. Dora & the Unicorn Adventure (Dora the Explorer) Golden Books Staff, illus. (p. 470)
—Dora & the Unicorn King (Dora the Explorer) Aikins, David, illus. (p. 470)
—Dora's Birthday Surprise! Aikins, David, illus. (p. 471)
—Dora's Princess Party. Aikins, Dave, illus. (p. 471)
—Halloween Hoedown! (p. 737)
—Halloween Hoedown! (Dora the Explorer) Aikins, David, illus. (p. 737)
Reisner, Molly & Ostrow, Kim. Camp Spongebob. Martinez, Heather, illus. (p. 257)
Reisner, Molly, et al. Nickelodeon Little Golden Book Collection (Nickelodeon) Golden Books, illus. (p. 1251)
Reisner, S. J. Left Horse Black. (p. 987)
Reiss, Christina, tr. see Jönsson, Maria.
Reiss, I. Boy in the Invisible Box. Katz, Avi, illus. (p. 218)
Reiss, James. Riff on Six: New & Selected Poems. (p. 1471)
Reiss, Johanna. Habitacion de Arriba. (p. 734)
Reiss, Kathryn. Bundle of Trouble: A Rebecca Mystery. Giovine, Sergio, illus. (p. 242)
—Dreadful Sorry. (p. 482)
—Paint by Magic. (p. 1318)
—Pale Phoenix. (p. 1319)
—Puzzle of the Paper Daughter. Hirsch, Jennifer, ed. (p. 1421)
—Riddle of the Prairie Bride. (p. 1470)
—Silver Guitar: A Julie Mystery. Ansfield, Elizabeth, ed. (p. 1576)
—Strange Case of Baby H. (p. 1665)
—Sweet Miss Honeywell's Revenge: A Ghost Story. (p. 1690)
—Tangled Web: A Julie Mystery. Tibbles, Jean-Paul, illus. (p. 1705)
Reiss, Mike. Boy Who Wouldn't Share. Catrow, David, illus. (p. 219)
—City of Hamburgers. Feinberg, Xeth, illus. (p. 324)
—How Murray Saved Christmas. Catrow, David, illus. (p. 811)
—Merry Un-Christmas. Catrow, David, illus. (p. 1129)
—Santa's Eleven Months Off Montgomery, Michael G., illus. (p. 1513)
Reiss, Mike, jt. auth. see Reiss, Mike.
Reiss, Mike & Reiss, Mike. Boy Who Looked Like Lincoln. Catrow, David, illus. (p. 219)
—Boy Who Wouldn't Share. Catrow, David, illus. (p. 219)
—Late for School Austin, Michael, illus. (p. 979)
Reiss, Stephen. Thomas Churchyard, 1798-1865. (p. 1738)
Reiss, William, illus. see Banks, Steven & Hillenburg, Stephen.
Reiss, William, illus. see Banks, Steven.
Reisz, Kristopher. Drowned Forest. (p. 486)
—Unleashed. (p. 1821)
Reiter, Cheryl, ed. see Hogan, Jayne.
Reiter, Chris. Blue Whale: A MyReportLinks.com Book. (p. 203)
—Delaware: A MyReportLinks.com Book. (p. 424)
—Gray Wolf: A MyReportLinks.com Book. (p. 713)
Reiter, Chris, jt. auth. see Katirgis, Jane.
Reiter, David P. Bringing down the Wall. Babajanyan, Sona, illus. (p. 229)
—Greenhouse Effect. (p. 723)
—Las Armas de Fuego. Rosales-Martinez, Guadalupe, tr. from ENG. (p. 976)
—Real Guns. Murphy, Patrick J., illus. (p. 1448)
—Tiger Takes the Big Apple. Bevin, Shane, illus. (p. 1748)
Reiter, David P., jt. auth. see Reiter, David P.
Reiter, David P. & Reiter, David P. Die Mauer Zu Fall Bringen. Beer, Michele, tr. from ENG. (p. 437)
Reiter, Douglas. Back to School in Cedar Heights. (p. 130)
Reiter, Mark, jt. auth. see Goldsmith, Marshall.
Reiter, Naomi. Sandy the Stingray. (p. 1511)
Reith, Sharon L. Infestation! Roaches, Bedbugs, Ants, & Other Insect Invaders (p. 873)
Reitmeyer, Hans. What People Eat. (p. 1892)
Reitmeyer, Shannon. Proud Inchworm. Reitmeyer, Shannon, illus. (p. 1412)
Reitz, Theresa, et al. Money Tree: A Financial Book for Children. (p. 1164)
Reitze, Glenn Logan. Ernie the Easter Hippopotamus: A Comic Adventure for Anytime. Reitze, Glenn Logan, illus. (p. 534)
—Ernie the Easter Hippotamus: A Comic Adventure for Anytime. (p. 534)
Reizer, Edwina, jt. auth. see Licata, Rosemarie.

Reizer, Edwina & Licata, Rosemarie. Magic Mountain. (p. 1072)
Rejent, Renee, illus. see DeVos, Janie.
Rejino, Mona. Just for Kids: HLSPL Composer Showcase NFMC 2014-2016 Selection Elementary Level. (p. 938)
Rekela, George R. Sports Great Kurt Warner. (p. 1632)
Reker, Martin, ed. see Shein, Daniel Erik.
Reker, Martin, ed. see Shein, Erik Daniel.
Reker, Martin, jt. auth. see Shein, Erik Daniel.
Relf, Adam, illus. see Clarke, Catriona.
Relf, Adam, illus. see Palfreman-Bunker, Claire.
Relf, Patricia. Magic School Plants Seeds. (p. 1073)
Relf, Sue. 100 Instant Children's Talks. (p. 1998)
Relin, David Oliver, jt. auth. see Mortenson, Greg.
Rell, G. Allegheny Doe Boy. Dean, Carla, ed. (p. 46)
Rellan, Clara, jt. auth. see Hernández, Guillermo.
Reller, Marcia Mattingly, illus. see Watson, Donn, ed.
Relota, Agatha. Carla & Leo's World of Dance. Perez, Thierry, illus. (p. 269)
Rely, Len. Y: Speculative Fkiction by Len Rely. (p. 1968)
Relyea, C. M., illus. see Jackson, Gabrielle E.
Relyea, C. M., illus. see Jackson, Gabrielle Emilie Snow.
Relyea, Charles M., illus. see Mathewson, Christy.
Rem, illus. see Schreiber, Ellen.
Remarque, Erich Maria. All Quiet on the Western Front. Bloom, Harold, ed. (p. 45)
—All Quiet on the Western Front. Wimperis, Sarah, illus. (p. 45)
Remarque, Erich-Maria. All Quiet on the Western Front: With Related Readings. Wheen, A. W., tr. from GER. (p. 45)
Rembert, Winfred. Don't Hold Me Back: My Life & Art. Rembert, Winfred, illus. (p. 467)
Rembisz, Linda. Count with Balloons. Liebeck, Lisa, illus. (p. 370)
Rembrandt Harmenszoon van Rijn, jt. auth. see Mason, Antony.
Remender, Rick. Castaway in Dimension Z (p. 276)
—Corps! (p. 368)
—Doll & Creature. (p. 463)
—Fear Agent Library Edition Volume 2. Thorpe, Patrick, ed. (p. 579)
—Fractured Fables HC. (p. 627)
—Girl Afraid (p. 678)
—Uncanny Avengers - Avenge the Earth (p. 1811)
Remey, Grace Anne. Lion's Pride: A Tail of Deployment. Remey, Grace Anne, illus. (p. 1021)
Reminders of Faith. Boy Scripture Theme. (p. 219)
—Girl Scripture Theme Pack. (p. 679)
—Mom Scripture Theme Pack. (p. 1161)
Remington, Frederic, jt. auth. see Longfellow, Henry Wadsworth.
Reminick, Gerald. Ollie Otter's Special Gift: A Story from Quiet Pond. Quintero, michelle, illus. (p. 1287)
Remkiewicz, illus. see Kline, Suzy & Remkiewicz, Frank.
Remkiewicz, F., illus. see London, Jonathan & Remkiewicz, Frank.
Remkiewicz, Frank. Gus Gets Scared. (p. 732)
—Gus Grows a Plant. (p. 732)
—Gus Loses a Tooth. (p. 732)
—Gus Makes a Gift. (p. 732)
—Twelve Days of Christmas in Florida. (p. 1800)
Remkiewicz, Frank, illus. see Kline, Suzy.
Remkiewicz, Frank, illus. see Lewis, J. Patrick.
Remkiewicz, Frank, illus. see London, Jonathan.
Remkiewicz, Frank, illus. see Martin, David Lozell.
Remkiewicz, Frank, illus. see Michalak, Jamie.
Remkiewicz, Frank, illus. see Murphy, Stuart J.
Remkiewicz, Frank, illus. see Riggs Vetter, Jennifer.
Remkiewicz, Frank, jt. auth. see Kline, Suzy.
Remkiewicz, Frank, jt. auth. see London, Jonathan.
Remland, Martin S. Nonverbal Communication in Everyday Life. (p. 1263)
Remler, Pat. Egyptian. (p. 506)
Remole, Arnulf. Island of Alphebia. (p. 892)
Remolina, Tere. Cambio de Piel. Martinez, Enrique, illus. (p. 255)
Rempel, Cherie J., ed. New Bridges - Book 1: Connecting People Through Language & Culture. (p. 1243)
—New Bridges - Book 2: Connecting People Through Language & Culture. (p. 1243)
—New Bridges - Book 4: Connecting People Through Language & Culture. (p. 1243)
—New Bridges - Book 5: Connecting People Through Language & Culture. (p. 1243)
Rempel, Jennifer. Lavi the Lion Finds His Pride. (p. 981)
Rempel, Judith K. Little Bear's Story. (p. 1024)
Rempel, Leah. Hey, Hmong Girl, Whassup? The Journal of Choua Vang. (p. 774)
Remphry, Martin. Pirates Are Stealing Our Cows. (p. 1363)
Remphry, Martin, illus. see Billam, Rosemary.
Remphry, Martin, illus. see Cassidy, Anne.
Remphry, Martin, illus. see Fischel, Emma.
Remphry, Martin, illus. see Harvey, Damian.
Remphry, Martin, illus. see Martin, Steve.
Remphry, Martin, jt. auth. see Harvey, Damian.
Rempt, Fiona. Snail's Birthday Wish. Smit, Noelle, illus. (p. 1596)
Rempt, Fione. Rico the Brave Sock Monkey. (p. 1470)
Remsburg, Rebecca. Camping Trip (p. 257)
—Night, Night, Knight (p. 1253)
Remson, Billie. Mississippi Autumn on Bluebird Hill: A True Story about our Little Farm in the Hills of Southern Mississippi. (p. 1154)
—Mississippi Autumn on Bluebird Hill: A true story about our little farm in the hills of Southern Mississippi. (p. 1154)
—Mississippi Spring on Bluebird Hill. Garraway, Kym W., illus. (p. 1154)
—Mississippi Summer on Bluebird Hill: A True Story about Our Little Farm in the Hills of Southern Mississippi. Garraway, Kym, illus. (p. 1154)
—Mississippi Winter on Bluebird Hill: A True Story about Our Little Farm in the Hills of Southern Mississippi. Garraway, Kym, illus. (p. 1154)
Remy, Jerry. Hello, Wally! Boston Red Sox. Moore, Danny, illus. (p. 765)
—Wally the Green Monster & His Journey Through Red Sox Nation. Moore, Danny, illus. (p. 1855)
Remy, Richard C. United States Government: Democracy in Action. (p. 1819)
Remy, Richard C., et al. Civics Today: Citizenship, Economics, & You. (p. 324)
Remza, Freddie. Journey to Mei. (p. 929)
—Ride the Wave. (p. 1471)
Ren, et al. Investigating Why Leaves Change Their Color. (p. 885)
Rena, Regina. Where Do Cows Moo? (p. 1906)
Renae, Cameo. Hidden Wings. (p. 776)
Renaissance Learning, Inc. Staff. Getting Started with Accelerated Math & Math Renaissance (Foundation & RP) Guide may be used by Foundaton or RP Customers. (p. 669)
—Math Power Lessons for Grade 4: Instruction for Accelerated Math Objectives. (p. 1107)
—STAR Early Literacy Made EZ (v 2. 1) RP: Quick Guide to Software. (p. 1640)
—STAR Math Made EZ (v 3. 1) RP: Quick Guide to the Software. (p. 1640)
Renard Roach, Marietta. Come, Bless the Baby. (p. 347)
Renaud, Andrea. Goal Keeper Journal. (p. 687)
—Sammy the Surfing Pelican Meets Steve the Surf Guru. (p. 1508)
Renaud, Anne. How the Sea Came to Marissa. Durland, Maud, illus. (p. 813)
—Into the Mist: The Story of the Empress of Ireland. (p. 881)
—Missuk's Snow Geese. Côté, Geneviève, illus. (p. 1154)
Renaud, Joanne, illus. see Coleman, Wim & Perrin, Pat.
Renaud, Katy. Guess Where I Was. (p. 729)
Renaud, Marguerite, jt. auth. see Parker, Emma.
Renaud, Sheilah. Veggi World Coloring Book. (p. 1834)
Renberg, Dalia Hardof. King Solomon & the Bee. Heller, Ruth, illus. (p. 959)
Renda, Joseph, illus. see Glenn, Judith.
Renda, Lori Epstein, photos by see Kostyal, Karen & Colonial Williamsburg Foundation Staff.
Rendall, John, jt. auth. see Bourke, Anthony.
Rendall, Richard & Abrams, Elise. Hand Painted Porcelain Plates: Nineteenth Century to the Present (p. 740)
Rende, Crystal, jt. auth. see Rende, Thomas.
Rende, Thomas & Rende, Crystal. Novel Ideas 3 Great Dog Stories. (p. 1268)
Rendeiro, Charlene, illus. see Hopkins, Lee Bennett.
Rendell, Ian, jt. auth. see Mott, Julian.
Rendell, Jane. Art & Architecture: A Place Between. (p. 101)
Rendell, Kingsley George. Samuel Rutherford: A New Biography of the Man & His Ministry. (p. 1509)
Rendina, Donna Rae. Golden Leaf. Bronowski, Karen Kmetz, illus. (p. 695)
Rendon, Daniel, illus. see Lobdell, Scott.
Rendon, Gilberto. Libro de Los Maravillosos Automatas de Juguete. Medina, Hector, illus. (p. 1006)
—saga de los jugadores de Pelota. Milagrito, El, illus. (p. 1502)
—Vampiro del Ropero. (p. 1832)
Rendon, Gilberto, jt. auth. see Ortiz, Gilberto Rendon.
Rendon, Gilberto, et al. Los Cuatro Amigos de Siempre. (p. 1053)
Rendon, Joel, illus. see Navarrete, Federico.
Rendon, Leah, ed. see Dzidrums, Christine.
Rendon, Leah, jt. auth. see Dzidrums, Christine.
Rendon, Marcie R. Powwow Summer: A Family Celebrates the Circle of Life. Walsh Bellville, Cheryl, photos by. (p. 1391)
René, Ellen. Investigating How Flowers Grow. (p. 884)
—Investigating Spiders & Their Webs. (p. 885)
—Investigating Volcanic Eruptions. (p. 885)
—Investigating Why Animals Shed Their Skin. (p. 885)
—Investigating Why It Rains. (p. 885)
—Investigating Why Leaves Change Their Color. (p. 885)
Rene, Ellen. Science Detectives. (p. 1525)
Rene, Perez, illus. see Heller, Andrew.
René, Richard. Edge of Mysterion: Another Tale of Mysterion. (p. 504)
Rene, Rochelle. Bella & the Bad Mood Busters: The Bad Mood Blues. (p. 162)
Reneaux, J. J. Cajun Folktales. (p. 252)
Renee Daeumler Thompson. I Made a Bad Choice. (p. 844)
Renee, Lindsey. What Kind of Fairy Is Merry Berry? (p. 1891)
Renee, Shawna. God... Why? (p. 690)
Renee, Sherry. Bye Bye Bed-Dy: Andrew Gets a Big Boy Bed. (p. 249)
Renehan, Edward J., Jr. Monroe Doctrine: The Cornerstone of American Foreign Policy. (p. 1166)
—Transcontinental Railroad: The Gateway to the West. (p. 1778)
—Treaty of Paris: The Precursor to a New Nation. (p. 1783)
Renek, Nava. Venice Is for Cats. (p. 1835)
Renero, Joaquin. Enchanted Scrapbook: Welcome to the Wilburton Society. (p. 523)
Renert, Gerry. Nathan & the Really Big Bully. Bradshaw, Carrie, illus. (p. 1231)
—Nathan Saves Summer. Bradshaw, Carrie Anne, illus. (p. 1231)
—Nathan Saves Summer/Nathan Rescata el Verano. Bradshaw, Carrie Anne, illus. (p. 1231)
Renfield, R. K. Venus. (p. 1836)
Renfrew, C. E. Bus Story Test. (p. 244)
Renfrew, C. E. & Hancox, Lucy. Action Picture Test. (p. 10)
Renfrew, Catherine. Word Finding Vocabulary Test. Mitchell, Polly, illus. (p. 1950)
Renfrew, Regan. Orphans of the Heart: A Young Girl & a Paint Filly Heal Each Other's Broken Hearts. (p. 1305)
Renfroe, Ann. Living Ice Cream Guys. Wilson, Alonza S., illus. (p. 1041)
Renfroe, Leisa, illus. see Trechsel, Kelli.
Renfroe, Marjorie. Doll Safari. (p. 463)
Renfroe, Vicki. Franklin. (p. 630)
Rengel, Marian. John Cabot: The Ongoing Search for a Westward Passage to Asia. (p. 921)
—Pakistan: A Primary Source Cultural Guide. (p. 1319)
Renick, Ricki & Swope, Gretchen. University of Mississippi College Prowler off the Record. (p. 1820)
Renick, Sam X. Adventures of Sammy the Saver In: Will Sammy Ride the World's First Space Coaster? Alvarado, Juan, illus. (p. 22)
Renier, Aaron. Spiral-Bound. (p. 1628)
—Unsinkable Walker Bean. Renier, Aaron, illus. (p. 1822)
Renier, Aaron, illus. see Morris, Gerald.
Renier, Aaron, jt. auth. see Pope, Paul.
Renier Nash, Oliver. Primate Puzzle: A tale of two friends & the missing long-nosed Monkeys. (p. 1400)
Renison, J. Secret History of Fairies. (p. 1541)
Renison, Jessica. Secret History of Dragons. (p. 1541)
—Secret History of Unicorns. (p. 1541)
Renn, Chantal, illus. see Walter Foster Custom Creative Team.
Renn, Chantal, jt. auth. see Clifford, Kathryn.
Renn, Diana. Tokyo Heist. (p. 1762)
Renn, Jürgen, ed. Einstein's Annalen Papers (Annalen der Physik) The Complete Collection, 1901-1922. (p. 507)
Renna, Diane M. Meghan's World: The Story of One Girl's Triumph Over Sensory Processing Disorder. Stark, Regina, illus. (p. 1124)
Renna, G. M. Meticulous Nicholas Goes to Camp. (p. 1130)
Renne. Ice Horse. (p. 850)
Renne, Philip K., illus. see O'Hearn, Michael.
Renner, C. J., et al. Soccer Longshot Maese, Fares, illus. (p. 1603)
—Soccer Longshot Maese, Fares & Aburto, Jesus, illus. (p. 1603)
Renner, Ed. When A Glass Breaks. (p. 1901)
Renner, Ellen. Castle of Shadows. (p. 277)
Renner, Sarah. Bouquet. (p. 216)
Rennert, Laura Joy. Emma, the Extra Ordinary Princess. Florian, Melanie, illus. (p. 520)
Rennert, Violette. Little Lions. (p. 1030)
—Little Whales. (p. 1037)
Rennich, Lori. When Cooper Got to Heaven. (p. 1901)
Rennie, Cliff. Goal Behind the Curtain. (p. 687)
—Offside in Ecuatina. (p. 1280)
—True Gold. (p. 1792)
Rennie, Richard, jt. auth. see Daintith, John.
Rennie-Pattison, Caroline. Law of Three. (p. 981)
Renninson, Lou. Frontalknutschen. (p. 644)
Rennison, Louise. Angus, Thongs & Full-Frontal Snogging. (p. 75)
—Angus, Thongs & Full-Frontal Snogging. (p. 76)
—Are These My Basoomas I See Before Me? Final Confessions of Georgia Nicolson. (p. 96)
—Away Laughing on a Fast Camel: Even More Confessions of Georgia Nicolson. (p. 120)
—Dancing in My Nuddy-Pants. (p. 403)
—Fabbity-Fab! A Big Box of Georgia: Angus, Thongs & Full-frontal Snogging; On the Bright Side I'm Now the Girlfriend of a Sex God; Knocked Out by My Nunga-Nungas. (p. 559)
—Knocked Out by My Nunga-Nungas: Further, Further Confessions of Georgia Nicolson. (p. 965)
—Knocked Out by My Nunga-Nungas. (p. 965)
—Love Is a Many Trousered Thing. (p. 1060)
—Midsummer Tights Dream. (p. 1139)
—On the Bright Side, I'm Now the Girlfriend of a Sex God: Further Confessions of Georgia Nicolson. (p. 1290)
—Startled by His Furry Shorts. (p. 1644)
—Stop in the Name of Pants! (p. 1653)
—Taming of the Tights. (p. 1704)
—Then He Ate My Boy Entrancers: More Mad, Marvy Confessions of Georgia Nicolson. (p. 1729)
—'...Then He Ate My Boy Entrancers' More Mad, Marvy Confessions of Georgia Nicolson. (p. 1729)
—Withering Tights: The Misadventures of Tallulah Casey. (p. 1942)
—Withering Tights. (p. 1942)
Renouf, Michael, illus. see Cattanach, Ann.
Renoult, Armelle. Basil Becomes a Big Brother. Frossard, Claire, illus. (p. 142)
Renshaw, Amanda. Art Book for Children. Kloet, Chris & Ace, Jane, eds. (p. 101)
Renshaw, Amanda & Phaidon Press Editors. Art Book for Children (p. 101)
Renshaw, D. M. Day to Remember. (p. 414)
Renshaw, Douglas. Around Our Feeder with George the Groundhog & Friends. Lamb, Janie, illus. (p. 100)
Rentala, Sita Kanaka Valli. Ocean Flows: In Prose: Zcumby's Judo (on Global Warming) (p. 1276)
Rentas, Donna. Leticia Goes to School. (p. 994)
Renteria, Justin, illus. see Dupont, Matthew.
Rentfro, Jeanne. Cowboy Country Coloring Book. (p. 374)
Renthrope, Damon, illus. see Wendel, Gretchen Schomel, et al.
Renthrope, Damon, illus. see Wendel, Gretchen Schomer & Schomer, Adam Anthomy.
Renthrope, Damon, illus. see Wendel, Gretchen Schomer & Schomer, Adam Anthony.
Rentschler, Ruth, jt. auth. see Fillis, Ian.
Rentta, Sharon, illus. see Nolan, Tina.
Reny, Anna. Dragon Tail: The Dragon of Legend Is Reborn. (p. 478)
Reny, Todd, illus. see MacGregor, Kim.
Reny, Todd, tr. see MacGregor, Kim.
Renzi, Pam. Global Christmas. (p. 684)
Reoch, Marcus. Dragons Chino para Ninos Libro 1 Spanish. (p. 479)
—Dragons Chinois Pour Enfants Livre 1 French. (p. 479)
Reoch, Martin. Primary School Chinese: Book 1. (p. 1399)
—Primary School Chinese: Book 3. (p. 1399)
Reonegro, Antonio, jt. auth. see Coy, John.
Repchuck, Caroline. Little Reindeer. (p. 1035)
Repchuk, Caroline. Fairy Colors. O'Neill, Rachael, illus. (p. 563)
Repetto, Laurie, illus. see Thomas, Charlene.
Repicci, Albert. Littlest Angel: A Christmas Story. (p. 1038)
Repka, Janice. Clueless Girl's Guide to Being a Genius. (p. 336)
Repka, Janice, jt. auth. see Rosensweig, Jay B.
Repkin, Mark. Mommy Breastfeeds My Baby Brother/ Mama Amamanta A Mi Hermanito. Moneysmith, David, illus. (p. 1162)
Repko, Marya. Historia de Everglades City. Gutierrez, Gloria, tr. from ENG. (p. 782)
—Story of Everglades City: A History for Younger Readers. (p. 1658)
Replogle, Steve & Carlsen, Wendy Vergoz, eds. From a Kid's Life: A Collection of Poetry by Bromwell Students. (p. 641)
Repp, Gloria. Story Shell: A Tale of Friendship Bog. Swaim, Michael, illus. (p. 1663)
Reppel, Phyllis, illus. see Martinez, Elsie & Stelly, Colette.
Reppert, Tom. Far Journey. (p. 572)
Repro. Amazing Grace Mazes & More. (p. 54)
Repta, Jennifer. Three Little Houses. (p. 1742)
Repun, Graceiela. Master of the Rings: Inside the World of J. R. R. Tolkein. (p. 1103)
Repun, Graciela. Monstruos de Visita. Fernandez, Luciana, illus. (p. 1170)
Rere The Storyteller. I Am a Wish. (p. 832)
Resau, Laura. Indigo Notebook. (p. 872)
—Red Glass. (p. 1454)
—Ruby Notebook. (p. 1493)
—Star in the Forest. (p. 1640)
—What the Moon Saw. (p. 1893)
Resau, Laura, jt. auth. see Farinango, Maria Virginia.
Rescek, Sanja. Bedtime Prayer. (p. 157)
—Bounce & Jiggle. (p. 216)
—Calm & Soothe. (p. 254)
—Easter Bunny's Helpers. (p. 499)
—One Elephant Went Out to Play. (p. 1294)
—Touch & Tickle. (p. 1772)
—Wiggle & Move. (p. 1927)
Rescek, Sanja, illus. see Dougherty, Brandi.
Rescek, Sanja, illus. see Fry, Sonali.
Rescek, Sanja, illus. see Harvey, Damian.
Rescek, Sanja, illus. see Mandy Ross.
Rescek, Sanja, illus. see Piper, Sophie.
Rescek, Sanja, illus. see Rock, Lois.
Rescek, Sanja, illus. see Schulz, Kathy.
Rescek, Sanja, illus. see Slater, Teddy.
Rescek, Sanja, illus. see Tiger Tales Staff, ed.
Rescek, Sanja, illus. see Tiger Tales, ed.
Rescek, Sanja, jt. illus. see Slater, Teddy.
Rescek, Sanja, et al. Itsy Bitsy Spider & Other Clap-along Rhymes. (p. 900)
Resch, Celeste. Alana's 12-Step Guide to Fun Golf: A How-to Book for Kids Who Want to Play Golf & Have Fun Doing It! (p. 33)
Reschke, Kathleen. Grandma, Mommy & Me. (p. 708)
—Monsters in My Basement. (p. 1169)
Reschofsky, Jean, illus. see Goff-Tuttle, Marie Jaume.
Research and Education Association Editors. MCAS Mathematics, Grade 10: Massachusetts Comprehensive Assessment System. (p. 1114)
—New York State Grade 8 English Language Arts. (p. 1248)
—Texas TAKS Exit-Level Mathematics. (p. 1724)
Research & Education Association Editors, illus. see Loeb, Jeph & Sale, Tim.
Research & Education Association Editors, illus. see Wagner, Matt.
Research Masters Staff & Barron's Educational Staff. Barron's Common Core Success Grade 5 ELA Workbook: Preparing Students for a Brilliant Future. (p. 140)
—Barron's Common Core Success Grade 5 Math Workbook: Preparing Students for a Brilliant Future. (p. 140)
Resh, Kimberly, ed. see Mikayla.
Resi, Putu, jt. auth. see Hawker, Frances.
Resl, Brigitte, jt. auth. see Mayer, Cassie.
Resman, Michael. Liliana Ageiraü. Cayetano, Eldred Roy, tr. (p. 1017)
—Villagers. Senelwa, Fred, tr. (p. 1842)
Resnicek, Tony, jt. auth. see Kershaw, Linda.
Resnick, Abraham. Lenin: Founder of the Soviet Union. (p. 991)
—Money. (p. 1163)
Resnick, Jacqueline. Daring Escape of the Misfit Menagerie. (p. 407)
Resnick, Yael, jt. auth. see Moscowitz, Moshe.
Resnicoff, Stan. BIG Parade: New York. (p. 183)
—BIG Parade: Los Angeles. (p. 183)
—BIG Parade: San Francisco. (p. 183)
—Stanley, the Seal of Approval. (p. 1640)
—Tom, the Talking Toilet. (p. 1764)
—Who'll Do the Moo? (p. 1920)
Resnikoff, Irene & Valas, Claudia. OG in Jerusalem. (p. 1280)
Respess, Beth. Autism & PDD Opposites Buddy Bear & Bonnie Bear. (p. 117)
—Autism & PDD Opposites Buddy Bear's Animals. (p. 117)
—Autism & PDD Opposites Buddy Bear's Food. (p. 117)
Respess, Beth, et al. Autism & PDD Concepts What Shape Is it, Becca Bunny? (p. 117)
Respess, Beth W. Autism & PDD Associations Buddy Bear Gets Ready for School. (p. 117)
—Autism & PDD Associations Buddy Bear Goes on a Picnic. (p. 117)
—Autism & PDD Associations Buddy Bear Has Fun. (p. 117)
—Autism & PDD Associations Buddy Bear Helps Mama Bear. (p. 117)
—Autism & PDD Associations Buddy Bear Likes Animals. (p. 117)
—Autism & PDD Categories Buddy Bear in the House. (p. 117)
—Autism & PDD Categories Buddy Bear in the Kitchen. (p. 117)
—Autism & PDD Categories Buddy Bear in the Yard. (p. 117)
—Autism & PDD Categories Buddy Bear Plays. (p. 117)
—Autism & PDD Comparatives/Superlatives What Buddy Bear Has. (p. 117)
—Autism & PDD Comparatives/Superlatives What Buddy Bear Does. (p. 117)
—Autism & PDD Comparatives/Superlatives What Buddy Bear Finds. (p. 117)

R

—Autism & PDD Yes/No Questions Buddy Bear at Home. (p. 117)
—Autism & PDD Yes/No Questions Buddy Bear at School. (p. 117)
—Autism & PDD Yes/No Questions Buddy Bear at the Park. (p. 117)
—Autism & PDD Yes/No Questions Buddy Bear at the Beach. (p. 117)
—Autism & PDD Yes/No Questions Buddy Bear at the Grocery Store. (p. 117)
Respondek, Kelly. Big Sister's Busy Day! (p. 183)
Ressler-Horst, Lara, illus. see Augsburger, A. Don.
Ressy-Nieves, Cynthia Ann. Keek-A-Poo's Adventures. (p. 946)
Restelli, Grazia, illus. see Krebs, Laurie.
Restivo, Andrea E. Arabella & the Perilous Pantheon. (p. 94)
Restle, Hope Madeline. Brianna in Pink. (p. 227)
Restrepo, Bettina. Illegal. (p. 856)
—Moose & Magpie Rogers, Sherry, illus. (p. 1173)
Restrepo, Bettina & Rogers, Sherry. Moose & Magpie (p. 1173)
Restrepo, Carlos Jose, tr. see Moreno-Velazquez, Juan A.
Restrepo, Felipe. Francis Bacon -Retrato de una Pesadilla. (p. 628)
Restrepo Gomez, Alonso. Ballena Jorobada: La Gran Viajera. (p. 134)
Retana, Maria, tr. see Crouch, Adele.
Retana, Maria Luisa. Tanili: An Afrocuban Folktale. (p. 1705)
Rethi, Lili, illus. see McKown, Robin.
Rethman, Hope. God Gives Us Jesus. (p. 688)
Rettenmund, Tamara, illus. see Charlip, Remy.
Rettig, Liz. Jumping to Confusions. (p. 934)
—My Desperate Love Diary. (p. 1201)
—My Rocky Romance Diary. (p. 1217)
Rettig, Shari. Night Before the First Christmas. (p. 1253)
Rettore. Elephant & Friends. (p. 511)
—Giraffe & Friends. (p. 677)
Retwick, Roy, illus. see Wood, Greg V. & Benchmark Education Co., LLC.
Retz, Zac, illus. see Lefebvre, Jason.
Retzlaff, Donald. Texas Instruments & Me (p. 1724)
Retzlaff, Shay, illus. see Shafer, Patty.
Reuben, Borgen, photos by see Learn As You Grow.
Reuben, Susan, et al. Food & Faith. (p. 613)
Reuille Irons, Rosemary. Frowning Clowns. (p. 645)
Reuker, Heidi. Queen of the Rats. (p. 1425)
Reul, Sarah Lynne, illus. see Potoma, Alison.
Reusch, Mister, illus. see Glenn, Joshua & Larsen, Elizabeth Foy.
Reusch, Mister, illus. see Larsen, Elizabeth Foy & Glenn, Joshua.
Reusser, Kayleen. Celebrities Giving Back: A Guide to Giving Back. (p. 285)
—Day by Day with Taylor Swift. (p. 412)
—Hades. (p. 735)
—Hephaestus. (p. 769)
—Hermes. (p. 771)
—Leona Lewis. (p. 992)
—Recipe & Craft Guide to Indonesia. (p. 1451)
—Selena Gomez. (p. 1549)
—Taylor Swift. (p. 1708)
Reusswig, William, illus. see Lowery, Lawrence F.
Reuter, Ted, ed. 267 Stupidest Things Democrats Ever Said: the 267 Stupidest Things Republicans Ever Said. (p. 2001)
Reuterstrand, Siri. Ellis Goes to the Doctor. Wik, Jenny, illus. (p. 514)
—Ellis Is Scared of the Dark. Wik, Jenny, illus. (p. 514)
Reva Jean Rohe. Adventures of Tomtom the Duck. (p. 24)
Révah, Noémie. Mister Horizontal & Miss Vertical. Zagnoli, Olimpia, illus. (p. 1155)
Revard, Carter. How the Songs Come Down: New & Selected Poems. (p. 813)
Revell, Cindy, illus. see Roberts, Jillian.
Revell, Cindy, illus. see StJohn, Amanda.
Revell, Cindy, illus. see Waldman, Debby & Feutl, Rita.
Revell, Cindy, illus. see Waldman, Debby.
Revell, Cindy, illus. see West, Tracey.
Revelle, Rick. I Am Algonquin: An Algonquin Quest Novel. (p. 832)
Revels, Robert, illus. see Shah, Idries.
Revenson, Jody. Fancy Nancy: Candy Bonanza. (p. 570)
Revere, John J. Little Brown Horse. Harvancik, Monica, illus. (p. 1025)
Revere, Paul, jt. auth. see Longfellow, Henry Wadsworth.
Reviejo, Carlos, jt. auth. see Reviejo, Carlos.
Reviejo, Carlos & Reviejo, Carlos. Dejame Que te Cuente: Cincuenta Cuentos de Animales para Ninos. (p. 424)
Reviejo, Carlos, et al. Cantares y Decires. (p. 262)
Reviejo Hernandez, Carlos. Platero y Juan Ramon. Wensell, Ulises, illus. (p. 1370)
Revilla, Daniel Juan. Dirt Road. (p. 446)
REVILLE, TONI-ANN, illus. see Signoretti, Brenda.
Revis, Beth. Across the Universe. (p. 9)
—Million Suns. (p. 1144)
—Shades of Earth. (p. 1557)
Revoir, Joyce, illus. see Foust, Cindy G.
Revoy, Antoine, illus. see San Souci, Robert D.
Revoy, Antoine, illus. see Shecter, Vicky Alvear.
Revoyr, Nina. Necessary Hunger: A Novel. (p. 1239)
Revutsky, Helen Ross, illus. see Zocchi, Judith Mazzeo, et al.
Revutsky, Helen Ross, illus. see Zocchi, Judith Mazzeo.
Rew, Jen, illus. see Hunter, Alex.
Rewa. Molly May on the High Seas. (p. 1160)
ReWalt, Nancy E. Aerial: A Spider's Tale. Cranford, Darren, illus. (p. 25)
—Aerial: A Trip to Remember. Cranford, Darren, illus. (p. 25)
Rewalt, Nancy E. Aerial Meets Farmer Fedamore. Cranford, Darren, illus. (p. 25)
—Lost & Found: Goldilocks & the Three Bears Revisited. Cranford, Darren, illus. (p. 1054)
Rex, Adam. Champions of Breakfast. (p. 289)
—Cold Cereal. (p. 338)
—Fat Vampire: A Never Coming of Age Story. (p. 577)
—Frankenstein Makes a Sandwich. (p. 629)
—Frankenstein Takes the Cake. (p. 629)
—Moonday. Rex, Adam, illus. (p. 1172)
—Smek for President! Rex, Adam, illus. (p. 1593)
—True Meaning of Smekday. (p. 1792)
—True Meaning of Smekday. Rex, Adam, illus. (p. 1792)
—Unlucky Charms. (p. 1821)
Rex, Adam, illus. see Barnett, Mac, et al.
Rex, Adam, illus. see Barnett, Mac.
Rex, Adam, illus. see Gaiman, Neil.
Rex, Adam, illus. see Kelly, Katy.
Rex, Adam, illus. see Scieszka, Jon, et al.
Rex, Adam, illus. see Timberlake, Amy.
Rex, Annmarie. Black's Adventure in the Big, Scary, Hairy World. (p. 197)
—Black's Adventure in the Big, Scary, Hairy World. Rex, Annmarie, illus. (p. 197)
Rex, Judith. Puppy Twins, Backyard Colors. Hitz, Dustin, illus. (p. 1418)
Rex, Michael. Egg of Misery: Fangbone, Third Grade Barbarian. Rex, Michael, illus. (p. 506)
—Egg of Misery. (p. 506)
—End of the World. Rex, Michael, illus. (p. 526)
—Fangbone! Third-Grade Barbarian. (p. 571)
—Fangbone! Third-Grade Barbarian. Rex, Michael, illus. (p. 571)
—Firefighter. Rex, Michael, illus. (p. 591)
—Furious George Goes Bananas: A Primate Parody. Rex, Michael, illus. (p. 650)
—Goodnight Goon: A Petrifying Parody. Rex, Michael, illus. (p. 701)
—Icky Ricky #3: the Dead Disco Raccoon. Rex, Michael, illus. (p. 851)
—Icky Ricky #4: the Hole to China. (p. 851)
—Runaway Mummy: A Petrifying Parody. (p. 1496)
—Toilet Paper Mummy. (p. 1762)
—Toilet Paper Mummy. Rex, Michael, illus. (p. 1762)
—Truck Duck. Rex, Michael, illus. (p. 1791)
—Two-Dollar Dirt Shirt. (p. 1803)
Rex, Michael, illus. see Branley, Franklyn M.
Rex, Michael, illus. see Branley, Franklyn Mansfield.
Rex, Michael, illus. see Bunting, Eve.
Rex, Michael, illus. see Murphy, Stuart J.
Rex, Michael, jt. auth. see Murphy, Stuart J.
Rex, Richard. Henry VIII & the English Reformation. (p. 768)
Rex, Sue, ed. see Geste, Mal, et al.
Rexing, Debbie. Writing Traits... My Perilous Journey, & I'm Only A 3rd Grader! (p. 1965)
Rexroad, Danese. Naked Baby. (p. 1228)
Rexroad, Fred. Whiz Tanner & the Phony Masterpiece: A Tanner-Dent Mystery. Rexroad, Susan, illus. (p. 1914)
Rexroad, Susan, illus. see Rexroad, Fred.
Rexroth, Sharon. America from the Sky. (p. 59)
—Ohio. (p. 1281)
—Ohio from the Sky. (p. 1281)
Rey. Attention aux Chiens. (p. 114)
—Panique a la Chocolaterie. (p. 1321)
—Vive le Cinema. (p. 1846)
Rey, jt. auth. see Gee.
Rey, Alain. Robert junior Poche. (p. 1479)
Rey and others, Rey and. Great Big Dinosaur Treasury. (p. 714)
Rey, Carol. Iris Wall, Cracker Cowgirl Lux, Eldon, illus. (p. 887)
Rey, H. A. Apple Harvest: Curious about Harvest Time. (p. 92)
—Around Town (p. 101)
—Awake-Asleep Cloth Book & Door Hanger. (p. 120)
—Builds a Home. (p. 239)
—Builds an Igloo. (p. 239)
—C Is for Curious. (p. 250)
—Car Wash. (p. 265)
—CG Puppies AMS Oversized Edition. (p. 288)
—Christmas Countdown. (p. 313)
—Complete Adventures of Curious George. (p. 352)
—Curious about Christmas. (p. 392)
—Curious Baby Counting. (p. 392)
—Curious Baby Everyday Shapes Puzzle Book: A Puzzle Play Book. (p. 392)
—Curious Baby My First Book of Color. (p. 392)
—Curious George a Home for Honeybees (CGTV Early Reader) (p. 393)
—Curious George & the Dump Truck. (p. 393)
—Curious George & the Hot Air Balloon. (p. 393)
—Curious George & the Ice Cream Surprise. (p. 393)
—Curious George Apple Harvest. (p. 393)
—Curious George at the Aquarium. (p. 393)
—Curious George at the Baseball Game (Jorge el Curioso en el Partido de Beisbol) (p. 393)
—Curious George at the Park. Meyer, Emily, ed. (p. 393)
—Curious George Builds an Igloo (CGTV Reader) (p. 393)
—Curious George Car Wash. (p. 393)
—Curious George Cleans Up. Canetti, Yanitzia, tr. (p. 393)
—Curious George Colors Eggs. (p. 393)
—Curious George Colors Eggs (CGTV Reader) (p. 393)
—Curious George Curious about Learning Boxed Set. (p. 393)
—Curious George Dance Party CGTV Reader. (p. 393)
—Curious George Discovers Germs (Science Storybook) (p. 393)
—Curious George Discovers the Ocean (Science Storybook) (p. 393)
—Curious George Discovers the Rainbow (Science Storybook) (p. 393)
—Curious George Discovers the Sun (Science Storybook) (p. 393)
—Curious George Flies a Kite. (p. 393)
—Curious George Gets a Medal. (p. 393)
—Curious George Goes to a Costume Party (Jorge el Curioso Va a una Fiesta de Disfraces) (p. 393)
—Curious George Goes to the Zoo. (p. 393)
—Curious George Grows a Garden. (p. 393)
—Curious George Haunted Halloween. (p. 393)
—Curious George Haunted Halloween (CGTV Reader) (p. 393)
—Curious George Home Run (Jorge el Curioso el Jonrón) (p. 393)
—Curious George Learns the Alphabet (p. 393)
—Curious George Learns to Count from 1 To 100. (p. 393)
—Curious George Magnetic Maze Book. (p. 393)
—Curious George Makes Maple Syrup (CGTV 8x8) (p. 393)
—Curious George Makes Pancakes. Rey, Margret, illus. (p. 393)
—Curious George Neighborhood Friends. (p. 393)
—Curious George Parade Day. (p. 393)
—Curious George Pat-A-Cake. (p. 393)
—Curious George Plants a Seed. (p. 393)
—Curious George Plants a Tree. Wilcox, Mary, ed. (p. 393)
—Curious George Saves His Pennies. (p. 393)
—Curious George Super Sticker Activity Book. (p. 393)
—Curious George Tool Time (CGTV Board Book) (p. 393)
—Curious George Travel Activity Kit. (p. 393)
—Curious George Visits the Library (Jorge el Curioso Va a la Biblioteca) (p. 393)
—Curious George What Do You See? (p. 393)
—Curious George's 5-Minute Stories. (p. 393)
—Curious George's Crane (mini Movers Shaped Board Books) (p. 394)
—Curious George's Dump Truck. (p. 394)
—Curious George's Fire Truck. (p. 394)
—Curious George's Train (mini Movers Shaped Board Books) (p. 394)
—Dance Party. (p. 402)
—Dinosaur Tracks. (p. 443)
—Feliz Navidad, Jorge el Curioso. Young, Mary O'Keefe, illus. (p. 581)
—Find the Constellations. (p. 587)
—Happy Halloween. (p. 745)
—Happy St. Patrick's Day, Curious George. (p. 746)
—Happy Thanksgiving. (p. 746)
—Happy Valentine's Day, Curious George! Young, Mary O'Keefe, illus. (p. 747)
—Home Run. (p. 792)
—Jorge el Curioso el Baile. (p. 926)
—Jorge el Curioso Huellas de Dinosaurio. (p. 926)
—Jorge el Curioso Siembra Una Semilla. Zappy, Erica, ed. (p. 926)
—Jorge el Curioso Va a una Fiesta de Disfraces/Curious George Goes to a Costume Party (Bilingual) (p. 926)
—Jorge el Curioso Visita el Acuario. (p. 926)
—Jorge el Curioso y la Pinata. (p. 926)
—Learns to Count from 1 to 100: Counting, Grouping, Mapping, & More! Hines, Anna Grossnickle, illus. (p. 986)
—Learns to Count from 1 to 100. (p. 986)
—Librarian for a Day. (p. 1005)
—Music Play. (p. 1193)
—My Curious Dreamer (p. 1200)
—My Curious World. (p. 1200)
—My Favorite Things. (p. 1203)
—My First Nursery Songs. (p. 1207)
—My First Words at the Farm (p. 1208)
—My Little Boat. (p. 1212)
—On the Go! (p. 1290)
—Perfect Carrot. (p. 1341)
—Pinata Party. (p. 1359)
—Plumber's Helper. Meyer, Emily, ed. (p. 1374)
—Race Day. (p. 1430)
—Stars: A New Way to See Them. (p. 1643)
—Storybook Collection. (p. 1663)
—Sweet Dreams, Curious George. (p. 1689)
—Tadpole Trouble. (p. 1695)
—Three Tales for a Winter's Night. (p. 1744)
—Time for School. (p. 1751)
—Treasury of Curious George (Coleccion de Oro Jorge el Curioso) (p. 1782)
—Up, Up, & Away. (p. 1824)
—Visits the Library / Jorge el Curioso Va a la Biblioteca. (p. 1846)
—Where Is Curious George? Around the Town: A Look-And-Find Book. (p. 1908)
—Windy Delivery. (p. 1936)
—Winter's Nap. (p. 1938)
—¡Eres Curioso Todo el Tiempo! (p. 533)
Rey, H. A., jt. auth. see Driscoll, Laura.
Rey, H. A., jt. auth. see Hapka, Catherine, pseud.
Rey, H. A., jt. auth. see Houghton Mifflin and Company Publishing Staff.
Rey, H. A., jt. auth. see Houghton Mifflin Harcourt Children's Group Staff.
Rey, H. A., jt. auth. see Houghton Mifflin Harcourt Publishing Company Staff.
Rey, H. A., jt. auth. see Rey, Margret.
Rey, H. A., jt. auth. see Zoehfeld, Kathleen Weidner.
Rey, H. A. & Berger, Sholem. [Dzshordzsh der Naygeriker/Fun H. A. Rey ; Yidish, Sholem Berger] George der Naygeriker. (p. 491)
Rey, H. A. & Houghton Mifflin Company Editors. Sweet Dreams 5-Minute Bedtime Stories. (p. 1689)
Rey, H. A. & Houghton Mifflin Company Staff. Bigger & Smaller. (p. 185)
Rey, H. A. & Margaret. Curious George Visits the Dentist. (p. 393)
Rey, H. A. & Rey, Margaret. Big Book of Adventures: 12 Beginning Readers in One. (p. 178)
—Chasing Waves. (p. 294)
—Curious George Goes to a Bookstore. (p. 393)
—Curious George Makes Maple Syrup. (p. 393)
—Curious George Saves His Pennies. (p. 393)
—Curious George Says Thank You. (p. 393)
—Curious George Visits the Library. (p. 393)
—Goes to the Beach. (p. 692)
—H. A. Rey Treasury of Stories. (p. 734)
—Where Is Curious George? A Look & Find Book. (p. 1908)
Rey, H. A. & Rey, Margret. At the Zoo. (p. 111)
—Before & After. (p. 158)
—Cecily G. & the 9 Monkeys. (p. 283)
—Circus Act. (p. 322)
—Complete Adventures of Curious George. (p. 352)
—Curious Baby My Growing World. (p. 392)
—Curious George (p. 393)
—Curious George & the Birthday Surprise. (p. 393)
—Curious George & the Birthday Surprise. Weston, Martha, illus. (p. 393)
—Curious George & the Dump Truck. (p. 393)
—Curious George & the Firefighters. (p. 393)
—Curious George & the Pizza Party. (p. 393)
—Curious George & the Pizza Party. Shalleck, Alan J., ed. (p. 393)
—Curious George & the Puppies. (p. 393)
—Curious George at the Aquarium. Hines, Anna Grossnickle, illus. (p. 393)
—Curious George Feeds the Animals. (p. 393)
—Curious George Finds a Friend. (p. 393)
—Curious George Flies a Kite (p. 393)
—Curious George Gets a Medal (p. 393)
—Curious George Goes Bowling (CGTV Lift-The-Flap 8x8) (p. 393)
—Curious George Goes to a Movie. (p. 393)
—Curious George Goes to the Movies. (p. 393)
—Curious George Hide-and-Seek. (p. 393)
—Curious George Home Run. (p. 393)
—Curious George in the Snow. (p. 393)
—Curious George Learns the Alphabet. (p. 393)
—Curious George - Librarian for a Day. (p. 393)
—Curious George Rides a Bike (p. 393)
—Curious George Says Thank You. (p. 393)
—Curious George Seasons Puzzle Book. (p. 393)
—Curious George Stories to Share. (p. 393)
—Curious George Super Sticker Coloring Book. (p. 393)
—Curious George Takes a Job. (p. 393)
—Curious George the Boat Show. (p. 393)
—Curious George to the Rescue. (p. 393)
—Curious George's 1 to 10 & Back Again. (p. 393)
—Curious George's ABCs. (p. 393)
—Curious George's Are You Curious? (p. 393)
—Curious George's Big Book of Curiosity. Paprocki, Greg, illus. (p. 393)
—Curious George's Dream. (p. 394)
—Curious George's First Day of School. (p. 394)
—Curious George's Neighborhood. Weston, Martha, illus. (p. 394)
—Curious George's Opposites. (p. 394)
—Dog Show. (p. 461)
—George O Curioso. (p. 663)
—Happy Hanukkah. (p. 745)
—Jorge el Curioso. Català, Josep Maria & Tusquets, Eugenia, trs. (p. 925)
—Jorge el Curioso Encuentra Trabajo. Canetti, Yanitzia, tr. (p. 926)
—Jorge el Curioso Vuela Una Cometa. (p. 926)
—Lost & Found. (p. 1054)
—My First Words at the Zoo (p. 1208)
—Plays Mini Golf. (p. 1373)
—Roller Coaster. (p. 1485)
—Seasons. (p. 1538)
—Shapes. (p. 1560)
—Surprise Gift. (p. 1686)
—Takes a Trip. (p. 1697)
—Three Tales for a Winter's Night. (p. 1744)
—Treasury of Curious George. (p. 1782)
Rey, H. A., et al. Curious George & the Firefighters. (p. 393)
—Curious George Cleans Up. (p. 393)
—Curious George Discovery Day. (p. 393)
—Curious George the Movie. (p. 393)
—Donut Delivery. (p. 469)
—Kite. (p. 962)
—Merry Christmas, Curious George. Young, Mary O'Keefe, illus. (p. 1128)
Rey, H.a. Curious George Visits the Dentist. (p. 393)
Rey, Hans Augusto. Schoolhouse Fun (p. 1523)
Rey Hazas, Antonio. Novela Picaresca. (p. 1268)
Rey, Luis, illus. see Chinsamy-Turan, Anusuya.
Rey, Luis, illus. see Hynson, Colin.
Rey, Luis, illus. see Mayes, Susan.
Rey, Luis, illus. see Staunton, Joseph & Flinthart, Dirk.
Rey, Luis V., illus. see Bakker, Robert T.
Rey, Luis V., illus. see Davidson, Susanna, et al.
Rey, Luis V., illus. see Holtz, Thomas R.
Rey, Margaret, jt. auth. see Rey, H. A.
Rey, Margret. Margret & H. A. Rey's Curious George Goes Camping. Vipah Interactive, illus. (p. 1092)
Rey, Margret, illus. see Rey, H. A.
Rey, Margret, jt. auth. see Rey, H. A.
Rey, Margret, jt. illus. see Rey, H. A.
Rey, Margret & Rey, H. A. Curious George & the Hot Air Balloon. (p. 393)
—Curious George at the Aquarium. (p. 393)
—Curious George Feeds the Animals. (p. 393)
—Curious George Goes Camping (p. 393)
—Curious George Goes Camping. (p. 393)
—Curious George Goes to the Hospital (p. 393)
—Curious George Takes a Train. (p. 393)
—Curious George Visits the Library. (p. 393)
—Curious George's First Day of School Vipah Interactive Staff, illus. (p. 394)
—Curious George's First Day of School. Hines, Anna Grossnickle, illus. (p. 394)
—Feeds the Animals Vipah Interactive Staff, illus. (p. 580)
—Goes to a Movie. Vipah Interactive Staff, illus. (p. 692)
—Makes Pancakes. (p. 1080)
—New Adventures of Curious George. Vipah Interactive Staff, illus. (p. 1243)
—Puppies. (p. 1417)
Rey, Maria Del. Institute. (p. 878)
Rey, Molly. Measuring with Footsteps: Measure Lengths. (p. 1117)
—Measuring with Footsteps. (p. 1117)
Reybold, Laura. Todo lo que necesitas saber sobre Los peligros del tatuaje y el body piercing (Everything You Need to Know about the Dangers of Tattooing & Piercing) (p. 1761)
Reyburn, Stanley S. Holmes Hiatus - The Parisian Affair. Landes, William-Alan, ed. (p. 789)
—Sherlock Holmes in the Case of the Crafty Cracksman. Landes, William-Alan, ed. (p. 1565)
—Sherlock Holmes in the Case of the Derailed Shipment. Landes, William-Alan, ed. (p. 1565)

—Sherlock Holmes in the Case of the Fatal Poppy. Landes, William-Alan, ed. (p. 1565)
—Sherlock Holmes in the Case of the Nervous Nanny. Landes, William-Alan, ed. (p. 1565)
—Sherlock Holmes in the Meiji Experience. Landes, William-Alan, ed. (p. 1565)
Reyburn, Susan. Amelia Earhart. (p. 58)
Reyes, Analisse. It Wasn't Me! (p. 894)
Reyes, Arlene, illus. see Zorka, Shawna.
Reyes, Blanca Matilde. Farm Animals. (p. 573)
—Insects. (p. 875)
—Sea Animals. (p. 1534)
—Wild Animals. (p. 1928)
Reyes, Cameron. In Your Heart. DeBroech, Sarah, illus. (p. 868)
Reyes, Carlos Jose. Dulcita y el Burrito. Redondo, Fernando, illus. (p. 489)
—Globito Manual. Parra, Rocio, illus. (p. 685)
—Piedra de la Felicidad. AZ, illus. (p. 1357)
Reyes, Gabrielle. Chugger of the Year. (p. 318)
—Dolphin Tale 2: The Junior Novel. (p. 464)
—Dolphin Tale 2: Movie Reader. (p. 464)
—Winter Friends. (p. 1938)
Reyes, Glendalys, illus. see Kittredge, James M.
Reyes, Jose & Reyes, Rhonda. I AM Alphabet Book. (p. 832)
Reyes, Laurisa White. Last Enchanter. (p. 977)
—Rock of Ivanore: Book One of the Celestine Chronicles. (p. 1482)
—Rock of Ivanore. (p. 1482)
Reyes, M. G. Emancipated. (p. 517)
Reyes, Maria Margarita, illus. see Aristizabal, Nora.
Reyes, Marily A. Reflexiones II/Reflections. Reyes, Marily A., ed. (p. 1456)
Reyes, Nikki. Unexpected Guest: It Started with a fish. It ended with a Friend. (p. 1817)
Reyes, Raquel, et al. I May Bien! Level E. (p. 844)
Reyes, Reyna. Chencha. (p. 297)
Reyes, Rhonda, jt. auth. see Reyes, Jose.
Reyes, S. L. Mommy Does a Lot So I Want to Too Taylor, Amber, illus. (p. 1162)
Reyes, Sharon D. Frank (p. 628)
Reyes, Shawntie L. I'm Two, So What Should I Do? Taylor, Amber L., illus. (p. 860)
Reyes, Victor, tr. see Laufer, Peter.
Reyes, Yazmin. Fairies vs. Wizards: The Last Battle (p. 563)
Reyes, Yolanda. Anos Terribles. (p. 87)
—Cama para Tres. Coll, Ivar Da, illus. (p. 255)
—Maria de los Dinosaurios. (p. 1093)
Reyes, Yolanda, jt. auth. see Ruiz, Clarisa.
Reymond, Robert L. Contending for the Faith: Lines in the Sand That Strengthen the Church. (p. 360)
—God-Centered Preacher: Developing a Pulpit Ministry Approved by God. (p. 688)
—Paul, Missionary Theologian: A Survey of His Missionary Labours & Theology. (p. 1330)
Reyna, A. Faith. Safari Girls: The Enchanted Beginning. (p. 1502)
Reynish, Jenny, illus. see Mordhorst, Heidi.
Reynolds, A. J. Chrysalid Conspiracy - the Sanddancer. (p. 317)
Reynolds, Aaron. Back of the Bus. Cooper, Floyd, illus. (p. 130)
—Buffalo Wings. Bogan, Paulette, illus. (p. 236)
—Carnivores. Newman, Jeff & Santat, Dan, illus. (p. 270)
—Chicks & Salsa. Bogan, Paulette, illus. (p. 301)
—Creepy Carrots! Brown, Peter, illus. (p. 381)
—Creepy Crawly Crime. Weaver, Brian M. & Numberman, Neil, illus. (p. 381)
—Dung Beetle Bandits Lervold, Erik, illus. (p. 490)
—Dung Beetle Bandits: Tiger Moth. Lervold, Erik, illus. (p. 490)
—Fortune Cookies of Weevil Lervold, Erik, illus. (p. 623)
—Fortune Cookies of Weevil: Tiger Moth. Lervold, Erik, illus. (p. 623)
—Here Comes Destructosaurus! Tankard, Jeremy, illus. (p. 770)
—In Big Hairy Drama. Numberman, Neil, illus. (p. 863)
—Insect Ninja: Tiger Moth. Lervold, Erik, illus. (p. 875)
—Kung Pow Chicken: Tiger Moth. Lervold, Erik, illus. (p. 968)
—Las Zanahorias Maléficas. (p. 977)
—Metal Man. Hoppe, Paul, illus. (p. 1130)
—Nerdy Birdy. Davies, Matt, illus. (p. 1241)
—Pest Show on Earth Lervold, Erik, illus. (p. 1345)
—Pest Show on Earth: Tiger Moth Lervold, Erik, illus. (p. 1345)
—Pirates vs. Cowboys. Barneda, David, illus. (p. 1364)
—Tiger Moth: Adventures of an Insect Ninja Lervold, Erik, illus. (p. 1748)
—Tiger Moth & the Dragon Kite Contest Lervold, Erik, illus. (p. 1748)
Reynolds, Aaron & Rash, Andy. Superhero School. Rash, Andy, illus. (p. 1683)
Reynolds, Adrian, illus. see Jarman, Julia.
Reynolds, Adrian, illus. see Oram, Hiawyn.
Reynolds, Adrian, illus. see Rosen, Michael.
Reynolds, Adrian, illus. see Ryan, Margaret & Reynolds, Ruth.
Reynolds, Adrian, illus. see Taylor, Thomas.
Reynolds, Adrian, illus. see Whybrow, Ian.
Reynolds, Adrian, illus. see Willis, Jeanne.
Reynolds, Alison. Let's Grow a Garden. Hopgood, Andrew, illus. (p. 998)
—Let's Save Water. Hopgood, Andrew, illus. (p. 1000)
—Let's Turn It Off. Hopgood, Andrew, illus. (p. 1001)
—Let's Use It Again. Hopgood, Andrew, illus. (p. 1001)
—New Friend for Marmalade. McKenzie, Heath, illus. (p. 1244)
—Why I Love My Mom. Geddes, Serena, illus. (p. 1925)
—Year with Marmalade. McKenzie, Heath, illus. (p. 1969)
Reynolds, Annette. First COLL of Bible Stories & Stickers: Daniel, Jonah, Jesus & Other Stories. MacLean, Moira, illus. (p. 593)
—First COLL of Bible Stories & Stickers: Noahn, Samson, Jesus & Other Stories. MacLean, Moira, illus. (p. 593)
Reynolds, Annette, ed. see Jeffs, Stephanie.
Reynolds, Annette, ed. see Lane, Leena.
Reynolds, Betty. Japanese Celebrations: Cherry Blossoms, Lanterns & Stars! (p. 909)
—Little Lies. (p. 1030)
—Tokyo Friends. (p. 1762)
Reynolds, Carl. Turkey Mountain Gang's... . Christmas Adventure! (p. 1797)
Reynolds, Carl Stanley. Turkey Mountain Gang: The Adventures Begin. (p. 1797)
Reynolds, Caroline. Bead Street-the Fable of Red Clover. (p. 149)
Reynolds, Cathy J. Little Mike Takes A Hike. (p. 1031)
Reynolds, Charles. Card Magic. (p. 265)
Reynolds, Cynthia Furlong. Across the Reach. (p. 9)
—Fishing for Numbers: A Maine Number Book. Brett, Jeannie, illus. (p. 599)
—Grammie's Secret Cupboard. Dodson, Bert, illus. (p. 706)
Reynolds, D. G. Moon Beam Walking: Dream Space Books Ward, Scott, illus. (p. 1171)
Reynolds, David West, et al. The Complete Visual Dictionary. Ivanov, Alex, photos by. (p. 1728)
Reynolds, Doris, illus. see Varble, Rachel McBrayer.
Reynolds, E. E. Behind the Ranges: Tales of Explorers, Pioneers & Travellers. Tresilian, S., illus. (p. 160)
—Unknown Ways: More Tales of Explorers, Pioneers & Travellers. Tresilian, S., illus. (p. 1821)
Reynolds, E. E., ed. see Belaney, Archibald Stansfeld.
Reynolds, Edith. We Are the Word People. (p. 1866)
—Working with Words. (p. 1953)
Reynolds, Eleanor Davenport. Why Aren't You My Friend? the Story of Bullying, Diversity, & Friendship. (p. 1922)
Reynolds, Emily C. S., illus. see Salas, Laura Purdie.
Reynolds, Emily C. S., tr. see Salas, Laura Purdie.
Reynolds, Evan. My Vacation. (p. 1220)
Reynolds, Gardiner John. Stone Fox. (p. 1652)
Reynolds, Grahame. Grafs of Arran Towers. (p. 705)
Reynolds, Hunter. Hunting with Great White Sharks. (p. 829)
Reynolds, Jan. Amazon Basin. (p. 56)
—Celebrate! Connections among Cultures Reynolds, Jan, photos by. (p. 283)
—Connections among Cultures. (p. 358)
—Cycle of Rice, Cycle of Life: A Story of Sustainable Farming. Reynolds, Jan, photos by. (p. 396)
—Down Under. (p. 474)
—Far North. (p. 572)
—Frozen Land (p. 645)
—Himalaya (p. 780)
—Mongolia (p. 1164)
—Only the Mountains Do Not Move: A Maasai Story of Culture & Conservation. Reynolds, Jan, photos by. (p. 1298)
—Sahara (p. 1503)
Reynolds, Janice, jt. auth. see Geye, Susan.
Reynolds, Jason. Boy in the Black Suit. (p. 218)
—When I Was the Greatest. Frost, Michael, photos by. (p. 1903)
Reynolds, Jason & Griffin, Jason. My Name Is Jason. Mine Too: Our Story. Our Way. Griffin, Jason, illus. (p. 1215)
—My Name Is Jason, Mine Too. (p. 1215)
Reynolds, Jean. Gwen & the Talking Napkin. (p. 733)
Reynolds, Jean B. Heather & the Talking Manger Scene. (p. 760)
Reynolds, Jeff E. Egypt. (p. 506)
—Puerto Rico. (p. 1415)
Reynolds, John & Hubbard, Julia. IGCSE Study Guide for First Language English. (p. 855)
Reynolds, John, et al. IGCSE English. (p. 855)
Reynolds, Johnny Sue. Hospitality Services: Food & Lodging. (p. 801)
Reynolds Jr., R. A. Simon's Big Move. Balek, Dayna Courtney, illus. (p. 1577)
Reynolds, Judy. Blue Jay's Choice. (p. 203)
Reynolds, K. Preston. You're Dead Meat, Sub. (p. 1982)
Reynolds, Laureen. Sight Word Poetry. Migliaccio, Eric, ed. (p. 1574)
Reynolds, Lauren F. Deep Sea Poetry: For Children. (p. 423)
Reynolds, Loralyn & Caldwell, Christiana Marie Melvin. Animals of the Ark: (for a boy named Clay) Foster, Trista, photos by. (p. 83)
Reynolds, Luke, ed. Break These Rules: 35 YA Authors on Speaking up, Standing Out, & Being Yourself. (p. 224)
Reynolds MacArthur, Anita. Royal Little Pest Roy, Karen, illus. (p. 1492)
Reynolds, Marilyn. World in Between. (p. 1956)
Reynolds, Mattie. Kids Making Money: An Introduction to Financial Literacy. (p. 954)
—Saving for the Future: An Introduction to Financial Literacy. (p. 1517)
—Sharing with Others: An Introduction to Financial Literacy. (p. 1561)
—Super-Smart Shopping: An Introduction to Financial Literacy. (p. 1682)
Reynolds, Michael, tr. see Erlbruch, Wolf.
Reynolds, Mignon C. Life as Bonkers. (p. 1008)
Reynolds, Mike. How to Analyze the Films of Spike Lee. (p. 814)
Reynolds, Pat, illus. see Reilly, Carmel.
Reynolds, Paul A. Going Places. Reynolds, Peter H., illus. (p. 692)
Reynolds, Paul A. & Reynolds, Peter. Sydney & Simon: To the Moon & Beyond! (p. 1692)
Reynolds, Paul & Reynolds, Paul, Jr. Sydney & Simon: Full Steam Ahead! (p. 1692)
Reynolds, Paul, Jr., jt. auth. see Reynolds, Paul.
Reynolds, Peter, illus. see McDonald, Megan.
Reynolds, Peter, illus. see Potter, Ellen.
Reynolds, Peter, illus. see Taylor, Sean.
Reynolds, Peter, jt. auth. see Reynolds, Peter H.
Reynolds, Peter, jt. illus. see Reynolds, Paul A.
Reynolds, Peter H. Animation-ish Classroom Edition CD-ROM Building License: Make Your Mark... Move! (p. 84)
—Best Kid in the World: A SugarLoaf Book. Reynolds, Peter H., illus. (p. 170)
—Big Screen Books: For Big Fans of Story Sharing: the Dot Download: the Dot - Download. (p. 183)
—Dot. Reynolds, Peter H., illus. (p. 472)
—Dot: Make Your Mark Kit. Reynolds, Peter H., illus. (p. 472)
—I'm Here. Reynolds, Peter H., illus. (p. 859)
—Ish. Reynolds, Peter H., illus. (p. 891)
—My Very Big Little World. Reynolds, Peter H., illus. (p. 1221)
—North Star. Reynolds, Peter H., illus. (p. 1265)
—Peter Reynolds Creatrilogy Box Set (Dot, Ish, Sky Color) (p. 1347)
—Punto. (p. 1417)
—Rose's Garden. Reynolds, Peter H., illus. (p. 1490)
—Sky Color. Reynolds, Peter H., illus. (p. 1586)
—Smallest Gift of Christmas. Reynolds, Peter H., illus. (p. 1592)
—So Few of Me. Reynolds, Peter H., illus. (p. 1602)
—Star Bright: A Christmas Story. (p. 1640)
Reynolds, Peter H., illus. see Brallier, Jess M.
Reynolds, Peter H., illus. see Emerson, Sharon.
Reynolds, Peter H., illus. see FableVision Staff.
Reynolds, Peter H., illus. see FableVision Studios Staff.
Reynolds, Peter H., illus. see FableVision.
Reynolds, Peter H., illus. see McDonald, Megan & Michalak, Jamie.
Reynolds, Peter H., illus. see McDonald, Megan.
Reynolds, Peter H., illus. see McGhee, Alison.
Reynolds, Peter H., illus. see New York Hall of Science Staff.
Reynolds, Peter H., illus. see O'Brien, Thomas C.
Reynolds, Peter H., illus. see Potter, Ellen.
Reynolds, Peter H., illus. see Reynolds, Paul A.
Reynolds, Peter H., illus. see Robinson, Michelle.
Reynolds, Peter H., illus. see Rosenthal, Amy Krouse.
Reynolds, Peter H., illus. see Stearns, Peggy Healy.
Reynolds, Peter H., illus. see Verde, Susan.
Reynolds, Peter H., jt. auth. see Raczka, Bob.
Reynolds, Peter H. & Reynolds, Peter. Ish. Reynolds, Peter H. & Reynolds, Peter, illus. (p. 891)
Reynolds, Ralph V. Dividing the Word of Truth. (p. 454)
—Usando Bien la Palabra de Verdad. Geissler, Darry & Geissler, Kimberly, eds. (p. 1826)
Reynolds, Rhonda, illus. see Ekberg, Nancy.
Reynolds, Rhonda, tr. see Ekberg, Nancy.
Reynolds, Ruth, jt. auth. see Ryan, Margaret.
Reynolds, Sarah, illus. see Pedrow, Debra A.
Reynolds, Shaye. I Am an American Citizen. (p. 832)
—Life Cycle of a Chicken. (p. 1009)
Reynolds, Shelly. Baby Steps. (p. 128)
Reynolds, Sue, jt. auth. see Neiman, Tommy.
Reynolds, Toby. Papercraft. (p. 1323)
—Printing. (p. 1407)
Reynolds, Tom. I Hate Myself & Want to Die: The 52 Most Depressing Songs You've Ever Heard. (p. 839)
—Rudy Becker, Stargazer. (p. 1494)
Reynolds, Virginia. Fine Art Scratch & Sketch: A Cool Art Activity Book for Budding Fine Artists of All Ages. (p. 589)
Reynolds, Wendy. Moby for Justice. (p. 1157)
Reynolds, Wendy A. & Hayes, Amy. Turning Apples into Applesauce. (p. 1798)
Reynoldson, Fiona. Geothermal Energy & Bioenergy. (p. 665)
—Home Front. (p. 792)
—Understanding Nuclear Power. (p. 1816)
—Understanding Solar Power. (p. 1816)
Reza, Connie. Leah Ann Adopta Un Perico. (p. 982)
Rezayazdi, Soheil, ed. see Adel, Kaveh N.
Reznicek, Curtis, illus. see Witt, Janice.
Reznick, Jenny. Eating Right: A Content Area Reader. (p. 501)
Reznicsek, Renee. Chucks. (p. 318)
Reznik, Anastassia, ed. Little Horse Gornok: Russian Fairy Tale. (p. 1029)
RH Disney Staff. Action Figures. RH Disney Staff, illus. (p. 10)
—Adventures in Andy's Room. RH Disney Staff, illus. (p. 15)
—Air Power! RH Disney Staff, illus. (p. 31)
—Alice in Wonderland. RH Disney Staff, illus. (p. 39)
—All Dressed Up. Legramandi, Francesco & Matta, Gabriella, illus. (p. 44)
—Amazing Ariel! (Disney Princess) RH Disney Staff, illus. (p. 53)
—Anna Is Our Babysitter (Disney Frozen) RH Disney Staff, illus. (p. 85)
—Anna's Icy Adventure. RH Disney Staff, illus. (p. 85)
—Ariel's Royal Wedding/Aurora's Royal Wedding (Disney Princess) RH Disney Staff, illus. (p. 98)
—Ariel's Undersea Adventures (Disney Princess) RH Disney Staff, illus. (p. 98)
—Ballet Dreams. (p. 134)
—Bambi. (p. 135)
—Be My Princess. RH Disney Staff, illus. (p. 148)
—Beauty & the Beast. (p. 154)
—Beck's Bunny Secret. (p. 156)
—Big Battle. RH Disney Staff, illus. (p. 178)
—Big Bear, Little Bear. RH Disney Staff, illus. (p. 178)
—Big Book of Princesses. (p. 179)
—Big Book of Toys. (p. 179)
—Big Hero 6. RH Disney Staff, illus. (p. 181)
—Big Hero 6 Big Golden Book (Disney Big Hero 6) RH Disney Staff, illus. (p. 181)
—Big Hero 6 Chapter Book (Disney Big Hero 6) RH Disney Staff, illus. (p. 181)
—Big Monsters on Campus. RH Disney Staff, illus. (p. 182)
—Big Race. RH Disney Staff, illus. (p. 183)
—Brave - A Mother's Love. RH Disney Staff, illus. (p. 223)
—Brave - A Twist of Fate. RH Disney Staff, illus. (p. 223)
—Brave Big Golden Book (Disney/Pixar Brave) RH Disney Staff, illus. (p. 223)
—Brave Chunky Crayon Book (Disney/Pixar Brave) RH Disney Staff, illus. (p. 223)
—Brave Little Golden Book (Disney/Pixar Brave) RH Disney Staff, illus. (p. 223)
—Burn Rubber! (p. 243)
—Buzz Off! - Showtime! RH Disney Staff, illus. (p. 248)
—Buzz's Space Adventure/Sunnyside Boot Camp (Disney/Pixar Toy Story) RH Disney Staff, illus. (p. 249)
—Cars 2 Big Golden Book. RH Disney Staff & Golden Books Staff, illus. (p. 272)
—Cars 2 Little Golden Book (Disney/Pixar Cars 2) RH Disney Staff, illus. (p. 272)
—Cars Little Golden Book Library (Disney/Pixar Cars) (p. 272)
—Cars Story Collection. (p. 272)
—Christmas in the Castle (Disney Princess) Legramandi, Francesco & Matta, Gabriella, illus. (p. 314)
—Christmas on Wheels! (Disney/Pixar Cars) RH Disney Staff, illus. (p. 315)
—Cinderella. RH Disney Staff, tr. (p. 320)
—Cinderella. Dias, Ron & Lorencz, Bill, illus. (p. 320)
—Cinderella (Diamond) Big Golden Book (Disney Princess) Disney Storybook Artists Staff, illus. (p. 320)
—Cinderella's Dream Wedding/Tiana's Royal Wedding (Disney Princess) RH Disney Staff, illus. (p. 320)
—Colorful Critters! (Disney Princess: Palace Pets) Disney Storybook Artists Staff, illus. (p. 344)
—Crown Jewels. (p. 386)
—Cute & Cuddly (Disney Princess) RH Disney Staff, illus. (p. 396)
—Cute Curls & Lovely Locks (Disney Princess) RH Disney Staff, illus. (p. 396)
—Dancing Cinderella/Belle of the Ball. RH Disney Staff, illus. (p. 402)
—Day at the Races/Night Vision. RH Disney Staff, illus. (p. 412)
—Dino Fun (Disney/Pixar Toy Story) RH Disney Staff, illus. (p. 441)
—Disney Frozen: Special Edition Junior Novelization (Disney Frozen) RH Disney Staff, illus. (p. 451)
—Disney Infinity Game Atlas (Disney Infinity) RH Disney Staff, illus. (p. 451)
—Disney Junior: Nine Favorite Tales (Disney Mixed Property) (p. 451)
—Disney Planes. RH Disney Staff, illus. (p. 452)
—Disney Planes the Junior Novelization. RH Disney Staff, illus. (p. 452)
—Disney/Pixar Little Golden Book Library (Disney/Pixar) (p. 453)
—Disney/Pixar Story Collection. RH Disney Staff, illus. (p. 453)
—Doc Mcstuffins Little Golden Book Library (Disney Junior: Doc Mcstuffins) (p. 459)
—Dreams Come True Forever. (p. 484)
—Dress-Up in Arendelle. RH Disney Staff, illus. (p. 485)
—Dumbo. Disney Storybook Artists Staff, illus. (p. 489)
—Dusty to the Rescue (Disney Planes: Fire & Rescue) RH Disney Staff, illus. (p. 490)
—Fast! RH Disney Staff, illus. (p. 576)
—Fearsome Friends. RH Disney Staff, illus. (p. 579)
—Fight to the Finish! RH Disney Staff, illus. (p. 585)
—Finding Nemo. (p. 588)
—Finding Nemo. Tilley, Scott & RH Disney Staff, illus. (p. 588)
—Finding Nemo Big Golden Book (Disney/Pixar Finding Nemo) RH Disney Staff, illus. (p. 588)
—Fish in a Box. (p. 598)
—Five Classic Tales (Disney Classics) (p. 600)
—Five Disney/Pixar Tales (Disney/Pixar) (p. 600)
—Five Tales from the Road (Disney/Pixar Cars) RH Disney Staff, illus. (p. 601)
—Five Toy Tales (Disney/Pixar Toy Story) (p. 601)
—Friend for Merida. RH Disney Staff, illus. (p. 637)
—Friends to the Finish. RH Disney Staff, illus. (p. 639)
—Frozen Big Golden Book (Disney Frozen) RH Disney Staff, illus. (p. 645)
—Frozen Junior Novelization (Disney Frozen) RH Disney Staff, illus. (p. 645)
—Frozen Story Collection (Disney Frozen) RH Disney Staff, illus. (p. 645)
—Furry, Fluffy & Fabulous! (Disney Princess: Palace Pets) Disney Storybook Artists Staff, illus. (p. 650)
—Girl & a Dragon. RH Disney Staff, illus. (p. 678)
—Give Us a Roar! RH Disney Staff, illus. (p. 681)
—Go, Team! RH Disney Staff, illus. (p. 687)
—Good Night, Lightning (Disney/Pixar Cars) RH Disney Staff, illus. (p. 699)
—Gorgeous Gems & Royal Crowns Kit (Disney Princess) RH Disney Staff, illus. (p. 702)
—Heart to Heart. Legramandi, Francesco & Disney Storybook Artists Staff, illus. (p. 760)
—Hiro to the Rescue! RH Disney Staff, illus. (p. 781)
—Hotshots! (Disney Planes: Fire & Rescue) RH Disney Staff, illus. (p. 802)
—Incredible Dash. (p. 869)
—Inside My Mind: A Book about Me! RH Disney Staff, illus. (p. 877)
—Inside Out Big Golden Book (Disney/Pixar Inside Out) RH Disney Staff, illus. (p. 877)
—Inside Out Full-Color C&a Plus Cardstock (Disney/Pixar Inside Out) RH Disney Staff, illus. (p. 877)
—Inside Out Junior Novelization (Disney/Pixar Inside Out) RH Disney Staff, illus. (p. 877)
—Jasmine & Aladdin. RH Disney Staff, illus. (p. 909)
—Jasmine & the Star of Persia (Disney Princess) RH Disney Staff, illus. (p. 910)
—Journey into the Mind. RH Disney Staff, illus. (p. 928)
—Jumbo Movie Mix! (Disney/Pixar) RH Disney Staff, illus. (p. 933)
—Jungle Book. (p. 935)
—Kind & Caring (Disney Princess) RH Disney Staff, illus. (p. 957)
—Let's Stick Together! (Disney Frozen) RH Disney Staff, illus. (p. 1000)
—Lightning Fast. Disney Storybook Artists Staff & RH Disney Staff, illus. (p. 1016)
—Lion King. (p. 1020)
—Little Heroes. (p. 1029)
—Little Man of Disneyland (Disney Classic) RH Disney Staff & Walt Disney Studios Staff, illus. (p. 1031)
—Little Mermaid Big Golden Book (Disney Princess) RH Disney Staff, illus. (p. 1031)
—Look Out for Mater! RH Disney Staff, illus. (p. 1049)
—Love at First Beep. (p. 1059)
—Lucky Fin! (Disney/Pixar Finding Nemo) RH Disney Staff, illus. (p. 1062)
—M Is for Monster (Disney/Pixar Monsters, Inc.) RH Disney Staff, illus. (p. 1067)
—Make-Believe Bride. (p. 1079)
—Mater & the Ghost Light. Luckey, Bud & Louis, Dominique, illus. (p. 1104)
—Mater's Big Mission. RH Disney Staff, illus. (p. 1104)

R

—Mater's Tall Tales. RH Disney Staff, illus. (p. 1104)
—Maximum Power. RH Disney Staff, illus. (p. 1112)
—Meet the Emotions. RH Disney Staff, illus. (p. 1122)
—Mega Movie Mix. RH Disney Staff, illus. (p. 1124)
—Merida's Challenge. RH Disney Staff, illus. (p. 1127)
—Mermaid Magic (Disney Princess) RH Disney Staff, illus. (p. 1128)
—Merry & Magical Christmas. RH Disney Staff & Legramandi, Francesco, illus. (p. 1128)
—Merry Princesses (Disney Princess) RH Disney Staff, illus. (p. 1129)
—Moments to Treasure (Disney Princess) (p. 1162)
—Monster Hide-and-Seek. RH Disney Staff, illus. (p. 1167)
—Monsters in Training. RH Disney Staff, illus. (p. 1169)
—Monsters, Inc. Big Golden Book (Disney/Pixar Monsters, Inc.) RH Disney Staff, illus. (p. 1169)
—Monsters, Inc. Little Golden Book (Disney/Pixar Monsters, Inc.) RH Disney Staff, illus. (p. 1169)
—Monsters University Big Golden Book (Disney/Pixar Monsters University) RH Disney Staff, illus. (p. 1169)
—Monsters University Little Golden Book (Disney/Pixar Monsters University) RH Disney Staff, illus. (p. 1169)
—Mother Goose. Walt Disney Company Staff & RH Disney Staff, illus. (p. 1177)
—Movie Madness! (Disney/Pixar) (p. 1183)
—My Hero. RH Disney Staff, illus. (p. 1211)
—Nemo's Big Adventure (Disney/Pixar Finding Nemo) (p. 1241)
—Never Girls Collection (p. 1243)
—Never Girls - In a Blink. Christy, Jana, illus. (p. 1243)
—Night to Sparkle (Disney Princess) RH Disney Staff, illus. (p. 1254)
—Ocean of Color. RH Disney Staff, illus. (p. 1276)
—Ocean's Treasures (Disney Princess) RH Disney Staff, illus. (p. 1277)
—Olaf's 1-2-3. RH Disney Staff, illus. (p. 1283)
—Oodles of Princess Doodles (Disney Princess) Disney Storybook Artists Staff, illus. (p. 1298)
—Palace Designs (Disney Princess) RH Disney Staff, illus. (p. 1319)
—Palace Paintings (Disney Princess) RH Disney Staff, illus. (p. 1319)
—Pedal to the Metal. RH Disney Staff, illus. (p. 1334)
—Perfect Princesses. RH Disney Staff, illus. (p. 1342)
—Peter Pan Step into Reading (Disney Peter Pan) RH Disney Staff, illus. (p. 1347)
—Pixie Hollow Paint Day. (p. 1365)
—Planes: Fire & Rescue (Disney Planes: Fire & Rescue) RH Disney Staff, illus. (p. 1367)
—Pretty Princess Paintings. RH Disney Staff, illus. (p. 1398)
—Princess Adventures (Disney Princess) RH Disney Staff, illus. (p. 1402)
—Princess & the Frog. RH Disney Staff, illus. (p. 1402)
—Princess Brides (Disney Princess) RH Disney Staff, illus. (p. 1403)
—Princess Doodle Book. (p. 1403)
—Princess Fun & Games (Disney Princess) Disney Storybook Artists Staff & Legramandi, Francesco, illus. (p. 1404)
—Princess Portraits (Disney Princess) (p. 1405)
—Princess Puzzlers (Disney Princess) RH Disney Staff, illus. (p. 1405)
—Princess Word Book. Legramandi, Francesco & Matta, Gabriella, illus. (p. 1406)
—Race Around the World. RH Disney Staff, illus. (p. 1430)
—Racing Rivals. RH Disney Staff, illus. (p. 1432)
—Racing Through the Snow. RH Disney Staff, illus. (p. 1432)
—Rainbow of Emotions. RH Disney Staff, illus. (p. 1435)
—Rapunzel's Royal Wedding/Belle's Royal Wedding (Disney Princess) RH Disney Staff, illus. (p. 1439)
—Rapunzel's Wedding Day (Disney Princess) RH Disney Staff, illus. (p. 1439)
—Razzle-Dazzle! (Disney Princess: Palace Pets) RH Disney Staff, illus. (p. 1441)
—Rescue Racers! (Disney Planes: Fire & Rescue) RH Disney Staff, illus. (p. 1462)
—Roaring Rivals. RH Disney Staff, illus. (p. 1478)
—Royal & Regal (Disney Princess) RH Disney Staff, illus. (p. 1492)
—Royal Ride. Artful Doodlers Limited Staff et al, illus. (p. 1492)
—Scares & Surprises! (Disney/Pixar Toy Story) RH Disney Staff, illus. (p. 1520)
—Scaring All-Stars (Disney/Pixar Monsters, Inc.) RH Disney Staff, illus. (p. 1520)
—Scaring Lessons. RH Disney Staff, illus. (p. 1520)
—Shape up! (Disney/Pixar Toy Story) RH Disney Staff, illus. (p. 1560)
—Shapes, Colors, Counting & More! RH Disney Staff, illus. (p. 1560)
—Sister Time! (Disney Frozen) RH Disney Staff, illus. (p. 1581)
—Sleeping Beauty Big Golden Book (Disney Princess) RH Disney Staff, illus. (p. 1589)
—Snow Days! RH Disney Staff, illus. (p. 1598)
—Snow White & the Seven Dwarfs. (p. 1600)
—Sparkle & Shine (Disney Princess) RH Disney Staff, illus. (p. 1622)
—Sparkle Magic! (Disney Frozen) RH Disney Staff, illus. (p. 1622)
—Spring Is in the Air. Artful Doodlers, illus. (p. 1635)
—Stick to the Road! (Disney Pixar/Cars) (p. 1650)
—Stuck on You (Disney/Pixar Toy Story) RH Disney Staff, illus. (p. 1669)
—Sugar Rush. RH Disney Staff, illus. (p. 1673)
—Super Princess Art Party (Disney Princess) RH Disney Staff, illus. (p. 1680)
—Super Spies. RH Disney Staff, illus. (p. 1682)
—Taking the Lead. RH Disney Staff, illus. (p. 1698)
—Team Lightning (Disney/Pixar Cars) RH Disney Staff, illus. (p. 1710)
—Team Up! RH Disney Staff, illus. (p. 1710)
—Time to Play. RH Disney Staff, illus. (p. 1753)
—Tinker Bell: Three Fairy Tales. (p. 1755)
—Too Fast! RH Disney Staff, illus. (p. 1766)
—Totally Tiaras! (Disney Princess) RH Disney Staff, illus. (p. 1771)
—Toy Christmas (Disney/Pixar Toy Story) RH Disney Staff, illus. (p. 1774)
—Toy Story. RH Disney Staff, illus. (p. 1774)
—Toy Story Little Golden Book Favorites. Golden Books Staff, illus. (p. 1774)
—Toy Story/Toy Story 2. RH Disney Staff, illus. (p. 1774)
—Toy Trouble. (p. 1774)
—Tricks, Treats, & Toys (Disney/Pixar Toy Story) RH Disney Staff, illus. (p. 1786)
—Triplet Trouble! RH Disney Staff, illus. (p. 1787)
—Up. RH Disney Staff, illus. (p. 1824)
—Welcome to Headquarters. RH Disney Staff, illus. (p. 1873)
—Wishes & Dreams. RH Disney Staff, illus. (p. 1940)
—World of Caring. RH Disney Staff, illus. (p. 1956)
—World's Greatest Racers (Disney/Pixar Cars) RH Disney Staff, illus. (p. 1960)
—Wreck-It Ralph (Disney Wreck-It Ralph) RH Disney Staff, illus. (p. 1962)
RH Disney Staff, illus. see Alberto, Daisy.
RH Disney Staff, illus. see Amerikaner, Susan.
RH Disney Staff, illus. see Arps, Melissa & Lagonegro, Melissa.
RH Disney Staff, illus. see Auerbach, Annie & Berrios, Frank.
RH Disney Staff, illus. see Belle, Sebastian.
RH Disney Staff, illus. see Berrios, Frank.
RH Disney Staff, illus. see Bobowicz, Pamela.
RH Disney Staff, illus. see Callahan, Patricia.
RH Disney Staff, illus. see Capozzi, Suzy & Finnegan, Delphine.
RH Disney Staff, illus. see Carbone, Courtney & Hands, Cynthia.
RH Disney Staff, illus. see Carbone, Courtney.
RH Disney Staff, illus. see David, Erica.
RH Disney Staff, illus. see Depken, Kristen L.
RH Disney Staff, illus. see Eberly, Chelsea.
RH Disney Staff, illus. see Francis, Suzanne.
RH Disney Staff, illus. see Hashimoto, Meika & Tillworth, Mary.
RH Disney Staff, illus. see Homberg, Ruth.
RH Disney Staff, illus. see Jordan, Apple.
RH Disney Staff, illus. see Julius, Jessica.
RH Disney Staff, illus. see Lagonegro, Melissa, et al.
RH Disney Staff, illus. see Lagonegro, Melissa.
RH Disney Staff, illus. see Man-Kong, Mary, et al.
RH Disney Staff, illus. see Man-Kong, Mary.
RH Disney Staff, illus. see Memling, Carl.
RH Disney Staff, illus. see Posner-Sanchez, Andrea & Julius, Jessica.
RH Disney Staff, illus. see Posner-Sanchez, Andrea & Weinberg, Jennifer Liberts.
RH Disney Staff, illus. see Posner-Sanchez, Andrea.
RH Disney Staff, illus. see Redbank, Tennant.
RH Disney Staff, illus. see Saxon, Victoria.
RH Disney Staff, illus. see Shealy, Dennis.
RH Disney Staff, illus. see Sky Koster, Amy.
RH Disney Staff, illus. see Thorpe, Kiki.
RH Disney Staff, illus. see Trimble, Irene.
RH Disney Staff, illus. see Webster, Christy.
RH Disney Staff, illus. see Weinberg, Jennifer Liberts.
RH Disney Staff, illus. see Winskill, John.
RH Disney Staff, illus. see Wrecks, Billy.
RH Disney Staff, jt. auth. see Awdry, Wilbert V.
RH Disney Staff, jt. auth. see Barrie, J. M.
RH Disney Staff, jt. auth. see Berrios, Frank.
RH Disney Staff, jt. auth. see Driscoll, Laura.
RH Disney Staff, jt. auth. see Golden Books Staff.
RH Disney Staff, jt. auth. see Jordan, Apple.
RH Disney Staff, jt. auth. see Lagonegro, Melissa.
RH Disney Staff, jt. auth. see Mackerel, Seymour.
RH Disney Staff, jt. auth. see Marsoli, Lisa Ann.
RH Disney Staff, jt. auth. see Poindexter, Katherine.
RH Disney Staff, jt. auth. see Random House Editors.
RH Disney Staff, jt. auth. see RH Disney Staff.
RH Disney Staff, jt. auth. see Richards, Kitty.
RH Disney Staff, jt. auth. see Saxon, Victoria.
RH Disney Staff, jt. auth. see Thorpe, Kiki.
RH Disney Staff, jt. auth. see Tyler, Amy J.
RH Disney Staff, jt. auth. see Vick-E.
RH Disney Staff, jt. auth. see Weinberg, Jennifer Liberts.
RH Disney Staff, jt. auth. see Weinberg, Jennifer.
RH Disney Staff, jt. illus. see Golden Books Staff.
RH Disney Staff & Auerbach, Annie. Toy Story 3. RH Disney Staff & Molina, Adrian H., illus. (p. 1774)
RH Disney Staff & Berrios, Frank. Fire Crew! (Disney Planes: Fire & Rescue) RH Disney Staff, illus. (p. 590)
—Shifting Gears! RH Disney Staff, illus. (p. 1566)
RH Disney Staff & Calmenson, Stephanie. Little Mermaid. Mateu, Francesca, illus. (p. 1031)
RH Disney Staff & Carbone, Courtney. Jet Set! RH Disney Staff, illus. (p. 916)
RH Disney Staff & Depken, Kristen L. My Never Land Journal (Disney: the Never Girls) Christy, Jana, illus. (p. 1216)
—Pet Problem (Disney/Pixar Toy Story) RH Disney Staff & Egan, Caroline, illus. (p. 1345)
RH Disney Staff & Disney Enterprises Inc. Staff. Best Dad in the Sea. (p. 168)
RH Disney Staff & Disney Pixar Staff. Play Day! RH Disney Staff & Disney Pixar Staff, illus. (p. 1371)
RH Disney Staff & Glum, Felicity. Simply Sadness/Joy's Greatest Joy. RH Disney Staff & Tyminski, Lori, illus. (p. 1578)
RH Disney Staff & Hall, Klay. Disney Planes. Golden Books Staff & Hand, Jason, illus. (p. 452)
RH Disney Staff & Hands, Cynthia. Arcade Brigade. RH Disney Staff, illus. (p. 95)
—High Score! RH Disney Staff, illus. (p. 778)
—Light up the Night. Disney Storybook Artists Staff, illus. (p. 1015)
—Once upon a Lily Pad. RH Disney Staff, illus. (p. 1293)
—Spring into Action! Disney Storybook Artists Staff et al, illus. (p. 1635)
RH Disney Staff & Jordan, Apple. Fast Kart, Slow Kart. RH Disney Staff, illus. (p. 576)
RH Disney Staff & Julius, Jessica. Anna's Birthday Surprise. RH Disney Staff, illus. (p. 85)
RH Disney Staff & Knowles, Heather. Picture Perfect. RH Disney Staff et al, illus. (p. 1356)
RH Disney Staff & Lagonegro, Melissa. Tale of Two Sisters. RH Disney Staff, illus. (p. 1701)
RH Disney Staff & O'Hara, Ellen. Flight to the Finish. RH Disney Staff, illus. (p. 604)
RH Disney Staff & Peymani, Christine. Tangled. Disney Storybook Artists Staff & Orpinas, Jean-Paul, illus. (p. 1705)
RH Disney Staff & Posner-Sanchez, Andrea. Bambi's Hide-and-Seek. Mones, Isidre, illus. (p. 135)
—Cinderella Is My Babysitter (Disney Princess) RH Disney Staff et al, illus. (p. 320)
—Treasure's Day at Sea (Disney Princess: Palace Pets) RH Disney Staff & DiCicco, Sue, illus. (p. 1782)
RH Disney Staff & Rabe, Tish. Big Snowman, Little Snowman. RH Disney Staff, illus. (p. 184)
—Frozen - Big Snowman, Little Snowman. RH Disney Staff, illus. (p. 645)
RH Disney Staff & Random House Staff. Thomas Breaks a Promise. Courtney, Richard, illus. (p. 1738)
RH Disney Staff & Redbank, Tennant. Toy to Toy. RH Disney Staff et al, illus. (p. 1774)
RH Disney Staff & RH Disney Staff. Mater's Mazes (Disney/Pixar Cars) (p. 1104)
—Princess Easter (Disney Princess) (p. 1403)
RH Disney Staff & Richards, Kitty. Great Toy Escape. RH Disney Staff, illus. (p. 718)
RH Disney Staff & Scollon, Bill. Wings Around the Globe. RH Disney Staff & Disney Storybook Artists Staff, illus. (p. 1936)
RH Disney Staff & Shealy, Dennis. Little Mermaid. (p. 1031)
RH Disney Staff & Smiley, Ben. Tangled. Disney Storybook Artists Staff & Ying, Victoria, illus. (p. 1705)
RH Disney Staff & Teitelbaum, Michael. Sleeping Beauty. DiCicco, Sue, illus. (p. 1589)
RH Disney Staff & Tillworth, Mary. Big Monster, Little Monster. RH Disney Staff, illus. (p. 182)
RH Disney Staff & Trimble, Irene. Big Hero 6 Junior Novelization (Disney Big Hero 6) RH Disney Staff, illus. (p. 181)
—Brave Junior Novelization (Disney/Pixar Brave) RH Disney Staff, illus. (p. 223)
RH Disney Staff & Weingartner, Amy. Toy Box Trouble! RH Disney Staff & Laguna, Fabio, illus. (p. 1774)
—Treasure Hunt! RH Disney Staff & Laguna, Fabio, illus. (p. 1781)
RH Disney Staff & Winkelman, Barbara Gaines. Pinocchio's Nose Grows. (p. 1361)
RH Disney Staff & Wooster, Devin Ann. Dazzling Day. Disney Storybook Artists Staff & Lee, Britney, illus. (p. 415)
RH Disney Staff, et al. First Flap-Book Library. Nelson, Mary Beth, illus. (p. 595)
Rhae, Sympne. My Name Is Johnson? (p. 1215)
Rhatigan, Joe. Don't Unravel When You Travel: Hold It Together with Goofy Games, Peculiar Puzzles, Atypical Activites, Droll Doodling, Fun Facts & Much More! (p. 469)
—Grow Your Own Giant Pumpkin. (p. 726)
—Ouch! The Weird & Wild Ways Your Body Deals with Agonizing Aches, Ferocious Fevers, Lousy Lumps, Crummy Colds, Bothersome Bites, Breaks, Bruises & Burns & Makes Them Feel Better! Owsley, Anthony, illus. (p. 1307)
—Ouch! The Weird & Wild Ways Your Body Deals with Agonizing Aches, Ferocious Fevers, Lousy Lumps, Crummy Colds, Bothersome Bites, Breaks, Bruises, & Burns & Makes Them Feel Better! Owsley, Anthony, illus. (p. 1307)
—People You Gotta Meet Before You Grow Up: Get to Know the Movers & Shakers, Heroes & Hotshots in Your Hometown. (p. 1340)
—Super Duper Most Ginormous Bubble Kit. (p. 1679)
Rhatigan, Joe, jt. auth. see Press, Applesauce.
Rhatigan, Joe & Owsley, Anthony. Inventions That Could Have Changed the World... But Didn't! (p. 884)
Rhatigan, Joe, et al. Craft It! 50 Fun Stamp, Paper & Polymer Clay Projects. (p. 375)
—Head Scratchers Trivia: 708 Numb-Your-Noggin Questions That'll Stump Ya! (p. 756)
—Mind Melting Trivia: 715 Head Thumpers That'll Sump Ya! (p. 1145)
—Trivia Goes Bananas: 711 Brain Bafflers That'll Stump Ya! (p. 1788)
—Wild & Wacky Trivia: 717 Brain Drainers That'll Stump Ya! (p. 1928)
Rhea, Carrie. I Will Miss You, Daddy! (p. 848)
Rhead, Louis, illus. see Stevenson, Robert Louis.
Rheaume, Sherry D. Lulu the Prairie Dog. (p. 1065)
Rheberg, Judy, illus. see Matthews, T. J.
Rheburg, Judy, illus. see Matthews, T. J.
Rhema, Dan. Bluegrass Breeze. Leonard, Michael, illus. (p. 204)
—One Tiny Twig Leonard, Michael, illus. (p. 1297)
Rhie, Gene S. & Jones, B. J. Mini Dictionary of English-Korean - Korean-English: Romanized. (p. 1146)
Rhiger, Tenna. Story about How the Spotted Wobblepig Got Its Spots. (p. 1656)
Rhijn, Patricia van & Alvarez, Rosanela. Cuentos de Animales Fantasticos para Ninos (Fantastic Animal Tales for Children) (p. 389)
Rhimer, Linda. Is He Really Coming Home! (p. 889)
Rhine, Karen C., illus. see Lilly, Melinda.
Rhine, Karen C., illus. see Taylor, Kay Lovelace.
Rhine, Linda H. Ivory Buttons. (p. 901)
—Ivory Buttons. (p. 901)
Rhines, Karin. Lupus. (p. 1066)
Rhoades, Heath, jt. auth. see Menge, Dawn.
Rhoades, Jacqueline. Rhoades to Reading Level II. (p. 1467)
—Rhoades to Reading Level II Teaching Guide. (p. 1467)
—Rhoades to Reading Level III. (p. 1467)
—Rhoades to Reading Level III Teaching Guide. (p. 1467)
—Rhoades to Reading Level V. (p. 1467)
—Rhoades to Reading Level V Teaching Guide. (p. 1467)
—Rhoades to Reading Teacher Handbook. (p. 1467)
—Rhoades to Reading Teacher's Answer Key Levels I-V. (p. 1467)
—Rhoades to Reading Teaching Guide Level I. (p. 1468)
Rhoades, Jacquelline. Rhoades to Reading Level I. (p. 1467)
Rhoads, JoAnn. Talisa Fashionista: Adventures in Paris Oh la La! (p. 1703)
Rhode, Paul. Presents for Phoebe: Growing Independent. Margolis, Al, illus. (p. 1396)
Rhoden, Chris J. B. How Niseag Became a Legend in Scotl. (p. 811)
Rhoden, Fletcher. Imagine Nathan on Supermarket Safari. (p. 861)
Rhodes, C. S. Bella Mouse at Mobberley Edge. (p. 162)
Rhodes, Carol. Gene the Pumpkin Man. (p. 660)
Rhodes, Corey L. Keep Your Head Up! (p. 947)
Rhodes, Danny W. I Know Tuff Luck. (p. 840)
Rhodes, David & Norris, Chad. Broken: When Life Falls Apart. (p. 230)
Rhodes, Evan. How Do Seeds Sprout? (p. 807)
Rhodes, Genee M. & Travers, Jasmine. Gloria Gets Glasses. (p. 685)
Rhodes, Immacula. Shoe Box Learning Centers: Addition & Subtraction: 30 Instant Centers with Reproducible Templates & Activities That Help Kids Practice Important Math Skills-Independently! (p. 1568)
Rhodes, Immacula A. Addition & Subtraction: 10 Ready-to-Go Games That Motivate Children to Practice & Strengthen Essential Math Skills-Independently! (p. 12)
—Alphabet Art Activities: Easy & Engaging Art Activities That Help Children Learn to Read & Write the Letters of the Alphabet. (p. 49)
—Alphabet Trees: 50+ Practice Pages That Help Kids Master the Letters a to Z & Build a Foundation for Reading Success. (p. 50)
—Grammar Games & Activities That Boost Writing Skills: Dozens of Engaging Grammar Manipulatives, Games, & Activities to Teach & Reinforce Parts of Speech, Capitalization, Punctuation, & More. (p. 706)
—No-Cook Snacks: Easy & Healthy Step-by-Step Recipes That Help Children Build Beginning Reading Skills. (p. 1258)
—Shoe Box Learning Centers - Science: 30 Instant Centers with Reproducible Templates & Activities That Help Kids Learn Important Science Skills & Concepts-Independently! (p. 1568)
—Teaching about Thanksgiving with Favorite Picture Books: Engaging Skill-Building Activities That Use the Very Best Fiction & Nonfiction Books to Teach about This Important Holiday. (p. 1709)
—Teaching about Winter Holidays with Favorite Picture Books. (p. 1709)
—Word Families, Grades K-2: 30 Easy-to-Make, Self-Checking Manipulatives That Teach Key Word Families & Put Kids on the Path to Reading Success. (p. 1950)
Rhodes, Immacula A., jt. auth. see Clarke, Jacqueline.
Rhodes, Immacula A., jt. auth. see Julio, Susan.
Rhodes, Immacula A. & Julio, Susan. Science: 10 Ready-to-Go Games That Help Children Learn Key Science Concepts & Vocabulary—Independently. (p. 1524)
—Social Studies: 10 Ready-to-Go Games That Help Children Learn Key Social Studies Concepts & Vocabulary - Independently. (p. 1604)
Rhodes, Immacula A. & Scholastic Teaching Resources Staff. Phonics Picture Puzzles for Little Learners: Dozens of Age-Perfect Practice Pages That Help Children Build Key Phonics Skills, Grades K-2. (p. 1352)
Rhodes, Jennifer. Adventures of Kirby. Balogh, Jared, illus. (p. 19)
Rhodes, Jewell Parker. Bayou Magic. (p. 147)
—Ninth Ward. (p. 1257)
—Sugar. (p. 1672)
Rhodes, Judith & Hodgson, Julie, eds. Games for the Early Years: 26 Games to Make & Play. (p. 655)
Rhodes, Julie & Quarto Generic Staff. Very Noisy House. Paul, Korky, illus. (p. 1838)
Rhodes, Karen. 7 Sensational Stories. (p. 1992)
—Do You Know Jesus? (p. 458)
—God's Word Then & Now Activity Book. (p. 692)
—Numeros en la Biblia. (p. 1273)
Rhodes, Karen, ed. see Egermeier, Elsie E.
Rhodes, Karen, ed. see Egermeier, Elsie.
Rhodes, Karen, ed. see Stoddard, Jeffery.
Rhodes, Katie, illus. see Powell, Richard.
Rhodes, Kenya. Luna's Birthday. (p. 1065)
Rhodes, Lilly, jt. auth. see Reader's Digest Staff.
Rhodes, Lisa. Animals of Africa. (p. 83)
—Animals of Alaska. (p. 83)
—Animals of Mountain West Region. (p. 83)
Rhodes, Lou. Phlunk's Worldwide Symphony. Elliott, Tori, illus. (p. 1351)
Rhodes, Mary Jo & Hall, David. Dolphins, Seals, & Other Sea Mammals. (p. 465)
—Octopuses & Squids. Hall, David, photos by. (p. 1278)
—Partners in the Sea. Hall, David, photos by. (p. 1325)
—Predators of the Sea. (p. 1395)
—Predators of the Sea. Hall, David, photos by. (p. 1395)
—Sea Turtles. Hall, David, photos by. (p. 1536)
—Seahorses & Sea Dragons. Hall, David, photos by. (p. 1536)
—Undersea Encounters Hall, David, photos by. (p. 1815)
Rhodes, Mary Wilson. Journey to Mercury (p. 929)
Rhodes, Morgan. Book of Spirits & Thieves. (p. 212)
—Falling Kingdoms. (p. 567)
—Gathering Darkness. (p. 658)
—Rebel Spring. (p. 1451)
Rhodes, O. K. Rock Holler Gang: Jr. Detectives Mystery of the Cornerstone. (p. 1482)
Rhodes, O. K. & Spencer, Octavia. Case of the Time-Capsule Bandit. To, Vivienne, illus. (p. 275)
Rhodes, R. A. W., et al. Decentralizing the Civil Service: From Unitary State to Differentiated Polity in the United Kingdom. (p. 421)

Rhodes, Sam. Native American Rhymes: The People of the Far North Howard, Kimberley, ed. (p. 1234)
Rhodes, Sean C., ed. see Adkins, Linda.
Rhodes, Shayla. I Know Who I Am. (p. 840)
Rhodes, Tamika. Francis & His Barnyard Friends. (p. 627)
Rhodes, Terry. Marley's Big Day. (p. 1095)
Rhodes, Tiffany. What I Learned This Christmas. (p. 1886)
—Where the Seeds Fall. (p. 1909)
Rhodes, Tim W. Story of the Bed Bear. (p. 1660)
Rhodes-Courter, Ashley. Three Little Words: A Memoir. (p. 1743)
Rhonda Lucas Donald, Rhonda Lucas. Dino Tracks Morrison, Cathy, illus. (p. 441)
Rhone, Alexus D. Secret Shame (p. 1543)
Rhoney, Anita, jt. auth. see Childres, Roger.
Rhose, Saga. Magdalene's Well. (p. 1071)
Rhoton, Lesa. Angus & the Triplets. Switzer, Bobby, illus. (p. 75)
Rhuday-Perkovich, Olugbemisola. 8th Grade Super Zero. (p. 1993)
Rhude, Steven. Natalie's Glasses (p. 1230)
Rhue, Morton. Die Welle: Bericht über einen Unterrichtsversuch, der zu weit ging. (p. 437)
Rhyason, Sharon. Utopia, Where Are You? (p. 1829)
Rhydderch, Gwyn, et al. Iesu'r Ffrind: 16 Seswn Yn Cyflwyno Bywyd Iesu Ar Gyfer Plant Cynradd Yn Seiliedig Ar Efengyl Luc. (p. 852)
Rhymes, Wriggly. No Place Like Home. (p. 1260)
Rhyne, Nancy. Crab Boys. (p. 375)
Rhynes, Martha E. Gwendolyn Brooks: Poet from Chicago. (p. 733)
—I, Too, Sing America: The Story of Langston Hughes. (p. 847)
—Ralph Ellison: Author of Invisible Man. (p. 1437)
Rhys, Ann Gruffydd & Bryntirion, Gwasg. Nansi Dolwar. (p. 1229)
Riachi, Ghassan Diab & Mitchell, Anna B. L. I. B. B. Y. The Green Dog. RJI Publishing, ed. (p. 969)
Riad, Hala. Haunted Backyard. (p. 753)
—There Is a Bully in My Tummy. (p. 1729)
—Twinkie Has a New Home. (p. 1802)
Riahi, Sep, jt. auth. see Maydell, Natalie.
Riamliw, J. S. To Fly Out. (p. 1759)
Rian, Jeff & Brooks, Rosetta. Richard Prince. (p. 1469)
Riano, Carlos, illus. see Espriella, Leopoldo Berdella De La.
Ribar, Lindsay. Art of Wishing. (p. 102)
—Fourth Wish. (p. 625)
Ribas, Meritxell, illus. see Sierra, Sergio A. & Shelley, Mary.
Ribay, Randy. Infinite Number of Parallel Universes. (p. 873)
Ribble, Karen. Beginning Hair Braiding Taught. (p. 159)
Ribble, S. Child's Book of Kitty-cat & Puppy-dog Tales. (p. 304)
Ribeira, Lili, illus. see Graham, Janice Barrett.
Ribeiro, Gustavo Lins & Escobar, Arturo, eds. World Anthropologies: Disciplinary Transformations Within Systems of Power. (p. 1954)
Ribeiro, Nelson. Jughead with Archie in Power Play. Gorelick, Victor, illus. (p. 932)
Ribeiro, Nelson & Spotlight Editors. Jughead with Archie in Fool Proof. Gorelick, Victor, illus. (p. 932)
—Jughead with Archie in Pup-Ularity Contest. Gorelick, Victor, illus. (p. 932)
—Jughead with Archie in Wish Fulfillment. Gorelick, Victor, illus. (p. 932)
Ribeiro, Nelson, et al. Betty & Veronica in Color Blind. (p. 172)
—Jughead with Archie in a Day to Remember. (p. 932)
—Jughead with Archie in Family Photos. (p. 932)
—Laugh with Fore! (p. 980)
Ribera Jorda, Antonio. Conquista del Polo Norte. (p. 358)
Ribera, Terry, illus. see Madonia, Kristen-Paige.
Ribero, J., jt. auth. see Martin, Andreu.
Ribic, Esad, illus. see Hickman, Jonathan.
Ribiero, Nelson & Spotlight Editors. Laugh with Mammoth Madness. Gorelick, Victor, illus. (p. 980)
—Laugh with Snack Swap. Gorelick, Victor, illus. (p. 980)
—Laugh with Stampede. Gorelick, Victor, illus. (p. 980)
Ribke, Simone T. Grouping at the Dog Show. (p. 725)
—I Have a Skeleton. (p. 839)
—I Have Allergies. (p. 839)
—I'll Do It Later. White, Lee, illus. (p. 856)
—Milton Hershey. (p. 1144)
—Ruby Bridges. (p. 1493)
—Shapes We Eat. (p. 1561)
—Thomas Jefferson. (p. 1739)
—Washington, D. C. (p. 1860)
—Washington, D. C. Hamilton, Harriet, tr. (p. 1860)
—William & Kate, Duke & Duchess of Cambridge. (p. 1933)
Ricahrdson, Brittany, illus. see Ricahrdson, Larry.
Ricahrdson, Larry. Metal Mike. Ricahrdson, Brittany, illus. (p. 1130)
Ricard, Anouk. Anna & Froga: Wanna Gumball? Dascher, Helge, tr. from FRE. (p. 85)
—Anna & Froga: I Dunno, What Do You Want to Do? Dascher, Helge, tr. from FRE. (p. 85)
—Anna & Froga: Thrills, Spills, & Gooseberries. Dascher, Helge, tr. from FRE. (p. 85)
—Anna & Froga - Fore! Dascher, Helge, tr. from FRE. (p. 85)
Ricard, Matthieu. Happiness: A Guide to Developing Life's Most Important Skill. Browner, Jesse, tr. (p. 744)
Ricaurte, Carmen Ortega. Campeonismo. (p. 257)
Riccards, Michael, jt. auth. see Frrich, Lewandowski.
Ricceri, David, illus. see Schwartz, Barry L. & Levine, Mark H.
Ricchi, Brenda. Grandchildren's Bible Journeys - the Creation Story. (p. 707)
—Grandchildren's Bible Journey-the Big Fall. (p. 707)
Ricchiazzi, Lisa Gail. Adventures of Fella & Dawn: Help One Another. (p. 18)
—Fella Finds a Friend: (You Are Never Alone) (p. 581)
—Little Lost Seashell: (Never Lose Hope) (p. 1031)
Ricchiuti, Paul B. Treasure on Spyglass Hill. (p. 1782)
Ricci, Andrés, illus. see Riley, Zach.
Ricci, Andres Martinez, illus. see Higgins, Nadia.
Ricci, Andrés Martínez, illus. see Slade, Suzanne.
Ricci, Andres Martinez, illus. see Slater, David Michael.
Ricci, Andrés Martínez, illus. see Weakland, Mark & Slade, Suzanne.
Ricci, Andres Martinez, jt. auth. see Higgins, Nadia.
Ricci, Christine. Animal Adventure. Aikins, Dave et al, illus. (p. 76)
—Be Nice, Swiper! Aikins, Dave & Miller, Victoria, illus. (p. 149)
—Best Friends Forever. (p. 169)
—Buenas Noches, Dora! Cuento Para Levantar la Tapita. Hall, Susan, illus. (p. 235)
—Diego's Sea Turtle Adventure. Maher, Alex, illus. (p. 437)
—Dora in the Deep Sea. Roper, Robert, illus. (p. 470)
—Dora's Book of Manners. Hall, Susan, illus. (p. 471)
—Dora's Costume Party! Saunders, Zina, illus. (p. 471)
—Dora's Nursery Rhyme Adventure. Fruchter, Jason, illus. (p. 471)
—Dora's Picnic. Hall, Susan, illus. (p. 471)
—Dora's Rainbow Picnic. Mangano, Tom et al, illus. (p. 471)
—Dora's Starry Christmas. Studios, A&J, illus. (p. 471)
—Dora's Valentine Adventure. A and J Studios Staff, illus. (p. 471)
—Follow Those Feet! Hall, Susan, illus. (p. 612)
—Great Big Parade. Aikins, Dave, illus. (p. 714)
—Helping Hands. Hall, Susan, illus. (p. 766)
—I Love My Abuela! Miller, Victoria, illus. (p. 842)
—Legend Hunters! McGee, Warner, illus. (p. 988)
—Meet the Animals! Aikins, Dave, illus. (p. 1122)
—Navidad Estelar de Dora. Ziegler, Argentina Palacios, tr. (p. 1238)
—Puppy Takes a Bath. Mangano, Tom, illus. (p. 1418)
—Say Cheese! Savitsky, Steven, illus. (p. 1518)
—Show Me Your Smile! Roper, Robert, illus. (p. 1570)
—Super Soccer Game. Hall, Susan & Roper, Robert, illus. (p. 1682)
Ricci, Christine & Golden Books Staff. Bug Hunt. Savitsky, Steve et al, illus. (p. 236)
Ricci, Christine, et al. Dora Loves Her Family. (p. 470)
Ricci, Dorothy. Through Goya's Eyes: The World of the Spanish Painter & His Friend & Mentor, Gaspar Jovellanos. (p. 1744)
Ricci, Laura. Dr. Mike's Adventures. (p. 475)
Riccio, Frank, illus. see Myers, Bill.
Riccio, Frank, illus. see Tolle, Eckhart & Friedman, Robert S.
Riccio, Frank, illus. see Walsch, Neale Donald.
Riccio, Nina M. Five Kids & a Monkey Blaze, Beth L., illus. (p. 600)
Ricciuti, Edward R. Federal Bureau of Investigation. (p. 580)
Riccobono, Michael P. Billy Balonie & the Belly Buttonie. (p. 187)
Rice, Adrienne. How Many? (p. 810)
Rice, Alice Caldwell Hegan. Mrs. Wiggs of the Cabbage Patch. (p. 1188)
Rice, Alice Hegan. Mrs. Wiggs of the Cabbage Patch. (p. 1188)
Rice, Anne & McCourt, Mariah. Anne Rice's Servant of the Bones. (p. 86)
Rice, Ashley. Adelante, niñA... Sigue soñando (You Go, Girl Keep Dreaming) Un libro especial sobre Cómo. (p. 12)
—For an Incredible Kid. (p. 615)
—Friends Rule: A Very Special Book of Friendship Especially for Girls. (p. 639)
—Girls Rule: A Very Special Book Created Especially for Girls. Rice, Ashley, illus. (p. 680)
—Girls Rule: A Very special book created especially for girls — UPDATED EDITION — (p. 680)
—You Are an Amazing Girl: A Very Special Book about Being You & Making Your Dreams Come True. (p. 1973)
—You Go, Girl... Keep Dreaming. (p. 1975)
Rice, Beth. I'm Adopted, I'm Special. Podgurski, Sharon, illus. (p. 858)
Rice, Bill. Endangered Animals of the Desert. (p. 526)
—Endangered Animals of the Sea. (p. 526)
—Survival! Desert. (p. 1686)
—Survival! Jungle. (p. 1686)
—Survival! Ocean. (p. 1686)
Rice, Bob, photos by see Vance, Vince.
Rice, Christopher. My First Body Book. (p. 1205)
—Snow Garden: A Novel. (p. 1599)
Rice, Cindy & Stolarski, Jerry. Mr. Mahaffy on Wisdom Pond: The Beginning. (p. 1185)
Rice, Clay. Lonely Shadow. (p. 1046)
—Mama, Let's Make a Moon. (p. 1084)
Rice, Condoleezza. Condoleezza Rice: A Memoir of My Extraordinary, Ordinary Family & Me. (p. 356)
Rice, Courtney, jt. auth. see Redford, Margorie.
Rice, Courtney, jt. auth. see Redford, Marjorie.
Rice, D. M. Visit to a Car Factory. (p. 1845)
—Visit to a Farm. (p. 1845)
Rice, Daniel. Pugs. (p. 1415)
Rice, David. Crazy Loco. (p. 377)
Rice, David & Garcia, Mike D. Heart-Shaped Cookies. (p. 760)
Rice, David & Rice, David Talbot. Crazy Loco. Clayton, Christian, illus. (p. 377)
Rice, David L. Because Brian Hugged His Mother. (p. 155)
—Lifetimes. Maydak, Michael S., illus. (p. 1014)
RICE, DAVID L., jt. auth. see Rice, David L.
Rice, David L. & Calvert, Trudy L. Do Animals Have Feelings Too? (p. 456)
Rice, David L. & RICE, DAVID L. ¿También Tienen Sentimientos Los Animales? Calvert, Trudy, tr. (p. 1704)
Rice, David Talbot, jt. auth. see Rice, David.
Rice, Dona. All in the Family. (p. 44)
—Always Growing. (p. 51)
—Environment: A World of Change. (p. 532)
—First Fire. (p. 595)
—Good Work. (p. 700)
—Growing Up. (p. 726)
—Growth & Change. (p. 727)
—Here Comes the Sun. (p. 770)
—Interdependence of Living Things. (p. 879)
—Marvelous Me: My Face. (p. 1099)
—Marvelous Me: My Feet. (p. 1099)
—Marvelous Me: My Hands. (p. 1099)
—Mohandas Gandhi. (p. 1160)
—Please Don't Feed the Animals. (p. 1373)
—Pollination. (p. 1381)
—Predict It! (p. 1395)
—Raising Babies: What Animal Parents Do (p. 1437)
—Roberto Clemente. (p. 1479)
—Science Detectives. (p. 1525)
—Sort It! (p. 1614)
—Teedie: The Boy Who Would Be President. (p. 1713)
—Too Much Trash! (p. 1767)
—Traits for Survival. (p. 1777)
—Use Math: Compare It. (p. 1827)
—Use Your Math Mind: Group It. (p. 1827)
—Use Your Math Mind: Describe It. (p. 1827)
—Water Bodies. (p. 1862)
—We Are Here. (p. 1865)
—What a Scientist Sees. (p. 1878)
—What Animal Parents Do. (p. 1879)
—What Kind of Weather? (p. 1891)
—What the Evidence Shows. (p. 1893)
—¿Qué Tipo de Tiempo? (p. 1424)
Rice, Dona, jt. auth. see Acosta, Jamey.
Rice, Dona, jt. auth. see Housel, Debra J.
Rice, Dona, jt. auth. see Rice, Dona Herweck.
Rice, Dona, jt. auth. see Smith, Jodene Lynn.
Rice, Dona & Petersen, Casey Null. School Around the World. (p. 1522)
Rice, Dona Herweck. Agua. (p. 30)
—American Through & Through. (p. 63)
—American Through & Through Lap Book. (p. 63)
—Animal Eyes. (p. 77)
—Animal Mothers & Babies. (p. 78)
—Bad Guys & Gals of the Ancient World (p. 131)
—Bad Guys & Gals of the High Seas. (p. 131)
—Bad Guys & Gals on the High Seas (p. 131)
—Batter Up! History of Baseball. (p. 145)
—Batter Up! History of Baseball. (p. 145)
—Bee's Life. (p. 158)
—Big & Little. (p. 177)
—Big Kid School. (p. 182)
—Butterfly's Life. (p. 248)
—Casas Alrededor Del Mundo. (p. 273)
—Colores. (p. 344)
—Colors. (p. 345)
—Comer Bien. (p. 348)
—Cómo Crecen las Plantas. (p. 350)
—Cosas con Alas. (p. 368)
—Day & Night: Time. (p. 412)
—Day & Night. (p. 412)
—Delicious & Nutritious. (p. 425)
—Dónde Ir. (p. 466)
—Eating Right. (p. 501)
—Esta Soy Yo. (p. 538)
—Figuras. (p. 586)
—Frog's Life. (p. 641)
—Going Buggy! (p. 692)
—Grande y Pequeño. (p. 707)
—Hit It! History of Tools. (p. 785)
—Hit It! - History of Tools (p. 785)
—Homes Around the World. (p. 793)
—How Plants Grow. (p. 812)
—I Can. (p. 834)
—I Can Be Anything. (p. 835)
—I Wear My Feelings. (p. 848)
—Into Space. (p. 881)
—Keeping Fit with Sports. (p. 947)
—Kids Around the World. (p. 952)
—Land. (p. 973)
—Lugares del Mundo. (p. 1064)
—Madres Animales y Sus Crías. (p. 1070)
—Mantenerse en Forma con Deportes. (p. 1088)
—Mantenerse Sano. (p. 1088)
—Mi Gran Familia. (p. 1132)
—Movimiento. (p. 1183)
—My Big Family. (p. 1197)
—Niños Alrededor del Mundo. (p. 1257)
—Ojos de Animales. (p. 1282)
—On the Go. (p. 1290)
—Physical Feats & Failures. (p. 1353)
—Places Around the World. (p. 1366)
—Places to Go. (p. 1366)
—Puedo Hacer Cualquier Cosa. (p. 1414)
—Sea Life. (p. 1534)
—Shapes. (p. 1560)
—Staying Healthy. (p. 1645)
—Terreno. (p. 1721)
—Things with Wings. (p. 1734)
—This Is Me. (p. 1736)
—Tiempo. (p. 1747)
—Trabajadores. (p. 1774)
—Unsolved! History's Mysteries (p. 1822)
—Unsolved! History's Mysteries. (p. 1822)
—Vida de una Abeja. (p. 1840)
—Vida de una Mariposa. (p. 1840)
—Vida de Una Rana. (p. 1840)
—Vida Marina. (p. 1841)
—Water. (p. 1862)
—Weather. (p. 1869)
—Workers. (p. 1952)
—Yo Sé. (p. 1971)
Rice, Dona Herweck, jt. auth. see Smith, Jodene Lynn.
Rice, Dona Herweck & Aucoin, Lee. All about Me. (p. 42)
Rice, Dona Herweck & Coan, Sharon. Special Me. (p. 1623)
Rice, Dona Herweck & Petersen, Casey Null. School Around the World. (p. 1522)
Rice, Dona Herweck & Rice, Dona. ¡Locos por Insectos y Arañas! (p. 1045)
Rice, Dona Herweck & Thompson, Chad. Old Mother Hubbard. (p. 1284)
Rice, Dona Herwick. Fox & the Crow. (p. 626)
—John Henry. (p. 922)
—Lion & the Mouse. (p. 1020)
—North Wind & the Sun. (p. 1265)
—Paul Bunyan. (p. 1330)
—Tortoise & the Hare. (p. 1771)
Rice, Dona Herwick, jt. auth. see Housel, Debra J.
Rice, Dona Herwick & Bradley, Kathleen. Chief Joseph & the Nez Perce. (p. 301)
—Goose That Laid the Golden Eggs. (p. 702)
—Lewis & Clark. (p. 1004)
—Molly Pitcher. (p. 1161)
Rice, Dona Herwick & Housel, Debra. Civil War Hero of Marye's Heights. (p. 325)
—Grasshopper & the Ants (p. 711)
—Town Mouse & the Country Mouse. (p. 1773)
Rice, Dona Herwick & Isecke, Harriet. Child Labor & the Industrial Revolution. (p. 301)
—Civil Rights: Freedom Riders. (p. 324)
—Remember the Alamo. (p. 1459)
Rice, Dona Herwick & Shannon, Catherine. Narcissa Whitman & the Westward Movement. (p. 1229)
Rice, Dona Herwick & Sugarman, Dorothy. Women's Suffrage. (p. 1947)
—World War II: Battle of Normandy. (p. 1959)
Rice, Donna. Magic Is Me. Rice, Doug, illus. (p. 1072)
Rice, Donna Herweck. I Can Be Anything. (p. 835)
Rice, Doug, illus. see Rice, Donna.
Rice, Earle. Billie Holiday. (p. 187)
—Careers in the US Army. (p. 268)
—Causes of the Mexican-American War. (p. 282)
—Causes of the Vietnam War. (p. 282)
—Charlie Parker. (p. 293)
—FDR & the New Deal. (p. 578)
—Korea 1950: From Pusan to Chosin. (p. 967)
—Life & Times of Attila the Hun. (p. 1008)
—Life & Times of Clovis. (p. 1008)
—Life & Times of Eleanor of Aquitaine. (p. 1008)
—Life & Times of Erik the Red. (p. 1008)
—Life & Times of Leif Eriksson. (p. 1008)
—Life & Times of the Brothers Custer: Galloping to Glory. (p. 1008)
—Overview of the Korean War. (p. 1314)
—Overview of the Persian Gulf War 1990. (p. 1314)
—Vietnam War Musteen, Jason R., ed. (p. 1841)
Rice, Earle & Camelo, Wilson. Careers in the US Air Force. (p. 268)
Rice, Earle & Rice, Earle, Jr. U. S. Army & Military Careers. (p. 1806)
Rice, Earle, Jr. Battle of Marathon. (p. 146)
—Blitzrieg! Hitler's Lightning War. (p. 199)
—Brief Political & Geographic History of Latin America: Where Are... Gran Colombia, la Plata, & Dutch Guiana. (p. 228)
—Canaletto. (p. 260)
—Empire in the East: The Story of Genghis Khan. (p. 521)
—John Cabot. (p. 921)
—Life & Times of Sir Walter Raleigh. (p. 1008)
—Point of No Return: Tonkin Gulf & the Vietnam War. (p. 1377)
—Robert E. Lee: First Soldier of the Confederacy. (p. 1479)
—Ulysses S. Grant: Defender of the Union. (p. 1810)
Rice, Earle, Jr., jt. auth. see Rice, Earle.
Rice, Earle, Jr., ed. Great Military Leaders of the 20th Century (p. 717)
Rice, Elizabeth. Genetic Engineering. (p. 660)
Rice, Elizabeth, jt. auth. see Ardia, Dan.
Rice, Ernestine. Mr Peacock. (p. 1186)
Rice, Franny L. Zip-Lock Zack. (p. 1987)
Rice, Howard. Step into the Desert. (p. 1648)
—Step into the Forest. (p. 1648)
—Step into the Rainforest. (p. 1648)
Rice, James. Gaston Joins the Circus. (p. 657)
—Gaston Lays an Offshore Pipeline Rice, James, illus. (p. 657)
—Gaston(r) Goes to Texas Rice, James, illus. (p. 657)
—Santa's Revenge Rice, James, illus. (p. 1513)
—Too Tall Thomas Rides the Grub Line Rice, James, illus. (p. 1767)
Rice, James, illus. see Blazek, Sarah.
Rice, James, illus. see Davis, David.
Rice, James, illus. see Layne, Steven.
Rice, James, illus. see McWilliams, Amanda & Moore, Clement C.
Rice, James, illus. see Turner, Thomas N.
Rice, James, Jr. Lyn & the Fuzzy Rice, James, Jr., illus. (p. 1066)
Rice, James, tr. Trail Boss: J. M. Daugherty. (p. 1776)
Rice, Joan W. Winter Sleep: A Story of Hibernation. Slimp, Gwen H., illus. (p. 1938)
Rice, John, illus. see Myers, Jack.
Rice Jr., Earle. Evolution of Government & Politics in China. (p. 547)
—Evolution of Government & Politics in North & South Korea. (p. 547)
—Ganges River. (p. 655)
—Tigris/Euphrates River. (p. 1749)
—Yangtze River. (p. 1968)
Rice, June K. Little Blue Tree. (p. 1024)
Rice, Kaleb, illus. see Porrata, Mayra.
Rice, Karen. Forbidden Sneeze. (p. 616)
Rice, Karen, des. Contemporary Native American Art: Reflections after Lewis & Clark. (p. 360)
Rice, Katie & Kuligowski, Stephanie. Dangerous Catch! Deep Sea Fishers. (p. 404)
Rice, Linda. Rhino's Special Ears (p. 1467)
Rice, Lisa A., jt. auth. see Feldhahn, Shaunti.
Rice, Liz. Bill Richardson. (p. 186)
Rice, M. L. Melody of Light. (p. 1125)
—Who I Am. (p. 1915)
Rice, Morgan. Charge of Valor. (p. 291)
—Grant of Arms. (p. 710)
—Land of Fire. (p. 973)
—Quest of Heroes. (p. 1426)
—Reign of Steel. (p. 1457)
—Rite of Swords. (p. 1475)
—Rule of Queens. (p. 1495)
—Vow of Glory. (p. 1850)
Rice, Myrtle Alley. Friends of Fur & Feather. (p. 638)
Rice, Racheal & Benchmark Education Co., LLC. Robert Ballard: Deepwater Explorer. (p. 1478)
Rice, Rob S. Ancient Greek Warfare. (p. 69)
—Ancient Roman Warfare. (p. 70)

R

Rice, Ruth Mason & Villar, Rose. Cycle, Children's Games & Other Songs. Browne, Anita, illus. (p. 396)
Rice, Sean Michael. Approach. (p. 93)
—Sunday. (p. 1676)
Rice, Sheila. Night Watchers. (p. 1254)
Rice, Simon. Discover Spain. (p. 448)
Rice, Simon & Campbell, Polly. Discover Spain. (p. 448)
Rice, Stanley A. Encyclopedia of Biodiversity. (p. 525)
Rice, Stephen Leon. League of Superheroes. (p. 982)
Rice, T. F. Wind Being. (p. 1935)
Rice, Tim & Webber, Andrew Lloyd. Joseph & the Amazing Technicolor Dreamcoat. Blake, Quentin, illus. (p. 926)
Rice, William B. Water Scientists. (p. 1863)
Rice, William. Our Sun. (p. 1310)
—Seasons. (p. 1538)
Rice, William & Franklin, Yvonne. Deserts. (p. 429)
—Forests. (p. 618)
—Oceans. (p. 1277)
—Ponds. (p. 1382)
—Rainforests. (p. 1436)
—Wetlands. (p. 1877)
Rice, William B. African Grasslands. (p. 27)
—Amazon Rainforest. (p. 56)
—Death Valley Desert. (p. 420)
—Earthquakes. (p. 497)
—Ecosystems. (p. 503)
—Endangered Animals of the Desert. (p. 526)
—Endangered Animals of the Sea. (p. 526)
—Fires. (p. 592)
—First Geologists. (p. 595)
—Geologists: From Pythias to Stock. (p. 662)
—Habitats. (p. 734)
—Huracanes. (p. 829)
—Incendios. (p. 868)
—Inside the Water Cycle (p. 878)
—Inundaciones y las Ventiscas. (p. 883)
—Jane Goodall. (p. 908)
—Landforms. (p. 974)
—Life & Non-Life in an Ecosystem. (p. 1007)
—Life & the Flow of Energy. (p. 1007)
—Our Resources. (p. 1309)
—Producers & Consumers. (p. 1409)
—Rocks & Minerals (p. 1483)
—Story of Fossil Fuels. (p. 1658)
—Survival! Desert. (p. 1686)
—Survival! Jungle. (p. 1686)
—Survival! Ocean. (p. 1686)
—Terremotos. (p. 1721)
—Tornadoes. (p. 1770)
—Tornados. (p. 1770)
—Volcanes. (p. 1848)
—Volcanoes. (p. 1849)
—World of Rocks & Minerals. (p. 1957)
Rice, William B., jt. auth. see Wolfe, Hillary.
Rice, William B. & Wolfe, Hillary. Blast off to Space Camp. (p. 198)
Rice, Yvette. Mountain Moving Faith. (p. 1181)
Rich, Anna, illus. see Barber, Barbara E.
Rich, Anna, illus. see Hru, Dakari.
Rich, Anna, illus. see Lundebrek, Amy.
Rich, Anna, illus. see Medearis, Angela Shelf.
Rich, Anna, illus. see Scholastic, Inc. Staff & Boyd, Dee.
Rich, Anna, illus. see Steenwyk, Elizabeth Van.
Rich, Bobbie, illus. see Rich, Carol Bak.
Rich, C. & Richardson, Carla R. Completely You: 12 Things Every Girl Needs to Know. (p. 353)
Rich, Carol Bak. Running Nose Book. Rich, Bobbie, illus. (p. 1497)
Rich, Deborah. Reindeer Luck. (p. 1457)
Rich, J. Milton. Heavenly Fathers Plan of Salvation Coloring Book. Knaupp, Andrew & Koford, Adam, illus. (p. 761)
Rich, Jamie S. Boy & a Girl. (p. 217)
—I Was Someone Dead. (p. 848)
—It Girl & the Atomics Round 2: the World Is Flat TP: The World Is Flat TP. (p. 894)
—Love the Way You Love (p. 1060)
—Spell Checkers Volume 3: Careless Whisper: Careless Whisper. (p. 1625)
Rich, Jillian, jt. auth. see Rawlins, George.
Rich, Juliann. Caught in the Crossfire. (p. 282)
—Searching for Grace. (p. 1537)
—Taking the Stand. (p. 1698)
Rich, K. L. From Roaches to Riches. (p. 643)
Rich, Karissa. Kit Carson: Legendary Mountain Man. (p. 962)
Rich, Lori. Smuggler's Flame: William Tyndale. (p. 1595)
Rich, Mari. Big-Animal Vets! (p. 177)
—Cyber Spy Hunters! (p. 396)
Rich, Steve. Mrs. Carter's Butterfly Garden. (p. 1187)
—My School Yard Garden. (p. 1218)
Rich, Susan. Half-Minute Horrors. (p. 736)
Rich, Winifred. Wake Up! To All You Are. (p. 1853)
Richa Kinra, illus. see Debra Maymon.
Richard Bellingham Edd. Fables of Boris: Invitations to Meaningful Conversations. (p. 559)
Richard, Elaine. 10 Critical Thinking Card Games: Easy-to-Play, Reproducible Card & Board Games That Build Kids' Critical Thinking Skills-And Help Them Succeed on Tests. (p. 1993)
—10 Reading Comprehension Card Games: Easy-to-Play, Reproducible Card & Board Games That Boost Kids' Reading Skills-And Help Them Succeed on Tests. (p. 1994)
—10 Vocabulary Card Games: Easy-to-Play, Reproducible Card & Board Games That Boost Kids' Vocabulary-And Help Them Succeed on Tests. (p. 1994)
Richard French. Secrets of Health. (p. 1545)
Richard, Ilene, illus. see Balsley, Tilda & Blalsey, Tilda.
Richard, Ilene, illus. see Balsley, Tilda.
Richard, Ilene, illus. see Mataya, Marybeth.
Richard, Ilene, illus. see Mishica, Clare.
Richard, Ilene, illus. see Williams, Rozanne Lanczak.
Richard, John. Big Book of Transport. Leeks, David, illus. (p. 179)
Richard, Keisha Luana, illus. see Lynch, Stephen D.
Richard, L. McBain. Cheating Hurts Yourself & Others: 8 Short Stories of Cheating & Consequences. (p. 295)
Richard, Laurent. Championship! Gauvin, Edward, tr. (p. 289)
—Clowns & Dragons! Gauvin, Edward, tr. (p. 335)
—Ninjas & Knock Outs! Gauvin, Edward, tr. from FRE. (p. 1256)
—Pranks & Attacks! Gauvin, Edward, tr. from FRE. (p. 1393)
—Wild Animals! Gauvin, Edward, tr. from FRE. (p. 1928)
Richard, Laurent, illus. see Hédelin, Pascale.
Richard, Lolita Louise. Walking with a B C Big Book Adventure. (p. 1854)
Richard, Martine. Chapeau, Camomille! Begin, Jean-Guy, illus. (p. 291)
Richard, Orlin. Bermuda Triangle. (p. 167)
—Ghosts. (p. 672)
—Investigating Seasons. (p. 885)
Richard, P. M., illus. see Mikowski, Tracy L.
Richard, P. M., illus. see Stanton, Laura.
Richard, Peck, jt. auth. see Peck, Richard.
Richard, Ramonda. Robert the Bully. (p. 1479)
Richard Richtmyer. Bit of Magic: A Novel. (p. 194)
Richard Scott Morris. Alphabet Soup with Anchovies. (p. 50)
—Irving the Duck in the Tortoise Shell Suit. (p. 888)
Richard, Southall. Printers Types in the Twentieth Century. (p. 1407)
Richard, Wright. Rite of Passage. (p. 1475)
Richard, Zachary, ed. History of the Acadians of Louisiana. (p. 784)
Richarde, jt. auth. see Russin, Nicole.
Richards, Aled. Stori Dda. (p. 1654)
Richards, Aled & Pritchard, Richard Huw. Am y Copa. (p. 51)
Richards, Andrea. Girl Director: A How-to-Guide for the First-Time, Flat-Broke Filmaker (and Videomaker) (p. 678)
Richards, Anna Matlack & Carroll, Lewis. New Alice in the Old Wonderland. (p. 1243)
Richards, Anthony Lee. Golden Bird (p. 694)
Richards, Arlene. That's Bingzy! Busy Building Self-Esteem. (p. 1726)
—That's Bingzy! Busy Building Self-Esteem. Zimmerman, Louis, illus. (p. 1726)
Richards, Beah E. Keep Climbing, Girls. Christie, R. Gregory, illus. (p. 946)
Richards, Brenda. Woodland Tale. (p. 1949)
Richards, C. E. King Arthur. (p. 958)
Richards, C. J. Junkyard Bot Fujita, Goro, illus. (p. 936)
—Lots of Bots. Fujita, Goro, illus. (p. 1057)
Richards, Carol. Ghostrider. (p. 672)
Richards, Charles. What Is a Space Probe? (p. 1888)
Richards, Charles, illus. see Richards, Pat.
Richards, Chip & De Alessi, O. B. Flutes in the Garden. (p. 608)
Richards, Christine. Bobby the Busy Body Boy. (p. 206)
Richards, Chuck. Catch That Cat! A Chase up & down & Through M.C. Escher's Art. (p. 279)
—Critter Sitter. Richards, Chuck, illus. (p. 384)
—Lulu's Magic Wand. (p. 1065)
Richards, Claire. Mai's Garden: Mickamoo's Rescue. (p. 1077)
Richards, Claude. Temple Letters: A Rewarding Path to Happiness on Earth & Everlasting Treasures in Heaven. (p. 1718)
Richards, Cliff, jt. auth. see Rodi, Robert.
Richards, Constance E., jt. ed. see Woodworth, Bradley.
Richards, Courtland William, jt. auth. see Mogavera, Cyndie Lepori.
Richards, Dan. Can One Balloon Make an Elephant Fly? Newman, Jeff, illus. (p. 258)
—Problem with Not Being Scared of Monsters. Neubecker, Robert, illus. (p. 1408)
Richards, David. Lady at Batoche. (p. 970)
Richards, Dawn. Duck's Easter Egg Hunt. D'hamers, Heidi, illus. (p. 488)
—My Dad Is a Hero. (p. 1200)
—My Mommy Is Magic. Massey, Jane, illus. (p. 1214)
Richards, Dillon H. & Stirling, Janet. Searching for UFOs. (p. 1538)
Richards, Douglas E. Trapped. Cabot, David, illus. (p. 1779)
Richards, Elisabeth, jt. auth. see Lord, Bruce.
Richards, Elizabeth. Black City. (p. 195)
—Phoenix. (p. 1351)
—Wings. (p. 1936)
Richards, Eugene. Fat Baby. (p. 576)
Richards, George. Great Australian Super-Hero: Now You See Him, Now You Don't. (p. 713)
Richards, J. Danielle Jennson, Life Lessons of a Little Clown. (p. 405)
Richards, J. Kirk. I'll Be There with Belzon. (p. 856)
Richards, J. Stuart. Hard Coal Times, Volume Two: Mules, Drivers & Spraggers (p. 748)
Richards, Jack C., et al. Connect (p. 357)
—Connect Level 2 Workbook. (p. 357)
Richards, Jame. Three Rivers Rising. (p. 1743)
Richards, Jane. Tombs, Temples, & Thrones. (p. 1764)
Richards, Jasmine. Book of Wonders. (p. 212)
Richards, Jean. Fruit Is a Suitcase for Seeds. Hariton, Anca, illus. (p. 645)
Richards, Jon. Air & Flight. (p. 31)
—Chemicals & Reactions. (p. 297)
—Clothes. (p. 334)
—Communication. (p. 349)
—Design It Yourself Supercars. Araujo, Paige Krul, ed. (p. 430)
—Forces & Simple Machines. (p. 617)
—Human Body. Simkins, Ed, illus. (p. 825)
—Human World. Simkins, Ed, illus. (p. 826)
—In the Home. (p. 866)
—Light & Sight. (p. 1014)
—Light & Sight. Moores, Ian & Thompson, Ian, illus. (p. 1014)
—Natural World. Simkins, Ed, illus. (p. 1236)
—Planet Earth. Simkins, Ed, illus. (p. 1367)
—Toys. (p. 1774)
—Transportation. (p. 1779)
—Vacations & Holidays. (p. 1830)
—Water & Boats. (p. 1862)
Richards, Jon, illus. see Arkin, Alan.
Richards, Jon & Flaherty, Michael. Science Factory (p. 1526)
Richards, Jon & Simkins, Ed. Record-Breaking Animals. (p. 1452)
—Record-Breaking Building Feats. (p. 1452)
—Record-Breaking Earth & Space Facts. (p. 1452)
—Record-Breaking People. (p. 1452)
Richards, Jon, text. Race Cars. (p. 1430)
Richards, Josie Aleardi. Grandma's Just Not Herself. Rowland, Lauri, illus. (p. 708)
Richards, Julian. Amazing Pop-Up Stonehenge: All the Questions You've Always Wanted to Ask... & Some of the Answers! Birkinshaw, Linda, illus. (p. 55)
Richards, Julie. Biofuels. (p. 188)
—Fossil Fuels. (p. 623)
—It's Sunny! (p. 899)
—Nuclear Energy. (p. 1269)
—Solar Energy. (p. 1606)
—Water Energy. (p. 1862)
—Wind Energy. (p. 1935)
Richards, Justin. Chaos Code. (p. 291)
—Licence to Fish (p. 1007)
—Rewind Assassin. (p. 1467)
—Sorted! (p. 1614)
—Thunder Raker. (p. 1746)
Richards, Justin, jt. auth. see Higgins, Jack.
Richards, Justin & BBC Education Staff. Doctor Who - Essential Guide. (p. 459)
Richards, Justin & Collins, Mike. Dalek Project. (p. 401)
Richards, Katherine. My Favorite Run. Fieldhouse, Vicky, illus. (p. 1203)
Richards, Keith. Gus & Me: The Story of My Granddad & My First Guitar. Richards, Theodora, illus. (p. 732)
Richards, Kirsten. My Little Beauty Shop: A Girly Girl Book. (p. 1212)
Richards, Kirsten, illus. see Cartaya, Pablo & Howard, Martin.
Richards, Kirsten, illus. see Dale, Jay.
Richards, Kirsten, illus. see Dougherty, Brandi.
Richards, Kirsten, illus. see Karr, Lily.
Richards, Kirsten, illus. see Manushkin, Fran.
Richards, Kirsten, illus. see Ranson, Erin.
Richards, Kirsten, illus. see Trowell, Michelle.
Richards, Kitty. Cinderella: The Lost Tiara. (p. 320)
—Meet the Sparkplugs, Level 3. Simard, Remy, illus. (p. 1123)
—New Friends. (p. 1244)
—Perfect Princess Tea Party. (p. 1342)
—Phineas & Ferb Laughapalooza Joke Book. (p. 1351)
—Phonics Comics: Twisted Tales - Level 3 Juarez, Fernando, illus. (p. 1352)
—SpongeBob AirPants: The Lost Episode (p. 1630)
—SpongeBob Airpants: The Lost Episode. Martinez, Heather, illus. (p. 1630)
Richards, Kitty, jt. auth. see Disney Book Group Staff.
Richards, Kitty, jt. auth. see RH Disney Staff.
Richards, Kitty & Disney Book Group Staff. Goodnight, Thumper! Tyminski, Lori & Gordon, Dean, illus. (p. 701)
Richards, Kitty & RH Disney Staff. Run, Remy, Run! Disney Storybook Artists Staff, illus. (p. 1496)
Richards, Kris, illus. see Springer, Audrey.
Richards, Kristen, illus. see Dougherty, Brandi.
Richards, Laura E. Captain January. (p. 264)
—Marie. (p. 1093)
—Wooing of Calvin Parks. (p. 1950)
Richards, Laura Elizabeth Howe. Hildegarde's Neighbors. (p. 779)
—Melody. (p. 1125)
—Queen Hildegarde. (p. 1424)
Richards, Laurae. Coming Home. (p. 348)
Richards, Lawrence O. Gospel of Mark (p. 703)
—King James Version Kids Study Bible (p. 958)
Richards, Lawrence O. & Richards, Sue. NIV Teen Study Bible (p. 1257)
—Teen Study Bible (p. 1714)
Richards, Lawrence O. & Zondervan Publishing Staff. King James Version Kids Study Bible (p. 958)
Richards, Linda L. Death Was in the Blood. (p. 420)
Richards, Lisa. Family Short Stories Book. (p. 568)
—Family Stories: A Collection of Short Stories by Lisa Richards (p. 568)
Richards, Lucy. Animal Antics (with Header Card) (p. 76)
—Busy Bugs (W/Header Card) (p. 246)
—Jumping Jungle (W/Hang Tag) (p. 934)
—Jumping Jungle (W/Header Card) (p. 934)
Richards, Lucy, illus. see Donaldson, Julia.
Richards, Lucy, illus. see Hunter, Jana Novotny, et al.
Richards, Lucy, illus. see Morpurgo, Michael.
Richards, Lucy, jt. auth. see Donaldson, Julia.
Richards, Lucy & Finn, Rebecca. Silly Sea (W/Hang Tag) (p. 1576)
—Silly Sea (W/Header Card) (p. 1576)
Richards, Lynne. Fearless Four: Braced for Battle. Semple, Dave, illus. (p. 579)
Richards, M. & Creese, S. Carry Me Rough N Tough - Emergency. (p. 271)
—Carry Me Rough N Tough - Trucks. (p. 271)
Richards, Mark & Creese, Sarah. Diggers & Dumpers. (p. 439)
Richards, Mark, et al. Tractors. (p. 1775)
Richards, Marlee. Johnstown Flood: Core Events of Deadly Disaster (p. 924)
Richards, Marlee, jt. auth. see Brill, Marlene Targ.
Richards, Mary, jt. ed. see American Girl Editors.
Richards, Mary & American Girl Editors, eds. Lists! A Year of Stuff about Me. (p. 1022)
Richards, Melissa. I Didn't Know I Was a Bully: A Meaningful & Memorable Reproducible Story Plus Six Literatur-Based Lessons on Bullying Behaviors. (p. 837)
Richards, Mose & Ferguson, Marfe Delano. Sea Monsters: A Prehistoric Adventure. (p. 1535)
Richards, Mose & U. S. National Geographic Society Staff. Sea Monsters: A Prehistoric Adventure. (p. 1535)
Richards, Mose, et al. Arctic Tale: Official Companion to the Major Motion Picture. (p. 96)
Richards, Natalie D. Gone Too Far. (p. 697)
—Six Months Later. (p. 1582)
Richards, Pat. Bardolph Bedivere Wolf Returns. Richards, Charles, illus. (p. 138)
Richards, Roy. En Movimiento. (p. 522)
—En Optica. (p. 522)
—En Papel. (p. 522)
Richards, Sonja. Comet Kid. (p. 348)
—My Maize & Blue Day. Viall, Pauline, illus. (p. 1214)
Richards, Stephen J. Twins First Snow. (p. 1802)
Richards, Sue, jt. auth. see Richards, Lawrence O.
Richards, Tanya, illus. see Paulin, Chrita.
Richards, Tanya Dawn. Squirrel's Peanut Allergy: A Peanut-Free Story. (p. 1637)
Richards, Theodora, illus. see Richards, Keith.
Richards, Tracy. My Navy Dad. (p. 1215)
Richards, V. H. First Christmas Color Act Bk. (p. 593)
Richards, Verity. Rhymes & Riddles to Rattle Your Reason. (p. 1468)
Richards, Virginia Helen. Ten Commandments. Richards, Virginia Helen & Halpin, D. Thomas, illus. (p. 1718)
Richards, Virginia Helen, illus. see Dateno, Maria Grace.
Richards, Virginia Helen, illus. see Halpin, D. Thomas.
Richards, Virginia Helen, illus. see Jenkins, Diana R.
Richards, Virginia Helen, illus. see MacDonald, Maryann.
Richards, Virginia Helen, illus. see Scarfi, Margaret Rose.
Richards, Virginia Helen, illus. see Tebo, Mary Elizabeth.
Richards, Virginia Helen, jt. auth. see Halpin, D. Thomas.
Richards, Virginia Helen & Halpin, D. Thomas. Blessed Miguel Pro. (p. 199)
—My Christmas Picture Book. (p. 1200)
Richards, Wayne, jt. auth. see Burris, Judy.
Richards, Wendy, jt. auth. see Delaney, Sally.
Richardson, Adele. Canada. (p. 260)
—China. (p. 306)
—Earth. (p. 495)
—Great Wall of China. (p. 719)
—Iran. (p. 886)
—Israel. (p. 893)
—Mars. (p. 1096)
—Mercury. (p. 1127)
—Mexico. (p. 1131)
—Michelangelo. (p. 1135)
—Saturn (p. 1515)
—Story of the San Francisco Giants. (p. 1662)
—Story of the Texas Rangers. (p. 1662)
—Venus (p. 1836)
Richardson, Adele & Richardson, Adele D. Alligators Rasch, Patricia, illus. (p. 47)
—Caring for Your Fish Garvin, Kelly, illus. (p. 269)
—Caring for Your Hamster Garvin, Kelly, illus. (p. 269)
—Electricity. Collins, Tami, illus. (p. 509)
—Jupiter. (p. 937)
Richardson, Adele D. Foxes Collins, Tami, illus. (p. 626)
—Freight Trains in Action (p. 635)
—Light: A Question & Answer Book Collins, Tami & Nei, Molly, illus. (p. 1014)
—Owls (p. 1315)
—Rocks (p. 1483)
—Seashells. (p. 1538)
—Story of Disney. (p. 1658)
—Story of Microsoft. (p. 1659)
Richardson, Adele D., jt. auth. see Haffmann, Janet.
Richardson, Adele D., jt. auth. see Richardson, Adele D.
Richardson, Adele D., jt. auth. see Richardson, Adele.
Richardson, Adele D. & Richardson, Adele D. Amphibians (p. 65)
—Balances (p. 133)
—Diana (p. 434)
—Fish (p. 598)
—Hades (p. 735)
—Hercules (p. 769)
—Thermometers (p. 1731)
Richardson, Adele D., et al. Birds. (p. 191)
Richardson, Alan. Platform Party. (p. 1370)
Richardson, Alex. Gladiator & the Legend of Auchinle. (p. 682)
—Gladiator & the legend of Auchinlea. (p. 682)
Richardson, Angelique. New Woman in Fiction & Fact: Fin-de-Siècle Feminisms. Richardson, Angelique & Willis, Chris, eds. (p. 1247)
Richardson, Arleta. More Stories from Grandma's Attic. (p. 1175)
—Still More Stories from Grandma's Attic (p. 1650)
—Treasures from Grandma. (p. 1782)
—Whistle Stop West. (p. 1912)
Richardson, Bernard. Freddy Weller's Holiday. (p. 633)
Richardson, Beth A. Child of the Light: Walking Through Advent & Christmas. (p. 301)
Richardson, Bill. Aunts Come Marching. Nugent, Cynthia, illus. (p. 115)
—I Would Have Gone to Woodstock. (p. 849)
—Sally Dog Little Undercover Agent. Malepart, Celine, illus. (p. 1505)
Richardson, Carla R., jt. auth. see Rich, C.
Richardson, Cathie, illus. see Eismann, Sheila F. & Putz, Ali F.
Richardson, Charisse K. Real Slam Dunk. Nelson, Kadir, illus. (p. 1449)
Richardson, Christopher. Beat Goes On. (p. 152)
—Pirates. (p. 1363)
—Special Effects. (p. 1623)
Richardson, Colin, jt. auth. see Harper, Glyn.
Richardson, D. L. Feedback. (p. 580)
Richardson, Deborra. Treasures at the Museum. (p. 1782)
Richardson, Dick. Oglin: A Hero's Journey Across Africa... Towards the Tomorrows. Feek, Cathy, illus. (p. 1280)
Richardson, Don. Secrets of the Koran: Revealing Insight into Islam's Holy Book. (p. 1545)
Richardson, Donna. Yellowstone: A Blast from the Past. (p. 1970)
Richardson, Donna Castle. Little Lilly Ladybug. (p. 1030)
Richardson, Donna Castle, ed. Teeny Tiny Tadpole. (p. 1715)
Richardson, Doris, illus. see Byj, Charlot.
Richardson, Dot. Go for It: Conversations on Being You. (p. 686)

Richardson, Duncan. Revenge. Edwards, Rebecca, illus. (p. 1465)
Richardson, E. E. Black Bones. (p. 195)
—Curse Box. (p. 394)
Richardson, Ellis. Common Short Vowel Syllables: Brown Sequence. Level 9 (p. 349)
—Sound of Short A: Green Sequence. Level 4 (p. 1615)
—Sound of Short U: Brown Sequence. Level 8 (p. 1615)
Richardson, Ellis & DiBenedetto, Barbara. Sound of Short E Level 10: Brown Sequence. (p. 1615)
Richardson, Faith. Angel Walker. (p. 74)
—Peacock's Stone. (p. 1332)
—Tree Root & River Rat. (p. 1783)
Richardson, Fay Lapka. Dark Is a Color. (p. 407)
—Hoverlight. (p. 804)
Richardson, Frederick. Best-Loved Children's Stories. (p. 170)
—Mother Goose: A Classic Collection of Children's Nursery Rhymes. (p. 1177)
Richardson, Frederick, illus. see Baum, L. Frank.
Richardson, Frederick, illus. see Faulkner, Georgene.
Richardson, Frederick, illus. see Maltby, Ethel H.
Richardson, Frederick, illus. see Thorne-Thomsen, Gudrun.
Richardson, Frederick, illus. see Treadwell, Harriette Taylor & Free, Margaret.
Richardson, George E. Brogee's Giant Bicycle. (p. 230)
Richardson, Gillian. 10 Plants That Shook the World. Rosen, Kim, illus. (p. 1994)
—10 Ships That Rocked the World. Rosen, Kim, illus. (p. 1994)
—Dan Gutman. (p. 402)
—Ecosystems. (p. 503)
—Ecosystems QandA. (p. 503)
—Hiking. (p. 779)
—Kaboom! Explosions of All Kinds. (p. 941)
—Machu Picchu. (p. 1068)
—Mountain Extremes. (p. 1180)
Richardson, Gillian & Kissock, Heather. Machu Picchu. (p. 1068)
Richardson, Hazel. Dinosaurs & Prehistoric Life. (p. 444)
—Life in Ancient Africa. (p. 1010)
—Life in Ancient Japan. (p. 1010)
—Life in Ancient South America. (p. 1010)
—Life in the Ancient Indus River Valley. (p. 1011)
—Life of the Ancient Celts. (p. 1012)
—Life of the Ancient Vikings. (p. 1012)
—Trade & Commerce in the Ancient World. Crabtree Publishing Staff, ed. (p. 1776)
Richardson, Hazel, jt. auth. see Miller, Reagan.
Richardson, Ida, compiled by. Survival Basics Guide to Nuclear, Biological or Chemical Terror Attack: The Companion Piece to the New Civil Defense: Survival Basics DVD & VHS. (p. 1686)
Richardson, J. J. It's about Time. (p. 896)
Richardson, Jane & Dawson, Ian. Dying for the Vote: Britain 1750-1900 - A Key Stage 3 Study on the Chartists & the Suffragettes. (p. 491)
Richardson, Jean, jt. auth. see Appling, Jeffrey R.
Richardson, Jeffery. Wormwood Adventures New Friends. (p. 1961)
Richardson, Jill. Hobbits, You, & the Spiritual World of Middle-Earth. (p. 786)
Richardson, Joy. Birds. (p. 191)
—Fish. (p. 598)
—Flowers. (p. 608)
—Insects. (p. 875)
—Mammals. (p. 1085)
—Mollusks. (p. 1160)
—Reptiles. (p. 1461)
—Trees. (p. 1784)
Richardson, Joy K. Helping Hand Series: I Love You. (p. 766)
Richardson, Justin & Parnell, Peter. And Tango Makes Three: 10th Anniversary Edition. Cole, Henry, illus. (p. 71)
—And Tango Makes Three. Cole, Henry, illus. (p. 71)
—Christian, the Hugging Lion. Bates, Amy June, illus. (p. 312)
Richardson, Kara, illus. see Moon, Catherine R. & Everette, Maureen C.
Richardson, Kara, illus. see Scherer, Catherine W.
Richardson, Kayla, illus. see Richardson, Levae.
Richardson, Kim, jt. auth. see Meissner, David.
Richardson, Kimberly Stanton. Gus Learns to Fly: Self-Defense Is Self-Discovery. Crowley, Adam A., photos by. (p. 732)
Richardson, Kiowa. Christmas Kangaroo: Written & Illustrated by Kiowa Richardson. (p. 314)
Richardson, KL. Heart Song. (p. 760)
Richardson, Lans. Calf Named Polly. Arndt, Charles T., illus. (p. 252)
Richardson, Larry. Metal Mike. (p. 1130)
Richardson, Levae. Skip & Marty. Richardson, Kayla, illus. (p. 1585)
Richardson, Lilith. TORO Special Edition Paperback. (p. 1770)
Richardson, Lin Douglas. Meaning of Me. (p. 1117)
Richardson, Linda. Gift. (p. 675)
Richardson, Linda, illus. see Evans, Sally.
Richardson, Linda A. Free Spirit. (p. 634)
Richardson, Matt, jt. auth. see Bdeir, Ayah.
Richardson, Michael. Surrealism & Cinema. (p. 1686)
Richardson, Michelle Y. Kaito: Shedding Tears. (p. 941)
Richardson, Mike. Return of the Gremlins. (p. 1464)
Richardson, Mike, illus. see Snyder, Susan E.
Richardson, Nigel. Finding Out about Life in Britain in the 1960's. (p. 588)
—Typhoid in Uppingham: Analysis of a Victorian Town & School in Crisis, 1875-1877 (p. 1805)
Richardson, Nikki. Beautiful Lie (p. 153)
Richardson, Owen, illus. see Hughes, Devon.
Richardson, Owen, illus. see Hunter, Erin, et al.
Richardson, Owen, illus. see Hunter, Erin.
Richardson, Peter, illus. see Jeffrey, Gary.
Richardson, Phillip, jt. auth. see Hom, Susan.
Richardson, R. Sarah & Charlesbridge Publishing Staff. Artist at Work. (p. 104)
Richardson, Rhiannon. Model Friendship. (p. 1157)
Richardson, Robert. Twin Hicks Noah's Ark. Hicks, Alan and Aaron, illus. (p. 1802)
Richardson, S. Lee. Backyard Series Volume Two: The Baby Bear Scare Story. (p. 131)
Richardson, Sandra Lee. Backyard Series: Volume One (p. 131)
Richardson, Sarah. Art in a Box. (p. 102)
—Make Your Mark: The Drawing Book for Children. (p. 1079)
Richardson, Sarah J. What If? The What Ifs of Childhood Safety (p. 1887)
Richardson, Sharde. Watched. (p. 1861)
Richardson, Steve. Alexander Trout's Amazing Adventure. Lowe, Wesley, illus. (p. 37)
—Billy's Mountain. Leonhard, Herb, illus. (p. 187)
Richardson, Timarlay A. Billy Bean & the Chocolate Dragon. (p. 187)
Richardson, Tom. Dominic Is Strong. (p. 465)
Richardson, Tracy. Field. (p. 583)
—Indian Summer. (p. 871)
Richardson, Travis. Lost in Clover. (p. 1055)
Richardson, William K. Grappler. (p. 711)
Richardson-Jones, Tessa, illus. see Stowell, Gordon.
Richardson-Jones, Tessa, illus. see Umansky, Kaye.
Richardville, Carol. Beau Bandit's Tale. Davis, Kaley, illus. (p. 153)
Richardville, Mandy, jt. auth. see Hashimoto, Daniel.
Richburg, Sheila. Story of Panhandle Pete Part One. (p. 1659)
Richelieu, Frank E. Art of Being Yourself: Discover Who You Are & Learn How to Live. (p. 102)
Richemont, Enid. Big Purple Wonderbook. Waldek, Kelly, illus. (p. 183)
—Jack the Fearless. (p. 903)
—Plop City. (p. 1374)
—Princess Frog. (p. 1404)
Richens, Carol & Smith, Lori. Lori's Summer Fun with Tamara! (p. 1053)
Richert, Catherine. Animal Rescue: Represent & Solve Problems Involving Addition. (p. 79)
Richert, Scott P. Bill Bryson. (p. 186)
—King Lear. (p. 958)
Richey, Denise. Four in a Fire. (p. 625)
—Handwriting on the Wall. (p. 741)
—King's Bad Dream. (p. 960)
Richey, Lisa. Manners to Go. (p. 1088)
Richie, Donald. Japanese Portraits: Pictures of Different People. (p. 909)
Richie, Jason. Iraq & the Fall of Saddam Hussein. (p. 887)
Richler, Mordecai. First Spy Case. Eyolfson, Norman, illus. (p. 597)
—Jacob Two-Two & the Dinosaur. Petricic, Dusan, illus. (p. 904)
—Jacob Two-Two & the Dinosaur. Eyolfson, Norman, illus. (p. 904)
—Jacob Two-Two Meets the Hooded Fang. Petricic, Dusan, illus. (p. 904)
—Jacob Two-Two's First Spy Case. Petricic, Dusan, illus. (p. 904)
Richman, Irwin. German Architecture in America: Folk House, Your House, Bauhaus, & More (p. 666)
Richman, Karyn. Land Where All Things Become Beautiful. (p. 974)
Richmond, Benjamin. What Are the Three Branches of the Government? And Other Questions about the U. S. Constitution. (p. 1880)
—Why Is the Sea Salty? And Other Questions about the Ocean. Azhderian, Cecelia, illus. (p. 1925)
—Why Is the Sea Salty? And Other Questions about the Oceans. Azhderian, Cecelia, illus. (p. 1925)
Richmond, Beulah. Anancy & Friends: A Grandmother's Anancy Stories for Her Grandchildren. Brown, Clovis, illus. (p. 67)
Richmond, Bob, illus. see Kennis, Don.
Richmond, Caroline Tung. Only Thing to Fear. (p. 1298)
Richmond, Dee & Colella, Cheryl. Dino Abc. (p. 441)
Richmond, Derek & Skindzier, Jon. Georgetown University College Prowler off the Record. (p. 665)
Richmond, Dick. Produced by Contemporary. (p. 1409)
Richmond, Jacob. Polly Perfect & the Tragic Fart. Pine, Hank, illus. (p. 1381)
Richmond, Jake. CrossRoads of Eternity RPG: Core Rule Book. (p. 385)
Richmond, Jamea, illus. see Little, Robert.
Richmond, John Francis. Mounds of Florida & Their Builders. (p. 1180)
richmond, keli. LIteracy Speaks 2. (p. 1022)
Richmond, Margie Hayes, ed. see Boyds Mills Press Staff.
Richmond, Margie Hayes, ed. see Highlights for Children Editorial Staff & Boyds Mills Press Staff.
Richmond, Marianne. Beautiful Blue Eyes. (p. 153)
—Big Boys Go Potty. Richmond, Marianne, illus. (p. 179)
—Big Brother. (p. 179)
—Big Girls Go Potty. Richmond, Marianne, illus. (p. 181)
—Big Sister. (p. 183)
—Daddy Loves Me! (p. 398)
—Dear Grandson. (p. 419)
—Dear Sister: A Message of Love. (p. 419)
—Friendly Floppy Fishie, What Do Wish For? (p. 637)
—Gift of an Angel: For Parents Welcoming a New Child. Vol. 1 (p. 675)
—Good Luck to You. (p. 698)
—Grandma Loves Me! (p. 708)
—Grand-O-Grams: Postcards to Keep in Touch with Your Grandkids All-Year-Round. (p. 707)
—Grandpa Loves Me! (p. 709)
—Hooray for You! A Celebration Of "You-Ness". (p. 796)
—I Love You So... (p. 844)
—I Love You So Much... (p. 844)
—If I Could Keep You Little. (p. 852)
—I'll Never Let You Go. (p. 856)
—I'm Not Tired Yet! (p. 859)
—Love-U-Grams: Postcards, Notes & Coupons to Connect with Your Kids. (p. 1060)
—My Journal about Me! A Keepsake Celebrating the Me-ness of Me. (p. 1211)
—Night Night Book. Richmond, Marianne, illus. (p. 1253)
—Oh, the Things My Mom Will Do. (p. 1281)
—Si Pudiera Conservarte Pequeño... (p. 1572)
—Thank You Mom. (p. 1725)
—With Heartfelt Sympathy. (p. 1942)
—You Are My Heart. (p. 1973)
Richmond, Marianne R. Dear Daughter. (p. 418)
—Dear Son: Simply Said... Little Books with Lots of Love. (p. 419)
—Do-it-yourself Guide to - Understanding a Wome. (p. 457)
—Goodbye, Faithful Friend: Remembering Your Dog with Love. (p. 700)
—Holiday Wishes. (p. 788)
—I Care about You. (p. 837)
—I Wished for You: An Adoption Story. (p. 849)
—It's a Boy! (p. 895)
—It's a Girl! (p. 895)
—Merry Christmas: Celebrating the True Gifts of the Season. (p. 1128)
—So Glad We're Sisters. (p. 1602)
—You Are My Wish Come True. (p. 1973)
Richmond, Peter. Always a Catch. (p. 51)
—Fever: The Life & Music of Miss Peggy Lee. (p. 583)
Richmond, Susan. Further Steps in Stagecraft. (p. 650)
—Junior Textbook of Stagecraft. (p. 936)
—Textbook of Stagecraft. (p. 1724)
Richmond, Wren. Apache. (p. 91)
Richoll, Stephanie, illus. see DeLong, Lucianne.
Richter, A. Boats that Float: Learning the OA Sound. (p. 205)
—By the Ocean: Learning the Long O Sound. (p. 249)
Richter, Abigail. Deadly Mosquitoes. (p. 417)
—Guide Dogs. (p. 730)
—I See a Horse! (p. 845)
—Mike the Bike. (p. 1141)
—Money: Saving & Spending. (p. 1164)
Richter, Al. Ocean Tides. (p. 1277)
Richter, Allen. America's Oldest Colony: The Story of St. Augustine. (p. 64)
Richter, Bernd & Richter, Susan. All Aboard the White Pass & Yukon Route Railroad. (p. 42)
—Cruising Alaska's Inside Passage. (p. 386)
—Discover Alaskas Denali Park. (p. 447)
—Gandma & Grandpa Cruise Alaska Inside Passage. (p. 655)
—Grandma & Grandpa Ride Alaska Train. (p. 708)
—Grandma & Grandpa Visit Denali. Drashner, Diane, illus. (p. 708)
—Listen to Alaskas Animals. Richter, Bernd, illus. (p. 1022)
—Little Bear Who Didn't Want to Hibernate. Green, Sue, illus. (p. 1024)
—There Was a Little Bear. (p. 1730)
—Touch & Feel Alaskas Animals. (p. 1772)
—Traveling Alaska. (p. 1780)
—When Grandma & Grandpa Cruised Through Alaska. (p. 1902)
—When Grandma & Grandpa Rode the Alaska Train. (p. 1902)
Richter, Cheryl R., photos by see Taus-Bolstad, Stacy.
Richter, Cindy. Pete's Big Paws - Hardcover. Peters, Rob, illus. (p. 1348)
Richter, Conrad. Light in the Forest. (p. 1015)
—Light in the Forest. Chappell, Warren, illus. (p. 1015)
Richter, Dana, adapted by. Disney Dinosaur Play-a-sound. (p. 451)
Richter, Danny. Big Gozonga. (p. 181)
Richter, Debra A. Hamster on the Run. LiveLearn, Robert, illus. (p. 740)
—Hamster on the Run, Let's Play in the Snow. LiveLearn, Robert, illus. (p. 740)
—Two Frogs & the Lost Wedding Band. (p. 1803)
Richter, Hank, illus. see Sio, Betsy Menson.
Richter, Ian. Chloe the Cat. (p. 308)
Richter, Jeff, photos by. White Deer: Ghost of the Forest. (p. 1912)
Richter, Joanne. Inventing the Camera. (p. 883)
—Inventing the Television. (p. 883)
—Iran: The Culture. (p. 886)
—Iran - The Culture. (p. 886)
Richter, Joanne, jt. auth. see Fast, April.
Richter, John J. & Zeller, Bob. Lincoln In 3-D. (p. 1018)
Richter, Judy. Riding for Kids: Stable Care, Equipment, Tack, Clothing, Longeing, Lessons, Jumping, Showing. (p. 1471)
Richter, Jutta. Beyond the Station Lies the Sea. Brailovsky, Anna, tr. from GER. (p. 174)
—Cat: Or, How I Lost Eternity. Brailovsky, Anna, tr. from GER. (p. 277)
—Summer of the Pike. Brailovsky, Anna, tr. from GER. (p. 1674)
Richter, Sandy. Grow a Plant Inch by Inch. (p. 726)
—Life of Florence Nightingale. (p. 1012)
Richter, Susan, jt. auth. see Bernd.
Richter, Susan, jt. auth. see Richter, Bernd.
Richter, W. D., jt. auth. see Rauch, Mac.
Richter, William. Dark Eyes. (p. 407)
Richterkessing, Suzanne. Time of Christmas. (p. 1752)
Rickabus, Ted. Ookie. (p. 1298)
Rickards, Lynne. Collins Big Cat - One Potato. Rowland, Andy, illus. (p. 340)
—Jack's Bed. Beardshaw, Rosalind, illus. (p. 904)
Rickenbaker, Becky Hyatt, illus. see Steele, D. Kelley.
Ricker, Jeffrey. Unwanted. (p. 1823)
Rickerty, Simon. Crayon: A Colorful Tale about Friendship. Rickerty, Simon, illus. (p. 377)
—Peanut: A Nutty Tale about Sharing. Rickerty, Simon, illus. (p. 1332)
Rickerty, Simon, illus. see Bently, Peter.
Rickerty, Simon, illus. see Bonwill, Ann.
Rickerty, Simon, illus. see Lewis, Jill.
Ricketson, Kathreen, ed. Kids' Crafternoon Sewing: 25 Projects for a Crafty Afternoon. (p. 953)
Rickett, Sally. Minky the Shoebox Monkey - a Little Monkey with a Long Way to Go. (p. 1147)
Ricketts, Harry. How to Catch a Cricket Match. (p. 815)
Ricketts, Mark. Night Trippers. Thorpe, Dan K., ed. (p. 1254)
Ricketts, William, illus. see Owen, Frank, ed.
Rickham, Elethia, tr. see Sherlock, Philip.
Rickis, Andrew. Magic Oak: (A Baseball Story) A Novel for Young Adults. (p. 1072)
Rickman, Jeanie Parker. Rising Star Ball. Taylor, Jennifer, illus. (p. 1475)
Ricks, Christopher, ed. see Milton, John.
Ricks, Kimber Orson. Discovering Santa: A Christmas Story. (p. 449)
Ricks, Melissa, illus. see Bess, Stacey.
Ricks, Sam, illus. see Adler, David A.
Ricks, Sam, illus. see Chabert, Jack.
Ricks, Thomas E. Fiasco: The American Military Adventure in Iraq, 2003-2005. (p. 583)
Rickus, Alexis & Saunder, Bev. OCR Home Economics for AS: Food, Nutrition & Health Today. (p. 1277)
Rickus, John. Animals of Alaska. (p. 83)
Ridddering, Marggie & Riddering, David. Atravesando el Valle. (p. 113)
Riddell, Andrew G. Curse of Blackbeard's Ghost. (p. 394)
Riddell, Chris. Mr Underbed. Riddell, Chris, illus. (p. 1186)
—Ottoline & the Yellow Cat. Riddell, Chris, illus. (p. 1307)
—Ottoline Goes to School. Riddell, Chris, illus. (p. 1307)
Riddell, Chris, illus. see Gaiman, Neil.
Riddell, Chris, illus. see McGough, Roger.
Riddell, Chris, illus. see Platt, Richard.
Riddell, Chris, illus. see Rosen, Michael.
Riddell, Chris, illus. see Stewart, Paul & Stewart, Paul.
Riddell, Chris, illus. see Stewart, Paul.
Riddell, Chris, illus. see Swift, Jonathan.
Riddell, Chris, jt. auth. see Cave, Kathryn.
Riddell, Chris, jt. auth. see Stewart, Paul.
Riddell, Chris & Stewart, Paul. Barnaby Grimes: Return of the Emerald Skull. (p. 139)
—Curse of the Gloamglozer. (p. 395)
—Curse of the Night Wolf. (p. 395)
—Edge Chronicles: Freeglader. (p. 504)
—Edge Chronicles: Vox. (p. 504)
Riddell, Fran, jt. auth. see Freese, Thomas.
Riddell, J. H. Open Door. (p. 1299)
Ridder, Elisabeth. Dear Grandpa, I Remember. (p. 419)
Riddering, David, jt. auth. see Ridddering, Marggie.
Riddering, David, jt. auth. see Riddering, Margie.
Riddering, Karenlie Anne. Puerto Rico: Encanto Oculto. (p. 1415)
Riddering, Margie & Riddering, David. Walking through the Valley. (p. 1854)
Riddle, A. Yogi & Me. (p. 1972)
Riddle, A. E. All about Blade (p. 42)
Riddle, Jamie. Beach Bum Babies & Sand Sisters Stormy. (p. 149)
Riddle, John. Coal Power of the Future: New Ways of Turning Coal into Energy. (p. 336)
—Marco Polo: 13th Century Italian Trader. (p. 1092)
—Marco Polo. (p. 1092)
—Pony Express. (p. 1382)
—Robert F. Scott: British Explorer of the South. (p. 1479)
—Robert F. Scott: British Explorer of the South Pole. (p. 1479)
Riddle, John & Simons, Rae. Firefighter. Riggs, Ernestine G. & Gholar, Cheryl, eds. (p. 591)
—Veterinarian. (p. 1839)
—Veterinarian. Gholar, Cheryl & Riggs, Ernestine G., eds. (p. 1839)
Riddle, Peter H. No Room: A Read-Aloud Story of Christmas. Hustins, Shelley, illus. (p. 1260)
—Painted Ponies of Partequineus & the Summer of the Kittens: Two Novels for Young Readers. (p. 1318)
Riddle, Sarah. ... & God Made Me! (p. 71)
Riddle, Scott, illus. see Stratton, Bart.
Riddle, Sharon Kay & Sanders, Nancy/Ida. King's Silverware. Lowe, Frank Allen, illus. (p. 961)
—Tony Loved to Learn. Mendoza, Megan Elizabeth, illus. (p. 1766)
Riddle, Sherry. Zippy & Me. (p. 1987)
Riddle, Sue, illus. see Swope, Sam.
Riddle, Tohby. Irving the Magician. Riddle, Tohby, illus. (p. 888)
Riddle, Tohby, illus. see Dubosarsky, Ursula.
Riddle, Waide. Chocolate Man: A Children's Horror Tale. (p. 309)
—Red River County from Short Story to Screenplay: From Short Story to Screenplay. (p. 1455)
Riddle, Waide Aaron. Chocolate Man A Children's Horror Tale. Aragon Art Studio, illus. (p. 309)
Riddleburger, Sam & Michael Hemphill. Stonewall Hinkleman & the Battle of Bull Run. (p. 1653)
Riddolls, Tom. Sally Ride: The First American Woman in Space. (p. 1505)
—Tigers. (p. 1749)
Riddolls, Tom, jt. auth. see Wearing, Judy.
Riddolls, Tom & Wearing, Judy. Hillary Clinton. (p. 779)
—Tiger Woods. (p. 1749)
—Zac Efron. (p. 1984)
Ride, Sally & O'Shaughnessy, Tam. Mission Planet Earth: Our World & Its Climate - And How Humans Are Changing Them. (p. 1153)
Ride, Sally & O'Shaughnessy, Tam E. Third Planet: Exploring the Earth from Space. (p. 1734)
—Voyager: An Adventure to the Edge of the Solar System. (p. 1850)
Rideau, J. & Asso, B. Falklands War. Chauvin, D. & Uderzo, M., illus. (p. 566)
Rideau, Joel, jt. auth. see Asso, Bernard.
Rideau, Nicole. What Is a Pookalaka? (p. 1888)
Ridell, Chris. Ottoline va al colegio/ Ottolina Goes To School. (p. 1307)
—Ottoline y la gata amarilla/ Ottolina & the Yellow Cat. (p. 1307)
Ridenour, Melissa. Bully & the Booger Baby: A Cautionary Tale. Crum, Shaun, illus. (p. 241)
Ridenour, Melissa Harker. What Would You Do? A Kid's Guide to Staying Safe in a World of Strangers. Fehling, Leslie, illus. (p. 1895)
Rideout, Henry. Dragons Blood. (p. 479)

R

Rideout, Sandy, jt. auth. see Collins, Yvonne.
Rider, Cynthia. Chatterbox Turtle. Petrlik, Andrea, illus. (p. 295)
—Circus. Aguilar, Sandra, illus. (p. 322)
—Explorers. Aguilar, Sandra, illus. (p. 551)
—Muddy Puddle. Evans, Nicola, illus. (p. 1189)
—Our Snowman. Evans, Nicola, illus. (p. 1310)
—Pirate Treasure Aguilar, Sandra, illus. (p. 1363)
—Spaceship. Aguilar, Sandra, illus. (p. 1620)
—Sunny Day. Evans, Nicola, illus. (p. 1677)
—What a Windy Day! Evans, Nicola, illus. (p. 1878)
Rider, Jason. Dawn of Hope. (p. 411)
Rider, John Russell. Adventures of Acorn & Pinecone. (p. 16)
Ridge, Sally, jt. auth. see Hildebrand, Jens.
Ridge, Yolanda. Road Block (p. 1476)
Ridgell, Earl W., Jr., illus. see Bye, K. A.
Ridgell, Regina. Baby Loggerhead's Long Journey. (p. 127)
Ridgers, Denise J. Elspeth's Great Adventure. (p. 516)
Ridges, Kedrick, illus. see Bruderer, Brooke.
Ridgley, Larry D. Dark Side of the Dragon. (p. 408)
Ridgley, Sara & Mole, Gavin. Sing It & Say - Ancient Egypt. (p. 1579)
—Sing It & Say - Ancient Rome. (p. 1579)
—Sing It & Say - France. (p. 1579)
Ridgley, Sara, et al. Sing It & Say - Festivals. (p. 1579)
Ridgway, Sam H., jt. auth. see Goldish, Meish.
Ridgway, Tom. Mad Cow Disease: Bovine Spongiform Encephalopathy. (p. 1069)
—Smallpox. (p. 1592)
Ridgway, Tom, jt. auth. see Lawrence, Lane.
Riding, Gale. Milo Is Not So Different after All. (p. 1144)
Riding, Will. Ebenezer's Tale. (p. 501)
Ridley, Alice, illus. see Emina, Peter.
Ridley, Frances. Amazing Jet Planes. (p. 54)
—Amazing Motorcycles. (p. 55)
—Awesome Supercars. (p. 121)
—Emergency Rescue! (p. 518)
—Lost at Sea. (p. 1055)
—Stunt Pros. (p. 1670)
Ridley, Frances J. Special Effects. (p. 1623)
—Stunt Pros. (p. 1670)
Ridley, K. F. Curse of Yama: The C. Walker Adventures. Maze, Ellen, illus. (p. 395)
Ridley, Kimberly. Secret Bay Raye, Rebekah, illus. (p. 1540)
Ridley, R. W. Banshee Worm King. (p. 136)
—Delon City: Book Two of the Oz Chronicles. (p. 425)
Ridley, Sarah. Anne Frank: ...And Her Diary. (p. 85)
—Chocolate Bar. (p. 309)
—Cotton T-Shirt. (p. 369)
—Glass Jar. (p. 682)
—In a Pond. (p. 863)
—In the Home. (p. 866)
—In the Soil. (p. 867)
—Life in Ancient Egypt. (p. 1010)
—Life in Ancient Greece. (p. 1010)
—Life in Roman Times. (p. 1011)
—Life in Viking Times. (p. 1011)
—Martin Luther King: ...And the Fight for Equality. (p. 1097)
—Metal Can. (p. 1130)
—On a Plant. (p. 1288)
—Rubber Tire. (p. 1493)
—Under a Stone. (p. 1813)
—Winston Churchill: ...And World War II. (p. 1937)
—Wooden Chair. (p. 1949)
Ridley, Sarah, jt. auth. see Barraclough, Sue.
Ridley, Sharon. My Wildflower Friends. Phillips, Marilyn, photos by. (p. 1221)
Ridley, Yvonne. God Made Me! Who Made You? (p. 689)
Ridling, Carole. Homerun Kid. (p. 793)
Ridolfi, Isabella, jt. auth. see Mills, Nathan.
Ridout. All Round English (p. 45)
Ridpath, Ian. Facts on File Stars & Planets Atlas: New Edition. (p. 561)
—Stars & Planets: The Most Complete Guide to the Stars, Planets, Galaxies, & the Solar System. Tirion, Wil, illus. (p. 1643)
Rie, Jannie. Community Food Tree. (p. 350)
Rieback, Milton. Adventures of Webb Ellis, a Tale from the Heart of Africa: The Return of the Protectors. Crowley, Cheryl, illus. (p. 24)
Riebe, C. V. Jonathan Jameson in the Crossroad Chronicles: Adventures in Heaven (p. 925)
Riebel, Jessica Mire. Katrina & the Rinky-Dink Sewing Machine. Herpin, K. K., illus. (p. 945)
Rieber, John Ney. Reloaded: In the Name of Patriotism. Vol. I Lim, Ron & Millet, Jason, illus. (p. 1458)
Riecks Goss, Carol, illus. see Holdman, Shirley Terrill.
Riedemann, Fran. Beatrice Baker: Bringer of Joy-BooK 1. (p. 153)
Rieder, E. & Toth, M. ABC-Haus: Schuelerbuch. (p. 3)
—ABC-Haus: Arbeitsheft 1. (p. 3)
—Das ABC-Haus. Arbeitsheft 2: Deutsch als Fremd- oder Zweitsprache mit wenigen oder keinen Vorkenntnissen. (p. 409)
Rieder, Floor, illus. see Schutten, Jan Paul.
Riedl, Sheila. Elijah & the Elephant. (p. 512)
Riedler, Amelia, ed. see Clark, M. H.
Riedler, Amelia, ed. see Yamada, Shale.
Riedling, Ann Marlow. Information Literacy: What Does It Look Like in the School Library Media Center? (p. 874)
Rief, Linda, et al. 100 Quickwrites: Fast & Effective Freewriting Exercises That Build Students' Confidence, Develop Their Fluency, & Bring Out the Writer in Every Student, Grades 5 & Up. (p. 1998)
Riege, Cheryl. Tracks Rivers Roads: Across Nebraska on the Meridian Highway. (p. 1775)
Riegelman, Rianna. Red Roger to the Rescue. Schorr, Bill, illus. (p. 1455)
Riegelman, Rianna & Accord Publishing Staff. Safari: A Build & Play Story. Chandler, Shannon, illus. (p. 1501)
Rieger, Linda. Dinosaur Party. Bianchi, John, illus. (p. 442)
—Flying Animals. Bianchi, John, illus. (p. 609)
—Good Heart. Rieger, Linda, illus. (p. 698)
—How Are We Alike? Bianchi, John, illus. (p. 805)
—Start the Clean Up. Bianchi, John, illus. (p. 1643)
—Water in Our House. Bianchi, John, illus. (p. 1863)
—Water Party. Bianchi, John, illus. (p. 1863)
Riegle, Janet. Piping Plover Summer. Riegle, Janet, illus. (p. 1362)
Riehecky, Janet. Camouflage & Mimicry: Animal Weapons & Defenses (p. 257)
—China. (p. 306)
—Citizenship (p. 323)
—Cobras: On the Hunt (p. 337)
—Diplodocus (p. 445)
—Giant Ground Sloth (p. 673)
—Giant Rhinoceros (p. 674)
—Giganotosaurus (p. 676)
—Great White Sharks: On the Hunt (p. 719)
—Iguanodon Saunders-Smith, Gail, ed. (p. 856)
—Killer Whales: On the Hunt (p. 956)
—Komodo Dragons: On the Hunt (p. 966)
—Komodo Dragons [Scholastic]: On the Hunt. (p. 966)
—Megalodon Saunders-Smith, Gail, ed. (p. 1124)
—Megalodon [Scholastic]. (p. 1124)
—Megalosaurus (p. 1124)
—Orangutans (p. 1302)
—Poisons & Venom: Animal Weapons & Defenses (p. 1377)
—Red Door Detective Club Mysteries Halverson, Lydia, illus. (p. 1453)
—Sabertooth Cat (p. 1499)
—Scorpions: On the Hunt (p. 1530)
—Settling of St. Augustine. (p. 1554)
—Show Me Dinosaurs: My First Picture Encyclopedia (p. 1570)
—Slime, Poop, & Other Wacky Animal Defenses. (p. 1590)
—Teeth, Claws, & Jaws: Animal Weapons & Defenses (p. 1715)
—Triceratops (p. 1785)
—Velociraptor (p. 1835)
Riehecky, Janet, jt. auth. see Crewe, Sabrina.
Riehecky, Janet, jt. auth. see O'Hern, Kerri.
Riehecky, Janet, jt. auth. see Williams, Gianna.
Riehecky, Janet & Capstone Press Staff. Diplodocus/Diplodocus Saunders-Smith, Gail, ed. (p. 445)
—Pteranodonte/Pteranodon Saunders-Smith, Gail, ed. (p. 1413)
Riehecky, Janet & Knowlton, MaryLee. Colonia de Jamestown. (p. 341)
Riehecky, Janet & O'Hern, Kerri. Battle of the Alamo. McHargue, D., illus. (p. 146)
Riehecky, Janet & Polydoros, Lori. Grizzly Bears: On the Hunt. (p. 724)
Riehecky, Janet & Rake, Jody Sullivan. Animal Weapons & Defenses. (p. 80)
Riehecky, Janet, et al. Endangered & Threatened Animals. (p. 526)
Riehle, Mary Ann McCabe. Is for Airplane: An Aviation Alphabet. Craig, David, illus. (p. 889)
—Little Kid's Table. Uhles, Mary, illus. (p. 1030)
—M Is for Mom: A Child's Alphabet. Ellison, Chris, illus. (p. 1067)
—M Is for Mountain State: A West Virginia Alphabet. Bryant, Laura J., illus. (p. 1067)
Rieken, Ethel Plaep. Growing Pains: A Childhood on Bear Creek. Zander, Julie McDonald, ed. (p. 726)
Riel, Jörn & Chodzin, Sherab. Raiders: The Inuk Quartet. Vol. 2 Cann, Helen, illus. (p. 1433)
Riel, Jörn & Mason, John. Shipwreck: The Inuk Quartet Cann, Helen & Fox-Davies, Sarah, illus. (p. 1567)
Riel, Jorn, et al. Snowstorm. Cann, Helen, illus. (p. 1601)
Rielly, Robin L. & Tok, Stephanie. Karate for Kids. (p. 943)
Riemer, Bernice. Old Straw Hat. (p. 1284)
Rienzi, Robert. Conspiritors Tale. (p. 359)
Riera, Ernest, tr. see Mignola, Mike.
Ries, Alex, illus. see Kids Can Press Staff & Becker, Helaine.
Ries, Lori. Aggie & Ben - Three Stories. Dormer, Frank W., illus. (p. 29)
—Aggie Gets Lost. Dormer, Frank W., illus. (p. 29)
—Aggie the Brave. Dormer, Frank W., illus. (p. 29)
—Good Dog, Aggie. Dormer, Frank W., illus. (p. 697)
—Super Sam! Rama, Sue, illus. (p. 1680)
Ries, Lori, et al. Tita y Ben: Tres Cuentos. Dormer, Frank W., illus. (p. 1757)
Rieser, Karen. Cat with Three Tales. (p. 278)
Rieth, Velvet. My First Little Workbook of Wicca: A Child's Guide to Wicca Through Interactive Play. (p. 1207)
Riette, Susanne, illus. see Conroe, Lindy.
Rietz, Kathleen, illus. see Berkes, Marianne.
Rietz, Kathleen, illus. see Halfmann, Janet.
Rietz, Kathleen, illus. see North, Sherry.
Rietz, Kathleen, illus. see Pattison, Darcy.
Rietz, Kathleen, illus. see Power, Teresa Anne.
Rieu, Jean-Philippe. Fairy Marie's New Home. Janssen, Mark, illus. (p. 563)
Rieu, Jean-Philippe & Janssen, Mark. Marie (p. 1093)
Rifa, Fina, illus. see Cormand, Bernat.
Rife, Ann Hollis, illus. see Leland, Debbie.
Rife, Douglas M. & Capaldi, Gina. American Revolution. Lyall, Dennis, illus. (p. 63)
—Arts & Crafts Across the USA. Mitchell, Judith, ed. (p. 104)
—Letters for Freedom: the Civil War. Lyall, Dennis, illus. (p. 1002)
Riffey, Rebecca, illus. see Pritchard, Heather.
Riffle, Sherry L. Where Did Mommy Go? (p. 1906)
Rifkin, L. Life Four. (p. 1010)
—Life One. Hartman, Kurt, illus. (p. 1012)
—Nine Lives of Romeo Crumb: Life One. (p. 1256)
—Nine Lives of Romeo Crumb: Life Seven. (p. 1256)
—Nine Lives of Romeo Crumb: Life 6. Hartman, Kurt, illus. (p. 1256)
Rifkin, L. (Lauren). Nine Lives of Romeo Crumb: Life Two. (p. 1256)
—Nine Lives of Romeo Crumb: Life Three. (p. 1256)
—Nine Lives of Romeo Crumb: Life Five. Hartman, Kurt, illus. (p. 1256)
Rifkin, Lauren l. Nine Lives of Romeo Crumb: Life Eight. (p. 1256)
Rifkin, Sherri & Bennett, Olivia. Allegra Biscotti Collection. (p. 46)
Rift. Wise Little Butterfly Rift, illus. (p. 1940)
Rigano, Giovanni, illus. see Colfer, Eoin & Donkin, Andrew.
Rigaud, Debbie. Perfect Shot. (p. 1342)
Rigaud, Louis, jt. auth. see Boisrobert, Anouck.
Rigaudie, Mylene, illus. see Benoit-Renard, Anne.
Rigaudie, Mylene, illus. see Husar, Jaco & Husar, Stephane.
RIGBY. Across the United States: Fourth Grade Class Collection Books. (p. 9)
—American Journeys: Fourth Grade Class Collection Books. (p. 62)
—Are We There Yet? Second Grade Big Books. (p. 96)
—By the People: Fifth Grade Class Collection Books. (p. 249)
—Can You Help Me Find My Puppy? Kindergarten Big Books. (p. 259)
—Complete Teacher's Guide: Fifth Grade. (p. 353)
—Complete Teacher's Guide: First Grade. (p. 353)
—Complete Teacher's Guide: Third Grade. (p. 353)
—Complete Teacher's Guide: Fourth Grade. (p. 353)
—Complete Teacher's Guide: Kindergarten. (p. 353)
—Complete Teacher's Guide: Second Grade. (p. 353)
—Diego Saves the Planet! Third Grade Big Books. (p. 437)
—Early Americas: Fourth Grade Class Collection Books. (p. 493)
—Earth, Moon, & Sun: Fifth Grade Class Collection Books. (p. 496)
—First Day of School: Kindergarten Big Books. (p. 594)
—Future Space Explorers: Third Grade Big Books. (p. 651)
—Getting Ready: Kindergarten Big Books. (p. 669)
Rigby. Golden Lasso. (p. 695)
RIGBY. Golden Opportunities: Fourth Grade Class Collection Books. (p. 695)
—Good News: First Grade Big Books. (p. 699)
—Growing Nation: Fifth Grade Class Collection Books. (p. 726)
—Guided Reading Teacher's Guide: First Grade. (p. 730)
—Guided Reading Teacher's Guide: Third Grade. (p. 730)
—Guided Reading Teacher's Guide: Kindergarten. (p. 730)
—Guided Reading Teacher's Guide: Second Grade. (p. 730)
—Hello! I'm Paty: Second Grade Big Books. (p. 764)
—How Bicycles Work: Second Grade Big Books. (p. 805)
—Ibis & Jaguar's Dinner: Second Grade Big Books. (p. 849)
—In the Deep: Fifth Grade Class Collection Books. (p. 865)
—Inside Our Bodies: Fourth Grade Class Collection Books. (p. 877)
—Just Like Me! First Grade. (p. 939)
—Little Kitten, Big Cat: First Grade Big Books. (p. 1030)
—Look Out the Window: First Grade Big Books. (p. 1050)
—Mainsails. (p. 1077)
—Making a Difference: Third Grade Big Books. (p. 1080)
—Moneybag: a Tale from Korea: Third Grade Big Books. (p. 1164)
—Mother Duck's Walk: First Grade Big Books. (p. 1177)
—My Grandmother's Hands: First Grade Big Books. (p. 1210)
—My Rooster Speaks Korean: Kindergarten Big Books. (p. 1218)
—Now Hear This! Fifth Grade Class Collection Books. (p. 1269)
—Now We Live in the USA! Third Grade Big Books. (p. 1269)
—Our Changing Earth: Fourth Grade Class Collection Books. (p. 1308)
—Phonics Teacher's Guide: First Grade. (p. 1352)
—Phonics Teacher's Guide: Third Grade. (p. 1352)
—Phonics Teacher's Guide: Second Grade. (p. 1352)
—Phonics teacher's Guide: Kindergarten. (p. 1352)
—Picture Cards: Package of 100 Cards First Grade. (p. 1355)
—Picture Cards: Package of 100 Cards Kindergarten. (p. 1355)
—PM Plus Emerald Teacher's Guide: For Chapter Books & Nonfiction Books. (p. 1374)
—PM Plus Sapphire. (p. 1374)
—Pocketful of Opossums: Second Grade Big Books. (p. 1375)
—Pulse of Life: Fifth Grade Class Collection Books. (p. 1416)
—Reading Strategy Cards: Complete Set of 40 Cards (K-5) (p. 1446)
—Reading Workshop Teacher's Guide. (p. 1447)
—Rice All Day: Kindergarten Big Books. (p. 1469)
—Rigby on Our Way to English: Leveled Reader Grade 2 (Level I) Desert Clowns. (p. 1472)
—Rigby PM Plus - Ruby Level, 27-28. (p. 1472)
—Road to Freedom: Fifth Grade Class Collection Books. (p. 1477)
—Rosita's Robot: Third Grade Big Books. (p. 1490)
—Sailing Solo at Blue. (p. 1503)
—Sailing Solo Green Teacher's Resource Book. (p. 1503)
—Technology Matters! Fifth Grade Class Collection Books. (p. 1711)
—Thematic Teacher's Guide: Fifth Grade. (p. 1728)
—Thematic Teacher's Guide: First Grade. (p. 1728)
—Thematic Teacher's Guide: Fourth Grade. (p. 1728)
—Thematic Teacher's Guide: Kindergarten. (p. 1728)
—Thematic Teacher's Guide: Second Grade. (p. 1728)
—Tran & the Beautiful Tree: First Grade Big Books. (p. 1778)
—Transportation: Then & Now: Third Grade Big Books. (p. 1779)
—Under the Canopy: Fourth Grade Class Collection Books. (p. 1813)
—Unearthing the Past: Fourth Grade Class Collection Books. (p. 1817)
—Water Detective: Second Grade. (p. 1862)
—What Are the Seasons Like? Kindergarten Big Books. (p. 1880)
—What Fine Gardeners: Second Grade. (p. 1884)
—What Is the Weather Outside? First Grade Big Books. (p. 1890)
Rigby. When Day Turned to Night. (p. 1901)
RIGBY. When I Grow Up: Kindergarten Big Books. (p. 1903)
—Word Study Teacher's Guide: Fifth Grade. (p. 1951)
—Word Study Teacher's Guide: Fourth Grade. (p. 1951)
—Word Wall Starters: Package of 100 Cards Third Grade. (p. 1951)
—Word Wall Starters: Package of 115 Cards First Grade. (p. 1951)
—Word Wall Starters: Package of 65 Cards Kindergarten. (p. 1951)
—Word Wall Starters: Package of 124 Cards Second Grade. (p. 1951)
Rigby, Christopher & Sail, Nicola. Let's Have a Christmas: Flip Quiz. (p. 998)
Rigby, Deborah, illus. see Baxter, Nicola.
Rigby, Deborah, illus. see Mahy, Margaret.
Rigby, Deborah, illus. see Scott, Janine.
Rigby, Ed & Dooley, Angela. Mouse of the Match. (p. 1182)
Rigby Education Staff. Activity Guide. (p. 10)
—Animal Advertisements. (p. 76)
—Animals: A Is for Animal. (p. 81)
—Animals Say... (p. 83)
—At the Big & Small Zoo. (p. 110)
—Bingo. (p. 188)
—Birdwoman Interview. (p. 192)
—Blends & Digraphs. (p. 199)
—Bugs on the Menu. (p. 237)
—Can You See The Eggs? (p. 259)
—Cargo Cat. (p. 268)
—Carrying Babies. (p. 271)
—Cat's Diary. (p. 281)
—Cinderella: Jumbled Tumble. (p. 320)
—Class Pet. (p. 327)
—Consonants. (p. 359)
—Custard's Cat Flap. (p. 395)
—Dad's Pasta. (p. 399)
—Daily Meow. (p. 400)
—Day on the Farm. (p. 414)
—Discovery World: My Body. (p. 450)
—Discovery World. (p. 450)
—Discovery World Orange Encyclopedia: Tiny Big Book. (p. 450)
—Discovery World Org Amazing Egg Big Book. (p. 450)
—Discovery World Org Fun Things. (p. 450)
—Discovery World Org Growing Plant. (p. 450)
—Discovery World Red Biography Ill. (p. 450)
—Discovery World Red Dictionary. (p. 450)
—Discovery World Red Insect Body. (p. 450)
—Discovery World Red Materials. (p. 450)
—Discovery World Yel Animl Leg. (p. 450)
—Discovery World Yel Seasons. (p. 450)
—Discovery World Yel Sizes. (p. 450)
—Dog's Diary. (p. 462)
—Egg Saga. (p. 506)
—Everything Changes: Little Red Riding Hood. (p. 544)
—Everything Changes Big Book: Little Red Riding Hood. (p. 544)
—Fans. (p. 571)
—Fat Ducks. (p. 577)
—Feathered Friends. (p. 579)
—Flying High. (p. 610)
—Follow the Paw Prints. (p. 612)
—Fox: Jumbled Tumble. (p. 626)
—Friends Together. (p. 639)
—Frog at Home. (p. 640)
—Frog Prince: Jumbled Tumble. (p. 640)
—From Here to There. (p. 642)
—Gardens of the Sea. (p. 656)
—Gliders & Sliders. (p. 683)
—Goldilocks: Jumbled Tumble. (p. 696)
—Goodness Me, Mr. Mageel (p. 701)
—Happy House. (p. 746)
—Head, Shoulders, Knees & Toes. (p. 756)
—Headline News. (p. 756)
—Hiders. (p. 777)
—Hot & Cold. (p. 801)
—Humpty Dumpty Bigbook: Rhyme 2. (p. 827)
—In the Jungle River. (p. 866)
—Island of Wingo. (p. 892)
—Jack & Jill Big Book: Rhyme 1. (p. 902)
—Jack Big Book. (p. 902)
—Jacko of Baker Street. (p. 904)
—John Henry. (p. 922)
—Jumble Tumble Old Woman. (p. 933)
—Jumbled Tumble Little Miss. (p. 933)
—Jumbled Tumble Little Tom. (p. 933)
—Jungle Sun. (p. 935)
—Kangaroo. (p. 942)
—Keep Tradition. (p. 947)
—Learning to Ride a Bicycle. (p. 986)
—Let's Sleep. (p. 1000)
—Little & Big. (p. 1023)
—Little Jack. (p. 1029)
—Look up, Look down, Look All Around. (p. 1050)
—Machines Around Your Home. (p. 1068)
—Mary Big Book: Rhyme 2. (p. 1100)
—Max. (p. 1110)
—McGinty's Friend. (p. 1114)
—Mickey Maloney's Mail. (p. 1136)
—Mouse Manual. (p. 1182)
—Mr. Merton's Vacation. (p. 1185)
—New Baby in the House. (p. 1243)
—Night Out. (p. 1254)
—Old King: Rhyme 1. (p. 1284)
—Old Mother Big Book. (p. 1284)
—Our Home on the Island. (p. 1309)
—Paul Bunyan: Jumbled Tumble. (p. 1330)
—Pebble Soup Ever Changing Big Book: Ants & Grasshoppers. (p. 1333)
—Peekaboo. (p. 1335)
—Peter Piper. (p. 1347)
—Pinocchio: Jumbled Tumble. (p. 1360)
—Queen of Hearts. (p. 1425)
—Real Prince: Jumbled Tumble. (p. 1448)
—Red Riding Hood: Jumbled Tumble. (p. 1454)
—Red Shoes. (p. 1455)
—Rhyme World Stage 2. (p. 1468)
—Rhyme World Stage 3. (p. 1468)
—Rhyme World Stage 4. (p. 1468)
—Robbers. (p. 1478)
—Roger's Best Friend. (p. 1484)
—Row, Row, Row Your Boat. (p. 1492)
—Rumpelstiltskin: Jumbled Tumble. (p. 1495)
—Sail Red Teacher Resource Guide. (p. 1503)
—Shapes. (p. 1560)

—Space Cat. (p. 1618)
—Spikes, Scales & Armor. (p. 1627)
—Spy Manual. (p. 1636)
—Stage 1 Components. (p. 1638)
—Stomachs. (p. 1652)
—Three Little Pigs. (p. 1743)
—Tom Sawyer: Jumbled Tumble. (p. 1763)
—Touching the Moon. (p. 1772)
—Two Eyes That See. (p. 1803)
—Using a Beak. (p. 1828)
—Using a Tail. (p. 1828)
—Vegetable Garden. (p. 1834)
—Very Noisy Family. (p. 1838)
—Visiting My Mom's Office. (p. 1845)
—Vowels. (p. 1850)
—Wake Up Dad! (p. 1853)
—What's in an Egg? (p. 1897)
—When I Go to School. (p. 1902)
—Where Do Elephants Stomp? (p. 1907)
—Where Do People Live? (p. 1907)
—Who Works in Your Neighborhood? (p. 1919)
—William Tell. (p. 1933)
Rigby Education Staff, jt. auth. see Brasch, Nicolas.
Rigby Education Staff, ed. Going to the Doctor. (p. 693)
—Rhyme World Stage 2: Components. (p. 1468)
—Rhyme World Stage 3: Components. (p. 1468)
—Rhyme World Stage 4: Components. (p. 1468)
Rigby, Jill. I Put It Right There! I Swear! The story of one boy's master plan to overcome executive functioning Difficulties! (p. 844)
Rigby, Robert. Goal! The Dream Begins. (p. 687)
—Goal - Glory Days. (p. 687)
—Goal II: Living the Dream. (p. 687)
Rigby, Robert & Cámara, Noemí. Gol II: Viviendo el Sueño. (p. 693)
Riger, Bob, illus. see Moody, Ralph.
Rigg, Annie & Woram, Catherine. Fun Christmas Crafts to Make & Bake: Over 60 Festive Projects to Make with Your Kids. (p. 647)
Rigg, Diana. Teach a Child to READ in... 3 Simple Steps. Walter, Deborah, illus. (p. 1708)
Rigg, Jo. Millie Moo. (p. 1144)
—Rocky Dog. (p. 1484)
Rigg, Jo & Priddy, Roger. My Little Animal Book. (p. 1212)
Rigg, Jo, et al. I Love Trucks. (p. 843)
Riggi, Samantha K. Wesley Reece: Fourth Grade Hero. (p. 1876)
Riggin, Lisa. Abigail & the Lost Purse. Calvert-Weyant, Linda, illus. (p. 5)
Riggio, Anita. Secret Signs: An Escape Through the Underground Railroad. Riggio, Anita, illus. (p. 1543)
Riggs, Darla L. Hooney Bacooney: Caught Red Handed. (p. 795)
Riggs, Ernestine G., ed. see Bonnice, Sherry.
Riggs, Ernestine G., ed. see Brinkerhoff, Shirley.
Riggs, Ernestine G., ed. see Intosh, Kenneth Mc & McIntosh, Kenneth.
Riggs, Ernestine G., ed. see Libal, Joyce & Simons, Rae.
Riggs, Ernestine G., ed. see Libal, Joyce.
Riggs, Ernestine G., ed. see Riddle, John & Simons, Rae.
Riggs, Ernestine G., ed. see Sanna, Ellyn.
Riggs, Ernestine G., ed. see Simons, Rae & Gommer, Viola Ruelke.
Riggs, Ernestine G., ed. see Vitale, Ann.
Riggs, Jenna, illus. see Engelman Berner, Beth.
Riggs, Jenna, illus. see Rizzi, Kathleen.
Riggs, Jenna, jt. auth. see Berner, Beth E.
Riggs, Jon & Evanoff, Corrine R. Little Blue Planet. Nazar, Alexandria, illus. (p. 1024)
Riggs, Kate. Across the Universe: Asteroids. (p. 9)
—Across the Universe: Comets. (p. 9)
—Across the Universe: Galaxies. (p. 9)
—Across the Universe: Moons. (p. 9)
—Across the Universe: Planets. (p. 9)
—Adjectives. (p. 13)
—Adverbs. (p. 25)
—Alligators. (p. 47)
—Amazing Animals: Whales. (p. 53)
—Amazing Animals: Alligators. (p. 53)
—Amazing Animals: Bats. (p. 53)
—Amazing Animals: Camels. (p. 53)
—Amazing Animals - Cheetahs. (p. 53)
—Amazing Animals: Cougars. (p. 53)
—Amazing Animals - Dolphins. (p. 53)
—Amazing Animals: Eagles. (p. 53)
—Amazing Animals - Elephants. (p. 53)
—Amazing Animals: Gorillas. (p. 53)
—Amazing Animals: Hummingbirds. (p. 53)
—Amazing Animals: Kangaroos. (p. 53)
—Amazing Animals: Killer Whales. (p. 53)
—Amazing Animals: Leopards. (p. 53)
—Amazing Animals: Moose. (p. 53)
—Amazing Animals: Sea Lions. (p. 53)
—Amazing Animals: Tortoises. (p. 53)
—Amazing Animals: Whales. (p. 53)
—Amazing Animals - Wolves. (p. 53)
—Amazing Animals: Woodpeckers. (p. 53)
—Amazing Animals: Zebras. (p. 53)
—Ambulances. (p. 57)
—Antelopes. (p. 89)
—Apatosaurus. (p. 91)
—Arctic Tundra. (p. 96)
—Armored Vehicles. (p. 100)
—Bats. (p. 144)
—Battleships. (p. 147)
—Beagles. (p. 150)
—Beavers. (p. 155)
—Bee. (p. 157)
—Brown Bears. (p. 231)
—Bulldogs. (p. 240)
—Bullet Trains. (p. 240)
—Butterfly. (p. 247)
—Camels. (p. 256)
—Cheetahs. (p. 296)
—Chimpanzees. (p. 306)
—Classical Music. (p. 328)
—Cougars. (p. 369)
—Country Music. (p. 372)
—Deserts. (p. 429)
—Dig It! Kubinyi, Laszlo, illus. (p. 438)
—Dolphins. (p. 464)
—Eagles. (p. 492)
—Easter Island. (p. 499)
—Egyptian Pyramids. (p. 507)
—Eiffel Tower. (p. 507)
—Elephants. (p. 511)
—Empire State Building. (p. 521)
—Enchanted Castles. (p. 523)
—Ernest Hemingway. (p. 533)
—Fairy Godmothers. (p. 563)
—Fire Trucks. (p. 591)
—Flamingos. (p. 602)
—Folk Music. (p. 611)
—French Revolution: Days of Change. (p. 636)
—French Revolution. (p. 636)
—Geckos. (p. 659)
—Giraffes. (p. 677)
—Gladiators. (p. 682)
—Golden Gate Bridge. (p. 694)
—Gorillas. (p. 703)
—Grammar Basics: Adjectives. (p. 706)
—Grammar Basics: Adverbs. (p. 706)
—Grammar Basics: Nouns. (p. 706)
—Grammar Basics: Verbs. (p. 706)
—Great Wall of China. (p. 719)
—Great Warriors - Samurai. (p. 719)
—Grow with Me: Bee. (p. 726)
—Grow with Me: Butterfly. (p. 726)
—Grow with Me: Frog. (p. 726)
—Grow with Me: Ladybug. (p. 726)
—Grow with Me: Sunflower. (p. 726)
—Grow with Me: Tomato. (p. 726)
—Hawks. (p. 755)
—Helicopters. (p. 763)
—Hippopotamuses. (p. 781)
—How Fast Can You Go? Williams, Nate, illus. (p. 809)
—Hummingbirds. (p. 826)
—Indy Cars. (p. 873)
—Jazz Music. (p. 911)
—Jets. (p. 916)
—Kangaroos. (p. 942)
—Killer Whales. (p. 956)
—Knights. (p. 964)
—Ladybug. (p. 971)
—Leopards. (p. 993)
—Lions. (p. 1021)
—Machu Picchu. (p. 1068)
—Magical Creatures. (p. 1074)
—Making Music: Drums. (p. 1081)
—Making Music: Flute. (p. 1081)
—Making Music: Guitar. (p. 1081)
—Making Music: Piano. (p. 1081)
—Making Music: Trumpet. (p. 1081)
—Making Music: Violin. (p. 1081)
—Michigan. (p. 1135)
—Monkeys. (p. 1165)
—Moons. (p. 1173)
—Moose. (p. 1173)
—Motorcycles. (p. 1179)
—Mount Rushmore. (p. 1180)
—Mountains. (p. 1181)
—Nouns. (p. 1268)
—Oceans. (p. 1277)
—Octopuses. (p. 1278)
—On the Farm. Dogi, Fiammetta & Kubinyi, Laszlo, illus. (p. 1290)
—Opera Music. (p. 1300)
—Pandas. (p. 1321)
—Penguins. (p. 1337)
—Pirates. (p. 1363)
—Planets. (p. 1368)
—Polar Bears. (p. 1379)
—Prairies. (p. 1393)
—Princes & Princesses. (p. 1401)
—Pterodactyls. (p. 1413)
—Pterodactylse. (p. 1414)
—Rainforests. (p. 1436)
—Release of Nelson Mandela. (p. 1458)
—Rescue Boats. (p. 1462)
—Rock 'n' Roll Music. (p. 1482)
—Samurai. (p. 1509)
—Sea Lions. (p. 1535)
—Sea Turtles. (p. 1536)
—Seed Needs Sun. Dogi, Fiammetta, illus. (p. 1547)
—Seedlings: Cheetahs. (p. 1547)
—Seedlings: Dolphins. (p. 1547)
—Seedlings: Eagles. (p. 1547)
—Seedlings: Elephants. (p. 1547)
—Seedlings: Giraffes. (p. 1547)
—Seedlings: Gorillas. (p. 1547)
—Seedlings: Koalas. (p. 1547)
—Seedlings: Lions. (p. 1547)
—Seedlings: Monkeys. (p. 1547)
—Seedlings: Penguins. (p. 1547)
—Seedlings: Sharks. (p. 1547)
—Seedlings: Snakes. (p. 1547)
—Seedlings: Tigers. (p. 1547)
—Seedlings: Wolves. (p. 1547)
—Sharks. (p. 1562)
—Snakes. (p. 1596)
—Speedboats. (p. 1624)
—Spells & Potions. (p. 1625)
—Stegosaurus. (p. 1646)
—Stock Cars. (p. 1651)
—Stonehenge. (p. 1653)
—Suez Canal. (p. 1672)
—Sun. (p. 1675)
—Sunflower. (p. 1676)
—Taj Mahal. (p. 1696)
—That's Creepy! Dogi, Fiammetta, illus. (p. 1726)
—Tigers. (p. 1749)
—Tomato. (p. 1764)
—Tortoises. (p. 1771)
—Trains. (p. 1777)
—Triceratops. (p. 1785)
—Tyrannosaurus Rex. (p. 1805)
—Velociraptor. (p. 1835)
—Verbs. (p. 1836)
—Vultures. (p. 1851)
—Whales. (p. 1878)
—What Is Cubism? (p. 1889)
—What Is Gothic Art? (p. 1889)
—What Is Impressionism? (p. 1889)
—What Is Modernism? (p. 1889)
—What Is Realism? (p. 1890)
—What Is Romanticism? (p. 1890)
—When Dinosaurs Lived: Apatosaurus. (p. 1902)
—When Dinosaurs Lived: Tyrannosaurus Rex. (p. 1902)
—When Dinosaurs Lived - Velociraptor. (p. 1902)
—Wicked Stepmothers. (p. 1927)
—Wild Horses. (p. 1929)
—Wolfgang Amadeus Mozart. (p. 1944)
—Wolves. (p. 1945)
—Woodpeckers. (p. 1949)
—Zebras. (p. 1985)
Riggs, Mary L. Dragon Forge the Ballad of Beighn. (p. 477)
Riggs, Nadine M. Judgement Line: A Christian's Greatest Challenge. (p. 930)
Riggs, Ransom. Hollow City. (p. 789)
—Hollow City. Riggs, Ransom, illus. (p. 789)
—Library of Souls. (p. 1006)
—Miss Peregrine's Home for Peculiar Children. (p. 1152)
Riggs, Ransom, et al. Miss Peregrine's Home for Peculiar Children. (p. 1152)
Riggs, Sandy. Habitats of Australia: Set Of 6. (p. 735)
—Habitats of Australia: Text Pairs. (p. 735)
—Joe Boat. Barr, Kristin, illus. (p. 920)
—LAN's Plant. Masheris, Bob, illus. (p. 975)
—Nick Is Sick. Koeller, Carol, illus. (p. 1251)
—Safe Streets. (p. 1502)
—Three Ancient Communities: Set Of 6. (p. 1741)
—Three Ancient Communities: Text Pairs. (p. 1741)
Riggs, Shannon. Not in Room 204: Breaking the Silence of Abuse. Zollars, Jaime, illus. (p. 1267)
Riggs, Thomas. Are Athletes Good Role Models? Greenhaven Press Editors & Gale Editors, eds. (p. 96)
—Are Players' Unions Good for Professional Sports Leagues? (p. 96)
—Book Banning. (p. 210)
—Reality TV. Greenhaven Press Editors, ed. (p. 1449)
Riggs, Thomas, ed. Democracy in the Poetry of Walt Whitman. (p. 425)
Riggs Vetter, Jennifer. Down by the Station. Remkiewicz, Frank, illus. (p. 474)
Riggs-Mayfield, Nellie. Collection of Short Stories for Children. (p. 340)
Righetti, Maggie. Knitting in Plain English. (p. 965)
Right, Emma. Keeper of Reign. (p. 947)
Right, Mike, illus. see Wolfe, Mike & Sprengelmeyer, Lily.
Right, U. B. Food for Life: Transitional Recipes for Food Combining & Blood Typing. (p. 613)
Righter, Kate, illus. see Sibley, Paul & Sibley, Paul.
Rights, Lenz-Mulligan, et al. Little Ladybug. (p. 1030)
Riglietti, Serena, illus. see Cooper, Susan.
Riglietti, Serena, illus. see d'Aquino, Alfonso.
Riglietti, Serena, illus. see Milbourne, Anna.
Riglietti, Serena, illus. see Ravel, Maurice, et al.
Rigo, L. Little Bunny. (p. 1025)
—Little Cow. (p. 1026)
—Little Dinosaur. (p. 1026)
—Little Duckling. (p. 1027)
—Little Elephant. (p. 1027)
—Little Kitten. (p. 1030)
—Little Lamb. (p. 1030)
—Little Lion. (p. 1030)
—Little Monkey. (p. 1032)
—Little Owl. (p. 1032)
—Little Panda. (p. 1033)
—Little Panda Bear. (p. 1033)
—Little Penguin. (p. 1033)
—Little Penguin. Rigo, L., illus. (p. 1033)
—Little Pig. (p. 1033)
—Little Polar Bear. (p. 1033)
—Little Pony. (p. 1033)
—Little Puppy. (p. 1034)
—Little Reindeer. (p. 1035)
Rigo, L., jt. illus. see Barron's Educational Series Staff.
Rigo, L. & Caviezel, Giovanni. Little Bunny. (p. 1025)
—Little Puppy. (p. 1034)
—Little Tiger. (p. 1037)
Rigo, L. & Pagnoni, Roberta. Little Elf. (p. 1027)
Rigo, Laura, illus. see Barron's Editorial Staff.
Rigo, Laura, illus. see Caviezel, Giovanni.
Rigo, Laura, illus. see Lorini, Andrea.
Rigo, Laura, illus. see Ravera, Giuseppe.
Rigo, Laura, jt. illus. see Pagnoni, Roberta.
Rigol, Francesc. Dan & Din Learn Colors. (p. 401)
—Dan & Din Learn Numbers. (p. 401)
—Dan & Din Learn Opposites. (p. 401)
—Dan & Din Learn Shapes. (p. 401)
Rigol, Francesc, illus. see Gaines, Isabel & Milne, A. A.
Rigsby, Annelle, jt. auth. see Raffa, Edwina.
Rigsby, Annelle & Raffa, Edwina. Race to Kitty Hawk. (p. 1431)
Rigsby, Mike. Amazing Rubber Band Cars: Easy-to-build Wind-up Racers, Models, & Toys. (p. 55)
—Doable Renewables: 16 Alternative Energy Projects for Young Scientists. (p. 458)
Rihani, Ina. Song to the Sun. (p. 1611)
Riipi, Sherida. Bunny Named Horse. (p. 242)
Riis, Jon. Something for Nothing: A Diploma for Your Life Experience. (p. 1610)
Riise, Joan. This Garden Grows A Goddess. (p. 1735)
Rijswijk, Cor van. John Is Not Afraid. (p. 922)
—Martin Shows the Way. (p. 1098)
Rijswijk, Cor van, see van Rijswijk, Cor.
Rikede, Victoria. Love Me, Love You: Manual for a Child's Self Esteem. (p. 1060)
Riker, Leigh. Curva Peligrosa. (p. 395)
Riker, Richard K. Scary Days Daze. (p. 1520)
—School Days Daze. (p. 1522)
Rikkers, Don. Jesus Loves Me. (p. 915)
Rikkers, Doris. Little Jesus, Little Me Stott, Dorothy, illus. (p. 1029)
Rikson, Paule. Daily Life on a Southern Plantation 1853. (p. 400)
Riley, Analynn. Legend of the Mountains & the Valleys: The Nine Gifts of Theodosia, the Final Question, Kenelm's Quest, Yedda Sings. (p. 989)
Riley, Andrew. Dawn of the Bunny Suicides. (p. 411)
Riley, Ange Belle Chandler. House in Which You Live. (p. 803)
Riley, Barbara. Grow, Grow, Grow. Guggenheim, Jaenet, illus. (p. 726)
Riley, Brad. Timothy: A Little Fish with a Big Purpose! Goodale, Krystahl, illus. (p. 1755)
Riley, Christine. Chester's Field O'Brien, Laurel, illus. (p. 298)
—Saving the Tooth Fairy. Warren, Mnetha, illus. (p. 1517)
Riley, Clifford. Operation Trinity. (p. 1300)
—Spymasters. (p. 1636)
Riley, Cooper. Absolutely Awesome Island Animals. (p. 7)
Riley, D. H. Mysterians (p. 1222)
Riley, David, illus. see Coleman, Evelyn.
Riley, David, illus. see Figley, Marty Rhodes.
Riley, Gail B., jt. auth. see Riley, Gail Blasser.
Riley, Gail Blasser. And Justice for All. (p. 71)
—Benjamin Franklin & Electricity. (p. 165)
—Delta Force in Action. (p. 425)
—Internet Piracy. (p. 880)
—Tower of London: England's Ghostly Castle. (p. 1773)
—Volcano! The 1980 Mount St. Helens Eruption. (p. 1848)
Riley, Gail Blasser & Riley, Gail B. NASCAR Chase for the Cup (p. 1230)
—NASCAR Greats (p. 1230)
—NASCAR Rules (p. 1230)
—NASCAR Technology (p. 1230)
—NASCAR Truck Series (p. 1230)
Riley, Glenda & Etulain, Richard W. Wild Women of the Old West (p. 1930)
Riley, J. D. Axel the Truck: Beach Race. (p. 121)
—Axel the Truck: Rocky Road. (p. 121)
—Axel the Truck: Beach Race. Dorman, Brandon, illus. (p. 121)
—Axel the Truck - Rocky Road. Dorman, Brandon, illus. (p. 121)
—Rocky Road. Dorman, Brandon, illus. (p. 1484)
Riley, James. Half upon a Time. (p. 737)
—Half upon a Time Trilogy: Half upon a Time; Twice upon a Time; Once upon the End. (p. 737)
—Once upon the End. (p. 1293)
—Twice upon a Time. (p. 1801)
Riley, James & Eberts, Marge. Math Challenge: Level 2 (p. 1105)
—Math Challenge: Level I. (p. 1105)
Riley, James Whitcomb. Rhymes of Childhood / by James Whitcomb Riley. (p. 1468)
—Riley Child-Rhymes. (p. 1472)
—Riley Child-Rhymes with Hoosier Pictures. Vawter, Will, illus. (p. 1472)
—Riley Farm-Rhymes. (p. 1472)
Riley, Janis, ed. see Wheatley, Abigail.
Riley, Jessica. Fearless Fifi: The Weedy Sea Dragon Coloring Book (Standard Version) (p. 579)
Riley, JillEllyn, jt. auth. see Levine, Deborah A.
Riley, Jim. Spiritual Grit: Pass It on to Kids (p. 1629)
Riley, Joelle. African Lions. (p. 27)
—Bats. (p. 144)
—Buzzing Bumblebees. (p. 249)
—Earthquakes. (p. 497)
—Examining Erosion. (p. 547)
—Hairy Tarantulas. (p. 736)
—Koalas. (p. 966)
—Quiet Owls. (p. 1428)
—Ring-Tailed Lemurs. (p. 1473)
—Sistema Nervioso. Translations.com Staff, tr. (p. 1581)
—Volcanoes. (p. 1849)
—Your Nervous System. (p. 1981)
Riley, Joelle, jt. auth. see Nault, Jennifer.
Riley, John B. Benjamin Franklin: A Photo Biography. (p. 164)
—George Washington Carver: A Photo Biography. (p. 664)
—Jane Addams: A Photo Biography. (p. 908)
—John Paul Jones: A Photo Biography. (p. 922)
Riley, Jon, illus. see Swindells, Robert.
Riley, Judi. When I Am Quiet on Maui. (p. 1902)
—When I Am Quiet on Oahu. (p. 1902)
Riley, Kana. Princess & the Wise Woman. Williams, Jenny, illus. (p. 1403)
Riley, Karen. Agarranderas Plasticas y Otras Cosas: Plastic Rings & Other Things. (p. 29)
—Don't Trash My Planet. (p. 469)
—Landfill Lunch Box. (p. 974)
Riley, Kellee. Happy Halloween, Kai-lan! A Lift-the-Flap Story. (p. 745)
—Tolee's Rhyme Time. (p. 1762)
Riley, Kellee, illus. see Betancourt, Jeanne.
Riley, Kellee, illus. see Black, Allyson.
Riley, Kellee, illus. see Cavalli, Frank.
Riley, Kellee, illus. see Frazer, Rebecca.
Riley, Kellee, illus. see Gallo, Tina.
Riley, Kellee, illus. see Golden Books Staff.
Riley, Kellee, illus. see Golden Books.
Riley, Kellee, illus. see Man-Kong, Mary.
Riley, Kellee, illus. see Nuhfer, Heather.
Riley, Kellee, illus. see Random House & Man-Kong, Mary.
Riley, Kellee, illus. see Random House Staff.
Riley, Kellee, illus. see Random House.
Riley, Kellee, illus. see Webster, Christy.
Riley, Kevin, illus. see Makeeff, Cyndi Sue.
Riley, Larry, illus. see Deighton-O'Flynn, Heather, et al.

R

Riley, Lehman & Austin, Megan. Life of Babe Didrikson: "Greatness Is Never Forgotten" Wallace, Joshua, illus. (p. 1011)
Riley, Lehman C. Meeting Dr. Martin Luther King. (p. 1123)
Riley, Lehman, et al. Adventures of Papa Lemon's Little Wanderers: The Dangerous Escape from Slavery. Bk. 2 (p. 21)
Riley, Margaret. Awesome Foam Craft: Quick & Easy Kids' Projects. (p. 121)
—Awesome Woodlets: Wooden Cut-Out Projects for Every Season. (p. 121)
—Crafty Parties for Kids: Creative Ideas, Invitations, Games, Favors, & More. (p. 376)
Riley, Matt. Making Shapes: Analyze, Compare, Create, & Compose Shapes. (p. 1082)
Riley, Melanie Ellis, illus. see Schamburg, Tracy M.
Riley, Michael, et al. Impact of Empire: A World Study of The British Empire - 1585 to The Present. (p. 862)
—Impact of Empire. (p. 862)
Riley, Penelope A. Christmas Away! A Duckie Dan Adventure Book. (p. 312)
—Duckie Dan the Traveling Man. (p. 488)
Riley, Peter. All about Gases. (p. 42)
—Changing Sounds. (p. 290)
—Earth, Moon & Sun. (p. 496)
—Journal of Discovery. (p. 927)
—Keeping Warm. (p. 948)
—Light & Seeing. (p. 1014)
—Plants. (p. 1369)
Riley, Peter & Lorimer, Lawrence. Solar System. (p. 1607)
Riley, Peter D. Checkpoint Biology. (p. 295)
—Checkpoint Chemistry. (p. 295)
—Checkpoint Physics. (p. 295)
—Electricity. (p. 509)
—Forces. (p. 617)
—Light. (p. 1014)
—Materials. (p. 1104)
—Sound. (p. 1615)
—Space. (p. 1618)
—Xtreme Drums. (p. 1967)
Riley, Peter D., jt. auth. see Farndon, John.
Riley, Roth. Managing Your Blood Pressure: Food or Medicine? Seven Easy Ways to Know for Sure. Vol. 2 (p. 1086)
Riley, Rowan. Great Careers with a High School Diploma: Hospitality, Human Services, & Tourism. (p. 714)
—Hospitality, Human Services, & Tourism. (p. 801)
Riley, Scott, illus. see Frey, Lisa A.
Riley, Steve. Little Ty Cooney & the Big Yosemite Race. (p. 1037)
Riley, Terry, illus. see Banks, Lynne Reid.
Riley, Terry, illus. see Jeffrey, Gary & Newport, Kate.
Riley, Terry, illus. see Jeffrey, Gary.
Riley, Terry, illus. see Shone, Rob.
Riley, Terry, illus. see West, David.
Riley, Terry, jt. illus. see Jeffrey, Gary.
Riley, Vicki. Squirt's Adventures: Episode 1. (p. 1637)
Riley, Zach. Down for the Count. Ricci, Andrés, illus. (p. 474)
—Quarterback Crisis. Ricci, Andrés, illus. (p. 1422)
—Sacred Stick. Ricci, Andrés, illus. (p. 1500)
—Surprise Kick. Ricci, Andrés, illus. (p. 1686)
Riley-Collins, Jennifer. Daddy God. (p. 398)
Riley-Webb, Charlotte, illus. see Brown, Tameka Fryer.
Riley-Webb, Charlotte, illus. see Buchanan, Jane.
Riley-Webb, Charlotte, illus. see Lindsey, Kathleen D.
Riley-Webb, Charlotte, illus. see Miller, William.
Rilla, Donald. Three Italian Foster Kids. (p. 1742)
Rillera, Catherine. Freedom. (p. 634)
Rillero, Peter, et al. Ecology. (p. 502)
Rillieux, Tina. Princess Nia & the Magic Flower. (p. 1404)
Rillo, Lori-Anne. Lorelei Finds a Home. (p. 1053)
Rim, Sujean. Birdie Plays Dress-Up. (p. 191)
—Birdie's Big-Girl Dress. (p. 191)
—Birdie's Big-Girl Hair. (p. 191)
—Birdie's Big-Girl Shoes. (p. 191)
—Birdie's First Day of School. (p. 191)
—Birdie's Happiest Halloween. (p. 191)
Rim, Sujean, illus. see Barham, Lisa.
Rim, Sujean, illus. see Schaefer, Laura.
Rimer, David, jt. auth. see Robertson, William P.
Rimer, David & Robertson, William P. Bucktails' Antietam Trials. (p. 234)
Rimes, Nicole, illus. see Lattak, Cheryl.
Rimes, Raleigh, jt. auth. see Fawcett, Jack.
Rimes, Rebecca. Hippie Hippopotamus. (p. 780)
Rimland, Jeff. Our Gift to Each Other: Heartfelt Poems of Our Love. (p. 1308)
Rimland, Mark. Secret Night World of Cats. (p. 1542)
Rimmer, Ian. Bootiful Game. Hansen, Jimmy & Williamson, Brian, illus. (p. 213)
—Whippet Vanishes. Hansen, Jimmy, illus. (p. 1911)
Rimmer, Ian, jt. auth. see Chilman-Blair, Kim.
Rimmington, Natasha. Wolf & the Seven Little Kids. (p. 1943)
Rinaldi, Angelo, illus. see Doyle, Malachy.
Rinaldi, Angelo, illus. see Hulme-Cross, Benjamin.
Rinaldi, Ann. Acquaintance with Darkness. (p. 9)
—Break with Charity: A Story about the Salem Witch Trials. (p. 224)
—Brooklyn Rose. (p. 231)
—Cast Two Shadows: The American Revolution in the South. (p. 276)
—Come Juneteenth. (p. 347)
—Education of Mary: A Little Miss of Color, 1832. (p. 505)
—Ever-After Bird. (p. 541)
—Family Greene. (p. 568)
—Fifth of March: A Story of the Boston Massacre. (p. 584)
—Finishing Becca: A Story about Peggy Shippen & Benedict Arnold. (p. 589)
—Hang a Thousand Trees with Ribbons: The Story of Phillis Wheatley. (p. 742)
—Juliet's Moon. (p. 932)
—Keep Smiling Through. (p. 947)
—Last Full Measure. (p. 977)
—Leigh Ann's Civil War. (p. 991)
—Letter Writer. (p. 1002)
—Mutiny's Daughter. (p. 1194)
—My Vicksburg. (p. 1221)
—Nine Days a Queen: The Short Life & Reign of Lady Jane Grey. (p. 1256)
—Numbering All the Bones. (p. 1271)
—Or Give Me Death: A Novel of Patrick Henry's Family. (p. 1301)
—Or Give Me Death. (p. 1301)
—Redheaded Princess. (p. 1455)
—Ride into Morning: The Story of Tempe Wick. (p. 1471)
—Sarah's Ground. (p. 1514)
—Secret of Sarah Revere. (p. 1542)
—Taking Liberty: The Story of Oney Judge, George Washington's Runaway Slave. (p. 1698)
—Taking Liberty: The Story of Oney Judge, George Washington's Runaway Slave. Dudash, C. Michael, illus. (p. 1698)
—Unlikely Friendship: A Novel of Mary Todd Lincoln & Elizabeth Keckley. (p. 1821)
Rinaldi, Francis. Brock Lee & the Salad Kids. (p. 230)
Rinaldi, Robin. Ballet. (p. 134)
—European Dance: Ireland, Poland, Spain, & Greece. (p. 540)
Rinaldo, Denise. Amelia Earhart: With a Discussion of Courage. (p. 58)
—Cesar Chavez: With a Discussion of Compassion. (p. 288)
—Cities of the Dead: Finding Lost Civilizations. (p. 322)
—Eleanor Roosevelt: With a Discussion of Respect. (p. 508)
—Jane Goodall: With a Discussion of Responsibility. (p. 908)
—Julius Caesar: Dictator for Life. (p. 933)
—Julius Caesar. (p. 933)
—Leonardo Da Vinci: With a Discussion of Imagination. (p. 992)
—Lost City Spotted from Space! Is There a Hidden Land under the Sand? (p. 1055)
—Rosa Parks: With a Discussion of Courage. (p. 1489)
—White House. (p. 1913)
Rinaldo, Jessica. Key to the Gate Book 1. (p. 950)
Rinaldo, Jim. Wally the Worm's Adventures on the Farm. (p. 1855)
Rinaldo, Luana. Matching Puzzle Cards - Colors. (p. 1104)
—Sleepy Farm. (p. 1589)
Rinaldo, Luana, illus. see Faglia, Matteo.
Rinaldo, Luana, illus. see Froeb, Lori C.
Rinaldo, Luana, illus. see Nash, C.
Rinaldo, Luana & Prasadam-Halls, Smriti. Who Am I? - This Is My Foot. (p. 1914)
—Who Am I? - This Is My Fur. (p. 1914)
—Who Am I? - This Is My Mouth. (p. 1914)
Rinck, Maranke. Hush Little Turtle. Van Der Linden, Martijn, illus. (p. 830)
—Prince Child. Linden, Martijn van der, illus. (p. 1401)
Rinck, Maranke & van der Linden, Martijn. I Feel a Foot. (p. 838)
Rincon, Fernando, illus. see Nino, Jairo Anibal.
Rinder, Lenore. Bones & Skin. Oszkay, Zulay, tr. (p. 209)
Rindone, Nancy L. Cars, Trucks, Planes, & Trains. SI Artists Staff, illus. (p. 272)
Rindt, Lindsay. Summer Time Carols. (p. 1675)
Rinehart, J. D., jt. auth. see Blackthorn, J. D.
Rinehart, Linda L. Train & Name Your Pup. (p. 1777)
Rinehart, Mary Roberts. Bab: A Sub-Deb. (p. 123)
Rinehart, Susie Caldwell. Eliza & Dragonfly. (p. 513)
—Eliza & the Dragonfly. Hovemann, Anisa Claire, illus. (p. 513)
Riner, Dax. Annika Sorenstam. (p. 87)
—Pelé. (p. 1335)
Riner, Dax & Savage, Jeff. Annika Sorenstam. (p. 87)
Riner, Kendall F. Rescue Adventures of Fireman Frank. (p. 1462)
Riner, Sherry. Wally the Whale Learns How to Be a Winner. Morris, Lillie, illus. (p. 1855)
Ring, Elizabeth. Loon at Northwood Lake. Oughton, Taylor, illus. (p. 1052)
—Monarch Butterfly of Aster Way. Lee, Katie, illus. (p. 1163)
Ring, Elizabeth & Smithsonian Institution Staff. onarch Butterfly of Aster Way (Mariposa Monarcha de la Calle Aster) (p. 1292)
Ring, Susan. Boats, Boats, Boats. (p. 205)
—Body: An Interactive & 3-D Exploration. Graham, Michele, illus. (p. 207)
—Caring for Your Cat. (p. 269)
—Caring for Your Cat. Kissock, Heather & Marshall, Diana, eds. (p. 269)
—Cat. (p. 277)
—Come to Mexico. (p. 347)
—Design It! Build It! (p. 430)
—Dinosaurs. Kendall, Gideon, illus. (p. 444)
—Earth. (p. 495)
—Elok. (p. 516)
—From Here to There (p. 642)
—From Here to There. (p. 642)
—Good Dog! (p. 697)
—Green Means Go (p. 722)
—Helping Hands. (p. 766)
—Herbie. (p. 769)
—Honeybees: An Amazing Insect Discovery BK. (p. 794)
—I See Shapes. (p. 845)
—Jupiter. (p. 937)
—Mammals. (p. 1085)
—Matemáticas y Dinero. Ramos, Gloria, tr. (p. 1104)
—Mercury. (p. 1127)
—Money Math. (p. 1164)
—Neptune. (p. 1241)
—Ocean (p. 1276)
—Ocean. (p. 1276)
—On the Farm. Melmon, Deborah, illus. (p. 1290)
—One Green Frog. (p. 1295)
—Pete's Surprise. (p. 1348)
—Places We Live. (p. 1366)
—Pluto. (p. 1374)
—Project Elephant. Kissock, Heather & Marshall, Diana, eds. (p. 1410)
—Project Hippopotamus. (p. 1410)
—Project Hippopotamus. Kissock, Heather & Marshall, Diana, eds. (p. 1410)
—Project Orangutan. Marshall, Diana & Nault, Jennifer, eds. (p. 1410)
—Project Otter. Kissock, Heather & Marshall, Diana, eds. (p. 1410)
—Project Tiger. Marshall, Diana & Nault, Jennifer, eds. (p. 1410)
—Saturn. (p. 1515)
—Scientists at Work. (p. 1528)
—Show Us Your Wings. (p. 1571)
—Snow (p. 1598)
—Snow. (p. 1598)
—Taking Care of Pets (p. 1698)
—Uranus. (p. 1825)
—Venus. (p. 1836)
—Verde Dice Adelante. (p. 1836)
—We Live in North America. (p. 1867)
—What Is Technology? (p. 1890)
—Where Should Turtle Be? Klein, Laurie Allen, illus. (p. 1909)
Ring, Susan, jt. auth. see Catala, Ellen.
Ring, Susan, jt. auth. see Dorling Kindersley Publishing Staff.
Ring, Susan, jt. auth. see VanVoorst, Jennifer Fretland.
Ringbom, Antonia, jt. auth. see Wiklund, Alison.
Ringbom, Antonia & Wiklund, Alison. Hiding Hyena. (p. 777)
—Hiding Hyena (Chichewa) (p. 777)
Ringeride, Karen. I Live in a House with a Cat & a Mouse & a Mom & a Dad & My Sisters. (p. 841)
Ringgold, Faith. Cassie's Word Quilt. Ringgold, Faith, illus. (p. 276)
—Harlem Renaissance. Ringgold, Faith, illus. (p. 749)
—Henry Ossawa Tanner: His Boyhood Dream Comes True. Ringgold, Faith, illus. (p. 768)
—If a Bus Could Talk: The Story of Rosa Parks. Ringgold, Faith, illus. (p. 852)
—O Holy Night: Christmas with the Boys Choir of Harlem. (p. 1274)
—Tar Beach. (p. 1706)
Ringgold, Faith, illus. see Boys Choir of Harlem Staff.
Ringgold, Faith, illus. see Brooks, Gwendolyn & Brooks.
Ringgold, Faith, illus. see Brooks, Gwendolyn.
Ringgold, Faith, illus. see Hurston, Zora Neale & Thomas, Joyce Carol.
Ringgold, Faith, illus. see Hurston, Zora Neale.
Ringgold, Faith, intro. What Will You Do for Your Peace? Impact of 9/11 on New York City Youth. (p. 1895)
Ringgold, Robyn. My Mom Hugs Trees. Vasudevan, Vidya, illus. (p. 1214)
Ringler, J. S. Family Guide to Classic Movies. Ringler, J. S., illus. (p. 568)
Ringler, Matt. It's Fall! Shearing, Leonie, illus. (p. 896)
—One Little, Two Little, Three Little Apples. Kennedy, Anne, illus. (p. 1295)
Ringley, Patrick & Brown, Anne Corbett. Adventures of the Nutters, the Tree Highway. Cotton, Sue Lynn, illus. (p. 23)
Ringo. Loss of a Friend. (p. 1054)
Ringo, Mary Lou. That's Not Fair. (p. 1727)
Ringstad, Arnold. Biking. (p. 186)
—Bizarre Origins of Kangaroo Court & Other Idioms. McGeehan, Dan, illus. (p. 194)
—Bobcats. (p. 206)
—Cheetahs. (p. 296)
—Compelling Histories of Long Arm of the Law & Other Idioms. McGeehan, Dan, illus. (p. 352)
—Constellation Orion: The Story of the Hunter. Morrow, J. T., illus. (p. 359)
—Constellation Scorpius: The Story of the Scorpion. Morrow, J. T., illus. (p. 359)
—Constellation Taurus: The Story of the Bull. Morrow, J. T., illus. (p. 359)
—Cougars. (p. 369)
—Desert Habitats. (p. 429)
—Fishing. (p. 599)
—Forest Habitats. (p. 618)
—Garbage Collector. (p. 655)
—Hunting. (p. 829)
—Intriguing Sources of Hold Your Horses & Other Idioms. McGeehan, Dan, illus. (p. 882)
—Jaguars. (p. 905)
—Kayaking. (p. 946)
—Leopards. (p. 993)
—Lions. (p. 1021)
—over-The-Top Histories of Chew the Scenery & Other Idioms. McGeehan, Dan, illus. (p. 1314)
—Portable Toilet Cleaner. (p. 1386)
—Rain Forest Habitats. (p. 1434)
—Sewer Inspector. (p. 1555)
—Shocking Stories Behind Lightning in a Bottle & Other Idioms. McGeehan, Dan, illus. (p. 1568)
—Thrilling Sources of Push the Envelope & Other Idioms. McGeehan, Dan, illus. (p. 1744)
—Tigers. (p. 1749)
—True Stories of Animal Antics. (p. 1792)
—True Stories of Animal Friends. (p. 1792)
—True Stories of Animal Oddities. (p. 1792)
—True Stories of Animal Tricks & Talents. (p. 1792)
—Unbelievable Origins of Snake Oil & Other Idioms. McGeehan, Dan, illus. (p. 1811)
—Underground Habitats. (p. 1814)
—Weird-But-True Facts about Inventions. Petelinsek, Kathleen, illus. (p. 1872)
—Weird-But-True Facts about Science. Petelinsek, Kathleen, illus. (p. 1872)
—Weird-But-True Facts about the U. S. Military. Petelinsek, Kathleen, illus. (p. 1872)
—Weird-But-True Facts about U. S. History. Gallagher-Cole, Mernie, illus. (p. 1872)
—Weird-But-True Facts about U. S. Presidents. Gallagher-Cole, Mernie, illus. (p. 1872)
Ringwald, Whitaker. Secret Box. (p. 1540)
—Secret Cipher: A Secret Box Book. (p. 1540)
Rininger, Alyce. Ka-Boom. Lucas, Diane, illus. (p. 941)
Rink, Cynthia A. Where Does the Wind Blow? (p. 1907)
—Where Does the Wind Blow? Rink, Cynthia A., illus. (p. 1907)
Rinkel, Ken. Giant Machines. (p. 673)
Rinkel, Ken, jt. auth. see Mitchell, Julie.
Rinker, Gary W. Very Best Toy. Rangel, Rawderson, illus. (p. 1837)
Rinker, Kimberly. Immigration from the Dominican Republic. (p. 861)
Rinker, Sherri Duskey. Goodnight, Goodnight, Construction Site. Lichtenheld, Tom, illus. (p. 701)
—Goodnight, Goodnight Construction Site Sound Book. Lichtenheld, Tom, illus. (p. 701)
—Steam Train, Dream Train. Lichtenheld, Tom, illus. (p. 1646)
—Steam Train, Dream Train Sound Book. Lichtenheld, Tom, illus. (p. 1646)
Rinker, Sherri Duskey & Lichtenheld, Tom. Goodnight, Goodnight, Construction Site. (p. 701)
Rinne, Teresa & Dillon, Preston. Snail Tails: Let's Play Ball! (p. 1596)
Rino. Buzz Buzz Rino, illus. (p. 248)
Rio, Adam del & Arroyo, David. Vines of the Earth. Rio, Adam del & Arroyo, David, illus. (p. 1843)
Rio, Adam del & Noel III. Teo & the Brick. Rio, Adam del & Noel III, illus. (p. 1720)
Rioja, Alberto Jimenez, tr. see Cronin, Doreen.
Rioja, Alberto Jimenez, tr. see Ganeri, Anita, et al.
Rioja, Alberto Jimenez, tr. see Harris, Dorothy Joan.
Rioja, Alberto Jimenez, tr. see Harris, Robie H.
Rioja, Alberto Jiménez, tr. see Joseph, Lynn.
Rioja, Alberto Jiménez, tr. see Pittar, Gill & Gill, Pittar.
Rioja, Alberto Jiménez, tr. see Silverstein, Shel.
Rioja, Alberto Jiménez, tr. see Smith, Doris Buchanan.
Rioja, Alberto Jiménez, tr. see Tibo, Gilles.
Riordan, Betty J. Imaginary Journeys of Bj & Dobbin. (p. 860)
Riordan, James. Blood Runner. (p. 200)
—Coming of Night: A Yoruba Creation Myth from West Africa. Stow, Jenny, illus. (p. 348)
—Jason & the Golden Fleece. Cockcroft, Jason, tr. (p. 910)
—Jason & the Golden Fleece. Cockcroft, Jason, illus. (p. 910)
—Sniper. (p. 1598)
Riordan, James, jt. auth. see Myers, Bill.
Riordan, James, jt. auth. see Tolstoy, Leo.
Riordan, Rick. Battle of the Labyrinth (p. 146)
—Battle of the Labyrinth. (p. 146)
—Blood of Olympus. (p. 200)
—Demigod Diaries. (p. 425)
—Demigod Files. James, Steve, illus. (p. 425)
—House of Hades (p. 803)
—House of Hades. (p. 803)
—Kane Chronicles Box Set. Rocco, John, illus. (p. 942)
—Kane Chronicles Hardcover Boxed Set: The Red Pyramid; The Throne of Fire; The Serpent's Shadow. (p. 942)
—Last Olympian (p. 978)
—Lightning Thief (p. 1016)
—Lightning Thief. (p. 1016)
—Lost Hero. (p. 1055)
—Mark of Athena. (p. 1095)
—Maze of Bones. (p. 1113)
—Percy Jackson & the Olympians. (p. 1341)
—Percy Jackson & the Olympians 3 Book Paperback Boxed Set with New Covers. Rocco, John, illus. (p. 1341)
—Percy Jackson's Greek Gods. (p. 1341)
—Percy Jackson's Greek Gods. Rocco, John, illus. (p. 1341)
—Percy Jackson's Greek Heroes. Rocco, John, illus. (p. 1341)
—Red Pyramid Collar, Orpheus, illus. (p. 1454)
—Red Pyramid. (p. 1454)
—Sea of Monsters (p. 1535)
—Sea of Monsters Tk, illus. (p. 1535)
—Sea of Monsters. (p. 1535)
—Serpent's Shadow. (p. 1552)
—Son of Neptune. (p. 1611)
—Throne of Fire (p. 1744)
—Throne of Fire. (p. 1744)
—Titan's Curse (p. 1758)
—Titan's Curse. (p. 1758)
—ULTIMO HEROE DEL OLIMPO: Percy Jackson y los Dioses del Olimpo V. (p. 1810)
Riordan, Rick, jt. auth. see Venditti, Robert.
Riordan, Rick & Collar, Orpheus. Red Pyramid: The Graphic Novel Collar, Orpheus, illus. (p. 1454)
Riordan, Rick & Scholastic, Inc. Staff. Black Book of Buried Secrets. (p. 195)
Riordan, Rick & Venditti, Robert. Heroes of Olympus, Book One the Lost Hero: the Graphic Novel. Powell, Nathan, illus. (p. 773)
—Lightning Thief. Futaki, Attila & Villarrubia, Jose, illus. (p. 1016)
—Sea of Monsters. Futaki, Attila & Gaspar, Tamas, illus. (p. 1535)
—Titan's Curse. (p. 1758)
—Titan's Curse. Futaki, Attila & Guilhaumond, Gregory, illus. (p. 1758)
Riordan, Rick, ed. Demigods & Monsters: Your Favorite Authors on Rick Riordan's Percy Jackson & the Olympians Series. (p. 425)
Riordan, Rick, et al. Vespers Rising. (p. 1839)
Riordan, Robert. Medicine for Wildcat: A Story of the Friendship between a Menominee Indian & Frontier Priest Samuel Mazzuchelli. (p. 1119)
Riordan, Timothy B. Prince of Quacks: The Notorious Life of Dr. Francis Tumblety, Charlatan & Jack the Ripper Suspect. (p. 1401)
Rios, Emma. Osborn: Evil Incarcerated. (p. 1305)
Rios, Emma, illus. see Deconnick, Kelly Sue.
Rios, Margarita, tr. see Rios, Yuri M.
Rios, Michael. Sudoku Puzzles for Kids. (p. 1672)
Rios, Yuri M. Kingdom of Ice. Rios, Margarita, tr. (p. 959)
Riosley, Lane. Attack of the Crab Nebula. (p. 113)
—Captives of the Dog Star. (p. 265)
—Polaris, the Robot King. (p. 1379)
—Revenge of the Dog Robber. (p. 1466)
Rioux, Jo. Golden Twine. Rioux, Jo, illus. (p. 695)
Rioux, Jo-Anne, illus. see Fan, Nancy Y.
Rioux, Jo-Anne, illus. see Fan, Nancy Yi.
Rioux, Jo-Anne, illus. see Labatt, Mary.
Rioux, Terry Lee. George W. Carroll: The Proof of an American Christian. (p. 664)
Riper, Guernsey Van, see Van Riper, Guernsey, Jr.

Ripes, Laura. Spaghetti-Slurping Sewer Serpent Zenz, Aaron, illus. (p. 1620)
Riphagen, Loes. Animals Home Alone. (p. 82)
Ripka, L. V. Plumbing Design & Installation: Answer Key. (p. 1374)
—Plumbing Design & Installation: Resource Guide. (p. 1374)
—Plumbing Design & Installation. (p. 1374)
Ripken, Cal. Cal Ripken, Jr. 's All-Stars Squeeze Play. (p. 252)
—Wild Pitch. Cowherd, Kevin, illus. (p. 1930)
Ripken, Cal, Jr. Hothead. (p. 802)
Ripken, Cal, Jr. & Cowherd, Kevin. Hothead. (p. 802)
—Super Slugger. (p. 1681)
—Wild Pitch. (p. 1930)
Ripken Jr., Cal. Cal Ripken, Jr. 's All-Stars Out at Home. (p. 252)
—Squeeze Play. (p. 1636)
Ripley, Catherine. Great Math Ideas. (p. 717)
—Why? The Best Ever Question & Answer Book about Nature, Science & the World Around You. Ritchie, Scot & Owlkids Books Inc. Staff, illus. (p. 1922)
Ripley County Historical Society (Ripley County, Mo.) Staff, contrib. by. Ripley County, Missouri: History & Heritage. (p. 1473)
Ripley, Ellen. Erosion. (p. 534)
—What Are Rules & Laws? (p. 1879)
Ripley, Ellen, jt. auth. see Mills, Nathan.
Ripley Entertainment. All Consuming. (p. 44)
—Amazing Earth. (p. 54)
—Beyond Belief. (p. 173)
—Beyond Understanding. (p. 174)
—Life in the Fast Lane. (p. 1011)
—Off the Wall. (p. 1279)
—Taking Life to Extremes. (p. 1698)
—Totally Obsessed. (p. 1771)
—Was That a Good Idea? (p. 1859)
—What Are You Like? (p. 1880)
—Wonders of Science. (p. 1948)
Ripley Entertainment, Inc Staff, jt. contrib. by see Ripley Publishing Staff.
Ripley Entertainment Staff & De la Bédoyère, Camilla. Oceans: Believe It or Not! (p. 1277)
Ripley Entertainment Staff, contrib. by. Animal Antics. (p. 76)
—Body & Mind. (p. 207)
—Extraordinary Animals. (p. 555)
—Fun & Games. (p. 647)
Ripley, Esther. Big Dinosaur Dig. (p. 181)
—Big Dinosaur Dig, Level 3. (p. 181)
Ripley, Frances, jt. auth. see Hughes, Mónica.
Ripley, Jill, ed. see Hunger, Bill.
Ripley Publishing Staff & Mason Crest Publishers Staff, contrib. by. Extraordinary Feats. (p. 555)
—Extreme Endeavors. (p. 556)
Ripley Publishing Staff & Ripley Entertainment, Inc Staff, contrib. by. Believe It! (p. 161)
—Beyond Reason. (p. 174)
—Body Tales. (p. 207)
—Crazy World. (p. 378)
—Strange Stories. (p. 1665)
—Wacky World. (p. 1852)
Ripley Publishing Staff, contrib. by. Extraordinary Art. (p. 555)
—Unbelievable Art. (p. 1811)
Ripley, Robert. Ripley's Believe it or Not! (p. 1474)
Ripley, T. P. Lily Lovebug & the Unconquered Planet. (p. 1018)
Ripley's. Burp! (p. 244)
—Roar! (p. 1478)
—Woof! (p. 1950)
—Zoom! (p. 1989)
Ripley's Believe It or Not Editors. Brutal Beasts. (p. 233)
—Danger Underground. (p. 404)
—Dragon's Triangle. (p. 479)
—Expect the Unexpected: Strange World. (p. 548)
—Expect the Unexpected: Amazing Animals. (p. 548)
—Expect the Unexpected: Impossible Feats. (p. 548)
—Expect the Unexpected: Larger than Life. (p. 548)
—Expect the Unexpected: Weird & Wonderful. (p. 548)
—Expect the Unexpected: Breaking Boundaries. (p. 548)
—Expect the Unexpected: Simply Unbelievable. (p. 548)
—Expect the Unexpected: The Final Reckoning. (p. 548)
—Haunted Hotel. (p. 753)
—Remarkable Revealed: Weird World. (p. 1459)
—Remarkable Revealed: Over the Top. (p. 1459)
—Remarkable Revealed: Unusual Tales. (p. 1459)
—Remarkable Revealed: Fantastic Feats. (p. 1459)
—Remarkable Revealed: Curious Creations. (p. 1459)
—Remarkable Revealed: Incredible Animals. (p. 1459)
—Remarkable Revealed: Life's Curiosities. (p. 1459)
—Remarkable Revealed: Extraordinary Endeavors. (p. 1459)
—Ripley: Amazing How to Draw Book. (p. 1473)
—Ripley: Awesome Activity Book. (p. 1473)
—Ripley Twists: Human Body PORTRAIT EDN. (p. 1474)
—Ripley Twists: Wild Animals PORTRAIT EDN. (p. 1474)
—Ripley: Wacky Word Search Book. (p. 1474)
—Ripley's Believe It or Not: Completely Awesome. (p. 1474)
—Ripley's Fun Facts & Silly Stories (p. 1474)
—Ripley's Fun Facts & Silly Stories 2. (p. 1474)
—Ripley's Remarkable & Unexpected (p. 1474)
—Ripley's Weirdities Slipcase 2. (p. 1474)
—Scaly Tale. (p. 1519)
—Sharks: And Other Scary Sea Creatures. (p. 1562)
—Sub-Zero Survival. (p. 1671)
—Wings of Fear. (p. 1936)
Ripley's Believe It or Not Editors, jt. auth. see De la Bédoyère, Camilla.
Ripley's Believe It or Not Editors, jt. auth. see Leroy, Robert.
Ripley's Believe It or Not Editors, jt. auth. see Tibballs, Geoff.
Ripley's Believe It or Not Editors & Matthews, Rupert. Dinosaurs: Fun, Facts, & Gore... It's Deadly Dinosaurs ... with a Ripley Twist! (p. 444)
Ripley's Believe It or Not Editors, compiled by. Ripley's Fun Facts & Silly Stories (p. 1474)
Ripley's Believe It or Not Editors, creator. Lost Island. (p. 1056)
—Running Wild. (p. 1497)
—Secrets of the Deep. (p. 1545)
—Shock Horror. (p. 1568)
Ripley's Believe It or Not Editors, et al. Extreme Earth: Fun, Facts, & Earth-Shattering Stories... (p. 556)
Ripley's Believe It Or Not! Staff. Amazing People. (p. 55)
—Animal Stories. (p. 79)
—Awesome Animals. (p. 120)
—Awesome Feats. (p. 121)
—Believe It! (p. 161)
—Beyond Reason. (p. 174)
—Body Bizarre. (p. 207)
—Body Tales. (p. 207)
—Crazy World. (p. 378)
—Curious Creatures. (p. 392)
—Curious Exploits. (p. 392)
—Eating Habits. (p. 501)
—Eccentric Tales. (p. 502)
—Extraordinary Art. (p. 555)
—Extraordinary Feats. (p. 555)
—Extreme Endeavors. (p. 556)
—Fun Animals. (p. 647)
—Incredible Feats. (p. 869)
—Incredibly Strange. (p. 870)
—Last Word. (p. 979)
—Prepare to Be Shocked: Epic Endeavors. (p. 1396)
—Ripley: Crazy Drawing Book. (p. 1474)
—Ripley Twists: Mighty Machines PORTRAIT EDN. (p. 1474)
—Ripley Twists: Space PORTRAIT EDN. (p. 1474)
—Ripley Twists: Spiders & Scary Creepy Crawlies. (p. 1474)
—Ripley: Zany Puzzle Book. (p. 1474)
—Ripley's Aquarium of Canada. (p. 1474)
—Seeing Is Believing. (p. 1548)
—Strange but True. (p. 1664)
—Strange Stories. (p. 1665)
—Unbelievable Art. (p. 1811)
—Unbelievable Feats. (p. 1811)
—Wacky World. (p. 1852)
—World Wonders. (p. 1960)
Ripley's Believe It Or Not! Staff, compiled by. Ripley's Believe It or Not: Impossibly Amazing. (p. 1474)
—Ripley's: Crazy Pets & Cute Animals. (p. 1474)
—Ripley's Fun Fact & Silly Stories 3. (p. 1474)
—Whales & Dolphins: Believe It or Not! (p. 1878)
Ripley's Belive It or Not! Staff. Ripley: Super Doodle Book. (p. 1474)
Ripley's Entertainment Inc Staff. Ripley's Believe It or Not! 2014. (p. 1474)
Ripley's Entertainment Inc Staff, jt. auth. see Scholastic, Inc. Staff.
Ripley's Entertainment Inc Staff, contrib. by. Arts & Entertainment. (p. 105)
Ripley's Inc. Staff. Burp! Graziano, John, illus. (p. 244)
—Ripley's Fun Facts & Silly Stories. (p. 1474)
—Roar! Graziano, John, illus. (p. 1478)
—Woof! Graziano, John, illus. (p. 1950)
—Zoom! Graziano, John, illus. (p. 1989)
Ripoll & Rovira. Hace un Buen Dia? Ideal Para Jugar! (p. 735)
Ripper, Georgie, illus. see Meadows, Daisy & Scholastic, Inc. Staff.
Ripper, Georgie, illus. see Meadows, Daisy.
Ripper, Peter, illus. see Hodgson, Joan.
Ripperton, Lisa M., ed. see Bigham, Madge A.
Rippey, Josie B. It's Ok to Be a Pre-Mie. (p. 898)
Rippin, Sally. Angel Creek. (p. 73)
—Bad Butterfly: Billie B. Brown. Fukuoka, Aki, illus. (p. 131)
—Bad Butterfly. Fukuoka, Aki, illus. (p. 131)
—Beautiful Haircut. Fukuoka, Aki, illus. (p. 153)
—Best Party Ever. Spartels, Stephanie, illus. (p. 171)
—Best Project. Fukuoka, Aki, illus. (p. 171)
—Big Sister: Billie B. Brown. Fukuoka, Aki, illus. (p. 183)
—Birthday Mix-Up: Billie B. Brown. Fukuoka, Aki, illus. (p. 192)
—Birthday Mix-Up. Fukuoka, Aki, illus. (p. 192)
—Bumpy Ride: Hey Jack! Spartels, Stephanie, illus. (p. 241)
—Circus Lesson: Hey Jack! Spartels, Stephanie, illus. (p. 322)
—Circus Lesson. Spartels, Stephanie, illus. (p. 322)
—Code Breakers. Fukuoka, Aki, illus. (p. 338)
—Crazy Cousins. Spartels, Stephanie, illus. (p. 377)
—Extra-Special Helper. Fukuoka, Aki, illus. (p. 555)
—Go Baby Go! James, Ann, illus. (p. 686)
—Hush Baby Hush. Smith, Craig, illus. (p. 830)
—Little Lie. Fukuoka, Aki, illus. (p. 1030)
—Midnight Feast. Fukuoka, Aki, illus. (p. 1138)
—New Friend: Hey Jack! Spartels, Stephanie, illus. (p. 1244)
—Playground Problem. Spartels, Stephanie, illus. (p. 1372)
—Robot Blues. Spartels, Stephanie, illus. (p. 1480)
—Scary Solo. Spartels, Stephanie, illus. (p. 1520)
—Second-Best Friend: Billie B. Brown. Fukuoka, Aki, illus. (p. 1539)
—Soccer Star. Fukuoka, Aki, illus. (p. 1603)
—Spooky House. Fukuoka, Aki, illus. (p. 1631)
—Spotty Vacation: Billie B. Brown. Fukuoka, Aki, illus. (p. 1634)
—Spotty Vacation. Fukuoka, Aki, illus. (p. 1634)
—Top Team. Spartels, Stephanie, illus. (p. 1769)
—Twin Trouble. (p. 1802)
—What's That Noise? Broekstra, Lorette, illus. (p. 1899)
—Where Is Baby? Rippin, Sally, illus. (p. 1908)
—Winning Goal. Spartels, Stephanie, illus. (p. 1937)
—Worry Monsters. Spartels, Stephanie, illus. (p. 1961)
—Worst Sleepover: Hey Jack! Spartels, Stephanie, illus. (p. 1961)
Rippin, Sally, illus. see Murray, Martine.
Rippin, Sally, illus. see Stewart, Whitney.
Rippin, Sally, illus. see Wang, Gabrielle.
Rippl, Terry. Tippy, Dog Gone Detective: From the Files of the World's Shortest Private Eye. (p. 1757)
Ripple, William J., jt. auth. see Ripple, William John.
Ripple, William John. Opossums Saunders-Smith, Gail, ed. (p. 1300)
—Porcupines Saunders-Smith, Gail, ed. (p. 1386)
—Raccoons Saunders-Smith, Gail, ed. (p. 1430)
—Wolves Saunders-Smith, Gail, ed. (p. 1945)
Ripple, William John & Ripple, William J. Camels (p. 256)
—Kangaroos (p. 942)
—Ostriches (p. 1306)
—Scorpions (p. 1530)
Rippley, P. U., jt. auth. see Grossblatt, Ben.
Rippon, Jor-El, illus. see Harris, Kandi.
Ripps, Robert A., photos by see Sewell, Amy & Ogilvie, Heather.
Rippy, Patricia J. Here Comes the Tornado. (p. 770)
Ripton, Kyle. Mourning Tree. (p. 1181)
Riquelme, Gabriel. Love & the Good Shepherd. (p. 1059)
Risby, Bonnie. Literature Companion. (p. 1023)
—Logic Countdown. (p. 1045)
—Logic Liftoff. (p. 1045)
—Logic Safari. (p. 1045)
Risby, Bonnie & Risby, Robby. Lollipop Logic: Critical Thinking Activities. (p. 1046)
Risby, Bonnie Lou. Great Honey Robbery: Using Critical Thinking to Solve Problems. (p. 716)
Risby, Robby, jt. auth. see Risby, Bonnie.
Risch, Christopher, illus. see Ammary, Neyal J.
Risch, Cynthia S. What Happened on Mrs. Mather's Roof? (p. 1885)
Rische, Stephanie. My Princesses Learn to Be Brave. Heyworth, Heather, illus. (p. 1217)
Risco, Elda del, tr. see Becker, Michelle Aki.
Risco, Elda del, tr. see Bredeson, Carmen.
Risco, Elda del, tr. see De Capua, Sarah.
Risco, Elle D. Dora Had a Little Lamb. Savitsky, Steve, illus. (p. 470)
Riseman, Daniel. They Return. (p. 1732)
Riseman, Daniel & D'Onofrio, J. J. Greatest Ride of All. (p. 720)
Rising, Heather. Is It Smooth or Rough? (p. 889)
Rising, Janet. Pony Rebellion: The Pony Whisperer. (p. 1383)
—Pony Whisperer. (p. 1383)
—Pony Whisperer: Team Challenge. (p. 1383)
—Prize Problems: The Pony Whisperer. (p. 1408)
—Runaway Rescue. (p. 1496)
—Secret Pony Society: The Pony Whisperer. (p. 1543)
—Stables S. O. S. The Pony Whisperer. (p. 1638)
—Team Challenge. (p. 1710)
—Word on the Yard. (p. 1951)
Rising Moon, creator. Great Colorado Activity Book. (p. 714)
Rising, Morgan. Maggie Moo the Holstein Cow. (p. 1071)
Rising Star Studios, illus. see Walton, Phillip.
Rising, Trudy L. Is It Magnetic or Nonmagnetic? (p. 889)
Risita, Sara. Lightning Bugs Strike Back. (p. 1016)
Riskin, Tim (Vadim). Language Resource Manual for Schools. (p. 975)
Risley, Ford. Civil War: Primary Documents on Events from 1860 to 1865 (p. 325)
Risley, Jacqueline & Tim. Alpha's ABC's Games: Spanish & English Ages 2-6. Risley, Jacqueline & Tim, illus. (p. 50)
Riso, Walter. Amar o Depender? Como Superar el Apego Afectivo y Hacer del Amor una Experiencia Plena y Saludable. (p. 52)
Risom, Ole. I Am a Bunny. Scarry, Richard, illus. (p. 832)
Risselada, Melissa. Seven Cats & the Big Gray Fence. Kalpart, illus. (p. 1554)
Risser, Terry. Sports Fun: Guide to Faith & God. (p. 1632)
Rissi, Anica Mrose. Anna, Banana, & the Big-Mouth Bet. Park, Meg, illus. (p. 85)
—Anna, Banana, & the Friendship Split. Park, Meg, illus. (p. 85)
—Anna, Banana, & the Monkey in the Middle. Park, Meg, illus. (p. 85)
—Anna, Banana, & the Puppy Parade. Park, Meg, illus. (p. 85)
Rissik, Maureen. Christmas Box: A Holiday Gift to Unlock & Treasure. (p. 313)
Rissing, Karen, illus. see Grosgebauer, Clare Ham.
Rissinger, Matt, jt. auth. see Yates, Philip.
Rissman, Angelica. Julius & the Lost Letter to Santa. (p. 932)
Rissman, Rebecca. ABCs at the Park (p. 4)
—ABCs at the Store (p. 4)
—Ahorrar Dinero (p. 30)
—Animal Spikes & Spines (p. 79)
—Animals (p. 81)
—Animals: Real Size Science (p. 81)
—Antlers (p. 89)
—Ants (p. 90)
—Arbor Day (p. 95)
—Aunts & Uncles (p. 115)
—Barn Owls: Nocturnal Hunters (p. 139)
—Bats: Nocturnal Flyers (p. 145)
—Beaks (p. 150)
—Bees (p. 158)
—Beetles (p. 158)
—Black Power Movement. (p. 196)
—Blue (p. 202)
—Brothers & Sisters (p. 231)
—Calm Girl: Yoga for Stress Relief. (p. 255)
—Caterpillars (p. 279)
—Cat's Day (p. 281)
—Centipedes (p. 287)
—Cheer Spirit. (p. 296)
—Chernobyl Disaster. (p. 298)
—Chernobyl Disaster Paperback. (p. 298)
—Cinco de Mayo (p. 319)
—Claws (p. 330)
—Cleaning Up: Comparing Past & Present (p. 330)
—Clothes (p. 334)
—Comparing Bodies of Water. (p. 351)
—Comparing Body Coverings. (p. 351)
—Comparing Past & Present (p. 352)
—Cooking & Eating: Comparing Past & Present (p. 361)
—Counting at Home (p. 370)
—Counting at the Park (p. 370)
—Counting in the Forest (p. 371)
—Counting in the Ocean (p. 371)
—Cousins (p. 373)
—Declaration of Independence. (p. 422)
—Día de Acción de Gracias (p. 433)
—Día de Árbol. (p. 433)
—Día de la Independencia (p. 433)
—Día de la Tierra (p. 433)
—Día de las Elecciones. (p. 433)
—Día de los Caídos. (p. 433)
—Día de los Veteranos. (p. 433)
—Día de Martin Luther King, Jr (p. 433)
—Día de Martin Luther King, Jr. (p. 433)
—Día del Árbol. (p. 433)
—Día del Presidente. (p. 433)
—Día del Trabajo. (p. 433)
—Dog's Day (p. 462)
—Dragonflies (p. 478)
—Earning Money (p. 494)
—Earth Day (p. 495)
—Eat (p. 501)
—Eddie & Ellie's Opposites at the Farm (p. 503)
—Election Day (p. 508)
—Excuses, Excuses! (p. 548)
—Exploring Citizenship (p. 551)
—Families (p. 567)
—Family (p. 568)
—Festivals (p. 582)
—Fit Girl: Yoga for Fitness & Flexibility. (p. 599)
—Five Senses (p. 601)
—Formas en el Arte. (p. 620)
—Formas en el Deporte. (p. 620)
—Formas en la Música. (p. 620)
—Formas en los Edificios. (p. 620)
—Formas en los Jardines. (p. 620)
—Foster Parents (p. 624)
—Ganar Dinero (p. 655)
—Gastar Dinero (p. 657)
—Going to a Beach (p. 693)
—Going to a Concert (p. 693)
—Going to a Farm (p. 693)
—Going to a Library (p. 693)
—Going to a Museum (p. 693)
—Going to a Park (p. 693)
—Going to a Stadium (p. 693)
—Going to a Zoo (p. 693)
—Going to School: Comparing Past & Present (p. 693)
—Going to the Doctor: Comparing Past & Present (p. 693)
—Grandparents (p. 709)
—Gusto (p. 733)
—Habitats. (p. 734)
—Hearing (p. 759)
—Hedgehogs: Nocturnal Foragers (p. 762)
—History of Fashion. (p. 784)
—Horns (p. 798)
—Horrible Habitats (p. 798)
—How We Get Around. (p. 823)
—I Can Count! (p. 835)
—Independence Day (p. 870)
—Insects. (p. 875)
—Is It Living or Nonliving? (p. 889)
—Jump, Tuck, Flip: Mastering Cheerleading Skills & Stunts. (p. 934)
—Kwanzaa (p. 968)
—Labor Day (p. 969)
—Living & Nonliving in the Desert (p. 1040)
—Living & Nonliving in the Grasslands (p. 1040)
—Living & Nonliving in the Mountains (p. 1040)
—Living & Nonliving in the Ocean (p. 1040)
—Living & Nonliving in the Polar Regions (p. 1040)
—Living & Nonliving in the Rain Forest (p. 1040)
—Make Some Noise: Chants & Cheers That Fire up the Crowd. (p. 1079)
—Martin Luther King, Jr. Day (p. 1098)
—Materials: Real Size Science (p. 1104)
—Memorial Day (p. 1125)
—Mice: Nocturnal Explorers (p. 1134)
—Night Safari (p. 1254)
—No Running in the House: Safety Tips Every Babysitter Needs to Know (p. 1260)
—Oído (p. 1282)
—Olfato (p. 1285)
—Orange (p. 1301)
—Parents (p. 1324)
—Parks (p. 1325)
—People Who Help Us. (p. 1340)
—Picture This! (p. 1356)
—Pirates (p. 1363)
—Plants. (p. 1369)
—Play (p. 1370)
—Playing with Friends: Comparing Past & Present (p. 1372)
—Presidents' Day (p. 1397)
—Quest for the Best: Conquering Cheerleading Tryouts & Competitions. (p. 1426)
—Real Size Science. (p. 1449)
—Red Foxes: Nocturnal Predators (p. 1454)
—Rocks & Soil. (p. 1483)
—Role Models (p. 1485)
—Saving Money (p. 1517)
—Say What You See. (p. 1519)
—Seasons (p. 1538)
—Seeing (p. 1548)
—Shapes in Art (p. 1560)
—Shapes in Music (p. 1560)
—Shapes in Sports (p. 1560)
—Shapes in the Garden (p. 1560)
—Should Bella Go to Bed? Staying Healthy (p. 1569)
—Should Billy Brush His Teeth? Taking Care of Yourself (p. 1569)
—Should Henry Wear a Helmet? Staying Safe (p. 1569)
—Should Theo Say Thank You? Being Respectful (p. 1570)
—Should Wendy Walk the Dog? Taking Care of Your Pets (p. 1570)
—Show Your Spirit: Cheerleading Basics You Need to Know. (p. 1571)
—Simple Machines: Real Size Science (p. 1578)
—Slavery in the United States. (p. 1588)
—Smart Girl: Yoga for Brain Power. (p. 1592)
—Smelling (p. 1593)
—Spending Money (p. 1625)
—Spines (p. 1628)
—Sports & My Body (p. 1632)

R

—Strong Girl: Yoga for Building Strength. (p. 1668)
—Tacto (p. 1695)
—Taking a Trip: Comparing Past & Present (p. 1698)
—Tasting (p. 1707)
—Teeth (p. 1715)
—Thanksgiving (p. 1725)
—Todos Aprendemos. (p. 1761)
—Todos Jugamos (p. 1761)
—Todos Leemos (p. 1761)
—Todos Nos Comunicamos (p. 1761)
—Todos Nos Movemos (p. 1761)
—Touching (p. 1772)
—Using Money. (p. 1828)
—Using Myplate. (p. 1828)
—Using Your Senses (p. 1829)
—Veterans Day (p. 1839)
—Vista (p. 1846)
—We All Communicate (p. 1865)
—We All Learn (p. 1865)
—We All Move (p. 1865)
—We All Play (p. 1865)
—We All Read (p. 1865)
—We Are All Different. (p. 1865)
—We Can Help the Environment. (p. 1866)
—We Can Stay Safe. (p. 1866)
—Werewolves (p. 1875)
—What Is a Family? (p. 1888)
—What Is a Landform? (p. 1888)
—What Is Money? (p. 1890)
—What Were Dinosaurs? (p. 1895)
—What Would You Do? (p. 1895)
—What's Great about Connecticut? (p. 1897)
—What's Great about New Hampshire? (p. 1897)
—World War I: Why They Fought. (p. 1959)
—Yoga for You. (p. 1972)
—Yoga for Your Mind & Body: A Teenage Practice for a Healthy, Balanced Life. (p. 1972)
—You're Hired! Business Basics Every Babysitter Needs to Know (p. 1982)
—¿Qué es el Dinero? (p. 1423)
Rissman, Rebecca, jt. auth. see Dallas, Justin.
Rissman, Rebecca, jt. auth. see Harris, Nancy.
Rissman, Rebecca, jt. auth. see Higgins, Melissa.
Rissman, Rebecca, jt. auth. see Nunn, Daniel.
Rissman, Rebecca, jt. auth. see Smith, Sian.
Rissman, Rebecca & Fandangleman, Rupert. Comparing Creatures. (p. 352)
Rissman, Rebecca & Nunn, Daniel. Everyday Alphabet (p. 543)
Rissman, Rebecca & Smith, Sian. Caring for Your Teeth (p. 269)
—Eating Well (p. 501)
—Fall (p. 566)
—Getting Exercise (p. 669)
—Getting Rest (p. 669)
—Keeping Clean (p. 947)
—Spring (p. 1634)
—Staying Safe in the Sun (p. 1645)
—Summer (p. 1673)
—What Is a Community? (p. 1888)
Rissman, Rebecca & Vigliano, Adrian. Weather. (p. 1869)
Risso, Eduardo. Mysteries of the Red Moon (p. 1222)
Risso, Eduardo & Trillo, Carlos. misterios de la Luna Roja (p. 1155)
—Misterios de la Luna Roja: El Ataque del Circo. Vol. 2 (p. 1155)
Risson, Toni. Licking Lizards. Danalis, John, illus. (p. 1007)
Rist, Stephen. Ladybirds Don't Like Scrambled Eggs. (p. 971)
Ristaino, Andy. Escape from Dullsville. (p. 534)
Ristas. Chistes para Ninos (p. 308)
Risteen, H. L. Montana Gold: Frontier Stories. (p. 1170)
Ristow, Trevor, illus. see Ehrenhaft, Daniel.
Ristuccia, Christine. Entire World of Attributes. (p. 531)
Ristuccia, Christine & Ristuccia, James. Entire World of S & Z Instructional Workbook: A Comprehensive Approach to Remediate Frontal & Lateral Lisps. (p. 531)
—Entire World of S & Z Screening Kit. (p. 531)
—Entire World of WH? Questions. (p. 531)
—Entire World of WH? Questions Flip Book. (p. 531)
Ristuccia, James, jt. auth. see Ristuccia, Christine.
Rita, Susan Adam, jt. auth. see Pedro, Coach.
Ritch, Catherine. Zipper Finds a Job. Trexler, Jennifer Suther, illus. (p. 1987)
Ritchey, Adam. Out-of-Sight Photo Puzzles: Spot the Differences & More! (p. 1311)
Ritchey, Carmil White. Adventures of Pine Cone the Cat. (p. 21)
Ritchey, Kate. Goofy's Sledding Contest. (p. 702)
—Huey, Dewey, & Louie's Rainy Day. (p. 824)
—Lion, Tiger, & Bear. (p. 1020)
—Lion, Tiger, & Bear, Level 4. (p. 1020)
—Mickey & Friends: A Perfect Picnic. (p. 1136)
Ritchey, Kate, jt. auth. see Disney Book Group Staff.
Ritchey, Kate, jt. auth. see Meister, Cari.
Ritchey, Kate & Disney Book Group Staff. Perfect Picnic. Disney Storybook Artists Staff & Disney Storybook Art Team, illus. (p. 1342)
Ritchey, Melissa. Kabeezles. (p. 941)
Ritchey, Richard I. True Adventures of the Reptileman. (p. 1791)
Ritchie, Alex, illus. see Ritchie, Jon.
Ritchie, Alison. Me & My Dad! Edgson, Alison, illus. (p. 1115)
—Tortoise & the Hare. Noj, Nahta, illus. (p. 1771)
—What Bear Likes Best! Kolanovic, Dubravka, illus. (p. 1880)
Ritchie, Ashley B. Mr. Pickles Paints the Town. (p. 1186)
Ritchie, David, jt. auth. see Gates, Alexander E.
Ritchie, Donald A. Congress of the United States: A Student Companion. (p. 357)
Ritchie, Fern J., jt. auth. see Ritchie, Ralph W.
Ritchie, Fern J. & Ritchie, Ralph W. Weaving with Rags & Leftovers: The Best of Recycling Ritchie, Fern J. & Ritchie, Ralph W., photos by. (p. 1870)
Ritchie, Helen. Dear Daddy. (p. 418)
Ritchie, James. Created by God: About Human Sexuality for Older Girls & Boys. (p. 378)
—Created by God. (p. 378)
Ritchie, Janet. Remember That I Love You. (p. 1459)
Ritchie, Jon. Babies Are Boring. Ritchie, Alex, illus. (p. 123)
Ritchie, Joseph. Peek-A-Boo! Valentine. Halverson, Lydia, illus. (p. 1334)
Ritchie, Joseph R. Baby Looney Tunes Visit a Haunted House. Halverson, Lydia, illus. (p. 127)
—Easter Basket Peek-A-Boo! Halverson, Lydia, illus. (p. 499)
—Frosty the Snowman Returns. Rose, Drew, illus. (p. 645)
—Knock, Knock, Who's There? Rose, Drew, illus. (p. 965)
—Peek-a-Boo! Halverson, Lydia, illus. (p. 1334)
—Peter Cottontail's Busy Day. Halverson, Lydia, illus. (p. 1346)
—Peter Cottontail's Easter Egg Hunt. Thornburgh, Rebecca McKillip, illus. (p. 1346)
—Peter Cottontail's Easter Surprise. Halverson, Lydia, illus. (p. 1346)
—Peter Cottontaol's Easter Egg Hunt. Thornburgh, Rebecca, illus. (p. 1346)
—Where's Santa? Halverson, Lydia, illus. (p. 1910)
Ritchie, Julie. Cal State Northridge College Prowler off the Record. (p. 252)
Ritchie, Mary, ed. see Dunning, Rebecca.
Ritchie, Polly. Pocket Full of Frogs. (p. 1375)
Ritchie, Ralph W. Emergency Power from Solar Electricity: The Operation & Application of the System Described in Volume 1 (p. 518)
—Emergency Power from Solar Electricity: Build Your Own System, Become Independent of the Grid, Competitive Substitute for Motor- Generators (p. 518)
Ritchie, Ralph W., jt. auth. see Ritchie, Fern J.
Ritchie, Ralph W. & Ritchie, Fern J. Farming Is Easy… And Other Tales from A Couple of City Kids Who Chose the Rural Life. (p. 574)
Ritchie, Robert. Historical Atlas of the Renaissance. (p. 783)
Ritchie, Scot. Connect the Dots Puzzle: Fun Is as Easy as 1-2-3 with These Cool & Crazy Follow-the-Numbers Puzzles. (p. 357)
—Follow That Map! Ritchie, Scot, illus. (p. 612)
—Kids' More Puzzles Book: From Mazes to Hidden Pictures - And Hours of Fun in Between. (p. 954)
—Look at That Building: A First Book of Structures. Ritchie, Scot, illus. (p. 1048)
—P'ésk'a & the First Salmon Ceremony (p. 1345)
—Up, up & Away! Ritchie, Scot, illus. (p. 1824)
Ritchie, Scot, illus. see Graves, Harmon.
Ritchie, Scot, illus. see Heidbreder, Robert.
Ritchie, Scot, illus. see Leatherdale, Mary Beth & Leatherdale, Mary.
Ritchie, Scot, illus. see Pearce, Emily Smith.
Ritchie, Scot, illus. see Ripley, Catherine.
Ritchie, Scot, jt. auth. see Wark, Laurie.
Ritchie, Scott. Ghouliest Ever Puzzle Book: Ghosts & Ghouls. (p. 673)
Ritchie, Thelma. Terra Nova: Settling the Red Planet. (p. 1721)
Riti, Marsha, illus. see Barkley, Callie.
Riti, Marsha, illus. see Brokamp, Elizabeth.
Ritland, Mike, et al. Navy SEAL Dogs: My Tale of Training Canines for Combat. (p. 1238)
Ritmeester, Peter. Sudoku Easy: 100 Wordless Crossword Puzzles. Vol. 1 (p. 1672)
Ritner, Amelia. Puppy Who Wasn't. Leidemer, Adam, illus. (p. 1418)
Rits, Susan Katherine. Pirates of Bair Island. (p. 1363)
Ritschel, John. Kickboxing Handbook. (p. 951)
Ritsema van Eck, Patricia. Dreaming of Paradise. (p. 484)
Ritsi, Renee. Mwangi: A Young African Boy's Journey of Faith. Thorp, Cameron, illus. (p. 1195)
Ritt, Sharon I. GQ GQ. Where Are You? Adventures of a Gambel's Quail. Komorova, Nadia, illus. (p. 704)
Rittel, Michael. Wake of the Wraith. (p. 1853)
Rittenhouse, Ralph, ed. see Donahue, Laurie.
Rittenhouse, Ralph, jt. auth. see Donahue, Laurie.
Ritter, Adam, illus. see Hsu, Stacey W.
Ritter, Christie R. Mother Teresa: Humanitarian & Advocate for the Poor. (p. 1178)
Ritter, Christie Rose. Obesity. (p. 1275)
—South Africa. (p. 1616)
Ritter, Erica, jt. auth. see Hoyt, Beth Caldwell.
Ritter, Helen E. And a Child Shall Lead Them… (p. 71)
Ritter, John H. Boy Who Saved Baseball. (p. 219)
—Choosing up Sides. (p. 310)
—Desperado Who Stole Baseball. (p. 430)
—Fenway Fever. (p. 581)
—Under the Baseball Moon. (p. 1813)
Ritter, Joshua & Ellis-Ritter, Karen. Be It Every Day! (p. 148)
Ritter, Lawrence S. Leagues Apart: The Men & Times of the Negro Baseball Leagues. Merkin, Richard, illus. (p. 982)
Ritter, Philip. Tales in Rhyme from Three Little Mischief Maker's Country Time: The Escapades of Three Little Mischief Makers. (p. 1702)
Ritter, William. Beastly Bones: A Jackaby Novel. (p. 152)
—Jackaby. (p. 903)
Ritter-Henley, Sharlene. 123 Count Drive Nursery Rhyme (p. 2000)
Ritthaler, Lynn. Pepper. (p. 1340)
Ritthaler, Sarah Pilcher, tr. see Hunter, Skillman
Rittmueller, Jeanne, illus. see Haave, Meghan.
Rittner, Don & Bailey, R. A. Encyclopedia of Chemistry. (p. 525)
Rittner, Don & McCabe, Timothy Lee. Encyclopedia of Biology. (p. 525)
Ritz, C. A. Tiger's World: Growing Up. (p. 1749)
Ritz, Karen. Windows with Birds. (p. 1936)
Ritz, Karen, illus. see Buchwald, Claire.
Ritz, Karen, illus. see Bunting, Eve.
Ritz, Karen, illus. see Lears, Laurie.
Ritz, Karen, illus. see Ransom, Candice.
Ritz, Karen, illus. see Wetterer, Margaret K.
Ritz, Lee F. Sun & the Wind. Hale, Randy, illus. (p. 1676)
Ritzmann, Mary B., illus. see Riachi, Ghassan Diab & Mitchell, Anna B.
Rius, Maria, illus. see Combel Editorial Staff & catalán, Cuento popular.
Rius, Maria, illus. see Orihuela, Luz, et al.
Rius, Maria, illus. see Sarfatti, Esther, tr.
Rius, Maria, jt. auth. see Sanchez, Isidro.
Rius, Maria, jt. auth. see Viza, Monserrat.
Rius, Roser, illus. see Trévol, S. A. & Produccions Editorials, Trèvol.
Rius, Roser, et al. Ruth es un Torbellino. Terzi, Marinella, tr. (p. 1498)
Riva, Jim. Marvin Mallard & the Magic Medallion. Steinmark, Sharyl, illus. (p. 1099)
Rivadeneira, Alexa. Confessions from the Heart of a Teenage Girl. (p. 356)
Rivais, Yak & Yak, Rivais. Rayos y Centellas! (p. 1441)
Rivard, Émilie & Quinn, Sarah. Really & Truly. Delisle, Anne-Claire & Owlkids Books Inc. Staff, illus. (p. 1449)
Rivard, Erin. Agattu: The Alaskan Caribou. (p. 29)
Rivard, Joanna, jt. auth. see Robin, Ink.
Rivard, Rebecca, illus. see Zolty, Meredith.
Rivas. Ca Alors. (p. 250)
Rivas, Duque de. Don Alvaro o la Fuerza del Sino. (p. 465)
Rivas, H. J. Word Sag: A Bedtime Story. (p. 1951)
Rivas, Spelile. Cucuy Stole My Cascarones / el Coco Me Robó Los Cascarones. Baeza Ventura, Gabriela, tr. (p. 389)
Rivas, Spelile & Plascencia, Amira. No Time for Monsters/No Hay Tiempo para Monstruos. Cervantes, Valeria, illus. (p. 1260)
Rivas, Victor. Red Riding Hood: The Graphic Novel. (p. 1454)
Rivas, Victor, illus. see Andersen, Hans Christian & Capstone Press Staff.
Rivas, Victor, illus. see Andersen, Hans Christian & Stone Arch Books Staff.
Rivas, Victor, illus. see Lyons, Jayne.
Rivas, Victor, illus. see Meister, Cari.
Rivas, Victor, illus. see Stone Arch Books Staff.
Rivas, Victor, illus. see Weston, Robert Paul.
Rive, Myrtle. Sam's Adventures. (p. 1509)
River, Fawn. Sophy & the River. (p. 1614)
River Lake Press. Osprey Summer. (p. 1306)
Rivera, Alane & Rivera, Raymundo. Rocks, Jeans, & Busy Machines: An Engineering Kids Storybook. (p. 1484)
Rivera, Alba Marina, illus. see Saki.
Rivera, Carmen & Maldonado, Victor. tres reyes a Caballo. Alvarez, Mrinali, illus. (p. 1784)
Rivera, Diego, illus. see Marin, Guadalupe Rivera.
Rivera, Donald S. LinguaFun! French. (p. 1019)
Rivera, Donna Dolcu. Simon the Magic Pen. (p. 1577)
Rivera Ferner, Marta & Marta, Rivera Ferner. Perfil de la Luna. (p. 1342)
Rivera Ferner, Marta, tr. León de Siete Colores. (p. 992)
Rivera, Gina Marie. Bee Safe. (p. 157)
Rivera, Hanae, illus. see Justice, William E.
Rivera, Isidro J., jt. auth. see Nance, Kimberly A.
Rivera, Jeff. Forever My Lady: Young Adult. (p. 619)
Rivera, Jose E. Voragine (The Vortex) (p. 1850)
Rivera, Kimberly. Boy Named Goose. (p. 218)
Rivera, Lassen. Mi Silla de Ruedas. Alvarez, Mrinali, illus. (p. 1133)
—Soy Gordito. Alvarez, Mrinali, illus. (p. 1618)
Rivera Lassén, Carmen & Maldonado, Víctor. tres reyes a Caballo. Alvarez, Mrinali, illus. (p. 1784)
Rivera, Mariano. Closer: Young Readers Edition. (p. 334)
—Closer. (p. 334)
Rivera, Mirabelle. What Is your favorite Color? (p. 1891)
Rivera, Monica O. Lola the Spider & the Purple Crayon. (p. 1046)
Rivera, Nicole. Glimpse into Max's World (Max's Mini Puzzle Book) (p. 683)
—Sweet Smell of Freedom (Max's Mini Coloring Book) (p. 1690)
Rivera Nieves, Irma N. Jenny y la silla Encantada. (p. 913)
Rivera, Paolo Manuel. Spider-Man: One Moment in Time. (p. 1626)
Rivera, Patsy Ann. Wendy & the Witch. (p. 1875)
Rivera, Rafael, et al. Baseball on Mars/Béisbol en Marte. Rivera, Rafael et al, illus. (p. 141)
Rivera, Raquel. Arctic Adventures: Tales from the Lives of Inuit Artists Marton, Jirina, illus. (p. 95)
—Orphan Ahwak (p. 1304)
—Tuk & the Whale Gerber, Mary Jane, illus. (p. 1796)
Rivera, Raymundo, jt. auth. see Rivera, Alane.
Rivera, Roberta, illus. see Krapp, JoAnn Vergona.
Rivera, Sheila. Above & Below. (p. 6)
—Assassination of John F. Kennedy. (p. 107)
—Balance. (p. 133)
—Behind & in Front. (p. 160)
—Bending. (p. 164)
—Bill of Rights. (p. 186)
—California Gold Rush. (p. 253)
—Compass. (p. 352)
—Cutting. (p. 396)
—Dalai Lama: A Life of Compassion. (p. 401)
—Desert. (p. 428)
—Dissolving. (p. 453)
—Doctor. (p. 459)
—Emergencies. (p. 518)
—Eyedropper. (p. 558)
—Fire Safety. (p. 590)
—Firefighter. Behrman, Carol H., ed. (p. 591)
—Forest. (p. 618)
—Gettysburg Address. (p. 670)
—Heating. (p. 761)
—Home Safety. (p. 792)
—How Does It Feel? (p. 808)
—I Know It Is Living. (p. 840)
—I Know It Is Nonliving. (p. 840)
—Is It Big or Little? (p. 889)
—Is It Heavy or Light? (p. 889)
—Is It Living or Nonliving? (p. 889)
—Magnifying Glass. (p. 1076)
—Martin Luther King Jr. Una Vida de Determinación. Translations.com Staff, tr. (p. 1098)
—Measuring Cup. (p. 1117)
—Media War. (p. 1118)
—Microscope. (p. 1136)
—Mixing. (p. 1156)
—Mohandas Ghandi: A Life of Integrity. (p. 1160)
—Ocean. (p. 1276)
—Operation Iraqi Freedom. (p. 1300)
—Pentagon. (p. 1338)
—Police Officer. (p. 1380)
—Rebuilding Iraq. (p. 1451)
—Rhombus. (p. 1468)
—Ruler. (p. 1495)
—Scale. (p. 1519)
—School Safety. (p. 1523)
—Tape Measure. (p. 1705)
—Teacher. (p. 1709)
—Thermometer. (p. 1731)
—Thunderbird. (p. 1746)
—Treaties & Resolutions. (p. 1783)
—Tweezers. (p. 1800)
—Weapons of Mass Destruction. (p. 1869)
—What Color Is It? (p. 1881)
—What Shape Is It? (p. 1893)
Rivera, Sheila, jt. auth. see Finlayson, Reggie.
Rivera, Sheila, jt. auth. see Kishel, Ann-Marie.
Rivera, Sheila & Kishel, Ann-Marie. Elizabeth Blackwell: A Life of Diligence. (p. 513)
Rivera, Ursula. Aretha Franklin. (p. 97)
—Fashion. (p. 575)
—Supremes. (p. 1685)
Rivera, Veronica. Mommy's Little Helper. (p. 1163)
Rivera-Ashford, Roni Capin. My Tata's Remedies - Los Remedios de Mi Tata. Castro L., Antonio, illus. (p. 1219)
Rivera-Ashford, Roni Capin & Johnson, Richard. Hip Hip Hooray, It's Monsoon Day! (p. 780)
Rivera-Lassen, Carmen Leonor. No estás. (p. 1258)
—Qué crees? Astacio, Mrinali Álvarez, illus. (p. 1423)
Rivera-Ortiz, Manuel, photos by see Carlson, Lori M., ed.
Rivera, Marcos Almada, illus. see Esperon, Maria Garcia.
Riveros, Gabriela. Encargo de Fernanda. Castillo, Jesus, illus. (p. 523)
—Mi Hermano Paco. Castillo, Jesus, illus. (p. 1132)
Rivers, C. Squirrel Dance's Plan to Relocate Buddy Raccoon: A Squirrel Dance Book. Barringer, Laura, illus. (p. 1637)
Rivers, Camilla Reghelini. Red-Line Blues (p. 1454)
Rivers, Debora Gossett. Working Mind of a Working Woman. (p. 1953)
Rivers, Francine. Warrior: Caleb. (p. 1858)
Rivers, Francine & Coibion, Shannon Rivers. Bible Stories for Growing Kids. Constantin, Pascale, illus. (p. 176)
—Historias Bíblicas para Niños Bilingüe. Constantin, Pascale, illus. (p. 782)
Rivers, Julia, jt. auth. see McCarthy, Peggy.
Rivers, Karen. Encyclopedia of Me. (p. 525)
—Finding Ruby Starling. (p. 588)
—What Is Real (p. 1890)
Rivers, Katie. Winter's Dream. (p. 1938)
Rivers, Moore Debbie & Henning, Heather. Cuddly Lion. Hayes, Fiona, illus. (p. 389)
Rivers, Phoebe. Ghost Town. (p. 672)
—Giving up the Ghost. (p. 681)
—Haunted Memories. (p. 753)
—Kindred Spirits. (p. 957)
—Mischief Night. (p. 1150)
—Moment of Truth. (p. 1161)
—Perfect Storm. (p. 1342)
—Playing with Fire. (p. 1372)
—Secrets Within. (p. 1546)
—Spirits of the Season. (p. 1629)
—Yesterday & Today. (p. 1971)
Rivers, Randi, tr. see Cali, Davide.
Rivers, Ruth, illus. see Bowman, Lucy.
Rivers, Ruth, illus. see Browne, Eileen.
Rivers, Ruth, illus. see Orme, David.
Rivers, Ruth, illus. see Rosenthal, Betsy R.
Rivers, Ruth, illus. see White, Kathryn.
Rivers, Tony. Wise Tales. (p. 1940)
Riverside Art Museum, des. Artifacts, Fall 2008: Riverside Art Museum Newsletter. (p. 104)
Rivers-Moore, Debbie. Colin Car: Bath Books That Float. Moulding, Lynne, illus. (p. 339)
—Danny Digger: Bath Books That Float. Moulding, Lynne, illus. (p. 405)
—Fairy Cake Contest. (p. 563)
—Farmyard Families. Tarbett, Debbie, illus. (p. 575)
—Firetruck Fred: Bath Books That Float. Moulding, Lynne, illus. (p. 592)
—First Christmas. (p. 593)
—Garden Games. Tarbett, Debbie, illus. (p. 656)
—Hugs for Little Bear: Valentine Shaker. Endersby, Frank, illus. (p. 825)
—Lamb Loves Springtime. Fox, Lisa, illus. (p. 972)
—Let's Go - Boat! Backhouse, Carolyn, illus. (p. 997)
—Let's Go - Rocket! Backhouse, Carolyn, illus. (p. 997)
—Let's Go - Tractor! Backhouse, Carolyn, illus. (p. 997)
—Little Bunny's Butterflies. Fox, Lisa, illus. (p. 1025)
—Max's Magical Potion. (p. 1112)
—Owl. Larranaga, Ana Martin, illus. (p. 1314)
—Pedro & the Pirate Puzzle. (p. 1334)
—Pig. Larranaga, Ana Martin, illus. (p. 1357)
—Playful Pets. Tarbett, Debbie, illus. (p. 1372)
—Pony. Larranaga, Ana Martin, illus. (p. 1382)
—Puppy. Larranaga, Ana Martin, illus. (p. 1418)
—Scrub-A-Dub Ducky: Bath Mitt & Bath Book Set. Jones, Anna, illus. (p. 1533)
—Story of Hanukkah. (p. 1658)
—Tractor Tim: Bath Books That Float. Moulding, Lynne, illus. (p. 1775)
—Woodland Adventure. Tarbett, Debbie, illus. (p. 1949)
Rives, J. G. Where Are My Christmas Presents? Young, Dot, illus. (p. 1906)
Rivett, Rachel. Are You Sad, Little Bear? A Book about Learning to Say Goodbye. Macnaughton, Tina, illus. (p. 97)
Riviello, Linda. Werewolves, Vampires & Ghosts… Oh My! (p. 1875)
Rivkah. Steady Beat (p. 1645)
Rivkin, Jennifer. All Ball: Basketball's Greatest Players. (p. 44)
—Baseball's Best: All-Time Greats. (p. 141)

—Hockey Superstars: Past, Present, & Future. (p. 787)
—Searching for Bigfoot. (p. 1537)
—Searching for el Chupacabra. (p. 1537)
—Searching for the Loch Ness Monster. (p. 1538)
—Searching for the Wendigo. (p. 1538)
—Searching for the Yeti. (p. 1538)
—Searching for UFOs. (p. 1538)
Rivkin, Jennifer, jt. auth. see Crabtree Publishing Company Staff.
Rivkin, Jennifer, jt. auth. see Crabtree Staff.
Rivoal, Marine, creator. Three Little Peas. (p. 1742)
Rivot, Jean Mahassel. Secret of Pet Heaven. (p. 1542)
Rix, Fred, illus. see Wyatt, Valerie.
Rix, James. Panda Panic. (p. 1320)
Rix, Jamie. Bendro Bach. Williams, Dylan, tr. from ENG. (p. 164)
—Panda Panic: Running Wild. (p. 1320)
—Superzeroes: Cautionary Tales for Lovers of Squeam! (p. 1684)
—Tough Turkey. (p. 1773)
Rix, Juliet. A-Maze-Ing Minotaur. Snape, Juliet, illus. (p. 1)
Rixon, Denise. Owl That Barked: Tammy (p. 1315)
Rizal, Clarissa, illus. see Lindoff, Hannah.
Rizvi, Farah, illus. see Kovacs, Lawrence.
Rizvi, Farah, illus. see Latham, Donna.
Rizvi, Farah, illus. see Reilly, Kathleen M.
Rizvi, Farah, illus. see Van Vleet, Carmella.
Rizvi, Sobia. Zebra Stripes. (p. 1985)
Rizy, Brock. Emily Edison: Volume 1. (p. 518)
Rizzi, Kathleen. Are You My Baby? (p. 97)
—Are You My Baby? (Hmong/English) (p. 97)
—Are You My Baby? (Portuguese/English) (p. 97)
—Are You My Baby? (Spanish/English) (p. 97)
—What's in My Dresser? Riggs, Jenna, illus. (p. 1897)
—What's up, Baby? (p. 1900)
—Who Lives Here? (p. 1916)
—Who Lives Here? (Arabic/English) (p. 1916)
—Who Lives Here? (Hmong/English) (p. 1916)
—Who Lives Here? (Portuguese/English) (p. 1916)
—Who Lives Here? (Spanish/English) (p. 1916)
Rizzi, Trefoni Michael, jt. auth. see De Bear, Tedrick.
Rizzitano, Kimberlee. Dragonairon: The Gathering. (p. 478)
Rizzo, Cynthia. Julie & the Unicorn 2. (p. 932)
Rizzo, Cynthia Marie. Angela & the Princess. (p. 74)
—Julie & the Unicorn. (p. 932)
—No No, Coco. (p. 1259)
Rizzo, Jerry, illus. see Heffernan, Anne Eileen.
Rizzo, Jerry, illus. see Heffernan, Eileen.
Rizzo, Joe. On the Same Frequency: A One-Act Comedy Play. (p. 1291)
Rizzo, Johnna, jt. auth. see National Geographic Editors.
Rizzo, Jorge, tr. see Paolini, Christopher.
Rizzo, M. Anthony. Sir Bentley the Beginning. (p. 1580)
Rizzo, Nicholas. Championship Nutrition & Performance: The Wrestler's Guide to Lifestyle, Diet & Healthy Weight Control. (p. 289)
Rizzuto, Katherine. Poodles Don't Play Tennis. Murphy, Liz, illus. (p. 1383)
RJF Publishing Staff & Burgan, Michael. Alamo. (p. 33)
—Fort McHenry. (p. 623)
RJF Publishing Staff & Hankins, Chelsey. Gateway Arch. (p. 658)
—Lincoln Memorial. (p. 1018)
RJF Publishing Staff & Schaffer, Julia. Washington Monument. (p. 1860)
RJF Publishing Staff & Staton, Hilarie. Ellis Island. (p. 515)
—Independence Hall. (p. 870)
—Statue of Liberty. (p. 1645)
RJF Publishing Staff & Thomas, William David. Mount Rushmore. (p. 1180)
RJF Publishing Staff & Todras, Ellen H. Gettysburg Battlefield. (p. 670)
RJI Publishing, ed. see Riachi, Ghassan Diab & Mitchell, Anna B.
Rjk. Little Hero's Frown. Stubbing, Lori, illus. (p. 1029)
Rml. Interesting Crew. (p. 879)
Roach. Attack of the Giant Hamster. (p. 113)
—Day the Mice Stood Still. (p. 414)
—Frogosaurus vs. the Bog Monster. (p. 641)
—Monstrous Stories #1: Night of the Zombie Goldfish. (p. 1169)
—Monstrous Stories #3: Frogosaurus vs. the Bog Monster. (p. 1169)
—Night of the Zombie Goldfish. (p. 1254)
Roach, David, illus. see Dickens, Charles.
Roach, Elizabeth. Secret Melody. (p. 1542)
Roach, Hesta. Friendship Thief. Dillingham, Charlene, illus. (p. 639)
Roach, James L. How to Put your Videos on the Internet Today! (p. 821)
Roach, Joyce Gibson. Horned Toad Canyon. Shaw, Charles, illus. (p. 798)
Roach, Joyce Gibson, tr. Cowgirl of the Rocking R. (p. 374)
Roach, Nicole. Private Parts. (p. 1407)
Roach, Sandra & Torowski, Dave. Alina's Options: Careers from A to Z. (p. 41)
Roach, Tregenza A. Lesson Box. Samuel, Karen L., illus. (p. 993)
Roache, Marjorie D. My Hair Is Too Big! (p. 1210)
—Night Flights. (p. 1253)
Roachford, Deidre. Rights for Animals? (p. 1472)
Roach-Langille, Nancy & Mitchell, Francis G. Fiddle Fantasy: A Selection of Fiddle Tunes by Maritime Composers. Mitchell, Francis G., ed. (p. 583)
Roadbloc. Vending MacHine Lunch. (p. 1835)
Roadhouse, Patricia. Gah Reen Galoshes. (p. 652)
Roam, Vanessa. Remnant Surprise. (p. 1460)
—Tippy Tip. (p. 1757)
Roane, E. M. Quincy's First Year. (p. 1428)
Roane, Wanda. Christmas Is a Birthday Story. (p. 314)
—Come & See: The Star of Christmas Is Shining in Me. (p. 347)
Roar, Kathy. Duckling That Learned to Swim. (p. 488)
Roark, Algernon Michael. Graylinger Grotto. Triplett, Ginger, illus. (p. 713)
Roark, Dann L., jt. auth. see Radcliff, R. Bruce.
Roash, Riki. Mom, I Can Sleep in My Bed Tonight! (p. 1161)
Roat, Sharon Huss. Between the Notes. (p. 173)
Roath, Tiffany R. I Call You Beautiful. (p. 834)
Roba, Jean. Bored Silly with Billy. (p. 214)
—Friends First. Roba, Jean, illus. (p. 638)
—It's a Dog's Life. (p. 895)
—Remember This, Billy? (p. 1459)
Robaard, Jedda. Little Book about Me & My Dad. (p. 1025)
—Little Lion Who Lost Her Roar. (p. 1030)
—Little Zebra Who Lost His Stripes. (p. 1038)
—Milo & Millie. Robaard, Jedda, illus. (p. 1144)
Robak, Raelinda. Cruzer the Crocodile. (p. 387)
—Herbie the Hippo. (p. 769)
Robar, Serena. Giving up the V. (p. 681)
Robards, Karen. Vanished. (p. 1833)
Robare, Jay. Pets in Heaven Activity Book: Children's Companion Book to: Do Pets & Other Animals Go to Heaven? (p. 1348)
Robateau, Lisa, jt. auth. see Epps, S. Emmanuel.
Robb, Andy. Ballistic Beginnings. (p. 135)
—Catastrophic Kings. (p. 278)
—Hodgepodge Hebrews. (p. 787)
—Hyper Holy Happenings. (p. 831)
—Magnificent Moses. (p. 1076)
—Super Son. (p. 1682)
Robb, Anina. 50 Reproducible Strategy Sheets That Build Comprehension During Independent Reading: Engaging Forms That Guide Students to Use Reading Strategies & Recognize Literary Elements-And Help You Assess Comprehension. (p. 1997)
—Graphic Organizers & Strategy Sheets: That Scaffold Writing from Paragraphs to Essays - Student Packets with Guided Lessons, Writing Models, Graphic Organizers, & Planning Sheets. (p. 711)
Robb, B. R. River Ghosts. (p. 1476)
Robb, Candace. Cross-Legged Knight. (p. 385)
Robb, Christina. This Changes Everything: The Relational Revolution in Psychology. (p. 1735)
Robb, Diane Burton. Alphabet War: A Story about Dyslexia. Piazza, Gail, illus. (p. 50)
Robb, Don. Hail to the Chief: The American Presidency. Witschonke, Alan, illus. (p. 735)
—Ox, House, Stick: The History of Our Alphabet. Smith, Anne, illus. (p. 1315)
—This Is America: The American Spirit in Places & People. Pratt, Christine Joy, illus. (p. 1735)
Robb, J. D., pseud. Strangers in Death. (p. 1665)
—Survivor in Death. (p. 1687)
Robb, Jackie. Miley Mania! Behind the Scenes with Miley Cyrus. (p. 1142)
Robb, Jackie & Stringle, Berny. Story of Armadillo. Duncan, Karen & Stringle, Sam, illus. (p. 1657)
—Story of Bat. Duncan, Karen & Stringle, Sam, illus. (p. 1657)
—Story of Cat. Duncan, Karen & Stringle, Sam, illus. (p. 1657)
—Story of Dog. Duncan, Karen & Stringle, Sam, illus. (p. 1658)
—Story of Pea Brain. Duncan, Karen & Stringle, Sam, illus. (p. 1659)
—Story of Plankton. Duncan, Karen & Stringle, Sam, illus. (p. 1659)
—Story of Slug. Duncan, Karen & Stringle, Sam, illus. (p. 1660)
—Story of Spider. Duncan, Karen & Stringle, Sam, illus. (p. 1660)
Robb, Jonathan, illus. see Wilkins, Nalini.
Robb, Laura. Music & Drum: Voices of War & Peace, Hope & Dreams. Lill, Debra, illus. (p. 1193)
—Teaching Reading in Social Studies, Science, & Math: Practical Ways to Weave Comprehension Strategies into Your Content Area Teaching. (p. 1710)
Robb, R. E. I Learned about Boating from This... (p. 840)
Robberecht, Thierry. Chick's Works of Art. Loufane, illus. (p. 301)
—Superhero School. Goossens, Philippe, illus. (p. 1683)
—¡Soy un Dragón! Goosens, Philippe, illus. (p. 1618)
Robberecht, Thierry & Goossens, Philippe. Perdí mi Sonrisa. Robberecht, Thierry, illus. (p. 1341)
Robbins, Alexandra. Overachievers: The Secret Lives of Driven Kids. (p. 1314)
—Secrets of the Tomb: Skulls & Bones, the Ivy League, & the Hidden Paths of Power. (p. 1546)
Robbins, Amanda, jt. auth. see Harrison, Paul.
Robbins, Ashley, illus. see Watson, Don.
Robbins, Brian. Denim Design Lab: A Tribute to the Beauty of Vintage Denim. (p. 426)
Robbins, Carrie, illus. see McDonough, Yona Zeldis.
Robbins, Dennis L. Soldier's Christmas. (p. 1607)
Robbins, Duffy. This Way to Youth Ministry: An Introduction to the Adventure (p. 1737)
Robbins, Duffy & Kageler, Len. This Way to Youth Ministry—Companion Guide: Readings, Case Studies, Resources to Begin the Journey (p. 1737)
Robbins, Eliza. Nana's New Room. (p. 1228)
—Popcorn Surprise. (p. 1384)
—Vegetables & How They Grow. (p. 1834)
—Which Holds More? Learning to Compare Volume. (p. 1911)
Robbins, Gerald. Azerbaijan. (p. 121)
—Ottoman & Qajar Empires in the Age of Reform. (p. 1307)
Robbins, Heather P., jt. auth. see Wolf, Kathryn Nider.
Robbins, Jacqui. New Girl... & Me. Phelan, Matt, illus. (p. 1244)
—Two of a Kind. Phelan, Matt, illus. (p. 1804)
Robbins, James L. Aristotle & Burgoo & the Ditto-Flake-Flu. (p. 98)
Robbins, Jann & Shachnow, Sidney. Hope & Honor. (p. 796)
Robbins, Karen. Care for Our World. Ball, Alexandra, illus. (p. 266)
—Care for Our World Play Set. (p. 266)
Robbins, Kathryn, illus. see Mccracken, Heather.
Robbins, Kathryn, illus. see McKracken, Heather.
Robbins, Ken. Apples. Robbins, Ken, photos by. (p. 92)
—For Good Measure: The Ways We Say How Much, How Far, How Heavy, How Big, How Old. Robbins, Ken, illus. (p. 615)
—Seeds. Robbins, Ken, illus. (p. 1547)
—Thunder on the Plains: The Story of the American Buffalo. Robbins, Ken, illus. (p. 1746)
—Trucks: Giants of the Highway. Robbins, Ken, illus. (p. 1791)
Robbins, Ken, illus. see Singer, Marilyn.
Robbins, Lynette. Gazelles. (p. 659)
—Grasshoppers. (p. 711)
—How to Deal with ADHD. (p. 816)
—How to Deal with Allergies. (p. 816)
—How to Deal with Asthma. (p. 816)
—How to Deal with Autism. (p. 816)
—How to Deal with Diabetes. (p. 816)
—How to Deal with Obesity. (p. 816)
—Jumping Spiders. (p. 934)
—Kangaroos. (p. 942)
—Rabbits & Hares. (p. 1430)
—Tree Frogs. (p. 1783)
Robbins, Maggie, et al. Enjoy the Silence: A 30 Day Experiment in Listening to God (p. 530)
Robbins, Maria Polushkin & Polushkin Robbins, Maria. Mother, Mother, I Want Another. Dawson, Diane & Goodell, Jon, illus. (p. 1178)
Robbins, Maureen. Cuentos de Pesca. (p. 390)
—En Sus Marcas, Listos, ¡Ya! (p. 523)
—Hábitat de los Murciélagos. (p. 734)
—Habitat for Bats. Reese, Bob, illus. (p. 734)
Robbins, Maureen & Steinkraus, Kyla. Fish Stories. Reese, Bob, illus. (p. 598)
—Ready, Set, Race! Reese, Bob, illus. (p. 1447)
Robbins, Michael W., jt. auth. see Art, Henry W.
Robbins, Michelle. Leaving the Scars Behind. (p. 986)
Robbins, Neal. Crimson Fish. Eisenfeld, Candice, illus. (p. 383)
—Island of the Three Sapphires. Mayfield, Helen, illus. (p. 892)
Robbins, R. Brian. Curse of the Jack o' Lantern. (p. 395)
Robbins, Sandra. Earth & Me. (p. 495)
—Earth & Me (Hard Cover Book & Tape Set) (p. 495)
Robbins, Sandra, told to. Earth & Me (Soft Cover Book & CD Set) (p. 495)
Robbins, Sarah F. George Eliot. Bloom, Harold, ed. (p. 663)
Robbins, Tom. B Is for Beer. Le Pere, Leslie, illus. (p. 122)
Robbins, Trina. Bark in Space. Page, Tyler, illus. (p. 139)
—Bessie Coleman: Daring Stunt Pilot Steacy, Ken, illus. (p. 168)
—Big Flush. Page, Tyler, illus. (p. 181)
—Drained Brains Caper. Page, Tyler, illus. (p. 479)
—Elizabeth Blackwell: America's First Woman Doctor. Martin, Cynthia & Timmons, Anne, illus. (p. 513)
—Florence Nightingale: Lady with the Lamp Timmons, Anne, illus. (p. 606)
—Freedom Songs: A Tale of the Underground Railroad Millet, Jason, illus. (p. 635)
—Hedy Lamarr & a Secret Communication System Martin, Cynthia, illus. (p. 762)
—Hedy Lamarr & a Secret Communication System Martin, Cynthia & Timmons, Anne, illus. (p. 762)
—Lily Renée, Escape Artist: From Holocaust Survivor to Comic Book Pioneer. Timmons, Anne & Oh, Mo, illus. (p. 1018)
—Maltese Mummy. Page, Tyler, illus. (p. 1084)
—Match Made in Heaven. Xian Nu Studio Staff, illus. (p. 1104)
—Match Made in Heaven. Ota, Yuko & Studio, Xian Nu, illus. (p. 1104)
—Midterm Night's Scheme. Page, Tyler, illus. (p. 1139)
—Night of the Living Dogs. Page, Tyler, illus. (p. 1254)
Robbins, Trina & Capstone Press Staff. Florence Nightingale: Lady with the Lamp Timmons, Anne, illus. (p. 606)
Robbins, Trina & Hess, Debra. Native Princess: Sarah Winnemucca. (p. 1235)
Robbins-Turner, Darlene. Wake up & Recognize: Life of a Stepdaughter. Hendricks, Tracey, illus. (p. 1853)
Robe, Adam D. Meeting My Cas. Robe, Kim A., ed. (p. 1123)
—Moving to Another Foster Home. Robe, Kim A., ed. (p. 1184)
—Robbie's Trail Through Adoption. Robe, Kim A., ed. (p. 1478)
—Robbie's Trail Through Adoption — Activity Book. Robe, Kim A., ed. (p. 1478)
—Robbie's Trail Through Adoption — Adult Guide. Robe, Kim A., ed. (p. 1478)
—Robbie's Trail Through Foster Care. Robe, Kim A., ed. (p. 1478)
—Robbie's Trail Through Foster Care — Activity Book. Robe, Kim A., ed. (p. 1478)
—Robbie's Trail Through Foster Care — Adult Guide. Robe, Kim A., ed. (p. 1478)
—Robbie's Trail Through Open Adoption. Robe, Kim A., ed. (p. 1478)
—Wanting to Belong. Robe, Kim A., ed. (p. 1857)
Robe, Kim. Robbie's Trail Through Divorce. Gavet, Nathalie, illus. (p. 1478)
—Robbie's Trail Through Divorce - Activity Book. Gavet, Nathalie, illus. (p. 1478)
—Robbie's Trail Through Divorce - Adult Guide. Gavet, Nathalie, illus. (p. 1478)
Robe, Kim A., ed. see Robe, Adam D.
Robello, Kimberly. Lilah in Love. (p. 1017)
Roberg, Robert & Whiting, Chuck. Littlest Star: A Musical Story. (p. 1039)
Roberge, Thomas, ed. see Carroll, Lewis, pseud.
Roberge, Tracy. Jacob & Alec Explore Shenzhen's Windows of the World. (p. 904)
—Jacob & Alec Move to Hong Kong. (p. 904)
Roberson, Bobby. Lillie Boy Willie Thompson. (p. 1017)
Roberson, Chris, jt. auth. see Rodriguez, Robert.
Roberson, Debbie. Can You Hear Me? Journey of the Letters. (p. 259)
Roberson, Erin. All about Money. (p. 43)
Roberson, Ibraim, illus. see Asmus, James.
Roberson, Karla, jt. auth. see Scholastic, Inc. Staff.
Roberson, Margaret. Maggie Poo the Kangaroo Adventures. (p. 1071)
Roberson, Ron, illus. see Irwin, Esther.
Roberson, T. S. Riley's Race. (p. 1472)
Robert, Belt & Harte, Lawrence. Sales Representative Agreements: How to Get Better Company/Rep Relationships, Increase Sales, & Reduce Conflicts. (p. 1504)
Robert, Bruno, illus. see Dolan, Penny.
Robert, Bruno, illus. see Peters, Andrew Fusek.
Robert, Bruno, illus. see Shaw, Stephanie.
Robert, Bulla Clyde. Chalk Box Kid. (p. 288)
Robert, Bulla Clyde & Bulla. Shoeshine Girl. (p. 1568)
Robert, Bulla Clyde & Clyde, Bulla. Lion to Guard Us. (p. 1020)
Robert, Cerny. My Kingdom Pal Adventure Color Activity Book. (p. 1211)
Robert, Cormier. Chocolate War. (p. 309)
Robert, Curtis. Buggee's Journal: A Boy's Book of Magic, Mystery & Monsters! (p. 236)
—Furry Mystery: The Story of the Disappearing Ferret. (p. 650)
Robert Green. Diseases & Disorders - SARS. (p. 450)
Robert, J. Martin, illus. see Fink, Thad.
Robert, Kraus. Leo the Late Bloomer. (p. 992)
Robert L. Drake. Boy Allies with the Victorious Fleets: The Fall of the German Navy. (p. 217)
Robert, Lipsyte. Contender. (p. 360)
Robert, Lytle. Mr. Blair's Labyrinth. Gayle, Vandercook, illus. (p. 1184)
Robert, Marstall, illus. see Pringle, Laurence.
Robert, Nadine. Joseph Fipps. Godbout, Geneviève, illus. (p. 926)
Robert, Na'ima B. Black Sheep. (p. 196)
—From Somalia with Love. (p. 643)
—Going to Mecca. Cavallini, Valentina, illus. (p. 693)
—Ramadan Moon. Adl, Shirin, illus. (p. 1437)
Robert, Na'ima B. & Quarto Generic Staff. Far from Home. (p. 572)
—Going to Mecca. Cavallini, Valentina, illus. (p. 693)
Robert, Na'ima bint. Don't Bully Me. Mistry, Nilesh, illus. (p. 467)
Robert, Na'ima Bint. Swirling Hijaab. Mistry, Nilesh, illus. (p. 1691)
—Welcome to the World Baby. Brazell, Derek, illus. (p. 1874)
Robert, Na'ima Bint & Petrova-Browning, Nina. Welcome to the World Baby. Brazell, Derek, illus. (p. 1874)
Robert, Naima Bint, tr. Swirling Hijaab: Le Foulard Qui Tourbillonne. Mistry, Nilesh, illus. (p. 1691)
Robert, Na'ima Bint, tr. Swirling Hijaab: Percja Valezuese. Mistry, Nilesh, illus. (p. 1691)
Robert Nielsen, Eric. Boo's Fantastic Journey & the Amazing Angel Nightlight. (p. 213)
Robert, Nolan. What Are Natural Resources? (p. 1879)
Robert, Peters. Da Goodie Monsta. Robert, Peters, illus. (p. 398)
Robert Quackenbush, jt. auth. see Robert, Quackenbush.
Robert, Quackenbush & Robert Quackenbush. Calling Doctor Quack. (p. 254)
Robert Sheldon Stradford. Dj's First Parade. (p. 455)
Robert, Thando Bint, adapted by. Macbeth: Dual Language Set. (p. 1068)
(Robert Thompson), Pau Pau. Santa's Secret Helpers (p. 1513)
Robert Williams Wood, jt. auth. see Phelps, Elizabeth Stuart.
Robert, Yannick, illus. see Husar, Stephane.
Robert, Yannick, illus. see Page, Nick & Page, Claire.
Roberta, Rogow. Problem of the Spiteful Spiritualist: A Charles Dodgson/Arthur Conandoyle Mystery. (p. 1408)
Roberti, Alessandra, illus. see Milbourne, Anna.
Roberti, Alessandra, jt. auth. see Milbourne, Anna.
Roberto, Brother. Don't Push! a Story of Cesar Franck. Jagodits, Carolyn Lee, illus. (p. 468)
—Music for Millions: A Story of Ignace Paderewski. Jagodits, Carolyn Lee, illus. (p. 1193)
Roberto, Nelsa. Illegally Blonde. (p. 857)
Roberton, Fiona. Wanted: The Perfect Pet. Roberton, Fiona, illus. (p. 1856)
Roberts, A. A. Bobo World. (p. 206)
Roberts, Allen F., jt. auth. see Roberts, Mary Nooter.
Roberts, Angela. Barbie Loves Ballet. Wolcott, Karen, illus. (p. 138)
—Nascar's Greatest Drivers. (p. 1230)
—Pig Tale. (p. 1357)
Roberts, Angela, jt. auth. see Man-Kong, Mary.
Roberts, Barbara. Adventures of Phoebe Flower: Stories of a Girl with ADHD. (p. 21)
Roberts, Barbara, jt. auth. see Jaffe, Charlotte.
Roberts, Bethany. Double Trouble Groundhog Day. Cauley, Lorinda Bryan, illus. (p. 473)
—Fourth of July Mice ! (p. 625)
—Halloween Mice! Cushman, Doug, illus. (p. 738)
—Thanksgiving Mice! Cushman, Doug, illus. (p. 1726)
—Valentine Mice! Board Book. Cushman, Doug, illus. (p. 1830)
Roberts, Bruce, photos by see Roberts, Nancy.
Roberts, Bruno, illus. see Peters, Andrew.
Roberts, Carmen. Inseparable: The Tale of the Amulet. (p. 876)
Roberts, Casey, tr. see Hotte, Sylvain.
Roberts, Catrin, et al. Mawredd Mawr Moses! 16 Sesiwn Beiblaidd Ar Gyfer Clwb Plant Neu'r Ysgol Sul. (p. 1110)
Roberts, Chaires G. D. Children of the Wild. (p. 303)
Roberts, Charles. Mini-Sudoku for Kids. (p. 1146)
Roberts, Charles G. D. Children of the Wild. (p. 302)
—Red Fox. (p. 1454)
Roberts, Chilena Marie. My Mama Called Me Chilie. (p. 1214)
Roberts, Chris. Mcspooky Halloween. (p. 1115)
Roberts, Christa. Living the Dream. (p. 1041)
—Rio 2: The Junior Novel. (p. 1473)
—Rio 2. (p. 1473)
Roberts, Christa, jt. auth. see Loggia, Wendy.
Roberts, Cokie. Founding Mothers: Remembering the Ladies. Goode, Diane, illus. (p. 624)
Roberts, Courtney. Uh-Oh! Cat. (p. 1808)
Roberts, Curt. Story of Scruffy of Smithfield, Virginia. Traylor, Waverley, ed. (p. 1660)
Roberts, D. W. Pep Squad Mysteries Book 1: Cavern in the Hills. (p. 1340)
—Pep Squad Mysteries Book 2:the Haunting of Townsand Hall. (p. 1340)
—Pep Squad Mysteries Book 4: Prediction of Danger. (p. 1340)
Roberts, Daniel. Adventures of Tumbleweed Smith. (p. 24)

R

—Boy & Dinosaur. (p. 217)
—Douglas Diggly Super Spy. (p. 473)
—Dragon, the Princess & the Peanut Butter Sandwiches. (p. 478)
—Ghost of Froggy's Swamp. (p. 671)
—Good Night Book: A Book of Animal Sounds. (p. 699)
—Harrison & His Dinosaur Robot. (p. 750)
—Harrison & His Dinosaur Robot & the Purple Spotted Sea Monster. (p. 750)
—Harrison & His Dinosaur Robot & the Super-Fast Race Car. (p. 750)
—Mouse & His Balloon. (p. 1181)
—Naughty Dog. (p. 1237)
—Penguin & the Polar Bear. (p. 1336)
—Super Hero Club. (p. 1680)
—Three Funky Monkeys. (p. 1742)
—Young Pep Squad Mysteries. (p. 1979)
Roberts, David, illus. see Beaty, Andrea.
Roberts, David, illus. see Blake, Jon.
Roberts, David, illus. see Crimi, Carolyn.
Roberts, David, illus. see Fleischman, Paul.
Roberts, David, illus. see Gardner, Sally.
Roberts, David, illus. see Grahame, Kenneth.
Roberts, David, illus. see King, Daren.
Roberts, David, illus. see MacDonald, Alan.
Roberts, David, illus. see Macdonald, Alan.
Roberts, David, illus. see MacDonald, Alan.
Roberts, David, illus. see Powell, Anna.
Roberts, David, illus. see Priestley, Chris.
Roberts, David, illus. see Roberts, Lynn.
Roberts, David, illus. see Smith, Linda.
Roberts, David, illus. see Sutherland, David, et al.
Roberts, David, illus. see Sutherland, David.
Roberts, David, illus. see Wong, Janet S.
Roberts, David, jt. auth. see Corbett, Susannah.
Roberts, David, jt. auth. see MacDonald, Alan.
Roberts, David, jt. auth. see Sutherland, David.
Roberts, David & Bently, Peter. Those Magnificent Sheep in Their Flying Machines. Roberts, David, illus. (p. 1740)
Roberts, David & Fletcher, Corina. Ghoul School. (p. 673)
Roberts, Deborah. Mr Otagiri's Promise. Ju-Young Im, Joy & Da-Young Im, Linda, illus. (p. 1186)
Roberts, Derek. English Precision Pendulum Clocks (p. 530)
Roberts, Dina. Thirty Cats. (p. 1735)
Roberts, Don & Roberts, Susan. Things That Scratch: The Story of Abrasives. (p. 1733)
Roberts, Dw. Pep Squad Mysteries Book: Cavern in the Hills. (p. 1340)
—Pep Squad Mysteries Book: Mystery in the Lions' Maze. (p. 1340)
—Pep Squad Mysteries Book: Trouble on Avalance Mountain. (p. 1340)
—Pep Squad Mysteries Book 7: The Deadly Doll. (p. 1340)
—Pep Squad Mysteries Book 8: Shock of the Scarecrow. (p. 1340)
Roberts, Ean, illus. see Roberts, Olivia.
Roberts Edd, Catherine L. That's the Second Time This Has Happened to Me, but It Was Only 57¢. (p. 1727)
Roberts, Eirlys. Dweud ein Dweud. (p. 491)
Roberts, Emily. Express Yourself: A Teen Girl's Guide to Speaking up & Being Who You Are. (p. 554)
Roberts, Emma Perry. Mrs. Murphy's Marvelous Mansion. Rogalski, Robert, illus. (p. 1187)
Roberts, Emrys. Loli-Pop Lili Puw: Cerddi Ar Gynghanedd I Blant. (p. 1046)
—Pwdin Semolina: Cerddi Cynganeddol I Blant. (p. 1421)
Roberts, Emrys & Knipping, Rod. Dau Gymro Dewr: A Storiau Gwir Eraill. (p. 409)
Roberts, Esyllt Nest, jt. auth. see Paulsen, Gary.
Roberts, Esyllt Nest & Owen, Carys Eurwen. Dinas Emrys. (p. 440)
—Elidir A'r Tylwyth Teg. (p. 512)
—Rhita Gawr. (p. 1467)
Roberts, Esyllt Nest, et al. 7 Dwynwen. (p. 1992)
Roberts, G. Gregory. S Is for Spirit Bear: A British Columbia Alphabet. Doucet, Bob, illus. (p. 1499)
Roberts, Gaylia. Giant Feathered Monsters. (p. 673)
Roberts, Gaylia, illus. see Bishop, Rhonda.
Roberts, Gill, illus. see Lewis, Siân.
Roberts, Gregory. Chin Music. (p. 306)
Roberts, Heather H. Raven & the Forest Angels. (p. 1441)
Roberts, Helen M. Miguel & the Pirates: A Tale of Mission Santa Cruz. Lawrence, Muriel, illus. (p. 1141)
Roberts, Heulwen. Anifeiliaid Anwes. (p. 76)
Roberts, In Pursuit of the Curious Bangle J. In Pursuit of the Curious Bangle. (p. 864)
Roberts, J. P., illus. see Lisbona, Margie Taylor.
Roberts, Jane & Mehta, Sonia. 101 Things You Should Know about Social Studies. (p. 2000)
Roberts, Jennifer, photos by see Coppola, Vanessa Rodriguez.
Roberts, Jennifer T., jt. auth. see Barrett, Tracy.
Roberts, Jeremy. Beatles: Music Revolutionaries. (p. 153)
—Bob Dylan: Voice of a Generation. (p. 205)
—Chinese Mythology A to Z, Second Edition. (p. 307)
—Drugs & Dieting. (p. 487)
—Japanese Mythology A to Z, Second Edition. (p. 909)
—Prescription Drug Abuse. (p. 1396)
—Real Deal: A Guy's Guide to Being a Guy. (p. 1448)
—Tiger Woods: Golf's Master. (p. 1749)
—U. S. Air Force Special Operations. (p. 1806)
—U. S. Army Special Operations Forces. (p. 1806)
Roberts, Jeremy, illus. see Auerbach, Annie & PopCap Games Staff.
Roberts, Jeremy, illus. see Lemke, Donald.
Roberts, Jeremy, illus. see Sazaklis, John.
Roberts, Jeremy, jt. auth. see Ellis, Catherine.
Roberts, Jeremy, jt. auth. see Leonard, Basia.
Roberts, Jeremy, jt. auth. see Lowery, Zoe.
Roberts, Jeremy, jt. auth. see Lynch, Patricia Ann.
Roberts, Jeremy, jt. auth. see Roscoe, Kelly.
Roberts, Jeremy, jt. auth. see Sazaklis, John.
Roberts, Jeremy & Lynch, Patricia Ann. African. (p. 26)
Roberts, Jeremy & Matson, Glenna. Celtic. (p. 286)
Roberts, Jerry. Roberto Clemente: Baseball Player. (p. 1479)
Roberts, Jeyn. Dark Inside. (p. 407)
—Rage Within. (p. 1433)
Roberts, Jillian. Where Do Babies Come From? Our First Talk about Birth Revell, Cindy, illus. (p. 1906)
Roberts, Jim. Strutter's Complete Guide to Clown Make-Up. (p. 1668)
Roberts, Jody, jt. auth. see Gelber, Lisa.
Roberts, Joel, illus. see Williams Jr., Floyd.
Roberts, Johanna Lonsdorf. Summer at the Cabin. Shaggy Dog Press, ed. (p. 1673)
Roberts, John Maddox. Nobody Loves a Centurion. (p. 1262)
—Saturnalia. (p. 1515)
Roberts, Justin & Robinson, Christian. Smallest Girl in the Smallest Grade. (p. 1592)
Roberts, Kayla. Frederick Douglass: Freedom Fighter. (p. 633)
Roberts, Kelly. Baseball Book for Kids. (p. 141)
—Baseball Boy. (p. 141)
Roberts, Kelly Hughes. Road to Chianti. (p. 1477)
Roberts, Ken. Hiccup Champion of the World (p. 775)
—Nothing Wright. (p. 1268)
—Thumb & the Bad Guys Franson, Leanne, illus. (p. 1745)
—Thumb & the Bad Guys. (p. 1745)
—Thumb in the Box. (p. 1745)
—Thumb on a Diamond Franson, Leanne, illus. (p. 1745)
—Thumb on a Diamond. (p. 1745)
Roberts, Ken, jt. auth. see Castellarin, Loretta.
Roberts, Kevin D., jt. auth. see Pobst, Sandy.
Roberts, LaDawna. Haunted Birthday Party. (p. 753)
Roberts, Laura Peyton. Green. (p. 721)
Roberts, Ley Honor, illus. see Kelly, Maoliosa.
Roberts, Ley Honor, illus. see Readman, Jo.
Roberts, Ley Honor, jt. auth. see Readman, Jo.
Roberts, Lisa, jt. auth. see Jett, Stephen C.
Roberts, Lisa Brown. How (Not) to Fall in Love. (p. 811)
Roberts, Lynn. Rapunzel: A Groovy Fairy Tale. Roberts, David, illus. (p. 1439)
Roberts, M. A., tr. Metamorphosis - Literary Touchstone. (p. 1130)
Roberts, Maggy, illus. see Lewis, Siân.
Roberts, Maggy, tr. see Lewis, Siân.
Roberts, Marc, jt. auth. see Roberts, P. J.
Roberts, Margiad & Owen, Carys Eurwen. Tecwyn y Ffergi Lwyd. (p. 1712)
—Tecwyn A'r Combein. (p. 1712)
—Tecwyn A'r Moto-Beic. (p. 1712)
—Tecwyn Yn Plannu Tatws. (p. 1712)
—Tecwyn Yn Teilo. (p. 1712)
Roberts, Marilyn, illus. see Larichev, Andrei Borisovich.
Roberts, Mary. Once upon A Monday. Lipe, Barbara, illus. (p. 1293)
Roberts, Mary Jo, illus. see Boyd, William T.
Roberts, Mary Nooter & Roberts, Allen F. Luba. (p. 1062)
Roberts, Mary Sue, photos by see Crow, Marilee.
Roberts, MarySue, jt. photos by see Burch, Lynda S.
Roberts, MarySue, photos by see Burch, Lynda S.
Roberts, MarySue, photos by see Crow, Marilee.
Roberts, MarySue, photos by see Reeg, Cynthia.
Roberts, Matthew, jt. auth. see Draper, Judith.
Roberts, Melva J. Mrs Moon's Pond. (p. 1187)
Roberts, Miranda, illus. see Meyer, Linda.
Roberts, Nancy. Ghosts of the Wild West: Enlarged Edition Including Five Never-Before-Published Stories. Roberts, Bruce, photos by. (p. 672)
—Ghosts of the Wild West. Roberts, Bruce, photos by. (p. 672)
Roberts, Nick H. Tyler the Tumbleweed & His Family Adventure. (p. 1805)
Roberts, Nora. Blue Smoke. (p. 203)
Roberts, Nora, see Robb, J. D., pseud.
Roberts, Olivia. Maylee Adventures: Facing the Sea Serpent. Roberts, Sara & Roberts, Ean, illus. (p. 1113)
—Maylee Adventures: the Adventure Begins. Roberts, Sara & Roberts, Ean, illus. (p. 1113)
Roberts, P. J. & Roberts, Marc. Mister Lee's Fantastic Football Dream. (p. 1155)
Roberts, Pam, illus. see Moses, Albert.
Roberts, Patricia Gaskins. My Friend Tommy Has a Daddy & a Mommy. (p. 1209)
Roberts, Paul. Betrayer: Prophecy of the Dragon. Bk. 1 (p. 172)
Roberts, Paula Carol. Good Morning Billy. (p. 698)
Roberts, Pauline. He Shined on Me. (p. 756)
—Miss Spider Misses Supper. (p. 1152)
—Oh! I Wish. Bates, Lindsey E. & Wiggan, Desmond, illus. (p. 1280)
—When I Was Just a Pea in a Pod: A True Story. (p. 1903)
Roberts, Pauline J. Girls Crying. (p. 680)
Roberts, Phyllis. Teeny Tiny Star. (p. 1715)
Roberts, Priscilla Mary, jt. ed. see Tucker, Spencer C.
Roberts, Rachel. All That Glitters. (p. 45)
—Avalon: Web of Magic - Full Circle. Bk. 12 (p. 118)
—Circles in the Stream. (p. 321)
—Fish & the Fisherman. (p. 598)
—Omnibus No. 1. (p. 1288)
—Song of the Unicorns. (p. 1611)
—Warlock Diaries Omnibus. Shiei, illus. (p. 1858)
Roberts, Ramona, illus. see Alexander, Troas.
Roberts, Rann. Adding Around the City (p. 11)
—Pizza Garden Patterns (p. 1365)
Roberts, Rebecca, illus. see Pigg, Theresa.
Roberts, Richard M. Computer Service & Repair a Guide to Upgrading, Configuring, Troubleshooting, & Networking Personal Computers. (p. 355)
Roberts, Ricky. You. (p. 1972)
Roberts, Robin. Bedtime Bear's Big Surprise. (p. 156)
Roberts, Roxanne. Angel Wings, Faery Dust & Other Magical Things: A Story about Merpeople. (p. 74)
—Angel Wings, Faery Dust & Other Magical Things: A Story about Guardian Angels. (p. 74)
—Angel Wings, Faery Dust & Other Magical Things: A Story about Witches, Warlocks & Such. (p. 74)
Roberts, Russell. 100 Baseball Legends Who Shaped Sports History. (p. 1998)
—African Union. (p. 28)
—African Union. Rotberg, Robert I., ed. (p. 28)
—Alicia Keys: Singer-Songwriter, Musician, Actress, & Producer. (p. 40)
—Ancient China. (p. 68)
—Ancient Greece. (p. 69)
—Apache of the Southwest: Apache. (p. 91)
—Athena. (p. 112)
—Battle of Hastings. (p. 146)
—Battle of Waterloo. (p. 147)
—Battle of Yorktown. (p. 147)
—Building the Panama Canal. (p. 239)
—C. C. Sabathia. (p. 249)
—Cyclopes. (p. 397)
—Daniel Boone. (p. 405)
—Davy Crockett. (p. 411)
—Dionysus. (p. 445)
—Elizabethan England. (p. 513)
—Evolution of Government & Politics in Egypt. (p. 547)
—Evolution of Government & Politics in Germany. (p. 547)
—History of the Democratic Party. (p. 785)
—Holidays & Celebrations in Colonial America. (p. 788)
—John Newbery & the Story of the Newbery Medal. (p. 922)
—Larry Fitzgerald. (p. 976)
—Life & Times of Alexander Hamilton. (p. 1007)
—Life & Times of George Rogers Clark. (p. 1008)
—Life & Times of Nostradamus. (p. 1008)
—Life & Times of Stephen F. Austin. (p. 1008)
—Life in Colonial America. (p. 1010)
—Lost Continent of Atlantis. (p. 1055)
—Manatees. (p. 1086)
—Medicine: A Matter of Life & Death. (p. 1119)
—Minotaur. (p. 1148)
—Mt. Vesuvius & the Destruction of Pompei, A. D. 79. (p. 1188)
—Nathaniel Hawthorne. (p. 1231)
—Philadelphia. (p. 1350)
—Poseidon. (p. 1387)
—Railroad Fuels Westward Expansion (1870s) (p. 1434)
—Rembrandt. (p. 1459)
—Sally Field. (p. 1505)
—Scott Joplin. (p. 1531)
—Texas Joins the United States. (p. 1724)
—Thomas Jefferson: The Life & Times Of. (p. 1739)
—Where Did All the Dinosaurs Go? (p. 1906)
—Zeus. (p. 1986)
Roberts, Russell, jt. auth. see Jacobs, Timothy.
Roberts, Sara, illus. see Roberts, Olivia.
Roberts, Sarah E. Lunch with Sam & Max. (p. 1065)
Roberts, Scott. Patty Cake & Friends. (p. 1329)
Roberts, Selyf, jt. auth. see Carroll, Lewis, pseud.
Roberts, Sheena. Birds & Beasts: Animal songs, games & Activities. Price, David & Ursell, Martin, illus. (p. 191)
—We All Go Traveling By. Bell, Siobhan, illus. (p. 1865)
Roberts, Sheena, jt. auth. see Sheena, Roberts.
Roberts, Sheena & Horn, Sandra Ann. Babushka. Bell, Siobhan & Fatus, Sophie, illus. (p. 124)
Roberts, Shelly. Sissy & the Old Crow. (p. 1581)
—Sissy & the Old Crow (Coloring Book) (p. 1581)
Roberts, Sherry J. Fundamentals of Business Communication. (p. 649)
Roberts, Smith. House for a Mouse. Roberts, Smith, illus. (p. 803)
Roberts, Steve, illus. see Hodge, Susie.
Roberts, Steve, illus. see Parker, Steve.
Roberts, Steve, illus. see Regan, Lisa.
Roberts, Steve, jt. auth. see Corporate Contibutor Staff.
Roberts, Steve, jt. auth. see Crabtree Staff.
Roberts, Steven. Chupacabras! (p. 318)
—Dragons! (p. 478)
—Francisco Vasquez de Coronado. (p. 628)
—Henry Ford. (p. 768)
—John Cabot. (p. 921)
—Loch Ness Monster! (p. 1044)
—Robert Fulton. (p. 1479)
—Vampires! (p. 1832)
—Yeti! (p. 1971)
Roberts, Steven & Gould, Jane H. United States in World War I: America's Entry Ensures Victory. (p. 1819)
Roberts, Susan, jt. auth. see Roberts, Don.
Roberts, Ted. Living Life Boldly: No Regrets, No What-Ifs-Selling Out to What Really Matters. (p. 1041)
Roberts, Temple, illus. see Brand, Mary.
Roberts, Tim. Portal to Chalicu. (p. 1386)
Roberts, Tina. Dream Watchman: Quest for the Missing Talisman Book I. (p. 484)
Roberts, Tom. Goldilocks. Kubinyi, Laszlo, illus. (p. 696)
—Red Riding Hood. Kubinyi, Laszlo, illus. (p. 1454)
—Twas the Night Before Christ. Hoffman, Steve, illus. (p. 1799)
Roberts, Tom & Asbjornsen, Peter Christen. Three Billy Goats Gruff. Jorgensen, David, illus. (p. 1741)
Roberts, Tony. Turquie the Turkey. (p. 1798)
Roberts, Trina. Lonley Little Birch. (p. 1047)
Roberts, Victoria. Best Pet Ever. Allwright, Deborah, illus. (p. 171)
—Market Day. Zlatic, Tomislav, illus. (p. 1095)
Roberts, Walter. Therapy Dogs. (p. 1729)
Roberts, William J. France: A Reference Guide from the Renaissance to the Present. (p. 627)
Roberts, Willo Davis. Blood on His Hands. (p. 200)
—Caught! (p. 281)
—Girl with the Silver Eyes. (p. 679)
—Jo & the Bandit. (p. 919)
—Nightmare. (p. 1255)
—One Left Behind. (p. 1295)
—Pawns. Pohl, David, illus. (p. 1331)
—Pet-Sitting Peril. (p. 1345)
—Rebel. (p. 1450)
—Sugar Isn't Everything. (p. 1673)
—To Grandmother's House We Go. (p. 1759)
—What Are We Going to Do about David? (p. 1880)
—What Could Go Wrong? (p. 1881)
Roberts, Willo Davis & Davis, Wayne R. Secrets at Hidden Valley. (p. 1544)
Robertshaw, Peter, jt. auth. see Rubalcaba, Jill.
Robertshaw, Peter & Rubalcaba, Jill. Early Human World. (p. 493)
Robertson, Allen. Timothy Tuttles Story Book. (p. 1755)
—Timothy Tuttles Story Book 11. (p. 1755)
Robertson, Amber. Runaway Doll. (p. 1496)
Robertson, Ann E. Militarization of Space. (p. 1142)
—Terrorism & Global Security. (p. 1722)
Robertson, Barbara, jt. auth. see Robertson, Craig.
Robertson, Barny. Kids Worship: 30 Great Worship Songs in 10 Useable Medleys for Kids in Worship. (p. 955)
Robertson, Barny & Robertson, Carter, told to. Christmas Puzzle: An Easy-to-Sing, Easy-to-Stage Kids' Christmas Musical about How We're All Part of God's Picture. (p. 315)
Robertson, Barny & Smith, Jeff. Pirates of the "I Don't Care" -Ibbean: A Kids' Musical about Storing up Treasures in Heaven. (p. 1364)
Robertson, Betsey. Frisky's Forest Friends: Robin Rescue. (p. 639)
Robertson, Brynn, compiled by. Standard Christmas Program Book: Poems & Programs for Christmas & Thanksgiving. (p. 1639)
—Standard Easter Program Book. (p. 1639)
Robertson, Carolyn & Salter, Wanda. Phonological Awareness Test 2 Forms. (p. 1352)
Robertson, Carter, jt. told to see Robertson, Barny.
Robertson, Catherine, illus. see Duggan, Janet.
Robertson, Chad, jt. auth. see Prueitt, Elisabeth M.
Robertson, Chris. My Yellow Umbrella. Robertson, Chris, illus. (p. 1222)
Robertson, Craig & Robertson, Barbara. Kids' Building Workshop: 15 Woodworking Projects for Kids & Parents to Build Together. (p. 953)
Robertson, Dan. Zoe Pencarrow & the River of Life. (p. 1987)
Robertson, Darick, jt. illus. see Capullo, Greg.
Robertson, David. 7 Generations: A Plains Cree Saga. Henderson, Scott B., illus. (p. 1992)
—Ballad of Nancy April: Shawnadithit. Henderson, Scott B., illus. (p. 134)
—Betty: The Helen Betty Osborne Story. Henderson, Scott B., illus. (p. 172)
—Land of Os: John Ramsay. Tien, Wai, illus. (p. 973)
—Poet: Pauline Johnson. Henderson, Scott B., illus. (p. 1376)
—Scout: Tommy Prince. Henderson, Scott B., illus. (p. 1532)
—Slave Woman: Thanadelthur. Tien, Wai, illus. (p. 1588)
Robertson, David Alexander. Ends/Begins. Henderson, Scott B., illus. (p. 527)
—Pact. Henderson, Scott B., illus. (p. 1317)
—Scars. Henderson, Scott B., illus. (p. 1520)
—Stone. Henderson, Scott B., illus. (p. 1652)
—Sugar Falls: A Residential School Story. Henderson, Scott B., illus. (p. 1672)
Robertson, Doc. I'm Glad Rancho Was There When I Got Hurt. (p. 859)
Robertson, Donald. Mitford at the Fashion Zoo. (p. 1156)
Robertson, Elysia. Birmingham Dixie Champagne: Southern Dixie Charm. (p. 192)
Robertson, Elysia Hill. Betsy Book: She Is A Smile. Robertson, Elysia Hill, illus. (p. 172)
—Charleston Savannah Rose: Pastel Yesteryears. (p. 292)
—D. J. 's Sneakers. Robertson, Elysia Hill & Bruce, Cindy, illus. (p. 398)
—Do Fish Cry ? Robertson, Elysia Hill, illus. (p. 456)
—Dottie Goes to School. Robertson, Elysia Hill, illus. (p. 472)
—Toley's Sleep over Learning Party. Robertson, Elysia Hill, illus. (p. 1762)
—Tool of Life My Pink School Books. Robertson, Elysia Hill, illus. (p. 1767)
—We Make the World A Special Place. Robertson, Elysia Hill & Bruce, Cindy, illus. (p. 1867)
Robertson, Harla H. Beatrice la Bat. (p. 153)
Robertson, Ian, ed. see Ragawa, Marimo & Marimo, Ragawa.
Robertson, J. Jean. Blimp in the Blue. Myer, Ed, illus. (p. 199)
—Charlie's Harmonica. Snape, Jenny, illus. (p. 293)
—Clam Beach. Myer, Ed, illus. (p. 326)
—Flipper Island. Myer, Ed, illus. (p. 605)
—Glaciers! Myer, Ed, illus. (p. 682)
—Green. (p. 721)
—Honeybee Hills. Anglicas, Louise, illus. (p. 794)
—Jungle Journey. Myer, Ed, illus. (p. 935)
—Kangaroo Country. Myer, Ed, illus. (p. 942)
—Meet My Grandmother. (p. 1121)
—My Capital. (p. 1200)
—My Community. (p. 1200)
—My Neighbors. (p. 1216)
—Off to Pluto! Myer, Ed, illus. (p. 1279)
—Sledding in Summer? Myer, Ed, illus. (p. 1588)
—To London to Visit the Queen. Allen, Marie, illus. (p. 1759)
—Tricky Triangles. (p. 1786)
—Volcano! Anglicas, Louise, illus. (p. 1848)
—Vote for Me! Mones, Marc, illus. (p. 1850)
—What Has Eight Legs And... ? (p. 1886)
Robertson, J. Jean, jt. auth. see Greve, Meg.
Robertson, J. Jean, jt. auth. see Karapetkova, Holly.
Robertson, Jacob Ryan. Far Away. (p. 572)
Robertson, James, tr. see McCall Smith, Alexander.
Robertson, James I., Jr. Robert E. Lee: Virginian Soldier, American Citizen. (p. 1479)
Robertson, Jean. Bedtime Battles. Dufalla, Anita, illus. (p. 156)
—Grandpa Comes to First Grade. Dufalla, Anita, illus. (p. 709)
—How Many Bites? Dufalla, Anita, illus. (p. 811)
—Monkey Business. Dufalla, Anita, illus. (p. 1165)
—My Community. (p. 1200)
—My Name Is Not... Dufalla, Anita, illus. (p. 1215)
—Pictures of America. (p. 1356)
—Team Captain. Dufalla, Anita, illus. (p. 1710)
—Vote for Me! Mones, Marc, illus. (p. 1850)
Robertson, Jean J. Off to Pluto! Myer, Ed, illus. (p. 1279)
Robertson, John. My Mean Old Dad. (p. 1214)
Robertson, Joyce. Meet the Magpie. (p. 1123)
Robertson, Karen. Treasure Kai & the Lost Gold of Shark Island: Treasure chest & toys Version. Guiza, Victor, illus. (p. 1782)
—Treasure Kai & the Lost Gold of Shark Island: Library Version (no chests or Toys) Guiza, Victor, illus. (p. 1782)

Robertson, Kathy & Hooker, Jennifer. Jasmine & Chad Make New Friends. (p. 909)
Robertson, Keith. Henry Reed, Inc. (p. 768)
—Henry Reed, Inc. McCloskey, Robert, illus. (p. 768)
—Ticktock & Jim: Famous Horse Stories. Dennis, Wesley, illus. (p. 1747)
Robertson, Korie & Howard, Chrys. Duck Commander Devotions for Kids (p. 488)
Robertson, Laura, illus. see Kurd, Tariq.
Robertson, M. P. Egg. (p. 506)
—Great Dragon Rescue. (p. 715)
Robertson, M. P., illus. see Quarto Generic Staff.
Robertson, M. P. & Quarto Generic Staff. Frank N Stan. (p. 629)
Robertson, Mary, jt. auth. see Chowdhury, Uttom.
Robertson, Michael, illus. see Bader, Bonnie.
Robertson, Michael, illus. see Frink-Hunter, Chene I.
Robertson, R. H., illus. see Gundel, Jean.
Robertson, Rachel. When You Just Have to Roar! Prentice, Priscilla, illus. (p. 1905)
Robertson, Robbie. Hiawatha & the Peacemaker. Shannon, David, illus. (p. 775)
Robertson, Robbie, et al. Legends, Icons & Rebels: Music That Changed the World. (p. 990)
Robertson, Robbin Davis. Sneaky Shoe Bug. Sexton, Jessa R., ed. (p. 1597)
Robertson, Ruth. Truck That Wouldn't! (p. 1791)
Robertson, Scott, ed. see Chan, Peter, et al.
Robertson, Sebastian. Rock & Roll Highway: The Robbie Robertson Story. Gustavson, Adam, illus. (p. 1481)
Robertson, Sheila. Fairhaven Forest: The Adventure Begins. (p. 562)
Robertson, Si & Nelson, Ashley Howard. Uncle Si, the Christmas Elf: Work Hard, Nap Hard. Gilpin, Stephen, illus. (p. 1812)
Robertson, Si, et al. Everything's Better with a Beard. (p. 546)
Robertson, Susan. Little Bunny. (p. 1025)
—Little Puppy. (p. 1034)
Robertson, Theda Robinson. Journey to a Free Land: The Story of Nicodemus, the First All Black Town West of the Mississippi. (p. 928)
Robertson, Warden Howard. 411 on Bullying, Gangs, Drugs & Jail: The Formula for Staying in School & Out of Jail. (p. 2001)
Robertson, William P., jt. auth. see Rimer, David.
Robertson, William P. & Rimer, David. Battling Bucktails at Fredericksburg. (p. 147)
Robertson, William R. Lurking in Pennsylvania. (p. 1066)
Robertson-Eletto, Joanne. Rocky: The Okeeheelee Bandit. (p. 1484)
Robes, Ruth & Almendro, Herminio. Habia una Vez: Libro Segundo de Lectura. (p. 734)
Robeson, K. S. Chloe & Bia: Tales from Wind Creek. Bk. 2 (p. 308)
—Chloe, Bia & the Little People: Tales from Wind Creek Book Three. (p. 308)
—Tales from Wind Creek: Activities & Worksheets for Grades 4 To 6. (p. 1702)
Robey, Katharine Crawford. Hare & the Big Green Lawn. MacDougall, Larry, illus. (p. 748)
Robey, Samantha, jt. auth. see Carney, Lacy.
Robey, Stephanie. My Favorite Food. Loeffelholz, Sarah, illus. (p. 1203)
Robichaud, Yves. Tomes of Tari: Kaylen's Rising. (p. 1764)
Robichaux-Koontz, Penny. I Thought You Had a Bigger Dream - Second Edition: The Legacy That Built Jacob's House. (p. 846)
Robico. My Little Monster 1. (p. 1212)
—My Little Monster 2. (p. 1212)
—My Little Monster 3. (p. 1212)
—My Little Monster 4. (p. 1212)
Robin, Emily, jt. auth. see Kempf, Molly.
Robin, Gulack, illus. see Garcia, Justine Marie.
Robin, Ink & Rivard, Joanna. Real Prince Is Hard to Find: A Modern Fairy Tale. (p. 1448)
Robin, Nicolas, jt. auth. see Benedetti, Hervé.
Robin, Theirry, jt. auth. see Trondheim, Lewis.
Robin, Thierry, illus. see Trondheim, Lewis & Robin, Theirry.
Robinet, Harriette Gillem. Missing from Haymarket Square. (p. 1152)
—Walking to the Bus-Rider Blues. (p. 1854)
Robinetie, Joseph & Tierney, Thomas. Fabulous Fable Factory. (p. 560)
Robinette, Joseph. Dorothy Meets Alice or the Wizard of Wonderland. (p. 472)
—Sarah, Plain & Tall. (p. 1514)
Robins, Arthur, illus. see Anholt, Laurence.
Robins, Arthur, illus. see Armitage, Ronda.
Robins, Arthur, illus. see Mayle, Peter.
Robins, Arthur, illus. see McDermid, Val.
Robins, Deri. Cartooning. (p. 273)
—Drawing & Sketching. (p. 481)
—Mixed Media. (p. 1156)
—Painting: Amazing Ideas & Techniques to Help You Create Fabulous Art. (p. 1318)
—Special Effects. (p. 1623)
—Stencils & Prints. (p. 1647)
Robins, Deri, jt. auth. see Nicholson, Sue.
Robins E. Be Fair. (p. 148)
Robins, E. Easy Way. (p. 500)
—Too Late. (p. 1766)
Robins, Eleanor. Art Show Mystery (p. 103)
—Aztec Ring Mystery (p. 122)
—Back-Up Quarterback (p. 130)
—Back-up Quarterback. (p. 130)
—Be Fair. (p. 148)
—Be Fair Teacher Resource Guide. (p. 148)
—Best Week Ever. (p. 171)
—Boy of Their Dreams (p. 218)
—Boy of Their Dreams. (p. 218)
—Break All Rules (p. 224)
—Broken Promise (p. 230)
—Don't Blame Me. (p. 467)
—Don't Blame Me 2011 (p. 467)
—Don't Get Caught (p. 467)
—Double-Cross (p. 472)
—Drama Club Mystery (p. 480)
—Easy Pass (p. 500)
—Easy Way (p. 501)
—Fastest Runner (p. 576)
—Fastest Runner. (p. 576)
—Field Trip Mystery (p. 584)
—Friend or Foe? (p. 637)
—It Does Matter (p. 894)
—It Does Matter. (p. 894)
—It Does Matter Teacher Resource Guide. (p. 894)
—It Is Not a Date (p. 894)
—It Is Not a Date. (p. 894)
—Just Be Yourself (p. 938)
—Just Be Yourself. (p. 938)
—Just Be Yourself Teacher Resource Guide. (p. 938)
—Last Time. (p. 979)
—Last Time Teacher Resource Guide. (p. 979)
—Library Book Mystery (p. 1006)
—Lucky Falcon Mystery (p. 1062)
—Missing Test Mystery (p. 1153)
—No Exceptions (p. 1258)
—No Limits (p. 1258)
—One Date Too Many (p. 1294)
—One Date Too Many. (p. 1294)
—One More Chance (p. 1296)
—One More Chance. (p. 1296)
—One More Chance Teacher Resource Guide. (p. 1296)
—Pay Back (p. 1331)
—Right Kind of Win (p. 1472)
—Right Kind of Win. (p. 1472)
—Secret Admirer Mystery (p. 1540)
—Secret Message (p. 1542)
—Someone to Count (p. 1609)
—Someone to Count on Teacher Resource Guide. (p. 1609)
—Time to Move On. (p. 1753)
—Too Late (p. 1766)
—Trust Me (p. 1793)
—Very Good Year (p. 1838)
—Very Good Year. (p. 1838)
—Very Good Year Teacher Resource Guide. (p. 1838)
—Where Is Mr. Zane? (p. 1908)
—Worst Year Ever (p. 1961)
—Worst Year Ever. (p. 1961)
—Wrong Way. (p. 1960)
Robins, Eleanor, ed. Time to Move on Teacher Resource Guide. (p. 1753)
Robins, James, illus. see Choiniere, Joseph & Golding, Claire Mowbray.
Robins, Jeannie. College Roadmap: Your Guide to Becoming A Freshman in Life. Grimes, Liz & Lindemann, Kara, eds. (p. 340)
Robins, Jim, illus. see West, David.
Robins, Jim, jt. auth. see Cox, Robert.
Robins, Maureen, jt. auth. see Karapetkova, Holly.
Robins, Maureen Picard. One Land, Many Cultures. (p. 1295)
—What Are the Us Regions? (p. 1880)
Robins, Sandy. For the Love of Cats: An A-to-Z Primer for Cat Lovers of All Ages. Anderson, Mark, illus. (p. 616)
Robins, Tudor. Objects in Mirror (p. 1275)
Robins, W., jt. auth. see Smith, S.
Robinson, A. M. Vampire Crush. (p. 1832)
Robinson, Alan James, illus. see Dunphy, Madeleine.
Robinson, Alise. Shining Stars: A Colors Book. Reich, Carin, illus. (p. 1566)
Robinson, Andrew. Satyajit Ray: A Vision of Cinema. Ray, Satyajit, illus. (p. 1516)
Robinson, Andrew. see Unwin, Mike.
Robinson, Ann. Gimme Five: Biblical Truths for Ages 9-12. Metcalf, Tania, illus. (p. 676)
Robinson, Anne & Saxby, Karen. Fun for Flyers Student's Book with Audio with Online Activities. (p. 647)
—Fun for Movers Student's Book with Audio with Online Activities. (p. 647)
—Fun for Starters Student's Book. (p. 647)
—Fun for Starters Student's Book with Audio with Online Activities. (p. 647)
Robinson, Anthony, jt. auth. see Collins Educational Staff.
Robinson, Anthony & Allan, June. Real Stories from Street Children Across the World. (p. 1449)
—Street Children. Robinson, Anthony, photos by. (p. 1666)
Robinson, Anthony & Young, Annemarie. Gervelie's Journey. Allan, June, illus. (p. 667)
Robinson, Anthony, et al. Hamzat's Journey: A Refugee Diary. Allan, June, illus. (p. 740)
Robinson, Aquila. Septic Zombie - a Short Story. (p. 1551)
Robinson, Arlene. Adventures of Wheelie Weenie & His Friends: A Brave & Wonderful Little Friend. (p. 24)
Robinson, B. J. LeBron James: King of the Court. (p. 987)
Robinson, Barbara. Best Christmas Pageant Ever. (p. 168)
—Best Christmas Pageant Ever. Cornell, Laura, illus. (p. 168)
—Best Halloween Ever. (p. 170)
—Best School Year Ever. (p. 171)
Robinson, Barbara J., illus. see Blotnick, Elihu.
Robinson, Beth. Safe Family Coloring Book. (p. 1502)
—Safe Touch Book. Green, Noel, illus. (p. 1502)
—Where Will I Grow Up? Green, Noel, illus. (p. 1910)
Robinson, Bill, illus. see Berrios, Frank.
Robinson, Bill, illus. see David, Erica.
Robinson, Bonita. Little Seed That Could. (p. 1036)
Robinson, Brenda. Monster Came to Our House. (p. 1166)
Robinson, C. Black Souls. (p. 197)
Robinson, C. L. MATH1on1 Add & Subtract Fractions. (p. 1107)
—MATH1on1 Algebra Foundation. (p. 1107)
—MATH1on1 Fractions & Decimals. (p. 1107)
—MATH1on1 Geometry Foundation. (p. 1107)
—MATH1on1 Graphing Foundation. (p. 1107)
—MATH1on1 Multiply & Divide Fractions. (p. 1107)
—MATH1on1 Numbers & Operations. (p. 1107)
—MATH1on1 Radicals Foundation. (p. 1107)
—MATH1on1 Statistics Foundation. (p. 1107)
—MATH1on1 Units of Measure. (p. 1107)

Robinson, Carole. On the Way to Cape May. (p. 1292)
Robinson, Charles, illus. see Buchwald, Emilie.
Robinson, Charles, illus. see Burnett, Frances Hodgson.
Robinson, Charles, illus. see Field, Eugene.
Robinson, Charles, illus. see Jerrold, Walter, ed.
Robinson, Charles, illus. see Stevenson, Robert Louis.
Robinson, Charles, illus. see Wilde, Oscar.
Robinson, Chris, ed. see Henson, Jim & Juhl, Jerry.
Robinson, Christian, illus. see Ashman, Linda.
Robinson, Christian, illus. see Barnett, Mac.
Robinson, Christian, illus. see Bieschke, Marke & Belge, Kathy.
Robinson, Christian, illus. see Brown, Margaret Wise.
Robinson, Christian, illus. see De la Peña, Matt.
Robinson, Christian, illus. see DiPucchio, Kelly.
Robinson, Christian, illus. see Powell, Patricia Hruby.
Robinson, Christian, illus. see Watson, Renée.
Robinson, Christian, jt. auth. see Roberts, Justin.
Robinson, Cindy. Baby Baobab. Robinson, Cindy, illus. (p. 125)
Robinson, Craig, jt. auth. see Reeves, Brian.
Robinson, Daphine. Brotherly Love & Betrayal. (p. 231)
Robinson, David. Mushroom Picker. (p. 1193)
—My Little Man. (p. 1212)
Robinson, Diane Mae. Sir Princess Petra: The Pen Pieyu Adventures. (p. 1580)
—Sir Princess Petra's Talent: The Pen Pieyu Adventures. (p. 1580)
Robinson, Dierdre. I Don't Look Like You & That's Ok. (p. 838)
Robinson, Dino. Gatherings: The History & Activities of the Emerson Street Branch YMCA Evanston, Illinois. West, Stan, ed. (p. 658)
Robinson, Don, illus. see Calma, Jocelyn.
Robinson, Don, illus. see Crowe, Ellie.
Robinson, Don, illus. see Gillespie, Jane.
Robinson, Don, illus. see Newsome, Tandy.
Robinson, Don, illus. see Paikai, Tammy.
Robinson, Don, illus. see Shapiro, Jane.
Robinson, Don Leonard. G Is for Gecko: An Alphabet Adventure in Hawaii. (p. 651)
Robinson, Donnell. Where's My L D 7 (p. 1910)
Robinson Ed. D., Shannon R. Adventures of Katie Koala: Oops! My Momma Is Lost! Swope, Brenda, illus. (p. 19)
Robinson, Elda L. Nathanial's Family. (p. 1231)
Robinson, Eliza Serena. Consequence. (p. 358)
Robinson, Elizabeth Keeler & Keeler Robinson, Elizabeth. Making Cents. McMahon, Bob & Mcmahon, Bob, illus. (p. 1080)
Robinson, Ella M. Happy Home Stories. (p. 746)
Robinson, Ella May. Stars in Her Heart. (p. 1643)
Robinson, Fay. Celebrating Chinese New Year. (p. 284)
—Christmas Crafts. (p. 313)
—Father's Day Crafts. (p. 577)
—Fish Wish. (p. 598)
—Fun Halloween Crafts. (p. 648)
—Halloween: Disfraces y Golosinas en la Vispera de Todos los Santos. (p. 737)
—Halloween Crafts. (p. 737)
—Hispanic-American Crafts Kids Can Do! (p. 781)
—In the Jungle. Lopez, Paul, illus. (p. 866)
Robinson, Fay, jt. auth. see Schafer, Susan.
Robinson, Fiona. 3-2-3 Detective Agency: The Disappearance of Dave Warthog. (p. 1991)
—Useful Moose: A Truthful, Moose-Full Tale. (p. 1828)
—Whale Shines: An Artistic Tale. (p. 1877)
—What Animals Really Like. (p. 1879)
Robinson, Fiona, illus. see Ibbotson, Eva.
Robinson, Francesca. Defenseless World. (p. 424)
—Song of the Seal. (p. 1611)
Robinson, Garrett, ed. see Bolger, Z. C.
Robinson, Garrick & Kjeldsen, Nell. Having A Ball: Youth Sports Done Right (p. 754)
Robinson, Gary. Danny Blackgoat, Rugged Road to Freedom. (p. 405)
—Little Brother of War. (p. 1025)
—Native American Night Before Christmas. Hummingbird, Jesse T., illus. (p. 1234)
—Native American Twelve Days of Christmas. Hummingbird, Jesse T., illus. (p. 1234)
—Paranormal: A Billy Buckhorn Supernatural Adventure. (p. 1324)
—Supranormal. (p. 1684)
—Tribal Journey. (p. 1753)
Robinson, Gary D. Who Pooped in the Park: Glacier. (p. 1917)
Robinson, George. Elmer the Elf & the Magical Jingle Bells Foster, Janet, illus. (p. 515)
Robinson, Gordon, illus. see Carroll, Lewis, pseud.
Robinson, Gwen. Renshaw Diversion. (p. 1460)
Robinson, Gwen G. Jensen Case. (p. 913)
Robinson, Hadley & Seaman, Jim. UC Santa Cruz College Prowler off the Record: Inside University of California Santa Cruz. (p. 1807)
Robinson, Heidi, ed. see Bumcrot, Curt & Dunlap, Shiree.
Robinson, Helen, ed. see Carlson, Glenn E.
Robinson, Helen Lee, compiled by. Guide's Greatest Christmas Stories. (p. 730)
Robinson, Helen Lee, ed. Guide's Greatest Angel Stories. (p. 730)
—Guide's Greatest Sabbath Stories. (p. 730)
Robinson, Hilary. Beauty & the Pea. Sanfilippo, Simona, illus. (p. 154)
—Cinderella & the Beanstalk. Sanfilippo, Simona, illus. (p. 320)
—Croc by the Rock. Gordon, Mike, illus. (p. 384)
—Croc Shock! Gordon, Mike, illus. (p. 384)
—Elves & the Emperor. Sanfilippo, Simona, illus. (p. 517)
—Goldilocks & the Wolf. Sanfilippo, Simona, illus. (p. 696)
—Hansel, Gretel, & the Ugly Duckling. Sanfilippo, Simona, illus. (p. 743)
—Mixed up Fairy Tales. Sharratt, Nick, illus. (p. 1156)
—Over the Moon. Abbott, Jane, illus. (p. 1314)
—Rapunzel & the Billy Goats. Sanfilippo, Simona, illus. (p. 1439)

—Snow White & the Enormous Turnip. Sanfilippo, Simona, illus. (p. 1599)
—Ted's Party Bus. (p. 1713)
—Three Pigs & a Gingerbread Man. Sanfilippo, Simona, illus. (p. 1743)
Robinson, Hilary & Catling, Andy. Aladdin & the Lamp. (p. 33)
Robinson, Hilda & Kunkel, Jeff. Didn't We Have Fun! Robinson, Hilda, illus. (p. 437)
Robinson, Ida. Sally's Doll. (p. 1505)
Robinson, J. d. & Robinson, J. Dennis. Striking Back: The Fight to End Child Labor Exploitation (p. 1667)
Robinson, J. Dennis, jt. auth. see Robinson, J. d.
Robinson, James. Jsa: The Golden Age. (p. 930)
Robinson, James & McCormick, Deborah J. Essentials of Health & Wellness. (p. 537)
Robinson, James, et al. Justice Be Done Bair, M. & Sadowski, Stephen, illus. (p. 940)
Robinson, James W. Because I'm Alive. (p. 155)
Robinson, Janice. Pride & Joy: African-American Baby Celebrations. Blander, Katy, illus. (p. 1398)
Robinson, Janie. Preston, the Not-So-Perfect-Pig. Snider, K. C., illus. (p. 1397)
Robinson, Jayme, illus. see Sapre, Reshme.
Robinson, Jeanette. Blueberry Bunny. (p. 204)
Robinson, Jeffrey, jt. auth. see Robinson, Jeffrey C.
Robinson, Jeffrey C. & Robinson, Jeffrey. Unfettering Poetry: The Fancy in British Romanticism. (p. 1817)
Robinson, Jennifer. Isabella's Shoes. (p. 891)
Robinson, Jeremy. Antarktos Rising. (p. 89)
—Last Hunter: Ascent. (p. 978)
—Rethinking Powys: Critical Essays on John Cowper Powys. (p. 1464)
Robinson, Jessie B., jt. auth. see Eisenberg, Azriel.
Robinson, Jill & Bekoff, Marc. Jasper's Story: Saving Moon Bears. Frankenhuyzen, Gijsbert van, illus. (p. 910)
Robinson, Jimmie. Evil & Malice - Save the World! (p. 546)
—Five Weapons: Make the Grade TP: Make the Grade TP. (p. 601)
Robinson, Jimmy. Mind Juice. (p. 1145)
Robinson, Jimmy D. Jimmyland. (p. 918)
—Lost Journey. (p. 1056)
—Pieces of Jimmy. (p. 1356)
—Tulips Painted Yellow. (p. 1796)
Robinson, Jimmy D. & Varela, John Owen. Tides Are Sailing...? (p. 1747)
Robinson, Joan G. Teddy Robinson Storybook. (p. 1712)
Robinson, Joanna J. Greece. (p. 720)
—Guatemala. (p. 728)
—Italy. (p. 894)
—Mexico. (p. 1131)
—Turkey. (p. 1797)
Robinson, Joanna Jarc. Andrew & Allen Learn about Adverbs. Boyer, Robin, illus. (p. 72)
—Phillip & Penny Learn about Pronouns. Hu, Caroline, illus. (p. 1350)
Robinson Jr., Charles Alexander. First Book of Ancient Mesopotamia & Persi. (p. 593)
Robinson, Julia Marie. Race, Religion, & the Pulpit: Rev. Robert L. Bradby & the Making of Urban Detroit. (p. 1431)
Robinson, Julie. Do Roosters Praise God. (p. 457)
Robinson, Julie Clark. Live in the Moment. (p. 1040)
Robinson, K. S. Mermaid's Tale. (p. 1128)
robinson, k. s. Mermaid's Tale. (p. 1128)
Robinson, K. S. No Lunch Money! (p. 1258)
robinson, k. s. No Lunch Money! (p. 1258)
Robinson, Kate. Lewis & Clark: Exploring the American West. (p. 1004)
—National Mall: A MyReportLinks.com Book. (p. 1233)
Robinson, Katherine, illus. see Sawyer, Kieran & Amodei, Michael.
Robinson, Kathleen Marie. Magic Doorknob (p. 1072)
—Snowflake Sandwiches. (p. 1600)
Robinson, Keith. Chamber of Ghosts. (p. 289)
—Valley of Monsters. (p. 1831)
Robinson, Keith, illus. see Imperato, Teresa.
Robinson, Keith, jt. auth. see Hughes, Pennie Jean.
Robinson, Kelley. Magic of Lo: Book 1, Lo Trilogy. (p. 1073)
—Naming: Book One of the Magic of Io Series. Curtiss, Melody, illus. (p. 1228)
Robinson, Kerby Mae. Give N Go. (p. 681)
Robinson, Kim. Unusual Experience. (p. 1823)
Robinson, Larry Jay. Stubborn Stanley. (p. 1668)
Robinson, Laura. Cyclist BikeList: The Book for Every Rider. Pérez, Ramón K., illus. (p. 397)
Robinson, Laura, illus. see Sargent, Dave & Sargent, Pat.
Robinson, Laura, illus. see Sargent, Dave & Sargent, Pat.
Robinson, Lenord, illus. see Speicher, Diane Carty.
Robinson, Linda, illus. see Shanker, Myrna Gelman.
Robinson, Linda M. Dear Grandchild, When You Come for a Visit. Larkins, Mona, illus. (p. 419)
Robinson, Lisa & Benchmark Education Co., LLC Staff. Can He See Me? (p. 258)
—I Zip to My Job. (p. 849)
Robinson, Lorna. Telling Tales in Latin: A New Course & Story Book for Children. De, Soham, illus. (p. 1717)
Robinson, Lynda S. Slayer of Gods. (p. 1588)
Robinson, Mabel L. Bright Island. Ward, Lynd, illus. (p. 228)
Robinson, Malcolm K. & Thomas, Abraham, eds. Obesity & Cardiovascular Disease. (p. 1275)
Robinson, Marcus, illus. see Branen, Kathy.
Robinson, Margaret Richardson. Wally's Wish. (p. 1855)
Robinson, Mark. Vile: A Cautionary Tale for Little Monsters. Horne, Sarah, illus. (p. 1842)
Robinson, Marquita E. Teddy's Bear Roscoe Robinson, illus. (p. 1713)
Robinson, Mary. Days of Terriers. (p. 415)
Robinson, Matthew. America Debates Global Warming: Crisis or Myth? (p. 59)
—America Debates-Global Warming: Crisis or Myth? (p. 59)
—Careers in Computer Gaming. (p. 720)
—Greatest NASCAR Tracks. (p. 720)
—Inhalant Abuse. (p. 874)
—Making Smart Choices about Relationships. (p. 1082)
Robinson, Melissa. Cheena Comes to Americ. (p. 295)

For book reviews, descriptive annotations, tables of contents, cover images, author biographies & additional information, updated daily, subscribe to www.booksinprint2.com

2641

R

—Special in Every Way. (p. 1623)
Robinson, Michael. Bloodline. (p. 201)
Robinson, Michael, illus. see Magnus, Kellie.
Robinson, Michelle. Bear Boar. Sim, David, illus. (p. 150)
—Ding Dong! Gorilla! Lord, Leonie, illus. (p. 440)
—How to Find a Fruit Bat. Tobia, Lauren, illus. (p. 819)
—How to Wash a Woolly Mammoth. Hindley, Kate, illus. (p. 822)
—There's a Lion in My Cornflakes. Field, Jim, illus. (p. 1731)
—What to Do If an Elephant Stands on Your Foot. Reynolds, Peter H., illus. (p. 1894)
—Yak Yuk. Sim, David, illus. (p. 1968)
Robinson, Nadolyn H. Boo! Hoo! Bluepurdue. (p. 209)
Robinson, Nick. Awesome Origami Pack: With Waterproof & Foil Papers, Plus 50 Sheets of Origami Papers. (p. 121)
—Halloween Origami. (p. 738)
—My First Origami Book — Paper Planes: With 24 Sheets of Origami Paper! (p. 1207)
—My First Origami Book—Christmas: With 24 Sheets of Origami Paper! (p. 1207)
—Origami Adventures: Animals. Quigley, Sebastian, illus. (p. 1303)
—Origami Adventures: Dinosaurs. Quigley, Sebastion, illus. (p. 1303)
Robinson, Nick, jt. auth. see Behar, Susan.
Robinson, Nick, jt. auth. see Harrison, Paul.
Robinson, Nick & Harrison, Paul. Secret Origami. (p. 1543)
Robinson, Nick & Origami. My First Origami Book-Animals. (p. 1207)
—My First Origami Book-Things That Go. (p. 1207)
Robinson, Nicola. Monster Machine. Robinson, Nicola, illus. (p. 1167)
Robinson, Nicola, illus. see Barrie, J. M.
Robinson, Nicola L., illus. see Safran, Sheri.
Robinson, Nikia. Lock-in. (p. 1045)
Robinson, P. J. True Prince. (p. 1792)
Robinson, P. J. & Atwood, Julie. Manners of a Princess. (p. 1088)
Robinson, Peewee. Spot. (p. 1633)
Robinson, Peter. Untitled Deeds. (p. 1823)
Robinson, R. M. Death by Paradox. (p. 420)
Robinson, Rachaell. Princess Karakul: The Runaway Bear. (p. 1404)
Robinson, Richard. Frequently Asked Questions about AIDS & HIV. (p. 636)
Robinson, Rina. Tarnished Threads: Australian Country Town Tales. (p. 1706)
Robinson, Rob. Princess & the Juggler. (p. 1402)
Robinson, Robin. L. Frank Baum's Wizard of Oz. (p. 969)
Robinson, Robin, text. Peeling the Onion: A Father/Daughter Journey Through A Revolutionary Medical Treatment for Stroke. (p. 1335)
Robinson, Roger, illus. see Jurgens, Dan.
Robinson, Ronnie D. Children Stories. (p. 303)
—Children's Stories. (p. 304)
—My Book of Poems (p. 1199)
Robinson, Sabra A. Micky, Ticky, Boo! Says Hello. (p. 1136)
Robinson, Shannon. Cubism: Movements in Art. (p. 389)
—Cubism. (p. 389)
Robinson, Sharon. Jackie Robinson: American Hero. (p. 904)
—Jackie Robinson: American Hero - Library Edition. (p. 904)
—Littlest Pumpkin. (p. 1039)
—Promises to Keep: How Jackie Robinson Changed America. (p. 1411)
—Slam Dunk! (p. 1587)
—Testing the Ice: A True Story about Jackie Robinson. Nelson, Kadir, illus. (p. 1723)
—Under the Same Sun. Ford, A. G., illus. (p. 1814)
Robinson, Sharon, et al. Home Economics. (p. 792)
Robinson, Shirley. Lion Who Thought He Was Handsome. (p. 1020)
—Singing Donkey. (p. 1579)
Robinson, Stephen. Duke of Cork. (p. 489)
Robinson, Stephen Edward. You Are Priceless: The Parable of the Bicycle. Sowards, Ben, illus. (p. 1973)
Robinson, Steve. Tool Town. (p. 1767)
Robinson, Sue. Bear in the Barnyard. Morris, Tony, illus. (p. 151)
Robinson, Susan, illus. see DuTemple, Leslie A.
Robinson, Susan, illus. see Langley, Jan.
Robinson, Susan G., illus. see Ramsay, Mark.
Robinson, T. H., illus. see Canton, William.
Robinson, T. H., illus. see Kingsley, Charles.
Robinson, T. J. Academy Defenders. (p. 7)
Robinson, Tanya, illus. see Merrick, Daniel.
Robinson, Tim, illus. see Schiller, David.
Robinson, Tim, illus. see Sheinkin, Steve.
Robinson, Tim, jt. auth. see Thryce, Marc.
Robinson, Timberly. Masterpiece Creation. (p. 1103)
Robinson, Timothy. What Happens When People Die? Reprint. (p. 1886)
Robinson, Tom. Andruw Jones: All-Star on & off the Field. (p. 72)
—Auto Racing: Math at the Racetrack. (p. 117)
—Barack Obama: 44th U. S. President. (p. 137)
—Basketball: Math on the Court. (p. 143)
—Basketball Skills: How to Play Like a Pro. (p. 143)
—Ben Roethlisberger: Gifted & Giving Football Star. (p. 163)
—David Beckham: Soccer's Superstar. (p. 410)
—Derek Jeter: Captain on & off the Field. (p. 427)
—Development of the Industrial United States: 1870-1900. (p. 432)
—Donovan Mcnabb: Leader on & off the Field. (p. 466)
—Evolution of News Reporting. (p. 547)
—Fibonacci Zoo Wald, Christina, illus. (p. 583)
—Football: Math on the Gridiron. (p. 615)
—Game Face: Handling Sports on & off the Field. (p. 654)
—Girls Play to Win Basketball. (p. 680)
—Hockey: Math at the Rink. (p. 786)
—Jeff Bezos: Amazon.com Architect. (p. 911)
—John McCain: POW & Statesman. (p. 922)
—Kevin Harvick: Racing to the Top. (p. 950)
—Malcolm X: Rights Activist & Nation of Islam Leader. (p. 1083)
—Mark Martin: Master Behind the Wheel. (p. 1095)
—Media Ownership. (p. 1118)
—New York Jets. (p. 1248)
—Pittsburgh Steelers. (p. 1365)
—Shaquille O'Neal: Giant on & off the Court. (p. 1561)
—Soccer: Math on the Field. (p. 1603)
—Tennessee Titans. (p. 1720)
Robinson, Tom & Blair, Beth L. Magical Science Experiments Book: Dazzle Your Friends & Family with Dozens of Science Tricks! (p. 1075)
Robinson, Tony. Bad Kids: The Naughtiest Children in History Vol. 1 (p. 131)
—Bad Kids: The Worst Behaved Children in History Vol. 1 Phillips, Mike, illus. (p. 131)
—Kings & Queens. (p. 960)
—Tony Robinson's Weird World of Wonders - World War I. (p. 1766)
—Weird World of Wonders - World War II. (p. 1873)
—Worst Children's Jobs in History. Phillips, Mike, illus. (p. 1961)
Robinson, Ty, et al. Ka-Choww! Blue Ramone. Bright, Todd et al, illus. (p. 941)
Robinson, Vickie J. Use Your Imagination. Long, Corey, illus. (p. 1827)
Robinson, Virgil E. Curse of the Cannibals. (p. 394)
Robinson, Virginia. Squid Kids. Doery, Marya, illus. (p. 1637)
Robinson, W. Heath. Adventures of Uncle Lubin. (p. 24)
Robinson, William, illus. see David, Erica.
Robinson, William E., illus. see David, Erica.
Robinson, Zan D. Ferdie the Fay Meets Flutterey the Butterfly: A Forest Fable. Maxwell, Jeremy, illus. (p. 581)
Robinson-Chavez, Kathryn A., illus. see Hayes, MJ.
Robison, C. Dan, Jr. Wind Seer: The Story of One Boy's Contribution to the Anasazi Culture. (p. 1935)
Robison, Christopher E., ed. see Pepin, Eric J.
Robison, Dan. Death Chant: Kimo's Battle with the Shamanic Forces. (p. 420)
—Kimo's Legacy: The Battle to Unite Hawaii. (p. 957)
Robison, Dan, Jr. Kimo's Escape: The Story of a Hawaiian Boy Who Learns to Believe in Himself. (p. 957)
Robison Gamble Creative, photos by. Dan & Louie: The Greatest Stories Ever Told Vol. 1 (p. 401)
Robison, Greg. Christian Rock Festivals. (p. 312)
—Coachella. (p. 336)
—Ozzfest. (p. 1316)
—Vans Warped Tour. (p. 1833)
Robison, Ken. Apolo Ohno. (p. 92)
Robison, Peggy. Prince Cody Meets A Monster. Clay, Doris, illus. (p. 1401)
—Prince Cody Runs Ahead of the Hurricane. Clay, Doris, illus. (p. 1401)
Robitaille, Jocelyn. Think Things: Book One. (p. 1734)
Robleda, Margarita. Este Soy Yo. Suarez, Maribel, illus. (p. 538)
—Jugando con Las Vocales. Suarez, Maribel, illus. (p. 931)
—Maria: Una Nina Latina en Estados Unidos. (p. 1093)
—Muneca de Trapo. Suarez, Maribel, illus. (p. 1191)
—Numeros Tragaldabas. Gurovich, Natalia, illus. (p. 1273)
—Paco: A Latino Boy in the U.S. (p. 1317)
—Patito, Donde Estas? Suarez, Maribel, illus. (p. 1328)
—Quien Soy? Adivinanzas Animales. Gurovich, Natalia, illus. (p. 1427)
—Ramon y Su Raton. Suarez, Maribel, illus. (p. 1438)
—Rebeca. Suarez, Maribel, illus. (p. 1450)
—Sana Ranita, Sana. Suarez, Maribel, illus. (p. 1510)
—Suenos. Suarez, Maribel, illus. (p. 1672)
Robleda, Maria. Jugando con Geometria. (p. 931)
Robledo, Emilia, illus. see Dale, Jay.
Robledo, Honorio, illus. see Black, Simon.
Robledo, Honorio, illus. see Hayes, Joe.
Robledo, Ronald J. Sasquatch for Dinner. Robledo, Victoria, ed. (p. 1515)
Robledo, Sol, tr. see Blair, Eric.
Robledo, Sol, tr. see Jones, Christianne C.
Robledo, Sol, tr. see Klein, Adria F.
Robledo, Sol, tr. see Meachen Rau, Dana & Picture Window Books Staff.
Robledo, Sol, tr. see Meachen Rau, Dana & Picture Window Books.
Robledo, Sol, tr. see Rosinsky, Natalie M.
Robledo, Sol, tr. see Rosinsky, Natalie M. & Picture Window Books Staff.
Robledo, Sol, tr. see Sherman, Josepha & Picture Window Books Staff.
Robledo, Sol, tr. see Sherman, Josepha.
Robledo, Sol, tr. see Stille, Darlene R.
Robledo, Sol, tr. see Stille, Darlene R. & Picture Window Books Staff.
Robledo, Sol, tr. see Thomas, Rick & Picture Window Books Staff.
Robledo Tapia, Honorio, illus. see Herrera, Juan Felipe & Herrera, Juan.
Robledo, Victoria, ed. see Robledo, Ronald J.
Robles, Anthony D. Lakas & the Makibaka Hotel /Si Lakas at Ang Makibaka Hotel. de Jesus, Eloisa D., tr. from TAG. (p. 972)
Robles, Anthony D. & Children's Book Press Staff. Lakas & the Manilatown Fish (Si Lakas at Ang Isdang Manilatown) de Jesus, Eloisa D. & de Guzman, Magdalena, trs. (p. 972)
Robles, D. & Minquini, Lourdes. 100 Mejores Acertijos Matematicos (The One Hundred Best Word Problems) (p. 1998)
Robles, David Alan. Natural History of Colorado. (p. 1235)
Robles Echeverria, Maria De Jesus & ALONSO CURIEL, Jorge David. Paisaje de Risas. DIVINCENZO, Yoselem G., illus. (p. 1319)
Robles, Eduardo. Computadora Maldita. (p. 354)
—Extrano en la Escuela. (p. 555)
—No Abras Esa Puerta! (p. 1257)
—Payaso Sin Rostro. (p. 1331)
—Sombra Vegetal. (p. 1608)
Robles, Tony. Joey Gonzalez, Great American. Pryor, Jim, illus. (p. 920)
Robley Blake, Colleen. I Can't Wait till I'm Five. (p. 837)
Robshaw, Brandon. Georgina & the Dragon. (p. 665)
—Livewire Chillers Ghost Dog. (p. 1040)
—Livewire Chillers the Underground. (p. 1040)
—Mirror. (p. 1149)
—Surgeon. (p. 1685)
Robshaw, Brandon & Scholar, Rochelle. Princess Diana. (p. 1403)
Robshaw, Brandon & Scholoar, Rochelle. Urban Myths. (p. 1825)
Robson & Kipling, Rudyard. Jungle Book (p. 935)
Robson, Claire. Outside Rules: Short Stories about Nonconformist Youth. (p. 1313)
Robson, David. Auschwitz. (p. 116)
—Black Arts Movement. (p. 195)
—Chris Rock. (p. 311)
—Colonial America. (p. 341)
robson, david. Cyclops. (p. 397)
Robson, David. Decade of The 2000s. (p. 421)
—Devil. (p. 432)
—Disaster Response. (p. 446)
—Encounters with Vampires. (p. 524)
—Israeli-Palestinian Conflict. (p. 893)
—Kennedy Assassination. (p. 948)
—Miley Cyrus. (p. 1142)
—Prince: Singer-Songwriter, Musician, & Record Producer. (p. 1401)
—Randy Moss. (p. 1438)
—Soledad O'Brien. (p. 1607)
Robson, David W. Brian Westbrook. (p. 226)
Robson, Eddie. Comic Books & Manga. (p. 348)
Robson, Eddie, jt. auth. see Pratchett, Rhianna.
Robson, Gary D. Who Pooped in Park: Grand Teton. (p. 1917)
—Who Pooped in the Black Hills? Scats & Tracks for Kids. Rath, Robert, illus. (p. 1917)
—Who Pooped in the Northwoods? (p. 1917)
—Who Pooped in the Park? Yellowstone. (p. 1917)
—Who Pooped in the Park? Clark, Elijah Brady, illus. (p. 1917)
—Who Pooped in the Park? Scat & Tracks for Kids. Rath, Robert, illus. (p. 1917)
—Who Pooped in the Park? Acadia National Park. Rath, Robert, illus. (p. 1917)
—Who Pooped in the Park? Grand Canyon National Park. Clark, Elijah Brady, illus. (p. 1917)
—Who Pooped in the Park? Red Rock Canyon National Conservation Area: Scats & Tracks for Kids. Rath, Robert, illus. (p. 1917)
—Who Pooped in the Park? Rocky Mountain National Park: Scats & Tracks for Kids. Clark, Elijah Brady, illus. (p. 1917)
—Who Pooped in the Park? Sequoia & Kings Canyon National Parks: Scats & Tracks for Kids. (p. 1917)
—Who Pooped in the Park? Shenandoah National Park: Scats & Tracks for Kids. Rath, Robert, illus. (p. 1917)
—Who Pooped in the Park? Yosemite National Park. Clark, Elijah Brady, illus. (p. 1917)
—Who Pooped in the Sonoran Desert? Scats & Tracks for Kids. Rath, Robert, illus. (p. 1917)
—Who Pooped on the Colorado Plateau? Scat & Tracks for Kids. Rath, Robert, illus. (p. 1917)
Robson, Gary D. & Rath, Robert. Who Pooped in the Park? Olympic National Park. (p. 1917)
Robson, Jenny. Savannah 2116 Ad. (p. 1516)
Robson, Kirsteen. Aliens Sticker Book. Burnett, Seb, illus. (p. 41)
—Mosaic Sticker Flowers. (p. 1176)
—My First Maze Book. (p. 1207)
—Third Big Maze Book. (p. 1734)
—Wipe-Clean Pirate Activities. (p. 1939)
—Wipe-Clean Vacation Activities. (p. 1939)
Robson, Kirsteen, ed. see Khan, Sarah.
Robson, Kirsteen & Clarke, Phil. 1000 Doodles. (p. 2001)
Robson, Kirsten. Big Maze Book. (p. 182)
Robson, Matthew, illus. see Kelleher, Damian.
Robson, Pam. First World War. (p. 597)
Robson, Pam, jt. auth. see Chapman, Gillian.
Robson, Samantha Eliza. Jack & the Cats. (p. 902)
Robus, Debbie. What to Say & Do... When You Don't Know What to Say & Do. (p. 1894)
Roby, Cynthia. Discovering STEM at the Airport. (p. 449)
—Discovering STEM at the Amusement Park. (p. 449)
—Werewolves. (p. 1875)
Roby, Cynthia A. Career As an Atf Agent. (p. 266)
Roby, Ian. Surface Diver Tommy & the Sea Critters (p. 1685)
Roby, Kinley. Death's Long Shadow. (p. 420)
Robyck, Michael. Where Is Lauren's Cat, Chaulky? (p. 1908)
Robyn Washburn. Singled Out in Center Field: Diamonds Are A Girl's Best Friend - Book One. Lisa Byers, illus. (p. 1579)
Roca, François, illus. see Brown, Tami Lewis.
Roca, François, illus. see Paterson, Katherine.
Roca, François, illus. see Prince, April Jones.
Roca, François, jt. auth. see Bernard, Fred.
Roca, Nuria. 5 Senses. Curto, Rosa Maria, illus. (p. 1992)
—Fall. (p. 566)
—Three R's: Reuse, Reduce, Recycle. Curto, Rosa Maria, illus. (p. 1743)
Roca, Nuria, jt. auth. see Moore-Mallinos, Jennifer.
Roca, Núria, et al. Earth. (p. 495)
—Moon. (p. 1171)
—Sun. (p. 1675)
Rocamore, Carol. Acts of Courage: Václav Havel's Life in the Theater. (p. 10)
Rocan, Susan. Withershins. (p. 1942)
Rocco, illus. see Gillot, Laurence & Sebaoun, Elisabeth.
Rocco, Joe, illus. see Diviny, Sean.
Rocco, John. Blackout. Rocco, John, illus. (p. 197)
—Blizzard. Rocco, John, illus. (p. 199)
—Fu Finds the Way. Rocco, John, illus. (p. 646)
—Super Hair-O & the Barber of Doom. Rocco, John, illus. (p. 1680)
Rocco, John, illus. see Eaton, Jason Carter.
Rocco, John, illus. see Kudlinski, Kathleen V.
Rocco, John, illus. see Paterson, Katherine & Paterson, John B.
Rocco, John, illus. see Paterson, Katherine & Paterson, John.
Rocco, John, illus. see Patten, E. J.
Rocco, John, illus. see Riordan, Rick.
Rocco, John, illus. see Tarpley, Todd.
Rocco, John & Primiano, Jay. Swim That Rock. Rocco, John, illus. (p. 1691)
Rocha, Toni. Magic in the Air. (p. 1072)
Rocha, Toni L. Careers in Magazine Publishing. (p. 268)
—Coping When Someone in Your Family Has Cancer. (p. 365)
Roche, Art. Art for Kids: Comic Strips - Create Your Own Comic Strips from Start to Finish. (p. 102)
—Art for Kids: Cartooning: The Only Cartooning Book You'll Ever Need to Be the Artist You've Always Wanted to Be. (p. 102)
Roche, Denis. Best Class Picture Ever! (p. 168)
Roche, Denis, illus. see Evans, Lezlie.
Roche, Denis, illus. see London, Jonathan.
Roche, Jackie. Derby Ram. (p. 427)
Roche, Judith, ed. Bottom of Heaven: Artwork & Poetry of the Remann Hall Women's Project. (p. 215)
Roche, Louise. Amazing Adventures of Libby Lightfoot: Book 1: Book 1. (p. 52)
Roche, Lynne. Happiest Christmas. (p. 744)
Roche, Maite. Beautiful Story of Jesus. Roche, Maite, illus. (p. 154)
—Bible for Little Ones. (p. 175)
—First Noel. Roche, Maite, illus. (p. 596)
—Gospel for Little Ones. (p. 703)
—My First Bedtime Prayers. (p. 1204)
—My First Pictures of Easter. (p. 1207)
—My First Pictures of Jesus. (p. 1207)
Roche, Patricia Jo. I Am More Than a Name. (p. 833)
Roche, Tim. Soldiers of the Civil War (p. 1607)
Rochea, Vanessa. Kamlyn's Journal (p. 942)
Rocheleau, Nicole. Ollie Ollie in Come Free! (p. 1287)
—Ryan, Me, & the Mysterious Book. (p. 1499)
Rocheleau, Paul, photos by see McLaughlin, David.
Rocheleau, Paul, photos by see Thorne-Thomsen, Kathleen.
Rochelin, Ghyslaine. Coconut Tree. Bertoni, Oliver, illus. (p. 337)
Rochelle, Maria. Jasmine at Work. Linsdell, Jo, illus. (p. 910)
Rochelle, Warren. Called. (p. 254)
Rocherolle, Eugenie. Eugenie Rocherolle Keyboard Capers. (p. 540)
Rochester, Andre. Sunflower & Rose. (p. 1676)
Rochester, B. Joey Jenkins Mysteries: Something Is Missing at Redding Lake. (p. 920)
Rochester, Geneva. Day at the Beach. (p. 412)
—Day at the Beach, a Colorful Version. (p. 412)
Rochester, Karen. Be Brave. Chadwick, Kat, illus. (p. 148)
Rochester, Mary Frances. Turquoise Monkey. (p. 1798)
Rochkind, Pat. McGooster & Mcgyman Begin Their Adventures. Wozniak, Patricia A., illus. (p. 1114)
Rochman, Hazel & McCampbell, Darlene Z., eds. Who do you Think you Are? (p. 1915)
Rocini, Mary L. Getting Ready. (p. 669)
Rocío, Martínez Pérez, jt. auth. see Martinez, Rocio.
Rocio, Mejia. Celebrando Dia de Muertos: Celebrating Day of the Dead. (p. 283)
Rock. My Angel. (p. 1196)
Rock & Piper, Sophie. Lion Read & Know Bible. Lewis, Anthony, illus. (p. 1020)
Rock, Brian. Deductive Detective Rogers, Sherry, illus. (p. 422)
—Don't Play with Your Food! Moerner, John, illus. (p. 468)
—With All My Heart. Banta, Susan, illus. (p. 1942)
Rock, Brian & Rogers, Sherry. Detective Deductivo Rogers, Sherry, illus. (p. 431)
Rock, Howard, illus. see Kittredge, Frances.
Rock, J. K. Camp Payback. (p. 257)
Rock, Jonathan. Night Riders (p. 1254)
—Out of Bounds Bk. 1 (p. 1311)
—Search & Rescue Bk. 2 (p. 1537)
—White Water (p. 1913)
Rock, Lois. Al Final del Dia. Rawlings, Louise, illus. (p. 32)
—Canoeing & Kayaking. (p. 261)
—Child's First Book of Prayers. Jay, Alison, illus. (p. 304)
—Estrella Que Brilló. Rawlings, Louise, illus. (p. 538)
—First Christmas. Allsopp, Sophie, illus. (p. 593)
—First Rainbow. Allsopp, Sophie, illus. (p. 596)
—Gift for Baby's Christening. Rescek, Sanja, illus. (p. 675)
—Gift for Baby's Dedication. Rescek, Sanja, illus. (p. 675)
—God Bless. Widdowson, Kay, illus. (p. 688)
—Goodnight. (p. 701)
—Gran Noticia. Rawlings, Louise, illus. (p. 707)
—Here I Am. Widdowson, Kay, illus. (p. 770)
—In the Beginning - Bible Stories for Little Hands. Bolam, Emily, illus. (p. 865)
—Jesus Is Born: A Spot-the-Difference Jigsaw Book. Bolam, Emily, illus. (p. 915)
—Journey into the Bible. Rowland, Andrew, illus. (p. 928)
—Lion Bible to Keep for Ever. Allsopp, Sophie, illus. (p. 1020)
—Lion Children's Bible: The World's Greatest Story Retold for Every Child. Cox, Carolyn, illus. (p. 1020)
—Lion First Book of Nursery Stories. Vagnozzi, Barbara, illus. (p. 1020)
—Lion First Book of Parables. Vagnozzi, Barbara, illus. (p. 1020)
—Little Life of Jesus. (p. 1030)
—Little Life of Jesus - To Read & Treasure. Langton, Roger W., illus. (p. 1030)
—Look Inside the Time of Jesus. Orlandi, Lorenzo, illus. (p. 1049)
—Lord's Prayer: And Other Classic Prayers for Children. Allsopp, Sophie, illus. (p. 1053)
—Lost Sheep & Other Bible Stories for Little Hands. Bolam, Emily, illus. (p. 1056)
—My Very First Bible & Prayers Ayliffe, Alex, illus. (p. 1221)
—My Very First Bible Stories Bumper Sticker Book. Ayliffe, Alex, illus. (p. 1221)
—My Very First Nativity Play. (p. 1221)
—Noah's Ark: A Spot-the-Difference Jigsaw Book. Bolam, Emily, illus. (p. 1261)
—Noah's Ark. Allsopp, Sophie, illus. (p. 1261)
—Now We Have a Baby. Massey, Jane, illus. (p. 1269)

—Our Father: And Other Classic Prayers for Children. Allsopp, Sophie, illus. (p. 1308)
—Prayers for Baby's Christening. Rescek, Sanja, illus. (p. 1393)
—Prayers for Your Confirmation. Firmin, Hannah, illus. (p. 1393)
—Saintly Tales & Legends. Balit, Christina, illus. (p. 1504)
—Thank You, God. Widdowson, Kay, illus. (p. 1725)
—Tiny Tots Bible. Widdowson, Kay, illus. (p. 1757)
—Todos los Dias Contigo. Rawlings, Louise, illus. (p. 1761)
—Viaje Por la Biblia. Pimentel, Alejandro, tr. (p. 1839)
—Who Is Jesus? (p. 1916)
Rock, Lois, jt. auth. see Archbold, Tim.
Rock, Lois, jt. auth. see Piper, Sophie.
Rock, Lois & Lush, Debbie. Lord's Prayer & Ten Commandments: Bible Words to Know & Treasure. (p. 1053)
Rock, Lois & Piper, Sophie. Noah & the Flood. Corke, Estelle, illus. (p. 1261)
Rock, Lois, et al. Beibl y Plant Lleiaf. (p. 160)
Rock, Maria. MiMi's Garden, It's a Kid Thing! A Guide for Beginning Gardeners. (p. 1145)
Rock, Maya. Scripted. (p. 1533)
Rock, Michelle L. Nighttime Adventures Counting Sheep. Longmore, Nickolai, illus. (p. 1255)
Rock 'N Learn, creator. Addition & Subtraction Rap. (p. 12)
Rock 'n' Roll Camp for Girls Staff. Rock 'n' Roll Camp for Girls: How to Start a Band, Write Songs, Record an Album, & Rock Out!! (p. 1482)
Rock, Nathaniel. Math for Everyone Combo Book: 7th Grade Math, Algebra I, Geometry I, Algebra II, Math Analysis, Calculus. (p. 1106)
Rock, Nathaniel Max. Math Is Easy So Easy, Combo Book. (p. 1106)
Rock, Nora. Fly Away (p. 609)
Rock Spring Elementary. Roadrunner Writing Rocks! (p. 1477)
Rock, Stella, ed. see Brinks, Jan Herman.
Rock, Zack. Homer Henry Hudson's Curio Museum. (p. 793)
Rockas, Leo. Mice Make War. (p. 1134)
Rockefeller, Matt, illus. see Heos, Bridget.
Rocker, Megan. How It Happens at the Cereal Company. Wolfe, Bob & Wolfe, Diane, photos by. (p. 810)
—How It Happens at the Fireworks Factory. Wolfe, Bob & Wolfe, Diane, photos by. (p. 810)
Rockett, Andrew M., jt. auth. see Berresford, Geoffrey C.
Rockett, Paul. 100 Trillion Good Bacteria Living in the Human Body. Ruffle, Mark, illus. (p. 1999)
—30 Million Different Insects in the Rain Forest. Ruffle, Mark, illus. (p. 1996)
—70 Thousand Million, Million, Million Stars in Space. Ruffle, Mark, illus. (p. 1998)
—Big Countdown. Ruffle, Mark, illus. (p. 180)
—Pieter Bruegel. (p. 1357)
—Seven Quintillion, Five Hundred Quadrillion Grains of Sand on Planet Earth. Ruffle, Mark, illus. (p. 1554)
—Ten Thousand, Eight Hundred & Twenty Endangered Species in the Animal Kingdom. Ruffle, Mark, illus. (p. 1719)
Rockey, Megan. Phantom. (p. 1349)
Rockfield, Darryl, illus. see Beeson, Lea Ann.
Rockford, Nancy, illus. see Surace, Joan.
Rockhill, Dennis. Meadow Dance. (p. 1116)
—Polar Slumber. (p. 1379)
—Polar Slumber. Rockhill, Dennis, illus. (p. 1379)
—Polar Slumber/Sueño Polar. Raven Tree Press Staff, ed. (p. 1379)
—Sueno Polar. (p. 1672)
Rockis, Gary. Solid State Fundamentals: Answer Key. (p. 1607)
—Solid State Fundamentals. (p. 1607)
Rockis, Gary & Mazur, Glen A. Electrical Motor Controls for Integrated Systems: Text. (p. 509)
—Electrical Motor Controls for Integrated Systems: Answer Key. (p. 509)
Rockitter, Leslie. Chester, the Water-Loving, Pool-Hopping, Salad-Eating, St Bernard Dog. (p. 298)
Rockley, Frank. Tinderbox Cottage. (p. 1755)
Rockliff, Mara. Al lado de una Hormiga: Next to an Ant. Constantin, Pascale, illus. (p. 32)
—Chik Chak Shabbat. Brooker, Kyrsten, illus. (p. 301)
—Get Real: What Kind of World Are You Buying? (p. 668)
—Gingerbread for Liberty! How a German Baker Helped Win the American Revolution. Kirsch, Vincent X., illus. (p. 677)
—Grudge Keeper Wheeler, Eliza, illus. (p. 727)
—Me & Momma & Big John. Low, William, illus. (p. 1115)
—Mesmerized: How Ben Franklin Solved a Mystery That Baffled All of France. Bruno, Iacopo, illus. (p. 1129)
—Next to an Ant. Constantin, Pascale, illus. (p. 1249)
—Pieces of Another World Alikhan, Salima, illus. (p. 1356)
Rocklin, Joanne. Five Lives of Our Cat Zook. (p. 601)
—Fleabrain Loves Franny. (p. 603)
—I Say Shehechiyanu. Filipina, Monika, illus. (p. 845)
—One Day & One Amazing Morning on Orange Street. (p. 1294)
—This Book Is Haunted. Adinolfi, JoAnn, illus. (p. 1735)
Rockne, Knute. Four Winners: The Head, the Hands, the Foot, the Ball. (p. 625)
Rocks, Tim. Bathroom Jokes: For Kids of All Ages. (p. 144)
—Gross-Out Jokes: For Kids of All Ages. (p. 725)
—Knock-Knock Jokes: For Kids of All Ages. (p. 965)
Rockwell, jt. auth. see Rockwell, Anne F.
Rockwell, Anne. Apples & Pumpkins. Rockwell, Lizzy, illus. (p. 92)
—Bugs Are Insects. Jenkins, Steve, illus. (p. 237)
—My Spring Robin. Rockwell, Harlow, illus. (p. 1219)
—One Bean. (p. 1293)
Rockwell, Anne & Iwai, Melissa. Truck Stop. (p. 1791)
Rockwell, Anne F. Apples & Pumpkins. Rockwell, Lizzy, illus. (p. 92)
—At the Beach. Rockwell, Harlow & Rockwell, Lizzy, illus. (p. 110)
—At the Firehouse. Rockwell, Anne F., illus. (p. 111)
—At the Police Station. (p. 111)
—Backyard Bear. Halsey, Megan, illus. (p. 130)
—Big George: How a Shy Boy Became President Washington. Trueman, Matthew & Phelan, Matt, illus. (p. 181)
—Big Wheels. (p. 184)
—Clouds. (p. 335)
—Clouds. Lessac, Frané, illus. (p. 335)
—Father's Day. Rockwell, Lizzy, illus. (p. 577)
—First Day of School. (p. 594)
—First Day of School. Rockwell, Lizzy, illus. (p. 594)
—Four Seasons Make a Year. Halsey, Megan, illus. (p. 625)
—Hey, Charleston! The True Story of the Jenkins Orphanage Band. Bootman, Colin, illus. (p. 774)
—How Kittens Grow. (p. 810)
—Katie Catz Makes a Splash. Meisel, Paul, illus. (p. 945)
—My Preschool. Rockwell, Anne F., illus. (p. 1217)
—Other Double Agent: The True Story of James Armistead Lafayette, the Revolutionary Spy No One Has Ever Heard of (Because He Didn't Get Caught) Cooper, Floyd, illus. (p. 1306)
—Presidents' Day. Rockwell, Lizzy, illus. (p. 1397)
—St. Patrick's Day. Rockwell, Lizzy, illus. (p. 1638)
—They Called Her Molly Pitcher. von Buhler, Cynthia, illus. (p. 1732)
—Trucks. (p. 1791)
—Welcome to Kindergarten. Rockwell, Anne F., illus. (p. 1873)
—What's So Bad about Gasoline? Fossil Fuels & What They Do. Meisel, Paul, illus. (p. 1899)
—Who Lives in an Alligator Hole? Rockwell, Lizzy, illus. (p. 1916)
—Why Are the Ice Caps Melting? The Dangers of Global Warming. Meisel, Paul, illus. (p. 1922)
Rockwell, Anne F. & Rockwell. 100 School Days. Rockwell, Lizzy, illus. (p. 1999)
—Brendan & Belinda & the Slam Dunk! Meisel, Paul, illus. (p. 226)
—Honey in a Hive. Schindler, S. D., illus. (p. 794)
—Who Lives in an Alligator Hole? Rockwell, Lizzy, illus. (p. 1916)
Rockwell, Anne F. & Rockwell, Harlow. Toolbox. Rockwell, Anne F. & Rockwell, Harlow, illus. (p. 1767)
Rockwell, Barry, illus. see Douglas, Babette.
Rockwell, Carey. On the Trail of Space Pirates. (p. 1291)
—On the Trail of Space Pirates. Ley, Willy, ed. (p. 1291)
—Revolt on Venus: The TOM CORBETT Space Cadet Adventure. (p. 1466)
—Revolt on Venus. (p. 1466)
—Sabotage in Space. (p. 1500)
—Space Pioneers. (p. 1619)
Rockwell, Carey & Ley, Willy. Space Pioneers: A Tom Corbett Space Cadet Adventure. Glanzman, Louis, illus. (p. 1619)
—Treachery in Outer Space: A Tom Corbett Space Cadet Adventure. Glanzman, Louis, illus. (p. 1781)
Rockwell, D. R. Jessicas: The Adventures of Five City Girls. (p. 914)
Rockwell, David, et al. Spectacle. (p. 1624)
Rockwell, Eve. Make Your Own Christmas Cards. (p. 1079)
Rockwell, Harlow, illus. see Rockwell, Anne F.
Rockwell, Harlow, illus. see Rockwell, Anne.
Rockwell, Harlow, jt. auth. see Rockwell, Anne F.
Rockwell, Joanna, illus. see Souliere, Lisa.
Rockwell, Lizzy. Bird Is a Bird. Rockwell, Lizzy, illus. (p. 190)
—Busy Body Book: A Kid's Guide to Fitness. Rockwell, Lizzy, illus. (p. 245)
—Busy Body Book: A Kid's Guide to Fitness. (p. 246)
—Good Enough to Eat: A Kid's Guide to Food & Nutrition. Rockwell, Lizzy, illus. (p. 698)
—Plants Feed Me. (p. 1370)
—Plants Feed Me. Rockwell, Lizzy, illus. (p. 1370)
Rockwell, Lizzy, illus. see Angelou, Maya.
Rockwell, Lizzy, illus. see Hulme, Joy N.
Rockwell, Lizzy, illus. see Jenkins, Priscilla Belz.
Rockwell, Lizzy, illus. see Rockwell, Anne F.
Rockwell, Lizzy, illus. see Rockwell, Anne F. & Rockwell.
Rockwell, Lizzy, illus. see Rockwell, Anne.
Rockwell, Lizzy & Fowler, Allan. What's the Weather? (p. 1900)
Rockwell, Norman, illus. see Public Domain Staff.
Rockwell, Norman & Public Domain Staff. You're a Grand Old Flag. (p. 1982)
Rockwell, Richard, illus. see Polsky, Milton & Gilead, Jack.
Rockwell, Scott, illus. see Barks, Carl.
Rockwell, Thomas. How to Eat Fried Worms. (p. 819)
—How to Eat Fried Worms. McCully, Emily Arnold, illus. (p. 819)
—How to Fight a Girl. (p. 819)
Rockwood, Leigh. Allosaurus. (p. 47)
—Ancient Egyptian Culture. (p. 68)
—Ancient Egyptian Daily Life. (p. 69)
—Ancient Egyptian Economy. (p. 69)
—Ancient Egyptian Geography. (p. 69)
—Ancient Egyptian Government. (p. 69)
—Ancient Egyptian Technology. (p. 69)
—Ankylosaurus. (p. 84)
—Brachiosaurus. (p. 221)
—Chimpanzees Are Smart! (p. 306)
—Creepy Crawlies (p. 381)
—Diplodocus. (p. 445)
—Dogs Are Smart! (p. 462)
—Dolphins Are Smart! (p. 465)
—Flies & Maggots Are Gross! (p. 604)
—Hadrosaurus. (p. 735)
—Horses Are Smart! (p. 800)
—Iguanodon. (p. 856)
—Parrots Are Smart! (p. 1325)
—Pigs Are Smart! (p. 1358)
—Plesiosaurus. (p. 1374)
—Pteranodon. (p. 1413)
—Slugs Are Gross! (p. 1591)
—Stegosaurus. (p. 1646)
—T. Rex. (p. 1694)
—Tell Me the Difference Between a Bee & a Wasp. (p. 1716)
—Tell Me the Difference Between a Frog & a Toad. (p. 1716)
—Tell Me the Difference Between a Porcupine & a Hedgehog. (p. 1716)
—Tell Me the Difference Between a Rabbit & a Hare. (p. 1716)
—Tell Me the Difference Between a Seal & a Sea Lion. (p. 1716)
—Tell Me the Difference Between an Alligator & a Crocodile. (p. 1716)
—Triceratops. (p. 1785)
—V Ancient Egyptian Geography. (p. 1829)
—Velociraptor. (p. 1835)
Rockwood, Leigh, jt. auth. see Clark, Willow.
Rockwood, Roy. Dave Dashaway & His Hydroplane. (p. 410)
—Jack North's Treasure Hunt: Or, Daring Adventures in South America. (p. 903)
—Lost on the Moon. (p. 1056)
—On a Torn-Away World: Or, the Captives of the Great Earthquake. (p. 1288)
—On a Torn-Away World. (p. 1288)
—Through Space to Mars. (p. 1745)
—Under the Ocean to the South Pole. (p. 1813)
—Under the Ocean to the South Pole. (p. 1814)
—Under the Ocean to the South Pole or the Strange Cruise of the Submarine Wonder. (p. 1814)
—Wizard of the Se. (p. 1943)
—Wizard of the Sea. (p. 1943)
Rockworth, Janice. Juelz Santana. (p. 931)
—Nas. (p. 1230)
—Wu-Tang Clan. (p. 1965)
Rocky Porch Moore. It's Farm Market Day! (p. 896)
Rocque, Rose, illus. see Mosher, Geraldine.
Rod and Staff Publishers, Inc Staff, contrib. by. My Little Bird Book. (p. 1212)
Rod and Staff Publishers Staff, contrib. by. My Little Flower Book. (p. 1212)
Rodanas, Kristina. Blind Hunter Rodanas, Kristina, illus. (p. 199)
—Yonder Mountain: A Cherokee Legend (p. 1972)
Rodanas, Kristina, illus. see London, Jonathan.
Rodari, Gianni. One & Seven. Anglin, David, tr. from ITA. (p. 1293)
Rodarmor, William, jt. auth. see Prévost, Guillaume.
Rodarmor, William, tr. see Audouin-Mamikonian, Princess Sophie.
Rodarmor, William, tr. see Lehmann, Christian.
Rodarmor, William, tr. see Place, Francois.
Rodarmor, William, tr. see Prevost, Guillaume.
Rodarmor, Williams, tr. see Audouin-Mamikonian, Princess Sophie.
Rodda, Bob. For the Fun of It: The Story of the 2001 Wooster, Ohio, Williamsport Little League Team's Tournament Run to the State Playoffs. (p. 616)
Rodda, Emily. Charm Bracelet Bk. 1. Vitale, Raoul, illus. (p. 294)
—Charm Bracelet. Vitale, Raoul, illus. (p. 294)
—City of the Rats. (p. 324)
—Dead End. (p. 416)
—Deltora Quest 1. Niwano, Makoto, illus. (p. 425)
—Deltora Quest 2. Niwano, Makoto, illus. (p. 425)
—Deltora Quest #2: the Lake of Tears. (p. 425)
—Deltora Quest 3. (p. 425)
—Deltora Quest 4. (p. 425)
—Deltora Quest #4: the Shifting Sands. (p. 425)
—Deltora Quest 5. (p. 425)
—Deltora Quest #5: Dread Mountain. (p. 425)
—Deltora Quest 6. (p. 425)
—Deltora Quest #6: the Maze of the Beast. (p. 425)
—Deltora Quest 7. (p. 425)
—Deltora Quest #7: the Valley of the Lost. (p. 425)
—Deltora Quest 8. (p. 425)
—Deltora Quest 9. (p. 425)
—Deltora Shadowlands. McBride, Marc, illus. (p. 425)
—Flower Fairies. Vitale, Raoul, illus. (p. 607)
—Ghost of Raven Hill. (p. 671)
—Golden Door. (p. 694)
—Isle of the Dead. (p. 893)
—Key to Rondo. (p. 950)
—Last Fairy-Apple Tree. Vitale, Raoul, illus. (p. 977)
—Rainbow Wand. Vitale, Raoul, illus. (p. 1436)
—Return to Del. (p. 1465)
—Rowan & the Ice Creepers. (p. 1492)
—Rowan & the Travelers. (p. 1492)
—Rowan & the Zebak. (p. 1492)
—Rowan of Rin. (p. 1492)
—Secrets of Deltora McBride, Marc, illus. (p. 1545)
—Shadowgate. (p. 1558)
—Silver Door. (p. 1576)
—Sister of the South. (p. 1581)
—Star Cloak. Vitale, Raoul, illus. (p. 1640)
—Third Door. (p. 1734)
—Third Wish. Vitale, Raoul, illus. (p. 1734)
—Unicorn. Vitale, Raoul, illus. (p. 1818)
—Water Sprites. Vitale, Raoul, illus. (p. 1863)
—Wizard of Rondo. (p. 1943)
Rodda, Geri. flu & You. (p. 608)
—Lyme in Rhyme. (p. 1066)
Roddam, Holly M. Forever I'll Be Thankful. (p. 619)
—Little Child of God: Growing the Fruit of the Spirit. (p. 1026)
Roddick, Melissa. Time for Gym Class: Count to Tell the Number of Objects. (p. 1751)
Roddie, Shen. Baby Goes Too. Stojic, Manya, illus. (p. 126)
—Gossipy Parrot. Terry, Michael, tr. (p. 703)
—Gossipy Parrot. Terry, Michael, illus. (p. 703)
—You're Too Small! Lavis, Steve, illus. (p. 1982)
Roddie, Shen & Quarto Generic Staff. Best of Friends! Lamb, Sally Ann, illus. (p. 170)
Roddy, Lauren S. My Scriptural Rosary. Darrenkamp, Julia Mary, illus. (p. 1218)
Roddy, Lee. Case of the Dangerous Cruise. (p. 274)
—City Bear's Adventures. (p. 323)
—Dangerous Canoe Race. (p. 404)
—Dooger, the Grasshopper Hound. (p. 470)
—Escape down the Raging Rapids. (p. 534)
—Eye of the Hurricane. (p. 557)
—Ghost Dog of Stoney Ridge. (p. 670)
—Ghost of the Moaning Mansion. (p. 671)
—Hair-Pulling Bear Dog. (p. 736)
—Hermit of Mad River. (p. 771)
—Hunted in the Alaskan Wilderness. (p. 828)
—Legend of Fire. (p. 988)
—Legend of the White Raccoon. (p. 989)
—Mad Dog of Lobo Mountain. (p. 1069)
—Mystery of the Black Hole Mine. (p. 1225)
—Mystery of the Island Jungle. (p. 1225)
—Mystery of the Wild Surfer. (p. 1226)
—Night of the Vanishing Lights. (p. 1254)
—Panic in the Wild Waters. (p. 1321)
—Peril at Pirate's Point. (p. 1343)
—Secret of the Shark Pit. (p. 1543)
—Secret of the Sunken Sub. (p. 1543)
—Stranded on Terror Island. (p. 1664)
—Terror at Forbidden Falls. (p. 1722)
—Tracked by the Wolf Pack. (p. 1775)
Roddy, Nikki. How to Fight, Lie & Cry Your Way to Popularity (And a Prom Date) Lousy Life Lessons from 50 Teen Movies. (p. 819)
Roddy, Ruth Mae. More Minute Monologues for Kids: Contemporary Scene-Study Pieces for Kids. (p. 1174)
Roddy-Worsham, Clara. Bear Baby & New Baby Forever. (p. 150)
—Bear Baby Goes Fishing. (p. 150)
—Bear Baby's Birthday Gift. (p. 150)
Rode, Linda & Moodie, Fiona. In the Never-Ever Wood. (p. 866)
Rode, Linda, et al. I, a Living Arrow. (p. 831)
Rode, Maureen. Day with Little Duke. Kinstle Nocera, Suzanne, illus. (p. 415)
Rode, Nikki, et al. Welcome to Suburbia/Bienvenido A Suburbia. (p. 1873)
Rodecker, Ron. Hello, Dragons! Hola, Dragones! Mathieu, Joe, illus. (p. 763)
Rodee, Marian. Weaving of the Southwest (p. 1870)
Rodell, Scott M. Chinese Swordsmanship - the Yang Family Taiji Jian Tradition. (p. 308)
Rodenas, Antonia. Punado de Besos. (p. 1416)
Rodenberg, Charlotte Vivian. Bronto, Friend of Ceratops: Friend of Ceratops. Rodenberg, Charlotte Vivian, illus. (p. 230)
Rodenbur, Susan. Boy Who Captured the Sun. Kirkpatrick, Karen, illus. (p. 219)
Rodenburg, Michelle. Good Germ. (p. 698)
Röder, Marlene. In the River Darkness. (p. 867)
—In the River Darkness. Reichel, Tammi, tr. (p. 867)
Roderick, Judith. Katie the Kangaroo & Her Five Acts of Kindness. (p. 945)
Roderick, Judith A. Charlie the Cat: Charlie Teaches Others a Lesson about Honesty. (p. 293)
—Connie the Caterpillar: Connie Teaches Others a Lesson of True Beauty. (p. 358)
Roderick, Stacey & Warwick, Ellen. Centsibility: The Planet Girl Guide to Money. Melnychuk, Monika, illus. (p. 287)
Roderick, Timothy. Briar Blackwood's Grimmest of Fairytales. (p. 227)
Roderman, Anna Marie. Two Tales of Courage. (p. 1804)
Rodger, Ellen. Biography of Potatoes. (p. 189)
—Biography of Spices. (p. 189)
—Bloodsucking Lice & Fleas. (p. 201)
—Building a Green Community. (p. 238)
—Fetal Alcohol Spectrum Disorder. (p. 582)
—How Does the Canadian Government Work? (p. 809)
—Hurricane Katrina. (p. 830)
—Is There a Future for Fossil Fuels? (p. 890)
—Lewis & Clark: Opening the American West. (p. 1004)
—Recycling Waste. (p. 1453)
—Reducing Your Foodprint: Farming, Cooking, & Eating for a Healthy Planet. (p. 1456)
—What Is the Judicial Branch? (p. 1890)
Rodger, Ellen, jt. auth. see Corporate Contributor Staff.
Rodger, Ellen, jt. auth. see Gleason, Carrie.
Rodger, Ellen & Field, Jon Eben. Social Justice Activist. (p. 1604)
Rodger, Ellen & Gleason, Carrie. Human Rights Activist. (p. 826)
Rodger, Ellen & Gowsell, Rosie. Fetal Alcohol Spectrum Disorder. (p. 582)
Rodger, Jessie, jt. auth. see Rodger, Marguerite.
Rodger, Marguerite. Autism Spectrum Disorder. (p. 117)
—Hydroelectric Power: Power from Moving Water. (p. 831)
—Party & Club Drugs. (p. 1326)
—Termites & Other Home Wreckers. (p. 1721)
Rodger, Marguerite & Rodger, Jessie. Racism & Prejudice. (p. 1432)
Rodger, Victor. Sons. (p. 1613)
Rodgers, Alan. Cloud Cover. (p. 334)
Rodgers, Alan & Streluk, Angella. Cloud Cover (p. 334)
—Forecasting the Weather (p. 617)
—Precipitation (p. 1394)
—Scotland. (p. 1530)
—Temperature (p. 1717)
—Wind & Air Pressure (p. 1935)
Rodgers and Hammerstein Organization Staff & Lindsay and Crouse Staff. Sound of Music: A Classic Collectible Pop-Up. Andreasen, Dan, illus. (p. 1615)
Rodgers, Barbara. Bible Activities in a Snap: Holidays. (p. 175)
—Bible Outreach Activities: Ages 4-5. (p. 175)
—Bible Outreach Activities: Grades 1-2. (p. 176)
—Bible Outreach Activities: Grades 3-4. (p. 176)
Rodgers, Catherine. Totally Cool Nails: 50 Fun & Easy Nail Art Designs for Kids. (p. 1771)
Rodgers, Dan. I Thought You Brought the Can Opener: And Other Tales of Outdoor Adventure. (p. 846)
Rodgers, Denise. Great Lakes Rhythm & Rhyme. Martin, Julie, illus. (p. 717)
—Great Lakes Rhythmn & Rhyme (p. 717)
—Little Bit of Nonsense. Martin, Julie, illus. (p. 1024)
Rodgers, Emily Puckett, jt. auth. see Roslund, Samantha.
Rodgers, Emily Puckett & Fontichiaro, Kristin. Creative Commons. (p. 379)
Rodgers, Frank. Little T & Lizard the Wizard Rodgers, Frank, illus. (p. 1037)
—Little T & the Royal Roar Rodgers, Frank, illus. (p. 1037)
—Mr. Croc's Silly Sock Rodgers, Frank, illus. (p. 1184)
—Mr. Croc's Walk Rodgers, Frank, illus. (p. 1184)

R

—Ruidos en la Noche. (p. 1494)
Rodgers, Frank, illus. see Ironside, Virgina & Ironside, Virginia.
Rodgers, Greg, as told by. Chukfi Rabbit's Big, Bad Bellyache: A Trickster Tale. (p. 318)
Rodgers Hill, Carol A. What Every Woman Wished She Had Known At 15: Plain Talk on God's Plan for Sex & Relationships. (p. 1884)
Rodgers, Ilona. Musgrove in Kensington Gardens. (p. 1193)
—Musgrove There's Something in My Shoe. (p. 1193)
—Nanny Musgrove & the New Baby. (p. 1229)
Rodgers, John, illus. see King, Mike.
Rodgers, Katherine, jt. auth. see Mills, Nathan.
Rodgers, Kelly. Byzantine Empire: A Society That Shaped the World. (p. 249)
—Doing Your Part: Serving Your Community (p. 463)
—Justinian I: Byzantine Emperor. (p. 940)
—Leaders in the Texas Revolution: United for a Cause. (p. 981)
—Lideres de la Revolucion de Texas (Leaders in the Texas Revolution) (p. 1007)
—Our Nation's Capital: Washington, DC (p. 1309)
—Remembering Our Heroes: Veterans Day (p. 1459)
—Revolucion de Texas. (p. 1466)
—Texas Revolution: Fighting for Independence. (p. 1724)
Rodgers, Kirsteen. Gran Libro del Microscopio. (p. 706)
Rodgers, Linda. King Joe's Garden: Unit 2: Data Analysis, Statistics & Probability (p. 958)
Rodgers, Maceo. Don't Mess with Grandmother. (p. 468)
Rodgers, Mary. Freaky Friday. (p. 632)
—Summer Switch. (p. 1675)
Rodgers, Mary & Hach, Heather. Freaky Monday. (p. 632)
Rodgers, Mary, ed. Freaky Friday. (p. 632)
Rodgers, Paul. Mind Books. (p. 1145)
Rodgers, Phillip W. When Was God Born? (p. 1905)
Rodgers, Phillip W., illus. see Cook, Julia.
Rodgers, Rebecca. Shanna Banana Shines. (p. 1559)
Rodgers, Richard & Hammerstein, Oscar, II. My Favorite Things. Graef, Renee, illus. (p. 1203)
Rodhe, Paul. Kids Meet the Dinosaurs. (p. 954)
Rodhe, Paul, jt. auth. see Beatrice, Paul.
Rodhe, Paul & Beatrice, Paul. Kids Meet the Dinosaurs. (p. 954)
—Kids Meet the Presidents 2nd Edition. (p. 954)
Rodhe, Paul & Wallas Reidy, Sarah. Little Plum Tree. Margolis, Al & Young, Bill, illus. (p. 1033)
Rodhe, Paul, et al. Kids Meet the Bugs. (p. 954)
Rodi, Rob. Crossovers. Mauricet et al, illus. (p. 385)
Rodi, Robert & Richards, Cliff. Rogue: Going Rogue. (p. 1485)
Rodkey, Geoff. Blue Sea Burning. (p. 203)
—Deadweather & Sunrise. (p. 418)
—Tapper Twins Go to War (with Each Other) (p. 1706)
Rodkin, Henry H. & Bernasconi, Pablo. Wizard, the Ugly & the Book of Shame. (p. 1943)
Rodman, Dennis & Warburton, Dustin. Dennis the Wild Bull. (p. 426)
Rodman, Mary Ann. Camp K-9 Hayashi, Nancy, illus. (p. 257)
—First Grade Stinks! Spiegel, Beth, illus. (p. 595)
—My Best Friend. Lewis, E. B., illus. (p. 1196)
—My Best Friend. Lewis, Earl & Lewis, E. B., illus. (p. 1196)
—Tree for Emmy Mai-Wyss, Tatjana, illus. (p. 1783)
—Yankee Girl. (p. 1968)
Rodman, Mercedes. My Blue Butterfly. (p. 1198)
Rodman, Sean. Dead Run (p. 417)
—Final Crossing (p. 586)
—Infiltration (p. 873)
Rodney, Janet, creator. Moon on an Oarblade Rowing: Crystals the Book of Craving Orphydice. (p. 1172)
Rodomista, Kim. 101 Cool Pool Games for Children: Fun & Fitness for Swimmers of All Levels. Patterson, Robin, illus. (p. 1999)
Rodomista, Kim & Patterson, Robin. 101 Cool Pool Games for Children: Fun & Fitness for Swimmers of All Levels. (p. 1999)
Rodrick, Anne Baltz. History of Great Britain (p. 784)
Rodricks, Marie. Razzle the Sunbeam. (p. 1441)
Rodrigo, Joaquin. Concierto de Aranjuez. (p. 355)
Rodrigue, illus. see Groot, Bob de.
Rodrigue, illus. see Groot, De.
Rodrigue, Michel. Amanite. Razzi, Manuela, illus. (p. 52)
—Nina. Razzi, Manuela & Dalena, Antonello, illus. (p. 1256)
—Princess Nina. Dalena, Antonello & Razzi, Manuela, illus. (p. 1404)
Rodrigue, Michel & Razzi, Manuela. Sybil the Backpack Fairy. Dalena, Antonello, illus. (p. 1692)
Rodrigue, Nancy Temple. Hidden Mickey Adventures 1: Peter & the Wolf (p. 776)
—Hidden Mickey Adventures 2: Peter & the Missing Mansion (p. 776)
Rodrigues, Carmen. 34 Pieces of You. (p. 1996)
—Not Anything. (p. 1267)
Rodrigues, Dulce. Once upon a Time ... a House: A Tale for Children & All Those Young at Heart. (p. 1293)
Rodrigues, Naomi. Molly Mouse & the Christmas Mystery. (p. 1161)
Rodriguez Aguilar, Christina, tr. see Janisch, Heinz.
Rodriguez, AJ. Cajun Crawfish Tale. (p. 252)
—Cycle of Life. (p. 396)
—Theodore Da Baer. (p. 1729)
—Theodore Da Baer II: A New Beginning. (p. 1729)
Rodriguez, Albert G., illus. see Clement, Janet.
Rodriguez, Alex. Jonron! Morrison, Frank, illus. (p. 925)
—Out of the Ballpark. Morrison, Frank, illus. (p. 1311)
Rodriguez, Alfredo. Redfoot. O'Reilly, Sean Patrick, ed. (p. 1455)
Rodriguez, Ana Maria. Autism & Asperger's Syndrome. (p. 117)
—Autism Spectrum Disorders. (p. 117)
—Day in the Life of the Brain. (p. 413)
Rodriguez, Ana Maria. Edward Jenner: Conqueror of Smallpox. (p. 505)
—Gray Foxes, Rattlesnakes, & Other Mysterious Animals of the Extreme Deserts. (p. 713)
RodriGuez, Ana María. Leatherback Turtles, Giant Squids, & Other Mysterious Animals of the Deepest Seas. (p. 986)
Rodriguez, Ana Maria. Leatherback Turtles, Giant Squids, & Other Mysterious Animals of the Deepest Seas. (p. 986)
RodriGuez, Ana Maria. Polar Bears, Penguins, & Other Mysterious Animals of the Extreme Cold. (p. 1379)
Rodríguez, Ana Maria. Polar Bears, Penguins, & Other Mysterious Animals of the Extreme Cold. (p. 1379)
—Secret of the Bloody Hippo ... & More! (p. 1542)
—Secret of the Puking Penguins ... & More! (p. 1542)
Rodriguez, Ana Maria. Secret of the Singing Mice... & More! (p. 1543)
Rodriguez, Ana Maria. Secret of the Sleepless Whales... & More! (p. 1543)
—Secret of the Suffocating Slime Trap... & More! (p. 1543)
RodriGuez, Ana Maria. Vampire Bats, Giant Insects, & Other Mysterious Animals of the Darkest Caves. (p. 1831)
Rodriguez, Ana Maria. Vampire Bats, Giant Insects, & Other Mysterious Animals of the Darkest Caves. (p. 1832)
Rodriguez, Ana Maria, jt. auth. see Rodriguez, Ana Maria.
Rodriguez, Ana Maria & Rodríguez, Ana María. Secret of the Plant-Killing Ants ... & More! (p. 1542)
Rodriguez, Angelica. Mia y Primos/Mia & Cousins: Yo grito,corro y grito / I scream, run & Scream. (p. 1133)
Rodriguez, Antonio Orlando. Cuento del Sinsonte Olvidadizo. (p. 389)
—Mi Bicicleta es un Hada y Otros Secretos Por el Estilo. (p. 1132)
—Que Extranos Son Los Terricolas/Earthlings, How Weird They Are! Cuellar, Olga, illus. (p. 1423)
Rodriguez, Art. Those Oldies but Goodies. (p. 1740)
Rodriguez, Artemio. King of Things/el Rey de Las Cosas. Rodriguez, Artemio, illus. (p. 959)
Rodriguez, Ashley. Mermaid Tale. (p. 1128)
Rodriguez, Béatrice. Chicken Thief. (p. 300)
—Fox & Hen Together. (p. 626)
—Rooster's Revenge. (p. 1488)
Rodriguez, Beatrix, illus. see Folk Tale Staff.
Rodriguez, Bobbie. How I Love My Dad. (p. 810)
Rodriguez Braojos, Alberto, illus. see Friden, Chris.
Rodriguez Braojos, Alberto, jt. auth. see Friden, Chris.
Rodriguez, Christina, illus. see Bernardo, Anilu.
Rodriguez, Christina, illus. see Gonzalez, Ada Acosta.
Rodriguez, Christina, illus. see Jackson, Bobby L.
Rodriguez, Christina, illus. see Maurer, Tracy.
Rodriguez, Christina, illus. see Redman, Mary.
Rodriguez, Christina Ann, illus. see Cofer, Judith Ortiz.
Rodriguez, Christina Ann, illus. see Troupe, Thomas Kingsley.
Rodriguez, Christina E., illus. see Bertrand, Diane Gonzales.
Rodriguez, Cindy. All about Chimps. (p. 42)
—Bats. (p. 145)
—Cougars. (p. 369)
—Flipper Friends. (p. 605)
—Gases. (p. 657)
—Gases with Code. (p. 657)
—Gases, with Code. (p. 657)
—Líquidos. (p. 1021)
—Liquids with Code. (p. 1021)
—Liquids, with Code. (p. 1021)
—New Mexico: The Land of Enchantment. (p. 1246)
—New York: The Empire State. (p. 1247)
—North Carolina: The Tar Heel State. (p. 1265)
—North Dakota: The Peach Garden State. (p. 1265)
—Ohio: The Buckeye State. (p. 1281)
—Sea Turtles. (p. 1536)
—Sólidos. (p. 1607)
—Utah: The Beehive State. (p. 1829)
—What's for Lunch? (p. 1897)
—Who's Listening? (p. 1920)
Rodriguez, Cindy L. Heroes Were Made On 9/11 Elliott, Joyce L., illus. (p. 773)
—When Reason Breaks. (p. 1904)
Rodriguez, Claudia Rodriguez & Ardila, Carlos. Pandra 2: Imaginar, Crear, Dibujar. Panamericana Staff, ed. (p. 1321)
Rodriguez, Cristian, illus. see Jones, Karen.
Rodriguez Cuadros, Evangelina, ed. see Calderón de la Barca, Pedro.
Rodriguez, Dave, illus. see May, Tessa.
Rodriguez, David. Finding Gossamyr Volume 1 HC. Nelson, Angela, ed. (p. 588)
—Shadowgirls - Season One. Nelson, Angela, ed. (p. 1558)
Rodriguez, Daynali Flores, tr. from ENG. Dora salva el Reino de Cristal (Dora Saves Crystal Kingdom) Aikins, Dave, illus. (p. 470)
Rodriguez, Ed. Kiki Kokí: La Leyenda Encantada del Coquí. (p. 955)
—Kiki Kokí: La Leyenda Encantada Del Coquí (Kiki Kokí: the Enchanted Legend of the Coquí Frog) (p. 955)
Rodriguez, Edarissa. Girl Who Took a Shower. Santiago, Claribel, ed. (p. 679)
Rodriguez, Edel, illus. see Achebe, Chinua.
Rodriguez, Edel, illus. see Crump, Marty.
Rodriguez, Edel, illus. see Winter, Jonah.
Rodriguez, Elaine M. Nerposito & Planet Earth. (p. 1241)
Rodriguez, Elizabeth. Hannah's Ayuna. (p. 742)
—Hannah's Fast. (p. 743)
Rodriguez, Emma Vera & Scogin, Connie. Blanca Rosa's Quinceaner. (p. 198)
Rodriguez, Evelyn, frwd. InvAsian: Growing up Asian & Female in the United States. (p. 883)
Rodriguez, Felix Manuel. Dad, Me, & Muhammad Ali: A Father-and-Son Story. (p. 398)
Rodriguez Ferrer, Janel. Arts-Angels Track 1: Drawn to You. (p. 105)
Rodriguez, Gaby. Pregnancy Project: A Memoir. (p. 1395)
Rodriguez Gonzalez, Tania. Adrián Beltré. (p. 13)
—Albert Pujols. (p. 34)
—Alex Rodriguez. (p. 36)
—Alfonso Soriano. (p. 37)
—Aramis Ramirez. (p. 94)
—Bartolo Colón. (p. 140)
—Carlos Beltrán. (p. 270)
—Carlos Peña. (p. 270)
—David Ortiz. (p. 411)
—Francisco Cordero. (p. 628)
—Francisco Liriano. (p. 628)
—Hanley Ramirez. (p. 742)
—Jhonny Peralta. (p. 917)
—José Bautista. (p. 926)
—José Reyes. (p. 926)
Rodriguez Gonzalez, Tania. Jose Valverde. (p. 926)
Rodriguez Gonzalez, Tania. José Valverde. (p. 926)
—Juan Uribe. (p. 930)
—Miguel Batista. (p. 1141)
—Miguel Tejada. (p. 1141)
—Nelson Cruz. (p. 1240)
—Placido Polanco. (p. 1366)
—Rafael Furcal. (p. 1433)
—Roberto Clemente. (p. 1479)
—Robinson Canó. (p. 1480)
—Ubaldo Jiménez. (p. 1807)
—Vladimir Guerrero. (p. 1846)
—Yadier Molina. (p. 1968)
Rodriguez Gonzalez, Tania & Rodriguez, Tania. Placido Polanco. (p. 1366)
Rodriguez, Gonzalo, illus. see Arciniegas, Triunfo.
Rodriguez, Grisell. Chaka the Cow. (p. 288)
Rodriguez Howard, Pauline, illus. see Armas, Teresa.
Rodriguez Howard, Pauline, illus. see Galindo, Mary Sue.
Rodriguez, Ingrid, illus. see Shah, Idries.
Rodriguez, Jason, ed. Colonial Comics: New England, 1620 ¿ 1750. (p. 341)
Rodriguez, Jill, et al. CliffsQuickReview Spanish II. (p. 332)
Rodriguez, Julia. Siriko y la Flauta. Parra, Rocio, illus. (p. 1581)
Rodriguez, Junius. Encyclopedia of Emancipation & Abolition in the Transatlantic World (p. 525)
Rodriguez, Leonardo, illus. see Tuck, Justin.
Rodriguez, Lisa G. Brave Little Hummingbird. (p. 223)
Rodriguez, Lorenzo, illus. see Imbernón, Teresa & Twain, Mark.
Rodriguez, Lorenzo, tr. see Imbernón, Teresa & Twain, Mark.
Rodriguez, Lourdes. Mandy, Princess of la la Land: The Green Monster. (p. 1087)
Rodriguez, Lucho, jt. auth. see Bustos, Eduardo.
Rodriguez, Luis J. It Doesn't Have to Be This Way. Galvez, Daniel, illus. (p. 894)
Rodriguez, Maite, tr. see Ray, Jane.
Rodriguez, Manny, illus. see Denzer, Barbara & Denzer, Missy.
Rodriguez, Marc, illus. see Martin, Kentrell.
Rodriguez, Mari, illus. see Molina, Silvia & Silvia, Molina.
Rodriguez, Marisela. Violet's Shoes. (p. 1843)
—Violet's Sweater. (p. 1843)
Rodriguez, Marisol. Princess & the Chocolate Castle. (p. 1402)
Rodriguez, Mary, illus. see Castaneda, Ricardo Chavez.
Rodriguez, Michelle. Never Far Away. (p. 1242)
Rodriguez, Odette B. Lezama. Last Golden Egg. (p. 977)
Rodriguez, Orlando A. Valores Morales y Buenos Hábitos—Rangel, Mario Hugo, illus. (p. 1831)
Rodriguez, Paul. Don't Do Drugs! Do Dance! Character Education/Prevention. Rodriguez, Paul, illus. (p. 467)
—Let's All Play! Character Education/ Anti-Bullying. Rodriguez, Paul, illus. (p. 994)
—What Color Are You? Rodriguez, Paul, illus. (p. 1881)
Rodriguez, Pedro. Chilling Tales of Horror: Dark Graphic Short Stories. (p. 306)
Rodriguez, Pedro, illus. see Kipling, Rudyard.
Rodriguez, Perfecto, illus. see Bevin, Teresa.
Rodriguez, Philippe L. All about Computers. (p. 42)
Rodriguez, Racer, jt. auth. see Rodriguez, Robert.
Rodriguez, Rachel Victoria. Building on Nature: The Life of Antoni Gaudí. Paschkis, Julie, illus. (p. 239)
—Through Georgia's Eyes. Paschkis, Julie, illus. (p. 1744)
Rodriguez, Raul. Mamma's Worm House. (p. 1085)
—Runaway Baby / el Bebe' Travieso. (p. 1496)
Rodriguez, Renae. Why You Are So Special. (p. 1927)
Rodriguez, Ricardo. Walter Benjamin -Salida de Emergencia. (p. 1856)
Rodriguez, Robert. Adventures of Shark Boy & Lava Girl in 3-D: The Illustrated Screenplay. Artists of Troublemaker Studios Staff, illus. (p. 22)
Rodriguez, Robert, illus. see Toader, Alex.
Rodriguez, Robert, jt. creator see Disney Staff.
Rodriguez, Robert & Roberson, Chris. Shark Boy & Lava Girl Adventures: The Deep Sleep. Toader, Alex, illus. (p. 1562)
—Shark Boy & Lava Girl Adventures: The Knight Mare. Toader, Alex, illus. (p. 1562)
—Shark Boy & Lava Girl Adventures: Return to Planet Drool. Toader, Alex, illus. (p. 1562)
Rodriguez, Robert & Rodriguez, Racer. Adventures of Shark Boy & Lava Girl: The Movie Storybook. (p. 22)
Rodriguez, Robert, et al. Day Dreamer. Toader, Alex, illus. (p. 412)
Rodriguez Salazar, Tania. Aramis Ramirez. (p. 94)
—Carlos Peña. (p. 270)
Rodriguez, Sergio R. Little Santa & Snowboy: The Childhood Adventures of Santa Claus. (p. 1036)
Rodriguez, Sonia & Browning, Kurt. T Is for Tutu: A Ballet Alphabet. Ong, Wilson, illus. (p. 1694)
Rodriguez, Susan & Monet, Claude. Travels with Monet: Travel in the Artist's Footsteps. (p. 1780)
Rodriguez, Susan R. Meadow of Mine. (p. 1116)
Rodriguez, Tania, jt. auth. see Rodriguez Gonzalez, Tania.
Rodriguez, Tia. Jackie Robinson: Baseball Legend. (p. 904)
Rodriguez, Tina, illus. see Bertrand, Diane Gonzales, et al.
Rodriguez, Tom, illus. see Aguiar, Judy Lee.
Rodriguez-Crawl, Tiah. Greatest Christmas Gift. (p. 719)
Rodriguez-Nora, Tere. En busca de la Paz. Gordo, Aleix, illus. (p. 522)
Rodriguez-Nora, Tere. Kikiwi y los desperdicios en el fondo del Mar. Guimarães, Santi Román i, illus. (p. 956)
Rodriquez, Daniel. Winning the Witnesses. (p. 1937)
Rodriquez, Pedro, illus. see Burgan, Michael.
Rodriquez, Pedro, illus. see Grimm, Jacob, et al.
Rodstrom, Terri, illus. see Morneau, Ronald E.
Rodwell, A. Juvenile Pianist (1836) (p. 941)
Rodwell, Timothy, illus. see O'Connell, Caitlin & Jackson, Donna M.
Rodwell, Timothy, illus. see O'Connell, Caitlin.
Rodwell, Timothy, photos by see O'Connell, Caitlin & Jackson, Donna M.
Roe, Chris. America: an Integrated Curriculum: And Every Gain Divine (p. 58)
—America: an Integrated Curriculum: May God Thy Gold Befine (p. 59)
—America: an Integrated Curriculum: 'Til All Success Be Nobleness (p. 59)
Roe, D. J. Impossible Dream. (p. 862)
Roe, David. DC Super Friends Mix & Match. (p. 415)
Roe, David, illus. see Aber, Linda Williams.
Roe, David, illus. see Aber, Linda.
Roe, David, illus. see Gilden, Mel.
Roe, David, jt. auth. see Reader's Digest Staff.
Roe, David & Reader's Digest Editors. Mix & Match. Milne, Alex & Ruffolo, Rob, illus. (p. 1156)
Roe, E. P. Three Thanksgiving Kisses. (p. 1744)
Roe, E. T. Fun & Frolic. (p. 647)
Roe, Monica M. Thaw. (p. 1728)
Roe, Monika, illus. see Wallach, Marlene.
Roecker, Laura, jt. auth. see Roecker, Lisa.
Roecker, Lisa & Roecker, Laura. Liar Society. (p. 1005)
—Third Lie's the Charm. (p. 1734)
Roedel, Michael & Kennedy, Gregory. Compact Guide to Kentucky Birds. (p. 351)
—Compact Guide to Missouri Birds. (p. 351)
—Compact Guide to Tennessee Birds (p. 351)
Roedel, Michael, et al. Compact Guide to Colorado Birds. (p. 351)
Roeder, Annette. 13 Buildings Children Should Know. (p. 1994)
—Art Coloring Book. (p. 101)
—Coloring Book Miro. (p. 344)
—Leonardo Da Vinci: Coloring Book. (p. 992)
—Vincent Van Gogh. Prestel, ed. (p. 1843)
Roeder, Annette, jt. auth. see Prestel Publishing.
Roeder, Mark. This Time Around. (p. 1737)
Roeder, Virginia, illus. see Wade, Mary Dodson.
Roeder, Virginia M., illus. see Chrismer, Melanie.
Roeder, Virginia Marsh, illus. see Wade, Mary Dodson.
Roederer, Charlotte, illus. see Echerique, Alfredo Bryce & Duenas, Ana Maria.
Roederer, Charlotte, illus. see Grimm, Jacob, et al.
Roegiers, Maud. Take the Time: Mindfulness for Kids. (p. 1697)
Roehler, Yvonne Fetig, illus. see Washburn, Sandi.
Roehlkepartain, Eugene C., ed. see Scales, Peter C. & Leffert, Nancy.
Roehlkepartain, Jolene L. 101 Great Games for Infants, Toddlers, & Preschoolers: Active, Bible-Based Fun for Christian Education. (p. 1999)
Roehlkepartain, Jolene L. & Leffert, Nancy. What Young Children Need to Succeed: Working Together to Build Assets from Birth to Age 11. (p. 1896)
Roehm, R. Curtis. My Dad's Gto. (p. 1201)
Roehrig, Catharine, jt. auth. see Metropolitan Museum of Art Staff.
Roelofsen, Marjorie. Where Have All the Puppies Gone? A Sequel to SAM. (p. 1907)
Roemer, Ann. Audio Cd: Used with ... Roemer-College Oral Communication 2. (p. 114)
—College Oral Communication (p. 340)
Roemer, Heidi. What Kind of Seeds Are These? Kassian, Olena, illus. (p. 1891)
Roemer, Heidi Bee. Whose Nest Is This? McLennan, Connie, illus. (p. 1921)
Roemer, Heidi Bee, ed. see Hoyte, Carol-Ann.
Roemermann, Jennifer. Long Grass Tunnel. (p. 1047)
Roemhildt, Mark. Gladiators. (p. 682)
—Jack Swagger. (p. 903)
Roensch, Greg. Bruce Lee. (p. 232)
—Furman V. Georgia: Cruel & Unusual Punishment. (p. 650)
—Lindbergh Baby Kidnapping Trial: A Primary Source Account. (p. 1019)
Roe-Pimm, Nancy. Colo's Story. (p. 346)
Roessel, David & Rampersad, Arnold, eds. Poetry for Young People: Langston Hughes. Andrews, Benny, illus. (p. 1376)
Roesser, Blanche. Story of Leo the Lion. (p. 1658)
—Story of Pegasus. (p. 1659)
—Story of Perseus. (p. 1659)
Roesser, Griffin. Digger Makes a Friend. (p. 438)
—Who Ate the Turkey? (p. 1914)
Roesti, Delores. Mareena Maree Mulligan & the Flying Wheel Chair: Book 1: School Days. (p. 1092)
—Mareena Maree Mulligan & the Flying Wheelchair: Book 2: The Busybodies. (p. 1092)
Roesti, Delores Anne. Mareena Maree Mulligan & the Flying Wheelchair Book #3: Temptation's Talking (p. 1092)
Roets, Lois F. Jumbo Reading Yearbook: Grade 1. (p. 933)
Roetzheim, William, ed. Modern Nursery Rhymes. (p. 1158)
Rofé, April. SENSEsational Alphabet: See-Read, Touch-Feel, Scratch & Smell, Hear-Learn, Have Fun! (p. 1551)
Rofé, Jennifer, jt. auth. see Peterson, Mary.
Roff, Don. Holiday Magic. (p. 788)
Roff, Jason T. Careers in E-Commerce: Software Development. (p. 267)
Roff, Jason T. & Roff, Kimberly A. Careers in E-Commerce Software Development. (p. 267)
Roff, Kimberly A., jt. auth. see Roff, Jason T.
Roffe Menhard, Francha. Cyberwar: Point. Click. Destroy. (p. 396)
Roffe, Michael, illus. see Wilkinson-Latham, Christopher.
Roffey, C. My Red Busy Book. (p. 1217)
Roffey, Chris. Coding Club Level 2 Python: Next Steps. (p. 338)
—Coding Club Level 3 Python: Building Big Apps. (p. 338)
Roffey, M. First Words Indoors. (p. 597)
Roffey, Maureen. 1 2 3 Count with Me! (p. 1990)

Rog, Lori Jamison. Guided Reading Basics: Organizing, Managing, & Implementing a Balanced Literacy Program in K-3. (p. 730)
Rogala, Jennifer. My Cat at Home in the Wild. (p. 1200)
—Ways to Say the Words You've Heard. (p. 1865)
—When My Nose Runs, Where Does It Go? Nicholas, Jacob, illus. (p. 1904)
Rogala, Judy. Dog Days of Christmas. Stroede, Paul, illus. (p. 461)
Rogalski, Robert, illus. see Roberts, Emma Perry.
Rogan, Bernie. Creatures of the Sea: Can You Guess Me. (p. 380)
Rog&eacute. French Fry King. Rogé, illus. (p. 635)
Rogasky, Barbara & Fisher, Leonard Everett. Dybbuk: A Version. (p. 491)
Rogé. Haiti My Country (p. 736)
—Mingan My Village (p. 1146)
Rogé, illus. see Chartrand, Lili.
Rogé, illus. see Todd, Barbara.
Roger, Marie-Sabine & Sol, Anne. Of Course They Do! Boys & Girls Can Do Anything. (p. 1279)
Roger, Moore & Ron, Kurtz. Arfie Plays Pirates. (p. 97)
Rogers, Aïda, jt. ed. see Lynn, Steve.
Rogers, Alan. Dai the Dragon-Keeper. Gruffudd, Robat, tr. from WEL. (p. 399)
—En Forme de Bateau. (p. 522)
—Higher & Higher. (p. 778)
—Ours Vert. (p. 1310)
—Vent Tourne! (p. 1836)
Rogers, Alan & Rogers, Lisa. Boston: City on a Hill. (p. 215)
Rogers, Amy B. Orion. (p. 1304)
—Que Hacen Los Bomberos? / What Do Firefighters Do? (p. 1423)
—Que Hacen Los Doctores? / What Do Doctors Do? (p. 1423)
—What Do Doctors Do? (p. 1882)
—What Do Firefighters Do? (p. 1882)
Rogers, Amy Keating. Journal of the Two Sisters: The Official Chronicles of Celestia & Luna. (p. 927)
Rogers, Andy. Puppy Brothers Adventures with Forest Friends - Children's Picture Book for Ages 3 To 8. (p. 1418)
—Who's Who of Pro Football: A Guide to the Game's Greatest Players. (p. 1921)
Rogers, Andy, et al. Who's Who of Pro Sports. (p. 1921)
Rogers, Anne. CAPTAIN DAN & SAILOR SAM. (p. 264)
—magic rainbow large Print. (p. 1073)
—magic rainbow very large Print. (p. 1073)
—PRINCE & the APPLE TREE. (p. 1401)
—Sooty Wooty Is a Cat. (p. 1613)
Rogers, Barbara. Screams from Childhood (p. 1533)
Rogers, Betsy, ed. see Trumbauer, Lisa.
Rogers, Betty Lou. Change Can Be Good. (p. 289)
—Paste & Gluey: A Sticky Tale. (p. 1327)
—Thimseagle Thievers: America's Thieviest Family. (p. 1732)
Rogers, Blessing. Gabby & Ralph Meet Their New Teacher. (p. 652)
Rogers, Brandy. It's Big, It's Little. (p. 896)
Rogers, Bryar Elizabeth. Special Bug Indeed Twigg, Craig, illus. (p. 1623)
Rogers, Bud, ed. see Krueger, Jim & Zondervan Publishing Staff.
Rogers, Bud, ed. see Martin, Gary & Zondervan Bibles Staff.
Rogers, Bud, jt. auth. see Avery, Ben.
Rogers, Bud, jt. auth. see Krueger, Jim.
Rogers, Bud, jt. auth. see Martin, Gary.
Rogers, Bud & Avery, Ben. Battle Between Wong, Scott & Merced, Eric, illus. (p. 145)
Rogers, Bud & Krueger, Jim. Battle for Argon Falls Padilla, Ariel, illus. (p. 145)
—Secret Alliance Padilla, Ariel, illus. (p. 1540)
Rogers, Bud & Lee, Young Shin. Trips, Ships, & the Ultimate Vision: Acts Pt. 2 Burner, Brett & Earls, J. S., eds. (p. 1787)
Rogers, Bud & Martin, Gary. Tears of Jehovah Cariello, Sergio, illus. (p. 1711)
—Witch of Endor Cariello, Sergio, illus. (p. 1941)
Rogers, Bud, et al. Truth Revealed Padilla, Ariel, illus. (p. 1794)
Rogers, Buddy, jt. auth. see Lee, Young Shin.
Rogers, Buddy & Avery, Ben. Power Play Wong, Scott, illus. (p. 1390)
Rogers, Carol, illus. see McCall, Edith S.
Rogers, Carol J. Adventures of Buttonballs' Trails. (p. 17)
Rogers, Christopher M. Homer the Helicopter Grand Canyon Adventures. (p. 793)
Rogers, David, illus. see Adams, Jesse.
Rogers, Denny, illus. see Cox, Judith.
Rogers, Denny, illus. see Hasling, Jack.
Rogers, Denny, illus. see Stonesifer, Gertrude.
Rogers, Derek G. Monstrous Myths & Fabulous Fables. (p. 1169)
Rogers, Diana. Critters of Grassy Green Plains: Got to Get the Critters Counted. (p. 384)
Rogers, Don. Adventures of Shawn & Jeremy. (p. 22)
—Adventures of Shawn & Jeremy with Sister Nicole & the Hot Air Balloon: Volume Two. (p. 22)
Rogers, Elizabeth E. Can of Magic Smiles. (p. 258)
Rogers, Fred. Many Ways to Say I Love You: Wisdom for Parents & Children from Mister Rogers. (p. 1089)
—Vamos a Jugar: Divertidos Juegos y Actividades para Estimular el Desarrollo de Tu Hijo. (p. 1831)
Rogers, Gil. Sally's Puppets Go to the Hospital: A Children's Play. (p. 1505)
Rogers, Ginger Weeks. MacDilleo Dude. (p. 1068)
Rogers, Gregory. Hero of Little Street. Rogers, Gregory, illus. (p. 772)
Rogers, Gregory, illus. see Chatterton, Martin.
Rogers, Gregory, illus. see Davis, Tony.
Rogers, Gregory, illus. see Gwynne, Phillip.
Rogers, Gregory, illus. see Wagner, Jenny.
Rogers, Gregory, illus. see Watts, Frances.
Rogers, Hal. Cherry Pickers. (p. 298)
—Tractors. (p. 1775)
—Trains. (p. 1777)
Rogers, J. Ellen. Hairy Legs & Wagon Wheels. (p. 736)
Rogers, Jacqueline. Jack Jones off to the Post Office. (p. 903)
Rogers, Jacqueline, illus. see Adams, Alison.
Rogers, Jacqueline, illus. see Cleary, Beverly.
Rogers, Jacqueline, illus. see Cullen, Lynn.
Rogers, Jacqueline, illus. see Gilman, Grace.
Rogers, Jacqueline, illus. see Herman, R. A.
Rogers, Jacqueline, illus. see Karr, Lily.
Rogers, Jacqueline, illus. see Levinson, Nancy Smiler.
Rogers, Jacqueline, illus. see Mayer, Kirsten.
Rogers, Jacqueline, illus. see Peterson, John & Slater, Teddy.
Rogers, Jacqueline, illus. see Salisbury, Graham.
Rogers, Jacqueline, illus. see San Souci, Robert D.
Rogers, Jacqueline, illus. see Sly, Alexandra.
Rogers, Jacqueline, illus. see Smith, Carrie.
Rogers, Jacqueline, illus. see Wallace, Bill.
Rogers, Jacqueline, illus. see Wallace, Carol.
Rogers, Jacqueline, illus. see Washington, Donna L. & Washington, Donna.
Rogers, Jacqueline, illus. see Wright, Betty Ren.
Rogers, Jacqueline, jt. illus. see Peterson, Joel.
Rogers, Jacqueline, tr. see Dumas, Alexandre.
Rogers, Jacqueline, tr. see Levinson, Nancy Smiler.
Rogers, Jane & Benchmark Education Co., LLC Staff. Best Nest. (p. 170)
—Get Well, Red Hen! (p. 668)
Rogers, Janelle. Penelope's Rainy Day Adventures. (p. 1336)
Rogers, Jaqueline, illus. see Wallace, Carol.
Rogers, Jean. Goodbye, My Island. Munoz, Rie, illus. (p. 701)
Rogers, Jennifer. While the Stars Are at Play. (p. 1911)
Rogers, Jennifer H. Chasing Grace. (p. 294)
Rogers, Jewels. Princess & the Dolphin. (p. 1402)
—Princess & the Parakeet. (p. 1402)
—Princess & the Puppy. (p. 1403)
—Princess & the Rabbit. (p. 1403)
Rogers, Joe, illus. see Hillert, Margaret.
Rogers, John. Dungeons & Dragons Volume 3: Down: Down. (p. 490)
Rogers, John & Di Vito, Andrea. First Encounters (p. 594)
Rogers, John, et al. Road Trip Albuquerque, Rafael, illus. (p. 1477)
Rogers, Jonathan. Charlatan's Boy. (p. 291)
Rogers, K. Complete Book of the Microscope. (p. 352)
—Light, Sound & Electricity. (p. 1015)
Rogers, Kara. Battling & Managing Disease. (p. 147)
—Cloning. (p. 333)
—Health & Disease in Society (p. 757)
—Infectious Diseases. (p. 873)
—Medicine & Healers Through History. (p. 1119)
—Substance Use & Abuse. (p. 1671)
Rogers, Kara, ed. 100 Most Influential Scientists of All Time. (p. 1998)
—Endocrine System. (p. 527)
—New Thinking about Genetics. (p. 1247)
Rogers, Kate. I Can Count To 10! Number Names & Count Sequence. (p. 835)
—Robert Fulton Invents the Steamboat. (p. 1479)
Rogers, Katherine. Dinosaur Dynasty: The Sternberg Fossil Hunters. (p. 442)
Rogers, Kenny & Junkerman, Kelly. Kenny Rogers Presents the Toy Shoppe. (p. 949)
Rogers, Kerima. Far from Far, Far Away: A Fractured Tale. (p. 572)
Rogers, Kirsteen. Christmas Coloring Book. (p. 313)
—Christmas Patterns Coloring Book. (p. 315)
—Complete Book of the Microscope. Dowswell, Paul, ed. (p. 352)
—First Illustrated Math Dictionary IR. (p. 595)
—Haunted House Sticker Book. (p. 753)
—Illustrated Elementary Science Dictionary IR. (p. 857)
—Monsters Sticker Book. (p. 1169)
—Mummies & Pyramids: Internet-Linked. (p. 1191)
—Spooky Coloring Book. (p. 1631)
—Under the Sea Jigsaw Book. Scott, Peter, illus. (p. 1814)
Rogers, Kirsteen, ed. see Clarke, Phillip & Khan, Sarah.
Rogers, Kirsteen, ed. see Dalby, Elizabeth.
Rogers, Kirsteen, ed. see Hickman, Clare & Meredith, Sue.
Rogers, Kirsteen, ed. see Large, Tori.
Rogers, Kirsteen, ed. see Marks, Anthony.
Rogers, Kirsteen, ed. see Stockley, Corinne, et al.
Rogers, Kirsteen, ed. see Stockley, Corinne.
Rogers, Kirsteen, ed. see Wertheim, Jane, et al.
Rogers, Kirsteen, jt. auth. see Howell, Laura.
Rogers, Kirsteen, jt. auth. see Tatchell, Judy.
Rogers, Kirsteen & Everall, Nayera. Patterns Coloring Book. (p. 1329)
Rogers, Kirsteen & Hickman, Clare. Religiones Del Mundo - Internet Linked. (p. 1458)
Rogers, Kirsteen & Large, Tori. Illustrated Elementary Math Dictionary. (p. 857)
Rogers, Kirsteen, et al. Usborne Science Encyclopedia: Internet-Linked. Bhachu, Verinder, illus. (p. 1827)
Rogers, Lauren. Skyler & the Se. Sexton, Jessa, ed. (p. 1587)
Rogers, Leeann. Ms Tulper Is Her Name. (p. 1188)
Rogers, Leigh Platt. Sticky Situations: Stories of Childhood Adventures Abroad. (p. 1650)
Rogers, Leslie E. It Is Me. Wilhelm, Doris L., illus. (p. 894)
Rogers, Lisa, jt. auth. see Rogers, Alan.
Rogers, Lon. Between Season. (p. 173)
Rogers, Lura, et al. Dominican Republic. (p. 465)
Rogers, Madalyn V., illus. see Liner, Robin.
Rogers, Marcus K., jt. auth. see Colt, James P.
Rogers, Martha. Bernie Finds a Friend. (p. 167)
—Bernie Goes to the Beach: Bernie's Journey. (p. 167)
—Bernie's Journey. (p. 167)
Rogers, Melissa, illus. see Waters, Galadriel, ed.
Rogers, Michelle Elizabeth. Adventures of Brutus & Baby: A Haunted Halloween. Collier, Kevin Scott, illus. (p. 17)
Rogers, Paul. What Will the Weather Be Like Today? Kazuko, illus. (p. 1895)
Rogers, Paul, illus. see Dylan, Bob.
Rogers, Paul, illus. see Marsalis, Wynton.
Rogers, Ramona. Buck & Penny. (p. 234)
Rogers, Robyn. No Lobster, Please! A Story of a Child with a Severe Seafood Allergy. (p. 1258)
Rogers, Roy. Roy Rogers & the Deadly Treasure. (p. 1492)
Rogers, Ruth W., illus. see Beck, William F.
Rogers, Sally, jt. auth. see McLeish, Mary.
Rogers, Shannon, jt. auth. see Batterson, Jason.
Rogers, Sherry, illus. see Cole, Carol A.
Rogers, Sherry, illus. see Fields, Terri.
Rogers, Sherry, illus. see Hutmacher, Kimberly.
Rogers, Sherry, illus. see Kapchinske, Pam.
Rogers, Sherry, illus. see Mariconda, Barbara.
Rogers, Sherry, illus. see Mayer, Lynne.
Rogers, Sherry, illus. see Mitchell, Susan K.
Rogers, Sherry, illus. see Rawson, Katherine.
Rogers, Sherry, illus. see Restrepo, Bettina.
Rogers, Sherry, illus. see Rock, Brian.
Rogers, Sherry, jt. auth. see Restrepo, Bettina.
Rogers, Sherry, jt. auth. see Rock, Brian.
Rogers, Simon. Information Graphics: Animal Kingdom. Blechman, Nicholas, illus. (p. 874)
—Information Graphics: Human Body. Grundy, Peter, illus. (p. 874)
—Information Graphics: Space. Daniel, Jennifer, illus. (p. 874)
Rogers, Siobain K. Champagne Roses. (p. 289)
Rogers, Stan. Northwest Passage James, Matt, illus. (p. 1266)
Rogers, Stillman, jt. auth. see Yomtov, Nelson.
Rogers, Suzanne. My Mother Can Do Anything. Rogers, Suzanne, photos by. (p. 1214)
—Pawsitive Tails. (p. 1331)
Rogers, Suzanne J. Cody Meets A Butterfly. (p. 338)
Rogers, Svetlana. Russian Picture Word Book: Learn over 500 Commonly Used Russian Words Through Pictures. Steadman, Barbara, illus. (p. 1498)
Rogers, Tara L. Diane's Fabulous Day at Preschool. (p. 434)
Rogers, Terry. Androcles & the Lion: A Roman Legend. (p. 72)
Rogers, Tony. Molly's Cat. (p. 1161)
Rogers, Tyrell. Hey, Bully. (p. 774)
Rogers, Virgil M., jt. auth. see Marks, John H.
Rogers, Walter S., illus. see Roy, Lillian Elizabeth.
Rogers, Wanda. Polliwog Pete. (p. 1381)
Rogers, Wanda Gayle. Miss Bean & the Great Tricycle Rescue: The Great Tricycle Rescue. (p. 1151)
Rogers Yaeger, Nancy. Constantine Goes to School. Grace, Bill, illus. (p. 359)
Rogers/Logsdon, Deborah J. Without Closure (p. 1942)
Rogers-Barnett, Cheryl, et al. All-American Cowboy Grill: Sizzlin' Recipes from the World's Greatest Cowboys (p. 43)
Rogers-Busboom, Kimberly. Angel Who Didn't Fit In. LeBlanc, Marc, illus. (p. 74)
—My Secret Best Friend. Dee, Kati, illus. (p. 1218)
Rogers-Hait, Nancy. Shark Puppies Adventures Book II: Nikki to the Rescue. (p. 1562)
Rogge, Rachel, illus. see Landstrom, Lee Ann & Shragg, Karen I.
Rogge, Rachel, illus. see Landstrom, Lee Ann & Shragg, Karen.
Rogge, Robie & Smith, Dian G. Animals in the Stars Lacing Cards. (p. 83)
Rogger. Fifty-Fifth Bear & the Awkward Rabbits: An Amazing Thick Blue Wood Bear Adventure. (p. 585)
Roginsky, Renata. Simulacrum & the Book of Spells. (p. 1578)
Rognoni, Yolani. Camino de Pecas/ Freckles' Path. (p. 256)
Rogora, Bernardo. Romanos. (p. 1486)
Rogow, Sally. Faces of Courage: Young Heroes of World War II. (p. 561)
Rogow, Sally M. Faces of Courage: Young Heroes of World War II. (p. 561)
Roguez, Jesus, illus. see Brozman, Dave.
Roh, Grace S. Booyoung & Sea Turtle's Adventure: God's Creatures' Adventures Series 1. Park, Mi-Ok, illus. (p. 213)
Rohan, Julia K. Weaverworld: Grimsnipe's Revenge. (p. 1870)
Rohan, Karen M., ed. see Lewinski, Marcel.
Rohan, Karen M., ed. Great Decisions 2007. (p. 715)
Rohan, Liz. Come Spring. (p. 347)
Rohan, Margaret de. Celia & Granny Meg go to Paris: A survival Guide. (p. 286)
—Celia & Granny Meg Return to Paris: The man with no Face. (p. 286)
Rohan, Rebecca Carey. Working with Electricity: Electrical Engineers. (p. 1953)
Rohde, Stephanie. Basic & Respectful Emailing Using Outlook Express. (p. 141)
Rohde, Stephen F. Freedom of Assembly. (p. 634)
Rohen, Sean. Unprincess Nermine. (p. 1822)
Roher, Michael, illus. see Steinkellner, Elisabeth.
Rohm, Robert, jt. auth. see Doyle, V. L.
Rohman, Stefanie, ed. see Dunning, Rebecca.
Rohmann, Eric. Bone Dog. Rohmann, Eric, illus. (p. 208)
—Kitten Tale. (p. 962)
—Mi Amigo Conejo. (p. 1132)
—My Friend Rabbit. Rohmann, Eric, illus. (p. 1209)
Rohmann, Eric, illus. see Fleming, Candace.
Rohmann, Eric, jt. auth. see Lowry, Lois.
Rohmann, Eric, creator. My Friend Rabbit & the Snow Geese. (p. 1209)
Rohmer, Harriet. Heroes of the Environment: True Stories of People Who Are Helping to Protect Our Planet. McLaughlin, Julie, illus. (p. 773)
—Uncle Nacho's Hat: El Sombrero Del to Nacho. Flor Ada, Alma & Zubizarreta, Rosalma, trs. (p. 1812)
Rohmer, Robert B., tr. see Suzuki, Koji.
Rohmer, Sax, pseud. Orchard of Tears. (p. 1302)
—Quest of the Sacred Slipper. (p. 1426)
—Sins of Severac Bablon. (p. 1580)
Rohmer, Sax, pseud, et al. Adventure Classics. Pomplun, Tom, ed. (p. 14)
Rohn, Eric, et al. Flashes of Life. (p. 602)
Rohner, Dorothia. Effie's Image. (p. 505)
Rohner, Dorothia, illus. see Patricia Pierce.
Rohr, Ian. Biggest, Highest, Fastest. (p. 185)
—Children's Celebrations. (p. 303)
—City & Country Celebrations. (p. 323)
—Dinosaur Dig. (p. 442)
—Emergency. (p. 518)
—Fighter Planes. (p. 585)
—Indigenous Celebrations. (p. 872)
—National & Global Celebrations. (p. 1231)
—Predators. (p. 1394)
—Religious Celebrations. (p. 1458)
—Snappers, Stingers & Stabbers of Australia. (p. 1597)
—Traditional Celebrations. (p. 1776)
Rohr, Ian, jt. auth. see Jones, Morris.
Rohr, Rebecca. Flocks: A Buster Bird Adventure. (p. 605)
Rohr, Stéphanie, illus. see Atherton, Isabel.
Röhr, Stéphanie, illus. see Rae, Philippa.
Rohrbach, Sophie, illus. see Doyle, Arthur.
Rohrbach, Sophie, illus. see Shaw, Murray & Cosson, M. J.
Rohrer, Kim. Adventures of Little Dooey: The Doctor. (p. 19)
Rohrer, Martha. Animals, Animals, Animals. (p. 82)
—Birds, Birds, Birds. (p. 191)
—Flowers, Flowers, Flowers. (p. 608)
Rohrer, Neal. Rohrer's Fun Coloring & Games. Rohrer, Neal, illus. (p. 1485)
Rohrig, Brian. 39 Dazzling Experiments with Dry Ice. (p. 1996)
—39 Dazzling Experiments with the Mega-Magnet. (p. 1996)
—Pure Slime: 50 Incredible Ways to Make Slime Using Household Substances. (p. 1419)
Rohwer/Lampstand Press, Lauren. South America: The Continent & Its Countries. Somerville/ Lampstand Press, David, illus. (p. 1616)
Roitman, Tanya. Do You Wear Diapers? (p. 458)
—More We Are Together. (p. 1175)
Roitman, Tanya, illus. see Linn, Margot.
Roitman, Tanya, illus. see Ziefert, Harriet.
Roizen, Michael F. & Oz, Mehmet C. Owner's Manual for Teens: A Guide to a Healthy Body & Happy Life. (p. 1315)
Roja, Alberto Jimenenz, tr. see Hijuelos, Oscar & Oscar, Hijuelos.
Rojankovsky, Feodor, illus. see Little Golden Books Staff.
Rojankovsky, Feodor, illus. see McGinley, Phyllis, et al.
Rojas Cardona, Javier, ed. Bob Dylan: Unscripted. Gilbert, Douglas R., photos by. (p. 205)
Rojas, Carlos. Yo, Goya. (p. 1971)
Rojas, Clare, illus. see Heti, Sheila.
Rojas, Emilio. Libro Mágico de los 101 Relatos para Niños: Fábulas, Cuentos y Leyendas. (p. 1006)
—Mitos, Leyendas, Cuentos, Fábulas, Apólogos y Parábolas. (p. 1156)
—Ortografía Real de la Lengua Española: Libro con Ejercicios. (p. 1305)
—Ortografía Real de la Lengua Española. (p. 1305)
—Pequeño Hombre. (p. 1341)
—Poemas de Amor de un Adolescente. (p. 1376)
—Simple Historia de un Cualquiera: No Siempre Es Cualquier Historia. (p. 1577)
Rojas, Fernando de. Celestina: Tragicomedia de Calisto y Melibea. (p. 286)
—Celestina. (p. 286)
Rojas, Fernando de, jt. auth. see Rojas, Fernando de.
Rojas, Fernando de & Rojas, Fernando de. Celestina: Tragicomedia de Calisto y Melibea. (p. 286)
Rojas, Jessica, illus. see Sipes, Peter.
Rojas, Mary, illus. see Allen, Margaret.
Rojas, Mary, illus. see Ekster, Carol Gordon.
Rojas, Mary, illus. see Geiser, Traci Ferguson & Boylan, Maureen McCourt.
Rojas, Mary, illus. see Lataif, Nicole.
Rojas, Mary Galan, illus. see Etringer, Kathy.
Rojas, Oscar. Dia, Una Abeja. (p. 433)
Rojas, Saul Oscar, illus. see Montes, Graciela.
Rojo, Andrea Szekasy. Arcoiris, Level 1 Activity Book: Spanish for Children. (p. 95)
Rojo, Andrea Szekasy & Bardsley, Maggie. I Love Spanish Songs: Songbook & CD. (p. 843)
Rojo, Sara. Baba Yaga: the Flying Witch. (p. 123)
—Why the Sea Is Salty. (p. 1926)
Rojo, Sara, illus. see White, Mark.
Rokhsar, Lillian. Babytionary. Bell, Liesl, illus. (p. 129)
Rokison, Abigail. Shakespeare for Young People: Productions, Versions & Adaptations. (p. 1559)
Rokkan, Elizabeth, tr. see Gaarder, Jostein.
Rokker, H. M. Adventures of Ralph in the Search for Blackbeard's Gold (p. 22)
Roland, Harry, illus. see Braun, Eric.
Roland, James. Ruth Bader Ginsburg: Iconic Supreme Court Justice. (p. 1498)
Roland, Mariko. Kijimuna & Shisa (Bilingual) (p. 955)
Roland, Timothy. Monkey Me #1: Monkey Me & the Golden Monkey (a Branches Book) Roland, Timothy, illus. (p. 1165)
—Monkey Me #1: Monkey Me & the Golden Monkey (a Branches Book) - Library Edition. (p. 1165)
—Monkey Me #2: Monkey Me & the Pet Show (a Branches Book) (p. 1165)
—Monkey Me #4: Monkey Me & the School Ghost (a Branches Book) (p. 1165)
—Monkey Me & the Golden Monkey. (p. 1165)
—Monkey Me & the New Neighbor. (p. 1165)
—Monkey Me & the New Neighbor. Roland, Timothy, illus. (p. 1165)
—Monkey Me & the Pet Show. (p. 1165)
—Monkey Me & the School Ghost. (p. 1165)
—Monkey Me & the School Ghost. Roland, Timothy, illus. (p. 1165)
—Our Crazy Class Election. (p. 1308)
—Silly Science Experiment. (p. 1576)
Roland-James, Patricia & James, Robert L. Something Wicked in the Land of Picatrix. Chidgey, Scarlett, ed. (p. 1610)
Rolando Elementary School. Children's Words of Wonder: A Poetry Anthology. (p. 304)
Rolbin, Cyrus. Art & Life in Rural Japan: Toho Village Throught the Eyes of Its Youth. (p. 101)
—Kana-OK! A New Approach to Learning the ABC's of Japanese: Hiragana & Katakana. (p. 942)

Roldan, Gustavo. Cuentos del Zorro. (p. 390)
Roldan, Patrict, illus. see Burns, Judith.
Rolde, Neil. Interrupted Forest: A History of Maine's Wildlands. (p. 881)
Roleff, Tamara. Alcoholism. (p. 35)
—English Language Learners. (p. 530)
—Is Torture Ever Justified? (p. 890)
Roleff, Tamara, ed. Cyberbullying. (p. 396)
—Homosexuality. (p. 794)
—What Limits Should Be Placed on Presidential Powers? (p. 1891)
Roleff, Tamara L. Alien Abductions. (p. 40)
—Beauty Pageants. Greenhaven Press Editors, ed. (p. 154)
—Civil Liberties. (p. 324)
—Cloning. (p. 333)
—Cocaine & Crack. (p. 337)
—Drug Abuse. (p. 486)
—Genetic Engineering. (p. 660)
Roleff, Tamara L., ed. Alien Abductions. (p. 40)
—Black Magic & Witches. (p. 196)
—Psychics. (p. 1413)
—World Trade Center Attack. (p. 1958)
Roles, Patricia. Facing Teenage Pregnancy: A Handbook for the Pregnant Teen. (p. 561)
Roley, Don, jt. auth. see Glaser, Jason.
Rolf, F. David. When Candy Bars Were a Nickel. (p. 1901)
Rolf, Heidi, illus. see Elefritz, Erin.
Rolf, Heidi, illus. see Pellegrin, Leeann.
Rolf, Pookie, tr. see Nakahara, Aya.
Rolfe, Helen, jt. auth. see Rolfe, Helen Y.
Rolfe, Helen Y. & Rolfe, Helen. Women Explorers: 100 Years of Mountain Adventure. (p. 1945)
Rolfe, John. Ken Griffey, Jr. Superstar Centerfielder. (p. 948)
Rolfe, John, et al. Ken Griffey, Jr. Superstar Centerfielder. (p. 948)
Rolfes, Nina. Examining Pandemics. (p. 547)
Rolfs, Judith. Adventures of Tommy Smurlee. (p. 24)
—Tommy Smurlee & the Missing Statue. (p. 1765)
Rolland, Carol, jt. auth. see Le Compte, David.
Rolland, Leonard Le, illus. see Hickman, Clare & Meredith, Sue.
Rolland, Leonard Le, illus. see Howell, Laura, ed.
Rolland, Will, illus. see Reilly, Pauline.
Rolland, Will, jt. auth. see Reilly, Pauline.
Rollans, Scott & Davis, Ken. Albertans. (p. 35)
Rollason, Jane. Alone! Level 3 Lower-intermediate. (p. 48)
—Freddie's War Level 6 Advanced. (p. 633)
—Freddie's War Level 6 Advanced Book with CD-ROM & Audio CDs (3) (p. 633)
—Killer Bees. (p. 956)
—Killer Bees Level 2 Elementary/Lower-intermediate. (p. 956)
—Killer Bees Level 2 Elementary/Lower-intermediate American English. (p. 956)
—London Level 2 Elementary. (p. 1046)
Rollason, Jane & Pearson Education Staff. Plpr2: Gandhi RLA. (p. 1374)
Rolle, Alexis, ed. see Boyd, Beverly L.
Rolle, Allison, ed. see Boyd, Beverly L.
Rolle, Ekkehard, tr. see Schulz, Charles M.
Rolle, Joan & Thompson, Tracey. I Am Special. (p. 834)
Rolle Williams, Joyce. Chris's Story: A Family Voting Secret Revealed. (p. 311)
Roller, Ellen. Trading Places. Shea, Gary, illus. (p. 1776)
Roller, John, photos by see Roller, Pat Kellogg.
Roller, Pat Kellogg. Pink Hat's Adventure with Kites. Salazar, Riana, illus. (p. 1360)
Rolleston-Cummins, Toni. Seven Stars of Matariki. Slade-Robinson, Nikki, illus. (p. 1555)
Rolli, Jennifer Hansen. Just One More. (p. 939)
Rolling, Beanic, illus. see Veremiah, Omari.
Rolling, Greg. First Time I Heard the Gospel. Dotty, Zens, illus. (p. 597)
Rolling, James Haywood, Jr. Come Look with Me: Discovering African American Art for Children. (p. 347)
Rolling Stone Magazine Staff. 500 Greatest Albums of All Times. (p. 2001)
Rollinger, Marsha, illus. see Klingensmith, Ryan Lee & Klingensmith, Sherri Ann.
Rollins, Barbara B. Syncopated Summer. (p. 1693)
Rollins, Barbara B. & Dahl, Michael. Cause of Death (p. 282)
—Fingerprint Evidence (p. 589)
Rollins, Berni, illus. see Jeremiah, Omari.
Rollins, Bernic, illus. see Jeremiatt, Omani.
Rollins, Bernie, illus. see Jeremiah, Omari.
Rollins, Brenda. How to Write a Book Report: 80 Interactive Screen Pages. (p. 822)
—How to Write a Paragraph: 80 Interactive Screen Pages. (p. 822)
—How to Write an Essay: 80 Interactive Screen Pages. (p. 823)
—Master Writing: 240 Interactive Screen Pages Big Box. (p. 1103)
Rollins, Ellie. Zip. (p. 1987)
Rollins, Jack, jt. auth. see Nelson, Steve.
Rollins, Jack & Nelson, Steve. Frosty the Snowman. Reed, Lisa, illus. (p. 645)
—Frosty the Snowman. Halverson, Lydia, illus. (p. 645)
—Frosty the Snowman. Thornburgh, Rebecca McKillip, illus. (p. 645)
—Frosty the Snowman Sticker Book. Thornburgh, Rebecca, illus. (p. 645)
Rollins, James. Jake Ransom & the Howling Sphinx. (p. 906)
—Jake Ransom & the Skull King's Shadow. (p. 906)
—Map of Bones. (p. 1090)
Rollins, Janice. Bunny's Dream. (p. 242)
Rollins, Joe, illus. see Crays, Lettie L.
Rollins, L. G. Shadows of Angels. (p. 1558)
Rollins, Michelle. Miss Dimples & the Big Stink. (p. 1151)
Rollins, Walter & Nelson, Steve. Frosty the Snowman. Williams, Sam, illus. (p. 645)
Rolls, Geoff, jt. auth. see Gross, Richard D.
Rollyson, Carl. Pablo Picasso: A Biography for Beginners. (p. 1316)
Rollyson, Carl E., ed. see Salem Press Staff.
Rolón, Rebecca Alisa. Rebecca's Tales. (p. 1450)
Rolseth, Ruthie, illus. see Hicks, Robert Z.
Rolston, Steve. One Bad Day. (p. 1293)
Rolston, Steve, illus. see Kyi, Tanya Lloyd.
Rolston, Steve, illus. see Lee, Cora.
Rolston, Steve, illus. see Torres, J.
Rolston, Steve, jt. auth. see Torres, J.
Rolt, Molly. Adventures of Marmaduke & Millicent Mouse & Other Stories. (p. 20)
—Chocci-Croc & Other Stories. (p. 309)
Rolt-Wheeler, Francis. Boy with the U. S. Census. (p. 220)
—Boy with the U S Foresters. (p. 220)
—Plotting in Pirate Seas. (p. 1374)
—TuskHunters. (p. 1799)
Roma, Ursula, illus. see Groner, Judyth Saypol & Wikler, Madeline.
Romagna, Karen, illus. see Collins, Billy.
Romagnoli, L. M. Memories of Me (p. 1126)
—Worn-Out Backpack. Campbell, Lisa, illus. (p. 1961)
Romain, Trevor. How to Do Homework Without Throwing Up. Verdick, Elizabeth, ed. (p. 816)
Romain, Trevor, jt. auth. see Verdick, Elizabeth.
Romaine, Deborah S., jt. auth. see Mosley, Anthony D.
Romaine, Deborah S. & Rothfeld, Glenn S. Encyclopedia of Men's Health. (p. 525)
Roman, Annette. 1 World Manga. Ng, Leandro, illus. (p. 1991)
—One World Manga Ng, Leandro & Wong, Walden, illus. (p. 1297)
—Passage 2: HIV/AIDS — First Love. Ng, Leandro, illus. (p. 1326)
Roman, Annette, ed. see Umezu, Kazuo.
Roman, Annette, ed. see Yuki, Kaori.
Roman, Annette, jt. auth. see World Bank Staff.
Roman, Celso. Amigos del Hombre. (p. 65)
—Arbol de Los Tucanes. (p. 94)
—Las Cosas de la Casa. Gonzalez, Henry, illus. (p. 976)
—Libro de las Cuidades. (p. 1006)
—Maravilloso Viaje de Rosendo Bucuru. Gonzalez, Henry, illus. (p. 1091)
Roman, Dave. Astronaut Academy - Re-Entry. Roman, Dave, illus. (p. 109)
—Teen Boat! Green, John, illus. (p. 1713)
—Zero Gravity. Roman, Dave, illus. (p. 1986)
Roman, Douglas T. How to Learn Phonics: Students' Workbook with More Than 3,000 Words to Make Good Readers. (p. 820)
Roman, Edward. My Busy Year. (p. 1200)
Roman, Javier. Adventures of Tinturu & Kumachan the M. (p. 24)
Roman, Lisa. Boots. Steckler, Megan, illus. (p. 213)
Roman, Luke & Roman, Monica. Encyclopedia of Greek & Roman Mythology. (p. 525)
Roman, Monica, jt. auth. see Roman, Luke.
Róman, Pedro. Perseo: El Joven que Venció a Medusa. Espinosa, Nuri, illus. (p. 1344)
Román, Pedro Josél. PANDORA -la portadora de todos los Dones- (p. 1321)
Roman Saint-Pierre, Erika. Hoppa's Big Move. Newman, J. Heidi, ed. (p. 797)
Roman, Santi, illus. see Lenam, Salva.
Roman, Stacey. Some of Us Want Wrinkles. Wurster, Laurie, illus. (p. 1609)
Roman, Steven A. Sunn. Preiss, Byron, ed. (p. 1677)
Romance, Trisha. Star for Christmas. (p. 1640)
Romanchick, Jennifer, ed. see Cassidy, Albert, Jr. & Bennedetti, Eric.
Romanek, Trudee. Achoo! Cowles, Rose, illus. (p. 9)
—Aha! The Most Interesting Book You'll Ever Read about Intelligence. Cowles, Rose, tr. (p. 30)
—Government & Law in the Early Islamic World. (p. 704)
—Great Ideas of the Renaissance. (p. 716)
—Life in a Commercial City. (p. 1010)
—Science, Medicine, & Math in the Early Islamic World. (p. 1526)
—Splash It Swimming. (p. 1629)
—Squirt! The Most Interesting Book You'll Ever Read about Blood. Cowles, Rose, illus. (p. 1637)
—Wow! The Most Interesting Book You'll Ever Read about the Five Senses. Cowles, Rose, illus. (p. 1962)
Romanek, Trudee, jt. auth. see Crabtree Editors.
Romanelli, Serena. Pequeno Coco. Lamas, Blanca Rose, tr. from GER. (p. 1341)
Romanenko, Vasilisa, illus. see Mermelstein, Yael.
Romanenko, Vitaliy, illus. see Mermelstein, Yael.
Romanes, Alexa. Dark River. (p. 408)
Romanet, Caroline, illus. see Longstaff, Abie.
Romango, Jim, illus. see Catalano, Tom.
Romano, Alexis, jt. ed. see Urban, Erin.
Romano, Amy. Cell Specialization & Reproduction: Understanding How Cells Divide & Differentiate. (p. 286)
—Cool Careers Without College for People Who Love Everything Digital. (p. 362)
—Germ Warfare. (p. 666)
—Historical Atlas of Afghanistan. (p. 782)
—Historical Atlas of Israel. (p. 782)
—Historical Atlas of Jordan. (p. 783)
—Historical Atlas of the United Arab Emirates. (p. 783)
—Historical Atlas of the United States & Its Territories. (p. 783)
—Historical Atlas of United Arab Emirates. (p. 783)
—Historical Atlas of Yemen. (p. 783)
Romano, Amy, jt. auth. see Simon, Alyssa.
Romano, Apamea. My Name Is Little-Flower. (p. 1215)
Romano, Danielle. Billy's First Haircut. (p. 187)
Romano, Elaine. Magic Potato - la Papa Magica: Story & coloring book in English & Spanish Nielsen, Emily, tr. (p. 1073)
Romano, Elaine Ambrose. Gators & Taters: A Week of Bedtime Stories (p. 658)
Romano, Jennifer. Saturday Morning. (p. 1515)
Romano, Juliana. First There Was Forever. (p. 597)
Romano, Melissa. Mama, Lions Don't Listen. (p. 1084)
Romano, Michael. My Max Score AP U. S. History: Maximize Your Score in Less Time. (p. 1214)
Romano, Ray. Raymie, Dickie, & the Bean: Why I Love & Hate My Brothers. Locke, Gary, illus. (p. 1441)
Romano, Tony, jt. auth. see Brett, Tyler.
Romansky, Sally Rosenberg. Invincible. Ott, Margot Janet, illus. (p. 885)
Romanuk, Paul. Hockey Ses Supervedettes 2004-2005. (p. 786)
—Hockey Superstars 2004-2005. (p. 787)
Romay, Alexis. Diego Saves the Sloth! Mawhinney, Art, illus. (p. 437)
Romay, Alexis, tr. see Field, Rachel.
Romay, Alexis, tr. OLIVIA Vende Galletas (OLIVIA Sells Cookies) Spaziante, Patrick, illus. (p. 1287)
—Olivia y el Regalo de Navidad. Johnson, Shane L., illus. (p. 1287)
Romberger, James, illus. see Lansdale, John L., et al.
Rombough, John, illus. see Highway, Tomson.
Rome, Ami Margolin, jt. auth. see Margolin, Phillip.
Rome, Jacqueline Thomas. Do I Have to Clean My Room? (p. 457)
—Do I Have to Clean My Room? Brown, Lillie Wyatt, illus. (p. 457)
—Do I Have to Go to Church Today? Thomas, Pamela L., illus. (p. 457)
Rome, Lori April. Adventures of Salt & Soap at Grand Canyon. Bauerle, Tanja, illus. (p. 22)
Romendik, Irena. Musical Muffin Man. (p. 1194)
Romendik, Irene. I've Been Working on the Railroad: Musical Book. (p. 900)
Romeo, Angelina, et al. Gooda & Goda. (p. 700)
Romeo, Fran, jt. auth. see Romeo, Fran.
Romeo, Fran & Romeo, Fran. Once upon A Dream. (p. 1292)
Romeo, Francesca. Leonardo Da Vinci. (p. 992)
Romer, John & Winston, Robert P. Egyptian Book of the Dead. Budge, E. A. Wallis, tr. from EGY. (p. 506)
Romer, Marcus & Hinton, S. E. Rumble Fish. (p. 1495)
Romer, Ruth. cuidadores de mascotas & Pet Care Kids. (p. 390)
—Great Lemonade Standoff. (p. 717)
—Jill Gets Fit. (p. 917)
—Pattern Hike Dufalla, Anita, illus. (p. 1329)
—Pet Care Kids. (p. 1345)
—Welcome to Waterworld. (p. 1874)
Romer, Ruth, jt. auth. see Kramer, Alan.
Romer, Ruth & Kramer, Candice. Farflings from Farflung. (p. 573)
Romero, Alfonso Suárez. Maraca. Alvarado, Dalia & Pacheco, Luis Gabriel, illus. (p. 1091)
Romero, Enric Badia, illus. see O'Donnell, Peter.
Romero, Gina, illus. see Altieri, Marion.
Romero Gutiérrez, Astrid. Cuentos de Angeles Para Ninos. (p. 389)
Romero, Jordan. No Summit Out of Sight: The True Story of the Youngest Person to Climb the Seven Summits. (p. 1260)
—No Summit Out of Sight. (p. 1260)
Romero, Jordan & Blanc, Katherine. Boy Who Conquered Everest: The Jordan Romero Story. (p. 219)
Romero, Kyle & Padron, Maria Lorena. Herbert Hoover Junior Ranger Activity Book. National Park Service (U.S.) & Herbert Hoover National Historic Site (U.S), eds. (p. 769)
Romero, Libby. Adaptation. (p. 11)
—Characteristics of Animals. (p. 291)
—Characteristics of People. (p. 291)
—Comets. (p. 348)
—Coral Reefs. (p. 366)
—Dinosaurs. (p. 444)
—Discover Animals. (p. 447)
—Discover Comets. (p. 447)
—Discover Forensic Chemistry. (p. 447)
—Discover Kitchen Chemistry. (p. 447)
—Discover Mars & Venus. (p. 447)
—Discover Medical Chemistry. (p. 447)
—Discover People. (p. 448)
—Discover Plants. (p. 448)
—Discover Stars. (p. 448)
—Dry as a Desert. (p. 487)
—Forensic Chemistry. (p. 617)
—Kitchen Chemistry. (p. 962)
—Mars & Venus. (p. 1096)
—Medical Chemistry. (p. 1118)
—Plant & Animal Fossils. (p. 1368)
—Stars. (p. 1643)
—Tropical Rain Forests. (p. 1789)
Romero, Sensi. Familia de Nieve. Serra, Armando, illus. (p. 567)
Romero, Victor Eclar. Learn Filipino: Book One Francisco, Manny, illus. (p. 983)
Romero, Vivian. On the Lam with Lambert. (p. 1290)
Romero-Robinette, Joella. Allie & Bailey Show: Meet Our Family. (p. 47)
Romeu, Emma. Ahi Viene el Lobo Gris. Sanchez Vigil, Luis Gerardo & VandenBroeck, Fabricio, illus. (p. 30)
—Bosque para la Mariposa Monarca. (p. 215)
—Flamingo's Legs. Vigil, Luis Gerardo Sanchez & Broeck, Fabricio Vanden, illus. (p. 602)
—Forest for the Monarch Butterfly. Vigil, Luis Gerardo Sanchez & Broeck, Fabricio Vanden, illus. (p. 618)
—Gregorio Vuelve a Mexico. (p. 723)
—Gregorio y el Mar. (p. 723)
—Gregorio y el Pirata. (p. 723)
—Here Comes the Grey Wolf. Vigil, Luis Gerardo Sanchez & Broeck, Fabricio Vanden, illus. (p. 770)
—Mi amigo el manatí. Sanchez Vigil, Luis Gerardo & VandenBroeck, Fabricio, illus. (p. 1132)
—My Manatee Friend. Vigil, Luis Gerardo Sanchez & Broeck, Fabricio Vanden, illus. (p. 1214)
—Naufragio en las Filipinas. (p. 1237)
—Patas del Flamenco. Sanchez Vigil, Luis Gerardo & VandenBroeck, Fabricio, illus. (p. 1328)
—Rey de las Octavas. Moreiro, Enrique S., illus. (p. 1467)
Romey, Elizabeth A. Dragon Magic. (p. 477)
Romeyn, Debra. Passage to Monterey. May, Dan, tr. (p. 1326)
Romig, Hilary. Meet Ruby & Louise. (p. 1122)
—Mrs Crumbs' Trunk. (p. 1187)
Romita, John. Avengers by Brian Michael Bendis Volume 1. (p. 118)
—Daredevil: The Man Without Fear. (p. 406)
—Marvel Art of John Romita Jr. (p. 1098)
Romita, John, illus. see Lee, Stan, et al.
Romita, John, illus. see Lee, Stan.
Romita, John & Ditko, Steve. X-Men - The Hidden Year (p. 1967)
Romita, John & Windsor-Smith, Barry. X-Men (p. 1967)
Romita, John, et al. Amazing Spider-Man: Origin of the Hobgoblin. (p. 55)
—Marvel Masterworks. (p. 1098)
—Origins of Marvel Comics. (p. 1304)
—Thor by Dan Jurgens & John Romita Jr. (p. 1739)
Romita, John, Jr. World War Hulk. David, Peter et al, illus. (p. 1958)
Romita, John, Jr., illus. see Aaron, Jason.
Romita, John, Jr., illus. see Nocenti, Ann.
Romita, John, Jr., illus. see O'Neil, Denny & Fleisher, Michael.
Romita, John, Jr., illus. see Straczynski, J. Michael.
Romita, John, Jr., et al. X-Men: Ghosts. (p. 1967)
Romney, Dixon. Who's Calling Now? Dr. Higgins & the Story of Mrs. Bea. (p. 1920)
Romney, Marshall B. & Schiff, Andrew D. Casebook in Accounting Information Systems. (p. 275)
Romney, T. S. Legend of the Bully Slayer: The Dishonor Roll. (p. 989)
Romo, Adriana, illus. see Newman, Lesléa.
Romo, Brandyn. Rustlings of an Old Tree. (p. 1498)
Romo, David Dorado. Ringside Seat to a Revolution: An Underground Cultural History of el Paso & Juarez: 1893-1923. (p. 1473)
Romolino, Kimberly. Day at Sea. (p. 412)
Romoulous. Katalambano: The Strong Survive. (p. 944)
—Katalambano: Its a Family Affair. (p. 944)
—Katalambano: 187 Warriors Killers. (p. 944)
—Katalambano: Rise & Fall of Power. (p. 944)
—Katalambano: By any Means Necessary. (p. 944)
—Katalambano: Invasion of the Terror Dome. (p. 944)
Rompella, Natalie. Edgar, Allan, & Poe, & the Tell-Tale Beets. (p. 504)
—Experiments in Light & Sound with Toys & Everyday Stuff. (p. 549)
—Experiments in Material & Matter with Toys & Everyday Stuff. (p. 549)
—Obsessive-Compulsive Disorder: The Ultimate Teen Guide. (p. 1275)
Rompella, Natalie, jt. auth. see Sohn, Emily.
Romulo, Liana. Filipino Celebrations: A Treasury of Feasts & Festivals. Dandan-Albano, Corazon, illus. (p. 586)
Romulo, Liana, jt. auth. see Dandan-Albano, Corazon.
Romulo, Liana, jt. auth. see Laurel, Jaime M.
Ron, Berry. Daddy Do You Love Me. (p. 398)
—Mommy Do You Love Me. (p. 1162)
Ron Cherney With Angel Logan. Coming Out of Her Shell. (p. 348)
Ron Frazier, photos by see Janice Turner & Colleen Connelly.
Ron, Kurtz, jt. auth. see Roger, Moore.
Ronald, Robrahn, illus. see Bodenstein, Dan.
Ronan, James & Schussel, Sara. Parks Portrayed in Pen & Paint. (p. 1325)
Ronay, Laura. Kids Like Me... Learn ABCs. Kishimoto, Jon Wayne, illus. (p. 954)
—Kids Like Me... Learn Colors. Kishimoto, Jon Wayne, illus. (p. 954)
Roncagliolo, Santiago. Matias y los Imposibles. Wensell, Ulises, illus. (p. 1109)
Ronchi, Susanna, illus. see Harwood, Beth.
Ronci, Kelli. Kids Crochet: Projects for Kids of All Ages. Corwin, Lena, illus. (p. 953)
Ronco, Dan. PeaceMaker. Pidlubny, Donna, illus. (p. 1332)
Ronda Eden, illus. see Steve Cormey.
Ronda, Gilger, illus. see Bell, Debora.
Rondeau, Amanda. Base + Ball = Baseball. (p. 140)
—Bed + Time = Bedtime. (p. 156)
—Cat + Fish = Catfish. (p. 277)
—Do Something in Your City. (p. 457)
—Do Something in Your Community. (p. 457)
—Do Something in Your Country. (p. 457)
—Do Something in Your State. (p. 457)
—Ed As in Bed. (p. 503)
—Food Pyramid. (p. 614)
—Foot + Stool = Footstool. (p. 614)
—Freedom. (p. 634)
—Fruits Are Fun. (p. 645)
—Grains Are Good. (p. 706)
—Justice. (p. 940)
—Key + Board = Keyboard. (p. 950)
—Milk Is Magnificent. (p. 1143)
—Ob As in Knob. (p. 1275)
—Ock As in Block. (p. 1277)
—Og As in Dog. (p. 1280)
—Op As in Top. (p. 1299)
—Ore As in Core. (p. 1302)
—Ot As in Knot. (p. 1306)
—Ow As in Cow. (p. 1314)
—Pan + Cake = Pancake. (p. 1320)
—Proteins Are Powerful. (p. 1412)
—Rain + Bow = Rainbow. (p. 1434)
—Rattle + Snake = Rattlesnake. (p. 1440)
—Skate + Board = Skateboard. (p. 1583)
—Snow + Shoe = Snowshoe. (p. 1598)
—Sun + Screen = Sunscreen. (p. 1675)
—Tea + Pot = Teapot. (p. 1708)
—Vegetables Are Vital. (p. 1834)
—Volunteering. (p. 1850)
Rondeau, Amanda, jt. auth. see ABDO Publishing Company Staff.
Rondeau, Amanda & ABDO Publishing Company Staff. Compound Words. (p. 354)
—Do Something about It! (Set of 5 Titles) (p. 457)
Rondeno, Lisa. Fly, Boys & Girls Fly! (p. 609)
Rondina, Catherine. 10 Worst Things about Internet. (p. 1994)
—Don't Touch That Toad & Other Strange Things Adults Tell You. Sylvester, Kevin, illus. (p. 469)

—Gossip: Before Word Gets Around Workman, Dan, illus. (p. 703)
—Gossip: Deal with It Before Word Gets Around Workman, Dan, illus. (p. 703)
—Lighting Our World: A Year of Celebrations. Oakley, Jacqui, illus. (p. 1015)
—Lying: Deal with It Straight Up Workman, Dan, illus. (p. 1066)
—Rudeness: Deal with It If You Please Workman, Dan, illus. (p. 1494)
Rondinone, Craig. Jeepers. Simonton, Tom, illus. (p. 911)
Rone, Trenton. Once upon a Bully. (p. 1292)
—Once upon a Hamster (p. 1292)
—Once upon the Land of Second Shells (p. 1293)
Roney, Carley. Knot Guide for the Groom. Luu, Cindy, illus. (p. 965)
—Knot Guide for the Mother of the Bride. Luu, Cindy, illus. (p. 965)
Rong, Yap Kun, illus. see Dahl, Michael.
Rong, Yu, illus. see Dowson, Nick.
Rongner, Bridget, ed. see Merline, Sharlene.
Ronne, Susan. Webster the Spelling Dog. (p. 1870)
Ronney, David, illus. see Potter, Maureen.
Ronney, Ronnie, illus. see Moncure, Jane Belk.
Ronney, Ronnie, illus. see Petersen, Christine.
Ronnholm, Ursula O. Mi Libro de Palabras, Oraciones y Cuentos. Deliz, Osdila O., ed. (p. 1132)
Ronnie, Purple. Purple Ronnie's Little Book for a Smashing Dad. (p. 1419)
—Purple Ronnie's Star Signs. (p. 1419)
Ronnie, Purple, jt. auth. see Andreae, Giles.
Ronnie, Purple & Purple Ronnie. Purple Ronnie's Little Book for a Lovely Mom. (p. 1419)
Ronnquist, Debby, illus. see Wall, Patricia Q.
Ronquillo, Karen, jt. auth. see Swensen, Karen.
Ronsley, Jill, ed. see Quest, Stacy.
Ronte, Dieter. Christo & Jeanne-Claude: International Projects. (p. 316)
Ronzani, Maggie, jt. auth. see Bloom.
Ronzio, Robert A. Encyclopedia of Nutrition & Good Health. (p. 525)
Ronzio, Robert & Kennedy Associates Staff. Encyclopedia of Nutrition & Good Health. (p. 525)
Roo, Peter De, see De Roo, Peter.
Rood, Brian. Art of Brian Rood. (p. 102)
Rood, Brian, illus. see Disney Book Group Staff & Thornton, Randy.
Rood, Phil, illus. see Ferris, Susan.
Roode, Daniel. Little Bea. Roode, Daniel, illus. (p. 1023)
—Little Bea & the Snowy Day. Roode, Daniel, illus. (p. 1023)
Roode, Daniel, illus. see Ainsworth, Kimberly.
Roode, Daniel, illus. see Beaumont, Karen.
Roode, Daniel, illus. see Eliot, Hannah.
Roode, Daniel, illus. see Frankel, Bethenny.
Roof, Judith. Understanding Fiction. (p. 1815)
Rooke, Thom. Germ's Journey Trimmer, Tony, illus. (p. 667)
Rooke, Veronica, illus. see Raffa-Mulligan, Teena.
Rooks, Elizabeth. Rayne: Queen Water Supplier of the World. (p. 1441)
—Where Does Santa Go on Vacation after Christmas? (p. 1907)
—Where Does Santa Work after Christmas? (p. 1907)
Rookstool, Yakiri. Christmas Star. (p. 315)
Roome, Anne Ross. Global Economy. (p. 684)
Roome, Anne Ross, jt. auth. see Roome, Hugh.
Roome, Anne Ross & Mattern, Joanne. Cesar Chavez. (p. 288)
Roome, Diana Reynolds. Elephant's Pillow: A Chinese Bedtime Story. Daly, Jude, illus. (p. 512)
Roome, Hugh & Roome, Anne Ross. Global Economy. (p. 684)
Rooney, Ann. Amazing Mysteries: Messages from Beyond. (p. 55)
Rooney, Anne. 1001 Horrible Facts: A Yukkopedia of Gross Truths about Everything. (p. 2002)
—1990s. (p. 2002)
—50 Amazing Things Kids Need to Know about Math. (p. 1997)
—501 1/2 Horrible Facts. (p. 2001)
—50s & 60s. (p. 1997)
—Aerospace Engineering & the Principles of Flight. (p. 25)
—Agricultural Engineering & Feeding the Future. (p. 30)
—Alan Turing & His Binary Computer Code. (p. 33)
—Albert Einstein & His Theory of Relativity. (p. 34)
—Alcohol. (p. 35)
—Alexander Fleming & the Discovery of Penicillin. (p. 36)
—Alien Abduction. (p. 40)
—Apples Grow on Trees. Taylor, Lauren, ed. (p. 93)
—Artificial Intelligence. (p. 104)
—Audio Engineering & the Science of Soundwaves. (p. 114)
—Berlin Wall. (p. 167)
—Bullying. (p. 241)
—Carrots Grow under the Ground. Taylor, Lauren, ed. (p. 271)
—China. (p. 306)
—Communicate Online. (p. 349)
—Computers. (p. 355)
—Creative & Media Careers. (p. 379)
—Dealing with Drugs. (p. 418)
—Dinosaurs. (p. 444)
—Drugs on the Street. (p. 487)
—Earthquake: Perspectives on Earthquake Disasters (p. 497)
—Eighteenth Century. Woolf, Alex, ed. (p. 507)
—Evolution: Why Did Fish Grow Feet? And Other Stories of Life on Earth. (p. 546)
—Fact Factory. (p. 561)
—Feeding the World. (p. 580)
—Finding Facts (p. 588)
—Genetic Engineering. (p. 660)
—Health & Medicine: The Impact of Science & Technology. (p. 757)
—History of Medicine. (p. 784)
—How Should We Deal with Crime? (p. 812)
—Infectious Diseases. (p. 873)
—Internet Safety. (p. 880)
—Is Our Climate Changing? (p. 889)
—James Watson & Francis Crick & the Discovery of Dna. (p. 907)
—Jonas Salk & the First Polio Vaccine. (p. 925)
—Keeping Healthy. (p. 947)
—Kidnaps. (p. 952)
—Lettuce Grows on the Ground. Taylor, Lauren, ed. (p. 1003)
—Machines in Medicine. (p. 1068)
—Making Charts (p. 1080)
—Making Pictures (p. 1082)
—Math Journey Through Planet Earth. (p. 1106)
—Math Journey Through Space. (p. 1106)
—Math Journey Through the Animal Kingdom. (p. 1106)
—Math Journey Through the Human Body. (p. 1106)
—Medicine Now. (p. 1119)
—Mega Machine Record Breakers. (p. 1124)
—Muffin. Julian, Sean, illus. (p. 1189)
—No Wobbly Teeth Fiorin, Fabiano, illus. (p. 1261)
—Optical Engineering & the Science of Light. (p. 1301)
—Picture This. (p. 1356)
—Race Hate. (p. 1431)
—Reducing the Carbon Footprint. (p. 1456)
—Responding to Emergencies (p. 1463)
—Secret Services. (p. 1543)
—So You Want a Pet? (p. 1602)
—Solar Power. (p. 1606)
—Sorting Information (p. 1614)
—Space Record Breakers. (p. 1619)
—Spies. (p. 1627)
—Stars & Planets Handbook: What's Out There? (p. 1643)
—Starting with Words (p. 1644)
—Strange Places. (p. 1665)
—Sustainable Water Resources. (p. 1688)
—Take Control. (p. 1696)
—Tomatoes Grow on Vines. Taylor, Lauren, ed. (p. 1764)
—UFOs & Aliens. (p. 1808)
—Using Instructions (p. 1828)
—Vampire Castle. (p. 1832)
—Volcanoes. (p. 1849)
—Wallace & Gromit's World of Mysteries. (p. 1855)
—What If? (p. 1887)
—Why Do People Make & Sell Drugs? (p. 1924)
—Working with Words. (p. 1953)
—World after Super-Plague. (p. 1953)
—You Wouldn't Want to Live Without Antibiotics. Antram, David, illus. (p. 1977)
—You Wouldn't Want to Live Without Insects! Antram, David, illus. (p. 1977)
—You Wouldn't Want to Live Without the Internet! Bergin, Mark, illus. (p. 1977)
—You Wouldn't Want to Live Without Vaccinations! Antram, David, illus. (p. 1977)
—Zombies on the Loose. (p. 1988)
Rooney, Anne, jt. auth. see Crabtree Staff.
Rooney, Anne, jt. auth. see Endsaff, Najoud.
Rooney, Anne & Savery, Annabel. Creative & Media Careers. (p. 379)
Rooney, Anne, et al. Disaster Dossiers (p. 446)
Rooney, Claire. As Far as Far Enough. (p. 105)
—Color of Dust. (p. 343)
Rooney, David, illus. see Simms, George Otto.
Rooney, Frances. Exceptional Women Environmentalists (p. 547)
—Extraordinary Women Explorers (p. 555)
Rooney, Frances, ed. see Planned Parenthood Toronto Staff.
Rooney, Jeff B. Abby Smiles. (p. 2)
Rooney, Jodie C. Feather in Your Cap (p. 579)
Rooney, M. A. Rudy the Rescue. (p. 1494)
Rooney Moreau, Maryellen & Welch, Brian Scott. Talk to Write, Write to Learn Kit. (p. 1703)
Rooney, Rachel. My Life As a Goldfish. (p. 1212)
—Patch of Black Allwright, Deborah, illus. (p. 1328)
Rooney, Ronnie. Thanksgiving Recipes Rooney, Ronnie, illus. (p. 1726)
—There Was a Crooked Man. Rooney, Ronnie, illus. (p. 1730)
Rooney, Ronnie, illus. see Calder, C. J.
Rooney, Ronnie, illus. see Cosson, J.
Rooney, Ronnie, illus. see Crow, Melinda Melton.
Rooney, Ronnie, illus. see Fauchald, Nick.
Rooney, Ronnie, illus. see Ingalls, Ann.
Rooney, Ronnie, illus. see Jones, Christianne C.
Rooney, Ronnie, illus. see Jones, Christianne C. & Kipling, Rudyard.
Rooney, Ronnie, illus. see Kesselring, Mari.
Rooney, Ronnie, illus. see Kramer, Janice.
Rooney, Ronnie, illus. see Lyons, Shelly.
Rooney, Ronnie, illus. see Moncure, Jane Belk.
Rooney, Ronnie, illus. see Petersen, Christine.
Rooney, Ronnie, illus. see Quinn, Lin.
Rooney, Ronnie, illus. see Sanders, Karen Nordberg.
Rooney, Ronnie, illus. see Slater, David Michael.
Rooney, Ronnie, illus. see St. John, Amanda.
Rooney, Ronnie, illus. see Tourville, Amanda Doering.
Rooney, Ronnie, jt. auth. see Dapre, Alan.
Rooney, Sandra, illus. see Young, Lauren.
Rooney, Sean. Paddy's First Day at Hilltop School. (p. 1317)
Rooney, Thomas L. Tobey Boland & the Blackstone Canal. Donovan, Patte, illus. (p. 1760)
Rooney-Freedman, Isabelle. Angus MacDream & the Roktopus Rogue. (p. 75)
Roop, Connie, jt. auth. see Roop, Peter.
Roop, Connie & Roop, Peter. Good-Bye for Today: The Diary of a Young Girl at Sea. Allen, Thomas B., illus. (p. 697)
—Millions of Monarchs. Maydak, Michael S., illus. (p. 1144)
Roop, Connie, et al. Extreme Survivors: (Level 2) (p. 557)
—Penguins Are Cool!, Level 2. (p. 1337)
Roop, James Q. Billy Brahman: The Story of A Calf. Pomerantz, Norman, illus. (p. 187)
Roop, Peter. Abe Lincoln's Dog. (p. 4)
—Houdini: Prince of Air. (p. 802)
—Lead Us to Freedom, Harriet Tubman! (p. 981)
—Take a Stand, Rosa Parks. (p. 1696)
Roop, Peter, jt. auth. see Roop, Connie.
Roop, Peter & Roop, Connie. Animal Families. (p. 77)
—Botones Para el General Washington. Hanson, Peter E., illus. (p. 215)
—Buttons for General Washington (p. 248)
—Buttons for General Washington Hanson, Peter E., illus. (p. 248)
—China (p. 306)
—China. (p. 306)
—Did Pilgrims Really Wear Black & White? And Other Questions about Colonial Times. (p. 436)
—Down East in the Ocean: A Maine Counting Book. (p. 474)
—Explore the Midwest. (p. 550)
—Explore the West. (p. 550)
—Eye for an Eye. (p. 557)
—Go Fly a Kite, Ben Franklin! (p. 686)
—India (p. 870)
—Israel. (p. 893)
—Japan (p. 909)
—Let's Dream, Martin Luther King, Jr.! (p. 996)
—Let's Drive, Henry Ford! (p. 996)
—Let's Fly Wilbur & Orville! (p. 996)
—Let's Ride, Paul Revere! (p. 1000)
—Louisiana Purchase. Comport, Sally Wern, illus. (p. 1058)
—Manten Las Luces Encendidas, Abbie. Hanson, Peter E., illus. (p. 1088)
—River Roads West: America's First Highways. (p. 1476)
—Stormy Adventure of Abbie Burgess, Lighthouse Keeper. (p. 1656)
—Stormy Adventure of Abbie Burgess, Lighthouse Keeper. Trover, Zachary, illus. (p. 1656)
—Tales of Famous Animals. (p. 1702)
—Top-Secret Adventure of John Darragh, Revolutionary War Spy. (p. 1769)
—Top-Secret Adventure of John Darragh, Revolutionary War Spy. Trover, Zachary, illus. (p. 1769)
—Vietnam (p. 1841)
—Who Conducted the Underground Railroad? And Other Questions about the Path to Freedom. (p. 1915)
—Who Cracked the Liberty Bell? And Other Questions about the American Revolution. (p. 1915)
Roop, Peter, et al. Baby Dolphin's First Day, Level 1. (p. 126)
Roorda, Julie. Wings of a Bee (p. 1936)
Roos, Am & Hamilton, A. Turning the Page: Frederick Douglass Learns to Read. Adams, Michael, illus. (p. 1798)
Roos, Maryn, illus. see Goldberg, Whoopi & Underwood, Deborah.
Roos, Maryn, illus. see Goldberg, Whoopi.
Roos, Maryn, illus. see Schall, Jane.
Roos, Maryn, illus. see Schulte, Mary.
Roos, Maryn, illus. see Wesley, Valerie Wilson.
Roos, Maryn, illus. see Zuckerman, Rory.
Roos, Stephen. Gypsies Never Came. Liepke, Peter, photos by. (p. 734)
—Recycling George. (p. 1453)
Roosa, Bertha. Hobert Bears' Great Ideas. (p. 786)
Roosa, Karen. Pippa at the Parade. Fortenberry, Julie, illus. (p. 1362)
Roosevelt, Michele Chopin, illus. see Harrington, Geri.
Roosevelt, Theodore, illus. see Selda, Toby.
Roosevelt, Theodore, IV. Man in the Arena: Selected Writings of Thoedore Roosevelt - A Reader. Thomsen, Brian M., ed. (p. 1085)
Root, Alice. Job for Deirdre. (p. 919)
—What Is a Mule? (p. 1888)
Root, Barry, illus. see Barber, Tiki & Barber, Ronde.
Root, Barry, illus. see Burleigh, Robert.
Root, Barry, illus. see Fleischman, Paul.
Root, Barry, illus. see Jordan, Deloris.
Root, Barry, illus. see Kay, Verla.
Root, Barry, illus. see Peck, Jan.
Root, Barry, illus. see Ray, Mary Lyn.
Root, Barry, illus. see Schroff, Laura & Tresniowski, Alex.
Root, Barry, illus. see Sullivan, Sarah.
Root, Betty & Langley, Jonathan. My First Dictionary. (p. 1206)
Root, Christine B., jt. auth. see Blanchard, Karen.
Root, Edwin R. & Stocker, Jeffrey D. Isn't This Glorious! The 15th, 19th & 20th Massachusetts Volunteer Infantry Regiments at Gettysburg's Copse of Trees. (p. 893)
Root, Jeff, illus. see Dumesnil, Phil & Sanchez, Asa.
Root, Kimberly Bulcken, illus. see Fletcher, Susan.
Root, Kimberly Bulcken, illus. see Kay, Verla.
Root, Kimberly Bulcken, illus. see Peterson, Jeanne Whitehouse.
Root, Kimberly Bulcken, illus. see Winter, Jonah.
Root, Laura L. Quail in My Garden: Book One of Adventures in My Garden. (p. 1422)
Root, Phyllis. Aunt Nancy & the Bothersome Visitors. Parkins, David, illus. (p. 115)
—Big Belching Bog. Bowen, Betsy, illus. (p. 178)
—Big Momma Makes the World. Oxenbury, Helen, illus. (p. 182)
—Creak! Said the Bed. Dunnick, Regan, illus. (p. 378)
—Flip, Flap, Fly! A Book for Babies Everywhere. Walker, David, illus. (p. 604)
—Gran Mamá Hace el Mundo. Oxenbury, Helen, illus. (p. 706)
—Hop! Meade, Holly, illus. (p. 796)
—House That Jill Built: A Pop-up Book. Durand, Delphine, illus. (p. 804)
—Kiss the Cow! (p. 961)
—Kiss the Cow! Hillenbrand, Will, illus. (p. 961)
—Lilly & the Pirates. Shepperson, Rob, illus. (p. 1017)
—Looking for a Moose. Cecil, Randy, illus. (p. 1051)
—Mouse Has Fun Big Book: Brand New Readers. Croft, James, illus. (p. 1182)
—One Duck Stuck: A Mucky Ducky Counting Book. Chapman, Jane, illus. (p. 1294)
—One Duck Stuck. (p. 1294)
—Plant a Pocket of Prairie. Bowen, Betsy, illus. (p. 1368)
—Rattletrap Car. Barton, Jill, illus. (p. 1440)
—Rattletrap Car Big Book. Barton, Jill, illus. (p. 1440)
—Scrawny Cat. Friend, Alison, illus. (p. 1532)
—Ten Sleepy Sheep. Gaber, Susan, illus. (p. 1719)
—Toot Toot Zoom! Cordell, Matthew, illus. (p. 1768)
—Who Said Boo? A Lift-the-Flap Book. Larrañaga, Ana Martín, illus. (p. 1917)
Root, Tiffany. How Loud Can a Dragonfly Roar? (p. 810)
—Panda Trouble: Association of Insect Researchers Book #2. (p. 1320)
Root, Wendy Wasson. Adventures of Willow's Closet: The Pilgrimage. (p. 24)
Rooth, Mike, illus. see Boyd, David.
Rooth, Mike, illus. see Low, Vicki.
Rooth, Mike, illus. see O'Donnell, Liam.
Rooth, Mike, illus. see Smillie, Bryan.
Roots, Adrian, illus. see Brook, Henry.
Roots, Arleen. Except Ye Abide in the Ship. (p. 547)
Roots, Robert. Prepararse para el Lobo: Los secretos del exito a partir de Los Tres Cerditos. (p. 1395)
Rooyackers, Paul. 101 More Dance Games for Children: New Fun & Creativity with Movement. Marix Evans, Amina, tr. from DUT. (p. 1999)
Rooyackers, Paul, et al. 101 Dialogues, Sketches & Skits: Instant Theatre for Teens & Tweens. (p. 1999)
Rooyen, Suzanne Van. Other Me [Library Edition]. (p. 1306)
Roozen, John. Stories to Make You Dream. Meyers, Mark, illus. (p. 1655)
Ropal, Monica. When You Leave. (p. 1905)
Roper, Bob, illus. see Golden Books Staff.
Roper, Bob, illus. see Miller, Marvin.
Roper, Bob, illus. see Random House.
Roper, Clyde F. E., photos by see Cerullo, Mary M.
Roper, M. Rat Bear & the Rabbits: The Rat Bear Adventures. (p. 1440)
Roper, Robert. Dolls of Danger. (p. 464)
—Dora Goes to School. (p. 470)
—Dora Goes to the Doctor/Dora Goes to the Dentist. (p. 470)
—Fatal Mountaineer: The High-Altitude Life & Death of Willi Unsoeld, American Himalayan Legend. (p. 577)
—Happy Birthday, Dora! (p. 744)
Roper, Robert, illus. see Beinstein, Phoebe.
Roper, Robert, illus. see Dominguez, Adriana, tr.
Roper, Robert, illus. see Fisch, Sarah.
Roper, Robert, illus. see Fisher, Doris & Gibbs, D. L.
Roper, Robert, illus. see Larsen, Kirsten.
Roper, Robert, illus. see Ricci, Christine.
Roper, Robert, illus. see Valdes, Leslie.
Roper, Robert, illus. see Willson, Sarah.
Roper, Robert, jt. auth. see Random House Staff.
Roper, Shannon L. Mommy's Garden. (p. 1162)
Ropes, Mary. Mary Jones & Her Bible. (p. 1100)
Roppelt, Donna. Women Go to Work, 1941-1945. (p. 1945)
—Women Go to Work, 1941-1945. Harrington, A. Page, ed. (p. 1945)
Roppelt, Donna J. & DeAngelis, Therese. General A.P. Hill: Light Division Leader. (p. 660)
Roques, Dominique. Anna Banana & the Chocolate Explosion. Dormal, Alexis, illus. (p. 85)
—Sleep Tight, Anna Banana! Dormal, Alexis, illus. (p. 1588)
Roque-Velasco, Ismael. Cuba for Kids: Illustrated History Book/Libro de Historia Ilustrado. Montes de Oca, Gonzalo, illus. (p. 388)
Roraback, Amanda. Afghanistan in a Nutshell. (p. 26)
—Iraq in a Nutshell. (p. 887)
—Iraq in a Nutshell. Gerber, Kathryn, illus. (p. 887)
—Islam in a Nutshell. (p. 891)
—Pakistan in a Nutshell. (p. 1319)
Roraback, Robin, illus. see Hoffmann, Sara E.
Rorby, Ginny. How to Speak Dolphin. (p. 821)
—Hurt Go Happy. (p. 830)
—Lost in the River of Grass. (p. 1055)
—Outside of a Horse. (p. 1313)
Rorer, Abigail, jt. auth. see Berry, Wendell.
Rorick, William. Society. (p. 1605)
Rorie, A. Godly Warrior. (p. 690)
Rorvik, Bjorn F. Little Paintbrush. Hansen, Thore, illus. (p. 1033)
Ros, Jordina & Estadella, Pere. Fun Crafts with 2D & 3D Figures. (p. 647)
—Fun Crafts with Colors. (p. 647)
—Fun Crafts with Dots & Lines. (p. 647)
—Fun Crafts with Shapes. (p. 647)
—Fun Crafts with Sizes & Spaces. (p. 647)
—Fun Crafts with Textures. (p. 647)
Ros, Laura, jt. contrib. by see Vittachi, Nury.
Ros, Rafael, tr. see Blake, Stephanie & Blake.
Ros, Rafael, tr. see Corentin, Philippe.
Ros, Rafael, tr. see d'Allancé, Mireille, et al.
Ros, Rafael, tr. see Solotareff, Gregoire & Solotareff.
Ros, Rafael, et al. Entonces? Ros, Rafael, illus. (p. 531)
Ros, Roser. Musicians of Bremen/Los Musicos de Bremen. Montserrat, Pep, illus. (p. 1194)
Rosa, A. S. Draco Brothers. (p. 476)
Rosa, Don, jt. auth. see Benjamin, Paul.
Rosa, Don, jt. auth. see Van Horn, William.
Rosa, Don, et al. Uncle Scrooge #350. Clark, John, ed. (p. 1812)
Rosa, Guy. Friends. (p. 638)
Rosa, Jean-Pierre, jt. auth. see Marchon, Benoit.
Rosa, M. Nina, ed. see Osborn School Students.
Rosa, Marrisa, photos by see Harris, Mark Jonathan.
Rosa-Casanova, Sylvia. Mama Provi & the Pot of Rice. (p. 1084)
Rosado, Jessica E. Princess. (p. 1402)
Rosado, Michael, illus. see Townsan, Judy.
Rosado, Puig, illus. see Gripari, Pierre.
Rosado, Rafael, illus. see Aguirre, Jorge.
Rosado, Tom. On the Elevator: Add & Subtract Within 20. (p. 1290)
Rosado, Will, illus. see Dixon, Chuck.
Rosado-Machain, Julian. Guardians Inc.: the Cypher. (p. 728)
Rosaler, Maxine. Botulism. (p. 215)
—Coping with Asperger Syndrome. (p. 365)
—Cystic Fibrosis. (p. 397)
—Department of Agriculture. (p. 427)
—Hamas: (Rev) Palestinian Terrorists. (p. 739)
—Listeriosis. (p. 1022)
—Measles. (p. 1117)

R

—Timeline of the First Continental Congress. (p. 1754)
Rosales, Irene González. Esmeralda Does Very Good Things. (p. 536)
Rosales, Mary, tr. see Shaw, Sandra Anne.
Rosales-Martinez, Guadalupe, tr. see Reiter, David P.
Rosales-Yeomans, Natalia, jt. auth. see Ruiz-Flores, Lupe.
Rosales-Yeomans, Natalia, tr. see Flores, Carolyn Dee.
Rosales- Yeomans, Natalia, tr. see Ortiz Cofer, Judith.
Rosales-Yeomans, Natalia, tr. see Saldaña, René.
Rosa-Mendoza, Gladys. Alphabet. Cifuentes, Carolina, ed. (p. 49)
—Animals at the Farm/Animales de la Granja. Wolff, Jason, illus. (p. 82)
—Animals at the Farm/Animales de la Granja Big Book. (p. 82)
—Cars, Trucks & Planes/Carros, Camiones y Aviones. Tugeau, Jeremy, illus. (p. 272)
—Colors & Shapes. Cifuentes, Carolina, ed. (p. 345)
—English-Spanish Foundations Series: The Alphabet; Numbers; Colors & Shapes. Cifuentes, Carolina, ed. (p. 530)
—I Live Here!/Yo Vivo Aqui! Gonzalez, Margarita E. & Weber, Amy, eds. (p. 841)
—I Take Care of Myself!/Me Se Cuidar! Powell, Luciana Navarro, illus. (p. 846)
—It's My Birthday!/Es Mi Cumpleanos! Simard, Remy, illus. (p. 897)
—Jobs Around My Neighborhood/Oficios en Mi Vecindario. Iosa, Ann, illus. (p. 919)
—Let's Go to the Zoo!/Vamos Al Zoolgico! Elkerton, Andy, illus. (p. 998)
—Lola. (p. 1045)
—Lupe Lupita, Where Are You?/Lupe Lupita, Donde Estas? Ochoa, Ana, illus. (p. 1066)
—Lupe Lupita, Where Are You?/Lupe Lupita Donde Estas? Ochoa, Ana, illus. (p. 1066)
—My Body/Mi Cuerpo. Butler, Chris, illus. (p. 1198)
—My Clothes/Mi Ropa. Abello, Patricia & Weber, Amy, eds. (p. 1200)
—My Family & I. Cifuentes, Carolina, ed. (p. 1202)
—My Family & I/Mi Familia y Yo. Snider, Jackie, illus. (p. 1202)
—My House/Mi Casa. Borlasca, Hector, illus. (p. 1211)
—My School/Mi Escuela. Murphy, Terri, illus. (p. 1218)
—My Senses/Mis Sentidos. Merer, Laura, illus. (p. 1218)
—My Week/Mi Semana. Wesley, Milliana, ed. (p. 1221)
—Numbers. Cifuentes, Carolina, ed. (p. 1271)
—Opposites. Cifuentes, Carolina, ed. (p. 1300)
—Opposites/Opuestos. Cifuentes, Carolina, ed. (p. 1301)
—Weather. Cifuentes, Carolina, ed. (p. 1869)
—What Time Is It? Cifuentes, Carolina, ed. (p. 1894)
—When I Am/Cuando Estoy. Regan, Dana, illus. (p. 1902)
—Who Lives in the Sea?/Qui'n Vive en el Mar? O'Neil, Sharron, illus. (p. 1916)
Rosa-Mendoza, Gladys, creator. Fruits & Vegetables. (p. 645)
—I Can! (p. 834)
—Jobs Around My Neighborhood. (p. 919)
—My Body. (p. 1198)
Rosamilia, Armand D., ed. Clash of Steel: Reluctant Hero. (p. 327)
Rosanbalm, Sunny. Gift for Baby. (p. 675)
Rosano, John. Molly Monkey. (p. 1160)
Rosario Irish. Ensueño. (p. 531)
Rosario, Joann. Bitty Witty Witty Witty Witty Monkey! Rosario, Joann, illus. (p. 194)
—Double Diddley WHaaat! Rosario, Joann, illus. (p. 472)
—Happy- Go -Lucky Giraffe!! Rosario, Joann, illus. (p. 744)
—Joey & His Famous Fish! Rosario, Joann, illus. (p. 920)
—PenguinThat Boom- Booms to a Ferret That Zoom-Zoomed. Rosario, Joann, illus. (p. 1337)
—Puddy Cat & the Chick Muck. Rosario, Joann, illus. (p. 1414)
—Secret Swan King. (p. 1544)
—Swiggly Swiggly Do! Rosario, Joann, illus. (p. 1690)
—Trick That Turned into Poop! Rosario, Joann, illus. (p. 1786)
—Where Did Sabrina Go? Rosario, Joann, illus. (p. 1906)
Rosario, Miguel. Backyard Math. (p. 131)
—Car Math. (p. 265)
—Kitchen Math. (p. 962)
—Paramedic's Job. (p. 1324)
Rosario, Miguel & Rosario, Miguel T. Paramedic's Job. (p. 1324)
Rosario, Miguel T., jt. auth. see Rosario, Miguel.
Rosario, Nicole & Williams, Tim. University of Wisconsin College Prowler off the Record. (p. 1821)
Rosario, Raymond Giovanni Ramos. Juan Makes Lemonade. (p. 930)
Rosario, Sherwin. Meet the Letters. (p. 1123)
—Meet the Numbers Lift the Flap Book. (p. 1123)
—Meet the Numbers One to Ten. (p. 1123)
—Meet the Vowels. (p. 1123)
Rosas, Alejandro. Diario de Aurora. (p. 434)
Rosas, Beverly. Hand That Scared Jenny. Davis, Jeff, illus. (p. 740)
Rosas, Heather. 1-2-3 Count with Me! (p. 1990)
—ABC What Will I Be? Rosas, Heather, illus. (p. 3)
—Red Riding Hood's Rainbow. (p. 1455)
Rosas, Marcelino. Afuera: A Young Latino's Journey. (p. 29)
Rosasco, Jose Luis. Mariposa Negra y Otros Cuentos. (p. 1094)
Rosati, Gina. Auracle. (p. 116)
Rosato, Albert. Reindeer Games. (p. 1457)
Rosato, Bruno, jt. auth. see Baldwin, Stephen.
Rosciti, Donna. Birthday Train: Book 1. (p. 193)
Roscoe, Kelly & Isle, Mick. Aristotle: The Father of Logic. (p. 98)
Roscoe, Kelly & Roberts, Jeremy. Joseph Goebbels. (p. 926)
Roscoe, Lily. Night Parade. Walker, David, illus. (p. 1254)
Roscoe, Lorraine, jt. auth. see Denenberg, Dennis.
Roscoe Robinson, illus. see Robinson, Marquita E.
Roscoe, Terry, jt. auth. see Wilson, Budge.
Rose, A. First Flight. (p. 595)
Rose, Alea. There's a Bear in my House. Witt, Rici, illus. (p. 1730)
Rose, Alexa. Prankster Handbook. (p. 1393)
—Spy Games. (p. 1636)
Rose, Alice. Maria Dracula: A Fantasy Novel for Children. (p. 1093)
Rose, Amber, jt. auth. see Klutz Press Staff.
Rose, Andrea. Home for Abby. (p. 792)
Rose, C. T. Don't Play with the Craft (p. 468)
Rose, Caroline. Over in the Wetlands: A Hurricane on the Bayou Story. Dunlavey, Rob, illus. (p. 1313)
Rose, Caroline Starr. Blue Birds. (p. 202)
—May B. (p. 1112)
Rose, Carolyn Maree, illus. see Harper, Julie-Ann.
Rose, Carolyn Maree, illus. see Pretreger, Lidija.
Rose, Chloe Gayle & Rose, Tammy Marie. Snake That Eats Cake. (p. 1596)
Rose, Christine & Rose, Ethan. Rowan of the Wood. (p. 1492)
Rose, Craig, jt. auth. see Mills, Nathan.
Rose, D. M. Tail of Friendship: The Psychiatrist Is In. (p. 1695)
Rose, Darlene Deibler. Evidence Not Seen: A Woman's Miraculous Faith in the Jungles of World War II. (p. 546)
Rose, Deborah. Joshua Wears A Red Cape. (p. 927)
Rose, Deborah Lee. All the Seasons of the Year. Chorao, Kay, illus. (p. 46)
—Ocean Babies. Nakata, Hiroe, illus. (p. 1276)
—Someone's Sleepy. Andreasen, Dan, illus. (p. 1609)
—Spelling Bee Before Recess. Armstrong-Ellis, Carey F., illus. (p. 1625)
—Twelve Days of Kindergarten: A Counting Book. Armstrong-Ellis, Carey, illus. (p. 1800)
—Twelve Days of Springtime: A School Counting Book. Armstrong-Ellis, Carey, illus. (p. 1800)
Rose, Deborah Lee, jt. auth. see Kelly, Susan.
Rose, Dilys. When I Wear My Leopard Hat: Poems for Young Children. Allan, Gill, illus. (p. 1903)
Rose, Dorothy. Haunted House. Oechsli, Kelly, illus. (p. 753)
—I Wish That I Could Have a Pet. (p. 849)
Rose, Drew. God's Heroes. (p. 691)
—God's Son, Jesus. (p. 691)
—God's World. (p. 692)
—John Henry. (p. 922)
Rose, Drew, illus. see Ciminera, Siobhan & Testa, Maggie.
Rose, Drew, illus. see DeGrie, Eve.
Rose, Drew, illus. see Fisher, Doris & Gibbs, D. L.
Rose, Drew, illus. see Gallo, Tina.
Rose, Drew, illus. see Goldsmith, Howard.
Rose, Drew, illus. see Pingry, Patricia A.
Rose, Drew, illus. see Poland, Pitch & Poland, Inglan.
Rose, Drew, illus. see Ritchie, Joseph R.
Rose, Eilidh. I'm Just a Little Horse. Orkrania, Alexia, illus. (p. 859)
Rose, Elizabeth. Animal Adaptations for Survival. (p. 76)
—Animal Adaptions for Survival. (p. 76)
—Classification. (p. 328)
—Classification of Living & Nonliving Things. (p. 328)
—Daft Doggerels. (p. 399)
—Dotty Ditties. (p. 472)
—Food & Nutrition. (p. 613)
—Human Impact on the Environment. (p. 826)
—Primary Source Guide to Australia. (p. 1399)
—Primary Source Guide to Ireland. (p. 1399)
—Primary Source Guide to Mexico. (p. 1399)
—Primary Source Guide to Portugal. (p. 1399)
Rose, Ella. Rihanna. (p. 1472)
Rose, Emma. Animal Habitats (p. 78)
—Energy Every Day (p. 528)
—Our Natural Resources (p. 1309)
—Warning!: Extreme Weather Set (p. 1858)
Rose, Emma, tr. see Collodi, Carlo.
Rose, Emma & Capstone Press Editors. Warning! Extreme Weather (p. 1858)
Rose, Emma & Capstone Press Staff. Energy Every Day (p. 528)
—Our Natural Resources (p. 1309)
Rose, Ethan, jt. auth. see Rose, Christine.
Rose, Eya. Magic Blanket. (p. 1071)
Rose, Gerald. Bad Boy Billy! ELT Edition. (p. 131)
—Cambridge Plays: The Little Red Hen. (p. 255)
—Clever Tortoise. (p. 331)
—Dad Goes Fishing ELT Edition. (p. 398)
—Horrible Melena. (p. 798)
—Lion & the Mouse. (p. 1020)
—Sam's Cafe. (p. 1509)
—Tortoise & the Hare ELT Edition. (p. 1771)
—We're Going on a Picnic ELT Edition. (p. 1875)
Rose, Gill. Pablo y el Conejillo de Indias. (p. 1317)
Rose, Hayley. Do's & Don'ts. (p. 472)
Rose, Heidi, illus. see Pharr, Nancy Elizabeth.
Rose, Heidi, illus. see Stihler, Cherie B.
Rose, Hilda, illus. see Browne, Susan Chalker.
Rose, Hilda, illus. see Safer, Catherine Hogan.
Rose, Hilda, illus. see Sullivan-Fraser, Deannie.
Rose, Imogen. Initiation: Japanese Language Edition. Galeano, Tomomi, tr. (p. 874)
Rose, Jasmine. Last Caterpillar Princess. (p. 977)
Rose, Jeremy. Frog & the Fly. (p. 640)
—If I Could Fly... (p. 852)
Rose, John. Wikker. (p. 1928)
Rose, John N. Direct Approach: Maya 5. (p. 445)
Rose, Joyce Ann. Potter's House. (p. 1388)
Rose, Judith Robbins. Look Both Ways in the Barrio Blanco. (p. 1049)
Rose, Julia, tr. see Taniguchi, Tomoko.
Rose, Julianna, illus. see KaBOOM!.
Rose, Karen. Count to Ten. (p. 370)
—Don't Tell. (p. 468)
—You Can't Hide. (p. 1974)
Rose, Katherine. Annie Oakley. (p. 87)
Rose, Kathryn. Avalon Rising. (p. 118)
—Camelot Burning. (p. 256)
Rose, Kim, jt. auth. see Allen-Conn, B. J.
Rose, Lance, illus. see Wasserman, Shannon & Wasserman, Curt.
Rose, Larkin. No Leavin' Love. (p. 1258)
Rose, Laura Lopez. Chester the Christmas Cookie Jar. (p. 298)
Rose, Lela. Truth in Stories for Children 4 Through 6. (p. 1794)
Rose, Lisa. Shmulik Paints the Town. Echeverri, Catalina, illus. (p. 1568)
Rose, Lyman Hinckley. Pure & Chased. (p. 1419)
Rose, Lynda J. Assignment Earth. (p. 107)
Rose, M. E. Kangaroo Christmas. Keenan, Brona, illus. (p. 942)
Rose, Maddy. Midnight Feast. (p. 1138)
Rose, Malcolm, jt. auth. see Fairley, Melissa.
Rose, Marie. Princess Silver Tears & One Feather. (p. 1405)
Rose, Marilyn C. Kylie Gets a Cochlear Implant. (p. 969)
Rose, Martin, jt. auth. see Huser, Glen.
Rose, Mary. Doctor, Doctor. Wright, Craig, ed. (p. 459)
—Little Helpers. Wright, Craig, ed. (p. 1029)
—My Family. Wright, Craig, ed. (p. 1202)
—Reading Comprehension & Fluency, Grade 1: 30 Reproducible High-Interest Readings for Kids to Read Aloud at Home - With Companion Activities. (p. 1445)
—Reading Comprehension & Fluency, Grades 2-3: 30 Reproducible High-Interest Passages for Kids to Read Aloud at Home - With Companion Activities. (p. 1445)
—Week-by-Week Homework for Building Math Skills. (p. 1871)
Rose, Mary Catherine. Clara Barton: Soldier of Mercy. Johnson, E. Harper, illus. (p. 326)
Rose, Mary Kline. Great Blessing: The First 150 Years of the Coupeville United Methodist Church. (p. 714)
Rose, Melanie, illus. see Browning, Kurt.
Rose, Melanie, illus. see Edwards, Pamela Duncan.
Rose, Melanie, illus. see Gorman, Lovenia.
Rose, Melanie, illus. see Herzog, Brad.
Rose, Melanie, illus. see Michaels, Pat.
Rose, Melanie, illus. see Napier, Matt.
Rose, Melanie, illus. see Scillian, Devin.
Rose, Melanie, illus. see Smith, Marie & Smith, Roland.
Rose, Melanie, illus. see Ulmer, Michael.
Rose, Melanie, illus. see Ulmer, Mike & Ulmer, Michael.
Rose, Melanie, illus. see Ulmer, Mike.
Rose, Melanie, jt. auth. see Napier, Matt.
Rose, Melanie M. Zak Makes a New Friend: Zak's World Book One. (p. 1984)
Rose, N. R. Griffin's Calling. (p. 724)
Rose, Nancy. Secret Life of Squirrels. (p. 1541)
Rose, Naomi. Tibetan Tales for Little Buddhas. (p. 1747)
Rose, Naomi C. Tibetan Tales from the Top of the World. (p. 1747)
Rose, Nathalie, illus. see Jeanne, Diana.
Rose, Noel R., jt. auth. see Cassell, Dana K.
Rose, Or N. Abraham Joshua Heschel: Man of Spirit, Man of Action. (p. 6)
Rose, Patricia M., illus. see Hallwood, Cheri L.
Rose, Peter. Rattus Rattus: New & Selected Poems. (p. 1440)
Rose, Peter I., et al. Sociology: Understanding Society. (p. 1605)
Rose, Phyllis, jt. auth. see de Brunhoff, Laurent.
Rose, Phyllis & de Brunhoff, Laurent. Babar & the New Baby. (p. 123)
—Babar's Lost & Found. (p. 123)
Rose Publishing. Reformation Time Line. (p. 1456)
Rose, Robert. Godintoxicated Becoming Paranoid. (p. 690)
Rose, Robin. Reaching for the Stars. (p. 1442)
Rose, S. J. Plant Agriculture Education: 2012 Edition. (p. 1368)
Rose Salih, Sara. Tales of a Sevie. (p. 1702)
Rose, Sandra. Doggone Grief. (p. 462)
—My Mom Has Wheels. Talbott, Sherri, illus. (p. 1214)
Rose, Shirley. Let's Discover the Bible Yerkes, Lane, illus. (p. 995)
Rose, Simon. Air Force. (p. 31)
—Air Force Special Operations. (p. 31)
—Alchemist's Portrait (p. 35)
—American Revolutionary War. (p. 63)
—Andromeda: The Myth & Science. (p. 72)
—Animal Caretaker. (p. 77)
—Army. (p. 100)
—Army Rangers. (p. 100)
—Aung San Suu Kyi. (p. 115)
—Belugas. (p. 163)
—Canada's Olympic Torch. (p. 260)
—Cardiovascular System. (p. 266)
—Civil War. (p. 325)
—Clone Conspiracy (p. 333)
—Coast Guard. (p. 336)
—Colosseum. (p. 346)
—Coral Reefs. (p. 366)
—Cygnus the Swan: The Myth & Science. (p. 397)
—Delta Force. (p. 425)
—Digestive System. (p. 438)
—Doomsday Mask (p. 470)
—Emerald Curse Nugent, Cynthia, illus. (p. 517)
—Estuaries. (p. 538)
—Family Groups. (p. 568)
—Fisher. (p. 598)
—Flambeau Olympique: Les Emblèmes Canadiens. McMann, Julie, tr. from ENG. (p. 602)
—Green Berets. (p. 721)
—Hercules: The Myth & Science. (p. 769)
—Heretic's Tomb (p. 771)
—House of Representatives. (p. 803)
—Loonies: Canadian Icons. (p. 1052)
—Loonies: Les Emblèmes Canadiens. McMann, Julie, tr. from ENG. (p. 1052)
—Marine Corps. (p. 1094)
—Marine Corps Special Operations. (p. 1094)
—Mechanic. (p. 1118)
—Meteors. (p. 1130)
—Mexican-American War. (p. 1131)
—Muscular System. (p. 1192)
—Navy. (p. 1238)
—Navy SEALs. (p. 1238)
—Nelson Mandela. (p. 1240)
—Nervous System. (p. 1241)
—Office of the President. (p. 1280)
—Orion: The Myth & Science. (p. 1304)
—Pegasus: The Myth & Science. (p. 1335)
—Plumber. (p. 1374)
—Polar Ice Caps. (p. 1379)
—Resource Conservation. (p. 1463)
—Respiratory System. (p. 1463)
—Sea Urchins. (p. 1536)
—Sheikh Zayed Al Nahyan Grand Mosque. (p. 1564)
—Skeletal System. (p. 1584)
—Sorcerer's Letterbox (p. 1614)
—Sources of Light. (p. 1616)
—Sphere of Septimus (p. 1626)
—Split History of World War II: A Perspectives Flip Book (p. 1630)
—Sri Harmandir Sahib. (p. 1637)
—Taxidermist. (p. 1707)
—Time Camera (p. 1751)
—Ursa Major: The Myth & Science. (p. 1826)
—Vietnam War: 1954-1975. (p. 1841)
—War of 1812. (p. 1857)
—What Is Light? (p. 1889)
—World War II: 1939-1945. (p. 1959)
—Zapotecs. (p. 1985)
Rose, Simon, jt. auth. see McDowell, Pamela.
Rose, Simon & McDowell, Pamela. Sea Urchins. (p. 1536)
Rose, Sue. Jinxed! (p. 919)
—Perfect Moment. (p. 1342)
—Starstruck. (p. 1643)
Rose, Susanna Van, see Van Rose, Susanna.
Rose, Tammy Marie. Majik the Black Unicorn (p. 1078)
—Munchkin. (p. 1191)
Rose, Tammy Marie, jt. auth. see Rose, Chloe Gayle.
Rose, Thomas & Schilling, Wilber H., III. Where do we Start? (p. 1907)
Rose, Thorina, illus. see Kenny, Allison.
Rose, Valerie. Family Reunion Is Not A Real Vacation. (p. 568)
Rose, Valerie, as told by. You Better Recognize! A Spiritual Guide - Because Life's A Trip. (p. 1973)
Rose, Wendy. Bonnie & Clyde's First Christmas. Ruddy, Limner, illus. (p. 209)
Rose, Whitney. Woo Hoo, the Growing You'll Do. (p. 1949)
Rose, Williams. Octavus Octopus. James, Estes, illus. (p. 1277)
—Rena Rhinoceros. James, Estes, illus. (p. 1460)
—Taurus Rex. James, Estes, illus. (p. 1707)
—Ursus et Porcus. James, Estes, illus. (p. 1826)
Rosebrock, Katie. Tabitha & Dundee: A Story of Friendship. (p. 1694)
Rosebrough, Amy & Malone, Bobbie. Water Panthers, Bears, & Thunderbirds: Exploring Wisconsin's Effigy Mounds. (p. 1863)
Rosebrough, Ellen. Dora's Chilly Day. (p. 471)
—Dora's Chilly Day (Dora the Explorer) Mcgee, Warner & MJ Illustrations Staff, illus. (p. 471)
Rose-Heim, Donna. Dream Walking for Kids: 21 Prayer Activities for Children & Adults. (p. 484)
Roselius, J. Chris. Dallas Cowboys. (p. 401)
—Danica Patrick: Racing to History. (p. 404)
—David Beckham: Gifted & Giving Soccer Star. (p. 410)
—Houston Astros. (p. 804)
—Houston Rockets. (p. 804)
—Houston Texans. (p. 804)
—Kevin Garnett: All-Star on & off the Court. (p. 950)
—Magic Johnson: Basketball Star & Entrepreneur. (p. 1072)
—Matt Kenseth: Speeding to Victory. (p. 1109)
—Michigan State Spartans. (p. 1135)
—Richard Petty: The King of Racing. (p. 1469)
—San Antonio Spurs. (p. 1510)
—Soccer Skills: How to Play Like a Pro. (p. 1603)
—Surviving School: Managing School & Career Paths. (p. 1687)
—Texas Longhorns. (p. 1724)
—Tim Duncan: Champion on & off the Court. (p. 1750)
Rosell, Joel Franz. Tremenda Bruja de la Habana Vieja. (p. 1784)
Rosellini, Eleanor. Mystery of the Ancient Coins. (p. 1225)
Rosely, Rose, illus. see Kroll, Virginia L.
Roseman, Kenneth D. Jeremiah's Promise: An Adventure in Modern Israel. (p. 913)
—Until the Messiah Comes. (p. 1823)
Roseman-Mendoza, Natalie. Maritza's Garden Path. (p. 1094)
Rosemary, Sutcliff. Black Ships Before Troy: The Story of the Iliad. (p. 196)
Rosemary Wells. McDuff & the Baby. Rusan Jeffers, illus. (p. 1114)
Rosemary, Wells, jt. auth. see Wells, Rosemary.
Rosen, Anne, illus. see Adams, David J.
Rosen, Anne, illus. see Adams, Megan Weeks & Gamble, Adam.
Rosen, Anne, illus. see Gamble, Adam & Jasper, Mark.
Rosen, Anne, illus. see Gamble, Adam & Mackey, Bill.
Rosen, Anne, illus. see Gamble, Adam.
Rosen, Anne, illus. see Jasper, Mark.
Rosen, Anne, illus. see Vrba, Christina.
Rosen, Anne, jt. auth. see McCarthy, Dan.
Rosen, Barry. Do You Know What a Stranger Is? Rosen, Barry & Bell, Greg, illus. (p. 458)
Rosen Central, creator. Careers in Forensics. (p. 268)
—Inside College Football. (p. 876)
Rosen, Chaya & Braverman, Rivkie. Our New Special Baby. (p. 1309)
Rosen Classroom, creator. Map Activities for Primary Sources of Immigration & Migration in America: Reproducible Blackline Masters. (p. 1089)
Rosen, Daniel. Battles of the Civil War: Set of 6: Antietam. (p. 147)
—Battles of the Civil War: Antietam: Text Pairs. (p. 147)
—Dred Scott & the Supreme Court: Set Of 6. (p. 484)
—Dred Scott & the Supreme Court: Text Pairs. (p. 484)
—Independence Now: The American Revolution 1763-1783. (p. 870)
—Independence Now: The American Revolution, 1763-1783. (p. 870)
—New Beginnings: Jamestown & the Virginia Colony 1607-1699. (p. 1243)
Rosen, Daniel & National Geographic Learning Staff. Fight for Freedom. (p. 585)
—Jamestown & the Virginia Colony. (p. 907)

Rosen, David & Kendall, R. T. Christian & the Pharisee: Two Outspoken Religious Leaders Debate the Road to Heaven. (p. 311)
Rosen, Devora. Mystery in Spain. (p. 1224)
Rosen Editors. Fighting Infectious Diseases. (p. 585)
—Tackling Cancer. (p. 1694)
Rosen, Ellis J., jt. auth. see Rosen, Lev Ac.
Rosen, Gail, ed. see Cohen, Hilda Stern & Gilcher, William Harry.
Rosen, Gary. Learning Land Desktop. (p. 985)
Rosen, Gary, illus. see Sloan, Holly Goldberg.
Rosen, Jane. Thread. (p. 1741)
Rosen, Joe. Encyclopedia of Physics. (p. 525)
Rosen, Jonathan. Joy Comes in the Morning. (p. 929)
Rosen, Karen. Great Moments in Olympic Swimming & Diving. (p. 717)
—Great Moments in Olympic Track & Field. (p. 717)
Rosen, Kim, illus. see Peters, Marilee.
Rosen, Kim, illus. see Richardson, Gillian.
Rosen, Kymberlee S. Do You Have Better Manners Than the Monkeys at the Zoo? (p. 457)
Rosen, Lev Ac & Rosen, Ellis J. Woundabout. Rosen, Lev Ac & Rosen, Ellis J., illus. (p. 1962)
Rosen, Lucy. Batman Phonics Fun! Farley, Rick et al, illus. (p. 144)
—Dark Knight Rises: Batman Versus Catwoman. (p. 407)
—Despicable Me 2: Meet the Minions. (p. 430)
—Disney Fairies: the Pirate Fairy: Meet Zarina the Pirate Fairy. (p. 451)
—Epic: Meet the Leafmen. (p. 532)
—Epic: M. K. Saves the Day. (p. 532)
—Friends & Foes. Gordon, Steven E. & Gordon, Eric A., illus. (p. 638)
—I Am Bane. Cohn, Scott, illus. (p. 832)
—Justice League: Meet the Justice League. Gordon, Eric A. & Gordon, Steven E., illus. (p. 940)
—M. K. Saves the Day. (p. 1067)
—Meet the Leafmen. (p. 1123)
—Meet the Teen Titans. (p. 1123)
—Minions: Dracula's Last Birthday. (p. 1147)
—Minions. (p. 1147)
—Minions: Dracula's Last Birthday. Miller, Ed, illus. (p. 1147)
—Muppets: Bunsen & Beaker Save the Show. (p. 1191)
—My Dad the Super Villain. (p. 1201)
—My Little Pony: Meet Princess Twilight Sparkle. (p. 1213)
—My Little Pony - Meet the Princess of Friendship. (p. 1213)
—Paranorman: Meet the Ghosts. (p. 1324)
—ParaNorman: Meet the Ghosts. (p. 1324)
—Parasite City. Gordon, Steven E. & Gordon, Eric A., illus. (p. 1324)
—Planet 51. (p. 1367)
—Super Hero Showdown! (p. 1680)
—Superman Phonics Fun. (p. 1683)
—Superman's Friends & Foes. (p. 1684)
—Superman's Superpowers. (p. 1684)
—Superman's Superpowers. Tong, Andie, illus. (p. 1684)
—Teen Titans Go!: Meet the Teen Titans! (p. 1714)
—Transformers Rescue Bots: Blast Off! (p. 1778)
—Transformers Rescue Bots: Bots' Best Friend. (p. 1778)
Rosen, Lucy, jt. auth. see Universal.
Rosen, Lucy & Auerbach, Annie. ParaNorman: Attack of the Pilgrim Zombies! (p. 1324)
Rosen, Lucy, et al. Squeakquel: Meet the 'Munks. (p. 1636)
Rosen, Lucy, text. Despicable Me 2: Meet the Minions. (p. 430)
Rosen, Lynn. Tomorrow's Vision. (p. 1765)
Rosen, Lynn, jt. auth. see Mourabiti, Hassan.
Rosen, Marvin. Becca in Cyberland (p. 155)
—Brain & Love. (p. 221)
—Demystifying Dreams. (p. 426)
—Meditation & Hypnosis. (p. 1120)
Rosen, Maureen. KIDSCA$H en Espanol. Nickerson, Sally, tr. (p. 955)
—MYCA$H LP en Espanol: Large Print Cash Management Workbook in Spanish. Nickerson, Sally, tr. (p. 1222)
Rosen, Michael. Aesop's Fables Hackyan, Talleen, illus. (p. 25)
—Bananas in My Ears: A Collection of Nonsense Stories, Poems, Riddles, & Rhymes. Blake, Quentin, illus. (p. 136)
—Bear Flies High. Reynolds, Adrian, illus. (p. 150)
—Bear's Day Out. Reynolds, Adrian, illus. (p. 151)
—Bob the Bursting Bear. Ross, Tony, illus. (p. 205)
—Burping Bertha. Ross, Tony, illus. (p. 244)
—Bus Is for Us. Tyler, Gillian, illus. (p. 244)
—Dickens: His Work & His World. Ingpen, Robert R., illus. (p. 436)
—Even My Ears Are Smiling. Cole, Babette, illus. (p. 541)
—Fantastic Mr. Dahl. (p. 571)
—Farmyard Read & Play Set Langley, Jonathan, illus. (p. 575)
—Great Big Cuddle: Poems for the Very Young. Riddell, Chris, illus. (p. 714)
—Happy Harry's Cafe. Holland, Richard, illus. (p. 745)
—I'm Number One. Graham, Bob, illus. (p. 859)
—Michael Rosen's Sad Book. Blake, Quentin, illus. (p. 1134)
—Mustard, Custard, Grumble Belly & Gravy. Blake, Quentin, illus. (p. 1194)
—Nonsense. Mackie, Clare, illus. (p. 1263)
—Poetry. Archbold, Tim, illus. (p. 1376)
—Red Ted & the Lost Things. Stewart, Joel, illus. (p. 1455)
—Ronquidos! Langley, Jonathan, illus. (p. 1487)
—Running with Trains: A Novel in Poetry & Two Voices. (p. 1497)
—Send for a Superhero! McEwen, Katharine, illus. (p. 1550)
—Shakespeare: His Work & His World. Ingpen, Robert R., illus. (p. 1559)
—Snore! Langley, Jonathan, illus. (p. 1598)
—This Is Our House. Graham, Bob, illus. (p. 1736)
—Tiny Little Fly. Waldron, Kevin, illus. (p. 1756)
—Vamos a Caca de Um Urso. Oxenbury, Helen, illus. (p. 1831)
—We're Going on a Bear Hunt: Sound Book. Oxenbury, Helen, illus. (p. 1875)
—We're Going on a Bear Hunt: Anniversary Edition of a Modern Classic. Oxenbury, Helen, illus. (p. 1875)
—We're Going on a Bear Hunt. Oxenbury, Helen, illus. (p. 1875)
—You Wait till I'm Older Than You! Rayner, Shoo, illus. (p. 1976)
—You're Thinking about Doughnuts. Tisdall, Sarah, illus. (p. 1982)
—You're Thinking about Tomatoes. (p. 1982)
Rosen, Michael, jt. auth. see Carthew, Mark.
Rosen, Michael & Langley, Jonathan. Oww! (p. 1315)
Rosen, Michael & Oxenbury, Helen. Chung Ta Di San Gau. (p. 318)
Rosen, Michael & Quarto Generic Staff. Lovely Old Roly. Lamont, Priscilla, illus. (p. 1061)
Rosen, Michael & Rosen, Michael J. My Dog! A Kids' Guide to Keeping a Happy & Healthy Pet. (p. 1202)
Rosen, Michael, ed. Classic Poetry. Howard, Paul, illus. (p. 328)
Rosen, Michael J. Balls! Round 2. Margeson, John, illus. (p. 135)
—Chanukah Lights. Sabuda, Robert, illus. (p. 291)
—Chanukah Lights Everywhere. (p. 291)
—Chanukah Lights Everywhere. Iwai, Melissa, illus. (p. 291)
—Cuckoo's Haiku: And Other Birding Poems. Fellows, Stan, illus. (p. 389)
—Don't Shoot! Chase R.'S Top Ten Reasons Not to Move to the Country. (p. 468)
—Drive in the Country. Burckhardt, Marc, illus. (p. 485)
—Forever Flowers. Danowski, Sonja, illus. (p. 619)
—Girls vs. Guys: Surprising Differences Between the Sexes. (p. 681)
—Hound Dog's Haiku: And Other Poems for Dog Lovers. Azarian, Mary, illus. (p. 802)
—If You're Like Me, & I Know I Am: The Dizzying Business of Personality Tests. (p. 855)
—Maine Coon's Haiku: And Other Poems for Cat Lovers. White, Lee, illus. (p. 1077)
—Place Hacking: Venturing off Limits. (p. 1365)
—Sailing the Unknown: Around the World with Captain Cook. Pritelli, Maria Cristina, illus. (p. 1503)
—Sailing the Unknown. Pritelli, Maria Cristina, illus. (p. 1503)
—School for Pompey Walker. (p. 1523)
—Urban Exploration. (p. 1825)
Rosen, Michael J., jt. auth. see Rosen, Michael.
Rosen, Michael J. & Kaboom! Staff. Let's Build a Playground. Kelson, Ellen & Cecil, Jennifer, illus. (p. 994)
Rosen, Michael J. & Kassoy, Ben. Bizarre Vehicles. Sandy, J. P., illus. (p. 194)
—Crazy Buildings. (p. 377)
—Crazy Buildings. Jones, Doug, illus. (p. 377)
—Odd Medical Cures. Sandy, Pat, illus. (p. 1278)
—Strange Foods. Jones, Doug, illus. (p. 1665)
—Wacky Sports. Jones, Doug, illus. (p. 1852)
—Weird Jobs. Sandy, Pat, illus. (p. 1872)
Rosen, Michael J., ed. Purr: Children's Book Illustrators Brag about Their Cats. (p. 1419)
Rosen Publishing Group. FAQ: Teen Life (p. 572)
—Get Outdoors (p. 668)
Rosen Publishing Group, creator. 21st-Century Robotics. (p. 1996)
—Extreme Engineering. (p. 556)
—Future of the Web. (p. 651)
—Mysteries of the Milky Way. (p. 1222)
—Nanotech Revolution. (p. 1229)
Rosen Publishing Staff. African American Quartet (p. 27)
—All about the Author: Set 3 (p. 43)
—American History Arts & Crafts (p. 61)
—Animal Cannibals (p. 77)
—Artists Through the Ages: Set 2 (p. 104)
—Best Job Ever (p. 170)
—Brain Games (p. 221)
—Britannica Beginner Bios (p. 229)
—Britannica Common Core Library: Set 2 (p. 229)
—Britannica Guide to Cell Biology (p. 229)
—Checkered Flag (p. 295)
—Conspiracies & Cover-Ups (p. 359)
—Core Language Skills: Set 2 (p. 367)
—Core Skills: Set 2 (p. 367)
—Creating Comics (p. 378)
—Digital & Information Literacy: Set 8 (p. 439)
—Drawing Is Awesome! (p. 482)
—Excellent Science Experiments (p. 547)
—Exploring Ancient Civilizations (p. 551)
—Exploring Food Chains & Food Webs (p. 552)
—Farmyard Friends (p. 575)
—Fitness for the Mind & Body (p. 599)
—Giants on the Road (p. 674)
—Glow-In-the-Dark Animals (p. 685)
—Greatest Records in Sports (p. 720)
—Guide for Curious Minds: Set 2 (p. 730)
—Heroes & Legends (p. 772)
—Holiday Origami: Set 2 (p. 788)
—How Kids Lived (p. 810)
—Infomax Common Core Math Readers: Levels I - L (p. 873)
—Infomax Common Core Math Readers: Levels I - O (p. 873)
—Inside Special Forces: Set 2 (p. 877)
—Inside Sports: Set 2 (p. 877)
—Internet Biographies: Set 3 (p. 880)
—Invaders from Earth (p. 883)
—Know Your Rights (p. 965)
—Let's Find Out! the Human Body (p. 996)
—Let's Find Out! Weather (p. 996)
—Let's Talk about It (p. 1001)
—Living Fossils (p. 1041)
—Media Literacy (p. 1118)
—Objects in Space (p. 1275)
—Original Thinkers (p. 1304)
—Remarkable Lgbtq Lives (p. 1458)
—Right Degree for Me (p. 1472)
—Save the Animals (p. 1516)
—Scatalog: A Kid's Field Guide to Animal Poop: Set 2 (p. 1521)
—Scientific Breakthroughs (p. 1528)
—Scientist's Guide to Physics: Set 2 (p. 1529)
—Service Learning for Teens (p. 1553)
—Sports Tips, Techniques, & Strategies: Set 2 (p. 1633)
—Spotlight on Space Science (p. 1634)
—Story of Math: Core Principles of Mathematics (p. 1659)
—Teen Life 411: Set 2 (p. 1713)
—Understanding the Paranormal (p. 1816)
—Wild Side (p. 1930)
Rosen, Rachel & Benchmark Education Co., LLC Staff. Rob, Ron, & I. (p. 1478)
—Sit, Sit, Sit. (p. 1582)
Rosen, Roger, ed. see Mahoney, Ellen Voelckers.
rosen, stan. Friendly Ghosts. (p. 638)
Rosen, Steven & Steventon, John. History of Rock. (p. 784)
Rosen, Suri. Playing with Matches. (p. 1372)
Rosen, Suri, jt. auth. see Miller, Reagan.
Rosen, Wendy & End, Jackie. Chicken Fingers, Mac & Cheese... Why Do You Always Have to Say Please? Tuck-Bernstein, Cheryl, illus. (p. 300)
Rosenau, James N., ed. see Hoffman, Aaron M.
Rosenbaum, Andria Warmflash. Grandma Like Yours. Bjornson, Barb, illus. (p. 708)
Rosenbaum, Andria Warmflash & Gill, Deirdre. Trains Don't Sleep. Rosenbaum, Andria Warmflash & Gill, Deirdre, illus. (p. 1777)
Rosenbaum, Bev, ed. see Brown, Natasha.
Rosenbaum, Elizabeth, photos by see Trooboff, Rhoda.
Rosenbaum, Jason & Weisgerber, Amy. University of Missouri College Prowler off the Record. (p. 1821)
Rosenbaum, Leann. MaMaw Pee Wee & the Dancing Chair. (p. 1084)
Rosenbaum, Stephanie. Fun Food. Williams, Chuck, ed. (p. 647)
Rosenberg, Aaron. 42: The Jackie Robinson Story: the Official Movie Novel. (p. 1997)
—Alpha & Omega. (p. 48)
—Case of the Bookstore Burglar #3 Harrington, David, illus. (p. 273)
—Case of the Secret Sauce Harrington, David, illus. (p. 275)
—Case of the Topsy-Turvy Toy. Harrington, David, illus. (p. 275)
—Colleen Doran. (p. 340)
—Cryptologists: Life Making & Breaking Codes. (p. 387)
—Gamal-Abdel Nasser. (p. 654)
—Kick Scooters: Techniques & Tricks. (p. 951)
—Madeleine L'Engle. (p. 1070)
—Madeline L'Engle. (p. 1070)
—Mountain Biking: Techniques & Tricks. (p. 1180)
—Mountain Biking. (p. 1180)
—Taïg Khris: In-Line Skating Superstar. (p. 1695)
—Taïg Khris:In-Line Skating. (p. 1695)
—Thomas Hobbes: An English Philosopher in the Age of Reason. (p. 1738)
—Vladimir Putin: President of Russia. (p. 1846)
—World War II. (p. 1959)
—Yom Kippur War. (p. 1972)
Rosenberg, Amye. Melly's Menorah. (p. 1125)
—Mitzvot. (p. 1156)
—Surprise in the Mail! Salanitro, Robert, illus. (p. 1686)
Rosenberg, Amye, illus. see Gootel, Rifka.
Rosenberg, Arthur D. & Hizer, David V. Resume Handbook. (p. 1464)
Rosenberg, Betsy, tr. see Grossman, David.
Rosenberg, Carol. Dragonfly,the Caterpillar,and the Honey Bee. (p. 478)
Rosenberg, Carol & Rosenberg, Gary. Jon & Jayne's Guide to Throwing, Going To, & Surviving Parties: Advice & More from Your Average but Xtraordinary Friends. (p. 924)
Rosenberg, concept. Reach Your Goal. (p. 1442)
Rosenberg, Donna & McGraw-Hill Staff. World Mythology. (p. 1956)
Rosenberg, Faigy & Weiss, Esti. Hot! Hot! Hot! David, Racheli, illus. (p. 801)
Rosenberg, Gary, jt. auth. see Rosenberg, Carol.
Rosenberg, Gary, et al. Jon & Jayne's Guide to Getting Through School. (p. 924)
Rosenberg, Joe, ed. Aplauso! Hispanic Children's Theater. (p. 91)
Rosenberg, Liz. Tyrannosaurus Dad. Myers, Matthew & Myers, Matt, illus. (p. 1805)
—What James Said. Myers, Matthew, illus. (p. 1891)
Rosenberg, Liz, jt. ed. see November, Deena.
Rosenberg, Madelyn. Canary in the Coal Mine. (p. 260)
—Happy Birthday, Tree! A Tu B'Shevat Story. Christy, Jana, illus. (p. 745)
—How to Behave at a Dog Show. Ross, Heather, illus. (p. 815)
—How to Behave at a Tea Party. Ross, Heather, illus. (p. 815)
—Nanny X. (p. 1229)
—Nanny X Returns. (p. 1229)
—Schmutzy Family. Meisel, Paul, illus. (p. 1521)
Rosenberg, Madelyn & Crockett, Mary. Dream Boy. (p. 483)
Rosenberg, Marsha Sarah. Coping When a Brother or Sister Is Autistic. (p. 365)
—Everything You Need to Know When a Brother or Sister Is Autistic. (p. 546)
Rosenberg, Mary. Math Review, Grade 3. (p. 1107)
—Math Review, Grade 4. (p. 1107)
—Math Review, Grade 6. (p. 1107)
—Place Value, Grade 2. (p. 1366)
ROSENBERG, Mary, jt. auth. see Rosenberg, Mary.
Rosenberg, Mary & ROSENBERG, Mary. Math Review, Grade 5. (p. 1107)
Rosenberg, Mathew T., jt. auth. see Tucci, Paul A.
Rosenberg, Matthew T. Handy Geography Answer Book. (p. 741)
Rosenberg, Michael. Chilly Goes to Hong Kong & China: Another Chilly the Toy Polar Bear Adventure. (p. 306)
—Little Lost Tune: More Adventures from Bendalot. (p. 1031)
—Story of Bendalot. (p. 1657)
—Story of Bendalot Part: The Return Home. (p. 1657)
Rosenberg, Moshe. Morality for Muggles: Ethics in the Bible & the World of Harry Potter. (p. 1173)
Rosenberg, Nancy Taylor & Pearson Longman Staff. Michael Jordan. (p. 1134)
Rosenberg, Natascha, illus. see Seltzer, Eric.
Rosenberg, Natascha & Kempter, Christa. When Mama Can't Sleep. (p. 1903)
Rosenberg, Pam. Ack! Icky, Sticky, Gross Stuff Underground. Ramos, Beatriz Helena, illus. (p. 9)
—Alexander Hamilton: Soldier & Statesman. (p. 36)
—Baseball Jokes. Ostrom, Bob, illus. (p. 141)
—Bug Jokes. Ostrom, Bob, illus. (p. 236)
—Cave Crawlers (p. 282)
—Dinosaur Jokes. Ostrom, Bob, illus. (p. 442)
—Doctor Jokes. Cole, Mernie & Gallagher-Cole, Mernie, illus. (p. 459)
—Eek! Icky, Sticky, Gross Stuff in Your Food. Ramos, Beatriz Helena, illus. (p. 505)
—Eew! Icky, Sticky, Gross Stuff in Your Body. Ramos, Beatriz Helena, illus. (p. 505)
—Eleanor Roosevelt: First Lady, Humanitarian, & World Citizen. (p. 508)
—Gross-Out Jokes. Ostrom, Bob, illus. (p. 725)
—Healing Plants. (p. 757)
—How Did That Get to My Table? Cereal. (p. 806)
—How Did That Get to My Table? Ice Cream. (p. 806)
—How Did That Get to My Table? Orange Juice. (p. 806)
—How Did That Get to My Table? Peanut Butter. (p. 806)
—Is It Still a Number? (p. 889)
—Knock-Knock Jokes. Ostrom, Bob, illus. (p. 965)
—Monster Jokes. Ostrom, Bob, illus. (p. 1167)
—Robert Fulton: Engineer & Inventor. (p. 1479)
—School Jokes. Ostrom, Bob, illus. (p. 1523)
—Sunny Weather Days. (p. 1677)
—Tongue Twisters. Ostrom, Bob, illus. (p. 1765)
—Ugh! Icky, Sticky, Gross Stuff in the Hospital. Ramos, Beatriz Helena, illus. (p. 1808)
—Volcano Explorers (p. 1848)
—Waterfall Watchers (p. 1863)
—Watershed Conservation. (p. 1864)
—What Is a Plant? (p. 1888)
—Working at a Hospital. (p. 1952)
—Yecch! Icky, Sticky, Gross Stuff in Your House. Ramos, Beatriz Helena, illus. (p. 1969)
—Yikes! Icky, Sticky, Gross Stuff Underwater. Ramos, Beatriz Helena, illus. (p. 1971)
—Yuck! Icky, Sticky, Gross Stuff in Your Garden. Ramos, Beatriz Helena, illus. (p. 1983)
Rosenberg, Pam, jt. auth. see Alter, Judy.
Rosenberg, Rachelle, illus. see Disney Book Group Staff & Thomas, Rich.
Rosenberg, Rachelle, illus. see Marvel Book Group & Wong, Clarissa S.
Rosenberg, Rachelle, illus. see Wyatt, Chris.
Rosenberg, Shelley Kapnek. Challenge & Change: Book 3: the Twentieth Century & Beyond: History of the Jews in America. (p. 288)
—Challenge & Change: Civil War Through the Rise of Zionism (p. 289)
—Challenge & Change: Early Settlement Through Central European Migration (p. 289)
Rosenberg, Tziporah. Round & Round the Jewish Year: Elul-Tishrei. Vol. 1 Beifus, Ruth, illus. (p. 1491)
—Round & Round the Jewish Year: Cheshvan-Shevat. Vol. 2 Gross, Sherie, tr. (p. 1491)
Rosenberry, Akiko, illus. see Donaki & Rosenberry, Donald.
Rosenberry, Donald, jt. auth. see Donaki.
Rosenberry, Susan, illus. see Donaki & Rosenberry, Donald.
Rosenberry, Vera. When Vera Was Sick Rosenberry, Vera, illus. (p. 1905)
Rosenberry, Vera, illus. see Guthrie, Woody.
Rosenberry, Vera, illus. see Jane, Pamela.
Rosenberry, Vera, illus. see McDonald, Megan.
Rosenblatt, Danielle. Ant in the Cellar. Kirk, Jacqueline, illus. (p. 88)
Rosenblatt, Joe. Tommy Fry & the Ant Colony (p. 1765)
Rosenbloom. Get Well Quick! Jokes & Riddles. (p. 668)
Rosenbloom, Joseph. Jokes. Hoffman, Sanford, illus. (p. 924)
—Riddles. Hoffman, Sanford, illus. (p. 1471)
Rosenbloom, Joseph, jt. auth. see Keller, Charles.
Rosenbloom, Joseph & Artell, Mike. Tongue Twisters. Artell, Mike & Kendrick, D., illus. (p. 1765)
Rosenblum, Gregg. City 1. (p. 323)
—Fugitive X. (p. 646)
—Revolution 19. (p. 1466)
Rosenblum, Jill, jt. auth. see Reader's Digest Editors.
Rosenbluth, Roz. Getting to Know Ruben Plotnick. Manning, Maurie J., illus. (p. 669)
Rosendahl, Melissa M., illus. see Budic, Hannah Purdy.
Rosendo, Joseph, ed. see Dorling Kindersley Publishing Staff.
Rosenfeld, D. L., ed. see Altein, Chani.
Rosenfeld, D. L., ed. see Fajnland, Leibel.
Rosenfeld, D. L., ed. see Hodakov, Levi.
Rosenfeld, D. L., ed. see Levy, Leah.
Rosenfeld, D. L., ed. see Lieberman, Naomi.
Rosenfeld, D. L., ed. see Weber, Rivka Doba.
Rosenfeld, Devorah Leah, ed. see Hodes, Loren.
Rosenfeld, Dina. All about Us. Agroff, Patti, illus. (p. 43)
—Chanukah Story for Night Number Three. (p. 291)
—It's Called Kibud Av Va'Eim: A Story about Honoring Parents. Ebert, Len, illus. (p. 896)
—Tan Grande como un Huevo. (p. 1704)
—Yossi & Laibel Learn to Help. Nodel, Norman, illus. (p. 1972)
Rosenfeld, Dina, ed. see Benenfeld, Rikki.
Rosenfeld, Dina, ed. see Mermelstein, Yael.
Rosenfeld, Dina, ed. see Peysin, Shainy.
Rosenfeld, Susan C., ed. Encyclopedia of American Historical Documents (p. 524)
Rosenfelder, Cheryl, illus. see Vos, Sharon.
Rosenfelt, David. Open & Shut. (p. 1299)
Rosenfield, Geraldine. Heroes of Masada. Sugarman, S. Allan, illus. (p. 773)
Rosenfield, Kat. Amelia Anne Is Dead & Gone. (p. 57)
—Inland. (p. 874)
Rosengarten, Philipp G., jt. auth. see Stuermer, Christoph B.
Rosengren, Gayle. Cold War on Maplewood Street. (p. 339)
Rosenkrantz, Linda, jt. auth. see Satran, Pamela Redmond.
Rosenlund, Ranee. Benny the Frog's Leap of Faith. (p. 165)
Rosenlund, Ranee Mercier. Benny the Frog & His New Friends. (p. 165)

Rosenow, Ty. Historical Adventures of Thomas Balfour. (p. 782)
Rosenstiehl, Agnes. Silly Lilly & the Four Seasons. (p. 1576)
—Silly Lilly & the Four Seasons. Mouly, Francoise, ed. (p. 1576)
—Silly Lilly in What Will I Be Today? (p. 1576)
—Silly Lilly in What Will I Be Today? Mouly, Francoise, ed. (p. 1576)
Rosenstiehl, Agnes, jt. auth. see Hayes, Geoffrey.
Rosenstock, Barb. Ben Franklin's Big Splash: The Mostly True Story of His First Invention. Schindler, S. D., illus. (p. 163)
—Camping Trip That Changed America: Theodore Roosevelt, John Muir, & Our National Parks. Gerstein, Mordecai, illus. (p. 257)
—Fearless: The Story of Racing Legend Louise Smith. Dawson, Scott, illus. (p. 579)
—Littlest Mountain. Hall, Melanie, illus. (p. 1039)
—Noisy Paint Box: The Colors & Sounds of Kandinsky's Abstract Art. GrandPré, Mary, illus. (p. 1263)
—Streak: How Joe DiMaggio Became America's Hero. Widener, Terry, illus. (p. 1666)
—Thomas Jefferson Builds a Library. O'Brien, John, illus. (p. 1739)
Rosenstock, Gabriel. I Met a Man from Artikelly: Verse for the Young & Young at Heart. Staunton, Mathew, illus. (p. 844)
Rosensweig, Jay B. & Repka, Janice. Stupendous Dodgeball Fiasco. Dibley, Glin, illus. (p. 1670)
Rosenthal, Adam. Adventures of Snizznsnozz. (p. 23)
Rosenthal, Amy Krouse. Al Pha's Bet. Durand, Delphine, illus. (p. 32)
—Bedtime for Mommy. Pham, LeUyen, illus. (p. 157)
—Chopsticks. Magoon, Scott, illus. (p. 310)
—Christmas Cookies: Bite-Size Holiday Lessons. Dyer, Jane, illus. (p. 313)
—Cookies: Bite-Size Life Lessons. Dyer, Jane, illus. (p. 361)
—Don't Blink! Light, Kelly, illus. (p. 467)
—Duck! Rabbit! Lichtenheld, Tom, illus. (p. 488)
—Exclamation Mark. Lichtenheld, Tom, illus. (p. 547)
—I Scream! Ice Cream! A Book of Wordles. Bloch, Serge, illus. (p. 845)
—I Wish You More. Lichtenheld, Tom, illus. (p. 849)
—It's Not Fair! Lichtenheld, Tom, illus. (p. 898)
—Little Hoot. Corace, Jen, illus. (p. 1029)
—Little Miss, Big Sis. Reynolds, Peter H., illus. (p. 1031)
—Little Oink. Corace, Jen, illus. (p. 1032)
—Little Pea. Corace, Jen, illus. (p. 1033)
—Little Pea - Little Hoot - Little Oink Corace, Jen, illus. (p. 1033)
—One of Those Days. Doughty, Rebecca, illus. (p. 1296)
—One Smart Cookie: Bite-Size Lessons for the School Years & Beyond. Dyer, Jane & Dyer, Brooke, illus. (p. 1297)
—Plant a Kiss. Reynolds, Peter H., illus. (p. 1368)
—Spoon. Magoon, Scott, illus. (p. 1631)
—Sugar Cookies: Sweet Little Lessons on Love. Dyer, Jane & Dyer, Brooke, illus. (p. 1672)
—This Plus That: Life's Little Equations. Corace, Jen, illus. (p. 1737)
—Uni the Unicorn. Barrager, Brigette, illus. (p. 1817)
—Wonder Book. Schmid, Paul, illus. (p. 1947)
—Wumbers. (p. 1966)
—Wumbers. Lichtenheld, Tom, illus. (p. 1966)
—Yes Day! Lichtenheld, Tom, illus. (p. 1970)
Rosenthal, Amy Krouse & Lichtenheld, Tom. Exclamation Mark. (p. 547)
—OK Book. Rosenthal, Amy Krouse & Lichtenheld, Tom, illus. (p. 1282)
—Ok Book. Rosenthal, Amy Krouse & Lichtenheld, Tom, illus. (p. 1282)
Rosenthal, Amy Krouse, narrated by. Spoon. (p. 1631)
Rosenthal, Beth. Are Executives Paid Too Much? Greenhaven Press Editors, ed. (p. 96)
—Atheism. (p. 112)
—Birth Control. (p. 192)
—Cheating. (p. 295)
—Gay Parenting. (p. 659)
Rosenthal, Beth & Des Chenes, Elizabeth, eds. Gun Control. (p. 732)
Rosenthal, Beth, ed. Gay Parenting. (p. 659)
Rosenthal, Betsy R. Ambush of Tigers: A Wild Gathering of Collective Nouns. Jago, illus. (p. 57)
—It's Not Worth Making a Tzimmes Over! Rivers, Ruth, illus. (p. 898)
—Looking for Me: In This Great Big Family. (p. 1051)
—Looking for Me. (p. 1051)
Rosenthal, Cathy M. Lucky Tale of Two Dogs. Warrick, Jessica, illus. (p. 1063)
Rosenthal, Cynthia. Day in Mexico. (p. 413)
—Matt Does Math at the Ball Game. (p. 1109)
Rosenthal, Eileen. Bobo the Sailor Man! Rosenthal, Marc, illus. (p. 206)
—I Must Have Bobo! Rosenthal, Marc, illus. (p. 844)
—I'll Save You Bobo! Rosenthal, Marc, illus. (p. 856)
Rosenthal, Howard L., et al, eds. What Do We Owe Each Other? Rights & Obligations in Contemporary American Society. (p. 1882)
Rosenthal, Marc. Archie & the Pirates. Rosenthal, Marc, illus. (p. 95)
—Big Bot, Small Bot: A Book of Robot Opposites. (p. 179)
—Phooey! Rosenthal, Marc, illus. (p. 1352)
Rosenthal, Marc, illus. see Appelt, Kathi.
Rosenthal, Marc, illus. see McGhee, Alison.
Rosenthal, Marc, illus. see Rosenthal, Eileen.
Rosenthal, Marc, illus. see Zimmerman, Andrea & Clemesha, David.
Rosenthal, Marc, illus. see Zimmerman, Andrea Griffing & Clemesha, David.
Rosenthal, Marc, tr. see Zimmerman, Andrea Griffing & Clemesha, David.
Rosenthal, Michele Marie. Frog & the Tadpole's Great Swamp Adventure (p. 640)
Rosenthal, Pamela. My Trip to the Zoo. (p. 1220)
Rosenthal, S. L. Mama, Where Do Our Butterflies Go in the Winter? (p. 1084)
Rosenthal, Sally. Matzo Frogs. Sheldon, David, illus. (p. 1110)
Rosenthal, Sue. Whales. McGinty, Mick, illus. (p. 1878)
Rosenthal, Zelda B. Precious Jewels: The Roadmap to a Child's Heart - a Delightful Resources for Mothers & Teachers. (p. 1394)
Rosenthal-Gazit, Roni. On Shapes & More. (p. 1289)
Rosenwasser, Rena, ed. see Kitrilakis, Thalia.
Rosenwasser, Robert, illus. see Kitrilakis, Thalia.
Rosenzweig, Charlotte, et al. Path to Research. (p. 1328)
Rosenzweig, Sharon, jt. auth. see Freeman, Aaron.
Rose-Popp, Melanie, illus. see Ulmer, Mike.
Roser, Nancy, jt. see deRubertis, Barbara.
Roser, Nancy & Gillet, Jean Wallace. SRA Spelling: Ball & Stick. (p. 1637)
—SRA Spelling: Continuous Stroke. (p. 1637)
Rosero, Evelio. Duenda. (p. 489)
—Juega el Amor. (p. 931)
—Teresita Cantaba. (p. 1721)
Rosero, Tucídides Perea. Reglamento Oficial Ilustrado Beisbol. (p. 1457)
Rosewald, Mary. Tara's Telescope. (p. 1706)
Rosewarne, Graham, illus. see Johnson, Jinny.
Rosewarne, Graham, et al. Discover the Amazing World of Animals. (p. 448)
Rosewood, Maya, tr. see Tezuka, Osamu.
Rosewood, Olivia. My French School: Mon École Francaise. (p. 1209)
Rosh, Mair, jt. auth. see DuBois, Jill.
Roshdi, Teymur. Solatium for the Child of Events! The Youth. (p. 1607)
Roshell, Starshine. Real-Life Royalty. (p. 1448)
Roshell, Starshine & Kelley, K. C. Day with a Fashion Designer. (p. 414)
Rosie, Maura & Gavlik, Sherry. Animal Adventures at the Farm. Johnson, Dolores Uselman, illus. (p. 76)
Rosier, Joan. Christmas Stilts. (p. 315)
Rosier, Maggie. Aliens. (p. 41)
—Dinosaurs. (p. 444)
—Robots. (p. 1481)
—Sharks. (p. 1562)
Rosier, Michelle. Elementary Spanish - Worktext Step 1. (p. 510)
—Elementary Spanish—Worktext Step 2. (p. 510)
Rosier, Paul C., jt. auth. see Bonvillain, Nancy.
Rosier, Paul C., jt. auth. see Jastrzembski, Joseph C.
Rosier, Paul C., jt. auth. see Lacey, Theresa Jensen.
Rosier, Paul C., jt. auth. see Pritzker, Barry M.
Rosier, Paul C., jt. auth. see Rzeczkowski, Frank.
Rosier, Paul C. & Crompton, Samuel Willard. Cheyenne. (p. 299)
Rosing, Norbert. Polar Bears. (p. 1379)
Rosing, Norbert, jt. auth. see Carney, Elizabeth.
Rosing, Norbert & Carney, Elizabeth. Face to Face with Polar Bears. (p. 560)
Rosinola, Anita Marie. Acorn for Emily: The True Story of One Remarkable Squirrel. (p. 9)
Rosinski, illus. see Hamme, Van.
Rosinski, illus. see Van Hamme, Jean.
Rosinski, Adolf, illus. see Rosinski & Van Hamme, Jean.
Rosinski & Van Hamme, Jean. Child of the Stars. Rosinski, Adolf, illus. (p. 308)
Rosinski, Carol. Getting Started: Discover Your Inner Artist as You Explore the Basic Theories & Techniques of Pencil Drawing. (p. 669)
Rosinski, Grzegorz, illus. see Dufaux, Jean.
Rosinski, Grzegorz, illus. see Van Hamme, Jean.
Rosinski, Grzegorz, illus. see van Hamme, Jean.
Rosinski, Grzegorz, illus. see Van Hamme, Jean.
Rosinsky, Natalie M. Aguas: Arriba, Abajo y en Todos Lados Robledo, Sol, tr. from ENG. (p. 30)
—Algonquin (p. 38)
—Ancient China (p. 68)
—California Ranchos Rosinsky, Natalie M., illus. (p. 253)
—Draft Lottery. (p. 476)
—Graphic Content! The Culture of Comic Books (p. 710)
—Hinduism (p. 780)
—Hospital. (p. 801)
—Imanes: Atraen y Rechazan Robledo, Sol, tr. from ENG. (p. 861)
—Judaism (p. 930)
—Kent State Shootings. (p. 949)
—Powhatan & Their History. (p. 1391)
—Sonido: Fuerte, Suave, Alto y Bajo Robledo, Sol, tr. from ENG. (p. 1612)
—Story of Pharmaceuticals: How They Changed the World (p. 1659)
—Story of the Atomic Bomb: How It Changed the World (p. 1660)
—Suelo: Tierra y Arena Robledo, Sol, tr. (p. 1672)
—Write Your Own Biography (p. 1964)
—Write Your Own Fable (p. 1964)
—Write Your Own Fairy Tale (p. 1964)
—Write Your Own Folktale (p. 1964)
—Write Your Own Graphic Novel (p. 1964)
—Write Your Own Legend (p. 1964)
—Write Your Own Myth (p. 1964)
—Write Your Own Nonfiction (p. 1964)
Rosinsky, Natalie M. & Picture Window Books Staff. Imanes: Atraen y Rechazan Robledo, Sol, tr. from ENG. (p. 861)
—Luz: Sombras, Espejos y Arco Iris Robledo, Sol, tr. from ENG. (p. 1066)
—Rocas: Duras, Blandas, Lisas y Ásperas. Robledo, Sol, tr. from ENG. (p. 1481)
—Sonido: Fuerte, Suave, Alto y Bajo Robledo, Sol, tr. from ENG. (p. 1612)
Roski, Gayle Garner, illus. see Olivas, John D.
Roski, Gayle Garner, illus. see Smith, Icy.
Roski, Gayle Garner, illus. see Smith, Michael.
Roski, Gayle Garner, jt. auth. see Smith, Michael.
Roskies, David G., jt. auth. see Roskies, Diane K.
Roskies, Diane K. & Roskies, David G. Shtetl Book. (p. 1571)
Roskifte, Kristin. Animal Beauty. (p. 76)
Roskilly, Jedda, jt. auth. see Russ, Tim.
Roskinski, Grzegorz, illus. see Van Hamme, Jean.
Roskos, Evan. Dr. Bird's Advice for Sad Poets. (p. 475)
Rosland, Linsey. How Much Do I Love You? (p. 811)
Rosler, O'Sullivan. It could be worse - oder? Eine deutsch-englische Geschichte. (p. 893)
Roslund, Samantha. Join Forces: Teaming up Online. (p. 924)
Roslund, Samantha & Fontichiaro, Kristin. Maker Faire. (p. 1080)
Roslund, Samantha & Rodgers, Emily Puckett. Makerspaces. (p. 1080)
Roslyn, Jacquelyn, illus. see Ureel, Jessica & Jacobs, Jessica.
Rosman, Yitz. Jerry Sets Sail. (p. 913)
Rosner, Gillian, tr. see Weil, Sylvie.
Rosner, Hannah. Ambulance Club. (p. 57)
Rosner, Linda, jt. auth. see Bowden, Mary Ellen.
Rosner, Marc Alan. Science Fair Success Using the Internet. (p. 1526)
Rosner, Mina. I Am a Witness. (p. 832)
Rosney, C., jt. auth. see Craig, A.
Rosno, Connie. This Is My Lucky Day. (p. 1736)
Rosoff, Iris, ed. see Dorling Kindersley Publishing Staff.
Rosoff, Meg. How I Live Now. (p. 810)
—Just in Case. (p. 938)
—Meet Wild Boars. Blackall, Sophie, illus. (p. 1123)
—Picture Me Gone. (p. 1355)
—There Is No Dog. (p. 1730)
—What I Was. (p. 1887)
Ross, Adam, illus. see Wainwright, Joann M.
Ross, Alan Eugene, compiled by. Genuine Jesus. (p. 661)
Ross, Alex, illus. see Busiek, Kurt.
Ross, Alex, illus. see Kruger, Jim.
Ross, Alex, et al. Absolute Kingdom Come. (p. 7)
—Cover to Cover: The Greatest Comic Book Covers of the Dark Knight. (p. 373)
Ross, Alice & Ross, Kent. Dama de Cobre. Bowman, Leslie, illus. (p. 401)
Ross, Allison J. Choosing a Career in Desktop Publishing. (p. 310)
—Coping When a Parent Is Mentally Ill. (p. 365)
—Everything You Need to Know about Anemia. (p. 545)
—Everything You Need to Know about Social Anxiety. (p. 546)
Ross, Allison J., jt. auth. see Harrison, Scott.
Ross, Allison J. & Harrison, Scott. Choosing a Career in Carpentry. (p. 310)
Ross, Andrea. Turtles Go Slow. Ross, Andrea, illus. (p. 1799)
Ross, Angus, ed. see Smollett, Tobias George.
Ross, Bakthi. Millipede Curl. (p. 1144)
Ross, Barbara & Beatty, Nicholas. Goops Circus: A Whimsical Telling of Do-Good Tales. Camille, Diana, illus. (p. 702)
Ross, Barbara, ed. Goops & How to Be Them: A Manual of Manners for Polite Children. (p. 702)
Ross, Betsy. Problem Solvers: Two Boys Solve Problems in Different Ways. (p. 1408)
Ross, Brad. Hocus Pocus Al I Mi Choo. Arnold, Michael, illus. (p. 787)
Ross, Brian, jt. auth. see Sacks, David.
Ross, C., illus. see Dorison, Xavier & Nury, Fabian.
Ross, C. M. Lotus Flower Girl. (p. 1057)
Ross, Casey. Vital Skills: How to Exercise Your Independence. (p. 1846)
Ross, Catherine Sheldrick. Shapes in Math, Science & Nature: Squares, Triangles & Circles. Slavin, Bill, illus. (p. 1560)
Ross, Cathy. Tater Town. (p. 1707)
Ross, Christine, illus. see Booth, David.
Ross, Christine, illus. see Holden, Pam.
Ross, Christine, illus. see Wallace, Jessica.
Ross, Chudney. Lone Bean. (p. 1046)
Ross, D. J., jt. auth. see Dumas, Bianca.
Ross, D. J., jt. auth. see Redmond, Jim.
Ross, Daisy. Peter's Pets. (p. 1347)
Ross, Daisy T. Ty & the Moon. (p. 1804)
Ross, Dalton. Top Teams Ever: Football, Baseball, Basketball & Hockey Winners. (p. 1769)
—Top Teams Ever: Football, Baseball, Basketball, & Hockey Winners. (p. 1769)
Ross, Damon, photos by see Weiss, Ellen.
Ross, Daniel Vaughn, illus. see Petrucha, Stefan, et al.
Ross, Darien. Carr House Cats at Christmas. (p. 271)
Ross, Dave. Not-so-Scary Monster Handbook: Halloween. Ross, Dave, illus. (p. 1267)
Ross, Dave, illus. see Scott, Greg.
Ross, David & Cattell, Bob. Bad Boys. (p. 131)
—Big Deal. (p. 181)
—World Cup. (p. 1954)
—Young Blood. (p. 1978)
Ross, Deborah, illus. see Jolly, Alison.
Ross, Dev. Los dos leemos-el Mejor Truco de Zorro: Nivel 1. Reinhart, Larry, illus. (p. 1053)
—Los dos leemos-el Mejor Truco de Zorro. Reinhart, Larry, illus. (p. 1053)
—Los dos leemos-Sapi y el Gigante. Reinhart, Larry, illus. (p. 1054)
—Los dos leemos-Sapi y el Gigante. Canetti, Yanitzia James, tr. (p. 1054)
—We Both Read Bilingual Edition-Frank & the Giant/Sapi y el Globo. Reinhart, Larry, illus. (p. 1866)
—We Both Read-Fox's Best Trick Ever: Level 1. Reinhart, Larry, illus. (p. 1866)
—We Both Read-Frank & the Balloon: Level K-1. Reinhart, Larry, illus. (p. 1866)
—We Both Read-Frank & the Giant. (p. 1866)
—We Both Read-Frank & the Giant (Picture Book) Reinhart, Larry, illus. (p. 1866)
—We Both Read-Frank & the Tiger. Reinhart, Larry, illus. (p. 1866)
—We Both Read-Oh No! We're Doing a Show! Johnson, Meredith, illus. (p. 1866)
—We Both Read-Soccer! Wenzel, David, illus. (p. 1866)
Ross, Dev & Canetti, Yanitzia. Frank & the Balloon: Sapi y el Globo. Reinhart, Larry, illus. (p. 628)
Ross, Diana. Little Red Engine & the Rocket. Wood, Leslie, illus. (p. 1034)
—Little Red Engine Goes to Town. Wood, Leslie, illus. (p. 1034)
Ross, Diane. Charlie Visits a Science Laboratory. (p. 293)
Ross, Elizabeth. Belle Epoque. (p. 162)
Ross, Eric. My Uncle's Wedding. Greene, Tracy, illus. (p. 1220)
Ross, Fiona. Chilly Milly Moo. (p. 306)
Ross, Garry. Timeshare College: The Secrets of Timeshare Sales. (p. 1754)
Ross, Gary. Bartholomew Biddle & the Very Big Wind. Myers, Matthew, illus. (p. 140)
Ross, Gary, illus. see Burrows, Roger & Gilligan, Jeff.
Ross, Gary, illus. see Edmonton Natural History Club.
Ross, Gayle. How Rabbit Tricked Otter: And Other Cherokee Trickster Stories. Jacob, Murv, illus. (p. 812)
Ross, Gayle, jt. auth. see Bruchac, Joseph, III.
Ross, Gayle L. Onyx Out Loud: Off to School I Go! (p. 1298)
Ross, Graham. Bible-Story Doodles: Favorite Scenes to Complete & Create. Running Press Staff, ed. (p. 176)
Ross, Graham, illus. see Attema, Martha.
Ross, Graham, illus. see Bar-el, Dan.
Ross, Graham, illus. see Brouwer, Sigmund.
Ross, Graham, illus. see Dickens, Ned.
Ross, Graham, illus. see Lewis, Wendy A.
Ross, Graham, illus. see Sharpe, Luke.
Ross, Graham, illus. see Skene, Pat.
Ross, Graham T., illus. see Skene, Pat.
Ross, H. K. Black American Women (p. 194)
Ross, H. K., ed. Great American Story Poems. (p. 713)
Ross, Harriet. Great American Heroes. (p. 713)
Ross, Harriet, ed. Great English Story Poems: Collections. (p. 715)
Ross, Heather, illus. see Calmenson, Stephanie & Cole, Joanna.
Ross, Heather, illus. see DiPucchio, Kelly.
Ross, Heather, illus. see Ransom, Candice.
Ross, Heather, illus. see Rosenberg, Madelyn.
Ross, Heather, illus. see Springstubb, Tricia.
Ross Houston, Anita. Frogs Don't Have Teeth. (p. 641)
—Listening to the Stars. (p. 1022)
—My Daddy Is a Tin Man. (p. 1201)
—My Granny's Baby. (p. 1210)
Ross, Jay. Bungalow 29. Klimko, Andrew, illus. (p. 242)
Ross, Jeff. Above All Else (p. 6)
—Coming Clean (p. 348)
—Dawn Patrol (p. 412)
—Drop (p. 485)
Ross, Jeffrey Ian, jt. auth. see Elwell, Jake.
Ross, Jesse Paul & Puzzling Sports Institute Staff. Slapshot Hockey Quizbook: 50 Fun Games Brought to You by the Puzzling Sports Institute. (p. 1588)
Ross, Jill. Blake Family Vacation. Pruitt, Gwendolyn, illus. (p. 198)
—Real Nitty-Gritty. Pruitt, Gwendolyn, illus. (p. 1448)
—What's the Matter, Mr. Ticklebritches? Pruitt, Gwendolyn, illus. (p. 1899)
Ross, Joel. Fog Diver. (p. 611)
Ross, John, ed. see IraqiGirl.
Ross, Jordan & Gohari, Omid. Emerson College College Prowler off the Record. (p. 518)
Ross, Julie, illus. see Pirnot, Karen Hutchins.
Ross, K. N. Daughters of the Lost World. (p. 410)
Ross, Katharine. Elmo & Grover, Come on over! (Sesame Street) Cooke, Tom, illus. (p. 515)
—Twinkle, Twinkle, Little Bug. Cooke, Tom & Brannon, Tom, illus. (p. 1802)
Ross, Kathleen Jayne. Hoo says Hoo! (p. 795)
Ross, Kathryn. Herencia Envenenada. (p. 771)
Ross, Kathryn & Pruitt, Kimberly. Artic Skits. Utley, David, illus. (p. 104)
Ross, Kathy. All New Crafts for Earth Day. Holm, Sharon Lane, illus. (p. 45)
—All New Crafts for Easter. Holm, Sharon Lane, tr. (p. 45)
—All New Crafts for Halloween. Leonard, Barbara & Holm, Sharon, illus. (p. 45)
—All New Crafts for Mother's Day & Father's Day. Holm, Sharon Lane, illus. (p. 45)
—All New Crafts for Thanksgiving. Holm, Sharon Lane, illus. (p. 45)
—All New Holiday Crafts for Mother's & Father's Day. Holm, Sharon Lane, illus. (p. 45)
—All-Girl Crafts. Garvin, Elaine, illus. (p. 44)
—Beautiful Beads. Bosch, Nicole in den, illus. (p. 153)
—Bedroom Makeover Crafts. Bosch, Nicole in den, illus. (p. 156)
—Community Workers. Barger, Jan, illus. (p. 350)
—Crafts for Kids Who Are Learning about Dinosaurs. Barger, Jan, illus. (p. 376)
—Crafts for Kids Who Are Learning about Farm Animals. Barger, Jan, illus. (p. 376)
—Crafts for Kids Who Are Learning about Insects. Barger, Jan, illus. (p. 376)
—Crafts to Make in the Fall. Enright, Vicky, illus. (p. 376)
—Crafts to Make in the Summer. Enright, Vicky, illus. (p. 376)
—Creative Kitchen Crafts. Bosch, Nicole in den, illus. (p. 379)
—Creative Kitchen Crafts. In Den Bosch, Nicole, illus. (p. 379)
—Earth-Friendly Crafts: Clever Ways to Reuse Everyday Items. Malépart, Céline, illus. (p. 496)
—Fairy World Crafts. Bosch, Nicole in den, illus. (p. 564)
—Fairy World Crafts. In Den Bosch, Nicole, illus. (p. 564)
—Girlfriends' Get-Together Craft Book. Bosch, Nicole in den, illus. (p. 679)
—Girlfriends' Get-Together Craft Book. In Den Bosch, Nicole, illus. (p. 679)
—Jazzy Jewelry, Pretty Purses, & More! Bosch, Nicole in den, illus. (p. 911)
—Kathy Ross Crafts Numbers. Barger, Jan, illus. (p. 944)
—Look What You Can Make with Plastic Bottles & Tubs: Over 80 Pictured Crafts & Dozens of Other Ideas. Schneider, Hank, photos by. (p. 1050)
—Look What You Can Make with Recycled Paper. Schneider, Hank & Filipski, J. W., photos by. (p. 1050)
—More of the Best Holiday Crafts Ever! Holm, Sharon Lane, illus. (p. 1174)

—One-of-a-Kind Stamps & Crafts. Bosch, Nicole, illus. (p. 1296)
—One-of-a-Kind Stamps & Crafts. Bosch, Nicole in den, illus. (p. 1296)
—Step-By-Step Crafts for Spring. Emery, Jennifer, illus. (p. 1647)
—Things to Make for Your Doll. Garvin, Elaine, illus. (p. 1733)
Ross, Kendric. Classic Children's Games from Scotland. Mackay, John, illus. (p. 328)
Ross Kennedy, illus. see Lihou, Gavin.
Ross, Kent, jt. auth. see Ross, Alice.
Ross Keyes, Joan, jt. auth. see Stamper, Judith Bauer.
Ross, Laura. Hand Puppets: How to Make & Use Them. (p. 740)
Ross, Leanna. Julie Simone. (p. 932)
Ross, Lesley & Shakespeare, William. 40 Minute Tempest. (p. 1997)
Ross, Linda B. 30 Pocket Chart Poems That Teach Phonics: Irresistible Poems with Ready-to-Use Picture Cards That Teach Initial Consonants, Long & Short Vowels, & More. (p. 1996)
—Big Book of Pocket Chart Poems - ABCs & 123s: Engaging Poems, Lessons, & Instant Templates to Teach the Alphabet, Number Concepts, & Phonics Skills. (p. 179)
Ross, Linda B., adapted by. Tom Sawyer: Read Aloud Classics Edition Big Book. (p. 1763)
Ross, Lionel. Baghdad Declaration. (p. 132)
Ross, M. K. Tiny the Teapot. (p. 1757)
Ross, M. T., illus. see Gordon, Elizabeth.
Ross, M. T., illus. see Kirkwood, Edith Brown.
Ross, Mandy. Animal Lullabies. Kallai, Nagy, illus. (p. 78)
—Animal Lullabies. Kallai Nagy, Krisztina, tr. (p. 78)
—Animal Lullabies. Kallai Nagy, Krisztina, illus. (p. 78)
—Chicken Licken. (p. 300)
—Dominic Grows Sweetcorn. Bartlett, Alison, illus. (p. 465)
—Rivers. (p. 1476)
—Wake up, Sleepyhead! Early Morning Poems. Kalanovic, Dubravka, illus. (p. 1853)
Ross, Margaret. Casey & the Amazing Good Finder: Teaching Adults & Children How to Succeed in School, Work, Life & Relationships. (p. 275)
Ross, Margaret Clark. Jumpy the Frog Learns the Meaning of Love McNeely, William, illus. (p. 934)
Ross, Marianne, jt. auth. see Ross, Marrianne.
Ross, Marlene. Adventures of Donny the Doorknob. Hallam, Colleen and Peggy, illus. (p. 17)
Ross, Marrianne & Ross, Marianne. Bible Detectives - Samuel. (p. 175)
Ross, Mary H. Primary Partners Singing Fun. Guymon-King, Jennette, illus. (p. 1399)
Ross, Melanie H., jt. auth. see Willis.
Ross, Melanie H. & Guymon-King. Primary Partners: New Testament. (p. 1399)
—Primary Partners: Ages 8 to 11 (Book of Mormon) (p. 1399)
—Primary Partners: Faith in God, We Love Activity Days. (p. 1399)
—Primary Partners. (p. 1399)
—Super Little Singers. (p. 1680)
Ross, Melanie H. & Guymon-King, Jennette. Primary Partners: Ages 8 to 11 (Book of Mormon) (p. 1399)
Ross, Melanie H. & Willis, Jeanne. Mayfly Day. Ross, Tony, illus. (p. 1113)
Ross, Melissa. Angels Watching over Us. (p. 75)
—Today I Am a Penguin. Ross, Melissa, illus. (p. 1760)
Ross, Melissa, illus. see Arbo, Barbara.
Ross, Michael. Boom: A Guy's Guide to Growing Up. (p. 213)
Ross, Michael & Johnson, Greg. 10 Reasons to Stay Christian in High School: A Guide to Staying Sane When Everyone Else Has Jumped off the Deep End. (p. 1994)
Ross, Michael & Koehler, Manfred. Tribe: A Warrior's Battles - A Purity Game Plan for Guys. (p. 1785)
Ross, Michael Elsohn. Baby Bear Isn't Hungry. Powell, Consie, illus. (p. 125)
—Body Cycles. Moore, Gustav, illus. (p. 207)
—Mama Me Alimenta. Wolff, Ashley, illus. (p. 1084)
—Re-Cycles. Moore, Gustav, illus. (p. 1441)
—Salvador Dali & the Surrealists: Their Lives & Ideas, 21 Activities. (p. 1506)
—She Takes a Stand: 16 Fearless Activists Who Have Changed the World. (p. 1564)
—What's the Matter in Mr. Whiskers' Room? (p. 1899)
—What's the Matter in Mr. Whiskers' Room? Meisel, Paul, illus. (p. 1899)
Ross, Michael, et al. Dating, Relating, Waiting: God's Word on Purity. (p. 409)
Ross, Nancy Wilson. Joan of Arc. (p. 919)
Ross, Neil M., jt. auth. see Mackenzie, Carine.
Ross, Nick. Fishing. (p. 599)
Ross, Patricia G. & Owens-Kristenson, Jodi. Take Charge of Your Life! (p. 1696)
—Take Charge of Your Life! Teaching Package Teacher's Resource Portfolio. (p. 1696)
Ross, Patrick. Joseph & Snowy Joe Blue Burcham, David, illus. (p. 926)
—Oliver: The Great Escape. Burcham, David, illus. (p. 1285)
—Runt River Rat's Wild Ride Burcham, David, illus. (p. 1497)
Ross, Paula. Classworks - Literacy Year 6. (p. 329)
Ross, Paula Kovacs, jt. auth. see Abramson, Andra Serlin.
Ross, Paula Kovacs, et al. Tractors & Trucks: An Exciting Mechanical & Educational Experience Awaits You When You Meet Tractors & Trucks. (p. 1775)
Ross, Peg, ed. see Buckey, Sarah Masters.
Ross, Philip. My First Book of Bible Prayers. (p. 1205)
Ross, Richard. Arctic Airlift. (p. 96)
Ross, Richhi. After the Alphabet. (p. 28)
Ross, Rose Laura, jt. auth. see Minciell, Rose Laura.
Ross, Samantha B. "Momby" Wears Combat Boots: Where did she Go? (p. 1161)
Ross, Samuel B., Jr. Extraordinary Spirit of Green Chimneys: Connecting Children & Animals to Create Hope. (p. 555)
Ross, Sarah C. E., jt. auth. see Acheson, James.
Ross, Sharon, illus. see Wilson, Sarah.
Ross, Sherry Lazarus. Light of Lucinda. (p. 1015)
Ross, Simon. Basic Mapwork Skills. (p. 142)
—Exploring Geography in a Changing World. (p. 552)
Ross, Steve. Marked. (p. 1095)
Ross, Stewart. Ancient Egypt. (p. 68)
—Clever Cleo. Shields, Sue, illus. (p. 331)
—Dear Mum, I Miss You! Clark, Linda, illus. (p. 419)
—Don't Say No to Flo: The Story of Florence Nightingale. Shields, Susan, illus. (p. 468)
—Henry VIII: Guilty or Innocent? (p. 768)
—Hiroshima. (p. 781)
—Home Front in World War II. (p. 792)
—Into the Unknown: How Great Explorers Found Their Way by Land, Sea, & Air. Biesty, Stephen, illus. (p. 881)
—Leaders of World War I. (p. 981)
—Medieval Europe (p. 1119)
—Point of Impact Series (p. 1377)
—Rich & Poor in Ancient Greece. (p. 1469)
—Science, History, & Mystery. (p. 1526)
—Seaside Holidays. (p. 1538)
—Sink the Armada! Sir Francis Drake & the Spanish Armada of 1588. Shields, Susan, illus. (p. 1579)
—Sport Technology. (p. 1631)
—Story of Wolfgang Amadeus Mozart. (p. 1663)
—Toys. (p. 1774)
—Will's Dream. Shields, Susan, illus. (p. 1934)
—World War I (p. 1958)
—World War I. (p. 1958)
Ross, Stewart & Woodward, Joe. Pearl Harbor. (p. 1333)
Ross, Susan. Kiki & Jacques. (p. 955)
Ross, Suzanne. BOOST Rain Forest Activity Book. (p. 213)
—Christmas: Follow-the-Dots. (p. 312)
—Nature Mazes. (p. 1236)
Ross, Sylvia. Blue Jay Girl. (p. 203)
—Lion Singer. Ross, Sylvia, illus. (p. 1020)
Ross, Thea. Lucy Loves Winter. (p. 1063)
—Lucy Wants to Help. (p. 1063)
—Molly Mole Loves to Garden. (p. 1160)
—Molly Mole Takes a Nature Walk. (p. 1160)
Ross, Theodore J. Lucy Wants to Play. (p. 1063)
Ross, Thomas A. Privileges of War: A Good Story of American Service in South Vietnam. (p. 1408)
Ross, Timothy & Whitt, Shannon. Clever Costumes. (p. 331)
Ross, Tony. Centipede's One Hundred Shoes. Ross, Tony, illus. (p. 287)
—Don't Do That! Ross, Tony, illus. (p. 467)
—Fairy Tale. (p. 564)
—Figuras. (p. 586)
—Hora de Dormir. (p. 797)
—I Don't Want to Go to Hospital. (p. 838)
—I Feel Sick! (p. 838)
—I Want a Cat! Ross, Tony, illus. (p. 847)
—I Want a Party! Ross, Tony, illus. (p. 847)
—I Want My Light On! Ross, Tony, illus. (p. 847)
—I Want My Mom! Ross, Tony, illus. (p. 847)
—I Want My Pacifier. Ross, Tony, illus. (p. 847)
—I Want to Do It Myself! Ross, Tony, illus. (p. 848)
—I Want to Go Home! Ross, Tony, illus. (p. 848)
—I Want to Win! Ross, Tony, illus. (p. 848)
—I Want Two Birthdays! Ross, Tony, illus. (p. 848)
—Is It Because... ? Ross, Tony, illus. (p. 889)
—Let's Visit the Louvre Museum. (p. 1001)
—Mascotas: La Pequena Princesa. (p. 1102)
—Mascotas. (p. 1102)
—My Favourite Fairy Tales. Ross, Tony, illus. (p. 1203)
—Naughty Nigel. Ross, Tony, illus. (p. 1237)
—No Quiero Ir al Hospital. (p. 1260)
—Oscar Got the Blame. (p. 1305)
—Oscar Got the Blame. Ross, Tony, illus. (p. 1305)
—Quiero un Gato (I Want a Cat) (p. 1428)
—Rita's Rhino. (p. 1475)
—Rizos de Oro y los Tres Osos: Little Books. (p. 1476)
—Super Dooper Jezebel. (p. 1679)
—Three Little Kittens & Other Favorite Nursery Rhymes. Ross, Tony, illus. (p. 1742)
—Tiempo. (p. 1747)
—Wash Your Hands! Ross, Tony, illus. (p. 1859)
Ross, Tony, illus. see Ahlberg, Allan.
Ross, Tony, illus. see Banks, Lynne Reid.
Ross, Tony, illus. see Barlow, Steve & Skidmore, Steve.
Ross, Tony, illus. see Beardsley, Martyn.
Ross, Tony, illus. see Blacker, Terence.
Ross, Tony, illus. see Bradman, Tony.
Ross, Tony, illus. see Camp, Lindsay.
Ross, Tony, illus. see Curtis, Philip.
Ross, Tony, illus. see Danziger, Paula & Mazer, Anne.
Ross, Tony, illus. see Danziger, Paula, et al.
Ross, Tony, illus. see Danziger, Paula.
Ross, Tony, illus. see Danzinger, Paula.
Ross, Tony, illus. see Grindley, Sally & Lucas, D J.
Ross, Tony, illus. see Grindley, Sally & Max, Querido.
Ross, Tony, illus. see Grindley, Sally.
Ross, Tony, illus. see Lawrence, Michael.
Ross, Tony, illus. see Lindgren, Astrid.
Ross, Tony, illus. see McCaughrean, Geraldine.
Ross, Tony, illus. see Page, Jan.
Ross, Tony, illus. see Rosen, Michael.
Ross, Tony, illus. see Ross, Melanie H. & Willis, Jeanne.
Ross, Tony, illus. see Simon, Francesca.
Ross, Tony, illus. see Skidmore, Steve & Barlow, Steve.
Ross, Tony, illus. see Townson, Hazel.
Ross, Tony, illus. see Waddell, Martin.
Ross, Tony, illus. see Whybrow, Ian.
Ross, Tony, illus. see Willis, Jeanne.
Ross, Tony, jt. auth. see Blacker, Terence.
Ross, Tony, jt. auth. see Ross, Tony.
Ross, Tony, jt. auth. see Willis, Jeanne.
Ross, Tony & Ross, Tony. I Want a Sister! (p. 847)
Ross, Tony & Willis, Jeanne. Dozy Mare. (p. 474)
Ross, Tony, et al. Paisajes. Ross, Tony, tr. (p. 1319)
Ross, Val. Road to There: Mapmakers & Their Stories. (p. 1477)
—You Can't Read This: Forbidden Books, Lost Writing, Mistranslations, & Codes. (p. 1975)
Ross, Veronica. Brain. (p. 221)
—Heart. (p. 759)
—Lungs. (p. 1065)
—Muscles. (p. 1192)
Ross Williamson, Hugh. Young People's Book of Saints: Sixty-Three Saints of the Western Church from the First to the Twentieth Century. Connelly, Sheila, illus. (p. 1979)
Rossacci, Jacob. Dinosaurs Live Together. (p. 445)
—Harold the Hippo Learns to Sing. (p. 749)
Rossbacher, John. From Father John's Story Book: Nine Fun Stories for Children & Grandchildren. (p. 642)
Rossbacher, John R. T. O. A. D. Trombone Ollie & Dyslexia. (p. 1694)
Rosseau, Paul. Lucifer, Mon Grand-Père Guénette, Geneviève, illus. (p. 1062)
Rossel, Seymour. Holocaust: An End to Innocence. (p. 789)
—Storybook Haggadah. (p. 1663)
—Storybook Haggadah. Zwebner, Janet, illus. (p. 1663)
—Torah Portion-by-Portion. (p. 1769)
Rossell, Judith. I Spy with Inspector Stilton. Rossell, Judith, illus. (p. 846)
—Inspector Stilton & the Missing Jewels. Rossell, Judith, illus. (p. 878)
—Jack Jones & the Pirate Curse. (p. 903)
—Oliver. Rossell, Judith, illus. (p. 1285)
—Ruby & Leonard & the Great Big Surprise. Rossell, Judith, illus. (p. 1493)
—Sam & the Killer Robot. (p. 1506)
—Withering-By-Sea. (p. 1942)
Rossell, Judith, illus. see Hanel, Wolfram.
Rossell, Judith, illus. see Holmes, Janet A.
Rossell, Judith, illus. see Kerr, Eleanor.
Rossell, Judith, illus. see Parker, Michael & Wiedmer, Caroline.
Rossell, Judith, illus. see Stills, Caroline & Stills-Blott, Sarcia.
Rossell, Judith, illus. see Stills, Caroline.
Rosselson, Leon. Gordon & the Giant Killers. (p. 702)
—Tom the Whistling Wonder. Haslam, John, illus. (p. 1764)
Rossendale, Helen. Tales from Pinocchio. Philpot, Graham, illus. (p. 1701)
Rosseter, Patrick W. Grampa Pat's Little Animal Tales. (p. 706)
Rossetti, Christina. What Is Pink? Carr, Holly, illus. (p. 1890)
Rossetti, Christina Georgina. Speaking Likenesses / by Christina Rossetti; with Pictures Thereof by Arthur Hughes. (p. 1623)
Rossetti, Rinsai. Girl with Borrowed Wings. (p. 679)
Rossetti-Shustak, Bernadette. I Love You Through & Through: Board Book & Plush. Church, Caroline Jayne, illus. (p. 844)
—I Love You Through & Through. Church, Caroline Jayne, illus. (p. 844)
—I Love You Through & Through (Te Quiero, Yo Te Quiero) Church, Caroline Jayne, illus. (p. 844)
Rossi, Andrea, illus. see Korobov, Kristine.
Rossi, Ann. Age of Inventions. (p. 29)
—Bright Ideas: The Age of Invention in America 1870-1910. (p. 228)
—Created Equal: Women Campaign for the Right to Vote 1840 - 1920. (p. 378)
—Cultures Collide: Native American & Europeans 1492-1700. (p. 391)
—Freedom Struggle: The Anti-Slavery Movement 1830-1865. (p. 635)
—India. (p. 870)
—Native Americans of the Southwest: Set Of 6. (p. 1234)
—Native Americans of the Southwest: Text Pairs. (p. 1234)
—Southeast: Set Of 6. (p. 1617)
—Southeast: Text Pairs. (p. 1617)
—Two Cultures Meet - Native American & European. (p. 1803)
Rossi, Ann, jt. auth. see National Geographic Learning, National Geographic Learning.
Rossi, Ann & National Geographic Learning Staff. Immigrants Today. (p. 861)
—Kids Communicate. (p. 953)
—Votes for Women. (p. 1850)
Rossi, Anna Maria. Struggle for Equality. (p. 1668)
Rossi, Anne. Bright Ideas: The Age of Invention in America 1870-1910. (p. 228)
Rossi, Christian, illus. see Dorison, Xavier & Nury, Fabien.
Rossi, Debra M. No Horsing Around: Kick off to Success in School. (p. 1258)
Rossi, Francesca. Aladdin. (p. 33)
—Beauty & the Beast. (p. 154)
—Cinderella. (p. 320)
—Little Mermaid. (p. 1031)
—Little Red Riding Hood. (p. 1035)
—Rapunzel. (p. 1439)
—Sleeping Beauty. (p. 1589)
—Snow White. (p. 1599)
Rossi, Ino, ed. see Kurtz, Jane.
Rossi, Joe, illus. see Oelschlager, Vanita & Durrant, Lynda.
Rossi, Joe, illus. see Oelschlager, Vanita.
Rossi, Joe, photos by. Minnesota's Hidden Alphabet. (p. 1147)
Rossi, Joyce. Gullywasher: El Chaparron Torrencial. (p. 731)
Rossi, Marty. Helpful Maxwell & the Missing Button. (p. 766)
Rossi, Michelle. Letters & sounds in Loveland. (p. 1002)
Rossi, Pamela, illus. see Bauer, Marion Dane.
Rossi, Regine & Dawson, Kai. Rensselaer Polytechnic Institute College Prowler off the Record: Inside RPI. (p. 1460)
Rossi, Regine & Nash, Kevin. University of Florida College Prowler off the Record. (p. 1820)
Rossi, Renzo. Age of the Book. Baldanzi, Alessandro, illus. (p. 29)
—Gift from the Gods. Baldanzi, Alessandro, illus. (p. 675)
—How Writing Began. Baldanzi, Alessandro, illus. (p. 823)
—In Nineteenth Century London with Dickens. Baldanzi, Alessandro, illus. (p. 864)
—In Renaissance Florence with Leonardo. Baldanzi, Alessandro, illus. (p. 864)
—In the Sun King's Paris with Molière. Baldanzi, Alessandro, illus. (p. 867)
—Los Egipcios: Historia, Sociedad, Religion. (p. 1054)
—Paris. (p. 1324)
—Revolution of the Alphabet. Baldanzi, Alessandro, illus. (p. 1466)
—Venice. (p. 1835)
Rossi, Rich. Pillow Fight. (p. 1359)
Rossi, Rich, illus. see Ziefert, Harriet.
Rossi, Richard, illus. see Woollatt, Margaret.
Rossi, Sophia. Buon Natale: Learning Songs & Traditions in Italian. Kelleher, Kathie, illus. (p. 243)
—Tale of Two Besties: A Hello Giggles Novel. (p. 1700)
Rossi, Veronica. Into the Still Blue. (p. 881)
—Through the Ever Night. (p. 1745)
—Under the Never Sky. (p. 1813)
Rössig, Wolfgang. Karl Marx. (p. 943)
Rossignol, Manon Éléonor & Lecor, Tex. Isory Poutch et le Sortilège de Cacouna. (p. 893)
Rossignol, Rosalyn. Chaucer: A Literary Reference to His Life & Work. (p. 295)
Rossignoli, Marco. Complete Pinball Book: Collecting the Game & Its History (p. 353)
Rossini, Gioacchino Antonio. Five Great Overtures in Full Score. (p. 600)
Rossini, Maia, jt. ed. see Lavender, Bee.
Rossiter, Nan Parson. Fo'c'sle: Henry Beston's Outermost House. (p. 610)
Rossiter, Sofia, jt. auth. see Kirk.
Rossitter, Derek. Greedy Pigeon & the Hungry Porcupine & Friends. (p. 720)
—Greedy Pigeon the Hungry Porcupine & Friends. Horne, Grace, illus. (p. 720)
Rossitto, Tamara. Alura. (p. 51)
Rossland, Ingelin. Minus Me. Dawkin, Deborah, tr. from NOR. (p. 1148)
Rossman, Alicia. Miss Lyla's Banana Pancakes to the Rescue! Harkins, Nathan, illus. (p. 1151)
Rossman, Martin L. Fighting Cancer from Within: How to Use the Power of Your Mind for Healing. (p. 585)
Rossman, Sherry. Miracle of Rain. (p. 1148)
Rosso, Norma, jt. auth. see Steele, Philip.
Rossoff, Donald. Perfect Prayer. Keiser, Tammy L., illus. (p. 1342)
Rossolovski, Lenny, tr. see Samarsky, Mikhail.
Rosson, Denise & Turnblacer, Margaret. Tadpole Dreams Etiquette & Good Manners Program Handbook. (p. 1695)
Rossouw, Andre J. & Bitline S. A. 1010. Natural Sciences Matters Grade 8 Learner's Book Afrikaans Translation. (p. 1236)
Rossouw, Andre J., et al. Natural Sciences Matters Grade 8 Learner's Book. (p. 1236)
Rosso-White, Gloria, ed. see Camarena, Cathy & Ruff, Gloria B.
Rost, Michael & Uruno, Munetsugu. Basics in Listening: Short Tasks for Listening Development. (p. 142)
Rosteck, Rachel, illus. see Speaker, Cathy.
Rostoker-Gruber, Karen. Bandit Nguyen, Vincent, illus. (p. 136)
—Bandit's Surprise Nguyen, Vincent, illus. (p. 136)
—Ferret Fun De Tagyos, Paul Rátz, illus. (p. 582)
—Tea Time Garófoli, Viviana, illus. (p. 1708)
Rostoker-Gruber, Karen & Isaacs, Ronald H. Farmer Kobi's Hanukkah Match. Decker, C. B., illus. (p. 574)
Rostom, Mustafa. Four Arabian Tales: Educating Children about Islam. (p. 624)
Rostrom, Laura Lee. My Church History Storybook. (p. 1200)
—My First Book of Mormon Activity Book. (p. 1205)
Roswell, Stacey, illus. see Alexander, Carmen.
Rosy. Tina's Doll. (p. 1755)
Roszel, Karen. Diamond Button. (p. 434)
Rota, Marco & Barks, Carl. Uncle Scrooge Clark, John, ed. (p. 1812)
Rotberg, Gene. Tess & the Dog Star. Barnard, Bryn, illus. (p. 1722)
Rotberg, Gene, et al. Quinn's Search for the Samurai. Barnard, Bryn, illus. (p. 1428)
Rotberg, Robert I. Governance & Leadership in Africa. (p. 704)
—Governance & Leadership in Africa. Rotberg, Robert I. & Ojakorotu, Victor, eds. (p. 704)
Rotberg, Robert I., ed. see Baughan, Brian.
Rotberg, Robert I., ed. see Baughan, Michael Gray.
Rotberg, Robert I., ed. see Brennan, Kristine.
Rotberg, Robert I., ed. see Cook, Diane.
Rotberg, Robert I., ed. see Corrigan, Jim.
Rotberg, Robert I., ed. see Friedenthal, Lora & Kavanaugh, Dorothy.
Rotberg, Robert I., ed. see Gelletly, LeeAnne.
Rotberg, Robert I., ed. see Habeeb, William Mark.
Rotberg, Robert I., ed. see Harmon, Daniel E.
Rotberg, Robert I., ed. see Hasday, Judy L.
Rotberg, Robert I., ed. see Kavanaugh, Dorothy.
Rotberg, Robert I., ed. see Koopmans, Andy.
Rotberg, Robert I., ed. see Kubuitsile, Lauri.
Rotberg, Robert I., ed. see Lewis, Susan Grant.
Rotberg, Robert I., ed. see MacDonald, Joan Vos.
Rotberg, Robert I., ed. see Marcovitz, Hal.
Rotberg, Robert I., ed. see Milios, Rita.
Rotberg, Robert I., ed. see Mulroy, Tanya.
Rotberg, Robert I., ed. see Noonan, Sheila Smith.
Rotberg, Robert I., ed. see Obadina, Elizabeth.
Rotberg, Robert I., ed. see Obadina, Tunde.
Rotberg, Robert I., ed. see Poisson, Barbara Aoki.
Rotberg, Robert I., ed. see Roberts, Russell.
Rotberg, Robert I., ed. see Shah, Anup.
Rotberg, Robert I., ed. see Staeger, Rob.
Rotberg, Robert I., ed. see Walker, Ida.
Rotberg, Robert I., ed. see Wittman, Kelly.
Rotberg, Robert I., ed. see Wittmann, Kelly.
Rotberg, Robert I., ed. Africa: Continent in the Balance (p. 26)
—Africa: Continent in the Balance 2 (p. 26)
Rotellar, Carlos. Little Red Monster: Tales of Monica. (p. 1035)
Roten, Lindsay Grace. Multicultural Cookbook for Students (p. 1190)
Roten, Lindsay Grace, jt. auth. see Webb, Lois Sinaiko.
Roten, Lindsay Grace & Webb, Lois Sinaiko. Multicultural Cookbook for Students (p. 1190)
Roter, Jordan. Camp Rules. (p. 257)
Roth, Adam J. Checking up on Daddy! (p. 295)

R

Roth, Alfred C. Small Gas Engines: Fundamentals, Service, Troubleshooting, Repair, Applications. (p. 1592)
Roth, Amy. Boy Who Wouldn't Toot. (p. 219)
—Captain Kale & the Super Foods. (p. 264)
Roth, Anthony H. Little Anthony Doesn't Want to Eat His Dinner. (p. 1023)
Roth, Ashley, jt. auth. see Gibson, Jennifer.
Roth, B. A. David Beckham: Born to Play. (p. 410)
Roth, Carol. Conejito No Puede Dormir. Fernandez, Queta, tr. (p. 356)
—Five Little Ducklings Go to Bed. Julian, Sean, illus. (p. 600)
—Five Little Ducklings Go to School. Julian, Sean, illus. (p. 600)
—Here Comes the Choo Choo! Cushman, Doug, illus. (p. 770)
—Little School Bus. Paparone, Pamela, illus. (p. 1036)
—Quien Me Arropara Esta Noche? Obregon, Jose Maria & Fernandez, Queta, trs. from SPA. (p. 1427)
—Ten Dirty Pigs: An Upside-Down Turn Around. Paparone, Pamela, illus. (p. 1718)
—Where's My Mommy? Julian, Sean, illus. (p. 1910)
—Who Will Tuck Me in Tonight? Gorbachev, Valeri, illus. (p. 1919)
Roth, Carol & Julian, Sean. Five Little Ducklings Go to Bed. (p. 600)
Roth, David. Adventures of the Magnificent Seven. (p. 23)
Roth, David, photos by see Ruth, Jamee.
Roth, Elana, et al. Allie Gator & the Easter Egg Hunt. (p. 47)
Roth, Irene. Courage. Turchan, Monique, illus. (p. 372)
Roth, Jennifer A. Backyard Laboratory. (p. 131)
—Just Add Water: Science Projects You Can Sink, Squirt, Splash, Sail. (p. 937)
Roth, Jerry D., jt. auth. see Helfinstine, Robert F.
Roth, John K., ed. see Salem Press Staff.
Roth, Judith. Goodnight, Dragons [padded Board Book]. Lemaitre, Pascal, illus. (p. 701)
Roth, Judith L. & Rothshank, Brooke. Julia's Words. (p. 932)
Roth, Judy Langemo, illus. see Livingston, Joshua.
Roth, Jurgen Philip Philip Philip Kevin Kevin P Geneen Philip Philip Philip Marie, Carol. Little Bunny's Sleepless Night. Gorbachev, Valeri, illus. (p. 1025)
Roth, Justin, illus. see Chin, Oliver Clyde.
Roth, Justin, illus. see Chin, Oliver.
Roth, Kapra Lynn. Healing Bugs. (p. 757)
Roth, Kate, jt. auth. see Minden, Cecilia.
Roth, Kendra. Scruffy, Moonlight, & German GO on VACATION. (p. 1533)
Roth, Matthue. Candy in Action: A Novel. (p. 261)
—Candy in Action. (p. 261)
Roth, Pam & Williams, Tim. Lafayette College College Prowler off the Record. (p. 971)
Roth, Philip. Philip Roth: Novels & Other Narratives. Miller, Ross, ed. (p. 1350)
—Zuckerman Bound The Ghost Writer - Zuckerman Unbound - The Anatomy Lesson - The Prague Orgy. Miller, Ross, ed. (p. 1990)
Roth, R. A. Tales of the Black Earth. (p. 1702)
Roth, R G, illus. see Ehrhardt, Karen.
Roth, R. G., illus. see Michelson, Richard.
Roth, R G, illus. see Staub, Leslie.
Roth, Rhonda. Most Important Thing. Grajczyk, Shane, illus. (p. 1177)
Roth, Robert, illus. see Albert, Burton.
Roth, Roger, illus. see Armstrong, Jennifer.
Roth, Roger, illus. see Friedman, Darlene.
Roth, Roger, illus. see Milton, Nancy.
Roth, Roger, Sr., illus. see Yolen, Jane & Stemple, Heidi E. Y.
Roth, Ruby. That's Why We Don't Eat Animals: A Book about Vegans, Vegetarians, & All Living Things. Roth, Ruby, illus. (p. 1727)
—V Is for Vegan: The ABCs of Being Kind. Roth, Ruby, illus. (p. 1829)
—Vegan Is Love: Having Heart & Taking Action. Roth, Ruby, illus. (p. 1834)
Roth, Ruchela, illus. see Schon, Ruchy.
Roth, Sarra J. Not the Quitting Kind. Bishop, Tracy, illus. (p. 1267)
Roth, Silke. Creak, Thump, Bonk! (p. 378)
Roth Sisson, Stephanie. Star Stuff: Carl Sagan & the Mysteries of the Cosmos. Roth Sisson, Stephanie, illus. (p. 1641)
Roth Sisson, Stephanie, illus. see Greene, Stephanie.
Roth, Stacy Schulstrom, illus. see Fenton, Karen B.
Roth, Stephanie, illus. see Demas, Corinne.
Roth, Stephanie, illus. see Nagda, Ann Whitehead.
Roth, Stephanie, illus. see O'Shaughnessy McKenna, Colleen.
Roth, Susan & Roth, Susan L. Do Re Mi: If You Can Read Music, Thank Guido D'Arezzo. Roth, Susan L., illus. (p. 457)
Roth, Susan L. Mi Amor Por Ti/My Love for You. (p. 1132)
Roth, Susan L., illus. see Aston, Dianna Hutts.
Roth, Susan L., illus. see Chapman, Cheryl.
Roth, Susan L., illus. see Laufer, Peter.
Roth, Susan L., illus. see Mortenson, Greg & Husain, Farzana.
Roth, Susan L., illus. see Trumbore, Cindy.
Roth, Susan L., illus. see Whitman, Walt.
Roth, Susan L., jt. auth. see Mortenson, Greg.
Roth, Susan L., jt. auth. see Roth, Susan.
Roth, Susan L. & Abouraya, Karen Leggett. Hands Around the Library: Protecting Egypt's Treasured Books. Roth, Susan L., illus. (p. 741)
Roth, Susan L. & Trumbore, Cindy. Mangrove Tree: Planting Trees to Feed Families. Roth, Susan L., illus. (p. 1087)
Roth, Veronica. Allegiant (p. 46)
—Divergent. (p. 454)
—Divergent; Insurgent; Allegiant (p. 454)
—Divergente. (p. 454)
—Four: A Divergent Collection: The Transfer; The Initiate; The Son; The Traitor. (p. 624)
—Insurgent. (p. 879)
Roth, Werner, et al. Essential X-Men (p. 537)
—Marvel Masterworks. (p. 1098)
Rothan, Ann, illus. see Atnip, Linda.
Rothan, Ann, illus. see Cheviot, Patrice.
Rothan, Ann, illus. see Fox, Sabrina & FOX, SABRINA.
Rothan, Ann, illus. see Fox, Sabrina.
Rothan, Ann, tr. see Fox, Sabrina & FOX, SABRINA.
Rothaus, Don P. Pythons. (p. 1422)
Rothbardt, Karen, jt. auth. see Sohn, Emily.
Rothbardt, Karen J., jt. auth. see Sohn, Emily.
Rothberg, Abraham. Pinocchio's Sister: A Feminist Fable. (p. 1361)
Rothberg, Kimmy. Saturdays with Daddy. (p. 1515)
Rothchild, Erik. Garden Adventures: The Mishaps of Martha & Matilda. Hief, Gina, illus. (p. 656)
Rothenberg, Annye. I Like to Eat Treats. Wenzel, David T., illus. (p. 841)
—Why Do I Have To? Wenzel, David T., illus. (p. 1923)
Rothenberg, B. Annye. I Want to Make Friends: A Story for Kids in Preschool & Kindergarten & a Guidance Section for Parents. Bright, Bonnie, illus. (p. 848)
—I'm Getting Ready for Kindergarten. Bright, Bonnie04, illus. (p. 859)
—Mommy & Daddy Are Always Supposed to Say Yes— Aren't They? Eldridge, Marion, illus. (p. 1162)
Rothenberg, Jess. Catastrophic History of You & Me. (p. 278)
Rothenberg, Joan. Matzah Ball Soup. Rothenberg, Joan, illus. (p. 1110)
Rothenberg, Joani, illus. see Sigal, Maxine Handelman.
Rothenberg, Joani Keller, illus. see Sasso, Sandy Eisenberg.
Rothenberger, Boyd, illus. see Rothenberger, Charlene.
Rothenberger, Charlene. Kara's Kapers with Katy Pillar. Rothenberger, Boyd & Bays, Gail, illus. (p. 943)
Rothenberger, Suzanne. Mattie: Life at Paddock Mansion. (p. 1110)
Rothenstein, Julian, ed. see Shrigley, David.
Rother, Beverly S., jt. auth. see Seigel, Jonathan.
Rothero, C. Moses in the Bulrushes. (p. 1176)
Rothero, Chris. Noah's Ark. Rothero, Chris, illus. (p. 1261)
—Strawberry Fair. (p. 1666)
Rothery, David A. Geology. (p. 662)
Rothfeld, Glenn S., jt. auth. see Romaine, Deborah S.
Roth-Fisch, Marla. Last Bedtime Story: That We Read Each Night. (p. 977)
—Sensitive Sam: Sam's Sensory Adventure Has a Happy Ending! (p. 1551)
Rothfuss, Patrick. Adventures of the Princess & Mr. Whiffle: The Thing Beneath the Bed. Taylor, Nate, illus. (p. 23)
Rothgery, Laura. My Brother's Heart. (p. 1199)
Rothkopf, Katherine. Pissarro: Creating the Impressionist Landscape. (p. 1364)
Rothman, Cynthia Anne. Funny Bugs. Lester, Mike, illus. (p. 649)
—I Love to Read (p. 843)
—Party for Nine. (p. 1326)
—Violets & Vegetables (p. 1843)
—What Does Sam Sell? Alley, R. W., illus. (p. 1884)
—Yes, You Can (p. 1971)
Rothman, Joel & Stein, Frank N. Shut up & Straighten the Bolt in Your Neck: For Monster Kids Ages 7-11. (p. 1572)
Rothman, Kevin F. Coping with Dangers on the Internet. (p. 365)
Rothman, Lorne. Southcrop Forest. (p. 1617)
Rothman, Michael, illus. see Clarke, Ginjer L.
Rothman, Michael, illus. see Dunphy, Madeleine.
Rothman, Seymour. Tales from the Imagi Nation. (p. 1701)
Rothrock, Megan H. LEGO Adventure Book: Spaceships, Pirates, Dragons & More! Vol. 2 (p. 990)
Rothschild, Jennifer. Walking by Faith: Lessons Learned in the Dark Member. (p. 1854)
Rothschild Moellers, Marcia. Model Markets of the World. DeLaney, Lynn, ed. (p. 1157)
Rothshank, Brooke. Cups Held Out. (p. 392)
Rothshank, Brooke, illus. see Selling, Rebecca.
Rothshank, Brooke, jt. illus. see Roth, Judith L.
Rothstein, Arminio & Brixler, Andreas. TOBY & TOBIAS: Die Abenteuer aus dem ZIRKUS HABAKUK. (p. 1760)
Rothstein, Barry & Rothstein, Betsy. Eye-Popping 3-D Bugs: Phantogram Creepy-Crawlies You Can Practically Touch! (p. 558)
Rothstein, Betsy, jt. auth. see Rothstein, Barry.
Rothstein, Evelyn. Clara Becomes a Citizen. Uhlig, Elizabeth, illus. (p. 326)
—Clara's Great War. Uhlig, Elizabeth, illus. (p. 326)
—Evelyn & the Two Evas. Uhlig, Elizabeth, illus. (p. 541)
—My Great Grandpa Dave. (p. 1210)
Rothstein, Gloria L. Sheep Asleep. (p. 1564)
Rothstein, Nancy, jt. auth. see Rothstein, Nancy H.
Rothstein, Nancy H. & Gilpin, Stephen. My Daddy Snores. (p. 1201)
Rothstein, Nancy H. & Rothstein, Nancy. My Daddy Snores. Gilpin, Stephen, illus. (p. 1201)
Rothwell, Barbara Yates. Boy from the Hulks. (p. 218)
Rothwell, David. Voyage of the Pilchard. (p. 1850)
Rothwell, Tammy. Adventures of Lewis the Dragon: The journey Begins... (p. 19)
Rotkowski, Judy. Journey to Christmas. (p. 928)
Rotman, Jeffrey L., illus. see Cerullo, Mary M.
Rotman, Jeffrey L., photos by see Cerullo, Mary M.
Rotman, Risa. Azoi Vi Ess Past Fahr a Princessen (Fit for a Princess) Flohr, Perel, tr. (p. 122)
Rotman, Stuart. Welcome to Trashtown. (p. 1874)
Rotner, Shelley. Body Actions. Rotner, Shelley & White, David A., illus. (p. 207)
—Body Bones. (p. 207)
—Body Bones. White, David, illus. (p. 207)
—Different Kinds of Good-Byes Rotner, Shelley, photos by. (p. 438)
—Different Kinds of Good-Byes. (p. 438)
—Feeling Thankful Rotner, Shelley, photos by. (p. 580)
—Feeling Thankful. (p. 580)
—Homer. deGroat, Diane, illus. (p. 793)
—Senses at the Seashore. Rotner, Shelley, photos by. (p. 1551)
—Senses in the City. Rotner, Shelley, photos by. (p. 1551)
—Shelley Rotner's World. (p. 1564)
—We All Do Something Well Rotner, Shelley, photos by. (p. 1865)
—We All Do Something Well. (p. 1865)
—What's Love? (p. 1898)
—Whose Eye Am I? (p. 1921)
Rotner, Shelley, photos by see Glaser, Linda.
Rotner, Shelley & Goldblas, Amy. Home. Rotner, Shelley, photos by. (p. 791)
Rotner, Shelley & Kelly, Sheila. Lots of Feelings. Rotner, Shelley, photos by. (p. 1057)
Rotner, Shelley & Kelly, Sheila M. De Muchas Maneras: Como las Familias Practican Sus Creencias y Religiones. Rotner, Shelley, photos by. (p. 416)
—Families. Rotner, Shelley, photos by. (p. 567)
—I'm Adopted! (p. 858)
—I'm Adopted! Rotner, Shelley, photos by. (p. 858)
—Lots of Grandparents. Rotner, Shelley, photos by. (p. 1057)
—Many Ways: How Families Practice Their Beliefs & Religions. Rotner, Shelley, photos by. (p. 1089)
—Shades of People. (p. 1557)
—Shades of People. Rotner, Shelley, photos by. (p. 1557)
—What's Love? Rotner, Shelley, photos by. (p. 1898)
—Yummy! Rotner, Shelley, photos by. (p. 1983)
Rotner, Shelley & Kreisler, Ken. Nature Spy. Rotner, Shelley, illus. (p. 1236)
Rotner, Shelley & Woodhull, Anne Love. Buzz on Bees: Why Are They Disappearing? (p. 248)
Rotsky, Leslie A. At Work in the Neighborhood: A Content Area Reader-Social Studies. (p. 111)
Rotstein, Adira. Little Jane & the Nameless Isle: A Little Jane Silver Adventure. (p. 1029)
—Little Jane & the Nameless Isle: A Little Jane Silver Adventure (Large Print 16pt) (p. 1029)
—Little Jane Silver. (p. 1029)
Rottenberg, David Ira, jt. auth. see Rottenberg, David Ira.
Rottenberg, David Ira & Rottenberg, David Ira. Gwendolyn Goes Hollywood. Anderson, Lesley, illus. (p. 733)
Rotter, Laura. Terratorv. (p. 1721)
Rotterdam, Erasmo de. Elogio de la Locura. Puyol, Julio, tr. (p. 516)
Rottinger, Amy, illus. see Chicatelli, Joy.
Rottinger, Amy, illus. see Consugar, Beth.
Rottinger, Amy, illus. see Gibson, Donovan.
Rottinger, Amy, illus. see Kail, Leanna.
Rottinger, Amy, illus. see Lloyd, Alicia.
Rottinger, Amy, illus. see Phelan, Anne.
Rottinger, Amy, illus. see Staehli, Melissa.
Rottinger, Amy, illus. see Torres, Veronica Hilda.
Rottinger, Amy, illus. see Turner, Darlene.
Rottman, Gordon L. Most Daring Raid of the Civil War: The Great Locomotive Chase. (p. 1177)
Rottman, S. L. Head above Water (p. 756)
—Hero (p. 772)
—Out of the Blue (p. 1311)
—Shadow of a Doubt (p. 1557)
Rottmann, Eric. Fruit of the Spirit. (p. 645)
—Rahab's Red Thread. (p. 1433)
Rottmann, Erik. Barabbas Goes Free. Kitchel, JoAnn E., illus. (p. 137)
—Deborah Saves the Day. Marchesi, Stephen, illus. (p. 421)
—Easter Victory. Billin-Frye, Paige, illus. (p. 499)
—Jesus, My Good Shepherd. Miyake, Yoski, illus. (p. 916)
—Meal for Many: My Gift for Jesus. Paris, Pat, illus. (p. 1116)
—Parable of the Prodigal Son. (p. 1323)
—Timothy Joins Paul. Snyder, Joel, illus. (p. 1755)
Rottmann, Erik J. Jesús alimenta a la multitud (A Meal for Many) - Bilingual. (p. 915)
Rotunda, Lucy. Mission. (p. 1153)
Rouba, Kelly. Juvenile Arthritis: The Ultimate Teen Guide. (p. 941)
Rouche, Jeffrey. Porcupines in the Wild. (p. 1386)
Roucoux, Katherine, jt. auth. see Malin, David.
Roucoux, Katherine & Malin, David. Heaven & Earth: Unseen by the Naked Eye. (p. 761)
Roudon Jr., James. Adventures of Ratsy & Kitten: Which Way Is Home? (p. 22)
Rouge, La Belle. Roscoe & the Secrets of Snow: Roscoe & His Boy Chandler Discover Magic. (p. 1489)
Rough Guides Staff. Rough Guide to the Caribbean. (p. 1491)
Rought, A. E. Broken. (p. 230)
Rougle, Eija, jt. auth. see Adler, Mary.
Rouillard, Wendy W. Barnaby's Tree House. (p. 139)
Roulaine, Katherine. Chang & Olan. (p. 289)
Roumain, Maryse Noel. Anacaona, Ayiti's Taino Queen/Anacaona, la Reine Taino D'Ayiti. (p. 66)
Roumanis, Alexis. Africa. (p. 26)
—Antarctica. (p. 88)
—Asia. (p. 106)
—Australia. (p. 116)
—Baboons. (p. 124)
—Blue Marlin. (p. 203)
—Coral Reefs. (p. 366)
—Deserts. (p. 429)
—Dwarf Planets. (p. 491)
—Earth. (p. 495)
—Europe. (p. 540)
—Giant Octopus. (p. 673)
—Grasslands. (p. 712)
—Jupiter. (p. 937)
—Mars. (p. 1096)
—Mercury. (p. 1127)
—Mountains. (p. 1181)
—Neptune. (p. 1241)
—North America. (p. 1264)
—Oceans. (p. 1277)
—Rainforests. (p. 1436)
—Saturn. (p. 1515)
—South America. (p. 1616)
—Uranus. (p. 1825)
—Venus. (p. 1836)
Rounce, Rebekah Barlow. Happy Hands. (p. 745)
Rounceville, Bibi. Bog Nymphs & Tiger Stones. (p. 207)
—Castle at Trail's End. (p. 276)
—Gimbels & Gooseberries. (p. 676)
—Sea Bugs & Moose Eggs. (p. 1534)
—Trouble at Binka Bridge. (p. 1789)
Round, Graham, illus. see Bryant-Mole, Karen & Tyler, Jenny.
Round, Graham, illus. see Bryant-Mole, Karen.
Round, Graham, illus. see Tatchell, Judy.
Round, Graham, illus. see Word Among Us Editorial Staff.
Round, J. Catcher. (p. 279)
Round, Suzanne. Dragonfire Crystal. (p. 478)
Rounds, Glen, illus. see Gage, Wilson.
Rounds, Harriet. Magic Stairway (p. 1073)
Rounds, Melissa M. Skeleton by the Bay. (p. 1584)
Roundtree, Abigail. Pathway to Statehood: The Territory of Colorado Joins the Union. (p. 1328)
Roundtree, Beth. Wilhamina Constance Winston Churchill Ingersol & the Cat. (p. 1932)
Roundtree, Rebecca. Fig the Dreaming Pig. (p. 585)
Rountree, Benjamin, jt. auth. see Allen, Alejandro.
Rountree, Elizabeth & Bauer, Susan Wise. Modern Age: From Victoria's Empire to the End of the USSR. Vol. 4 (p. 1158)
Rountree, Harry, illus. see Carroll, Lewis, pseud.
Rountree, Helen C. Pocahontas, Powhatan, Opechancanough: Three Indian Lives Changed by Jamestown. (p. 1375)
Rountree, Monica, tr. see Biel, Timothy Levi.
Rountree, Monica, tr. see Quality Productions Staff.
Rountree, Monica, tr. see Wexo, John Bonnett.
Rountree, Monica, tr. Ballenas. (p. 134)
Rountree, Wendy. Lost Soul. (p. 1056)
Roure, Luis A. Antonio el manati de Aqui. (p. 90)
Rourke, Brigid. Tools of Science. (p. 1767)
Rourke, Janet W. New Baby: Featuring Marta the Mouse. (p. 1243)
Rourke Publishing Staff. Rourke's World of Science Encyclopedia: Animal Life Vol. 2 (p. 1491)
Rourke Publishing Staff, ed. see Cooper, Jason.
Rourke Publishing Staff, ed. see Greve, Tom.
Rourke Publishing Staff, ed. see Ohare, Ted.
Rous, Sheri, ed. see Callella, Trisha.
Rous, Sheri, ed. see Cernek, Kim & Shiotsu, Vicky.
Rous, Sheri, ed. see Cernek, Kim, et al.
Rous, Sheri, ed. see Cernek, Kim.
Rous, Sheri, ed. see Hults, Alaska.
Rous, Sheri, ed. see Jacks, Cyndie & Lewis, Dawn.
Rous, Sheri, ed. see Jennett, Pamela.
Rous, Sheri, ed. see Kim, Hy.
Rous, Sheri, ed. see Lewis, Dawn & Jacks, Cyndie.
Rous, Sheri, ed. see Lewis, Sue & Abrams, Suzanne.
Rous, Sheri, ed. see Shiotsu, Vicky.
Rous, Sheri, ed. United States History. (p. 1819)
Rousay II, Richard A. Choose the Right & Walk with Noah. (p. 310)
—Choose the Right 'Walk with Alma' (p. 310)
—Choose the Right! Walk with Ruth. (p. 310)
Rouse, Andy, photos by see Schindel, John.
Rouse, Betty Munn. Adventures of the Phillyfab Family. (p. 23)
Rouse, Bonna, illus. see Crossingham, John.
Rouse, Bonna, illus. see Kalman, Bobbie & Smithyman, Kathryn.
Rouse, Bonna, illus. see Kalman, Bobbie.
Rouse, Bonna, illus. see Levigne, Heather.
Rouse, Bonna, jt. auth. see Calder, Kate.
Rouse, Bonna, jt. auth. see Crossingham, John.
Rouse, Bonna, jt. auth. see Sotzek, Hannelore.
Rouse, Ciona. CIC for Older Youth & Young Adults: The Bible: Travel Guide for Pilgrimage. (p. 318)
Rouse, Jacob. Pam's Adventure. (p. 1320)
Rouse, Jeff. Jovenes Nadadores. Cabré, María Ángeles, tr. (p. 929)
Rouse, Lidany, compiled by. Children's Letters to Their Hero. (p. 303)
Rouse, Marisa K. JoJo the Troll. (p. 924)
Rouse, W. H. D. Giant Crab & Other Tales from Old Indi. (p. 673)
Rouse, W. H. D., jt. auth. see Homer.
Rouse, W. H. D., tr. see Fagles, Robert & Homer.
Rouse, W. H. D., ed. Giant Crab & Other Tales from Old Indi. (p. 673)
Rouse, Walt. Adventures of Clever Kitty. Bowker, Margie, illus. (p. 17)
Rouse, William Bower Julie A. Pet Tales: Back to School. (p. 1346)
Rouseau, Jasmine. Bizzy Bee Goes to School. (p. 194)
Roush, April, illus. see D'Andrea, Deborah.
Roush, April, illus. see Hapka, Cathy, pseud.
Roush, April, illus. see Wolf, Jackie.
Rouss, Shannan, jt. auth. see Rouss, Sylvia A.
Rouss, Sylvia. God's World. Zwebner, Janet, illus. (p. 692)
—Holiday for Ari Ant. (p. 788)
—Littlest Pair. Hannon, Holly, illus. (p. 1039)
—Littlest Tree. Binus, Ari, illus. (p. 1039)
—Sammy Spider's First Haggadah. Kahn, Katherine, illus. (p. 1508)
—Sammy Spider's First Mitzvah. Janus Kahn, Katherine, illus. (p. 1508)
—Sammy Spider's Shabbat Fun Book. Kahn, Katherine Janus, illus. (p. 1508)
—Touch of Chanukah: A Touch & Feel Book. Becker, Boruch, illus. (p. 1772)
Rouss, Sylvia A. Aaron's Bar Mitzvah. Dubois, Liz Goulet, tr. (p. 2)
—Circle of Smiles: A Story about Beit Issie Shapiro, Israel's Leading Organization in the Field of Disability. (p. 321)
—Jaekob, the Dreamer. (p. 905)
—Littlest Candlesticks. Hannon, Holly, illus. (p. 1039)
—Littlest Frog. Hannon, Holly, illus. (p. 1039)
—Littlest Maccabee: An Original Story. Cohen, Greg A., illus. (p. 1039)
—Littlest Pair. Hannon, Holly, illus. (p. 1039)
—No Rules for Michael. Simon, Susan, illus. (p. 1260)
—Reach for the Stars. (p. 1442)
—Sammy Spider's First Book of Jewish Holidays. Kahn, Katherine, illus. (p. 1508)

—Sammy Spider's First Day of School. Kahn, Katherine, illus. (p. 1508)
—Sammy Spider's First Day of School. Kahn, Katherine Janus, illus. (p. 1508)
—Sammy Spider's First Haggadah. Kahn, Katherine Janus, illus. (p. 1508)
—Sammy Spider's First Shavuot. Kahn, Katherine Janus, illus. (p. 1508)
—Sammy Spider's First Sukkot. Kahn, Katherine Janus, illus. (p. 1508)
—Sammy Spider's First Yom Kippur. (p. 1508)
—Sammy Spider's First Yom Kippur. Kahn, Katherine, illus. (p. 1508)
—Sammy Spider's First Yom Kippur. Kahn, Katherine Janus, illus. (p. 1508)
—Tali's Jerusalem Scrapbook. Oppenheimer, Nancy, illus. (p. 1703)
Rouss, Sylvia A. & Janus Kahn, Katherine. Sammy Spider's New Friend. (p. 1508)
Rouss, Sylvia A. & Kahn, Katherine. Sammy Spider's Israel Fun Book. (p. 1508)
Rouss, Sylvia A. & Lanton, Sandy. Lots of Latkes: A Hanukkah Story. Kahn, Katherine Janus & Redenbaugh, Vicki Jo, illus. (p. 1057)
Rouss, Sylvia A. & Rouss, Shannan. Watermelon in the Sukkah. Iosa, Ann, illus. (p. 1863)
Rouss, Sylvia A. & Turndorf, Genene Levy. Sammy Spider's First Taste of Hanukkah: A Cookbook. Kahn, Katherine Janus, illus. (p. 1508)
Rouss, Sylvia & Avalone, C. Littlest Fish. (p. 1039)
Rousseau, Craig, illus. see McCool, Ben.
Rousseau, Craig, illus. see Thomas, Rich.
Rousseau, Henri, jt. auth. see Markel, Michelle.
Rousseau, Jean-Jacques. Contrato Social. Alingue, Andebeng-Abeu, tr. (p. 361)
Rousseau, Leon. Fritz Deelman en die Woestynrowers. (p. 639)
Rousseau, Paul. Lucifer, Mon Grand-Pere: Tome 2. Guenette, Genevieve, illus. (p. 1062)
Rousselow, Jeff. Bury the Dead. (p. 244)
Roussey, Christine. My Beastly Book of Tangled Tinsel: 140 Ways to Doodle, Scribble, Color & Draw. (p. 1196)
Roussey, Christine, illus. see Witek, Jo.
Roussy de Sales, Richard de. French Grammar Puzzles. (p. 635)
Route 52 Staff & Jackson, Carol A. Follow Jesus: 52 Bible Lessons from the Life of Christ for Ages 6-8. (p. 612)
Route 52 Staff & Lingo, Susan L. Study Jesus' Teachings: 52 Bible Lessons from the Gospels for Ages 8-12. (p. 1670)
Route 52 Staff & Standard Publishing Staff. Discover God's Word: 52 Bible Lessons for Ages 3 & 4. (p. 447)
—Explore Bible Stories: 52 Bible Lessons for Ages 4-6. (p. 550)
—Study God's Plan: 52 Bible Lessons That Build Bible Skills for Ages 8-12. (p. 1670)
Routenburg, Rise' & Wasser, Barbara. Divine Kosher Cuisine: Catering to Family & Friends. Keen, Annette, ed. (p. 454)
Routh, Kristina. AIDS. (p. 30)
Routley, Becky. Moon Golf. (p. 1172)
Routt, Bill. Introduction to XHTML. (p. 882)
Roux, Lindy. Czech Republic. (p. 397)
Roux, Madeleine. Asylum. (p. 109)
—Catacomb. (p. 278)
—Sanctum. (p. 1510)
Roux, Stephane, illus. see Disney Book Group Staff & Siglain, Michael.
Rouzer, Walter. Rebel Stone & the Ghost Whisperers. (p. 1451)
Rovan, Joan. Patches the Cow-Cat. (p. 1328)
Rovere, Amy. And Still They Bloom: A Family's Journey of Loss & Healing. Spector, Joel, illus. (p. 71)
Rovetch, L. Bob. 1,2,3 Octopus & Me. Gévry, Claudine, illus. (p. 2000)
—And the Surprisingly Slobbery Attack of the Dog-Wash Doggies. Whamond, Dave, illus. (p. 71)
—Frog Went A-Dancing. Berry, Holly, illus. (p. 640)
—Hot Dog & Bob: And the Dangerously Dizzy Attack of the Hypno Hamsters. Whamond, Dave, illus. (p. 801)
—Hot Dog & Bob: And the Particularly Pesky Attack of the Pencil People. Whamond, Dave, illus. (p. 801)
—I Need a Kazoot! Castillon, Carly, illus. (p. 844)
—TLC Grow with Me! McLeod, Chum, illus. (p. 1758)
Rovetch, L. Bob & Whitman, Emily. Sir Henry, the Polite Knight. Barnard, Bryn, illus. (p. 1580)
Rovin, Jeff, jt. auth. see Clancy, Tom.
Rovinson, Solon. Selected Writings. (p. 1549)
Rovira, jt. auth. see Ripoll.
Rovira, Francesc, illus. see Grimm, Jacob, et al.
Rovira, Francesc, illus. see Sarfatti, Esther, tr.
Rovira, Francesc, jt. auth. see Viza, Monserrat.
Rovner, Michal, illus. see Grossman, David.
Rovolio, Jimothy, illus. see Knapman, Tim.
Row, Richard, illus. see Stuchner, Joan Betty.
Rowan, Charles A. I Like to Love. (p. 841)
Rowan, Dave, jt. auth. see Collins, Max Allan.
Rowan, Heather, jt. auth. see Rowan, John.
Rowan, John & Rowan, Heather. Jake the Bombed Out Bomb Dog. (p. 906)
Rowan, Ron, jt. auth. see Johnson, D. C.
Rowan, William. Incident at Roan High Bluff. (p. 869)
Rowand, Phyllis. It Is Night. Dronzek, Laura, illus. (p. 894)
Rowden, Justine. Paint Me a Poem: Poems Inspired by Masterpieces of Art. (p. 1318)
Rowe, Alan, illus. see Locke, Ian.
Rowe, Anne Burgess. Newest Angel. (p. 1249)
Rowe, Barry & Doyle, Garry. Atmosphere & Light: The Automotive Paintings of Barry Rowe. (p. 113)
Rowe, Ben. Can an Alligator Drive a Nail with His Tail? (p. 258)
Rowe, Brian. Mentor. (p. 1127)
Rowe, Brooke. What Club Should You Try? (p. 1881)
—What Creature Are You Most Like? (p. 1881)
—What Decade Do You Belong In? (p. 1881)
—What Kind of Friend Are You? (p. 1891)
—What Kind of Spender Are You? (p. 1891)
—What Pet Should You Get? (p. 1892)
—What TV Show Should You Be On? (p. 1894)
—What's Your Dream Job? (p. 1900)
—What's Your Perfect Vacation? (p. 1900)
—What's Your Spirit Animal? (p. 1900)
Rowe, Dana. Pavo Explores the Solar System. (p. 1331)
Rowe, Eric F., jt. auth. see Sutton, Rosalind, et al.
Rowe, Eva McKenzie & Hodge, Darren. Harrison Bean. (p. 750)
Rowe, Gordon J. Showdown at Pecos. (p. 1571)
Rowe, Harriet. L Is for London. (p. 969)
Rowe, Harriet, illus. see Hodgson, Karen J.
Rowe, Jeannette. Bruce the Brachiosaurus. (p. 232)
—Rex the Tyrannosaurus. (p. 1467)
—Tip the Triceratops. (p. 1757)
—Tracy the Pterodactyl. (p. 1776)
—YoYo Goes Next Door. Rowe, Jeannette, illus. (p. 1982)
—YoYo Goes to the Park. Rowe, Jeannette, illus. (p. 1982)
Rowe, Jodye P. & Pileggi, Steven. Once upon a Time a Fairy Tale ABC Book. (p. 1293)
Rowe, John. Little Stories for Little People. (p. 1037)
Rowe, John, ed. see Kipling, Rudyard.
Rowe, John, illus. see Harris, Annaka.
Rowe, John, illus. see Kipling, Rudyard & Landolf, Diane Wright.
Rowe, John, ed. Jungle Book. (p. 935)
—Jungle Book. Alexander, Gregory, illus. (p. 935)
Rowe, K. Secret Box Society: in Search of Bigfoot: In Search of Bigfoot. (p. 1540)
Rowe, Kysha D. What Creatures Teach Us (p. 1881)
Rowe, Louise. Sleeping Beauty: A Pop-Up Book. (p. 1589)
Rowe, Louise, illus. see Grimm, Jacob, et al.
Rowe, Louise, et al. Red Riding Hood: A Pop-Up Book. (p. 1454)
Rowe, Michael, jt. auth. see Dale, Jenny.
Rowe, Michael Langham, illus. see Batten, Mary.
Rowe, Nicholas. Tragedy of Jane Shore. Landes, William-Alan, ed. (p. 1776)
Rowe, Papa. Itchy Lee & Itchy Dee Mcgee. Wilkins, Kevan & Mason, Shannon, eds. (p. 895)
Rowe, Percy. Toronto. (p. 1770)
Rowe, Percy & Coster, Patience. Delhi. (p. 424)
—Montreal. (p. 1170)
Rowe, Ruth & Anderson, Alan. Simple Maintenance for Archery: Easy Things You Can Do to Maintain Your Equipment (p. 1578)
Rowe, Stephanie. Date Me, Baby, One More Time. (p. 409)
—Must Love Dragons. (p. 1194)
Rowe, Susan, jt. auth. see Thomas, John.
Rowe, Thereza. Hearts. (p. 760)
Rowe, Vicki J. Yellow Roses. (p. 1970)
Rowe, W. W. Amy & Gully with Aliens. (p. 66)
—Jerry's Madness. (p. 914)
—Robber Chief: A Tale of Vengeance & Compassion. Banigan, Chris, illus. (p. 1478)
—Wand Goes Wild. (p. 1856)
—Wizard's Wayward Wand. (p. 1943)
Rowe, W. W. & Filius, Charles A. Things Alive! & Other Freaky Secrets. (p. 1733)
Rowell, Coralynn, illus. see King, M.
Rowell, Judith, jt. auth. see Ellermeyer, Deborah.
Rowell, Judy, jt. auth. see Ellermeyer, Deborah.
Rowell, Rainbow. Eleanor & Park. (p. 508)
—Fangirl. (p. 571)
Rowell, Rebecca. 12 Most Amazing American Inventions. (p. 1994)
—12 Most Amazing American Natural Wonders. (p. 1994)
—Ancient India. (p. 69)
—Charles Lindbergh: Groundbreaking Aviator. (p. 292)
—Energy & Waves Through Infographics. Sciuto, Alex, illus. (p. 528)
—Forces & Motion Through Infographics. Dean, Venitia, illus. (p. 617)
—Iraq. (p. 887)
—John F. Kennedy's Presidency. (p. 921)
—Natural Gas. (p. 1235)
—Perspectives Flip Books: Issues. (p. 1344)
—Randolph Caldecott: Renowned British Illustrator. (p. 1438)
—Switzerland. (p. 1692)
—US Marine Corps. (p. 1826)
—Weather & Climate Through Infographics. Dean, Venitia, illus. (p. 1869)
—Wildfires. (p. 1931)
—YouTube: The Company & Its Founders. (p. 1982)
Rowell, Victoria, jt. auth. see Tukey, Paul.
Rowen, Amy & Rowen, Tyla Marie. Waggin' Tails. (p. 1852)
—Waggin' Tales. (p. 1852)
Rowen, Beth, ed. see Time for Kids Magazine Staff.
Rowen, Michelle. Angel with Attitude. (p. 74)
—Reign Check. (p. 1457)
—Reign or Shine. (p. 1457)
Rowen, Michelle & Mead, Richelle. Vampire Academy: The Ultimate Guide. (p. 1831)
Rowen, Tyla Marie, jt. auth. see Rowen, Amy.
Rowh, Mark. Life of W. E. B. du Bois: Civil Rights Champion. (p. 1012)
Rowland, Andrew, illus. see Cleary, Brian P.
Rowland, Andrew, illus. see Crow, Melinda Melton.
Rowland, Andrew, illus. see Klein, Adria F.
Rowland, Andrew, illus. see Rock, Lois.
Rowland, Andrew, illus. see Wallace, Karen.
Rowland, Andy, illus. see Cleary, Brian P.
Rowland, Andy, illus. see Cleary, Brian.
Rowland, Andy, illus. see Goodhart, Pippa.
Rowland, Andy, illus. see Rickards, Lynne.
Rowland, Andy, illus. see Sutton, Jane.
Rowland, Dawn. Adventures of Little Sprout. Oliver, Angel, illus. (p. 20)
Rowland, Jada, illus. see Gray, Libba Moore.
Rowland, Joanna. Always Mom, Forever Dad. Weber, Penny, illus. (p. 51)
Rowland, Lauri, illus. see Richards, Josie Aleardi.
Rowland, Marcus L., ed. see Griffith, George.
Rowland, Michael J., illus. see Kasony_O'Malley, Michael R.
Rowland, Patty. Marvelous Max, the Mansion Mouse. Rasmussen, Wendy, tr. (p. 1099)
Rowland, Teresa. Blusher's First Christmas. (p. 204)
Rowland, Wickie. Good Morning Piscataqua. (p. 698)
—Good Morning, Strawbery Banke. (p. 698)
Rowland, Wil. Wise & Silly. (p. 1939)
Rowland, Wilmer. Wise & Silly: The Reason for Christmas. (p. 1939)
Rowland-Hill, Hugo, illus. see Broz, Jon.
Rowlands, Andy, illus. see Crow, Melinda Melton.
Rowlands, Avril. All the Tales from the Ark. (p. 46)
—Rainbow's End & Other Tales from the Ark. Moran, Rosslyn, illus. (p. 1436)
Rowlands, Caroline. Ballet Creativity Book: With Games, Cut-Outs, Art Paper, Stickers, & Stencils. (p. 134)
—Dare to Doodle: Can You Complete over 100 Drawings & Let Your Pencils Loose? (p. 406)
—Daydream Doodles: Let Your Mind Drift & Your Pencil Scribble with over 100 Drawings to Complete & Color. (p. 415)
—Do It Yourself Beauty Diary: With Pretty Stickers, Body Art Stencils, & a Skin Color Guide. (p. 457)
—Do It Yourself Fashion Diary. (p. 457)
—Halloween Tattoo Book: With 24 Spooky Play Tattoos to Wear & Share! (p. 739)
Rowlands, Samuel. Bride. (p. 227)
Rowland-Warne, L. Trajes. (p. 1778)
Rowles, Charles G., 3rd. Gods of Arr-Kelaan: Going Home (Book 1) (p. 691)
—Gods of Arr-Kelaan: Going Home (Book 2) Pezzino, Martha, ed. (p. 691)
Rowles, Chuck, et al. Drunk & Disorderly: The Drunk Duck Collection. Vol. 2 Rowles, Chuck et al, illus. (p. 487)
Rowles, Louis. Ida Claire Decorates with Flair. Brownlee, Sunny, illus. (p. 851)
Rowles, Steve, illus. see Rowles, Charles G., 3rd.
Rowlett, Dana. Treasures from a Kindergarten Room. (p. 1782)
Rowley, Alexandra, photos by see Strauss, Elisa & Matheson, Christie.
Rowley, B. J. What Makes Guys Tick? (p. 1892)
Rowley, Deborah. Miracle of the Wooden Shoes. (p. 1148)
Rowley, Deborah Pace. Easter Walk: A Treasure Hunt for the Real Meaning of Easter. Burr, Dan, illus. (p. 499)
—My Wedding Day. Harmon, Glenn, illus. (p. 1221)
—White Dresses: A Baptism Keepsake for Girls. Hodson, Jewel, illus. (p. 1912)
—White Shirts: A Baptism Keepsake for Boys. Call, Brian, illus. (p. 1913)
Rowley, Jillian, illus. see Saavedra, Eusebio.
Rowley, Maryann (Mimi). Frankie & His Muse. (p. 629)
Rowley, Melissa. Falcon Shield. (p. 565)
Rowley, M'lin. Knights of Right, BK 4: The Fiery Gloves. (p. 964)
—Silver Coat. (p. 1576)
Rowleym'Lin. Knights of Right, BK 3: The Warrior's Guard. (p. 964)
Rowling, J. K. Harrius Potter et Camera Secretorum. Needham, Peter, tr. from ENG. (p. 750)
—Harrius Potter et Philosophi Lapis. Needham, Peter, tr. from ENG. (p. 750)
—Harry Potter 65c Color/Act Sidekick Flr Display. (p. 750)
—Harry Potter à l'École des Sorciers. Menard, Jean-François, tr. from ENG. (p. 750)
—Harry Potter & the Chamber of Secrets. (p. 750)
—Harry Potter & the Deathly Hallows. (p. 750)
—Harry Potter & the Deathly Hallows. (p. 750)
—Harry Potter & the Deathly Hallows. GrandPré, Mary, illus. (p. 750)
—Harry Potter & the Deathly Hallows. Bar-hillel, Gili, tr. from ENG. (p. 750)
—Harry Potter & the Goblet of Fire. (p. 750)
—Harry Potter & the Goblet of Fire. GrandPré, Mary, illus. (p. 750)
—Harry Potter & the Half Blood Prince - Chinese Language. (p. 751)
—Harry Potter & the Half-Blood Prince (p. 750)
—Harry Potter & the Half-Blood Prince. GrandPré, Mary, illus. (p. 750)
—Harry Potter & the Half-Blood Prince. (p. 751)
—Harry Potter & the Half-Blood Prince. GrandPré, Mary, illus. (p. 751)
—Harry Potter & the Order of the Phoenix (p. 751)
—Harry Potter & the Order of the Phoenix. (p. 751)
—Harry Potter & the Order of the Phoenix. GrandPré, Mary, illus. (p. 751)
—Harry Potter & the Prisoner of Azkaban (p. 751)
—Harry Potter & the Prisoner of Azkaban. (p. 751)
—Harry Potter & the Sorcerer's Stone. (p. 751)
—Harry Potter Coffret: Harry Potter à l'École des Sorciers; Harry Potter et la Chambre des Secrets; Harry Potter et le Prisonnier d'Azkaban. (p. 751)
—Harry Potter e a Camara Secreta. (p. 751)
—Harry Potter e a Pedra Filosofal. (p. 751)
—Harry Potter e o Prisioneiro de Azkaban. (p. 751)
—Harry Potter e il Prigioniero di Azkaban. (p. 751)
—Harry Potter e la camera dei segreti. (p. 751)
—Harry Potter e la Pietra Filosofale. (p. 751)
—Harry Potter e o Cálice de Fogo. (p. 751)
—Harry Potter et la Coupe de Feu. (p. 751)
—Harry Potter et l'Ordre du Phenix. (p. 751)
—Harry Potter I Czara Ognia. (p. 751)
—Harry Potter I Kamie D. (p. 751)
—Harry Potter I Komnata Tajem. (p. 751)
—Harry Potter I wi Zied Azkab. (p. 751)
—Harry Potter y el Caliz de Fuego. (p. 751)
—Harry Potter y el Prisionero de Azkaban. (p. 751)
—Harry Potter y la Camara Secreta. (p. 751)
—Harry Potter Y la Orden del Fenix. (p. 751)
—Harry Potter Y la Orden del Fenix. Ortega, Gemma Rovira, tr. from ENG. (p. 751)
—Harry Potter y la Piedra Filosofal. (p. 751)
—Harrys Zauberbox: Books 1 - 4. (p. 751)
—Hogwarts Library (p. 787)
—Sorcerer's Stone. Grand Pre, Mary, illus. (p. 1614)
—Tales of Beedle the Bard. GrandPré, Mary, illus. (p. 1702)
Rowling, J. K., see Scamander, Newt, pseud.
Rowling, J. K., see Whisp, Kennilworthy, pseud.
Rowling, J. K. & Xocuasvili, Cico. Hari Poteri Da Sikvdilis Sacukrebi. (p. 748)
Rowlinson, Joanne. Catching Boo. Brown, Mari, illus. (p. 279)
Rowntree, G. M. Wizards Spell Magic in the Legends of Mere Leander. (p. 1943)
—Wizards Spell Magic in the Legends of Mere Leander - US Trade Size. (p. 1943)
Rowohlt, Harry & Trier, Walter. Jolly Steamship. Trier, Walter, illus. (p. 924)
Rowold, Shirley. Big Bear. (p. 178)
Rowsell, Cyrilla & Vinden, David. Music Handbook - Level 3: A Handbook for Teaching Key Music Skills (inc. 7 Audio CDs) Lamb, Karen, illus. (p. 1193)
Rowton, Caitlin, illus. see Pruett, Nichole Lee.
Rox, John. I Want a Hippopotamus for Christmas. Whatley, Bruce, illus. (p. 847)
Roxas, Isabel, illus. see Berger, Samantha.
Roxas, Isabel, illus. see Lê, Minh.
Roxas, Isabel, illus. see McGhee, Alison.
Roxbee Cox, Phil. Phonics Stories for Young Readers (p. 1352)
—Say Please, Louise! Tyler, Jenny, ed. (p. 1518)
Roxbee-Cox, Phil. Find the Bird. Cartwright, Stephen, illus. (p. 587)
—Find the Kitten. Cartwright, Stephen, illus. (p. 587)
—Find the Puppy. Cartwright, Stephen, illus. (p. 587)
—Find the Teddy. Cartwright, Stephen, illus. (p. 587)
—Ted's Shed. (p. 1713)
Roxbee-Cox, Phil, et al. Reino de los Juguetes. (p. 1457)
Roxburgh, Ellis. Abraham Lincoln vs. Jefferson Davis: Presidents of a Divided Nation. (p. 7)
—Adolf Hitler vs. Winston Churchill: Foes of World War II. (p. 13)
—Aztec Empire. (p. 122)
—British Empire. (p. 229)
—Chinese Empire. (p. 307)
—Cleopatra vs. the Roman Empire: Power, Conquest, & Tragedy. (p. 331)
—Egyptian Empire. (p. 506)
—Elizabeth I of England vs. Mary, Queen of Scots: Battle for the Throne. (p. 513)
—Founding Fathers vs. King George III: The Fight for a New Nation. (p. 624)
—John F. Kennedy vs. Nikita Khrushchev. (p. 921)
—Mauryan Empire of India. (p. 1110)
—Mesopotamian Empires. (p. 1129)
—Sitting Bull vs. George Armstrong Custer: The Battle of the Little Bighorn. (p. 1582)
—Thomas Jefferson vs. John Adams: Founding Fathers & Political Rivals. (p. 1739)
—Ulysses S. Grant vs. Robert E. Lee: Civil War Rivals. (p. 1810)
Roxy. Adventure of Benny Franklin: A Boy Tale. (p. 14)
Roy, Alene Adele. Legend of Dragonfly Pond: Book Three. (p. 988)
—Legend of Dragonfly Pond: Volume One. (p. 988)
—Legend of Dragonfly Pond: Coloring Book. (p. 988)
Roy, Anita. India. (p. 870)
Roy, Arundhati. Dieu des Petits Riens. (p. 437)
Roy, Brenda & Lantis, Lora. Night Noise. (p. 1253)
Roy, Claude. Chat qui parlait malgre Lui. (p. 295)
Roy, Deryl. Just Like Dad. (p. 939)
Roy, Gregory, jt. auth. see Roy, Jennifer Rozines.
Roy, Gregory & Roy, Jennifer Rozines. Graphing in the Desert. (p. 711)
Roy, Indrapramit, illus. see Euripides.
Roy, Indrapramit, illus. see Wolf, Gita.
Roy, James. Anonymity Jones. (p. 87)
—Billy Mack's War. (p. 187)
—Chaz & the Missing Mayo. Gorissen, Dean, illus. (p. 295)
—Chaz at the Fish Market. Gorissen, Dean, illus. (p. 295)
—Chaz, Superbarf Surprise. Gorissen, Dean, illus. (p. 295)
—Chaz, TV Superstar? Gorissen, Dean, illus. (p. 295)
—Gimlet Eye. (p. 676)
—Ichabod Hart & the Lighthouse Mystery. (p. 851)
—Legend of Big Red. Dale, Rae, illus. (p. 988)
—Max Quigley: Technically Not a Bully. (p. 1111)
—Miss Understood. (p. 1152)
—Queasy Rider. (p. 1424)
Roy, Jennifer. Cordially Uninvited. (p. 366)
—Jars of Hope: How One Woman Helped Save 2,500 Children During the Holocaust. Owenson, Meg, illus. (p. 909)
—Mindblind (p. 1145)
—Yellow Star (p. 1970)
Roy, Jennifer, jt. auth. see DeVillers, Julia.
Roy, Jennifer Rozines. Cordially Uninvited. (p. 366)
—Sharpen Your Good Grammar Skills. (p. 1563)
—Sharpen Your Report Writing Skills. (p. 1563)
—Sharpen Your Story or Narrative Writing Skills. (p. 1563)
—You Can Write a Report. (p. 1974)
—You Can Write a Story or Narrative. (p. 1974)
—You Can Write Using Good Grammar. (p. 1974)
Roy, Jennifer Rozines, jt. auth. see DeVillers, Julia.
Roy, Jennifer Rozines, jt. auth. see Roy, Gregory.
Roy, Jennifer Rozines & Gordon, Sherri Mabry. Sharpen Your Business Letter Writing Skills. (p. 1563)
—You Can Write a Business Letter. (p. 1974)
Roy, Jennifer Rozines & Haney, Johannah. Sharpen Your Debate & Speech Writing Skills. (p. 1563)
—Sharpen Your Essay Writing Skills. (p. 1563)
—You Can Write an Essay. (p. 1974)
—You Can Write Speeches & Debates. (p. 1974)
Roy, Jennifer Rozines & Roy, Gregory. Addition in the Forest. (p. 12)
—Division with Toys. (p. 455)
—Graphing in the Desert. (p. 711)
—Holiday Fractions. (p. 788)
—How Does the Wind Blow? (p. 809)
—Math All Around (p. 1105)
—Math All Around Group 2 (p. 1105)
—Measuring at Home. (p. 1117)

R

—Money at the Store. (p. 1164)
—Multiplication on the Farm. (p. 1190)
—Numbers on the Street. (p. 1272)
—Patterns in Nature. (p. 1329)
—Shapes in Transportation. (p. 1561)
—Sorting at the Ocean. (p. 1614)
—Subtraction at School. (p. 1671)
Roy, Karen, illus. see Reynolds MacArthur, Anita.
Roy, Kasi. Elizabeth Dreams: And the Christmas House Clock. (p. 513)
Roy, Katherine. Neighborhood Sharks: Hunting with the Great Whites of California's Farallon Islands. Roy, Katherine, illus. (p. 1240)
Roy, Katherine, illus. see Aveni, Anthony.
Roy, Katherine, illus. see Taylor, S. S.
Roy, Kelsey. Nemanee. Roy, Kelsey, illus. (p. 1241)
Roy, Keri Anne & Holt, K. A. Brains for Lunch: A Zombie Novel in Haiku?! Wilson, Gahan, illus. (p. 222)
Roy, Lillian Elizabeth. Alice in Beeland: A Tale of Cornwall, Inspired by Lewis Carroll's Wonderland. (p. 39)
—Girl Scouts in Arizona & New Mexico. Lehman, A. C., illus. (p. 679)
—Little Woodcrafters' Fun on the Farm. Rogers, Walter S., illus. (p. 1038)
—Polly in Egypt: The Polly Brewster Series. Barbour, H. S., illus. (p. 1381)
—Polly in New York. Barbour, H. S., illus. (p. 1381)
—Polly's Southern Cruise: The Polly Brewster Series. Barbour, H. S., illus. (p. 1381)
—Woodcraft Girls at Camp. Barbour, H. S., illus. (p. 1949)
Roy, Oscar. I Was Captured by Pirates. (p. 848)
Roy, Pat & Roy, Sandy. Jonathan Park: a New Beginning. (p. 925)
—Jonathan Park: a Startling Discovery. (p. 925)
—Jonathan Park: Return to the Hidden Cave. (p. 925)
Roy, Philip. Jellybean Mouse. Torrey Balsara, Andrea, illus. (p. 912)
—Journey to Atlantis. (p. 928)
—Me & Mr. Bell: A Novel (p. 1115)
—Mouse Tales. Torrey Balsara, Andrea, illus. (p. 1182)
—Seas of South Africa. (p. 1538)
—Submarine Outlaw. (p. 1671)
Roy Rockwood. Through the Air to the North Pole: Or the Wonderful Cruise of the Electric Monarch. (p. 1745)
Roy, Ron. Absent Author. Gurney, John Steven, illus. (p. 7)
—April Adventure. (p. 93)
—April Adventure. Gurney, John Steven, illus. (p. 93)
—August Acrobat. (p. 115)
—August Acrobat. Gurney, John Steven, illus. (p. 115)
—Bald Bandit. Gurney, John Steven, illus. (p. 133)
—Calendar Mysteries: April Adventure. Gurney, John Steven, illus. (p. 252)
—Calendar Mysteries #8: August Acrobat. Gurney, John Steven, illus. (p. 252)
—Canary Caper. Gurney, John Steven, illus. (p. 260)
—Capital Mysteries #13: Trapped on the D. C. Train! Bush, Timothy, illus. (p. 262)
—Castle Crime. (p. 276)
—Detective Camp. Gurney, John Steven, illus. (p. 431)
—Election-Day Disaster. Bush, Timothy, illus. (p. 508)
—February Friend. Gurney, John Steven, illus. (p. 580)
—Fireworks at the FBI. Bush, Timothy, illus. (p. 592)
—Ghost at Camp David. (p. 670)
—Ghost at Camp David. Bush, Timothy, illus. (p. 670)
—January Joker. Gurney, John Steven, illus. (p. 908)
—July Jitters. (p. 933)
—July Jitters. Gurney, John Steven, illus. (p. 933)
—June Jam. Gurney, John Steven, illus. (p. 934)
—March Mischief. (p. 1091)
—March Mischief. Gurney, John Steven, illus. (p. 1091)
—May Magic. Gurney, John Steven, illus. (p. 1112)
—Mayflower Treasure Hunt. Gurney, John Steven, illus. (p. 1113)
—Mystery at the Washington Monument. Bush, Timothy, illus. (p. 1224)
—New Year Dragon Dilemma. Gurney, John Steven, illus. (p. 1247)
—October Ogre. (p. 1277)
—October Ogre. Gurney, John Steven, illus. (p. 1277)
—Operation Orca. Gurney, John Steven, illus. (p. 1300)
—School Skeleton. Gurney, John Steven, illus. (p. 1523)
—Secret at Jefferson's Mansion. (p. 1540)
—Secret at Jefferson's Mansion. Bush, Timothy, illus. (p. 1540)
—September Sneakers. (p. 1551)
—September Sneakers. Gurney, John Steven, illus. (p. 1551)
—Skeleton in the Smithsonian. Bush, Timothy, illus. (p. 1584)
—Sleepy Hollow Sleepover. Gurney, John Steven, illus. (p. 1589)
—Sleepy Hollow Sleepover. (p. 1590)
—Spy in the White House. Bush, Timothy, tr. (p. 1636)
—Talking T. Rex. Gurney, John Steven, illus. (p. 1703)
—Thief at the National Zoo. Bush, Timothy, illus. (p. 1732)
—to Z Mysteries Collection Gurney, John Steven, illus. (p. 1759)
—Trouble at the Treasury. Bush, Timothy, illus. (p. 1789)
—Unwilling Umpire. Gurney, John Steven, illus. (p. 1823)
—Vampire's Vacation. Gurney, John Steven, illus. (p. 1832)
—White House White-Out. Gurney, John Steven, illus. (p. 1913)
—White Wolf. Gurney, John Steven, tr. (p. 1914)
—Who Broke Lincoln's Thumb? Bush, Timothy, illus. (p. 1914)
—X'ed-Out X-Ray. Gurney, John Steven, illus. (p. 1967)
—Yellow Yacht. Gurney, John Steven, illus. (p. 1970)
—Zombie Zone. Gurney, John Steven, illus. (p. 1988)
Roy, Ronald. Calendar Mysteries #11: November Night. Gurney, John Steven, illus. (p. 252)
—Calendar Mysteries #12: December Dog. Gurney, John Steven, illus. (p. 252)
—Calendar Mysteries #13: New Year's Eve Thieves. Gurney, John Steven, illus. (p. 252)
—Capital Mysteries #14: Turkey Trouble on the National Mall. Bush, Timothy, illus. (p. 262)
—December Dog. (p. 421)
—New Year's Eve Thieves. (p. 1247)
—November Night. (p. 1268)
—to Z Mysteries Super Edition #6: the Castle Crime. Gurney, John Steven, illus. (p. 1759)
—Turkey Trouble on the National Mall. (p. 1797)
Roy, Sandrine Dumas. Hot Air. Ardizzone, Sarah, tr. from FRE. (p. 801)
Roy, Sandy, jt. auth. see Roy, Pat.
Roy Shah, Amita. It's Time for Holi! Lucas, Diane, illus. (p. 899)
Roy, Simon, jt. auth. see Graham, Brandon.
Roy, Tamba. Gift for Anansi. (p. 675)
Roy, Wendy. Kelly Confident Shows You Why... It's POWERFUL to be a GIRL! It's POWERFUL to be a GIRL! (p. 948)
Roy Windham, Windham & Windham, Roy. Uncle Fuddy-Duddy & the Big Bad Bear. (p. 1811)
Royal Air Force, creator. Gloster Meteor Pilot's Flight Operating Instructions. (p. 685)
—Hawker Hurricane Pilot's Flight Operating Manual. (p. 755)
—Supermarine Spitfire Pilot's Flight Operating Instructions. (p. 1684)
Royal British Columbia Museum Staff, photos by see Swanson, Diane.
Royal Observatory Greenwich Staff & Collins Maps Staff. Stars & Planets. (p. 1643)
Royal, Randal. Spirit Mountain: Wounded-Fox. (p. 1628)
Royal, Stephen. Journey Inside the Womb. (p. 928)
Roybal, Laura. Blood Brothers. Warner, Christopher, ed. (p. 200)
Royce Conant, Jan. Children of Light. Royce Conant, Jan, illus. (p. 302)
Royce, Phillip. Shiny Egg-Shaped Stone. (p. 1567)
Royce, Ralph, jt. auth. see Knight, Clayton.
Royce, Richard. Hard Day for Harry. (p. 748)
Royce, Ron. At the Butterfly Conservatory: Represent & Interpret Data (p. 110)
Royce, Ruth. Children of France. (p. 302)
Royce, Topher. Nez Perce. (p. 1249)
Roychoudhury, Upendrakishore. Goopy Gyne Bagha Byne. (p. 702)
Roycroft, Mitch. Chris Moneymaker. (p. 311)
—Daniel Kid Poker Negreanu. (p. 405)
—Greg Fossilman Raymer. (p. 723)
—Jennifer Harman. (p. 912)
—Johnny Orient Express Chan. (p. 923)
—Phil the Poker Brat Hellmuth. (p. 1350)
—Phil Tiger Woods of Poker Ivey. (p. 1350)
Royde-Smith, N. G. and the Red Cross Knight & Other T. (p. 71)
Roydhouse, Sally. Find & Seek Singapore. (p. 587)
Roydhouse, Sandy. Oceans of the World. (p. 1277)
Roydon, Michael, illus. see Smith, Marie & Smith, Roland.
Royer, Anne. Little Ducks. (p. 1027)
—Little Guinea Pigs. (p. 1028)
—Little Marmots. Castle, Muriel, tr. from FRE. (p. 1031)
—Patitos. (p. 1328)
Royer, Danielle, jt. auth. see Rudolph, Shaina.
Royer, France & Dickinson, Richard. Plants of Alberta. (p. 1370)
Royka, Paul A. Mission Furniture: From the American Arts & Crafts Movement. (p. 1153)
Royle, Nicholas. E. M. Forster. (p. 492)
Royo, Luis, illus. see Martin, George R. R.
Royo-Horodynska, Irena. Mnie Stworzye Bog - Ciebie Euolucya. Royo-Horodynska, Irena, illus. (p. 1157)
Royoux, Jean-Christophe, et al. Tacita Dean. (p. 1694)
Royovej, Kristiny. Sunshine Country: A Story of Family Love & Home. (p. 1678)
Roys, Julie. Outside the Window. (p. 1313)
Royse, Jane, illus. see Morton, Jane & Dreier, Ted.
Royster, D. A. Adoption Is... (p. 13)
Royster, Ka-Sandra. Cough Syrup in Mommy's Hair. (p. 369)
Royster, Mia. Manual: Which Being Interpreted Is, God with Us. (p. 1088)
Royston, Angela. Adapted to Survive (p. 11)
—Adapted to Survive: Animals That Climb (p. 11)
—Adapted to Survive: Animals That Dig (p. 11)
—Adapted to Survive: Animals That Hide (p. 11)
—Aire Contaminado (p. 31)
—Alien Neighbors? The Solar System (p. 41)
—Allergies. (p. 46)
—Alligator. (p. 47)
—Alligators & Crocodiles. (p. 47)
—Amphibians. (p. 65)
—Ancient Greek Adventure. (p. 69)
—Animal Classification. (p. 77)
—Animal Classifications. (p. 77)
—Animals under Threat (p. 84)
—Asthma. (p. 108)
—Astronauts Working in Space (p. 109)
—Ballet (p. 134)
—Ballroom (p. 135)
—Bean's Life. (p. 150)
—Birds. (p. 191)
—Blue Whales. (p. 203)
—Bones & Muscles. (p. 209)
—Bosques en Peligro (p. 215)
—Broad Bean (p. 230)
—Butterfly (p. 247)
—Calentamiento Global (p. 252)
—Canguro (p. 261)
—Chicken (p. 299)
—Colds, the Flu, & Other Infections. (p. 339)
—Color (p. 342)
—Conductors & Insulators (p. 356)
—Conejillo de Indias (p. 356)
—Cuts, Bruises, & Breaks. (p. 396)
—Day the Sun Went Out: The Sun's Energy (p. 414)
—Desert Food Chains (p. 429)
—Diary of A... (p. 434)
—Diary of a Ballerina. (p. 434)
—Diary of a Circus Performer (p. 434)
—Diary of a Dog Walker (p. 434)
—Diary of a Farmer. (p. 434)
—Diary of A... Farmer. (p. 434)
—Diary of a Firefighter (p. 434)
—Diary of a Pilot (p. 434)
—Diet. (p. 437)
—Disappearing Forests (p. 446)
—Disappearing Wildlife (p. 446)
—Disgusting Body Facts (p. 450)
—Dog (p. 460)
—Electricity. (p. 509)
—Energy for the Future (p. 528)
—Explaining Asthma. (p. 549)
—Explaining Down's Syndrome. (p. 549)
—Fighting Smallpox. (p. 586)
—Fire Fighter! (p. 590)
—Fish. (p. 598)
—Flexible & Rigid (p. 603)
—Floods. (p. 605)
—Flora y la Fauna en Peligro. (p. 606)
—Flowers. (p. 608)
—Food Chains & Webs (p. 613)
—Forces: Pushes & Pulls. (p. 617)
—Forces & Motion (p. 617)
—Frog (p. 639)
—Get Some Exercise! (p. 668)
—Get Some Rest! (p. 668)
—Girasol (p. 678)
—Glass: Let's Look at Marbles. (p. 682)
—Global Warming (p. 684)
—Grassland Food Chains (p. 712)
—Guinea Pig (p. 731)
—Gun Crimes. (p. 732)
—Head Lice. (p. 756)
—Heavy & Light (p. 761)
—Heroes of Medicine & Their Discoveries. (p. 773)
—Homes That Move (p. 793)
—Homicide. (p. 794)
—Hongo (p. 795)
—Hoping for Peace in the Middle East. (p. 797)
—Hostile Homes: Extreme Habitats. (p. 801)
—How to Survive in the Desert. (p. 822)
—How to Survive in the Rain Forest. (p. 822)
—Human Growth (p. 826)
—Hurricanes! (p. 830)
—Hurricanes & Tornadoes. (p. 830)
—Imanes (p. 861)
—Insects. (p. 875)
—Inventors Who Changed the World. (p. 884)
—Invertebrates. (p. 884)
—Itches & Scratches (p. 895)
—Kangaroo (p. 942)
—Las Habas (p. 976)
—Let's Look at Marbles (p. 999)
—Levers. (p. 1003)
—Life & Times of a Drop of Water: The Water Cycle (p. 1007)
—Life Cycles. (p. 1009)
—Light & Dark. (p. 1014)
—Living & Nonliving (p. 1040)
—Looking at Forces & Motion: How Do Things Move? (p. 1050)
—Looking at Life Cycles: How Do Plants & Animals Change? (p. 1050)
—Looking at Weather & Seasons: How Do They Change? (p. 1051)
—Love to Dance. (p. 1060)
—Magnetic & Nonmagnetic (p. 1075)
—Magnets (p. 1076)
—Mammals. (p. 1085)
—Manzana (p. 1089)
—Mariposa (p. 1094)
—Materials (p. 1104)
—Metal: Let's Look at a Knife & Fork. (p. 1130)
—Mountain Food Chains (p. 1180)
—Mushroom (p. 1193)
—Natural & Man-Made (p. 1235)
—Oak Tree (p. 1274)
—Ocean Explorer! (p. 1276)
—Ocean Food Chains (p. 1276)
—Ocean It's My Home! (p. 1276)
—Ocean - It's My Home! (p. 1276)
—Océanos y Ríos en Peligro (p. 1277)
—Oceans & Rivers in Danger (p. 1277)
—Ooze & Goo (p. 1299)
—Paper: Let's Look at a Comic Book. (p. 1322)
—Pencil. (p. 1336)
—Perro (p. 1343)
—Plastic: Let's Look at the Frisbee. (p. 1370)
—Polar Bears & Their Homes (p. 1379)
—Pollo (p. 1381)
—Polluted Air (p. 1381)
—Proteins for a Healthy Body (p. 1412)
—Puke & Poo (p. 1415)
—Pulleys & Gears (p. 1416)
—Rabbit. (p. 1429)
—Race That Bike! Forces in Vehicles. (p. 1431)
—Race to Survive Climate Change. (p. 1431)
—Rain Forest Food Chains (p. 1434)
—Rana (p. 1438)
—Read Me! Love to Dance: Ballroom. (p. 1443)
—Reptiles. (p. 1461)
—River Food Chains (p. 1475)
—Roble (p. 1480)
—Rock: Let's Look at a Pebble. (p. 1481)
—Salmon (p. 1505)
—Salmón (p. 1505)
—Science of Hurricanes. (p. 1527)
—Science of Volcanoes. (p. 1527)
—Science vs. Crime. (p. 1528)
—Science vs. Natural Disasters. (p. 1528)
—Senses. (p. 1551)
—Shark: Killer King of the Ocean. (p. 1561)
—Shark. (p. 1561)
—Shiny & Dull (p. 1567)
—Sir Isaac Newton: Overlord of Gravity. (p. 1580)
—Smooth & Rough (p. 1595)
—Smooth & Rough. (p. 1595)
—Soft & Hard (p. 1605)
—Soft & Hard. (p. 1606)
—Soil: Let's Look at a Garden. (p. 1606)
—Solids, Liquids, & Gases (p. 1608)
—Sound & Hearing (p. 1615)
—Sound & Hearing. (p. 1615)
—Space Blog. (p. 1618)
—Storms! (p. 1656)
—Sunflower (p. 1676)
—Sustainable Cities. (p. 1688)
—Sustainable Energy. (p. 1688)
—Tadpole Story. (p. 1695)
—Tap (p. 1705)
—Teeth & Hair. (p. 1715)
—Tooth Decay. (p. 1768)
—Transparent & Opaque (p. 1779)
—Truck Trouble, Level 1. (p. 1791)
—Twitches & Sneezes (p. 1803)
—Using Electricity (p. 1828)
—Vida Silvestre en Peligro de Extincion. (p. 1841)
—Vitamins & Minerals for a Healthy Body (p. 1846)
—Water (p. 1862)
—Water: Let's Look at a Puddle (p. 1862)
—Water & Fiber for a Healthy Body (p. 1862)
—What Happens If We Overfish the Oceans? (p. 1886)
—What Happens When an Ice Cap Melts? (p. 1886)
—Why Do Bones Break? And Other Questions about Movement. (p. 1923)
—Why Do I Brush My Teeth? (p. 1923)
—Why Do I Get a Toothache? And Other Questions about the Nervous System. (p. 1923)
—Why Do I Run? (p. 1923)
—Why Do I Sleep? (p. 1923)
—Why Do I Wash My Hands? (p. 1923)
—Why Do My Eyes Itch? And Other Questions about Allergies. (p. 1924)
—Why Do We Need to Eat? (p. 1924)
—Why We Need Proteins. (p. 1926)
—Why We Need Water & Fiber. (p. 1926)
—Win That Sprint! Forces in Sport. (p. 1935)
—Wolf. (p. 1943)
—Wolves. (p. 1945)
—Wood: Let's Look at a Sports Bat. (p. 1949)
Royston, Angela, jt. auth. see Hewitt, Sally.
Royston, Angela & Dussling, Jennifer. Slinky, Scaly Snakes. (p. 1590)
Royston, Angela & Heinemann Library Staff. Apple (p. 92)
—Butterfly (p. 247)
—Chicken (p. 299)
—Dog (p. 460)
—Frog (p. 639)
—Guinea Pig (p. 731)
—Mushroom (p. 1193)
—Sunflower (p. 1676)
Royston, Angela, et al. Essential Physical Science. (p. 537)
Royther, Chris. Abi's First Camping Days (p. 5)
—Zippy's Christmas Tree. (p. 1987)
Roytman, Arkady. Adventures of King Arthur Coloring Book. (p. 19)
—Build-a-Window Halloween Stained Glass Coloring Book. (p. 238)
—Extreme Sports. (p. 557)
—Fairy Princess. (p. 563)
—Fantasy Warriors Stained Glass Coloring Book. (p. 572)
—GOAL! the Hockey Coloring Book. (p. 687)
—Greek & Roman Gods Stained Glass Coloring Book. (p. 720)
—How to Beat a Bully Sticker Activity Book. (p. 815)
—Knights & Dragons. (p. 964)
—Maneki Neko Lucky Cat Coloring Book. (p. 1087)
—Martial Arts Coloring Book. (p. 1097)
—Pixelations Coloring Book. (p. 1365)
—Secret Agent Sticker Activity. (p. 1540)
—Treasure Hunter Sticker Activity Book. (p. 1781)
—Treasures of King Tut's Tomb Stained Glass Coloring Book. (p. 1782)
—Vampire Nights. (p. 1832)
—World of Dragons Coloring Book. (p. 1956)
Roytman, Arkady, jt. auth. see Dutton, Michael.
Roytman, Arkady & Coloring Books Staff. Outer Space. (p. 1312)
Roytman, Arkady & Paper Dolls for Grownups Staff. Glow-in-the-Dark Ghouls Paper Action Figures. (p. 685)
Roytman, Arkady, et al. Build a 3-D Poster Coloring Book—Outer Space. (p. 237)
—Build a Poster Coloring Book—Atlantis. (p. 238)
—Build a Poster Coloring Book—Space. (p. 238)
Roza, Autumn & Roza, Greg. Miranda Cosgrove. (p. 1149)
Roza, G. Lots of Leaves: Learning the L Sound. (p. 1057)
—On Flat Land: Learning the FL Sound. (p. 1288)
Roza, Greg. Adena, Hopewell, & Fort Ancient of Ohio. (p. 12)
—America's First Highway. (p. 64)
—America's Transition from Agriculture to Industry: Drawing Inferences & Conclusions. (p. 64)
—Analyzing the Boston Tea Party: Establishing Cause-and-Effect Relationships. (p. 67)
—Arctic Ecosystem. (p. 96)
—Armed & Dangerous (p. 99)
—Arsenic. (p. 101)
—Bacteria up Close. (p. 131)
—Basketball in the SEC (Southeastern Conference) (p. 143)
—Beastly Beetles. (p. 152)
—Beavers. (p. 155)
—Beneath Earth's Surface. (p. 164)
—Bill & Melinda Gates. (p. 186)
—Bizarre Life Cycle of a Cicada. (p. 194)
—Bo Diddley: Rock-And-Roll All-Star. (p. 205)
—Bromine. (p. 230)
—Calcium. (p. 252)
—Career as a Carpenter. (p. 266)
—Careers in the Coast Guard's Search & Rescue Units. (p. 268)
—Careers in the Military. (p. 268)
—Checkmate! the Game of Chess: Applying Strategies from Simple to Complex Problems. (p. 295)
—Checkmate! The Game of Chess: Applying Strategies from Simpler Problems to Complex Problems. (p. 295)

—Chomp! The Great White Shark & Other Animals That Bite. (p. 309)
—Choosing a Career in the Military. (p. 310)
—Chromium. (p. 317)
—Colony of New York. (p. 342)
—Colony of Rhode Island. (p. 342)
—Comets & Asteroids: Space Rocks. (p. 348)
—Cool Careers Without College for People Who Love to Write. (p. 363)
—Dale Earnhardt Jr: NASCAR Driver. (p. 401)
—Dale Earnhardt Jr. NASCAR Driver. (p. 401)
—David Beckham: Soccer Superstar. (p. 410)
—Day for Dad. (p. 412)
—Deadly Bacteria. (p. 417)
—Deadly Black Widows. (p. 417)
—Deadly Pufferfish. (p. 418)
—Decomposers. (p. 422)
—Día de San Valentín (Valentines for Vinnie) (p. 433)
—Disaster Relief Workers. (p. 446)
—Drawing Dracula. (p. 481)
—Drawing Frankenstein. (p. 481)
—Drawing Godzilla. (p. 482)
—Drawing King Kong. (p. 482)
—Early Explorers of Texas. (p. 493)
—Earthquake: True Stories of Survival. (p. 497)
—Eighth Amendment: Preventing Cruel & Unusual Punishment. (p. 507)
—Evaluating the Articles of Confederation: Determining the Validity of Information & Arguments. (p. 540)
—Exploring Rocks & Minerals. (p. 553)
—Famous Flights: Understanding & Using Variables. (p. 569)
—Freaky Flies. (p. 632)
—Frequently Asked Questions about Driving & the Law. (p. 636)
—Frequently Asked Questions about Emergency Lifesaving Techniques. (p. 636)
—Galapagos Islands. (p. 653)
—Game of Chess: Applying Strategies from Simple to Complex Problems. (p. 654)
—Geometry. (p. 662)
—Getting the Most Out of Makerspaces to Make Musical Instruments. (p. 669)
—Goal! (p. 687)
—Great Lakes. (p. 716)
—Great Networking Skills. (p. 717)
—Gross Things on Buses, Trains, & Planes. (p. 725)
—Gross Things under Your Feet. (p. 725)
—Guide My Pen: The Poems of Phillis Wheatley. (p. 730)
—Halogen Elements. (p. 739)
—Happy New Year! (p. 746)
—Harley-Davidson: An All-American Legend. (p. 749)
—Heads or Tails: Exploring Probability Through Games. (p. 757)
—Heads or Tails? Exploring Probability Through Games. (p. 757)
—Henry Ford: Pioneer of Modern Industry. (p. 768)
—Hockey. (p. 786)
—Hoover Dam: Applying Problem-Solving Strategies. (p. 796)
—How Are Stars Born? (p. 805)
—Hubble Space Telescope: Understanding & Representing Numbers in the Billions. (p. 824)
—Immigration & Migration. (p. 861)
—Incredible Story of Aircraft Carriers. (p. 869)
—Incredible Story of Trains. (p. 869)
—Indian Ocean Tsunami. (p. 871)
—Inside the Human Body: Using Exonential & Scientific Notation. (p. 872)
—Inside an Ant Colony. (p. 876)
—Inside the Human Body: Using Scientific & Exponential Notation. (p. 877)
—It's Electric! (p. 896)
—Jellyfish. (p. 912)
—Karankawa of Texas. (p. 943)
—Kevin Harvick: NASCAR Driver. (p. 950)
—Landfills: Habitat Havoc. (p. 974)
—Listen Up: Knowing When & When Not to Speak. (p. 1022)
—Looking at Differences Between Living & Nonliving Things with Graphic Organizers. (p. 1050)
—Looking at the Differences Between Living & Nonliving Things with Graphic Organizers. (p. 1051)
—Lucy's Lunch. (p. 1063)
—Mapping Antarctica. (p. 1090)
—Measurement. (p. 1117)
—Messy Robot. (p. 1130)
—Missouri: Past & Present. (p. 1154)
—Murder of Crows. (p. 1192)
—Murder of Crows / una Bandada de Cuervos. (p. 1192)
—Muscular System. (p. 1192)
—Mysterious Mantises. (p. 1223)
—Neptune: The Stormy Planet. (p. 1241)
—Nevada: Past & Present. (p. 1242)
—Olympic Math: Working with Percentages & Decimals. (p. 1287)
—Olympic Math: Working with Percents & Decimals. (p. 1288)
—Optical Artist: Exploring Patterns & Symmetry. (p. 1301)
—Oregon: Past & Present. (p. 1303)
—Ossuaries & Charnel Houses. (p. 1306)
—Out & About. (p. 1310)
—OutKast. (p. 1312)
—Paintball: Rules, Tips, Strategy, & Safety. (p. 1318)
—Patterns in Poetry: Recognizing & Analyzing Poetic Form & Meter. (p. 1329)
—Peanut Butter Party. (p. 1332)
—Phew! The Skunk & Other Stinky Animals. (p. 1350)
—Piggy Bank for Pedro. (p. 1358)
—Pluto: The Dwarf Planet. (p. 1374)
—Poison! The Spitting Cobra & Other Venomous Animals. (p. 1377)
—Poke! The Sea Urchin & Other Animals with Spikes. (p. 1377)
—Potassium. (p. 1388)
—Powerful Earthquakes. (p. 1390)
—Primary Source Guide to China. (p. 1399)
—Reducing Your Carbon Footprint on Vacation. (p. 1456)
—Repulsive Roaches. (p. 1462)
—Severe Storms: Measuring Velocity. (p. 1555)
—Sidney Crosby. (p. 1573)
—Skeletal System. (p. 1584)
—Space Math. (p. 1619)
—Sting! The Scorpion & Other Animals That Sting. (p. 1651)
—Strange Spiders. (p. 1665)
—Tasmanian Devil vs. Hyena. (p. 1707)
—Terry Labonte. (p. 1722)
—Texas Cities: Then & Now. (p. 1724)
—Thomas Alva Edison (p. 1737)
—Titanium. (p. 1758)
—Tony Stewart. (p. 1766)
—Tundra: Life in a Frozen Landscape. (p. 1796)
—Valentines for Vinnie. (p. 1830)
—Venus & Serena Williams: The Sisters of Tennis. (p. 1836)
—Wedges. (p. 1871)
—Weird Walking Sticks. (p. 1872)
—Westward Expansion. (p. 1876)
—What Happens When I Throw Up? (p. 1886)
—What Is a Black Hole? (p. 1888)
—What Is Fiction? (p. 1889)
—Where We Play Sports: Measuring the Perimeters of Polygons. (p. 1910)
—Where's the Spaghetti? (p. 1911)
—Why People Work. (p. 1925)
—Your Neighbor the Alley Cat. (p. 1981)
—Your Neighbor the Coyote. (p. 1981)
—Your Neighbor the Mouse. (p. 1981)
—Your Neighbor the Pigeon. (p. 1981)
—Your Neighbor the Raccoon. (p. 1981)
—Your Neighbor the Squirrel. (p. 1981)
—Zap! The Electric Eel & Other Electric Animals. (p. 1985)
—Zirconium. (p. 1987)
Roza, Greg, jt. auth. see Mclendon, Jacquelyn.
Roza, Greg, jt. auth. see Mills, Nathan.
Roza, Greg, jt. auth. see Power, Bob.
Roza, Greg, jt. auth. see Roza, Autumn.
Roza, Greg, jt. auth. see Schimel, Kate.
Roza, Greg & Burdick, Mason. Soccer. (p. 1603)
Roza, Greg & Leigh, Autumn. Primary Source Guide to India. (p. 1399)
Rozakis, Laurie. Get Test Smart! The Ultimate Guide to Middle School Standardized Tests. (p. 668)
Rozanski, Bonnie. Borderline. (p. 214)
Rozanski, Lillian. House of Shod. (p. 803)
Rozarena, P., tr. see Lechermeier, Philippe.
Rozarena, P., tr. see McDonald, Megan.
Rozarena, P., tr. see Patricelli, Leslie.
Rozario, Paul. Liberia. (p. 1005)
—Libya. (p. 1007)
Rozario, Paul A., jt. auth. see Gomez, Leticia.
Rozelaar, Angie, illus. see Prasadam-Halls, Smriti.
Rozelle, Catheryne Izeklow & Siegman, Greg Forbes. Place to Sit. (p. 1366)
Rozen, Anna. Merchant of Noises. Scarbrough, Carl W., tr. from FRE. (p. 1127)
Rozen, Beti. Heart Alone in the Land of Darkness. Lima, Graca, illus. (p. 759)
—Stolen Spirit. Lima, Graca, illus. (p. 1652)
Rozett, Louise. Confessions of an Almost-Girlfriend. (p. 356)
—Ice Queen: Catherine the Great Seizes Power in Russia. (p. 850)
Rozevskis, Diana. Crystal Waters & on to North America. (p. 387)
Rozier, Dana. Natural Hawai'i: An Inquisitive Kid's Guide. (p. 1235)
Rozier, Lucy Margaret. Jackrabbit McCabe & the Electric Telegraph. Espinosa, Leo, illus. (p. 904)
Rozinski, Bob, photos by see Jackson, Donna M.
Rozman, Jennifer Blue. With You Forever. (p. 1942)
Rozum, John. Scooby-Doo in Yankee Doodle Danger. (p. 1529)
RR. Priscilla. (p. 1407)
Rsm Ma, Anne Frances Pulling. Tales from the Pumpkin Patch Spooky: Kitten Who Wanted to Fly. (p. 1702)
RSPB Staff. RSPB Garden Nature Colouring Book. (p. 1493)
—RSPB Wild Nature Colouring Book. (p. 1493)
RSPCA Australia Staff. Pet Isn't Just for Christmas. (p. 1345)
Ruano, Alfonso, illus. see Amado, Elisa.
Ruano, Alfonso, illus. see Skármeta, Antonio & Skarmeta, Antonio.
Ruark Gibb, Paula, jt. auth. see Ballard Beath, Ernest, III.
Ruark, Robert C. I Didn't Know It Was Loaded. (p. 837)
Rubalcaba, Jill. Ancient Egypt: Archaeology Unlocks the Secrets of Egypt's Past. (p. 68)
—Empires of the Maya. (p. 521)
—Wadjet Eye. (p. 1852)
Rubalcaba, Jill, jt. auth. see Cline, Eric H.
Rubalcaba, Jill, jt. auth. see Robertshaw, Peter.
Rubalcaba, Jill & Pei, I.M. I. M. Pei: Architect of Time, Place, & Purpose (p. 844)
Rubalcaba, Jill & Robertshaw, Peter. Every Bone Tells a Story: Hominin Discoveries, Deductions, & Debates. (p. 542)
Rubanenko, Diana, tr. see Shahak, Bat-Chen.
Rubay, Donnell. Emma & the Oyster Pirate. (p. 519)
Rubbino, Salvatore. Walk in London. Rubbino, Salvatore, illus. (p. 1853)
—Walk in New York. Rubbino, Salvatore, illus. (p. 1853)
—Walk in Paris. Rubbino, Salvatore, illus. (p. 1853)
Rubbino, Salvatore, illus. see Davies, Nicola.
Rubcic, Michael. Native Soul. (p. 1235)
Rubel, David. Carpenter's Gift: A Christmas Tale about the Rockefeller Center Tree. LaMarche, Jim, illus. (p. 271)
—If I Had a Hammer: Building Homes & Hope with Habitat for Humanity. (p. 853)
—Scholastic Encyclopedia of the Presidents & Their Times. (p. 1522)
Rubel, Doris, illus. see Caballero, D., tr.
Rubel, Mike. Big Feet, the Story. (p. 181)
Rubel, Nicole, illus. see Gantos, Jack.
Rubel, Nicole, illus. see Hall, Katy, pseud & Eisenberg, Lisa.
Rubel, Nicole, tr. see Gantos, Jack.
Ruben, Anthony R., ed. see Ruben, Pamela J.
Ruben, Maryann. Which Way Today? (p. 1911)
Ruben, Pamela. Lessons from the Bubbe & Zayde Tree. (p. 993)
—Lessons from the Grandma & Grandpa Tree. (p. 993)
Ruben, Pamela J. Don't Pick on Pepper! Take a Journey with Pepper as She Takes on a Schoolyard Bully with Brainpower, Humor, & a Dash of Spice! Ruben, Anthony R., ed. (p. 468)
—Yenta the Chicken & Other Fowl Tales! Ruben, Anthony R., ed. (p. 1970)
Ruben, Paul L., photos by see Karr, Susan Schott.
Ruben, Ruben, illus. see Dumas, Alexandre.
Rubens, Michael. Sons of The 613. (p. 1613)
Rubenstein, Glenn. Sports Gamer: The Best in Sports Video Games. (p. 1632)
Rubenstein, Lauren. Visiting Feelings. Hehenberger, Shelly, illus. (p. 1845)
Rubenstein, Laurence Z. Visiting Feelings. Hehenberger, Shelly, illus. (p. 1845)
Rubenstein, Lauri. My Friendly Giant. Adams, Mark W., illus. (p. 1209)
Rubenstein, Reva, illus. see Finkelstein, Ruth.
Rubenz, Sima. Bringing up Parents: A Biography in Verse. (p. 229)
Ruberto, Carolyn. There Was a Monkey. (p. 1730)
Rubi, Nicholas. My Mom's Not Cool. Maia, Chavez Larkin, illus. (p. 1214)
Rubiano, Roberto. Robert Capa -Imágenes de Guerra. (p. 1478)
Rubin, Adam. Big Bad Bubble. Salmieri, Daniel, illus. (p. 177)
—Dragons Love Tacos. Salmieri, Daniel, illus. (p. 479)
—Secret Pizza Party. Salmieri, Daniel, illus. (p. 1543)
—Those Darn Squirrels! Salmieri, Daniel, illus. (p. 1740)
—Those Darn Squirrels & the Cat Next Door. Salmieri, Daniel, illus. (p. 1740)
—Those Darn Squirrels Fly South. Salmieri, Daniel, illus. (p. 1740)
Rubin, Alan. Esta Granja. (p. 538)
—How Many Fish? (p. 811)
Rubin, Barnett R. Fragmentation of Afghanistan: State Formation & Collapse in the International System. (p. 627)
Rubin, Barry A. Iranian Revolution & the Resurgence of Islam. (p. 887)
—Middle East in the Age of Uncertainty, 1991-Present. (p. 1137)
Rubin, Barry M. & Garton, Leora. History of Islam. (p. 784)
Rubin, Bruce Joel & Michaels, Julie. Stuart Little 2: El Libro de la Pelicula. Vol. 2 (p. 1668)
Rubin, Daniel. Orchestra. (p. 1302)
Rubin, David, illus. see Pope, Paul & Petty, J. T.
Rubin, Diana. King Choco the Great. (p. 958)
Rubin, Donna. Log Cabin Kitty. Halbower, Susan J., illus. (p. 1045)
Rubin, Elizabeth. Curies & Radium. Moyler, Alan, illus. (p. 392)
Rubin, Ellen. Hanakkah Puzzle Book. (p. 740)
Rubin, Judith, jt. auth. see Rubin, Susan Ellen.
Rubin, Julian. Orchid Grower. (p. 1302)
Rubin, Ken. Volcanoes & Earthquakes. (p. 1849)
Rubin, Lance. Denton Little's Deathdate. (p. 427)
Rubin, Laurie. Do You Dream in Color? Insights from a Girl Without Sight. (p. 457)
Rubin, Sarah. Someday Dancer. (p. 1609)
Rubin, Scott & Oestreicher, Mark. My Future (p. 1209)
Rubin, Sean, illus. see Jacques, Brian.
Rubin, Susan Ellen & Rubin, Judith. Bee Yourself: The Story of Bernard the Bee. (p. 157)
Rubin, Susan Goldman. Andy Warhol: Pop Art Painter. (p. 73)
—Andy Warhol's Colors. (p. 73)
—Anne Frank Case: Simon Wiesenthal's Search for the Truth. Farnsworth, Bill, illus. (p. 86)
—Counting with Wayne Thiebaud. (p. 372)
—Degas & the Dance: The Painter & the Petits Rats, Perfecting Their Art. (p. 424)
—Delicious: The Life & Art of Wayne Thiebaud. (p. 425)
—Diego Rivera: An Artist for the People. (p. 437)
—Everyone Paints! The Lives & Art of the Wyeth Family. (p. 544)
—Fireflies in the Dark: The Story of Friedl Dicker-Brandeis & the Children of Terezin. (p. 592)
—Flag with Fifty-Six Stars: A Gift from the Survivors of Mauthausen. Farnsworth, Bill, illus. (p. 602)
—Freedom Summer: The 1964 Struggle for Civil Rights in Mississippi. (p. 635)
—Hot Pink: The Life & Fashions of Elsa Schiaparelli. (p. 802)
—Irena Sendler & the Children of the Warsaw Ghetto. Farnsworth, Bill, illus. (p. 887)
—Jacob Lawrence in the City. (p. 904)
—Jean Laffite: The Pirate Who Saved America. Howell, Troy & Himmelman, Jeff, illus. (p. 911)
—Matisse Dance for Joy. (p. 1109)
—Music Was IT: Young Leonard Bernstein. (p. 1193)
—Stand There! She Shouted: The Invincible Photographer Julia Margaret Cameron. Ibatoulline, Bagram, illus. (p. 1639)
—Whaam! The Art & Life of Roy Lichtenstein. (p. 1877)
—Wideness & Wonder: The Life & Art of Georgia O'Keeffe. (p. 1927)
Rubin, Susan Goldman & Magritte, Rene. Magritte's Imagination. (p. 1076)
Rubin, Susan Goldman & Weissberger, Ela. Cat with the Yellow Star: Coming of Age in Terezin. (p. 278)
Rubinacci, Mary Ellen. Srepsihw: The Land of Quiet? (p. 1637)
Rubine, illus. see Smith, Owen & Smith, Anne.
Rubinger, Ami. Big Cat, Small Cat. Baitner, Ray, tr. from HEB. (p. 180)
—Dog Number 1, Dog Number 10. (p. 461)
—I Dream of an Elephant. Rubinger, Ami, illus. (p. 838)
Rubino, Alisa A., illus. see Serafin, Jordan.
Rubino, Alisa A., illus. see Stryker, Robin.
Rubino, Alisa A., jt. illus. see Brudos, Susan E.
Rubino, M. Gayle. Truth about Scuttlebutt. (p. 1794)
Rubino, Michael. Bang! How We Came to Be. (p. 136)
Rubino, Tony. Animal Farm. (p. 77)
—Who Ate the Brownies. (p. 1914)
Rubino-Bradway, Caitlen. Ordinary Magic. (p. 1302)
Rubins, Diane Teitel. Sarah the Best Bridesmaid: Paper Doll Storybook. Shanahan, Sue, illus. (p. 1514)
Rubins, Diane Teitel & Daste, Larry. Nature Search-a-Words. (p. 1236)
Rubinstein, Gary, jt. auth. see Pett, Mark.
Rubinstein, Murray A. Taiwan: A New History. (p. 1696)
Rubinstein, Robert. Zishe the Strongman. Miller, Woody, illus. (p. 1987)
Rubinstein, Robert E. Zishe the Strongman. Miller, Woody, illus. (p. 1987)
Rubio, Adrian, jt. auth. see Benatar, Raquel.
Rubio, Adriana. Jim Morrison Ceremony: '... Exploring the Shaman Possession...' (p. 917)
Rubio, Antonio. Pollito de la Avellaneda. Pacheco, Gabriel, illus. (p. 1381)
Rubio, Esther, jt. auth. see Child, Lauren.
Rubio, Esther, tr. see Child, Lauren.
Rubio, Esther, tr. see Cowan, Catherine & Buehner, Mark.
Rubio, Esther, tr. see Crebbin, June.
Rubio, Esther, tr. see Hest, Amy.
Rubio, Esther, tr. see Matthews, Andrew.
Rubio, Esther, tr. see Stimson, Joan.
Rubio, Gabriela. Terrible/Terrible. (p. 1721)
Rubio, Gabriela, illus. see Miracles, Max & Brigitte, Smadja.
Rubio, Gabriela, illus. see Smadja, Bridgitte & Brigitte, Smadja.
Rubio, Gabriela & Rubio Márquez, Gabriela. Se Acabo! (p. 1534)
Rubio Márquez, Gabriela, jt. auth. see Rubio, Gabriela.
Rubio, Mary Henley, ed. see Montgomery, L. M.
Ruble, Eugene. Ancient Symbols, Artwork, Carvings & Alphabets. Burch, Lynda S., ed. (p. 70)
—Counting 1 to 10 with Professor Hoot. Ruble, Eugene, illus. (p. 370)
—Learning the Basics of Color. Ruble, Eugene, illus. (p. 985)
Ruble, Eugene, illus. see Berger, Susan J.
Ruble, Eugene, illus. see Cairn, Barbara.
Ruble, Eugene, illus. see Cairns, Barbara.
Ruble, Eugene, illus. see Collins, Janet Ann.
Ruble, Eugene, illus. see Cox, Tracey M.
Ruble, Eugene, illus. see Kirk, Bill.
Ruble, Eugene, illus. see Lyle-Soffe, Shari.
Ruble, Eugene, illus. see Malandrinos, Cheryl C.
Ruble, Eugene, illus. see McNamee, Kevin.
Ruble, Eugene, illus. see Vishpriya.
Ruble, Kam. Princess Annado Tandy's Versery Rhymes. McMullen, T. C., illus. (p. 1403)
Ruble, Stephanie, illus. see Ryan, Candace.
Rubow, Carol. God Loves You. (p. 689)
—God Loves You Mini Book. (p. 689)
Rubright, Lynn. Mama's Window. Smith, Duane, illus. (p. 1084)
Rubsam, Lee Ann. Character Building for Families. (p. 291)
Ruby, Anne. Children of the Sea. Meier, Ty, illus. (p. 302)
Ruby, Carl, jt. auth. see Fajardo, Renee.
Ruby, India. Three Twentieth Century Dictators: Set Of 6. (p. 1744)
—Three Twentieth Century Dictators & Tres dictadores del siglo XX: 6 English, 6 Spanish Adaptations. (p. 1744)
Ruby, Laura. Bad Apple. (p. 131)
—Bone Gap. (p. 208)
—Good Girls. (p. 698)
—Lily's Ghosts. (p. 1018)
—Play Me. (p. 1371)
Ruby, Lois. Doll Graveyard. (p. 463)
—Rebel Spirits. (p. 1451)
—Secret of Laurel Oaks. (p. 1542)
—Shanghai Shadows. (p. 1559)
—Strike! Mother Jones & the Colorado Coal Field War. (p. 1667)
Ruchlis, Hyman. Wonder of Light: A Picture Story of How & Why We See. Hirsh, Alice, illus. (p. 1947)
Ruchman, Laura, jt. auth. see Thomas, Wendy Russell.
Rucinski, Sandra. Story of Jesus According to Tobin. (p. 1658)
Ruck, jt. auth. see Deluc, Yves.
Ruck, Colleen. Cars. (p. 272)
—Diggers. (p. 439)
—Helicopters. (p. 763)
—Motorcycles. (p. 1179)
—Planes. (p. 1367)
—Submarines. (p. 1671)
—Trucks. (p. 1791)
Rucka, Greg. Declassified (p. 422)
—Operation: Blackwall (p. 1300)
Rucka, Greg & Brubaker, Ed. Dead Robin. Kano & Lieber, Steve, illus. (p. 417)
Rucka, Greg, et al. Bruce Wayne Fugitive. (p. 232)
—Checkmate: A King's Game. Vol. 1 (p. 295)
—Land of the Dead. (p. 973)
—No Man's Land. Land, Greg & Eaglesham, Dale, illus. (p. 1259)
—Omac Project. (p. 1288)
—Quick & the Dead. (p. 1427)
—Sacrifice. (p. 1501)
Ruckdeschel, Liz & James, Sara. All Your Dreams Came True. (p. 46)
Ruckel, Izidor. Abandoned for Life: The Incredible Story of One Romanian Orphan, Hidden from the World. His Life. His Words. Bramsch, Joan, ed. (p. 2)
Rucker, David. Valley of the Christmas Trees: A Legend. Laster, Brenda, illus. (p. 1831)
Rucker, Georgia, illus. see Merberg, Julie.
Rucker, Jeffrey A. historia de Toro Sentado (the Story of Sitting Bull) (p. 782)
—Story of Sitting Bull. (p. 1660)
—Trip to the Fire Station. (p. 1787)
Rucker, Justin, jt. auth. see Bauer, Marion Dane.
Rucker, Justin, jt. auth. see Silverman, Erica.
Rucker, Mike. Terry & the Beaver Dam Fiasco. (p. 1722)
—Terry & the Earthquake. (p. 1722)

R

—Terry & the Elephant. (p. 1722)
—Terry & The South Pole Breakdown. (p. 1722)
—Terry & the Super Powerful Fuel. (p. 1722)
Rucker, Noah. Mystery of the Shadows. (p. 1226)
Ruckman, Ivy. Night of the Twisters. (p. 1254)
Ruckman, Kathleen. God's Amazing Book. Davies, Lauretta, illus. (p. 690)
Ruck-Pauquet, Gina. Ninos Mas Encantadores del Mundo. (p. 1257)
Rud, Jeff. Crossover (p. 385)
—First & Ten (p. 593)
—High & Inside (p. 777)
—In the Paint: South Side Sports (p. 867)
—Paralyzed (p. 1966)
Rudd, Benton, illus. see Adair, Tammi.
Rudd, Benton, illus. see Faber, Toni Tuso.
Rudd, Benton, illus. see Ferguson, Scott.
Rudd, Bill. Broken Circle: The Black-footed Ferrets. (p. 230)
Rudd, Brandon Kyle. Cooper's Pack — New York City: New York City McCann, Martin, illus. (p. 365)
—Cooper's Pack Travel Guide to Alaska. McCann, Martin, illus. (p. 365)
—Cooper's Pack Travel Guide to New York City. McCann, Martin, illus. (p. 365)
Rudd, Kelly, ed. see Thomson Gale Staff & Hermsen, Sarah.
Ruddell, Deborah. Today at the Bluebird Café: A Branchful of Birds. Rankin, Joan E. & Rankin, Joan, illus. (p. 1760)
—Whiff of Pine, a Hint of Skunk: A Forest of Poems. Rankin, Joan E., illus. (p. 1911)
—Who Said Coo? Luebs, Robin, illus. (p. 1917)
Ruddock, Evie. Mozart the Singing Frog. (p. 1184)
Ruddra, Anshumani. Dorje's Stripes. A-Park, Gwangjo & A-Park, Jung, illus. (p. 471)
Ruddy, Limner, illus. see Rose, Wendy.
Rude, Steve. Spider-Man Through the Decades. Ditko, Steve et al, illus. (p. 1626)
Rude, Steve, illus. see Jones, Bruce.
Rudel-Tessier, Melanie. Caillou: Happy Easter! Brignaud, Pierre, illus. (p. 251)
Ruden, Jenny. Camp Utopia: & the Forgiveness Diet. (p. 257)
Rudenko, Dennis. Look Out for the Pufferfish! (p. 1050)
—Planning My Farm: Reason with Shapes & Their Attributes. (p. 1368)
—Sea Turtles. (p. 1536)
Rudetsky, Seth. My Awesome - Awful Popularity Plan. (p. 1196)
—Rise & Fall of a Theater Geek. (p. 1474)
Rudge, Glen. Sun Rose & the Wind Blue. (p. 1676)
Rudge, Leila. Perfect Place for Ted. Rudge, Leila, illus. (p. 1342)
Rudge, Leila, illus. see McKinlay, Meg.
Rudgers, Stephanie. How We Use Maps. (p. 823)
Rudi, Julie A. That's How Much I Love You. Beeke, Tiphanie, illus. (p. 1727)
Rudick, Dina. Barnyard Kids: A Family Guide for Raising Animals. (p. 140)
Rudin, Ronald. Founding Fathers: The Celebration of Champlain & Laval in the Streets of Quebec, 1878-1908. (p. 624)
Rudisill, J. J. Hickory Dickory Dock. (p. 775)
Ruditis, P. J. Love, Hollywood Style. (p. 1059)
Ruditis, Paul. Charmed: Season 9 Volume 1 (p. 294)
—Devil's in the Diva: The Four Dorothys - Everyone's a Critic. (p. 432)
—Entrances & Exits. (p. 531)
—Everyone's a Critic. (p. 544)
—Four Dorothys. (p. 624)
—Rainbow Party. (p. 1435)
—Ready to Glow. Choi Sung Hwan, Aragon Noel, illus. (p. 1447)
Ruditis, Paul, jt. auth. see Gregory, Raven.
Rudkin, Shawn, ed. see Polk, James G.
Rudkin, Tracy, illus. see Polk, James G.
Rudko, Che, jt. auth. see Mitter, Matt.
Rudland, Joanne. Short-Term Memory Difficulties in Children: A Practical Resource. (p. 1569)
Rudman, Jack, ed. see Standish, Burt L.
Rudman, Jack, jt. auth. see Standish, Burt L.
Rudman, Mark. Motel en Route to Life Out There: Selections from the Rider Quintet. (p. 1177)
Rudner, Barry. Silent Voice. Trabalka, Pegy, illus. (p. 1575)
Rudnick, Arnold. Little Green. Gorenman, Marcelo, illus. (p. 1028)
Rudnick, Elizabeth. Cinderella: Junior Novel. (p. 320)
—Cinderella. (p. 320)
—Hulk Versus the World. Marvel Illustrators, illus. (p. 825)
—Iron Man Is Born. Marvel Illustrators, illus. (p. 888)
—Maleficent. (p. 1083)
—Thor the Mighty. Marvel Illustrators, illus. (p. 1740)
Rudnick, Lois Palken, et al. Instructor's Guide for American Identities. (p. 878)
Rudnick, Paul. Gorgeous. (p. 702)
Rudnicki, Richard. Christmas Dollhouse (p. 313)
Rudnicki, Richard, illus. see Dudar, Judy.
Rudnicki, Richard, illus. see Kulling, Monica.
Rudnicki, Richard, illus. see Laxer, James.
Rudnicki, Richard, illus. see Meyrick, Judith.
Rudnicki, Richard, illus. see Warner, Jody Nyasha.
Rudolph, Aaron. Mystery of the Bermuda Triangle. (p. 1225)
—Unsolved Mystery of the Bermuda Triangle. (p. 1822)
Rudolph, Allyson & Gohari, Omid. Colby College College Prowler off the Record. (p. 338)
Rudolph, Ellen K. Willi Gets a History Lesson: In Virginia's Historic Triangle. Rudolph, Ellen K., photos by. (p. 1933)
Rudolph, Jessica. American Shorthairs: Pioneers. (p. 63)
—Beaver. (p. 154)
—CIA Paramilitary Operatives in Action. (p. 318)
—Erased by a Tornado! (p. 533)
—Flu of 1918: Millions Dead Worldwide! (p. 608)
—Gecko. (p. 659)
—Guatemala. (p. 728)
—Guide Dogs. (p. 730)
—Huracan. (p. 829)
—Hurricane. (p. 829)
—Labrador Retriever: Most Popular. (p. 970)
—Mexico. (p. 1131)
—Mi Cuerpo Es Rayado y Parece Lleno de Hojas. (p. 1132)
—Mi Pelambre es Gruesa y Moteada. (p. 1133)
—Mi Piel Tiene Bultos y es Babosa. (p. 1133)
—MIS Colmillos Son Blancos y Afilados. (p. 1150)
—MIS Garras Son Largas y Curvas. (p. 1150)
—My Body Is Striped & Leafy (Leafy Sea Dragon) (p. 1198)
—My Claws Are Large & Curved (Komodo Dragon) (p. 1200)
—My Fangs Are White & Sharp (Vampire Bat) (p. 1203)
—My Fur Is Thick & Spotted (Snow Leopard) (p. 1209)
—My Skin Is Bumpy & Slimy (Fire Salamander) (p. 1219)
—Rockhopper Penguin. (p. 1483)
—Saint Bernard: Mountain Retriever. (p. 1503)
—Search-And-Rescue Dogs. (p. 1537)
—Service Dogs. (p. 1553)
—South Korea. (p. 1617)
—Tornado. (p. 1770)
Rudolph, Jessica & Pushies, Fred J. Marine Scout Snipers in Action. (p. 1094)
—Today's Navy Heroes. (p. 1761)
Rudolph, Miriam. Frozen Dream. (p. 645)
Rudolph, Nancy Lyn. Paper Animal Masks from Northwest Tribal Tales. (p. 1322)
Rudolph, Shaina & Royer, Danielle. All My Stripes: A Story for Children with Autism. Zivoin, Jennifer, illus. (p. 45)
Rudolph, Tammy. Lucy's Mysterious Paint Brush. (p. 1063)
Rudy, Carol-Ann. Coral Gables, Gateway to the Sun. George, Paul S., ed. (p. 366)
—Crossing to Freedom. George, Paul S., ed. (p. 385)
Rudy, Lisa Jo. Bioterror: Deadly Invisible Weapons. (p. 190)
—Eyes in the Sky: Satellite Spies Are Watching You! (p. 558)
—Micro Spies: Spy Planes the Size of Birds! (p. 1136)
—Snakes! (p. 1596)
Rudy, Maggie. I Wish I Had a Pet. Rudy, Maggie, illus. (p. 848)
Rudy, Maggie & Abrams, Pam. House That Mouse Built. Wolf, Bruce, photos by. (p. 804)
Rudy, Patricia, ed. see Payer-Smith, Heather.
Rue, Ginger. Brand-New Emily. (p. 222)
Rue, Leonard Lee. Wolves - Pb: A Portrait of the Animal World. (p. 1945)
Rue, Nancy. So Not Okay (p. 1602)
—Sorry I'm Not Sorry: An Honest Look at Bullying from the Bully (p. 1614)
—You Can't Sit with Us - Mean Girl Makeover (p. 1975)
Rue, Nancy N. Body Talk (p. 207)
—Boyfriends, Burritos & an Ocean of Trouble (p. 220)
—Everybody Tells Me to Be Myself but I Don't Know Who I Am. (p. 543)
—Everything You Need to Know about Peer Mediation. (p. 545)
—False Friends & True Strangers (p. 567)
—Fun-Finder Book: It's a God Thing! (p. 647)
—Lily's in London?! (p. 1018)
—Lily's in London?! It's a God Thing! (p. 1018)
—Lily's Passport to Paris (p. 1018)
—Lucy Doesn't Wear Pink (p. 1063)
—Lucy Finds Her Way (p. 1063)
—Lucy Out of Bounds (p. 1063)
—Lucy's Perfect Summer (p. 1063)
—Motorcycles, Sushi & One Strange Book (p. 1180)
—Skin You're In: Discovering True Beauty (p. 1585)
—Sophie & the New Girl (p. 1613)
—Sophie Gets Real (p. 1613)
—Sophie Loves Jimmy (p. 1613)
—Sophie Steps Up (p. 1613)
—Sophie under Pressure (p. 1613)
—Sophie's Drama (p. 1613)
—Sophie's First Dance Chen, Grace, illus. (p. 1613)
—Sophie's Friendship Fiasco. (p. 1613)
—Sophie's Secret (p. 1613)
—Sophie's Stormy Summer Chen, Grace, illus. (p. 1613)
—Sophie's World (p. 1613)
—Totally Unfair (p. 1771)
—Tournaments, Cocoa & One Wrong Move (p. 1773)
Rue, Nancy N., jt. auth. see Carlson, Melody.
Rue, Nancy N., et al. Beauty of Believing: 365 Devotions That Will Change Your Life (p. 154)
Ruebartsch, John, photos by see Cole, Kenneth.
Ruebartsch, John, photos by. All about Wisconsin: Todo Acerca de Wisconsin. (p. 43)
Rueda, Claudia. Huff & Puff: Can You Blow down the Houses of the Three Little Pigs? (p. 824)
—I Know an Old Lady Who Swallowed a Fly. (p. 840)
—No Amado, Elisa, tr. from SPA. (p. 1257)
—Suerte de Ozu. (p. 1672)
Rueda, Claudia, illus. see Flor Ada, Alma.
Rueda, Claudia, illus. see Underwood, Deborah.
Rueda, Claudia, illus. see Wang, Margaret.
Rueda, Claudia, jt. auth. see Underwood, Deborah.
Rueda, Marty. Emma Stone. (p. 520)
Ruell, L J, illus. see Patrick, B. & Schotz, Leo D.
Ruellan, Susan. Lost Treasure of Finistere. (p. 1057)
Ruelle, Karen Gray. April Fool! (p. 93)
—Bark Park Ruelle, Karen Gray, illus. (p. 139)
—Crunchy, Munchy Christmas Tree. (p. 386)
—Crunchy, Munchy Christmas Tree. Ruelle, Karen Gray, illus. (p. 386)
—Dear Tooth Fairy: A Harry & Emily Adventure. Ruelle, Karen Gray, illus. (p. 419)
—Dear Tooth Fairy. Ruelle, Karen Gray, illus. (p. 419)
—Easter Egg Disaster: A Harry & Emily Adventure. (p. 499)
—Easter Egg Disaster: A Harry & Emily Adventure. Ruelle, Karen Gray, illus. (p. 499)
—Easy As Apple Pie: A Harry & Emily Adventure. (p. 500)
—Grand Mosque of Paris: A Story of How Muslims Rescued Jews During the Holocaust. DeSaix, Deborah Durland, illus. (p. 707)
—Grand Mosque of Paris: A Story of How Muslims Rescued Jews During the Holocaust. Desaix, Deborah Durland, illus. (p. 707)
—Great Groundhogs! (p. 716)
—Great Groundhogs! A Harry & Emily Adventure. Ruelle, Karen Gray, illus. (p. 716)
—Hidden on the Mountain: Stories of Children Sheltered from the Nazis in le Chambon. DeSaix, Deborah Durland, illus. (p. 776)
—Just in Time for New Year's! (p. 938)
—Just in Time for New Year's! A Harry & Emily Adventure. Ruelle, Karen Gray, illus. (p. 938)
—Monster in Harry's Backyard. Ruelle, Karen Gray, illus. (p. 1167)
—Mother's Day Mess. (p. 1178)
—Spookier Than a Ghost. (p. 1631)
—Thanksgiving Beast Feast: A Holiday House Reader. Level 2 Ruelle, Karen Gray, illus. (p. 1726)
—Thanksgiving Beast Feast. (p. 1726)
Ruelle, Karen Gray, jt. auth. see DeSaix, Deborah Durland.
Ruesga, Rita Rosa & Scholastic, Inc. Staff. Cantaba la Rana. Sebastián, Soledad, illus. (p. 262)
Ruf, Beatrix, ed. see Warren, Rebecca.
Rufener, Meadow Rue. Everything Round. (p. 545)
Ruff, Carolyn. Keystones of the Stone Arch Bridge. Washam, Christie, illus. (p. 951)
Ruff, Gloria B., jt. auth. see Camarena, Cathy.
Ruff, Jim, illus. see Ruff, Zeata P.
Ruff, Karen S. Cooney. Sensory Pen: Unique Writing Prompts for Journalism Students & Other Writers. (p. 1551)
Ruff, Kimberly & Sheets, Leslie. Brave Just Like Me. (p. 223)
Ruff, Kimberly & Venturi-Pickett, Stacy. Brave Just Like Me. Sheets, Leslie, illus. (p. 223)
Ruff, Zeata P. Gumdrop Tree. Ruff, Zeata P. & Ruff, Jim, illus. (p. 731)
Ruffell, Ann & Orme, David. Treachery by Night. (p. 1781)
Ruffenach, France, photos by see Klivans, Elinor.
Ruffenach, France, photos by see Maggipinto, Donata.
Ruffenach, France, photos by see Prueitt, Elisabeth M. & Robertson, Chad.
Ruffenach, France, photos by see Willan, Anne.
Ruffenach, Jessie, ed. see Blue, Martha.
Ruffenach, Jessie, ed. see John, Roberta.
Ruffenach, Jessie, ed. see Parsons Yazzie, Evangeline.
Ruffenach, Jessie, ed. see Powell, Patricia Hruby.
Ruffenach, Jessie, ed. see Thomas, Marjorie.
Ruffenach, Jessie E., ed. see Flood, Nancy Bo.
Ruffenach, Jessie E., et al. Learn along with Ashkii: First Grade Level 1. Whitethorne, Bahe, Jr., illus. (p. 982)
—Learn along with Ashkii: Third Grade Level 1. Whitethorne, Bahe, Jr., illus. (p. 982)
—Learn along with Ashkii: Second Grade Level 1. Whitethorne, Bahe, Jr., illus. (p. 982)
Ruffenach, Jessie, ed. Baby Learns about Animals. Thomas, Peter, tr. from NAV. (p. 127)
—Baby Learns about Colors. Thomas, Peter, tr. from NAV. (p. 127)
—Baby Learns about Seasons. Thomas, Peter, tr. from ENG. (p. 127)
—Baby Learns about Senses. Thomas, Peter, tr. from ENG. (p. 127)
—Baby Learns about Time. Thomas, Peter, tr. from ENG. (p. 127)
—Baby Learns about Weather. Thomas, Peter, tr. from ENG. (p. 127)
—Baby Learns to Count. Thomas, Peter, tr. (p. 127)
—Baby's First Laugh. Thomas, Peter, tr. from ENG. (p. 129)
Ruffenach, Jessie Eve, ed. see Yazzie, Seraphine G.
Ruffin, Aurzella, illus. see Stevenson-Spurgon, Barbara J.
Ruffin, David C. Duties & Responsibilities of the Secretary of Defense. (p. 490)
—Duties & Responsibilities of the Secretary of Education. (p. 490)
—Duties & Responsibilities of the Secretary of Homeland Security. (p. 490)
—Duties & Responsibilities of the Secretary of Health & Human Services. (p. 490)
—Duties & Responsibilities of the Secretary of State. (p. 490)
—Duties & Responsibilities of the Secretary of the Treasury. (p. 490)
Ruffin, Fran. Cats. (p. 280)
—Whales / Ballenas. (p. 1878)
Ruffin, Frances & Phillips, Ellen Blue. Abraham Lincoln: From Pioneer to President. (p. 6)
Ruffin, Frances E. Alamo. (p. 33)
—Annie Oakley. (p. 87)
—Clara Barton. (p. 326)
—Creating a City Park: Dividing Three-Digit Numbers by One-Digit Numbers Without Remainders. (p. 378)
—Creating a City Park: Dividing Three-digit Numbers by One-digit Numbers Without Remainders. (p. 378)
—Ellis Island. (p. 515)
—Gateway Arch. (p. 658)
—Her Story, Her Words: The Narrative of Sojourner Truth. (p. 769)
—How to Draw the Life & Times of Theodore Roosevelt. (p. 819)
—Jamestown. (p. 907)
—Kitchen Smarts: Food Safety & Kitchen Equipment. (p. 962)
—Let's Have a Bake Sale: Calculating Profit & Unit Cost. (p. 998)
—Lincoln Memorial. (p. 1018)
—Martin Luther King & the March on Washington. (p. 1097)
—Medical Detective Dogs. (p. 1118)
—Meet Lois Lowry. (p. 1121)
—Meet Patricia MacLachlan. (p. 1122)
—Meet Paula Danziger. (p. 1122)
—Meet Sid Fleischman. (p. 1122)
—Military Dogs. (p. 1142)
—Molly Pitcher. (p. 1161)
—Police Dogs. (p. 1380)
—Polycystic Ovary Syndrome. (p. 1381)
—Sally Hemings. (p. 1505)
—Sojourner Truth: Early Abolitionist. (p. 1606)
—St. Augustine. (p. 1637)
—Unsinkable Molly Brown. (p. 1822)
—Water Rescue Dogs. (p. 1863)
—Whales: Ballenas. Beullens, Nathalie, tr. (p. 1878)
Ruffin, Frances E., jt. auth. see Brown, Jonatha A.
Ruffing, Eric, jt. auth. see Parmley, Dave.
Ruffing, Faith Elizabeth. Lewis & Clark Bicentenial Corps of Discovery Journal & Record Book. (p. 1004)
Ruffins, Reynold, illus. see Cartier, Wesley.
Ruffins, Reynold, illus. see Gleeson, Brian.
Ruffle, Mark, illus. see Naish, Darren.
Ruffle, Mark, illus. see Rockett, Paul.
Ruffle, Mark, illus. see Taylor, Barbara.
Ruffle, Mark, illus. see Walker, Richard.
Ruffler, Walter. Paper Automata Mechanisms: A Handbook. (p. 1322)
Ruffner, Melissa. Whatever Happened to Baby Harry: The True Story of the First Child Born to an Officer's Family at Camp Apache, Arizona Territory. Summerhayes, Roger, photos by. (p. 1896)
Ruffner, Peter & Hillstrom, Kevin. Worker's Unite! The American Labor Movement. (p. 1952)
Ruffolo, Rob, illus. see Roe, David & Reader's Digest Editors.
Rugg, Frederick E. 20 More Tips on the Colleges - 12th Edition. (p. 1995)
—30 Questions & Answers on the Colleges 12th Edition. (p. 1996)
—40 Tips on the Colleges - 12th EDition. (p. 1997)
—Financial Aid in Less Than 3,000 Words. (p. 587)
—Financial Aid in Less Than 3000 Words. (p. 587)
—Forty Tips on the Colleges. (p. 623)
—Rugg's Recommendations on the Colleges. (p. 1494)
—Thirty Questions & Answers on the Colleges. (p. 1735)
—Twenty More Tips on the Colleges. (p. 1801)
Rugg, Jim. Dr. Horrible. Whedon, Zack, illus. (p. 475)
Rugg, Jim, illus. see Seagle, Steven T.
Rugg, Michael. Bigfoot Discovery Book. (p. 185)
Rugg, Michael & Kieffer, Steve. Dinosaur Coloring Book. (p. 441)
Ruggieri, J. G. Weather Changes, Mountains Move, & Islands Disappear. (p. 1870)
Ruggiero, Adriane. Judaism. Szumski, Bonnie & Cothran, Helen, eds. (p. 930)
—Reconstruction. (p. 1452)
Ruggiero, Adriane, ed. Confucianism. (p. 357)
Ruggiero, David, jt. auth. see Tarantino, Scott.
Ruggiero, Lorenzo, illus. see Carey, Mike.
Ruggiero, M. Wild Flowers of North America. (p. 1929)
Ruggiero, Wilma. Orange Barnge. (p. 1301)
Ruhl, Greg, illus. see Tanaka, Shelley.
Rui, Paolo, illus. see Pettenati, Jeanne.
Rui, Zhou, et al. Children's Stories: By Contemporary Shanghai Writers. (p. 304)
Rui-An, Wen. Four Constables. (p. 624)
Ruijters, Marcel & Morse, Scott. Barefoot Serpent. (p. 139)
Ruin Mist Publications Staff, jt. auth. see Stanek, Robert, pseud.
Ruis, Maria, illus. see Sánchez, Isidro.
Ruiz Abello, Margarita, illus. see Combel Editorial Staff.
Ruiz Abello, Margarita, jt. illus. see Ruiz, Margarita.
Ruiz, Alfonso, illus. see Gonzalez, Jorge & Collodi, Carlo.
Ruiz, Alfonso, illus. see Gunderson, Jessica & Gonzalez, Jorge.
Ruiz, Alfonso, illus. see Hoena, Blake A. & Gonzalez, Jorge.
Ruiz, Alfonso, illus. see Protobunker Studio Staff & Wells, H. G.
Ruiz, Alfonso, illus. see Stoker, Bram.
Ruiz, Amanda Mae. So Big: A Cricket's Journey to His Purpose. (p. 1601)
Ruiz, Ana, jt. illus. see Gonzalez, Ralfka.
Ruiz, Aristides, illus. see Golden Books Staff.
Ruiz, Aristides, illus. see Golden Books.
Ruiz, Aristides, illus. see Rabe, Tish & Seuss, Dr.
Ruiz, Aristides, illus. see Rabe, Tish.
Ruiz, Aristides, illus. see Seuss, Dr.
Ruiz, Aristides, illus. see Thomas, Jim.
Ruiz, Aristides, illus. see Worth, Bonnie.
Ruiz, Carlos, tr. see Blackaby, Susan & Haugen, Ryan.
Ruiz, Carlos, tr. see Blackaby, Susan & Jones, Christianne C.
Ruiz, Carlos, tr. see Blackaby, Susan.
Ruiz, Carlos, tr. see Jones, Christianne C.
Ruiz, Carlos, tr. see Meachen Rau, Dana.
Ruiz, Celia & Stevenson, Robert Louis. Isla del Tesoro. Solé, Francisco, tr. (p. 891)
Ruiz, Clarisa & Reyes, Yolanda. Noche en el Tejado. Ruiz, Pedro, illus. (p. 1262)
Ruiz, Derek, ed. see Fitzpatrick, Becca.
Ruiz, Emilio. Waluk. (p. 1856)
—Waluk. Oliverio, Daniel, tr. (p. 1856)
Ruiz, Fernando, illus. see McCarthy, Rebecca.
Ruiz, Frances. Fairy Bond: Book Two of the Key to Embralia. (p. 563)
Ruiz, Jackson. It's Cool in the Furnace: The first graphic novel by Jackson Ruiz. (p. 896)
Ruiz, Jaime Alejandro Rodriguez. Johannes Kepler -Del otro lado está Dios. (p. 921)
Ruiz, Jeanette, tr. see Turton, Karalynn Teresa.
Ruiz, John. Squirrel, the Eagle & the Red Hawk. (p. 1637)
Ruiz, Jorge, illus. see Velasquez, Leonor Bravo.
Ruiz, Jose Alfonso Ocampo, illus. see Fuentes, Benny & Stoker, Bram.
Ruiz, Jose Alfonso Ocampo, illus. see Gunderson, J.
Ruiz, Joseph J. Angel on Daniel's Shoulder. (p. 74)
—Manuel & the Magic Ring. (p. 1089)
Ruiz, Margarita. Boda del Ratón y la Ratita. (p. 206)
—Indio Errante. (p. 872)
—Pinocho. (p. 1361)
Ruiz, Margarita, illus. see catalán, Cuento popular.
Ruiz, Margarita, illus. see Combel Editorial Staff & Menotti, Gian Carlo.
Ruiz, Margarita, illus. see Combel Editorial Staff & árabe, Cuento popular.
Ruiz, Margarita, illus. see Combel Editorial Staff, et al.
Ruiz, Margarita, illus. see Combel Editorial Staff.
Ruiz, Margarita, illus. see griego, Mito.
Ruiz, Margarita & Ruiz Abello, Margarita. Pez de Oro. (p. 1349)
—Sastrecillo Valiente. (p. 1515)

Ruiz, Maria Emilia Beyer. Enfermedad del Beso. Sada, Margarita, illus. (p. 529)
—Sonidos, Olores y Colores - la Comunicacion en el Mundo Animal. Pelaez, Ricardo, illus. (p. 1612)
Ruiz Navarro, Jose, illus. see González, Lola, et al.
Ruiz, Olivia, et al. Amiga Nueva De Roberto: Guias De Observacion, Level 12. (p. 65)
—Cajas De Zapatos: Guias De Observacion, Level 10. (p. 252)
—Debes Ser Atento Con Jesefina: Resumen Del Cuento, Level 34. (p. 421)
—Debes Ser Atento Con Josefina: Guias De Observacion, Level 34. (p. 421)
—Dia Mas Maravilloso: Guias De Observacion, Level 24. (p. 433)
—Donde Esta Mi Gorra? Guias De Observacion, Level 4. (p. 466)
—Duque: Guias De Observacion, Level 8. (p. 490)
—Evaluacion Del Desarrollo De la Lectura Package. (p. 540)
—Gigante En El Bosque: Guias De Observacion, Level 18. (p. 676)
—Mas Astuto Que El Viejo Camilo Canoso: Guias De Observacion, Level 40. (p. 1101)
—Mas Astuto Que El Viejo Camilo Canoso: Registro De la Lectura Oral, Level 40. (p. 1101)
—Olla De Oro: Guias De Observacion, Level 16. (p. 1287)
—Peligro En las Profundidades: Guias De Observacion, Level 44. (p. 1336)
—Por Que Paramos? Guias De Observacion, Level 6. (p. 1385)
—Que Te Gusta? Guias De Observacion, Level 3. (p. 1424)
—Reni la Rana: Guias De Observacion, Level 20. (p. 1460)
—Sabes Cantar? Mira Lo Que Se Va: Registro De la Lectura Oral. (p. 1500)
—Sabes Cantar? Mira Lo Que Se Va Yo Veo: Guias De Observacion (p. 1500)
—Vagon: Guias De Observacion, Level 14. (p. 1830)
—Yo No Te Veo Hermosa: Guias De Observacion, Level 28. (p. 1971)
—Yo Veo Que Te Gusta? Registro De la Lectura Oral, Level 3. (p. 1971)
Ruiz, Pedro, illus. see Ruiz, Clarisa & Reyes, Yolanda.
Ruiz, Ruth Ann. Coping with the Death of a Brother or Sister. (p. 365)
Ruiz, Ruth Anne. Coping with the Death of a Brother or Sister. (p. 365)
Ruiz Zafón, Carlos. Marina. (p. 1094)
—Prince of Mist. (p. 1401)
Ruiz-Flores, Lupe. Alicia's Fruity Drinks / Las Aguas Frescas de Alicia. Baeza Ventura, Gabriela, tr. from ENG. (p. 40)
—Battle of the Snow Cones/La Guerra de las Raspas. (p. 147)
—Lupita's First Dance / el Primer Baile de Lupita. Baeza Ventura, Gabriela, tr. (p. 1066)
—Woodcutter's Gift/el Regalo del Lenador. Ventura, Gabriela Baeza, tr. from ENG. (p. 1949)
Ruiz-Flores, Lupe & Rosales-Yeomans, Natalia. Let's Salsa. Rosales-Yeomans, Natalia, tr. (p. 1000)
Rujin, Ma, illus. see Ma, Zheng & Li, Zheng.
Ruka, Greg. Eyes of the Gorgon. Johnson, Drew & Raiz, James, illus. (p. 558)
Rukl, Antonin, illus. see Storm, Dunlop.
Ruland, Patty J. From Painted Scrolls to Anime: Literature & the Arts of Japan. (p. 643)
Rule, Adi. Strange Sweet Song. (p. 1665)
Rule, Rebecca. Iciest, Diciest, Scariest Sled Ride Ever! Thermes, Jennifer, illus. (p. 851)
Ruley, Garrett. Hollin. (p. 789)
Ruley, Rose. Quest for a Moose: An Alaska Tale of Searching for an Animal that Doesn't Exist — until it Is Found. (p. 1426)
Rulnick, Mary Jo. Frantic Woman's Guide to Feeding Family & Friends: Shopping Lists, Recipes, & Tips for Every Dinner of the Year. (p. 631)
Rulnick, Mary Jo & Schneider, Judith Burnett. Frantic Woman's Guide to Life: A Year's Worth of Hints, Tips, & Tricks. (p. 631)
Rumaner, Marc. Let's Play Soccer! Incl. 2 1/2" Soccer Ball. (p. 1000)
—Play Ball! Incl. 2 1/2" Baseball. (p. 1371)
—Tundra Finds Her Howler. (p. 1796)
Rumbaugh, Melinda. Great Easter Egg Hunt. Reed, Lisa, illus. (p. 715)
—Somebunny Loves You! Biscoe, Cee, illus. (p. 1609)
Rumble, Chris. Moby Stink. (p. 1157)
—My Dad Is Coming to Career Day but Hopefully the Earth Will Be Destroyed. (p. 1201)
—Stink Trek: The Adventures of Uncle Stinky #2. Rumble, Chris, illus. (p. 1651)
Rumble, Coral. My Teacher's As Wild As a Bison: Poems Based on the Great Outdoors. (p. 1220)
Rumble, P. Barry. Full Moon. (p. 646)
Rumbley, Rose-Mary. Dear Santa: Thanks for the Piano. (p. 419)
Rumford, James. Beo-Bunny. (p. 166)
—Beowulf: A Hero's Tale Retold. (p. 166)
—From the Good Mountain: How Gutenberg Changed the World. Rumford, James, illus. (p. 644)
—Rain School. (p. 1435)
—Seeker of Knowledge: The Man Who Deciphered Egyptian Hieroglyphs. (p. 1548)
—Sequoyah: The Cherokee Man Who Gave His People Writing. Huckaby, Anna Sixkiller, tr. (p. 1552)
—Silent Music: A Story of Baghdad. Rumford, James, illus. (p. 1575)
—Traveling Man: The Journey of Ibn Battuta, 1325-1354. (p. 1780)
Rumi. Two Parrots. Rashin, illus. (p. 1804)
Rumi, M. Jan, jt. auth. see Feldman, Reynold.
Ruminski, Jeff, illus. see Mullican, Judy.
Rummel, Jack & Wagner, Heather Lehr. Malcolm X: Civil Rights Leader. (p. 1083)
Rummel, Tim, jt. auth. see Fearing, Mark.
Rummel, Verna. I Can Too (p. 836)
—My School (p. 1218)
—Time for Bed. (p. 1751)
Rumpf, Wolfgang. Taekwondo Kids: From White Belt to Yellow/Green Belt. Dornemann, Volker, illus. (p. 1695)
Rumpf, Wolfgang & Dornemann, Volker. Taekwondo Kids Volume 2: From Green Belt to Blue Belt. (p. 1695)
Rumph-Geddis, Ashlye V. Tori Finds Shapes All Around. (p. 1769)
Rumsch, BreAnn. Abraham Lincoln. (p. 6)
—Bill Clinton. (p. 186)
—Franklin Pierce. (p. 630)
—George W. Bush. (p. 664)
—Grover Cleveland. (p. 725)
—Herbert Hoover. (p. 769)
—James K. Polk. (p. 907)
—Martin Van Buren. (p. 1098)
—Money Matters. (p. 1164)
—Rutherford B. Hayes. (p. 1499)
—Saving & Investing. (p. 1517)
—Ulysses S. Grant. (p. 1810)
—William Taft. (p. 1933)
—Woodrow Wilson. (p. 1949)
Rumsey, Frances. My Very Own Organic Cookbook: Bananas. (p. 1221)
—My Very Own Organic Cookbook: Potatoes. (p. 1221)
—My Very Own Organic Cookbook: The Teen, Book 1. (p. 1221)
Rumstuckle, Cornelius. Book of Wizardry: The Apprentice's Guide to the Secrets of the Wizards' Guild. (p. 212)
Runberg, Sylivain. Orbital: Ruptures. Vol. 2 Saincatin, Jerome, tr. from FRE. (p. 1302)
Runberg, Sylvain. Nomads Pellé, Serge, illus. (p. 1263)
—Orbital: Scars. Vol. 1 Saincatin, Jerome, tr. from FRE. (p. 1302)
—Orbital Vol. 5: Justice. Pelle, Serge, illus. (p. 1302)
Runcorn, Scott, illus. see Dumesnil, Phil & Sanchez, Asa.
Rund, Christopher. Indiana Rail Road Company: America's New Regional Railroad. (p. 871)
Rundell, Katherine. Cartwheeling in Thunderstorms. Castrillón, Melissa, illus. (p. 273)
—Rooftoppers. Fan, Terry, illus. (p. 1487)
—Wolf Wilder. (p. 1944)
Rundgren, Helen. World's Best Noses, Ears, & Eyes. Arrhenius, Ingela P., illus. (p. 1960)
Rundquist, Thomas J., ed. Drug Addict Trials Before the US Supreme Court: An Educational Prevention Game. (p. 486)
Rundstrom, T. S. Baribold Jones & Big Big Booger Grabber. (p. 139)
Rundstrom, Teressa. Adventures of Tommy Toad. Marshall, Setsu, illus. (p. 24)
—Cherry the Sheep Finds Her Sheep Sound. Miller, Bryan & Marshall, H. Keene, illus. (p. 298)
—I Love to Leap! Miller, Bryan, illus. (p. 843)
Runels, Margie "B". Talon. (p. 1704)
Runholt, Susan. Adventure at Simba Hill. (p. 14)
—Mystery of the Third Lucretia. (p. 1226)
—Rescuing Seneca Crane. (p. 1462)
Runion, Laura K. Sleepy Faces in Sleeping Places. (p. 1589)
Runkle, Toni & Webb, Stephen. Glitter Girl. (p. 684)
Runnells, Patricia, illus. see DePrisco, Dorothea.
Runnells, Treesha. Afraid of the Dark? Runnells, Treesha, illus. (p. 26)
—Five Wishing Stars: Disappearing Die Cut. Dillard, Sarah, illus. (p. 601)
—Forest Friends: A Fold-Out Fun Book. Runnells, Treesha, illus. (p. 618)
—Safari Friends: Fold-Out Fun. Runnells, Treesha, illus. (p. 1502)
—Ten Wishing Stars: A Countdown to Bedtime Book. Dillard, Sarah, illus. (p. 1719)
Runnells, Treesha, illus. see DePrisco, Dorothea.
Runnells, Treesha, illus. see O'Brien, Melanie.
Runnentrom, Bengt-Arne, illus. see Zak, Monica.
Runnerstrom, Bengt-Arne, illus. see Zak, Monica.
Running Press Staff. Berry Best Friends. (p. 167)
—Fabulous Doodles: Over 100 Pictures to Complete & Create. Ryan, Nellie, illus. (p. 560)
—Gumby & Pokey (p. 731)
—Harry Potter Time Turner Sticker Kit (p. 751)
—Meerkat Manners. (p. 1120)
—Numbers. (p. 1271)
—Olivia's Adventure Doodles: Fantastic Full-Color Pictures to Create & Complete. (p. 1287)
—One Little Meerkat. (p. 1295)
—Oodles of Doodles: Over 200 Pictures to Complete & Create. Catlow, Nikalas, illus. (p. 1298)
—Opposites. (p. 1300)
—Peanuts Gang Loves to Doodle: Create & Complete Full-Color Pictures with Charlie Brown, Snoopy, & Friends. (p. 1332)
Running Press Staff, ed. see Alexander, Heather.
Running Press Staff, ed. see Bagdasarian, Ross & Karman, Janice.
Running Press Staff, ed. see Barclay, Adrian.
Running Press Staff, ed. see Crook, Lydia.
Running Press Staff, ed. see Deere, John & Berg, Ron.
Running Press Staff, ed. see Deere, John & Hill, Dave.
Running Press Staff, ed. see Deere, John.
Running Press Staff, ed. see John, Deere & Berg, Ron.
Running Press Staff, ed. see John, Deere & Hill, Dave.
Running Press Staff, ed. see Poitier, Anton.
Running Press Staff, ed. see Ross, Graham.
Running Press Staff, ed. see Schulz, Charles M.
Running Press Staff, ed. see Tusman, Jordana.
Running Press Staff, ed. see Wald, Christina.
Running Press Staff, jt. auth. see Neusner, Dena.
Running Press Staff, jt. auth. see Phillips, Sara.
Running Press Staff, jt. auth. see Speregen, Devra Newberger.
Running Press Staff & Berg, Ron. Danny Dozer & the Haunted House. (p. 405)
Running Press Staff & Pinder, Andrew. Goodnight, Johnny Tractor. (p. 701)
Running Press Staff & Speregen, Devra Newberger. Busy Days in Deerfield Valley. Wakelin, Bob, illus. (p. 246)
Running Press Staff & Tussman, Jordana. Orange Doodle Book. (p. 1301)
Running Press Staff, ed. A Chipmunk Christmas: With Sound & Music. (p. 1)
—Allie Gator & the Mixed-Up Scarecrow. (p. 47)
—Apollo Has a Bad Day. (p. 91)
—Batman & Superman Doodles: Fearless Pictures to Complete & Create. (p. 144)
—Care Bears - Together Is Better. (p. 266)
—Cowbella & the Bad Dream. (p. 373)
—CreARTivity: Chunky Chalk. (p. 378)
—CreARTivity: Perfect Pattern Art. (p. 378)
—Frozen: Melting Olaf the Snowman Kit. (p. 645)
—Harry Potter Golden Snitch Sticker Kit (p. 751)
—Harry Potter Hogwarts Castle Snow Globe & Sticker Kit. (p. 751)
—Harry Potter Wizard's Wand & Sticker Book. (p. 751)
—Hello Kitty Fun, Friendly Doodles: Supercute Full-Color Pictures to Create & Complete. (p. 764)
—Johnny Tractor's Rain-and-Shine Farm. (p. 923)
—Justice League Doodles: Amazing Adventures to Complete & Create. (p. 940)
—Madeline & Genevieve. (p. 1070)
—No Fun Without Sleep! A Lift-the-Flap Story. (p. 1258)
—Olivia Loves to Doodle: Extraordinary Full-Color Pictures to Create & Complete. (p. 1286)
—Paint, Print & Roll. (p. 1318)
—Pajanimals: It's Apollo's Special Day. (p. 1319)
—Pajanimals: Let's Bundle up & Go! A Lift-The-Flap Guessing Game. (p. 1319)
—Pajanimals: Squacky & the Gift of Christmas. (p. 1319)
—Pajanimals: Squacky Is Afraid of the Dark. (p. 1319)
—Pajanimals: Sweet Pea Sue Misses Mom & Dad. (p. 1319)
—Peanuts Finger Puppet Theater: Starring Charlie Brown & Snoopy! (p. 1332)
—Scratch & Draw: Christmas. (p. 1532)
—Scratch & Stencil - Outer Space. (p. 1532)
—Scratch & Stencil: Ponies. (p. 1532)
—Sweet Pea Sue Makes a New Friend. (p. 1690)
—Treasury of Christmas Classics: Includes the Night Before Christmas, the Twelve Days of Christmas, & the Nutcracker. (p. 1782)
—Wintery White: Draw Beautiful Sparkly Pictures. (p. 1939)
Running Press Staff, et al. Classic Treasury of Bulfinch's Mythology. (p. 328)
Runstadler, Nancy. Pay It Forward Kids: Small Acts, Big Change (p. 1331)
Runstedler, Nancy. Beautiful Goodbye. (p. 153)
Runton, Andy. Flying Lessons (p. 610)
—Just a Little Blue. (p. 937)
—Owly 04: Time to Be Brave. (p. 1315)
—Owly & Wormy, Bright Lights & Starry Nights. Runton, Andy, illus. (p. 1315)
—Owly & Wormy, Friends All Aflutter! Runton, Andy, illus. (p. 1315)
—Owly Volume 1: the Way Home & the Bittersweet Summer: The Way Home & the Bittersweet Summer. (p. 1315)
—Time to Be Brave. (p. 1753)
—Tiny Tales. (p. 1756)
Runyan, Brandy. Year of You: Journal of My Child. (p. 1969)
Runyen, Elizabeth. Watch Me Draw Disney's Mickey Mouse Clubhouse. (p. 1861)
Runyon, Anne Marshall. Sheltering Cedar. Runyon, Anne Marshall, illus. (p. 1565)
Runyon, Brent. Burn Journals. (p. 243)
Ruocco, L. A. Nothing: Literal Nothing Lite(r)ªL TM Volume 0 (0pages) There Is No End As There Is No Beginning to This Book, Nothing Between U & I on the Keyboard -La Ru(c)&co. Enterprises 2014 * (p. 1268)
Ruocco, Paul, illus. see Amarone, Morgan.
Ruotsala, Charity Alli, jt. auth. see Thorp, Gloria J.
Rupe, Heather, jt. auth. see Wolstenholm, Jessica.
Rupert, Chris, illus. see Bledsoe, Michele.
Rupert, Matthews. Visual Factfinder Bugs. (p. 1846)
—Visual Factfinder Dinosaurs & Prehistoric Life. (p. 1846)
—Visual Factfinder HIST Timelines. (p. 1846)
—Visual Factfinder Rocks & Fossils. (p. 1846)
—What about Dinosaurs. (p. 1878)
Rupert, Rona. Straw Sense. (p. 1666)
Rupnik, Louise & Priddy, Roger. Puppy Love. (p. 1418)
Rupp, Cecelia, ed. How to Be #1 Kid at Table Manners: Activity Book. (p. 814)
Rupp, Dain Chistopher. Greatest Saint Stories A-Z: (Book 1 of 2: A-M) (p. 720)
Rupp, Kristina, illus. see Fleischer, Jayson & Lynch, Michelle.
Rupp, Kristina, illus. see Fleischer, Jayson.
Rupp, Kristina, jt. auth. see Taylor, Trace.
Rupp, Rebecca. After Eli. (p. 28)
—Dragon of Lonely Island. (p. 477)
—Journey to the Blue Moon: In Which Time Is Lost & Then Found Again. (p. 929)
—Octavia Boone's Big Questions about Life, the Universe & Everything. (p. 1277)
—Return of the Dragon. (p. 1464)
—Rocks. (p. 1483)
—Sarah Simpson's Rules for Living. (p. 1514)
—Weather! A Book about Pink Snow, Fighting Kites, Lightning Rods, Rains of Frogs, Typhoons, Tornadoes, & Ice Balls from Space. Nap, Dug & Sweet, Melissa, illus. (p. 1869)
Ruppaport, Aviva, tr. see Fried, Leah.
Ruppel, Maxine. Vostaas: White Buffalo's Story of the Plains Indians. (p. 1850)
Ruppelius, Conrad, jt. auth. see Ruppelius, Jeffrey.
Ruppelius, Jeffrey & Ruppelius, Conrad. Conrad's Hiking Adventure. Ruppelius, Conrad, illus. (p. 358)
Ruppert, Larry, illus. see Hope, Laura Lee.
Rupprecht, Karen & Minor, Pamela. Months of Music & More. (p. 1170)
Ruprecht, Jennifer L. Crayon Kids' Art Adventure. Shaw-Peterson, Kimberly, illus. (p. 377)
Rusackas, Francesca. Daddy All Day Long. Burris, Priscilla, tr. (p. 398)
—I Love You All Day Long. Burris, Priscilla, illus. (p. 843)
Rusan Jeffers, illus. see Rosemary Wells.
Rusch, Brian. Bear Who Barked Like a Dog. (p. 151)
Rusch, Elizabeth. Day with No Crayons. Cameron, Chad, illus. (p. 415)
—Electrical Wizard: How Nikola Tesla Lit up the World. Dominguez, Oliver, illus. (p. 509)
—Eruption! Volcanoes & the Science of Saving Lives. Uhlman, Tom, illus. (p. 534)
—For the Love of Music: The Remarkable Story of Maria Anna Mozart. Fancher, Lou & Johnson, Steve, illus. (p. 616)
—Mighty Mars Rovers: The Incredible Adventures of Spirit & Opportunity. (p. 1140)
—Muddy Max: The Mystery of Marsh Creek. Lawrence, Mike, illus. (p. 1188)
—Next Wave: The Quest to Harness the Power of the Oceans. (p. 1249)
—Will It Blow? Become a Volcano Detective at Mount St. Helens. Lewis, K. E., illus. (p. 1932)
Rusch, Elizabeth & Capstone Press Staff. Girls' Tennis: Conquering the Court (p. 681)
Rusch, Elizabeth & Swan, Susan. Volcano Rising. (p. 1848)
Ruschmann, Paul. Energy Policy. (p. 528)
—FCC/Broadcast Regulations. Marzilli, Alan, ed. (p. 578)
—Legalizing Marijuana. (p. 988)
—Mandatory Military Service. (p. 1087)
—Prescription & Non-Prescription Drugs. (p. 1396)
—Regulating Violence in Entertainment. (p. 1457)
Ruschmann, Paul & Nasiatska, Maryanne. Social Security. (p. 1604)
Ruscoe, Michael. Kick Ball Capitalization. (p. 951)
—Skating to Spelling Success. (p. 1584)
Ruscoe, Michael, jt. auth. see Barchers, Suzanne I.
Ruscoe, Michael & Voege, Debra. Pit Stop Prefixes. (p. 1364)
—Soccer Goal Suffixes. (p. 1603)
Rusczyk, Richard, jt. auth. see Lehoczky, Sandor.
Ruse, Jill, illus. see Long, John.
Ruse, Jill, jt. auth. see Long, John.
Rush, Barbara & Stratton, Jane. Boat in the Attic. (p. 205)
Rush, Christopher. Will. (p. 1932)
Rush, Diana. Where Does Your Bread Come From? (p. 1907)
Rush, Elizabeth. M Is for Myanmar. (p. 1067)
Rush, Jennifer. Altered. (p. 50)
—Erased. (p. 533)
—Reborn. (p. 1451)
Rush, Ken. Seltzer Man. (p. 1550)
Rush, Locke. Finding the Way Home. (p. 588)
Rush, Peter, illus. see Derwent, Lavinia.
Rush, Rickie, jt. auth. see Winans, Vickie.
Rush, Ryan. Home on Time: Life Management by the Book. (p. 792)
Rushall, Chris. Do Cows Lay Eggs? (p. 456)
Rushby, Allison. Blondetourage. (p. 200)
—Diamonds Are a Teen's Best Friend. (p. 434)
—Heiresses. (p. 762)
—How to Date a Millionaire. (p. 816)
—Seven Month Itch. (p. 1554)
—Shooting Stars. (p. 1568)
Rushby, Pamela. Ben Franklin: Printer, Author, Inventor, Politician. (p. 163)
—Circles of Stone. (p. 321)
—Discovering SuperCroc. (p. 449)
—Haunted Houses: Footsteps, Shadows in the Garden, the Midnight Children. (p. 753)
—Mysteries of the Fossil Dig: How Paleontologists Learn about Dinosaurs. (p. 1222)
—Rosie & the Audition. Konye, Paul, illus. (p. 1490)
—Rosie Goes Home. Konye, Paul, illus. (p. 1490)
Rushdie, Salman. Luka & the Fire of Life. (p. 1064)
Rushford, Betty. Best Buddies: And the Fruit of the Spirit. (p. 168)
Rushford, Patricia H. Danger at Lakeside Farm. (p. 403)
—Secrets of Ghost Island. (p. 1545)
—Trouble with Max. (p. 1790)
Rushforth, Cathy. Citizenship Studies for AQA GCSE Short Course. (p. 323)
Rushforth, Keith & Hollis, Charles. National Geographic Field Guide to Trees of North America. (p. 1231)
Rushing, John Alan. A. J. Puppy Learns to Swim. Fay, David, illus. (p. 1)
Rushton, Jenna. Simple Flower. (p. 1577)
Rushton, Rhian Wyn, jt. auth. see Greenslade, David.
Rushton, Rosie. Friends, Enemies & Other Tiny Problems. (p. 638)
—How Could You Do This to Me, Mum? (p. 806)
—I Think I'll Just Curl up & Die. (p. 846)
—Just Don't Make a Scene, Mum! (p. 938)
—Last Seen Wearing Trainers. (p. 978)
—Where Do We Go from Here? (p. 1907)
Rushworth, Gary. Body Systems: Set of 6: Skeletal & Muscular. (p. 207)
—Body Systems Human Cells: Set Of 6. (p. 207)
—Body Systems: Human Cells: Text Pairs. (p. 207)
—Body Systems: Skeletal & Muscular: Text Pairs. (p. 207)
—Life Cycle of Trees: Set Of 6. (p. 1009)
—Life Cycle of Trees: Text Pairs. (p. 1009)
—Life Cycle of Water Plants: Set Of 6. (p. 1009)
—Life Cycle of Water Plants: Text Pairs. (p. 1009)
—Our Solar System Earth: Set Of 6. (p. 1310)
—Our Solar System: Earth: Text Pairs. (p. 1310)
—Our Solar System the Moon: Set Of 6. (p. 1310)
—Our Solar System: the Moon: Text Pairs. (p. 1310)
—Our Solar System the Sun: Set Of 6. (p. 1310)
—Our Solar System: the Sun: Text Pairs. (p. 1310)
—What Makes a Human a Human: Text Pairs. (p. 1892)
—What Makes a Human a Human? Set Of 6. (p. 1892)
—What Makes a Plant a Plant: Text Pairs. (p. 1892)
—What Makes a Plant a Plant? Set Of 6. (p. 1892)
—What Makes an Animal an Animal: Text Pairs. (p. 1892)
—What Makes an Animal an Animal? Set Of 6. (p. 1892)
Rushworth, Victoria. Battles of the American Revolution: Set of 6: Saratoga. (p. 147)
—Battles of the American Revolution: Saratoga: Text Pairs. (p. 147)
Rusinek, Catherine. So Many Maps! Reading Different Kinds of Maps. (p. 1602)

Ruskin, John. Famous Stories Every Child Should Know. (p. 569)
—King of the Golden River. (p. 959)
—King of the Golden River. Ghiuselev, Iassen, illus. (p. 959)
—King of the Golden River or the Black Brothers: A Legend of Stiria. (p. 959)
Rusky, Ann G., illus. see Vachon, Mary Beth.
Rusling, Annette. Farm Sticker Activities. Cunliffe, Ian, illus. (p. 574)
—No Time for Bed! Edgson, Alison, illus. (p. 1260)
Rusnell, Gwendlyn. Poppie & Paydro, the Adventurous Coyote Pups. (p. 1384)
Russ Cardona, illus. see Jewell, Beverly.
Russ, John Paul. Monster Hunters Survival Guide. Brusha, Joe, ed. (p. 1167)
Russ, Tim & Roskilly, Jedda. Bugsters! (p. 237)
Russ, Tony. Bear Hunting in Alaska: How to Hunt Brown & Grizzly Bears. O'Loughlin, Diane, ed. (p. 150)
—Sheep Stalking in Alaska: A Step-by-Step Guide. O'Loughlin, Diane, ed. (p. 1564)
Russ, Tony, ed. see Hackenberg, Richard.
Russ-Ayon, Angela. We Eat Food That's Fresh. June, Cathy, illus. (p. 1867)
Russel, Angela, jt. auth. see von Botefuhr, Andrea.
Russel, Mary. Fickertail & Paint, Barnyard Sleuths (p. 603)
Russel, Takeria. Little Brown Skin. (p. 1025)
Russell, Alessia. Princess Jaycee: The Little Princess with down Syndrome. (p. 1404)
Russell, Allyson. Lizard Who Wanted to Be a Mouse. Bubp, Jennifer, illus. (p. 1042)
Russell, Ann. Little Truff & the Siamese Cat. Morris, Adrienne, ed. (p. 1037)
Russell, B. M. My Friend Bianca. (p. 1209)
Russell, Bill. Bruno the Red Ear Slider. (p. 232)
Russell Brown, Eleanor. C Robat Goes to Circus School. (p. 250)
—Ring of Rats: An Other World Dimension. (p. 1473)
Russell, Bruce L. Channelling Henry. (p. 290)
Russell, Burt R. Cleo & the Coin. (p. 331)
Russell, Carol, illus. see Sanger, Rick.
Russell, Carol & Russell, Tally. I Like Rocks! Russell, Fletch, photos by. (p. 841)
Russell, Ching Yeung. Tofu Quilt. (p. 1761)
Russell, Ching Yeung & Boyds Mills Press Staff. Moon Festival. Zhang, Christopher Zhong-Yuan, illus. (p. 1172)
Russell, Christine, jt. auth. see Russell, Christopher.
Russell, Christine, jt. auth. see Sauder, B. L.
Russell, Christopher. Dogboy. (p. 462)
—Hunted. (p. 828)
Russell, Christopher & Russell, Christine. Quest of the Warrior Sheep. (p. 1426)
—Warrior Sheep down Under. (p. 1859)
—Warrior Sheep Go Jurassic. (p. 1859)
—Warrior Sheep Go West. (p. 1859)
Russell, Craig. Alternatives to Prison: Rehabilitation & Other Programs. (p. 50)
—Antidepressants & Side Effects: Managing the Risks. (p. 89)
—Incarceration Around the World. (p. 868)
—Psychostimulants as Antidepressants: Worth the Risk? (p. 1413)
—Psychostimulants as Antidepressants: Worth the Risk? (p. 1413)
Russell, D. Z. Amazing Adventures of Andy Owl: A Children's Guide to Understanding Music. Stone, John, illus. (p. 52)
Russell, David. Who'z Who at the Zoo. (p. 1922)
Russell, David O. & Auseon, Andrew. Alienated. (p. 41)
Russell, Dorothy, jt. auth. see Christian Focus Publications (CFP) Staff.
Russell, Elaine. Martin Mcmillan & the Lost Inca City. Cornell du Houx, Emily M. D., illus. (p. 1098)
—Shack That Dad Built. Russell, Elaine, illus. (p. 1556)
Russell, Elaine, illus. see Stewart, Lolla.
Russell, Elizabeth. Adaptable Stage Costume for Women: A Hundred-in-One Costumes. (p. 11)
Russell, Fletch, photos by see Russell, Carol & Russell, Tally.
Russell, Freedman. Boston Tea Party. Malone, Peter, illus. (p. 215)
—Immigrant Kids. (p. 861)
Russell, Gayle, illus. see Reilly, Pauline.
Russell, Gloria. Taylor's Talent Show: Use Place Value Understanding & Properties of Operations to Add & Subtract (p. 1708)
Russell, Greta. Olive Boone: Frontier Woman. Hare, John, illus. (p. 1285)
Russell, Harriet, illus. see Weinstein, Bruce D.
Russell, Henry. Germany. (p. 666)
—Russia. (p. 1498)
Russell, Henry & Cooke, Tim. Ancient Aztec: Archaeology Unlocks the Secrets of the Mexico's Past. (p. 68)
Russell, J. L. Sugabear Goes to Bed. (p. 1672)
Russell, Jane, et al. Practical Intervention for Cleft Palate Speech. (p. 1392)
Russell, Jay, et al. Street Life & Hard Time. (p. 1666)
Russell, Jesse & Cohn, Ronald, eds. Five Go off to Camp. (p. 600)
—Ice Age: Continental Drift. (p. 850)
—Nick & Norah's Infinite Playlist. (p. 1251)
Russell, John. Sam & Socrates. (p. 1506)
Russell Johnson, Charlotte. Grace under Fire: The Journey Never Ends. (p. 705)
—Journey to Hell & Back: The Flip Side. (p. 928)
Russell, Joyce. My First Bus Ride to School. (p. 1206)
Russell, Joyce, illus. see Gmeyner, Elizabeth.
Russell, Julia & Wigens, Lynne. Introduction to Psychology for Health Carers. (p. 882)
Russell, K. Buddy's Tail. (p. 235)
Russell, Katherine. Imagine the Butterfly Within Me. (p. 861)
Russell, Kay, illus. see Macy-Mills, Phyllis.
Russell, Ken & Carter, Philip. Bumper Quiz Book for Kids. (p. 241)
Russell, Kerri G., illus. see Foster, Kelli C. & Erickson, Gina Clegg.
Russell, Kirk. Night Game. (p. 1253)
Russell, Kitty, compiled by. Fairy Hearts & Charms: Stories of Yesteryear. (p. 563)
—Fairy Lovely: Stories of Yesteryear. (p. 563)
Russell, Krista. Chasing the Nightbird (p. 294)
—Other Side of Free (p. 1306)
Russell, L. November in Salem: The Bargain of Witches. (p. 1268)
Russell, Lisa. Farm Puppy. (p. 574)
—Sam Is Angry. (p. 1506)
Russell, Lyndsay & Hanson, Tippi. Rainbow Weaver. Russell, Lyndsay & Hanson, Tippi, illus. (p. 1436)
Russell, Marcia. Visit to a Marine Base. (p. 1845)
Russell, Margaret. Exploring the Native Plant World: A Life Science Curriculum, 5th-6th Grade: Adaptations in the Native Plant World. Thompson, Maria, illus. (p. 554)
Russell, Mark James. Young-Hee & the Pullocho. (p. 1978)
Russell, Michael L. Lolabell, the Good Little Helper along with Patsy Poopoo & Friends. (p. 1046)
Russell, Natalie. Brown Rabbit in the City. (p. 232)
—Donkey's Busy Day. Russell, Natalie, illus. (p. 466)
—Hamish the Highland Cow. (p. 739)
—Home Sweet Hamish. (p. 793)
—Lost for Words Russell, Natalie, illus. (p. 1055)
Russell, P. Craig. Fairy Tales of Oscar Wilde: The Selfish Giant & the Star Child Russell, P. Craig, illus. (p. 564)
—Isolation & Illusion: Collected Short Stories of P. Craig Russell. (p. 893)
Russell, P. Craig, illus. see Augustyn, Brian.
Russell, P. Craig, illus. see Gaiman, Neil.
Russell, P. Craig, illus. see Sale, Tim, et al.
Russell, P. Craig, illus. see Wilde, Oscar.
Russell, P. Craig, jt. auth. see Gaiman, Neil.
Russell, P. Craig & Howard, Robert E. Conan & the Jewels of Gwahlur. (p. 355)
Russell, P. Craig & Wilde, Oscar. Devoted Friend, the Nightengale, & the Rose. Russell, P. Craig, illus. (p. 432)
Russell, P. M. Wormhole Adventures: Travel Is Relative. (p. 1961)
Russell, Pamela L. R. Bee Careful! My Big Kid Safety Manual. (p. 157)
Russell, Patricia C. Discovery - in the Beginning: Genesis. (p. 450)
Russell, Patricia Constance. Beginnings II - God's Promises: Old Testament Lessons for Young Readers. Murtha, Dee M., ed. (p. 160)
—Beginnings II - Jesus, My Shepherd: New Testament Lessons for Young Readers. Murtha, Dee M., ed. (p. 160)
Russell, Patricia Yates, jt. auth. see Garcha, Rajinder.
Russell, Paul. Immaculate Blue. (p. 861)
—Sea of Tranquility. (p. 1535)
Russell, Paula. My Sister Olive. Chapman, Gaye, illus. (p. 1218)
—My Sister, Olive. Chapman, Gaye, illus. (p. 1218)
Russell, Peggy. Patsy Goes to a New Home: The Patsy Adventures Volume 1. Scott, Larry, illus. (p. 1329)
Russell, Philip. Sunny Day for Snails. (p. 1677)
Russell, R. R. Unicorn Thief. (p. 1818)
—Wonder Light: Unicorns of the Mist. (p. 1947)
Russell, Rachel. How the Hare Saved the Animals of the Savanna from a Drought. (p. 813)
Russell, Rachel Renée. Dork Diaries Russell, Rachel Renée, illus. (p. 471)
—Dork Diaries Set Russell, Rachel Renée, illus. (p. 471)
—How to Dork Your Diary. Russell, Rachel Renée, illus. (p. 816)
—OMG!:All about Me Diary! Russell, Rachel Renée, illus. (p. 1288)
—Tales from a Not-So-Dorky Drama Queen (p. 1701)
—Tales from a Not-So-Dorky Drama Queen. (p. 1701)
—Tales from a Not-So-Dorky Drama Queen. Russell, Rachel Renée, illus. (p. 1701)
—Tales from a Not-So-Fabulous Life. (p. 1701)
—Tales from a Not-So-Fabulous Life. Russell, Rachel Renée, illus. (p. 1701)
—Tales from a Not-So-Glam TV Star. (p. 1701)
—Tales from a Not-So-Glam TV Star. Russell, Rachel Renée, illus. (p. 1701)
—Tales from a Not-So-Graceful Ice Princess. Russell, Rachel Renée, illus. (p. 1701)
—Tales from a Not-So-Happily Ever After. (p. 1701)
—Tales from a Not-So-Happy Heartbreaker. Russell, Rachel Renée, illus. (p. 1701)
—Tales from a Not-So-Smart Miss Know-It-All. Russell, Rachel Renée, illus. (p. 1701)
Russell, Randy. Dead Rules. (p. 417)
—Ghost Cats of the South. (p. 670)
Russell, Robyn. Eden's Flesh. (p. 504)
Russell, Romina. Zodiac. (p. 1987)
Russell, Shane. Phloomp! (p. 1351)
Russell, Sharman Apt. Frederick Douglass: Abolitionist Editor. (p. 633)
—Teresa of the New World. (p. 1721)
Russell, Shelle. Mind Twisters, Grade 1. (p. 1145)
Russell, Solveig Paulson. From Barter to Gold: The Story of Money. Cary, illus. (p. 642)
Russell, Tally, jt. auth. see Russell, Carol.
Russell, Terry, illus. see Leonard, Mary T.
Russell, Wendy Thomas & Goodman, Sarah. MEdia. (p. 1118)
Russell, Willy & Gunton, Mark. Our Day Out: Improving Standards in English Through Drama at Key Stage 3 & GCSE. (p. 1308)
Russell-Brown, Katheryn. Little Melba & Her Big Trombone. Morrison, Frank, illus. (p. 1031)
Russell-Gilmer, Phyllis A. Where Do Crickets Go When Winter Comes? Jones, Chamira, illus. (p. 1907)
Russell-Peter, Jasmine. Biddle in the Middle. (p. 177)
Russert, Tim & Russert, Timothy J. Big Russ & Me: Father & Son - Lessons of Life. (p. 183)
Russert, Timothy J., jt. auth. see Russert, Tim.
Russett, Bruce, ed. see Docalavich, Heather.
Russett, Bruce, ed. see Nelson, Sheila.
Russett, Bruce, ed. see Smith, Roger.
Russett, Bruce, ed. see Walker, Ida.
Russik, Michael, illus. see Polette, Keith.
Russin, Nicole & Richarde. Big Bad Wolf Strikes It Rich! Fairy Tale Wall Street Memoirs. Richarde, illus. (p. 178)
Russin, Nicole & Richárde. Ingrid Has Two Dads: My Family Is Normal! (p. 874)
Russo, Angela B. Beautiful. (p. 153)
Russo, Anthony. Abby. Sampson, Jody, illus. (p. 2)
Russo, Blythe, illus. see Adhikary, Anita B.
Russo, Bud. Magic Picture. (p. 1073)
Russo, David Anson. Around the World: The Great Treasure Hunt. Russo, David Anson, illus. (p. 100)
—Great Treasure Hunt. Russo, David Anson, illus. (p. 719)
Russo, Domenic J. Oh My Gosh, Josh! (p. 1281)
Russo, Frank M. Sleigh. Cittadino, Kyle & Cittadino, Kristen, illus. (p. 1590)
Russo, Gina & Benchmark Education Co., LLC Staff. Big Job. (p. 182)
Russo, Joseph Anthony. For My Love Endures Forever: Poetry & Prose. (p. 616)
Russo, M. Great Book of Dot to Dot: Omnibus Edition. (p. 714)
Russo, Mallory Kate. Hotel Christmas. (p. 802)
Russo, Marisabina. Always Remember Me: How One Family Survived World War II. Russo, Marisabina, illus. (p. 51)
—Bunnies Are Not in Their Beds. (p. 242)
—Bunnies Are Not in Their Beds. Russo, Marisabina, illus. (p. 242)
—I Will Come Back for You. (p. 848)
—Little Bird Takes a Bath. (p. 1024)
—Peter Is Just a Baby. (p. 1346)
—Sophie Sleeps Over. Russo, Marisabina, illus. (p. 1613)
—Trouble with Baby. Russo, Marisabina, illus. (p. 1790)
—Very Big Bunny. Russo, Marisabina, illus. (p. 1837)
Russo, Mary. Adventures of Wizahickon. (p. 24)
Russo, Michael, jt. auth. see Brehm, Mike.
Russo, Monica. Birdology: 30 Activities & Observations for Exploring the World of Birds. Byron, Kevin, photos by. (p. 191)
—Mythical Animals Dot-to-Dot. (p. 1227)
Russo, Richard. Bridge of Sighs. (p. 227)
Russo, Steve. Fear No Evil? Shining God's Light on the Forces of Darkness. (p. 579)
Russo, Steve, jt. auth. see Phillips, Bob.
Russon, Anne E., photos by see Smith, Dale.
Russon, Penni. Breathe. (p. 226)
Rust, Graham, illus. see Burnett, Frances Hodgson.
Rust, Ned, jt. auth. see Patterson, James.
Rustad, Alan & Isaac, Andrew. Cooks & Kids: 11 Top Chefs & Children Cook up a Storm in the Kitchen with Their Favourite Recipes. (p. 362)
Rustad, Mark & Utter, Mark. BrainerdBound: Landmarks to the Lakes. Johnson, Curtis, photos by. (p. 222)
Rustad, Martha. Can We Ring the Liberty Bell? Poling, Kyle, illus. (p. 258)
—Can You Sing the Star-Spangled Banner? Poling, Kyle, illus. (p. 259)
—Is a Bald Eagle Really Bald? Conger, Holli, illus. (p. 888)
—What Is Inside the Lincoln Memorial? Poling, Kyle, illus. (p. 1889)
—Why Are There Stripes on the American Flag? Poling, Kyle, illus. (p. 1922)
—Why Is the Statue of Liberty Green? Conger, Holli, illus. (p. 1925)
Rustad, Martha & Adamson, Heather. School in Many Cultures (p. 1523)
Rustad, Martha E. Dolphins [Scholastic]. (p. 465)
—Foxes & Their Dens [Scholastic]. (p. 626)
—Rays [Scholastic]. (p. 1441)
—Sea Turtles [Scholastic]. (p. 1536)
Rustad, Martha E., jt. auth. see Harris, Calvin.
Rustad, Martha E., jt. auth. see Rustad, Martha E. H.
Rustad, Martha E. H. African Animals (p. 27)
—Airplanes (p. 32)
—Algunos Niños Tienen Autismo. (p. 38)
—All about Animals in Winter. (p. 42)
—All about Christmas. (p. 42)
—All about Spring. (p. 43)
—Animal Camouflage in the Desert (p. 77)
—Animal Camouflage in the Desert [Scholastic]. (p. 77)
—Animal Camouflage in the Ocean (p. 77)
—Animal Camouflage in the Snow (p. 77)
—Animal Camouflage in the Snow [Scholastic]. (p. 77)
—Animales en Invierno/Animals in Winter (p. 81)
—Animals in Fall: Preparing for Winter. Enright, Amanda, illus. (p. 83)
—Animals in Spring. (p. 83)
—Animals in Winter (p. 83)
—Animals Working Together (p. 84)
—Ants & Aphids Work Together (p. 90)
—Baby Duck Story (p. 126)
—Baby Penguin Story (p. 127)
—Baby Polar Bear Story (p. 127)
—Baby Sea Otter Story (p. 128)
—Baby Seal Story (p. 128)
—Beavers & Their Lodges. (p. 155)
—Birthdays in Many Cultures (p. 193)
—Black Holes (p. 196)
—Bullfrogs. (p. 240)
—Butterflies. (p. 247)
—Christmas. (p. 312)
—Christmas in Many Cultures (p. 314)
—Clown Fish & Sea Anemones Work Together (p. 335)
—Cockroaches (p. 337)
—Constellations (p. 359)
—Cool Caper. (p. 362)
—Do Chicks Ask for Snacks? Noticing Animal Behaviors. Morandin, Mike, illus. (p. 456)
—Does the Sun Sleep? Noticing Sun, Moon, & Star Patterns. Conger, Holli, illus. (p. 460)
—Dogs (p. 462)
—Driest Places on Earth. (p. 485)
—Earth's Hottest Place & Other Earth Science Records (p. 498)
—Elephants Are Awesome! (p. 511)
—En el Espacio. (p. 522)
—Estrellas. (p. 538)
—Exploring Space. (p. 553)
—Fall Apples: Crisp & Juicy. Enright, Amanda, illus. (p. 566)
—Fall Harvests: Bringing in Food. Enright, Amanda, illus. (p. 566)
—Fall Leaves: Colorful & Crunchy. Enright, Amanda, illus. (p. 566)
—Fall Pumpkins: Orange & Plump. Enright, Amanda, illus. (p. 566)
—Fall Weather: Cooler Temperatures. Enright, Amanda, illus. (p. 566)
—Foxes. (p. 626)
—Foxes & Their Dens. (p. 626)
—Goldfish (p. 695)
—Great Leaders & Thinkers of Ancient Greece (p. 717)
—Helicopters (p. 763)
—Highest Places on Earth. (p. 779)
—Historia de un Pato Bebé) Strictly Spanish Translation Services Staff, tr. from ENG. (p. 126)
—Historia de un Pingüino Bebé) Strictly Spanish Translation Services Staff, tr. (p. 127)
—Historia de una Foca Bebé. Strictly Spanish Translation Services Staff, tr. from ENG. (p. 782)
—How Books Are Made (p. 805)
—Hurricanes (p. 830)
—Insects (p. 875)
—Jellyfish Saunders-Smith, Gail, ed. (p. 912)
—Ladybugs. (p. 971)
—Language Arts (p. 974)
—Las Estrellas. (p. 976)
—Learning about Ads. (p. 984)
—Learning about Fact & Opinion. (p. 984)
—Learning about Fiction Doerrfeld, Cori, illus. (p. 984)
—Learning about Folktales, Fables, & Fairy Tales (p. 984)
—Learning about Media Literacy. (p. 984)
—Learning about Nonfiction (p. 984)
—Learning about Privacy. (p. 984)
—Let's Go to the Library (p. 997)
—Little Scientists (p. 1036)
—Lobsters. (p. 1044)
—Lowest Places on Earth. (p. 1061)
—Luna. (p. 1065)
—Luna/the Moon (p. 1065)
—Manatees Saunders-Smith, Gail, ed. (p. 1086)
—Martin Luther King, Jr: A Life of Fairness. (p. 1098)
—Mealworms (p. 1116)
—Media Literacy for Kids. (p. 1118)
—Mice. (p. 1134)
—Milkweed Bugs (p. 1143)
—Milky Way (p. 1143)
—Moon. (p. 1171)
—Moon [Scholastic]: Revised Edition. (p. 1172)
—Moray Eels & Cleaner Shrimp Work Together (p. 1173)
—Mosquitoes. (p. 1176)
—Mother Teresa: A Life of Kindness. (p. 1178)
—Moths. (p. 1179)
—My Body (p. 1198)
—NASA (p. 1230)
—Navidad. (p. 1237)
—Owls. (p. 1315)
—Painted Lady Butterflies (p. 1318)
—Parrotfish. (p. 1325)
—Parts of a Book (p. 1325)
—People in Spring (p. 1339)
—People in Winter (p. 1339)
—Planetas. (p. 1368)
—Planets. (p. 1368)
—Planets [Scholastic]. (p. 1368)
—Plants in Spring (p. 1370)
—Prairie Dogs & Their Burrows. (p. 1392)
—Raccoons. (p. 1430)
—Reading Is Everywhere (p. 1446)
—Saltwater Stumper: A Zoo Animal Mystery (p. 1506)
—Sea Anemones. (p. 1534)
—Sea Snakes (p. 1535)
—Sea Urchins. (p. 1536)
—Sharks [Scholastic]. (p. 1563)
—Shopping in Many Cultures (p. 1569)
—Silkworms (p. 1575)
—Snails (p. 1596)
—Snakes (p. 1596)
—Snowflakes. (p. 1600)
—Snowflakes (Copos de Nieve) (p. 1600)
—Sol/the Sun (p. 1608)
—Some Kids Have Autism Saunders-Smith, Gail, ed. (p. 1609)
—Space (p. 1618)
—Space Stations (p. 1620)
—Space Vehicles (p. 1620)
—Squirrels & Their Nests. (p. 1637)
—Stars. (p. 1643)
—Stars [Scholastic]. (p. 1643)
—Stingrays. (p. 1651)
—Sun. (p. 1675)
—Sun [Scholastic]. (p. 1676)
—Termites. (p. 1721)
—This Book Might Blow Your Mind: A Collection of Awesome Trivia. (p. 1735)
—Todo Sobre el Invierno. (p. 1761)
—Transportation in Many Cultures (p. 1779)
—Volcanoes (p. 1849)
—Walruses (p. 1855)
—Wasps. (p. 1860)
—Water (p. 1862)
—Weather in Spring (p. 1870)
—Wettest Places on Earth (p. 1877)
—What Is It Made Of? Noticing Types of Materials. Schneider, Christine M., illus. (p. 1889)
—What's in a Cave? (p. 1897)
—What's in a Pond? (p. 1897)
—What's in a Tree? (p. 1897)
—What's in the Dirt? (p. 1898)
—When Will It Rain? Noticing Weather Patterns. Conger, Holli, illus. (p. 1905)
—Why Do Puddles Disappear? Noticing Forms of Water. Schneider, Christine M., illus. (p. 1924)
—Why Is the Statue of Liberty Green? Conger, Holli, illus. (p. 1925)

—Wonderful World of Reading. (p. 1948)
—World's Longest Snake & Other Animal Records. (p. 1960)
—Zebras & Oxpeckers Work Together (p. 1985)
Rustad, Martha E. H., jt. auth. see Capstone Press Staff.
Rustad, Martha E. H., jt. auth. see Frost, Helen.
Rustad, Martha E. H., jt. auth. see Gray-Wilburn, Renée.
Rustad, Martha E. H., jt. auth. see Peterson, Megan Cooley.
Rustad, Martha E. H., jt. auth. see Sweeney, Alyse.
Rustad, Martha E. H., jt. auth. see Wittrock, Jeni.
Rustad, Martha E. H. & Kalz, Jill. Droughts: Be Aware & Prepare (p. 486)
—Tornadoes: Be Aware & Prepare (p. 1770)
Rustad, Martha E. H. & Morey, Allan. Awesome Asian Animals. (p. 121)
Rustad, Martha E. H. & Rustad, Martha E. Animals in Fall Saunders-Smith, Gail, ed. (p. 83)
—Beavers & Their Lodges (p. 155)
—Cockroaches (p. 337)
—Foxes & Their Dens (p. 626)
—Leaves in Fall Saunders-Smith, Gail, ed. (p. 986)
—Manatees. (p. 1086)
—People in Fall Saunders-Smith, Gail, ed. (p. 1339)
—Prairie Dogs & Their Burrows (p. 1392)
—Sea Snakes (p. 1535)
—Squirrels & Their Nests (p. 1637)
Rustad, Martha E. H. & Wittrock, Jeni. Animales Bebé. Strictly Spanish, LLC., tr. (p. 80)
Rustad, Marthe E. H. Bats. (p. 144)
Rustrian, Edvin E. Adventures of Timmy & Jay. (p. 24)
Rusu, Meredith, jt. auth. see Disney Book Group Staff.
Rusu, Meredith L., jt. auth. see Disney Book Group Staff.
Ruta, Angelo, illus. see Ferguson, Sinclair B.
Ruta, Angelo, illus. see Piper, Sophie.
Ruta, Angelo, illus. see Sims, Lesley.
Ruta, Angelo, illus. see Skevington, Andrea.
Rutberg, Jim, jt. auth. see Carmichael, Chris.
Rutch, Joe. Grampa & the Roller Coaster. (p. 706)
Ruth, Angie. My Adventure at a Lighthouse. (p. 1195)
—My Adventure Bug Collecting. (p. 1195)
—My Adventure Camping. (p. 1195)
—My Adventure in Australia. (p. 1195)
—My Adventure in Canada. (p. 1195)
—My Adventure in the Snow. (p. 1195)
Ruth, Ann. Wonderfully Made. (p. 1948)
Ruth, Annie. I Can Read. Ruth, Annie, illus. (p. 836)
Ruth, Greg. Coming Home. Ruth, Greg, illus. (p. 348)
—Lost Boy. (p. 1055)
Ruth, Greg, illus. see Avi.
Ruth, Greg, illus. see Golden, Christopher & Lebbon, Tim.
Ruth, Greg, illus. see Jiang, Ji-Li.
Ruth, Greg, illus. see Obama, Barack.
Ruth, Greg, illus. see Preller, James.
Ruth, Jamee. Grill Pan Cookbook: Great Recipes for Stovetop Grilling. Roth, David, photos by. (p. 724)
Ruth, Krauss & Krauss. Carrot Seed. (p. 271)
Ruth, Nick. Breezes of Inspire. Concannon, Sue, illus. (p. 226)
—Dark Dreamweaver. Concannon, Sue, illus. (p. 407)
Ruth, Peggy Joyce. My Own Psalm 91 Book: German. (p. 1216)
—My Own Psalm 91 Book: Russian. (p. 1216)
—My Own Psalm 91 Book: Ukrainian. (p. 1216)
—My Own Psalm 91 Book: Vietnamese English. (p. 1216)
—My Own Psalm 92 Book: Simplified Chinese-English. (p. 1216)
Ruth, Pekida. Tuffie's Heartrending Decision: Lessons from Meme. (p. 1796)
Ruth, Terry. Tattered Clad: A Novel Written by Terry Ruth. (p. 1707)
Rutherford, Alexa, illus. see Klehm, Eve Begley.
Rutherford, Clarice. Dog Is a Dog: And That's Why He's So Special. (p. 461)
Rutherford, David B. Froglogic, Field Manuals for Kids, Get Squared Away (p. 641)
Rutherford, Fran. Ancient Rome Student Book: Questions for the Thinker. Rutherford, James, illus. (p. 70)
Rutherford, James, illus. see Rutherford, Fran.
Rutherford, Kris. Batting Ninth. (p. 145)
Rutherford, Lucy. Demi Lovato & Selena Gomez: The Complete Unofficial Story of the BFFs. (p. 425)
Rutherford, Margaret. Timothy Helps Out. (p. 1755)
Rutherford, Meg, illus. see Stimson, Joan.
Rutherford, Peter. Baby's Bible Stories: Noah's Ark. (p. 128)
—Giant Fun-to-Find Puzzles Busy Animals: Search for Pictures in Eight Exciting Scenes. (p. 673)
—Let's Look on the Move. Spong, Clive, illus. (p. 999)
Rutherford, Peter, illus. see Crosbie, Duncan.
Ruth-Kilgore, Chanacee. Alphabet Soup. (p. 50)
Rutigliano, Tony, jt. auth. see Smith, Benson.
Rutkoski, Marie. Cabinet of Wonders. (p. 250)
—Celestial Globe. (p. 285)
—Celestial Globe. (p. 286)
—Jewel of the Kalderash. (p. 917)
—Shadow Society. (p. 1558)
—Winner's Crime. (p. 1937)
—Winner's Curse. (p. 1937)
Rutkowski, Chris A. I Saw It Too! Real UFO Sightings. (p. 845)
Rutland, J. I Love You No Matter What: A Prince Chirpio Story (p. 844)
Rutland, Jarrett, illus. see Fair, Sherry W.
Rutland, Jarrett, illus. see Fair, Sherry.
Rutland, Mirium. Miss Pistachios Big Day. (p. 1152)
Rutledge, Eddie. Amani's World: Amani & Friends Go to New York City. (p. 52)
—Amani's World: Amani Goes to Washington D. C. Anderson, Susan, illus. (p. 52)
Rutledge, Jill Zimmerman. Dealing with the Stuff That Makes Life Tough: The 10 Things That Stress Teen Girls Out & How to Cope with Them. (p. 418)
—Picture Perfect: What You Need to Feel Better about Your Body. (p. 1356)
Rutledge, Mary. Toothless Tooth Fairy. (p. 1768)
Rutley, Erika L. Adventures in Pup-A-Dupping. (p. 15)
Rutman, Meredyth & Rutman, Rhett. Couch Potato Classroom. (p. 369)
Rutman, Rhett, jt. auth. see Rutman, Meredyth.
Rutnik, Robert. Barkersville, a Town Built from Love: The Beginning. (p. 139)
Rutsky, R. L. Global Sport Sponsorship. Amis, John M. & Cornwell, T. Bettina, eds. (p. 684)
Rutten, Nicole, illus. see Conan, Sally Anne.
Rutten, Nicole, illus. see Hill, Susanna Leonard.
Rutter, Carol. Burying the Secret: The Road to Ruin Is Paved with Books about the Law of Attraction. (p. 244)
Rutter, Michael. Fly Fishing for the Compleat Idiot: A No-Nonsense Guide to Fly Casting. Ort, Kathleen, ed. (p. 609)
Rutter, Sue. Fluffy Flower Seeds. (p. 608)
Ruttle, Kate, jt. auth. see Budgell, Gill.
Ruttle, Keith. Lord Mount Dragon. (p. 1052)
Ruttledge, Nancy. If I Were My Mommy & Daddy. (p. 853)
Rutzky, Ivy. See-Inside Science Mini Posters. (p. 1546)
Ruud, Curtis D. Zero at the Bone. (p. 1986)
Ruud, Jay. Encyclopedia of Medieval Literature. (p. 525)
Ruurs, Margriet. Amazing Animals: The Remarkable Things That Creatures Do. Hancock, W. Allan, illus. (p. 53)
—Animal Alphabed. Emery, Jennifer, illus. (p. 76)
—Emma at the Fair Spurll, Barbara, illus. (p. 519)
—Emma's Cold Day Spurll, Barbara, illus. (p. 520)
—In My Backyard. Broda, Ron, illus. (p. 864)
—Logan's Lake. (p. 1045)
—Mountain Alphabet. Kiss, Andrew, illus. (p. 1180)
—My Librarian Is a Camel: How Books Are Brought to Children Around the World. (p. 1211)
—My School in the Rain Forest: How Children Attend School Around the World. (p. 1218)
—Pacific Alphabet Bonder, Dianna, illus. (p. 1317)
—Virtual Maniac: Silly & Serious Poems for Kids. Tanselle, Eve, illus. (p. 1844)
—Wake up, Henry Rooster! Cassidy, Sean, illus. (p. 1853)
—When We Go Camping. (p. 1905)
—When We Go Camping. Kiss, Andrew, illus. (p. 1905)
—Wild Babies. Kiss, Andrew, illus. (p. 1928)
Ruurs, Margriet & Gooderham, Andrew. Ms. Bee's magical bookcase. (p. 1188)
Ruyle, Susan. Lily's Art Adventures with God. (p. 1018)
RUZICKA, Carol, illus. see Baker, Bill.
Ruzicka, Delores F., illus. see Zachmeyer, Mary L.
Ruzicka, Oldrich. Maya, Aztecs & Incas. Kleinova, Pavla, illus. (p. 1112)
—Time Traveler Prehistory. Klimes, Jan, illus. (p. 1753)
Ruzicka, Oldrich & Kolcavova, Klara. Princess Tales. Neradova, Maria, illus. (p. 1405)
Ruzicka, Oldrich & Sanza, Silvie. Time Traveler Inventions. Klimes, Jan, illus. (p. 1753)
Ruzima, Keza. Girl Power: The Adventures of a Teenage Circle. (p. 679)
Ruzycki, Dan Dan. Adventures of Pillow Head: The Fallen Star. Hunter, Robbie Chase, illus. (p. 21)
—Adventures of Pillow Head & the Bubble Boys. Hunter, R. Chase, illus. (p. 21)
Ruzycki, Dandan. Adventures of Pillow Head: The Fallen Star. Hunter, R., illus. (p. 21)
Ruzzier, Sergio. Bear & Bee. Ruzzier, Sergio, illus. (p. 150)
—Letter for Leo. (p. 1002)
—Little Giant. (p. 1028)
—Too Busy. Ruzzier, Sergio, illus. (p. 1766)
—Two Mice. (p. 1804)
Ruzzier, Sergio, illus. see Bunting, Eve.
Ruzzier, Sergio, illus. see Cohen, Caron Lee.
RV 1960 Staff. Biblia Tu Andar Diario. (p. 176)
Rwakasisi, Rose. How Goats Lost Their Beautiful Tails. (p. 809)
Ryall, Chris. I Am Optimus Prime. (p. 833)
Ryall, Chris, ed. see Niles, Steve.
Ryall, Chris, ed. see Oprisko, Kris.
Ryall, Chris & Waltz, Tom. Kiss Kids. (p. 961)
Ryall, Jeanette. Clay Art. (p. 330)
—Food Art. (p. 613)
—Junk Art. (p. 936)
—Nature Art. (p. 1236)
—Paper Art. (p. 1322)
—Sand Art. (p. 1510)
Ryall, Michael. China Long Ago. (p. 306)
—Empire of Egypt. (p. 521)
—Empires of Mesopotamia. (p. 521)
—Greece Long Ago. (p. 720)
—Kingdom of Kush. (p. 959)
—Rome Long Ago. (p. 1486)
Ryall, Rich. Classic Fall: The Journal of a 2002 Giants Fan. (p. 328)
Ryals, Katherine. Storytime Stickers: Baby Animals at Play. Berlin, Rose Mary, illus. (p. 1664)
Ryals, Lexi. Little Misses' Fabulous Book of Nail Art. (p. 1032)
—Liv & Maddie: Double Trouble. (p. 1039)
—Liv & Maddie: Sisters Forever. (p. 1039)
—Mirror Mirror. (p. 1149)
Ryals, Lexi, jt. auth. see Disney Book Group Staff.
Ryals, Lexi, jt. auth. see Scholastic, Inc. Staff.
Ryals, Lexi & Hargreaves, Roger. Mr. Men Little Miss All Year Round. (p. 1185)
Ryals, Marie M. Mama, Tell about It: The Helen Stories. (p. 1084)
Ryals, Mary Jane. Moving Waters. (p. 1184)
Ryan. Lost: Big Book: Level Q. Group 1. (p. 1054)
Ryan, illus. see Ryan, Ann Marie.
Ryan, Amanda. Anna's Spring Day. (p. 85)
Ryan, Amber. Diary of a Kindergartner: Day One. (p. 434)
Ryan, Amy Kathleen. Flame. (p. 602)
—Spark: A Sky Chasers Novel. (p. 1622)
—Vibes. (p. 1839)
—Zen & Xander Undone. (p. 1986)
Ryan, Ann. Little Wannabee. Ryan, Ann, illus. (p. 1037)
Ryan, Ann Marie. Best Gift. Denis, Florencia, illus. (p. 170)
—Top Dog. Ryan & Marie, Anne, illus. (p. 1769)
Ryan, Anne Marie. ILR Phonics - the Best Gift. (p. 858)
Ryan, Ashley, illus. see Hall, Melissa.
Ryan, Bernard. Hillary Rodham Clinton: First Lady & Senator. (p. 780)
—Jimmy Carter: U. S. President & Humanitarian. (p. 918)
—Secret Service. (p. 1543)
—Stephen Hawking: Physicist & Educator. (p. 1648)
Ryan, Bernard, jt. auth. see Ryan, Bernard, Jr.
Ryan, Bernard Jr. Warren Buffett: Financier. (p. 1858)
Ryan, Bernard, Jr. & Ryan, Bernard. Tyler's Titanic. (p. 1805)
Ryan Books Ltd. Staff, ed. see Norris, Roger & Ryan, Lawrie.
Ryan, Brittney. Legend of Holly Claus. Long, Laurel, illus. (p. 988)
Ryan, Candace. Animal House. Hale, Nathan, illus. (p. 78)
—Ewe & Aye. Ruble, Stephanie, illus. (p. 547)
—Moo Hoo. Lowery, Mike, illus. (p. 1171)
—Ribbit Rabbit. Lowery, Mike, illus. (p. 1469)
Ryan, Carol. Bridge Through Time (p. 227)
Ryan, Carrie. Dark & Hollow Places. (p. 407)
—Daughter of Deep Silence. (p. 409)
—Dead-Tossed Waves. (p. 417)
—Divide & Conquer. (p. 454)
—Divide & Conquer (Infinity Ring, Book 2) (p. 454)
—Forest of Hands & Teeth. (p. 618)
Ryan, Carrie & Davis, John Parke. Map to Everywhere. (p. 1090)
Ryan, Carrie, ed. Foretold: 14 Tales of Prophecy & Prediction. (p. 619)
Ryan, Cheryl, jt. auth. see Harshman, Marc.
Ryan, Cheryl, et al. My Christmas Treasury. Bassett, Jeni et al, illus. (p. 1200)
Ryan, Christopher. Moon & the Mouse. Tillson, Linda L., illus. (p. 1171)
Ryan, Chuck. Full Circle. (p. 646)
Ryan, Connie. Gary the Gator. (p. 657)
Ryan, Darlene. Cuts Like a Knife (p. 396)
—Five Minutes More (p. 601)
—Pieces of Me (p. 1356)
—Responsible (p. 1463)
—Rules for Life (p. 1495)
—Saving Grace (p. 1517)
Ryan, Darlene & Fernández, Queta. De Nadie Mas (p. 416)
Ryan, Darlene & Manchester, Peter. Kisses, Kisses, Kisses. (p. 962)
Ryan, Emma. Animal Disguises. (p. 77)
—Surprising Swimmers. (p. 1686)
Ryan, Evelyn. Guinea Pigs Are Not Pigs! (p. 731)
Ryan, Frank P. Snowmelt River. (p. 1601)
Ryan, G. William. Little Donkey: A Palm Sunday/Easter Story for All Ages. (p. 1027)
Ryan, George, jt. auth. see Futterweit, Walter.
Ryan, Hugh. Hunt. (p. 828)
—Spy Academy: Mission Twinpossible. (p. 1635)
Ryan, James D., jt. auth. see Jones, Constance A.
Ryan, James Daniel, jt. auth. see Jones, Constance.
Ryan, James G. & Schlup, Leonard, eds. Historical Dictionary of The 1940s. (p. 783)
Ryan, James R. & Schwartz, Joan, eds. Picturing Place: Photography & the Geographical Imagination. (p. 1356)
Ryan, Jeanne. Charisma. (p. 291)
—Nerve. (p. 1241)
Ryan, Jerome F. Road to Baghdad: A Soldier's Story. (p. 1477)
Ryan, Jerome T. On Foreign Soil. (p. 1288)
Ryan, Jerry & Ryan, Roberta. Preparing for Career Success. (p. 1396)
—Preparing for Career Success ExamView(r) Test Generator. (p. 1396)
—Preparing for Career Success Student Activity Book. (p. 1396)
—Preparing for Career Success Teacher's Wraparound Edition. (p. 1396)
Ryan, Jessica. Mystery of Arroyo Seco. Stone, David, illus. (p. 1224)
Ryan, John. Captain Pugwash: A Pirate Story. (p. 264)
—Captain Pugwash Comic Book Collection. (p. 264)
—Pugwash & the Sea Monster. (p. 1415)
—Pugwash the Smuggler. (p. 1415)
Ryan, Jone. Sadie the Little Elephant. (p. 1501)
Ryan, Karlene Kay. Genevieve & the Moon. Johnson, Meredith, illus. (p. 661)
—Genevieve Goes to School. Johnson, Meredith, illus. (p. 661)
Ryan, Kate Moira. Expeditioner's Club: Rio Roosevelt. Vol. 1 (p. 548)
Ryan, Kathleen. Oscar the Dragon. (p. 1305)
Ryan, Kevin. Nightscape. (p. 1255)
Ryan, Lawrie. New Chemistry for You. (p. 1244)
Ryan, Lawrie, jt. auth. see Norris, Roger.
Ryan, Lawrie, et al. Biology. (p. 189)
—Chemistry. (p. 297)
—Physics. (p. 1353)
Ryan, Leslie. I Am Flippish! (p. 833)
Ryan, Linda, ed. see Turkovitiz, Karen.
Ryan, Margaret. Calamity & Chaos. (p. 252)
—Confusion & Catastrophe. (p. 357)
—Madness & Mayhem. (p. 1070)
—Magic Mess! Murfin, Teresa, illus. (p. 1072)
—Magic Mistakes! Murfin, Teresa, illus. (p. 1072)
—Wild Kat Mccrumble. (p. 1929)
Ryan, Margaret & Reynolds, Ruth. Canterbury Tales: Big Sister's Tales. (p. 262)
—Canterbury Tales: Little Brother Tale. Reynolds, Adrian, illus. (p. 262)
Ryan, Maria Felkins & Schmittroth, Linda, eds. Abenaki. (p. 4)
—Chinook. (p. 308)
Ryan, Mary C. Twitcher Mcgee & the Wonderful Tree. (p. 1803)
Ryan, Matthew. Box. (p. 216)
—Move. (p. 1183)
Ryan, Meg. Hat for Markie. (p. 752)
Ryan, Michael. Dead End Kids. (p. 416)
—Living in Colonial America. (p. 1041)
Ryan, Michael, illus. see David, Peter.
Ryan, Michaela. Taiwan. (p. 1696)
Ryan, Mike. Mayda Saves the Day. Ralph, Karin, illus. (p. 1113)
Ryan, Muriel Drake. Innkeeper's Wife. (p. 875)
Ryan, Nancy. Bookworm & His New Book. (p. 213)
—Follow the Star. (p. 612)
Ryan, Nancy, jt. auth. see McMahon, James P.
Ryan, Nellie. Beautiful Doodles: Over 100 Pictures to Complete & Create. (p. 153)
—Beautiful Doodles. (p. 153)
—Designer Doodles: Over 100 Designs to Complete & Create. (p. 430)
—Designer Doodles. (p. 430)
—Doodles Dancing: Graceful & Gorgeous Pictures to Create & Complete. (p. 469)
—Dream House Doodles. (p. 483)
—Fabulous Doodles. (p. 560)
—Fabulous Fashion. Ryan, Nellie, illus. (p. 560)
Ryan, Nellie, illus. see Bailey, Ellen.
Ryan, Nellie, illus. see Running Press Staff.
Ryan, Nellie, illus. see Scholastic, Inc. Staff & Bailey, Ellen.
Ryan, Nellie, jt. illus. see Davies, Hannah.
Ryan, Nellie, et al. Girls' World of Doodles: Over 100 Pictures to Complete & Create. (p. 681)
—Gorgeous Doodles: Pretty, Full-Color Pictures to Create & Complete. (p. 702)
Ryan, Nelly & Jackson, Katy. Sticker Style Studio Runway Fashion. (p. 1650)
Ryan, Nikki Joyce. Grandma Cookie's Treasure Box. (p. 708)
Ryan, P E. Saints of Augustine. (p. 1504)
Ryan, Pam Muñoz. Becoming Naomi Leon. (p. 156)
—Dreamer. (p. 484)
—Dreamer. Sis, Peter, illus. (p. 484)
—Echo. (p. 502)
—Esperanza Rising. (p. 536)
—Flag We Love. Masiello, Ralph, illus. (p. 602)
—Hello Ocean. Astrella, Mark, illus. (p. 764)
—Hello, Ocean (Hola Mar) Canetti, Yanitzia, tr. from ENG. (p. 764)
—How Do You Raise a Raisin? Brown, Craig McFarland & Astrella, Mark, illus. (p. 808)
—Mice & Beans. Cepeda, Joe, illus. (p. 1134)
—Nuestra California. López, Rafael, illus. (p. 1270)
—Our California. López, Rafael, illus. (p. 1308)
—Pinta el Viento. (p. 1361)
—Soñador. Sis, Peter, illus. (p. 1611)
—Tony Baloney: Pen Pal. Fotheringham, Ed, illus. (p. 1766)
—Tony Baloney: Buddy Trouble. Fotheringham, Ed, illus. (p. 1766)
—Tony Baloney: School Rules. Fotheringham, Edwin, illus. (p. 1766)
—Tony Baloney: Buddy Trouble. Fotheringham, Edwin, illus. (p. 1766)
—Tony Baloney. Fotheringham, Edwin, illus. (p. 1766)
—Tony Baloney: Pen Pal. Fotheringham, Edwin, illus. (p. 1766)
—When Marian Sang: The True Recital of Marian Anderson. Selznick, Brian, illus. (p. 1903)
—Yo, Naomi León. (p. 1971)
Ryan, Pam Muñoz & McInerney, Kathleen. Paint the Wind. (p. 1318)
Ryan, Pat. Car Racing Greats (p. 265)
—Iowa. (p. 886)
—Kansas. (p. 943)
Ryan, Patrick. Gemini Bites. (p. 660)
—In Mike We Trust. (p. 864)
—Shakespeare's Storybook: Folk Tales That Inspired the Bard. Mayhew, James, illus. (p. 1559)
Ryan, Patrick, jt. auth. see Mayhew, James.
Ryan, Paul, et al. Iron Man Epic Collection: War Games. (p. 888)
—Squadron Supreme. (p. 1636)
Ryan, Peter. Online Bullying. (p. 1298)
Ryan, Peter K. Black Ops & Other Special Missions of the U. S. Air Force Combat Control Team. (p. 196)
—Careers in Electronic Publishing. (p. 267)
—How the Gold Standard Works. (p. 813)
—Powering up a Career in Robotics. (p. 1391)
—Social Networking. (p. 1604)
Ryan, Phillip. Freight Trains. (p. 635)
—Monorails. (p. 1166)
—Passenger Trains. (p. 1326)
—Steam-Powered Trains. (p. 1646)
—Streetcars. (p. 1667)
—Subways. (p. 1671)
Ryan, Randy. My First Baseball Game. (p. 1204)
Ryan, Regina Sara, jt. auth. see April, Elyse.
Ryan, Rob, illus. see Duffy, Carol Ann.
Ryan, Rob, jt. auth. see Duffy, Carol Ann.
Ryan, Roberta, jt. auth. see Ryan, Jerry.
Ryan, Ruth. In the Swamp, Oh Yeah, in the Swamp. Seahorse, Risa, illus. (p. 867)
Ryan, Sara. Bad Houses. Hahn, Sierra, ed. (p. 131)
—Empress of the World. (p. 521)
Ryan, Sean. Spain in Our World. (p. 1620)
Ryan, Shaun, jt. auth. see Michelson, Grant.
Ryan, Shawn. Right Now I'm Small, & I Have a Long Time to Grow. (p. 1472)
Ryan, Shirley Ann. Searching for the Waters of Antiquity (p. 1538)
Ryan, Susan Jane & Tornatore, Carol. Florida a to Z. (p. 607)
Ryan, Susannah, illus. see Maestro, Betsy.
Ryan, Tammy. Music Lesson. (p. 1193)
Ryan, Tom. Big Time (p. 184)
—Tag Along (p. 1695)
—Totally Unrelated (p. 1771)
—Way to Go (p. 1864)
Ryan, Tracy, jt. auth. see Kinsella, John.
Ryan, Victoria. When Your Pet Dies: A Healing Handbook for Kids. Ryan, Victoria & Alley, R. W., illus. (p. 1906)
Ryback, Carol. Hurricanes. (p. 830)
—Moon. (p. 1171)
—Planets. (p. 1368)
—Scuba Diving. (p. 1533)
—Stars. (p. 1643)
—Sun. (p. 1675)
Ryback, Carol, jt. auth. see Blashfield, Jean F.
Ryback, Carol, jt. auth. see Somervill, Barbara A.
Ryback, Carol, jt. auth. see Stille, Darlene R.
Ryback, Carol & Mezzanotte, Jim. Liquids. (p. 1021)

R

—Solids. (p. 1607)
Ryback, Jeffrey W. Many Faces of William Shakespeare. Landes, William-Alan, ed. (p. 1089)
Rybakov, Vladimir. Afghans. (p. 26)
Rybolt, Leah M., jt. auth. see Rybolt, Thomas R.
Rybolt, Thomas R. Soda Pop Science Fair Projects. (p. 1605)
—Soda Pop Science Projects: Experiments with Carbonated Soft Drinks. (p. 1605)
Rybolt, Thomas R. & Mebane, Robert C. Environmental Science Fair Projects: Using Water, Feathers, Sunlight, Balloons, & More. (p. 532)
—Environmental Science Fair Projects, Revised & Expanded Using the Scientific Method. LaBaff, Tom & LaBaff, Stephanie, illus. (p. 532)
—Science Experiments for Young People. (p. 1525)
Rybolt, Thomas R. & Rybolt, Leah M. Smelly Science Fair Projects. (p. 1593)
Rycroft, Frederick. Young World: Book Two - Friends 'Til the End. (p. 1979)
Rycroft, Nina, illus. see Cummings, Phil.
Rycroft, Nina, illus. see Harris, Stephen.
Rycroft, Nina, illus. see Wild, Margaret.
Rydaker, Ewa. Lucia Morning in Sweden. Lewis, Anne Gillespie, ed. (p. 1062)
Rydberg, Viktor & Reaves, William P. Our Fathers' Godsaga: Retold for the Young. (p. 1308)
Rydberg, Viktor & Reeves, William P. Our Fathers' Godsaga: Retold for the Young. Rydberg, Viktor, tr. (p. 1308)
Ryden, David. Andy the Ambulance: My Two Partners. (p. 73)
Ryder, jt. auth. see Ryder, Joanne.
Ryder, Chloe. Best Friends Forever! (p. 169)
—Dream Come True. (p. 483)
—Magical Friend. (p. 1074)
—Princess Ponies: An Amazing Rescue. (p. 1405)
—Princess Ponies 3: the Special Secret. (p. 1405)
—Princess Ponies 4: a Unicorn Adventure! (p. 1405)
—Princess Ponies 7: a Special Surprise. (p. 1405)
—Princess Ponies 8: a Singing Star. (p. 1405)
Ryder, Joanne. Bear of My Heart. Moore, Margie, illus. (p. 151)
—Dance by the Light of the Moon. Francis, Guy, illus. (p. 402)
—Little Panda: The World Welcomes Hua Mei at the San Diego Zoo. World-Famous San Diego Zoo Staff, photos by. (p. 1033)
—My Father's Hands. Graham, Mark, illus. (p. 1203)
—Night Flight. Schwartz, Amy, illus. (p. 1253)
—Pair of Polar Bears: Twin Cubs Find a Home at the San Diego Zoo. San Diego Zoological Society Staff, photos by. (p. 1318)
—Panda Kindergarten. (p. 1320)
—Panda Kindergarten. Feng, Katherine, illus. (p. 1320)
—Panda Kindergarten. Feng, Katherine, photos by. (p. 1320)
—Waterfall's Gift. Watson, Richard Jesse, illus. (p. 1863)
—Where Butterflies Grow. Cherry, Lynne, illus. (p. 1906)
—Wild Birds. Kwas, Susan Estelle, illus. (p. 1929)
—Won't You Be My Kissaroo? Sweet, Melissa, illus. (p. 1949)
Ryder, Joanne, jt. auth. see Yep, Laurence.
Ryder, Joanne & Ryder. My Mother's Voice. Catalanotto, Peter, illus. (p. 1215)
Ryder, Michael. Moon Below. (p. 1172)
Ryder, Michael/Todd. Twins. (p. 1802)
Ryder, Rob. Blood, Sweat & Cheers: Athletes Speak Out. (p. 200)
Ryder, Verdene & Decker, Celia A. Parents & Their Children: Teaching Package Teacher's. (p. 1324)
—Parents & Their Children: Teaching Package Teacher's Resource Guide. (p. 1324)
—Parents & Their Children: Teaching Package Teacher's Resource Portfolio. (p. 1324)
Ryder, Verdene & Harter, Marjorie B. Contemporary Living: Teaching Package Teacher's Resource Guide. (p. 360)
—Contemporary Living: Teaching Package Teacher's Resource Portfolio. (p. 360)
Ryder, Verdene & Smith, Peggy B. Human Sexuality: Responsible Life Choices. (p. 826)
Rydholm, Fred, frwd. Ancient Mines of Kitchi-Gummi: Cypriot/Minoan Traders in Norty America. (p. 70)
Ryerson, Richard A., jt. ed. see Fremont-Barnes, Gregory.
Rygg, Kathy. Tall Tales with Mr. K. (p. 1704)
Rygiel, Maria E. Purple Boots. (p. 1419)
Ryherd, Saundra. Adventures of Sparky. (p. 23)
Ryherd, Tim. My Hurricane Book. (p. 1211)
Ryken, Philip Graham. Ecclesiastes (Redesign) Why Everything Matters. (p. 502)
Rykken, Cheryl. My Shaky Grandma. (p. 1218)
Rykken, John. Bloodwood: The Chronicles of Max Mayhem. (p. 201)
Rylance, Dan. Quentin Burdick: The Gentle Warrior. (p. 1425)
Rylance, Maureen. Spur on the Plate. (p. 1635)
Rylance, Ulrike. Emma in Buttonland. Morby, Connie Stradling, tr. from GER. (p. 519)
Rylance, Ulrike, jt. auth. see Adamson, Ged.
Ryland, John B., told to. Wisdom for the Little People. (p. 1939)
Ryland Peters and Small Staff, creator. Now I Am a Fairy. (p. 1269)
—Now I am a Pirate. (p. 1269)
—Now I Am a Princess. (p. 1269)
Rylander, Chris. Codename Zero. (p. 338)
—Countdown Zero. (p. 370)
—Fourth Stall. (p. 625)
Rylander, Emily, jt. auth. see Meil, Gabriel.
Rylant, Cynthia. All in a Day. McClure, Nikki, illus. (p. 44)
—Annie & Snowball & the Book Bugs Club. (p. 86)
—Annie & Snowball & the Book Bugs Club. Stevenson, Suçie, illus. (p. 86)
—Annie & Snowball & the Cozy Nest. Stevenson, Suçie, illus. (p. 86)
—Annie & Snowball & the Dress-Up Birthday. (p. 86)
—Annie & Snowball & the Dress-Up Birthday. Stevenson, Suçie, illus. (p. 86)
—Annie & Snowball & the Magical House. Stevenson, Suçie, illus. (p. 86)
—Annie & Snowball & the Prettiest House. Stevenson, Suçie, illus. (p. 86)
—Annie & Snowball & the Shining Star. Stevenson, Suçie, illus. (p. 86)
—Annie & Snowball & the Surprise Day. (p. 86)
—Annie & Snowball & the Teacup Club. Stevenson, Suçie, illus. (p. 86)
—Annie & Snowball & the Thankful Friends. (p. 86)
—Annie & Snowball & the Thankful Friends. Stevenson, Suçie, illus. (p. 86)
—Annie & Snowball & the Wedding Day: The Thirteenth Book of Their Adventures. Stevenson, Suçie, illus. (p. 86)
—Annie & Snowball & the Wedding Day. (p. 86)
—Baby Face: A Book of Love for Baby. Goode, Diane, illus. (p. 126)
—Beautiful Stories of Life: Six Greek Myths, Retold. Ellis, Carson, illus. (p. 154)
—Brownie & Pearl Get Dolled Up. (p. 232)
—Brownie & Pearl Get Dolled Up. Biggs, Brian, illus. (p. 232)
—Brownie & Pearl Go for a Spin. Biggs, Brian, illus. (p. 232)
—Brownie & Pearl Grab a Bite. Biggs, Brian, illus. (p. 232)
—Brownie & Pearl Hit the Hay. Biggs, Brian, illus. (p. 232)
—Brownie & Pearl Make Good. Biggs, Brian, illus. (p. 232)
—Brownie & Pearl See the Sights. Biggs, Brian, illus. (p. 232)
—Brownie & Pearl Step Out. Biggs, Brian, illus. (p. 232)
—Brownie & Pearl Take a Dip. Biggs, Brian, illus. (p. 232)
—Case of the Baffled Bear. Karas, G. Brian, illus. (p. 273)
—Case of the Climbing Cat. Karas, G. Brian, illus. (p. 273)
—Case of the Desperate Duck. (p. 274)
—Case of the Desperate Duck. Karas, G. Brian, illus. (p. 274)
—Case of the Fidgety Fox. Karas, G. Brian, illus. (p. 274)
—Case of the Missing Monkey. Karas, G. Brian, illus. (p. 274)
—Case of the Puzzling Possum. Karas, G. Brian, illus. (p. 275)
—Case of the Sleepy Sloth. Karas, G. Brian, illus. (p. 275)
—Caso de la Perezosa Dormilona. (p. 276)
—Caso del Gato Escalador. (p. 276)
—Eagle. McDaniels, Preston, illus. (p. 492)
—Family Stories You Can Relate To: A Reading Rainbow Reader. Stevenson, Suçie, illus. (p. 568)
—Fine White Dust. (p. 589)
—Give Me Grace: A Child's Daybook of Prayers. Rylant, Cynthia, illus. (p. 681)
—God Got a Dog. Frazee, Marla, illus. (p. 689)
—God Went to Beauty School. (p. 690)
—Gooseberry Park. Howard, Arthur, illus. (p. 702)
—Gooseberry Park & the Master Plan. Howard, Arthur, illus. (p. 702)
—Henry & Mudge & a Very Merry Christmas. Stevenson, Suçie, illus. (p. 767)
—Henry & Mudge & Mrs. Hopper's House. Bracken, Carolyn, illus. (p. 767)
—Henry & Mudge & the Big Sleepover Stevenson, Suçie, illus. (p. 767)
—Henry & Mudge & the Big Sleepover. Stevenson, Suçie, illus. (p. 767)
—Henry & Mudge & the Big Sleepover. Stevenson, Suçie & Stevenson, Suçie, illus. (p. 767)
—Henry & Mudge & the Funny Lunch. Bracken, Carolyn, illus. (p. 767)
—Henry & Mudge & the Great Grandpas. Stevenson, Suçie, illus. (p. 767)
—Henry & Mudge & the Great Grandpas. Stevenson, Suçie & Stevenson, Suçie, illus. (p. 767)
—Henry & Mudge & the Tumbling Trip. Bracken, Carolyn, illus. (p. 767)
—Henry & Mudge & the Wild Goose Chase. Bracken, Carolyn, illus. (p. 767)
—Henry & Mudge Get the Cold Shivers. Stevenson, Suçie, illus. (p. 767)
—Henry & Mudge Ready-To-Read Value Pack #2: Henry & Mudge & the Long Weekend; Henry & Mudge & the Bedtime Thumps; Henry & Mudge & the Big Sleepover; Henry & Mudge & the Funny Lunch; Henry & Mudge & the Great Grandpas; Henry & Mudge & the Tall Tree House. Stevenson, Suçie, illus. (p. 767)
—High-Rise Private Eye: The\Case of the Troublesome Turtle. Karas, G. Brian, illus. (p. 778)
—High-Rise Private Eyes Series. Karas, G. Brian, illus. (p. 778)
—I Had Seen Castles. (p. 838)
—If You'll Be My Valentine. Kosaka, Fumi, illus. (p. 855)
—In November. Kastner, Jill, illus. (p. 864)
—Kindness. (p. 957)
—Let's Go Home: The Wonderful Things about a House. Halperin, Wendy Anderson, illus. (p. 997)
—Little Whistle. Bowers, Tim, illus. (p. 1037)
—Little Whistle's Christmas. Bowers, Tim, illus. (p. 1037)
—Little Whistle's Dinner Party. Bowers, Tim, illus. (p. 1037)
—Little Whistle's Medicine. Bowers, Tim, illus. (p. 1037)
—Missing May. (p. 1152)
—Moonlight: The Halloween Cat. Sweet, Melissa, illus. (p. 1172)
—Mr. Putter & Tabby Catch the Cold. Howard, Arthur, illus. (p. 1186)
—Mr. Putter & Tabby Clear the Decks. Howard, Arthur, illus. (p. 1186)
—Mr. Putter & Tabby Dance the Dance. (p. 1186)
—Mr. Putter & Tabby Dance the Dance. Howard, Arthur, illus. (p. 1186)
—Mr. Putter & Tabby Drop the Ball. (p. 1186)
—Mr. Putter & Tabby Drop the Ball. Howard, Arthur, illus. (p. 1186)
—Mr. Putter & Tabby Feed the Fish. Howard, Arthur, illus. (p. 1186)
—Mr. Putter & Tabby Make a Wish. Howard, Arthur, illus. (p. 1186)
—Mr. Putter & Tabby Ring the Bell. Howard, Arthur, illus. (p. 1186)
—Mr. Putter & Tabby Run the Race. Howard, Arthur, illus. (p. 1186)
—Mr. Putter & Tabby See the Stars. Howard, Arthur, illus. (p. 1186)
—Mr. Putter & Tabby Smell the Roses. Howard, Arthur, illus. (p. 1186)
—Mr. Putter & Tabby Turn the Page. Howard, Arthur, illus. (p. 1186)
—Mr. Putter & Tabby Walk the Dog. Howard, Arthur, illus. (p. 1186)
—Mr. Putter & Tabby Write the Book. Howard, Arthur, illus. (p. 1186)
—Night in the Country. Szilagyi, Mary, illus. (p. 1253)
—Octopus. McDaniels, Preston, illus. (p. 1278)
—Old Town in the Green Groves. (p. 1285)
—Old Woman Who Named Things. Brown, Kathryn, illus. (p. 1285)
—Poppleton. Teague, Mark, illus. (p. 1384)
—Poppleton in Spring. Teague, Mark, illus. (p. 1384)
—Poppleton in Winter. Teague, Mark, illus. (p. 1385)
—Poppleton in Winter, Level 3. Teague, Mark, illus. (p. 1385)
—Poppleton Se Divierte. Teague, Mark, illus. (p. 1385)
—Puppy Mudge Finds a Friend. Stevenson, Suçie, illus. (p. 1418)
—Puppy Mudge Has a Snack. Mones, Isidre, illus. (p. 1418)
—Puppy Mudge Loves His Blanket. Mones, Isidre, illus. (p. 1418)
—Puppy Mudge Wants to Play. Stevenson, Suçie, illus. (p. 1418)
—Scarecrow. Stringer, Lauren, illus. (p. 1519)
—Sleeping Beauty. McGuire, Erin, illus. (p. 1589)
—Snow. Stringer, Lauren, illus. (p. 1598)
—Stars Will Still Shine. Beeke, Tiphanie, illus. (p. 1643)
—Storm. (p. 1655)
—Storm. McDaniels, Preston, illus. (p. 1655)
—Tall Tree House. (p. 1704)
—Thimbleberry Stories. Kneen, Maggie, illus. (p. 1732)
—Tormenta. (p. 1770)
—Turtle. McDaniels, Preston, illus. (p. 1798)
—Van Gogh Cafe. (p. 1833)
—Van Gogh Café. (p. 1833)
—Walt Disney's Cinderella. Blair, Mary, illus. (p. 1855)
—Wedding Flowers. Halperin, Wendy Anderson, illus. (p. 1870)
—Whale. McDaniels, Preston, illus. (p. 1877)
—Wonderful Happens. Dowley, Coco, illus. (p. 1948)
Rylant, Cynthia, jt. auth. see Lobel, Arnold.
Rylant, Cynthia & Andersen, Hans Christian. Steadfast Tin Soldier. Corace, Jen, illus. (p. 1645)
Rylant, Cynthia & Bracken, Carolyn. Henry & Mudge & Mrs. Hopper's House. (p. 767)
—Henry & Mudge & the Funny Lunch. Bracken, Carolyn, illus. (p. 767)
—Henry & Mudge & the Tall Tree House. (p. 767)
—Henry & Mudge & the Tumbling Trip. (p. 767)
—Henry & Mudge & the Wild Goose Chase. (p. 767)
—Henry & Mudge & the Wild Goose Chase. Bracken, Carolyn, illus. (p. 767)
Rylant, Cynthia & Halperin, Wendy Anderson. Wedding Flowers. (p. 1871)
Rylant, Cynthia & Howard, Arthur. Mr. Putter & Tabby Catch the Cold. Howard, Arthur, illus. (p. 1186)
—Mr. Putter & Tabby Dance the Dance. Howard, Arthur, illus. (p. 1186)
Rylant, Cynthia & Mones, Isidre. Puppy Mudge Takes a Bath. Mones, Isidre, illus. (p. 1418)
Rylant, Cynthia & Siegel, Mark. Long Night Moon. Siegel, Mark, illus. (p. 1047)
Ryle, J. C. Children's Stories. (p. 304)
—Regeneration: Being 'Born Again' - What It Means & Why It's Necessary. (p. 1457)
Ryles, Briony & Hall, Derek. Ages of Steam & Electricity. (p. 29)
—Early 20th Century. (p. 493)
—Medieval Period & the Renaissance. (p. 1119)
—Modern World. (p. 1159)
—Prehistory & the Classical Period. (p. 1395)
—Scientific Revolution. (p. 1528)
Ryles, Donald. Magic Holiday Forest. (p. 1072)
Ryley, David, illus. see Kovacs, Victoria.
Rymas-Loomis, Cathy. Calamity Clancey: The Calamity Cat from Kalvesta Kansas. (p. 252)
Rymer, Alta M. Stars of Obron: Chambo Returns. Rymer, Alta M., illus. (p. 1643)
—Up from Uzam. Rymer, Alta M., illus. (p. 1824)
Rymer, Nan, tr. see Akamatsu, Ken.
Rymer, Nan, tr. see Donbo, Koge.
Rymer, Nan, tr. see Iida, Haruko.
Rymer, Nan, tr. see Ken, Akamatsu.
Rymer, Nan, tr. see Matoh, Sanami.
Ryndak, Rob. Alligator or Crocodile? (p. 47)
—Bats. (p. 144)
—Crocodiles. (p. 384)
—Dolphin or Porpoise? (p. 464)
—Frog or Toad? (p. 640)
—Jungle Animals. (p. 935)
—Leopard or Jaguar? (p. 993)
—Monkeys. (p. 1165)
—Parrots. (p. 1325)
—Sloths. (p. 1591)
—Toucans. (p. 1772)
—Turtle or Tortoise? (p. 1798)
Rynders, Dawn, jt. auth. see Wallingford, Stephanie.
Ryniak, Christopher, illus. see Amato, Mary.
Rynning, Sten. NATO Renewed: The Power & Purpose of Transatlantic Cooperation. (p. 1235)
Ryrie, Alec, ed. Palgrave Advances in the European Reformations. (p. 1320)
Rys, John Van, see Van Rys, John.
Ryser, Nicolas, illus. see Richard, Laurent.
Ryshpan-Harris, Joanne. Great Adventures of Bottom the Bassett Hound. Bouganim, Revital, illus. (p. 713)
Ryskind, Sam, illus. see Drake, Tim.
Ryton, Charlotte. Lion Book of Five-Minute Parables. Wickenden, Nadine, illus. (p. 1020)
Ryu, Ki Woon. Yongbi, the Invincible 1 Moon, Jung Who, illus. (p. 1972)
Ryu, Youngju, tr. see Hyung, Min-Woo.
Ryu, Youngju, tr. see Lee, Kang-Woo.
Ryzewski, Deborah. Yoga ABC's with Alvin, Beatrice & Conner. (p. 1972)
Rzasa, Jennifer, illus. see Bolte, Mari.
Rzeczkowski, Frank & Rosier, Paul C. Lakota Sioux. (p. 972)

S

S., Bijan, jt. illus. see Mukherjee, Aiswarya.
S. I. Artists Staff. Fun & Games. (p. 647)
S. I. Artists Staff, illus. see Mitter, Matt.
S. I. Artists Staff, illus. see Reader's Digest Staff & Tomaselli, Doris.
S. I. International, jt. auth. see Brooke, Samantha.
S. I. International, jt. auth. see Olsen, Leigh.
S. I. International Staff, jt. auth. see Gallo, Tina.
S., John, jt. auth. see Des Forges, Roger V.
S. K. Mrs. Emerson. (p. 1187)
S., LaTisha & Lee, Mykle. One Giant Leap: Love Poems. Blob, Anjali & Beverly-Patterson, Sylvia Dianne, eds. (p. 1295)
S., Lisa Hamilton Ed. From Plot to Plate: "a Story of Ambition & Dedication" (p. 643)
—Tale of the Talking Trees: The Tale of the Talking Trees a Story of Suspense & Surprise. (p. 1700)
S. P. C. K. Stories from the History of Sweden. (p. 1654)
S, Peter. 12 Minutes: So Short Stories. (p. 1994)
S, Shemayne. Journey into Grace. (p. 928)
S, Shemayne. Leap of Faith. (p. 982)
S. Surges, Carol. Food Chains. (p. 613)
S. Wong, Derrick & Varacalli, Lauren. Bowdoin College College Prowler off the Record. (p. 216)
Sa, Rachel. Lewton Experiment (p. 1004)
Saab, Carl Y. Seeing, Hearing, & Smelling the World. (p. 1548)
Saab, Julie. Little Lola. Gothard, David, illus. (p. 1030)
—Little Lola Saves the Show. Gothard, David, illus. (p. 1030)
Saab, Tarek. Gut Check: Confronting Love, Work, & Manhood in Your Twenties. (p. 733)
Saada, Nicholas, ed. see Cinema, Cahiers du.
Saada, Nicholas, jt. ed. see Cinema, Cahiers du.
Saaf, Donald. ABC Animal Orchestra. Saaf, Donald, illus. (p. 3)
Saari, Danial. Tales with Tails: Bed Time Stories. (p. 1703)
Saari, Holly. Is This Really My Body? Embracing Physical Changes. (p. 890)
—Rhode Island. (p. 1468)
—South Dakota. (p. 1617)
—Tennessee. (p. 1720)
—Texas. (p. 1724)
—Utah. (p. 1829)
—Vermont. (p. 1837)
—Violins. (p. 1843)
—Virginia. (p. 1844)
—Washington. (p. 1859)
—West Virginia. (p. 1876)
—Wyoming. (p. 1966)
Saari, Peggy. Biography, Space Exploration. (p. 189)
—Primary Sources - Space Exploration. (p. 1400)
Saathoff, Deborah, jt. auth. see Jarrell, Jane.
Saavedra, Anthony, illus. see Cox, Steven.
Saavedra, Eusebio. Tree & Annly el Árbol y Annly. Rowley, Jillian, illus. (p. 1783)
Saavedra, Patricia, jt. auth. see Cardenas, Ernesto.
Saavedra, Scott. Dr. Radium & the Gizmos of Boola Boola! (p. 475)
—Flee, Puny Humans! (p. 603)
Sabado, Joe. Mommy Teach Us to Pray. Fujii, Jason, photos by. (p. 1162)
Sabaka, Donna, illus. see Hansen, Judith.
Sabanski, Helen, illus. see Fedderesen, Jill.
Sabate, Hernan, tr. see Donelly, Joe & Donnelly, Joe.
Sabatier-Morel, Francoise & Pellegrini, Isabelle. Marie from Paris. Camcam, Princesse, illus. (p. 1093)
Sabatini, Clare Barone. Stevielephant. (p. 1649)
Sabatini, Kety. Joseph's Hands. Sabatini, Marie, illus. (p. 926)
Sabatini, Key. Isabel's Sister. (p. 891)
Sabatini, Kimberly. Touching the Surface. (p. 1772)
Sabatini, Marie, illus. see Sabatini, Kety.
Sabatini, Rafael. King's Messenger. (p. 960)
Sabatini, Rafael, et al. Rafael Sabatini Pomplun, Tom, ed. (p. 1433)
Sabatino, Chris. Animal Doodles for Kids (p. 77)
—City Doodles - Boston. (p. 323)
—Dinosaur Doodles (p. 442)
—Monster Doodles for Kids (p. 1167)
—Pocketdoodles for Boys (p. 1375)
—Superhero Doodles for Kids (p. 1683)
Sabatino, Chris, illus. see Ficocelli, Elizabeth.
Sabatino, Chris, jt. auth. see King, Bart.
Sabatino, Chris, jt. auth. see Wood, Anita.
Sabatino, Michael. 20 Fun Facts about Galaxies. (p. 1995)
—Being an Orangutan. (p. 161)
—How Long Will the Sun Last? (p. 810)
—Legend of Dracula. (p. 988)
—T. Rex vs. Crocodile. (p. 1694)
Sabatino, N. S. Tiny Donut with a Big Heart (p. 1756)
Sabatino, Nick. Paint Stripes Stop Traffic Dead (p. 1318)
Sabato, George F. New Improved Santa. Landes, William-Alan, ed. (p. 1245)
Sabato, Larry J. & Ernst, Howard R. Encyclopedia of American Political Parties & Elections. (p. 524)
Sabbagh, Tatiana, illus. see Boutros, Jill, et al.
Sabbeth, Carol. Frida Kahlo & Diego Rivera: Their Lives & Ideas, 24 Activities. (p. 637)
—Van Gogh & the Post-Impressionists for Kids: Their Lives & Ideas, 21 Activities. (p. 1833)
Sabean, Maurice. Atomic Structure. (p. 113)
—Forces & Machines. (p. 617)
Sabeca International Investment Corp. Todo Mexico 2004. (p. 1761)
Sabeca International Investment Corp. Staff. Enciclopedia de Mexico (p. 524)
Sabeca International Investment, Corp. Staff. Enciclopedia de Mexico. (p. 524)
Sabeca International Investment Corp. Staff. Todo Mexico 2005. (p. 1761)
Sabeca International Investment Staff. Enciclopedia de Mexico. (p. 524)
Sabel, Lauren. Vivian Divine Is Dead. (p. 1846)

Sabella, Elisa, illus. see Zelinger, Laurie & Zelinger, Jordan.
Sabella, Elisa, illus. see Zelinger, Laurie E. & Zelinger, Jordan.
Sabin, Edwin L. Boys' Book of Border Battles. (p. 220)
Sabin, Ellen. Giving Book: Open the Door to a Lifetime of Giving. (p. 681)
—Healing Book: Facing the Death-and Celebrating the Life-of Someone You Love. (p. 757)
—Hero Book: Learning Lessons from the People You Admire. Barbas, Kerren, illus. (p. 772)
—Special Needs Acceptance Book: Being a Friend to Someone with Special Needs. (p. 1623)
Sabin, Francene & Macken, JoAnn Early. Abigail Adams: Young Patriot. Miyake, Yoshi, illus. (p. 5)
—Elizabeth Blackwell, the First Woman Doctor. Toulmin-Rothe, Ann, illus. (p. 513)
Sabin, Francene & Mattern, Joanne. Helen Keller, Girl of Courage. Meyer, Jean, illus. (p. 763)
Sabin, Louis & Macken, JoAnn Early. Thomas Edison: Incredible Inventor. (p. 1738)
Sabin, Patricia T. If I Could Fly I Would Play among the Clouds. (p. 852)
Sabina, C. Frosted August. (p. 644)
Sabio & Prudente. Libro de Caligrafia (p. 1006)
—Libro de Caligrafia (p. 1006)
—Numeros, Conceptos y Figuras Geometricas. (p. 1273)
Sabiston, Susan, illus. see Gunther, Joseph.
Sable, Katherine, illus. see Aryal, Aimee.
Sabnani, Nina, illus. see Rao, Sandhya.
Sabnani, Nina, illus. see Shukla, Subir.
Sabo, J. Mamma's Boy. (p. 1085)
—Train Wrecker. (p. 1777)
Sabol, Elizabeth. Day Is Done: A Lullaby (p. 413)
Sabo-Western, Deborah. Peter Penny: Discovers the Gift. (p. 1347)
Sabuda, Robert. 12 Days of Christmas. Sabuda, Robert, illus. (p. 1994)
—America the Beautiful. Sabuda, Robert, illus. (p. 59)
—Beauty & the Beast: A Pop-Up Adaptation of the Classic Tale. Sabuda, Robert, illus. (p. 154)
—Little Mermaid. Sabuda, Robert, illus. (p. 1031)
—Peter Pan: A Pop-Up Adaptation of J. M. Barrie's Original Tale. (p. 1347)
—Uh-Oh, Leonardo! The Adventures of Providence Traveler. Sabuda, Robert, illus. (p. 1808)
—Winter in White: A Mini Pop-Up Treat. Sabuda, Robert, illus. (p. 1938)
—Winter's Tale: An Original Pop-Up Journey. (p. 1938)
Sabuda, Robert, illus. see dePaola, Tomie.
Sabuda, Robert, illus. see Rosen, Michael J.
Sabuda, Robert, illus. see Whitman, Walt.
Sabuda, Robert, jt. auth. see Carroll, Lewis, pseud.
Sabuda, Robert, jt. auth. see Reinhart, Matthew.
Sabuda, Robert & Reinhart, Matthew. Encyclopedia Prehistorica Mega-Beasts. Sabuda, Robert & Reinhart, Matthew, illus. (p. 526)
Saccheri, Briana, illus. see Saccheri, Josephine.
Saccheri, Josephine. Magic on the Wall Carrescia, Reid, illus. (p. 1073)
—Secret to Easter Eggs. Saccheri, Briana, illus. (p. 1544)
Sacco, Christopher & Haehnel, Alan. Education of Janet O'Malley: One-Act Comedy Play. (p. 505)
Sacco, Joe, illus. see Kesey, Ken.
Sach, Jacqueline. Wham-O Hacky Sack Handbook: The Tips & Tricks for Becoming an Expert Shredder! (p. 1878)
Sachar, Louis. Buchi nel Deserto. (p. 234)
—Buracos. (p. 243)
—Cardturner. (p. 266)
—Fuzzy Mud. (p. 651)
—Gets a Little Stranger. (p. 668)
—Holes. (p. 788)
—Hoyos. (p. 824)
—Marvin Redpost #1: Kidnapped at Birth? Record, Adam, illus. (p. 1099)
—Marvin Redpost #2: Why Pick on Me? Record, Adam, illus. (p. 1099)
—Marvin Redpost #3: Is He a Girl? Record, Adam, illus. (p. 1099)
—Marvin Redpost #5: Class President. Record, Adam, illus. (p. 1099)
—Marvin Redpost #6: a Flying Birthday Cake? Record, Adam, illus. (p. 1099)
—Marvin Redpost #8: a Magic Crystal? Record, Adam, illus. (p. 1100)
—Passage. (p. 1326)
—Sideways Stories from Wayside School. (p. 1573)
—Sideways Stories from Wayside School. McCauley, Adam, illus. (p. 1573)
—Small Steps. (p. 1592)
—Someday Angeline. Samuels, Barbara, illus. (p. 1609)
—Super Fast, Out of Control. Record, Adam, illus. (p. 1680)
—There's a Boy in the Girls' Bathroom. (p. 1730)
—Wayside School Gets a Little Stranger. McCauley, Adam, illus. (p. 1865)
—Wayside School Gets a Little Stranger. Schick, Joel & McCauley, Adam, illus. (p. 1865)
—Wayside School Is Falling Down. (p. 1865)
—Wayside School Is Falling Down. McCauley, Adam, illus. (p. 1865)
Sachar, Louis, jt. auth. see Sachar, Louis.
Sachar, Louis & Sachar, Louis. Hoyos. Abos, Elena, tr. (p. 824)
Sachedina, Shenin. Metu & Lee Learn about Breast Cancer. (p. 1130)
Sachi Miller, Crisalyn. Me & My Skateboard: Story & Coloring Book. (p. 1115)
Sachiko, Lorraine. Brothers Banyans Bones. (p. 231)
Sachs, Andrew. Teddybear Tales. (p. 1713)
Sachs, Barry, illus. see Reese Martin, Faith.
Sachs, Bernard, illus. see Fox, Gardner, et al.
Sachs, Harley L. Troll for Christmas & Other Stories. (p. 1788)
Sachs, Jim. I Knew a Gnu! (p. 840)
Sachs, Lloyd. American Country: Bluegrass, Honky-Tonk, & Crossover Sounds. (p. 60)
Sachs, Marilyn. Bears' House. (p. 152)
—Fat Girl. (p. 577)
Sachs, Ruth. Adolf Eichmann: Engineer of Death. (p. 13)
Sachs, Ruth, jt. auth. see Oshiro, Beverly.
Sachse, Dina. My Body: 12 Lift-N-Learn Flashcards about the Human Body (p. 1198)
—My Clothes: 12 Lift-N-Learn Flashcards about Clothes (p. 1200)
—My Food: 12 Lift-N-Learn Flashcards about Food! (p. 1208)
Sachtleben, William Lewis, jt. auth. see Allen, Thomas Gaskell, Jr.
Sack, Nancy. Puppies & Poems. Fuchs, Kaitlyn, illus. (p. 1418)
Sackanay, Kathleen. Adventures in the Forest. Wood, Morgan, illus. (p. 15)
Sackett, Frances. Misadventures of the Magician's Dog. (p. 1150)
Sackett-Smith, Lucy. Giraffes: Towering Tall. (p. 677)
—Gorillas: Beasts of the Wild. (p. 703)
—Grizzly Bears: Fierce Hunters. (p. 724)
—Hippos: Huge & Hungry. (p. 781)
Sackier, Shelley. Dear OPL. (p. 419)
Sacks, David & Ross, Brian. Vigfus the Viking. (p. 1842)
Sacks, David & Savel, Dava. Town of Zack. (p. 1773)
Sacks, Janet. Brain Booster Pack. (p. 221)
—Mysterious Case of Magic & Trickery: Tricks & Tales from the Masters of Magic. (p. 1222)
—Optical Illusion Pack. (p. 1301)
Sacks, Nathan. American Hip-Hop: Rappers, Djs, & Hard Beats. (p. 61)
—Big Fix. (p. 181)
—Duel: Mitsubishi Eclipse. (p. 489)
Sacks, Raymond J. & Bohnart, Edward R. Welding: Principles & Practices. (p. 1874)
Sackstein, Starr. Simply May. (p. 1578)
Sacre, Antonio. Mango in the Hand: A Story Told Through Proverbs. Serra, Sebastia, illus. (p. 1087)
—Noche Buena: A Christmas Story. Dominguez, Angela, illus. (p. 1262)
Sacred Friends. I Found the Answer. (p. 838)
Sacui, Alexandru, illus. see Fiore, Keith M.
Sad, Elizabeth Levy & Eliaszevich, Esteban. Gonzalo Higuain. (p. 697)
—Luis Amaranto Perea. (p. 1064)
—Radamel Falcao. (p. 1432)
Sada, Margarita, illus. see Arciniegas, Triunfo.
Sada, Margarita, illus. see Argueta, Jorge & Amado, Elisa.
Sada, Margarita, illus. see Caban, Jose Alberto.
Sada, Margarita, illus. see Cardenas, Teresa.
Sada, Margarita, illus. see Flores, Enrique.
Sada, Margarita, illus. see Ruiz, Maria Emilia Beyer.
Sada, Margarita, et al. De Principios y Princesas. (p. 416)
Sadamoto, Yoshiyuki. Neon Genesis Evangelion. Sadamoto, Yoshiyuki, illus. (p. 1241)
Sadan, Dana. Animals of the Rain Forest. (p. 83)
Sadar, Albin. Hamster Holmes: A Mystery Comes Knocking. (p. 739)
—Hamster Holmes: A Mystery Comes Knocking. Fabbretti, Valerio, illus. (p. 739)
—Hamster Holmes, Combing for Clues. Fabbretti, Valerio, illus. (p. 739)
—Mystery Comes Knocking. Fabbretti, Valerio, illus. (p. 1224)
Sadd, Kenn. Crazy Cracked Pots. (p. 377)
Saddleback, creator. Animal World. (p. 80)
—Earth. (p. 495)
—Human Body. (p. 825)
—Machines & Inventions. (p. 1068)
Saddleback Educational Publishing. 50 Cent (p. 1997)
—Beyonce (p. 173)
—Chris Brown (p. 311)
—Drake (p. 479)
—Jay-Z (p. 910)
—Kanye West (p. 943)
—Lifeskills Vocabulary 1 (p. 1013)
—Lifeskills Vocabulary 2 Reproducible Book with CD (p. 1013)
—Lil Wayne (p. 1017)
—Nicki Minaj (p. 1251)
—Pitbull (p. 1364)
—Rihanna (p. 1472)
—Sean Combs (p. 1536)
—Usher (p. 1828)
Saddleback Educational Publishing, ed. Adventure (p. 14)
—American History 1 (p. 61)
—American History 2 (p. 61)
—Creature (p. 380)
—Dark Suspicions (p. 408)
—Detective (p. 431)
—Earth Science (p. 496)
—Life Science (p. 1013)
—Mathematics for New English Speakers of English (p. 1108)
—Mudslide (p. 1189)
—Physical Science (p. 1353)
—Ransom (p. 1438)
—Read Reflect Respond (p. 1443)
—Shelter (p. 1565)
—Treasure (p. 1781)
Saddleback Educational Publishing Staff. 50 Cent. (p. 1997)
—Beyonce. (p. 173)
—Chris Brown. (p. 311)
—Dr. Dre. (p. 475)
—Drake. (p. 479)
—Jay-Z. (p. 910)
—Kanye West. (p. 943)
—Lil Wayne. (p. 1017)
—Nicki Minaj. (p. 1251)
—Pharrell Williams. (p. 1350)
—Pitbull. (p. 1364)
—Rihanna. (p. 1472)
—Sean Combs. (p. 1536)
—Usher. (p. 1828)
Saddleback Educational Publishing Staff, ed. see Dickens, Charles.
Saddleback Educational Publishing Staff, ed. see Dumas, Alexandre.
Saddleback Educational Publishing Staff, ed. see Hutchinson, Emily.
Saddleback Educational Publishing Staff, ed. see Norvell, Candyce & Gregg, Paula.
Saddleback Educational Publishing Staff, ed. see Pizer, Carol.
Saddleback Educational Publishing Staff, ed. see Quinley, Elliott.
Saddleback Educational Publishing Staff, ed. see Schraff, Anne.
Saddleback Educational Publishing Staff, ed. see Suter, Joanne.
Saddleback Educational Publishing Staff, ed. see Verne, Jules.
Saddleback Educational Publishing Staff, jt. auth. see Duncan, John.
Saddleback Educational Publishing Staff, jt. ed. see Doyle, Arthur.
Saddleback Educational Publishing Staff, jt. ed. see Laurel Associates Inc.
Saddleback Educational Publishing Staff, creator. Barclay Family Adventures Resource Guide. (p. 138)
—Machines & Inventions. (p. 1068)
—Plants. (p. 1369)
—Saddleback's Dark Man Full Set. (p. 1501)
—Universe. (p. 1820)
—Viking Life Teacher Resource Guide. (p. 1842)
Saddleback Educational Publishing Staff, ed. 20,000 Leagues under the Sea (p. 2003)
—Abraham Lincoln (p. 6)
—Adventures of Huckleberry Finn (p. 18)
—Adventures of Tom Sawyer (p. 24)
—Albert Einstein (p. 34)
—Alexander Graham Bell (p. 36)
—Amelia Earhart (p. 58)
—Around the World in 80 Days (p. 100)
—Babe Ruth (p. 123)
—Back-Up Quarterback 2011 (p. 130)
—Be Fair (p. 148)
—Beatles (p. 153)
—Benjamin Franklin (p. 164)
—Best Week Ever (p. 171)
—Blizzard (p. 199)
—Boy of Their Dreams (p. 218)
—Call of the Wild (p. 254)
—Camp (p. 257)
—Captains Courageous (p. 264)
—Charles Lindbergh (p. 292)
—Christmas Carol (p. 313)
—Comprehension Skill-Boosters (p. 354)
—Comprehension Spell-Boosters (p. 354)
—Count of Monte Cristo (p. 369)
—Crash (p. 376)
—Daniel Boone (p. 405)
—Davy Crockett (p. 411)
—Dive (p. 454)
—Don't Blame Me (p. 467)
—Dr. Jekyll & Mr. Hyde (p. 475)
—Dracula (p. 476)
—Easy Way (p. 501)
—Elvis Presley (p. 517)
—Everyday Life Math 2011 (p. 544)
—Fastest Runner (p. 576)
—Frankenstein (p. 629)
—Franklin Roosevelt (p. 630)
—George Washington (p. 664)
—Great Expectations (p. 715)
—Gulliver's Travels (p. 731)
—Hamlet (p. 739)
—Heights Series Sample Set (1 ea of 20 titles) (p. 762)
—Home & School Math (p. 791)
—Houdini (p. 802)
—Hunchback of Notre Dame (p. 827)
—It Does Matter (p. 894)
—It Is Not a Date (p. 894)
—Jackie Robinson (p. 904)
—Jane Eyre (p. 908)
—Julius Caesar (p. 933)
—Jungle Book (p. 935)
—Just Be Yourself (p. 938)
—Kidnapped (p. 952)
—King Lear (p. 958)
—Last of the Mohicans (p. 978)
—Macbeth (p. 1067)
—Man in the Iron Mask (p. 1085)
—Marie Curie (p. 1093)
—Martin Luther King Jr. (p. 1098)
—Mathematics for New Speakers of English (p. 1108)
—Merchant of Venice (p. 1127)
—Midsummer Night's Dream (p. 1139)
—Moby Dick (p. 1157)
—Mystery (p. 1223)
—Neptune (p. 1241)
—Oliver Twist (p. 1286)
—On the Job Math (p. 1290)
—One Date Too Many (p. 1294)
—One More Chance (p. 1296)
—Othello (p. 1306)
—Pride & Prejudice (p. 1399)
—Prince & the Pauper (p. 1401)
—Quickreads (p. 1427)
—Read, Reflect, Respond (p. 1443)
—Red Badge of Courage (p. 1453)
—Red Rhino Set Sample Set (1 ea of 9 titles) (p. 1454)
—Right Kind of Win (p. 1472)
—River (p. 1475)
—Robinson Crusoe (p. 1480)
—Romeo & Juliet (p. 1486)
—Sail (p. 1503)
—Scarlet Letter (p. 1520)
—Science Fiction (p. 1526)
—Score (p. 1530)
—Smart Shopping Math (p. 1593)
—Someone to Count On (p. 1609)
—Spy (p. 1635)
—Suspense (p. 1688)
—Swamp (p. 1688)
—Swiss Family Robinson (p. 1691)
—Tale of Two Cities (p. 1700)
—Tempest (p. 1717)
—Thomas Edison (p. 1738)
—Thomas Jefferson (p. 1739)
—Three Musketeers (p. 1743)
—Time Machine (p. 1752)
—Time to Move (p. 1753)
—Too Late (p. 1766)
—Treasure Island (p. 1781)
—Twelfth Night (p. 1800)
—Twister (p. 1802)
—Very Good Year (p. 1838)
—Walt Disney (p. 1855)
—War of the Worlds (p. 1857)
—White Fang (p. 1913)
Saddleback Publishing, creator. Chinese Life Teacher Resource Guide. (p. 307)
—Egyptian Life Teacher Resource Guide. (p. 506)
—Greek Life Teacher Resource Guide. (p. 720)
—Inca Life Teacher Resource Guide. (p. 868)
—Math Computation Skills & Strategies: Level 3. (p. 1105)
—Math Computation Skills & Strategies: Level 4. (p. 1105)
—Math Computation Skills & Strategies: Level 5. (p. 1105)
—Math Computation Skills & Strategies: Level 6. (p. 1105)
—Math Computation Skills & Strategies: Level 7. (p. 1105)
—Math Computation Skills & Strategies: Level 8. (p. 1105)
—Native American Life Teacher Resource Guide. (p. 1234)
Saddler, Gloria. Dewan! Oh, Nuts! (p. 432)
Saddler-Reed, Gloria. Dewan!! "Ooh,Nuts" (p. 432)
Saddlewick, A. B. Horror Holiday. Horne, Sarah, illus. (p. 799)
—Monstrous Maud: Scary Show. Horne, Sarah, illus. (p. 1169)
—Monstrous Maud: School Scare. Horne, Sarah, illus. (p. 1169)
—Monstrous Maud: Freaky Sleepover. Horne, Sarah, illus. (p. 1169)
—Monstrous Maud - Big Fright. Horne, Sarah, illus. (p. 1169)
Sade, Orly, jt. auth. see Neuborne, Ellen.
Sadeghian, Alireza. Knight, the Princess, & the Magic Rock: A Classic Persian Tale. (p. 964)
Sadeghian, Alireza, illus. see York Lumbard, Alexis.
Sadek, Ademola O. & Indovino, Shaina C. Italy. Bruton, John, ed. (p. 894)
Sadi. Careless King & Other Stories. (p. 268)
Sadie, Stanley & Macy, Laura, eds. Grove Book of Operas. (p. 725)
Sadig bai Afshar, illus. see Laird, Elizabeth.
Sadik, Ademola O. & Indovino, Shaina Carmel. Italy. (p. 894)
Sadler, Ann. Sewing. (p. 1556)
Sadler, Dale, illus. see Fussell, Bonnie.
Sadler, Judy, jt. auth. see Sadler, Judy Ann.
Sadler, Judy Ann. Beads. (p. 149)
—Embroidery. Bradford, June, illus. (p. 517)
—New Jumbo Book of Easy Crafts. Price, Caroline, illus. (p. 1245)
—Sandwiches for Duke Bennett. Lorna, illus. (p. 1511)
Sadler, Judy Ann & Sadler, Judy. Hemp Jewelry. Bradford, June, illus. (p. 767)
—Knotting: Make Your Own Basketball Nets, Guitar Straps, Sports Bags & More. Gagnon, Cileste & Gagnon, Celeste, illus. (p. 965)
—Simply Sewing. Kurisu, Jane, illus. (p. 1578)
Sadler, Judy Ann, et al. Jumbo Book of Needlecrafts. Bradford, June et al, illus. (p. 933)
Sadler, Marilyn. Alice from Dallas. Hoyt, Ard, illus. (p. 39)
—P. J. Funnybunny's Bag of Tricks. (p. 1316)
—P. J. Funnybunny's Bag of Tricks. Bollen, Roger, illus. (p. 1316)
—Pass It On! Slack, Michael, illus. (p. 1326)
—Ten Eggs in a Nest. Fleming, Michael, illus. (p. 1718)
—Tony Baroni Loves Macaroni. Crovatto, Lucie et al, illus. (p. 1766)
Sadler, Marilyn & Bollen, Roger. Money, Money, Honey Bunny! (p. 1164)
Sadler, Marilyn & Comstock, Eric. Charlie Piechart & the Case of the Missing Pizza Slice. Comstock, Eric, illus. (p. 293)
Sadler, Martin. Crystal Universe. (p. 387)
Sadler, R. D. Littlest Bell. (p. 1038)
Sadler, Sonia Lynn, illus. see Johnson, Jen Cullerton.
Sadler, Sonia Lynn, illus. see Patrick, Denise Lewis.
Sadler, Stefani, jt. auth. see Jarboe, Tracy.
Sadler, Wendy. Electricity: Turn It On! (p. 509)
—Magnets: Sticking Together! (p. 1076)
—Sound: Listen Up! (p. 1615)
—Using Levers (p. 1828)
Sadler, Wesley L. Saada - His Story. (p. 1499)
Sadlier, Rosemary. Kids Book of Black Canadian History. Wang, Qijun, illus. (p. 952)
Sadorus, Lauri. Pacific Halibut Flat or Fiction? Soderlund, Birgit, illus. (p. 1317)
Sadowski, Frank, ed. see Vasari, Giorgio.
Sadowski, Jeff, illus. see Tully, Sandra M.
Sadowski, Stephen, illus. see Robinson, James, et al.
Sadrozinski, Priya. Priya Said See Ya: Illustrated Rhymes. (p. 1408)
Sadu, Itah. Touch of the Zebras. (p. 1772)
Sadu, Itah & Condy, Roy. Christopher Changes His Name. (p. 316)
Saeed, Aisha. Written in the Stars. (p. 1965)
Saeed, Mahmud S. Model of the Muslim Youth in the Story of Prophet Yusuf. (p. 1157)
Saefkow, Hans, jt. auth. see Sudbury, Dave.
Saenagi, Ryo, et al. Sequence (p. 1552)
Saenger, Diana. Everyone Wants My Job! The ABCs of Entertainment Writing. Fife, Bruce, ed. (p. 544)
Saenger, Stefanie. Grow Healthy Little One. (p. 726)
Saenz, Benjamin Alire. Aristotle & Dante Discover the Secrets of the Universe. (p. 98)
Sáenz, Benjamin Alire. Aristotle & Dante Discover the Secrets of the Universe. (p. 98)

—Gift from Papa Diego: Un Regalo de Papa Diego. Garcia, Geronimo, illus. (p. 675)
—He Forgot to Say Goodbye. (p. 756)
—Last Night I Sang to the Monster. (p. 978)
—Perfect Season for Dreaming (Un Tiempo Perfecto para Soñar) Andrade Valencia, Esau, illus. (p. 1342)
—Perrita Que le Encantaban las Tortillas. Garcia, Geronimo, illus. (p. 1343)
—Sammy & Juliana in Hollywood. (p. 1507)
—Tiempo Perfecto para Sonar. Valencia, Esau Andrade, illus. (p. 1748)
Sáenz, Miguel, tr. see Ende, Michael.
Saenz, Moises. Indian, Citizen of America. (p. 871)
Saenz, Sandra C. Lot the Tot & the Beautiful Pearl. (p. 1057)
—Precious Gift. (p. 1394)
Saez Castan, Javier. Tres Erizos. (p. 1784)
Saez, Fernando, illus. see de Cervantes, Miguel.
Saez, Javier, illus. see Murugarren, Miguel.
Saez, Sofia, illus. see De Matos, Isabel Freire.
Safai, Nasrin. Gifts from the Masters of Light: Journeys into the Inner Realms of Consciousness - Gifts III. (p. 675)
—Path to Enlightenment, The Pillar of Light (p. 1328)
Safar, Lina, illus. see Barberi, Gladys.
Safar, Lina, illus. see Maillis, Nicole.
Safar, Lina, illus. see Shein, Erik Daniel & Reker, Martin.
Safar, Lina, illus. see Shein, Erik Daniel.
Safarewicz, Evie, illus. see Tatchell, Judy.
Safari Press Staff, ed. Book Buddy - Elephant with Story Book. (p. 210)
—Book Buddy - Hippo with Story Book. (p. 210)
—Book Buddy - Lion with Story Book. (p. 210)
—Book Buddy - Tiger with Story Book. (p. 210)
Safe Kids USA Staff. Self-Defense for Kids: Learn Practical & Effective Techniques to Help You Defend Yourself. (p. 1549)
Safeblade, Evelyn. Summer Cottage. (p. 1674)
—White Birch. (p. 1912)
Safer, Catherine Hogan. What If Your Mom Made Raisin Buns? Rose, Hilda, illus. (p. 1887)
Saferstein, Mark J., compiled by. Oh, Ranger! True Stories from our National Parks. (p. 1281)
Saffell, Robert. Farm Boy. (p. 573)
Saffer, Barbara. ABC Science Riddles. Johnson, Jennifer, illus. (p. 3)
—Harry S. Truman. (p. 751)
Saffer, Sally. Friend in Need Is a Friend Indeed: A Lesson Within a Story from the Series, Learning to Be Wise. (p. 637)
—It's No Use Crying over Spilled Milk: A Lesson Within a Story from the Series, Learning to be Wise. (p. 897)
Saffiedine, Amanda. Goodnight Sweet Baby: A Collection of Short Stories. (p. 701)
—I Don't Understand. (p. 838)
Saffioti, Trina. Old Frangipani Tree at Flying Fish Point. Prewett, Maggie, illus. (p. 1283)
Saffter, Sally. Every Cloud Has a Silver Lining: A Lesson Within a Story from the Series Learning to Be Wise. (p. 542)
Safley, Beverly M. Tale of a Crab. (p. 1699)
Safran, Faigy. Uncle Moishy Visits Torah Island. Snowden, Linda, illus. (p. 1812)
Safran, Sheri. All Kinds of Babies. Damon, Emma, illus. (p. 44)
—All Kinds of Beliefs. Damon, Emma, illus. (p. 44)
—All Kinds of Fears. Brownjohn, Emma, illus. (p. 44)
—All Kinds of Feelings. Brownjohn, Emma, illus. (p. 44)
—All Kinds of Festivals. Fuller, Rachel, illus. (p. 45)
—All Kinds of People. Damon, Emma, illus. (p. 45)
—Bully. Tipping, Naomi, illus. (p. 241)
—Let's Dress! Fuller, Rachel, illus. (p. 996)
—Magic Carousel: A Book & Removable 3-D Play Carousel. Safran, Sheri, illus. (p. 1072)
—Orchestra! Robinson, Nicola L., illus. (p. 1302)
Safren, Hannah. Dive: The Life & Fight of Reba Tutt. (p. 454)
Safro, Jill. 5-Minute Proofreading Practice: 180 Quick & Motivating Activities Students Can Use to Practice Essential Proofreading Skills-Every Day of the School Year. (p. 1992)
—Math Word Problems Made Easy: Surefire Strategies-With 100+ Guided & Independent Practice Problems-That Give Kids the Tools to Tackle All Kinds of Word Problems. (p. 1107)
Safro, Jill, ed. see Sweeny, Sheila.
Safro, Jill, ed. Birnbaum's Walt Disney World Dining Guide. (p. 192)
—Disney Cruise Line 2008. Wright, Alex, illus. (p. 451)
Saft, Lauren. Those Girls. (p. 1740)
Sagar, Marie. Cuddly Sam. (p. 389)
—Jimmy's Adventures: I'm Bored & Mr. Gray Bat. (p. 918)
—Magical Snowman. (p. 1075)
—Pirate Hill. (p. 1362)
—Princess Samantha? (p. 1405)
SAGARA, S. O. U. Hentai Prince & the Stony Cat. (p. 769)
Sagasti, Miriam, illus. see Kolodny, Cynthia.
Sagasti, Miriam, illus. see Lundy, Charlotte.
Sagasti, Miriam, illus. see Metzger, Steve.
Saga-Whyte. Why the Naiads Dance: Book One of the Naiad Legends Saga-Whyte, illus. (p. 1926)
Sage, Alison. Stop That Robot! Band 00/Lilac. Dunn, Gary, illus. (p. 1653)
—What Is CGI? Band 06/Orange. Stuart, Jon, illus. (p. 1889)
Sage, Angie. Araminta Spookie: The Sword in the Grotto. Pickering, Jimmy, illus. (p. 94)
—Darke (p. 408)
—Darke. Zug, Mark, illus. (p. 408)
—Flyte. (p. 610)
—Flyte. Zug, Mark, illus. (p. 610)
—Frognapped. Pickering, Jimmy, illus. (p. 641)
—Fyre. (p. 651)
—Fyre. Zug, Mark, illus. (p. 651)
—Gargoyle Hall: An Araminta Spookie Adventure. (p. 657)
—Ghostsitters. Pickering, Jimmy, illus. (p. 673)
—Magyk. (p. 1076)
—Magyk. Zug, Mark, illus. (p. 1076)
—Magykal Papers. Zug, Mark, illus. (p. 1076)
—My Haunted House. Pickering, Jimmy, illus. (p. 1210)
—Physik (p. 1353)
—Physik. (p. 1353)
—Physik. Zug, Mark, illus. (p. 1353)
—Queste. Zug, Mark, illus. (p. 1426)
—Sandrider. (p. 1511)
—Septimus Heap Zug, Mark, illus. (p. 1551)
—Septimus Heap, Book Seven: Fyre. Zug, Mark, illus. (p. 1551)
—Septimus Heap - Todhunter Moon. Zug, Mark, illus. (p. 1551)
—Sword in the Grotto. Pickering, Jimmy, illus. (p. 1692)
—Syren. Zug, Mark, illus. (p. 1693)
—Todhunter Moon. Zug, Mark, illus. (p. 1761)
—Vampire Brat. Pickering, Jimmy, illus. (p. 1832)
Sage, C. O. Nitro: A Wild Mustang. (p. 1257)
—Patches, A Bucking Bull: Son of Mabel. (p. 1328)
—Pete Goes on Vacation. (p. 1346)
Sage, Cathryn. Destiny's Secret. (p. 431)
Sage, David. Adzul, the Heirs of the Medallion Book 1. (p. 25)
Sage, Lorna. Angela Carter. (p. 74)
Sage, Molly. At the Beach. Sage, Molly, illus. (p. 110)
Sage, Molly, illus. see Gilpin, Rebecca.
Sage, Molly, illus. see Gulliver, Amanda & Turnbull, Stephanie.
Sage, Molly, illus. see Pratt, Leonie & Atkinson, Catherine.
Sage, Molly, illus. see Watt, Fiona.
Sage, Trina, illus. see Krohn, Kathryn T.
Sage-Midgorden, Lucinda. Scottosaurus the Little Dinosaur. Midgorden, Barry, illus. (p. 1532)
Sagendorph, Jean. Starry Night, Hold Me Tight. Siebold, Kim, illus. (p. 1642)
Sager, Michelle, illus. see Delaney, Lawrence.
Sagerman, Evan. Giraffe Rescue Company. Chou, Joey, illus. (p. 677)
Saghafi, Majid, tr. see Akbarpour, Ahmad.
Saguchi, Kensaku. Biographical Comics: Christopher Columbus: The Merchant Adventurer. Miyazoe, Ikuo, illus. (p. 188)
Sah, Anup, photos by see Ledu-Frattini, Stephanie.
Saha, Tulika. 'Kosho & Sid on the Rainbow' (p. 967)
Sahai, Supriya, illus. see Patel, Mukul.
Sahgal, Lara & Levy, Janey. Primary Source Investigation of the Erie Canal. (p. 1400)
Saia, Karla, ed. see Coy, Steven.
Saia, Stephanie. Hunting with Crocodiles. (p. 829)
Saichann, Alberto, illus. see Lagonegro, Melissa & RH Disney Staff.
Said. Snow Bears Never Lie. Ludin, Marine, illus. (p. 1598)
Said, S. F. Varjak Paw. McKean, Dave, illus. (p. 1833)
Said, Taunya D. Smart Alec- Alex: The 5th Grade Schedule Change. (p. 1592)
Saidens, Amy, illus. see Zeer, Darrin.
Saidens, Amy, jt. auth. see Burnham, Niki.
Saiga, Reiji & Inoue, Sora. Real Bout High School Kennedy, Ai, tr. (p. 1448)
Saigeon, Lori. Fight for Justice (p. 585)
Saijiyo, Shinji & Saijyo, Shinji. Iron Wok Jan! (p. 888)
Saijyo, Shinji. Iron Wok Jan! (p. 888)
—Iron Wok Jan! Saijyo, Shinji, illus. (p. 888)
Saijyo, Shinji, jt. auth. see Saijiyo, Shinji.
Saikal, Amin. Modern Afghanistan: A History of Struggle & Survival. (p. 1158)
Saikia, Mayur. Anansi & His Children. (p. 67)
Sail, Nicola, jt. auth. see Rigby, Christopher.
Saillard, Remi. Funny Machines for George the Sheep: A Children's Book Inspired by Leonardo Da Vinci. (p. 650)
Sailors, Misty, jt. ed. see Hiebert, Elfrieda H.
Sain, Judy L. Daily Math SKills Review Grade 4: Practice for Mastery of Math Standards. (p. 400)
Saincantin, Jerome, tr. see Dorison, Xavier.
Saincantin, Jerome, tr. see Gilson.
Saincantin, Jerome, tr. see Tome.
Saincatin, Jerome, tr. see Runberg, Sylivain.
Saincatin, Jerome, tr. see Runberg, Sylvain.
Saincilus, Larimer, illus. see Jeune, Marie Carole.
Sainlouis, Kercise. Danielle's Amazing Day. (p. 405)
Sainsbury, Adam. Coin. (p. 338)
Sainsbury, Kylee. Anna Banana Goes to Se. (p. 85)
Sainsilus, Ismer, illus. see Hudicourt, Caroline.
Saint Cyr, Vanessa. Straggly Smile. Petch, Fionn, tr. (p. 1664)
Saint James, Synthia, illus. see Barnwell, Ysaye M.
Saint James, Synthia, illus. see Nikola-lisa, W. & Nikola-lisa, W.
Saint James, Synthia, illus. see Sneve, Virginia Driving Hawk.
Saint, Mimi. Bride's Price. Wendt, Yohanna, illus. (p. 227)
Sainte Croix, Judith. Everything You Need to Know about Meditation. (p. 545)
Saint-Exupéry, Antoine de. Little Prince. (p. 1033)
—Little Prince 70th Anniversary Gift Set (Book/CD/Downloadable Audio) Howard, Richard, tr. (p. 1033)
—Little Prince Graphic Novel. Sfar, Joann, illus. (p. 1033)
Saint-Exupery, Antoine De, see de Saint-Exupéry, Antoine.
Saint-James, Synthia, illus. see Hull, Bunny.
Saint-Lot, Katia Novet. Amadi's Snowman. Tokunbo, Dimitrea, illus. (p. 51)
Saint-Onge, Danielle, jt. auth. see Szpirglas, Jeff.
Saint-Saens, Camille. Aquarium: Hands-on Music: an iconic listening experience in Felt. (p. 94)
—Aquarium (Craft Kit) Hands-on Music: an Iconic Listening Experience in Felt. (p. 94)
SAINZ DE LA MAZA, ARO, et al. Cuentos de Todos Los Colores. (p. 390)
Saito, Chiho. Revolutionary Girl Utena: To Sprout. Vol. 3 (p. 1466)
—Revolutionary Girl Utena: To Till Saito, Chiho, illus. (p. 1466)
—Revolutionary Girl Utena: The Adolescence of Utena. Saito, Chiho, illus. (p. 1466)
—Revolutionary Girl Utena. Be-Papas, illus. (p. 1466)
Saito, Ioe, illus. see McCarthy, Ralph F.
Saito, Kazu, photos by see Pace, Teruko, tr.
Saito, Masamitsu, illus. see Konagaya, Kiyomi.
Saito, Ryusuke & Takidaira, Jiro. Tree of Courage. Laughlin, Sako, tr. (p. 1783)
Saito, Taeko. Kiss the Frog. (p. 961)
Saito, Takao. Orbital Hit. (p. 1302)
Saitou, Chiho, illus. see Be-Papas.
Saitta, Kevin. 2007 a Poetic Journey. (p. 2003)
Saiyjo, Shinji. Iron Wok Jan! (p. 888)
Sajewel, Jamie. Do Watermelons Grow on Trees? (p. 457)
Sajjad, Mohammad. Insecticide Resistance Management in Tomato Fruit Borer. (p. 875)
Sak., M. J. Stone Summons. (p. 1653)
Sakade, Florence. Japanese Children's Favorite Stories. Kurosaki, Yoshisuke, illus. (p. 909)
—More Japanese Children's Favorite Stories. Hayashi, Yoshio, illus. (p. 1174)
Sakade, Florence & Hayashi, Yoshio. Kintaro's Adventures & Other Japanese Children's Favorite Stories. (p. 961)
—Urashima Taro & Other Japanese Children's Favorite Stories. Kurosaki, Yoshisuke, illus. (p. 1825)
Sakade, Florence & Kurosaki, Yoshisuke. Little One-Inch & Other Japanese Children's Favorite Stories. (p. 1032)
—Peach Boy & Other Japanese Children's Favorite Stories. (p. 1332)
Sakadolsky, Kimberly. Jeff Jinxed Me. (p. 912)
Sakai, Komako. Emily's Balloon. (p. 519)
—Hannah's Night. (p. 743)
—Mad at Mommy. Sakai, Komako, illus. (p. 1068)
—Snow Day. (p. 1598)
Sakai, Komako, illus. see Kato, Yukiko.
Sakai, Komako, illus. see Nakawaki, Hatsue.
Sakai, Komako, creator. Velveteen Rabbit. (p. 1835)
Sakai, Stan. Adventures of Nilson Groundthumper & Hermy. Wright, Brendan, ed. (p. 21)
—Usagi Yojimbo: Segadora. Vol. 5 (p. 1826)
—Usagi Yojimbo: Estaciones. Vol. 4 (p. 1826)
—Usagi Yojimbo: Primeras Andanzas. Vol. 6 (p. 1826)
—Usagi Yojimbo: Samurai (en Español) Vol. 7 (p. 1826)
—Usagi Yojimbo: Al Filo de la Vida y la Muerte. Vol. 3 (p. 1826)
—Usagi Yojimbo Saga (p. 1826)
—Usagi Yojimbo Saga Volume 3. Sakai, Stan, illus. (p. 1826)
—Usagi Yojimbo Saga Volume 3 Ltd. Ed. Sakai, Stan, illus. (p. 1826)
—Usagi Yojimbo Volume 26: Traitors of the Earth: Traitors of the Earth. Schutz, Diana, ed. (p. 1826)
Sakakura, Yoshinobu, illus. see Yasuda, Yuri & Yasuda, Yuri Old tales of Japan.
Sakamoto, Miki, illus. see Dunn, Todd.
Sakamoto, Miki, illus. see Froeb, Lori C.
Sakamoto, Miki, illus. see Froeb, Lori.
Sakamoto, Miki, illus. see Gainer, Cindy.
Sakamoto, Miki, illus. see Lewison, Wendy Cheyette.
Sakamoto, Miki, illus. see Metzger, Steve.
Sakamoto, Miki, illus. see Singer, Marilyn.
Sakamoto, Miki, illus. see Zobel-Nolan, Allia.
Sakanakun. Gensundai Suizokukan. Matsuzawa, Yoji, photos by. (p. 661)
Sakany, Lois. Canada: A Primary Source Cultural Guide. (p. 260)
—Cell Regulation: Understanding How Cell Functions, Growth, & Division Are Regulated. (p. 286)
—Joe DiMaggio. (p. 920)
—Joe Dimaggio. (p. 920)
—Progressive Leaders: The Platforms & Policies of America's Reform Politicians. (p. 1410)
—Women Civil War Spies of the Union. (p. 1945)
Sakany, Lois, jt. auth. see Tucker, Clementine.
Saker, Linda, illus. see Sills, Elizabeth & Patrice, Elena.
Sakevich, C. J., illus. see Sakevich, Linda & C. J.
Sakevich, Linda & C. J. Sister-Brother Adoption Day: Updated Edition. Sakevich, C. J., illus. (p. 1581)
—Sister-Sister Adoption Day: Updated Edition. Sakevich, C. J., illus. (p. 1581)
Sakhavarz, Nazy, illus. see Brass, Alice.
Saki. Contador de Cuentos. Canales, Veronica & Guix, Juan Gabriel Lopez, trs. (p. 360)
Saki, Lily. Alien Attack. (p. 40)
Sakkai, Yohei. Dinosaur King. Sakkai, Yohei, illus. (p. 442)
Sakmar-Sullivan, Eva M. Kangaroo's Out of This World Restaurant Sakmar-Sullivan, Eva M., illus. (p. 942)
—Silly Looking Thing (p. 1576)
—Willie the Taxi Cat (p. 1934)
Sakolsky, Josh. Copernicus & Modern Astronomy. (p. 365)
—Critical Perspectives on the Industrial Revolution. (p. 383)
Sakowicz, G. Rosary. (p. 1489)
Sakowski, Nadeen. Adventures of Bailey Wiggins. (p. 16)
Sakprayoonpong, Worachet Boon, illus. see Friedlander, Mark P., Jr.
Saksena, Salini. Anthony Horowitz. (p. 89)
Sakura, Ken-Ichi. Dragon Drive, Volume 5. Sakura, Ken-Ichi, illus. (p. 477)
Sakuragi, Yukiya. Inubaka - Crazy for Dogs Vol. 1. Sakuragi, Yukiya, illus. (p. 883)
Sakurai, Ami. Innocent World. Clark, Steven, tr. from JPN. (p. 875)
Sakurakoji, Kanoko. Black Bird. Sakurakoji, Kanoko, illus. (p. 195)
Sakurazawa, Erica. Between the Sheets. (p. 173)
Sakurazawa, Erika. Erika Sakurazawa: Angel Nest. (p. 533)
Sakya, Kalden D. Life of the Great Mahasiddha Virupa. (p. 1012)
Sala, George Augustus. Captain Dangerous. (p. 264)
Sala, Richard. Cat Burglar Black. Sala, Richard, illus. (p. 277)
—Hidden. (p. 775)
Sala, Sharon. Amen Trail. (p. 58)
—Lunatic Detective. (p. 1065)
—Lunatic Revenge. (p. 1065)
Salaam, Kiini Ibura, ed. see Wolos-Fonteno, Mary, et al.
Sala-I-Martin, Xavier. Global Competitiveness Report 2006-2007. Porter, Michael E. et al, eds. (p. 684)
Salamoff, Paul J. Bo Obama: The White House Tails. (p. 205)
Salamon, Julie. Cat in the City. Weber, Jill, illus. (p. 278)
Salamunic, Tim, illus. see Anderson, Kirsten.
Salan, Felipe Lopez. Jack & the Beanstalk. (p. 902)
Salandria, Vincent J. False Mystery: Essays on the Assassination of JFK. Kelin, John, ed. (p. 567)
Salane, Jeffrey. Justice. (p. 940)
—Lawless. (p. 981)
—Lawless: Book 1. (p. 981)
—Lego Movie. Kiernan, Kenny, illus. (p. 990)
Salanitro, Robert, illus. see Benhamu, Margaret.
Salanitro, Robert, illus. see Rosenberg, Amye.
Salant, Dawnelle. Smile. (p. 1593)
Salardino, Nicholas. I Can Paint a Rainbow of Words. Hughes, Serifati, illus. (p. 836)
Salariya, David. Ancient Greek Myths. (p. 69)
Salariya, David, illus. see Legg, Gerald.
Salariya, David, jt. auth. see Cook, Peter.
Salariya, David, jt. auth. see Ford, Michael.
Salariya, David, jt. auth. see Matthews, Rupert.
Salariya, David, jt. auth. see Morley, Jacqueline.
Salariya, David & Williams, Mark. Animal Atlas. (p. 76)
Salariya, David, creator. Scary Creatures (p. 1520)
Salas, Laura Purdie. Amphibians: Water-to-Land Animals. Kest, Kristin, illus. (p. 65)
—And Then There Were Eight: Poems about Space (p. 71)
—Are You Living? A Song about Living & Nonliving Things Garofoli, Viviana, illus. (p. 97)
—BookSpeak! Poems about Books. Bisaillon, Josée, illus. (p. 213)
—C Is for Cake! A Birthday Alphabet (p. 249)
—Canoeing. (p. 261)
—Catch Your Breath: Writing Poignant Poetry. (p. 279)
—Chatter, Sing, Roar, Buzz: Poems about the Rain Forest. (p. 295)
—Colors of Fall (p. 345)
—Colors of Insects (p. 345)
—Colors of Sports (p. 345)
—Colors of the Ocean (p. 345)
—Colors of Weather (p. 345)
—Coral Reefs: Colorful Underwater Habitats Yesh, Jeff, illus. (p. 366)
—Deserts: Thirsty Wonderlands Yesh, Jeff, illus. (p. 429)
—Desiertos: Tierras Secas Abello, Patricia, tr. from ENG. (p. 429)
—Discovering Nature's Laws: A Story about Isaac Newton. Reynolds, Emily C. S., tr. (p. 449)
—Do Buses Eat Kids? Poems about School (p. 456)
—Do Crocodiles Dance? A Book about Animal Habits. Yesh, Jeff, illus. (p. 456)
—Do Polar Bears Snooze in Hollow Trees? A Book about Animal Hibernation. Ouren, Todd, illus. (p. 457)
—Do Turtles Sleep in Treetops? A Book about Animal Homes Yesh, Jeff, illus. (p. 457)
—Eight Great Planets! A Song about the Planets De Giorgi, Sergio, illus. (p. 507)
—Flashy, Clashy, & Oh-So Splashy: Poems about Color (p. 602)
—From Beginning to End: A Song about Life Cycles Garofoli, Viviana, illus. (p. 642)
—From Mealworm to Beetle: Following the Life Cycle Yesh, Jeff, illus. (p. 643)
—From Seed to Daisy: Following the Life Cycle Yesh, Jeff, illus. (p. 643)
—From Seed to Maple Tree: Following the Life Cycle Yesh, Jeff, illus. (p. 643)
—Fuzzy-Fast Blur: Poems about Pets. (p. 651)
—Home on the Earth: A Song about Earth's Layers Garofoli, Viviana, illus. (p. 792)
—Humedales: Hábitats Húmedos. Abello, Patricia, tr. from ENG. (p. 826)
—Ice Fishing. (p. 850)
—I'm Exploring with My Senses: A Song about the Five Senses De Giorgi, Sergio, illus. (p. 858)
—Is for Arrr! A Pirate Alphabet (p. 889)
—J Is for Jingle Bells: A Christmas Alphabet (p. 901)
—Leaf Can Be- Dabija, Violeta, illus. (p. 982)
—Lettuce Introduce You: Poems about Food. (p. 1003)
—Mammals: Hairy, Milk-Making Animals. Solomon, Rosiland, illus. (p. 1085)
—Many Creatures: A Song about Animal Classifications De Giorgi, Sergio, illus. (p. 1089)
—Océanos: Mundos Submarinos. Abello, Patricia, tr. from ENG. (p. 1277)
—P Is for Pom Pom! A Cheerleading Alphabet (p. 1316)
—Pastizales: Campos Verdes y Dorados. Abello, Patricia, tr. from ENG. (p. 1327)
—Picture Yourself Writing Poetry: Using Photos to Inspire Writing (p. 1356)
—Rain Forests: Gardens of Green Yesh, Jeff, illus. (p. 1434)
—Reptiles: Scaly-Skinned Animals. Solomon, Rosiland, illus. (p. 1461)
—Rock Can Be . . Dabija, Violeta, illus. (p. 1482)
—S Is for Score! A Sports Alphabet (p. 1499)
—Saltwater Fishing. (p. 1506)
—Selvas Tropicales: Mundos Verdes Abello, Patricia, tr. from ENG. (p. 1550)
—Shrinking Days, Frosty Nights: Poems about Fall (p. 1571)
—Snowmobiling. (p. 1601)
—Taking the Plunge. (p. 1698)
—Temperate Deciduous Forests: Lands of Falling Leaves Yesh, Jeff, illus. (p. 1717)
—There Goes the Water: A Song about the Water Cycle De Giorgi, Sergio, illus. (p. 1729)
—Tiny Dreams, Sprouting Tall: Poems about the United States (p. 1756)
—Tundras: Frosty, Treeless Lands Yesh, Jeff, illus. (p. 1796)
—Water Can Be ... Dabija, Violeta, illus. (p. 1862)
—Whose Gloves Are These? A Look at Gloves Workers Wear - Leather, Cloth, & Rubber Muehlenhardt, Amy Bailey, illus. (p. 1921)
—Whose Shoes Are These? A Look at Workers' Footwear - Slippers, Sneakers, & Boots Muehlenhardt, Amy Bailey, illus. (p. 1922)
—Write Your Own Poetry. (p. 1964)
—Y Is for Yak: A Zoo Alphabet (p. 1968)
—Y Is for Yowl! A Scary Alphabet (p. 1968)
—Z Is for Zoom! A Race Car Alphabet. (p. 1984)
Salas, Laura Purdie, jt. auth. see Menhard, Francha Roffe.
Salas, Laura Purdie & Nichols, Cheyenne. Sad Is... (p. 1501)
—Sad Is ... (p. 1501)
—Scared Is... (p. 1519)
—Scared Is ... (p. 1519)

Salas, Laura Purdie & Purdie Salas, Laura. Phillis Wheatley: Colonial American Poet (p. 1351)
Salas, Laura Purdie & Weakland, Mark. Bubbles Float, Bubbles Pop (p. 233)
Salas-Tristan, M. U. Rocky's ABC Book with His Friends: Photographic Bilingual. (p. 1484)
Salati, Giorgio, jt. auth. see Secchi, Richard.
Salaver, Jillianne & Williams, Tim. UC Irvine College Prowler off the Record: Inside University of California Irvine. (p. 1807)
Salazar, L. J. Chin & the Magic Stones: Book One - Becoming Guardians. (p. 306)
Salazar, Martinez Lydia. Lily, the Lost & Found Lamb. (p. 1018)
Salazar, Riana, illus. see Roller, Pat Kellogg.
Salazar, Sam. Jordin Sparks. (p. 925)
—One Direction. (p. 1294)
Salazar, Sam & Kennon, Michou. Jordin Sparks. (p. 925)
Salazar, Sharon, jt. auth. see LaRoe, Locki.
Salazar, Souther. Destined for Dizzyness. Salazar, Souther, illus. (p. 430)
Salazar, Vivian, illus. see Bass, William E.
Salazar, Vivian Rose, illus. see Bass, William E.
Salcedo, Betsy. Together we Can. (p. 1762)
Salch, Megan. 100+ Activities for Houston Kids 2006. (p. 1998)
Saldaña, Jr. Good Long Way. (p. 698)
Saldana, Rene. Case of Pen Gone Missing/El Caso de la Pluma Perdida. Villarroel, Carolina, tr. from ENG. (p. 273)
—Dale, Dale, Dale / Hit It, Hit It, Hit It: Una Fiesta de Numeros / a Fiesta of Numbers. Flores, Carolyn Dee, illus. (p. 401)
Saldaña, René. Dancing with the Devil & Other Tales from Beyond / Bailando con el Diablo y Otros Cuentos del Más Allá. Baeza Ventura, Gabriela, tr. from ENG. (p. 403)
—Lemon Tree Caper: A Mickey Rangel Mystery / la Intriga del limonero: Colección Mickey Rangel, detective Privado. Rosales-Yeomans, Natalia, tr. from ENG. (p. 991)
—Mystery of the Mischievous Marker / el Misterio Del Malvado Marcador: A Mickey Rangel Mystery / Colección Mickey Rangel, Detective Privado. Villarroel, Carolina, tr. from ENG. (p. 1225)
Saldana, Rene. Whole Sky Full of Stars. (p. 1920)
Saldana, Rene, Jr. Jumping Tree. (p. 934)
Saldana, Theresa. Almost Murder & Other Stories. (p. 48)
Saldin, Erin. Girls of No Return. (p. 680)
Saldivar, Jose A. Adventures of Oskar: Oskar's New School. Nilsson, Janet Busbey, ed. (p. 21)
Sale, Carolyn. How to Read a Dinosaur & Other Museum Tales. Dubinsky, Lon, ed. (p. 821)
Sale, Graham, illus. see Boritzer, Etan.
Sale, Tim, illus. see Loeb, Jeph.
Sale, Tim, jt. auth. see Loeb, Jeph.
Sale, Tim, et al. Buffy the Vampire Slayer: Tales of the Slayers: Tales of the Slayers. Russell, P. Craig, illus. (p. 236)
Saleem-Muhammad, Rasheedah. My Friend Michael: A Short Story about Autism - A Pedro Collection. Harris, - Crystal, illus. (p. 1209)
Saleff, Olga. Baba's Bedtime Stories. (p. 123)
Saleh, Amal Kamal Ali. Guess Who My Best Friend Is. (p. 729)
Salem, I., jt. auth. see Wigden, Susan.
Salem, Iosi. Mitzva for Zelda Coloring Book. (p. 1156)
—Mr. Mentch Coloring Book. (p. 1185)
Salem, Iosi, illus. see Fridman, Sashi.
Salem Press Editors, ed. Cyclopedia of Young Adult Authors (p. 397)
Salem Press Staff. American Presidents Magill, Frank N., ed. (p. 62)
—Ancient Greece Sienkewicz, Thomas J., ed. (p. 69)
—Drama Rollyson, Carl E. & Magill, Frank N., eds. (p. 480)
—Masterplots II: Christian Literature Roth, John K., ed. (p. 1103)
—United States at War Super, John C., ed. (p. 1819)
—World Conflicts, Asia & the Middle East Bankston, Carl L., ed. (p. 1954)
Salem Press Staff, jt. auth. see Herrera-Sobek, Maria.
Salem Press Staff, jt. auth. see Link, Eric Carl.
Salem Press Staff, jt. auth. see Lynch, Jack.
Salem Press Staff, jt. auth. see Murdoch, Brian.
Salem Press Staff, jt. auth. see Mustazza, Leonard.
Salem Press Staff, jt. auth. see Newlin, Keith.
Salen, Jill. Corsets: Historic Patterns & Techniques. (p. 368)
Salenas, Bobbi. Cinderella Latina - Cinicienta Latina. La Madrid, Enriquee, tr. (p. 320)
Salerni, Dianne K. Caged Graves. (p. 251)
—Eighth Day. McClellan, David, illus. (p. 507)
—Inquisitor's Mark: Book 2 in the Eighth Day Series. (p. 875)
—Inquisitor's Mark. (p. 875)
—We Hear the Dead. (p. 1867)
Salerno, Dorsey P. Latin for Beginners. (p. 979)
Salerno, John, illus. see Messinger, Robert.
Salerno, Steven. Little Tumbo (p. 1037)
—Wild Child. (p. 1929)
Salerno, Steven, illus. see Brown, Margaret Wise.
Salerno, Steven, illus. see Elya, Susan Middleton.
Salerno, Steven, illus. see Franco, Betsy.
Salerno, Steven, illus. see Freeman, Martha.
Salerno, Steven, illus. see Orgill, Roxane & Orgill.
Salerno, Steven, illus. see Vernick, Audrey.
Salerno, Steven, jt. auth. see Franco, Betsy.
Salerno, Steven, tr. see Orgill, Roxane & Orgill.
Salerno, Tony. Dog Tired: A Learning Adventure in Perseverance (p. 461)
—Sticky Situation: A Learning Adventure in Honesty. (p. 1650)
—Where's Beeper? A Learning Adventure in Helpfulness (p. 1910)
—Wise Quacks: A Learning Adventure in Self-Control (p. 1940)
Salerno, Tony, et al. Tony Salerno's Good News Express. Thompson, Del et al, illus. (p. 1766)
Sales, Bob. Day Jesus Came to Town. (p. 413)
Sales, Jordi, illus. see García, César Fernández.
Sales, Kyle M. On Our Way to Fontinasi. (p. 1289)
Sales, Leila. Mostly Good Girls. (p. 1177)
—Past Perfect. (p. 1327)
—This Song Will Save Your Life. (p. 1737)
—Tonight the Streets Are Ours. (p. 1765)
Sales, Virginia. Prairie Flours. (p. 1392)
Salesman, Awel P. Jo-Dene's Little Feet. (p. 919)
Salesse, Alain, illus. see Chihak, Sheena.
Salg, Bert, illus. see Edwards, Leo.
Salg, Bert, illus. see Heyliger, William.
Salg, Bert, illus. see Lloyd, Hugh.
Salgado. Nuevas Canciones Infantiles. (p. 1270)
Salgado, Tono. Versos y Rimas para Ninos. (p. 1837)
Salgari, Emilio, jt. auth. see Salgari, Emilio.
Salgari, Emilio & Salgari, Emilio. Pirates de Malasia. (p. 1363)
—Tigres de Mom Pracem. (p. 1749)
Salib Salibi, Nuha. Palm Tree & the Fir. (p. 1320)
Saliba, Theresa. Surviving HIV/AIDS. (p. 1687)
Salicrup, Jim & Gladir, George. Bed Bugged. Goldberg, Stan, illus. (p. 156)
—Three Stooges Graphic Novels #1: Bed Bugged. Goldberg, Stan, illus. (p. 1744)
Salicrup, Jim, et al. My Name Is Orange - Secret Agent Orange! Parker, Rick, illus. (p. 1215)
—Orange You Glad You're Not Me? Parker, Rick, illus. (p. 1302)
—Orange You Glad You're Not Me? No. 2. Parker, Rick, illus. (p. 1302)
—Secret Agent Orange. Parker, Rick, illus. (p. 1540)
Salimena, Kathleen Elizabeth. Royal Yacht. (p. 1492)
Salinas, Alex, illus. see Martin, Bob.
Salinas, Eva. Inventaron los Latinoamericanos: Innovaciones Asombrosas. (p. 883)
—Latin Americans Thought of It: Amazing Innovations. (p. 979)
Salinas, Robert C., et al. Encyclopedia of Death & Dying. (p. 525)
Salinas, Sonia. Muu muuu dice una Vaca. Alfaro, Luis, illus. (p. 1195)
Salinas, Veronica. Voyage Eirheim, Jeanne, tr. from NOR. (p. 1850)
Salina-Thompson, Andrea. D. D. the Cross-Eyed Kitty. (p. 397)
Salinger, J. D. Guardian Entre el Centeno. (p. 728)
Salin-Pascual, Rafael. espectro del seÑor Amok. (p. 536)
Salisbury, Graham. Calvin Coconut: Man Trip. Rogers, Jacqueline, illus. (p. 255)
—Calvin Coconut: Zoo Breath. Rogers, Jacqueline, illus. (p. 255)
—Calvin Coconut: Rocket Ride. Rogers, Jacqueline, illus. (p. 255)
—Calvin Coconut: Dog Heaven. Rogers, Jacqueline, illus. (p. 255)
—Calvin Coconut: Man Trip. Rogers, Jacqueline, illus. (p. 255)
—Calvin Coconut: Rocket Ride. Rogers, Jacqueline, illus. (p. 255)
—Calvin Coconut: Zoo Breath. Rogers, Jacqueline, illus. (p. 255)
—Extra Famous. Rogers, Jacqueline, illus. (p. 555)
—Hero of Hawaii. Rogers, Jacqueline, illus. (p. 772)
—House of the Red Fish. (p. 803)
—Hunt for the Bamboo Rat. (p. 828)
—Kung Fooey. Rogers, Jacqueline, illus. (p. 968)
—Lord of the Deep: A Novel. (p. 1052)
—Lord of the Deep. (p. 1052)
—Night of the Howling Dogs. (p. 1254)
—Trouble Magnet. Rogers, Jacqueline, illus. (p. 1790)
—Under the Blood Red Sun. (p. 1813)
—Under the Blood-Red Sun. (p. 1813)
—Zippy Fix. Rogers, Jacqueline, illus. (p. 1987)
Salisbury, Laurie. Reins of Love. (p. 1457)
Salisbury, Linda. Earthquake Surprise: A Bailey Fish Adventure. Tornatore, Carol, illus. (p. 497)
Salisbury, Linda G. Mudd Saves the Earth: Booger Glue, Cow Diapers & Other Good Ideas. (p. 1188)
—Mysterious Jamestown Suitcase: A Bailey Fish Adventure. Grotke, Christopher A., illus. (p. 1223)
—No Sisters Sisters Club: A Bailey Fish Adventure. Grotke, Christopher A., illus. (p. 1260)
—Thief at Keswick Inn: A Bailey Fish Adventure. Grotke, Christopher A., illus. (p. 1732)
—Trouble in Contrary Woods: A Bailey Fish Adventure. Tornatore, Carol, illus. (p. 1789)
—Wild Women of Lake Anna: A Bailey Fish Adventure. (p. 1930)
Salisbury, Melinda. Sin Eater's Daughter. (p. 1578)
Salkeld, Audrey. Climbing Everest: Tales of Triumph & Tragedy on the World's Highest Mountain. (p. 333)
Salkey, Andrew. Drought. (p. 486)
—Earthquake. (p. 497)
—Hurricane. (p. 829)
—Riot. (p. 1473)
Salkin, Jeffrey K. For Kids - Putting God on Your Guest List: How to Claim the Spiritual Meaning of Your Bar or Bat Mitzvah. (p. 615)
Salko, Donna. Gertie's Birdies: A Children's Guide to Friends That Fly. (p. 667)
Salladay, Brenda. Jungle Friends: Mack the Missing Monkey. (p. 935)
—Jungle Friends. (p. 935)
Sallah, Michael & Weiss, Mitch. Tiger Force: A True Story of Men & War. (p. 1748)
Salle, Katherine Talmadge. Daily Life Around the World: Text Pairs. (p. 399)
Sallen-Jackson, April. Away: An Adventure Just on the Other Side of Mysteria Bridge. (p. 120)
Salley, Coleen. Epossumondas Plays Possum. Stevens, Janet, illus. (p. 532)
—Epossumondas Saves the Day. Stevens, Janet, illus. (p. 532)
—Why Epossumondas Has No Hair on His Tail. Stevens, Janet, illus. (p. 1924)
Sallis, Zoe. Ten Eternal Questions: Wisdom, Insight, & Reflection for Life's Journey. (p. 1718)
Sallows, Lee C. F. Geometric Magic Squares: A Challenging New Twist Using Colored Shapes Instead of Numbers. (p. 662)
Sally Ride Science Editors, Sally Ride Science. What Do You Want to Be? Explore Earth Sciences. (p. 1883)
—What Do You Want to Be? Explore Engineering. (p. 1883)
—What Do You Want to Be? Explore Health Sciences. (p. 1883)
Sally Spencer. Juanita's Flowers. Phil Brannan & Sunni Brannan, illus. (p. 930)
Sally, Zak. Sammy the Mouse #1 (Ignatz) (p. 1508)
—Sammy the Mouse #2 (Ignatz) (p. 1508)
Salm, Arthur. Anyway: A Story about Me with 138 Footnotes, 27 Exaggerations, & 1 Plate of Spaghetti. (p. 91)
—Anyway* *a Story about Me with 138 Footnotes, 27 Exaggerations, & 1 Plate of Spaghetti. (p. 91)
Salm, René. Myth of Nazareth: The Invented Town of Jesus. (p. 1227)
Salma, Hammad. I am Beautiful. (p. 832)
Salma, Sergio. Penguins on Ice. (p. 1337)
Salmansohn, Pete & Kress, Stephen W. Giving Back to the Earth: Teacher's Guide to Project Puffin & Other Seabird Studies. Gagliardo, Lucy, illus. (p. 681)
—Saving Birds: Heroes Around the World (p. 1517)
Salmaso, Valentina, illus. see Piumini, Roberto.
Salmassian, Jennifer. Sally Saves the Mice. (p. 1505)
—Sally the Firefighter. (p. 1505)
Salmeron, Carmelo, jt. auth. see Narváez, Concha López.
Salmerón Carmelo, et al. leyenda del viajero que no podía detenerse. (p. 1004)
Salmeron Lopez, Rafael, illus. see Cruz-Contarini, Rafael & Rafael, Cruz-Contarini.
Salmeron, Rafael, illus. see Cruz-Contarini, Rafael & Rafael, Cruz-Contarini.
Salmeron, Rafael, illus. see Narváez, Concha López & Concha, López Narváez.
Salmieri, Daniel, illus. see Pennypacker, Sara.
Salmieri, Daniel, illus. see Rubin, Adam.
Salmon, Casey. Adventures of Mabel & Stinky: Mabel, Stinky, & the Terrified Toad. (p. 20)
Salmon, Charles Ray, afterword by. Adventures of Pittypat & Tippytoe (p. 21)
Salmon, Michael. Dinosaur. (p. 441)
Salmon, Nina. Nola & the Sprickle. (p. 1263)
Salmon, Peg. Percy & His Family. (p. 1341)
Salmon, Richard. William Makepeace Thackeray. (p. 1933)
Salmon, Sheryl. Adventures of Kaptain Kristian. (p. 19)
Salmon, Shirley. Hello Children: A Collection of Songs & Related Activities for Children Aged 4-9. (p. 763)
Salom, Andree. When the Anger Ogre Visits. Salom, Ivette, illus. (p. 1904)
Salom, Ivette, illus. see Salom, Andree.
Salomon, Peter Adam. All Those Broken Angels. (p. 46)
Salomon, Ron. Suicide. (p. 1673)
Salomons, Elizabeth. 1900: Canadian Decades. (p. 2002)
Salonen, Roxane B. P Is for Peace Garden: A North Dakota Alphabet. Yardley, Joanna, illus. (p. 1316)
Salopek, Kirk, illus. see Sumner, Christine.
Salote, Ana. Oy Yew. (p. 1316)
Salqueiro, Adolfo. Carlos Gonzalez. (p. 270)
Salsedo, Greg, jt. auth. see Dauvillier, Loïc.
Salsi, Lynn. Jack & the Giants. Young, James, illus. (p. 902)
Salsi, Lynn Sims. Young Ray Hicks: Learns the Jack Tales. (p. 1979)
Salt, Allan, jt. auth. see James, Soloman.
Salt, Chrys. Methuen Book of Contemporary Monologues for Women. (p. 1130)
Salten, Felix. Bambi: A Life in the Woods. Chambers, Whittaker, tr. (p. 135)
—Bambi: A Life in the Woods. Cowdrey, Richard, illus. (p. 135)
—Bambi: A Life in the Woods. Cowdrey, Richard & Johnson, Steve, illus. (p. 135)
—Bambi - Life in the Woods. (p. 135)
—Bambi's Children: The Story of a Forest Family. Tilley, R. Sudgen, ed. (p. 135)
—Bambi's First Day. van Frankenhuyzen, Gijsbert, illus. (p. 135)
—Forest World. Greenburger, Sanford Jerome & Milton, Paul R., trs. (p. 618)
—Hound of Florence. Paterson, Huntley, tr. from GER. (p. 802)
—Renni the Rescuer. Kaufman, Kenneth C., tr. from GER. (p. 1460)
Salten, Felix & Dusikova, Maja. Bambi. (p. 135)
Salter, Christopher L. North Korea. (p. 1265)
—South Korea. (p. 1617)
—Taiwan. (p. 1696)
Salter, Christopher L. & Whiteford, Gary T. China. (p. 306)
Salter, Helen. Does Snogging Count as Exercise? (p. 460)
Salter, Kay. Fifteenth Summer: The Sarah Bowers Series. (p. 584)
—Fourteenth Summer: So begins the search for a suitable Bride. Noe, Amy, ed. (p. 625)
—Thirteenth Summer: More fun & adventure on the Carolina Coast. Noe, Amy, ed. (p. 1735)
—Twelfth Summer: Coming of age in a time of War. Noe, Amy, ed. (p. 1800)
Salter, Michelle Lewis. Kitty Who Found His Meeooww. Stone, Jonny, illus. (p. 963)
Salter, Safaya, illus. see Handford, S. A.
Salter, Safaya, illus. see Kipling, Rudyard.
Salter, Sydney. My Big Nose & Other Natural Disasters. (p. 1197)
—Swoon at Your Own Risk. (p. 1692)
Salter, Wanda, jt. auth. see Robertson, Carolyn.
Salter-Mathieson, Nigel C. S. Little Chief Mischief: From Tales of the Menehune. Gruen, Chuck, illus. (p. 1026)
Salti, Kim. Riley's Imagination Super Highway - Adventures in Dreamworld. (p. 1472)
Saltman, Judith, jt. auth. see Edwards, Gail.
Salton, Liz. Eelfish, a Rock & Roll King. Hathaway, Karen, illus. (p. 505)
Saltz, Gail. Amazing You! Getting Smart about Your Private Parts. Cravath, Lynne Avril, illus. (p. 56)
—Changing You! A Guide to Body Changes & Sexuality. Cravath, Lynne Avril, illus. (p. 290)
Saltzberg, Barney. All Around the Seasons. Saltzberg, Barney, illus. (p. 44)
—Andrew Drew & Drew. (p. 72)
—Arlo Needs Glasses. (p. 99)
—Beautiful Oops! (p. 154)
—Chengdu Could Not, Would Not, Fall Asleep. Saltzberg, Barney, illus. (p. 297)
—Cornelius P. Mud, Are You Ready for Baby? Saltzberg, Barney, illus. (p. 367)
—Cornelius P. Mud, Are You Ready for School? (p. 367)
—Crazy Hair Day (p. 377)
—Crazy Hair Day. Saltzberg, Barney, illus. (p. 377)
—Crazy Hair Day Big Book. Saltzberg, Barney, illus. (p. 377)
—Good Egg. (p. 698)
—I Love Cats. (p. 842)
—Inside This Book. (p. 878)
—Little Bit of Oomph! (p. 1024)
—Redbird: Friends Come in Different Sizes. (p. 1455)
—Redbird: Colors, Colors, Everywhere! (p. 1455)
—Star of the Week. Saltzberg, Barney, illus. (p. 1641)
—Tea with Grandpa. Saltzberg, Barney, illus. (p. 1708)
Saltzwedel, Hans H. Hans' Journal: A Young German's Memories of His Family's Survival During Germany's Darkest Days. (p. 743)
Salu, Yehuda. Physics for Architects. (p. 1353)
Salum, Rose Mary. Sirol. Simon, Loris, illus. (p. 1581)
Salus, Diane, illus. see Do, Elisa Shipon-Blum.
Salusso, S. T. Billy the Roly Poly Bug. (p. 187)
Salvador, Ana, jt. auth. see Jeunese, Gallimard.
Salvador, Ana & Quarto Generic Staff. Draw with Pablo Picasso. (p. 481)
Salvador, Martin, illus. see Leighton, Marian.
Salvadori, Mario, jt. auth. see Levy, Matthys.
Salvaggio, Tony, jt. auth. see Henderson, Jason.
Salvagnini, Rudy, et al. Uncle Scrooge Clark, John, ed. (p. 1812)
Salvas, Jay Peter, illus. see Shaw, Tucker.
Salvati, Elizabeth A. Counting Your Way down the Toccoa River Canoe Trail. (p. 372)
—Tony Trout of the Toccoa River. (p. 1766)
Salvati, Urbano. Anthology of a Childhood Dream. (p. 89)
Salvatierra, Dante. Latchkey Kids & the Escape from California. (p. 979)
Salvatore, R. A. Crimson Shadow: The Sword of Bedwyn - Luthien's Gamble - The Dragon King. (p. 383)
—Demon Spirit. (p. 426)
—Legacy. (p. 987)
—Road of the Patriarch. (p. 1477)
—Trial by Fire. Ciencin, Scott et al, illus. (p. 1785)
Salvatore, R. A., et al. Worlds of Dungeons & Dragons (p. 1960)
Salvatore, Wilsin. Picky Joshy. (p. 1355)
Salvatus III, Mark Ramsel N., illus. see Olizon-Chikiamco, Norma, et al.
Salvatus, Mark, illus. see Olizon-Chikiamco, Norma, et al.
Salvi, Francesco. Impressionists. (p. 862)
Salvidge, Guy. Yellowcake Summer. (p. 1970)
Salvucci, Richard J., illus. see Joachim, Jean C.
Salway, Ruth. Through Rose Coloured Glasses. (p. 1745)
Salwey, Kenny. Muskrat for Supper: Exploring the Natural World with the Last River Rat. (p. 1194)
Salwi, Dilip. Meet the Four Elements (English) (p. 1122)
—Meet the Four Elements (Hindi) (p. 1122)
Salyards, Jeffrey. Dino Thunder. (p. 441)
Salyer, Adam Ernest, illus. see Salyer, Jennifer Marie.
Salyer, Jennifer Marie. My Shadow. Salyer, Adam Ernest, illus. (p. 1218)
Salyers, Rita. Too Many Choices. Melvin, Anita, illus. (p. 1766)
—Wood's New Collar. Stafford, Rosalee, illus. (p. 1950)
Salyers, Wendy. Verdict Is In: Destination Reality. (p. 1836)
Salzano, Tammi. I Love You Just the Way You Are. Grey, Ada, illus. (p. 843)
—One Little Blueberry. Whelan, Kat, illus. (p. 1295)
—One Rainy Day. Wood, Hannah, illus. (p. 1296)
—One Snowy Day. Wood, Hannah, illus. (p. 1297)
—One Sunny Day. (p. 1297)
—Poison. (p. 1377)
—Truck Party. Wood, Hannah, illus. (p. 1791)
Salzano, Tammi J. Destination, Space. (p. 430)
—Night Sky. Myers, Lawrence E., illus. (p. 1254)
—One Sunny Day. Wood, Hannah, illus. (p. 1297)
—One Windy Day. Wood, Hannah, illus. (p. 1297)
—Rocks, Minerals, & Gemstones. Jankowski, Daniel, illus. (p. 1484)
Salzano, Tammi J., et al. Animal Friends. (p. 77)
Salzberg, Helen, illus. see Falzon, Adrienne.
Salzman, Jeremiah. Day of the Sandwich. Smith, Stephan, illus. (p. 414)
—Mike's Adventure Packs: England. Smith, Stephan, illus. (p. 1141)
Salzman, Mary Brigid. Ding Goes the Happy Cat. (p. 677)
Salzmann, Ann. Kids Do Grown Up. (p. 953)
—Rainbow Rhymes. (p. 1435)
Salzmann, Mary Elizabeth. Accordion to Zeppelin: Inventions from A to Z. (p. 8)
—Ad As in Dad. (p. 10)
—Ag As in Flag. (p. 29)
—Aircraft. (p. 31)
—Airedale to Zuchon: Dogs from A to Z. (p. 31)
—Albatross to Zebra Finch: Birds from A to Z. (p. 34)
—Alcott to Zaharias: Famous Women from A to Z. (p. 35)
—Alex & Max. (p. 35)
—Alley to Zippy: Cats from A to Z. (p. 47)
—Am As in Ham. (p. 51)
—Am I Happy? (p. 51)
—Amy & Abe. (p. 66)
—Angling to Zorbing: Sports from A to Z. (p. 75)
—Ann & Alan. (p. 84)
—Ant Farm to Zebra Fish: Pets from A to Z. (p. 88)
—Ap As in Cap. (p. 91)
—Appleseed to Zamboni: Famous Men from A to Z. (p. 93)
—Arctic Ocean to Zimbabwe: Geography from A to Z. (p. 96)
—As in Fan. (p. 105)
—Astronauts. (p. 109)
—At As in Cat. (p. 110)
—Automobile. (p. 117)
—Ay As in Clay. (p. 121)
—Baby Alligators. (p. 124)
—Baby Eagles. (p. 126)
—Baby Goats. (p. 126)

S

—Baby Gorillas. (p. 126)
—Baby Polar Bears. (p. 127)
—Baby Tigers. (p. 128)
—Balls, Birdies & Pucks. (p. 135)
—Baseball by the Numbers. (p. 141)
—Basketball by the Numbers. (p. 143)
—Bats, Sticks & Rackets. (p. 145)
—Bee & Flea Go to the Sea. (p. 157)
—Bess & Bill. (p. 168)
—Biggest, Baddest Book of Flight. (p. 185)
—Blair & Blaine. (p. 198)
—Boards, Skis & Skates. (p. 205)
—Brandi & Brent. (p. 222)
—Brilliant Birds. (p. 228)
—Brush Your Teeth! Healthy Dental Habits. (p. 232)
—Busy Bumblebees. (p. 246)
—Camera. (p. 256)
—Can a Giraffe Cry or Laugh? (p. 258)
—Can You Go Fast or Slow? (p. 259)
—Caracol de la Tortuga. Nobens, C. A., illus. (p. 265)
—Cash for Trash. (p. 276)
—Cassie & Carl. (p. 276)
—Chap & the Cap. (p. 291)
—Chelsey & Chad. (p. 297)
—Cindy & Cecil. (p. 321)
—Come Home with Me! (p. 347)
—Cristy & Craig. (p. 383)
—Dandy Dogs. (p. 403)
—Dashing Dragonflies. (p. 409)
—Deb & Dan. (p. 420)
—Dentist's Tools. (p. 427)
—Did I Hear a Hello from above or Below? (p. 436)
—Did You See One Jump? (p. 437)
—Doctor's Tools. (p. 459)
—Does It Fly Away in the Night or Day? (p. 460)
—Don't Sneeze on Skis. (p. 468)
—Drew & Drake. (p. 485)
—Eat Your Vegetables! Healthy Eating Habits. (p. 501)
—Eating Right. (p. 501)
—Ell As in Well. (p. 513)
—Fan in the Can. (p. 570)
—Fay Loves Ballet. (p. 578)
—Flashy Fish. Craig, Diane, ed. (p. 602)
—Fluttering Butterflies. (p. 609)
—Football by the Numbers. (p. 615)
—Getting Enough Sleep. (p. 669)
—Goldfish Bowl. Chawla, Neena, illus. (p. 695)
—Goldfish Bowl (6-pack) Chawla, Neena, illus. (p. 695)
—Goofy Guinea Pigs. Craig, Diane, ed. (p. 702)
—Great Lei Race: A Story about Hawaii. Doucet, Bob, illus. (p. 717)
—Healthy Habits. (p. 758)
—Here Are Toys! (p. 770)
—Here Is a Zoo. (p. 770)
—Humming Hummingbird. (p. 826)
—I Am a Good Citizen. (p. 832)
—I Am a Kitten. (p. 832)
—I Am Caring. (p. 832)
—I Am Fair. (p. 832)
—I Am Honest. (p. 833)
—I Am Respectful. (p. 833)
—I Am Responsible. (p. 833)
—I Had a Great Time! (p. 838)
—I See a Costume. (p. 845)
—Is It a Day for Work or Play? (p. 889)
—Is the Treat Sour or Sweet? (p. 890)
—It's A! (p. 895)
—It's F! (p. 896)
—It's I! (p. 897)
—It's J! (p. 897)
—It's Not Good, It's Great! (p. 898)
—It's P! (p. 898)
—It's U! (p. 899)
—It's W! (p. 899)
—It's Z! (p. 900)
—Kangaroo & the Crew. (p. 942)
—Keeping Your Body Clean. (p. 948)
—Know Your Numbers: Food. (p. 965)
—Know Your Numbers: Toys. (p. 965)
—Know Your Numbers: Nature. (p. 965)
—Know Your Numbers: Animals. (p. 965)
—Kyle Wears a Smile. (p. 969)
—Lady Bauer in the Tower. (p. 970)
—Leaping Lizards. Chawla, Neena, illus. (p. 982)
—Look at the Playground! (p. 1049)
—Lucky Ladybugs. (p. 1062)
—Money for Clothes. (p. 1164)
—Money for Entertainment. (p. 1164)
—Money for Food. (p. 1164)
—Money for Hobbies. (p. 1164)
—Money for School. (p. 1164)
—Money for Toys. (p. 1164)
—Nate, Let's Skate. (p. 1230)
—No Pigs on the Farm! (p. 1259)
—Out for the Summer! (p. 1311)
—Parade Is Here! (p. 1323)
—Paw That Can Draw. (p. 1331)
—Pesky Houseflies. (p. 1345)
—Pete the Parakeet. (p. 1346)
—Phonograph. (p. 1352)
—Presidential Seal. (p. 1397)
—Race for the Vase. (p. 1431)
—Rachel's Home on Bear Mountain: A Story about Connecticut. Doucet, Bob, illus. (p. 1432)
—RAM & the Clam. (p. 1437)
—Ram & the Clam. (p. 1437)
—Robin Hoods. Haberstroh, Anne, illus. (p. 1480)
—Run! Jump! Play! Healthy Active Habits. (p. 1496)
—Scat the Fat Cat. (p. 1521)
—Sea Horse Races. (p. 1534)
—See the Farm! (p. 1547)
—See the Farm! Craig, Diane, ed. (p. 1547)
—Shoes, Boots & Cleats. (p. 1568)
—Sleep All Night! Healthy Sleeping Habits. (p. 1588)
—Snack for Jack. (p. 1595)
—Snail Tale. (p. 1596)
—Snake by the Lake. (p. 1596)
—Snow & More Snow! (p. 1598)
—Stag in the Bag. (p. 1638)
—Super Saint Bernards. Doucet, Bob, illus. (p. 1680)
—Take a Bath! Healthy Body Habits. (p. 1696)
—Taking Care of Your Teeth. (p. 1698)
—Taking Time to Relax. (p. 1698)
—Telegraph. (p. 1716)
—Telephone. (p. 1716)
—Thad & His Dad. (p. 1724)
—They Are the Best! (p. 1732)
—Train to Spain. (p. 1777)
—Turtle Shells. Nobens, C. A., illus. (p. 1798)
—Turtle Shells. Nobens, Cheryl A., illus. (p. 1798)
—Veterinarian's Tools. (p. 1839)
—Way to Go! (p. 1864)
—We All Like It! (p. 1865)
—We Are at the Park. (p. 1865)
—We Are Playing! (p. 1865)
—We Look at Food. (p. 1867)
—We See the Beach! (p. 1868)
—Wear a Helmet! Healthy Safety Habits. (p. 1869)
—What a Day in the Park! (p. 1878)
—What Has a Shell? (p. 1886)
—What Has a Tail? (p. 1886)
—What Has Claws? (p. 1886)
—What Has Fur? (p. 1886)
—What Has Hooves? (p. 1886)
—What Has Horns? (p. 1886)
—What Has Paws? (p. 1886)
—What Has Scales? (p. 1886)
—What Has Spots? (p. 1886)
—What Has Stripes? (p. 1886)
—What Has Webbed Feet? (p. 1886)
—What Has Wings? (p. 1886)
—What in the World Is a Clarinet? (p. 1887)
—What in the World Is a Cup? (p. 1887)
—What in the World Is a Cup? CD & Book. (p. 1887)
—What in the World Is a Cup? Site CD & Book. (p. 1887)
—What in the World Is a Drum? (p. 1887)
—What in the World Is a Flute? (p. 1887)
—What in the World Is a Foot? CD & Book. (p. 1887)
—What in the World Is a Foot? Site CD & Book. (p. 1887)
—What in the World Is a Gallon? (p. 1887)
—What in the World Is a Gallon? CD & Book. (p. 1887)
—What in the World Is a Gallon? Site CD & Book. (p. 1887)
—What in the World Is a Pound? CD & Book. (p. 1887)
—What in the World Is a Pound? Site CD & Book. (p. 1887)
—What in the World Is a Violin? (p. 1888)
—What in the World Is an Inch? (p. 1888)
—What in the World Is an Inch? CD & Book. (p. 1888)
—What in the World Is an Inch? Site CD & Book. (p. 1888)
—What in the World Is an Ounce? CD & Book. (p. 1888)
—What in the World Is an Ounce? Site CD & Book. (p. 1888)
—Who Is This at the Beach? (p. 1916)
Salzmann, Mary Elizabeth, jt. auth. see ABDO Publishing Company Staff.
Sam, Ackerman. Language Quest Spanish B Blue. (p. 975)
Sam, Hundley, illus. see Suhay, Lisa.
Sam, Joan. I Have Cancer. (p. 839)
Sam, Joe. Invisible Hunters (Los Cazadores Invisibles) (p. 885)
Sam, Kagan. Mr. Duz Solves a Mystery. (p. 1185)
Sam, Kagan, illus. see Patrick, Wellman.
Sam, Kurutsi Dan'azumi. Big Photograph of Sir Ahmadu Bello: And Other Short Stories for Children & Young Adults. (p. 183)
Sama, Kent. Fruit of the Spirit - Love. Moody, Julie, illus. (p. 645)
Samanich, John G., jt. auth. see Powell, Jillian.
Samaniego, Fabián A. Quia Online Student Activities Manual with Smarthinking: Used with ... Samaniego-Mundo 21. (p. 1427)
Samaniego, Félix María, jt. auth. see Combel Editorial Staff.
Samantha May Cerney, illus. see Oldenburg, Richard.
Samantha Nowak, illus. see Jessica Hoel.
Samarasinghe, Sara. Dalaina. (p. 401)
Samarrippas, Gloria. In Search for Lucky's Lost Toys. (p. 864)
Samarsky, Mikhail. Rainbow for a Friend. Payne, Lawrence, ed. (p. 1435)
Sambar, Syma. This Is Olivia. Spaziante, Patrick, illus. (p. 1736)
Sambrone, Erika Elizabeth. Heavenly Angel Bugs: God Answers Prayers. (p. 761)
Sami. Baby Animals. (p. 124)
—Colors. (p. 344)
—Colors - Shapes. (p. 345)
—Count. (p. 369)
SAMi. Flip-a-Face: Colors. (p. 604)
—Let's Learn Colors & Shapes. (p. 998)
Sami. Yum! (p. 1983)
Sami, illus. see Doodler, Todd H.
Sami & Dwell Studio Staff. Go! Flip-a-Shape. (p. 686)
SAMi Staff. Big, Bigger, Biggest Book. (p. 178)
—Look, Baby! (p. 1049)
—Play! (p. 1370)
SAMi Staff, jt. auth. see Ziefert, Harriet.
Sammarco, Teresa "T". What If Book. Curley, Carol, illus. (p. 1887)
Sammartino, Joseph & Ozimkowski, Edward. Legend of Kringle. (p. 988)
Sammel, Rochelle. Tales of Two Mouse Brothers. (p. 1703)
Sammons, Sandra Wallus. Henry Flagler, Builder of Florida. (p. 768)
—Marjorie Kinnan Rawlings & the Florida Crackers. (p. 1094)
—Marjory Stoneman Douglas & the Florida Everglades. (p. 1094)
—Ponce de Leon & the Discovery of Florida. (p. 1382)
—Zora Neale Hurston: Wrapped in Rainbows. (p. 1990)
—Zora Neale Hurston. (p. 1990)
Samms, Olivia. Sketchy. (p. 1584)
Samol, Nanette, photos by see Ogle, Jennifer, et al.
Samos (Amos Amir). Nemo the Mole Rat: Stories from the Woodland. (p. 1241)
Samoun, Abigail. How Gator Says Good-Bye! Watts, Sarah, illus. (p. 809)
—How Hippo Says Hello! Watts, Sarah, illus. (p. 809)
—How Penguin Says Please! Watts, Sarah, illus. (p. 811)
—How Tiger Says Thank You! Watts, Sarah, illus. (p. 814)
—What's in Your Purse? Dion, Nathalie, illus. (p. 1898)
Sampar, illus. see Bergeron, Alain M.
Sampar, illus. see Bergeron, Alain M. & Quintin, Michel.
Sampar, illus. see Quintin, Michel & Bergeron, Alain.
Sampar, illus. see Quintin, Michel, et al.
Sampar, jt. auth. see Bergeron, Alain M.
Sample, Jewel. Besos y Abrazos Al Aire. Tenorio-Gavin, Lucero, tr. (p. 168)
—Flying Hugs & Kisses Activity Book. Kiplinger Pandy, Lori, illus. (p. 610)
Sample, Matthew, illus. see Cone, Stephanie M.
Sample, Matthew C. What a Day! (p. 1878)
Sample, Matthew II, illus. see Cutrera, Melissa.
Sample, Vincent W. Reach to Your Youth Mentor Project: Reaching Your Potential Student's Workbook. Vol. 1 (p. 1442)
Samples, Suzanne. Pivot. (p. 1365)
Sampson, Ajpril. Margarita y la Mariposa. Sampson, Ajpril, illus. (p. 1092)
Sampson, Ana, jt. auth. see Kennedy, Caroline.
Sampson, Anne, ed. see Bahamon, Claire.
Sampson, April, illus. see Stockton, Lucille.
Sampson, Brent. Aidan's Shoes. Switzer, Bobbi, illus. (p. 30)
—One Wacky Wasp: The Perfect Children's Book for Kids Ages 3-6 Who Are Learning to Read. (p. 1297)
Sampson, Fay. Finnglas & the Stones of Choosing (p. 589)
—Sorcerer's Daughter. (p. 1614)
—Them. (p. 1728)
Sampson, Jeff. Havoc: A Deviants Novel. (p. 755)
—Ravage: A Deviants Novel. (p. 1440)
—Vesper: A Deviants Novel. (p. 1839)
—Vesper. (p. 1839)
Sampson, Jody, illus. see Kelly, Theresa.
Sampson, Jody, illus. see Russo, Anthony.
Sampson, Juliet M. Bon Voyage! A Young Girl's Search for Friendship, Love & Life. (p. 208)
Sampson, Kathleen, illus. see Abbruzzi, Danielle.
Sampson, Michael, jt. auth. see Martin, Bill, Jr.
Sampson, Michael & Martin, Bill, Jr. Kitty Cat, Kitty Cat, Are You Waking Up? Bryant, Laura J., illus. (p. 963)
Sampson, Michael R. & Martin, Bill, Jr. Kitty Cat, Kitty Cat, Are You Waking Up? Bryant, Laura & Bryant, Laura J., illus. (p. 963)
Sampson, Sally. Chop Chop: The Kids' Guide to Cooking Real Food with Your Family. Tremblay, Carl, photos by. (p. 310)
Sams, B. B., illus. see Gaydos, Nora.
Sams, Carl R., 2nd, photos by see Llewellyn, Bridget McGovern.
Sams, Carl R. & Stoick, Jean. Tea with Lady Sapphire. (p. 1708)
Sams, Carl R., II. Stranger in the Woods. (p. 1665)
Sams, Carl R., II, jt. photos by see Stoick, Jean.
Sams, Carl R., II & Stoick, Jean. Find My Friends. (p. 587)
—Happy Bird Day! Sams, Carl R., II & Stoick, Jean, photos by. (p. 744)
—Lost in the Woods: A Photographic Fantasy. Herrick, Mark J., illus. (p. 1056)
—Winter Friends. McDiarmid, Karen, ed. (p. 1938)
Sams, Carl R., II & Stoick, Jean, photos by. Lost in the Woods: A Photographic Fantasy. (p. 1056)
Sams II, Carl R., jt. photos by see Stoick, Jean.
Sams II, Carl R. & Stoick, Jean, photos by. When Snowflakes Fall. (p. 1904)
Sams, Laura & Sams, Robert. Pirate's Quest: For His Family Heirloom Peg Leg. Herting, Heiner, illus. (p. 1364)
Sams, Robert, jt. auth. see Sams, Laura.
Samson, David. American Idle: The Anti-Motivation Handbook. (p. 61)
—Men Who Hate Themselves - And the Women Who Agree with Them. (p. 1126)
—Wake up & Smell the Coffin: 387 Ways to Know You're Aging Disgracefully. (p. 1853)
Samson, Don. Teenage Aviation Stories. (p. 1714)
Samson, Donald, tr. see Streit, Jakob.
Samson, John M., ed. Star Trek Crosswords (p. 1641)
Samson, Lisa E. Songbird. (p. 1611)
Samson, Tess. Animals on the Farm. (p. 83)
—Going up & Down. (p. 693)
—Look & See. (p. 1048)
—See the Birds. (p. 1547)
—Snack Time. (p. 1595)
—They Grow Plants. (p. 1732)
—We Like Vegetables. (p. 1867)
—What Goes Up? (p. 1885)
Samuel, Adele. Wild World of Sports. (p. 1931)
Samuel, Anna, ed. Glitter Butterflies Stickers. (p. 683)
—Glitter Old-Time Christmas Stickers. (p. 684)
Samuel, Charlie. Entertainment in Colonial America. (p. 531)
—Government & Politics in Colonial America. (p. 704)
—Medicine in Colonial America. (p. 1119)
—Solving the Mysteries of Pompeii. (p. 1608)
Samuel, Dot, illus. see Woodruff, Ellen Larkin.
Samuel, Hiti, jt. auth. see Midthun, Joseph.
Samuel, Janet. One Sneaky Sheep: A Touch-and-Feel Fluffy Tale. (p. 1297)
—One Sneaky Sheep: The Sheep Who Didn't Want to Get Sheared. (p. 1297)
Samuel, Janet, illus. see Goodings, Christina.
Samuel, Janet, illus. see Hartman, Bob.
Samuel, Janet, illus. see McKendry, Sam.
Samuel, Janet, illus. see Moore, Clement C.
Samuel, Janet, illus. see Mumme, Sarah.
Samuel, Janet, illus. see Nolan, Allia Zobel.
Samuel, Janet, illus. see Pierpont, James Lord.
Samuel, Janet, illus. see Sully, Katherine.
Samuel, Josiah C. Mr. Tortoise Funny Life (p. 1186)
Samuel, Karen, illus. see Sewer, Anecia.
Samuel, Karen L., illus. see Roach, Tregenza A.
Samuel, Kyrie. Kyrie Loves Grandma Soooo Much. (p. 969)
Samuel, Lynette M. Mommy's Hat. Capps, Leigh, illus. (p. 1162)
Samuel, Nancy K. Recruiting Game. (p. 1452)
Samuel, Nigel. 10 Coolest Wonders of the Universe. (p. 1993)
—10 Mightiest Mountains. (p. 1993)
—Creatures of the Deep. (p. 380)
Samuel, Quentin. Where's Everybody Going? Corr, Christopher, illus. (p. 1910)
—Why Is Everybody So Excited. Corr, Christopher, illus. (p. 1925)
Samuel, R. Skull & Bones: A Pirate's Odyssey. (p. 1586)
Samuel, Tankersley. Alone. (p. 48)
Samuel, Y. D. Learning with Strawberry & Friends: C o l o u r S. (p. 986)
Samuels, Arthur. Old Flames: Teen Bullies & Prep School Cruelty. (p. 1283)
Samuels, Barbara. Canada's Immigrant Cultures: Multiculturalism in Canada. (p. 260)
—Canada's Multicultural Society Today: Multiculturalism in Canada. (p. 260)
—Fred's Beds. Samuels, Barbara, illus. (p. 633)
—Multiculturalism in Early Canada: Multiculturalism in Canada. (p. 1190)
—Trucker. Samuels, Barbara, illus. (p. 1791)
Samuels, Barbara, illus. see Sachar, Louis.
Samuels, Carolee S., jt. auth. see Liddell, Louise A.
Samuels, Charlie. Advent of Electricity, 1800-1900. (p. 14)
—Age of the Atom (1900-1946) (p. 29)
—Ancient Science: Prehistory-A.D. 500. (p. 70)
—Astonishing Bodies. (p. 108)
—Civil War. (p. 325)
—Conspiracy! (p. 359)
—Digital Age (1947-Present Day) (p. 439)
—Forgotten Cities. (p. 619)
—Home Front. (p. 792)
—Iraq. (p. 887)
—Life under Occupation. (p. 1013)
—Machines & Weaponry of the Vietnam War. (p. 1068)
—Machines & Weaponry of World War I. (p. 1068)
—Machines & Weaponry of World War II. (p. 1068)
—Medieval Science (500-1500) (p. 1119)
—Propaganda. (p. 1411)
—Revolutions in Science: 1550-1700. (p. 1467)
—Rise of Industry (1700-1800) (p. 1474)
—Soldiers. (p. 1607)
—Spying & Security. (p. 1636)
—Technology in Ancient China. (p. 1711)
—Technology in Ancient Greece. (p. 1711)
—Technology in Ancient Mesopotamia. (p. 1711)
—Technology in Ancient Rome. (p. 1711)
—Technology in Mesopotamia. (p. 1711)
—Technology in the Ancient Americas. (p. 1711)
—Timeline of the Classical World. (p. 1754)
—Timeline of the Colonial World. (p. 1754)
—Timeline of the Industrial Revolution. (p. 1754)
—Timeline of the Middle Ages. (p. 1754)
—Timeline of the Muslim World. (p. 1754)
—Timeline of the Renaissance. (p. 1754)
—Timeline of the Revolutionary War. (p. 1754)
—Timeline of the Vietnam War. (p. 1754)
—Timeline of the War on Terror. (p. 1754)
—Timeline of World War I. (p. 1754)
—World War II. (p. 1959)
Samuels, Charlie & George, Enzo. Civil War: The War Between Brothers. (p. 325)
—Vietnam Conflict: War with Communism. (p. 1841)
Samuels, Gregory Robert. Mommy, Where Does Everything Come From? Brennan, Craig, illus. (p. 1162)
Samuels, Jack. Town of Masquerade. Snider, K. C., illus. (p. 1773)
Samuels, Linda Nissen. Cuando Elly Fue a la Reserva Ecologica. Samuels, Linda Nissen, illus. (p. 388)
—Elly e il Parco Degli Animali. Samuels, Linda Nissen, illus. (p. 515)
—When Elly Went to the Animal Park... Samuels, Linda Nissen, illus. (p. 1902)
Samuels, Nancy. How to Prepare for the State Standards Grade 2. (p. 821)
Samuels, Ryan, illus. see W, Maurice.
Samuels, Suzanne. Law, Politics, & Society: An Introduction to American Law. (p. 981)
Samuels, Vallerie. Village of Time. (p. 1842)
Samuels, Vyanne. Carry Go Bring Come. (p. 271)
Samuels, Wilfred D. Encyclopedia of African-American Literature. Woodard, Loretta Gilchrist & Guzzio, Tracie Church, eds. (p. 524)
Samuelson, Jazlyn. Dream Big. (p. 483)
Samuil, Marshak. Baggage. (p. 132)
Samura, Hiroaki. Blade of the Immortal - Fall Frost. (p. 198)
—Last Blood. Lewis, Dana & Smith, Toren, trs. (p. 977)
Samura, Juliet Tumoe. Animal Town: Fishing Trip. (p. 80)
Samwell, Cynthia A. Witches Anonymous. (p. 1941)
Samworth, Kate. Aviary Wonders Inc. Spring Catalog & Instruction Manual. (p. 119)
San Antonio Museum of Art Staff. Colores Everywhere! Colors in English & Spanish. (p. 344)
—Hello, Circulos! Shapes in English & Spanish. (p. 763)
San Antonio Museum of Art Staff, creator. Animal Amigos! Artsy Creatures in English y Espanol. (p. 76)
—Black & Blanco! Engaging Art in English y Español. (p. 195)
San Diego Zoo Staff. Animal ABC's San Diego Zoo. (p. 76)
—Count to 10 & Back Again: San Diego Zoo. (p. 370)
San Diego Zoo Staff, photos by see Pingry, Patricia A.
San Diego Zoological Society Staff, photos by see Ryder, Joanne.
San Francisco Bay Area Staff, illus. see Students of Wallenberg Traditional High School Staff.
San Francisco Bay Area Students Staff. 826 Quarterly (p. 2001)
—Show of Hands: Young Authors Reflect on the Golden Rule. (p. 1571)
San Francisco Bay Area Students Staff & 826 Valencia Writing Project Student Staff. Apprentices Issue. (p. 93)

S

San Francisco, Carolina Diaz. Fantastic Herbs. (p. 571)
San Francisco School, illus. see Moog, Bob.
San Giacomo, Renee. Herbie's Star. (p. 769)
San Jorge, José. Variedades Poéticas. Hernández, René Mario, ed. (p. 1833)
San José, Miguel Angel, jt. auth. see Batchelor, R. E.
San Román, Sonsoles, jt. ed. see Cortina, Regina.
San Souci, Daniel. Rabbit & the Dragon King: Based on a Korean Folk Tale. Neilan, Eujin Kim, illus. (p. 1429)
San Souci, Daniel, illus. see Kimmel, Eric A.
San Souci, Daniel, illus. see Wadsworth, Ginger.
San Souci, Daniel, jt. illus. see San Souci, Robert D.
San Souci, Robert D. Cendrillon: A Caribbean Cinderella. (p. 286)
—Cinderella Skeleton. Catrow, David, illus. (p. 320)
—Cut from the Same Cloth: American Women of Myth, Legend, & Tall Tale. Pinkney, Brian, illus. (p. 396)
—Dare to Be Scared: Thirteen Stories to Chill & Thrill. Ouimet, David, illus. (p. 406)
—Dare to Be Scared 4: Thirteen More Tales of Terror. Ouimet, David, illus. (p. 406)
—Double-Dare to Be Scared: Another Thirteen Chilling Tales. Ouimet, David, illus. (p. 472)
—Even More Short & Shivery: Thirty Spine-Tingling Tales. Rogers, Jacqueline, illus. (p. 541)
—Haunted Houses. Murphy, Kelly & Revoy, Antoine, illus. (p. 753)
—More Short & Shivery: Thirty Terrifying Tales. Coville, Katherine, illus. (p. 1174)
—Robin Hood & the Golden Arrow. Lewis, Earl B., illus. (p. 1480)
—Six Foolish Fishermen Kennedy, Doug, illus. (p. 1582)
—Triple-Dare to Be Scared: Thirteen Further Freaky Tales. Ouimet, David, illus. (p. 1787)
—Twins & the Bird of Darkness: A Hero Tale from the Caribbean. Widener, Terry, illus. (p. 1802)
—Zigzag. Czernecki, Stefan, illus. (p. 1986)
San Souci, Robert D. & Burroughs, Edgar Rice. Tarzan. McCurdy, Michael, illus. (p. 1706)
San Souci, Robert D. & San Souci, Daniel. Sister Tricksters: Rollicking Tales of Clever Females. (p. 1581)
San Vicente, Luis. Festival of Bones / el Festival de Las Calaveras. (p. 582)
Sananmuang, Chatree, illus. see Pujari, M. Nathalie.
Sanborn, Casey, illus. see McIntosh, Kenneth.
Sanborn, Casey, illus. see Rader, Mark.
Sanborn, F. C., illus. see Lindsay, Maud.
Sanborn, Franklin Benjamin. Hawthorne & His Friends. (p. 755)
—Ralph Waldo Emerson. (p. 1437)
Sanborn, Perry F. Little Ant A Wright, Spencer, illus. (p. 1023)
Sanburn, Douglas. Stellar Revelations. (p. 1647)
SanCartier, Emma, illus. see James, Tamara.
Sanches, Sharon. Flexi Bility: A Superhero in My Brain! (p. 603)
Sánchez Abulí, Enrique, tr. see Bateson, Maggie.
Sanchez Abuli, Enrique, tr. see Gribbin, Mary & Gribbin, John.
Sánchez Abulí, Enrique, tr. see Handford, Martin & Geddes, Anne.
Sánchez Abulí, Enrique, tr. see Handford, Martin.
Sanchez, Alex. Bait. (p. 133)
—Boyfriends with Girlfriends. (p. 220)
—Getting It. Mehta, Sangeeta, ed. (p. 669)
—God Box. Del Rosario, Michael, ed. (p. 688)
—Rainbow Boys. (p. 1435)
—Rainbow High. (p. 1435)
—Rainbow Road. (p. 1435)
—So Hard to Say. Weiss, Jennifer, ed. (p. 1602)
Sanchez, Alex & Louth, Jack. Rainbow Road. (p. 1435)
Sanchez Almara, Dono, illus. see Dickens, Charles.
Sánchez, Alvaro Iglesias, illus. see Cooper, Sharon Katz.
Sánchez, Andres, illus. see Abodehman, Ahmed.
Sanchez, Andres, illus. see Peredo, Roberto.
Sanchez, Andres, illus. see Soci Et E de La Faune Et Des Parcs Du Qu Ebec.
Sanchez, Anita. Invasion of Sandy Bay. (p. 883)
—Karl, Get Out of the Garden! Carolus Linnaeus & the Naming of Everything. Stock, Catherine, illus. (p. 943)
—Leaflets Three, Let It Be! The Story of Poison Ivy. Brickman, Robin, illus. (p. 982)
Sanchez, Asa, jt. auth. see Dumesnil, Phil.
Sánchez Beras, César. Sapito Azul. Diaz, Raquel, illus. (p. 1514)
Sánchez, Celeste. Familia 1: Nuestro Primer Grupo Social. Burgos, Mayda, ed. (p. 567)
—Familia 1 Guía: Nuestro Primer Grupo Social Burgos, Mayda, ed. (p. 567)
—Nuestro País 3: Su gente, su historia y su Cultura. Burgos, Mayda, ed. (p. 1270)
Sánchez, Celeste & Burgos, Mayda. Nuestro País 3 Cuaderno: Su gente, su historia y su Cultura. (p. 1270)
Sanchez, Chani. There Are No Animals in This Book (Only Feelings) (p. 1729)
Sanchez, Claudia. Cuidador de Pajaros (Bird Trainer & Other Legends) (p. 390)
Sánchez, Consuelo. Claudet Monet. (p. 329)
Sánchez, Edmundo, illus. see Villanueva, David.
Sanchez, Elizabeth. Jesus, It's Me Nicholas! Gutierrez, Chris, illus. (p. 915)
Sanchez, Enrique O., illus. see Castañeda, Omar S.
Sanchez, Enrique O., illus. see de la Vega, Elda, tr.
Sanchez, Enrique O., illus. see Gonzalez Jensen, Margarita.
Sanchez, Enrique O., illus. see Jaffe, Nina.
Sanchez, Enrique O., illus. see Mora, Pat.
Sanchez, Enrique O., illus. see O'Neill, Alexis.
Sanchez, Enrique O., illus. see Santiago, Esmeralda.
Sanchez, Enrique O., jt. auth. see Mora, Pat.
Sanchez, Enrique O., jt. auth. see O'Neill, Alexis.
Sanchez, Evan, illus. see Shonka, Maria.
Sanchez Gallego, Maria Isabel, jt. auth. see Litchfield, Jo.
Sanchez, Gervasio, et al. Cinco Anos Despues: Vidas Minadas. (p. 319)
Sánchez, Gilberto. Poesía Coral. (p. 1376)
Sánchez, Gloria. Siete Casas, Siete Brujas y un Huevo. López Domínguez, Xan, tr. (p. 1573)
Sánchez, Haroldo & McCaughrean, Geraldine. Juegos de la Mente: La\Vida de un Periodista Guatemalteco en 30 Días. (p. 931)
Sanchez, Helen. Buddy Boys. (p. 234)
Sánchez, Isidro. Mi Gato. Ruis, Maria, illus. (p. 1132)
—Mi Hamster. Ruis, Maria, illus. (p. 1132)
—Mi Pajaro. Ruis, Maria, illus. (p. 1133)
—Mi Perro. Ruis, Maria, illus. (p. 1133)
Sanchez, Isidro & Bordoy, Irene. Cuando: Cuando Como (When I Eat) (p. 388)
—Cuando: Cuando Me Bano (When I Take a Bath) (p. 388)
—Cuando: Cuando Estoy Engermo (When I'm Sick) (p. 388)
—Cuando: Cuando Me Visto (When I Get Dressed) (p. 388)
—Dia en la Escuela: El Recreo (Recess) (p. 433)
—Dia en la Escuela: La Clase (In Class) (p. 433)
—Dia en la Escuela: Salimos a la Escuela (Going to School) (p. 433)
—Dia en la Escuela: Mi Primer Dia de Colegio (My First School Day) (p. 433)
Sanchez, Isidro & Rius, Maria. Mis Animales Preferidos: Mi Gato (My Cat) (p. 1149)
—Mis Animales Preferidos: Mi Perro (My Dog) (p. 1149)
—Mis Animales Preferidos: Mi Pajaro (My Bird) (p. 1149)
Sanchez, Israel, illus. see Brockenbrough, Martha.
Sanchez, Javier G., illus. see Monkman, Olga.
Sanchez, Jenny Torres. Death, Dickinson, & the Demented Life of Frenchie Garcia. (p. 420)
Sanchez, Jimena, illus. see Simonson, Louise.
Sanchez, John Joseph P. Illuminating the Legacy: A Coloring & Activity Book of the CNMI's History. Ogo, Luis S., illus. (p. 857)
Sanchez, Juanita L. Pancho the Green Parrot Lays an Egg Ramirez, Samuel, illus. (p. 1320)
Sánchez, Juanvi. Cinco. (p. 319)
—Cuatro. (p. 388)
Sánchez, Juanvi, jt. auth. see Sánchez, Juanvi.
Sánchez, Juanvi & Sánchez, Juanvi. Dos Con Lunares. (p. 472)
—Tres de Lunares. (p. 1784)
—Uno. (p. 1822)
Sanchez, Kevin & Sanchez, Laura. Nikki's Hurricane Adventure. (p. 1255)
Sanchez, La Tania. Day Out with Grammie. (p. 414)
Sanchez, Laura, jt. auth. see Sanchez, Kevin.
Sanchez, Lorrie Christel & Blank, Carol. Virgil: The Bully from Cyberspace. Margolis, Al, illus. (p. 1844)
—Virgil: The Bully from Cyberspace Teacher Edition. Margolis, Al, illus. (p. 1844)
Sánchez, Lucía M. Viento. Taylor, Trace, illus. (p. 1841)
Sánchez, Lucía M., jt. auth. see Dibble, Traci.
Sánchez, Lucía M., jt. auth. see Johnson, Gee.
Sánchez, Lucía M., jt. auth. see Pitt, Marilyn.
Sánchez, Lucía M., jt. auth. see Taylor, Trace.
Sánchez, Lucía M., jt. auth. see Washington, Joi.
Sánchez, Lucía M., jt. auth. see Zorzi, Gina.
Sánchez, Lucía M. & Cline, Gina. Vida de la Tortuga de Mar. (p. 1840)
Sánchez, Lucía M. & Taylor, Trace. Guinea (Spanish) (p. 731)
Sanchez, Maria, illus. see Lazaro, Georgina.
Sanchez, Maria Jesús, tr. see Meyer, Stephenie.
Sánchez, Miriam. Donde Perdio Luna la Risa? (p. 466)
Sanchez, Monica A. Twinkle, Sparkle, Watch Me Grow. (p. 1802)
Sanchez, Pete. Friend for Petro. (p. 637)
Sánchez Priede, José María. Don Tancleto Trotamundos: Cuentos y Fabulas. (p. 465)
Sanchez, Priscilla. Champ the Boxing Boxer. (p. 289)
Sanchez, Ricardo. Spotlight Soccer Waryanto, Ian, illus. (p. 1634)
Sanchez, Richard. Animales (Animals) (p. 80)
—Colores (Colors) (p. 344)
—Numeros (Numbers) (p. 1273)
Sanchez, Sara, illus. see Zur Muehlen, Nersel.
Sánchez, Sergio García, illus. see Spiegelman, Nadja.
Sánchez, Sonia, illus. see Kim, Patti.
Sánchez, Sonia, illus. see Mantchev, Lisa.
Sanchez Vicario, Arantxa. Jovenes Tenistas. (p. 929)
Sanchez Vigil, Luis Gerardo, illus. see Romeu, Emma.
Sánchez-Korrol, Virginia. Feminist & Abolitionist: The Story of Emilia Casanova. (p. 581)
Sanchez-Silva, Jose Maria. Adios, Josefina (Goodbye, Josephine) (p. 12)
Sancton, Sylvaine. Some Birds ... Sancton, Sylvaine, photos by. (p. 1609)
Sand, George. What Flowers Say: And Other Stories. Erskine Hirko, Holly, tr. from FRE. (p. 1884)
Sand, Marc. Sheltered. (p. 1565)
Sanda-Ebosh, Mary, illus. see Merriweather-Beech, Myrtle.
Sandage, Charley. ALL AROUND ARKANSAS Big Book. (p. 43)
—ALL AROUND ARKANSAS student Edition. (p. 43)
—Big Bear's Arkansas ABCs. Przybylek, Leslie, illus. (p. 178)
—Big Bear's Arkansas ABCs Big Book. (p. 178)
—"I Can Tell You Stories, If You Gather Near"... The Big Bear of Arkansas. Daniel, R. F., illus. (p. 836)
—I can tell you stories, if you gather round Big Book. (p. 836)
—Where did we come from, Grandpa? Big Book. (p. 1906)
—Where did we come from, Grandpa? student Edition. (p. 1906)
Sandall, Anne. Small Graces. Sandall, Diane, illus. (p. 1592)
Sandall, Barbara R., et al. Algebra Practice: Examples & Practice. (p. 38)
Sandall, Diane, illus. see Sandall, Anne.
Sandall, Ellie. Copycat Bear! Sandall, Ellie, illus. (p. 366)
—Daisy Plays Hide-and-Seek. Sandall, Ellie, illus. (p. 400)
Sandau, Carol E. 10 Puzzling Pieces. (p. 1994)
—Prairie Patchwork. (p. 1392)
Sandbeck, Fletcher, jt. auth. see Sanders, Susan.
Sandberg, Winter. Private Display of Affection [Library Edition]. (p. 1407)
Sandburg, Carl. Abe Lincoln Grows Up. Daugherty, James, illus. (p. 4)
—Carl Sandburg. Berman, Paul, ed. (p. 269)
—Huckabuck Family: And How They Raised Popcorn in Nebraska & Quit & Came Back. Small, David, illus. (p. 824)
—Rootabaga Stories. (p. 1488)
—Rootabaga Stories. Petersham, Maud & Petersham, Miska, illus. (p. 1488)
Sande, Ana. Patito Feo. (p. 1328)
Sande, Carter, jt. auth. see Sande, Warren.
Sande, Hans. Snake in the Grass. Vetleseter, Tonje, tr. from NOR. (p. 1596)
Sande, Warren & Sande, Carter. Hello World! Computer Programming for Kids & Other Beginners. (p. 765)
Sandell, Lisa Ann. Map of the Known World. (p. 1090)
—Song of the Sparrow. (p. 1611)
Sandemose, Iben. Gracie & Grandma. Sandemose, Iben, illus. (p. 705)
—Gracie & Grandma & the Itsy, Bitsy Seed. Vetleseter, Tonje, tr. from NOR. (p. 705)
—Underwater. Vetleseter, Tonje, tr. from NOR. (p. 1817)
Sander, Heather. Robbie Packford - Alien Monster (p. 1478)
Sander, Hedda & Deling, Bjorn. Judo: From White/Yellow Belt to Brown Belt. (p. 931)
Sander, Sonia. 3, 2, 1, Liftoff! (p. 1991)
—All Aboard! (p. 41)
—Andrea Takes the Stage. (p. 72)
—Big-Top Scooby-Doo! Duendes Del Sur Staff, illus. (p. 184)
—Big-Top Scooby-Doo! Movie Reader. (p. 184)
—Calling All Cars! (p. 254)
—Chill Out, Scooby-Doo! Duendes Del Sur Staff, illus. (p. 305)
—Easter Egg Dash! A Lift-The-Flap Book with Stickers. Shannon, David et al, illus. (p. 499)
—Fire Truck to the Rescue! (p. 591)
—Help Is on the Way! (p. 765)
—LEGO City Reader Collection: LEGO City Emergency. (p. 990)
—Plant a Garden. Moore, Saxton & McGee, Warner, illus. (p. 1368)
—Scooby-Doo & the International Express. (p. 1529)
—Scooby-Doo Reader #31: Werewolf Watch. Duendes Del Sur Staff, illus. (p. 1529)
—Scooby-Doo!: Untitled TV Reader. (p. 1529)
—Werewolf Watch. (p. 1875)
—Witching Hour. (p. 1941)
Sander, Sonia, jt. auth. see Scholastic, Inc. Staff.
Sander, Sonia, adapted by. Dragon's Snowy Day. (p. 479)
Sander, Sonia & Bridwell, Norman. Clifford Helps Santa. Cuddy, Robbin, illus. (p. 332)
Sander, Sonia & Scieszka, Jon. Smash That Trash! Shannon, David et al, illus. (p. 1593)
Sander, Sonia, told to. Dog: New You for the New Year: The Dogs Share Their Health Secrets! (p. 460)
Sander, Sonya & Scholastic, Inc. Staff. Inkheart. (p. 874)
Sanders, Addie Meyer. I Don't Want to Go. (p. 838)
Sanders, Alex. Lobo! (p. 1044)
—Lolo. (p. 1046)
—Maxibano. (p. 1112)
Sanders, Brian, illus. see Jenkins, Martin.
Sanders, Bruce. Death & Dying. (p. 420)
Sanders, Carly. Whitman College College Prowler off the Record. (p. 1914)
Sanders, Cecilia. Tale of the Perfect Whitetails. (p. 1700)
—Wanted Dead or Alive. (p. 1856)
Sanders, D. J. Metatheatre: A Ten-Minute Comedy Duet. (p. 1130)
—(un)Comfortable Silence: A Ten-Minute Comedy Duet. (p. 1812)
Sanders, D. J., tr. see Clua, Guillem.
Sanders, D. M., jt. auth. see Sanders, D. m.
Sanders, D. m. & Sanders, D. M. Fin the Godsend. (p. 586)
Sanders, Dori. Clover. (p. 335)
Sanders, Doug. Idaho. (p. 852)
—Missouri. (p. 1154)
—Nebraska. (p. 1239)
—North Dakota. (p. 1265)
—Oklahoma. (p. 1282)
—Superstorm Sandy. (p. 1684)
Sanders, Doug & Boehme, Gerry. Missouri. (p. 1154)
Sanders, Doug & Gorman, Jacqueline Laks. Idaho. (p. 852)
Sanders, Doug & Horn, Geoffrey M. Oklahoma. (p. 1283)
Sanders, Doug, et al. Idaho. (p. 852)
—Utah. (p. 1829)
Sanders, E. T. Ninja Grandm. (p. 1256)
Sanders, Esther, tr. see Ochiai, Midori & Oyama, Shigeki.
Sanders, Esther, tr. see Yoshida, Yuko.
Sanders, Francesca. Miss Wonderling's History Class: A Comedy Monologue. (p. 1152)
Sanders, Gaye Lynn. Chameleon Girl. (p. 289)
—Chameleon Girl Again. (p. 289)
Sanders, Jane & Grainger, Ragnil. Youth Justice: Your Guide to Cops & Courts in New South Wales. (p. 1982)
Sanders, Jayneen. Algunos Secretos Nunca Deben Guardarse. Smith, Craig, illus. (p. 38)
—Some Secrets Should Never Be Kept. Smith, Craig, illus. (p. 1609)
Sanders, Jeane F. Ramón. (p. 1438)
Sanders, Jeff & Sanders, Nancy I. Readers Theatre for African American History (p. 1444)
Sanders, Jennifer. My Student Teacher's Last Day. (p. 1219)
—Tail Tales. (p. 1695)
Sanders, Joe Sutliff, tr. see Brontë, Charlotte.
Sanders, Joe Sutliff, tr. see Shakespeare, William.
Sanders, Karen Nordberg. Ruth & Naomi. Rooney, Ronnie, illus. (p. 1498)
Sanders, Kathy. After Oklahoma City: A Grieving Grandmother Uncovers Shocking Truths about the Bombing... & Herself. (p. 28)
Sanders, Lynn Bogen. Social Justice: How You Can Make a Difference (p. 1604)
Sanders, Marcus. Dante's Paradiso Birk, Sandow, illus. (p. 406)
Sanders, Mark, ed. see Aoki, Shoichi.
Sanders, Martin B., jt. auth. see Xavier, Imbeus.
Sanders, Mary. Case of the Missing Alphabet. (p. 274)
Sanders, Michael J. Preteen Challenges: Hurdling to Your Success. (p. 1398)
Sanders, Nancy I. America's Black Founders: Revolutionary Heroes & Early Leaders with 21 Activities. (p. 64)
—Apostle Paul (p. 92)
—Bible Crafts & More, Ages 6-8. (p. 175)
—Bible Crafts on a Shoestring Budget. (p. 175)
—Cut & Paste Mini-Books: Math: 15 Fun, Interactive Mini-Books That Reinforce Key Math Concepts & Boost Reading Skills. (p. 396)
—D Is for Drinking Gourd: An African American Alphabet. Lewis, E. B., illus. (p. 397)
—Fall into Sin: Genesis 2-3 for Children. Van Severen, Joe, illus. (p. 566)
—Frederick Douglass for Kids: His Life & Times, with 21 Activities. (p. 633)
—Jesus (p. 914)
—Jesus Walks on the Water. Swisher, Elizabeth, illus. (p. 916)
—Kid's Guide to African American History: More Than 70 Activities. (p. 953)
—King David (p. 958)
—Mary (p. 1100)
Sanders, Nancy I., jt. auth. see Hering, Marianne.
Sanders, Nancy I., jt. auth. see Sanders, Jeff.
Sanders, Nancy I. & Kuhn, Pamela J. Favorite Bible Heroes: Ages 4&5. Galey, Chuck, illus. (p. 578)
Sanders, Nancy/Ida, jt. auth. see Riddle, Sharon Kay.
Sanders, Norman, ed. see Shakespeare, William.
Sanders, Pete. What You Need to Know about Bullying (p. 1896)
Sanders, Rob. Cowboy Christmas. Manders, John, illus. (p. 373)
—Ruby Rose on Her Toes. Ohi, Debbie Ridpath, illus. (p. 1493)
Sanders, Robert L. Outer Space Bedtime Race. Won, Brian, illus. (p. 1312)
Sanders, Robert S., Jr. Mis Propios Terminos: Mi Jornada Con Asperger's. (p. 1150)
—On My Own Terms: My Journey with Asperger's. (p. 1289)
Sanders, Roy E. Land of Pink. Patzelt, Kasie, illus. (p. 973)
Sanders, Sammy. Bryce's Bike Race: Add Within 20. (p. 233)
Sanders, Sandy. Ms. Goozenpopa's Crazy Alphabet Show & Tell. (p. 1188)
Sanders, Scott, jt. auth. see d'Errico, Camilla.
Sanders, Scott Russell. Bad Man Ballad. (p. 132)
—Floating House. Cogancherry, Helen, illus. (p. 605)
—Warm as Wool. Cogancherry, Helen, illus. (p. 1858)
Sanders, Shauna. Oscar & Eddie's Search for the Golden Bone. (p. 1305)
Sanders, Shelly. Rachel's Promise (p. 1432)
Sanders, Stephanie. Q. T. Pie Meets Smart E. Pauling, Galen T., illus. (p. 1422)
Sanders, Stephanie & Pauling, Galen T. Q. T. Pie's Rescue Adventure. (p. 1422)
Sanders, Stephanie S. Villain School: Good Curses Evil. (p. 1842)
—Villain School: Hero in Disguise. (p. 1842)
Sanders, Steven. Snaggle. (p. 1595)
Sanders, Susan & Sandbeck, Fletcher. Coffee Roasting at Home: The Magic Bean. (p. 338)
Sanders, Ted. Box & the Dragonfly. Bruno, Iacopo, illus. (p. 216)
Sanders, Terri L. Night Flies. (p. 1253)
—Rainbow Spider. (p. 1436)
Sanders, Todd, tr. see Desnos, Robert.
Sanders, Vivienne. Race Relations in the USA since 1900. (p. 1431)
Sanders, Walter. England Explores the Americas. (p. 529)
—France Explores the Americas. (p. 627)
—Spain Explores the Americas. (p. 1620)
Sanderson, Ana. Banana Splits: Ways into Part-Singing. Jude, Connie & Dobson, Phil, illus. (p. 136)
Sanderson, Brandon. Elantris. (p. 508)
—Firefight. (p. 591)
—Hero of Ages (p. 772)
—Rithmatist. (p. 1475)
—Rithmatist. McSweeney, Ben, illus. (p. 1475)
—Steelheart. (p. 1646)
Sanderson, CarolAnn. Two Nativities for Emilee: A Chronology of the Biblical Christmas Story. (p. 1804)
Sanderson, Caroline. Pick Your Brains about Greece. Williams, Caspar, illus. (p. 1354)
Sanderson, Constance, illus. see Webb, Heather.
Sanderson, Geoff. What Color Is It? (p. 1881)
Sanderson, Harvelene. Hello, Jesus Loves You. (p. 764)
Sanderson, Ian, jt. auth. see Crawford, Sheryl Ann Saunders.
Sanderson, Jeanette. Robin Hood Shoots for the Queen: A Legend from England. (p. 1480)
—Visit to the New Amsterdam. (p. 1845)
Sanderson, Jeannette. Odyssey: A Greek Myth. (p. 1279)
—Sword in Stone: A King Arthur Legend. (p. 1692)
Sanderson, Jeannette & Benchmark Education Co., LLC. Echo & Narcissus. Ramos, José, illus. (p. 502)
Sanderson, Jessica B., illus. see Symington, Martha M.
Sanderson, Krystyna. Light at Ground Zero: St. Paul's Chapel After 9/11. Bustard, Ned, ed. (p. 1015)
Sanderson, Nancy. Horse of the Four Winds. (p. 800)
—Summer of the Dancing Horse. (p. 1674)
—Summer of the Painted Horse. (p. 1674)
Sanderson, Ruth. Castle Full of Cats. (p. 276)
—More Saints: Lives & Illuminations. Sanderson, Ruth, illus. (p. 1174)
—Nativity. (p. 1235)
—Papa Gatto: An Italian Fairy Tale. (p. 1322)
—Rose Red & Snow White. (p. 1489)
—Saints: Lives & Illuminations. Sanderson, Ruth, illus. (p. 1504)
—Snow Princess. (p. 1599)
Sanderson, Ruth, illus. see Doty, Jean Slaughter.
Sanderson, Ruth, illus. see Hapka, Catherine, pseud & Hapka, Cathy.
Sanderson, Ruth, illus. see Hapka, Catherine, pseud.
Sanderson, Ruth, illus. see Hart, Alison.
Sanderson, Ruth, illus. see Hermes, Patricia.
Sanderson, Ruth, illus. see Kendall, Jane F.

Sanderson, Ruth, illus. see Sanderson, Whitney.
Sanderson, Ruth, illus. see Yolen, Jane.
Sanderson, Sean, illus. see Scand, Sandra.
Sanderson, Whitney. Darcy. (p. 406)
—Darcy. Sanderson, Ruth, illus. (p. 406)
—Golden Sun. Sanderson, Ruth, illus. (p. 695)
Sanders-Wells, Linda. Maggie's Monkeys. Carter, Abby, illus. (p. 1071)
Sand-Eveland, Cyndi. Dear Toni. (p. 419)
—Tinfoil Sky. (p. 1755)
Sandford, Barbara, illus. see Anderson, P. G.
Sandford, Chester M. Modern Americans: A Biographical School. (p. 1158)
Sandford, John. Little House Hotel. Sandford, John, illus. (p. 1029)
Sandford, John, illus. see Arnold, Caroline.
Sandford, John, illus. see MacNeil, Stephen.
Sandford, John, illus. see Tucker, Kathy.
Sandford, John, illus. see Wallace, Barbara Brooks.
Sandford, John, pseud. Hidden Prey (p. 776)
Sandford, John, pseud & Cook, Michele. Outrage (the Singular Menace, 2) (p. 1313)
—Uncaged. (p. 1811)
—Uncaged (the Singular Menace, 1) (p. 1811)
Sandham, Henry, illus. see Burnett, Frances Hodgson.
Sandheim, May, illus. see Jacob, Violet.
Sandi A. Why, Pops? (p. 1925)
Sandifer, Audie Cavett. Exciting Adventures of Eekie & Squeeky. (p. 547)
Sandifer, Theresa M., jt. auth. see Pelosi, Marilyn K.
Sandiford, Ted, illus. see Bousquet, Anthea.
Sandilands, Joyce. 3 on a Moonbeam. Padur, Simone, illus. (p. 1991)
Sandilands, Joyce, jt. auth. see Whittle, J. Robert.
Sandin, Joan, jt. auth. see Anderson, Lena.
Sandin, Joan, tr. see Björk, Christina.
Sandin, Joan, tr. see Cohen, Peter.
Sandin, Joan, tr. see Dahlin, Adam A.
Sandin, Joan, tr. see Kruusval, Catarina.
Sandin, Joan, tr. see Landstrom, Lena.
Sandin, Joan, tr. see Landstrom, Olof, et al.
Sandin, Joan, tr. see Milde, Jeanette.
Sandland, Reg, illus. see Ulmer, Louise.
Sandler, Karen. Awakening. (p. 120)
Sandler, Martin W. America's Great Disasters. Sandler, Martin W., illus. (p. 64)
—Civil War. (p. 325)
—Dust Bowl Through the Lens: How Photography Revealed & Helped Remedy a National Disaster. (p. 490)
—Flying over the USA: Airplanes in American Life. (p. 610)
—How the Beatles Changed the World. (p. 812)
—Immigrants. (p. 861)
—Impossible Rescue: The True Story of an Amazing Arctic Adventure. (p. 862)
—Imprisoned: The Betrayal of Japanese Americans During World War II. (p. 862)
—Inventors. (p. 884)
—Iron Rails, Iron Men, & the Race to Link the Nation: The Story of the Transcontinental Railroad. (p. 888)
—Kennedy Through the Lens: How Photography & Television Revealed & Shaped an Extraordinary Leader. (p. 948)
—Lincoln Through the Lens: How Photography Revealed & Shaped an Extraordinary Life. (p. 1019)
—Secret Subway: The Fascinating Tale of an Amazing Feat of Engineering. (p. 1544)
—What Was America's Deadliest War? And Other Questions about the Civil War. Hunt, Robert, illus. (p. 1894)
—Who Were the American Pioneers? And Other Questions about Westward Expansion. Barrett, Robert, illus. (p. 1919)
—Why Did the Whole World Go to War? And Other Questions about... World War II. Barrett, Robert, illus. (p. 1923)
Sandler, Martin W., et al. Contemporary Art: World Currents. (p. 360)
Sandler, Michael. Aaron Rodgers & the Green Bay Packers: Super Bowl XLV. (p. 2)
—Adrian Peterson. (p. 13)
—Army Rangers in Action. (p. 100)
—Baseball: The 2004 Boston Red Sox. (p. 140)
—Basketball: The Return of Bernard King. (p. 143)
—Ben Roethlisberger. (p. 163)
—Bethany Hamilton: Follow Your Dreams! (p. 171)
—Brett Favre. (p. 226)
—Brian Urlacher. (p. 226)
—Catastrophic Storms: Set Of 6. (p. 278)
—Catastrophic Storms: Text Pairs. (p. 278)
—Cool Snowboarders. (p. 364)
—Cycling: Lance Armstrong's Impossible Ride. (p. 397)
—Daring BMXers. (p. 406)
—David Eckstein & the St. Louis Cardinals: 2006 World Series. (p. 411)
—Derek Jeter & the New York Yankees: 2000 World Series. (p. 427)
—Deserts: Surviving in the Sahara. (p. 429)
—Donovan Mcnabb. (p. 466)
—Drew Brees & the New Orleans Saints. (p. 485)
—Dynamic Drag Racers. (p. 491)
—Electrifying Eco Race Cars. (p. 509)
—Eli Manning & the New York Giants: Super Bowl Xlvi. (p. 512)
—Enter the Speed Zone. (p. 531)
—Explorers of the Americas: Set Of 6. (p. 551)
—Explorers of the Americas: Text Pairs. (p. 551)
—Fast Rides (p. 576)
—Gnarly Skateboarders. (p. 685)
—Hines Ward & the Pittsburgh Steelers. (p. 780)
—Hockey: Miracle on Ice. (p. 786)
—Hot Hot Rods. (p. 801)
—Ice Skating: The Incredible Michelle Kwan. (p. 850)
—Jean Driscoll: Dream Big, Work Hard! (p. 911)
—Jermaine Dye & the Chicago White Sox: 2005 World Series. (p. 913)
—Jet-Powered Speed. (p. 916)
—Joe Flacco & the Baltimore Ravens: Super Bowl XLVII. (p. 920)
—Joe Montana & the San Fransisco 49ers. (p. 920)
—John Cena. (p. 921)
—John Elway & the Denver Broncos. (p. 921)
—Josh Beckett & the Florida Marlins: 2003 World Series. (p. 926)
—Kurt Warner & the St. Louis Rams. (p. 968)
—Ladainian Tomlinson. (p. 970)
—Larry Fitzgerald. (p. 976)
—LeBron James: I Love Challenges! (p. 987)
—Malcolm Smith & the Seattle Seahawks: Super Bowl XLVIII. (p. 1083)
—Manny Ramirez & the Boston Red Sox: 2004 World Series. (p. 1088)
—Marine Force Recon in Action. (p. 1094)
—Mark Sanchez. (p. 1095)
—Matt Hasselbeck. (p. 1109)
—Mighty MotoXers. (p. 1140)
—Mike Lowell & the Boston Red Sox: 2007 World Series. (p. 1141)
—Military Horses. (p. 1143)
—Most Spectacular Quarterbacks. (p. 1177)
—Mountains: Surviving on Mt. Everest. (p. 1181)
—Oceans: Surviving in the Deep Sea. (p. 1277)
—Pararescuemen in Action. (p. 1324)
—Peyton Manning. (p. 1349)
—Peyton Manning & the Indianapolis Colts. (p. 1349)
—Pro Football's Dream Teams. (p. 1408)
—Pro Football's Stars of the Defense. (p. 1408)
—Race Horses. (p. 1431)
—Rain Forests: Surviving in the Amazon. (p. 1435)
—Rally Car Dudes. (p. 1437)
—Randy Johnson & the Arizona Diamondbacks: 2001 World Series. (p. 1438)
—Rock. (p. 1481)
—Soccer: The Amazing U. S. World Cup Team. (p. 1603)
—Stupendous Sports Stadiums. (p. 1670)
—Super Surfers. (p. 1682)
—Tennis: Victory for Venus Williams. (p. 1720)
—Tim Tebow. (p. 1750)
—Tom Brady & the New England Patriots. (p. 1762)
—Tony Gonzalez. (p. 1766)
—Tony Romo. (p. 1766)
—Troy Aikman & the Dallas Cowboys. (p. 1790)
—Troy Glaus & the Anaheim Angels: 2002 World Series. (p. 1790)
—Troy Polamalu. (p. 1790)
Sandler, Michael & Cohen, Eric. Randy Orton. (p. 1438)
—Triple H. (p. 1787)
Sandler, Michael & Hess, Debra. Checkered Flag! (p. 295)
Sandler, Michael & Pushies, Fred J. Today's Marine Heroes. (p. 1761)
Sandler, Michael & Zegers, Charlie. Amar'E Stoudemire. (p. 52)
—Derrick Rose. (p. 427)
—Dwyane Wade. (p. 491)
—Kevin Durant. (p. 950)
Sandler, Steve. My Uncle Rob. Cunningham, Rob, illus. (p. 1220)
Sandlin, Pauline. Mannequins. (p. 1088)
Sandmann, Alexa L. Civil War. (p. 325)
—Performing Arts (p. 1343)
Sandner, Lionel. What Is Electromagnetism? (p. 1889)
Sandom, J. Two Teen Terrors: Kiss Me, I'm Dead & Confessions of a Teenage Body Snatcher. (p. 1804)
Sandon, Gina, illus. see Proulx, Roxanna Darling.
Sandoval, Alex. Zack Goes to School. (p. 1984)
Sandoval, Ana Valay, jt. auth. see Valay, Ana Patricia.
Sandoval, Anna. Tickle a Daisy. (p. 1747)
Sandoval, Anthony J. Unusual Animals from A to Z. (p. 1823)
Sandoval, Gerardo, illus. see Bowen, Carl & Fuentes, Benny.
Sandoval, Gerardo, illus. see Ciencin, Scott & Fuentes, Benny.
Sandoval, Gerardo, illus. see Fein, Eric & Fuentes, Benny.
Sandoval, Gerardo, illus. see Fuentes, Benny & Hoena, Blake A.
Sandoval, Gerardo, illus. see Hoena, Blake A. & Fuentes, Benny.
Sandoval, Gerardo, illus. see Stevens, Eric & Fuentes, Benny.
Sandoval, Gerardo, illus. see Terrell, Brandon & Fuentes, Benny.
Sandoval, Gerardo, illus. see Wyss, Johann D. & Fuentes, Benny.
Sandoval, Gerardo, illus. see Yomtov, Nel & Fuentes, Benny.
Sandoval, Gerardo, illus. see Yomtov, Nel, et al.
Sandoval, Gerardo, jt. auth. see Andersen, Hans Christian.
Sandoval, Jaime Alfonso, et al. Confidencias de un Superhéroe. Jotave, Jazmin Velasco, illus. (p. 356)
Sandoval, John. Witches of Ruidoso. (p. 1941)
Sandoval, Kate & Keller, Carolyn. UC Santa Barbara College Prowler off the Record: Inside University of California Santa Barbara. (p. 1807)
Sandoval, Lynda. Father Knows Best. (p. 577)
—Who's Your Daddy? (p. 1921)
Sandoval, Migs. Beauty & the Beast: Level 3: Learn Chinese Mandarin Through Fairy Tales. (p. 154)
—Cinderella: Level 1: Learn French Through Fairy Tales. (p. 320)
—Goldilocks & the 3 Bears: Level 2: Learn French Through Fairy Tales. (p. 696)
Sandoval, Migs, illus. see Bobrick, Julie, ed.
Sandoval, Migs, illus. see Burke, David.
Sandoval, Rafa. Ultimate Comics Doomsday. (p. 1809)
Sandoval, Sam, illus. see Confederated Salish and Kootenai Tribes Staff.
Sandoval, Sergio, illus. see Gallardo, Adam.
Sandoval, Victor. Roll over, Big Toben. (p. 1485)
Sandoz, Matt, illus. see Howard, Assuanta.
Sandquist, Brittney D. Take Me to Your Leader. (p. 1696)
Sandra De Mos. Cleo's Playground Adventure. (p. 331)
Sandrey, Alexander & Sellers, Carolyn. Cold Weather Bro's Arctic Adventure. (p. 339)
Sands, Emily. Egyptology: Search for the Tomb of Osiris. Andrew, Ian et al, illus. (p. 507)
—Egyptology Handbook: A Course in the Wonders of Egypt. Steer, Dugald A., ed. (p. 507)
Sands, Emily & Anderson, Wayne. Egyptology: Search for the Tomb of Osiris. Andrew, Ian P. et al, illus. (p. 507)
Sands, Kathryn Ann. How Chili Willie Got His Name. (p. 805)
Sands, Kathryn N. Billy's Big Adventure. (p. 187)
Sands, Kevin. Blackthorn Key. (p. 198)
Sands, Maria. Sanjee & Her Delightful Hats. (p. 1511)
Sands, Monty. King of Nine Mile Canyon. (p. 959)
Sands, Nora. Crunch & Munch. (p. 386)
Sandstrom, Eve K., see Carl, JoAnna, pseud.
Sandstrom, Heather. Brenda Badbroom & the Very Best Pet Yet. (p. 226)
Sandstrom, Karen, illus. see Holbrook, Sara E.
Sandstrom, Karen, illus. see Holbrook, Sara.
Sandstrom, Ulf. Magic Silver Coin: The Secret to a Balanced Life. (p. 1073)
Sandu, Anca. Astonishing Case of the Stolen Stories. (p. 108)
—Churchill's Tale of Tails Sandu, Anca, illus. (p. 318)
Sandusky, Ian. Five Words in Black. (p. 601)
Sandusky, Thomas. Frogs Stopped Singing. (p. 641)
Sandusky, Thomas & Hill, Kathy. Gracie, the Glass Tree Frog. Johnson, Gretchen, illus. (p. 705)
—Peter the Poison Dart Frog, Stories of the Rainforest. Johnson, Gretchen, illus. (p. 1347)
—Spidy the Spider Monkey. Johnson, Gretchen, illus. (p. 1627)
Sandviks HOP, Inc. Staff. Discover Reading: Baby Edition. (p. 448)
—Discover Reading Toddler Edition. (p. 448)
—Hooked on English. (p. 795)
—Hooked on First Grade. (p. 795)
—Hooked on French: Premium Edition. (p. 795)
—Hooked on Kindergarten. (p. 795)
—Learn to Read: Localized Spanish for U. S. (p. 984)
Sandviks HOP, Inc. Staff, contrib. by. Hooked on Second Grade Super Workbook. (p. 795)
—Hooked on Spelling Super Workbook. (p. 795)
—My Colors Wipe-off Board Book with DVD. (p. 1200)
Sandviks HOP, Inc. Staff, ed. Hooked on Baby: Learn to Sign. (p. 795)
Sandvold, Lynnette B. & Capstone Press Editors. Time for Kids Super Science (p. 1751)
Sandvold, Lynnette Brent. Genetics. (p. 661)
—Revolution in Construction. (p. 1466)
—Revolution in Medicine. (p. 1466)
Sandvold, Rolf, jt. auth. see Torpie, Kate.
Sandwall-Bergstrom, Martha. Goldie at the Farm. Stalsjo, Eva, illus. (p. 695)
Sandwall-Bergström, Martha. Goldie at the Orphanage. Stålsjö, Eva, illus. (p. 695)
Sandy, J. P., illus. see Cleary, Brian P.
Sandy, J. P., illus. see Rosen, Michael J. & Kassoy, Ben.
Sandy, John, illus. see Cleary, Brian P.
Sandy Marie Russell. Abc's of Fun Activities. (p. 4)
Sandy, Pat, illus. see Rosen, Michael J. & Kassoy, Ben.
Sandy Taylor, jt. auth. see Asafo-Agyei Okrah, Kwadwo.
Sandys, Jon. Movie Mavericks: Trivia from the Filmmaking Fringes. (p. 1183)
—Movie Mistakes Take. (p. 1183)
Sane, Justin. Heart of a Corpse; an Undead Engagement Part One. Sane, Justin, illus. (p. 759)
Saneshige, Norio. Wu-lung & I-lung: Color Edition. (p. 1965)
—Wu-lung & I-lung: Deluxe Edition. (p. 1965)
Sanfield, Steve. Adventures of High John the Conqueror. (p. 18)
—Feather Merchants, & Other Tales of the Fools of Chelm. Magaril, Mikhail, illus. (p. 579)
Sanfilippo, Simona. Rapunzel. (p. 1439)
Sanfilippo, Simona, illus. see Robinson, Hilary.
Sanfilippo, Simona, illus. see Wilding, Valerie.
Sanford. Today's Teen. (p. 1761)
Sanford, Agnes. Melissa & the Little Red Book. Heinen, Sandy, illus. (p. 1125)
Sanford, Barry. Shoes. (p. 1568)
Sanford, Candace. Captain Nathaniel Brown Palmer. Scala, Susan, illus. (p. 264)
Sanford, Carl R. & Sanford, William R. Outlaws & Lawmen of the Wild West (p. 1312)
Sanford, Joyce. Goldenlocks & Her 3 Homes. (p. 695)
Sanford, Lidia. Children's Diabetes. (p. 303)
Sanford, Lori Hood, illus. see Wean, Sarah.
Sanford, Rob. Self-Centering Manual: How to Align Your Outward Behavior with Your Inner Belief. (p. 1549)
Sanford, Timothy L. Tengo que Ser Perfecto: (y otras herejias de la casa Pastoral) Rdm, tr. from ENG. (p. 1720)
Sanford, William. Margo's Pen (p. 1092)
Sanford, William R. Apache Chief Geronimo. (p. 91)
—Comanche Chief Quanah Parker. (p. 346)
—Hunkpapa Lakota Chief Sitting Bull. (p. 828)
—Nez Percé Chief Joseph. (p. 1249)
—Oglala Lakota Chief Red Cloud. (p. 1280)
—Oglala Sioux Chief Crazy Horse. (p. 1280)
—Seminole Chief Osceola. (p. 1550)
Sanford, William R., jt. auth. see Green, Carl R.
Sanford, William R., jt. auth. see Sanford, Carl R.
Sanford, William R. & Green, Carl R. Bill Pickett: Courageous African-American Cowboy. (p. 186)
—Brigham Young: Courageous Mormon Leader. (p. 228)
—Buffalo Bill Cody: Courageous Wild West Showman. (p. 235)
—Calamity Jane: Courageous Wild West Woman. (p. 252)
—Daniel Boone: Courageous Frontiersman. (p. 405)
—Davy Crockett: Courageous Hero of the Alamo. (p. 411)
—John C. Frémont: Courageous Pathfinder of the Wild West. (p. 921)
—Kit Carson: Courageous Mountain Man. (p. 962)
—Richard King: Courageous Texas Cattleman. (p. 1469)
—Sacagawea: Courageous American Indian Guide. (p. 1500)
—Sam Houston: Courageous Texas Hero. (p. 1506)
—Zebulon Pike: Courageous Rocky Mountain Explorer. (p. 1985)
Sang, David, et al. Scientifica. (p. 1528)
Sang, Francesca Ho, compiled by. Wisdom of Frogs. (p. 1939)
—Wisdom of Kittens. (p. 1939)
—Wisdom of Pandas. (p. 1939)
—Wisdom of Penguins. (p. 1939)
Sanger, Amy Wilson. Mangia! Mangia! (p. 1087)
—Yum Yum Dim Sum. Sanger, Amy Wilson, illus. (p. 1983)
Sanger, Amy Wilson & Wilson Sanger, Amy. Little Bit of Soul Food. Wilson Sanger, Amy, illus. (p. 1024)
Sanger, Rick. No Eat Not Food: The Search for Intelligent Food on Planet Earth. Russell, Carol, illus. (p. 1258)
Sangha Mitra, Ms Janice. Golden Bear: The Story of a Flowering Heart. Sangha Mitra, Ms Janice, illus. (p. 694)
Sangregorio, Fernando, illus. see Santillana.
Sangster, Alan, jt. auth. see Wood, Frank.
Sangster, Margaret. Splendid Times. (p. 1630)
Sangster, Margaret Elizabeth, ed. Holiday Stories for Young People. (p. 788)
Sangster, Margret Elizabeth, jt. auth. see Noonan, Shelley.
Sang-Sun, Park, illus. see Eun-Ha, Jo.
Sanguedolce, Patty & Cowne, Chris. In the Belly of an Elephant. (p. 865)
Sanjo, Riku. Beet the Vandel Buster Inada, Koji, illus. (p. 158)
—Beet the Vandel Buster (p. 158)
—Beet the Vandel Buster Inada, Koji, illus. (p. 158)
—Beet the Vandel Buster. Inada, Koji, illus. (p. 158)
Sanjo, Riku, jt. auth. see Inada, Koji.
Sanjo, Riku & Inada, Koji. Beet the Vandel Buster. (p. 158)
San-Joyz, Naweko. Acne Messages: Crack the Code of Your Zits & Say Goodbye to Acne. (p. 9)
—Skinny Fat Girls: Why we're still not getting this dieting Thing. (p. 1585)
Sankaranarayanan, Ayswarya, illus. see Subramaniam, Manasi.
Sankey, Alice. Roy Rogers & the Desert Treasure. Souza, Paul, illus. (p. 1492)
—Roy Rogers' Surprise for Donnie. Steel, John, illus. (p. 1492)
Sankey, Erica. Magic Dust. (p. 1072)
Sankey, Tom, illus. see Gryski, Camilla.
Sanmiguel, Rosario, tr. see Bernardo, Anilu.
Sanmiguel, Rosario, tr. see Bertrand, Diane Gonzales.
Sanmugam, Devagi & Den Ouden, Marijke. Fun with Asian Food: A Kids' Cookbook. (p. 648)
Sanna, Alessandro, creator. River. (p. 1475)
Sanna, Charles A. Daddy. Daddy There's a Mouse in the House. Hill, Dave, illus. (p. 398)
Sanna, E. J. Heroin & Other Opioids: Poppies' Perilous Children. Henningfield, Jack E., ed. (p. 773)
—Lloyd Banks. (p. 1043)
—Marijuana: Mind-Altering Weed. (p. 1094)
—Marijuana: Mind-Altering Weed. Henningfield, Jack E., ed. (p. 1094)
Sanna, Ellyn. Big Portions, Big Problems. Garcia, Victor, ed. (p. 183)
—Childcare Worker. Riggs, Ernestine G. & Gholar, Cheryl, eds. (p. 302)
—Ethnic Folklore. (p. 539)
—Firefighters' Folklore. (p. 591)
—Folk Customs. (p. 611)
—Folk Festivals. (p. 611)
—Folk Religion. (p. 611)
—Folk Tales & Legends. (p. 611)
—Food Folklore. (p. 613)
—Gallup Guides for Youth Facing Persistent Prejudice Muslims. (p. 653)
—Homeland Security Officer. Riggs, Ernestine G. & Gholar, Cheryl, eds. (p. 793)
—Mary, Mother of Jesus. (p. 1101)
—Mexican Americans' Role in the United States: A History of Pride, a Future of Hope. (p. 1131)
—Mexican Facts & Figures. (p. 1131)
—Mexico: Facts & Figures. (p. 1131)
—Native North American Indians. (p. 1235)
—Nature's Wrath: Surviving Natural Disasters. (p. 1237)
—People with Mental & Physical Challenges. (p. 1340)
—Politician. (p. 1380)
—Politician. Riggs, Ernestine G. & Gholar, Cheryl, eds. (p. 1380)
—Potawatomi. (p. 1388)
—Special Education Teacher. (p. 1623)
—Special Education Teacher. Riggs, Ernestine G. & Gholar, Cheryl, eds. (p. 1623)
—Those Who Remain: What It Means to Be a Survivor. (p. 1740)
—Women in the World of China. (p. 1946)
Sanna, Ellyn, jt. auth. see Seba, Jaime.
Sanna, Emily. Gay Believers: Homosexuality & Religion. (p. 659)
—Pop Monsters: The Modern-Day Craze for Vampires & Werewolves. (p. 1384)
Sanna, Gabriel. Baseball & Softball. (p. 141)
Sanna, Jeanine. Austria. (p. 116)
Sanna, Jeanine & Indovino, Shaina C. Austria. Bruton, John, ed. (p. 116)
—France. Bruton, John, ed. (p. 627)
Sanna, Jeanine & Indovino, Shaina Carmel. Austria. (p. 116)
—France. (p. 627)
Sanna, Lindsey. Game. (p. 654)
Sanne, Don, illus. see Coons, Susan Anderson.
Sanner, Catie. Cooking with Catie: The 3ABN Kids Time Cookbook. Walsh, Brenda, ed. (p. 362)
Sanner, Jennifer Jackson, ed. Three Little Jayhawks. Pearson, Larry Leroy, illus. (p. 1742)
Sannes, Dorothy L. Simple Things You Can Do to Carry Your Child Through School (p. 1578)
Sanoja, Kira Shanell. Ducks from the Block. (p. 488)
Sanrio. Best Friends: Hello Kitty & Me. (p. 169)
—Easter Bonnet Surprise. (p. 499)
—Happy St. Patrick's Day, Hello Kitty. (p. 746)
—Hello Kitty Goes to Camp. (p. 764)
—Hello Kitty, Hello Halloween! (p. 764)
—Hello Kitty, Hello Love! (p. 764)
—Hello Kitty Storybook Collection. (p. 764)
—Hello Kitty: What Will You Be a to Z? (p. 764)
—Hugs: Hello Kitty & Me. (p. 825)
—Let's Go to School. (p. 997)
—Merry Christmas, Hello Kitty! (p. 1128)

—Trick or Treat: Hello Kitty & Me. (p. 1786)
Sanrio Company, LTD. Hello Kitty, Hello Winter! Hirashima, Jean, illus. (p. 764)
Sanrio Company, Ltd Staff. Happy Birthday, Hello Kitty. (p. 744)
—Hello Kitty, Hello Fall! Hirashima, Jean, illus. (p. 764)
—Hello Kitty, Hello New York! Hirashima, Jean, illus. (p. 764)
—I Heart Hello Kitty Activity Book: Read, Write, Count, & Draw with Hello Kitty & Friends! (p. 839)
Sanrio Company, Ltd Staff, illus. see Becker and Mayer! Books Staff.
Sanrio Company, Ltd Staff, jt. auth. see Hirashima, Jean.
Sanrio Company, Ltd Staff & Hirashima, Jean. Hello Kitty, Hello Summer! (p. 764)
Sanroman, Susana. Senora Reganona: A Mexican Bedtime Story. (p. 1550)
—Senora Reganona: A Mexican Bedtime Story. Domi, illus. (p. 1550)
Sanschagrin, Joceline. At Grandma & Grandpa's. Brignaud, Pierre & Depratto, Marcel, illus. (p. 110)
—Caillou: Potty Time. Brignaud, Pierre, illus. (p. 251)
—Caillou: The Broken Castle. Brignaud, Pierre, illus. (p. 251)
—Caillou at the Doctor. Brignaud, Pierre, illus. (p. 251)
—Caillou, Be Careful! Brignaud, Pierre, illus. (p. 251)
—Caillou: It's Mine! Brignaud, Pierre, illus. (p. 251)
—Caillou Takes a Bath. Brignaud, Pierre, illus. (p. 251)
—Hora del Bano. (p. 797)
—Osito de Peluche. (p. 1305)
—Visage Masqué. Brignaud, Pierre, illus. (p. 1844)
Sanserl, Wanda. Play by the Sea. (p. 1371)
—SWR Chart Pack. (p. 1692)
Sansevero, Tony, illus. see Cockrum, James L.
Sansevero, Tony, illus. see Morris, Kimberly & Burke, Kathleen.
Sansevero, Tony, illus. see Wermund, Jerry.
Sansom, Anthony. Thirsty Horse of Mongolia. (p. 1734)
Sansom, Fiona, illus. see Claybourne, Anna.
Sansom, Fiona, illus. see Elgin, Kathy.
Sansom, Fiona, illus. see Morris, Neil.
Sansom, Fiona, illus. see Williams, Suzanne.
Sansom, Fiona, jt. auth. see Bingham, Jane.
Sansone, Adele. Little Green Goose. Faust, Anke, illus. (p. 1028)
Sansone, Emma. Getting to Know Italy & Italian. Woolley, Kim, illus. (p. 669)
Sansone, Leslie. Walking the Walk: Getting Fit with Faith. (p. 1854)
Sansone, V. K. Carpenter & His Wife. (p. 271)
—Daunting Quest for Quincy & Quigley. (p. 410)
—Heavenly Hannah's Little Black Hat. (p. 761)
—Katie Bear: Fun Days at School. WillowRaven, Aidana, illus. (p. 945)
—Katie Bear & Friends (Book One) (p. 945)
—Katie Bear & Friends (Book Three) (p. 945)
—Pandora's Incredible Journey. (p. 1321)
—Strange Day at the Zoo. (p. 1665)
—Tweens Book of Shorts. (p. 1799)
—WANTED: Children for Toys. (p. 1856)
Sansum, Vicki, jt. auth. see Enderle, Dotti.
Sansweet, Stephen J. & Hidalgo, Pablo. Prequels. (p. 1396)
Sant, Geoff, tr. see Yamada, Futaro.
Sant, Sharon. Runners. (p. 1497)
Santa, Carlos Piedra. Animales Mensajeros. (p. 81)
Santa, Carlos Piedra, illus. see Zea, Amilcar.
Santa Elena, Antonio E. Babba Has Golden Feathers. (p. 123)
Santa Niclaus. Hay Baggins: The Little Scarecrow Boy. (p. 755)
—Letter from Sant: The Original. (p. 1002)
Santacroce, John P. Running Across the Moon. (p. 1497)
Santacruz, Juan, illus. see Parker, Jeff.
Santamaria, Jenni Currie & Keyes, Joan Ross. Content Areas for Kids: Accelerates Academic Language Development. (p. 360)
Santamaria, Jenni Currie, et al. Oxford Picture Dictionary Content Area for Kids. (p. 1315)
Santan. Good & Evil: The Princess & Devil. (p. 697)
Santana, Andrea, illus. see Castelli, Jeanette.
Santana, Elaina. Tania: Volume 1 (p. 1705)
Santana, Rachel. Who's Older? Understand & Apply Properties of Operations. (p. 1921)
Santana, Sr. Sabina Stella. Happy Ending Children's Stories, & More: Poems, Tongue-Twisters, Proverbs, & Brain-Teasers. (p. 745)
Santana, Sr. Stella. We Are the People of This World: Book One. Bear, Andrea, illus. (p. 1866)
Santanach, Tino, illus. see Beakman, Onk.
Santanach, Tino, illus. see Golden Books Staff.
Santaniello, Shelly W. Tommy's Needham Rocket. (p. 1765)
Santat, Dan. Adventures of Beekle: The Unimaginary Friend. (p. 16)
—Mighty Robot vs. the Stupid Stinkbugs from Saturn. (p. 1140)
—Sidekicks. (p. 1573)
—Stupid Stinkbugs from Saturn. (p. 1670)
Santat, Dan, illus. see Barnett, Mac.
Santat, Dan, illus. see Beaty, Andrea.
Santat, Dan, illus. see Berger, Samantha.
Santat, Dan, illus. see Buckley, Michael.
Santat, Dan, illus. see Diesen, Deborah.
Santat, Dan, illus. see Elya, Susan Middleton.
Santat, Dan, illus. see Esbaum, Jill.
Santat, Dan, illus. see Going, K. L.
Santat, Dan, illus. see Gutman, Dan.
Santat, Dan, illus. see Isaacs, Anne.
Santat, Dan, illus. see Marsoli, Lisa Ann.
Santat, Dan, illus. see Perlman, Rhea.
Santat, Dan, illus. see Pilkey, Dav.
Santat, Dan, illus. see Reynolds, Aaron.
Santat, Dan, illus. see Sauer, Tammi.
Santat, Dan, illus. see Schwartz, Corey Rosen.
Santat, Dan, illus. see Scieszka, Jon, et al.
Santat, Dan, illus. see Selfors, Suzanne.
Santat, Dan, illus. see Spratt, R. A.
Santat, Dan, illus. see Yee, Lisa.
Santat, Dan, illus. see Zappa, Ahmet.
Sante, Andrew R. Silver Heart Chronicles: The Voyage. (p. 1576)
Santella, Andrew. All Around Illinois: Regions & Resources (p. 43)
—Aztec. (p. 122)
—Building the New York Subway. (p. 239)
—First Thanksgiving. (p. 597)
—French & Indian War. (p. 635)
—Hopi. (p. 797)
—Illinois History (p. 857)
—Illinois Native Peoples (p. 857)
—Illinois Plants & Animals (p. 857)
—Kentucky. (p. 949)
—Library of Congress Santella, Andrew, illus. (p. 1006)
—Millard Fillmore. (p. 1143)
—Mountain Men. (p. 1181)
—Navajo. (p. 1237)
—Navajo Code Talkers (p. 1237)
—Pearl Harbor. (p. 1333)
—People of Illinois (p. 1339)
—Persian Gulf War. (p. 1344)
—Plains Indians (p. 1366)
—Rutherford B. Hayes. (p. 1499)
—Southeast Indians (p. 1617)
—Uniquely Illinois (p. 1818)
Santella, Andrew, jt. auth. see Davis, Marc.
Santella, Sheila. Simons Gift. (p. 1577)
Santella, Thomas & Triggle, David J. Hallucinogens. (p. 739)
Santella, Tom. Body Enhancement Products. Triggle, David J., ed. (p. 207)
Santelli, Bob & Santelli, Robert. Greetings from E Street: The Story of Bruce Springsteen & the E Street Band. (p. 723)
Santelli, Robert, jt. auth. see Santelli, Bob.
Santhosh, Lekshmi, ed. see Schimler, Stuart.
Santiago Baca, Jimmy. En Suelo Firme: El Nacimiento de un Poeta. Berástegui, Manu, tr. (p. 523)
Santiago, Brianna A. Why Is the Moon Following Us? (p. 1925)
Santiago, Carmen. Fun & Easy Spanish for You (p. 647)
Santiago, Carmen Angelica. Fun & Easy Spanish for You (p. 647)
Santiago, Chiori. Home to Medicine Mountain. (p. 793)
—Home to Medicine Mountain. Lowry, Judith, illus. (p. 793)
Santiago, Claribel, ed. see Rodriguez, Edarissa.
Santiago, Danielle & Whitaker, Tu-Shonda L. Cream. (p. 378)
Santiago, Esmeralda. Muneca para el Dia de Reyes. Torres-Vidal, Nina, tr. from ENG. (p. 1191)
Santiago, Roberto. Ultimo Sordo. (p. 1810)
Santiago, Rose Mary, illus. see Shah, Idries.
Santiago, Rose Mary, illus. see Shah, Indries.
Santiago, Rose Mary, tr. see Shah, Idries.
Santiago, Shelly. Fairies of Tythian. (p. 563)
Santiago, Tony. Greyhound's Tale: Running for Glory, Walking for Home. (p. 723)
Santiago, Tony, illus. see Pierce, Craig.
Santillan, Jorge. When's the Doctor? (p. 1906)
Santillan, Jorge, illus. see Eason, Sarah.
Santillan, Jorge, illus. see Schwaeber, Barbie Heit.
Santillan, Jorge, jt. auth. see Jones, Richard.
Santillan, Jorge & British Broadcasting Corporation Staff. When's the Doctor? (p. 1906)
Santillan, Jorge & Eason, Sarah. Drawing Dinosaurs. (p. 481)
—Drawing Dragons. (p. 481)
—Drawing Fairies, Mermaids, & Unicorns. (p. 481)
—Drawing Knights & Castles. (p. 482)
—Drawing Pirates & Pirate Ships. (p. 482)
Santillan, Jorge H. Sports Illustrated Kids Victory School Superstars (p. 1632)
Santillan, Jorge H., illus. see Gassman, Julie A.
Santillan, Jorge H., illus. see Gunderson, Jessica.
Santillan, Jorge H., illus. see Kreie, Chris.
Santillan, Jorge H., illus. see LeBoutillier, Nate.
Santillan, Jorge H., illus. see Nickel, Scott.
Santillan, Jorge H., illus. see Priebe, Val.
Santillan, Jorge H., illus. see Yasuda, Anita.
Santillan, Maria Luisa. Circuito Interior: Los Deportistas Por Dentro. Cuevas, Andres Mario Ramirez, illus. (p. 321)
Santillan, Mariano, illus. see Edison, Richard E.
Santillan, Mariano, illus. see Sirois, Celia.
Santillan, Suzanne. Grandma's Pear Tree. Pernisco, Atilio, illus. (p. 709)
—Grandma's Pear Tree/El Peral de Abuela. Pernisco, Atilio, illus. (p. 709)
Santillana. Nuevo Diccionario Escolar de la Lengual Espanola. (p. 1270)
—Pictodiccionario: Diccionario en Im Genes. Sangregorio, Fernando et al, illus. (p. 1355)
Santillana & Dorling Kindersley Publishing Staff. Colores. (p. 344)
—Figuras. (p. 586)
—Numeros. (p. 1273)
—Tamanos. (p. 1704)
Santillana U. S. A. Publishing Co, Inc. Staff. David Crockett. Alvarez, Jose M. & Alonso, Jesus, illus. (p. 410)
Santillana USA. Dreams. Suarez, Maribel, illus. (p. 484)
Santillan-Cruz, Silvia R., tr. see Frontiera, Deborah K.
Santillan-Cruz, Sylvia R., tr. see Van Scoyoc, Pam.
Santilli, Shirley. Trouble in Treeville. Santilli Wolfinger, Lorrie, illus. (p. 1790)
Santilli Wolfinger, Lorrie, illus. see Santilli, Shirley.
Santillo, LuAnn. At the Beach Santillo, LuAnn, ed. (p. 110)
—At the Circus Santillo, LuAnn, ed. (p. 111)
—Bad Crab. Santillo, LuAnn, ed. (p. 131)
—Ball. Santillo, LuAnn, ed. (p. 134)
—Barnyard Buddies Santillo, LuAnn, ed. (p. 139)
—Bee. Santillo, LuAnn, ed. (p. 157)
—Best Show. Santillo, LuAnn, ed. (p. 171)
—Best Tricks. Santillo, LuAnn, ed. (p. 171)
—Big Hunt. Santillo, LuAnn, ed. (p. 181)
—Big Job. Santillo, LuAnn, ed. (p. 182)
—Big Top. Santillo, LuAnn, ed. (p. 184)
—Blends & Ends - Level B Santillo, LuAnn, ed. (p. 199)
—Bluejay. Santillo, LuAnn, ed. (p. 204)
—Buzz. Santillo, LuAnn, ed. (p. 248)
—Cat. Santillo, LuAnn, ed. (p. 277)
—Chick. Santillo, LuAnn, ed. (p. 299)
—Chip. Santillo, LuAnn, ed. (p. 308)
—Community Helpers Santillo, LuAnn, ed. (p. 350)
—Cop. Santillo, LuAnn, ed. (p. 365)
—Dentist. Santillo, LuAnn, ed. (p. 426)
—Digging for Clams. Santillo, LuAnn, ed. (p. 439)
—Dip & Sip. Santillo, LuAnn, ed. (p. 445)
—Doctor. Santillo, LuAnn, ed. (p. 459)
—Dog. Santillo, LuAnn, ed. (p. 460)
—Down on the Farm Santillo, LuAnn, ed. (p. 474)
—Duck. Santillo, LuAnn, ed. (p. 488)
—Eggs. Santillo, LuAnn, ed. (p. 506)
—Family Fun Santillo, LuAnn, ed. (p. 568)
—Fire Fighter. Santillo, LuAnn, ed. (p. 590)
—Fishing. Santillo, LuAnn, ed. (p. 599)
—Flap. Santillo, LuAnn, ed. (p. 602)
—Flipper. Santillo, LuAnn, ed. (p. 605)
—Fred & Ed. Santillo, LuAnn, ed. (p. 632)
—Fun Trip. Santillo, LuAnn, ed. (p. 648)
—Fun with Phonemes. Santillo, LuAnn, ed. (p. 649)
—Funny Clowns. Santillo, LuAnn, ed. (p. 649)
—Go West. Santillo, LuAnn, ed. (p. 687)
—Good Food. Santillo, LuAnn, ed. (p. 698)
—Gum. Santillo, LuAnn, ed. (p. 731)
—I Have Fun. Santillo, LuAnn, ed. (p. 839)
—In the Meadow Santillo, LuAnn, ed. (p. 866)
—Jack. Santillo, LuAnn, ed. (p. 902)
—Jake's Big Day. Santillo, LuAnn, ed. (p. 906)
—Jane. Santillo, LuAnn, ed. (p. 907)
—Jim & the Thug. Santillo, LuAnn, ed. (p. 917)
—King. Santillo, LuAnn, ed. (p. 958)
—Kiss. Santillo, LuAnn, ed. (p. 961)
—Level A- Take Home Readers. Santillo, LuAnn, ed. (p. 1003)
—Level B Take Home Readers. Santillo, LuAnn, ed. (p. 1003)
—Level C - Take Home Readers. Santillo, LuAnn, ed. (p. 1003)
—Lift-Off. Santillo, LuAnn, ed. (p. 1014)
—Lion Tamer. Santillo, LuAnn, ed. (p. 1020)
—Liz. Santillo, LuAnn, ed. (p. 1042)
—Look at Me. Santillo, LuAnn, ed. (p. 1048)
—Lots More Fun with Phonemes. Santillo, LuAnn, ed. (p. 1057)
—Mailman. Santillo, LuAnn, ed. (p. 1077)
—Medieval Magic Santillo, LuAnn, ed. (p. 1119)
—Mike. Santillo, LuAnn, ed. (p. 1141)
—Mole. Santillo, LuAnn, ed. (p. 1160)
—More Fun with Phonemes. Santillo, LuAnn, ed. (p. 1174)
—Moving A-Long Level C Santillo, LuAnn, ed. (p. 1183)
—Outerspace Santillo, LuAnn, ed. (p. 1312)
—Packing. Santillo, LuAnn, ed. (p. 1317)
—Picnic. Santillo, LuAnn, ed. (p. 1355)
—Pig. Santillo, LuAnn, ed. (p. 1357)
—Pioneer Days Santillo, LuAnn, ed. (p. 1361)
—Rags. Santillo, LuAnn, ed. (p. 1433)
—Rose. Santillo, LuAnn, ed. (p. 1489)
—Running Fox. Santillo, LuAnn, ed. (p. 1497)
—Seeds. Santillo, LuAnn, ed. (p. 1547)
—Shag. Santillo, LuAnn, ed. (p. 1558)
—Sights & Sounds - Level Santillo, LuAnn, ed. (p. 1574)
—Six Jobs. Santillo, LuAnn, ed. (p. 1582)
—Snack Shack. Santillo, LuAnn, ed. (p. 1595)
—Snail. Santillo, LuAnn, ed. (p. 1595)
—Steve & Pete. Santillo, LuAnn, ed. (p. 1649)
—Stop Hopping. Santillo, LuAnn, ed. (p. 1653)
—Stubs. Santillo, LuAnn, ed. (p. 1668)
—Sun. Santillo, LuAnn, ed. (p. 1675)
—Suntan. Santillo, LuAnn, ed. (p. 1679)
—Ted's Job. Santillo, LuAnn, ed. (p. 1713)
—Tight Rope. Santillo, LuAnn, ed. (p. 1749)
—Toad. Santillo, LuAnn, ed. (p. 1759)
—Tracks. Santillo, LuAnn, ed. (p. 1775)
—Trip. Santillo, LuAnn, ed. (p. 1787)
—Trot, Trot. Santillo, LuAnn, ed. (p. 1789)
—Tune. Santillo, LuAnn, ed. (p. 1796)
—UFO. Santillo, LuAnn, ed. (p. 1807)
—Under the Sea Santillo, LuAnn, ed. (p. 1814)
—Vet. Santillo, LuAnn, ed. (p. 1839)
—Wet Dock. Santillo, LuAnn, ed. (p. 1877)
—Wild West Santillo, LuAnn, ed. (p. 1930)
—Wish. Santillo, LuAnn, ed. (p. 1940)
Santini, Debrah L., illus. see Santucci, Barbara.
Santini, Linda. Solving the Mystery of ADHD—Naturally. (p. 1608)
Santini, Nicky. Christes y Sorpresas prar Ninos. (p. 311)
Santini, Philip. Harvey's Adventures. Chambers, Z., illus. (p. 752)
Santirso, Liliana. Capitan. (p. 262)
—Me Gusta Jugar Con los Libros. Gomez, Patricio & Villagomez, Raul, illus. (p. 1116)
Santitoro, Theresa, illus. see Isler, Linda Germano.
Santolaya, Antonia, illus. see Alonso, Manuel L. & Alonso Gómez, Manuel L.
Santolaya, Antonia, tr. see Alonso, Manuel L. & Alonso Gómez, Manuel L.
Santoli, Christie. Zodiac for Kids. (p. 1987)
Santomauro, Fabio, illus. see Elvgren, Jennifer.
Santomenna, Joan E. & Santomenna, Marco D. Caribbean Capers. (p. 268)
Santomenna, Marco D., jt. auth. see Santomenna, Joan E.
Santomero, Angela. Daniel's First Sleepover. (p. 405)
Santomero, Angela C. Big Brother Daniel. Fruchter, Jason, illus. (p. 179)
—Blue Va a la Escuela. Levy, David B., illus. (p. 203)
—Daniel Tiger: The Baby Is Here! (p. 405)
—Goodnight, Daniel Tiger. (p. 701)
—Goodnight, Daniel Tiger. Style Guide Staff, illus. (p. 701)
—Happy Halloween, Daniel Tiger! Style Guide Staff & Fruchter, Jason, illus. (p. 745)
Santomero, Angela C., adapted by. You Are Special, Daniel Tiger! (p. 1973)
Santopolo, Jill. All That Glitters. (p. 45)
—Bad News Nails. (p. 132)
—Love on the Lifts. (p. 1060)
—Nina, the Pinta, & the Vanishing Treasure. (p. 1256)
—Purple Nails & Puppy Tails. (p. 1419)
—Summer Love. (p. 1674)
—True Colors. (p. 1792)
Santora, Bud, illus. see Wooten, Arthur.
Santora, L. Steven. Touched by an Angel's Tear. Connors, Clare & Szitas, Kathie, eds. (p. 1772)
Santora, Maureen Crethan. Day the Towers Fell: The Story of September 11, 2001. (p. 414)
—Day the Towers Fell: The Story of September 11, 2001. Santora, Maureen Crethan, illus. (p. 414)
—My Son Christopher: A 9/11 Mother's Tale of Remembrance. (p. 1219)
Santore, Charles. Aesop's Fables. (p. 25)
—Cuento de Nochebuena: Una Visita de San Nicolas. (p. 389)
—Night Before Christmas. (p. 1252)
—Stowaway on Noah's Ark. (p. 1664)
—William the Curious: Knight of the Water Lilies. (p. 1933)
—William the Curious: Knight of the Water Lilies. Santore, Charles, illus. (p. 1933)
Santore, Charles, illus. see Anderson, Hans Christian.
Santore, Charles, illus. see Grimm, Jacob & Grimm, Wilhelm.
Santore, Charles, illus. see Longfellow, Henry Wadsworth.
Santore, Charles, illus. see Moore, Clement C.
Santore, Charles, illus. see Potter, Beatrix.
Santore, Charles, illus. see Williams, Margery.
Santore, Charles & Potter, Beatrix. Peter Rabbit Board Book. Encarnacion, Elizabeth, ed. (p. 1347)
Santoro. My Secret Place: A Simply Gorjuss Journal. Santoro, illus. (p. 1218)
Santoro, Christopher. It's Haunted! (p. 897)
Santoro, Christopher, illus. see Baker, Ken.
Santoro, Christopher, illus. see Evans, Nate & Brown, Stephanie Gwyn.
Santoro, Christopher, illus. see Milton, Joyce.
Santoro, Christopher, illus. see Stephens, Amanda.
Santoro, Frank, jt. auth. see Millar, Mark.
Santoro, Lucio & Santoro, Meera. Wild Oceans: A Pop-Up Book with Revolutionary Technology. (p. 1930)
Santoro, Matt, jt. auth. see Niles, Steve.
Santoro, Meera, jt. auth. see Santoro, Lucio.
Santoro, Scott. Farm-Fresh Cats. (p. 574)
—Which Way to Witch School? Santoro, Scott, illus. (p. 1911)
Santorum, Karen. Everyday Graces: Child's Book of Good Manners. Torode, Sam, illus. (p. 543)
Santos, Angel David. Love Story Written in the Stars. (p. 1060)
Santos, Antonio. Pancho. (p. 1320)
—Viaje de Pancho. (p. 1839)
Santos, Care. Como Nos Hicimos Amigas. (p. 351)
—Dime la Verdad. (p. 440)
—Prohibido Enamorarse. (p. 1410)
—Ser Feliz Es Facil. (p. 1552)
Santos, Carriel Ann, illus. see Bortnick, Lori.
Santos, D. Friends: Learning the FR Sound. (p. 638)
—I Can Draw: Learning the DR Sound. (p. 835)
—My New Glasses: Learning the GL Sound. (p. 1216)
Santos de las Heras, José María. Cachicos. (p. 250)
Santos, Dennis. Earl the Pearl. (p. 492)
Santos, Edson. Cool Careers Without College for People who Love to Buy Things. (p. 363)
—People Who Love to Buy Things. (p. 1340)
Santos, Edward J. Everything You Need to Know If You & Your Parents Are New Americans. (p. 546)
Santos, Jordan, jt. auth. see Ching, Brent.
Santos, Ma Jesus, illus. see O'Callaghan, Elena.
Santos, Marisa de los, see de los Santos, Marisa.
Santos, Martha. Littlest Fairy. (p. 1039)
Santos, Nuria G., tr. see Hagen, Oddmund.
Santos, Patti Higdon. Bobby, the Blue-Footed Booby. (p. 206)
Santos, Penelope. Fireman & Fire. (p. 592)
—Peas for Pat. (p. 1333)
Santos, Ray. Justice League Classic: I Am Green Lantern. (p. 940)
—Justice League Classic: I Am Green Lantern. Gordon, Steven E. & Gordon, Eric A., illus. (p. 940)
—Meet the Rangers. (p. 1123)
—Transformers Prime: Optimus Prime & the Secret Mission. (p. 1778)
Santos, Ray & Landers, Ace. Power Rangers Samurai: Armed for Battle. (p. 1390)
Santoso, Charles, illus. see Eyre, Lindsay.
Santoso, Charles, illus. see Ferrell, Sean.
Santoso, Charles, illus. see McGee, Joe.
Santoso, Charles, illus. see Young, Jessica.
Santow, Dan. Millard Fillmore. (p. 1143)
Santrey, Laurence, jt. auth. see Mattern, Joanne.
Santrey, Laurence & Macken, JoAnn Early. Davy Crockett: Young Pioneer. Livingston, Francis, illus. (p. 411)
Santrey, Laurence & Mattern, Joanne. Genio Creativo. Beier, Ellen, illus. (p. 661)
Santucci, Barbara. Abby's Chairs. Santini, Debrah L., illus. (p. 2)
—Loon Summer. (p. 1052)
—Loon Summer. Shine, Andrea, illus. (p. 1052)
Santy, Elizabeth, illus. see Debeer, Kristen.
Sanvageau, Juan. Stories, Fables & Poems for You (p. 1654)
Sanz Falcon, Maria Teresa, tr. see Griswood, John, ed.
Sanz, Jesús, illus. see Dahl, Roald.
Sanz, Jesús, tr. see Dahl, Roald.
Sanz, Ma Pilar, jt. auth. see Gonzales, Doreen.
Sanz, Ma Pilar, illus. see Vaughn, Inés.
Sanz, Ma Pilar, tr. see Hollihan, Kerrie Logan.
Sanz, Maria Teresa, tr. see Baines, Francesca.
Sanz, Pilar, tr. see Franks, Katie.
Sanz, Pilar, tr. see Von Zumbusch, Amelie.
Sanza, Silvie, jt. auth. see Ruzicka, Oldrich.
Sanzi, Desiderio, illus. see Ganeri, Anita & Johnson, Jinny.
Sanzi, Desiderio, illus. see Johnson, Jinny.
Sanzi, Desiderio, illus. see Martineau, Susan & Jinny, Johnson.
Sanzo, Stephen. Cranky Pants. Whitlock, Matt, illus. (p. 376)
Sao, Jennifer, illus. see Cecca, John.
Sapara, Jim. Money Freedom: Achieve the Millionaire Lifestyle of Your Dreams. (p. 1164)

Saper, Lee & Lee, Brian. Tales of Tranquility. (p. 1703)
Sapergia, Barbara, ed. see Draper, Penny.
Sapet, Kerrily. Al Gore. (p. 32)
—Eleanor of Aquitaine: Medieval Queen. (p. 508)
—Elizabeth I of England. (p. 513)
—Halle Berry: Academy Award Winning Actress. (p. 737)
—Halle Berry. (p. 737)
—Jeff Gordon. (p. 911)
—John Lewis. (p. 922)
—Maria Sharapova. (p. 1093)
—Mariah Carey: Singer, Songwriter, Record Producer, Actress. (p. 1093)
—Mariah Carey: Singer, Songwriter, Record Producer, & Actress. (p. 1093)
—Rhythm & Folklore: The Story of Zora Neale Hurston. (p. 1468)
—Salma Hayek. (p. 1505)
—Suzanne Collins. (p. 1688)
Saphin, Wendy. Rosie's Box: A Box Full of Surprises. Saphin, Wendy, illus. (p. 1490)
Sapir, Edward. Time Perspective in Aboriginal American Culture, a Study in Method. (p. 1752)
Saponaro, Dominick, illus. see Strickland, Brad & Fuller, Thomas E.
Saport, Linda, illus. see Williams, Karen Lynn.
Saport, Linda, jt. auth. see Carlstrom, Nancy White.
Sapp, Allen, illus. see Bouchard, David & Bouchard, David.
Sapp, Allen, illus. see Bouchard, David.
Sapp, Allen, jt. auth. see Bouchard, David.
Sapp, Brent. Teknon & the Champion Warriors. Cariello, Sergio, illus. (p. 1716)
Sapp, Eric. World Geography Student Activity Book. (p. 1955)
Sapp, Karen. Christmas Is... (p. 314)
—Ellie's Christmas. (p. 514)
—Who Is Sleeping? (p. 1916)
Sapp, Karen, illus. see Bedford, David.
Sapp, Karen, illus. see Stier, Catherine.
Sapp, Karen, illus. see Top That Publishing Staff, ed.
Sapp, Richard. Lewis & Clark on Their Journey to the Pacific. (p. 1004)
—Ulysses S. Grant & the Road to Appomattox. (p. 1810)
Sappenfield, Heather. View from Who I Was. (p. 1842)
Sappey, Maureen Stack. Letters from Vinnie. (p. 1002)
Sappington, Ray, illus. see Randolph, Robert.
Sapre, Reshma. Patnaxi's Crezy Long Journey Home. (p. 1328)
Sapre, Reshma & Vargus, Nanci Reginelli. Iowa. (p. 886)
Sapre, Reshme. Unfortunate Tale of Kachuva the Tortoise: As Told by Chukwa Sulcata. Robinson, Jayme, illus. (p. 1817)
Sapulich, Joseph, illus. see Henley, Karyn.
Saqr, Abdul B. How to Call People to Islam. Ahmad, Shakil, tr. (p. 815)
Saraceni, Claudia, illus. see Jeffrey, Gary.
Saraceni, Claudia, illus. see Shone, Rob.
Saracino, Luciano & Bernatene, Poly. Monster Diaries. Bernatene, Poly, illus. (p. 1167)
Saracuse, Tara. Island Kids (p. 892)
Sarago-Kendrick, Delphine. Nana's Land. Sarago-Kendrick, Delphine, illus. (p. 1228)
Sarago-Kendrick, Delphine, illus. see Fry, Christopher.
Sarah Taylor. Teddy That Went to Iraq. Baker, David, illus. (p. 1712)
Sarah Withers, jt. auth. see Browne, Hetty S.
Saramago, José. Flor Mas Grande del Mundo. Caetano, Joao, illus. (p. 606)
Saranam, Sankara. God Without Religion: Questioning Centuries of Accepted Truths. (p. 690)
—God Without Religion: Questioning Centuries of Accepted Truths. Ellen, Kleiner, ed. (p. 690)
Sarandon, Susan, narrated by. Dying to Be Thin. (p. 491)
Saraniti, Carlos, illus. see Carvajal, Mario.
Sarao, Mary Russell, jt. auth. see Pitts, Barbara Russell.
Sarcone-Roach, Julia. Bear Ate Your Sandwich. (p. 150)
—Subway Story. (p. 1671)
Sarcone-Roach, Julia, illus. see Hopkins, Lee Bennett.
Sardelli, Darren. Galaxy Pizza & Meteor Pie. (p. 653)
Sardinha, Rick, illus. see Farmer, Nancy.
Sardo, Cindy. Cooking's Cool in the Spring. (p. 362)
Sardon, Vincent, jt. auth. see Baraou, Anne.
Sarduy, Severo. Gatico-Gatico. Gomez, Patricio, illus. (p. 658)
Sare, Etta. Dominic Ties His Shoes. (p. 465)
Sarecky, Melody, illus. see Bennett, Andrea T. & Kessler, James H.
Sareva, Ibrahim. West of Kilimanjaro 1: Book 1. (p. 1876)
Sarfati, Sonia. Comédienne Disparue. (p. 347)
—Comme une Peau De Chagrin. (p. 349)
—Ville Engloutie. (p. 1842)
Sarfati, Sonia, tr. see Nielandt, Dirk.
Sarfatti, Esther. Colors: Red. (p. 345)
—Colors: Blue. (p. 345)
—Colors: Green. (p. 345)
—Colors: Yellow. (p. 345)
—Counting By: Tens. (p. 371)
—Counting By: Twos. (p. 371)
—Counting By: Threes. (p. 371)
—Shapes: Circles. (p. 1560)
—Shapes: Squares. (p. 1560)
—Shapes: Triangles. (p. 1560)
—Shapes: Rectangles. (p. 1560)
Sarfatti, Esther, jt. auth. see Brown, Marc.
Sarfatti, Esther, jt. auth. see Krensky, Stephen.
Sarfatti, Esther, tr. see Blackstone, Stella.
Sarfatti, Esther, tr. see Brown, Marc.
Sarfatti, Esther, tr. see d'Allancé, Mireille, et al.
Sarfatti, Esther, tr. see Higginson, Mel.
Sarfatti, Esther, tr. see Sheehan, Thomas F.
Sarfatti, Esther, tr. see Stuve-Bodeen, Stephanie.
Sarfatti, Esther, tr. see Ziefert, Harriet & Harriet, Ziefert.
Sarfatti, Esther, tr. Caperucita Roja. Rovira, Francesc, illus. (p. 262)
—Patito Feo. Bordoy, Irene, illus. (p. 1328)
Sarfatti, Esther, tr. from ENG. Berto Da la Talla. (p. 168)
—Lechera. Pierola, Mabel, illus. (p. 987)
—Tres Cerditos (The Three Little Pigs) Rius, Maria, illus. (p. 1784)
Sarg, Tony. Up & down New York. (p. 1824)
Sargant, Pam. Mother's Survival Kit. (p. 1179)
Sargeant, Glen. Finders Keepers (p. 587)
—Ghost Ship: A y-Files Mystery. (p. 671)
Sargeant, Theresa. Drainpipe Gang - the Adventures of Chris & Andy Smy. (p. 479)
Sargemt, Dave & Sargent, Pat. Batley Needs Glasses Robinson, Laura, illus. (p. 144)
Sargent, Alan E. Do You Know What I Like about Bugs? (p. 458)
—Fortitude: The Adventures of the Esteem Team. Wade, Jerry, illus. (p. 623)
Sargent, Brian. Altruism: What's in It for Me? (p. 50)
—Gold: Greed & Glory Intermediate Book with Online Access. (p. 693)
—Grandfather's Shape Story. (p. 707)
—Guess the Order. (p. 729)
—How Heavy Is It? (p. 809)
—How Much Does It Hold? (p. 811)
—Life in Mumbai. (p. 1010)
—Life on the Edge. (p. 1012)
—Losing It: The Meaning of Loss. (p. 1054)
—Mark Your Territory Intermediate Book with Online Access. (p. 1095)
—Pen Pals Compare. (p. 1336)
—Placebo Effect: The Power of Positive Thinking. (p. 1366)
—Places along the Way. (p. 1366)
—Slumber Party Problem Solving. (p. 1591)
—Traditions of Death Intermediate Book with Online Access. (p. 1776)
Sargent, Claudia Karabaic, illus. see Goldish, Meish.
Sargent, Daina. Alaska: Be Brave Lenoir, Jane, illus. (p. 33)
—Arkansas: Dream Big. Lenoir, Jane, illus. (p. 99)
—Colors & the Number 1 Lenoir, Jane, illus. (p. 345)
—Colors & the Number 1/Los Colores y el Número 1 Lenoir, Jane, illus. (p. 345)
—Colors & the Number 10 Lenoir, Jane, illus. (p. 345)
—Colors & the Number 10/Los Colores y el Número 10 Lenoir, Jane, illus. (p. 345)
—Introduction to Colors & Numbers Lenoir, Jane, illus. (p. 882)
—Introduction to Colors & Numbers Lenoir, Jane, illus. (p. 882)
—Introduction to Colors & Numbers (BL) Introduccion a los colores y a los Numeros Lenoir, Jane, illus. (p. 882)
—Introduction to Colors & Numbers/Introduccion a los Colores Numeros Lenoir, Jane, illus. (p. 882)
—Kansas: Conquer Fear. Lenoir, Jane, illus. (p. 943)
—Missouri: Teamwork. Lenoir, Jane, illus. (p. 1154)
Sargent, Daina & Lenoir, Jane. Colors & the Number 6/Los colores y el Número 6 (p. 345)
Sargent, Dave. Baldy Eagle: Honor. (p. 134)
—Baldy Eagle: Honor. Lenoir, Jane, illus. (p. 134)
—Blackie Crow: Tell the Truth Lenoir, Jane, illus. (p. 197)
—Bogart Blue Jay: Be Thoughtful Lenoir, Jane, illus. (p. 207)
—Finding Sammy #1 (PB) (p. 588)
—Hiding Place #4 (p. 777)
—Hiding Place #4 (PB) (p. 777)
—I Named Him Sammy #7 (p. 844)
—I Named Him Sammy #7 (PB) (p. 844)
—Sammy Goes to School #8 (p. 1508)
—Sammy Goes to School #8 (PB) (p. 1508)
—Sammy's First Winter #10 (p. 1508)
—Sammy's First Winter #10 (PB) (p. 1508)
—Sammy's Hiding Place #9 (p. 1508)
—Sammy's Hiding Place #9 (PB) (p. 1508)
—Storky Stork: Be Trustworthy Lenoir, Jane, illus. (p. 1655)
—Tornado & Sweep Bowen, Debbie, ed. (p. 1770)
Sargent, Dave & Denton, Ivan. Blizzard: Don't Give Up. No. 5 Denton, Ivan, illus. (p. 200)
—Misty's Miracle: Overcome Fear No. 4 Denton, Ivan, illus. (p. 1155)
—My Grandpa Is a Cowboy: Learning Is Fun #1 Denton, Ivan, illus. (p. 1210)
Sargent, Dave & Sargent, David, Jr. Hoot Owl: Mind Your Mamma Lenoir, Jane, illus. (p. 796)
—Hummer Hummingbird: Being Small Is Okay Lenoir, Jane, illus. (p. 826)
—Kitty Hawk: Stealing Lenoir, Jane, illus. (p. 963)
—Petie Pelican: Be Proud of Yourself Lenoir, Jane, illus. (p. 1348)
—Pinkie Flamingo: Leaving Home Lenoir, Jane, illus. (p. 1360)
—Sandy Sea Gull: Making Friends Lenoir, Jane, illus. (p. 1511)
—Storky Stork: Be Trustworthy Lenoir, Jane, illus. (p. 1655)
—Tin Wren: Be Nice Lenoir, Jane, illus. (p. 1755)
—Tom Turkey: Don't Bully Lenoir, Jane, illus. (p. 1764)
Sargent, Dave & Sargent, David M. Bob White: Use Good Judgement Lenoir, Jane, illus. (p. 205)
—Bogart Blue Jay: Be Thoughtful Lenoir, Jane, illus. (p. 207)
—Buzz Buzzard: Obey the Rules Lenoir, Jane, illus. (p. 248)
—Cindy Sparrow: Respect the Property of Others Lenoir, Jane, illus. (p. 321)
—Dinky Duck: Be Prompt Lenoir, Jane, illus. (p. 440)
Sargent, Dave & Sargent, David M., Jr. Dinky Duck: Be Prompt Lenoir, Jane, illus. (p. 440)
—Glenda Goose: Sharing Lenoir, Jane, illus. (p. 683)
—Hoot Owl: Mind Your Mamma Lenoir, Jane, illus. (p. 796)
—Pammie Pigeon: Keep Your Cool Lenoir, Jane, illus. (p. 1320)
—Penny Penguin: Be Kind to Others Lenoir, Jane, illus. (p. 1338)
—Petie Pelican: Be Proud of Yourself Lenoir, Jane, illus. (p. 1348)
—Speedy Roadrunner: Helping Others Lenoir, Jane, illus. (p. 1624)
Sargent, Dave & Sargent, Pat. Amy Armadillo: Mind Your Mama Huff, Jeane, illus. (p. 66)
—Bandit: I Help Others Huff, Jeane, illus. (p. 136)
—Bashful: (Dusty Dun) Be Brave. Lenoir, Jane, illus. (p. 141)
—Batley Needs Glasses Robinson, Laura, illus. (p. 144)
—Big Jake: I'm Very Curious Huff, Jeane, illus. (p. 182)
—Billy Beaver: A New Beginning Huff, Jeane, illus. (p. 187)
—Bo: (Linebacked Orange Dun) Be Happy Lenoir, Jane, illus. (p. 204)
—Bo Bo's Big Imagination Robinson, Laura, illus. (p. 205)
—Bo Bo's Big Imagination/la Gran Imaginacion de Bo Bo Robinson, Laura, illus. (p. 205)
—Bobby Bobcat: Be a Friend Huff, Jeane, illus. (p. 206)
—Brandy: (Blue Roan) Beauty Is Inside Lenoir, Jane, illus. (p. 222)
—Brutus the Bear: Show Respect Huff, Jeane, illus. (p. 233)
—Buddy Badger: I'm a Little Bully Huff, Jeane, illus. (p. 234)
—Buttons: (Muddy Dun) Have Courage Lenoir, Jane, illus. (p. 248)
—Cat Who Barked Robinson, Laura, illus. (p. 278)
—Cat Who Barked/el gato que Ladró Robinson, Laura, illus. (p. 278)
—Chick: (Chocolate Chestnut) Be Loyal Lenoir, Jane, illus. (p. 299)
—Chrissy Cottontail: Mind Your Mama Huff, Jeane, illus. (p. 311)
—Chuck Wagon: Don't Be Stubborn Lenoir, Jane, illus. (p. 318)
—Colorado Blizzard: Be Determined Lenoir, Jane, illus. (p. 343)
—Cricket: (Seal Brown) Do Your Best Lenoir, Jane, illus. (p. 382)
—Dawn the Deer: Family & Friends Huff, Jeane, illus. (p. 412)
—Dike the Wolf: Teamwork Huff, Jeane, illus. (p. 440)
—Do All Ducks Quack? Robinson, Laura, illus. (p. 456)
—Do All Ducks Quack?/¿Granznan todos los Patos? Robinson, Laura, illus. (p. 456)
—Do Frogs Have Tails? Robinson, Laura, illus. (p. 456)
—Do Frogs Have Tails?/Tienen Colas las Ranas? Robinson, Laura, illus. (p. 456)
—Drought: Have Faith Lenoir, Jane, illus. (p. 486)
—Duke: (Dappled Palomino) Good Behavior Lenoir, Jane, illus. (p. 489)
—Dusty: (Grey Sabino) Be Helpful Lenoir, Jane, illus. (p. 490)
—Fire: A Second Chance Lenoir, Jane, illus. (p. 590)
—Freckles: (Flea-bitten Grey) Be Proud of Old Glory Lenoir, Jane, illus. (p. 632)
—Fuzzy Bunny Robinson, Laura, illus. (p. 651)
—Fuzzy Bunny/el conejito Velloso Robinson, Laura, illus. (p. 651)
—Ginger: (Lilac Roan) Be Likeable Lenoir, Jane, illus. (p. 676)
—Goober: (Silver Dapple) Appreciate Others Lenoir, Jane, illus. (p. 697)
—Goober: (Silver Dapple) Appreciate Others Lenoir, Jane, illus. (p. 697)
—Grady: Proud to Be an American Lenoir, Jane, illus. (p. 705)
—Grady: (Dappled Grey) Proud to Be an American Lenoir, Jane, illus. (p. 705)
—Greta Groundhog: I'm Special! Huff, Jeane, illus. (p. 723)
—Gus: (Slate Grullo) Be Thankful Lenoir, Jane, illus. (p. 732)
—Hondo: (Silver Dun) Look for Good in Others Lenoir, Jane, illus. (p. 794)
—Hoot: (Grullo) Be Creative Lenoir, Jane, illus. (p. 796)
—I Can Read, Too/Puedo Leer, Tambien Robinson, Laura, illus. (p. 836)
—Lily: (Lilac Dun) A Second Chance Lenoir, Jane, illus. (p. 1017)
—Little Big Cat Robinson, Laura, illus. (p. 1024)
—Little Big Cat/Gato pequeño y Grande Robinson, Laura, illus. (p. 1024)
—Little Tadpole Robinson, Laura, illus. (p. 1037)
—Little Tadpole/el Renacuajo Pequeño Robinson, Laura, illus. (p. 1037)
—Lizzy Lightning Bug Robinson, Laura, illus. (p. 1043)
—Lizzy Lightning Bug/Lizzy la Luciérnaga Robinson, Laura, illus. (p. 1043)
—Mack: (Medicine Hat Paint) Be a Leader Lenoir, Jane, illus. (p. 1068)
—Mad Jack: I Throw Fits Huff, Jeane, illus. (p. 1069)
—Molly's Journey: I'm Getting Older Huff, Jeane, illus. (p. 1161)
—Nick: (Linebacked Claybank Dun) Crime Does Not Pay Lenoir, Jane, illus. (p. 1251)
—Nubbin: (Linebacked Apricot Dun) Freedom Lenoir, Jane, illus. (p. 1269)
—Peggy Porcupine: Don't Wander Off Huff, Jeane, illus. (p. 1335)
—Pete: Pink-skinned Palomino) Be a Hero Lenoir, Jane, illus. (p. 1346)
—Pete: (Pink-skinned Palomino) Be a Hero Lenoir, Jane, illus. (p. 1346)
—Pokey Opossum: I'm Kinda Slow Huff, Jeane, illus. (p. 1378)
—Puppy for Bobby/un cachorro para Robertito Robinson, Laura, illus. (p. 1418)
—Ranger: (Olive Grullo) Be Honest Lenoir, Jane, illus. (p. 1438)
—Rascal: (Red Dun) Responsible Leadership Lenoir, Jane, illus. (p. 1439)
—Redi Fox: Friendship Huff, Jeane, illus. (p. 1455)
—Rocky: (Blue-eyed Palomino) Be Free Lenoir, Jane, illus. (p. 1484)
—Roy Raccoon: I Love Adventure Huff, Jeane, illus. (p. 1492)
—Rusty: (Red Roan) Be Strong & Brave Lenoir, Jane, illus. (p. 1498)
—Sammy Skunk: I'm a Little Stinker Huff, Jeane, illus. (p. 1508)
—Sonny: (Linebacked Yllow Dun) Have Orderly Manners Lenoir, Jane, illus. (p. 1612)
—Sonny: (Linebacked Yellow Dun) Have Orderly Manners Lenoir, Jane, illus. (p. 1612)
—Sweetpea: (Purple Corn Welsh) Be Happy Lenoir, Jane, illus. (p. 1690)
—Tunnel King: I Work Hard Huff, Jeane, illus. (p. 1797)
—Valley Oak Acorns: (Maidu) Be Helpful Lenoir, Jane, illus. (p. 1831)
—Whiskers: (Roan) Pride & Peace Lenoir, Jane, illus. (p. 1912)
—White Thunder: I'm a Leader Huff, Jeane, illus. (p. 1913)
—Young Billy: A New Beginning! Woodward, Elaine, illus. (p. 1978)
—Young Dawn: Friends Care! Woodword, Elaine, illus. (p. 1978)
—Young Dike: Teamwork! Woodward, Elaine, illus. (p. 1978)
—Young Redi: Friendship! Woodward, Elaine, illus. (p. 1979)
—Young Sammy: I'm a Little Stinker! Woodword, Elaine, illus. (p. 1979)
—Young White Thunder: I'm a Leader! Woodword, Elaine, illus. (p. 1979)
—Zeb: (Zebra Dun) Be Prepared Lenoir, Jane, illus. (p. 1985)
Sargent, Dave, et al. Berry Picking Time: (Apache) Be Brave Vol. 3 Lenoir, Jane, illus. (p. 167)
—Bundle Keeper: (Pawnee) Be Responsible Lenoir, Sue, illus. (p. 242)
—Bundle Keeper: (Pawnee) Be Responsible Lenoir, Jane, illus. (p. 242)
—Counting Coup: (Cheyenee) Be Proud Vol. 4 Lenoir, Jane, illus. (p. 371)
—Fields of Golden Corn: (Navajo) Be Energetic Vol. 6 Lenoir, Jane, illus. (p. 584)
—Fierce Warriors: (Comanche) Learn Skills Vol. 7 Lenoir, Jane, illus. (p. 584)
—Grubby: (Smutty Olive Grullo) Have a Good Disposition (p. 727)
—Hole in the Sun: (Choctaw) Be Independent Lenoir, Jane, illus. (p. 788)
—Keeping Ghosts Away: (Creek) Be Respectful Vol. 8 Lenoir, Jane, illus. (p. 947)
—Knocking the Rice: (Chippewa) Be Powerful Vol. 9 Lenoir, Jane, illus. (p. 965)
—Ladder at the Door: (Hopi) Be Curious Vol. 10 Lenoir, Jane, illus. (p. 970)
—Land of the Sun: (Ute) Respect Elders Vol. 11 Lenoir, Jane, illus. (p. 973)
—Little One: (Cherokee) Be Inventive Vol. 12 Lenoir, Jane, illus. (p. 1032)
—On the Banks of the Wallowa River: (Nez Perce) Use Your Talent Lenoir, Jane, illus. (p. 1289)
—Once upon a Totem Pole: (Haida) Be Creative Vol. 14 Lenoir, Jane, illus. (p. 1293)
—Puppy for Bobby (p. 1418)
—Rays of the Sun: (Shoshone) Learn Lessons Vol. 15 Lenoir, Jane, illus. (p. 1441)
—Rays of the Sun: (shoshone) Learn Lessons Vol. 15 Lenoir, Jane, illus. (p. 1441)
—Strand of Wampum: Be Honest Vol. 2 Lenoir, Sue, illus. (p. 1664)
—Strand of Wampum: Be Honest Vol. 2 Lenoir, Jane, illus. (p. 1664)
—Summer Milky Way: (Blackfeet) Be Compassionate Lenoir, Jane, illus. (p. 1674)
—Tattoos of Honor: (Osage) Be Gentle & Giving Vol. 17 Lenoir, Jane, illus. (p. 1707)
—Truth, Power & Freedom: (Sioux) Show Respect Vol. 19 Lenoir, Jane, illus. (p. 1794)
—Valley Oaks Acorns: (Maidu) Be Helpful Vol. 20 Lenoir, Jane, illus. (p. 1831)
—Young Chrissy: Mind Your Mama! (p. 1978)
Sargent, Dave M., Jr. Bones: Hidden Talent #1 (p. 209)
—Duke: Friends #4 (p. 489)
—Liza: Good Work #3 (p. 1042)
—Misty: Manners #5 (p. 1155)
—Spot: Helpful #2 (p. 1633)
—Vicious Vera Huff, Jeane Lirley, illus. (p. 1840)
Sargent, David, Jr., jt. auth. see Sargent, Dave.
Sargent, David M. Bob White: Use Good Judgement Lenoir, Jane, illus. (p. 205)
—Emma! Huff, Jeane, illus. (p. 519)
Sargent, David M., jt. auth. see Sargent, Dave.
Sargent, David M., Jr. Autumn's Emergency. Huff, Jeane Lirley, illus. (p. 118)
—Buffy's Anger. (p. 236)
—Buffy's Revenge. Huff, Jeane Lirley, illus. (p. 236)
—Emma's Law (p. 520)
—Guard Dog Mary Huff, Jeane Lirley, illus. (p. 728)
—Portia's Prank Huff, Jeane Lirley, illus. (p. 1386)
—Vera's Talent (p. 1836)
Sargent, Mandy And Ben. Best Ted & Ben. (p. 171)
Sargent, Pamela. Farseed. (p. 575)
—Homesmind (Watchstar Trilogy: Book 3) (p. 793)
Sargent, Pat. Black Panther Lenoir, Jane, illus. (p. 196)
—Bobcat Lenoir, Jane, illus. (p. 206)
—Timber Wolf Lenoir, Jane, illus. (p. 1750)
Sargent, Pat, jt. auth. see Sargemt, Dave.
Sargent, Pat, jt. auth. see Sargent, Dave.
Sargent, Pat L. Cheetah Lenoir, Jane, illus. (p. 296)
—Grizzly Lenoir, Jane, illus. (p. 724)
—Jaguar Lenoir, Jane, illus. (p. 905)
—Jaguar #8 (PB) (p. 905)
—Topper: Son of Barney Lenoir, Jane, illus. (p. 1769)
—Topper, Son of Barney #7 (p. 1769)
Sargent, Shannon Marie, illus. see Wilt, Gerri Ann, et al.
Sargent, Shelly. My Dad the Hero. (p. 1201)
Sargent-Barker, Erika. Casey Moore, the Littlest Leprechaun (p. 275)
—Living with a Legend. (p. 1042)
Sargisson, Lisa. Quick Connect Articulation 1. (p. 1427)
Sari. Jeanne-Marie Goes to Market: A Story of the West Indies. (p. 911)
Sari, illus. see Govan, Christine Noble.
Sariola, Eulalia, illus. see Castells, Margarita.
Sarja, Jennifer. When Watute Wants Some Water. Phan, Henry et al, illus. (p. 1905)
Sarja, Jennifer, ed. How to Cook with a Pencil: Youth Inkwell Anthology: Volume One (p. 816)
Sarkan, Carole. And Candy Smiled. (p. 71)
Sarkar, Dona. How to Salsa in a Sari. (p. 821)
Sarkar, Maria. Have Fun with Words. (p. 754)
Sarkar, Soumitro, illus. see Moorthy, Anita.
Sarkees-Wircenski, Michelle & Scott, John L. Special Populations in Career & Technical Education. (p. 1623)
Sarker, Sheena. Doctor Is Always In. (p. 459)
Sarkisian, K. I Go to the Garden: Learning the Hard G Sound. (p. 838)
—I Have a Horse: Learning the H Sound. (p. 839)
—You Need Your Nose: Learning the N Sound. (p. 1976)
Sarkisov, Anton G. Curse of the Gemini. (p. 395)
Sarkis-Scalzo, Hanney. My Magical Unicorn Mi Unicornio Mágico Ma Licorne Magique. (p. 1213)
Sarl Aky-Aka Creations, illus. see Golden Books Staff.
Sarmiento, R. One Race Kids New Beginnings. (p. 1296)
Sarmiento-Waring, D. Meet the One Race Kids. (p. 1123)
—One Race Kids Fun Book. (p. 1296)
—We Are the One Race Kids. (p. 1866)
Sarn, Amélie & Trouillot, Virgile. Argument. (p. 98)

—Audition. (p. 115)
—Day of Surprises. (p. 414)
—Everyone on Stage. (p. 544)
—Happy Holidays. (p. 746)
—Looking for Trouble. (p. 1051)
—Love Is in the Air. Ducrest, Olivier, illus. (p. 1060)
—New Girl. (p. 1244)
—Recipe for Happiness. (p. 1451)
Sarna, Billy, illus. see Champagne, Elena.
Sarnat, Marjorie. Creativity Unhinged. (p. 380)
Sarnella, Jeanette. Santini's Magic Castle. (p. 1513)
Sarno, J. P. Little Paddle the Platypus & His First Day Outing Adventure. (p. 1033)
Sarno-Doyle, Christine. Your Inside Shape. (p. 1980)
Sarnon, Benendikt. Stop Being Surprised! Vignettes from Soviet Literary & other Life. (p. 1653)
Saroff, Phyllis, illus. see Corlett, Mary Lee.
Saroff, Phyllis, illus. see Friday, Stormy.
Saroff, Phyllis, illus. see Goodman, Susan E.
Saroff, Phyllis, illus. see Jennings, Terry Catasús.
Saroff, Phyllis, illus. see Plotz, John.
Saroff, Phyllis, illus. see Stuckey, Denise.
Saroff, Phyllis, illus. see Weber, Rivka Doba.
Saroff, Phyllis V., illus. see Collard, Sneed B., III.
Saroff, Phyllis V., illus. see Goodman, Susan E.
Saroff, Phyllis V., illus. see Johnson, Rebecca L.
Sarquis, Mickey. Squishy, Squashy Sponges: Early Childhood Science Guide for Teachers. (p. 1637)
Sarquis, Mickey, ed. see Taylor, Beverley, et al.
Sarrasin, Alex. Guardians of Neoegypti: Book One. (p. 674)
Sarratt, Carla. Freshman Focus Carter G Woodson High Sc. (p. 636)
Sarratt, Carla R. Just Be. (p. 938)
Sarrazin, Jean-charles, illus. see Teulade, Pascale.
Sarrazin, Jean-charles & Teulade, Pascale. Mas Bonito De Todos Los Regalos Del Mundo. (p. 1101)
—Porque Te Quiero... (p. 1386)
Sarrazin, Marisol, illus. see Butcher, Kristin & Labatt, Mary.
Sarrazin, Marisol, illus. see Labatt, Mary.
Sarrazin, Marisol, illus. see Wiebe, Trina.
Sarrazin, Marisol, jt. auth. see Anfousse, Ginette.
Sarrazin, Marisol, tr. see Anfousse, Ginette.
Sarrazin, Marisol, tr. see Labatt, Mary.
Sarreshtedari, Mehdi, narrated by. Hasht Ketab/ Sohrab Sepehri: Eight Books (p. 752)
Sarrgisson, Lisa. Quick Connect Articulaton 2. (p. 1427)
Sarris, Eno, jt. ed. see Aihara, Masaaki.
Sarris, Eno, jt. ed. see Akaishi, Shinobu.
Sarris, Eno & Aihara, Masaaki, eds. Long Vowels Write & Wipe. (p. 1047)
Sarris, Eno & Masaaki, Aihara, eds. Short Vowels Write & Wipe. (p. 1569)
Sarris, Eno, ed. Animals: Dog & Cat (p. 81)
—Dinosaurs: Triceratops & Pteranodon (p. 444)
Sarro, Ashley. Lost in the Library. (p. 1055)
Sarta, Jon. Your Adoption Story. (p. 1979)
Sartarelli, Stephen, jt. auth. see Camilleri, Andrea.
Sartell, Debra. Time for Bed, Baby Ted. Chorao, Kay, illus. (p. 1751)
Sarti, Roland. Italy: A Reference Guide from the Renaissance to the Present. (p. 895)
Sartin, Barbara J. Betty Butterfly to the Rescue: A Hero's Story. (p. 172)
—When Will I Be Able to Fly? (p. 1905)
Sartin, Laurence, jt. auth. see Brezina, Thomas.
Sarton, George. Ancient Science Through the Golden Age of Greece. (p. 70)
Sartor, Amanda, illus. see Weidt, Maryann N.
Sartor, Amanda, tr. see Weidt, Maryann N.
Sartore, Joel. Face to Face with Grizzlies. (p. 560)
—Face to Face with Grizzlies. Sartore, Joel, illus. (p. 560)
Sartori, Gloria. Papá Guillermo y los Pájaros. Brignole, Giancarla, tr. (p. 1322)
Sartori, Rosanne Sheritz. New Start: One Child's Struggle with Obesity. (p. 1247)
—Tales of Temper: Grades 3-6. Barber, David L., illus. (p. 1702)
Sartorius, Evohn. Bobbie, His Family & Dog Bingo (p. 206)
Sartre, Jean-Paul. Mur (p. 1191)
Sarvady, Andrea, et al. Baby-Gami: Baby Wrapping for Beginners. Stislow, John, illus. (p. 126)
Sarver, Amy. Science at the Airport. (p. 1525)
—Science at the Grocery. (p. 1525)
Sarver, Amy & National Geographic Learning Staff. Science at the Mall. (p. 1525)
Sarwari, Zohra. Inheritance: A Journey to China (Book 1) (p. 874)
Sas, Alfredo C., ed. Reformation Hymnal. (p. 1456)
Sasa, Fungisayi. Search for the Perfect Head. (p. 1537)
Sasabuchi, Tyler. Stealing Snake. (p. 1646)
Sasaki, Akane. Princess Ninja Scroll Tenka Muso. (p. 1404)
Sasaki, Chie, illus. see Moran, Maggie A.
Sasaki, Chris & Wells, H. G. War of the Worlds. Akib, Jamel, illus. (p. 1857)
Sasaki, Ellen Joy, illus. see Bateman, Teresa.
Sasaki, Haruko. Maya & the Dragon. (p. 1112)
Sasaki, Joh. Zero over Berlin. Yoda, Hiroko & Alt, Matt, trs. from JPN. (p. 1986)
Sasaki, Youko. Pilipala: 7 Volumes. (p. 1359)
Sasakishonen. Blue Blue Glass Moon, under the Crimson Air (p. 202)
Sasakishonen, jt. auth. see Chiaki, Taro.
Saseen, Sharon. Patience & the Flower Girl. (p. 1328)
Sasek, M. This Is Ireland. (p. 1736)
—This Is Venice. (p. 1736)
Sasek, Miroslav. This Is Australia. (p. 1735)
—This Is Britain. (p. 1735)
—This Is Edinburgh. (p. 1735)
—This Is Greece. (p. 1736)
—This Is Hong Kong. (p. 1736)
—This Is Israel. (p. 1736)
—This Is London. (p. 1736)
—This Is Munich. (p. 1736)
—This Is New York (p. 1736)
—This Is Paris. (p. 1736)
—This Is Rome. (p. 1736)
—This Is San Francisco. (p. 1736)
—This Is Texas. (p. 1736)
—This Is the Way to the Moon. (p. 1736)
—This Is the United Nations: A Global Treasury. (p. 1736)
—This Is Washington, D. C. (p. 1736)
Sasheva, Iva, illus. see Isaacs, Sally Senzell.
Sasic, Natasha, illus. see Banks, Steven.
Saslavsky, Irene, tr. see Harris, Robie H. & Cousins, Lucy.
Sasley, Brent. Cold War in the Middle East, 1950-1991. (p. 339)
Saslow, Joan M. & Collins, Tim. Living & Working in English (p. 1040)
—Workplace Plus 1 with Grammar Booster (p. 1953)
—Workplace Plus 2 with Grammar Booster (p. 1953)
—Workplace Plus 3 with Grammar Booster (p. 1953)
Sasscer, Abby. Sophie's Stuff. Cayless, Sophie, illus. (p. 1613)
Sasscer, Glenn, Jr. Suffering Madness. (p. 1672)
Sasse, Connie R. & McGraw-Hill Education Staff. Families Today (p. 567)
Sasseville, Jim, jt. auth. see Schulz, Charles M.
Sassi, Laura. Goodnight, Ark Chapman, Jane, illus. (p. 701)
Sassin, Eva, illus. see Crow, Melinda Melton.
Sassin, Eva, illus. see Oxlade, Chris.
Sassin, Eva, jt. auth. see Crow, Melinda Melton.
Sassman, Charlotte, jt. auth. see Diffily, Deborah.
Sasso, illus. see Bannerji, Himani.
Sasso, illus. see Trotman, Althea.
Sasso, Emilie. Cystic Fibrosis & You. (p. 397)
Sasso, Sandy Eisenberg. Adam & Eve's First Sunset: God's New Day. Rothenberg, Joani Keller, illus. (p. 11)
—Adam & Eve's New Day. Rothenberg, Joani Keller, illus. (p. 11)
—But God Remembered: Stories of Women from Creation to the Promised Land. Andersen, Bethane, illus. (p. 246)
—Butterflies under Our Hats. Rothenberg, Joani Keller, illus. (p. 247)
—God's Paintbrush. Compton, Annette, illus. (p. 691)
—I Am God's Paintbrush. Compton, Annette, illus. (p. 833)
—In God's Name. Stone, Phoebe, illus. (p. 863)
—Shema in the Mezuzah: Listening to Each Other. Rothenberg, Joani Keller, illus. (p. 1565)
Sasso, Sandy Eisenberg & Schmidt, Donald. God's Paintbrush Celebration Kit: A Spiritual Activity Kit for Teachers & Students of All Faiths, All Backgrounds. (p. 691)
Sassoli de Bianchi, Massimiliano. What weighs more: 1 kg of iron or 1 kg of Feathers? (p. 1895)
Sassone, Richard. Galangous. Sassone, Richard, illus. (p. 653)
Sassone, Terri. Circus. (p. 322)
—Littlest Princess. (p. 1039)
Sastrias, Marta. Cuentos de Todo y de Nada. Martinez y Luis San Vicente, Enrique, illus. (p. 390)
Sastrias, Martha. Como Motivar a los Ninos a Leer: Lecto-Juegos y Algo Mas. (p. 351)
Sastrías, Martha. Lecto-Juego-Acertijos: Para Motivar a los Niños a Leer el Mundo Natural. (p. 987)
—Uso Del Folklore Para Motivar a los Ninos a Leer y Escribir. (p. 1829)
Sasturain, Juan. Brooklin y Medio. (p. 231)
Sataram, Nikita. Zatheria: The Hidden Realm. (p. 1985)
Satcher, David, tr. see Drew, Alejandrina.
Satchwell, Sm. Len Stories. (p. 991)
Satera, Diane. Angel of Wild Springs: Jaiden & the Sacred Stones. (p. 74)
Sateren, Shelley Swanson. Fearless Freddie. Melmon, Deborah, illus. (p. 579)
—Growling Gracie. Melmon, Deborah, illus. (p. 727)
—Homesick Herbie. Melmon, Deborah, illus. (p. 793)
—Lunchroom Fight. Sullivan, Mary, illus. (p. 1065)
—Max & Zoe. Sullivan, Mary, illus. (p. 1110)
—Max & Zoe at Recess Sullivan, Mary, illus. (p. 1110)
—Max & Zoe at School Sullivan, Mary, illus. (p. 1111)
—Max & Zoe at Soccer Practice Sullivan, Mary, illus. (p. 1111)
—Max & Zoe at the Dentist Sullivan, Mary, illus. (p. 1111)
—Max & Zoe at the Doctor Sullivan, Mary, illus. (p. 1111)
—Max & Zoe at the Library Sullivan, Mary, illus. (p. 1111)
—Max & Zoe Celebrate Mother's Day Sullivan, Mary, illus. (p. 1111)
—Max & Zoe: the Lunchroom Fight Sullivan, Mary, illus. (p. 1111)
—Max & Zoe: the Science Fair Sullivan, Mary, illus. (p. 1111)
—Max & Zoe: the Very Best Art Project Sullivan, Mary, illus. (p. 1111)
—Max & Zoe: Too Many Tricks Sullivan, Mary, illus. (p. 1111)
—Mudball Molly. Melmon, Deborah, illus. (p. 1188)
—School Concert. Sullivan, Mary, illus. (p. 1522)
—Science Fair. Sullivan, Mary, illus. (p. 1526)
—Too Many Tricks. Sullivan, Mary, illus. (p. 1767)
—Very Best Art Project. Sullivan, Mary, illus. (p. 1837)
Sateren, Shelley Swanson & Swanson Sateren, Shelley. New Jersey Facts & Symbols. (p. 1245)
Sather, Connie. Sadie the Sled Dog? (p. 1501)
Sathre, Vivian. J. B. Wigglebottom & the Parade of Pets: True Ringside Tales, BBQ, & down-Home Recipes. O'Neill, Catharine, illus. (p. 901)
Satifka, Erica L., et al. Triangulation 2005: A Confluence of Speculative Fiction. Carlson, Barbara, ed. (p. 1785)
Satkamp, Diana. Woodpile Kitty. (p. 1949)
Sato. Animals: Super-Deformed Characters. (p. 81)
Sato, Alice Ogura, jt. auth. see Sato, Shozo.
Sato, Anna & Sato, Eriko. My First Japanese Kanji Book: Learning Kanji the Fun & Easy Way! Sato, Anna & Sato, Eriko, illus. (p. 1207)
Sato, Eriko, jt. auth. see Sato, Anna.
Sato, Koichi. Infinite Coloring Dazzling Designs. (p. 873)
Sato, Kunio, illus. see Miyazawa, Kenji.
Sato, Shozo. Tea Ceremony: Explore the Unique Japanese Tradition of Sharing Tea. (p. 1708)
Sato, Shozo & Sato, Alice Ogura. Ikebana: Create Beautiful Flower Arrangements with This Traditional Japanese Art. (p. 856)
Sato, Yuki, illus. see Ando, Yuma.
Sato, Yuki, jt. auth. see Ando, Yuma.
Satoru, Akahori. Sorcerer Hunter Satoru, Akahori, illus. (p. 1614)
Satoshi, Yamamoto, illus. see Kusaka, Hidenori.
Satran, Pamela Redmond & Rosenkrantz, Linda. Baby Name Bible: The Ultimate Guide by America's Baby-Naming Experts. (p. 127)
Satrapi, Marjane. Ajdar. (p. 32)
—Bordados. Domínguez, Manuel, tr. from FRE. (p. 213)
Satriani, Zack. Assassin (p. 107)
—Hidden Enemy. (p. 775)
—Invasion. (p. 883)
Satterfield, April. Leah Bug & Her Flying Friends. Guthrie, Lewis, illus. (p. 982)
Satterfield, Barbara. Answer Why for Mee Mee. (p. 88)
Satterfield, Kathryn Hoffman. Benjamin Franklin A Man of Many Talents. (p. 165)
Satterfield, Kathryn Hoffman, jt. auth. see Time for Kids Magazine Staff.
Satterfield, Mary & Satterfield, Nathaniel. Leaping Lady: A Tall Tale from Mary & Nathaniel Satterfield. (p. 982)
Satterfield, Nathaniel, jt. auth. see Satterfield, Mary.
Satterlee, Chuck. Smoke & Mirror: Time & Again. Vol. 1 (p. 1594)
Satterly, Denise B. Adventures of Icky & Weezy: Fall Has Arrived. (p. 19)
Satterwhite, William. Stealth (p. 1646)
Sattgast, L. J. Rhyme Bible Storybook for Toddlers Cleyet-Merle, Laurence, illus. (p. 1468)
Sattgast, L. J. & Sattgast, Linda. Rhyme Bible Storybook Bible Cleyet-Merle, Laurence, illus. (p. 1468)
Sattgast, Linda, jt. auth. see Sattgast, L. J.
Sattler, Colleen. Bear with Me. (p. 151)
Sattler, Jennifer. Chick 'n' Pug. (p. 299)
—Chick 'n' Pug Christmas. (p. 299)
—Chick 'n' Pug Meet the Dude. (p. 299)
—Pig Kahuna. (p. 1357)
—Pig Kahuna Pirates! (p. 1357)
—Sylvie. (p. 1693)
—Uh-Oh, Dodo! Sattler, Jennifer, illus. (p. 1808)
—Who's That Pig? (p. 1921)
Sattler, Jennifer Gordon. Chick 'n' Pug. (p. 299)
—Chick 'n' Pug Christmas. (p. 299)
—Pig Kahuna Pirates! (p. 1357)
—Sylvie. (p. 1693)
Saturen, Myra. Journey to a New World: Mystic River of the West. (p. 928)
—Journey to a New World. (p. 928)
—Julietta. (p. 932)
Sauber, Tim & Tschirky, Hugo. Structured Creativity: Formulating an Innovation Strategy. (p. 1668)
Sauceda, Vickie. Doobie Kind & Mean Gene. (p. 469)
Saucedo, Jaime Garcia. Diccionario de Literatura Colombiana en el Cine. (p. 435)
Saucedo, Rudy E. Old '39 & the Eight Mice from Wisconsin. (p. 1283)
Saucerman, Linda. Carbon. (p. 265)
—Chlorine. (p. 309)
—Hydrogen: The Fuel for Life. (p. 831)
—Hydrogen. (p. 831)
—Ozzy & Kelly Osbourne. (p. 1316)
—Ozzy Osbourne & Kelly Osbourne. (p. 1316)
Saucier, Kimberly. Tweet Dreams. (p. 1799)
Sauder, B. L. & Russell, Christine. Year of the Golden Dragon (p. 1969)
Saudo, Coralie. My Dad Is Big & Strong, But... A Bedtime Story. Di Giacomo, Kris, illus. (p. 1201)
Sauer, Abe. Goodnight Loon. Davauer, Nathaniel, illus. (p. 701)
Sauer, Cat. Flip Flop & Hoot. Jankowski, Daniel, illus. (p. 605)
—Gwendolyn the Ghost. Jankowski, Daniel, illus. (p. 733)
—Possum in the Roses. Jankowski, Daniel, illus. (p. 1387)
—What's a Jaybird to Do? Jankowski, Dan, illus. (p. 1896)
Sauer, Drake & Sauer, Katheryn. Betsy the Brachiosaurus. (p. 172)
Sauer, Katheryn, jt. auth. see Sauer, Drake.
Sauer, Michelle. Facts on File Companion to British Poetry Before 1600. (p. 561)
Sauer, Tammi. Chicken Dance. Santat, Dan, illus. (p. 300)
—Cowboy Camp. Reed, Mike, illus. (p. 373)
—Dear Jack. (p. 419)
—Ginny Louise & the School Field Day. Munsinger, Lynn, illus. (p. 677)
—Ginny Louise & the School Showdown. Munsinger, Lynn, illus. (p. 677)
—Me Want Pet! Shea, Bob, illus. (p. 1116)
—Mostly Monsterly. Magoon, Scott, illus. (p. 1177)
—Mr. Duck Means Business. Mack, Jeff, illus. (p. 1185)
—Nugget & Fang: Friends Forever—Or Snack Time? Slack, Michael, illus. (p. 1270)
—Nugget & Fang: Friends Forever - Or Snack Time? Slack, Michael, illus. (p. 1270)
—Nugget & Fang. (p. 1270)
—Oh, Nuts! Krall, Dan, illus. (p. 1281)
—Princess in Training. Berger, Joe, illus. (p. 1404)
—Twelve Days of Christmas in Oklahoma. Hutto, Victoria, illus. (p. 1800)
—Your Alien. Fujita, Goro, illus. (p. 1979)
Sauers, Charlotte. Bee in Bonnie Bondelle's Bow. Jasuna, Aija, illus. (p. 157)
Sauers, Joey. How to Make a Snowman. (p. 820)
Sauers, Richard A., jt. auth. see Books, D. W. J.
Sauerwein, Leigh. Song for Eloise. (p. 1611)
Sauerwein, Stan. Ma Murray: The Story of Canada's Crusty Queen of Publishing. (p. 1067)
Saufley, Ted & Schreiner, Paul B. AutoCAD LT 2004 Fundamentals: Drafting Abd Design Applications. (p. 117)
Saugstad, Edward. Oakee Doakee & the Ego Bomb. (p. 1274)
—Oakee Doakee & the Hate Wave. (p. 1274)
Saul, "Aunt" Laya. You Don't Have to Learn Everything the Hard Way: What I Wish Someone Had Told Me. (p. 1975)
Saul, Laya. Meet Our New Student from Israel. (p. 1122)
—Recipe & Craft Guide to Israel. (p. 1451)
—Ways to Help after a Natural Disaster: A Guide to Giving Back. (p. 1865)
—Ways to Help Disadvantaged Youth: A Guide to Giving Back. (p. 1865)
—We Visit Israel. (p. 1868)
Saules, Tony de, jt. auth. see Arnold, Nick.
Saull, Eve, illus. see Muse, Elizabeth St. Cloud.
Saulles, Tony De, see Arnold, Nick & De Saulles, Tony.
Saulmon, Greg. Genital Herpes. (p. 661)
—Linkin Park. (p. 1019)
Sauls, Debra A. Angel Quest. (p. 74)
Sauls, Lynn B. Gabriel Goes to Washington: Through Big Brown Eyes; the Adventures of Gabriel the Poodle. Sauls, Lynn B., illus. (p. 652)
Saumande, Juliette. In Search of Happiness. Weller, Andrew, tr. from FRE. (p. 864)
Saumande, Juliette, et al. No Me da Miedo! 10 Historias Escalofriantes. (p. 1259)
Saumell, Marina, illus. see Canady, Mary Monica.
Saumier, Chantelle. Vinnie! Star of the Show. (p. 1843)
—Vinnie! the Hurricane. (p. 1843)
Saunder, Bev, jt. auth. see Rickus, Alexis.
Saunders. Saunders 2. (p. 1516)
Saunders, Barbara R. Ivan Pavlov: Exploring the Mysteries of Behavior. (p. 900)
Saunders, Brianna. Magic Marble. (p. 1072)
Saunders, Catherine. Are Ewoks Scared of Stormtroopers? (p. 96)
—Character Encyclopedia. (p. 291)
—Legendary Yoda. (p. 989)
—LEGO Friends Character Encyclopedia. (p. 990)
Saunders, Catherine, jt. auth. see Beecroft, Simon.
Saunders, Catherine, jt. auth. see Casey, Joe.
Saunders, Catherine, jt. auth. see Dorling Kindersley Publishing Staff.
Saunders, Catherine & Stock, Lisa. Are Ewoks Scared of Storm Troopers? (p. 96)
Saunders, Craig. What Is the Theory of Plate Tectonics? (p. 1890)
Saunders, George P. Last Elf. (p. 977)
Saunders, Hal. When Are We Ever Gonna Have to Use This? (p. 1901)
Saunders, Harry M. Teenagers on an Adventure: Journey of Two Boys & a Girl. (p. 1714)
Saunders, Helen. Good Night Little Man. Groshelle, Dave, illus. (p. 699)
—So, Where do all the teeth Go? Bolick, Brian, illus. (p. 1602)
Saunders, Helen B. Sweet Faces Story Book. (p. 1689)
Saunders, Helen B., creator. Sweet Faces Coloring Book. (p. 1689)
Saunders, Jami Lynn. Feral: Book I of the Werecat Saga. (p. 581)
—Rabid: Book II of the Werecat Saga. (p. 1430)
Saunders, Joanne D. Secret at the Winthrop House. (p. 1540)
—Secret at the Winthrop House, Independence Day. (p. 1540)
Saunders, Kackie L. Hazel & Daemon. (p. 756)
Saunders, Kate. Beswitched. (p. 171)
—Magicalamity. (p. 1075)
—Whizz Pop Chocolate Shop. (p. 1914)
Saunders, Katie. Little Reindeer. (p. 1035)
—Preschool Days Treasury: Preschool Learning Friendships & Fun. (p. 1396)
—Toddler Christmas: Activities, Games, & Stories for Excited Toddlers. (p. 1761)
—Toddler Time Teddy Hunt. (p. 1761)
—Toddler Treasury: 5 Lively Sections for Toddlers on the Move. (p. 1761)
—Toddler World: Includes 24 Exciting Flaps! (p. 1761)
Saunders, Katie, illus. see Bicknell, Joanna & Page, Nick.
Saunders, Katie, illus. see Bullard, Lisa.
Saunders, Katie, illus. see Page, Nick & Page, Claire.
Saunders, Katie & Little Bee Books Staff. Color Fun! An Abacus Book. Saunders, Katie, illus. (p. 342)
—Counting Fun! An Abacus Book. Saunders, Katie, illus. (p. 371)
Saunders, Len. Joey the Kangaroo: An Adventure in Exercise. (p. 920)
—Spunky the Monkey: An Adventure in Exercise. (p. 1635)
Saunders, Louise. Knave of Hearts. Parrish, Maxfield, illus. (p. 964)
Saunders, Lucy S., jt. auth. see Willis, Carrie (Hunter).
Saunders, M. D., illus. see Wisdom, Eileen Mary.
Saunders, Maggie. Adventures of Morgan & Malyk: The Lost Dog Mystery. (p. 20)
Saunders, Margaret Marshall. Beautiful Joe: Der Hund, der die Menschen verändert hat. (p. 153)
—Tilda Jane: A Rambunctious Orphan's Misadventures Finding a Home in the Early 1900s. (p. 1750)
Saunders, Marshall. Beautiful Joe: An AutoBiography of a Dog. (p. 153)
—Beautiful Joe a Dog's Own Story. (p. 153)
—Pussy BlackFace or the Story of A Kitten. (p. 1420)
Saunders, Mike, illus. see Dicker, Katie.
Saunders, Mike, illus. see Dickler, Katie.
Saunders, N. Who Invented the Periodic Table? (p. 1915)
Saunders, N. & Saunders, Nigel. Geothermal Energy. (p. 665)
Saunders, Nicholas & Faber, Laurie. Times Table Rap. (p. 1754)
Saunders, Nicholas J. & Saunders, Nick. Inca City of Cuzco. (p. 868)
Saunders, Nick, jt. auth. see Saunders, Nicholas J.
Saunders, Nigel. Exploring Atoms & Molecules. (p. 551)
—Exploring Chemical Reactions. (p. 551)
—Geothermal Energy. (p. 665)
—Nuclear Energy. (p. 1269)
—Wind Power. (p. 1935)
Saunders, Nigel, jt. auth. see Saunders, N.
Saunders, Nigel, jt. auth. see Solway, Andrew.
Saunders, Nigel & Chapman, Steven. Energía Renovable. (p. 528)
—Energy Transfers (p. 528)
—Fossil Fuel (p. 623)
—Nuclear Energy (p. 1269)
—Renewable Energy (p. 1460)

S

—Transferencias de Energía. (p. 1778)
Saunders, Nigel J. & Chapman, Steven. Combustibles Fósiles. (p. 347)
—Energía Nuclear. (p. 528)
Saunders, Sara. Swirly. Pierce, Matthew, illus. (p. 1691)
Saunders, Tom. I Want to Go to the Moon. Nugent, Cynthia, illus. (p. 848)
Saunders, Vivien. Adventures of Annika. Muckle, Christine, illus. (p. 16)
Saunders, Zina. Say Please! A Book about Manners. (p. 1518)
—Trouble at the Krusty Krab! (p. 1789)
Saunders, Zina, illus. see Banks, Steven.
Saunders, Zina, illus. see Beechen, Adam.
Saunders, Zina, illus. see Beinstein, Phoebe.
Saunders, Zina, illus. see Fuqua, Nell & Jankowki, Dan.
Saunders, Zina, illus. see Inches, Alison & Weiner, Eric.
Saunders, Zina, illus. see Inches, Alison.
Saunders, Zina, illus. see Ricci, Christine.
Saunderson, Chris, illus. see Jeffs, Stephanie.
Saunderson, Chris, illus. see Lane, Leena.
Saunders-Smith, Gail. Animal Robots (p. 79)
—Countries. (p. 372)
—Leaves. (p. 986)
—Robots in Space (p. 1481)
—Robots on the Job (p. 1481)
—Seeds. (p. 1547)
—Tiny Robots (p. 1756)
—Ultimate Small Group Reading How-To Book: Building Comprehension Through Small-Group Instruction. (p. 1810)
—You'll Love Chorkies (p. 1977)
—You'll Love Cockapoos (p. 1977)
—You'll Love Labradoodles (p. 1978)
—You'll Love Morkies (p. 1978)
Saunders-Smith, Gail, ed. see Adamson, Heather.
Saunders-Smith, Gail, ed. see Adamson, Thomas K.
Saunders-Smith, Gail, ed. see Adamson, Thomas K. & Capstone Press Editors.
Saunders-Smith, Gail, ed. see Adamson, Thomas K. & Capstone Press Staff.
Saunders-Smith, Gail, ed. see Allen, Kathy.
Saunders-Smith, Gail, ed. see Bodach, Vijaya Khisty & Bodach, Vijaya.
Saunders-Smith, Gail, ed. see Bodach, Vijaya Khisty.
Saunders-Smith, Gail, ed. see Braun, Eric.
Saunders-Smith, Gail, ed. see Bullard, Lisa.
Saunders-Smith, Gail, ed. see Capstone Press Editors & Rake, Jody Sullivan.
Saunders-Smith, Gail, ed. see Carlson, Cheryl.
Saunders-Smith, Gail, ed. see DeGezelle, Terri & Capstone Press Staff.
Saunders-Smith, Gail, ed. see DeGezelle, Terri.
Saunders-Smith, Gail, ed. see Doeden, Matt & Capstone Press Editors.
Saunders-Smith, Gail, ed. see Doeden, Matt & Capstone Press Staff.
Saunders-Smith, Gail, ed. see Doeden, Matt.
Saunders-Smith, Gail, ed. see Emerson, Judy.
Saunders-Smith, Gail, ed. see Frost, Helen.
Saunders-Smith, Gail, ed. see Glaser, Rebecca Stromstad.
Saunders-Smith, Gail, ed. see Hall, Margaret C.
Saunders-Smith, Gail, ed. see Hall, Margaret C. & Hall, Margaret.
Saunders-Smith, Gail, ed. see Hall, Margaret.
Saunders-Smith, Gail, ed. see Harris, Calvin & Rustad, Martha E.
Saunders-Smith, Gail, ed. see Ipcizade, Catherine.
Saunders-Smith, Gail, ed. see Knox, Barbara.
Saunders-Smith, Gail, ed. see Lindeen, Carol K.
Saunders-Smith, Gail, ed. see Lindeen, Carol K. & Capstone Press Editors.
Saunders-Smith, Gail, ed. see Lindeen, Carol K. & Capstone Press Staff.
Saunders-Smith, Gail, ed. see Lindeen, Carol K. & Lugtu, Carol J.
Saunders-Smith, Gail, ed. see Lindeen, Carol K., et al.
Saunders-Smith, Gail, ed. see Macken, JoAnn Early.
Saunders-Smith, Gail, ed. see Meltzer Kleinhenz, Sydnie & Kleinhenz, Sydnie M.
Saunders-Smith, Gail, ed. see Miller, Connie Colwell & Capstone Press Editors.
Saunders-Smith, Gail, ed. see Miller, Connie Colwell & Capstone Press Staff.
Saunders-Smith, Gail, ed. see Miller, Connie Colwell.
Saunders-Smith, Gail, ed. see Nuzzolo, Deborah.
Saunders-Smith, Gail, ed. see Olson, Gillia M.
Saunders-Smith, Gail, ed. see Perkins, Wendy & Capstone Press Editors.
Saunders-Smith, Gail, ed. see Perkins, Wendy & Capstone Press Staff.
Saunders-Smith, Gail, ed. see Rake, Jody Sullivan.
Saunders-Smith, Gail, ed. see Riehecky, Janet & Capstone Press Staff.
Saunders-Smith, Gail, ed. see Riehecky, Janet.
Saunders-Smith, Gail, ed. see Ripple, William John.
Saunders-Smith, Gail, ed. see Rustad, Martha E. H.
Saunders-Smith, Gail, ed. see Rustad, Martha E. H. & Rustad, Martha E.
Saunders-Smith, Gail, ed. see Schaefer, Lola M.
Saunders-Smith, Gail, ed. see Schaefer, Lola M. & Schaefer, Wyatt S.
Saunders-Smith, Gail, ed. see Schaefer, Lola M., et al.
Saunders-Smith, Gail, ed. see Schuette, Sarah L.
Saunders-Smith, Gail, ed. see Schuette, Sarah L. & Capstone Press Editors.
Saunders-Smith, Gail, ed. see Schuette, Sarah L. & Capstone Press Staff.
Saunders-Smith, Gail, ed. see Schuh, Mari C.
Saunders-Smith, Gail, ed. see Schuh, Mari C. & Schuh, Mari.
Saunders-Smith, Gail, ed. see Sullivan Rake, Jody & Rake, Jody Sullivan.
Saunders-Smith, Gail, ed. see Sullivan Rake, Jody, et al.
Saunders-Smith, Gail, ed. see Tagliaferro, Linda & Capstone Press Staff.
Saunders-Smith, Gail, ed. see Townsend, Emily Rose.
Saunders-Smith, Gail, ed. see Trumbauer, Lisa.
Saunders-Smith, Gail, illus. see Czeskleba, Abby.
Saunders-Smith, Gail, jt. auth. see Doyle, Sheri.
Saunders-Smith, Gail, jt. auth. see Edison, Erin.
Saunders-Smith, Gail, jt. auth. see Fandel, Jennifer.
Saunders-Smith, Gail, jt. auth. see Shores, Lori.
Saunders-Smith, Gail & Hoena, Blake A. Farms ABC: An Alphabet Book (p. 575)
Saunders-Smith, Gail, contrib. by. Extreme Animals (p. 556)
—Rev It Up! (p. 1465)
Saunders-Smith, Gail, ed. Famous Americans (p. 569)
—First Biographies (p. 593)
—Helpers in Our Community (p. 766)
Saundra Luchs. Wait for the Sunrise. (p. 1852)
Saupé, Rick. Moses P Rose Has Broken His Nose. DeBroeck, Sarah, illus. (p. 1176)
—Tyler Tiger Has Tonsillitis. (p. 1805)
Saur, Gregory. Strange New People: Book II of Finding Innocence (p. 1665)
Sauri, Trudy. Gift of Yucatan Nouns A-Z. (p. 675)
—Gift of Yucatan Pancho's Quest. (p. 675)
Sauro, Joan. Does God Ever Sleep? (p. 460)
Sautai, Raoul, illus. see Fuhr, Ute & Allaire, Caroline.
Sautai, Raoul, illus. see Fuhr, Ute.
Sautai, Raoul, illus. see Fuhr, UteSautai & Allaire, Caroline.
Sautai, Raoul, illus. see Moonlight Publishing Ltd Staff, et al.
Sautai, Raoul, jt. auth. see Fuhr, Ute.
Sautai, Raoul, jt. auth. see Krawczyk, Sabine.
Sautai, Raoul, tr. see Fhur, Ute, et al.
Sautai, Raoul, tr. see Fuhr, Ute, et al.
Sauter, Cynthia M. Birds Nest Outside My Bedroom Window. (p. 191)
Sautereau, Francois. Extrana Navidad de Jonas. (p. 555)
Sautter, A. J. Fantasy Field Guides McGrath, Tom & Juta, Jason, illus. (p. 572)
—Field Guide to Dragons, Trolls, & Other Dangerous Monsters Ashcroft, Colin Michael et al, illus. (p. 583)
—Field Guide to Elves, Dwarves, & Other Magical Folk Ashcroft, Colin Michael et al, illus. (p. 583)
—Field Guide to Goblins, Gremlins, & Other Wicked Creatures Ashcroft, Colin Michael et al, illus. (p. 583)
—Field Guide to Griffins, Unicorns, & Other Mythical Beasts Juta, Jason, illus. (p. 583)
Sautter, Aaron. Boys' Guide to Drawing: Aliens, Warriors, Robots & Other Cool Stuff. (p. 220)
—Boys' Guide to Drawing [LTD Commodities]. (p. 220)
—Drawing DC Super Heroes. Doescher, Erik & Levins, Tim, illus. (p. 481)
—How to Draw Amazing Motorcycles Smith, Tod, illus. (p. 816)
—How to Draw Batman & His Friends & Foes. Doescher, Erik, illus. (p. 817)
—How to Draw Batman, Superman, & Other DC Super Heroes & Villains. Doescher, Erik & Levins, Tim, illus. (p. 817)
—How to Draw Comic Heroes Martin, Cynthia, illus. (p. 817)
—How to Draw Crazy Fighter Planes Whigham, Rod, illus. (p. 817)
—How to Draw Disgusting Aliens Lentz, Bob, illus. (p. 817)
—How to Draw Ferocious Animals Erwin, Steve & Barnett, Charles, III, illus. (p. 817)
—How to Draw Ferocious Dinosaurs Martin, Cynthia, illus. (p. 817)
—How to Draw Grotesque Monsters Bascle, Brian, illus. (p. 817)
—How to Draw Incredible Cars Bascle, Brian, illus. (p. 817)
—How to Draw Indestructible Tanks Whigham, Rod, illus. (p. 817)
—How to Draw Manga Warriors Martin, Cynthia, illus. (p. 818)
—How to Draw Monster Trucks Whigham, Rod, illus. (p. 818)
—How to Draw Superman & His Friends & Foes. Doescher, Erik, illus. (p. 818)
—How to Draw the Joker, Lex Luthor, & Other DC Super-Villains. Levins, Tim, illus. (p. 818)
—How to Draw Unreal Spaceships Bascle, Brian, illus. (p. 819)
—How to Draw Wonder Woman, Green Lantern, & Other DC Super Heroes. Levins, Tim, illus. (p. 819)
—Sea Monsters (p. 1535)
—Werewolves (p. 1875)
Sautter, Aaron, jt. auth. see Jenson-Elliott, Cynthia L.
Sautter, Aaron & Capstone Press Staff. Hovercrafts (p. 804)
—Speedboats (p. 1624)
Sautter, Aaron, et al. Searching for UFOs: An Isabel Soto Investigation (p. 1538)
Sauvageau-Smestad, Sheila. Cassie's Creepy Candy Store. Berg, Kelly, illus. (p. 276)
—Rain, Rain, What a Pain! (p. 1435)
Sauvageot, Claude, photos by see Sein, Dominique.
Sauve, Gordon, illus. see Edmonston, Phil & Sawa, Maureen.
Sauza, Saul, jt. auth. see Hourglass Press, Hourglass.
Sava, Scott Christian. Animal Crackers. (p. 77)
—Cameron & His Dinosaurs. (p. 256)
—Ed's Terrestrials. (p. 505)
—Gary the Pirate. (p. 657)
—Hyperactive. (p. 831)
—Magic Carpet. (p. 1072)
—My Grandparents Are Secret Agents. (p. 1210)
Sava, Scott Christian & Bergin, Joseph. Luckiest Boy. (p. 1062)
Savadier, Elivia, illus. see Flor Ada, Alma.
Savage, Andrea. Famous Structures. (p. 570)
—On Safari. (p. 1289)
Savage, Annastaysia. Any Witch Way. (p. 90)
Savage, Bridgette Z. Fly Like the Wind. Savage, Charles J., ed. (p. 609)
Savage, Carol. Left Behind Kitty. (p. 987)
Savage, Charles J., ed. see Savage, Bridgette Z.
Savage, Charles J., photos by see Savage, Bridgette Z.
Savage, Christine Lyseng, et al. Halloween Recipes & Crafts (p. 738)
Savage, Derek. Cool Cat Loves Baseball. (p. 363)
—Cool Cat Loves Biodiesel. (p. 363)
—Cool Cat Loves Going Green. (p. 363)
—Cool Cat Loves Wrestling. (p. 363)
Savage, J. Scott. Air Keep. (p. 31)
—Evil Twins. Holgate, Doug, illus. (p. 546)
—Fires of Invention. (p. 592)
—Land Keep. (p. 973)
—Making the Team. Holgate, Doug, illus. (p. 1082)
—Water Keep. (p. 1863)
—Zombie Kid. Holgate, Doug, illus. (p. 1988)
Savage, Jeff. Aaron Rodgers. (p. 2)
—Adrian Peterson. (p. 13)
—Albert Pujols. (p. 34)
—Alex Ovechkin. (p. 36)
—American Cowboys: True Tales of the Wild West. (p. 60)
—ATVs (p. 114)
—Barry Bonds. (p. 140)
—Brett Favre. (p. 226)
—Brian Urlacher. (p. 226)
—California: A MyReportLinks. Com Book. (p. 253)
—Calvin Johnson. (p. 255)
—Carly Patterson. (p. 270)
—Choppers (p. 310)
—Chris Paul. (p. 311)
—Clay Matthews. (p. 330)
—Dale Earnhardt Jr. (p. 401)
—Dale Earnhardt, Jr. (p. 401)
—Dallas Friday. (p. 401)
—Danica Patrick. (p. 404)
—Danica Patrick (Revised Edition) (p. 404)
—Daring Pony Express Riders: True Tales of the Wild West. (p. 407)
—Dave Mirra. (p. 410)
—David Beckham. (p. 410)
—David Ortiz. (p. 411)
—Drew Brees. (p. 485)
—Dwight Howard. (p. 491)
—Dwyane Wade. (p. 491)
—Eli Manning. (p. 512)
—Fearless Scouts: True Tales of the Wild West. (p. 579)
—Freddy Adu. (p. 633)
—Georgia: A MyReportLinks. Com Book. (p. 665)
—Ichiro Suzuki. (p. 851)
—James Stewart. (p. 907)
—Jeff Gordon. (p. 911)
—Jeremy Lin. (p. 913)
—Josh Hamilton. (p. 926)
—Justin Verlander. (p. 940)
—Kevin Durant. (p. 950)
—Kobe Bryant. (p. 966)
—Kobe Bryant (Revised Edition) (p. 966)
—LaDainian Tomlinson. (p. 970)
—Lebron James. (p. 987)
—Lisa Leslie: Slam Dunk Queen. (p. 1022)
—Maria Sharapova. (p. 1093)
—Mark Sanchez. (p. 1095)
—Maryland: A MyReportLinks.com Book. (p. 1101)
—Maya Moore. (p. 1112)
—Michael Vick. (p. 1135)
—Michael Vick (Revised Edition) (p. 1135)
—Monster Trucks (p. 1168)
—Motorcycles. (p. 1179)
—Mountain Bikes (p. 1180)
—Muhammad Ali: The Greatest (p. 1189)
—Oscar de la Hoya: The Golden Boy. (p. 1305)
—Peyton Manning. (p. 1349)
—Pioneering Women: True Tales of the Wild West. (p. 1361)
—Prince Fielder. (p. 1401)
—Quick-Draw Gunfighters: True Tales of the Wild West. (p. 1427)
—Roger Federer. (p. 1484)
—Roy Halladay. (p. 1492)
—Rugged Gold Miners: True Tales of the Wild West. (p. 1494)
—Ryan Howard. (p. 1499)
—Ryan Howard (Revised Edition) (p. 1499)
—Sammy Sosa. (p. 1508)
—Sidney Crosby. (p. 1573)
—South Dakota: A MyReportLinks. Com Book. (p. 1617)
—Stephen Strasburg. (p. 1648)
—Steve Nash. (p. 1649)
—Street Skating: Grinds & Grabs (p. 1666)
—Super Basketball Infographics. Schuster, Rob, illus. (p. 1679)
—Super Hockey Infographics. (p. 1680)
—Super Hockey Infographics. Kulihin, Vic, illus. (p. 1680)
—Thrill Rides! All about Roller Coasters. (p. 1744)
—Tiger Woods. (p. 1749)
—Tim Duncan. (p. 1750)
—Tim Lincecum. (p. 1750)
—Tim Tebow. (p. 1750)
—Tom Brady. (p. 1762)
—Tony Hawk: Skateboarding Legend (p. 1766)
—Tony Romo. (p. 1766)
—Top 25 Gymnastics Skills, Tips, & Tricks. (p. 1768)
—Top 25 Hockey Skills, Tips, & Tricks. (p. 1768)
—Top 25 Soccer Skills, Tips, & Tricks. (p. 1768)
—Travis Pastrana. (p. 1781)
—Tuner Cars (p. 1796)
—Usain Bolt. (p. 1826)
—X-Games. (p. 1967)
Savage, Jeff, jt. auth. see Doeden, Matt.
Savage, Jeff, jt. auth. see Pendleton, Ken.
Savage, Jeff, jt. auth. see Riner, Dax.
Savage, Jeffrey. Fourth Nephite. (p. 625)
Savage, Jeffrey S. Fourth Nephite: Return to Palmyra (p. 625)
Savage, Jill & Savage, Mark. Living with Less So Your Family Has More. (p. 1042)
Savage, Joshua, illus. see Smith, Stephen.
Savage, Julie Hemming, jt. auth. see Hemming, Heidi.
Savage, Leah, et al. POW Wow: Niimiwin Everyone Dance. (p. 1389)
Savage, Lily. Sort of A-Z Thing. (p. 1614)
Savage, Lorraine. Eating Disorders. (p. 501)
—Mental Illness. (p. 1126)
Savage, Mark, jt. auth. see Savage, Jill.
Savage, Sam. Criminal Life of Effie O. An Entertainment. Beverley, Virginia, illus. (p. 382)
Savage, Stephen. British Animals - Bat. (p. 229)
—Duck. (p. 488)
—Focus on Amphibians. (p. 610)
—Focus on Birds. (p. 610)
—Focus on Fish. (p. 610)
—Focus on Insects. (p. 610)
—Focus on Mammals. (p. 610)
—Focus on Reptiles. (p. 611)
—Little Tug. (p. 1037)
—Little Tug. Savage, Stephen, illus. (p. 1037)
—Mole. (p. 1160)
—Mouse. (p. 1181)
—Rat. (p. 1440)
—Seven Orange Pumpkins Board Book. (p. 1554)
—Supertruck. Savage, Stephen, illus. (p. 1684)
—Swallow. (p. 1688)
—Ten Orange Pumpkins: A Counting Book. (p. 1719)
—Toad. (p. 1759)
—Where's Walrus? Savage, Stephen, illus. (p. 1911)
Savage, Stephen, illus. see Brown, Margaret Wise.
Savage, Stephen, illus. see Thompson, Lauren.
Savage, Steven. Duck. (p. 488)
Savage, Tawanna. Anna Mischievous: The Early Years. (p. 85)
Savage, Virginia, illus. see Tenenbaum, Frances & Peterson, Roger Tory.
Savageau, Cheryl. Muskrat Will Be Swimming Hynes, Robert, illus. (p. 1194)
Savageau, Tony. Mud House Mystery: A Wild Bunch Adventure. Raditz, JoAnne, illus. (p. 1188)
Savaget, Luciana. 1,2,3 y Ya. (p. 2000)
Savannah. Silly Sally Sometime. Seay, Christina, illus. (p. 1576)
Savard, Remi, et al. First Spring: An Innu Tale of North America. (p. 597)
Savary, Fabien. Caillou: Que Faita? Tipeo, illus. (p. 251)
Savary, Fabien & Vadeboncoeur, Isabelle. Caillou: Sorpresa! Tipeo, illus. (p. 251)
—Caillou: Los Contrarios. Tipeo, illus. (p. 251)
Savary, Louis M. Rosary for Children. (p. 1489)
—Way of the Cross. (p. 1864)
Save A Gato, as told by. Old San Juan Cat Tales: Cuentos de Gatos del Viejo San Juan. (p. 1284)
Save, Ken, illus. see Bateman, Jordan.
Savedoff, Barbara E. & Elissa, Barbara. Remarkable Journey of Josh's Kippah. Jamana, Pharida & Zaman, Farida, illus. (p. 1458)
Savel, Dava, jt. auth. see Sacks, David.
Saveley, Barb. Curse of Moonstone Island. (p. 394)
—Dusky: The Lost Unicorn. (p. 490)
—Dusky II: Journey of Tears. (p. 490)
Savelle, Jerry. Don't Let Go of Your Dreams. (p. 468)
Savers, Richard A. Guide to Civil War Philadelphia. (p. 730)
Savery, Annabel. Brazil. (p. 224)
—Dinosaurs. (p. 444)
—Fairies. (p. 562)
—Monsters. (p. 1168)
—Pirates. (p. 1363)
—Supercars. (p. 1682)
—Superheroes. (p. 1683)
Savery, Annabel, jt. auth. see Barker, Geoff.
Savery, Annabel, jt. auth. see Rooney, Anne.
Savery, Annabel, jt. auth. see Senker, Cath.
Savery, Annabel, jt. auth. see Stearman, Kaye.
Saville, Kathy Dee, illus. see Aragón, Carla, et al.
Savino, Bob. Black Butterfly: Poems for a Muse. (p. 195)
Saviola, Ava. Dinosaur ABCs. (p. 441)
—Dinosaur Colors. (p. 441)
—Dinosaur Opposites. (p. 442)
—Dinosaur Shapes. (p. 442)
—Dinosaurs Count! (p. 444)
—Dinosaur's First Words. (p. 444)
—Story of Johnny Appleseed. (p. 1658)
Saviola, Erin. Airplane Jane. (p. 32)
—Biggest Fish. (p. 185)
Saviola, Joseph A. Tour de France: Solving Addition Problems Using Regrouping. (p. 1773)
—Tour de France: Solving Addition Problems Involving Renaming. (p. 1773)
Savitskas, Margaret. Totally Lent! A Kid's Journey to Easter 2006. Larkin, Jean K., ed. (p. 1771)
Savitskas, Margaret & Behe, Mary. Totally Lent! A Child's Journey to Easter 2006. Larkin, Jean K., ed. (p. 1771)
Savitsky, Steve. Dora's Pirate Treasure Hunt. (p. 471)
Savitsky, Steve, illus. see Ricci, Christine & Golden Books Staff.
Savitsky, Steve, illus. see Risco, Elle D.
Savitsky, Steven. Dora Had a Little Lamb. (p. 470)
Savitsky, Steven, illus. see Echeverria, Jessica.
Savitsky, Steven, illus. see Golden Books Staff.
Savitsky, Steven, illus. see Ricci, Christine.
Savitsky, Steven, illus. see Thorpe, Kiki.
Savitsky, Steven, illus. see Willson, Sarah.
Savitt, Sam, illus. see Davidson, Mary Richmond.
Savitz, Harriet May. Dear Daughters & Sons: Three Essays on the American Spirit... a Tribute. (p. 418)
Savitz, Harriet May, jt. auth. see Wolff, Ferida.
Savo, Jimmy. Little World, Hello! Birnbaum, A., illus. (p. 1038)
Savoie, Jacques & Zekina, Daniela. Chapeau Qui Tournait Autour de la Terre. (p. 291)
Savory, Phyllis. Best of African Folklore. (p. 170)
Savoy, Darryl, jt. auth. see Raymond, Roger.
Savoy, Simona. Faerwald's Secret (p. 562)
Savoy, Tom. Champions of the Dead. (p. 289)
Sawa, Maureen, jt. auth. see Edmonston, Phil.
Sawada, Hajime, illus. see Akita, Yoshinobu.
Sawada, Hajime, jt. auth. see Akita, Yoshinobu.
Sawai, Gloria. Song for Nettie Johnson. (p. 1611)
Sawai, Yoshio. Bobobo-Bo Bo-Bobo. Sawai, Yoshio, illus. (p. 206)
Sawaski, James H. Next Chess Team: A Novel. (p. 1249)
Sawka, Searra. Ghost Stories: John, Are You down There? (p. 671)
Sawler, Kimberly. Rocket & the Magical Cosmic Candies. Walls, Ty, illus. (p. 1482)

Sawvel, Patty Jo. Water Resource Management. (p. 1863)
Sawyer, Charles, et al. One Man Show: Henry Miller in the San Joaquín. (p. 1296)
Sawyer, Darren, photos by see Rayner, Matthew.
Sawyer, Debra D. Let Me Speak You A Secret. (p. 994)
Sawyer, J. Clark. Los Cometas Helados: A Veces Tienen Colas. (p. 1053)
—Nuestra Luna: El Objeto MÁS Brillante Del Cielo Nocturno. (p. 1270)
—Our Moon: Brightest Object in the Night Sky. (p. 1309)
—PlutÓN: No Es un Planeta. (p. 1374)
Sawyer, J. Clark, jt. auth. see Glaser, Chaya.
Sawyer, J. Scott. Broccoli Bush. Bozeman, Gary, illus. (p. 230)
Sawyer, Jacqueline. Little Racer Big Heart. (p. 1034)
Sawyer, Jocelyn, illus. see Lorenzen, Margaret.
Sawyer, Judith L. This Is How I Pray. Sawyer, Judith L., illus. (p. 1736)
Sawyer, Kem Knapp. Amazing Underground Railroad: Stories in American History. (p. 56)
—Amazing Underground Railroad. (p. 56)
—Eleanor Roosevelt. (p. 508)
—Grace Akallo & the Pursuit of Justice for Child Soldiers. (p. 704)
—Harriet Tubman - A Photographic Story of a Life. (p. 750)
—Mohandas Gandhi. (p. 1160)
Sawyer, Kieran & Amodel, Michael. Confirming Faith: Candidate Book. . Faith Development Program for High School Students Preparing to Celebrate the Sacrament of Confirmation with the Support of the Entire Faith Community. Robinson, Katherine, illus. (p. 357)
—Confirming Faith: Director's Manual... Faith Development Program for High School Students Preparing to Celebrate the Sacrament of Confirmation with the Support of the Entire Faith Community. Robinson, Katherine, illus. (p. 357)
Sawyer, Kim. Trial with No Exit. (p. 1785)
Sawyer, Kim Vogel. Katy's Debate (p. 946)
—Katy's Decision (p. 946)
—Katy's Homecoming (p. 946)
—Katy's New World (p. 946)
Sawyer, Louise. Mother's Storybook Signs. (p. 1179)
—Phantom. (p. 1349)
Sawyer, Odessa, illus. see Bracken, Beth & Fraser, Kay.
Sawyer, Parker K. Potty Time! Moroney, Christopher, illus. (p. 1388)
Sawyer, Peter, illus. see Miller, Karen.
Sawyer, Ruth. Primrose Ring. (p. 1401)
—This Way to Christmas. (p. 1737)
Sawyer, Sarah. Avril Lavigne. (p. 120)
—Body Piercing & Tattooing: The Hidden Dangers of Body Art. (p. 207)
—Career Building Through Podcasting. (p. 266)
—Careers in DNA Analysis. (p. 267)
—Denny Hamlin: NASCAR Driver. (p. 426)
—Fall Out Boy. (p. 566)
—Florida: Past & Present. (p. 606)
—Frequently Asked Questions about Body Piercing & Tattooing. (p. 636)
Sawyer, Timothy L., jt. auth. see Torres, Eliseo.
Sawyer-Aitch, Anne. Nalah & the Pink Tiger. Sawyer-Aitch, Anne, illus. (p. 1228)
Sawyers, Carol. Trapped At 13. (p. 1779)
Sawyers, William. Nest That Could Fly. (p. 1242)
—What Am I? Book. (p. 1879)
—What Am I? Bugs. (p. 1879)
Sax, Aline. War Within These Walls. (p. 1858)
Sax, Anita. One Step at a Time. Jasuna, Aija, illus. (p. 1297)
—Oscar & the Zoo. Jasuna, Aija, illus. (p. 1305)
Saxby, Claire. Big Red Kangaroo. Byrne, Graham, illus. (p. 183)
—Emu. Byrne, Graham, illus. (p. 521)
—Meet the ANZACs. Berry, Max, illus. (p. 1122)
—Meet Weary Dunlop. Lord, Jeremy, illus. (p. 1123)
—Seadog. Jellett, Tom, illus. (p. 1536)
Saxby, Karen. Storyfun for Flyers Student's Book. (p. 1663)
—Storyfun for Movers Student's Book. (p. 1663)
—Storyfun for Starters Student's Book. (p. 1663)
Saxby, Karen, jt. auth. see Robinson, Anne.
Saxena, Shalini. Legend of King Arthur. (p. 988)
—Legend of Sleepy Hollow. (p. 988)
—Saving the Endangered Gray Wolf. (p. 1517)
—Volleyball & Its Greatest Players (p. 1849)
Saxena, Shalini, ed. Dictatorship, Fascism, & Totalitarianism. (p. 436)
Saxon, John. Algebra 1-2. (p. 38)
—Handbook for County Social Services Boards. (p. 740)
—Home Study Packet for Calculus: Test Forms. (p. 793)
Saxon, John, jt. auth. see Hake, Stephen.
Saxon, John H., Jr. Algebra 2: An Incremental Development. (p. 38)
Saxon, John L. Social Services in North Carolina. (p. 1604)
Saxon, Lucy. Take Back the Skies. (p. 1696)
Saxon, Maddie. Black Lace Sexy Quiz Book. (p. 196)
Saxon Publishers, creator. Advanced Math Test Forms: Homeschool Packet For. (p. 13)
Saxon Publishers, Inc. Staff. Algebra 1-2. (p. 38)
Saxon Publishers Staff, tr. see Larson, Nancy.
Saxon Publishers Staff & Hake, Stephen. Saxon Math 5/4 Homeschool: Solutions Manual. (p. 1518)
—Saxon Math 5/4 Homeschool. (p. 1518)
—Saxon Math 6/5 Homeschool Kit (p. 1518)
Saxon, Terrill. Baby's Noah's Ark. (p. 129)
—Now I Lay Me down to Sleep. (p. 1269)
Saxon, Victoria. Frozen (Disney Frozen) Lee, Grace & Cagol, Andrea, illus. (p. 645)
—Ready to Play! (Disney Infinity) RH Disney Staff & Doescher, Erik, illus. (p. 1448)
Saxon, Victoria & RH Disney Staff. Frozen Fever. RH Disney Staff, illus. (p. 645)
—Ratatouille. Tilley, Scott & Orpinas, Jean-Paul, illus. (p. 1440)
Saxon, Victoria & Smiley, Ben. Disney-Pixar Little Golden Book Favorites. Golden Books Staff, illus. (p. 452)
Saxon-Ford, Stephanie. Czech Americans: The Immigrant Experience. (p. 397)
Saxton, Brenda. Reading Pals: Alphabet Recognition Gr. Pre K-K. (p. 1446)
Saxton, Curtis, et al. Complete Cross-Sections. (p. 352)
Saxton, Jo. Snail Trail: In Search of a Modern Masterpiece. (p. 1596)
Saxton, Patricia. Book of Fairies. Saxton, Patricia, illus. (p. 211)
—Book of Mermaids. Saxton, Patricia, illus. (p. 211)
Say, Allen. Allison. (p. 47)
—Boy in the Garden. (p. 218)
—Drawing from Memory. (p. 481)
—Drawing from Memory. Say, Allen, illus. (p. 481)
—Emma's Rug. (p. 520)
—Favorite Daughter. (p. 578)
—Favorite Daughter. Say, Allen, illus. (p. 578)
—Grandfather's Journey. (p. 707)
—Grandfather's Journey. Say, Allen, illus. (p. 707)
—Ink-Keeper's Apprentice. (p. 874)
—Kamishibai Man. (p. 942)
—Sign Painter. (p. 1574)
—Tea with Milk. Say, Allen, illus. (p. 1708)
—Tree of Cranes. Say, Allen, illus. (p. 1783)
Sayegh, R. J. Dividing Line. (p. 454)
Sayer, Ann Marie Mulhearn, jt. auth. see Slobodkina, Esphyr.
Sayer, Chloe. Incan Empire. (p. 868)
Sayer, Geoff, jt. auth. see Marshall, David.
Sayer, Marjorie. Girl Mechanic of Wanzhou. (p. 678)
Sayer, Melissa, jt. auth. see Cronin, Ali.
Sayer, Melissa & Naik, Anita. Too Fat? Too Thin? The Healthy Eating Handbook. (p. 1766)
Sayers, Mary. Franky: The Cranky Crab. (p. 631)
Sayers, Myrna, illus. see John Blake Publishing Staff.
Sayers, Rachel, illus. see Heeney, Bronwyn.
Sayle, Stephen. Cam & Zara the Travel Bugs: Egypt. (p. 255)
—Cam & Zara the Travel Bugs. (p. 255)
Sayler, Machelle. Folkeminnevitskap II. (p. 611)
Sayler, Mary Harwell. Encyclopedia of Muscle & Skeletal Systems & Disorders. (p. 525)
—Prescription Pain Relievers. (p. 1396)
Sayles, Alayne. Alphie & the Alphabets: A Fun Way to Learn to Read. Platt, Greg, illus. (p. 50)
Sayles, Carol L. Turn the Turtle Rightside. (p. 1797)
Sayles, Elizabeth, illus. see Bauer, Marion Dane.
Sayles, Elizabeth, illus. see Blackmore, Jeanne C.
Sayles, Elizabeth, illus. see Teltelbaum, Michael.
Sayles, Elizabeth, illus. see Cohlene, Terri.
Sayles, Elizabeth, illus. see Crystal, Billy.
Sayles, Elizabeth, illus. see Kohuth, Jane.
Sayles, Elizabeth, illus. see Krilanovich, Nadia.
Sayles, Elizabeth, illus. see Mora, Pat.
Sayles, John, illus. see Lyons, Wendy Ackerman.
Sayles, Kristi. Jacob's Monkey-the Trouble with Lying. (p. 904)
Saylor-Marchant, Linda. From Sea to Shining Sea: Oklahoma. (p. 643)
—Hip Hop into Reading Series: It's easy to read & rap/read & rap like the President. (p. 780)
—Oklahoma. (p. 1282)
Sayre, April Pulley. Ant, Ant, Ant! An Insect Chant. Park, Trip, illus. (p. 88)
—Bird, Bird, Bird! A Chirping Chant. Locke, Gary, illus. (p. 190)
—Bumblebee Queen. Wynne, Patricia J., illus. (p. 241)
—Eat Like a Bear. Jenkins, Steve, illus. (p. 501)
—Exploring Earth's Biomes (p. 552)
—Go, Go, Grapes! A Fruit Chant. Sayre, April Pulley, illus. (p. 686)
—Here Come the Humpbacks! Hogan, Jamie, illus. (p. 770)
—Honk, Honk, Goose! Canada Geese Start a Family. Lee, Huy Voun, illus. (p. 795)
—If You're Hoppy. Urbanovic, Jackie, illus. (p. 855)
—Let's Go Nuts! Seeds We Eat. Sayre, April Pulley, illus. (p. 997)
—Meet the Howlers! Miller, Woody, illus. (p. 1122)
—Rah, Rah, Radishes! A Vegetable Chant. Sayre, April Pulley, photos by. (p. 1433)
—Raindrops Roll. Sayre, April Pulley, photos by. (p. 1436)
—Stars Beneath Your Bed: The Surprising Story of Dust. Jonas, Ann, illus. (p. 1643)
—Trout Are Made of Trees. Endle, Kate, illus. (p. 1790)
—Trout, Trout, Trout: (A Fish Chant) Park, Trip, illus. (p. 1790)
—Trout, Trout, Trout! (p. 1790)
—Turtle, Turtle, Watch Out! Patterson, Annie, illus. (p. 1798)
—Vulture View. Jenkins, Steve, illus. (p. 1851)
—Woodpecker Wham! Jenkins, Steve, illus. (p. 1949)
Sayre, April Pulley, jt. auth. see Sayre, Jeff.
Sayre, April Pulley & Sayre, Jeff. One Is a Snail, Ten Is a Crab: A Counting by Feet Book. Cecil, Randy, illus. (p. 1295)
Sayre, Hilda L. Kids, Quilts & Reading. (p. 955)
Sayre, Jeff, jt. auth. see Sayre, April Pulley.
Sayre, Jeff & Sayre, April Pulley. One Is a Snail, Ten Is a Crab Big Book: A Counting by Feet Book. Cecil, Randy, illus. (p. 1295)
Sayre, Jill K. Fairies of Turtle Creek. (p. 563)
Sayre, Tamara, illus. see DeStrulle, Arlene & Johnson, Tora.
Sayres, Brianna Caplan. Tiara Saurus Rex. Boldt, Mike, illus. (p. 1747)
—Where Do Diggers Sleep at Night? Slade, Christian, illus. (p. 1907)
Sayres, David. Flatland. Emberley, Rebecca, ed. (p. 603)
Sazaklis, John. Barnyard Brainwash Baltazar, Art, illus. (p. 139)
—Batman: An Origin Story. Baltazar, Art & Vecchio, Luciano, illus. (p. 144)
—Batman Classic: The Batman Reusable Sticker Book. (p. 144)
—Batman Classic: Gotham's Villains Unleashed! Mada Design Staff, illus. (p. 144)
—Batman Classic: Dawn of the Dynamic Duo. Gordon, Eric A. & Gordon, Steven E., illus. (p. 144)
—Batman Classic - Eternal Enemies. Tong, Andie, illus. (p. 144)
—Battle - Battle in Metropolis. Smith, Andy & Vancata, Brad, illus. (p. 145)
—Battle in Metropolis. (p. 146)
—Biggest Little Hero Baltazar, Art, illus. (p. 185)
—Candy Store Caper Baltazar, Art, illus. (p. 261)
—Day of Doom. (p. 414)
—Deep-Sea Duel Baltazar, Art, illus. (p. 423)
—Design & Draw. (p. 429)
—Disney Fairies: the Pixie Dust Doodle Book. (p. 451)
—Fate of Krypton. (p. 577)
—Fate of Krypton. Roberts, Jeremy, illus. (p. 577)
—Feline Felonies: With Wonder Woman. Gordon, Steven E., illus. (p. 581)
—Fowl Play. Gordon, Steven E. & Gordon, Eric A., illus. (p. 625)
—Ghosts of Griffin Rock. (p. 672)
—Goat on a Boat Bradley, Jessica, illus. (p. 687)
—Hopping Hero Baltazar, Art, illus. (p. 797)
—I Am the Flash. (p. 834)
—Justice League Classic - I Am the Flash. Gordon, Steven E., illus. (p. 940)
—Land Before Prime. (p. 973)
—Man of Steel. (p. 1085)
—Mystery of the Maze Monster Neely, Scott, illus. (p. 1225)
—Optimus Prime Versus Predaking. (p. 1301)
—Return of the Dinobot. (p. 1464)
—Royal Rodent Rescue Baltazar, Art, illus. (p. 1492)
—Salamander Smackdown. Baltazar, Art, illus. (p. 1504)
—Superman: Escape from the Phantom Zone. Gordon, Steven E., illus. (p. 1683)
—Superman Alliance of Heroes - Freezeframe (p. 1683)
—Superman Classic - Day of Doom. Smith, Andy & Vancata, Brad, illus. (p. 1683)
—Superman Saves Smallville. Roberts, Jeremy, illus. (p. 1683)
—Superman Saves Smallville. (p. 1684)
—Superman vs. Bizarro Vecchio, Luciano, illus. (p. 1684)
—Super-Villain Smackdown! Beavers, Ethen, illus. (p. 1682)
—Swamp Thing vs the Zombie Pets Baltazar, Art, illus. (p. 1688)
—Transformers Prime Beast Hunters: Optimus Prime Versus Predaking. (p. 1778)
—Transformers: Rescue Bots: the Ghosts of Griffin Rock. (p. 1778)
—Wonder Woman: An Origin Story. Baltazar, Art & Vecchio, Luciano, illus. (p. 1947)
Sazaklis, John, illus. see McVeigh, Mark W.
Sazaklis, John, illus. see Rao, Lisa.
Sazaklis, John, illus. see Teitelbaum, Michael.
Sazaklis, John, jt. auth. see Manning, Matthew K.
Sazaklis, John, jt. auth. see Sutton, Laurie S.
Sazaklis, John & Farley, John. Attack of the Toyman. (p. 114)
—Attack of the Toyman. Smith, Andy, illus. (p. 114)
Sazaklis, John & Merkel, Joe F. Day of the Undead. (p. 414)
—Day of the Undead. Tong, Andie, illus. (p. 414)
Sazaklis, John & Phillips, Ruby Ann. Krystal Ball (p. 968)
Sazaklis, John & Roberts, Jeremy. Fright Club. Farley, Rick & Smith, Andy, illus. (p. 639)
Sazaklis, John & Vancata, Brad. Superman: Day of Doom. Smith, Andy, illus. (p. 1683)
Scacco, Linda. Always My Grandpa: A Story for Children about Alzheimer's Disease. Wong, Nicole, illus. (p. 51)
Scace, Orsolya Lorincz & McEwen, Sarah. What Do Frogs Eat? (p. 1882)
Scadden, Kathryn, illus. see Nolan, Nancy.
Scafuro, Lisa. Adventures at Cedar Hollow: Tigre Encounters the Great Horned Owl. (p. 15)
Scagell, Robin & Dorling Kindersley Publishing Staff. Night Sky Atlas. (p. 1254)
Scaglione, Dapos & Maria. Unique Bunny. (p. 1818)
Scaglione, Joanne & Small, Gail. Big Squeal: A Wild, True, & Twisted Tail. Endelman, David, illus. (p. 184)
—Life's Little Lessons: An Inch-by-Inch Tale of Success. (p. 1013)
Scaglione, Rebecca L. Jack: The trilogy ... the Truth. (p. 902)
Scala, Susan, illus. see Sanford, Candace.
Scala, Vincent. Beep Beep Goes the Bus Driver (p. 157)
Scalawag: (A Kathy Dubetz Production). Unicorns in the Mist: Books One & Two. (p. 1818)
Scalera, Buddy. Decoy: Storm of the Century. Huddleston, Courtney, illus. (p. 422)
Scales, Barbara a. Wally the Whale with the Crazy Wavy Hair. (p. 1855)
Scales, Peter C. & Leffert, Nancy. Developmental Assets: A Synthesis of the Scientific Research on Adolescent Development. Roehlkepartain, Eugene C. & Tyler, Kate, eds. (p. 432)
Scales, Simon, illus. see Spurr, Elizabeth.
Scales, Simon, jt. auth. see Millett, Peter.
Scaletta, Jane. Kimbo's First Horse Show (p. 957)
Scaletta, Kurtis. 823rd Hit Bk. 4. Wight, Eric, illus. (p. 2001)
—Batter Up! Beavers, Ethen, illus. (p. 145)
—Jinxed! Wight, Eric, illus. (p. 919)
—Mudville. (p. 1189)
—Steal That Base! Wight, Eric, illus. (p. 1645)
—Tanglewood Terror. (p. 1705)
—Topps League Story: Book Three: Zip It! Wight, Eric, illus. (p. 1769)
—Winter of the Robots. (p. 1938)
—You're Out! Beavers, Ethen, illus. (p. 1982)
Scalf, Chris, illus. see Bailey, Gerry.
Scalf, Chris, illus. see Nussbaum, Ben & McIntosh, G. B.
Scalf, Chris, illus. see Nussbaum, Ben.
Scalf, Christopher, illus. see Nussbaum, Ben.
Scali, Jacob, et al. Sprucy: The Tallest Christmas Tree. Carrier, Jason, illus. (p. 1635)
Scaling, Sam. Rabbit Talk. (p. 1429)
Scaling, Sam T. Marv the Moose Is on the Loose. Stanley, Susan, illus. (p. 1098)
—Marv the Moose... Is on the Loose: A Primer for Young People. (p. 1098)
Scalise, David. SAT Advantage with Professor Dave (p. 1515)
Scalise, Frank. Hardest Hit: A Sam the Hockey Player Novel. (p. 748)
Scally, Robert. Jeff Bezos: Founder of Amazon & the Kindle. (p. 911)
Scalzo, Linda V. Carazona's Coloring Book. (p. 265)
—circo llega al Pueblo: Version de Lectura Temprana. Torres, Marcela H., tr. (p. 321)
—Circus Is Coming to Town: Full-Length Version. (p. 322)
—Circus Is coming to Town: Early Reader Version. Spalinski, Amanda, illus. (p. 322)
Scam, Busta. Kingdom of Nome. (p. 959)
Scamander, Newt, pseud. Fantastic Beasts & Where to Find Them. (p. 571)
Scamihorn, Aaron, illus. see Hearst, Michael.
Scammon, Richard M., et al. America Votes 2001-2002: A Handbook of Contemporary American Election Statistics Vol. 25 (p. 59)
—America Votes 26 2003-2004 (p. 59)
Scand, Sandra. Time for Bed Little Red. Sanderson, Sean, illus. (p. 1751)
Scandella, Alessandra, illus. see Capriolo, Paola.
Scandiffio, Laura. Aztec. Holdcroft, Tina, illus. (p. 122)
—Crusades. Mantha, John & Holdcroft, Tina, illus. (p. 386)
—Escapes! MacEachern, Stephen, illus. (p. 535)
—Evil Masters: The Frightening World of Tyrants. (p. 546)
—Martial Arts Book. Debon, Nicolas, illus. (p. 1097)
—Outlaws, Spies, & Gangsters: Chasing Notorious Criminals. Williams, Gareth, illus. (p. 1313)
—People Who Said No: Courage Against Oppression. (p. 1340)
Scandiffio, Laura, jt. auth. see Gray, Nick.
Scandinavia Publishing House Staff, ed. see Alex, Ben.
Scandinavia Publishing House Staff, ed. see Garwin, Elaine & Youd, Pauline.
Scandora, Julie. Rules Are Rules. (p. 1495)
Scanes, Amy. Chosen: Book Two of the Abon Trilogy. (p. 310)
Scanlan, John M. Dink-Gadink. (p. 440)
Scanlan, Lawrence. Big Red Horse: The Story of Secretariat & the Loyal Groom Who Loved Him. (p. 183)
Scanlan, W. J. Rebellion (p. 1451)
Scanlon, Allison. Great Grilled Cheese! My Sandwich Is on Fire! (p. 716)
Scanlon, Cara. Where Did Grandma Go? Mattes-Ruggiero, Lynn, illus. (p. 1906)
—Where Did Grandpa Go? Mattes-Ruggiero, Lynn, illus. (p. 1906)
Scanlon, Elizabeth G., jt. auth. see Scanlon, Elizabeth Garton.
Scanlon, Elizabeth Garton & Scanlon, Elizabeth G. Sock Is a Pocket for Your Toes. Glasser, Robin Preiss, illus. (p. 1605)
Scanlon, Jack. Rainbow Zoo. (p. 1436)
Scanlon, Jody. Lonely Little Fish. (p. 1046)
Scanlon, Liz Garton. All the World. Frazee, Marla, illus. (p. 46)
—Good-Pie Party. Denton, Kady MacDonald, illus. (p. 700)
—Great Good Summer. (p. 716)
—Happy Birthday, Bunny! Graegin, Stephanie, illus. (p. 744)
—In the Canyon. Wolff, Ashley, illus. (p. 865)
—Noodle & Lou. Howard, Arthur, illus. (p. 1263)
—Think Big. Newton, Vanessa & Magnette, Paul, illus. (p. 1734)
Scanlon, Michael. How We Met! Little Airplane Productions Staff, illus. (p. 823)
Scanlon, Michael, illus. see McDoogle, Farrah.
Scanlon, Michael, illus. see Seiss, Ellie.
Scanlon, Michael, jt. illus. see Little Airplane Productions.
Scanlon, Rachel. Operation Reverse April Fools' (p. 1300)
Scanziani, Emanuele. To Market! to Market! (p. 1759)
Scaperrotta, Kirstyn. I Lost My Cracker to the Big Cheese: A Collection of Voices. (p. 841)
Scarboro, Dale. England, 1625-1660: Charles I, the Civil War & Cromwell. Dawson, Ian, ed. (p. 529)
Scarborough. Target Spelling 1020. (p. 1706)
—Target Spelling 180. (p. 1706)
—Target Spelling 360. (p. 1706)
—Target Spelling 540. (p. 1706)
—Target Spelling 780. (p. 1706)
Scarborough, Casey, illus. see Hollis, Ginger.
Scarborough, Casey, illus. see Ondrias, Rachel.
Scarborough, Kate. Extreme Sports. (p. 557)
Scarborough, Kate, jt. auth. see Brown, Roland.
Scarborough, Kate, jt. auth. see Brush, Jim.
Scarborough, Kate, jt. auth. see Hyland, Tony.
Scarborough, Kate, jt. auth. see Palmer, Tom.
Scarborough, Ken, jt. auth. see Fallon, Joe.
Scarborough, R. A. Starblade: The Beginning (p. 1642)
Scarborough, Rob, illus. see Arvidson, Douglas.
Scarbro, Maxine. One Room Schoolgames: Children's Games of Yesteryear. (p. 1296)
Scarbrough, Carl W., tr. see Rozen, Anna.
Scarbrough, Mary Hertz. African American Writers & Journalists. (p. 27)
—African American Writers & Journalists. Hill, Marc Lamont, ed. (p. 27)
—Heroes of the American Revolution. (p. 773)
Scardamaglia, Christine. Paso Joe. (p. 1326)
Scardamalia, Marlene, et al. Writing for Results. (p. 1964)
Scardina, Tom, illus. see England, Don.
Scardina, Tom, illus. see Nunnery, Donna.
Scarff, Ruth. Floating Zoo. Combs, Paul, illus. (p. 605)
Scarfi, Margaret Rose. I Pray the Rosary! Richards, Virginia Helen & Dick, Regina Frances, illus. (p. 844)
Scarfone, Dorothy, ed. see Basso, Michael.
Scaris, Maria. Ollie & Jumper. (p. 1287)
Scarlett, Cat. College Girls. (p. 340)
—Player. (p. 1372)
Scarlett Giblin, Alison. Children of Conygre & the Time Capsule. (p. 302)
Scaro, Diego, ed. see Sudjic, Deyan.
Scarpa, Daniel, illus. see Courtauld, Sarah.
Scarpa, Romano & Block, Pat and Shelly. Walt Disney's Uncle Scrooge Clark, John, ed. (p. 1856)
Scarpa, Romano, et al. Uncle Scrooge #380. Clark, John, ed. (p. 1812)
Scarpaci, Mark, ed. see Dryland, David.
Scarpati, Kevin. Minnesota Vikings. (p. 1147)
Scarpulla, Caren, illus. see Fitterman, Lisa.
Scarrone, Gustavo, illus. see Villalba Casas, Consuelo.
Scarrow, Alex. Day of the Predator. (p. 414)
—TimeRiders. (p. 1754)
—TimeRiders: Day of the Predator. (p. 1754)
—TimeRiders: the Doomsday Code. (p. 1754)

—TimeRiders: the Eternal War. (p. 1754)
Scarrow, Alex & Bale, Tim. TimeRiders. (p. 1754)
Scarrow, Kristine. Throwaway Girl. (p. 1745)
Scarrow, Simon. Fight for Freedom. (p. 585)
Scarry, Huck. Life on a Farm: A Sketchbook. (p. 1012)
Scarry, Huck, illus. see Farber, Erica.
Scarry, Huck, illus. see Scarry, Richard & Farber, Erica.
Scarry, Huck, jt. auth. see Scarry, Richard.
Scarry, Huck & Scarry, Richard. Day at the Police Station. Scarry, Richard, illus. (p. 412)
Scarry, Janet. Land of Whodunnit. (p. 973)
Scarry, Patricia M. Sweet Smell of Christmas. Miller, J. P., illus. (p. 1690)
Scarry, Patricia M. & Scarry, Patsy. Bunny Book. Scarry, Richard, illus. (p. 242)
Scarry, Patsy. Richard Scarry's Good Night, Little Bear. Scarry, Richard, illus. (p. 1469)
—Richard Scarry's the Bunny Book. Scarry, Richard, illus. (p. 1469)
Scarry, Patsy, jt. auth. see Scarry, Patricia M.
Scarry, Patsy, et al. Richard Scarry's Best Little Golden Books Ever! Scarry, Richard, illus. (p. 1469)
Scarry, Richard. Best Busytown. (p. 168)
—Best Little Board Book Ever. Random House Staff, illus. (p. 170)
—Best Lowly Worm Book Ever! (p. 170)
—Biggest, Busiest Storybook Ever. Scarry, Richard, illus. (p. 185)
—Busy, Busy World. Scarry, Richard, illus. (p. 246)
—Christmas Mice. Scarry, Richard, illus. (p. 314)
—Cosas Que Nos Gustan. (p. 368)
—Cosas Que Se Mueven. (p. 368)
—Counting to Ten Jigsaw Book: With Six 24-Piece Jigsaws Inside. (p. 371)
—Day at the Fire Station. (p. 412)
—Egg in the Hole. Golden Books Staff, illus. (p. 506)
—Lowly Worm Meets the Early Bird. (p. 1061)
—Mi Casa. (p. 1132)
—Mi Casa. Scarry, Richard, illus. (p. 1132)
—Mixed-up Mail Mystery: Richard Scarry's Readers Level 3. (p. 1156)
—My School Backpack. (p. 1218)
—Nicky Va al Doctor. (p. 1251)
—Night Before the Night Before Christmas! Scarry, Richard, illus. (p. 1253)
—Pie Rats Ahoy! Scarry, Richard, illus. (p. 1356)
—Richard Scarry Mr. Paint Pig's ABC's. Random House Staff, illus. (p. 1469)
—Richard Scarry's ABC Word Book. (p. 1469)
—Richard Scarry's All the Colors of Busytown. (p. 1469)
—Richard Scarry's Be Careful, Mr. Frumble! Scarry, Richard, illus. (p. 1469)
—Richard Scarry's Best Bunny Book Ever! Scarry, Richard, illus. (p. 1469)
—Richard Scarry's Best Busy Year Ever. (p. 1469)
—Richard Scarry's Best Christmas Book Ever! (p. 1469)
—Richard Scarry's Best Counting Book Ever. (p. 1469)
—Richard Scarry's Best Counting Book Ever. Scarry, Richard, illus. (p. 1469)
—Richard Scarry's Best Ever Color, Shapes, & Numbers: Includes Giant Poster & 80+ Stickers! (p. 1469)
—Richard Scarry's Best Word Book Ever. Scarry, Richard, illus. (p. 1469)
—Richard Scarry's Big Busy Sticker & Activity Book. (p. 1469)
—Richard Scarry's Boats. Scarry, Richard, illus. (p. 1469)
—Richard Scarry's Books on the Go. Scarry, Richard, illus. (p. 1469)
—Richard Scarry's Bunnies. Scarry, Richard, illus. (p. 1469)
—Richard Scarry's Busiest Pop-Up Ever! (p. 1469)
—Richard Scarry's Busytown on the Go! (p. 1469)
—Richard Scarry's Cars. (p. 1469)
—Richard Scarry's Cars & Trucks. (p. 1469)
—Richard Scarry's Early Words Sticker Book: With 101 Stickers! (p. 1469)
—Richard Scarry's Favorite Christmas Carols. (p. 1469)
—Richard Scarry's from 1 To 10. (p. 1469)
—Richard Scarry's Good Morning, Busytown! (p. 1469)
—Richard Scarry's Good Night, Little Bear: With Stickers! Scarry, Richard, illus. (p. 1469)
—Richard Scarry's Good Night, Little Bear Pictureback. (p. 1469)
—Richard Scarry's Great Big Schoolhouse. (p. 1469)
—Richard Scarry's Hop Aboard! Here We Go! (p. 1469)
—Richard Scarry's Just Right Word Book! Scarry, Richard, illus. (p. 1469)
—Richard Scarry's Let's Count with Lowly. (p. 1469)
—Richard Scarry's Lowly Worm Word Book. Scarry, Richard, illus. (p. 1469)
—Richard Scarry's Lowly Worm's Applecar. (p. 1469)
—Richard Scarry's Mixed-Up Cars & Trucks. (p. 1469)
—Richard Scarry's Mr. Frumble's Big, Flat Hat. (p. 1469)
—Richard Scarry's My First School Journal. (p. 1469)
—Richard Scarry's Nicky Goes to the Doctor. (p. 1469)
—Richard Scarry's Pig Will & Pig Won't. Scarry, Richard, illus. (p. 1469)
—Richard Scarry's Planes. Scarry, Richard, illus. (p. 1469)
—Richard Scarry's Postman Pig & His Busy Neighbors. (p. 1469)
—Richard Scarry's Postman Pig & His Busy Neighbors. Scarry, Richard, illus. (p. 1469)
—Richard Scarry's Smokey the Fireman. Scarry, Richard, illus. (p. 1469)
—Richard Scarry's the Adventures of Lowly Worm. (p. 1469)
—Richard Scarry's the Great Pie Robbery. (p. 1469)
—Richard Scarry's the Great Pie Robbery & Other Mysteries. (p. 1469)
—Richard Scarry's the Great Steamboat Mystery. (p. 1470)
—Richard Scarry's the Rooster Struts. (p. 1470)
—Richard Scarry's the Supermarket Mystery. (p. 1470)
—Richard Scarry's This Is Me. (p. 1470)
—Richard Scarry's Trucks. (p. 1470)
—Richard Scarry's Welcome to Busytown! Includes Giant Poster & 80+ Stickers! (p. 1470)
—Richard Scarry's What Do People Do All Day? (p. 1470)
—Scarry Busy Week - Four in One Bind-Up. (p. 1520)
—School Bus Box Set. (p. 1522)
—Snowstorm Surprise. (p. 1601)
—Splish-Splash. (p. 1630)
Scarry, Richard, illus. see Golden Books Staff.
Scarry, Richard, illus. see Jackson, Kathryn.
Scarry, Richard, illus. see Nolte, Nancy.
Scarry, Richard, illus. see Risom, Ole.
Scarry, Richard, illus. see Scarry, Patricia M. & Scarry, Patsy.
Scarry, Richard, illus. see Scarry, Patsy, et al.
Scarry, Richard, illus. see Scarry, Patsy.
Scarry, Richard, jt. auth. see Scarry, Huck.
Scarry, Richard & Farber, Erica. Cake Soup. Scarry, Huck, illus. (p. 252)
—Go, Huckle, Go! Scarry, Huck, illus. (p. 686)
—Ice Cream for Breakfast. Scarry, Huck, illus. (p. 850)
—Smelly Story, Level 2. Scarry, Huck, illus. (p. 1593)
Scarry, Richard & Golden Books Staff. Nicky Goes to the Doctor. (p. 1251)
—Richard Scarry's Favorite Storybook Ever. (p. 1469)
Scarry, Richard & Scarry, Huck. Day at the Fire Station. (p. 412)
Scarsbrook, M. Poison in the Blood: The Memoirs of Lucrezia Borgia. (p. 1377)
Scarsbrook, Richard. Cheeseburger Subversive. (p. 296)
—Featherless Bipeds. (p. 579)
Scatina, Michael. Goby & the Shrimp. (p. 688)
Scattergood, Augusta. Glory Be. (p. 685)
—Way to Stay in Destiny. (p. 1864)
Scauzillo, Tony, illus. see Alvarez, Michel J.
Scavuzzo, Wendy. Tornado Alert! (p. 1770)
Scearcy, Steve, jt. auth. see Shuchart, John.
Scelsa, Greg. Granny's Coming 'Round the Mountain' Faulkner, Stacey, ed. (p. 710)
—I Like Potatoes. Faulkner, Stacey, ed. (p. 841)
—Months of the Year. Faulkner, Stacey, ed. (p. 1170)
—Muffin Man. Faulkner, Stacey, ed. (p. 1189)
—Rainbow of Colors. Faulkner, Stacey, ed. (p. 1435)
—Rhyme Time. Faulkner, Stacey, ed. (p. 1468)
—World Is a Rainbow. Faulkner, Stacey, ed. (p. 1956)
Scelsa, Greg, jt. auth. see Leto, Frank.
Scelsa, Greg & Debney, John. Friends Forever. Faulkner, Stacey, ed. (p. 638)
Scelsa, Kate. Fans of the Impossible Life. (p. 571)
Schaaf, Fred. Seeing the Sky: 100 Projects, Activities & Explorations in Astronomy. Myers, Doug, illus. (p. 1548)
Schaaf, Ron. BearClaw: Finding Courage Within. (p. 151)
—Tiger's Quest: Rounding Cape Horn. (p. 1749)
Schaal, Patty. Nighttide on a Vineyard Farm. Datz, Margot, illus. (p. 1255)
Schab, Lisa. Divorce Workbook for Teens: Activities to Help You Move Beyond the Break Up. (p. 455)
Schab, Lisa & Gardner, Richard. Helping, Caring, & Sharing. Schader, Karen, ed. (p. 766)
Schab, Lisa M. Beyond the Blues: A Workbook to Help Teens Overcome Depression. (p. 174)
—Cool, Calm, & Confident: A Workbook to Help Kids Learn Assertiveness Skills. (p. 362)
—Self-Esteem Workbook for Teens: Activities to Help You Build Confidence & Achieve Your Goals. (p. 1549)
Schabert, Kyrill, tr. see Winterfeld, Henry.
Schabram, Dennis W. Sugar & Me (p. 1672)
Schach, David. Comanche Warriors. (p. 346)
—Loch Ness Monster. (p. 1044)
—Sea Dragons. (p. 1534)
—Sea Monsters. (p. 1535)
Schacher, Joe. For Where Your Treasure Is: An Adventure Story. (p. 616)
Schacher, Tracey, illus. see Powell, Joyce.
Schachner, Judy. Bits & Pieces. (p. 194)
—Color Crazy. Schachner, Judy, illus. (p. 342)
—Costume Crazee. (p. 368)
—Dewey Bob. Schachner, Judy, illus. (p. 432)
—Doghouse. (p. 462)
—Get Busy with Skippyjon Jones! Schachner, Judy, illus. (p. 667)
—Grannyman. (p. 710)
—Great Bean Caper. (p. 714)
—Knock, Knock! Schachner, Judy et al, illus. (p. 965)
—Say It With/Diga Con Skippyjon Jones. (p. 1518)
—Shape Up. (p. 1560)
—Skippydoodle-Do & Draw! Schachner, Judy, illus. (p. 1586)
—Skippyjon Jones. (p. 1586)
—Skippyjon Jones. (p. 1586)
—Skippyjon Jones. Schachner, Judy, illus. (p. 1586)
—Skippyjon Jones 1-2-3. (p. 1586)
—Skippyjon Jones & the Big Bones. (p. 1586)
—Skippyjon Jones & the Treasure Hunt. (p. 1586)
—Skippyjon Jones Book & Toy Set Schachner, Judy, illus. (p. 1586)
—Skippyjon Jones Cirque de Ole. (p. 1586)
—Skippyjon Jones, Class Action. (p. 1586)
—Skippyjon Jones in Mummy Trouble. (p. 1586)
—Skippyjon Jones in Mummy Trouble. (p. 1586)
—Skippyjon Jones in Mummy Trouble. Schachner, Judy, illus. (p. 1586)
—Skippyjon Jones in the Doghouse. (p. 1586)
—Skippyjon Jones in the Doghouse. Wilhelm, James J., ed. (p. 1586)
—Skippyjon Jones in the Doghouse. Schachner, Judy, illus. (p. 1586)
—Skippyjon Jones Keepin' Busy Kit. Schachner, Judy, illus. (p. 1586)
—Skippyjon Jones, Lost in Spice. (p. 1586)
—Skippyjon Jones, Lost in Spice. Schachner, Judy, illus. (p. 1586)
—Skippyjon Jones Presto-Change-O. (p. 1586)
—Skippyjon Jones Snow What. (p. 1586)
—Surprise for Mama. (p. 1685)
—Up & Down. Schachner, Judy, illus. (p. 1824)
—Up, up, & Away! (p. 1824)
Schacht, Carol. Timmy Turtle's Journey to the Light. (p. 1755)
Schachter, Esty. Anya's Echoes: A Novel. (p. 90)
Schachter, Martin. Environmental Science. (p. 532)
Schacter, Bernice. Genetics in the News. (p. 661)
Schad, Anna, jt. auth. see Burris, Andrea.
Schad, Anna M., jt. auth. see Burris, Andrea M.
Schad, Kristine. Do You Love Me Best? Timmons, Gayle, illus. (p. 458)
Schade, Susan. Riff Raff Sails the High Cheese. Kennedy, Anne, illus. (p. 1471)
—Riff Raff the Mouse Pirate. Kennedy, Anne, illus. (p. 1471)
—Simon's Dream. Buller, Jon, illus. (p. 1577)
—Travels of Thelonious. Buller, Jon, illus. (p. 1780)
Schade, Susan, jt. auth. see Buller, Jon.
Schade, Susan & Buller, Jon. Faradawn. (p. 572)
Schader, Karen, ed. see Bryant, John E.
Schader, Karen, ed. see Huebner, Dawn.
Schader, Karen, ed. see Schab, Lisa & Gardner, Richard.
Schader, Karen, ed. see Schneider, Elaine Ernst.
Schader, Karen, ed. see Shore, Hennie & Gardner, Richard.
Schader, Kim, et al. Loom Band It: 60 Rubberband Projects for the Budding Loomineer. (p. 1051)
Schadler, Susan, et al. Adopting the Euro in Central Europe: Challenges of the Next Step in European Integration. (p. 13)
Schaedler, Kimberly. My Freaky Family. (p. 1209)
Schaedler, Peggy. Dagger & Dash: The Scrimshaw Medallion. (p. 399)
Schaefer, A. Help Me Find Something. (p. 765)
Schaefer, A. R. Healthy Food (p. 758)
—Jaguar (p. 905)
—Jaguar/Jaguar (p. 905)
—Maserati (p. 1102)
—Maserati - Maserati. (p. 1102)
—Roller Coasters (p. 1485)
—Spotlight on Africa (p. 1633)
—Spotlight on Antarctica (p. 1634)
—Spotlight on Asia (p. 1634)
—Talladega Superspeedway. (p. 1704)
Schaefer, A. R., jt. auth. see Heinemann Library Staff.
Schaefer, A. R., jt. auth. see Schaefer, Adam R.
Schaefer, A. R. & Schaefer, Adam R. Triangle Shirtwaist Factory Fire. (p. 1785)
Schaefer, Adam. Alimentos Saludables (p. 41)
—Ejercicio (p. 507)
—Harlem Renaissance (p. 749)
—Mantenerse Fuera de Peligro (p. 1088)
—Mantenerse Sano (p. 1088)
—Modern Immigration & Expansion (p. 1158)
—Steroids. (p. 1649)
Schaefer, Adam, jt. auth. see Crewe, Sabrina.
Schaefer, Adam R. Food Around the World. (p. 613)
—Help Me Find Something. Freeman, Marcia S., ed. (p. 765)
—Homes Around the World. Freeman, Marcia S., ed. (p. 793)
Schaefer, Adam R., jt. auth. see Schaefer, A. R.
Schaefer, Adam R. & Schaefer, A. R. Dale Earnhardt (p. 401)
—Racing with the Pit Crew (p. 1432)
Schaefer, Carole Lexa. Down in the Woods at Sleepytime. Cabban, Vanessa, illus. (p. 474)
—Monkey & Elephant. Bernstein, Galia, illus. (p. 1164)
—Monkey & Elephant & a Secret Birthday Surprise. Bernstein, Galia, illus. (p. 1164)
—Monkey & Elephant Get Better. Bernstein, Galia, illus. (p. 1164)
—Monkey & Elephant Go Gadding. Bernstein, Galia, illus. (p. 1164)
Schaefer, Carole Lexa, et al. Dragon Dancing. Morgan, Pierr, illus. (p. 477)
Schaefer, Elizabeth. Ballet Lesson. (p. 134)
—Peppa Pig: Ballet Lesson. (p. 1340)
Schaefer, Elizabeth A., jt. auth. see Disney Book Group Staff.
Schaefer, Laura. Secret Ingredient. Rim, Sujean, illus. (p. 1541)
—Teashop Girls. Rim, Sujean, illus. (p. 1711)
Schaefer, Lola. One Special Day. Meserve, Jessica, illus. (p. 1297)
Schaefer, Lola M. Acorn. Preston-Gannon, Frann, illus. (p. 9)
—Airplanes in Action (p. 32)
—Alexander Graham Bell Saunders-Smith, Gail, ed. (p. 36)
—Algunos Niños Son Sordos. (p. 38)
—Algunos Niños Usan Sillas de Ruedas. (p. 38)
—Arrowhawk: A True Survival Story. Swiatkowska, Gabi, illus. (p. 101)
—Arrowhawk. Swiatkowska, Gabi, illus. (p. 101)
—Aunts. (p. 115)
—Aunts. Saunders-Smith, Gail, ed. (p. 115)
—Beep-Beep! Honk! (p. 157)
—Boo Who? A Foldout Halloween Adventure. Frost, Michael, photos by. (p. 210)
—Booker T. Washington Saunders-Smith, Gail, ed. (p. 212)
—Brothers. Saunders-Smith, Gail, ed. (p. 231)
—Carta para Mi Amigo: Set Of 6. (p. 272)
—Cotton Plant to Cotton Shirt. (p. 369)
—Cotton Plant to Cotton Shirt & de una planta a una camisa de Algodón: 6 English, 6 Spanish Adaptations (p. 369)
—Cousins. (p. 373)
—Cousins. Saunders-Smith, Gail, ed. (p. 373)
—De una Planta a una Camisa de Algodón: Set Of 6. (p. 416)
—Erosión: Set Of 6. (p. 534)
—Family Pets. Saunders-Smith, Gail, ed. (p. 568)
—Fathers. Saunders-Smith, Gail, ed. (p. 577)
—Follow Me, Mittens. Hartung, Susan Kathleen, illus. (p. 612)
—Frankie Stein Atteberry, Kevan, illus. (p. 630)
—Frankie Stein Starts School Atteberry, Kevan, illus. (p. 630)
—Grandfathers. Saunders-Smith, Gail, ed. (p. 707)
—Grandmothers. Saunders-Smith, Gail, ed. (p. 709)
—Happy Halloween, Mittens. Hartung, Susan Kathleen, illus. (p. 745)
—How Did This City Grow? (p. 806)
—Island Grows. Felstead, Cathie, illus. (p. 892)
—Johnny Appleseed Saunders-Smith, Gail, ed. (p. 923)
—Las Máquinas Simples: Set Of 6. (p. 976)
—Letter to a Friend. (p. 1002)
—Letter to a Friend & una carta para mi Amigo: 6 English, 6 Spanish Adaptations (p. 1002)
—Lifetime: The Amazing Numbers in Animal Lives. Neal, Christopher Silas, illus. (p. 1014)
—Loose Tooth. Wickstrom, Sylvie K., tr. (p. 1052)
—Loose Tooth. Wickstrom, Sylvie Kantorovitz, illus. (p. 1052)
—Mi Corazón: Set Of 6. (p. 1132)
—Mi Cuerpo: Set Of 6. (p. 1132)
—Mittens. (p. 1156)
—Mittens. Hartung, Susan Kathleen, illus. (p. 1156)
—Mittens at School. (p. 1156)
—Mittens at School. Hartung, Susan Kathleen, illus. (p. 1156)
—Mittens, Where Is Max? Hartung, Susan Kathleen, illus. (p. 1156)
—Mother Teresa (p. 1178)
—Mothers. Saunders-Smith, Gail, ed. (p. 1178)
—My Body & Mi Cuerpo: 6 English, 6 Spanish Adaptations (p. 1198)
—One Busy Day: A Story for Big Brothers & Sisters. Meserve, Jessica, illus. (p. 1294)
—Pick, Pull, Snap! Where Once a Flower Bloomed. George, Lindsay Barrett, illus. (p. 1354)
—Please Pass the Manners! Mealtime Tips for Everyone. Lewis, Kellie, illus. (p. 1373)
—Run for Your Life! A Day on the African Savanna. Meisel, Paul, illus. (p. 1496)
—Sea Stars [Scholastic]. (p. 1535)
—Semitrucks in Action (p. 1550)
—Simple Machines & Las máquinas Simples: 6 English, 6 Spanish Adaptations (p. 1578)
—Sisters. Saunders-Smith, Gail, ed. (p. 1581)
—Some Kids Are Blind (p. 1609)
—Some Kids Are Blind. Saunders-Smith, Gail, ed. (p. 1609)
—Some Kids Are Deaf (p. 1609)
—Some Kids Are Deaf. Saunders-Smith, Gail, ed. (p. 1609)
—Some Kids Use Wheelchairs (p. 1609)
—Some Kids Use Wheelchairs. Saunders-Smith, Gail, ed. (p. 1609)
—Some Kids Wear Leg Braces (p. 1609)
—Some Kids Wear Leg Braces. Saunders-Smith, Gail, ed. (p. 1609)
—Somos Iguales: Set Of 6. (p. 1611)
—Swamp Chomp. Meisel, Paul, illus. (p. 1688)
—Tow Trucks in Action. (p. 1773)
—Uncles. Saunders-Smith, Gail, ed. (p. 1812)
—We are All Alike. (p. 1865)
—Welcome Home And ¡Bienvenidos!: 6 English, 6 Spanish Adaptations (p. 1873)
—What Is Matter? (p. 1889)
—What Is Matter? & ¿Qué es la Materia? 6 English, 6 Spanish Adaptations (p. 1889)
—What's That, Mittens? Hartung, Susan Kathleen, illus. (p. 1899)
—Who Makes the Rules? (p. 1917)
—Who Makes the Rules? & ¿Quién hace las Reglas? 6 English, 6 Spanish Adaptations (p. 1917)
—Writing Lessons for the Overhead: 20 Transparencies That Show Models of Strong Writing with Companion Mini-Lessons. (p. 1965)
—Your Heart. (p. 1980)
—¡Bienvenidos! Set Of 6. (p. 177)
—¿Como Crecio Esta Ciudad? Set Of 6. (p. 350)
—¿Qué Es la Materia? Set Of 6. (p. 1423)
—¿Quién Hace Las Reglas? Set Of 6. (p. 1427)
Schaefer, Lola M., jt. auth. see Schaefer, Ted.
Schaefer, Lola M. & Endres, Hollie J. Push & Pull (p. 1420)
Schaefer, Lola M. & Hanel, Rachael. Japanese-American Internment: An Interactive History Adventure. (p. 909)
Schaefer, Lola M. & McCue, Lisa. Easter Surprises. (p. 499)
Schaefer, Lola M. & Miller, Heather Lynn. Look Behind! Tales of Animal Ends. Manning, Jane K., illus. (p. 1049)
Schaefer, Lola M. & Schaefer, Wyatt S. Albert Einstein Saunders-Smith, Gail, ed. (p. 34)
—Jane Goodall Saunders-Smith, Gail, ed. (p. 908)
—Marie Curie Saunders-Smith, Gail, ed. (p. 1093)
Schaefer, Lola M., et al. Albert Einstein Saunders-Smith, Gail, ed. (p. 34)
—Florence Nightingale (p. 606)
—Jane Goodall (p. 908)
Schaefer, Nikki. Potty Train. Schaefer, Nikki, illus. (p. 1389)
Schaefer, Peggy. Bob & Larry's Book of Prayers. Reed, Lisa, illus. (p. 205)
—Haunted Halloween Activity Book. Arif, Tasneem & Reed, Lisa, illus. (p. 753)
—More Stories of Cats. (p. 1175)
—More Stories of Dogs. (p. 1175)
—Trick or Treat! Halverson, Lydia, illus. (p. 1786)
Schaefer, Ted. Exploring the Americas (p. 553)
—Harvest Time. (p. 752)
—Machines Large & Small. (p. 1068)
—Ready for School. (p. 1447)
—Westward to the Pacific: From the Trail of Tears to the Transcontinental Railroad. (p. 1876)
Schaefer, Ted & Schaefer, Lola M. Arlington National Cemetery (p. 99)
Schaefer, Todd, jt. auth. see Brooker, Russell.
Schaefer, Todd M. & Birkland, Thomas A. Encyclopedia of Media & Politics (p. 525)
Schaefer, Valorie. Care & Keeping of You 1: The Body Book for Younger Girls. (p. 266)
Schaefer, Wyatt. Addiction. (p. 11)
Schaefer, Wyatt S., jt. auth. see Schaefer, Lola M.
Schaeffer, Bob, illus. see Heller, Pete.
Schaeffer, Julia. Midwest States: Set Of 6. (p. 1139)
Schaeffer, Teresa. Questions Within (p. 1426)
—Questions Within. (p. 1426)
Schaeffer-Stumpf, Dawn. Fluttah Fluttah Butterfly. (p. 608)
Schaenen, Inda. All the Cats of Cairo. (p. 45)
Schaerer, Kathrin, illus. see Pauli, Lorenz.
Schafer, Albert. Illusionology: The Secret Science of Magic. Wyatt, David & Pinfold, Levi, illus. (p. 857)
Schafer, Christopher. Attack in Iraq. (p. 113)
—War Protesters. (p. 1858)
Schafer, Gary. Passing Moments of the Mind. (p. 1326)
Schafer, Holden J., illus. see Steininger-Moore, Cheryl A.
Schafer, Kevin. Penguins 123. (p. 1337)
—Penguins ABC. (p. 1337)
Schafer, Milton. I'm Big! Lew-Vriethoff, Joanne, illus. (p. 858)
Schafer, Rick, photos by see King, William.

Schafer, Rick, photos by see Puetz, Gary Rainer.
Schafer, Susan. Capybaras. (p. 265)
—Chinese Giant Salamanders. (p. 307)
—DNA & Genes. (p. 456)
—Heredity. (p. 771)
—Saltwater Crocodiles. (p. 1506)
Schafer, Susan & Meredith, Susan Markowitz. Lions. (p. 1021)
Schafer, Susan & Robinson, Fay. Tigers. (p. 1749)
Schaffer, Angel Boi. Blessed Child. (p. 199)
Schaffer, David. Bono. (p. 209)
—Discovering South America's Land, People, & Wildlife: A MyReportLinks. com Book. (p. 449)
—Idaho: A MyReportLinks. Com Book. (p. 852)
—Kentucky: A MyReportLinks. Com Book. (p. 949)
—Louisiana Purchase: The Deal of the Century That Doubled the Nation. (p. 1059)
—Saudi Arabia in the News: Past, Present, & Future. (p. 1516)
—Vermont: A MyReportLinks.com Book. (p. 1837)
Schaffer, David, ed. Iraq. (p. 887)
Schaffer, Donna. Mealworms. (p. 1116)
Schaffer, Jacqueline. Porsha & the Great Snowmen Adventure. (p. 1386)
Schaffer, Julia. Midwest States: Text Pairs. (p. 1139)
Schaffer, Julia, jt. auth. see RJF Publishing Staff.
Schaffter, Ehren. Through the Curtain. (p. 1745)
Schafrath, Ty, illus. see McCullough, Myrina D.
Schall, Jane. Jump at the Sun Bible Classics David & Goliath. Roos, Maryn, illus. (p. 934)
—Jump at the Sun Bible Classics Jonah & the Whale. Roos, Maryn, illus. (p. 934)
Schall, Rebecca. Historic Photos of Paris. (p. 782)
Schaller, Bob & Harnish, Coach Dave. Kids' Basketball Book: The All-Time Greats, Legendary Teams, Today's Superstars - And Tips on Playing Like a Pro. (p. 952)
Schaller, James A. Death by Prescription. (p. 420)
Schaller, Michael, et al. Present Tense: The United States Since 1945. (p. 1396)
Schaller, Tandy & Makenzie. Little Red Conquers Her Fear of Flying (HARDBACK) (p. 1034)
Schallert, Ann. Message for Woman: The Teenage Girl. (p. 1129)
Schallmo, Carolyn, illus. see Lamb, Jim.
Schalow, Al. Adventure down Crunchy Road. (p. 14)
Schambach, R. W., frwd. This Charge, This Generation: Could This Be the Generation That Brings about Change in the Earth? (p. 1735)
Schamburg, Tracy M. Catie the Caterpillar: A Story to Help Break the Silence of Sexual Abuse. Riley, Melanie Ellis, illus. (p. 280)
Schamerhorn, Ronna. Dreamy Navy Boy. (p. 484)
Schanback, Mindy. Princess from Another Planet. (p. 1404)
Schanck, Agnes, illus. see Rehm, Carolyn.
Schandle, Julie. Little Wishes Big Dreams: Around the World. (p. 1038)
Schandy, Rosita, illus. see Mitchell, Malinda.
Schanen, Adriana Brad. Quinny & Hopper. Swearingen, Greg, illus. (p. 1428)
Schanker, Harry H., et al. Stage & the School. (p. 1638)
Schantin, Diane. Parables from Twilight: A Bible Study. (p. 1323)
Schantz, Becky. How to Grow a Hippo! Mitchell, Anne, illus. (p. 820)
Schanzer, Olivia. B'chol L'vavcha: With All Your Heart. (p. 147)
Schanzer, Rosalyn. George vs. George: The Revolutionary War as Seen by Both Sides. (p. 663)
—George vs. George: The American Revolution as Seen from Both Sides. (p. 663)
—Gold Fever! Tales from the California Gold Rush. (p. 693)
—How Ben Franklin Stole the Lightning. Schanzer, Rosalyn, illus. (p. 805)
—How We Crossed the West: The Adventures of Lewis & Clark. (p. 823)
—John Smith Escapes Again! (p. 922)
Schanzer, Rosalyn, illus. see Lauber, Patricia.
Schanzer, Rosalyn & Darwin, Charles. What Darwin Saw: The Journey That Changed the World. (p. 1881)
Schapira, Leah & Dwek, Victoria. Kids Cooking Made Easy. Lailah, Daniel, photos by. (p. 953)
Scharer, Kathrin. All Aboard with Joanna! (p. 42)
Schärer, Kathrin, illus. see Pauli, Lorenz.
Scharer, Niko. Emily's House Fitzgerald, Joanne, illus. (p. 519)
Scharer, Patricia L., jt. auth. see Pinnell, Gay Su.
Scharf, Greg. Prepared to Preach: God's Work & Ours in Proclamation. (p. 1396)
Scharf, J. L. Grace & the Ice Prince: The Diamond Heart Quest. (p. 704)
Scharff-Kniemeyer, Marlis. Gute Nacht, Meine Mauschen. (p. 733)
Scharfglass, Matt. Starting Guitar: The Number One Method for Young Guitarists. (p. 1644)
Scharschmidt, Sherry, illus. see Hacohen, Dean.
Scharschmidt, Sherry, jt. auth. see Hacohen, Dean.
Schart, Elizabeth, jt. auth. see Schart, Elizabeth.
Schart, Elizabeth & Schart, Elizabeth. Ralph Simian, I've Had It! (p. 1437)
Schartup, Adam, illus. see Aryal, Naren.
Schartup, Adam, illus. see Milani, Joan.
Schatell, Brian. Owl Boy. (p. 1315)
Schatell, Brian, illus. see Kaiser, Cecily.
Schatz, Dennis. Al Descubierto T Rex. (p. 32)
—King of the Dinosaurs. (p. 959)
Schatz, Dennis & Bonadonna, Davide. Uncover a T. Rex: Take a Three-Dimensional Look Inside a T. Rex! Keitzmueller, Christian, illus. (p. 1812)
Schatz, Kate. Rad American Women A-Z: Rebels, Trailblazers, & Visionaries Who Shaped Our History ... & Our Future! Stahl, Miriam Klein, illus. (p. 1432)
Schatz, Letta. So Many Henrys. (p. 1602)
Schatzel, Tom. Continuous & Amazing Adventures of Eddie the Edgy Elephant: Adventure 60,259: The Big Maze. (p. 361)
Schatzer, Jeffrey L. Bird in Santa's Beard: How a Christmas Legend Was Forever Changed. (p. 190)
Schaub, Michelle. Bee Puzzle. (p. 157)
—Honeybees Help Flowers. (p. 795)
—Lost Pirate. (p. 1056)
—This or That Sports Debate: A Rip-Roaring Game of Either/or Questions. (p. 1737)
—Vehicles of World War I (p. 1834)
—Where Are We? (p. 1906)
Schaub, Stephen, photos by. Through a Glass Darkly: Photographs by Stephen M. Schaub. (p. 1744)
Schauer, Donald D. Careers in Trucking. (p. 268)
Schauer, Jane. Fantasy Park Book 1: The Doorman. Schauer, Jane, illus. (p. 572)
Schauer, M. RIP, M. D. Vosburg, M., illus. (p. 1473)
Schauer, Pete. Russell Wilson: Super Bowl Sensation. (p. 1498)
Schauer, Peter J. Russell Wilson: Super Bowl Sensation. (p. 1498)
—What You Need to Know about Violent Crimes, Felonies, & the Law (p. 1896)
Schauer, S., jt. auth. see Di Gregorio, Robert.
Schauer, Tosca M. J. J. Bear. (p. 901)
Schaumberg, Emily Rose, jt. auth. see Schaumberg, Rose Mary.
Schaumberg, Rose Mary & Schaumberg, Emily Rose. I'll Miss My Grandma, Wouldn't You? (p. 856)
Scheber, George. Earl Joins the Circus. Spicer, Bridgett, illus. (p. 492)
—Earl the Squirrel. Spicer, Bridgett, illus. (p. 492)
Schechter, Lynn R. My Big Fat Secret: How Jenna Takes Control of Her Emotions & Eating. Chin, Jason, illus. (p. 1197)
Schecter, Deborah. 25 Reproducible Mini-Books in English & Spanish That Give Kids a Great Start in Reading. (p. 1996)
—Easy Origami: Adorable Folded Paper Projects with Super-Easy Directions & Rebus Support That Build Beginning Reading Skills. (p. 500)
—Nursery Rhymes: Adorable Art Projects with Easy Directions & Rebus Support That Build Beginning Reading Skills. (p. 1273)
—Sight Word Manipulatives for Reading Success: Wheels, Pull-Throughs, Puzzles, & Dozens of Other Easy-to-Make Manipulatives That Help Kids Read, Write, & Really Learn High-Frequency Words. (p. 1574)
Schecter, Deborah, jt. auth. see Charlesworth, Liza.
Schecter, Deborah & Charlesworth, Liza. My First Little Readers: 25 Reproducible Mini-Books That Give Kids a Great Start in Reading. (p. 1207)
Schedeen, Minnie, illus. see Arthur, Clint.
Scheele, Charel. Old World Breads from Your Bread Machine. (p. 1285)
Scheele, William E. Ancient Elephants. (p. 69)
Scheer, Ruth D. Mouse & the Angel. (p. 1181)
Scheerger, Sarah Lynn. Opposite of Love. (p. 1300)
Scheets, Sonny. At the Car Show. (p. 111)
Scheff, Anna. Shopping Smarts: How to Choose Wisely, Find Bargains, Spot Swindles, & More. (p. 1569)
Scheff, Matt. ATVs. (p. 114)
—Best Extreme Sports Stars of All Time. (p. 169)
—Best NFL Quarterbacks of All Time. (p. 170)
—Best NFL Running Backs of All Time. (p. 170)
—Brock Lesnar. (p. 230)
—Dirt Bikes. (p. 446)
—Dolph Ziggler. (p. 464)
—Eli Manning: Football Superstar (p. 512)
—Hovercraft. (p. 804)
—Indy Cars. (p. 873)
—Jamie Bestwick. (p. 907)
—Jeff Gordon. (p. 911)
—Jets. (p. 916)
—Kelly Slater. (p. 948)
—Kyle Busch. (p. 969)
—Lyn-Z Adams Hawkins Pastrana. (p. 1066)
—Shaun White. (p. 1563)
—Snowmobiles. (p. 1601)
—Speed Machines. (p. 1624)
—Speedboats. (p. 1624)
—Superbikes. (p. 1682)
—Tom Brady: Football Superstar. (p. 1762)
—Tom Brady: Football Superstar. (p. 1762)
—Tony Hawk. (p. 1766)
—Tony Stewart. (p. 1766)
—Torah Bright. (p. 1769)
Scheff, Matt & Frederick, Shane. Superstar Athletes (p. 1684)
Scheff, William, jt. auth. see Koestler, Larry.
Scheff, William, jt. auth. see Singer, Jenny.
Scheff, William, jt. auth. see Wiedrich, Merrick.
Scheffler, Axel. Axel Scheffler's Noisy Jungle. (p. 121)
—Freddy the Frog. Scheffler, Axel, illus. (p. 633)
—Katie the Kitten. (p. 945)
—Lizzy the Lamb. (p. 1043)
—Pip & Posy: the Big Balloon. Scheffler, Axel, illus. (p. 1361)
—Pip & Posy: the Little Puddle. Scheffler, Axel, illus. (p. 1361)
—Pip the Puppy. (p. 1361)
—Pip the Puppy Bath Book. (p. 1361)
—Rhyming Stories: Pip the Dog & Freddy the Frog. (p. 1468)
—Rhyming Stories: Katie the Kitten; Lizzy the Lamb. Bk. 2 (p. 1468)
Scheffler, Axel, illus. see Collins, Mark, et al.
Scheffler, Axel, illus. see Crow, Nosy.
Scheffler, Axel, illus. see Donaldson, Julia.
Scheffler, Axel, illus. see Green, Alison.
Scheffler, Axel, illus. see Morgan, Gaby.
Scheffler, Axel, illus. see Nosy Crow.
Scheffler, Axel, illus. see Prasadam-Halls, Smriti.
Scheffler, Axel & Green, Alison. Mother Goose's Storytime Nursery Rhymes. (p. 1178)
Scheffler, Axel & Nosy Crow Staff. Pip & Posy: the Snowy Day. Scheffler, Axel, illus. (p. 1361)
Scheffler, Stephanie. Elise the Patriot: A Revolutionary War Story. (p. 513)
—Elizabeth & the War of 1812. (p. 513)
Scheffrin-Falk, Gladys. Another Celebrated Dancing Bear. Garrison, Barbara, illus. (p. 87)
Scheft, Bill. Best of the Show: A Classic Collection of Wit & Wisdom. (p. 171)
Scheibe, Nancy, illus. see Murray-Gibson, Lynnette A.
Scheibe, Nancy, illus. see Strauss, Kevin.
Scheid, Petra Maria. DIARY for lovers: Tagebuch für Verliebte. (p. 434)
—Fairy Tales, Elves & Magicans. (p. 564)
Scheidegger, Evan. I Was a Superhero Last Night! (p. 848)
Scheidies, Carolyn R. heart of Christmas. (p. 759)
—Let's Fly Away Little Blue Car. (p. 996)
—My Summer Journel: the Rescue. (p. 1219)
—WHERE IS CAT? She's Obviously Been Here! (p. 1908)
Scheiding, Marcia L., illus. see Sundberg, Angela M., et al.
Scheie, Jesse. I'm Still Shinin' On. (p. 860)
—Kisses to Heaven Scheie, Jesse, illus. (p. 962)
Scheler, Leah. Secret Letters. (p. 1541)
—Your Voice Is All I Hear. (p. 1981)
Scheinberg, Shepsil, illus. see Lazewnik, Libby.
Scheiner, A., illus. see Hoffmann, E. T. A.
Schell, Steve, ed. Mujeres en el Ministerio de Liderazgo. (p. 1189)
Schellenbach, Pete, illus. see Kissane, sheela.
Schellpeper, Kathy, photos by see Manton, Charlotte.
Schelly, Bill. Words of Wonder: The Life & Times of Otto Binder. (p. 1952)
Schelvis, Jules. Sobibor: A History of a Nazi Death Camp. Moore, Bob, ed. (p. 1603)
Schembra, John. Vince Torelli Novel Book 2: Retribution. Cummins, Sandy, ed. (p. 1842)
Schembri, Pamela, jt. auth. see Catalanotto, Peter.
Schemenauer, Patty Ann. Alphabet Fun at the Zoo. (p. 49)
Schemery, Beau. Last Blade. (p. 977)
—Unlikely Hero. (p. 1821)
—Unlikely Hero [Library Edition]. (p. 1821)
Schena, Maghan. When I Grow Up. (p. 1902)
Schenbeck, Sharon. Barky & Bill's Rocky Road. (p. 139)
—Barky's Belch. (p. 139)
—Barky's Big Number Book: 1 Through 10. (p. 139)
—Barky's Blizzard. (p. 139)
—Barkys Bone. (p. 139)
schenbeck, sharon. Barky's Buddy. (p. 139)
Schenbeck, Sharon. Barky's Buffalo: The Trip Out West. (p. 139)
—Little Dog Who Knew Jesus. (p. 1027)
Schenck, Deborah. Blooms: 20 Assorted Notecards & Envelopes. (p. 201)
Schenck, Emily, jt. auth. see Glasser, Debbie.
Schenck, Linda, jt. auth. see Thor, Annika.
Schenck, Linda, tr. see Thor, Annika.
Schendlinger, Mary. Prepare to Be Amazed: The Geniuses of Modern Magic. Clark, Warren, illus. (p. 1396)
Schenke, Heiner, et al. Basic German: Grammar & Workbook. (p. 141)
Schenker, Hilary, illus. see House, Silas & Vaswani, Neela.
Schenkman, Richard. Girl from Atlantis. Braga, Humberto, illus. (p. 678)
Schense, Deb & Burt-Westvig, Molly. Adventures of Molly Sue & Buster Too: A Trip to the Vet. (p. 20)
Schepper, Denise Marie. My Dad the Navy Hero (p. 1201)
Scheppler, Bill. Al-Biruni: Master Astronomer & Muslim Scholar of the Eleventh Century. (p. 32)
—British Royal Marines: Amphibious Division of the United Kingdom's Royal Navy. (p. 230)
—Careers with Click-and-Mortar Businesses. (p. 268)
—Guantanamo Bay & Military Tribunals: Detention Center for Terrorists. (p. 728)
—Guantánamo Bay & Military Tribunals: The Detention & Trial of Suspected Terrorists. (p. 728)
—How a Law Is Passed. (p. 804)
—Iraqi Insurgents: Resisting America's Nation-Building in Iraq. (p. 887)
—Iron Man Triathlon. (p. 888)
—Mississippi Burning Trial: A Primary Source Account. (p. 1154)
—USA Patriot Act: Antiterror Legislation in Response To 9/11. (p. 1826)
Scher, Linda. Texas City Disaster. (p. 1724)
Scherberger, Patrick, illus. see Marvel Comics Staff.
Scherberger, Patrick, illus. see Yost, Christopher.
Scherberger, Patrick, jt. illus. see Wegener, Scott.
Scherer, Catherine W. Simon & Barklee in China, Book 1 - the Southeast. (p. 1577)
—Simon & Barklee in China, Book 3 - the North. (p. 1577)
—Simon & Barklee in Egypt. Richardson, Kara, illus. (p. 1577)
—Simon & Barklee in West Africa. Richardson, Kara, illus. (p. 1577)
Scherer, Donovan Harold. Fear & Sunshine. Scherer, Donovan Harold, illus. (p. 579)
Scherer, Glenn, jt. auth. see Fletcher, Marty.
Scherer, Glenn & Fletcher, Marty. American Crocodile: Help Save This Endangered Species! (p. 60)
—J. Robert Oppenheimer: The Brain Behind the Bomb. (p. 902)
—Neptune: A MyReportLinks. com Book. (p. 1241)
—Primary Source Accounts of World War I. (p. 1399)
—Uranus: A MyReportLinks. com Book. (p. 1825)
—Who on Earth Is Aldo Leopold? Father of Wildlife Ecology. (p. 1917)
—Who on Earth Is Rachel Carson? Mother of the Environmental Movement. (p. 1917)
Scherer, Glenn & Library. True Mountain Rescue Stories. (p. 1792)
Scherer, Lauri S. Artificial Ingredients. Friedman, Lauri S., ed. (p. 104)
—Autism. Greenhaven Press Editors, ed. (p. 117)
—Cyber Bullying. Greenhaven Press Staff, ed. (p. 396)
—Dating. Gale, ed. (p. 409)
—Death & Dying. Greenhaven Press Editors, ed. (p. 420)
—Fast Food. Greenhaven Press Editors, ed. (p. 576)
—Gun Violence. Friedman, Lauri S., ed. (p. 732)
—Human Rights. Greenhaven Press Editors & Gale Editors, eds. (p. 826)
—Obesity. (p. 1275)
—Privacy. Gale Editors, ed. (p. 1407)
—Recycling. Greenhaven Press Editors, ed. (p. 1453)
—Social Protest. Gale, ed. (p. 1604)
—Taliban. (p. 1703)
Scherer, Lauri S., jt. ed. see Friedman, Lauri S.
Scherer, Randy. Kelly Slater. Greenhaven Press Staff, ed. (p. 948)
—Political Scandals. (p. 1380)
Scherer, Viki, ed. see Henneberry, Dottie.
Scherm, Deedra. ABC Bible Verse Book. Dreyer, Laura, illus. (p. 3)
—Cinco Panes y un Par de Peces: Una Historia de la Fe y de Dar. Dreyer, Laura, illus. (p. 319)
—Five Loaves & a Couple of Fish: A Story of Faith & Giving. Dreyer, Laura, illus. (p. 601)
—Only One Me: A Sweet Little Rhyme to Help Your Light Shine. Dreyer, Laura, illus. (p. 1298)
—Solo uno Como Yo: Una Rima Dulce y Pequeñita para Ayudar Hacer Brillar Tu Lucecita. Dreyer, Laura, illus. (p. 1608)
—Whale & Jonah: A Story of Obedience & Forgiveness. Dreyer, Laura, illus. (p. 1877)
Schermbrucker, Reviva. African Christmas Cloth. (p. 27)
—Lucky Fish. (p. 1062)
—Taking the Cows Home. Lomofsky, Lynne & Laubscher, André, illus. (p. 1698)
Scherrer, David L. & Klepacki, Linda M. Celebrating Changes: Everything You Always Wanted to Know about Sex in Middle School. (p. 284)
—Fearless Love: Making Sexual Choices That Honor God. (p. 579)
Schertle, Alice. Adventures of Old Bo Bear. Parkins, David, illus. (p. 21)
—All You Need for a Snowman. Lavallee, Barbara, illus. (p. 46)
—Button Up! Wrinkled Rhymes. Mathers, Petra, illus. (p. 248)
—Button up! Wrinkled Rhymes. (p. 248)
—Camioncito Azul. McElmurry, Jill, illus. (p. 256)
—Little Blue Truck. McElmurry, Jill, illus. (p. 1024)
—Little Blue Truck Farm Sticker Fun! McElmurry, Jill, illus. (p. 1024)
—Little Blue Truck Leads the Way. McElmurry, Jill, illus. (p. 1024)
—Little Blue Truck's Christmas. McElmurry, Jill, illus. (p. 1024)
—Lucky Thing: Poems & Paintings. Minor, Wendell, illus. (p. 1063)
—Skeleton in the Closet. Jobling, Curtis, illus. (p. 1584)
—Such a Little Mouse. Yue, Stephanie, illus. (p. 1672)
—Very Hairy Bear. Phelan, Matt, illus. (p. 1838)
—We Addison, Kenneth, illus. (p. 1865)
—When the Moon Is High. (p. 1905)
Schertle, Alice, jt. auth. see McCully, Emily Arnold.
Schertle, Alice & McElmurry, Jill. Little Blue Truck's Beep-Along Book. McElmurry, Jill, illus. (p. 1024)
Scherzer, Cecilia. Close Encounter of a Bug. (p. 333)
Schettle, Jane, illus. see Maslyn, Stacie K. B. & Maslyn, Stacie K.
Schettler, Amanda. Adventures of Mike & Fanny: A Story about A Dog & A Goat. (p. 20)
Scheuer, Lauren, illus. see Lynch, Amy.
Scheuer, Lauren, illus. see Raymer, Dottie.
Scheuer, Lauren, illus. see Walton, Rick.
Scheunemann, Pam. -Ack As in Snack. (p. 9)
—Acting with Kindness. (p. 10)
—Animal Sounds Set 2 (p. 79)
—Ape Cape. (p. 91)
—Ash As in Trash. (p. 105)
—Aw As in Paw (p. 120)
—Band in the Sand. (p. 136)
—Bear Claws. Chawla, Neena, illus. (p. 150)
—Bees Buzz! (p. 158)
—Being a Peacekeeper. (p. 160)
—Big Bug, Little Bug. (p. 180)
—Bolígrafo del Cerdo. Nobens, C. A., illus. (p. 208)
—Cat Tails. Chawla, Neena, illus. (p. 278)
—Cats Meow! (p. 281)
—Chick on the Thick Brick. (p. 299)
—Chipper Flipper. (p. 308)
—Come & See My Game! (p. 347)
—Come for a Party! (p. 347)
—Cool Fabric Projects: Creative Ways to Upcycle Your Trash into Treasure. (p. 363)
—Cool Glass & Ceramic Projects: Creative Ways to Upcycle Your Trash into Treasure. (p. 363)
—Cool Metal Projects: Creative Ways to Upcycle Your Trash into Treasure. (p. 364)
—Cool Odds & Ends Projects: Creative Ways to Upcycle Your Trash into Treasure. (p. 364)
—Cool Paper Projects: Creative Ways to Upcycle Your Trash into Treasure. (p. 364)
—Cool Plastic Projects: Creative Ways to Upcycle Your Trash into Treasure. (p. 364)
—Cooler Ruler. (p. 364)
—Coping with Anger. (p. 365)
—Courage. (p. 372)
—Cow Licks. Haberstroh, Anne, illus. (p. 373)
—Cow Said Meow! (p. 373)
—Crane Loves Grain. (p. 376)
—Crocodile Tears. Chawla, Neena, illus. (p. 384)
—Daring Dalmatians. Doucet, Bob, illus. (p. 407)
—Dealing with Bullies. (p. 418)
—Dill Spill. (p. 440)
—Dogs Bark! (p. 462)
—Dolphins Click! (p. 465)
—Drew & the Crew. (p. 485)
—Ducks Quack! (p. 488)
—Elephants Trumpet! (p. 512)
—Emma Is Cooking! Word Building with Prefixes & Suffixes. (p. 519)
—Ent As in Cent. (p. 531)
—Four Soar & Roar. (p. 625)
—Frenchy's Float: A Story about Louisiana. Doucet, Bob, illus. (p. 636)
—Frog in the Clog. (p. 640)
—Frogs Croak! (p. 641)
—Ick As in Kick. (p. 851)
—Ing As in King. (p. 874)
—Ink As in Drink. (p. 874)

S

—Is This a Flower? (p. 890)
—Jumping Jack Russell Terriers. Doucet, Bob, illus. (p. 934)
—King on a Spring. (p. 959)
—Learning about Differences. (p. 984)
—Lena & the Lady's Slippers: A Story about Minnesota. Doucet, Bob, illus. (p. 991)
—Look at Me! (p. 1048)
—Lou Flew Too! (p. 1057)
—Loud Crowd. (p. 1057)
—Lovely Labrador Retrievers. Doucet, Bob, illus. (p. 1061)
—Marvelous Maine Coons. Doucet, Bob, illus. (p. 1099)
—Meg & I. (p. 1124)
—Mice Squeak! (p. 1134)
—One-Cent Tent. (p. 1294)
—Overdue Kangaroo. (p. 1314)
—Parrots Talk! (p. 1325)
—Patriotism. (p. 1329)
—Peacock Fan. Chawla, Neena, illus. (p. 1332)
—Peas & Cheese. (p. 1333)
—Pelican's Pouch. (p. 1336)
—Perky Poodles. Doucet, Bob, illus. (p. 1343)
—Pig Pens. Nobens, C. A., illus. (p. 1357)
—Pig Pens. Nobens, Cheryl A., illus. (p. 1357)
—Popular Persians. Doucet, Bob, illus. (p. 1385)
—Pot with a Dot. (p. 1388)
—Pug with a Mug. (p. 1415)
—Puppy Is for Me! (p. 1418)
—Raccoon & the Balloon. (p. 1430)
—Rainy Day. (p. 1436)
—Rare Fair. (p. 1439)
—Repainted School: Word Building with Prefixes & Suffixes. (p. 1460)
—Silky Is the Luckiest Cat! Word Building with Prefixes & Suffixes. (p. 1575)
—Skunk & His Junk. (p. 1586)
—Skye & Skip. (p. 1587)
—Sloane & Sly. (p. 1591)
—Snakes Hiss! (p. 1597)
—Spelling Bee. (p. 1625)
—Stacy & Steve. (p. 1638)
—Sub Club. (p. 1670)
—Tam & Tom. (p. 1704)
—Ted's Red Sled. (p. 1713)
—Tennis in Venice. (p. 1720)
—This Is Not My Dog! (p. 1736)
—Tigers Roar! (p. 1749)
—Time - 6 Titles. (p. 1751)
—Time to Learn about Measuring Time. (p. 1753)
—Time to Learn about Past, Present & Future. (p. 1753)
—Time to Learn about Seasons & Years. (p. 1753)
—Time to Learn about Seconds, Minutes & Hours. (p. 1753)
—Tolerance. (p. 1762)
—Tracy & Treavor. (p. 1776)
—Tracy & Trevor (6-pack) (p. 1776)
—Trash to Treasure: A Kid's Upcycling Guide to Crafts. (p. 1780)
—Ulma & Umberto. (p. 1809)
—Ulma & Umberto (6-pack) (p. 1809)
—Unity & Uri. (p. 1820)
—Unk As in Skunk. (p. 1821)
—Unknown Ballplayer: Word Building with Prefixes & Suffixes. (p. 1821)
—Val & Vince. (p. 1830)
—We Like Music! (p. 1867)
—We Like to Play! (p. 1867)
—Wendy & Wally. (p. 1875)
—Whitney & Wheeler. (p. 1914)
—Working Together. (p. 1953)
—Yana & Yosef. (p. 1968)
—Zoe & Zach. (p. 1987)
Scheunemann, Pam, jt. auth. see ABDO Publishing Company Staff.
Scheunemann, Pam & ABDO Publishing Company Staff. Keeping the Peace. (p. 947)
—Rhyming Riddles. (p. 1468)
Scheve, Janice Rose. Grandma Rocks! (p. 708)
—Grandma Rocks! Lewis, Benjamin E., illus. (p. 708)
—Grandpa Rolls! (p. 709)
Schexnayder, Paul. Kajun Kween. (p. 941)
Schexnayder, Paul, illus. see Clement, Maryceleste.
Scheyder, Jacob P., illus. see Scheyder, S. Jane.
Scheyder, S. Jane. One More Thing. Scheyder, Jacob P., illus. (p. 1296)
Schiavello, Arlene, photos by see Schiavello, Kira.
Schiavello, Kira. My Chosen Path: A Poetic Reflection of Teenage Emotions. Schiavello, Arlene, photos by. (p. 1200)
Schiavi, Sherry. Chelsea's Healthy Secrets. Huffmaster, Elizabeth, illus. (p. 297)
Schick, Joel. Jungle Book: A Story about Loyalty. (p. 935)
Schick, Joel, illus. see Albee, Sarah.
Schick, Joel, illus. see Beech, Linda Ward.
Schick, Joel, illus. see Sachar, Louis.
Schick-Jacobowitz, Jeannie, et al. Bit of Applause for Mrs. Claus. (p. 194)
—Bit of Applause for Mrs. Claus. Malinow, Wendy, illus. (p. 194)
Schickle, Ian, illus. see Cameron, Kristy.
Schieber, Barry J. Open Heart: A Story about Moritz. (p. 1299)
Schieber, Jennifer. Animals in Motion: Small Book. (p. 83)
—Animals in Motion. (p. 83)
—Burt's Counting Stew: Small Book. (p. 244)
—Burt's Counting Stew. (p. 244)
—contar con la sopa de Beto: Fiction-to-Fact Big Book. May, Gillie, illus. (p. 360)
—contar en las Olimpiadas: Fiction-to-Fact Big Book. (p. 360)
—Counting at the Olympics. (p. 370)
—Insects Measure Up! (p. 876)
—movimiento de los Animales: Fiction-to-Fact Big Book. (p. 1183)
Schieber, Jennifer, jt. auth. see Hartley, Susan.
Schiebold, Olivia, jt. illus. see Thomas, Leanne.
Schiefelbein, Betty. Shingle Nail: A Parable of Worth. (p. 1566)
Schiefelbein, Janis, jt. auth. see Seglie, Susan.
Schiel, Katy. Inside Germany's BND: The Federal Intelligence Service. (p. 876)
—Monarchy: A Primary Source Analysis. (p. 1163)
—Whiskey Rebellion: An Early Challenge to America's New Government. (p. 1912)
Schield, Allie Schield. Solomon & Lily. Jerome, Barb, illus. (p. 1608)
Schieldt, Corine. Somebody's Gotta Get Rid of That Vacuum. Schieldt, Jodi, illus. (p. 1609)
Schieldt, Jodi, illus. see Schieldt, Corine.
Schiemann, John W. Politics of Pact-Making: Hungary's Negotiated Transition to Democracy in Comparative Perspective. (p. 1381)
Schier, Helga. Cuban Missile Crisis. (p. 388)
—Endangered Oceans. Gale, G., ed. (p. 527)
—George Washington Carver: Agricultural Innovator. (p. 664)
Schier, Helga, tr. see Masannak, Joachim.
Schiff, Andrew D., jt. auth. see Romney, Marshall B.
Schiff, Stacy. Great Improvisation: Franklin, France, & the Birth of America. (p. 716)
Schiffer, Howard B. First Love: Remembrances. (p. 596)
—How to Be the Best Lover - a Guide for Teenage Boys. (p. 815)
Schiffer, Miriam B. Stella Brings the Family. Clifton-Brown, Holly, illus. (p. 1647)
Schiffer, Nancy N. Contemporary Hopi Kachina Dolls (p. 360)
—Rhinestones! A Collector's Handbook & Price Guide (p. 1467)
—Silver Jewelry Treasures. (p. 1576)
Schifferli, Paul Phillip. Darryl's Daring Deed. Schifferli, Paul Phillip, illus. (p. 409)
Schiffman, Jessica. Sybil Ludington: Freedom's Brave Rider. (p. 1692)
Schiffman, Jessica, illus. see Fridman, Sashi.
Schiffman, Lawrence H. Understanding Second Temple & Rabbinic Judaism. (p. 1816)
Schiffmiller, Robin, jt. auth. see Frender, Sam.
Schiffner, Frederick A. My Back Yard: Poems to Read to Your Children. Guenther, Kim, illus. (p. 1196)
Schifini, Alfredo, jt. auth. see Burt, Barbara.
Schifini, Alfredo, jt. auth. see Johnson, Rebecca L.
Schifini, Alfredo, jt. auth. see Keller, Ellen.
Schifini, Alfredo, jt. auth. see Leacock, Elspeth.
Schifini, Alfredo, jt. auth. see McClellan, Adam.
Schifini, Alfredo, jt. auth. see Stephens, Catherine.
Schifino, Angela. I Miss You When You Sleep: Edition 1. (p. 844)
Schigiel, Gregg. Feel the Love. (p. 580)
Schigiel, Gregg, illus. see Bird, Benjamin.
Schigiel, Gregg, illus. see Bright, J. E. & Loughridge, Lee.
Schigiel, Gregg, illus. see Dahl, Michael & Loughridge, Lee.
Schigiel, Gregg, illus. see Dahl, Michael, et al.
Schigiel, Gregg, illus. see Fein, Eric & Loughridge, Lee.
Schigiel, Gregg, illus. see Golden Books Staff.
Schigiel, Gregg, illus. see Greenberger, Robert, et al.
Schigiel, Gregg, illus. see Kupperberg, Paul, et al.
Schigiel, Gregg, illus. see Lemke, Donald B. & Loughridge, Lee.
Schigiel, Gregg, illus. see Pass, Erica.
Schigiel, Gregg, illus. see Stevens, Eric, et al.
Schilb, Nancy. Animal Cop Adventures: Wise Wiley. (p. 77)
—Animal Cop Adventures: Forrest the Hero. (p. 77)
Schiller Brenz, Jeanne. Hannah y Molly. Sullivan, Elizabeth, illus. (p. 742)
Schiller, Caitlin, ed. see Canas-Jovel, Lourdes E. & Acock, Anthony W.
Schiller, David. All American Car-I-Oke. (p. 43)
—All American Car-i-oke (8 Disp) (p. 43)
—Christmas Sing-Along Car-I-Oke. Robinson, Tim, illus. (p. 315)
Schiller, Dawn. Tommy the Turtle: And His Angry Feelings. Earnhart, Jeanine, illus. (p. 1765)
Schiller, Fred, et al. Racer X (p. 1431)
Schiller, Friedrich. Guillermo Tell. (p. 730)
Schiller, Melissa. 100th Day of School. (p. 1999)
—April Fool's Day. (p. 93)
Schilling, Christine, tr. see Armand, Villavert.
Schilling, Christine, tr. see Kazumi, Yuana.
Schilling, Deborah, illus. see Davis, Beth.
Schilling, Mark, tr. see Kitakata, Kenzo.
Schilling, Michael A. Jackson Adventure Goes Cow Fishing. (p. 904)
Schilling, Sarah Phillips, ed. see Phillips, Shannon & Garland, Nick.
Schilling, Vincent. Native Athletes in Action: Sports Stars Past & Present. Peterson, Gary, illus. (p. 1234)
—Native Defenders of the Environment (p. 1234)
—Native Musicians in the Groove (p. 1234)
Schilling, Vincent & Benjamin, Michelle. Native Men of Courage (p. 1234)
Schilling, Wilber H., III, jt. see Rose, Thomas.
Schillow, Ned W. and Schillow. Titanic Hearts. (p. 1758)
Schimel, Kate, jt. auth. see George, Lynn.
Schimel, Kate & Adams, Colleen. Colonial Leaders in New York. (p. 341)
Schimel, Kate & Alagna, Magdalena. New York's Government. (p. 1248)
Schimel, Kate & Cefrey, Holly. New York's Industrial Growth. (p. 1249)
Schimel, Kate & Collins, Kathleen. Economic Growth of New York. (p. 502)
Schimel, Kate & George, Lynn. Native Americans: The First Peoples of New York. (p. 1234)
Schimel, Kate & Khu, Jannell. British Colony of New York. (p. 229)
Schimel, Kate & Levy, Janey. New York: The Dutch Colony of New Amsterdam. (p. 1247)
Schimel, Kate & Roza, Greg. Land & Resources of New York. (p. 973)
Schimel, Kate & Zuravicky, Orli. New York's Role in the New Nation. (p. 1249)
Schimel, Lawrence. Is That a Bat? (p. 890)
Schimel, Lawrence, jt. auth. see Ikids Staff.
Schimel, Lawrence, jt. auth. see Nesquens, Daniel.
Schimler, Amy. Splish Splash! A Touch & Hear Book. Schimler, Amy, illus. (p. 1630)
Schimler, Amy, illus. see Krensky, Stephen.
Schimler, Stuart. Reaching the Ivory Tower: College Admissions & Beyond. Santhosh, Lekshmi, ed. (p. 1442)
Schimmel, Beth, illus. see Taylor, Dorothy L.
Schimmel, David, illus. see Hillert, Margaret.
Schimmel, Schim. Magic Planet: Pop-Up Fun. (p. 1073)
Schimmel, Schim, illus. see Book Company Staff.
Schimmell, David. Alice in Wonderland. (p. 39)
—Sherlock Holmes Activity Book. (p. 1565)
—Wizard of Oz. (p. 1943)
Schimmell, David, illus. see Hillert, Margaret & Fernández, Queta.
Schimmell, David, illus. see Hillert, Margaret.
Schimmelman, Alex, illus. see Zsikai-Spiker, Lisa Marie.
Schindel, John. Busy Barnyard. Holt, Steven, photos by. (p. 245)
—Busy Bear Cubs. Husar, Lisa & Husar, Mike, photos by. (p. 245)
—Busy Birdies. Holt, Steven, photos by. (p. 245)
—Busy Bunnies. Holt, Steven, photos by. (p. 246)
—Busy Doggies. Sparks, Beverly, photos by. (p. 246)
—Busy Elephants. Harvey, Martin, photos by. (p. 246)
—Busy Gorillas. Rouse, Andy, photos by. (p. 246)
—Busy Horsies. Lark, Casi, photos by. (p. 246)
—Busy Kitties. Franzen, Sean, photos by. (p. 246)
—Busy Pandas. Husar, Lisa & Husar, Mike, photos by. (p. 246)
—Busy Piggies. Holt, Steven, illus. (p. 246)
Schindel, John & Holt, Steven. Busy Chickens. Holt, Steven, photos by. (p. 246)
Schindel, John & Woodward, Molly. Babies & Doggies Book. (p. 123)
Schindelman, Joseph, illus. see Dahl, Roald.
Schindler, Anton Felix, jt. auth. see Macardle, Donald W.
Schindler, Holly. Blue So Dark. (p. 203)
—Feral. (p. 581)
—Junction of Sunshine & Lucky. (p. 934)
—Playing Hurt. (p. 1372)
Schindler, John. Rock Climbing. (p. 1482)
—Triathlons. (p. 1785)
Schindler, John E. Extreme Skiing. (p. 556)
—Hang Gliding & Parasailing. (p. 742)
—Skydiving. (p. 1587)
Schindler, Nina. Amores Enredados. Alonso, Maria, tr. (p. 65)
—Order of Amelie, Hold the Fries. Barrett, Robert, tr. from GER. (p. 1302)
Schindler, Roslyn. Zeon. Schindler, Roslyn, illus. (p. 1986)
Schindler, S. D., illus. see Armstrong, Alan W.
Schindler, S. D., illus. see Berger, Melvin.
Schindler, S. D., illus. see Bildner, Phil.
Schindler, S. D., illus. see Borden, Louise.
Schindler, S. D., illus. see Cuyler, Margery.
Schindler, S. D., illus. see Davies, Jacqueline.
Schindler, S. D., illus. see Davis, Kenneth C.
Schindler, S. D., illus. see Demuth, Patricia Brennan.
Schindler, S. D., illus. see Dragonwagon, Crescent.
Schindler, S. D., illus. see Fleming, Candace.
Schindler, S. D., illus. see Kay, Verla.
Schindler, S. D., illus. see Krensky, Stephen.
Schindler, S. D., illus. see Kroll, Steven.
Schindler, S. D., illus. see Kudlinski, Kathleen V.
Schindler, S. D., illus. see Kurlansky, Mark.
Schindler, S. D., illus. see Le Guin, Ursula K.
Schindler, S. D., illus. see O'Connor, Jane.
Schindler, S. D., illus. see Pearson, Susan.
Schindler, S. D., illus. see Pelley, Kathleen T.
Schindler, S. D., illus. see Rockwell, Anne F. & Rockwell.
Schindler, S. D., illus. see Rosenstock, Barb.
Schindler, S. D., illus. see Walters, Virginia.
Schinske, Kris. Stinky Chair. (p. 1651)
Schippe, Cullen, jt. ed. see Cannizzo, Karen.
Schippe, Cullen & Cannizzo, Karen, eds. Learning How to Live: Grade 4 (p. 985)
Schippe, Cullen W., jt. ed. see Cannizzo, Karen.
Schippers, Mary Kay. Year on the Family Farm: And the Life Lessons Learned. (p. 1969)
Schirack, Timm, illus. see Beres, Nancy.
Schirmer, Jodi L. Dear Deer Friend. (p. 418)
—It Is a Good Day: Clay. (p. 894)
Schirmer, Susan, illus. see Frazin, Julian.
Schiro, Michael. Treasure Hunt: Level R (p. 1781)
Schisgal, Zachary. Man, a Can, a Tailgate Plan: 50 Easy Game Time Recipes That Are Sure to Please. Men's Health Staff, ed. (p. 1085)
Schiti, Valerio, illus. see Lynch, Brian & Waltz, Tom.
Schizas, Lea. Bubba & Giganto: Odds Against Us. (p. 233)
Schkade, Jonathan. Get up, Lazarus! Dorenkamp, Michelle, illus. (p. 668)
—Icky, Sticky, Hairy Scary Bible Stories: 60 Poems for Kids. Mourning, Tuesday, illus. (p. 851)
—Jesus Shows His Glory. (p. 916)
—Nicodemus & Jesus. Miyake, Yoshi, illus. (p. 1251)
Schkolnik, Saul. Cuentos de Terror, de Magia y de Otras Cosas Extranas. (p. 390)
—Cuentos Ecologicos. Cardemil, Carmen, illus. (p. 390)
Schlabach, Amy. Times of Trial: Poem Stories of Anabaptist Martyrs for Children. Schlabach, Amy, illus. (p. 1754)
Schlachter, Gail Ann, jt. auth. see Weber, R. David.
Schlaepfer, Gloria G. Butterflies. (p. 247)
—Hyenas. (p. 831)
Schlafer, Linda. Gift for the Christ Child: A Christmas Folktale. Wilson, Anne, illus. (p. 675)
Schlafman, Dave, illus. see Dower, Laura.
Schlager, Neil, et al, eds. Grzimek's Student Animal Life Resource: Cumulative Index. (p. 728)
Schlaht, Kim. Ronnie's Rotten Recipes. Tijerina, Arnold G., III, ed. (p. 1487)
Schlangen, DVM, Mary. Zoe's Good-Bye. (p. 1987)
Schlechter, Annie, photos by see Rains, Valerie & Real Simple Magazine Staff.
Schlegel, Elfi & Dunn, Claire Ross. Gymnastics Book: The Young Performer's Guide to Gymnastics. (p. 734)
—Thr Gymnastics Book: The Young Performer's Guide to Gymnastics. (p. 1740)
Schlegel, Paula. Christmas Potato. (p. 315)
Schlegel, William. Miracle Puzzlers. Moran, Edna, illus. (p. 1148)
Schlegl, Abigail, jt. auth. see Schlegl, Stacey Lynn.
Schlegl, Stacey Lynn. Little Frog. (p. 1028)
Schlegl, Stacey Lynn & Schlegl, Abigail. MerMountain. (p. 1128)
Schlegl, William. Bible Alphabet Puzzles. (p. 175)
—Parable Puzzlers: Word Puzzles from Jesus' Parables. (p. 1323)
Schleich, James J. Sound Man. (p. 1615)
Schleich, Mary B., illus. see Heisinger, Denise.
Schleichert, Elizabeth. Peces. (p. 1333)
Schleifer, Jay. Everything You Need to Know about Weapons in School & at Home. (p. 546)
—Todo lo que necesitas saber sobre Cuando alguien a quien conoces ha mureto (Everything You Need to Know When Someone You Know Has Been Killed) (p. 1761)
Schleifer, Jay, jt. auth. see Huddle, Lorena.
Schleifer, Martha Furman, jt. ed. see Glickman, Sylvia.
Schleifstein, Mark, jt. auth. see McQuaid, John.
Schleihs, Kristin, illus. see Hubbard, Sharron/Y.
Schleihs, Krostin, illus. see Hubbard, Sharron/Y.
Schlein, Miriam. Hello, Hello! Kirk, Daniel, illus. (p. 764)
—Little Raccoon's Big Question. Schoenherr, Ian, illus. (p. 1034)
Schlembach, Audrey. Stinky Winky Bear. (p. 1651)
Schleper, Frank, tr. see Rebscher, Susanne.
Schlesinger, Arthur M., et al. History of American Presidential Elections, 1789-2008 (p. 783)
Schlesinger, Arthur M., Jr. Education of the Presidents (p. 505)
Schlesinger, Arthur M., Jr., ed. see Darraj, Susan Muaddi.
Schlesinger, Arthur M., Jr., ed. see Greenberg, David.
Schlesinger, Arthur M., Jr., ed. see Lange, Brenda.
Schlesinger, Arthur M., Jr., ed. see Lashnits, Tom.
Schlesinger, Arthur M., Jr., ed. see Phillips, Kevin.
Schlesinger, Arthur M., Jr., ed. see Wagner, Heather Lehr.
Schlesinger, Arthur M., Jr. & Israel, Fred L., eds. Taught to Lead: The Education of the Presidents. (p. 1707)
Schlesinger, Arthur M., Jr., ed. Major World Leaders. (p. 1078)
Schlesinger, Arthur M., Jr., intro. Ancient World Leaders. (p. 71)
Schlesinger, Ethan. AC/DC. (p. 8)
—Aerosmith. (p. 25)
—Billy Joel. (p. 187)
—Elton John. (p. 516)
—Led Zeppelin. (p. 987)
—Rolling Stones. (p. 1485)
Schlesinger, Gretchen. Send Me the Soap #1: The Emerald Isle Adventure. Pietila, David, illus. (p. 1550)
—Send Me the Soap #1: The Emerald Isle Adventure (lib. Bdg.) Pietila, David, illus. (p. 1550)
—Send Me the Soap #2: The Amazon Adventure. Pietila, David, illus. (p. 1550)
Schlesinger, Roger, et al. Global Passage: Sources in World History, since 1500. Vol. II (p. 684)
—Global Passages: Sources in World History. Vol. 1 (p. 684)
Schlesinger, Sarah, jt. auth. see Barringer, Janice.
Schlessinger, Laura. Dr. Laura Schlessinger's Where's God? McFeeley, Daniel, illus. (p. 475)
—Where's God? (p. 1910)
Schlessinger Media Staff, prod. My Family from Japan. (p. 1202)
Schleuning, Cheryl, jt. auth. see Schleuning, Todd.
Schleuning, Todd & Schleuning, Cheryl. Misphits: Story of Snake. Vene, Alessandro, illus. (p. 1151)
Schley, Cheri, illus. see Marshall, Denise.
Schley, Michael. Heart of Prague. (p. 759)
Schliesman, Matthew. Nimbus. (p. 1256)
Schliewen, Richard. Paulina's Teddy Bear Journey. Visaya, Artemio, illus. (p. 1331)
Schliewen, Richard D. Paulina, Girl of the Pacific. (p. 1331)
Schliewen, Ulrich. My Aquarium. Bye, Eric A., tr. from GER. (p. 1196)
Schlimm, John. Stand Up! 75 Young Activists Who Rock the World & How You Can, Too! (p. 1639)
Schlingman, Dana, illus. see Brown, Suzanne.
Schlitt, Christine. Journey into the Invisible: The World from under the Microscope. Brandt, Chris, tr. from GER. (p. 928)
—Perfectly Hidden: The Animal Kingdom's Fascinating Camouflage. Brandt, Chris, tr. from GER. (p. 1342)
Schlitt, D. Celebrate the Holidays with Scripture. (p. 284)
—Celebrate the Names of Jesus. (p. 284)
—Celebrate the World God Made. (p. 284)
Schlitt, Jayme & Schlitt, Ron. Rags, Riches & the Robe. (p. 1433)
Schlitt, RaRa, illus. see Hayton, Althea.
Schlitt, Ron, jt. auth. see Schlitt, Jayme.
Schlitz, Laura Amy. Bearskinner: A Tale of the Brothers Grimm. Grafe, Max, illus. (p. 152)
—Drowned Maiden's Hair. (p. 486)
—Good Masters! Sweet Ladies! Voices from a Medieval Village. Byrd, Robert, illus. (p. 698)
—Hero Schliemann: The Dreamer Who Dug for Troy. (p. 772)
—Hero Schliemann: The Dreamer Who Dug up Troy. Byrd, Robert, illus. (p. 772)
—Hero Schliemann: The Dreamer Who Dug for Troy. Byrd, Robert, illus. (p. 772)
—Hired Girl. (p. 781)
—Night Fairy. (p. 1253)
—Night Fairy. Barrett, Angela, illus. (p. 1253)
—Splendors & Glooms. (p. 1630)
Schlitz, Matt, jt. auth. see Brus, Mischa.
Schloesser, Natalie. Donkey's Ear. (p. 466)
Schloss, Andrew & Joachim, David. Mastering the Grill: The Owner's Manual for Outdoor Cooking. Miksch, Alison, photos by. (p. 1103)
Schloss, E., illus. see Goldstein, Rose B.
Schloss, Eva & Kent, Evelyn. Eva's Story: A Survivor's Tale by the Stepsister of Anne Frank. (p. 541)

S

Schloss, Neil W. Christmas Tree Stan. (p. 316)
Schlossberg, Elizabeth, illus. see Kroll, Virginia.
Schlosser, Bobbi. Pilgrim: A True Story. (p. 1358)
Schlosser, Eric. Chew on This: Everything You Don't Want to Know about Fast Food. (p. 299)
Schlosser, Eric & Wilson, Charles. Chew on This: Everything You Don't Want to Know about Fast Food. (p. 299)
Schlosser, Jeffrey A. Little Jacky Yooper: Kid Fisherman. (p. 1029)
Schlosser, S. E. Spooky Texas: Tales of Hauntings, Strange Happenings, & Other Local Lore. Hoffman, Paul G., illus. (p. 1631)
Schluenderfritz, Ted, illus. see Kavanagh, Herminie Templeton.
Schluenderfritz, Theodore, illus. see Hicks, Clifford B.
Schlueter, Rachel, illus. see Pappas, Charles.
Schlund, Mackenzie, illus. see Mcinnes, Lisa.
Schlup, Leonard, jt. ed. see Ryan, James G.
Schmaedek, Robert, photos by see Crockett, Sonja Michelle.
Schmaltz, Joanne, photos by see Disney Book Group Staff & Littlefield, Cynthia.
Schmalzbauer, Adam. History of the Denver Broncos. (p. 785)
—History of the Miami Dolphins. (p. 785)
—History of the Philadelphia Eagles. (p. 785)
—History of the Pittsburgh Steelers. (p. 785)
—History of the San Diego Chargers. (p. 785)
Schmatjen, Marc. My Giraffe Makes Me Laugh. (p. 1209)
Schmatz, Pat. Bluefish. (p. 204)
—Circle the Truth. (p. 321)
—Lizard Radio. (p. 1042)
—Mousetraps. Hauser, Bill, illus. (p. 1182)
Schmauss, Judy Kentor. Caterpillar. Collier, Mary, illus. (p. 279)
—Just the Right Home. Harrald-Pilz, Marilee, illus. (p. 940)
—Luke's Mule. Costello, Shawn, illus. (p. 1064)
—Parade Day. Chewning, Randy, illus. (p. 1323)
—People on My Street. (p. 1339)
—Ted Saw an Egg. Epstein, Len, illus. (p. 1712)
—Too, Too Hot! (p. 1767)
—Too, Too Hot! Kaminski, Karol, illus. (p. 1767)
—Truck Can Help. (p. 1791)
—Wicked & Wonderful Water. (p. 1927)
—World's Toughest Machines (p. 1961)
Schmauss, Judy Kentor, et al. Reader's Clubhouse Long Vowels Level 2 Valu-Pak (p. 1444)
Schmertz Navarro, Christine, ed. Student Activity Workbook for Breakthrough! the Bible for Young Catholics: Getting to Know Jesus. (p. 1669)
—Student Activity Workbook for Breakthrough! the Bible for Young Catholics: An Introduction to People of Faith. (p. 1669)
Schmicker, Michael. Old Mcdonald-San's Farm. Kenyon, Tony, illus. (p. 1284)
Schmickl, Angela. Matador Who Ran Away from the Spider. (p. 1104)
Schmid, A, HC;Nemet, jt. auth. see Schmidt, Hans-Christian.
Schmid, Christoph von. Basket of Flowers. (p. 143)
Schmid, Diana J. Samule the Worthless White Mule. (p. 1509)
Schmid, Evan. Cardinal from Oxford: A Story of John Henry Newman. (p. 266)
Schmid, Katie Kelley. Nat Turner & Slave Life on a Southern Plantation. (p. 1230)
Schmid, Paul. Hugs from Pearl. Schmid, Paul, illus. (p. 825)
—Oliver & His Alligator. Schmid, Paul, illus. (p. 1285)
—Oliver & His Egg. Schmid, Paul, illus. (p. 1285)
—Perfectly Percy. Schmid, Paul, illus. (p. 1342)
—Pet for Petunia. (p. 1345)
—Pet for Petunia. Schmid, Paul, illus. (p. 1345)
—Petunia Goes Wild. Schmid, Paul, illus. (p. 1349)
Schmid, Paul, illus. see de Seve, Randall.
Schmid, Paul, illus. see Levine, Gail Carson.
Schmid, Paul, illus. see Rosenthal, Amy Krouse.
Schmid, Paul, illus. see Thompson, Laurie Ann.
Schmid, Susan Maupin. One Hundred Dresses. (p. 1295)
Schmid, Teresa Anne Marie. Teresa & the Bananas. (p. 1721)
Schmidt, Alejandra, tr. see Fleming, Candace.
Schmidt, Alex & Schmidt, Steve. Our Federal Constitution, Our Missouri Constitution. Schmidt, Dennis, ed. (p. 1308)
—Our Federal Constitution, Our New Jersey Constitution. Schmidt, Dennis, ed. (p. 1308)
—Our Federal Constitution, Our Texas Constitution. Schmidt, Dennis, ed. (p. 1308)
—Our Federal Constitution, Our Wisconsin Constitution. Schmidt, Dennis, ed. (p. 1308)
Schmidt, Alex J. & Schmidt, Steven L. Our Federal Constitution, Our Michigan Constitution. Schmidt, Dennis, ed. (p. 1308)
Schmidt, Amy. Dog-Gone School. Schmidt, Ron, photos by. (p. 461)
Schmidt, Andy & Barr, Mike W. Star Trek: Motion Picture Trilogy: Motion Picture Trilogy. (p. 1641)
Schmidt, Andy & Jourdan, Diego. We Are G. I. Joe. (p. 1865)
Schmidt, Annie M. G. Miaou. (p. 1134)
Schmidt, Bryan Thomas. Abraham Lincoln Dinosaur Hunter. (p. 7)
Schmidt, Caleb, illus. see Paulding, Steve.
Schmidt, Carol. Butterfly Alphabet Coloring Book. (p. 247)
—Butterfly Fairies Stained Glass Coloring Book. (p. 247)
—Creative Haven Kaleidoscope Designs Stained Glass Coloring Book. (p. 379)
—Creative Haven Patchwork Quilt Designs Coloring Book. (p. 379)
—Witches Stained Glass Coloring Book. (p. 1941)
Schmidt, Carol & Coloring Books Staff. Japanese Stencil Designs Stained Glass Coloring Book. (p. 909)
Schmidt, Carter, illus. see Paulding, Steve.
Schmidt, Dennis, ed. see Schmidt, Alex & Schmidt, Steve.
Schmidt, Dennis, ed. see Schmidt, Alex J. & Schmidt, Steven L.
Schmidt, Dennis, illus. see Schmidt, Alex & Schmidt, Steve.
Schmidt, Dennis, illus. see Schmidt, Alex J. & Schmidt, Steven L.
Schmidt, Dennis & Schmidt, Esther. Baby Wild Animals: An Altitude Kid's Own Naturebook. (p. 128)
—Baby Wild Animals. (p. 128)
Schmidt, Denyse. Denyse Schmidt Quilts: 30 Colorful Quilt & Patchwork Projects. Cushner, Susie, photos by. (p. 427)
—What a Bunch of Squares. (p. 1878)
Schmidt, Donald, jt. auth. see Sasso, Sandy Eisenberg.
Schmidt, Elton. Colorado's Changing Cities: Then & Now. (p. 343)
Schmidt, Erica Lyn, illus. see McGowan, Chris.
Schmidt, Erin. Lo Que Hacen los Bomberos. (p. 1044)
—What Does a Firefighter Do? (p. 1883)
Schmidt, Esther, jt. auth. see Schmidt, Dennis.
Schmidt, Gary, jt. auth. see Kushner, Lawrence.
Schmidt, Gary D. Anson's Way. (p. 88)
—First Boy. (p. 593)
—Lizzie Bright & the Buckminster Boy. (p. 1043)
—Mara's Stories: Glimmers in the Darkness. (p. 1091)
—Martin de Porres: The Rose in the Desert. Diaz, David, illus. (p. 1097)
—Okay for Now. (p. 1282)
—Orbiting Jupiter. (p. 1302)
—Pilgrim's Progress. Moser, Barry, illus. (p. 1359)
—Straw into Gold. (p. 1666)
—Trouble. (p. 1789)
—Wednesday Wars. (p. 1871)
—What Came from the Stars. (p. 1880)
—William Bradford: Plymouth's Faithful Pilgrim. (p. 1933)
Schmidt, Gary D., ed. Poetry for Young People: Robert Frost. Sorensen, Henri, illus. (p. 1376)
—Robert Frost. Sorensen, Henri, illus. (p. 1479)
Schmidt, Hans-Christian. Are You Sleeping Little One. Lindgren, Laura, tr. from GER. (p. 97)
Schmidt, Hans-Christian & Bieber, Hartmut. Wondrous Day. (p. 1949)
Schmidt, Hans-Christian & Schmid, A, HC;Nemet. When a Coconut Falls on Your Head. Nemet, Andreas, illus. (p. 1901)
Schmidt, Heidi. Too Many Murkles. Byrne, Mary Gregg, illus. (p. 1766)
Schmidt, J. Marc. Egg Story. (p. 506)
Schmidt, Jacqueline. Patchwork Goes under Cover. (p. 1328)
Schmidt, Jacqueline, illus. see Greiner, Gail.
Schmidt, Jeremy, jt. auth. see Schmidt, Thomas.
Schmidt, Jessica, jt. auth. see Schmidt, Julie.
Schmidt, Jonathon, ed. see Yolen, Jane.
Schmidt, Julie. My Piggy Bank: Number Names & Count Sequence. (p. 1217)
Schmidt, Julie & Schmidt, Jessica. My Piggy Bank: Number Names & Count Sequence. (p. 1217)
Schmidt, Karen. Gingerbread Man. (p. 677)
Schmidt, Karen, jt. auth. see Schmidt, Karen Lee.
Schmidt, Karen Lee & Schmidt, Karen. Gingerbread Man. (p. 677)
Schmidt, Karen, retold by. Gingerbread Man. (p. 677)
Schmidt, Karenlee, illus. see Paxton, Tom.
Schmidt, Katen, illus. see Nolen, Jerdine.
Schmidt, Kristin. Give Your Song a Voice. (p. 681)
Schmidt, Kristina Edelkamp. Miss Flavia & the Cookie Cottage. Cologne, Starla, illus. (p. 1151)
Schmidt, Maegan. US Constitution & Bill of Rights. (p. 1826)
—Us Constitution & Bill of Rights. (p. 1826)
Schmidt, Marcia Binder, ed. see Padmasambhava.
Schmidt, Maria T. Fire Trucks. (p. 591)
Schmidt, Marsha & Schmidt, Matt. Santa Claus Project: Stories of Discovery about a Man in a Red Suit. (p. 1511)
Schmidt, Matt, jt. auth. see Schmidt, Marsha.
Schmidt, Mollie. Children of Courage. (p. 302)
—It Happened in Maine. Wood, Madeline, illus. (p. 894)
Schmidt, Nancy Li. Little Spark That Grew. (p. 1036)
Schmidt, Nathan. Zoey & the Zones: Coloring Book (p. 1987)
Schmidt, Norman. Best Ever Paper Airplanes. (p. 169)
Schmidt, Rebecca C., contrib. by. My Book about Cancer: A Workbook to Help Children Deal with the Diagnosis & Treatment of a Father with Cancer. (p. 1198)
Schmidt, René. Leaving Fletchville (p. 986)
Schmidt, Roderic. How to Draw the Life & Times of Abraham Lincoln. (p. 818)
—How to Draw the Life & Times of George W. Bush. (p. 819)
—How to Draw the Life & Times of James Madison. (p. 819)
—How to Draw the Life & Times of Martin Van Buren. (p. 819)
Schmidt, Roderic D. Infantry of the Future. (p. 873)
—Land Warfare of the Future. (p. 974)
Schmidt, Ron, photos by see Schmidt, Amy.
Schmidt, Sharon Vanek, jt. auth. see Vanek, Karen.
Schmidt, Shawntay. Invincible Me. Du Pont, Brittany, illus. (p. 885)
Schmidt, Steve, jt. auth. see Schmidt, Alex.
Schmidt, Steven L., jt. auth. see Schmidt, Alex J.
Schmidt, Susie, jt. auth. see Schultheiss, Amy.
Schmidt, Thomas & Schmidt, Jeremy. National Geographic Yosemite National Park Road Guide. (p. 1233)
Schmidt, Tiffany. Bright Before Sunrise. (p. 228)
—Hold Me Like a Breath. (p. 787)
—Send Me a Sign. (p. 1550)
Schmidt, Troy. Donkey & Jesus. Jones, Cory, illus. (p. 466)
—Donkey Tells His Side of the Story: Hey God, I'm Sorry to Be Stubborn, but I Just Don't Like Anyone Riding on My Back! Jones, Cory, illus. (p. 466)
—Frog & the Plagues. Jones, Cory, illus. (p. 640)
—Lion & Daniel. Jones, Cory, illus. (p. 1019)
—Lion Tells His Side of the Story: Hey God, I'm Starving in This Den So Why Won't You Let Me Eat This Guy Named Daniel?! Jones, Cory, illus. (p. 1020)
—Raven & Noah's Ark. Jones, Cory, illus. (p. 1441)
—Whale & Jonah. Jones, Cory, illus. (p. 1877)
Schmidt, Troy, jt. auth. see Lucado, Max.
Schmidt, Ulf. Justice at Nuremberg: Leo Alexander & the Nazi Doctors' Trial. (p. 940)
Schmidt, Werner. Forests of Adventure. (p. 618)
—Prisoners of the Witchaliks. (p. 1407)
Schmidt-Kyanka, Anita. Sapsucker Blues: The Story of an Endearing Family of Great Blue Herons. (p. 1514)
Schmitt & McGraw-Hill Staff. Invitation to Languages. (p. 886)
Schmitt, Betsy & Sokolava, Valerie. Promise of Abraham. (p. 1411)
Schmitt, Conrad. Así Se Dice 2009, Level 1A. (p. 106)
—¡Así Se Dice! (p. 106)
Schmitt, Conrad J. Como Te Va?, B: Glencoe Middle School Spanish. (p. 351)
—Glencoe Middle School Spanish Como Te Va? Audio Activities. (p. 683)
—Glencoe Middle School Spanish Level a Como Te Va?: A, Audio Activities. (p. 683)
—Invitation to Languages: Foreign Language Exploratory Program. (p. 886)
—¿Cómo Te Va? (p. 351)
—¿Cómo te Va? (p. 351)
Schmitt, Conrad J. & Glencoe McGraw-Hill Staff. Invitation to Languages: Exploratory Program. (p. 886)
Schmitt, Conrad J. & McGraw-Hill Education Staff. Glencoe Middle School Spanish - ¿Cómo Te Va? (p. 683)
—¿Cómo Te Va? (p. 351)
Schmitt, Conrad J. & Woodford. Cómo te va? B Nivel Azul. (p. 351)
Schmitt, Conrad J., et al. Español para Nosotros, Level 2: Curso para Hispanohablantes. (p. 536)
—Glencoe French 1B Bon Voyage! (p. 683)
—Glencoe Middle School Spanish: ¿Cómo Te Va? A Nivel Verde. (p. 683)
Schmitt, et al. Buen Viaje! (p. 235)
—Canta con Justo: Products for all three levels: Intro, Book A, Book B. (p. 262)
—Glencoe Middle School Spanish: Cómo te va? Intro Nivel Rojo. (p. 683)
—¡En Vivo! (p. 523)
Schmitt, Gary. R. O. Dents in the School. (p. 1429)
Schmitt, H. D. Pee Wee Pickle Goes to Kinder-Garden. Spears, Sheri, illus. (p. 1334)
Schmitt, Laura, jt. auth. see Hendrix, Jennifer.
Schmitt, Louis J., illus. see Landry, Cornell P.
Schmitt, Michel-Yves. Snowball Truce! Caut, Vincent, illus. (p. 1600)
—Your Pajamas Are Showing! (p. 1981)
—Your Pajamas Are Showing! Caut, Vincent, illus. (p. 1981)
Schmitt, Michel-Yves & Burrell, Carol Klio. Snowball Truce! Caut, Vincent, illus. (p. 1600)
Schmitt, Nannette Toups. Remember Last Island. Gorman, Carolyn Portier, ed. (p. 1459)
Schmitt, Sarah. It's a Wonderful Death. (p. 896)
Schmitthenner, Sam. Between the Lines of the Bible. (p. 173)
Schmittroth, Linda, jt. ed. see Ryan, Marla Felkins.
Schmitz, Barbara. How Much Our Dancing Has Improved. (p. 811)
Schmitz, Cecile & Mouchet, Klutt. Father Damien Hawaii's Saint. (p. 577)
Schmitz, Don. New Face of Grandparenting: Why Parents Need Their Own Parents. (p. 1244)
Schmitz, James H. Other Likeness. (p. 1306)
—Trigger & Friends. (p. 1786)
Schmitz, John. Funny Thing Happened on My Way Out of Church. (p. 650)
Schmitz, Mark. Creative Haven Manga Coloring Book. (p. 379)
—Manga Boys Coloring Book. (p. 1087)
—Manga Paper Dolls. (p. 1087)
Schmitz, Mary Brittany. P. U. Stew. (p. 1316)
Schmitz, Michael. Jellatto the Christmas Mouse. (p. 912)
Schmitz, Tamara. Standing on My Own Two Feet: A Child's Affirmation of Love in the Midst of Divorce. Schmitz, Tamara, illus. (p. 1639)
Schmitz, Tamara, illus. see Friedman, Laurie.
Schmitz, Tamara, illus. see Tangvald, Christine Harder.
Schmitz, Tamara, tr. see Friedman, Laurie.
Schmitz, Troy G., et al. E-Commerce in Agribusiness. (p. 492)
Schmoll, Edie. Holly, the Christmas Tree Fairy. (p. 789)
Schmolze, Ian, illus. see Larner, Eric.
Schnapp, Eric Cesar, et al. First Aid Clueless: An Emergency Guide for Young People. (p. 592)
Schnee, Silke. Prince Who Was Just Himself. Sistig, Heike, illus. (p. 1401)
Schneeberger, Thomas M. Catch the Wind & Spin, Spin, Spin (p. 279)
Schnee-Bosch, Penny. Mommy Always Comes Back. Bosch, David, illus. (p. 1162)
Schneersohn, Yosef Yitzchak. Notations on the Arrest: By Rabbi Yosef Y. Schneersohn. Gurevich, David A., tr. from HEB. (p. 1267)
Schneid, Frances E., illus. see Storper, Barbara.
Schneider, Antonie. Advent Storybook: 24 Stories to Share Before Christmas. Miller, Marisa, tr. from GER. (p. 14)
Schneider, Antonie & Bansch, Helga. Leo's Dream. Cole, Alyson, tr. from GER. (p. 993)
Schneider, Antonie & Maccarone, Grace. Mr. Happy & Miss Grimm. Strasser, Susanne, illus. (p. 1185)
Schneider, Barbara Hoss, illus. see Berman, Gina Dalpra.
Schneider, Carl J., jt. auth. see Schneider, Dorothy.
Schneider, Cheryl & Olson, Carole. Bunnaby Bunny (L) Toddler Reader. Schneider, Cheryl, illus. (p. 242)
Schneider, Christine, illus. see Bullard, Lisa.
Schneider, Christine, illus. see Perez, Jessica.
Schneider, Christine, illus. see Scelsa, Greg.
Schneider, Christine, illus. see Wang, Margaret.
Schneider, Christine, illus. see Williams, Rozanne Lanczak.
Schneider, Christine M., illus. see Bullard, Lisa.
Schneider, Christine M., illus. see Harrast, Tracy L.
Schneider, Christine M., illus. see Rustad, Martha E. H.
Schneider, Claude, illus. see Jeffers, Dawn.
Schneider, David. Dillan Mcmillan, Please Eat Your Peas. Shelly, Jeff, Sr., illus. (p. 440)
Schneider, Dianna. Rocky Ford Stories: Sleepytime at Rocky Ford. (p. 1484)
Schneider, Dorothy & Schneider, Carl J. Slavery in America. (p. 1588)
—World War II. (p. 1959)
Schneider, Elaine. 52 Children's Moments: A Treasure for Every Week of the Year. (p. 1997)
Schneider, Elaine Ernst. Taking Hearing Impairment to School. Schader, Karen, ed. (p. 1698)
Schneider, Hank, photos by see Boyds Mills Press Staff.
Schneider, Hank, photos by see Burke, Judy, ed.
Schneider, Hank, photos by see Halls, Kelly Milner.
Schneider, Hank, photos by see Highlights for Children Editorial Staff.
Schneider, Hank, photos by see Highlights for Children Editorial Staff & Boyds Mills Press Staff.
Schneider, Hank, photos by see Ross, Kathy.
Schneider, Hank, photos by see Slomades, Lorianne, ed.
Schneider, Herman & Schneider, Nina. Rocks, Rivers & the Changing Earth: A First Book about Geology. Herron, Edwin, illus. (p. 1484)
Schneider, Ingrid E., jt. ed. see Allison, Maria T.
Schneider, Jack. Allagash River Towboat: A Maine Logging Adventure. (p. 46)
Schneider, John Lee. Extinction: Dragons of Earth: A Novel. (p. 555)
Schneider, Josh. Bedtime Monsters. (p. 157)
—Everybody Sleeps (but Not Fred) (p. 543)
—Meanest Birthday Girl. (p. 1116)
—Princess Sparkle-Heart Gets a Makeover. (p. 1405)
—Tales for Very Picky Eaters. Schneider, Josh, illus. (p. 1701)
Schneider, Judith Burnett, jt. auth. see Rulnick, Mary Jo.
Schneider, Judy. But Not Quite. Weeks, Mary, illus. (p. 246)
Schneider, Katy, illus. see MacLachlan, Patricia & Charest, Emily MacLachlan.
Schneider, Katy, illus. see MacLachlan, Patricia & MacLachlan, Emily.
Schneider, Maxwell. Do You Hear Me? Laughs for the Hard of Hearing by the Hard of Hearing (p. 457)
Schneider, Melissa. G. U. M. Drops 1-2. (p. 651)
—G. U. M. Drops 3. (p. 651)
—G. U. M. Drops 4. (p. 651)
Schneider, Nina, jt. auth. see Schneider, Herman.
Schneider, Peter. Der Mauerspringer. (p. 427)
Schneider, Rebecca J. Why Can't Turtle Play? (p. 1923)
Schneider, Rex, illus. see Burk, Rachelle.
Schneider, Rex, illus. see Carroll, Lewis, pseud.
Schneider, Rex, tr. see Carroll, Lewis, pseud.
Schneider, Richard H. Blue Angel Ornament: A Story of Love & Loyalty. Davis, Florence S., illus. (p. 202)
—Christmas Pea Coat. Bond, Higgins, illus. (p. 315)
—Lighthouse Boy: A Story about Courage. Petrov, Anton, illus. (p. 1015)
—Zeek, the Christmas Tree Mouse. Davies, Florence S., illus. (p. 1985)
Schneider, Robin, illus. see Smith-Eubanks, Jennifer.
Schneider, Robin, illus. see Weaver, Amy Garrett.
Schneider, Robyn. Beginning of Everything. (p. 159)
—Extraordinary Means. (p. 555)
Schneider, Rosemary. Bully Paws. (p. 241)
schneider, Sandra. Secrets of the Symbols: Advanced Phonics Book including 54 skill Cards. Hoppe, Gail, ed. (p. 1546)
Schneider, Sherrie, jt. auth. see Fein, Ellen.
Schneider, Stephen A. Chess Basics. (p. 298)
—Chess Openings 1. (p. 298)
—Color My Chess World. (p. 343)
—Endgame Strategies 1: 2nd Edition. (p. 527)
—Endgame Strategies 1. (p. 527)
Schneithorst, Penny. Milestones & More. (p. 1142)
Schneithorst, Penny Pohrer & Mills, Nikki Holder. I Wake up in the Morning & What Do I See... Is That You Dad? (p. 847)
—I Wake up in the Morning & What Do I See... Is That You Grandma? (p. 847)
Schnell, David. Night Before Baseball at the Park by the Bay. Pamintuan, Macky, illus. (p. 1252)
Schnell, Robert W. Bonko. Wilkon, Jozef, illus. (p. 209)
Schnell, Selynn. Backpack Jungle. (p. 130)
Schneller, Candace. Jayden's Magic Door. (p. 910)
Schneller, Lisa, illus. see Mather, Kelly.
Schnetzler, Pattie. Earth Day Birthday. Wallace, Chad, illus. (p. 495)
—Ten Little Dinosaurs. Harris, Jim, illus. (p. 1719)
Schnitt, Deborah. Petey's Angel. (p. 1348)
Schnitzlein, Danny. Monster Who Ate My Peas Faulkner, Matt, illus. (p. 1168)
—Monster Who Did My Math Mayer, Bill, illus. (p. 1168)
—Trick or Treat on Monster Street Faulkner, Matt, illus. (p. 1786)
Schnitzler, Arthur. Anatol. Landes, William-Alan, ed. (p. 67)
—Meistererzählungen. Weigel, Hans, ed. (p. 1124)
Schnobrich, Emily. Delaware. (p. 424)
—New York. (p. 1247)
Schnupp, Al. Censored. (p. 286)
Schnur, Dawn. Bailey's Tree House Adventures. (p. 133)
Schnur, Steven. Henry David's House. Fiore, Peter M., illus. (p. 768)
—Mrs. Popham's Library. (p. 1187)
Schnur, Susan & Schnur-Fishman, Anna. Tashlich at Turtle Rock. Steele-Morgan, Alex, illus. (p. 1706)
Schnurbush, Barbara. Striped Shirts & Flowered Pants: A Story about Alzheimer's Disease for Young Children. Pillo, Cary, illus. (p. 1667)
Schnur-Fishman, Anna, jt. auth. see Schnur, Susan.
Schnurr, J., ed. Specialities from German-Russian Cuisine. Herzog, Alex, tr. from GER. (p. 1623)
Schoberle, Cecile. Day Lights, Night Lights. (p. 413)
—Everyday Heroes. Ewers, Joe & Lopez, Paul, illus. (p. 543)
—Morning Sounds, Evening Sounds. (p. 1175)
—To the Rescue! SI Illustrators, illus. (p. 1759)
Schoch, Robert M. & Yonavjak, Logan. Parapsychology Revolution: A Concise Anthology of Paranormal & Psychical Research. (p. 1324)
Schochet, Jacob Immanuel, tr. Selichot with English Translation: According to Chabad-Lubavitch Custom. (p. 1550)
Schoeder, Alan. In Daddy's Arms I Am Tall: African Americans Celebrating Fathers. Steptoe, Javaka, illus. (p. 863)

Schoedl, Mark A. It's a New Day. (p. 895)
Schoeffield, Susan. Basset Goes to Boston: A Beau & Cornelius Adventure. (p. 143)
Schoell, William. Giuseppe Verdi & Italian Opera. (p. 681)
—H. P. Lovecraft: Master of Weird Fiction. (p. 734)
—"I Can Do Anything" The Sammy Davis, Jr. Story. (p. 835)
—Mystery & Terror: The Story of Edgar Allan Poe. (p. 1223)
—Remarkable Journeys: The Story of Jules Verne. (p. 1458)
Schoeller, Jen. Biggest, Baddest Book of Sea Creatures. (p. 185)
—Biggest, Baddest Book of Space. (p. 185)
Schoeman, Chris. Somme Chronicles: South Africans on the Western Front 1916. (p. 1610)
Schoen, Ben, jt. auth. see Spartz, Emerson.
Schoen, Ben, et al. What Will Happen in Harry Potter 7: Who Lives, Who Dies, Who Falls in Love & How Will the Adventure Finally End? (p. 1895)
Schoen, Harold L. Teaching Mathematics Through Problem Solving: Grades 6-12. (p. 1710)
Schoen, Robin. Grandmother's Guest: The Blue Lady of Wilton. Hoar, Gail, illus. (p. 709)
Schoen, Sarah. Omar the Smiling Labrador (p. 1288)
Schoenbauer, Lauren. Leppy & the Magic Pot. (p. 993)
Schoenberg, Jane. Baby Hustle: An Interactive Book with Wiggles & Giggles! Conrad, Liz, illus. (p. 126)
—One & Only Stuey Lewis: Stories from the Second Grade. Evans, Cambria, illus. (p. 1293)
—Stuey Lewis Against All Odds: Stories from the Third Grade. Evans, Cambria, illus. (p. 1670)
—Stuey Lewis Against All Odds: Stories from the Third Grade. Evans, Cambria, illus. (p. 1670)
Schoenberg, Jill. Journal Buddies: A Girl's Journal for Sharing & Celebrating Magnificence. (p. 927)
Schoenberg, Richard. Boot Camp - A Marine Legacy. Schoenberg, Richard, photos by. (p. 213)
Schoenberg, Thomas J. & Trudeau, Lawrence J., eds. Twentieth-Century Literary Criticism, Volume 199 (p. 1801)
Schoenberger, Megan. Ella Fitzgerald: First Lady of Jazz (p. 514)
Schoenberger, Megan, jt. auth. see Schoeneberger, Megan.
Schoenberg-Lam, Dahlia, illus. see Person, Hara & Lewy, Faye Tillis.
Schoendfeld, Steve. Jake Plummer: The Comeback Cardinal. (p. 906)
Schoene, Kerstin. Monsters Aren't Real. Schoene, Kerstin, illus. (p. 1169)
Schoene, Kerstin & Gunetsreiner, Nina. Milo Is Not a Dog Today. (p. 1144)
—Milo Is Not a Dog Today. Schoene, Kerstin & Gunetsreiner, Nina, illus. (p. 1144)
Schoeneberger, Megan & Schoenberger, Megan. Diego Rivera: Artist & Muralist (p. 437)
Schoenfeld, Dustin, jt. auth. see Schoenfeld, Owen.
Schoenfeld, Jeff. Information: A Ten-Minute Comedy Duet. (p. 873)
Schoenfeld, Owen & Schoenfeld, Dustin. It Isn't Just a Game. (p. 894)
Schoenfeld, Wayne. Almost Perfect: An American Volunteer Medical Mission to Vietnam. (p. 48)
Schoenfeld, Wayne, photos by see Weiner, Rex.
Schoenherr, Ian. Cat & Mouse. Schoenherr, Ian, illus. (p. 277)
—Don't Spill the Beans! Schoenherr, Ian, illus. (p. 468)
—Pip & Squeak. Schoenherr, Ian, illus. (p. 1361)
—Read It, Don't Eat It! Schoenherr, Ian, illus. (p. 1443)
Schoenherr, Ian, illus. see Almhjell, Tone.
Schoenherr, Ian, illus. see Cashore, Kristin.
Schoenherr, Ian, illus. see Harnick, Sheldon.
Schoenherr, Ian, illus. see Jacques, Brian.
Schoenherr, Ian, illus. see Meloy, Maile.
Schoenherr, Ian, illus. see Schlein, Miriam.
Schoenherr, Jeffrey. Lillie Saves the Day. (p. 1017)
—Lillie's Big Parade. (p. 1017)
Schoenherr, John, illus. see George, Jean Craighead.
Schoenherr, John, illus. see Morey, Walt.
Schoenherr, John, illus. see Plourde, Lynn.
Schoening, Dan. Green Lantern (p. 722)
Schoening, Dan, illus. see Acampora, Michael V.
Schoening, Dan, illus. see Acampora, Michael Vincent.
Schoening, Dan, illus. see Bright, J. E.
Schoening, Dan, illus. see Carbone, Courtney.
Schoening, Dan, illus. see Crawford, Philip & Crawford, Philip Charles.
Schoening, Dan, illus. see Dahl, Michael.
Schoening, Dan, illus. see Hoena, B. A.
Schoening, Dan, illus. see Hoena, Blake A.
Schoening, Dan, illus. see Hoena, Blake A. & Hoena, B. A.
Schoening, Dan, illus. see Kupperberg, Paul.
Schoening, Dan, illus. see Mason, Jane B.
Schoening, Dan, illus. see Simonson, Louise.
Schoening, Dan, illus. see Sonneborn, Scott.
Schoening, Dan, illus. see Steele, Michael A.
Schoening, Dan, illus. see Steele, Michael Anthony.
Schoening, Dan, illus. see Stephens, Sarah Hines & Hines-Stephens, Sarah.
Schoening, Dan, illus. see Stephens, Sarah Hines.
Schoening, Dan, illus. see Sutton, Laurie S.
Schoening, Dan, illus. see Tullen, Sean, et al.
Schoening, Dan, illus. see Wrecks, Billy.
Schoeningh, Debby. Little Raindrop. Brown, Margaret, illus. (p. 1034)
Schoen-Smith, Sieglinde, illus. see von Olfers, Sibylle.
Schoenthaler, Robin, jt. auth. see Pierce, Charlotte.
Schoettler, Joan. Good Fortune in a Wrapping Cloth. Lanan, Jessica, illus. (p. 698)
Schofer, Yvonne, ed. Literary Feast: Recipes & Writings by American Women Authors from History. (p. 1022)
Schoff, Bill. If Life Were a Hollywood Movie: Still More Humorous Poems for Kids & Adults. (p. 853)
Schoffman, Stuart, tr. see Grossman, David.
Schofield, Angela, illus. see Nourigat, Paul.
Schofield, Brent R. Hairballs & Sticky Things. (p. 736)
Schofield, Christina Diane, illus. see Gunn, Robin Jones.
Schofield, Jo, jt. auth. see Danks, Fiona.
Schofield Sr., Derrick. Frog's Tale. (p. 641)
Schofield-Farmer, Twila, illus. see Entinger, Chad.
Schofield-Morrison, Connie. I Got the Rhythm. Morrison, Frank, illus. (p. 838)
Scholar, Rochelle, jt. auth. see Robshaw, Brandon.
Scholastic / LeapFrog, jt. auth. see Kirk, David.
Scholastic / LeapFrog, jt. auth. see Marzollo, Jean.
Scholastic Book Editors. Sign Language: My First 100 Words. Nelson, Michiyo, illus. (p. 1574)
Scholastic Book Editors, jt. auth. see Guarino, Deborah.
Scholastic Book Editors, et al. Scooby-Doo! Franken Creepy. (p. 1529)
Scholastic Canada Ltd. Staff, jt. auth. see Baicker, Karen.
Scholastic Canada Ltd. Staff, jt. auth. see Charlesworth, Liza.
Scholastic Canada Ltd. Staff, jt. auth. see Fleming, Maria.
Scholastic Canada Ltd. Staff, jt. auth. see Pilkey, Dav.
Scholastic Canada Ltd. Staff, jt. auth. see Zuravicky, Orli.
Scholastic Coach Magazine Staff & Beech, Linda Ward. 180 Essential Vocabulary Words: Independent Learning Packets That Help Students Learn the Most Important Words They Need to Succeed in School. (p. 2000)
Scholastic Editors. Battle for the Bolt Badge. (p. 145)
—Scholastic Almanac for Kids 2014. (p. 1521)
Scholastic Editors & Wiltshire, Alex. Minecraft: Blockopedia. (p. 1146)
Scholastic Editors, ed. Last Laugh! (p. 978)
Scholastic, Inc. Staff. 39 Clues: the Black Book of Buried Secrets - Library Edition. (p. 1996)
—ABC. (p. 3)
—Awkward! Your Stars' Oops, Goofs & Blushes. (p. 121)
—Books of the Bible! (p. 212)
—Brain Play 1st-3rd. (p. 221)
—Brain Play Preschool-1st. (p. 221)
—Brilliant Butterflies! (p. 228)
—Carry & Learn Colors. Ward, Sarah G., illus. (p. 271)
—Carry & Learn Numbers. Ward, Sarah G., illus. (p. 271)
—Children's Dictionary. (p. 303)
—Circus Big Top! (p. 322)
—Clifford Forever Friends. (p. 332)
—Clifford Musical Memory Games. (p. 332)
—Colors & Shapes. (p. 345)
—Construir la Ciudad! (p. 360)
—Counting to 100. (p. 371)
—Create & Trace Sinnoh Heroes. (p. 378)
—Cursive Alphabet. (p. 395)
—Dazzling Daisies! (p. 415)
—Dear Mrs. Larue. (p. 419)
—Dolphin Rescue. (p. 464)
—Drama-Free Life. Bokram, Karen, ed. (p. 480)
—Ever after High: Yearbook. (p. 541)
—Fantastic Ants! (p. 571)
—Friends Forever. (p. 638)
—Gingerbread Man Fairy Tale Masks. (p. 677)
—Girls' Life Guide to Being the Most Amazing You. Bokram, Karen, ed. (p. 680)
—Goldilocks & the Three Bears Fairy Tale Masks with Easy-to-Read Play! (p. 696)
—Good Character Kids! (p. 697)
—Heroes - Harry Potter (p. 772)
—How to Draw Goosebumps. (p. 817)
—Hunger Games Official Illustrated Movie Companion. (p. 828)
—I Spy Fantasy. (p. 846)
—I Spy Riddle Master. (p. 846)
—I Spy Treasure Hunt. (p. 846)
—International Flags! (p. 880)
—Lego DC Super Heroes: Space Justice! (p. 990)
—LEGO Duplo: Animal Sounds. (p. 990)
—LEGO DUPLO: My Town. (p. 990)
—Lego Ninjago Reader. (p. 990)
—Lightsabers: A Guide to Weapons of the Force. (p. 1016)
—Little Lamb: A Pull-The Tab Cloth Book. Mills, Liz, ed. (p. 1030)
—Me by Me. Any Kid, ed. (p. 1115)
—Merry Christmas, Lego City! (p. 1128)
—Mexico Borders with Corners. (p. 1131)
—Mi Primera Biblia. (p. 1133)
—Modern Manuscript Alphabet. (p. 1158)
—My Backpack! Swanson, Weldon, illus. (p. 1196)
—My First 100 Words. Nelson, Michiyo, illus. (p. 1203)
—My First Book of Sign Language. Holub, Joan, illus. (p. 1205)
—My Mommy. (p. 1214)
—Mystery Incorporated. (p. 1224)
—Nursery Rhyme Flip Chart: 20 Favorite Nursery Rhymes That Build Phonemic Awareness & Inspire a Love of Reading. (p. 1273)
—Old Testament Characters! (p. 1284)
—Our Birthday Graph! (p. 1307)
—Peppa Goes Swimming. (p. 1340)
—Peppa Pig: The Tooth Fairy. (p. 1340)
—Peppa Pig: Peppa's First Sleepover. Eone, François René, illus. (p. 1340)
—Peppa Pig: the Tooth Fairy. (p. 1340)
—Peppa's Chalk ABCs. (p. 1340)
—Peppa's First Sleepover. (p. 1340)
—Peppa's Windy Fall Day. Scholastic, Inc. Staff, illus. (p. 1340)
—Perfect Poems with Strategies for Building Fluency: Easy-to-Read Poems with Effective Strategies to Help Students Build Word Recogniton. (p. 1342)
—Perfect Poems with Strategies for Building Fluency: Easy-to-Read Poems with Effective Strategies to Help Students Build Word Recognition. (p. 1342)
—Perfect Poems with Strategies for Building Fluency, Grades 3-4: Easy-to-Read Poems with Effective Strategies to Help Students Build Word Recognition Fluency, & Comprehension. (p. 1342)
—Phonics (p. 1351)
—Pirates Treasure. (p. 1364)
—Plan Your Destiny: A Spellbinding School Planner. (p. 1366)
—Pokemon: Kalos Region Handbook. (p. 1377)
—Pokemon All-New Collector's Sticker. (p. 1378)
—Pokemon Deluxe Essential Handbook. (p. 1378)
—Pokemon: Kalos Region Handbook. (p. 1378)
—Potholders. (p. 1388)
—Preschool Basic Skills: Visual Perception & Drawing Activities. (p. 1396)
—Rainbow Stars! (p. 1436)
—Ready for Takeoff! (p. 1447)
—Real Mother Goose. Maccarone, Grace, ed. (p. 1448)
—Ripley's Believe It or Not! 2011. (p. 1474)
—Safari. (p. 1501)
—Safari Animals! (p. 1501)
—Scholastic Almanac for Kids 2015. (p. 1521)
—Scholastic Pocket Dictionary. (p. 1522)
—Scooby-Doo: Frankencreepy Movie Reader. (p. 1529)
—Seasons & Holidays: 40 Instant & Adorable Patterns for Bulletin Boards, Class Books, Newsletters, Stationery, & More. (p. 1538)
—Sight Word Tales Interactive E-Storybooks: 25 e-Books with Engaging Interactive Whiteboard Activities That Teach the Top 100 High-Frequency Words. (p. 1574)
—Sirenita (The Little Mermaid) Bordoy, Irene, illus. (p. 1580)
—Space Justice! (p. 1619)
—Sport Kids! (p. 1631)
—Spy vs. Spy. (p. 1636)
—Stop That Heist! (p. 1653)
—Sunflowers! (p. 1676)
—Sunny Rainbow! (p. 1677)
—Super Sinnoh. (p. 1681)
—Super Sports. (p. 1682)
—Super Sunshine! (p. 1682)
—Three Little Pigs Fairy Tale Masks with Easy-to-Read Play! (p. 1743)
—Tickety Toc: Let's Tell Time! (p. 1747)
—Vowel Sounds. (p. 1850)
—We are Thankfull (p. 1865)
—Weather Kids! (p. 1870)
—Welcome to Chuggington. (p. 1873)
—Welcome to Horrorland: A Survival Guide. (p. 1873)
—Welcome to Sinnoh. (p. 1873)
—Wolf-Pack Attack! (p. 1944)
—Write-and-Learn Number Practice Pages: Engaging Reproducible Activity Pages That Help Kids Recognize, Write, & Really Learn the Numbers 1 Through 30. (p. 1963)
—Zombie Apocalypse Survival Guide. (p. 1988)
Scholastic, Inc. Staff, ed. see Ackerman, Jill & Landers, Ace.
Scholastic, Inc. Staff, ed. see Beech, Linda Ward, et al.
Scholastic, Inc. Staff, ed. see Beech, Linda, et al.
Scholastic, Inc. Staff, ed. see Heinst, Marie.
Scholastic, Inc. Staff, ed. see Landers, Ace & Cartwheel Editors.
Scholastic, Inc. Staff, ed. see Smith, Justine & Ackerman, Jill.
Scholastic, Inc. Staff, illus. see Farshtey, Greg.
Scholastic, Inc. Staff, illus. see Hernandez, Christopher.
Scholastic, Inc. Staff, illus. see Holmes, Anna.
Scholastic, Inc. Staff, illus. see Howard, Lee.
Scholastic, Inc. Staff, illus. see Landers, Ace.
Scholastic, Inc. Staff, illus. see Margles, Samantha.
Scholastic, Inc. Staff, jt. auth. see Baicker, Karen.
Scholastic, Inc. Staff, jt. auth. see Bridwell, Norman.
Scholastic, Inc. Staff, jt. auth. see Brooke, Samantha.
Scholastic, Inc. Staff, jt. auth. see Bugbird, Tim.
Scholastic, Inc. Staff, jt. auth. see Carman, Patrick.
Scholastic, Inc. Staff, jt. auth. see Cecil, Lauren.
Scholastic, Inc. Staff, jt. auth. see Charlesworth, Liza.
Scholastic, Inc. Staff, jt. auth. see Easton, Marilyn J.
Scholastic, Inc. Staff, jt. auth. see Farshtey, Greg.
Scholastic, Inc. Staff, jt. auth. see Holmes, Anna.
Scholastic, Inc. Staff, jt. auth. see London, C. Alexander.
Scholastic, Inc. Staff, jt. auth. see Martin, Steve.
Scholastic, Inc. Staff, jt. auth. see McAllister, Angela.
Scholastic, Inc. Staff, jt. auth. see Meadows, Daisy.
Scholastic, Inc. Staff, jt. auth. see Pokemon Staff.
Scholastic, Inc. Staff, jt. auth. see Riordan, Rick.
Scholastic, Inc. Staff, jt. auth. see Ruesga, Rita Rosa.
Scholastic, Inc. Staff, jt. auth. see Sander, Sonya.
Scholastic, Inc. Staff, jt. auth. see Sevaly, Karen.
Scholastic, Inc. Staff, jt. auth. see Silver, Ivy.
Scholastic, Inc. Staff, jt. auth. see Slater, Teddy.
Scholastic, Inc. Staff, jt. auth. see Stiefvater, Maggie.
Scholastic, Inc. Staff, jt. auth. see Teague, Mark.
Scholastic, Inc. Staff, jt. auth. see Warhola, James.
Scholastic, Inc. Staff, jt. auth. see Watson, Jude.
Scholastic, Inc. Staff, jt. auth. see Whitehill, Simcha.
Scholastic, Inc. Staff, jt. auth. see Yolen, Jane.
Scholastic, Inc. Staff, jt. contrib. by see Children's Press (New York, N.Y.) Staff.
Scholastic, Inc. Staff, jt. contrib. by see Childrens Press Staff.
Scholastic, Inc. Staff, jt. contrib. by see Franklin Watts.
Scholastic, Inc. Staff, jt. contrib. by see Piney Grove Elementary School (Kernsville, N.C.) Staff.
Scholastic, Inc. Staff, jt. contrib. by see Tangerine Press Staff.
Scholastic, Inc. Staff & Ackerman, Jill. Snuggly Bunny. Wildish, Lee, illus. (p. 1601)
Scholastic, Inc. Staff & Alexander, Rosemary. Poetry Place Anthology: More Than 600 Kid-Pleasing Poems to Celebrate Seasons & Holidays. (p. 1376)
Scholastic, Inc. Staff & American Bible Society Staff. Lee y Aprende: La Biblia. (p. 987)
Scholastic, Inc. Staff & Arion, Penelope. The Ultimate Book of Randomly Awesome Facts. (p. 1728)
Scholastic, Inc. Staff & Bailey, Ellen. Girls' Book of Secrets. Ryan, Nellie, illus. (p. 679)
Scholastic, Inc. Staff & Barnes, Derrick D. Low-Down Bad-Day Blues. Boyd, Aaron, illus. (p. 1061)
—Stop, Drop, & Chill. Phillips-Duke, Barbara Jean & Duke, Barbara, illus. (p. 1653)
Scholastic, Inc. Staff & Beech, Linda Ward. 180 Essential Vocabulary Words: Independent Learning Packets That Help Students Learn the Most Important Words They Need to Succeed in School. (p. 2000)
—180 Essential Vocabulary Words for 6th Grade: Independent Learning Packets That Help Students Learn the Most Important Words They Need to Succeed in School. (p. 2000)
Scholastic, Inc. Staff & Bermiss, Aamir Lee. I Hate to Be Sick! Wilson-Max, Ken, illus. (p. 839)
Scholastic, Inc. Staff & Black, Sonia. Jumping the Broom. Hu, Ying-Hwa & Van Wright, Cornelius, illus. (p. 934)
—Mommy's Bed. Kindert, Jennifer, illus. (p. 1162)
Scholastic, Inc. Staff & Blade, Adam. Dark Realm: Skor the Winged Stallion. Tucker, Ezra, illus. (p. 408)
—Skor the Winged Stallion. (p. 1586)
Scholastic, Inc. Staff & Boyd, Dee. Only the Stars. Rich, Anna, illus. (p. 1298)
Scholastic, Inc. Staff & Brooks, Regina. Never Finished, Never Done! Borgella, Marjorie, illus. (p. 1242)
Scholastic, Inc. Staff & Brooks, Riley. All Access. (p. 43)
—Edward or Jacob? Quick Quizzes for Fans of the Twilight Saga. (p. 505)
Scholastic, Inc. Staff & Campbell, Guy. Boys' Book of Survival: How to Survive Anything, Anywhere. (p. 220)
Scholastic, Inc. Staff & Cannon, Nick. Neon Aliens Ate My Homework: And Other Poems. Cannon, Nick et al, illus. (p. 1241)
Scholastic, Inc. Staff & Chapman, Cindy. Baby Animals (p. 124)
Scholastic, Inc. Staff & Chorba, April. Pom-Pom Monster Salon. (p. 1381)
Scholastic, Inc. Staff & de la Bretesche, Genevieve. Scholastic First Picture Dictionary. (p. 1522)
Scholastic, Inc. Staff & Dougherty, Martin. Drones: From Insect Spy Drones to Bomber Drones. (p. 485)
Scholastic, Inc. Staff & DreamWorks Animation Staff, contrib. by. Over the Hedge: Animal Antics. (p. 1314)
Scholastic, Inc. Staff & Duendes Del Sur Staff, contrib. by. Scooby-Doo! & the Mummy's Curse. (p. 1529)
Scholastic, Inc. Staff & Easton, Marilyn. All Hands on Deck! (p. 44)
Scholastic, Inc. Staff & Farshtey, Greg. Lego Ninjago. (p. 990)
Scholastic, Inc. Staff & Ford, Juwanda G. Shop Talk. Hoston, Jim, illus. (p. 1568)
Scholastic, Inc. Staff & Fry, Jason. Darth Maul - Shadow Conspiracy. (p. 409)
Scholastic, Inc. Staff & George, Olivia. Bravest Girls in the World. DuBurke, Randy, illus. (p. 223)
Scholastic, Inc. Staff & Giovanni, Nikki. Girls in the Circle. Johnson, Cathy Ann, illus. (p. 680)
Scholastic, Inc. Staff & Glass, Calliope. Annie - A True Family. (p. 86)
Scholastic, Inc. Staff & Grimes, Nikki. Day with Daddy. Tadgell, Nicole, illus. (p. 415)
Scholastic, Inc. Staff & Hapka, Cathy. Jungle Adventure Ameet Studio, Ameet, illus. (p. 935)
Scholastic, Inc. Staff & Hooks, Gwendolyn. Mystery of the Missing Dog. Devard, Nancy, illus. (p. 1225)
—Three's a Crowd. Walker, Sylvia, illus. (p. 1744)
Scholastic, Inc. Staff & Hudson, Cheryl Willis. What Do You Know? Snow! Walker, Sylvia, illus. (p. 1883)
Scholastic, Inc. Staff & Karr, Lily. Chanukah Present for Me! McDonald, Jill, illus. (p. 291)
Scholastic, Inc. Staff & Keenan, Sheila. O, Say Can You See? America's Symbols, Landmarks, & Important Words. Boyajian, Ann, illus. (p. 1274)
Scholastic, Inc. Staff & Kelley, K. C. Football Superstars 2014. (p. 615)
Scholastic, Inc. Staff & King, Trey. Detective Chase McCain - Stop That Heist! Kiernan, Kenny, illus. (p. 431)
Scholastic, Inc. Staff & Landers, Ace. Power Rangers Megaforce: Alien Attack! (p. 1390)
Scholastic, Inc. Staff & Malone, Sydney. For Me & U! Fun for BFFs. (p. 616)
Scholastic, Inc. Staff & Medearis, Angela Shelf. Singing for Dr. King. Van Wright, Cornelius & Hu, Ying-Hwa, illus. (p. 1579)
Scholastic, Inc. Staff & Melwani, Mona. 201 Report Card Comments: Short Narrative Comments, Word Lists, & Sentence Starters That Cover Any Situation, Let Parents Know How Their Kids Are Doing-And Save You Time! (p. 2001)
Scholastic, Inc. Staff & Negley, Sam. Hot Wheels: the Ultimate Handbook. (p. 802)
Scholastic, Inc. Staff & Northrop, Michael. Book of the Dead. (p. 212)
Scholastic, Inc. Staff & Norton, Sally. Girls' Book of Excellence: Even More Ways to Be the Best at Everything. (p. 679)
Scholastic, Inc. Staff & Oliver, Martin. Boys' Book of Greatness: Even More Ways to Be the Best at Everything. (p. 220)
Scholastic, Inc. Staff & Ripley's Entertainment Inc Staff. Ripley's Believe It or Not! (p. 1474)
Scholastic, Inc. Staff & Roberson, Karla. My Shoelaces Are Hard to Tie! Holley, Vanessa, illus. (p. 1218)
Scholastic, Inc. Staff & Ryals, Lexi. Annie. (p. 86)
Scholastic, Inc. Staff & Sander, Sonia. Ready for Takeoff! (p. 1447)
Scholastic, Inc. Staff & Sevaly, Karen. Bulletin Board Wild West Ranch (p. 240)
Scholastic, Inc. Staff & Simon, Jenne. Welcome to Shopville. Scholastic, Inc. Staff, illus. (p. 1873)
Scholastic, Inc. Staff & Steele, Michael Anthony. Fix That Truck! Dynamo Limited Staff, illus. (p. 601)
Scholastic, Inc. Staff & Stevens, Chris. Thirty Days Has September: Cool Ways to Remember Stuff. Horne, Sarah, illus. (p. 1735)
Scholastic, Inc. Staff & Stine, R. L. Write Your Fright. (p. 1964)
Scholastic, Inc. Staff & Taylor-Butler, Christine. Mom Like No Other. Devard, Nancy, illus. (p. 1161)
—No Boys Allowed! Page, Mark, illus. (p. 1257)
Scholastic, Inc. Staff & Watson, Jude. Doublecross - Mission Titanic (p. 473)
Scholastic, Inc. Staff & West, Tracey. Snake Attack! (p. 1596)
Scholastic, Inc. Staff & Wheeler, Alex. Hostage. (p. 801)

Scholastic, Inc. Staff & Whitehill, Simcha. Amazing Scenes in 3-D. (p. 55)
Scholastic, Inc. Staff & Windham, Ryder. Fire Ring Race. (p. 590)
—Return of the Jedi. (p. 1464)
Scholastic, Inc. Staff & Zalme, Ron. How to Draw Goosebumps. (p. 817)
Scholastic, Inc. Staff, contrib. by. 1, 2, 3. (p. 1990)
—100 Day Count up Calendar with100 Open & Peek Door. (p. 1998)
—ABC. (p. 3)
—ABC's & 123's Note Pads. (p. 4)
—Addition & Subtraction. (p. 12)
—Addition, Subtraction, Multiplication & Division. (p. 12)
—Adventures in LEGO City. (p. 15)
—Alice in Pop up Wondrland 6cp Solid Counter Disp. (p. 39)
—America, Land That I Love. (p. 59)
—Animal Babies. (p. 76)
—Apples. (p. 92)
—Baby Animals. (p. 124)
—Baby Animals at the Zoo. (p. 124)
—Baby Animals on the Farm. (p. 125)
—Bee Proud. (p. 157)
—Beginning Sounds. (p. 159)
—Big & Little: Things That Go. (p. 177)
—Big News! (p. 182)
—Bionicle 42 Copy Floor Display. (p. 190)
—Bookworm & Books. (p. 213)
—Build This City! (p. 238)
—Cahills vs. Vespers (p. 251)
—Can You Say Please? (p. 259)
—Care Bears Floor Display 36 Copy. (p. 266)
—Children of the Lamp: 18-Copy Solid Floor Display. (p. 302)
—Chuggington: Snowstruck Wilson. (p. 318)
—Class News. (p. 327)
—Clifford Paw Print. (p. 332)
—Color with Clifford the Big Red Dog. (p. 343)
—Colors. (p. 344)
—Contemporary Cursive, Grades 2-4. (p. 360)
—Contemporary Manuscript. (p. 360)
—Counting 1 to 10. (p. 370)
—Counting 1 To 20. (p. 370)
—Counting in the Garden Dog: Magalina the Dog Plush. (p. 371)
—Counting Tools 1 to 10. (p. 371)
—Country Apple Basket Border with Corners. (p. 372)
—Day in Heartlake City. (p. 413)
—Dinosaurs. (p. 444)
—Early Math: 25 Ready-to-Go Manipulative Wheels That Help Children Practice & Master Key Early Math Skills. (p. 493)
—Ears, Eyes, Nose. (p. 494)
—Ella the Elegant Elephant 8-Copy Floor Display. (p. 514)
—Entering Kindergarten. (p. 531)
—Entering Pre-K. (p. 531)
—Fantastic Ants! (p. 571)
—Fiesta Stripes. (p. 584)
—Fractions. (p. 626)
—Fractions & Decimals. (p. 626)
—Geronimo Stilton: 12-copy Solid Shelf Shipper. 12 (p. 667)
—Geronimo Stilton 12-Copy Self-Shipper. (p. 667)
—Gingerbread Kids. (p. 677)
—Go, Go, Samurai! (p. 686)
—Hack Attack! (p. 735)
—Handprints Note Pads. (p. 741)
—Happy 100th Day! (p. 744)
—Happy Valentine's Day Trimmer. (p. 747)
—Head to Head. (p. 756)
—Hello, Spring! (p. 765)
—Hop, Hop. Hooray for You! (p. 796)
—Hot Wheels: The Collector's Handbook. (p. 802)
—I Am Bigger Than... (p. 832)
—I Love You, Little Bear. (p. 843)
—I'am a Good Apple. (p. 849)
—I'm A Shining Star. (p. 858)
—Is It Hot Enough for You? Global Warming Heats Up. (p. 889)
—It Is Time For... (p. 894)
—Johto Handbook. (p. 924)
—Lalaloopsy: Dress-Up Day! (p. 972)
—LEGO Friends: Meet the Friends. (p. 990)
—Lego Ninjago. (p. 990)
—Let's Go to the Library. (p. 997)
—Lions & Eagles. (p. 1021)
—Math Picture Puzzles for Little Learners: Dozens of Age-Perfect Practice Pages That Help Children Build Key Early Math Skills, Grades PreK-K. (p. 1107)
—Months of the Year. (p. 1170)
—More or Less. (p. 1174)
—Nice Work! (p. 1250)
—Olivia's Great Idea. (p. 1287)
—Opposites. (p. 1300)
—Out of This World. (p. 1311)
—Patchwork Squares. (p. 1328)
—Penguins. (p. 1337)
—Peppa Pig: Class Trip. (p. 1340)
—Peppa Pig: Fun with Friends. (p. 1340)
—Peppa Pig: the Story of Peppa Pig. (p. 1340)
—Pioneer Quilt. (p. 1361)
—Pokemon. (p. 1377)
—Pokemon Sneak. (p. 1378)
—Population 1.3 Billion: China Becomes a Super Superpower. (p. 1385)
—Red Apple, Green Pear: A Book of Colors. (p. 1453)
—Red Pepper, Yellow Squash: A Book of Colors. (p. 1454)
—Red Truck, Yellow Bus: A Book of Colors. (p. 1455)
—Reward Pad Lovely Work. (p. 1467)
—Romeo Rabbit Counting in the Garden. (p. 1486)
—Rookie Reader Boxed: Go-With Words Messy Bessey The Secret Code (p. 1487)
—Rookie Reader Boxed Level B (p. 1487)
—Rudy Cat Counting in the Garden. (p. 1494)
—Schol Banners All Ideas Are Welcome Here. (p. 1521)
—Schol Banners Take Time to Be Kind. (p. 1521)
—Schol Banners We Treasure Our Friends. (p. 1521)
—Schol Design Paper Peppermint Stick. (p. 1521)
—Scholastic Almanac for Kids 2014. (p. 1521)
—Scholastic Discover More: Penguins Stickerbook. (p. 1521)
—Scholastic Pocket Dictionary of Synonyms, Antonyms & Homonyms. (p. 1522)
—Scholastic Success with Addition & Subtraction. (p. 1522)
—School Days. (p. 1522)
—School Supplies. (p. 1523)
—Scooby Doo Halloween 42c Display. (p. 1529)
—Seasons. (p. 1538)
—Shapes. (p. 1560)
—Shapes at Home. (p. 1560)
—Shapes That Go. (p. 1561)
—Short Plays for Building Fluency: Famous Americans - 22 Reproducible Plays That Build Fluency, Vocabulary, & Comprehension. (p. 1569)
—Smiley Faces. (p. 1594)
—Smiley Faces Borders with Corners. (p. 1594)
—Special Helper. (p. 1623)
—Springtime Gingham! (p. 1635)
—Stars & Stripes. (p. 1643)
—Stars Note Pads. (p. 1643)
—Star-Spangled Citizen! (p. 1641)
—Stats & Facts on over 150 Brand-New Pokémon! (p. 1644)
—Sunflowers! Borders with Corners. (p. 1676)
—Teddy Bear, Teddy Bear, Turn Around. (p. 1712)
—Traditional Manuscript, Grades K-1. (p. 1776)
—Trucks Around the City. (p. 1791)
—Turn-to-Learn Wheels in Color - Phonics: 25 Ready-to-Go Manipulative Wheels That Help Children Practice & Master Key Phonics Skills to Become Successful Readers. (p. 1798)
—USA Road Trip! (p. 1826)
—Very Scary Halloween 2004 40 Copy Floor Display. (p. 1838)
—We're a Team. (p. 1875)
—What Happens Next? Caterpillar to Butterfly. (p. 1886)
—What Happens Next? Seed to Plant. (p. 1886)
—What Is the Weather Today? (p. 1890)
—What Rhymes? (p. 1893)
—Wheels on the Truck Go 'Round & 'Round. (p. 1901)
—Which Is Different? (p. 1911)
—Who Is in Your Family? (p. 1916)
—Wolf-Pack Attack! (p. 1944)
—World of Harry Potter: Harry Potter Poster Book. (p. 1956)
—Zoo Animals. (p. 1988)
Scholastic, Inc. Staff, ed. Chicken Soup for Little Souls: The Never Forgotten Doll. (p. 300)
—Children's Visual Dictionary. (p. 304)
—Close-Up Colors. (p. 334)
—Comptons les Animaux Grandeur Nature. (p. 354)
—Lego DC Superheroes: Save the Day. (p. 990)
—Lifesize Animal Counting Book. (p. 1013)
—Peppa Pig: Class Trip. (p. 1340)
—Scholastic First Encyclopedia (p. 1522)
—Secret Shapes. (p. 1543)
Scholastic, Inc. Staff, et al. Alphabet: 10 Ready-to-Go Games That Help Children Learn & Practice Letter-Recognition Skills-Independently. (p. 49)
—Don't Hit Me! Grier, Gary, illus. (p. 467)
—Sunday Best. Bootman, Colin, illus. (p. 1676)
Scholastic Library Publishing. Ancient World. (p. 71)
—Cornerstones of Freedom. (p. 367)
—Cornerstones of Freedom, Third Series. (p. 367)
—Enchantment of the World. (p. 523)
—Nature's Children. (p. 1237)
—Quite Enough Hot Dogs & Other Silly Stories. (p. 1429)
—Rookie Read: About Safety. (p. 1487)
—Rookie Read: About Community. (p. 1487)
—Rookie Read: About Geography—Continents. (p. 1487)
—Rookie Read-about(r) Dinosaurs. (p. 1487)
—Rookie Read-about(r) Sports. (p. 1487)
—Rookie Ready to Learn (p. 1487)
—Rookie Ready to Learn Español. (p. 1487)
—Three Little Kittens Get Dressed. (p. 1742)
—True Book—Civics. (p. 1792)
—True Book—Earth Science. (p. 1792)
—True Book-Experiments. (p. 1792)
—True Book—Information Literacy. (p. 1792)
—True Book-Physical Science. (p. 1792)
—True Book-the Civil War. (p. 1792)
—True Book-the Thirteen Colonies. (p. 1792)
—True Book-the U. S. Regions. (p. 1792)
—War in Iraq: From the Front Lines to the Home Front. (p. 1857)
—You Wouldn't Want To... (p. 1976)
Scholastic Library Publishing Staff, contrib. by. African American Biographies (p. 26)
Scholastic Teaching Resources Staff. Essential Questions Handbook, Grades 4-8: Hundreds of Guiding Questions That Help You Plan & Teach Successful Lessons in the Content Areas. (p. 537)
—Kindergarten Basic Skills: Alphabet & Fine-Motor Skills. (p. 957)
—Kindergarten Basic Skills: Numbers & Counting. (p. 957)
—Kindergarten Basic Skills: Visual Perception, Classifying & More. (p. 957)
—Preschool Basic Skills: Colors, Shapes & More. (p. 1396)
—Preschool Basic Skills: Fine-Motor & Scissor Skills. (p. 1396)
Scholastic Teaching Resources Staff, jt. auth. see Rhodes, Immacula A.
Scholes, Katherine. Nino y la Ballena. (p. 1257)
Scholl, Elizabeth. Ancient Mesopotamia. (p. 70)
—David Archuleta. (p. 410)
—Independence Day/Dia de la Independencia. de la Vega, Eida, tr. from ENG. (p. 870)
—New York City. (p. 1248)
—Organic Gardening for Kids. (p. 1303)
—Shontelle Layne. (p. 1568)
Scholl, Elizabeth J. Mayan Civilization. (p. 1113)
—New Jersey. (p. 1245)
Scholl, Jenny. Four Farm Boys: Turkey Times. Casto, Christina, illus. (p. 625)
Scholma, Vicki. Hippoty Hop. (p. 781)
Scholoar, Rochelle, jt. auth. see Robshaw, Brandon.
Scholten, Cheri, illus. see Vescio, Robert.
Scholtz, Pieter. Tales of the Tokoloshe. Treweek, Cherie, illus. (p. 1703)
Scholz, Barbara. Abc-Duden. (p. 3)
Scholz, Susie. I'm Not Going to School Today. (p. 859)
Scholzen, Barbara. Jolanta & Her 2,500 Kids12. (p. 924)
Schomberger, Mary. Adventures of Goldy the Mouse. (p. 18)
Schombs, James. Little Boy in a Dog Suit Weidman, James, illus. (p. 1025)
Schomburg, Sue. Baby Sue Meets Lollygag. (p. 128)
—Day with Baby Sue. (p. 414)
Schomer, Adam Anthony, jt. auth. see Wendel, Gretchen Schomer.
Schomer, Adam Anthony, jt. auth. see Schomer-Wendel, Gretchen.
Schomer, Adam Anthony, jt. auth. see Wendel, Gretchen Schomer.
Schomer-Wendel, Gretchen & Schomer, Adam Anthony. All Around Town. (p. 44)
—Becka Goes to Chicago. (p. 155)
—Becka Goes to India. (p. 155)
—Becka Goes to San Diego. (p. 155)
—Becka Goes to San Francisco. (p. 155)
—Becka Goes to the North Pole. (p. 156)
Schomp, Virginia. 24 Hours in a Pond. (p. 1996)
—24 Hours in a Tropical Rain Forest. (p. 1996)
—24 Hours in the Desert. (p. 1996)
—24 Hours on a Coral Reef. (p. 1996)
—American Voices from the Women's Movement. (p. 64)
—Ancient Africans. (p. 67)
—Ancient Chinese. (p. 68)
—Ancient Egyptians. (p. 69)
—Ancient Greeks. (p. 69)
—Ancient India. (p. 69)
—Ancient Maya. (p. 69)
—Ancient Mesopotamians. (p. 70)
—Ancient Romans. (p. 70)
—Aztecs. (p. 122)
—Brer Rabbit & the Goober Patch. (p. 226)
—Ceratosaurus: And Other Horned Meat-Eaters. (p. 287)
—Church. (p. 318)
—City. (p. 323)
—Countryside. (p. 372)
—Hiawatha & the Great Peace. (p. 775)
—Iguanodon: And Other Spiky-Thumbed Plant-Eaters. (p. 856)
—Marching Toward Freedom. (p. 1092)
—Myths of the World (p. 1227)
—Myths of the World - Group 2 (p. 1227)
—Native Americans. (p. 1234)
—New York. (p. 1247)
—Norsemen. (p. 1264)
—Ornithomimus: And Other Speedy Ostrich Dinosaurs. (p. 1304)
—Plateosaurus: And Other Early Long-Necked Plant-Eaters. (p. 1370)
—Prehistoric World (p. 1395)
—Stegosaurus: And Other Plate-Backed Plant-Eaters. (p. 1646)
—Therizinosaurus: And Other Colossal-Clawed Plant-Eaters. (p. 1731)
—Victoria & Her Court. (p. 1840)
Schomp, Virginia, jt. auth. see Johnson, Dolores.
Schomp, Virginia, jt. auth. see McClaurin, Irma.
Schomp, Virginia & Firdawsi. Ancient Persians. (p. 70)
Schomp, Virginia & Harris, Joel Chandler. Brer Rabbit & the Number-Nine Shoes. (p. 226)
Schomp, Virginia & Hinds, Kathryn. Mermaids. (p. 1128)
Schon, Isabel. Best of Latino Heritage, 1996-2002: A Guide to the Best Juvenile Books about Latino People. (p. 170)
Schon, Nick, illus. see Clarke, Jane.
Schon, Nick, illus. see Cullimore, Stan.
Schon, Ruchy. Who Am I? Roth, Ruchela, illus. (p. 1914)
Schönberg, John, illus. see Fenn, George Manville.
Schönberg, John, illus. see Fenn, George.
Schonberg, Marcia. All Around Ohio: Regions & Resources (p. 43)
—Discover Ohio Langton, Bruce, illus. (p. 447)
—I Is for Idea: An Inventions Alphabet. Radzinski, Kandy, illus. (p. 839)
—Little Ohio. Monroe, Michael Glenn, illus. (p. 1032)
—Ohio History (p. 1281)
—Ohio Native Peoples (p. 1281)
—Ohio Plants & Animals (p. 1281)
—Ohio Reader. Darnell, K. L., illus. (p. 1281)
—People of Ohio (p. 1339)
—Uniquely Ohio (p. 1818)
Schonberg, Marcia & Heinemann Library Staff. All Around Ohio: Regions & Resources (p. 43)
—Ohio History (p. 1281)
—Ohio Native Peoples (p. 1281)
—Ohio Plants & Animals (p. 1281)
—People of Ohio (p. 1339)
—Uniquely Ohio (p. 1818)
Schonewill, Lisa. Tell Me Mama, Is Santa Claus Real? (p. 1716)
Schonfeld, Shaya, illus. see Spero, Yechiel.
Schongut, Emanuel, illus. see Curtis, Jennifer Keats.
Schongut, Emanuel, illus. see Vlahakis, Andrea.
Schonhorst, Elizabeth, ed. see Gulberson, Brenda Z.
Schonour, Sarah Jane, jt. auth. see Phelan, Thomas W.
Schons, Chris, illus. see Vizzini, Ned.
Schonwalder, Helmut. Napkin Folding. (p. 1229)
Schonzeit, Miriam. Sweetest Song & other Stories. (p. 1690)
School, Blue Mountain. Colored Pencils. (p. 343)
School, Liberty, illus. see Webb, Dirk.
School, Liberty, jt. auth. see Webb, Dirk.
School Mathematics Project. SMP Interact for Two-Tier Projectable PDFs Key Stage 3 Tier S CD-ROM. (p. 1595)
School Mathematics Project Staff. Core 2 for AQA. (p. 367)
—SMP GCSE Interact 2-tier Foundation 2. (p. 1595)
—SMP Interact Book 8S. (p. 1595)
—SMP Interact Book 9C. (p. 1595)
—SMP Interact - For the Mathematics Framework. (p. 1595)
—SMP Interact Practice for Book 7C: For the Mathematics Framework. (p. 1595)
—SMP Interact Teacher's Guide to Book 7S: For the Mathematics Framework. (p. 1595)
School Mathematics Project Staff, contrib. by. For the Mathematics Framework. (p. 616)
—SMP Interact: For the Mathematics Framework. Bk. 7S (p. 1595)
—SMP Interact Book 8T: For the Mathematics Framework. (p. 1595)
—SMP Interact Practice for Book 8S: For the Mathematics Framework. (p. 1595)
—SMP Interact Teacher's Guide to Book 7C: For the Mathematics Framework. (p. 1595)
—Statistics 2 for Edexcel. (p. 1644)
School Specialty Publishing Staff & Carson-Dellosa Publishing Staff. 70 Must-Know Word Problems. (p. 1998)
—70 Must-Know Word Problems, Level 3. (p. 1998)
—Beetle Bug Ball. (p. 158)
—Sight Words. (p. 1574)
School Students, Tuttle Elementary. Respect, a Global Vision by the Students of Tuttle Elementary School. (p. 1463)
School, Waverly. Waverly Review: Spring 2003, Issue 1. (p. 1864)
School Zone. Animal Alphabet Pop-up Flash Cards. (p. 76)
—Wonder Words Flash Action Software. (p. 1947)
School Zone, ed. Transition Math K-1. (p. 1778)
School Zone Interactive Staff. Dot-to-Dots. Boyer, Robin, illus. (p. 472)
—First Grade. (p. 595)
—Flash Action Software Go Fish / Old Maid. (p. 602)
—Hidden Pictures. Sullivan, Mary, illus. (p. 776)
—Kindergarten. (p. 957)
—Math Basics. (p. 1105)
—Mazes. Simard, Remy, illus. (p. 1113)
—Phonics Review. (p. 1352)
—Preschool. (p. 1396)
—Second Grade. (p. 1539)
—Time, Money & Fractions. (p. 1752)
School Zone Interactive Staff, et al. Spelling 1-2. (p. 1625)
School Zone Publishing. Alphabet Express. (p. 49)
—Beginning Reading. (p. 159)
—Builds Skills & Confidence for Success in School. (p. 239)
—Kindergarten. (p. 957)
—Math 1. (p. 1105)
—Math 2. (p. 1105)
—Math 3. (p. 1105)
—Mazes Animals. (p. 1113)
—Multiplication & Division. (p. 1190)
—Phonics. (p. 1351)
—Reading Readiness. (p. 1446)
—Same or Different. (p. 1507)
—Spelling Puzzles. (p. 1625)
—Third Grade: Builds Skills & Confidence for Success in Schooll. (p. 1734)
—Third Grade. (p. 1734)
—Transition Math. (p. 1778)
—Vocabulary Puzzles. (p. 1847)
—Word Search Challenges. (p. 1951)
School Zone Publishing Co. Alphabet Bingo Game. (p. 49)
—Make-A-Word Bingo Game. (p. 1079)
—Numbers Bingo Game. (p. 1272)
School Zone Publishing Company Staff. 1-25 Punto-a-Punto 1-25 Dot-to-Dot. (p. 1990)
—3D Think & Blink Alphabet. (p. 1992)
—ABC Punto-a-Punto ABC Dot to Dot. (p. 3)
—Addition & Subraction 1-2. (p. 12)
—Addition & Subtraction 2. (p. 12)
—Addition & Subtraction Grade 1-2 A Wipe-off Book: Hours of Reusable Fun. (p. 12)
—Alfabeto Mayusculas Uppercase Alphabet. (p. 37)
—Alphabet Fun A Wipe-off Book: Hours of Reusable Fun! (p. 49)
—Basic Sight Word Fun! (p. 142)
—Beginning Reading. (p. 159)
—Big Activity Ages 8-Up: Word Searches, Crosswords, Puzzles, & Codes. (p. 177)
—Big Alphabet. (p. 177)
—Bilingual Addition & Subtraction. (p. 186)
—Bilingual Preschool Big Get Ready! (p. 186)
—Contando 1-10 Counting 1-10. (p. 360)
—Counting 1-10. (p. 370)
—Cursive Writing. (p. 395)
—English: Grades 1 & 2. (p. 529)
—English: Grades 3 & 4. (p. 529)
—Following Directions. (p. 612)
—Insects & Spiders. (p. 876)
—Japanese - Alphabet Game. (p. 909)
—Japanese - Colors & Shapes. (p. 909)
—Japanese - Dominoes Game. (p. 909)
—Japanese - Make a Word Bingo Game. (p. 909)
—Japanese Numbers Game. (p. 909)
—Japanese - Three Letter Words. (p. 909)
—Japanese - Three Word Rhyme. (p. 909)
—Language Arts 1. (p. 974)
—Language Arts 2. (p. 974)
—Los Sonidos para Empezar Beginning Sounds. (p. 1054)
—Lowercase Alphabet. (p. 1061)
—Mammals. (p. 1085)
—Manuscript Writing. (p. 1089)
—Matematicas Basicas Math Basics. (p. 1104)
—Math: Grades 5 & 6. (p. 1105)
—Math 1-2 Software. (p. 1105)
—Math 4. (p. 1105)
—Math Readiness: Hours of Reusable Fun! (p. 1107)
—Math Readiness. (p. 1107)
—Multiplication: Hours of Reusable Fun! (p. 1190)
—Multiplication & Division. (p. 1190)
—Multiplication Facts. (p. 1190)
—Numbers 1-12. (p. 1272)
—Phonics Review. (p. 1352)
—Reading Comprehension 1. (p. 1445)
—Reading Readiness (p. 1446)
—Reading Skills-1: And Language Activities. (p. 1446)
—Reptiles & Amphibians. (p. 1461)
—School Time Fun. (p. 1523)
—Seeds & Plants. (p. 1547)

—Shapes & Colors. (p. 1560)
—Spelling 2. (p. 1625)
—Story Problems: Grades 1 & 2. (p. 1663)
—Think & Blink Numbers & Shapes. (p. 1734)
—Thinking Skills Bilingual. (p. 1734)
—Vocabulary Puzzles 2. (p. 1847)
School Zone Publishing Interactive Staff. Colors, Shapes & More. (p. 345)
—Phonics Made Easy. (p. 1352)
School Zone Staff. Addition. (p. 12)
—Alphabet. (p. 49)
—Alphabet Match. (p. 49)
—Animals of All Kinds. (p. 83)
—Beginning Sight Words. (p. 159)
—Big Hidden Pictures & More. (p. 181)
—Big Mazes & More. (p. 182)
—Big Science: Hours of Fun! (p. 183)
—Colors, Shapes & More. (p. 345)
—Division. (p. 455)
—Fun & Festive. (p. 647)
—Go Fish. (p. 686)
—Math War Addition & Subtraction. (p. 1107)
—Math War Multiplication. (p. 1107)
—Multiplication. (p. 1190)
—My First Dot-to-Dots. (p. 1206)
—My First Hidden Pictures. (p. 1206)
—My First Mazes. (p. 1207)
—My First Smart Art Alphabet. (p. 1208)
—Nouns, Verbs & More. (p. 1268)
—Numbers 0-25. (p. 1272)
—Old Maid. (p. 1284)
—On the Farm. (p. 1290)
—Picture Words. (p. 1356)
—Puzzle Cards - Match & Mix. (p. 1420)
—Readiness. (p. 1444)
—Subtraction. (p. 1671)
—Things That Go. (p. 1733)
—Time & Money. (p. 1751)
School Zone Staff, jt. auth. see Poitier, Antonine.
School Zone Staff, ed. Baby Faces Infant Mirror Cards. (p. 126)
—Busy Puzzle People P-K Peg Puzzle Cards. (p. 246)
—Crosswords Challenges. (p. 385)
—Dot-to-Dot Alphabet. (p. 472)
—Farm Friends Peek-A-Boo Cards. (p. 574)
—Guess Who? Peek-A-Boo Cards. (p. 729)
—Happy Faces Infant Mirror Cards. (p. 745)
—Hidden Pictures Discovery. (p. 776)
—Hide & Seek Peek-A-Boo Cards. (p. 777)
—Kindergarten Spelling Bee. (p. 957)
—Mazes Preschool. (p. 1113)
—Multiplication & Division 3-4. (p. 1190)
—My First 100 Magnetic Words. (p. 1203)
—Preschool Counting Farm. (p. 1396)
—Preschool Shapes & Words. (p. 1396)
—Surprise Party Peek-A-Boo Cards. (p. 1686)
—Talking Telephone. (p. 1703)
—Time & Money. (p. 1751)
—Time, Money & Fractions. (p. 1752)
Schooler, Cindy. Creative Ministry Bulletin Boards: Fall. (p. 380)
—Creative Ministry Bulletin Boards: Spring. (p. 380)
—Creative Ministry Bulletin Boards: Summer. (p. 380)
—Creative Ministry Bulletin Boards: Winter. (p. 380)
—Creative Ministry Bulletin Boards: Special Days. (p. 380)
Schooler, Cindy, jt. auth. see Julio, Susan.
Schooley, Bob. Kim Possible Cine-Manga McCorkle, Mark, illus. (p. 956)
—Kim Possible Cine-Manga: Sink or Swim & Number One McCorkle, Mark, illus. (p. 956)
—Kim Possible Cine-Manga: Animal Attraction & All the News McCorkle, Mark, illus. (p. 956)
Schooley, Bob, jt. auth. see Disney Staff.
Schooley, Bob, jt. auth. see McCorkle, Mark.
Schooley, Bob & McCorkle, Mark. Liar of Kudzu. (p. 1005)
Schoombee, Cherese. Frilly Lilly. (p. 639)
Schoon, Christian. Under Nameless Stars. (p. 1813)
—Zenn Scarlett. (p. 1986)
Schoonen, Josephine Connolly. Losing Weight Permanently with the Bull's-Eye Food Guide: Your Best Mix of Carbs, Proteins, & Fats. (p. 1054)
Schoonmaker, Christina, illus. see Farrow, Nancy L.
Schoonmaker, Elizabeth. Square Cat. Schoonmaker, Elizabeth, illus. (p. 1636)
Schoonmaker, Frances, ed. Poetry for Young People: Henry Wadsworth Longfellow. Wallace, Chad, illus. (p. 1376)
—Robert Louis Stevenson. Corvino, Lucy, illus. (p. 1479)
Schoonmaker, Gail, illus. see Piper, Noël.
Schoonover, Brent, illus. see Gunderson, J.
Schoonover, Brent, illus. see Niz, Xavier & Niz, Xavier W.
Schoonover, Brent, illus. see Olson, Nathan & Glaser, Jason.
Schoonover, Brent, illus. see Olson, Nathan.
Schoonover, Brent, illus. see Trumbauer, Lisa.
Schopp, Bernice Frances. Legend of Moon-Goblin Town. (p. 988)
Schories, Pat. Biscuit Visits the Farm. (p. 193)
—Biscuit's Fourth of July. (p. 193)
—Biscuit's Graduation Day. (p. 193)
—Breakfast for Jack. (p. 224)
—Jack & the Missing Piece. (p. 902)
—Jack & the Night Visitors. (p. 902)
—Jack Wants a Snack. (p. 903)
—Pants for Chuck. Schories, Pat, illus. (p. 1321)
—Pie for Chuck. (p. 1356)
—When Jack Goes Out. (p. 1903)
Schories, Pat, illus. see Capucilli, Alyssa Satin.
Schories, Pat, illus. see O'Garden, Irene.
Schories, Pat & Capucilli, Alyssa Satin. Biscuit & the Little Pup. Schories, Pat, illus. (p. 193)
Schorr, Andrew. Advantage Grammar Grade 4: High Interest Skill Building for Home & School. Vol. 8140 Hamaguchi, Carla, ed. (p. 13)
—Advantage Math Grade 8: High Interest Skill Building for Home & School Hamaguchi, Carla, ed. (p. 14)
Schorr, Bill, illus. see Riegelman, Rianna.
Schorr, Loretta. Attacked (p. 114)
Schorr, Loretta Jean. Sash: The Life of a Little Toy Poodle. (p. 1515)
Schorr, Rachel. What a Golem. (p. 1878)
Schott, Diana. Aztecs & Nature. (p. 122)
Schott, Edward. Dogs of King Park. (p. 463)
Schott, Elizabeth. Jake & Sam at the Empty Abbey. (p. 905)
Schott, George. Half Emm. (p. 736)
Schott, Gretchen Victoria, jt. auth. see Black, Cary.
Schott, Jane A. Abraham Lincoln. (p. 6)
Schott, Joanna. Bellows in Hell. (p. 163)
Schott, Sandy. Travels of T. Tommy Turtle: A Day with the Desert Dwellers. (p. 1780)
Schotter, Roni. All about Grandmas. Nadeau, Janice, illus. (p. 42)
—Boy Who Loved Words. Potter, Giselle, illus. (p. 219)
—Doo-Wop Pop. Collier, Bryan, illus. (p. 469)
—Hanukkah! Hafner, Marylin, illus. (p. 743)
—Hanukkah! (p. 744)
—Mama, I'll Give You the World. Gallagher, S. Saelig, illus. (p. 1084)
—Nothing Ever Happens on 90th Street. Brooker, Kyrsten, illus. (p. 1268)
—Passover Magic Hafner, Marylin, illus. (p. 1327)
—Purim Play Hafner, Marylin, illus. (p. 1419)
—When the Wizzy Foot Goes Walking. Wohnoutka, Mike, illus. (p. 1905)
Schotz, Leo D. Rooftop. (p. 1487)
Schotz, Leo D., jt. auth. see Patrick, B.
Schouest, Stacey. Very 1st Christmas Tree. (p. 1837)
Schouwenberg, Louise, jt. auth. see Jongerius, Hella.
Schow, Betsy. Spelled. (p. 1625)
Schpitalnik, Vladimir, illus. see Evans, Connie.
Schrader, Constance A. Sense of Dance: Exploring Your Movement Potential. (p. 1551)
Schrader, Jessica R. Carrie's New Puppy. (p. 271)
Schrader, Kimberly, illus. see Schrader, Margaret.
Schrader, Margaret. Green Knee-High Farm. Schrader, Kimberly, illus. (p. 722)
Schrader, Mark, illus. see Furlong, Michelle.
Schrader, Missy W., jt. auth. see Schrader, Missy Wolgemuth.
Schrader, Missy Wolgemuth & Schrader, Missy W. Hooray! I Obeyed! Nuffer, Bruce, ed. (p. 796)
Schrader, Racheal. Doodlebugs: Trouble On Moss Farm. Schrader, Racheal, illus. (p. 469)
Schraer, William D. Biology: Study of Life. (p. 189)
Schraff, jt. auth. see Schraff, Anne.
Schraff, Anne. Accuser (p. 8)
—And We Will Be No More. (p. 71)
—Black Widow Beauty (p. 197)
—Blackout (p. 197)
—Bluford 03: Secrets in the Shadows. (p. 204)
—Bluford 04: Someone to Love Me. (p. 204)
—Boy Called Twister (p. 217)
—Boy Called Twister. (p. 217)
—Burning of the Valley. (p. 244)
—Case of the Bad Seed (p. 273)
—Case of the Dead Duck (p. 274)
—Case of the Wanted Man (p. 275)
—Charles Drew: Pioneer in Medicine. (p. 292)
—Cold, Cold Shoulder (p. 338)
—Daredevil American Heroes of Exploration & Flight. (p. 406)
—Dark Secrets (p. 408)
—Darkest Secret. (p. 408)
—Dr. Charles Drew: Blood Bank Innovator. (p. 475)
—Experiment (p. 549)
—Facing It (p. 561)
—Fairest (p. 562)
—Fairest. (p. 562)
—Freedom Knows No Color. (p. 634)
—Ghost Mountain (p. 671)
—Gingerbread Heart. (p. 677)
—Going for Gold. (p. 692)
—Haunting of Hawthorne. (p. 754)
—Hero at Crow's Crossing (p. 772)
—Howling House. Miller, Fujiko, illus. (p. 824)
—Hunter (p. 828)
—Hurting Time (p. 830)
—Hyena Laughs at Night. (p. 831)
—I Am Underdog. (p. 834)
—If You Really Loved Me (p. 854)
—If You Really Loved Me. (p. 854)
—If You Were Mine (p. 855)
—Just Another Name for Lonely. (p. 937)
—Leap of Faith (p. 982)
—Life of Dr. Charles Drew: Blood Bank Innovator. (p. 1011)
—Life of Frederick Douglass: Speaking Out Against Slavery. (p. 1012)
—Life of Harriet Tubman: Moses of the Underground Railroad. (p. 1012)
—Like a Broken Doll (p. 1016)
—Like a Broken Doll. (p. 1016)
—Lost (p. 1054)
—Lost & Found. (p. 1054)
—Lost & Found. Langan, Paul, ed. (p. 1054)
—Marcus Garvey: Controversial Champion of Black Pride. (p. 1092)
—Matter of Trust. (p. 1109)
—Matter of Trust. Langan, Paul, ed. (p. 1109)
—Memories Are Forever. (p. 1126)
—No Fear (p. 1258)
—Once upon a Crime (p. 1292)
—One for Me (p. 1295)
—One of Us (p. 1296)
—One of Us. (p. 1296)
—Outrunning the Darkness (p. 1313)
—Outrunning the Darkness. (p. 1313)
—Petition. (p. 1348)
—Philippines. (p. 1350)
—Please Don't Ask Me to Love You. (p. 1373)
—Power of the Rose. (p. 1389)
—Price of Friendship. (p. 1398)
—Quality of Mercy (p. 1422)
—Quality of Mercy. (p. 1422)
—Roses Red as Blood (p. 1490)
—Second Chances (p. 1539)
—Secrets in the Shadows. (p. 1544)
—Secrets in the Shadows. Langan, Paul, ed. (p. 1544)
—Shadow Man. (p. 1557)
—Shadows of Guilt (p. 1558)
—Shadows of Guilt. (p. 1558)
—Shining Mark. (p. 1566)
—Something Dreadful down Below (p. 1609)
—Song to Sing. (p. 1611)
—Sounds of Terror (p. 1615)
—Stolen Treasure. (p. 1652)
—Stranger (p. 1665)
—Time of Courage (p. 1752)
—To Be a Man (p. 1758)
—To Be a Man. (p. 1758)
—To Be Somebody. (p. 1758)
—To Catch a Dream (p. 1758)
—Unbroken (p. 1811)
—Under the Mushroom Cloud. (p. 1813)
—Unforgiven (p. 1817)
—Until We Meet Again. (p. 1823)
—Urban Underground Class Set. (p. 1825)
—Urban Underground Complete Set. (p. 1825)
—Urban Underground Sample Set. Saddleback Educational Publishing Staff, ed. (p. 1825)
—Vandal. (p. 1833)
—Vengeance (p. 1835)
—Very Bad Dream (p. 1837)
—Walk in the Park (p. 1853)
—Waters Edge (p. 1864)
—Whatever Happened to Megan Marie? (p. 1896)
—Where's Dudley? (p. 1910)
—Wildflower (p. 1931)
—Wildflower. (p. 1931)
—Wilma Rudolph: The Greatest Woman Sprinter in History. (p. 1934)
—Winners & Losers (p. 1937)
Schraff, Anne, jt. auth. see Langan, Paul.
Schraff, Anne, jt. auth. see Schraff, Anne E.
Schraff, Anne & Schraff. Terrible Orchid Sky (p. 1721)
Schraff, Anne E. Bad Blood. (p. 131)
—Booker T. Washington: Character Is Power. (p. 212)
—Case of the Cursed Chalet (p. 274)
—Case of the Watery Grave (p. 275)
—Daredevil American Heroes of Exploration & Flight. (p. 406)
—Dark Suspicions (p. 408)
—Dark Suspicions. (p. 408)
—Deliverance (p. 425)
—Don't Think about Tomorrow. (p. 468)
—Ellen Ochoa: Astronaut & Inventor. (p. 514)
—Facing It. (p. 561)
—Guilt Trip. (p. 730)
—Hero at Crow's Crossing. (p. 772)
—Horse Called Courage (p. 799)
—Hurting Time. (p. 830)
—Ida B. Wells-Barnett: Strike a Blow Against Glaring Evil. (p. 851)
—If You Were Mine. (p. 855)
—I'll Be There. (p. 856)
—Jaime Escalante: Inspirational Math Teacher. (p. 905)
—John Brown: We Came to Free the Slaves. (p. 921)
—Life of Dr. Charles Drew: Blood Bank Innovator. (p. 1011)
—Life of Frederick Douglass: Speaking Out Against Slavery. (p. 1012)
—Martin Luther King, Jr: We Shall Overcome. (p. 1098)
—Misjudged. (p. 1150)
—One for Me. (p. 1295)
—Out of Love for You. (p. 1311)
—Outcasts. (p. 1312)
—Philippines. (p. 1350)
—Planet Doom (p. 1367)
—Rescuers. (p. 1462)
—Rosa Parks: Tired of Giving In. (p. 1489)
—Second Chances. (p. 1539)
—See No Evil. (p. 1547)
—Someone to Love Me. (p. 1609)
—To Die For. (p. 1758)
—Unbroken. (p. 1811)
—Up Rattler Mountain (p. 1824)
—Vengeance. (p. 1835)
—Walk in the Park. (p. 1853)
—When Sleeping Dogs Awaken (p. 1904)
—Who Has Seen the Beast? (p. 1915)
—Winners & Losers. (p. 1937)
Schraff, Anne E. & Schraff, Anne. Someone to Love Me. (p. 1609)
Schraffenberger, J. D. Saint Joe's Passion. (p. 1503)
Schram, Kristina. Chronicles of Anaedor: The Uprising. (p. 317)
—Chronicles of Anaedor: The Lost Ones. (p. 317)
—Chronicles of Anaedor. (p. 317)
Schram, Peninnah. Chanukah Blessing. Allon, Jeffrey, illus. (p. 291)
—Magic Pomegranate: A Jewish Folktale. Hall, Melanie, illus. (p. 1073)
—Magic Pomegranate. Hall, Melanie, illus. (p. 1073)
—Purim Costume. Keiser, Tammy L., illus. (p. 1419)
Schram, Peninnah, jt. auth. see Oren, Miriam.
Schram, Peninnah & Davis, Rachayl Eckstein. Apple Tree's Discovery. Lee, Wendy W., illus. (p. 92)
Schram, Peninnah, comment. Solomon & the Ant: And Other Jewish Folktales. (p. 1608)
Schram, Ruth Elaine, et al. Sing & Celebrate 2! Sacred Songs for Young Voices. (p. 1579)
Schram, Scott. Last Noel: A Christmas Musical for Children. (p. 978)
—Last Noel, Director's Score: A Christmas Musical for Children. (p. 978)
Schramm, Linda Anette. Don't Let the Ziglers into the Zoo! (p. 468)
Schrantz, Joseph. Do Whatever He Tells You. (p. 457)
Schrantz, Joseph A. Three Gods. (p. 1742)
Schrecengost, Maity. High above the Hippodrome. (p. 777)
Schreck, Bob. Redemption (p. 1455)
Schreck, Karen Haluorsen. While He Was Away. (p. 1911)
Schreck, Karen Halvorsen. Lucy's Family Tree Gassler, Stephen, III, illus. (p. 1063)
Schreck, Tabatha M. Welcome to God's Big Backyard: Little Mouse's Adventure. (p. 1873)
Schrefer, Eliot. Deadly Sister. (p. 418)
—Endangered. (p. 526)
—Fall of the Beasts (p. 566)
—Rise & Fall. (p. 1474)
—School for Dangerous Girls. (p. 1522)
—Threatened. (p. 1741)
Schreiber, Angela, jt. auth. see Mitchell, Joan.
Schreiber, Ann. Twister Trouble. Speirs, John, illus. (p. 1803)
Schreiber, Anne. National Geographic Readers: Monkeys. (p. 1233)
—Pandas. (p. 1321)
—Penguins! (p. 1337)
—Sharks! (p. 1562)
—Volcanoes! (p. 1849)
Schreiber, Anne, et al. National Geographic Readers: Cutest Animals Collection. (p. 1233)
Schreiber, Elisheva. Miniature Puppet Theater Book. Pollack, Gadi & Markovitch, Evegeny, illus. (p. 1146)
Schreiber, Ellen. Coffin Club. (p. 338)
—Cryptic Cravings. (p. 387)
—Dance with a Vampire. (p. 402)
—Full Moon Kisses. (p. 646)
—Graveyard Games Xian Nu Studio, illus. (p. 712)
—Immortal Hearts. (p. 861)
—Kissing Coffins. (p. 962)
—Love Bites. (p. 1059)
—Magic of the Moonlight. (p. 1073)
—Once in a Full Moon. (p. 1292)
—Royal Blood No. 6. (p. 1492)
—Teenage Mermaid. (p. 1714)
—Vampire Kisses: Finstere Sehnsucht. (p. 1832)
—Vampire Kisses: Finstere Sehnsucht / Dunkle Ahnung / Düsteres Versprechen. (p. 1832)
—Vampire Kisses. (p. 1832)
—Vampire Kisses - Blood Relatives Rem, illus. (p. 1832)
—Vampire Kisses - Blood Relatives Kwon, Elisa & Rem, illus. (p. 1832)
—Vampire Kisses Boxed Set: Vampire Kisses; Kissing Coffins; Vampireville. (p. 1832)
—Vampire Kisses - Kissing Coffins. (p. 1832)
—Vampire Kisses - The Beginning. (p. 1832)
—Vampireville. (p. 1832)
Schreiber, Flora Rheta. Sybil. (p. 1692)
Schreiber, Hannah & Hartsock, Conner. One in a Buzzillion. Foster, Jack, illus. (p. 1295)
Schreiber, Joe. Au Revoir, Crazy European Chick. (p. 114)
—Con Academy. (p. 355)
—Game over, Pete Watson. Rash, Andy, illus. (p. 654)
—Lenny Cyrus, School Virus. Smith, Matt, illus. (p. 991)
—Perry's Killer Playlist. (p. 1344)
Schreiber, Sam. Raise Your Voice. (p. 1436)
Schreiber, Sophia. Greek Thought. Miller, Zachary N., ed. (p. 721)
Schreiber-Wicke, Edith. Cuando Decir No. (p. 388)
—Cuidado! Palabra Terrible! (Careful! Terrible Word!) (p. 390)
Schreier, Alta. Cuba. (p. 388)
Schreier, Carl. Cookie Book. (p. 361)
Schreiner, Paul B., jt. auth. see Saufley, Ted.
Schrewe, Suzanne. Hello Little Snowflake: A Christmas Miracle. (p. 764)
Schrey, Sophie, ed. see Carter, Andrew.
Schrey, Sophie & Buster Books Staff. I Love Louis. Schrey, Sophie, illus. (p. 842)
Schreyer. Empress Blaze Moon: A Story. (p. 521)
Schreyer, Karmel. Bounce! The Wonderful World of Rubber. (p. 216)
—Tragedy on the Slopes. (p. 1776)
Schriemer, Peter, jt. auth. see Zondervan.
Schrier, Alfred, illus. see McHugh, Erin.
Schrier, Allyson Valentine. Eat Right: Your Guide to Maintaining a Healthy Diet (p. 501)
—Fast as a Cheetah, Slow as a Sloth. (p. 576)
—First in Line. (p. 595)
—Gaming Safely (p. 655)
—Girl's Guide to Basketball (p. 680)
—Girl's Guide to Soccer (p. 680)
—How Many Baby Animals? (p. 811)
—How Many in All? (p. 811)
—Is It Heavier Than an Elephant? (p. 889)
Schrier, Allyson Valentine, et al. Get in the Game. (p. 667)
—Healthy Me. (p. 758)
—Tech Safety Smarts. (p. 1711)
Schrock, Cynthia. Ultimate Gift of a Birthday. (p. 1809)
Schrocke, Kathrin. Freak City. Tammi Reichel, tr. (p. 631)
—Freak City. Reichel, Tammi, tr. from GER. (p. 631)
Schroder, Fred. Run for the Money. (p. 1496)
Schroder, Jack. Dugout. (p. 489)
—Fun Day at the Beach. (p. 647)
Schroder, Jennifer Michaels. Fish Food: Skimmer Catches His Spirit. (p. 598)
Schroder, Mark, illus. see Krensky, Stephen.
Schroder, Mark, illus. see Nelson, Vaunda Micheaux & Nelson, Drew.
Schroder, Mark, illus. see Wadsworth, Ginger.
Schröder, Monika. Dog in the Wood. (p. 461)
Schroedel, Jenny. Blackbird's Nest: Saint Kevin of Ireland. Montross, Doug, illus. (p. 197)
Schroeder, Abraham. Too Many Tables. Chambers-Goldberg, Micah & Monkey, Micah, illus. (p. 1767)
Schroeder, Alan. Abe Lincoln: His Wit & Wisdom from A to Z. O'Brien, John, illus. (p. 4)
—Baby Flo: Florence Mills Lights up the Stage. Van Wright, Cornelius & Hu, Ying-Hwa, illus. (p. 126)
—Ben Franklin: His Wit & Wisdom from A-Z. O'Brien, John, illus. (p. 163)
—Ben Franklin: His Wit & Wisdom from A to Z. O'Brien, John, illus. (p. 163)
—Booker T. Washington: Educator & Racial Spokesman. (p. 212)

—In Her Hands: The Story of Sculptor Augusta Savage. Bereal, JaeMe, illus. (p. 863)
—Over the Falls with Granny. (p. 1314)
Schroeder, Alan & Wagner, Heather Lehr. Josephine Baker: Entertainer. (p. 926)
Schroeder, Andreas. Duped! True Stories of the World's Best Swindlers. Simard, Remy, illus. (p. 490)
—Robbers! True Stories of the World's Most Notorious Thieves. Simard, Remy, illus. (p. 1478)
—Scams! (p. 1519)
—Thieves! (p. 1732)
Schroeder, Binette. Sir Lofty & Sir Tubb. Schroeder, Binette, illus. (p. 1580)
Schroeder, Binette, illus. see Grimm, J. & W. & Grimm, J.
Schroeder, Binnette, illus. see Kipling, Rudyard.
Schroeder, Brock E. Ecstasy. (p. 503)
Schroeder, Doris. Annie Oakley in the Ghost Town Secret. Sgroi, Tony, illus. (p. 87)
Schroeder, Doug. Does the Bunny Lay Easter Eggs. (p. 460)
Schroeder, Erin. Oh no! it's the helpful hound... & the days of the Week. (p. 1281)
Schroeder, Frauna. Elwood: A Dog with Heart. Carlson, Kim, illus. (p. 517)
Schroeder, Heather Lee. Reader's Guide to Marjane Satrapi's Persepolis. (p. 1444)
Schroeder, Holly. Israel ABCs: A Book about the People & Places of Israel. Wolf, Claudia, illus. (p. 893)
—New Zealand ABCs: A Book about the People & Places of New Zealand. Wolf, Claudia, illus. (p. 1249)
—United States ABCs: A Book about the People & Places of the United States. Yesh, Jeff, illus. (p. 1819)
Schroeder, Judith, ed. see Swallow, Pamela C.
Schroeder, Judith, ed. see Swallow, Pamela Curtis.
Schroeder, Lisa. All We Have Is Now. (p. 46)
—Bridge from Me to You. (p. 227)
—Caitlin's Lucky Charm. (p. 252)
—Charmed Life #1: Caitlin's Lucky Charm. (p. 294)
—Charmed Life #2: Mia's Golden Bird. (p. 294)
—Charmed Life #3: Libby's Sweet Surprise. (p. 294)
—Charmed Life #4: Hannah's Bright Star. (p. 294)
—Chasing Brooklyn. (p. 294)
—Day Before. (p. 412)
—Falling for You. (p. 566)
—Far from You. (p. 572)
—Frosting & Friendship. (p. 645)
—I Heart You, You Haunt Me. (p. 839)
—It's Raining Cupcakes. (p. 898)
—Libby's Sweet Surprise. (p. 1005)
—Mia's Golden Bird. (p. 1134)
—My Secret Guide to Paris. (p. 1218)
—Sprinkles & Secrets. (p. 1635)
Schroeder, Lisa & Dion, Nathalie. Sprinkles & Secrets. (p. 1635)
Schroeder, Louise, illus. see Malnor, Carol & Fuller, Sandy F.
Schroeder, Louise, illus. see Malnor, Carol L. & Fuller, Sandy F.
Schroeder, Niels Olaf. Berlin Brain Odyssee - a trip into the Brain. (p. 167)
Schroeder, Patrick & Maria, ed. see Wickman, Don.
Schroeder, Peter W. & Schroeder-Hildebrand, Dagmar. Six Million Paper Clips: The Making of a Children's Holocaust Memorial. (p. 1582)
Schroeder-Hildebrand, Dagmar, jt. auth. see Schroeder, Peter W.
Schroeder-Lein, Glenna R. Encyclopedia of Civil War Medicine. (p. 525)
Schroeppel, John. Power of Proverbs: A Daily Devotional Guide for young Adults. (p. 1389)
Schroeter, Chloe. Sharks. (p. 1562)
—Why Why Why... Are Sharks so Scary? (p. 1926)
—Why Why Why... Were Mammoths Wooly? (p. 1926)
Schroff, Laura & Tresniowski, Alex. Invisible Thread Christmas Story: A True Story Based on the New York Times Bestseller. Root, Barry, illus. (p. 886)
Schrom, Garren, illus. see Lacy, Sandy Allbee.
Schronk, Julie. Grass Grows Green. (p. 711)
Schrotter, Gustav, illus. see Sootin, Harry.
Schrowang, Irene. Sam & Joey's Pirate Ship Adventure. (p. 1506)
Schrum, Kelly. Some Wore Bobby Sox: The Emergence of Teenage Girls' Culture, 1920-1945. (p. 1609)
Schubach, Alanna & Pecsenye, Jessica. American University College Prowler off the Record. (p. 63)
Schubert, Barbara. George Washington. (p. 664)
Schubert, Charles, jt. auth. see Soni, Jaymee.
Schubert, Dieter. Opposites. Schubert, Dieter, illus. (p. 1300)
—Umbrella. (p. 1810)
—Umbrella Doodle Book. (p. 1810)
Schubert, Dieter, jt. auth. see Schubert, Ingrid.
Schubert, Ingrid & Schubert, Dieter. Elephant Soup. (p. 511)
—Hammer Soup. (p. 739)
—Like People. (p. 1017)
—My Hero. (p. 1211)
—Ophelia. (p. 1300)
Schubert, Jan. Sun Seed. Schubert, Jan, illus. (p. 1676)
Schubert, Karin, illus. see Alonso, Manuel L.
Schubert, Leda. Feeding the Sheep. U'Ren, Andrea, illus. (p. 580)
—Monsieur Marceau: Actor Without Words. Dubois, Gérard, illus. (p. 1166)
—Reading to Peanut. Haley, Amanda, illus. (p. 1446)
Schuck, Jenna, photos by see Skinner, Tina.
Schuck, Philip. Ricochet from Circumstance. (p. 1470)
Schudel, Matt, jt. auth. see Schulke, Flip.
Schueler, Donald G. Gopher Tortoise: A MyReportLinks.com Book. (p. 702)
Schueler, M. A. Penny the Beach Westie Big Trouble for a Little Dog. (p. 1338)
Schueller, Gretel. Rivers, Lakes, & Oceans. (p. 1476)
Schueller, Gretel H. Cnidarians: Jellyfish, Corals, Sea Anemones, & Their Relatives. (p. 336)
Schueller, Gretel H. & Schueller, Sheila K. Animal Migration. (p. 78)
Schueller, Sheila K., jt. auth. see Schueller, Gretel H.
Schuelmann, Bettina, jt. auth. see Wenzel, Angela.
Schuepbach, Lynnette. Cat Time. (p. 278)
—Froggy Hollow. Schuepbach, Lynnette, illus. (p. 641)
—Shhhh!!! Schuepbach, Lynnette, illus. (p. 1566)
Schuepbach, Lynnette, illus. see Dwyer, Cynthia.
Schuerger, Andrew, jt. auth. see Leedy, Loreen.
Schuett, Stacey, illus. see Ashford, Jeron.
Schuett, Stacey, illus. see Borden, Louise.
Schuett, Stacey, illus. see Brown, Barbara.
Schuett, Stacey, illus. see Creech, Sharon.
Schuett, Stacey, illus. see Edwards, Michelle.
Schuett, Stacey, illus. see Hopkins, Lee Bennett.
Schuett, Stacey, illus. see Katz, Susan.
Schuett, Stacey, illus. see Levinson, Nancy Smiler.
Schuett, Stacey, illus. see McCain, Becky Ray.
Schuett, Stacey, illus. see Miller, Debbie S.
Schuett, Stacey, illus. see Murphy, Claire Rudolf.
Schuett, Stacey, illus. see Silverman, Erica.
Schuett, Stacey, illus. see Sklansky, Amy.
Schuett, Stacey, illus. see Smucker, Anna.
Schuett, Stacey, illus. see Williams, Rozanne Lanczak.
Schuett, Stacey, illus. see Wong, Janet S.
Schuett, Stacey, illus. see Younger, Barbara.
Schuette, Eva. Kingdom of the Wild Gootsies: Meet the Wild Gootsies. (p. 960)
Schuette, Leslie Elaine. Adventures of Little Autumn. Walker, Bradley, illus. (p. 19)
—Adventures of Little Autumn. Walker, Bradley, illus. (p. 19)
—Kristina's Shoes. (p. 967)
—Little Autumn's Adventure in the Smoky Mountains. (p. 1023)
Schuette, Sarah L. 100th Day: A Spot-It Challenge (p. 1999)
—3, 2, 1 Go! A Transportation Countdown. (p. 1991)
—3, 2, 1 ¡Vamos!/3, 2, 1, Go! Contemos Hacia Atrás Usando el Transporte. (p. 1991)
—Adoptive Families (p. 13)
—Alphabet Salad: Fruits & Vegetables from A to Z. (p. 50)
—Animal Fun. (p. 78)
—Animals Everywhere: A Spot-It Challenge (p. 82)
—Ballerina Cookbook: Simple Recipes for Kids (p. 134)
—Birthday Cakes (p. 192)
—Birthday Customs Around the World (p. 192)
—Birthday Parties & Celebrations (p. 193)
—Birthday Party Games (p. 199)
—Blended Families (p. 199)
—Character Values. (p. 291)
—Character Values Bilingual. Saunders-Smith, Gail, ed. (p. 291)
—Christmas Cookbook: Simple Recipes for Kids (p. 313)
—Círculos: Círculos a Nuestro Alrededor. (p. 322)
—Color Camouflage: A Spot-It Challenge (p. 342)
—Colors & Patterns! A Spot-It, Learn-It Challenge (p. 345)
—Communities (p. 349)
—Cuadrados: Cuadrados a Nuestro Alrededor. (p. 388)
—Dinosaur Cookbook: Simple Recipes for Kids (p. 441)
—Downhill BMX (p. 474)
—Eating Pairs: Counting Fruits & Vegetables by Twos (p. 501)
—Eating Pairs (Comer Pares) Counting Fruits & Vegetables by Two (Contar Frutas y Vegetales de DOS en DOS) (p. 501)
—Families (p. 567)
—Figuras Geométricas/Shapes. (p. 586)
—First Cookbooks (p. 594)
—First Cookbooks. (p. 594)
—Football Cookbook: Simple Recipes for Kids (p. 615)
—Football Frenzy (p. 615)
—Football Frenzy: A Spot-It Challenge (p. 615)
—Formula One Cars (p. 620)
—Foster Families (p. 624)
—Garrett Morgan (p. 657)
—Halloween Cookbook: Simple Recipes for Kids (p. 737)
—Halloween Hunt: A Spot-It Challenge (p. 737)
—Happy Birthday! A Spot-It Challenge (p. 744)
—Hockey Scramble: A Spot-It Challenge (p. 786)
—How to Carve Freakishly Cool Pumpkins (p. 815)
—I Am Friendly (p. 833)
—I Am Generous Saunders-Smith, Gail, ed. (p. 833)
—I Am Patient Saunders-Smith, Gail, ed. (p. 833)
—I Am Patriotic (p. 833)
—I Am Polite (p. 833)
—I Have Self-Respect (p. 839)
—I Have Self-Respect Saunders-Smith, Gail, ed. (p. 839)
—Let's Look at Winter Saunders-Smith, Gail, ed. (p. 999)
—Loads of Letters! A Spot-It, Learn-It Challenge. (p. 1044)
—Milton Hershey (p. 1144)
—Monster Cookbook: Simple Recipes for Kids (p. 1167)
—Morado: Mira el Morado Que Te Rodea. (p. 1173)
—Mountain Biking (p. 1180)
—My Family (p. 1202)
—Pets All Around: A Spot-It Challenge (p. 1348)
—Pirate Cookbook: Simple Recipes for Kids (p. 1362)
—Princess Cookbook: Simple Recipes for Kids (p. 1403)
—Princesses & Fairy Tales: A Spot-It Challenge (p. 1406)
—Rectángulos: Rectángulos a Nuestro Alrededor. (p. 1452)
—Réctangulos: Rectángulos a Nuestro Alrededor. (p. 1452)
—Science Fun: A Spot-It Challenge (p. 1526)
—Season Search: A Spot-It Challenge (p. 1538)
—Single-Parent Families (p. 1579)
—So Many Shapes! (p. 1602)
—So Many Shapes! A Spot-It, Learn-It Challenge (p. 1602)
—Sports Zone: A Spot-It Challenge (p. 1633)
—Spot It. (p. 1633)
—Spot It, Learn It! (p. 1633)
—Superhero Cookbook: Simple Recipes for Kids (p. 1683)
—Taking Care of My Ears (p. 1698)
—Tons of Numbers! A Spot-It, Learn-It Challenge. (p. 1765)
—Triángulos: Triángulos a Nuestro Alrededor. (p. 1785)
—Tuner Cars (p. 1796)
—Veamos el Invierno. (p. 1834)
—Veamos el Otono. (p. 1834)
—Veamos el Verano. (p. 1834)
—Veamos la Primavera. (p. 1834)
—Wallace Famous Amos (p. 1855)
Schuette, Sarah L., jt. auth. see Knox, Barbara.
Schuette, Sarah L. & Capstone Press Editors. Hot Rods (p. 802)
—Let's Look at Fall Saunders-Smith, Gail, ed. (p. 998)
Schuette, Sarah L. & Capstone Press Staff. Cómo Cuidar Mis Oídos. Saunders-Smith, Gail, ed. (p. 350)
—Let's Look at Spring Saunders-Smith, Gail, ed. (p. 999)
—Let's Look at Summer Saunders-Smith, Gail, ed. (p. 999)
—Motocicletas Harley-Davidson/Harley-Davidson Motorcycles (p. 1179)
Schuette, Sarah L. & Davis, Rebecca F. Counting Books (Vamos a Contar) (p. 370)
—Vamos a Contar / Counting Books. (p. 1831)
Schuette, Sarah L. & Marks, Jennifer L. Spot It. (p. 1633)
Schuette, Sarah L., et al. Great African-Americans (p. 713)
Schuetz, Kar. Scorpions. (p. 1530)
Schuetz, Kari. African Elephants. (p. 27)
—Amphibians. (p. 65)
—Argentina. (p. 97)
—Armadillos. (p. 99)
—Baby Bears. (p. 125)
—Baby Cows. (p. 125)
—Baby Dogs. (p. 125)
—Baby Goats. (p. 126)
—Baby Monkeys. (p. 127)
—Baby Penguins. (p. 127)
—Baby Sloths. (p. 128)
—Bats. (p. 144)
—Birds. (p. 191)
—Caring for Your Fish. (p. 269)
—Centipedes. (p. 287)
—Charles Schulz. (p. 292)
—Dr. Seuss. (p. 475)
—Eagles. (p. 492)
—Fire Ants. (p. 590)
—Fish. (p. 598)
—Giant Pandas. (p. 674)
—Giraffes. (p. 677)
—Guatemala. (p. 728)
—Hawks. (p. 755)
—Hedgehogs. (p. 762)
—Hippopotamuses. (p. 781)
—Hissing Cockroaches. (p. 781)
—Hyenas. (p. 831)
—Insects. (p. 875)
—Kangaroos. (p. 942)
—Karate. (p. 943)
—Koalas. (p. 966)
—Lemurs. (p. 991)
—Mammals. (p. 1085)
—Mealworms. (p. 1116)
—Meerkats. (p. 1120)
—Millipedes. (p. 1144)
—Ostriches. (p. 1306)
—Owls. (p. 1315)
—Portugal. (p. 1387)
—Reptiles. (p. 1461)
—Rhinoceroses. (p. 1467)
—Tarantulas. (p. 1706)
—Termites. (p. 1721)
—Toads. (p. 1760)
—Venezuela. (p. 1835)
—Woodpeckers. (p. 1949)
Schuetz, Kristin. Cloud Cover. (p. 334)
—Forecasts. (p. 617)
—Humidity. (p. 826)
—Moose. (p. 1173)
—Mountain Lions. (p. 1181)
—Prairie Dogs. (p. 1392)
—Precipitation. (p. 1394)
—Severe Weather. (p. 1555)
—South Carolina. (p. 1616)
—Temperature. (p. 1717)
—Wild Turkeys. (p. 1930)
Schuetz, Rachael Law. Long Road to Change: An American Story of Civil Rights & Barack Obama's Journey to the White House. (p. 1047)
Schuff, Nicolás & Fraticelli, Damin. Ana y la Maldicion de Las Pecas. Mey, illus. (p. 66)
Schuh, Eileen. Traz. (p. 1781)
Schuh, Leesa, jt. auth. see Gilbert, Keith.
Schuh, Mari. Aaron Rodgers. (p. 2)
—Aircraft. (p. 31)
—All about Matter (p. 42)
—All Kinds of Gardens (p. 45)
—All Kinds of Gardens [Scholastic]. (p. 45)
—Animals in Fall. (p. 83)
—Animals in the Garden (p. 83)
—Animals in the Garden [Scholastic]. (p. 83)
—Anteaters. (p. 89)
—Ants. (p. 90)
—Apples Grow on a Tree (p. 93)
—Apples in Fall. (p. 93)
—Backyard Animals. (p. 130)
—Beagles. (p. 150)
—Beavers. (p. 155)
—Beetles. (p. 158)
—Blueberries Grow on a Bush (p. 203)
—Butterflies. (p. 247)
—Camels. (p. 256)
—Carrots Grow Underground (p. 271)
—Cicadas. (p. 318)
—Cockroaches. (p. 337)
—Compost Basics (p. 354)
—Counting Money. (p. 371)
—Crickets. (p. 382)
—Dachshunds. (p. 398)
—Dairy on Myplate (p. 400)
—Earning Money. (p. 494)
—Electricity. (p. 509)
—Fireflies. (p. 592)
—French Bulldogs. (p. 635)
—Fruits on Myplate (p. 646)
—German Shepherds. (p. 666)
—Get Moving! (p. 667)
—Glaciers (p. 682)
—Golden Retrievers. (p. 695)
—Grains on Myplate (p. 706)
—Grasshoppers. (p. 711)
—Growing a Garden. (p. 726)
—Growing a Garden [Scholastic]. (p. 726)
—Harvest in Fall. (p. 751)
—Healthy Snacks on Myplate (p. 759)
—Honeybees. (p. 794)
—Hot Air Balloons (p. 801)
—Jet Planes (p. 916)
—Kangaroos. (p. 942)
—Labrador Retrievers. (p. 970)
—Ladybugs. (p. 971)
—Leaves in Fall. (p. 986)
—Lettuce Grows on the Ground (p. 1003)
—Light. (p. 1014)
—Magnetism. (p. 1075)
—Manatees. (p. 1086)
—Mira Dentro de Una Cabaña. (p. 1148)
—Mira Dentro/Look Inside. (p. 1148)
—Mosquitoes. (p. 1176)
—Moths. (p. 1179)
—Poodles. (p. 1383)
—Praying Mantises. (p. 1393)
—Protein on Myplate (p. 1412)
—Pufferfish. (p. 1415)
—Pumpkins in Fall. (p. 1416)
—Saving Money. (p. 1517)
—Sea Life. (p. 1534)
—Sea Otters. (p. 1535)
—Sea Slugs. (p. 1535)
—Seaplanes (p. 1537)
—Sense of Hearing. (p. 1551)
—Sense of Sight. (p. 1551)
—Sense of Smell. (p. 1551)
—Sense of Taste. (p. 1551)
—Sense of Touch. (p. 1551)
—Show Me Insects: My First Picture Encyclopedia (p. 1570)
—Show Me Transportation: My First Picture Encyclopedia (p. 1570)
—Soil Basics (p. 1606)
—Special Diets (p. 1623)
—Spending Money. (p. 1625)
—Squids. (p. 1637)
—Stars of Baseball (p. 1643)
—Stars of Football (p. 1643)
—Stink Bugs. (p. 1651)
—Sugars & Fats (p. 1673)
—Termites. (p. 1721)
—Tomatoes Grow on a Vine (p. 1764)
—Tools for the Garden (p. 1767)
—Tools for the Garden [Scholastic]. (p. 1767)
—Troy Polamalu. (p. 1790)
—Types of Money. (p. 1805)
—U. S. Government. (p. 1806)
—Vegetables on Myplate (p. 1834)
—Walkingsticks. (p. 1854)
—Wasps. (p. 1860)
—Waterfalls (p. 1863)
—Weather in Fall. (p. 1870)
—What's on Myplate? (p. 1899)
—Yorkshire Terriers. (p. 1972)
Schuh, Mari, jt. auth. see Doeden, Matt.
Schuh, Mari, jt. auth. see Marx, Mandy R.
Schuh, Mari, jt. auth. see Schuh, Mari C.
Schuh, Mari & Alpert, Barbara. Science Builders. (p. 1525)
Schuh, Mari & Schuh, Mari C. All Kinds of Gardens (p. 45)
—Growing a Garden (p. 726)
Schuh, Mari C. All about Matter (p. 42)
—All about Teeth Saunders-Smith, Gail, ed. (p. 43)
—Antojitos para Dientes Sanos. (p. 89)
—Apples Grow on a Tree (p. 93)
—Assistance Dogs (p. 107)
—At the Dentist Saunders-Smith, Gail, ed. (p. 111)
—Avalanches (p. 118)
—Blueberries Grow on a Bush (p. 203)
—Brushing Teeth Saunders-Smith, Gail, ed. (p. 233)
—Butterflies. (p. 247)
—Carrots Grow Underground (p. 271)
—Cats on the Farm (p. 281)
—Chipmunks. (p. 308)
—Clown Fish. (p. 335)
—Compost Basics. (p. 354)
—Dairy on Myplate (p. 400)
—Dairy-Free Diets (p. 400)
—Diabetes-Aware Diets (p. 433)
—Diente Está Flojo. Guzman Ferrer, Martin Luis, tr. from ENG. (p. 437)
—Dragonflies. (p. 478)
—Ducks on the Farm (p. 488)
—Earthquakes (p. 497)
—Earthquakes [Scholastic]. (p. 498)
—Electricity. (p. 509)
—Fire Safety in Action (p. 590)
—Fire Stations in Action (p. 591)
—Fire Trucks in Action (p. 591)
—Fireboats in Action (p. 591)
—Flossing Teeth Saunders-Smith, Gail, ed. (p. 607)
—Full Speed Ahead: The Science of Going Fast. (p. 646)
—Geese on the Farm (p. 659)
—Get Moving! (p. 667)
—Gluten-Free Diets (p. 685)
—Going Ice Fishing: Lever vs. Screw. (p. 692)
—Grains on Myplate (p. 706)
—Growing a Garden (p. 726)
—Hang Gliders (p. 742)
—Hauling a Pumpkin: Wheels & Axles vs. Lever. (p. 753)
—Healthy Snacks on Myplate (p. 759)
—Holding a Door Open: Wedge vs. Wheels & Axles. (p. 788)
—How Fruits & Vegetables Grow (p. 809)
—Huracanes. Translation Services Staff & Translations.com Staff, trs. from ENG. (p. 829)
—Hurricanes (p. 830)
—Hurricanes [Scholastic]. (p. 830)
—Jellyfish. (p. 912)
—K-9 Police Dogs (p. 941)
—Learning about Rocks (p. 984)

—Let's Find Ads in Magazines. (p. 996)
—Let's Find Ads on Clothing. (p. 996)
—Let's Find Ads on the Internet. (p. 996)
—Let's Find Ads on TV. (p. 996)
—Lettuce Grows on the Ground (p. 1003)
—Look Inside a Log Cabin (p. 1049)
—Look Inside a Pyramid (p. 1049)
—Look Inside a Tepee (p. 1049)
—Look Inside an Igloo (p. 1049)
—Loose Tooth Saunders-Smith, Gail, ed. (p. 1052)
—Making a Salad: Wedge vs. Inclined Plane. (p. 1080)
—Meet a Baby Chimpanzee. (p. 1120)
—Milk Group (p. 1143)
—Mira Dentro de un Iglú. (p. 1148)
—Mira Dentro de una Pirámide. (p. 1148)
—Nut-Free Diets (p. 1273)
—On the Farm. (p. 1290)
—Perros de Ayuda. (p. 1344)
—Perros Policías (K-9 Police Dogs) (p. 1344)
—Playing a Game: Inclined Plane vs. Lever. (p. 1372)
—Protein on Myplate (p. 1412)
—Proteínas en MiPlato. Strictly Spanish LLC. Staff, tr. (p. 1412)
—Rabbits. (p. 1430)
—Raccoons. (p. 1430)
—Raising a Bag of Toys: Pulley vs. Inclined Plane. (p. 1437)
—Regal Tangs. (p. 1457)
—Sea Stars. (p. 1535)
—Search & Rescue Dogs (p. 1537)
—Show Me Transportation: My First Picture Encyclopedia (p. 1570)
—Sloths (p. 1591)
—Snacks for Healthy Teeth Saunders-Smith, Gail, ed. (p. 1595)
—Soil Basics. (p. 1606)
—Squirrels. (p. 1637)
—Stars of Stock Car Racing (p. 1643)
—Sugars & Fats (p. 1673)
—Termites (p. 1721)
—Terremotos. Translations.com Staff, tr. from ENG. (p. 1721)
—Todo Sobre los Dientes. Guzman Ferrer, Martin Luis, tr. from ENG. (p. 1761)
—Tomatoes Grow on a Vine (p. 1764)
—Tornadoes (p. 1770)
—Tornadoes [Scholastic]. (p. 1770)
—Tsunamis (p. 1795)
—Tsunamis [Scholastic]. (p. 1795)
—U. S. House of Representatives (p. 1806)
—U. S. Presidency (p. 1807)
—U. S. Senate (p. 1807)
—Uso del Hilo Dental. (p. 1829)
—Vamos al Dentista. (p. 1831)
—Vegetables on Myplate (p. 1834)
—Volcanoes (p. 1849)
—Volcanoes. Translation Services Staff & Translations.com Staff, trs. from ENG. (p. 1849)
—Waterfalls (p. 1863)
—¡Muévete! Strictly Spanish LLC. Staff, tr. from ENG. (p. 1189)
Schuh, Mari C., jt. auth. see Frost, Helen.
Schuh, Mari C., jt. auth. see Schuh, Mari.
Schuh, Mari C. & Adamson, Heather. My World. (p. 1221)
Schuh, Mari C. & Leavitt, Amie Jane. Declaration of Independence in Translation: What It Really Means (p. 422)
Schuh, Mari C. & Olson, Kay Melchisedech. Gettysburg Address in Translation: What It Really Means (p. 670)
Schuh, Mari C. & Raum, Elizabeth. Pledge of Allegiance in Translation: What It Really Means (p. 1374)
—Star-Spangled Banner in Translation: What It Really Means. (p. 1641)
Schuh, Mari C. & Schuh, Mari. Agua Potable. (p. 30)
—All about Teeth Saunders-Smith, Gail, ed. (p. 43)
—Being Active Saunders-Smith, Gail, ed. (p. 161)
—Cats on the Farm. (p. 281)
—Drinking Water (p. 485)
—Ducks on the Farm (p. 488)
—Fruit Group (p. 645)
—Grain Group (p. 705)
—Grupo de la Leche. (p. 728)
—Grupo de las Carnes y los Frijoles. (p. 728)
—Grupo de las Frutas. (p. 728)
—Grupo de las Verduras. Guzman Ferrer, Martin Luis, tr. from ENG. (p. 728)
—Grupo de los Cereales. (p. 728)
—Healthy Snacks (p. 759)
—In My Home. (p. 864)
—In My Neighborhood (p. 864)
—In My State. (p. 864)
—In My Town (p. 864)
—Labor Day. (p. 969)
—Mantenerse Activo. (p. 1088)
—Meat & Beans Group (p. 1118)
—Meriendas Saludables. Guzman Ferrer, Martin Luis, tr. from ENG. (p. 1127)
—National Holidays (p. 1233)
—On the Farm (p. 1290)
Schujer, Silvia. Palabras para Jugar (Word Play) (p. 1319)
Schulbaum, Michael, illus. see Singh, Rajinder.
Schuldt, Lori Meek. Martin Luther King, Jr: With Profiles of Mohandas K. Gandhi & Nelson Mandela. (p. 1098)
Schuler, Betty Jo. Brainman & Double Trouble Ditto Box. Cummins, Sandy, ed. (p. 222)
Schuler, Christoph. Kiki. Eisenring, Rahel Nicole, illus. (p. 955)
Schuler, Harold H. Fort Sisseton. (p. 623)
Schuler, Kimberly B. I Will Remember You: My Catholic Guide Through Grief. (p. 848)
Schuler, Lou & King, Ian. World's Most Authoritative Guide to Building Your Body. (p. 1960)
Schuler, Marilyn. Big Day for Jack. (p. 180)
—Giraffes on a Cruise. (p. 678)
—Lions' Silent Night: Animals of the Bible Book. (p. 1021)
—Mia's Night Adventure. (p. 1134)
—Ravens' Mission. (p. 1441)
Schuler, Stanley. Architectural Details from Victorian Homes (p. 95)
Schuler, Susan, tr. see Stoker, Bram.
Schulke, Flip & Schudel, Matt. Witness to Our Times: My Life As a Photojournalist. (p. 1942)
Schulkers, Robert. Stormie the Dog Stealer: Seckatary Hawkins. (p. 1656)
Schulkins, Laura. Happy to be Mia. (p. 747)
Schuller, Kathleen. How to Be a Hero - for Boys: Inspiration from Classic Heroes. (p. 814)
—How to Be a Heroine-For Girls: Inspiration from Classic Heroines. Bailey, Melissa, illus. (p. 814)
—How to Be a Heroine—For Girls: Inspiration from Classic Heroines. (p. 814)
Schuller, Robert H. Dr. Robert Schuller's Children's Daily Devotional Bible: With Positive Thoughts for Each Day. (p. 475)
Schuller, Sheldon V., jt. auth. see Pennington, Norma C.
Schulman, Bruce J. Lyndon B. Johnson & American Liberalism: A Brief Biography with Documents. (p. 1066)
Schulman, Janet. 10 Easter Egg Hunters: A Holiday Counting Book. Davick, Linda, illus. (p. 1993)
—10 Easter Egg Hunters. (p. 1993)
—10 Trick-or-Treaters: A Halloween Counting Book. Davick, Linda, illus. (p. 1994)
—10 Trim-the-Tree'ers. Davick, Linda, illus. (p. 1994)
—10 Valentine Friends. Davick, Linda, illus. (p. 1994)
—Nutcracker: The Untold Story. Graef, Renee, illus. (p. 1274)
—Pale Male: Citizen Hawk of New York City. So, Meilo, illus. (p. 1319)
Schulman, L. B. League of Strays. (p. 982)
Schulman, Robert A., et al. Solve It with Supplements: The Best Herbal & Nutritional Supplements to Help Prevent & Heal More Than 100 Common Health Problems. (p. 1608)
Schult, Sherry. Adventures of Didi & Mr Taco. Banks, Sandra, illus. (p. 17)
—There's a Horse in My Closet... (p. 1731)
Schulte, Christa. Tantric Sex for Women: A Guide for Lesbian, Bi, Hetero, & Solo Lovers. (p. 1705)
Schulte, Jeanne Baca. Full-Color Phonics Word Sorts. (p. 646)
Schulte, Mary. Amazon River. (p. 56)
—Dover Demon. (p. 473)
—Eva Longoria. (p. 540)
—Helen Griener: Cofounder of iRobot Corporation. (p. 762)
—Minotaur. (p. 1148)
—Piranhas & Other Fish. (p. 1362)
—Sirens. (p. 1580)
—Who Do I Look Like? Roos, Maryn, illus. (p. 1915)
Schulte, Mary E. Final Four: All about College Basketball's Biggest Event (p. 586)
Schultheiss, Amy & Schmidt, Susie. Grocery Shopping: In Five Easy Steps (p. 725)
Schultz. Geometry: Premier Online Edition. (p. 662)
Schultz, Agnes Szenozicska. Little Tree. (p. 1037)
Schultz, Aronka. Dinosaur on the Loose. (p. 442)
Schultz, Ashlee, illus. see Dreier, David.
Schultz, Ashlee, illus. see Gray, Susan H.
Schultz, Ashlee, illus. see Nardo, Don.
Schultz, Ashlee, illus. see Stille, Darlene R.
Schultz, Barbara, illus. see Gunderson, Jessica Sarah.
Schultz, Brenda. Wanda & Willie. Albano, Jennifer, illus. (p. 1856)
Schultz, Caleb. Keela & Capone's Take That Dog Back! (p. 946)
Schultz, Charles M. Love Is Walking Hand in Hand. (p. 1060)
Schultz, Diana, ed. see Miller, Frank, et al.
Schultz, Doreen. Days of Noah. (p. 415)
Schultz, Edward L. Pix (p. 1365)
Schultz, Gary, photos by see Fleisher, Paul.
Schultz, George M., jt. auth. see Thompson, John M.
Schultz, Heidi. Twelve Dreams of Christmas. (p. 1800)
Schultz, Jacque Lynn, jt. auth. see Pavia, Audrey.
Schultz, James Willard. Floating on the Missouri: 100 Years after Lewis & Clark. (p. 605)
Schultz, Jan Neubert. Battle Cry. Allen, Rick, illus. (p. 145)
Schultz, Jana. God Always Loves Me. (p. 688)
Schultz, Jeffrey. Critical Companion to John Steinbeck: A Literary Reference to His Life & Work. (p. 383)
Schultz, Jeffrey & Li, Luchen. Critical Companion to John Steinbeck: A Literary Reference to His Life & Work. (p. 383)
Schultz, Joani, et al. Easter Extras: Faith-Filled Ideas for Easter Week. Creyts, Patrick, illus. (p. 499)
Schultz, Jolene, illus. see Slade, Suzanne.
Schultz, Leslie & Braulick, J. J. M. And Sometimes Y. Newman, Heather, illus. (p. 71)
Schultz, Linda. Tales of the Awesome Foursome: Beatles Fans Share Their Personal Stories. Vol 1 (p. 1702)
Schultz, Lizzie. My Father's House. (p. 1203)
Schultz, Lucy & Shultz, Lucy. Zoo Faces. Larranaga, Ana, illus. (p. 1989)
Schultz, Michael, illus. see Fort, Gary W.
Schultz Nicholson, Lorna. Against the Boards (p. 29)
—Big Air (p. 177)
—Fighting for Gold: The Story of Canada's Sledge Hockey Paralympic Gold (p. 585)
—Interference (p. 879)
—Northern Star (p. 1266)
—Pink Power: The First Women's Hockey World Champions (p. 1360)
—Roughing (p. 1491)
—Too Many Men (p. 1766)
Schultz Nicholson, Lorna, jt. auth. see Nicholson, Lorna Schultz.
Schultz, Randy. Dwight D. Eisenhower: A MyReportLinks. Com Book. (p. 491)
—Richard M. Nixon: A MyReportLinks. Com Book. (p. 1469)
—Warren G. Harding: A MyReportLinks. Com Book. (p. 1858)
Schultz, Robert, jt. auth. see Delisle, James R.
Schultz, Shelley & English, Jill. TurkeyDog. (p. 1797)
Schultz, Susan M. And Then Something Happened. (p. 71)
Schultz, Terry L. & Sorenson, Linda M. Organic Puppet Theatre. (p. 1303)
Schultz, Walter A., jt. auth. see Schulz, Walter A.
Schultze, Gwendolyn. Dog That's Not a Poodle. Cameron, Ed, illus. (p. 461)
Schultze, Miriam. Dime Dónde Crece la Pimienta: Culturas Exóticas Explicadas a Los Niños. Knipping, Jutta, illus. (p. 440)
Schultze, Reimar A. C. I Am Love: From Nothing... to All Things. (p. 833)
Schultz-Ferrell, Karren, et al. Introduction to Reasoning & Proof, Grades 3-5. (p. 882)
Schulz. Buon San Valentino Dolce. (p. 243)
—Permetti Questo Ballo Charl. (p. 1343)
—Tutti qui Biscotti. (p. 1799)
Schulz, Barbara, illus. see Biskup, Agnieszka, et al.
Schulz, Barbara, illus. see Biskup, Agnieszka.
Schulz, Barbara, illus. see Burgan, Michael & Hoena, Blake A.
Schulz, Barbara, illus. see Burgan, Michael.
Schulz, Barbara, illus. see Collins, Terry, et al.
Schulz, Barbara, illus. see Fontes, Justine & Fontes, Ron.
Schulz, Barbara, illus. see Fontes, Ron & Fontes, Justine.
Schulz, Barbara, illus. see Gianopoulos, Andrea.
Schulz, Barbara, illus. see Gunderson, Jessica Sarah.
Schulz, Barbara, illus. see Jacobson, Ryan.
Schulz, Barbara, illus. see Limke, Jeff.
Schulz, Barbara, illus. see Olson, Kay Melchisedech.
Schulz, Barbara, illus. see Sohn, Emily.
Schulz, Barbara, jt. auth. see Biskup, Agnieszka.
Schulz, Barbara, jt. auth. see Collins, Terry.
Schulz, Carol D., jt. auth. see Soumerai, Eve Nussbaum.
Schulz, Charles M. Alle Achtung. Herbst, Gabriele & Rolle, Ekkehard, trs. from ENG. (p. 46)
—Alles Peanuts. Herbst, Gabriele & Rolle, Ekkehard, trs. from ENG. (p. 46)
—Allzeit Bereit. Herbst, Gabriele & Rolle, Ekkehard, trs. from ENG. (p. 48)
—An der Langen Leine. Herbst, Gabriele & Rolle, Ekkehard, trs. from ENG. (p. 66)
—Auf den Hund Gekommen. Herbst, Gabriele & Rolle, Ekkehard, trs. from ENG. (p. 115)
—Batter up, Charlie Brown! (p. 145)
—Be Active. (p. 148)
—Be Joyful: Peanuts Wisdom to Carry You Through. (p. 148)
—Be My Valentine, Charlie Brown. (p. 148)
—Be Thankful: Peanuts Wisdom to Carry You Through. (p. 149)
—Be Unique: Peanuts Wisdom to Carry You Through. (p. 149)
—Charlie Brown Christmas: A Book & Tree. Kit (p. 292)
—Charlie Brown Christmas: With Sound & Music. (p. 292)
—Charlie Brown Christmas: The Making of a Tradition. (p. 292)
—Charlie Brown Christmas. (p. 292)
—Charlie Brown Christmas. Running Press Staff, ed. (p. 292)
—Charlie Brown Seasonal. (p. 292)
—Charlie Brown Thanksgiving. (p. 292)
—Christmas Is Together-Time. Schulz, Charles M., illus. (p. 314)
—Den Wind im Ruecken. Herbst, Gabriele & Rolle, Ekkehard, trs. from ENG. (p. 426)
—Easter Beagle Egg Hunt. (p. 499)
—Einfach Genial. Herbst, Gabriele & Rolle, Ekkehard, trs. from ENG. (p. 507)
—Einfach Unschlagbar. Herbst, Gabriele & Rolle, Ekkehard, trs. from ENG. (p. 507)
—Felicidad Es... Un Perrito Cariñoso. (p. 581)
—Good Grief! Charlie Brown Doodles: Create & Complete Pictures with the Peanuts Gang. (p. 698)
—Grundlos Gluecklich. Herbst, Gabriele & Rolle, Ekkehard, trs. from ENG. (p. 727)
—Gut Aufgelegt. Herbst, Gabriele & Rolle, Ekkehard, trs. from ENG. (p. 733)
—Happiness Is a Warm Blanket, Charlie Brown. (p. 744)
—Herzlich Unverschaemt. Herbst, Gabriele & Rolle, Ekkehard, trs. from ENG. (p. 774)
—Himmel & Hoelle. Herbst, Gabriele & Rolle, Ekkehard, trs. from ENG. (p. 780)
—Hoch die Tassen. Herbst, Gabriele & Rolle, Ekkehard, trs. from ENG. (p. 786)
—Hogar Está Encima de Una Caseta de Perro. (p. 787)
—I Need All the Friends I Can Get. (p. 844)
—Immer Dabei. Herbst, Gabriele & Rolle, Ekkehard, trs. from ENG. (p. 861)
—It's the Easter Beagle, Charlie Brown. (p. 899)
—It's the Easter Beagle, Charlie Brown: with Sound & Music. (p. 899)
—It's the Great Pumpkin, Charlie Brown. (p. 899)
—It's the Great Pumpkin, Charlie Brown: with Sound & Music. (p. 899)
—Kaum zu Bremsen. Rolle, Ekkehard, tr. from ENG. (p. 946)
—Linus Learns to Share: A Book & Blanket. Kit (p. 1019)
—Many Faces of Snoopy. (p. 1089)
—Necesito Todos los Amigos Que Pueda Tener. (p. 1239)
—Peanuts: Be Brave: Peanuts Wisdom to Carry You Through. (p. 1332)
—Peanuts: Be Friends. (p. 1332)
—Peanuts Grand Piano Book. (p. 1332)
—Peanuts Guide to the Seasons: A Jumbo Activity Book. Bennett, Elizabeth, illus. (p. 1332)
—Pfoten Hoch! Herbst, Gabriele & Rolle, Ekkehard, trs. from ENG. (p. 1349)
—Schwer in Fahrt. Herbst, Gabriele & Rolle, Ekkehard, trs. from ENG. (p. 1524)
—Security Is a Thumb & a Blanket. (p. 1546)
—Seguridad es un Pulgar y una Manta. (p. 1548)
—Snoopy & Woodstock: Best Friends. (p. 1598)
—Snoopy at the Bat. (p. 1598)
—Snoopy - Cowabunga! A Peanuts Collection. (p. 1598)
—Snoopy's Thanksgiving. (p. 1598)
—Suppertime! (p. 1684)
—Trick or Treat: A Peanuts Halloween. (p. 1786)
—Ultimate Box (p. 1809)
—Voll auf die Schnauze. Herbst, Gabriele & Rolle, Ekkehard, trs. from ENG. (p. 1849)
—Voll im Griff. Herbst, Gabriele & Rolle, Ekkehard, trs. from ENG. (p. 1849)
—Von der Rolle. Herbst, Gabriele & Rolle, Ekkehard, trs. from ENG. (p. 1850)
—Waiting for the Great Pumpkin. (p. 1853)
—Where Did Woodstock Go? (p. 1906)
—Where Is Woodstock? (p. 1909)
Schulz, Charles M. & Bennett, Elizabeth. Peanuts Guide to Sports: A Jumbo Activity Book. (p. 1332)
Schulz, Charles M. & Houghton, Shane. Peanuts Braddock, Paige, illus. (p. 1332)
Schulz, Charles M. & Mendelson, Lee. It's the Great Pumpkin: The Making of a Tradition. (p. 899)
Schulz, Charles M. & Pastis, Stephan. Happiness Is a Warm Blanket, Charlie Brown! Scott, Bob, illus. (p. 744)
Schulz, Charles M. & Sasseville, Jim. It's Only a Game. Bang, Derrick, ed. (p. 898)
Schulz, Charles M. & Scott, Vicki. It's Tokyo, Charlie Brown! Braddock, Paige, illus. (p. 899)
Schulz, Charles M., creator. Be Kind: Peanuts Wisdom to Carry You Through. (p. 148)
—Be Yourself! (p. 149)
—Snoopy Loves to Doodle: Create & Complete Pictures with the Peanuts Gang. (p. 1598)
—You Can Be Anything! (p. 1974)
Schulz, Christian Dahl. Professional Sports Organizations. (p. 1409)
Schulz, Hal. Dak's Country Visit: The Painter & His Cat. (p. 401)
Schulz, Heidi. Hook's Revenge. (p. 795)
—Hook's Revenge. Hendrix, John, illus. (p. 795)
Schulz, Janet, illus. see Schulz, Walter A.
Schulz, Karen. Crime Scene Detective: Using Science & Critical Thinking to Solve Crimes. (p. 382)
Schulz, Karen K. Csi Expert! Forensic Science for Kids. Parker, David, illus. (p. 387)
Schulz, Kathy. Always Be Safe. (p. 51)
—Always Be Safe. Potter, Katherine, illus. (p. 51)
—I Do Not Want To. Rescek, Sanja, illus. (p. 837)
—I Need a Little Help. Iosa, Ann, illus. (p. 844)
—Necesito una Ayudita. Iosa, Ann, illus. (p. 1239)
Schulz, Lori. Papa's Plan for Buddy Bee. (p. 1322)
Schulz, Monte. This Side of Jordan. (p. 1737)
Schulz, Walter A. Johnny Moore & the Wright Brothers' Flying Machine. Bowles, Doug, illus. (p. 923)
—Will y Orv. Translations.com Staff, tr. from ENG. (p. 1932)
Schulz, Walter A. & Schultz, Walter A. Johnny Moore & the Wright Brothers' Flying Machine. Bowles, Doug, illus. (p. 923)
Schulz, Wendy Anderson, jt. auth. see Shasek, Judy.
Schulze, G. L. Secret Treasure of Pirate's Cove: The Young Detectives' Mystery. (p. 1544)
Schulze, Marc-Alexander. Child Is Born: The Nativity Story. (p. 301)
Schumacher, Anna. Children of the Earth. (p. 302)
—End Times. (p. 526)
Schumacher, Bev. Body Parts / Las Partes Del Cuerpo: Partes Del Cuerpo. (p. 207)
—Body Parts (Chinese-English) (p. 207)
—Count on Me! (p. 369)
—Count on Me!/ Cuenta Conmigo! (p. 369)
—Critters. (p. 384)
—Critters (Chinese/English) (p. 384)
—Dress Up. (p. 485)
—Dress Up (Chinese/English) (p. 485)
—Letters Aa to Zz. (p. 1002)
—Patterns. (p. 1329)
—Patterns (Chinese/English) (p. 1329)
—Play Action (Chinese-English) (p. 1370)
—Play Action/ Juego en Accion: Juego en Acción. (p. 1370)
—Shape Land. (p. 1560)
—Shapeland / Figuralandia. (p. 1560)
—What Color Is It? (p. 1881)
—What Color Is It? / de Que Color Es? (p. 1881)
—What Color Is It? (Chinese/English) (p. 1881)
—Where Will You Find Me? (p. 1910)
—Where Will You Find Me? / Donde Me Encontraras. (p. 1910)
—Where Will You Find Me? (Chinese/English) (p. 1910)
—Which Way? (p. 1911)
—Which Way? / Por Donde? (p. 1911)
—Which Way? (Chinese-English) (p. 1911)
Schumacher, Bev, creator. Body Parts. (p. 207)
—Play Action. (p. 1370)
Schumacher, Dan, jt. auth. see Kuczenski, Tyler.
Schumacher, Julie. Black Box. (p. 195)
—Book of One Hundred Truths. (p. 211)
—Unbearable Book Club for Unsinkable Girls. (p. 1811)
Schumacher, Philip, tr. see Knecht, F. J.
Schumacher, Stef. Amazing Blue Animals (p. 54)
Schumacher, Tyler. Cesar Chavez: Champion of Workers (p. 288)
—Georgia Colony. (p. 665)
Schumaker, Ward, illus. see Zeiler, Freddi.
Schuman, Burt E. Chanukah on the Prairie. Kaye, Rosalind Charney, illus. (p. 291)
Schuman, Jo Miles. Art from Many Hands: Multicultural Art Projects. (p. 102)
Schuman, Michael. Alexander Graham Bell: Scientist & Inventor. (p. 36)
—Halle Berry: A Biography of an Oscar-Winning Actress. (p. 737)
—Will Smith: A Biography of Rapper Turned Movie Star. (p. 1932)
Schuman, Michael A. Adam Sandler: Celebrity with Heart. (p. 11)
—Alexander Graham Bell: Scientist & Inventor. (p. 36)
—Angelina Jolie: Celebrity with Heart. (p. 74)
—Barack Obama: We Are One People. (p. 137)
—Barack Obama: We Are One People, Revised & Expanded. (p. 137)
—Beyonc: A Biography of a Legendary Singer. (p. 173)
—Bill Clinton. (p. 186)
—Bill Gates: Computer Mogul & Philanthropist. (p. 186)
—Bob Dylan: The Life & Times of an American Icon. (p. 205)
—Emma! Amazing Actress Emma Stone. (p. 519)
—Frederick Douglass: Truth Is of No Color. (p. 633)
—Halle Berry: Beauty Is Not Just Physical. (p. 737)
—Halle Berry: A Biography of an Oscar-Winning Actress. (p. 737)

—Harry S. Truman. (p. 751)
—Jim Thorpe: "There's No Such Thing as 'Can't" (p. 918)
—Led Zeppelin: Legendary Rock Band. (p. 987)
—Life of Martin Luther King, Jr: Leader for Civil Rights. (p. 1012)
—Louis Armstrong: Jazz Is Played from the Heart. (p. 1058)
—Maya & Aztec Mythology Rocks! Bock, William Sauts, illus. (p. 1112)
—Richard M. Nixon. (p. 1469)
—Rihanna: Music Megastar. (p. 1472)
—Robert Pattinson: Shining Star. (p. 1479)
—Scarlett Johansson: Hollywood Superstar. (p. 1520)
—Tina Fey: TV Comedy Superstar. (p. 1755)
—Will Smith: I Like Blending a Message with Comedy. (p. 1932)
—Will Smith: A Biography of a Rapper Turned Movie Star. (p. 1932)
Schuman, Michael A., jt. auth. see Schuman, Michael.
Schuman, Michael & Brill, Marlene Targ. Delaware. (p. 424)
Schuman, Michael & Schuman, Michael A. Write Science Fiction in 5 Simple Steps. (p. 1963)
Schumann, Erik. All While the Gods Watched. (p. 46)
Schumann, Marc. Ha Jin. (p. 734)
Schumer, Angela. What Do Your Ears Look Like? the Listening Ladybug. (p. 1883)
Schumer, Angela Points. Million Kisses to the Moon. (p. 1144)
Schumm, Jeanne Shay, ed. Reading Assessment & Instruction for All Learners. (p. 1445)
Schumman, Nani, tr. see Stamm, Peter & Bauer, Jutta.
Schuna, Ramona, illus. see Brown, Elizabeth.
Schuna, Sam, illus. see Bathroom Readers' Institute Staff.
Schunemann, Ryan, illus. see Bush, Randall B.
Schuon, Catherine & Fitzgerald, Michael Oren, eds. King James Christmas: Biblical Selections with Illustrations from Around the World. (p. 958)
Schuon, Karl, jt. auth. see Pierce, Philip N.
Schupack, Sara. Indira Gandhi. (p. 872)
—Merchant of Venice. (p. 1127)
Schuppert, David, illus. see Kudlinski, Kathleen V.
Schur, Joan Brodsky. Arabs. (p. 94)
Schur, Maxine Rose. Story of Ruth. Connelly, Gwen, illus. (p. 1659)
—There's a Babirusa in My Bathtub: Fact & Fancy about Curious Creatures. Maydak, Michael, illus. (p. 1730)
—There's a Babirusa in My Bathtub: Fact & Fancy about Curious Creatures. Maydak, Michael S., illus. (p. 1730)
Schurch, Maylan. Sword of Denis Anwyck. (p. 1692)
Schurch, Maylan Henry. Meatless Mayhem Mystery. (p. 1118)
Schurch, Vicky. Little Songbird Named Annie. (p. 1036)
Schurr, Cathleen. Shy Little Kitten: Classic Edition. Tenggren, Gustaf, illus. (p. 1572)
—Shy Little Kitten. Tenggren, Gustaf, illus. (p. 1572)
Schurr, Cathleen, jt. auth. see Depken, Kristen L.
Schurr, Sandra, jt. auth. see Forte, Imogene.
Schurz, Carl. Reminenisence of Carl Schurz (p. 1460)
—Reminiscences. (p. 1460)
—Speeches, Correspondence, & Political Papers. (p. 1624)
Schussel, Sara, jt. auth. see Ronan, James.
Schuster, Judith A. No Place to Call Home: Book Two-the Eddie Brewster Adventures. (p. 1260)
Schuster, Rob, illus. see Savage, Jeff.
Schuster-Grossman, Margaret. God's Greatest Miracle. (p. 691)
Schusterman, Michelle. Crushes, Codas, & Corsages Kote, Geneviève, illus. (p. 387)
—Friends, Fugues, & Fortune Cookies. Kote, Genevieve, illus. (p. 638)
—I Heart Band #1. Kote, Genevieve, illus. (p. 839)
Schusterman, Michelle & Kote, Geneviève. Sleepovers, Solos, & Sheet Music. (p. 1589)
Schut, Jessie. Telling Your Friends about Jesus. (p. 1717)
Schutte, Hellmut, jt. auth. see Lasserre, Philippe.
Schutten, Jan Paul. Mystery of Life: How Nothing Became Everything. Watkinson, Laura, tr. from DUT. (p. 1224)
Schutz, Diana, ed. see Marder, Larry.
Schutz, Diana, ed. see Sakai, Stan.
Schutz, Samantha. You Are Not Here. (p. 1973)
Schutzer, Dena, illus. see England, Linda.
Schuurman, Donna. Never the Same: Coming to Terms with the Death of a Parent. (p. 1243)
Schuurmans, Hilde. Sidney Won't Swim. Schuurmans, Hilde, illus. (p. 1573)
Schuvent, Julia & Skindzier, Jon. Rice University College Prowler off the Record. (p. 1469)
Schwab, Jessica. Adventures of Joey: A Guinea Pig Rescue Tale. (p. 19)
Schwab, Jordan, illus. see Delrusso, Diana.
Schwab, Victoria. Archived. (p. 95)
—Everyday Angel #1: New Beginnings. (p. 543)
—Everyday Angel #2: Second Chances. (p. 543)
—Everyday Angel #3: Last Wishes. (p. 543)
—New Beginnings. (p. 1243)
—Unbound. (p. 1811)
—Unbound (An Archived Novel) (p. 1811)
Schwabach, Karen. Hope Chest. (p. 796)
—Storm Before Atlanta. (p. 1655)
Schwabacher, Martin & Kummer, Patricia K. Minnesota. (p. 1147)
Schwabacher, Martin & Mortensen, Lori. Elephants. (p. 511)
Schwabacher, Martin & Otfinoski, Steven. Puerto Rico. (p. 1415)
Schwabacher, Martin & Shannon, Terry Miller. Bears. (p. 151)
Schwabacher, Martin, et al. Flies with the Dinosaurs. Bracken, Carolyn, illus. (p. 604)
Schwabauer, Daniel. Runt the Hunted. (p. 1497)
Schwaber, Ken. Agile Project Management with Scrum. (p. 29)
—Enterprise & Scrum. (p. 531)
Schwabsky, Barry. Vitamin P: New Perspectives in Painting. (p. 1846)
Schwacber, Barbie Helt. Alphabet of Earth. Vitsky, Sally, illus. (p. 49)
Schwaeber, Barbie. Alphabet of Earth. Vitsky, Sally, illus. (p. 49)
—Grand Old Flag. Nussbaum, Ben, ed. (p. 707)
—Make New Friends. Brooks, Nan, illus. (p. 1079)
—Star-Spangled Banner. (p. 1641)
Schwaeber, Barbie, jt. auth. see Cohan, George M.
Schwaeber, Barbie H. Grand Old Flag. Nussbaum, Ben, ed. (p. 707)
—Princess: A Lucky Kitten. Huerta, Catherine, illus. (p. 1402)
—She'll Be Comin Round the Mountain. Beaky, Suzanne, illus. (p. 1564)
Schwaeber, Barbie H., ed. see Bentley, Dawn, et al.
Schwaeber, Barbie H., ed. see Galvin, Laura Gates & Soundprints Editorial Staff.
Schwaeber, Barbie H., ed. see Galvin, Laura Gates & Studio Mouse Staff.
Schwaeber, Barbie H., ed. see Smithsonian Institution Staff.
Schwaeber, Barbie H., ed. She'll Be Comin' Round the Mountain. Beaky, Suzanne, illus. (p. 1564)
Schwaeber, Barbie Helt. Alphabet of Bears. Nelson, Will et al, illus. (p. 49)
—Alphabet of Dance. Ward, Damian, illus. (p. 49)
—Alphabet of Dance. Wood, Damian, illus. (p. 49)
—Alphabet of Dinosaurs. Buchs, Thomas, illus. (p. 49)
—Alphabet of Dinosaurs. Buchs, Thomas et al, illus. (p. 49)
—Alphabet of Insects. Buchs, Thomas, illus. (p. 49)
—Alphabet of Insects. Bratun, Katy et al, illus. (p. 49)
—Alphabet of Music. Clark, Debbie, illus. (p. 49)
—Alphabet of Music. Santillan, Jorge, illus. (p. 49)
—Alphabet of Music. Santillan, Jorge & Clark, Debbie, illus. (p. 49)
—Alphabet of Sports. Lowe, David, illus. (p. 50)
—Princess: A Lucky Kitten. Huerta, Catherine, illus. (p. 1402)
—Princess a Lucky Kitten. Huerta, Catherine, illus. (p. 1402)
Schwaeber, Barbie Helt, ed. see Bentley, Dawn.
Schwaeber, Barbie Helt, ed. see Galvin, Laura Gates.
Schwaeber, Barbie Helt, ed. see Gates Galvin, Laura.
Schwaeber, Barbie Helt, ed. see Soundprints Staff.
Schwake, Rainer, photos by see Schwake, Susan.
Schwake, Susan. 3D Art Lab for Kids: 32 Hands-On Adventures in Sculpture & Mixed Media - Including Fun Projects Using Clay, Plaster, Cardboard, Paper, Fiber Beads & More! Schwake, Rainer, photos by. (p. 1992)
—Art for All Seasons. (p. 102)
—Art Lab for Kids: 52 Creative Adventures in Drawing, Painting, Printmaking, Paper, & Mixed Media - For Budding Artists of All Ages. Schwake, Rainer, photos by. (p. 102)
Schwalbach, Pamela. Happiest Day for Simeon & Sula. (p. 744)
Schwalm, Claudia. Folk Art of Mexico Book & Game. Martinez Aydelott, Carmen, tr. (p. 611)
Schwaner, Lynne, illus. see Hapka, Cathy, pseud.
Schwark, Mike. Van Von Hunter. (p. 1833)
Schwartau, Winn. Shit: A Shitload of Practical Uses for the Most Flexible Word in the English Language (p. 1567)
Schwartz, Allan A., jt. auth. see Edson, Ann.
Schwartz, Alvin. Gold & Silver, Silver & Gold: Tales of Hidden Treasure. Christiana, David, illus. (p. 693)
—More Scary Stories to Tell in the Dark. (p. 1174)
—More Scary Stories to Tell in the Dark. Helquist, Brett, illus. (p. 1174)
—Scary Stories 3: More Tales to Chill Your Bones. Helquist, Brett, illus. (p. 1520)
—Scary Stories Box Set Helquist, Brett, illus. (p. 1520)
—Scary Stories to Tell in the Dark. Helquist, Brett, illus. (p. 1521)
Schwartz, Alvin & Alvin, Schwartz. Historias de Miedo. Irving, George S., illus. (p. 782)
—Historias de Miedo 2: Relatos Espeluznantes para No Dejarte Dormir. Irving, George S., illus. (p. 782)
—Historias de Miedo 3: Relatos Aterradores para Helarte la Sangre. Irving, George S., illus. (p. 782)
Schwartz, Amy. 100 Things That Make Me Happy. (p. 1999)
—Begin at the Beginning: A Little Artist Learns about Life. Schwartz, Amy, illus. (p. 159)
—Boys Team. Schwartz, Amy, illus. (p. 220)
—Dee Dee & Me. (p. 422)
—Dee Dee & Me. Schwartz, Amy, illus. (p. 422)
—Glorious Day. Schwartz, Amy, illus. (p. 685)
—Oma & Bobo. (p. 1288)
—Polka Dots. (p. 1381)
—What James Likes Best. Schwartz, Amy, illus. (p. 1891)
—Willie & Uncle Bill. (p. 1934)
Schwartz, Amy, illus. see Feder, Jane.
Schwartz, Amy, illus. see Ryder, Joanne.
Schwartz, Amy & Marcus, Leonard S. Oscar: The Big Adventure of a Little Sock Monkey. Schwartz, Amy, illus. (p. 1305)
Schwartz, Arthur, ed. see Evers, Alf.
Schwartz, B. J. Adventures of Max & I: Dream Pirates. (p. 20)
—Adventures of Max & I. (p. 20)
Schwartz, Barry L. & Levine, Mark H. Judaism's Great Debates. Klossner, John & Ricceri, David, illus. (p. 930)
Schwartz, Bennett L. Khadim & the Wanderers. (p. 951)
Schwartz, Betty & Seresin, Lynn. Busy Little Dinosaurs: A Touch-And-Feel Alphabet Book. Powell, Luciana Navarro, illus. (p. 246)
—Puppies, Puppies, Everywhere! A Back-And-Forth Opposites Book. Powell, Luciana Navarro, illus. (p. 1418)
—Ten Playful Tigers: A Touch-And-Feel Counting Book. Powell, Luciana Navarro, illus. (p. 1719)
—You're It, Little Red Fish! A Back-And-Forth Color Book. Powell, Luciana Navarro, illus. (p. 1982)
Schwartz, Betty Ann. De Que Esta Hecho el Arco Iris? Turner, Dona, illus. (p. 416)
—One to Ten... & Back Again. Shakir, Susie, illus. (p. 1297)
—What Makes a Rainbow: (British Version) Turner, Dona, illus. (p. 1892)
—What Makes a Rainbow? Turner, Dona, illus. (p. 1892)
—What Makes Music? A Magic Ribbon Book. Turner, Dona, illus. (p. 1892)
Schwartz, Betty Ann, jt. auth. see Seresin, Lynn.
Schwartz, Betty Ann & Seresin, Lynn. My Barnyard! A Read & Play Book! Bendall-Brunello, John, illus. (p. 1196)
—My Dinosaurs! A Read & Play Book. Bendall-Brunello, John, illus. (p. 1202)
—Run, Run Piglet. Ng, Neiko, illus. (p. 1496)
Schwartz, Carol. Old Mother Hubbard. Schwartz, Carol, illus. (p. 1284)
Schwartz, Carol, illus. see Bryant, Megan E.
Schwartz, Carol, illus. see Carson, Mary Kay.
Schwartz, Carol, illus. see Edwards, Roberta.
Schwartz, Carol, illus. see Hulme, Joy N.
Schwartz, Carol, illus. see Moss, Deborah.
Schwartz, Carol, illus. see Norman, Kim & American Museum of Natural History Staff.
Schwartz, Carol, illus. see Slade, Suzanne.
Schwartz, Carol, illus. see Stewart, Melissa.
Schwartz, Carol & Edwards, Roberta. Emperor Penguins. Schwartz, Carol, illus. (p. 521)
Schwartz, Charles. Originators: A Novel. (p. 1304)
Schwartz, Corey Rosen. Ninja Red Riding Hood. Santat, Dan, illus. (p. 1256)
—Three Ninja Pigs. Santat, Dan, illus. (p. 1743)
Schwartz, Corey Rosen & Coulton, Beth. Goldi Rocks & the Three Bears. Wragg, Nate, illus. (p. 695)
Schwartz, Corey Rosen & Gomez, Rebecca J. What about Moose? Yamaguchi, Keika, illus. (p. 1879)
Schwartz, David, jt. auth. see Schwartz, David M.
Schwartz, David, jt. auth. see Schy, Yael.
Schwartz, David & Schwartz, David M. Q Is for Quark: A Science Alphabet Book. Doner, Kim, illus. (p. 1422)
Schwartz, David M. Animal Noses. Kuhn, Dwight, photos by. (p. 79)
—Bean. Kuhn, Dwight, photos by. (p. 150)
—Cuanto Es un Millon? Kellogg, Steven, illus. (p. 388)
—Fighting Fish. Kuhn, Dwight, photos by. (p. 585)
—Green Snake. Kuhn, Dwight, photos by. (p. 722)
—How Much Is a Million? Kellogg, Steven, illus. (p. 811)
—Look Once Look Again Collection Box Set. Kuhn, Dwight, photos by. (p. 1049)
—Millions to Measure. Kellogg, Steven, illus. (p. 1144)
—Superabuelo. Guzman, Martin Luis, tr. (p. 1682)
Schwartz, David M., jt. auth. see Schwartz, David.
Schwartz, David M. & Pascoe, Elaine. Life Cycles, How & Why Collection. (p. 1010)
Schwartz, David M. & Schwartz, David. Millions to Measure. Kellogg, Steven, illus. (p. 1144)
Schwartz, David M. & Schy, Yael. Where Else in the Wild? Kuhn, Dwight, illus. (p. 1907)
—Where in the Wild? Camouflaged Creatures Concealed... & Revealed. Kuhn, Dwight, photos by. (p. 1908)
Schwartz, David M., et al. Where in the Wild? Camouflaged Creatures Concealed... & Revealed. Kuhn, Dwight, photos by. (p. 1908)
Schwartz, Ellen. Abby's Birds Shefrin, Sima Elizabeth, illus. (p. 2)
—Avalanche Dance. (p. 118)
—Case of the Missing Deed. (p. 274)
—Cellular. (p. 286)
—I Love Yoga: A Source Book for Teens. Hodson, Ben, illus. (p. 843)
—Stealing Home. (p. 1646)
—Yossi's Goal (p. 1972)
Schwartz, Eric. Central American Immigrants to the United States: Refugees from Unrest. (p. 287)
—What Makes America America? (p. 1892)
—World Contender. (p. 1954)
Schwartz, Evan I. Last Lone Inventor: A Tale of Genius, Deceit, & the Birth of Television. (p. 978)
Schwartz, Fletcher. Willim was a Dancer. (p. 1934)
Schwartz, Heather. Ariana Grande: From Actress to Chart-Topping Singer. (p. 98)
—Austin Mahone: Vocals Going Viral. (p. 116)
—French Revolution: Terror & Triumph. (p. 636)
—Guerra, Ganado y Vaqueros. (p. 728)
—Gymnastics. (p. 734)
—Little Mix: Singers with X-Tra Success. (p. 1032)
—Lizzie Johnson: Texan Cowgirl. (p. 1043)
—Lizzie Johnson: Vaquera Texana. (p. 1043)
—Maia Mitchell: Talent from down Under. (p. 1076)
—Marie Antoinette: The Controversial Queen of France. (p. 1093)
—War, Cattle, & Cowboys: Texas as a Young State. (p. 1857)
—Zendaya: Capturing the Stage, Screen, & Modeling Scene. (p. 1986)
Schwartz, Heather E. Adele: Soulful Singer. (p. 12)
—Ariana Grande: From Actress to Chart-Topping Singer. (p. 98)
—Bank Wisely. (p. 136)
—Civil Rights Act of 1964: A Primary Source Exploration of the Landmark Legislation. (p. 324)
—Cody Simpson: Pop Star from down Under. (p. 338)
—Cool Engineering Activities for Girls (p. 363)
—Cyberbullying (p. 396)
—Emma Stone: Star of the Stage, TV, & Film. (p. 520)
—Foul, Filthy American Frontier: The Disgusting Details about the Journey Out West. (p. 624)
—Freedom Riders: A Primary Source Exploration of the Struggle for Racial Justice (p. 635)
—Gangsters, Bootleggers, & Bandits. (p. 655)
—Girls Rebel! Amazing Tales of Women Who Broke the Mold (p. 680)
—Girls' Snowboarding: Showing off Your Style. (p. 680)
—Girls' Softball: Winning on the Diamond (p. 680)
—Idina Menzel: Vocal Superpower. (p. 852)
—Jaden Smith: Actor, Rapper, & Activist. (p. 905)
—Justin Timberlake: From Mouseketeer to Megastar. (p. 940)
—Lorde: Songstress with Style. (p. 1052)
—Maia Mitchell: Talent from down Under. (p. 1076)
—Make Good Choices: Your Guide to Making Healthy Decisions (p. 1079)
—March on Washington: A Primary Source Exploration of the Pivotal Protest (p. 1091)
—Miley Ray Cyrus (p. 1142)
—Miranda Cosgrove (p. 1149)
—Morkie: A Cross Between a Maltese & a Yorkshire Terrier (p. 1175)
—Outlaws, Gunslingers, & Thieves. (p. 1313)
—Rebel Wilson: From Stand-Up Laughs to Box-Office Smash. (p. 1451)
—Safe Social Networking (p. 1502)
—Save Wisely. (p. 1517)
—Science of a Race Car: Reactions in Action (p. 1527)
—Seeking Freedom: Causes & Effects of the Flight of the Nez Perce. (p. 1548)
—Selena Gomez. (p. 1549)
—Shailene Woodley: Divergent's Daring Star. (p. 1558)
—Steal the Scene: Writing Amazing Drama. (p. 1646)
—Stress Less: Your Guide to Managing Stress (p. 1667)
—Taylor Swift. (p. 1708)
—Theodore Roosevelt's Presidency. (p. 1729)
—Wanted: British Boy Band Sensation. (p. 1856)
—Women of the U. S. Air Force: Aiming High (p. 1946)
—Women of the U. S. Marine Corps: Breaking Barriers. (p. 1946)
—Yourspace: Questioning New Media (p. 1982)
—Zendaya: Capturing the Stage, Screen, & Modeling Scene. (p. 1986)
Schwartz, Heather E., jt. auth. see Greenhaven Press Editors.
Schwartz, Heather E., jt. auth. see Higgins, Nadia.
Schwartz, Heather E. & Capstone Press Editors. Girls' Volleyball: Setting up Success (p. 681)
Schwartz, Heather E. & Capstone Press Staff. Girls' Figure Skating: Ruling the Rink (p. 680)
Schwartz, Heather E. & Meinking, Mary. Star Biographies. (p. 1640)
Schwartz, Heather E., et al. Star Biographies. (p. 1640)
—We Shall Overcome (p. 1868)
Schwartz, Howard. Day the Rabbi Disappeared: Jewish Holiday Tales of Magic. Passicot, Monique, illus. (p. 414)
—Gathering Sparks. Swarner, Kristina, illus. (p. 658)
—Journey to Paradise: And Other Jewish Tales. Carmi, Giora, illus. (p. 929)
Schwartz, Howard, jt. auth. see Olson, Arielle North.
Schwartz, Jaime. See the U. S. A. (p. 1547)
Schwartz, Jean. Snake with a Bellyache. Fisher, Todd, illus. (p. 1596)
Schwartz, Joan, jt. ed. see Ryan, James R.
Schwartz, Joanne. City Alphabet Beam, Matt, illus. (p. 323)
—Our Corner Grocery Store. Beingessner, Laura, illus. (p. 1308)
Schwartz, Joel. Extraordinary Pupfish of Calaveras County. (p. 555)
—Noses are Red. (p. 1266)
Schwartz, Josh, jt. auth. see Van Syckle, A.
Schwartz, Julie & Tanenbaum, Teri. Haz-Mat Attack Pack. (p. 756)
Schwartz, Katherine. Sex in the Texts. (p. 1556)
Schwartz, Katherine, ed. see Yedwab, Paul Michael.
Schwartz, Kristi. Divorced Together: For teh Sake of the Children. (p. 455)
Schwartz, Laura. Willamen. (p. 1933)
Schwartz, Lesley, jt. auth. see Moss, Samantha.
Schwartz, Linda. Conquer Spelling: Word Lists, Roles, & Activities to Help Kids Become Spelling Heros. Scott, Kelly, ed. (p. 358)
—Following Directions 1-2. Scott, Kelly, ed. (p. 612)
—Following Directions 3-4. Martin, Kelly, ed. (p. 612)
—Language Arts Quiz Whiz. Larson, Eric, ed. (p. 974)
—Language Arts Quiz Whiz 3-5 VanBlaricum, Pam, ed. (p. 974)
—Language Critical Thinking, Grades 2-4: Creative Puzzles to Challenge the Brain. Armstrong, Bev & Grayson, Rick, illus. (p. 975)
—Math Critical Thinking, Grades 2-4: Creative Puzzles to Challenge the Brain. VanBlaricum, Pam, ed. (p. 1105)
—Math Quiz Whiz 3-5 VanBlaricum, Pam, ed. (p. 1107)
—Picture Prompts for Writing. Larson, Eric, ed. (p. 1356)
—Primary Math Quiz Whiz VanBlaricum, Pam, ed. (p. 1399)
—Primary Science Quiz Whiz VanBlaricum, Pam, ed. (p. 1399)
—Science Quiz Whiz. Larson, Eric, ed. (p. 1527)
—Social Studies & Science Quiz Whiz 3-5 VanBlaricum, Pam, ed. (p. 1604)
—Social Studies Quiz Whiz. Larson, Eric, ed. (p. 1604)
Schwartz, Linda, ed. see Klawitter, Pamela Amick.
Schwartz, Lloyd, ed. see Bishop, Elizabeth.
Schwartz, Marcia. Lobo & the Rabbit Stew. Campbell, Brent, illus. (p. 1044)
—Lobo & the Rabbit Stew/El Lobo y el Caldo de Conejo. Campbell, Brent, illus. (p. 1044)
Schwartz, Marian, jt. auth. see Wilke, Daria.
Schwartz, Marty. What Makes Sense? Fun Deck: Fd60. (p. 1892)
Schwartz, Marty, illus. see Foster, Beverly & Foster, Stacy Lynn.
Schwartz, Marty, illus. see Webber, Sharon.
Schwartz, Pepper & Capello, Dominic. 10 Charlas que los Padres Deben Tener con sus Hijos Sobre Caracter y Sexo. (p. 1993)
Schwartz, Richard Alan. 1990s. (p. 2002)
Schwartz, Richard Evan. You Can Count on Monsters: The First 100 Numbers & Their Characters. (p. 1974)
Schwartz, Robert, jt. auth. see Schwartz, Suzanne.
Schwartz, Robert, jt. auth. see Skewes, John.
Schwartz, Robert, jt. illus. see Schwartz, Suzanne.
Schwartz, Roslyn. Complete Adventures of the Mole Sisters. Schwartz, Roslyn, illus. (p. 352)
—Mole Sisters & the Fairy Ring. Schwartz, Roslyn, illus. (p. 1160)
—Mole Sisters & the Way Home. Schwartz, Roslyn, illus. (p. 1160)
—Tales from Parc la Fontaine. Schwartz, Roslyn, illus. (p. 1701)
—Vole Brothers. Schwartz, Roslyn & Owlkids Books Inc. Staff, illus. (p. 1849)
Schwartz, Sara Leah. Let's Use Them Right: Social Skills for My Hands, Feet, & Mouth. David, Racheli, illus. (p. 1001)
Schwartz, Sheila. Lies Will Take You Somewhere. (p. 1007)

Schwartz, Simon. First Man: The Voyages of Matthew Henson. Watkinson, Laura, tr. from GER. (p. 596)
—Other Side of the Wall. Watkinson, Laura, tr. (p. 1306)
Schwartz, Staci J. New Bear on the Block. (p. 1243)
Schwartz, Stephanie. Miranda & the Magic Shoes: The Land of the Rising Sun. (p. 1149)
Schwartz, Steven. Mega Picture Puzzles: Challenge Yourself to Spot the Differences. (p. 1124)
Schwartz, Suzanne & Schwartz, Robert. Christmas Palm Tree: A Storybook to Color. Schwartz, Suzanne & Schwartz, Robert, illus. (p. 315)
—Hibby's Coloring Book. (p. 775)
—My Friend Hibby: A Tropical Adventure. Schwartz, Suzanne & Schwartz, Robert, illus. (p. 1209)
—My Friend Hibby Picture & Coloring Book Set (p. 1209)
Schwartz, Tina P. Bass Fishing. (p. 143)
—Deep-Sea Fishing. (p. 423)
—Depression: The Ultimate Teen. (p. 427)
—Fly-Fishing. (p. 609)
—Freshwater Fishing. (p. 637)
—Ice Fishing. (p. 850)
—Motocross Freestyle (p. 1179)
—Salmon Fishing. (p. 1505)
—Writing & Publishing: The Ultimate Teen Guide. (p. 1964)
Schwartz, Tom. How Mother Nature Dealt with Creatures of the Earth. (p. 811)
—How Mother Nature Flowered the Fields. (p. 811)
—Spaceship Earth: A Beginning Without End. (p. 1620)
Schwartz, Virginia Frances. 4 Kids in 5E & 1 Crazy Year. (p. 1992)
—Initiation (p. 874)
—Initiation Morin, Paul, tr. (p. 874)
—Messenger (p. 1129)
—Nutz! Leist, Christina, illus. (p. 1274)
—Send One Angel Down (p. 1550)
Schwartz, Wendy, illus. see Beloat, Betty.
Schwartzenberger, Tina. Don Cherry. (p. 465)
Schwartzenberger, Tina, ed. see Lomberg, Michelle.
Schwartzenberger, Tina, ed. Substance Use & Abuse. (p. 1671)
Schwartzkopf, Jere, jt. auth. see Miller, Holly.
Schwarz, Alan. Baseball All-Stars: Today's Greatest Players. (p. 141)
—Rising Stars: The 10 Best Young Players in Baseball. (p. 1475)
Schwarz, Evelyn. Hummingbird Garden. Quinn, Kitty, illus. (p. 826)
Schwarz, Jacob D., ed. In the Land of Kings & Prophets. (p. 866)
Schwarz, Jacob David & Gamoran, Emanuel, eds. Into the Promised Land: The Bible Story in Bible Words, Book 3. (p. 881)
Schwarz, Manuela, illus. see Hay, Louise L. & Tracy, Kristina.
Schwarz, Patrick, jt. auth. see Kluth, Paula.
Schwarz, Philip, ed. see Burgan, Michael.
Schwarz, Philip, ed. see DeFord, Deborah H.
Schwarz, Philip, ed. see Doak, Robin Santos.
Schwarz, Philip, ed. see Kachur, Matthew.
Schwarz, Philip, ed. see Worth, Richard.
Schwarz, Renee. Birdfeeders. Schwarz, Renee, illus. (p. 190)
—Birdhouses. Schwarz, Renee, illus. (p. 190)
—Funky Junk: Cool Stuff to Make with Hardware. Schwarz, Renee, illus. (p. 649)
—Wind Chimes & Whirligigs. Schwarz, Renee, illus. (p. 1935)
Schwarz, Susan, jt. auth. see Sprague, Susan.
Schwarz, Thies, jt. illus. see Style Guide, Style.
Schwarz, Thies & Style Guide, Style. Tip's Tips on Friendship. (p. 1757)
Schwarz, Viviane. Is There a Dog in This Book? Schwarz, Viviane, illus. (p. 890)
—Shark & Lobster's Amazing Undersea Adventure. Stewart, Joel, illus. (p. 1562)
—Welcome to Your Awesome Robot. (p. 1874)
Schwarz, Viviane, illus. see Deacon, Alexis.
Schwarzer, Marie. Wizard of Math. (p. 1943)
Schwarzkopf, Tom. Danger at Mason's Island (p. 403)
—Ghost at Mahone Bay (p. 670)
—Secrets of Dynamite Point (p. 1545)
—Trouble Twins Save Christmas (p. 1790)
Schwarzschild, Barbara. Guppy Grebe. (p. 732)
Schweitzer, Albert. J. S. Bach Newman, Ernest, tr. from GER. (p. 902)
Schweitzer, Arlette. Whatever It Takes: One Woman's Gift of Motherhood to Her Daughter. Grosinger, Paula, ed. (p. 1896)
Schweitzer, C. V. Making of an Angel. (p. 1082)
Schweitzer, Karen. Americans of South American Heritage. (p. 64)
—Cocker Spaniel. (p. 337)
—Dachshund. (p. 398)
—Making the Band. (p. 1082)
—Real World. (p. 1449)
—Shaun White. (p. 1563)
—Sheryl Swoopes. (p. 1566)
—Soulja Boy Tell 'Em. (p. 1614)
Schweitzer, Patty, illus. see Wolcott, P. A.
Schweitzer-Johnson, Betty, illus. see Coffey, Ethel.
Schweizer, Chris. Creeps: Book 1: Night of the Frankenfrogs. (p. 381)
—Crogan Adventures. (p. 384)
—Crogan's Loyalty. (p. 384)
—Tricky Coyote Tales. Thomas, Chad, illus. (p. 1786)
—Tricky Fox Tales Paroline, Shelli & Paroline, Michelle, illus. (p. 1786)
—Tricky Fox Tales. Paroline, Shelli, illus. (p. 1786)
—Tricky Fox Tales. Paroline, Shelli & Paroline, Michelle, illus. (p. 1786)
—Tricky Monkey Tales. Thomas, Chad, illus. (p. 1786)
—Tricky Rabbit Tales. Giallongo, Zack, illus. (p. 1786)
—Tricky Raven Tales. Witt, David, illus. (p. 1786)
—Tricky Spider Tales. Huddleston, Courtney, illus. (p. 1786)
Schwemm, Diane. Year I Turned Sixteen: Rose, Daisy, Laurel, Lily. (p. 1969)
Schweninger, Ann, illus. see Van Leeuwen, Jean.
Schweppe, Deirdre. Migrating Animals: Use Place Value Understanding & Properties of Operations to Add & Subtract. (p. 1140)
Schwettmann, Gail L. Tangle Mangle Mess. (p. 1705)
Schwiebert, John E. Reading & Writing from Literature. (p. 1445)
Schwiebert, Pat. We Were Gonna Have a Baby, but We Had an Angel Instead. Bills, Taylor, illus. (p. 1868)
Schwiebert, Pat & DeKlyen, Chuck. Tear Soup: A Recipe for Healing after Loss. Bills, Taylor, illus. (p. 1711)
Schwieder, Dorothy, et al. Iowa Past to Present: The People & the Prairie. (p. 886)
Schwind, Beverly Lahote. Patches & Her Backpack Adventures. (p. 1328)
Schwinn, Aleaha. What Happens When I Yawn? (p. 1886)
Schwinn, Ruth E. Henry & Dale. Flores, Justin, illus. (p. 767)
Schwortz, Anna M. B C Rhymetime. Schwortz, Anna M., ed. (p. 122)
Schy, Yael, jt. auth. see Schwartz, David M.
Schy, Yael & Schwartz, David. What in the Wild? Mysteries of Nature Concealed... And Revealed. Kuhn, Dwight, photos by. (p. 1887)
Schyffert, Bea Uusma. Man Who Went to the Far Side of the Moon: The Story of Apollo 11 Astronaut Michael Collins. (p. 1086)
Schynert, Mark. Women of the Vietnam War. (p. 1946)
Sciarra, John. Shoestrings-Paradox. (p. 1568)
Sciarrino, Stephanie. Multiplication at the Marina: Multiply Within 100. (p. 1190)
Sciarrone, Claudio, illus. see Carbone, Courtney.
Sciarrone, Claudio, illus. see Golden Books.
Sciascia, Salvatore, illus. see Sartori, Gloria.
Science & Voege, Debra. Energy Today (p. 528)
Science Applications, Inc Staff, jt. auth. see Voege, Debra.
Science, Punk & Punk Science Staff. Punk Science - Intergalactic, Supermassive Space Book (p. 1417)
Science Readers Staff & Jankowski, Connie. From Hubble to Hubble: Astromers & Outer Space. (p. 643)
—Wonder of Outer Space. (p. 1947)
Science Readers Staff & Van Gorp, Lynn. World of Genetics. (p. 1956)
Scientifi, Pasco, et al. Pasco Laboratory Manual to Accompany Fundamentals of Physics, by Halliday, Resnick, & Walker, Student Version. (p. 1326)
Scientific American Editors, creator. Endangered Earth. (p. 526)
—What Makes a Genius? (p. 1892)
Scientific American Staff. 21st Century Robotics. (p. 1996)
—Beyond Extreme Physics. (p. 174)
—Endangered Earth. (p. 526)
—Extreme Engineering. (p. 556)
—Extreme Physics. (p. 556)
—Fighting Infectious Diseases. (p. 585)
—Future of the Web. (p. 651)
—Mysteries of the Milky Way. (p. 1222)
—Nanotech Revolution. (p. 1229)
—Tackling Cancer. (p. 1694)
Scieszka, Casey. To Timbuktu: Nine Countries, Two People, One True Story. Weinberg, Steven, illus. (p. 1759)
Scieszka, Jon. 2095. Smith, Lane, illus. (p. 2003)
—Ay, Samuray! (p. 121)
—Baloney (Henry P.) Smith, Lane, illus. (p. 135)
—Baloney (Henry P.) Smith, Lane, illus. (p. 135)
—Caballeros de la Mesa de la Cocina. Smith, Lane, illus. (p. 250)
—Da Wild, Da Crazy, Da Vinci McCauley, Adam & Adam, Mccauley, illus. (p. 398)
—Da Wild, Da Crazy, Da Vinci. McCauley, Adam, illus. (p. 398)
—Dizzy Izzy. Gordon, David et al, illus. (p. 455)
—Dizzy Izzy. Shannon, David et al, illus. (p. 455)
—Domingo, el Dia del Vikingo. (p. 465)
—Frank Einstein & the Antimatter Motor. Biggs, Brian, illus. (p. 628)
—Frank Einstein & the BrainTurbo. Biggs, Brian, illus. (p. 628)
—Frank Einstein & the Electro-Finger. Biggs, Brian, illus. (p. 628)
—Frog Prince. Johnson, Steve, illus. (p. 640)
—Frog Prince, Continued (p. 640)
—Frog Prince, Continued. (p. 640)
—Frog Prince, Continued. Johnson, Steve, illus. (p. 640)
—Garage Tales. Gordon, David et al, illus. (p. 655)
—Good, the Bad, & the Goofy. Smith, Lane, illus. (p. 700)
—Great Truck Rescue. Shannon, David et al, illus. (p. 719)
—Guys Read: Thriller. Helquist, Brett, illus. (p. 733)
—Hey Kid, Want to Buy a Bridge? McCauley, Adam, illus. (p. 774)
—It's All Greek to Me Smith, Lane, illus. (p. 896)
—It's All Greek to Me. Smith, Lane, illus. (p. 896)
—Kat's Maps. Long, Loren et al, illus. (p. 945)
—Kat's Maps. Shannon, David et al, illus. (p. 945)
—Kat's Mystery Gift. Gordon, David et al, illus. (p. 945)
—Kat's Mystery Gift. Shannon, David et al, illus. (p. 945)
—Knights of the Kitchen Table. (p. 964)
—Knucklehead: Tall Tales & Almost True Stories about Growing up Scieszka. (p. 965)
—Marco? Polo! McCauley, Adam, illus. (p. 1092)
—Math Curse. (p. 1105)
—Math Curse. Smith, Lane, illus. (p. 1105)
—Me Oh Maya. McCauley, Adam, illus. (p. 1116)
—Melvin Might? Gordon, David et al, illus. (p. 1125)
—Melvin's Valentine. Shannon, David et al, illus. (p. 1125)
—Oh Say, I Can't See McCauley, Adam, illus. (p. 1281)
—Pete's Party. Gordon, David et al, illus. (p. 1348)
—Pirata Barbanegra. Smith, Lane, illus. (p. 1362)
—Race from A to Z Gordon, David et al, illus. (p. 1431)
—Robot Zot! Shannon, David, illus. (p. 1480)
—Sam Samurai. McCauley, Adam, illus. (p. 1507)
—Science Verse. Smith, Lane, illus. (p. 1528)
—See You Later, Gladiator. McCauley, Adam, illus. (p. 1547)
—Seen Art? Smith, Lane, illus. (p. 1548)
—Smash! Crash! Shannon, David et al, illus. (p. 1593)
—Snow Trucking! Gordon, David et al, illus. (p. 1599)
—Spaceheadz (p. 1620)
—Spaceheadz. Prigmore, Shane, illus. (p. 1620)
—Sphdz 4 Life! (p. 1625)
—SPHDZ 4 Life! Prigmore, Shane, illus. (p. 1625)
—SPHDZ Book #1! Prigmore, Shane, illus. (p. 1625)
—SPHDZ Book #2! Prigmore, Shane, illus. (p. 1626)
—Spooky Tire. Shannon, David et al, illus. (p. 1631)
—Squids Will Be Squids: Fresh Morals, Beastly Fables. Smith, Lane, illus. (p. 1637)
—Summer Reading Is Killing Me! Smith, Lane, illus. (p. 1674)
—Thriller. Helquist, Brett, illus. (p. 1744)
—Truckery Rhymes. (p. 1791)
—Truckery Rhymes. Gordon, David et al, illus. (p. 1791)
—Trucks Line Up. Gordon, David et al, illus. (p. 1791)
—Trucks Line Up. Shannon, David et al, illus. (p. 1791)
—Trucksgiving. Shannon, David et al, illus. (p. 1791)
—True Story of the 3 Little Pigs. Smith, Lane, illus. (p. 1793)
—Tu Mama Era Neanderthal. Smith, Lane, illus. (p. 1795)
—Tut, Tut Smith, Lane, illus. (p. 1799)
—Tut, Tut. Smith, Lane, illus. (p. 1799)
—Uh-Oh, Max. Shannon, David et al, illus. (p. 1808)
—Viking It & Liking It. (p. 1842)
—Viking It & Liking It. McCauley, Adam, illus. (p. 1842)
—Welcome to Trucktown! Shannon, David et al, illus. (p. 1874)
—Who Done It? (p. 1915)
—Your Mother Was a Neanderthal. Smith, Lane, illus. (p. 1981)
—Zoom! Boom! Bully. Shannon, David et al, illus. (p. 1989)
—¡La Verdadera Historia de los Tres Cerditos! (p. 969)
Scieszka, Jon, jt. auth. see Harper, Benjamin.
Scieszka, Jon, jt. auth. see Sander, Sonia.
Scieszka, Jon, jt. auth. see Teitelbaum, Michael.
Scieszka, Jon, jt. narrated by see Willems, Mo.
Scieszka, Jon & Barnett, Mac. Battle Bunny. Myers, Matthew, illus. (p. 145)
Scieszka, Jon & Brown, Dustin, eds. Sports Pages. (p. 1633)
Scieszka, Jon & Smith, Lane. Cowboy & Octopus. Smith, Lane, illus. (p. 373)
Scieszka, Jon, et al. Funny Business. Rex, Adam, illus. (p. 649)
—Guys Read: Terrifying Tales. (p. 733)
—Guys Read: True Stories. (p. 733)
—Sports Pages. Santat, Dan, illus. (p. 1633)
—Terrifying Tales. Grimly, Gris, illus. (p. 1721)
Scillian, Corey, jt. auth. see Scillian, Devin.
Scillian, Devin. Brewster the Rooster. White, Lee, illus. (p. 226)
—Cosmo's Moon. Braught, Mark, illus. (p. 368)
—D Is for down Under: An Australia Alphabet. Cook, Geoff, illus. (p. 397)
—H Is for Honor: A Military Family Alphabet. Juhasz, Victor, illus. (p. 734)
—Johnny Kaw: A Tall Tale. Sneed, Brad, illus. (p. 923)
—Memoirs of a Goldfish. Bowers, Tim, illus. (p. 1125)
—Memoirs of a Hamster. Bowers, Tim, illus. (p. 1125)
—Memoirs of an Elf. Bowers, Tim, illus. (p. 1125)
—One Nation: America by the Numbers. Carroll, Pam, illus. (p. 1296)
—P Is for Passport: A World Alphabet. Rose, Melanie, illus. (p. 1316)
—Pappy's Handkerchief. Ellison, Chris, illus. (p. 1323)
—S Is for Sooner: An Oklahoma Alphabet. Doner, Kim, illus. (p. 1499)
Scillian, Devin & Scillian, Corey. One Kansas Farmer: A Kansas Number Book. Bowles, Doug, illus. (p. 1295)
—S Is for Sunflower: A Kansas Alphabet. Bowles, Doug, illus. (p. 1499)
Scillian, Devin & Young, Judy. Westward Journeys. Ellison, Chris et al, illus. (p. 1876)
Scimone, Diana. Adventures with Pawpaw: China. Wiedemer, Leah, illus. (p. 25)
—Adventures with Pawpaw: France. Wiedemer, Leah, illus. (p. 25)
—Adventures with Pawpaw: Costa Rica. Wiedemer, Leah, illus. (p. 25)
Scipio, Laurise. I Wish. (p. 848)
Sciulli, Erika, illus. see Brant, Dennis, Jr.
Sciuto, Alex, illus. see Higgins, Nadia.
Sciuto, Alex, illus. see Rowell, Rebecca.
Sclafani, Terry. Thompson Twins Cruise Adventure. (p. 1739)
—Thompson Twins Western Adventure. (p. 1739)
Scoble, Andrea, illus. see Waldman, Alan/A.
Scoble, Andrea, illus. see Yontz-Oetting, Carolyn.
Scoffham, Stephen. World in Maps. (p. 1956)
Scoffham, Stephen & Bridge, Colin. Primary Geography - Collins Primary Geography (p. 1399)
—Primary Geography - Collins Primary Geography Pupil Book 3. (p. 1399)
—Primary Geography - Collins Primary Geography Pupil Book 1 & 2. (p. 1399)
Scoffham, Stephen & Collins Maps Staff. UK in Maps. (p. 1808)
Scoffham, Stephen, ed. Junior World Atlas. (p. 936)
Scofield, Chris. Shark Curtain. (p. 1562)
Scoggins, Jocelyn, illus. see Achilles, Carole.
Scoggins, Terry. Electric Ellie & Lightning Lucy: Firefly Friends Forever. (p. 508)
Scogin, Connie, jt. auth. see Rodriguez, Emma Vera.
Scognamiglio, John, jt. auth. see James, Sabrina.
Scoles, Candie, illus. see Throckmorton, Sylvestra.
Scollen, C. My Big Book for Boys. (p. 1197)
—My Big Book for Girls. (p. 1197)
—My Giant Sticker Stencil. (p. 1209)
Scollen, Chris. 1000 Stickers Sweet Treats. (p. 2001)
—Busy Kids Baby Animals Sticker Activity Book. (p. 246)
—Busy Kids Farm Animals Sticker Activity Book. (p. 246)
—Busy Kids Kittens & Puppies Sb. (p. 246)
—Busy Kids Sticker Storybook Gingerbread Fred. (p. 246)
—Busy Kids Sticker Storybook Goldilocks. (p. 246)
—Busy Kids Sticker Storybook Little Mermaid. (p. 246)
—Busy Kids Sticker Storybook Sleeping Beauty. (p. 246)
—Busy Kids Sticker Storybook Three Billy Goats. (p. 246)
—Busy Kids Tractors & Trucks Sticker Activity Book. (p. 246)
Scollen, Chris, et al. Diggers & Dumpers. (p. 439)
Scollon, Bill. Dreamworks Dragons: A Tale of Two Dragons. (p. 484)
—Jake & the Never Land Pirates: Battle for the Book. (p. 905)
—Mickey Mouse Clubhouse: A Goofy Fairy Tale. (p. 1136)
—Minnie: Case of the Missing Sparkle-Izer. Loter Inc. Staff, illus. (p. 1147)
—Minnie's Winter Bow Show. (p. 1148)
—Moshi Monsters Super Search. (p. 1176)
—Pirate Pup. (p. 1363)
—Super Adventure. Disney Book Group Staff & Disney Storybook Artists Staff, illus. (p. 1679)
—Wings Around the Globe. (p. 1936)
Scollon, Bill, jt. auth. see Disney Book Group Staff.
Scollon, Bill, jt. auth. see RH Disney Staff.
Scollon, Bill & Nee, Chris. Engine Nine, Feelin' Fine! (p. 529)
Scollon, William. Case of the Missing Sparkle-Izer. (p. 274)
—Doc Mcstuffins: Brave Dragon. (p. 459)
—Doc Mcstuffins: Starry, Starry Night. (p. 459)
—Jake & the Never Land Pirates: Pirate Campout. (p. 905)
—Minnie: Be My Sparkly Valentine. (p. 1147)
—Minnie's Pet Salon. (p. 1148)
—Minnie's Summer Vacation. (p. 1148)
Scollon, William, jt. auth. see Disney Book Group Staff.
Scollon, William & Disney Book Group Staff. Case of the Missing Sparkle-Izer, Level Pre-1. Disney Storybook Art Team, illus. (p. 274)
—Great Treasure Hunt. Disney Storybook Art Team, illus. (p. 719)
—Jake Saves Bucky. Disney Storybook Artists Staff & Disney Storybook Art Team, illus. (p. 906)
—Key to Skull Rock, Level 1. Disney Storybook Art Team, illus. (p. 950)
—Mickey & Donald Have a Farm. Disney Storybook Art Team, illus. (p. 1135)
—Minnie's Pet Salon. Disney Storybook Art Team, illus. (p. 1148)
—World of Reading: Doc Mcstuffins Starry, Starry Night: Level 1. Disney Storybook Art Team, illus. (p. 1957)
Scollon, William & Parent, Nancy. Blooming Bows. Disney Storybook Artists Staff, illus. (p. 201)
Scollon, William, et al. Easter Bonnet Parade. Disney Storybook Artists Staff, illus. (p. 499)
—Engine Nine, Feelin' Fine! Disney Storybook Artists Staff, illus. (p. 529)
—Minnie Be My Sparkly Valentine. Disney Storybook Art Team Staff, illus. (p. 1147)
—Trouble Times Two. Disney Storybook Artists Staff, illus. (p. 1790)
—World of Reading: Jake & the Never Land Pirates Pirate Campout: Level 1. Disney Storybook Artists Staff, illus. (p. 1957)
Sconnely, Martha. When Toby Lost His Yard. (p. 1905)
Sconyers, Jennifer. John Bunny Goes on Vacation. (p. 921)
—Map. (p. 1089)
Scooby Doo & Balaban, Mariah. Scooby-Doo & the Scary Snowman. (p. 1529)
Scoones, Simon. Focus on Brazil. (p. 610)
—Rio de Janeiro. Parker, Edward, photos by. (p. 1473)
—South America. (p. 1616)
Scoppettone, Sandra. Happy Endings Are All Alike. (p. 745)
Scorey, John, illus. see Mayes, Susan.
Scotford, Groenewald & Scotford, Tina. Bush Buffet in the Land of Kachoo: The Land of Kachoo Series. (p. 244)
—Mighty Elephant in the Land of Kachoo: The Land of Kachoo Series. Groenewald, Frans, illus. (p. 1140)
Scotford, Tina. Saving the Rhino in the Land of Kachoo: The Land of Kachoo Series. Groenewald, Frans, illus. (p. 1517)
Scotford, Tina, jt. auth. see Scotford, Groenewald.
Scotland, James. Day of Wrath. (p. 414)
Scott. Heinle Rdg Lib Ivanhoe. (p. 762)
Scott, A. O., illus. see Kessler, Ramon Wilke.
Scott, Aaron Sharon. Dark Divide. (p. 407)
Scott, Adrian. Road Gets Better from Here. (p. 1476)
Scott, Amanda. Highland Bride. (p. 779)
—Highland Princess. (p. 779)
—Knight's Treasure. (p. 964)
—Lady's Choice. (p. 971)
Scott, Angela, jt. auth. see Scott, Johnathan.
Scott, Angela, jt. auth. see Scott, Jonathan.
Scott, Ann, ed. see Murdin, Lesley.
Scott, Ann, illus. see Seyderhelm, Amanda.
Scott, Ann Herbert. Las Piernas de Mama. Coalson, Glo, illus. (p. 977)
Scott, Autrilla W. Stories from the Past. (p. 1654)
Scott B, Bryon. School by Blue Lake. (p. 1522)
Scott, B. L. Adventures of Babadoodle Kit Kit. (p. 16)
Scott, Bart. Balaam. (p. 133)
Scott, Bill. Next Steps: A Student Devotional. (p. 1249)
Scott, Bob, illus. see Schulz, Charles M. & Pastis, Stephan.
Scott, Brandon James. Justin Time: the Big Pet Story. (p. 940)
—Pancake Express. (p. 1320)
Scott, Brandy. Because I Am an American Girl: An Early Lesson on Women's Rights. (p. 155)
Scott, Brigett, jt. auth. see Scott, Sabrina.
Scott, Caitlin. Condemned (p. 355)
—Treasure Hunting: Looking for Lost Riches. (p. 1781)
—Treasure Hunting: Looking for Lost Riches Set (p. 1781)
Scott, Carey. Magic & Mystery. (p. 1071)
Scott, Cassandra. Boys & Girls Are Created2Produce. (p. 220)
Scott, Catherine, ed. see Holbrook, John Robert.
Scott, Cathy. Lily Mouse. (p. 1018)
Scott, Cavan. Machine of Doom. (p. 1068)
Scott, Cavan & Snider, Brandon T. Complete Collection. (p. 352)
Scott, Cavan, et al. Penguins of Madagascar: Operation Heist. Vol. 2 Bartolini, Egle, illus. (p. 1337)
Scott, Celicia. Dangerous Depressants & Sedatives. Borus, Joshua, ed. (p. 404)
—Doping: Human Growth Hormone, Steroids, & Other Performance-Enhancing Drugs. Borus, Joshua, ed. (p. 470)
—Energy Drinks, Coffee, Soda, & Pills. Borus, Joshua, ed. (p. 528)
—Facebook(Tm) How Mark Zuckerberg Connected More Than a Billion Friends. (p. 560)

—Hard Drugs: Cocaine, LSD, PCP, & Heroin. Borus, Joshua, ed. (p. 748)
—Ludacris. (p. 1063)
—Mariah Carey. (p. 1093)
—My Daily Diet: Proteins. Prock, Lisa Albers, ed. (p. 1201)
—My Daily Diet: Vegetables. Prock, Lisa Albers, ed. (p. 1201)
—New Drugs: Bath Salts, Spice, Salvia, & Designer Drugs. Borus, Joshua, ed. (p. 1244)
—Sports & Fitness. Hart, Diane H., ed. (p. 1632)
—Twitter: How Jack Dorsey Changed the Way We Communicate. (p. 1803)
—Weight Lifting & Strength Building. Hart, Diane H., ed. (p. 1872)
—YouTube: How Steve Chen Changed the Way We Watch Videos. (p. 1982)
Scott, Chad H. Bad Pups: Club Life. (p. 132)
Scott, Chay L. Henry the Hippo. (p. 768)
Scott, Chelsey, illus. see Jahn, Benny.
Scott, Chris. Unseen. (p. 1822)
Scott, Christina. All in A Night's Work. (p. 44)
—Chimney. (p. 306)
—North Pole. (p. 1265)
Scott, Christopher L., illus. see Pendleton, Claudette M.
Scott, Clark C., jt. auth. see Bennett, Doraine.
Scott, Clarke C., jt. auth. see Donohue, Moira Rose.
Scott, Colin. Children's Secret Diary. (p. 304)
—Speedy Kids Coloring Book. (p. 1624)
Scott, Concetta C., illus. see Dowell, Ruth I.
Scott, Crissy. Toast Is the Most. (p. 1760)
Scott, D. P. Christmas Elf. Hayward, Roy, illus. (p. 313)
Scott, Damion, illus. see Jenkins, Paul.
Scott, Dan. Secret of Fort Pioneer: A Bret King Mystery. Beeler, Joe, illus. (p. 1542)
Scott, Daniel. Classical Greats: Junior Guest Spot. (p. 328)
—Classical Greats: Easy Playalong for Flute. (p. 328)
—Classical Greats: Easy Playalong for Clarinet. (p. 328)
Scott, Daniel, ed. see Snicket, Lemony, pseud.
Scott, Dee Mary. Adventures of Charles & Camilla Chinchilla. (p. 17)
Scott, Denise & Disney Book Group Staff. Nursery Rhymes. Disney Storybook Art Team, illus. (p. 1273)
Scott, Donald Iain. Letters of the Alphabet - Celtic Art Designs. (p. 1002)
Scott, Douglas. Adventures of Turtle Boy & Beaver Girl: Tales of the Little People. (p. 24)
Scott, E., illus. see Lee, G.
Scott, Earnestine E. Little Mike's Family: A Novel for Second & Third Graders. (p. 1031)
Scott, Eileen. For the Love of Padah: The Transforming Touch of the Shepherd's Love. (p. 616)
Scott, Elaine. Buried Alive! How 33 Miners Survived 69 Days Deep under the Chilean Desert. (p. 243)
—Secrets of the Cirque Medrano. (p. 1545)
—Space, Stars, & the Beginning of Time: What the Hubble Telescope Saw. (p. 1620)
—Spanish Web: An Encounter with Picasso. (p. 1621)
Scott, Elizabeth. Between Here & Forever. (p. 172)
—Bloom. (p. 201)
—Living Dead Girl. (p. 1040)
—Love You Hate You Miss You. (p. 1060)
—Miracle. (p. 1148)
—Perfect You. (p. 1342)
—Something, Maybe. (p. 1610)
—Stealing Heaven. (p. 1646)
—Unwritten Rule. (p. 1824)
Scott, Elizabeth M. Adventures with Mama Scottie & the Kids. Jackson, Kay Whytock, illus. (p. 25)
—It's Rodeo Time! With Mamma Scottie & the Kids. (p. 898)
Scott, Emmett J. Scott's Official History of the American Negro in the World War: American Black in World War I. (p. 1532)
Scott, Eric. Day the Rainbow Ended. (p. 414)
—Great Fairytale Robbery. (p. 716)
—Island of Lost Dolls. (p. 892)
—Santa & the Cyberspace Plot. (p. 1511)
Scott, Foresman and Company Staff. Discover Science. (p. 448)
—Fun with Dick & Jane. (p. 648)
—Read with Dick & Jane (p. 1444)
—Up & over, Thrills & Spills. (p. 1824)
—Work & Play, Big & Little, You & Me. (p. 1952)
Scott, Fred & Southworth, Gordon. English for the Thoughtful Child Vol 2 (p. 530)
Scott, G. C. At the End of Her Tether. (p. 111)
Scott, Gavin, illus. see Corderoy, Tracey.
Scott, Gavin, illus. see Freedman, Claire.
Scott, Gavin, jt. auth. see Freedman, Claire.
Scott, Geoffrey. Fairy Tales for Adults. (p. 564)
Scott, Greg. Captain America by Dan Jurgens Scott, Greg & Ross, Dave, illus. (p. 263)
Scott, Greg, illus. see Cosby, Andrew & Nelson, Michael Alan.
Scott, Gwen. Blackberry Junction. Baker, David, illus. (p. 197)
—Dog That Wore Glasses. (p. 461)
—In Between the Cracks: The Search for Zar. (p. 863)
Scott, Heather, jt. auth. see Dorling Kindersley Publishing Staff.
Scott, James. Indian in the Cupboard: Activity Pack. (p. 871)
—Indian in the Cupboard: Response Journal. (p. 871)
—Jane Eyre: A Student Response Journal. (p. 908)
—Johnny Tremain: Response Journal. (p. 923)
—Macbeth: Activity Pack. (p. 1068)
Scott, James, adapted by. Othello - Side by Side. (p. 1306)
Scott, James W. Sourface Kids. (p. 1616)
Scott, Jane Beecher. Amazing Mosquito Bridge Secret. Scott, Jane Beecher, ed. (p. 55)
Scott, Jane Wooster, illus. see Raffin, Deborah.
Scott, Janice B. Children's Stories from the Village Shepherd. (p. 304)
Scott, Janine. Café Cosmos. Wood, Hannah, illus. (p. 250)
—Growing a Plant. (p. 726)
—Kids Have Rights Too! (p. 954)
—Living in Hong Kong: Set Of 6. (p. 1041)
—Mars Mouse. Wood, Hannah, illus. (p. 1096)
—Noisy Parrot. Rigby, Deborah, illus. (p. 1263)
—Ocean of Animals (p. 1276)
—Rain Forest Life (p. 1434)
—Two Great Wars. (p. 1803)
Scott, Jeanette B. Three Story House. (p. 1744)
Scott, Jeanne Ann. Raining Worms. (p. 1436)
Scott, Jeff. Becoming the King: Where's my Father? (p. 156)
—Discovery of Monkey Island. (p. 450)
Scott, Jennifer, illus. see Harney Jr., Robert.
Scott, Jeremy. P. T. A. Night. (p. 1316)
Scott, Jerry. Chillax. Borgman, Jim, illus. (p. 305)
—Shredded. Borgman, Jim, illus. (p. 1571)
—Zits: Carretera y Manta. Vol. 7 (p. 1987)
Scott, Jerry & Borgman, Jim. El Estiron. Falcó, Roberto, tr. from ENG. (p. 507)
—Zits: ¿Existe un "Nosotros"? Falcó, Roberto, tr. from ENG. (p. 1987)
—Zits: Mframe Cuando Te Hablo, Jovencito. Falcó, Roberto, tr. from ENG. (p. 1987)
—Zits Descomprimido: Volume 5 (p. 1987)
—Zits (En Español) Estefanía, Oscar, tr. from ENG. (p. 1987)
Scott, Joanna. Liberation. (p. 1005)
—Tourmaline: A Novel. (p. 1773)
Scott, Joanna I. Stanley the Moose: Book One of the Woodsie Tails Series. (p. 1640)
Scott, John L., jt. auth. see Sarkees-Wircenski, Michelle.
Scott, John, suppl. How to Study. (p. 821)
Scott, John, text. Athletic Quest Total Sports System. (p. 112)
—How to Financially Fund Your College Education. (p. 819)
—Juniors: How to Make the Team. (p. 936)
—Seniors: How to Get Recruited. (p. 1550)
—Sophomore: How to Make the Team. (p. 1614)
Scott, Johnathan & Scott, Angela. Big Cat Babies. Moon, Cliff, ed. (p. 180)
Scott, Jonathan, illus. see Scott, Johnathan & Scott, Angela.
Scott, Jonathan & Scott, Angela. Africa's Big Three. Scott, Jonathan & Scott, Angela, illus. (p. 28)
—Antarctica: Land of the Penguins Band 11/Lime. (p. 88)
—Kings of the Wild. Scott, Jonathan & Scott, Angela, illus. (p. 960)
—Living Dinosaurs. Scott, Jonathan & Scott, Angela, illus. (p. 1040)
—Masai: Tribe of Warriors. Scott, Jonathan & Scott, Angela, illus. (p. 1102)
Scott, Judy, illus. see Floyd, Gina.
Scott, Julie, illus. see Ward, Jennifer.
Scott, Karen. Endangered Species & Friends in the U. S. A. Seamans, Amanda, illus. (p. 527)
Scott, Karen, jt. auth. see Smith, Kathryn.
Scott, Kathleen. TEEN's Self-Discovery Workbook in Astrology: All the World's a Stage... Know Your Chart... You'll Know Your Part! (p. 1715)
Scott, Kathy. Beacon Hill. (p. 149)
Scott, Katie, illus. see Broom, Jenny.
Scott, Keith. Bear Man. Hill, Steve, illus. (p. 151)
Scott, Kelly, ed. see Schwartz, Linda.
Scott, Kevin. Stevie Wonderboy. (p. 1649)
Scott, Kieran. Geek Magnet. (p. 659)
—He's So Not Worth It. (p. 774)
—I Was a Non-Blonde Cheerleader. (p. 848)
—Non-Blonde Cheerleader in Love. (p. 1263)
—Only Everything. (p. 1298)
—She's So Dead to Us. (p. 1566)
—Something True. (p. 1610)
—This Is So Not Happening. (p. 1736)
—What Waits in the Woods. (p. 1894)
Scott, Kieran, see Brian, Kate, pseud.
Scott, Kieran & Scott, Kiernan. Brunettes Strike Back. (p. 232)
Scott, Kiernan, jt. auth. see Scott, Kieran.
Scott, Kimberley. Wipe-Clean First Math. (p. 1939)
—Wipe-Clean First Words. (p. 1939)
Scott, Kimberley, illus. see Gallo, Tina.
Scott, Kimberley, illus. see Greenwell, Jessica.
Scott, Kimberley, illus. see MacLaine, James.
Scott, Kimberley, illus. see McKay, Hilary.
Scott, Kimberley, illus. see Ostrove, Karen.
Scott, Kimberley G., illus. see McKay, Hilary.
Scott, Kimberly, illus. see Claybourne, Anna.
Scott, Kimberly Ann. Mommy! There's a Snot Man Standing Next to You! (p. 1162)
Scott, Kitty, et al. Peter Doig. (p. 1346)
Scott, Korey, illus. see Frontiera, Deborah K.
Scott, Korey, illus. see Frontiera, Deborah.
Scott, Korey, illus. see Gordon, Jon.
Scott, Korey, illus. see Hansen, Amy S.
Scott, Korey, illus. see Hansen, Amy S. & Olien, Rebecca.
Scott, Korey, illus. see Osterkamp, Oie.
Scott, L. K. Snakes. Mangiat, Jeff, illus. (p. 1596)
Scott, Ladena Mae. Bossy Rossy. (p. 215)
Scott, Larry, illus. see Russell, Peggy.
Scott, Laurian. Thisbe's Promise. Sharp, Kelley, illus. (p. 1737)
Scott, Laurie, jt. auth. see Dick, William.
Scott, Leah. Tincup & the Tornado. (p. 1755)
Scott, Lee, et al. Where Is It Going. (p. 1908)
Scott, Linda. How to Be the Best Bubblewriter in the World ... Ever! (p. 815)
—My Bubble Writer Christmas Book. (p. 1199)
—My Monster Bubblewriter Book. (p. 1214)
Scott, Lisa Ann. School of Charm. (p. 1523)
Scott, Liz. Bear Story: Just a Silly Man Who Wears a Fur Coat & Needs a Shave. (p. 151)
Scott, Liz, et al. Alex & the Amazing Lemonade Stand. Howard, Pam, illus. (p. 35)
Scott, Luke. Through a Crystal Doorknob. (p. 1744)
Scott, Mairghread, jt. auth. see Johnson, Mike.
Scott, Maisie. Coloured Detectives. (p. 346)
Scott, Marc, illus. see McKay, Sindy.
Scott, Maren J., illus. see Heno, Christy C.
Scott, Margaret. Medieval Clothing & Costumes: Displaying Wealth & Class in Medieval Times. (p. 1119)
—Medieval Clothing & Costumes. (p. 1119)
Scott, Marilyn. Lightening Bug's Message of Love. (p. 1015)
—Little Christmas Fairy. (p. 1026)
Scott, Martha. Honey Bee, Where Are You? (p. 794)
—Timeless Sea Turtles. (p. 1754)
Scott, Martin J. Boy Knight. (p. 218)
Scott, Mary Ann. New Girl (p. 1244)
—New Girl. (p. 1244)
Scott, Matthew. Search & Find Puzzle Island: Picture Puzzles, Number Games, Amazing Mazes, Treasure Hunt. (p. 1537)
Scott, Michael. Alchemyst. (p. 35)
—Enchantress. (p. 523)
—Magician. (p. 1075)
—Necromancer. (p. 1239)
—Necromancer the Secrets of the Immortal Nicholas Flamel. (p. 1239)
—Sorceress. (p. 1614)
—Sorceress the Secrets of the Immortal Nicholas Flamel. (p. 1614)
—Warlock. (p. 1858)
—Warlock the Secrets of the Immortal Nicholas Flamel. (p. 1858)
Scott, Michael, jt. auth. see Scott, Michael.
Scott, Michael & Scott, Michael. Hechicera: Los Secretos del Immortal Nicolas Flamel. Fernandez, Maria Angulo, tr. (p. 761)
Scott, Michael Rhys. Island's unto Himself. (p. 892)
Scott, Michele. Dark Harmony: A Vivienne Taylor Horse Lover's Mystery (p. 407)
—Perfect Harmony: A Vivienne Taylor Horse Lover's Mystery (p. 1342)
—Silent Harmony (p. 1575)
Scott, Mindi. Freefall. (p. 635)
—Live Through This. (p. 1040)
Scott, Molly. Broken Bones Are No Fun, but Broken Bones Won't Stop My Play! Baker, David, illus. (p. 230)
Scott, Natalie. Wheels Make it Work. (p. 1901)
Scott, Nathan Kumar. Mangoes & Bananas. Balaji, T., illus. (p. 1087)
—Sacred Banana Leaf. (p. 1500)
Scott, Nathan Kumar & Chitara, Jagdish. Great Race. (p. 718)
Scott, Norm. Hsu & Chan (p. 824)
Scott, Peter, illus. see Clarke, Phillip.
Scott, Peter, illus. see Frith, Alex.
Scott, Peter, illus. see Greenwell, Jessica.
Scott, Peter, illus. see Khan, Sarah.
Scott, Peter, illus. see Rogers, Kirsteen.
Scott, Peter, illus. see Segal, Andrew.
Scott, Peter, illus. see Tatchell, Judy & Rogers, Kirsteen.
Scott, Peter, illus. see Tatchell, Judy.
Scott, Peter, illus. see Turnbull, Stephanie.
Scott, Peter & Justine, Torode. Box of Bugs. (p. 216)
Scott, Peter David. A to Z Book of Wild Animals: An Alphabet Adventure. (p. 1)
—Amazing Animals: A Nature Adventure. (p. 53)
—Dinosaur. (p. 441)
Scott, Peter David, illus. see Clarke, Phillip & Furnival, Keith.
Scott, Peter David, illus. see Kahn, Sarah.
Scott, Peter David, illus. see Smith, Alastair & Tachell, Judy.
Scott, Peter David, illus. see Smith, Alastair & Tatchell, Judy.
Scott, Peter David, illus. see Tatchell, Judy.
Scott, Richard, illus. see David, Juliet.
Scott, Robbie. Mystery of Rascal Pratt. Gary Cianciarulo, Gary, illus. (p. 1225)
Scott, Robert. Justin Bieber Confidential. (p. 940)
—Shades of Monte Christo & Other Short Stories. (p. 1557)
Scott, Ron. Latte's Counting Book (p. 980)
Scott, Rosanna. Peter & Friends at Camp. Fargo, Todd, illus. (p. 1346)
Scott, Rose Marie. Gentle Ones. Scott, Rose Marie, illus. (p. 661)
Scott, Rosseau, illus. see Ivan, Benson.
Scott, Sabrina & Scott, Brigett. What's That in Mom's Belly? (p. 1899)
Scott, Sally. Time for Tea. (p. 1751)
Scott, Sara, ed. see Arnauld, D. S.
Scott, Sarah C., illus. see Day, Ed D.
Scott, Sarah Chamberlin, illus. see Green, Holly G.
Scott, Shirley A. Adventures of Jack & Dobbie: Happy Tails. (p. 19)
—Adventures of Jack & Dobbie: The Beginning. (p. 19)
—Adventures of Jack & Dobbie: Doggie Holidays. (p. 19)
—Adventures of Jack & Dobbie: Traveling Buddies. (p. 19)
Scott, Sirag. Fall (p. 566)
Scott, Stephen K. Grunions with Onions: A Children's Food Fantasy. (p. 727)
Scott, Steve, illus. see Martinez, Victor.
Scott, Steve, illus. see Parker, Jeff.
Scott, Steve, illus. see Williams, Rob.
Scott, Susan, illus. see Cohen-Spence, Susan.
Scott, Susan, illus. see O'Connell, Isabel.
Scott, Terrence. Bryce Coris Blessing. (p. 233)
Scott, Thomas F., jt. auth. see Harrison, Geoffrey C.
Scott, Trevor, illus. see Simone, Gail.
Scott, Vicki, jt. auth. see Schulz, Charles M.
Scott, Victoria. Fire & Flood. (p. 590)
—Liberator. (p. 1005)
—Salt & Stone. (p. 1505)
Scott, Victoria Joan Groves, jt. auth. see Weishaar, Mary Konya.
Scott, Walter. Ivanhoe. (p. 900)
—Ivanhoe. Lago, Ray, illus. (p. 900)
—Rob Roy. (p. 1478)
Scott, Walter, et al. Ivanhoe. (p. 900)
Scott, Wanda L. Lifetime of Relationships: Letters, Poems & Words of Love. (p. 1014)
Scott, William. Bouncy Bear. (p. 216)
Scott, Winston. We Can Count! (p. 1866)
Scott, Xavier. Great Diary Planner for Teens: Diary. (p. 715)
Scott-Barrett, Fiona, jt. auth. see O'Driscoll, Nina.
Scott-Branagan, Bronwen. Chips Quackety. (p. 308)
Scott-Branagan, Browmen. Pandanuspeople. (p. 1320)
Scott-Brown, Anna. Creation Song. Gomez, Elena, illus. (p. 379)
Scott-Cameron, Nancy. Santa Claus Is on a Diet! Conlan, Craig, illus. (p. 1511)
Scott-Coleman, Brenda. Girl with Many Faces. (p. 679)
Scott-Daniel, Toni, illus. see Jackson, Gwendolyn.
Scott-Dixon, Valerie. My Fuzzy Wuzzy Hair. (p. 1209)
Scott-Goodman, Barbara. Beach House Cookbook. Maas, Rita, photos by. (p. 149)
Scott-Hughes, Brian, jt. auth. see Lambert, Alan.
Scotti, Alberto Douglas. Cocina y Ciencia. (p. 337)
Scotti, Douglas & Pelagotti, Alessandra. Nail Art. (p. 1227)
Scotto, Michael. Buck's Bad Dreams. Gabriel, Evette, illus. (p. 234)
—Builda the Re-Bicycler. Gabriel, Evette, illus. (p. 238)
—Just Flash. Gabriel, Evette et al, illus. (p. 938)
—Sweet Tooth Bun. Gabriel, Evette, illus. (p. 1690)
Scotton, Rob. Back to School, Splat! Scotton, Rob, illus. (p. 130)
—Big Helper. (p. 181)
—Big Helper. Scotton, Rob, illus. (p. 181)
—Blow, Snow, Blow. (p. 202)
—Doodle & Draw. Scotton, Rob, illus. (p. 469)
—Fishy Tales. (p. 599)
—Funny Valentine. Scotton, Rob, illus. (p. 650)
—Good Night, Sleep Tight. Scotton, Rob & Eberz, Robert, illus. (p. 700)
—I Scream for Ice Cream. Scotton, Rob, illus. (p. 845)
—Love, Splat. Scotton, Rob, illus. (p. 1060)
—Merry Christmas, Splat. Scotton, Rob, illus. (p. 1129)
—Name of the Game. (p. 1228)
—Name of the Game. Scotton, Rob, illus. (p. 1228)
—On with the Show. Scotton, Rob, illus. (p. 1292)
—Oopsie-Daisy. Scotton, Rob, illus. (p. 1299)
—Perfect Present for Mom & Dad. (p. 1342)
—Perfect Present for Mom & Dad. Scotton, Rob, illus. (p. 1342)
—Rain Is a Pain. (p. 1435)
—Rain Is a Pain. Scotton, Rob, illus. (p. 1435)
—Russell & the Lost Treasure. Scotton, Rob, illus. (p. 1498)
—Russell the Sheep. Scotton, Rob, illus. (p. 1498)
—Russell's Christmas Magic. Scotton, Rob, illus. (p. 1498)
—Scaredy-Cat, Splat! Scotton, Rob, illus. (p. 1519)
—Secret Agent Splat! Scotton, Rob, illus. (p. 1540)
—Sings Flat. Scotton, Rob, illus. (p. 1579)
—Splat & Seymour, Best Friends Forevermore. (p. 1629)
—Splat & the Cool School Trip. Scotton, Rob, illus. (p. 1629)
—Splat Says Thank You! Scotton, Rob, illus. (p. 1629)
—Splat the Cat: On with the Snow. (p. 1629)
—Splat the Cat: Up in the Air at the Fair. (p. 1629)
—Splat the Cat: What Was That? Scotton, Rob, illus. (p. 1629)
—Splat the Cat: Twice the Mice. Scotton, Rob, illus. (p. 1629)
—Splat the Cat: Blow, Snow, Blow. Scotton, Rob, illus. (p. 1629)
—Splat the Cat: A Whale of a Tale. Scotton, Rob, illus. (p. 1629)
—Splat the Cat: Big Reading Collection. Scotton, Rob, illus. (p. 1629)
—Splat the Cat: Up in the Air at the Fair. Scotton, Rob, illus. (p. 1629)
—Splat the Cat: And the Snowy Day Surprise. Scotton, Rob, illus. (p. 1629)
—Splat the Cat: Good Night, Sleep Tight. Scotton, Rob & Eberz, Robert, illus. (p. 1629)
—Splat the Cat: Splat & Seymour, Best Friends Forevermore. Scotton, Rob, illus. (p. 1629)
—Splat the Cat. (p. 1629)
—Splat the Cat. Scotton, Rob, illus. (p. 1629)
—Splat the Cat & the Duck with No Quack. Scotton, Rob, illus. (p. 1629)
—Splat the Cat & the Hotshot. Scotton, Rob, illus. (p. 1629)
—Splat the Cat & the Pumpkin-Picking Plan. Scotton, Rob, illus. (p. 1629)
—Splat the Cat Dreams Big. Scotton, Rob, illus. (p. 1629)
—Splat the Cat - Fishy Tales. Scotton, Rob, illus. (p. 1629)
—Splat the Cat Goes to the Doctor. Scotton, Rob, illus. (p. 1629)
—Splat the Cat - I Scream for Ice Cream. Scotton, Rob, illus. (p. 1629)
—Splat the Cat Makes Dad Glad. (p. 1629)
—Splat the Cat Makes Dad Glad. Scotton, Rob, illus. (p. 1629)
—Splat the Cat Sings Flat. Scotton, Rob, illus. (p. 1630)
—Splat the Cat - Sticker Fun. Scotton, Rob, illus. (p. 1629)
—Splat the Cat Storybook Collection. Scotton, Rob, illus. (p. 1630)
—Splat the Cat Takes the Cake. (p. 1630)
—Splat the Cat Takes the Cake. Scotton, Rob, illus. (p. 1630)
—Splat the Cat - The Rain Is a Pain. Scotton, Rob, illus. (p. 1629)
—Splat the Cat Treasure Box. Scotton, Rob, illus. (p. 1630)
—Splat the Cat - Twice the Mice. Scotton, Rob, illus. (p. 1629)
—Splat the Cat with a Bang & a Clang. (p. 1630)
—Splat the Cat with a Bang & a Clang. Scotton, Rob, illus. (p. 1630)
—Splish, Splash, Splat! Scotton, Rob, illus. (p. 1630)
—Up in the Air at the Fair. Scotton, Rob, illus. (p. 1824)
—Whale of a Tale. (p. 1877)
—Whale of a Tale. Scotton, Rob, illus. (p. 1877)
—Where's the Easter Bunny? Scotton, Rob, illus. (p. 1911)
Scotton, Rob & Driscoll, Laura. I Scream for Ice Cream. (p. 845)
Scottorosano, Deborah, illus. see Columbro, Judy.
Scott-Waters, Marilyn, jt. auth. see Everett, J. H.
Scott-Waters, Marilyn, creator. Toymaker: Paper Toys That You Can Make Yourself (p. 1774)
Scow, Alfred, jt. auth. see Spalding, Andrea.
Scowen, Kate, ed. I. D. Stuff That Happens to Define Us. Mitchell, Peter, illus. (p. 837)
Scrace, Carolyn. Life in the Wetlands. (p. 1011)
Scrace, Carolyn, illus. see Legg, Gerald.
Scrambly, Crab. 13th of Never. (p. 1995)
Scrambly, Crab, illus. see Thompson, Colin.
Scranton, Philip B., jt. auth. see Blaszczyk, Regina Lee.
Scraper, Katherine. Boy Who Cried Wolf: An Aesop's Fable. (p. 219)
—Fox in the Forest. (p. 626)
—Garden Lunch. (p. 656)
—George Washington Carver. (p. 664)

—Gift-Guessing Kid. (p. 675)
—Kids Can Have Jobs. (p. 953)
—Laura Ingalls Wilder. (p. 980)
—Laura Ingalls Wilder & Laura Ingalls Wilder (Spanish) 6 English, 6 Spanish Adaptations. (p. 980)
—Matthew Henson. (p. 1109)
—Max's Job. (p. 1112)
—Pen Pal Penguin. Callen, Liz, illus. (p. 1336)
—Remember the Rules. (p. 1459)
—Rules at School. (p. 1495)
—Save the Fairy Penguins. (p. 1516)
—Seed Needs Help. (p. 1547)
—Tag Sale Today. (p. 1695)
—What Is in a Forest? (p. 1889)
—Yard Sale. (p. 1968)
—You Can Sort Boats. (p. 1974)
Scraper, Katherine, et al. Around Town: Things You Can Do in Your Community. (p. 101)
—Boredom Busters! Try This! Free & Inexpensive Things to Make & Do. (p. 214)
Scratch N Sniff Staff. Scratch N Sniff Food. (p. 1532)
—Scratch N Sniff Fruit. (p. 1532)
—Scratch N Sniff Gang. (p. 1532)
Scratchmann, Max, illus. see Durant, Alan.
Scremin, Lauren. 10 Most Amazing Skyscrapers. (p. 1993)
Scretching, Dorothy/Janis. Story Time with Princess Dorothy. Walters, Steve, ed. (p. 1663)
Scribens, Sunny & Barefoot Books Staff. Space Song Rocket Ride. (p. 1619)
Scribens, Sunny, et al. Space Song Rocket Ride. Sim, David, illus. (p. 1619)
Scriber, Christian. Adventures of Almighty Mouse: And Tales of His Friends. (p. 16)
Scribner, Ashley, jt. auth. see Scribner, Curtis.
Scribner, Belding. Kidney Treatment: A Patient's Guide to a Better Life. (p. 952)
Scribner, Carol A. To Life in the Small Corners Scribner, Carol A., photos by. (p. 1759)
Scribner, Curtis & Scribner, Ashley. Findlay: A Cincinnati Pig Tale. (p. 588)
Scribner, Don. Bennie & Thomas & the Battle at Worldsend (p. 165)
—Bennie & Thomas & the Rescue at Razor's Edge: Volume I. Scribner, Peter, illus. (p. 165)
—Bennie & Thomas & the Rescue at Razor's Edge: Volume II. Scribner, Peter, illus. (p. 165)
Scribner, Joanne, illus. see Zolotow, Charlotte.
Scribner, Meagen & Jensen, Angelina. Princess & the Peasant. (p. 1403)
Scribner, Peter, illus. see Scribner, Don.
Scrimger, Richard. Boy from Earth. (p. 217)
—Bun Bun's Birthday. Johnson, Gillian, illus. (p. 241)
—Eugene's Story. Johnson, Gillian, illus. (p. 540)
—Ink Me (p. 874)
—Into the Ravine. (p. 881)
—Me & Death: An Afterlife Adventure. (p. 1115)
—Wolf & Me (p. 1943)
Scrimger, Richard, jt. auth. see Jocelyn, Marthe.
Scrimshire, Hazel. Big Crash. (p. 180)
—God Cares: A Colouring Book. (p. 688)
—God Is Good. (p. 689)
—God's Little Guidebooks (p. 691)
—Jesus Loves You: A Colouring Book. (p. 916)
Scrimshire, Hazel, jt. auth. see Christian Focus Publications (CFP) Staff.
Scrimshire, Hazel, jt. auth. see Evangelical Press Staff.
Scrimshire, Hazel, jt. auth. see Woodman, Rosalind.
Scripps, Robert. Second Chance: Life in a Continuing Care Retirement Community. (p. 1539)
Script, Roseanne D'Erasmo. I AM a Rainbow. (p. 832)
Scripts Publishing Staff, jt. see Hamilton, Patricia Birdsong.
Scripture Union Staff, contrib. by. Landlubbers: Holiday Club Programme for 5- to 11-Year-Olds. (p. 974)
Scrivanich, Kerry Ann. My Gifted & Talented Adventure. (p. 1209)
Scriven, Maggie. Short & Sweet Skits for Student Actors: 55 Sketches for Teens. (p. 1569)
Scroggs, Kirk. Monster Book of Creature Features: Wiley & Grampa's First Three Adventures. (p. 1166)
—Snoop Troop: Attack of the Ninja Potato Clones. (p. 1598)
—Snoop Troop - It Came from Beneath the Playground. (p. 1598)
—Snoop Troop - Sloppy Joe Stink-O-Rama. (p. 1598)
Scruggs, Kathy. Espanol Con Senora Scruggs! (p. 536)
Scruggs, Sheldon. Tyler: The Strongest Boy on the Block. (p. 1805)
Scruggs, Stephanie. Deer Can't Dance. (p. 423)
Scruggs, Trina, illus. see Cook, Deena & McIntosh, Cherie.
Scruton, Clive, illus. see Goldish, Meish.
Scruton, Clive, illus. see Gray, Keith.
Scudamore, Beverly. Foul Play (p. 624)
—Ice Dreams (p. 850)
—Misconduct (p. 1150)
—Pure Fake (p. 1419)
—Ready to Run (p. 1448)
Scudder, Horace Elisha. James Russell Lowell: A Biography. (p. 907)
Scudder, James A. Son of Satan: The Coming Economic Prosperity. (p. 1611)
Scuderi. Lo Que el Lobo le Conto a la Luna. (p. 1044)
Scuderi, Lucia. Si Oigo. Turrion, Celia, tr. (p. 1572)
—Si Sabe A. Turrion, Celia, tr. (p. 1572)
—Si Toco. Turrion, Celia, tr. (p. 1572)
Scull, Marie-Louise, illus. see MacDonald, Margaret.
Scull, Paul E. Animals Tell His Story. (p. 84)
—Los Animales Cuentan Su Histori. (p. 1053)
Scullin, Sara. Tiki the Prima Donn. (p. 1749)
Scully, Michael & Donovan, Patrick. Reaching Teens Through Film Cannizzo, Karen A., ed. (p. 1442)
Scully, Michael & Donovan, Patrick J. Reaching Teens Through Film Cannizzo, Karen, ed. (p. 1442)
Scurman, Ike & Malam, John. Ancient Roman Civilization. D'Ottavi, Francesca, illus. (p. 70)
Scurr, Ruth. Fatal Purity: Robespierre & the French Revolution. (p. 577)
SD, Agent, et al. Secret Discussions. (p. 1540)
Sea Breeze Productions, ed. see Harris, Tumeka.
Seabag-Montefiore, Mary. Black Beauty (Picture Book) Marks, Alan, illus. (p. 195)
—Secret Garden. (p. 1541)
Seabag-Montefiore, Mary, retold by. Black Beauty with CD. (p. 195)
—David Copperfield. (p. 410)
Seabaugh, Jan, illus. see Chukovsky, Kornei.
Seabaugh, Jan, illus. see Shookuhi, Aminjon.
Seabaugh, Jan, tr. see Chukovsky, Kornei.
Seaberg, Richard Leonard. Elmoson the Christmas Goat. (p. 516)
Seaborn, Ron. Children's Health Food Book. (p. 303)
Seabrook, Heather. Heroes' Quest. (p. 773)
—Lego Chima - Heroes' Quest. (p. 990)
Seabrook, Heather & Dorling Kindersley Publishing Staff. Lego Chima — Heroes' Quest. (p. 990)
Seabrook, Jane. Furry Logic: Parenthood. (p. 650)
Seabrook, Lochlainn. Honest Jeff & Dishonest Abe: A Southern Children's Guide to the Civil War. (p. 794)
—Quotable Nathan Bedford Forrest: Selections from the Writings & Speeches of the Confederacy's Most Brilliant Cavalryman. (p. 1429)
—Saddle, Sword, & Gun: A Biography of Nathan Bedford Forrest for Teens. (p. 1501)
Seabrooke, Brenda. Cemetery Street. (p. 286)
—Stonewolf. (p. 1653)
Seabrooks, Lydia, illus. see Young, Elizabeth.
Seaburn, Paul. Jestercises & Gamestorms. (p. 914)
Seaby, David. BADD: Menace to Hero. Bk. 1 (p. 132)
Seager, Maryann, illus. see LaBerge, Margaret M.
Seagle, Edward E., Jr. & Smith, Ralph W. Internships in Recreation & Leisure Services: A Practical Guide for Students. (p. 880)
Seagle, Steven, jt. auth. see Wagner, Matt.
Seagle, Steven T. American Virgin - Going Down (p. 63)
—Frankie Stein HC. (p. 630)
—Head Rugg, Jim, illus. (p. 756)
—Solstice. Norman, Justin & Starkings, Richard, illus. (p. 1608)
Seagraves, Randy, jt. auth. see Whittlesey, Lisa.
Seagreaves, Kelly E. Best Pet. Zoller, Jayson D., illus. (p. 171)
Seagull, Robert. Adventure to Septumus Sevusere & the Magic Glowing Rings. (p. 15)
—Mindbender's Revenge Book One. (p. 1145)
Seah, Audrey & Nair, Charissa M. Vietnam. (p. 1841)
Seah, Audrey, et al. Vietnam. (p. 1841)
Seahorse, Risa, illus. see Ryan, Ruth.
Seal, Frances Thurber. Our Journey Toward True Selfhood. (p. 1309)
Seal, Julia. Three Little Pigs. (p. 1743)
Seal, Kerry. Five Silly Pumpkins: A Pop-up Halloween Book. Smith, Jane, illus. (p. 601)
Seal, Vickie Di-Ann. Edgar Tells the Truth. (p. 504)
Seale McCrory, Brooke. Our Firecracker: Bringing David Home. (p. 1308)
Sealey, Edmund J. Toast. (p. 1760)
Sealey, Nanlie, jt. auth. see Gardener, Amanda.
Sealey, Philip. Sorcerer's Tome. (p. 1614)
Sealls, Arthur. Three Little Heroes: Book One of Kirk, Chelsea, & Samantha's Adventures. (p. 1742)
Seals, David. Seventh Generation: Images of the Lakota Today. Freisager, Katrin, photos by. (p. 1555)
Seals, Hollie. When You Can't Find the Words. (p. 1905)
Seals, Loretta & Ravarra, Katana. Shoebeeville. (p. 1568)
Seaman, Alison, jt. auth. see Brown, Alan.
Seaman, Alison & Brown, Alan. My Christian Faith. (p. 1200)
Seaman, Augusta Huiell. Boarded-Up House. (p. 205)
Seaman, Hannah. Micro Polo: Adventures. Bk. 1 (p. 1136)
—Micro Polo: Acrobatics. Bk. III (p. 1136)
—Micro Polo. (p. 1136)
—Micro Polo (Spanish) Una Serie de Tres Partes - Aventuras, Monstruos y Acrobacia. (p. 1136)
Seaman, Jim, jt. auth. see Fried, Alyssa.
Seaman, Jim, jt. auth. see Garrett, Tiffany.
Seaman, Jim, jt. auth. see Keller, Carolyn.
Seaman, Jim, jt. auth. see Niekerk, Katie.
Seaman, Jim, jt. auth. see R, Sarah.
Seaman, Jim, jt. auth. see Robinson, Hadley.
Seaman, Jim, jt. auth. see Treadway, Kathryn.
Seaman, John E. Captain's Secret: A Lost Boy's Odyssey in Old New York. (p. 264)
—On the Road with Ruben Doyle. (p. 1291)
Seaman, Kathleen. Annycole (p. 87)
Seaman, Lucy. Mr Mouse Morgan. Swope, Brenda, illus. (p. 1185)
Seaman, P. David. Bootstraps & Blessings: From Poverty to Success. (p. 213)
Seaman, Paul, illus. see Bell, Frank & Bowler, Colin.
Seaman, Paul, illus. see Bell, Frank.
Seamans, Amanda, illus. see Scott, Karen.
Seamon, Hollis. Somebody up There Hates You: A Novel. (p. 1609)
Seamons, Karen. Child of Virtue: SamiTales Relationship Series. (p. 301)
Sean, Harmon Casey. My Daddy Has Ptsd. (p. 1201)
Seapics.com Staff, photos by see Horsman, Paul.
Searcy, Doc. Jimmy Jack & Jilly Jan, the Fireman. (p. 918)
Searcy, Margaret Zehmer. Charm of the Bearclaw Necklace. Brough, Hazel, illus. (p. 294)
Searight Dibert, Tracy. Detective Pancake. (p. 431)
Searl, Duncan. Beagle: A Howling Good Time. (p. 150)
—Cairn Terrier: Hero of Oz. (p. 252)
—Elephants. (p. 511)
—Ellen Tebbits. Friedland, Joyce & Kessler, Rikki, eds. (p. 514)
—Jamie & Angus Stories: A Study Guide. Friedland, Joyce & Kessler, Rikki, eds. (p. 907)
—Maiasaura Nests: Jack Horner's Dinosaur Eggs. (p. 1076)
—Pigs. (p. 1358)
—Trapped! (p. 1779)
—Wolves. (p. 1945)
Searl, Duncan, et al. Keep the Lights Burning, Abbie. Friedland, Joyce & Kessler, Rikki, eds. (p. 947)
Searle, Carole, jt. see Hollingworth, Denise.
Searle, Gleneta E. Mr. Tedd Fredd: The Intellectual Pioneer from Phew. (p. 1186)
Searle, Ken, illus. see Wheatley, Nadia.
Searle, Rodney, jt. auth. see Pohlman, Jennifer.
Searle, Ronald, illus. see Forbes, Robert L.
Searle, Ronald, illus. see Forbes, Robert.
Searleman, Eric, ed. see Miyazaki, Hayao.
Searleman, Eric, ed. see Morita, Hiroyuki.
Searles, H. Louise. Sit Down little Sister & Let me Talk to You: The Voices of the Sparkletts. Vol. 1 (p. 1581)
Searles, Rachel. Lost Planet. (p. 1056)
—Stolen Moon. (p. 1652)
Searley, Kevin. Hello, God. (p. 764)
Sears, Bart, illus. see Marz, Ron.
Sears, Bart, illus. see Way, Daniel.
Sears, Cynthia A. Dragon Lord: The Fairy Princess Chronicles - Book 2. (p. 477)
Sears, Dovid, illus. see Estrin, Leibel.
Sears, Evelyn. Muslims & the West. (p. 1194)
Sears, Gale. Missing Christmas Treasure. Johnson, Meredith, illus. (p. 1152)
Sears, James, et al. Healthiest Kid in the Neighborhood: Ten Ways to Get Your Family on the Right Nutritional Track. (p. 758)
Sears, Mary A., jt. auth. see Pakizer, Debi.
Sears, Robert. Pictorial History of the American Revolution; with a Sketch of the Early History of the Country. the Constitution of the United States, & a Chronological Index. (p. 1355)
Sears, Stanley. Olivia Desiree & the Mystic East: Classic Mythology. (p. 1286)
Sears, Stephen W. Air War Against Hitler's Germany. (p. 31)
—Battle of the Bulge. (p. 146)
Seaton, Kristen, jt. auth. see Herman, George.
Seatter, Pamela, illus. see Douglass Thom, Kara.
Seatter, Robert. On the Beach with Chet Baker. (p. 1289)
Seaver, Barton. National Geographic Kids Cookbook: A Year-Round Fun Food Adventure. (p. 1232)
Seaver, C. H. American Boys' Book of Electricity. (p. 60)
Seaver Keith, Emily. Home for Webby. Seaver Keith, Emily, illus. (p. 792)
Seaver, Richard, jt. auth. see Spooner, J. B.
Seaworld, photos by see Pingry, Patricia A.
Seaworld, photos by see Shively, Julie.
Seaworld, Chris, illus. see Shivley, Julie.
Seaworld, Chris, photos by see Shivley, Julie.
Seaworthy, Oscar. Port Side Pirates. (p. 1386)
Seaworthy, Oscar & Collins, Mark. Port Side Pirates! Harter, Debbie, illus. (p. 1386)
Seay, Christina, illus. see Savannah.
Seay, Dave, illus. see Counce, Betty.
Seba, Jaime. Being Gay, Staying Healthy. (p. 161)
—Coming Out: Telling Family & Friends. (p. 348)
—Ellen DeGeneres: From Comedy Club to Talk Show. (p. 514)
—Gallup Guides for Youth Facing Persistent Prejudice: Blacks. (p. 653)
—Gallup Guides for Youth Facing Persistent Prejudice. (p. 653)
—Gallup Guides for Youth Facing Persistent Prejudice - The LGBT Community. (p. 653)
—Gay & Lesbian Role Models. (p. 659)
—Gay Characters in Theatre, Movies, & Television: New Roles, New Attitudes. (p. 659)
—Gay Issues & Politics: Marriage, the Military, & Work Place Discrimination. (p. 659)
—Gay People of Color: Facing Prejudices, Forging Identities. (p. 659)
—Gays & Mental Health: Fighting Depression, Saying No to Suicide. (p. 659)
—Homosexuality Around the World: Safe Havens, Cultural Challenges. (p. 794)
Seba, Jaime A. Feeling Wrong in Your Own Body: Understanding What It Means to Be Transgender. (p. 580)
—Gay & Lesbian Role Models. (p. 659)
—Gay Issues & Politics: Marriage, the Military, & Work Place Discrimination. (p. 659)
—Smashing the Stereotypes: What Does It Mean to Be Gay, Lesbian, Bisexual, or Transgender? (p. 1593)
Seba, Jaime & Sanna, Ellyn. Gallup Guides for Youth Facing Persistent Prejudice. (p. 653)
Sebag-Montefiore, Hugh & Dorling Kindersley Publishing Staff. China. (p. 306)
Sebag-Montefiore, Mary. Railway Children. Marks, Alan, illus. (p. 1434)
Sebag-Montefiore, Mary, ed. Tale of Two Cities: Internet-Referenced. Ablett, Barry, illus. (p. 1700)
Sebaoun, Elisabeth, jt. auth. see Gillot, Laurence.
Sebastian, illus. see Cabanillas, Laura Sabin.
Sebastian Bianchi, A., jt. auth. see Bianchi, Sebastian.
Sebastian, Emily. Armadillos. (p. 99)
—Badgers. (p. 132)
—Chipmunks. (p. 308)
—Foxes. (p. 626)
—Moles. (p. 1160)
—Mongooses. (p. 1164)
—My Brothers & Sisters: MIS Hermanos. (p. 1199)
—My Brothers & Sisters. (p. 1199)
—My Cousins: MIS Primos. (p. 1200)
—My Cousins. (p. 1200)
—My Dad. (p. 1200)
—My Dad(Mi Papá) (p. 1201)
—Technology of the Medieval & Early Modern Worlds. (p. 1712)
Sebastian Quigley, Sebastian, illus. see Harris, Nicholas.
Sebastián, Soledad, illus. see Ruesga, Rita Rosa & Scholastic, Inc. Staff.
Sebastian, Teresa L. & Harrell, Angel R. Kootie Kids & the Attack of the Poot Troop. (p. 967)
Sebastiani, Laura, creator. Penny & Drew's Penciltips (p. 1338)
—Penny & Drew's Penciltips: Idioms. (p. 1338)
—Penny & Drew's Penciltips: Draw THIS! (p. 1338)
—Penny & Drew's Penciltips: Transportation. (p. 1338)
—Penny & Drew's Penciltips: Animal Alliteration. (p. 1338)
Sebba, Jane. Abracadabra Piano Edwards, Gunvor & Felstead, Cathie, illus. (p. 6)
—Abracadabra Piano 3: Graded Pieces for the Young Pianist. Vol. 3 (p. 6)
Sebba, Jane, ed. see Davey, Peter.
Sebe, Masayuki. 100 Animals on Parade! Sebe, Masayuki, illus. (p. 1998)
—100 Hungry Monkeys! Sebe, Masayuki, illus. (p. 1998)
—Let's Count to 100! Sebe, Masayuki, illus. (p. 995)
Sebern, Brian, illus. see Mills, Joyce C.
Sebhatu, Temnete, ed. Best Teen Writing of 2008. (p. 171)
Sebra, Diane. Making Mountains Out of Moles. (p. 1081)
Sebring, Janet And Jordan. Every Child Can Be a Hero. (p. 542)
Sebring Lowrey, Janette. Little Golden Book Poky Little Puppy Tales. Tenggren, Gustaf, illus. (p. 1028)
Sebring, Ruthie. Charlie, Itty's Guinea Pig (p. 293)
—Itty's Guinea Pig. (p. 900)
Secakuku, Susan. Meet Mindy: A Native Girl from the Southwest. Harrington, John, photos by. (p. 1121)
Secakuku, Susan, photos by see Harrington, John, illus.
Secchi, Riccardo, illus. see Ghiglione, Marco & Randolph, Grace.
Secchi, Riccardo, illus. see Ghiglione, Marco.
Secchi, Richard & Salati, Giorgio. Race for the Ultrapods Turconi, Stefano et al, illus. (p. 1431)
Sechan, Olivier. Zorro. (p. 1990)
Secheret, Jessica. Dolls of the World Coloring Book. (p. 464)
—Kokeshi Dolls Coloring Book. (p. 966)
Secheret, Jessica, illus. see Young, Jessica.
Sechrist, Darren. Air Pollution. (p. 31)
—Inventions & Inventors. (p. 884)
—Powerful Planet: Can Earth's Renewable Energy Save Our Future? (p. 1390)
—Supercross & Arenacross: Taking MX Indoors. (p. 1683)
—Taming the West. (p. 1704)
—Westward, Ho! (p. 1876)
Seckel, Al, illus. see Taplin, Sam.
Seco, Manuel, ed. Diccionario de Dudas y Dificultades de la Lengua Espanola. (p. 435)
Seco, Nina S. & Pilutik, Anastasia D. Saints Adrian & Natalie. Duckworth, Ruth, illus. (p. 1504)
Second and Fourth Grade Franklin Elementary. Cat Has Class! (p. 278)
Second Story Press Staff, illus. see Foggo, Cheryl.
Second Story Press Staff, illus. see Handy, Femida & Carpenter, Carole H.
Second Story Press Staff, illus. see Hearn, Emily.
Second Story Press Staff, illus. see Jennings, Sharon.
Second Story Press Staff, illus. see Simard, Danielle.
Second Story Press Staff, illus. see Souza, Cláudia.
Second Story Press Staff, illus. see Stehlik, Tania Duprey.
Second Story Press Staff, illus. see Upjohn, Rebecca.
Second Story Press Staff, jt. auth. see Bryant, Jill.
Second Story Press Staff, jt. auth. see Crysdale, Joy.
Second Story Press Staff, jt. auth. see Dublin, Anne.
Second Story Press Staff, jt. auth. see Lundgren, Jodi.
Second Story Press Staff, jt. auth. see Plaxton, Judith.
Second Story Press Staff, jt. auth. see Posesorski, Sherie.
Second Story Press Staff, jt. auth. see Reid, Donalda.
Second Story Press Staff, jt. auth. see Wilson, Janet.
Secor, Julie. Counting Flowers Is Fun: Number Names & Count Sequence. (p. 371)
Secuban, Andy S. Papagayo: Magical Bird of Paradise. (p. 1322)
Seda, Alison, illus. see Finch, Susan M.
Seda, Gus. Prohex the Cat. (p. 1410)
—Sally & the Four Wizards. (p. 1505)
Sedaka, Neil, et al. Dinosaur Pet. (p. 442)
—Waking up Is Hard to Do. Miyares, Daniel, illus. (p. 1853)
Sedalia, Rajan, illus. see Dunn, Kevin Ikim.
Seddon, Jane. Tales of Bermy Wood (p. 1702)
Seddon, Leigh, jt. auth. see Seddon, Wayne.
Seddon, Rhea, et al. Rise to the Challenge: Memoir of an Astronaut. (p. 1475)
Seddon, Richard, ed. see Steiner, Rudolf.
Seddon, Viola Anne, illus. see Mahoney, Jean.
Seddon, Wayne & Seddon, Leigh. Scribbles: Using your eyes to see with your Mind. (p. 1533)
Sedell, Kirsten J. Remembering Sarah: A Child's Story. (p. 1460)
Seder, Isaac. Alaska: The Last Frontier. (p. 34)
Seder, Rufus Butler. Gallop! (p. 653)
—Gallop! Cards: 8 Scanimation Gift Cards. (p. 653)
—Santa! A Scanimation Picture Book. (p. 1511)
—Star Wars: A Scanimation Book - 11 Iconic Scenes from a Galaxy Far, Far Away... (p. 1641)
—Swing! (p. 1691)
—Waddle! (p. 1852)
—Waddle! Seder, Rufus Butler, illus. (p. 1852)
—Wizard of Oz: A Scanimation Book. (p. 1943)
—¡Al Galope! Un Libro de Scanimation. (p. 32)
Sederman, Marty & Epstein, Seymour. Magic Box: When Parents Can't Be There to Tuck You In. Brooks, Karen Stormer, illus. (p. 1071)
Sedgwick, Chantele. Love, Lucas. (p. 1060)
Sedgwick, Marcus. Book of Dead Days. (p. 211)
—Floodland. (p. 605)
—Ghosts of Heaven. (p. 672)
—Midwinterblood. (p. 1139)
—She Is Not Invisible. (p. 1564)
Sedgwick, Michael. Cars of the Fifties: Goodbye Seller's Market. (p. 272)
—Cars of the Forties: The Years after the War. (p. 272)
—Cars of the Thirties: The Dawn of Automation. (p. 272)
Sedgwick, Patricia Louise. Santa's Key. (p. 1513)
Sedita, Francesco. Miss Popularity. (p. 1152)
—Miss Popularity Candy Apple. (p. 1152)
—Miss Popularity Goes Camping. (p. 1152)
Sedlacek, Jan Gill. Colors of a City: Philadelphia. Oudinot, Wanda & Baum, Kipley, photos by. (p. 345)
Sedrak, Asham. Santa Claus Fox. (p. 1511)
Sedwick, Daniel & Sedwick, Frank. Practical Book of Cobs. (p. 1392)
Sedwick, Frank, jt. auth. see Sedwick, Daniel.

S

Sedwick, Helen. Coyote Winds. (p. 374)
See, Betty. Electing the President: The Electoral Process in Action. (p. 508)
See, Ee Lin. My Kiasu Teenage Life in Singapore. (p. 1211)
See, Jonny. On the Walk Trail - Japan. (p. 1291)
See, Marcia A. Candy Cane Rain. (p. 261)
See, Mary Jo, creator. Art Plus Science: A tribute to the 100th Anniversary of Albert Einstein's "Theory of Relativity" (p. 103)
See, Sharon. God Gives Us Work. (p. 688)
Seeberger, Beverley. Razzle Dazzler. (p. 1441)
Seed Faith Books LLC, prod. Lord Is My Shepherd Curriculum CD: 23 Psalm Curriculum CD- 2 Sets of Lessons. (p. 1052)
Seeger, K R. Asa-Birdie Corn. (p. 105)
Seeger, Laura Vaccaro. Bully. Seeger, Laura Vaccaro, illus. (p. 241)
—Dog & Bear: Two's Company. Seeger, Laura Vaccaro, illus. (p. 460)
—Dog & Bear: Tricks & Treats. Seeger, Laura Vaccaro, illus. (p. 460)
—Dog & Bear: Three to Get Ready. Seeger, Laura Vaccaro, illus. (p. 460)
—Dog & Bear: Two Friends, Three Stories. Seeger, Laura Vaccaro, illus. (p. 460)
—Dog & Bear, Level 2: Two Friends, Three Stories. Seeger, Laura Vaccaro, illus. (p. 460)
—First the Egg. (p. 597)
—First the Egg. Seeger, Laura Vaccaro, illus. (p. 597)
—Green. Seeger, Laura Vaccaro, illus. (p. 721)
—I Used to Be Afraid. (p. 847)
—Lemons Are Not Red. Seeger, Laura Vaccaro, illus. (p. 991)
—One Boy. Seeger, Laura Vaccaro, illus. (p. 1294)
—Walter Was Worried. Seeger, Laura Vaccaro, illus. (p. 1856)
—What If? Seeger, Laura Vaccaro, illus. (p. 1887)
Seeger, Pete. One Grain of Sand: A Lullaby. Wingerter, Linda, illus. (p. 1295)
Seeger, Pete & Jacobs, Paul DuBois. Abiyoyo Returns. Hays, Michael, illus. (p. 5)
Seegmuller, Stephanie, jt. auth. see Gutman, Colas.
Seelen, Christopher. Daddy Is That the Best You Got? Moen, Tyler, illus. (p. 398)
Seeley, Bonnie L. Chincoteague Daisy Chain. Lidard, Kelly & Seeley, Douglas A., illus. (p. 307)
—Sun & Ponies, Wind & Sky. Seeley, Douglas A., illus. (p. 1676)
Seeley, Douglas A., illus. see Seeley, Bonnie L.
Seeley, Laura L., illus. see Deedy, Carmen Agra.
Seeley, Scott, illus. see New York City Students Staff.
Seeley, Steve, jt. auth. see Moreci, Michael.
Seeley, Terre Lamb, illus. see Spooner, J. B.
Seeley, Terre Lamb, illus. see Spooner, J. B. & Seaver, Richard.
Seeley, Terre Lamb, jt. auth. see Spooner, J. B.
Seeley, Tim. Bloodstrike Volume 1: Reborn under a Bad Sign TP: Reborn under a Bad Sign TP. (p. 201)
—Hack/Slash Slasher Diary/Journal. (p. 735)
—Revival: You're among Friends. Vol. 1 (p. 1466)
—Witchblade Rebirth (p. 1941)
—Witchblade: Rebirth Volume 4 TP: Rebirth Volume 4 TP. (p. 1941)
Seeley, Tim, illus. see Limke, Jeff.
Seelig, Renate. Mein Kleiner Brockhaus: Jahreszeiten. (p. 1124)
—Mein Kleiner Brockhaus: Erste Woerter. (p. 1124)
Seeling, Caleb. Battle Begins: The Story of Creation. Cariello, Sergio, illus. (p. 145)
Seely, Tim, illus. see Spears, Rick.
Seerattan, Tanya. Uncle Noel's Journey to Americ. (p. 1812)
Seese, Ellen. Waking Up. Kolding, Richard Max, illus. (p. 1853)
Seever, Berni. Supernatural Tale. (p. 1684)
Seevers, Tim. Love, Grandp. (p. 1059)
Seewald, Jacqueline. Clair's Curse. (p. 326)
Sefchovich, Sara. Vivir la Vida. (p. 1846)
Sefcik, Wendy, illus. see Brown, Tiffany M.
Sefcik, Wendy, illus. see Thomas, Terri.
Seffal, Rabah & Spilling, Jo-Ann. Niger. (p. 1252)
Sefusatti, Emiliano & Hamann, Hilary. Categories - On the Beauty of Physics: Essential Physics Concepts & Their Companions in Art & Literature. (p. 279)
Sega. Valkyria Chronicles 2: World Artworks: World Artworks. (p. 1830)
Segal, Abraham, jt. auth. see Charry, Elias.
Segal, Andrew. Clarissa the Clown. Scott, Peter & JessT, Grant, illus. (p. 327)
—Roberto the Robot. Scott, Peter & JessT, Grant, illus. (p. 1479)
Segal Block, Marta. Egypt (p. 506)
—Graphing Global Politics (p. 711)
—Tunisia (p. 1797)
Segal Diascro, Jennifer & Ivers, Gregg. Inside the Judicial Process: A Contemporary Reader in Law, Politics, & the Courts. (p. 877)
Segal, Douglas. Dolphin's Day. (p. 465)
—I Can Go to School: An I-Can-Do-It Book. Widdowson, Kay, illus. (p. 835)
Segal, Erich. Oliver's Story. (p. 1286)
Segal, Erna. Memoirs in Toe Shoes: The Unabashed Autobiography of Chiquita of the World-Famous Dance Team Chiquita & Johnson. (p. 1125)
Segal, Howard. My Daddy the Lawyer: Mommy-Daddy Books. (p. 1201)
Segal, John. Alistair & Kip's Great Adventure! Segal, John, illus. (p. 41)
—Carrot Soup. Segal, John, illus. (p. 271)
—Pirates Don't Take Baths. Segal, John, illus. (p. 1363)
—Sopa de Zanahoria. Mlawer, Teresa, tr. from ENG. (p. 1613)
Segal, John, illus. see Wilson, Karma.
Segal, Kevin & Levy, Nathan. 101 Things Everyone Should Know about Math — TEST BOOKLET. (p. 2000)
Segal, Lore. Story of Mrs. Lovewright & Purrless Her Cat. Zelinsky, Paul O., illus. (p. 1659)
—Tell Me a Mitzi. (p. 1716)
Segal, Lore, et al. Juniper Tree: And Other Tales from Grimm. Segal, Lore & Jarrell, Randall, trs. from GER. (p. 936)
Segal, Nechamy. Torah Book of Opposites. Lumer, Marc, illus. (p. 1769)
Segal, Robin. ABC in Albuquerque. (p. 3)
—ABC in Boston. (p. 3)
—ABC in Chicago. (p. 3)
—ABC in Miami: And the Beaches. (p. 3)
—ABC in Montreal. (p. 3)
—ABC in San Antonio. (p. 3)
—ABC in San Francisco. (p. 3)
—ABC in the City. (p. 3)
—ABC in Tulsa. (p. 3)
—ABC in Washington, DC. (p. 3)
Segal, Robin & Adler, Tasha. ABC in Los Angeles: And la County. (p. 3)
Segal, Yocheved. Our Sages Showed the Way (p. 1310)
Segal, Zoe. Confessions of a Tenth-Grade Social Climber. (p. 356)
Segall, Grant. John D Rockefeller: Anointed with Oil. (p. 921)
Segall, Miriam. Career Building Through Digital Moviemaking. (p. 266)
—Career Building Through Fan Fiction Writing: New Work Based on Favorite Fiction. (p. 266)
—Fan Fiction Writing: New Work Based on Favorite Fiction. (p. 570)
—Pandemics: Epidemics in a Shrinking World. (p. 1321)
Segalove, Llene. List Your Self: Discover Your Own True Self by Making Lists. (p. 1022)
Segamu. Sokora Refugees. DeJesus, Melissa, illus. (p. 1606)
Segarra, Angelo M. Coca Finds a Shell. Segarra, Kirstie, ed. (p. 337)
Segarra, Kirstie, ed. see Segarra, Angelo M.
Segarra, Mercedes. Fun Party Food: Little Chef Recipes. (p. 648)
—Pizza & Pasta: Little Chef Recipes. (p. 1365)
—Tasty Desserts: Little Chef Recipes. (p. 1707)
—Yummy Snacks: Little Chef Recipes. (p. 1983)
Segawa, Michael, illus. see Wells, Tina.
Segawa, Yasuo, illus. see Matsutani, Miyoko.
Segel, Jason & Miller, Kirsten. Nightmares! Kwasny, Karl, illus. (p. 1255)
Segel, Robert G. Machine Gun Inventors: A Military History Coloring Book. Pajot, Lauren, illus. (p. 1068)
Segerberg, Ebba, tr. see Eriksson, Kjell.
Segerberg, Ebba, tr. see Stark, Ulf.
Seggio, Monica Maria. Treasures of Emmanuel's Kingdom: Rose's New Discoveries. (p. 1782)
Seghetti, Nancy & Esseveld, Nelson. Day Mom Quit. (p. 413)
Seglie, Susan & Schiefelbein, Janis. Sissy's Christmas Program. Zagorski, Astrid, tr. (p. 1581)
Segner, Ellen, illus. see Grew, David.
Segovia, Carmen, illus. see Blackaby, Susan.
Segovia, Gertrudis. Spanish Fairy Book. (p. 1621)
Segovia, Patty. Skate Girls. (p. 1583)
Segovia, Patty & Meredith Books Staff. On the Edge Skateboarding/on the Edge Snowboarding: Tips & Tricks from Six of the Coolest Skateboarders/Tips & Tricks from Six of the Coolest Snowboarders. (p. 1290)
Segovia, Silvia. De Aqui para Alla. Palacios G., Sara Helena, illus. (p. 416)
Segovia, Stephen, et al. Silver Surfer Devolution. (p. 1577)
Segrelles, Vicente. Agua Magica. (p. 30)
Segriff, Larry, jt. auth. see Perry, Steve.
Seguin, Marilyn. No Ordinary Lives: Four 19th Century Teenage Diaries. (p. 1259)
—Young & Courageous: American Girls Who Made History. (p. 1978)
Segur, Comtesse De, see De Segur, Comtesse.
Segur, Sophie. Old French Fairy Tales. Sterrett, Virginia Frances, illus. (p. 1283)
Segvic-Boudreaux, Ivana. Desperately Seeking Talent: A Puppy's Journey. (p. 430)
Sehel Tahir, Alisha Menon. Bff? (Best Friends Forgotten) (p. 174)
Sehgal, Kabir & Sehgal, Surishtha. Bucket of Blessings. Tsong, Jing Jing, illus. (p. 234)
Sehgal, Surishtha, jt. auth. see Sehgal, Kabir.
Sehlin, Gunhild. Mary's Little Donkey: And the Flight to Egypt Latham, Hugh & Maclean, Donald, trs. from SWE. (p. 1101)
Seib, Anke & Cameron, Emma. Out of This Place. (p. 1311)
Seib, Philip. Beyond the Front Lines: How the News Media Cover a World Shaped by War. (p. 174)
Seibers, Elexis. Jasmine & the Mystery of the Disappearing Shoes. (p. 910)
—Zoac Moves to Jugabh. (p. 1987)
Seibert, Brian. George Balanchine. (p. 663)
—Jerome Robbins. (p. 913)
Seibert, Jerry. Dan Beard: Boy Scout Pioneer. Bjorklung, Lorence, illus. (p. 401)
Seibert, Patricia. Three Little Pigs, Grades Pk - 3. (p. 1743)
Seibold, J. Otto. Count, Dagmar! (p. 369)
—Lost Sloth. (p. 1056)
—Other Goose: Re-Nurseried!! & Re-Rhymed!! Childrens Classics. (p. 1306)
—Quincy, the Hobby Photographer: Dogs. Vol. 1 (p. 1428)
Seibold, J. Otto, illus. see Chronicle Books Staff.
Seibold, J. Otto, illus. see Edgemon, Darcie.
Seibold, J. Otto, illus. see Sierra, Judy.
Seidel, Jeff. Alabama Crimson Tide. (p. 33)
Seidel, Kathleen Gilles. Most Uncommon Degree of Popularity. (p. 1177)
Seiden, Abraham. Particle Physics: A Comprehensive Introduction. (p. 1325)
Seiden, Art, illus. see Berg, Jean Horton.
Seiden, Art, illus. see Daly, Kathleen.
Seiden, Art, illus. see Glazer, Tom.
Seiden, Art, illus. see Grosset and Dunlap Staff.
Seiden, Art, illus. see Kean, Edward.
Seidenberg, Mark & Milky, D. J. Kung Fu Klutz & Karate Cool Owen, Erich, illus. (p. 968)
Seidensticker, John & Lumpkin, Susan. Predators. (p. 1394)
Seider, Sharon J. Door in the Garden Wall. (p. 470)
Seiders, Marian, illus. see Ali, Anila & Gottlieb, Karen.
Seidler, Rena. Can You Imagine? LaDuca, Michael, illus. (p. 259)
Seidler, Tor. Dulcimer Boy. Selznick, Brian, illus. (p. 489)
—Firstborn. Sheban, Chris, illus. (p. 598)
—Gully's Travels. Cole, Brock, illus. (p. 731)
—Rat's Tale. (p. 1440)
—Rat's Tale. Marcellino, Fred, illus. (p. 1440)
—Toes. Beddows, Eric, illus. (p. 1761)
Seidler, Tor & Tor, Seidler. Hermanos Bajo Cero. McCarty, Peter, illus. (p. 771)
Seidlitz, Lauri. 1990: Canadian Decades. (p. 2002)
—Animals. (p. 81)
—Human Body. (p. 825)
—Legacy of World War II. (p. 987)
Seidman, Amy. Adventures of Bebop Bunny. (p. 16)
Seidman, David. Cesar Chavez: Labor Leader. (p. 288)
—Creating a New Future: 1986 to Present. Overmyer-Velazquez, Mark, ed. (p. 378)
—F/A-18 Hornet. (p. 559)
—Katharine Mcphee. (p. 944)
—Teens in South Africa (p. 1715)
—What If I'm an Atheist? A Teen's Guide to Exploring a Life Without Religion. (p. 1887)
Seidman, David, jt. auth. see Ball, Madeline K.
Seidman, David, jt. auth. see January, Brendan.
Seidman, David, jt. auth. see Kootz, Russell.
Seidman, David & Williams, Keith. Samuel Morse & the Telegraph Whigham, Rod & Barnett, Charles, III, illus. (p. 1509)
Seidman, David, et al. Deadly Double. (p. 417)
—Samuel Morse & the Telegraph Whigham, Rod, illus. (p. 1509)
Seidman, Lauren. What Makes Someone a Jew? (p. 1892)
Seidon, Bonnie Bale. Adventures of Trevor & the Tiger. (p. 24)
Seif, Adam, creator. Tacos, Beans & Rice... the Episodes: From the Beginning. (p. 1695)
Seif, Adam/Jeffrey. Tacos, Beans & Rice Episode 2: Lights, Camera, Action! (p. 1695)
Seif Simpson, Martha. What NOT to Give Your Mom on Mother's Day (p. 1892)
Seife, Emily. Hunger Games: Tribute Guide. (p. 828)
Seife, Emily & Collins, Suzanne. Hunger Games - Tribute Guide. (p. 828)
Seifert, Brandon. Disney Kingdoms: Seekers of the Weird. (p. 451)
—Witch Doctor Volume 2: Mal Practice TP: Mal Practice TP. (p. 1941)
Seifert, Christine. Predicteds. (p. 1395)
Seifert, Sheila. Happy Birthday Jesus. (p. 744)
Seifert, Sheila, jt. auth. see Naylor, Beth.
Seifert, Sheila & Naylor, Beth. And the Winner Is. (p. 71)
—Getting to Know God. (p. 669)
—Stepping up, Stepping Out. (p. 1648)
Seifert, Sheila, et al. Lead the Way, Jesus. (p. 981)
Seifrit, Brian T. Absolute Anger. (p. 7)
—Bloodlines. (p. 201)
Seigel, Andrea & Bradshaw, Brent. Everybody Knows Your Name. (p. 543)
Seigel, Jonathan & Rother, Beverly S. Myrtle the Turtle & Popeye the Mouse: Learning about Our Solar System. (p. 1222)
Seigel, Mike. Latin: A Fresh Approach. Harrison, T., illus. (p. 979)
Seigerman, Michelle. Christmastime Book of Rhymes. (p. 316)
Seigman, Reshea. Woody Goes to Grandma's. (p. 1950)
Seignobosc, Francoise. Springtime for Jeanne-Marie. (p. 1635)
Seiler, Jason, illus. see Bannister, Barbara.
Seiling, Rebecca. Plant a Seed of Peace. Rothshank, Brooke, illus. (p. 1368)
Seim, Donna Marie. Hurricane Mia: A Caribbean Adventure. Spellman, Susan, illus. (p. 830)
Sein, Dominique. Poland. Sauvageot, Claude, photos by. (p. 1378)
Seinfeld, Jerry. Halloween. Bennett, James, illus. (p. 737)
Seip, Shannon Payette. Pop Quiz Book: Tons of Trivia! Sheuer, Lauren, illus. (p. 1384)
Seip, Shannon Payette, jt. auth. see Parthen, Kelly.
Seiple, Samantha. Byrd & Igloo: A Polar Adventure. (p. 249)
—Ghosts in the Fog: The Untold Story of Alaska's WWII Invasion. (p. 672)
Seiple, Samantha, jt. auth. see Seiple, Todd.
Seiple, Samantha & Seiple, Todd. Giant Anteaters. (p. 673)
Seiple, Todd, jt. auth. see Seiple, Samantha.
Seiple, Todd & Seiple, Samantha. Mutants, Clones, & Killer Corn: Unlocking the Secrets of Biotechnology. (p. 1194)
Seiss, Ellie. Best Friends: A Chock-a-Block Book. Scanlon, Michael, illus. (p. 169)
—Dora's Princess Pals. (p. 471)
Seiss, Ellie, adapted by. It's Okay, Try Again! (p. 898)
Seiss, Ellie & Random House Staff. Dora & the Unicorn King. (p. 470)
Seitler, Travis, illus. see Erickson, Byron, et al.
Seitz, J. B. Freddy the Flea. (p. 633)
Seitz, Melissa. Stewie Meets New Friends. Accrocco, Anthony, illus. (p. 1649)
Seitzinger, Victoria, illus. see Baum, Roger S.
Seivwright, Leonard, illus. see Landy, Adrienne.
Seix, Merce, jt. auth. see Comella, Maria Angeles.
Seki, Sunny. Last Kappa of Old Japan: A Magical Journey of Two Friends. (p. 978)
—Tale of the Lucky Cat. (p. 1700)
—Tale of the Lucky Cat. Seki, Sunny, illus. (p. 1700)
—Yuko-Chan & the Daruma Doll: The Adventures of a Blind Japanese Girl Who Saves Her Village. (p. 1983)
Seki, Sunny, illus. see Moon, Josephine.
Sekowsky, Mike, illus. see Fox, Gardner & DC Comics Staff.
Sekowsky, Mike, illus. see Fox, Gardner.
Sekowsky, Mike, jt. auth. see Haney, Bob.
Sekulic, Goran, photos by see Sullivan, Marija.
Selber, Danielle. Pope Francis Bobblehead. (p. 1384)
Selby, John. Meditation the Cool Way to Calm: Solve Your Problems, Find Peace of Mind, & Discover the Real You. (p. 1120)
Selby, Shannon, illus. see Coffey, Joe.
Selby, Vicki L. Sleepy Sierra & the Great Blanket Adventure. (p. 1590)
Selcer, Richard F. Civil War America, 1850 To 1875. Balkin, Richard, ed. (p. 325)
Selda, Toby. Simply Father: Life with Theodore Roosevelt As Seen through the Eyes of His Children. Roosevelt, Theodore, illus. (p. 1578)
Selden, George. Cricket in Times Square. (p. 382)
—Cricket in Times Square. Williams, Garth, illus. (p. 382)
—Harry Kitten & Tucker Mouse; Chester Cricket's Pigeon Ride. Williams, Garth, illus. (p. 750)
—Tucker's Countryside. Williams, Garth, illus. (p. 1796)
Selden, Mark, ed. see Hamashita, Takeshi.
Selden, Samuel, ed. see Shakespeare, William.
Seles, Monica. Love Match. (p. 1060)
Seles, Monica & LaRosa, James. Game On. (p. 654)
Seletzky, Valentina. Mosaic: A Child's Recollections of the Russian Revolution. (p. 1176)
Self, David. Christianity. (p. 312)
—Drama & Theatre Arts Course Book. (p. 480)
—Islam. (p. 891)
—Lion Encyclopedia of Christianity. (p. 1020)
—Lion Encyclopedia of World Religions. (p. 1020)
—Loyola Treasury of Saints: From the Time of Jesus to the Present Day. Hall, Amanda, illus. (p. 1061)
Self, Timothy. Davy the Dolphin. (p. 411)
Selfors, Suzanne. Coffeehouse Angel. (p. 338)
—Ever after High: General Villainy: A Destiny Do-Over Diary. (p. 541)
—Ever after High: Hero Training: A Destiny Do-Over Diary. (p. 541)
—Ever after High: Science & Sorcery: a Destiny Do-Over Diary. (p. 541)
—Fortune's Magic Farm. (p. 623)
—Griffin's Riddle. Santat, Dan, illus. (p. 724)
—Kiss & Spell. (p. 961)
—Lonely Lake Monster. Santat, Dan, illus. (p. 1046)
—Mad Love. (p. 1069)
—Next Top Villain. (p. 1249)
—Order of the Unicorn: The Imaginary Veterinary. Santat, Dan, illus. (p. 1302)
—Order of the Unicorn. Santat, Dan, illus. (p. 1302)
—Sasquatch Escape. Santat, Dan, illus. (p. 1515)
—Saving Juliet. (p. 1517)
—Semi-Charming Kind of Life. (p. 1550)
—Smells Like Dog. (p. 1593)
—Smells Like Pirates. (p. 1593)
—Smells Like Treasure. (p. 1593)
—Sweetest Spell. (p. 1690)
—To Catch a Mermaid. (p. 1758)
Selfridge, Benjamin. Kid's Guide to Creating Web Pages for Home & School. (p. 953)
Selfridge, Benjamin & Selfridge, Peter. Kid's Guide to Creating Web Pages for Home & School. (p. 953)
Selfridge, Peter, jt. auth. see Selfridge, Benjamin.
Selig, Josh. Go, Wonder Pets! Little Airplane Productions, illus. (p. 687)
—Ride the Potato Train. (p. 1471)
—Ride the Potato Train. Gibbons, Cassandra, illus. (p. 1471)
—Small Potatoes Go Camping. Gibbons, Cassandra, illus. (p. 1592)
Selig, Julian W., Jr. Cousins, A True Story. (p. 373)
Seligson, Sherri. Exploring Creation with Marine Biology: Student Text. Wile, Jay L., ed. (p. 552)
—Exploring Creation with Marine Biology. Wile, Jay L., ed. (p. 552)
Sell, Jeff. Quarry Cave. (p. 1422)
Sellard, Parke. Glass Fish. (p. 682)
—Three Score & Ten. (p. 1743)
Sellaro, Brendan. Space Santa Holiday Hero. (p. 1619)
Sellaro, Brendan, illus. see Hamilton, Lily & Myers, Barbara.
Sellars, Rodney, jt. auth. see Snelson, Brian.
Sellars, Roy & Allen, Graham, eds. Salt Companion to Harold Bloom. (p. 1505)
Selleck, Michael. UMY Handbook: United Methodist Handbook. (p. 1810)
Selleck, Richelle. Little Red Riding Hood. Myer, Ed, illus. (p. 1035)
Sellen, Sandi. Splendiddly Fazztabulous Grandmas. Maltman Dinwoodie, Heather, illus. (p. 1630)
Sellers, Amy. Miss Amy's: Hurray for Rhyme It's Story Time: Contemporary Rhyming Stories for Children of All Ages. (p. 1151)
Sellers, Amy, illus. see Gallucci, Susie.
Sellers, Amy, illus. see Hanson, Paige & Hanson, Jon.
Sellers, Amy C., ed. Finding Jesus: Contemporary Children's Story. Behan, Rachel A., illus. (p. 588)
Sellers, Carolyn, jt. auth. see Sandrey, Alexander.
Sellers, Charles. Subtracting with Seals. (p. 1671)
Sellers, Jackie. Adventures of Harley the Turtle. (p. 18)
Sellers, Kathy Lacey. Willie Chaff. (p. 1934)
Sellers, Melonie. Harry the Happy Frog. (p. 751)
Sellers, Sandra. Gran's Story II: A Shy Maiden Finds Her Voice in the Tune of an Old Fiddle. (p. 710)
—Gran's Story III: The Long Awaited Trip to the Haunted House. (p. 710)
—Gran's Story IV: Gathering Wild Violets. (p. 710)
—Gran's Story V: Roxanne in Europe. (p. 710)
Sellier, Marie. Legend of the Chinese Dragon. Kazeroid, Sibylle, tr. from FRE. (p. 989)
—Renoir's Colors. (p. 1460)
—What the Rat Told Me. Louis, Catherine, illus. (p. 1893)
Sellier, Marie & Bright Connections Media. My First 10 Paintings. (p. 1203)
Sellke, Ron. Life's Little Lessons. (p. 1013)
Sellmeyer, Mark, jt. des. see Martin, Rob.
Sellmeyer, Susan. Time for Preschool: An Early Developmental Tool Designed for Toddlers. (p. 1751)
Selman, Sheri. I Love You for Real. (p. 843)

Selous, Edmund. Tommy Smith's Animals. Ord, G. W., illus. (p. 1765)
Selover, Arthur, illus. see Linkowski, Tami Leli.
Selover, Lisa, illus. see Linkowski, Tami Leli.
Selsam, Millicent E. & Hunt, Joyce. First Look at Animals with Backbones & a First Look at Animals Without Backbones. (p. 596)
Seltzer, Donna Lee & Thorne, Lawrence R., creators. Carnival Cookbook: From the Kitchen of the Hurricane Grille. (p. 270)
Seltzer, Eric. Bake, Mice, Bake! (p. 133)
—Bake, Mice, Bake! Rosenberg, Natascha, illus. (p. 133)
—Doodle Dog. Seltzer, Eric, illus. (p. 469)
—Granny Doodle Day. Seltzer, Eric, illus. (p. 710)
Seltzer, Eric & Hall, Kirsten. Dog on His Bus. Braun, Sebastien, illus. (p. 461)
Seltzer, Erin, ed. see Thompson, Sharon & Booth, Vanessa.
Seltzer, Jerry, illus. see Abbott, Rosalind.
Seltzer, Jerry, illus. see Bogardus, Ray & Bogardus, Karin.
Seltzer, Jerry, illus. see Collins, Charles.
Seltzer, Jerry, illus. see Yaldezian, Lisa M.
Seltzer, Jerry Joe. There Are Fairies in My Tub. Seltzer, Jerry Joe, illus. (p. 1729)
Seltzer, Jerry Joe, illus. see Abbott, Roz.
Seltzer, Sara Leah. Day Full of Mitzvos. Katz, Avi, illus. (p. 413)
Selucky, Oldrich. Adventures of Saint Paul. Trouve, Marianne Lorraine, tr. from CZE. (p. 22)
Selvadurai, Shyam. Swimming in the Monsoon Sea. (p. 1691)
Selway, Martina, illus. see Whitford, Rebecca.
Selwyn, Josephine. How Can I Get Fit? (p. 805)
—How Do I Move? (p. 807)
—How Do You Measure Rain & Wind? (p. 808)
—What Do Plants Need? (p. 1882)
—What Holidays Do You Have? (p. 1886)
—When Does Water Turn into Ice? (p. 1902)
—Who Uses This Machine? (p. 1918)
Selwyn, Josephine & Smart Apple Media Staff. Don't Touch. (p. 469)
Selyov, Trebor E., ed. see Fox, Lee White.
Selzer, Adam. I Kissed a Zombie, & I Liked It. (p. 840)
—Smart Aleck's Guide to American History. (p. 1592)
Selzer, Edwin, ed. see Baker, Paul R. & Hall, William H.
Selznick, Brian. Houdini Box. Selznick, Brian, illus. (p. 802)
—Invention of Hugo Cabret. (p. 883)
—Invention of Hugo Cabret. Selznick, Brian, illus. (p. 883)
—Wonderstruck. Selznick, Brian, illus. (p. 1949)
Selznick, Brian, illus. see Clements, Andrew.
Selznick, Brian, illus. see Kerley, Barbara.
Selznick, Brian, illus. see Levithan, David.
Selznick, Brian, illus. see Martin, Ann M. & Godwin, Laura.
Selznick, Brian, illus. see Ryan, Pam Muñoz.
Selznick, Brian, illus. see Seidler, Tor.
Semadini, Tomassino. Lukie the Astro-Dog. (p. 1064)
Sember, Brette McWhorter, jt. auth. see Morris, Rick A.
Sembos, Evangelos C. Solo Piano for Children. (p. 1608)
Semchuk, Rosann. Tennessee. (p. 1720)
Semeiks, Val, illus. see Disney Book Group Staff & Dworkin, Brooke.
Semeiks, Val, illus. see Thomas, Rich.
Semerad, Emma & Semerad, Johnnie. Josh W. Time Out. Semerad, Johnnie, illus. (p. 926)
Semerad, Johnnie, jt. auth. see Semerad, Emma.
Semionov, Vladimir. Silver Wings. (p. 1577)
Semionov, Vladimir, illus. see Montgomery, Anson.
Semionov, Vladimir, illus. see Montgomery, R. A.
Semionov, Vladimir & Louie, Wes. Forecast from Stonehenge. (p. 617)
Semkiw, Walter, jt. auth. see Pluto Project Staff.
Sempe & Goscinny. Recreos del Pequeno Nicolas. (p. 1452)
Sempe, Goscinny. Joaquin Tiene Problemas. (p. 919)
—Vacaciones del Pequeno Nicolas. (p. 1829)
Sempé, Jean-Jacques. Everything Is Complicated. Bell, Anthea, tr. from FRE. (p. 545)
—Mixed Messages. Bell, Anthea, tr. from FRE. (p. 1156)
—Notes from the Couch. (p. 1268)
—Nothing Is Simple. Bell, Anthea, tr. from FRE. (p. 1268)
—Sunny Spells. Bell, Anthea, tr. from FRE. (p. 1677)
Sempé, Jean-Jacques, illus. see Bell, Anthea, tr.
Sempé, Jean-Jacques, illus. see Goscinny, Ren&eacute.
Sempé, Jean-Jacques, illus. see Goscinny, René & Bell, Anthea.
Sempé, Jean-Jacques, illus. see Goscinny, René.
Sempé, Jean-Jacques, jt. auth. see Goscinny, René.
Sempé, Jean-Jacques & Bell, Anthea. Martin Pebble. (p. 1098)
—Monsieur Lambert. (p. 1166)
—Raoul Taburin Keeps a Secret. (p. 1438)
Sempebwa, Christina. Art of Hope. (p. 102)
—Tales of Zindan. (p. 1703)
Sempeck, Tina. Widdly Diddly Doo Could Not Tie His Shoe. (p. 1927)
Semper, Lothar. Auf einer Harley Davidson möchte ich sterben. (p. 115)
Sempill, illus. see Storm, Michael.
Semple, Dave, illus. see Bergen, Lara Rice.
Semple, Dave, illus. see Richards, Lynne.
Semple, David, illus. see Doyle, Malachy.
Semple, David, illus. see Punter, Russell.
Semple, J. J., jt. auth. see Semple, Veronique.
Semple, Veronique & Semple, J. J. Halloween Ooga-Ooga Ooum. Semple, J. J., ed. (p. 738)
Sen, Benita. Polar Creatures. (p. 1379)
—Rainforest Creatures. (p. 1436)
Sena, Hideaki. Parasite Eve. Grillo, Tyran, tr. from JPN. (p. 1324)
Senabre, Ricardo, ed. see Baroja y Nessi, Pio.
Sénac, Jean-Vincent. How to Draw a Chicken. (p. 816)
Senac, Jean-Vincent. Meet Matisse. (p. 1121)
Senchyne, Jonathan & Sikorskyj, Jerod, eds. Living Forge. (p. 1041)
Sendak, J., jt. auth. see Sendak, Jack.
Sendak, Jack & Sendak, J. Happy Rain. Sendak, Maurice, illus. (p. 746)
Sendak, Maurice. Alligators All Around Board Book: An Alphabet. Sendak, Maurice, illus. (p. 47)
—Bumble-Ardy. Sendak, Maurice, illus. (p. 241)
—Chicken Soup with Rice Board Book: A Book of Months. Sendak, Maurice, illus. (p. 300)
—Cocina de Noche. Sendak, Maurice, illus. (p. 337)
—Didola Pidola Pon! O la Vida Debe Ofrecer Algo Mas. (p. 437)
—Donde Viven los Monstruos. (p. 466)
—In the Night Kitchen. (p. 867)
—Kenny's Window. Sendak, Maurice, illus. (p. 949)
—My Brother's Book. Sendak, Maurice, illus. (p. 1199)
—One Was Johnny Board Book: A Counting Book. Sendak, Maurice, illus. (p. 1297)
—Pierre Board Book: A Cautionary Tale in Five Chapters & a Prologue. Sendak, Maurice, illus. (p. 1357)
—Very Far Away. Sendak, Maurice, illus. (p. 1838)
—We Love You, Mama! (p. 1867)
—Where the Wild Things Are. (p. 1909)
—Where the Wild Things Are. Sendak, Maurice, illus. (p. 1909)
—Where the Wild Things Are Collector's Edition. Sendak, Maurice, illus. (p. 1909)
Sendak, Maurice, illus. see Engvick, William.
Sendak, Maurice, illus. see Grimm, Wilhelm K.
Sendak, Maurice, illus. see Hoffmann, E. T. A.
Sendak, Maurice, illus. see Joslin, Sesyle.
Sendak, Maurice, illus. see Krauss, Ruth.
Sendak, Maurice, illus. see Kushner, Tony.
Sendak, Maurice, illus. see Minarik, Else Holmelund & Tashlin, Frank.
Sendak, Maurice, illus. see Minarik, Else Holmelund.
Sendak, Maurice, illus. see Orgel, Doris.
Sendak, Maurice, illus. see Segal, Lore, et al.
Sendak, Maurice, illus. see Sendak, Jack & Sendak, J.
Sendak, Maurice, illus. see Sendak, Philip.
Sendak, Maurice, illus. see Stockton, Frank R. & Stockton.
Sendak, Maurice, illus. see Stockton, Frank Richard.
Sendak, Maurice, illus. see Udry, Janice May.
Sendak, Maurice, illus. see Wahl, Jan.
Sendak, Maurice, illus. see Yorinks, Arthur.
Sendak, Maurice, tr. see Minarik, Else Holmelund.
Sendak, Maurice & Grimm, Jacob. Marchen der Bruder Grimm. (p. 1091)
Sendak, Maurice & Knussen, Oliver. Higglety Pigglety Pop! & Where the Wild Things Are. (p. 777)
Sendak, Philip. In Grandpa's House. Sendak, Maurice, illus. (p. 863)
Sendelbach, Brian. Underpants Zoo. Sendelbach, Brian, illus. (p. 1815)
Sendelbach, Brian, illus. see Johnston, Teresa.
Sendrowski, Brian, Jr. & Gohari, Omid. Connecticut College College Prowler off the Record. (p. 358)
Send-up, Maurice. Where the Mild Things Are: A Very Meek Parody. Leick, Bonnie, illus. (p. 1909)
Senelwa, Fred, tr. see Resman, Michael.
Senese, Frederick, jt. auth. see Brady, James.
Senge, Peter, et al. Escuelas Que Aprenden: Un Manual de la Quinta Disciplina para Educadores, Padres de Familiar y Todos los Que Se Interesen en la Educacion. Nannetti, Jorge Cardenas, tr. (p. 535)
Sengele, Mark. Inside the Reformation. (p. 877)
Sengelmann, Jennifer. Discovering the Best Me I Can Be! (p. 449)
Sengupta, Anita, tr. see Clamp Staff.
Sengupta, Anita, tr. see Takahashi, Kazuki.
Sengupta, Anita, tr. from JPN. Magic Knight Rayearth II (p. 1072)
Sengupta, Monalisa. Discover Big Cats. (p. 447)
—Discover Bugs. (p. 447)
—Discover Sharks. (p. 448)
—Volcanoes & Earthquakes. (p. 1849)
—Wild Weather. (p. 1930)
Senior, Kathryn. Life in a Rain Forest. (p. 1010)
—Volcanoes. (p. 1849)
—What on Earth? - Wild Weather (p. 1892)
—You Wouldn't Want to Be a Nurse During the American Civil War! A Job That's Not for the Squeamish. (p. 1976)
—You Wouldn't Want to Be Sick in the 16th Century! (Revised Edition) (p. 1977)
Senior, Kathryn, et al. Photography. (p. 1353)
Senior, Kevin. One Step Away. (p. 1297)
Senior, Olive. Anna Carries Water James, Laura, illus. (p. 85)
Senior, Patricia. Mischief on Mumpit Mountain. (p. 1150)
—Pip & the Magic Flute. (p. 1361)
Senior, Suzy. Teddy Bear Says Goodnight. Mitchell, Melanie, illus. (p. 1712)
—Teddy Bear Says I Love You. Mitchell, Melanie, illus. (p. 1712)
—Teddy Bear Says Let's Hug. Mitchell, Melanie, illus. (p. 1712)
—Teddy Bear Says Wake Up! Mitchell, Melanie, illus. (p. 1712)
Senior, Trevor & Kaye, Jacqueline. New Maths Frameworking: Matches the Revised KS3 Framework. (p. 1246)
Senisi, Ellen B. Berry Smudges & Leaf Prints: Finding & Making Colors from Nature. Senisi, Ellen B., photos by. (p. 168)
Senisi, Ellen B., jt. auth. see Marx, Trish.
Senisi, Ellen B., photos by see Marx, Trish.
Senkel, Nicholas, illus. see Teare, Nellie.
Senker, Cath. Arab-Israeli Conflict. (p. 94)
—Avoiding Harmful Substances. (p. 120)
—Christianity: Signs, Symbols, Stories. (p. 312)
—Construction Careers. (p. 359)
—Debate about Immigration. (p. 421)
—Everyday Life in Ancient Greece. (p. 543)
—Everyday Life in the Bible Lands. (p. 543)
—Exercise & Play. (p. 548)
—Fashion Designers. (p. 575)
—Fs: On the Frontline Surviving the Holocaust. (p. 646)
—Germany. (p. 666)
—Healthy Eating. (p. 758)
—Hinduism: Signs, Symbols, Stories. (p. 780)
—Immigrants & Refugees. (p. 861)
—Improving Healthcare (p. 862)
—Islam: Signs, Symbols, Stories. (p. 891)
—Israel & the Middle East. (p. 893)
—J. K. Rowling: Creator of Harry Potter. (p. 901)
—Judaism: Signs, Symbols, Stories. (p. 930)
—Judaism. (p. 930)
—Keeping Clean. (p. 947)
—Keeping Safe. (p. 947)
—Kennedy & the Cuban Missile Crisis: Days of Decision (p. 948)
—Lebanon. (p. 986)
—Mapping Global Issues: Immigrants & Refugees. (p. 1090)
—Migration & Refugees. (p. 1141)
—My Buddhist Year. (p. 1199)
—My Christian Year. (p. 1200)
—My Hindu Year. (p. 1211)
—My Jewish Year. (p. 1211)
—My Muslim Year. (p. 1215)
—My Sikh Year. (p. 1218)
—Nelson Mandela. (p. 1240)
—North & South Korea. (p. 1264)
—Plant Reproduction: How Do You Grow a Giant Pumpkin? (p. 1369)
—Poverty. (p. 1389)
—Poverty & Hunger. (p. 1389)
—Refugees. (p. 1456)
—Relationships (p. 1457)
—Saudi Arabia. (p. 1516)
—Self-Harm (p. 1549)
—South Africa. (p. 1616)
—Stephen Hawking. (p. 1648)
—Stories about Asylum Seekers. (p. 1654)
—Surviving the Holocaust (p. 1687)
—Sustainable Transportation. (p. 1688)
—Taking Action Against Racism. (p. 1698)
—Vietnam War (p. 1841)
—Who Traveled the Underground Railroad? (p. 1917)
—Why Did World War II Happen? (p. 1923)
—Why Do People Seek Asylum? (p. 1924)
—World War II. (p. 1959)
—Year of Religious Festivals (p. 1969)
Senker, Cath, jt. auth. see Bailey Association Staff.
Senker, Cath & Savery, Annabel. Construction Careers. (p. 359)
Senker, Cath & Throp, Claire. Against the Odds Biographies. (p. 29)
Senker, Cath, et al. Eco Guides. (p. 502)
Senkungu, Dinah. How the Tortoise Got His Scars. (p. 813)
—Wishing Needle. (p. 1940)
Senneff, John A. Apastron Reports: Quest for Life Hausmann, Rex, illus. (p. 91)
Sennell, Joles. Yuyo, Nino No Podia... (Yuyo, Boy Who...) (p. 1983)
Senner, Katja, illus. see Cuno, Sabine.
Senning, Cindy Post, jt. auth. see Post, Peggy.
Senning, Cindy Post & Post, Emily. Emily Post's the Guide to Good Manners for Kids. Björkman, Steve, illus. (p. 519)
Senning, Cindy Post & Post, Peggy. Emily's New Friend. Björkman, Steve, illus. (p. 519)
Senning, Susan, illus. see Turnbull, Betty J.
Senning, Susan, illus. see Turnbull, Betty.
Senno, Knife, jt. auth. see Kakinuma, Hideki.
Senno, Knife, jt. auth. see Shimazaki, Kento.
Senopati, Erik, illus. see Smith, Brian.
Sensel, Joni. Bears Barge In. Bivins, Christopher, illus. (p. 151)
—Farwalker's Quest. (p. 575)
—Garbage Monster. Bivins, Christopher, illus. (p. 655)
—Timekeeper's Moon. (p. 1754)
Sensenig, Janet Martin. Maria de Guatemala y Otras Historias. (p. 1093)
—Missing Bible: And Other Stories. (p. 1152)
Senshu, Noriko. Year of the Beloved Animal: Story of the Chinese zodiac Animals. (p. 1969)
Sente, Yves. Sarcophagi of the Sixth Coninent Juillard, André, illus. (p. 1514)
Sente, Yves & Juillard, Andre. Gondwana Shrine. (p. 697)
—Sarcophagi of the Sixth Continent (p. 1514)
—Voronov Plot. (p. 1850)
Sentek, Kimberly. Oh Brother! A Nico & Tugger Tale. (p. 1280)
Senter, Denise. Chosen Lady. (p. 310)
Senturk, Burak, illus. see Redmond, Shirley Raye.
Senuta, Michael. Puzzling over Sherlock. Earlenbaugh, Dennis, illus. (p. 1421)
—Second Thoughts about Sherlock Holmes. Earlenbaugh, Dennis, illus. (p. 1539)
Senzai, N. H. Saving Kabul Corner. (p. 1517)
—Shooting Kabul. (p. 1568)
Seo & So, Chong-O. Toad Bridegroom & Other Fantastic Tales Retold. Kim, Sung-Min, illus. (p. 1759)
Seo, Hong-Seock. Dragon Hunter Seo, Hong-Seock, illus. (p. 477)
Seo, Kaila Eunhye. Fred. (p. 632)
Seock Seo, Hong. Dragon Hunter. (p. 477)
Seock Seo, Hong, illus. see Im, Hye-Young, tr.
Seock Seo, Hong & Redstone Press Staff. Dragon Hunter (p. 477)
Seock Seo, Hong & Studio Redstone. Dragon HunterTM Im, Hye-Young, tr. (p. 477)
Seock Seo, Hong, creator. Dragon Hunter (p. 477)
Seok, Boin. Itchy! Itchy! My Wings Must Be Growing! (p. 895)
Seomeng, Judah. Dimo & the Little Bush Doctor. (p. 440)
Seon, JeongHyeon, illus. see Kim, JiYu.
Sepahban, Lois. Floods. (p. 605)
—Mongol Warriors. (p. 1164)
—Samurai Warriors. (p. 1510)
—Spartan Warriors. (p. 1622)
—Temple Grandin: Inspiring Animal-Behavior Scientist. (p. 1718)
Sepe, Kim A. Crouching Cat, Hidden Kitten. (p. 385)
Sepehri, Sandy. Continents. (p. 360)
—Rourke's Native American History & Culture Encyclopedia. (p. 1491)
Sepesi, Laura. Master of Kelmar. (p. 1103)
—Secrets of Kelmar. (p. 1545)
Sepetys, Ruta. Between Shades of Gray. (p. 173)
—Out of the Easy. (p. 1311)
Sepheri, Sandy. Continents. (p. 360)
—Glaciers. (p. 682)
Seplowitz, P'Nina. Once upon a Vegetable. (p. 1293)
Sepulveda, Luis. Gaviota y del Gato. (p. 658)
Sepulveda, Sandra. Adventures of Halo & Manny: Lost in the City. (p. 18)
Sequeira, Michele & Westphal, Michael. Cell Phone Science: What Happens When You Call & Why. (p. 286)
Sequin, Tamiko. Potato Chip Club. (p. 1388)
—Yes, I Do Love You, Jordan Magoo. (p. 1970)
Sera, Lucia. Another Tree in the Yard. Lonergan Iorio, John, illus. (p. 88)
Serafin, Jordan. Bella: The Crooked Hat Witch. Rubino, Alisa A., illus. (p. 162)
Serafin, Kim. Mission San Antonio de Padua. (p. 1153)
Serafin, Michael. 4 Seasons of Baghdad. (p. 1992)
Serafin, Mike. 7 Stories from Baghdad. (p. 1993)
Serafin, Shan. Seventeen. (p. 1555)
Serafin, Steven & Bendixen, Alfred, eds. Continuum Encyclopedia of American Literature. (p. 361)
Serafini, Estela, tr. see Stone, Lynn.
Serafini, Frank. Garden. Serafini, Frank, illus. (p. 656)
—Looking Closely Across the Desert. Serafini, Frank, illus. (p. 1051)
—Looking Closely along the Shore. Serafini, Frank, illus. (p. 1051)
—Looking Closely Around the Pond. (p. 1051)
—Looking Closely in the Rain Forest. Serafini, Frank, illus. (p. 1051)
—Looking Closely Through the Forest Serafini, Frank, illus. (p. 1051)
Serazio, Audrey. Cocker Tales. (p. 337)
Serban, Milica. Little Bag with Two Gold Coins. (p. 1023)
Serber, Michael & Peiser, Andrew. U. S. History & Government. (p. 1806)
Serdula, Anne P. Healing Truths: Ten Truths that Lead to Joy, Well-Being & Wisdom. (p. 757)
Sereda, Maja, illus. see Gumede, William.
Serediuk, J. L. Tales of Nottoway: Balak's Reign: Book 1. (p. 1702)
Seredy, Kate. Chestry Oak. (p. 298)
—Philomena. Seredy, Kate, illus. (p. 1351)
—Tree for Peter. Seredy, Kate, illus. (p. 1783)
Seredy, Kate, illus. see Blanco, Margery Williams.
Sereno, Paul C., jt. auth. see Lunis, Natalie.
Seres, Frank & Seres, Nancy. Jacob Series: Book #1 Fearfully & Wonderfully Made. (p. 904)
Seres, Nancy, jt. auth. see Seres, Frank.
Seresin, Lynn, jt. auth. see Schwartz, Betty Ann.
Seresin, Lynn, jt. auth. see Schwartz, Betty.
Seresin, Lynn & Schwartz, Betty Ann. Hop, Hop Bunny. Ng, Neiko, illus. (p. 796)
Serfass, Jim, illus. see Link, C. Edward.
Serfozo, Mary. Plumply, Dumply Pumpkin. Petrone, Valeria, illus. (p. 1374)
Serfozo, Mary & Petrone, Valeria. Plumply, Dumply Pumpkin. (p. 1374)
Sergeant, Kate. It's a Very Good Night. (p. 896)
Sergeyeva, Marina. Nikki & Nick Are Great Friends to Pick. Sergeyeva, Marina, illus. (p. 1255)
Sergis, Diana K. Bush vs. Gore: Controversial Presidential Election Case. (p. 244)
Serich, Mary, jt. auth. see Martin, Jack.
Serino, Robert. Adventures of Pea-Shooter: Into the Forbidden Forest. Lally, Cory, illus. (p. 21)
Serio, John N., ed. Poetry for Young People: the Seasons. Crockett, Robert, illus. (p. 1376)
—Seasons. Crockett, Robert, illus. (p. 1538)
Serio, Marie L. Hello Autumn Goodbye Autumn. (p. 763)
Serizawa, Naoki. Samurai Man Serizawa, Naoki, illus. (p. 1510)
Serkis, Andy. Gollum: How We Made Movie Magic. (p. 696)
Serle, Rebecca. Edge of Falling. (p. 504)
—Famous in Love. (p. 569)
—When You Were Mine. (p. 1905)
Serling, Rod, jt. auth. see Kneece, Mark.
Serluca-Foster, Rosemary. Genevieve's Gift: A Child's Joyful Tale of Connecting with Her Intuitive Heart. (p. 661)
Serman, Gina L., ed. see Fast, Suellen M.
Sermons, Faye. My Granma Lives at the Airport. (p. 1210)
—No Ordinary Cat. Becket, Nancy, illus. (p. 1259)
Serna, Ana. Cuentos y Recetas de la Abuela. (p. 390)
Serofilli, Loretta, et al. Provisiones del Raton Roblito. Brignole, Giancarla, tr. (p. 1413)
Seroney, Kibny'aanko Arap. Cheebtabuut, Blue Berries & the Monsters Den. (p. 295)
Seroya, Tea, illus. see Allen, Teresa R.
Seroya, Tea, illus. see Alpert, Sherri.
Seroya, Tea, illus. see Downie, David.
Seroya, Tea, illus. see Lefkowits, John.
Serpa, Dylon J. Moosey's Adventures: The Way Home. (p. 1173)
Serpentelli, John, illus. see Kelso, Susan.
Serra, Alexander, illus. see Torres, J., et al.
Serra, Armando, illus. see Romero, Sensi.
Serra Huerta, Luis, tr. see Meyer, Kai.
Serra, Louis. Reluctant Vampire. (p. 1458)
Serra, Sebastia, illus. see Compestine, Ying Chang.
Serra, Sebastia, illus. see Garcia, Cristina.
Serra, Sebastia, illus. see Grimm, Jacob, et al.
Serra, Sebastià, illus. see Kudlinski, Kathleen V.
Serra, Sebastia, illus. see Sacre, Antonio.
Serra, Sebastiá, illus. see Yates, Philip.
Serraino, Pierluigi. NorCalMod: Icons of Northern California Modernist Architecture. (p. 1264)
Serrano, Alfonso, illus. see Serrano, Berta.
Serrano, Berta. Born from the Heart. Serrano, Alfonso, illus. (p. 214)
Serrano, Francisco. Malinche: The Princess Who Helped Cortés Conquer the Aztec Empire Ouriou, Susan, tr. from SPA. (p. 1083)
—Our Lady of Guadalupe Davalos, Felipe, illus. (p. 1309)

—Poet King of Tezcoco: A Great Leader of Ancient Mexico Balch, Trudy & Engelbert, Jo Anne, trs. from SPA. (p. 1376)
—Virgen de Guadalupe. Dávalos, Felipe, illus. (p. 1844)
Serrano, Javier, illus. see Sierra I. Fabra, Jordi & Sierra i Fabra, Jordi.
Serrano, Javier, tr. see Sierra I. Fabra, Jordi & Sierra i Fabra, Jordi.
Serrano, Javier U., illus. see Pascual, Emilio.
Serrano, Monica, jt. auth. see Fawcett, Louise.
Serrano, Pablo, illus. see Ramos, Maria Cristina.
Serrano, Pablo, illus. see Serrano, Francisco.
Serrano, Pet. Best Friends No Matter What. (p. 169)
Serrano, Shea. Bun B's Rap Coloring. (p. 241)
Serrano, Tina. Catfish Caper. (p. 280)
—Urban Scavenger Hunt (p. 1825)
Serrano, Tomas. Salfon el Limpiador de Tejados. (p. 1504)
Serratosa, Miquel, illus. see Despeyroux, Denise & Poe, Edgar Allen.
Serres, Alain. And Picasso Painted Guernica. Price, Rosalind, tr. from FRE. (p. 71)
—I Have the Right to Be a Child Mixter, Helen, tr. from FRE. (p. 839)
Serros, Michele. Honey Blonde Chica. (p. 794)
—¡Scandalosa! A Honey Blonde Chica Novel. (p. 1519)
Serrurier, Jane, illus. see Plummer, Deborah.
Sertori, J. M. Monsters. (p. 1168)
Sertori, Trisha. Dairy Foods. (p. 400)
—Fats & Oils. (p. 577)
—Fruits, Vegetables, & Legumes. (p. 646)
—Grains, Bread, Cereal & Pasta. (p. 706)
—Meats, Fish, Eggs, Nuts, & Beans. (p. 1118)
—Vitamins & Minerals. (p. 1846)
Servatius, John Jerome. Unspeakable. (p. 1822)
Servello, Joe, illus. see Kotzwinkle, William.
Server, David, jt. auth. see Lanzing, Jackson.
Server, David & Lanzing, Jackson. Madagascar Digest Prequel: Long Live the King! Long Live the King! (p. 1069)
—Penguins of Madagascar. (p. 1337)
—Penguins of Madagascar Digest: Operation Weakest Link & Other Stories: Operation Weakest Link & Other Stories. (p. 1337)
Server, Lee. Lions - Pb: A Portrait of the Animal World. (p. 1021)
—Tigers - Pb: A Portrait of the Animal World. (p. 1749)
Servi Machlin, Edda. My Puppy Marrano. (p. 1217)
Service, Pamela F. #4 Alien Encounter. Gorman, Mike, illus. (p. 1992)
—#5 Alien Contact. Gorman, Mike, illus. (p. 1992)
—Alien Contact. Gorman, Mike, illus. (p. 40)
—Alien Encounter. Gorman, Mike, illus. (p. 40)
—Alien Envoy. Gorman, Mike, illus. (p. 40)
—Alien Expedition. (p. 40)
—Alien Expedition. Gorman, Mike, illus. (p. 40)
—Camp Alien. (p. 257)
—Camp Alien. Gorman, Mike, illus. (p. 257)
—Escape from Planet Yastol Gorman, Mike, illus. (p. 535)
—My Cousin, the Alien. (p. 1200)
—My Cousin, the Alien. Gorman, Mike, illus. (p. 1200)
—Not-So-Perfect Planet. Gorman, Mike, illus. (p. 1267)
—Wizards of Wyrd World. Gorman, Mike, illus. (p. 1943)
Service, Regina. Ginger Family. (p. 677)
Serwacki, Anita, jt. auth. see Karwowski, Chris.
Serwacki, Kevin & Pallace, Chris. Joey & Johnny - The Ninjas - Get Mooned. Serwacki, Kevin & Pallace, Chris, illus. (p. 920)
Serwer-Berstein, Blanche. Let's Steal the Moon: Jewish Tales, Ancient & Recent. Hyman, Trina Schart, illus. (p. 1000)
Sesa, jt. auth. see Beck, Lynn G.
Sesame Street. Sesame Street Elmo's Musical Hugs. (p. 1553)
Sesame Street, Sesame. Sesame Street Elmo's 1 2 3. (p. 1553)
—Sesame Street Elmo's ABC: Lift-The-Flap. (p. 1553)
Sesame Street Staff. Fairly Furry 2 bk Big Red Riding Hood 3 Little Grouches. (p. 563)
—Fairly Furry 2 bk Rhyming Rapunzel Rosita & Beanstalk. (p. 563)
—Fairly Furry Fairy Tales 3 bk Pack. (p. 563)
—Sesame Street Count with Elmo! A Look, Lift, & Learn Book. (p. 1553)
—Sesame Street Elmo's Boo Boo Book. (p. 1553)
—Sesame Street Hide & Seek, Elmo! (p. 1553)
Sesame Street Staff, jt. auth. see Albee, Sarah.
Sesame Street Staff & Studio Mouse Staff. Learning Fun. (p. 985)
Sesame Street Staff, creator. Sesame Street: Elmo & Me! Boxed Set. (p. 1553)
—Sesame Street: Early Learning Boxed Set. (p. 1553)
—Sesame Street: My First Manners Boxed Set. (p. 1553)
Sesame Street Workshop Staff. Shalom Sesame DVD Set (p. 1559)
Sesame Workshop. Abby Cadabby up & Down: Brand New Readers. Kwiat, Ernie, illus. (p. 2)
—All Tucked in on Sesame Street! (p. 46)
—Bert & Ernie Go Camping: Brand New Readers. Kwiat, Ernie, illus. (p. 168)
—Bert & Ernie Go Camping. (p. 168)
—Brand New Readers. (p. 222)
—Cookie Monster's Busy Day: Brand New Readers. Kwiat, Ernie, illus. (p. 361)
—Cookie Monster's Busy Day. (p. 361)
—Elmo Loves You! (p. 515)
—Happy Halloween! (p. 745)
—Here Comes Super Grover! Brand New Readers. Kwiat, Ernie, illus. (p. 770)
—I Am a Friend. (p. 832)
—I Like School. (p. 841)
—Just One You! (p. 939)
—Off to School! (p. 1279)
—Sesame Play-N-Learn 123S. (p. 1553)
—Sesame Play-N-Learn Dot to Dots. (p. 1553)
—Sesame Play-N-Learn Mazes. (p. 1553)
—Sesame Street (p. 1553)
—Toddler Time Explore Animals with Elmo. (p. 1761)
—Toddler Time Explore Seasons with Cookie Monster. (p. 1761)
—'Twas the Night Before Christmas on Sesame Street! (p. 1799)
Sesame Workshop, ed. ABC Sesame Street Flash Cards. (p. 3)
—Pets Elmos World Flash Cards. (p. 1348)
—Your Body Elmos World Flash Cards. (p. 1980)
Sesame Workshop, Sesame & McQuillan, Susan. Sesame Street Let's Cook! (p. 1553)
Sesame Workshop Staff. Big Bird at Home: Brand New Readers. Kwiat, Ernie, illus. (p. 178)
—Elmo & His Friends: Brand New Readers. Brannon, Tom, illus. (p. 515)
—Shalom Sesame Set. (p. 1559)
Sesame Workshop Staff, jt. auth. see McQuillan, Susan.
Sesame Workshop Staff, ed. My First Library Sesame Street: 12 Board Books. (p. 1207)
Sesen, Cihan. Stop the Rain, Issue #1. (p. 1654)
Seskin, Steve & Shamblin, Allen. Chance to Shine. Christie, R. & Christie, Gregory, illus. (p. 289)
Sesko, Frank & Sesko, Mary Ann. Santa & Sam's Big Secret. (p. 1511)
Sesko, Mary Ann, jt. auth. see Sesko, Frank.
Sesma, C. Basic ESL Workbook: Level 1 (p. 141)
—Basic ESL Workbook: Level 2 (p. 141)
—Basic ESL Workbook: Level 3 (p. 141)
Session, Garry. Odessa Bluegill & The Star Ship: Odessa Bluegill & The Space Ship. (p. 1278)
—Odessa Bluegill - Out Shovels a Yellow Tractor. Warren, Pamela, ed. (p. 1278)
Sessions, Nancy Marie. Across the Bridge. (p. 9)
Sesso, Karen A. Off They Swam (p. 1279)
Sessoms, Bob. Buscar Arriba para Alcanzar Alrededor: Guia para Lideres. (p. 244)
Sester, Richard, jt. auth. see Bowling, Joyce E.
Setaro, John F., jt. auth. see Hyde, Margaret O.
Setford, Steve. Scholastic Discover More: Human Body. (p. 1521)
Seth, illus. see Snicket, Lemony, pseud.
Seth, jt. auth. see Snicket, Lemony, pseud.
Seth, jt. auth. see Stanley, John.
Seth, Shantum. Siddhartha Gautama: The Life of the Buddha - Based on Original Sources. Mukherjee, Aniruddha, illus. (p. 1573)
Seth, Shaun. Economics: The Study of Production, Distribution, & Consumption. (p. 502)
—Key Figures of the Korean War. (p. 950)
Seth, Shaun, ed. Key Figures of the Korean War. (p. 950)
Seth, Vikram. Arion y el Delfin. Dieguez Dieguez, Remedios, tr. (p. 98)
Sethi, Maneesh. Game Programming for Teens. (p. 654)
—Web Design for Teens. (p. 1870)
Sethi, Maneesh & Harbour, Jonathan. Game Programming Kit for Teens. (p. 654)
Seto, Alex. What Do You See? Touch My Nose, It Feels Funny. (p. 1883)
—Whose Hat? (p. 1921)
Seto, Lillian, illus. see Reed, Rosemary.
Seto, Loretta. Mooncakes Benoit, Renne, illus. (p. 1172)
Seton, Ernest Thompson. Biography of a Grizzly. (p. 189)
—Biography of a Grizzly. Seton-Thompson, Grace Gallatin, illus. (p. 189)
—Biography of a Silver Fox. (p. 189)
—Johnny Bear. (p. 923)
—Monarch, the Big Bear of Tallac. (p. 1163)
—Rolf in the Woods: The Adventures of a Boy Scout with Indian Quonab & Little Dog Skookum. (p. 1485)
—Trail of the Sandhill Stag. Seton, Ernest Thompson, illus. (p. 1776)
—Two Little Savages: Being the Adventures of Two Boys Who Lived As Indians & What They Learned. (p. 1804)
—Two Little Savages: The Adventures of Two Boys Who Lived As American Indians. Seton, Ernest Thompson, illus. (p. 1804)
—Two Little Savages. (p. 1804)
—Wild Animal Ways. (p. 1928)
—Wild Animals I Have Known. (p. 1928)
—Woodmyth & Fable. (p. 1949)
Seton, Ernest Thompson, et al. Books about Animals. (p. 212)
Seton Press, prod. Book of Friendliness. (p. 211)
—English 3 for Young Catholics. (p. 529)
—Kindergarten Handwriting for Young Catholics. (p. 957)
Seton-Thompson, Ernest. Biography of a Grizzly & Drawing. (p. 189)
Seton-Thompson, Grace Gallatin, illus. see Seton, Ernest Thompson.
Settel, Jim. Things I See & the Things I Do. Han, Mylene, illus. (p. 1733)
Settel, Joanne. Amazing Skin from Outside In. Timmons, Bonnie, illus. (p. 55)
Setterington, Ken. Branded by the Pink Triangle (p. 222)
—Mom & Mum Are Getting Married! Priestley, Alice, illus. (p. 1161)
Settino, Erica. I Am Everything & Everything Is Me. (p. 832)
Settle, Melissa A. Firefighters Then & Now. (p. 591)
—Police Then & Now (p. 1380)
Setzer, Lee Ann. I Am a Child of God. Harmon, Glenn, illus. (p. 832)
—I Am Ready for Baptism. (p. 833)
—Sariah McDuff: Primary Program Diva. Officer, Robyn, illus. (p. 1515)
—Sariah Mcduff: Book Three of the Sariah Mcduff Series: Valentine's Day Scrooge. Bonham, Bob, illus. (p. 1515)
—Tiny Talks: My Savior, Jesus Christ (p. 1756)
—Tiny Talks #6: I will Trust in Heavenly Father & His Son, Jesus Christ-Their Promises are Sure (p. 1756)
Setzer, LeeAnn. Tiny Talks 2009: My Eternal Family. Harmon, Glenn, illus. (p. 1756)
Seuil Staff, contrib. by. Mad Professor. (p. 1069)
Seuling, Barbara. Ancient Coins Were Shaped Like Hams: And Other Freaky Facts about Coins, Bills, & Counterfeiting. Skeens, Matthew, illus. (p. 68)
—Cows Sweat Through Their Noses: And Other Freaky Facts about Animal Habits, Characteristics, & Homes. Skeens, Matthew, illus. (p. 374)
—Cows Sweat Through Their Noses [Dollar General]: And Other Freaky Facts about Animal Habits, Charac. Skeens, Matthew, illus. (p. 374)
—Earth Is Like a Giant Magnet: And Other Freaky Facts about Planets, Oceans. Skeens, Matthew, illus. (p. 496)
—Earth Is Like a Giant Magnet: And Other Freaky Facts about Planets, Oceans, & Volcanoes. Skeens, Matthew, illus. (p. 496)
—Earth Is Like a Giant Magnet [Dollar General]: And Other Freaky Facts about Planets, Oceans, And. Skeens, Matthew, illus. (p. 496)
—Flick a Switch: How Electricity Gets to Your Home. Tobin, Nancy, illus. (p. 603)
—How Does a Fish Take a Bath? (p. 808)
—One President Was Born on Independence Day: And Other Freaky Facts about the 26th Through 43rd Presidents. Skeens, Matthew, illus. (p. 1296)
—Robert & the Attack of the Giant Tarantula. Brewer, Paul, illus. (p. 1478)
—Robert & the Great Escape. Brewer, Paul, illus. (p. 1478)
—Robert & the Happy Endings. Brewer, Paul, illus. (p. 1478)
—Robert & the Lemming Problem. Brewer, Paul, illus. (p. 1478)
—Robert & the Practical Jokes. Brewer, Paul, illus. (p. 1478)
—Robert Finds a Way. Brewer, Paul, illus. (p. 1479)
—Robert Goes to Camp. Brewer, Paul, illus. (p. 1479)
—Robert Takes a Stand. Brewer, Paul, illus. (p. 1479)
—There Are Millions of Millionaires: And Other Freaky Facts about Earning, Saving, & Spending Haugen, Ryan, illus. (p. 1729)
—There are Millions of Millionaires [Scholastic]: And Other Freaky Facts about Earning, Saving, And. Haugen, Ryan, illus. (p. 1729)
—You Blink Twelve Times a Minute: And Other Freaky Facts about the Human Body Haugen, Ryan, illus. (p. 1973)
—Your Skin Weighs More Than Your Brain: And Other Freaky Facts about Your Skin, Skeleton, & Other Body Parts. Skeens, Matthew, illus. (p. 1981)
Seung-Man, Hwang, illus. see Eun-Jeong, Kim.
Seupel, Celia. Performing Arts. (p. 1343)
Seurat, Georges, jt. auth. see Venezia, Mike.
Seurat, Georges Pierre. Make a Masterpiece — Seurat's a Sunday Afternoon on the Island of la Grande Jatte. (p. 1078)
Seus. Wie der Grinch Weihnachten. (p. 1927)
Seuss, Dr. All Aboard the Circus McGurkus. (p. 42)
—Bartholomew & the Oobleck. (p. 140)
—Battaglia dell Burro. (p. 145)
—Big Box of Bright & Early Board Books about Me. (p. 179)
—Big Green Book of Beginner Books. Stevenson, James et al, illus. (p. 181)
—Big Orange Book of Beginner Books. (p. 183)
—Bippolo Seed & Other Lost Stories. (p. 190)
—Cat in the Hat. (p. 278)
—Cat in the Hat Book & Hat. (p. 278)
—Cat in the Hat Cloth Book. (p. 278)
—Cat in the Hat Comes Back. (p. 278)
—Cat in the Hat in English & French. Vallier, Jean, tr. (p. 278)
—Cat in the Hat/el Gato Ensombrerado: Bilingual Edition. (p. 278)
—Cat in the Hat's. Ruiz, Aristides, illus. (p. 278)
—Circus McGurkus 1, 2, 3! (p. 322)
—Comment le Grinch a Vvolé Noël! (p. 349)
—Do You Like Green Eggs & Ham? Seuss, Dr., illus. (p. 458)
—Dr. Seuss Horton Collection (p. 475)
—Dr. Seuss Pops Up. (p. 475)
—Dr. Seuss's ABC: An Amazing Alphabet Book! (p. 475)
—Dr. Seuss's ABC Book & CD (p. 475)
—Dr. Seuss's Sleep Softly Book. (p. 475)
—Fox in Socks: Dr. Seuss's Book of Tongue Tanglers. (p. 626)
—Fox in Socks. (p. 626)
—Fox in Socks & Socks in Box. (p. 626)
—Fox in Socks, Bricks & Blocks. Gerardi, Jan, illus. (p. 626)
—Gato con Sombrero Viene de Nuevo! Canetti, Yanitzia, tr. from ENG. (p. 658)
—Gato Ensombrerado. (p. 658)
—Gatola da Cartola. (p. 658)
—Gerald McBoing Boing. Seuss, Dr., illus. (p. 666)
—Green Eggs & Ham (p. 721)
—Grinch's Great Big Flap Book. (p. 724)
—Happy Birthday, Baby! Gerardi, Jan, illus. (p. 744)
—Happy Birthday to You! (p. 745)
—Hay un Molillo en Mi Bolsillo! Canetti, Yanitzia, tr. from ENG. (p. 755)
—Hooper Humperdink... ? Not Him! Nash, Scott, illus. (p. 795)
—Hop on Pop. (p. 796)
—Horton & the Kwuggerbug & More Lost Stories. (p. 801)
—Horton Entend un Zou! (p. 801)
—Horton Hears a Who Pop-Up! (p. 801)
—How the Grinch Stole Christmas! Seuss, Dr., illus. (p. 813)
—How the Grinch Stole Christmas! Jonaitis, Alice, ed. (p. 813)
—I Can Draw It Myself, by Me, Myself. (p. 835)
—If I Ran the Zoo. (p. 853)
—In a People House. (p. 863)
—Little Blue Box of Bright & Early Board Books by Dr. Seuss. (p. 1024)
—Lorax. Seuss, Dr., illus. (p. 1052)
—Many Mice of Mr. Brice. McKie, Roy, illus. (p. 1089)
—McElligot's Pool. (p. 1114)
—Mr. Brown Can Moo! Can You? (p. 1184)
—Oeufs Verts Au Jambon: The French Edition of Green Eggs & Ham. (p. 1279)
—Oh, Baby! Go, Baby! Gerardi, Jan, illus. (p. 1280)
—Oh, the Places You'll Go! (p. 1281)
—Oh, the Places You'll Go Pop-Up. (p. 1281)
—Oh, the Thinks You Can Think! (p. 1281)
—One Fish, Two Fish, Red Fish, Blue Fish Book & CD (p. 1295)
—One Fish, Two Fish, Three, Four, Five Fish. (p. 1295)
—Pez, Dos Peces, Pez Rojo. Canetti, Yanitzia, tr. from ENG. (p. 1349)
—Poisson Un - Poisson Deux - Poisson Rouge - Poisson Bleu. (p. 1377)
—Seuss-Isms! A Guide to Life for Those Just Starting Out... & Those Already on Their Way. (p. 1554)
—Sneetches on Beaches. (p. 1597)
—Snicci e Altre Storie. (p. 1597)
—There's a Zamp in My Lamp! (p. 1731)
—Tonho Choca o Ovo. (p. 1765)
—Tooth Book. Mathieu, Joe, illus. (p. 1768)
—Virent Ova! Viret Perna! Tunberg, Jennifer Morrish & Tunberg, Terence O., trs. from ENG. (p. 1844)
—Wet Pet, Dry Pet, Your Pet, My Pet. (p. 1877)
—What Pet Should I Get? (p. 1892)
—What Was I Scared Of? A Glow-in-the-Dark Encounter. (p. 1894)
—Who's Who in the Dr. Seuss Crew (p. 1921)
—Would You Rather Be a Bullfrog? (p. 1962)
—Would You Rather Be a Bullfrog? Seuss, Dr. & McKie, Roy, illus. (p. 1962)
—Y Pensar Que lo Vi Por la Calle Porvenir Canetti, Yanitzia James, tr. from ENG. (p. 1968)
—Yo Puedo Leer con los Ojos Cerrados! Canetti, Yanitzia, tr. (p. 1971)
—Yoruga la Tortuga y Otros Cuentos Canetti, Yanitzia, tr. from ENG. (p. 1972)
—Your Favorite Seuss: A Baker's Dozen by the One & Only Dr. Seuss. (p. 1980)
Seuss, Dr., illus. see Brennan, Georgeanne.
Seuss, Dr., illus. see Rabe, Tish.
Seuss, Dr., jt. auth. see Brooke, Susan Rich.
Seuss, Dr., jt. auth. see Cohen, Charles.
Seuss, Dr., jt. auth. see Rabe, Tish.
Seuss, Dr. & Berger, Sholem. [Eyn Fish, Tsvey Fish, Royter Fish, Bloyer Fish. (p. 559)
Seuss, Dr., tr. Come Over to My House. (p. 347)
Seva, illus. see Fridman, Sashi.
Seva, illus. see Glazer, Devorah.
Sevaly, Karen, jt. auth. see Scholastic, Inc. Staff.
Sevaly, Karen & Scholastic, Inc. Staff. Counting Money Puzzles. (p. 371)
—Short Vowels Mats. (p. 1569)
—Word Family Words Mats. (p. 1950)
Sevaly, Karen, ed. Alphabet Mats. (p. 49)
—Beginning Sound Puzzles. (p. 159)
—Classifying Puzzles. (p. 328)
—Match, Trace, & Write Numbers Mats: 30 Activities. (p. 1104)
—Rhyming Puzzles. (p. 1468)
—Sight Word Mats. (p. 1574)
—Vowel Puzzles: 20 Activities. (p. 1850)
Seven, John. Alchemist War Phillips, Craig, illus. (p. 35)
—Dragon of Rome Phillips, Craig, illus. (p. 477)
—Happy, Sad, Silly, Mad. Christy, Jana, illus. (p. 746)
—Ocean Story Christy, Jana, illus. (p. 1276)
—Outlaw of Sherwood Forest Hans, Stephanie, illus. (p. 1312)
—Terror of the Tengu Hans, Stephanie, illus. (p. 1722)
—Time-Tripping Faradays Phillips, Craig, illus. (p. 1753)
Seven, John & Christy, Jana. Happy Punks 1 2 3: A Counting Story. (p. 746)
—Rule Is to Break: A Child's Guide to Anarchy. (p. 1495)
Seven, John & Phillips, Craig. Dragon of Rome (p. 477)
Seventeen Magazine Editors, jt. auth. see Shoket, Ann.
Severance, Charles R. & Fontichiaro, Kristin. Raspberry Pi. (p. 1439)
Severance, Lyn, illus. see Older, Jules, et al.
Severance, Lyn, illus. see Older, Jules.
Severe, Doreese. ABC's See What They Say. (p. 4)
—Beginning See ABC'S Package. (p. 159)
Severin, Carol. Rhode Island. (p. 1468)
Severin, E. Hoover. North Dakota. (p. 1265)
Severin, Marie, illus. see Gallagher, Michael.
Severin, Marie, illus. see Kay, Stan.
Severine Rugumamu. Further Adventures of the Black Hand Gang. (p. 650)
Severino, Philip, illus. see Burke, Patrick J.
Sevig-Fajardo, Mari Elise, tr. see Louise, Märtha.
Sevig-Fajardo, Mari Elise, tr. see Märtha Louise, Princess.
Sevigny, Eric. As Good as New. (p. 105)
Sévigny, Éric. Caillou: Watches Rosie. (p. 251)
—Caillou: Happy Halloween. (p. 251)
—Caillou: Accidents Happen. (p. 251)
—Caillou: The Birthday Party. (p. 251)
Sévigny, Éric. Caillou: Fresh from the Farm. (p. 251)
—Caillou & the Big Slide. (p. 251)
Sévigny, Eric. Caillou & the Rain. (p. 251)
Sévigny, Éric. Caillou - At the Beach. (p. 251)
Sévigny, Éric. Caillou Borrows a Book. (p. 251)
—Caillou Dances with Grandma. (p. 251)
—Caillou, Emma's Extra Snacks: Living with Diabetes. (p. 251)
—Caillou: Family Fun Story Box (p. 251)
Sévigny, Eric. Caillou Gets the Hiccups! (p. 251)
Sévigny, Éric. Caillou Goes Apple Picking. (p. 251)
—Caillou Gone Fishing. (p. 251)
—Caillou Is Sick. (p. 251)
Sévigny, Éric. Caillou - Learns to Recycle. (p. 251)
—Caillou Learns to Swim. (p. 251)
Sévigny, Eric. Caillou Makes a Snowman. (p. 251)
—Caillou: My First Sticker Book: Includes 400 Fun Stickers. (p. 251)
—Caillou: Mystery Valentine. (p. 251)
Sevigny, Eric. Caillou Plants a Tree. (p. 251)
Sévigny, Éric. Caillou Puts Away His Toys. (p. 251)
—Caillou Sends a Letter. (p. 251)
—Caillou - The Captain. (p. 251)
Sévigny, Eric. Caillou: the Doodle Artist. (p. 251)
Sévigny, Éric. Caillou - The Firefighter. (p. 251)
—Caillou - Training Wheels. (p. 251)
Sevigny, Eric. Every Drop Counts. (p. 542)
—In the Garden. (p. 866)
Sévigny, Eric. Jungle Explorer. (p. 935)
Sévigny, Eric. Missing Sock. (p. 1153)
—Phone Call. (p. 1351)
Sévigny, Éric. Show & Tell. (p. 1570)
Sevigny, Eric, illus. see Chouette Publishing Staff.
Sevigny, Eric, illus. see Johanson, Sarah Margaret.
Sevigny, Eric, illus. see Paradis, Anne.

Sévigny, Éric, jt. auth. see Harvey, Roger.
Sévigny, Eric, jt. illus. see Sevigny, Eric.
Sevigny, Eric & Sévigny, Eric. My Imaginary Friend. (p. 1211)
Sevonna. Simon, the Christmas Tree Fle. (p. 1577)
S.E.W. Year at Widows' Creek: The Beginning. (p. 1969)
Sewall, Marcia. People of the Breaking Day. (p. 1339)
Sewall, Marcia, illus. see Gardiner, John Reynolds.
Sewall, Marcia, illus. see Hesse, Karen.
Sewall, Samuel. Diary of Samuel Sewall, 1674-1729 (p. 435)
Seward, Daniel, illus. see Fox, Nancy.
Seward, Pat & Hargraves, Orin. Morocco. (p. 1176)
Seward, Pat & Lal, Sunandini Arora. Netherlands. (p. 1242)
Seward, Prudence, illus. see Parker, Richard.
Seward, Toni Gibson. Kloey & the Ladybug. (p. 963)
Sewell, Amy. Mad Hot Adventures of an Unlikely Documentary Filmmaker. (p. 1069)
Sewell, Amy & Ogilvie, Heather. She's Out There! Essays by 35 Young Women Who Aspire to Lead the Nation - The Next Generation of Presidential Candidates. Ripps, Robert A., photos by. (p. 1566)
Sewell, Anna. Black Beauty. (p. 195)
—Black Beauty: The Autobiography of a Horse. (p. 195)
—Black Beauty: And a Discussion of Kindness. Martin, Richard, illus. (p. 195)
—Black Beauty. (p. 195)
—Black Beauty. Marks, Alan, illus. (p. 195)
—Black Beauty. Aldous, Kate, illus. (p. 195)
—Black Beauty. Brigman, June, illus. (p. 195)
—Black Beauty. Corvino, Lucy, illus. (p. 195)
—Black Beauty. Shaffer, Bren, illus. (p. 195)
—Black Beauty. McKowen, Scott, illus. (p. 195)
—Black Beauty. Hough, Charlotte, illus. (p. 195)
—Black Beauty, Young Folks' Edition - Abridged with Original Illustrations. (p. 195)
—Black Beauty's Early Days in the Meadow. Donovan, Jane Monroe, illus. (p. 195)
Sewell, Anna, jt. auth. see Hill, Susan.
Sewell, Anna, jt. auth. see Lerner, Sharon.
Sewell, Anna & Anna, Sewell. Belleza Negra. (p. 163)
Sewell, Anna, et al. Enchanted Collection: Alice's Adventures in Wonderland; The Secret Garden; Black Beauty; The Wind in the Willows; Little Women Macdonald, Ross, illus. (p. 523)
Sewell, Byron W. Alix's Adventures in Wonderland: Lewis Carroll's Nightmare. (p. 41)
—Snarkmaster: A Destiny in Eight Fits. a Tale Inspired by Lewis Carroll's the Hunting of the Snark. Sewell, Byron W., illus. (p. 1597)
Sewell, Byron W. & Carroll, Lewis. Álpok's Adventures in Goatland. (p. 48)
Sewell, Byron W. & Everson, Michael. Alice's Bad Hair Day in Wonderland: A Tangled Tale. (p. 40)
Sewell, Deborah. You Want Me to Do What? (p. 1976)
Sewell, E. M. Child's History of Rome. (p. 305)
Sewell, Earl. Back to Me. (p. 130)
—Decision Time. (p. 421)
—If I Were Your Boyfriend. (p. 853)
—Keysha's Drama. (p. 951)
—Lesson Learned. (p. 993)
—Maya's Choice. (p. 1113)
—Myself & I. (p. 1222)
—Way Too Much Drama. (p. 1864)
Sewell, Earl, et al. Boyfriend Shopping: Shopping for My Boyfriend My Only Wish All I Want for Christmas Is You. (p. 220)
Sewell, Elizabeth. Bible Activity Book. (p. 175)
Sewell, Helen, illus. see Coatsworth, Elizabeth Jane.
Sewell, Helen, illus. see Coatsworth, Elizabeth.
Sewell, Helen, illus. see Cregan, Mairin.
Sewell, Jaime. When Mommy Went on Strike. (p. 1903)
Sewell, James C. Jesus Loves Me!, Grades K - 4: Scriptures & Songs in Sign Language. (p. 916)
—Signs of Wisdom: Expressing God's Wisdom in Sign Language. Huffine, Erik, illus. (p. 1574)
Sewell, James Witt. Classical Grammar. (p. 328)
Sewell, Kele. Beewee & Meager to the Rescue! the Underbed Entertainment Network. (p. 158)
Sewell, Kristin. Collection of Seven Children's Stories. (p. 340)
Sewell, Sue. Poppy the Three-Legged Puppy. (p. 1385)
Sewer, Anecia. Why Transfer Day, Anyway? Samuel, Karen, illus. (p. 1926)
Sexauer, Donald E. Kramer Makes David Smile. (p. 967)
—Standoff & Kramer Too! (p. 1639)
Sexton, Brenda. Have a Silly Easter! (p. 754)
—Little Jackie Rabbit. (p. 1029)
—Little Sleepy Eyes. (p. 1036)
—You Can Draw Fairies & Princesses Sexton, Brenda, illus. (p. 1974)
—You Can Draw Pets Sexton, Brenda, illus. (p. 1974)
Sexton, Brenda, illus. see Abrams, Majella.
Sexton, Brenda, illus. see Allen, Margaret.
Sexton, Brenda, illus. see Allen, Molly.
Sexton, Brenda, illus. see Charlesworth, Liza & Scholastic, Inc. Staff.
Sexton, Brenda, illus. see Fleming, Maria.
Sexton, Brenda, illus. see Ho, Jannie, et al.
Sexton, Brenda, illus. see LaRochelle, David.
Sexton, Brenda, illus. see Scelsa, Greg.
Sexton, Brenda, jt. auth. see Bruning, Matt.
Sexton, Brenda, jt. auth. see Cerato, Mattia.
Sexton, Brenda & Ho, Jannie. Easy-To-Draw Animals: A Step-By-Step Drawing Book. Sexton, Brenda & Ho, Jannie, illus. (p. 500)
Sexton, Brenton, illus. see Simeon, S. & Golden Books Staff.
Sexton, Clarence. Parables of Jesus: The Greatest Stories Ever Told. (p. 1323)
Sexton, Colleen. African Elephant. (p. 27)
—Anacondas. (p. 66)
—Angelfish. (p. 74)
—Aphids. (p. 91)
—Astronauts. (p. 109)
—Australia. (p. 116)
—Barracudas. (p. 140)
—Beetles. (p. 158)
—Bengal Tiger. (p. 164)
—Blastoff! Readers - Oceans Alive (p. 198)
—Boa Constrictors. (p. 205)
—Box Jellyfish. (p. 216)
—Brazil. (p. 224)
—Bunnies. (p. 242)
—Canada. (p. 260)
—Caring for Your Horse. (p. 269)
—Caring for Your Parakeet. (p. 269)
—Caring for Your Rabbit. (p. 269)
—Caring for Your Turtle. (p. 269)
—China. (p. 306)
—Cicadas. (p. 318)
—Clown Fish. (p. 335)
—Cobras. (p. 337)
—Copperheads. (p. 366)
—Coral Reefs. (p. 366)
—Coral Snakes. (p. 366)
—Cottonmouths. (p. 369)
—Cuba. (p. 388)
—Cuttlefish. (p. 396)
—Damselflies. (p. 401)
—Ducklings. (p. 488)
—Earwigs. (p. 498)
—Egypt. (p. 506)
—England. (p. 529)
—France. (p. 627)
—Frogfish. (p. 640)
—Germany. (p. 666)
—Glaciers. (p. 682)
—Honey Bees. (p. 794)
—India. (p. 870)
—Ireland. (p. 887)
—Israel. (p. 893)
—Italy. (p. 894)
—Jackie Robinson: A Life of Determination. (p. 904)
—Japan. (p. 909)
—Kittens. (p. 963)
—Life Cycle of a Bee. (p. 1008)
—Life Cycle of a Butterfly. (p. 1008)
—Life Cycle of a Cat. (p. 1009)
—Life Cycle of a Chicken. (p. 1009)
—Life Cycle of a Cow. (p. 1009)
—Life Cycle of a Dog. (p. 1009)
—Life Cycle of a Frog. (p. 1009)
—Life Cycle of a Ladybug. (p. 1009)
—Life Cycle of a Penguin. (p. 1009)
—Life Cycle of a Salmon. (p. 1009)
—Life Cycle of a Sea Horse. (p. 1009)
—Life Cycle of a Turtle. (p. 1009)
—Lionfish. (p. 1021)
—Mambas. (p. 1084)
—Manta Rays. (p. 1088)
—Mexico. (p. 1131)
—Moon. (p. 1171)
—Piglets. (p. 1358)
—Pluto. (p. 1374)
—Ponds. (p. 1382)
—Praying Mantises. (p. 1393)
—Puffer Fish. (p. 1415)
—Puffins. (p. 1415)
—Puppies. (p. 1417)
—Pythons. (p. 1422)
—Rat Snakes. (p. 1440)
—Rattlesnakes. (p. 1440)
—Russia. (p. 1498)
—Saltwater Crocodile. (p. 1506)
—Sea Lions. (p. 1535)
—Sea Snakes. (p. 1535)
—Seal Pups. (p. 1536)
—Seals. (p. 1536)
—Sharks. (p. 1562)
—Shrimp. (p. 1571)
—Sidewinders. (p. 1573)
—Solar System. (p. 1607)
—Space Shuttles. (p. 1619)
—Space Stations. (p. 1620)
—Spain. (p. 1620)
—Sponges. (p. 1631)
—Squids. (p. 1637)
—Stink Bugs. (p. 1651)
—Sun. (p. 1675)
—Sweden. (p. 1689)
—Swordfish. (p. 1692)
—Thailand. (p. 1724)
—Tide Pools. (p. 1747)
—Tundra. (p. 1796)
—Uranus. (p. 1825)
—Venus. (p. 1836)
—Vietnam. (p. 1841)
—Walruses. (p. 1855)
Sexton, Colleen A. Japan. (p. 909)
—Philippines in Pictures. (p. 1350)
Sexton, Jessa, ed. see Rogers, Lauren.
Sexton, Jessa R. Mobert's Irish Experience. Sexton, Jessa R., photos by. (p. 1157)
—Saturday. (p. 1515)
Sexton, Jessa R., ed. see Cutrer, Elisabeth.
Sexton, Jessa R., ed. see Robertson, Robbin Davis.
Sexton, Jessa Rose. Eldy & Ohi. Miele, Brianna, illus. (p. 508)
—Rose-Pie. Morozova, Anastasia, illus. (p. 1489)
Sexton, Kris, illus. see Forte, Imogene.
Sexton, Kris, illus. see Hunt-Ullock, Kathy, et al.
Sexton, Richard, photos by. In the Victorian Style. (p. 867)
—New Orleans: Elegance & Decadence. (p. 1246)
Sexton, Shirley. Fairy with an Attitude. (p. 564)
Sexton, Susan. Sprint Car Racing: Unleashing the Power. (p. 1635)
—Sprint Car Racing: Unleashing the Power. (p. 1635)
—Stock Car Racing: Running with the Big Boys. (p. 1651)
Seybold, Celisa. Keys to Adventure. (p. 950)
—Keys to Adventure Take Flight. (p. 950)
Seyderhelm, Amanda. Isaac & the Red Jumper. Scott, Ann, illus. (p. 890)
Seydou, Garba B. One Man Army. (p. 1296)
Seyfert, Ella Maie. Amish Moving Day. Jones, Henrietta, illus. (p. 65)
Seyforth, Edward L. Horribly Frightening Deception (p. 798)
Seykora, Teresa. Case of the Missing Peanut Butter: The Adventures of Peanut Butter Bob. Drewes, Dan, illus. (p. 274)
Seykora, Teresa M. Peanut Butter Bob's Alphabet Book: The Adventures of Peanut Butter Bob. (p. 1332)
Seymour, Alta Halverson. Toward Morning: A Story of the Hungarian Freedom Fighters. (p. 1773)
Seymour, Arlene. Moon Book: A Lunar Pop-up Celebration. Seymour, Arlene, illus. (p. 1172)
Seymour, Dale. Balanced Assessment for the Mathematics Curriculum. (p. 133)
—Developing Skills in Estimation (p. 432)
Seymour, Gloria, told to. ABC Sing-along. (p. 3)
Seymour, Isobel. I am Mexican American. (p. 833)
Seymour, Jane. Good King Wenceslas. Rayyan, Omar, illus. (p. 698)
Seymour, Jane & Keach, James. And Then There Were Three. Planer, Geoffrey, illus. (p. 71)
—Boing! No Bouncing on the Bed. Planer, Geoffrey, illus. (p. 208)
—Fried Pies & Roast Cake. Planer, Geoffrey, illus. (p. 637)
—Other One: You Make Me Happy. Planer, Geoffrey, illus. (p. 1306)
—Splat! The Tale of a Colorful Cat. Planer, Geoffrey, illus. (p. 1629)
—Yum! A Tale of Two Cookies. Planer, Geoffrey, illus. (p. 1983)
Seymour, Kristen. No Thank You, I'm Allergic: A Story Agout Food Allergy Awareness. (p. 1260)
Seymour, Malcolm. And Fight for Bread. (p. 71)
Seymour, Mary Sue. Friends in a Storm. Flynn, Samantha, illus. (p. 638)
Seymour, Marysue. Where Will We Fly. Spadaccini, Cheryl, illus. (p. 1910)
Seymour, Sharon & Walsh, Laura. Essentials of Teaching Academic Reading. (p. 537)
Seymour, Simon. Wolves. (p. 1945)
Seyvos, Florence. Pockety: The Tortoise Who Lived As She Pleased. Provata-Carlone, Mika, tr. from FRE. (p. 1375)
Sezgin, Orhan. Adventures of Little Selim. (p. 20)
Sfair, Antonio Chalita, tr. see Gibran, Khalil.
Sfakianos, Jeffrey N. Avian Flu. Alcamo, I. Edward, ed. (p. 119)
Sfar, Joann, illus. see de Saint-Exupéry, Antoine.
Sfar, Joann, illus. see Guibert, Emmanuel.
Sfar, Joann, illus. see Saint-Exupéry, Antoine de.
Sfar, Joann, jt. auth. see Guibert, Emmanuel.
Sfar, Joann & Trondheim, Lewis. Dungeon Too Many. Larcenet, Manu, illus. (p. 490)
—Mazmorra: El Camison. Abuli, Enrique Sanchez, tr. from FRE. (p. 1113)
—Mazmorra: Corazón de Pato. Abuli, Enrique Sanchez, tr. from FRE. (p. 1113)
—Mazmorra: El Cementerio de los Dragones. Abuli, Enrique Sanchez, tr. from FRE. (p. 1113)
—Mazmorra: El rey de la Pelea. Abuli, Enrique Sanchez, tr. (p. 1114)
—Mazmorra: Un Justiciero en Apuros. Abuli, Enrique Sanchez, tr. from FRE. (p. 1114)
—Mazmorra: Sortilegios e Infortunios. Abuli, Enrique Sanchez, tr. from FRE. (p. 1114)
—Mazmorra: La Princesa de los Barbaros. Abuli, Enrique Sanchez, tr. from FRE. (p. 1114)
Sforza, Daniella, ed. Savannah Blue's Activity Book/Libro de Actividades de Savannah Azul. Spagnoli, Maria Eugenia, tr. (p. 1516)
SFX Fantasy. Tween Tales - Robots, Dragons & the Interworld Machine. (p. 1799)
Sganga, Francis. Essentials of Electricity for Gifted Students: Preparation for High School Physics, Grades 4-8. (p. 537)
—Introducing Gifted Students to the Wonders of Mathematics: Preparation for High School & Higher Mathematics, Grades 4-8. (p. 882)
Sganga, Francis T. Essential Chemistry for Gifted Students: Preparation for High School Chemistry, Grades 4-8. (p. 536)
Sgarlato, Dawn. Big Sister. (p. 183)
Sgouros, Yorgos, illus. see James, Bethan.
Sgroi, Tony, illus. see Schroeder, Doris.
S.H., Addan. Guardabosque Del Ano 3000: Canis Familiaris Evolucion. (p. 728)
Shabazz, Ilyasah. Malcolm Little: The Boy Who Grew up to Become Malcolm X. Ford, A. G., illus. (p. 1083)
Shabazz, Ilyasah & Magoon, Kekla. X. (p. 1966)
Shabazz, Phillip. XYZoom: Poems. (p. 1967)
Shaber, Mark. Animals & Stuff. LaGrange, Tiffany, illus. (p. 82)
Shaboo, Joseph R. Shalamazoo. Churchill, Jessica, photos by. (p. 1559)
Shachat, Andrew, illus. see Armour, Peter.
Shachnow, Sidney, jt. auth. see Robbins, Jann.
Shackelford, David, illus. see Henderson, Richard.
Shackelford, Mary. Cinnamon's Quest. (p. 321)
Shackell, John, illus. see Davies, Helen.
Shackell, John, illus. see Mayes, Susan.
Shackleford, Maudie. Upside-Down Tale. (p. 1825)
Shackleton, Caroline & Turner, Nathan Paul. Avalanche! (p. 118)
—Deep Blue: Discovering the Sea Intermediate Book with Online Access. (p. 422)
—Down to Earth Intermediate Book with Online Access. (p. 474)
—Get Smart: Our Amazing Brain Intermediate Book with Online Access. (p. 668)
—Lift off - Exploring the Universe, High Intermediate. (p. 1014)
—Money Tree: the Business of Organics High Intermediate Book with Online Access. (p. 1164)
—Poison: Medicine, Murder, & Mystery. (p. 1377)
—Robots: the Next Generation? High Intermediate Book with Online Access. (p. 1481)
—Skin. (p. 1585)
—Trapped! (p. 1779)
—Up in the Air: Our Fight Against Gravity Intermediate Book with Online Access. (p. 1824)
—Wheel Low Intermediate Book with Online Access. (p. 1900)
Shacter, Sara F. Heading to the Wedding: You're Invited to Join Patrick & Evie on the Great Adventure of Becoming (Almost) Perfect Guests. Thornton, Christine, illus. (p. 756)
Shaddix, M. K. Aisling's Summer Diary. (p. 32)
Shade, Jeff. Unusual Education. (p. 1823)
Shadick, Stan. Skywatcher's Companion: Constellations & Their Mythology (p. 1587)
Shadow, Jak. Crime Lord. (p. 382)
—F. E. A. R. Agency. (p. 559)
—Space Plague. (p. 1619)
Shadow, Stone. Faithful John. (p. 565)
Shadrick, Crystal Star. My Name Was Fear. Stone, Karen, ed. (p. 1215)
Shady, Bethany, jt. auth. see Shady, Justin.
Shady, Justin & Chinsang, Wayne. Lava Is a Floor. (p. 980)
Shady, Justin & Shady, Bethany. I Beg Your Pardon. (p. 834)
Shady, Leigh, jt. auth. see James, Bethany.
Shae, Jordan. Handy Measuring: Measuring Lengths. (p. 742)
Shafaeddin, Mehdi. Trade Policy at the Crossroads: The Recent Experience of Developing Countries. (p. 1776)
Shafer, Anders C. Fantastic Journey of Pieter Bruegel. Shafer, Anders C., illus. (p. 571)
Shafer, Audrey. Mailbox. (p. 1077)
Shafer, Jan. Where's Rascal? / A Surprise for Rascal. (p. 1910)
Shafer, Janet. Woof: The Story of a Girl & Her Dog. (p. 1950)
Shafer, Jean. Learning from Charts & Graphs: Lessons in History, Civics, Geography, & Economics (p. 985)
Shafer, Patty. Annie the Texas Ranch Dog - Danger at Lost Maples. Retzlaff, Shay, illus. (p. 87)
—Annie the Texas Ranch Dog - Injured Hero. Retzlaff, Shay, illus. (p. 87)
—Annie the Texas Ranch Dog - New Life in Utopia. Retzlaff, Shay, illus. (p. 87)
Shafer, Susan. Jesse Owens: Fastest Human. (p. 914)
—Ponce de Leon & the Fountain of Youth. (p. 1382)
—Thomas Edison Invents the Lightbulb. (p. 1738)
Shaffer, Bren, illus. see Sewell, Anna.
Shaffer, Christy. Fairies Around the World. (p. 562)
—Glitter Dragons Stickers. (p. 684)
—Glitter Tattoos Dolphins. (p. 684)
—Glitter Unicorns Stickers. (p. 684)
—Glow-in-the-Dark Snowflakes. (p. 685)
—Glow-in-the-Dark Tattoos Dragons. (p. 685)
—Glow-In-the-Dark Tattoos Snowflakes. (p. 685)
—Glow-in-the-Dark Tattoos Unicorns. (p. 685)
—Learning about Mythical Creatures. (p. 984)
—Magical Horses Stained Glass Coloring Book. (p. 1074)
—Magical Unicorns Stained Glass Coloring Book. (p. 1075)
—Mini Dragons Tattoos. (p. 1146)
—Shiny Dragonflies Stickers. (p. 1567)
—Shiny Snowflakes Stickers. (p. 1567)
Shaffer, Dale E. Marbles: A Forgotten Part of Salem History Shaffer, Dale E., ed. (p. 1091)
Shaffer, J. E. Mrs. Mugsy & Nolan Grant's Island Adventure (p. 1187)
Shaffer, Jan. Summoning Stone Book Two: Vision Caster. (p. 1675)
Shaffer, Jason. Quick Brown Fox Jumps over the Lazy Dog. (p. 1427)
Shaffer, Jeanne E. Swimmer with a Rope in His Teeth: A Shadow Fable. Cruse, Howard, illus. (p. 1691)
Shaffer, Jeffrey P. Boris the Spider. (p. 214)
Shaffer, Jennifer. I Want to Play! (p. 848)
Shaffer, Jody Jensen. Bearded Dragons. (p. 151)
—Black-Footed Ferrets. (p. 196)
—Bread Before the Store. McGeehan, Dan, illus. (p. 224)
—Demi Lovato: Taking Another Chance. (p. 425)
—Grizzly Bear. (p. 724)
—Grizzly Bear Paperback. (p. 724)
—Josh Hutcherson: The Hunger Games' Hot Hero. (p. 926)
—Lea Michele. (p. 981)
—Liam Hemsworth: The Hunger Games' Strong Survivor. (p. 1004)
—Liam Hemsworth. (p. 1004)
—My Heart. Alberini, Teresa, illus. (p. 1210)
—My Lungs. Alberini, Teresa, illus. (p. 1213)
—My Muscles. Alberini, Teresa, illus. (p. 1215)
—Ninja Warriors. (p. 1256)
—Taylor Lautner. (p. 1708)
—Vampires & Light Gervasio, illus. (p. 1832)
—Victoria Justice: Television's It Girl. (p. 1840)
—What's Your Story, Frederick Douglass? (p. 1900)
—What's Your Story, Sequoyah? (p. 1900)
Shaffer, Jody Jensen, et al. Monster Science. Gervasio et al, illus. (p. 1168)
Shaffer, Neal. Last Exit Before Toll. (p. 977)
Shafferman, Jean Anne, jt. see Page, Anna Laura.
Shaffert, Charles. Googus, the Toothless Alligator. Stringer, Margaret, illus. (p. 702)
Shaffert, Charles F. Googus to the Rescue. Stringer, Margaret, illus. (p. 702)
Shaffner, Randolph P. Heart of the Blue Ridge: Highlands, North Carolina. (p. 759)
Shafran, Michael. Extreme Sports Skate! Your Guide to Blading, Aggressive, Vert, Street, Roller Hockey, Speed & More. (p. 557)
Shafran, Michael, jt. auth. see Donovan, Amy.
Shafran, Nigel, photos by see Collings, Matthew.
Shafto, Daniel & Matters, Print. Carnival. (p. 270)
Shagam, Rodger. Stories from My Gramps. (p. 1654)
Shaggy Dog Press, ed. see Roberts, Johanna Lonsdorf.
Shah, Amina. Tales from the Bazaars. (p. 1701)
Shah, Anup. Helping Africa Help Itself: A Global Effort. (p. 766)
—Helping Africa Help Itself: A Global Effort. Ojakorotu, Victor & Rotberg, Robert I., eds. (p. 766)
Shah, Aram, text. Super Cody & Ernie the Eggplant: Vs. the Walloping Rancids. (p. 1679)
Shah, Bharat S. Sanskrit: An Appreciation Without Apprehension. (p. 1511)
Shah, Idries. Boy Without a Name. Caron, Mona, illus. (p. 220)

—Boy Without a Name / el Nino Sin Nombre. Wirkala, Rita, tr. (p. 220)
—Clever Boy & the Terrible, Dangerous Animal. Santiago, Rose Mary, illus. (p. 331)
—Clever Boy & the Terrible, Dangerous Animal/el Muchachito Listo y el Terrible y Peligroso Animal. Wirkala, Rita, tr. (p. 331)
—Farmer's Wife. Santiago, Rose Mary, illus. (p. 574)
—Farmer's Wife (La Esposa del Granjero) Santiago, Rose Mary, illus. (p. 574)
—Farmer's Wife/la Esposa del Granjero. Santiago, Rose Mary, illus. (p. 574)
—Farmer's Wife/la Esposa del Granjero. de Gonzales, Angelica Villagran, tr. (p. 574)
—Lion Who Saw Himself in the Water. Rodriguez, Ingrid, illus. (p. 1020)
—Lion Who Saw Himself in the Water/el Leon Que Se Vio en el Aqua. Rodriguez, Ingrid, illus. (p. 1020)
—Man & the Fox. Mallam, Sally, illus. (p. 1085)
—Man with Bad Manners. Santiago, Rose Mary, tr. (p. 1086)
—Man with Bad Manners. Santiago, Rose Mary, illus. (p. 1086)
—Neem el Media Nino. Wirkala, Rita, tr. (p. 1240)
—Neem the Half-Boy. Mori, Midori & Revels, Robert, illus. (p. 1240)
—Old Woman & the Eagle. Delmar, Natasha, illus. (p. 1285)
—Silly Chicken. Jackson, Jeff, illus. (p. 1575)
—Silly Chicken/el Pollo Bobo. Wirkala, Rita, tr. (p. 1575)
—Thinkers of the East: Studies in Experientialism. (p. 1734)
—World of Nasrudin. (p. 1957)
Shah, Indries. Farmer's Wife/la Esposa Del Granjero. Santiago, Rose Mary, illus. (p. 574)
Shah, Keiran. Making Pictographs. (p. 1082)
Shah, Lara A. Freedom of Innocence: A Journey into the Heart of All That Is. (p. 634)
Shah, Meera. And, Then Came Katrina. (p. 71)
Shah, Nupur. In the Woods. Shah, Nupur, illus. (p. 868)
—Let's Go Camping. (p. 997)
Shah, Sapna Jaiswal. Sapna Aunty's Hindi Book of Colors: Rang. (p. 1514)
Shah, Syeda Mleeha. Peace in My World. (p. 1331)
Shah, Yasmin. Abby & the Feather Quest. (p. 2)
Shahak, Bat-Chen. Bat-Chen Diaries. Rubanenko, Diana, tr. from HEB. (p. 143)
Shahan, Sherry. Cool Cats Counting. Barragán, Paula, illus. (p. 363)
—Death Mountain (p. 420)
—Feeding Time at the Zoo. Shahan, Sherry, illus. (p. 580)
—Fiesta! A Celebration of Latino Festivals. Barragán, Paula, illus. (p. 584)
—Fountain of Weird. (p. 624)
—Jazzy Alphabet. Thelen, Mary, illus. (p. 911)
—Little Butterfly. Shahan, Sherry, illus. (p. 1025)
—Skin & Bones. (p. 1585)
—That's Not How You Play Soccer, Daddy! Mai-Wyss, Tatjana, illus. (p. 1727)
—Willie Covan Loved to Dance. Van Wright, Cornelius & Ha, Ying-Hwa, trs. (p. 1934)
Shahan, Sherry, photos by. Dashing Through the Snow: The Story of the Jr. Iditarod. (p. 409)
Shahbaz, Zak Iman. Ameerah & the Missing Lunchbox. (p. 57)
—Ameerah's First Day. (p. 57)
Shahbaz, Zakia. Ramadan & the Three R's. (p. 1437)
Shahegh, Mahvash. Green Musician. Ewart, Claire, illus. (p. 722)
Shahn, Ben, illus. see Ish-Kishor, Sulamith.
Shahn, Ben, illus. see Reid, Alastair.
Shahrukh Husain. Greece. (p. 720)
Shahrukh Husain & Willey, Bee. Egypt. (p. 506)
Shaikh, Rianna. Milly Goes to Montauk. (p. 1144)
Shajardoust, Masoumeh. Neaty Mitty. (p. 1239)
Shakarian, Lorraine & Huggins, Pat. Helping Kids Handle Conflict (Intermediate Version) Teaching Self-control. (p. 766)
ShakeB company Staff. Cooking Fun for Children. (p. 361)
Shakes, Suzanne, et al. Maths in Practice. (p. 1108)
—Maths in Practice Year 7 (p. 1108)
Shakespeare, Nancy. Benjamin the Bear. Clouette, Katie, illus. (p. 165)
—Benjamin the Bear Gets a Sister. Clouette, Katie, illus. (p. 165)
—Benjamin the Bear Goes on a Picnic. Clouette, Katie, illus. (p. 165)
—Benjamin the Bear Goes to Kindergarten. Clouette, Katie, illus. (p. 165)
—Benjamin the Bear Rides on an Airplane. Clouette, Katie, illus. (p. 165)
Shakespeare, Strawberry. Hope's Horse: The Mystery of Shadow Ridge. (p. 797)
Shakespeare, William. All's Well That Ends Well. (p. 48)
—Antony & Cleopatra. (p. 90)
—Antony & Cleopatra. Frost, Adam, ed. (p. 90)
—Antony & Cleopatra. Heims, Neil & Bloom, Harold, eds. (p. 90)
—As You Like It: Classicscript. Landes, William-Alan, ed. (p. 105)
—As You Like It. (p. 105)
—As You Like It. Kutsuwada, Chie, illus. (p. 105)
—Comedy of Errors: Graphic Novel. Espinosa, Rod, illus. (p. 348)
—Cymbeline: Graphic Novel. Perry, Fred, illus. (p. 397)
—Hamlet (p. 739)
—Hamlet: With Reader's Guide. (p. 739)
—Hamlet. (p. 739)
—Hamlet. Gill, Roma, ed. (p. 739)
—Hamlet. Moliken, Paul, ed. (p. 739)
—Hamlet. De Moratín, Leandro Fernandez, tr. (p. 739)
—Hamlet the Graphic Novel Quick Text: American English. (p. 739)
—Henry V: The Graphic Novel. (p. 768)
—Henry V Hort, John & Hort, Leela, eds. (p. 768)
—Henry V: Classicscript. Landes, William-Alan, ed. (p. 768)
—Henry V. (p. 768)
—Henry V. Howell, Keith, tr. (p. 768)
—Henry VIII: Graphic Novel. Allen, Chris, illus. (p. 768)
—Julius Caesar Garcia, Eduardo, illus. (p. 933)
—Julius Caesar: Graphic Novel. Perry, Fred, illus. (p. 933)
—Julius Caesar. Mahbab, Mustashrik, illus. (p. 933)
—Julius Caesar 2010. (p. 933)
—Julius Caesar - Literary Touchstone. (p. 933)
—King Lear: Classicscript. Landes, William-Alan, ed. (p. 958)
—King Lear. (p. 958)
—King Lear. Ilya, illus. (p. 958)
—Life of Henry V. Castaldo, Annalisa & Lake, James H., eds. (p. 1012)
—Macbeth Pérez, Daniel & Ferran, Daniel, illus. (p. 1067)
—Macbeth. Gill, Roma, ed. (p. 1067)
—Macbeth. Deas, Robert, illus. (p. 1067)
—Macbeth. Cheung, Charly, illus. (p. 1067)
—Macbeth. Sutliff Sanders, Joe, tr. (p. 1067)
—Macbeth: The Graphic Novel. (p. 1068)
—Macbeth Ferran, Daniel, illus. (p. 1068)
—Macbeth: Classicscript. Landes, William-Alan, ed. (p. 1068)
—Macbeth: The Inessential Shakespeare. Hort, John & Hort, Leela, eds. (p. 1068)
—Macbeth: Including Stage Directions for All Levels of Experience. Newlin, Nick, ed. (p. 1068)
—Measure for Measure. (p. 1117)
—Merchant of Venice. (p. 1127)
—Merry Wives of Windsor. Monahan, Jerome & Gibson, Rex, eds. (p. 1129)
—Midsummer Night's Dream: Classicscript. Landes, William-Alan, ed. (p. 1139)
—Midsummer Night's Dream: Prestwick House Literary Touchstone Edition. (p. 1139)
—Midsummer Night's Dream: Including Stage Directions for All Levels of Experience. Newlin, Nick, ed. (p. 1139)
—Midsummer Night's Dream. (p. 1139)
—Midsummer Night's Dream. Bryant, Clive, ed. (p. 1139)
—Midsummer Night's Dream. Cheung, Charly, illus. (p. 1139)
—Midsummer Night's Dream. Hort, John & Hort, Leela, eds. (p. 1139)
—Much Ado about Nothing. (p. 1188)
—Much Ado about Nothing. Vieceli, Emma, illus. (p. 1188)
—Othello: Classicscript. Landes, William-Alan, ed. (p. 1306)
—Othello. Osada, Ryuta, illus. (p. 1306)
—Othello. Pechter, Edward, ed. (p. 1306)
—Othello. Sanders, Norman, ed. (p. 1306)
—Othello - Literary Touchstone. (p. 1306)
—Pericles. (p. 1343)
—Pyramus & Thisbe: A Dramatization Arranged from Shakespeare's A Midsummer Night's Dream. Landes, William-Alan, ed. (p. 1421)
—Romeo & Juliet: The Inessential Shakespeare. (p. 1486)
—Romeo & Juliet. Bryant, Clive, ed. (p. 1486)
—Romeo & Juliet. Moliken, Paul, ed. (p. 1486)
—Romeo & Juliet. Cheung, Charly, illus. (p. 1486)
—Romeo & Juliet. Fearon Globe Staff, ed. (p. 1486)
—Romeo & Juliet. Evans, G. Blakemore, ed. (p. 1486)
—Romeo y Julieta. (p. 1486)
—Shakespeare's Quotations: A Players Press Guide. (p. 1559)
—Short Scenes from Shakespeare: Nineteen Cuttings for the Classroom. Selden, Samuel, ed. (p. 1569)
—Taming of the Shrew. (p. 1704)
—Taming of the Shrew - Literary Touchstone. (p. 1704)
—Taming of the Shrew - Side by Side. (p. 1704)
—Tempest: Adaptation. (p. 1717)
—Tempest. (p. 1717)
—Tempest. Cheung, Charly, illus. (p. 1717)
—Tempest. Hulme, Peter & Sherman, William H., eds. (p. 1717)
—Tempest Study Guide. (p. 1717)
—Three Great Plays of Shakespeare (p. 1742)
—Tragedy of Macbeth. (p. 1776)
—Tragedy of Macbeth. Bloom, Harold, ed. (p. 1776)
—Treasury of Shakespeare's Verse. Pollinger, Gina, ed. (p. 1783)
—Twelfth Night: Or, What You Will. (p. 1800)
—Twelfth Night: Classicscript. Landes, William-Alan, ed. (p. 1800)
—Twelfth Night: The Inessential Shakespeare. Hort, John & Hort, Leela, eds. (p. 1800)
—Twelfth Night. (p. 1800)
—Twelfth Night 2010. (p. 1800)
—Twelfth Night Paperback Book. (p. 1800)
—Twelfth Night Study Guide. (p. 1800)
—Two Gentlemen of Verona. (p. 1803)
—Winter's Tale: Shakespeare Series Level 2. (p. 1938)
—Winter's Tale: Graphic Novel. Espinosa, Rod, illus. (p. 1938)
Shakespeare, William, jt. auth. see Bauer, A. C. E.
Shakespeare, William, jt. auth. see Bevington, David.
Shakespeare, William, jt. auth. see Birch, Beverley.
Shakespeare, William, jt. auth. see Cooney, Caroline B.
Shakespeare, William, jt. auth. see Farrens, Brian.
Shakespeare, William, jt. auth. see Gibson, Rex.
Shakespeare, William, jt. auth. see Gill, Roma.
Shakespeare, William, jt. auth. see Gonzalez, Jorge.
Shakespeare, William, jt. auth. see Goodwin, Vincent.
Shakespeare, William, jt. auth. see Hinds, Gareth.
Shakespeare, William, jt. auth. see Maese, Fares.
Shakespeare, William, jt. auth. see Marion, Dominique.
Shakespeare, William, jt. auth. see Ross, Lesley.
Shakespeare, William, jt. auth. see Williams, Marcia.
Shakespeare, William & Appignanesi, Richard. Hamlet. Vieceli, Emma, illus. (p. 739)
—Romeo & Juliet. Leong, Sonia, illus. (p. 1486)
Shakespeare, William & Birch, Beverley. Macbeth. Chesterton, Peter, illus. (p. 1068)
Shakespeare, William & Gabel, Claudia. Romeo & Juliet & Vampires. (p. 1486)
Shakespeare, William & Gill, Roma. As You Like It. (p. 105)
—Midsummer Night's Dream. (p. 1139)
—Othello. (p. 1306)
Shakespeare, William & Marlowe, Christopher. Hamlet, Volume 1: The Play Jack, Alex, ed. (p. 739)
—Hamlet, Volume 2: History & Commentary Jack, Alex, ed. (p. 739)
Shakespeare, William & McDonald, John. Henry V the Graphic Novel Original Text Hardback: American English. Howell, Keith, tr. (p. 768)
Shakespeare, William & SparkNotes Staff. Hamlet. Crowther, John, ed. (p. 739)
—King Lear. Crowther, John, ed. (p. 958)
—Macbeth. Crowther, John, ed. (p. 1068)
—Merchant of Venice. Crowther, John, ed. (p. 1127)
—Much Ado about Nothing. (p. 1188)
—No Fear Shakespeare: Othello. Crowther, John, ed. (p. 1258)
—Romeo & Juliet. Crowther, John, ed. (p. 1486)
—Twelfth Night. Crowther, John, ed. (p. 1800)
Shakespeare, William, et al. Hamlet. (p. 739)
—One Hundred & Eleven Shakespeare Monologues for Teens. Swanson, Jill K., tr. (p. 1295)
—Sixty Shakespeare Scenes for Teens. (p. 1583)
—Tempest. (p. 1717)
Shakir, Susie, illus. see Nels, Izzy.
Shakir, Susie, illus. see Poitier, Anton.
Shakir, Susie, illus. see Schwartz, Betty Ann.
Shalaby, Asharaf, illus. see Vanasse, Patricia.
Shalansky, Len, illus. see Brinton, Margaret.
Shalansky, Len, illus. see Enderle, Dotti.
Shalant, Phyllis. Beware of Kissing Lizard Lips. (p. 173)
—Look What We've Brought You from Korea: Crafts, Games, Recipes, Stories & Other Cultural Activities from Korean-Americans. Park, Soyoo H., illus. (p. 1050)
—When Pirates Came to Brooklyn. (p. 1904)
Shalaway, Linda. Learning to Teach ... Not Just for Beginners: The Essential Guide for All Teachers. (p. 986)
Shale, Erin. Complete Survival Guide for High School & Beyond. (p. 353)
Shaler, Robert. Boy Scouts As Country Fair Guides. (p. 218)
—Boy Scouts in the Great Flood. (p. 218)
—Boy Scouts of the Flying Squadron. (p. 218)
—Boy Scouts of the Geological Survey. (p. 218)
—Boy Scouts on Picket Duty. (p. 218)
—Boy Scouts with the Motion Picture P. (p. 219)
—Boy Scouts with the Motion Picture Playe. (p. 219)
Shalhout, Ahlam. For the Love of My Dreams (p. 616)
Shalin, Mike. Drew Bledsoe: Patriot Rifle. (p. 485)
—Nomar Garciaparra: High 5! Rains, Rob, ed. (p. 1263)
—Pedro Martinez: Throwing Strikes. Rains, Rob, ed. (p. 1334)
Shalit, Willa. Becoming Myself: Reflections on Growing up Female. (p. 156)
Shalleck, Alan J., ed. see Rey, H. A. & Rey, Margret.
Shallop, Laura. Pacific Northwest: Set Of 6. (p. 1317)
—Pacific Northwest: Text Pairs. (p. 1317)
Shally, Celeste. Since We're Friends: An Autism Picture Book. Harrington, David, illus. (p. 1578)
Shaloshvili, Natasha, illus. see Friedman, Laurie B.
Shalvey, Declan, illus. see Bryant, Clive, ed.
Shalvey, Declan, jt. illus. see Walker, Kev.
Shalvey, Declan & Walker, Kev. Shadowland: Thunderbolts. (p. 1558)
Sham And Geri Mahabir. Freddie Learns Responsibility. (p. 632)
Shamaley, Rochelle. Buddy Finds a Home. (p. 235)
Shamane, Aunty. Grandma of the Gardens. (p. 708)
Shamberger, Lindsey. I, I, I for Iguan. (p. 839)
Shambles, Shorty. Computer Ganguconnie Computer. (p. 354)
Shamblin, Allen, jt. auth. see Seskin, Steve.
Shames, Stephen. Transforming Lives: Turning Uganda's Forgotten Children into Leaders. Shames, Stephen, photos by. (p. 1778)
Shami, Susan, ed. see Florido, Lorraine.
Shami, Susan, ed. see Lorraine, Florido.
Shamir, O'Shea. Tales of Maddness: A Rare Collection of Short Stories. (p. 1702)
Shammas, Anna. Recorder Karate. Guiza, Victor, illus. (p. 1452)
Shamp, Danielle, illus. see Tabor, Stephen A.
Shams, K. Piggle. Spears, Ashley E., illus. (p. 1358)
Shamshirsaz, Shahab, illus. see McRae, J. R.
Shamsiddeen, Abdul. Long Jeffery & the Backboard. (p. 1047)
Shan, Darren, pseud. Allies of the Night. (p. 47)
—Angels. (p. 75)
—Bec. (p. 155)
—Birth of a Killer. (p. 192)
—Blood Beast. (p. 200)
—Brothers to the Death. (p. 231)
—Dark Calling. (p. 407)
—Death's Shadow. (p. 420)
—Demon Apocalypse. (p. 426)
—Demon Thief. (p. 426)
—Gladiator. (p. 682)
—Hell's Heroes. (p. 765)
—Hunters of the Dusk. (p. 828)
—Hunters of the Dusk. (p. 829)
—Killers of the Dawn. (p. 956)
—Lake of Souls. (p. 972)
—Lord Loss. (p. 1052)
—Lord of the Shadows. (p. 1052)
—Ocean of Blood. (p. 1276)
—Palace of the Damned. (p. 1319)
—Slawter. (p. 1588)
—Sons of Destiny. (p. 1613)
—Thin Executioner. (p. 1732)
—Trials of Death. (p. 1785)
—Tunnels of Blood. (p. 1797)
—Vampire Destiny Trilogy: The Lake of Souls; Lord of the Shadows; Sons of Destiny. (p. 1832)
—Vampire Mountain. (p. 1832)
—Vampire Prince. (p. 1832)
—Vampire War Trilogy. (p. 1832)
—Wolf Island. (p. 1944)
—Zom-B. (p. 1987)
—Zom-B Baby. (p. 1987)
—Zom-B Chronicles. (p. 1987)
—Zom-B Chronicles #2. (p. 1987)
—Zom-B City. (p. 1987)
—Zom-B Family. (p. 1987)
—Zom-B Underground. (p. 1987)
Shan Shan, Kathryn. Everyday Circus. Wilson, Lynda Farrington, illus. (p. 543)
Shan Shan, Kathryn Velikanje. E Is for Elephant. Wilson, Lynda Farrington, illus. (p. 492)
—Is for Alligator. Wilson, Lynda Farrington, illus. (p. 889)
Shanahan, Danny, illus. see Edwards, Pamela Duncan.
Shanahan, Lisa. My Mom Tarzan. Guthridge, Bettina, illus. (p. 1214)
Shanahan, Sue. Cut & Color Paper Dolls: Maria & Megan. (p. 395)
—Glitter Angel Babies Stickers. (p. 683)
Shanahan, Sue, illus. see Rubins, Diane Teitel.
Shanbhag, Arun. Prarthana: A Book of Hindu Psalms. (p. 1393)
Shand, Jennifer. Why Do Computers Know So Much? (p. 1923)
—Why Do Feet Get So Stinky? (p. 1923)
—Why Do Rainbows Have So Many Colors? (p. 1924)
—Why Do Rainbows Have So Many Colors? Paiva, Johannah Gilman, ed. (p. 1924)
—Why Do Tractors Have Such Big Tires? (p. 1924)
—Why Do Tractors Have Such Big Tires? Paiva, Johannah Gilman, ed. (p. 1924)
Shanddaramon. 12 Days of Yule. (p. 1994)
—Pagan Book of ABCs. (p. 1317)
—Pagan Sabbats of the Northern Hemisphere. (p. 1318)
—Pagan Stories for Children: A Fairy's First Year in the Forest of Songs. (p. 1318)
Shandler, Jeffrey, tr. see Glatshteyn, Yankev.
Shandley, Pandré, jt. auth. see Greenberg, Doris.
Shane, Bill. Hey Batter Batter: A Collection of Baseball Poems for Kids. (p. 774)
Shane, C. J. Mexicans. (p. 1131)
Shane, Molly G. Butterfly Wishes & Popsicle Dreams Deseos de Mariposas y Sue±Os de Paletas: A Collection of Children's Silly Poems una Colecci=n de poemas raros Par. (p. 248)
Shane, Rachel, jt. auth. see Silver, Shana.
Shane, Sam. Rocky the Mudhen: Baseball & Humble Pie. (p. 1484)
Shane, Victor. Book of Life: God, Cosmos & Man - A New Understanding of Human Nature. Ansell, Maggi, ed. (p. 211)
—In God We Trust: Understanding the Culture War in a Scientific Age: the Pitched Battle for the Soul of America. (p. 863)
Shang, Anthony. When Jack Meets Jill: A Backstory to the Nursery Rhyme. (p. 1903)
Shang, Wendy Wan-Long. Great Wall of Lucy Wu. (p. 719)
—Way Home Looks Now. (p. 1864)
Shange, Ntozake. Coretta Scott. Nelson, Kadir, illus. (p. 367)
—Ellington Was Not a Street. Nelson, Kadir, illus. (p. 514)
—Freedom's a-Callin Me. Brown, Rod, illus. (p. 635)
—We Troubled the Waters. Brown, Rod, illus. (p. 1868)
Shanghai Animation Studio Staff & Tang, Sanmu. Attempt to Scoop up the Moon. Ying, Wu, tr. from CHI. (p. 114)
—Deer of Nine Colors. Lee, Yawtsong, tr. from CHI. (p. 423)
—Monkey Makes Havoc in Heaven. Xiaozhen, Wu, tr. from CHI. (p. 1165)
—Nezha Conquers the Dragon King. Yawtsong, Lee, tr. from CHI. (p. 1249)
—Tadpoles Looking for Their Mother. Xiaozhen, Wu, tr. from CHI. (p. 1695)
—Three Monks. Ying, Wu, tr. from CHI. (p. 1743)
Shank, Carol. U. S. Military Assault Vehicles (p. 1806)
—U. S. Military Weapons & Artillery (p. 1806)
Shank, Carol, jt. auth. see Alpert, Barbara.
Shank, Cathy, et al. Collaborations Literacy: Newbury Dictionary. (p. 339)
—Collaborations Literacy. (p. 339)
Shank, Cheryl. And God Said, Let There Be Chickenpox . (p. 71)
Shank, Diane S. Minnow Kisses. Bailey, Terri L., illus. (p. 1148)
Shank, Jon A., jt. auth. see Hoggatt, Jack P.
Shank, Marilyn Sue. Child of the Mountains. (p. 301)
Shank, Ronald L. Grandpa's Stories: A Compilation of Short Stories Written to Be Read by Grandpa or Grandma to Their Grand Children. (p. 710)
Shanker, Myrna Gelman. Lazar, the Good Deed Dog. Robinson, Linda, illus. (p. 981)
Shankland, Hugh, tr. Prettiest Love Letters in the World: Letters Between Lucrezia Borgia & Pietro Bembo 1503 to 1519. Smith, Richard Shirley, illus. (p. 1398)
Shanklin, Sandra, told to. Tales of Cat Canyon. (p. 1702)
Shankman, Ed. Boston Balloonies. O'Neill, Dave, illus. (p. 215)
—Bourbon Street Band Is Back. O'Neill, Dave, illus. (p. 216)
—Champ & Me by the Maple Tree. O'Neill, Dave, illus. (p. 289)
—Cods of Cape Cod. O'Neill, Dave, illus. (p. 338)
—I Met a Moose in Maine One Day. O'Neill, Dave, illus. (p. 844)
—I Went to the Party in Kalamazoo. Frank, Dave, illus. (p. 848)
—My Grandma Lives in Florida. O'Neill, Dave, illus. (p. 1210)
Shanks, Cindy. Alfonso Grows up on the Sheep Trail. (p. 37)
—Emilia Camina la Vereda de Borregos. (p. 518)
—Emily Walks the Sheep Trail. (p. 519)
Shanks, Elizabeth. Momma, Will I Ever? (p. 1162)
Shanks Jr. Father's Stories for His Children: A Christian Reader for Students Grades 5-9. (p. 577)
Shanks, Melanie. Squints. (p. 1637)
Shanks, Ronnie. Oh Where, Oh Where Is My Teddy Bear? (p. 1281)
Shann, Taylor. Strange Day. (p. 1665)
Shannon, jt. auth. see Shannon, George.
Shannon, Ann. Wilder Kids: I Really Want to Go to College!! (p. 1931)
Shannon, Ben, illus. see Mototsune, Kat.
Shannon, Ben, illus. see Peters, Diane.
Shannon, Ben, illus. see Slavens, Elaine.
Shannon, Ben, illus. see Staunton, Ted.
Shannon, Carol. Dusky Langurs at the Zoo. (p. 490)
Shannon, Carole. Melody's Surprise. (p. 1125)
Shannon, Catherine, jt. auth. see Rice, Dona Herwick.
Shannon, Chelsey. Chelsey: My True Story of Murder, Loss, & Starting Over. (p. 297)
Shannon, David. Alice the Fairy. (p. 39)
—Alice the Fairy. Shannon, David, illus. (p. 39)

—Bad Case of Stripes. (p. 131)
—Bad Case of Stripes. Shannon, David, illus. (p. 131)
—Bugs in My Hair! Shannon, David, illus. (p. 237)
—David Smells! Shannon, David, illus. (p. 411)
—Duck & a Book. (p. 488)
—Good Boy, Fergus! Shannon, David, illus. (p. 697)
—How Georgie Radbourn Saved Baseball. Shannon, David, illus. (p. 809)
—It's Christmas, David! Shannon, David, illus. (p. 896)
—Jangles: A Big Fish Story. Shannon, David, illus. (p. 908)
—Oh, David! A Diaper David Book. Shannon, David, illus. (p. 1280)
—Oops! A Diaper David Book. Shannon, David, illus. (p. 1299)
—Rain Came Down. (p. 1434)
—Too Many Toys. Shannon, David, illus. (p. 1767)
—Uh-Oh, David! A David Sticker Book. Shannon, David, illus. (p. 1808)
Shannon, David, illus. see Auerbach, Annie.
Shannon, David, illus. see Bergen, Lara.
Shannon, David, illus. see Harper, Benjamin & Scieszka, Jon.
Shannon, David, illus. see Long, Melinda.
Shannon, David, illus. see Mason, Tom & Danko, Dan.
Shannon, David, illus. see Mason, Tom, et al.
Shannon, David, illus. see McKown, Hunter.
Shannon, David, illus. see Parker, Sydney.
Shannon, David, illus. see Rao, Lisa.
Shannon, David, illus. see Robertson, Robbie.
Shannon, David, illus. see Sander, Sonia & Scieszka, Jon.
Shannon, David, illus. see Sander, Sonia.
Shannon, David, illus. see Scieszka, Jon.
Shannon, David, illus. see Teitelbaum, Michael & Scieszka, Jon.
Shannon, David, illus. see Teitelbaum, Michael.
Shannon, David, illus. see Testa, Maggie.
Shannon, David, illus. see Wood, Audrey.
Shannon, Donald H. Boise Massacre on the Oregon Trail: Attack on the Ward Party in 1854 & Massacres Of 1859. (p. 208)
Shannon, Doug, illus. see Shannon, Jennifer.
Shannon, George. Hands Say Love. Yoo, Taeeun, illus. (p. 741)
—Lizard's Guest. Aruego, Jose & Dewey, Ariane, illus. (p. 1043)
—One Family. Gomez, Blanca, illus. (p. 1295)
—Red All Over. (p. 1453)
—Tippy-Toe Chick, Go! Dronzek, Laura, illus. (p. 1757)
—Turkey Tot. Mann, Jennifer K., illus. (p. 1797)
—Very Witchy Spelling Bee. Fearing, Mark, illus. (p. 1839)
—White Is for Blueberry. Dronzek, Laura, illus. (p. 1913)
—Who Put the Cookies in the Cookie Jar? Paschkis, Julie, illus. (p. 1917)
—Wise Acres. Zemke, Deborah, illus. (p. 1939)
Shannon, George & Shannon. White Is for Blueberry. Dronzek, Laura, illus. (p. 1913)
Shannon, Jacqueline, jt. auth. see Carson, Nancy.
Shannon, Jason. Three Things about Animals... And Only One of Them's True! Hartter, Sean, illus. (p. 1744)
—Three Things about Bugs... And Only One of Them's True! Hartter, Sean, illus. (p. 1744)
Shannon, Jennifer. Anxiety Survival Guide for Teens: CBT Skills to Overcome Fear, Worry, & Panic. Shannon, Doug, illus. (p. 90)
Shannon, Kate, illus. see Bennett, Paul.
Shannon, Kate, illus. see Cooper, Diana.
Shannon, Kelsey, jt. auth. see Gunter, Miles.
Shannon, Kenyon, illus. see Hyler, Nelson W.
Shannon, L. L. On Fairy Wings: Tselina. (p. 1288)
Shannon, Marilyn, jt. auth. see Wile, Jay L.
Shannon, Molly. Tilly the Trickster. Hoyt, Ard, illus. (p. 1750)
Shannon, Patrick. Viva Cisco. (p. 1846)
Shannon, R. J. Rita Rain & the Shadow Apprentice: Book 1. (p. 1475)
Shannon, Ronnie Jay. Samurai Force: the Final Hope: The Junior Novel. (p. 1509)
Shannon, Rosemarie, jt. auth. see Kids Can Press Staff.
Shannon, Rosemarie & Southern, Shelley, adapted by. Franklin's Picture Dictionary. (p. 631)
Shannon, Sarah. Despacio (p. 430)
—Empujar (p. 521)
—Fast (p. 576)
—Jalar (p. 906)
—Pulls (p. 1416)
—Pushes (p. 1420)
—Rápido (p. 1439)
—Slow (p. 1591)
Shannon, Sarah, jt. auth. see Smith, Sian.
Shannon, Sarah & Heinemann Library Staff. Despacio (p. 430)
—Empujar (p. 521)
—Jalar (p. 906)
—Rápido (p. 1439)
Shannon Simmons. Community Club: #1 Aubrey & the Fight for Life. (p. 349)
Shannon, Star Erian. Erian's Friend Jeremiah the Owl. (p. 533)
Shannon, Terry Miller. New Hampshire. (p. 1244)
—Oregon. (p. 1302)
Shannon, Terry Miller, jt. auth. see Blackwood, Gary L.
Shannon, Terry Miller, jt. auth. see Schwabacher, Martin.
Shannon-Riddle, Deidre. Peeka's Perseverance. (p. 1335)
Shanower, Eric. Adventures in Oz. (p. 15)
—Adventures in Oz. Shanower, Eric, illus. (p. 15)
—Adventures in Oz Volume 1. (p. 15)
—Betrayal Shanower, Eric, illus. (p. 171)
—Betrayal: The Story of the Trojan War. Pt. 1 (p. 171)
—Marvelous Land of Oz: Vol. 1. (p. 1099)
—Oz: Road to Oz. (p. 1316)
—Oz: The Emerald City of Oz. (p. 1316)
—Oz: Dorothy & the Wizard in Oz. (p. 1316)
—Salt Sorcerer of Oz & Other Stories. Shanower, Eric, illus. (p. 1505)
—Wonderful Wizard of Oz: Vol. 1. (p. 1948)
Shanower, Eric, illus. see Einhorn, Edward.
Shanower, Eric & Baum, L. Frank. Marvelous Land of Oz: Adapted from the Novel by L. Frank Baum. Young, Skottie, illus. (p. 1099)
—Wonderful Wizard of Oz. Young, Skottie, illus. (p. 1948)
Shanta, N. D. He's My Brother. (p. 774)
Shantz-Hilkes, Chloe, ed. Hooked: When Addiction Hits Home. (p. 795)
Shapard, Sandra Gales. Nick's Guardian Angel. (p. 1251)
Shapera, Paul M. Iran's Religious Leaders. (p. 887)
Shapira, Amy & Chadwick, Douglas H. Growing up Grizzly: The True Story of Baylee & Her Cubs. (p. 726)
Shapiro, Alison Bonds, illus. see Phillips, Jan.
Shapiro, Alla, illus. see Lopatina, Irina.
Shapiro, Arnold. Mice Squeak, We Speak. (p. 1134)
Shapiro, Brett, tr. see Gallavotti, Barbara.
Shapiro, Brigette. Tale of the Tooth Fairy. (p. 1700)
Shapiro, Cynthia. Corporate Confidential: 50 Secrets Your Company Doesn't Want You to Know—And What to Do about Them. (p. 368)
Shapiro D., Brian. Plaquetooth. (p. 1370)
Shapiro, Daniel. Conflict & Communication: A Guide Through the Labyrinth of Conflict Management. (p. 357)
Shapiro, David I. Gigolo & the Gold Digger. (p. 676)
Shapiro, David L. Sara's Journey. (p. 1514)
Shapiro, David R. Flowers by Number. Vair, Hayley, illus. (p. 608)
—Terra Tempo: The Four Corners of Time. Herndon, Christopher, illus. (p. 1721)
—Terra Tempo: The Academy of Planetary Evolution. Vol. 3 Herndon, Christopher, illus. (p. 1721)
Shapiro, Dean & Sheen, Barbara. Prostate Cancer. (p. 1412)
Shapiro, Deborah & Daniel, Lea. Letters from the Sea. Shapiro, Deborah & Daniel, Alan, illus. (p. 1002)
Shapiro, Gordon & Crafts, Gregory. Super Sidekick: The Musical. (p. 1681)
Shapiro, Howard. Hockey Player for Life. (p. 786)
Shapiro, Howard M. Dr. Shapiro's Picture Perfect Weight Loss: The Visual Program for Permanent Weight Loss. (p. 475)
Shapiro, J. H. Magic Trash. Brantley-Newton, Vanessa, illus. (p. 1074)
Shapiro, Jane. Daddy, What Is Love? Robinson, Don, illus. (p. 399)
Shapiro, Jody Fickes. Family Lullaby. Felstead, Cathie, illus. (p. 568)
—Up, up, up! It's Apple-Picking Time. Harvill, Kitty, illus. (p. 1824)
Shapiro, Karen Jo. Because I Could Not Stop My Bike: And Other Poems. Faulkner, Matt, illus. (p. 155)
Shapiro, Lawrence, jt. auth. see Shapiro, Lawrence E.
Shapiro, Lawrence. Ethan Has Too Much Energy: An Emotional Literacy Book. Harpster, Steve, illus. (p. 539)
—Stopping the Pain: A Workbook for Teens Who Cut & Self Injure. (p. 1654)
Shapiro, Lawrence & Holmes, Julia. Let's Be Friends: A Workbook to Help Kids Learn Social Skills & Make Great Friends. (p. 994)
Shapiro, Lawrence E. ADHD Workbook for Kids: Helping Children Gain Self-Confidence, Social Skills, & Self-Control. (p. 12)
—Freddy Fights Fat: An Emotional Literacy Book. Harpster, Steve, illus. (p. 633)
Shapiro, Lawrence E. & Shapiro, Lawerence. Stopping the Pain: A Workbook for Teens Who Cut & Self-Injure. (p. 1654)
Shapiro, Lawrence, et al. I'm Not Bad, I'm Just Mad: A Workbook to Help Kids Control Their Anger. (p. 859)
Shapiro, Lindy. Moon Mangoes. Peterson, Kathleen, illus. (p. 1172)
Shapiro, Marc. Infamous: Lindsay Lohan. (p. 873)
—J. K. Rowling: The Wizard Behind Harry Potter. (p. 901)
—Stephenie Meyer: The Unauthorized Biography of the Creator of the Twilight Saga. (p. 1648)
Shapiro, Michelle, illus. see Jules, Jacqueline.
Shapiro, Michelle, illus. see Kroll, Steven.
Shapiro, Michelle, illus. see Sugarman, Brynn Olenberg.
Shapiro, Neil, illus. see Dresner, Hal.
Shapiro, Ouisie. Autism & Me: Sibling Stories Vote, Steven, photos by. (p. 117)
—Bullying & Me: Schoolyard Stories Vote, Steven, photos by. (p. 241)
Shapiro, Pepper, illus. see Meyer, Kim Shapiro.
Shapiro, Phylis Stacey. Open Your Eyes. (p. 1299)
Shapiro, Rebecca, illus. see Brody, Lazer.
Shapiro, Sara. What Do You See? A Book about the Seasons. (p. 1883)
Shapiro, Sheryl, jt. auth. see Shapiro, Simon.
Shapiro, Sheryl & Shapiro, Simon. Better Together. Petricic, Dusan, illus. (p. 172)
—Ladybugs Have Lots of Spots. (p. 971)
—Zebra Stripes Go Head to Toe. (p. 1985)
Shapiro, Simon, jt. auth. see Shapiro, Sheryl.
Shapiro, Simon & Shapiro, Sheryl. What Can You Do with Only One Shoe? Reuse, Recycle, Reinvent. Blake, Francis, illus. (p. 1881)
Shapiro, Stephen. It's a Feudal, Feudal World: A Different Medieval History. Kinnaird, Ross, illus. (p. 895)
—Siege: Under Attack in Renaissance Europe. Mantha, John, illus. (p. 1573)
Shapiro, Stephen & Forrester, Tina. Ultra Hush-Hush: Espionage & Special Missions. Craig, David, illus. (p. 1810)
Shapiro, Susan G., ed. see Caratsev, Serghei I., et al.
Shaposhnik, Alina. Warm Yellow Pancake (p. 1858)
shapouri, naiyer. Sweet Dreams Buggy. (p. 1689)
Shara, Diana, jt. auth. see Mills, Susan.
Sharafeddine, Fatima. Amazing Discoveries of Ibn Sina Ali, Intelaq Mohammed, illus. (p. 54)
—Servant (p. 1552)
—Servant. (p. 1552)
Shardlow, Tom & Wysotski, Chrissie. Mapping the Wilderness: The Story of David Thompson. (p. 1090)
Share, Brian, illus. see Sharfe, Elaine.
Sharenow, Robert. Berlin Boxing Club. (p. 167)
—Girl in the Torch. (p. 678)
—My Mother the Cheerleader. (p. 1214)
Sharer, Avigail. Here, There, Everywhere: Kids' True Stories about Finding Hashem in Their Lives. (p. 770)
Sharf, Frederic A., 1st. Lary Salk: The Evolution of American Fashion Art: 1945-1965. (p. 976)
Sharfe, Elaine. There's a Dinosaur in My Room. Share, Brian, illus. (p. 1730)
Sharhonda, jt. auth. see Sharhonda.
Sharhonda & Sharhonda. Lunchroom Delight: Peanut Butter & Jelly. (p. 1065)
Shariati, Karen Allison. Meet Arzeen, Citizen of the World. Kim, Jay Jiyeon, illus. (p. 1120)
Sharif, Medeia. Bestest. Ramadan. Ever. (p. 171)
Sharifi, David & Sharifi, Jason. Moonlight Valley: The Great Race. (p. 1173)
Sharifi, Jason, jt. auth. see Sharifi, David.
Sharipovas, Alesja, ed. see AZ Books Staff.
Sharkawy, Azza. Observe It! (p. 1275)
—Predict It! (p. 1395)
—Question It! (p. 1426)
—Share It! (p. 1561)
Sharkey, Alex. Classic Bikes (p. 327)
—Classic Cars (p. 327)
Sharkey, Niamh. Dreams of Old Ireland. (p. 484)
—"Finally he reached the land of the clouds" (Jack & the Beanstalk) (p. 587)
—I'm a Happy Hugglewug: Laugh & Play the Hugglewug Way. Sharkey, Niamh, illus. (p. 858)
—"King Lorcan" (Tales from Old Ireland) (p. 958)
—"Niamh's fairy horse" (Tales from Old Ireland) (p. 1250)
—Ravenous Beast. (p. 1441)
—Santasaurus. Sharkey, Niamh, illus. (p. 1513)
—Tales of Wisdom & Wonder. (p. 1703)
Sharkey, Niamh, illus. see Doyle, Malachy.
Sharkey, Niamh, illus. see Lupton, Hugh.
Sharkey, Niamh, illus. see Tolstoy, Aleksei.
Sharkey, Niamh, jt. auth. see Doyle, Malachy.
Sharkey, Niamh, jt. auth. see Tolstoy, Aleksei.
Sharkey, Niamh & Walker, Richard. Jack & the Beanstalk. Sharkey, Niamh, illus. (p. 902)
Sharkey-Wilmot. Mysterious Golden Horse. (p. 1223)
Sharki, Nicolina & Walid. Bon Voyage Starsky & Davey: The Gulf Oil Explosion Rocks Their World. (p. 208)
Sharky & George. Don't You Dare. (p. 469)
Sharma, Lalit Kumar, illus. see Cowsill, Alan.
Sharma, Lalit Kumar, illus. see Deshpande, Sanjay.
Sharma, Lalit Kumar, illus. see Helfand, Lewis.
Sharma, Neal, jt. auth. see Maya, Valorie.
Sharma, Radhika. Princess & the Unicorn Prince. (p. 1403)
Sharma, Shivan. Castle, Dragons & a Cricket Ball. (p. 276)
Sharma, Vicky, jt. auth. see Delios, Louis.
Sharman, Lydia. Amazing Book of Shapes. (p. 54)
Sharman, Margaret. 1950s. (p. 2002)
—Take Ten Years 1900s. (p. 1697)
Sharmat, Marjorie Weinman. Nate the Great. Simont, Marc, illus. (p. 1230)
—Nate the Great & the Halloween Hunt. (p. 1230)
—Nate the Great & the Halloween Hunt. Simont, Marc, illus. (p. 1230)
—Nate the Great & the Missing Key. Simont, Marc, illus. (p. 1230)
—Nate the Great & the Snowy Trail. (p. 1230)
—Nate the Great Goes Undercover. Simont, Marc, illus. (p. 1230)
—Nate the Great on the Owl Express. Sharmat, Mitchell & Weston, Martha, illus. (p. 1230)
—Yo, el Gran Fercho. (p. 1971)
—Yo, el Gran Fercho y el Ladron. (p. 1971)
Sharmat, Marjorie Weinman & Sharmat, Mitchell. Green Toenails Gang. Brunkus, Denise, illus. (p. 722)
—Nate the Great & the Big Sniff. Weston, Martha, illus. (p. 1230)
—Nate the Great & the Hungry Book Club. Wheeler, Jody, illus. (p. 1230)
—Nate the Great Talks Turkey: With Help from Olivia Sharp. Wheeler, Jody, illus. (p. 1231)
—Nate the Great Talks Turkey. Wheeler, Jody, illus. (p. 1231)
—Nate the Great, Where Are You? Wheeler, Jody, illus. (p. 1231)
—Pizza Monster. Brunkus, Denise, illus. (p. 1365)
—Princess of the Fillmore Street School. Brunkus, Denise, illus. (p. 1404)
—Sly Spy. Brunkus, Denise, illus. (p. 1591)
Sharmat, Mitchell. Gregory, the Terrible Eater. Dewey, Ariane & Aruego, Jose, illus. (p. 723)
—Nate the Great, Where Are You? Wheeler, Jody, illus. (p. 1231)
Sharmat, Mitchell, illus. see Sharmat, Marjorie Weinman.
Sharmat, Mitchell, jt. auth. see Sharmat, Marjorie Weinman.
Sharon, Callen. This Is the Tower That Frank Built. (p. 1736)
Sharon, Creech. Love That Dog. (p. 1060)
Sharon, Janusz. When Horses Could Fly: And Other Fantastic Tales. Kathy, Newell-Worby, illus. (p. 1902)
Sharon, P. On Thin Ice. (p. 1292)
Sharona, Tel-Oren, tr. see Regelson, Abraham.
Sharp, Alice, illus. see Harrast, Tracy.
Sharp, Andre L. I Don't Talk Funny, I Stutter: A Children's Motivational Book. (p. 838)
Sharp, Anna Layton. Rudy Giuliani. (p. 1494)
—Taking Godly Care of My Money: Stewardship Lessons in Money Matters, Grades 2-5. Flint, Russ, illus. (p. 1698)
Sharp, Anne. Jigsaw Minibeasts: With Six Fantastic 24-Piece Jigsaws! (p. 917)
—Pop-up Dinosaur Danger! (p. 1384)
Sharp, Anne, jt. illus. see Denchfield, Nick.
Sharp, Anne Wallace. Coretta Scott King. (p. 367)
—Ice Hockey. (p. 850)
—Lebron James. (p. 987)
—Nancy Lopez. (p. 1229)
—Separate but Equal: The Desegregation of America's Schools. (p. 1551)
—Women Civil Rights Leaders. (p. 1945)
—Women of Ancient Egypt. (p. 1946)
Sharp, Anne Wallace, jt. auth. see Burns, Kate.
Sharp, Anne Wallace, ed. Freedom Rides. (p. 635)
Sharp, Cecil James. English Folk-Chanteys: With Pianoforte Accompaniment, Introduction & Notes. (p. 530)
Sharp, Chris, illus. see Barry, Ron & Fitzgerald, Paula.
Sharp, Chris, illus. see Berry, Ron & Mead, David.
Sharp, Chris, illus. see Berry, Ron.
Sharp, Chris, illus. see Lashbrook, Marilyn.
Sharp, Chris, illus. see Mead, David & Berry, Ron.
Sharp, Chris, illus. see Mead, David.
Sharp, Chris, illus. see Pingry, Patricia A.
Sharp, Chris, illus. see Shively, Julie.
Sharp, Chris, illus. see Shivley, Julie.
Sharp, Chris, illus. see Smart Kids Publishing Staff.
Sharp, Chris, illus. see Synder, Bernadette.
Sharp, Chris, illus. see Weimer, Heidi R.
Sharp, Chris, illus. see Weimer, Heidi.
Sharp, Chris, jt. auth. see Berry, Ron.
Sharp, Chris, jt. auth. see Pingry, Patricia A.
Sharp, Constance. America Is Born, 1770-1800. (p. 59)
—America Is Born, 1770-1800. Rakove, Jack N., ed. (p. 59)
—Beyond Our Shores: America Extends Its Reach,1890-1899. (p. 174)
—Beyond Our Shores: America Extends Its Reach,1890-1899. Rakove, Jack N., ed. (p. 174)
—Thomas Jefferson & the Growing United States (1800-1811) (p. 1739)
—Thomas Jefferson & the Growing United States (1800-1811) Rakove, Jack N., ed. (p. 1739)
Sharp, Craig, illus. see Bishop, Michele.
Sharp, D. L. M. Pocket of Magic on Beechwood Street. (p. 1375)
Sharp, Euan. Diggedy Dozer in Ned at Night. (p. 438)
—Diggedy Dozer in Treetop Troubles. (p. 438)
Sharp, Gene, illus. see Greene, Carol.
Sharp, Gene, illus. see Matthias, Catherine.
Sharp, Gene, jt. auth. see Matthias, Catherine.
Sharp, J. L. Persephia. (p. 1344)
Sharp, J. Michael. Directory of Congressional Voting Scores & Interest Group Ratings (p. 445)
Sharp, Jean. Contando Por la Ciudad. Walter, Lorin, illus. (p. 360)
—Counting in the City. Walter, Lorin, illus. (p. 371)
—Telling Time All the Time. (p. 1717)
—Vamos a Decir La Hora Todo el Tiempo. (p. 1831)
—Vamos a Decir la Hora Todo el Tiempo. (p. 1831)
Sharp, Julis, jt. auth. see Allen, Lisa.
Sharp, Katie. Soil. (p. 1606)
Sharp, Katie, jt. auth. see Sohn, Emily.
Sharp, Katie John. Smokeless Tobacco: Not a Safe Alternative. (p. 1594)
—Teenagers & Tobacco: Nicotine & the Adolescent Brain. (p. 1714)
Sharp, Katie John, jt. auth. see Burke, Melissa Blackwell.
Sharp, Kelley, illus. see Scott, Laurian.
Sharp, Kerri, ed. Sex...At The Sports Club: The Sexiest Wicked Words Stories Ever! (p. 1556)
—Wicked Words. (p. 1927)
—Wicked Words 10: The Best of Wicked Words. (p. 1927)
—Wicked Words 8: An Erotic Short-Story Collection. (p. 1927)
Sharp, Kevin. Amazing Adventures of Ted Shuttle: Book One. (p. 52)
Sharp, Laura. Key Prince. (p. 950)
SHARP Literacy, compiled by. Growing up Strong: Healthy Children can Change the World. (p. 727)
SHARP Literacy Students. American Dream. (p. 60)
Sharp, M. Theory of Music for Young Musicians. (p. 1729)
Sharp, Maggie. Growing Roses in the Rocky Mountains & High Plains: Limiting Factors of Gardening. (p. 726)
Sharp, Margery. Rescuers. Williams, Garth, illus. (p. 1462)
Sharp, Mary, ed. see Brenner, Vida.
Sharp, Melanie, illus. see Collins Educational Staff & Cronick, Mitch.
Sharp, Melanie, illus. see Cronick, Mitch.
Sharp, Melanie, illus. see Cunningham, Anna.
Sharp, Meredith. Frogs for William. (p. 641)
Sharp, Michael. Book of Life: Ascension & the Divine World Order. (p. 211)
—Captain Tristan Am I. Van Tine, Laura, illus. (p. 264)
—Vayda Jane Bean. (p. 1833)
—Vayda Jane Bean - Chocolate. Van Tine, Laura, illus. (p. 1833)
—Vayda Jayne Bean - Vanilla. Van Tine, Laura, illus. (p. 1833)
Sharp, Michael D., ed. Popular Contemporary Writers: Index Volume. (p. 1385)
Sharp, N. L. Effie's Image. (p. 505)
—Flower Girl / the Ring Bear. Hantula, Timothy James, illus. (p. 607)
Sharp, Paul. Pablo el Lanzador. Sharp, Paul, illus. (p. 1316)
—Paul the Pitcher. (p. 1330)
Sharp, Paul, illus. see Greene, Carol.
Sharp, Paul, illus. see Hapka, Cathy, pseud.
Sharp, Paul, illus. see Harrast, Tracy.
Sharp, Rhonda Winchell. Nine Most Famous Reindeer of All. Vandewater, Rena, illus. (p. 1256)
Sharp, Robert P. & Glazner, Allen F. Geology Underfoot in Death Valley & Owens Valley. (p. 662)
—Geology Underfoot in Southern California. (p. 662)
Sharp, S. Pearl. Slave Trade & the Middle Passage. (p. 1588)
Sharp, Sharon. Planet Chaos (p. 1367)
Sharp, Stephanie. Bird That Couldn't. (p. 190)
Sharp, Todd, illus. see Edgar, Robert.
Sharp, Todd, illus. see Mosher, Jennifer.
Sharp, Zoe. I Help My Dad. (p. 839)
Sharp, Zoe, et al. In the Tree. (p. 867)
Sharpe, Angeles. Quiz Spinners: Book #1: Fun-Filled Facts & Brain-Teasers! (p. 1429)
Sharpe, Cathy. Jayne Sullivan, Army Brat. (p. 910)
Sharpe, Charlotte. Jasper & Jesus at the Well. Ettinger, Charles, illus. (p. 910)
Sharpe, Gerald. Parade of Lights. Moya, Patricia, illus. (p. 1323)
—Tommy's Tales. Moya, Patricia, illus. (p. 1765)
—What Lies Beneath the Bed: Tommy's Tales (Revised) (p. 1891)
Sharpe, Jaime, jt. auth. see Thompson, Jan.

Sharpe, Jean Ann, ed. Saving Name of God the Son. (p. 1517)
Sharpe, Jeannie w. Once There Was an Orange Truck. (p. 1292)
Sharpe, Jesse. Pictures Poetry & ABCs: my alphabet Learning Book. (p. 1356)
Sharpe, Jim, illus. see Gillooly, Eileen, ed.
Sharpe, Katie & Sharpe, Tony. Wake up Sun. (p. 1853)
Sharpe, Leah Marinsky. Goat-Faced Girl: A Classic Italian Folktale. Marinsky, Jane, illus. (p. 687)
Sharpe, Luke. And the Stink Spectacular. Ross, Graham, illus. (p. 71)
—Billy Sure, Kid Entrepreneur. Ross, Graham, illus. (p. 187)
—Stink Drink. Ross, Graham, illus. (p. 1651)
Sharpe, Margaret, jt. auth. see Bombay, Cal.
Sharpe, Paula A. Maria Montessori. Ward, Patricia R. & Pigford, Grady A., illus. (p. 1093)
Sharpe, Roseanne, illus. see Pellowski, Anne.
Sharpe, Stuart. Mouse & Kat & the Evil One. (p. 1181)
Sharpe, Susan. Waterman's Boy. (p. 1863)
Sharpe, Tess. Far from You. (p. 572)
Sharpe, Tony, jt. auth. see Sharpe, Katie.
Sharples, Ann. Violet Jelly: Unillustrated Version. (p. 1843)
Sharpless, Rick. Bees: Trouble on the Throne. (p. 158)
Sharpless, Sheila M. Mystery on Bear's Island: A Short Adventure Novel for Girls Aged 8-11. (p. 1226)
Sharpley, Kate, illus. see Hughes, Julie.
Sharpnack, Joe, illus. see Brenner, Vida.
Sharps, Angelique, ed. see Alston, Stanley E.
Sharrar, Jack, jt. ed. see Slaight, Craig.
Sharratt, Nick, illus. see Goodhart, Pippa.
Sharratt, Mary, jt. auth. see Hawes, Louise.
Sharratt, Nick. What's in the Witch's Kitchen? Sharratt, Nick, illus. (p. 1898)
Sharratt, Nick, illus. see Andreae, Giles.
Sharratt, Nick, illus. see Donaldson, Julia.
Sharratt, Nick, illus. see Gray, Kes.
Sharratt, Nick, illus. see Morgan, Michaela.
Sharratt, Nick, illus. see Robinson, Hilary.
Sharratt, Nick, illus. see Strong, Jeremy.
Sharratt, Nick, illus. see Symes, Sally.
Sharratt, Nick, illus. see Taylor, Sean.
Sharratt, Nick, illus. see Wilson, Jacqueline.
Sharratt, Nick, jt. auth. see Bennett, Jill.
Sharratt, Nick, jt. auth. see Goodhart, Pippa.
Sharratt, Nick & Tucker, Stephen. Cinderella. (p. 320)
—Little Red Riding Hood (p. 1035)
—Three Billy Goats Gruff. (p. 1741)
Sharyn, November, ed. see Alexander, Lloyd, et al.
Shasek, Judy. Generation FIT. (p. 660)
Shasek, Judy & Schulz, Wendy Anderson. E-Wally & the Renegades. (p. 492)
Shasha, Mark. Night of the Moonjellies: 15th Anniversary Edition. (p. 1254)
Shashaani, Avideh, ed. Something Deeper Happened: Young Voices & the 2008 U.S. Election. (p. 1609)
Shaskan, Kathy. How Underwear Got under There: A Brief History. Dunnick, Regan, illus. (p. 823)
Shaskan, Stephen. Dog Is a Dog. (p. 461)
—Three Triceratops Tuff. Shaskan, Stephen, illus. (p. 1744)
Shaskan, Stephen, illus. see Shaskan, Trisha Speed.
Shaskan, Trisha Speed. Around the World with the Percussion Family! Meganck, Robert & Communication Design (Firm) Staff, illus. (p. 101)
—Art Panels, BAM! Speech Bubbles, POW! Writing Your Own Graphic Novel Shaskan, Stephen, illus. (p. 102)
—Ava the Angelfish Mackey, James, illus. (p. 118)
—Brass Family on Parade! Meganck, Robert & Communication Design (Firm) Staff, illus. (p. 222)
—Fair Game Christenson, Erik, illus. (p. 562)
—Green Park Loopstra, Esther Dawn, illus. (p. 722)
—Honestly, Red Riding Hood Was Rotten! The Story of Little Red Riding Hood As Told by the Wolf Guerlais, Gérald, illus. (p. 794)
—Honestly, Red Riding Hood Was Rotten! The Story of Little Red Riding Hood as Told by the Wolf. Guerlais, Gérald, illus. (p. 794)
—I Am a Sea Horse: The Life of a Dwarf Sea Horse Ouren, Todd, illus. (p. 832)
—I Am an Octopus: The Life of a Common Octopus Ouren, Todd, illus. (p. 832)
—If You Were a Capital Letter Gray, Sara, illus. (p. 854)
—If You Were a Compound Word Gray, Sara, illus. (p. 854)
—If You Were a Contraction Gray, Sara, illus. (p. 854)
—If You Were a Divided-By Sign Dillard, Sarah, illus. (p. 854)
—If You Were a Fraction Carabelli, Francesca, illus. (p. 855)
—If You Were a Minus Sign Carabelli, Francesca, illus. (p. 855)
—If You Were a Minus Sign [LTD Commodities]. Carabelli, Francesca, illus. (p. 855)
—If You Were a Minus Sign [Scholastic]. Carabelli, Francesca, illus. (p. 855)
—If You Were a Minute Carabelli, Francesca, illus. (p. 855)
—If You Were a Plural Word Gray, Sara, illus. (p. 855)
—If You Were a Plus Sign Carabelli, Francesca, illus. (p. 855)
—If You Were a Plus Sign [LTD Commodities]. Carabelli, Francesca, illus. (p. 855)
—If You Were a Plus Sign [Scholastic]. Carabelli, Francesca, illus. (p. 855)
—If You Were a Times Sign Dillard, Sarah, illus. (p. 855)
—If You Were Alliteration. Gray, Sara, illus. (p. 855)
—If You Were Onomatopoeia. Gray, Sara, illus. (p. 855)
—Keyboard Family Takes Center Stage! Meganck, Robert & Communication Design (Firm) Staff, illus. (p. 950)
—Opening Night with the Woodwind Family! Meganck, Robert & Communication Design (Firm) Staff, illus. (p. 1300)
—Princess Bella's Birthday Cake Eroglu, Aysin D., illus. (p. 1403)
—Seriously, Cinderella Is So Annoying! The Story of Cinderella as Told by the Wicked Stepmother. Guerlais, Gérald, illus. (p. 1552)
—String Family in Harmony! Meganck, Robert & Communication Design (Firm) Staff, illus. (p. 1667)
—Truly, We Both Loved Beauty Dearly! The Story of Sleeping Beauty as Told by the Good & Bad Fairies. Tayal, Amit, illus. (p. 1793)
—What's the Difference Between a Dolphin & a Porpoise? Bandelin, Debra et al, illus. (p. 1899)
—What's the Difference Between a Turtle & a Tortoise? Bandelin, Debra et al, illus. (p. 1899)
Shaskan, Trisha Speed, jt. auth. see Aboff, Marcie.
Shaskan, Trisha Speed, jt. auth. see Clark, Claire.
Shaskan, Trisha Speed & Loewen, Nancy. Truly, We Both Loved Beauty Dearly! The Story of Sleeping Beauty, As Told by the Good & Bad Fairies. Tayal, Amit & Alsonso, Denis, illus. (p. 1793)
Shats, Marina. Nature Knows (Paperback) (p. 1236)
Shattil, Wendy, photos by see Jackson, Donna M.
Shattil, Wendy, et al, photos by. Sierra Babies. (p. 1573)
Shattuck, Jason. Civil War. (p. 325)
Shauger, Daniel. How to Kill the Ball - the Mike Austin Method: The Formula for Power & Accuracy. (p. 820)
Shaughnessy, Adam. Entirely True Story of the Unbelievable FIB. (p. 531)
Shaughnessy, Annie L. Morning Glory & Music. (p. 1175)
Shaughnessy, Brian. Man Under. (p. 1086)
Shaughnessy, Dan. Legend of the Curse of the Bambino. Payne, C. F., illus. (p. 989)
Shaughnessy, Dick. Road to Barker's Farm. (p. 1477)
Shaughnessy, Edward L. Exploring the Life, Myth, & Art of Ancient China. (p. 554)
Shaughnessy, Mara. LEGO Man in Space: A True Story. (p. 990)
Shaughnessy, Mara, illus. see Martin, Emily.
Shaughnessy, Nicola. Gertrude Stein. (p. 667)
Shaughnessy, Robert. Four Renaissance Comedies. (p. 625)
Shavell, Lauren, illus. see Dreyfuss, Katy.
Shaver, Susan M. Flying Cowboys. (p. 609)
Shavick, Andrea. Roald Dahl. (p. 1477)
Shaw, Alexander William. Adventures of A Teenage Time Traveller. (p. 16)
Shaw, Alyx J. Merry Executioner Returns. (p. 1129)
—Strange Place in Time Book Ii: The White Palace Awakens. (p. 1665)
Shaw, Antony. World War II. (p. 1959)
Shaw, Bill. If Baby Bucking Bulls Could Talk. Wells, Jack J., illus. (p. 852)
Shaw, Brian, jt. auth. see McGrath, Barbara Barbieri.
Shaw, Carol Anne. Hannah & the Spindle Whorl. (p. 742)
Shaw, Cathleen, jt. auth. see Prostova, Elena.
Shaw, Charles, illus. see McKenzie, Tim A.
Shaw, Charles, illus. see Roach, Joyce Gibson.
Shaw, Charles, illus. see Smalley, Roger.
Shaw, Charles D. Stories of the Ancient Greeks. Harker, George A., illus. (p. 1655)
Shaw, Chrysie. Cat & the Goldfish. (p. 277)
Shaw, Dana Alton, III. My Friend Zundel. (p. 1209)
Shaw, Daniel. Eco-Tracking: On the Trail of Habitat Change. (p. 502)
—Journey to Pansophigus. (p. 929)
—Southwest Aquatic Habitats: On the Trail of Fish in a Desert. (p. 1617)
Shaw, David, illus. see Blair, Eric, et al.
Shaw, David, illus. see Blair, Eric.
Shaw, Dawn. Anthony's First Ant March. (p. 89)
Shaw, Debra. Riley & Ginger's Big Adventure. (p. 1472)
Shaw, Deirdre. Fair Play. (p. 562)
Shaw, Diana. Dias de Terror. (p. 435)
Shaw, Elizabeth. Little Black Sheep. (p. 1024)
—T-Uan Beag Dubh. MacPhaidan, Daire, tr. from ENG. (p. 1694)
Shaw, Ellie. Together Again. (p. 1761)
Shaw, Esther. Winter Mare. (p. 1938)
Shaw, Frank. Birds of the United States & Canada. (p. 192)
Shaw, George Bernard. Androcles & the Lion. Landes, William-Alan, ed. (p. 72)
—Annajanska. Landes, William-Alan, ed. (p. 85)
—Arms & the Man. Landes, William-Alan, ed. (p. 100)
—Augustus Does His Bit. Landes, William-Alan, ed. (p. 115)
—Caesar & Cleopatra. (p. 250)
—Candida. (p. 261)
—Captain Brassbound's Conversion. Landes, William-Alan, ed. (p. 263)
—Dark Lady of the Sonnets. (p. 407)
—Devil's Disciple. (p. 432)
—Doctor's Dilemma. Landes, William-Alan, ed. (p. 459)
—Getting Married. Landes, William-Alan, ed. (p. 669)
—Great Catherine. Landes, William-Alan, ed. (p. 714)
—Heartbreak House. Landes, William-Alan, ed. (p. 760)
—Inca of Perusalem. Landes, William-Alan, ed. (p. 868)
—Major Barbara. Landes, William-Alan, ed. (p. 1078)
—Man of Destiny. Landes, William-Alan, ed. (p. 1085)
—Mrs. Warren's Profession. Landes, William-Alan, ed. (p. 1188)
—O'Flaherty V. C. Landes, William-Alan, ed. (p. 1280)
—Overruled. (p. 1314)
—Philanderer. (p. 1350)
—Shewing-up of Blanco Posnet. Landes, William-Alan, ed. (p. 1566)
—Widowers' Houses. Landes, William-Alan, ed. (p. 1927)
—You Never Can Tell. (p. 1976)
Shaw, George Bernard, jt. auth. see Sherwood, Mary.
Shaw, Gina. Build My Own Main Street: Build My Own Books with Building Bricks. Wood, Steven, illus. (p. 238)
—Dinosaurs in a Box. (p. 444)
—Dolphins & Whales in a Box. (p. 465)
—Oh My! Ginny Fry! Barton, Patrice, illus. (p. 1280)
—Waiting for Snow. Barton, Patrice, illus. (p. 1853)
—Welcome, Bao Bao. (p. 1873)
Shaw, Gregory. Spirit. (p. 1628)
Shaw, Hannah. Rainbow. (p. 1435)
Shaw, Hannah, illus. see Davies, Katie.
Shaw, Hannah, illus. see Taylor, Sean & Quarto Generic Staff.
Shaw, Hannah, illus. see Taylor, Sean, et al.
Shaw, Hannah, illus. see Taylor, Sean.
Shaw, Hannah, jt. auth. see Taylor, Sean.
Shaw, Hannah, et al. Crocodiles Are the Best Animals of All! Shaw, Hannah, illus. (p. 384)
Shaw, Heather. Smallfish Clover. (p. 1592)
Shaw, Helen. Five Cents Worth. (p. 600)
Shaw, Henry. Creative Haven Geometric Genius Stained Glass Coloring Book. (p. 379)
Shaw, Holly & Gluck, Leanne. Mirror, Mirror: Discover Your Inner Beauty, a Guide for Girls 14-17. (p. 1149)
Shaw, Irene. Cosy Cottage. (p. 369)
Shaw, J. D. Leave No Footprints. (p. 986)
—Secrets of Loon Lake. (p. 1545)
Shaw, J. M. Molly's Stallion. (p. 1161)
Shaw, Jacob, jt. auth. see Kobliner Shaw, Beth.
Shaw, Janet. Kirsten Story Collection. Graef, Renee, illus. (p. 961)
—Kirsten's Short Story Collection. Lewis, Kim & Graef, Renee, illus. (p. 961)
Shaw, Katie & Nash, Kevin. University of Washington College Prowler off the Record. (p. 1821)
Shaw, Laura. Priscilla & the Big Red Ball Shaw, Yvonne, illus. (p. 1407)
Shaw, LaVerne. Mesa Magic. (p. 1129)
Shaw, Liane. Fostergirls (p. 624)
—Thinandbeautiful. Com (p. 1732)
Shaw, Luci. Genesis of It All. Miao, Huai-Kuang, Sr. & Miao, Huai-Kuang, illus. (p. 660)
Shaw, M. Beatryce. Mr. Browne & the Rose Show: A Child's Perception of "Different" (p. 1184)
—Mr. Browne & the Rose Show. (p. 1184)
Shaw, Marie-Jose. Jumbo English Yearbook: Grade 2. (p. 933)
—Jumbo English Yearbook: Grade 3. (p. 933)
—Jumbo English Yearbook: Grade 4. (p. 933)
—Jumbo English Yearbook: Grade 5. (p. 933)
—Jumbo English Yearbook: Grade 6. (p. 933)
—Jumbo English Yearbook: Grade 7. (p. 933)
—Jumbo English Yearbook: Grade 8. (p. 933)
—Jumbo English Yearbook: Grade 9. (p. 933)
—Jumbo English Yearbook: Grade 10. (p. 933)
—Jumbo English Yearbook: Grade 11. (p. 933)
—Jumbo English Yearbook: Grade 12. (p. 933)
—Jumbo Reading Yearbook: Grade 2. (p. 933)
—Jumbo Reading Yearbook: Grade 3. (p. 933)
—Jumbo Reading Yearbook: Grade 4. (p. 933)
—Jumbo Reading Yearbook: Grade 5. (p. 933)
—Jumbo Reading Yearbook: Grade 6. (p. 933)
—Jumbo Reading Yearbook: Grade 7. (p. 933)
—Jumbo Spelling Yearbook: Grade 3. (p. 933)
—Jumbo Spelling Yearbook: Grade 4. (p. 933)
—Jumbo Spelling Yearbook: Grade 6. (p. 933)
—Jumbo Vocabulary Development Yearbook: Grade 3. (p. 933)
—Jumbo Vocabulary Development Yearbook: Grade 4. (p. 933)
—Jumbo Vocabulary Development Yearbook: Grade 5. (p. 933)
Shaw, Marilyn Bishop. Solomon. (p. 1608)
Shaw, Mary. Brady Brady & the B Team Temple, Chuck, illus. (p. 221)
—Brady Brady & the Ballpark Bark. Temple, Chuck, illus. (p. 221)
—Brady Brady & the Big Mistake Temple, Chuck, illus. (p. 221)
—Brady Brady & the Cleanup Hitters. Temple, Chuck, illus. (p. 221)
—Brady Brady & the Great Exchange Temple, Chuck, illus. (p. 221)
—Brady Brady & the Great Rink Temple, Chuck, illus. (p. 221)
—Brady Brady & the Most Important Game Temple, Chuck, illus. (p. 221)
—Brady Brady & the MVP Temple, Chuck, illus. (p. 221)
—Brady Brady & the Puck on the Pond Temple, Chuck, illus. (p. 221)
—Brady Brady & the Runaway Goalie Temple, Chuck, illus. (p. 221)
—Brady Brady & the Singing Tree Temple, Chuck, illus. (p. 221)
—Brady Brady & the Super Skater Temple, Chuck, illus. (p. 221)
—Brady Brady & the Twirlin' Torpedo Temple, Chuck, illus. (p. 221)
—Max - a Griggstown Mystery. Cornilliat, Francois, tr. (p. 1110)
Shaw, Maura D. Dorothy Day: A Catholic Life of Action. Marchesi, Stephen, illus. (p. 471)
—Gandhi: India's Great Soul. Marchesi, Stephen, illus. (p. 655)
—Thich Nhat Hanh: Buddhism in Action. Marchesi, Stephen, illus. (p. 1732)
Shaw, Michael. Slider: The Leo Butterburger Story. (p. 1590)
Shaw, Mick, illus. see McKay, Hilary.
Shaw, Murray & Cosson, M. J. Sherlock Holmes & a Scandal in Bohemia. Rohrbach, Sophie, illus. (p. 1565)
—Sherlock Holmes & the Adventure at the Abbey Grange. Rohrbach, Sophie, illus. (p. 1565)
—Sherlock Holmes & the Adventure of the Blue Gem. Rohrbach, Sophie, illus. (p. 1565)
—Sherlock Holmes & the Adventure of the Dancing Men. Rohrbach, Sophie, illus. (p. 1565)
—Sherlock Holmes & the Adventure of the Speckled Band. Rohrbach, Sophie, illus. (p. 1565)
—Sherlock Holmes & the Adventure of the Sussex Vampire. Rohrbach, Sophie, illus. (p. 1565)
Shaw, Nancy. Elena's Story. (p. 511)
—Me First. Apple, Margot, illus. (p. 1116)
—Sheep Go to Sleep. Apple, Margot, illus. (p. 1564)
Shaw, Nancy E. Sheep Blast Off! Apple, Margot, illus. (p. 1564)
—Sheep in a Jeep. Apple, Margot, illus. (p. 1564)
—Sheep in a Shop Apple, Margot, illus. (p. 1564)
—Sheep Out to Eat. Apple, Margot, illus. (p. 1564)
Shaw, Nancy, et al. Sheep Blast Off! Apple, Margot, illus. (p. 1564)
Shaw, Nancy J. Bats. (p. 144)
Shaw, Nancy J., jt. auth. see Gish, Melissa.
Shaw, Natalie. Be Careful, Friend! Craig, Karen, illus. (p. 148)
—Busy Day in Busytown. Style Guide Staff, illus. (p. 246)
—Get Your Shell On. (p. 668)
—Good Po, Bad Po. (p. 700)
—Great Mom Rescue. (p. 717)
—Guide to Being a Big Sister. (p. 730)
—Guide to Being a Friend. (p. 730)
—Guide to Life. (p. 730)
—Hilda Hippo's Big Surprise! Style Guide Staff, illus. (p. 779)
—It's Nice to Meet You. Giles, Mike, illus. (p. 897)
—Journey to Dragon Mountain. (p. 928)
—Meet the Neighbors! Style Guide Staff, illus. (p. 1123)
—OLIVIA & the Butterfly Adventure. Spaziante, Patrick, illus. (p. 1286)
—Olivia & the Perfect Valentine. (p. 1286)
—OLIVIA & the Perfect Valentine. Johnson, Shane L., illus. (p. 1286)
—OLIVIA Dances for Joy. Spaziante, Patrick, illus. (p. 1286)
—Olivia Leaps! Osterhold, Jared, illus. (p. 1286)
—Olivia Sells Cookies. (p. 1287)
—Snack Attack! Style Guide Staff, illus. (p. 1595)
—Special Day with Dad. (p. 1623)
—Special Day with Dad. Johnson, Shane L., illus. (p. 1623)
—Tale of Dragons. (p. 1699)
—Who Is Huckle? (p. 1916)
Shaw, Natalie, jt. auth. see Barton, Elizabeth.
Shaw, Natalie, adapted by. In a Pickle. (p. 863)
—Mixed-Up Message. (p. 1156)
—Pizza Delivery Mystery. (p. 1365)
Shaw, Natalie & Barton, Elizabeth Dennis. Smurfin' Guide to the Smurfs. (p. 1595)
Shaw, Patricia. Gilly the Duck Meets the Magical Lady. (p. 676)
Shaw, Peter, illus. see Wild, Margaret.
Shaw, Rebecca. Elisha's Great Mission. (p. 513)
Shaw, S. B. Children's Edition of Touching Incidents. (p. 303)
Shaw, Sandra Anne. Mary's Gift. Rosales, Mary, tr. (p. 1101)
Shaw, Sandy. Do You Know Where the Bus Driver Will Go? (p. 458)
Shaw, Sarah, illus. see Chand, Emlyn.
Shawl, Scott. Shrek - Living Green (p. 1571)
Shawl, Scott, jt. auth. see Shrek.
Shawl, Scott & Kaplan, Arie. Shrek (p. 1571)
Shawl, Scott & Kazaleh, Mike. Annoying Orange #4: Tales from the Crisper. (p. 87)
—Pulped Fiction. (p. 1416)
Shaw, Scott & Kazaleh, Mike. Tales from the Crisper. (p. 1701)
Shaw, Sherry. I'm a Christian Now, Older Child. (p. 858)
—I'm a Christian Now Younger Child. (p. 858)
—I'm a Christian Now,Leader Resources. (p. 858)
Shaw, Stan, illus. see Wilde, Oscar, et al.
Shaw, Stephanie. Bedtime in the Meadow. Watkins, Laura, illus. (p. 157)
—Cookie for Santa. Robert, Bruno, illus. (p. 361)
Shaw, Steven. Five & a Brass Pair. (p. 599)
Shaw, Susan. Black-Eyed Suzie. (p. 196)
—Boy from the Basement. (p. 218)
—One of the Survivors. (p. 1296)
—Safe. (p. 1502)
—Star. (p. 1640)
—Tunnel Vision. (p. 1797)
Shaw, Toshia. High Stakes. (p. 778)
Shaw, Tucker. Anxious Hearts. (p. 90)
—Gentlemen, Start Your Ovens: Killer Recipes for Guys. Salvas, Jay Peter, illus. (p. 661)
—Girls. (p. 679)
—Oh Yeah, Audrey! (p. 1281)
Shaw, Tucker & Luce, Clare Boothe. Girls. (p. 679)
Shaw, V. Lost Sock. (p. 1056)
Shaw, Victoria. Coping with Sexual Harassment & Gender Bias. (p. 365)
Shaw, Wendy M. How Much Do I Love You? Hemby, Margaret, illus. (p. 811)
Shaw Wolf, Jennifer. Dead Girls Don't Lie. (p. 416)
Shaw, Yvonne, illus. see Shaw, Laura.
Shaw-Burns, Carol. Grandma's House: Jacob's Adventure. (p. 708)
Shaw-Lott, Karen. Binky Fairy. Marquez, Erick, illus. (p. 188)
Shaw-MacKinnon, Margaret. Tiktala Gal, Laszlo, illus. (p. 1750)
Shawntel, Ashley. Heart's Flames. (p. 760)
Shaw-Peterson, Kimberly, illus. see Hakala, Joann.
Shaw-Peterson, Kimberly, illus. see Lewandowski, Lisa & Trost, Shannon.
Shaw-Peterson, Kimberly, illus. see Ruprecht, Jennifer L.
Shaw-Russell, Susan. Animal ABC Super Sticker Book. (p. 76)
—Build Your Own Breakfast Sticker Activity Book. (p. 238)
—Build Your Own Burger Sticker Activity Book. (p. 238)
—Cinderella Activity Book. (p. 320)
—Create Your Own Aliens Sticker Activity Book. (p. 378)
—Day with the Dinosaurs Sticker Activity Book. (p. 415)
—Deep Sea Diner Sticker Activity Book. (p. 423)
—Make Your Own Bookmark Sticker Activity Book: Monsters, Robots & More! (p. 1079)
—Make Your Own Bookmark Sticker Activity Book: Princesses, Mermaids & More! (p. 1079)
—Pampered Pooches Sticker Activity Book. (p. 1320)
—Robots Activity Book. (p. 1481)
—Seek, Sketch & Color — Alphabet. (p. 1548)
—Seek, Sketch & Color — Animals. (p. 1548)
—Smiley Robot Tattoos. (p. 1594)
—Snow White Activity Book. (p. 1599)
—Three Bears Activity Book. (p. 1741)
—Three Little Pigs. (p. 1743)
—Under the Sea Party Sticker Activity Book. (p. 1814)
Shaw-Russell, Susan & Activity Books Staff. Bee Cool! Sticker Activity Book. (p. 157)
—Build Your Own Cupcake Sticker Activity Book. (p. 238)
—Tortoise & the Hare. (p. 1771)
Shaw-Russell, Susan, et al. Animals on Parade Find & Color. (p. 83)
Shaw-Smith, Emma, illus. see Gershator, David & Gershator, Phillis.
Shawver, Amanda Nicole. Lily's Rag Doll. (p. 1018)
Shawver, Margaret. What's Wrong with Grandma? A Family's Experience with Alzheimer's. Bagby, Jeffrey K., illus. (p. 1900)
Shawyer, Jo. Legend of the Paymaster's Gold. (p. 989)
Shay, Cynthia K. 32 Libritos de Rimas: 32 Spanish Rhyming Flip Books. (p. 1996)

Shay Locomotive Works, creator. 1921 Shay Geared Locomotive Engine & Parts Catalog. (p. 2002)
—Shay Patent & Direct Locomotive Catalog. (p. 1563)
Shay, Mary Bernard. Friend for Bobby. (p. 637)
Shayne, Maggie. Eternal Love. (p. 539)
Shazak. Out of Egypt. (p. 1311)
Shazak Productions Inc. Staff, Shazak Productions. Miracle Lights: The Complete Story of Chanukah... Like You've Never Seen Before! (p. 1148)
She, Liu, illus. see Ma, Zheng & Li, Zheng.
Shea. Working with Numbers (p. 1953)
—Working with Numbers. (p. 1953)
Shea, Abigail. Victoria Justice. (p. 1840)
—Wolves in Danger. (p. 1945)
Shea, Adele. Wolves in Danger. (p. 1945)
Shea, Betty. Animals of the Desert: Adapting to Survive. (p. 83)
Shea, Bob. Ballet Cat: The Totally Secret Secret. Shea, Bob, illus. (p. 134)
—Cheetah Can't Lose. Shea, Bob, illus. (p. 296)
—Dinosaur vs. Bedtime. Shea, Bob, illus. (p. 443)
—Dinosaur vs. Mommy. Shea, Bob, illus. (p. 443)
—Dinosaur vs. Santa. Shea, Bob, illus. (p. 443)
—Dinosaur vs. School. Shea, Bob, illus. (p. 443)
—Dinosaur vs. the Library. Shea, Bob, illus. (p. 443)
—Dinosaur vs. the Potty. Shea, Bob, illus. (p. 443)
—Don't Play with Your Food! (p. 468)
—I'm a Shark. Shea, Bob, illus. (p. 858)
—Kid Sheriff & the Terrible Toads. Smith, Lane, illus. (p. 951)
—Oh, Daddy! Shea, Bob, illus. (p. 1280)
—Race You to Bed. Shea, Bob, illus. (p. 1431)
—Unicorn Thinks He's Pretty Great. Shea, Bob, illus. (p. 1818)
Shea, Bob, illus. see DiPucchio, Kelly.
Shea, Bob, illus. see Harper, Charise Mericle.
Shea, Bob, illus. see John, Jory.
Shea, Bob, illus. see Sauer, Tammi.
Shea, Bobby Kennedy. Patterns with Pandas. (p. 1329)
Shea, Bobby Kennedy & Kennedy Shea, Bobby. Patterns with Pandas. (p. 1329)
Shea, C. O. Conductors & Insulators. (p. 356)
Shea, Chris. That's How Much God Loves You! Shea, Chris, illus. (p. 1726)
Shea, Christine. Las Aventuras de Max, el Camión Volteador: El Mejor Día de Nieve! = the Adventures of Max the Dump Truck: The Greatest Snow Day Ever! Chase, Michelle B. & Chase, Tanor R., illus. (p. 976)
Shea, Denise, illus. see Allen, Nancy Kelly.
Shea, Denise, illus. see Bridges, Sarah.
Shea, Denise, illus. see Dahl, Michael.
Shea, Denise, illus. see Meachen Rau, Dana & Picture Window Books.
Shea, Denise, illus. see Meachen Rau, Dana & Picture Window Books Staff.
Shea, Denise, illus. see Meachen Rau, Dana.
Shea, Denise, illus. see Thomas, Rick & Picture Window Books Staff.
Shea, Denise, illus. see Thomas, Rick.
Shea, Gary, illus. see Roller, Ellen.
Shea, George. First Flight: The Story of Tom Tate & the Wright Brothers. Bolognese, Don, illus. (p. 595)
Shea, George Beverly. Grandpa's Sleepy-Time Bible Stories with George Beverly Shea. (p. 710)
Shea, Jerry. Where Does the Recycling Go? (p. 1907)
Shea, John. Canticle: Biblical Songs Illuminated. Mullan, G. E., illus. (p. 262)
—Combating Computer Viruses. (p. 346)
—Declaration of Independence. (p. 422)
—If I Wasn't Me. (p. 853)
—Outsiders. (p. 1313)
—Respiratory System. (p. 1463)
Shea, John & Harmon, Michael B. Kid from Southie. (p. 951)
Shea, John & Shea, John M. Declaration of Independence. (p. 422)
Shea, John M. Digestive System. (p. 438)
—DNA up Close. (p. 456)
—Franklin D. Roosevelt in His Own Words. (p. 630)
—Gross Things about Your Body. (p. 725)
—Heroes of the US Coast Guard. (p. 773)
—Self-Injury & Cutting: Stopping the Pain. (p. 1549)
—Syracuse Basketball. (p. 1693)
—Tuskegee Airmen. (p. 1799)
—Viruses up Close. (p. 1844)
Shea, John M., jt. auth. see Shea, John.
Shea, Kevin. H Is for Hockey: An NHL Alumni Alphabet. Dewar, Ken, illus. (p. 734)
—H Is for Hockey. (p. 734)
Shea, Kevin Pearce. Snoop Dogg. (p. 1598)
Shea, Kitty. Out & about at the Newspaper. Trover, Zachary, illus. (p. 1310)
—Out & about at the Post Office. Shipe, Becky, illus. (p. 1310)
—Out & about at the Science Center. Shipe, Becky, illus. (p. 1310)
—Wright Brothers (p. 1963)
Shea, Lisa. Transformers: Rescue Bots: Meet Chase the Police-Bot. (p. 1778)
—Transformers: Rescue Bots: Meet Heatwave the Fire-Bot. (p. 1778)
—Transformers: Rescue Bots: Meet Heatwave the Fire-Bot. (p. 1778)
Shea, Lisa, jt. auth. see Hasbro.
Shea, Mary Molly. Being a Manatee. (p. 160)
—Foods of India. (p. 614)
—Giraffes. (p. 677)
—Lions. (p. 1021)
—Making Line Graphs. (p. 1081)
—Taylor Swift. (p. 1708)
—Wildebeests. (p. 1931)
Shea, Molly. Alicia Keys. (p. 40)
—Black Eyed Peas. (p. 196)
Shea, Nicole. American Revolution. (p. 63)
—Animals & Climate Change. (p. 82)
—Be an Astronomer. (p. 148)
—Creepy Amphibians. (p. 381)
—Creepy Birds. (p. 381)
—Creepy Bugs. (p. 381)
—Creepy Mammals. (p. 381)
—Creepy Sea Creatures. (p. 381)
—Elizabeth Cady Stanton in Her Own Words. (p. 513)
—Poaching & Illegal Trade. (p. 1374)
Shea, Pegi Deitz. Liberty Rising: The Story of the Statue of Liberty. Zahares, Wade, illus. (p. 1005)
—Liberty Rising. (p. 1005)
—Noah Webster: Weaver of Words. Vachula, Monica, illus. (p. 1261)
Shea, Pegi Deitz, jt. auth. see Van Rynbach, Iris.
Shea, Pegi Deitz & Deitz Shea, Pegi. Carpet Boy's Gift Morin, Leane, illus. (p. 271)
Shea, Pegi Deitz, ed. African American Picture-Poetry Collection for Children. (p. 27)
Shea, Robert Kennedy. Hunting. (p. 829)
Shea, Ryan. Adventures of Bob: To Doodledip for Soup. (p. 16)
—Adventures of Bob: Bongo & the Great Donut Chase. (p. 16)
Shea, Shawn, illus. see Evangelista, Gloria.
Shea, Steve, ed. see Tamayo, Alex.
Shea, Steve, ed. see Vinson, Haley.
Shea, Susan A. Do You Know Which Ones Will Grow? Slaughter, Tom, illus. (p. 458)
Shea, Tess & Pohlen, Jerome. San Francisco Baby: A Local Baby Book. Lemay, Violet, illus. (p. 1510)
Shea, Therese. 20 Fun Facts about Hippos. (p. 1995)
—20 Fun Facts about Spiders. (p. 1995)
—20 Fun Facts about the US Constitution. (p. 1995)
—alboroto en el autobús (A Fuss on the Bus) (p. 35)
—America's Electoral College: Choosing the President Comparing & Analyzing Charts, Graphs, & Tables. (p. 64)
—America's Electoral College: Choosing the President: Comparing & Analyzing Charts, Graphs, & Tables. (p. 64)
—Arctic Hares. (p. 96)
—Around the Globe: Where Are Your Ancestors From? (p. 100)
—At the Luau. (p. 111)
—Avoiding Online Hoaxes. (p. 120)
—Basketball Stars. (p. 143)
—Bear Likes to Share. (p. 151)
—Bears. (p. 151)
—Becoming a Pro Basketball Player. (p. 156)
—Bigfoot. (p. 184)
—Bigfoot Trail. (p. 185)
—Biosphere 2: Solving Word Problems. (p. 190)
—Bird Watcher's Guide to Cardinals. (p. 190)
—Bizarre Life Cycle of an Octopus. (p. 194)
—Black Ops & Other Special Missions of the U. S. Army Green Berets. (p. 196)
—Bloodsucking Vampire Bats. (p. 201)
—Bobcats in the Dark. (p. 206)
—Brad Paisley. (p. 221)
—Britannica Beginner BIOS: Set 2. (p. 229)
—Career As a Secret Service Agent. (p. 266)
—Carmen's Photo Album. (p. 270)
—CC Sabathia. (p. 283)
—Climbing Mount Everest: Understanding Commutative, Associative & Distributive Properties. (p. 333)
—Climbing Mount Everest: Understanding Commutative, Associative, & Distributive Properties. (p. 333)
—Creepy Reptiles. (p. 381)
—Crocodiles (p. 384)
—Crocodiles & Alligators. (p. 384)
—Crypts & Tombs. (p. 387)
—Dead Sea. (p. 417)
—Dementia. (p. 425)
—Digger Has a Bath. (p. 438)
—Discovering Egyptian Dynasties. (p. 449)
—Discovering STEM at the Zoo. (p. 449)
—Flag Day. (p. 602)
—Flags & Fireworks. (p. 602)
—Foods of China. (p. 614)
—Freaky Weather Stories. (p. 632)
—Fuss on the Bus. (p. 650)
—Getting to Know Lego Mindstorms. (p. 669)
—Godzilla. (p. 692)
—Great Barrier Reef: Using Graphs & Charts to Solve Word Problems. (p. 714)
—Grizzly Bears. (p. 724)
—Hammerhead Sharks. (p. 739)
—Haunted! the Queen Mary. (p. 754)
—Heat in Action. (p. 760)
—History of the Chesapeake Bay. (p. 784)
—House for Mouse. (p. 803)
—How Do I Use an Atlas? (p. 807)
—How Dolphins & Other Animals Use Sonar. (p. 809)
—Immigration to America: Identifying Different Points of View about an Issue. (p. 861)
—Interpreting America's Civil War: Organizing & Interpreting Information in Outlines, Graphs, Timelines, Maps, & Charts. (p. 880)
—Investigating UFOs & Aliens (p. 885)
—John Lee Hooker: King of the Blues. (p. 922)
—Kate DiCamillo: Newbery Medal-Winning Author. (p. 944)
—Kwanzaa Surprise. (p. 969)
—Lions. (p. 1021)
—Louisiana Purchase. (p. 1059)
—Lunch Bunch. (p. 1065)
—lunch muy especial (the Lunch Bunch) (p. 1065)
—Meet the House of Representatives. (p. 1122)
—Mummies of Ancient Egypt. (p. 1191)
—One More Floor! (p. 1296)
—Overfishing. (p. 1314)
—Racing Horses. (p. 1432)
—Reading Map Keys. (p. 1446)
—Real-Life Monsters? (p. 1448)
—Robotics Club: Teaming up to Build Robots. (p. 1481)
—Rock & Ice Climbing. (p. 1481)
—Rosa Parks (p. 1488)
—Sam's New Shoes. (p. 1509)
—Saving the Endangered American Bald Eagle. (p. 1517)
—School Bus Mystery. (p. 1522)
—Scorpions. (p. 1530)
—Sharks. (p. 1562)
—Sinking of the Titanic. (p. 1580)
—Sixth Amendment: The Rights of the Accused in Criminal Cases. (p. 1583)
—Snakes. (p. 1596)
—Soccer Stars. Shea, Therese, illus. (p. 1603)
—Solving Real World Problems with Civil Engineering. (p. 1608)
—Solving Real World Problems with Mechanical Engineering. (p. 1608)
—Spider Biters. (p. 1626)
—Steve Jobs & Apple. (p. 1649)
—Summer Job. (p. 1674)
—Texas Wildfires. (p. 1724)
—Toby Keith. (p. 1760)
—Top 10 Secrets for Managing Credit Cards & Paying Bills Successfully. (p. 1768)
—Transcontinental Railroad: Using Proportions to Solve Problems. (p. 1778)
—Transcontinental Railroad: Using Algebra to Represent Situations & Solve Problems. (p. 1778)
—Trip to the White House. (p. 1787)
—United States Constitution. (p. 1819)
—Usher. (p. 1828)
—Watch Peas Grow. (p. 1861)
—Watch Peas Grow / ¡Mira cómo crecen los Guisantes! (p. 1861)
—Watch Pine Trees Grow. (p. 1861)
—Watch Pine Trees Grow / ¡Mira cómo crecen los Pinos! (p. 1861)
—We Need Spiders. (p. 1867)
—What Is Animal Migration? (p. 1889)
—When Blizzards Blow. (p. 1901)
—When Tornadoes Touch Down. (p. 1905)
—Wild Cats. (p. 1929)
—Yao Ming: International Basketball Star. (p. 1968)
Sheafer, Silvia Anne. Aimee Semple McPherson. (p. 30)
—Life of Aretha Franklin: Queen of Soul. (p. 1011)
—Ramses the Great. (p. 1438)
—Roh Moo-Hyun. (p. 1485)
Sheaffer, C. H. Soccer Heart: A Story & Guide for the Friendly Contender. (p. 1603)
Shea-Gass, Lucille. How Animals Sleep: In Africa. Vol. 1 (p. 805)
Sheahan, Michael. Roof Top Hop (with CD & DVD) (p. 1487)
Shealeya, Mildred. Pookie Lookie: The Pink Spotted Panda Bear. Gang, Jobie, illus. (p. 1383)
Shealy, Dennis. I'm a Bulldozer. (p. 858)
—I'm a T. Rex! Biggs, Brian, illus. (p. 858)
—I'm a Truck. (p. 858)
—I'm a Truck. Staake, Bob, illus. (p. 858)
—Joker's Joyride - Built for Speed. Random House Editors, illus. (p. 924)
—Mater Takes off! (Disney/Pixar Cars) RH Disney Staff, illus. (p. 1104)
—Might of Doom. Spaziante, Patrick, illus. (p. 1139)
—Overdrive! RH Disney Staff, illus. (p. 1314)
—Terrific Trains. (p. 1721)
Shealy, Dennis, jt. auth. see RH Disney Staff.
Shealy, Dennis & Little Golden Books Staff. I'm a Monster Truck. Staake, Bob, illus. (p. 858)
Shealy, Dennis & Miryam. Favorites: I'm a Truck/The Happy Man & His Dump Truck/I'm a Monster Truck. Staake, Bob et al, illus. (p. 578)
Shealy, Dennis & Random House Staff. Heroes United! - Attack of the Robot! Doescher, Erik et al, illus. (p. 773)
Shealy, Dennis R., jt. auth. see Random House.
Shealy, Larry. Kid-Jitsu: Children Learning the Art of Brazilian Jiu-Jitsu. (p. 951)
Shealy, Larry & Dos Anjos, Charles. Kid-Jitsu: Teaching Children the Art of Brazilian Jiu-Jitsu. (p. 951)
Shear, Dani. Foodie Club. Weinstein, Holly, illus. (p. 614)
Sheard, Jean. Chinese Fantasy - Cave in a Casket. (p. 307)
Shearer, Alex. Canned. (p. 261)
—Cloud Hunters. (p. 334)
—Sea Legs. (p. 1534)
—Sky Run. (p. 1587)
—Wilmot & Chips. (p. 1934)
—Wilmot & the Pops. (p. 1934)
Shearer, Amelia. God Made Seasons. Marlin, Kathryn, illus. (p. 690)
—God's Armor for Me. Burroughs, Scott, illus. (p. 690)
Shearer, Cyndy, jt. auth. see Arthur, Kay.
Shearer, Cynthia & Washington, George. Handwriting by George 28-55: Rules of Civility & Decent Behaviour in Company & Conversation: Rules 28-53 to Draw & Write (p. 741)
Shearer, Janet. Artist's Guide to Perspective. (p. 104)
Shearer, Susan. Wacky Rhymes: Three-Letter A, E, I, O & U Words. (p. 1852)
Shearer, Tony. Praying Flute: Song of the Earth Mother. (p. 1393)
Shearin, Effie Mae. Pedro Menendez: The Adelantado of Florida. (p. 1334)
Shearin, Mary A. Is for All of Us: Earth Friendly ABC's. (p. 889)
Shearing, Leonie. Guess Who Says Moo? Shearing, Leonie, illus. (p. 729)
Shearing, Leonie, illus. see Ringler, Matt.
Shearon, Lillian Nicholson. Little Mixer. (p. 1032)
Shears, William. My Little Pony. Utopia, illus. (p. 1213)
Sheath, Irene. Lippy Lime Juice. (p. 1021)
Sheban, Chris, illus. see Alsdurf, Phyllis.
Sheban, Chris, illus. see Bateman, Teresa.
Sheban, Chris, illus. see Bernheimer, Kate.
Sheban, Chris, illus. see Clifton, Lutricia.
Sheban, Chris, illus. see DiCamillo, Kate.
Sheban, Chris, illus. see Frisch, Aaron.
Sheban, Chris, illus. see Greene, Stephanie.
Sheban, Chris, illus. see Heinz, Brian J.
Sheban, Chris, illus. see Hesse, Karen.
Sheban, Chris, illus. see Seidler, Tor.
Sheban, Chris, illus. see Wahl, Jan.
Sheckels, Astrid. Nic & Nellie (p. 1250)
Sheckels, Astrid, illus. see Baldwin, Robert F.
Sheckels, Astrid, illus. see Freeberg, Jane.
Sheckels, Astrid, illus. see Hermes, Patricia.
Sheckels, Astrid, illus. see Kendall, Jane F.
Shecter, Vicky Alvear. Anubis Speaks! A Guide to the Afterlife by the Egyptian God of the Dead. Revoy, Antoine, illus. (p. 90)
—Cleopatra Rules! The Amazing Life of the Original Teen Queen. (p. 331)
—Cleopatra's Moon. (p. 331)
—Curses & Smoke: A Novel of Pompeii. (p. 395)
—Hades Speaks! A Guide to the Underworld by the Greek God of the Dead. Larson, J. E., illus. (p. 735)
Shed, Greg, illus. see Bowen, Anne M.
Shed, Greg, illus. see Bruchac, Joseph.
Shed, Greg, illus. see Martin, Bill, Jr.
Shed, Greg, illus. see Wood, Douglas.
Shedd, Blair, illus. see Brown, Cynthia Light.
Shedd, Blair, illus. see Van Vleet, Carmella.
Sheehan, Anna. Long, Long Sleep. (p. 1047)
Sheehan, J. Kevin. Leader Becomes a Leader: Inspirational Stories of Leadership for a New Generation. (p. 981)
Sheehan, Jennifer E. Chicky Dickey's Animal Pancakes. (p. 301)
—Miss Bumples Lands on Earth. (p. 1151)
Sheehan, Kevin. Dandelion's Tale. Dunlavey, Rob, illus. (p. 403)
Sheehan, Linda Clarke. Chronicles of Mr. Kitty Mozart. (p. 317)
Sheehan, Monica. Be Happy! Sheehan, Monica, illus. (p. 148)
—Love Is You & Me. Sheehan, Monica, illus. (p. 1060)
Sheehan, Nicholas, et al. Geographical Enquiry (p. 662)
Sheehan, P. J. Gabby's Big Game. (p. 652)
Sheehan, Patricia. And So I Did. (p. 71)
Sheehan, Patricia & Dhilawala, Sakina. Luxembourg. (p. 1066)
Sheehan, Patricia & Ong, Jacqueline. Côte D'Ivoire. (p. 369)
Sheehan, Patricia & Quek, Lynette. Moldova. (p. 1160)
Sheehan, Peter. Maze of Twisted Tales. (p. 1113)
—Willy Wagtail grows Up. (p. 1934)
Sheehan, Peter, illus. see Measday, Stephen.
Sheehan, Peter, illus. see Morgan, Sally, et al.
Sheehan, Robert. Conquering Mount Everest. (p. 358)
—Francis Drake: Patriot or Pirate? (p. 628)
Sheehan, S. & Ali, Sharifah Enayat. Afghanistan. (p. 26)
Sheehan, Sean. Ancient African Kingdoms. (p. 67)
—Auschwitz. (p. 116)
—Cold War. (p. 339)
—Endangered Species. (p. 527)
—From Beatlemania to Watergate: The Early 1960s to the Mid 1970s. (p. 642)
—From Jessie Owens to Hiroshima: The Mid 1930s to 1945. (p. 643)
—From Television to the Berlin Wall: The Mid-1940s to the Early 1960s. (p. 644)
—From the Wright Brothers to the Treaty of Versailles: The 1900s to 1918. (p. 644)
—Holocaust. (p. 789)
—Jamaica. (p. 906)
—Modern Eras Uncovered: From Jesse Owens to Hiroshima. (p. 1158)
—Modern Eras Uncovered: From Speakeasies to Stalinism. (p. 1158)
—Modern Eras Uncovered: From Television to the Berlin Wall. (p. 1158)
—Modern Eras Uncovered: From the Wright Brothers to the Treaty of Versailles. (p. 1158)
—Why Did the Holocaust Happen? (p. 1923)
—World War II: The Pacific. (p. 1959)
Sheehan, Sean, jt. auth. see Levy, Patricia.
Sheehan, Sean & Cooke, Barbara. Cambodia. (p. 255)
Sheehan, Sean & Elias, Josie. Cameroon. (p. 256)
Sheehan, Sean & Jermyn, Leslie. Cuba. (p. 388)
Sheehan, Sean & Koh, Magdalene. Guatemala. (p. 728)
Sheehan, Sean & Latif, Zawiah Abdul. Lebanon. (p. 986)
Sheehan, Sean & Levy, Pat. Modern Eras Uncovered: From Speakeasies to Stalinism. (p. 1158)
—Modern Eras Uncovered: From Television to the Berlin Wall. (p. 1158)
Sheehan, Sean & Levy, Patricia. Ancient Rome. (p. 70)
Sheehan, Sean & Nevins, Debbie. Romania. (p. 1486)
Sheehan, Sean & Spilling, Michael. Zimbabwe. (p. 1986)
Sheehan, Sean & Yong, Jui Lin. Angola. (p. 75)
—Malta. (p. 1084)
—Trinidad & Tobago. (p. 1786)
Sheehan, Sean, et al. Jamaica. (p. 906)
—Pakistan. (p. 1319)
Sheehan, Thomas F. Islands. (p. 892)
—Para Calentarse, para Refrescarse (Keeping Warm, Keeping Cool) Sarfatti, Esther, tr. (p. 1323)
—Playground Science. (p. 1372)
—Trees Don't Freeze: A Book about Adaptations. (p. 1784)
Sheehy, Shawn. Welcome to the Neighborwood. Sheehy, Shawn, illus. (p. 1874)
Sheehy-Culhane, Roisin. WHEN MAMA GOES to WORK: DEVIN'S STORY. (p. 1903)
Sheeler, Jim. Obit: Inspiring Stories of Ordinary People Who Led Extraordinary Lives. (p. 1275)
Sheely, Robert. In the Hands of the Enemy. Killcoyne, Hope L., ed. (p. 866)
Sheely, Tiffany. Captain William Clark's Great Montana Adventure. (p. 264)
Sheen, Barbara. Acne. (p. 9)
—ADHD. (p. 12)
—Asthma. (p. 108)
—Birth Defects. (p. 192)
—Careers in Architecture & Construction. (p. 267)
—Careers in Education. (p. 267)
—Careers in Healthcare. (p. 268)
—Careers in Sales & Marketing. (p. 268)
—Cerebral Palsy. (p. 287)
—Chile. (p. 305)
—Cuba. (p. 388)
—Danica Patrick. (p. 404)
—Derek Jeter. (p. 427)
—Flu. (p. 608)
—Foods of Afghanistan. (p. 614)
—Foods of Australia. (p. 614)
—Foods of China. (p. 614)

—Foods of Egypt. (p. 614)
—Foods of Ethiopia. (p. 614)
—Foods of Greece. (p. 614)
—Foods of India. (p. 614)
—Foods of Iran. (p. 614)
—Foods of Ireland. (p. 614)
—Foods of Japan. (p. 614)
—Foods of Kenya. (p. 614)
—Foods of Mexico. (p. 614)
—Foods of Scandinavia. (p. 614)
—Foods of Spain. (p. 614)
—Foods of Thailand. (p. 614)
—Foods of the Caribbean. (p. 614)
—J. J. Abrams. (p. 901)
—Janet Guthrie: Racing Pioneer. (p. 908)
—Kanye West. (p. 943)
—Korea. (p. 967)
—Lung Cancer. (p. 1065)
—Nuclear Weapons. (p. 1270)
—Peru. (p. 1345)
—Pope Benedict XVI. (p. 1384)
—Stephenie Meyer: Twilight Saga Author. (p. 1648)
—Steve Jobs. (p. 1649)
—Teen Alcoholism. (p. 1713)
—Tony Hawk. (p. 1766)
—Yoga. (p. 1972)
Sheen, Barbara, jt. auth. see Marcovitz, Hal.
Sheen, Barbara, jt. auth. see Shapiro, Dean.
Sheen, Barbara, ed. Childhood Obesity. (p. 302)
—Foods of Canada. (p. 614)
—Foods of Colombia. (p. 614)
—Foods of England. (p. 614)
—Foods of Ghana. (p. 614)
—Foods of Israel. (p. 614)
—Foods of Morocco. (p. 614)
—Foods of Pakistan. (p. 614)
—Foods of Poland. (p. 614)
—Foods of South Africa. (p. 614)
—Michael Phelps. (p. 1134)
—Natalie Coughlin. (p. 1230)
—Paul Cezanne. (p. 1330)
Sheen, C. D. McKnight. Morphani: And the Valley of the Coloured Doorway's. (p. 1176)
Sheen, Fulton J. You. (p. 1972)
Sheena, Roberts & Roberts, Sheena. We All Go Traveling By. Siobhan, Bell, illus. (p. 1865)
Sheene, Chris. Painted Footsteps: A Creative Collection of Poetry. (p. 1318)
Sheeran, Beth. Child's Book of Prayer. (p. 304)
Sheesley, Brian, illus. see Carman, Patrick.
Sheets, Bethany Pease. Doodle Designs. (p. 469)
Sheets, Dutch. Beginner's Guide to Intercession: How to Pray Effectively. (p. 159)
—Intercessory Prayer Study Guide: How God Can Use Your Prayers to Move Heaven & Earth. (p. 879)
Sheets, Judy. Gift. Nausley, Kathy, illus. (p. 675)
Sheets, Katherine. Captured by Henrey (p. 265)
Sheets, Leslie, illus. see Ruff, Kimberly & Venturi-Pickett, Stacy.
Sheets, Leslie, jt. auth. see Ruff, Kimberly.
Sheets, Scott & Vanover, Howard. Day at the Ballpark: The Wannabe Kids. (p. 412)
Shefelman, Janice J. & Shefelman, Tom. Son of Spirit Horse. (p. 1611)
Shefelman, Janice Jordan. Anna Maria's Gift. Papp, Robert, illus. (p. 85)
Shefelman, Janice Jordan, et al. I, Vivaldi. Shefelman, Janice Jordan & Shefelman, Tom, illus. (p. 847)
Shefelman, Tom, illus. see Shefelman, Janice Jordan, et al.
Shefelman, Tom, jt. illus. see Shefelman, Janice J.
Sheff, Nic. Schizo. (p. 1521)
—Tweak: Growing up on Methamphetamines. (p. 1799)
—We All Fall Down: Living with Addiction. (p. 1865)
Sheffer, Donnel Gloster. Seacil the Sea Turtle. (p. 1536)
Sheffield, Bill. Beginnings under Attack. (p. 160)
Sheffield, Marilyn. Fizza the Flamingo. Al-Fakhri, Patricia, illus. (p. 601)
Sheffield, S. Train on the Track: Learning the TR Sound. (p. 1777)
—When Leaves Turn: Learning the UR Sound. (p. 1903)
Sheffield, Sarah. Life During the American Civil War. (p. 1010)
Sheffield, Sherry Overton. Children's Choices: What Would YOU Do? (p. 303)
Sheffield, Stephanie, jt. auth. see Burns, Marilyn.
Sheffield, Stephanie & Gallagher, Kathleen. Math & Nonfiction, Grades 3-5. (p. 1105)
Sheffler, Axel, illus. see Donaldson, Julia.
Shefield, April, ed. see Lumpkin, Kenya.
Shefrin, Jill. Such Constant Affectionate Care: Lady Charlotte Finch - Royal Governess & the Children of George III. (p. 1672)
Shefrin, Sima Elizabeth, illus. see Goss, Sheila M. & Hughes, Vi.
Shefrin, Sima Elizabeth, illus. see Schwartz, Ellen.
Shefrin, Sima Elizabeth, illus. see Yolen, Jane & Stemple, Heidi E. Y.
Shegog, Jakeenya. My Friend Jesus. (p. 1209)
Sheh, Stephanie, tr. see Hongo, Akiyoshi.
Shehadeh, Y. I. Legendary Heroes: The Beginning. (p. 989)
Shehan, Terece, illus. see Thompson, Shannon Raines.
Shehane, Kristen. Chomp! (p. 309)
Sheik, Mayra & Varacalli, Lauren. Caltech College Prowler off the Record: Inside California Institute of Technology. (p. 255)
Sheikh-Miller, J. & Turnbull, S. Big Cats. (p. 180)
Sheikh-Miller, Jonathan. Latin Words Sticker Book. Cartwright, Stephen, illus. (p. 979)
—Sharks. (p. 1562)
—Snakes. (p. 1596)
Sheikh-Miller, Jonathan, jt. auth. see Kalbag, Asha.
Sheils, Christine M. Owen Has Burgers & Drum: Helping to Understand & Befriend Kids with Asperger's Syndrome. DuFalla, Anita, illus. (p. 1314)
Shein, Daniel Erik. Aurora Spirit Bear of the North: Aurora. (p. 116)
—Seedkrakers: MytStoryland Friends. Reker, Martin, ed. (p. 1547)
Shein, Erik. Pillow Princess: Mystoryland Friends Brand. (p. 1359)
Shein, Erik Daniel. Apple the Racing Cow: My Storyland Friends. (p. 92)
—Forgotton Ornament. Reker, Martin, ed. (p. 620)
Shein, Erik Daniel & Reker, Martin. Forgotten Ornament. Safar, Lina, illus. (p. 620)
Sheinkin, Steve. Bomb: The Race to Build — & Steal — the World's Most Dangerous Weapon. (p. 208)
—King George: What Was His Problem? - The Whole Hilarious Story of the American Revolution. Robinson, Tim, illus. (p. 958)
—Lincoln's Grave Robbers. (p. 1019)
—Most Dangerous: Daniel Ellsberg & the Secret History of the Vietnam War. (p. 1177)
—Notorious Benedict Arnold: A True Story of Adventure, Heroism & Treachery. (p. 1268)
—Notorious Benedict Arnold. (p. 1268)
—Port Chicago 50: Disaster, Mutiny, & the Fight for Civil Rights. (p. 1386)
—Storyteller's History: The American Revolution. (p. 1664)
—Two Miserable Presidents: The Amazing, Terrible, & Totally True Story of the Civil War. Robinson, Tim, illus. (p. 1804)
Sheinkin, Steve & National Geographic Learning Staff. North America - Geography & Environments. (p. 1264)
Sheinkopf, Barry. Collected Poems. (p. 339)
Sheinmel, Alyssa B. Beautiful Between. (p. 153)
—Lucky Kind. (p. 1062)
—Stone Girl. (p. 1652)
Sheinmel, Courtney. All the Things You Are. (p. 46)
—Edgewater. (p. 504)
—My So-Called Family. (p. 1219)
—Positively. (p. 1387)
—Sincerely: Sincerely, Sophie; Sincerely, Katie. (p. 1578)
—Stella Batts: Pardon Me. Bell, Jennifer A., illus. (p. 1647)
—Stella Batts: Needs a New Name. Bell, Jennifer A., illus. (p. 1647)
—Stella Batts: None of Your Beeswax. Bell, Jennifer A., illus. (p. 1647)
—Stella Batts: A Case of the Meanies. Bell, Jennifer A., illus. (p. 1647)
—Stella Batts: Hair Today, Gone Tomorrow. Bell, Jennifer A., illus. (p. 1647)
—Stella Batts Something Blue. Bell, Jennifer A., illus. (p. 1647)
—Stella Batts - Who's in Charge? Bell, Jennifer A., illus. (p. 1647)
Sheinmel, Courtney & Bell, Jennifer A. Stella Batts: Needs a New Name. (p. 1647)
—Stella Batts: Hair Today, Gone Tomorrow. (p. 1647)
Shekailo, Pamela, illus. see Edwards-Wright, Tracy.
Shekell, Dustin. LL Cool J. (p. 1043)
Shekerow, Mark D., ed. see Polley, J. Patrick & Polley, JoAnn.
Shekhter, Eli. Crosswalk: A Novel of Espionage & Intrigue. (p. 385)
—Most Wanted List: An Action Packed Mystery Novel. (p. 1177)
—Plan B. (p. 1366)
Shekinah Productions, des. Nursing Student Prayer Book: Working Your Dreams into a Reality. (p. 1273)
Shekunov, Vladimir. Nature & Us: Whether Ants Can Think. (p. 1236)
Shelby, Anne. Adventures of Molly Whuppie & Other Appalachian Folktales. McArdle, Paula, illus. (p. 20)
—Man Who Lived in a Hollow Tree. Hazelaar, Cor, illus. (p. 1086)
Shelby, Fay, jt. auth. see Drexler, Sam.
Sheldon. Not Just Another Alphabet Book. (p. 1267)
Sheldon, Annette. Big Brother Now: A Story about Me & Our New Baby. Maizel, Karen, illus. (p. 179)
—Big Sister Now: A Story about Me & Our New Baby. Maizel, Karen, illus. (p. 183)
Sheldon, Camilla & Skinner, Tony. Popular Music Theory: Grade 1. (p. 1385)
Sheldon, David. Barnum Brown: Dinosaur Hunter. Sheldon, David, illus. (p. 139)
Sheldon, David, illus. see Brown, Peggy.
Sheldon, David, illus. see Day, Nancy.
Sheldon, David, illus. see Namm, Diane.
Sheldon, David, illus. see Rosenthal, Sally.
Sheldon, Dyan. Confessions of a Teenage Drama Queen. (p. 356)
—Confessions of a Teenage Hollywood Star. (p. 356)
—Crazy Things Girls Do for Love. (p. 378)
—Deep & Meaningful Diaries from Planet Janet. (p. 422)
—I Conquer Britain. (p. 837)
—Moon Dragons. Blythe, Gary, illus. (p. 1172)
—My Worst Best Friend. (p. 1222)
—One or Two Things I Learned about Love. (p. 1296)
—Planet Janet. (p. 1367)
—Sophie Pitt-Turnbull Discovers America. (p. 1613)
—Truth about My Success. (p. 1794)
Sheldon, Ian. Seashore of Southern California. Sheldon, Ian, illus. (p. 1538)
Sheldon, Ian, illus. see Acorn, John Harrison.
Sheldon, Ian, illus. see Acorn, John.
Sheldon, Kaylene Kauwila. Day with Makana. (p. 415)
Sheldon, Ken. Alphabet: Easy Learning Songs & Instant Activities That Teach Each Letter of the Alphabet. (p. 49)
—Sing-Along & Learn - Science: 12 Lively Learning Songs & Instant Activities That Teach Key Science Concepts. (p. 1578)
Sheldon, Ken, ed. see Cricket Books Staff & Cobblestone Publishing, Inc. Staff.
Sheldon, Ken, ed. see Cricket Books Staff & Cobblestone Publishing Staff.
Sheldon, Kristin, illus. see Hicks, Greg & Foster, Rick.
Sheldon, Ruth. Verminators. (p. 1837)
Sheldon, Sam, jt. auth. see Dicker, Katie.
Sheldon, Tamia. What Is a Family? Sheldon, Tamia, illus. (p. 1888)
Sheldon, Tamia, illus. see Nelson, M. R.
Sheldon, Tamia, jt. auth. see Belshaw, Yvonne.
Sheldon, Tom. Big Match Manager Burton, Nathaniel, illus. (p. 182)
Sheldon, William D., et al. Social Work: A Profession of Many Faces. (p. 1605)
Sheldrake, Missy, illus. see Peine, Jan.
Sheldrake, Rupert, jt. auth. see Banks, Kate.
Sheley, Kristen. Partners in Time #4: Family Matters. (p. 1325)
—Partners in Time #5: A Change of Course. (p. 1325)
ShelFish. Dots Dots Polka Dots (p. 472)
Sheljagovich, Yana, ed. see AZ Books Staff.
Sheikh-Miller, Jonathan. Big Cats II. (p. 180)
—Snakes II. (p. 1597)
Shell, S. E. Coffee with Orange Sherbert: Friendship Can Be Found Where Eyes & Hearts Are Open. Smith, Mary Elizabeth, illus. (p. 338)
Shell-Aurora, Callie, photos by see Ignatius, Adi, et al, eds.
Shellenberger, Susie. How to Help Your Hurting Friend: Clear Guidance for Messy Problems (p. 820)
—One Year Devos for Teens 2. (p. 1297)
Shellenberger, Susie & Weber, Kristin. Smart Girl's Guide to God, Guys, & the Galaxy: Save the Drama! & 100 Other Practical Tips for Teens. (p. 1592)
Shelley Ann Boutcher-Caldwell. Naughty Little Birdie & the Surprise Cake. (p. 1237)
Shelley, Jeff, illus. see Pearson, Mary E.
Shelley, John, illus. see Bauer, Marion Dane.
Shelley, John, illus. see Danneberg, Julie.
Shelley, John, illus. see Evans, Douglas.
Shelley, John, illus. see Mason, Jane B. & Stephens, Sarah Hines.
Shelley, John, illus. see Sutcliffe, Jane.
Shelley, John, illus. see Wynne-Jones, Tim.
Shelley, John, jt. auth. see Solomon, Elena Vestri.
Shelley, Mary. Frankenstein: The Graphic Novel. (p. 629)
—Frankenstein: With a Discussion of Tolerance. Clift, Eva, tr. (p. 629)
—Frankenstein. (p. 629)
—Frankenstein. Ho, Jason, illus. (p. 629)
—Frankenstein. Akib, Jamel, illus. (p. 629)
—Frankenstein. Irving, Frazer, illus. (p. 629)
—Frankenstein. Williams, Anthony, illus. (p. 629)
—Gris Grimly's Frankenstein. Grimly, Gris, illus. (p. 724)
—Timeless Classics Low Level: Frankenstein (p. 1754)
Shelley, Mary, jt. auth. see Reed, Gary.
Shelley, Mary, jt. auth. see Shelley, Mary.
Shelley, Mary, jt. auth. see Sierra, Sergio A.
Shelley, Mary & Shelley, Mary. Frankenstein Calero, Dennis, illus. (p. 629)
—Frankenstein. (p. 629)
—Frankenstein. Moliken, Paul, ed. (p. 629)
—Frankenstein. Cruz, Nardo, illus. (p. 629)
—Frankenstein. Jones, Barry, illus. (p. 629)
—Frankenstein. Sutliff Sanders, Joe, tr. (p. 629)
Shelley, Rebecca. All I Got for Christmas: Smartboys Club. Goldsmith, Abby, illus. (p. 44)
—Bees in My Butt: The Smartboys Club: Book 1. Goldsmith, Abby, illus. (p. 158)
—I Lost My Head: Smartboys Club Book 4. Goldsmith, Abby, illus. (p. 841)
—I Took a Burp. Goldsmith, Abby, illus. (p. 847)
—Mist Warriors. (p. 1155)
—My Stomach Explodes: The Smartboys Club Book 5. Goldsmith, Abby, illus. (p. 1219)
Shelley, Rebecca, jt. auth. see Shelley, Rebecca.
Shelley, Rebecca & Shelley, Rebecca. Aos Si. (p. 91)
Shelley, Rex. Japan. (p. 909)
Shellly, Jeff, jt. illus. see LaPadula, Tom.
Shells, B. Malone. Henry Has a Head Cold. (p. 768)
Shelly, Christina. Company of Slaves. (p. 351)
—Silken Servitude. (p. 1575)
Shelly, Jeff. Cars & Trucks: Step by Step Instructions for 28 Different Vehicles. (p. 272)
—Draw & Color Dinosaurs: Step-by-Step Instructions for 27 Prehistoric Creatures. (p. 480)
—Learn to Draw Cars & Trucks. (p. 983)
—Learn to Draw Dinosaurs. (p. 983)
Shelly, Jeff, illus. see Bateman, Teresa.
Shelly, Jeff, illus. see Black, Dave & Houghton, Steve.
Shelly, Jeff, illus. see Manus, Ron & Harnsberger, L. C.
Shelly, Jeff, illus. see Montgomery, Claire & Montgomery, Monte.
Shelly, Jeff, illus. see Perez, Jessica.
Shelly, Jeff, illus. see Walter Foster Creative Team.
Shelly, Jeff, jt. auth. see LaPadula, Tom.
Shelly, Jeff, jt. auth. see Pearson, Mary E.
Shelly, Jeff, jt. illus. see Fisher, Diana.
Shelly, Jeff, Sr., illus. see Schneider, David.
Shelly, Susan, jt. auth. see Stettler, Nicolas.
Shelton, A., jt. auth. see Brown, Bruce.
Shelton, Angela. Tilda Pinkerton's Magical Hats. (p. 1750)
—Tilda Pinkerton's Magical Hats. Murray, James, illus. (p. 1750)
Shelton, C. H., jt. auth. see Shelton, C. H.
Shelton, C. H. & Shelton, C. H. Kid's Guide to Being a Winner. Gillespie, Greg G., illus. (p. 953)
Shelton, Carter. Adventures of Hagel the Hound: And Lito the Dove Homework. Andreasen, Tim, illus. (p. 18)
—Adventures of Hagel the Hound: And Dandy the Cat Friendship. Andreasen, Tim, illus. (p. 18)
—Adventures of Hagel the Hound: And Marble the Mouse Okay to Be Small. Andreasen, Tim, illus. (p. 18)
—Adventures of Hagel the Hound: And Louie the Fish Watching Too Much T. V. Andreasen, Tim, illus. (p. 18)
Shelton, Cherrelle. Feedies. (p. 580)
—Princess Curl. (p. 1403)
Shelton, Crystal G. Theodore's Rings. (p. 1729)
Shelton, Danny & Quinn, Shelley J. Antichrist Agenda: Ten Commandments Twice Removed. (p. 89)
Shelton, Dave. Boy & a Bear in a Boat. (p. 217)
—Thirteen Chairs. (p. 1734)
Shelton, Dierdre A. Angels Surrounding Me. (p. 75)
Shelton, Donna. Breaking Dawn (p. 225)
—Breaking Dawn. (p. 225)
Shelton, Giulia M., jt. auth. see Nourse, Audrey S.
Shelton, Jayne C. In Grandma's Arms. Katz, Karen, illus. (p. 863)
Shelton, Karen. Famous Americans: Ready-to-Go Units That Include Mini-Books, Read-Aloud Plays, Graphic Organizers, & Writing Activities That Teach about 12 Important Americans. (p. 569)
Shelton, Michael. Secret Encounters: Addressing Sexual Behaviors in Group Settings. (p. 1540)
Shelton, Nathan. Mystery of Cambria. (p. 1224)
Shelton, Paula Young. Child of the Civil Rights Movement. Colón, Raúl, illus. (p. 301)
Shelton, Rick. Hoggle's Christmas. Gates, Donald, illus. (p. 787)
Shelton, Ricky V. Quacker Meets His Dad the Squirrel: Tales from a Duck Named Quacker. Williams, Shan, illus. (p. 1422)
Shelton, Sherry, jt. auth. see Burgo, Ann.
sheltrown, karen, illus. see Jones, Rachel.
Shemayne S. Place Called There. (p. 1365)
Shemin, Craig. Families Are Forever McCoy, John, illus. (p. 567)
—Families Are Forever. McCoy, John, illus. (p. 567)
Shems, Ed. First Word Search: Phonics, Phonics, Phonics! (p. 597)
Shems, Ed, illus. see Hovanec, Helene.
Shems, Ed, illus. see Wiese, Jim.
Shems, Ed, illus. see Yates, Philip & Rissinger, Matt.
Shems, Ed, jt. auth. see Wiese, Jim.
Shemtov, Yael. Sadie's Funny Feeling. (p. 1501)
Shen, Alexander, jt. auth. see Gelfand, I. M.
Shen, Kristy & Leung, Bryce. Little Miss Evil. (p. 1031)
Shen, Prudence. Nothing Can Possibly Go Wrong. Hicks, Faith Erin, illus. (p. 1268)
Shen-Chow, Lulu. Silly Girl Adventures. (p. 1576)
Shene, Paula. Mandy - The Alpha Dog: The Chronicles of the K-9 Boys & Girls on Locus Street. Shene, Prescott, illus. (p. 1087)
Shene, Prescott, illus. see Shene, Paula.
Sheng, Y. Karen, tr. see Mycek-Wodecki, Anna.
Shenhav. Raspberry Juice. (p. 1439)
Sheninger, Rick. Buddy the Duck Gets Lost. (p. 235)
Shenkman, David Mark. Buddy the Talking Cat. (p. 235)
Shenton, Tim. Life of Abraham: Faith, Courage, Children, God. (p. 1011)
—Readings from James: Trials + Faith + Riches + Prayer. (p. 1447)
Shepard, Aaron. Adventures of Mouse Deer: Favorite Folktales of Southeast Asia. Gamble, Kim, illus. (p. 20)
—Folktales on Stage: Children's Plays for Readers Theater, with 16 Reader's Theatre Play Scripts from World Folk & Fairy Tales & Legends, Including Asian, African, Middle Eastern, & Native American. (p. 611)
—Hija del Rey de los Mares. Spirin, Gennady, illus. (p. 779)
—King o' the Cats. Sorra, Kristin, illus. (p. 958)
—Legend of Lightning Larry. Goffe, Toni, illus. (p. 988)
—Magic Flyswatter: A Superhero Tale of Africa, Retold from the Mwindo Epic. (p. 1072)
—Monkey King: A Superhero Tale of China, Retold from the Journey to the West. (p. 1165)
—Mountain of Marvels: A Celtic Tale of Magic, Retold from the Mabinogion. (p. 1181)
—One-Eye! Two-Eyes! Three-Eyes! A Very Grimm Fairy Tale. Clement, Gary, illus. (p. 1294)
—Princess Mouse: A Tale of Finland. Gore, Leonid, illus. (p. 1404)
—Songs of Power: A Finnish Tale of Magic, Retold from the Kalevala. (p. 1612)
—Timothy Tolliver & the Bully Basher. (p. 1755)
Shepard, Allan. Story of Creation & Adam & Eve: Scripture Rhymes. (p. 1658)
Shepard, Betty Bruce. Virginia: An Alphabetical Journey Through History. Lederman, Marsha, illus. (p. 1844)
Shepard, C. Lori & the Sky of Colors. (p. 1053)
Shepard, Daniel. All Kinds of Farms. (p. 44)
—Solid Shapes. (p. 1607)
—What Do People Use Long Ago? (p. 1882)
Shepard, Ernest H., illus. see Ellison, Virginia H.
Shepard, Ernest H., illus. see Grahame, Kenneth & Williams, Nicholas.
Shepard, Ernest H., illus. see Grahame, Kenneth.
Shepard, Ernest H., illus. see Milne, A. A.
Shepard, Ernest H., illus. see Milne, A. A. & Soman, David.
Shepard, Jon M., et al. Sociology & You. (p. 1605)
Shepard, Kathy. Recovering Drama Queen: How to Keep from Going over the Edge & Have a Fabulous Life in the Center! (p. 1452)
Shepard, Mark. Bully Proof Kid: Bullying Prevention from the Inside Out. (p. 241)
Shepard, Mary, illus. see Travers, P. L.
Shepard, Sara. Ali's Pretty Little Lies. (p. 41)
—Burned. (p. 243)
—Cross My Heart, Hope to Die. (p. 385)
—Crushed. (p. 386)
—Deadly. (p. 417)
—Flawless. (p. 603)
—Good Girls. (p. 698)
—Heartless. (p. 760)
—Hide & Seek. (p. 776)
—Killer. (p. 956)
—Lying Game. (p. 1066)
—Never Have I Ever. (p. 1243)
—Perfect. (p. 1341)
—Perfectionists. (p. 1342)
—Pretty Little Liars. (p. 1398)
—Pretty Little Liars Bind-Up #1: Pretty Little Liars & Flawless. (p. 1398)
—Pretty Little Liars Bind-Up #2: Perfect & Unbelievable. (p. 1398)
—Pretty Little Secrets. (p. 1398)
—Ruthless. (p. 1499)
—Seven Minutes in Heaven. (p. 1554)
—Stunning. (p. 1670)
—Toxic. (p. 1774)
—Twisted. (p. 1802)
—Two Truths & a Lie. (p. 1804)

—Unbelievable. (p. 1811)
—Vicious. (p. 1840)
—Wanted. (p. 1856)
—Wicked. (p. 1927)
Shepard, William, adapted by. Our Young Folks' Josephus: Antiquities of the Jews, the Jewish Wars. (p. 1310)
Shephard, Colin, jt. auth. see Rees, Rosemary.
Shephard, Esther. Paul Bunyan. Kent, Rockwell, illus. (p. 1330)
Shephard, H. Ferebee. Dad's Birthday Present. (p. 399)
—Jonathan & Roscoe. (p. 925)
Shepherd, Amanda, illus. see Pearson, Susan.
Shepherd, Angela. Through the Lens #1: Ava's Big Surprise. (p. 1745)
Shepherd, Anita. Easter Rabbit's Magic. (p. 499)
—Santa Genie. (p. 1512)
—Scareboo's Halloween Trick. (p. 1519)
Shepherd, Audrey. Morgana the Recession Witch. (p. 1175)
Shepherd, C. A., et al. Sly Fox (Playscript) (p. 1591)
Shepherd, Cody Ryan. GLM Investigators: Mystery at Wilderness High. (p. 684)
Shepherd, David. That Movie in Your Head: Guide to Improvising Stories on Video. (p. 1726)
Shepherd, David & Plummer, William K. We Were There at the Driving of the Golden Spike. (p. 1868)
Shepherd, Deborah. Thread Through Time. (p. 1741)
Shepherd, Donna J. Ava's Secret Tea Party. Sinclair, Bella, illus. (p. 118)
—Bradybug. Grady, Kit, illus. (p. 221)
—Chizzy's Topsy Tale. Collier, Kevin Scott, illus. (p. 308)
—Dotty's Topsy Tale. Collier, Kevin Scott, illus. (p. 472)
—Lonely Lightning Bug. (p. 1046)
—OUCH! Sunburn. Collier, Kevin Scott, illus. (p. 1307)
—Sully's Topsy Tale. Collier, Kevin Scott, illus. (p. 1673)
Shepherd, Donna J. & Foster, Jack. Where Is Salami. (p. 1909)
Shepherd, Donna Walsh. Earth. (p. 495)
Shepherd, Good. Our Almighty God: A Bible Study. (p. 1307)
Shepherd, J. A. Old Hendrik's Tales - 13 South African Folk Tales. (p. 1284)
Shepherd, JaiLeen. Anan: Lea's Special Friend—Part II of the Lea Trilogy. (p. 67)
—Lea's Song: The Life of a Special Little Horse. (p. 986)
Shepherd, Jeremy, jt. auth. see Churilla, Bryan.
Shepherd, Jessica. Grandma. (p. 707)
Shepherd, Joanne. What I Look Like When I Am Scared: Como Me Veo Cuando Estoy Asustado. (p. 1887)
—What I Look Like When I Am Scared. (p. 1887)
—What I Look Like When I am Scared / Cómo me veo cuando estoy Asustado. (p. 1887)
—What I Look Like When I Am Surprised: Como Me Veo Cuando Estoy Sorprendido. (p. 1887)
—What I Look Like When I Am Surprised. (p. 1887)
—What I Look Like When I am Surprised / Cómo me veo cuando estoy Sorprendido. (p. 1887)
Shepherd, Jodie. Day with Doctors. (p. 415)
—Day with Firefighters. (p. 415)
—Day with Librarians. (p. 415)
—Day with Mail Carriers. (p. 415)
—Day with Paramedics. (p. 415)
—Day with Police Officers. (p. 415)
—Days of the Week. (p. 415)
—Hillary Clinton. (p. 779)
—It's a Good Thing There Are Earthworms. (p. 895)
—Jane Goodall. (p. 908)
—Johnny Appleseed. Furukawa, Masumi, illus. (p. 923)
—Kindness & Generosity: It Starts with Me! (p. 957)
—Mae Jemison. (p. 1070)
—Merry Christmas, Rarity! Fletcher, Lyn, illus. (p. 1129)
—Ocean Friends. Ovresat, Laura, illus. (p. 1276)
—Olivia & the Haunted Hotel. (p. 1286)
—Olivia & the Haunted Hotel. Spaziante, Patrick, illus. (p. 1286)
—Optimism: Sunny-Side Up! (p. 1301)
—Perseverance: I Have Grit! (p. 1344)
—Sacagawea - Brave Explorer. (p. 1500)
—Sesame Street Elmo Goes to School. Moroney, Christopher, illus. (p. 1553)
—Where Can That Silly Monkey Be? Your Turn, My Turn Reader. Haefele, Steve, illus. (p. 1906)
Shepherd, Jodie, jt. auth. see Artifact Group, The.
Shepherd, Jodie, jt. auth. see Kimmelman, Leslie.
Shepherd, Jodie, jt. auth. see Reader's Digest Staff.
Shepherd, Jodie, jt. auth. see Twin Sister Produtions Staff.
Shepherd, Jodie, jt. auth. see Twin Sister Produtions.
Shepherd, Keith D. Kumba & Kambili: A Tale from Mali. (p. 968)
Shepherd, Keith D., illus. see LaFaye, A.
Shepherd, Lauren. Bebé Elefante Se Olvida: The Story of Elephant Baby Forgets en Español for Spanish Speakers & Learners! (p. 155)
Shepherd, Lee Walker. Gingerhaus & the Runaway Gingerboy. (p. 677)
Shepherd, Matthew, et al. Pollinator Conservation Handbook: A Guide to Understanding, Protecting, & Providing Habitat for Native Pollinator Insects (p. 1381)
Shepherd, Megan. Cage. (p. 251)
—Her Dark Curiosity. (p. 769)
—Madman's Daughter. (p. 1070)
Shepherd, Melissa L. On Mother's Day. (p. 1289)
Shepherd Mountain Press Staff. What Can You See on the Coast? A Shepherd Mountain Press Coloring Book. (p. 1881)
Shepherd, Nicole Leigh, jt. auth. see Mikulski, Keri.
Shepherd, Pamela. Zach at Risk. (p. 1984)
Shepherd, Paul, photos by see Robinson, Janice.
Shepherd, Rosalie M., illus. see Collins, David R.
Shepherd, Rosalie M., illus. see Homan, Lynn M. & Reilly, Thomas.
Shepherd, Rosalie M., tr. see Homan, Lynn M. & Reilly, Thomas.
Shepherd, Sandra. Kangapoo & the Monster at Kakadu. (p. 942)
Shepherd, Sandra & Hughes, Jenny. Tail of Kangapoo: Dinkidi Aussie Books. (p. 1695)
Shepherd, Sheri Rose. His Little Princess: Treasured Letters from Your King. Browning, Lisa Marie, illus. (p. 781)
—His Mighty Warrior: A Treasure Map from Your King. Browning, Lisa Marie, illus. (p. 781)
Shepherd, Wendy & Hershenson, Ken. Ernie's Special Summer Day: An Ernie the Sock Monkey Adventure. Shepherd, Wendy & Hershenson, Ken, photos by. (p. 534)
Shepherd, Wilf. Behind the Whiskers: Tales for the Young at Heart. (p. 160)
Shepherd-Guenette, C. Lost & Found. (p. 1054)
Shepherd-Guenette, Claire. Creation, Christian Stories, Crafts, Puzzles & Projects. (p. 379)
Shepherd-Harvey, M. Neville the Froad. (p. 1243)
Sheppard, Bonnie. 10 Greatest Art Forgers. (p. 1993)
Sheppard, Bonnie, jt. auth. see Harper, Suzanne.
Sheppard, Caroline H. Shadow Moves: A Story for Families & Children Experiencing a Difficult or Traumatic Move. Manikoff, John, illus. (p. 1557)
Sheppard, Daniela, jt. auth. see Hawthorne, Kate.
Sheppard, Hazel A. Inchy Books: Inch Worm Goes a Mile; Inchy Goes the Extra Mile; Inchy Goes the Distance (p. 869)
—Inchy Goes the Distance. (p. 869)
Sheppard, Kate, illus. see Childs, Rob.
Sheppard, Kate, illus. see Newman, Marjorie.
Sheppard, Keith. In the Kingdom of the Fair-Eyes. (p. 866)
—Welcome to the Crazyverse: A Collection of Comic Poems about Famous People in History. (p. 1874)
—Wonderland Revisited & the Games Alice Played There. (p. 1948)
Sheppard, Paul. Access to Geography: Economic Activity & Change. (p. 8)
Sheppard, Robert. Tin Pan Arcadia. (p. 1755)
Sheppard, Robert, ed. Salt Companion to Lee Harwood. (p. 1505)
Sheppard, Si. Heroes & Legends: Set 2. (p. 772)
—Heroes of the Trojan War. (p. 773)
Shepperson, Claude A., illus. see Wiggin, Kate Douglas.
Shepperson, Jacqueline. Martins of the Everglades. (p. 1098)
Shepperson, Jacqueline Ruth. Blue Jay Tales. (p. 203)
Shepperson, Rob, illus. see Coman, Carolyn.
Shepperson, Rob, illus. see Davis, Kenneth C.
Shepperson, Rob, illus. see Harrison, David L.
Shepperson, Rob, illus. see Lewis, J. Patrick.
Shepperson, Rob, illus. see Mills, Claudia.
Shepperson, Rob, illus. see Pomerantz, Charlotte.
Shepperson, Rob, illus. see Rauss, Ron.
Shepperson, Rob, illus. see Root, Phyllis.
Shepperson, Rob, illus. see White, Andrea & Mimi, Vance.
Shepple, Sue Ann. Christopher & Grammy Join the Circus. (p. 316)
Sheps, Sheldon G., ed. Mayo Clinic on Prostrate Health: Answers from the World-Renowned Mayo Clinic on Prostate Inflammation, Enlargement, Cancer. (p. 1113)
Sher, Abby. Kissing Snowflakes. (p. 962)
Sher, Barbara. Refuse to Choose! Use All of Your Interests, Passions, & Hobbies to Create the Life & Career of Your Dreams. (p. 1456)
Sher, Emil, jt. ed. see Barrie, Shirley.
Sher, Geoffrey, et al. In Vitro Fertilization: The A.R.T. of Making Babies. (p. 868)
Sher, Steven. Where the Shouting Began. (p. 1909)
Sherab, Chodzin & Langham, Tony. Creepy Crawly Calypso. (p. 381)
Sheras, Peter. I Can't Believe You Went Through My Stuff! How to Give Your Teens the Privacy They Crave & the Guidance They Need. (p. 837)
Sherayko, Peter. Travels of Oso & Neo. Liljeblad, Lynn, illus. (p. 1780)
Shereda, Laura. Spectacular Space Trivia. (p. 1624)
Sherer, Mary (Huston). Ho Fills the Rice Barrel. Greenwood, Marion, illus. (p. 786)
Sherfinski, Julie, jt. auth. see Wirth, Margie.
Sheridan, Celi. Tolly & Maisie's Ghastly Adventure. (p. 1762)
Sheridan, Luke. Luke & His Amazing Space Bed. McCartney, Jen, illus. (p. 1064)
Sheridan, Richard Brinsley. Ketelitian Peta Rencana Tata Ruang (PP No. 8 Tahun 2013) Dan Pedoman Penyusunan Peraturan Daerah Tentang Tata Ruang Wilayah Provinsi Dan Kabupaten/Kota: Dilengkapi Undang-Undang Tentang Tata Ruang, Peraturan Pemerintah Tentang Rencana Tata Ruang Wilayah Nasional. Landes, William-Alan, ed. (p. 949)
—School for Scandal. Loftis, John, ed. (p. 1523)
Sheridan, Sara. I'm Me! Chamberlain, Margaret, illus. (p. 859)
Sheriff, Jeanne. Walkabout Kid. (p. 1854)
Sheriff, Marcia. God's Great Big Love. (p. 691)
Sherlock, Patti. Letters from Wolfie. (p. 1002)
Sherlock, Philip. Anansi & the Alligator Eggs y Los Huevos Del Caimán. Rickham, Elethia, tr. (p. 67)
Sherman, Alexie. Flight. (p. 604)
Sherman, Aliza. Everything You Need to Know about Placing Your Baby for Adoption. (p. 545)
Sherman, Arthur. Atomic Layer Deposition for Nanotechnology: An enabling process for Nanotechnology Fabrication. (p. 113)
Sherman, Benjamin. Gregory's Paper Airplane. (p. 723)
Sherman, Brandi. Sweetest Dreams. (p. 1690)
Sherman, Caroline. Dog's Life Wu, Donald, illus. (p. 463)
Sherman, Casey, jt. auth. see Tougias, Michael J.
Sherman, David & Cragg, Dan. Lazarus Rising. (p. 981)
Sherman, Dean. Relationships: The Key to Love, Sex, & Everything Else. (p. 1457)
Sherman, Deborah. Triple Chocolate Brownie Genius (p. 1787)
Sherman, Delia. Changeling. (p. 290)
Sherman, Gisela. Early Harvest (p. 493)
Sherman, Harold M. Ding Palmer, Air Detective. (p. 440)
—Get 'Em Mayfield. Anderson, Harold, illus. (p. 667)
—Strike Him Out. (p. 1667)
—Tahara, Boy Mystic of Indi. (p. 1695)
Sherman, Harold Morrow. Fight 'Em Big Three. (p. 585)
—Flying Heels & Other Hockey Stories. (p. 610)
Sherman, Harold Morrow & Townsend, Ernest N. Batter Up: A Story of American Legion Junior Baseball. (p. 145)
Sherman, Howard, jt. auth. see Fox, Gardner.
Sherman, Jan, ed. see Munroe, Myles.
Sherman, Janice. Colorful Critters. (p. 344)
—Colorful Critters Color Match Coloring Book. (p. 344)
—Counting Critters. (p. 371)
—Critter Zoo. (p. 384)
—Critters A-Z. (p. 384)
—Draco the Dragonfly. (p. 476)
—Kyle the Caterpillar. (p. 969)
—Ocean Critters. (p. 1276)
—Rainforest Critters. (p. 1436)
—Where Critters Live. (p. 1906)
Sherman, Janine, jt. auth. see Rapini, Mary Jo.
Sherman, Jill. Drug Trafficking. (p. 487)
—Hindenburg Disaster. (p. 780)
—Melvil Dewey: Library Genius. (p. 1125)
—Vaccination Debate. (p. 1830)
Sherman, Josepha. Amazing Science - Weather (p. 55)
—Asteroids, Meteors, & Comets. (p. 108)
—Charles Babbage & the Story of the First Computer. (p. 291)
—Copos y Cristales: Un Libro Sobre la Nieve Robledo, Sol, tr. from ENG. (p. 365)
—Flakes & Flurries: A Book about Snow. Yesh, Jeff, illus. (p. 602)
—Fossil Fuel Power (p. 623)
—Geothermal Power. (p. 666)
—Gusts & Gales: A Book about Wind Wesley, Omarr, illus. (p. 733)
—Gusts & Gales: A Book about Wind. Wesley, Omarr, illus. (p. 733)
—Henry Cavendish & the Discovery of Hydrogen. (p. 767)
—Henry Hudson: Exploring the Northwest Passage. (p. 768)
—Henry Hudson: English Explorer of the Northwest Passage. (p. 768)
—How Do We Know the Nature of the Cell. (p. 808)
—How Do We Know the Nature of Time. (p. 808)
—Hydroelectric Power. (p. 831)
—J. J. Thomson & the Discovery of Electrons. (p. 901)
—Land of Endless Night. (p. 973)
—Magic Hoofbeats: Horse Tales from Many Lands. Wingerter, Linda, illus. (p. 1072)
—Mark Twain. (p. 1095)
—Neptune. (p. 1241)
—Nuclear Power. (p. 1270)
—Rachel the Clever & Other Jewish Folktales. (p. 1432)
—Sampler of Jewish-American Folklore. (p. 1509)
—Samuel de Champlain: Explorer of the Great Lakes Region & Founder of Quebec. (p. 1509)
—Shapes in the Sky: A Book about Clouds. Wesley, Omarr, illus. (p. 1561)
—Solar Power. (p. 1606)
—Splish! Splash! A Book about Rain Yesh, Jeff, illus. (p. 1630)
—Sunshine: A Book about Sunlight. Yesh, Jeff, illus. (p. 1677)
—Trickster Tales: Forty Stories from Around the World. (p. 1786)
—Uranus. (p. 1825)
—War Against Germs. (p. 1857)
—Wind Power. (p. 1935)
—Your Travel Guide to Ancient China. (p. 1981)
Sherman, Josepha, jt. auth. see Becker, Jack.
Sherman, Josepha, jt. auth. see Faulkner, Nicholas.
Sherman, Josepha, jt. auth. see Kagayame, Johnny.
Sherman, Josepha, jt. auth. see Pierce, Tamora.
Sherman, Josepha & Picture Window Books Staff. Sopla y Silba: Un Libro Sobre el Viento Robledo, Sol, tr. from ENG. (p. 1614)
Sherman, Linda. Art Fair for Grandma. (p. 102)
Sherman, M. Zachary. Blood Brotherhood Casas, Fritz, illus. (p. 200)
—Bloodlines Casas, Fritz, illus. (p. 201)
—Control under Fire Casas, Fritz, illus. (p. 361)
—Fall Line Majado, Caio & Emery, Thomas, illus. (p. 566)
—Fighting Phantoms Casas, Fritz, illus. (p. 586)
—Heart of War. (p. 760)
—Impulse Majado, Caio et al, illus. (p. 862)
—Time for War Casas, Fritz, illus. (p. 1752)
—Unchained Majado, Caio & Emery, Thomas J., illus. (p. 1811)
Sherman, M. Zachary & Iligan, Marlon. Damage Control Cage, Josef, illus. (p. 401)
—Heart of the Enemy Cage, Josef, illus. (p. 759)
Sherman, M. Zachary & Lee, Raymund. Depth Charge Bermudez, Raymund, illus. (p. 427)
—Emergency Ops Bermudez, Raymund, illus. (p. 518)
Sherman, M. Zachary & Lemke, Donald. Tony Hawk's 900 Revolution. (p. 1766)
Sherman, M. Zachary & Martinek, Tom. Harry Walton: Henchman for Hire: Henchman for Hire. O'Reilly, Sean Patrick, ed. (p. 751)
Sherman, Marcia A. Splendid, Blended Family. (p. 1630)
Sherman, Michael. Suction Cup Critters: Make Your Own Window Grabbers. (p. 1672)
Sherman, Michael, jt. auth. see Torres, Laura.
Sherman, Michael & Klutz Editors. Me vs. You: Head to Head Pencil Puzzles! (p. 1116)
Sherman, Patrice. Ben & the Emancipation Proclamation. Cooper, Floyd, illus. (p. 163)
—Boston. (p. 215)
—Case of the Train Without Wheels & Other True History Mysteries for You to Solve (p. 275)
—Colonial America. (p. 341)
—Enlightenment: A Revolution in Reason. (p. 530)
—George W. Bush: Texan Governor & U. S. President. (p. 664)
—George W. Bush: Gobernado de Texas y Presidente de los Estados Unidos / George W. Bush - Texan Governor & U. S. President. (p. 664)
—John Locke: Philosopher of the Enlightenment. (p. 922)
—Legendary Creatures. (p. 989)
—Secret, Mystifying, Unusual History of Magic (p. 1542)
—What It's Like to Be President Barack Obama? Vega, Eida de la, tr. (p. 1891)
Sherman, Patrice & Murica, Rebecca Thatcher. What It's Like to Be Ryan Howard: Como Es Ser Ryan Howard. de la Vega, Eida, tr. from ENG. (p. 1891)
Sherman, Patrice & Wood, Elaine. John James Audubon. (p. 922)
Sherman, Paulette Kouffman. Shekhinah. Vine, Rachel Shana, illus. (p. 1564)
Sherman, Rose. Danielle the Duck. (p. 405)
Sherman, Shandel, illus. see Early, Kelly.
Sherman, Susan & Poryes, Michael. That's So Raven (p. 1727)
Sherman, Suzanne. Milky Way: A River of Stars. (p. 1143)
Sherman, V. T. Call of the Beaver Patrol: Or A Break in the Glacier. (p. 254)
—Call of the Beaver Patrol: Or a Break in the Glacier. (p. 254)
Sherman, William H., ed. see Shakespeare, William.
Shermer, Michael. How We Believe: Science, Skepticism, & the Search for God. (p. 823)
Shernock, Judith. Sammi the Seahorse. (p. 1507)
Sherouse, J. Neil. Burden of Evil Times. (p. 243)
Sherrard, Brent, jt. auth. see Brignall, Richard.
Sherrard, Brent R. Wasted (p. 1860)
Sherrard, Laura, illus. see Innis-Weisseneder, Emma May.
Sherrard, Valerie. Accomplice. (p. 8)
—Chasing Shadows. (p. 294)
—Driftwood (p. 485)
—Eyes of a Stalker. (p. 558)
—Glory Wind (p. 685)
—Hiding in Plain Sight: A Shelby Belgarden Mystery. (p. 777)
—In Too Deep: A Shelby Belgarden Mystery. (p. 868)
—Kate. (p. 944)
—Miss Wondergem's Dreadfully Dreadful Pie Whittingham, Wendy, illus. (p. 1152)
—Rain Shadow (p. 1435)
—Sam's Light. (p. 1509)
—Searching for Yesterday: A Shelby Belgarden Mystery. (p. 1538)
—Speechless. (p. 1624)
—Testify. (p. 1723)
—There's a Cow under My Bed Jardine, David, illus. (p. 1730)
—There's a Goldfish in My Shoe! Jardine, David, illus. (p. 1730)
—Three Million Acres of Flame. (p. 1743)
—Tumbleweed Skies (p. 1796)
—Vanessa Hudgens. (p. 1833)
—Watcher. (p. 1861)
Sherratt, Andrew. International Mathematics (p. 880)
Sherratt, Tana. Santa's Magic Dust. (p. 1513)
Sherrell, Craig, illus. see Kowen, Dorothy.
Sherrell, Deborah. Baby Lauren & Theodore,hardcover. (p. 127)
Sherrer, Quin, Sr. & Garlock, Ruthanne. Woman's Guide to Spiritual Warfare. (p. 1945)
Sherrerd, Chris S. Christian Marriage: A Sixfold Covenant of Love-Motivated Servanthood. (p. 312)
—Profiles in Sanctification: Maturing in One's Personal Relationship with Christ. (p. 1409)
—Spiritual Dynamics in the Body of Christ: Dynamic Interactions with Christ Indwelling. (p. 1629)
—Unto the Mountain Pass: A Theology of the End Time Purposes of God. (p. 1823)
Sherri L. Berner. Healthy Fun with Benjamin & Jasmine: ABCs of the Human Body. Michael A. Cicchetti, illus. (p. 758)
Sherrill, Cathy, ed. see Sherrill, Rusty & Miers, Doug.
Sherrill, Rusty & Miers, Doug. Kid Nitro & the Sinister Slorp. Sherrill, Cathy, ed. (p. 951)
Sherritt-Fleming, Lori, jt. auth. see Winters, Kari-Lynn.
Sherrod, Elbert L. Soul's Sweet Simple Music. (p. 1614)
Sherrod, Leslie J. Like Sheep Gone Astray. (p. 1017)
Sherrow, Victoria. Ancient Africa: Archaeology Unlocks the Secrets of Africa's Past. (p. 67)
—Bottlenose Dolphin. Wertheim, Anne, illus. (p. 215)
—Chipmunk at Hollow Tree Lane. Davis, Allen, illus. (p. 308)
—Connecticut. (p. 357)
—Food Safety. (p. 614)
—Foster Care System. (p. 624)
—Galapagos Fur Seal: At Home in the Tropics. Wertheim, Anne, illus. (p. 653)
—Galapagos Fur Seal. (p. 653)
—Guglielmo Marconi: Inventor of Radio & Wireless Communication. (p. 729)
—Homegrown Terror: The Oklahoma City Bombing. (p. 793)
—Jonas Salk: Beyond the Microscope. (p. 925)
—Medical Imaging. (p. 1118)
—Ohio. (p. 1281)
—Product Liability. (p. 1409)
—Tennis. (p. 1720)
—Wilma Rudolph. Translations.com Staff, tr. (p. 1934)
Sherry. Always & Forever: Angel's Ladybugs. (p. 51)
Sherry, Clifford. Inhalants. (p. 874)
Sherry, Clifford J. Inhalants. (p. 874)
Sherry, Kevin. I'm the Best Artist in the Ocean! (p. 860)
—I'm the Biggest Thing in the Ocean. (p. 860)
—I'm the Scariest Thing in the Castle. (p. 860)
—Meet the Bigfeet. (p. 1122)
—Turtle Island. (p. 1798)
Sherry, Maureen. Walls Within Walls. (p. 1855)
—Walls Within Walls. Stower, Adam, illus. (p. 1855)
Sherry, Raymond. Adventures of Kyree & Kyere: The Basement. Williams, Deshantren, illus. (p. 19)
Shertzer, Twilene & Eshbach, Karen. No Glass Between: A Boy's Journey with Loving & Then Losing His Baby Brother. (p. 1258)
Sherup, illus. see Benson, Sandra.
Sherven, Judith & Sniechowski, James. Be Loved for Who You Really Are: How the Differences Between Men & Women Can Be Turned into the Source of the Very Best Romance You'll Ever Know. (p. 148)
Sherwin, Frank. Ocean Book. (p. 1276)
Sherwin, Frank J. Guide to Animals. (p. 730)
Sherwin, Michael, tr. see Pinckaers, Servais.
Sherwood, C. A. Aj's Easter Surprise. (p. 32)
Sherwood, George. Legends in Their Time: Young Heroes & Victims of Canada. Sherwood, Stewart, illus. (p. 990)
Sherwood, K. C. Midnight at Moonglow's. (p. 1138)
Sherwood, Lance. Grandpa Tales. (p. 709)
Sherwood, Mary & Shaw, George Bernard. Little Woodmand & Other Stories. (p. 1038)

Sherwood, Mary Marth. History of Lucy Clare. (p. 784)
Sherwood, Mary Martha. History of Lucy Clare. (p. 784)
Sherwood, Stewart, illus. see Sherwood, George.
Sherwood-Sitts, Herm. Fox & Farmer Beeching. (p. 626)
—Secret of Cypress Swamp. (p. 1542)
Sheryl the pearl productions, Sheryl Clayton. Teeny the Magic Genie. (p. 1715)
Shestakova, Anna, ed. see AZ Books Staff.
Sheth, Kashmira. Blue Jasmine. (p. 203)
—Boys Without Names. (p. 220)
—Keeping Corner. (p. 947)
—Koyal Dark, Mango Sweet. (p. 967)
—Monsoon Afternoon Jaeggi, Yoshiko, illus. (p. 1166)
—My Dadima Wears a Sari Jaeggi, Yoshiko, illus. (p. 1201)
—No-Dogs-Allowed Rule. Pearce, Carl, illus. (p. 1258)
—Sona & the Wedding Game Jaeggi, Yoshiko, illus. (p. 1611)
—Tiger in My Soup Ebbeler, Jeffrey, illus. (p. 1748)
Shetterly, Robert. Americans Who Tell the Truth. (p. 64)
Shetterly, Robert, illus. see Keyser, Samuel Jay & Boyds Mills Press Staff.
Shetterly, Will. Elsewhere. (p. 516)
—Nevermever. (p. 1243)
Shettleworth, Earle, jt. auth. see Malone, Richard.
Shetty, B. Vithal. World as Seen under the Lens of a Scientist: Negro Zero to American Hero Who Changed United States from American Hypocrisy to Greatest Democracy. (p. 1954)
Shetty, Lakshmi, illus. see Shetty, Lalitha A.
Shetty, Lalitha A. Tales of Toy World. Shetty, Lakshmi, illus. (p. 1703)
Sheuer, Lauren, illus. see Seip, Shannon Payette.
Sheva, Marie, mem. Year of the Dogs: A Chronicle of Redemption, a Story of Love. (p. 1969)
Shevick, Ed. Great Scientists in Action. Wheeler, Ron, illus. (p. 718)
Shew, David & Ottenburger, Rhonda Shew. Midway Dreams. (p. 1139)
Shewan, Edward. Manual of Christian Doctrine, Answer Key. (p. 1089)
Shewmaker, Eugene F. Shakespeare's Language: A Glossary of Unfamiliar Words in His Plays & Poems. (p. 1559)
Shewver, Margaret. Without a Trace & Other Stories. (p. 1942)
Shi, Anshen, et al. Essentials of Chinese Medicine: Internal Medicine (p. 537)
Shi, Charleston. Quest of the Phoenix: Book 3, Rage of the Serpents. (p. 1426)
—Quest of the Phoenix: Book Two, Storm of the Kraken. (p. 1426)
—Quest of the Phoenix: Book 1, the Phoenix & the Yeti. (p. 1426)
Shi, Lily L., tr. see Youjun, Sun.
Shi, Shannon. English. (p. 529)
Shibaja, Calixto, jt. auth. see Cueva, Susana.
Shibamoto, Thores, illus. see Suzukaze, Ryo.
Shibley, Joe, illus. see Forte, Imogene & Schurr, Sandra.
Shichtman, Sandra H. Colin Powell: Have a Vision. Be Demanding. (p. 339)
—Michael Bloomberg. (p. 1134)
—Nancy Pelosi. (p. 1229)
—Sonia Sotomayor. (p. 1612)
Shichtman, Sandra H. & Indenbaum, Dorothy. Joy of Creation: The Story of Clara Schumann. (p. 929)
Shickle, Ian, illus. see Cameron, Kristy.
Shickman, Allan Richard. Dael & the Painted People. (p. 399)
—Zan-Gah: A Prehistoric Adventure. (p. 1984)
—Zan-Gah & the Beautiful Country. (p. 1984)
Shieber, Jennifer. Insects Measure Up! Small Book. (p. 876)
Shiei, illus. see Arnold, Adam.
Shiei, illus. see DeFilippis, Nunzio & Weir, Christina.
Shiei, illus. see Roberts, Rachel.
Shiei, Shiei, illus. see Arnold, Adam.
Shield ARP, Peter J. Don Quixote & the Windmills (p. 465)
Shield, Sophie. Pupitukaar. Smart, George, illus. (p. 1417)
Shields, Amy. Best Friends Forever: And More True Stories of Animal Friendships. (p. 169)
—Best Friends Forever! And More True Stories of Animal Friendships. (p. 169)
—National Geographic Little Kids First Big Book of Why. (p. 1232)
—National Geographic Readers - Planes. (p. 1233)
—National Geographic Readers: Saving Animal Babies. (p. 1233)
—Planes. (p. 1367)
—Trains. (p. 1777)
Shields, Amy & Stewart, Melissa. National Geographic Readers: Robots. (p. 1233)
Shields, Bonnie, illus. see Hodges, Meredith.
Shields, Brooke. Welcome to Your World, Baby. Doerrfeld, Cori, illus. (p. 1874)
Shields, Carol Diggory. After the Bell Rings: Poems about After-School Time. Meisel, Paul, illus. (p. 28)
—Baby's Got the Blues. Tobia, Lauren, illus. (p. 129)
—Bugliest Bug. Nash, Scott, illus. (p. 237)
—Saturday Night at the Dinosaur Stomp. Nash, Scott, illus. (p. 1515)
—Science, Fresh Squeezed! Thompson, Richard, illus. (p. 1526)
—Wombat Walkabout. Blackall, Sophie, illus. (p. 1945)
Shields, Carrie. Sweet Dreams. (p. 1689)
Shields, Charles J. Argentina. (p. 97)
—Argentina Henderson, James D., ed. (p. 98)
—Belize Henderson, James D., ed. (p. 162)
—Belize. (p. 162)
—Brazil Henderson, James D., ed. (p. 224)
—Brazil. (p. 224)
—Central America: Facts & Figures. (p. 287)
—Central America: Facts & Figures Henderson, James D., ed. (p. 287)
—Central America Today (p. 287)
—Chile Henderson, James D., ed. (p. 305)
—Chile. (p. 305)
—Costa Rica Henderson, James D., ed. (p. 368)
—Costa Rica. (p. 368)
—Guatemala Henderson, James D., ed. (p. 728)
—Guatemala. (p. 728)
—Honduras Henderson, James D., ed. (p. 794)
—Honduras. (p. 794)
—I Am Scout: The Biography of Harper Lee. (p. 833)
—Nicaragua Henderson, James D., ed. (p. 1250)
—Nicaragua. (p. 1250)
—Panama Henderson, James D., ed. (p. 1320)
—Panama. (p. 1320)
—Peru Henderson, James D., ed. (p. 1345)
—Peru. (p. 1345)
—Saddam Hussein. (p. 1501)
—Salvador Henderson, James D., ed. (p. 1506)
—Salvador. (p. 1506)
—Uruguay Henderson, James D., ed. (p. 1826)
—Uruguay. (p. 1826)
—Venezuela Henderson, James D., ed. (p. 1835)
—Venezuela. (p. 1835)
—Vladimir Putin. (p. 1846)
Shields, Charles J. & Koestler-Grack, Rachel A. Saddam Hussein. (p. 1501)
Shields, Chris, illus. see Kilpatrick, Cathy.
Shields, Chris, illus. see Watt, Fiona.
Shields, Christine. Tiny Little Scary Mouse. (p. 1756)
Shields, Clarissa & O'Shea, Mick. Beyond District 12: The Stars of the Hunger Games. (p. 174)
Shields, Dave. Tour. (p. 1773)
Shields, Erik P., illus. see Aunt Darla.
Shields, Gillian. Amber's First Clue. Turner, Helen, illus. (p. 57)
—Betrayal. (p. 171)
—DogFish. Taylor, Dan, illus. (p. 462)
—Elephantantrum! Johnson-Isaacs, Cally, illus. (p. 511)
—Eternal. (p. 539)
—Holly Takes a Risk. Turner, Helen, illus. (p. 789)
—Immortal. (p. 861)
—Library Lily. Chessa, Francesca, illus. (p. 1006)
—Perfect Bear. Blythe, Gary, illus. (p. 1341)
—Puppy Love: The Story of Esme & Sam. Harbour, Elizabeth, illus. (p. 1418)
—Sophie Makes a Splash. Turner, Helen, illus. (p. 1613)
—When the World Is Ready for Bed. Currey, Anna, illus. (p. 1905)
—When the World Was Waiting for You. Currey, Anna, illus. (p. 1905)
—When the World Was Waiting for You Baby Book. Currey, Anna, illus. (p. 1905)
Shields, Gillian, jt. auth. see Angelini, Josephine.
Shields, Gillian & Reed, Nathan. Angel Baby. (p. 73)
Shields, Kathleen J. Hamilton Troll Meets Chatterton Squirrel. Klug, Leigh A. & Bryant, Carol W., illus. (p. 739)
—Hamilton Troll Meets Dinosaurs. Klug, Leigh A. & Bryant, Carol W., illus. (p. 739)
—Hamilton Troll Meets Elwood Woodpecker. Klug, Leigh A. & Bryant, Carol W., illus. (p. 739)
Shields, Laurie, illus. see Tartakoff, Katy.
Shields, Lew. Legend of Pleasant Island. (p. 988)
Shields, Mary & Grace, Susan. What's a Shrew to You? Van Zyle, Jon, illus. (p. 1896)
Shields, Ruth, illus. see Zyrro, Roggen.
Shields, Sarah D., jt. auth. see U. S. National Geographic Society Staff.
Shields, Scott & West, Nancy. Bear - Heart of a Hero. (p. 150)
Shields, Sue, illus. see Jenkins, Martin.
Shields, Sue, illus. see Ross, Stewart.
Shields, Susan, illus. see Ross, Stewart.
Shields, Vicki. Mooshka the Bear. (p. 1173)
Shiels, Tony "Doc". Monstrum! a Wizard's Tale. (p. 1169)
Shier, David, et al. Human Anatomy & Physiology with OLC Bind-In Card. (p. 825)
—Student Study Guide to Accompany Hole's Human Anatomy & Physiology. (p. 1669)
Shier, David N., et al. Hole's Essentials of Human Anatomy & Physiology with OLC bind-In Card. (p. 788)
Shifflett, Stephen. Josie Unlimited. (p. 927)
Shiffman, Lena, illus. see Snyder, Marilyn.
Shiffman, Lena, jt. auth. see McNulty, Faith.
Shifler, Ann. Lone, Lone Cloud. Birky, Rachael, illus. (p. 1046)
Shifrin, Joshua. Study Skills 365: A Study Skill for Every Day of the Year. (p. 1670)
Shifrine, Moshe & Dorian, Camille. I Have Diabetes Too: Molly's Story (p. 839)
Shiga, Jason. Meanwhile: Pick Any Path. 3,856 Story Possibilities. (p. 1117)
Shigeno, Shuichi. Initial D (p. 874)
—Initial D Shigeno, Shuichi, illus. (p. 874)
—Initial D Hagihara, Rie, tr. from JPN. (p. 874)
—Initial D: Volume 17 Shigeno, Shuichi, illus. (p. 874)
—Initial D: Volume 6. Shigeno, Shuichi, illus. (p. 874)
—Initial D. Shigeno, Shuichi, illus. (p. 874)
Shigeno, Shuichi & Papia, Dan. Initial D (p. 874)
Shigeno, Shuichi, creator. Initial D (p. 874)
Shigeno, Suichi. Initial D (p. 874)
—Initial D Papia, Dan, tr. from JPN. (p. 874)
—Initial D Kanemitsu, Dan, tr. from JPN. (p. 874)
Shih, Lin, illus. see Caro, Joe.
Shiina, Karuho. From Me to You. Shiina, Karuho, illus. (p. 643)
—Kimi Ni Todoke: From Me to You. Vol. 5 Shiina, Karuho, illus. (p. 957)
—Kimi Ni Todoke: From Me to You. Vol. 10 Shiina, Karuho, illus. (p. 957)
—Kimi Ni Todoke - From Me to You. Shiina, Karuho, illus. (p. 957)
Shilliam, Jo-Anne, illus. see Nystrom, Carolyn.
Shillitoe, Tony. Caught in the Headlights. (p. 282)
Shiloh, Ramon. Guidance Through an Illustrative Alphabet: Written & Illustrated by Ramon Shiloh. Shiloh, Ramon, illus. (p. 730)
Shiloh, Ramon, illus. see Hausman, Gerald.
Shimabukuro, Mitsutoshi. Toriko Shimabukuro, Mitsutoshi, illus. (p. 1769)
Shimalla, Jen. Heaven Cent. (p. 761)
Shimamoto, Kazuhiko. Skull Man (p. 1586)
Shimano, Chie. BioGraphic Novel: Che Guevara. (p. 188)
Shimazaki, Kento & Senno, Knife. Depicting Humans (p. 427)
Shimberg, Elaine Fantle. Helga, the Hippopotamouse. Walling, Sandy Seeley, illus. (p. 763)
—Herman, the Hermit Crab. Walling, Sandy Seeley, illus. (p. 771)
Shimin, Symeon, illus. see Hamilton, Virginia.
Shimizu, Aki. Qwan (p. 1429)
—Successor of Fate (p. 1672)
—Suikoden III: Successor of Fate (p. 1673)
—Suikoden III: The Successor of Fate (p. 1673)
—Suikoden III: Successor of Fate Coffman, Patrick, tr. from JPN. (p. 1673)
Shimizu, Aki, illus. see Kiefl, Mike, tr.
Shimizu, Aki, creator. Suikoden III: The Successor of Fate (p. 1673)
Shimizu, Aki, ed. Suikoden III: The Successor of Fate. (p. 1673)
Shimizu, Michio. Ding Dong. McLaughlin, Sako, tr. (p. 440)
Shimizu, Yuki. Love Mode (p. 1060)
Shimizu, Yuko, illus. see Moss, Marissa.
Shimizu, Yuko, illus. see Uehashi, Nahoko & Hirano, Cathy.
Shimizu, Yuko, illus. see Uehashi, Nahoko.
Shimko, Bonnie. You Know What You Have to Do (p. 1975)
Shimmen, Cathy, illus. see Adeney, Anne.
Shimmen, Cathy, illus. see Milbourne, Anna.
Shimmen, Cathy, illus. see Page, Nick & Page, Claire.
Shimohara, Heisuke. Let's Draw Manga- Sexy Gals. (p. 996)
Shimokawa, Emi, tr. see Ekuni, Kaori.
Shimokawa, Emi, tr. see Kitakata, Kenzo.
Shimokawa, Melanie. Family for Madison. (p. 568)
Shimon, Diana, illus. see Water, Mark.
Shimony, Yaniv, illus. see Plaisted, Caroline.
Shimpi, Shekhar, jt. auth. see Turner, Ginger.
Shin, Chi Sup. Three Little Turtles & the Big Bad Pelican. (p. 1743)
Shin, Eui-Cheol. Chrono Code Choi, Il-Ho, illus. (p. 317)
Shin, Hayoung, illus. see Gunderson, Jessica.
Shin, Hwan, illus. see Noh, Mi Young.
Shin, Hwan, jt. auth. see Lee, Jong-Kyu.
Shin, Hwan & Lee, Jong-Kyu. Evil's Return (p. 546)
Shin, Janet Jaywan, tr. see Lee, T. S.
Shin, Ji-Sang. Chocolat (p. 309)
—Chocolat. Geo, illus. (p. 309)
Shin, Ji-Soo, illus. see Kim, Young-Ah.
Shin, Simone, illus. see Doering, Amanda F. & Higgins, Melissa.
Shin, Simone, illus. see Doering, Amanda.
Shin, Simone, illus. see Higgins, Melissa.
Shin, Simone, illus. see Isabella, Jude.
Shin, Sun Yung. Cooper's Lesson. Cogan, Kim & Paek, Min, trs. from ENG. (p. 365)
Shinba, Rize. Juicy Cider. (p. 932)
—Mister Mistress (p. 1155)
Shindel, Allan R. Duel Identity. (p. 489)
Shindo, Hikaru, jt. auth. see Hotta, Yumi.
Shine, Andrea, illus. see Brisson, Pat.
Shine, Andrea, illus. see Clark, Clara.
Shine, Andrea, illus. see Quattlebaum, Mary.
Shine, Andrea, illus. see Santucci, Barbara.
Shine, Ian, jt. ed. see Siler, Deborah.
Shine, Joe. I Become Shadow. (p. 834)
Shiner, Jack. Raking Leaves: Poems. (p. 1437)
—Stunning Jagged Edges of Precise Malfunction. (p. 1670)
Shingle, Jude, illus. see Moodey, Mary.
Shingleton, Todd. Point of You: From the Empty Nest. (p. 1377)
Shingu, Fumiaki. Easy Origami. (p. 500)
Shingu, Susumu. Traveling Butterflies. (p. 1780)
—Wandering Whale Sharks. (p. 1856)
Shinjo, Mayu. Sensual Phrase (p. 1551)
—Sensual Phrase Shinjo, Mayu, illus. (p. 1551)
—Sensual Phrase. Yamazaki, Joe, tr. (p. 1551)
—Sensual Phrase. Shinjo, Mayu, illus. (p. 1551)
Shinjo, Shelly, illus. see Terasaki, Stanley Todd.
Shinn, Samantha. Ollie. (p. 1287)
Shinn, Sharon. Dream-Maker's Magic. (p. 483)
—Gateway. (p. 658)
—General Winston's Daughter. (p. 660)
—Safe-Keeper's Secret. (p. 1502)
—Truth-Teller's Tale. (p. 1794)
Shinno, Stephanie. Syler & the Sandpaper Towel. Douglas, Vannick, illus. (p. 1692)
Shino, Natsuho. Oh My God! (p. 1280)
Shinoda, Anna. Learning Not to Drown. (p. 985)
Shinohara, Chie. Red River (p. 1455)
—Red River. Shinohara, Chie, illus. (p. 1455)
Shinozawa, Kelly. Manga Metamorphosis. (p. 1087)
Shiono, Nanami. Fall of Constantinople. Yasar, Kerim, tr. (p. 566)
Shiotsu, Vicky. Build-A-Skill Instant Books: Synonyms & Antonyms. (p. 238)
—Build-a-Skill Instant Books Beginning & Ending Consonant Sounds. Faulkner, Stacey, ed. (p. 238)
—Comprehension Crosswords Grade 1 McMahon, Kelly, illus. (p. 354)
—Comprehension Crosswords Grade 3 Tunell, Ken, illus. (p. 354)
—Preschool Math: Learning Basic Concepts Through Experimenting & Play. (p. 1396)
—Rocks & Minerals. Rous, Sheri, ed. (p. 1483)
Shiotsu, Vicky, ed. see Callella, Kim.
Shiotsu, Vicky, ed. see Cernak, Kim.
Shiotsu, Vicky, ed. see Cernek, Kim & Williams, Rozanne Lanczak.
Shiotsu, Vicky, ed. see Lubben, Amy & Williams, Rozanne Lanczak.
Shiotsu, Vicky, jt. auth. see Cernek, Kim.
Shioya, Hitoshi. Dinosaur Hour. (p. 442)
Shiozaki, Yuji. Battle Vixens Shiozaki, Yuji, illus. (p. 147)
—Battle Vixens. (p. 147)
Shiozaki, Yuji, creator. Battle Vixens. (p. 147)
Shiozu, Shuri. Eerie Queerie! (p. 505)
—Eerie Queerie! Yamaguchi, Heidi, tr. from JPN. (p. 505)
Shiozu, Shuri, creator. Eerie Queerie! (p. 505)
Shipe, Becky, illus. see Nettleton, Pamela Hill.
Shipe, Becky, illus. see Shea, Kitty.
Shiplett, Danaye. Paint My World with Colors. (p. 1318)
Shipley, Jocelyn, jt. auth. see Loughead, Deb.
Shipley, Marie, illus. see Skoor, Susan.
Shipley, Nan & Anthony, Jason. Is Your Straight Man Gay Enough? The Ultimate Renovation Guide. (p. 890)
Shipley, Space. Extraordinary Sam. (p. 555)
Shiply, Lyn, jt. auth. see Ballard, John E.
Shipman, Carol Ann. Seafood Cookbook (p. 1536)
Shipman, Gary. Pakkins' Land: Tavitah (p. 1319)
Shipman, James & Barker, Clyde D. Introduction to Physical Science. (p. 882)
Shipman, Josie, illus. see Kruse, Donald W.
Shipman, Talitha, illus. see Sklansky, Amy E.
Shipman, Todd. Morse the Horse Gets His Chance. (p. 1176)
Shipp, Josh. Teen's Guide to World Domination: Advice on Life, Liberty, & the Pursuit of Awesomeness. (p. 1715)
Shipton, Jonathan. Baby Baby Blah Blah Blah! Chessa, Francesca, illus. (p. 125)
Shipton, Paul. Clown School. Blake, Beccy, illus. (p. 335)
—Collins Big Cat - What's for Breakfast? Stuart, Jon, illus. (p. 340)
—Games Player of Zob. McCafferty, Jan, illus. (p. 655)
—Get the Fruit! Moon, Cliff, ed. (p. 668)
—Guinea Pigs. Dunton, Trevor, illus. (p. 731)
—I Can Do It! Elworthy, Antony, illus. (p. 835)
—In the Boat. Dunton, Trevor, illus. (p. 865)
—Pig Who Saved the World. (p. 1357)
Shipton, Paul & Henry, O. Ransom of Red Chief. Oxford University Press Staff & Bassett, Jennifer, eds. (p. 1438)
Shipton, Paul & Pearson Education Staff. Charles Dickens (p. 292)
Shipton, Rigby. Monster Is Coming: Individual Title Six-Packs. (p. 1167)
Shipton, Rosemary. 1960: Canadian Decades. (p. 2002)
Shirane, Haruo. Classical Japanese: A Grammar. (p. 328)
Shiras, Wilmar H. Children of the Atom: Facsimile Reproduction of the 1953 First Edition. (p. 302)
Shirasu, Nori, illus. see Nono, Auntie.
Shiraz, Yasmin. Blueprint for My Girls in Love: 99 Rules for Dating, Relationships, & Intimacy. (p. 204)
Shire, Poppy. Flame the Desert Pony. Berg, Ron, illus. (p. 602)
—Jewel the Midnight Pony. Berg, Ron, illus. (p. 917)
—Sparkle the Circus Pony. Berg, Ron, illus. (p. 1622)
—Star the Western Pony. Berg, Ron, illus. (p. 1641)
Shireen, Nadia. Good Little Wolf. (p. 698)
—Hey, Presto! (p. 774)
—Yeti & the Bird. Shireen, Nadia, illus. (p. 1971)
Shireen, Nadia, illus. see Puttock, Simon.
Shireman, Abbie. Fish Tank. (p. 598)
Shirey, Dave. Off the Street: Hiring on with Amtrak As a Passenger Conductor (p. 1279)
Shirin Yim, Bridges. Ruby's Wish. Blackall, Sophie, illus. (p. 1494)
Shiring, Jeff. Pizza by the Numbers. (p. 1365)
Shirk, Lois Marie. Bible 101: New Testament Volume 1. (p. 175)
Shirley, Alice. Aesop's Fables. (p. 25)
—Gentle Lion & the Little Owlet. Shirley, Alice, illus. (p. 661)
Shirley, David. Alex Haley: Author. (p. 36)
Shirley, David & Hart, Joyce. Alabama. (p. 33)
—North Carolina. (p. 1264)
Shirley, David & Kummer, Patricia K. Mississippi. (p. 1154)
Shirley, Debra. Best Friend on Wheels. Stead, Judy, illus. (p. 169)
Shirley, Donna. Land That Lost Its Green. (p. 974)
Shirley, Evans. Green Like Me. (p. 722)
Shirley, Grandma. Rudy. (p. 1494)
Shirley, Hoskins, illus. see Mary, Mize.
Shirley, John, illus. see Tudhope, Simon.
Shirley, John, et al. Classics Mutilated. (p. 328)
Shirley, Rachel. Ben's Little Big Adventure. (p. 165)
—Katie & the Cosmic Pandas' Deep Sea Voyage. (p. 944)
—Katie's Magic Teapot & the Cosmic Pandas. (p. 945)
Shirley, Rebekah Joy. Dressing up Fun: Make Your Own Costumes at Home. Fairclough, Chris, photos by. (p. 485)
—I Want to Be a Fairy. (p. 847)
—I Want to Be a Knight. (p. 847)
—I Want to Be a Pirate. (p. 847)
—I Want to Be a Princess. (p. 847)
—I Want to Be a Robot. (p. 847)
—I Want to Be an Astronaut. (p. 847)
Shirley Russak Wachtel. Howie Rocket—World Traveler-Detective: The Search for the Lovely Precious. (p. 823)
Shirley-Smith, Sanette, illus. see Smith, Pieter Ernst.
Shiro, S. P. Postcards from the Beyond. (p. 1388)
Shirodaira, Kyo. Bonds of Reasoning (p. 208)
—Bonds of Reasoning Vol. 11 (p. 208)
Shirodaira, Kyo & Mizuno, Eita. Bonds of Reasoning Vol. 6. (p. 208)
Shirodkar, Suhag. Captured in Miniature. (p. 265)
Shirow, Masamune. Intron Depot. (p. 883)
Shirt, Virginia. Angels of Clover Farm. Lane, Rob, ed. (p. 75)
Shirtliffe, Leanne. Change Your Name Store. Kügler, Tina, illus. (p. 290)
Shirtliffe, Leanne, jt. auth. see Lecis, Alessandro.
Shirvington, Jessica. Emblaze. (p. 517)
—Embrace. (p. 517)
—Empower. (p. 521)
—Endless. (p. 527)
—Entice. (p. 531)
—One Past Midnight. (p. 1296)
Shivack, Nadia. Inside Out: Portrait of an Eating Disorder. Shivack, Nadia, illus. (p. 877)
Shiveley, Lorie. Chester Church Mouse & Ash Wednesday. (p. 298)
—Chester Church Mouse & Lent. (p. 298)
Shively, Julie. Baby Elephant. Johnson, Meredith, illus. (p. 126)
—Baby Orangutan. Johnson, Meredith, illus. (p. 127)

—Baby Orca. Sharp, Chris, illus. (p. 127)
—Baby Polar Bear. Johnson, Meredith, illus. (p. 127)
—What Belongs? Kurtz, John, illus. (p. 1880)
Shively, Julie, illus. see Kurtz, John.
Shively, Julie D. Baby Penguin. (p. 127)
Shivers, Holly Hawkins. I Can Learn the Bible: The Joshua Code for Kids: 52 Scriptures Every Kid Should Know (p. 836)
Shivers, Joseph P. & Shivers, Paul L. Harriers: The Making of a Championship Cross Country Team. (p. 749)
Shivers, Juliette. Brenda Doesn't Like Broccoli. (p. 226)
Shivers, Paul L., jt. auth. see Shivers, Joseph P.
Shivley, Julie. Baby Dolphin. Sharp, Chris & Seaworld, Chris, illus. (p. 126)
—Baby Seal. Sharp, Chris & Seaworld, Chris, illus. (p. 128)
Shkhyan, Maria. Funny Day. (p. 649)
Shlasko, Robert. Molly & the Sword Diamond, Donna, illus. (p. 1160)
Shlichta, Joe. Strongheart Jack & the Beanstalk. (p. 1668)
Shlichta, Joe, illus. see DeSpain, Pleasant.
Shlomo, Pia. Thank You for Everything: A Book about Thanking Hashem. (p. 1725)
Shloss, Carol Loeb. Lucia Joyce: To Dance in the Wake. (p. 1062)
Shmaefsky, Brian R. Gonorrhea. (p. 697)
—Meningitis. (p. 1126)
—Rubella & Rubeola. (p. 1493)
—Toxic Shock Syndrome. (p. 1774)
Shmakov, Efim. Return of Hezzord. (p. 1464)
Shneiderman, Ben, photos by see Beck, Tom.
Shoaf, Molly Spencer, jt. auth. see Cunningham, Raymond Kelly, Jr.
Shoals, Cinda. Ashley Says. (p. 106)
Shoals, Melinda, jt. illus. see Worthington, Jennifer.
Shock, Tanya & Thomson, Roger. Walking in Courage: Stories of Virtue's Forest. (p. 1854)
Shockey, Marilyn. What's a Wolf to Do? (Musical) (p. 1896)
Shodell, Elly, ed. Particles of the Past: Sandmining on Long Island, 1870s-1980s. (p. 1325)
Shoebridge-Bloom, Melanie. Eleanor. (p. 508)
Shoemacher, Paul, jt. auth. see Herrington, Russel M.
Shoemaker, Craig. What You Have Now What Your Mommy Had Then. Kushner, Sarah, illus. (p. 1896)
Shoemaker, E. W. Mother Nature & the Tales of North Fork. (p. 1178)
Shoemaker, Eleanor B., ed. see DiSesa, Verdi J.
Shoemaker, H. Stephen. Finding Jesus in His Prayers. (p. 588)
Shoemaker, Kate. Octopus Ink. (p. 1278)
—Skunk Stench. (p. 1586)
Shoemaker, Kathryn, illus. see Stephens, R. David.
Shoemaker, Kathryn, illus. see Stone, Tiffany.
Shoemaker, Kathryn E., illus. see Watts, Irene N.
Shoemaker, Maria K., jt. auth. see Friedland, Katy.
Shoemaker, Marla K., jt. auth. see Friedland, Katy.
Shoemaker, Sharon. Sir Waltie of Shoe. Whiting, Sandra, illus. (p. 1580)
Shoemaker, Terry, illus. see Gillis, Peter & Alexander, Larry.
Shoemaker, Terry, illus. see Simonson, Louise & Engelhart, Steve.
Shoemaker, Tim. Below the Surface (p. 163)
Shoen, Melinda. Invisible Me: A Walking Stick's Wish. (p. 885)
Shoesmith-Bateman, Amanda. Magic Tree House Beitz-Grant, Heather, illus. (p. 1074)
Shofner, Shawndra. Alabama. (p. 33)
—Arkansas. (p. 99)
—Georgia. (p. 665)
—Hawaii. (p. 755)
—How it Happens: At the T. V. Station. (p. 810)
—How it Happens: At the Ice Cream Factory. (p. 810)
—How It Happens at the Motorcycle Plant. Wolfe, Bob & Wolfe, Diane, photos by. (p. 810)
—How It Happens at the Pizza Company. Wolfe, Bob & Wolfe, Diane, photos by. (p. 810)
—Illinois. (p. 857)
—Indiana. (p. 871)
—Louisiana. (p. 1058)
—Mississippi. (p. 1154)
—Stonehenge. (p. 1653)
—Story of the Tampa Bay Devil Rays. (p. 1662)
—Story of the Toronto Blue Jays. (p. 1662)
—Sydney Opera House. (p. 1692)
—Taj Mahal. (p. 1696)
Shogakukan, ed. see Mitsui-Kids.
Shogakukan & Mitsui-Kids. Duel Masters: The Champion of Tomorrow. Vol. 3 (p. 489)
Shohat, Ella. Israeli Cinema: East/West & the Politics of Representation. (p. 893)
Shoket, Ann & Seventeen Magazine Editors. Seventeen Ultimate Guide to Beauty: The Best Hair, Skin, Nails & Makeup Ideas for You. (p. 1555)
—Seventeen Ultimate Guide to Style: How to Find Your Perfect Look. (p. 1555)
Sholander, Graciela, jt. auth. see Cook, Sharon.
Sholevar, Bahman, ed. see Tabibzadeh, M. R.
Sholl, Anna. Faery Tales of Weir. (p. 562)
Shollar, Leah Pearl. Shadow Play: A True Story of Tefillah. Gerber, Pesach, illus. (p. 1557)
Shollar, Leah Perl & Klineman, Harvey. Key under the Pillow: A Story about Honoring Parents. (p. 950)
Sholtes, Andrew, tr. see Crouch, Adele.
Sholto, Walker, illus. see Jarman, Julia.
Shomon, Mary J. & Marjama-Lyons, Jill. Parkinson's Disease: A Holistic Program for Optimal Wellness. (p. 1325)
Shon. Henry Boothill: The Return of Nidagall (p. 767)
Shonda. My Soul Fainted Within Me: Second Edition. (p. 1219)
Shondalae. Great Giver of Life (p. 716)
Shondeck, Betty, illus. see Palmer, Pat.
Shone, Rob. Alexander the Great: The Life of a King & Conqueror. (p. 36)
—Allosaurus: The Strange Lizard. Riley, Terry, illus. (p. 47)
—Ancient Treasures. (p. 71)
—Ancient Treasures. Spender, Nick, illus. (p. 71)
—Archaeopteryx: The First Bird. (p. 95)
—Atlantis & Other Lost Cities. (p. 112)
—Atlantis & Other Lost Cities. Eldridge, Jim, illus. (p. 112)
—Avalanches & Landslides. (p. 118)
—Avalanches & Mudslides. (p. 118)
—Bigfoot & Other Strange Beasts. (p. 185)
—Bigfoot & Other Strange Beasts. Spender, Nik, illus. (p. 185)
—Bigfoot & Other Strange Beasts. Spender, Nick, illus. (p. 185)
—Brachiosaurus: The Long-Limbed Dinosaur. Riley, Terry, illus. (p. 221)
—Chinese Myths. Saraceni, Claudia, illus. (p. 307)
—Corpses & Skeletons: The Science of Forensic Anthropology. (p. 368)
—Corpses & Skeletons: The Science of Forensic Anthropology. Spender, Nick, illus. (p. 368)
—Crime Scene Investigators. (p. 382)
—Crime Scene Investigators. Saraceni, Claudia, illus. (p. 382)
—Defying Death in the Mountains. Spender, Nik, illus. (p. 424)
—Defying Death in the Mountains. Spender, Nick, illus. (p. 424)
—Defying Death in the Wilderness. Field, James, illus. (p. 424)
—Diplodocus: The Whip-Tailed Dinosaur. Field, James, illus. (p. 445)
—Earthquakes. (p. 497)
—Earthquakes. Spender, Nick, illus. (p. 497)
—Elizabeth I: The Life of England's Renaissance Queen. (p. 513)
—Giganotosaurus: The Giant Southern Lizard. Riley, Terry, illus. (p. 676)
—Greek Myths. (p. 720)
—Hadrosaurus: The Duck-Billed Dinosaur. Riley, Terry, illus. (p. 735)
—Harriet Tubman: The Life of an African-American Abolitionist. (p. 750)
—Ichthyosaurus: The Fish Lizard. (p. 851)
—Muhammad Ali: The Life of a Boxing Hero. (p. 1189)
—Muhammad Ali: The Life of a Boxing Hero. Spender, Nick, illus. (p. 1189)
—Nelson Mandela: The Life of an African Statesman. (p. 1241)
—Nelson Mandela: The Life of an African Statesman. Reed, Neil, illus. (p. 1241)
—Oviraptor: The Egg Thief. (p. 1314)
—Pachycephalosaurus: The Thick Headed Lizard. (p. 1317)
—Rosa Parks: The Life of a Civil Rights Heroine. (p. 1489)
—Rosa Parks: The Life of a Civil Rights Heroine. Spender, Nik, illus. (p. 1489)
—Rosa Parks: The Life of a Civil Rights Heroine. Spender, Nick, illus. (p. 1489)
—Solving Crimes Through Criminal Profiling. Spender, Nick, illus. (p. 1608)
—Spartacus: The Life of a Roman Gladiator. (p. 1622)
—Triceratops: The Three Horned Dinosaur. (p. 1785)
—Triceratops: The Three Horned Dinosaur. Riley, Terry & Ball, Geoff, illus. (p. 1785)
—Tyrannosaurus: The Tyrant Lizard. (p. 1805)
—Tyrannosaurus: The Tyrant Lizard. Field, James, illus. (p. 1805)
—Volcanoes. (p. 1849)
—Volcanoes. Riley, Terry, illus. (p. 1849)
—War Correspondents. (p. 1857)
—War Correspondents. Forsey, Chris, illus. (p. 1857)
Shone, Rob, illus. see Ganeri, Anita.
Shone, Rob, jt. auth. see Jeffrey, Gary.
Shone, Rob & Field, James. Diplodocus: The Whip-Tailed Dinosaur. (p. 445)
Shone, Rob & Ganeri, Anita. Elizabeth I: The Life of England's Renaissance Queen. (p. 513)
—Harriet Tubman: The Life of an African-American Abolitionist. (p. 750)
—Spartacus: The Life of a Roman Gladiator. (p. 1622)
Shone, Rob & Spender, Nick. Solving Crimes Through Criminal Profiling. (p. 1608)
Shongo Jr., Earl. Chippie the Squirrel. (p. 308)
Shonka, Maria. Snail with Two Slippers. Sanchez, Evan, illus. (p. 1596)
Shonkwiler, Martha, illus. see Miller, Ruth L.
Shontae, Tanisha. I Am Eagle: Look up & Fly. (p. 832)
Shook, Charles Augustus. Cumorah Revisited: Or, the Book of Mormon & the Claims of the Mormons Re-Examined from the Viewpoint of American Archaeology & Ethnology. (p. 392)
Shook, Karl. Family Thing. (p. 568)
Shook, Rachael, jt. auth. see Penna, Christina.
Shook, Vicci. Silly Bubba & the Llama. (p. 1575)
Shookhoff, Carol, jt. auth. see Metzl, Jordan D.
Shookuhi, Aminjon. Where Does the Water Come From? (p. 1907)
—Where Does the Water Come From? Khodjibaev, Karim & Khodjibaeva, Moukhabbat, trs. (p. 1907)
Shoop, Johanna, illus. see Lindeman, Craig.
Shoopik, Marina, illus. see Wilson, Nathaniel.
Shoopman, Jim. Cowboy Zack & the Monkey from the Muggletown Zoo. (p. 374)
—Zachary Hamm in the Land of Eggs. (p. 1984)
Shooter, Darlene D. Adventures of the Tree Frog Family: My Favorite Little Critters. (p. 24)
Shooter, Howard, photos by see Dorling Kindersley Publishing Staff & Ibbs, Katharine.
Shooter, Howard, photos by see Graimes, Nicola.
Shooter, Jim & Wolfman, Marv. Essential Avengers Perez, George et al, illus. (p. 536)
Shooter, Jim, et al. Secret Wars. (p. 1544)
Shooter, Sam. Goat in the Coat. (p. 687)
Shope, Lois, jt. auth. see Shope, Ray.
Shope, Ray & Shope, Lois. Sandy Claws & Chris Mouse. White, Michael, illus. (p. 1511)
Shope, Sam. Donkey's Tale. (p. 466)
Shoquist, Jennifer & Stafford, Diane. Encyclopedia of Sexually Transmitted Diseases. (p. 525)
Shorack, Todd. Hero in the Mirror. (p. 772)
Shore, Diane Z. Bus-a-Saurus Bop. Clark, David, illus. (p. 244)
—How to Drive Your Sister Crazy. Rankin, Laura, illus. (p. 819)
—This Is the Feast. Lloyd, Megan, illus. (p. 1736)
Shore, Diane Z., jt. auth. see Alexander, Jessica.
Shore, Diane Z. & Alexander, Jessica. This Is the Dream. Ransome, James E., illus. (p. 1736)
Shore, Diane ZuHone. This Is the Feast. Lloyd, Megan, illus. (p. 1736)
Shore, Diane ZuHone & Alexander, Jessica. This Is the Game. Smith, Owen, illus. (p. 1736)
Shore, Elayne. Candy Girl. (p. 261)
Shore, Hennie & Gardner, Richard. Helping, Caring, & Sharing Scriptbook. Schader, Karen, ed. (p. 766)
Shore, Judie, illus. see Hickman, Pamela & Federation of Ontario Naturalists.
Shore, Marguerite, tr. see Bacchin, Matteo & Signore, Marco.
Shore, Marguerite, tr. from ITA. Journey: Plateosaurus. Bacchin, Matteo, illus. (p. 927)
Shore, Stephen. Nature of Photographs. Shore, Stephen, photos by. (p. 1236)
Shores, Erika L. All about Beagles (p. 42)
—All about Boxers (p. 42)
—All about Chihuahuas (p. 42)
—All about German Shepherds (p. 42)
—All about Poodles (p. 43)
—All about Rottweilers (p. 43)
—All about Yorkshire Terriers (p. 43)
—Apples. (p. 92)
—Canada Lynx (p. 260)
—Deadliest Animals on Earth. (p. 417)
—Deadliest Bugs on Earth. (p. 417)
—Harvest Time. (p. 752)
—How to Make Bubbles (p. 820)
—Leaves. (p. 986)
—More Funny Knock-Knock Jokes (p. 1174)
—Mountain Lions (p. 1181)
—Pebble First Guide to Whales (p. 1333)
—Pet Dogs up Close. (p. 1345)
—Pumpkins. (p. 1416)
—Sam Walton (p. 1507)
—Silly Classroom Jokes (p. 1575)
—Snow Leopards (p. 1599)
Shores, Erika L., jt. auth. see Clay, Kathryn.
Shores, Erika L., jt. auth. see Winter, Judy A.
Shores, Erika L. & Wittrock, Jeni. Dogs, Dogs, Dogs. (p. 462)
Shores, Erika L., et al. Business Leaders (p. 245)
Shores, Lloyd. Adventures of Mr. Ant. (p. 20)
Shores, Lori. Cómo Hacer Slime. (p. 351)
—Cómo Hacer un Cohete Efervescente. (p. 351)
—Cómo Hacer un Globo con Olor Misterioso. Translations.com Staff, tr. from ENG. (p. 351)
—Cómo Hacer un Tornado en una Botella. Translations.com Staff, tr. from ENG. (p. 351)
—Ghosts: Truth & Rumors. Doty, Eldon, illus. (p. 672)
—Hands-On Science Fun. (p. 741)
—How to Build a Fizzy Rocket (p. 815)
—How to Build a Tornado in a Bottle (p. 815)
—How to Build Flipsticks (p. 815)
—How to Make a Liquid Rainbow (p. 820)
—How to Make a Mystery Smell Balloon (p. 820)
—How to Make Slime (p. 820)
Shores, Lori & Capstone Press Staff. Hands-On Science Fun (p. 741)
Shores, Lori & Compass Point Books Staff. Teens in India (p. 1715)
Shores, Lori & Saunders-Smith, Gail. Pebble First Guide to Butterflies (p. 1333)
Shores, Randall. Starting & Managing a Small Business. (p. 1644)
Shorkey, Cde. Jake Gets Diabetes. (p. 906)
Shorrock, Anne. Secret Adventures of Amelia & Rainbow. (p. 1540)
Shors, John. Beside a Burning Sea. (p. 168)
Short, Carol. Robert & the Princess. (p. 1478)
—Todd's Nine Lives. (p. 1761)
Short, Elizabeth, tr. see Johnson, Sandi.
Short, Gregory T., illus. see Weathers, Regina Lorick.
Short, Jody. Adventures of Sam & Penny: a New Home & Night Patrol. (p. 22)
Short, Kasey, illus. see Elmore, Amber.
Short, Mike, jt. auth. see Goldfield, Rebecca.
Short M.S., Jeff. Kid's World (p. 955)
Short, Robbie. I Want One Too! (p. 847)
Short, Robbie, illus. see Ehrmantraut, Brenda.
Short, Robbie, illus. see Weiss, Bobbi & Weiss, David.
Short, Robert Edward. Out of the Stars: A Message from Extraterrestrial Intelligence. (p. 1311)
Short, Robyn & Williams, Nanon McKewn. Peace People. Bailey, Lindsey, illus. (p. 1331)
Shortall, Leonard, illus. see Sobol, Donald J.
Shortall, Leonard W., illus. see Sobol, Donald J.
Shortcake 99. Beach Day. (p. 149)
Shortell, Stephen, illus. see Rowe, Papa.
Shortelle, Dennis, jt. auth. see Gardner, Robert.
Shorter-Gooden, Kumea, jt. auth. see Jones, Charisse.
Shortland. Busy Bees. (p. 245)
Shortle, Stacy & Mooney, Dean J. M. Train Ride to Grandma's (with NO Chocolate Donut!) Wulfing, Amy J., illus. (p. 1777)
Shortley, Michele, illus. see Krensky, Stephen.
Shortridge, Retha. Baby & Meow. (p. 124)
Shortt, Yvonne. New York City Public School Goes Green. (p. 1248)
Shortt, Yvonne M., jt. auth. see West, Richard A.
Shorty. Tad, the Sad Tadpole Evans, Margaret, illus. (p. 1695)
Shortz, Will. I Love Sudoku: 100 Wordless Crossword Puzzles. (p. 843)
—Puzzlemaster Deck: 75 Brain Twisters. (p. 1421)
—Ultimate Sudoku Challenge: 100 Wordless Crossword Puzzles. (p. 1810)
Shortz, Will, ed. see New York Times Staff.
Shortz, Will, jt. auth. see Creators of the Hit Documentary.
Shortz, Will & New York Times Staff. New York Times Crosswords in the Sun: Easy, Enjoyable Puzzles. (p. 1248)
—New York Times Favorite Day Crosswords: Monday: 75 of Your Favorite Very Easy Monday Crosswords from the New York Times. Shortz, Will, ed. (p. 1248)
—New York Times Weekend at Home Crossword Puzzle Omnibus: 200 Relaxing Puzzles. (p. 1248)
Shortz, Will, ed. Giant Book of Sudoku. (p. 673)
—Sudoku to Boost Your Brainpower: 100 Wordless Crossword Puzzles. (p. 1672)
—Will Shortz Presents the First World Sudoku Championship: 100 Wordless Crossword Puzzles. (p. 1932)
—Will Shortz Presents the Little Black Book of Sudoku: 400 Puzzles. (p. 1932)
—Will Shortz Presents the Monster Book of Sudoku: 300 Wordless Crossword Puzzles. (p. 1932)
Shortz, Will, intro. Will Shortz Presents the Monster Book of Sudoku for Kids: 150 Fun Puzzles. (p. 1932)
Shoshan, Beth. If You Can...we Can! Brown, Petra, illus. (p. 854)
—Little Rabbit Waits for the Moon. Peel, Stephanie, illus. (p. 1034)
—Mess Monsters at Christmas. (p. 1129)
—That's When I'm Happy. East, Jacqueline, illus. (p. 1727)
Shoshan, Beth, jt. auth. see Strathie, Chae.
Shostak, Arthur B., ed. Defeating Terrorism/Developing Dreams: Beyond 9/11 & the Iraq War. (p. 423)
—Tackling Tomorrow Today. (p. 1694)
Shostak, Jerome. Vocabulary Workshop, Student Text, Level A. (p. 1847)
Shotwell, Mary Sue. Summer Expedition. (p. 1674)
Shouji, Gatou. Full Metal Panic! - Into the Blue. (p. 646)
Shoulders, Debbie, jt. auth. see Shoulders, Michael.
Shoulders, Debbie & Shoulders, Michael. G Is for Gladiators: An Ancient Rome Alphabet. Juhasz, Victor, illus. (p. 651)
—T Is for Titanic: A Titanic Alphabet. van Frankenhuyzen, Gijsbert, illus. (p. 1694)
Shoulders, Michael. 1 Mississippi 2 Mississippi: A Mississippi Number Book. Anderson, Rick, illus. (p. 1991)
—Count on Us: A Tennessee Number Book. Langton, Bruce, illus. (p. 370)
—Discover Tennessee: Count on Us; V is for Volunteer Langton, Bruce, illus. (p. 448)
—Goodnight Baby Bear. Weidner, Teri, illus. (p. 701)
—Little Tennessee. (p. 1037)
—M Is for Magnolia: A Mississippi Alphabet. Anderson, Rick, illus. (p. 1067)
—N Is for Natural State: An Arkansas Alphabet. Anderson, Rick, illus. (p. 1227)
—Natural Numbers: An Arkansas Number Book. Anderson, Rick, illus. (p. 1235)
—Say Daddy! Weidner, Teri, illus. (p. 1518)
Shoulders, Michael, jt. auth. see Shoulders, Debbie.
Shoulders, Michael & Shoulders, Debbie. D Is for Drum: A Native American Alphabet. Toddy, Irving, illus. (p. 397)
Shoule, Michael, jt. auth. see Read Together Books Inc. Staff.
Shoup, Andrew J. Andy & Elmer's Apple Dumpling Adventure. (p. 72)
—Andy & Elmer's Apple Dumpling Adventure Coloring & Activity Book. Shoup, Andrew J., illus. (p. 72)
Shoup, Barbara. Wish You Were Here. (p. 1940)
Shoup, Dolores, jt. auth. see Bersson, Robert.
Shoup, Gary. Suma the Elephant. (p. 1673)
Shoup, Kate. Egypt. (p. 506)
—India. (p. 870)
—Life As a Soldier in the Civil War. (p. 1008)
—Life As an Engineer on the First Railroads in America. (p. 1008)
—Rohypnol. (p. 1485)
—Texas & the Mexican War. (p. 1724)
Shouse, Eric. Good Shepherd. (p. 700)
Shoushen, Jin. Bejing Legends. Yang, Gladys, tr. (p. 161)
Shoutarou, Harada. Na Na Na Na. Shoutarou, Harada, illus. (p. 1227)
Shoveller, Herb. Ryan & Jimmy: And the Well in Africa That Brought Them Together. (p. 1499)
Shovlin, Paul, ed. Lake Monsters. (p. 972)
Show What You Know Publishing, creator. Show What You Know on the TAKS, Grade 3 Spanish Math Flash Cards. (p. 1571)
—Show What You Know on the TAKS, Grade 3 Spanish Reading Flash Cards. (p. 1571)
Show What You Know Publishing, ed. Show What You Know on the CSAP 7, Reading/Writing Student Workbook. (p. 1571)
—Show What You Know on the CSAP for Grade 5, Student Workbook. (p. 1571)
—Show What You Know on the CSAP for Grade 6, Mathematics Student Workbook. (p. 1571)
—Show What You Know on the CSAP for Grade 9 Reading Student Self-Study Workbook. (p. 1571)
Showalter, Elaine, ed. see Alcott, Louisa May.
Showalter, Gena. Alice in Zombieland. (p. 39)
—Intertwined. (p. 881)
—Mad Zombie Party. (p. 1069)
—Oh My Goth. (p. 1281)
—Queen of Zombie Hearts. (p. 1425)
—Red Handed. (p. 1454)
—Through the Zombie Glass. (p. 1745)
—Twisted. (p. 1802)
—Unraveled. (p. 1822)
Showalter, Kristin, illus. see Olsen, S. R.
Showalter, Sarah Evelyn. Animals of the Bible from A to Z. (p. 83)
Showell, Isaiah, Sr. Faith Found New Nichols, Clayton, illus. (p. 565)
Showers, Barbara. Angel Jubilee. (p. 73)
Showers, Paul. Drop of Blood. Miller, Edward, illus. (p. 485)
—How a Baby Begins. (p. 804)
—Where Does the Garbage Go? Chewning, Randy, illus. (p. 1907)
Showler, Dave, jt. auth. see Whittley, Sarah.
Showstack, Richard. Gift of the Magic: And Other Enchanting Character-Building Stories for Smart Teenage Girls Who

S

Want to Grow up to Be Strong Women. Eric, Whitfield, illus. (p. 675)
—Peggy: And Other Enchanting Character-Building Stories for Smar Boys Who Want to Grow up to Be Strong Men. Whitfrid, Eric, illus. (p. 1335)
Shpitalnik, Vladimir, jt. auth. see Evans, Cornelia.
Shpitalnik, Vladimir & Evans, Connie. Sasha & Babushka: A Story of Russia. (p. 1515)
Shpitalnik, Vladimir & Evans, Cornelia. Sasha & Babushka: A Story of Russia. (p. 1515)
Shragg, Karen, jt. auth. see Landstrom, Lee Ann.
Shragg, Karen I. Lucy's Hero: Remembering Paul Wellstone. Klotz, Bryan, illus. (p. 1063)
Shragg, Karen I., jt. auth. see Landstrom, Lee Ann.
Shraya, Vivek. God Loves Hair. Neufeld, Juliana, illus. (p. 689)
Shreder, Etienne, illus. see Van Hamme, Jean.
Shreeve, Elizabeth. Hector Afloat. Levy, Pamela R., illus. (p. 761)
—Hector Finds a Fortune. Levy, Pamela R., illus. (p. 761)
—Hector Springs Loose. Levy, Pamela R., illus. (p. 761)
—Oliver at the Window. McDonald, Candice Hartsough, illus. (p. 1285)
Shrek & Shaw!, Scott. Shrek. (p. 1571)
Shrestha, Anuj, illus. see Aryal, Aimee.
Shrestha, Romio, jt. auth. see Shrestha, Sophie.
Shrestha, Sophie & Shrestha, Romio. In Search of the Thunder Dragon. Shrestha, Sophie & Shrestha, Romio, illus. (p. 865)
Shreve, Anita. All He Ever Wanted. (p. 44)
—Body Surfing. (p. 207)
—Sea Glass. (p. 1534)
Shreve, Steve. Adventures of Benny (p. 16)
—Adventures of Charlie: Bigfoot or the Value of a Smelly Friend. Shreve, Steve, illus. (p. 17)
—Bogey Man: Or a Good Argument for Not Picking Your Nose. Shreve, Steve, illus. (p. 207)
—Monkey Island: Or the Advantage of Opposable Thumbs. Shreve, Steve, illus. (p. 1165)
—Mummy: Or Another Great Use for Toilet Paper. (p. 1191)
—Pirates: Or the Truth about Life on the High Seas. Shreve, Steve, illus. (p. 1363)
—Stan & the Toilet Monster (p. 1639)
Shreve, Susan. Search for Baby Ruby. (p. 1537)
Shreve, Susan Richards. Kiss Me Tomorrow. (p. 961)
Shrigley, David. Book of Shrigley. Gooding, Mel & Rothenstein, Julian, eds. (p. 211)
Shrimpton, Nicholas, ed. see Trollope, Anthony.
Shriver, Chelsea & Grey, Chelsea Gillian. Ema the Rhinoceros. (p. 517)
—Ema the Rhinoceros. Leeper, Christopher, illus. (p. 517)
Shriver, Maria. What's Happening to Grandpa? Speidel, Sandra, illus. (p. 1897)
—What's Heaven? (p. 1897)
—What's Heaven. Speidel, Sandra, illus. (p. 1897)
Shroades, John, illus. see Klimo, Kate.
Shroades, John, illus. see Lawler, Janet & Moore, Clement C.
Shroades, John, illus. see Torpie, Kate.
Shroades, John / W., illus. see Lowell, Susan.
Shrode, Donna. Fun with Nan: A Trip to the Zoo. (p. 648)
—Fun with Nana: Let's Play. (p. 648)
Shroder, John F., et al. Afghanistan. (p. 26)
Shropshire, Sandy, illus. see Webber, Desiree Morrison.
Shrubshall & Free. Around the Pind in 80 Days: A Musical for Children. (p. 100)
Shrum, Edgar, illus. see Cortez, Linda.
Shrum-Williams, Heather. Dreamwalker. (p. 484)
Shryer, Donna. Body Fuel: A Guide to Good Nutrition. (p. 207)
—Peak Performance: Sports Nutrition. (p. 1332)
Shryer, Donna & Dawson, Stephen. Body Fuel: A Guide to Good Nutrition. (p. 207)
Shryer, Donna & Forschmiedt, Jodi. Peak Performance: Sports Nutrition. (p. 1332)
Shu, Sammy. There's a Season for All. Cone, Carl, illus. (p. 1731)
Shub, Elizabeth, tr. see Singer, Isaac Bashevis.
Shubert, Samantha, jt. auth. see Maisel, Grace Ragues.
Shubin, Jon, illus. see Shubin, Masha.
Shubin, Masha. Camp Caper: A Shubin Cousins Adventure. Hayes, Kathy & Hayes, David, illus. (p. 257)
—Fairytale Fracas: A Shubin Cousins Adventure. Shubin, Jon, illus. (p. 565)
Shubrook Bros Creative Staff. Skylanders Sypro's Adventure. (p. 1587)
Shubuck, Sheila. I Love You All Year Round. Padron, Alicia, illus. (p. 843)
Shucart, Deborah. ABC Scripts. (p. 3)
Shuchart, John & Scearcy, Steve. Kids' Letters to Terrorists. (p. 954)
Shuckburgh, Emily & Chambers, Catherine. Polar Scientist: The Coolest Jobs on the Planet HL Studios Staff, illus. (p. 1379)
Shue, Jenna. Animal Island. Herzog, Inge, illus. (p. 78)
Shuemann, Cynthia & Benz, Cheryl. College Reading (p. 340)
Shuert, Randy. Randy Ray & Easy Jay: Court Day Adventure. (p. 1438)
—Randy Ray & Easy Jay: The Wood House Adventure. (p. 1438)
Shufelberger, Amanda, jt. auth. see Livingston, Mary A.
Shufen, Li. Questions about the Human Body. (p. 1426)
Shuff, Chrissi. Dancing Tree & other Stories. (p. 403)
Shuff, Lana Tanaka. Kira Helps A Friend. (p. 961)
Shugaar, Antony & International Spy Museum Staff. I Lie for a Living: Greatest Spies of All Time. Guarnaccia, Steven, illus. (p. 840)
Shugars, Betty. Smokey the Tailess Dog. (p. 1594)
Shugart, Alden. Marvelous Misadventures of the Fab Five. (p. 1099)
Shughart-Knecht, Kimberly. Princess Kiali & the Purple Box. (p. 1404)
Shughry, Salam, tr. see Gillespie, Frances.
Shuh, Mari. Adrian Peterson. (p. 13)
Shukert, Rachel. Starstruck. (p. 1643)
Shukin, Barbara. Ancient History Portfolio: A History of First Civilizations Through the Classical Age. (p. 69)
—Medieval History Portfolio: A History of Early Christianity, Byzantium, & Medieval Europe. (p. 1119)
—Modern History Portfolio: A History of America & the World from the 17th to the 21st Centuries. (p. 1158)
—Renaissance History Portfolio: A History of Europe & the Americas from the 14th -18th Centuries. (p. 1460)
Shukla, Shubhda, jt. auth. see Shukla, Shubhda.
Shukla, Shubhda & Shukla, Shubhda. Naughty GOLDIE. (p. 1237)
Shukla, Subir. Boy Who Loved Colour. Sabnani, Nina, illus. (p. 219)
Shulda, Daron M. Dragon Boots. (p. 476)
Shuler, Curtis, illus. see Shuler, Melissa.
Shuler, Kala. Do You Love Me? (p. 458)
—I've Got the Boy. (p. 901)
Shuler, Melissa. Safiya's Garden. Shuler, Curtis, illus. (p. 1502)
Shuler, Nancy. Nick the Basset Hound. (p. 1251)
Shulevitz, Uri. Dusk. Shulevitz, Uri, illus. (p. 490)
—How I Learned Geography. Shulevitz, Uri, illus. (p. 810)
—One Monday Morning. (p. 1296)
—One Monday Morning. Shulevitz, Uri, illus. (p. 1296)
—Rain Rain Rivers. Shulevitz, Uri, illus. (p. 1435)
—Snow Shulevitz, Uri, illus. (p. 1598)
—Snow. (p. 1598)
—Snow. Shulevitz, Uri, illus. (p. 1598)
—Snow Storytime Set. Shulevitz, Uri, illus. (p. 1599)
—Troto & the Trucks. (p. 1789)
Shulimson, Sarene. Lights Out Shabbat. Ebbeler, Jeff, illus. (p. 1016)
—Lights Out Shabbat. Ebbeler, Jeffrey, illus. (p. 1016)
Shull, Jodie. Words of Promise: A Story about James Weldon Johnson. Stetz, Ken, illus. (p. 1951)
Shull, Jodie A. Georgia O'Keeffe: Legendary American Painter. (p. 665)
—Langston Hughes: Life Makes Poems. (p. 974)
—Words of Promise: A Story about James Weldon Johnson. Stetz, Ken, illus. (p. 1951)
Shull, Megan. Amazing Grace. (p. 54)
—Penelope. (p. 1336)
—Swap. (p. 1689)
Shulman, Dee. My Totally Secret Diary - Reality TV Nightmare. (p. 1220)
—On Stage in America. (p. 1289)
—Polly Price's Totally Secret Diary: Mum in Love. (p. 1381)
Shulman, Dee, illus. see Morgan, Michaela.
Shulman, Goldie. Way Too Much Challah Dough. (p. 1864)
Shulman, Holly. Dolley Madison: Her Life, Letters, & Legacy. (p. 464)
Shulman, Holly Cowan & Mattern, David B. Dolley Madison: Her Life, Letters, & Legacy. (p. 464)
Shulman, Lisa. How Penguins & Butterflies Grow (p. 811)
—Library (p. 1005)
—Matzo Ball Boy. Litzinger, Rosanne, illus. (p. 1110)
—Old MacDonald Had a Woodshop. Wolff, Ashley, illus. (p. 1284)
Shulman, Lisa & Capstone Press Staff. How Penguins & Butterflies Grow (p. 811)
—Library (p. 1005)
Shulman, Mark. Ann & Nan Are Anagrams: A Mixed-Up Word Dilemma. McCauley, Adam, illus. (p. 84)
—Are You Normal? Wild Questions That Will Test Your Weirdness. (p. 97)
—Are You Normal ? 2: More Than 100 Questions That Will Test Your Weirdness. (p. 97)
—Big Bagel, Little Bagel. Miline, Bill, photos by. (p. 178)
—Big Cat. Chambers, Sally, illus. (p. 180)
—Dinosaurs Then & Wow! Ostrom, Bob, illus. (p. 445)
—Fillmore & Geary Take Off! The Adventures of a Robot Boy & a Boy Boy. Fickling, Phillip, illus. (p. 586)
—Foxy Fox. Chambers, Sally, illus. (p. 626)
—Gorilla Garage Nguyen, Vincent, illus. (p. 703)
—Horsing Around. Nethery, Susan, illus. (p. 801)
—I'll Take a Dozen! Miline, Bill, photos by. (p. 856)
—Mom & Dad Are Palindromes. (p. 1161)
—My Square Breakfast. Miline, Bill, photos by. (p. 1219)
—Scrawl. (p. 1532)
—Shark Attack: Top 10 Attack Sharks. (p. 1562)
—Super Storms That Rocked the World: Hurricanes, Tsunamis, & Other Disasters. (p. 1682)
—There's No Blue on a Bagel. Miline, Bill, photos by. (p. 1731)
—Wicked Weather. (p. 1927)
Shulman, Mark, illus. see Fickling, Phillip.
Shulman, Mark, jt. auth. see De La Hoya, Oscar.
Shulman, Mark, jt. auth. see Heckschler, Melissa.
Shulman, Mark, jt. auth. see McCauley, Adam.
Shulman, Mark & Krog, Hazlitt. Attack of the Killer Video Book: Tips & Tricks for Young Directors. Newbigging, Martha, illus. (p. 113)
Shulman, Mark & Lamison, C. Mayhem Manual. (p. 1113)
Shulman, Mark & Meredith Books Staff. Super Storms That Rocked the World: Hurricanes, Tsunamis, & Other Disasters. (p. 1682)
Shulman, Neil, et al. Germ Patrol: All about Shots for Tots... & Big Kids, Too! (p. 666)
Shulman, Polly. Enthusiasm. (p. 531)
—Grimm Legacy. (p. 724)
—Poe Annex. (p. 1375)
Shulman, Stephanie J. Nose Pickers. (p. 1266)
Shulman, Terrence Daryl. Something for Nothing: Shoplifting Addiction & Recovery. (p. 1610)
Shulte, Sara, illus. see Shulte, Sharon.
Shulte, Sharon. Sandy's Aunt. Shulte, Sara, illus. (p. 1511)
Shults, Anna, ed. see Meyer, Jan.
Shults, Sylvia. Double Double Love & Trouble. (p. 472)
Shultz, Cara Lynn. Dark World. (p. 408)
—Spellbound. (p. 1625)
—Spellcaster. (p. 1625)
Shultz, Carrie. V. I. P. Stepkid. (p. 1829)
Shultz, Charles M. Peanuts Ready-to-Reads Lo Bianco, Nick, illus. (p. 1332)
Shultz, Charles M. & Bailer, Darice. Lose the Blanket, Linus! Lo Bianco, Peter, illus. (p. 1054)
—Make a Trade, Charlie Brown! Lo Bianco, Peter, illus. (p. 1079)
—Snoopy: Flying Ace to the Rescue. Lo Bianco, Peter, illus. (p. 1598)
Shultz, Charles M. & Katschke, Judy. It's a Home Run, Charlie Brown! Lo Bianco, Nick, illus. (p. 895)
—It's Time for School, Charlie Brown. Lo Bianco, Nick, illus. (p. 899)
—Kick the Football, Charlie Brown! (p. 951)
—Lucy's Advice. Lo Bianco, Peter, illus. (p. 1063)
—Take a Hike, Snoopy. (p. 1696)
Shultz, D. B. World Adventures of Sahara the Mummy: The Magical Exploration of Ancient Egypt. (p. 1953)
Shultz, Karl A. St. Joseph Guide to Lectio Divina. (p. 1638)
Shultz, Kirsten, photos by see Beery, Barbara.
Shultz, Lucy, jt. auth. see Schultz, Lucy.
Shulz, Rebecca. Drake the Dragon Boy. (p. 480)
Shum, Chi Wan. SVC Chaos: SNK vs. Capcom. Vol. 3 (p. 1688)
—Svc Chaos: Snk vs. Capcom. Vol. 2 (p. 1688)
Shum, Chi Wan & Chen, Wah. SNK vs. Capcom. (p. 1598)
Shum, Howard M. Gun Fu. (p. 732)
Shumaker, Terence M. Process Pipe Drafting. (p. 1408)
—Process Pipe Drafting Instructor's Guide. (p. 1408)
Shumaker, Terence M. & Madsen, David A. AutoCAD & Its Applications: Basics 2005. (p. 117)
—AutoCad & Its Applications: Basics 2004. (p. 117)
—AutoCAD & Its Applications: Comprehensive 2005. (p. 117)
—AutoCAD & Its Applications: Basics Solution Manual. (p. 117)
—AutoCAD & Its Applications: Advanced Solution Manual, 2000/2000i Edition. (p. 117)
—AutoCad & Its Applications 2009. (p. 117)
—AutoCAD & Its Applications, Advanced 2005. (p. 117)
Shuman, Carol. Jenny Is Scared! When Sad Things Happen in the World. Pillo, Cary, tr. (p. 913)
Shumate, A. M. True-Color Book. (p. 1792)
Shumate, Robert O. Snuffley. Sutherland, Nicholas, illus. (p. 1601)
Shumer, Christine. Can You Find It? Identify & Describe Shapes. (p. 258)
Shumovich, Nadegda, ed. see AZ Books Staff.
Shumovich, Nadezhda, ed. see AZ Books Staff & Evans, Olivia.
Shumovich, Nadezhda, ed. see AZ Books Staff.
Shumsky, Ron, et al. Survival Guide for School Success: Use Your Brain's Built-In Apps to Sharpen Attention, Battle Boredom, & Build Mental Muscle. (p. 1686)
Shumway, Gail. Stripey Follows His Dream. (p. 1667)
Shumway, Lindsey. I Chose You. (p. 837)
Shupe, Bobbi, illus. see Sprick, Marilyn, et al.
Shure, Myrna B. I Can Problem Solve (Kindergarten & Primary Grades) An Interpersonal Cognitive Problem-Solving Program for Children. (p. 836)
—I Can Problem Solve (Preschool) An Interpersonal Cognitive Problem-Solving Program for Children. (p. 836)
Shurei, Kouyu. Alichino. Shurei, Kouyu, illus. (p. 40)
Shurei, Kouyu, illus. see Forbes, Jake T. & Jake, T. F.
Shurin, Masha. Great Time: Children's Poems in Russian & English. Morris, Brian, ed. (p. 718)
Shurtliff, Liesl. Jack: The True Story of Jack & the Beanstalk. (p. 902)
—Rump: The True Story of Rumpelstiltskin. (p. 1495)
Shurtliff, William, illus. see Ahern, Dianne.
Shushushu, Sakurai. Mandayuu & Me. (p. 1087)
Shuster, Joe, jt. creator see Siegel, Jerry.
Shuster, Joe, creator. Superman (p. 1683)
Shuster, Kate, jt. auth. see Meany, John.
Shusterman, Brendan, illus. see Shusterman, Neal.
Shusterman, Danielle, illus. see Cline, Gina.
Shusterman, Neal. Antsy Does Time. (p. 90)
—Bruiser. (p. 232)
—Challenger Deep. Shusterman, Brendan, illus. (p. 289)
—Complete Unwind Dystology: Unwind; Unwholly; Unsouled; Undivided. (p. 353)
—Dark Side of Nowhere. (p. 408)
—Darkness Creeping: Twenty Twisted Tales. (p. 408)
—Downsiders. (p. 474)
—Dread Locks. (p. 482)
—Duckling Ugly. (p. 488)
—Everfound. (p. 542)
—Everlost. (p. 542)
—Everwild. (p. 542)
—Eyes of Kid Midas. (p. 558)
—Full Tilt. (p. 646)
—Red Rider's Hood. (p. 1454)
—Schwa Was Here. (p. 1524)
—Scorpion Shards. (p. 1530)
—Shadow Club Rising. (p. 1557)
—Shattered Sky. (p. 1563)
—Ship Out of Luck. (p. 1567)
—Skinjacker Trilogy: Everlost; Everwild; Everfound. (p. 1585)
—Speeding Bullet. (p. 1624)
—Thief of Souls. (p. 1732)
—UnDivided. (p. 1817)
—UnSouled. (p. 1822)
—Unsouled. (p. 1822)
—UnWholly. (p. 1823)
—Unwind. (p. 1823)
—Unwind. (p. 1824)
Shusterman, Neal & Elfman, Eric. Edison's Alley. (p. 504)
—Tesla's Attic. (p. 1722)
Shute, A. B., illus. see Optic, Oliver, pseud.
Shute, A. B., illus. see Stratemeyer, Edward.
Shute, Henry. Sequil or Things Whitch Aint Finished in The. (p. 1552)
Shute, Henry A. Real Diary of A Real Boy. (p. 1448)
Shute, Henry Augustus. Real Diary of a Real Boy. (p. 1448)
Shute, Linda, illus. see Jones, Rebecca C.
Shute, Nevil. On the Beach. (p. 1289)
Shuter, Jane. Ancient China. (p. 68)
—Ancient Egypt. (p. 68)
—Ancient Egyptians (p. 69)
—Ancient West African Kingdoms (p. 71)
—Aztecs (p. 122)
—How the Ancient Egyptians Lived. (p. 812)
—Incas (p. 868)
—Indus Valley (p. 872)
—Life along the River Nile. (p. 1007)
—Life in a Greek Temple (p. 1010)
—Life in a Greek Trading Port (p. 1010)
—Life in a Medieval Castle (p. 1010)
—Life in Ancient Athens (p. 1010)
—Life on a Viking Ship (p. 1012)
—Maya (p. 1112)
—Middle Ages (p. 1137)
—Renaissance (p. 1460)
—Resistance to the Nazis. (p. 1463)
—Shakespeare & the Theater (p. 1559)
—Shakespeare Today (p. 1559)
—Sumerians (p. 1673)
—Vikings (p. 1842)
Shuter, Jane & Shuter, Paul. Shakespeare Alive (p. 1559)
Shuter, Jane & Taylor, Pat. Renaissance (p. 1460)
Shuter, Paul. William Shakespeare: A Man for All Times (p. 1933)
Shuter, Paul, jt. auth. see Shuter, Jane.
Shutt, Susan R. Four Seasons in the Spring House: Book 1. (p. 625)
Shutt, Vickie Lee. Mountain Mermaid. (p. 1181)
Shuttlewood, Anna, illus. see Lehman-Wilzig, Tami.
Shuttlewood, Craig. Who's in the Tree? And Other Lift-The-Flap Surprises. (p. 1920)
Shuttleworth, Cathie. Children's Treasury of Classic Poetry. (p. 304)
—Classic Collection of Fairy Tales & Poems (p. 328)
—Little Tales for Toddlers: 35 Stories about Adorable Teddy Bears, Puppies & Bunnies. (p. 1037)
Shuttleworth, Cathie, illus. see Baxter, Nicola.
Shuttleworth, Cathie, jt. auth. see Baxter, Nicola.
Shuttleworth, Cathy. Classic Poems for Children: Classic Verse from the Great Poets, Including Lewis Carroll, John Keats & Walt Whitman. (p. 328)
Shuttleworth, Cathy, illus. see Grimm, Jacob & Grimm, Wilhelm.
Shutz, Ashley. Little Ricky Roo. (p. 1035)
Shyam, Bhajju, illus. see Devadasan, Rashmi Ruth.
Shyam, Bhajju. London Jungle Book. (p. 1046)
Shyam, Bhajju, illus. see Wolf, Gita & Anastasio, Andrea.
Shyba, Jessica. Naptime with Theo & Beau. (p. 1229)
Shyu, Theresa. Bilingual Songs - English-Mandarin-Chinese (p. 186)
Shyun, James & Cimino, Michael. Ancient Ways for Modern Times: Paths to Health & Longevity. (p. 71)
SI Artists Staff, illus. see Froeb, Lori C.
SI Artists Staff, illus. see Mitter, Matt & Reader's Digest Editors.
SI Artists Staff, illus. see Packard, Mary.
SI Artists Staff, illus. see Reader's Digest Editors & Mitter, Matt.
SI Artists Staff, illus. see Reader's Digest Editors.
SI Artists Staff, illus. see Rindone, Nancy L.
SI Artists Staff, illus. see Weiss, Ellen.
SI Illustrators, illus. see Schoberle, Cecile.
Sia, Cress. Bamboo Dance. Butler, Lisa, illus. (p. 135)
Sia, Nicole. Finland. (p. 589)
Sia, Nicole & Indovino, Shaina Carmel. Finland. (p. 589)
Siadhail, Michael O. Learning Irish (p. 985)
Siamon, Sharon. Brave Horse (p. 223)
—Coyote Canyon (p. 374)
—Dinosaurs! Battle of the Bones. (p. 444)
—Fire Horse (p. 590)
—Free Horse Vol. 7 (p. 634)
—Haunted Hotel Sleepover (p. 753)
—Heartbreak Hills (p. 760)
—Lost Attic (p. 1055)
—Mystery Stallion (p. 1226)
—Night Horse (p. 1253)
—Rodeo Horse (p. 1484)
—Secrets in the Sand (p. 1544)
—Secrets in the Sand. (p. 1544)
—Shivering Sea (p. 1567)
—Sky Horse (p. 1586)
—Sleepover: Secret Room. (p. 1589)
—Stone Horse (p. 1652)
—Swift Horse (p. 1690)
—Wild Horse (p. 1929)
Sias, Ryan. Sniff! Sniff! (p. 1597)
—Zoe & Robot, Let's Pretend! (p. 1987)
Sias, Ryan, illus. see Blue Apple Staff.
Siau, John, illus. see Harp, Susan.
Siau, Jon, illus. see Harp, Susan.
Sibbett, Ed JR. & Sibbett, Jr., Ed, Ed. Birds GemGlow Stained Glass Coloring Book. (p. 191)
Sibbett, Ed, Jr., et al. 3-D Coloring Book—Merry Christmas. (p. 1991)
—Japanese Prints. (p. 909)
Sibbett, Joyce, jt. auth. see Derrick, Patricia.
Sibbett, Jr., Ed, Ed. Butterfly GemGlow Stained Glass Coloring Book. (p. 247)
Sibbett, Jr., Ed, Ed, jt. auth. see Sibbett, Ed JR.
Sibbick, John. My Favorite Dinosaurs. (p. 1203)
Sibbick, John, illus. see Ashby, Ruth.
Sibert, Stephanie Grace, illus. see Boyce, Catherine & Boyce, Peter.
Sibila, Tom. LeBron James: King of the Court. (p. 987)
—SpaceShipOne: Making Dreams Come True. (p. 1620)
Sibille, Lucinda. Dragon Swirl: Book II. (p. 478)
—Dragon Swirl: Book IV. (p. 478)
—Dragon Swirl: Book III. (p. 478)
—Dragon Swirl: In the Beginning. (p. 478)
Sibley, Linda. David Joins the California Gold Rush. (p. 411)
Sibley, Linda & Marks, Dea. David Takes Part in the Battle of the Alamo. (p. 411)
Sibley, Paul, jt. auth. see Sibley, Paul.
Sibley, Paul & Sibley, Paul. Perry the Great Leaping Bullfrog of Orleans Parish. Righter, Kate, illus. (p. 1344)
Sibley, Steve. Teaching & Assessing Skills in Geography. (p. 1709)
Siburt, Ruth, jt. auth. see Blackwood, Gary L.
Sica, Diane. Adventures of Sammy & Vinney. (p. 22)

Sichel, Harold, illus. see Gates, Josephine Scribner.
Sicinski-Skeans, Sharon. Heath Social Studies Data Disks. (p. 760)
—Write Direction. (p. 1963)
Sicinski-Skeans, Sharon & Baron, Lindamichelle. Big Book & Teacher Resource Guide Package. (p. 178)
—Hardcover Student Book. (p. 748)
—Skills for Super Writers Softcover: Grade 3. (p. 1585)
—Skills for Super Writers Softcover. (p. 1585)
—Skills for Super Writers Softcover Student Book. (p. 1585)
—Skills for Super Writers Softcover Teacher Guide. (p. 1585)
—Teacher Resource Guide. (p. 1709)
—Transparencies. (p. 1779)
—Write Direction: Hardcover Student Book. (p. 1963)
—Write Direction. (p. 1963)
Sickels, Amy. Adrienne Rich. (p. 13)
—African-American Writers. (p. 27)
—Laura Ingalls Wilder. (p. 980)
—Mark Twain. (p. 1095)
—Mythmaker: The Story of J. K. Rowling. (p. 1227)
—Richard Peck. (p. 1469)
—Walter Dean Myers. (p. 1856)
Sickler, Jonas, jt. see Pixton, Kaaren.
Sickler, Jonas & Pixton, Amy. Frere Jacques: Hey Baby! Look Where Jacques is Sleeping—and Dreaming—in Paris! Sickler, Jonas & Pixton, Kaaren, illus. (p. 636)
—Hickory Dickory Dock: Hey Baby! Look at the Mouse that Went up the Clock—Big Ben in London! Pixton, Kaaren, illus. (p. 775)
—Old Macdonald Had a Farm: Hey Baby! Look at These Animals on the Farm—in Bolivia! Pixton, Kaaren, illus. (p. 1284)
Sickman, Kari. Rhyming & Sight Words. (p. 1468)
—Sounds & Letters. (p. 1615)
Sicks, Linda. How Different Is Good: Nick the Wise Old Cat. Messing, Dave, illus. (p. 806)
—Nick the Wise Old Cat: How I Found My Family. Messing, Dave, illus. (p. 1251)
—Nick the Wise Old Cat How I Found My Family. Messing, Dave, illus. (p. 1251)
—Nick's Holiday Celebration: Nick the Wise Old Cat. Messing, Dave, illus. (p. 1251)
Siclari, Theresa. Case of the Missing Hairpin (p. 274)
—Pond Behind Grandmother's House. (p. 1382)
Siculan, Dan, illus. see Hillert, Margaret.
Sid, Fleischman. Whipping Boy. (p. 1912)
Sidaris-Green, Hannah, ed. see Kelso, Brendan P.
Siddall, Ann, jt. auth. see Stuckey, Gary.
Siddall, James W. Weekend Wilderness: A Connoisseur's Guide to Canoe Camping. (p. 1872)
Siddals, Mary McKenna. Compost Stew: An A to Z Recipe for the Earth. Wolff, Ashley, illus. (p. 354)
—Compost Stew: An a to Z Recipe for the Earth. Wolff, Ashley, illus. (p. 354)
—Shivery Shades of Halloween. Pickering, Jimmy, illus. (p. 1567)
Siddell, Thomas. Gunnerkrigg Court - Reason Vol. 3 Siddell, Thomas, illus. (p. 732)
—Orientation Siddell, Thomas, illus. (p. 1303)
—Research Siddell, Thomas, illus. (p. 1462)
Siddiqa, Juma. My Arabic Words Book. (p. 1196)
Siddons, Brian. Crispus Attucks & African American Patriots of the American Revolution. (p. 383)
Siddoway, Ramona. Grit. (p. 724)
—Self-Control. (p. 1549)
Siddoway, Richard M. Cottage Park Puzzle. (p. 369)
Sideman, Jill, intro. Women in Science. (p. 1946)
Sider, Sandra. Handbook to Life in Renaissance Europe. (p. 740)
Sideri, Simona. Let's Look at Eyes. Noble, Sheilagh, illus. (p. 998)
—Let's Look at Mouths. Noble, Sheilagh, illus. (p. 999)
Sideri, Simona, tr. see van Lieshout, Ted.
Siderovski, Susan. Tularemia. Alcamo, I. Edward, ed. (p. 1796)
Sidinger, Jim. Eternal Companions: Faces of the Pere Lachaise, Paris. (p. 539)
Sidman, Joyce. Butterfly Eyes & Other Secrets of the Meadow. Krommes, Beth, illus. (p. 247)
—Dark Emperor & Other Poems of the Night. (p. 407)
—Dark Emperor & Other Poems of the Night. Allen, Rick, illus. (p. 407)
—Red Sings from Treetops: A Year in Colors. (p. 1455)
—Red Sings from Treetops: A Year in Colors. Zagarenski, Pamela, illus. (p. 1455)
—Song of the Water Boatman & Other Pond Poems. Prange, Beckie, illus. (p. 1611)
—Swirl by Swirl: Spirals in Nature. Krommes, Beth, illus. (p. 1691)
—This Is Just to Say: Poems of Apology & Forgiveness. Zagarenski, Pamela, illus. (p. 1736)
—Ubiquitous: Celebrating Nature's Survivors. Prange, Beckie, illus. (p. 1807)
—What the Heart Knows: Chants, Charms, & Blessings. Zagarenski, Pamela, illus. (p. 1893)
Sidney, James, jt. auth. see Sidney, Margaret.
Sidney, Maragret. Five Little Peppers Abroad. (p. 600)
Sidney, Margaret. Adventures of Joel Pepper. (p. 19)
—Five Little Peppers & How They Grew. (p. 600)
—Five Little Peppers & How They Grew. Andreasen, Dan, illus. (p. 600)
—Five Little Peppers at School. (p. 600)
—Five Little Peppers Grown Up. (p. 600)
—Margaret Sidney: Little Peppers. (p. 1092)
—Polly Pepper's Book. (p. 1381)
Sidney, Margaret & Sidney, James. Five Little Peppers & How They Grew. (p. 600)
Sido, Barbi, illus. see Priddy, Roger & Powell, Sarah.
Sidon, Ephraim. Animated Menorah: Travels on a Space Dreidel. Oren, Rony, illus. (p. 84)
Sidwell, Beth. Zack the Zombie. (p. 1984)
Sidwell, Kathy, illus. see Bell, Holly.
Siebel, Fritz, illus. see McClintock, Mike.
Siebel, Fritz, illus. see Parish, Peggy & Parish, Herman.
Siebel, Fritz, illus. see Parish, Peggy.
Siebenmorgan, Toni. St. Joseph's Catholic School Presents. (p. 1638)
Sieber, Antonia, jt. auth. see Barth, Katrin.
Siebert, Anne & Clark, Raymond C. All Around America: The Time Traveler's Talk Show. (p. 43)
—All Around America Activities: The Time Traveler's Talk Show. (p. 43)
Siebert, Diane. Motorcycle Song. Jenkins, Leonard, illus. (p. 1179)
—Spring, Summer, Autumn, Winter. Burckhardt, Marc, illus. (p. 1635)
Siebold, J. Otto, illus. see Wilbur, Richard.
Siebold, Jan. Doing Time Online. (p. 463)
Siebold, Kim, illus. see Sagendorph, Jean.
Siede Preis Photography (Firm) Staff & Brian Warling Photography (Firm) Staff, contrib. by. First Words. (p. 597)
Siedler, Maurya. Ethics of Genetic Engineering. (p. 539)
Sieegenthaler, Pfist, jt. auth. see Siegenthaler, Kathrin.
Siefker, Eunice. Crocodile Song. Grimm, Debi & Eadie, Inger Sommer, illus. (p. 384)
Siegal, Aranka. Grace in the Wilderness: After the Liberation, 1945-1948. (p. 704)
—Upon the Head of the Goat: A Childhood in Hungary, 1939-1944. (p. 1825)
Siegal, Ida. Big News! (p. 182)
Siegel, Adam, ed. see Kaye, Terry, et al.
Siegel, Alexis, tr. see Guibert, Emmanuel & Sfar, Joann.
Siegel, Alexis, tr. see Jolivet, Joelle.
Siegel, Alexis, tr. see Stassen.
Siegel, Alice. Girlwonder: Every Girl's Guide to the Fantastic Feats, Cool Qualities, & Remarkable Abilities of Women & Girls. Hartman, Holly et al, eds. (p. 681)
Siegel, Barbara, jt. auth. see Siegel, Scott.
Siegel, Elizabeth. Dinosaurs. (p. 444)
—Taj. Toye, Derek, illus. (p. 1696)
Siegel, James. Deceit. (p. 421)
—Derailed. (p. 427)
Siegel, Jan. Devil's Apprentice. (p. 432)
Siegel, Jay. Forensic Science at Work. (p. 617)
Siegel, Jay A., ed. see Bauchner, Elizabeth.
Siegel, Jay A., ed. see Esherick, Joan.
Siegel, Jay A., ed. see Ford, Jean.
Siegel, Jay A., ed. see Hunter, William.
Siegel, Jay A., ed. see Libal, Angela.
Siegel, Jay A., ed. see Walker, Maryalice.
Siegel, Jennifer Semple. Are You ever Going to be Thin & Other Stories. (p. 97)
Siegel, Jerry. Superman. Gold, M. & Hill, M., eds. (p. 1683)
—Superman Archives (p. 1683)
—Superman Chronicles (p. 1683)
—Superman Chronicles. (p. 1683)
—World's Finest Comics (p. 1960)
Siegel, Jerry, jt. auth. see Bird, Benjamin.
Siegel, Jerry & Binder, Otto. Supergirl (p. 1683)
Siegel, Jerry & Cameron, Don. Superman Archives. (p. 1683)
—Superman - The Action Comics. (p. 1683)
Siegel, Jerry & Shuster, Joe, creators. Amazing Transformation of Jimmy Olsen. (p. 56)
—Daily Planet. (p. 400)
—Superman. (p. 1683)
Siegel, Jerry, et al. Superman: The Action Comics Archives. Vol. 5 (p. 1683)
Siegel, Katy & Heiser, Jorg, contrib. by. Dana Schutz: Paintings 2002-2005 (p. 402)
Siegel, Mark, illus. see Messner, Kate.
Siegel, Mark, illus. see Siegel, Siena Cherson.
Siegel, Mark, illus. see Simon, Tanya & Simon, Richard.
Siegel, Mark, illus. see Wheeler, Lisa.
Siegel, Mark, jt. auth. see Rylant, Cynthia.
Siegel, Melanie, illus. see Dyer, Wayne W. & Tracy, Kristina.
Siegel, Melanie, illus. see Horton, Joan.
Siegel, Melanie, illus. see Ingalls, Ann.
Siegel, Melanie, tr. see Horton, Joan.
Siegel, Pete. Light Switch to Heaven. (p. 1015)
Siegel, Philip. Break-Up Artist. (p. 224)
Siegel, R. V. Seagull & the Starfish. (p. 1536)
—Son of Olympia. (p. 1611)
Siegel, Randy. My Snake Blake. Bloch, Serge, illus. (p. 1219)
Siegel, Rv. Bee Called Kangaroo. (p. 157)
Siegel, Scott & Siegel, Barbara. Encyclopedia of Hollywood. (p. 525)
Siegel, Siena Cherson. To Dance: A Ballerina's Graphic Novel. Siegel, Mark, illus. (p. 1758)
Siegel, Terri. Goodnight Princess Scharazad. (p. 701)
Siegel, William, illus. see McNeely, Marian Hurd.
Siegen-Smith, Nikki, ed. Songs for Survival: Songs & Chants from Tribal Peoples Around the World. Lodge, Bernard, illus. (p. 1612)
Siegenthaler, Kathrin & Sieegenthaler, Pfist. Hopper's Easter Surprise. Pfister, Marcus, illus. (p. 797)
Siegfried Holtz, Eric & Barenblat, Rachel. Texas. (p. 1724)
Siegman, Greg Forbes, jt. auth. see Paxson, Jillip Naysinthe.
Siegman, Greg Forbes, jt. auth. see Rozelle, Catheryne Izeklow.
Siegrist, Bonnie. Little Farm down the Lane -Book IV. (p. 1027)
Siegrist, Bonnie Bedi. Little Farm down the Lane Book V. (p. 1027)
Siegrist, Vicky. Our Magical House. (p. 1309)
Siegrist, Wes, illus. see Costello, Emily.
Sieling, Peter. Folk Medicine. (p. 611)
—Folk Music. (p. 611)
—Folk Songs. (p. 611)
—Growing up on a Farm: Responsibilities & Issues. (p. 727)
Siemasz, Greg. Hockey (p. 786)
Siembieda, Kevin. Heroes Unlimited. Marciniszyn, Alex, ed. (p. 773)
—Rifts Adventure Guide. Breaux, Wayne, Jr. et al, illus. (p. 1471)
—Rifts Book of Magic. (p. 1471)
—Rifts Game Master Guide. (p. 1471)
Siembieda, Kevin & Coffin, Bill. Rifts Coalition Wars: Cyber-Knights Vol. 4 (p. 1471)
Siemens, Cindy Louetta. Adventures of Mr Grizz. (p. 20)
Siemens, Jared. City. (p. 323)
—Doctors. (p. 459)
—Firefighters. (p. 591)
—Librarians. (p. 1005)
—Police Officers. (p. 1380)
—Teachers. (p. 1709)
—Veterinarians. (p. 1839)
Siemens, Mary, tr. see Football, Virginia & Mantla, Rosa.
Siemers, Robert, jt. auth. see Blay, Chuck.
Siems, Dorthy R. Fairy's Wings: Set 1. (p. 565)
Siems, Thomas F. Dangerous Pet. (p. 404)
Siemsen, Nancy. Girl Who Loved Jupiter. (p. 679)
Sienkewicz, Thomas J., ed. see Salem Press Staff.
Sienkiewicz, Bill, illus. see Mack, David.
Sienkiewicz, Henryk. Quo Vadis: A Narrative of the Time of Nero. (p. 1429)
Sieplinga, Drew. Paint Your Own Piggy Bank. (p. 1318)
Sierra, Donn. Candin Book 2: The Visitors. (p. 261)
Sierra, Holly, illus. see Hiris, Monica.
Sierra, Holly, illus. see Sweet, J. H.
Sierra, Holly, illus. see Sweet, J. H., et al.
Sierra i Fabra, Jordi. Asombrosa Historia del Viajero de las Estrellas. (p. 107)
—Aydin. (p. 121)
—Disco Magico. (p. 447)
—Guardian de la Luna. Núñez, Pablo, tr. (p. 728)
—John Lennon - Imagina que esto fue Real. (p. 922)
—Kafka y la Muneca Viajera. Montserratt, Pep, illus. (p. 941)
—Martes XXIII. (p. 1097)
—Nave Fantastica. (p. 1237)
—Nino Que Vivia en las Estrellas. (p. 1257)
—Niño Que Vivía en Las Estrellas. (p. 1257)
Sierra i Fabra, Jordi. Sala de Conflictos. (p. 1504)
Sierra i Fabra, Jordi, jt. auth. see Sierra i Fabra, Jordi.
Sierra i Fabra, Jordi, jt. auth. see Sierra I. Fabra, Jordi.
Sierra i Fabra, Jordi, jt. auth. see Sierra I. Fabra, Jordi.
Sierra I. Fabra, Jordi & Sierra i Fabra, Jordi. Hombre Que Perdió Su Imagen. Cañas, Alicia, tr. (p. 791)
—¡¡¡Lambertooo!!! Serrano, Javier, tr. (p. 972)
Sierra i Fabra, Jordi & Sierra i Fabra, Jordi. Fabrica de Nubes. (p. 559)
Sierra, Juan, illus. see Arciniegas, Triunfo.
Sierra, Juan Ramon, illus. see Bastidas Padilla, Carlos.
Sierra, Juan Ramon, illus. see Nino, Jairo Anibal.
Sierra, Judy. Antarctic Antics: A Book of Penguin Poems. Aruego, Jose & Dewey, Ariane, illus. (p. 88)
—Ballyhoo Bay. Anderson, Derek, illus. (p. 135)
—Beautiful Butterfly: A Folktale from Spain. Chess, Victoria, illus. (p. 153)
—Born to Read. Brown, Marc, illus. (p. 214)
—Gruesome Guide to World Monsters. Drescher, Henrik, illus. (p. 727)
—Mind Your Manners, B. B. Wolf. (p. 1145)
—Mind Your Manners, B. B. Wolf. Seibold, J. Otto, illus. (p. 1145)
—Never Kick a Ghost & Other Silly Chillers. Constantin, Pascale, illus. (p. 1243)
—Secret Science Project That Almost Ate the School. Gammell, Stephen, illus. (p. 1543)
—Sleepy Little Alphabet: A Bedtime Story from Alphabet Town. Sweet, Melissa, illus. (p. 1590)
—Suppose You Meet a Dinosaur: A First Book of Manners. Bowers, Tim, illus. (p. 1684)
—Tell the Truth, B. B. Wolf. Seibold, J. Otto, illus. (p. 1717)
—Thelonius Monster's Sky-High Fly Pie. (p. 1728)
—We Love Our School! A Read-Together Rebus Story. Davick, Linda, illus. (p. 1867)
—What Time Is It, Mr. Crocodile? Cushman, Doug, illus. (p. 1894)
—Wild about Books. Brown, Marc, tr. (p. 1928)
—Wild about You! Brown, Marc, illus. (p. 1928)
—ZooZical. Brown, Marc, illus. (p. 1990)
Sierra, JulieAnn. Legacy & the Dark Prince (p. 987)
Sierra Martinez, Martha. Eva's Two Houses. (p. 541)
Sierra, Sergio A. & Shelley, Mary. Frankenstein by Mary Shelley. Ribas, Meritxell, illus. (p. 629)
Siesel, Barbara, jt. auth. see Torgan, Keith.
Sieveking, Anthea, photos by see Buczacki, Stefan & Buczacki, Beverley.
Sieveking, Anthea, photos by see Buczacki, Stefan & Buczacki, Beverly.
Sievers, Lee, illus. see Follett, Ross C.
Sievert, Antonio R. Across the Seas. (p. 9)
Sievert, Claus, illus. see Tolstoy, Leo & Riordan, James.
Sievert, Jean & Cloninger, Shirley. Gabriel the Gordian Angel. (p. 652)
Sievert, Terri. Dirt Bike History (p. 446)
—Forecasting Weather (p. 617)
—Loch Ness Monster (p. 1044)
—Motocross Racing (p. 1179)
—Prairie Plants (p. 1392)
—Travis Pastrana: Motocross Legend (p. 1781)
—UFOs (p. 1807)
—Unsolved Mystery of the Loch Ness Monster (p. 1822)
—Unsolved Mystery of UFOs (p. 1822)
—Valentine's Day: A Day of Friendship & Love (p. 1830)
Sievert, Terri, jt. auth. see Dougherty, Terri.
Sievert, Terri & Dougherty, Terri. Illinois. (p. 857)
—Texas. (p. 1724)
—Wind Williams, Ted, illus. (p. 1935)
Siewart, Pauline. Look What I Can Do! (p. 1050)
—Look What I Can Make! (p. 1050)
—Look What I Can Play! (p. 1050)
—See What I Can Do! (p. 1547)
—See What I Can Make! (p. 1547)
—See What I Can Play! (p. 1547)
Siewart, Pauline, illus. see Baxter, Nicola.
Sieweke, Susan. Annie Nell Meets the Sock Gnomes. (p. 87)
—Spirit of Hope. (p. 1628)
Siewert, Pauline. It's Valentine's Day! A Valentine Book & Activity Kit. (p. 899)
Siewert, Pauline, illus. see Adams, Michelle Medlock.
Siewert, Pauline, illus. see David, Juliet.
Siewert, Pauline, illus. see Pierpont, James Lord.
Siewert, Pauline, jt. auth. see Baxter, Nicola.
Sif, Birgitta. Frances Dean Who Loved to Dance & Dance. Sif, Birgitta, illus. (p. 627)
—Oliver. Sif, Birgitta, illus. (p. 1285)
Sif, Birgitta, illus. see Potter, Alicia.
Sif, Birgitta, jt. auth. see Monroe, Sue.
Sifakis, Carl. Mafia Encyclopedia. (p. 1071)
Sigafoose, Dick & Sigafoose, Richard. American Art Pottery. (p. 59)
Sigafoose, Richard, jt. auth. see Sigafoose, Dick.
Sigafus, Kim & Ernst, Lyle. Native Writers-Voices of Power (p. 1235)
Sigal, Maxine Handelman. Shabbat Angels. Rothenberg, Joani, illus. (p. 1556)
Sigersmith, L. J. Looking a Little Closer at Things. (p. 1050)
Siggins, Gerard. Rugby Warrior: Back in School. Back in Sport. Back in Time. (p. 1494)
Siglain, Michael. Breakout! Marvel Illustrators, illus. (p. 225)
—Captain America: The Winter Soldier 8X8. (p. 263)
—Captain America - The Winter Soldier: Rescue at Sea. (p. 263)
—Thor: The Dark World Junior Novel. (p. 1739)
Siglain, Michael, jt. auth. see Disney Book Group Staff.
Siglain, Michael, jt. auth. see Thomas, Rich, Jr.
Sigmar Staff. Sinonimos - Ant - Paraonimos (Synonyms - Ant - Homonyms) (p. 1580)
Sigmon, Cheryl, jt. auth. see Ford, Sylvia.
Sigmon-Heck, Christina. Birthday Wish. (p. 193)
—Smile for Only You! (p. 1594)
Sign2Me, creator. Pick Me up! (Music & ASL) Fun Songs for Learning Signs. (p. 1354)
Signer, Billie Touchstone. Ozarks with a Dog Named Bo. (p. 1316)
Signor, Priscilla M. Adventures of Hooch & Mile-A-Minute-Freebee: Buehrle, Jacquelyn, illus. (p. 18)
Signor Sr., S. Ernest. Book of David: Volume One. (p. 211)
—Book of Esther. (p. 211)
—Book of Ruth. (p. 211)
Signore, Marco. Giant vs. Giant: Argentinosaurus & Giganotosaurus. Bacchin, Matteo, illus. (p. 674)
—Growing up in the Cretaceous: Scipionyx. Bacchin, Matteo, illus. (p. 726)
—Hunting Pack: Allosaurus. Bacchin, Matteo, illus. (p. 829)
—T. Rex & the Great Extinction. Bacchin, Matteo, illus. (p. 1694)
Signore, Marco, jt. auth. see Bacchin, Matteo.
Signoretti, Brenda. Freddie the Frog & Friends. REVILLE, TONI-ANN, illus. (p. 632)
Signorino, John. Billy & the Aliens of Alpha-C (p. 187)
Signorino, Slug. I Know an Old Lady Who Swallowed a Fly: A Traditional Rhyme. (p. 840)
Sigurdsson, Rev. Rupert. Lifetime of Pets (p. 1014)
Siivola, Liz. Little Mouse Finds a New Home. DuPont, Brittany, illus. (p. 1032)
Sijercic, Hedina. Unusual Family: A Romani Folktale. Greven, Doris, illus. (p. 1823)
Sikes, Richard. Laughing with Uncle Adolph. (p. 980)
Sikora, Frank & Batcheler, Michelle. Frank M. Johnson, Jr. Courageous Judge. (p. 628)
Sikorski, Lorna D. Consonant Variations of American English (p. 359)
—Intonation Patterns of American English CD Series (p. 881)
—Vowel System of American English (p. 1850)
—Vowel System of American English CD Series (p. 1850)
Sikorski, Lorna D., jt. auth. see Feinstein-Whittaker, Marjorie.
Sikorskyj, Jerod, jt. ed. see Senchyne, Jonathan.
Sikoryak, Bob, illus. see Sturm, James.
Siks, Geraldine B. Ali Baba & the Forty Thieves. (p. 39)
Siku, illus. see Burne, Cristy.
Silas, Elizabeth & Goodney, Diane. Yoga. (p. 1972)
Silas, Steve. Where Do Bubbles Go? (p. 1906)
Silas, Thony, illus. see Slott, Dan & Caselli, Stefano.
Silate, Jennifer. American Flag. (p. 60)
—Bald Eagle. (p. 133)
—Betsy Ross: Creator of the American Flag. (p. 172)
—Betsy Ross: Creadora de la bandera Estadounidense. (p. 172)
—Betsy Ross: Creator of the American Flag / Creadora de la bandera Estadounidense. (p. 172)
—Betsy Ross: Creadora de la bandera estadounidense (Betsy Ross: Creator of the American Flag) (p. 172)
—Betsy Ross. (p. 172)
—Calhoun-Randolph Debate on the Eve of the War of 1812: A Primary Source Investigation. (p. 253)
—Language Development Writing Process. (p. 975)
—Last Stand: The Final Military Campaign of General George Armstrong Custer. (p. 978)
—Liberty Bell. (p. 1005)
—Little Sure Shot: Annie Oakley & Buffalo Bill's Wild West Show. (p. 1037)
—Planning & Preparing Healthy Meals & Snacks: A Day-to-Day Guide to a Healthier Diet. (p. 1368)
—Seeing the Future: The Final Vision of Sitting Bull. (p. 1548)
—Statue of Liberty. (p. 1645)
—Terrorist Attack: True Stories of Survival. (p. 1722)
—United States Capitol. (p. 1819)
—White House. (p. 1913)
—Your Mayor: Local Government in Action. (p. 1981)
Silbaugh, Michael John. Crosseyed Puzzle. (p. 385)
Silber, Jere. Tree Story. (p. 1783)
Silber, Lee. Organizing from the Right Side of the Brain: A Creative Approach to Getting Organized. (p. 1303)
Silber, Sherman J. How to Get Pregnant. (p. 820)
Silberberg, Alan. Awesome, Almost 100% True Adventures of Matt & Craz. Silberberg, Alan, illus. (p. 120)
—Milo: Sticky Notes & Brain Freeze. Silberberg, Alan, illus. (p. 1144)
Silberg, Jackie. Trescientos Juegos de 3 Minutos. (p. 1784)
Silbering, Shelly. Killer! Deadly Insects & Spiders. (p. 956)
Silberman, Dani. Three Monkey Brothers. (p. 1743)
Silbermintz, Marvin, jt. auth. see Fuhrer, David.

Silberstein, James. Night Crystal Mcgoober Had Seven Heads. (p. 1253)
Silbert, Jack. Honest Abe's Funny Money Book. (p. 794)
Silbert, Jack, jt. auth. see D'Agnese, Joseph.
Silbey, Robyn. Math Hooks. (p. 1106)
Silcox, Beth Douglass. Little Rumely Man. Peters, Darcy, illus. (p. 1036)
Silcox, Diane. Light to Keep. Moates, Carol Meetze, illus. (p. 1015)
Sileo, Frank J. Don't Put Yourself down in Circus Town: A Story about Self-Confidence. Cornelison, Sue, illus. (p. 468)
—Sally Sore Loser: A Story about Winning & Losing. Pillo, Cary, illus. (p. 1505)
Siler, D. Danger Cave. (p. 403)
Silin-Palmer, Pamela, illus. see Loehr, Mallory.
Silivanch, Annalise. Career as a Teacher. (p. 266)
—Making the Right College Choice: Technical, 2 Year, 4 Year. (p. 1082)
—Rebuilding America's Infrastructure. (p. 1451)
Silk, Courtney. Barbie - From the Heart. Duarte, Pamela, illus. (p. 138)
Silk, Max V. Whiskers. Hirsch, Kerry, illus. (p. 1912)
Silkman, Anne. Country Songbird. Doghouse Press Inc. Staff, ed. (p. 372)
Sill, Cathryn. About Amphibians: A Guide for Children Sill, John, illus. (p. 5)
—About Arachnids: A Guide for Children Sill, John, illus. (p. 5)
—About Birds: A Guide for Children Sill, John, illus. (p. 5)
—About Birds: A Guide for Children / Sobre Los Pajaros: una Guia para Niños Sill, John, illus. (p. 5)
—About Birds. (p. 5)
—About Crustaceans: A Guide for Children Sill, John, illus. (p. 5)
—About Crustaceans: A Guide for Children Sill, John & Sill, John, illus. (p. 5)
—About Fish: A Guide for Children Sill, John, illus. (p. 5)
—About Habitats: Polar Regions Sill, John, illus. (p. 5)
—About Habitats: Deserts. Sill, John, illus. (p. 5)
—About Habitats-Deserts Sill, John, illus. (p. 5)
—About Habitats-Oceans Sill, John, illus. (p. 5)
—About Habitats-Wetlands Sill, John, illus. (p. 5)
—About Hummingbirds: A Guide for Children Sill, John, illus. (p. 6)
—About Insects: A Guide for Children Sill, John, illus. (p. 6)
—About Insects. (p. 6)
—About Insects / Sobre Los Insectos: A Guide for Children / una Guia para Niños Sill, John, illus. (p. 6)
—About Mammals: A Guide for Children Sill, John, illus. (p. 6)
—About Marsupials: A Guide for Children Sill, John, illus. (p. 6)
—About Mollusks: A Guide for Children Sill, John, illus. (p. 6)
—About Penguins: a Guide for Children: A Guide for Children Sill, John, illus. (p. 6)
—About Raptors: A Guide for Children Sill, John, illus. (p. 6)
—Wetlands Sill, John, illus. (p. 1877)
Sill, Cathryn, jt. auth. see Batten, Mary.
Sill, Cathryn, jt. auth. see Sill, Cathryn P.
Sill, Cathryn, jt. auth. see Sill, John.
Sill, Cathryn & Sill, John. About Rodents: A Guide for Children (p. 6)
Sill, Cathryn P. About Habitats-Grasslands Sill, John, illus. (p. 5)
—About Penguins: A Guide for Children Sill, John, illus. (p. 6)
Sill, Cathryn P., illus. see Torre, Cristina de la.
Sill, Cathryn P., jt. auth. see Sill, Cathryn P.
Sill, Cathryn P. & Sill, Cathryn. About Reptiles: A Guide for Children Sill, John, illus. (p. 6)
Sill, Cathryn P. & Sill, Cathryn P. About Habitats-Mountains Sill, John & Sill, John, illus. (p. 5)
Sill, Cathryn P. & Sill, John. About Hummingbirds Sill, Cathryn P. & Sill, John, illus. (p. 6)
Sill, Cathryn P., et al. About Arachnids: A Guide for Children Sill, Cathryn P. & Sill, John, illus. (p. 5)
Sill, John, illus. see Alden, Peter C. & Peterson, Roger Tory.
Sill, John, illus. see Batten, Mary & Sill, Cathryn.
Sill, John, illus. see Sill, Cathryn P.
Sill, John, illus. see Sill, Cathryn P. & Sill, Cathryn P.
Sill, John, illus. see Sill, Cathryn P. & Sill, Cathryn.
Sill, John, illus. see Sill, Cathryn P., et al.
Sill, John, illus. see Sill, Cathryn.
Sill, John, illus. see Torre, Cristina de la.
Sill, John, jt. auth. see Sill, Cathryn P.
Sill, John, jt. auth. see Sill, Cathryn.
Sill, John & Sill, Cathryn. About Mollusks: A Guide for Children Sill, John, illus. (p. 6)
Siller, Dianne. Driver Billy & Amazing Grace, the Tanker Truck. (p. 485)
Siller, Germin, illus. see Fuentes, Claudia Luna & Fuente, Claudia Luna.
Sillet, Helen. Awesome Power of Volcanoes & Earthquakes. (p. 121)
—Understanding Volcanoes & Earthquakes. (p. 1816)
Sillett, Helen. Whatever It Takes: The Lance Armstrong Story. (p. 1896)
Sillifant, Alec. Farmer Ham. Spoor, Mike, illus. (p. 574)
Silliman, Elaine R., jt. ed. see Mody, Maria.
Silliman, Elaine R. & Wilkinson, Louise C., eds. Language & Literacy Learning in Schools. (p. 974)
Silliman, Lee, ed. see Clawson, Calvin C.
Silliman, Ron. Under Albany. (p. 1813)
Sills, Elizabeth & Patrice, Elena. Nana Star. Saker, Linda, illus. (p. 1228)
—Nana Star & the Moonman. Saker, Linda, illus. (p. 1228)
Sills, Karen, jt. auth. see Sills, Kathy.
Sills, Kathy & Sills, Karen. Feelings, Feelings, Feelings. (p. 580)
Sills, Leslie. From Rags to Riches: A History of Girls' Clothing in America. (p. 643)
—In Real Life: Stories about Women Photographers. (p. 864)
—In Real Life: Six Women Photographers. Cunningham, Imogen et al, photos by. (p. 864)
Silman, Roberta. Astronomers & Los Astrónomos: 6 English, 6 Spanish Adaptations (p. 109)
—Los Astrónomos: Set Of 6. (p. 1053)
Silsbe, Brenda. Bears We Know. van Kampen, Vlasta, illus. (p. 152)
Siltman, Mike L. Hoodles. (p. 795)
Silva, Abbey. She Came to Heal. (p. 1564)
Silva, Amanda. Day That Jack Became a Jack O'Lantern. (p. 414)
Silva, Angel R. Morenit. (p. 1175)
Silva, Augusto Alves da, illus. see MacCracken, Joan.
Silva, Carlos. Diario de Fernando. (p. 434)
Silva, Daniel. Prince of Fire. (p. 1401)
Silva, David, illus. see Flor Ada, Alma.
Silva, Eliseo Art, illus. see Montoya, Carina Monica.
Silva, Erika, illus. see Close, Rosa.
Silva Escalera, Manuel. Ale y Su Estrellit. (p. 35)
Silva, Gabriel, adapted by. HERACLES -Doce años tras la Inmortalidad. (p. 769)
—POSIDÓN -el dios del Mar- (p. 1387)
—ZEUS -el padre de los Dioses. (p. 1986)
Silva, Jose Asuncion. Aserrin Aserran. (p. 105)
—Poemas y Prosas. (p. 1376)
Silva, Kenny. Card. (p. 265)
Silva Lee, Alfonso. Mi Isla y Yo: La Naturaleza de Cuba. Hayskar, Bonnie J., ed. (p. 1132)
—Mi Isla y Yo: La Naturaleza de Puerto Rico. Hayskar, Bonnie J., ed. (p. 1132)
—Mi Isla y Yo: La Naturaleza de Republica Dominicana. Hayskar, Bonnie J., ed. (p. 1132)
—Mi isla y yo/My Island & I: La naturaleza de Puerto Rico/The Nature of Puerto Rico. Hayskar, Bonnie J., ed. (p. 1132)
—Mon Ile et Moi: La Nature d'Haiti: Lanati an Ayti: Peyrn Avern. Hayskar, Bonnie, ed. (p. 1163)
—My Island & I: The Nature of the Caribbean. Hayskar, Bonnie J., ed. (p. 1211)
Silva, Linda Kay. Just Killing Time. (p. 939)
Silva, Luna. Pescado en la Olla! Landinez, Jairo Linares, illus. (p. 1345)
Silva, Patricia. Modern Times. Baldanzi, Alessandro, illus. (p. 1159)
—Reading & Writing Today. Baldanzi, Alessandro, illus. (p. 1445)
Silva, Paula M. Ice Cream Dream. (p. 850)
Silva, Simon, illus. see Jiménez, Francisco.
Silva, Tom, illus. see Hahn, Beverly.
Silva Vallejo, Fabio. Mitos y Leyendas Colombianos. Panamericana Staff, ed. (p. 1156)
Silva-Barbeau, Irma. Crown on Her Head. (p. 386)
Silvani, James. Draw-A-Saurus: Everything You Need to Know to Draw Your Favorite Dinosaurs. (p. 480)
Silvani, James, jt. auth. see Petrucha, Stefan.
Silvano, Wendi. Just One More. Gamboa, Ricardo, illus. (p. 939)
—Turkey Trouble (p. 1797)
—What Does the Wind Say? Delehanty, Joan M., illus. (p. 1884)
Silvano, Wendi J. Turkey Claus Harper, Lee, illus. (p. 1797)
Silveira, Terri & Combs, Sharon. Puppy Pen Pals. (p. 1418)
Silver, Alex, et al. Our Mom Is Getting Better. (p. 1309)
Silver, Annira, tr. see Parkkola, Seita.
Silver, Charlotte. Summer Invitation. (p. 1674)
Silver, Connie. Story Book for Beginning Readers. (p. 1656)
Silver Dolphin Books, Silver Dolphin, ed. see Ahmed, Suhel.
Silver Dolphin en Español Editors. Amigos del Mar. (p. 65)
—Dia con los Dinosaurios. (p. 433)
—Dia en la Granja. (p. 433)
—Dinosaurios. (p. 443)
—Disney Animales Cine en Casa. (p. 451)
—Disney Princesa Cine en Casa. (p. 452)
—Disney Serie Aprendizaje: Disney Learn to Count. (p. 453)
—Disney Serie Aprendizaje: Disney Princesses Learn to Write. (p. 453)
—Disney Serie Aprendizaje: Disney Winnie the Pooh Learning Shapes. (p. 453)
—Disney Tesoro de libros de Calcomanias: Disney Sticker Book Treasury, Spanish-Language Edition. (p. 453)
—Fairies Forever Imanes Magicos. (p. 563)
—Figuras Magicas: Disney Magical Magnets. (p. 586)
—Figuras Magicas: Disney Princesses Magical Magnets. (p. 586)
—Figuras Magicas: Disney Winnie the Pooh Magical Magnets. (p. 586)
—Girlfriends Imanes Magicos. (p. 679)
—Libro de actividades con plantillas: Disney Animales: Animals Stencil. (p. 1006)
—Llegs la hora del baile: Time for the Ball, Spanish-Language Edition. (p. 1043)
—Magical Magnets: Pixar. (p. 1074)
—Magical Magnets: Chicken Little. (p. 1074)
—Mi Pequeno Pony Dibuja con los Ponys. (p. 1133)
—Mi Pequeno Pony Figuras Magicas: Las Maravillosas Estaciones. (p. 1133)
Silver Dolphin en Espanol Editors. Mundo a Mi Alrededor: El Oceano. Zaidi, Nadeem, illus. (p. 1191)
Silver Dolphin en Español Editors. Seqorita Cmrculo: Miss Circle, Spanish-Language Edition. (p. 1551)
—Serie Aprendizaje: Drawing with Fairies. (p. 1552)
—Serie Aprendizaje: Let's Draw with Pixar. (p. 1552)
—Tesoro de Libros de Calcomanias Princesas. (p. 1722)
—Tesoros para llevar Disney: Disney Princess CarryAlong Treasury, Spanish-Language Edition. (p. 1722)
—Todo Sobre los Perros: Libro Interactivo con Marioneta. (p. 1761)
—Tonka Vehiculos Robustos y Sensacionales. (p. 1765)
Silver Dolphin en Español Editors, creator. Felices para Siempre/Happily Ever After. (p. 581)
Silver Dolphin en Español Staff. Disney Tesoro de Libros de Calcomanias, Volume 6 (p. 453)
—Figuras magicas: Cars: Magical Magnets: Cars, Spanish-Language Edition. (p. 586)
Silver Dolphin en Español Staff, creator. Aprende con Tus Amigas. (p. 93)
—Baile de las Princesas. (p. 132)
—Bichos y Mas. (p. 177)
—Camiones a la Obra! (p. 256)
—Caritas Felices. (p. 269)
—Disney Favoritos 2: Libro de Actividades con Plantillas. (p. 451)
—Disney Princesa Libro de Actividades con Plantillas. (p. 452)
—Gusto. (p. 733)
—Mickey Mouse: Tesoros para Llevar: Una Coleccion de Cuentos Adaptada de los Dibujos Animados Clasicos de Mickey. (p. 1136)
—Mis Figuras Geometricas. (p. 1150)
—Mis Figuras Geometricas, Srita Estrella. (p. 1150)
—Musica en Casa Libro de Cuentos. (p. 1194)
—Olfato. (p. 1285)
—Vista. (p. 1846)
Silver Dolphin en Español Staff, ed. Cine en casa: Cars: Movie Theater: Cars. (p. 321)
Silver Dolphin Staff. Cuerpo humano/Human Body. (p. 390)
Silver Dolphin Staff, creator. Disney Caritas Felices: Dumbo. (p. 451)
Silver, Donald, jt. auth. see Wynne, Patricia J.
Silver, Donald & Wynne, Patricia J. Geographic Terms: 15 Engaging Mini-Books That Students Read-And Interact With-To Really Learn about Key Landforms. (p. 662)
Silver, Donald M., jt. auth. see Wynne, Patricia J.
Silver, Donald M. & Wynne, Patricia J. Adorable Wearables That Teach about the Human Body: Reproducible Patterns for Hear Muffs, Vision Goggles, & Other Easy-to-Make Paper Projects That Kids Can Wear. (p. 13)
—Body Book: Easy-To-Make Hands-on Models That Teach. (p. 207)
—Interactive 3-D Maps - American History: Easy-to-Assemble 3-D Maps That Students Make & Manipulate to Learn Key Facts & Concepts - In a Kinesthetic Way! (p. 879)
—Interactive Science Wheels: Reproducible, Easy-To-Make Manipulatives That Teach about Life Cycles, Animals, Plants, Weather, Space, & More. (p. 879)
—Northeast Indians: Reproducible Models That Help Students Build Content Area Knowledge & Vocabulary & Learn about the Traditional Life of Native American Peoples. (p. 1265)
Silver Dragon Books Staff & Edmund, Neo. Jump Start. (p. 934)
Silver, Emily, et al. Our Dad Is Getting Better. (p. 1308)
Silver, Eve. Crash. (p. 376)
—Rush. (p. 1497)
Silver, Gail. Anh's Anger. Kromer, Christiane, illus. (p. 76)
—Anh's Anger. Krömer, Christiane, illus. (p. 76)
—Peace, Bugs, & Understanding: An Adventure in Sibling Harmony. Ly, Youme Nguy?n, illus. (p. 1331)
—Steps & Stones: An Anh's Anger Story. Krömer, Christiane, illus. (p. 1648)
Silver, Ivy. Dragon's Apple-Picking Day. (p. 479)
—Dragon's Easter Egg Hunt. (p. 479)
Silver, Ivy & Scholastic, Inc. Staff. Lights, Camera, Action Chuggerl, Level 1. (p. 1016)
Silver, Jago. Mr. Aesop's Story Shop. (p. 1184)
Silver, Jago, illus. see Balsley, Tilda.
Silver, Jane, illus. see Matsakis, Cynthia.
Silver, Joanne, jt. auth. see Herbert, Denis.
Silver, Joanne S., ed. see Herbert, Denis.
Silver, Joanne S., tr. see Idrac, Armand.
Silver, Maggie, illus. see Helbrough, Emma.
Silver, Marc, jt. auth. see Silver, Maya.
Silver, Maya & Silver, Marc. My Parent Has Cancer & It Really Sucks. (p. 1216)
Silver Moon Press Staff, ed. Family Ties Set (p. 568)
Silver, Pattie. Kitty's Barn. (p. 963)
Silver Phoenix Staff & Pon, Cindy. Fury of the Phoenix. (p. 650)
Silver, Rhonda Graff. First Graphic Organizers: Reading - 30 Reproducible Graphic Organizers That Build Early Reading & Comprehension Skills. (p. 595)
—Graphic Organizer Booklets for Reading Response: Guided Response Packets for Any Fiction or Nonfiction Book That Boost Students' Comprehension - And Help You Manage Independent Reading. (p. 711)
Silver, Ruth. Aberrant. (p. 5)
—Isaura. (p. 891)
Silver, Shana & Shane, Rachel. Alice in Wonderland High. (p. 39)
Silver, Sheree. Voice from Heaven. (p. 1848)
Silver, Tony. What's the Big Idea? The Story of Thomas Edison. (p. 1899)
Silvera, Adam. More Happy Than Not. (p. 1174)
Silvera, Elvia. Candida. Peli, Peli, illus. (p. 261)
Silverberg, Beth. Adventures of Mattie Mae: Life Lessons Through the Eyes of A Puppy. (p. 20)
Silverberg, Cory. Sex Is a Funny Word: A Book about Bodies, Relationships, & YOU. Smyth, Fiona, illus. (p. 1556)
—What Makes a Baby. Smyth, Fiona, illus. (p. 1892)
Silverberg, Larry. 7 Simple Truths of Acting for the Teen Actor. (p. 1993)
Silverberg, Robert A. Treasures Beneath the Sea. (p. 1782)
Silverberg, Selma Kritzer. Naomi's Song. (p. 1229)
Silverberg-Kiss, Esti, illus. see Biers-Ariel, Matt.
Silverberry, A. R. Wyndano's Cloak. (p. 1966)
Silverhardt, Lauryn. Dia en la Playa. Ziegler, Argentina Palacios, tr. (p. 433)
—Happy Easter, Sprinkles! Kanemoto, Dan, illus. (p. 745)
—OLIVIA Blasts Off! Wolek, Guy, illus. (p. 1286)
—SpongeBob SpookyPants. Style Guide Staff, illus. (p. 1630)
—Surprise Party. Yee, Josie, illus. (p. 1686)
Silverhardt, Lauryn, jt. auth. see Beinstein, Phoebe.
Silverhardt, Lauryn, jt. auth. see Tuchman, Lauryn.
Silveria, Gordon, illus. see Burns, Marilyn.
Silverman, Buffy. Amazing Facts about Sound. (p. 54)
—Birds. (p. 191)
—Blame Your Parents: Inherited Traits (p. 198)
—Body Parts: Double-Jointedness, Hitchhiker's Thumb, & More. (p. 207)
—Bonobos (p. 209)
—Can an Old Dog Learn New Tricks? And Other Questions about Animals. (p. 258)
—Can You Tell a Bee from a Wasp? (p. 259)
—Can You Tell a Brachiosaurus from an Apatosaurus? (p. 259)
—Can You Tell A Butterfly from A Moth? (p. 259)
—Can You Tell a Butterfly from a Moth? (p. 259)
—Can You Tell a Cheetah from a Leopard? (p. 259)
—Can You Tell a Coyote from a Wolf? (p. 259)
—Can You Tell a Cricket from a Grasshopper? (p. 259)
—Can You Tell A Dolphin from A Porpoise? (p. 259)
—Can You Tell a Dolphin from a Porpoise? (p. 259)
—Can You Tell A Frog from A Toad? (p. 259)
—Can You Tell a Frog from a Toad? (p. 259)
—Can You Tell a Gecko from a Salamander? (p. 259)
—Can You Tell a Giganotosaurus from a Spinosaurus? (p. 260)
—Can You Tell a Horse from a Pony? (p. 260)
—Can You Tell a Seal from a Sea Lion? (p. 260)
—Can You Tell a Stegosaurus from an Ankylosaurus? (p. 260)
—Can You Tell a Triceratops from a Protoceratops? (p. 260)
—Can You Tell a Tyrannosaurus from an Allosaurus? (p. 260)
—Can You Tell a Velociraptor from a Deinonychus? (p. 260)
—Can You Tell an Alligator from a Crocodile? (p. 260)
—Can You Tell an Ostrich from an Emu? (p. 260)
—Composting: Decomposition (p. 354)
—Desert Food Chains (p. 429)
—Do You Know about Amphibians? (p. 457)
—Do You Know about Birds? (p. 457)
—Do You Know about Fish? (p. 458)
—Do You Know about Insects? (p. 458)
—Do You Know about Mammals? (p. 458)
—Do You Know about Reptiles? (p. 458)
—Energy All Around. (p. 528)
—Exploring Dangers in Space: Asteroids, Space Junk, & More. (p. 552)
—Fleas. (p. 603)
—Grassland Food Chains (p. 712)
—Grasslands (p. 712)
—Gravity! Do You Feel It? (p. 712)
—Hair Traits: Color, Texture, & More. (p. 736)
—How Do Big Rigs Work? (p. 806)
—How Do Hot Air Balloons Work? (p. 807)
—How Do Jets Work? (p. 807)
—How Do Space Vehicles Work? (p. 807)
—How Do Trains Work? (p. 807)
—I Use Simple Machines. (p. 847)
—Let's Investigate Light. (p. 998)
—Lightning Bolt Books: Meet the Animal Groups (p. 1016)
—Lightning Bolt Books#8482; - Animal Look-Alikes: 6Pack Set. (p. 1016)
—Lightning Bolt Books#8482; - Animal Look-Alikes: Single Copy Set. (p. 1016)
—Magnet Power. (p. 1075)
—Me & My Shadow: A Book about Light. (p. 1115)
—Orangutans (p. 1302)
—Pull It, Push It. (p. 1415)
—Recycling: Reducing Waste (p. 1453)
—Saving Energy: Earth's Resources (p. 1517)
—Saving Water: The Water Cycle (p. 1518)
—Simple Machines: Forces in Action. (p. 1578)
—State of Confusion: Solids, Liquids, & Gases (p. 1644)
—Stop & Go, Fast & Slow: Moving Objects in Different Ways. (p. 1653)
—Stop & Go, Fast & Slow. (p. 1653)
—Unusual Traits: Tongue Rolling, Special Taste Sensors, & More. (p. 1823)
—Wetlands (p. 1877)
—Zap! It's Electricity! (p. 1985)
—¿Sabes Algo Sobre Anfibios? (Do You Know about Amphibians?) (p. 1500)
—¿Sabes Algo Sobre Aves? (Do You Know about Birds?) (p. 1500)
—¿Sabes Algo Sobre Insectos? (Do You Know about Insects?) (p. 1500)
—¿Sabes Algo Sobre MamiFeros? (Do You Know about Mammals?) (p. 1500)
—¿Sabes Algo Sobre Peces? (Do You Know about Fish?) (p. 1500)
—¿Sabes Algo Sobre Reptiles? (Do You Know about Reptiles?) (p. 1500)
Silverman, Dianne, illus. see Blair, Eric & Aesop Enterprise Inc. Staff.
Silverman, Dianne, illus. see Blair, Eric.
Silverman, Drew. Atlanta Hawks. (p. 112)
—Basketball. (p. 143)
—Indiana Hoosiers. (p. 871)
—Kansas Jayhawks. (p. 943)
—Nba Finals. (p. 1238)
—Orlando Magic. (p. 1304)
—Syracuse Orange. (p. 1693)
—UCLA Bruins. (p. 1807)
Silverman, Elisa. Understanding Israel Today. (p. 1815)
Silverman, Erica. Cowgirl Kate & Cocoa. Lewin, Betsy, illus. (p. 374)
—Cowgirl Kate & Cocoa: Horse in the House. Lewin, Betsy, illus. (p. 374)
—Cowgirl Kate & Cocoa: Partners. Lewin, Betsy, illus. (p. 374)
—Cowgirl Kate & Cocoa: Rain or Shine. Lewin, Betsy, illus. (p. 374)
—Favorite Stories from Cowgirl Kate & Cocoa: Partners. Lewin, Betsy, illus. (p. 578)
—Favorite Stories from Cowgirl Kate & Cocoa: School Days. Lewin, Betsy, illus. (p. 578)
—Favorite Stories from Cowgirl Kate & Cocoa: Rain or Shine. Lewin, Betsy, illus. (p. 578)
—Favorite Stories from Cowgirl Kate & Cocoa. (p. 578)
—Favorite Stories from Cowgirl Kate & Cocoa. Lewin, Betsy, illus. (p. 578)
—Favorite Stories from Cowgirl Kate & Cocoa Partners. Lewin, Betsy, illus. (p. 578)
—Hanukkah Hop! D'Amico, Steven, illus. (p. 744)
—Horse in the House. Lewin, Betsy, illus. (p. 799)
—Lana's World - Let's Have a Parade! Jess Golden, Jess, illus. (p. 973)
—Liberty's Voice: The Story of Emma Lazarus. Schuett, Stacey, illus. (p. 1005)
—Liberty's Voice the Story of Emma Lazarus. Schuett, Stacey, illus. (p. 1005)
—Mrs. Peachtree & the Eighth Avenue Cat. Beier, Ellen, illus. (p. 1187)

S

—On the Morn of Mayfest. Frazee, Marla, illus. (p. 1291)
—Partners. Lewin, Betsy, illus. (p. 1325)
—School Days. Lewin, Betsy, illus. (p. 1522)
Silverman, Erica & Lewin, Betsy. Favorite Stories from Cowgirl Kate & Cocoa. (p. 578)
—Favorite Stories from Cowgirl Kate & Cocoa Partners. (p. 578)
Silverman, Erica & Rucker, Justin. Lana's World - Let's Go Fishing! Jess Golden, Jess, illus. (p. 973)
Silverman, Hillel, jt. auth. see Silverman, Morris.
Silverman, Maida. Snow Search Dogs. (p. 1599)
Silverman, Morris, jt. auth. see Greenberg, Sidney.
Silverman, Morris & Silverman, Hillel. Prayer Book for Summer Camps. (p. 1393)
Silverman, Robin Landew. North Dakota. (p. 1265)
—Reaching Your Goals. (p. 1442)
Silverman, Steve. Performance-Enhancing Drugs. (p. 1343)
—Story of the Indiana Pacers. (p. 1661)
—Story of the Phoenix Suns. (p. 1662)
—Story of the Sacramento Kings. (p. 1662)
—Story of the Washington Wizards. (p. 1662)
Silverman, Toby. Garbage Grandma. Strapec, Amy, illus. (p. 655)
Silvermetz, Marcia A. Gertrude the Albino Frog & Her Friend Rupert the Turtle. Doyel, Ginger, illus. (p. 667)
Silvers, Terry, jt. auth. see Cheung, Theresa.
Silverstein, jt. auth. see Silverstein, Shel.
Silverstein, Alvin. Diseases & People. (p. 450)
Silverstein, Alvin & Silverstein, Virginia. Metamorphosis: Nature's Magical Transformations. (p. 1130)
Silverstein, Alvin, et al. Adaptation. (p. 11)
—ADHD Update: Understanding Attention-Deficit/Hyperactivity Disorder. (p. 12)
—AIDS Update. (p. 30)
—Asthma Update. (p. 108)
—Boas & Pythons: Cool Pets! Kelley, Gerald, illus. (p. 205)
—Breast Cancer Update. (p. 225)
—Cells. (p. 286)
—Chocolate Ants, Maggot Cheese, & More: The Yucky Food Book. Kelley, Gerald, illus. (p. 309)
—Creepy Crawlies. (p. 381)
—Curious Cats. (p. 392)
—Depression & Bipolar Disorder Update. (p. 427)
—Diabetes Update. (p. 433)
—DNA. (p. 456)
—Dung Beetles, Slugs, Leeches, & More: The Yucky Animal Book. Kelley, Gerald, illus. (p. 490)
—Earthquakes: The Science Behind Seismic Shocks & Tsunamis. (p. 497)
—Eating Disorders Update: Understanding Anorexia, Bulimia, & Binge Eating. (p. 501)
—Energy. (p. 528)
—Fabulous Fish. (p. 560)
—Ferrets: Cool Pets! Kelley, Gerald, illus. (p. 582)
—Floods: The Science Behind Raging Waters & Mudslides. (p. 605)
—Flu & Pneumonia Update. (p. 608)
—Food Chains. (p. 613)
—Food Poisoning Update. (p. 614)
—Forces & Motion. (p. 617)
—Global Warming. (p. 684)
—Hairless Cats: Cool Pets! Kelley, Gerald, illus. (p. 736)
—Hairless Dogs: Cool Pets! (p. 736)
—Handy Health Guide to Headaches. (p. 742)
—Hermit Crabs: Cool Pets! Kelley, Gerald, illus. (p. 771)
—Hissing Cockroaches: Cool Pets! Kelley, Gerald, illus. (p. 781)
—Hurricanes: The Science Behind Killer Storms. (p. 830)
—Iguanas: Cool Pets! Kelley, Gerald, illus. (p. 856)
—Miniature Horses: Cool Pets! Kelley, Gerald, illus. (p. 1146)
—Pains & Strains. (p. 1318)
—Plate Tectonics. (p. 1370)
—Poison Dart Frogs: Cool Pets! Kelley, Gerald, illus. (p. 1377)
—Poisoning. (p. 1377)
—Poop Collectors, Armpit Sniffers, & More: The Yucky Jobs Book. Kelley, Gerald, illus. (p. 1383)
—Potbellied Pigs: Cool Pets! Kelley, Gerald, illus. (p. 1388)
—Rats: Cool Pets! Kelley, Gerald, illus. (p. 1440)
—Science Concepts, Second Series (p. 1525)
—Scoliosis. (p. 1529)
—Sickle Cell Anemia Update. (p. 1572)
—Smog, Oil Spills, Sewage, & More: The Yucky Pollution Book. Kelley, Gerald, illus. (p. 1594)
—Snot, Poop, Vomit, & More: The Yucky Body Book. Kelley, Gerald, illus. (p. 1598)
—STDs Update. (p. 1645)
—Stomachaches. (p. 1652)
—Tapeworms, Foot Fungus, Lice, & More: The Yucky Disease Book. Kelley, Gerald, illus. (p. 1705)
—Tarantulas: Cool Pets! Kelley, Gerald, illus. (p. 1706)
—Tornadoes: The Science Behind Terrible Twisters. (p. 1770)
—Tuberculosis Update. (p. 1795)
—Universe. (p. 1820)
—Volcanoes: The Science Behind Fiery Eruptions. (p. 1849)
—What Are Germs? (p. 1879)
—Wildfires: The Science Behind Raging Infernos. (p. 1931)
Silverstein, Grant, illus. see Mason, David.
Silverstein, Janna. Close Encounters with Aliens. (p. 333)
Silverstein, Janna, jt. auth. see Goldfarb, Ian M.
Silverstein, Laura. Buttered Beetle Bugs: Short Poems & Silly Rhymes. (p. 247)
Silverstein, Ruth J., et al. Spanish Now! Level 1. Quinones, Nathan, ed. (p. 1621)
Silverstein, Shel. Cayendo Hacia Arriba. (p. 282)
—Different Dances. Silverstein, Shel, illus. (p. 438)
—Don't Bump the Glump! And Other Fantasies. Silverstein, Shel, illus. (p. 467)
—Every Thing on It. Silverstein, Shel, illus. (p. 543)
—Falling Up: Poems & Drawings. (p. 567)
—Falling Up: Poems & Drawings. Silverstein, Shel, illus. (p. 567)
—Falling up Special Edition. Silverstein, Shel, illus. (p. 567)
—Giraffe & a Half. Silverstein, Shel, illus. (p. 677)
—Giving Tree. (p. 681)
—Giving Tree. Silverstein, Shel, illus. (p. 681)
—Hay Luz en el Desvan. Alonso Blanco, Victoria, tr. (p. 755)
—Lafcadio, el Leon Que Disparo al Cazador. Rioja, Alberto Jimenez, tr. from ENG. (p. 971)
—Lafcadio, the Lion Who Shot Back. (p. 971)
—Lafcadio, the Lion Who Shot Back. Silverstein, Shel, illus. (p. 971)
—Light in the Attic. Silverstein, Shel, illus. (p. 1015)
—Missing Piece Meets the Big O. Silverstein, Shel, illus. (p. 1152)
—Runny Babbit: A Billy Sook. Silverstein, Shel, illus. (p. 1497)
—Shel Silverstein Pop-up Treasury. Silverstein, Shel, illus. (p. 1564)
—Where the Sidewalk Ends: Poems & Drawings. Silverstein, Shel, illus. (p. 1909)
—Who Wants a Cheap Rhinoceros? Silverstein, Shel, illus. (p. 1918)
Silverstein, Shel & Margolin, Phillip. Donde el Camino se Corta: Nuevos Poemas para Reirse. Alonso Blanco, Victoria et al, trs. (p. 466)
Silverstein, Shel & Silverstein. Missing Piece. Silverstein, Shel, illus. (p. 1152)
Silverstein, Virginia. Handy Health Guide to ADHD. (p. 741)
—Handy Health Guide to Asthma. (p. 741)
—Handy Health Guide to Better Sleep. (p. 742)
—Handy Health Guide to Bites & Stings. (p. 742)
—Handy Health Guide to Burns & Blisters. (p. 742)
—Handy Health Guide to Colds & Flu. (p. 742)
—Handy Health Guide to Diabetes. (p. 742)
—Handy Health Guide to Headaches. (p. 742)
—Handy Health Guide to Your Teeth. (p. 742)
Silverstein, Virginia, jt. auth. see Silverstein, Alvin.
Silverstein, Virginia & Nunn, Laura Silverstein. Handy Health Guide to Better Sleep. (p. 742)
—Handy Health Guide to Burns & Blisters. (p. 742)
—Handy Health Guide to Colds & Flu. (p. 742)
—Handy Health Guide to Diabetes. (p. 742)
—Handy Health Guide to Headaches. (p. 742)
—Handy Health Guide to Your Teeth. (p. 742)
Silverstein, Virginia B. & Nunn, Laura Silverstein. Handy Health Guide to ADHD. (p. 741)
—Handy Health Guide to Asthma. (p. 742)
—Handy Health Guide to Bites & Stings. (p. 742)
Silver-Stock, Carrie. Secrets Girls Keep: What Girls Hide (And Why) & How to Break the Stress of Silence. (p. 1544)
Silverston, Sondra, tr. see Orgad, Dorit.
Silverstone, Michael. Latino Legends: Hispanics in Major League Baseball. (p. 979)
—Latino Legends: Hispanics in Major League Baseball Set (p. 979)
—Paramedics to the Rescue: When Every Second Counts (p. 1324)
Silverstru, Emil. Cave Book. (p. 282)
Silver-Thompson, Pattie, illus. see Wang, Margaret.
Silverthorne, Elizabeth. Anorexia & Bulimia. (p. 87)
—Louisa May Alcott. (p. 1058)
—Plants. (p. 1369)
—Sarah Bernhardt. (p. 1514)
Silverthorne, Elizabeth & Hardman, Lizabeth. Cancer. (p. 260)
Silverthorne, Jill. SOS Titanic. (p. 1614)
Silverthorne, Judith. Dinosaur Blackout (p. 441)
—Dinosaur Breakout (p. 441)
—Dinosaur Stakeout (p. 443)
—Secret of Sentinel Rock (p. 1542)
—Secret of Sentinel Rock. (p. 1542)
—Secret of the Stone Circle (p. 1543)
—Secret of the Stone House (p. 1543)
Silverthorne, Judith & Coteau Books Staff. Dinosaur Hideout (p. 442)
Silverthorne, Sandy. Surviving Middle School: How to Manage the Maze. (p. 1687)
—Surviving When You're Home Alone: How to Avoid Being Grounded for Life. Silverthorne, Sandy, illus. (p. 1687)
—Surviving Zits: How to Cope with Your Changing Self. Silverthorne, Sandy, illus. (p. 1687)
—Wild & Wacky Bible Adventures for Kids. (p. 1928)
Silverwood, Sarah. Double-Edged Sword. (p. 472)
—London Stone. (p. 1046)
—Traitor's Gate. (p. 1777)
Silves, Kate. Jamie the Giraffe Learns to Dance. (p. 907)
Silvestre, R. Quique lo Salvo y Otras Historias. (p. 1428)
—Secreto en la Tormenta. (p. 1544)
Silvestri, Cris. Pokemon. (p. 1377)
—Pokemon Ultimate Handbook. (p. 1378)
—Test Your Sinnoh Smarts. (p. 1723)
Silvestri, Cris & Alfano, Maria B. Eye See It! (p. 558)
Silvestri, Enzo & Silvestri, Karen Hamilton. War in the Heavens: Episode 6. (p. 1857)
Silvestri, Eric & Silvestri, Mark. Cyber Force Origins (p. 396)
Silvestri, Karen Hamilton, jt. auth. see Silvestri, Enzo.
Silvestri, Linda. Clementina & the Hooey-Phooey Circus Troupe. (p. 330)
Silvestri, Marc, illus. see Claremont, Chris & Austin, Terry.
Silvestri, Marc, illus. see Waid, Mark & Chinsang, Wayne.
Silvestri, Marc, jt. auth. see Silvestri, Eric.
Silvestri, Marc & Hawkins, Matt. Cyber Force Rebirth Volume 1 TP. (p. 396)
Silvestri, Marc, et al. Essential X-Factor Volume 4. (p. 537)
—X-Men vs. Avengers/Fantastic Four. (p. 1967)
Silvestri, Mark, jt. auth. see Silvestri, Eric.
Silvestro, Martha Jo. to Z My Alphabet Zoo. (p. 1759)
Silvey, Allen, ed. see Silvey, Joan.
Silvey, Allen, illus. see Silvey, Joan.
Silvey, Anita. Henry Knox: Bookseller, Soldier, Patriot. Minor, Wendell, illus. (p. 768)
—I'll Pass for Your Comrade: Women Soldiers in the Civil War. (p. 856)
—Plant Hunters: True Stories of Their Daring Adventures to the Far Corners of the Earth (p. 1369)
—Untamed: The Wild Life of Jane Goodall. (p. 1823)
Silvey, Craig. Jasper Jones. (p. 910)
Silvey, Diane. Kids Book of Aboriginal Peoples in Canada. Mantha, John, illus. (p. 952)
—Spirit Quest. (p. 1628)
—Time of the Thunderbird. Mantha, John, illus. (p. 1752)
Silvey, Joan. Help Me Learn: Counting 1 - 10 in American Language Silvey, Allen, ed. (p. 765)
Silvia, Dubovoy, jt. auth. see Dubovoy, Silvia.
Silvia, Molina, jt. auth. see Molina, Silvia.
Silvoso, Ed. Anointed for Business: How Christians Can Use Their Places of Influence to Make a Profound Impact on the World. (p. 87)
Sim, Dave, jt. auth. see Neal, Nate.
Sim, David. Jump Freddy, Jump! Sim, David, illus. (p. 934)
—Matt's Hat: A Find the Hat Color Book Sim, David, illus. (p. 1110)
—Matt's Mat: A Touch & Feel Counting Book Sim, David, illus. (p. 1110)
—Panda's Pants. Sim, David, illus. (p. 1321)
Sim, David, illus. see Dobbins, Jan & Songs, Steve.
Sim, David, illus. see Dobbins, Jan.
Sim, David, illus. see Laird, Elizabeth & Davison, Roz.
Sim, David, illus. see Robinson, Michelle.
Sim, David, illus. see Scribens, Sunny, et al.
Sim, David, illus. see SteveSongs Staff.
Sim, Stephanie. Copycat. (p. 366)
Sima, Judy & Cordi, Kevin. Raising Voices: Creating Youth Storytelling Groups & Troupes (p. 1437)
Simandan, Voicu Mihnea. Ironman. A Play. (p. 888)
Simanu-Klutz, Luafata, tr. see Carroll, Lewis, pseud.
Simard, Danielle. Little Word Catcher Côté, Geneviève & Second Story Press Staff, illus. (p. 1038)
Simard, Remy. Bottine Magique de Pipo. (p. 215)
—Busy Day Coloring Storybook. (p. 246)
—Favorite Places Coloring Storybook. (p. 578)
—Mon Chien Est un Elephant. (p. 1163)
—Monsieur Iletaitunefois. (p. 1166)
Simard, Rémy, illus. see Desrosiers, Sylvie.
Simard, Remy, illus. see Fienberg, Anna.
Simard, Remy, illus. see Hall, Kirsten.
Simard, Remy, illus. see Jones, Christianne C.
Simard, Remy, illus. see Korb, Rena B. & Weinhaus, Anthony J.
Simard, Remy, illus. see Meister, Carl.
Simard, Remy, illus. see Mortensen, Lori.
Simard, Remy, illus. see Murphy, Stuart J.
Simard, Remy, illus. see Richards, Kitty.
Simard, Remy, illus. see Rosa-Mendoza, Gladys.
Simard, Remy, illus. see School Zone Interactive Staff.
Simard, Remy, illus. see Schroeder, Andreas.
Simard, Tim. Haunted Hikes of Vermont. (p. 753)
Simatoribus, Alessandra, illus. see Patacrúa.
Simblet, Sarah & Dorling Kindersley Publishing Staff. Sketch Book for the Artist. (p. 1584)
Simcic, Christina, illus. see Cameron-Gallo, Vivian.
Simcox, Hazel P. Happy Halloween (Coloring Book) (p. 745)
—Hello, Autumn. (p. 763)
—Hooray for Summer (Coloring Book) (p. 796)
—Hoppin' into Easter. (p. 797)
—Let It Snow. (p. 994)
—Welcome Springtime. (p. 1873)
—Wild for Animals. (p. 1929)
Simcox, Lorraine. Single Red Thread. (p. 1579)
Simcox, M. A. Adventures Abroad: The Pearl of Africa. (p. 15)
—Adventures Abroad: The Eden of the Caribbean. (p. 15)
Simee. Giggles Feel Good (p. 676)
Simekova, Jela, ed. see Krcmár, Karol.
Simendinger, Ted. 12 Miles to Paradise: A People Story about Horses & Horseracing. (p. 1994)
—Jurassic Trout: A Flyfishing Comedy. (p. 937)
Simens, Dov S-S. From Reel to Deal: Everything You Need to Create a Successful Independent Film. (p. 643)
Simeon, S. & Golden Books Staff. Little Golden Bible Storybook. Sexton, Brenton, illus. (p. 1028)
Simeone, Angelique, jt. auth. see Pirzada, Nefes.
Simer, Carolyn Christopher. Goat in the Boat. (p. 687)
Simermeyer, Genevieve. Meet Christopher: An Osage Indian Boy from Oklahoma. Fogden, Katherine, photos by. (p. 1120)
Simeton, Julia. Mom, Why Can't I Catch Up? (p. 1161)
Simhaee, Rebeka. Avi's Choice: A Story about Bikur Cholim-Visiting the Sick. Hechter, Janice, illus. (p. 120)
—Sara Finds A Mitzva. Leverton, Yossi, ed. (p. 1514)
Simhananda, B. Jyoti for Kids: A Meditative Technique of Purification by the Light. (p. 941)
Simhoni, S. Legends of Queen Esther. Lask, I. M., tr. (p. 990)
Simi, Gillingham & Gillingham, Sara. In My Patch. Siminovich, Lorena, illus. (p. 864)
Siminovich, Lorena. Alex & Lulu: Two of a Kind. Siminovich, Lorena, illus. (p. 35)
—I Like Bugs. Siminovich, Lorena, illus. (p. 841)
—I Like Toys. Siminovich, Lorena, illus. (p. 841)
—Monkey See, Look at Me! (p. 1165)
—You Are My Baby - Farm. (p. 1973)
—You Are My Baby: Garden. (p. 1973)
—You Are My Baby: Meadow. (p. 1973)
—You Are My Baby: Ocean. (p. 1973)
—You Are My Baby: Pets. (p. 1973)
—You Are My Baby - Safari. (p. 1973)
—You Are My Baby: Woodland. (p. 1973)
—You Know What I Love? (p. 1975)
Siminovich, Lorena, illus. see Chronicle Books Staff.
Siminovich, Lorena, illus. see Gillingham, Sara & Chronicle Books Staff.
Siminovich, Lorena, illus. see Gillingham, Sara.
Siminovich, Lorena, illus. see Simi, Gillingham & Gillingham, Sara.
Siminovich, Lorena, jt. auth. see Gillingham, Sara.
Simione, Allen, illus. see Simione, Ruth.
Simione, Ruth. Mike the Microbe. Simione, Allen, illus. (p. 1141)
Simkins, Aron. Dream Big: The Journey of the Jazz Bear. (p. 483)
Simkins, Ed, illus. see Richards, Jon.
Simkins, Ed, jt. auth. see Richards, Jon.
Simkins, Kate & Dorling Kindersley Publishing Staff. I Want to Be a Gymnast, Level 2. (p. 847)
Simko, Danielle, illus. see Martinez, Genevieve.
Simko, Joe. Sweet Rot: The Purple Meltdown Book 3 Simko, Joe, illus. (p. 1690)
—Sweet Rot, Book 2: Raiders of the Lost Art (p. 1690)
Simko, Joe, illus. see Baldwin, Stephen & Rosato, Bruno.
Simko, Joe, illus. see Baldwin, Stephen.
Simko, Joe, illus. see Consiglio, Joe.
Simmans, Sean, illus. see Wells, H. G.
Simmel, Mike, jt. auth. see Skead, Robert.
Simmers, Louise. Health Science Career Exploration. (p. 758)
Simmers, Louise M. Health Science Career Exploration. (p. 758)
Simmie, Lois. Mister Got to Go: The Cat that Wouldn't Leave Nugent, Cynthia, illus. (p. 1155)
—Mr Got to Go Where Are You Nugent, Cynthia, illus. (p. 1185)
Simmie, Lois & Coteau Books Staff. They Shouldn't Make You Promise That. (p. 1732)
Simmions, Glenn. My Father's Work. (p. 1203)
Simmonds, Frank H., illus. see Caudle, P. L.
Simmonds, Posy. Baker Cat. Simmonds, Posy, illus. (p. 133)
—Fred. (p. 632)
Simmons, Alex. Mysteries of the Past: A Chapter Book. (p. 1222)
Simmons, Allan H., ed. see Conrad, Joseph.
Simmons, Andra. What Anna Loves. Capaldi, Gina, illus. (p. 1879)
Simmons, Andrew & Averdonz, N. R. I Was an Eighth-Grade Ninja Padilla, Ariel, illus. (p. 848)
Simmons, Ann, illus. see Jones, Cheryl & Joseph, Rahzheena.
Simmons, Anthea. Bestest Baby. Birkett, Georgie, illus. (p. 171)
—Share! Birkett, Georgie, illus. (p. 1561)
Simmons Bell, Linda. Kylie & Mr Whiskers. (p. 969)
Simmons, Beth E., jt. auth. see Cerullo, Mary M.
Simmons, Bethany, illus. see Osborne, Erin.
Simmons, Carl & Alexander, Heather. Bending over Backwards. (p. 164)
Simmons, Carl & Douglas, Lola. You First. (p. 1975)
Simmons, Carl & Zulkey, Claire. Best Frenemies. (p. 169)
Simmons, Celeste. Adventures of Booger Malone: Busted in the Backseat. (p. 16)
Simmons, Derek. Flash of Life. (p. 602)
Simmons, H. Two Tales from Our Corner Lot. (p. 1804)
Simmons, H. J. Little House on the Corner. (p. 1029)
Simmons, J. A. Hannah's First Airplane Ride. (p. 743)
Simmons, Jane. Beryl: A Pig's Tale. (p. 168)
—Come On, Daisy! (p. 347)
—Daisy & the Egg. (p. 400)
—Que Valiente Eres, Daisy! (p. 1424)
—Ship's Cat Doris. Simmons, Jane, illus. (p. 1567)
—Ven Aqui, Daisy! (p. 1835)
Simmons, Jane, illus. see Moss, Miriam.
Simmons, Jeff. Vital Skills: How to be a Godly Man. (p. 1846)
—Vital Skills: How to Have a Quiet Time. (p. 1846)
Simmons, John M. All the Little Things: A Thanksgiving Prayer. (p. 46)
—Katya's Prayer. (p. 946)
Simmons, Joy. I Can't Wait to Be on TV! (p. 837)
Simmons, Judy. Where Is Heaven? (p. 1906)
Simmons, Justine, et al. God, Can You Hear Me? (p. 688)
Simmons, Kantis Andrew. Playing Your A Game: Biblical Principles for Academic Success. (p. 1373)
Simmons, Kenneth. Mr Ken's Rhymes. (p. 1185)
Simmons, Kristen. Article 5. (p. 104)
—Glass Arrow. (p. 682)
—Three. (p. 1741)
Simmons, Lynn. Bo & the Christmas Bandit Lyne, Alison, illus. (p. 204)
—Bo & the Night Intruder (p. 204)
Simmons, Lynn Sheffield. Bo & the Missing Dogs Hampton, Lin, illus. (p. 204)
—Bo & the Roaring Pines Lyne, Alison Davis, illus. (p. 204)
—Bo, the Famous Retriever Hampton, Lin, illus. (p. 205)
—Jack Crow Said Hello Lopez, Willie, illus. (p. 903)
—Sugar Lump, the Orphan Calf (p. 1673)
—Sugar Lump's Night Before Christmas Ward, Sue Marshall, illus. (p. 1673)
Simmons, Marc. New Mexico! (p. 1246)
Simmons, Marjorie. Gift Box That Meant Everything. (p. 675)
Simmons, Mark, illus. see Bolte, Mari.
Simmons, Mark, illus. see Collins, Terry, et al.
Simmons, Mark, illus. see Yomtov, Nelson.
Simmons, Martha. Grandma Perkido & Sidney. (p. 708)
Simmons, Mary Louise. Little Fir Tree Who Wanted a Friend. (p. 1027)
Simmons, Matt J. Jackie Robinson: Breaking the Color Line in Baseball. (p. 904)
Simmons, Michael. Alien Feast. O'Connor, George, illus. (p. 40)
—Pool Boy. (p. 1383)
Simmons, Nancy B., ed. Exploring the World of Mammals (p. 554)
Simmons, Pat. Vietnam. (p. 1841)
Simmons, Philip. Aprendiendo a Caer: Elogio de la vida Imperfecta. (p. 93)
Simmons, Richard. Adventures of John & Alex. (p. 19)
Simmons, Robert, illus. see Hancock, Susan G.
Simmons, Rulon E. & Littlehales, Bates. National Geographic Photographing Birds. (p. 1233)
Simmons, Russell, illus. see Mayer, Nicole & Mayer, Ryan.
Simmons, Sukether Williams. Deep in My Soul Poems by Sukether Simmons. (p. 423)
Simmons, Ted. Diablo Creek. (p. 433)
—Sandstorm. (p. 1511)
Simmons, Vikk. Divided Loyalties. (p. 454)
—Video Magic. (p. 1841)
Simmons, Walter. Cambodia. (p. 255)
—Colombia. (p. 341)
—Czech Republic. (p. 397)
—Dominican Republic. (p. 465)
—Egypt. (p. 506)
—Iran. (p. 886)
—Morocco. (p. 1176)
—Pakistan. (p. 1319)
—Poland. (p. 1378)

S

—Salvador. (p. 1506)
—Vietnam. (p. 1841)
Simmons-Moake, Jane. Excelling at Dog Agility - Book 1: Obstacle Training - Updated Second Edition. (p. 547)
—Excelling at Dog Agility - Book 3 Advanced Skills Training - Updated Second Edition Bk. 3. (p. 547)
Simms, Abigail & Gabrielle. Let's Turn Our World Upside Down. (p. 1001)
Simms, Albert Clint. My Values & Morales Treasury. (p. 1221)
Simms, B. D. Place in My Heart. (p. 1365)
Simms, Donna A. Hillsborough Tales. (p. 780)
Simms, George Otto. Saint Patrick: Ireland's Patron Saint. Rooney, David, illus. (p. 1504)
Simms, L. Glenn. Reflections of A. P. K. (Preacher's Kid) During the 20th Century. (p. 1456)
Simms, Laura. Stories to Nourish the Hearts of Our Children. Krizmanic, Tatjana, illus. (p. 1655)
Simms, Mattie. Q. (p. 1422)
—(Q) Kids Help Center. (p. 1422)
Simms, Rk. Me & My Dog, Petey. (p. 1115)
Simms, Rosie. Read, Think, & Write about It - Binder 1. (p. 1443)
Simner, Janni Lee. Bones of Faerie. (p. 209)
—Faerie After. (p. 562)
—Faerie Winter. (p. 562)
—Secret of the Three Treasures. (p. 1543)
—Thief Eyes. (p. 1732)
Simolke, Duane. Degranon: A Science Fiction Adventure. (p. 424)
Simon, jt. auth. see Simon, Seymour.
Simon, Alonzo, jt. ed. see Eisinger, Justin.
Simon, Alyssa & Romano, Amy. How Cells Divide, Reproduce, & Specialize. (p. 805)
Simon & Schuster Audio Firm Staff, jt. auth. see Falconer, Ian.
Simon and Schuster Children's Staff, ed. see Burge, Constance M.
Simon and Schuster Staff. Colour in One Direction! (p. 346)
—Macmillan Dictionary for Children: 4th Revised Edition. (p. 1068)
—Macmillan Dictionary for Children. Morris, Christopher G., ed. (p. 1068)
—Macmillan First Dictionary. Morris, Christopher G., ed. (p. 1068)
—NASCAR Jeff Gordon: Stock Car Superstar. (p. 1230)
—NASCAR Tony Stewart: Racing to Victory Lane. (p. 1230)
—Simon & Schuster Thesaurus for Children: The Ultimate Student Thesaurus. (p. 1577)
Simon and Schuster UK Staff. Colour in 5 SOS! (p. 346)
—Ultimate Boy Band Pack! (p. 1809)
Simon and Schuster/LeapFrog Staff, jt. auth. see Cronin, Doreen.
Simon and Schuster/LeapFrog Staff, jt. auth. see Falconer, Ian.
Simon, Annette. Mocking Birdies. (p. 1157)
—Robot Zombie Frankenstein! Simon, Annette, illus. (p. 1480)
Simon, Barbara Brooks. Escape to Freedom: The Underground Railroad Adventures of Callie & William. (p. 535)
—Underground Railroad: Voices from America's Past. (p. 1815)
Simon, Barney. Pass Math: Arithmetic. Bk. 1 (p. 1326)
Simon, Carly, jt. auth. see Norworth, Jack.
Simon, Charnan. Ancient Euphrates. (p. 69)
—Dance Team. (p. 402)
—Earth. (p. 495)
—Luna the Wake-Up Cat. Huang, Benrei, illus. (p. 1065)
—Mars. (p. 1096)
—Me Gusta Ganar! Translations.com Staff, tr. from ENG. (p. 1116)
—Me Gusta Ganar; I Like to Win. (p. 1116)
—Mighty Mississippi. (p. 1140)
—Mysterious Amazon. (p. 1222)
—Noble Yangtze. (p. 1262)
—Plan B. (p. 1366)
—Pumpkin Fever. Bryan-Hunt, Jan, illus. (p. 1416)
—Rachel Carson: Author & Environmentalist. (p. 1431)
—Sacred Ganges. (p. 1500)
—Sam the Dog: Guard the House, Sam!/Sam's Pet/Show-and-Tell Sam. (p. 1507)
—Secrets of the Nile. (p. 1545)
—Shattered Star. (p. 1563)
—Super Cool Science Experiments: Compounds & Mixtures. (p. 1679)
—Tressa the Musical Princess. Allen, Joy, illus. (p. 1785)
—Wolves. (p. 1945)
Simon, Charnan, jt. auth. see Kazunas, Ariel.
Simon, Charnan & Kazunas, Ariel. Killer Whales. (p. 956)
—Super Cool Science Experiments: Water. (p. 1679)
Simon, Charnan & Kazunis, Ariel. Experiment with Water. (p. 549)
Simon, Clea. Feline Mystique: On the Mysterious Connection Between Women & Cats. (p. 581)
Simon, Coco. Alexis: The Icing on the Cupcake. (p. 37)
—Alexis & the Missing Ingredient. (p. 37)
—Alexis & the Perfect Recipe. (p. 37)
—Alexis Cool As a Cupcake. (p. 37)
—Alexis Cool as a Cupcake. (p. 37)
—Alexis Gets Frosted. (p. 37)
—Alexis the Icing on the Cupcake. (p. 37)
—Alexis's Cupcake Cupid. (p. 37)
—Cupcake Diaries Collection: Katie & the Cupcake Cure; Mia in the Mix; Emma on Thin Icing; Alexis & the Perfect Recipe. (p. 392)
—Emma: Lights! Camera! Cupcakes! (p. 519)
—Emma: Sugar & Spice & Everything Nice. (p. 519)
—Emma All Stirred Up! (p. 519)
—Emma: Lights! Camera! Cupcakes! Halpin, Abigail, illus. (p. 520)
—Emma on Thin Icing. (p. 520)
—Emma, Smile & Say Cupcake! (p. 520)
—Emma, Smile & Say "Cupcake!" (p. 520)
—Emma Sugar & Spice & Everything Nice. (p. 520)
—Emma's Not-So-Sweet Dilemma. (p. 520)
—Katie & the Cupcake Cure. (p. 944)
—Katie & the Cupcake War. (p. 944)
—Katie, Batter Up! (p. 945)
—Katie Sprinkled Secrets. (p. 945)
—Katie Sprinkles & Surprises. (p. 945)
—Katie Starting from Scratch. (p. 945)
—Katie's New Recipe. (p. 945)
—Mia: A Matter of Taste. (p. 1133)
—Mia: Fashion Plates & Cupcakes. (p. 1133)
—Mia a Matter of Taste. (p. 1133)
—Mia Fashion Plates & Cupcakes. (p. 1133)
—Mia in the Mix. (p. 1133)
—Mia's Baker's Dozen. (p. 1134)
—Mia's Boiling Point. (p. 1134)
—Mia's Recipe for Disaster. (p. 1134)
Simon, Daniel. Cosmic Motors: Spaceships, Cars & Pilots of Another Galaxy. (p. 368)
Simon, Eleanor. Little Girl Found. (p. 1028)
Simon, Elizabeth. Caring for Your Iguana. (p. 269)
—Caring for Your Rat. (p. 269)
—Iguana. (p. 856)
—Rat. (p. 1440)
—Tyler Adams & the Adventures of Bravura: the First Quest. (p. 1805)
Simon, Emma & Streissguth, Thomas. Raoul Wallenberg. (p. 1438)
Simon, Eric M., illus. see Kaufmann, Helen L.
Simon, Francesca. Gets a Shock. Lucas, James, illus. (p. 668)
—Hello, Moon! Cort, Ben, illus. (p. 764)
—Helping Hercules. Ross, Tony, illus. (p. 766)
—Horrid Henry. (p. 798)
—Horrid Henry. Ross, Tony, illus. (p. 798)
—Horrid Henry & the Abominable Snowman. (p. 798)
—Horrid Henry & the Abominable Snowman. Ross, Tony, illus. (p. 798)
—Horrid Henry & the Mega-Mean Time Machine. (p. 799)
—Horrid Henry & the Mega-Mean Time Machine. Ross, Tony, illus. (p. 799)
—Horrid Henry & the Mummy's Curse. (p. 799)
—Horrid Henry & the Mummy's Curse. Ross, Tony, illus. (p. 799)
—Horrid Henry & the Scary Sitter. Ross, Tony, illus. (p. 799)
—Horrid Henry & the Soccer Fiend. (p. 799)
—Horrid Henry & the Zombie Vampire. Ross, Tony, illus. (p. 799)
—Horrid Henry Robs the Bank. Ross, Tony, illus. (p. 799)
—Horrid Henry Rocks. Ross, Tony, illus. (p. 799)
—Horrid Henry Tricks the Tooth Fairy. (p. 799)
—Horrid Henry Tricks the Tooth Fairy. Ross, Tony, illus. (p. 799)
—Horrid Henry Wakes the Dead. Ross, Tony, illus. (p. 799)
—Horrid Henry's Christmas. (p. 799)
—Horrid Henry's Christmas. Ross, Tony, illus. (p. 799)
—Horrid Henry's Joke Book. Ross, Tony, illus. (p. 799)
—Horrid Henry's Monster Movie. Ross, Tony, illus. (p. 799)
—Horrid Henry's Stinkbomb. (p. 799)
—Horrid Henry's Stinkbomb. Ross, Tony, illus. (p. 799)
—Horrid Henry's Underpants. (p. 799)
—Horrid Henry's Underpants. Ross, Tony, illus. (p. 799)
—Jogger's Big Adventure. Bolam, Emily, illus. (p. 920)
—Little Yellow Dog Bites the Builder. Lucas, James E., illus. (p. 1038)
—Little Yellow Dog Says Look at Me. Lucas, James E., illus. (p. 1038)
—Look at Me. Bolam, Emily, illus. (p. 1048)
—Miaow Miaow Bow Wow. Bolam, Emily, illus. (p. 1134)
—Pablo Diablo y el Dinero. (p. 1316)
—Pablo Diablo Y la Bomba Fetida. (p. 1316)
—Pablo Diablo Y la Cangura Fantasma. Ross, Tony, illus. (p. 1316)
—Pablo Diablo y la Maldicion de la Momia. (p. 1316)
—Pablo Diablo Y Los Piojos. Ross, Tony, illus. (p. 1316)
—Rampage in Prince's Garden. Bolam, Emily, illus. (p. 1438)
—Venganza de Pablo Diablo. (p. 1835)
—Yum Yum. Bolam, Emily, illus. (p. 1983)
Simon, Jay. Deep Freeze. (p. 423)
Simon, Jenne. Andrea's New Horse. (p. 72)
—Ballet Recital. (p. 134)
—Double Trouble. (p. 473)
—Jungle Party. (p. 935)
—Lalaloopsy: Chasing Rainbows. (p. 972)
—Lalaloopsy: Let's Pick Apples! (p. 972)
—Lalaloopsy: Easter Eggs-Travaganza. (p. 972)
—Lalaloopsy: Easter Eggs-Travaganza. Hill, Prescott, illus. (p. 972)
—Lalaloopsy: School Day! Hill, Prescott, illus. (p. 972)
—Lalaloopsy: the Ballet Recital. (p. 972)
—LEGO Friends: Andrea's New Horse. Ku, Min Sung, illus. (p. 990)
—Lego Friends - Double Trouble. Ameet Studio Staff, illus. (p. 990)
—Let's Pick Apples. Hill, Prescott, illus. (p. 999)
—Mirror Mirror: The Movie Storybook. (p. 1149)
—Moody Monsters. (p. 1171)
—Shopkins. (p. 1569)
—Snow Day. (p. 1598)
—Snow Day!, Level 2. Hill, Prescott, illus. (p. 1598)
Simon, Jenne, jt. auth. see Scholastic, Inc. Staff.
Simon, Jenne & Cole, Joanna. Magic School Bus: Dinosaur Rescue. Degen, Bruce, illus. (p. 1073)
Simon, Jim, jt. auth. see Simon, Joe.
Simon, Jo Ann, see Campbell, Joanna, pseud.
Simon, Joe. Adventures of the Fly. Davis, Jack & Williamson, Al, illus. (p. 23)
Simon, Joe & Simon, Jim. Comic Book Makers (p. 348)
Simon, John Oliver, tr. see Luján, Jorge.
Simon, John Oliver, ed. Cyclops Wearing Flip-Flops. (p. 397)
Simon, Kitty. Preschool Here I Come! (p. 1396)
Simon, Kristen Koerner. Bruce: The Little Blue Spruce. (p. 232)
—Jack's Knack: Book Three of the Blue Forest Series: Book Three of the Blue Forest Series. (p. 904)
—Tiffany's Epiphany. (p. 1748)
Simon, Les. How To: Have Money & Avoid & Dump Debt. (p. 814)
Simon, Leslie & Kelley, Trevor. Wish You Were Here: An Essential Guide to Your Favorite Music Scenes - From Punk to Indie & Everything in Between. Dobi, Rob, illus. (p. 1940)
Simon, Loris, illus. see Salum, Rose Mary.
Simon, M. Ed. Parrots 2 Peacocks Pattern Book. (p. 1325)
Simon, Madeline Gerstein, illus. see Nunez, Ralph da Costa & Ellison, Jesse Andrews.
Simon, Margaret. Blessen. (p. 199)
Simon, Martin P., jt. auth. see Jahsmann, Allan Hart.
Simon, Mary. Ay Que Lio. (p. 121)
—Oh Oh. (p. 1281)
Simon, Mary Mans. David & Goliath: Read & Learn the Bible. (p. 410)
—Fishes & Loaves: Read & Learn the Bible. (p. 599)
—Good Samaritan: Read & Learn the Bible. (p. 700)
—Jesus Blesses the Children: Read & Learn the Bible. (p. 915)
—Jesus Fills the Nets: Read & Learn the Bible. (p. 915)
—Jonah & the Big Fish: Read & Learn the Bible. (p. 925)
—Noah's Ark: Read & Learn the Bible. (p. 1261)
—See What God Made! Read & Learn the Bible. (p. 1547)
—Too Tall, Too Small: Read & Learn the Bible. (p. 1767)
Simon, Mary Manz. Anytime Bible. Duendes Del Sur Staff, illus. (p. 91)
—Bear Obeys. Clearwater, Linda & Couri, Kathy, illus. (p. 151)
—Build A Tower. (p. 238)
—Bunny Loves Others. Stott, Dorothy, illus. (p. 242)
—Countdown to Christmas. (p. 370)
—Duckling Is Patient. Clearwater, Linda, illus. (p. 488)
—Hear Me Read Bible. (p. 759)
—Kitty Shows Kindness. Clearwater, Linda, illus. (p. 963)
—Koala Does His Best. Harris, Phyllis & Clearwater, Linda, illus. (p. 966)
—Lamb Is Joyful. Harris, Phyllis & Clearwater, Linda, illus. (p. 972)
—Lion Can Share. Harris, Phyllis & Clearwater, Linda, illus. (p. 1020)
—Little Visits for Toddlers. Munger, Nancy, illus. (p. 1037)
—Little Visits with Jesus. Warren, Beverly, illus. (p. 1037)
—Mis Primeros Versículos de la Biblia. Duendes Del Sur Staff, illus. (p. 1150)
—My First Read & Learn Book of Prayers. Duendes Del Sur Staff, illus. (p. 1207)
—Panda Is Polite. (p. 1320)
—Piglet Tells the Truth. Stott, Dorothy, illus. (p. 1358)
—Puppy Makes Friends. Couri, Kathy & Clearwater, Linda, illus. (p. 1418)
—Set of eight Books. (p. 1554)
—Sit Down. (p. 1581)
—Squirrel Says Thank You. Couri, Kathy & Clearwater, Linda, illus. (p. 1637)
—Tiger Forgives. Clearwater, Linda & Couri, Kathy, illus. (p. 1748)
—Where Is Jesus? (p. 1908)
—Young Learner's Bible Storybook: 52 Stories with Activities for Family Fun & Learning. Harper, Piers, illus. (p. 1979)
Simon, Mary Manz, et al. I Love Fall! Nakata, Hiroe, illus. (p. 842)
Simon, Morris. Wizards Keep. (p. 1943)
Simon, Nadine. Flickers of True Destiny. (p. 603)
—Treasured Dream. (p. 1782)
Simon, Norma. All Families Are Special. Flavin, Teresa, illus. (p. 44)
—Every Friday Night. Weiss, Harvey, illus. (p. 542)
—Happy Purim Night. Gordon, Ayala, illus. (p. 746)
Simon, Philip, ed. see Bates, Cary, et al.
Simon, Philip, ed. see Brancatelli, Joe, et al.
Simon, Philip, ed. see Clamp Staff.
Simon, Philip, ed. see CLAMP.
Simon, Philip, ed. see Hogan, Peter.
Simon, Philip, ed. see Hughes, Richard E.
Simon, Philip, ed. see Melo, Filipe.
Simon, Philip, ed. see Tobin, Paul.
Simon, Philip, ed. see Yun, Mi-Kyung.
Simon, Philip, ed. Art of Plants vs. Zombies: A Visual Book. (p. 102)
Simon, Richard, jt. auth. see Simon, Tanya.
Simon, Romain. Forest Animals. (p. 618)
Simon, Sandy. Sylvie. (p. 1693)
Simon, Seymour. Big Cats. (p. 180)
—Body Sense, Body Nonsense. (p. 207)
—Brain: Our Nervous System. (p. 221)
—Butterflies. (p. 247)
—Cats. Simon, Seymour, illus. (p. 280)
—Coral Reefs. (p. 366)
—Creepy Creatures. (p. 381)
—Deadly Ants. Downey, William, illus. (p. 417)
—Destination: Space. (p. 430)
—Destination Space. (p. 430)
—Destination: Space. (p. 430)
—Destination - Space. (p. 430)
—Dogs. Simon, Seymour, illus. (p. 462)
—Dolphins. (p. 464)
—Earth: Our Planet in Space. (p. 495)
—Earthquakes. (p. 497)
—Extreme Earth Records. (p. 556)
—Eyes & Ears. (p. 558)
—Frogs. (p. 641)
—Ghosts. (p. 672)
—Giant Snakes. (p. 674)
—Global Warming. (p. 684)
—Gorillas. (p. 703)
—Guts: Our Digestive System. (p. 733)
—Heart: Our Circulatory System. (p. 759)
—Horses. (p. 800)
—Horses. Simon, Seymour, illus. (p. 800)
—Hurricanes. (p. 830)
—Incredible Sharks. (p. 869)
—Knights & Castles. (p. 964)
—Lightning. (p. 1016)
—Lungs: Your Respiratory System. (p. 1066)
—Mars. (p. 1096)
—Moon. (p. 1171)
—Oceans. (p. 1277)
—Our Solar System. (p. 1310)
—Our Solar System (revised Edition) (p. 1310)
—Penguins. (p. 1337)
—Planets. (p. 1368)
—Poisonous Animals. (p. 1377)
—Poisonous Snakes. Downey, William, illus. (p. 1377)
—Science Dictionary. (p. 1525)
—Secret Clocks: Time Senses of Living Things. Brett, Jan, illus. (p. 1540)
—Seymour Simon's Extreme Earth Records. (p. 1556)
—Seymour Simon's Extreme Oceans. (p. 1556)
—Seymour Simon's Silly Riddles & Jokes Coloring Book. Kendrick, D., illus. (p. 1556)
—Sharks. (p. 1562)
—Space Travelers. (p. 1620)
—Spiders. (p. 1627)
—Stars. (p. 1643)
—Stars & Constellations. (p. 1643)
—Strange Mysteries from Around the World. (p. 1665)
—Sun. (p. 1675)
—Tropical Rainforests. (p. 1789)
—Under the Sea. (p. 1814)
—Universe. (p. 1820)
—Vampire Bats: Extreme Animals. (p. 1831)
—Volcanoes. (p. 1849)
—Weather. (p. 1869)
—Wolves. (p. 1945)
Simon, Seymour & Carle, Eric. La Cabeza a los Pies. Carle, Eric, illus. (p. 969)
Simon, Seymour & Fauteux, Nicole. Let's Try It Out in the Air. Cushman, Doug, illus. (p. 1001)
—Let's Try It Out in the Water: Hands-on Early-Learning Science Activities. Cushman, Doug, illus. (p. 1001)
Simon, Seymour & Simon. Seymour Simon's Book of Trains. (p. 1556)
—Snakes. (p. 1596)
Simon, Shane. Prophecy: Book One (p. 1411)
Simon, Solomon & Bial, Morrison D. Rabbi's Bible: Torah Vol. 1 (p. 1429)
Simon Spotlight, creator. Adventures to Go! (p. 25)
—Dora & Diego's Adventures! (p. 470)
Simon, Stephen. Casey at the Bat. (p. 275)
Simon, Steven, jt. auth. see Benjamin, Daniel.
Simon, Sue A., illus. see Cicola, Amanda, et al.
Simon, Sue A., illus. see Estice, Rose Mary & Fried, Mary.
Simon, Sue A., illus. see Pinnell, Gay Su, et al.
Simon, Susan, illus. see Rouss, Sylvia A.
Simon, T. R., jt. auth. see Bond, Victoria.
Simon, Tanya & Simon, Richard. Oskar & the Eight Blessings. Siegel, Mark, illus. (p. 1305)
Simon, Toby L., et al. Don't Wake the Baby! (p. 469)
Simon, Tom. Traje Azul de Papa Noel. (p. 1777)
Simon, Ute, illus. see Norwich, Grace.
Simon, Veronica, jt. ed. see Applin, Barbara.
Simon, Veronica & Applin, Barbara, eds. Treasure House 2: A Caribbean Anthology. (p. 1781)
Simonds, Kevin. Tomb of Father Time. (p. 1764)
Simonds, Lucy. Celebrations. (p. 285)
—Indoor Sports. (p. 872)
—Olympics. (p. 1288)
—People & Pets. (p. 1339)
—Sky Is the Limit. (p. 1586)
—Wonders of the World. (p. 1949)
Simonds, William. Ella; or, Turning over a New Leaf by Walter Aimwell [Pseud]. (p. 514)
—Marcus; or, the Boy-Tamer by Walter Aimwell [Pseud]. (p. 1092)
—Whistler; or, the Manly Boy by Walter Aimwell [Pseud]. (p. 1912)
Simone. Things I Should Have Said. (p. 1733)
Simone, Gail. Birds of Prey: Sensei & Student. (p. 192)
—My Life in Miniature. Scott, Trevor, illus. (p. 1212)
—Of Like Minds. (p. 1279)
Simone, Gail, jt. auth. see Verheiden, Mark.
Simone, Jacquelyn. Clara. (p. 318)
—Outkast. (p. 1312)
Simone, Kriss. Fairy Forest. (p. 563)
Simone, Ni-Ni. No Boyz Allowed. (p. 1257)
—Shortie Like Mine. (p. 1569)
—Teenage Love Affair. (p. 1714)
Simone, Ni-Ni & Abrams, Amir. Get Ready for War. (p. 668)
—Hollywood High. (p. 789)
—Lights, Love & Lip Gloss. (p. 1016)
—Lights, Love, & Lip Gloss. (p. 1016)
—Put Your Diamonds Up. (p. 1420)
Simone, Ni-Ni & London, Kelli. Break-Up Diaries. (p. 224)
Simone, Val Edward. Proton Gator & Friends Coloring Book. McGill, Joshua, illus. (p. 1412)
Simone, Yve. Little Valentine. (p. 1037)
Simoneau, D. K. We're Having a Tuesday. Cornelius, Brad, illus. (p. 1875)
Simoneau, Shelly. Cows Came Running & the Horses Did Too! (p. 374)
Simonet, Evan. Jake & the Sailing Tree. (p. 906)
Simoni, Suzanne. Fantastic Female Filmmakers (p. 571)
Simonian, Andrew. Bi-Curious George: An Unauthorized Parody. (p. 174)
Simonis, Cheryl, illus. see Lind, Kathleen.
Simon-Kerr, Julia. Princess Party Paint Book. Edwards, Ken, illus. (p. 1405)
Simonnet, Aurore, illus. see Prasad, Kamal S.
Simons, Alan L. Incredible Adventures of Captain Cameron MacDuddyfunk in Cuggermuggerland. Boggelen-Heutink, Ellen van, illus. (p. 869)
Simons, Barbara Brooks. Escape to Freedom the Underground Railroad: Set Of 6. (p. 535)
—Escape to Freedom: the Underground Railroad: Text Pairs. (p. 535)
Simons, D. M. Keep Her Safe. (p. 946)
Simons, Joseph. Under a Living Sky (p. 1813)
Simons, Lisa M. B. Amazing Animal Stunts. (p. 53)
—From Egg to Spider. (p. 642)
Simons, Lisa M. Bolt. Acrostic Poems. Petelinsek, Kathleen, illus. (p. 9)
—Airmen de la Fuerza Aérea de EE. UU. (p. 31)
—Airmen of the U. S. Air Force (p. 31)

—Airmen of the U. S. Air Force [Scholastic]. (p. 31)
—Cinquain Poems. Petelinsek, Kathleen, illus. (p. 321)
—Daily Life in Ancient Greece (p. 400)
—First Olympics of Ancient Greece (p. 596)
—Haikus. Petelinsek, Kathleen, illus. (p. 735)
—Kids' Guide to Military Vehicles (p. 953)
—Rev up Your Writing in Letters & E-Mails. Gallagher-Cole, Mernie, illus. (p. 1465)
—Rev up Your Writing in Opinion Pieces. Gallagher-Cole, Mernie, illus. (p. 1465)
—Rhyming Poems. Petelinsek, Kathleen, illus. (p. 1468)
—Soldados del Ejército de EE. UU. (p. 1607)
—Soldiers of the U. S. Army (p. 1607)
—Soldiers of the U. S. Army [Scholastic]. (p. 1607)
—Transportation Long Ago & Today (p. 1779)
—U. S. Air Force by the Numbers (p. 1806)
—U. S. Army by the Numbers (p. 1806)
—Unusual & Awesome Jobs Using Math: Stunt Coordinator, Cryptologist, & More. (p. 1823)
Simons, Lisa M. Bolt, et al. Long Ago & Today (p. 1046)
—Military by the Numbers (p. 1142)
—U. S. Military by the Numbers (p. 1806)
Simons, Marijke, illus. see Payzant, Joan M.
Simons, Marijke, tr. see Payzant, Joan M.
Simons, Moya. Hello God. Coutts, Lisa, illus. (p. 764)
Simons, Paullina. I Love My Baby Because... Thomas, Cassia, illus. (p. 842)
Simons, Phillida Brooke, jt. auth. see BHB International Staff.
Simons, Rae. Adoptive Parents. (p. 13)
—All about Money: The History, Culture, & Meaning of Modern Finance. (p. 43)
—At Home in Your Body: Care for the Shape You're In. (p. 110)
—Bigger Isn't Always Better: Choosing Your Portions. (p. 185)
—Blended Families. (p. 199)
—Bruce Springsteen. (p. 232)
—Business Math. (p. 245)
—Does Television Make You Fat? Lifestyle & Obesity. (p. 460)
—Doors. (p. 470)
—Entrepreneurship. (p. 531)
—Fashion Math. (p. 575)
—Grandparents Raising Kids. (p. 709)
—Guide to Teaching Young Adults about Money. (p. 730)
—Healthy Skin. McDonnell, Mary Ann & Forman, Sara, eds. (p. 759)
—I Eat When I'm Sad: Food & Feelings. (p. 838)
—Kanye West. (p. 943)
—Luxembourg. (p. 1066)
—Money & Relationships. (p. 1164)
—Single Parents. (p. 1579)
—Spending Money. (p. 1625)
—Sports Math. (p. 1633)
—Sustainable Lifestyles in a Changing Economy. (p. 1688)
—Teen Parents. (p. 1713)
—Texas Hold'em: The Learning Curve of Life. (p. 1724)
—Texas Hold'em: the Learning Curve of Life. (p. 1724)
—Too Many Sunday Dinners: Family & Diet. (p. 1767)
Simons, Rae, jt. auth. see Libal, Joyce.
Simons, Rae, jt. auth. see Riddle, John.
Simons, Rae, jt. auth. see Stewart, Sheila.
Simons, Rae & Gommer, Viola Ruelke. Nurse. Riggs, Ernestine G. & Gholar, Cheryl, eds. (p. 1273)
Simons, Rae & Indovino, Shaina C. Spain. Bruton, John, ed. (p. 1620)
Simons, Rae & Indovino, Shaina Carmel. Luxembourg. (p. 1066)
—Spain. (p. 1620)
—United Kingdom. (p. 1819)
—United Kingdom. Bruton, John, ed. (p. 1819)
Simons, Sally, illus. see Walker, Colin.
Simonson, Audrey. Where Is Your Mousey? (p. 1909)
Simonson, Bill. Itt 'N' Ott's Pizza Journey. (p. 900)
Simonson, Lona. Noodles by Mcnoodle. Herges, Connie, illus. (p. 1264)
Simonson, Lona Marie. Grandma Lucy Feeds the Birds Herges, Connie, illus. (p. 708)
Simonson, Louise. Battling Bigfoot. Elston, James W., illus. (p. 147)
—Fall of the Mutants - X-Men. Brigman, June et al, illus. (p. 566)
—Lex Luthor's Power Grab! Vecchio, Luciano, illus. (p. 1004)
—Marvel Universe Thor Comic Reader 1. (p. 1099)
—Meet Mr. Hydeous Elston, James W., illus. (p. 1121)
—Monster Magic Schoening, Dan, illus. (p. 1167)
—Snow White & the Seven Robots. Sanchez, Jimena, illus. (p. 1600)
—What's with Wulf? Elston, James W., illus. (p. 1900)
—X-Force: Cable & the New Mutants. Liefeld, Rob & Hall, Bob, illus. (p. 1967)
Simonson, Louise, illus. see Simonson, Walter.
Simonson, Louise, jt. auth. see Claremont, Chris.
Simonson, Louise & Engelhart, Steve. Evolutionary War. Shoemaker, Terry et al, illus. (p. 547)
Simonson, Louise & Hendricks, Damion. Magnus, Robot Fighter Steranko, illus. (p. 1076)
Simonson, Louise & Sutton, Laurie S. Superman: Comic Chapter Books Vecchio, Luciano, illus. (p. 1683)
Simonson, Louise, et al. Bizarro Is Born! Doescher, Erik, illus. (p. 194)
Simonson, Roy W. Six Months along the Missouri. (p. 1582)
Simonson, Walter. Jurassic Park: Danger: Vol. 1. (p. 937)
—Jurassic Park: Don't Move!: Vol. 3. (p. 937)
—Jurassic Park: Leaving Jurassic Park: Vol. 4. (p. 937)
—Jurassic Park: The Miracle of Cloning: Vol. 2. (p. 937)
—Meltdown Simonson, Louise et al, illus. (p. 1125)
—Thor by Walter Simonson Volume 2. Buscema, Sal, illus. (p. 1739)
Simonson, Walter & Englehart, Steve. Jurassic Park. (p. 937)
Simonson, Walter, et al. Fantastic Four Epic Collection: Into the Timestream. Buckler, Rich et al, illus. (p. 571)
Simont, Marc. Perro Vagabundo. Simont, Marc, illus. (p. 1344)
—Perro Vagabundo. Simont, Marc, illus. (p. 1344)
—Stray Dog. Simont, Marc, illus. (p. 1666)
Simont, Marc, illus. see Krauss, Ruth.
Simont, Marc, illus. see Lord, Bette Bao.
Simont, Marc, illus. see Sharmat, Marjorie Weinman.
Simont, Marc, illus. see Thurber, James.
Simont, Marc, illus. see Udry, Janice May & Udry, Janice M.
Simonton, Tom, illus. see Furr, L. David.
Simonton, Tom, illus. see Hood, Douglas.
Simonton, Tom, illus. see Rondinone, Craig.
Simpkins, Debra Burke. Luna Tuna. (p. 1065)
Simpkins, Iravis, illus. see Buzzy.
Simpkins, Philip. PJ & the Crazy Squirrels. (p. 1365)
Simplicity, Barberella. Uh-Oh, My Foogle Flopped! (p. 1808)
Simpon, Tj. Tiny Paul the Tarantula Takes a Walk Register, J. R., illus. (p. 1756)
Simpson, Albert. Adventures of Billy, Ras, & Al. (p. 16)
Simpson, Amy, jt. auth. see Arbuckle, Katrina.
Simpson, Audrey. Cambridge O Level Mathematics: Volume 1. (p. 255)
—Teaching & Assessing Skills in Mathematics. (p. 1710)
Simpson, B. G. Winds of Time: Oracles of the Great-Gulf-Book One. (p. 1936)
Simpson, C. E. & Smith, C. E. Eighth Grade Witch. Utomo, Gabhor, illus. (p. 507)
Simpson, Caroll. First Beaver (p. 593)
—First Mosquito (p. 596)
Simpson, Carolyn. Coping with Post-Traumatic Stress Disorder (PTSD) Dealing with Tragedy. (p. 365)
—Understanding Compulsive Eating. (p. 1815)
Simpson, Carolyn & Simpson, Dwain. Coping with Post-Traumatic Stress Disorder (PTSD) Dealing with Tragedy. (p. 365)
Simpson, Carrie. Jungle Jack. (p. 935)
Simpson, Charles B. North Fork Verses. (p. 1265)
Simpson, Craig. Resistance. (p. 1463)
—Wolf Squadron. (p. 1944)
Simpson, D. C. Closer to the Void: Ozy & Millie 2006-2007. (p. 334)
Simpson, Dana. Phoebe & Her Unicorn: A Heavenly Nostrils Chronicle. (p. 1351)
—Phoebe & Her Unicorn. (p. 1351)
—Unicorn on a Roll: Another Heavenly Nostrils Chronicle. (p. 1818)
—Unicorn on a Roll. (p. 1818)
Simpson, Deb. Pink Place Paperback. (p. 1360)
Simpson, Dorothy. Lesson for Janie. (p. 993)
—Matter of Pride. (p. 1109)
—Visitors from the Sea. (p. 1846)
Simpson, Dwain, jt. auth. see Simpson, Carolyn.
Simpson, Howard. Through Loona's Door: A Tammy & Owen Adventure with Carter G. Woodson. (p. 1745)
Simpson, Howard, illus. see Brown, Margery W.
Simpson, Howard, illus. see Foster, William H.
Simpson, Howard, illus. see Hudson, Cheryl Willis.
Simpson, Howard, illus. see Hudson, Katura J.
Simpson, Jeff. Access to Algebra Simpson, Marilyn, ed. (p. 8)
—Addition, Subtraction & Place Value Student Edition: Count, Notice & Remember Math Intervention Volume I, AS. Simpson, Marilyn, ed. (p. 12)
—Best Stuff for Multiplying & Dividing, Student Edition: Count, Notice & Remember Math Intervention MD-1. Simpson, Marilyn, ed. (p. 171)
—Sharing Big Numbers, 2nd Edition, Student Edition: Count, Notice & Remember Math Intervention Volume I, MD-2. Simpson, Marilyn, ed. (p. 1561)
Simpson, Jeffrey L. Core Processes of Mathematics, Student Edition: Count, Notice & Remember Math Intervention, Volume 4. Simpson, Marilyn Bohlen, ed. (p. 367)
—Fractions & Decimals, Student Edition: Count, Notice & Remember Math Intervention, Volume 2. Simpson, Marilyn Bohlen, ed. (p. 627)
—Functions & Equations, Student Edition: Count, Notice & Remember Math Intervention, Volume 5. Simpson, Marilyn Bohlen, ed. (p. 649)
—Measurement & Geometry, Student Edition: Count, Notice & Remember Math Intervention, Volume 6. Simpson, Marilyn Bohlen, ed. (p. 1117)
Simpson, Joe & Bembibre, Cecilia. Tocando el Vacío. (p. 1760)
Simpson, John. Condor One. (p. 356)
Simpson, John H. Everafter. (p. 542)
Simpson, Judith. Indonesia. (p. 872)
Simpson, Judith, jt. auth. see Whitecap Books Staff.
Simpson, Kathleen. Extreme Weather: Science Tackles Global Warming & Climate Change. (p. 557)
—Genetics: From DNA to Designer Dogs. (p. 661)
—Geography of Mexico: Set Of 6. (p. 662)
—Geography of Mexico: Text Pairs. (p. 662)
—Human Brain: Inside Your Body's Control Room. (p. 826)
—Women in the Renaissance: Set Of 6. (p. 1946)
—Women in the Renaissance: Text Pairs. (p. 1946)
Simpson, Lesley. Hug. Yayo, illus. (p. 824)
—Yuvi's Candy Tree. Porter, Janice Lee, illus. (p. 1983)
Simpson, Louie. My Mom Votes! (p. 1214)
Simpson, Marilyn, ed. see Simpson, Jeff.
Simpson, Marilyn Bohlen, ed. see Simpson, Jeffrey L.
Simpson, Marilyn Bohlen, ed. Percents, Ratios, & Rates, Student Edition: Count, Notice & Remember Math Intervention, Volume 3. (p. 1341)
Simpson, Marilyn, ed. Best Stuff for Multiplying & Dividing, Teacher's Edition: Count, Notice & Remember Math Intervention MD-1. (p. 171)
Simpson, Martha Seif. Dreidel That Wouldn't Spin: A Toyshop Tale of Hanukkah. Bernhard, Durga Yael, illus. (p. 484)
Simpson, Mary. 31 Girl. (p. 1996)
Simpson, Mary, illus. see Merrill, Yvonne Y.
Simpson, Matt, creator. Happy Heart: English Book 1. (p. 746)
Simpson McLellan, Stephanie. Leon's Song Bonder, Dianna, illus. (p. 992)
Simpson, N. J. Not So Random. (p. 1267)
Simpson, Pat. Compilation of Tales to Thrill & Chill. (p. 352)
Simpson, Patrica Ann. Flick the little Runt. (p. 603)
Simpson, Patricia Ann. Frog, the Birds & the Trout. (p. 640)
—Twinkle Collection. (p. 1802)
Simpson, Phillip. All about Tigers: A Description Text (p. 43)
—Big Cats Head to Head: A Compare & Contrast Text (p. 180)
—How Can We Save the Cheetah? A Problem & Solution Text (p. 805)
—Life Cycle of a Leopard: A Sequence & Order Text (p. 1009)
—Lion Habitats under Threat: A Cause & Effect Text (p. 1020)
Simpson, Richard. Squirrel Who Was Afraid to Climb Trees. Hoch, Kevin, illus. (p. 1637)
Simpson, Roberta. Nana's Bible Stories. Mitchell, Susan, illus. (p. 1228)
Simpson, Rodney. Frannie Fern Goes to Kindergarten. (p. 631)
Simpson, Ron. Quick Revision KS3 English. (p. 1427)
Simpson, S. E. Ginger & the Bully. (p. 676)
Simpson, Sandra. Mina Fox Meets the Lady of the Library. (p. 1145)
Simpson, Steve. Farmer in the Dell. (p. 574)
Simpson, Steve, illus. see Galan, Alvaro.
Simpson, Steve, illus. see Jones, Karl.
Simpson, Sue, illus. see Sonnenberg, Lois.
Simpson, Susan. Little Tree Learns a Lesson about Sharing. (p. 1037)
Simpson, Wanda. Jupiter the Space Donkey (p. 937)
—Sammy, the Earth Traveling Turtle (p. 1508)
Simpson, William, illus. see Davis, Mike.
Simpson, Yvonne. When Spring Comes. (p. 1904)
Simpson-Enock, Sarah & Quarto Generic Staff. Mummy, Mummy, What's in Your Tummy? West, Linzi, illus. (p. 1191)
Simpson-Tweedie, Karen. Treasure on Chincoteague Island. (p. 1782)
Sims, Agnes, illus. see Travers, P. L.
Sims, Anthony. Princess Zoe. (p. 1406)
Sims, Blanche, illus. see Alberto, Daisy.
Sims, Blanche, illus. see Charney, Steve.
Sims, Blanche, illus. see Driscoll, Laura.
Sims, Blanche, illus. see Dussling, Jennifer A.
Sims, Blanche, illus. see Giff, Patricia Reilly.
Sims, Blanche, illus. see Jackson, Ellen.
Sims, Blanche, illus. see Knudsen, Michelle.
Sims, Blanche, illus. see May, Eleanor.
Sims, Blanche, illus. see McGillian, Jamie Kyle.
Sims, Blanche, illus. see Walker, Nan.
Sims, C. Bailey. Candlewax. (p. 261)
Sims, Chris & Bowers, Chad. Down Set Fight. (p. 474)
Sims, Frances. Princess Mina's Sound of Joy. (p. 1404)
Sims, Guy A. & Myers, Walter Dean. Monster. Anyabwile, Dawud, illus. (p. 1166)
Sims, Harold "Catman". Kevin Tames the Bullies. (p. 950)
Sims, Janet G. Cristy & Her Amazing Friends. (p. 383)
Sims, Janice. Grandma's Basket. Storr, Nicola, illus. (p. 708)
Sims, Julee. A. J. Loses a Tooth. (p. 1)
—A. J.'s Big Move. (p. 1)
Sims, Kathy C. Louisiana Potpourri from A to Z. (p. 1058)
Sims, Kristin. Patrick's Space Adventure. (p. 1329)
Sims, L. Castles. (p. 277)
—Puzzle Journey Around the World. (p. 1421)
—Puzzle Journey into Space. (p. 1421)
—Puzzle Journey under the Sea. (p. 1421)
Sims, L., jt. auth. see Dickens, Charles.
Sims, L., jt. auth. see Edom, H.
Sims, L., jt. auth. see Millard, A.
Sims, Lesley. Agent Arthur's Island Adventures. Mounter, Paddy, illus. (p. 29)
—Castle That Jack Built. Gordon, Mike, illus. (p. 277)
—Christmas Around the World. Ruta, Angelo et al, illus. (p. 312)
—Delightful Illustrated Stories (was Illustrated Stories for Girls) (p. 425)
—Enchanted Castle. Marks, Alan, illus. (p. 523)
—Goat in a Boat. (p. 687)
—Gran Libro de Los Castillos - Internet Linked. Groebner, Dominic, illus. (p. 706)
—How Zebras Got Their Stripes. (p. 823)
—Illustrated Classics Action & Adventure Stories for Young Readers. (p. 857)
—Illustrated Classics Enchanting Stories for Young Readers. (p. 857)
—Illustrated Classics for Children. (p. 857)
—Illustrated Classics for Girls. Mason, Conrad, illus. (p. 857)
—Island Adventures. (p. 892)
—Magical Book. Tavares, Victor, illus. (p. 1074)
—Magical Stories for Little Children. (p. 1075)
—Midsummer Night's Drem. (p. 1139)
—Roman Soldier's Handbook: Everything a Beginner Soldier Needs to Know. McNee, Ian, illus. (p. 1486)
—Snow Queen. (p. 1599)
—Snow white & the seven Dwarfs. (p. 1600)
—Story of Castles. (p. 1657)
—Story of Castles. Gower, Teri, illus. (p. 1657)
—Story of Flying. Cartwright, Stephen, illus. (p. 1658)
Sims, Lesley, ed. see Dickins, Rosie & Pratt, Leonie.
Sims, Lesley, jt. auth. see Dickens, Charles.
Sims, Lesley, jt. auth. see Dickins, Rosie.
Sims, Lesley, jt. auth. see Sims, Lesley.
Sims, Lesley & Sims, Lesley. Stories from Around the World for Children. (p. 1654)
Sims, Lesley & Stowell, Louie. Illustrated Stories for Boys. McNee, Ian, illus. (p. 858)
Sims, Lesley, ed. Illustrated Adventure Stories. (p. 857)
—Illustrated Animal Stories. Mason, Conrad, illus. (p. 857)
Sims, Leslie B., jt. auth. see Firth, Rachel.
Sims, Lori. Starvin' Marvin & Skinny Minnie Melt Minnesota. (p. 1644)
—Starvin' Marvin & Skinny Minnie Shake up San Francisco. (p. 1644)
Sims, Nat. Peekaboo Barn. Tabor, Nathan, illus. (p. 1335)
Sims, Roger A. Wise Thin King. (p. 1940)
Sims, Rudine. Bishop Daniel A. Payne: Great Black Leader. (p. 193)
Sims, Stacy. Rainbow Butterflies. (p. 1435)
Sims, Steve. Drawing Dungeon Creatures. (p. 481)
—Drawing Heroic Warriors. (p. 482)
Sims, Tom. Repo Elf. Perri, Anthony F., illus. (p. 1461)
Simson, Dana. Colors. (p. 345)
—Numbers. (p. 1271)
—Princess Ruby's Rainbow Day. (p. 1405)
—Shapes. (p. 1560)
—Zooballie. (p. 1989)
Simson, Dana & Book Company Staff. Dreamland. Simson, Dana, illus. (p. 484)
Simula, Laura. Broken Yesterday. (p. 230)
Simwenyi, Robbinson Namasaka. Death, the Only Gift (p. 420)
—Young Detectives. (p. 1978)
Sin Fronteras (Without Borders), tr. see Kannenberg, Stacey.
Sin I Si Tou. Child's Creation: Stories & Poems. (p. 304)
Sina-Ataanda, Moyin. Phenomenal Four: Four on a Mission to Save the Animals. (p. 1350)
Sinclair, Alex, illus. see Azzarello, Brian & Loeb, Jeph.
Sinclair, Alison. Lightborn. (p. 1015)
Sinclair, Angie, ed. see Herzog, Joyce.
Sinclair, Bella, illus. see O'Connor, Jane.
Sinclair, Bella, illus. see Shepherd, Donna J.
Sinclair, Dan, ed. see Herzog, Joyce.
Sinclair, Donna, jt. auth. see Kyle, Margaret.
Sinclair, Gardine. Keira at Stageschool. (p. 948)
—Mystery at Stageschool. (p. 1224)
—Stageschool by the Sea. (p. 1638)
Sinclair, Howard. Ego: And the Chocolate-Covered Worms. (p. 506)
Sinclair, James, illus. see Mignola, Mike.
Sinclair, Jean. Tender Touch. Landes, William-Alan, ed. (p. 1719)
Sinclair, Jeff, illus. see Gardner, Martin.
Sinclair, Jeff, illus. see Pellowski, Michael J.
Sinclair, Kerrie, jt. auth. see Fyke, Laurie.
Sinclair, Lynn. Key to Aten (p. 950)
Sinclair, Mehded Maryam. Miraculous Happenings in the Year of the Elephant. (p. 1149)
—Trust of Treasures. Desira, Angela, illus. (p. 1793)
—When Wings Expand. (p. 1905)
Sinclair, Nicholas, et al. Cookie Story. Wall, Randy Hugh, ed. (p. 361)
Sinclair, Pembroke. Dealing with Devils. (p. 418)
Sinclair, Peter, illus. see Reeves, Barbara.
Sinclair, Scott & Penner, Jim. Come as a Child 3: Children's Sermons to See & Hear (p. 347)
Sinclair, Sydney. Curse of Crion: Book 1: the World of Fyedybar Series. (p. 394)
Sinclair, Tim. Run. (p. 1496)
Sinclair, Upton. Jungle: Literary Touchstone Edition. (p. 934)
—Jungle. Burns, Charles, illus. (p. 934)
—Oil! (p. 1282)
Sinclair, Upton, et al. Jungle. (p. 934)
Sinclair, Valerie, jt. auth. see Evans, D. L.
Sinclair, William John. Recent Investigations Bearing on the Question of the Occurrence of Neocene Man in the Auriferous Gravels of the Sierra Nevada. (p. 1451)
Sinden, David, jt. auth. see Catlow, Nikalas.
Sinden, David, jt. auth. see Matthews, Morgan.
Sinden, David, et al. Bang Goes a Troll Duddle, Jonny, illus. (p. 136)
—Jungle Vampire. Duddle, Jonny, illus. (p. 935)
—Sea Monsters & Other Delicacies. Duddle, Jonny, illus. (p. 1535)
—Werewolf Versus Dragon. Duddle, Jonny, illus. (p. 1875)
Sinelli, Todd Andrew. Until Now. (p. 1823)
Sinex, Roxana Faith. Colby's New Home. Cowper-Thomas, Wendy, illus. (p. 338)
Sinfield, Irene. Julia & her Bears on Holiday. (p. 932)
Singal, Sudesh. Moongi & Mohan: A Story from India As Told to Me by My Mother. Kinra, Richa, illus. (p. 1172)
Singer, Alexis. Alexis: My True Story of Internet Sex with a Married Man. (p. 37)
Singer, Allie, ed. see Kaye, Megan.
Singer, Beth & Benchmark Education Co., LLC Staff. Red Bird Chirps. (p. 1453)
—We Can Fix It! (p. 1866)
Singer, Bill, jt. auth. see Ward-Singer, Tonya.
Singer, Cindy & Gurrentz, Sheryl. If Your Child Is Bipolar: The Parent-to-Parent Guide to Living with & Loving a Bipolar Child. (p. 855)
Singer, Dani & Hunter, Myra, eds. Assisted Human Reproduction: Psychological & Ethical Dilemmas. (p. 107)
Singer, David. Yisrael Sheli/My Israel: People & Places. (p. 1971)
Singer, Edmund, ed. see Kreutzer, Rudolph.
Singer, Ellen, jt. auth. see de Posada, Joachim.
Singer, Flora M. Flora - I Was but A Child. (p. 606)
Singer, Howard. With Mind & Heart. (p. 1942)
Singer, Isaac Bashevis. Cuentos Judios de la Aldea de Chelm. (p. 390)
—Mazel y Schlimazel. (p. 1113)
—Parakeet Named Dreidel. Berkson, Suzanne Raphael, illus. (p. 1323)
—Short Friday & Other Stories. (p. 1569)
—Singer: Collected Stories - Gimple the Fool to the Letter Writer. Stavans, Ilan, ed. (p. 1579)
—Why Noah Chose the Dove. (p. 1925)
—Why Noah Chose the Dove. Shub, Elizabeth, tr. (p. 1925)
Singer, Jane. DNA & Body Evidence (p. 456)
Singer, Jane, jt. auth. see Innes, Brian.
Singer, Jane, jt. auth. see Wright, John D.
Singer, Jane E. Meat. (p. 1117)
—Rice. (p. 1469)
—Soybeans. (p. 1618)
—Wheat. (p. 1900)
Singer, Jenny & Scheff, William. Marquette University College Prowler off the Record. (p. 1096)
Singer, Marilyn. Animales a Tu Alrededor. Zaidi, Nadeem, illus. (p. 80)
—Brushes with Religion. (p. 233)
—Caterpillars. (p. 279)
—City Lullaby. Cneut, Carll, illus. (p. 323)
—Eggs. Stevenson, Emma, illus. (p. 506)
—Every Day's a Dog's Day: A Year in Poems. Sakamoto, Miki, illus. (p. 542)
—Fireflies at Midnight. Robbins, Ken, illus. (p. 592)

—Follow Follow: A Book of Reverso Poems. Masse, Josée, illus. (p. 612)
—Full Moon is Rising. (p. 646)
—Fun with Animals Friendship Box. Zaidi, Nadeem, illus. (p. 648)
—I'm Gonna Climb a Mountain in My Patent Leather Shoes. Avril, Lynne, illus. (p. 859)
—Mirror Mirror. Masse, Josée, illus. (p. 1149)
—On the Same Day in March. (p. 1291)
—Rutherford B., Who Was He? Poems about Our Presidents. Hendrix, John, illus. (p. 1499)
—Stick Is an Excellent Thing: Poems Celebrating Outdoor Play. Pham, LeUyen, illus. (p. 1649)
—Strange Place to Call Home: The World's Most Dangerous Habitats & the Animals That Call Them Home. Young, Ed, illus. (p. 1665)
—Superheroes Employment Agency. Jones, Noah Z., illus. (p. 1683)
—Tallulah's Nutcracker. Boiger, Alexandra, illus. (p. 1704)
—Tallulah's Solo. Boiger, Alexandra, illus. (p. 1704)
—Tallulah's Tap Shoes. Boiger, Alexandra, illus. (p. 1704)
—Tallulah's Toe Shoes. Boiger, Alexandra, illus. (p. 1704)
—Tallulah's Tutu. Boiger, Alexandra, illus. (p. 1704)
—Twosomes: Love Poems from the Animal Kingdom. Wildish, Lee, illus. (p. 1804)
—Venom. (p. 1835)
—What Is Your Dog Doing? Habbley, Kathleen, illus. (p. 1891)
Singer, Marilyn & Cairns, Julia. Full Moon Is Rising. (p. 646)
Singer, Marilyn, ed. Face Relations: 11 Stories about Seeing Beyond Color. (p. 560)
Singer, Maurene, et al. Place in the Sky. Marino, Natalie & Marino, Illustrator, Natalie, Natalie, illus. (p. 1365)
Singer, Neal. Wonders of Nuclear Fusion: Creating an Ultimate Energy Source. (p. 1948)
Singer, Nicky. Innocent's Story. (p. 875)
—Under Shifting Glass. (p. 1813)
Singer, Rhona Stein. There Can't Be Two Queens in the Same Hive. Singer, Rhona Stein, illus. (p. 1729)
Singer, Ryan, illus. see Tsinajinnie, Veronica.
Singer, Sarah Jane. Two Bullets for Sergeant Franks. (p. 1803)
Singer, Thom, jt. auth. see Morris, Paris.
Singer, Thomas & Kimbles, Samuel L., eds. Cultural Complex: Contemporary Jungian Perspectives on Psyche & Society. (p. 391)
Singer-Towns, Brian, ed. Catholic Youth Bible: Pray It, Study It, Live It. (p. 280)
—Catholic Youth Bible. (p. 280)
Singer-Towns, Brian, et al. Catholic Faith Handbook for Youth. (p. 280)
Singh, Asavari. Drawing. (p. 481)
—How to Draw the Craziest, Creepiest Characters James, Martin et al, illus. (p. 818)
—How to Draw the Darkest, Baddest Graphic Novels Mudgal, Nishant et al, illus. (p. 818)
—How to Draw the Fastest, Coolest Cars James, Martin et al, illus. (p. 818)
—How to Draw the Most Exciting, Awesome Manga James, Martin et al, illus. (p. 819)
Singh, Balwant. Jako - The Dog That Survived The 9/11. (p. 906)
—Old Man & the Donkey. (p. 1284)
Singh, Belveen. Kaleidoscopic Life: Poems for the Childrens' Heart. (p. 942)
Singh, Bilveer. Papua: Geopolitics & the Quest for Nationhood. (p. 1323)
Singh, Devika, jt. auth. see Singh, Raghubir.
SINGH, H. Happy peace Day. (p. 746)
Singh, Jay. Once upon a Time in a Forest Far Away. (p. 1293)
Singh, Jen, illus. see Buffington, Perry W.
Singh, Jen, illus. see Butcher, Nancy.
Singh, Kanwaljit Kaur, jt. auth. see A&C Black Staff.
Singh, Lalit Kumar, illus. see Helfand, Lewis.
Singh, Lee. ABC & Do. Wall, Karen, illus. (p. 3)
Singh, Mahendra, jt. auth. see Uttley, Alison.
Singh, Nalini. Angels' Blood (p. 75)
Singh, Navneet. Key to Light & Darkness: Everything Can Feel Like a Dream... (p. 950)
Singh, Nikhil, jt. auth. see Dunning, John Harris.
Singh, Raghubir & Singh, Devika. River of Colour the India of Raghubir Singh. Singh, Raghubir, photos by. (p. 1476)
Singh, Rajinder. Journey of the Phoenix. Bergen, Brenda, illus. (p. 928)
—Jyoti Meditation for Children. Schulbaum, Michael, illus. (p. 941)
—King's Mascot. Williams-El, Belinda Irene, illus. (p. 960)
Singh, Rina. Forest of Stories: Magical Tree Tales from Around the World. Cann, Helen, illus. (p. 618)
—Forest of Stories. Cann, Helen, illus. (p. 618)
—Magic Braid. Zaman, Farida, illus. (p. 1072)
—Nearly Nonsense: Hoja Tales from Turkey. Zaman, Farida, illus. (p. 1239)
—Pitseolak Ashoona: Une Artiste Inuite. (p. 1364)
Singh, Sara, illus. see Brontë, Emily.
Singhal, Sheetal. Counting. Sona & Jacob, illus. (p. 370)
—Opposites. Sona & Jacob, illus. (p. 1300)
Singhose, Rose. Granny's Giggles. (p. 710)
—Granny's GIGGLES BOOK EIGHT. (p. 710)
—Granny's GIGGLES BOOK FIVE. (p. 710)
—Granny's giggles book Four. (p. 710)
—Granny's GIGGLES BOOK SIX. (p. 710)
—Granny's giggles book Three. (p. 710)
—Granny's giggles book Two. (p. 710)
Singhose, Rose & StGermain, Annetta. Gramma's Sure Fire Cure for Insomnia in the Very Young. (p. 706)
Singlehurst, Naomi. Grandpa, What's That Sound in the Middle of the Night? Ellen Koski, Rachel, ed. (p. 709)
Singletary, Gladys Renae. Snowman with a Heart. (p. 1601)
Singletary, Mabel, jt. auth. see Singletary, Mabel Elizabeth.
Singletary, Mabel Elizabeth. Just Jump! (p. 939)
—Promise & a Rainbow. (p. 1411)
—Run, Jeremiah Run! (p. 1496)
—Something to Jump About. (p. 1610)
Singletary, Mabel Elizabeth & Singletary, Mabel. Coming Across Jordan (p. 348)
Singletary, Nicole. My Grandmamma's X-Ray. (p. 1210)
Singleton, Clayton. Dream an Awesome Dream. (p. 483)
Singleton, Clive. City through the Clouds. (p. 324)
Singleton, Crystal. Princess of Pilayzha. (p. 1404)
Singleton, David & Martin, Loyce. Us Mail. (p. 1826)
Singleton, Debbie. King Who Wouldn't Sleep. Swain, Holly, illus. (p. 959)
Singleton, Glen. 1001 Cool School Yard Jokes. (p. 2002)
—1001 Even More Cool Jokes. (p. 2002)
—101 Cool Magic Tricks. (p. 1999)
—Crazy Book of Gross Jokes. (p. 377)
Singleton, Glynn. Buddy Boy Brooks Takes the Wheel: A Mile Wide Tale from the Mighty Mississippi. Carisse, Carissa, illus. (p. 234)
Singleton, Harry. Silver Saddle. (p. 1576)
Singleton, Jennifer. That magnificent Medallion. (p. 1726)
Singleton, Linda Joy. Buried: A Goth Girl Mystery. (p. 243)
—Curious Cat Spy Club. (p. 392)
—Dead Girl Dancing. (p. 416)
—Dead Girl in Love. (p. 416)
—Dead Girl Walking. (p. 416)
—Don't Die, Dragonfly. Karre, Andrew, ed. (p. 467)
—Fatal Charm. (p. 577)
—Last Dance. (p. 977)
—Magician's Muse. (p. 1075)
—Melissa's Mission Impossible. (p. 1125)
—Melissa's Mission Impossible/Mail Order Monster: Twin Spins. (p. 1125)
—My Sister the Ghost #1 Twin Again. (p. 1218)
—Snow Dog, Sand Dog. Golden, Jess, illus. (p. 1599)
—Sword Play. (p. 1692)
—Witch Ball. (p. 1941)
Singleton, Paul. Sometimes Mama's Just Like That. (p. 1610)
Singleton, Sarah. Hodder Reading Project 5-6 Reader: Century. (p. 787)
Singley, George. Mutation. (p. 1194)
Singley, George T. Silent Ghost. (p. 1575)
Singley, Judith M. B C Trees. (p. 122)
Singmaster, Elsie. Rifles for Washington. (p. 1471)
Sinha, Rhea. Latte's Vacation. Sinha, Rhea, illus. (p. 980)
Siniard, Ricky, illus. see Fenton, Geleta.
Sinish, Peter. Your Cookbook with Chef Peter. (p. 1980)
Sink, Christopher A. Contemporary School Counseling: Theory, Research, & Practice. (p. 360)
Sink, Cynthia, illus. see Pritchard, Herman S.
Sinke, Grandma Janet Mary. Grandma's Christmas Tree. Pennington, Craig, illus. (p. 708)
—I Wanna Go to Grandma's House. Pennington, Craig, illus. (p. 847)
Sinke, Janet Mary. I Wanna Go to Grandma's House & Grandma's Treasure Chest Pennington, Craig, illus. (p. 847)
—Priscilla Mcdoodlenut Doodle Mcmae Asks, Why? Pennington, Craig, illus. (p. 1407)
Sinker, Alice, illus. see Bourgeois, Paulette & Clark, Brenda.
Sinkler, Adrian. Iraq. (p. 887)
Sinkner, Alice, jt. adapted by see McIntyre, Sasha.
Sinkovec, Igor, illus. see Dahl, Michael.
Sinkovec, Igor, illus. see Gunderson, Jessica & Weakland, Mark.
Sinkovec, Igor, illus. see Gunderson, Jessica.
Sinkovec, Igor, illus. see Weakland, Mark.
Sinnott, Adrian C., illus. see Steinberg, D. J.
Sinnott, Adrian C., tr. see Steinberg, D. J.
Sinnott, Bruce. Special Place. (p. 1623)
Sinnott, Joe, et al. Fantastic Four (p. 571)
Sinois, Latrice J. You Are My Sunshine. (p. 1973)
Sinykin, Sheri. Giving up the Ghost (p. 681)
Sio, Betsy Menson. Little Critters. Richter, Hank, illus. (p. 1026)
Siobhan, Bell, illus. see Sheena, Roberts & Roberts, Sheena.
Siobhan, Dowd. London Eye Mystery. (p. 1046)
Siomades, Lorianne. Cuckoo Can't Find You. Siomades, Lorianne, illus. (p. 389)
—Katy Did It! (p. 945)
Siomades, Lorianne, ed. Look What You Can Make with Boxes: Creative Crafts from Everyday Objects. Schneider, Hank, photos by. (p. 1050)
Sioras, Efstathia & Spilling, Michael. Czech Republic. (p. 397)
Sioux Rose. Cassandra's Tale: Invitation to the Circle. (p. 276)
Sioux, Tracee. African American Migration. (p. 27)
—Immigrants & the Westward Expansion. (p. 861)
—Immigrants in Colonial America. (p. 861)
—Immigrants, Migration, & the Growth of the American City. (p. 861)
—Immigrants, Migration, & the Industrial Revolution. (p. 861)
—Immigration, Migration, & the Growth of the American City. (p. 861)
—Immigration, Migration, & the Industrial Revolution. (p. 861)
—Native American Migration. (p. 1234)
Sipe, Antoinette Leonard. Alamo. (p. 33)
Sipe, Kelly. What It Takes to Be a Hero. (p. 1891)
Sipe, S. Anthony. Was Bug. (p. 1859)
—Wishing Star. (p. 1940)
Sipes, Peter. Abecedarium Latinum. Rojas, Jessica, illus. (p. 4)
Sipi, Claire. One Direction Doodles: Color, Doodle, & Daydream about the Gorgeous Boys. (p. 1294)
—One Direction Dress-Up Sticker Book. (p. 1294)
—One Direction Party Pack. Carlton Books Staff, ed. (p. 1294)
Siple, Greg, illus. see Rutter, Michael.
Sipp, Caroline M., jt. auth. see Carayannis, Elias G.
Sipp, Leora Janson. Emma & Sara Learn about Harvest Time. (p. 519)
—Nathan & Tori Visit Ohio: And Learn about Wild Animals. (p. 1231)
Sipperley, Keli. Old Fort at St. Augustine. (p. 1283)
—St. Louis Gateway Arch. (p. 1638)
—Statue of Liberty. (p. 1645)
—White House. (p. 1913)
Sipple, Dan, illus. see Krieger, Emily.
Siqueiros, Paula, jt. auth. see Lasky, Ricki.
Siraj-Blatchford, John & Whitebread, David. Supporting ICT in the Early Years. (p. 1684)
—Supporting Information & Communications Technology in the Early Years. (p. 1684)
Siravo, Christina E., illus. see Davis, Dan.
Sirch, Willow Ann. Eco-Women: Protectors of the Earth. (p. 502)
Sire, Storma. Lessons in Magic. (p. 993)
Sireau, Christine. Theo: The Blue Rider Pigeon. Tannenbaum, Rose, illus. (p. 1729)
Sirett, Dawn, ed. see Dorling Kindersley Publishing Staff.
Sirett, Dawn & Dorling Kindersley Publishing Staff. All about Me! 6 Fun Flaps to Flap. (p. 42)
—Baby Animals. (p. 124)
—Beep! Beep! Peekaboo! Quasha, Jennifer, ed. (p. 157)
—Farm. Quasha, Jennifer, ed. (p. 573)
—My First Christmas Board Book. (p. 1206)
—My First Words: Let's Get Talking! Quasha, Jennifer, ed. (p. 1208)
Siriano, A. M. Nod. (p. 1262)
Sirimarco, Elizabeth. Time of Slavery. (p. 1752)
Siris-Winchester, Elizabeth, jt. auth. see Winchester, Elizabeth Siris.
Sirkis, Rafael. Wacky Facts. (p. 1852)
Sirko, Teodora. Aesop's Fables. (p. 25)
Sirod, G. P., jt. auth. see Sirod, G. p.
Sirod, G. p. & Sirod, G. P. Scabs. (p. 1519)
Sirois, Celia. My Jewish Friend: A Young Catholic Learns about Judaism. Santillan, Mariano, illus. (p. 1211)
Sirois, Celia M. Jesus Is the Promise (p. 915)
Siroka, Eva. Maddalena. (p. 1069)
Sirota, Lyn. Pink. (p. 1359)
—Screws. Butler, Reginald, illus. (p. 1533)
Sirota, Lyn A. Acropolis Museum. (p. 9)
—Bandicoots (p. 136)
—Bearded Dragons (p. 151)
—Bengal Tigers (p. 164)
—Camels (p. 256)
—Capitol. (p. 263)
—Crocodiles (p. 384)
—Dingoes (p. 440)
—Giant Pandas (p. 674)
—Horned Lizards (p. 798)
—Out of Control: The Science of Wildfires (p. 1311)
—Science Lab: Technological Design. (p. 1526)
—South America. (p. 1616)
—Tasmanian Devils. (p. 1707)
Sirota, Lyn A., jt. auth. see Mattern, Joanne.
Sirota, Lyn A., jt. auth. see Sirota, Lyn.
Sirota, Lyn & Sirota, Lyn A. Capitol. (p. 263)
Sirota Rosenberg, Shirley, jt. auth. see Bulger, Roger J.
Sirotowitz, Sandi, et al. Study Strategies for Early School Success: Seven Steps to Improve Your Learning. Dimatteo, Richard, illus. (p. 1670)
—Study Strategies Made Easy: A Practical Plan for School Success. DiMatteo, Richard A., illus. (p. 1670)
Sirotzky, Sara. Red Rose & Blue Butterfly. Weber, Andra, illus. (p. 1455)
Sirowy, Alexandra. Creeping: If You Hunt for Monsters, You'll Find Them. (p. 381)
Sirr, Peter. Black Wreath: The Stolen Life of James Lovett. (p. 197)
Sirrell, Terri, illus. see Cole, Bob.
Sirrell, Terri, jt. auth. see Cole, Bob.
Sirrell, Terry, illus. see Masoff, Joy.
Sirrell, Terry, illus. see Meister, Cari.
Sirrell, Terry, jt. auth. see Meister, Cari.
Sirrine, Carol. Cool Crafts with Old CDs: Green Projects for Resourceful Kids. (p. 363)
—Cool Crafts with Old Jeans: Green Projects for Resourceful Kids. (p. 363)
—Cool Crafts with Old T-Shirts: Green Projects for Resourceful Kids (p. 363)
—Cool Crafts with Old Wrappers, Cans, & Bottles: Green Projects for Resourceful Kids. (p. 363)
Sirrine, Carol, jt. auth. see Jones, Jen.
Sirvaitis, Karen. Barack Obama: A Leader in a Time of Change. (p. 137)
—European American Experience. (p. 540)
—Guyana in Pictures. (p. 733)
—Nevada. (p. 1242)
—Seven Wonders of Green Building Technology. (p. 1555)
Sís, Peter. Ballerina! (p. 134)
—Dinosaur! Sís, Peter, illus. (p. 441)
—Fire Truck. Sís, Peter, illus. (p. 591)
—Follow the Dream: The Story of Christopher Columbus. Sís, Peter, illus. (p. 612)
—Ice Cream Summer. (p. 850)
—Madlenka. Sís, Peter, illus. (p. 1070)
—Madlenka's Dog (p. 1070)
—Pilot & the Little Prince: The Life of Antoine de Saint-Exupéry. Sís, Peter, illus. (p. 1359)
—Play, Mozart, Play! Sís, Peter, illus. (p. 1371)
—Small Tall Tale from the Far Far North. (p. 1592)
—Train of States. (p. 1777)
—Train of States. Sís, Peter, illus. (p. 1777)
—Tree of Life: Charles Darwin. (p. 1783)
—Tree of Life: Charles Darwin. Sís, Peter, illus. (p. 1783)
—Trucks Trucks Trucks. Sís, Peter, illus. (p. 1791)
—Wall: Growing up Behind the Iron Curtain. Sís, Peter, illus. (p. 1854)
Sís, Peter, illus. see Banks, Kate.
Sís, Peter, illus. see Fleischman, Sid.
Sís, Peter, illus. see Kipling, Rudyard.
Sís, Peter, illus. see Prelutsky, Jack.
Sís, Peter, illus. see Ryan, Pam Muñoz.
Sís, Peter, illus. see Taravant, Jacques.
SISA CHINESE CULTURE CENTER, compiled by. Fun Chinese for Kids. (p. 647)
Sisco, Joann Ellen. Bison of the High Meadow: 1. (p. 193)
—Bonnie from Blue Mountain: 1. (p. 209)
—Midnight at Faraway Farm. (p. 1138)
—Priscilla, the Graceful Greased Pig: 11. (p. 1407)
—Search for the Porcupine: 2. (p. 1537)
—Story of Many Blankets: 3. (p. 1659)
Sisco, K. B. Jackpot's Tail. (p. 904)
Sise, Katie. Boyfriend App. (p. 220)
—Pretty App. (p. 1398)
Sisemore, Timothy A. Of Such Is the Kingdom: Nurturing Children in the Light of Scripture. (p. 1279)
Sisk, Clay, illus. see Wax, Wendy & Wax, Naomi.
Sisk, Liza. Clay Birds of Jesus. (p. 330)
Sisk, Maeve T. Arctic Foxes. (p. 96)
—Arctic Wolves. (p. 96)
—Caving. (p. 282)
—Fractions with Fish. (p. 627)
—Mount Terror. (p. 1180)
—Polar Bears. (p. 1379)
Siskind, Ellyn, jt. auth. see Levin, Ina.
Siskind, Fred, photos by see Lewis, J. Patrick.
Sisler, Celeste. Disney Fairies: Meet Rosetta. (p. 451)
—Disney Fairies: Bedtime Fairy Stories: a Treasury. (p. 451)
—Disney Fairies: Love, Tinker Bell. (p. 451)
—Disney Fairies: Meet the Fairies: A Collection of Reading Adventures. (p. 451)
—Disney Fairies: the Perfect Pumpkin. (p. 451)
—Disney Fairies: Tink & Friends Story Collection. (p. 451)
—Disney Fairies: Very Short Fairy Stories: a Treasury. (p. 451)
—Disney Fairies: Winter Wonderland Reusable Sticker Book. (p. 451)
—Fairies' New Forest Friend. (p. 563)
—Legend of the NeverBeast - Fawn's Field Guide: A Reusable Sticker Book. (p. 989)
—My Little Pony: the Rainbow Power Sticker Book. (p. 1213)
Sisler, Celeste, jt. auth. see Disney.
Sisler, Celeste & Fox, Jennifer. Meet Fawn. (p. 1121)
Sisler, Stephanie. Gravy on My Mashed Potatoes: A Creative Exploration of Special Relationships. Grzelak, Kyle, illus. (p. 713)
—Matthews Monsters, a Creative Comprehensive Exercise. Grzelak, Kyle, illus. (p. 1110)
—One Bright Monster. Holcomb, Nicholas, illus. (p. 1294)
Sisneros, Shawn, illus. see Nyikos, Stacy Ann.
Sisneros, Shawn, illus. see Nyikos, Stacy.
Sisoj, Natalja, ed. see AZ Books Staff.
Sisperova, Iva. Travel Through Towns with Bernie & Ben. (p. 1780)
Sissom, Carol, jt. auth. see Raquel, Israel.
Sisson, Debbie, illus. see Sisson, Mark & Sisson, Wesley.
Sisson, Kathryn Cleven. Eddie Rickenbacker: Boy Pilot & Racer Morrison, Cathy, illus. (p. 503)
—Eddie Rickenbacker: Boy Pilot & Racer Underdown, Harold D., ed. (p. 503)
—John Hancock: Independent Boy. Underdown, Harold D., ed. (p. 922)
Sisson, Mark & Sisson, Wesley. Alaskan Railroad Adventure: Messy Macie Where Have You Been Today? Sisson, Mark et al, illus. (p. 34)
Sisson, Stephanie Roth, illus. see Greene, Stephanie.
Sisson, Stéphanie Roth, illus. see Pulver, Robin.
Sisson, Stéphanie Roth, illus. see Ward, Jennifer.
Sisson, Stéphanie Roth, jt. auth. see Hirsch, Jennifer.
Sisson, Wesley, jt. auth. see Sisson, Mark.
Sissung, Ingrid. Hiccup. (p. 775)
Sister Flowers. When Boo Boo Wakes Up! Smith, Brenda, illus. (p. 1901)
Sister Mary of the Compassion, illus. see Windeatt, Mary F.
Sisters of Notre Dame, Chardon, Ohio. God Cares for Us: Grade 2. (p. 688)
—We Believe: Grade 3. (p. 1866)
Sisters, Write, jt. auth. see Buell, Janet.
Sisters, Write, jt. auth. see Mayr, Diane.
Sistig, Heike, illus. see Schnee, Silke.
Sistrunk, Pat A. Bunny Kisses from Thumperlen. (p. 242)
Sisung, Peter, illus. see Wildman, Dale.
Sita, Lisa. Pocahontas: The Powhatan Culture & the Jamestown Colony. (p. 1375)
Sita, Lisa, jt. auth. see Krizner, L. J.
Sitaraman, Soumya, illus. see Krishnaswami, Uma.
Sitarski, Anita. Cold Light: Creatures, Discoveries, & Inventions That Glow. (p. 338)
Sitarz, Paula Gaj. Curtain Rises: A History of the European Theatre from 18th Century to the Present. Vol. II Landes, William-Alan, ed. (p. 395)
—Curtain Rises: A History of Theatre from Its Origins in Greek & Roman Times Through the English Restoration. Vol. 1 Landes, William-Alan, ed. (p. 395)
Sites, Jennifer, illus. see Glover, Rosanne Harper.
Sithole, Thelma. Little Monkey & the Crocodile. Montague, Christine, illus. (p. 1032)
—Little Shoko & the Crocodile. Holmes, Rebecca, illus. (p. 1036)
Sitner, Nechama. What Did Pinny Do? An Upsherin Story. Leff, Tova, illus. (p. 1882)
Sitomer, Alan Lawrence. Caged Warrior. (p. 251)
—Daddies Do It Different. Carter, Abby, illus. (p. 398)
—Daddy's Back-To-School Shopping Adventure. Carter, Abby, illus. (p. 399)
—Daddy's Zigzagging Bedtime Story. Carter, Abby, illus. (p. 399)
—Hip-Hop High School. (p. 780)
—Homeboyz. (p. 793)
—Hoopster (p. 795)
—Nerd Girls: A Catastrophe of Nerdish Proportions. (p. 1241)
—Noble Warrior. (p. 1262)
—Secret Story of Sonia Rodriguez. (p. 1544)
—Teaching Teens & Reaping Results in a Wi-Fi, Hip-Hop,Where-Has-All-the-Sanity-Gone World: Stories, Strategies, Tools, & Tips from a Three-Time Teacher of the Year Award Winner. (p. 1710)
Sitomer, Alan Lawrence & Cirelli, Michael, texts. Hip-Hop Poetry & the Classics for the Classroom. (p. 780)
Sitton, Rebecca. Rebecca Sitton's Practice Book for Learning Spelling & Word Skills Level 1 (p. 1450)
—Rebecca Sitton's Practice Book for Learning Spelling & Word Skills, Level 3 (p. 1450)
—Word Skills in Rhythm & Rhyme Level 1. Bernard, Donna, illus. (p. 1951)
Sitzenstock, Gabriele. Raising Puppy. (p. 1437)
Siu-Chong, Ken. Chun-Li. (p. 318)

—Darkstalkers: the Ultimate Edition: The Ultimate Edition. (p. 409)
—Fighter's Destiny (p. 585)
—Street Fighter (p. 1666)
—Street Fighter Classic Volume 3: Psycho Crusher: Psycho Crusher. (p. 1666)
—Street Fighter Legends Volume 1: Sakura: Sakura. (p. 1666)
Siuda, Erik. Creative Haven Asian Tattoo Design Coloring Book. (p. 379)
—Creative Haven Floral Tattoo Designs Coloring Book. (p. 379)
—Creative Haven Polynesian Designs Coloring Book. (p. 379)
—Dolphin Dream Designs Coloring Book. (p. 464)
Siuda, Erik & Creative Haven. Creative Haven Modern Tattoo Designs Coloring Book. (p. 379)
Sivertsen, Linda & Sivertsen, Tosh. Generation Green: The Ultimate Teen Guide to Living an Eco-Friendly Life. (p. 660)
Sivertsen, Tosh, jt. auth. see Sivertsen, Linda.
Sivier, Janet. Charlotte & Jackson: The Butterfly. (p. 293)
—Charlotte & Jackson: The Strange Flowers. (p. 293)
Siwak, Brenda S. Counting on the Bay. Dodge, Barbara A., illus. (p. 371)
Siwanowicz, Igor. Animals up Close: Zoom in on the World's Most Incredible Creatures. (p. 84)
Siwinski, Deborah. Adventures of Teddy & Freddy Summer Safari. Siwinski, Deborah, illus. (p. 23)
Sixtus, Albert. Rabbit School: A Light-Hearted Tale. Freischlad, Roland, tr. from GER. (p. 1429)
Siy, Alexandra. Bug Shots: The Good, the Bad, & the Bugly. Kunkel, Dennis, illus. (p. 236)
—Cars on Mars: Roving the Red Planet. (p. 272)
—Mosquito Bite. Kunkel, Dennis, illus. (p. 1176)
—One Tractor: A Counting Book. Rogers, Jacqueline, illus. (p. 1297)
—One Tractor. Rogers, Jacqueline, illus. (p. 1297)
—Spidermania: Friends on the Web. Kunkel, Dennis, photos by. (p. 1626)
Si-Young, Lee. Real Lies (p. 1448)
Sizemore, Carmen, illus. see Pitman, Sandra.
Sizemore, Robert Anthony. For Douglas - a Final Word on the Korean War. (p. 615)
Sizer, Ralph Robuck. Rashad & Rameen. (p. 1439)
Sjogren, Steve. Conspiracy of Kindness: A Refreshing New Approach to Sharing the Love of Jesus. (p. 359)
Sjonger, Rebecca. Biomedical Engineering & Human Body Systems. (p. 189)
—Do Your Bit to Be Physically Fit! (p. 458)
—Geotechnical Engineering & Earth's Materials & Processes. (p. 665)
—Knockout! How "Little Giant" Tommy Burns Became the World Heavyweight Champion (p. 965)
—On a Mission for Good Nutrition! (p. 1288)
—Raies. (p. 1433)
—Shailene Woodley. (p. 1558)
—Stress Less! A Kid's Guide to Managing Emotions. (p. 1667)
—You Need Rest to Be at Your Best! (p. 1976)
Sjonger, Rebecca, jt. auth. see Kalman, Bobbie.
Sjonger, Rebecca & Kalman, Bobbie. Aves de Todo Tipo. (p. 119)
—Birds of All Kinds. (p. 191)
—Cachorros. Crabtree, Marc, photos by. (p. 250)
—Gerbils. Crabtree, Marc, illus. (p. 666)
—Hamsters. Crabtree, Marc, illus. (p. 740)
—Hamsters. Crabtree, Marc, photos by. (p. 740)
—Life Cycle of a Bat. (p. 1008)
—Life Cycle of a Polar Bear. (p. 1009)
—Life of the Powhatan. (p. 1012)
—Los Hámsters. Crabtree, Marc, photos by. (p. 1054)
—Mice. Crabtree, Marc, illus. (p. 1134)
—Monkeys & Other Primates. (p. 1166)
—Nations of the Eastern Great Lakes. (p. 1234)
—Oiseaux. (p. 1282)
—Ours Polaires. Briere, Marie-Josee, tr. from ENG. (p. 1310)
—Puppies. (p. 1417)
—Singes et Autres Primates. (p. 1579)
—Skates & Rays. (p. 1584)
Sjonger, Rebecca, et al. Chiots. (p. 308)
—Hamsters. (p. 740)
—Souris. (p. 1616)
Sjostrom, Nicole, illus. see Carey-Costa, Denise.
Skae, Hilda T. Adventure League. (p. 14)
Skafish, Brad. Outnumbered! the Bad Cats Learn about Numbers. (p. 1313)
—Red Letter Day: The Bad Cats Learn about Letters! (p. 1454)
Skahill, Carolyn. Historical Atlas of Lebanon. (p. 783)
Skahill, Carolyn M. Historical Atlas of Lebanon. (p. 783)
—Socialist Party: Eugene V. Debs & the Radical Politics of the American Working Class. (p. 1605)
Skalak, Daniel. All Summer's Fun. Skalak, Daniel, illus. (p. 45)
Skaletski, Roslyn, jt. auth. see Zielinski, Valerie.
Skalitza, Anne. Lost & Found Love. (p. 1054)
Skalla, Nancy. Grandma's Telos Boxes of Wishes. (p. 709)
Skancke, Jennifer. Alternatives to Prisons. (p. 50)
—History of Indie Rock. (p. 784)
Skancke, Jennifer, jt. auth. see Woodward, John.
Skancke, Jennifer, ed. Alternatives to Prisons. (p. 50)
Skandle, D. L. Little Duckie's Day. (p. 1027)
Skardarasy, Doreen L., illus. see Hereford, L. F.
Skarmeas, Nancy. My First Day of School. (p. 1206)
Skarmeas, Nancy J. Story of Thanksgiving. Venturi-Pickett, Stacy, illus. (p. 1660)
Skarmeta, Antonio, jt. auth. see Skármeta, Antonio.
Skármeta, Antonio & Skarmeta, Antonio. Composition Ruano, Alfonso, illus. (p. 354)
Skaug, James. Holiday Recipes. Skaug, Terry, ed. (p. 788)
—My Favorite Mexican Recipes. Skaug, Terry, ed. (p. 1203)
Skaug, Joshua. Kooking for Kids. Skaug, Terry, ed. (p. 967)
Skaug, Terry, ed. see Skaug, James.
Skaug, Terry, ed. see Skaug, Joshua.
Skead, Robert. Elves Can't Kick. (p. 517)
—Elves Can't Tackle. (p. 517)
—Something to Prove: Rookie Joe Dimaggio vs. the Great Satchel Paige. Cooper, Floyd, illus. (p. 1610)
Skead, Robert & Simmel, Mike. Mighty Mike Bounces Back: A Boy's Life with Epilepsy. (p. 1140)
Skead, Robert J. Patriots, Redcoats & Spies (p. 1329)
—Submarines, Secrets & a Daring Rescue (p. 1671)
Skedgell, Marian. Double Exposure. (p. 472)
Skeens, Matthew, illus. see Firestone, Mary & Picture Window Books Staff.
Skeens, Matthew, illus. see Firestone, Mary, et al.
Skeens, Matthew, illus. see Firestone, Mary.
Skeens, Matthew, illus. see Jones, Christianne C.
Skeens, Matthew, illus. see Mortensen, Lori.
Skeens, Matthew, illus. see Pearl, Norman & Picture Window Books Staff.
Skeens, Matthew, illus. see Pearl, Norman.
Skeens, Matthew, illus. see Seuling, Barbara.
Skeens, Matthew, illus. see Suen, Anastasia.
Skeens, Matthew, illus. see Troupe, Thomas Kingsley.
Skeens, R. Going to the Dentist with Major Taylor. (p. 693)
Skeers, Linda. Impossible Patriotism Project. Hoyt, Ard, illus. (p. 862)
Skeete, D. C., creator. Hip Hop Wordsearch. (p. 780)
Skeffington, Miranda. My Little Pony: Friendship Is Magic: Collectible Poster Book. (p. 1213)
—My Little Pony: Mini Pony Collector's Guide with Exclusive Figure. (p. 1213)
Skehan, Krista, illus. see Spieker, Diana.
Skele, Shari. Sea Shells. (p. 1535)
Skelley, Paula, jt. auth. see Loewen, Nancy.
Skelly-Caporal, Ellen. Tales of Mr. B. (p. 1702)
Skelton, Holly. Perfect You. (p. 1342)
Skelton, J. R., illus. see Marshall, H. E.
Skelton, John. Band of Acadians. (p. 136)
Skelton, K. Magic from the Wishing Well. (p. 1072)
Skelton, Matthew. Endymion Spring. (p. 527)
Skelton, Renee. Forecast Earth: The Story of Climate Scientist Inez Fung. (p. 617)
—Harriet Tubman A Woman of Courage. (p. 750)
—Kid's Guide to Exploring Black Canyon of the Gunnison National Park. (p. 953)
—Time for Kids Readers: the Chumash. (p. 1751)
—Woman of Courage. (p. 1945)
Skelton, Renee & Time for Kids Editors. Time for Kids: A Woman of Courage. (p. 1751)
Skelton, Sandra. Dancing Tree: And Other Short Stories to Capture the Imagination of Young Children. (p. 403)
Skelton, Stephen. Lucy Show Bible Study. (p. 1063)
Skelton, Vonda Skinner. Bitsy & the Mystery at Amelia Island. (p. 194)
—Bitsy & the Mystery at Hilton Head Island. (p. 194)
—Bitsy & the Mystery at Tybee Island. (p. 194)
Skene, Catling Patrick & Catling, Patrick S. Chocolate Touch. (p. 309)
Skene, Pat. Monster Lunch Ross, Graham T., illus. (p. 1167)
—Rhyme Stones Ross, Graham, illus. (p. 1468)
—What a Hippopota-Mess! Ross, Graham, illus. (p. 1878)
Skerl, Jennie, ed. Reconstructing the Beats. (p. 1452)
Skerry, Brian. Face to Face with Manatees. (p. 560)
Skerry, Brian, photos by see Lawler, Janet.
Skerry, Brian, photos by see Mallory, Kenneth.
Skerry, Brian & Zoehfeld, Kathleen Weidner. Whale Who Stole Hearts: And More True Stories of Adventures with Animals. (p. 1877)
—Whale Who Won Hearts. (p. 1877)
Skerwarski, N. D. Freddy Freckles: Friends, Flags, Facts & Fun. Wooten, Neal, illus. (p. 633)
Skevington, Andrea. Little Red Riding Hood. Hersey, Bob, illus. (p. 1035)
—Story of Jesus. Ruta, Angelo, illus. (p. 1658)
Skewes, John. Alaska Doodles: Over 200 Doodles to Create Your Own Northern Frontier! (p. 34)
—Larry Loves Chicago! Skewes, John, illus. (p. 976)
—Larry Loves New York City! Skewes, John, illus. (p. 976)
—Larry Loves Portland! Skewes, John, illus. (p. 976)
—Larry Loves San Francisco! Skewes, John, illus. (p. 976)
—Portland ABC. (p. 1386)
Skewes, John, jt. auth. see Mullin, Michael.
Skewes, John & Fox, Andrew. Larry Gets Lost in Prehistoric Times: From Dinosaurs to the Stone Age. Skewes, John, illus. (p. 976)
—Larry Gets Lost in Washington, D. C. Skewes, John, illus. (p. 976)
Skewes, John & Mullin, Michael. Larry Gets Lost in Alaska. Skewes, John, illus. (p. 976)
—Larry Gets Lost in Boston. Skewes, John, illus. (p. 976)
—Larry Gets Lost in Chicago. Skewes, John, illus. (p. 976)
—Larry Gets Lost in Los Angeles. Skewes, John, illus. (p. 976)
—Larry Gets Lost in New York City. Skewes, John, illus. (p. 976)
—Larry Gets Lost in Philadelphia. Skewes, John, illus. (p. 976)
—Larry Gets Lost in Portland. Skewes, John, illus. (p. 976)
—Larry Gets Lost in San Francisco. Skewes, John, illus. (p. 976)
—Larry Gets Lost in Texas. Skewes, John, illus. (p. 976)
Skewes, John & Ode, Eric. Elliott the Otter: The Totally Untrue Story of Elliott Bay. Skewes, John, illus. (p. 514)
—Larry Gets Lost under the Sea. Skewes, John, illus. (p. 976)
Skewes, John & Schwartz, Robert. Larry Gets Lost in Seattle. Skewes, John & Mullin, Michael, illus. (p. 976)
—Seattle ABC. Skewes, John, illus. (p. 1539)
Skiadas, Melissa, illus. see McMachan, Susan K.
Skiadas, Stephanie, illus. see McMachan, Susan K.
Skidmore, Lauren. What Is Lost. (p. 1889)
Skidmore, Louis H. Purple Fuzzballs. (p. 1419)
Skidmore, Marlene. In Trouble Again! (p. 868)
—Wesley's Swoo-Foo. (p. 1876)
Skidmore, Sharon, et al. Balanced Literacy Grade 5. (p. 133)
Skidmore, Steve, jt. auth. see Barlow, Steve.
Skidmore, Steve & Barlow, Steve. Football Fanatic. (p. 615)
—Mind the Door! Ross, Tony, illus. (p. 1145)
Skies, Apryl. Skye the Troll: & Other Fairy Tales for Children. Morino, Brandon et al, illus. (p. 1587)
Skilbeck, Carol. Adventures of Melonhead. (p. 20)
Skiles, Janet. Crafts Around the House. (p. 376)
Skiles, Janet, illus. see Cecchini, Marie E.
Skiles, Janet, illus. see Standard Publishing Staff.
Skiles, Janet & Coloring Books Staff. How to Care for Your Cat: A Color & Learn Guide for Kids. (p. 815)
Skillen, Roy. Three Wise Men. (p. 1744)
Skillet, Helen. Mummies! Unwrapping the Secrets of Ancient Egypt. (p. 1191)
Skillicorn, Helen. Friendship Crafts. (p. 639)
—Spooky Crafts. (p. 1631)
Skillicorn, Phillipa, et al. Primary Science. (p. 1399)
Skilton, Sarah. Bruised. (p. 232)
—High & Dry. (p. 777)
Skinas, John. Pictures of God: A Child's Guide to Understanding Icons. (p. 1356)
Skinas, John Kosmas. Getting to Know God. (p. 669)
Skinder-Strauss Staff. 2006 New York Lawyers Diary & Manual Including Bar Directory of the State of New York. (p. 2003)
Skindzier, Jon. Southern Methodist University College Prowler off the Record. (p. 1617)
Skindzier, Jon, jt. auth. see Baier, Ellen.
Skindzier, Jon, jt. auth. see Bist, Richard.
Skindzier, Jon, jt. auth. see Brown, Antoinette.
Skindzier, Jon, jt. auth. see C.Laird, Elizabeth.
Skindzier, Jon, jt. auth. see Davis, Jenny.
Skindzier, Jon, jt. auth. see DuPree, Ben.
Skindzier, Jon, jt. auth. see Gordon, Julie.
Skindzier, Jon, jt. auth. see Granberry, Debra.
Skindzier, Jon, jt. auth. see Hall, Erin.
Skindzier, Jon, jt. auth. see Hansen, Peter.
Skindzier, Jon, jt. auth. see Hein, Michelle.
Skindzier, Jon, jt. auth. see Helmer, Jay.
Skindzier, Jon, jt. auth. see Hofius, Sarah.
Skindzier, Jon, jt. auth. see Hood, Dominic.
Skindzier, Jon, jt. auth. see Krakauer, Steve.
Skindzier, Jon, jt. auth. see L, Jessica.
Skindzier, Jon, jt. auth. see Lee, Susie.
Skindzier, Jon, jt. auth. see Lexa, Katrina.
Skindzier, Jon, jt. auth. see McRobert, Megan.
Skindzier, Jon, jt. auth. see Pommer, Christina.
Skindzier, Jon, jt. auth. see Pope-Roush, Jordan.
Skindzier, Jon, jt. auth. see Richmond, Derek.
Skindzier, Jon, jt. auth. see Schuvent, Julia.
Skindzier, Jon, jt. auth. see Trousdale, Jonathan.
Skindzier, Jon, jt. auth. see Tylevich, Katherine.
Skindzier, Jon, jt. auth. see Valhouli, Alex.
Skinner. Instructor Presentation to Accompany Dynami C Earth. (p. 878)
Skinner, Ada & Wickes, Frances. Child's Own Book of Verse, Book One (Yesterday's Classics) Petersham, Maud & Petersham, Miska, illus. (p. 305)
—Child's Own Book of Verse, Book Three (Yesterday's Classics) Petersham, Maud & Petersham, Miska, illus. (p. 305)
Skinner, Ada M., jt. auth. see Dickinson, Asa Don.
Skinner, Brian J., et al. Dynamic Earth: An Introduction to Physical Geology. (p. 491)
Skinner, Christine Way. Jesus Invites Me to the Feast: My First Eucharist Journal. (p. 915)
Skinner, Constance Lindsay. Becky Landers: Frontier Warrior. (p. 156)
Skinner, Daphne. Albert Keeps Score. Melmon, Deborah, illus. (p. 34)
—All Aboard! Smath, Jerry, illus. (p. 41)
—Henry Lleva la Cuenta. O'Rourke, Page Eastburn, illus. (p. 768)
—Henry Lleva la Cuenta; Henry Keeps Score. (p. 768)
—Palapalooza. Smath, Jerry, illus. (p. 1319)
—Right Place for Albert. Melmon, Deborah, illus. (p. 1472)
—Tod el Apretado: Math Matters en Espanol. Nez, John, illus. (p. 1760)
Skinner, Daphne, et al. Tim Burton's the Nightmare Before Christmas. (p. 1750)
Skinner, Gard. Game Slaves. (p. 654)
Skinner, Gayle, illus. see Turner, Daniel.
Skinner, J. C. Ringo & the Fruit Tree. (p. 1473)
Skinner, Kerry L., ed. see Harned, Bert.
Skinner, Lynn C. Eugene & His Go-Kart Machine, Second Edition: A Tale of a Creative Mouse. (p. 540)
Skinner, Malcolm. Hazards. (p. 756)
Skinner, Malcolm, et al. Complete A-Z Geography Handbook. (p. 352)
Skinner, Michael, illus. see Heidhausen, Bud.
Skinner, Michelle Cruz. Balikbayan: A Filipino Homecoming. (p. 134)
Skinner, Patricia. Jordan. (p. 925)
—Syria. (p. 1693)
Skinner, Teresa. Casaq the Eagle. (p. 273)
Skinner, Tina. Christopher Wren Avian Architect LouLou, illus. (p. 317)
—Fashionable Clothing from the Sears Catalogs: Early 1940s. Schuck, Jenna, photos by. (p. 576)
—Fashionable Clothing from the Sears Catalogs, Mid-1940s (p. 576)
—Home, Office, Library, & Den Design (p. 792)
—Hot Tubs & Spas: An Inspirational Design Guide (p. 802)
—Log & Timber Frame Homes (p. 1045)
—Story of Story Book Land. (p. 1660)
Skinner, Tina & National Concrete Masonry Association Staff. Retaining Walls: A Building Guide & Design Gallery (p. 1464)
Skinner, Tina & Palecko-Schuck, Jenna. Trademarks of The 1950s. (p. 1776)
Skinner, Tony. Electric Guitar Playing: Grade 5. (p. 508)
Skinner, Tony, jt. auth. see Browne, Anton.
Skinner, Tony, jt. auth. see Sheldon, Camilla.
Skinner, Tony, compiled by. Electric Guitar Playing: Grade 1. (p. 508)
Skip Press Staff. Kuwaiti Oil Fires. Miller, Zachary N., ed. (p. 968)
Skipper, Angelic. Launching Out into the Deep. (p. 980)
Skipper, Cecil. Deer Lick. (p. 423)
Skipper, John C. Frank Robinson: A Baseball Biography. (p. 629)
Skipworth, Kelly. Twelve Ordinary Men. (p. 1800)
Skipworth, Kelly & Fernández, Cecilia. Los doce disipulos (The Twelve Ordinary Men) (p. 1053)
Skirvan, Pamela. Bad Day. Skirvan, Ted, 3rd, illus. (p. 131)
Skirvan, Ted, 3rd, illus. see Skirvan, Pamela.
Skirving, Janet. P Is for Puffin: A Newfoundland & Labrador Alphabet. Archibald, Odell, illus. (p. 1316)
Sklansky, Amy. Out of This World: Poems & Facts about Space. Schuett, Stacey, illus. (p. 1311)
Sklansky, Amy E. Where Do Chicks Come From? Paparone, Pam, illus. (p. 1906)
—Where Do Chicks Come From? Paparone, Pamela, illus. (p. 1906)
—You Are My Little Cupcake. Shipman, Talitha, illus. (p. 1973)
—You Are My Little Pumpkin Pie. (p. 1973)
Sklar, Andy, illus. see Kidd, Ronald.
Sklar, David. Day at the Zoo with My Daddy. (p. 412)
Sklar, Tanya. Islamic-Jewish Relations Before 1947. (p. 892)
Sklaver, Ellen. Aleph Finds Her Voice. (p. 35)
Sklyar, Igor. King & the Star. (p. 958)
Skocz, Anita Joyce. Kite Tale. (p. 962)
Skofield, James. Bear & Bird. Thermes, Jennifer, illus. (p. 150)
—Detective Dinosaur Undercover. Alley, R. W., illus. (p. 431)
Skog, Jason. Acting: A Practical Guide to Pursuing the Art (p. 9)
—Chicago - Blackhawks. (p. 299)
—Citizenship Brown, Kelly, illus. (p. 323)
—Dolphins. (p. 464)
—Dred Scott Decision. (p. 484)
—Kurt Angle: From Olympian to Wrestling Machine (p. 968)
—Legacy of the Holocaust (p. 987)
—NHL: The\Story of the Chicago Blackhawks. (p. 1250)
—Screenwriting: A Practical Guide to Pursuing the Art (p. 1533)
—Setting up the Shot: Photography Volume 1 (p. 1554)
—Taking the Shot: Photography Volume 2 (p. 1698)
—Taking the Shot. (p. 1698)
—Weeping Time (p. 1872)
Skog, Jason, jt. auth. see Nemeth, Jason D.
Skog, Jason & Compass Point Books. Yellow Journalism (p. 1970)
Skog, Jason & Kalz, Jill. Displaying the Shot. (p. 453)
Skog, Jason, et al. Pro Wrestling Stars. (p. 1408)
Skogen, J. M. Dallas Mavericks. (p. 401)
—Memphis Grizzlies. (p. 1126)
—Oklahoma City Thunder. (p. 1283)
—Portland Trail Blazers. (p. 1386)
—Utah Jazz. (p. 1829)
—Washington Wizards. (p. 1860)
Skogen, J. M., jt. auth. see Skogen, J. m.
Skogen, J. m. & Skogen, J. M. Memphis Grizzlies. (p. 1126)
Skogen, Jenny. Film. (p. 586)
Skolmoski, Stephanie. Paper Hug. Bennion, Anneliese, illus. (p. 1322)
Skolsky, Mindy Warshaw. Love from Your Friend, Hannah. (p. 1059)
Skon, Sandy, illus. see Lamb.
Skoor, Susan. Lion & the Lamb. Shipley, Marie, illus. (p. 1020)
Skorackiji, Olga, ed. see Fitzgerald, Josephine.
Skordy, Anne Marie. Start with Your Heart. Collier, Kevin, illus. (p. 1643)
Skorlinski, Cynthia. My Little Erica. (p. 1212)
Skorpen, Liesel Moak. Outside My Window. Mayer, Mercer, illus. (p. 1313)
Skorpen, Neal, illus. see Klug, Kirsten.
Skortcheva, Rossitza, illus. see Pearl, Sydelle.
Skot, Joelle. Legend of the Blue Squid. (p. 989)
Skotko, Brian & Levin, Sue. Fasten Your Seatbelt: A Crash Course on Down Syndrome for Brothers & Sisters. (p. 576)
Skotnicki, Jill. Ham & Beans: Have You Seen the Color Green? (p. 739)
Skou, Nick, illus. see Jordan, Claire.
Skoubye, Daniel. Perceptions. (p. 1341)
Skougaard, Shari. Grumpy Goo, I Love You. (p. 727)
Skovron, Jon. Man Made Boy. (p. 1085)
—Misfit. (p. 1150)
—Struts & Frets. (p. 1668)
—This Broken Wondrous World. (p. 1735)
Skrbic, Melissa, illus. see Mumaugh, Lene.
Skrbina, Daniel William. Knight to Remember: Gulliver's Journey Continues (p. 964)
Skrentny, Jan. Christmas Moose. (p. 314)
Skrepnick, Michael, illus. see Bakker, Robert T.
Skrepnick, Michael, illus. see Holtz, Thomas R. & Random House Staff.
Skrepnick, Michael W. Sinosauropteryx: Mysterious Feathered Dinosaur. (p. 1580)
Skrepnick, Michael W., illus. see Williams, Judith.
Skrepnick, Michael William. Diplodocus—Gigantic Long-Necked Dinosaur. Skrepnick, Michael William, illus. (p. 445)
—Triceratops—Mighty Three-Horned Dinosaur. Skrepnick, Michael William, illus. (p. 1785)
—Tyrannosaurus Rex—Fierce King of the Dinosaurs. Skrepnick, Michael William, illus. (p. 1805)
Skrepnick, Michael William, illus. see Holmes, Thom & Holmes, Laurie.
Skrepnick, Michael William, illus. see Williams, Judith.
Skreslet, Laurie & MacLeod, Elizabeth. To the Top of Everest. (p. 1759)
Skrimager, R. J. Making: Volume One of the Golden Isle. (p. 1080)
Skroce, Steve, illus. see Kavanagh, Terry, et al.
Skrypuch, Marsha. Call Me Aram Wood, Muriel, illus. (p. 254)
—Enough Martchenko, Michael, illus. (p. 531)
Skrypuch, Marsha Forchuk. Aram's Choice Wood, Muriel, illus. (p. 94)
—Best Gifts MacKay, Elly, illus. (p. 170)
—Dance of the Banished (p. 402)
—Daughter of War (p. 409)
—Kobzar's Children: A Century of Untold Ukranian Stories (p. 966)
—Last Airlift: A Vietnamese Orphan's Rescue from War. (p. 977)
—One Step at a Time: A Vietnamese Child Finds Her Way. (p. 1297)

Skrypuch, Marsha Forchuk & Forchuk Skrypuch, Marsha. Nobody's Child. (p. 1262)
Skrypuch, Marsha Forchuk & Martchenko, Michael. Silver Threads (p. 1577)
Skues, Richard, jt. auth. see Skues, Richard A.
Skues, Richard A. & Skues, Richard. Sigmund Freud & the History of Anna O. Reopening a Closed Case. (p. 1574)
Skulski, Monica Fitch, jt. auth. see Kulig, Ann.
Skultety, Nancy. From Here to There. Lyon, Tammie, illus. (p. 642)
Skultety, Nancy Laney. 101 Words Your Child Will Read by the End of Grade 1. (p. 2000)
Skurnick, Lizzie. Girls' Life Big Book of Friendship Fiction. (p. 680)
Skurzynski, Gloria. Afterwar. (p. 29)
—Are We Alone? Scientist Search for Life in Space. (p. 96)
—Are We Alone? Scientists Search for Life in Space. (p. 96)
—Clones Bk. 2. (p. 333)
—Good-Bye, Billy Radish. (p. 697)
—Sweat & Blood: A History of U. S. Labor Unions. (p. 1689)
—This Is Rocket Science: True Stories of the Risk-Taking Scientists Who Figure Out Ways to Explore Beyond. (p. 1736)
—Virtual War: The Virtual War Chronologs—Book 1. (p. 1844)
Skurzynski, Gloria, jt. auth. see Ferguson, Alane.
Skurzynski, Gloria & Ferguson, Alane. Buried Alive. (p. 243)
—Cliff-Hanger: A Mystery in Mesa Verde National Park. (p. 332)
—Ghost Horses. (p. 670)
—Hunted. (p. 828)
—Night of the Black Bear: A Mystery in Great Smoky Mountains National Park. (p. 1253)
—Night of the Black Bear. (p. 1253)
—Out of the Deep. (p. 1311)
—Over the Edge. (p. 1314)
—Valley of Death: A Mystery in Death Valley National Park. (p. 1831)
—Wolf Stalker: A Mystery in Yellowstone National Park. (p. 1944)
Skuse, C. J. Pretty Bad Things. (p. 1398)
—Rockoholic. (p. 1483)
Skuy, David. Off the Crossbar. (p. 1279)
—Striker (p. 1667)
Skvarch, Angela & Skvarch, Jeffrey. Dinosaurs in Space. (p. 444)
Skvarch, Jeffrey, jt. auth. see Skvarch, Angela.
Skwara, Malke Lena. Diogo the Little Dinosaur. Barr, Bailey, illus. (p. 445)
Skwarck, Skip, ed. Tails: An Interactive Book. (p. 1695)
Skwarek, Skip, ed. see Van Fleet, Matthew.
Sky Koster, Amy. Cute, Sweet, & Petite! (Disney Princess: Palace Pets) RH Disney Staff, illus. (p. 396)
—Petite's Winter Wonderland. RH Disney Staff, illus. (p. 1348)
Sky, Lucinda. At the Amusement Park: Understand & Apply Properties of Operations. (p. 110)
Skyberg, Andrea, creator. Snickeyfritz. (p. 1597)
Skye. Beyond Foo, Book 1: Geth & the Return of the Lithens. (p. 174)
Skye, Ione. My Yiddish Vacation. Menchin, Scott, illus. (p. 1222)
Skye, Obert. Beyond Foo: Geth & the Return of the Lithens. (p. 174)
—Beyond Foo, Book 2: Geth & the Deception of Dreams. (p. 174)
—Choke. (p. 309)
—Eyes of the Want. Sowards, Ben, illus. (p. 558)
—Gateway. Sowards, Ben, illus. (p. 658)
—Katfish. Skye, Obert, illus. (p. 944)
—Leven Thumps 5 Volume Set. (p. 1003)
—Leven Thumps & the Eyes of the Want. (p. 1003)
—Leven Thumps & the Gateway to Foo. (p. 1003)
—Leven Thumps & the Ruins of Alder. (p. 1003)
—Leven Thumps & the Wrath of Ezra. (p. 1003)
—Pillage. (p. 1359)
—Pillagy: The Complete Trilogy. (p. 1359)
—Pinocula. Skye, Obert, illus. (p. 1361)
—Potterwookiee. Skye, Obert, illus. (p. 1388)
—Ruins of Alder. Sowards, Ben, illus. (p. 1494)
—Whispered Secret. (p. 1912)
—Whispered Secret. Sowards, Ben, illus. (p. 1912)
—Witherwood Reform School. Thompson, Keith, illus. (p. 1942)
—Wonkenstein. Skye, Obert, illus. (p. 1949)
—Wrath of Ezra. Sowards, Ben, illus. (p. 1962)
Skye Toggles. Bella the Witch & Her Worries. (p. 162)
Skylark, Lollie. My Mommy's Accident. (p. 1214)
SL Resources Staff, prod. Inhabit Student Book. (p. 874)
—SEQUENCE Student Work Book. (p. 1552)
Slaby, Nette. Movies I've Seen. (p. 1183)
Slachman, Virginia. North American Indians. (p. 1264)
Slack, Alex, illus. see Poulter, J. R.
Slack, Michael. Elecopter. Slack, Michael, illus. (p. 508)
—Wazdot? (p. 1865)
Slack, Michael, illus. see Goodman, Susan E.
Slack, Michael, illus. see Hale, Dean & Hale, Shannon.
Slack, Michael, illus. see Hale, Dean.
Slack, Michael, illus. see Lewis, J. Patrick.
Slack, Michael, illus. see Sadler, Marilyn.
Slack, Michael, illus. see Sauer, Tammi.
Slack, Michael H. Gross Body Science (p. 725)
Slack, Michael H., illus. see Donovan, Sandy.
Slack, Michael H., illus. see Goodman, Susan E.
Slack, Michael H., illus. see Kelley, Ellen A.
Slack, Michael H., illus. see Larsen, C. S.
Slack, Michael H., illus. see Lew, Kristi & Lewandowski, Laura C.
Slack, Michael H., illus. see Lew, Kristi.
Slack, Michael H. & Slack, Mike. Monkey Truck. Slack, Michael H. & Slack, Mike, illus. (p. 1165)
Slack, Mike, jt. auth. see Slack, Michael H.
Slade, Arthur. Empire of Ruins: the Hunchback Assignments 3. (p. 521)
—Island of Doom: Hunchback Assignments 4. (p. 892)
—Monsterology: Fabulous Lives of the Creepy, the Revolting, & the Undead. Mah, Derek, illus. (p. 1168)
—Northern Frights Trilogy. (p. 1265)
—Villainology: Fabulous Lives of the Big, the Bad, & the Wicked. Mah, Derek, illus. (p. 1842)
Slade, Arthur G. Dark Deeps. (p. 407)
—Empire of Ruins. (p. 521)
—Hunchback Assignments. (p. 827)
Slade, Christian. Korgi (p. 967)
Slade, Christian, illus. see Hannigan, Paula & Accord Publishing Staff.
Slade, Christian, illus. see Sayres, Brianna Caplan.
Slade, Christian, illus. see Smith, Clete Barrett.
Slade, Christian, illus. see Tebo, Mary Elizabeth.
Slade, Christian, illus. see Wharton, Kate.
Slade, Elena. Bigfoot Lives in My Bathroom. (p. 185)
—Plant Out of Place. (p. 1369)
Slade, Joseph W., III & Lee, Judith, eds. Midwest (p. 1139)
Slade, Mark. Week of Mushrooming Book One. (p. 1871)
Slade, Nicholas. Joon the Zsun & His Magical Spoon. (p. 925)
Slade, Roger. Cambridge Checkpoints VCE Chemistry Unit 3 2005. (p. 255)
Slade, Suzanne. Adventures Outdoors (p. 25)
—Albert Einstein: Scientist & Genius. Schultz, Jolene, illus. (p. 34)
—Ants. (p. 90)
—Atoms & Chemical Reactions. (p. 113)
—Basketball: How It Works (p. 143)
—Bees. (p. 158)
—Bill's Journey into Law Trimmer, Tony, illus. (p. 187)
—Birds: Winged & Feathered Animals Kest, Kristin, illus. (p. 191)
—Butterflies. (p. 247)
—Carbon Cycle. (p. 265)
—Cesar Chavez: Champion & Voice of Farmworkers. Thompson, Jeffrey, illus. (p. 288)
—Climbing Lincoln's Steps: The African American Journey. Bootman, Colin, illus. (p. 333)
—Cool Physics Activities for Girls (p. 364)
—Cycles in Nature (p. 397)
—Do All Bugs Have Wings? And Other Questions Kids Have about Bugs Pillo, Cary, illus. (p. 456)
—Dollar Bill's Journey Swan, Susan, illus. (p. 463)
—Dragonflies. (p. 478)
—Elements & the Periodic Table. (p. 510)
—Elements Common to Most Living Organisms. (p. 510)
—Elements in Living Organisms. (p. 510)
—Feel the G's: The Science of Gravity & G-Forces (p. 580)
—Fencing for Fun! (p. 581)
—Four Seasons. (p. 625)
—Friends for Freedom: The Story of Susan B. Anthony & Frederick Douglass. (p. 638)
—Friends for Freedom: The Story of Susan B. Anthony & Frederick Douglass. Tadgell, Nicole, illus. (p. 638)
—From Caterpillar to Butterfly: Following the Life Cycle Yesh, Jeff, illus. (p. 642)
—From Egg to Snake: Following the Life Cycle Yesh, Jeff, illus. (p. 642)
—From Pup to Rat: Following the Life Cycle Yesh, Jeff, illus. (p. 643)
—From Puppy to Dog: Following the Life Cycle Yesh, Jeff, illus. (p. 643)
—From Seed to Apple Tree: Following the Life Cycle Yesh, Jeff, illus. (p. 643)
—From Seed to Pine Tree: Following the Life Cycle Yesh, Jeff, illus. (p. 643)
—From Tadpole to Frog: Following the Life Cycle Yesh, Jeff, illus. (p. 644)
—Grasshoppers. (p. 711)
—Great Divide Hunter, Erin E., illus. (p. 715)
—House That George Built. Bond, Rebecca, illus. (p. 803)
—How Do Tornadoes Form? And Other Questions Kids Have about Weather Pillo, Cary, illus. (p. 807)
—Inventor's Secret: What Thomas Edison Told Henry Ford. Reinhardt, Jennifer Black, illus. (p. 884)
—Jackie Robinson: Hero & Athlete Spence, Thomas, illus. (p. 904)
—Kids' Guide to Money in Sports (p. 953)
—Ladybugs. (p. 971)
—Let's Go Camping. (p. 997)
—Let's Go Canoeing & Kayaking. (p. 997)
—Let's Go Fishing. (p. 997)
—Let's Go Hiking. (p. 997)
—Let's Go Snowboarding. (p. 997)
—Look at Jupiter. (p. 1048)
—Look at Neptune. (p. 1048)
—Look at Saturn. (p. 1048)
—Look at Uranus. (p. 1049)
—Looking at Atoms & Molecules. (p. 1050)
—Monarch Butterfly's Journey Swan, Susan, illus. (p. 1163)
—Multiply on the Fly Hunter, Erin E., illus. (p. 1190)
—Nitrogen Cycle. (p. 1257)
—OxyContin Abuse. (p. 1315)
—Phases of the Moon. (p. 1350)
—Plastic Bottle's Journey Wickenden, Nadine, illus. (p. 1370)
—Raindrop's Journey Conger, Holli, illus. (p. 1436)
—Rock Cycle. (p. 1482)
—Science of Bicycle Racing (p. 1527)
—Scientific Instruments: Looking at Atoms & Molecules. (p. 1528)
—Scientific Instruments for Studying Atoms & Molecules. (p. 1528)
—Sojourner Truth: Preacher for Freedom & Equality Blanks, Natascha Alex, illus. (p. 1606)
—Splat! Wile E. Coyote Experiments with States of Matter Cornia, Christian, illus. (p. 1629)
—States of Matter. (p. 1644)
—Structure of Atoms. (p. 1668)
—Technology of Basketball (p. 1712)
—Water on the Move. (p. 1863)
—What Can We Do about Endangered Animals? (p. 1880)
—What Can We Do about Pollution? (p. 1881)
—What Can We Do about the Energy Crisis? (p. 1881)
—What Do You Know about Animal Adaptations? (p. 1883)
—What Do You Know about Food Chains & Food Webs? (p. 1883)
—What Do You Know about Fossils? (p. 1883)
—What Do You Know about Life Cycles? (p. 1883)
—What Do You Know about Plant Life? (p. 1883)
—What Do You Know about World Habitats? (p. 1883)
—What Eats What in a Desert Food Chain Wertheim, Anne, illus. (p. 1884)
—What Eats What in an Ocean Food Chain McLaughlin, Zack, illus. (p. 1884)
—What If There Were No Bees? A Book about the Grassland Ecosystem Schwartz, Carol, illus. (p. 1887)
—What If There Were No Gray Wolves? A Book about the Temperate Forest Ecosystem Schwartz, Carol, illus. (p. 1887)
—What If There Were No Lemmings? A Book about the Tundra Ecosystem Schwartz, Carol, illus. (p. 1887)
—What If There Were No Sea Otters? A Book about the Ocean Ecosystem Schwartz, Carol, illus. (p. 1887)
—What's the Difference? An Endangered Animal Subtraction Story Waites, Joan, illus. (p. 1899)
—Who Invented Basketball? And Other Questions Kids Have about Sports Pillo, Cary, illus. (p. 1915)
—Why Do Dogs Drool? And Other Questions Kids Have about Dogs Pillo, Cary, illus. (p. 1923)
—With Books & Bricks: How Booker T. Washington Built a School. Tadgell, Nicole, illus. (p. 1942)
—Zap! Wile E. Coyote Experiments with Energy Ricci, Andrés Martínez, illus. (p. 1985)
Slade, Suzanne, jt. auth. see Weakland, Mark.
Slade, Suzanne & Kutner, Laura. Soda Bottle School. Darragh, Aileen, illus. (p. 1605)
Slade, Suzanne & Picture Window Books Staff. Frederick Douglass: Writer, Speaker, & Opponent of Slavery McGuire, Robert, illus. (p. 633)
—Susan B. Anthony: Fighter for Freedom & Equality. Orback, Craig, illus. (p. 1688)
Slade, Suzanne & Waites, Joan. What's New at the Zoo? An Animal Adding Adventure (p. 1898)
Slade, Suzanne Buckingham. Adopted: The Ultimate Teen Guide. Papile, Christopher et al, illus. (p. 13)
Slade, Suzanne, et al. High-Tech Sports. (p. 778)
—Science of Speed (p. 1527)
—SI Kids Guide Books (p. 1572)
Slade-Robinson, Nikki, illus. see Rolleston-Cummins, Toni.
Slaghekke, Harry, illus. see Atwood, Grace.
Slagle, Clark. Axel Cecil & the Rising Sun Adventures: the Janwah. (p. 121)
Slahor, Stephenie. Tales from Merrie England I & Tales from Merrie England II (p. 1701)
Slaight, Craig & Sharrar, Jack, eds. Great Monologues for Young Actors (p. 717)
Slaight, Craig, ed. New Plays from A. C. T. 's Young Conservatory (p. 1246)
Slamp, Kathy. Little House in the Arctic: An Adventure Story. (p. 1029)
Slane, Andrea, illus. see Clarke, Catriona.
Slanina, Anne M. Baby Brother Goes to the Hospital. Agnew, Alicia, illus. (p. 125)
Slanina, Anne Maro. Annie Mouse's Route 66 Adventure: A Photo Journal Collins, Kelsey, illus. (p. 87)
Slapa, April. Why Do Dancers Only Count To 8? (p. 1923)
Slate, jt. auth. see Slate, Joseph.
Slate, Jenny & Fleischer-Camp, Dean. Marcel the Shell with Shoes On: Things about Me (p. 1091)
—Most Surprised I've Ever Been. (p. 1177)
Slate, Joseph. I Want to Be Free. Lewis, E. B., illus. (p. 848)
—Miss Bindergarten & the Best Friends. Wolff, Ashley, illus. (p. 1151)
—Miss Bindergarten & the Secret Bag. (p. 1151)
—Miss Bindergarten & the Secret Bag. Wolff, Ashley, illus. (p. 1151)
—Miss Bindergarten Celebrates the 100th Day of Kindergarten. (p. 1151)
—Miss Bindergarten Celebrates the Last Day of Kindergarten. Wolff, Ashley, illus. (p. 1151)
—Miss Bindergarten Has a Wild Day in Kindergarten. Wolff, Ashley, illus. (p. 1151)
—Miss Bindergarten Plans a Circus with Kindergarten. Wolff, Ashley, illus. (p. 1151)
—Miss Bindergarten Stays Home from Kindergarten. Wolff, Ashley, illus. (p. 1151)
—Miss Bindergarten Takes a Field Trip with Kindergarten. Wolff, Ashley, illus. (p. 1151)
Slate, Joseph & Slate. Secret Stars Dávalos, Felipe, illus. (p. 1544)
Slate, Kelly. Adventures of Santa Claws: At Amelia Island. (p. 22)
Slater, Barbara B. When Wishes Come True. (p. 1905)
Slater, Calvin. Hold Me Down. (p. 787)
—Lovers & Haters. (p. 1061)
Slater, Dashka. Baby Shoes. Nakata, Hiroe, illus. (p. 128)
—Dangerously Ever After. Docampo, Valeria, illus. (p. 404)
Slater, David Michael. Battle of the Books. Ebbeler, Jeff, illus. (p. 146)
—Boy & the Book. Kolar, Bob, illus. (p. 217)
—Comin' Through. Rooney, Ronnie, illus. (p. 348)
—David Michael Slater: Missy Swiss & More (p. 411)
—David Michael Slater: Missy Swiss & More - 6 Titles (p. 411)
—Flour Girl: A Recipe for Disaster. Brooks, S. G., illus. (p. 607)
—Milo & the Monster. Ebbeler, Jeff, illus. (p. 1144)
—Missy Swiss. Reibeling, Brandon, illus. (p. 1154)
—Ned Breaks His Heart. Brooks, S. G., illus. (p. 1239)
—Ned Loses His Head. (p. 1239)
—Ned's Nose Is Running. Brooks, S. G., illus. (p. 1239)
—Seven Ate Nine. Trover, Zachary, illus. (p. 1554)
—Sharpest Tool in the Shed. Reibeling, Brandon, illus. (p. 1563)
—Westley the Wicked & the Rascally Ring Bear. Brooks, S. G., illus. (p. 1876)
—Wrench in the Works. Ricci, Andres Martinez, illus. (p. 1962)
Slater Iii, John D. Monkey & the Dragon Meet. (p. 1165)
Slater, Jean M. Adventures of Hopper. Slater, Jean M., illus. (p. 18)
—At the Fire Station: An Interactive Book. (p. 111)
—Mixed up Morning. Slater, Jean M., illus. (p. 1156)
—Monkey Business: At the Market. Slater, Jean M., illus. (p. 1165)
—Wonderful Snow! Slater, Jean M., illus. (p. 1948)
Slater, Kate. Magpie's Treasure. Slater, Kate, illus. (p. 1076)
Slater, Kate, illus. see Bateson-Hill, Margaret.
Slater, Kate, illus. see Calhoun, Dia.
Slater, Kate, illus. see Dunn, James & Quarto Generic Staff.
Slater, Kate, illus. see Dunn, James.
Slater, Kate, illus. see Finch, Mary & Messing, Debra.
Slater, Kate, jt. auth. see Finch, Mary.
Slater, Lee. Army Rangers. (p. 100)
—Delta Force. (p. 425)
—Green Berets. (p. 721)
—Marine Force Recon. (p. 1094)
—Navy SEALs. (p. 1238)
—Pararescue Jumpers. (p. 1324)
Slater, Mandy. Spoken Prayers: An Introduction. (p. 1630)
Slater, Nicola. We're Bored. (p. 1875)
Slater, Nicola, illus. see Anderson, Sorrel.
Slater, Nicola, illus. see Ganny, Charlee.
Slater, Nicola, illus. see Joy, Angela.
Slater, Nigel. Real Fast Food. (p. 1448)
Slater, Robert. Great Jews in Sports. (p. 716)
Slater, Teddy. 75 Sing-Along e-Songs That Teach Essential Early Reading Skills. (p. 1998)
—Beauty & the Beast. Dias, Ron et al, illus. (p. 154)
—Best Thanksgiving Ever! Long, Ethan, illus. (p. 171)
—Dottie & the Dog Show. (p. 472)
—Emergency, Call 911. Lewis, Anthony, illus. (p. 518)
—Fire Prevention. Lewis, Anthony, illus. (p. 590)
—Four Fiddlers. Kennedy, Kelly, illus. (p. 625)
—Goldilocks & the Three Bears: Pop-up Storybook Theater. Yerkes, Lane, illus. (p. 696)
—Home Safe Home. Smith, Jamie, illus. (p. 792)
—Luckiest St. Patrick's Day Ever! Long, Ethan, illus. (p. 1062)
—Patty & the Pink Princesses. Springer, Sally, illus. (p. 1329)
—Safety in the Bus. Smith, Jamie, illus. (p. 1502)
—Stranger Danger. Lewis, Anthony, illus. (p. 1665)
—Street Safety. Smith, Jamie, illus. (p. 1666)
—Tim Feels Scared. Rescek, Sanja, illus. (p. 1750)
—Word Family Sing-Along: 25 Fun Songs Set to Your Favorite Tunes That Build Phonemic Awareness & Teach the Top Word Families. (p. 1950)
Slater, Teddy, jt. auth. see Peterson, John.
Slater, Teddy & Harrald-Pilz, Marilee. Here Comes Smelly Nellie. (p. 770)
—Jake's Secret. (p. 906)
Slater, Teddy & Rescek, Sanja. I Can Say Please. (p. 836)
Slater, Teddy & Scholastic, Inc. Staff. Nine Bright Pennies. Lewis, Stephen, illus. (p. 1256)
Slater, Teddy & Springer, Sally. Trouble for Trudy. (p. 1789)
Slater, Teddy, text. I Love Korky. (p. 842)
Slater, Timothy F., ed. see Chaple, Glenn F.
Slattery, Karen. Piper's Diapers. (p. 1362)
Slattery, Kathryn. If I Could Ask God Anything: Awesome Bible Answers for Curious Kids (p. 852)
—My Friend Jesus (p. 1209)
Slaughter, Charles E. Golden Tusk. Horvath, Ferdinand H., illus. (p. 695)
Slaughter, Jane & Bokovoy, Melissa K. Sharing the Stage: Biography & Gender in Western Civilization. Vol. 1 (p. 1561)
Slaughter, Kristi. Emma & Allie. Hanks, Carol, illus. (p. 519)
Slaughter, Mark. Christian Boy & the Lion. (p. 311)
Slaughter, Nathan E. & Lewis, Kevin. Clear Perceptions. (p. 330)
—Fresh Foundations. (p. 636)
—Pure Reflections. (p. 1419)
Slaughter, Tom. 1 2 3. (p. 1990)
—1 2 3. Slaughter, Tom, illus. (p. 1990)
—Boat Works. (p. 205)
—One, Two, Three. (p. 1297)
Slaughter, Tom, illus. see Jocelyn, Marthe.
Slaughter, Tom, illus. see Shea, Susan A.
Slaughter, Tom, illus. see Ziefert, Harriet.
Slavens, Elaine. Arguing: Word by Word Murray, Steven, illus. (p. 98)
—Bullying: Deal with It Before Push Comes to Shove. Kerrigan, Brooke, illus. (p. 241)
—Fighting: Without Coming to Blows Murray, Steven, illus. (p. 585)
—Peer Pressure: Deal with It Without Losing Your Cool Shannon, Ben, illus. (p. 1335)
Slavens, Elaine & James Lorimer and Company Ltd. Staff. Fighting: Without Coming to Blows Murray, Steven, illus. (p. 585)
Slavens, Elaine & Pitt, Steve. Teasing: Before the Joke's on You Geoffroi, Remie, illus. (p. 1711)
Slavens, Rick, photos by see Rieken, Ethel Plaep.
Slavicek, Louise Chipley. Anne Hutchinson. (p. 86)
—Black Death. (p. 195)
—Boer War. (p. 207)
—Carlos Santana. (p. 270)
—Chinese Cultural Revolution. (p. 307)
—Daniel Inouye. (p. 405)
—Establishment of the State of Israel. (p. 538)
—Great Wall of China. (p. 719)
—Harriet Tubman & the Underground Railroad. (p. 750)
—I. M. Pei. (p. 844)
—Israel. (p. 893)
—Jane Addams. (p. 907)
—Juan Ponce de Leon. (p. 930)
—Mexican Revolution. (p. 1131)
—Mother Teresa: Caring for the World's Poor. (p. 1178)
—Paul Robeson. (p. 1330)
—Run-DMC. (p. 1496)
—Salem Witch Trial: Hysteria in Colonial America. (p. 1504)
—San Francisco Earthquake & Fire Of 1906. (p. 1510)
—Treaty of Versailles. (p. 1783)
Slavin, Bill. Stone Lion Slavin, Bill, illus. (p. 1652)
—Transformed: How Everyday Things Are Made. Slavin, Bill, illus. (p. 1778)
Slavin, Bill, illus. see Ashby, Ruth.
Slavin, Bill, illus. see Bailey, Linda.

Slavin, Bill, illus. see Beiser, Tim.
Slavin, Bill, illus. see Bourgeois, Paulette.
Slavin, Bill, illus. see Drake, Jane & Love, Ann.
Slavin, Bill, illus. see Heidbreder, Robert.
Slavin, Bill, illus. see Jackson, Ellen B.
Slavin, Bill, illus. see Kulling, Monica.
Slavin, Bill, illus. see Leedahl, Shelley A.
Slavin, Bill, illus. see Levy, Janice.
Slavin, Bill, illus. see Love, Ann & Drake, Jane.
Slavin, Bill, illus. see Nicolson, Cynthia Pratt & Nicolson, Cynthia.
Slavin, Bill, illus. see Nicolson, Cynthia Pratt, et al.
Slavin, Bill, illus. see Nicolson, Cynthia Pratt.
Slavin, Bill, illus. see Nicolson, Cynthia.
Slavin, Bill, illus. see Ross, Catherine Sheldrick.
Slavin, Bill, illus. see Spinelli, Eileen.
Slavin, Bill, illus. see Staunton, Ted.
Slavin, Bill, illus. see Whitehouse, Howard.
Slavin, Bill, jt. auth. see Bourgeois, Paulette.
Slavin, Bill, jt. auth. see Nicolson, Cynthia Pratt.
Slavin, Bill & Melo, Esperanca. Big Top Otto. Slavin, Bill, illus. (p. 184)
Slavin, John Mark. My Friend Dad. (p. 1209)
SLAY, Jenette. ABBY, the Easter Chicken. (p. 2)
Slayton, Fran. When the Whistle Blows. (p. 1905)
Slayton, Shonna. Cinderella's Dress. (p. 320)
Slayton-Mitchell, Joyce, jt. auth. see Brooks, Walter R.
Sleator, William. Blackbriar (p. 197)
—Boy Who Couldn't Die. (p. 219)
—Hell Phone. (p. 763)
—Interstellar Pig. (p. 881)
—Test. (p. 1723)
Sleator, William & Monticone, Ann. Phantom Limb. (p. 1349)
Sled, Robert A. Adventures of Daisy Snowball: The Journey Begins. (p. 17)
Sledden, S. E. Tillie Winslow & the Castle of Courage. (p. 1750)
Sledge-Yancy, Barbara. Red Haired Hare. (p. 1454)
Slee, Natasha. Design Line: History of Women's Fashion. Mander, Sanna, illus. (p. 430)
Sleep, Betty. Purrlock Holmes, & the Case of the Vanishing Valuables. (p. 1419)
Sleeper, Amanda A. Speech & Language. (p. 1624)
Sleeping Bear Editor, ed. Diary of an American Kid. (p. 435)
Sleeping Bear Press. Diary of a Canadian Kid. Moore, Cyd, illus. (p. 434)
—Diary of a Pennsylvania Kid. (p. 434)
—Little Dance. Benoit, Renné, illus. (p. 1026)
Slegers, Liesbet. Andy & Sam. Slegers, Liesbet, illus. (p. 72)
—Bathing. (p. 144)
—Child in the Manger. Slegers, Liesbet, illus. (p. 301)
—Clothes. (p. 334)
—Eating. (p. 501)
—Fall Leaves. (p. 566)
—Funny Ears. (p. 649)
—Funny Feet. (p. 649)
—Funny Tails. (p. 650)
—Guess What I Feel. Slegers, Liesbet, illus. (p. 729)
—Guess What I Hear. Slegers, Liesbet, illus. (p. 729)
—Guess What I See. (p. 729)
—Guess What I'm Doing? (p. 729)
—Guess Where I Am. (p. 729)
—Guess Who Eats What. Slegers, Liesbet, illus. (p. 729)
—Guess Who I Am. (p. 729)
—Guess Who Lives Where. (p. 729)
—Happy Easter! Slegers, Liesbet, illus. (p. 745)
—Happy Halloween! Slegers, Liesbet, illus. (p. 745)
—Hooray, I Am a Boy! (p. 796)
—Hooray, I Am a Girl! (p. 796)
—It's My Birthday. (p. 897)
—Katie Discovers Summer. Slegers, Liesbet, illus. (p. 945)
—Katie Discovers Winter. Slegers, Liesbet, illus. (p. 945)
—Katie Goes to the Doctor. Slegers, Liesbet, illus. (p. 945)
—Katie Helps Mom. Slegers, Liesbet, illus. (p. 945)
—Katie Moves. (p. 945)
—Katie's Day with Grandma. (p. 945)
—Kevin & Katie. (p. 949)
—Kevin Discovers Autumn. Slegers, Liesbet, illus. (p. 950)
—Kevin Discovers Spring. Slegers, Liesbet, illus. (p. 950)
—Kevin Goes to School. Slegers, Liesbet, illus. (p. 950)
—Kevin Goes to the Hospital. Slegers, Liesbet, illus. (p. 950)
—Kevin Goes to the Library. Slegers, Liesbet, illus. (p. 950)
—Kevin Helps Dad. Slegers, Liesbet, illus. (p. 950)
—Kevin's Big Book of the Five Senses. Slegers, Liesbet, illus. (p. 950)
—Kevin's Christmas. Slegers, Liesbet, illus. (p. 950)
—Laura Ayuda a Su Mama/ Laura Helps Her Mom. (p. 980)
—Move! (p. 1183)
—Nacho. Turrion, Celia, tr. (p. 1227)
—Playing. (p. 1372)
—Puppy for Kevin. Slegers, Liesbet, illus. (p. 1418)
—Que Veo?/ What Do I See? (p. 1424)
—Sleeping. (p. 1588)
—Surprise! (p. 1685)
—Take a Look, Bear. (p. 1696)
—Take a Look, Buzz. (p. 1696)
—Winter Snow. (p. 1938)
Sleigh, Barbara. Carbonel: The King of the Cats. Drummond, V. H., illus. (p. 265)
—Carbonel & Calidor: Being the Further Adventures of a Royal Cat. Front, Charles, illus. (p. 265)
—Kingdom of Carbonel. Kennedy, Richard, illus. (p. 959)
Sleiman, Dina L. Dauntless. (p. 410)
Sleith III, Eric. You & Me = We. (p. 1973)
Slepian, Curtis, ed. see Time for Kids Magazine Staff.
Sletcher, Michael. New England: The Greenwood Encyclopedia of American Regional Cultures (p. 1244)
Sleva, Michael, illus. see Wechsler, Kimberly.
Slezak, Roy E. Marsha the Manatee. (p. 1096)
Slider-Baker, Belinda. Lost Stripes, Please Return. (p. 1056)
Slier, Debby. Babies, Babies (p. 123)
—Babies on the Go! (p. 124)
—Cradle Me (p. 375)
—Loving Me (p. 1061)
Slier, Deborah & Shine, Ian, eds. Hidden Letters Van Binsbergen-Pritchard, Marion, tr. from DUT. (p. 776)
Slifka, Linda. Where's My Puppy? (p. 1910)
Slike, Janet. Take a Closer Look at Your Eyes. (p. 1696)
—Take a Closer Look at Your Heart. (p. 1696)
Slim Goodbody Corp. What's on Myplate? A Guide to Good Nutrition. (p. 1899)
Slim Goodbody Corp., creator. What's on Myplate? A Guide to Good Nutrition. (p. 1899)
Slim, Lillian, et al. Subsistence Adventures. Slim, Lillian et al, illus. (p. 1671)
Slimp, Gwen H., illus. see Rice, Joan W.
Slingerland, Janet. Secret Lives of Plants! Kemarskaya, Oksana, illus. (p. 1541)
—Werewolves & States of Matter Mosquito, Angel, illus. (p. 1875)
Slingsby, Janet. Hetty's 100 Hats Dodd, Emma, illus. (p. 774)
Slingsby, Miki, photos by see Erickson, Paul.
Slinkard, Doreen. Wicky Wacky Farm Stories: Peppi Goes to China. (p. 1927)
Slipperjack, Ruby. Dog Tracks (p. 461)
Sloan, Andy & Benchmark Education Co., LLC. Opinions about Ocean Health. (p. 1300)
Sloan, Brian. Really Nice Prom Mess. (p. 1450)
—Tale of Two Summers. (p. 1701)
Sloan, Chris & Sloan, Christopher. Mummies: Tanned, Dried, Sealed, Drained, Frozen, Embalmed, Stuffed, Wrapped, & Smoked... & We're Dead Serious. (p. 1190)
Sloan, Christopher. Baby Mammoth Mummy: Frozen in Time: A Prehistoric Animal's Journey into the 21st Century. (p. 127)
—How Dinosaurs Took Flight: The Fossils, the Science, What We Think We Know, & Mysteries yet Unsolved. (p. 806)
—Mummies: Dried, Tanned, Sealed, Drained, Frozen, Embalmed, Stuffed, Wrapped, & Smoked... & We're Dead Serious. (p. 1190)
—Tracking Tyrannosaurs: Meet T. Rex's Fascinating Family, from Tiny Terrors to Feathered Giants. Lida, Xing & Yi, Liu, illus. (p. 1775)
Sloan, Christopher, jt. auth. see Sloan, Chris.
Sloan, Glenna Davis. Give Them Poetry! A Guide for Sharing Poetry with Children K-8. (p. 681)
Sloan, Holly Goldberg. Appleblossom the Possum (p. 92)
—Appleblossom the Possum. Rosen, Gary, illus. (p. 92)
—Counting by 7s. (p. 371)
—I'll Be There. (p. 856)
—Just Call My Name. (p. 938)
—Keeper. (p. 947)
Sloan, Jodi Probst. Wonderful Paisley. (p. 1948)
Sloan, Kacey. Farmer Phil's Scarecrow. (p. 574)
Sloan, L. Bridges. (p. 227)
Sloan, Lucinda. Harvest Town USA: Children's Christian Edition. (p. 752)
—Lemon Tree: John Henry Plumb. (p. 991)
Sloan, Megan S. Teaching Young Writers to Elaborate: Mini-Lessons & Strategies That Help Students Find Topics & Learn to Tell More. (p. 1710)
—Trait-Based Mini-Lessons for Teaching Writing, Grades 2-4. (p. 1777)
Sloan, Michael, illus. see Lane, Andy.
Sloan, Michael, illus. see Tompkins, Michael A. & Martinez, Katherine A.
Sloan, Monty, photos by see Hillert, Margaret.
Sloan, Peter, illus. see Carroll, Lewis, pseud.
Sloan, PH.D., Phyllis E. Unknown Connection: Spirituality, the Paranormal & You. (p. 1821)
Sloan, William. Of Bees & Bats of Crocodiles & Cats. (p. 1279)
Sloane, Eric. Age of Barns: An Illustrated Review of Classic Barn Styles & Construction. Sloane, Eric, illus. (p. 29)
Sloane, Richard. Back to the Dark Ages! (p. 130)
Sloane, Roxy. Missing: The Heather Harding Mysteries. (p. 1152)
Sloane, Roxy, illus. see Erin, K. c.
Sloane, William, ed. Space, Space, Space: Stories about the Time When Men Will Be Adventuring to the Stars. (p. 1619)
Sloat, Teri. I'm a Duck! Sloat, Teri, illus. (p. 858)
—There Was an Old Man Who Painted the Sky. Vitale, Stefano, illus. (p. 1730)
Sloat, Teri, illus. see Alexie, Oscar.
Sloat, Teri, illus. see Blanchard, Patricia & Suhr, Joanne.
Sloat, Teri, illus. see Winslow, Barbara.
Sloat, Teri & Huffmon, Betty. Berry Magic. (p. 167)
Sloate, Susan. Ray Charles: Find Another Way! (p. 1441)
—Ray Charles: Young Musician. Henderson, Meryl, illus. (p. 1441)
Slobodchikoff, Michael O. Building Hegemonic Order Russia's Way: Order, Stability, & Predictability in the Post-Soviet Space. (p. 239)
Slobodkin, Louis, illus. see Estes, Eleanor.
Slobodkina, jt. auth. see Esphyr, Slobodkina.
Slobodkina, jt. auth. see Slobodkina, Esphyr.
Slobodkina, Esphyr. Caps for Sale: A Tale of a Peddler, Some Monkeys & Their Monkey Business. Slobodkina, Esphyr, illus. (p. 263)
—Caps for Sale. Slobodkina, Esphyr, illus. (p. 263)
—Circus Caps for Sale. Slobodkina, Esphyr, illus. (p. 322)
Slobodkina, Esphyr & Sayer, Ann Marie Mulhearn. More Caps for Sale: Another Tale of Mischievous Monkeys. Slobodkina, Esphyr, illus. (p. 1174)
Slobodkina, Esphyr & Slobodkina. Caps for Sale: A Tale of a Peddler, Some Monkeys & Their Monkey Business. Slobodkina, Esphyr, illus. (p. 263)
—Circus Caps for Sale. Slobodkina, Esphyr, illus. (p. 322)
Slocombe, Megan. Trip to Italy. (p. 1787)
Slocum, Bradley, illus. see Wax, Wendy & Weiss, Bobbi.
Slocum, James. Shadow of War. (p. 1557)
Slodovnick, Avi. Tooth. Gauthier, Manon, illus. (p. 1768)
Slomba, Gregory. Deliverers: Sharky & the Jewel. (p. 425)
Slomba, Gregory S. Deliverers 2: Order of the Crystal Lion. (p. 425)
Slomski, Genevieve T. Living with Cancer. (p. 1042)
Slonecker, Chris, jt. auth. see Slonecker, William T.
Slonecker, William T. & Slonecker, Chris. Parenting Principles from the Heart of a Pediatrician. (p. 1324)
Sloniker, Phyllis. Quest for the Golden Flower. (p. 1426)
Slonim, David. He Came with the Couch. Slonim, David, illus. (p. 756)
—I Loathe You. Slonim, David, illus. (p. 841)
—Oh, Ducky! A Chocolate Calamity. Slonim, David, illus. (p. 1280)
—Patch. Slonim, David, illus. (p. 1328)
Slonim, David, illus. see Bell-Rehwoldt, Sheri.
Slonim, David, illus. see Collins, Pat Lowery.
Slonim, David, illus. see Goodman, Susan E.
Slonim, David, illus. see Melmed, Laura Krauss.
Slonim, David, illus. see Nesbitt, Kenn.
Slonim, David, illus. see Newman, Lesléa.
Slonim, David, illus. see Noullet, Georgette.
Slonim, David, illus. see Pearson, Susan & Pearson.
Slonim, David, illus. see Pearson, Susan.
Slonim, David, illus. see Quest for the Golden Flower.
Slonim, David, illus. see Spinelli, Eileen.
Slonim, David, illus. see Sturgis, Brenda Reeves.
Slonim, David, illus. see Vestergaard, Hope.
Slonim, David, illus. see Yacowitz, Caryn.
Slote, Alfred. Hang Tough, Paul Mather. (p. 742)
—Jake. (p. 905)
—My Trip to Alpha I. (p. 1220)
Sloth, Coach. Hank the Bully. (p. 742)
—Sammy Sloth: Sport Superstar. (p. 1508)
—Sammy Sloth & the Iowa State Cyclones. (p. 1508)
—Sammy Sloth's Big Fish. (p. 1508)
—Sammy Sloth's Big Golf Tourney. (p. 1508)
—Tucker Turtle's Soooo Silly Jungle Safari. (p. 1795)
Sloth, Lia, jt. auth. see Keuss, Jeff.
Slott, Dan. Arkham Asylum: Living Hell. (p. 99)
—Misassembled. (p. 1150)
—Spider-Man: Big Time. Ramos, Humberto, illus. (p. 1626)
—The Return of Anti-Venom. Stegman, Ryan, illus. (p. 1728)
Slott, Dan, jt. auth. see Templeton, Ty.
Slott, Dan & Busiek, Kurt. Spider-Man - Lizard: No Turning Back. Frenz, Ron, illus. (p. 1626)
Slott, Dan & Caselli, Stefano. Ends of the Earth. Silas, Thony et al, illus. (p. 527)
Slott, Dan & Templeton, Ty. Batman Adventures. Templeton, Ty, illus. (p. 144)
Slott, Dan & Waid, Mark. Amazing Spider-Man - Flying Blind. Camuncoli, Giuseppe et al, illus. (p. 56)
Slott, Dan, et al. Masquerade in Red! (p. 1102)
—Phantasm Strikes! Burchett, Rick, illus. (p. 1349)
—Playing with Matches Burchett, Rick, illus. (p. 1372)
—Target: Deadshot! Templeton, Ty, illus. (p. 1706)
Slovacek, Joe. Apple Chase. (p. 92)
Slowik, M. L. 9-11-2002: The Children of the World Save Planet Earth. Larry & Orion. (p. 1993)
Sloyer, Elliot. Safety Pin: Summer Camp Stories. Guiza, Victor, illus. (p. 1502)
Slupskiy, Leon. Volleyball with the Family: Fife Steps to Success. Synepolsky, I. & Belominsky, M., illus. (p. 1849)
Slusar, Julia, ed. see AZ Books Staff.
Slusher, Randall. Day in the Life. (p. 413)
Slusher-Haas, Kathy Jo. Southeast Indians: Daily Life in The 1500s (p. 1617)
Slusser, Janet S. Smokey & the Big Snow. (p. 1594)
Slutz, Stephani, illus. see Thompson, Richard & Thompson, Ofa.
Sluzhaev, Viktor. Lute Player: A Tale from Russia. (p. 1066)
Sly, Debby. Fun with Ponies & Horses: Training, Riding, Grooming, Games. (p. 649)
Sly, Stacey. What Should I Eat? Gentry, Susana, photos by. (p. 1893)
Slyke, Rebecca Van, see Van Slyke, Rebecca.
Slyman, Jody. Bloodline of a Serial Killer. (p. 201)
Slywotzky, Adrian J. Art of Profitability. (p. 102)
Smacchia Patrick. Practical . Net2 & C#2. (p. 1391)
Smadja, Bridgitte & Brigitte, Smadja. He Decidido Llamarme Max. Rubio, Gabriela, illus. (p. 756)
Smadja, Brigitte. Tarte aux Escargots. (p. 1706)
Smailes, Arthur, jt. auth. see Smailes, Arthur E.
Smailes, Arthur E. & Smailes, Arthur. Geography of Towns. (p. 662)
Smalbach, Richard, ed. Capitalism. (p. 262)
Smale, Denise L. Santa I Moved! (p. 1512)
—What If the Sun Didn't Rise. Smale, Denise L. & Blowers, Ryan, illus. (p. 1887)
Smale, Holly. Geek Girl. (p. 659)
Small, Amare & Kelly, Apryl. Operation Back to the Field. (p. 1300)
Small, Bertrice. Border Lord's Bride. (p. 213)
—Dangerous Pleasures. (p. 404)
Small, Cathleen. Computer Animation. (p. 354)
—How to Start an Online Business. (p. 821)
—Make the Most of Facebook & Other Social Media. (p. 1079)
—Mike Lupica. (p. 1141)
Small, Charlie. Daredevil Desperados of Destiny. (p. 406)
—Hawk's Nest. (p. 755)
—Piratas de la Isla Perfidia. Isern, Carol, tr. (p. 1362)
Small, David. Eulalie & the Hopping Head. (p. 540)
—Eulalie & the Hopping Head. Small, David, illus. (p. 540)
Small, David, illus. see Appelt, Kathi.
Small, David, illus. see Armstrong, Jennifer.
Small, David, illus. see Ashman, Linda.
Small, David, illus. see Broach, Elise.
Small, David, illus. see Buzzeo, Toni.
Small, David, illus. see Durand, Hallie.
Small, David, illus. see Henson, Heather.
Small, David, illus. see Howland, Naomi.
Small, David, illus. see Kennedy, Edward M.
Small, David, illus. see Kennedy, Edward.
Small, David, illus. see Sandburg, Carl.
Small, David, illus. see St. George, Judith.
Small, David, illus. see Stewart, Sarah.
Small, David, illus. see Weeks, Sarah.
Small, David, illus. see Yolen, Jane.
Small, Gail, jt. auth. see Scaglione, Joanne.
Small, Gary. Memory Bible: An Innovative Strategy for Keeping Your Brain Young. (p. 1126)
Small, Gary & Vorgan, Gigi. Memory Prescription: Dr. Gary Small's 14-Day Plan to Keep Your Brain & Body Young. (p. 1126)
Small, Jan, illus. see Dicello, Bob.
Small, Larry. Sandstone Rock. (p. 1511)
Small, Lily. Bella the Bunny. (p. 162)
—Chloe the Kitten. (p. 308)
—Mia the Mouse. (p. 1133)
—Paddy the Puppy. (p. 1317)
Small, Mary. Being a Good Citizen: A Book about Citizenship Previn, Stacey, illus. (p. 160)
—Being Fair: A Book about Fairness Previn, Stacey, illus. (p. 161)
—Being Respectful: A Book about Respectfulness Previn, Stacey, illus. (p. 161)
—Being Responsible: A Book about Responsibility Previn, Stacey, illus. (p. 161)
—Being Trustworthy: A Book about Trustworthiness Previn, Stacey, illus. (p. 161)
—Caring: A Book about Caring Previn, Stacey, illus. (p. 269)
—Ser Digno de Confianza. Previn, Stacey, illus. (p. 1552)
Small, Mary, jt. auth. see Donahue, Jill Lynn.
Small Object Staff. I Like to Draw/I Like to Write. (p. 841)
Small, Rachel, jt. auth. see Kissock, Heather.
Small, Roberta Lee. Down by the Pond. (p. 474)
Small, Tanya. What You Say Is What You Are. (p. 1896)
Small, VTaylor. Maggie the Shih Tzu Detective: Volume I: Faith. (p. 1071)
Small, Wylie J. Great Prune Caper. (p. 718)
Smallcomb, Pam. Camp Buccaneer. Lichtenheld, Tom, illus. (p. 257)
Smalley, Carol. Exploring Earth's Biomes. (p. 552)
—Green Changes You Can Make Around the House. (p. 721)
—Project Guide to Fishes & Amphibians. (p. 1410)
—Project Guide to Sponges, Worms, & Mollusks. (p. 1410)
Smalley, Carol Parenzan. Care for a Pet Hamster. (p. 266)
—Fats, Oils, & Sweets. (p. 577)
—Henry Hudson. (p. 768)
—Lewis & Clark. (p. 1004)
—Ride the Giant Waves with Garrett Mcnamara. (p. 1471)
—Threat to the Spotted Owl. (p. 1741)
Smalley, Roger. Adventures of Marco Polo Bascle, Brian, illus. (p. 20)
—Adventures of Marco Polo Carter, Greg & Bascle, Brian, illus. (p. 20)
—Aventuras de Marco Polo. Bascle, Brian, illus. (p. 119)
—Aztecs: Rise & Fall of a Great Empire (p. 122)
—Big Cat Trouble. Shaw, Charles, illus. (p. 180)
—Gorilla Guardian. Shaw, Charles, illus. (p. 703)
—Rick's Dream Adventure. (p. 1470)
Smalley, Roger, adapted by. Big-Hearted Monkey & the Lion. (p. 181)
Smalley, Ruth Ann. Sheila Says We're Weird Emery, Jennifer, illus. (p. 1564)
Smalley, Ryan. Valus: A Fantasy Role-Playing World Sourcebook. (p. 1831)
Smallfield, Graeme, illus. see Smallfield, Jane.
Smallfield, Jane. Bedtime Treasury of Real Fairy Tales. Smallfield, Greeme, illus. (p. 157)
Smalling, Curtis & Kagume, Krista, contrib. by. Compact Guide to South Carolina Birds. (p. 351)
Smalling, Curtis & Kennedy, Gregory. Compact Guide to North Carolina Birds. (p. 351)
Smalling, Curtis G. & Kennedy, Gregory. Compact Guide to Virginia Birds. (p. 351)
Smallman, Claire. Outside-In: A Lift-the-Flaps Body Book. (p. 1313)
Smallman, Jeff. Stump's in the Cellar. (p. 1670)
Smallman, Steve. Bear's Big Bottom Yarlett, Emma, illus. (p. 151)
—Bumbletum. Warnes, Tim, illus. (p. 241)
—Daisy Dinosaur Gets Lost. Howarth, Daniel, illus. (p. 400)
—Don't Wake the Bear! Pedler, Caroline, illus. (p. 469)
—Lamb Who Came for Dinner. Dreidemy, Joëlle, illus. (p. 972)
—My Friend the Weather Monster. Merz, Bruno, illus. (p. 1209)
—Santa Is Coming to Alabama. Dunn, Robert, illus. (p. 1512)
—Santa Is Coming to Alaska. Dunn, Robert, illus. (p. 1512)
—Santa Is Coming to Albuquerque. Dunn, Robert, illus. (p. 1512)
—Santa Is Coming to Arkansas. Dunn, Robert, illus. (p. 1512)
—Santa Is Coming to Asheville. Dunn, Robert, illus. (p. 1512)
—Santa Is Coming to Bellingham. Dunn, Robert, illus. (p. 1512)
—Santa Is Coming to Bentonville. Dunn, Robert, illus. (p. 1512)
—Santa Is Coming to Boise. Dunn, Robert, illus. (p. 1512)
—Santa Is Coming to Boston. Dunn, Robert, illus. (p. 1512)
—Santa Is Coming to Bozeman. Dunn, Robert, illus. (p. 1512)
—Santa Is Coming to Brooklyn. Dunn, Robert, illus. (p. 1512)
—Santa Is Coming to Calgary. Dunn, Robert, illus. (p. 1512)
—Santa Is Coming to California. Dunn, Robert, illus. (p. 1512)
—Santa Is Coming to Canada. Dunn, Robert, illus. (p. 1512)
—Santa Is Coming to Cape Cod. Dunn, Robert, illus. (p. 1512)
—Santa Is Coming to Charlotte. Dunn, Robert, illus. (p. 1512)
—Santa Is Coming to Connecticut. Dunn, Robert, illus. (p. 1512)
—Santa Is Coming to Dallas. Dunn, Robert, illus. (p. 1512)
—Santa Is Coming to Delaware. Dunn, Robert, illus. (p. 1512)
—Santa Is Coming to Durango. Dunn, Robert, illus. (p. 1512)
—Santa Is Coming to Edmonton. Dunn, Robert, illus. (p. 1512)
—Santa Is Coming to Florida. Dunn, Robert, illus. (p. 1512)
—Santa Is Coming to Georgia. Dunn, Robert, illus. (p. 1512)
—Santa Is Coming to Green Bay. Dunn, Robert, illus. (p. 1512)
—Santa Is Coming to Hawaii. Dunn, Robert, illus. (p. 1512)
—Santa Is Coming to Idaho. Dunn, Robert, illus. (p. 1512)
—Santa Is Coming to Illinois. Dunn, Robert, illus. (p. 1512)
—Santa Is Coming to Indiana. Dunn, Robert, illus. (p. 1512)
—Santa Is Coming to Iowa. Dunn, Robert, illus. (p. 1512)
—Santa Is Coming to Jefferson City. Dunn, Robert, illus. (p. 1512)
—Santa Is Coming to Kansas. Dunn, Robert, illus. (p. 1512)
—Santa Is Coming to Kansas City. Dunn, Robert, illus. (p. 1512)
—Santa Is Coming to Kentucky. Dunn, Robert, illus. (p. 1512)
—Santa Is Coming to Las Vegas. Dunn, Robert, illus. (p. 1512)
—Santa Is Coming to Los Angeles. Dunn, Robert, illus. (p. 1512)

—Santa Is Coming to Lubbock. Dunn, Robert, illus. (p. 1512)
—Santa Is Coming to Madison. Dunn, Robert, illus. (p. 1512)
—Santa Is Coming to Maine. Dunn, Robert, illus. (p. 1512)
—Santa Is Coming to Manchester. Dunn, Robert, illus. (p. 1512)
—Santa Is Coming to Maryland. Dunn, Robert, illus. (p. 1512)
—Santa Is Coming to Massachusetts. Dunn, Robert, illus. (p. 1512)
—Santa Is Coming to Minnesota. Dunn, Robert, illus. (p. 1512)
—Santa Is Coming to Mississippi. Dunn, Robert, illus. (p. 1512)
—Santa Is Coming to Naperville. Dunn, Robert, illus. (p. 1512)
—Santa Is Coming to Naples. Dunn, Robert, illus. (p. 1512)
—Santa Is Coming to Nashville. Dunn, Robert, illus. (p. 1512)
—Santa Is Coming to Nebraska. Dunn, Robert, illus. (p. 1512)
—Santa Is Coming to New Brunswick. Dunn, Robert, illus. (p. 1512)
—Santa Is Coming to New England. Dunn, Robert, illus. (p. 1512)
—Santa Is Coming to Newfoundland. Dunn, Robert, illus. (p. 1512)
—Santa Is Coming to North Carolina. Dunn, Robert, illus. (p. 1512)
—Santa Is Coming to Nova Scotia. (p. 1512)
—Santa Is Coming to Ohio. Dunn, Robert, illus. (p. 1512)
—Santa Is Coming to Oklahoma. Dunn, Robert, illus. (p. 1512)
—Santa Is Coming to Omaha. Dunn, Robert, illus. (p. 1512)
—Santa Is Coming to Oregon. Dunn, Robert, illus. (p. 1512)
—Santa Is Coming to Pennsylvania. Dunn, Robert, illus. (p. 1512)
—Santa Is Coming to Pittsburgh. Dunn, Robert, illus. (p. 1512)
—Santa Is Coming to Portland. Dunn, Robert, illus. (p. 1512)
—Santa Is Coming to Rhode Island. Dunn, Robert, illus. (p. 1512)
—Santa Is Coming to San Diego. Dunn, Robert, illus. (p. 1512)
—Santa Is Coming to San Francisco. Dunn, Robert, illus. (p. 1512)
—Santa Is Coming to Santa Cruz. Dunn, Robert, illus. (p. 1512)
—Santa Is Coming to Santa Fe. Dunn, Robert, illus. (p. 1512)
—Santa Is Coming to South Carolina. Dunn, Robert, illus. (p. 1512)
—Santa Is Coming to South Dakota. Dunn, Robert, illus. (p. 1512)
—Santa Is Coming to Tampa Bay & St. Petersburg. Dunn, Robert, illus. (p. 1512)
—Santa Is Coming to Tennessee. Dunn, Robert, illus. (p. 1512)
—Santa Is Coming to Texas. Dunn, Robert, illus. (p. 1512)
—Santa Is Coming to the Carolinas. Dunn, Robert, illus. (p. 1512)
—Santa Is Coming to the Great Smoky Mountains. Dunn, Robert, illus. (p. 1512)
—Santa Is Coming to the Jersey Shore. Dunn, Robert, illus. (p. 1512)
—Santa Is Coming to the Quad Cities. Dunn, Robert, illus. (p. 1512)
—Santa Is Coming to the Rockies. Dunn, Robert, illus. (p. 1512)
—Santa Is Coming to Toronto. Dunn, Robert, illus. (p. 1512)
—Santa Is Coming to Tucson. Dunn, Robert, illus. (p. 1512)
—Santa Is Coming to Utah. Dunn, Robert, illus. (p. 1512)
—Santa Is Coming to Vancouver. Dunn, Robert, illus. (p. 1512)
—Santa Is Coming to Vermont. Dunn, Robert, illus. (p. 1512)
—Santa Is Coming to Virginia. Dunn, Robert, illus. (p. 1512)
—Santa Is Coming to Washington. Dunn, Robert, illus. (p. 1512)
—Santa Is Coming to Washington DC. Dunn, Robert, illus. (p. 1513)
—Santa Is Coming to Wisconsin. Dunn, Robert, illus. (p. 1513)
—Santa Is Coming to Wyoming. Dunn, Robert, illus. (p. 1513)
—Smelly Peter: The Great Pea Eater. Dreidemy, Joëlle, illus. (p. 1593)
—Super Ben. Smallman, Steve, illus. (p. 1679)
—Troll Two— Three— Four. Temairik, Jaime, illus. (p. 1788)
—Very Special Hug. Warnes, Tim, illus. (p. 1838)
Smallman, Steve, illus. see Ellis, Gwen.
Smallman, Steve, illus. see Freedman, Claire.
Smalls, David, illus. see Stewart, Sarah.
Smalls, Irene. I Can't Take a Bath! Boyd, Aaron, illus. (p. 837)
Smallwood, Edward. J. Frankles: Space Adventures. (p. 901)
Smallwood, John, jt. auth. see Hareas, John.
Smallwood, John, jt. auth. see Ladewski, Paul.
Smallwood, Sally. Cool as a Cucumber. (p. 362)
—Sweet as a Strawberry. Smallwood, Sally, illus. (p. 1689)
—We Are What We Eat! (p. 1866)
Smallwood, Sally & Jones, Bryony. Circle. Fox, Rebecca, illus. (p. 321)
—Rectangle. Fox, Rebecca, illus. (p. 1452)
—Square. Fox, Rebecca, illus. (p. 1636)
—Triangle. Fox, Rebecca, illus. (p. 1785)
Smart, Andy. Bob'n Joe Book One: Lunch Time. Smart, Andy, illus. (p. 206)
Smart, Andy, illus. see Brown, Adam.
Smart, Andy, jt. auth. see Brown, Adam.
Smart Apple Media Staff, jt. auth. see Gallagher, Debbie.
Smart Apple Media Staff, jt. auth. see Hyland, Tony.
Smart Apple Media Staff, jt. auth. see Jakab, Cheryl.
Smart Apple Media Staff, jt. auth. see MacDonald, Margaret.
Smart Apple Media Staff, jt. auth. see Mason, Paul.
Smart Apple Media Staff, jt. auth. see Park, Louise.
Smart Apple Media Staff, jt. auth. see Pryor, Kimberley Jane.
Smart Apple Media Staff, jt. auth. see Selwyn, Josephine.
Smart, Bradford D. & Alexander, Greg. Topgrading for Sales: World-Class Methods to Interview, Hire, & Coach Top Sales Representatives. (p. 1769)
Smart, Dominic. 40 Days with Jesus: A Journey Through Mark's Gospel. (p. 1997)
Smart, George, illus. see Shield, Sophie.
Smart, Jamie. Where's the Doctor? (p. 1910)
Smart Kids Publishing. Scary Sounds of Halloween. (p. 1520)
Smart Kids Publishing Staff. David & Goliath: A Story about Courage. Sharp, Chris, illus. (p. 410)
—Jonah & the Whale: A Story about Responsibility. Sharp, Chris, illus. (p. 925)
—My Snuggle up Bedtime Book. Smart Kids Publishing Staff, illus. (p. 1219)
—Noah's Ark Story of Being Thankful. (p. 1261)
—What's That Sound. Sharp, Chris, illus. (p. 1899)
Smart Kids Publishing Staff, ed. see Berry, Ron.
Smart Kids Publishing Staff, creator. Adam & Eve: A Story about Making the Right Choices. (p. 11)
—Down on the Farm Bath Book. (p. 474)
—Everybody Takes a Bath. (p. 543)
—God Loves.... (p. 689)
—My Christmas Photo Album! A Personal Photo Storybook. (p. 1200)
—My Princess Bath Book. (p. 1217)
—Noah & the Ark: A Story about Being Thankful. (p. 1261)
Smart Kidz, creator. 123s of How I Love You. (p. 2000)
—ABC's of How I Love You: You're My Alphabet of Love! (p. 4)
—I'm a Little Teapot. (p. 858)
—It's Potty Time for Boys. (p. 898)
—Itsy Bitsy Spider. (p. 900)
—Jesus Loves Me! (p. 915)
—Jesus Loves the Little Children. (p. 916)
—Jingle Bells. (p. 918)
—This Is the Way We Take a Bath. (p. 1736)
—This Little Piggy Went to Market. (p. 1737)
Smart Kidz Media. Love Bug: Sad. (p. 1059)
Smart Kidz Media, creator. O Christmas Tree! (p. 1274)
—Silent Night. (p. 1575)
—Up on the Housetop! (p. 1824)
Smart Kidz Media Studios Staff, ed. It's Bedtime! (p. 896)
Smart, Kimberly. New Home for Gabril. (p. 1245)
Smart, Margaret & Tuel, Patricia. Focus on Fractions (p. 610)
Smart, Ross, illus. see Turner, Dale.
Smartink Books Staff. CityBLOCKS Stacking Blocks. Crisp, Dan, illus. (p. 324)
SmartLab. SmartLab Catalog Fall 2005. (p. 1593)
SMARTLAB Creative Team. Indoor Outdoor Science Lab. (p. 872)
—Inside Out! the Human Body. (p. 877)
—Mega 3D Puzzle Play Dinosaurs. (p. 1124)
—Mega 3D Puzzle Play Sharks. (p. 1124)
—Space Exploration. (p. 1619)
SmartLab, creator. Custom Car Design Shop. (p. 395)
—Fashion Designer. (p. 575)
—Fashion Studio. (p. 576)
—Glitter Spa Lab. (p. 684)
—It's Alive! T. Rex. (p. 896)
—Secret Formula Lab. (p. 1540)
Smarto, Don. Family Secrets. (p. 568)
Smarto, Luke. Donde Te Vas? (p. 466)
Smath, Jerry, illus. see Alberto, Daisy.
Smath, Jerry, illus. see Broughton, Pamela & Watson, Jane Werner.
Smath, Jerry, illus. see Ditchfield, Christin.
Smath, Jerry, illus. see Driscoll, Laura.
Smath, Jerry, illus. see Haskins, Lori & Ramirez, Alma.
Smath, Jerry, illus. see Haskins, Lori.
Smath, Jerry, illus. see Hays, Anna Jane.
Smath, Jerry, illus. see Herman, Gail.
Smath, Jerry, illus. see Hudson, Iris.
Smath, Jerry, illus. see Kassirer, Sue.
Smath, Jerry, illus. see Kulling, Monica & Walker, Nan.
Smath, Jerry, illus. see Larsen, Kirsten.
Smath, Jerry, illus. see Marks, Burton.
Smath, Jerry, illus. see Penner, Lucille Recht.
Smath, Jerry, illus. see Skinner, Daphne.
Smath, Jerry, illus. see Thaler, Mike.
Smath, Jerry, illus. see Watson, Jane Werner.
Smath, Jerry, illus. see Weiss, Ellen.
Smath, Jerry, et al. Merry Christmas: A Storybook Collection. (p. 1128)
Smead, Rosemarie. Skills for Living-Adolescent-Vol. 2: Group Counseling Activities for Young Adolescents. Vol. 2 (p. 1585)
Smedes, Marty. Goldie Bear & the Three Lockes. (p. 695)
Smedley, jt. auth. see Cox, Michael.
Smedley, Chris, illus. see Umansky, Kaye.
Smedley, Frank E. Frank Fairlegh: Scenes from the Life of a Private Pupil. (p. 628)
—Frank Fairlegh. (p. 628)
Smedley, Garrett. Adventures of Chi Chi. (p. 17)
Smedley, Gord. Orcas Calling. Hammond, Gaye, illus. (p. 1302)
Smedley, Mike. Emily & the Mysterious Potato. (p. 518)
Smedman, Lisa. Creature Catchers. Baldwin, Alisa, illus. (p. 380)
—From Boneshakers to Choppers: The Rip-Roaring History of Motorcycles. (p. 642)
—Sacrifice of the Widow. (p. 1501)
Smeds, Dave. Chuck Norris. (p. 318)
Smedstad, Shannon. Tomorrow Is My Birthday. (p. 1765)
Smee, Nicola. Clip-Clop. (p. 333)
—Jingle-Jingle. (p. 918)
—Sleepyhead. (p. 1590)
—Sleepyhead. Smee, Nicola, illus. (p. 1590)
—Two-Minute Bedtime Stories. (p. 1804)
Smee, Nicola, illus. see Dann, Penny.
Smee, Nicola, illus. see Pasquali, Elena.
Smekhov, Zely, illus. see Elkins, Dov Peretz.
Smelcer, John. Edge of Nowhere. (p. 504)
—Great Death. (p. 715)
—Savage Mountain. (p. 1516)
—Trap. (p. 1779)
Smelcer, John E., et al. Native American Classics Pomplun, Tom & Smelcer, John E., eds. (p. 1234)
Smeldt, H. W., jt. auth. see Chapman, Jared.
Smelser, Lynne M. Noodles & Goo: All over Baby. (p. 1264)
Smelt, Roselynn. New Zealand. (p. 1249)
Smeltzer, Jennifer. Scrolls & Coals. (p. 1533)
Smerek, Kim. What Is Zazu? Smerek, Kim, illus. (p. 1891)
Smet, Margaret. Exploring Amsterdam from A to Z. (p. 551)
Smet, Marian De, see De Smet, Marian.
Smethurst, Julia. Finclucky from Kentucky: A Picture Book. (p. 587)
Smi. Screams in the Night. (p. 1533)
Smibert, Angie. Amazing Feats of Aerospace Engineering. (p. 54)
—Forgetting Curve (p. 619)
—Meme Plague (p. 1125)
Smidlap, Harley, jt. auth. see Smurd, John.
Smiler, Andrew M. Dating & Sex: A Guide for the 21st Century Teen Boy. (p. 409)
Smiley, Ben, jt. auth. see RH Disney Staff.
Smiley, Ben, jt. auth. see Saxon, Victoria.
Smiley, Bob & Florea, Jesse. Devotions for Super Average Kids 2. (p. 432)
Smiley, Diane. Ollie. (p. 1287)
Smiley, Jane. Gee Whiz (p. 659)
—Gee Whiz. Clayton, Elaine, illus. (p. 659)
—Georges & the Jewels. (p. 665)
—Good Horse. (p. 698)
—Pie in the Sky. (p. 1356)
—True Blue. (p. 1791)
Smiley, Jeremy. Chester: Little Turtle, Big Adventure (p. 298)
—Flood of Mice City 2 (p. 605)
—Mice City. (p. 1134)
Smiley, Jess Smart. Rumpus on the Run: A Monster Look-N-Find Book. (p. 1496)
—Upside down: a Vampire Tale: A Vampire Tale. (p. 1825)
Smiley, Kendra. One Rehearsal Christmas Plays: The Easiest Christmas Plays Ever. (p. 1296)
Smiley, Lucy Ireland. Bass-Fishing Bears. (p. 143)
Smiley, Mark. Journey Far Away. (p. 928)
Smiley, Mary Anne, illus. see Griffin, Martha & Griffin, Grant.
Smiley, Norene. Simon & Catapult Man's Perilous Playground Adventure Jones, Brenda, illus. (p. 1577)
Smiley, Patricia. Cover Your Assets. (p. 373)
Smiley, Sophie. Team Trouble. Foreman, Michael, illus. (p. 1710)
Smiley, Sophie & Foreman, Michael. Man of the Match. (p. 1085)
Smileyworld Ltd. Staff. Where's Smiley? Smileyworld Ltd. Staff, illus. (p. 1910)
Smillie, Bryan. Time for Evron. Rooth, Mike, illus. (p. 1751)
Sminkey, Paul, tr. see Haitani, Kenjiro.
Smirl, Mike. Crysta Lun. (p. 387)
Smishliaev, Anatoli, illus. see Konnikova, Svetlana.
Smit, Anika. Taxi. (p. 1707)
Smit, Dawn. Rainbow Editing (tm) A Colorful New Take on the Editing Experience. (p. 1435)
—Rainbow Editing (tm) with Macros: A Colorful New Take on the Editing Experience. (p. 1435)
Smit, Nina. My First Book about God. (p. 1205)
Smit, Noelle, illus. see Rempt, Fiona.
Smith, jt. auth. see Smith, Doris Buchanan.
Smith, A. Big Book of Science Experiments. (p. 179)
—Book of Astronomy & Space. (p. 210)
—Energy, Forces & Motion. (p. 528)
—Materials. (p. 1104)
—Papercraft. (p. 1323)
Smith, A. & Clarke, P. Mixtures & Compounds. (p. 1156)
Smith, A. & Tatchell, J. Complete Book of Drawing. (p. 352)
—How are Babies Made? How do Your Senses Work? What Happens to Your Food? (p. 805)
Smith, A. G. Abraham Lincoln Sticker Paper Doll. (p. 7)
—Abraham Lincoln Stickers. (p. 7)
—Arabic Patterns Stained Glass Coloring Book. (p. 94)
—Beautiful Butterflies Stained Glass Coloring Book. (p. 153)
—BOOST Story of the Vikings Coloring Book. (p. 213)
—Celtic Knotwork Stained Glass Colouring Book. (p. 286)
—Creative Haven Geometric Star Designs Coloring Book. (p. 379)
—Creative Haven Tiffany Designs Stained Glass Coloring Book. (p. 379)
—Cut & Assemble an Old-Fashioned Train. (p. 395)
—Cut & Make a Human Skeleton. (p. 395)
—Decorative Chinese Designs. (p. 422)
—Easy Kaleidoscope Stained Glass Coloring Book. (p. 500)
—FRENCH EDITION of Gargoyles & Medieval Monsters Coloring Book. (p. 635)
—Glow-in-the-Dark Dinosaurs Stickers. (p. 685)
—Green Power: Earth-Friendly Energy Through the Ages. (p. 722)
—Historic American Landmarks. (p. 782)
—Little Mandalas Stained Glass Coloring Book. (p. 1031)
—Masks of the World Coloring Book. (p. 1102)
—Mounties Livesey, Robert, illus. (p. 1181)
—Snowflake Designs Stained Glass Coloring Book. (p. 1600)
—Starbursts Stained Glass Coloring Book. (p. 1642)
—Tallest Building in the World - Burj Khalifa: Cut & Assemble. (p. 1704)
—Visual Illusions Stained Glass Coloring Book. (p. 1846)
—Wonders of the World Coloring Book. (p. 1949)
Smith, A. G., jt. auth. see Livesey, Robert.
Smith, A. G., jt. auth. see Noble, Marty.
Smith, A. G., jt. auth. see Smith, A. g.
Smith, A. G. & Mason, Randy. History of American Automobile Coloring Book. (p. 783)
Smith, A. g. & Smith, A. G. White House Cut & Assemble. (p. 1913)
Smith, A. J. Even Monsters... (p. 541)
Smith, A. Valentine. Circle of Three: Book of Newport. Smith, Frederick J. & Davis, Cynthia, eds. (p. 321)
Smith, Abby, illus. see Toombs, Tom.
Smith, Adam. Other People's Shoes. (p. 1306)
Smith, Adelene Keeler. Sophie Gets Curtains! (p. 1613)
Smith, Al. Koala & Bunny: Instilling Protective Behaviours in Children. (p. 966)
Smith, Alan. Modular Maths for Edexcel Statistics 2 (p. 1159)
Smith, Alastair. Baby Animals. (p. 124)
—Baby Animals Lift-the-Flap. Butler, John, illus. (p. 124)
—Clothes & Fashion Then & Now. (p. 334)
—Nighttime. (p. 1255)
—Nighttime Lift-the-flap. Butler, John, illus. (p. 1255)
—On the Farm Lift-the-Flap. Torode, Justine, illus. (p. 1290)
—What Happens to Your Food. Wheatley, Maria, illus. (p. 1886)
Smith, Alastair, illus. see Tatchell, Judy.
Smith, Alastair, jt. auth. see Le Rolland, L.
Smith, Alastair, jt. auth. see Miles, Lisa.
Smith, Alastair & Clarke, Phillip. Weather: With Internet Links. (p. 1869)
—Weather Spotter's Guide - Internet Referenced. (p. 1870)
Smith, Alastair & Howell, Laura. On the Beach. (p. 1289)
Smith, Alastair & Tachell, Judy. Under the Sea. Scott, Peter David, illus. (p. 1814)
Smith, Alastair & Tatchell, Judy. Dinosaurs. (p. 444)
—Dinosaurs. Scott, Peter David, illus. (p. 444)
Smith, Alastair, ed. Homes & Houses Then & Now. (p. 793)
—Travel & Transport Then & Now. (p. 1780)
Smith, Alene L., jt. auth. see Smith, George Bundy.
Smith, Alex. Home. Smith, Alex, illus. (p. 791)
Smith, Alex, jt. auth. see Kingsbury, Karen.
Smith, Alex T. Claude at the Beach Smith, Alex T., illus. (p. 329)
—Claude at the Circus Smith, Alex T., illus. (p. 329)
—Claude in the City Smith, Alex T., illus. (p. 329)
—Foxy & Egg: Starring Vivien Vixen As Foxy Dubois - Introducing Edward I'Ouef As Egg. Smith, Alex T., illus. (p. 626)
—Happy Birthday, Bunny! (p. 744)
—Little Red & the Very Hungry Lion. (p. 1034)
Smith, Alex T., illus. see Cottringer, Anne.
Smith, Alex T., illus. see Kemp, Anna.
Smith, Alex T., illus. see McAllister, Angela.
Smith, Alexander Gordon. Death Sentence. (p. 420)
—Execution: Escape from Furnace 5. (p. 548)
—Execution. (p. 548)
—Fugitives. (p. 646)
—Fury. (p. 650)
—Lockdown. (p. 1045)
—Solar System: A Breathtaking Tour of the Universe & How It Works with More Than 300 Incredible Photographs & Illustrations. (p. 1607)
—Solar System. (p. 1607)
—Solitary. (p. 1608)
Smith, Alexander O., tr. see Kamijyo, Akimine.
Smith, Alexander O., tr. see Kurimoto, Kaoru.
Smith, Alexander O., tr. see Miyabe, Miyuki.
Smith, Ali, jt. auth. see Howson, Imogen.
Smith, Alice, jt. auth. see Smith, James.
Smith, Alice & Smith, Eddie. Spiritual Housecleaning: Protect Your Home & Family from Spiritual Pollution. (p. 1629)
Smith, Alisha. More Than What I See. (p. 1175)
Smith, Alison, illus. see DeVillers, Julia & Roy, Jennifer Rozines.
Smith, Alison, jt. auth. see Dorling Kindersley Publishing Staff.
Smith, Althea. Clashes: Lessons in Class. (p. 327)
Smith, Amber. Way I Used to Be. (p. 1864)
Smith, Andrea, jt. auth. see Smith, Scott.
Smith, Andrea Claire Harte. Effects of Farming. (p. 505)
—Food Safety & Farming. (p. 614)
Smith, Andrea Helen. Catholic How-to-Draw. (p. 280)
Smith, Andrea Joy. Gladys Blackmon-Morrow: Let the Words from My Mouth... Be Acceptable in Thy Sight, O Lord... Psalms 19:14: the Woman, the Wife, the Mother. (p. 682)
—We Live Spend Our Years As A Tale That Is Told Psalms 90: Tales of the Life of Mr. Andrew Lee Morrow, R. :9. (p. 1867)
Smith, Andrea Nelle. Who Aiden Was. (p. 1914)
Smith, Andrea P. Casey Jones. (p. 275)
—Daniel Boone. (p. 405)
—Davy Crockett. (p. 411)
—Day in the Life of Colonial Silversmith Paul Revere. (p. 413)
—First Thanksgiving. (p. 597)
—Jim Bowie. (p. 917)
—Johnny Appleseed. (p. 923)
—Journey of the Mayflower. (p. 928)
—Mystery of Roanoke, the Lost Colony. (p. 1225)
—Paul Bunyan. (p. 1330)
—Pocahontas & John Smith. (p. 1375)
—Salem Witch Trials. (p. 1504)
Smith, Andrew. 100 Sideways Miles. (p. 1999)
—Alex Crow. (p. 36)
—Ghost Medicine. (p. 671)
—Grasshopper Jungle. (p. 711)
—In the Path of Falling Objects. (p. 867)
—Marbury Lens. (p. 1091)
—Passenger. (p. 1326)
—Stand-off. Bosma, Sam, illus. (p. 1639)
—Winger. Bosma, Sam, illus. (p. 1936)
Smith, Andrew Christopher John. Soi. (p. 1606)
Smith, Andy, illus. see Kesel, Barbara.
Smith, Andy, illus. see Lemke, Donald.
Smith, Andy, illus. see Mayer, Kirsten.
Smith, Andy, illus. see Sazaklis, John & Farley, John.
Smith, Andy, illus. see Sazaklis, John & Roberts, Jeremy.
Smith, Andy, illus. see Sazaklis, John & Vancata, Brad.
Smith, Andy, illus. see Sazaklis, John.
Smith, Andy, illus. see Sonneborn, Scott.
Smith, Andy J. Fang Fairy Smith, Andy J., illus. (p. 571)
Smith, Andy J., illus. see Nickel, Scott.
Smith, Angie. For Such a Time As This: Stories of Women from the Bible, Retold for Girls. Brookshire, Breezy, illus. (p. 616)
Smith, Ann Pierce. Esmerelda Hedgepath's First Date. (p. 536)
Smith, Anne, illus. see Candlewick Press, Candlewick.
Smith, Anne, illus. see Robb, Don.
Smith, Anne, illus. see Smith, John D. H.
Smith, Anne, jt. auth. see Smith, Owen.
Smith, Anne, tr. see Cerami, Matteo, et al.
Smith, Anne, tr. see Costi, Vincent.
Smith, Anne, tr. see De Bonneval, Gwen.
Smith, Anne, tr. see Dubos, Delphine.
Smith, Anne, tr. see Gaudin, Thierry.
Smith, Anne & Smith, Owen. Safari Survivor. Rayas, Rubén, illus. (p. 1502)
Smith, Anne Collins, tr. see Bonneval, Gwen de & Smith, Owen.
Smith, Anne Collins, tr. see Dobel, Jean-Marc, et al.
Smith, Anne Collins, et al. Planet of Music. (p. 1367)

Smith, Annette. Saturday Morning Soccer. Hoit, Richard, illus. (p. 1515)
Smith, Annie Laura. Legacy of Bletchley Park. (p. 987)
—Legacy of Bletchley Park. Hamilton, Dianne, ed. (p. 987)
—Saving da Vinci. (p. 1517)
Smith Annie, Laura. Whispers in the Wind. (p. 1912)
Smith, Annie Laura. Will Paris Burn? Casteel, Kay, illus. (p. 1932)
Smith, Anya. Respect - Companion Book. Cesena, Denise, illus. (p. 1463)
Smith, Archibald Nora, jt. auth. see Wiggin, Kate Douglas.
Smith, Argile. Jbs 2005 Planning/Promo Pack Hope When Believers Struggle: Mark. (p. 911)
Smith, Ashley, illus. see Holzer, Angela.
Smith, Aubrey. How to Build a Robot (With Your Dad) 20 Easy-to-Build Robotic Projects. (p. 815)
Smith, Audrey. Halloween Misfits. (p. 738)
Smith, Audrey Christine. Clementine. (p. 330)
Smith, B. Good Night Jonathan - Good Morning Laura. (p. 699)
Smith, B. M. Evan & Cassie Go on a Train Meet Smith, Mandy M., illus. (p. 540)
—My Very Own Picnic Basket: An Evan & Cassie Adventure. (p. 1221)
Smith, Barb, ed. see Tenpas, Steve.
Smith, Barbara. Animal Phantoms: Fin, Fur & Feather Ghosts Vol. 1 (p. 79)
—Dream Come True. (p. 483)
—Ghost Riders: Planes, Trains & Automobiles. Vol. 1 (p. 671)
—Ghost Stories of the Rocky Mountains (p. 671)
—Ghost Stories of the Sea (p. 671)
—Great Canadian Romances: Love, Scandal, Deceit & Passion. (p. 714)
—Haunted Hearts: True Ghostly Love Stories. Vol. 1 (p. 753)
—Horribly Haunted Houses (p. 798)
—Lost Diary Secrets. (p. 1055)
Smith, Barbara, jt. auth. see Adanac, Victoria.
Smith, Barbara Maxine. God Loves You & You Love Yourself -To God You Are Special. (p. 689)
Smith, Barry, illus. see Redmond, Diane.
Smith, Bart, photos by. Appalachian Trail: Calling Me Back to the Hills. (p. 92)
Smith, Ben. How Are Oceans & Lakes Alike? (p. 805)
—What Makes the Air Dirty? (p. 1892)
—Where Can You Find Hard & Soft Things? (p. 1906)
—Where Do Big Cats Live? (p. 1906)
—Who Listens to the Weather Forecast? (p. 1916)
—Why Do We Celebrate? (p. 1924)
—Why Does This Float? (p. 1924)
Smith, Benjamin Eric, jt. auth. see Ramrattan Smith, Sherry.
Smith, Benson & Rutigliano, Tony. Discover Your Sales Strengths: How the World's Greatest Salespeople Develop Winning Careers. (p. 448)
Smith, Bernard & Pearson Education Staff. Blue Cat Club. (p. 202)
Smith, Bethany. Hiding Sunrise. (p. 777)
Smith, Betsi H., jt. auth. see Flegal, Daphna.
Smith, Bill D. Freshwater or Salt Water? (p. 637)
Smith, Bill D. & Machajewski, Sarah. Freshwater or Salt Water? (p. 637)
Smith, Bill O. Chickadees At Night. Murphy, Charles R., illus. (p. 299)
Smith, Blanche Z. Gift from God. (p. 675)
Smith, Bonnie G. & Kelley, Donald R. Medieval & Early Modern World: Primary Sources & Reference Volume. (p. 1119)
Smith, Brady A., jt. auth. see Smith-Rogers.
Smith, Brenda. Football Goalpost Killed My Son. (p. 615)
Smith, Brenda, illus. see Sister Flowers.
Smith, Brenda J. Where Did Mommy Go? A Spiritual Tool to Help Children Grow from Grief to Peace. Smith, Brenda J. & Cloud, Olivia, eds. (p. 1906)
Smith, Brendan Powell. Assassination! The Brick Chronicle of Attempts on the Lives of Twelve US Presidents. (p. 107)
—Brick Bible (p. 227)
—Christmas Story: The Brick Bible for Kids. (p. 315)
—Complete Brick Bible for Kids: Six Classic Bible Stories. (p. 352)
—Jonah & the Whale: The Brick Bible for Kids. (p. 925)
—Joseph & the Colorful Coat: The Brick Bible for Kids. (p. 926)
—Noah's Ark: The Brick Bible for Kids. (p. 1261)
Smith Bresciani, Cathleen & Eldredge, Richard. Sassafrass Jones & the Search for a Forever Home. (p. 1515)
Smith, Brian. Intrepid EscapeGoat: Curse of the Buddha's Tooth. Conkling, Jon & DeVito, Michael A., eds. (p. 881)
—Moto Mutants Senopati, Erik et al, illus. (p. 1179)
Smith, Brian, illus. see Steinberg, D. J.
Smith, Brian, jt. auth. see Lucado, Max.
Smith, Brian, jt. auth. see Viz Media Staff.
Smith, Brian & Levine, Cory. Revenge/Sacrifice Prasetya, Erwin & Campidelli, Maurizio, illus. (p. 1466)
Smith, Brian & Moore, B. Clay. Hero Overload. Carreres, Albert et al, illus. (p. 772)
Smith, Brian W. S. W. A. P. Game: Some Games Shouldn't Be Played! (p. 1499)
Smith, Brock R., illus. see Smith, Brenda J.
Smith, Brody, illus. see Barbre, Mark.
Smith, Bron, illus. see Fisher, Ann Richmond.
Smith, Bron, illus. see Myers, R. E.
Smith, Brooke. Mimi & Maty to the Rescue!: Roger the Rat Is on the Loose! Bk. 1 Arnold, Alli, illus. (p. 1145)
—Mimi & Maty to the Rescue! Book 1: Roger the Rat Is on the Loose! Arnold, Alli, illus. (p. 1145)
—Mimi & Maty to the Rescue! Book 3: C. C. the Parakeet Flies the Coop! Arnold, Alli, illus. (p. 1145)
—Mimi & Maty to the Rescue! Book 2: Sadie the Sheep Disappears Without a Peep! Arnold, Alli, illus. (p. 1145)
Smith, Bruce. Poppies in Bloom (p. 1384)
Smith, Bruce L. Song of Life. (p. 1611)
—When My Dad Was Little. (p. 1904)
Smith, Bryan. If Winning Isn't Everything, Why Do I Hate to Lose? Martin, Brian, illus. (p. 854)
—Is There an App for That? Wish, Katia, illus. (p. 890)
Smith, Bryan L. Bear That 8 My Flashlight. (p. 151)
Smith, Buckley. Moonsailors. Smith, Buckley, illus. (p. 1173)
Smith, C. Christopher. Water, Faith & Wood: Stories of the Early Church's Witness for Today. (p. 1862)
Smith, C. E. Draupner's Curse. (p. 480)
—Giants of Anglesey. (p. 674)
Smith, C. E., jt. auth. see Simpson, C. E.
Smith, C. Michelle. Skeeter Sneeter Doodlebop. Foreman, A., illus. (p. 1584)
—Skeeter Uses Manners. Foreman, A., illus. (p. 1584)
Smith, Caroline. Writing & Developing Social Stories: Practical Interventions in Autism. (p. 1964)
Smith, Carrie. Baby Animals: Lap Book. (p. 124)
—Bird Homes: Lap Book. (p. 190)
—Boy Who Cried Wolf: Classic Tales Edition. Kelley, Gerald, illus. (p. 219)
—Chicken Little: Classic Tales Series. Harpster, Steve, illus. (p. 300)
—Cinderella: Classic Tales Edition. Greenhead, Bill, illus. (p. 320)
—Counting Insects: Lap Book. (p. 371)
—Crow & the Pitcher: Classic Tales Series. Greenhead, Bill, illus. (p. 385)
—Enormous Turnip: Classic Tales Edition. Rogers, Jacqueline, illus. (p. 531)
—Finding Shapes: Lap Book. (p. 588)
—Going to the Beach: Small Book. (p. 693)
—Going to the Beach. (p. 693)
—Goldilocks & the Three Bears: Classic Tales Edition. Greenhead, Bill, illus. (p. 696)
—Human Emotions & Las emociones Humanas: 6 English, 6 Spanish Adaptations Hanner, Albert, illus. (p. 826)
—Humpty Dumpty's Fall. (p. 827)
—Jobs at School. (p. 919)
—Jumping Monkeys. Harpster, Steve, illus. (p. 934)
—Las emociones Humanas. Hanner, Albert, illus. (p. 976)
—Lion & the Rabbit: Classic Tales Edition. Greenhead, Bill, illus. (p. 1020)
—Little Bo Peep. Abbott, Jason, illus. (p. 1024)
—Little Red Hen: Classic Tales Series. Palmer, James, illus. (p. 1034)
—Little Red Riding Hood: Classic Tales Edition. Kelley, Gerald, illus. (p. 1035)
—Mary Has a Little Lamb. (p. 1100)
—One Silly Hey Diddle Day. (p. 1297)
—Our Family Stories: Small Book. (p. 1308)
—Our Family Stories. (p. 1308)
—Princess & the Pea: Classic Tales Edition. Harpster, Steve, illus. (p. 1402)
—Stone Soup: Classic Tales Edition. Rogers, Jacqueline, illus. (p. 1653)
—Ugly Duckling: Classic Tales Edition. Rogers, Jacqueline, illus. (p. 1808)
—We See with Our Eyes: Lap Book. (p. 1868)
—Where Are Bo Peep's Sheep? Abbott, Jason, illus. (p. 1906)
Smith, Carrie, jt. auth. see Jones, Tammy.
Smith, Carrie & Swain, Cameron. Fun at the Beach. (p. 647)
—Life at the Beach. (p. 1008)
Smith, Carrie Myers. Fitastic Kids: A Complete Guide to Health & Wellness for Children of All Ages. (p. 599)
Smith, Carter. Presidents: Every Question Answered. (p. 1397)
Smith, Carter, jt. auth. see Ochoa, George.
Smith, Carter, jt. ed. see Nash, Gary B.
Smith, Cat Bowman, illus. see Freeman, Martha.
Smith, Cat Bowman, illus. see Gardiner, John Reynolds.
Smith, Cat Bowman, illus. see Levitin, Sonia.
Smith, Cat Bowman, illus. see Thomas, Peggy.
Smith, Cat Bowman, illus. see Thomassie, Tynia.
Smith, Cat Bowman, illus. see Voigt, Cynthia.
Smith, Catharine Bowman, illus. see Gardiner, John Reynolds.
Smith, Catherine. On My Knees. (p. 1289)
Smith, Cathy Jo. Seamus Mcseamus, an Irish Rover. (p. 1536)
Smith, Charles. Out at First. (p. 1310)
Smith, Charles, Jr. Reel to Real: Making the Most of the Movies with Youth. Vol. 3, No. 4 (p. 1456)
—Two Terrific Christmas Plays: Two Plays for Children, Ages 3 to Older Elementary. (p. 1804)
Smith, Charles R., Jr. 28 Days: Moments in Black History That Changed the World. Evans, Shane W., illus. (p. 1996)
—Black Jack: The Ballad of Jack Johnson. Evans, Shane W., illus. (p. 196)
—Brick by Brick. Cooper, Floyd, illus. (p. 227)
—Chameleon. (p. 289)
—Hoop Kings. (p. 795)
—Hoop Queens. (p. 795)
—I Am the World. (p. 834)
—Stars in the Shadows: The Negro League All-Star Game of 1934. Morrison, Frank, illus. (p. 1643)
—Twelve Rounds to Glory: The Story of Muhammad Ali. Collier, Bryan, illus. (p. 1800)
—Twelve Rounds to Glory. (p. 1800)
Smith, Charles R., Jr., illus. see Hughes, Langston.
Smith, Charles R., Jr., jt. ed. see Aronson, Marc.
Smith, Charles R., Jr., photos by see Kipling, Rudyard.
Smith, Charles R., Jr. & La Raso, Carlo. I Am America. (p. 832)
Smith, Charlie E. T., illus. see MacNeil, Ben.
Smith, Charlotte, jt. auth. see Buscemi, Santi V.
Smith, Cheryl Jean. Journal. (p. 927)
—Offering. (p. 1279)
Smith, Chris. One City, Two Brothers. Fronty, Aurélia, illus. (p. 1294)
Smith, Chris & Ansell, Dave. Spectacular Science: Exciting Experiments to Try at Home. (p. 1624)
Smith, Chris & McGrath, Marci. Business Leaders: Twitter: Jack Dorsey, Evan Williams & Biz Stone. (p. 245)
Smith, Chrysa. Adventures of the Poodle Posse: [happy Tales 1 & 2]. Achilles, Pat, illus. (p. 23)
Smith, Claire, illus. see Smith, Gloria.
Smith, Clara Batton. Elliott & Anastaci. Smith, Clara Batton, illus. (p. 514)
Smith, Claude Clayton. Gull That Lost the Sea. Cathcart, Sharyn, illus. (p. 731)
Smith, Clete Barrett. Alien on a Rampage. (p. 41)
—Aliens in Disguise. (p. 41)
—Aliens in Disguise. Slade, Christian, illus. (p. 41)
—Aliens on Vacation. Slade, Christian, illus. (p. 41)
—Magic Delivery. Dziekan, Michal, illus. (p. 1072)
Smith, Cleveland W. Billabongo. (p. 187)
Smith, Cliff. New Magical Holiday Stories. (p. 1246)
Smith, Clint. Infusion. (p. 874)
Smith, Clyde. Bashful Bull of Buchanan County. (p. 141)
—Hen That Couldn't Lay an Egg. Bainbridge, Shane & Bainbridge, Bob, illus. (p. 767)
Smith, Clyde R. Bully of Glendale Pond. Perin, Pauline, illus. (p. 241)
Smith, Constance. Pea Soup Fog. Cart, Jen, illus. (p. 1331)
Smith, Cordellya. Kawoni's Journey Across the Mountain: A Cherokee Little Red Riding Hood. (p. 946)
Smith, Craig. Wonky Donkey. Cowley, Katz, illus. (p. 1949)
Smith, Craig, illus. see Ball, Duncan.
Smith, Craig, illus. see Condon, Bill.
Smith, Craig, illus. see Dumbleton, Mike.
Smith, Craig, illus. see Eggleton, Jill.
Smith, Craig, illus. see MacLeod, Doug.
Smith, Craig, illus. see McKinlay, Helen.
Smith, Craig, illus. see Mueller, Ross.
Smith, Craig, illus. see Rippin, Sally.
Smith, Craig, illus. see Sanders, Jayneen.
Smith, Craig, jt. auth. see Bell, Krista.
Smith, Craig, jt. auth. see Osterweil, Adam.
Smith, Crystal. Lioness. (p. 1021)
Smith, Crystal, illus. see Smith, Michael.
Smith, Cyncie. Joyful Shepherd. (p. 930)
Smith, Cynthia & Wishbone. Dogs Get Cancer Too: A True Story. (p. 463)
Smith, Cynthia Leitich. Blessed. (p. 199)
—Diabolical. (p. 433)
—Eternal. (p. 539)
—Feral Curse. (p. 581)
—Feral Pride. (p. 581)
—Tantalize: Kieren's Story. Doyle, Ming, illus. (p. 1705)
—Tantalize. (p. 1705)
Smith, D. I Am Complete. (p. 832)
Smith, D. A. Axis Mundi Sum. (p. 121)
Smith, D. James. Boys of San Joaquin. (p. 220)
—It Was September When We Ran Away the First Time. (p. 894)
—Probably the World's Best Story about a Dog & Th. (p. 1408)
—Probably the World's Best Story about a Dog & the Girl Who Loved Me. (p. 1408)
Smith, D. K. Sock 'n Boots - Share. (p. 1605)
Smith, D. Preston. Bedwetting Handbook. (p. 157)
Smith, Dale. What the Orangutan Told Alice: A Rain Forest Adventure. Smith, Dale & Russon, Anne E., photos by. (p. 1893)
Smith, Dan. My Brother's Secret. (p. 1199)
Smith, Dan, illus. see Bustamante, Frank & Gray, Dan, eds.
Smith, Dan & Nickoloff, Michael, eds. Portable Adventures: 8th Grade. Smith, Dan, illus. (p. 1386)
—Portable Adventures: Lair of the Rat King. Smith, Dan, illus. (p. 1386)
Smith, Dana C. & McClure, Denise. Monkey Learns to Potty. (p. 1165)
Smith, Daniel. My Friend the Enemy. (p. 1209)
—World Cultures Explained (p. 1954)
Smith, Danna. Dos en el Zoológico: Un Libro para Contar. Petrone, Valeria, illus. (p. 472)
—Pirate Nap: A Book of Colors. Petrone, Valeria, illus. (p. 1362)
—Two at the Zoo. Petrone, Valeria, illus. (p. 1803)
Smith, Darshiel & Haddi, Javon. Introducing the Rollies. (p. 882)
Smith, David. Nature's Garden. (p. 1237)
Smith, David, illus. see Blasing, George & Blasing, George.
Smith, David, jt. auth. see Milligan, Chris.
Smith, David, jt. auth. see Newton, Derek.
Smith, David, jt. auth. see Somerville, Louisa.
Smith, David J. If America Were a Village: A Book about the People of the United States. Armstrong, Shelagh, illus. (p. 852)
—If the World Were a Village: A Book about the World's People. Armstrong, Shelagh, illus. (p. 854)
—This Child, Every Child: A Book about the World's Children. Armstrong, Shelagh, illus. (p. 1735)
Smith, David L. Animals of Christmas. (p. 83)
Smith, David Preston, illus. see Bawtree, Michael.
Smith, David Preston, illus. see Kessler, Deirdre & Montgomery, L. M.
Smith, David Preston, illus. see Vaughan, Garth.
Smith, David R. Door to Andara. (p. 470)
Smith, David Thomas. Frenchie the Grass Seed's Journey Around the World to Learn How to Sow a Lawn. (p. 636)
Smith, David, told to. Cart. (p. 272)
Smith, Dawn K. Hulk of Cranberry Lake: Don't Be a Bully. (p. 825)
Smith, Debbie. Israel: The Land. (p. 893)
—Israel: The Culture. (p. 893)
—Israel - The Culture. (p. 893)
—Israel - The People. (p. 893)
Smith, Debora Ann Baker. Magnificent Fairy Party. (p. 1076)
Smith, Debra. Hattie Marshall & the Dangerous Fire (p. 753)
—Young Heroes of the Confederacy (p. 1978)
Smith, Debra West. Hattie Marshall & the Prowling Panther (p. 753)
Smith, Dee. Pigs of Pineapple Beach Anthology. (p. 1358)
Smith, DeLinda. Mommy, Who Made Me? Creation Series: 100% Handmade. (p. 1162)
Smith, Derek. Bob the Builder Manual. (p. 205)
—Kamallah's Bracelet. (p. 942)
Smith, Devin, illus. see Dunning, Rebecca.
Smith, Dian G., jt. auth. see Rogge, Robie.
Smith, Diana, jt. illus. see Last, Ian.
Smith, Diana M. Every Sock Needs a Mate. (p. 543)
Smith, Dianne M. Cyanne Rose & Sherbet Are Best Friends. (p. 396)
—Happy Birthday to You! (p. 745)
—I Don't Want To! (p. 838)
—Stuck! (p. 1668)
Smith, Dietrich, illus. see Winick, Judd, et al.
Smith Dinbergs, Holly. Diary Disaster. Stewart, Chantal, illus. (p. 434)
—Pool Pals. Maddock, Monika, illus. (p. 1383)
Smith, Dineen. So, You Think I Am Too Little To Bake! (p. 1602)
Smith, Dodie. 101 Dalmatians. (p. 1999)
Smith, Don F. Collapse of Unity, Sanity & Democracy in the USA. (p. 339)
Smith, Donald A., illus. see Adler, David A.
Smith, Donald M., Jr. Haze Gray Odyssey. (p. 756)
Smith, Donna. Tommy Tell. (p. 1765)
Smith, Donna Campbell. Independent Spirit: The Tale of Betsy Dowdy & Black Bess. (p. 870)
Smith, Donna R. Room for One More. (p. 1488)
Smith, Doris Buchanan. Sabor a Moras. Rioja, Alberto Jiménez, tr. (p. 1500)
—Taste of Blackberries. (p. 1707)
Smith, Doris Buchanan & Smith. Taste of Blackberries. Wimmer, Michael, illus. (p. 1707)
Smith, Dororthy. Noah's Ark Coloring Book. (p. 1261)
Smith, Douglas W. Classical Guitar for Young Children, Ages 5-12: For Development of Technique, Musicianship, & Memory, Rote Book 1. (p. 328)
—Doug Smith's Classical Guitar Method, Reading Book 2: Beginning Pieces for the First Position. (p. 473)
Smith, Duane. Heritage Revealed Series (p. 771)
Smith, Duane, illus. see Halfmann, Janet.
Smith, Duane, illus. see Rubright, Lynn.
Smith, Duane, jt. auth. see Halfmann, Janet.
Smith, Duane A., illus. see Masters, Susan Rowan.
Smith, Duane A., jt. auth. see Noel, Thomas J.
Smith, Duncan, illus. see Clarke, Ann.
Smith, Duriel, illus. see Alexander, David E.
Smith, Dwight, illus. see Archambault, Jeanne.
Smith, E. Adventures of Sir Ambrose Elephant: A Visit to the City. Apa, Ivy Marie, illus. (p. 23)
Smith, E. Boyd. Noah's Ark: The Story of the Flood & After. (p. 1261)
Smith, E. Boyd, illus. see Brown, Abbie Farwell.
Smith, E. Boyd, illus. see Dutton, Maude Barrows.
Smith, E. K. Alien Dude! & the Attack of Wormzilla!! Grosshauser, Peter, illus. (p. 40)
—Alien Dude! Mr. Evil Potato Man & the Food Fight. Grosshauser, Peter, illus. (p. 40)
Smith, E. Norbert. Al-the-Gator & Honey Bunny. (p. 33)
—Al-the-Gator & Sneaky Snake. (p. 33)
Smith, Earl. Mainu & the Prince of Bakara: And Other Stories from Africa. (p. 1077)
Smith, Eddie, jt. auth. see Smith, Alice.
Smith, Eileen M. ElectriCity Beyond the Curve of Deregulation: Neighborhood Energy Watch Groups & the Ethos of Commerce. (p. 509)
Smith, Elise & Smith, Kimanne. Missing Trumpet Blues. (p. 1153)
Smith, Elizabeth. Magic School Bus & the Shark Adventure. Bracken, Carolyn, illus. (p. 1073)
Smith, Elizabeth, jt. auth. see Mullins, Lisa.
Smith, Elva S. Christmas in Legend & Story. (p. 314)
Smith, Elva S. & Hazeltine, Alice I. Christmas in Legend & Story: A Book for Boys & Girls. (p. 314)
Smith, Elwood. How to Draw with Your Funny Bone. Smith, Elwood, illus. (p. 819)
—I'm Not a Pig in Underpants. Smith, Elwood, illus. (p. 859)
Smith, Elwood, illus. see Goodman, Susan E.
Smith, Elwood, illus. see Laínez, René Colato.
Smith, Elwood H., illus. see Goodman, Susan E.
Smith, Elwood H., illus. see Katz, Alan.
Smith, Elwood H., illus. see Laínez, René Colato.
Smith, Elwood H., illus. see Mandel, Peter.
Smith, Elwood H., illus. see Sylver, Adrienne.
Smith, Elwood H., illus. see Weeks, Sarah.
Smith, Elwyn Allen. Men Called Him Master. (p. 1126)
Smith, Emilie & Tejada, Marguerita. Viva Zapata! Czernecki, Stefan, illus. (p. 1846)
Smith, Emily. Stain on the Stone. (p. 1638)
Smith, Emily R. Life in the Colonies. (p. 1011)
—Phillis Wheatley. (p. 1350)
Smith, Emma. Othello. (p. 1306)
Smith, Eric, illus. see Carr, Stephen.
Smith, Eric, illus. see Chandler, Pauline.
Smith, Eric, illus. see Faulkner, Keith.
Smith, Eric, illus. see Freidman, Mel.
Smith, Eric, et al. This Little Piggy: And Other Favorite Rhymes. (p. 1737)
Smith, Erica. Making Music with Stringed Instruments. (p. 1082)
—Solid, Liquid, Gas: What Is Matter? (p. 1607)
Smith, Ernest Lynnwood. It's All God. (p. 896)
—Raw Poetry & Prose in Transition. (p. 1441)
—Road to Oneness. (p. 1477)
Smith, Eunice Geil. Treasure Hunt. (p. 1781)
Smith, Evans. Christmas Angel. (p. 312)
Smith, Eveline Maria. Christmas to Remember. (p. 316)
Smith, Evelyn. First Fifth Form. Wiles, Frank, illus. (p. 595)
—Seven Sisters at Queen Anne's. Collier, H., illus. (p. 1555)
—Small Sixth Form. Wiles, Frank, illus. (p. 1592)
Smith, Farhanna. Rivers of the United States. (p. 1476)
Smith, Felipe. MBQ (p. 1114)
Smith, Florence B. Bitter Revenge. (p. 194)
Smith Ford, Deborah. Little Apple. (p. 1023)
Smith, Frank. Little Kid Named Billy. (p. 1029)
Smith, Frank Dabba & Quarto Generic Staff. My Secret Camera: Life in the Lodz Ghetto. Grossman, Mendel, photos by. (p. 1218)
Smith, Frederick D. Black Premiere (p. 196)
Smith, Frederick J., ed. see Smith, A. Valentine.
Smith, G., tr. see Stockley, Corinne, et al.
Smith, Gail. Journey. (p. 927)

Smith, Geof. Star Wars: a New Hope (Star Wars) Meurer, Caleb, illus. (p. 1641)
—Star Wars: Return of the Jedi (Star Wars) Cohee, Ron, illus. (p. 1642)
—Star Wars: Revenge of the Sith (Star Wars) Spaziante, Patrick, illus. (p. 1642)
—Star Wars: the Empire Strikes Back (Star Wars) Kennett, Chris, illus. (p. 1642)
Smith, Geof, jt. auth. see Golden Books Staff.
Smith, George. Journey of the Little Red Boat: A Story from the Coast of Maine. (p. 928)
Smith, George Bundy & Smith, Alene L. You Decide! Applying the Bill of Rights to Real Cases. (p. 1975)
—You Decide! Instruction/Answer Guide: Applying the Bill of Rights to Real Cases. (p. 1975)
Smith, Gibbs, jt. auth. see Williams, Nate.
Smith, Glenn C. Tybee Island Terror Plot. (p. 1804)
Smith, Gloria. Annie Elf & Bo Bo Robin. (p. 86)
—Annie Elf & Flippy Butterfly. (p. 86)
—Annie Elf Meets Mitty Mouse. Smith, Claire, illus. (p. 86)
Smith, Grace. Granddaughter of the Heart: Search for Identity. (p. 707)
Smith, Graham. Karting. (p. 944)
Smith, Graham, illus. see Dale, Jay.
Smith, Grahame Baker. George's Magic Day. (p. 665)
Smith, Greg Leitich. Chronal Engine. Henry, Blake, illus. (p. 317)
—Little Green Men at the Mercury Inn. Arnold, Andrew, illus. (p. 1028)
—Ninjas, Piranhas, & Galileo. (p. 1257)
Smith, Gregory. Those Are the Breaks. (p. 1740)
Smith, Guy, illus. see Stockley, Corinne, et al.
Smith, Guy, illus. see Stockley, Corinne.
Smith, Guy, illus. see Tatchell, Judy.
Smith, H. Student Oriented Approach to Topology. (p. 1669)
Smith, Hannah Whitall. Christian's Secret of a Happy Life. (p. 312)
Smith, Harriet. Pollyanna's Debt of Honor. (p. 1381)
Smith, Harriet Lummis. Pollyanna's Debt of Honor. (p. 1381)
Smith, Heather. Baygirl (p. 147)
Smith, Heidi. Thirty Pieces of Gold. (p. 1735)
Smith, Helen. Pirates, Swashbucklers & Buccaneers of London. (p. 1364)
Smith, Helen, illus. see Baxter, Nicola.
Smith, Helen, illus. see St. John, Patricia.
Smith, Helene. Dreamstone. Guinard, Geraldine, illus. (p. 484)
Smith, Hilary T. Sense of the Infinite. (p. 1551)
Smith, Holly C. Tyler the Monkey & Andy the Mouse. (p. 1805)
Smith, Hope Anita. Keeping the Night Watch. Lewis, E. B., illus. (p. 947)
—Mother Poems. Smith, Hope Anita, illus. (p. 1178)
—Way a Door Closes. Evans, Shane W., illus. (p. 1864)
Smith Howard, Alycia, jt. auth. see Heintzelman, Greta.
Smith, Howard Bud, jt. auth. see Wagner, Willis H.
Smith, Hugh. On Clausewitz: A Study of Military & Political Ideas. (p. 1288)
Smith, Huhana, illus. see Tipene, Tim.
Smith, I. J. Legend of Scary Mary: The Journey to Leadership Collection Adventure 2. Pollard, Deborah Hanna, illus. (p. 988)
—Musical Fort. Pollard, Deborah Hanna, illus. (p. 1194)
Smith, Iain. Angel Fish: A Pull & Lift Book. Smith, Iain, illus. (p. 73)
Smith, Ian. First Experiences: Going to the Doctor. (p. 594)
—Going to the Doctor. (p. 693)
—How Does it Grow? From Seed to Sunflower. (p. 809)
—Scholastic Clubs Animal Kingdom Pack (5 x PB QAL Titles) (p. 1521)
—What's in the Sky? (p. 1898)
Smith, Ian & Julian, Sean. Rooster's Alarm. Smith, Ian, illus. (p. 1488)
Smith, Icy. Daddy, My Favorite Guy. (p. 398)
—Half Spoon of Rice: A Survival Story of the Cambodian Holocaust. Nhem, Sopaul, illus. (p. 737)
—Mystery of the Giant Mask of Sanxingdui. Roski, Gayle Garner, illus. (p. 1225)
—Three Years & Eight Months. Kindert, Jennifer C., illus. (p. 1744)
Smith, Ivy. Roxie & the Deer. (p. 1492)
—Stickers VIP. (p. 1650)
—Sully's New Home. (p. 1673)
Smith, J. Batty about Texas Coates, Kathy, illus. (p. 147)
Smith, J. Albert. Adventures of the Molly Dollys. (p. 23)
—Goosey Green. (p. 702)
Smith, J. D. Best Mariachi in the World. de la Vega, Eida, tr. (p. 170)
—Best Mariachi in the World/El Mejor Mariachi del Mundo. de la Vega, Eida, tr. (p. 170)
Smith, J. D. & Jones, Dani. Best Mariachi in the World/El Mejor Mariachi del Mundo. (p. 170)
Smith, J. E. Complex City: All in a Day's Work. (p. 354)
Smith, J. L. Abominators: And My Amazing Panty Wanty Woos! Hearn, Sam, illus. (p. 5)
—Abominators & the Forces of Evil. Hearn, Sam, illus. (p. 5)
—Blue & Purple Egg. Baker, David, illus. (p. 202)
Smith, J. W. Economic Democracy Pbk: A Grand Strategy for World Peace & Prosperity, 2nd Edition. (p. 502)
—Money Pbk: A Mirror Image of the Economy, 2nd Edition. (p. 1164)
Smith, Jack K., illus. see Collins, David R.
Smith, Jackie. Cat Who Wanted to Fly. (p. 278)
Smith, Jacquelyn. Pitty the City Kitty; Tokyo. Smith, Jacquelyn & Kalafatis, John, illus. (p. 1365)
Smith, Jacqui, illus. see Lincoln, James.
Smith, Jada. Touched by an Angel. (p. 1772)
Smith, James. Wonderer of Time. (p. 1948)
Smith, James & Smith, Alice. I'm So over Fairies: Really - I Hate Them. Smith, Alice, illus. (p. 860)
Smith, James J. Mikey's Monster. (p. 1141)
Smith, James J. & James, Hollis. Mikey's Monster (Teenage Mutant Ninja Turtles) Spaziante, Patrick, illus. (p. 1141)
Smith, James K. David Thompson (p. 411)
Smith, James Noel, illus. see Hale, Shannon.
Smith, James V., Jr. Creative Corporate Writer. (p. 379)
Smith, Jamie, illus. see Barbo, Maria S. & Preller, James.
Smith, Jamie, illus. see Bauer, Marion Dane.
Smith, Jamie, illus. see Orloff, Karen Kaufman.
Smith, Jamie, illus. see Preller, James.
Smith, Jamie, illus. see Slater, Teddy.
Smith, Jan, illus. see David, Juliet.
Smith, Jan, illus. see Holub, Joan.
Smith, Jane. Adventure on White High Island. (p. 14)
—Fairytale Mix-up. Raynor, Jackie, illus. (p. 565)
—Starlight Starbright. (p. 1642)
Smith, Jane, illus. see Seal, Kerry.
Smith, Jane Burnett. Spanish Crossword Puzzles: 48 Word Puzzles for Beginning Students of Spanish. (p. 1621)
Smith, Jane Denitz. Fairy Dust. (p. 563)
Smith, Jane H. Living Tale Series: Star & the Book of Treasures. (p. 1041)
Smith, Janet Kay. Sing A Song of Science: Lyrics for Kids From 1-99. (p. 1578)
Smith, Janine, jt. auth. see Manger, Barbara.
Smith, Jason. We Share When We Sleep. (p. 1868)
Smith, Jay F. Day to Remember: A Sam & Coco Story. Smith, Jay F., illus. (p. 414)
Smith, J.C. Deja, Where's My Shoe? (p. 424)
Smith, Jeff. Bone: Los Ojos de la Tormenta. Vol. 3 (p. 208)
—Bone: La Gran Carrera de Vacas. Vol. 2 (p. 208)
—Bone Handbook. Hamaker, Steve, illus. (p. 208)
—Bone Handbook. (p. 209)
—Crown of Horns. Smith, Jeff, illus. (p. 386)
—Dragonslayer. Smith, Jeff, illus. (p. 479)
—Eyes of the Storm. Smith, Jeff & Hamaker, Steve, illus. (p. 558)
—Ghost Circles. (p. 670)
—Ghost Circles. Smith, Jeff & Hamaker, Steve, illus. (p. 670)
—Graphix Collection Smith, Jeff, illus. (p. 711)
—Great Cow Race. Smith, Jeff & Hamaker, Steve, illus. (p. 715)
—Little Mouse Gets Ready. (p. 1032)
—Little Mouse Gets Ready, Level 1. (p. 1032)
—Old Man's Cave. (p. 1284)
—Old Man's Cave. Smith, Jeff & Hamaker, Steve, illus. (p. 1284)
—Out from Boneville. Smith, Jeff, illus. (p. 1311)
—Out from Boneville. Smith, Jeff & Hamaker, Steve, illus. (p. 1311)
—Rock Jaw: Master of the Eastern Border. Hamaker, Steve & Smith, Jeff, illus. (p. 1482)
—Rock Jaw: Master of the Eastern Border. Smith, Jeff & Hamaker, Steve, illus. (p. 1482)
—Rock Jaw Master: Master of the Eastern Border. (p. 1482)
—Rose. Vess, Charles, illus. (p. 1489)
Smith, Jeff, illus. see Lester, Sharon.
Smith, Jeff, illus. see Sniegoski, Tom.
Smith, Jeff, jt. auth. see Robertson, Barry.
Smith, Jeff, jt. auth. see Sniegoski, Tom.
Smith, Jeff & Sniegoski, Tom. Tall Tales. Smith, Jeff, illus. (p. 1704)
Smith, Jeffrey, illus. see Metaxas, Eric.
Smith, Jeffrey B. Stubby. (p. 1668)
Smith, Jeffrey Chipps. Northern Renaissance. (p. 1266)
Smith, Jen, illus. see Kent, Alex.
Smith, Jenni, illus. see Branch, Jennifer.
Smith, Jennifer. Diary of a Parent Trainer. (p. 434)
—Gay Rights Movement. (p. 659)
Smith, Jennifer & Morgan, Andre. Zelza Zero. (p. 1986)
Smith, Jennifer Crown. Dad's Falling Apart: Keeping It Together When a Family Member Has Multiple Sclerosis. Williams, Ron, illus. (p. 399)
Smith, Jennifer Dawn Deconinck. If I Could Float on A Cloud, Where Would I Go? (p. 852)
Smith, Jennifer E. Comeback Season. (p. 347)
—Hello, Goodbye, & Everything in Between. (p. 764)
—Statistical Probability of Love at First Sight. (p. 1644)
—Storm Makers. Helquist, Brett, illus. (p. 1656)
—This Is What Happy Looks Like. (p. 1736)
Smith, Jennifer Lynne. Things I Wonder. Perez, Angela J., ed. (p. 1733)
Smith, Jeremy, illus. see Thomas, John Ira.
Smith, Jerry, illus. see Janowski, Alice.
Smith, Jessica Gillis. Charlotte's Halloween. (p. 293)
Smith, Jessie Carney & Wynn, Linda T. Freedom Facts & Firsts: 400 Years of the African American Civil Rights Experience. (p. 634)
Smith, Jessie Willcox, illus. see Coussens, Penrhyn W.
Smith, Jessie Willcox, illus. see Crothers, Samuel McChord.
Smith, Jessie Willcox, illus. see Moore, Clement C.
Smith, Jessie Willcox & Moore, Clement C. 'Twas the Night Before Christmas. Smith, Jessie Willcox, illus. (p. 1799)
Smith, Jill & Diller, Howard. Consonant Primer II. (p. 359)
—Nat the Fat Cat: Workbook. (p. 1230)
—Nat the Fat Cat. (p. 1230)
Smith, Jim. Barry Loser & the Case of the Crumpled Carton. (p. 140)
—Barry Loser & the Holiday of Doom. (p. 140)
—I Am So over Being a Loser. (p. 834)
—I Am Sort of a Loser. (p. 834)
Smith, Jim, illus. see Waddell, Dan.
Smith, Jim, jt. auth. see Loser, Barry.
Smith, Jim & Beresford, Nicholas A. Chernobyl: Catastrophe & Consequences (p. 297)
Smith, Jim & Loser, Barry. I Am Still Not a Loser. (p. 834)
Smith, Jim W. W., illus. see Loxton, Daniel.
Smith, Jimmie. Jonas Little Donkey, Big Job. (p. 925)
Smith, Joanie, ed. see Meyell, Lenaise.
Smith, Jodene. Activities for Fine Motor Skills Development. (p. 10)
—Activities for Gross Motor Skills Development. (p. 10)
—Cut & Paste - Language Arts. (p. 395)
—Cut & Paste - Math, Grades 1-3. (p. 395)
—Cut & Paste - Science. (p. 395)
—Day the Crayons Quit: An Instructional Guide for Literature (p. 414)
Smith, Jodene Lynn & Garbani, Tony. Oats, Peas, Beans, & Barley Grow. (p. 1275)
Smith, Jodene Lynn & Reid, Stephanie. Animales. (p. 80)
—Animals. (p. 81)
—Plantas. (p. 1369)
—Plants. (p. 1369)
Smith, Jodene Lynn & Rice, Dona. Animal Homes. (p. 78)
—Hogares de los Animales. (p. 787)
—Si Fuera un Árbol. (p. 1572)
Smith, Jodene Lynn & Rice, Dona Herweck. Animal Homes. (p. 78)
—Hogares de los Animales. (p. 787)
—If I Were a Tree. (p. 853)
—Si Fuera un Árbol. (p. 1572)
Smith, Jodene Lynn & Thompson, Chad. Baa, Baa, Black Sheep. (p. 123)
—Beh, Beh, Borreguito Negro. (p. 160)
Smith, Joe. Single with Six. (p. 1579)
Smith, Joe, jt. auth. see Nasu, Yukie.
Smith, Joel D. Santa's Secret Deal: Who Else Signed It, & Where You Can Find Proof of the Deal in Your Room Right Now. (p. 1513)
Smith, Johanna, jt. auth. see Carabine, Sue.
Smith, John A. Special Christmas for Oscar (p. 1623)
Smith, John C. Popee the Purple Pig-a-Saurus. (p. 1384)
Smith, John D. & Warburton, Fiona. Cambridge IGCSE Travel & Tourism. (p. 255)
Smith, John D. H. Whale Whisperers Smith, Anne, illus. (p. 1877)
Smith, John David. We Ask Only for Even-Handed Justice: Black Voices from Reconstruction, 1865-1877. (p. 1866)
Smith, Jonathan. White Hat Hacking. (p. 1913)
Smith, Jonathan, illus. see Meed, Douglas V.
Smith, Jordyn, illus. see McHaney, Eric & McHaney, Mandy.
Smith, Jos. A., illus. see Bardoe, Cheryl.
Smith, Jos. A., illus. see Fleischman, Sid.
Smith, Jos. A., illus. see Yorinks, Arthur.
Smith, Joseph K. Substitute Kid. (p. 1671)
Smith, Josephine A. It's Okay on a Winters Day! Hickle Pickle Books Presents Adventures of Hickle the Pickle. (p. 898)
Smith, Joshua T. Frog's Van. (p. 641)
Smith, Joy V. Why Won't Anyone Play with Me? (p. 1927)
Smith, Joye. What Does It Mean to Be Poor? (p. 1884)
Smith, Judah. Jesus Is Student Edition (p. 915)
Smith, Julie. Hearts for the Homeless. (p. 760)
—Magic Pencil: Happy Birthday Kuser Elementary School 1909-2009. (p. 1073)
—Samuel, God's Helper. (p. 1509)
Smith, Justin R. Mills of God. (p. 1144)
Smith, Justine. My Daddy Says. Stevens, Angie, illus. (p. 1201)
—Zak Zoo & the Baffled Burglar. Elsom, Clare, illus. (p. 1984)
—Zak Zoo & the Birthday Bang. Elsom, Clare, illus. (p. 1984)
—Zak Zoo & the Hectic House. Elsom, Clare, illus. (p. 1984)
—Zak Zoo & the School Hullabaloo. Elsom, Clare, illus. (p. 1984)
—Zak Zoo & the Seaside SOS. Elsom, Clare, illus. (p. 1984)
—Zak Zoo & the TV Crew. Elsom, Clare, illus. (p. 1984)
Smith, Justine, jt. auth. see Ackerman, Jill.
Smith, Justine, jt. auth. see Doodlemum.
Smith, Justine & Ackerman, Jill. Playtime. Scholastic, Inc. Staff, ed. (p. 1373)
Smith, Justine & Elsom, Clare. Zak Zoo & the Birthday Bang. (p. 1984)
—Zak Zoo & the Hectic House. (p. 1984)
—Zak Zoo & the Peculiar Parcel. (p. 1984)
Smith, K. Be Safe on the Bus: Learning the B Sound. (p. 149)
Smith, Kallis. Finger & Thumb. (p. 589)
Smith, Karen Barker, jt. auth. see Malam, John.
Smith, Karen Cecil. Old Salem Christmas, 1840. Phipps, Bebe, illus. (p. 1284)
Smith, Karen Kelley. Even Though I'm Small. (p. 541)
Smith, Karen Lynn. Popular Dance: From Ballroom to Hip-Hop. (p. 1385)
Smith, Karen S. Sleazy Rider. (p. 1588)
Smith, Karla. All Around Texas: Regions & Resources. (p. 43)
—All Around Virginia: Regions & Resources. (p. 44)
—People of Virginia. (p. 1339)
—Uniquely Virginia (p. 1818)
—Virginia History. (p. 1844)
—Virginia Native Peoples. (p. 1844)
—Virginia Plants & Animals. (p. 1844)
Smith, Kath. Let's Make a Movie. Dodd, Emma, illus. (p. 999)
Smith, Kathie Billingslea. Rainforest Animals. Bonforte, Lisa, illus. (p. 1436)
Smith, Kathie Billingslea & Munro, Alice. Moons of Jupiter. (p. 1173)
Smith, Kathleen. Puppy for the White House. Hansen, Laurie, illus. (p. 1418)
Smith, Kathryn, jt. auth. see Lawson, Peter.
Smith, Kathryn & Scott, Karen. King Murray's Royal Tail: The True Story of an Easter Bunny. (p. 958)
Smith, Kathy. Helping Hannah. (p. 766)
—Let's Go to the Bank. (p. 997)
—New Shoes for Chili Bean: Adventures of a Little Red Mule. (p. 1247)
Smith, Kathy Jo. Come Play with Me. (p. 347)
Smith, Katrina M. This Is My Flag. (p. 1736)
Smith, Keeley. First Soul. (p. 597)
Smith, Keith, illus. see Blue, Martha.
Smith, Keith, illus. see John, Roberta.
Smith, Keith A. Quick Leather Bindings: Non-Adhesive Binding Volume V. (p. 1427)
—Structure of the Visual Book. (p. 1668)
Smith, Kelly. Sticker Fashionista: Vintage Style. (p. 1650)
—Sticker Fashionista: A Year of Fashion. (p. 1650)
Smith, Keri. Tear up This Book! The Sticker, Stencil, Stationery, Games, Crafts, Doodle, & Journal Book for Girls! Magruder, Trula, ed. (p. 1711)
Smith, Kevin. Sounds of Violence (p. 1615)
Smith, Kim. Leroy's Long Journey: Leroy Baxter, the near-Sighted Spider Volume I (p. 993)
—Sunny Summer Lapbook. Assembled. Kinney, Cyndi, ed. (p. 1677)
—Sunny Summer Lapbook. Kinney, Cyndi, ed. (p. 1677)
Smith, Kim, illus. see Diaz, Natalia & Owens, Melissa.
Smith, Kim, illus. see Jules, Jacqueline.
Smith, Kim, illus. see Lewis, Marion.
Smith, Kimanne, illus. see Ferris, Jeri Chase.
Smith, Kimanne, jt. illus. see Smith, Elise.
Smith, Kimberly. Monkeying Around: Meet Chippey & His Friends. Goris, Laura, illus. (p. 1165)
Smith, Kirsten. Geography of Girlhood. (p. 662)
—Trinkets. (p. 1787)
Smith, Kourtney. Adventures of Stanley the Staple. (p. 23)
Smith, Kristie Lyn. Dottie & Dots See Animal Spots: Learning Braille with Dots & Dottie. (p. 472)
Smith, Kristy. Princess Crowns: Kindness. (p. 1403)
Smith, Kuleigh, illus. see Vermillion, Patricia.
Smith, L. Survival Skills. (p. 1687)
—Usborne Book of Horses & Ponies. (p. 1827)
Smith, L. & Mcgee, B. Clappity clap all through the Town. (p. 326)
Smith, L. J. Awakening & The Struggle (p. 120)
—Awakening & the Struggle (p. 120)
—Captive Part II & the Power. (p. 264)
—Craving. (p. 376)
—Dark Angel - The Chosen - Soulmate (p. 407)
—Dark Visions: The Strange Power - The Possessed - The Passion. (p. 408)
—Destiny Rising. (p. 431)
—Forbidden Game: The Hunter - The Chase - The Kill. (p. 616)
—Fury & Dark Reunion (p. 650)
—Fury & Dark Reunion. (p. 650)
—Heart of Valor. (p. 759)
—Heart of Valor. (p. 760)
—Hunt. (p. 828)
—Huntress, Black Dawn, Witchlight (p. 829)
—Initiation & the Captive. (p. 874)
—Midnight. (p. 1138)
—Moonsong Vol. 9. (p. 1173)
—Moonsong. (p. 1173)
—Night of the Solstice. (p. 1254)
—Night World: Secret Vampire; Daughters of Darkness; Spellbinder. (p. 1254)
—Nightfall. (p. 1255)
—Passion. (p. 1326)
—Phantom. (p. 1349)
—Secret Circle: The Divide. Vol.4 (p. 1540)
—Secret Circle - The Divide (p. 1540)
—Shadow Souls. (p. 1558)
—Strange Fate. (p. 1665)
—Struggle. (p. 1668)
—Temptation (p. 1718)
—Temptation. (p. 1718)
Smith, L. J. & Clark, Aubrey. Unmasked (p. 1821)
—Unseen (p. 1822)
—Unspoken (p. 1822)
Smith, L. J. & Kevin Williamson & Julie Plec. Asylum. (p. 109)
—Compelled. (p. 352)
Smith, L. J. & Pollert, Annette. Night World: The Ultimate Fan Guide. (p. 1254)
Smith, L. J. & Smith, Tom. Night of the Solstice. (p. 1254)
Smith, L. J. & Williamson, Kevin. Asylum. (p. 109)
—Compelled. (p. 352)
Smith, L. J., et al. Bloodlust. (p. 201)
—Ripper. (p. 1474)
Smith, Landa, illus. see Johnson, Kimberly P.
Smith, Lane. Abe Lincoln's Dream. Smith, Lane, illus. (p. 4)
—Grandpa Green. Smith, Lane, illus. (p. 709)
—Inaho Kitab. Smith, Lane, illus. (p. 868)
—It's a Book. Smith, Lane, illus. (p. 895)
—It's a Little Book. (p. 895)
—John, Paul, George & Ben. (p. 922)
—John, Paul, George & Ben. Smith, Lane, illus. (p. 922)
—Madam President. (p. 1069)
—Madam President. Smith, Lane, illus. (p. 1069)
—Return to Augie Hobble. (p. 1465)
Smith, Lane, illus. see Heide, Florence Parry.
Smith, Lane, illus. see Scieszka, Jon.
Smith, Lane, illus. see Shea, Bob.
Smith, Lane, illus. see Viorst, Judith.
Smith, Lane, jt. auth. see Scieszka, Jon.
Smith, Larry. Cloud Realm. (p. 334)
Smith, Latisha. Mama Always Knows Best. (p. 1084)
Smith, Latoya K. My Favorite Trey. (p. 1203)
Smith, Laura. Book Bunch: Developing Elementary Book Clubs. (p. 210)
Smith, Laura Ann. Murder in T-Town. (p. 1192)
Smith, Laura L., contrib. by. Skinny. (p. 1585)
Smith, Laura Lundgren. Sending down the Sparrows. (p. 1550)
Smith, Laura R. & Fearis, J. S. Little Sir Echo. Faulkner, Stacey, ed. (p. 1036)
Smith, Laura Rountree. Fairy Babies. Dulin, Dorothy, illus. (p. 563)
—Snubby Nose & Tippy Toes. (p. 1601)
Smith, Lauren. Ashley Enright & the Mystery at Miller's Pond. (p. 106)
Smith, Lauren E. Ashley Enright & the Darnell Diamonds (p. 106)
—Ashley Enright Investigations. (p. 106)
Smith, Laurie Chance. Snapshots: Nature Stories in the Bible. (p. 1597)
Smith, Laverne Byrd. Pokey the Playful Whale: (who wanted to live on Land) (p. 1378)
Smith, Lawrence Beall, illus. see Meyer, Franklyn E.
Smith, Lee, jt. auth. see Collett, Jo.
Smith, Lee A. Dobee the Littlest Dragon. (p. 458)
Smith, Leone. Jasmine Finds a Doctor. Smith, Marcelle, illus. (p. 910)
Smith, Lesley. My Big Book of Rhymes. (p. 1197)
Smith, Lesley, illus. see Andrews, Jackie.
Smith, Lesley & Award Publications Staff. Brer Rabbit & Brer Fox. (p. 226)
—Brer Rabbit & the Honey Pot. (p. 226)
—Brer Rabbit & the Tar Baby. (p. 226)
Smith, Lesley, et al. Brer Rabbit & the Great Race. (p. 226)
Smith, Levi. Sparkie's Great Adventures: The Great Space Adventure. (p. 1622)
Smith, Linda. Broken Thread (p. 230)

—Dat's New Year. (p. 409)
—Inside Tree. Brown, Kathryn, illus. (p. 878)
—Inside Tree. Parkins, David, illus. (p. 878)
—Kelly's Cabin Krasulja, Corina, illus. (p. 948)
—Mrs. Biddlebox: Her Bad Day & What She Did about It. Frazee, Marla, illus. (p. 1187)
—Mrs. Crump's Cat. Roberts, David, illus. (p. 1187)
—Piper of Shadonia (p. 1361)
—Sea Change. (p. 1534)
—Smith Picture Book. (p. 1594)
—Wind Shifter. (p. 1935)
Smith, Linda J. Willie Mays: The Say Hey Kid. (p. 1934)
Smith, Linda L. Have You Ever Seen a Bird Skip? (p. 754)
Smith, Linda Wasmer. Louis Pasteur: Disease Fighter. (p. 1058)
—Louis Pasteur: Genius Disease Fighter. (p. 1058)
Smith, Lindsay. Sekret. (p. 1549)
—Skandal. (p. 1583)
Smith, Lindsay, ed. see Wood, Beatrice.
Smith, Lisa. Makini, the Impala with a Crooked Horn. (p. 1082)
—Not So Very Far Away. (p. 1267)
Smith, Lisa, illus. see Dolan, Penny.
Smith, Lisa R. There's a Monster in My Washing MacHine. (p. 1731)
Smith, Liz. Girl's Guide to Growing up - Booklet Perry, Gala, illus. (p. 680)
Smith, Loretta. Bela & the Gold Medallion. Marconi, Gloria, illus. (p. 161)
Smith, Lori, jt. auth. see Richens, Carol.
Smith, Lori Joy. Goodnight Book. (p. 701)
Smith, Louis. How Do I Talk to My Child about Sex: If I Don't the Devil Will. (p. 807)
—Sexual Sins of the Bible: Everything You Want to Know, but Wouldn't Ask! (p. 1556)
Smith, Louise C. Mr. Stubbs: Autobiography of a Clever Cat. (p. 1186)
Smith, Lucy. Giraffes: Towering Tall. (p. 677)
—Gorillas: Beasts of the Wild. (p. 703)
—Grizzly Bears: Fierce Hunters. (p. 724)
—Hippos: Huge & Hungry. (p. 781)
—How to Draw Horses. Chapman, Chris et al, illus. (p. 817)
—Usborne Book of Horses & Ponies. Gray, Miranda & Trotter, Stuart, illus. (p. 1827)
Smith, Lucy, jt. auth. see Evans, Cheryl.
Smith, Lucy Sackett. Elephants: From Trunk to Tail. (p. 511)
—Mighty Mammals (p. 1140)
—Tigers: Prowling Predators. (p. 1749)
Smith, Lurs Schwarz, illus. see Thienes-Schunemann, Mary.
Smith, Lynda Faye. Revenge of the Big Bad Wolf. (p. 1465)
Smith, Lynn & Faust Kalscheur, Jann. ABC's Naturally: A Child's Guide to the Alphabet Through Nature. Faust Kalscheur, Jann, photos by. (p. 4)
Smith, M. A., jt. auth. see Smith, M. a.
Smith, M. a. & Smith, M. A. Boy & His Wizard. Freeland, Devon & Contreras-Freeland, Gina, illus. (p. 217)
Smith, M. Jane. First Fry Bread: A Gitxsan Story. Wheeler, Jordan, ed. (p. 595)
Smith, Maggie. Christmas with the Mousekins. (p. 316)
—Counting Our Way to Maine. (p. 371)
—My Blue Bunny, Bubbit. (p. 1198)
—One Naked Baby. (p. 1296)
—Pigs in Pajamas. (p. 1358)
Smith, Maggie, illus. see Berry, Joy.
Smith, Maggie, illus. see Bottner, Barbara.
Smith, Maggie, illus. see Bunting, Eve.
Smith, Maggie, illus. see George, Kristine O'Connell.
Smith, Maggie, illus. see Greene, Rhonda Gowler.
Smith, Maggie, illus. see Markes, Julie & Markes.
Smith, Maggie, illus. see Park, Linda Sue.
Smith, Maggie Caldwell. Tommy Wilson, Junior Veterinarian: The Case of the Wounded Jack Rabbit. McHose, Jean, illus. (p. 1765)
—Tommy Wilson, Junior Veterinarian: The Case of the Orphaned Bobcat. Heyer, Carol & White, Charlotte L., illus. (p. 1765)
Smith Management Associates Staff, jt. auth. see Peterson, Eugene H.
Smith, Mandy M., illus. see Smith, B. M.
Smith, Marcelle, illus. see Smith, Leone.
Smith, Margaret Ann. New Kind of Life for Eddie Eagle. (p. 1245)
Smith, Margie Fulton. Chicken Kate's Visit to Church. (p. 300)
Smith, Marie, jt. auth. see Smith, Roland.
Smith, Marie & Smith, Roland. B Is for Beaver: An Oregon Alphabet. Roydon, Michael, illus. (p. 122)
—T Is for Time. Graef, Renée, illus. (p. 1694)
—W Is for Waves: An Ocean Alphabet. Megahan, John & Rose, Melanie, illus. (p. 1851)
Smith, Marie, et al. N Is for our Nation's Capital: A Washington, DC Alphabet. Gibson, Barbara Leonard, illus. (p. 1227)
Smith, Marilyn. Kingdom Lifestyles for Children: Kingdom Lifestyles for Successful Living. (p. 959)
Smith, Mark Andrew. Gladstone's School for World Conquerors. (p. 682)
Smith, Marla. Little Miracles: Book of Prayers. (p. 1031)
Smith, Martha, jt. auth. see Knowles, Elizabeth.
Smith, Martin. In-Line Skating. (p. 864)
Smith, Martina. Story of Creation: A Spark Bible Story. Grosshauser, Peter, illus. (p. 1657)
—Story of Jesus' Teaching & Healing: A Spark Bible Story. Grosshauser, Peter, illus. (p. 1658)
—Story of Moses & God's Promise: A Spark Bible Story. Grosshauser, Peter, illus. (p. 1659)
Smith, Marvelyn A. Kangaroo & the Crocodile. (p. 942)
Smith, Mary Ann Free, illus. see Newell, Karmel H.
Smith, Mary C. Day in the Life of William Bray Goat. Smith, Mary C., illus. (p. 413)
Smith, Mary Claire, illus. see Petty, Kate.
Smith, Mary Elizabeth, illus. see Shell, S. E.
Smith, Mary L. Ramblings of Clyde Frog & Jasmine. Bermejo, Hilbert, illus. (p. 1437)
Smith, Mary Lou. Celebrate Easter. (p. 283)
—Celebrate Halloween. (p. 283)
—Celebrate Saint Patrick's Day. (p. 284)
—I See Squares. (p. 845)
—I See Triangles. (p. 845)
Smith, Mary P. Boy Captive of Old Deerfield. (p. 217)
Smith, Mary P. Wells. Young Puritans in King Philip's War. Bridgman, L. J., illus. (p. 1979)
Smith, Mary-Lou. I See Stars. (p. 845)
Smith, Mason, jt. auth. see Mitchell, Marie.
Smith, Matt. Barbarian Lord. Smith, Matt, illus. (p. 137)
Smith, Matt, illus. see Derico, Laura Ring.
Smith, Matt, illus. see Derico, Laura.
Smith, Matt, illus. see Schreiber, Joe.
Smith, Matt & Tilton, David. Tale of Despereaux: The Graphic Novel. Tilton, David, illus. (p. 1699)
Smith, Matthew, illus. see Marz, Ron.
Smith, Mavis, illus. see McMullan, Kate.
Smith, Maximilian. History of Juneteenth. (p. 784)
—Story of Cinco de Mayo. (p. 1657)
—What Is Groundhog Day? (p. 1889)
Smith, M.D., Jane H. Living Tale Series: Henley & the Book of Heroes. (p. 1041)
Smith, Melanie. Beginner Cello Theory for Children, Book One (p. 159)
—Beginner Violin Theory for Children, Book One (p. 159)
Smith, Melinda. Soldiers for Battle. (p. 1607)
Smith Meyer, Ruth. Tyson's Sad Bad Day. (p. 1805)
Smith, Michael. Beyond the Basics DataCad 10 Advanced Construction Drawing & Visualization- Student's Guide: A Student's Guide & Activities for the Official DataCad User's Guide Text. (p. 174)
—My Ducky Buddy. Oliva, Octavio, illus. (p. 1202)
—My Ducky Buddy/Mi Amigo el Pato. Oliva, Octavio, illus. (p. 1202)
—Questions for Kids: A Book to Discover a Child's Imagination & Knowledge. Lin, Albert & Smith, Crystal, illus. (p. 1426)
—Questions for Kids: A Book to Discover a Child's Imagination & Knowledge. Smith, Crystal & Lin, Albert, illus. (p. 1426)
—Relativity. Oliva, Octavio, illus. (p. 1457)
—Shackleton - the Boss: The Remarkable Adventures of Ernest Shackleton. Brady, Annie, illus. (p. 1556)
—Thomas the T. Rex: The Journey of a Young Dinosaur to Los Angeles. Roski, Gayle Garner, illus. (p. 1739)
Smith, Michael, jt. auth. see Nasman, Leonard.
Smith, Michael & Aguiler, Manny. Smile: B una Sonrisa. Aguiler, Manny, illus. (p. 1594)
Smith, Michael & Oliva, Octavio. Grasshopper Buddy. Oliva, Octavio, illus. (p. 711)
—Relativity: Relatividad. Oliva, Octavio, illus. (p. 1457)
Smith, Michael & Roski, Gayle Garner. Thomas the T. Rex: The Journey of a Young Dinosaur to Los Angeles. Roski, Gayle Garner, illus. (p. 1739)
Smith, Michael & Wang, Emily. My Ducky Buddy. Oliva, Octavio, illus. (p. 1202)
Smith, Michael Bennett. Dawn of Awareness. (p. 411)
Smith, Michael Ray. FeatureWriting. Net: Timeless Feature Story Ideas in an Online World. (p. 580)
Smith, Michael W., Jr., jt. auth. see Goodman, Susan E.
Smith, Michelle. Duck in the Hedge: Jeremy & the Big Pond. (p. 488)
—Play On. (p. 1371)
Smith, Mildred M. Louie the Blue Frog. (p. 1058)
Smith, Mindy, illus. see Holladay, Shirley.
Smith, Miranda. Navigators: Ancient Egypt. (p. 1238)
—Plant Propagator's Bible. (p. 1369)
Smith, Miranda, jt. auth. see Steele, Philip.
Smith, Miriam & Fraser, Afton. Point to Happy: A Book for Kids on the Autism Spectrum. Smithwick, Margo, photos by. (p. 1377)
Smith, Miss Diane Pearl. Princess S Magickal Christmas. (p. 1405)
Smith, Molly. Border Breakdown: The Fall of the Berlin Wall. (p. 213)
—Border Breakdown: The Fall of the Berlin Wall. Opie, David, illus. (p. 213)
—Don't Worry, Mason. Poole, Helen, illus. (p. 469)
—Don't Worry, Mason Lap Book. Poole, Helen, illus. (p. 469)
—Green Anaconda: The World's Heaviest Snake. (p. 721)
—Helpful Ladybugs. (p. 766)
—Roly-Poly Pillbugs. (p. 1485)
—Speedy Dragonflies. (p. 1624)
Smith, Molly, jt. auth. see Chronicle Books Staff.
Smith, Molly, et al. World Almanac for Kids Workbook. (p. 1953)
Smith, Molly K. Cassie's Guardian Angel. (p. 276)
Smith, Montez Roller. Growing Pains. (p. 726)
—Growing Tall. (p. 726)
—Summer to Grow On. House upon a Hill Series - Book 1. (p. 1675)
Smith, N. L. Elle's Silly Hats. (p. 514)
Smith, Naiya. Pinky Swear: The Heart Wants What the Heart Wants. (p. 1360)
Smith, Nancy. Christmas Duck. (p. 313)
Smith, Nancy, jt. auth. see Milligan, Lynda.
Smith, Nancy Cain. Someday Adventures of Robin Kane. (p. 1609)
Smith, Naniloa. Children Are Happy Activity Book with Animals from the Southwest. (p. 302)
—Children are Happy CD with Animals from the Southwest. Smith, Naniloa, ed. (p. 302)
Smith, Natalie. Habitat Protection. (p. 734)
Smith, Nathan, illus. see Wakefield, Nelida.
Smith, Neil. Jason & the Argonauts (p. 910)
—Robin Hood (p. 1479)
Smith, Nerissia. Prince de'Mario's Adventure Dartes, Staci, illus. (p. 1401)
Smith, Nial, illus. see Steven, Kenneth C.
Smith, Nicole. Allie the Allergic Elephant: A Children's Story of Peanut Allergies. (p. 47)
—Chad the Allergic Chipmunk: A Children's Story of Nut Allergies. (p. 288)
Smith, Nicole Elizabeth. Healthy Black Hair: Step-by-Step Instructions for Growing Longer, Stronger Hair. (p. 758)
Smith, Nikki. Five Little Speckled Frogs Activity Guide. (p. 601)
Smith, Nikki Shannon. Little Christmas Elf. Mitchell, Susan, illus. (p. 1026)
Smith, Nikki Siegen. Welcome to the World: A Celebration of Birth & Babies from Many Cultures. (p. 1874)
Smith, Nina, illus. see Nelson, Thea.
Smith, Nora Archibald, jt. auth. see Wiggin, Kate Douglas.
Smith Novelty Company Staff. Clyde the Cable Car. (p. 336)
—Monterey & Carmel Coloring Book. (p. 1170)
Smith, Ophia D. True Story of Johnny Appleseed. (p. 1793)
Smith, Owen, illus. see Armstrong, Jennifer.
Smith, Owen, illus. see Shore, Diane ZuHone & Alexander, Jessica.
Smith, Owen, jt. auth. see Bonneval, Gwen de.
Smith, Owen, jt. auth. see Smith, Anne.
Smith, Owen, tr. see Bruneau, Clotilde, et al.
Smith, Owen, tr. see Cerami, Matteo, et al.
Smith, Owen, tr. see Constantine, Clélia.
Smith, Owen, tr. see Costi, Vincent.
Smith, Owen, tr. see Dobel, Jean-Marc, et al.
Smith, Owen, tr. see Dubos, Delphine.
Smith, Owen, tr. see Gaudin, Thierry.
Smith, Owen, tr. see Loisillier, Maud & Morel, Diane.
Smith, Owen & Smith, Anne. Safari Survivor. Rubine, illus. (p. 1502)
Smith, Ozzie, jt. auth. see Rains, Rob.
Smith, P. Athene, jt. tr. see Cooper, John E.
Smith, Pamela. It's Worth the Wait. (p. 899)
Smith, Pamela Colman. Annancy Stories. (p. 85)
Smith, Paris. Shafi Doldi. (p. 1558)
Smith, Patricia T. Miss Elly & the Gift of a Lifetime. (p. 1151)
Smith, Patty. Children's Hour. Gage, James, illus. (p. 303)
Smith, Paul, illus. see Claremont, Chris, et al.
Smith, Paul, illus. see Waid, Mark & Porter, Howard.
Smith, Paul, et al. Avengers: Falcon. (p. 118)
Smith, Paula. Attention-Deficit & Other Behavior Disorders. (p. 114)
—Autism & Other Pervasive Developmental Disorders. (p. 117)
—Be the Change for the Environment. (p. 149)
—Be the Change in the World. (p. 149)
—Be the Change in Your Community. (p. 149)
—Be the Change in Your School. (p. 149)
—Birthdays in Different Places. (p. 193)
—Clothing in Different Places. (p. 334)
—Depression & Other Mood Disorders. (p. 427)
—Foods in Different Places. (p. 614)
—Homes in Different Places. (p. 793)
—How Do Wind & Water Change Earth? (p. 808)
—Measure It! (p. 1117)
—Model It! (p. 1157)
—Phobias & Other Anxiety Disorders. (p. 1351)
—Plan & Investigate It! (p. 1366)
—Protecting Earth's Surface. (p. 1412)
—Prove It! (p. 1413)
—Schizophrenia & Other Psychotic Disorders. (p. 1521)
—Schools in Different Places. (p. 1524)
—Transportation in Different Places. (p. 1779)
—What Are Idioms, Adages, & Proverbs? (p. 1879)
—What Is a Metaphor? (p. 1888)
—What Is a Simile? (p. 1888)
—What Is Personification? (p. 1890)
Smith, Paula & Colozza Cocca, Lisa. Calendar Math. (p. 252)
—Time Word Problems. (p. 1753)
Smith, Paula & Mason, Helen. Length Word Problems. (p. 991)
—Word Problems: Mass & Volume. (p. 1951)
Smith, Peggy. Champ: The Adventures of a Boy & His New Puppy. Told in One-syllable Words for the Barton Reading & Spelling System. (p. 289)
—Job for Jeff: The Story of a Teen Who Applies for a Job as a Summer Camp Counselor, for the Barton Reading & Spelling System. (p. 919)
—Kingdom of Nod: A Sweet Tale about an Unlucky Young Queen, & the Men Who Try to Win Her Hand, for the Barton Reading & Spelling System. (p. 959)
Smith, Peggy B., jt. auth. see Ryder, Verdene.
Smith, Penny, ed. see Kei, Rose.
Smith, Penny & Dorling Kindersley Publishing Staff. A Trip to the Dentist Level 1. (p. 2)
—Animal Hide & Seek. (p. 78)
Smith, Peter. Monsieur Albert Rides to Glory. Graham, Bob, illus. (p. 1166)
Smith, Phil, illus. see Lowery, Lawrence F.
Smith, Pieter Ernst. Donkey Is Not Stupid, a Donkey Can Think. Shirley-Smith, Sanette, illus. (p. 466)
Smith, Pohla. Shaquille O'Neal: Superhero at Center. (p. 1561)
Smith, Pohla, jt. auth. see Cantwell, Lois.
Smith, Pohla & Wilson, Steve. Shaquille O'Neal: Superhero at Center. (p. 1561)
Smith, R. Cadwallader. Within the Deep. (p. 1942)
Smith, R. J. Mantassa Murders. (p. 1088)
Smith, R. L. Journals of Underwich: Book One. (p. 927)
Smith, R. M. A to Z Walk in the Park (Animal Alphabet Book) Smith, R. M., illus. (p. 2)
—Peep in the Deep - Sea Creature Counting Book: Sea Creature Counting Book. (p. 1335)
Smith, Rachael, illus. see Stephas, Kristi.
Smith, Rachel, illus. see Maurer, Amy J.
Smith, Rad, text. Distant Early Warning. (p. 453)
Smith, Raissa B., illus. see Smith, Brenda J.
Smith, Ralph W., jt. auth. see Seagle, Edward E., Jr.
Smith, Raven, illus. see Smith, Scott.
Smith, Raven, photos by see Waley, Safiya & Woodcock, Victoria.
Smith, Raymond R. Righteous Ray-Ray Has a Bad Day. (p. 1472)
—Righteous Ray-Ray Has a Bad Day Beginning Readers Edition. Davis, Alan, illus. (p. 1472)
Smith, Rebekah, jt. auth. see Sullivan, Davina.
Smith, Regina Faith. When Sam Cries. (p. 1904)
Smith, Reta Hucks. Vision Quest of Little Feather. (p. 1845)
Smith, Rich. Alabama. (p. 33)
—Arkansas. (p. 99)
—Bill of Rights (p. 186)
—Bill of Rights: Defining Our Freedoms. (p. 186)
—California. (p. 253)
—Eighth Amendment: The Right to Mercy. (p. 507)
—Fifth Amendment: The Right to Fairness. (p. 584)
—First Amendment: The Right of Expression. (p. 592)
—Fourth Amendment: The Right to Privacy. (p. 625)
—Georgia. (p. 665)
—How Amendments Are Adopted. (p. 804)
—Illinois. (p. 857)
—Indiana. (p. 871)
—Kentucky. (p. 949)
—Louisiana. (p. 1058)
—Massachusetts. (p. 1102)
—Mississippi. (p. 1154)
—Ninth & Tenth Amendments: The Right to More Rights. (p. 1257)
—North Carolina. (p. 1264)
—Oklahoma. (p. 1283)
—Oregon. (p. 1302)
—Second & Third Amendments: The Right to Security. (p. 1539)
—Seventh Amendment: The Right to a Trial by Jury. (p. 1555)
—Sixth Amendment: The Right to a Fair Trial. (p. 1583)
Smith, Richard, illus. see Bancroft, Myles.
Smith, Richard A., jt. auth. see Citrin, James M.
Smith, Richard G. Wanda Jean's Face. (p. 1856)
—When the Moon Fell Down. (p. 1905)
Smith, Richard G., illus. see Murphy, Emily.
Smith, Richard Shirley, illus. see Shankland, Hugh, tr.
Smith, Rita & Baish, Vanessa. Self-Image & Eating Disorders. (p. 1549)
Smith, Robert. American Revolution. (p. 63)
—Pre-Algebra, Grade 3. (p. 1394)
—Pre-Algebra, Grade 4. (p. 1394)
—Pre-Algebra, Grade 5. (p. 1394)
—Spotlight on America: The Lewis & Clark Expedition & the Louisiana Purchase. (p. 1633)
—Word Problems, Grade 5. (p. 1951)
Smith, Robert, jt. auth. see Smith, Robert W.
Smith, Robert Bruce. McGowan's Call. (p. 1114)
Smith, Robert Earl, Sr. New Man: Study Guide for True Biblical Reconciliation (p. 1246)
Smith, Robert F. Bitten: A Romantic Comedy. (p. 194)
Smith, Robert J., jt. auth. see Ostrowski, Thaddeus.
Smith, Robert Kimmel. Chocolate Fever. (p. 309)
—Chocolate Fever. Fiammenghi, Gioia, illus. (p. 309)
—Jelly Belly. (p. 912)
—Squeaky Wheel. (p. 1636)
—War with Grandpa. (p. 1858)
Smith, Robert Kimmel, ed. Chocolate Fever. (p. 309)
Smith, Robert W. 20th Century Wars. Hoffman, Nancy, ed. (p. 1996)
—Constitution. (p. 359)
—Great Depression. (p. 715)
—Spotlight on America: Industrial Revolution. (p. 1633)
Smith, Robert W. & Smith, Robert. Westward Movement. (p. 1876)
—Word Problems, Grade 6. (p. 1951)
Smith, Robin Deneen. Celina the Ballerina: King Megethos & the Kingdom of Tiqvah Series. (p. 286)
Smith, Robin L. Lies at the Altar: The Truth about Great Marriages. (p. 1007)
Smith, Robin Wayne. If You Got It, a Truck Brought It. Smith, Robin Wayne, illus. (p. 854)
Smith, Rodney Gipsy. Lost Christ. (p. 1055)
Smith, Roger. Adventures of Xavier Winfield & His Pal Oggie, the Great Camping Adventure. (p. 24)
—Human Rights & Protecting Individuals Russett, Bruce, ed. (p. 826)
—Humanitarian Relief & Lending a Hand Russett, Bruce, ed. (p. 826)
—Humanitarian Relief Operations: Lending a Helping Hand. (p. 826)
—Political Prisoners. (p. 1380)
—Prison Conditions: Overcrowding, Disease, Violence, & Abuse. (p. 1407)
—Prisoners on Death Row. (p. 1407)
—Rural Teens on the Move: Cars, Motorcycles, & off-Road Vehicles. (p. 1497)
—UNICEF & Other Human Rights Efforts: Protecting Individuals. (p. 1818)
Smith, Roger & McIntosh, Marsha & Smith. Youth in Prison. (p. 1982)
Smith, Roland. Beneath. (p. 164)
—Captain's Dog: My Journey with the Lewis & Clark Tribe. (p. 264)
—Chupacabra. (p. 318)
—Cryptid Hunters. (p. 387)
—Edge. (p. 504)
—Elephant Run. (p. 511)
—Eruption. (p. 534)
—Independence Hall. (p. 870)
—Jack's Run. (p. 904)
—Kitty Hawk. (p. 963)
—Mutation. (p. 1194)
—Peak. (p. 1332)
—Shatterproof. (p. 1563)
—Storm Runners. (p. 1656)
—Surge. (p. 1685)
—Tentacles. (p. 1720)
—Walkabout. (p. 1854)
—White House. (p. 1913)
—Zach's Lie. (p. 1984)
Smith, Roland, jt. auth. see Smith, Marie.
Smith, Roland, jt. auth. see Spradlin, Michael P.
Smith, Roland & Smith, Marie. E Is for Evergreen: A Washington State Alphabet. Holt Ayriss, Linda, illus. (p. 492)
—S Is for Smithsonian: America's Museum Alphabet. Frankenhuyzen, Gijsbert van, illus. (p. 1499)
—Z Is for Zookeeper: A Zoo Alphabet. Cole, Henry, illus. (p. 1984)
Smith, Roland & Spradlin, Michael P. Windy City (p. 1936)
Smith, Ron, jt. auth. see Butchart, Francis.
Smith, Ronald J. Expository of Expression. (p. 554)

Smith, Ronald L. Hoodoo. (p. 795)
Smith, Ronn, adapted by. Nothing but the Truth. (p. 1268)
Smith, Rosemarie. Meet the Bubblechomps - & the Bubblechomps Go Skiing. (p. 1122)
Smith, Rosemary. Lizard Tales: Lizzie Walks on the Wild Side. (p. 1042)
—Lizzie Goes to Tea. (p. 1043)
—Three Wishes for Maddy. (p. 1744)
—Woody Gets Dunked. (p. 1950)
Smith, Rosie. My Mom's the Best. Whatley, Bruce, illus. (p. 1214)
Smith, Roy. Louphole Forest Tells Its Tale of Enchantment. Magpie, ed. (p. 1059)
Smith, Rupert. Poets of World War I (p. 1376)
Smith, Ruth. Buddy Bear: Visits Michigan Lighthouses. (p. 234)
Smith, Ruth J. Divine Providence: A Child's History of the United States. Mikler, Lisa M., illus. (p. 454)
—Liberty & Justice for All: A Child's History of the United States of America. Mikler, Lisa M., illus. (p. 1005)
—Liberty & Justice for All Teacher's Guide: Liberty & Justice for All. (p. 1005)
Smith, Ryan A. Surfboards: From Start to Finish. Howard, Devon, photos by. (p. 1685)
—Surfboards. (p. 1685)
Smith, S. Billy Blue the Caribou. (p. 187)
—Hey Silly Cat! Dont Tease the Dog! (p. 774)
Smith, S. & Robins, W. Airport Sticker Book. (p. 32)
Smith, S. C. Mabell. Ethel Morton's Holidays. (p. 539)
Smith, Sandra. Dilemm. (p. 440)
Smith, Sandra, illus. see Allgood, Jean.
Smith, Sandra S. Cost of Eggs: Hill House Farm Series. Mason, Turning Bear, illus. (p. 368)
Smith, Sarah. Butterfly House. (p. 248)
—Other Side of Dark. (p. 1306)
—Where's My Mommy? (p. 1910)
Smith, Scott. God Loves to Color Too! Smith, Raven et al, illus. (p. 689)
Smith, Scott & Smith, Andrea. Teach a Donkey to Fish. (p. 1708)
Smith, Shane W. Lesser Evil, Book 3 Comic Book. Smith, Shane W., illus. (p. 993)
Smith, Sharon. Queen Diva. (p. 1424)
—Speedy the Squirrel. (p. 1625)
Smith, Shelley, jt. auth. see Wall, Pauline.
Smith, Shelli. Grammy Goes Green. (p. 706)
Smith, Sherri. Counting with Mike the Tiger. Walsh, D. T., illus. (p. 372)
—Mike the Tiger Teaches the Alphabet. Walsh, D. T., illus. (p. 1141)
—Where's the Baby??? (p. 1910)
Smith, Sherri Graves. Bully's Game Day Rules. Danielson, Damon, illus. (p. 241)
—Cimarron's Game Day Rules. Danielson, Damon, illus. (p. 319)
—Cocky's Game Day Rules. Danielson, Damon, illus. (p. 337)
—Nittany Lion's Game Day Rules. Danielson, Damon, illus. (p. 1257)
—Reveille's Game Day Rules. Danielson, Damon, illus. (p. 1465)
—Tiger's Game Day Rules. Danielson, Damon, illus. (p. 1749)
—UGA Teaches the Alphabet. Walsh, D. T., illus. (p. 1808)
Smith, Sherri L. Flygirl. (p. 609)
—Orleans. (p. 1304)
Smith, Sherrie. Not Another Dog. (p. 1267)
Smith, Sherry L. & Frehner, Brian. Indians & Energy: Exploitation & Opportunity in the American Southwest. (p. 871)
Smith, Sherwood. Emerald Wand of Oz. Stout, William, illus. (p. 518)
—Over the Sea: CJ's First Notebook. (p. 1314)
Smith, Shirleen L. Not All Heroes Are on TV. (p. 1267)
Smith, Shuford. ABC All-American Riddles. (p. 3)
Smith, Sian. Big & Small (p. 177)
—Changing Direction (p. 290)
—Changing Seasons. (p. 290)
—City Homes (p. 323)
—Fall (p. 566)
—Flies (p. 604)
—Grasshoppers (p. 711)
—Hard & Soft (p. 748)
—Homes in the Past (p. 793)
—Homes That Move (p. 793)
—Hot & Cold (p. 801)
—Invierno (p. 885)
—Ladybugs (p. 971)
—Levers (p. 1003)
—Life Cycles (p. 1009)
—Machines at the Airport (p. 1068)
—Machines at Work. (p. 1068)
—Machines on a Construction Site (p. 1068)
—Machines on the Farm (p. 1068)
—Machines on the Road (p. 1068)
—Making Things Move. (p. 1082)
—Night & Day (p. 1252)
—Old & New (p. 1283)
—Opposites (p. 1300)
—Opposites Big Book (p. 1301)
—Otoño (p. 1307)
—Primavera (p. 1400)
—Pulleys (p. 1416)
—Ramps & Wedges (p. 1438)
—Rural Homes (p. 1497)
—Screws, Nuts, & Bolts (p. 1533)
—Sea Mysteries (p. 1535)
—Seasons. (p. 1538)
—Spiders (p. 1627)
—Spring (p. 1634)
—Springs (p. 1635)
—Summer (p. 1673)
—Verano (p. 1836)
—Wet & Dry (p. 1877)
—What Can You See in Fall? (p. 1881)
—What Can You See in Spring? (p. 1881)
—Wheels & Axles (p. 1900)
—Where We Live. (p. 1910)
—Winter (p. 1937)
—Woodlice (p. 1949)
—Worms (p. 1961)
Smith, Sian, jt. auth. see Nunn, Daniel.
Smith, Sian, jt. auth. see Rissman, Rebecca.
Smith, Sian & Guillain, Charlotte. How Does My Body Work? (p. 809)
Smith, Sian & Heinemann Library Staff. Invierno (p. 885)
—Otoño (p. 1307)
—Primavera (p. 1400)
—Verano (p. 1836)
Smith, Sian & Rissman, Rebecca. Winter (p. 1937)
Smith, Sian & Shannon, Sarah. Cambiar de Dirección (p. 255)
—Changing Direction (p. 290)
Smith, Sian, et al. Cambiar de Dirección (p. 255)
Smith, Simon. Reverdy Road. (p. 1466)
Smith, Simon, illus. see Fandel, Jennifer, et al.
Smith, Simon, illus. see Kalz, Jill.
Smith, Simon, illus. see Knudsen, Shannon.
Smith, Simon, illus. see Miller, Connie Colwell, et al.
Smith, Sindy. Charlie the Chipmunk & the Lost Goldmine. (p. 293)
—Charlie the Chipmunk & the Lost Goldmine. Smith, Sindy, illus. (p. 293)
—Dadu the Dolphin. Smith, Sindy, illus. (p. 399)
—Ervin & Alma's Little Mouse House. (p. 534)
—Indy the Unicorn Prince. (p. 873)
—Indy the Unicorn Prince. Smith, Sindy, illus. (p. 873)
—Little Lucy Lou. Smith, Sindy, illus. (p. 1031)
—Mr. Minko. Smith, Sindy, illus. (p. 1185)
—Rosie the Rottweiler. (p. 1490)
—Rosie the Rottweiler. Smith, Sindy, illus. (p. 1490)
—Tale of Pinky Wink Possum. (p. 1700)
Smith, Soonboke. Origami. (p. 1303)
Smith, Sr. Every Time I Look Up. (p. 543)
Smith Sr., Ernest Lee. Which Animal Am I? (p. 1911)
Smith, Stacy & Davis, Cristine. University of Rhode Island College Prowler off the Record. (p. 1821)
Smith, Stan. Five-Minute Mini-Mysteries. O'Malley, Kathleen, illus. (p. 601)
Smith, Stephan, illus. see Salzman, Jeremiah.
Smith, Stephanie. Snowshoe Hare's Family. Hynes, Robert, illus. (p. 1601)
Smith, Stephanie A., jt. auth. see Smith, Stephanie.
Smith, Stephanie & Smith, Stephanie A. Gray Wolf Pup's Adventure. Hynes, Robert, illus. (p. 713)
Smith, Stephanie Harms. For Everything There Is a Season in God's Time. (p. 615)
Smith, Stephen. Game on Boxed Set Series for Boys. (p. 654)
—JogNog: The Story of How a Small Creature Made a Big Difference & Everyone Got Smarter. Savage, Joshua, illus. (p. 920)
Smith, Stephen, photos by. Choosing a Dance School: What Every Parent Should Consider. (p. 310)
Smith, Steven. Charlie the T-Rex. (p. 293)
Smith, Steven K. Summer of the Woods. (p. 1674)
Smith, Steven Michael. New Carissa: The Ship That Refused to Die. (p. 1244)
Smith, Stuart. My School's a Zoo! Catrow, David, illus. (p. 1218)
Smith, Sue Millar, illus. see Reid, Joy.
Smith, Susan K. Carla & Annie. (p. 269)
Smith, Susan Mathias. Booford Summer. Glass, Andrew, illus. (p. 210)
Smith, Suzanne C. Ande-Lu & Grampa, Too. (p. 71)
—Peter Cottontail & the Easter Bunny Imposter. Brittingham, Geoffrey, illus. (p. 1346)
Smith, Sydney, illus. see Barber, Jill.
Smith, Sydney, illus. see Barkhouse, Joyce & Barkhouse, Janet.
Smith, Sydney, illus. see Fitch, Sheree.
Smith, Sydney, illus. see Inglis, Kate.
Smith, Sydney, jt. auth. see Lawson, JonArno.
Smith, T. A. Pocketful of Kindness. (p. 1375)
Smith, Tamara. Story of Ulysses S. Grant. Britt, Stephanie, illus. (p. 1662)
Smith, Tamara Ellis. Another Kind of Hurricane. (p. 88)
Smith, Tammie L. Crystal Haven- a Safe Place for Zoe. (p. 387)
Smith, Tammy. Boy & Me Go to the Zoo. (p. 217)
Smith, Tammy, illus. see Driscoll, Laura.
Smith, Tana. DIY Bedroom Decor: 50 Awesome Ideas for Your Room. (p. 455)
Smith, Tanika L. Cause And (E)Affect: A Screenplay Text. (p. 282)
Smith, Tara C. Ebola & Marburg Virus. (p. 501)
—Streptococcus (Group B) Alcamo, I. Edward, ed. (p. 1667)
Smith, Terri Peterson. Paper. (p. 1322)
Smith, Terri Peterson, et al. Junior Drug Awareness: Alcohol. (p. 936)
Smith, Terri Smith. Jessica Simpson. (p. 914)
—Tony Hawk: Flying High. (p. 1766)
Smith, Terry L. Asthma. (p. 108)
—Modern Genetic Science: New Technology, New Decisions. (p. 1158)
Smith, Terry L., jt. auth. see Tomczyk, Tara.
Smith, Thomasina. Amazing Masks to Make Yourself: 25 Projects for Funny & Frightening Faces to Wear! (p. 55)
—Crafty Fun with Clay! 25 Brilliant Ideas, from Pretty Pots to Scary Monsters. (p. 376)
—Fantastic Finger Puppets to Make Yourself: 25 Fun Ideas for Your Fingers, Thumbs & Even Feet! (p. 571)
Smith, Tiffany Nicole. Bex Carter: Middle School Disaster (and Reluctant Fairy Protector) (p. 173)
Smith, Tim. Buck Wilder's Animal Wisdom. Herrick, Mark, illus. (p. 234)
Smith, Tim, illus. see Dunn, Joeming W.
Smith, Timothy R. Ants Dig to China. (p. 90)
—Owls Don't Give a Hoot. (p. 1315)
—Salmon Stop Running. (p. 1505)
—Work Bees Go on Strike. (p. 1952)
Smith, Timothy Ryan, tr. see Christin, Pierre & Mezieres, Jean-Claude.
Smith, Tina. Secret Love of Lone Wolf & Sarah. (p. 1542)
Smith, Tod, illus. see Fuentes, Benny & Stoker, Bram.
Smith, Tod, illus. see Gutierrez, Dave & Irving, Washington.
Smith, Tod, illus. see Harbo, Christopher L.
Smith, Tod, illus. see Sautter, Aaron.
Smith, Tod, illus. see Verne, Jules & Fuentes, Benny.
Smith, Tod, illus. see Wells, H. G.
Smith, Tod, ed. Legend of Sleepy Hollow. (p. 988)
Smith, Tod G., illus. see Biskup, Agnieszka.
Smith, Tod G., illus. see Doeden, Matt.
Smith, Tod G., illus. see Glaser, Jason.
Smith, Tod G., illus. see Gutierrez, Dave & Irving, Washington.
Smith, Tod G., illus. see Harbo, Christopher L.
Smith, Tod G., illus. see Irving, Washington & Gutierrez, Dave.
Smith, Tod G., illus. see Krohn, Katherine E.
Smith, Tod G., illus. see Krohn, Katherine.
Smith, Tod G., illus. see Lemke, Donald B.
Smith, Tod G., illus. see Lemke, Donald B., et al.
Smith, Tod G., illus. see Olson, Kay Melchisedech.
Smith, Tod G., illus. see Peschke, Marci.
Smith, Tod G., illus. see Verne, Jules & Lokus, Rex.
Smith, Tod G., illus. see Yomtov, Nel, et al.
Smith, Tod G., contrib. by. Graphic Expeditions Schulz, Barbara, illus. (p. 711)
Smith, Todd Aaron. Average Monkey. Smith, Todd Aaron, illus. (p. 119)
—Higby Throws a Fit. Smith, Todd Aaron, illus. (p. 777)
Smith, Todd Aaron, illus. see Biskup, Agnieszka.
Smith, Tom. Discovery of the Americas, 1492-1800. (p. 450)
Smith, Tom, jt. auth. see Smith, L. J.
Smith, Tony. CM Punk. (p. 336)
—Shaolin Monks. (p. 1560)
Smith, Toren, tr. see Fujishima, Kosuke.
Smith, Toren, tr. see Miyazaki, Hayao.
Smith, Toren, tr. see Samura, Hiroaki.
Smith, Tracy, illus. see Derke, Connie Butterfield.
Smith, Trevor. Earth's Changing Climate. (p. 498)
Smith Turner, Jennifer. Lost & Found: Rhyming Verse Honoring African American Heroes. (p. 1054)
Smith, Valerie H. Spirit Stories: A Series of Short Stories for Children. (p. 1628)
Smith van Frankenhuyzen, Robbyn. Saving Samantha: A True Story. van Frankenhuyzen, Gijsbert, illus. (p. 1517)
Smith, Vicki. Jamaican Adventure with Tori & Paul. (p. 906)
Smith, Virginia. Silly Adventures of Gail the Snail & the Chocolate Cake. (p. 1575)
—Silly Adventures of Gail the Snail & the Disco Ball. (p. 1575)
Smith, Vivian. Along the Line. (p. 48)
Smith, W. J. Gorte 2: The Awakening. (p. 703)
Smith, Walter. Grandad's Ashes. (p. 707)
Smith, Wayne, ed. Rifter Number Twenty Four. (p. 1471)
Smith Weber, Terri. Dixie Chicks. (p. 455)
Smith, Wendy, illus. see Hollenbeck, Kathleen M.
Smith, Wendy, illus. see McKay, Sindy.
Smith, Wendy, tr. see Hollenbeck, Kathleen M.
Smith Whatley, Ben, jt. auth. see Whatley, Bruce.
Smith, William. Frankie & Earnie Meet (p. 629)
Smith, William, illus. see Tennant Iain Staff.
Smith, William, tr. see Minh Quoc.
Smith, William, tr. see Song Hà.
Smith, William, tr. see Tran, Quoc.
Smith, William D. Becoming a Superhero: Adventures of an American Superhero. (p. 156)
Smith, William E., illus. see Snowden, Gary.
Smith, William Herbert Cecil. Twentieth Century Europe. (p. 1801)
Smith, William J. Savior. (p. 1518)
Smith, Yeardley. I, Lorelei. (p. 841)
Smith, Yolanda L. Differently Able Me. (p. 438)
Smith-Armand, Kristie. Diamond in the Rough: More Fun Adventures with Abby Diamond. (p. 434)
Smithee, Allan. Dinosaurs. (p. 444)
Smithem, Beth. Cocoa Bean & Squirt. (p. 337)
—Dust Bunny's Mission. (p. 490)
—Misadventures of Dust Bunny. (p. 1150)
Smither, Ethel L. Stories of Jesus. Wiese, Kurt, illus. (p. 1655)
Smithers, J. Megan. Emma: An Interactive Storybook. (p. 519)
Smitherton, Jeb, illus. see Marsoli, Lisa Ann.
Smith-Eubanks, Jennifer. Balloons for Grandpa Schneider, Robin, illus. (p. 135)
Smithey, Donna. Nichisan & the Ancient Ones. (p. 1250)
Smith-Henderson, Susie. Adventures of Snorro & the Keepers from Sleep. (p. 23)
Smith-Leckie, Nina. Fall & Rise of Abuse-a-Saurus Rex. Gordon, Danny, illus. (p. 566)
Smith-Llera, Danielle. Cherokee: The Past & Present of a Proud Nation. (p. 298)
—Iroquois: The Past & Present of the Haudenosaunee. (p. 888)
—Presidency of George Washington: Inspiring a Young Nation (p. 1396)
—Revolutionary War: A Chronology of America's Fight for Independence. (p. 1467)
—River Communities Past & Present (p. 1475)
—Stranded in the Sierra Nevada: The Story of the Donner Party. (p. 1664)
—Teens in Argentina (p. 1715)
—Vietnam War POWs. (p. 1841)
Smith-Llera, Danielle & Bowman, Donna Janell. American Indian Life. (p. 62)
—Navajo: The Past & Present of the Dine. (p. 1237)
Smith-Llera, Danielle, et al. Adventures on the American Frontier (p. 25)
—Ancient Greece (p. 69)
—Who Lived Here? (p. 1916)
Smith-Mansell, Dana. Smith Family's New Puppy: Helping Children Cope with a New Family Member. Voerg, Kathy, illus. (p. 1594)
Smith-Marshall, Donna Ann. Time on the Inside: Behind the Walls in a Maximum Security Women's Prison from an Insiders View. (p. 1752)
Smith-Moore, J. J., illus. see Hay, Louise L.
Smith-Ready, Jeri. Shade. (p. 1556)
—Shift. (p. 1566)
—Shine. (p. 1566)
—This Side of Salvation. (p. 1737)
Smith-Rogers & Smith, Brady A. Culinary Capers of Canon & Lily: Canon Grows a Garden. (p. 390)
Smithrud, Norma. Mucky Yucky Swamp. Miles, Peregrine B., illus. (p. 1188)
Smithson, Colin. What the Bible Is. (p. 1893)
Smithson, Melissa. Bennie the Squirrel. (p. 165)
Smithson, Ryan. Ghosts of War: The True Story of a 19-Year-Old GI. (p. 673)
Smithsonian Institution, ed. Dinosaurs & More! Write-with-Me Alphabet. (p. 444)
—Insects A to Z. (p. 876)
—Oh Where, Oh Where Has My Little Dog Gone? (p. 1281)
Smithsonian Institution Staff. Home on the Range. Schwaeber, Barbie H., ed. (p. 792)
Smithsonian Institution Staff, jt. auth. see Galvin, Laura Gates.
Smithsonian Institution Staff, jt. auth. see Halfmann, Janet.
Smithsonian Institution Staff, jt. auth. see Hammerslough, Jane.
Smithsonian Institution Staff, jt. auth. see Hollenbeck, Kathleen.
Smithsonian Institution Staff, jt. auth. see Ring, Elizabeth.
Smithsonian Institution Staff, jt. auth. see Zoehfeld, Kathleen Weidner.
Smithsonian Institution Staff, contrib. by. Destined for Space: Our Story of Exploration (p. 430)
Smithsonian Institution Staff, creator. Astronauts & Other Space Heroes. (p. 109)
—Extreme Aircraft! Q&A. (p. 556)
Smithwick, John. All-Star Players (p. 45)
—Meet Alex Rodriguez: Baseball's Lightning Rod. (p. 1120)
—Meet David Ortiz: Baseball's Top Slugger. (p. 1120)
—Meet Dwyane Wade: Basketball's Rising Star. (p. 1121)
—Meet Lebron James: Basketball's King James. (p. 1121)
—Meet Peyton Manning: Football's Top Quarterback. (p. 1122)
—Meet Shaun Alexander: Football's Top Running Back. (p. 1122)
Smithwick, John W. Drift. (p. 485)
Smithwick, Margo, photos by see Smith, Miriam & Fraser, Afton.
Smithyman, Kathryn. Ocean Biome. (p. 1276)
Smithyman, Kathryn, jt. auth. see Kalman, Bobbie.
Smithyman, Kathryn & Kalman, Bobbie. Active Kids: Fun Ways to Be Active. (p. 10)
—Arthropodes. (p. 103)
—Bioma Marino. (p. 189)
—Biome Marin. (p. 189)
—Insects in Danger. (p. 876)
—Native North American Foods & Recipes. (p. 1235)
—Trains on the Tracks. (p. 1777)
—Trenes en las Vias. (p. 1784)
Smithyman, Kathryn, et al. Nations of the Northwest Coast. (p. 1234)
Smits, Josh, illus. see Drewery, Melanie.
Smitten, Susan. Ghost Stories of New England Wangler, Chris, ed. (p. 671)
—Ghost Stories of New York State (p. 671)
—Ghosts of the World: True Tales of Ghostly Hauntings. (p. 672)
—Guardian Angels: True Stories of Guidance & Protection. Vol. 1 Norell, Aaron, illus. (p. 728)
Smitten, Susan, et al. Canadian Ghost Stories (p. 260)
Smittenaar, H. G., tr. see Jer, Baant.
Smoak, I. W., illus. see Washington, Ida H.
Smolanoff, Michael. Scary Kids Clubt. (p. 1520)
Smolik, Jane Petrlik. Currents. (p. 394)
—Great Massachusetts Puzzle Book: Over 75 Puzzles about Life in the Bay State. (p. 717)
—Great State of Maine Activity Book: Over 75 Puzzles about Life in Maine. (p. 718)
Smolin, Lori A. & Grosvenor, Mary B. Nutrition & Eating Disorders. (p. 1274)
Smolinski, Diane & Smolinski, Henry. Battles of the French & Indian War (p. 147)
—Battles of the War of 1812. (p. 147)
Smolinski, Henry, jt. auth. see Smolinski, Diane.
Smolka, Bo. Baseball. (p. 140)
—Florida Marlins. (p. 607)
—Girls Play to Win Lacrosse. (p. 680)
—Jackie Robinson Breaks the Color Barrier. (p. 904)
—Miami Marlins. (p. 1134)
—Negro Leagues' Integration Era. (p. 1240)
—Story of the Negro Leagues. (p. 1661)
Smollett, Tobias George. Humphry Clinker. Ross, Angus, ed. (p. 827)
Smollin, Michael, illus. see Stone, Jon.
Smoot, Madeline, compiled by. Summer Shorts: A Short Story Collection. (p. 1675)
Smothers, Ethel F., jt. auth. see Smothers, Ethel Footman.
Smothers, Ethel Footman. Auntee Edna. Clay, Wil, illus. (p. 115)
—Down in the Piney Woods. (p. 474)
Smothers, Ethel Footman & Smothers, Ethel F. Hard-Times Jar. Holyfield, John, illus. (p. 748)
Smouse, Phil. Born Again! (p. 214)
—Lord Is My Shepherd. (p. 1052)
—Lost Sheep. (p. 1056)
—Treasures in Heaven. (p. 1782)
Smouse, Phil A. Jesus Wants All of Me. (p. 916)
Smouse, Phil A., illus. see Chambers, Oswald.
Smucker, Anna. History of West Virginia. (p. 785)
—No Star Nights. Johnson, Steve & Fancher, Lou, illus. (p. 1260)
—Outside the Window. Schuett, Stacey, illus. (p. 1313)
Smucker, Anna Egan. Brother Giovanni's Little Reward. Hall, Amanda, illus. (p. 231)
—Golden Delicious: A Cinderella Apple Story. Kemly, Kathleen, illus. (p. 694)
—To Keep the South Manitou Light. (p. 1759)
Smucker, Barbara. Days of Terror. (p. 415)

—Nubes Negras. (p. 1269)
—Selina & the Bear Paw Quilt. (p. 1550)
Smucker, Emily. Emily: My True Story of Chronic Illness & Missing Out on Life. (p. 518)
Smurd, John & Smidlap, Harley. 707 Book: (707 Questions-707 Answers) (p. 2001)
Smuskiewicz, Alfred J. Earth's Resources. (p. 498)
—Properties of Water. (p. 1411)
Smutny, Joan Franklin. Stand up for Your Gifted Child: How to Make the Most of Kids' Strengths at School & at Home. (p. 1639)
Smy, Pam, illus. see Cattell, Bob & Agard, John.
Smy, Pam, illus. see Donaldson, Julia.
Smy, Pam, illus. see Henderson, Kathy & Quarto Generic Staff.
Smyer, Lori. Journey Through Galaxies (p. 928)
Smyers, David D. & Knuckles, Tiffany S. Youth Offender's Golden Rules of Guidance. (p. 1982)
Smyth, Bambi. Favourite Nursery Rhymes. (p. 578)
Smyth, Bethinna & Winkelmann, Rachele. Sleepy Monk. (p. 1590)
Smyth, Fiona. Never Weres. (p. 1243)
Smyth, Fiona, illus. see Silverberg, Cory.
Smyth, Iain. Eye of the Pharaoh: A Pop-up Whodunit. Smyth, Iain, illus. (p. 557)
Smyth, Iain, illus. see Ratnett, Michael.
Smyth, Jennifer. Abc's for Silver Spoon Babies: A Couture Alphabet Learning Book. (p. 4)
Smyth, Jimmy. Causeway Coast. (p. 282)
—Fairy Princess. (p. 563)
—Leprechaun. Ozzy, illus. (p. 993)
—Lost Fairy. (p. 1055)
—Magic Garden. (p. 1072)
—Titanic the Untold Story. (p. 1758)
Smyth, T. R. Principles of Writing in Psychology. (p. 1406)
Smythe, Cheryl, et al. S. M. A. R. T. Pre-K: Program Guide: Get to the CORE of Readiness. Kulp, Jodee, illus. (p. 1499)
Smythe, E. Louise. Primary Reader: Old Time Stories, Fairy Tales & Myths Retold by Children. (p. 1399)
Smythe, I. H. Poetry for Animals. (p. 1376)
—Stories for Animals. (p. 1654)
Smythe, R. R. Into the Woods. (p. 881)
Smythe, Savannah. Cream of the Crop. (p. 378)
—Hot Gossip. (p. 801)
Smythe, Theresa. Chester's Colorful Easter Eggs. Smythe, Theresa, illus. (p. 298)
Snader, Gregory, illus. see Krone, Thelma Smith.
Snadowsky, Daria. Anatomy of a Boyfriend. (p. 67)
—Anatomy of a Single Girl. (p. 67)
Snaith, Andy, photos by see Bicknell, Joanna & Page, Nick.
Snaith, Andy, photos by see Boon, Fiona, ed.
Snaith, Andy, photos by see Donoghue, Stella.
Snaith, Andy, photos by see Gordon, Bob.
Snaith, Andy, photos by see Holmen, Lene.
Snaith, Andy, photos by see Phillips, Sarah.
Snaith, Tal. Family Hour Through Australia (p. 568)
Snapdragon Group, Rebecca Currington. Reindeer Games: Bible-Based Christmas Activities for Kids. (p. 1457)
Snape, Charles & Snape, Juliet. Brain Busters: Games, Puzzles & More! (p. 221)
—Count Your Way Out! Math Mazes. (p. 370)
—Mind Twisters: Games, Puzzles & More! (p. 1145)
Snape, Jenny, illus. see Mckenzie, Precious.
Snape, Jenny, illus. see Robertson, J. Jean.
Snape, Juliet, illus. see Rix, Juliet.
Snape, Juliet, jt. auth. see Snape, Charles.
Snare, Todd Tariq. KIDS CAN PLAY HIP HOP DRUMS! Book Series: Volume One: the Snare Drum. Snare, Todd Tariq, illus. (p. 953)
Snavlin, Joyce Burgess. Adirondack ABCs. Reed, Linda Davis, illus. (p. 12)
Snead, Anna. Bird That Sang the Prettiest Song. (p. 190)
Snead, D. J. E. D. Nasty Nathan (the No-good Gnat who Never Listened to Nobody) (p. 1230)
Snead, Kathi. My Mom Has a Job. Christine, Grove, illus. (p. 1214)
—My Mom Has a Job. Grove, Christine, illus. (p. 1214)
Snedden, Genevra Sis. Docas the Indian Boy of Santa Clara. (p. 459)
Snedden, Robert. Adaptation & Survival (p. 11)
—Amphibians. (p. 65)
—Ancient China. (p. 68)
—Ancient Egypt. (p. 68)
—Ancient Greece. (p. 69)
—Ancient Rome. (p. 70)
—Animals: Multicelled Life (p. 81)
—Aztec, Inca & Maya. (p. 122)
—Aztec, Inca, & Maya. (p. 122)
—Birds. (p. 191)
—Cell Division & Genetics (p. 286)
—Chemical Engineering & Chain Reactions. (p. 297)
—DNA & Genetic Engineering (p. 456)
—Exploring Space (p. 553)
—Fish. (p. 598)
—Flowers. (p. 608)
—Fungi. (p. 649)
—Growth of Cities. (p. 727)
—How Do Scientists Explore Space? (p. 807)
—Insects. (p. 875)
—Mammals. (p. 1085)
—Mary Anning: Fossil Hunter. (p. 1100)
—Materials Engineering & Exploring Properties. (p. 1104)
—Medical Technology. (p. 1118)
—Medieval World. (p. 1119)
—Nutrition: From Birth to Old Age (p. 1274)
—Protecting Mountain Habitats. (p. 1412)
—Reptiles. (p. 1461)
—Scientists Behind Living Things (p. 1529)
—Scientists Behind the Environment (p. 1529)
—Stephen Hawking: Master of the Cosmos. (p. 1648)
—Understanding Food & Digestion. (p. 1815)
—Understanding Muscles & the Skeleton. (p. 1816)
—Understanding the Brain & the Nervous System. (p. 1816)
—Variation in Living Things (p. 1833)
—Who Eats Who in the Rainforest? (p. 1915)
—Who Invented the Computer? (p. 1915)
—World of the Cell: Life on a Small Scale (p. 1957)
Snedden, Robert, jt. auth. see Corporate Contibutor.
Snedden, Robert, jt. auth. see Crabtree Staff.
Snedden, Robert, jt. auth. see Gibbons, Tony.
Snedden, Robert, jt. auth. see Graf, Mike.
Snedden, Robert & Heinemann Library Staff. Earth's Shifting Surface (p. 498)
—Exploring Space (p. 553)
Snedegar, Eugenia. Ellie Goes Potty (p. 514)
Snedeker, Caroline. Downright Dencey. Barney, Maginel Wright, illus. (p. 474)
Snedeker, Caroline Dale. Forgotten Daughter. Elkorek, Alexander, illus. (p. 619)
—Lysis Goes to the Play. Clark, Elizabeth Palmer, illus. (p. 1067)
—Spartan. Elkorek, Alexander, illus. (p. 1622)
—Triumph for Flavius. (p. 1788)
Snedeker, Erin. Littlest Elf: Marvin Mcgee & the Candle of Fate. Drotleff, David J., illus. (p. 1039)
Snedeker, Gus. Apple a Day: Folk Proverbs & Riddles. (p. 92)
—Apple a Day: Folk Proverbs & Riddles. Jabbour, Alan, ed. (p. 92)
—Campfire Songs, Ballads, & Lullabies: Folk Music. (p. 257)
—Campfire Songs, Ballads, & Lullabies: Folk Music. Jabbour, Alan, ed. (p. 257)
—Celebrations Throughout the Year: Holiday Folklore. (p. 285)
—Celebrations Throughout the Year: Holiday Folklore. Jabbour, Alan, ed. (p. 285)
—Heroes, Fools, & Ghosts: Folk Tales & Legends. (p. 772)
—Heroes, Fools, & Ghosts: Folk Tales & Legends. Jabbour, Alan, ed. (p. 772)
—Quilts, Rag Dolls, & Rocking Chairs: Folk Arts & Crafts. (p. 1428)
—Quilts, Rag Dolls, & Rocking Chairs: Folk Arts & Crafts. Jabbour, Alan, ed. (p. 1428)
—Tell Me a Story: Family Folklore. (p. 1716)
—Tell Me a Story: Family Folklore. Jabbour, Alan, ed. (p. 1716)
Snedeker, Joe. Everything Kids Weather Book: From Tornadoes to Snowstorms, Puzzles, Games, & Facts That Make Weather for Kids Fun! (p. 545)
Sneed, Brad. Boy Who Was Raised by Librarians. Sneed, Brad, illus. (p. 219)
Sneed, Brad, illus. see Aylesworth, Jim.
Sneed, Brad, illus. see Bunting, Eve.
Sneed, Brad, illus. see Clark, Stacy.
Sneed, Brad, illus. see Krensky, Stephen.
Sneed, Brad, illus. see Morris, Carla.
Sneed, Brad, illus. see Scillian, Devin.
Sneed, Brad, illus. see Walton, Rick.
Sneed, Brad & Andersen, Hans Christian. Thumbelina. Sneed, Brad, illus. (p. 1745)
Sneed, Dani. Ferris Wheel! George Ferris & His Amazing Invention. (p. 582)
—Man Who Invented the Ferris Wheel: The Genius of George Ferris. (p. 1086)
Sneed, Dani, jt. auth. see Fisher, Doris.
Sneed, Dani & Fisher, Doris. My Half Day Lee, Karen, illus. (p. 1210)
Sneed, Elouise M. Who Is Mr Buzz? (p. 1916)
Sneed, Nancy Glascock. Grains of Sand: Beach Poems. (p. 706)
Sneed, Patty, illus. see Kuhns, Jennifer.
Sneesby, Frederick. Believer's Christmas. (p. 162)
Sneideman, Joshua & Twamley, Erin. Climate Change: Discover How It Impacts Spaceship Earth. Crosier, Mike, illus. (p. 332)
Sneider, Cary I., photos by see Gould, Alan.
Sneider, Marian, jt. auth. see Vander Zee, Ruth.
Sneidern, Maja-Lisa Von, see Canfield, J. Douglas & Von Sneidern, Maja-Lisa.
Snelbaker, Carmela. Thank You for Your Service, Sheep! (p. 1725)
Snell, Gordon. King of Quizzical Island. McKee, David, illus. (p. 959)
—Tina & the Tooth Fairy. Blodau, Peter, illus. (p. 1755)
—Twas the Day after Christmas. Delonas, Sean, illus. (p. 1799)
—Twelve Days: A Christmas Countdown. O'Malley, Kevin, illus. (p. 1800)
—Twelve Days of Christmas. (p. 1800)
Snell, Gordon & Askin, Corrina. Supermarket Ghost. Byrne, Bob, illus. (p. 1684)
Snell, Roy F. Wings for Victory. (p. 1936)
Snell, Roy J. Blue Envelope. (p. 202)
—Curlie Carson Listens In. (p. 394)
—Little White Fox & His Arctic Friends. (p. 1037)
—Lost in the Air. (p. 1055)
—Triple Spies. (p. 1787)
Snell, Roy Judson. Curlie Carson Listens In. (p. 394)
—Sparky Ames of the Ferry Command. Darwin, Erwin L., illus. (p. 1622)
Snell, Ted. Pippin Drysdale: Lines of Site. (p. 1362)
Snellenberger, Bonita, jt. auth. see Snellenberger, Earl.
Snellenberger, Earl & Snellenberger, Bonita. Noah's Ark Pre-School Activity Book. Snellenberger, Earl & Snellenberger, Bonita, illus. (p. 1261)
—Wonders of God's World Dinosaur Activity Book. Snellenberger, Earl & Snellenberger, Bonita, illus. (p. 1948)
Snellenberger, Tracy. Tyler the Toddler Feeds the Cows. (p. 1805)
Snelling, Carolyn. BBall, Zip, & Sock: An Easter Story. (p. 147)
—Christ's Cake. (p. 317)
—Mystery of the Golden Christmas Trees. (p. 1225)
Snelling, Lauraine. Golden Filly (p. 694)
—Golden Filly Collection 2. (p. 694)
—What about Cimmaron? (p. 1878)
Snelson, Bob. Riding into Glory: An Introduction to the Battle of the Little Bighorn. (p. 1471)
Snelson, Brian & Sellars, Rodney. Shaturanga: The Story of Onus. (p. 1563)
Snelson, Doug. Who's Got the Face? (p. 1920)
Snerling, Tina, illus. see McCartney, Tania.
Sneve, Virginia, jt. auth. see Sneve, Virginia Driving Hawk.
Sneve, Virginia Driving Hawk. Bad River Boys. Farnsworth, Bill, illus. (p. 132)
—Chichi Hoohoo Bogeyman. Agard, Nadema, illus. (p. 299)
—Christmas Coat: Memories of My Sioux Childhood. Beier, Ellen, illus. (p. 313)
—Enduring Wisdom: Sayings from American Indians. Saint James, Synthia, illus. (p. 527)
—High Elk's Treasure. (p. 777)
—Standing Bear of the Ponca. (p. 1639)
Sneve, Virginia Driving Hawk & Sneve, Virginia. Lana's Lakota Moons. (p. 973)
Snezhana, Ivinskaya, ed. see AZ Books Staff.
Sniad, Tamara, jt. auth. see Weisburd, Claudia.
Snicket, Lemony, pseud. 13 Words. (p. 1995)
—13 Words. Kalman, Maira, illus. (p. 1995)
—29 Myths on the Swinster Pharmacy. Brown, Lisa, illus. (p. 1996)
—Academia Muy Austera. (p. 7)
—Ascensor Artificioso. (p. 105)
—Austere Academy. Helquist, Brett, illus. (p. 116)
—Bad Beginning: Or, Orphans! No. 1 Helquist, Brett & Kupperman, Michael, illus. (p. 131)
—Bad Beginning. (p. 131)
—Beatrice Letters. Helquist, Brett, illus. (p. 153)
—Cauchemar a la Scierie. (p. 281)
—Complete Wreck Helquist, Brett, illus. (p. 353)
—Dark. Klassen, Jon, illus. (p. 407)
—Dilemma Deepens Helquist, Brett, illus. (p. 440)
—End. Helquist, Brett, illus. (p. 526)
—End. Helquist, Brett & Kupperman, Michael, illus. (p. 526)
—File Under - 13 Suspicious Incidents. Seth, illus. (p. 586)
—Funesta Finestra. (p. 649)
—Gloom Looms Helquist, Brett, illus. (p. 685)
—Grim Grotto. Helquist, Brett, illus. (p. 724)
—Grim Grotto. Helquist, Brett & Kupperman, Michael, illus. (p. 724)
—Infausto Inizio. (p. 873)
—Laboratoire aux Serpents. (p. 969)
—Latke Who Couldn't Stop Screaming: A Christmas Story. Scott, Daniel, ed. (p. 980)
—Lemony Snicket: The Unauthorized Autobiography. (p. 991)
—Lemony Snicket: The Unauthorized Autobiography. Helquist, Brett, illus. (p. 991)
—Loathsome Library Helquist, Brett, illus. (p. 1044)
—Lump of Coal. Helquist, Brett, illus. (p. 1065)
—Miserable Mill Helquist, Brett, illus. (p. 1150)
—Ouragan sur le Lac. (p. 1310)
—Penultimate Peril. Helquist, Brett & Kupperman, Michael, illus. (p. 1338)
—Piege au College. (p. 1357)
—Reptile Room: Or, Murder! Helquist, Brett & Kupperman, Michael, illus. (p. 1461)
—Schlimme Anfang. (p. 1521)
—Series of Unfortunate Events: The Bad Beginning; The Reptile Room; The Wide Window. Helquist, Brett, illus. (p. 1552)
—Shouldn't You Be in School? Seth, illus. (p. 1570)
—Slippery Slope. Helquist, Brett, illus. (p. 1590)
—Slippery Slope. Helquist, Brett & Kupperman, Michael, illus. (p. 1590)
—Tout Commence Mal. (p. 1773)
—Trouble Begins. Helquist, Brett, illus. (p. 1789)
—When Did You See Her Last? Seth, illus. (p. 1902)
—Who Could That Be at This Hour? Seth, illus. (p. 1915)
—Wide Window - Or, Disappearance! Helquist, Brett & Kupperman, Michael, illus. (p. 1927)
Snicket, Lemony, pseud & Seth. Who Could That Be at This Hour? (p. 1915)
Snicket, Lemony, pseud & Stookey, Nathaniel. Composer Is Dead. Ellis, Carson, illus. (p. 354)
Snider, Ann. Giant Sea & Me. (p. 674)
Snider, Brandon T. Be the Brush Doodle Book. Johnson, Shane L., illus. (p. 149)
—BMO's Character File. (p. 204)
—Brain Food. (p. 221)
—Game Night! Quips's Book of Questions, Quizzes & Games. (p. 654)
—Good Morning, UG-RV! An Unfoldable Journey Through the World of Uncle Grandpa. (p. 698)
—How to Be Annoying: A Joke Book. (p. 815)
—Mordecai & the Rigbys - The Experience. (p. 1173)
—Scribble & Sketch. (p. 1533)
—Transformers: Kre-O Character Encyclopedia: With Special Figure. (p. 1778)
—Who in the Land of Ooo Are You? (p. 1915)
Snider, Brandon T., jt. auth. see Dorling Kindersley Publishing Staff.
Snider, Brandon T., jt. auth. see Scott, Cavan.
Snider, Cindy Gay. Finding Anna Bee. Chambers, Mary, illus. (p. 587)
Snider, Fred. Bonds of Antiquity: Making Christianity Relevant Today. (p. 208)
Snider, Jackie, illus. see Baker, Courtney.
Snider, Jackie, illus. see Charlesworth, Liza & Scholastic Canada Ltd. Staff.
Snider, Jackie, illus. see Cifuentes, Carolina, ed.
Snider, Jackie, illus. see Cifuentes, Carolina.
Snider, Jackie, illus. see Horsfall, Jacqueline.
Snider, Jackie, illus. see Pellowski, Michael J.
Snider, Jackie, illus. see Rosa-Mendoza, Gladys.
Snider, Jesse Blaze. Muppet Snow White. Paroline, Shelli, illus. (p. 1191)
—Return of Buzz Lightyear Watson, Nathan, illus. (p. 1464)
—Return of Buzz Lightyear Vol. 2. Watson, Nathan, illus. (p. 1464)
—Toy Story: Toy Overboard. Watson, Nathan, illus. (p. 1774)
—Toy Story: Some Assembly Required. Watson, Nathan, illus. (p. 1774)
Snider, K. C., illus. see Calvani, Mayra.
Snider, K. C., illus. see Crow, Marilee.
Snider, K. C., illus. see Finke, Margot.
Snider, K. C., illus. see Glover, Emma M.
Snider, K. C., illus. see Kelso, Mary Jean.
Snider, K. C., illus. see Luce, Catherine.
Snider, K. C., illus. see McNamee, Kevin.
Snider, K. C., illus. see Phillips, Dixie.
Snider, K. C., illus. see Reece, Colleen L. & DeMarco, Julie Reece.
Snider, K. C., illus. see Robinson, Janie.
Snider, K. C., illus. see Samuels, Jack.
Snider, K. C., illus. see Stephenson, Susan.
Snider, K. C., jt. auth. see Crow, Marilee.
Snider, K. C., jt. auth. see Kelso, Mary Jean.
Snider, K. C., jt. auth. see Phillips, Dixie.
Snider, Kc. Silence. Snider, Kc, illus. (p. 1575)
Snider, Kc, illus. see Kelso, Mary Jean.
Snider, Kc, illus. see McDine, Donna M.
Snider, Lori L. Little Princess. Longmore, Nickolai, illus. (p. 1033)
Snider, Sharon, illus. see Dunlap, Sonya.
Snider, Sharon, illus. see MacGregor, Kim.
Snider, Sharon, tr. see MacGregor, Kim.
Sniechowski, James, jt. auth. see Sherven, Judith.
Sniegoski, Thomas E. Aerie & Reckoning. (p. 25)
—Brimstone Network. (p. 228)
—End of Days Vol. 3. (p. 526)
—Fallen 5: Armageddon. (p. 566)
—Fallen & Leviathan. (p. 566)
—Forsaken. (p. 623)
—Leviathan. (p. 1004)
—Shroud of A'Ranka. Howard, Zachariah, illus. (p. 1571)
—Specter Rising. (p. 1624)
Sniegoski, Thomas E., jt. auth. see Golden, Christopher.
Sniegoski, Thomas E. & Golden, Christopher. Battle for Arcanum. (p. 145)
—Dragon Secrets. (p. 478)
—Ghostfire. (p. 672)
—Magic Zero. (p. 1074)
Sniegoski, Tom. Legacy. (p. 987)
—Quest for the Spark. (p. 1426)
—Quest for the Spark. Smith, Jeff, illus. (p. 1426)
—Quest for the Spark 2. (p. 1426)
Sniegoski, Tom, jt. auth. see Smith, Jeff.
Sniegoski, Tom & Smith, Jeff. Quest for the Spark Smith, Jeff, illus. (p. 1426)
—Tall Tales. Smith, Jeff, illus. (p. 1704)
Sniffin, Bill. High Altitudes, Low Multitudes: More Stories about Wyoming, the Best Part of America (p. 777)
Snipes, Carol. Mary's Rockin' ABC's. (p. 1101)
Snitkin, Harvey R. Practicing for Young Musicians: You Are Your Own Teacher. (p. 1392)
Snively, Carolyn. Zippo's First Christmas. (p. 1987)
Snoddy, Brian & Wilson, Matt, creators. Iron Kingdoms World Guide: Full Metal Fantasy; Volume 2. (p. 888)
Snoddy, Gillian, ed. see Hex, Kathleen.
Snodgrass, Kimberly J. I Am a Foster Child, & That's Okay with Me. (p. 832)
Snodgrass, Lady Cecily. Really Rotten Princess. Lester, Mike, illus. (p. 1450)
—Really Rotten Princess & the Cupcake Catastrophe. Lester, Mike, illus. (p. 1450)
Snodgrass, Mary Ellen. Encyclopedia of Feminist Literature. (p. 525)
—Facts on File Encyclopedia of Gothic Literature. (p. 561)
—Melville's Billy Budd & Typee. (p. 1125)
Snook, Randy, photos by. Many Ideas Open the Way: A Collection of Hmong Proverbs. (p. 1089)
Snopek, Roxanne Willems. Wildlife in the Kitchen: ... & Other Great Animal Tales (p. 1931)
Snorradottir, Asthildur Bj. Raphael: The Angel Who Decided to Visit Earth. Bjarnason, Bjarni Thor, illus. (p. 1439)
Snortum, Marty, photos by see Beery, Barbara.
Snow, Alan. Here Be Monsters! Snow, Alan, illus. (p. 770)
—How Dinosaurs Really Work! Snow, Alan, illus. (p. 806)
—How Kids Really Work. Snow, Alan, illus. (p. 810)
—How Santa Really Works. Snow, Alan, illus. (p. 812)
—Worse Things Happen at Sea! A Tale of Pirates, Poison, & Monsters. Snow, Alan, illus. (p. 1961)
Snow, Alan, illus. see Bowvayne.
Snow, Alan, illus. see Murray, Andrew.
Snow, Alan, illus. see Perry, Andrea J. & Perry, Andrea.
Snow, Alan, illus. see Perry, Andrea.
Snow, Carol. Bubble World. (p. 233)
—Placed: Karesansui Poems. (p. 1366)
—Snap. (p. 1597)
—Switch. (p. 1691)
Snow, D. C. Champ Bailey. (p. 289)
Snow, Dorothea J. Roy Rogers' Favorite Western Stories. Ushler, John, illus. (p. 1492)
—Secret of the Stone Frog. Burns, Raymond, illus. (p. 1543)
Snow, Eliza R. Story of Jesus. (p. 1658)
Snow, Elliot, ed. Adventures at Sea in the Great Age of Sail: Five Firsthand Narratives. (p. 15)
Snow, Jeff. Beasts in the Closet. Snow, Jeff, illus. (p. 152)
Snow, Judith E. How It Feels to Have a Gay or Lesbian Parent: A Book by Kids for Kids of All Ages. (p. 810)
Snow, Maya. Blade's Edge. (p. 198)
—Chasing the Secret. (p. 294)
—Journey Through Fire. (p. 928)
—Sisters of the Sword. (p. 1581)
—Sisters of the Sword - Chasing the Secret. (p. 1581)
Snow, Pegeen. Eat Your Peas, Louise! Venezia, Mike, illus. (p. 501)
Snow, Peggy. My Favorite Places from A to Z. Barber, Brian, illus. (p. 1203)
—My Favorite Sounds from A to Z. (p. 1203)
Snow, Peggy, jt. auth. see Snow, Todd.
Snow, Philip. Animals of the Bible. Snow, Philip, illus. (p. 83)
—Birds of the Bible. Snow, Philip, illus. (p. 192)
—Places of the Bible. Snow, Philip, illus. (p. 1366)
—Plants of the Bible. Snow, Philip, illus. (p. 1370)
Snow, Ravay L. Hildegarde & the Great Green Shirt Factory. Snow, Ravay L., illus. (p. 779)
Snow, Sarah, illus. see Formento, Alison.
Snow, Scott, illus. see Kimmel, E. Cody.
Snow, Scott, illus. see Kimmel, Elizabeth Cody.
Snow, Susie. Old Cookie Jar. Motz, Mike, illus. (p. 1283)
Snow, Todd. Kindness to Share from A to Z. (p. 957)

—Manners Are Important. Hartman, Carrie, illus. (p. 1088)
—You Are Beautiful. Strong, Melodee, illus. (p. 1973)
—You Are Brave. (p. 1973)
—You Are Creative. (p. 1973)
—You Are Friendly. (p. 1973)
—You Are Friendly. Strong, Melodee, illus. (p. 1973)
—You Are Healthy. (p. 1973)
—You Are Helpful. Strong, Melodee, illus. (p. 1973)
—You Are Important. Strong, Melodee, illus. (p. 1973)
Snow, Todd & Snow, Peggy. Feelings to Share from A to Z. Hartman, Carrie, illus. (p. 580)
Snow, Virginia Brimhall. Fall Walk (p. 566)
—Winter Walk (p. 1938)
Snow, Virginia Brimhall, jt. auth. see Williams, Nate.
Snow, Wesley. Tree's Life. (p. 1784)
Snow, William, jt. auth. see Andre, Richard.
Snowden, Gary. Hank & Kale Visit the Aquarium. Smith, William E., illus. (p. 742)
—Lost Treasure of Hawkins Cave. Pierce Clark, Donna, illus. (p. 1057)
Snowden, Linda, illus. see Safran, Faigy.
Snowden, Maxine. Polar Explorers for Kids: Historic Expeditions to the Arctic & Antarctic with 21 Activities. (p. 1379)
Snowden, Susan, ed. see Stevens, Tracey.
Snowe, Olivia. Beauty & the Basement Lamoreaux, Michelle, illus. (p. 154)
—Cassie & the Woolf Lamoreaux, Michelle, illus. (p. 276)
—Dandelion & the Witch Lamoreaux, Michelle, illus. (p. 403)
—Girl & the Seven Thieves Lamoreaux, Michelle, illus. (p. 678)
—Glass Voice Lamoreaux, Michelle, illus. (p. 682)
—Hansen & Gracie Lamoreaux, Michelle, illus. (p. 743)
—Home in the Sky Lamoreaux, Michelle, illus. (p. 792)
—Sealed-Up House Lamoreaux, Michelle, illus. (p. 1536)
—Twicetold Tales Lamoreaux, Michelle, illus. (p. 1801)
Snowman, Sally R. Sammy the Boston Lighthouse Dog. (p. 1508)
Snozek, Lee Anne. Infinite Coloring Circles & Squares CD & Book. (p. 873)
—Simply Square Designs. (p. 1578)
—Terrific Triangles. (p. 1721)
Snozek, Lee Anne & Coloring Books for Adults. Outrageous Octagons. (p. 1313)
—Simply Circular Designs Coloring Book. (p. 1578)
Snure, Roger, illus. see Denham, Joyce.
Snyder. Instructor's Resource to Accompany the Extraordinary Chemistry of Ordinary Things. (p. 879)
Snyder, Anthony, illus. see Trivelli, John.
Snyder, Barb, ed. see Harris, Janice L. & Lisech, Howard.
Snyder, Barb, ed. see Harris, Janice L., et al.
Snyder, Bernadette McCarver. 110 Fun Facts about God's Creation: Is It Animal, Vegetable, or Mineral? (p. 2000)
Snyder, Betsy E. Haiku Baby. Snyder, Betsy E., illus. (p. 735)
—Have You Ever Tickled a Tiger? (p. 754)
—I Can Dance. (p. 835)
—I Can Play. (p. 836)
—I Haiku You. (p. 838)
—Lily's Potty. (p. 1018)
—Sweet Dreams Lullaby. (p. 1689)
Snyder, Betsy E., illus. see Bergen, Lara.
Snyder, Betsy E., illus. see Cleary, Brian P.
Snyder, Betsy E., illus. see Fliess, Sue.
Snyder, Carl H. Extraordinary Chemistry of Ordinary Things, Lab Manual. (p. 555)
Snyder, Carol. One up, One Down. Chambliss, Maxie, illus. (p. 1297)
Snyder, Carrie A., jt. auth. see Crocker, Carter.
Snyder, Casey. Adventures of Food. (p. 18)
—Miss Fit the Dog & the Football Eating Tree. (p. 1151)
—Miss Fit the Dog Saves Christmas. (p. 1151)
Snyder, Deanna Sytek. Lee the Pe. (p. 987)
Snyder, Diana, illus. see Chauvin, Belinda N.
Snyder, Don, photos by see La Prade, Erik.
Snyder, Donna. Rose & Rosey. (p. 1489)
Snyder, Edward B., et al. Through Tiger's Eyes. (p. 1745)
Snyder, Elaine. Anna & Solomon. Bliss, Harry, illus. (p. 85)
Snyder, Elizabeth. Tink the Christmas Cat. (p. 1755)
Snyder, Gail. Angry Girl? Girls Dealing with Feelings. (p. 75)
—Brooke Knows Best. (p. 230)
—David Cook. (p. 410)
—Filipino Americans. (p. 586)
—George Washington. (p. 664)
—Jake Gyllenhaal. (p. 906)
—Jealous Girl? Girls Dealing with Feelings. (p. 911)
—Kelly Clarkson. (p. 948)
—Korean Americans. (p. 967)
—Lonely Girl? Girls Dealing with Feelings. (p. 1046)
—Malia. (p. 1083)
—Marriage & Family Issues. (p. 1096)
—Queen Latifah. (p. 1424)
—Sasha. (p. 1515)
—Seth Mcfarlane Family Guy: Family Guy. (p. 1554)
—Sudan. (p. 1672)
—Teens & Alcohol. Developed in Association with the Gallup Organization Staff, ed. (p. 1714)
Snyder, Gail, jt. auth. see Marcovitz, Hal.
Snyder, Geraldine Ann. Johnny Appleseed: Musical. (p. 923)
Snyder, Harold E., illus. see Curtis, Alice Turner.
Snyder, III, illus. see Snyder, Max.
Snyder, Inez. Apples. (p. 92)
—Berries to Jelly. (p. 167)
—Milk to Ice Cream. (p. 1143)
—Oranges to Orange Juice: How Things Are Made. (p. 1302)
—Sap to Syrup. (p. 1514)
—Trees to Paper. (p. 1784)
—Wax to Crayons. (p. 1864)
—Welcome Books: Grains to Bread: How Things Are Made. (p. 1873)
Snyder, J. M. Journey to Venus (p. 929)
Snyder, Jane. Days of the Week: Learning Ordinal Numbers. (p. 415)
—Desert Animals. (p. 428)
Snyder, Jane McIntosh. Sappho. (p. 1514)
Snyder, Jeffrey B. Hull Pottery: Decades of Design (p. 825)

Snyder, Jennifer. Grandad's Book. Bruner, Tammy, illus. (p. 707)
Snyder, Joe, illus. see Heisel, Sandra.
Snyder, Joel, illus. see Heinrichs, Ann.
Snyder, Joel, illus. see Konzen, Lisa M.
Snyder, Joel, illus. see Lamm, C. Drew.
Snyder, Joel, illus. see Petrie, Catherine.
Snyder, Joel, illus. see Rottmann, Erik.
Snyder, Joel, illus. see Trueit, Trudi Strain.
Snyder, Joel, illus. see Walker, Sally M.
Snyder, Joel, illus. see Zoehfeld, Kathleen Weidner.
Snyder, John. Mets Journal: Year by Year & Day by Day with the New York Mets Since 1962. (p. 1130)
Snyder, John A. Writing the Vision: Releasing the Prophetic Dimension into Today's New Testament Church. (p. 1965)
Snyder, John K., III, jt. auth. see Conrad, Joseph.
Snyder, Judi. Emily's First Visit to the Dentist. (p. 519)
Snyder, Karen. Camp Charlie, the Adventures of Grandma Lipstick. LaGrange, Tiffany, illus. (p. 257)
—Mona Lisa's Makeover. LaGrange, Tiffany, illus. (p. 1163)
—Safari Smooches. LaGrange, Tiffany, illus. (p. 1502)
Snyder, Karen Lee. Loony Lori. (p. 1052)
Snyder, Laurel. Any Which Wall. Pham, LeUyen, illus. (p. 90)
—Baxter, the Pig Who Wanted to Be Kosher. (p. 147)
—Baxter, the Pig Who Wanted to Be Kosher. Goldin, David, illus. (p. 147)
—Bigger Than a Bread Box. (p. 185)
—Camp Wonderful Wild Whitt, Carlynn, illus. (p. 257)
—Charlie & Mouse. (p. 292)
—Longest Night: A Passover Story. Chien, Catia, illus. (p. 1047)
—Penny Dreadful. Halpin, Abigail, illus. (p. 1338)
—Seven Stories Up. (p. 1555)
—Swan: The Life & Dance of Anna Pavlova. Morstad, Julie, illus. (p. 1688)
—Up & down the Scratchy Mountains. Dorman, Brandon & Call, Greg, illus. (p. 1847)
Snyder, Lavinia Branca. Going Home: The Little Stories of Manoosh & Baloosh. (p. 692)
—Mission in Space: Sofi's Adventures. (p. 1153)
—Treasure of Lodian: The Kyss Family Mysteries. (p. 1782)
Snyder, Lydia. Rhinos in Danger. (p. 1467)
Snyder, Maria V. Inside Out. (p. 877)
—Outside In. (p. 1313)
—Storm Watcher. (p. 1656)
Snyder, Marilyn. Second Chance for Tina. Shiffman, Lena, illus. (p. 1539)
Snyder, Maryhelen. No Hole in the Flame: A Story of Love & Loss in Prose & Poetry (p. 1258)
Snyder, Matthew. How to Survive in a World with Two or More People. (p. 822)
Snyder, Max. King with No Kingdom. Snyder, Max & Snyder, III, illus. (p. 959)
Snyder, Peter Etril, illus. see Forler, Nan.
Snyder, R. Bradley & Engelsgjerd, Marc. What Every Child Needs to Know about Cancer. Kempe, Barbara, ed. (p. 1884)
—What Every Child Needs to Know about Coffee. (p. 1884)
Snyder, R. Bradley, et al. What Every Child Needs to Know about Elvis Presley. (p. 1884)
Snyder, Rebecca. Two Hearts Are Better Than One. (p. 1803)
Snyder, Robert. Itsy Bitsy Spider. Snyder, Robert, illus. (p. 900)
Snyder, Robert, illus. see Hanby, Benjamin Russell.
Snyder, Robert M. More Unbeatable Chess Lessons for Juniors. (p. 1175)
—Unbeatable Chess Lessons for Juniors. (p. 1811)
—Winning Chess Tournaments for Juniors. (p. 1937)
Snyder, Ronda, illus. see Milliner, Donna L.
Snyder, Sally. Hold the Fort. Snyder, Sally, illus. (p. 788)
Snyder, Sandy. New Orleans Dogs Allowed. (p. 1246)
—There's Only One I in Charlie. Ferrenburg, Susie, illus. (p. 1731)
Snyder, Sarah Kovin. Skippit the Cricket. (p. 1586)
Snyder, Scott. Batman Vol. 5: Zero Year—Dark City. (p. 144)
Snyder, Sharon J. Zeus Comes Home. (p. 1986)
Snyder, Susan. There's a Frog Trapped in the Bathroom. Johanson, Anna, illus. (p. 1730)
—Very Stubborn Centipede. Johanson, Anna, illus. (p. 1839)
Snyder, Susan E. Grandma's Crazy Chickens. Richardson, Mike, illus. (p. 708)
—Shivers & Shakes. (p. 1567)
Snyder, Suzanne, illus. see Flegal, Daphna.
Snyder, Trish. Alligator & Crocodile Rescue: Changing the Future for Endangered Wildlife. (p. 47)
Snyder, Vicki & West, Lois. Lighten up Lenny. Karn, Mike, illus. (p. 1015)
Snyder, Zilpha Keatley. Bronze Pen. (p. 230)
—Egypt Game. (p. 506)
—Egypt Game. Raible, Alton, illus. (p. 506)
—Famous Stanley Kidnapping Case. (p. 569)
—Headless Cupid. Raible, Alton, illus. (p. 756)
—Treasures of Weatherby. (p. 1782)
—Unseen. (p. 1822)
—William S. & the Great Escape. (p. 1933)
—William's Midsummer Dreams. (p. 1934)
—Witches of Worm. (p. 1941)
—Witches of Worm. Raible, Alton, illus. (p. 1941)
Snyders, Natalie & Stuckey, Kevin. Articulation Quick Take along Mini-Book: Ta120. (p. 104)
Snyders, Natalie, et al. Vocabulary Quick Take along Mini-Book: Ta230. (p. 1847)
So, Chong-O, jt. auth. see Seo.
So, Meilo. Read a Rhyme, Write a Rhyme. (p. 1442)
So, Meilo, illus. see Coombs, Kate.
So, Meilo, illus. see Cummings, E. E.
So, Meilo, illus. see Gibson, Amy.
So, Meilo, illus. see Hoberman, Mary Ann.
So, Meilo, illus. see Look, Lenore.
So, Meilo, illus. see Moore, Julianne.
So, Meilo, illus. see Mora, Pat & Dominguez, Adriana.
So, Meilo, illus. see Mora, Pat, et al.
So, Meilo, illus. see O Flatharta, Antoine.
So, Meilo, illus. see Schulman, Janet.
So, Meilo, illus. see Spinner, Stephanie.

So, Meilo, illus. see Thong, Roseanne Greenfield.
So, Meilo, jt. auth. see Wilson, Barbara Ker.
So, Patty. So Simple at-Home A Month of Ideas: 31 Fun & Simple Activities to Reinforce Your Child's Reading Success! (p. 1602)
—So Simple Sightwords (p. 1602)
—So Simple Sightwords At-Home: 31 Fun Sightword Activities. (p. 1602)
—So Simple Sightwords at-Home Volume 1. (p. 1602)
—So Simple Sightwords at-Home Volume 3. So, Patty, illus. (p. 1602)
So, Po-Lin. Skin Cancer. (p. 1585)
So, Sungwan & Quarto Generic Staff. C Is for China. So, Sungwan, photos by. (p. 249)
Soard, Lori. Housebreaking A Husband. (p. 804)
Soares, Lise. What Will Christine Do? (p. 1895)
Soares, Maria Fernanda, photos by see Williamson, Kate T.
Soares, Valérie I. O. Lily & Kayden's 1969 Woodstock Adventure. Tzekov, Jack, illus. (p. 1017)
Sobania, Neal. Culture & Customs of Kenya (p. 391)
Sobat, Gail Sidonie. Chance to Dance for You. (p. 289)
—Glass Darkly. (p. 682)
—Gravity Journal. (p. 713)
—Winter's Tale. (p. 1938)
Sobel, Bobbi. Mandle the Candle: A Drippy Tale for Chanukah. (p. 1087)
Sobel, David S. What's the Catch: How to Avoid Getting Hooked & Manipulated. Jackson, Jeff, illus. (p. 1899)
Sobel, Deane. Philip the Sea Lion. (p. 1350)
Sobel Frieder, Barbara. My Friend Penelope. (p. 1209)
Sobel, Gerrie. Jacob & His Magical Flying Bears. Torres, Dottie, illus. (p. 904)
—Jacob & His Magical Flying Bears, a Halloween Story. Torres, Dottie, illus. (p. 904)
Sobel J. D., Syl, jt. auth. see Sobel, Syl.
Sobel, June. B Is for Bulldozer: A Construction ABC. Iwai, Melissa, illus. (p. 123)
—Goodnight Train. Huliska-Beith, Laura, illus. (p. 701)
—Shiver Me Letters: A Pirate ABC. Cole, Henry, illus. (p. 1567)
Sobel, June & Iwai, Melissa. B Is for Bulldozer: A Construction ABC. Iwai, Melissa, illus. (p. 123)
Sobel, M., et al. Poison Plate Cunningham, Kelley, illus. (p. 1377)
Sobel, Syl. How the U. S. Government Works. (p. 813)
Sobel, Syl & Sobel J. D., Syl. Bill of Rights: Protecting Our Freedom Then & Now. (p. 186)
Soberijaski. Red Snow. (p. 1455)
Soberon, Cecilia, jt. auth. see Gamboa, Norma.
Sobey, Ed. Build Your Own Robot Science Fair Project. (p. 238)
—Loco-Motion: Physics Models for the Classroom. (p. 1045)
—Motorboat Book: Build & Launch 20 Jet Boats, Paddle-Wheelers, Electric Submarines & More. (p. 1179)
—Rocket-Powered Science: Invent to Learn! Create, Build & Test Rocket Designs. (p. 1483)
Sobey, Ed, ed. Electric Motor Experiments. (p. 508)
—Radio-Controlled Car Experiments. (p. 1433)
—Robot Experiments. (p. 1480)
—Solar Cell & Renewable Energy Experiments. (p. 1606)
Sobey, Edwin J. C. Young Inventors at Work! Learning Science by Doing Science. (p. 1979)
Sobha, Geeta. Green Technology: Earth-Friendly Innovations. (p. 722)
—Green Technology: Earth-friendly Innovations. (p. 722)
Sobol, Donald J. Encyclopedia Brown Shortall, Leonard W., illus. (p. 524)
—Encyclopedia Brown. (p. 524)
—Encyclopedia Brown & His Best Cases Ever. (p. 524)
—Encyclopedia Brown & the Case of the Dead Eagles. Shortall, Leonard, illus. (p. 524)
—Encyclopedia Brown & the Case of the Dead Eagles. Shortall, Leonard W., illus. (p. 524)
—Encyclopedia Brown & the Case of the Jumping Frogs. (p. 524)
—Encyclopedia Brown & the Case of the Jumping Frogs. Papp, Robert, illus. (p. 524)
—Encyclopedia Brown & the Case of the Midnight Visitor. Brandi, Lillian, illus. (p. 524)
—Encyclopedia Brown & the Case of the Secret Pitch. (p. 524)
—Encyclopedia Brown & the Case of the Secret Pitch. Shortall, Leonard, illus. (p. 524)
—Encyclopedia Brown & the Case of the Secret Pitch. Shortall, Leonard W., illus. (p. 524)
—Encyclopedia Brown & the Case of the Secret UFOs. (p. 524)
—Encyclopedia Brown & the Case of the Secret UFOs. Bernardin, James, illus. (p. 524)
—Encyclopedia Brown & the Case of the Slippery Salamander. Chang, Warren, illus. (p. 524)
—Encyclopedia Brown & the Case of the Soccer Scheme. Bernadin, James, illus. (p. 524)
—Encyclopedia Brown, Boy Detective. (p. 524)
—Encyclopedia Brown, Boy Detective. Shortall, Leonard, illus. (p. 524)
—Encyclopedia Brown, Boy Detective. Shortall, Leonard W., illus. (p. 524)
—Encyclopedia Brown Cracks the Case. (p. 524)
—Encyclopedia Brown Finds the Clues. (p. 524)
—Encyclopedia Brown Finds the Clues. Shortall, Leonard, illus. (p. 524)
—Encyclopedia Brown Finds the Clues. Shortall, Leonard W., illus. (p. 524)
—Encyclopedia Brown Gets His Man. (p. 524)
—Encyclopedia Brown Gets His Man. Shortall, Leonard, illus. (p. 524)
—Encyclopedia Brown Gets His Man. Shortall, Leonard W., illus. (p. 524)
—Encyclopedia Brown Keeps the Peace. Shortall, Leonard, illus. (p. 524)
—Encyclopedia Brown Keeps the Peace. Shortall, Leonard W., illus. (p. 524)
—Encyclopedia Brown Lends a Hand. Shortall, Leonard, illus. (p. 524)

—Encyclopedia Brown Lends a Hand. Shortall, Leonard W., illus. (p. 524)
—Encyclopedia Brown Saves the Day. Shortall, Leonard, illus. (p. 524)
—Encyclopedia Brown Saves the Day. Shortall, Leonard W., illus. (p. 524)
—Encyclopedia Brown Solves Them All. Shortall, Leonard, illus. (p. 524)
—Encyclopedia Brown Solves Them All. Shortall, Leonard W., illus. (p. 524)
—Encyclopedia Brown, Super Sleuth. (p. 524)
—Encyclopedia Brown Takes the Case. Shortall, Leonard, illus. (p. 524)
—Encyclopedia Brown Takes the Case. Shortall, Leonard W., illus. (p. 524)
—Encyclopedia Brown Tracks Them Down. Shortall, Leonard, illus. (p. 524)
—Encyclopedia Brown Tracks Them Down. Shortall, Leonard W., illus. (p. 524)
—Secret Agents Four. Shortall, Leonard W., illus. (p. 1540)
—Two-Minute Mysteries Collection: Two-Minute Mysteries; More Two-Minute Mysteries; Still More Two-Minute Mysteries. (p. 1804)
Sobol, Joseph Daniel. House Between Earth & Sky: Harvesting New American Folktales (p. 803)
Sobol, Laurel Marie. Fairytales Do Come True: A Lovely Christmas Story. (p. 565)
—Nez Perce Nimiipuu Stories & Legends. Sobol, Laurel Marie, illus. (p. 1249)
Sobol, Laurel Marie, jt. auth. see Sobol, Laurel Marie.
Sobol, Laurel Marie & Sobol, Laurel Marie. Fairytales Do Come True a Christmas Heirloom Story. (p. 565)
Sobol, Richard. Breakfast in the Rainforest: A Visit with Mountain Gorillas. Sobol, Richard, photos by. (p. 225)
—Elephant Twins. (p. 511)
—Life of Rice: From Seedling to Supper. Sobol, Richard, photos by. (p. 1012)
—Story of Silk: From Worm Spit to Woven Scarves. Sobol, Richard, illus. (p. 1660)
Sobol, Richard, photos by see Hudson, Cheryl Willis.
Sobol, Richard, photos by. Elephant in the Backyard. (p. 511)
Sobran, Joseph. Henry IV, Part 1. (p. 768)
—Twelfth Night. (p. 1800)
Sobrino, Javier. Me Gusta. Villamuza, Noemí, tr. (p. 1116)
Sochor, Lesia, illus. see Love, Pamela.
Soci Et E de La Faune Et Des Parcs Du Qu Ebec. Sarah de Cordoba. Sanchez, Andres & Tagle, illus. (p. 1514)
Socias, Marcel. Secretos de la Tierra. (p. 1544)
Sociedades Biblicas Unidas, creator. Biblia Hazme un Instrumento. (p. 176)
—Pedro: Pescador de Hombres. (p. 1334)
—Pedro y la Duda. (p. 1334)
Society for the Study of Manga Techniques Staff & The Society For The Study Of Manga Techniques. Dressing Your Characters in Suits & Sailor Suits. (p. 485)
—Maids & Miko (p. 1077)
Sockabasin, Allen. Thanks to the Animals Raye, Rebekah, illus. (p. 1725)
Socks, Loretta. Welcome to Clown Town: Book One. (p. 1873)
Socolovsky, Gisela, jt. auth. see Martin, Manuela.
Soda, Cynthia. Lolly's Basement Crawlies. (p. 1046)
Soda, Masahito. Firefighter: Daigo of Fire Company M. Soda, Masahito, illus. (p. 591)
—Firefighter! Vol. 14. (p. 591)
—Firefighter! Soda, Masahito, illus. (p. 591)
—Firefighter! Daigo of Fire Company M. (p. 591)
—Firefighter! Daigo of Fire Company M. Soda, Masahito, illus. (p. 591)
—Firefighter!: Daigo of Fire Company M. Vol. 10 Soda, Masahito, illus. (p. 591)
—Privileged to Kill. Soda, Masahito, illus. (p. 1408)
Sodaro, Craig. Blazing Hot Rods: By Craig Sodaro. (p. 199)
—Civil War Spies (p. 325)
—Dangerous, Disastrous, Unusual History of War (p. 404)
—U. S. Marines Special Operations Regiment: The Missions. (p. 1806)
Sodaro, Craig, jt. auth. see Raatma, Lucia.
Sodaro, Craig, et al. Dream Cars. (p. 483)
Soderberg, Erin. Dinosaur Dig. (p. 442)
—Monkey See, Monkey Zoo. Francis, Guy, illus. (p. 1165)
—Quirks & the Quirkalicious Birthday. Light, Kelly, illus. (p. 1428)
—Quirks in Circus Quirkus. (p. 1428)
—Quirks - Welcome to Normal. (p. 1428)
Soderberg, Erin, jt. auth. see Wasserman, Robin.
Soderberg, Erin & Munford, Rebecca. Welcome to Normal. (p. 1873)
Soderberg, Erin & Wasserman, Robin. Stowaway! (p. 1664)
Soderlund, Birgit, illus. see Sadorus, Lauri.
Sodré, Julie, illus. see Grimm, Sandra.
Soederberg, Susanne, et al, eds. Internalizing Globalization: The Rise of Neoliberalism & the Decline of National Varieties of Capitalism. (p. 880)
Soenen, Chantal. Sally: And the Wheel of the Year. (p. 1505)
Soentgen, Beate, et al. Peter Fischli - David Weiss. Laner, Melissa, ed. (p. 1346)
Soentpiet, Chris K., illus. see Bunting, Eve.
Soentpiet, Chris K., illus. see Farris, Christine King.
Soentpiet, Chris K., illus. see Hopkins, Lee Bennett.
Soentpiet, Chris K., illus. see King Farris, Christine.
Soentpiet, Chris K., illus. see Laminack, Lester L.
Soentpiet, Chris K., illus. see Raven, Margot Theis.
Soentpiet, Chris K., illus. see Yin.
Soentpiet, Chris K., et al. Molly Bannaky. (p. 1160)
Soetoro-Ng, Maya. Ladder to the Moon. Morales, Yuyi, illus. (p. 970)
—Ladder to the Moon with CD. Morales, Yuyi, illus. (p. 970)
Sofer, Barbara. Keeping Israel Safe: Serving the Israel Defense Forces. (p. 947)
—Keeping Israel Safe: Serving in the Israel Defense Forces. (p. 947)
Sofer, Rochel, jt. auth. see Feder, Aliza.

S

Soffe, Caroline Dawn. Billy Barnet & the House of Fern: An Environmental Story. (p. 187)
—Bluebell Wood. (p. 203)
—Burrows of Trother. (p. 244)
Soffer, Allison. Apple Days: A Rosh Hashanah Story. McMahon, Bob, illus. (p. 92)
Soffer, Allison Sarnoff. Apple Days: A Rosh Hashanah Story. McMahon, Bob, illus. (p. 92)
Soffer, Gilad. Duck's Vacation. (p. 488)
Soffer, Ruth. Amazing Birds. (p. 54)
—Animal Illustrations to Paint or Color. (p. 78)
—Baby Animals Coloring Book. (p. 124)
—Birds Alphabet Coloring Book. (p. 191)
—Birds in Flight Coloring Book. (p. 191)
—BOOST Arctic & Antarctic Life Coloring Book. (p. 213)
—BOOST North American Desert Life Coloring Book. (p. 213)
—Butterflies & Flowers to Paint or Color. (p. 247)
—Cat Lovers. (p. 278)
—Cats Stained Glass Coloring Book. (p. 281)
—Creative Haven in Full Bloom Coloring Book. (p. 379)
—Dogs Stained Glass Coloring Book. (p. 463)
—Favorite Birds Stained Glass Coloring Book. (p. 578)
—Flower Garden Coloring Book. (p. 607)
—Garden Flowers Alphabet Coloring Book. (p. 656)
—Glitter Tattoos Flowers & Birds. (p. 684)
—Great Barrier Reef Coloring Book. (p. 714)
—Nature Alphabets Coloring Book. (p. 1236)
—Sea Life Alphabet Coloring Book. (p. 1534)
—Swampland Plants & Animals Coloring Book. (p. 1688)
—Woodpeckers Stickers. (p. 1949)
Soffer, Ruth, jt. auth. see DuneCraft.
Soffer, Ruth & Coloring Books Staff. Beautiful Birds in Mated Pairs Stained Glass Coloring Book. (p. 153)
Soffer, Ruth, et al. Big Book of Sea Life to Color. (p. 179)
Soffritti, Donald, illus. see Enna, Bruno.
Sofilas, Mark, illus. see Graham, Mark.
Sofilas, Mark, illus. see Husar, Stephane.
Sofka, Amy E., jt. auth. see Justice, Laura M.
Sofocles & Euripides. Edipo Rey Antigona Medea. (p. 504)
Sofranac, Rodo. Polly & the Peanut Pull. (p. 1381)
Soft Spots. Holy Halo. (p. 791)
SoftPlay Staff, contrib. by. Dora's Happy Dance. (p. 471)
Sogabe, Aki, illus. see Lachenmeyer, Nathaniel.
Soggie, Neil. Young-Dogs of Elbow. (p. 1978)
Sohaili, Monira. Stories from Earth & Beyond: Enchanting & Inspirational Stories. (p. 1654)
Sohl, Marcia & Dackerman, Gerald. Two Years Before the Mast: Student Activity Book. Cruz, Ernesto R, illus. (p. 1804)
Sohmer, Ryan. Gutters: The Absolute Ultimate Complete Omnibus. Vol. 2 (p. 733)
—Least I Could Do Beginnings Volume 1: Look at Me: Look at Me. (p. 986)
Sohn, Coby. Peach Named Parker. (p. 1332)
Sohn, Emily. Crash Course in Forces & Motion with Max Axiom, Super Scientist Erwin, Steve & Barnett, Charles, III, illus. (p. 376)
—Experiments in Earth Science & Weather with Toys & Everyday Stuff. (p. 549)
—Experiments in Forces & Motion with Toys & Everyday Stuff. (p. 549)
—Illuminating World of Light with Max Axiom, Super Scientist Derington, Nick, illus. (p. 857)
—Journey Through the Digestive System with Max Axiom, Super Scientist (p. 928)
—Journey Through the Digestive System with Max Axiom, Super Scientist Martin, Cynthia & Schulz, Barbara, illus. (p. 928)
—Skateboarding: How It Works. (p. 1583)
Sohn, Emily, jt. auth. see Biskup, Agnieszka.
Sohn, Emily & Ash Sullivan, Erin. New Plants: Seeds in the Soil Patch. (p. 1246)
—Weather & the Water Cycle: Will it Rain? (p. 1870)
Sohn, Emily & Bair, Diane. Food & Nutrition: Eating to Win. (p. 613)
—Pebbles, Sand & Silt: The Neighbor's Garden. (p. 1333)
Sohn, Emily & Barnett III, Charles. Crash Course in Forces & Motion with Max Axiom, Super Scientist Erwin, Steve et al, illus. (p. 376)
—Curso Intensivo Sobre Fuerzas y Movimiento con Max Axiom, Supercientífico. Strictly Spanish, LLC., tr. from ENG. (p. 395)
Sohn, Emily & Brennan, Joseph. Balance & Motion: Toying with Gravity. (p. 133)
—Magnetism & Electricity: The Broken Toy Car. (p. 1076)
—Mixtures & Solutions: The Sugar in the Tea. (p. 1156)
Sohn, Emily & Fellows, Fred. Levers & Pulleys: Lift Anything! (p. 1003)
Sohn, Emily & Fellows, Frederick. Variables & Experiments: Getting Across the River. (p. 1833)
Sohn, Emily & Gendler, Joel. Solids & Liquids: Who Messed up My Sand? (p. 1608)
Sohn, Emily & Hansen, Anya. Models & Designs: It's a Roller Coaster Ride! (p. 1158)
Sohn, Emily & Harter, Adam. Landforms: The Ever-changing Earth. (p. 974)
—Sun, Moon, & Stars: A Cosmic Case. (p. 1676)
Sohn, Emily & Kentor Schmauss, Judy. Air & Weather: Where'd My Hat Go? (p. 31)
—Structures of Life: What Is this Fossil? (p. 1668)
Sohn, Emily & Klobuchar, Lisa. Fabric: It's Got You Covered! (p. 559)
Sohn, Emily & Linde, Barbara. Environments: Beetles in the Garden. (p. 532)
Sohn, Emily & Ohlenroth, Patricia. Living Systems: Life's Inside Story. (p. 1041)
—Solar Energy: Saving the School Budget. (p. 1606)
Sohn, Emily & Rompella, Natalie. Fun Science. (p. 648)
Sohn, Emily & Rothbardt, Karen. Insects: Which One Doesn't Belong? (p. 875)
—Trees: Worlds Within Leaves. (p. 1784)
Sohn, Emily & Rothbardt, Karen J. Insects: Which One Doesn't Belong? (p. 875)
Sohn, Emily & Sharp, Katie. Human Body: Train it Right. (p. 825)
—Measurement: The Measured Mystery. (p. 1117)
Sohn, Emily & Timmons, Anne. Adventures in Sound with Max Axiom, Super Scientist Martin, Cynthia, illus. (p. 15)
—Adventures in Sound with Max Axiom, Super Scientist. Martin, Cynthia & Timmons, Anne, illus. (p. 15)
—Aventuras con el Sonido con Max Axiom, Supercientífico. Martin, Cynthia, illus. (p. 119)
Sohn, Emily & Townsend, Laura. Animal Needs: Who's New at the Zoo? (p. 79)
—Patterns & Textures: Who Took the Pets? (p. 1329)
—Water: Watch It Change. (p. 1862)
Sohn, Emily & Tsang, Nina. Matter & Energy: Finding the Power. (p. 1109)
Sohn, Emily & Wright, Pam. Earth Materials: The Mystery Rocks. (p. 496)
—Paper from Wood: Dollhouse Decisions. (p. 1322)
—Sound: Music to Your Ears. (p. 1615)
Sohn, Emily, et al. Investigating Machu Picchu: An Isabel Soto Archaeology Adventure (p. 884)
—Rescue in Antarctica: An Isabel Soto Geography Adventure Timmons, Anne, illus. (p. 1462)
Sohn, Emily, frwd. Health & Medicine. (p. 757)
Sohn, Jeana, illus. see Bee, Granny.
Sohn, Ruth H. Crossing Cairo: A Jewish Woman's Encounter with Egypt. (p. 385)
Sohn, Tonia. Socks! Sohn, Tonia, illus. (p. 1605)
Sohrabi, Behzad. Legend of Sigh: A Collection of Fairy Tales. (p. 988)
Soileau, Hodges. Black Widow Spider Mystery. (p. 197)
—Comic Book Mystery. (p. 348)
—Great Shark Mystery. (p. 718)
—Mystery at Skeleton Point. (p. 1224)
—Mystery in the Fortune Cookie. (p. 1224)
—Mystery of the Haunted Boxcar. (p. 1225)
—Mystery of the Runaway Ghost. (p. 1226)
—Radio Mystery. (p. 1433)
Soileau, Hodges, illus. see Warner, Gertrude Chandler.
Soisson, Chelsea. Tate's Wayward Voyage. (p. 1707)
Soissons-Segal, Arthur. Disability Experience: A Healing Journey. (p. 446)
Sojo, Cecilia I. Everything Kids' Learning Spanish Book: Exercises & Puzzles to Help You Learn Espanol. (p. 545)
Sojos, Catalina. Ecuador. Bladimir, Trejo, illus. (p. 503)
Sokol, Bill, illus. see Hicks, Clifford B.
Sokol, Dawn DeVries. Doodle Circle: A Fill-In Journal for BFFs to Share. (p. 469)
—Doodle Diary: Art Journaling for Girls (p. 469)
—Doodle Sketchbook: Art Journaling for Boys (p. 469)
Sokol, Ron. Retrieval. (p. 1464)
Sokolava, Valerie, illus. see McFadden, Deanna.
Sokolava, Valerie, illus. see Olmstead, Kathleen, et al.
Sokolava, Valerie, jt. auth. see Schmitt, Betsy.
Sokoloff, David. Classic Jewish Tales. (p. 328)
Sokoloff, David, illus. see Moscowitz, Moshe & Resnick, Yael.
Sokolov, Raymond. Fading Feast: A Compendium of Disappearing American Regional Foods. (p. 562)
Sokolova, Valerie, illus. see Bowman, Crystal.
Sokolova, Valerie, illus. see Davis, Holly.
Sokolova, Valerie, illus. see Garn, Laura Aimee.
Sokolova, Valerie, illus. see Spinner, Stephanie.
Sol & K'naan. When I Get Older: The Story Behind Wavin' Flag. Gutierrez, Rudy, illus. (p. 1902)
Sol, Anne, jt. auth. see Roger, Marie-Sabine.
Sola, Emilio, jt. auth. see Garcia, Marina.
Sola, Lawrence H. Jeremy's Adventures: Miracle on Main Street. (p. 913)
Solages, Mahalia. What Morning Is This? (p. 1892)
Solal, Marc, tr. see David, Francois.
Solana, Guillermo, ed. Cézanne: Site/Non-Site. (p. 288)
Solana, Javier, illus. see Fuertes, Gloria.
Solana, Javier, tr. see Fuertes, Gloria.
Solana, Maria T., tr. see French, Vivian.
Solanet & Bergandi. ¿Que Hace Llover? (p. 1423)
Solange, Helene. Lala the Little Princess. (p. 972)
Solari, Jordi. Love Doodle. (p. 1059)
Solari, Maria J., jt. auth. see Kipling, Rudyard.
Solberg, Jessica. First Dog: Unleashed in the Montana Capital. Rath, Robert, illus. (p. 594)
Solberg, Jessica L. First Dog: Unleashed in the Montana Capitol. Rath, Robert, illus. (p. 594)
Solbert, Ronni, illus. see Merrill, Jean.
Soldevilla, Juan Manuel, jt. auth. see Hain-Jun, Yue.
Sole, Francisco, illus. see Molina, Maria Isabel.
Solé, Francisco, illus. see Ruiz, Celia & Stevenson, Robert Louis.
Solé, Francisco, tr. see Ruiz, Celia & Stevenson, Robert Louis.
Soleilhac, Aude, illus. see Verne, Jules.
Soleim, Heather. God's Incredible Creatures: The Gift of Sharing. Greisen, Steve, ed. (p. 691)
Soleiman, Serg, illus. see Strange, Jason.
Solensten, John M. Swing. (p. 1691)
Soler Blanch, Carmen. Hernan Cortes. (p. 771)
Soler, Michael. Ladybug & Me. Eisenberg, Serge, illus. (p. 971)
Soles, Henry, ed. NEW Children of Color Holy Bible Hardcover Edition. Carter, Fred et al, illus. (p. 1244)
Solesbee, Mary Ann. Sal & Amanda Take Morgan's Victory March to the Battle of Cowpens. Waters, Tony, illus. (p. 1504)
Soley, Liesel. Can You Be an Artist? Soley, Liesel, illus. (p. 258)
Solga, Kim, jt. auth. see Kohl, MaryAnn F.
Solheim, James. Only Alex Addleston in All These Mountains. Ebbeler, Jeffrey, illus. (p. 1298)
Solheim, Kermit, illus. see Hogan, Jayne.
Solheim, Tracy. Risky Game. (p. 1475)
Soli, Doris. Jango the Little Dragon: The Wondrous Adventures of Little Dragon. (p. 908)
Soli, Tina, illus. see Bringsvaerd, Tor Age.
Solice, Deborah. Eye of the Undead: The Hidden Channel: an Adventure Series in Time. (p. 558)
Solid, Silas, photos by see Jaime, Catherine.
Solimene, Laura, ed. see Stowe, Harriet Beecher.
Soling, Cevin. Boris the Dog. Kille, Steve, illus. (p. 214)
Solis, Javier Rene. Adventures of Tony the Turtle: La Familia the Family. (p. 24)
Solis, Lisa V. Classroom Cupboard: Lessons, Activities & Culinary Concoctions for Kids (p. 329)
Soliz, Adela. Alzheimer's Disease. (p. 51)
—Bullying. (p. 241)
Sollano, Carolyn. Tree Top Angels. (p. 1784)
Sollee, Anne. Scripture Scrapbook for Children. (p. 1533)
Sollenne, Ava. Ava & Happy's Awesome Adventures. (p. 118)
Sollers, Jim, illus. see Bloxam, Frances.
Sollers, Jim, illus. see Plourde, Lynn.
Sollinger, Emily. Diego's Ocean Adventure: A Book of Facts about Ocean Animals. Mawhinney, Art, illus. (p. 437)
—OLIVIA Plants a Garden. Osterhold, Jared, illus. (p. 1287)
—Owls: Birds of the Night. Rallis, Chris, illus. (p. 1315)
—This Is Our World: A Story about Taking Care of the Earth. Brown, Jo, illus. (p. 1736)
Sollish, Ari. Toque de Pesaj: A Touch of Passover. Becker, Boruch, illus. (p. 1769)
—Touch of Passover: A Touch & Feel Book. Becker, Boruch, illus. (p. 1772)
Soll-Tauchert, Sabine, jt. auth. see Neysters, Silvia.
Solly, Gloria, jt. illus. see Cruzan, Patricia.
Solly, Gloria D., illus. see Cruzan, Patricia.
Solner Heimer, Patricia. Li'l Earth. Solner Heimer, Patricia, illus. (p. 1017)
Solo, Hope. Hope Solo: My Story. (p. 796)
—Hope Solo: My Story (Young Readers' Edition) (p. 796)
Solod, Margo. Coyote Summer: A Summerhood Island Book. (p. 374)
Solodar, Marisol. Bailey's Band: Develop Understanding of Fractions & Numbers (p. 133)
Solodky, M. Technology of Ancient Egypt. (p. 1711)
Soloman, Debra. Don't Look under the Bridge. (p. 468)
Soloman, Ana Weston. Introduction to Multimedia. (p. 882)
Solomon, Annie. Blackout. (p. 197)
—Tell Me No Lies. (p. 1716)
Solomon, Barbara. Girl Who Wanted to Become a Princess. (p. 679)
Solomon, Carl, Sr. Do Animals Believe in God? (p. 456)
Solomon, Chad. Adventures of Rabbit & Bear Paws: The Voyageurs. (p. 22)
Solomon, Debra, illus. see Wollard, Kathy.
Solomon, Debra, jt. auth. see Wollard, Kathy.
Solomon, Elena Vestri & Shelley, John. Listening, Note Taking, & Speaking Across the Disciplines Bk. 1 (p. 1022)
—Listening, Note Taking, & Speaking Across the Disciplines Bk. 2. (p. 1022)
Solomon, Enid. Toby Visits Mommy: A Book for Children Who See Their Parents Only During Scheduled Visitations. (p. 1760)
Solomon, Harry. Day Silver Snowed. Solomon, Harry, illus. (p. 414)
Solomon, Heather, illus. see Wheeler, Lisa.
Solomon, Heather M., illus. see Coombs, Kate.
Solomon, Heather M., illus. see Del Negro, Janice M. & Del Negro.
Solomon, Heather M., illus. see Weeks, Sarah.
Solomon, Heather M., illus. see Willey, Margaret.
Solomon, Iris L. & Solomon, Ron. Friendz Pakz: Love. (p. 639)
—Friendz Pakz: Future. (p. 639)
—Friendz Pakz: Friends. (p. 639)
—Friendz Pakz: Showbiz. (p. 639)
—Invisible Secrets. (p. 886)
Solomon, Jef. Right in My Own Neighborhood. (p. 1472)
Solomon, Martha. Christmas in Da Hood. (p. 314)
Solomon, Michelle & Pereira, Lavinia. Cow Cake. Faust, Laurie A., illus. (p. 373)
—Too Big! Faust, Laurie A., illus. (p. 1766)
—Uh - Oh! Faust, Laurie A., illus. (p. 1808)
Solomon, Philippa. Settle down for Tiger. (p. 1554)
Solomon, Ron, jt. auth. see Solomon, Iris L.
Solomon, Rosiland, illus. see Salas, Laura Purdie.
Solomon, Sharon. Cathy Williams, Buffalo Soldier Lorenzetti, Doreen, illus. (p. 280)
—Lewis Tewanima: Born to Run Fields, Lisa, illus. (p. 1004)
—Walk With Grandpa/Un Paseo con el Abuelo. Del Risco, Eida, tr. (p. 1854)
Solomon, Sharon K. Christopher Newport: Jamestown Explorer Bridy, Dan, illus. (p. 317)
—Walk with Grandpa. Barcita, Pamela, illus. (p. 1854)
Solomon, Steven. Homophobia: Deal with It & Turn Prejudice into Pride Johnson, Nick, illus. (p. 794)
Solomons. Computerized Test Bank to Accompany Organic Chemistry. (p. 355)
—Instructor's Resource to Accompany Organic Chemistry. (p. 878)
Solomons, David. My Brother Is a Superhero. (p. 1199)
Solotareff, jt. auth. see Solotareff, Gregoire.
Solotareff, Gregoire. Edu, El Pequeno Lobo. (p. 505)
—Nieve. (p. 1252)
—Que Mas Quisieras! Vicens, Paula, tr. (p. 1424)
Solotareff, Gregoire & Le Saux, Alain - Solotareff. Pequeno Museo. (p. 1341)
Solotareff, Gregoire & Solotareff. Rey Cocodrilo. Ros, Rafael, tr. (p. 1467)
Soloway, Cindy. Mommy, What's an MRI? Steve, Sumner, ed. (p. 1162)
Soltero, Emilio. Draw the Line. (p. 481)
Soltero, Emilio, illus. see Flynn, Dale Bachm.
Soltis, Sue. Nothing Like a Puffin. Kolar, Bob, illus. (p. 1268)
Soltz, Sheri. Finn Gets a Dog: Teaching Children the Responsibility of Having a Pet. (p. 589)
Soltz, Sheri, jt. auth. see Soltz, Sheri.
Soltz, Sheri & Soltz, Sheri. Finn Learns to Surf. Soltz, Sheri, illus. (p. 589)
Solway, Andrew. Aircraft (p. 31)
—Biofuels. (p. 188)
—Buildings & Structures (p. 239)
—Cadenas y Redes Alimentarias. (p. 250)
—Castle under Siege! Simple Machines (p. 277)
—Chemistry. (p. 297)
—Civil Engineering & the Science of Structures. (p. 324)
—Classifying Birds (p. 328)
—Classifying Insects (p. 328)
—Classifying Mammals (p. 328)
—Climate Change. (p. 332)
—Communication: The Impact of Science & Technology. (p. 349)
—Designing Greener Vehicles & Buildings (p. 430)
—Energy & Matter. (p. 528)
—Environmental Technology. (p. 532)
—Exploring Electricity & Magnetism. (p. 552)
—Exploring Energy. (p. 552)
—Exploring Forces & Motion. (p. 552)
—Exploring Sound, Light, & Radiation. (p. 553)
—Food & Digestion. (p. 613)
—Food Chains & Webs (p. 613)
—Fossil Fuels. (p. 623)
—From Crashing Waves to Music Download: An Energy Journey Through the World of Sound. (p. 642)
—From Sunlight to Blockbuster Movies: An Energy Journey Through the World of Light. (p. 643)
—Generating & Using Electricity (p. 660)
—Genetics. (p. 661)
—Genetics in Medicine. (p. 661)
—Graphing Energy (p. 711)
—Graphing Immigration (p. 711)
—Graphing War & Conflict (p. 711)
—Growing. (p. 726)
—Heart & Lungs. (p. 759)
—History of Super Science: Atoms & Elements (p. 784)
—Human Body: Investigating an Unexplained Death. Stayte, James, illus. (p. 825)
—Hydrogen Fuel. (p. 831)
—Inventions & Investigations (p. 884)
—Jupiter & the Outer Planets (p. 937)
—Pirate Adventure: Weather (p. 1362)
—Renewable Energy Sources (p. 1460)
—Resources. (p. 1463)
—Science of a Loaf of Bread: The Science of Changing Properties. (p. 1527)
—Scientists Behind Earth's Processes (p. 1528)
—Scientists Behind Energy (p. 1528)
—Secrets of Animal Life Cycles. (p. 1545)
—Secrets of Flight. (p. 1545)
—Secrets of Habitats. (p. 1545)
—Secrets of Heat & Cold. (p. 1545)
—Secrets of Pollution & Conservation. (p. 1545)
—Seeing Inside the Body. (p. 1548)
—Sustainable Tourism. (p. 1688)
—Transportation (p. 1779)
—Understanding Cycles & Systems (p. 1815)
—Universe. (p. 1820)
—Voyage of a Light Beam: Light Energy (p. 1850)
—Waste Disposal. (p. 1860)
—Water Power. (p. 1863)
—Why Is There Life on Earth? (p. 1925)
Solway, Andrew, jt. auth. see Crabtree Staff.
Solway, Andrew & Graham, Ian. Energy Journeys. (p. 528)
—Energy Transfers. (p. 529)
Solway, Andrew & Heinemann Library Staff. Classifying Birds (p. 328)
—Classifying Insects (p. 328)
—Classifying Mammals (p. 328)
—Inventions & Investigations (p. 884)
—Renewable Energy Sources (p. 1460)
—Understanding Cycles & Systems (p. 1815)
Solway, Andrew & Saunders, Nigel. Exploring Physical Science. (p. 553)
Solway, Jeff, illus. see Vernon, Steve.
Somaiah, Ranjan & Somaiah, Rosemarie. Indian Children's Favorite Stories. (p. 871)
Somaiah, Rosemarie, jt. auth. see Somaiah, Ranjan.
Soman, David. Three Bears in a Boat. Soman, David, illus. (p. 1741)
Soman, David, illus. see Davis, Jacky.
Soman, David, illus. see Heller, Maryellen.
Soman, David, jt. auth. see Davis, Jacky.
Soman, David, jt. auth. see Milne, A. A.
Soman, David & Davis, Jacky. Doodle All Day with Ladybug Girl. Soman, David, illus. (p. 469)
—Happy Halloween, Ladybug Girl! Soman, David, illus. (p. 745)
—Happy Holidays, Ladybug Girl! Gift Set. Soman, David, illus. (p. 746)
—Little Box of Ladybug Girl Soman, David, illus. (p. 1025)
—Play All Day with Ladybug Girl. Soman, David, illus. (p. 1371)
—Who Can Play? (p. 1914)
Soman, Pascal K. & Soman, Vickie A. A-B-C for Alex, Bash, & Company: A to Z Animal Tales from Around the World. (p. 1)
Soman, Vickie A., jt. auth. see Soman, Pascal K.
Somaschini, jt. auth. see Gabbi.
Sombart, Elisabeth, et al. Doce Vidas para la Musica. (p. 459)
Some, Inir Raissa. David Has a Purpose. (p. 411)
Somers, Dayle. Sergeant Steve's Station. (p. 1552)
Somers, Ian. Secret Gift. (p. 1541)
Somers, Kevin, illus. see Puck.
Somers, Kevin & Puck. 1 2 3 New York. Somers, Kevin, illus. (p. 1990)
Somerville, Barbara. Actor. (p. 10)
—Africanized Honey Bee. (p. 28)
—Asian Carp. (p. 106)
—Brown Treesnake. (p. 232)
—Commercial Fisher. (p. 349)
—Dental Hygienist. (p. 426)
—Ethiopia. (p. 539)
—Fire Ant. (p. 590)
—Florida Panther. (p. 607)
—Food Scientist. (p. 614)
—Gray Squirrel. (p. 713)
—Gray Wolf. (p. 713)
—Green General Contractor. (p. 721)
—Grizzly Bear. (p. 724)
—Japan. (p. 909)
—Marine Biologist. (p. 1094)

S

—Mexico. (p. 1131)
—Monitor Lizard. (p. 1164)
—Musician. (p. 1194)
—Python. (p. 1421)
—Sea Lamprey. (p. 1534)
—Small Indian Mongoose. (p. 1592)
Somervill, Barbara A. Abigail Adams: Courageous Patriot & First Lady. (p. 5)
—Alabama. (p. 33)
—American Bison. (p. 60)
—Ancient Maya. (p. 70)
—Andrew Jackson. (p. 72)
—Animal Cells & Life Processes (p. 77)
—Arizona. (p. 98)
—Arizona (Revised Edition) (p. 98)
—Awesome Alps. (p. 120)
—Cane Toad. (p. 261)
—Cells & Disease (p. 286)
—Colorado. (p. 343)
—Distance, Area, & Volume (p. 453)
—Does This Make Sense? Constructing Explanations. (p. 460)
—Does This Make Sense? Constructing Explanations. (p. 460)
—Electrical Circuits & Currents (p. 509)
—Elizabeth Blackwell: America's First Female Doctor. (p. 513)
—Empire of Ancient Mesopotamia. (p. 521)
—Empire of the Aztecs. (p. 521)
—Empire of the Incas, Revised Edition. (p. 521)
—First Response - By Air. (p. 596)
—Fleas: Feasting on Blood. (p. 603)
—Florida. (p. 606)
—Francisco Pizarro: Conqueror of the Incas (p. 628)
—Glaciers. (p. 682)
—Graphing Crime (p. 711)
—Graphing Health & Disease (p. 711)
—Graphing Natural Disasters (p. 711)
—Hong Kong. (p. 795)
—How Life Changes. (p. 810)
—Hurricanes. (p. 830)
—Iceland. (p. 851)
—Ida Tarbell: Pioneer Investigative Reporter. (p. 851)
—Iran. (p. 886)
—Japan. (p. 909)
—Land of the Andes. (p. 973)
—Leeches: Waiting in the Water. (p. 987)
—Lice: Head Hunters. (p. 1007)
—Life & Times of James Madison. (p. 1008)
—Magnificent Himalayas. (p. 1076)
—Martin Luther: Father of the Reformation (p. 1097)
—Mary McLeod Bethune: African-American Educator. (p. 1101)
—Maryland. (p. 1101)
—Mass & Weight (p. 1102)
—Mississippi. (p. 1154)
—Mosquitoes: Hungry for Blood. (p. 1177)
—Mountain Gorilla. (p. 1180)
—New York. (p. 1247)
—Oral Reports (p. 1301)
—Pennsylvania (Revised Edition) (p. 1338)
—Pennsylvania. (p. 1338)
—Pierre-Auguste Renoir. (p. 1357)
—Plains & Plateaus. (p. 1366)
—Plant Cells & Life Processes (p. 1368)
—Plant Reproduction (p. 1369)
—Producing Fish (p. 1409)
—Producing Grains (p. 1409)
—Rugged Rockies. (p. 1494)
—Sorting It Out: Evaluating Data. (p. 1614)
—South Carolina (Revised Edition) (p. 1616)
—South Korea. (p. 1617)
—Spain. (p. 1620)
—Speed & Acceleration (p. 1624)
—Story Behind Coal (p. 1656)
—Story Behind Glass (p. 1656)
—Story Behind Maps (p. 1656)
—Story Behind Paper (p. 1656)
—Story Behind Rubber (p. 1656)
—Taiwan. (p. 1696)
—Team Projects (p. 1710)
—Teens in Egypt (p. 1715)
—Tennessee. (p. 1720)
—Texas. (p. 1724)
—Texas (Revised Edition) (p. 1724)
—Ticks: Digging for Blood. (p. 1747)
—Timeworn Urals. (p. 1754)
—United Arab Emirates. (p. 1818)
—Vampire Bats: Hunting for Blood. (p. 1831)
—Veterinarian. (p. 1839)
—Votes for Women! The Story of Carrie Chapman Catt. (p. 1850)
—West. (p. 1876)
—West Virginia. (p. 1876)
—What Are the Facts? Collecting Information. (p. 1880)
—What Are the Facts? Collecting Information. (p. 1880)
—What Did You Find Out? Reporting Conclusions. (p. 1882)
—What Did You Find Out? Reporting Conclusions. (p. 1882)
—What Do You Want to Prove? Planning Investigations. (p. 1883)
—What Do You Want to Prove? Planning Investigations. (p. 1883)
—What's the Big Idea? Forming Hypotheses. (p. 1899)
—What's the Big Idea? Forming Hypotheses. (p. 1899)
—Wildlife Photographer. (p. 1931)
—William Penn: Founder of Pennsylvania Somervill, Barbara A., illus. (p. 1933)
Somervill, Barbara A., jt. auth. see Gray, Susan H.
Somervill, Barbara A. & Capstone Press Staff. Measure It! (p. 1117)
Somervill, Barbara A. & Compass Point Books Staff. Clara Barton: Founder of the American Red Cross (p. 326)
—Indira Gandhi: Political Leader in India (p. 872)
Somervill, Barbara A. & Ryback, Carol. Human Body. (p. 825)
Somervill, Barbara & Gray, Susan H. Wild Boar. (p. 1929)
Somerville, Charles C. E Is for Egypt. Somerville, Charles C., illus. (p. 492)
Somerville, Charles C., jt. auth. see Elliott, Ned.
Somerville, Clive. Drug Enforcement Administration. (p. 486)
Somerville, Louisa. Rescue Vehicles. Jensen, Hans, illus. (p. 1462)
—Sharks. (p. 1562)
—Snakes. (p. 1596)
Somerville, Louisa & Smith, David. Preparing for Times Tables. Tulip, Jenny, illus. (p. 1396)
Somerville, Louisa, et al. Times Tables. (p. 1754)
Somerville, Mary Ann. Traveler & the Flower. (p. 1780)
Somerville, Sheila, illus. see Copeland, Colene.
Somerville, Sheila, illus. see Dashney, John.
Somerville, Sunshine. Kota. (p. 967)
Somerville/ Lampstand Press, David, illus. see Rohwer/Lampstand Press, Lauren.
Somme, Kate. Very Active Alphabet Book: And Other Alphabet Rhymes. (p. 1837)
Sommer, Bill & Tilghman, Natalie. 52-Hertz Whale. (p. 1997)
Sommer, Carl. Androcles & the Lion. Martinez, Jorge, illus. (p. 72)
—Ant & the Grasshopper. Noé, illus. (p. 88)
—Boy Who Cried Wolf. Bogdan, Enache, illus. (p. 219)
—Can You Help Me Find My Smile? (p. 259)
—Can You Help Me Find My Smile? Budwine, Greg, illus. (p. 259)
—Can You Help Me Find My Smile? Me Puedes Ayudar a Encontrar Mi Sonrisa? Budwine, Greg, illus. (p. 259)
—Chicken Little. Mercado, Jorge, illus. (p. 300)
—Country Mouse & the City Mouse. Noe, Ignacio, illus. (p. 372)
—Dare to Dream! Martinez, Jorge et al, illus. (p. 406)
—Dare to Dream! Martínez, Jorge et al, illus. (p. 406)
—Dare to Dream! ¡Atrévete a Soñar! Martínez, Jorge et al illus. (p. 406)
—Donkey, Fox, & the Lion. Noé, illus. (p. 466)
—Dream. Martínez, Jorge et al, illus. (p. 483)
—Dream (Sueña) Martínez, Jorge et al, illus. (p. 484)
—Eagle & the Chickens. Noé, illus. (p. 492)
—Emperor & the Seed. Martinez, Jorge, illus. (p. 520)
—Emperor's New Clothes. Noe, Ignacio, illus. (p. 521)
—Fast Forward. Budwine, Greg, illus. (p. 576)
—Fast Forward(Avance Acelarado) Budwine, Greg, illus. (p. 576)
—Great Deception. Noé, illus. (p. 715)
—Great Deception(El Gran Engaño) Noé, illus. (p. 715)
—Great Royal Race. (p. 718)
—Great Royal Race. Westbrook, Dick, illus. (p. 718)
—Great Royal Race(La Gran Carrera Real) Westbrook, Dick, illus. (p. 718)
—Hopeless to Hopeful. Vignolo, Enrique, illus. (p. 797)
—I Am a Lion! (p. 832)
—I Am a Lion! Budwine, Greg, illus. (p. 832)
—I Am a Lion!(Yo Soy un León!) Budwine, Greg, illus. (p. 832)
—If Only I Were... (p. 853)
—If Only I Were... James, Kennon, illus. (p. 853)
—If Only I Were. . . (p. 853)
—If Only I Were. . . James, Kennon, illus. (p. 853)
—If Only I Were- James, Kennon, illus. (p. 854)
—If Only I Were...(Si Yo Fuese...) James, Kennon, illus. (p. 854)
—It's Not Fair! (p. 898)
—It's Not Fair! Budwine, Greg, illus. (p. 898)
—It's Not Fair!(No Es Justo) ! Budwine, Greg, illus. (p. 898)
—King of the Pond. (p. 959)
—King of the Pond. Budwine, Greg, illus. (p. 959)
—King of the Pond(El Rey Del Estanque) Budwine, Greg, illus. (p. 959)
—Light Your Candle. (p. 1015)
—Light Your Candle. James, Kennon, illus. (p. 1015)
—Light Your Candle(Enciende Tu Vela) James, Kennon, illus. (p. 1015)
—Lion & the Mouse. Mercado, Jorge, illus. (p. 1020)
—Lion & the Three Bulls. Mercado, Jorge, illus. (p. 1020)
—Little Red Hen. Noe, Ignacio, illus. (p. 1034)
—Little Red Riding Hood. Noe, Ignacio, illus. (p. 1035)
—Little Red Train. (p. 1035)
—Little Red Train. James, Kennon, illus. (p. 1035)
—Little Red Train(El Trenecito Rojo) James, Kennon, illus. (p. 1035)
—Lost & Found. Budwine, Greg, illus. (p. 1054)
—Lost & Found(Perdida y Encontrada) Budwine, Greg, illus. (p. 1054)
—Mayor for a Day: Alcalde Por un Dia. Westbrook, Dick, illus. (p. 1113)
—Mayor for a Day. (p. 1113)
—Mayor for a Day. Westbrook, Dick, illus. (p. 1113)
—Mayor for A Day Read-along (p. 1113)
—Miller, His Son & Their Donkey. Denman, Michael, illus. (p. 1143)
—Miserable Millie. Vignolo, Enrique, illus. (p. 1150)
—Miserable Millie(La Pobrecita Mili) Vignolo, Enrique, illus. (p. 1150)
—No Longer a Dilly Dally (p. 1258)
—No Longer a Dilly Dally James, Kennon, illus. (p. 1258)
—No Longer a Dilly Dally. James, Kennon, illus. (p. 1258)
—No Longer a Dilly Dally Read-Along (p. 1258)
—No Longer a Dilly Dally Read-Along James, Kennon, illus. (p. 1258)
—No Longer a Dilly Dally(Nunca Mas a Troche y Moche) James, Kennon, illus. (p. 1258)
—No One Will Ever Know. (p. 1259)
—No One Will Ever Know. Budwine, Greg, illus. (p. 1259)
—No One Will Ever Know. Westbrook, Dick, illus. (p. 1259)
—No One Will Ever Know Read-Along Westbrook, Dick, illus. (p. 1259)
—No One Will Ever Know Read-Along. (p. 1259)
—No One Will Ever Know(Nadie Se Va a Enterar) Westbrook, Dick, illus. (p. 1259)
—Noise! Noise! Noise! (p. 1262)
—Noise! Noise! Noise! James, Kennon, illus. (p. 1262)
—Noise! Noise! Noise! Read-along (p. 1262)
—Noise! Noise! Noise!(Ruido! Ruido! Ruido!) James, Kennon, illus. (p. 1262)
—Proud Rooster & Little Hen (p. 1412)
—Proud Rooster & Little Hen. (p. 1412)
—Proud Rooster & Little Hen. Budwine, Greg, illus. (p. 1412)
—Proud Rooster & Little Hen(Gallito Orgulloso y Gallinita) Budwine, Greg, illus. (p. 1413)
—Race. Budwine, Greg, illus. (p. 1430)
—Race(La Carrera) Budwine, Greg, illus. (p. 1431)
—Racing Fools. Budwine, Greg, illus. (p. 1432)
—Rebel. Vignolo, Enrique, illus. (p. 1450)
—Rebel(El Rebelde) Vignolo, Enrique, illus. (p. 1451)
—Revolt. Budwine, Greg, illus. (p. 1466)
—Revolt(La Revuelta) Budwine, Greg, illus. (p. 1466)
—Richest Poor Kid. Martinez, Jorge, illus. (p. 1470)
—Richest Poor Kid. Martínez, Jorge, illus. (p. 1470)
—Roar. Budwine, Greg, illus. (p. 1478)
—Roar(El Rugido) Budwine, Greg, illus. (p. 1478)
—Runaway(La Escapada) Vignolo, Enrique, illus. (p. 1497)
—Sly Fox & the Chicks. (p. 1591)
—Sly Fox & the Chicks. James, Kennon, illus. (p. 1591)
—Sly Fox & the Chicks Read-along. (p. 1591)
—Sly Fox & the Chicks Read-along. James, Kennon, illus. (p. 1591)
—Sly Fox & the Chicks(El Zorro Astuto y los Pollitos) James, Kennon, illus. (p. 1591)
—Spike the Rebel! Vignolo, Enrique, illus. (p. 1627)
—Spike the Rebel!(pua, el Rebelde!) Vignolo, Enrique, illus. (p. 1627)
—Stone Soup. Denman, Michael, illus. (p. 1652)
—Three Little Pigs. (p. 1743)
—Three Little Pigs. Budwine, Greg, illus. (p. 1743)
—Three Little Pigs Read-Along. (p. 1743)
—Three Little Pigs(Los Tres Cerditos) Budwine, Greg & Vignolo, Enrique, illus. (p. 1743)
—Tied up in Knots. (p. 1747)
—Tied up in Knots. Budwine, Greg, illus. (p. 1747)
—Tied up in Knots Read-along (p. 1747)
—Tied up in Knots Read-along. Budwine, Greg, illus. (p. 1747)
—Tied up in Knots(Enredados) Budwine, Greg, illus. (p. 1747)
—Time Remote! (p. 1752)
—Time Remote! Budwine, Greg, illus. (p. 1752)
—Time Remote! Read-along. (p. 1752)
—Time Remote! Read-along. Budwine, Greg, illus. (p. 1752)
—Time Remote!(El Control Del Tiempo!) Budwine, Greg, illus. (p. 1752)
—Tortoise & the Hare. Vignolo, Enrique, illus. (p. 1771)
—Town Musicians of Bremen. Denman, Michael L., illus. (p. 1773)
—Ugly Caterpillar. (p. 1808)
—Ugly Caterpillar. Budwine, Greg, illus. (p. 1808)
—Ugly Caterpillar Read-along (p. 1808)
—Ugly Caterpillar Read-along. Budwine, Greg, illus. (p. 1808)
—Ugly Caterpillar(La Oruga Fea) Budwine, Greg, illus. (p. 1808)
—Ugly Princess. Martinez, Jorge, illus. (p. 1808)
—You Move You Lose (p. 1976)
—You Move You Lose James, Kennon, illus. (p. 1976)
—You Move You Lose. (p. 1976)
—You Move You Lose. James, Kennon, illus. (p. 1976)
—You Move You Lose(El Que Se Mueva, Pierde) James, Kennon, illus. (p. 1976)
—Your Job Is Easy. James, Kennon, illus. (p. 1980)
—Your Job Is Easy. (p. 1981)
—Your Job Is Easy Read-along. (p. 1981)
—Your Job Is Easy Read-along. James, Kennon, illus. (p. 1981)
—Your Job Is Easy(Tu Trabajo Es Facil) James, Kennon, illus. (p. 1981)
Sommer, Carl & Aesop. Divide to Conquer. Mercado, Jorge, illus. (p. 454)
—Divide to Conquer(Divide y Venceras) Mercado, Jorge, illus. (p. 454)
—Silent Scream. Bogdan, Enache, illus. (p. 1575)
—Silent Scream(El Grito Silencioso) Bogdan, Enache, illus. (p. 1575)
—Tiny Giant. Mercado, Jorge, illus. (p. 1756)
—Tiny Giant(La Gigante Pequeña) Mercado, Jorge, illus. (p. 1756)
Sommer, Carl, narrated by. It's Not Fair! (p. 898)
Sommer, Isabell & Reinhardt, Swen. CHIP CHIPS JAM - 4: Der Schatz in der Elbe. (p. 308)
Sommer, Kathryn. Passion of Her Own: Life-Path Journeys with Women of Kansas. (p. 1327)
Sommer, Patricia, tr. see Mycek-Wodecki, Anna.
Sommer, Sharon. Adventures of Summer Hills: Rowdy Red's Lesson. (p. 23)
Sommer, Shelley. Hammerin' Hank Greenberg: Baseball Pioneer. (p. 739)
—John F. Kennedy: His Life & Legacy. (p. 921)
Sommer, Xiaolan, tr. see Blackington, Debbie.
Sommer-Bodenburg, Angela. Pequeno Vampiro. Glienke, Amelie, illus. (p. 1341)
Sommerdorf, Norma. Red River Girl. (p. 1455)
Sommerfeld, Monika, tr. see Jensen, Elizabeth.
Sommerhalder, Benjamin. Ghost Knigi. (p. 671)
Sommers, Annie. College Athletics: Steroids & Supplement Abuse. (p. 340)
Sommers, Annie Leah. Everything You Need to Know about Looking & Feeling Your Best: A Guide for Girls. (p. 545)
—Frequently Asked Questions about Foster Care. (p. 636)
—Great National Soccer Teams. (p. 717)
Sommers, Annie Leah, jt. auth. see Sommers, Michael A.
Sommers, Audrey. Mickey the Monarch. Mattie, Dugan, ed. (p. 1136)
Sommers, Faith & Burkholder, Diane. Helping Mama. (p. 766)
Sommers, Jackie Lea. Truest. (p. 1793)
Sommers, Katy, jt. auth. see Allegretti, Jan.
Sommers, Michael. Basketball in the Big 12 Conference. (p. 143)
—Cocaine. (p. 337)
—Ehud Olmert: Prime Minister of Israel. (p. 507)
—Football in the Big 12. (p. 615)
—NFL: Steroids & Human Growth Hormone. (p. 1249)
—Silicon. (p. 1575)
—Tsunami: True Stories of Survival. (p. 1795)
—Vermont: Past & Present. (p. 1837)
—Wildlife Photographers: Life Through a Lens. (p. 1931)
Sommers, Michael A. Antarctic Melting: The Disappearing Antarctic Ice Cap. (p. 88)
—Avi. (p. 119)
—Basketball in the Big 12 Conference. (p. 143)
—Chris Crutcher. (p. 311)
—Cocaine. (p. 337)
—Ehud Olmert: Prime Minister of Israel. (p. 507)
—Everything You Need to Know about Bipolar Disorder & Manic Depressive Illness. (p. 545)
—Everything You Need to Know about Looking & Feeling Your Best: A Guide for Guys. (p. 545)
—France: A Primary Source Cultural Guide. (p. 627)
—Great Interpersonal Skills. (p. 716)
—J. D. Salinger. (p. 901)
—Snowmobiling: Have Fun, Be Smart. (p. 1601)
—Tsunamis: True Stories of Survival. (p. 1795)
—Wildlife Photographers: Life Through a Lens. (p. 1931)
—Yeast Infections, Trichomoniasis, & Toxic Shock Syndrome. (p. 1969)
Sommers, Michael A., jt. auth. see Cross, Nathaniel.
Sommers, Michael A., jt. auth. see Orr, Tamra.
Sommers, Michael A., jt. auth. see Winters, Adam.
Sommers, Michael A., jt. auth. see Zahensky, Kenneth.
Sommers, Michael A. & Sommers, Annie Leah. Everything You Need to Know about Virginity. (p. 546)
Sommerville, L. & Pells, T. Guitar. (p. 731)
Somoskey, Rebecca. Say What? Kool Kids Stories from Appalachia. (p. 1518)
—Summer of the Buckeye Whistle. (p. 1674)
Somper, Justin. Allies & Assassins. (p. 47)
—Black Heart. (p. 196)
—Blood Captain. (p. 200)
—Conspiracy of Princes. (p. 359)
—Dead Deep. (p. 416)
—Demons of the Ocean. (p. 426)
—Empire of Night. (p. 521)
—Immortal War. (p. 861)
—Pyramid Plot. Wingham, Peter, illus. (p. 1421)
—Tide of Terror. (p. 1747)
Son, Eugene, jt. illus. see Mosier, Scott.
Son, Hee-Joon. iD_eNTITY Kim, Yoon-Kyung, illus. (p. 852)
—iD_eNTITY Kim, Youn-Kyung, illus. (p. 852)
—Phantasy Degree Son, Hee-Joon, illus. (p. 1349)
Son, John. Finding My Hat. (p. 588)
Sona & Jacob. Varnamala Geet. (p. 1833)
Sona and Jacob, illus. see Darling, Helen.
Sona & Jacob, illus. see Kumar, Monica & Kumar, Manisha.
Sona & Jacob, illus. see Kumar, Monica.
Sona & Jacob, illus. see Singhal, Sheetal.
Sonandres, Thomas William & Peterson, Marilyn A. DreamLady.com: Guidance from Your Dreams. (p. 484)
Sonberg, Caryn. Six Dogs & a Police Officer. Dorenkamp, Michelle, illus. (p. 1582)
Sonday, Arlene. Sonday System - Let's Play Learn: Alphabet Book. Breckman, Cindy, ed. (p. 1611)
Sonder, Ben. Parrots: A Portrait of the Animal World. (p. 1325)
—Parrots - Pb: A Portrait of the Animal World. (p. 1325)
Sondheim, Alan. Wayward. (p. 1865)
Sonenklar, Carol. AIDS. (p. 30)
—Anorexia & Bulimia. (p. 87)
Sones, S. Stop Pretending: What Happened When My Sister Went Crazy. (p. 1653)
Sones, Sonya. One of Those Hideous Books Where the Mother Dies. (p. 1296)
—Sonya Sones Collection: One of Those Hideous Books Where the Mother Dies; What My Mother Doesn't Know; What My Girlfriend Doesn't Know. (p. 1613)
—Stop Pretending: What Happened When My Big Sister Went Crazy. (p. 1653)
—To Be Perfectly Honest: A Novel Based on an Untrue Story. (p. 1758)
—What My Girlfriend Doesn't Know. (p. 1892)
—What My Mother Doesn't Know. (p. 1892)
Sones, Sonya & Tramer, Ava. Night Before College. Dalton, Mar, illus. (p. 1253)
Song, Amira. Horse Lovers Forever. (p. 799)
Song, Aram, illus. see Kelman, Marcy.
Song, Danielle, illus. see Payne, Jody.
Song Hà. Indebted As Lord Chom/No Nhu Chua Chom: The Legend of the Forbidden Street. Smith, William, tr. from VIE. (p. 870)
Song, Jennifer, illus. see Posner-Sanchez, Andrea.
Song, Jennifer, illus. see Tillworth, Mary.
Songhurst, Hazel & Breeden, Neil. Activators Drawing. (p. 10)
Song-I, Yoon. Saint Teresa of Avila, God's Troublemaker. (p. 1504)
Songs, Steve, illus. see Engel, Christiane.
Songs, Steve, jt. auth. see Dobbins, Jan.
Songs, Steve, jt. auth. see Engel, Christiane.
Soni, Jaymee & Schubert, Charles. Kid at Art - Paul Cezanne. (p. 951)
—Kid at Art - Vincent Van Gogh. (p. 951)
—Kid at Art - Wassily Kandinsky. (p. 951)
Soni, Parwinder Singh. Little Red Riding Hood. (p. 1035)
Sonic Scribes Staff. Best of Sonic the Hedgehog 2: Villains. (p. 170)
—Knuckles the Echidna Archives (p. 965)
—Sonic Saga Series 2: Order from Chaos. (p. 1612)
—Sonic Saga Series 3: Eggman Empire. (p. 1612)
—Sonic Saga Series 4: House of Cards. (p. 1612)
—Sonic Select Spaziante, Patrick 'Spaz', illus. (p. 1612)
—Sonic Select Book 10. (p. 1612)
—Sonic Select Book 7. (p. 1612)
—Sonic Select Book 8. (p. 1612)
—Sonic Select Book 9: the Games. (p. 1612)
—Sonic the Hedgehog Archives 20. (p. 1612)
—Sonic the Hedgehog: Legacy Vol. 3. (p. 1612)
—Sonic the Hedgehog Presents Knuckles the Echidna Archives 4. (p. 1612)
—Sonic Universe 4: Journey to the East. (p. 1612)
—Sonic Universe 5: the Tails Adventure. (p. 1612)
—Sonic Universe 6: Treasure Team Tango. (p. 1612)
—Sonic Universe 7: Silver Saga. (p. 1612)

Sonic Scribes Staff, jt. auth. see Flynn, Ian.
Sonic Scribes Staff, jt. auth. see Spaziante, Patrick Spaz.
Sonic/Mega Man Scribes Staff. Sonic / Mega Man: Worlds Collide 1. (p. 1612)
Sonik, Madeline. Belinda & the Dustbunnys. Bridal, Grania, tr. (p. 162)
Sonishi, Kenji. Leave It to Pet! (p. 986)
—Leave It to PET! Sonishi, Kenji, illus. (p. 986)
Sonja. Clear Vision: Finding Peace in a Trouble World. (p. 330)
Sonja Johannesen & Alice Johannesen. Ola & Jens' Christmas Adventure. (p. 1283)
Sonkin, Jessica, illus. see Weissman, Elissa Brent.
Sonne, Lisa T. E., jt. text see Moore, Katharine.
Sonnebeyatta, Kemba. P'nut Butter & Rubber. Charles, Simpson, illus. (p. 1374)
Sonneborn, Liz. Acquisition of Florida: America's Twenty-Seventh State. (p. 9)
—America the Beautiful: The Story Behind Our National Hymn. (p. 59)
—American Indian Experience. (p. 62)
—Ancient China. (p. 68)
—Articles of Confederation. (p. 104)
—California Gold Rush. (p. 253)
—California Indians. (p. 253)
—Canada. (p. 260)
—Choctaws. (p. 309)
—Chronology of American Indian History. (p. 317)
—Chumash. (p. 318)
—Colony of Maryland. (p. 342)
—District of Columbia: Past & Present. (p. 454)
—Electric Light: Thomas Edison's Illuminating Invention. (p. 508)
—End of Apartheid in South Africa. (p. 526)
—Environmental Movement: Protecting Our Natural Resources. (p. 532)
—Fantasia Barrino. (p. 571)
—Far Out Fashion: Bringing 1960s & 1970s Flair to Your Wardrobe. (p. 572)
—Forces in Nature: Understanding Gravitational, Electrical, & Magnetic Force. (p. 617)
—France. (p. 627)
—Frequently Asked Questions about Plagiarism. (p. 636)
—Frequently Asked Questions about Shoplifting & Theft. (p. 636)
—German Americans. (p. 666)
—Great Irish Famine. (p. 716)
—Harriet Beecher Stowe. (p. 749)
—How to Beat Verbal Bullying. (p. 815)
—Iraq. (p. 887)
—James Lincoln Collier. (p. 907)
—John Paul Jones: American Naval Hero. (p. 922)
—Kuwait. (p. 968)
—Mark Twain. (p. 1095)
—Mexican-American War: A Primary Source History of the Expansion of the Western Lands of the United States. (p. 1131)
—Mexican-American War. (p. 1131)
—Murder at the 1972 Olympics in Munich. (p. 1192)
—Native Peoples of the Northeast. (p. 1235)
—Nonverbal Communication: The Art of Body Language. (p. 1263)
—North Korea. (p. 1265)
—Northwest Coast Indians. (p. 1266)
—Oregon. (p. 1302)
—Pakistan. (p. 1319)
—Pizarro: Conqueror of the Mighty Incas. (p. 1365)
—Pledge of Allegiance: The Story Behind Our Patriotic Promise. (p. 1374)
—Pompeii. (p. 1382)
—Primary Source History of the Colony of Georgia. (p. 1400)
—Primary Source History of the Colony of Maryland. (p. 1400)
—Romans: Life in Ancient Rome. Hiti, Samuel, illus. (p. 1486)
—Sherman Alexie. (p. 1566)
—Star-Spangled Banner: The Story Behind Our National Anthem. (p. 1641)
—United States Constitution. (p. 1819)
—War of 1812: A Primary Source History of America's Second War with Britain. (p. 1857)
—War of 1812. (p. 1857)
—Wild Bill Hickok. (p. 1929)
—Wilma Mankiller. (p. 1934)
—Yemen. (p. 1970)
Sonneborn, Scott. Attack of the Invisible Cats Baltazar, Art, illus. (p. 113)
—Attack of the Zom-Bees! Esparza, Andres et al, illus. (p. 114)
—Batman & the Villainous Voyage. Vecchio, Luciano, illus. (p. 144)
—Beware Our Power! Schoening, Dan, illus. (p. 173)
—Captain Cold & the Blizzard Battle McManus, Shawn, illus. (p. 263)
—Catwoman's Classroom of Claws. Schoening, Dan, illus. (p. 281)
—Computer Meltdown. Lozano, Omar, illus. (p. 355)
—Danger on Deck! Vecchio, Luciano & DC Comics Staff, illus. (p. 404)
—Deep Space Hijack. Schoening, Dan, illus. (p. 423)
—Feet First. Banks, Timothy, illus. (p. 580)
—Frankenstein Journals Banks, Timothy, illus. (p. 629)
—Frankenstein Journals: Guts or Bust. Banks, Timothy, illus. (p. 629)
—Good, the Bad, & the Monkeys Bradley, Jessica, illus. (p. 700)
—I for an Eye. Banks, Timothy, illus. (p. 838)
—Meet the South Police. Lozano, Omar, illus. (p. 1123)
—Moon Bandits. Cavallaro, Mike, illus. (p. 1171)
—Moon Bandits. Cavallaro, Mike & DC Comics Staff, illus. (p. 1171)
—Mystery of Santa's Sleigh. Lozano, Omar, illus. (p. 1225)
—No Guts, No Gloria. Banks, Timothy, illus. (p. 1258)
—Pain in the Butt. Banks, Timothy, illus. (p. 1318)
—Partners in Peril. Smith, Andy & Vancata, Brad, illus. (p. 1325)
—Pete Bogg: King of the Frogs. Aburtov, illus. (p. 1346)
—Prisoner of the Penguin! Vecchio, Luciano, illus. (p. 1407)
—Prisoner of the Ring Schoening, Dan, illus. (p. 1407)
—Reindeer Games. Lozano, Omar, illus. (p. 1457)
—Supergirl vs. Brainiac Vecchio, Luciano, illus. (p. 1683)
—Tiger Moth: Attack of the Zom-Bees! Esparza, Andres, illus. (p. 1748)
Sonneborn, Scott & Loughridge, Lee. Captain Cold & the Blizzard Battle McManus, Shawn, illus. (p. 264)
Sonneborn, Scott, et al. Killer Croc Hunter (p. 956)
—Shell Shocker Doescher, Erik, illus. (p. 1564)
Sonnemair, Jan, illus. see Flood, Nancy Bo.
Sonneman, Alan. Clouds & Skyscapes: Explore Techniques for Painting Splendid Skies. (p. 335)
Sonnenberg, Lois. Grave Tales: A Mother Goose Spoof. Simpson, Sue, illus. (p. 712)
Sonnenberg, Matthew Martin. Clown Closet. Cagle, Terry R., illus. (p. 335)
Sonnenblick, Jordan. After Ever After. (p. 28)
—Are You Experienced? (p. 97)
—Curveball: The Year I Lost My Grip. (p. 395)
—Dodger & Me. (p. 460)
—Dodger for President. (p. 460)
—Drums, Girls, & Dangerous Pie. (p. 487)
—Notes from the Midnight Driver. (p. 1268)
—Zen & the Art of Faking It. (p. 1986)
Sonnenburg, Chris, jt. auth. see Moshier, Joe.
Sonner, Barbara. Watch for Bright Pumpkin Faces. (p. 1860)
Sonneveld, Stephen. Prince of Destiny. (p. 1401)
Sonnichsen, A. L. Red Butterfly. Bates, Amy June, illus. (p. 1453)
Sonnier, Suzanne. Shinto, Spirits, & Shrines: Religion in Japan. (p. 1567)
Sonntag, Steven. Learning, the Hardest Job You'll Ever Love: Helpful Ideas for Students & Parents. (p. 985)
Sonoda, Hideki. Zoroark: Master of Illusions. (p. 1990)
Sonoda, Konami. Choco Mimi. Sonoda, Konami, illus. (p. 309)
—Chocomimi. Sonoda, Konami, illus. (p. 309)
—ChocoMimi , Vol. 5. Sonoda, Konami, illus. (p. 309)
Sonsino, Rifat. Many Faces of God: A Reader of Modern Jewish Theologies. (p. 1089)
Sonsino, Rifat & Syme, Daniel B. Finding God: Selected Responses. (p. 588)
Sonsky, Kim, jt. auth. see Garry-McCord, Kathleen.
Sontag, Mary G. Bruno's Adventures. (p. 232)
Soo, Kean. Baker's Run. (p. 133)
—Great Desert Rally. (p. 715)
—Jellaby (p. 912)
—Lost Monster. (p. 1056)
—March Grand Prix: The Fast & the Furriest. (p. 1091)
—Monster in the City. (p. 1167)
—Race at Harewood. (p. 1430)
Sood, Malini. Hurricanes & Tornadoes. (p. 830)
Sood, Sana Hoda. Diwali: A Cultural Adventure. Hoda, Rubina, illus. (p. 455)
Sookraj, Esther. Good with Words Bueno con las Palabras. (p. 700)
Sooner, Jeffrey. Rascal Flatts. (p. 1439)
Soos, Eva, photos by see Greenfield, Anne.
Sootin, Harry. Experiments with MacHines & Matter. Aloise, Frank, illus. (p. 549)
—Robert Boyle, Founder of Modern Chemistry. Schrotter, Gustav, illus. (p. 1478)
Soper, Nan, jt. auth. see Westfield, Patricia.
Soper, Sandra. Punctuation Practice: Capital. (p. 1417)
—Reading & Writing (p. 1445)
Soper, Stuart A. Milky Saves Christmas. (p. 1143)
—P. U'Trid & S. Pooky Pickles Company. (p. 1316)
Soper, Vernon, illus. see Buchan, John.
Sophia Hansen, Hansen & Hansen, Sophia. Crow & the Raven. (p. 385)
Sophocles. Antigone. Landes, William-Alan, ed. (p. 89)
—Electra. Landes, William-Alan, ed. (p. 508)
—Oedipus at Colonus. Landes, William-Alan, ed. (p. 1279)
—Oedipus Rex - Literary Touchstone Edition. (p. 1279)
—Sophocles: Antigone. (p. 1614)
—Sophocles: Oedipus Tyrannus. (p. 1614)
Sophocles, et al. Ajax. Landes, William-Alan, ed. (p. 32)
Soprano, Sophie. Laughing All the Way. (p. 980)
Sorachi, Hideaki. Gin Tama. (p. 676)
Sorba, Richard, illus. see Dombrower, Jan.
Sorbier, Frederic. Impressionists. Chabot, Jean-Phillipe, illus. (p. 862)
Sorbier, Frédéric, jt. auth. see Philippe Chabot, Jean.
Sorel, Edward. Johnny on the Spot. (p. 923)
Sorel, Edward, illus. see Metaxas, Eric.
Sorensen. Curious Missie C. (p. 394)
—Curious Missie P. (p. 394)
Sorensen, A. A. Turner's Worms.... Realizing Expectations. (p. 1798)
Sorensen, Heather, illus. see Davies, Kathern.
Sorensen, Henri, illus. see Huling, Jan.
Sorensen, Henri, illus. see McCutcheon, John.
Sorensen, Henri, illus. see Melmed, Laura Krauss.
Sorensen, Henri, illus. see Schmidt, Gary D., ed.
Sorensen, Henri, illus. see Tobias, Tobi.
Sorensen, Henri, illus. see Uhlberg, Myron.
Sorensen, Henri, illus. see Weidt, Maryann N.
Sorensen, Henri, tr. see Uhlberg, Myron.
Sorensen, Launa. King's First Journey (p. 960)
—My Adventure in China. (p. 1195)
Sorensen, Lita. Bryan Talbot. (p. 233)
Sorensen, "Miss Nancy". Alexa's Rainbow. (p. 37)
Sorensen, Pamela. Help Me Draw A Rainbow, Help Me Draw an Airplane. (p. 765)
Sorensen, Peter, illus. see Hein, Simeon.
Sorensen, Rebekah M., jt. auth. see Doonan, Gladys.
Sorensen, Stephanie A. Flash: The Amazing Basset Hound. (p. 602)
—Flash el Increíble Basset Ayuda a Santa / Flash: The Amazing Basset Hound Helps Santa. (p. 602)
—Flash the Amazing Basset Hound Helps Santa. (p. 602)
—Flash the Amazing Basset Hound Visits the Spa. (p. 602)
—Threads of Love. (p. 1741)
Sorensen, Virginia. Miracles on Maple Hill. Krush, Joe & Krush, Beth, illus. (p. 1149)
—Plain Girl. Geer, Charles, illus. (p. 1366)
Sorenson, E. Randy. First Reindeer Couldn't Fly. (p. 596)
Sorenson, Jack R. Eibhlin & Her Dragon (p. 507)
Sorenson, Linda M., jt. auth. see Schultz, Terry L.
Sorenson, Margo. Aloha for Carol Ann. Burris, Priscilla, illus. (p. 48)
—Ambrose & the Cathedral Dream. Szegedi, Katalin, illus. (p. 57)
—Ambrose & the Princess. Szegedi, Katalin, illus. (p. 57)
—Hurricane! Nature's Most Destructive Force. (p. 829)
—Spaghetti Smiles Harrington, David, illus. (p. 1620)
Sorenson, Toni. I Will Go, I Will Do: A Book of Mormon Story. (p. 848)
Sorenson, Vanessa, illus. see Libbrecht, Kenneth.
Sorenson, Verona. Pumpkin Patch. (p. 1416)
Sorey, Barbara J. Florida Girl: Short Stories of Family, Community & History. (p. 607)
Soria, Angeles Jimenez & Angeles, Jiménez Soria. Atasco! (p. 111)
Soriano, Al. Excursions Gr 1 Sp. (p. 547)
—Excursions Gr 2 Sp. (p. 547)
—Excursions Gr 3 Sp. (p. 547)
—Excursions Grade 1. (p. 547)
—Excursions Grade 2. (p. 547)
—Excursions Grade 3. (p. 547)
—Excursions Grade 4. (p. 547)
—Excursions Grade 5. (p. 547)
—Metro Math Voyages Kindergarten Kit Sp. (p. 1130)
—Nat'L Voyages Grade 1 Subtopic Tests Tg. (p. 1235)
—Voyages Gr 1 Anchors & Subtopic Tests Nat'L. (p. 1850)
—Voyages Gr 1 Anchors & Subtopic Tests Sp. (p. 1850)
—Voyages Gr 1 Instruction Kit Sp. (p. 1850)
—Voyages Gr 1 Sp Subtopic Tests. (p. 1850)
—Voyages Gr 1 Sp Topic Tests Blm & Te. (p. 1850)
—Voyages Gr 1 Student Kit Sp. (p. 1850)
—Voyages Gr 2 Anchors & Subtopic Tests Nat'L. (p. 1850)
—Voyages Gr 2 Anchors & Subtopic Tests Sp. (p. 1851)
—Voyages Gr 2 Instruction Kit Sp. (p. 1851)
—Voyages Gr 2 Sp Subtopic Tests. (p. 1851)
—Voyages Gr 2 Sp Topic Tests Blm & Te. (p. 1851)
—Voyages Gr 2 Student Kit Sp. (p. 1851)
—Voyages Gr 3 Anchors & Subtopic Tests Nat'L. (p. 1851)
—Voyages Gr 3 Anchors & Subtopic Tests Sp. (p. 1851)
—Voyages Gr 3 Instruction Kit Sp. (p. 1851)
—Voyages Gr 3 Sp Subtopic Tests. (p. 1851)
—Voyages Gr 3 Sp Topic Tests Blm & Te. (p. 1851)
—Voyages Gr 3 Student Kit Sp. (p. 1851)
—Voyages Gr 4 Anchors & Subtopic Tests Nat'L. (p. 1851)
—Voyages Gr 5 Anchors & Subtopic Tests Nat'L. (p. 1851)
—Voyages Grade 1 Subtopic Tests. (p. 1851)
—Voyages Grade 1 Topic Tests Te Nat'L. (p. 1851)
—Voyages Grade 2 Complete Program Sp. (p. 1851)
—Voyages Grade 2 Subtopic Tests. (p. 1851)
—Voyages Grade 2 Topic Tests Te Nat'L. (p. 1851)
—Voyages Grade 3 Complete Program Sp. (p. 1851)
—Voyages Grade 3 Subtopic Tests. (p. 1851)
—Voyages Grade 3 Topic Tests Te Nat'L. (p. 1851)
—Voyages Grade 4 Subtopic Tests. (p. 1851)
—Voyages Grade 4 Topic Tests Te Nat'L. (p. 1851)
—Voyages Grade 5 Subtopic Tests. (p. 1851)
—Voyages Grade 5 Topic Tests Te Nat'L. (p. 1851)
—Voyages Kinder Sp Activity Cards Deck a Sp. (p. 1851)
—Voyages Kinder Sp Student. (p. 1851)
—Voyages Kindergarten Teacher Resource Book Nat'L. (p. 1851)
—Voyages Kindergarten Teacher's Guide Nat'L. (p. 1851)
Soriano, Osvaldo. Negro de Paris. (p. 1240)
Soriano Puche, Lola, jt. auth. see Torres Moliner, Isabel.
Soriao, S. T., Jr. Tale of an Embattled Chairman of the Board. (p. 1699)
Sorin, Sergey. Power Principle: The Mind-Body-Spirit Approach to Ultimate Weight Loss. (p. 1390)
Sorkin, Louis N., jt. auth. see Goodman, Sarah.
Sornson, Bob. Essential Math Skills: Over 250 Activities to Develop Deep Learning. (p. 537)
—Math Moms & Dads Home Program: Developing Symbolic Math Skills for Ages 5 to 8. (p. 1106)
Sornson, Kathy, jt. auth. see Stinson, Aimee.
Sornson, Robert. Juice Box Bully: Empowering Kids to Stand up for Others. (p. 932)
—Math Moms & Dads Home Program: Preschool & Kindergarten Level, for ages 3 to 6. (p. 1106)
Soros, Barbara. Tenzin's Deer: A Tibetan Tale. Mayer, Danuta, illus. (p. 1720)
—Tenzin's Deer. Mayer, Danuta, illus. (p. 1720)
Sorpreso, Linda. Cassandra Behind Closed Doors: A Teenager's Struggle into Adulthood. (p. 276)
Sorra, Kristin, illus. see Doering Tourville, Amanda.
Sorra, Kristin, illus. see Holub, Joan.
Sorra, Kristin, illus. see Loewen, Nancy.
Sorra, Kristin, illus. see Shepard, Aaron.
Sorra, Kristin, illus. see Tourville, Amanda Doering.
Sorra, Kristin, jt. auth. see Ashman, Linda.
Sorra, Kristin, jt. auth. see Tourville, Amanda Doering.
Sorrell, Connie. Our Family's Darlene. (p. 1308)
Sorrells, Aaron. Trip through the Solar System. (p. 1787)
Sorrells, W. A. Florence Fiasco. Bancroft, Tom & Corley, Rob, illus. (p. 606)
—Nairobi Nightmare. Bancroft, Tom & Corley, Rob, illus. (p. 1227)
Sorrells, Walter. Book Three of the Travelers. (p. 212)
—Club Dread. (p. 335)
—Fake ID. (p. 565)
—First Shot. (p. 596)
—Travelers (p. 1780)
—White-Out. (p. 1913)
Sorrells/Sorrells. Scratch. (p. 1532)
Sorrels, Roy. Legend of the Alamo: Stories in American History. (p. 989)
—Legend of the Alamo. (p. 989)
Sorrentino, Alessandra, illus. see Corral, Alberto.
Sorrentino, Dawn. I Wish I Were. (p. 849)
—Look at Me. (p. 1048)
Sorrentino, Michela, illus. see Watterson, Carol.
Sorrow, Casey, illus. see Joyce, James.
Sosa, Carlos. Celebrations. (p. 285)
—Cultures. (p. 391)
—Lionel Messi. (p. 1021)
Sosa, Carlos & Castaneda, Patricia. Celebrations: La Familia Banderas. (p. 285)
—Cultures: La Familia Banderas. (p. 391)
Sosa, Cynthia. Sebastian, the Small Trunk Elephant. (p. 1539)
Sosa, Hernan, illus. see Fine, Edith Hope & Josephson, Judith Pinkerton.
Sosa, Hernan, illus. see Gil, Lydia M.
Sosa, Joe. Lonely Little World. (p. 1046)
Sosa, Maritza, concept. Formas - Shapes. (p. 620)
Sosebee, Cheryl, illus. see Hamilton, Matthew.
Sosieski, Shanti. Who's Next: The Hottest Young Stars in Action Sports. (p. 1920)
Sosin, Deborah. Charlotte & the Quiet Place. Woolley, Sara, illus. (p. 293)
Soske, Becky. Just the Way He Wanted Me to Be. Haisch, Joshua, illus. (p. 940)
Sosna, Marvin. Brandon's Trail. (p. 222)
Sosnowski, Saul, ed. see Mansilla, Lucio V.
Sosnowski, Tiffany, illus. see Written By Kimberly M Sosnowski; Illustr.
Sotherden, Nora, jt. auth. see Mills, Nathan.
Sotirovski, Aleksandar, illus. see Aboff, Marcie & Gray-Wilburn, Renée.
Sotirovski, Aleksandar, illus. see Aboff, Marcie.
Sotirovski, Aleksandar, illus. see Gray-Wilburn, Renée & Beehive Illustrations Staff.
Sotirovski, Aleksandar, illus. see Gray-Wilburn, Renée.
Sotnik, Katherine. Choir of Angels Coloring Book. (p. 309)
Soto Aparicio, Fernando. Mientras Llueve. (p. 1139)
—Viajeros de la Eternidad. (p. 1839)
Soto, G., et al. Multicultural Collection. Byrd, S., illus. (p. 1190)
Soto, Gary. Accidental Love. (p. 8)
—Afterlife. (p. 28)
—Buried Onions. (p. 243)
—Canto Familiar. Nelson, Annika & Diaz, David, illus. (p. 262)
—Cebollas Enterradas. (p. 283)
—Cesar Chavez: A Hero for Everyone. Lohstoeter, Lori, illus. (p. 288)
—Chato & the Party Animals. Guevara, Susan, illus. (p. 295)
—Chato Goes Cruisin' Guevara, Susan, illus. (p. 295)
—Chato y los Amigos Pachangueros. Guevara, Susan, illus. (p. 295)
—Chato's Kitchen. Guevara, Susan, illus. (p. 295)
—Crazy Weekend. (p. 378)
—Facts of Life. (p. 561)
—Fire in My Hands. (p. 590)
—Help Wanted: Stories. (p. 766)
—Hey 13! (p. 774)
—Jesse. (p. 914)
—Local News: Stories. (p. 1044)
—Mercy on These Teenage Chimps. (p. 1127)
—Neighborhood Odes. Diaz, David, illus. (p. 1240)
—Novio Boy: A Play. (p. 1268)
—Pacific Crossing. (p. 1317)
—Partly Cloudy: Poems of Love & Longing. (p. 1325)
—Petty Crimes. (p. 1349)
—Taking Sides. (p. 1698)
Soto, Jasmine, photos by see Irvin, Feliza & irvin, Feliza.
Soto, Luisa & Benchmark Education Co., LLC Staff. Bob, Tab, & I. (p. 205)
—Yes, Cubs! (p. 1970)
Soto, Manuel. Mi & Two. Duggan, Micheal, illus. (p. 1132)
Soto, Maritza. Mystery of Fairy Tales. (p. 1224)
Soto, Michael, jt. auth. see Knittel, John.
Soto Moore, Llasmin. Oso the Rainbow Bear. (p. 1305)
Soto, Nayda. Yo - Guía: Mi familia, la escuela y la Comunidad. Burgos, Mayda, ed. (p. 1971)
—Yo - Kinder: Mi familia, la escuela y la Comunidad. Burgos, Mayda, ed. (p. 1971)
Soto, Nibi. Beyond the Map's Boundary, 2nd Edition: A Timely Sort of Adventure. (p. 174)
Sottolichio, Rafael, jt. auth. see Massicotte, Sylvie.
Sotzek, Hannelore, jt. auth. see Kalman, Bobbie.
Sotzek, Hannelore & Rouse, Bonna. Golf. (p. 696)
Soud. Beginner Biographies (p. 159)
Soud, illus. see Cosson, Jody.
Soud, illus. see Hall, M. C.
Soud, illus. see Hall, Margaret.
Soud, illus. see Lindeen, Mary.
Soud, illus. see Wilson, Wayne L.
Souder, Patricia. Blindness & Vision Impairment. Albers, Lisa et al, eds. (p. 199)
Souder, Patti. Different Way of Seeing: Youth with Blindness & Vision Impairment. (p. 438)
—Different Way of Seeing: Youth with Visual Impairments & Blindness. (p. 438)
—On the Edge of Disaster: Youth in the Juvenile Court System (p. 1290)
Souders, J. A. Renegade. (p. 1460)
—Revelations. (p. 1465)
Souders, Taryn. Whole-Y Cow! Fractions Are Fun. Mai-Wyss, Tatjana, illus. (p. 1920)
Souhami, Jessica. Foxy! (p. 626)
—King Pom & the Fox. (p. 959)
—Leopard's Drum: An Asante Tale from West Africa. (p. 993)
—Piglet's Picnic: A Story about Food & Counting. (p. 1358)
—Rama & the de Mon King: An Ancient Tale from India. (p. 1437)
—Rama & the Demon King. (p. 1437)
—Sausages. (p. 1516)
Souhami, Jessica & Quarto Generic Staff. Little, Little House. (p. 1030)
—Strongest Boy in the World. (p. 1668)
Soule, Charles. Strongman (p. 1668)
Soule, Jean Conder. Never Tease a Weasel. Booth, George, illus. (p. 1243)
Soule, Lesley Wade. As You Like It. (p. 105)
Souleiman, Serg, illus. see Dahl, Michael.
Soulier, Daniel, illus. see Berocay, Roy.
Souliere, Lisa. Guess What? I Have Diabetes. (p. 729)
—Toasters Are Easy, School Not So Much. Rockwell, Joanna, illus. (p. 1760)
Soumagnac, Virginie, illus. see Monari, Manuela.

Soumeral, Eve Nussbaum & Schulz, Carol D. Voice from the Holocaust (p. 1848)
So-un, Kim. Korean Children's Favorite Stories. (p. 967)
So-Un, Kim. Tigers of the Kumgang Mountains: A Korean Folktale. Kyoung-Sim, Jeong, illus. (p. 1749)
So-Un, Kim & Kyoung-Sim, Jeong. Korean Children's Favorite Stories. (p. 967)
Soundar, Chitra. Chasing the Pot of Gold. Amrein, Paul, illus. (p. 294)
Soundprints. Grizzly Bear Cub's First Fish: Wilderness Adventures. (p. 724)
—Panda Cub in the Bamboo Forest: Wilderness Adventures. (p. 1320)
—Polar Bear Cub & Mommy: Wilderness Adventures. (p. 1378)
—Prickly Porcupine: Wilderness Adventures. (p. 1398)
Soundprints, creator. Flamingo Grows Up. (p. 602)
—New Baby Giraffe. (p. 1243)
—Orang Utan's Playtime. (p. 1301)
—Panda's Busy Day. (p. 1321)
—Rhinoceros's Bathtime. (p. 1467)
—Tiger Cub See-and-Do. (p. 1748)
Soundprints Editorial Staff, jt. auth. see Galvin, Laura Gates.
Soundprints Staff. Big Book of Alphabet Songs. (p. 178)
—Cinderella's Birthday. (p. 320)
—Elephant & Mommy. (p. 511)
—Fairy Tales. (p. 564)
—Farmer in Dell. (p. 574)
—Hey Diddle Diddle & Other Favorites. (p. 774)
—Humpty Dumpty: And Other Favorites. (p. 827)
—If You're Happy & You Know It & Other Favorites. (p. 855)
—I'm a Little Teapot & Other Favorites. (p. 858)
—Itsy Bitsy Spider: And Other Favorites. (p. 900)
—I've Been Workin on Railroad. (p. 900)
—Little Miss Muffet & Other Favorites. (p. 1032)
—Make New Friends. Schwaeber, Barbie Heit & Williams, Tracee, eds. (p. 1079)
—Mother Goose Bitsy Board Book Travel Pack (p. 1178)
—Mother Goose's Hide n' Seek Book. (p. 1178)
—My Princess Treasury. (p. 1217)
—Nursery Rhymes: Story Time Treasury. (p. 1273)
—Ocean Adventures: Story-Time Treasury. (p. 1276)
—Old MacDonald: And Other Favorites. (p. 1284)
—Pat-a-Cake: And Othe Favorites. (p. 1327)
—Pat-a-Cake: And Other Favorites. (p. 1327)
—Piglet's Feelings Pack. (p. 1358)
—Pooh & Piglet's Colors & Shapes. (p. 1383)
—Smithsonian Oceanic Collection Micro 4 Book Set. (p. 1594)
—Smithsonian's Backyard Collection Micro 4 Book Set. (p. 1594)
—Wheels on the Bus: Move-Alongs. (p. 1901)
Soundprints Staff, ed. see Studio Mouse Staff.
Soundprints Staff, jt. auth. see Odierno, Lisa.
Soundprints Staff & Galvin, Laura Gates. First Look at Aircraft. (p. 596)
Soundprints Staff & Studio Mouse Staff. Hickory Dickory Dock & Other Silly-Time Rhymes. (p. 775)
—This Little Piggy & Other Favorite Rhymes. (p. 1737)
Soundprints Staff, creator. Head, Shoulders, Knees & Toes: And Other Move-along Rhymes. (p. 756)
Soundprints Staff, ed. Backyard Collection: Daddy Longlegs, Owl, Armadillo & Ladybug Books (p. 131)
—Oceanic Collection III: Beluga Whale, Harp Seal, Walrus & Lobster Books (p. 1277)
Soup, Cuthbert. Another Whole Nother Story. Timmins, Jeffrey Stewart, illus. (p. 88)
—No Other Story. (p. 1259)
—Whole Nother Story. (p. 1920)
—Whole Nother Story. Timmins, Jeffrey Stewart, illus. (p. 1920)
Sourcebooks, Inc. My Little Valentine: Coupons & Stickers for the Sweetest Girl I Know. (p. 1213)
Sourcebooks, Inc Staff. Baby's First Mother Goose Treasury. (p. 129)
—Easter Bunny Coupons. (p. 499)
Sourcebooks, Inc Staff, jt. auth. see Cheyney, Arnold.
Sourcebooks, Inc Staff, jt. auth. see Dellasega, Cheryl.
Sourdais, Clèmentine, illus. see Grimm, Jacob & Grimm, Wilhelm.
Sourwine, David, illus. see Blum, Vicki.
Sousa, Jay, photos by see Campodonica, Carol A.
Soussana, Nathalie, et al. Songs from the Garden of Eden: Jewish Lullabies & Nursery Rhymes. Alemagna, Beatrice, illus. (p. 1612)
Souter, Gerry. Battle Tanks: Power in the Field. (p. 147)
—Military Rifles: Fierce Firepower. (p. 1143)
—Secret Service Agent: And Careers in Federal Protection. (p. 1543)
Souter, Gerry, jt. auth. see Kiland, Taylor Baldwin.
Souter, Gerry & Souter, Janet. Herbert Hoover. (p. 769)
—James Buchanan. (p. 907)
—John Quincy Adams. (p. 922)
—War in Afghanistan & Iraq: The Daily Life of the Men & Women Serving in Afghanistan & Iraq. Carlton Books Staff, ed. (p. 1857)
Souter, Gerry, et al. Bringing Photos, Music, & Video into Your Web Page. (p. 229)
—Creating Animation for Your Web Page. (p. 378)
—Creating e-Reports & Online Presentations. (p. 378)
—Researching on the Internet Using Search Engines, Bulletin Boards, & Listservs. (p. 1463)
Souter, Janet. Air Marshal: And Careers in Transportation Security. (p. 31)
Souter, Janet, jt. auth. see Souter, Gerry.
South, Coleman. Jordan. (p. 925)
South, Coleman & Jermyn, Leslie. Syria. (p. 1693)
South, Victor. America in the 20th Century (1913-1999) (p. 59)
—America in the 20th Century (1913-1999) Rakove, Jack N., ed. (p. 59)
—Remember the Alamo: Americans Fight for Texas, 1820-1845. (p. 1459)
—Remember the Alamo: Americans Fight for Texas, 1820-1845. Rakove, Jack N., ed. (p. 1459)
—Shifting Role: America & the World, 1900-1912. (p. 1566)
—Shifting Role: America & the World, 1900-1912. Rakove, Jack N., ed. (p. 1566)
Southall, Donna. Buibble Trailer. (p. 237)
Southall, Ivan. Ash Road. (p. 105)
—Hills End. (p. 780)
—Josh. (p. 926)
Southall, M. Renee. My Daddy Loves Me & He Can Do Anything. (p. 1201)
Southall, Margo. Differentiated Small-Group Reading Lessons: Scaffolded & Engaging Lessons for Word Recognition, Fluency, & Comprehension That Help Every Reader Grow. (p. 438)
—Ready-To-Go Differentiated Literacy Centers: Grade 1: Engaging Centers Designed to Help Every Student Meet the Common Core. (p. 1447)
Southam, Phil, jt. auth. see Needler, Matthew.
Southard, Ashley. Maddie. (p. 1069)
Southard, Jan, illus. see Stoll, Emily.
Southard, Patricia. Captain Andre's Adventure in the Sky. (p. 263)
Southerland, Taylor, illus. see Halpert, Ben.
Southern Lion Books, ed. see McClain, Charles.
Southern, Randy, et al. Revolution Devotional: 90 Daily Devotions for Guys (p. 1466)
Southern, Shelley, illus. see Bourgeois, Paulette & Clark, Brenda.
Southern, Shelley, jt. adapted by see Shannon, Rosemarie.
Southern, Shelley, tr. see Bourgeois, Paulette & Clark, Brenda.
Southey, Robert. Goldilocks & the Three Bears. (p. 696)
Southgate, Anna & Li, Yishan. Drawing Manga Faces & Bodies. (p. 482)
—Drawing Manga Mecha, Weapons, & Wheels. (p. 482)
—Drawing Manga Men. (p. 482)
—Drawing Manga Women. (p. 482)
Southgate, Anna & Sparrow, Keith. Drawing Manga Boys. (p. 482)
—Drawing Manga Expressions & Poses. (p. 482)
—Drawing Manga Weapons, Vehicles, & Accessories. (p. 482)
Southwell, David. Unsolved Political Mysteries. (p. 1822)
Southwell, David & Twist, Sean. Secret Societies. (p. 1544)
—Unsolved Political Mysteries. (p. 1822)
Southwestern Press. Speak English on the Job: Hable Ingles en el Trabajo. (p. 1622)
Southwick Elementary Students. Soaring on the Wings of Eagles. (p. 1603)
Southwick, Terre' Dyer. Kenny: A Foster Child's Story. (p. 949)
Southworth, Gordon, jt. auth. see Scott, Fred.
Souto, Jose, illus. see Ibarrola, Begonia.
Souvestre, Emile. Peronnik: A French Fairy Tale of the Grail Quest. (p. 1343)
Souviney, Randall. Solving Math Problems Kids Care About. (p. 1608)
Souviney, Randall J., et al. Mathematical Investigations (p. 1107)
Souza, Cláudia. Princess to the Rescue Ammirati, Christelle & Second Story Press Staff, illus. (p. 1406)
Souza, D. M. John C. Fremont. (p. 921)
—Look What Whiskers Can Do. (p. 1050)
—Packed with Poison! Deadly Animal Defenses. Harris, Jack, illus. (p. 1317)
—Volcanoes Inside & Out. Drew-Brook, Deborah & Cormack, Allan, illus. (p. 1849)
Souza, Dorothy M. John Wesley Powell. (p. 923)
—Plant Invaders. (p. 1369)
Souza, Paul, illus. see Sankey, Alice.
Souza, Sandy. Kirby & the Coyote. (p. 961)
Sovago-Royal, Sandra. Magimus. (p. 1075)
Sovak, Jan. 3-D Coloring Book—Dangerous Animals. (p. 1991)
—3-D Coloring Book—Dinosaurs. (p. 1991)
—Alaskan Wildlife Coloring Book. (p. 34)
—Build a Giant Poster Coloring Book—Under the Sea. (p. 237)
—Deadly Creatures Coloring Book. (p. 417)
—Deadly Insects & Arachnids. (p. 417)
—Dinosaurs! Coloring Book. (p. 444)
—Dinosaurs of the Cretaceous Era. (p. 445)
—Dinosaurs of the Jurassic Era. (p. 445)
—Dinosaurs of the Triassic Era. (p. 445)
—Dinosaurs Stained Glass Coloring Book. (p. 445)
—Endangered Animals. (p. 526)
—Fairy World. (p. 564)
—Giants & Ogres Coloring Book. (p. 674)
—Glow-in-the-Dark Tattoos Butterflies. (p. 685)
—Invisible Prehistoric Animals Magic Picture Book. (p. 886)
—Learning about Swamp Animals. (p. 984)
—Let's Explore! Sea Animals. (p. 996)
—Lizards. (p. 1043)
—Lost in the Amazon: Hidden Pictures. (p. 1055)
—Manatees Coloring Book. (p. 1086)
—Prehistoric Man Coloring Book. (p. 1395)
—Rain Forest Wildlife. (p. 1434)
—Shiny Sharks Stickers. (p. 1567)
—Shiny Whales Stickers. (p. 1567)
—T-Rex Sticker Picture Puzzle. (p. 1694)
Sovak, Jan & Coloring Books Staff. Build a Poster Coloring Book—Dinosaurs. (p. 238)
Sovak, Jan, et al. Build a 3-D Poster Coloring Book — Fairies. (p. 237)
Sovak, Jean-Marc Superville, illus. see Chibbaro, Julie.
Sovern, Megan Jean. Meaning of Maggie. (p. 1117)
Sowa, Elizabeth. Hexagon . (p. 774)
Sowach, Rick. Critters, Flitters & Spitters: 24 Amazing Ohio Animal Tales. (p. 384)
Sowards, Ben. Asleep on the Hay: A Dust Bowl Christmas. Sowards, Ben, illus. (p. 106)
—Christmas Oranges. (p. 315)
—He Took My Lickin' for Me: A Classic Folk Tale. (p. 756)
Sowards, Ben, illus. see Robinson, Stephen Edward.
Sowards, Ben, illus. see Skye, Obert.
Sowards, Ben, illus. see Wright, Jason F.
Sowards, Ellen. Ellie Lou Leaves the Ditch. (p. 514)
Sowards, Penny. Naper & the Missing News Paper Caper. (p. 1229)
Sowash, Bradley, jt. auth. see Houston, Scott.
Sowash, Rick. Critters, Flitters & Spitters: 24 Amazing Ohio Animal Tales. (p. 384)
—Heroes of Ohio: 23 True Tales of Courage & Character. (p. 773)
—Heroes of Ohio Coloring Book. (p. 773)
—Ripsnorting Whoppers! A Book of Ohio Tall Tales. (p. 1474)
Sowchek, Ellen, tr. see Bessen, Luc.
Sowchek, Ellen, tr. see Besson, Luc.
Sowder, G. Wesley & Sowder, Joseph, told to. Hunter-Lee & the Toy Monster: Book One. (p. 828)
Sowder, Joseph, jt. told to see Sowder, G. Wesley.
Sowerby, Dale. Adventures of Baggy & Paxton: Trouble in Dawlish Warren. (p. 16)
Sowerby, Githa & Sowerby, Millicent. Cinderella. (p. 320)
Sowerby, Millicent, jt. illus. see Sowerby, Githa.
Sowers, Sherry. Tallulah & the Three Cowgirls. (p. 1704)
Sowers, Susan. Dotsie Bug Finds Her Purpose. (p. 472)
Sowles, Joann I. Martin. Darkness (the Brookehaven Vampires Series #2) The Brookehaven Vampires. (p. 409)
—Tainted Blood (the Brookehaven Vampires #3): The Brookehaven Vampires. Vol. 3 (p. 1696)
Sowunmi, Lakeysha. Apple Leaves. (p. 92)
So-Yong, Lee. Model (p. 1157)
—Model Na, Lauren, tr. from KOR. (p. 1157)
So-Young, Lee. Model (p. 1157)
—Model Min, Grace, tr. (p. 1157)
—Model So-Young, Lee, illus. (p. 1157)
So-young, Lee, creator. Model (p. 1157)
Sozapato, illus. see Williams, Ricardo.
Spachner, Karen D., illus. see Jackson, Kimberly.
Spackman, Jeff, illus. see Hubbell, Patricia & Hubbell.
Spada, Alberto, jt. auth. see Tagliaferri, Sarla.
Spadaccini, Cheryl, illus. see Seymour, Marysue.
Spady, Angela & Thomas Nelson Publishing Staff. Channing O'Banning & the Rainforest Rescue (p. 290)
—Channing o'Banning & the Turquoise Trail (p. 290)
Spady, Angie. Catie Conrad: Faith, Friendship & Fashion Disasters. Everidge, Channing, illus. (p. 280)
—Catie Conrad: How to Become the Most (un)Popular Girl in Jr. High. Everidge, Channing, illus. (p. 280)
Spaeth, Heidi. Cici Finds a Home. (p. 318)
Spafford, Suzy. Helping-Out Day? Hooray! Spafford, Suzy, illus. (p. 766)
—My Little Book of Prayers. (p. 1212)
—Witzy's Fall Collection. (p. 1942)
Spafford-Fitz, Karen. Dog Walker (p. 462)
Spagnol, Estelle Billon. Little Benguin. Spagnol, Estelle Billon, illus. (p. 1024)
Spagnol, Estelle Billon, illus. see Collet, Géraldine.
Spagnoli, Cathy. Nine-In-One:Grr! Grr! Horn, Nancy, illus. (p. 1256)
Spagnoli, Maria Eugenia, tr. see Sforza, Daniella, ed.
Spahn, Jerrold, illus. see White, Steve D.
Spahn, Jerrold, illus. see White, Steve.
Spaht-Gill, Janie. Gator's Out, Said the Trout. Reese, Bob, illus. (p. 658)
—Monster Stew. Reese, Bob, illus. (p. 1168)
—Socks. Lambson, Elizabeth, illus. (p. 1605)
Spain, Jack, Jr. Retracing Marco Polo: A Tale of Modern Travelers Who Locate & Follow Marco Polo's Route to China & Burma (p. 1464)
Spain, Susan. Deep Cut (p. 422)
Spain, Susan Rosson. Deep Cut (p. 422)
—Twelve Days of Christmas in Georgia. Dulemba, Elizabeth O., illus. (p. 1800)
Spalding, Amy. Ink Is Thicker Than Water. (p. 874)
—Kissing Ted Callahan (And Other Guys) (p. 962)
—Reece Malcolm List. (p. 1456)
Spalding, Andrea. Behind the Sorcerer's Cloak (p. 160)
—Dance Baby Dance (p. 402)
—Dance of the Stones (p. 402)
—Finders Keepers. (p. 587)
—Heart of the Hill (p. 759)
—Island of My Own. (p. 892)
—Most Beautiful Kite in the World Watts, Leslie Elizabeth, illus. (p. 1177)
—Sarah May & the New Red Dress. (p. 1514)
—Seal Song Milelli, Pascal, illus. (p. 1536)
—Solomon's Tree Wilson, Janet, illus. (p. 1608)
Spalding, Andrea & Scow, Alfred. Secret of the Dance Gait, Darlene, illus. (p. 1542)
Spalding, Andrea & Spalding, David. Silver Boulder. (p. 1576)
Spalding, Andrea & Spalding, David A. E. Klondike Ring. (p. 963)
Spalding, Arthur W. Pioneer Stories. (p. 1361)
Spalding, Bethany Brady, jt. auth. see Krishna, McArthur.
Spalding, Brenda M. Hayden's Garden. (p. 755)
—Just Batty. Teagle, Caitlyn, illus. (p. 938)
Spalding, David, jt. auth. see Spalding, Andrea.
Spalding, David A. E., jt. auth. see Spalding, Andrea.
Spalding, Frank. Catastrophic Climate Change & Global Warming. (p. 278)
—Genocide in Rwanda. (p. 661)
—Methamphetamine: The Dangers of Crystal Meth. (p. 1130)
—Nuclear Annihilation. (p. 1269)
—Plane Crash: True Stories of Survival. (p. 1366)
Spalding, Frank, jt. auth. see Norquist, Lara.
Spalding, Lee-Anne T. Go-Kart Racing. (p. 686)
Spalenka, Greg, illus. see Bateman, Teresa.
Spalinski, Amanda, illus. see Scalzo, Linda V.
Spanabel, H. A. Skyler & the Skunks. (p. 1587)
Spang, Janine, photos by see Ferone, Jen.
Spangenberg, Greg. Christmas Eve Victory. Lodwick, Sarah, illus. (p. 313)
—Churchy & the Light on Christmas Eve. Lodwick, Sarah, illus. (p. 318)
Spangenburg, Ray & Moser, Diane. Birth of Science: Ancient Times to 1699. (p. 192)
—Genetic Engineering. (p. 660)
—Science Frontiers, 1946-2001. (p. 1526)
Spangenburg, Ray & Moser, Diane Kit. Barbara Mcclintock: Pioneering Geneticist. (p. 137)
—Niels Bohr: Atomic Theorist. (p. 1251)
—Wernher Von Braun: Out of the Fire, the Stars. (p. 1875)
Spangenburg, Ray & Moser, Kit. Carl Sagan: A Biography (p. 269)
—Civil Liberties. (p. 324)
—Teen Fads: Fun, Foolish, or Fatal? (p. 1713)
—TV News: Can It Be Trusted? (p. 1799)
Spangenburg, Ray, et al. African Americans in Science, Math, & Invention. (p. 27)
—Alan Turing: Computing Genius & Wartime Code Breaker. (p. 33)
—Alfred Wegener: Puzzle of the Continents. (p. 37)
—Chien-Shiung Wu: The Elegance of Experiment. (p. 301)
—Makers of Modern Science (p. 1080)
—Richard Feynman: Quarks, Bombs, & Bongos. (p. 1469)
—Rita Levi-Montalcini: Discoverer of Nerve Growth Factor. (p. 1475)
—Robert Ballard. (p. 1478)
Spangler, Brie. We Both Read-The Mystery of Pirate's Point: Level 3. (p. 1866)
—We Both Read-the Mystery of Pirate's Point. (p. 1866)
Spangler, David. Mathematics Explorations. (p. 1108)
Spangler, Jon. Sky Princess. (p. 1587)
—Sky Princess Moves to the Land of Peaches. (p. 1587)
Spangler, Lois. Fort on Fourth Street Wald, Christina, illus. (p. 623)
Spangler, Paula Jeanne. Abigail's Christmas: Christmas Morn Reveals A Newborn. (p. 5)
—Abigail's Christmas ~ Christmas Morn Reveals A Newborn. (p. 5)
Spanish Educational Publishers Staff, tr. see Suen, Anastasia.
Spanish House Inc. Staff. Sp Little Bible Reader. (p. 1618)
Spanjer, Kendra, illus. see Oceanak, Karla.
Spann, Bill. Agents of Little Woods. (p. 29)
Spanos, Seva, retold by. Goldilocks & the Three Bears. (p. 696)
—Thumbelina's Song. (p. 1745)
Spanton, Elizabeth & Bright, Laren. Golden Voyages. (p. 695)
Spanyol, Jessica. Keith & His Super-Stunt Rally Racer. Spanyol, Jessica, illus. (p. 948)
—Little Neighbors on Sunnyside Street. Spanyol, Jessica, illus. (p. 1032)
Sparacia, Roseann. Angel & Jackie Meet Sweetheart: Angel Inspired. (p. 73)
—Angel Inspired. (p. 73)
—Ngel Inspirado / Angel Inspired. (p. 1250)
Sparhawk, Bud. Sam Boone: Front to Back. (p. 1506)
Sparkes, Ali. Alligator Action. Collins, Ross, illus. (p. 47)
—Anaconda Adventure. Collins, Ross, illus. (p. 66)
—Ant Attack. Collins, Ross, illus. (p. 88)
—Beetle Blast. Collins, Ross, illus. (p. 158)
—Chameleon Chaos. Collins, Ross, illus. (p. 289)
—Crane Fly Crash. Collins, Ross, illus. (p. 376)
—Fly Frenzy. Collins, Ross, illus. (p. 609)
—Frog Freakout. Collins, Ross, illus. (p. 640)
—Gecko Gladiator. Collins, Ross, illus. (p. 659)
—Grasshopper Glitch. Collins, Ross, illus. (p. 711)
—Lizard Loopy. Collins, Ross, illus. (p. 1042)
—Newt Nemesis. Collins, Ross, illus. (p. 1249)
—Spider Stampede. Collins, Ross, illus. (p. 1626)
—Turtle Terror. Collins, Ross, illus. (p. 1798)
Sparkes, Amy. Hodge the Hedgehog. (p. 787)
Sparkes, Wendy. Sunny Day. (p. 1677)
Sparkles. Awesome Opossum: Everything You Wanted to Know about Opossums! (p. 121)
—Itty Bitty Kitty: The Cutest Little Kitty in the World. (p. 900)
Sparklington, Madame & Gurney, Stella. Princess: A Glittering Guide for Young Ladies. Allsop, Sophie et al, illus. (p. 1402)
Sparkman, Winette. Tennessee Trailblazers. Laughbaum, Steve & Crutchfield, Jim, illus. (p. 1720)
SparkNotes Staff. Hamlet. Babra, Neil, illus. (p. 739)
—Literature. (p. 1023)
—Macbeth. Hoshine, Ken, illus. (p. 1068)
—Romeo & Juliet. Wiegle, Matt, illus. (p. 1486)
SparkNotes Staff, jt. auth. see Cisneros, Sandra.
SparkNotes Staff, jt. auth. see Hesse, Hermann.
SparkNotes Staff, jt. auth. see Shakespeare, William.
SparkNotes Staff, jt. auth. see Wilde, Oscar.
Sparks, Barry. Rick Riordan. (p. 1470)
Sparks, Beatrice. Annie's Baby: The Diary of Anonymous, a Pregnant Teenager. (p. 87)
—It Happened to Nancy: A True Story from Her Diary. (p. 894)
Sparks, Beatrice, ed. see Anonymous.
Sparks, Beverly, photos by see Schindel, John.
Sparks, Candi. Max Gets It! William, Graf, illus. (p. 1111)
—Of Course You Can! Educating Children about Money. Graf, William, illus. (p. 1279)
Sparks, Candi, et al. Nacho Money. Bill, Graf, illus. (p. 1227)
Sparks, David. Flat-Top Sam & the Junkyard Elephant. Sparks, David, illus. (p. 603)
Sparks, Emmet. Sanibel Island under Siege. (p. 1511)
Sparks, Evan. Freddy's Tale. (p. 633)
Sparks, Favre. Agnes, the Eggless Quail. (p. 30)
—Katie. (p. 944)
—Ugly Brown Cup. (p. 1808)
Sparks, Fredda. One October Night. (p. 1296)
Sparks, Janet. Do Mice Like Mushrooms? (p. 457)
Sparks, Joanna Susan. Marvelous! (p. 1099)
Sparks, Joanne. Mr. Squirrel. Sparks, Jolene, illus. (p. 1186)
Sparks, John. Game. (p. 654)
Sparks, Jolene, illus. see Sparks, Joanne.
Sparks, Jordan Rae. Dream Lagoon. (p. 483)
Sparks, Kerry. Frost Bites. (p. 644)
—Jen & the Frosted Friends: Book #2 of the Get Frosted Series. (p. 912)
Sparks, Lanny L. & Patterson, Blenna Rae Sparks. Sugar for Christmas. (p. 1673)
Sparks, Marilyn, jt. auth. see Aitchison, Jim.
Sparks, Matthew Landon. Little Hoss Adventures. (p. 1029)
Sparks, Megan. Boot Camp Blues (p. 213)
—Falling Hard (p. 567)
—Hell's Belles (p. 765)
—Hell's Belles/By Megan Sparks. (p. 765)

—In a Jam (p. 863)
Sparks, Melissa. Courageous Abe. (p. 372)
Sparks, Michal, illus. see TerKeurst, Lysa.
Sparks, Nicholas. True Believer. (p. 1791)
Sparks, Ruthilyn. I Worked Hard for You: (Sweet-Pea-Pie-Boy-Face) (p. 849)
Sparks, Sarah Constance. Omfg: Owning My Future Greatness. (p. 1288)
Sparks, Shanti. Honey & the Sunset. (p. 794)
Sparks, Stacey. Clean up, Everybody Lap Book. Patton, Julia, illus. (p. 330)
—Let's Get It Started. Evans, Antony, illus. (p. 997)
—Let's Get It Started Lap Book. Evans, Antony, illus. (p. 997)
Sparks Taylor, Chandra. Promise. (p. 1411)
Sparling, Bren M., illus. see Reintjes, Susan B.
Sparling, Eric. Tantramar. (p. 1705)
Sparling, Rebecca. Amendment XIII: Abolishing Slavery. Biscontini, Tracey Vasil, ed. (p. 58)
—Gerbils. (p. 666)
Sparrow, Giles. Astronauts. (p. 109)
—Book of Beasts. (p. 210)
—Destination Asteroids, Comets, & Meteors. (p. 430)
—Destination Jupiter. (p. 430)
—Destination Mars. (p. 430)
—Destination Mercury. (p. 430)
—Destination Saturn. (p. 430)
—Destination the Moon. (p. 430)
—Destination the Sun. (p. 430)
—Destination Uranus, Neptune, & Pluto. (p. 430)
—Destination Venus. (p. 430)
—Earth & the Inner Planets. (p. 495)
—Exploring the Universe. (p. 554)
—Nickel. (p. 1251)
—Night Sky. (p. 1254)
—Observing the Universe. (p. 1275)
—Outer Planets. (p. 1312)
—Planets & Moons. (p. 1368)
—Probing Deep Space. (p. 1408)
—Space Exploration. (p. 1619)
—Stars & Galaxies. (p. 1643)
—Sun & Stars. (p. 1676)
Sparrow, Keith, jt. auth. see Southgate, Anna.
Sparrow, Rebecca. Find Your Feet (the 8 Things I Wish I'D Known Before I Left High School) (p. 587)
Sparrow, Steve. Wooden Tiger. (p. 1949)
Sparshott, Francis. Naming of the Beasts (p. 1228)
Spartels, Stephanie, illus. see Rippin, Sally.
Spartz, Emerson & Schoen, Ben. Mugglenet. Com's Harry Potter Should Have Died: Controversial Views from the #1 Fan Site. (p. 1189)
Spat, Eszter. Yezidis. (p. 1971)
Spath, Carolyn E. W. Making a Budget. (p. 1080)
—Savvy Saving. (p. 1518)
Spatrisano, Kimberly, illus. see Novara, Joe.
Spatt, Leslie E. Sleeping Beauty: Behind the Scenes at the Ballet. (p. 1589)
Spatz, Caroline, ed. see Chandler, Samuel.
Spaulding & Namowitz. Earth Science. (p. 496)
Spaulding, Jeffrey. Career Building Through Digital Sampling & Remixing. (p. 266)
—Careers in Fingerprint & Trace Analysis. (p. 267)
—Matt Kenseth: NASCAR Driver. (p. 1109)
—Most Victorious Cars of NASCAR Racing. (p. 1177)
Spaulding, Jeffrey & Gisnash, Sahara. Career Building Through Digital Sampling & Remixing. (p. 266)
Spay, Anthony, illus. see Anderson, Dale & Goff, Elizabeth Hudson.
Spay, Anthony, illus. see Holland, Gini & O'Hern, Kerri.
Spay, Anthony, illus. see O'Hern, Kerri & Holland, Gini.
Spay, Anthony, illus. see Raatma, Lucia & O'Hern, Kerri.
Spaziano, Layna. Shane & Molly's Magical Journey (p. 1559)
Spaziante, Patrick. Look Out! It's Turtle Titan! (p. 1050)
—Meet Casey Jones. (p. 1120)
—Olivia Acts Out. (p. 1286)
—OLIVIA & Her Alien Brother. (p. 1286)
—OLIVIA & the Fashion Show. (p. 1286)
—OLIVIA & the Kite Party. (p. 1286)
—OLIVIA Learns to Surf. (p. 1286)
—Olivia Plans a Tea Party: From the Fancy Keepsake Collection. (p. 1287)
—OLIVIA Sells Cookies. (p. 1287)
—Sokka, the Sword Master. (p. 1606)
—Too Much Ooze! (p. 1767)
Spaziante, Patrick, illus. see Black, Allyson.
Spaziante, Patrick, illus. see David, Erica.
Spaziante, Patrick, illus. see Evans, Cordelia.
Spaziante, Patrick, illus. see Flynn, Ian & Sonic Scribes Staff.
Spaziante, Patrick, illus. see Gallo, Tina.
Spaziante, Patrick, illus. see Gerver, Jane E.
Spaziante, Patrick, illus. see Gilbert, Matthew.
Spaziante, Patrick, illus. see Golden Books Staff.
Spaziante, Patrick, illus. see Harvey, Alex.
Spaziante, Patrick, illus. see Lewman, David.
Spaziante, Patrick, illus. see Mason, Tom & Danko, Dan.
Spaziante, Patrick, illus. see Mattern, Joanne.
Spaziante, Patrick, illus. see Mayer, Kirsten.
Spaziante, Patrick, illus. see McDoogle, Farrah & Pulliam, Gabe.
Spaziante, Patrick, illus. see McDoogle, Farrah.
Spaziante, Patrick, illus. see Peterson, Scott.
Spaziante, Patrick, illus. see Random House Editors.
Spaziante, Patrick, illus. see Random House Staff & Webster, Christy.
Spaziante, Patrick, illus. see Random House Staff.
Spaziante, Patrick, illus. see Random House.
Spaziante, Patrick, illus. see Romay, Alexis, tr.
Spaziante, Patrick, illus. see Sambar, Syma.
Spaziante, Patrick, illus. see Shaw, Natalie.
Spaziante, Patrick, illus. see Shealy, Dennis.
Spaziante, Patrick, illus. see Shepherd, Jodie.
Spaziante, Patrick, illus. see Smith, Geof.
Spaziante, Patrick, illus. see Smith, James J. & James, Hollis.
Spaziante, Patrick, illus. see Teitelbaum, Michael.
Spaziante, Patrick, illus. see Testa, Maggie.
Spaziante, Patrick, illus. see Thomas, Jim.
Spaziante, Patrick, illus. see Wax, Wendy.
Spaziante, Patrick, illus. see Webster, Christy.
Spaziante, Patrick, jt. auth. see Flynn, Ian.
Spaziante, Patrick, et al. Sonic the Hedgehog Archives. (p. 1612)
Spaziante, Patrick Spaz, illus. see Bates, Ben, et al.
Spaziante, Patrick Spaz, illus. see Flynn, Ian & Sonic Scribes Staff.
Spaziante, Patrick Spaz, illus. see Gallagher, Mike, et al.
Spaziante, Patrick 'Spaz', illus. see Sonic Scribes Staff.
Spaziante, Patrick Spaz & Sonic Scribes Staff. Beginning. (p. 159)
—Sonic the Hedgehog Archives (p. 1612)
SPCK. I Can Join in Common Worship: A Children's Communion Book. (p. 836)
Speak, Steven. Skip & L, Guardian Angel. (p. 1585)
Speaker, Cathy. Road Home. Rosteck, Rachel, illus. (p. 1476)
Speaker-Yuan, Margaret. Avi. (p. 119)
Speaker-Yuan, Margaret & Yuan, Margaret Speaker. Phillip Pullman. (p. 1350)
Speakes, Leslie. Hygiene Mystery. (p. 831)
Speakman, David. Adventures of Sierra Rae: The Forgotten Map (p. 23)
Speakman, Peter, jt. auth. see Galvin, Michael M. B.
Spear, Barbara. Little Red's Neighborhood. (p. 1035)
—Three Little Puggies & the Huff'n Puff Hound. (p. 1743)
Spear, Kevin. David & the Giant. (p. 410)
—Itty-bitty Bible Activity Book, Easter. (p. 900)
—My Very Own Activity Pages: Spring 2004. (p. 1221)
—What's a Bathtub Doing in My Church? Fifteen Questions Kids Ask about Baptism, Salvation & Snorkels. Spear, Kevin, illus. (p. 1896)
Spear, Kevin, des. Favorite Bible Stories Puzzle Book. (p. 578)
Spear, Lisa D. Thunderburps. Baker, David, illus. (p. 1746)
Spear, Luke, jt. auth. see Goscinny, Rene.
Spear, Luke, tr. see De Gieter, Lucien.
Spear, Luke, tr. see Goscinny, René.
Spear, Luke, tr. see Groot, De.
Spear, Luke, tr. see Zidrou.
Speare, E., jt. auth. see Colvin, L.
Speare, Elizabeth George. Estanque de Mirlo. (p. 538)
—Sign of the Beaver. (p. 1574)
—Witch of Blackbird Pond. (p. 1941)
Speare, Janie. ABC's for Christ. (p. 4)
—Standing up & Standing Out: A Teen's Guide to Godly Characteristics. (p. 1639)
Speare, Jean. Candle for Christmas Blades, Ann, illus. (p. 261)
Spearing, Craig J., illus. see Hopkins, Jackie Mims.
Spearing, Darwin R. Roadside Geology of Louisiana. (p. 1477)
—Roadside Geology of Texas. (p. 1477)
Spearman, David. What Will I Grow up to Be? Spearman, Davidx & Spearman, Terry, illus. (p. 1895)
Spearman, Davidx, illus. see Spearman, David.
Spearman, Terry, illus. see Spearman, David.
Spears, Ashley, illus. see Clayton, Lisa.
Spears, Ashley E., illus. see Forester, MaMa Eagle.
Spears, Ashley E., illus. see Shams, K.
Spears, Ashley E., illus. see Stover, Anne Long.
Spears, Aubrey, jt. auth. see Peele, Chandra.
Spears, James, jt. auth. see Perritano, John.
Spears, James, jt. auth. see U. S. National Geographic Society Staff.
Spears, Jr. Derek's Dilemm. (p. 427)
Spears, Kat. Sway. (p. 1689)
Spears, Rick. Black Metal Volume 2. (p. 196)
—Black Metal Volume 3: Darkness Enthroned: Darkness Enthroned. (p. 196)
—Filler. (p. 586)
—Jennifer's Body. Seely, Tim et al, illus. (p. 913)
Spears, Rick, illus. see Halls, Kelly Milner.
Spears, Sheri, illus. see Schmitt, H. D.
Spears-Johnson, Dedra. Remember Who You Are. (p. 1459)
Speas, Joann, illus. see Leduc-Lenmark, MaryAlice.
Speceal, Edetha. Lost Egg & Other Stories. (p. 1055)
Specht, Jessica, illus. see Michaels, Joanna.
Specht, Judy. Aliens Please! Adventures of Lili, Zeke, & Bella. (p. 41)
—Appetizers, Please. (p. 92)
Specht, Roland H., et al. Deutsch Aktuell 3: Junge Leute. (p. 431)
Specialty Press & Goodstat, Alan. Put Yourself in Thier Shoes: Understanding Teenagers with Attention Deficit Hyperactivity Disorder. (p. 1420)
Specialty Publishing Company, illus. see Newmark, Rachel J.
Speck, Catherine. Painting Ghosts: Australian Women Artists in Wartime. (p. 1318)
Speck, Dave, ed. see Prince Rupert Writers' Group Staff.
Speck, Katie. Maybelle Goes to School. Tagyos, Paul Rátz de, illus. (p. 1113)
—Maybelle Goes to Tea. De Tagyos, Paul Rátz, illus. (p. 1113)
—Maybelle in the Soup / Maybelle Goes to Tea. Tagyos, Paul Rátz de, illus. (p. 1113)
Speck, Katie & De Tagyos, Paul Rátz. Maybelle & the Haunted Cupcake. (p. 1113)
Specter, Baron. All in a Night's Work. Kneupper, Setch, illus. (p. 44)
—Chasing Whales Aboard the Charles W. Morgan Evans, Dustin, illus. (p. 294)
—Dodging Danger on the Dartmouth Evans, Dustin, illus. (p. 460)
—Drama at Dungeon Rock: #6 Evans, Dustin, illus. (p. 480)
—How Not to Be Killed by a Zombie. Kneupper, Setch, illus. (p. 811)
—Lighthouse of Terror Evans, Dustin, illus. (p. 1015)
—Spooky Short Sands Shipwreck: #4 Evans, Dustin, illus. (p. 1631)
—Star Island Spirits: #5 Evans, Dustin, illus. (p. 1640)
—To Werewolf or Not to Werewolf. Kneupper, Setch, illus. (p. 1759)
—Vampires Are Not Your Friends. Kneupper, Setch, illus. (p. 1832)
Spector, Baron. Approaching the Undead. Kneupper, Setch, illus. (p. 93)
—Tracking Your Nightmare. Kneupper, Setch, illus. (p. 1775)
Spector, Diveda. Olivias Adventure with Frick & Frack. (p. 1287)
Spector, Joel, illus. see Gillooly, Eileen, ed.
Spector, Joel, illus. see Jones, Stan & Jones, Brenna.
Spector, Joel, illus. see Rovere, Amy.
Spector, Todd. How to Pee: Potty Training for Boys. Chung, Arree, illus. (p. 821)
Spectrum, compiled by. Spectrum Math & Language Arts Kit, Grade 3. (p. 1624)
Spectrum (Institute) Staff. Ready to Read. (p. 1448)
Spectrum Staff. Language Arts, Grade K. (p. 974)
—Ready for School. (p. 1447)
Spectrum Staff, ed. see Douglas, Vincent.
Spectrum Staff, jt. auth. see Carson-Dellosa Publishing Staff.
Spectrum Staff, et al. Awesome! Reader, Grades Preschool - 1. (p. 121)
Spedding, Steven. Boriscat & the Quest for the Golden Carp. (p. 214)
Spee, Gitte, illus. see Nilsson, Ulf.
Speechley, Greta. Arts & Crafts for Myths & Tales. (p. 104)
—Backyard Crafts. (p. 131)
—Bead Crafts. (p. 149)
—Birthday Crafts. (p. 192)
—Step-by-Step Clay Modelling. (p. 1647)
—Valentine Crafts. (p. 1830)
—World Crafts. (p. 1954)
Speechmark. Familiar Verbs: In Context. (p. 567)
—Heads & Tails. (p. 757)
—How Many? (p. 810)
—How's Teddy? (p. 824)
—Sequencing Sounds. (p. 1552)
—Shape & Size. (p. 1560)
—Sport & Leisure. (p. 1631)
—What Is It? (p. 1889)
—What's Wrong? (p. 1900)
Speed, Bryan W. Little Bent Cedar. Todd, Sheri, illus. (p. 1024)
Speed, Evelyn. Digger Rabbit & the First Easter. (p. 438)
Speed, Nakesha. Yucky Brother. (p. 1983)
Speed Shaskan, Trisha, jt. auth. see Loewen, Nancy.
Speelman, Helen, jt. auth. see Hardiman, Richard.
Speer, Beth. LuLa. (p. 1064)
Speer, Cindy Lynn. Unbalanced. (p. 1811)
Speer, Julie, illus. see Adams, Jesse.
Speer, Laura Y. Good Ground Seeds. (p. 698)
Speer, Scott. Battle Angel. (p. 145)
—Natural Born Angel: An Immortal City Novel. (p. 1235)
Spees, Melanie. Run for Hawk's Bay. (p. 1496)
Speicher, Diane Carty. Brighton One Star's Journey to Shine. Robinson, Lenord, illus. (p. 228)
Speicher, Helen Ross, jt. auth. see Borland, Kathryn Kilby.
Speicher, Helen Ross & Borland, Kathryn Kilby. Phillis Wheatley: Young Revolutionary Poet. Morrison, Cathy, illus. (p. 1351)
Speidel, Sandra, illus. see Nystrom, Carolyn.
Speidel, Sandra, illus. see Shriver, Maria.
Speigel, Beth, illus. see Pincus, Donna & Kaplow, Julie.
Speight, Peter. Wally the Whale. (p. 1855)
Speir, Nancy, illus. see Hubbell, Patricia.
Speir, Nancy, illus. see McGinty, Alice B.
Speirs, John. Best Halloween Hunt Ever. Speirs, John, illus. (p. 170)
Speirs, John, illus. see Capeci, Anne.
Speirs, John, illus. see Carmi, Rebecca.
Speirs, John, illus. see Ghigna, Charles.
Speirs, John, illus. see Murphy, Stuart J.
Speirs, John, illus. see Schreiber, Ann.
Speirs, John, illus. see Stamper, Judith Bauer.
Speirs, John, illus. see Stamper, Judith.
Speirs, John, tr. see Ghigna, Charles.
Spelbring, J. L. Perfection. (p. 1342)
Spellman, David & Lutz, Lisa. How to Negotiate Everything. Temairik, Jaime, illus. (p. 821)
Spellman, Frankie. Pinky & Bubs' Stinky Night Out. Spellman, Susan, illus. (p. 1360)
Spellman, Rhonda J., as told by. When I Was a Little Boy, by Jesus: Written for Children, Illustrated by Children: Experience the Life Jesus Lived When Jesus Was a Little Boy. (p. 1903)
Spellman, Susan, illus. see Hunter, Sara Hoagland.
Spellman, Susan, illus. see Seim, Donna Marie.
Spellman, Susan, illus. see Spellman, Frankie.
Spellman, Susan, illus. see Stiegemeyer, Julie.
Spellman, Susan, illus. see Towle, Barbara E.
Spellmeyer, William. Ick-N-Pog: The Encounter Book 2. (p. 851)
—Ick-n-Pog: How it all Began Book 1. (p. 851)
Spelman, Annette. Fountain That Uncle John Built: A True Story about Five Birds That Live in New Mexico. (p. 624)
Spelman, Cornelia. When I Feel Angry. Cote, Nancy, illus. (p. 1902)
—When I Feel Scared. Parkinson, Kathy, illus. (p. 1902)
Spelman, Cornelia Maude. When I Feel Good about Myself. Parkinson, Kathy, illus. (p. 1902)
—When I Feel Jealous. Parkinson, Kathy, illus. (p. 1902)
—When I Feel Scared. Parkinson, Kathy, illus. (p. 1902)
—When I Feel Worried. Parkinson, Kathy, illus. (p. 1902)
—When I Miss You. Parkinson, Kathy, illus. (p. 1903)
—Your Body Belongs to You Weidner, Teri, illus. (p. 1980)
Spelman, Cornelia Maude, jt. auth. see Maude Spelman, Cornelia.
Spelman, Lucy H., jt. auth. see U. S. National Geographic Society Staff.
Speltz, Ann. Year My Mother Was Bald. Sternberg, Kate, illus. (p. 1969)
Spelvin, Justin. Blue's Big Parade! Chernichaw, Ian, illus. (p. 204)
—Deep-Sea Countdown. McGee, Warner, illus. (p. 423)
—Riding the Range. (p. 1471)
Spena, Jud. Echoes in the Valley. (p. 502)
Spence, Ann. Elmo's Play Day. (p. 516)
Spence, Bob, illus. see Stalker, Aileen.
Spence, Christine, compiled by. Christmas Programs for Children. (p. 315)
Spence, Cliff. Noah C. (p. 1261)
Spence, Craig. Einstein Dog. Tucker, Diane, ed. (p. 507)
—Josh & the Magic Vial. (p. 926)
Spence, David. Crime & Punishment. (p. 382)
—Gauguin: Huida al Eden. (p. 658)
—Gauguin. (p. 658)
—Impressionists: Monet, Cezanne, Renoir, Degas. (p. 862)
—Manet. (p. 1087)
—Michelangelo. (p. 1135)
—Monet: Impresionismo. (p. 1163)
—Monet. (p. 1163)
—Picasso: Una Revolucion en el Arte. (p. 1354)
—Picasso. (p. 1354)
—Pirates. (p. 1363)
—Rembrandt. (p. 1459)
—Renoir: Color y Naturaleza. (p. 1460)
—Renoir. (p. 1460)
—Van Gogh. (p. 1833)
—Vincent Van Gogh: Arte y Emocion. (p. 1843)
Spence, David & Spence, Susan. History of Shipwrecks. (p. 784)
Spence, David & Ticktock Media, Ltd. Staff. Michelangelo. (p. 1135)
—Picasso. (p. 1354)
Spence, Eleanor. Jamberoo Road. (p. 906)
—Switherby Pilgrims: A Tale of the Australian Bush. (p. 1692)
Spence, Jim, illus. see Pingry, Patricia A.
Spence, Kelly. Emma Stone. (p. 520)
Spence, Kenlyn Foster. Astronaut Noodle on Planet Velocity. (p. 109)
Spence, Lyndsylee. My Neighbour Peejay. (p. 1216)
Spence, Nancy & Connell, Jane. From BC to PC: A Guide for Using Computers with Children in Christian Education. (p. 642)
Spence, Paul B. Red Shift Equipment Guide. (p. 1455)
Spence, Robert, jt. auth. see Evans, Charlene.
Spence, Stephen Mark. African Knights. (p. 27)
Spence, Susan, jt. auth. see Spence, David.
Spence, Thomas, illus. see Donahue, Jill Urban.
Spence, Thomas, illus. see Slade, Suzanne.
Spence, Tom. Tough Day at the Plate. (p. 1772)
Spenceley, Angela. Virgin Islands Coloring Book. (p. 1844)
Spenceley, Angela, compiled by. Pirate Coloring & Sticker Book: Your Complete Guide to Famous Pirates. (p. 1362)
Spenceley, Annabel. Beauty & the Beast. (p. 154)
—Faber Book of Nursery Rhymes. (p. 559)
Spenceley, Annabel, illus. see Amos, Janine.
Spenceley, Annabel, illus. see Elliot, Rachel.
Spenceley, Annabel, illus. see Heddle, Rebecca.
Spenceley, Annabel, illus. see Needham, Kate.
Spenceley, Annabel, illus. see Perrault, Charles.
Spenceley, Annabel, illus. see Piper, Sophie.
Spenceley, Annabel, illus. see Taylor, Kenneth N.
Spenceley, Annabel, illus. see Unwin, Mike & Woodward, Kate.
Spenceley, Annabel, jt. auth. see Amos, Janine.
Spenceley, Annabel, jt. auth. see Amos, Janine.
Spencer, Adam. Green Zone Kicker. (p. 722)
Spencer, Alison, illus. see Stewart, Maddie.
Spencer, Alison Hill. Bird Color (p. 190)
—Bird Count (p. 190)
Spencer, Anne & Lee, Jordan. I Get Panic Attacks. Now What? (p. 838)
Spencer, Betty. Life Is Fragile: One Girl's Story of the Bath School Disaster. Gallinger, Jared, illus. (p. 1011)
Spencer, Carolyn Royer, jt. auth. see Davis, Regina.
Spencer, Chip, illus. see Hays, Phillip.
Spencer, Eve. Stories of America (p. 1654)
Spencer, Frances Mcneil. Dee & the Dog: Home at Last. (p. 422)
Spencer, Hannah. With All Best Wishes, Mrs Butterbean. (p. 1942)
Spencer, Henry Cecil, et al. Basic Technical Drawing. (p. 142)
Spencer, James. Sally Small & the Judith-Situation. (p. 1505)
Spencer, James N. Physical Chemistry: A Guided Inquiry - Thermodynamics. (p. 1353)
Spencer, Jamie. Train to Maine. Reed, Rebecca, illus. (p. 1777)
Spencer, Janet. Montana Trivia. (p. 1170)
Spencer, Jean W. Careers & Opportunities: Great Career Opportunities (p. 267)
—Careers Inside the World of Technology. (p. 268)
Spencer, Jeffrey. Building for the Ages: Omaha's Architectural Landmarks. (p. 239)
Spencer, John Nicholas. Sleigh Ride with Santa. Spencer, Kay Kincannon, illus. (p. 1590)
Spencer, Karl. Money Guide: Basic Money How-to for Teenagers & Young Adults: Personal Finance for Teens & Generation Debt. (p. 1164)
Spencer, Katherine. More Than Friends: A Saving Grace Novel. (p. 1175)
—Saving Grace. (p. 1517)
Spencer, Kathlynn, jt. auth. see Spencer, Russell.
Spencer, Kay Kincannon, illus. see Spencer, John Nicholas.
Spencer, Lauren. Assassination of John F. Kennedy. (p. 107)
—Everything You Need to Know about Falling in Love. (p. 545)
—Hank Aaron. (p. 742)
—Iran: A Primary Source Cultural Guide. (p. 886)
—Step-by-Step Guide to Informative Writing. (p. 1647)
Spencer, Lauren, jt. auth. see Beutel, Roger.
Spencer, Lauren, jt. auth. see Cook, Jaye E.
Spencer, Lauren, jt. auth. see Hubbard, Frances K.
Spencer, Lauren, jt. auth. see McGuinness, Denis E.
Spencer, Lauren, jt. auth. see Nolan, Chris.
Spencer, Leslie. Social Stories for Children with Disabilities (p. 1604)
—Social Stories for Children with Disabilities. (p. 1604)
Spencer, Linda. War at Home: Japan During World War II. (p. 1857)

Spencer, Liv. Love Bites: The Unofficial Saga of Twilight. (p. 1059)
—Miranda Cosgrove & iCarly Spectacular! Unofficial & Unstoppable. (p. 1149)
—Taylor Swift: Every Day Is a Fairytale - The Unofficial Story. (p. 1708)
Spencer, Mariko Ando, illus. see Swanson, Diane.
Spencer, Mary A. Daddy's Girl. (p. 399)
Spencer, Mignon. I'm Living My Dream: An inspirational Rhyme for all Ages in English & Spanish. Mack, Travis, illus. (p. 859)
Spencer, Monica, illus. see Kline, Karen E.
Spencer, Nick. Asymmetry. Kano & Olivetti, Ariel, illus. (p. 110)
—Morning Glories (p. 1175)
—Palmer Addley Is Dead. Kitson, Barry, illus. (p. 1320)
Spencer, Nick & Hickman, Jonathan. Avengers - Prelude to Infinity Caselli, Stefano, illus. (p. 118)
Spencer, Nigel, tr. see Michel, Pauline.
Spencer, Octavia, jt. auth. see Rhodes, O. K.
Spencer, Pamela. Timeless Treasures. (p. 1754)
Spencer, Peter A. Musicals: The Guide to Amateur Production. (p. 1194)
Spencer, Rose-Maree. What Was That. (p. 1895)
Spencer, Russell & Spencer, Kathlynn. California's Highway SR 1 Windshield Adventures: From Santa Monica to Monterey Peninsula (p. 253)
Spencer, Trevor, illus. see Burnham, Molly B.
Spencer-Johnson, Laura A. Geoville School & the New Student. (p. 666)
Spencer-Lahman, Vickie K. Biscuit Steals a Fish: The Adventures of Sailor the Farm Dog. (p. 193)
Spencer-Longhurst, Paul. Moonrise over Europe: J. C. Dahl & Romantic Landscape. (p. 1173)
Spencer-Wood, Sophie. Family: Photographers Photograph Their Families. (p. 568)
Spender, Nick, illus. see Jeffrey, Gary.
Spender, Nick, illus. see Shone, Rob.
Spender, Nick, jt. auth. see Shone, Rob.
Spender, Nik, illus. see Jeffrey, Gary & Shone, Rob.
Spender, Nik, illus. see Jeffrey, Gary.
Spender, Nik, illus. see Shone, Rob.
Spender, Nik, illus. see West, David.
Spender, Nik, jt. illus. see Jeffrey, Gary.
Spendlove, Joanna. Adventures of Gooky & Spinnet: The Universe, Our Wonderland. (p. 18)
Spendlove, Owen. Stanley Brambles & the Pirate's Treasure. (p. 1639)
Spengler, Kenneth, illus. see Fredericks, Anthony D.
Spengler, Kenneth, illus. see Ghigna, Charles.
Spengler, Kenneth, illus. see Napoli, Donna Jo & Johnston, Shelagh.
Spengler, Kenneth, illus. see Stephenson, Midji.
Spengler, Kenneth, tr. see Napoli, Donna Jo & Johnston, Shelagh.
Spengler, Kenneth J., illus. see Fredericks, Anthony D.
Spengler, Kenneth J., illus. see Sudduth, Brent H.
Spengler, Kenneth J., illus. see Ulmer, Wendy K.
Spengler, Kenneth J., illus. see Ward, Jennifer.
Spengler, Kremena T. Caring for Your Guinea Pig (p. 269)
—Chile. (p. 305)
—Dominican Republic: A Question & Answer Book (p. 465)
—France: A Question & Answer Book (p. 627)
—Germany: A Question & Answer Book (p. 666)
—Hieroglyphs (p. 777)
—Illustrated Timeline of Inventions & Inventors Morgan, Rick, illus. (p. 858)
—Illustrated Timeline of Transportation Doty, Eldon, illus. (p. 858)
—Louis Pasteur. (p. 1058)
—Mummies (p. 1190)
—Pyramids (p. 1421)
—South Africa: A Question & Answer Book (p. 1616)
—Spain: A Question & Answer Book (p. 1620)
Spengler, Kremena T. & Capstone Press Editors. Greece: A Question & Answer Book (p. 720)
Spengler, Margaret. One, Two, Buckle My Shoe. (p. 1297)
Spengler, Margaret, illus. see Buzzeo, Toni.
Spengler, Margaret, illus. see Hawksley, Gerald.
Spengler, Margaret, illus. see Tekavec, Heather.
Spengler, Margaret, illus. see Wilson, Karma.
Spengler, Margaret, tr. see Buzzeo, Toni.
Spengler, Margaret L., illus. see Greene, Rhonda Gowler.
Spengler, Ray. Always Yearning. (p. 51)
Spens, Michael, et al. Modern Landscape. (p. 1158)
Spenser & Brooks, Melanie. Spenser Via a el Paso. Jacobsen, Amie, illus. (p. 1625)
Spenser & Mom. Spenser Goes to Portland. Jacobsen, Amie, illus. (p. 1625)
Spenser and Mom Staff, jt. auth. see Brooks, Melanie.
Spensley, Joe. Home Thoughts from A Broader Perspective. (p. 793)
Sper, Devin. Future of Israel. (p. 651)
Sper, Emily. Kids' Fun Book of Jewish Time. Sper, Emily, illus. (p. 953)
Spera, Carole. Oh My Goodness! (p. 1281)
Spera, Massimiliano, tr. see Crouch, Adele.
Sperber, Dan, jt. ed. see Noveck, Ira A.
Sperber, Susie. 'Geee' Giggles My Grammy Who Glides down Giraffes. (p. 659)
Speregen, Devra Newberger. Girl Style: Get Your Glam On. (p. 679)
—Got Class? A GF's Guide to School Style. (p. 703)
—Ilan Ramon: Jewish Star. (p. 856)
—Party Girl: How to Throw a Fab Fest. Tallardy, Laura, illus. (p. 1326)
Speregen, Devra Newberger, jt. auth. see Running Press Staff.
Speregen, Devra Newberger & Running Press Staff. Snow Day! Vincent, Benjamin & DePew, Robert, illus. (p. 1598)
Spergel, Heather. Cloud City: A Child's Journey Through Bereavement. Stylou, Georgia, illus. (p. 334)
—Free to Be Gluten Free! Martino, Anita, illus. (p. 634)
—Gabi Babaroni on Broadway. Vene, Alessandro, illus. (p. 652)
—NiNi Spergelini: Guitar-Ific! Perla, Brian, illus. (p. 1256)
Sperling, Alia, illus. see Kabbani, Shaykh Muhammad & Kabbani, Muhammad Hisham.
Sperling, Karima, illus. see Kabbani, Shaykh Muhammad & Kabbani, Muhammad Hisham.
Sperling, Karima, jt. auth. see Adil, Hajjah Amina.
Sperling, S. David, illus. see Steinbock, Steven E.
Sperling, Thomas. Chicken Licken. (p. 300)
—Little Red Hen. (p. 1034)
—Little Red Riding Hood. (p. 1035)
—Stone Cheese. (p. 1652)
—Three Little Pigs. (p. 1743)
Sperling, Thomas, illus. see Asbjornsen, Peter Christen.
Sperling, Thomas, illus. see DeRubertis, Barbara.
Sperling, Thomas, illus. see deRubertis, Barbara.
Sperling, Thomas, illus. see DeRubertis, Barbara.
Sperling, Tom, illus. see Allen, Kathy.
Sperling, Vatsala. Ganga: The River That Flows from Heaven to Earth. Johari, Harish & Weltevrede, Pieter, illus. (p. 655)
—Hanuman's Journey to the Medicine Mountain. Johari, Sandeep, illus. (p. 744)
—Karna: The Greatest Archer in the World. Johari, Sandeep, illus. (p. 944)
—Magical Adventures of Krishna: How a Mischief Maker Saved the World. Weltevrede, Pieter, illus. (p. 1074)
—Ram the Demon Slayer. Weltevrede, Pieter, illus. (p. 1437)
Sperling, Vatsala, jt. auth. see Johari, Harish.
Spero, Maria, jt. auth. see Spero, Mitch.
Spero, Mitch & Spero, Maria. Florida the Turtle: Who Thinks He's a Dog Finds His Feelings. (p. 607)
Spero, Yechiel. Touched by a Story: For Children. Schonfeld, Shaya, illus. (p. 1772)
Sperounis, Kathy. J. A. M. S. & the Case of the Missing Tennessee Walking Horse. McRae, Angel, illus. (p. 901)
Sperring, Mark. Dino-Baby. Lloyd, Sam, illus. (p. 441)
—How Many Sleeps 'til Christmas? Braun, Sebastein, illus. (p. 811)
—Mabel & Me - Best of Friends. Warburton, Sarah, illus. (p. 1067)
—Max & the Won't Go to Bed Show. Warburton, Sarah, illus. (p. 1110)
—Shape of My Heart. Paterson, Alys, illus. (p. 1560)
—Sunflower Sword. Latimer, Miriam, illus. (p. 1676)
Sperry, Amanda. Let's Be Friends. Krone, Mike, illus. (p. 994)
Sperry, Armstrong. Call It Courage. (p. 254)
—Wagons Westward: The Old Trail to Santa Fe. Sperry, Armstrong, illus. (p. 1852)
Sperry, Brendan. Captain Dino & the Revenge of Roberto. (p. 264)
Sperry, John Lamont. Where Is Home? (p. 1908)
Speth, Brandilyn, illus. see Garner, Linda.
Spetter, Jung-Hee, illus. see Kaufmann, Nancy.
Spetzler, Carl. Goldilocks Meets Desidero. Meyers, Mark, illus. (p. 696)
Speyer, Silvia. Baldo's Awesome Adventures: A Balloon's Search for a Friend. (p. 134)
Spezialy, Millie. Binky's Trophy. (p. 188)
Spicer, Bridgett, illus. see Scheber, George.
Spicer, Candace. Hopper & the Happy Houses. (p. 797)
Spicer, Carolyn, jt. auth. see Swanberg, Arvon.
Spicer, Lin. Faerie Baby. (p. 562)
Spicer, Maggee, jt. auth. see Thompson, Richard.
Spickert, Diane Nelson. Earthsteps: A Rock's Journey Through Time. Wallace, Marianne D., illus. (p. 498)
Spickett, D. M. Adventures of Sarah the Seahorse (p. 22)
Spickler, Valerie. God Is for Every Day(r) - Stories & Songs for Children: Teach-a-Child Book/CD/Midi Set. (p. 689)
Spicuzza, Jeanne Marie. Beautiful Terrible & True: Writings by Jeanne Marie Spicuzza. (p. 154)
Spiegel, Al. Ideas. Mortimer, Mitch, illus. (p. 852)
Spiegel, Beth, illus. see Bottner, Barbara.
Spiegel, Beth, illus. see Bunting, Eve.
Spiegel, Beth, illus. see Rodman, Mary Ann.
Spiegel, Beth, tr. see Bottner, Barbara.
Spiegelman, Art. Jack & the Box. (p. 902)
—Jack & the Box. Hayes, Geoffrey, illus. (p. 902)
—Sin la Sombra de las Torres. Ferrer, Maria, tr. (p. 1578)
Spiegelman, Art & Mouly, Françoise. It Was a Dark & Silly Night... Spiegelman, Art & Mouly, Françoise, illus. (p. 894)
Spiegelman, Art & Mouly, Françoise, eds. Toon Treasury of Classic Children's Comics. (p. 1767)
Spiegelman, Nadja. Lost in NYC: A Subway Adventure. Sánchez, Sergio García, illus. (p. 1055)
—Zig & Wikki in Something Ate My Homework. (p. 1986)
—Zig & Wikki in Something Ate My Homework. Mouly, Francoise, ed. (p. 1986)
—Zig & Wikki in the Cow. (p. 1986)
Spiegelman, Nadja & Loeffler, Trade. Zig & Wikki in Something Ate My Homework. (p. 1986)
Spieker, Diana. Alphabetica: Odes to the Alphabet. Skehan, Krista, illus. (p. 50)
Spieler, Leah. ThumBle Character Kit. Spieler, Leah, illus. (p. 1745)
Spieler, Leah, ed. see Wiens, Patti.
Spieler, Marlena. Grilled Cheese: 50 Recipes to Make You Melt. Giblin, Sheri, photos by. (p. 724)
—Macaroni & Cheese. Barnhurst, Noel, photos by. (p. 1067)
Spieler, Marlena, jt. auth. see Ballingall, Peter.
Spieler, Marlena, jt. auth. see Douglas, Paul.
Spieler, Marlena & Oxmoor House Staff. Paris: Authentic Recipes Celebrating the Foods of the World. Hall, Jean-Blaise, photos by. (p. 1324)
Spielman, Gloria. Marcel Marceau: Master of Mime. Gauthier, Manon, illus. (p. 1091)
Spielman, Howard, jt. auth. see Fine, Arnold.
Spielman, Madison. Build It: Skyscrapers (p. 238)
—Build It: Skyscrapers. (p. 238)
—Craft It: Hand-Blown Glass (p. 375)
—Craft It: Hand-Blown Glass. (p. 375)
—Make It: Chocolate. (p. 1079)
—Make It - Chocolate. (p. 1079)
Spielvogel, Jackson J. Glencoe World History. (p. 683)
Spielvogel, Jackson J. & McGraw-Hill Editors. Glencoe World History. (p. 683)
Spielvogel, Jackson J. & McGraw-Hill Education Staff. Journey Across Time: The Early Ages. (p. 927)
—World History: Modern Times. (p. 1955)
Spielvogel, Jackson J. & McGraw-Hill Staff. World History: Journey Across Time: The Early Ages, Course 2 (p. 1955)
Spielvogel, Jackson J., et al. Glencoe World History: Modern Times. (p. 683)
—Journey Across Time: The Early Ages. (p. 927)
—Journey Across Time. (p. 927)
—World History Journey Across Time: The Early Ages, Course 1. (p. 1955)
Spier, Jo, illus. see Malkus, Alida Sims.
Spier, Peter. Fox Went Out on a Chilly Night. (p. 626)
—Star-Spangled Banner. (p. 1641)
Spier, Peter E. Book of Jonah. (p. 211)
Spiero, Simon. Delights of Reading: Written for My Grandchildren. (p. 425)
Spies, Karen Bornemann. Buffalo Bill Cody: Legend of the Wild West. (p. 235)
—Heroes in Greek Mythology Rock! Bock, William Sauts, illus. (p. 773)
—Mythology of the Iliad & the Odyssey. (p. 1227)
—Pan Am Flight 103: Terrorism over Lockerbie. (p. 1320)
Spiewak, Chet. Ornament's Tale. (p. 1304)
—Vinney the Bug Man: The Journey Begins. (p. 1843)
Spika, Jana. Locket & the Mask. (p. 1045)
Spiker, Sue Ann, illus. see Chambers, Melinda.
Spiker, Sue Ann Maxwell, illus. see Hedrick, Helen Groves.
Spiker, Ted, jt. auth. see Fernstrom, Madelyn H.
Spiker, Ted, jt. auth. see Zinczenko, David.
Spikes, James L. Adventures of LemonHead & Mudd Duck: What to do if Someone Tries to Grab You. (p. 19)
—Taffey Pop Kids Presents the Adventures of Lemmon Head & Mudd Duck: What to Do if Someone Tries to Grab YOU!!! Spikes, Leon, Jr., illus. (p. 1695)
Spikes, Leon, Jr., illus. see Spikes, James L.
Spillane, Lisa. Six Healing Sounds with Lisa & Ted: Qigong for Children. Spillane, Lisa, illus. (p. 1582)
—Smiling Heart Meditations with Lisa & Ted (And Bingo) (p. 1594)
Spillane, Michael. Anthony's Nightmare. (p. 89)
Spillebeen, Geert. Kipling's Choice. Edelstein, Terese, tr. (p. 961)
Spiller, John, et al. United States, 1763-2001. (p. 1819)
Spiller, Michael, illus. see Milligan, Domino.
Spiller, Yuko, tr. see Crouch, Adele.
Spilling, Jo-Ann, jt. auth. see Hestler, Anna.
Spilling, Jo-Ann, jt. auth. see Seffal, Rabah.
Spilling, Jo-Ann, jt. auth. see Spilling, Michael.
Spilling, Michael. Estonia. (p. 538)
Spilling, Michael, jt. auth. see Brown, Roslind Varghese.
Spilling, Michael, jt. auth. see Levy, Patricia.
Spilling, Michael, jt. auth. see McGaffey, Leta.
Spilling, Michael, jt. auth. see O'Shea, Maria.
Spilling, Michael, jt. auth. see Sheehan, Sean.
Spilling, Michael, jt. auth. see Sioras, Efstathia.
Spilling, Michael & Lark, Liz. Yoga Step-by-Step. (p. 1972)
Spilling, Michael & Spilling, Jo-Ann. Cyprus. (p. 397)
Spilling, Michael & Wong, Winnie. Georgia. (p. 665)
Spillman, Ken, jt. auth. see Doust, Jon.
Spilsbury, Louise. Animal Bodies: Extreme Anatomies. (p. 76)
—Baboon (p. 124)
—Backyard Bugs. (p. 131)
—Bean. (p. 150)
—Boa Constrictor. (p. 205)
—Butterfly. (p. 247)
—Caterpillar Capers. (p. 279)
—Clean & Healthy. (p. 330)
—Coastal Treasure Hunter. (p. 336)
—Coyote (p. 374)
—Creeping Killers: Extreme Plants. (p. 381)
—Cristales. (p. 383)
—Dams & Hydropower. (p. 401)
—Day in the Life: Grassland Animals Set (p. 413)
—Dolphin (p. 464)
—Eat or Be Eaten: Extreme Food Chains. (p. 501)
—Environment (p. 531)
—Family & Friends. (p. 568)
—Flight (p. 604)
—Fósiles. (p. 623)
—Foxes (p. 626)
—Frog. (p. 639)
—Fruits (p. 645)
—Garbage Can. Hanna, Gary, illus. (p. 655)
—Get Active! (p. 667)
—Harmful Substances. (p. 749)
—Head-to-Toe Body Questions. (p. 756)
—How Bees Make Honey (p. 805)
—How Community Gardens Work. (p. 806)
—How to Survive in the Arctic & Antarctica. (p. 822)
—How to Survive in the Ocean. (p. 822)
—How to Survive on a Mountain. (p. 822)
—Hyena (p. 831)
—Ice Age Animals (p. 850)
—Igloos & Inuit Life (p. 856)
—Industrialization & Empire, 1783 to 1914. (p. 873)
—Jellyfish (p. 912)
—Kill or Die: Extreme Life Cycles. (p. 956)
—Kori Bustard (p. 967)
—Lion. (p. 1019)
—Mapping (p. 1090)
—Minerales. (p. 1146)
—Mob of Meerkats: And Other Mammal Groups (p. 1157)
—Natural Resources (p. 1235)
—Octopus (p. 1278)
—Octopus Set. (p. 1278)
—One Egg. (p. 1294)
—Ostrich (p. 1306)
—Polar Bear: Killer King of the Arctic. (p. 1378)
—Polar Bear. (p. 1378)
—Pond. Hanna, Gary, illus. (p. 1382)
—Projects with Recycling & Reusing. (p. 1411)
—Projects with Space. (p. 1411)
—Protecting & Caring for Children (p. 1412)
—Respiration & Circulation. (p. 1463)
—Same-Sex Marriage. (p. 1507)
—Say No to Bullying. (p. 1518)
—Science of Avalanches. (p. 1527)
—Sea Otters (p. 1535)
—Sea Turtle (p. 1535)
—Seal (p. 1536)
—Shark (p. 1561)
—Sight (p. 1574)
—Skeleton & Muscles. (p. 1584)
—Suelo. (p. 1672)
—Superstar Birds. (p. 1684)
—Superstar Mammals. (p. 1684)
—Superstar Plants. (p. 1684)
—Superstar Reptiles. (p. 1684)
—Survival of the Fittest: Extreme Adaptations. (p. 1686)
—Tapestries & Textiles. (p. 1705)
—Threats to Our Water Supply. (p. 1741)
—Tide Pool. Hanna, Gary, illus. (p. 1747)
—True Cost of Fashion. (p. 1792)
—Walruses (p. 1855)
—Waste & Recycling Challenges. (p. 1860)
—Wildebeest (p. 1931)
—World Cultures (p. 1954)
—World Wars & Globalization, 1914 to 2010. (p. 1959)
—Zoologists in the Field (p. 1989)
Spilsbury, Louise, jt. auth. see Spilsbury, Richard.
Spilsbury, Louise, jt. auth. see Whitehouse, Patricia.
Spilsbury, Louise A., jt. auth. see Spilsbury, Richard.
Spilsbury, Louise & Heinemann Library Staff. Environment (p. 532)
—Mapping (p. 1090)
—Natural Resources (p. 1235)
—World Cultures (p. 1954)
Spilsbury, Louise & Spilsbury, Richard. Airplane (p. 31)
—Arctic Ocean. (p. 96)
—Atlantic Ocean. (p. 112)
—Awesome Forces of Nature (p. 121)
—Bengal Tiger (p. 164)
—Cells (p. 286)
—Chimpanzee Troops. (p. 306)
—Classifying Amphibians (p. 328)
—Classifying Fish (p. 328)
—Crystals (p. 387)
—Electricity (p. 509)
—Energy (p. 528)
—Exploring Light. (p. 552)
—Exploring Sound (p. 553)
—Florida Manatee (p. 607)
—Fly to Mars! Forces in Space. (p. 609)
—Food Chains & Webs: From Producers to Decomposers (p. 613)
—Fossils (p. 624)
—Houses & Homes. (p. 804)
—Howling Hurricanes (p. 824)
—Hurricanes & Tornadoes in Action. (p. 830)
—Indian Ocean. (p. 871)
—Life Processes (p. 1012)
—Light & Dark. (p. 1014)
—Light & Sound (p. 1014)
—Making Noise!: Making Sounds (p. 1082)
—Materials (p. 1104)
—Microorganisms (p. 1136)
—Minerals (p. 1146)
—Nature Walk in the City (p. 1236)
—Nature Walk in the Woods (p. 1236)
—Nature Walk on the Beach (p. 1236)
—Nature Walk on the Farm (p. 1236)
—Nature Walks (p. 1236)
—Oceans of the World. (p. 1277)
—Pacific Ocean. (p. 1317)
—Plant Classification (p. 1369)
—Raging Floods (p. 1433)
—Reflecting Light. (p. 1456)
—Robots in Industry. (p. 1481)
—Robots in Law Enforcement. (p. 1481)
—Robots in Medicine. (p. 1481)
—Robots in Space. (p. 1481)
—Robots in the Military. (p. 1481)
—Robots Underwater. (p. 1481)
—Shadows. (p. 1558)
—Shattering Earthquakes (p. 1563)
—Shhh! Listen!: Hearing Sounds HL Studios, H. L., illus. (p. 1566)
—Soil (p. 1606)
—Solids & Liquids. (p. 1608)
—Solids, Liquids, & Gases (p. 1608)
—Sources of Light. (p. 1616)
—Southern Ocean. (p. 1617)
—Submarine (p. 1671)
—Sweeping Tsunamis (p. 1689)
—Telephone (p. 1716)
—Terrifying Tornadoes (p. 1722)
—Tsunamis in Action. (p. 1795)
—Turn It up!; Turn It down!: Volume HL Studios Staff, illus. (p. 1797)
—Violent Volcanoes (p. 1843)
—Why Can't I Hear That?: Pitch & Frequency HL Studios Staff, illus. (p. 1923)
Spilsbury, Louise, et al. Classifying Amphibians (p. 328)
—Classifying Fish (p. 328)
—Essential Physical Science (p. 537)
—Feel the Force. (p. 580)
Spilsbury, Richard. Adaptation & Survival. (p. 11)
—Air & Water Pressure (p. 31)
—Animal Variation & Classification. (p. 80)
—Ask an Expert: Climate Change. (p. 106)
—Bones Speak! Solving Crimes from the Past. (p. 209)
—Brain & Nervous System. (p. 221)
—Burrow. Hanna, Gary, illus. (p. 244)
—Cave. Hanna, Gary, illus. (p. 282)
—Cells, Tissues, & Organs. (p. 286)
—Chemical Reactions: Investigating an Industrial Accident (p. 297)
—Climate Change Catastrophe. (p. 332)
—Debate about Energy Resources. (p. 421)
—Decorated Pottery. (p. 422)

—Deep Sea Exploration. (p. 423)
—Deforestation. (p. 424)
—Deforestation Crisis. (p. 424)
—Discover Afghanistan. (p. 447)
—Discover Greece. (p. 447)
—Forming a Band (p. 620)
—Geronimo (p. 667)
—Geronimo Faure, Florence, illus. (p. 667)
—Global Economy (p. 684)
—Great Aircraft Designs 1900-Today. (p. 713)
—Great Car Designs 1900-Today. (p. 714)
—Great Outdoors: Saving Habitats (p. 717)
—Health & Disease: Investigating a TB Outbreak (p. 757)
—Hi-Tech Clothes (p. 775)
—I'm Good at English... What Job Can I Get? (p. 859)
—I'M Good at Math... What Job Can I Get? (p. 859)
—I'M Good at Science... What Job Can I Get? (p. 859)
—I'm Good with Computers... what Job Can I Get? (p. 859)
—Invaders from Earth (p. 883)
—Jay-Z (p. 910)
—Life Cycles. (p. 1009)
—Performing Live (p. 1343)
—Pharmaceutical Industry. (p. 1350)
—Pod of Dolphins: And Other Sea Mammal Groups (p. 1375)
—Ramesses II (p. 1438)
—Reproduction & Genetics. (p. 1461)
—Sculpture. (p. 1534)
—Shaka Zulu (p. 1558)
—Simon Cowell (p. 1577)
—Slavery & the Slave Trade (p. 1588)
—Speed & Acceleration (p. 1624)
—Stained Glass Windows. (p. 1638)
—Tree. Hanna, Gary, illus. (p. 1783)
—Troop of Chimpanzees: And Other Primate Groups (p. 1788)
—Who Marched for Civil Rights? HL Studios Staff, illus. (p. 1917)
—Who Protested Against the Vietnam War? (p. 1917)
—Zoom in on Bizarre Bugs. (p. 1989)
—Zoom in on Body Invaders. (p. 1989)
—Zoom in on Crime Scenes. (p. 1989)
—Zoom in on House of Horrors. (p. 1989)
Spilsbury, Richard, jt. auth. see Spilsbury, Louise.
Spilsbury, Richard & Graham, Ian. Iconic Designs. (p. 851)
Spilsbury, Richard & Spilsbury, Louise. Animals in Danger. (p. 83)
—Animals in Danger in Africa (p. 83)
—Animals in Danger in Asia (p. 83)
—Animals in Danger in Australia (p. 83)
—Animals in Danger in North America (p. 83)
—Ant Colonies. (p. 88)
—Biomass Power. (p. 189)
—Blue Whale (p. 203)
—Classifying Reptiles (p. 328)
—Clock (p. 333)
—Dog Packs. (p. 461)
—Dolphin & Whale Pods. (p. 464)
—Estonia (p. 538)
—Farming & the Environment. (p. 574)
—Feeding the World. (p. 580)
—Fossil Fuel Power. (p. 623)
—From Farm to Table. (p. 642)
—Iran (p. 886)
—Lion Prides. (p. 1020)
—Look Inside. (p. 1049)
—Magnetism (p. 1075)
—Mountain Gorilla (p. 1180)
—Nuclear Power. (p. 1270)
—Oil Industry. (p. 1282)
—Plant Growth (p. 1369)
—Plant Reproduction (p. 1369)
—Printing Press (p. 1407)
—Pros & Cons of Water Power. (p. 1412)
—Pros & Cons of Wind Power. (p. 1412)
—Radio (p. 1432)
—Ride That Rollercoaster! Forces at an Amusement Park. (p. 1471)
—Solar Power. (p. 1606)
—Television (p. 1716)
—Water, Waves, & Tidal Power. (p. 1863)
—What Are Forces & Motion? Exploring Science with Hands-on Activities. (p. 1879)
—What Are Solids, Liquids, & Gases? Exploring Science with Hands-on Activities. (p. 1879)
—What Is Electricity & Magnetism? Exploring Science with Hands-on Activities. (p. 1889)
—What Is Energy? Exploring Science with Hands-on Activities. (p. 1889)
—What Is Light? Exploring Science with Hands-on Activities. (p. 1889)
—What Is Sound? Exploring Science with Hands-on Activities. (p. 1890)
—Wind Power. (p. 1935)
—Wolf Packs. (p. 1944)
—WWII Survival Tips. (p. 1966)
Spilsbury, Richard & Spilsbury, Louise A. Atoms & Molecules (p. 113)
—Chemical Reactions (p. 297)
—Classifying Amphibians. (p. 328)
—Elements & Compounds (p. 510)
—Mixtures & Solutions (p. 1156)
—Murder of Crows. (p. 1192)
—Pack of Wolves. (p. 1317)
—Plant Parts (p. 1369)
—Pod of Whales. (p. 1375)
—Troop of Chimpanzees. (p. 1788)
—What Is a Plant? (p. 1888)
Spilsbury, Richard, et al. Anatomy of an Investigation. (p. 67)
—Classifying Reptiles (p. 328)
—Disappearing Mountain & Other Earth Mysteries: Erosion & Weathering (p. 446)
—Future - Bleak or Bright? (p. 651)
—How Do Plants Grow? (p. 807)
—I'm in the Band (p. 859)
—Islamic Empires (p. 891)
—Journal of a Fossil Hunter: Fossils (p. 927)
—Shark Snacks: Food Chains & Webs (p. 1562)
—War in Your Backyard: Life in an Ecosystem (p. 1857)
—Where Do Plants Grow? (p. 1907)
—Why Do Plants Have Flowers? (p. 1924)
—Your Body for Life. (p. 1980)
Spina Dixon, Debra, illus. see Wheeler, Annie.
Spina, Janice. Louey the Lazy Elephant. (p. 1058)
Spinden, Herbert Joseph. Ancient Civilizations of Mexico & Central America. (p. 68)
Spindler, Brenda Lee. Night Granny Came. (p. 1253)
Spindler, Madelyn, jt. auth. see Spindler, Rebecca Williams.
Spindler, Rebecca Williams & Spindler, Madelyn. Life According to Liz. (p. 1007)
Spinelle, Nancy Louise. Moose's Loose Tooth. Gedeon, Gloria, illus. (p. 1173)
Spinelli, jt. auth. see Spinelli, Eileen.
Spinelli, Eileen. Another Day As Emily. Lew-Vriethoff, Joanne, illus. (p. 87)
—Baby Loves You So Much! Wenzel, David, illus. (p. 127)
—Best Story. (p. 171)
—Best Story. Wilsdorf, Anne, illus. (p. 171)
—Big Boy Now. Lloyd, Megan, illus. (p. 179)
—Boy, Can He Dance! Yalowitz, Paul, illus. (p. 217)
—Buzz. Nguyen, Vincent, illus. (p. 248)
—Callie Cat, Ice Skater. Kennedy, Anne, illus. (p. 254)
—Cold Snap. Priceman, Marjorie, illus. (p. 338)
—Dancing Pancake. Lew-Vriethoff, Joanne, illus. (p. 403)
—Do You Have a Cat? Valério, Geraldo, illus. (p. 457)
—Do You Have a Dog? Valério, Geraldo, illus. (p. 457)
—Do You Have a Hat? Valério, Geraldo, illus. (p. 457)
—God's Amazing World! Florian, Mlanie, illus. (p. 690)
—Hero Cat Stammen, Jo Ellen McAllister, illus. (p. 772)
—How to Clean Your Room. Leonard, David, illus. (p. 816)
—Hug a Bug. Andreasen, Dan, illus. (p. 824)
—I Know It's Autumn. Hayashi, Nancy, tr. (p. 840)
—I Like Noisy, Mom Likes Quiet. Halverson, Lydia, illus. (p. 841)
—Jonah's Whale. Ferri, Giuliano, illus. (p. 925)
—Love My Shoes! (p. 1060)
—Miss Fox's Class Earns a Field Trip Kennedy, Anne, illus. (p. 1151)
—Miss Fox's Class Earns a Field Trip. Kennedy, Anne, illus. (p. 1151)
—Miss Fox's Class Gets It Wrong. Kennedy, Anne, illus. (p. 1151)
—Miss Fox's Class Goes Green. Kennedy, Anne, illus. (p. 1151)
—Miss Fox's Class Shapes Up. Kennedy, Anne, illus. (p. 1151)
—Nora's Ark Hilb, Nora, illus. (p. 1264)
—Now It Is Summer. DePalma, Mary Newell, illus. (p. 1269)
—Now It Is Winter. DePalma, Mary Newell, illus. (p. 1269)
—Obra de Sofia. Dyer, Jane, illus. (p. 1275)
—Peace Week in Miss Fox's Class. Kennedy, Anne, illus. (p. 1332)
—Perfect Thanksgiving. Adinolfi, JoAnn, illus. (p. 1342)
—Polar Bear, Arctic Hare: Poems of the Frozen North. Fernandes, Eugenie, illus. (p. 1378)
—Silly Tilly Slonim, David, illus. (p. 1576)
—Someday. Winstead, Rosie, illus. (p. 1609)
—Something to Tell the Grandcows. Slavin, Bill, illus. (p. 1610)
—Song for the Whooping Crane. Warnick, Elsa, illus. (p. 1611)
—Sophie's Masterpiece: A Spider's Tale. Dyer, Jane, illus. (p. 1613)
—Summerhouse Time. Lew-Vriethoff, Joanne, illus. (p. 1675)
—Thanksgiving at the Tappletons' Lloyd, Megan, illus. (p. 1725)
—Thanksgiving at the Tappletons' Cocca-Leffler, Maryann, illus. (p. 1725)
—Thanksgiving at the Tappletons' Lloyd, Megan, illus. (p. 1726)
—Together at Christmas. Lee, Bin, illus. (p. 1761)
—Two to Cuddle. Logan, Laura, illus. (p. 1804)
—When Christmas Came. Parmenter, Wayne, illus. (p. 1901)
—When No One Is Watching. Johnson, David, illus. (p. 1904)
—When Papa Comes Home Tonight. McPhail, David, illus. (p. 1904)
—When You Are Happy. Valério, Geraldo, illus. (p. 1905)
—Where I Live. Matt, Phelan & Phelan, Matt, illus. (p. 1908)
—Where Is the Night Train Going? Bedtime Poems. Moore, Cyd, illus. (p. 1909)
Spinelli, Eileen & Spinelli. Bath Time Pedersen, Janet, illus. (p. 144)
—I Know It's Autumn. Hayashi, Nancy, tr. (p. 840)
Spinelli, Jami. David's Tractor. Margolis, Lois, illus. (p. 411)
Spinelli, Jerry. Eggs. (p. 506)
—Fourth Grade Rats. (p. 625)
—Hokey Pokey. (p. 787)
—I Can Be Anything! (p. 835)
—Jake & Lily. (p. 905)
—Knots in My Yo-Yo Strong. Gentieu, Penny, photos by. (p. 965)
—Loser. (p. 1054)
—Love, Stargirl. (p. 1060)
—Mama Seeton's Whistle. (p. 1084)
—Maniac Magee. (p. 1087)
—Milkweed. (p. 1143)
—My Daddy & Me. Chwast, Seymour, illus. (p. 1201)
—Smiles to Go. (p. 1594)
—Stargirl. (p. 1642)
—Stargirl. Tino, illus. (p. 1642)
—There's a Girl in My Hammerlock. (p. 1730)
—Third Grade Angels. (p. 1734)
—Third Grade Angels. Bell, Jennifer, illus. (p. 1734)
—Tooter Pepperday. (p. 1768)
—Wringer. (p. 1963)
—Zinkoff, el Inutil. (p. 1987)
Spinelli, Patti. Alphabet Book with Mackenzie & Emma. Spinelli, Patti, illus. (p. 49)
—Mackenzie & Emma Get a Puppy. (p. 1068)
—Mackenzie & Emma Visit York Beach. Spinelli, Patti, illus. (p. 1068)
Spinelli, Rhonda. Thank You, God, for Making Me! (p. 1725)
Spinks, Sarah, jt. auth. see Polizzotto, Carolyn.
Spinks, Scott, illus. see Lazurek, Michelle S.
Spinks, Stefphany (Snider), illus. see Eubanks-Adkison, Eufa.
Spinner, Stephanie. Alex the Parrot: No Ordinary Bird. So, Meilo, illus. (p. 36)
—Atlanta, la Cazadora. Holguin, Magdalena, tr. (p. 112)
—Damosel: In Which the Lady of the Lake Renders a Frank & Often Startling Account of Her Wondrous Life & Times. (p. 401)
—It Came from Outer Space. Gott, Barry, illus. (p. 893)
—It's a Miracle! A Hanukkah Storybook. McElmurry, Jill, illus. (p. 895)
—Magic of Merlin. Sokolova, Valerie, illus. (p. 1073)
—Nutcracker. Malone, Peter, illus. (p. 1274)
—Paddywack. Howarth, Daniel, illus. (p. 1317)
—Quicksilver. (p. 1427)
—Quiver. (p. 1429)
—Who Is Steven Spielberg? (p. 1916)
—Who Is Steven Spielberg? Mather, Daniel & Harrison, Nancy, illus. (p. 1916)
—Who Was Annie Oakley? Day, Larry, illus. (p. 1918)
—Who Was Clara Barton? (p. 1918)
—Who Was Clara Barton? Groff, David, illus. (p. 1918)
—Who Was Clara Barton? Harrison, Nancy & Groff, David, illus. (p. 1918)
—Who Was Sitting Bull? (p. 1919)
—Who Was Sitting Bull? Eldridge, Jim & Harrison, Nancy, illus. (p. 1919)
Spino, Bonnie, illus. see Lorraine, Loria.
Spiotta-DiMare, Loren. Draft Horses: Horses That Work. (p. 476)
—Performing Horses: Horses That Entertain. (p. 1343)
—Police Horses: Horses That Protect. (p. 1380)
—Therapy Horses: Horses That Heal. (p. 1729)
Spiotto, Joey, illus. see Barton, Chris.
Spires, Ashley. Binky: License to Scratch. Spires, Ashley, illus. (p. 188)
—Binky Takes Charge. Spires, Ashley, illus. (p. 188)
—Binky the Space Cat. Spires, Ashley, illus. (p. 188)
—Binky to the Rescue. Spires, Ashley, illus. (p. 188)
—Edie's Ensembles. (p. 504)
—Larf. Spires, Ashley, illus. (p. 975)
—Penguin & the Cupcake. (p. 1336)
—Small Saul. Spires, Ashley, illus. (p. 1592)
Spires, Ashley, illus. see Glass, Eleri.
Spires, Ashley, illus. see Gomes, Filomena.
Spires, Ashley, illus. see Jennings, Sharon.
Spires, Ashley, illus. see Levine, Shar & Johnstone, Leslie.
Spires, Ashley, illus. see Lloyd, Jennifer.
Spires, Elizabeth. I Am Arachne: Fifteen Greek & Roman Myths. Gerstein, Mordicai, illus. (p. 832)
—I Heard God Talking to Me: William Edmondson & His Stone Carvings. (p. 839)
Spires, Jeanette, ed. What Do You Know? Wisdom for the Road Ahead. (p. 1883)
Spires, Sharlene. Grandsisters. (p. 710)
Spires, Sidney, jt. auth. see Mangum, James A.
Spires, Sidney, jt. auth. see Mangum, James.
Spiridellis, Evan, illus. see Moore, Clement C.
Spiridellis, Gregg, illus. see Moore, Clement C.
Spirin, Gennady. Goldilocks & the Three Bears (p. 696)
—Martha. Spirin, Gennady, illus. (p. 1097)
—Night Before Christmas (p. 1252)
—Twelve Days of Christmas Spirin, Gennady, illus. (p. 1800)
—Twelve Days of Christmas. Spirin, Gennady, illus. (p. 1800)
—We Three Kings. (p. 1868)
Spirin, Gennady, illus. see Andrews, Julie & Hamilton, Emma Walton.
Spirin, Gennady, illus. see Andrews, Julie, et al.
Spirin, Gennady, illus. see Cuyler, Margery.
Spirin, Gennady, illus. see Guiberson, Brenda Z.
Spirin, Gennady, illus. see Perkins, John.
Spirin, Gennady, illus. see Shepard, Aaron.
Spirin, Gennady, illus. see Williams, Margery.
Spirin, Gennady, jt. auth. see Pogorelsky, Antony.
Spirin, Ilya, illus. see Guiberson, Brenda Z.
Spirin, Ilya, illus. see London, Jonathan.
Spirit Press, creator. Lord Told Noah. (p. 1052)
—Ultimate Bible Fun Book. (p. 1809)
Spiritworks. Dreamtime. (p. 484)
—Sleep Foster, Jonathan, illus. (p. 1588)
Spirko, Robert. Palestine Conspiracy. (p. 1319)
Spirn, M. S. Poison Plate Cunningham, Kelley, illus. (p. 1377)
Spirn, Michele. Octopuses. (p. 1278)
—Ripley's Cold-Blooded Creatures. (p. 1474)
Spirn, Michele S., jt. auth. see Spirn, Michele Sobel.
Spirn, Michele Sobel. Bridges in Edinburgh. (p. 227)
—I Am the Turkey. Allen, Joy, illus. (p. 834)
—Mysterious People. (p. 1223)
Spirn, Michele Sobel & Spirn, Michele S. I Am the Turkey. Allen, Joy, illus. (p. 834)
Spiro, Ian & Jendrey, Julie. Stanford University College Prowler off the Record. (p. 1639)
Spiro, Ruth. Baby Loves Aerospace Engineering! Chan, Irene, illus. (p. 127)
—Baby Loves Quarks! Chan, Irene, illus. (p. 127)
Spittle, Elsie. Wisdom for Life: Three Principles for Well-Being (p. 1939)
Spitz, Clarita. Enrique Tiene Cinco Anos. (p. 531)
Spitz, Eleanor. Phoenix the Rising Star. (p. 1351)
Spitz, Marc. Nobody Likes You: Inside the Turbulent Life, Times, & Music of Green Day. (p. 1262)
Spitz, Mary Y. Mint's Christmas Message. Pierce, Joanne Y., illus. (p. 1148)
Spitzer, Linda. Friend in Freezeville. (p. 637)
Spitzer, Linda & Myers, Sarah. Tales of the Paper Bag Fairies/Color Version. (p. 1702)
Spivak, Dawnine. Grass Sandals: The Travels of Basho. Demi, illus. (p. 711)
Spivak, Samuel. Children's Cowboy Songs for Piano. Barbelle, illus. (p. 303)
Spivet, Bonnie. Avoiding Predators Online. (p. 120)
—Playing Games Online. (p. 1372)
—Protecting Your Privacy Online. (p. 1412)
—Stopping Cyberbullying. (p. 1654)
—Using Social Networks. (p. 1828)
Spivey, Clark. Danger in the Nest. (p. 404)
Spivey, Mark. Spot in the Road: My Personal Adventu. (p. 1633)
Spizman, Robyn F. Lollipop Grapes & Clothespin Critters: Quick on the Spot Remedies for Restless Children. (p. 1046)
Spizman, Robyn Freedman, jt. auth. see Johnston, Mark.
Spizman, Robyn Freedman & Johnston, Mark. Secret Agent. (p. 1540)
—Secret Agents Strike Back. (p. 1540)
Spizzirri, Linda. Dogs of the Wild: An Educational Coloring Book. (p. 463)
Spizzirri, Linda, ed. see Spizzirri, Peter M.
Spizzirri, Linda, ed. Cats of the Wild. (p. 281)
—Counting & Coloring Dinosaurs. (p. 370)
—Dinosaurs. Kohn, Arnie, illus. (p. 444)
—Endangered Species. (p. 527)
—Northeast Indians. (p. 1265)
—Northwest Indians. (p. 1266)
—Prehistoric Birds. Spizzirri, Peter M., illus. (p. 1395)
—Prehistoric Sea Life. Kohn, Arnie, illus. (p. 1395)
—Space Craft. Spizzirri, Peter M., illus. (p. 1618)
Spizzirri, Peter M. Aircraft. Spizzirri, Linda, ed. (p. 31)
Spizzirri, Peter M., illus. see Spizzirri, Linda, ed.
Splawn, "E". Planting Fruitful Seeds. (p. 1369)
Splho, Michal, illus. see McKinnon, Margie.
Splink, illus. see Gormally, Eleanor.
Spoerl, Amber, illus. see Dusablon, David.
Spoerl, Heinrich. Man Kann Ruhig Darüber Sprechen (p. 1085)
Spohn, Bruce. Christmas Hope. (p. 314)
Spohn, David, illus. see Audia, John P.
Spohn, Kate. Turtle & Snake's Day at the Beach. Spohn, Kate, illus. (p. 1798)
—Turtle & Snake's Spooky Halloween. Spohn, Kate, illus. (p. 1798)
Spohn, Onna J., illus. see Walley, Judith L. & Faith, Virginia T.
Spohn, Rebecca. Ready, Set, Create! A Kid's Guide to Crafting. (p. 1447)
—Ready Set Grow. (p. 1447)
Spoilyourhorse Com Staff. SpoilYourHorse. com Horse Bits: A Study Guide for Beginning Rider & Instructor. (p. 1630)
Spomer, Ron. Predator Hunting: Proven Strategies That Work from East to West. (p. 1394)
Sponaugle, Kim, illus. see Buckley, Colleen.
Sponaugle, Kim, illus. see Gresham, Evelyn.
Sponaugle, Kim, illus. see Keys, Dalen.
Sponaugle, Kim, illus. see Matulewicz, Elisabeth Ann.
Sponaugle, Kim, illus. see Phillips, Dixie.
Sponaugle, Kim, illus. see Spoonmore, Scott.
Spong, Clive, illus. see McCafferty, Catherine.
Spong, Clive, illus. see Rutherford, Peter.
Sponheimer, Katheryne, illus. see Callahan, Ann Marie.
Spookytooth, T. S., illus. see Levine, Sara (Veterinarian).
Spookytooth, T. S., illus. see Levine, Sara.
Spoon, Cynthia. Ice Angel. Harr, Lynn, illus. (p. 850)
Spooner, Carol. I Love You Best. (p. 843)
Spooner, F. M. Granny Spooner's Christian Bedtime Stories. (p. 710)
Spooner, J. B. Little Black Dog Buccaneer. Seeley, Terre Lamb, illus. (p. 1024)
Spooner, J. B. & Seaver, Richard. Story of the Little Black Dog. Seeley, Terre Lamb, illus. (p. 1661)
Spooner, J. B. & Seeley, Terre Lamb. Little Black Dog Has Puppies. Seeley, Terre Lamb, illus. (p. 1024)
Spooner, Joe. Elephant Walk. McCann, Michelle, ed. (p. 511)
—N Is for Nostril—and Other Alphabet Silliness. (p. 1227)
Spooner, Joe, illus. see Till, Danelle.
Spooner, Luke, illus. see Kneff, Steff F.
Spooner, M. Entr@pment: A High School Comedy in Chat. (p. 531)
—Entrapment. (p. 531)
Spooner, Meagan. Lark Ascending. (p. 975)
—Shadowlark. (p. 1558)
—Skylark. (p. 1587)
Spooner, Meagan, jt. auth. see Kaufman, Amie.
Spoonmore, Scott. Seymour the Semi- Space Truckin' Sponaugle, Kim, illus. (p. 1556)
Spoor, Mike. Desperate Measures: Units of Measurement in Action. (p. 430)
—Emperor's Guards: Concepts of Time. (p. 521)
—Emperor's Last Command: Problem-Solving in Action. (p. 521)
—Emperor's Last Command: Problem-solving in Action. (p. 521)
—Hidden Valley: Reasoning in Action. (p. 776)
—Lightning Flash: Probability in Action. (p. 1016)
Spoor, Mike, illus. see Dhami, Narinder.
Spoor, Mike, illus. see Kennemore, Tim.
Spoor, Mike, illus. see Law, Felicia & Way, Steve.
Spoor, Mike, illus. see Law, Felicia.
Spoor, Mike, illus. see O'Donnell, Liam.
Spoor, Mike, illus. see Sillifant, Alec.
Spoor, Mike, illus. see Taylor, Dereen.
Sporn, Jessica. Old Enough to do Good in the World. (p. 1283)
Sporteller Staff. Race to Win (Auto Racing) (p. 1431)
Sportelli-Rehak, Angela. Moving Again Mom! Hinlicky, Gregg, illus. (p. 1183)
—Uncle Sam's Kids: When Duty Calls. Hinlicky, Gregg, illus. (p. 1812)
—Uncle Sam's Kids: Moving Again Mom. Hinlicky, Gregg, illus. (p. 1812)
Sports Illustrated Editors. Basketball Book. (p. 143)
—Sports Illustraded Kids Wow! Pop-Up Book of Sports. (p. 1632)
Sports Illustrated for Kids Editors. Race Day: Behind the Scenes at NASCAR. (p. 1430)
—Sports Illustrated Kids 1st And 10: Top 10 Lists of Everything in Football. (p. 1632)
—Sports Illustrated Kids Stats! The Greatest Numbers in Sports. (p. 1632)
Sports Illustrated for Kids Editors, creator. All-Star Picture Puzzles. (p. 45)

Sports Illustrated Kids Magazine Staff. Sports Illustrated Kids Top Dogs: Babe Ruff & the Legendary Canines of Sports. (p. 1632)
—Top 10 of Everything in Sports. (p. 1768)
Spotd, Donald. Diana: The Last Year. (p. 434)
Spotlight Editors. Laugh with a Test Case. Gorelick, Victor, illus. (p. 980)
—Quiet Please. (p. 1428)
Spotlight Editors, jt. auth. see Ribeiro, Nelson.
Spotlight Editors, jt. auth. see Ribiero, Nelson.
Spoto, Donald. Reluctant Saint: The Life of Francis of Assisi. (p. 1458)
Spotswood, Jessica. Born Wicked. (p. 214)
—Sisters' Fate. (p. 1581)
Spotted Eagle, Douglas. Digital Video Basics: Your Guide to Making Great Movies. (p. 440)
Spowart, Robin, illus. see O'Keefe, Susan Heyboer.
Spowart, Robin, jt. auth. see Modesitt, Jeanne.
Spradlin, Joe. Sugar. (p. 1672)
Spradlin, Leslie, illus. see Gilbert, Drexel.
Spradlin, Mark. Thumper & the Squirrels. (p. 1746)
—Thumper Meets Santa Claus. (p. 1746)
Spradlin, Michael. Orphan of Destiny: Book 3 (p. 1304)
Spradlin, Michael P. Baseball from A to Z. Pamintuan, Macky, illus. (p. 141)
—Daniel Boone's Great Escape. Hoyt, Ard, illus. (p. 405)
—Feeding Frenzy. (p. 580)
—Into the Killing Seas. (p. 881)
—Jack & Jill Went up to Kill: A Book of Zombie Nursery Rhymes. Weigel, Jeff, illus. (p. 902)
—Keeper of the Grail (p. 947)
—Killer Species #1: Menace from the Deep. (p. 956)
—Killer Species #2: Feeding Frenzy. (p. 956)
—Killer Species #3: Out for Blood. (p. 956)
—Killer Species #4: Ultimate Attack. (p. 956)
—Live & Let Shop. (p. 1039)
—Menace from the Deep. (p. 1126)
—Off Like the Wind! The First Ride of the Pony Express. Johnson, Layne, illus. (p. 1279)
—Out for Blood. (p. 1310)
—Out for Blood. (p. 1311)
—Texas Rangers: Legendary Lawmen. Munro, Roxie, illus. (p. 1724)
—Trail of Fate (p. 1776)
—Ultimate Attack. (p. 1809)
Spradlin, Michael P., jt. auth. see Smith, Roland.
Spradlin, Michael P. & Smith, Roland. Alcatraz. (p. 35)
Spragg, Patrick. KnightBeard. (p. 964)
Spraggett, Daphne. Window on the World: Prayer Atlas for All. (p. 1936)
Spraggett, Daphne, jt. auth. see Johnstone, Jill.
Sprague, Cate. My Dog Bauer Is a Thief. (p. 1202)
Sprague, Dean, illus. see Trimble, Marcia.
Sprague, Gary. Cowboy Saved Christmas. (p. 374)
Sprague, Howard Lee. Snowflake's Vacation. Borrajero, Judy, illus. (p. 1600)
Sprague, Jeff & Golly, Annemieke. Best Behavior: Building Positive Behavior Support in Schools. (p. 168)
Sprague, Lois, illus. see Pelley, Kathleen.
Sprague, Lois Rosio, illus. see Hurst, Rich.
Sprague, Susan & Schwarz, Susan. Coping with Cliques: A Workbook to Help Girls Deal with Gossip, Put-Downs, Bullying & Other Mean Behavior. (p. 365)
Sprangers, Heather, jt. auth. see Marsh, Kathleen Marie.
Spratt, Niall, jt. auth. see Meehan, Patrick.
Spratt, Niall & Meehan, Patrick. Shamrogues: First Challenge. (p. 1559)
Spratt, R. A. Adventures of Nanny Piggins. Santat, Dan, illus. (p. 21)
—Nanny Piggins & the Accidental Blast-Off. (p. 1229)
—Nanny Piggins & the Rival Ringmaster. (p. 1229)
—Nanny Piggins & the Runaway Lion. (p. 1229)
—Nanny Piggins & the Wicked Plan. (p. 1229)
Spray, Michelle. My ABCs: An ABC Book for Any Age. Pasternack, Susan, ed. (p. 1195)
Spraycar, Marjory A. This, I Do for Me. (p. 1735)
Sprecher, John. Eric & the Angrrry Frog Forrest, James, illus. (p. 533)
—Tori & Cassandra & the Pelican in Peril. Forrest, James, illus. (p. 1769)
—Zoe & the Very Unmerry Bear. Forrest, James, illus. (p. 1987)
Spreekmeester, Kevin, jt. auth. see Walters, Eric.
Spreen, Kathe, illus. see Kalar, Bonnie.
Spremulli, Pam. Letter Birds. (p. 1002)
Spremulli, Pam, illus. see Markey, Neil.
Spreng, Robert. Goin' Great in the Lone Star State. (p. 692)
Spreng, Robert C. Tahoe Tiger & the Lahontan Lion. (p. 1695)
Sprengelmeyer, Lily, jt. auth. see Wolfe, Mike.
Sprenger, Luke. Sommer in Canvas Bay. (p. 1611)
Sprenkle, Connie L. My Shining Star. (p. 1218)
Sprick, Jessica. Kangaroos: Read Well Level K Unit 15 Storybook. Crum, Anna-Maria, illus. (p. 942)
Sprick, Jessica, jt. auth. see Dunn, Richard.
Sprick, Jessica, jt. auth. see Sprick, Marilyn.
Sprick, Marilyn. Monkey Business: Read Well Level K Unit 3 Storybook. Nolte, Larry, illus. (p. 1165)
Sprick, Marilyn, jt. auth. see Jones, Shelley V.
Sprick, Marilyn & Lemieux, Aurora, adapted by. Race: Read Well Level K Unit 13 Storybook. (p. 1430)
Sprick, Marilyn & Sprick, Jessica. Hey Diddle Diddle: Read Well Level K Unit 16 Storybook. Clark, Steve, illus. (p. 774)
Sprick, Marilyn, et al. All about Eels: Read Well Level K Unit 2 Storybook. Clark, Steve, illus. (p. 42)
—All about Eels: Read Well Level K Unit 2 Teacher Storybook. Clark, Steve, illus. (p. 42)
—Amazing Insects: Read Well Level K Unit 4 Storybook. Weber, Phillip A., Jr., illus. (p. 54)
—Cats: Read Well Level K Unit 12 Storybook. Zilis, Tom, illus. (p. 281)
—Man's Best Friend: Read Well Level K Unit 5 Storybook. Zilis, Tom, illus. (p. 1088)
—Read Well K Magazine Prelude F: Plain Text. (p. 1443)
—Read Well Magazine Prelude A: Plain Text. (p. 1443)
—Read Well Magazine Prelude A: Slanted Text. (p. 1443)
—Read Well Magazine Preude F: Slanted Text. (p. 1443)
—Read Well Magazine Unit 1: Plain Text. (p. 1443)
—Read Well Magazine Unit 1: Slanted Text. (p. 1443)
—Read Well Magazine Unit 10: Plain Text. (p. 1443)
—Read Well Magazine Unit 10: Slanted Text. (p. 1443)
—Read Well Magazine Unit 16. (p. 1443)
—Read Well Teacher's Guide: Level K; Whole Class: Units 25-26 Plus Vowel Units. (p. 1443)
—Read Well Teacher's Guide Units 10-15: Level K Whole Class. (p. 1443)
—Read Well Teacher's Guide Units 1-6: Level K Whole Class. (p. 1443)
—Rescue Workers: Read Well Level K Unit 11 Storybook. Zilis, Tom, illus. (p. 1462)
—Rhyming Fun: Read Well Level K Unit 6 Storybook. Jerde, Susan, illus. (p. 1468)
—Spiders: Read Well Level K Unit 1 Storybook. Shupe, Bobbi & Crum, Anna-Maria, illus. (p. 1627)
—Spiders: Unit 1 Read Well Level K Teacher's Storybook. Shupe, Bobbi & Crum, Anna-Maria, illus. (p. 1627)
—Student Workbook 1 (Plain Text) Units 1-9 Plus Review Unit. (p. 1669)
—Student Workbook 2 (Plain Text) Units 10-18 Plus Review Unit. (p. 1669)
—Student Workbook 3 (Plain Text) Unit 19 through Vowel Review Unit. (p. 1669)
—Teacher's Guide Small Group Prelude A: Read Well Level K. (p. 1709)
—Teacher's Guide Small Group Unit 1: Read Well Level K. (p. 1709)
—Teacher's Guide Small Group Unit 10: Read Well Level K. (p. 1709)
—Teacher's Guide Small Group Unit 5: Read Well K. (p. 1709)
Sprick, Randall S. Solution Book. (p. 1608)
Spring, Albert. M. E. Kerr. (p. 1067)
Spring, Debbie. Breathing Soccer (p. 226)
—Righteous Smuggler (p. 1472)
Spring, Jill, jt. auth. see Delamain, Catherine.
Spring, Manda. Emerald & the Magic of Raynon. (p. 517)
—Emerald & the Withered Willow. (p. 517)
Spring, Melanie. Practice Makes Perfect. (p. 1392)
—Turn It Up. (p. 1797)
Springer, Alan. E-KidZ in Cyberspace. (p. 492)
Springer, Audrey. Rusty's Gift. Richards, Kris, illus. (p. 1498)
Springer, David. Patch Quilt Santa. (p. 1328)
—Samhain in the Kitchen. (p. 1507)
Springer, Jane. Genocide (p. 661)
Springer, Jane, tr. from POR. Amazonia: Indigenous Tales from Brazil Popov, Nikolai, illus. (p. 56)
Springer, Kristina. Espressologist. (p. 536)
—My Fake Boyfriend Is Better Than Yours. (p. 1202)
Springer, Lisa. Art & Culture of Ancient Egypt. (p. 101)
Springer, Lisa & Morris, Neil. Art & Culture of Ancient Egypt. (p. 101)
Springer, Michael. Bootlegger's Secret. (p. 213)
Springer, Nancy. Blood Trail. (p. 200)
—Boy on a Black Horse. (p. 218)
—Case of the Bizarre Bouquets. (p. 273)
—Case of the Cryptic Crinoline. (p. 274)
—Case of the Gypsy Goodbye. (p. 274)
—Case of the Left-Handed Lady. (p. 274)
—Case of the Missing Marquess. (p. 274)
—Case of the Peculiar Pink Fan: An Enola Holmes Mystery. (p. 274)
—Lionclaw: A Tale of Rowan Hood. (p. 1021)
—Possessing Jessie. (p. 1387)
—Somebody. (p. 1609)
—Wild Boy: A Tale of Rowan Hood. (p. 1929)
—Wild Boy. (p. 1929)
Springer, Paul. Ink Thief. (p. 874)
Springer, Sally, illus. see Gold-Vukson, Marji.
Springer, Sally, illus. see Slater, Teddy.
Springer, Sally, illus. see Stamper, Judith Bauer & Keyes, Joan Ross.
Springer, Sally, illus. see Stamper, Judith Bauer & Ross Keyes, Joan.
Springer, Sally, jt. auth. see Slater, Teddy.
Springer, Susan K. Child Can Hear God's Voice. (p. 301)
Springer, Susan Woodward. Seldovia Sam & the Blueberry Bear Meissner, Amy, illus. (p. 1549)
—Seldovia Sam & the Sea Otter Rescue. Meissner, Amy, illus. (p. 1549)
—Seldovia Sam & the Very Large Clam. Meissner, Amy, illus. (p. 1549)
—Seldovia Sam & Wildfire Escape. Meissner, Amy, illus. (p. 1549)
Springer, T. S. Tyler Builds a Birdhouse. (p. 1805)
Springett, Isobel, photos by see Springett, Martin.
Springett, Martin. Breakfast on a Dragon's Tail: And Other Book Bites. (p. 225)
—Jousting with Jesters: An ABC for the Younger Dragon (p. 929)
—Kate & Pippin: An Unlikely Love Story. Springett, Isobel, photos by. (p. 944)
Springett, Martin, illus. see Katz, Welwyn W.
Springett, Martin, illus. see Thompson, Springett & Thompson, Richard.
Springham, James. Earth-n-Bones: Toxic. (p. 496)
—Earth-n-Bones: Blue Things. (p. 496)
Springman, I. C. More. Lies, Brian, illus. (p. 1173)
SpringSprang Studio Staff, illus. see Poth, Karen.
Springsteen, Cindy. Waffles & Pancakes. (p. 1852)
Springstubb, Tricia. Cody & the Fountain of Happiness. Wheeler, Eliza, illus. (p. 338)
—Mo Wren, Lost & Found. Ross, Heather, illus. (p. 1157)
—Moonpenny Island. Ford, Gilbert, illus. (p. 1173)
—Phoebe & Digger. Newman, Jeff, illus. (p. 1351)
—What Happened on Fox Street. Ross, Heather, illus. (p. 1885)
Sprinkel, Katy. Big Book of Bieber: All-in-One, Most-Definitive Collection of Everything Bieber. (p. 179)
Sprinkel, Katy, jt. auth. see Boone, Mary.
Sprinkle, Alicia. Clementine Is Fairy Special. (p. 330)
—Lolly & the Holly Berry Tree. (p. 1046)
Sprinkle, Charleeda. Jesus's First Birthday Party. (p. 916)
Sprott, Jeffrey. Long Walk to the Park. (p. 1047)
Sproul, R. C. Barber Who Wanted to Pray. Fluharty, T. Lively, illus. (p. 138)
—Priest with Dirty Clothes. Gerard, Justin, illus. (p. 1399)
—Prince's Poison Cup. Gerard, Justin, illus. (p. 1402)
—Ultimate Issues. (p. 1809)
Sproule, Acquanetta M. Scamp. (p. 1519)
Sproule, Anna. Wright Brothers. (p. 1963)
Sproule, Gail. Singing the Dark Lott, Sheena, illus. (p. 1579)
Sprouse, A. R. Guardian Alva: Awakening: Second Edition. (p. 728)
Sprouse, Jackie. Orry & Izzy's Perfect Worm. (p. 1305)
Sprowell, Tom. Wilma & Pester's Genie Brew. (p. 1934)
Spruill, Beverle. Dream Box. (p. 483)
Spruill, Ed. Jordan Wants a Brother. (p. 925)
Spruill, Edward L. & Spruill, Sonya. Jordan's Hair. Peringer, Stephen Mercer, illus. (p. 925)
Spruill, Patricia Thomas. Josie Is Afraid. (p. 927)
Spruill, Sonya, jt. auth. see Spruill, Edward L.
Sprunger, Reed. Albert Einstein: Brilliant Scientist. (p. 34)
—Thomas Edison: Incredible Inventor. (p. 1738)
Sprunger, Reed, illus. see Stille, Darlene R.
Spudvilas, Anne, illus. see Hartnett, Sonya.
Spudvilas, Anne, illus. see Walters, Celeste.
Spudvilas, Anne, jt. auth. see Walters, Celeste.
Spungin, Jennifer. Susan B. Anthony & Justice for All. (p. 1688)
Spurgeon, Aaron, illus. see DiSiena, Laura Lyn & Eliot, Hannah.
Spurgeon, Charles H. God Loves You. (p. 689)
—Queen Victoria's Request: A Story of Grace & Mercy. Anderson, Jeff, illus. (p. 1425)
Spurgeon, Maureen. Big Book of Animals. (p. 178)
Spurgeon, S. Great Kitten Mystery. (p. 716)
Spurlin, Barbara & Bernhardt, Michael J. Jellyfish on the Menu. (p. 912)
Spurling, Wesley. Books for Jacob. (p. 212)
—Gerry the Giraffe. (p. 667)
Spurll, Barbara, illus. see Haight, Angela.
Spurll, Barbara, illus. see Jones, Carolyn.
Spurll, Barbara, illus. see Metzger, Steve.
Spurll, Barbara, illus. see Ruurs, Margriet.
Spurll, Barbara, illus. see Zaretsky, Evan.
Spurlock, Cathy. Toby, the Two-Toed Tiger. (p. 1760)
Spurlock, Jefferson. Clemente's Dream. (p. 330)
Spurlock, Necole. Rocky & Rudy's Wild Adventure (p. 1484)
Spurr, Debbie. Quilly from Philly: The Pen that Helped Found a Nation. (p. 1428)
—Where Do Butterflies Go When it Rains? (p. 1906)
Spurr, Elizabeth. At the Beach Oliphant, Manelle, illus. (p. 110)
—Farm Life. Björkman, Steve, illus. (p. 574)
—Halloween Sky Ride. Long, Ethan, illus. (p. 738)
—Happy Sparkling Halloween. Madden, Colleen, illus. (p. 746)
—Happy Sparkling Hanukkah. Madden, Colleen, illus. (p. 746)
—In the Garden Oliphant, Manelle, illus. (p. 866)
—In the Woods Oliphant, Manelle, illus. (p. 868)
—Monsters, Mind Your Manners! Scales, Simon, illus. (p. 1169)
—Pumpkin Hill. Martin, Whitney, illus. (p. 1416)
Spurr, Judy. Trapped. (p. 1779)
Spurr, Pam. Sex Dreams & Symbols. (p. 1556)
Spurrier, Simon & Swierczynski, Duane. X-Men: Second Coming Revelations. Davidson, Paul et al, illus. (p. 1967)
Spusta, Marq, illus. see Harper, Joel.
Spyer, Jonathan & Brown, Cameron. Rise of Nationalism: The Arab World, Turkey, & Iran. (p. 1474)
Spykman, E. C. Terrible, Horrible Edie. (p. 1721)
Spyri, Johanna. Erick & Sally. (p. 533)
—Gritli's Children. (p. 724)
—Heidi: With a Discussion of Optimism. Clift, Eva, illus. (p. 762)
—Heidi. (p. 762)
—Heidi. Akib, Jamel, illus. (p. 762)
—Heidi. Marks, Alan, illus. (p. 762)
—Heidi. Hunsicker, Ranelda Mack, ed. (p. 762)
—How Wiseli Was Provided For. (p. 823)
—Maezli. (p. 1070)
—Moni, the Goat Boy & What Sami Sings with the Birds. (p. 1164)
—Otra Vez Heidi. (p. 1307)
—Rico & Stineli. (p. 1470)
—Uncle Titus & His Visit to the Country. (p. 1812)
—Veronica. (p. 1837)
—Veronica & Other Friends. (p. 1837)
—What Sami Sings with the Birds. (p. 1893)
Spyri, Johanna, jt. auth. see Dusikova, Maja.
Spyri, Johanna & Blaisdell, Robert. Heidi: Adapted for Young Readers. Kliros, Thea, illus. (p. 762)
Spyri, Johanna & Stork, Elisabeth P. Heidi. Kirk, Maria L., illus. (p. 762)
Spyropolous, Angelo. RV. (p. 1499)
Squadrito, Vanessa. Girl & Her Cat. Iwanaga, Kent, illus. (p. 678)
Squamish Nation Education Department. Hussa. (p. 830)
Square Fish Staff. Kisses & Curses. Burniac, Lauren, ed. (p. 962)
Squareman, Clarence. My Book of Indoor Games. (p. 1199)
Squatrito, J. Michael, Jr. Talisman of Unification: The Overlords. (p. 1703)
Squier, Emma-Lindsay. On Autumn Trails & Adventures in Captivity. (p. 1288)
Squier, Robert. Follow the Drinking Gourd: An Underground Railroad Story (p. 612)
—Sensational Senses (p. 1551)
—Story of Cassiopeia: A Roman Constellation Myth (p. 1657)
Squier, Robert, illus. see Bangs, Edward.
Squier, Robert, illus. see Berendes, Mary.
Squier, Robert, illus. see Braun, Eric.
Squier, Robert, illus. see Capstone Press Staff.
Squier, Robert, illus. see Frith, Margaret.
Squier, Robert, illus. see Gray, Susan H.
Squier, Robert, illus. see Heinrichs, Ann.
Squier, Robert, illus. see Herman, Gail.
Squier, Robert, illus. see Prince, April Jones.
Squier, Robert, illus. see Temple, Teri.
Squier, Robert, illus. see Troupe, Thomas Kingsley.
Squier, Robert, illus. see Vogel, Julia.
Squier, Robert, illus. see Vogel, Julie & Vogel, Julia.
Squier, Robert, illus. see Vogel, Julie.
Squiers, Connie. Copper Colt. (p. 365)
Squillace, Elisa. Aladdin: Flip-up Fairy Tales. (p. 33)
—Aladdin. (p. 33)
—Down in the Jungle. (p. 474)
—Three Wishes. (p. 1744)
Squire, Ann O. Allergies. (p. 46)
—Animals Helping at Work. (p. 82)
—Animals Helping with Healing. (p. 82)
—Ants. (p. 90)
—Asthma. (p. 108)
—Autism. (p. 117)
—Beetles. (p. 158)
—Birds. (p. 191)
—Bobcats. (p. 206)
—Cancer. (p. 260)
—Cheetahs. (p. 296)
—Chinese Giant Salamander: The World's Biggest Amphibian. (p. 307)
—Crickets & Grasshoppers. (p. 382)
—Ebola. (p. 501)
—Extreme Bridges. (p. 556)
—Extreme Experiments. (p. 556)
—Extreme Laboratories. (p. 556)
—Extreme Science Careers. (p. 556)
—Extreme Weather. (p. 557)
—Fossils. (p. 624)
—Gemstones. (p. 660)
—Hydrofracking. (p. 831)
—Mammals. (p. 1085)
—Minerals. (p. 1146)
—Planet Jupiter. (p. 1367)
—Planet Mars. (p. 1367)
—Planet Mercury. (p. 1367)
—Planet Neptune. (p. 1367)
—Planet Saturn. (p. 1368)
—Reptiles. (p. 1461)
—Rocks. (p. 1483)
—Sinkholes. (p. 1579)
—Termites. (p. 1721)
—Tsunamis. (p. 1795)
—Volcanic Eruptions. (p. 1848)
Squire, M H, illus. see Kingsley, Charles.
Squire, Maud Hunt, illus. see Williston, Teresa Peirce.
Squire, Stan, illus. see Thompson, Lisa.
Squires, jt. auth. see Squires, Claire.
Squires, Amanda, jt. auth. see Gaster, Lucy.
Squires, Claire & Squires. Philip Pullman, Master Storyteller: A Guide to the Worlds of His Dark Materials. (p. 1350)
Squires, Janet. Gingerbread Cowboy. Berry, Holly, illus. (p. 677)
Squires, Mary L. Margaret Who Dared to Dream. (p. 1092)
Squires, Patricia. Enter Here. (p. 531)
Squires, R. L. Peaches & Cream Collier, Kevin Scott, illus. (p. 1332)
Squires, Ricky. Lily & Ike (p. 1017)
Squires, Susanne. When I Lose My Tooth. (p. 1903)
Squyres, Steven. Roving Mars: Spirit, Opportunity, & the Exploration of the Red Planet. (p. 1492)
Sr. Harlette. Princess Frisky. (p. 1403)
SRA Publications Staff. Get Set. (p. 668)
—Grade: Gr 6 CDs Share the Music. (p. 705)
Sra/Mcgraw-Hill. Art Connections: Student Edition. (p. 101)
—Come Play with Me Today: (Long A) (p. 347)
—Hopeless Homer: (Long O) (p. 797)
—I Like Surprises: (Long I) (p. 841)
—If You Are Sick: (Short I) (p. 854)
SRA/McGraw-Hill. Open Court Phonemic Awareness & Phonics Kit. (p. 1299)
Sra/Mcgraw-Hill. Shenette Gets the Perfect Pet: (Short E) (p. 1565)
SRA/McGraw-Hill. Specific Skill Series for Language Arts: Middle Set. (p. 1624)
—Specific Skill Series for Language Arts: Primary Set. (p. 1624)
—Specific Skill Series for Language Arts: Level A Starter Set. (p. 1624)
—Specific Skill Series for Language Arts: Level B Starter Set. (p. 1624)
—Specific Skill Series for Language Arts: Level C Starter Set. (p. 1624)
—Specific Skill Series for Language Arts: Level G Starter Set. (p. 1624)
—Specific Skill Series for Language Arts: Level H Starter Set. (p. 1624)
Sra/McGraw-Hill. Specific Skill Series for Language Arts: Level E Starter Set. (p. 1624)
—Specific Skill Series for Language Arts: Level F Starter Set. (p. 1624)
SRA/McGraw-Hill. Specific Skill Series for Language Arts: Upper Elementary Set. (p. 1624)
—Specific Skill Series for Language Arts: Complete Elementary Set. (p. 1624)
Sra/Mcgraw-Hill. Time for Lunch: (Short U) (p. 1751)
Sra/Mcgraw-Hill Staff. Specific Skill Series for Language Arts: Level D Starter Set. (p. 1624)
Sreekumar, T. T. ICTs & Development in India: Perspectives on the Rural Network Society. (p. 851)
Sretaw. Aussie Animal Friends. (p. 116)
—Homonym Hunt. (p. 794)
Sridhar, Kala Seetharam. Incentives for Regional Development: Competition among Sub-National Governments. (p. 868)
Sridharan, Sona. Slip in the Summer. (p. 1590)
Srinivasan, Divya. Little Owl's 1-2-3. Srinivasan, Divya, illus. (p. 1033)
—Little Owl's Colors. Srinivasan, Divya, illus. (p. 1033)
—Little Owl's Day. Srinivasan, Divya, illus. (p. 1033)
—Little Owl's Night. (p. 1033)
—Octopus Alone. (p. 1278)
Srinivasan, Krishnan. Rise, Decline & Future of the British Commonwealth. (p. 1474)

S

Srinivasan, Radhika, et al. India. (p. 870)
Srivi, illus. see Mahadevan, Madhavi S.
Sroda, George. Facts about Nightcrawlers: Redworms & Garden Worms. (p. 561)
—Life Story of TV Star Herman the Worm. Hughes, Janet, illus. (p. 1013)
Sschweiger-dmiel, Izhak. Hanna's Sabbath Dress. Eitan (tchernov), Ora, illus. (p. 743)
Ssebulime, John, illus. see Cohen, Warren Lee.
SSPB Staff, prod. Townsend Press SS Commentary Work-Book 2003-2004. (p. 1773)
St. Amand, R. Paul & Marek, Claudia Craig. Fibromyalgia Fatigue: The Powerful Program That Helps You Boost Your Energy & Reclaim Your Life. (p. 583)
St. Amant, Shayna. Boy in the Forest. (p. 218)
St. Angelo, Ron, photos by see Hitzges, Norm.
St Anthony, Gus, illus. see Marcucci, Vince.
St. Anthony, Jane. Grace above All. (p. 704)
—Isabelle Day Refuses to Die of a Broken Heart. (p. 891)
—Summer Sherman Loved Me. (p. 1675)
St. Antoine, Sara, ed. see Milkweed Editions Staff.
St. Antoine, Sara & Milkweed Editions Staff. Great Lakes: A Literary Field Guide. (p. 716)
St. Antoine, Sara, ed. Great North American Prairie: A Literary Field Guide. Mirocha, Paul & Nicholson, Trudy, illus. (p. 717)
—North Atlantic Coast: A Literary Field Guide. Mirocha, Paul & Nicholson, Trudy, illus. (p. 1264)
St. Antoine, Sarah. Three Bird Summer. (p. 1741)
St. Aubin, Anne. Drafus the Daring Dragon. (p. 476)
St. Aubin, Bruno, illus. see Tibo, Gilles.
St. Aubin, Bruno, jt. auth. see Croteau, Marie-Danielle.
St. Aubin, Claude, illus. see Lemke, Donald B. & Pattison, Ronda.
St. Aubin, Claude, illus. see Patton, Chris.
St. Aubyn, Douglas. Caribbean Fables. (p. 268)
St. Clair, Noel. Unofficial Divergent Aptitude Test: Discover Your True Faction! (p. 1822)
St Clair, Stephen. ORBS: A Haunting at the Claxton Mansion. (p. 1302)
St. Clair, Stephen. ORBS: A Haunting at Five Falls Plantation. (p. 1302)
St. Claire, Erin, pseud & Brown, Sandra. Kiss Remembered. (p. 961)
—Words of Silk. (p. 1952)
St. Claire, Roxanne. They All Fall Down. (p. 1732)
St. Croix, Sammy, jt. auth. see Ganzer, Diane.
St. Crow, Lili. Betrayals. (p. 171)
—Betrayals. (p. 172)
—Betrayals. (p. 172)
—Defiance. (p. 424)
—Jealousy. (p. 911)
—Jealousy. (p. 911)
—Kin. (p. 957)
—Reckoning. (p. 1452)
—Strange Angels. (p. 1664)
—Strange Angels. (p. 1664)
—Wayfarer. (p. 1865)
St. Francis, Susan. Tale of the Bug Fairies: The Two Christmas Year. (p. 1700)
St. George, Carolyn, illus. see Hakowski, Maryann.
St George, Colleen. Don't Pollute Our Island. (p. 468)
St. George, Judith. Duel: The Parallel Lives of Alexander Hamilton & Aaron Burr. (p. 489)
—Ghost, the White House & Me. (p. 672)
—Journey of the One & Only Declaration of Independence. Hillenbrand, Will, illus. (p. 928)
—Sacagawea. (p. 1500)
—So You Want to Be an Inventor? Small, David, illus. (p. 1602)
—So You Want to Be President? Small, David, illus. (p. 1602)
—Stand Tall, Abe Lincoln. Faulkner, Matt, illus. (p. 1639)
—What Was the Lewis & Clark Expedition? (p. 1895)
—What Was the Lewis & Clark Expedition? Foley, Tim, illus. (p. 1895)
St. George, Judith & Faulkner, Matt. You're on Your Way, Teddy Roosevelt. (p. 1982)
St. George, Victoria. Barnyard Bandits. (p. 139)
St. Germain, Mark. Three Cups: Teaching Children How to Save, Spend & Be Charitable with Money Is As Easy As 1, 2, 3. Willy, April, illus. (p. 1741)
—Tres Tazas. Willy, April, illus. (p. 1784)
St. Germain, Wendy. Talking about Exercise. (p. 1703)
St. Jacques, Philip M., jt. auth. see Caron, Lucille.
St. James, Cassidy. Finding a Mate: Animal Companions. (p. 587)
—Teaming Up: Animal Partners. (p. 1710)
St. James, James. Freak Show. (p. 631)
St. James, Leah. Lights of Imani. Morse, Nessa Neilson, illus. (p. 1016)
St. James, Rebecca. 40 Days with God: A Devotional Journey. (p. 1997)
—Friendly Beasts: An Old English Christmas Carol Vojtech, Anna, illus. (p. 637)
St. James, Rebecca, jt. auth. see Bjorklund, Lynda Hunter.
St. Jean, Alan. Aidan of Oren: The Journey Begins. Friedman, Judith, illus. (p. 30)
—Legend of OinkADoodleMoo. St. Jean, Alan, ed. (p. 988)
St. Jean, Catherine. Caleb Takes a Ride on the Staten Island Ferry. Frahm, Paul, illus. (p. 252)
St Jean, Catherine Avery. Staten Island Ferry Tale. Frahm, Paul, illus. (p. 1644)
St. John, Amanda. Bridget & Bo Build a Blog. McDee, Katie, illus. (p. 227)
—Evan & Erin Build an Essay. Rooney, Ronnie, illus. (p. 540)
St. John, Bonnie. How Strong Women Pray. (p. 812)
St. John, Charlotte, ed. see Johnson, Kathryn T. & Balczon, Mary-Lynne J.
St. John, Chris. Wrestling. (p. 1962)
St. John, Justine. Wilbur the Zucchini-Eating Dragon. (p. 1928)
St. John, Kelley. Real Women Don't Wear Size 2. (p. 1449)
St. John, Lauren. Dolphin Song. (p. 464)
—Elephant's Tale. (p. 512)
—Last Leopard. (p. 978)
—White Giraffe. (p. 1913)
St. John, Lauren, jt. auth. see St John, Lauren.
St John, Lauren & St. John, Lauren. Kentucky Thriller. Dean, David, illus. (p. 949)
St. John, Laurence. Metatron: The Angel Has Risen. (p. 1130)
St. John, P. Historias Que Jesus Conto (Stories That Jesus Told) (p. 782)
St. John, Patricia. Friska My Friend & the Other Kitten. (p. 639)
—Home for Virginia. Smith, Helen, illus. (p. 792)
—I Needed a Neighbour. (p. 844)
—Missing the Way: How Israel Missed God's Rest. (p. 1153)
—Nothing Else Matters. (p. 1268)
St John, Patricia. Other Kitten. (p. 1306)
St. John, Patricia. Safe Place. (p. 1502)
—Secret of the Fourth Candle. (p. 1542)
—Talking & Listening to God. (p. 1703)
—Until the Letter Came. Brownlie, Ian D., illus. (p. 1823)
—Victor. (p. 1840)
St. John, Patricia, et al. No Darkness at All: An Adaptation of Patricia St. John's Star of Light. Hertzler, Frances et al, illus. (p. 1258)
St John, Patroca. Friska My Friend. (p. 639)
St. John, Sally. Polar Regions. (p. 1379)
St. John Taylor, Jeannie, illus. see Mehl, Ron, et al.
St. John Taylor, Jeannie, jt. auth. see Taylor, Jeannie St. John.
St. John, Warren. Outcasts United: The Story of a Refugee Soccer Team That Changed a Town. (p. 1312)
St. Julian, Ska. Basket of Seeds. Cameron, Eugenia, illus. (p. 143)
St. Lawrence, Genevieve. Hopi. (p. 797)
—Iroquois & Their History (p. 888)
—Pueblo & Their History (p. 1414)
St. Marcus, Marcus. Tiger & the Turtle. (p. 1748)
St. Mark Kindergarten. Kindergarten Goes to Outer Space for the Day. (p. 957)
St. Peter Chanel High School Staff, compiled by. Phoenix Rising: A Book of Hope. (p. 1351)
St. Peters, Dovie. Snaggletail. (p. 1595)
St. Pierre, Connie. Camping with Mommy. (p. 258)
St. Pierre, Joe, creator. Bold Blood. (p. 208)
St. Pierre, Stephanie. Jesus, the Good Shepherd. Bolam, Emily, illus. (p. 916)
—What the Sea Saw Doyle, Beverly, illus. (p. 1893)
St. Pierre, Todd-Michael. Woolly Mammoth on Amelia Street: Read Aloud Poems4Kids (and Grownups Too!) Douglas, Keith Cartoon Man, illus. (p. 1950)
St. Pierre-Ford, Hillary & Ford, Xander. Z & the Cancer Meanie. LoParco, Chris, illus. (p. 1984)
St. Romain, Rose Anne. Monsieur Durand's Grosse Affaire Waites, Joan, illus. (p. 1166)
—Moon's Cloud Blanket. Waites, Joan C., illus. (p. 1173)
St. Stephen's Community House Staff. It's Not All Black & White: Multiracial Youth Speak Out. (p. 898)
—Little Black Book for Guys: Guys Talk about Sex. (p. 1024)
Staake, Bob. Bluebird. (p. 204)
—Donut Chef. Staake, Bob, illus. (p. 469)
—First Pup: The Real Story of How Bo Got to the White House. Staake, Bob, illus. (p. 596)
—Look! a Book! (p. 1048)
—Look! Another Book! (p. 1048)
—My Pet Book. (p. 1217)
—Red Lemon. (p. 1454)
—Red Lemon. Staake, Bob, illus. (p. 1454)
—This Is Not a Pumpkin. Staake, Bob, illus. (p. 1736)
Staake, Bob, illus. see Bell, Babs.
Staake, Bob, illus. see Fliess, Sue.
Staake, Bob, illus. see Muldrow, Diane.
Staake, Bob, illus. see Shealy, Dennis & Little Golden Books Staff.
Staake, Bob, illus. see Shealy, Dennis & Miryam.
Staake, Bob, illus. see Shealy, Dennis.
Staake, Bob, illus. see Stainton, Sue.
Staake, Bob, illus. see Stein, Peter.
Staake, Bob, illus. see Thomas, Stephen, ed.
Staat, Blaine. Finding Liberty. (p. 588)
Stabenfeldt. Secrets in the Sand. (p. 1544)
Stabenfeldt, prod. Starshine Legacy 2: Comic Book. (p. 1643)
Stabile, Nicolette, illus. see Meissner, Jacqueline.
Stabler, David. Kid Presidents: True Tales of Childhood from America's Presidents. Horner, Doogie, illus. (p. 951)
Stabler, Jane, jt. auth. see Austen, Jane.
Stabler, Ken. Roll Tide! De Angel, Miguel, illus. (p. 1485)
Stables, Gordon. Cruise of the Snowbird - a Story of Arctic Adventure. (p. 386)
Stacey, Alan, illus. see Crane, Carol.
Stacey, Gill. London. (p. 1046)
—Paris. (p. 1324)
—Religions of the Middle East. (p. 1458)
Stacey International Staff, ed. see Johnson, Julia.
Stacey, Mark, illus. see McIntee, David.
Stacey, W., illus. see Leslie, Emma.
Stacey, W. S., illus. see Stretton, Hesba.
Stack, David Martin. Good Morning Captain. (p. 698)
Stack, Edward. Food, Spirits, Lodging. (p. 614)
—Ily's Dream. (p. 858)
Stack, Jocelyn, illus. see Steiner, Stan, et al.
Stack, Kevin W. Great Oak Tree. (p. 717)
Stacy, Alan, illus. see Brown, Tricia.
Stacy, Alan, illus. see Collison, Cathy & Campbell, Janis.
Stacy, Alan, illus. see Crane, Carol.
Stacy, Alan, illus. see Davis, David.
Stacy, Alan, illus. see Herzog, Brad.
Stacy, Alan, illus. see Williamson, Chet.
Stacy, Alan F., illus. see Dailey, Reid.
Stacy, Dorothy. Erie Canal Cousins. Stacy, Dorothy, illus. (p. 533)
—Three Weeks in Utica. Stacy, Dorothy, illus. (p. 1744)
Stacy, Heidi. Hoppy Feelings. (p. 797)
Stacy, Lee. Jaguar. (p. 905)
Stacy, Lori, jt. auth. see White, Kelly.
Stacy, Susan. Talent Machine. (p. 1701)
Stade, George. Love Is War. (p. 1060)
Stader, Kristina, illus. see Stadler, Kristina.
Stadlen, Naomi. What Mothers Do: Especially When It Looks Like Nothing. (p. 1892)
Stadler, Alexander. Invasion of the Relatives. (p. 883)
—Trash Crisis on Earth. (p. 1780)
—What Willie Wore: Scenes from the Life & Wardrobe of a Very Fashionable Dog. (p. 1895)
Stadler, Charlotte. About How Many? (p. 5)
—About How Many? & ¡Adivina cuántos Hay! 6 English, 6 Spanish Adaptations (p. 6)
—Building a Castle. (p. 238)
—Building a Castle & Nuestro Castillo: 6 English, 6 Spanish Adaptations (p. 238)
—Coin Magic. (p. 338)
—Dos Hipopotamos con Hambre: Set Of 6. (p. 472)
—Dulces Sabrosos: Set Of 6. (p. 489)
—Frijolitos Dulces: Set Of 6. (p. 639)
—Jellybeans & Frijolitos Dulces: 6 English, 6 Spanish Adaptations (p. 912)
—Las Lagartijas: Set Of 6. (p. 976)
—Leaping Lizards & Las Lagartijas: 6 English, 6 Spanish Adaptations (p. 982)
—Making Patterns. (p. 1082)
—Making Patterns & ¿Qué son Patrones? 6 English, 6 Spanish Adaptations (p. 1082)
—Nuestro Castillo: Set Of 6. (p. 1270)
—Origami. (p. 1303)
—Penny Candy. (p. 1338)
—Penny Candy & Dulces Sabrosos: 6 English, 6 Spanish Adaptations (p. 1338)
—¡Adivina Cuántos Hay! Set Of 6. (p. 12)
—¿Qué Son Patrones? Set Of 6. (p. 1424)
Stadler, John. Catilda. Stadler, John, illus. (p. 280)
—Cats of Mrs. Calamari (p. 281)
—Snail Saves the Day (p. 1596)
—Three Cheers for Hippo! (p. 1741)
Stadler, Kristina. Frog on my Head. Stader, Kristina & Stroede, Paul, illus. (p. 640)
Stadler, Terrie. Who's Knocking at My Door? A Country Pond Tale. (p. 1920)
Stadther, Michael. 101 New Puzzles Clues, Maps, Tantalizing Tales: And Stories of Real Treasure. Stadther, Michael, illus. (p. 1999)
—Secrets of the Alchemist Dar. Stadther, Michael, illus. (p. 1545)
Stadtlander, Becca, illus. see Doyle, Eugenie.
Stadtlander, Becca, illus. see Elliott, David.
Stadtler, Bea. Adventures of Gluckel of Hameln. (p. 18)
Stadtler, M. Melvin Twitcher Book of Stories & Poems: M J Stadtler. (p. 1125)
Stadtman, Shep. Dollhouse Furnishings for the Bedroom & Bath: Complete Instructions for Sewing & Making 44 Miniature Projects. (p. 464)
Staeger, Rob. Angola. (p. 75)
—Angola. Rotberg, Robert I., ed. (p. 75)
—Asylees. (p. 109)
—Boom Towns. (p. 213)
—Deported Aliens. (p. 427)
—Hunting with the Native Americans. Johnson, Troy, ed. (p. 829)
—Native American Religions. Johnson, Troy, ed. (p. 1234)
—Native American Sports & Games. Johnson, Troy, ed. (p. 1234)
—Native American Tools & Weapons. Johnson, Troy, ed. (p. 1234)
Staehli, Melissa. Charlie's Gingerbread House. Rottinger, Amy, illus. (p. 293)
—I Love You to the Moon. (p. 844)
Staehr, Linda, jt. auth. see Fleury, Rick.
Staf, Edie. Christmas Novena: For Home or Classroom. (p. 314)
Staff, Di I., jt. auth. see Francesc Bargada Studios Staff.
Staffen, Julie. Krista Kay MacKinac Island Adventures. (p. 967)
—Krista Kay Summer Adventures. (p. 967)
Staffi, Iginio, jt. auth. see VIZ Media Staff.
Stafford, Andy, ed. see Barthes, Roland.
Stafford, Andy, tr. see Barthes, Roland.
Stafford, Anika. Aisha's Moonlit Walk: Stories & Celebrations for the Pagan Year. (p. 32)
Stafford, Diane, jt. auth. see Shoquist, Jennifer.
Stafford, Emma. Exploring the Life, Myth, & Art of Ancient Greece. (p. 554)
Stafford, Gerry. Young Canaller. Wanecski, Erica Joan, illus. (p. 1978)
Stafford, James. Malta. (p. 1084)
Stafford, James & Indovino, Shaina Carmel. Malta. (p. 1084)
Stafford, Jean & Van Draanen, Wendelin. Villain's Lair. Blegvad, Erik & Gilpin, Stephen, illus. (p. 1842)
Stafford, Jordan, illus. see Gambini, Josephine.
Stafford, Jordan, illus. see Mitchell, Shirley Lipscomb.
Stafford, Lesa. Then Came Samuel. (p. 1729)
Stafford, Liliana. Snow Bear. Davis, Lambert, illus. (p. 1598)
Stafford, Lonnie. I'm a Child of God: Songs & Activities for Preschool Choirs & School Programs. Tyree, Debra, ed. (p. 858)
Stafford, Mark & Davenport, John, texts. W. E. B. Du Bois: Scholar & Activist. (p. 1851)
Stafford, Mary. Lincoln & the Lilac Lilies. Dennis, Nadine, illus. (p. 1018)
—Lincoln's Day of Discovery Dennis, Nadine, illus. (p. 1019)
—Lincoln's Journey of Journeys Dennis, Nadine, illus. (p. 1019)
Stafford, Paul. 101 Damnations. (p. 1999)
—Feral Peril. (p. 581)
—Great Brain Robbery. (p. 714)
—Interghouls Cricket Cup. (p. 880)
Stafford, Rosalee, illus. see Salyers, Rita.
Stafford, Susan. Pocket Pegasus. (p. 1375)
Stafford, Susan, ed. see Archer, Colleen Rutherford.
Stafford, Susan, ed. Dog Tales for the Soul (p. 461)
—Horse Tales for the Soul (p. 800)
Stafford-Crandall, Bectoria. Hunt for Christmas Treasure. (p. 828)
Staggenborg, Kim, illus. see Woodfield, Elaine.
Staggs, Kelley, jt. auth. see Hutson-Thompson, Holliday.
Staggs, Sam. When Blanche Met Brando: The Scandalous Story of a Streetcar Named Desire. (p. 1901)
Stagliano, Katie. Katie's Cabbage. Heid, Karen, illus. (p. 945)
Stagliano, Michael F. Wesley's Stories: Afterschool Adventures. (p. 1876)
Stagnaro, Angelo. Catechist's Magic Kit: 80 Simple Tricks for Teaching Catholicism to Kids. Pryor, Sean, illus. (p. 279)
Stagnitti, Karen. Playthings: 101 Used for Everyday Objects. Treffry, Teresa, illus. (p. 1373)
Stagno, Laura, illus. see Anónimo.
Stahel, Merry Kesner. Jennifer's Christmas Gift. (p. 913)
Stahell, Bee, ed. Owl Who Couldn't Say Whoo. Clish, Lori, illus. (p. 1315)
Stahl, Daniel. Who Knows What God Knows. (p. 1916)
Stahl, Deborah Joan. Man Called Christmas. (p. 1085)
Stahl, Hilda. Big Trouble for Roxie. (p. 184)
Stahl, J. D., tr. see Kästner, Erich.
Stahl, Joan Christine. Pathway to the Son: On a Journey to His Kingdom. (p. 1328)
Stahl, Katherine A. Dougherty & McKenna, Michael C., eds. Reading Research at Work: Foundations of Effective Practice. (p. 1446)
Stahl, Mary L. Accumulating Cats. (p. 8)
Stahl, Mary Louise. Louie. (p. 1058)
Stahl, Matt. Fuzzy Winkerbane: The Boy Who Would Never Change. (p. 651)
Stahl, Michael. Early to Rise: A Young Adult's Guide to Investing... & Financial Decisions That Can Shape Your Life. (p. 494)
Stahl, Miriam Klein, illus. see Schatz, Kate.
Stahl, Richard O. Back to Basics, Back to School. (p. 130)
Stahl, Richard Otto. United States Army Europe: One Soldier's Story. (p. 1819)
Stahl, Stephanie. Best Snowman Ever! Vasylenko, Veronica, illus. (p. 171)
Stahlberg, Carina, illus. see Lewis, Anne G.
Stahlberg, Carina, illus. see Rydaker, Ewa.
Stahlberg, Whitney, tr. see DeMonfreid, Dorothée.
Stahler, David, Jr. Doppelganger. (p. 470)
—Gathering of Shades. (p. 658)
—Seer. (p. 1548)
—Spinning Out. (p. 1628)
—Truesight. (p. 1793)
Stahnke, Rich. Furious Fist of the Drunken Monkey: Origin of the Species #3. (p. 650)
Staige, Pat, jt. auth. see Banicki, Patsy.
Staines, Bill. All God's Critters. Nelson, Kadir, illus. (p. 44)
Staino, Franco. Adventures of Pinocchio. (p. 21)
Staino, Franco, illus. see Collodi, Carlo.
Stainton, Sue. Chocolate Cat. Mortimer, Anne, illus. (p. 309)
—Christmas Magic. Melhuish, Eva, illus. (p. 314)
—I Love Dogs. Truesdell, Sue, illus. (p. 842)
—I Love Dogs! Truesdell, Sue & Staake, Bob, illus. (p. 842)
—Lighthouse Cat. Mortimer, Anne, illus. (p. 1015)
Stair, Karen Smith. Glasses, Glasses Oh What Do I See. (p. 682)
Stair, Nancy. Choosing a Career in Mortuary Science & the Funeral Industry. (p. 310)
—Michelle Yeoh. (p. 1135)
Stair, Nancy L. Choosing a Career in Mortuary Science & the Funeral Industry. (p. 310)
—Michelle Yeoh. (p. 1135)
Stair, Nancy L., jt. auth. see Wolfe, James.
Stairs-Oberlick, Anita Ruth. Helen the Transartist. (p. 763)
Staker, Sara. My Baptism Keepsake. (p. 1196)
Stakes, Mary E., jt. auth. see Jackson, Edwin L.
Stalcup, Ann. Brazil in Colors. (p. 224)
—Guatemala in Colors (p. 728)
—Hungary. (p. 827)
—Mexico in Colors (p. 1131)
Stalcup, Ann & Politi, Leo. Leo Politi: Artist of the Angels. (p. 992)
Stalcup, Brenda. Late Middle Ages. (p. 979)
Stalder, Erika. Fashion 101: A Crash Course in Clothing. Kreitzman, Ariel, illus. (p. 575)
—Look Book: 50 Iconic Beauties & How to Achieve Their Signature Styles. Pesce, Carol, illus. (p. 1049)
Stalder, Päivi. Advent Elf. Korthues, Barbara, illus. (p. 14)
—Ernest's First Easter. Weldin, Frauke, illus. (p. 534)
—My Wish Tonight. Wolferman, Iris, illus. (p. 1221)
Stalder, Paula A. I Wish I Had Curly Hair. (p. 848)
Staler-Kucholtz, Kristin. Marlin, Harry, & the Great River Rescue. (p. 1096)
Staley, Erin. Career Building Through Creating Mobile Apps. (p. 266)
—Careers in Hospitality (p. 268)
—Defeating Stress & Anxiety. (p. 423)
—Improving Community Health & Safety Through Service Learning (p. 862)
—Maggie Stiefvater. (p. 1071)
—Martin Luther King Jr. & the Speech That Inspired the World. (p. 1098)
—Nick Swinmurn, Tony Hsieh, & Zappos. (p. 1251)
—What Is Animal Camouflage? (p. 1889)
Staley, Loretta B. They Had to Die! (p. 1732)
Staley, S. Little Tommie. (p. 1037)
Staley, Samuel. Pirate of Panther Bay Classroom Guide. (p. 1362)
Stalfelt, Pernilla. Death Book. (p. 420)
Stalick, Garyanna. Cocoa's Collar Goodwin, Wendy, illus. (p. 337)
Stalikas, Jimmy. Rocket & the Construction Worker. (p. 1482)
Stalio, Ivan, illus. see Starry Dog Books.
Stalker, Aileen. One & Only Sam: A Story Explaining Idioms for Children with Asperger Syndrome & Other Communication Difficulties. Spence, Bob, illus. (p. 1293)
Staller, Mary J. Meet Sandy Gull. (p. 1122)
Stalling-Patton, Deborah. Shypoodle: Getting to Know You. (p. 1572)
Stallings, Gary. Mario's Golden Locket. (p. 1094)
Stallop, Christy, illus. see Pluta, K.
Stallworth, Rachel. SaSsy SaRaH: A Children's Book. (p. 1515)
Stalsjo, Eva, illus. see Sandwall-Bergstrom, Martha.
Stålsjö, Eva, illus. see Sandwall-Bergström, Martha.

Staman, A. Louise. Rupert & the Bag. Adams, Rich, illus. (p. 1497)
Sta.Maria, Ian, illus. see Caputo, Antonella, et al.
Stamatinos, Lucy. Nicholas. (p. 1250)
Stamatis, Alexis. Seventh Elephant. Connolly, David, tr. (p. 1555)
Stamaty, Mark Alan. Alia's Mission: Saving the Books of Iraq. (p. 39)
—Muhimat Al Sayyda Alia: Inkaz Kuttub Al Iraq. (p. 1189)
—Shake, Rattle & Turn That Noise Down! How Elvis Shook up Music, Me & Mom. (p. 1558)
—Who Needs Donuts? (p. 1917)
Stamey, Marsha. Man in the Clouds Jones, Seth, illus. (p. 1085)
Stamford, Tasha. Monet (p. 1163)
Stamm, Linda J. Lilly & Zander: A Children's Story about Equine-Assisted Activities. Whitaker, Suzanne, illus. (p. 1017)
Stamm, Peter & Bauer, Jutta. When We Lived in Uncle's Hat. Schumman, Nani & Connolly, Kate, trs. from GER. (p. 1905)
Stamm, Stephanie. Gift of Wings. (p. 675)
Stammen, Jo Ellen McAllister, illus. see Spinelli, Eileen.
Stammen, JoEllen McAllister, illus. see Mason, Cherie.
Stamp, Jeffrey. Red & Slim: One Hot Day. Bohrer, Joe, illus. (p. 1453)
Stamp, Jorgen. Volando Alto. (p. 1848)
Stamp, Jorgen & Buckley, William F., Jr. Flying High. (p. 610)
Stamper, G. C. Nelson Mandela. (p. 1240)
Stamper, Judith. Polar Bear Patrol. Haefele, Steve, illus. (p. 1378)
—Voyage to the Volcano. Speirs, John, illus. (p. 1850)
Stamper, Judith, jt. auth. see Stamper, Judith Bauer.
Stamper, Judith B. Polar Bear Patrol. Haefele, Steve, illus. (p. 1378)
Stamper, Judith Bauer. 5-Minute Grammar Practice: 180 Quick & Motivating Activities Students Can Use to Practice Essential Grammar Skills-Every Day of the School Year. (p. 1992)
—Breakfast at Danny's Diner: A Book about Multiplication. Demarest, Chris L., illus. (p. 224)
—Buildings, Buildings, Buildings. (p. 239)
—Caves. (p. 282)
—Earthquakes. (p. 497)
—Eco Dogs. (p. 502)
—Growing Trees. Lowe, Wesley, illus. (p. 726)
—House, Sweet House. (p. 803)
—Quinceañera. Varma, Ishan, illus. (p. 1428)
—Ragdolls: Alien Cats. (p. 1433)
—Rocks & Minerals. (p. 1483)
—Rocky Road Trip. Gangloff, Hope, illus. (p. 1484)
—Sam Helps Recycle. (p. 1506)
—Text-Marking Lessons for Active Nonfiction Reading: Reproducible Nonfiction Passages with Lessons That Guide Students to Read Strategically, Identify Text Structures, & Activate Comprehension. (p. 1724)
—Tree Is For- (p. 1783)
—Volcanoes. (p. 1849)
—Voyage to the Volcano. Speirs, John, illus. (p. 1850)
—Who Wears What? (p. 1919)
Stamper, Judith Bauer & Bauer-Stamper, Judith. Rocky Road Trip. Gangloff, Hope, illus. (p. 1484)
Stamper, Judith Bauer & Keyes, Joan Ross. Diego's Big Day. (p. 437)
—Fun on the Farm. Springer, Sally, illus. (p. 648)
—Monster Parade. (p. 1168)
—Out the Window! (p. 1311)
—Snow Tracks. (p. 1599)
—Sweet Surprise. (p. 1690)
—Trip to Toy Town. (p. 1787)
—What's for Breakfast? Springer, Sally, illus. (p. 1897)
Stamper, Judith Bauer & Ross Keyes, Joan. Hide & Seek. Springer, Sally, illus. (p. 776)
—Hop, Hop, Jump! (p. 796)
Stamper, Judith Bauer & Stamper, Judith. Go, Fractions! Demarest, Chris L., illus. (p. 686)
—Polar Bear Patrol. (p. 1379)
—Voyage to the Volcano. (p. 1850)
Stamper, Judith Bauer & Willows, Vicky. Fossils. (p. 624)
Stamper, Judith Bauer, et al. Polar Bear Patrol. Haefele, Steve, illus. (p. 1378)
Stampler, Ann Redisch. Afterparty. (p. 29)
—Cats on Ben Yehuda Street. Carabelli, Francesca, illus. (p. 281)
—Where It Began. (p. 1909)
Stamps, Caroline, jt. auth. see Dorling Kindersley Publishing Staff.
Stamps, Paula. Learning Makes Friends Fun (p. 985)
Stamps, Sarah. Our Gang & the Shrinking Machine. Workman, Paula J., illus. (p. 1308)
Stamps, Stephanie J. Earnest the Duck with the Wide Feet. (p. 494)
Stamschror, Robert P., ed. see Aresenault, Jane & Cedor, Jean.
Stamschror, Robert P., ed. see Arsenault, Jane & Cedor, Jean.
Stamschror, Robert P., ed. see Hakowski, Maryann.
Stan, Adrianna. Letters. (p. 1002)
Stan, Andreea. Cloud Fairy Tales: The Clouds Are Our Feelings. (p. 334)
Stan, Jaskiel. Families are Forever Learning & Activity Guide. (p. 567)
Stan, Jaskiel, illus. see Deb, Capone.
Stan, N. Tales from Elisa's Garden. (p. 1701)
Stanbridge, Joanne. Extraordinary Music of Mr. Ives: The True Story of a Famous American Composer. Stanbridge, Joanne, illus. (p. 555)
—Maurice Ruddick: Un Survivant. (p. 1110)
Stanbro, Heather. Lion Without A Roar. (p. 1020)
Stanbury, Jean. How to Dazzle at Being a Scientist. (p. 816)
Stanbury, Sarah & Mehta, Sonia. 101 Things You Should Know about Geography. (p. 2000)
Stanchfield, Justin. Timewalker. (p. 1754)
Stanchfield, Ronald M., jt. auth. see Chepokas, Rebecca.
Stancic, Giselle M. Paganini Curse. (p. 1318)
Stancil, Kristina. One Boy, One Girl. (p. 1294)
Standard, Carole K. Arizona. (p. 98)
Standard Publishing Staff. 20 Bible Stories Every Child Should Know. (p. 1995)
—Bible Crafts & More, Ages 3-6. (p. 175)
—Bible Puzzles for Kids, Ages 6-8. (p. 176)
—Bible Puzzles for Kids, Ages 8-10. (p. 176)
—Bible Stories to Color & Tell, Ages 3-6. Grossmann, Dan, illus. (p. 176)
—Bible Stories to Color & Tell, Ages 6-8. Ebert, Len, illus. (p. 176)
—Church Programs for Special Days: Plays, Poems, & Ideas for 10 Celebrations! (p. 318)
—Discover God's Love: 52 Bible Lessons for Ages 3 & 4. (p. 447)
—Follow the Bible: 52 Bible Lessons for Beginning Readers Ages 6-8. (p. 612)
—God Loves Me Coloring Pages: For Toddlers & 2s. Bausman, Mary, illus. (p. 689)
—Grow up in Christ: 52 Bible Lessons from the New Testament for Ages 8-12. (p. 726)
—Léeme Historias de la Biblia (Read to Me Bible Stories) Ebert, Len, illus. (p. 987)
—Maps & Charts. (p. 1090)
—Self Esteem. (p. 1549)
—Standard Bible Atlas. (p. 1639)
—Thru-the-Bible Coloring Pages, (Ages 3-6) Skiles, Janet, illus. (p. 1745)
—Thru-the-Bible Coloring Pages, Ages 6-8. Skiles, Janet, illus. (p. 1745)
—Time Lines & Activities. (p. 1752)
Standard Publishing Staff, jt. auth. see Route 52 Staff.
Standard Publishing Staff, creator. What a Wonderful Life for Dads: Tackling the Awesome Responsibilities & Joys of Fatherhood. (p. 1878)
—What a Wonderful Life for Graduates. (p. 1878)
—What a Wonderful Life for Moms: Celebrating the Wonder & Joy of Motherhood. (p. 1878)
Standfield, Robert. Little Tacker's Guide to Opposites. (p. 1037)
Standifer, Charlcy. Butch the One-Of-a-Kind Dog. (p. 246)
Standifer, Lauren, et al. Grinnell College College Prowler off the Record. (p. 724)
Standiford, Natalie. Boy on the Bridge. (p. 218)
—Breaking up Is Really, Really Hard to Do. (p. 225)
—Confessions of the Sullivan Sisters. (p. 356)
—Countdown (p. 370)
—Dating Game (p. 409)
—Ex-Rating. (p. 547)
—How to Say Goodbye in Robot. (p. 821)
—Parallel Parking. (p. 1324)
—Secret Tree. (p. 1544)
—Speed Dating. (p. 1624)
—Switched at Birthday. (p. 1692)
Standingdeer, John, Jr., illus. see Duncan, Barbara, ed.
Standish, Burt L. Dick Merriwell Abroad. Rudman, Jack, ed. (p. 435)
—Dick Merriwell Adrift. Rudman, Jack, ed. (p. 435)
—Dick Merriwell at Fardale. Rudman, Jack, ed. (p. 435)
—Dick Merriwell Doubted. Rudman, Jack, ed. (p. 435)
—Dick Merriwell, Freshman. Rudman, Jack, ed. (p. 435)
—Dick Merriwell in the Wilds. Rudman, Jack, ed. (p. 435)
—Dick Merriwell on the Gridiron. Rudman, Jack, ed. (p. 435)
—Dick Merriwell, the Wizard. Rudman, Jack, ed. (p. 435)
—Dick Merriwell's Ability. Rudman, Jack, ed. (p. 435)
—Dick Merriwell's Assurance. Rudman, Jack, ed. (p. 436)
—Dick Merriwell's Backers. Rudman, Jack, ed. (p. 436)
—Dick Merriwell's Backstop. Rudman, Jack, ed. (p. 436)
—Dick Merriwell's Best Work. Rudman, Jack, ed. (p. 436)
—Dick Merriwell's Black Star. Rudman, Jack, ed. (p. 436)
—Dick Merriwell's Cleverness. Rudman, Jack, ed. (p. 436)
—Dick Merriwell's Close Call. Rudman, Jack, ed. (p. 436)
—Dick Merriwell's Dare. Rudman, Jack, ed. (p. 436)
—Dick Merriwell's Dash. Rudman, Jack, ed. (p. 436)
—Dick Merriwell's Day. Rudman, Jack, ed. (p. 436)
—Dick Merriwell's Debt. Rudman, Jack, ed. (p. 436)
—Dick Merriwell's Defense. Rudman, Jack, ed. (p. 436)
—Dick Merriwell's Delivery. Rudman, Jack, ed. (p. 436)
—Dick Merriwell's Diamond. Rudman, Jack, ed. (p. 436)
—Dick Merriwell's Disguise. Rudman, Jack, ed. (p. 436)
—Dick Merriwell's Downfall. Rudman, Jack, ed. (p. 436)
—Dick Merriwell's Example. Rudman, Jack, ed. (p. 436)
—Dick Merriwell's Five. Rudman, Jack, ed. (p. 436)
—Dick Merriwell's Glory. Rudman, Jack, ed. (p. 436)
—Dick Merriwell's Grit. Rudman, Jack, ed. (p. 436)
—Dick Merriwell's Home Run. Rudman, Jack, ed. (p. 436)
—Dick Merriwell's Honors. Rudman, Jack, ed. (p. 436)
—Dick Merriwell's Influence. Rudman, Jack, ed. (p. 436)
—Dick Merriwell's Joke. Rudman, Jack, ed. (p. 436)
—Dick Merriwell's Long Slide. Rudman, Jack, ed. (p. 436)
—Dick Merriwell's Magnetism. Rudman, Jack, ed. (p. 436)
—Dick Merriwell's Marked Money. Rudman, Jack, ed. (p. 436)
—Dick Merriwell's Mastery. Rudman, Jack, ed. (p. 436)
—Dick Merriwell's Model. Rudman, Jack, ed. (p. 436)
—Dick Merriwell's Mystery. Rudman, Jack, ed. (p. 436)
—Dick Merriwell's Narrow Escape. Rudman, Jack, ed. (p. 436)
—Dick Merriwell's Persistence. Rudman, Jack, ed. (p. 436)
—Dick Merriwell's Polo Team. Rudman, Jack, ed. (p. 436)
—Dick Merriwell's Pranks. Rudman, Jack, ed. (p. 436)
—Dick Merriwell's Promise. Rudman, Jack, ed. (p. 436)
—Dick Merriwell's Racket. Rudman, Jack, ed. (p. 436)
—Dick Merriwell's Regret. Rudman, Jack, ed. (p. 436)
—Dick Merriwell's Reputation. Rudman, Jack, ed. (p. 436)
—Dick Merriwell's Rescue. Rudman, Jack, ed. (p. 436)
—Dick Merriwell's Resource. Rudman, Jack, ed. (p. 436)
—Dick Merriwell's Return. Rudman, Jack, ed. (p. 436)
—Dick Merriwell's Revenge. Rudman, Jack, ed. (p. 436)
—Dick Merriwell's Ruse. Rudman, Jack, ed. (p. 436)
—Dick Merriwell's Stanchness. Rudman, Jack, ed. (p. 436)
—Dick Merriwell's Stand. Rudman, Jack, ed. (p. 436)
—Dick Merriwell's Staying Power. Rudman, Jack, ed. (p. 436)
—Dick Merriwell's Stroke. Rudman, Jack, ed. (p. 436)
—Dick Merriwell's Team Mate. Rudman, Jack, ed. (p. 436)
—Dick Merriwell's Test. Rudman, Jack, ed. (p. 436)
—Dick Merriwell's Threat. Rudman, Jack, ed. (p. 436)
—Dick Merriwell's Trap. Rudman, Jack, ed. (p. 436)
—Dick Merriwell's Way. Rudman, Jack, ed. (p. 436)
—Dick Merriwell's Western Mission. Rudman, Jack, ed. (p. 436)
—Dick Merriwell's Wonders. Rudman, Jack, ed. (p. 436)
—Frank Merriwell as Coach. Rudman, Jack, ed. (p. 628)
—Frank Merriwell down South. Rudman, Jack, ed. (p. 628)
—Frank Merriwell Facing His Foes. Rudman, Jack, ed. (p. 628)
—Frank Merriwell in Camp. Rudman, Jack, ed. (p. 628)
—Frank Merriwell in England. Rudman, Jack, ed. (p. 628)
—Frank Merriwell in Europe. Rudman, Jack, ed. (p. 628)
—Frank Merriwell in Kentucky. Rudman, Jack, ed. (p. 628)
—Frank Merriwell in Maine. Rudman, Jack, ed. (p. 628)
—Frank Merriwell in the Rockies. Rudman, Jack, ed. (p. 628)
—Frank Merriwell in Wall Street. Rudman, Jack, ed. (p. 628)
—Frank Merriwell on the Boulevards. Rudman, Jack, ed. (p. 628)
—Frank Merriwell on the Road. Rudman, Jack, ed. (p. 628)
—Frank Merriwell on Top. Rudman, Jack, ed. (p. 628)
—Frank Merriwell's Air Voyage. Rudman, Jack, ed. (p. 628)
—Frank Merriwell's Alarm. Rudman, Jack, ed. (p. 628)
—Frank Merriwell's Athletes. Rudman, Jack, ed. (p. 628)
—Frank Merriwell's Auto. Rudman, Jack, ed. (p. 628)
—Frank Merriwell's Backers. Rudman, Jack, ed. (p. 628)
—Frank Merriwell's Baseball Victories. Rudman, Jack, ed. (p. 628)
—Frank Merriwell's Bicycle Tour. Rudman, Jack, ed. (p. 628)
—Frank Merriwell's Bravery. (p. 628)
—Frank Merriwell's Bravery. Rudman, Jack, ed. (p. 628)
—Frank Merriwell's Challengers. Rudman, Jack, ed. (p. 628)
—Frank Merriwell's Champions. Rudman, Jack, ed. (p. 628)
—Frank Merriwell's Chase. Rudman, Jack, ed. (p. 628)
—Frank Merriwell's Chums. (p. 628)
—Frank Merriwell's Club. Rudman, Jack, ed. (p. 628)
—Frank Merriwell's College Chums. Rudman, Jack, ed. (p. 628)
—Frank Merriwell's Confidence. Rudman, Jack, ed. (p. 628)
—Frank Merriwell's Courage. Rudman, Jack, ed. (p. 628)
—Frank Merriwell's Cruise. Rudman, Jack, ed. (p. 628)
—Frank Merriwell's Danger. Rudman, Jack, ed. (p. 628)
—Frank Merriwell's Double Shot. Rudman, Jack, ed. (p. 628)
—Frank Merriwell's Duel. Rudman, Jack, ed. (p. 628)
—Frank Merriwell's Encounter. Rudman, Jack, ed. (p. 628)
—Frank Merriwell's Encouragement. Rudman, Jack, ed. (p. 628)
—Frank Merriwell's Faith. Rudman, Jack, ed. (p. 628)
—Frank Merriwell's False Friend. Rudman, Jack, ed. (p. 628)
—Frank Merriwell's Fame. Rudman, Jack, ed. (p. 628)
—Frank Merriwell's First Job. Rudman, Jack, ed. (p. 628)
—Frank Merriwell's Fortune. Rudman, Jack, ed. (p. 628)
—Frank Merriwell's Fun. Rudman, Jack, ed. (p. 628)
—Frank Merriwell's Generosity. Rudman, Jack, ed. (p. 628)
—Frank Merriwell's Great Scheme. Rudman, Jack, ed. (p. 628)
—Frank Merriwell's Happy Camp. Rudman, Jack, ed. (p. 628)
—Frank Merriwell's Hard Case. Rudman, Jack, ed. (p. 629)
—Frank Merriwell's Honor. Rudman, Jack, ed. (p. 629)
—Frank Merriwell's Hunting Tour. Rudman, Jack, ed. (p. 629)
—Frank Merriwell's Iron Nerve. Rudman, Jack, ed. (p. 629)
—Frank Merriwell's Leaguers. Rudman, Jack, ed. (p. 629)
—Frank Merriwell's Lesson. Rudman, Jack, ed. (p. 629)
—Frank Merriwell's Loyalty. Rudman, Jack, ed. (p. 629)
—Frank Merriwell's Luck. Rudman, Jack, ed. (p. 629)
—Frank Merriwell's Marriage. Rudman, Jack, ed. (p. 629)
—Frank Merriwell's Marvel. Rudman, Jack, ed. (p. 629)
—Frank Merriwell's New Boy. Rudman, Jack, ed. (p. 629)
—Frank Merriwell's New Comedian. Rudman, Jack, ed. (p. 629)
—Frank Merriwell's Nomads. Rudman, Jack, ed. (p. 629)
—Frank Merriwell's Opportunity. Rudman, Jack, ed. (p. 629)
—Frank Merriwell's Own Company. Rudman, Jack, ed. (p. 629)
—Frank Merriwell's Party. Rudman, Jack, ed. (p. 629)
—Frank Merriwell's Peril. Rudman, Jack, ed. (p. 629)
—Frank Merriwell's Phantom. Rudman, Jack, ed. (p. 629)
—Frank Merriwell's Power. Rudman, Jack, ed. (p. 629)
—Frank Merriwell's Pride. Rudman, Jack, ed. (p. 629)
—Frank Merriwell's Problem. Rudman, Jack, ed. (p. 629)
—Frank Merriwell's Prosperity. Rudman, Jack, ed. (p. 629)
—Frank Merriwell's Pupils. Rudman, Jack, ed. (p. 629)
—Frank Merriwell's Pursuit. Rudman, Jack, ed. (p. 629)
—Frank Merriwell's Races. (p. 629)
—Frank Merriwell's Races. Rudman, Jack, ed. (p. 629)
—Frank Merriwell's Rescue. Rudman, Jack, ed. (p. 629)
—Frank Merriwell's Return to Yale. Rudman, Jack, ed. (p. 629)
—Frank Merriwell's Rough Deal. Rudman, Jack, ed. (p. 629)
—Frank Merriwell's Search. Rudman, Jack, ed. (p. 629)
—Frank Merriwell's Setback. Rudman, Jack, ed. (p. 629)
—Frank Merriwell's Shrewdness. Rudman, Jack, ed. (p. 629)
—Frank Merriwell's Skill. Rudman, Jack, ed. (p. 629)
—Frank Merriwell's Son. Rudman, Jack, ed. (p. 629)
—Frank Merriwell's Sports Afield. Rudman, Jack, ed. (p. 629)
—Frank Merriwell's Stage Hit. Rudman, Jack, ed. (p. 629)
—Frank Merriwell's Steadying Hand. Rudman, Jack, ed. (p. 629)
—Frank Merriwell's Strategy. Rudman, Jack, ed. (p. 629)
—Frank Merriwell's Strong Arm. Rudman, Jack, ed. (p. 629)
—Frank Merriwell's Support. Rudman, Jack, ed. (p. 629)
—Frank Merriwell's Talisman. Rudman, Jack, ed. (p. 629)
—Frank Merriwell's Temptation. Rudman, Jack, ed. (p. 629)
—Frank Merriwell's Tigers. Rudman, Jack, ed. (p. 629)
—Frank Merriwell's Tricks. Rudman, Jack, ed. (p. 629)
—Frank Merriwell's Trip West. Rudman, Jack, ed. (p. 629)
—Frank Merriwell's Triumph. Rudman, Jack, ed. (p. 629)
—Frank Merriwell's Trump Card. Rudman, Jack, ed. (p. 629)
—Frank Merriwell's Trust. Rudman, Jack, ed. (p. 629)
—Frank Merriwell's Vacation. Rudman, Jack, ed. (p. 629)
—Frank Merriwell's Victories. Rudman, Jack, ed. (p. 629)
—Frank Merriwell's Winners. Rudman, Jack, ed. (p. 629)
—Frank Merriwell's Wizard. Rudman, Jack, ed. (p. 629)
—Frank Merriwell's Worst Boy. Rudman, Jack, ed. (p. 629)
Standish, Burt L. & Rudman, Jack. Frank Merriwell on the Boulevards. (p. 628)
Standish, Ella, jt. auth. see Standish, Russell R.
Standish, Joyce, ed. see Tika.
Standish, Joyce, ed. Adventures of Ryan Lincoln. Cooper, Nicole, illus. (p. 22)
Standish, Marilyn, jt. auth. see Landes, William-Alan.
Standish, Russell R. & Standish, Ella. Gwanpa & Nanny's Home. (p. 733)
Standish, Sharon L. Ganly Delivers Parcel & Post: Bountiful Blessing Township. (p. 655)
Standke, Linda. Hidden Pictures: Explore Hidden Treasures in God's Word. (p. 776)
—Hidden Pictures, Grades 1 - 3: Explore Hidden Treasures in God's Word. (p. 776)
—Hidden Pictures, Grades Pk - K: Explore Hidden Treasures in God's Word. (p. 776)
—Play & Learn Bible Games: 16 Reproducible Games to Help Children Grow in Their Faith. (p. 1371)
Standley, Andrew. My Old Cat. (p. 1216)
Standley, Peter, illus. see Jacques, Brian.
Standridge, T. L. Melanie Marie Mary Mowry & the Sugar Plum Fairies. (p. 1125)
Standring, Richard. Dangerous Encounters. (p. 404)
Stanek, Gerald. Sarah 'n' Dippity. Stanek, Joyce Huntington, illus. (p. 1514)
Stanek, Joyce Huntington, illus. see Stanek, Gerald.
Stanek, Linda. Beco's Big Year: A Baby Elephant Turns One. (p. 156)
—Pig & Miss Prudence Castillo, Lauren, illus. (p. 1357)
Stanek, Linda, photos by see Stanek, Mary Beth.
Stanek, Mary Beth. Fire Keepers: Mystery at Manitou Beach. Stanek, Mary Beth, illus. (p. 590)
Stanek, Muriel. We Came from Vietnam. McMahon, Wm. Franklin, photos by. (p. 1866)
Stanek, Robert, pseud. Adventures with Letters & Words (Buster Bee's Learning Series #1, the Bugville Critters) (p. 25)
—Art of Ruin Mist: Heroes & Villains. (p. 102)
—Break Their Bad Habits: (the Bugville Critters, Lass's Adventures Series #2) (p. 224)
—Break Their Bad Habits. (p. 224)
—Bugville Critters & Catching a Cup of Sunshine. (p. 237)
—Bugville Critters & Every Day Is Different. (p. 237)
—Bugville Critters Explore the Solar System. (p. 237)
—Bugville Critters Go on Vacation. (p. 237)
—Bugville Critters Go to Camp. (p. 237)
—Bugville Critters Go to School. (p. 237)
—Bugville Critters Have a Sleepover. (p. 237)
—Bugville Critters Make New Friends: Buster Bee's School Days #2. (p. 237)
—Bugville Critters Play Their First Big Game. (p. 237)
—Bugville Critters Remember Their Manners. (p. 237)
—Bugville Critters Rush to the Hospital. (p. 237)
—Bugville Critters Save Their Allowance. (p. 237)
—Bugville Critters So Many Lessons to Learn. (p. 237)
—Bugville Critters Start Summer Vacation. (p. 237)
—Bugville Critters Too Much Sweets: Buster Bee's School Days #1. (p. 237)
—Bugville Critters Vacation Surprise: Buster Bee's School Days #3. (p. 237)
—Bugville Critters Visit Dad & Mom at Work. (p. 237)
—Bugville Critters Visit Garden Box Farms. (p. 237)
—Bugville Critters Visit the Library. (p. 237)
—Buster Bee's Adventures with Letters & Words. (p. 245)
—Catching a Cup of Sunshine. (p. 279)
—Elf Queen & the King III. (p. 512)
—Elf Queen & the King IV. (p. 512)
—Every Day Is Different. (p. 542)
—Explore the Solar System. (p. 550)
—Go on Vacation. (p. 687)
—Go to Camp. (p. 687)
—Go to School. (p. 687)
—Have a Backyard Picnic. (p. 754)
—Have a Bad Day. (p. 754)
—Have a Sleepover. (p. 754)
—Have a Surprise Party. (p. 754)
—Have Trouble at School. (p. 754)
—Illustrated Encyclopedia of Ruin Mist. (p. 857)
—In the Service of Dragons: Keeper Martin's Tales, Book 5. (p. 867)
—In the Service of Dragons. (p. 867)
—In the Service of Dragons II: Keeper Martin's Tales, Book 6. (p. 867)
—In the Service of Dragons II. (p. 867)
—In the Service of Dragons III: Keeper Martin's Tales, Book 7. (p. 867)
—In the Service of Dragons III. (p. 867)
—Into the Stone Land. (p. 881)
—Journey Beyond the Beyond. (p. 928)
—Kingdoms & the Elves of the Reaches: Keeper Martin's Tales, Book 1. (p. 960)
—Kingdoms & the Elves of the Reaches: Signature, Keeper Martin's Tales (p. 960)
—Kingdoms & the Elves of the Reaches. Stanek, Robert, illus. (p. 960)
—Kingdoms & the Elves of the Reaches II: Keeper Martin's Tales, Book 2. (p. 960)
—Kingdoms & the Elves of the Reaches II: Signature, Keeper Martin's Tales (p. 960)
—Kingdoms & the Elves of the Reaches II. Stanek, Robert, illus. (p. 960)
—Kingdoms & the Elves of the Reaches Ii (Reader's Choice Edition, Keeper Martin's Tales Book 2) (p. 960)
—Kingdoms & the Elves of the Reaches III: Keeper Martin's Tales (p. 960)
—Kingdoms & the Elves of the Reaches III: Keeper Martin's Tales, Book 3. (p. 960)
—Kingdoms & the Elves of the Reaches III: Signature, Keeper Martin's Tales (p. 960)
—Kingdoms & the Elves of the Reaches III. Stanek, Robert, illus. (p. 960)
—Kingdoms & the Elves of the Reaches Iii (Reader's Choice Edition, Keeper Martin's Tales Book 3) (p. 960)
—Kingdoms & the Elves of the Reaches Iv. (p. 960)
—Kingdoms & the Elves of the Reaches (Reader's Choice Edition, Keeper Martin's Tales Book 1) (p. 960)
—Lineswom: Battle for Ruin Mist. (p. 1019)
—Play Their First Big Game. (p. 1371)

—Reinos y los Elfos de las Quimeras. (p. 1457)
—Reinos y los Elfos de las Quimeras II. (p. 1457)
—Reinos y los Elfos de las Quimeras III. (p. 1457)
—Remember Their Manners. (p. 1459)
—Rise of the Fallen: Dawn of the Ages. (p. 1475)
—Robert Stanek's Bugville Critters Storybook Treasury. (p. 1479)
—Robert Stanek's Bugville Critters Storybook Treasury Volume 2 (the Bugville Critters Storybook Collection, Volume 2) (p. 1479)
—Ruin Mist Journal: The Alliance. (p. 1494)
—Ruin Mist Journal: The Kingdoms. (p. 1494)
—Rush to the Hospital. (p. 1498)
—Save Their Allowance. (p. 1517)
—Secrets, Mysteries & Magic of Robert Stanek's Ruin Mist. (p. 1545)
—Start Summer Vacation. (p. 1643)
—Stay after School. (p. 1645)
—Student's Classroom Handbook for Robert Stanek's Magic Lands. (p. 1669)
—Student's Classroom Handbook for the Kingdoms & the Elves of the Reaches. (p. 1669)
—Student's Classroom Handbook for the Kingdoms & the Elves of the Reaches II. (p. 1669)
—Visit City Hall. (p. 1845)
—Visit Dad & Mom at Work. (p. 1845)
—Visit Garden Box Farms. (p. 1845)
—Visit the Library. (p. 1845)
Stanek, Robert, pseud & Ruin Mist Publications Staff. Magic of Ruin Mist: A Candid Look at Robert Stanek's Life, Work & Books. (p. 1073)
Stanek, William, see Stanek, Robert, pseud.
Stanek, William, see Stanek, Robert, pseud.
Stanfield, James, ed. see Walker-Hirsch, Leslie & Champagne, Marklyn.
Stanfield, Michael. Bucky & Becky - the Magic of Wigglepoo Mountain. (p. 234)
Stanford, Cody L. Sinews of the Heart. (p. 1578)
Stanford, Eleanor. Interracial America. (p. 881)
Stanford, Elisa, jt. auth. see Basaluzzo, Constanza.
Stanford, Halle, jt. auth. see Allen, Elise.
Stanford, J. K. Twelfth & After (p. 1800)
Stanford, K. B. Sixteen Wishes (paperback) (p. 1583)
Stang, Debra L. Visiting Grandma. (p. 1845)
Stang, Virginia. Baroness & Her Wandering Pearls. (p. 140)
Stanger, Rob. I Love Golf! (p. 842)
Stangherlin, Tonia. T-Bird & the Island of Lost Cats. (p. 1693)
Stanglin, Jackie A. Mami, Que Es una Carcel? McGuckie, Cierra Jade, illus. (p. 1084)
—What Is Jail, Mommy? McGuckie, Cierra Jade, illus. (p. 1889)
Stango, Diane. Too Many Tomatoes. (p. 1767)
—Vicky's Vegetables. (p. 1840)
Stango, Diane E. City Life. (p. 323)
Stanford, Linda. Clothes. (p. 334)
—Food & Drink. (p. 613)
—Place to Live. (p. 1365)
—Possessions. (p. 1387)
—Wants vs Needs. (p. 1857)
Staniland, C., illus. see Leslie, Emma.
Stanisha, Terésa (Tracey). Especially for Rachel - Butterflies Abound. (p. 536)
Stanislaus, Justin. Purple Elephant in the Room. (p. 1419)
Stanislawski, J., ed. McKay's English-Polish Polish-English Dictionary. (p. 1114)
Staniszewski, Anna. Dirt Diary. (p. 446)
—Gossip File. (p. 703)
—I'm with Cupid. (p. 860)
—My Epic Fairy Tale Fail. (p. 1202)
—My Sort of Fairy Tale Ending. (p. 1219)
—My Very Unfairy Tale Life. (p. 1221)
—Power down, Little Robot. Zeltner, Tim, illus. (p. 1389)
—Prank List. (p. 1393)
Stankard, Paul. No Green Leaves or Berries: The Creative Journey of an Artist in Glass. (p. 1258)
Stankard, Paul J. No Green Berries or Leaves: The Creative Journey of an Artist in Glass. (p. 1258)
Stanké, Claudie. Bisous. Malépart, Céline, illus. (p. 193)
Stankiewicz, Steven, illus. see Kenney, Karen.
Stanlake, George. Starting Economics. (p. 1644)
Stanley, Amanda, illus. see Morgan, Randolph & Morgan, Niclas.
Stanley, Andy. Go Fish: Because of What's on the Line. (p. 686)
Stanley, Andy & Bennett, Heath. Up to You: It's Your Life, Choose Wisely. (p. 1824)
Stanley, Andy & Hall, Stuart. Max Q Student Journal: How to Be Influential Without Being Influenced. Buckingham, Michele, ed. (p. 1111)
Stanley, Anne. Listen in Addition. (p. 1022)
Stanley, Barb. What Catholics Teens Should Know When Dating Turns Violent. Larkin, Jean K., ed. (p. 1881)
Stanley, Barbara, ed. see Sullivan, Sonja.
Stanley, Baron. Brewed in America: A History of Beer & Ale in the United States. (p. 226)
Stanley, Betty J. Dupree Family Says No to Bullying. (p. 490)
Stanley, Brenda. I Am Nuchu. (p. 833)
Stanley, Christopher Heath, illus. see Stanley, Phillip Orin, 2nd.
Stanley, Dan. Danny the Fisherman LaRue, Athena Mariah, illus. (p. 406)
Stanley, David. Kanga Santa. Stanley, Stephen, illus. (p. 942)
Stanley, David J. Lovely Day for Knitting. (p. 1061)
Stanley, Dean. Horsosaurus. France, Mark, illus. (p. 801)
Stanley, Debbie. Coping with Vision Disorders. (p. 365)
—Everything You Need to Know about Student-on-Student Sexual Harassment. (p. 546)
—Everything You Need to Know about Vision Disorders. (p. 546)
—Understanding Sports & Eating Disorders. (p. 1816)
Stanley, Diane. Bella at Midnight. Ibatoulline, Bagram, illus. (p. 162)
—Caballero y la Doncella. (p. 250)
—Chosen Prince. (p. 311)
—Cup & the Crown. (p. 392)
—Elena. (p. 511)
—Giant & the Beanstalk. Stanley, Diane, illus. (p. 673)
—Goldie & the Three Bears. Stanley, Diane, illus. (p. 695)
—Michelangelo. Stanley, Diane, illus. (p. 1135)
—Mozart: The Wonder Child - A Puppet Play in Three Acts. Stanley, Diane, illus. (p. 1184)
—Mysterious Case of the Allbright Academy. (p. 1223)
—Princess of Cortova. (p. 1404)
—Raising Sweetness Stanley, Diane, illus. (p. 1437)
—Raising Sweetness Karas, G. Brian, illus. (p. 1437)
—Raising Sweetness. (p. 1437)
—Saving Sky. (p. 1517)
—Silver Bowl. (p. 1576)
—Sweetness Series. Karas, G. Brian, illus. (p. 1690)
—Thanksgiving on Plymouth Plantation. Berry, Holly, illus. (p. 1726)
—Trouble with Wishes. Stanley, Diane, illus. (p. 1790)
Stanley, Ed. Grand Central Terminal: Gateway to New York City. (p. 707)
Stanley, Elizabeth. Tyger! Tyger! (p. 1805)
Stanley, George E. Case of the Bank-Robbing Bandit. Murdocca, Salvatore, illus. (p. 273)
—Case of the Dirty Clue. Murdocca, Sal, illus. (p. 274)
—Clue of the Left-Handed Envelope. Murdocca, Sal, illus. (p. 336)
—Coretta Scott King: First Lady of Civil Rights. Madsen, Jim & Henderson, Meryl, illus. (p. 367)
—Crazy Horse: Young War Chief. Henderson, Meryl, illus. (p. 377)
—Frederick Douglass: Abolitionist Hero. Henderson, Meryl, illus. (p. 633)
—George S. Patton: War Hero. Henderson, Meryl, illus. (p. 663)
—Harry S. Truman: Thirty-Third President of the United States. Henderson, Meryl, illus. (p. 751)
—Leonardo Da Vinci: Young Artist, Writer, & Inventor. (p. 992)
—Mr. Rogers: Young Friend & Neighbor. Henderson, Meryl, illus. (p. 1186)
—Mystery of the Stolen Statue. Murdocca, Salvatore, illus. (p. 1226)
—Night Fires. (p. 1253)
—Pope John Paul II: Young Man of the Church. (p. 1384)
—Riddle of the Stolen Sand. Murdocca, Salvatore, illus. (p. 1470)
—Secret of the Green Skin. Murdocca, Sal, illus. (p. 1542)
—Secret of the Wooden Witness. Murdocca, Salvatore, illus. (p. 1543)
—Teddy Kennedy: Lion of the Senate. Fancy, Patrick, illus. (p. 1712)
Stanley, George Edward. America & the Cold War (1949-1969) (p. 59)
—America in Today's World (1969-2004) (p. 59)
—Andrew Jackson: Young Patriot. Henderson, Meryl, illus. (p. 72)
—Case of the Dirty Clue. Murdocca, Sal, illus. (p. 274)
—Crisis of the Union (1815-1865) (p. 383)
—Emerging World Power, 1900-1929. (p. 518)
—Era of Reconstruction & Expansion (1865-1900) (p. 533)
—European Settlement of North America (1492-1754) (p. 540)
—Great Depression & World War II (1929-1949) (p. 715)
—New Republic (1763-1815) (p. 1247)
—Night Fires. (p. 1253)
—Secret of the Green Skin. Murdocca, Sal, illus. (p. 1542)
—Sitting Bull: Great Sioux Hero. (p. 1582)
Stanley, Glen F. & Porterfield, Jason. Insider's Guide to Baseball. (p. 878)
Stanley, Glen F & Wesley, Ann. Gymnastics: Girls Rocking It. (p. 734)
Stanley, Jan. If I Could Breathe Like Fishes Do Wennekes, Ron, illus. (p. 852)
Stanley, John. Collecting Vinyl. (p. 339)
—Idaho: Past & Present. (p. 852)
—Melvin Monster (p. 1125)
—Melvin Monster: The John Stanley Library (p. 1125)
Stanley, John & Seth. Nancy (p. 1228)
Stanley, John P. Mickey Price - Journey to Oblivion. (p. 1136)
Stanley, Joseph. Big Dipper. (p. 181)
—Half-Dollars! (p. 736)
—Is It Flat or Is It Solid? Identify & Describe Shapes. (p. 889)
—Little Dipper. (p. 1026)
—Magnet Magic! (p. 1075)
Stanley, Karen, ed. see Manton, Charlotte.
Stanley, Karen Andersen. Busy & Sticky: Two Tiny Bees: Second Edition. (p. 245)
Stanley, Lesa, told to. You Have That in Your Purse, Mrs. Connor? (p. 1975)
Stanley, Malaika Rose. Baby Ruby Bawled. Wilson-Max, Ken, illus. (p. 128)
—Dance Dreams. (p. 402)
—Spike & Ali Enson. Horne, Sarah, illus. (p. 1627)
—Spike in Space. (p. 1627)
Stanley, Mandy. Baby Blessings Baby's Bible. (p. 125)
—Birthday Party. Stanley, Mandy, illus. (p. 193)
—Fairy Ball. Stanley, Mandy, illus. (p. 563)
—Jack & Jill & Other Nursery Favourites. (p. 902)
—Lift & Look Daniel. (p. 1014)
—My First French Book: A Bilingual Introduction to Words, Numbers, Shapes, & Colors. (p. 1206)
—This Little Piggy & Other Action Rhymes. (p. 1737)
—Three Little Kittens & Other Number Rhymes. (p. 1742)
—Twinkle, Twinkle, Little Star & Other Nursery Favourites. (p. 1802)
—Who Do You Love? Stanley, Mandy, illus. (p. 1915)
—Who Tickled Tilly? (p. 1917)
—Who Tickled Tilly? Stanley, Mandy, illus. (p. 1917)
Stanley, Mandy, illus. see Davidson, Alice Joyce.
Stanley, Mandy, illus. see Hawksley, Gerald.
Stanley, Mandy, illus. see Moore, Karen.
Stanley, Mandy & Kingfisher Publications, Inc. Staff. Vamos a la Granja. (p. 1831)
Stanley, Mary. Bruno, Peanut & Me. (p. 232)
Stanley, P. "Olivia". Dreadful Noises of Landoshar. (p. 482)
Stanley, Pauline. Children & the Witches Magic. (p. 302)
Stanley, Phillip Orin, 2nd. Castle Rock Critter. Stanley, Christopher Heath & Parsons, Arielle, illus. (p. 277)
Stanley, Phyllis M. Elizabeth Terwilliger - Someone Special: A Biography of the Celebrated Naturalist. (p. 513)
Stanley, Robert. Nelly Goes Out to Sea (p. 1240)
Stanley, Robert E., Sr. Northwest Native Arts: Creative Colors 1 (p. 1266)
Stanley, Robin, ed. see Stevens, Joy.
Stanley, Sanna, illus. see McKissack, Patricia C.
Stanley, Shalanda. Drowning Is Inevitable. (p. 486)
Stanley, Sharina & Stowbridge, Amarri. Pritsy & Purrdy: Pritsy Moves to Kickapoo. (p. 1407)
Stanley, Sheryl. Hank Becomes a Hero. (p. 742)
Stanley, Stephen. City of Lost Mazes. (p. 324)
—Haunted Maze. (p. 753)
Stanley, Stephen, illus. see Stanley, David.
Stanley, Susan, illus. see Scaling, Sam T.
Stanley, Tracy. Alphabet Appreciation Book. (p. 49)
Stanmore, Tony. Tide of Chance: A Holiday Adventure. (p. 1747)
Stannard, Russell. Curious History of God. Davies, Taffy, illus. (p. 394)
—www.Here-I-Am. Pugh, Jonathan, illus. (p. 1966)
Stanos, Dimi & Lesaux, Nonie K. Taking Care of Farm Animals. (p. 1698)
Stanos, Dimi, et al. Plants in the Park. (p. 1370)
Stansberry, Don. Inky & the Missing Gold. (p. 874)
Stansberry, Don & Cluster Springs Elementary School Staff. Skipping Through the ABC's of History. Barczak, Mariss & Long, Lisa, eds. (p. 1586)
Stansfield, Anita. Captain of Her Heart. (p. 264)
Stansfield, John. Enos Mills: Rocky Mountain Naturalist. (p. 531)
Stanton, Andy. Mr Gum & the Biscuit Billionaire. Tazzyman, David, illus. (p. 1185)
—Mr Gum & the Cherry Tree. Tazzyman, David, illus. (p. 1185)
—Mr Gum & the Dancing Bear. Tazzyman, David, illus. (p. 1185)
—Mr. Gum & the Goblins. Tazzyman, David, illus. (p. 1185)
—Mr Gum & the Power Crystals. Tazzyman, David, illus. (p. 1185)
—Mr Gum & the Secret Hideout. Tazzyman, David, illus. (p. 1185)
—Sterling & the Canary. (p. 1648)
—What's for Dinner, Mr Gum? Tazzyman, David, illus. (p. 1897)
—You're a Bad Man. Tazzyman, David, illus. (p. 1981)
—You're a Bad Man, Mr Gum! Tazzyman, David, illus. (p. 1981)
—You're a Bad Man, Mr. Gum! Tazzyman, David, illus. (p. 1981)
Stanton, Angie. Rock & a Hard Place. (p. 1481)
—Royally Lost. (p. 1492)
—Snapshot. (p. 1597)
—Under the Spotlight. (p. 1814)
Stanton, Brandon. Little Humans. Stanton, Brandon, photos by. (p. 1029)
Stanton, Brian, illus. see Van Fleet, Matthew.
Stanton, Brian, photos by see Van Fleet, Matthew.
Stanton, Elizabeth Rose. Henny. Stanton, Elizabeth Rose, illus. (p. 767)
Stanton, Ilene. Kristen's Bears. Stanton, Martin, illus. (p. 967)
Stanton, Janet, illus. see Banicki, Patsy & Staige, Pat.
Stanton, Jeanne. Put on Your Glasses Grandma, I Can't See You. (p. 1420)
Stanton, Karen. Monday, Wednesday, & Every Other Weekend. Stanton, Karen, illus. (p. 1163)
—Papi's Gift. Moreno, Rene King, illus. (p. 1323)
Stanton, Laura. Animals Animales: A Bilingual ABC Book for all Readers. Richard, P. M., illus. (p. 82)
Stanton, Martin, illus. see Stanton, Ilene.
Stanton, Mary & Hyma, Albert. Streams of Civilization: Earliest Times to the Discovery of the New World. Vol. 1 (p. 1666)
Stanton, Melissa. My Pen Pal, Santa. Bell, Jennifer A., illus. (p. 1216)
Stanton, Nicholas Sheridan. KK Undercover Mystery: The Cookie Caper. (p. 963)
Stanton, Philip, illus. see Hopkins, Lee Bennett.
Stanton, Sue. Child's Guide to Baptism. Blake, Anne Catharine, illus. (p. 305)
—Child's Guide to the Stations of the Cross. Blake, Anne Catharine, illus. (p. 305)
—Great Women of Faith: Inspiration for Action. (p. 719)
Stanton, Terence M. Bill of Rights: What It Means to You. (p. 186)
—Branches of the U. S. Government. (p. 222)
—Declaration of Independence. (p. 422)
Stanwood, Jane. Squeak Jr's Short Stories; Comments & Information. (p. 1636)
—Squeak's Bus Company. (p. 1636)
Stanwood Pier, Arthu. Jester of St. Timothy's. (p. 914)
Stape, J. H., ed. see Conrad, Joseph.
Staple, Sandra. Drawing Dragons: Learn How to Create Fantastic Fire-Breathing Dragons. (p. 481)
Staples, Edna. Wolf over the Ridge: Games We Used to Play. (p. 1944)
Staples, Erika. Spirals of Nature. (p. 1628)
Staples, Suzanne Fisher. Haveli. (p. 754)
—House of Djinn. (p. 803)
—Shabanu: Daughter of the Wind. (p. 1556)
—Under the Persimmon Tree. (p. 1814)
Staples, Val, illus. see Balaban, Mariah, ed.
Stapleton, Merv, et al. OCR Technology: A2 Level. (p. 1277)
Stapleton, Rhonda. Flirting with Disaster. (p. 605)
—Pucker Up. (p. 1414)
—Stupid Cupid. (p. 1670)
Stapley, Craig, illus. see Nielson, Mark S.
Stapley, Giles. Plinktus, the Little Pink Dinosaur. (p. 1374)
Stapley, Michele. Death of Art. (p. 420)
Stapylton, K. E. Terror of Prism Fading. (p. 1722)
Star, Brenda, illus. see Errico, Jessica / C.
Star Bright Books. Carry Me (Portuguese/English) Icibaci, Neusa, tr. (p. 271)
—Families (Portuguese/English) Icibaci, Neusa, tr. (p. 567)
—Families (Spanish/English) Fiol, Maria A., tr. (p. 567)
—My First Words at Home (p. 1208)
—My First Words at Home (Burmese Karen/English) (p. 1208)
—My First Words at Home (Burmese/English) (p. 1208)
—My First Words at HOME (Spanish/English) (p. 1208)
Star Bright Books, creator. Carry Me (Somali/English) (p. 271)
—Carry Me (Vietnamese/English) (p. 271)
—Eating the Rainbow (Vietnamese/English) (p. 501)
—Families (Vietnamese/English) (p. 568)
star, celina. Paw Prints on the Road. (p. 1331)
Star, Eloney. Heavy Duty Trucker. (p. 761)
Star, Ian. Breakfast at the Farm. (p. 224)
Star, L. J. Lydia's First Christmas (p. 1066)
Star, Nancy. Case of the April Fool's Frogs. (p. 273)
—Case of the Kidnapped Cupid. Bernardin, James, illus. (p. 274)
—Case of the Sneaky Strangers. (p. 275)
—Case of the Thanksgiving Thief. Bernardin, James, illus. (p. 275)
—Mystery of the Snow Day Bigfoot. Bernardin, James, illus. (p. 1226)
Star, Pat, jt. auth. see Mills, Nathan.
Star Wars Staff & Valois, Rob. Sticker Storyteller. (p. 1650)
Star Wars Staff, et al. Renegade. (p. 1460)
Star Wars, Star. Star Wars Movie Theater Storybook & Lightsaber Projector. (p. 1641)
Starace, Tom, illus. see Knudsen, Michelle.
Starbird, Caroline, jt. auth. see Justus, Barbara.
Starbright Foundation Staff, jt. auth. see Andersen, Hans Christian.
Starbuck-McMillan, Elizabeth, illus. see Briggs, Martha Wren.
Starcher, Michele. Ornery Angel. (p. 1304)
Stardoll. Cover Girl Handbook: What Every Stardoll Needs to Know! (p. 373)
—Stardoll: Top Trends - Autumn/Winter. (p. 1642)
—Stardoll: Sticker Red Carpet Dress Up. (p. 1642)
—Stardoll: Style Bible. (p. 1642)
—Sticker Catwalk Dress Up. (p. 1650)
—Sticker Holiday Dress Up. (p. 1650)
—Superstar Stylist. (p. 1684)
Starfall Education. Level I Reading & Writing Journal: Starfall Manuscript. Starfall Education, ed. (p. 1003)
—Level I Reading & Writing Journal - Block Print: WK201b. Starfall Education, ed. (p. 1003)
—My Starfall Dictionary. (p. 1219)
—My Starfall Writing Journal. (p. 1219)
—Starfall Learn to Read 15 Phonics Books: Zac the Rat & Other Tales! Starfall Education, ed. (p. 1642)
Starfall Education, ed. see Hillert, Margaret.
Starfall Education, photos by see Hillert, Margaret.
Starfall Education, creator. Level II Reading & Writing Journal: Second Edition. (p. 1003)
StarFields, Nick. In Serein: Sorceror & Apprentice. (p. 865)
Stargeon, Bobbi, illus. see Johnson, Sandi, et al.
Starishevsky, Jill. My Body Belongs to Me: A Book about Body Safety. Padrón, Angela, illus. (p. 1198)
Stark, illus. see Stark, Ken.
Stark, Andrew. 5th Brother. (p. 1992)
Stark, Barbara. Blue Dinosaur's Friends. (p. 202)
Stark, Clifford D., jt. auth. see Bowers, Elizabeth Shimer.
Stark, Dan, jt. auth. see Estes, Allison.
Stark Draper, Allison. Historical Atlas of Syria. (p. 783)
Stark, Evan. Todo lo que necesitas saber sobre Pandillas (Everything You Need to Know about Street Gangs) (p. 1761)
Stark, Freddy. Gray's Anatomy: A Fact-Filled Coloring Book. (p. 713)
Stark, Henry. Heart Lessons. (p. 759)
Stark, Ken. Marching to Appomattox: The Footrace That Ended the Civil War. Stark, Ken, illus. (p. 1092)
—Marching to Appomattox: The Footrace That Ended the Civil War. Stark, Ken & Stark, illus. (p. 1092)
Stark, Kristy, ed. see Bradley, Timothy.
Stark, Lynn. With Cherry on Top. (p. 1942)
Stark, Mindy C., illus. see Bringhurst, Nancy J.
Stark, Paula Allene. Abraham the Alligator. (p. 7)
—Babe the Bear (p. 123)
Stark, Regina, illus. see Renna, Diane M.
Stark, Robin. Haldona: Land of Mignon. (p. 736)
Stark, Ryan. Why Do Seasons Change? (p. 1924)
Stark, Ryan, illus. see Dunham, Bandhu Scott.
Stark, Sam. Diderot: French Philosopher & Father of the Encyclopedia. (p. 437)
Stark, Teri. Alison's Helmet. (p. 41)
Stark, Ulf. Can You Whistle, Johanna? A Boy's Search for a Grandfather. Segerberg, Ebba, tr. from SWE. (p. 260)
—When Dad Showed Me the Universe. Eriksson, Eva, illus. (p. 1901)
Stark, William N. Aerosmith: Living the Rock 'n' Roll Dream. (p. 25)
Stark, William N., et al. Legends of Rock. (p. 990)
Starke, John. Speed Machines: Mission Xtreme 3D. (p. 1624)
Starke, Katherine. Cats & Kittens. (p. 281)
—Dogs & Puppies. Watt, Fiona, ed. (p. 462)
Starke, Katherine & Watt, Fiona. Cats & Kittens. Fox, Christyan, illus. (p. 281)
—Dogs & Puppies. Fox, Christyan, illus. (p. 462)
Starke, Ruth. Noodle Pie. (p. 1264)
Starkey, Anna, jt. auth. see Child, Lauren.
Starkey, Fiona, illus. see White, June.
Starkey, Ines. Chrichi & the Little Blue Bird: A Lesson Learned Book. Acayen, Alex, illus. (p. 311)
Starkey, R. Hawk. Mysterious Magical Circus Family Kids: The Chocolate Cake Turkey Lip Crumb Trail Mystery Adventure. (p. 1223)
Starkey, Richard, see Starr, Ringo, pseud.
Starkey, Scott. Call of the Bully: A Rodney Rathbone Novel. (p. 254)
—Call of the Bully. (p. 254)
—How to Beat the Bully Without Really Trying. 3: (p. 815)
Starkings, Richard. Elephantmen Volume 3: Dangerous Liasons TP: Dangerous Liasons TP. (p. 511)
Starkings, Richard, illus. see Loeb, Jeph & Sale, Tim.
Starkings, Richard, illus. see Seagle, Steven T.

S

Starkings, Richard & Kelly, Joe. Elephantmen Volume 1: Wounded Animals Revised Edition TP: Wounded Animals Revised Edition TP. (p. 511)
Starks, Nicole. Childrens Story Book Rainbow. (p. 304)
Starks, Shirley. Inspiration for Every Occasion: An Inspiring Collection of Poems, Topics, Scriptures & Prayers. (p. 878)
Starks-Johnson, Annie. Doggie Day Care. (p. 462)
—Dottie Meets Gilda the Old Oak Tree. (p. 472)
Starlight, Cyandria. Daydreams of a Little Girl. (p. 415)
Starlin, Jim. Cosmic Odyssey. Kahan, Bob, ed. (p. 368)
—Death in the Family. O'Neil, Dennis, ed. (p. 420)
—Dreadstar. (p. 482)
—Jim Starlin's Cosmic Guard. (p. 918)
—Marvel Universe: The End. (p. 1099)
—Thanos: Epiphany. Vol. 4 Youngquist, Jeff, ed. (p. 1726)
—Thanos: Marvel Universe - The End Vol. 3 Starlin, Jim, illus. (p. 1726)
Starlin, Jim, et al. Cult. Thorsland, Dan & O'Neill, Dennis, eds. (p. 390)
Starling, Landa. If You Sleep with a Cat on Your Head. Formelio, Lorri, illus. (p. 854)
Starmer, Aaron. Riverman. (p. 1476)
—Whisper. (p. 1912)
Starmer, Anika, illus. see Thomas, Wendy Russell & Ruchman, Laura.
Starnes, Sandy. Finley the Fish with Tales from the Sea of Galilee: A Story of Faith. (p. 589)
Starno, Nancy. HTML 2 Student Activity Book. Matthews, Douglas L., ed. (p. 824)
Starns, Ayesha. Buddy Bully: Overcome Being Bullied. Feel Happy & Empowered. (p. 234)
Starosta, Paul. Bee: Friend of the Flowers. (p. 157)
—Face-to-Face with the Hamster. (p. 560)
Starp. Anancy's Magic. (p. 67)
Starr, Barbara May. Home for Finn: The Tail of an Alaska Rescue Dog (p. 792)
Starr, Branka, illus. see Bodecker, N. M.
Starr, Debra, compiled by. Book of Christmas: A Collection of Holiday Verse, Prose, & Carols. (p. 211)
Starr, Fredro. Lil Freddy: The Red Sock. (p. 1017)
Starr, Joyce, ed. see Frances, Ethel & Miller, Marcia.
Starr, L. Lee. Huggily Buggily & the Magical Fart of Wind. (p. 825)
Starr, Lara, jt. auth. see Davis, Robin.
Starr, Lisa, illus. see McGuinness, Jeff.
Starr, Meg. Alicia's Happy Day Hu, Ying-Hwa & Van Wright, Cornelius, illus. (p. 40)
—Alicia's Happy Day Van Wright, Cornelius & Hu, Ying-Hwa, illus. (p. 40)
—Alicia's Happy Day (Spanish/English) Fiol, Maria, tr. from ENG. (p. 40)
—día más feliz de Alicia Fiol, Maria A., tr. from ENG. (p. 433)
Starr, Ringo, pseud. Octopus's Garden. Cort, Ben, illus. (p. 1278)
Starr, Robert. Apple Lady. (p. 92)
—Sophistry by Degrees. (p. 1613)
Starr Taylor, Bridget, illus. see Williams, Rozanne Lanczak.
Starr, Will. Circus Math. (p. 322)
Starrenburg, Hasko. Queen's Orb. (p. 1425)
Starry Dog Books. Human Body. Stalio, Ivan, illus. (p. 825)
Starwolf. Dance of the Fire Fairies: Book 1-Just Beginning. (p. 402)
—Tiny Dancer. (p. 1756)
—Where Sand Castles Go. (p. 1909)
Starwoman, Athena & Gray, Deborah. How to Turn Your Ex-Boyfriend into a Toad Kit. (p. 822)
Stary, Mary Lu. Charlie, la Tortuguita Valiente / Charlie, the Brave Little Turtle. (p. 293)
—Charlie, the Brave Little Turtle: A Grandma's Barnyard Tale. (p. 293)
—Cricket, the Unhappy Frog: A Grandma's Barnyard Tale. (p. 382)
—Sage, the Little Brown Pony: A Grandma's Barnyard Tale. (p. 1502)
Stasco, Raymond. Adventures of Mr Mccroak. (p. 20)
Stasiak, Krystyna, illus. see Hillert, Margaret.
Stasik, Eric. Strategic Patent Planning for Software Companies. (p. 1666)
Stasio, M. L. Imagine If. (p. 861)
Stasiuk, Max, illus. see Kopczynski, Megan.
Staska, H. M. How George Became King. (p. 809)
Stasolla, Mario, illus. see Peck, Judith.
Stasse, Lisa M. Defiant: The Forsaken Trilogy. (p. 424)
—Defiant. (p. 424)
—Forsaken. (p. 623)
—Uprising: The Forsaken Trilogy. (p. 1825)
Stassen. Deogratias: A Tale of Rwanda. Siegel, Alexis, tr. from FRE. (p. 427)
Stassen, Jean-Philippe. Deogratias. (p. 427)
Stastny, Peter & Lehmann, Peter, eds. Alternatives Beyond Psychiatry. Christine Holzhausen et al, trs. from GER. (p. 50)
Stasyuk, Max, illus. see Levine, Karen R.
Stasyuk, Max, illus. see Edwards, Garth.
Stasyuk, Maz, jt. auth. see Edwards, Garth.
State, Paul. France. (p. 627)
State, Paul F. Brief History of Ireland. (p. 227)
—Brief History of Netherlands. (p. 227)
States, Anna, illus. see Yamada, Rikako.
Stathis, Roberta, jt. auth. see Blanch, Gregory.
Stathis, Roberta & Blanch, Gregory. Daring Explorers Who Sailed the Oceans. (p. 407)
—Women Who Ruled. (p. 1946)
—Writers Who Inspired the World. (p. 1964)
Stathis, Stephen W. Landmark Legislation, 1774-2002: Major U. S. Acts & Treaties. (p. 974)
Staton, Debbie. Twiggle. Patzelt, Kasie, illus. (p. 1801)
Staton, Hilarie, jt. auth. see RJF Publishing Staff.
Staton, Hilarie & Compass Point Books Staff. Progressive Party: The Success of a Failed Party (p. 1410)
Staton, Hilarie N. Civil Rights. (p. 324)
Staton, Hilarie N. & McCarthy, Tara. Science & Stories Grade K-3: Integrating Science & Literature. (p. 1525)
Staton, Joe, illus. see Fisch, Sholly & Ottolini, Horacio.
Staton, Rebecca McKown & Butler-Moore, Nylea L. Follow That Star! (p. 612)
Statt, David A. Student's Dictionary of Psychology. (p. 1669)
Statyuk, Max, jt. auth. see Edwards, Garth.
Staub, Frank. America's Mountains. (p. 64)
—Food Chain. (p. 613)
—Photosynthesis. (p. 1353)
Staub, Frank J. Running Free: America's Wild Horses. Staub, Frank J., photos by. (p. 1497)
Staub, Frank J., photos by. America's Forests & Woodlands. (p. 64)
Staub, Leslie. Everybody Gets the Blues. Roth, R G, illus. (p. 543)
Staub, Leslie, illus. see Danticat, Edwidge.
Staub, Leslie, illus. see Fox, Mem.
Staub, Rusty. Hello, Mr. Met. Moore, Danny, illus. (p. 764)
Staub, Wendy Corsi. Awakening. (p. 120)
—Believing. (p. 162)
—Discovering. (p. 448)
St-Aubin, Bruno, illus. see Croteau, Marie-Danielle.
St-Aubin, Bruno, illus. see Ellis, Sarah.
Staudacher, Carol. Getting Ahead at Work. (p. 669)
—Job Search. (p. 919)
Staudenmeier, Kelley Anne, jt. auth. see Medlyn, Lynda Lee.
Stauffacher, Sue. Animal Rescue Team: Gator on the Loose! Lamont, Priscilla, illus. (p. 79)
—Animal Rescue Team: Hide & Seek. Lamont, Priscilla, illus. (p. 79)
—Animal Rescue Team: Show Time. Lamont, Priscilla, illus. (p. 79)
—Animal Rescue Team: Special Delivery! Lamont, Priscilla, illus. (p. 79)
—Bessie Smith & the Night Riders. Holyfield, John, illus. (p. 168)
—Cassidy's Guide to Everyday Etiquette (and Obfuscation) (p. 276)
—Donuthead. (p. 469)
—Gator on the Loose! Lamont, Priscilla, illus. (p. 658)
—Nothing but Trouble: The Story of Althea Gibson. Couch, Greg, illus. (p. 1268)
—Show Time. Lamont, Priscilla, illus. (p. 1571)
—Special Delivery! Lamont, Priscilla, illus. (p. 1623)
—Tillie the Terrible Swede: How One Woman, a Sewing Needle, & a Bicycle Changed History. McMenemy, Sarah, illus. (p. 1750)
Stauffer, Alysia. God Is with You, Little One. (p. 689)
Stauffer, Lori & Deblinger, Esther. Let's Talk about Coping & Safety Skills: A Workbook about Taking Care of Me! Stauffer, Lori, illus. (p. 1001)
—Let's Talk about Safety Skills for Kids: A Personal Safety Activity Book for Children. Stauffer, Lori, illus. (p. 1001)
—Let's Talk about Taking Care of Me: An Educational Book about Body Safety. Stauffer, Lori & Moyer, Brett, illus. (p. 1001)
—Let's Talk about Taking Care of Me: An Educational Book about Body Safety for Young Children. Stauffer, Lori, illus. (p. 1001)
Stauffer, Sharon. Cornfield Baby: And Other Nature Surprises. (p. 367)
Staunton, Joseph. Dinosaurs in the Sea. (p. 445)
—Dinosaurs in the Sky. (p. 445)
—Meat-Eating Dinosaurs. (p. 1118)
—Plant-Eating Dinosaurs. (p. 1369)
Staunton, Joseph, illus. see Hynson, Colin.
Staunton, Joseph & Flinthart, Dirk. Dinosaurs in the Sea. Rey, Luis, illus. (p. 445)
—Meat Eating Dinosaurs. Rey, Luis, illus. (p. 1118)
Staunton, Joseph & Hynson, Colin. Dinosaurs in the Sky. (p. 445)
Staunton, Mathew, illus. see Rosenstock, Gabriel.
Staunton, Ted. Accord de Puissance: (Power Chord) (p. 8)
—Ace's Basement (p. 8)
—Acting Up (p. 10)
—Campfire Morgan Slavin, Bill, illus. (p. 257)
—Coda (p. 338)
—Confederation. Pilsworth, Graham, illus. (p. 356)
—Dreadful Truth: Building the Railway. Goff, Brian, illus. (p. 482)
—Dreadful Truth: Canadian Crime. Geoffroi, Remie, illus. (p. 482)
—Gold Rush. Geoffroi, Remie, illus. (p. 694)
—Great Play, Morgan. Slavin, Bill, illus. (p. 718)
—Great Play, Morgan! Slavin, Bill & Shannon, Ben, illus. (p. 718)
—Jump Cut (p. 934)
—Morgan & the Dune Racer. Slavin, Bill, illus. (p. 1175)
—Morgan & the Money Shannon, Ben, illus. (p. 1175)
—Morgan & the Money. Slavin, Bill, illus. (p. 1175)
—Morgan Makes a Deal Slavin, Bill & Shannon, Ben, illus. (p. 1175)
—Morgan Makes a Deal. Slavin, Bill, illus. (p. 1175)
—Morgan Makes a Splash Slavin, Bill & Shannon, Ben, illus. (p. 1175)
—Morgan Makes a Splash. Slavin, Bill, illus. (p. 1175)
—Morgan on Ice Slavin, Bill, illus. (p. 1175)
—Morgan's Pet Plot Slavin, Bill & Shannon, Ben, illus. (p. 1175)
—Morgan's Pet Plot. Slavin, Bill, illus. (p. 1175)
—Music by Morgan Slavin, Bill, illus. (p. 1193)
—Northwest Passage. (p. 1266)
—Power Chord (p. 1389)
—Pucker up, Morgan Slavin, Bill, illus. (p. 1414)
—Sounding Off (p. 1615)
—Stinky Gardos, Susan, illus. (p. 1651)
—Stinky. (p. 1651)
—Super Move, Morgan! Slavin, Bill, illus. (p. 1680)
—Trouble with Girls Gardos, Susan, illus. (p. 1790)
Staunton, Ted & Clark, Brenda. Homme De Boue (p. 794)
Staunton, Ted & Gardos, Susan. Princess (p. 1402)
—Second Banana (p. 1539)
Stavans, Ilan. Golemito. Villegas, Teresa, illus. (p. 696)
Stavans, Ilan, ed. see Singer, Isaac Bashevis.
Stave, Mel. How Harry Found the Meaning of Friendship. (p. 809)
Stavely, John F. Ghosts & Gravestones in St. Augustine Florida. (p. 672)
Stavreva, Kirilka & Quek, Lynette. Bulgaria. (p. 240)
Stawell, Rodolph. Fairies I Have Met. Dulac, Edmund, illus. (p. 563)
Stawicki, Matt. How to Draw & Paint Fantasy Combat: A Step-By-Step Guide to Epic Combat Scenes. (p. 816)
Stawski, Paul. Both Sides. (p. 215)
Stayer, Elizabeth. Get off My Corner!! (p. 667)
—Santa's Magic Stardust. (p. 1513)
Stayte, James, illus. see Graham, Ian.
Stayte, James, illus. see Solway, Andrew.
Stayton, Claudia Grace. Day by Day the Jesus Way: What Jesus Has to Say about Life, Love, & the Way to God. (p. 412)
Stckvagn. AC Ems Decimals & Percents. (p. 7)
—AC Ems Fractions. (p. 7)
—AC Ems Whole Numbers. (p. 7)
—AC Reading for Today. (p. 7)
—Americas Story Complete Book S. (p. 64)
St.Clair, Jennifer. Beth-Hill Novel: Full Moon. Cummins, Sandy, ed. (p. 171)
Steacy, Ken, illus. see Robbins, Trina.
Stead, April-Nicole, illus. see Stevens, Gary J.
Stead, Emily. On the Farm. (p. 1290)
—Things That Go! With 200 Stickers, Puzzles & Games, Fold-Out Pages, & Creative Play. (p. 1733)
Stead, Erin E., illus. see Fogliano, Julie.
Stead, Erin E., illus. see Stead, Philip C.
Stead, Judy. Mister Sun. (p. 1155)
—Twelve Days of Christmas in North Carolina. Stead, Judy, illus. (p. 1800)
Stead, Judy, illus. see Bair, Sheila.
Stead, Judy, illus. see Jules, Jacqueline.
Stead, Judy, illus. see MacDonald, Maryann.
Stead, Judy, illus. see Raczka, Bob.
Stead, Judy, illus. see Shirley, Debra.
Stead, Kevin, illus. see Whitecap Books Staff.
Stead, Philip C. Bear Has a Story to Tell. Stead, Erin E., illus. (p. 150)
—Creamed Tuna Fish & Peas on Toast. Stead, Philip C., illus. (p. 378)
—Hello, My Name Is Ruby. Stead, Philip C., illus. (p. 764)
—Home for Bird. Stead, Philip C., illus. (p. 792)
—Indama Marada Al Am Nooh. Stead, Erin E., illus. (p. 870)
—Jonathan & the Big Blue Boat. Stead, Philip C., illus. (p. 925)
—Sebastian & the Balloon. Stead, Philip C., illus. (p. 1539)
—Sick Day for Amos McGee. Stead, Erin E., illus. (p. 1572)
—Special Delivery. Cordell, Matthew, illus. (p. 1623)
Stead, Rebecca. Cuando Me Alcances. (p. 388)
—First Light. (p. 596)
—Goodbye Stranger. (p. 701)
—Liar & Spy. (p. 1005)
—When You Reach Me. (p. 1905)
Stead, Tony. Reality Checks: Teaching Reading Comprehension with Nonfiction K-5. (p. 1449)
—Should There Be Zoos? A Persuasive Text. (p. 1570)
Stead, Vince. Rusty the Runaway Golden Retriever. (p. 1498)
—Sammy, the Runaway Mastiff: Sammy Breaks Out of His Kennel. (p. 1508)
Steadman, Barbara. Christmas Princess Sticker Paper Doll. (p. 315)
—Fairy Princess Sticker Paper Doll. (p. 563)
—Glitter Ballerina Sticker Paper Doll. (p. 683)
—Glitter Figure Skater Sticker Paper Doll. (p. 684)
—Glitter Flower Girl Sticker Paper Doll. (p. 684)
—Little Flower Girls Sticker Paper Dolls. (p. 1027)
—Little Scandinavian Girls Sticker Paper Dolls. (p. 1036)
—Storybook Princess Sticker Paper Doll. (p. 1663)
—Sweet Valentine Sticker Paper Doll. (p. 1690)
Steadman, Barbara, illus. see Rogers, Svetlana.
Steadman, Barbara, jt. auth. see Alcott, Louisa May.
Steadman, Pamela M. Hannah Savannah's Favorite Tales. (p. 742)
Steadman, Ralph. Flowers for the Moon. (p. 608)
—Jelly Book. Steadman, Ralph, illus. (p. 912)
—Little. com. (p. 1026)
—Little Red Computer. (p. 1034)
Steadman, Ralph, illus. see Carroll, Lewis, pseud.
Steadman, Ralph, illus. see Damjan, Mischa.
Steadman, Ralph, illus. see Dickens, Frank.
Stealey, Bryan. Motorcross. (p. 1179)
—Powerhouse MX Nations: USA, Belgium, UK, Netherlands, France & Germany. (p. 1391)
—Powerhouse MX Nations: USA, Belgium, UK, Netherlands, France, & Germany. (p. 1391)
Stearman, G. G., ed. see Church, J. R.
Stearman, Kaye. Debate about Cosmetic Surgery. (p. 421)
—Debate about Euthanasia. (p. 421)
—Debate about Military Intervention. (p. 421)
—Debate about the Death Penalty. (p. 421)
—Freedom of Information. (p. 634)
—Taking Action Against Homelessness. (p. 1698)
—Travel & Tourism Careers. (p. 1780)
Stearman, Kaye & Savery, Annabel. Travel & Tourism. (p. 1780)
Stearman, Kaye, et al. Ethical Debates. (p. 539)
Stearns, Dan. Harriet Tubman & the Underground Railroad. (p. 750)
Stearns, Debra, ed. see Pence, Shari A.
Stearns, Forest, illus. see Dohlke, Nora.
Stearns, Megan, jt. auth. see Mooney, Carla.
Stearns, Peggy Healy. Stationery Studio Writing Collection Deluxe CD-ROM Single Computer License: The Irresistible Tool to Encourage Writing. Reynolds, Peter H., illus. (p. 1644)
Stearns, Precious. Manatees. (p. 1086)
—Steller Sea Lions. (p. 1647)
—Whooping Cranes. (p. 1920)
Stearns, Richard. God's Love for You Bible Storybook (p. 691)
Stebakova, Elena, illus. see Yacoubou, Jeanne.
Stebbins, Erec. Caterpillar & the Stone: A Love Storybook for Not-Quite Grown-Ups. (p. 279)
Stebbins, Robert A. Serious Leisure: A Perspective for Our Time. (p. 1552)
Steccati, Eve, illus. see Barba, Rick.
Steck, Jim, illus. see Bellen-Berthézène, Cyndie.
Steckel, Michele, illus. see Steckel, Richard, et al.
Steckel, Michele, jt. auth. see Steckel, Richard.
Steckel, Michele, jt. photos by see Steckel, Richard.
Steckel, Michele, photos by see Stromberg, Betsy, et al.
Steckel, Richard, photos by see Stromberg, Betsy, et al.
Steckel, Richard & Steckel, Michele. Faith. Steckel, Richard & Steckel, Michele, illus. (p. 565)
Steckel, Richard & Steckel, Michele, photos by. My Teeth. (p. 1220)
Steckel, Richard, et al. Wise at Heart: Children & Adults Share Words of Wisdom. Steckel, Richard et al, illus. (p. 1940)
Steckler, Elaine, illus. see Nick, Barbara.
Steckler, Kerren Barbas, illus. see Conlon, Mara.
Steckler, Kerren Barbas, illus. see Paulding, Barbara.
Steckler, Megan, illus. see Ayres, S. C.
Steckler, Megan, illus. see Fitzsimmons, Christy.
Steckler, Megan, illus. see Roman, Lisa.
Steckling, Deon M., II. What Is Allot? (p. 1888)
—Who Am I? (p. 1914)
STECK-VAUGHN. Mountain Man & the President. (p. 1181)
Steck-Vaughn Company, creator. Fitness. (p. 599)
—Health. (p. 757)
—Measure Mints, Grades K-6. (p. 1117)
—Taste Like Math!, Grades K-6. (p. 1707)
Steck-Vaughn, creator. Cast Your Vote!: High School: National, State, & Local Government. (p. 276)
—Using Information Resources, Grade 2. (p. 1828)
Steck-Vaughn Staff. Access Math. (p. 8)
—Access Reading. (p. 8)
—Access Writing. (p. 8)
—Analogies. (p. 66)
—Animal Eyes. (p. 77)
—Applied Math Intermediate. (p. 93)
—Applied Math Introductory. (p. 93)
—Applied Math Introductory 8-Pack. (p. 93)
—Arctic People. (p. 96)
—At-Home Workbooks: Time. (p. 110)
—At-Home Workbooks: Money. (p. 110)
—At-Home Workbooks: Vowels. (p. 110)
—At-Home Workbooks: Numbers. (p. 110)
—At-Home Workbooks: Reading. (p. 110)
—At-Home Workbooks: Division. (p. 110)
—At-Home Workbooks: Fractions. (p. 110)
—At-Home Workbooks: Subtraction. (p. 110)
—At-Home Workbooks: The Alphabet. (p. 110)
—At-Home Workbooks: Multiplication. (p. 110)
—Bones! The Frame Inside Us. (p. 209)
—Computational & Applied Mathematics. (p. 354)
—Core Skills - At Home with Phonics. (p. 367)
—Core Skills, Grade 3: At Home with Phonics. (p. 367)
—Creepy Creatures. (p. 381)
—Cycles Go: Quests. Bk. FA (p. 397)
—Cycles Go: Choices. Bk. GA (p. 397)
—Cycles Go: Visions. Bk. HA (p. 397)
—Cycles Go - Reflections. (p. 397)
—Early Math: Addition. (p. 493)
—Early Math: 2 Digit Addition & Subtraction. (p. 493)
—Early Math: 2 Digit Addition with Regrouping. (p. 493)
—Early Math: 2 Digit Subtraction with Regrouping. (p. 493)
—Early Math: 3 Digit Addition & Subtraction with Regrouping. (p. 493)
—Early Math: Shapes (p. 494)
—Early Math: Time I. (p. 494)
—Early Math: Money I. (p. 494)
—Early Math: Time II. (p. 494)
—Early Math: Money II. (p. 494)
—Early Math: Readiness. (p. 494)
—Early Math: Fractions I. (p. 494)
—Early Math: Place Value. (p. 494)
—Early Math: Subtraction. (p. 494)
—Early Math: Fractions II. (p. 494)
—Early Math: Number Sense. (p. 494)
—Early Math: Place Value 1 (p. 494)
—Early Math: Shapes. Set 1 (p. 494)
—Early Math: Measurement I. (p. 494)
—Early Math: Measurement II. (p. 494)
—Early Math: Place Value II. (p. 494)
—Early Math: Mixed Operations. (p. 494)
—Early Math: Problem Solving I. (p. 494)
—Early Math: Problem Solving II. (p. 494)
—Early Math: Readiness for Problem Solving. (p. 494)
—Early Math 10-pack: Subtraction. (p. 494)
—Early Math 10-pack: Place Value II. (p. 494)
—Early Measurement 10-pack: Measurement I. (p. 494)
—Early Reading Program: Professional Development. (p. 494)
—ESL: Building English Proficiency. (p. 536)
—ESL - Building English Proficiency, Grades 2-3. (p. 536)
—Esl/Ell. (p. 536)
—Exactly the Right Egg. (p. 547)
—Fact Family Fun. (p. 561)
—Focus on Math Level C: Decimals. (p. 610)
—Focus on Math Level C: Geometry. (p. 610)
—Focus on Math Level C: Measurement. (p. 610)
—Focus on Math Level C: Addition & Subtraction. (p. 610)
—Focus on Math Level C: Problem Solving. (p. 611)
—Focus on Math Level C: Multiplication & Division. (p. 611)
—Focus on Math Level C 10-pack: Decimals. (p. 611)
—Focus on Math Level C 10-pack: Geometry. (p. 611)
—Focus on Math Level C 10-pack: Fractions. (p. 611)
—Focus on Math Level C 10-pack: Measurement. (p. 611)
—Focus on Math Level C 10-pack: Problem Solving. (p. 611)
—Focus on Math Level C 10-pack: Addition & Subtractions. (p. 611)
—Focus on Math Level C 10-pack: Multiplication & Division. (p. 611)
—Focus on Math Level D: Decimals. (p. 611)
—Focus on Math Level D: Geometry. (p. 611)
—Focus on Math Level D: Fractions. (p. 611)
—Focus on Math Level D: Measurement. (p. 611)
—Focus on Math Level D: Mixed Operations. (p. 611)
—Focus on Math Level E: Ratio Percent. (p. 611)
—Focus on Math Level E 10-pack: Ratio Percent. (p. 611)
—Focus on Math Level F: Ration Percent. (p. 611)
—Focus on Science. (p. 611)

—Focus on Science 2004 (p. 611)
—Grade Level Math. (p. 705)
—Head for Home: Colors & Shapes. (p. 756)
—Head for Home: Consonant Blends. (p. 756)
—Head for Home: Handwriting - Cursive. (p. 756)
—Head for Home: Handwriting - Manuscript. (p. 756)
—Hey Theres Math in My Literature. (p. 774)
—History of Our World. (p. 784)
—How Much Is 100? (p. 811)
—Interpreting Visual Information. (p. 880)
—Interpreting Visual Information 10-Pack. (p. 880)
—Just-a-Minute Math: Build Math Strength Through Timed Drills. (p. 937)
—Language Art & Spelling. (p. 974)
—Language Arts & Spelling. (p. 974)
—Language Exercises. (p. 975)
—Language Exercises, Grade 3, Level C. (p. 975)
—Language Exercises, Level D. (p. 975)
—Life on the Tallest Tree. (p. 1012)
—Looking for Patterns. (p. 1051)
—Mastering Math. (p. 1103)
—Mastering Math, Level F. (p. 1103)
—Math: Data Analysis & Statistics. (p. 1105)
—Math: How Big Is a Cat? Level H-J (p. 1105)
—Math: Graphing the Rain Forest. Level J-M (p. 1105)
—Math 10-Pack: Data, Analysis & Statistics. (p. 1105)
—Math Computation Intermediate. (p. 1105)
—Math Computation Intermediate 8-Pack. (p. 1105)
—Math Remediation: Number Concepts. (p. 1107)
—Math Remediation 10-Pack: Fractions. (p. 1107)
—Matter All Around Us. (p. 1109)
—Measure That Tongue! (p. 1117)
—Measurement & Geometry. (p. 1117)
—National Parks. (p. 1233)
—Nonfiction Comprehension. (p. 1263)
—Nonfiction Comprehension, Middle School. (p. 1263)
—People & Places Nearby Level B. (p. 1339)
—Phonics: Sounds, Words, & Meanings. (p. 1351)
—Phonics + (p. 1351)
—Phonics Decoding Skills Handbook. (p. 1352)
—Phonics+Sounds, Words, & Meanings. (p. 1352)
—Poetry Comprehension. (p. 1376)
—Pre-GED Complete Preparation. (p. 1394)
—Primary Grades, Grades 1-3. (p. 1399)
—Reading & Language Arts. (p. 1445)
—Reading & Language Arts 8-Pack. (p. 1445)
—Reading Comprehension: Building Vocabulary & Measurement. (p. 1445)
—Reading Intermediate (p. 1446)
—Science: Hello, Hello! Level H-J (p. 1524)
—Science: Earth & Space Life, Physical. (p. 1524)
—Science: Life, Physical, Earth & Spac. (p. 1524)
—Science: Life, Physical, Earth & Space. (p. 1524)
—Science - Earth & Space Life - Physical. (p. 1524)
—Shutterbug: Add to Package. (p. 1572)
—Skip-Count by Threes. (p. 1585)
—Social Studies: World Cultures. Level F (p. 1604)
—Social Studies: America Is... Level H-J (p. 1604)
—Social Studies: People & Places. Level B (p. 1604)
—Social Studies: Homes & Families. Level A (p. 1604)
—Social Studies: Living in Communities. Level C (p. 1604)
—Social Studies: Regions of the Country. Level D (p. 1604)
—Social Studies: History of Our Country. Level E (p. 1604)
—Social Studies: History of the Country. Level E (p. 1604)
—Stormy Weather. (p. 1656)
—Stuck on You. (p. 1669)
—Super Sizes! (p. 1681)
—Test Best Success Math Level I: High School Edition. (p. 1723)
—Test Best Success Math Level J. (p. 1723)
—Test Best Success Reading Level J. (p. 1723)
—That Makes Ten! (p. 1726)
—Three Cheers for May. (p. 1741)
—Three Cheers for November. (p. 1741)
—Top Line Math: Algebra. (p. 1769)
—Top Line Math: Decimals. (p. 1769)
—Top Line Math: Geometry. (p. 1769)
—Top Line Math: Fractions. (p. 1769)
—Top Line Math: Measurement. (p. 1769)
—Top Line Math: Probability. (p. 1769)
—Top Line Math: Proportions. (p. 1769)
—Top Line Math: Tables & Maps. (p. 1769)
—Top Line Math: Special Topics in Math. (p. 1769)
—Vocabulary Connections (p. 1847)
—Vocabulary Skills. (p. 1847)
—Vocabulary Skills, Grade 3. (p. 1847)
—Vocabulary Ventures. (p. 1847)
—What Goes up Must Come Down. (p. 1885)
—What's the Question? (p. 1899)
Steck-Vaughn Staff & Coulter, Barbara. Vocabulary Connections, Level C. (p. 1847)
Steck-Vaughn Staff, creator. Cast Your Vote! Grades 3-5: National, State, & Local Government. (p. 276)
—Mathematics, Level J. (p. 1108)
—Reading & Language Arts, Level 1. (p. 1445)
—Sensational Seasons: Spring. (p. 1551)
—Test Fundamentals Math Computation: Basic. (p. 1723)
—Test Fundamentals: Reading: Basic (p. 1723)
Steck-Vaughn Staff, ed. Early Math: Addition. (p. 493)
Stedjee, James V. Dawn of the Third Moon. (p. 412)
Stedman, Edmund Clarence. Master Corkonata. (p. 1103)
—Rip Van Winkle & His Wonderful Nap. (p. 1473)
Steed, K. A. We Can't Do It. (p. 1866)
Steed, Tobias, ed. see Hench, Larry.
Steed, Tobias, ed. see Molloy, Sheila.
Steedley-Tolan, Chopper. I'm Not Sick! Chopper's Tails of the Doctor. (p. 859)
—I've Been Picked! Chopper's Tail of Adoption. (p. 900)
Steedman, Amy. In God's Garden: Stories of the Saints for Children. (p. 863)
—In God's Garden (Yesterday's Classics) (p. 863)
—Nursery Book of Bible Stories. (p. 1273)
—Our Island Saints (Yesterday's Classics) (p. 1309)
—Read-Aloud Book of Bible Stories. (p. 1442)
Steedman, Judith, illus. see Mitchell, Robin.
Steedman, Judith & Mitchell-Cranfield, Robin. Foggy. (p. 611)
Steedman, Scott. History News: the Egyptian News. (p. 783)
Steege, Joanna, illus. see Cole, Hana.
Steege, Mark W. & Watson, T. Steuart. Conducting School-Based Functional Behavioral Assessments: A Practitioner's Guide. (p. 356)
Steel, Abigail, jt. auth. see Wiedemer.
Steel, Danielle. Pretty Minnie in Paris. Valiant, Kristi, illus. (p. 1398)
Steel, Flora. Adventures of Akbar. (p. 16)
Steel, Flora Annie. English Fairy Tales. (p. 530)
Steel, John, illus. see Sankey, Alice.
Steel, Joleen. Sparky the Super Pig. Wanaselja, Patricia, illus. (p. 1622)
Steel, Kathy. Sally Saves Our Seas: Teaching Children How We Can Save Our Oceans Using the 3 R's! (p. 1505)
Steel, Lindsey J. Wanda the Cow. (p. 1856)
Steel, S. Spilt Milk. (p. 1627)
Steele, Andrea M., illus. see Brower, Sandra Shane.
Steele, Andrea M., illus. see Brower.
Steele, Andrew. Galaxy Boys & the Sphere. (p. 653)
Steele, Andrew, illus. see Young, Francis Kerr.
Steele, Anne. Using the Standards, Grade 4: Building Grammar & Writing Skills. (p. 1828)
Steele, Anne L. Using the Standards, Grade 5: Building Grammar & Writing Skills. (p. 1828)
Steele, Ashton. Master Luthier. (p. 1103)
Steele, Blake. Radical Forgiveness: A Handbook for Spiritual Growth. (p. 1432)
Steele, Cameron. Funny Cars. (p. 649)
Steele, Cheryl. Cranky Pants. (p. 376)
—Do Lions Wear Pajamas? (p. 457)
—Mouse in God's House. (p. 1182)
—What If... ? Questions to Delight & Inspire Children. (p. 1887)
Steele, Christy. California & the Southwest Join the United States. (p. 253)
—Famous Wagon Trails. (p. 570)
—Louisiana Purchase. (p. 1059)
—Pioneer Life in the American West. (p. 1361)
—Texas Joins the United States. (p. 1724)
Steele, Christy Lee. Uniquely Wisconsin (p. 1818)
Steele, Cynthia W., jt. auth. see Reamy, Donna W.
Steele, D. Kelley. Would You Salute? One Child's Story of the Holocaust. Rickenbaker, Becky Hyatt, illus. (p. 1962)
Steele, Giselle. off-Limits Watermelon Patch. (p. 1279)
Steele, Giselle V. Nicholas & the Magical Wind. (p. 1250)
Steele, Gregory D., illus. see Tvelte, William P.
Steele, Howard L. Bushels & Bales: A Food Soldier in the Cold War. (p. 244)
Steele, Irene J. Some Glad Morning. (p. 1609)
Steele, James M. Sadie Listens: An Inward Journey. (p. 1501)
Steele, John F. & Kachmar, Lilliam. Boomer's Eldercare Handbook. (p. 213)
Steele, Julia P., jt. auth. see Winkleby, Marilyn A.
Steele, Kaila Capehart. My Blankie. (p. 1198)
Steele, Kathleen Marie. Legend of the Angel Wing Shell. Chylak, Jolie Catherine, illus. (p. 989)
Steele, Kathryn. Stones & Bones: Archaeology in Action. (p. 1653)
Steele, Kris. Journey to Cahokia. Steele, Kris, illus. (p. 928)
Steele, Linda. Creating a Prosperous Practice Spending Little or No Money Marketing. (p. 378)
Steele, Margaret. Wuz Da Nite Befo: A Pidgin Christmas Story in Hawaii. Chang, Roy, illus. (p. 1966)
Steele, Mark. Flashbang: How I Got over Myself. (p. 602)
Steele, Michael A. At Large Cano, Fernando, illus. (p. 110)
—At Large. (p. 110)
—High-Tech Terror Schoening, Dan, illus. (p. 778)
—On Cue Cano, Fernando, illus. (p. 1288)
—Revive Cano, Fernando, illus. (p. 1466)
—Web of Doom Schoening, Dan, illus. (p. 1870)
Steele, Michael A., et al. Tony Hawk: Live2Skate (p. 1766)
Steele, Michael Anthony. Apagar el Incendio! (p. 91)
—At Large Cano, Fernando, illus. (p. 110)
—Catch That Crook! (p. 279)
—Catch That Crook! Wang, Sean, illus. (p. 279)
—Chugger Championship. (p. 318)
—Fight This Fire! (p. 585)
—Fix That Truck! (p. 601)
—Fresh Cano, Fernando, illus. (p. 636)
—Friends Forever. (p. 638)
—Koko on Call. (p. 966)
—LEGO City: Catch That Crook! (p. 990)
—Look Out Below! Kiernan, Kenny, illus. (p. 1049)
—Night at the Museum: Secret of the Tomb. (p. 1252)
—Web of Doom Schoening, Dan, illus. (p. 1870)
—Work This Farm! (p. 1952)
Steele, Michael Anthony, jt. auth. see Scholastic, Inc. Staff.
Steele, Michael Anthony & Oda, Eiichiro. Shonen Jump's One Piece. (p. 1568)
Steele, Paul, illus. see Baran, Robert J.
Steele, Philip. Activists. (p. 10)
—Afghanistan: From War to Peace? (p. 26)
—Ancient Egypt. (p. 68)
—Ancient Greece. (p. 69)
—Chinese Empire. (p. 307)
—Did Anything Good Come Out of the Civil War? (p. 436)
—Did Anything Good Come Out of World War I? (p. 436)
—Documenting Slavery & Civil Rights. (p. 460)
—Documenting World War I. (p. 460)
—Freedom of Speech. (p. 634)
—Galileo: The Genius Who Faced the Inquisition. (p. 653)
—Hail! Ancient Romans. (p. 735)
—Hail! Tudors. (p. 735)
—Hands-On History! Ancient China: Step into the Time of the Chinese Empire, with 15 Step-by-step Projects & over 300 Exciting Pictures. (p. 741)
—Hands-On History! Ancient Egypt: Find Out about the Land of the Pharaohs, with 15 Step-by-Step Projects & over 400 Exciting Pictures. (p. 741)
—Hands-On History! Ancient Rome: Step into the Time of the Roman Empire, with 15 Step-by-step Projects & over 370 Exciting Pictures. (p. 741)
—Hands-On History! Incas: Step into the Spectacular World of Ancient South America, with 340 Exciting Pictures & 15 Step-By-Step Projects. (p. 741)
—Hands-On History! Viking World: Learn about the Legendary Norse Raiders, with 15 Step-by-step Projects & More Than 350 Exciting Pictures. (p. 741)
—I Wonder Why Castles Had Moats: And Other Questions about Long Ago. (p. 849)
—I Wonder Why Pyramids Were Built. (p. 849)
—Incredible Quests: Epic Journeys in Myth & Legend. Climpson, Sue, illus. (p. 869)
—Iran & the West. (p. 886)
—Isaac Newton: Mi Mejor Amigo Es la Verdad. (p. 890)
—Kingfisher Readers L3: Vikings. (p. 960)
—Knight's City: With Amazing Pop-Ups & an Interactive Tour of Life in a Medieval City! (p. 964)
—Marie Curie: La Mujer Que Cambio el Curso de la Ciencia. (p. 1093)
—Marie Curie: The Woman Who Changed the Course of Science. (p. 1093)
—Medieval World. Woolf, Alex, ed. (p. 1119)
—Moscow. (p. 1176)
—My Body. (p. 1198)
—Navigators: Ancient Greece. (p. 1238)
—Nineteenth Century. (p. 1256)
—Roman Empire. (p. 1485)
—Saving Water & Energy. (p. 1518)
—Sudan, Darfur & the Nomadic Conflicts. (p. 1672)
—Sydney. (p. 1692)
—Vikings. (p. 1842)
—Wow! Surprising Facts about Pirates. Aspinall, Marc, illus. (p. 1962)
Steele, Philip, jt. auth. see Feldman, Thea.
Steele, Philip, jt. auth. see Jacobs, Pat.
Steele, Philip, jt. auth. see MacDonald, Fiona.
Steele, Philip, jt. auth. see Morris, Neil.
Steele, Philip & Dorling Kindersley Publishing Staff. City Through Time. Noon, Steve, illus. (p. 324)
Steele, Philip & Goldsmith, Mike. My Body. (p. 1198)
Steele, Philip & Lavery, Brian. Legendary Journeys: Ships. Quigley, Sebastian, illus. (p. 989)
Steele, Philip & MacDonald, Fiona. Vikings & the Celts: Ancient Warriors & Raiders. (p. 1842)
Steele, Philip & Morris, Neil. Inside Volcanoes. (p. 878)
Steele, Philip & Philip, Steele. Piramides Fueron Construidas. (p. 1362)
Steele, Philip & Powell, Anton. History News: the Greek News. (p. 783)
Steele, Philip & Rosso, Norma. History News: the Aztec News. (p. 783)
Steele, Philip & Smith, Miranda. Medieval World. (p. 1119)
—World of Pirates. (p. 1957)
Steele, Philip, et al. Mesopotamia. (p. 1129)
—Weird & Wacky History Book Box: Find Out What Is Fact or Fantasy in 8 Amazing Books (p. 1872)
Steele, Phillip. Amazing World Of: Pirates. (p. 56)
—Step Into: The Chinese Empire. (p. 1648)
Steele, Phillip W. Changing Coastlines. (p. 290)
Steele, Robert, illus. see Wilbur, Helen.
Steele, S. Tell Me a Story Book. (p. 1716)
Steele, Samantha. Teenagers: An Alaska Teen Novel. Mercie, Melodye, ed. (p. 1714)
Steele, Tara. Medieval Warfare. (p. 1119)
Steele, William O. Buffalo Knife. (p. 235)
—Flaming Arrows. (p. 602)
—Perilous Road. (p. 1343)
—We Were There with the Pony Express. (p. 1868)
—Winter Danger. (p. 1938)
Steele-Card, Adrianna, illus. see Handy, Femida & Carpenter, Carole H.
Steele-Kurtin, Christina. Elbee Mclittle's Donkey Delivery. (p. 508)
Steele-Morgan, Alex, illus. see Nolan, Allia Zobel.
Steele-Morgan, Alex, illus. see Schnur, Susan & Schnur-Fishman, Anna.
Steele-Morgan, Alexandra, illus. see Fischer, Jean & Thomas Nelson Publishing Staff.
Steele-Saccio, Eva. Headbands & Hairstyles: Make & Wear Super Stylish Headbands. (p. 756)
—Marvelous Book of Magical Mermaids. (p. 1099)
—Nail Style Studio: Simple Steps to Painting 25 Stunning Designs. (p. 1227)
—Ribbon Bangles: Make 5 Beautiful Wrapped Bracelets. (p. 1469)
Steele-Saccio, Eva & Johnson, Anne Akers. Beaded Bands: Super Stylish Bracelets Made Simple. (p. 149)
Steele-Saccio, Eva & Klutz Editors. Thumb Wars: The Ultimate Guide. (p. 1745)
—Twisted Critters: The Pipe Cleaner Book. (p. 1802)
Steele-Staccio, Eva. String Art: Turn String & Pins into Works of Art. Klutz Press Staff, ed. (p. 1667)
Steele-Staccio, Eva & Klutz Editors. Marvelous Book of Magical Horses: Dress up Paper Horses & Their Fairy Friends. (p. 1099)
Steelhammer, Ilona, illus. see Cosgrove, Stephen.
Steelsmith, Mary. Bedside Companion. (p. 156)
—Old Man & the Seed. (p. 1284)
—They's Weywulves. (p. 1732)
Steen, Joel. Home Room 7b. (p. 792)
Steen, Rob, illus. see Gervais, Ricky.
Steenholdt, Jeff, illus. see Hoeksema, Gertrude.
Steenhuis, Peter Henk, jt. auth. see Prins, Marcel.
Steenkamer, Paul. Sports Great Donovan Mcnabb. (p. 1632)
Steensland, Mark. Behind the Bookcase. Murphy, Kelly, illus. (p. 160)
Steenwyk, Carrie & Witvliet, John D. At Your Baptism. (p. 111)
Steenwyk, Elizabeth Van. Blacksmith's Song. Rich, Anna, illus. (p. 197)
Steer, Deirdre Clancy, jt. auth. see Bailey Publishing Staff.
Steer, Dugald A. Dragon Diary Carrel, Douglas, illus. (p. 477)
—Dragon Prophecy. Carrel, Douglas, illus. (p. 477)
—Snappy Little Halloween. Matthews, Derek, illus. (p. 1597)
Steer, Dugald A., ed. see Blake, Spencer.
Steer, Dugald A., ed. see De Lesseps, Ferdinand Zoticus.
Steer, Dugald A., ed. see Drake, Ernest.
Steer, Dugald A., ed. see Evans, Hestia.
Steer, Dugald A., ed. see Grey, Allan.
Steer, Dugald A., ed. see Hardcastle, Henry.
Steer, Dugald A., ed. see Lubber, William.
Steer, Dugald A., ed. see Merlin, Master.
Steer, Dugald A., ed. see Merlin.
Steer, Dugald A., ed. see Sands, Emily.
Steer, Dugald A., jt. auth. see Lubber, William.
Steer, Dugald A. & Master Merlin. Wizardology Handbook: A Course for Apprentices. (p. 1943)
Steer, Malcolm. Christian's Evangelistic Pocket Guide to Islam. (p. 312)
Steere, Jay & Gamble, Adam. Good Night Seattle. Veno, Joe, illus. (p. 700)
Steere, Marcia. Tales from My Coloring Book. (p. 1701)
Steers, Amanda . M. Old's Cool. (p. 1285)
Steers, Billy. Lift-The-Flap Tab: Tractor Mac: Friends on the Farm. (p. 1014)
—Tractor Mac Arrives at the Farm. (p. 1775)
—Tractor Mac Builds a Barn. (p. 1775)
—Tractor Mac Fall Harvest. (p. 1775)
—Tractor Mac Family Reunion. (p. 1775)
—Tractor Mac Farmers Market: Farmer's Market: Steers, Billy, illus. (p. 1775)
—Tractor Mac Farmers' Market. (p. 1775)
—Tractor Mac Harvest Time. (p. 1775)
—Tractor Mac Learns to Fly. (p. 1775)
—Tractor Mac New Friend. (p. 1775)
—Tractor Mac Parade's Best. (p. 1775)
—Tractor Mac Saves Christmas. (p. 1775)
—Tractor Mac Tune-Up. (p. 1775)
—Tractor Mac You're a Winner. (p. 1775)
Steever, Sarah, illus. see Porras, Nikki Jo & Hix, Jax.
Stef. Be Careful What You Wish For. (p. 148)
Stefanescu, Estera. Megan's Great Day. (p. 1124)
Stefano, Tony. Tommy & the Dream MacHine — What a Trip! a Boy, a Soda MacHine & a Voyage to Save the Planet. (p. 1764)
Stefans, Brian Kim. Before Starting Over: Selected Writings & Interviews 1994-2005. (p. 158)
Stefanski, Daniel. How to Talk to an Autistic Kid. (p. 822)
Stefansson, Vilhjalmur & Irwin, Violet. Shaman's Revenge: Based on the Arctic Diaries of Vilhjalmur Stefansson. Grier, Geoffrey, illus. (p. 1559)
Steffek, Tracey H. Coloring Fun with Words: Learn to Spell & Remember Difficult Words Through Coloring. (p. 344)
Steffen, Jennifer, illus. see Becker, Laura.
Steffen, Jeremy, illus. see Terry, Alana.
Steffen, Randy, illus. see Beecher, Elizabeth.
Steffen, Tim. Big Book of Birds. (p. 179)
—Mom's Cup of Coffee: The (Incr)Edible Adventures of Allie Quirk. (p. 1163)
Steffen, Tim & Thornton, Susan. Adventures of Baby Cat in Cherry Grove: Home Sweet Home. (p. 16)
Steffen, Tim & Thornton, Susan Ann. Adventures of Baby Cat in Cherry Grove: Finding Faith. Thornton, Susan Ann, illus. (p. 16)
—Golden Dragonfly: The Adventures of Baby Cat in Cherry Grove. Thornton, Susan Ann, illus. (p. 694)
Steffens, Bradley. Free Speech. (p. 634)
—Free Speech Movement. (p. 634)
—Giants. (p. 674)
—Ibn Al-Haytham: First Scientist. (p. 849)
Steffensmeier, Alexander. Millie & the Big Rescue. (p. 1144)
—Millie in the Snow. Steffensmeier, Alexander, illus. (p. 1144)
—Millie to the Rescue. (p. 1144)
—Millie Waits for the Mail. Steffensmeier, Alexander, illus. (p. 1144)
Steffibauer, Thomas, illus. see Panev, Aleksandar.
Steffora, Tracey. Adding with Ants (p. 11)
—Animal Math. (p. 78)
—Animal Math: Adding, Taking Away, & Skip Counting (p. 78)
—Animal Math: Comparing & Measuring (p. 78)
—Clocks & Calendars (p. 333)
—Comparing with Cats (p. 352)
—Counting in the City (p. 371)
—Days of the Week (p. 415)
—Días de la Semana. (p. 435)
—Estaciones del Año. (p. 538)
—Horas del Día. (p. 797)
—Horas, Minutos y Segundos. (p. 797)
—Hours, Minutes, & Seconds (p. 802)
—Math Around Us (p. 1105)
—Math at the Airport (p. 1105)
—Math at the Hospital (p. 1105)
—Math at the Store (p. 1105)
—Math at the Train Station (p. 1105)
—Math at the Vet (p. 1105)
—Math on the Farm (p. 1106)
—Math on the Job. (p. 1106)
—Measuring in the Garden (p. 1117)
—Measuring Time (p. 1117)
—Measuring with Monkeys (p. 1117)
—Medir el Tiempo. (p. 1120)
—Meses del Año. (p. 1129)
—Months of the Year (p. 1170)
—My Five Senses (p. 1208)
—Patterns at the Museum (p. 1329)
—Relojes y Calendarios. (p. 1458)
—Seasons of the Year (p. 1538)
—Shapes in the Kitchen (p. 1560)
—Shapes with Snakes (p. 1561)
—Skip Counting with Meerkats (p. 1586)
—Sorting at the Market (p. 1614)
—Taking Away with Tigers (p. 1698)
—Times of the Day (p. 1754)
—Using Addition at Home (p. 1828)
—Using Subtraction at the Park (p. 1828)
—What Is Math? (p. 1889)
—What Is Time? (p. 1891)
Stefoff, Rebecca. Al Gore: Fighting for a Greener Planet. (p. 32)
—Alaska. (p. 33)
—Alchemy & Chemistry. (p. 35)

S

—Amphibian Class. (p. 65)
—Ancient Mediterranean World. (p. 70)
—Ancient Near East. (p. 70)
—Arachnid Class. (p. 94)
—Asian Empires. (p. 106)
—Astrology & Astronomy. (p. 109)
—Astrology or Astronomy: Is Your Fate in the Stars? (p. 109)
—Bakke Case: Challenge to Affirmative Action. (p. 133)
—Bird Class. (p. 190)
—Building Bridges. (p. 239)
—Building Dams. (p. 239)
—Building Roads. (p. 239)
—Building Skyscrapers. (p. 239)
—Building Tunnels. (p. 239)
—Camera. (p. 256)
—Captain Kidd. (p. 264)
—Century of Immigration: 1820-1924. (p. 287)
—Chimpanzees. (p. 306)
—Cities & Towns. (p. 322)
—Conifer Division. (p. 357)
—Crime Labs. (p. 382)
—Criminal Profiling. (p. 382)
—Cybercrime. (p. 396)
—Deer. (p. 423)
—Earth or Sun: Which One Is in the Center? (p. 496)
—Exploration & Settlement. (p. 550)
—Faisal: World Leaders: Past & Present. (p. 565)
—Family Trees - Group 2 (p. 569)
—Famous Forensic Cases. (p. 569)
—First Humans. (p. 595)
—Fish Classes. (p. 598)
—Flat Earth & Round Earth. (p. 602)
—Flowering Plant Division. (p. 608)
—Forensic Techniques. (p. 617)
—Forensics & Medicine. (p. 617)
—Forensics & Modern Disasters. (p. 617)
—Four Elements & the Periodic Table. (p. 624)
—Fungus Kingdom. (p. 649)
—Furman V. Georgia: Debating the Death Penalty. (p. 650)
—Ghosts & Spirits. (p. 672)
—Giants. (p. 674)
—How Animals Communicate. (p. 804)
—How Animals Feel. (p. 804)
—How Animals Play. (p. 804)
—How Animals Think. (p. 805)
—Humans: An Evolutionary History (p. 826)
—Ice Age Neanderthals. (p. 850)
—Idaho. (p. 852)
—John Brown & Armed Resistance to Slavery. (p. 921)
—Lions. (p. 1021)
—Magic. (p. 1071)
—Magic & Medicine. (p. 1071)
—Managing Land Use. (p. 1086)
—Marriage. (p. 1096)
—Marsupial Order. (p. 1096)
—Medieval World. (p. 1119)
—Microscopes & Telescopes. (p. 1136)
—Modern Humans. (p. 1158)
—Monarchy. (p. 1163)
—Moneran Kingdom. (p. 1163)
—Nevada. (p. 1242)
—Oregon. (p. 1303)
—Origins. (p. 1304)
—Patriot ACT. (p. 1329)
—Penguins. (p. 1337)
—Polar Bears. (p. 1379)
—Primate Order. (p. 1400)
—Prophets & Prophecy. (p. 1411)
—Pros & Cons of Coal. (p. 1412)
—Redbeard. (p. 1455)
—Right to Die. (p. 1472)
—Robots. (p. 1481)
—Rodent Order. (p. 1484)
—Sea Mammals. (p. 1535)
—Secrets of the Supernatural (p. 1546)
—Security V. Privacy. (p. 1546)
—Smart Spending. (p. 1593)
—Solving History's Mysteries. (p. 1608)
—Stephen King. (p. 1648)
—Submarines. (p. 1671)
—Sun & the Earth. (p. 1676)
—Surviving the Oregon Trail: Stories in American History. (p. 1687)
—Surviving the Oregon Trail. (p. 1687)
—Telephone. (p. 1716)
—Turtles. (p. 1799)
—U. S. v. Nixon: The Limits of Presidential Privilege. (p. 1807)
—Vampires, Zombies, & Shape-Shifters. (p. 1832)
—Washington. (p. 1859)
—Whale Sharks. (p. 1877)
—Wild West. (p. 1930)
—Witches & Witchcraft. (p. 1941)
Stefoff, Rebecca, adapted by. Third Chimpanzee for Young People: On the Evolution & Future of the Human Animal. (p. 1734)
Stefoff, Rebecca & Mead, Wendy. Utah. (p. 1829)
Stegall, Billy Mark. Pat & Pea Soup. Archambault, Matthew, illus. (p. 1327)
Stegall, Joel E., illus. see Johns, Isabel G.
Stegall, Kim. Mumsi Meets a Lion. Batti, Kimberly Rose, illus. (p. 1191)
—Rodney Robbins & the Rainy-Day Pond. Day, Bruce, illus. (p. 1484)
Stegenga, Wil. Pinwheel Designs. (p. 1361)
—Sacred Yantra Coloring Book. (p. 1500)
—Spectacular Star Designs. (p. 1624)
Stegenga, Wil & Coloring Books for Adults. Geometric Whirlwind Coloring Book. (p. 662)
—Heart Designs. (p. 759)
Stegenga, Wil & Coloring Books Staff. Geometric Motifs. (p. 662)
Stegen-Hanson, Tania, jt. auth. see Ernsperger, Lori.
Steger, Volker. Buzz. (p. 248)
Steggall, Susan. Diggers Are Coming! (p. 439)
—On the Road. (p. 1291)
—Rattle & Rap. (p. 1440)
—Red Car, Red Bus. (p. 1453)
Steggall, Susan & Quarto Generic Staff. Busy Boats. (p. 245)
—Following the Tractor. (p. 612)
Steggall, Vicki. Lunchtime Rules. Oswald, Ash, illus. (p. 1065)
Stegmaier, Laura J. Ling-Ling Turner, Ppi: Mystery of the Rising Island. (p. 1019)
Stegman, Ryan, illus. see Slott, Dan.
Stegman-Bourgeois, Karen M. Trollerella. Long, Ethan, illus. (p. 1788)
Stegmann, Lisa, jt. auth. see Meinke, Amanda.
Stegos, Daniel, illus. see Halfmann, Janet.
Stegos, Daniel, illus. see Hollenbeck, Kathleen.
Stegos, Daniel, illus. see Korman, Susan.
Stegos, Daniel, jt. auth. see Halfmann, Janet.
Stegos, Daniel J., illus. see Halfmann, Janet.
Stegos, Daniel J., illus. see Hollenbeck, Kathleen M.
Stegos, Daniel J., illus. see Korman, Susan.
Stehlik, Tania Duprey. Violet Jovanovic, Vanja Vuleta & Second Story Press Staff, illus. (p. 1843)
Stehr, jt. auth. see Broutin.
Stehr, Frederic. Soy Yo Cuac-Cuac. (p. 1618)
Steier, John, ed. see Diggs, Linda.
Steig, jt. auth. see Steig, William.
Steig, Jeanne. Tales from Gizzard's Grill. Turner, Sandy, illus. (p. 1701)
Steig, William. Abel's Island. (p. 4)
—Abel's Island. Steig, William, illus. (p. 4)
—Amazing Bone. Steig, William, illus. (p. 54)
—Amos & Boris. (p. 65)
—Amos & Boris. Steig, William, illus. (p. 65)
—Brave Irene. Steig, William, illus. (p. 223)
—C D B! Steig, William, illus. (p. 249)
—C D C ? Steig, William, illus. (p. 249)
—Doctor de Soto. (p. 459)
—Doctor de Soto. Steig, William, illus. (p. 459)
—Doctor de Soto Book & CD Storytime Set Steig, William, illus. (p. 459)
—Dominic. (p. 465)
—Dominic. Steig, William, illus. (p. 465)
—Farmer Palmer's Wagon Ride. Steig, William, illus. (p. 574)
—Grown-Ups Get to Do All the Driving. Steig, William, illus. (p. 727)
—Pedro Es una Pizza. (p. 1334)
—Pete's a Pizza. Steig, William, illus. (p. 1347)
—Pete's a Pizza. (p. 1348)
—Potch & Polly. (p. 1388)
—Potch & Polly. Agee, Jon, illus. (p. 1388)
—Real Thief. (p. 1449)
—Real Thief. Steig, William, illus. (p. 1449)
—Shrek! (p. 1571)
—Shrek! Steig, William, illus. (p. 1571)
—Spinky Sulks. Steig, William, illus. (p. 1628)
—Sylvester & the Magic Pebble. Steig, William, illus. (p. 1692)
—Toby, Who Are You? Euvremer, Teryl, illus. (p. 1760)
—When Everybody Wore a Hat. Steig, William, illus. (p. 1902)
—Wizzil. (p. 1943)
—Wizzil. Blake, Quentin, illus. (p. 1943)
Steig, William & Steig. Which Would You Rather Be? Bliss, Harry, illus. (p. 1911)
Steigemeyer, Julie. Mommy Promises. Ong, Wilson, illus. (p. 1162)
—My Little Easter Book. Regan, Dana, illus. (p. 1212)
Steiger, A. J. Mindwalker. (p. 1145)
Steigvilas, Nemira. Mini Eva Lovvves Ballet. (p. 1146)
Steimle, James. New Adventures of Stephen Crown. (p. 1243)
Steimle, Robert, illus. see Dawson, Dylan.
Stein, A. K. EZEKIEL MAYHILL & the Crystal of God. (p. 559)
Stein, Ben P., jt. auth. see Karam, P. Andrew.
Stein, Catherine. Madley Doesn't Want To. (p. 1070)
Stein, Clem. Scotty's Feeder & the Secret Tower. Prouix, Denis, illus. (p. 1532)
Stein, David & Klutz Press Staff. How to Make Monstrous, Huge, Unbelievably Big Bubbles (p. 820)
Stein, David Ezra. Because Amelia Smiled. Stein, David Ezra, illus. (p. 155)
—Cowboy Ned & Andy. Stein, David Ezra, illus. (p. 374)
—Dinosaur Kisses. Stein, David Ezra, illus. (p. 442)
—I'm My Own Dog. (p. 859)
—I'm My Own Dog. Stein, David Ezra, illus. (p. 859)
—Interrupting Chicken. (p. 881)
—Interrupting Chicken. Stein, David Ezra, illus. (p. 881)
—Leaves. Stein, David Ezra, illus. (p. 986)
—Love, Mouserella. Stein, David Ezra, illus. (p. 1060)
—Nice Book. Stein, David Ezra, illus. (p. 1250)
—Ol' Mama Squirrel. Stein, David Ezra, illus. (p. 1283)
—Pouch! Stein, David Ezra, illus. (p. 1389)
—Tad & Dad. Stein, David Ezra, illus. (p. 1695)
Stein, Deborah Jiang, jt. auth. see Free Spirit Publishing Staff.
Stein, Deborah Jiang, jt. auth. see Free Spirit Publishing.
Stein, Eric, jt. auth. see Bandy, Michael S.
Stein, Erin, ed. see Hasbro.
Stein, Erin, ed. see R, Disney.
Stein, Erin & Rau, Zachary, eds. Madagascar (p. 1069)
Stein, Erin K. I Am Wonder Woman. Farley, Rick, illus. (p. 834)
—Peppa Pig: Paint Book. (p. 1340)
—Peppa Pig: Family Fun Reusable Sticker Book. (p. 1340)
Stein, Ethel. Jewish Holiday Adventures. Kaye, Donna M., illus. (p. 917)
Stein, Evaleen. Christmas Porringer (Yesterday's Classics) Everhart, Adelaide, illus. (p. 315)
—Gabriel & the Hour Book (Yesterday's Classics) (p. 652)
—Our Little Crusader Cousin of Long Ago. Meister, Charles E., illus. (p. 1309)
—Our Little Frankish Cousin of Long Ago. Landau, Helena Von & Meister, Charles, illus. (p. 1309)
—Our Little Norman Cousin of Long Ago. Goss, John, illus. (p. 1309)
Stein, Frank N., jt. auth. see Rothman, Joel.
Stein, Garth. Enzo & the Christmas Tree Hunt! Alley, R. W., illus. (p. 532)
—Enzo - Races in the Rain! Alley, R. W., illus. (p. 532)
—Racing in the Rain: My Life as a Dog. (p. 1432)
Stein, Gertrude. Everybody's Autobiography (p. 543)
—Three Lives. (p. 1743)
—Three Lives & Tender Buttons. (p. 1743)
—To Do: A Book of Alphabets & Birthdays. (p. 1758)
Stein, Gertrude & Hurd, Thacher. World Is Round. Hurd, Clement, illus. (p. 1956)
Stein, Harve, illus. see Bell, Marion R. & Geyer, Donna M.
Stein, Jeanne C. Becoming (p. 156)
—Blood Drive. (p. 200)
—Legacy. (p. 987)
—Watcher. (p. 1861)
Stein, Joshua. Chasing the King. (p. 294)
Stein, Kristen. Oh Sweet Child of Mine. (p. 1281)
—Vegetarian Lion. (p. 1834)
Stein, Larry. Josh Discovers Passover! Goodman, Marlene K., illus. (p. 926)
—Really! Fun Family Haggadah. (p. 1449)
Stein, Laurie, illus. see Landman, Yael & Hill, Barbara.
Stein, Lee. Generation Communication: For Teens Who Want to Get Ahead in the World. (p. 660)
Stein, Lori. Butterfly Treats & Hummingbird Sweets. (p. 248)
Stein, Mathilde. Brave Ben. Van Hout, Mies, illus. (p. 223)
—Child Cruncher. Van Hout, Mies, illus. (p. 301)
—Dear Daisy Dunnington. Groenink, Chuck, illus. (p. 418)
—Mine! Van Hout, Mies, illus. (p. 1145)
—Monstersong. Van Der Linden, Gerdien, illus. (p. 1169)
Stein, Paul. Droughts of the Future. (p. 486)
—Floods of the Future. (p. 606)
—Global Warming: A Threat to Our Future. (p. 684)
—Ice Ages of the Future. (p. 850)
—Library of Future Weather & Climate (p. 1006)
—Storms of the Future. (p. 1656)
Stein, Peter. Bugs Galore. Staake, Bob, illus. (p. 237)
—Cars Galore. Staake, Bob, illus. (p. 272)
—Little Red's Riding 'Hood. Gall, Chris, illus. (p. 1035)
—Toys Galore. Staake, Bob, illus. (p. 1774)
Stein, R. Conrad. Ancient Mexico. (p. 70)
—Annapolis. (p. 85)
—Austria. (p. 117)
—Benito Juarez & the French Intervention. (p. 164)
—Conquistadors: Building a Spanish Empire in the Americas. (p. 358)
—Cortes & the Spanish Conquest. (p. 368)
—Cuban Missile Crisis: In the Shadow of Nuclear War. (p. 388)
—David Farragut: First Admiral of the U. S. Navy. (p. 411)
—Emiliano Zapata & the Mexican Revolution. (p. 518)
—Escaping Slavery on the Underground Railroad. (p. 535)
—Great Chicago Fire. (p. 714)
—Harriet Tubman: On My Underground Railroad I Never Ran My Train off the Track. (p. 750)
—Hernando Cortés: Conquistador & Empire Builder. (p. 772)
—Hernando de Soto: A Life of Adventure. (p. 772)
—Home Front During World War II in American History. (p. 792)
—Incredible Transcontinental Railroad: Stories in American History. (p. 869)
—Industrial Revolution: Manufacturing a Better America. (p. 872)
—Mexican Revolution. (p. 1131)
—Mexican War of Independence. (p. 1131)
—Mexican-American War. (p. 1131)
—Mexico. (p. 1131)
—Modern Mexico. (p. 1158)
—Montana (Revised Edition) (p. 1170)
—National Archives. (p. 1231)
—New Deal: Pulling America Out of the Great Depression. (p. 1244)
—Oklahoma City National Memorial. (p. 1283)
—Sioux: A Proud People. (p. 1580)
—Someone Talked! (p. 1609)
—Spanish Missionaries: Bringing Spanish Culture to the Americas. (p. 1621)
—Story of Mexico (p. 1659)
—U. S. Marine Corps & Military Careers. (p. 1806)
—Washington (Revised Edition) (p. 1860)
—World War II. (p. 1959)
—World War II D-Day Invasion in American History. (p. 1959)
—World War II in Europe: From Normandy to Berlin. (p. 1959)
—World War II in the Pacific: From Pearl Harbor to Nagasaki. (p. 1959)
Stein, R. Conrad, jt. auth. see Kiland, Taylor Baldwin.
Stein, R. Conrad, jt. auth. see Taylor, Charlotte.
Stein, Renea. Wise Old Owl & Those Tricky Times Tables. (p. 1940)
Stein, Robert. Jewish Americans: Coming to America. (p. 917)
Stein, Tammar. High Dive. (p. 777)
—Kindred. (p. 957)
—Spoils. (p. 1630)
Stein, Uriel Von. Gretta's & Graci's Bright, Bright, Moonlit Night. (p. 723)
Steinagle, Jason. Citizenship: What It Means to Be from Texas. (p. 323)
—Understanding the Texas Constitution. (p. 1816)
Steinbach, Coreen, illus. see Hoese, Ray.
Steinbach, Hans. Midnight Opera: Act 2 Steinbach, Hans, illus. (p. 1139)
Steinbach, Hanzo. Midnight Opera (p. 1139)
Steinbacher, Philip A. Quotation Quizzlers: Puzzling Your Way Through Famous Quotations. (p. 1429)
Steinbauer, Larry, illus. see Swartz, Neva.
Steinberg, Alfred. Admiral Richard E Byrd. Beck, Charles, illus. (p. 13)
Steinberg, Barbara, jt. auth. see Tabs, Judy.
Steinberg, D. J. Grasshopper Pie & Other Poems. Sinnott, Adrian C., tr. (p. 711)
—Grow Up! Smith, Brian, illus. (p. 726)
—Kindergarten, Here I Come! Chambers, Mark, illus. (p. 957)
—Mac Attack! Smith, Brian, illus. (p. 1067)
Steinberg, Don, jt. auth. see History Channel, History.
Steinberg, Harriet. Tooth with a Hole. (p. 1768)
Steinberg, Howard. Jackie's Got Game! A Story about Diabetes. Chris, Healey, illus. (p. 904)
Steinberg, Jon L. "Eye" See My Alphabet. (p. 558)
Steinberg, Lane, jt. auth. see Pollack, Jeff.
Steinberg, Laya. All Around Me I See. Arbo, Cris, illus. (p. 43)
—All Around Me, I See. Arbo, Cris, illus. (p. 43)
—Thesaurus Rex. Harter, Debbie, illus. (p. 1731)
—Thesaurus Rex Finds a Friend. Harter, Debbie, illus. (p. 1731)
Steinberg, Lynnae D. What Are Taxes? (p. 1879)
—What Is Weather Forecasting? (p. 1891)
Steinberg, Peter K. Sylvia Plath. (p. 1693)
Steinberg, Ruth, jt. auth. see Vogel, Eva.
Steinberg, Sari. King Solomon Figures It Out. Taulo, Tuija, illus. (p. 959)
Steinbock, Steven E. Gift of Wisdom: The Books of Prophets & Writings. Mantell, Ahuva & Sperling, S. David, illus. (p. 675)
—Gift of Wisdom. (p. 675)
—Words upon Your Heart: Concepts & Ideas That Shape Judaism & World Religions. (p. 1952)
Steiner. Murder Takes a Fast Track. (p. 1192)
Steiner, Barbara. 23 Shadow Street: Deadly Dreams. (p. 1996)
—Cry of the Loon: A Samantha Mystery. Tibbles, Jean-Paul, illus. (p. 387)
—Mystery at Chilkoot Pass. (p. 1223)
Steiner, Christina. Sad Tree & Pronuba. (p. 1501)
Steiner, Dawn. Silver Squirrel & Friends: The Original Book. (p. 1577)
—Silver Squirrel & Friends I Can Read Edition: For Beginner Readers. (p. 1577)
Steiner, Edward A. My Doctor Dog. (p. 1202)
Steiner, Elke, jt. auth. see Guillain, Adam.
Steiner, Gerda & Lenzlinger, Jorg. Gerda Steiner & Jörg Lenzlinger: Stupid & Good Miracles. (p. 666)
Steiner, Hartley. This Is Gabriel - Making Sense of School: A Book about Sensory Processing Disorder. (p. 1735)
Steiner, Howard. Declaration of Independence. (p. 422)
Steiner II, Michael, jt. auth. see Steiner, Michaela.
Steiner, Joan. Look-Alikes: The More You Look, the More You See! Steiner, Joan, illus. (p. 1048)
—Look-Alikes Christmas: The More You Look, the More You See! Steiner, Joan, illus. (p. 1048)
—Look-Alikes Jr. The More You Look, the More You See! Steiner, Joan, illus. (p. 1048)
—Look-Alikes Seek-and-Search Puzzles. (p. 1048)
Steiner, Jörg. Bear Who Wanted to Be a Bear. Müeller, Jörg, illus. (p. 151)
Steiner, Lana. Thor's Tummy. (p. 1740)
Steiner, Maria, illus. see Newswanger, Rebecca.
Steiner, Matt. Mission Possible. (p. 1153)
Steiner, Michaela & Steiner II, Michael. Mike Lost His Bike. (p. 1141)
Steiner, Nancy. On This Night: The Steps of the Seder in Rhyme. Leff, Tova, illus. (p. 1292)
Steiner, Naomi. 7 Steps to Raising a Bilingual Child. (p. 1993)
Steiner, Roger J. New College French & English Dictionary. (p. 1244)
Steiner, Rudolf. Cinderella at the Ball. (p. 320)
—Fun Days. (p. 647)
—Rudolf Steiner. Seddon, Richard, ed. (p. 1494)
—Three Grimms' Fairy Tales. Wagner, Gerard, illus. (p. 1742)
Steiner, Stan, et al. P Is for Potato: An Idaho Alphabet. Stack, Jocelyn, illus. (p. 1316)
Steinfeld, Alan. Careers in Alternative Medicine. (p. 267)
Steingress, Frederick M. Low Pressure Boilers: Text. (p. 1061)
—Low Pressure Boilers: Workbook. (p. 1061)
—Low Pressure Boilers: Answer Key. (p. 1061)
—Low Pressure Boilers: Resource Guide. (p. 1061)
Steingress, Frederick M., et al. High Pressure Boilers: Text. (p. 778)
—High Pressure Boilers: Answer Key. (p. 778)
—High Pressure Boilers: Resource Guide. (p. 778)
—Stationary Engineering. (p. 1644)
Steinhardt, Marge, illus. see Mills Inc.
Steinhardt, Nancy S., ed. see Kwong-Chiu, Chiu.
Steinhardt, Nancy S., ed. see Tse, Brian.
Steinhauer, Olen, see Steinhauer, Olen, pseud.
Steinhauer, Olen, pseud. 36 Yalta Boulevard. (p. 1996)
Steinhöfel, Andreas. Elk Dropped In. Jaffa, Alisa, tr. from GER. (p. 513)
Steinhöfel, Andreas & Wright, Chantal. Spaghetti Detectives. (p. 1620)
Steinhorn, Leonard. Greater Generation: In Defense of the Baby Boom Legacy. (p. 719)
Steininger-Moore, Cheryl A. Blue Tooth Sleuth. Schafer, Holden J., illus. (p. 203)
Steinitz, Andy, jt. auth. see Bjorklund, Ruth.
Steinitz, Andy, jt. auth. see Gaines, Ann.
Steinitz, Andy, jt. auth. see Otfinoski, Steven.
Steinke, Aron Nels. Super Crazy Cat Dance. (p. 1679)
—Super Duper Dog Park. (p. 1679)
Steinke, Aron Nels, illus. see Cohn, Ariel.
Steinke, Gord. Crossing the Line: Mobsters & Rumrunners (p. 385)
—Mobsters & Rumrunners of Canada: Crossing the Line (p. 1157)
Steinke, Misty. Who Hung the Moon. (p. 1915)
Steinke, Theodore R., jt. ed. see Kovacik, Charles F.
Steinkellner, Elisabeth. My New Granny. Roher, Michael, illus. (p. 1216)
Steinkellner, Teddy. Trash Can Days: A Middle School Saga. (p. 1780)
—Trash Can Nights: The Saga Continues. (p. 1780)
Steinkraus, Kyla. Camping Out. Reese, Bob, illus. (p. 257)
—Casita Del Arbol. (p. 276)
—Constitution. (p. 359)
—Ducks on the Farm. (p. 488)
—Giant Gas Planets: Jupiter, Saturn, Uranus, & Neptune. (p. 673)
—How a Bill Becomes a Law. (p. 804)
—In the Doghouse. Myer, Ed, illus. (p. 865)
—Let's Work Together. (p. 1001)
—Los Problemas Del Intercambio. (p. 1054)
—May I Please? (p. 1112)
—Money down the Drain. Myer, Ed, illus. (p. 1164)
—Nobody's Watching. Dufalla, Anita, illus. (p. 1262)

—Rabbits on the Farm. (p. 1430)
—Rocky Planets: Mercury, Venus, Earth, & Mars. (p. 1484)
—Table Wars! Dufalla, Anita, illus. (p. 1694)
—Tree Fort. Reese, Bob, illus. (p. 1783)
—Trouble with Trading. Reese, Bob, illus. (p. 1790)
—Vamos a Acampar. (p. 1831)
—¡Paren de Discutir! (p. 1324)
Steinkraus, Kyla, jt. auth. see Robbins, Maureen.
Steinkraus, Kyla & Moreta, Gladys. Stop Arguing! Reese, Bob, illus. (p. 1653)
Steinkühler, Martina. First Good Shepherd: Psalm 23 for Children. Holzmann, Angela, illus. (p. 595)
Steinlage, Ben. Bird Boy. (p. 190)
Steinlage, Kelly, illus. see Ramsey, Charmaine J.
Steinman, Joshua & Nash, Kevin. University of Chicago College Prowler off the Record. (p. 1820)
Steinmann, Donna. Hello, Grand Mamoon! Guion, Tamara, illus. (p. 764)
Steinmark, Sharyl, illus. see Riva, Jim.
Steinmeyer, Petra, illus. see Combel Editorial Staff.
Steinsiek, Sabra Brown. Tale of the Pronghorned Cantaloupe. Chilton, Noel, illus. (p. 1700)
—Tale of the Pronghorned Cantaloupe. Chilton, Noel Dora, illus. (p. 1700)
Steinwart, Coe, illus. see Aebersold, Carol V. & Bell, Chanda.
Steinwart, Coe, illus. see Aebersold, Carol V. & Chanda, Bell.
Steinwart, Coe, illus. see Bell, Chanda & Aebersold, Carol.
Steinwender, Cherry. Bread Is a Simple Food: Teaching Children about Cultures. (p. 224)
Stejskal, Susan. Little Dog Who Did Big Things. (p. 1027)
Stella, Heather. Get Ready for Kindergarten: Numbers, Time & Opposites - 251 Fun Exercises for Mastering Skills for Success in School. (p. 668)
—Get Ready for Kindergarten - Letters & Sight Words: 247 Fun Exercises for Mastering Skills for Success in School. (p. 668)
—Get Ready for Pre-K: Numbers, Shapes & Colors - 249 Fun Exercises for Mastering Basic Skills. (p. 668)
—Get Ready for School Kindergarten Laptop Workbook: Uppercase Letters, Phonics, Lowecase Letters, Spelling, Rhyming. (p. 668)
Stella, Heather, jt. auth. see Carole, Jane.
Stella, Lennon & Stella, Maisy. In the Waves. Björkman, Steve, illus. (p. 867)
Stella, Leslie. Permanent Record (p. 1343)
Stella M. Reese. Princess of Topaz: An African American Saga. (p. 1405)
Stella, Maisy, jt. auth. see Stella, Lennon.
Stella, Pilar. Seeking Serenity. Cummings, Maris, illus. (p. 1548)
Stellinga, Mark. Buster Boogernose & the Bank Robbers. (p. 245)
—Buster Boogernose & the Boxcar. (p. 245)
—Buster Boogernose & the Bully. (p. 245)
—Buster Boogernose & the Copper Mine. (p. 245)
—Buster Boogernose & the Junkyard. (p. 245)
—Buster Boogernose & the Liar. (p. 245)
—Satellite Detectives. (p. 1515)
Stellings, Caroline. Contest (p. 360)
—Skippers at Cape Spear. (p. 1586)
Stelljes, Susan. Wonder Dog: The Story of Silverton Bobbie. (p. 1947)
Stelly, Colette, jt. auth. see Martinez, Elsie.
Stelmach, Orest. Boy Who Stole from the Dead (p. 219)
Stelten, Gene. House for Wally & Me. Johnson, Chelsea, illus. (p. 803)
Steltzer, Ulli. Building an Igloo. Steltzer, Ulli, photos by. (p. 238)
Stelzer, Cameron. Forgotten Map (p. 620)
—Island of Destiny. (p. 892)
Stelzer, Christina Papalas. Susan Paley Lady Vases Collection: Susan Paley Lady Vases Reference Guide. (p. 1688)
Stem, J. David, et al. Eloise in Hollywood. Enik, Ted, illus. (p. 516)
Stem, Jacqueline. Ghosts of Goliad. (p. 672)
—Haunted Tunnel. (p. 754)
—Mystery of the Whispering Walls. (p. 1226)
Stem, Jacqueline C. Secret of the Dragonfly Pin. (p. 1542)
Stemen, Jeffrey. Critter Giggles. (p. 384)
Stemke, Kathy. Sh Sh Sh Let the Baby Sleep. Foster, Jack, illus. (p. 1556)
Stemmer, Gerhard, jt. auth. see Prien, Jochen.
Stemple, Adam, jt. auth. see Yolen, Jane.
Stemple, Heidi, jt. auth. see Yolen, Jane.
Stemple, Heidi E. Y. One If by Land: A Massachusetts Number Book. Brett, Jeannie, illus. (p. 1295)
—Ready for Anything! Training Your Brain for Expert Espionage. (p. 1447)
Stemple, Heidi E. Y., jt. auth. see Yolen, Jane.
Stemple, Heidi E. Y. & Yolen, Jane. Dance Stories. Cann, Helen, illus. (p. 402)
Stemple, Heidi Elisabet Y., jt. auth. see Yolen, Jane.
Stemple, Jason, illus. see Yolen, Jane.
Stemple, Jason, jt. auth. see Yolen, Jane.
Stemple, Jason, photos by see Yolen, Jane.
Stempleski. Aladdin & the Magic Lamp. (p. 33)
Stenberg, Dick, illus. see Kristiansson, Leif.
Stender, Joshua. Na Makana a Na I'a: The Fish & Their Gifts. (p. 1227)
Stendhal. Red & the Black: A Chronicle of the Nineteenth Century. (p. 1453)
Stengel, Joyce A. St. Patrick & the Three Brave Mice Leonhard, Herb, illus. (p. 1638)
Stengel, Michelle, photos by see Darnell, Yolanda.
Stensaas, Martin, illus. see Holbrook, John Robert.
Stensen, Cindy, illus. see Knutson, Eric.
Stensland, Doris. Advent - Daily Meditations Throughout the Advent Season. (p. 14)
—Country Style - Living the Farm Life. (p. 372)
Stenson, Marcia. Illustrated History of the South Pacific. (p. 857)
Stenstrup, Allen. Forests. (p. 618)

Stent, Amanda & Lewis, Philip. Princess at the Keyboard: Why Girls Should Become Computer Scientists. (p. 1403)
Stentiford, Tyler Michael. Darker Secret. (p. 408)
Stenton, Murray, illus. see Kats, Jewel.
Stentz, Zack, jt. auth. see Miller, Ashley Edward.
Stenzel, Myron James. Save the Next Dance. (p. 1516)
Stenzel, Pam. Sex Has a Price Tag: Discussions about Sexuality, Spirituality, & Self-Respect (p. 1556)
Stenzel, Pam, et al. Sex Has a Price Tag: Discussions about Sexuality, Spirituality, & Self Respect. (p. 1556)
Stepanian, Isabel H. Cat Paws Through History: Ko-Ko the Cat Meets Napoleon Bonaparte. (p. 278)
Stephaan, Kynza. Empress Kynza of Skrollz: You Are Special. (p. 521)
Stephan, Danette. Letter Sound Yoga: For All the Beautiful Children. (p. 1002)
Stephan, Eric G., jt. auth. see Pace, R. Wayne.
Stephanie. Beginning of Gerald. (p. 159)
Stephanie K. McMahan. Sylvan Tales: The Secret of Elfenore. (p. 1692)
Stephanie Longfoot Staff. God Bless 2001. (p. 688)
Stephanie Wheeler Maier. Vincent VanDersnoot Finds His Purpose! Why God Made the Earth, Why He Made People, & the Meaning of Everything. (p. 1843)
Stephas, Kristi. Flying Solo Smith, Rachael, illus. (p. 610)
Stephen, Kevin Paul. Realms of Glory: Encountering God in the Last Days. (p. 1450)
Stephen, Lib, illus. see Fyke, Laurie & Sinclair, Kerrie.
Stephen, Lib, illus. see Lloyd, Sue & Wernham, Sara.
Stephen, Lib, illus. see Lloyd, Sue.
Stephen, Lib, illus. see Wernham, Sara & Lloyd, Sue.
Stephen, Lib, illus. see Wernham, Sara.
Stephen, Marchesi, jt. illus. see Pukac, Michael.
Stephen, Sheila. Preparing for Church: Integrating into the Body of Christ. (p. 1396)
Stephens, Aarti D. Is Racism a Serious Problem? (p. 889)
Stephens, Aarti, ed. Is Racism a Serious Problem? (p. 889)
—Teenage Sexuality. (p. 1714)
Stephens, Amanda. Peter Cottontail. Santoro, Christopher, illus. (p. 1346)
Stephens, Andrea. True Beauty. (p. 1791)
Stephens, Ann Marie. Christmas for Bly & Ray. Bolan, Michael P., illus. (p. 314)
—Stella Eats Out. Bolan, Michael, illus. (p. 1647)
—Surprise for Ray. Bolan, Michael P., illus. (p. 1686)
Stephens, Autumn, ed. Roar Softly & Carry a Great Lipstick: 28 Women Writers on Life, Sex, & Survival. (p. 1478)
Stephens, Berin L. Time Gangsters. (p. 1752)
Stephens, Billie. White of Snow: An Fairie Tale Extraordinaire. (p. 1913)
Stephens, Catherine. Classification Clues. (p. 328)
—Volcanoes. (p. 1849)
Stephens, Catherine & National Geographic Learning Staff. Inside the Internet. (p. 877)
—Life Cycles. (p. 1009)
Stephens, Catherine & Schifini, Alfredo. Looking at Light. (p. 1051)
Stephens, Charles Asbury. Busy Year at the Old Squire's. (p. 246)
Stephens, Chris S. Christmas Box. (p. 313)
—Rapping on the Window. Carpenter, Suzanne, illus. (p. 1439)
—Wartime Scrapbook: The Teachers' Pack. (p. 1859)
—Wartime Scrapbook. (p. 1859)
Stephens, Courtney. My Christmas Child. (p. 1200)
Stephens, David. Coastal Habitats. (p. 336)
—Sharks: Predators of the Ocean. (p. 1563)
Stephens, David R. Treasure Hunters. (p. 1781)
Stephens, Dawn. Little Pot. (p. 1033)
Stephens, Edna Cucksey. Core Democratic Values with Rock U. S. A. Herrick, Mark J., illus. (p. 367)
—Rock U. S. A. & the American Way! A Freedom Handbook. Herrick, Mark J., illus. (p. 1482)
Stephens, Edna Cucksey, et al. You & Me Make Three. Drescher, Heather, illus. (p. 1973)
—You & Me Make Three & Accompanying Plush B. B. the Bear. Drescher, Heather, illus. (p. 1973)
Stephens, Edna, et al. B. B. the Bear: Helps Kids with Divorce. (p. 122)
Stephens, Elaine C., jt. ed. see Brown, Jean E.
Stephens, Evelyn. Five Little Yaks. (p. 601)
Stephens, Harold. Tales from the Pacific Rim. (p. 1702)
Stephens, Heather. Cabbage & Other Scenes. (p. 250)
Stephens, Helen. Betsy Goes to School. (p. 172)
—Betsy Goes to the Doctor. (p. 172)
—Betsy Makes a Splash. (p. 172)
—Betsy Visits Her Grandparents. (p. 172)
—Big Adventure of the Smalls. Stephens, Helen, illus. (p. 177)
—How to Hide a Lion. Stephens, Helen, illus. (p. 820)
—Witchety Sticks & the Magic Buttons. Stephens, Helen, illus. (p. 1941)
Stephens, Helen, illus. see Morpurgo, Michael.
Stephens, James. Traditional Irish Fairy Tales. (p. 1776)
Stephens, Jane. Katie's Too-Big Coat. (p. 945)
Stephens, Jay. Freaky Fun Activities. (p. 632)
Stephens, Jay, illus. see de Mariaffi, Elisabeth.
Stephens, Joan Wilson, illus. see Catalani, Dorothy Kon & Catalani, Jim.
Stephens, John. Black Reckoning. (p. 196)
—Emerald Atlas. (p. 517)
—Fire Chronicle. (p. 590)
Stephens, Juanita. Martha the Multiplying Magician. (p. 1097)
Stephens, Karen & Hammonds-Smith, Maxine. Child & Adult Care Professionals. (p. 301)
Stephens, Kat. Where Did Gypsy Go? (p. 1906)
Stephens, Kate. College, Quicker: 24 Practical Ways to Save Money & Get Your Degree Faster. (p. 340)
Stephens, Kathleen, compiled by. Secrets of a Good Life as Told by Saints & Sinners. (p. 1545)
Stephens Landoll, Mary. Vision from Heaven. (p. 1844)
Stephens, Leigh F., jt. auth. see Disney Book Group Staff.
Stephens, Malcolm B. How to Double Your Solidworks Productivity. (p. 816)
Stephens, Melissa. Little Miss & Spirit Bear's Kiss: A Simple Story of Rediscovering One's Light. (p. 1031)
—Many Adventures of Filbert the Frog. (p. 1089)

Stephens, Michael. Mudlark. (p. 1189)
Stephens, Michael, jt. auth. see Cook, Jessica.
Stephens, Monique Z. Fantastic Four: The Fantastic Four Versus Doctor Doom. (p. 571)
Stephens, Nia. Boy Shopping. (p. 219)
Stephens, Nicholas. Plant Cells & Tissues. Hopkins, William G., ed. (p. 1369)
Stephens, Pam. Dropping in on Rousseau. (p. 486)
Stephens, Pamela. Dropping in on Grandma Moses. McNeill, Jim, illus. (p. 486)
Stephens, Pamela Geiger. Dropping in on Andy Warhol. McNeill, Jim, illus. (p. 486)
—Dropping in on Impressionists. McNeill, Jim, illus. (p. 486)
—Dropping in on Matisse. McNeill, Jim, illus. (p. 486)
—Dropping in on Picasso. McNeill, Jim, illus. (p. 486)
—Dropping in on Romare Bearden. McNeill, Jim, illus. (p. 486)
Stephens, Pamela Greiger. Dropping in on Grant Wood. McNeill, Jim, illus. (p. 486)
Stephens, Pat, illus. see Hickman, Pamela.
Stephens, Pat, illus. see Hodge, Deborah.
Stephens, Pat, illus. see Kaner, Etta.
Stephens, R. David. My Animal Friends Shoemaker, Kathryn, illus. (p. 1196)
Stephens, Ronald, ed. see Etingoff, Kim.
Stephens, Ronald, ed. see Marlowe, Christie.
Stephens, Ronald, ed. Peer Pressure & Relationships. (p. 1335)
—Road Safety. (p. 1477)
—Sports. (p. 1632)
—Stranger Danger. (p. 1665)
—Terrorism & Perceived Terrorism Threats. (p. 1722)
Stephens, Sarah. Midway Monkey Madness Baltazar, Art, illus. (p. 1139)
—Pooches of Power! Baltazar, Art, illus. (p. 1383)
Stephens, Sarah, jt. auth. see Mason, Jane B.
Stephens, Sarah Hines. Backward Bowwow Baltazar, Art, illus. (p. 130)
—Creature of Chaos. Schoening, Dan, illus. (p. 380)
—Lights Out. (p. 1016)
—Night of the Scaredy Crows Baltazar, Art, illus. (p. 1254)
—Pranks for Nothing! (p. 1393)
—Show Off: How to Do Absolutely Everything. One Step at a Time. Mann, Bethany, illus. (p. 1571)
—Sleepy Time Crime Baltazar, Art, illus. (p. 1590)
—Spring Break-Up. (p. 1635)
—Superman Classic: Superman & the Mayhem of Metallo. Mada Design Staff, illus. (p. 1683)
—Super-Pets Showdown Baltazar, Art, illus. (p. 1680)
—Superpowered Pony Baltazar, Art, illus. (p. 1684)
Stephens, Sarah Hines, jt. auth. see Mason, Jane B.
Stephens, Sarah Hines & Hines-Stephens, Sarah. Rumble in the Rainforest Schoening, Dan, illus. (p. 1495)
Stephens, Sarah Hines & Mann, Bethany. Do It Now! Crafts: Cool Art Projects & Tasty Snacks. (p. 457)
—Do It Now! Tricks: Rad Stunts & Sneaky Pranks. (p. 457)
Stephens, Sherry, illus. see Argo, Sandi & Argo, Kaitlyn.
Stephens, Tara. Mouse. (p. 1181)
Stephens, Torrance. Matter of Attention. (p. 1109)
—Rockstar, Stud, Gigolo. (p. 1484)
Stephens, Wayne. Building Character Through Music - Elementary Song Book. (p. 239)
—Building Character Through Music - High School Song Book. (p. 239)
—Building Character Through Music - High School Teacher's Manual. (p. 239)
—Building Character Through Music-Middle School Teacher's Guide. (p. 239)
Stephens, William R. Finding Food in the Wild. (p. 588)
Stephenson, Alan. Adventures of Roy & Rosie Rabbit. (p. 22)
Stephenson, Anna. Good Apple, Bad Apple. (p. 697)
Stephenson, Caitlin, jt. auth. see Flanery, Alicia.
Stephenson, Donald Grier, ed. see Glenn, Richard A.
Stephenson, Eric. Long Hot Summer. (p. 1047)
Stephenson, Karen F., jt. auth. see Anderson, Margaret J.
Stephenson, Kenniqueca. Magical Land of Norms. (p. 1074)
Stephenson, Kristina. Baby Boy Bible (p. 125)
—Baby Girl Bible. (p. 126)
—Sir Charlie Stinky Socks & the Really Frightful Night. (p. 1580)
—Sir Charlie Stinky Socks & the Terrible Secret. (p. 1580)
—Sir Charlie Stinky Socks & the Terrible Secret. Stephenson, Kristina, illus. (p. 1580)
—Sir Charlie Stinkysocks & the Really Big Adventure. Stephenson, Kristina, illus. (p. 1580)
—Sir Charlie Stinkysocks - The Pirate's Curse. (p. 1580)
Stephenson, Kristina, illus. see Bauer, Marion Dane.
Stephenson, Kristina, illus. see Freedman, Claire.
Stephenson, Kristina, illus. see Piper, Sophie.
Stephenson, Kristina, illus. see Stromberg, Ronica.
Stephenson, Kristina, illus. see Toulmin, Sarah.
Stephenson, Kristina, jt. auth. see Toulmin, Sarah.
Stephenson, Lynda. Dancing with Elvis. (p. 403)
Stephenson, Mary. Naven's Dream. (p. 1237)
Stephenson, Midji. Ravenous Raven. Gray, Steve, illus. (p. 1441)
—Whose Tail on the Trail at Grand Canyon. Spengler, Kenneth, illus. (p. 1922)
Stephenson, Nancy. Three Little Kittens. Faris, Eva, illus. (p. 1742)
Stephenson, Nancy Ann. Ducks' New Friends. Coffin, Marilyn, illus. (p. 488)
Stephenson, Norman E. God's Blood: The Fate of the Lost Templar Treasure. (p. 691)
Stephenson, Omri. Freddie Finds Out. (p. 632)
Stephenson, Omri, jt. auth. see Reid Banks, Lynne.
Stephenson, Stone. Somewhere among the Stars & Snowflakes. (p. 1610)
Stephenson, Susan. Monster Maddie. Snider, K. C., illus. (p. 1167)
Stephenson, Wendy. Idaa Trail: In the Steps of Our Ancestors Downey, Autumn, illus. (p. 851)
Stephenson, William. John Fowles. (p. 921)
Stepp, Laura Sessions. Como Guiar a su Hijo a Traves de los Primeros anos de la Adolescencia. (p. 351)
Stepp, Lindsey F. Politely Percy. (p. 1380)

Stepp, Shirley. Pongo Penguin's Whale of a Tale. (p. 1382)
—Santa Lost His Cell Phone. (p. 1513)
Steps To Literacy, compiled by. Bilingual Fairy Tales for Young Readers. (p. 186)
Steps To Literacy Staff, compiled by. Advanced Chapter Books: Lib794. (p. 13)
—Adventures of the Bailey School Kids Set 1: Lib501. (p. 23)
—Adventures of the Bailey School Kids Set 2: Lib500. (p. 23)
—Alexander Series: Lib987. (p. 36)
—Aliki Author Study: Ast045. (p. 41)
—All Aboard Reading Level 1: Lib713. (p. 42)
—All Aboard Reading Level 2: Lib418. (p. 42)
—All about Pets Variety Pack. (p. 43)
—Alphabet Books: Alphabet Picture Books Set 1 (5 Titles) (p. 49)
—Amanda & Oliver Series: Lib018. (p. 52)
—Amazing Athletes: Gen025. (p. 53)
—Amazing Days of Abby Hayes Set of 5 Titles: Rfl006. (p. 54)
—Amelia Bedelia Books: Stl939. (p. 57)
—American Girls Collection: Lib055. (p. 61)
—American Symbols: Lib155. (p. 63)
—Anastasia & Sam Series. (p. 67)
—Andrew Clements Collection: Lib708. (p. 72)
—Animals Variety Pack. (p. 84)
—Ann Cameron Collection: Ast439. (p. 84)
—Arthur Books Collection of 10 Titles, 1 Each: Stl936. (p. 103)
—Audrey Wood Author Study: Ast520. (p. 115)
—Avi Author Study: Ast219. (p. 119)
—A-Z Mysteries Books: Lib711. (p. 2)
—Baseball Card Adventure Collection. (p. 141)
—Beast Quest Collection Grades 2-5: Class Pack (6 Titles, 6 Each) (p. 152)
—Beast Quest Collection Grades 2-5: Variety Pack (6 Titles, 1 Each) (p. 152)
—Betsy Byars Author Study: Ast259. (p. 172)
—Beverly Cleary Books Collection #1 Set of 5 Titles: Stl969. (p. 173)
—Beverly Cleary Books Set 2: Lib023. (p. 173)
—Bill Martin, Jr. Author Study: Ast020. (p. 186)
—Biscuit Series: Rem001. (p. 193)
—Black Lagoon Laugh-Alouds: Lib870. (p. 196)
—Boxcar Children: Lib580. (p. 216)
—Bruce Coville Author Studies Collection: Ast119. (p. 232)
—Bruce Lansky School Poems Collection of 2 Titles: Pro534. (p. 232)
—Caldecott Winners Collection Set 1: Lib368. (p. 252)
—Caldecott Winners Collection Set 2: Lib369. (p. 252)
—Cam Jansen Books: Lib930 (p. 255)
—Cam Jansen Set 2: Lib931. (p. 255)
—Capitol Mysteries: Gen014. (p. 263)
—Captain Underpants: Rfl010. (p. 264)
—Carol Marsh Mysteries: Lib530. (p. 270)
—Catwings Adventures: Rfl004. (p. 281)
—Character Education Variety Pack: Ced005. (p. 291)
—Charlotte Zolotow Author Study: Ast309. (p. 293)
—Childhood of Famous Americans: Lib709. (p. 302)
—Classic Big Books. (p. 327)
—Classroom Classics Set 1: Hcb046. (p. 328)
—Classroom Classics Set 2: Hcb059. (p. 328)
—Classroom Classics Set 3: Hcb069. (p. 328)
—Classroom Paperback Library: Lib011. (p. 329)
—Clyde Robert Bulla Collection: Ast109. (p. 336)
—Community Series Level H Variety Pack. (p. 350)
—Countries of the World Set 1 Variety Pack. (p. 372)
—Countries of the World Set 2 Variety Pack: Capv250. (p. 372)
—Curious George Paperback Series: Lib554. (p. 393)
—Cynthia Rylant Author Study: Ast289. (p. 397)
—Cynthia Rylant Collection: Lib119. (p. 397)
—David Mcphail Author Study: Ast249. (p. 411)
—Donald Crews Author Study: Ast179. (p. 465)
—Donald Freeman Collection: Lib224. (p. 466)
—Dr. Seuss Set 1: Lib326. (p. 475)
—Dr. Seuss Set 2: Lib336. (p. 475)
—Dr. Seuss Set 3: Lib346. (p. 475)
—E. B. White Collection: Lib264. (p. 492)
—Early Step into Reading: Stl940. (p. 494)
—Encyclopedia Brown Series: Lib509. (p. 524)
—Eragon/Eldest Box Set: Variety Pack (2 Titles, 1 Each) (p. 533)
—Eric Carle Collection: Lib206. (p. 533)
—Eva Ibbotson Author Studies: Ast229. (p. 540)
—Eve Bunting Author Studies: Ast209. (p. 541)
—Eve Bunting Author Study: Ast169. (p. 541)
—Explore Space Collection: Capv220. (p. 550)
—Ezra Jack Keats Collection: Lib270. (p. 559)
—Ezra Keats Author Study Set 2: Ast029. (p. 559)
—Fables & Tales Leveled Readers - Set of 6 Titles: Lib686. (p. 559)
—Fairy Tales for Young Readers. (p. 564)
—Faith Ringgold Author Study: Ast379. (p. 565)
—Families Variety Pack Collection of 6 Titles, 1 Each: Capv201. (p. 567)
—Fantasy Collection: Lib548. (p. 572)
—Favorite Animal Big Books. (p. 578)
—Favorite Chapter Books: Lib416. (p. 578)
—First Biographies Set 1: Lib701. (p. 593)
—First Biographies Set 2: Lib702. (p. 593)
—First Chapter Books: Lib788. (p. 593)
—Fox Series: Lib552. (p. 626)
—Freaky Joe Club: Gen027. (p. 632)
—Froggy Series Variety Pack (5 Titles) Lib479. (p. 641)
—Gail Gibbons Collection: Gen003. (p. 652)
—Gary Paulsen Author Study: Ast299. (p. 657)
—George & Martha: Lib511. (p. 663)
—Grade 1 Classroom Library Set 1: Lib749. (p. 705)
—Grade 1 Classroom Library Set 2: Lib752. (p. 705)
—Grade 2 Chapter Books: Lib792. (p. 705)
—Grade 2 Classroom Library Set 1: Lib758. (p. 705)
—Grade 3 Chapter Books: Lib793. (p. 705)
—Grade 3 Classroom Set 2: Lib762. (p. 705)
—Grade 3 Leveled Lit Circle: Lib072. (p. 705)
—Grade 4 Classroom Library: Lib074. (p. 705)
—Grade 5 Classroom Library: Lib076. (p. 705)
—Grade 5-6 Classroom Library: Glc047. (p. 705)
—Grade Leveled 2 Lit Circles Variety Pack: Lib070. (p. 705)

—Grades 1-2 Big Books - Set of 4 Titles: Bgb065. (p. 705)
—Grades 1-2 Classroom Library: Lib755. (p. 705)
—Grades PK-1 Big Books - Set of 4 Titles: Lib919. (p. 705)
—Green Light Readers, Level 2 Set A: Lib565. (p. 722)
—Green Light Readers, Level 2 Set B: Lib564. (p. 722)
—Green Light Readers, Level 2 Set B: Lib566. (p. 722)
—Guided Reading Level A Variety Pack: Gra000. (p. 730)
—Guided Reading Level B Variety Pack: Grb000. (p. 730)
—Guided Reading Level C Variety Pack: Grc000. (p. 730)
—Guided Reading Level D Variety Pack: Grd000. (p. 730)
—Guided Reading Level F Variety Pack: Grf000. (p. 730)
—Guided Reading Level G Variety Pack: Grg000. (p. 730)
—Guided Reading Level H Variety Pack: Grh000. (p. 730)
—Guided Reading Level I Variety Pack. (p. 730)
—Guided Reading Level L Variety Pack: Grl000. (p. 730)
—Guided Reading Level M Variety Pack: Grm000. (p. 730)
—Guided Reading Packs - Level J - 8 Titles: Grj000. (p. 730)
—Hank Zipzer Collection: Rfl009. (p. 742)
—Henry & Mudge Books: Lib013. (p. 767)
—High-Rise Private Eyes: Lib948. (p. 778)
—Historical Fiction Series Set 1. (p. 783)
—Historical Fiction-Collection of 7 Titles, 1 Each: Lib407. (p. 783)
—Holiday Picture Books: Lib032. (p. 788)
—Horrible Harry Chapter Books: Stl993. (p. 798)
—Humor-Genre Studies Collection of 6 Titles: Lib779. (p. 827)
—I Can Read: HFC004. (p. 836)
—I Can Read Arthur Books: Stl932. (p. 836)
—I Can Read Books Level 3 Set B: Lib576. (p. 836)
—I Can Read Chapter Books: Lib575. (p. 836)
—I Can Read! Level 1 Set A: Stl958. (p. 836)
—I Can Read Level 1 Set C: Lib574. (p. 836)
—I Can Read Level 2 Read-Alongs Variety Pack (5 Titles - 1 Book 1 Cass Each) Lvp008. (p. 836)
—I Can Read Level 2 Set B: Stl934. (p. 836)
—I Can Read Level 3 Set A: Stl957. (p. 836)
—I Can Read Lvl 3 Read-Alongs Class Pack (5 Titles - 4 Books 1 Cassette Each) Lis018. (p. 836)
—I Want to Be A ... Series Set 1 (6 Titles) Lib289. (p. 847)
—I Wonder Series: Lib065. (p. 849)
—If You Lived Then Series: Lib134. (p. 854)
—Indian in the Cupboard Series Collection of 4 Titles: Rfl011. (p. 871)
—Iris & Walter Collection of 5 Titles: Lib066. (p. 887)
—Jan Brett Collection: Ast359. (p. 907)
—Jean Fritz Collection: Nfs119. (p. 911)
—Jerry Spinelli Author Study: Ast189. (p. 913)
—Jigsaw Jones Mystery Books: Lib010. (p. 917)
—Joey Pigza Series. (p. 920)
—Judy Blume Collection: Lib254. (p. 931)
—Julian & More Julian: Lib056. (p. 932)
—Junie B. First Grader: Rtr004. (p. 935)
—Junie B Jones Set Of 10: Stl953. (p. 936)
—Just Kids Chapter Books: Lib200. (p. 939)
—Kaeden Super Value Pack. (p. 941)
—Kaeden Variety Pack A-B. (p. 941)
—Kaeden Variety Pack C. (p. 941)
—Katie Kazoo, Switcheroo: Rtr001. (p. 945)
—Kevin Henkes Collection: Lib218. (p. 950)
—Kids of the Polk Street School: Lib514. (p. 954)
—Kindergarten Classroom Collection Set 2: Lib745. (p. 957)
—Leo Lionni Collection: Lib212. (p. 992)
—Level 1 Big Books: Svp001. (p. 1003)
—Level 1 Guided Reading Collection: Lib858. (p. 1003)
—Level 2 Big Books: Svp002. (p. 1003)
—Level 3 Big Books: Svp003. (p. 1003)
—Level A Guided Readidng Class Pack: Lib850. (p. 1003)
—Level B Guided Reading Classroom Packs: Lib851. (p. 1003)
—Level C Guided Reading Classroom Packs. (p. 1003)
—Level C Variety Books for Young Learners: Roc000. (p. 1003)
—Level D Variety Books for Young Learners: Rod000. (p. 1003)
—Level E-F Variety Books for Young Learners: Rof000. (p. 1003)
—Level G Variety Books for Young Learners: Rog000. (p. 1003)
—Level H Variety Books for Young Learners: Roh000. (p. 1003)
—Level I Variety Books for Young Learners: Roi000. (p. 1003)
—Level K Variety Books for Young Learners: Rok000. (p. 1003)
—Level L Variety Books for Young Learners: Rol000. (p. 1003)
—Level M Variety Books for Young Learners: Rom000. (p. 1003)
—Little Critters Collection: Lib667. (p. 1026)
—Little Critters First Readers Level 1: Lib467. (p. 1026)
—Little Critters First Readers Level 2: Lib468. (p. 1026)
—Little Critters First Readers Level 3: Lib469. (p. 1026)
—Little Leveled Readers Levels D-E: Lib569. (p. 1030)
—Little Readers Levels F-G: Lib570. (p. 1034)
—Little Readers Levels H-J: Lib571. (p. 1034)
—Littles Series: Lib516. (p. 1038)
—Louis Sachar Collection: Ast139. (p. 1058)
—M & M Series: Lib517. (p. 1067)
—Magic School Bus Science Chapter Books: Lib014. (p. 1073)
—Magic Tree House Chapter Book Series: Lib518. (p. 1074)
—Margaret Wise Brown Collection: Ast389. (p. 1092)
—Marvin Redpost: Lib519. (p. 1099)
—Math Big Books: Mbb007. (p. 1105)
—Math Big Books - Set 1 - 4 Titles: Lib620. (p. 1105)
—Math Start Series Set 1A: Mat102. (p. 1107)
—Math Start Series Set 1B: Mat103. (p. 1107)
—Math Start Series Set 2A: Mat104. (p. 1107)
—Math Start Series Set 2B: Mat105. (p. 1107)
—Math Start Series Set 3A. (p. 1107)
—Math Start Series Set 3B: Mat107. (p. 1107)
—Matt Christopher Sport Collection: Lib009. (p. 1109)
—Mercer Mayer Author Studies Collection: Lib095. (p. 1127)
—Messy Bessy Series: Lib550. (p. 1130)
—Modern Biographies: Lib196. (p. 1158)
—Mr. Putter & Tabby Series: Lib556. (p. 1186)
—Mrs. Piggle Wiggle Collection of 4 Titles: Lib425. (p. 1187)
—Multicultural Legends & Tales. (p. 1190)
—My America Series: Lib186. (p. 1196)
—My First I Can Read Book: Stl935. (p. 1207)
—Mysterious Benedict Society Collection: Class Pack (3 titles, 6 Each) (p. 1222)
—Mysterious Benedict Society Collection: Variety Pack (3 titles, 1 Each) (p. 1222)
—Mystery-Genre Studies: Lib405. (p. 1224)
—Nancy Carlson Author Study: Ast239. (p. 1228)
—Nate the Great Series: Lib520. (p. 1231)
—Ocean Life Set 1 Variety Pack: Capv205. (p. 1276)
—Ocean Life Set 2 Variety Pack: Capv206. (p. 1276)
—One Day in the ... Series: Rfl002. (p. 1294)
—Our World Variety Pack: Capv208. (p. 1310)
—Pat Hutchins Collection: Lib276. (p. 1327)
—Patricia MacLachlan Collection: Lib104. (p. 1328)
—Patricia Polacco Author Study: Ast279. (p. 1328)
—Patricia Polacco Collection: Lib248. (p. 1329)
—Pee Wee Scouts: Lib522. (p. 1334)
—Percy Jackson & the Olympians Series: Variety Pack (5 Titles, 1 Each) (p. 1341)
—Phonemic Awareness Library Complete Set: Hcb039. (p. 1351)
—Phonemic Awareness Paperback Library: Lib770. (p. 1351)
—Photo Illustrated Biographies: Cap270. (p. 1352)
—Picture Book Biographies - Set 1 - 6 Titles: Lib839. (p. 1355)
—Pinky & Rex Collection: Lib478. (p. 1360)
—Planets: Lib312. (p. 1368)
—Plays for Fluency - Set of 5 Titles: Lib531. (p. 1373)
—Puffin Easy to Read Books Level 1-2: Stl928. (p. 1415)
—Puffin Easy-to-Ready Level 2. (p. 1415)
—Question & Answer Series: Lib797. (p. 1426)
—Read about the Five Sense Collection: Lib052. (p. 1442)
—Read-along Classics Class Pack (4 Titles - 4 Books 1 Cassette Each) Lis541. (p. 1442)
—Real People Series set Of 6: Lib057. (p. 1448)
—Realistic Fiction-Family & Friends COllection of 7 Titles, 1 Each: Lib406. (p. 1449)
—Rhythm & Rhyme Big Books: Lib600. (p. 1468)
—Rigby Collection Level M: Rig180. (p. 1471)
—Rigby Collections D & E: Rig120. (p. 1471)
—Rigby Collections Level C: Rig110. (p. 1471)
—Rigby Collections Level J: Rig150. (p. 1471)
—Rigby Collections Level K: Rig160. (p. 1471)
—Rigby Collections Level L: Rig170. (p. 1471)
—Rigby Collections Levels A & B: Rig100. (p. 1471)
—Rigby Collections Levels F & G: Rig130. (p. 1471)
—Rigby Collections Levels H & I: Rig140. (p. 1471)
—Rigby Collections Levels N & O: Rig190. (p. 1472)
—Roald Dahl Collection: Lib590. (p. 1478)
—Robert Munsch Series: Lib068. (p. 1479)
—Rookie Readers Space Science: Spa553. (p. 1487)
—Rosemary Wells Collection: Lib230. (p. 1489)
—Russell Chapter Books: Lib523. (p. 1498)
—Ruth Heller World of Language: Pro405. (p. 1498)
—Secrets of Droom: Lib526. (p. 1545)
—Sharon Creech Author Studies: Ast199. (p. 1563)
—Sheep Series: Lib555. (p. 1564)
—Sid Fleischman Author Study: Ast129. (p. 1572)
—Silly Animal Read along Stories Variety Pack of 5 TItles: Lvp031. (p. 1575)
—Somos Latinos/We are Latin: Spa554. (p. 1611)
—Song Lee Series: Lib527. (p. 1611)
—Spanish Early Concept Books: Spa014. (p. 1621)
—Spanish Paperback Library: Lib012. (p. 1621)
—Sport Hero Chapter Books: Lib476. (p. 1631)
—Sports Hero Books: Lib902. (p. 1632)
—Spot Series: Stl992. (p. 1633)
—Step into Reading Step 2 Set B: Lib577. (p. 1648)
—Step into Reading Step 3 Set A: Stl911. (p. 1648)
—Step into Reading Step 3 Set B: Lib578. (p. 1648)
—Step into Reading Step 4 Set A: Stl912. (p. 1648)
—Step into Reading Step 4 Set B: Lib579. (p. 1648)
—Step into Reading Step 5: Lib020. (p. 1648)
—Steven Kellogg Collection: Lib377. (p. 1649)
—Stories of Famous Americans: Nfs001. (p. 1655)
—Stories to Go Collection of 10 Titles 1 Each: Rsp015. (p. 1655)
—Storybook Big Books Set 1 (4 Titles) Lib434. (p. 1663)
—Storybook Big Books Set 3 (4 Titles) Lib464. (p. 1663)
—Suzy Kline Collection: Ast429. (p. 1688)
—Tales for the House of Bunnicula: Lib710. (p. 1701)
—Time Warp Trio: Lib636. (p. 1753)
—Tomie Depaola Author Study: Ast269. (p. 1764)
—Tomie dePaola Collection: Lib236. (p. 1764)
—True Stories: Lib781. (p. 1792)
—Wayside School Stories Collection of 3 Titles: Lib030. (p. 1865)
—Weather Series: Capv210. (p. 1870)
—Welcome Books Colonial America: Rnf004. (p. 1873)
—Welcome Books, Hard Work Series: Stl951. (p. 1873)
—Welcome Books My Body: Rnf002. (p. 1873)
—Welcome Books - Sports Series: Lib596. (p. 1873)
—What Kind of Day Is It? Collection: Capv204. (p. 1891)
—William Steig Collection: Lib545. (p. 1933)
—Wordless Books Set 1 (6 Titles) Lib397. (p. 1951)
—Young Cam Jansen Series: Lib528. (p. 1978)
—Zack Chapter Books: Lib003. (p. 1984)
Steps To Literacy Staff, creator. My Writing Journal: Stl077. (p. 1222)
Steptoe, Javaka. Radiant Child: The Story of Young Artist Jean-Michel Basquiat. (p. 1432)
Steptoe, Javaka, illus. see Golio, Gary.
Steptoe, Javaka, illus. see Pearsall, Shelley.
Steptoe, Javaka, illus. see Schoeder, Alan.
Steptoe, John, illus. see Greenfield, Eloise.
Ster, Caroline Rose. Face 2 Face. Jones, Emily, illus. (p. 560)
Steranko, illus. see Simonson, Louise & Hendricks, Damion.
Steranko, Jim, illus. see Anderson, Lars.
Sterguiz, Richard, illus. see Stille, Darlene R.
Sterling, Amber. Little Mud Bear. (p. 1032)
Sterling Casil, Amy. Bomb Scares. (p. 208)
—Pancreatic Cancer: Current & Emerging Trends in Detection & Treatment. (p. 1320)
—Tony Hawk: Skateboard Mogul. (p. 1766)
Sterling Children's, Sterling. Airport. Finn, Rebecca, illus. (p. 32)
—Builders. Finn, Rebecca, illus. (p. 238)
—My First Baseball Book. (p. 1204)
—My First Basketball Book. (p. 1204)
—My First Football Book. (p. 1206)
—My First Soccer Book. (p. 1208)
—Railway. Finn, Rebecca, illus. (p. 1434)
Sterling Children's, Sterling, ed. Sleepy Kitty. (p. 1590)
—Sleepy Puppy. (p. 1590)
Sterling, Christina. What Makes a Sandwich... (p. 1892)
Sterling, Dorothy. Forever Free: The Story of the Emancipation Proclamation. Crichlow, Ernest, illus. (p. 619)
Sterling Editors, creator. Dot to Dot Count To 30. (p. 472)
Sterling, James Milton. Willy the Mountain Climber. (p. 1934)
Sterling, Joyce Bea. Guide to Passing the AMP Real Estate Exam. (p. 730)
Sterling, Kristin. Addition. (p. 12)
—Black Everywhere. (p. 196)
—Blue Everywhere. (p. 202)
—Brown Everywhere. (p. 232)
—Exploring Flowers. (p. 552)
—Exploring Leaves. (p. 552)
—Exploring Roots. (p. 553)
—Exploring Seeds. (p. 553)
—Exploring Stems. (p. 553)
—Fractions. (p. 626)
—Gray Everywhere. (p. 713)
—Green Everywhere. (p. 721)
—It's Cloudy Today. (p. 896)
—It's Rainy Today. (p. 898)
—It's Snowy Today. (p. 899)
—It's Sunny Today. (p. 899)
—It's Windy Today. (p. 899)
—Jane Goodall: A Life of Loyalty. (p. 908)
—Lightning Bolt Books: Colors Everywhere (p. 1016)
—Lightning Bolt Books: What's the Weather Like? (p. 1016)
—Living in Rural Communities. (p. 1041)
—Living in Suburban Communities. (p. 1041)
—Living in Urban Communities. (p. 1041)
—Mary Mcleod Bethune: A Life of Resourcefulness. (p. 1101)
—Mary Mcleod Bethune. (p. 1101)
—Money. (p. 1163)
—Orange Everywhere. (p. 1301)
—Ordinal Numbers. (p. 1302)
—Pink Everywhere. (p. 1359)
—Purple Everywhere. (p. 1419)
—Red Everywhere. (p. 1453)
—Silver & Gold Everywhere. (p. 1576)
—Subtraction. (p. 1671)
—White Everywhere. (p. 1912)
—Yellow Everywhere. (p. 1970)
Sterling, Laurie A. Bloom's How to Write about Nathaniel Hawthorne. (p. 201)
Sterling, Mary Jane. Trigonometry Workbook for Dummies. (p. 1786)
Sterling Publishing Co., Inc. Baby Animals. (p. 124)
—Bebes Animales(Bebes Animales) (p. 155)
—Colors. (p. 345)
—Colors/Colores. (p. 346)
—First Words. (p. 597)
—First Words/Primeras Palabras. (p. 597)
—Numbers. (p. 1272)
—Numbers/Numeros. (p. 1272)
—Oink, Moo, Meow. (p. 1282)
—Oink, Moo, Meow - Oink, Muu, Miau. (p. 1282)
—Things That Go. (p. 1733)
—Things That Go/Cosas Que Se Mueven. (p. 1733)
Sterling Publishing Co., Inc & Verlag, Arena. Kids' First Mandalas. (p. 953)
Sterling Publishing Co., Inc Staff. Dinosaur Sticker Book. (p. 443)
—Garage. Finn, Rebecca, illus. (p. 655)
Sterling Publishing Company Staff. Pocket Factfiles: Dinosaurs. (p. 1375)
—Scrabble Word Search Puzzles for Kids. (p. 1532)
Sterling Publishing Company Staff, ed. see Barry, Sheila Anne, et al.
Sterling Publishing Company Staff, ed. see Blum, Raymond, et al.
Sterling Publishing Company Staff, ed. see Kurchan, Rodolfo, et al.
Sterling Publishing Company Staff & Natural History Museum Staff. Dinosaur Dot to Dot. (p. 442)
Sterling Publishing Company Staff & Ward, Adam, contrib. by. Birds. (p. 191)
Sterling Publishing Company Staff & Ward, Adam. Endangered Animals. (p. 526)
Sterling Publishing Company Staff & Ward, Adam, contrib. by. Pocket Factfiles: Mammals. (p. 1375)
Sterling Publishing Company Staff, creator. Dot to Dot Count To 25. (p. 472)
Sterling, Zack, illus. see Corsetto, Danielle.
Sterling-Orth, Angela. Sound Reading: Literature Lists for Phonology & Articulation. (p. 1615)
Stern, A. J. Check, Please! Marts, Doreen Mulryan, illus. (p. 295)
—Doggy Day Care Marts, Doreen Mulryan, illus. (p. 462)
—Fashion Frenzy. Marts, Doreen Mulryan, illus. (p. 575)
—Frankly, Frannie Marts, Doreen Mulryan, illus. (p. 631)
—Frankly, Frannie: Books 1-3. Marts, Doreen Mulryan, illus. (p. 631)
—Funny Business Marts, Doreen Mulryan, illus. (p. 649)
—Here Comes the... Trouble! Marts, Doreen Mulryan, illus. (p. 770)
—Miss Fortune Marts, Doreen Mulryan, illus. (p. 1151)
—Miss Fortune. (p. 1151)
—Principal for the Day. Marts, Doreen Mulryan, illus. (p. 1406)
—Rocking Out! (p. 1483)
—Rocking Out! Marts, Doreen Mulryan, illus. (p. 1483)
Stern, Amy, jt. auth. see Lewis, Sue.
Stern, Ariella. Chanukah Guess Who? A Lift the Flap Book. Argoff, Patti, illus. (p. 291)
Stern, Beth. Yoda: The Story of a Cat & His Kittens. Crane, Devin, illus. (p. 1972)
Stern, D. G. Disappearing Diamonds: An Upton Charles Adventure. Bartlett, Rebecca, illus. (p. 446)
Stern, Evan, jt. auth. see Stern, Zoe.
Stern, G. B. Duck to Water. (p. 488)
Stern, Judith M., jt. auth. see Quinn, Patricia O.
Stern, Judith M. & Ben-Ami, Uzi. Many Ways to Learn: A Kid's Guide to LD. Chesworth, Michael, illus. (p. 1089)
Stern, Leonard. Mad Libs Worst-Case Scenario Survival Handbook. (p. 1069)
—School Rules! Mad Libs Junior. (p. 1523)
Stern, Leonard, jt. auth. see Price, Roger.
Stern, Leonard, jt. creator see Price, Roger.
Stern, Leonard & Price, Roger. Christmas Carol Mad Libs: Very Merry Songs & Stories. (p. 313)
—Dance Mania Mad Libs. (p. 402)
—Escape from Detention Mad Libs. (p. 534)
—Hello Kitty Loves Mad Libs. (p. 764)
—Letters to Mom & Dad Mad Libs. (p. 1002)
—Luck of the Mad Libs. (p. 1062)
—More Best of Mad Libs. (p. 1174)
—Peace, Love, & Mad Libs. (p. 1331)
—You've Got Mad Libs. (p. 1982)
Stern, Leonard, et al. Animals, Animals, Animals! (p. 82)
—Under the Sea Mad Libs Junior. (p. 1814)
Stern, Linda. Service & Retail. (p. 1553)
Stern, Margaret, creator. Fraction Set. (p. 626)
Stern, Marie Simchow. Favorite Psalms for Children. (p. 578)
Stern, Peggy Poe. Tamarack: The Beekeepers Daughter. (p. 1704)
Stern, Ricki. Mission Impossible. (p. 1153)
Stern, Ricki & Worcester, Heidi P. Adventure: Lonely Leader. Bates, Amy, illus. (p. 14)
Stern, Robin. We Follow the Rules. (p. 1867)
Stern, Robin, jt. auth. see Mills, Nathan.
Stern, Roger. Avengers: Heavy Metal. (p. 118)
—Avengers: Absolute Vision. Akin, Ian et al, illus. (p. 118)
Stern, Roger & Defalco, Tom. Avengers Epic Collection: Judgement Day. Pollard, Keith et al, illus. (p. 119)
Stern, Roger & Layton, Bob. X-Men - Phoenix Rising. Byrne, John et al, illus. (p. 1967)
Stern, Roger, et al. Spider-Man by Roger Stern Omnibus. Zeck, Mike et al, illus. (p. 1626)
—X-Factor Byrne, John, illus. (p. 1967)
Stern, Sam & Stern, Susan. Get Cooking. Campbell, Lorne, photos by. (p. 667)
Stern, Steven L. Building Green-Scrapers. (p. 239)
—Cursed Grounds. (p. 395)
—Witchcraft in Salem. (p. 1941)
—Wretched Ruins. (p. 1963)
Stern, Susan, jt. auth. see Stern, Sam.
Stern, Zoe & Stern, Evan. Divorce Is Not the End of the World: Zoe's & Evan's Coping Guide for Kids. (p. 455)
Sternal, Mark John. BASS GUITAR Total Scales Techniques & Applications BOOK & CD. (p. 143)
—GUITAR Probable Chords: A Chord Key Encyclopedia. (p. 731)
—GUITAR Total Scales Techniques & Applications BOOK & CD: Lessons for beginner through Professional! (p. 731)
—Twelve Notes of Music: Music Theory Simplified: Ear Training & Interval Study Course. (p. 1800)
Sternberg, Demetria. Hey, What's Going on down There? (p. 774)
Sternberg, Ilene & Beck, Allison. Best Garden Plants for Pennsylvania. (p. 169)
—Perennials for Pennsylvania. (p. 1341)
Sternberg, Julie. Bedtime at Bessie & Lil's. Gudeon, Adam, illus. (p. 156)
—Friendship Over. Wright, Johanna, illus. (p. 639)
—Like Bug Juice on a Burger. Cordell, Matthew, illus. (p. 1017)
—Like Carrot Juice on a Cupcake. Cordell, Matthew, illus. (p. 1017)
—Like Pickle Juice on a Cookie. Cordell, Matthew, illus. (p. 1017)
Sternberg, Kate, illus. see Hale, Natalie.
Sternberg, Kate, illus. see Speltz, Ann.
Sternberg, Kate, tr. see Hale, Natalie.
Sternberg, Libby. Case Against My Brother. (p. 273)
—Finding the Forger. (p. 588)
—Uncovering Sadie's Secrets: A Bianca Balducci Mystery. (p. 1812)
Sterne, Laurence, jt. auth. see Barrie, J. M.
Sterne, René, illus. see Van Hamme, Jean.
Sterner, Nathan. Onami: The Great Wave. Dutchak, Shelly, illus. (p. 1292)
Sterner, Wendy L. Seymore Monster. (p. 1556)
Sternfeld, Nathan. Adventures with Rebbe Mendel. Pomerantz, Riva, tr. (p. 25)
—All about Motti & His Adventures with Rebbe Mendel. Bichman, David, illus. (p. 43)
Sterngass, Jon. Brian Urlacher. (p. 226)
—Crazy Horse: The Wild West for Kids. (p. 377)
—Crazy Horse. (p. 377)
—Dan Marino. (p. 402)
—Filipino Americans. (p. 586)
—Frederick Douglass. (p. 633)
—Geronimo. (p. 667)
—Great Careers with a High School Diploma: Armed Forces. (p. 714)
—Great Careers with a High School Diploma: Public Safety, Law, & Security. (p. 714)
—Jerry Rice. (p. 913)
—John Brown. (p. 921)
—Reproductive Technology. (p. 1461)
—Same Sex Marriage. (p. 1507)
—Steroids. (p. 1649)
—Terrorism. (p. 1722)
—U.S. Acquisition of Alaska: Seward's Folly. (p. 1826)
Sterngass, Jon, jt. auth. see Kachur, Matthew.
Sterngass, Jon, jt. auth. see Katchur, Matthew.
Sterngass, Jon & Kachur, Matthew. Plastics. (p. 1370)
Sternhagen, Mimi, illus. see Gorler, Rosemarie & Piscitelli, Donna.

Sternhagen, Mimi, illus. see Gortler, Rosemarie & Piscitelli, Donna.
Sternhagen, Mimi, illus. see Piscitelli, Donna & Gortler, Rosemarie.
Sternick, Michele J. Charged up Twins. (p. 291)
Sternin, Joshua & Ventimilla, Jeffrey. Teenage Mutant Ninja Turtles: Pizza Party! (p. 1714)
Sterns, Megan, illus. see Mooney, Carla.
Sterns, Michael. Kokopelli & the Island of Change. Hageman, Erik, illus. (p. 966)
Sterrett, Nicole. 1-2 Recycling's for You! (p. 1990)
Sterrett, Virginia, illus. see Hawthorne, Nathaniel.
Sterrett, Virginia Frances, illus. see Segur, Sophie.
Sterry, Nedra. When the Meadowlark Sings: The Story of a Montana Family. (p. 1904)
Sterry, Paul. Insects - Pb: A Portrait of the Animal World. (p. 876)
Stetson, Emily. Create a Wildlife Habitat for Urban & Suburban Small Spaces. (p. 378)
Stetson, Raymond. Math Mage: A Position in Addition (p. 1106)
Stetter, tr. see Tullet, Hervé.
Stettler, Linda, jt. auth. see Mauk, Susan.
Stettler, Nicolas & Shelly, Susan. Living with Obesity. (p. 1042)
Stetz, Ken, illus. see Leeds, Robert X.
Stetz, Ken, illus. see Shull, Jodie A.
Stetz, Ken, illus. see Shull, Jodie.
Steuerwald, Joy, illus. see Harper, Stephen J.
Steuerwald, Shannon B. From Scrawny to Brawny. (p. 643)
Stevanovic, Ivica, illus. see Aronson, Deborah.
Stevanovic, Ivica, illus. see Doan, Lisa.
Stevanovic, Ivica, illus. see Joseph, Lisa.
Stevanovic, Ivica, illus. see Harris, Trudy.
Stevanovic, Ivica, illus. see Kimmel, Eric A.
Stevanovic, Ivica, illus. see Olson, Gillia M.
Stevans, Joy. Hugs in a Lunch Box. Stanley, Robin, ed. (p. 825)
Steve Chering. There's Something in Granny's Garden! (p. 1731)
Steve Cormey. Brothers Foot: A Hare Raising Story. Ronda Eden, illus. (p. 231)
Steve, Crain, Larry. Bible Fun Book No. 1. (p. 175)
Steve, Lavigne, illus. see Janis, Tim.
Steve, Parker. What about Science & Technology. (p. 1879)
Steve, Smallman. Very Greedy Bee. Jack, Tickle, illus. (p. 1838)
Steve, Sumner, ed. see Soloway, Cindy.
Steve Van Der Merwe. Policeman Bobby & Stinky. (p. 1380)
Steven, Kenneth. Fergus Finds a Friend Crowe, Louise, illus. (p. 582)
—Ghostwing. (p. 673)
—Imagining Things & Other Poems. (p. 861)
—Raven's Tale: & other Stories. Wake, Katherine, illus. (p. 1441)
—Sea Mice & the Stars Ho, Louise, illus. (p. 1535)
—Stories for a Fragile Planet: Traditional Tales about Caring for the Earth. Ray, Jane, illus. (p. 1654)
Steven, Kenneth, jt. auth. see Torseter, Oyvind.
Steven, Kenneth C. Biggest Thing in the World. Mitchell, Melanie, illus. (p. 185)
—Lord's Prayer: Explained for Children. Smith, Nial, illus. (p. 1053)
Steven, Michaan. American Fish Decoy Note Cards, Set 3. the Master Carver Series: Beautiful American Folk Art Blank Note Cards, 4x6 printed on museum-grade stock, packed in heavy, reusable gift Boxes. (p. 60)
Steven, Peter. News (p. 1249)
Steven, Rhoades. Grover's Favorite Day. (p. 725)
Stevens, illus. see Gardner, L. S.
Stevens, A. P. Volcano: The Adventures of Antboy & Mr Cricket. Finn, N. K., ed. (p. 1848)
Stevens, Alex, jt. auth. see Mills, Nathan.
Stevens, Angie, illus. see Doodlemum & Smith, Justine.
Stevens, Angie, illus. see Smith, Justine.
Stevens, April. Edwin Speaks Up. Blackall, Sophie, illus. (p. 505)
Stevens, arthur, illus. see Meuse, Theresa.
Stevens, B. Pistolero. (p. 1364)
Stevens, Betsy T. Sea Soup: Discovering the Watery World of Phytoplankton. Glebfried, Rosemary, illus. (p. 1535)
Stevens, Beverly. This Dog Team Lives in the House. (p. 1735)
Stevens, C. J. Supernatural Side of Maine. (p. 1684)
Stevens, C. M. Wonderful Story of Washington & Th. (p. 1948)
Stevens, Cara. Let's Save Pirate Day! (Dora & Friends) Aikins, David, illus. (p. 1000)
Stevens, Carla & Stevens, Chapman. Who's Knocking at the Door? Chapman, Lee, illus. (p. 1920)
Stevens, Catrin. Hywel Dda / Hywel the Good. (p. 831)
Stevens, Catrin, et al. Yr Oesoedd Canol. (p. 1983)
Stevens, Chambers. Magnificent Monologues for Kids 2: More Kids' Monologues for Every Occasion! (p. 1076)
—Sensational Scenes for Kids: The Scene Study-Guide for Young Actors! (p. 1550)
—Ultimate Commercial Book for Kids & Teens: The Young Actors' Commercial Study-guide! Stevens, Chambers, ed. (p. 1809)
Stevens, Chapman, jt. auth. see Stevens, Carla.
Stevens, Charles McCellan. Adventures of Uncle Jeremiah & Family at the Great Fair: Their Observations & Triumphs. (p. 24)
Stevens, Chris, illus. see Jerwa, Brandon.
Stevens, Chris, jt. auth. see Scholastic, Inc. Staff.
Stevens, Courtney C. Faking Normal. (p. 565)
—Lies about Truth. (p. 1007)
Stevens Crummel, Susan, jt. auth. see Stevens, Janet.
Stevens Crummel, Susan, see Crummel, Susan Stevens.
Stevens Crummel, Susan, see Stevens, Janet & Crummel, Susan Stevens.
Stevens, Dan. Magic of the Brass Ring. (p. 1073)
Stevens, Daniel, illus. see Fabian, Cynthia.
Stevens, Danielle. Minibeasts. (p. 1146)
Stevens, David. Romanticism. (p. 1486)
Stevens, David S., illus. see Stevens, Margaret M.
Stevens, Debra, illus. see Van Kersen, Elizabeth.
Stevens, Deon. Frankie's Kingdom: Winning in Face of Uncertainty. (p. 630)
Stevens, Dylan. Wooded Sanctuary. (p. 1949)
Stevens, E. How I Feel: WeeMoods. (p. 810)
Stevens, Elizabeth. Mister D. Frongia, Daniela, illus. (p. 1155)
Stevens, Emily & Graham, Sadie. Drama Diaries - the Alice Adventure. (p. 480)
Stevens, Eric. Classic: '69 Chevy Camaro. (p. 327)
—Finn Reeder, Flu Fighter: How I Survived a Worldwide Pandemic, the School Bully, & the Craziest Game of Dodge Ball Ever. Fraser, Kay, illus. (p. 589)
—Flu Fighter: How I Survived a Worldwide Pandemic, the School Bully, & the Craziest Game of Dodge Ball Ever. Fraser, Kay, illus. (p. 608)
—Jacked: Ford Focus ST. (p. 903)
Stevens, Eric & Fuentes, Benny. Skateboard Sonar Sandoval, Gerardo, illus. (p. 1583)
Stevens, Eric & Maddox, Jake. Playing Forward. Tiffany, Sean, illus. (p. 1372)
Stevens, Eric, et al. Menace of Metallo (p. 1126)
—Revenge of Clayface Schigiel, Gregg, illus. (p. 1465)
Stevens, Gareth, jt. auth. see Connors, Kathleen.
Stevens, Garrett. Who Cloned the President? Friedland, Joyce & Kessler, Rikki, eds. (p. 1915)
Stevens, Gary J. If I Called You a Hippopotamus! Stead, April-Nicole, illus. (p. 852)
Stevens, Helen, illus. see Beckhorn, Susan Williams.
Stevens, Helen, illus. see Keyes, Diane.
Stevens, Helen, illus. see Patten, Elizabeth & Lyons, Kathy.
Stevens, James A. Duke, the Duchess, & the Labyrinth: A Continuation of Robert Browning's Verse My Last Duchess. (p. 489)
Stevens, Jan Romero. Carlos Digs to China. Arnold, Jeanne, illus. (p. 270)
Stevens, Jane. Walking with Dinosaurs: A Reusable Sticker Book. (p. 1854)
Stevens, Janet. Anansi & the Magic Stick. (p. 67)
Stevens, Janet, illus. see Beaumont, Karen.
Stevens, Janet, illus. see Crummel, Susan Stevens.
Stevens, Janet, illus. see Kimmel, Eric A.
Stevens, Janet, illus. see Levitt, Paul M., et al.
Stevens, Janet, illus. see Salley, Coleen.
Stevens, Janet, jt. auth. see Crummel, Susan Stevens.
Stevens, Janet & Crummel, Susan Stevens. Find a Cow Now! (p. 587)
—Find a Cow Now! Stevens, Janet, illus. (p. 587)
—Great Fuzz Frenzy. (p. 716)
—Help Me, Mr. Mutt! Expert Answers for Dogs with People Problems. (p. 765)
—Help Me, Mr. Mutt! Expert Answers for Dogs with People Problems. Stevens, Janet, illus. (p. 765)
—Jackalope. (p. 903)
—Little Red Pen. Stevens, Janet, illus. (p. 1035)
—Tumbleweed Stew/Sopa de Matojos. Flor Ada, Alma & Campoy, F. Isabel, trs. from ENG. (p. 1796)
Stevens, Janet & Stevens Crummel, Susan. My Big Dog. Stevens, Janet, illus. (p. 1197)
Stevens, Jennifer. Love You More. (p. 1060)
Stevens, Jon Ellis. Old Softy & Angel (p. 1284)
Stevens, Judy, illus. see Denham, Joyce.
Stevens, K. T. Christmas Stories for Children & the Young at Heart! (p. 315)
—Stories for Children. (p. 1654)
Stevens, Kathryn. Bugs Rule! (p. 237)
—Cats. (p. 280)
—Christmas Trees. (p. 316)
—Dogs. (p. 462)
—Fish. (p. 598)
—Gorillas. (p. 703)
—Halloween Jack-O'-Lanterns. (p. 738)
—Hamsters. (p. 740)
—Hermit Crabs. (p. 771)
—Lizards. (p. 1043)
—Night Creatures. (p. 1253)
—Parakeets. (p. 1323)
—Positively Penguins! (p. 1387)
—Turtles. (p. 1799)
Stevens, Kim. Salon Success Secrets (p. 1505)
Stevens, Larry. Clown Games. (p. 335)
Stevens, Linda M. Unlocking the Hidden Treasures. (p. 1821)
Stevens, Lynda. Lawn Monster: A Book to Help Kids Learn to Be Brave. (p. 981)
Stevens, Madeline. Discovering Mission San José. (p. 449)
—Discovering Mission San Juan Bautista. (p. 449)
—Orange Around Me. (p. 1301)
—Red Around Me. (p. 1453)
Stevens, Madeline, jt. auth. see McGinty, Alice B.
Stevens, Margaret M. Stepping Stones for Boys & Girls. Stevens, David S., illus. (p. 1648)
—Stepping Stones for Little Feet. Stevens, David S., illus. (p. 1648)
Stevens, Mark. Tailspin Tommy: The Mystery of the Midnight Patrol. Beebe, Robb, illus. (p. 1695)
Stevens, Mary, illus. see Campbell, Julie.
Stevens, Mary, illus. see Parkinson, Ethelyn.
Stevens, Mary, illus. see Sutton, Margaret.
Stevens, Matt, illus. see Peterson, Megan Cooley & Rustad, Martha E. H.
Stevens, Michael J. Silver Spitfire. (p. 1577)
Stevens, Mitchell. Hey! Follow Your Dreams: 7 Steps to Dream Followin' (p. 774)
Stevens, Neil, jt. auth. see Cossons, Malcolm.
Stevens, Neil & Isles, Deborah. Phonological Screening Assessment. (p. 1352)
Stevens, Noel. From the Farthest Hills of Elsewhere. (p. 644)
—In the Never-Never-Converse with an Archangel. (p. 867)
—Tin Gods. (p. 1755)
Stevens, Paul D., ed. Congressional Medal of Honor: The Names, the Deeds. (p. 357)
Stevens, R. Bacon Is a Vegetable, Coffee Is a Vitamin (p. 131)
—Diesel Sweeties: I'm a Rocker, I Rock Out: I'm a Rocker, I Rock Out. (p. 437)
Stevens, Rita. Glumpkins. (p. 685)
Stevens, Robin. Murder Is Bad Manners. (p. 1192)
Stevens, Roger, jt. auth. see Dean, Jan.
Stevens, Roger, jt. auth. see Moses, Brian.
Stevens, Roger & Moses, Brian. What Are We Fighting For? New Poems about War. (p. 1880)
Stevens, Roger & Quarto Generic Staff. Comic Café. (p. 348)
Stevens, Samantha. Creating Love: A Guide to Finding & Attracting Love. (p. 378)
—Creating Money: Spiritual Prescriptions for Prosperity. (p. 378)
Stevens, Serita. Adventure Begins. (p. 14)
Stevens, Sherri. Where Is God? Freeman, Patricia, illus. (p. 1908)
—Where Is God on My Bad Days? (p. 1908)
Stevens, Sky. Looking Close: Teaching Kids to Love the Earth. (p. 1051)
Stevens, Stefan. Understanding Civilizations. (p. 1815)
Stevens, Terry. Battle at Longshore Causeway. (p. 145)
—Tommy, the Wizard & the Magic Umbrella. (p. 1765)
Stevens, Tim, illus. see Cross, Gillian.
Stevens, Tim, illus. see Langrish, Katherine.
Stevens, Torrance. Foe U Who Left Me While I Slept. (p. 611)
Stevens, Tracey. Chalice of the Goddess. Snowden, Susan, ed. (p. 288)
Stevens, Travis. I Ain't Mad at YA. (p. 831)
Stevens-Egerton, Drema. Three Wishes for Christmas: A Stevens Children Adventure. (p. 1744)
Stevenski, Linda. Chetty T Chipmunk's Journey to Aunt Ella's. (p. 298)
—Collection of Small Animal Stories. (p. 340)
Stevens-Marzo, Bridget, illus. see Cocagne, Marie-Pascale.
Stevenson, Augusta. George Washington: Our First Leader. Dreany, E. Joseph, illus. (p. 664)
—Wilbur & Orville Wright: Boys with Wings. Laune, Paul, illus. (p. 1928)
Stevenson, Charles. Adventures of the Glo-Worm Family. (p. 23)
Stevenson, D. E. Miss Buncle's Book. (p. 1151)
—Two Mrs. Abbotts. (p. 1804)
Stevenson, Daryl, illus. see Nathan, Helen.
Stevenson, Dave, illus. see Hunter, Erin.
Stevenson, Dave, illus. see Wolverton, Barry.
Stevenson, Emma. Hide-and-Seek Science: Animal Camouflage. (p. 777)
—Hide-and-Seek Science: Animal Camouflage. Stevenson, Emma, illus. (p. 777)
Stevenson, Emma, illus. see Kirkpatrick, Katherine.
Stevenson, Emma, illus. see Nirgiotis, Nicholas.
Stevenson, Emma, illus. see Singer, Marilyn.
Stevenson, Geoff, illus. see Karst, Patrice.
Stevenson, Harvey. Looking at Liberty. Stevenson, Harvey, illus. (p. 1050)
Stevenson, Harvey, illus. see Brown, Elizabeth Ferguson & Boyds Mills Press Staff.
Stevenson, Harvey, illus. see Carter, Dorothy.
Stevenson, James. Flying Feet: A Mud Flat Story. Stevenson, James, illus. (p. 610)
—Night after Christmas. (p. 1252)
—Peor Que Willy. (p. 1340)
—Runaway Horse! (p. 1496)
—Tiovivo de Don Ramiro. (p. 1757)
—Zampano y Su Oso. (p. 1984)
Stevenson, James, illus. see Blume, Judy.
Stevenson, James, illus. see Prelutsky, Jack.
Stevenson, James, illus. see Seuss, Dr.
Stevenson, Jennifer. Little Hands Story Bible. (p. 1029)
Stevenson, Jennifer Laughlin. Daddy's Week at Antique Acres. (p. 399)
—My Mommy's Keys. (p. 1214)
Stevenson, John, illus. see Stevenson, Paula.
Stevenson, Juliet, jt. auth. see Duffy, Carol Ann.
Stevenson, Kris Coffin. God's Mighty Champions. (p. 691)
Stevenson, L. Harold & Wyman, Bruce C. Facts on File Dictionary of Environmental Science. (p. 561)
Stevenson, May. Brilliant Activities for Reading Non-Fiction: Comprehension Activities for 7-11 Year Olds. (p. 228)
Stevenson, Mónica. Tradiciones Mexicanas Para Ninos. (p. 1776)
Stevenson, Noelle. Nimona. Stevenson, Noelle, illus. (p. 1256)
Stevenson, Patricia. Z Family Coloring Book. (p. 1984)
Stevenson, Paula. Twig Pencil: A Story of Perseverance. Stevenson, John & Davidson, Dawn, illus. (p. 1801)
Stevenson, Peggy. Meet the Spencers & the Smart Knots. (p. 1123)
Stevenson, Peter, illus. see Zobel-Nolan, Allia.
Stevenson, R. L. Adventure Classics for Boys: Robinson Crusoe, Treasure Island, Kidnapped! Egmont UK, ed. (p. 14)
Stevenson, Richard. Alex Anklebone & Andy the Dog. Masi, P. J., illus. (p. 36)
Stevenson, Robert L. & Facio, Sebastian. Extraño Caso del Dr. Jekyll y Mr. Hyde. Ferran, Adriana et al, illus. (p. 555)
Stevenson, Robert Louis. Artfolds: Sun: Treasure Island & Other Adventures. (p. 103)
—Bed in Summer. Reisch, Jesse, illus. (p. 156)
—Black Arrow: A Tale of the Two Roses. (p. 195)
—Black Arrow. (p. 195)
—Block City. Kirk, Daniel, illus. (p. 200)
—Child's Garden of Verses: A Collection of Scriptures, Prayers & Poems. (p. 305)
—Child's Garden of Verses: A Collection of Scriptures, Prayers & Poems. Fujikawa, Gyo, illus. (p. 305)
—Child's Garden of Verses: A Collection of Scriptures, Prayers & Poems Wildsmith, Brian, illus. (p. 305)
—Child's Garden of Verses: A Collection of Scriptures, Prayers & Poems. Robinson, Charles, illus. (p. 305)
—Child's Garden of Verses. McClintock, Barbara, illus. (p. 305)
—Child's Garden of Verses Shape Book. Peat, Fern Bisel, illus. (p. 305)
—Classics Illustrated #7: Dr. Jekyll & Mr. Hyde. (p. 328)
—Dr Jekyll & Mr Hyde. Lubach, Vanessa, illus. (p. 475)
—Dr. Jekyll & Mr. Hyde. (p. 475)
—Dr. Jekyll & Mr. Hyde. (p. 475)
—Flecha Negra. (p. 603)
—Isla del Tesoro. (p. 891)
—Kidnapped: Bring the Classics to Life. (p. 952)
—Kidnapped: Adapted for Young Readers. Kliros, Thea, illus. (p. 952)
—Kidnapped. (p. 952)
—Kidnapped. Harvey, Bob, illus. (p. 952)
—Kidnapped. Kennedy, Cam, illus. (p. 952)
—Kidnapped. Kumar, Naresh, illus. (p. 952)
—Kidnapped & Catriona. (p. 952)
—Kidnapped (Quality Library Classics) (p. 952)
—Land of Counterpane. Harrison, Nancy, illus. (p. 973)
—Little Land. Thornburgh, Rebecca McKillip, illus. (p. 1030)
—Memoir of Fleeming Jenkin. (p. 1125)
—Merry Men. (p. 1129)
—Michael Foreman's Treasure Island. Foreman, Michael, illus. (p. 1134)
—My Shadow. Idle, Molly, illus. (p. 1218)
—On the Island. Comport, Sally Wern, illus. (p. 1290)
—Pirate Attack. Comport, Sally Wern, illus. (p. 1362)
—Poetry For Young People: Robert Louis Stevenson. (p. 1376)
—Robert Louis Stevenson/Treasure Island. Cruz, Nardo, illus. (p. 1479)
—Strange Case of Dr. Jekyll & Mr. Hyde: With a Discussion of Moderation. Clift, Eva, tr. (p. 1665)
—Strange Case of Dr. Jekyll & Mr. Hyde. (p. 1665)
—Strange Case of Dr. Jekyll & Mr. Hyde. Akib, Jamel, illus. (p. 1665)
—Strange Case of Dr. Jekyll & Mr. Hyde. Kennedy, Cam, illus. (p. 1665)
—Strange Case of Dr. Jekyll & Mr. Hyde. Andrews, Gary, illus. (p. 1665)
—Strange Case of Dr. Jekyll & Mr. Hyde. McKowen, Scott, illus. (p. 1665)
—Strange Case of Dr. Jekyll & Mr. Hyde (Quality Library Classics) (p. 1665)
—Treasure Island. (p. 1781)
—Treasure Island. Rhead, Louis, illus. (p. 1781)
—Treasure Island. Corvino, Lucy, illus. (p. 1781)
—Treasure Island. Lawrence, John, illus. (p. 1781)
—Treasure Island. McKowen, Scott, illus. (p. 1781)
—Treasure Island: With a Discussion of Courage. (p. 1782)
—Treasure Island: A Classic Story about Responsibility. (p. 1782)
—Treasure Island: With Story of the Treasure of Normon Island. (p. 1782)
—Treasure Island: The Treasure Map. Comport, Sally Wern, illus. (p. 1782)
—Treasure Island. (p. 1782)
—Treasure Island. Todd, Justin, illus. (p. 1782)
—Treasure Island. Chapman, Neil, illus. (p. 1782)
—Treasure Island. Corvino, Lucy, illus. (p. 1782)
—Treasure Island. Ingpen, Robert R., illus. (p. 1782)
—Treasure Island. Stevenson, Robert Louis & Timothy, Hamilton Baird, illus. (p. 1782)
—Treasure Island (Quality Library Classics) (p. 1782)
—Treasure Map. Comport, Sally Wern, illus. (p. 1782)
Stevenson, Robert Louis, jt. auth. see Andersen, Hans Christian.
Stevenson, Robert Louis, jt. auth. see De Grift Stevenson, Fanny Van.
Stevenson, Robert Louis, jt. auth. see Ruiz, Celia.
Stevenson, Robert Louis, jt. auth. see Stevenson, Robert Louis.
Stevenson, Robert Louis & Ballaz, Jesus. Treasure Island. (p. 1782)
Stevenson, Robert Louis & Louis Stevenson, Robert. Flecha Negra. (p. 603)
Stevenson, Robert Louis & Louis Stevenson Robert. Isla del Resoro. (p. 891)
Stevenson, Robert Louis & Louis Stevenson, Robert. Isla del Tesoro. (p. 891)
Stevenson, Robert Louis & Louis, Stevenson Robert. Secuestrado. (p. 1546)
Stevenson, Robert Louis & Peat, Fern Bisel. Child's Garden of Verses: A Collection of Scriptures, Prayers & Poems. (p. 305)
Stevenson, Robert Louis & Stevenson, Robert Louis. Kidnapped. McFarlan, Donald, ed. (p. 952)
Stevenson, Robert Louis & Venable, Alan. Strange Case of Dr. Jekyll & Mr. Hyde. (p. 1665)
Stevenson, Robert Louis & Vosburg, Mike. Kidnapped. (p. 952)
Stevenson, Robert Louis & Wyeth, N. C. Kidnapped. Wyeth, N. C., illus. (p. 952)
—Treasure Island. (p. 1782)
Stevenson, Robert, photos by. Already Legends: Stevenson Studios Sports Photo Journal. (p. 50)
Stevenson, Robin. Attitude (p. 114)
—Ben the Inventor Parkins, David, illus. (p. 163)
—Ben's Robot Parkins, David, illus. (p. 165)
—Big Guy (p. 181)
—Dead in the Water (p. 416)
—Desolación (p. 430)
—Escape Velocity (p. 535)
—Hummingbird Heart (p. 826)
—Impossible Things (p. 862)
—Inferno (p. 873)
—Liars & Fools (p. 1005)
—Out of Order (p. 1311)
—Outback (p. 1312)
—Record Breaker (p. 1452)
—Thousand Shades of Blue (p. 1740)
—World Without Us. (p. 1960)
Stevenson, S. Roy. Magic Act: A Mystery by S. Roy Stevenson. (p. 1071)
Stevenson, Sarah Jamila. Latte Rebellion. (p. 980)
—Truth Against the World. (p. 1794)
Stevenson, Seline, illus. see Tóth-Jones, Dee S.
Stevenson, Sharry. Gibby's Story. (p. 674)
Stevenson, Steve. Crown of Venice Turconi, Stefano, illus. (p. 386)
—Crown of Venice. (p. 386)
—Curse of the Pharaoh Turconi, Stefano, illus. (p. 395)
—Curse of the Pharaoh. (p. 395)
—Eiffel Tower Incident. (p. 507)
—Eiffel Tower Incident #5. Turconi, Stefano, illus. (p. 507)

—Heist at Niagara Falls. (p. 762)
—Heist at Niagara Falls. Turconi, Stefano, illus. (p. 762)
—Kenyan Expedition. (p. 949)
—Kenyan Expedition #8. Turconi, Stefano, illus. (p. 949)
—King of Scotland's Sword. (p. 959)
—King of Scotland's Sword. Turconi, Stefano, illus. (p. 959)
—Pearl of Bengal Turconi, Stefano, illus. (p. 1333)
—Pearl of Bengal. (p. 1333)
—Treasure of the Bermuda Triangle Turconi, Stefano, illus. (p. 1782)
—Treasure of the Bermuda Triangle. (p. 1782)
Stevenson, Suçie, illus. see Rylant, Cynthia.
Stevenson, Tysheia E. Jude (p. 930)
Stevenson, William. Ricky's Dream Trip to Ancient Egypt. (p. 1470)
—Ricky's Dream Trip to Ancient Greece. (p. 1470)
—Ricky's Dream Trip under the Sea. (p. 1470)
Stevenson-Ringo, Angela. Keith's Shoes. (p. 948)
—Where Are My Shoes? (p. 1906)
Stevenson-Spurgon, Barbara J. Have You Ever Made Mud Pies on a Hot Summer Day? This Is a Bitty Book. Ruffin, Aurzelia, illus. (p. 754)
—Old Silent One & Fresh Water Fishing: This Is a Bitty Book. (p. 1284)
Steventon, John. DJing. (p. 455)
Steventon, John, jt. auth. see Rosen, Steven.
Stever, Karen Malloy. Jabin, the Talking Donkey: In Jerusalem. (p. 902)
Stever, Susan. When Fairies Die. (p. 1902)
Stevermer, Caroline. Magic below Stairs. (p. 1071)
Stevermer, Caroline, jt. auth. see Wrede, Patricia C.
Stevermer, Caroline & Collin, Francesca. River Rats. (p. 1476)
Stevermer, Caroline & Wrede, Patricia C. Grand Tour: Being a Revelation of Matters of High Confidentiality & Greatest Importance, Including Extracts from the Intimate Diary of a Noblewoman & the Sworn Testimony of a Lady of Quality. (p. 707)
—Sorcery & Cecelia or the Enchanted Chocolate Pot: Being the Correspondence of Two Young Ladies of Quality Regarding Various Magical Scandals in London & the Country. (p. 1614)
Steverson, Sylvia. I LOVE YOU Means... (p. 843)
SteveSongs Staff. Shape Song Singalong. Sim, David, illus. (p. 1560)
Stevos, Joyce L., jt. auth. see Currie, David P.
Steward, Jennifer. Choreganizers: The Visual Way to Organize Household Chores. (p. 310)
Steward, Kimberly. Color of Secrets: Encouraging Children to Talk about Abuse. (p. 343)
Steward, Margaret. Tamsi: The Errant Lamb. (p. 1704)
Steward, Martha. Bangle Bear: The Tale of a Tailless Cat. (p. 136)
—Darby's Story: The Life of an Adopted Dog. (p. 406)
Steward, Tod B. Juliet's Opera: An Evelyn Burke Adventure. (p. 932)
—Painting Aalesund. (p. 1318)
Stewart, A. W. Rooktime. (p. 1487)
Stewart, Aileen. Fern Valley: A Collection of Short Stories. (p. 582)
Stewart, Alex. Gladiators. (p. 682)
—Greek Soldiers. (p. 721)
—Pirates. (p. 1363)
Stewart, Amber. Rabbit Ears. Rankin, Laura, illus. (p. 1429)
—Too Small for My Big Bed: Sleep Tight in Your Own Bed Tonight! Marlow, Layn, illus. (p. 1767)
Stewart, Amber & Rankin, Laura. Rabbit Ears. Rankin, Laura, illus. (p. 1429)
Stewart, Andrew. There Is a Boy on Top of My Bed. Langille, Rob, illus. (p. 1729)
Stewart, Angela. Curious Adventures of India Sophia. Stuart, Mitchell, illus. (p. 392)
Stewart, Anne. I Saw a Moose Today. (p. 845)
Stewart, Audrey. Our Natural Resources. (p. 1309)
Stewart, Barbara. In-Between. (p. 863)
—What We Knew. (p. 1895)
Stewart, Bob. Baily Bumble Bee. (p. 133)
Stewart, Carolyn, illus. see Flynn, Lesley, et al.
Stewart, Cathy. Hat Trick. (p. 752)
—Sassy Sparrow & the Hungry Owl. (p. 1515)
Stewart, Celia, et al. Going Live in 3, 2, 1: Have You Got What It Takes to Be a TV Producer? (p. 692)
Stewart, Chantal. Tortoise Soup! (p. 1771)
Stewart, Chantal, illus. see Abela, Donna.
Stewart, Chantal, illus. see Dinbergs, Holly Smith.
Stewart, Chantal, illus. see Flynn, Pat.
Stewart, Chantal, illus. see Smith Dinbergs, Holly.
Stewart, Chantal, illus. see Zail, Suzy.
Stewart, Christen, jt. auth. see Ellis, Julie.
Stewart, Christen, jt. auth. see Reilly, Carmel.
Stewart, Chuck. Angels at Rickwood. (p. 75)
—Gay & Lesbian Issues: A Reference Handbook Vasan, Mildred, ed. (p. 658)
—Queer History & Politics Word Games. (p. 1425)
Stewart, Colin, et al. Media & Meaning: An Introduction. (p. 1118)
Stewart, Colina. Wild Flower. (p. 1929)
Stewart, Crista R. Jealousy of Little Frog. (p. 911)
—Little Frog. (p. 1028)
—Little Frog Learns the Golden Rule. (p. 1028)
Stewart, Dave, illus. see Mignola, Mike.
Stewart, Dave, jt. auth. see Cooke, Darwyn.
Stewart, David. Amaze Franklin, Carolyn, illus. (p. 52)
—Creepy Egyptian Mummies. (p. 381)
—Dinosaurs. Hewetson, Nick, illus. (p. 444)
—How a Seed Grows into a Sunflower. Franklin, Carolyn, illus. (p. 804)
—How a Tadpole Grows into a Frog. Franklin, Carolyn, illus. (p. 804)
—How Your Body Works: A Good Look Inside You Insides. Franklin, Carolyn, illus. (p. 823)
—How Your Body Works: A Good Look Inside Your Insides. Franklin, Carolyn, illus. (p. 823)
—Inside Ancient Rome. James, John et al, illus. (p. 876)
—Tutankhamen! A Mummy Who Really Got Meddled With. Antram, David, illus. (p. 1799)
—World of Wonder Franklin, Carolyn, illus. (p. 1957)
—You Wouldn't Want to Be an Egyptian Mummy! Disgusting Things You'd Rather Not Know. Antram, David, illus. (p. 1977)
—You Wouldn't Want to... Be an Egyptian Mummy! Antram, David, illus. (p. 1977)
—You Wouldn't Want to Be in a Medieval Dungeon! Antram, David, illus. (p. 1977)
—You Wouldn't Want to Explore with Sir Francis Drake! A Pirate You'd Rather Not Know. Antram, David, illus. (p. 1977)
—You Wouldn't Want to Sail on the Titanic! (p. 1977)
—You Wouldn't Want to Sail on the Titanic! One Voyage You'D Rather Not Make. Antram, David, illus. (p. 1977)
Stewart, David, illus. see Morley, Jacqueline.
Stewart, David, jt. auth. see Franklin, Carolyn.
Stewart, Dianne. Who's Afraid of the Dark? Rankin, Joan, illus. (p. 1920)
Stewart, Dianne & Heale, Jay. African Myths & Legends. (p. 27)
Stewart, Dianne & Pienaar, Kathy. Zebra's Stripes: And Other African Animal Tales. (p. 1985)
Stewart, Dianne & Quarto Generic Staff. Dove. Daly, Jude, illus. (p. 473)
Stewart, Dianne C. Longitude - Zero Degrees. (p. 1047)
—Quimbaya. (p. 1428)
—Season of the Cold Moon. (p. 1538)
Stewart, Don, illus. see Vazquez, Ana Maria & Dean, Jennings.
Stewart, Dorothy M. It's Hard to Hurry When You're a Snail. Taylor, Thomas, illus. (p. 897)
Stewart, E. J. Lyre Birds. (p. 1066)
—Wayfaring Dolphin. (p. 1865)
Stewart, Ed, jt. auth. see McDowell, Josh.
Stewart, Ed & McDowell, Josh. Conflicts with Others. (p. 357)
—Finding True Love. (p. 588)
—Thoughts of Suicide. (p. 1740)
Stewart, Edgar, illus. see Williamson, Ray A. & Monroe, Jean Guard.
Stewart, Elaine, ed. see Lynn, Tammy.
Stewart, Elizabeth. Angel Named Love. (p. 73)
—Blue Gold: A Novel. (p. 202)
—Lynching of Louie Sam. (p. 1066)
Stewart, Emma. Adventures of Fillmore the Gerbil. (p. 18)
Stewart, Es. Who Made the Moon, Mummy? (p. 1916)
Stewart, Faith. Teens & Rural Education: Opportunities & Challenges. (p. 1715)
Stewart, Fion, illus. see Chen, Julia.
Stewart, Gail. Fat in America. (p. 577)
—Graphic Art. (p. 710)
—Illegal Immigration. (p. 857)
stewart, gail. Trolls. (p. 1788)
—Urban Legends. (p. 1825)
—Water Monsters. (p. 1863)
Stewart, Gail B. Alexandra Scott: Champion for Cancer Research. (p. 37)
—Anorexia. (p. 87)
—Bermuda Triangle. (p. 167)
—Bulimia. (p. 240)
—Cesar Milan. (p. 288)
—Cold Cases. Gale Editors, ed. (p. 338)
—Crime Scene Photographer. (p. 382)
—Defending the Borders: The Role of Border & Immigration Control. (p. 423)
—Drowning in a Bottle: Teens & Alcohol Abuse (p. 486)
—Fetal Alcohol Syndrome. (p. 582)
—Fighting for Freedom: Blacks in the American Military. (p. 585)
—Han Dynasty. (p. 740)
—Hauntings. (p. 754)
—Identity Theft. (p. 852)
—Jennifer Lawrence. (p. 912)
—Life of a Soldier in Washington's Army. (p. 1011)
—Missing Persons. (p. 1152)
—Population. (p. 1385)
—Revolutionary War. (p. 1466)
—Ripped from the Headlines: Smoking. (p. 1474)
—Ripped from the Headlines: Population. (p. 1474)
—Salem Witch Trials. (p. 1504)
—Stephanie Kwolek: Creator of Kevlar. (p. 1648)
—Teens & Bullying. (p. 1714)
—Ukraine: Then & Now. (p. 1808)
—Vampires: Do They Exist? (p. 1832)
Stewart Gordon, Allecia. Alphabet & Numbers. Alfabeto y los Números: Spanish & English. (p. 49)
—Niños para Niños: English & Spanish. Abc 123. Inglés y Español. (p. 1257)
Stewart, Grandmother. George the Rooster Goes to the Apple Orchard. (p. 663)
Stewart, Gregory J. Immune System. (p. 861)
—Skeletal & Muscular Systems. (p. 1584)
Stewart, H. E. Patched Heart: A Gift of Friendship & Caring (p. 1328)
—TreeSong (p. 1784)
—Walrus's Gift (p. 1855)
Stewart, Hal D. Nineteenth Hole. (p. 1256)
Stewart, Henry. He Created Me. (p. 756)
Stewart, Ian. Math Hysteria: Fun & Games with Mathematics. (p. 1106)
Stewart III, Freddie Leonard. Night Night Birmingham. (p. 1253)
Stewart, Isaac, jt. auth. see Pike, Kenneth.
Stewart, James. Shipwrecks. (p. 1567)
—Spies & Traitors. (p. 1627)
Stewart, James, illus. see Turner, Gary.
Stewart, Jan. Getting along with Others. (p. 669)
—How Drugs & Alcohol Affect Us. (p. 809)
—Knowing Yourself. (p. 965)
—Learning about Anger. (p. 984)
—Learning More about Anger. (p. 985)
—Respecting the Rights of Others. (p. 1463)
—Teacher - Counselor Manual. (p. 1709)
Stewart, Jane. Island Escapade. (p. 892)
Stewart, Jane L. Camp Fire Girls at Long Lake: Bessie King in Summer Camp. (p. 257)
—Camp Fire Girls at Long Lake. (p. 257)
—Camp Fire Girls at Long Lake or Bessie King in Summer Camp. (p. 257)
—Campfire Girl's Test of Friendship. (p. 257)
Stewart, Jennifer J. Close Encounters of a Third World Kind. (p. 333)
—Twelve Days of Christmas in Arizona. Avril, Lynne, illus. (p. 1800)
Stewart, Joel. Addis Berner Bear Forgets. Stewart, Joel, illus. (p. 12)
—Dexter Bexley & the Big Blue Beastie. Stewart, Joel, illus. (p. 432)
—Dexter Bexley & the Big Blue Beastie on the Road. (p. 432)
—Tree Soup. (p. 1783)
Stewart, Joel, illus. see Andersen, Hans Christian.
Stewart, Joel, illus. see Rosen, Michael.
Stewart, Joel, illus. see Schwarz, Viviane.
Stewart, Joel, illus. see Willis, Jeanne.
Stewart, John. Baseball Clinic: A Handbook for Players & Coaches. (p. 141)
Stewart, Judy. 'Twas the Two Weeks of Christmas Break. (p. 1799)
Stewart, Justus. Kyle Oaks: A Traitor on Nighta. (p. 969)
Stewart, K. L., illus. see Hoyes, Amy & Reimann, A. J.
Stewart, Kara. City Street. (p. 324)
Stewart, Kathy & Effe Team. Earth Facts for Earthlings: The World. Bk. 1 (p. 496)
Stewart, Kellie. Journey to Pluto & Other Dwarf Planets (p. 929)
Stewart, Kelly, ed. Readers' Theater: Scripts for Young Readers. Palacios, John, illus. (p. 1444)
—Readers' Theater: Scripts for Young Readers: the Peach Boy. Palacios, John, illus. (p. 1444)
—Readers' Theater: Scripts for Young Readers: the Monkey & the Crocodile. Palacios, John, illus. (p. 1444)
Stewart, Kelly, retold by. Readers' Theater Stone Soup: Scripts for Young Readers. (p. 1444)
—Readers' Theater the Magic Porridge Pot: Scripts for Young Readers: the Magic Porridge Pot. (p. 1444)
—Readers' Theater the Mitten: Scripts for Young Readers: the Mitten. (p. 1444)
Stewart, Kelsey. Best for You. (p. 169)
Stewart, Kenneth. Drop of the Puck. (p. 486)
—Kickball Kid. (p. 951)
Stewart, Kiera. Fetching. (p. 583)
Stewart, Kimberly Lord. Eating Between the Lines: The Supermarket Shopper's Guide to the Truth Behind Food Labels. (p. 501)
Stewart, Kymberly M. Play It Again, Rachel. (p. 1371)
Stewart, Linda. Great Catsby: A Sam the Cat Mystery. (p. 714)
Stewart, Lisa, illus. see Kelly, Deborah.
Stewart, Lolla. Savannah Dreams. Russell, Elaine, illus. (p. 1516)
Stewart, Maddie. Bertie Rooster. Aggs, Patrice, tr. (p. 168)
—Cinders. Spencer, Alison, illus. (p. 321)
Stewart, Margaret Taylor, jt. auth. see Baker, David G.
Stewart, Maria. Omelet Fit for a King. Cost, Steve, illus. (p. 1288)
Stewart, Marilyn. Footprint's & Fragrance in the Outback. (p. 615)
Stewart, Mark. Alabama Crimson Tide. (p. 33)
—Alamo: February 23-March 6, 1836. (p. 33)
—All Around New York: Regions & Resources (p. 43)
—Arizona Cardinals. (p. 98)
—Arizona Diamondbacks. (p. 98)
—Atlanta Braves. (p. 112)
—Atlanta Falcons. (p. 112)
—Atlanta Hawks. (p. 112)
—Auburn Tigers. (p. 114)
—Baltimore Orioles. (p. 135)
—Baltimore Ravens. (p. 135)
—Baseball. (p. 140)
—Basketball. (p. 143)
—Blizzards & Winter Storms. (p. 200)
—Boston Bruins. Gibbons, Denis, ed. (p. 215)
—Boston Red Sox. (p. 215)
—Brooklyn Nets. (p. 231)
—Carolina Panthers. (p. 270)
—Charlotte Bobcats. (p. 293)
—Chicago Bears. (p. 299)
—Chicago Blackhawks. Gibbons, Denis, ed. (p. 299)
—Chicago Bulls. (p. 299)
—Chicago Cubs. (p. 299)
—Chicago White Sox. (p. 299)
—Cincinnati Bengals. (p. 319)
—Cincinnati Reds. (p. 319)
—Classic Rivalries. (p. 328)
—Cleveland Cavaliers. (p. 331)
—Cleveland Indians. (p. 331)
—Clutch Performers. (p. 336)
—Colorado Avalanche. Gibbons, Denis, ed. (p. 343)
—Colorado Rockies. (p. 343)
—Dallas Cowboys. (p. 401)
—Dallas Mavericks. (p. 401)
—Denver Nuggets. (p. 427)
—Detroit Lions. (p. 431)
—Detroit Pistons. (p. 431)
—Detroit Red Wings. Gibbons, Denis, ed. (p. 431)
—Detroit Tigers. (p. 431)
—Edmonton Oilers. Gibbons, Denis, ed. (p. 504)
—Eli Manning. (p. 512)
—Florida Gators. (p. 607)
—Football. (p. 615)
—Georgia Bulldogs. (p. 665)
—Golden State Warriors. (p. 695)
—Houston Astros. (p. 804)
—Houston Rockets. (p. 804)
—Houston Texans. (p. 804)
—Indiana Pacers. (p. 871)
—Jacksonville Jaguars. (p. 904)
—Kansas City Chiefs. (p. 943)
—Kansas City Royals. (p. 943)
—Los Angeles Angels of Anaheim. (p. 1053)
—Los Angeles Clippers. (p. 1053)
—Los Angeles Dodgers. (p. 1053)
—Los Angeles Kings. Gibbons, Denis, ed. (p. 1053)
—Los Angeles Lakers. (p. 1053)
—Los Heat de Miami. Kalmanovitz, Manuel, tr. from ENG. (p. 1054)
—Los Lakers de los Angeles. Kalmanovitz, Manuel, tr. from ENG. (p. 1054)
—Maria Sharapova. (p. 1093)
—Memphis Grizzlies. (p. 1126)
—Mets de Nueva York. Kalmanovitz, Manuel, tr. from ENG. (p. 1130)
—Miami Heat. (p. 1134)
—Miami Marlins. (p. 1134)
—Michigan Wolverines. (p. 1135)
—Milwaukee Brewers. (p. 1144)
—Milwaukee Bucks. (p. 1145)
—Minnesota Timberwolves. (p. 1147)
—Minnesota Twins. (p. 1147)
—Minnesota Vikings. (p. 1147)
—Montreal Canadiens. Gibbons, Denis, ed. (p. 1170)
—Movie Blockbusters. (p. 1183)
—Movie Characters. (p. 1183)
—Music Legends. (p. 1193)
—NBA Finals. Kennedy, Mike, ed. (p. 1238)
—New England (p. 1244)
—New Jersey Devils. Gibbons, Denis, ed. (p. 1245)
—New Orleans Hornets. (p. 1246)
—New York History (p. 1248)
—New York Knicks. (p. 1248)
—New York Mets. (p. 1248)
—New York Native Peoples (p. 1248)
—New York Plants & Animals (p. 1248)
—New York Rangers. Gibbons, Denis, ed. (p. 1248)
—New York Yankees. (p. 1248)
—Notre Dame Fighting Irish. (p. 1268)
—Oakland A's. (p. 1274)
—Ohio State Buckeyes. (p. 1281)
—Oklahoma City Thunder. (p. 1283)
—Olympics. (p. 1288)
—Orlando Magic. (p. 1304)
—People of New York (p. 1339)
—Philadelphia 76ers. (p. 1350)
—Philadelphia Eagles. (p. 1350)
—Philadelphia Flyers. Gibbons, Denis, ed. (p. 1350)
—Philadelphia Phillies. (p. 1350)
—Phoenix Suns. (p. 1351)
—Pittsburgh Penguins. Gibbons, Denis, ed. (p. 1364)
—Pittsburgh Pirates. (p. 1364)
—Portland Trail Blazers. (p. 1386)
—Rafael Nadal. (p. 1433)
—Sacramento Kings. (p. 1500)
—San Antonio Spurs. (p. 1510)
—San Diego Chargers. (p. 1510)
—San Diego Padres. (p. 1510)
—San Francisco 49ers. (p. 1510)
—San Francisco Giants. (p. 1510)
—Seattle Mariners. (p. 1539)
—Seattle Seahawks. (p. 1539)
—Southwest (p. 1617)
—St. Louis Cardinals. (p. 1638)
—St. Louis Rams. (p. 1638)
—Tampa Bay Buccaneers. (p. 1704)
—Tampa Bay Rays. (p. 1704)
—Television Moments. (p. 1716)
—Tennessee Titans. (p. 1720)
—Texas Rangers. (p. 1724)
—Toronto Blue Jays. (p. 1770)
—Toronto Maple Leafs. Gibbons, Denis, ed. (p. 1770)
—Toronto Raptors. (p. 1770)
—Ultimate 10: Sports - Fall 2009 Release Set (p. 1809)
—Uniquely New York (p. 1818)
—United States & Canada (p. 1819)
—Utah Jazz. (p. 1829)
—Vancouver Canucks. Gibbons, Denis, ed. (p. 1833)
—Washington Nationals. (p. 1860)
—Washington Redskins. (p. 1860)
—Washington Wizards. (p. 1860)
—White Sox de Chicago. Kalmanovitz, Manuel, tr. from ENG. (p. 1913)
—World Cup. Kennedy, Mike, ed. (p. 1954)
Stewart, Mark, ed. see Harrison, Geoffrey C. & Scott, Thomas F.
Stewart, Mark, jt. auth. see Doeden, Matt.
Stewart, Mark, jt. auth. see Kennedy, Mike.
Stewart, Mark & Dodson Wade, Mary. New York History (p. 1248)
—People of New York. (p. 1339)
Stewart, Mark & Heinemann Library Staff. Uniquely New Jersey (p. 1818)
Stewart, Mark & Kennedy, Mike. Goal: The Fire & Fury of Soccer's Greatest Moment. (p. 687)
—Long Ball: The Legend & Lore of the Home Run. (p. 1047)
—NASCAR at the Track. (p. 1230)
—NASCAR in the Driver's Seat. (p. 1230)
—Nascar in the Driver's Seat. (p. 1230)
—NASCAR in the Pits. (p. 1230)
—Nascar in the Pits. (p. 1230)
—Science of NASCAR (p. 1527)
—Science of Nascar. (p. 1527)
—Score! The Action & Artistry of Hockey's Magnificent Moment. (p. 1530)
—Swish: The Quest for Basketball's Perfect Shot. (p. 1691)
—Touchdown: The Power & Precision of Football's Perfect Play. (p. 1772)
Stewart, Mark & Wade, Mary Dodson. New York Native Peoples (p. 1248)
—New York Plants & Animals (p. 1248)
—Uniquely New York (p. 1818)
Stewart, Mark R. Malcolm's Cubby House. Swope, Brenda, illus. (p. 1083)
Stewart, Martha. Martha Stewart's Favorite Crafts for Kids. (p. 1097)
Stewart, Mary. Little Broomstick. (p. 1025)

Stewart, Melissa. Alligator or Crocodile? How Do You Know? (p. 47)
—Amazing Eyes up Close. (p. 54)
—Ants. (p. 90)
—Baboons. (p. 124)
—Beneath the Sun Bergum, Constance R., illus. (p. 164)
—Bird-Acious. (p. 190)
—Blasts of Gas: The Secrets of Breathing, Burping, & Farting. (p. 198)
—Blue Animals. (p. 202)
—Bone Zone: The Secrets of Muscles & Bones. (p. 209)
—Butterflies. Recher, Andrew, illus. (p. 247)
—Butterfly or Moth? How Do You Know? (p. 248)
—Cell Biology. (p. 286)
—Classification of Life. (p. 328)
—Creepy, Crawly Jokes about Spiders & Other Bugs: Laugh & Learn about Science. Kelley, Gerald, illus. (p. 381)
—Daddy Longlegs Isn't a Spider. Himmelman, John, illus. (p. 398)
—Deadliest Animals. U. S. National Geographic Society Staff, photos by. (p. 417)
—Dino-Mite Jokes about Prehistoric Life: Laugh & Learn about Science. Kelley, Gerald, illus. (p. 441)
—Do People Really Have Tiny Insects Living in Their Eyelashes? And Other Questions about the Microscopic World. (p. 457)
—Dolphins. (p. 464)
—Earthquakes & Volcanoes. (p. 497)
—Energy in Motion. (p. 528)
—Extreme Coral Reef! (p. 556)
—Extreme Rocks & Minerals! (p. 556)
—Eyes Have It: The Secrets of Eyes & Seeing. Hamlin, Janet, illus. (p. 558)
—Fantastic Feet up Close. (p. 571)
—Feathers: Not Just for Flying. Brannen, Sarah S., illus. (p. 579)
—Fossils (p. 624)
—Frog or Toad? How Do You Know? (p. 640)
—Germ Wars! The Secrets of the Immune System. (p. 666)
—Give Me a Hand: The Secrets of Hands, Feet, Arms, & Legs. (p. 681)
—Green Animals. (p. 721)
—Gross & Goofy Body (p. 725)
—Here We Grow: The Secrets of Hair & Nails. (p. 771)
—How Do Bats Fly in the Dark? (p. 806)
—How Do Bees Make Honey? (p. 806)
—How Do Birds Fly? (p. 806)
—How Do Chameleons Change Color? (p. 806)
—How Do Fish Breathe Underwater? (p. 807)
—How Do Plants Grow? (p. 807)
—How Do Spiders Make Webs? (p. 807)
—How Does a Bone Become a Fossil? (p. 808)
—How Does a Caterpillar Become a Butterfly? And Other Questions about Butterflies. Patterson, Annie, illus. (p. 808)
—How Does a Seed Sprout? And Other Questions about Plants. Schwartz, Carol, illus. (p. 808)
—How Does Sand Become Glass? (p. 809)
—How Does the Ear Hear? And Other Questions about the Five Senses. Madsen, Jim, illus. (p. 809)
—How Is My Brain Like a Supercomputer? And Other Questions about the Human Body. Bull, Peter, illus. (p. 810)
—How Is My Brain Like a Supercomputer? And Other Questions about ... the Human Body. Bull, Peter, illus. (p. 810)
—Hurricane Watch. Morley, Taia, illus. (p. 830)
—Incredible Ears up Close. (p. 869)
—Insect or Spider? How Do You Know? (p. 875)
—Inside Earthquakes. (p. 876)
—Inside Volcanoes. (p. 878)
—Is the Bermuda Triangle Really a Dangerous Place? And Other Questions about the Ocean. (p. 890)
—It's Spit-Acular! The Secrets of Saliva. Hamlin, Janet, illus. (p. 899)
—Life in a Wetland. Maka, Stephen, photos by. (p. 1010)
—Meteors. (p. 1130)
—Mountains of Jokes about Rocks, Minerals, & Soil: Laugh & Learn about Science. Kelley, Gerald, illus. (p. 1181)
—National Geographic Kids - Ants. (p. 1231)
—National Geographic Readers: Deadly Predators. (p. 1233)
—National Geographic Readers - Snakes! (p. 1233)
—National Geographic Readers: Water. (p. 1233)
—New World Monkeys. (p. 1247)
—Nifty Noses up Close. (p. 1252)
—Now Hear This! The Secrets of Ears & Hearing. Hamlin, Janet, illus. (p. 1269)
—Orange Animals. (p. 1301)
—Out of This World Jokes about the Solar System: Laugh & Learn about Science. Kelley, Gerald, illus. (p. 1311)
—Place for Bats Bond, Higgins, illus. (p. 1365)
—Place for Birds Bond, Higgins, illus. (p. 1365)
—Place for Birds (revised Edition) Bond, Higgins, illus. (p. 1365)
—Place for Butterflies Bond, Higgins, illus. (p. 1365)
—Place for Butterflies, Revised Edition Bond, Higgins, illus. (p. 1365)
—Place for Fish Bond, Higgins, illus. (p. 1365)
—Place for Frogs Bond, Higgins, illus. (p. 1365)
—Place for Turtles Bond, Higgins, illus. (p. 1365)
—Pump It Up! The Secrets of the Heart & Blood. Hamlin, Janet, illus. (p. 1416)
—Purple Animals. (p. 1419)
—Rabbits. (p. 1430)
—Rainbow of Animals. (p. 1435)
—Red Animals. (p. 1453)
—Salamander or Lizard? How Do You Know? (p. 1504)
—Shark or Dolphin? How Do You Know? (p. 1562)
—Shockingly Silly Jokes about Electricity & Magnetism: Laugh & Learn about Science. Kelley, Gerald, illus. (p. 1568)
—Skin You're In: The Secrets of Skin. (p. 1585)
—Snakes! (p. 1596)
—Swans. (p. 1689)
—Talented Tails up Close. (p. 1701)
—Tell Me Why, Tell Me How - Group 2 (p. 1717)
—Terrific Tongues up Close. (p. 1721)
—Under the Snow Bergum, Constance Rummel, illus. (p. 1814)
—Up Your Nose! The Secrets of Schnozes & Snouts. Hamlin, Janet, illus. (p. 1824)
—Wacky Weather & Silly Season Jokes: Laugh & Learn about Science. Kelley, Gerald, illus. (p. 1852)
—When Rain Falls Bergum, Constance R., illus. (p. 1904)
—Why Are Animals Blue? (p. 1922)
—Why Are Animals Green? (p. 1922)
—Why Are Animals Orange? (p. 1922)
—Why Are Animals Purple? (p. 1922)
—Why Are Animals Red? (p. 1922)
—Why Are Animals Yellow? (p. 1922)
—Why Do the Seasons Change? (p. 1924)
—Why Do We See Rainbows? (p. 1924)
—Why Does T. Rex Have Such Short Arms? And Other Questions about Dinosaurs. Csotonyi, Julius, illus. (p. 1924)
—Why Does the Moon Change Shape? (p. 1924)
—Yellow Animals. (p. 1970)
—You've Got Nerve! The Secrets of the Brain & Nerves. (p. 1982)
—Zoom in on Bees. (p. 1989)
—Zoom in on Butterflies. (p. 1989)
—Zoom in on Dragonflies. (p. 1989)
—Zoom in on Fireflies. (p. 1989)
—Zoom in on Grasshoppers. (p. 1989)
—Zoom in on Ladybugs. (p. 1989)
Stewart, Melissa, jt. auth. see Shields, Amy.
Stewart, Melissa, jt. auth. see U. S. National Geographic Society Staff.
Stewart, Melissa & American Museum of Natural History Staff. World's Fastest Animals, Level 2. (p. 1960)
Stewart, Melissa & Heinemann Library Staff. How Does a Bone Become a Fossil? (p. 808)
—How Does Sand Become Glass? (p. 809)
Stewart, Melissa & Young, Allen M. No Monkeys, No Chocolate. Wong, Nicole, illus. (p. 1259)
Stewart, Michael & Black, Garry. Jet Pack Pets. (p. 916)
Stewart, Michael F. Assured Destruction. (p. 107)
Stewart, Michael G., illus. see Polisar, Barry Louis.
Stewart, Muriel, illus. see Chambers, Pamela G.
Stewart, Nancy. Bella Saves the Beach. Bell, Samantha, illus. (p. 162)
—Katrina & Winter: Partners in Courage. (p. 945)
—One Pelican at a Time: A Story of the Gulf Oil Spill. Bell, Samantha, illus. (p. 1296)
Stewart, Nicolette & Nash, Kevin. Skidmore College College Prowler off the Record. (p. 1584)
Stewart, Pat. Hans Christian Andersen Fairy Tales Stained Glass Coloring Book. (p. 743)
—Invisible Bugs Magic Picture Book. (p. 885)
—Invisible Fairy Tales Magic Picture Book. (p. 885)
—Learning about the Zodiac. (p. 985)
—Little Circus Stained Glass Coloring Book. (p. 1026)
—Wedding Stained Glass Coloring Book. (p. 1871)
Stewart, Pat, illus. see Burgess, Thornton W.
Stewart, Pat, jt. auth. see Burgess, Thornton W.
Stewart, Pat L. Hans Christian Andersen Storybook Stickers. (p. 743)
—Zoo Animals Coloring Fun. (p. 1988)
Stewart, Pat Ronson, illus. see Burgess, Thornton W.
Stewart, Pat Ronson, tr. see Burgess, Thornton W.
Stewart, Paul. Curse of Magoria. (p. 394)
—Far-Flung Adventures: Hugo Pepper. (p. 572)
—In the Dark of the Night. Vyner, Tim, illus. (p. 865)
—Little Bit of Winter. Riddell, Chris, illus. (p. 1024)
—Regalo de Cumpleanos. Riddell, Chris, illus. (p. 1457)
—The Nameless One. Riddell, Chris, illus. (p. 1728)
Stewart, Paul, jt. auth. see Riddell, Chris.
Stewart, Paul, jt. auth. see Stewart, Paul.
Stewart, Paul & Riddell, Chris. Barnaby Grimes: Curse of the Night Wolf. (p. 139)
—Barnaby Grimes: Legion of the Dead. (p. 139)
—Barnaby Grimes: Phantom of Blood Alley. (p. 139)
—Beyond the Deepwoods. (p. 174)
—Bloodhoney. (p. 201)
—Dragon's Hoard. Riddell, Chris, illus. (p. 479)
—Edge Chronicles: Clash of the Sky Galleons. (p. 504)
—Edge Chronicles: the Winter Knights. (p. 504)
—Far-Flung Adventures: Corby Flood. (p. 572)
—Far-Flung Adventures: Fergus Crane. (p. 572)
—Fergus Crane. (p. 582)
—Immortals. (p. 861)
—Joust of Honor. Riddell, Chris, illus. (p. 929)
—Lake of Skulls. Riddell, Chris, illus. (p. 972)
—Last of the Sky Pirates. (p. 978)
—Midnight over Sanctaphrax. (p. 1139)
—Returner's Wealth. (p. 1465)
—Stormchaser. (p. 1656)
Stewart, Paul & Stewart, Paul. Poquito de Invierno. Riddell, Chris, illus. (p. 1385)
Stewart, Peter, jt. auth. see Foster, John.
Stewart, Rachel M. Angel Inside Me. (p. 73)
Stewart, Rhea A., jt. auth. see Egan, Jill.
Stewart, Rhea A. & Technology Education Design Forum Staff. Math in the Real World Set, 10-Volumes. (p. 1106)
Stewart, Roger, illus. see Biskup, Agnieszka.
Stewart, Samara. Solomon's Smile. (p. 1608)
Stewart, Sarah. Gardener. Small, David, illus. (p. 656)
—Journey. Small, David, illus. (p. 927)
—Journey. Smalls, David, illus. (p. 927)
—Library. Small, David, illus. (p. 1005)
—Quiet Place Small, David, illus. (p. 1428)
Stewart, Scott. Calculus. (p. 252)
Stewart, Scott, illus. see Black, Jake & Meredith Books Staff.
Stewart, Sean. Perfect Circle. (p. 1341)
Stewart, Sean & Weisman, Jordan. Cathy's Book: If Found Call (650) 266-8283. (p. 280)
—Cathy's Key: If Found Call 650-266-8202. (p. 280)
—Cathy's Ring: If Found, Please Call 650-266-8263. (p. 280)
—Cathy's Ring: If Found, Please Call 650-266-8263. Brigg, Cathy, illus. (p. 280)
Stewart, Shannon. Captain Jake Hodson, Ben, illus. (p. 264)
Stewart, Sharon. Raven Quest. (p. 1441)
Stewart, Shawn. Donny & the Doorman's Nightmare. (p. 466)
Stewart, Shawna. Amazing Tails of Zomber Doodles & Buttons (p. 56)
Stewart, Sheila. Celebrity Families. (p. 285)
—Finding My Voice: Kids with Speech Impairment. (p. 588)
—Growing up in Religious Communities. (p. 726)
—Hidden Child: Kids with Autism. (p. 775)
—House Between Homes: Kids in the Foster Care System. (p. 803)
—I Can Do It! Kids with Physical Challenges. (p. 835)
—I Don't Keep Secrets. (p. 837)
—I Like Me. (p. 841)
—I Live in Two Homes: Adjusting to Divorce & Remarriage. (p. 841)
—Kids Have Troubles Too (p. 954)
—Listening with Your Eyes: Kids Who Are Deaf & Hard of Hearing. (p. 1022)
—My Feelings Have Names. (p. 1203)
—My Name Is Not Slow: Kids with Intellectual Disabilities. (p. 1215)
—Place Called Dead. (p. 1365)
—Psychology of Our Dark Side: Humans' Love Affair with Vampires & Werewolves. (p. 1413)
—Something's Wrong! Kids with Emotional Disturbance. (p. 1610)
—Sometimes My Mom Drinks Too Much. (p. 1610)
—Speed Racer: Kids with Attention-Deficit/Hyperactivity Disorder. (p. 1624)
—What Is a Family? (p. 1888)
—What's Wrong with My Brain? Kids with Brain Injury. (p. 1900)
—When Daddy Hit Mommy. (p. 1901)
—When Life Makes Me Mad. (p. 1903)
—When My Brother Went to Prison. (p. 1904)
—When My Dad Lost His Job. (p. 1904)
—Why Can't I Learn Like Everyone Else? Kids with Learning Disabilities. (p. 1923)
Stewart, Sheila & Flath, Camden. Finding My Voice: Kids with Speech Impairment. (p. 588)
—Hidden Child: Kids with Autism. (p. 775)
—House Between Homes: Kids in the Foster Care System. (p. 803)
—I Can Do It! Kids with Physical Challenges. (p. 835)
—Listening with Your Eyes: Kids Who Are Deaf & Hard of Hearing. (p. 1022)
—My Name Is Not Slow: Kids with Intellectual Disabilities. (p. 1215)
—Seeing with Your Fingers: Kids with Blindness & Visual Impairment. (p. 1548)
—Speed Racer: Kids with Attention-Deficit/Hyperactivity Disorder. (p. 1624)
—What's Going to Happen Next? Kids in the Juvenile Court System. (p. 1897)
—What's Wrong with My Brain? Kids with Brain Injury. (p. 1900)
—Why Can't I Learn Like Everyone Else? Kids with Learning Disabilities. (p. 1923)
Stewart, Sheila & Simons, Rae. I Live in Two Homes: Adjusting to Divorce & Remarriage. (p. 841)
Stewart, Sheryl. Friendly Beasts: Stories of Jesus. (p. 637)
Stewart, Sue, jt. auth. see Bassett, Jennifer.
Stewart, Tobi. Colonial Teachers. (p. 341)
Stewart, Tobi Stanton. Colonial Teachers. (p. 341)
—Primary Source Guide to Japan. (p. 1399)
—Solar Storms. (p. 1607)
Stewart, Trenton Lee. Extraordinary Education of Nicholas Benedict. (p. 555)
—Extraordinary Education of Nicholas Benedict. Sudyka, Diana, illus. (p. 555)
—Mr. Benedict's Book of Perplexing Puzzles, Elusive Enigmas, & Curious Conundrums. Sudyka, Diana, illus. (p. 1184)
—Mysterious Benedict Society. (p. 1222)
—Mysterious Benedict Society. Ellis, Carson, illus. (p. 1222)
—Mysterious Benedict Society & the Perilous Journey. (p. 1222)
—Mysterious Benedict Society & the Perilous Journey. Sudyka, Diana, illus. (p. 1222)
—Mysterious Benedict Society & the Prisoner's Dilemma. Tingley, Megan, ed. (p. 1222)
—Mysterious Benedict Society & the Prisoner's Dilemma. Sudyka, Diana, illus. (p. 1222)
—Mysterious Benedict Society Collection. (p. 1222)
—Mysterious Benedict Society Complete Collection. (p. 1222)
Stewart, Trudy & Turnbull, Jackie. Working with Dysfluent Children. (p. 1953)
Stewart, Vicky. Heide Loves to Cheer. (p. 762)
Stewart, Virginia. Visionary: An Elmhurst Retrospective. (p. 1845)
Stewart, Whitney. Catfish Tale: A Bayou Story of the Fisherman & His Wife. Guerlais, Gérald, illus. (p. 280)
—Marshall: A Nantucket Sea Rescue. Lyall, Dennis, illus. (p. 1096)
—Marshall, the Sea Dog. (p. 1096)
—Meditation Is an Open Sky: Mindfulness for Kids. Rippin, Sally, illus. (p. 1120)
—Mr. Lincoln's Gift: A Civil War Story. Dunham Akiyama, Laine, illus. (p. 1185)
—Who Was Walt Disney? (p. 1919)
—Who Was Walt Disney? Harrison, Nancy, illus. (p. 1919)
Stewart, Willa. Forever Bed. (p. 619)
Stewart, Wilson N. Cock-a-Doodle-Who? (p. 337)
Stewart, Yale. Alien Superman! Stewart, Yale, illus. (p. 41)
—Amazing Adventures of Superman Stewart, Yale, illus. (p. 52)
—Battle of the Super Heroes! Stewart, Yale, illus. (p. 147)
—Creatures from Planet X! Stewart, Yale, illus. (p. 380)
—Escape from Future World! Stewart, Yale, illus. (p. 535)
Stewart-Goodair, Madonna. Key to the Golden Gates: The Mystic Soldier, Book 1 (p. 950)
—Mystic Soldier: Warlock of Fire (p. 1226)
Stewig, John Warren. Animals Watched: An Alphabet Book. Litzinger, Rosanne, illus. (p. 84)
—Nobody Asked the Pea. Van Wright, Cornelius, illus. (p. 1262)
Steyert, Bill, illus. see Brodsky, Irene.
Steyn, Mark. Mark Steyn's American Songbook: Words by Dorothy Fields, Music by Jule Styne, Song by Cole Porter. Vol. 1 (p. 1095)
—Song for the Season. (p. 1611)
StGermain, Annetta, jt. auth. see Singhose, Rose.
Stibbens, Steve. Knights over the Delta: An Oral History of the 114th Aviation Company in Vietnam, 1963-72. Stibbens, Steve, ed. (p. 964)
Stiberth, Elizabeth. Halloween Mystery. (p. 738)
Stich, Bill. Let's Make Art! (p. 999)
Stich, Carolyn R., illus. see Henry, Regene.
Stich, Carolyn R., illus. see McKinney, Barbara Shaw.
Stich, Carolyn R., illus. see Stroschin, Jane H.
Stich, Paul, ed. see Milanese, Celestine Marie & Peck, Carolyn.
Stich, Paul, ed. see Moreau, Nancy & Moreau, Wayne.
Stich, Paul, ed. see Pickles, Jonathan & Van Ackooy, Maureen.
Stich, Tim. Paper Crafts: Shapes & Their Attributes. (p. 1322)
Stichter, Jami McDaniel. When You Don't Clean Your Room. (p. 1905)
Stickels, Terry, jt. auth. see Honeycutt, Brad.
Stickels, Terry & Immanuvel, Anthony. Sudoku. (p. 1672)
Sticker Family Staff, jt. auth. see Hardie Grant Books Staff.
Stickers, jt. auth. see Dahlen, Noelle.
Stickers, jt. auth. see Maderna, Victoria.
Stickers, jt. auth. see Rechlin, Ted.
Stickland, Eugene. Two Plays: Sitting on Paradise & a Guide to Mourning. (p. 1804)
Stickland, Henrietta. Dinosaur More! A First Book of Dinosaur Facts. Stickland, Paul, illus. (p. 442)
Stickland, Paul. Big Bug, Little Bug: A Book of Opposites. (p. 180)
—Dinosaur Colors. (p. 441)
—Dinosaur Numbers. (p. 442)
—Dinosaur Opposites. (p. 442)
—Dinosaur Shapes. (p. 442)
Stickland, Paul, illus. see Stickland, Henrietta.
Stickland, Shadra, illus. see Bandy, Michael S. & Stein, Eric.
Stickland, Shadra, illus. see Watson, Renée.
Stickler, John. Land of Morning Calm: Korean Culture Then & Now. Han, Soma, illus. (p. 973)
Stickler, John C. & Han, Soma. Maya & the Turtle: A Korean Fairy Tale. (p. 1112)
Stickler, LeeDell, jt. auth. see Preston, Rhoda.
Stickler, LeeDell & Newman, Judy. Footprints on the Wall. (p. 615)
—From Bags to Bushes. (p. 642)
—Jailhouse Rocked. (p. 905)
Stickler, LeeDell, compiled by. Mystery of the Shaking Ground: Dramas, Speeches, & Recitations for Children. (p. 1226)
Stickler, LeeDell, ed. Busy Boogie: And Other Dramas for Preschool. (p. 246)
Stickler, LeeDell, et al. Ring 'Round Jericho. (p. 1473)
Stickley, Kelly, illus. see Mysak, Mary.
Stickmon, Janet Christine. Crushing Soft Rubies: A Memoir. (p. 387)
Stidwell O'Boyle, Carrie, ed. see Carey, Becky.
Stidworthy, John. Queen Alexandra's Birdwing: The World's Largest Butterfly. (p. 1424)
Stieber, Joel, illus. see MacDonald, Tom.
Stiefel, Chana. Chickens on the Family Farm. (p. 300)
—Comets & Meteors: Shooting Through Space. (p. 348)
—Cows on the Family Farm. (p. 374)
—Fingerprints: Dead People Do Tell Tales. (p. 589)
—Goats on the Family Farm. (p. 688)
—Lives of Stars: From Supernovas to Black Holes. (p. 1040)
—Pigs on the Family Farm. (p. 1358)
—Sheep on the Family Farm. (p. 1564)
—Sky High. (p. 1586)
—Sweaty Suits of Armor: Could You Survive Being a Knight? Kelley, Gerald, illus. (p. 1689)
—There's a Rat in My Soup: Could You Survive Medieval Food? Kelley, Gerald, illus. (p. 1731)
—Thunderstorms. (p. 1746)
—Tsunamis. (p. 1795)
—Turkeys on the Family Farm. (p. 1797)
—Ye Castle Stinketh: Could You Survive Living in a Castle? Kelley, Gerald, illus. (p. 1968)
Stiefvater, Maggie. Ballad: A Gathering of Faerie. (p. 134)
—Blue Lily, Lily Blue. (p. 203)
—Dream Thieves. (p. 484)
—Forever. (p. 619)
—Hunted (p. 828)
—Lament: The Faerie Queen's Deception. (p. 972)
—Linger. (p. 1019)
—Raven Boys. (p. 1441)
—Scorpio Races. (p. 1530)
—Shiver. (p. 1567)
—Sinner. (p. 1580)
Stiefvater, Maggie & Pearce, Jackson. Pip Bartlett's Guide to Magical Creatures. (p. 1361)
Stiefvater, Maggie & Scholastic, Inc. Staff. Shiver; Linger; Forever. (p. 1567)
Stieg, Megan & Myers, Lawrence Eddie. How to Be a Harmonica Hero. (p. 814)
Stiegemeyer, Julie. Baby in a Manger. Wong, Nicole, illus. (p. 126)
—Bright Easter Day. Spellman, Susan, illus. (p. 228)
—Cheep! Cheep! Balcker-McKee, Carol, illus. (p. 295)
—Dorothea Creamer. Martin, John, illus. (p. 471)
—Fear Not, Joseph. Bladholm, Cheri, illus. (p. 579)
—Gobble-Gobble Crash! A Barnyard Counting Bash. Gorbachev, Valeri, illus. (p. 688)
—Jesus Teaches Us Not to Worry. (p. 916)
—Saint Nicholas: The Real Story of the Christmas Legend. Ellison, Chris, illus. (p. 1504)
—Seven Little Bunnies Bryant, Laura J., illus. (p. 1554)
—Stephen Stands Strong. Myers, Glenn, illus. (p. 1648)

—Thanksgiving: A Harvest Celebration. Benoit, Renne, illus. (p. 1725)
—Things I Hear in Church. Mitter, Kathy, illus. (p. 1733)
—Things I See at Baptism. Mitter, Kathryn, illus. (p. 1733)
—Things I See at Christmas. Mitter, Kathryn, illus. (p. 1733)
—Things I See at Easter. Mitter, Kathy, illus. (p. 1733)
—Things I See in Church. Mitter, Kathy, illus. (p. 1733)
—Under the Baobab Tree Lewis, E. B., illus. (p. 1813)
Stiegemeyer, Julie & Mitter, Kathy. Things I Do in Church. (p. 1733)
Stiegler, Lorraine. Space Probes. (p. 1619)
Stiegler, Lorraine, jt. auth. see Mills, Nathan.
Stiekel, Bettina, ed. Nobel Book of Answers: A the Dalai Lama, Mikhail Gorbachev, Shimon Peres. (p. 1262)
Stiekel, Bettina, et al. Nobel Book of Answers: The Dalai Lama, Mikhail Gorbachev, Shimon Peres, & Other Nobel Prize Winners Answer Some of Life's Most Intriguing Questions for Young People. Stiekel, Bettina, ed. (p. 1262)
Stier, Catherine. Barnaby the Bedbug Detective. Sapp, Karen, illus. (p. 139)
—Bugs in My Hair?! Lyon, Tammie, illus. (p. 237)
—If I Ran for President. Avril, Lynne, illus. (p. 853)
—If I Were President. DiSalvo-Ryan, DyAnne, illus. (p. 853)
—Terrible Secrets of the Tell-All Club. (p. 1721)
—Today on Election Day. Leonard, David, illus. (p. 1761)
—Welcome to America, Champ. Ettlinger, Doris, illus. (p. 1873)
—What's Bugging Nurse Penny? A Story about Lice. Beaky, Suzanne, illus. (p. 1896)
Stier, Roy E. Son of Bunyan & the Sacred Moonstone. (p. 1611)
Stierle, Cynthia. Build My Own Farm Machines. (p. 238)
—Build My Own Spacecraft. (p. 238)
—Cars 2 CarryAlong(r) Play Book. Disney Artists Staff, illus. (p. 272)
—Diego in the Dark: Being Brave at Night. Maher, Alex, illus. (p. 437)
—Grand Prix Garage: Storybook & Garage. (p. 707)
—Together Forever. (p. 1762)
Stierle, Cynthia & Crawley, Annie. Ocean Life: From A to Z. (p. 1276)
Stietencron, Bettina, illus. see Grimm, Jacob & Grimm, Wilhelm K.
Stiff, Brenda K. Erica the Eagle: I Believe I Can Fly. (p. 533)
Stiffler, Michael, illus. see Malavolti, Angela.
Stig Gjerlaug & Dallas Stebanuk, jt. auth. see Stig Gjerlaug & Dallas Stebanuk, Gjerla.
Stig Gjerlaug & Dallas Stebanuk, Gjerla & Stig Gjerlaug & Dallas Stebanuk. Good Morning Mr Frubus. (p. 698)
Stigler, Marilyn, illus. see Franz, Kevin.
Stiglich, Tom, illus. see Adams, William J.
Stiglich, Tom, illus. see O'Conner, Patricia T.
Stihler, Cherie. Giant Cabbage: An Alaska Folktale. Trammell, Jeremiah, illus. (p. 673)
Stihler, Cherie B. Cabin That Moose Built. Trammell, Jeremiah, illus. (p. 250)
—Polar Polka: Counting Polar Bears in Alaska. Brooks, Erik, illus. (p. 1379)
—Sourdough Man: An Alaska Folktale. Lavallee, Barbara, illus. (p. 1616)
—Squishy, Squishy: A Book about My Five Senses. Rose, Heidi, illus. (p. 1637)
—Wiggle-Waggle Woof: Counting Sled Dogs in Alaska. Bania, Michael, illus. (p. 1927)
Stihler, Chérie B. Wiggle-Waggle Woof 1, 2, 3. Bania, Michael, illus. (p. 1927)
Stileman, Kali. Big Book of My World. (p. 179)
—Roly Poly Egg. (p. 1485)
—Snack Time for Confetti. (p. 1595)
Stiles, Amanda. Runaway Soccer Ball. Torrey, Rich, illus. (p. 1496)
Stiles, Dan. Baby's First Bloox: Colors, Shapes, & Patterns. (p. 129)
—Put on Your Shoes! (p. 1420)
—Today I'm Going to Wear ... (p. 1760)
Stiles, David. Forts for Kids. (p. 623)
Stiles, Erinn. Monkey & the Rainbow. (p. 1165)
Stiles, Gannett Ruth. My Father's Dragon. (p. 1203)
Stiles, Helen E. Pottery of the American Indians; Illustrated with Halftone Photographs, Endpapers, Jacket & Line Drawings by Marion Downer. (p. 1388)
Stiles, Martha Bennett. Sailing to Freedom. (p. 1503)
Stiles, Mary & Mills, Barbara. Rookie's Guide to Research. (p. 1487)
Stiles, Michelle. Different Way. (p. 438)
Stiles, Norman. On My Very First School Day I Met... Mayer, Bill, illus. (p. 1289)
Stiles, Tim, illus. see Jacobson, Ryan.
Still, Cynthia W. Gypsy Travels the World. (p. 734)
Still, Teresa B. Tessa Has Two Homes. (p. 1722)
Still, Teresa Brooks. Sarah Lucele's Ordeals: Dolly's Dilemma. (p. 1514)
Still, Wayne A., illus. see Chandler, Alton.
Still, Wayne A., illus. see Howell, Ann C. & Chandler, Alton.
Stille, Darlene R. Air: Outside, Inside, & All Around Boyd, Sheree, illus. (p. 31)
—Aire: Afuera, Adentro y en Todos Lados Robledo, Sol, tr. from ENG. (p. 31)
—Altering the Biological Blueprint: The Science of Genetic Engineering (p. 50)
—Anne Hutchinson: Puritan Protester Stille, Darlene R., illus. (p. 86)
—Architects of the Holocaust (p. 95)
—Barack Obama: 44th U.S. President. Sterguiz, Richard, illus. (p. 137)
—Capitol Building. Ouren, Todd, illus. (p. 263)
—Case of the Soda Explosion & Other True Science Mysteries for You to Solve (p. 275)
—Cells. (p. 286)
—Changing Habits, Living Green. (p. 290)
—Civil War Through Photography (p. 326)
—Classifying Living Things. (p. 328)
—DNA: The Master Molecule of Life Hoffmann, Eric, illus. (p. 456)
—Eleanor Roosevelt: First Lady & Civil Rights Activist. Sprunger, Reed, illus. (p. 508)
—Electricity: Bulbs, Batteries, & Sparks. Boyd, Sheree, illus. (p. 509)
—Emergence of Modern America: 1890-1930. (p. 518)
—Energy: Heat, Light, & Fuel. Boyd, Sheree, illus. (p. 528)
—Forensic Evidence: Blood. (p. 617)
—Good Food, Good for Earth. (p. 698)
—Great Shakes: The Science of Earthquakes Hoffmann, Erich, illus. (p. 718)
—Hadrosaurus. (p. 735)
—Heat (p. 760)
—I Am a Sea Turtle: The Life of a Green Sea Turtle Ouren, Todd, illus. (p. 832)
—I Live in the Ocean Ouren, Todd, illus. (p. 841)
—Igneous Rocks: From Fire to Stone Schultz, Ashlee, illus. (p. 856)
—Indiana. (p. 871)
—Invisible Exposure: The Science of Ultraviolet Rays Hossain, Farhana, illus. (p. 885)
—Jackie Robinson: Amazing Athlete & Activist. Sterguiz, Richard, illus. (p. 904)
—Journals of Lewis & Clark (p. 927)
—Life Cycle of Amphibians (p. 1009)
—Life Cycle of Fish (p. 1009)
—Life Cycle of Reptiles (p. 1009)
—Lunch Lady Science: Understanding the Food That Goes in Your Body (p. 1065)
—Manipulating Light: Reflection, Refraction, & Absorption Hossain, Farhana, illus. (p. 1087)
—Matter: See It, Touch It, Taste It, Smell It Boyd, Sheree, illus. (p. 1109)
—Metamorphic Rocks: Recycled Rock Schultz, Ashlee, illus. (p. 1130)
—Minerals: From Apatite to Zinc Hossain, Farhana, illus. (p. 1146)
—Motion: Push & Pull, Fast & Slow. Boyd, Sheree, tr. (p. 1179)
—Movimiento: Tira y Empuja, Rápido y Despacio. Robledo, Sol, tr. from ENG. (p. 1183)
—Natural Resources: Using & Protecting Earth's Supplies Hossain, Farhana, illus. (p. 1235)
—Nature Interrupted: The Science of Environmental Chain Reactions (p. 1236)
—North Dakota (Revised Edition) (p. 1265)
—Ohio (Revised Edition) (p. 1281)
—Outbreak! The Science of Pandemics (p. 1312)
—Percy Lavon Julian: Pioneering Chemist (p. 1341)
—Physical Change: Reshaping Matter Hossain, Farhana, illus. (p. 1353)
—Protecting Animals. (p. 1412)
—Protecting Land. (p. 1412)
—Puerto Rico. (p. 1415)
—Recipe for Disaster: The Science of Foodborne Illness (p. 1451)
—Science of Gym Class: More Than Just Dodgeball & Sweatpants (p. 1527)
—Sedimentary Rocks: A Record of Earth's History Schultz, Ashlee, illus. (p. 1546)
—Ships (p. 1567)
—Soil: Digging into Earth's Vital Resource Hossain, Farhana, illus. (p. 1606)
—Space Shuttle (p. 1619)
—Statue of Liberty. Ouren, Todd, illus. (p. 1645)
—Temperature: Heating up & Cooling Down Boyd, Sheree, illus. (p. 1717)
—Temperature: Heating up & Cooling Down. Boyd, Sheree, illus. (p. 1717)
—Weather (p. 1869)
Stille, Darlene R. & Compass Point Books Staff. Atoms & Molecules: Building Blocks of the Universe Hossain, Farhana, illus. (p. 113)
—Madam C. J. Walker: Entrepreneur & Millionaire (p. 1069)
Stille, Darlene R. & Picture Window Books Staff. Electricidad: Focos, Pilas y Chispas Robledo, Sol, tr. (p. 509)
—Energía: Calor, Luz y Combustible. Robledo, Sol, tr. from ENG. (p. 527)
—Materia: Mira, Toca, Prueba, Huele Robledo, Sol, tr. from ENG. (p. 1104)
—Temperatura: Caliente y Frío. Robledo, Sol, tr. from ENG. (p. 1717)
Stille, Darlene R. & Ryback, Carol. Cells. (p. 286)
—Heredity. (p. 771)
—Simple Life Forms. (p. 1577)
Stille, Ljuba & Mundt, Anja. Mia's Thumb. Stille, Ljuba, illus. (p. 1134)
Stillerman, Marci. Something Terrible Happened on Kenmore. (p. 1610)
Stillerman, Robbie. Amusement Park Stickers. (p. 66)
—Animal Mix & Match Sticker Activity Book. (p. 78)
—Ballerina Friends Sticker Paper Dolls. (p. 134)
—Best Friends Sticker Paper Dolls. (p. 169)
—Birthday Girls Sticker Paper Dolls. (p. 192)
—Color Your Own Zoo Animals Stickers. (p. 343)
—Easy Old MacDonald's Farm Sticker Picture Puzzle. (p. 500)
—Ghoulish Girls Paper Dolls. (p. 673)
—Glitter Jewelry Sticker Activity Book. (p. 684)
—Glitter Pretty in Pink Sticker Paper Doll. (p. 684)
—Kati & Kayla. (p. 944)
—Little King & Queen Sticker Paper Dolls. (p. 1030)
—Mix & Match Jewelry Sticker Activity Book. (p. 1156)
—Monster Mix & Match Sticker Activity Book. (p. 1168)
—Pretty Jewelry Sticker. (p. 1398)
—Princess Mix & Match. (p. 1404)
—Princess the Pony Sticker Activity Book. (p. 1406)
—Shiny Girl Stuff Stickers. (p. 1567)
—Wendy Works Out Sticker Paper Doll. (p. 1875)
Stillerman, Robbie, illus. see Pearlstein, Don.
Stillinger, Doug. Aviones de Papel. (p. 120)
—Ball Games. (p. 134)
—Baterias en Accion. (p. 143)
—Espirales de Colores. (p. 536)
—Klutz Book of Paper Airplanes. (p. 963)
—Spiral Draw. (p. 1628)
Stillinger, Doug, ed. Battery Science: Make Widgets That Work & Gadgets That Go. (p. 145)
Stillman, Andrea G., ed. see Adams, Ansel.
Stillman, David. Repaso: Answer Key. (p. 1460)
Stillman, David M., jt. auth. see Gordon, Ronni L.
Stillman, David M. & Gordon, Ronni L. Cuadorno 2: An Intermediate Workbook for Grammar & Communication (p. 388)
Stillman, Josh. Chinese Finger Trap. (p. 307)
Stillman, Lorry & Holocaust Human Rights Center of Maine. Spirit That Moves Us: Using Literature, Art, & Music to Teach about the Holocaust at the Secondary & College Level (p. 1628)
Stillman, Norma. Forest Adventures: Book # 1 - Digger the Gopher & Hoppity the Frog. (p. 618)
Stillman, Sarah. Soul Searching: A Girl's Guide to Finding Herself. Gross, Susan, illus. (p. 1614)
Stillman, Steve L., 3rd. Effects & Their Uses. (p. 505)
Stills, Caroline. A to Z of Fairies. McKenzie, Heath, illus. (p. 2)
—ABC of Pirates. McKenzie, Heath, illus. (p. 3)
—Mice Mischief: Math Facts in Action. Rossell, Judith, illus. (p. 1134)
Stills, Caroline & Stills-Blott, Sarcia. House of 12 Bunnies. Rossell, Judith, illus. (p. 803)
Stills-Blott, Sarcia, jt. auth. see Stills, Caroline.
Stillview, photos by see Top That! Team Staff.
Stillwell, Alexander. Green Berets: What It Takes to Join the Elite. (p. 721)
—Military Jobs: Navy SEALs. (p. 1143)
Stillwell, Heath, illus. see Johnson, Sandi.
Stillwell, Jennifer, illus. see Loveland-Coen, Victoria.
Stilson, E. C. How to Lose a Tooth. (p. 820)
Stilson, Linda J. Sew Easy Felt Puppets. (p. 1555)
Stilton, Geronimo. Alien Escape. (p. 40)
—All Because of a Cup of Coffee. Wolf, Matt, illus. (p. 44)
—Amazing Voyage. Barozzi, Danilo, illus. (p. 56)
—Attack of the Bandit Cats. Wolf, Matt, illus. (p. 113)
—Back in Time. (p. 130)
—Cat & Mouse in a Haunted House. (p. 277)
—Cat & Mouse in a Haunted House. Wolf, Matt & Keys, Larry, illus. (p. 277)
—Cavemice: Surfing for Secrets. (p. 282)
—Cheese-Colored Camper. (p. 296)
—Christmas Catastrophe. (p. 313)
—Christmas Tale. (p. 316)
—Christmas Toy Factory. (p. 316)
—Curse of the Cheese Pyramid. (p. 395)
—Curse of the Cheese Pyramid. Wolf, Matt & Keys, Larry, illus. (p. 395)
—Dinosaurs in Action. (p. 444)
—Don't Wake the Dinosaur! (p. 469)
—Down & Out down Under. (p. 474)
—Dragon Prophecy. (p. 477)
—Enormouse Pearl Heist. (p. 531)
—Fabumouse School Adventure. (p. 560)
—Fabumouse Vacation for Geronimo. Keys, Larry, illus. (p. 560)
—Fast & the Frozen. (p. 576)
—Fastest Train in the West. (p. 576)
—Field Trip to Niagara Falls. (p. 584)
—Field Trip to Niagara Falls. Keys, Larry et al, illus. (p. 584)
—First Samurai. (p. 596)
—Flight of the Red Bandit. (p. 604)
—Following the Trail of Marco Polo (p. 612)
—Four Mice Deep in the Jungle. Wolf, Matt & Keys, Larry, illus. (p. 625)
—Fright Night. (p. 639)
—Galactic Goal. (p. 652)
—Geronimo & the Gold Medal Mystery. (p. 667)
—Geronimo Stilton: Welcome to Moldy Manor. Bk. 59 (p. 667)
—Geronimo Stilton: Red Pizzas for a Blue Count, Attack of the Bandit Cats, a Fabumouse Vacation for Gernimo. Bks. 7-9 (p. 667)
—Geronimo Stilton 12-Copy Prepack. (p. 667)
—Geronimo Stilton 12-Copy Self-Shipper. (p. 667)
—Geronimo Stilton 12-Copy Solid Self-Shipper. Wolf, Matt, illus. (p. 667)
—Geronimo Stilton 30 Mouse Island Marathon. (p. 667)
—Geronimo Stilton Cavemice: I¿m a Scaredy-Mouse! Bk. 7 (p. 667)
—Geronimo Stilton Saves the Olympics. (p. 667)
—Geronimo's Valentine (p. 667)
—Geronimo's Valentine. (p. 667)
—Get into Gear, Stilton! (p. 667)
—Ghost Pirate Treasure. (p. 671)
—Giant Diamond Robbery. (p. 673)
—Golden Statue Plot. (p. 695)
—granizado de moscas para el Conde. Wolf, Matt, illus. (p. 710)
—Great Ice Age. (p. 716)
—Great Mouse Race. (p. 717)
—Haunted Castle. (p. 753)
—Help, I'm in Hot Lava! (p. 765)
—Hunt for the Curious Cheese. (p. 828)
—Hunt for the Golden Book. (p. 828)
—Ice Planet Adventure. (p. 850)
—I'm Not a Supermouse! (p. 859)
—I'm Too Fond of My Fur! (p. 860)
—I'm Too Fond of My Fur! Wolf, Matt, illus. (p. 860)
—I'm Too Fond of My Fur! Wolf, Matt & Keys, Larry, illus. (p. 860)
—It's Halloween, You 'Fraidy Mouse! Wolf, Matt, illus. (p. 897)
—Journey Through Time. (p. 928)
—Karate Mouse. (p. 943)
—Kingdom of Fantasy. (p. 959)
—Lost Treasure of the Emerald Eye. Wolf, Matt, illus. (p. 1057)
—Lost Treasure of the Emerald Eye. Wolf, Matt & Keys, Larry, illus. (p. 1057)
—Meet Me in Horrorwood. (p. 1121)
—Merry Christmas, Geronimo! Wolf, Matt, illus. (p. 1128)
—Mighty Mount Kilimanjaro. (p. 1140)
—Misterio Del Ojo Esmeralda. (p. 1155)
—Mona Mousa Code. Wolf, Matt, illus. (p. 1163)
—Mouse Island Marathon. (p. 1182)
—Mummy with No Name. (p. 1191)
—My Name Is Stilton, Geronimo Stilton. (p. 1215)
—Mysterious Cheese Thief. (p. 1223)
—Mystery in Venice. (p. 1224)
—Paws Off, Cheddarface! Wolf, Matt & Keys, Larry, illus. (p. 1331)
—Peculiar Pumpkin Thief. (p. 1334)
—Phantom of the Subway. (p. 1349)
—Phantom of the Subway. Wolf, Matt, illus. (p. 1349)
—Play It Again, Mozart! (p. 1371)
—Quest for Paradise. (p. 1426)
—Race Across America. (p. 1430)
—Red Pizzas for a Blue Count. Wolf, Matt & Keys, Larry, illus. (p. 1454)
—Return of the Vampire. (p. 1464)
—Ride for Your Life! (p. 1471)
—Rumble in the Jungle. (p. 1495)
—Run for the Hills, Geronimo! (p. 1496)
—Save the White Whale! (p. 1517)
—Search for Sunken Treasure. (p. 1537)
—Search for Sunken Treasure. Wolf, Matt, illus. (p. 1537)
—Search for Treasure. (p. 1537)
—Secret Agent. (p. 1540)
—Secret of Cacklefur Castle. (p. 1542)
—Shipwreck on the Pirate Islands. (p. 1567)
—Singing Sensation. (p. 1579)
—Stinky Cheese Vacation. (p. 1651)
—Stone of Fire. (p. 1652)
—Suitcase Full of Ghosts. (p. 1673)
—Super Chef Contest. (p. 1679)
—Surfing for Secrets. (p. 1685)
—Surf's up Geronimo. (p. 1685)
—Temple of the Ruby of Fire. (p. 1718)
—Temple of the Ruby of Fire. Wolf, Matt, illus. (p. 1718)
—The Golden Statue Plot. (p. 1728)
—Thea Stilton & the Dragon's Code. (p. 1728)
—Thirteen Ghosts. (p. 1735)
—This Hotel Is Haunted! (p. 1735)
—Treasure of Easter Island. (p. 1782)
—Valentine's Day Disaster. (p. 1830)
—Valentine's Day Disaster. Keys, Larry et al, illus. (p. 1830)
—Valley of the Giant Skeletons. (p. 1831)
—Very Merry Christmas. (p. 1838)
—Volcano of Fire. (p. 1848)
—Watch Your Tail! (p. 1861)
—Watch Your Whiskers, Stilton! (p. 1861)
—Way of the Samurai. (p. 1864)
—Wedding Crasher. (p. 1870)
—Weird Book Machine. (p. 1872)
—Welcome to Moldy Manor. (p. 1873)
—We'll Always Have Paris. (p. 1874)
—Who Stole the Mona Lisa? (p. 1917)
—Wild, Wild West. (p. 1930)
—You're Mine, Captain! (p. 1982)
Stilton, Geronimo, jt. auth. see Bargellini, Demetrio.
Stilton, Geronimo, jt. auth. see Stilton, Thea.
Stilton, Geronimo & Dami, Elisabetta. Enchanted Charms: The Seventh Adventure in the Kingdom of Fantasy. Barozzi, Danilo, illus. (p. 523)
Stilton, Geronimo & Mckeon, Kathryn. Mouse in Space! (p. 1182)
Stilton, Geronimo & Stilton, Thea. Blue Scarab Hunt. (p. 203)
—Cherry Blossom Adventure. (p. 298)
—Thea Stilton & the Dragon's Code. (p. 1728)
—Thea Stilton & the Ghost of the Shipwreck. (p. 1728)
—Thea Stilton & the Ice Treasure. (p. 1728)
—Thea Stilton & the Mountain of Fire. (p. 1728)
—Thea Stilton & the Mystery on the Orient Express. (p. 1728)
—Thea Stilton & the Prince's Emerald. (p. 1728)
—Thea Stilton & the Secret of the Old Castle. (p. 1728)
—Thea Stilton & the Star Castaways. (p. 1728)
Stilton, Geronimo & Wolf, Matt. All Because of a Cup of Coffee. (p. 44)
Stilton, Thea. Big Trouble in the Big Apple. (p. 184)
—Journey to Atlantis. (p. 928)
—Revenge of the Lizard Club. (p. 1466)
—Secret of the Fairies. (p. 1542)
—Secret of Whale Island (p. 1543)
—Spanish Dance Mission. (p. 1621)
—Thea Stilton & the Blue Scarab Hunt. (p. 1728)
—Thea Stilton & the Chocolate Sabotage. (p. 1728)
—Thea Stilton & the Dancing Shadows. (p. 1728)
—Thea Stilton & the Great Tulip Heist. (p. 1728)
—Thea Stilton & the Journey to the Lion's Den. (p. 1728)
—Thea Stilton & the Legend of the Fire Flowers. (p. 1728)
—Thea Stilton & the Lost Letters. (p. 1728)
—Thea Stilton & the Missing Myth. (p. 1728)
—Thea Stilton & the Mystery on the Orient Express. (p. 1728)
—Thea Stilton & the Prince's Emerald. (p. 1728)
—Thea Stilton & the Secret City. (p. 1728)
—Thea Stilton & the Secret of the Old Castle. (p. 1728)
—Thea Stilton & the Spanish Dance Mission. (p. 1728)
Stilton, Thea, jt. auth. see Stilton, Geronimo.
Stilton, Thea & Stilton, Geronimo. Secret of the Snow: A Geronimo Stilton Adventure. (p. 1543)
Stilwell, Alexander. Army Rangers. (p. 100)
—Navy SEALs: What It Takes to Join the Elite. (p. 1238)
Stilwell, Debra. Where Does Our Food Come From? (p. 1907)
Stilwell, Dwayne. Levers. (p. 1003)
Stilwell, Norma. It Was Powwow Time in Plymouth. (p. 894)
Stilwell, Norma Minturn. Making Beautiful Music. LaGrange, Tiffany, illus. (p. 1080)
—Thought for Thanksgiving. Bingham, Pamela E., illus. (p. 1740)
Stim, R. I Didn't Kill Your Cat. (p. 837)
Stimola, Aubrey. Brain Injuries. (p. 221)
—Cell Biology. (p. 286)
Stimpson, Aaron & Stimpson, Sarah. Story Builders. (p. 1657)
Stimpson, Colin. Jack & the Baked Beanstalk. Stimpson, Colin, illus. (p. 902)
Stimpson, Colin, illus. see Howard, Martin.
Stimpson, Sarah, jt. auth. see Stimpson, Aaron.
Stims, Robert. Chain of Wisdom (p. 288)
Stimson, Aaron. From Stone to Steel. (p. 643)

Stimson, James. Bully Goat Grim: A Maynard Moose Tale. (p. 241)
—Thirteen O'Clock. Stimson, James, illus. (p. 1735)
Stimson, James, illus. see Claflin, Willy.
Stimson, Joan. Brave Lion, Scared Lion. Rubio, Esther, tr. (p. 223)
—Dinosaur Next Door. (p. 442)
—Jake's Cake. (p. 906)
Stinchecum, Amanda M., tr. see Cho, Shinta.
Stinchecum, Amanda Mayer, jt. auth. see Yagyu, Genichiro.
Stine, Fay. Star Ship Fantasy: The New Frontier of Space. (p. 1641)
Stine, Faye. Golden Goblet: 200 Years in a Medieval Castle. (p. 694)
—Magic Forest: The Magic of Childhood. (p. 1072)
—Wolf: A Story of the Wild. (p. 1943)
Stine, Megan. Where Is Niagara Falls? (p. 1909)
—Where Is the White House? (p. 1909)
—Where Is the White House? Groff, David, illus. (p. 1909)
—Who Is Michelle Obama? (p. 1916)
—Who Is Michelle Obama? O'Brien, John & Harrison, Nancy, illus. (p. 1916)
—Who Was Marie Curie? (p. 1918)
—Who Was Marie Curie? Hammond, Ted & Harrison, Nancy, illus. (p. 1918)
—Who Was Sally Ride? (p. 1919)
—Who Was Ulysses S. Grant? (p. 1919)
—Who Was Ulysses S. Grant? Harrison, Nancy & Geyer, Mark Edward, illus. (p. 1919)
Stine, Megan, et al. Boy Crazy. (p. 217)
—Girl Talk. (p. 679)
—Likes Me, Likes Me Not. (p. 1017)
—Now You See Him, Now You Don't. (p. 1269)
—Sealed with a Kiss. (p. 1536)
—Surprise Surprise! (p. 1686)
—War of the Wardrobes. (p. 1857)
Stine, R. L. 12 Screams of Christmas. (p. 1994)
—13th Warning (p. 1995)
—30 Tales to Give You Goosebumps. (p. 1996)
—Adventures of Shrinkman (p. 23)
—All-Night Party. (p. 45)
—Attack of the Aqua Apes & Nightmare in 3-D: Twice Terrifying Tales. (p. 113)
—Attack of the Graveyard Ghouls. (p. 113)
—Battle of the Dum Diddys. Park, Trip, illus. (p. 146)
—Be Careful What You Wish For. (p. 148)
—Best Friend. (p. 169)
—Beware! R. L. Stine Picks His Favorite Scary Stories. (p. 173)
—Beware, the Snowman. (p. 173)
—Bienvenido Al Campamento de Las Serpientes. (p. 177)
—Big Blueberry Barf-Off! Park, Trip, illus. (p. 178)
—Birthday Party of No Return! (p. 193)
—Bitten: Dangerous Girls & the Taste of Night. (p. 194)
—Blob That Ate Everyone. (p. 200)
—Bound Galley - Haunted Mask Lives! (p. 216)
—Boy Who Ate Fear Street. (p. 219)
—Broken Hearts. (p. 230)
—Calling All Birdbrains. Park, Trip, illus. (p. 254)
—Chicas Peligrosas. Garde, Dora, tr. (p. 299)
—Classic Goosebumps #32: Please Don't Feed the Vampire! A Give Yourself Goosebumps Book. (p. 328)
—Claws! (p. 330)
—Confession. (p. 356)
—Creature Teacher: The Final Exam. (p. 380)
—Creatures from Beyond Beyond (p. 380)
—Creep from the Deep. (p. 380)
—Creep from the Deep. (p. 381)
—Creepy Creatures. Hernandez, Gabriel et al, illus. (p. 381)
—Curse of the Mummy's Tomb. (p. 395)
—Dangerous Girls. (p. 404)
—Darkest Dawn. (p. 408)
—Deep Trouble. (p. 423)
—Don't Scream! (p. 468)
—Don't Stay up Late: A Fear Street Novel. (p. 468)
—Dr. Maniac vs. Robby Schwartz. (p. 475)
—Dr. Maniac Will See You Now. (p. 475)
—Dudes, the School Is Haunted! Park, Trip, illus. (p. 489)
—Dumb Clucks. Park, Trip, illus. (p. 489)
—Escape from HorrorLand. (p. 535)
—Escape from Horrorland. (p. 535)
—Espanto Marino. (p. 536)
—Fear: 13 Stories of Suspense & Horror. (p. 579)
—Fear Street Super Thriller: Party Games & Don't Stay up Late. (p. 579)
—Final de la Noche. Alonso, Victoria, tr. (p. 586)
—First Date. (p. 594)
—First Evil. (p. 594)
—Five Masks of Dr. Scream. (p. 601)
—Frankenstein's Dog. (p. 629)
—Fright Knight & the Ooze: Twice Terrifying Tales. (p. 639)
—Ghost Beach. (p. 670)
—Ghost Camp. (p. 670)
—Ghost Next Door. (p. 671)
—Ghouls Gone Wild. (p. 673)
—Girlfriend. (p. 679)
—Good, the Bad & the Very Slimy. Park, Trip, illus. (p. 700)
—Goosebumps Graphix 02: Terror Trips. (p. 702)
—Goosebumps Wanted: the Haunted Mask. (p. 702)
—Got Cake? Park, Trip, illus. (p. 703)
—Great Smelling Bee. Park, Trip, illus. (p. 718)
—Grito de la Mascara Maldita. (p. 724)
—Halloween Party. (p. 738)
—Haunted Car. (p. 753)
—Haunted Mask. (p. 753)
—Haunting Hour. (p. 754)
—Have You Met My Ghoulfriend? (p. 754)
—Heads, You Lose. (p. 757)
—Heinie Prize. Park, Trip, illus. (p. 762)
—Help! We Have Strange Powers! (p. 766)
—Hide & Shriek & Who's Been Sleeping in My Grave? Twice Terrifying Tales. (p. 777)
—Hora de Las Pesadillas. Batlles Vinn, Camila, tr. (p. 797)
—Horror at Camp Jellyjam. (p. 799)
—Horror at Chiller House. (p. 799)
—How I Got My Shrunken Head. (p. 810)
—How I Met My Monster. (p. 810)
—How to Be a Vampire. (p. 815)
—It Came from Beneath the Sink! (p. 893)
—It Came from Ohio! - My Life as a Writer. (p. 893)
—It's the First Day of School... Forever! (p. 899)
—Killer's Kiss. (p. 956)
—Little Shop of Hamsters. (p. 1036)
—Little Shop of Monsters. Brown, Marc, illus. (p. 1036)
—Lose, Team, Lose! Park, Trip, illus. (p. 1054)
—Midnight Games. (p. 1138)
—Midsummer Night's Scream. (p. 1139)
—Mis Amigos Me llaman Monstruo. (p. 1149)
—Mis Amigos Me Llaman Monstruo (My Friends Call Me Monster) (p. 1149)
—Monster Blood. (p. 1166)
—Monster Blood for Breakfast! (p. 1166)
—Monstruos en el Campamento. (p. 1170)
—Mutacion Fatal. (p. 1194)
—My Alien Parents (p. 1195)
—My Friends Call Me Monster. (p. 1209)
—New Girl. (p. 1244)
—Night in Terror Tower. (p. 1253)
—Night of the Creepy Things. Park, Trip, illus. (p. 1254)
—Night of the Giant Everything. (p. 1254)
—Night of the Living Dummy. (p. 1254)
—Night of the Werecat. (p. 1254)
—Nightmare Hour. (p. 1255)
—Nightmare on Clown Street. (p. 1255)
—One Day at Horrorland. (p. 1294)
—Padres de Otra Dimension. (p. 1317)
—Party Games: A Fear Street Novel. (p. 1326)
—Party Poopers. Park, Trip, illus. (p. 1326)
—Perfect Date. (p. 1341)
—Phantom of the Auditorium. (p. 1349)
—Planet of the Lawn Gnomes. (p. 1368)
—Please Don't Feed the Vampire a Give Yourself Goosebumps Book. (p. 1373)
—Punk'd & Skunked. Park, Trip, illus. (p. 1417)
—Red Rain. (p. 1454)
—Return of the Mummy. (p. 1464)
—Revenge of the Lawn Gnomes. (p. 1466)
—Revenge of the Living Dummy. (p. 1466)
—Revenge of the Shadow People & the Bugman Lives! Twice Terrifying Tales. (p. 1466)
—Rich Girl. (p. 1469)
—Rotten School Park, Trip, illus. (p. 1490)
—Rotten School #12: Battle of the Dum Diddys. Park, Trip, illus. (p. 1491)
—Rotten School #15: Calling All Birdbrains. Park, Trip, illus. (p. 1491)
—Rotten School #16: Dumb Clucks. Park, Trip, illus. (p. 1491)
—Rotten School - Dudes, the School Is Haunted! Park, Trip, illus. (p. 1491)
—Rottenest Angel. Park, Trip, illus. (p. 1491)
—Say Cheese & Die. (p. 1518)
—Say Cheese & Die Screaming! (p. 1518)
—Say Cheese - And Die Screaming! (p. 1518)
—Scarecrow Walks at Midnight. (p. 1519)
—Scary Summer. (p. 1521)
—Scream of the Haunted Mask. (p. 1532)
—Secret Admirer. (p. 1540)
—Shake, Rattle, & Hurl! Park, Trip, illus. (p. 1558)
—Shocker on Shock Street. (p. 1568)
—Slappy New Year! (p. 1588)
—Son of Slappy. (p. 1611)
—Stay Away from the Tree House & Eye of the Fortuneteller: Twice Terrifying Tales. (p. 1645)
—Stay Out of the Basement. (p. 1645)
—Stepsister. (p. 1648)
—Streets of Panic Park. (p. 1667)
—Switched. (p. 1691)
—Taste of Night. (p. 1707)
—Teacher from Heck. Park, Trip, illus. (p. 1709)
—Temptation. (p. 1718)
—Terror Trips. Thompson, Jill et al, illus. (p. 1722)
—Three Faces of Me (p. 1742)
—Trick or Trap. (p. 1786)
—Vampire Breath. (p. 1832)
—Wanted: The Haunted Mask. (p. 1856)
—Weirdo Halloween. (p. 1873)
—Welcome to Camp Nightmare. (p. 1873)
—Welcome to Camp Slither. (p. 1873)
—Welcome to Dead House. (p. 1873)
—Werewolf of Fever Swamp. (p. 1875)
—When the Ghost Dog Howls. (p. 1904)
—Who's Your Mummy? (p. 1921)
—Why I Quit Zombie School. (p. 1925)
—Why I'm Afraid of Bees. (p. 1925)
—Wizard of Ooze. (p. 1943)
—Yo Fui un Zombi. (p. 1971)
—You Can't Scare Me! (p. 1975)
—Zombie Halloween. (p. 1988)
—Zombie Town (p. 1988)
Stine, R. L., ed. see International Thriller Writers Association Staff.
Stine, R. L., jt. auth. see Classic Goosebumps.
Stine, R. L., jt. auth. see Keenan, Sheila.
Stine, R. L., jt. auth. see Scholastic, Inc. Staff.
Stine, R. L., jt. auth. see Windham, Ryder.
Stine, R. L., ed. Fear: 13 Stories of Suspense & Horror. (p. 579)
—!Peligro! Las Historias de Terror Favoritas Del Autor de Pesadillas. Alonso Blanco, Victoria, tr. (p. 1336)
Stingley, Quinton. My Little Adventure. (p. 1212)
Stingley, Tanya. Jonas & the Legend of the Dark Forest. (p. 925)
—Jonas & the Pride of Fiona. (p. 925)
Stinnett, Leia A. In the Mirror I See, God's Reflection Within Me: A Workbook for Teenagers. (p. 866)
—Other Me. (p. 1306)
Stinson, Aimee. Championship Game (p. 289)
Stinson, Aimee & Sornson, Kathy. Bearless City (p. 151)
Stinson, Doug. Protecting the Nation's Borders. (p. 1412)
Stinson, Douglass, ed. Protecting America's Borders. (p. 1412)
Stinson, Jim. Video - Digital Communication & Production. (p. 1841)
Stinson, June. Basset Named Fred. (p. 143)
—Milton Hears a Train. (p. 1144)
—Yellow Kitty Rags. (p. 1970)
Stinson, Kathy. 101 Ways to Dance (p. 2000)
—Bare Naked Book. Collins, Heather, illus. (p. 139)
—Big or Little? Goffe, Toni, illus. (p. 183)
—Big or Little? Bell, Jennifer, illus. (p. 183)
—Fish House Secrets. (p. 598)
—Great Bike Race (p. 714)
—Highway of Heroes (p. 779)
—Man with the Violin. Petricic, Dusan, illus. (p. 1086)
—Mom & Dad Don't Live Together Anymore. Oelofsen, Vian, illus. (p. 1161)
—One More Clue (p. 1296)
—One Year Commencing. (p. 1297)
—Parfois Grand, Parfoit Petit. Homel, David, tr. from ENG. (p. 1324)
—Pocket Can Have a Treasure in It. Betteridge, Deirdre, illus. (p. 1375)
—Red Is Best. Lewis, Robin Baird, illus. (p. 1454)
—Seven Clues (p. 1554)
—What Happened to Ivy (p. 1885)
Stinson, Paul. Sales, Marketing, Business & Finance. (p. 1504)
Stinson, Rick. Kyle Busch: NASCAR Driver. (p. 969)
Stipe, Michael, et al. Haiku Year. (p. 735)
Stirewalt, Robert A. Memories of Growing Up (p. 1126)
Stirling, Janet, jt. auth. see Richards, Dillon H.
Stirling, S. M. Sunrise Lands. (p. 1677)
Stirling, Tricia. When My Heart Was Wicked. (p. 1904)
Stirnkorb, Patricia. All about Me! Regular Version. (p. 43)
—All about Me! Inspirational Version (p. 43)
—Place for the King: Christmas from the Angels Point of View. Bock, Suzanne, illus. (p. 1365)
—Stranger Danger: The reluctantly written but absolutely necessary book for todays boys & Girls. (p. 1665)
Stislow, John, illus. see Sarvady, Andrea, et al.
Stites, Bill. Democracy: A Primary Source Analysis. (p. 425)
Stites, Clara. Lixia of Gold Mountain: A Story of Early California. (p. 1042)
Stites, Ranae & Buethe, Amanda. Cooperative Mathematics. (p. 365)
Stites, Richard. History of Russia: Peoples, Legends, Events, Forces: Since 1800. (p. 784)
Stites, Theresa. Orange Peel. (p. 1302)
Stites, Theresa, illus. see Porter, Harry.
Stith, Jennifer, ed. see Armstrong, Linda.
Stith, Jennifer, ed. see Mullarkey, Lisa.
Stitt, Sue, illus. see Chisholm, Jane & Reid, Straun.
Stitt, Sue, illus. see Gibson, Ray.
Stivender, Ed. Raised Catholic (Can You Tell?) (p. 1436)
Stiver, Joan. Door in the Floor: An Underground Railroad Adventure. (p. 470)
Stiver, Megan. Great Bellybutton Cover-Up. (p. 714)
—Say Please to the Honeybees. (p. 1518)
StJohn, Amanda. 5 Steps to Drawing Dogs & Cats. Regan, Dana, illus. (p. 1992)
—5 Steps to Drawing Monsters. Girouard, Patrick, illus. (p. 1992)
—5 Steps to Drawing Sea Creatures. Close, Laura Ferraro, illus. (p. 1992)
—Bouki Cuts Wood: A Haitian Folktale. Revell, Cindy, illus. (p. 216)
—Frog King: An African Folktale. Perrins, Karen, illus. (p. 640)
—Frog Went A-Traveling: A Russian Folktale. Wenzel, David, illus. (p. 640)
—How a Library Works. Ostrom, Bob, illus. (p. 804)
—How an e-Book Works. Ostrom, Bob, illus. (p. 804)
—How to Check Out a Book. Ostrom, Bob, illus. (p. 816)
—How to Find a Book. Ostrom, Bob, illus. (p. 819)
—How to Find Information Online. Ostrom, Bob, illus. (p. 819)
—How to Treat a Book. Ostrom, Bob, illus. (p. 822)
—Medio Pollito (Half-Chick) A Mexican Folktale. Todd, Sue, illus. (p. 1120)
—Pied Piper of Hamelin: A German Folktale. Bonder, Dianna, illus. (p. 1356)
—Sophie & Sadie Build a Sonnet. Marten, Luanne, illus. (p. 1613)
St.John, Sue. Everybody Knows Emma. (p. 543)
St-Laurent, Christina. Macaroni's Midnight Madness. (p. 1067)
St-Laurent, Sebastien. COMPLETE Effect & HLSL Guide. Engel, Wolfgang, ed. (p. 352)
—Complete HLSL Reference. Wolfgang, Engel, ed. (p. 353)
sto, illus. see Bontempelli, Massimo.
Stobaugh, James. American Literature Student. (p. 62)
—British Literature Student. (p. 230)
—Skills for Literary Analysis Student: Encouraging Thoughtful Christians to be World Changers. (p. 1585)
—Skills for Rhetoric: Encouraging Thoughtful Christians to Be World Changers. (p. 1585)
—Skills for Rhetoric Student. (p. 1585)
—World Literature Student. (p. 1956)
Stock, Catherine. Porc in New York. (p. 1386)
—Vinnie & Abraham. (p. 1843)
Stock, Catherine, illus. see Figley, Marty Rhodes.
Stock, Catherine, illus. see FitzGerald, Dawn.
Stock, Catherine, illus. see Lunde, Darrin P.
Stock, Catherine, illus. see Mohammed, Khadra & Williams, Karen Lynn.
Stock, Catherine, illus. see Moreillon, Judi.
Stock, Catherine, illus. see Sanchez, Anita.
Stock, Catherine, illus. see Walter, Mildred Pitts.
Stock, Catherine, illus. see Whitaker, Suzanne George.
Stock, Catherine, illus. see Williams, Karen Lynn.
Stock, Catherine, jt. auth. see Lunde, Darrin P.
Stock, Gregory. Kids' Book of Questions. (p. 952)
—Kids' Book of Questions. (p. 955)
Stock, Jennifer York, jt. auth. see Benson, Sonia.
Stock, Jonathan. World Sound Matters. (p. 1958)
Stock, Lisa. Battle for Naboo. (p. 145)
—Lego Friends Perfect Pets. (p. 990)
—Perfect Pets. (p. 1342)
Stock, Lisa, jt. auth. see Dorling Kindersley Publishing Staff.
Stock, Lisa, jt. auth. see Saunders, Catherine.
Stock, Lisa & Dorling Kindersley Publishing Staff. Friends Perfect Pets, Level 2. (p. 638)
Stock, Rose, illus. see Freeman, Marcia S.
Stockburger, Susan. Adventures of Sugar Pie! (p. 23)
Stockdale, Patricia Ann, jt. auth. see Mullen, Michael.
Stockdale, Sean, jt. auth. see Strick, Alex.
Stockdale, Sean & Strick, Alex. Max the Champion. Asquith, Ros, illus. (p. 1111)
Stockdale, Stephanie. Sidney Visits Australi. (p. 1573)
Stockdale, Susan. Bring on the Birds Stockdale, Susan, illus. (p. 229)
—Carry Me! Animal Babies on the Move Stockdale, Susan, illus. (p. 271)
—Fabulous Fishes Stockdale, Susan, illus. (p. 560)
—Spectacular Spots Stockdale, Susan, illus. (p. 1624)
—Stripes of All Types Stockdale, Susan, illus. (p. 1667)
—Stripes of All Types: Rayas de Todas Las Tallas. (p. 1667)
—Stripes of All Types / Rayas de Todas Las Tallas Stockdale, Susan, illus. (p. 1667)
Stockel, Martin T., jt. auth. see Johanson, Chris.
Stockel, Martin W., et al. Auto Diagnosis, Service, & Repair. (p. 117)
—Auto Diagnosis, Service, & Repair Instructor's Manual. (p. 117)
—Auto Fundamentals. (p. 117)
—Auto Fundamentals Instructor's Manual. (p. 117)
Stockelbach, Ed, illus. see Dupuy, Diane.
Stocker, Jeffrey D., jt. auth. see Root, Edwin R.
Stockham, Jess. Baby Sitter. (p. 128)
—Beauty & the Beast: Flip up Fairy Tales. (p. 154)
—Beauty & the Beast. (p. 154)
—Big Day Out. (p. 181)
—Boy Who Cried Wolf. (p. 219)
—Cinderella. (p. 320)
—Cockerel, the Mouse & the Little Red Hen. (p. 337)
—Feeling Great!/Sentirse Bien! (p. 580)
—Frog Prince. (p. 640)
—Little Red Riding Hood. (p. 1035)
—Looking Good!/Lucir Bien! (p. 1051)
—Moving House! (p. 1183)
—Nursery. (p. 1273)
—Oh Baby! (p. 1280)
—On the Go!/a Moverse! (p. 1290)
—Party! (p. 1325)
—Peekaboo- Forest. (p. 1335)
—Peekaboo-Jungle. (p. 1335)
—Peekaboo- Ocean. (p. 1335)
—Peekaboo- Safari. (p. 1335)
—Peep-O! (p. 1335)
—Princess & the Pea. (p. 1402)
—Puss in Boots. (p. 1420)
—Recycling! (p. 1453)
—Rumpelstiltskin. (p. 1495)
—Shopping! (p. 1569)
—Sleepover. (p. 1589)
—Steadfast Tin Soldier. (p. 1645)
—Stone Soup. (p. 1652)
—Town Mouse, Country Mouse. (p. 1773)
Stockham, Jess, illus. see Baker, Sue & Stockham, Jessica.
Stockham, Jess, illus. see Peters, Polly.
Stockham, Jess, illus. see Twinn, A.
Stockham, Jess, et al. Frog Prince. (p. 640)
Stockham, Jessica. Having Fun! (p. 755)
—Little Red Riding Hood. (p. 1035)
—Making Friends! (p. 1081)
—Princess & the Pea. (p. 1402)
—Rumpelstiltskin. (p. 1495)
—Runaway Train. (p. 1496)
—Taking It Easy! (p. 1698)
—Together! (p. 1761)
—Visiting the Dentist. (p. 1845)
—Visiting the Doctor. (p. 1845)
—Visiting the Hospital. (p. 1845)
—Visiting the Vet. (p. 1845)
Stockham, Jessica, jt. auth. see Baker, Sue.
Stockham, Jessica, tr. Down by the Station. (p. 474)
Stockings, J. B. Stubborn Princess. (p. 1668)
Stockland, Patricia M. Anthill Home Repair. Haugen, Ryan, illus. (p. 89)
—Assassination of John F. Kennedy. (p. 107)
—Barnyard Buddies Ouren, Todd, illus. (p. 139)
—Big Banana Hunt. Haugen, Ryan, illus. (p. 178)
—Black. Woolf, Julia, illus. (p. 194)
—Blue. Woolf, Julia, illus. (p. 202)
—Brown. Woolf, Julia, illus. (p. 231)
—Clean up the Watering Hole! Haugen, Ryan, illus. (p. 330)
—Colors Woolf, Julia, illus. (p. 345)
—Colors - 6 Titles Woolf, Julia, illus. (p. 345)
—Gray. Woolf, Julia, illus. (p. 713)
—Green. Woolf, Julia, illus. (p. 721)
—In the Buffalo Pasture. Ouren, Todd, illus. (p. 865)
—In the Cattle Yard. Ouren, Todd, illus. (p. 865)
—In the Chicken Coop. Ouren, Todd, illus. (p. 865)
—In the Goat Yard. Ouren, Todd, illus. (p. 866)
—In the Goose Pen. Ouren, Todd, illus. (p. 866)
—In the Horse Stall. Ouren, Todd, illus. (p. 866)
—In the Llama Yard. Ouren, Todd, illus. (p. 866)
—In the Pig Pen. Ouren, Todd, illus. (p. 867)
—In the Rabbit Hutch. Ouren, Todd, illus. (p. 867)
—In the Sheep Pasture. Ouren, Todd, illus. (p. 867)
—In the Turkey Pen. Ouren, Todd, illus. (p. 867)
—Look at a Birch Tree. (p. 1048)
—Look at a Maple Tree. (p. 1048)
—Look at a Palm Tree. (p. 1048)
—Look at a Pine Tree. (p. 1048)
—Look at an Ash Tree. (p. 1048)
—Look at an Oak Tree. (p. 1048)
—On the Duck Pond. Ouren, Todd, illus. (p. 1290)
—Orange. Woolf, Julia, illus. (p. 1301)

—Peanut Picking. Haugen, Ryan, illus. (p. 1332)
—Pink. Woolf, Julia, illus. (p. 1359)
—Purple. Woolf, Julia, illus. (p. 1419)
—Red. Woolf, Julia, illus. (p. 1453)
—Red Eyes or Blue Feathers: A Book about Animal Colors Ouren, Todd, illus. (p. 1454)
—Sand, Leaf, or Coral Reef: A Book about Animal Habitats. Ouren, Todd, illus. (p. 1510)
—Stop the Grassfires! Haugen, Ryan, illus. (p. 1653)
—Strange Dances & Long Flights: A Book about Animal Behavior. Ouren, Todd, illus. (p. 1665)
—Stripes, Spots, or Diamonds: A Book about Animal Patterns. Ouren, Todd, illus. (p. 1667)
—Tan. Woolf, Julia, illus. (p. 1704)
—Tiger Toothache. Haugen, Ryan, illus. (p. 1748)
—White. Woolf, Julia, illus. (p. 1912)
—Yellow. Woolf, Julia, illus. (p. 1970)
Stockland, Patricia M., jt. auth. see Brecke, Nicole.
Stockley, C., jt. auth. see Oxlade, C.
Stockley, Corinne. Illustrated Dictionary of Biology. Rogers, Kirsteen, ed. (p. 857)
Stockley, Corinne, ed. see Watt, Fiona.
Stockley, Corinne, jt. auth. see Oxlade, Chris.
Stockley, Corinne, et al. Illustrated Dictionary of Physics. Johnson, Fiona, illus. (p. 857)
—Usborne Illustrated Dictionary of Science: A Complete Reference Guide to Physics, Chemistry & Biology. Rogers, Kirsteen, ed. (p. 1827)
—Usborne Illustrated Dictionary of Science. Rogers, Kirsteen, ed. (p. 1827)
Stockley, Gerry, illus. see Arnone, Marilyn P. & Coatney, Sharon.
Stockman, Hollie. Leon the Lizard. (p. 992)
Stockman, Jack, illus. see Carlson, Melody.
Stockman Opat, Jamie. Uniquely Nebraska (p. 1818)
Stockman, Steve. Walk On: The Spiritual Journey of U2. (p. 1853)
Stocks, David. Moon Rabbit. (p. 1172)
Stocks, Mike, jt. auth. see Grant, John.
Stocksdale, Rosie (aka Rosemary). Roxy from the Bronx (p. 1492)
Stockstill. Jesus Nacio en Belen. (p. 916)
Stockstill, Gloria McQueen. Basket in the River. Girouard, Patrick, illus. (p. 143)
—Blind Man by the Road. Girouard, Patricia L., illus. (p. 199)
—Jesus Rose on Easter Morn: A Listen! Look! Book. Durrell, Julie, illus. (p. 916)
—To the Town of Bethlehem. Durrell, Julie, illus. (p. 1759)
Stockton, jt. auth. see Stockton, Frank R.
Stockton, Dede. Sammi Jo & the BEST Day EVER! (p. 1507)
—Sammi Jo & the Best Day Ever. (p. 1507)
Stockton, Frank, illus. see Kurlansky, Mark.
Stockton, Frank R. Buccaneers & Pirates. Varian, George & Clinedinst, B. West, illus. (p. 234)
—John Gayther's Garden & the Stories Told Therein. (p. 921)
—Ting-A-Ling. (p. 1755)
—What Might Have Been Expected. (p. 1892)
Stockton, Frank R. & Stockton. Griffin & the Minor Canon. Sendak, Maurice, illus. (p. 724)
Stockton, Frank Richard. Associate Hermits. (p. 107)
—Bee-Man of Orn. (p. 157)
—Bee-Man of Orn. Lynch, P. J., illus. (p. 157)
—Bee-Man of Orn. Sendak, Maurice, illus. (p. 157)
—Bee-Man of Orn & Other Fanciful Tales. (p. 157)
—Buccaneers & Pirates of Our Coasts. (p. 234)
—Buccaneers & Pirates of Our Coasts. Varian, George & Clinedinst, B. West, illus. (p. 234)
—Captain's Toll-Gate. (p. 264)
—Jolly Fellowship. (p. 924)
—Kate Bonnet: The Romance of a Pirate's Daughter. (p. 944)
—Lady or the Tiger. (p. 971)
—Round-about Rambles in Lands of Fact & Fancy. (p. 1491)
—Ting-a-Ling Tales. (p. 1755)
—What Might Have Been Expected. (p. 1892)
Stockton, Frank Richard, et al. Simply Suspense. (p. 1578)
Stockton, Greta, illus. see Toutz-Hager, Tanya.
Stockton, Kevin, illus. see Batcher, Jack.
Stockton, Lucille. God in a Child's World & King Catfish Roonie & His Neighbors. (p. 689)
—Hallo, Mallo & Pallo: The Ostracized Ostrich Family. Sampson, April, illus. (p. 737)
Stockum, Hilda Van, see Van Stockum, Hilda.
Stockwell, Gail Provost, jt. auth. see Provost, Gary.
Stockwell, Jeff. Fandango: The Key to the Wind. Stockwell, Pel, illus. (p. 570)
Stockwell, Pel, illus. see Stockwell, Jeff.
Stockwell-Moniz, Marc & Moniz, Teresa. George Washington's Unsung Heroes: He Couldn't Have Done It Without Them. the Men & Women Who Helped Win the American Revolution. (p. 665)
Stoddard, Chad L. Why Is Santa Fat? (p. 1925)
Stoddard, Charles Warren. Exits & Entrances. (p. 548)
—For the Pleasure of His Company. (p. 616)
—Island of Tranquil Delights. (p. 892)
—Poems of Charles Warren Stoddard. (p. 1376)
Stoddard, Jack. Cowboy Dreams. (p. 374)
Stoddard, Jeff, illus. see Bishop, Jennie.
Stoddard, Jeffery. Pete & Pillar: A Story of Friendship Based on John 15:13: the Big Rain. Stoddard, Jeffery, illus. (p. 1346)
—Skid & the Too Tiny Tunnel: A Story of Courage Based on Deuteronomy 31:6. Fogle, Robin & Rhodes, Karen, eds. (p. 1584)
Stoddard, Jutta. Miss Elli. (p. 1151)
Stoddard, Laura. Dreamosphere. (p. 484)
Stoddard, Rosie & Marshall, Phillip. Horse: The Essential Guide for Young Equestrians. Hamilton, Libby, ed. (p. 799)
Stoddard, T. R. Don't Ask, Don't Tell. (p. 466)
Stoddard, William O. Dab Kinzer: A Story of a Growing Boy. (p. 398)
—Dab Kinzer A Story of A Growing Boy. (p. 398)
Stoddart, Heidi Jardine. Back to the Beach (p. 130)
—East to the Sea (p. 498)
—Return to the Sea (p. 1465)
Stoddart, Lady. Eskdale Herd Boy: A Scottish Tale for the Instruction & Amusement of Young Persons. (p. 535)
Stodden, Lindsay, illus. see Powell, Anthony.
Stoeber, Michael. Reclaiming Theodicy: Reflections on Suffering, Compassion & Spiritual Transformation. (p. 1452)
Stoebner, Ben E. Learning How to Read & to Write. (p. 985)
Stoehr, Shelley. Crosses. (p. 385)
—Tomorrow Wendy: A Love Story. (p. 1765)
—Weird on the Outside. (p. 1872)
Stoeke, Janet Morgan. Letting Go. Stoeke, Janet Morgan, illus. (p. 1003)
—Loopy Coop Hens. (p. 1052)
—Loopy Coop Hens. Stoeke, Janet Morgan, illus. (p. 1052)
—Loopy Coop Hens: Oh No! a Fox! (p. 1052)
—Loopycoop Hens. (p. 1052)
—Minerva Louise on Christmas Eve. Stoeke, Janet Morgan, illus. (p. 1146)
—Minerva Louise on Halloween. Stoeke, Janet Morgan, illus. (p. 1146)
—Pip's Trip. (p. 1362)
—Pip's Trip. Stoeke, Janet Morgan, illus. (p. 1362)
Stoeker, Fred. Tactics: Securing the Victory in Every Young Man's Battle. (p. 1695)
Stoff, Laurie. Rise & Fall of the Soviet Union. (p. 1474)
Stoff, Laurie S., ed. Rise & Fall of the Soviet Union. (p. 1474)
Stoff, Michael B., jt. auth. see Davidson, James West.
Stoffel, Dominique, photos by see Gomel, Luc.
Stoffels, Karlijn. Heartsinger. (p. 760)
—Heartsinger. Watkins, Laura, tr. from DUT. (p. 760)
Stofko, Michael D. Has Anybody Seen Me? (p. 752)
—Tale of Taylor the Tailor. (p. 1700)
—Visit from the Zoo. (p. 1845)
Stoh, Emily. Roger Meets Sam. Stoh, Judy, illus. (p. 1484)
Stoh, Judy, illus. see Stoh, Emily.
Stohl, Kevin. Time Chronicles Ozone (p. 1751)
Stohl, Margaret. Icons. (p. 851)
—Idols. (p. 852)
Stohl, Margaret, jt. auth. see Garcia, Kami.
Stohner, Anu. Brave Charlotte. Wilson, Henrike, illus. (p. 223)
—Brave Charlotte & the Wolves. Wilson, Henrike, illus. (p. 223)
Stohner, Anu & Wilson, Henrike. Brave Charlotte. Wilson, Henrike, illus. (p. 223)
Stohr, Cynthia, et al. Easy Does it Articulation: A Language Approach Materials Book. (p. 500)
Stohs, Anita. Here Is the Church. Mitter, Kathy, illus. (p. 770)
—Praise God with Puppets. (p. 1393)
Stohs, Anita Reight. Manualidades Faciles con Vasos de Papel. Beckmann, Ewaldo, tr. (p. 1089)
Stohs, Anita Reith. Hush Little One: A Lullaby for God's Children. Kanzler, John, illus. (p. 830)
—Hush, Little One: A Lullaby for God's Children. Kanzler, John, tr. (p. 830)
—Manualidades Faciles con Platos de Papel. (p. 1089)
—Oh, Come, Little Children. Huang, Benrei, illus. (p. 1280)
—Praise God with Banners. (p. 1393)
—Praise God with Paper Bags. (p. 1393)
—Praise God with Paper Cups: 45 Easy Bible Crafts; Grades 1-5. Koehler, Ed, illus. (p. 1393)
—Praise God with Shapes. (p. 1393)
Stoicheff, Peter & Taylor, Andrew, eds. Future of the Page. (p. 651)
Stoick, Jean, jt. auth. see Sams, Carl R.
Stoick, Jean, jt. auth. see Sams, Carl R., II.
Stoick, Jean, jt. auth. see Sams, Carl R., II.
Stoick, Jean, jt. photos by see Sams II, Carl R.
Stoick, Jean, jt. photos by see Sams, Carl R., II.
Stoick, Jean, photos by see Llewellyn, Bridget McGovern.
Stoick, Jean & Sams, Carl R., II, photos by. First Snow in the Woods. (p. 596)
Stoick, Jean & Sams II, Carl R., photos by. Stranger in the Woods: Snowflake Edition. (p. 1665)
Stojanova, Elena, illus. see Zake, Daiga.
Stojanovic, Laura, photos by see Hellmich, Mittie.
Stojic, Manya. Rain. Stojic, Manya, illus. (p. 1434)
Stojic, Manya, illus. see Collins Educational Staff & Hawes, Alison.
Stojic, Manya, illus. see Hawes, Alison.
Stojic, Manya, illus. see Roddie, Shen.
Stojic, Manya, illus. see Wilson-Max, Ken.
Stokely, Ted. Yaya & Uncle Ted Go Walk! (p. 1968)
Stoker, Bram. Bram Stoker/Dracula. Redondo, Nestor, illus. (p. 222)
—Count Dracula. (p. 369)
—Dracula: Retold from the Bram Stoker Original. Akib, Jamel, illus. (p. 476)
—Dracula. (p. 476)
—Dracula. Bryant, Clive, ed. (p. 476)
—Dracula. Schuler, Susan, tr. (p. 476)
—Drácula. Schuler, Susan, tr. (p. 476)
—Dracula. Jones, Barry, illus. (p. 476)
—Dracula. Kliros, Thea, illus. (p. 476)
—Dracula. McKowen, Scott, illus. (p. 476)
—Dracula. DiTerlizzi, Tony, illus. (p. 476)
—Dracula. Williams, Anthony, illus. (p. 476)
—Dracula. Gilbert, Anne Yvonne, illus. (p. 476)
—Mummy. Miroglio, Brian, illus. (p. 1191)
Stoker, Bram, jt. auth. see Fuentes, Benny.
Stoker, Bruce, ed. see Lingo, Susan L.
Stokes, Betty Southard. Postcards from George, 1763-1781: George Rogers Clark Writes Home to Virginia from the Kentucky Wilderness. Cable, Annette, illus. (p. 1388)
Stokes, Brenda. Bella's Blessings. DesRosiers, Trisha, illus. (p. 162)
Stokes, Carolyn Ashe. Multy: The Search to Belong. . . a Story of Hope. (p. 1190)
Stokes, Donald & Stokes, Lillian. Stokes Field Guide to Warblers. (p. 1651)
Stokes, Erica M. Economy of Mexico. (p. 503)
—Finding a Financial Balance: The Economy of Mexico. (p. 587)
—Sports of Mexico. (p. 1633)
—Victoria! the Sports of Mexico. (p. 1840)
Stokes, Gary. Dinosaur Drool. (p. 442)
Stokes, Jamie. Muslim World. (p. 1194)
Stokes, Jeffery D. Que Bien Suena: Mastering Spanish Phonetics & Phonology. (p. 1423)
—!Qué Bien Suena! Text. (p. 1423)
—World Languages. (p. 1956)
Stokes, Johanna, jt. auth. see Cosby, Andrew.
Stokes, John, illus. see Wilde, Oscar.
Stokes, John A., et al. Students on Strike: Jim Crow, Civil Rights, Brown, & Me. (p. 1669)
Stokes, Jordan & Belinkie, Matt. Gilded Delirium. (p. 676)
Stokes, K. Lynn. Clouded Visions. (p. 334)
Stokes, Katherine. Motor Maids in Fair Japan. (p. 1179)
Stokes, Kathy. Insurance Operations. (p. 879)
Stokes, Kathy E. Insurance Operations. (p. 879)
Stokes, Kirstin, jt. auth. see Clark, Cherith.
Stokes, Lillian, jt. auth. see Stokes, Donald.
Stokes, Mark. Prostate Cancer: Current & Emerging Trends in Detection & Treatment. (p. 1412)
Stokes, N. L. Mystery of the Missing Teacup. (p. 1225)
Stokes, Paula. Art of Lainey. (p. 102)
—Liars, Inc. (p. 1005)
Stokes, Phil. Phillip & Dickie. (p. 1350)
Stokes, Roy Eliot. Andy at Yale: Or the Great Quadrangle Mystery. (p. 73)
Stokes, Tanya C. 101 Ways You Can Save Money: Take Control of Your Financial Future. (p. 2000)
Stokes, Tawny. Static. (p. 1644)
Stokholm, Susan Mary. Between a Shadow & the Moon. (p. 172)
Stoklasa, JoAnne. Oliver & I: The Long Way Home. (p. 1285)
—Travels of Timmy & Thomas: A Tale of Two Turtles. (p. 1780)
—Travels of Timmy & Thomas: Trouble in Tumbletown. (p. 1780)
Stolarski, Jerry, jt. auth. see Rice, Cindy.
Stolarz, Laurie Faria. Black Is for Beginnings. (p. 196)
—Blue Is for Nightmares. Zins, Rebecca, ed. (p. 203)
—Deadly Little Games. (p. 417)
—Deadly Little Lessons. (p. 417)
—Project 17. (p. 1410)
—Red Is for Remembrance. (p. 1454)
—Return to the Dark House. (p. 1465)
—Silver Is for Secrets. (p. 1576)
—Welcome to the Dark House. (p. 1874)
—White Is for Magic. Karre, Andrew, ed. (p. 1913)
Stolarz, Laurie Faria, jt. auth. see Valentino, Amanda.
Stolberg, Tina. Little Shrew Caboose. O'Neill, Philomena, illus. (p. 1036)
Stolfo, Paul. Wright Brothers. (p. 1963)
Stolinski, Eddie Ree, jt. auth. see Eddie Ree Stolinski, Ree Stolinski.
Stoll, Annie, illus. see Wallace, Daniel.
Stoll, Emily. Ookie! Southard, Jan, illus. (p. 1298)
Stoll, Krisit, jt. auth. see Clayton, Gidget.
Stoll, Kristen, jt. auth. see Stoll, Scott.
Stoll, Mark, jt. auth. see Boomgaard, Peter.
Stoll, Scott. Cupcake Boy. Amy Belle Elementary School, illus. (p. 392)
Stoll, Scott & Stoll, Kristen. God's Garden Friends. (p. 691)
Stolle, Dietlind, jt. auth. see Hooghe, Marc.
Stolle, Rachel Jeanette Hall. Why Do Our Loved Ones Die, Aunt Lou? (p. 1924)
Stollers, Veronica & Keyishian, Elizabeth. Frequently Asked Questions about Smoking. (p. 636)
Stollinger, Heide, illus. see Dahiméne, Adelheid.
Stoloff, Maxene. Maxy Poppinz: A Contemporary Tale about a Girl & Her New Nanny. Stoloff, Maxene, illus. (p. 1112)
Stoltenberg, Nathan, illus. see Marler, Jerilyn.
Stoltz, Adrienne & Bass, Ron. Let Me Wake. (p. 994)
—Lucid. (p. 1062)
Stoltz, Donald R. Bubble Flight. Wiesner, Al, illus. (p. 233)
Stoltz, Susan. Sharkey Helps ChooChoo. Sylvester, Suzanne, photos by. (p. 1562)
Stoltzfus, Sherman Matthew. Little Bear Builds a Wigwam. Zimmerman, Edith Fay Martin & Kanagy, Audrey Ann Zimmerman, illus. (p. 1024)
Stolz, Donald R. Classroom Times: Charactoons & Rhymes. Thornton, Barbara, illus. (p. 329)
Stolz, Joelle. Shadows of Ghadames. Temerson, Catherine, tr. (p. 1558)
Stolz, Mary. Emmett's Birthday Pig. (p. 520)
—Pigeon Flight. Tinkelman, Murray, illus. (p. 1357)
Stolze, Greg. Rites of the Dragon. (p. 1475)
Stolzenberg, Mark. Be a Clown. (p. 148)
Stomann, Allan, illus. see Ball, Duncan.
Stone. Lucky 13 Card Game. (p. 1062)
Stone, A. R., illus. see McKinna, Caelaach.
Stone, Adam. Apollo 13 Mission. (p. 91)
—Bermuda Triangle. (p. 167)
—Big Show. (p. 183)
—Challenger Explosion. (p. 289)
—Deepwater Horizon Oil Spill. (p. 423)
—Edge. (p. 504)
—ESP. (p. 536)
—Ghosts. (p. 672)
—Haunted Houses. (p. 753)
—John Cena. (p. 921)
—Kane. (p. 942)
—Near-Death Experiences. (p. 1239)
—Randy Orton. (p. 1438)
—Titanic Disaster. (p. 1757)
—Triple H. (p. 1787)
—Undertaker. (p. 1816)
Stone, Amy. Creek. (p. 380)
—Jackie Chan. (p. 903)
—Jewish Americans. (p. 917)
—Jim Carrey. (p. 917)
—Oneida. (p. 1298)
Stone, Amy M., jt. auth. see Dwyer, Helen.
Stone, Amy Wingrove. I Love You Every Minute. Lennhoff, Andrew, illus. (p. 843)
Stone, Andrew & Bryan, Jessica. Well... What's All That Drilling About? Pender, Rachel, illus. (p. 1874)
Stone Arch Books. April Showers & Cinco de Mayo Nguyen, Dustin, illus. (p. 93)
—Batman: Li'l Gotham Nguyen, Dustin Tri, illus. (p. 144)
—Christmas & New Year's Eve Nguyen, Dustin, illus. (p. 312)
—Halloween & Thanksgiving Nguyen, Dustin, illus. (p. 737)
—Mother's Day & Father's Day Nguyen, Dustin, illus. (p. 1178)
—St. Patrick's Day & Easter Nguyen, Dustin, illus. (p. 1638)
—Valentine's Day & the Lunar New Year Nguyen, Dustin, illus. (p. 1830)
Stone Arch Books & Fisch, Sholly. DC Super Friends (p. 415)
Stone Arch Books (Firm : Afton, Minn.) Staff. Hansel & Gretel: The Graphic Novel Dietrich, Sean, illus. (p. 743)
Stone Arch Books Staff. Beauty & the Beast: The Graphic Novel Feldman, Luke, illus. (p. 154)
—Cinderella: The Graphic Novel Timmins, Jeffrey Stewart, illus. (p. 320)
—Jack & the Beanstalk: The Graphic Novel Tercio, Ricardo, illus. (p. 902)
—John Henry - Hammerin' Hero. Evergreen, Nelson, illus. (p. 922)
—Legend of Johnny Appleseed. Lamoreaux, M. A. & Lamoreaux, Michelle, illus. (p. 988)
—Pecos Bill: Colossal Cowboy. Weber, Lisa K., illus. (p. 1334)
—Red Riding Hood: The Graphic Novel Rivas, Victor, illus. (p. 1454)
—Robin Hood Tobon, Sara, tr. (p. 1480)
—Robin Hood Tobon, Sara, tr. from ENG. (p. 1480)
—Rumpelstiltskin: The Graphic Novel Alanis, Erik Valdez Y., illus. (p. 1495)
—Tall Tale of Paul Bunyan. Blecha, Aaron, illus. (p. 1704)
Stone Arch Books Staff, jt. auth. see Andersen, Hans Christian.
Stone Arch Books Staff, jt. auth. see Meister, Cari.
Stone Arch Books Staff & Sutton, Laurie S. Superman: Comic Chapter Books Vecchio, Luciano, illus. (p. 1683)
Stone Arch Books Staff, et al. Batman: Comic Chapter Books Vecchio, Luciano, illus. (p. 144)
Stone, B. J. Girl on the Bluff. (p. 678)
Stone, Benjamin, ed. see Ma, Wing Shing & Lau, Ding Kin.
Stone, Bryan, illus. see Blobaum, Cindy.
Stone, Bryan, illus. see Brown, Cynthia Light & Brown, Nick.
Stone, Bryan, illus. see Diehn, Andi.
Stone, Bryan, illus. see Fisher, Verna.
Stone, Bryan, illus. see Latham, Donna.
Stone, Bryan, illus. see Mooney, Carla.
Stone, Bryan, illus. see Reilly, Kathleen M.
Stone, Bryan, illus. see Van Vleet, Carmella.
Stone, Bryan, illus. see Yasuda, Anita.
Stone, Bryan, jt. auth. see Yasuda, Anita.
Stone, Caroline, jt. auth. see Dorling Kindersley Publishing Staff.
Stone, Charlene. Greatest Fishing Adventure of a Lifetime: American Kids Greatest Adventures. (p. 719)
Stone, Chuck. Squizzy the Black Squirrel: A Fabulous Fable of Friendship. Jackson, Jeannie, tr. (p. 1637)
Stone, Connie. Tractor Green Day. Barnes, Garry, illus. (p. 1775)
Stone, Dan. Historiography of the Holocaust. (p. 783)
Stone, Danton. Basketball. (p. 143)
Stone, David, illus. see Evatt, Harriet.
Stone, David, illus. see Ryan, Jessica.
Stone, David Lee. Shadewell Shenanigans. (p. 1557)
Stone, Diane, illus. see Evangelista, Colette.
Stone, Dori. Beyond the Fence: A Journey to the Roots of the Migration Crisis. (p. 174)
Stone, Elaine Murray. Dorothy Day: Champion of the Poor. Kelley, Patrick, illus. (p. 471)
Stone, Elaine Murray, jt. auth. see Rayburn, Cathy.
Stone, Emma. Loholt Scrimminge & the Moor-Land Quest. (p. 1045)
Stone, Ethel B. Wild Bill Hickok & Deputy Marshal Joey. Timmins, William, illus. (p. 1929)
Stone, Forrest. Ant & Grasshopper Show. (p. 88)
—Fox & Grapes at Belleville Elementary. (p. 626)
—Loki & the Magic Hammer: A Norse Myth. (p. 1045)
Stone, George. Muscle: A Minor League Legend. (p. 1192)
Stone, Glyn A., jt. auth. see Stone, Glyn.
Stone, Glyn & Stone, Glyn A. Spain, Portugal & the Great Powers, 1931-1941. (p. 1620)
Stone, Heather Duffy. Fighter's Alley. (p. 585)
—Over the Tracks. (p. 1314)
—This Is What I Want to Tell You. (p. 1737)
Stone, Helen, illus. see Bennett, Anna Elizabeth.
Stone, Ilene & Grenz, Suzanna M. Jessie Benton Fremont: Missouri's Trailblazer. (p. 914)
Stone, Jade. Whispering Willow Woods. (p. 1912)
Stone, James, jt. auth. see Stone, Sandra.
Stone, Jamie, ed. Danny Dino Ventures Out. (p. 405)
Stone, Janet, jt. auth. see Barone, Deborah.
Stone, Janet, jt. auth. see Miller, Reagan.
Stone, Jasmine. Stripped to the Bone. (p. 1668)
—Symphony X. (p. 1693)
Stone, Jeff. Crane. (p. 376)
—Five Ancestors Book 6: Mouse. (p. 599)
—Five Ancestors Out of the Ashes #1: Phoenix. (p. 599)
—Five Ancestors Out of the Ashes #2: Lion. (p. 599)
—Five Ancestors Out of the Ashes #3: Jackal. (p. 599)
—Monkey. (p. 1164)
—Snake. (p. 1596)
—Tiger. (p. 1748)
Stone, Jennifer Arlene. Freud's Body Ego or Memorabilia of Grief: Lucian Freud & William Kentridge. (p. 637)
Stone, Jessica J. Picnic at the Zoo. (p. 1355)
Stone, Jodi. I Want to Catch a Dragonfly. (p. 848)
—Lady Bug. Herring, Kip, illus. (p. 970)
Stone, John, illus. see Russell, D. Z.
Stone, Jon. Another Monster at the End of This Book. Smollin, Michael, illus. (p. 88)
—Monster at the End of This Book. Smollin, Michael, illus. (p. 1166)
Stone, Jonny, illus. see Salter, Michelle Lewis.
Stone, Joyce M., illus. see Stone, Kelly P.
Stone, Judith. Billie the Buffalo Goes to Great Sand Dunes National Park. (p. 187)
—Billie the Buffalo Goes to Town. (p. 187)
Stone, Julia. Lion Book of Nursery Rhymes. (p. 1020)
—Little Bear's Sparkly Christmas. Muss, Angela, illus. (p. 1024)

Stone, Juliana. Boys Like You. (p. 220)
—Some Kind of Normal. (p. 1609)
Stone, Karen, ed. see Shadrick, Crystal Star.
Stone, Karen P., ed. see Parker, James S.
Stone, Kate. ABC Train. (p. 3)
—Happy Birthday, Mouse! (p. 745)
—Heads & Tails. (p. 757)
—Mouse Goes to School. (p. 1182)
Stone, Kate, illus. see Andrews McMeel Publishing, LLC Staff.
Stone, Kate, jt. auth. see Accord Publishing Staff.
Stone, Kate, jt. auth. see Cole, Jeff.
Stone, Kate & Accord Publishing Staff. Bunnies for Tea. (p. 242)
Stone, Kathrine Thompson, ed. see Thompson, Shannon Raines.
Stone, Kazuko G., illus. see Gollub, Matthew.
Stone, Kazuko G. & Keido, Ippo. Butterfly's Dream: Children's Stories from China. (p. 248)
Stone, Kelly P. What Do Pets Do When They Go up to Heaven? Stone, Kelly P. & Stone, Joyce M., illus. (p. 1882)
Stone, Kelsey. Predahil Chronicles. (p. 1394)
Stone, Kyle M., illus. see Esbaum, Jill.
Stone, Kyle M., illus. see Lewis, J. Patrick.
Stone, L. Creepy Crawlers Discovery Library. (p. 381)
Stone, Larry. Ken Griffey, Jr. The Home Run Kid. Rains, Rob, ed. (p. 948)
Stone, Laura. Little Lulu Learns a Lesson. (p. 1031)
—Miss Clarissa & Her Musical Shoes. (p. 1151)
—Tulia Turtle Finds Her Talents. (p. 1796)
Stone, Lori. Bubba Bullfrog for Sheriff. (p. 233)
Stone, Lyn, illus. see Taylor, Dereen.
Stone, Lynn. Cocker Spaniels. (p. 337)
—Como Usan Los Animales Sus Alas?/How Do Animals Use Their Wings ? Serafini, Estela, tr. from ENG. (p. 351)
—Flowers. (p. 608)
—Fruit. (p. 645)
—How Do Animals Use Their Ears? (p. 806)
—How Do Animals Use Their Flippers? (p. 806)
—Leaves. (p. 986)
—Roots. (p. 1488)
—Seeds. (p. 1547)
—Space (Skywatch) (p. 1619)
—Stems. (p. 1647)
Stone, Lynn M. A-10 Thunderbolt II. (p. 1)
—Aircraft Carriers. (p. 31)
—American Quarter Horses. (p. 63)
—Amphibious Assault Ships. (p. 66)
—Arabian Horses. (p. 94)
—Bald Eagles. (p. 133)
—Basset Hounds. (p. 143)
—Battleships. (p. 147)
—Border Collies. (p. 213)
—Box Turtles. Stone, Lynn M., photos by. (p. 216)
—Códigos de Color: Color Codes. (p. 338)
—Deserts. (p. 429)
—Exotic Cats. (p. 548)
—F/A-22 Raptor. (p. 559)
—Forests. (p. 618)
—Giant Pandas. Su, Keren, photos by. (p. 674)
—Goalies. (p. 687)
—Grasslands. (p. 712)
—Grizzlies. Stone, Lynn M., photos by. (p. 724)
—Horns, Humps, & Hooks. (p. 798)
—Jellyfish. (p. 912)
—Labradoodles. (p. 970)
—Nighthawk F-117A. (p. 1255)
—Oceans. (p. 1277)
—Paint Horses. (p. 1318)
—Pitchers. (p. 1364)
—Predators Discovery Library (p. 1395)
—Pugs. (p. 1415)
—Quarterbacks. (p. 1423)
—Rodeo. (p. 1484)
—Rodeo Bronc Riders. (p. 1484)
—Sea Stars. (p. 1535)
—Shortstops. (p. 1569)
—Strikers. (p. 1667)
—Submarines. (p. 1671)
—Tigers. (p. 1749)
—Wetlands. (p. 1877)
—Wild Horses. (p. 1929)
—Zebras. (p. 1985)
Stone, Marie. On Their Own: A Journey to Jamestown. (p. 1292)
Stone, Monica. Thank You, Mrs. Mel! (p. 1725)
Stone, Nancy Medaris, jt. auth. see Loendorf, Lawrence L.
Stone, Natalie. Monkey in a Tree Counts 1-2-3. Stone, Natalie, illus. (p. 1165)
Stone, Oliver & Kuznick, Peter J. Untold History of the United States: Young Readers Edition. (p. 1823)
Stone, Pam. Oscar's Adventures in the Woods: True story about a turtle that comes back every year to find his Friend. (p. 1305)
—Watermelon Party. (p. 1864)
Stone, Penny. Complicated Mourning & Grief Blocks: How to Move Forward Past Our Pain. (p. 354)
—How to Help Someone Who Is Grieving. (p. 820)
—My World Is Upside Down: Making Sense of Life after Confronting Death. (p. 1221)
—Surviving the Loss of a Parent. (p. 1687)
—Taste of Cultures: Italy. (p. 1707)
Stone, Phoebe. Boy on Cinnamon Street. (p. 218)
—Deep down Popular. (p. 423)
—Romeo & Juliet Code. (p. 1486)
—Romeo Blue. (p. 1486)
Stone, Phoebe, illus. see Sasso, Sandy Eisenberg.
Stone, Reuben. Guardians of the Cambrian Lode: An Ancient People - A Timeless Quest. (p. 728)
Stone, Russell, ed. see Hoffman, Aaron M.
Stone, Sandra & Stone, James. Alaska We Love. Stone, Sandra & Stone, James, photos by. (p. 34)
Stone, Sandra J. Playing: A Kid's Curriculum. Kizer, Fran, illus. (p. 1372)
Stone, Steve. Warriors Verses Warriors. Stone, Steve, illus. (p. 1859)
Stone, Summer. Lobster Trips. (p. 1044)
Stone, Susan, jt. auth. see Hughes, Karyn.
Stone, Susheila. Eid Ul-Fitr. (p. 507)
Stone, Suzanne. Lake Tahoe: The Guidebook with a point of View. (p. 972)
Stone, Tamara Ireland. Every Last Word. (p. 542)
—Time after Time. (p. 1751)
—Time Between Us. (p. 1751)
Stone, Tanya Lee. A Is for America: A Patriotic Alphabet Book. Kelley, Gerald, illus. (p. 1)
—Abraham Lincoln - A Photographic Story of a Life. Dorling Kindersley Publishing Staff, ed. (p. 6)
—Almost Astronauts: 13 Women Who Dared to Dream. (p. 48)
—Amelia Earhart. (p. 58)
—Bad Boy Can Be Good for a Girl. (p. 131)
—Chickens. (p. 300)
—Courage Has No Color: The True Story of the Triple Nickles - America's First Black Paratroopers. (p. 372)
—Elephants. (p. 511)
—Elizabeth Leads the Way: Elizabeth Cady Stanton & the Right to Vote. Gibbon, Rebecca, illus. (p. 513)
—Frogs. (p. 641)
—Good, the Bad, & the Barbie: A Doll's History & Her Impact on Us. (p. 700)
—Gorillas. (p. 703)
—Hippos. (p. 781)
—House That Jane Built: A Story about Jane Addams. Brown, Kathryn, illus. (p. 804)
—Lobsters. (p. 1044)
—Octopuses. (p. 1278)
—P Is for Passover. Lucas, Margeaux, illus. (p. 1316)
—Peacocks. (p. 1332)
—Pigs. (p. 1358)
—Polar Bears. (p. 1379)
—Rhinos. (p. 1467)
—Sandy's Circus: A Story about Alexander Calder. Kulikov, Boris, illus. (p. 1511)
—Sharks. (p. 1562)
—Snakes. (p. 1596)
—T Is for Turkey: A True Thanksgiving Story. Kelley, Gerald, illus. (p. 1694)
—Tigers. (p. 1749)
Stone, Tanya Lee & Dorling Kindersley Publishing Staff. Laura Ingalls Wilder. (p. 980)
Stone, Tiffany. Floyd the Flamingo: And His Flock of Friends Shoemaker, Kathryn, illus. (p. 608)
Stone, Vicki L. Why Should I Stay A Virgin? (p. 1926)
Stone, Vicky. Jamaica. (p. 906)
Stone, Wendy, illus. see Williams, Karen Lynn.
Stone-Barker, Holly, illus. see De Las Casas, Dianne.
Stone-Barker, Holly, illus. see De Las Casas, Dianne.
Stone-Barker, Holly, illus. see De Las Casas, Dianne.
Stone-Barker, Holly, illus. see de Las Casas, Dianne.
Stone-Barker, Holly, illus. see Horning, Sandra.
Stonebraker Wright, Susan. Enchanted Costume Shop. (p. 523)
Stonehouse, Bernard. & Bertram, Esther. Truth about Animal Communication. Francis, John, illus. (p. 1794)
Stonehouse, Frederick. My Summer at the Lighthouse: A Boy's Journal. (p. 1219)
Stonelake, Rebecca. Tale of Ella & Cinder: Legend One, Book One of the Mosaic Tales. (p. 1699)
Stoneman, Sonya. First Aid in Reading: Program Book. (p. 592)
—First Aid in Reading. (p. 592)
—First Aid in Spelling. (p. 592)
Stoner, Alexis, illus. see Gerbracht, Edie.
Stoner, David. Dancer's Story. (p. 402)
—Historia de Dancer / Dancer's Story. (p. 782)
Stoner, Denise, jt. auth. see Marden, Kathleen.
Stoner, Diane. Do You Know My Friend, Jesus? (p. 458)
Stoner, Eileen M. Inky & Dinky: Mindy .... A Tale of Change. (p. 874)
Stoner, Gary, jt. auth. see DuPaul, George J.
Stoner, Marcia. Signs of Faith: Bible Verses for Teens. (p. 1574)
Stoner, Marcia, compiled by. Teaching Tips for Terrified Teachers: A Must Have for Children's Sunday School. (p. 1710)
Stoner, Mark R., jt. auth. see Perkins, Sally J.
Stones, Brenda, jt. auth. see Feldman, Thea.
Stones, Brenda & Feldman, Thea. Kingfisher Readers L2 What We Eat. (p. 960)
Stones, Yvonne. Olivia's Magical Moment. (p. 1287)
Stonesifer, Gertrude. Peanut Butter Kid. Rogers, Denny, illus. (p. 1332)
—Sister & Me. (p. 1581)
—Then & Now Stories. Nelson, William, illus. (p. 1729)
St-Onge, Claire. Caillou: L'anniversaire. (p. 251)
St-Onge, Donna Na-Tasa Katherine. Eye of Isis (p. 557)
St-Onge, Julie-Ann. Passage to Fairywell. (p. 1326)
Stontz, Karen & Malone, Kelly. Autism & PDD Concepts How Does Becca Bunny Feel? (p. 117)
—Autism & PDD Concepts How Many, Becca Bunny. (p. 117)
—Autism & PDD Concepts What Time Is it, Becca Bunny. (p. 117)
—Autism & PDD Concepts Where are they Hiding, Becca Bunny? (p. 117)
Stooke, Andrew, illus. see Blacklaws, Troy.
Stookey, Nathaniel, jt. auth. see Snicket, Lemony, pseud.
Stoop, David A. Forgiving the Unforgivable. (p. 619)
Stoop, David & Stoop, Jan. When Couples Pray Together. (p. 1901)
Stoop, Jan, jt. auth. see Stoop, David.
Stoop, Naoko. All Creatures Great & Small. (p. 44)
—Red Knit Cap Girl. (p. 1454)
—Red Knit Cap Girl & the Reading Tree. (p. 1454)
—Red Knit Cap Girl to the Rescue. (p. 1454)
Stoop, Naoko, illus. see Collins Thoms, Susan.
Stoppard, Miriam. Nuevo Libro del Embarazo y Nacimiento: Guia Practica y Completa para Todos los Futuros Padres. McKenna, Nancy Durrell, photos by. (p. 1270)
Storad, Conrad J. Aparato Circulatorio. Translations.com Staff, tr. from ENG. (p. 91)
—Aparato Circulatorio (the Circulatory System) Translations.com Staff, tr. (p. 91)
—Circulatory System. (p. 322)
—Day & Night. (p. 412)
—Desert Night Shift: A Pack Rat Story. Jensen, Nathaniel P., illus. (p. 429)
—Don't Ever Cross That Road! An Armadillo Story. Jensen, Nathaniel P., illus. (p. 467)
—Earth Is Tilting! (p. 496)
—Earth's Changing Surface. (p. 498)
—Earth's Crust. (p. 498)
—Fossil Fuels. (p. 623)
—Galápagos Tortoises. (p. 653)
—Hippos. (p. 781)
—Javelinas. (p. 910)
—Large Sitting Armadillo Character. Jensen, Nathaniel P., illus. (p. 975)
—Lizards for Lunch: A Roadrunner's Tale. (p. 1043)
—Mars. (p. 1096)
—Our Sun Brings Life. (p. 1310)
—Piranhas. (p. 1362)
—Rattlesnake Rules. Hagelberg, Michael & Jensen, Nathaniel P., illus. (p. 1440)
—Small Standing Armadillo Character. Jensen, Nathaniel P., illus. (p. 1592)
—Studying Weather & Climates. (p. 1670)
—Uncovering Earth's Crust. (p. 1812)
—What's the Weather Like Today? (p. 1900)
—Your Circulatory System. (p. 1980)
Storch, Ellen N. Here We Go! Storch, Ellen N., illus. (p. 770)
Storch, Ellen N., illus. see Heady, Heather.
Storch, Ellen N., illus. see Hensley, Sarah M.
Storch, Ellen N., illus. see Jarrell, Pamela R.
Storch, Ellen N., illus. see Muench-Williams, Heather & Jarrell, Pamela R.
Storch, Ellen N., illus. see Muench-Williams, Heather.
Storch, Ellen N., illus. see Mullican, Judy & Williams, Heather L.
Storch, Ellen N., illus. see Mullican, Judy.
Storch, Ellen N., illus. see Vonthron, Satanta C.
Storch, Ellen N., illus. see Williams, Heather L. & Muench-Williams, Heather.
Storck, Patrick. Muppet Sherlock Holmes. Mebberson, Amy, illus. (p. 1191)
Storden, Thom. Amazing Baseball Records (p. 54)
—Amazing Basketball Records (p. 54)
—Amazing Football Records (p. 54)
—Amazing Hockey Records (p. 54)
—Epic Sports Records (p. 532)
Storeby, Jordan. Boy's Book of Daily Thoughts: For Ages 8 To 12. (p. 220)
Storer, Florence, illus. see Field, Eugene.
Storer, Jen. Quincy Jordan. (p. 1428)
Storer, June. Kip, Brenda & Emong's Adventure. (p. 961)
Storer, Megan. Cowbelle - Snow Day. (p. 373)
Storer, Wendy. Bring Me Sunshine. (p. 228)
Stores, Teresa. Backslide. (p. 130)
Storey, Andrea. Heavens Gate Secrets Revealed. (p. 761)
Storey, Charles H. National Chess Syllabus Featuring the Bandana Martial Art Exam System. (p. 1231)
Storey, Jim, illus. see Eggleton, Jill.
Storey, Jim, illus. see Holden, Pam.
Storey, Lela Belle, illus. see Lozzi, Annette.
Storey, Linda, illus. see Carlson, Glenn E.
Storey, Mags, jt. auth. see Storey, Margaret.
Storey, Margaret & Storey, Mags. If Only You Knew (p. 854)
Storey, Melinda. Volcanoes: A Comprehensive Hands-on Science Unit. Mitchell, Judy & Lindeen, Mary, eds. (p. 1849)
Storey Publishing Staff. Eye See You. Balmuth, Deborah L. & Guare, Sarah, eds. (p. 558)
—Horses in Action! (p. 800)
—Petting Farm Poster Book. (p. 1349)
—Under the Sea Poster Book. (p. 1814)
Storey Publishing Staff & Danks, Hugh. Bug Book & Bug Bottle. (p. 236)
Storey, Rita. Animals. (p. 81)
—Christmas Book. (p. 313)
—Clay. (p. 330)
—Dinosaurs. (p. 444)
—Drum & Other Percussion Instruments. (p. 487)
—Fairies. (p. 562)
—Irish Dancing: And Other National Dances. (p. 887)
—Knights & Castles. (p. 964)
—Make Your Own Creative Cards. (p. 1079)
—Make Your Own Creative Cards (Do It Yourself Projects!) (p. 1079)
—Make Your Own Toys. (p. 1080)
—Make Your Own Toys (Do It Yourself Projects!) (p. 1080)
—Metal. (p. 1130)
—Piano & Other Keyboard Instruments. (p. 1354)
—Pirates. (p. 1363)
—Recorder & Other Wind Instruments. (p. 1452)
—Rock 'n' Roll: And Other Dance Crazes. (p. 1482)
—Rocks & Stones. (p. 1483)
—Street Jazz. (p. 1666)
—Tractors & Trucks. (p. 1775)
—Violin & Other Stringed Instruments. (p. 1843)
—Voice & Singing. (p. 1847)
—Wool & Cotton. (p. 1950)
Storey, Tony & Lidbury, Alan. Criminal Law. (p. 382)
Storey, William, jt. auth. see Kantor, Stuart.
Storie Tree Inc, Staff. Pocket Pearl of Light: Twinkle & Shinmet Come Home. (p. 1375)
Stories Of The Bible. Bedtime Bear Bible Stories. (p. 156)
storiesbypj.com. Willow, Too Soon, Too Late. Manny, illus. (p. 1934)
Storino, Sara, illus. see Hilgenberg, Bob & Muir, Roberto.
Storino, Sara, illus. see Posner-Sanchez, Andrea.
Stork, Elisabeth P., jt. auth. see Spyri, Johanna.
Stork, Francisco X. Irises. (p. 887)
—Last Summer of the Death Warriors. (p. 979)
—Marcelo in the Real World. (p. 1091)
Storm, Dunlop. Atlas of the Night Sky. Tirion, Wil & Rukl, Antonin, illus. (p. 113)
Storm, Falcon. Natalie the Not-So-Nasty: Tales from upon A. Time Series. (p. 1230)
—Persnickety Princess (Tales from upon A. Time - Book 1) (p. 1344)
Storm, Hannah, frwd. Buddy Booby's Birthmark. (p. 234)
Storm, Jeff. Petrified World, Determine Your Destiny No. 1: You Are the Hero of This Book! Chan, Harvey, illus. (p. 1348)
Storm, Jennifer. Deadly Loyalties. (p. 417)
Storm, Michael. Pulp7: A Sweet Deal, a Killer Calling, & a Man Inside. (p. 1416)
—Pulp7 Quartereader Sempill, illus. (p. 1416)
—Roboshop. (p. 1480)
Storm, Raen. God's Palette. (p. 691)
Storm, Rayne. Elemental Tarot for Kids (p. 510)
—In the Night Sky: The Astrological Zodiac for Children (p. 867)
Storm, Wilda. Write up A Storm! Take Rewarding Revisions by Storm. (p. 1964)
—Write up A Storm! ¿ Practice for Proficiency: Student Handbook 3rd Grade. (p. 1964)
—Write up A Storm! ¿ Writing Tools: A Student Guide ¿ Grade 2-3. (p. 1964)
Storm, Zed. Will Solvit & the Cannibal Cavemen. (p. 1932)
—Will Solvit & the Deadly Gladiator. (p. 1932)
—Will Solvit & the Dreaded Droids. (p. 1932)
—Will Solvit & the Mission of Menace. (p. 1932)
—Will Solvit & the Mummy's Curse. (p. 1932)
—Will Solvit & the T-Rex Terror. (p. 1932)
Stormer, Kate. Casey's Unexpected Friend. Lowes, Tom, illus. (p. 275)
—Rescue of Little Red. Lowes, Tom, illus. (p. 1462)
—Stranger in Casey's World. Lowes, Tom, illus. (p. 1665)
Storms, Patricia. Pirate & the Penguin. Storms, Patricia & Owlkids Books Inc. Staff, illus. (p. 1362)
Storms, Patricia, illus. see Jenkins, Diana R.
Storms, Patricia, illus. see Montgomery, Monte.
Storms, Patricia, illus. see Todd, Barbara.
Storper, Barbara. Janey Junkfood's Fresh Adventure! Making Good Eating Great Fun! Schneid, Frances E., illus. (p. 908)
Storr, Catherine. Chinese Egg. (p. 307)
Storr, Nicola, illus. see Sims, Janice.
Storr, Robert, et al. Alex Katz. (p. 36)
Storrie, Paul. Perseus: The Hunt for Medusa's Head [A Greek Myth]. Yeates, Thomas, illus. (p. 1344)
Storrie, Paul D. #02 Made for Each Other. Cowgur, Eldon, illus. (p. 1991)
—Amaterasu: Return of the Sun. Randall, Ron, illus. (p. 52)
—Amaterasu: Return of the Sun - A Japanese Myth. Randall, Ron, illus. (p. 52)
—Amaterasu. (p. 52)
—Beowulf: Monster Slayer. (p. 166)
—Beowulf: Monster Slayer. Randall, Ron, illus. (p. 166)
—Hercules: The Twelve Labors - A Greek Myth. Kurth, Steve, illus. (p. 769)
—Hercules. (p. 769)
—Made for Each Other Cowgur, Eldon, illus. (p. 1070)
—Nightmare on Zombie Island. Witt, David, illus. (p. 1255)
—Peril at Summerland Park. Carruthers, Sandy, illus. (p. 1343)
—Perseus: The Hunt for Medusa's Head. (p. 1344)
—Perseus: The Hunt for Medusa's Head. Yeates, Thomas, illus. (p. 1344)
—Robin Hood: Outlaw of Sherwood Forest. Yeates, Thomas, illus. (p. 1480)
—Terror in Ghost Mansion. Carruthers, Sandy, illus. (p. 1722)
—William Tell: A Swiss Legend. Yeates, Thomas, illus. (p. 1933)
—William Tell: One against an Empire [A Swiss Legend]. Yeates, Thomas, illus. (p. 1933)
—Yu the Great: Conquering the Flood. Carruthers, Sandy, illus. (p. 1983)
—Yu the Great: Conquering the Flood - A Chinese Legend. Carruthers, Sandy, illus. (p. 1983)
—Yu the Great. (p. 1983)
Storrs, Landon & Storrs, Landon R. Y. Second Red Scare & the Unmaking of the New Deal Left. (p. 1539)
Storrs, Landon R. Y., jt. auth. see Storrs, Landon.
Storti, Jill. Keiko the Koala. (p. 948)
Stortz, Diane. Adam Named the Animals from a to Z. Reed, Lisa, illus. (p. 11)
—Four Faithful Friends. (p. 625)
—I Can Praise God! (p. 836)
—Let's Shine Jesus' Light on Halloween. (p. 1000)
—Obeying God at Jericho. (p. 1275)
—Sweetest Story Bible for Toddlers Bailey, Sheila, illus. (p. 1690)
—Words to Dream On: Bedtime Bible Stories & Prayers Feyer, Diane Le, illus. (p. 1952)
Stortz, Diane & Holder, Jennifer. I Can Pray! Nobens, C. A., illus. (p. 836)
Stortz, Diane & Thomas Nelson & Sons Staff. Say & Pray Bible (p. 1518)
Stortz, Diane M. Sweetest Story Bible: Sweet Thoughts & Sweet Words for Little Girls Bailey, Sheila, illus. (p. 1690)
Story And Pictures By Neenie. Rachel & the Rose Silk Unicorn. (p. 1431)
Story, Dan. Where Wild Things Live: Wildlife Watching Techniques & Adventures. (p. 1910)
Story, Ken, jt. auth. see Pearce, Richard.
Story Rhyme Staff. Self-Esteem: Stories, Poetry & Activity Pages. Story Rhyme Staff, illus. (p. 1549)
Story, Rita. Belly Garden. Galluzzo, Madeline, illus. (p. 163)
Story, Ros. Pera Pera. (p. 1341)
Story Time Staff. Vowel Sounds: Rapping, Word Mapping & Rhyming. Doyle, Alfreda C., ed. (p. 1850)
Story Time Stories That Rhyme, prod. Kids Rhyme Stories Games & More- Teacher's Edition. (p. 955)
Stosch, Dawn. Science Math. (p. 1526)
Stossel, Sage. On the Loose in Boston. (p. 1290)
—On the Loose in Washington, D. C. (p. 1290)
Stossel, Sage, illus. see Wile, Mary Lee.
Stott, Ann. Always. Phelan, Matt, illus. (p. 51)

—I'll Be There. Phelan, Matt, illus. (p. 856)
—What to Do When You're Sent to Your Room. Gilpin, Stephen, illus. (p. 1894)
Stott, Apryl, illus. see Lazurek, Michelle S.
Stott, Apryl, illus. see Monchamp, Genny.
Stott, Carole. I Wonder Why Stars Twinkle. (p. 849)
—Stars & Planets. Bull, Peter, illus. (p. 1643)
Stott, Colin. Victorian Transport. (p. 1840)
Stott, Darrel E. Gods Joy Can Make A Difference. (p. 691)
—Indonesian Revival. (p. 872)
Stott, Dorothy. Ten in the Bed. (p. 1718)
Stott, Dorothy, illus. see Capucilli, Alyssa Satin.
Stott, Dorothy, illus. see Rikkers, Doris.
Stott, Dorothy, illus. see Simon, Mary Manz.
Stott, Jon C. Book of Tricksters: Tales from Many Lands (p. 212)
—Gerald McDermott & You McDermott, Gerald, illus. (p. 666)
Stott, Rebecca. Oyster. (p. 1316)
Stotter, Michael. Native Americans: Find Out About the World of North American Indians, with 400 Exciting Pictures & 15 Step-by-step Projects. (p. 1234)
Stotter, Mike. World of North American Indians. (p. 1957)
Stotter, Ruth. Loop of String: String Stories & String Stunts: Traditional & Original String Figures & Stories. Coffey, Kevin, illus. (p. 1052)
Stotts, Jasmyn & Jayda, illus. see Toles-Stotts, LaShunda.
Stotts, Stuart. Books in A Box: Lutie Stearns & the Traveling Libraries of Wisconsin. (p. 212)
—Curly Lambeau: Building the Green Bay Packers. (p. 394)
—Father Groppi: Marching for Civil Rights. (p. 577)
—Lucius Fairchild: Civil War Hero. (p. 1062)
—We Shall Overcome: A Song That Changed the World. Cummings, Terrance, illus. (p. 1868)
Stott-Thornton, Janet. Shadows. Barrett, Virginia, illus. (p. 1558)
Stouch, Ryan, illus. see Klick, Lisa.
Stoudemire, Amar'e. Double Team. Jessell, Tim, illus. (p. 473)
—Home Court. (p. 792)
—Home Court. Jessell, Tim, illus. (p. 792)
—Most Valuable. (p. 1177)
—Schooled. (p. 1523)
—Slam Dunk: Standing Tall & Talented. Jessell, Tim, illus. (p. 1587)
—Slam Dunk. (p. 1587)
—Standing Tall & Talented - Most Valuable. (p. 1639)
—Stat: Schooled. (p. 1644)
—STAT #4: Schooled. (p. 1644)
Stoughton, K. Come along on a Tour: With Angel & Henry. (p. 347)
Stout, C. Then Sings My Soul. (p. 1729)
Stout, Carol A. Proud to Be an American (p. 1413)
Stout, Frankie. Bats: Nature's Night Flyers. (p. 145)
—Bugs: In Flight. (p. 237)
—Bugs in Flight. (p. 237)
—Extreme Animals. (p. 556)
—Hummingbirds: Hovering in Nature. (p. 826)
—Nature's Best Jumpers. (p. 1237)
—Nature's Deadliest Animals. (p. 1237)
—Nature's Fastest Animals. (p. 1237)
—Nature's Nastiest Biters. (p. 1237)
—Nature's Slowest Animals. (p. 1237)
—Nature's Strongest Animals. (p. 1237)
—Ostriches: Nature's Biggest Birds. (p. 1306)
—Pelicans: Soaring the Seas. (p. 1335)
—Penguins: Nature's Coolest Birds. (p. 1337)
Stout, Glenn. Able to Play: Overcoming Physical Challenges. (p. 5)
—Baseball Heroes. (p. 141)
—Soldier Athletes. (p. 1607)
—Yes, She Can! Women's Sports Pioneers. (p. 1970)
Stout, Glenn, jt. auth. see Christopher, Matt.
Stout, Glenn & Christopher, Matt. Jackie Robinson: Legends in Sports. (p. 904)
—Muhammad Ali: Legends in Sports. (p. 1189)
Stout, Glenn & Williams, Ike. Against All Odds: Never Give Up. (p. 29)
—From Hardships to Championships. (p. 642)
Stout, Katie M. Hello, I Love You: A Novel. (p. 764)
—Hello, I Love You. (p. 764)
Stout, M. H. Day at the Zoo with Grandma. (p. 412)
—Saturdays at Grandma's House. (p. 1515)
Stout, Mary. Atlanta. (p. 112)
—Blackfoot. (p. 197)
—Blackfoot History & Culture. (p. 197)
—Shoshone History & Culture. (p. 1569)
Stout, Mary, jt. auth. see Dwyer, Helen.
Stout, Mary A. Aztec. (p. 122)
—Cree. (p. 380)
—Native American Boarding Schools (p. 1234)
Stout, Mary A., jt. auth. see Dwyer, Helen.
Stout, Mary A., jt. auth. see Stout, Mary.
Stout, Mary & Stout, Mary A. Hopi. (p. 797)
—Shoshone. (p. 1569)
Stout, Mary Gallagher & Gascot, John. Usa to Z. (p. 1826)
Stout, Shawn K. Ballerina Weather Girl. Martini, Angela, illus. (p. 134)
—Don't Chicken Out. Ying, Victoria, illus. (p. 467)
—Fiona Finkelstein, Big-Time Ballerina!! Martini, Angela, illus. (p. 589)
—Fiona Finkelstein Meets Her Match!! Martini, Angela, illus. (p. 589)
—Miss Matched. Martini, Angela, illus. (p. 1151)
—Penelope Crumb. (p. 1336)
—Penelope Crumb Is Mad at the Moon. (p. 1336)
—Penelope Crumb Never Forgets. Docampo, Valeria, illus. (p. 1336)
Stout, Shawn K. & Docampo, Valeria. Penelope Crumb Finds Her Luck. (p. 1336)
Stout, Timothy G. Japanese for Kids (p. 909)
Stout, William. William Stout - Animal Sketches from Around the World. (p. 1933)
—William Stout - Tribute to Ray Harryhausen. (p. 1933)
Stout, William, illus. see Matheson, Richard.
Stout, William, illus. see Smith, Sherwood.
Stout, William, text. Charles R. Knight Sketchbook (p. 292)
Stoutland, Allison. Take a Deep Breath: Little Lessons from Flowers for a Happier World. Hofner, Cathy, illus. (p. 1696)
—What Can I Do Today? To Make This World a Happier Place. Hofner, Cathy, illus. (p. 1880)
Stovall, Jo Ann Goldman. Do Dot, Family, & Friends: A Premier Story/Coloring Book. (p. 456)
Stovall, Sue A. Dream Valley. (p. 484)
Stover, Anne Long. Cloudy. Spears, Ashley E., illus. (p. 335)
Stover, Beth, illus. see Bentley, Dawn.
Stover, Elizabeth, jt. auth. see Morton, Debra.
Stover, Jo Ann. If Everybody Did. (p. 852)
Stover, Melissa Henry. Monkeys Taste Like Chocolate. (p. 1166)
Stow, Jenny, illus. see Riordan, James.
Stowasser, Peter & Burnett, James. Cupcake Capers: A Book about Take-Away Subtraction. (p. 392)
Stowbridge, Amarri, jt. auth. see Stanley, Sharina.
Stowe, Betsy. Calico Tales. . . & Others. (p. 253)
Stowe, Cynthia M. Understanding Special Education: A Helpful Handbook for Classroom Teachers. (p. 1816)
Stowe, Harriet Beecher. Betty's Bright Idea. (p. 172)
—First Christmas of New England & O. (p. 593)
—Key to Uncle Tom's Cabin (large Facsimile) Presenting the Original Facts & Documents upon which the Story Is Founded. (p. 950)
—Queer Little Folks. (p. 1425)
—Uncle Tom's Cabin: Or, Life among the Lowly. Vol. 1 Solimene, Laura, ed. (p. 1812)
—Uncle Toms Cabin Young Folks Edition Ill. (p. 1812)
Stowell, Brian, jt. auth. see Carroll, Lewis, pseud.
Stowell, Charlotte. God's Wonderful World (p. 692)
Stowell, Cinci, jt. auth. see Miller, Reagan.
Stowell, Gordon. Libro de Actividades Biblicas (Bible Story Activities) (p. 1006)
—Y Ddihangfa Anhygoel! Llyfr Drysfa Beiblaidd. Davies, Aled, ed. (p. 1968)
Stowell, Louie. Astronaut's Handbook IR. (p. 109)
—Brer Rabbit down the Well. Muszynski, Eva, illus. (p. 226)
—Look Inside Your Body. (p. 1049)
—Samurai. Engle, Jason, illus. (p. 1509)
—School for Super Villans. (p. 1523)
—Spooky Sticker Dressing. (p. 1631)
—Sticker Dressing Second World War. (p. 1650)
—Story of Astronomy & Space: Internet-Referenced. Allen, Peter, illus. (p. 1657)
—Usborne Big Book of Big Monsters. Fiorin, Fabiano, illus. (p. 1827)
—Wind-Up Pirate Ship. Fox, Christyan, illus. (p. 1935)
—Write & Draw Your Own Comics IR. (p. 1963)
Stowell, Louie, ed. see Leigh, Susannah.
Stowell, Louie, jt. auth. see Davidson, Susanna.
Stowell, Louie, jt. auth. see Davies, Kate.
Stowell, Louie, jt. auth. see Milbourne, Anna.
Stowell, Louie, jt. auth. see Pratt, Leonie.
Stowell, Louie, jt. auth. see Reid, Struan.
Stowell, Louie, jt. auth. see Sims, Lesley.
Stowell, Louie & Pearcey, Alice. Diggers Stencil Book. Doherty, Gillian, ed. (p. 439)
Stowell, Walton. Hopper's Furry. (p. 797)
Stower, Adam. Den. (p. 426)
—Naughty Kitty! Stower, Adam, illus. (p. 1237)
—Silly Doggy! Stower, Adam, illus. (p. 1575)
—Troll & the Oliver. Stower, Adam, illus. (p. 1788)
Stower, Adam, illus. see Baker, Kenneth, ed.
Stower, Adam, illus. see Clements, Andrew.
Stower, Adam, illus. see Johnson, Jane.
Stower, Adam, illus. see Jones, Marcia Thornton & Dadey, Debbie.
Stower, Adam, illus. see Pinkwater, Daniel M.
Stower, Adam, illus. see Sherry, Maureen.
Stowers, B. J. & Stowers, Hal. Hal Stowers & the Art of Life Blending: How to Keep Your Creative Juices Flowing Stowers, B. J., photos by. (p. 736)
Stowers, Hal, jt. auth. see Stowers, B. J.
Stoyanof, Debbie. Little Sock Monster. (p. 1036)
Stoyles, Pennie. A-Z of Health. (p. 2)
Stoyles, Pennie & Mulvany, Christine. A to Z of Scientific Discoveries. (p. 2)
Stoyles, Pennie & Pentland, Peter. Earth & Space. (p. 495)
—Everyday Technology. (p. 544)
—Human Body. (p. 825)
—Life on Earth. (p. 1012)
—Medicine & Health. (p. 1119)
—Power & Fuel. (p. 1389)
Straaten, Harmen Van, jt. auth. see Van Straaten, Harmen.
Strachan, Linda. Hamish Mchaggis & the Edinburgh Adventure. Collins, Sally J., illus. (p. 739)
—Hamish Mchaggis & the Ghost of Glamis. Collins, Sally J., illus. (p. 739)
—Hamish Mchaggis & the Search for the Loch Ness Monster. Collins, Sally J., illus. (p. 739)
—Hamish Mchaggis & the Skye Surprise. Collins, Sally J., illus. (p. 739)
Strachan-Davidson, J. R. Appian Civil Wars (p. 92)
Strachen, Iona. Adventures in a Red Tartan Duffle Coat. (p. 15)
Stracher, Cameron. Water Wars. (p. 1863)
Strack, Beth. Sammy the Snail's Bright Ideas. (p. 1508)
Strack, Jay. Identity Theft: The Thieves Who Want to Rob Your Future (p. 852)
Strack, Jay & Edwards, David. Life: How to Get There from Here (p. 1007)
Strack, Jay & Land, Richard. Mercury Rising: 8 Issues That Are Too Hot to Handle (p. 1127)
Strack, Jay & Lucado, Max. Leadership Rocks: Becoming a Student of Influence (p. 981)
Straczynski, J. Michael. Best of Spider-Man Youngquist, Jeff, ed. (p. 170)
—Book of Ezekiel Romita, John, Jr., illus. (p. 211)
—Fantastic Four (p. 571)
—Happy Birthday. Romita, John, Jr. & Romita, John, Sr., illus. (p. 744)
—Superman: Earth One 2. (p. 1683)
—Ten Grand Volume 1. (p. 1718)
Strader, Irm. What Came First. (p. 1880)
Stradley, Don. Schooled. (p. 1523)
Stradling, Jan. Animal Babies: Level H (p. 76)
—Buildings for a Purpose: Level K (p. 239)
—Earth Materials: Level I (p. 496)
—Erosion & Weathering: Level K (p. 534)
—Food for All: Level I (p. 613)
—Handle with Care: Level I (p. 740)
—Lights On: Level K (p. 1016)
—Look Up: Level I (p. 1050)
—Nests & Shelters: Level H (p. 1242)
—People & Places: Level I (p. 1339)
—Plants all Around: Level H (p. 1369)
—Ponds & Rivers: Level I (p. 1382)
—Rain Forest Life: Level I (p. 1434)
—Sense This: Level I (p. 1551)
—Sounds all Around: Level K (p. 1615)
—Spy on Spiders: Level K (p. 1636)
—Under Attack: Level I (p. 1813)
—You are Special: Level I (p. 1973)
Strady, Sophie. Memory of an Elephant: An Unforgettable Journey. Martin, Jean-Francois, illus. (p. 1126)
Straffi, Iginio. Winx Club: Magic Collection. (p. 1939)
Straffi, Iginio, jt. auth. see VIZ Media Staff.
Straffi, Iginio, jt. auth. see VIZ Media, .
Stragford, Robert. My Place in History: From Africa to America. (p. 1217)
Strahan, Jonathan. Life on Mars: Tales from the New Frontier. Strahan, Jonathan, ed. (p. 1012)
—Under My Hat: Tales from the Cauldron. (p. 1813)
Strahm, Jake, illus. see Strahm, Luke.
Strahm, Luke. Island of Beginnings. Strahm, Jake, illus. (p. 892)
Strain, Connie Rae. Perfect Imperfections: For Animal lovers of all Ages (p. 1342)
—Perfect Imperfections: For animal lovers of all Ages. (p. 1342)
Strain, Jim, jt. auth. see Chiodo, Stephen.
Strain Trueit, Trudi. Massachusetts. (p. 1102)
Strain-Trueit, Trudi. Christmas. (p. 312)
—Keeping a Journal. (p. 947)
—Valentine's Day. (p. 1830)
Strain-Trueit, Trudi, jt. auth. see Trueit, Trudi Strain.
Strait, Mark, et al, creators. Webber Interactive WH Questions Level 1: Whcd11. (p. 1870)
Straker, Bethany. Funny Bunny Fly. (p. 649)
Straker, Bethany, illus. see Atherton, Isabel.
Straker, Bethany, illus. see Duffett-Smith, James.
Straker, Bethany, illus. see Mannering, Rose.
Straker, Bethany, illus. see Ormand, Kate & Louise, Kate.
Straker, Bethany, jt. auth. see Atherton, Isabel.
Straley, Linda. Boundaries: To celebrate the joy of childhood & protect the Children. (p. 216)
Stram, Dawn. Fat Ladies Shouldn't Have Orange Hair! (p. 577)
Strambini, Karla. Extraordinary Mr. Qwerty. Strambini, Karla, illus. (p. 555)
Stranaghan, Crystal. 13th Floor: Colouring Outside the Lines. Bzymek, Izabela, illus. (p. 1995)
Stranaghan, Crystal J. Then It Rained. Espadaler, Rosa, illus. (p. 1729)
Stranaghan, Crystal J. & Bzymek, Izabela. Safety Superheroes: Preventing Grandparents from Falling. (p. 1502)
Strand, Angel & Black Lace Staff. Undressing the Devil. (p. 1817)
Strand, Claudia. Look at Me! The Art of the Portrait for Children. (p. 1048)
Strand, Jeff. Bad Day for Voodoo. (p. 131)
—Elrod McBugle on the Loose. (p. 516)
—I Have a Bad Feeling about This. (p. 839)
—Mandibles. (p. 1087)
Strand, Jessica. Dinner Parties: Simple Recipes for Easy Entertaining. Pearson, Victoria, photos by. (p. 441)
—Holiday Crafting & Baking with Kids: Gifts, Sweets, & Treats for the Whole Family! Herring, Aimée, photos by. (p. 788)
Strand, Jessica & Massman-Johnson, Tammy. Kids in the Holiday Kitchen. (p. 954)
Strand, Jessica, et al. Kids in the Holiday Kitchen. (p. 954)
Strand, John. Diaries. (p. 434)
Strand, Kai. Save the Lemmings. (p. 1516)
—Wishing Well. (p. 1941)
Strand, Mike. Meditations on Brain Injury (p. 1120)
Strand, Robert. Simple Tips for Simple Living - For Teens. (p. 1578)
Strand, Vibeke, jt. auth. see Johnson, Kent R.
Strand, Vivian, illus. see Larson, Elaine M., et al.
Strand, Vivian, illus. see Larson, Elaine Marie.
Strandberg, Mats, jt. auth. see Elfgren, Sara B.
Strang, Herbert. Round the World in Seven Days. (p. 1491)
—With Marlborough to Malplaquet. (p. 1942)
Strang, Kay, ed. see Lamb, Charles & Lamb, Mary.
Strange, Cordelia. Environmental Science & Protection: Keeping Our Planet Green. (p. 532)
—Medical Technicians: Health-Care Support for the 21st Century. (p. 1118)
—Physicians Assistants & Nurses: New Opportunities in the 21st-Century Health System. (p. 1353)
Strange, David. Why Grandpa Rides a Harley. (p. 1925)
Strange, David, jt. auth. see Vogl, Nancy.
Strange, Derek & Pearson Longman Staff. Girl Meets Boy. (p. 678)
Strange, J. R. Tree & the Light. Massivebrain.com, illus. (p. 1783)
Strange, Jason. 23 Crow's Perch Evergreen, Nelson & Kendall, Bradford, illus. (p. 1996)
—Basement of the Undead Parks, Phil, illus. (p. 141)
—Demon Card Evergreen, Nelson & Kendall, Bradford, illus. (p. 426)
—Faceless Friend Parks, Phil, illus. (p. 561)
—Full Moon Horror Parks, Phil & Dal Lago, Alberto, illus. (p. 646)
—Graveyard Plot Evergreen, Nelson & Kendall, Bradford, illus. (p. 712)
—Mothman's Shadow Parks, Phil, illus. (p. 1179)
—Mothman's Shadow Soleiman, Serg & Parks, Phil, illus. (p. 1179)
—Realm of Ghosts Parks, Phil, illus. (p. 1450)
—Strays Evergreen, Nelson & Kendall, Bradford, illus. (p. 1666)
—Text 4 Revenge Parks, Phil & Dal Lago, Alberto, illus. (p. 1724)
—To Wake the Dead Parks, Phil, illus. (p. 1759)
—Zombie Winter Parks, Phil, illus. (p. 1988)
—Zombie Winter Soleiman, Serg & Parks, Phil, illus. (p. 1988)
Strange, Jo. Justin Bieber Test Your Super-Fan Status: All New. (p. 940)
Strange, Katie, illus. see Hoffmann, Sara E.
Strange, Matthew. America at War: Military Conflicts, Home & Abroad in the 1800s. (p. 59)
—Bleeding, Blistering, & Purging: Health & Medicine in The 1800s. (p. 199)
—Guardians of the Home: Women's Lives in The 1800s. (p. 728)
—Jump Ropes, Jacks, & Endless Chores: Children's Lives in The 1800s. (p. 934)
Strange, Spencer. Operation Billion Gazillion. (p. 1300)
Strangway, Melissa. 56 Water Street. (p. 1997)
—Finding Hope. (p. 588)
Strapec, Amy, illus. see Silverman, Toby.
Strapp, James. Science & Technology. (p. 1525)
Strasburg, Sunny, illus. see Holbrook, John Robert.
Strasnick, Lauren. Her & Me & You. (p. 769)
—Nothing Like You. (p. 1268)
—Then You Were Gone. (p. 1729)
Strassburg, Brian, illus. see Humphrey, Sandra McLeod & Barker, Dan.
Strasser, Dirk. Lost in Space. (p. 1055)
Strasser, Myrna A. Saint Francis & the Nativity Bianchi, Fausto, illus. (p. 1503)
Strasser, Stephanie. Blue Bananas. (p. 202)
—Pink Peanut Butter. (p. 1360)
Strasser, Susanne, illus. see Schneider, Antonie & Maccarone, Grace.
Strasser, Todd. Abe Lincoln for Class President. (p. 4)
—Boot Camp. (p. 213)
—Can't Get There from Here. (p. 262)
—Close Out. (p. 333)
—Con-fidence. (p. 355)
—Count Your Blessings. (p. 370)
—Cut Back. (p. 396)
—Fallout. (p. 567)
—Famous. (p. 569)
—For Money & Love. (p. 616)
—Give a Boy a Gun. (p. 681)
—If I Grow Up. (p. 853)
—Is That an Angry Penguin in Your Gym Bag? (p. 890)
—Is That an Unlucky Leprechaun in Your Lunch? Swearingen, Greg, illus. (p. 890)
—Nighttime: Too Dark to See. Cushman, Doug, illus. (p. 1255)
—No Place. (p. 1259)
—Sidewayz Glory. Phillips, Craig, illus. (p. 1573)
—Slide or Die. Phillips, Craig, illus. (p. 1590)
—Stolen Kisses, Secrets, & Lies. (p. 1652)
—Take Off. (p. 1696)
—Too Dark to See. Cushman, Doug, illus. (p. 1766)
—Wave. (p. 1864)
Strasser, Todd & Thacker, Nola. Shore: Shirt & Shoes Not Required; LB (Laguna Beach) (p. 1569)
Stratemeyer, Edward. Dave Porter at Star Ranch. (p. 410)
—Marching on Niagara: The Soldier Boys of the Old Frontier. (p. 1092)
—Mystery at Putnam Hall: Or the School Chums' Strange Discovery. (p. 1223)
—Richard Dare's Venture. (p. 1469)
—Rover Boys at Colby Hall: Or the Struggles of the Young Cadets. (p. 1491)
—Rover Boys at College: The Right Road & the Wrong. (p. 1491)
—Rover Boys at College or the Right R. (p. 1491)
—Rover Boys at College or the Right Road & the Wrong. (p. 1491)
—Rover Boys at School: Or the Cadets of Putnam Hall. (p. 1491)
—Rover Boys in Business or the Search. (p. 1491)
—Rover Boys in Business or the Search for the Missing Bonds. (p. 1491)
—Rover Boys in Camp. (p. 1491)
—Rover Boys in the Air: From College Campus to the Clouds. (p. 1491)
—Rover Boys on a Hunt: Or the Mysterious House in the Woods. (p. 1491)
—Rover Boys on the Ocean: Or, a Chase for a Fortune. (p. 1491)
—Rover Boys on Treasure Isle. (p. 1491)
—With Washington in the West: A Soldier Boy's Battles in the Wilderness. (p. 1942)
—With Washington in the West or A Soldier Boy's Battles in the Wilderness. Shute, A. B., illus. (p. 1942)
Stratemeyer, Edward, jt. auth. see Alger, Horatio.
Stratford, Ann. Tara Toad Meets Roman the Robot Soldier. (p. 1706)
Stratford, Anne Margaret. My Daddy Is A Soldier. (p. 1201)
Stratford, Jordan. Case of the Missing Moonstone (the Wollstonecraft Detective Agency, Book 1) Murphy, Kelly, illus. (p. 274)
Stratford, S. J., jt. auth. see Matters, Print.
Stratford, Stevan, illus. see Qamaruddin, Rizwana.
Stratford, Stevan, jt. auth. see Radwan, Hassan.
Strathearn, Chris. Ant-Man: The Incredible Shrinking Suit. (p. 88)
—Marvel's Guardians of the Galaxy: Friends & Foes. (p. 1099)
—Superman Versus Bizarro. Mada Design, Inc Staff, illus. (p. 1684)
Strathearn, Chris, jt. auth. see Marvel Books Staff.
Strathergyffe, Paul. Curie & Radioactivity: The Big Idea. (p. 392)
Strathgryffe, Alexander. Drizzleys. (p. 485)
Strathie, Chae. Tickle Tree. Bernatene, Poly, illus. (p. 1747)
Strathie, Chae & Shoshan, Beth. My Dad! (p. 1200)
—My Mom! (p. 1214)

S

Strathy, Glen C. Dancing on the Inside. (p. 403)
Stratievsky, Adam. Classics for Children & Adults: Four-hand Piano Arrangements of Popular Works of Classical Music. (p. 328)
Stratman, Kay, illus. see Martin, Maria G.
Stratten, Lou. Hello, I'm Sir Frettirick! Let's Say Hello to Our New Friends! Bennett, Judy, ed. (p. 764)
Stratton, Allan. Borderline. (p. 214)
—Chanda's Secrets. (p. 289)
—Chanda's Wars. (p. 289)
—Grave Robber's Apprentice. (p. 712)
—Leslie's Journal. (p. 993)
Stratton, Bart. Arctic Mall Adventure. Riddle, Scott, illus. (p. 96)
Stratton, Erin. There's Nothing Wrong with Boys. Gregeory, Vicki, illus. (p. 1731)
Stratton, Helen, illus. see MacDonald, George.
Stratton, Jane, jt. auth. see Rush, Barbara.
Stratton, Steve. Plainridge. (p. 1366)
Stratton-Porter, Gene. At the Foot of the Rainbow. (p. 111)
—Birds of the Limberlost. (p. 192)
—Daughter of the Land. (p. 409)
—Freckles. (p. 632)
—Girl of the Limberlost. (p. 678)
—Girl of the Limberlost. Benda, Wladyslaw T., illus. (p. 678)
—Harvester. (p. 752)
—Strike at Shane's. (p. 1667)
Straub-Martin, Susan M. Legends, Loves & Great Lakes. (p. 990)
Strauch, Brenda. Tragic Endings: The Unwritten Series. (p. 1776)
Straumanis, Andrei. Organic Chemistry: A Guided Inquiry. (p. 1303)
Straus, Jane. Blue Book of Grammar & Punctuation: The Mysteries of Grammar & Punctuation Revealed. (p. 202)
Straus, Marc J., jt. auth. see Turkington, Carol.
Straus, Susan Farber. Healing Days: A Guide for Kids Who Have Experienced Trauma. Bogade, Maria, illus. (p. 757)
—Somebody Cares: A Guide for Kids Who Have Experienced Neglect. Keay, Claire, illus. (p. 1609)
Strausner, Marcia. Brady Does Christmas. (p. 221)
—Destination San Antonio, TX: A guide for the Journey. (p. 430)
Strauss, Bob. Field Guide to Dinosaurs of North America: And Prehistoric Megafauna. (p. 583)
Strauss, David, jt. ed. see Reddy, Prerana.
Strauss, Ed. Bible Freaks & Geeks Haya, Erwin, illus. (p. 175)
—Big Bad Bible Giants Carpenter, Anthony, illus. (p. 177)
—Big Bible Guide: Kids' Bible Facts & Q&a: Fun & Fascinating Bible Reference for Kids Ages 8-12. (p. 178)
—Devotions to Make You Smarter (p. 432)
—Devotions to Make You Stronger (p. 432)
—Devotions to Take You Deeper (p. 432)
—Good Always Wins—Kids' Edition: Through Bad Times, Through Sad Times, Through All Time. (p. 697)
—Heaven for Kids: My First Bible Reference for 5-8 Year Olds. (p. 761)
—Know Your Bible for Kids: Noah's Ark: My First Bible Reference for 5-8 Year Olds. (p. 965)
—Seriously Sick Bible Stuff Haya, Erwin, illus. (p. 1552)
Strauss, Ed, jt. auth. see Osborne, Rick.
Strauss, Elisa & Matheson, Christie. Confetti Cakes Cookbook: Spectacular Cookies, Cakes, & Cupcakes from New York City's Famed Bakery. Rowley, Alexandra, photos by. (p. 356)
Strauss, Greg. Eleven Minute Workout: Total Fitness in 11 Minutes a Day. (p. 512)
Strauss, Holden. Chef's Tools. (p. 297)
—Jobs in Science: Solve Problems Involving Measurement & Estimation. (p. 919)
Strauss, Joanne. Charlie & His Friends. (p. 292)
Strauss, Kevin. Loon & Moon: And Other Animal Stories. Scheibe, Nancy, illus. (p. 1052)
—Pecos Bill Invents the Ten-Gallon Hat Harrington, David, illus. (p. 1334)
Strauss, Kim, jt. auth. see Strauss, Kurt.
Strauss, Kurt & Strauss, Kim. Little Boy's Lullaby: A Songbook. (p. 1025)
Strauss, Linda Leopold. Best Friends Pretend. Munsinger, Lynn, illus. (p. 169)
—Elijah Door. Natchev, Alexi, illus. (p. 512)
Strauss, Michael J. Investigating the Natural World of Chemistry with Kids: Experiments, Writing, & Drawing Activities for Learning Science. (p. 885)
Strauss, Peggy Guthart. Getting the Boot. (p. 669)
Strauss, Rochelle. One Well: The Story of Water on Earth. Woods, Rosemary, illus. (p. 1297)
—Tree of Life: The Incredible Biodiversity of Life on Earth. Thompson, Margot, illus. (p. 1783)
Strauss, Victoria. Passion Blue (p. 1327)
Strausser, A., jt. auth. see Wasson, E.
Strausser, Jeffrey. Painless American Government. (p. 1318)
—Painless Writing. (p. 1318)
Stravinskas, Janice. Pam the Dog: A Hawaiian Adventure. (p. 1320)
Straw, Eileen Jones. Choir Starters. (p. 309)
Strawn, Jim, jt. auth. see Stump, Chuck.
Strawn, W. Gregg. Interactive Parables: Play Through the Parables. (p. 879)
Strayer, Beverly, jt. auth. see Strayer, Troy.
Strayer, Beverly & Strayer, Troy. Strategies for Differentiating in the Content Areas: Easy-to-Use Strategies, Scoring Rubrics, Student Samples, & Leveling Tips to Reach & Teach Every Middle-School Student. (p. 1666)
Strayer, Susan. Right Job, Right Now: The Complete Toolkit for Finding Your Perfect Career. (p. 1472)
Strayer, Troy, jt. auth. see Strayer, Beverly.
Strayer, Troy & Strayer, Beverly. Check-In Assessments for Differentiated Lessons: Quick, Engaging Activities That Help You Find Out What Students Know at the Beginning & End of Your Lessons So You Can Plan Your Next Instructional Steps. (p. 295)
Strayhorn, Willa. Way We Bared Our Souls. (p. 1864)
Strayton, George R. Tales of the Jedi Companion. (p. 1702)
Strazzabosco, Jeanne M. Learning about Responsibility. (p. 984)
—Learning about Responsibility from the Life of Colin Powell. (p. 984)
Strazzabosco, John. Aircraft Carriers Supplies for a City at Sea: Multiplying Multidigit Numbers with Regrouping. (p. 31)
—Aircraft Carriers, Supplies for a City at Sea: Multiplying Multidigit Numbers with Regrouping. (p. 31)
—Extreme Temperatures: Learning about Positive & Negative Numbers. (p. 557)
—Mathematical Thinking Reasoning Proof. (p. 1107)
—Measurement. (p. 1117)
Streatfeild, N., jt. auth. see Streatfeild, Noel.
Streatfeild, Noel. Bell Family. Hughes, Shirley, illus. (p. 162)
—Party Shoes. (p. 1326)
—Skating Shoes. (p. 1584)
Streatfeild, Noel & Streatfeild, N. Ballet Shoes. (p. 134)
Streb, Marla. Bicycling Magazine's Century Training Program: 100 Days to 100 Miles. (p. 177)
Streblow, Mary. Family of Man. (p. 568)
—Martian for Christmas. (p. 1097)
Strecker, Darren, illus. see Fettig, Pamela.
Streep, Meryl, jt. auth. see Pennybacker, Mindy.
Street, James, illus. see Garner, Ellen.
Street, Julia Montgomery, jt. auth. see Walser, Richard.
Street Level Studio, illus. see Bartch, Marian.
Street, Pat, jt. auth. see Leedy, Loreen.
Street, Sesame. Elmo's Guessing Game about Colors/Elmo y Su Juego de Adivinar Los Colores. (p. 515)
Street, Sharon & National Geographic Learning Staff. Living Things Need Water. (p. 1042)
—My Friend & I. (p. 1209)
Street, Wayne J. Summer of the Goose. (p. 1674)
Streeten, Roz. Rosie Flo's Kitchen. (p. 1490)
—Rosie Flo's Sticky. (p. 1490)
Streeten, Roz, jt. auth. see Cosmic Debris Etc., Inc. Staff.
Streeter, Lord Ronald. Grumpy Brother Christmas. (p. 727)
Streeter, Michael. Ice Skating. (p. 850)
Streetman, Al. 20 Patterns for Santa Carvers (p. 1995)
Streib, Sally. Octopus Encounter. (p. 1278)
Streich, Michel. Grumpy Little King. Streich, Michel, illus. (p. 727)
Streiffert, Kristi, jt. auth. see Kott, Jennifer.
Streissguth, Thomas. Albania in Pictures. (p. 34)
—Bangladesh. (p. 136)
—Denmark in Pictures. (p. 426)
—Egypt. (p. 506)
—Hernan Cortes Streissguth, Thomas, tr. (p. 771)
—Japan. (p. 909)
—Kickboxing. (p. 951)
—Media Bias. (p. 1118)
—Mini Bikes. (p. 1146)
—Myanmar in Pictures. (p. 1222)
—Namibia in Pictures. (p. 1228)
—Napoleonic Wars: Defeat of the Grand Army. (p. 1229)
—Off-Road Motorcycles. (p. 1279)
—Pocket Bikes. (p. 1375)
—Rwanda in Pictures. (p. 1499)
—Scooters. (p. 1529)
—Skateboard Vert. (p. 1583)
—Skateboarding Street Style. (p. 1583)
—Standard Motorcycles. (p. 1639)
—Suriname in Pictures. (p. 1685)
—Trials Bikes. (p. 1785)
—United States in Pictures. (p. 1819)
—Women of the French Revolution. (p. 1946)
Streissguth, Thomas, jt. auth. see Simon, Emma.
Streissguth, Thomas & Streissguth, Tom. Senegal in Pictures. (p. 1550)
Streissguth, Tom. Adolf Eichmann: Executing the Final Solution. (p. 13)
—America's Security Agencies: The Department of Homeland Security, FBI, NSA, & CIA. (p. 64)
—Belize in Pictures. (p. 162)
—China in the 21st Century: A New World Power. (p. 306)
—Clay V. United States & How Muhammad Ali Fought the Draft: Debating Supreme Court Decisions. (p. 330)
—Colombia in Pictures. (p. 341)
—D. B. Cooper Hijacking. (p. 397)
—District of Columbia V. Heller: The Right to Bear Arms Case. (p. 454)
—Edgar Allan Poe. (p. 504)
—Extreme Weather. (p. 557)
—Fashion & Dress Codes: A How-to Guide. (p. 575)
—Fashion & Dress Codes. (p. 575)
—France. (p. 627)
—India. (p. 870)
—Jesse Owens. (p. 914)
—John Glenn. (p. 922)
—Korean War. (p. 967)
—Liberia in Pictures. (p. 1005)
—P. T. Barnum: Every Crowd Has a Silver Lining. (p. 1316)
—Panama in Pictures. (p. 1320)
—Richard the Lionheart: Crusader King of England. (p. 1470)
—Russia. (p. 1498)
—Science Fiction Pioneer: A Story about Jules Verne. Ramstad, Ralph L., illus. (p. 1526)
—Security Agencies of the United States: How the CIA, FBI, NSA, & Homeland Security Keep Us Safe. (p. 1546)
—U. S. Navy. (p. 1807)
—Vietnam War. (p. 1841)
—Welfare & Welfare Reform. (p. 1874)
—Wilma Rudolph. (p. 1934)
Streissguth, Tom, jt. auth. see Streissguth, Thomas.
Streit, Jakob. Brother Francis: The Life of Francis of Assisi. Kuettel, Nina, tr. (p. 231)
—Puck the Gnome. Mitchell, David S., ed. (p. 1414)
—Three Knight Tales (p. 1742)
—We Will Build A Temple: The Path of Israel from King Solomon to John the Baptist. Mitchell, David, ed. (p. 1868)
Strelecky, John. Why Are You Here Cafe Audio Book. (p. 1922)
Strelitski, Mies & de Hartog, Arnold. Woobie Paints: A Discovery of Color. (p. 1949)
Strelitski, Mies & Hartog, Arnold. Woobie Dreams Hc. (p. 1949)
Strelkoff, Tatiana. Jeremy & the Crow Nation. Martin, Bobi, ed. (p. 913)
Streluk, Angella, jt. auth. see Rodgers, Alan.
Stremanos, A. M. Rosemary's Taken over My Potatoes. (p. 1489)
Strempke, Maria Elena. What's a Hafta? (p. 1896)
Stren, Patti. Hug Me. (p. 824)
Strenge, Kelly. Truth about Cancer. (p. 1794)
Strenkowski, Lorraine. Mickey the Cat. (p. 1136)
Strepponi, Blanca. Claudia y Daniel. Muller, Cristina, illus. (p. 329)
Stretch, Ian. Marty the Mailbox. McNevin, Dale, illus. (p. 1098)
Stretton, Hesba. Cassy. Hymper, W. & Stacey, W. S., illus. (p. 276)
—Jessica's First Prayer. (p. 914)
—Jessica's First Prayer. Doe, Charles J., ed. (p. 914)
—Lost Gip. (p. 1055)
Streul, Cathy. Adventures from the Farm: The Beginning. (p. 15)
Strevens-Marzo, Bridget. Bridget's Book of Nursery Rhymes. (p. 227)
Strevens-Marzo, Bridget, illus. see Bedford, David.
Strevens-Marzo, Bridget, illus. see Dempsey, Kristy.
Strevens-Marzo, Bridget, illus. see Sturges, Philemon.
Strevens-Marzo, Bridget, illus. see Wild, Margaret.
Strevens-Marzo, Bridget, jt. auth. see Wild, Margaret.
Stribling, Anne & Benchmark Education Co., LLC Staff. Get up, Meg! (p. 668)
Strichman, John Galt. How Not to Lose at Spades. (p. 811)
Strick, Alex, jt. auth. see Stockdale, Sean.
Strick, Alex & Stockdale, Sean. Max the Champion. Asquith, Ros, illus. (p. 1111)
Strickland, A. W. Adventures of Ralph & Elmer This Potato Is for You. (p. 22)
Strickland, AdriAnne. Lifeless. (p. 1013)
—Wordless. (p. 1951)
Strickland, Brad. Dragon's Plunder. (p. 479)
—Flight of the Outcast. (p. 604)
—House Where Nobody Lived. (p. 804)
—When Mack Came Back. (p. 1903)
Strickland, Brad & Fuller, Thomas E. Guns of Tortuga. Saponaro, Dominick, illus. (p. 732)
—Marooned! (p. 1096)
—Missing! (p. 1152)
Strickland, Deborah. Mary Reeder, Prairie Girl. (p. 1101)
Strickland, Della. Emma's Moments. (p. 520)
Strickland, Dorothy S. & Alvermann, Donna E. Bridging the Literacy Achievement Gap. (p. 227)
Strickland, James R. Lincoln's Lost Papers. (p. 1019)
Strickland, Jennifer. Pretty from the Inside Out: Discover All the Ways God Made You Special. (p. 1398)
Strickland, Karen L., jt. auth. see Leighton, Davis L.
Strickland, Shadra, illus. see Bandy, Michael S. & Stein, Eric.
Strickland, Shadra, illus. see Derby, Sally.
Strickland, Shadra, illus. see Morrison, Toni & Morrison, Slade.
Strickland, Shadra, illus. see Nolen, Jerdine.
Strickland, Shadra, illus. see Randall, Alice & Williams, Caroline Randall.
Strickland, Shadra, illus. see Watson, Renée.
Strickland, Shadra, jt. auth. see Elliott, Zetta.
Strickland, Sharon. Even Though: A Story about Being Different (p. 541)
Strickler, Ashley. Once upon A Time. (p. 1293)
Strickler, LeeDell. Super Simple Bible Lessons: 60 Ready-to-Use Bible Activities for Ages 3-5. (p. 1681)
Strictly Spanish, LLC., tr. see Biskup, Agnieszka, et al.
Strictly Spanish, LLC., tr. see Edison, Erin.
Strictly Spanish, LLC., tr. see Gianopoulos, Andrea.
Strictly Spanish, LLC., tr. see Harbo, Christopher L.
Strictly Spanish, LLC., tr. see McCormick, Lisa Wade & Miller, Connie Colwell.
Strictly Spanish, LLC., tr. see McCormick, Lisa Wade.
Strictly Spanish, LLC., tr. see Miller, Connie Colwell, et al.
Strictly Spanish, LLC., tr. see Miller, Connie Colwell.
Strictly Spanish, LLC., tr. see Monahan, Erin & O'Brien, Kim.
Strictly Spanish, LLC., tr. see Olson, Nathan.
Strictly Spanish, LLC., tr. see Rustad, Martha E. H. & Wittrock, Jeni.
Strictly Spanish, LLC., tr. see Sohn, Emily & Barnett III, Charles.
Strictly Spanish LLC. Staff, tr. see Biskup, Agnieszka, et al.
Strictly Spanish LLC. Staff, tr. see Clay, Kathryn & Czeskleba, Abby.
Strictly Spanish LLC. Staff, tr. see Clay, Kathryn.
Strictly Spanish LLC. Staff, tr. see Edison, Erin & Saunders-Smith, Gail.
Strictly Spanish LLC. Staff, tr. see Miller, Connie Colwell.
Strictly Spanish LLC. Staff, tr. see Nichols, Cheyenne.
Strictly Spanish LLC. Staff, tr. see O'Brien, Kim.
Strictly Spanish LLC. Staff, tr. see Schuh, Mari C.
Strictly Spanish Translation Services Staff, tr. see Biskup, Agnieszka, et al.
Strictly Spanish Translation Services Staff, tr. see Biskup, Agnieszka.
Strictly Spanish Translation Services Staff, tr. see Clay, Kathryn.
Strictly Spanish Translation Services Staff, tr. see Czeskleba, Abby.
Strictly Spanish Translation Services Staff, tr. see Monahan, Erin.
Strictly Spanish Translation Services Staff, tr. see Nichols, Cheyenne.
Strictly Spanish Translation Services Staff, tr. see O'Brien, Kim.
Strictly Spanish Translation Services Staff, tr. see Rustad, Martha E. H.
Strictly Spanish Translation Services Staff, tr. see Wittrock, Jeni.
Stride, Lottie. Meerkat Mischief. Stride, Lottie, illus. (p. 1120)
—Write (or Is It Right?) Every Time: Cool Ways to Improve Your English. (p. 1963)
Stride, Lottie & Oliver, Martin. Girls Only: How to Survive Anything! Geremia, Daniela & Ecob, Simon, illus. (p. 680)
Striker, Fran. Lone Ranger Traps Smugglers. (p. 1046)
—Lone Ranger Traps the Smugglers. Laune, Paul, illus. (p. 1046)
Striker, Oliver & Varacalli, Lauren. Cornell University College Prowler off the Record. (p. 367)
Striker, Randy, pseud & White, Randy Wayne. Deadlier Sex. (p. 417)
Strindberg, August. Father. Landes, William-Alan, ed. (p. 577)
—Miss Julie. Landes, William-Alan, ed. (p. 1151)
Stringam, Jean. How Not to Cry in Public. (p. 811)
Stringer. Fairies of Spencer Meadow: Fairy Tales. (p. 563)
Stringer, Bruce. Earlihee the Turtle. (p. 493)
Stringer, John. Magnetism: An Investigation. (p. 1076)
Stringer, Karen, illus. see Glowatsky, Phyllis.
Stringer, Lauren. When Stravinsky Met Nijinsky: Two Artists, Their Ballet, & One Extraordinary Riot. (p. 1904)
—Winter Is the Warmest Season. (p. 1938)
Stringer, Lauren, illus. see Fox, Mem.
Stringer, Lauren, illus. see George, Kristine O'Connell.
Stringer, Lauren, illus. see Orr, Wendy.
Stringer, Lauren, illus. see Peters, Lisa Westberg.
Stringer, Lauren, illus. see Ray, Mary Lyn.
Stringer, Lauren, illus. see Rylant, Cynthia.
Stringer, Lynne. Crown. (p. 386)
Stringer, Margaret, illus. see Shaffert, Charles F.
Stringer, Margaret, illus. see Shaffert, Charles.
Stringfield, Joni, illus. see Brokamp, Elizabeth.
Stringham, Jean. Balance. (p. 133)
Stringle, Berny, jt. auth. see Robb, Jackie.
Stringle, Sam, illus. see Robb, Jackie & Stringle, Berny.
Stripland, Rubye Weldon. Lucy Bell, Queen of the Pasture. (p. 1063)
—Lucy Bell, Queen of the Pasture Book Four. (p. 1063)
—Lucy Bell, Queen of the Pasture, Book Three. (p. 1063)
—Lucy Bell, Queen of the Pasture Book Two. (p. 1063)
Stripling, Ashley. No clothes for Ashley. (p. 1258)
Stripling, Joe. See You in Heaven. Carroll, Joan, ed. (p. 1547)
Striveildi, Cheryl. Asia. (p. 106)
—Australia. (p. 116)
Strnad, George J. Adventures of Colonel Bob B Beagle Us Army Canine Corp: The Adventures of Colonel Bob. (p. 17)
Strnad, Jan. Grimwood's Daughter. (p. 724)
Strobel, Christoph, jt. auth. see Nash, Alice.
Strobel, Lee. Case for a Creator for Kids (p. 273)
—Case for Faith: A Journalist Investigates the Toughest Objections to Christianity (p. 273)
—Case for Faith for Kids (p. 273)
—Case for Grace for Kids (p. 273)
—Case for the Real Jesus: A Journalist Investigates Current Challenges to Christianity (p. 273)
—Case for the Real Jesus: A Journalist Investigates Scientific Evidence That Points Toward God. (p. 273)
Strobel, Lee, et al. Case for Christ for Kids (p. 273)
—Secret Survivors: Real-Life Stories to Give You Hope for Healing (p. 1544)
Strobel Morrow, Alison, jt. auth. see Morrow, Daniel.
Strobel-Cort, Joanne. Emillee Kart & the Seven Saving Signs: The Tale of Beasley's Bonnet. (p. 518)
Stroble, Chris. There IS Hope after a Teen Pregnancy: A Collection of Inspiring Mother-Daughter Success Stories plus the Handbook for Teen Moms Anonymous. (p. 1730)
Strodder, Chris. Wish Book. (p. 1940)
Strode, James. Norma Defeats the Aliens. (p. 1264)
Stroede, Paul, illus. see Rogala, Judy.
Stroede, Paul, illus. see Stadler, Kristina.
Stroeher, Susan. 25 Best-Ever Collaborative Books for Young Writers: Ready-to-Use Templates to Help Develop Early Writing Skills & Meet the Common Core State Standards. (p. 1996)
Strogatz, Steven H. Sync: How Order Emerges from Chaos in the Universe, Nature, & Daily Life. (p. 1693)
Stroh, Debbie, jt. auth. see Boston, Vicki.
Stroh, Debbie & Boston, Vicki. Christ's Kids Create: Volume 1. (p. 317)
Stroh, Mary, jt. auth. see Woodward, John.
Strohm, Keith Francis. Bladesinger. (p. 198)
Strohm, Stephanie Kate. Confederates Don't Wear Couture: A Tale of Heartache, Haunting, & Hoop Skirts. (p. 356)
—Pilgrims Don't Wear Pink. (p. 1358)
Strohmeier, jt. auth. see Strohmeier, Lenice.
Strohmeier, Lenice & Strohmeier. Mingo Farnsworth, Bill, illus. (p. 1146)
Strohmenger, Marie. Smart Bunny: A Story about Big & Small, Smart & Stupid, Winning & Losing. (p. 1592)
Strohmeyer, Sarah. How Zoe Made Her Dreams (Mostly) Come True. (p. 823)
—Secrets of Lily Graves. (p. 1545)
—Sleeping Beauty Proposal. (p. 1589)
—Smart Girls Get What They Want. (p. 1592)
Strole, Jennifer R. Mommy says Jesus Is Coming! (p. 1162)
Strom, Chris. 3D Game Programming for Kids: Create Interactive Worlds with JavaScript. (p. 1992)
Strom, Kay Marshall, jt. auth. see Kline, Daniel.
Strom, Laura Layton. Built below Sea Level: New Orleans. (p. 239)
—Caught with a Catch: Poaching in Africa. (p. 282)
—Don't Try This at Home: The Science of Extreme Behaviors. (p. 469)
—Dr. Medieval: Medicine in the Middle Ages. (p. 475)
—Egyptian Science Gazette. (p. 507)
—From Bugbots to Humanoids: Robotics. (p. 642)
—Leonardo Da Vinci. (p. 992)
—Mirror Power. (p. 1149)
—Racing on the Wind: Steve Fossett. (p. 1432)
—Rock We Eat - Salt. (p. 1482)
Strom, Laura Layton, et al. Opinions about Two Fairy Tales: Baba Yaga & Hansel & Gretel. Czernichowska, Joanna, illus. (p. 1300)

Strom, Maria Diaz. Joe Arco Iris y Yo. Strom, Maria Diaz, illus. (p. 920)
—Rainbow Joe & Me. (p. 1435)
Strom, Yale. Wedding That Saved a Town. Prosmitsky, Jenya, illus. (p. 1871)
Stroman, Larry. Peter David (p. 1346)
Stromberg, Betsy, et al. Happy Birthday! Steckel, Richard & Steckel, Michele, photos by. (p. 744)
Stromberg, Ronica. Living It up to Live It Down. (p. 1041)
—Shadow in the Dark. (p. 1557)
—Time-for-Bed Angel. Stephenson, Kristina, illus. (p. 1751)
Stromoski, Rick, illus. see Cappetta, Cynthia.
Stromoski, Rick, illus. see Curry, Don L.
Stromoski, Rick, illus. see Meltzer Kleinhenz, Sydnie.
Strong, Abigail. Troggins Tales. (p. 1788)
Strong, Amy. Lee Bennett Hopkins: A Children's Poet. (p. 987)
Strong, Austin. Drums of Oude. Landes, William-Alan, ed. (p. 487)
Strong, B. L. Troll & His Bridge. (p. 1788)
Strong, Belinda. Hold & Touch Bedtime. (p. 787)
Strong, Beth. Meet the Jaspers. (p. 1122)
Strong, Cynda. Resurrection. (p. 1464)
—Where Do Angels Sleep? Denos, Julia, illus. (p. 1906)
Strong, Frances Dinkins. Beth's Fella. Payne, Kay, illus. (p. 171)
—Pat, the Cat. Lee, Linda, illus. (p. 1327)
Strong, Jeremy. Bungleman. Mosedale, Julian, illus. (p. 242)
—Chicken Licken. Blundell, Tony, illus. (p. 300)
—Dinosaur Pox. (p. 442)
—Giant Jim & the Hurricane. (p. 673)
—Indoor Pirates on Treasure Island. Sharratt, Nick, illus. (p. 872)
—Sneezles. Blundell, Tony, illus. (p. 1597)
Strong, Louise. Island Adventures of Frodo Mcadoo. (p. 892)
Strong, Melodee, illus. see Snow, Todd.
Strong, Pam. Turbo Gets Stuck. (p. 1797)
Strong, Terri. Wee Wisdom. (p. 1871)
Stroniarz, Christina V. Let's Sing & Celebrate! 105 Original Songs for Seasons & Festivals. (p. 1000)
Stroschin, Jane H. Atsa & Ga: A Story from the High Desert. Stich, Carolyn R., illus. (p. 113)
Strother, Ruth. B Is for Blue Planet: An Earth Science Alphabet. Marstall, Robert, illus. (p. 122)
—Bill Gates. (p. 186)
—Red Foxes. (p. 1454)
—Smithsonian Everything You Need to Know: Grades 2-3. (p. 1594)
—Tarantula. (p. 1706)
—Tarantula Paperback. (p. 1706)
—W Is for Woof: A Dog Alphabet. Frankenhuyzen, Gijsbert van, illus. (p. 1851)
—W Is for Woof: A Dog Alphabet. van Frankenhuyzen, Gijsbert, illus. (p. 1851)
Strother, Ruth & Van Valkenburgh, Blaire. Coyote. (p. 374)
Strother, Scott. Adventurous Book of Outdoor Games: Classic Fun for Daring Boys & Girls. (p. 25)
Stroud, Bettye. Patchwork Path: A Quilt Map to Freedom. Bennett, Erin Susanne, illus. (p. 1328)
—Reconstruction Era. (p. 1452)
—World's Wide Open. Cummings, Pat, illus. (p. 1961)
Stroud, Bettye & Ramsey, Calvin Alexander. Belle, the Last Mule at Gee's Bend: A Civil Rights Story. Holyfield, John, illus. (p. 163)
Stroud, Brenda, illus. see Ennis, Ryan R.
Stroud, Brenda D., illus. see Finley, Ucal P.
Stroud, Cassie, jt. auth. see Latter, Kym.
Stroud, Cynthia. Carolina Children: The Sandhills. (p. 270)
Stroud, David Wayne. Funny, Dust & Honey & the Giant Carrot. Nardandrea, Swannee, illus. (p. 649)
—Wiggles the White Blood Cell. Stroud, David Wayne, illus. (p. 1928)
Stroud, G. J. Measuring Up. (p. 1117)
Stroud, Joanne, illus. see West, Tracey.
Stroud, Jonathan. Amulet of Samarkand (p. 66)
—Amulet of Samarkland. (p. 66)
—Bartimaeus (p. 140)
—Buried Fire. (p. 243)
—Golem's Eye (p. 696)
—Heroes of the Valley. (p. 773)
—Hollow Boy. (p. 789)
—Lockwood & Co. the Screaming Staircase. (p. 1045)
—Ptolemy's Gate (p. 1414)
—Screaming Staircase. (p. 1533)
—Whispering Skull. (p. 1912)
Stroud, Jonathan & Stroudjonathan. Amuleto de Samarkanda. (p. 66)
Stroud, Scott. Baby Kong. Hunt, Jim, illus. (p. 127)
—Grumpy Mr. Grady. Hunt, Jim, illus. (p. 727)
Stroudjonathan, jt. auth. see Stroud, Jonathan.
Stroud-Peace, Glenda. Pearlie. Larkin, Paige A., illus. (p. 1333)
Stroun, Fabrice, jt. ed. see Bovier, Lionel.
Strouss, Jessica & Strouss, Stephen. There's a Dog at My Feet when I Eat. (p. 1730)
Strouss, Stephen, jt. auth. see Strouss, Jessica.
Strout, Anton. Dead to Me. (p. 417)
Strout, Morgan. Petri's Adventures. (p. 1348)
Strow, Lorie. Shimmers. (p. 1566)
Strozier, M. Stefan, ed. see Phillips, Louis.
Strub, Scott Richard. Otto the Outerspace Octopus. (p. 1307)
Struble, S. Steven. Li'l Depressed Boy (p. 1017)
Struck, Mary Dowd, jt. auth. see Brown, Sylvia.
Struck, Mike. Larry Lives Forever: A Story to Help Children Cope with Loss. (p. 976)
Strudwick, Leslie. Alaska. (p. 33)
—Inuit. (p. 883)
—Inuit with Code. (p. 883)
—Maori. (p. 1089)
—Maori with Code. (p. 1089)
—Oklahoma. (p. 1283)
—Science of Seasons. (p. 1527)
—South Dakota. (p. 1617)
—Washington. (p. 1859)
Strudwick, Leslie & Webster, Christine. Indigenous Peoples Series (p. 872)
Struer, Kameron. Simon the Snowball. (p. 1577)
Strugnell, Ann, illus. see Cameron, Ann.
Strum, Richard. Henry Knox: Washington's Artilleryman. (p. 768)
Strum, Richard M. Causes of the American Revolution. (p. 282)
—Henry Knox: Washington's Artilleryman. (p. 768)
Strungis, Elaine. Sammi & Danny Learn about Jupiter. (p. 1507)
—Sammi & Danny Learn about the Earth. (p. 1507)
—Sammi & Danny Learn about Uranus. (p. 1507)
—Sammi & Danny Learn about Venus. (p. 1507)
Strunk, Crisman. Elemental Fources #3. Mullarky, Eric, ed. (p. 510)
Strunk, Peter. Two Inch Hero: The Adventures of Lorenzo Lizard. (p. 1803)
Strunk, William, Jr. & White, E. B. Elements of Style. (p. 511)
Strutz, Amuel U. Santa's New Reindeer Team. (p. 1513)
Struyk-Bonn, Chris. Whisper (p. 1912)
Stryer, Andrea Stenn. Kami & the Yaks. Dodson, Bert, illus. (p. 942)
Stryk, Suzanne, illus. see Person, Naomi, et al.
Stryker, Dale, jt. auth. see Stryker, Stephanie.
Stryker, Laura Kirby. Incredibly Tall Mrs. Tippet. (p. 870)
Stryker, Robin. Goldie, the Homeless Calico Cat. Rubino, Alisa A., illus. (p. 696)
Stryker, Stephanie. Speech Illustrated Cards- Set 1: Pictured Nouns & Verbs. (p. 1624)
—Speech Illustrated Cards- Set 5: Where & What? (p. 1624)
—Speech Illustrated Cards- Set 6: More Nouns & Verbs. (p. 1624)
Stryker, Stephanie & Stryker, Dale. Speech Illustrated Numero Uno: Pictured Nouns & Verbs. Stryker, Stephanie & Stryker, Dale, illus. (p. 1624)
Strykowski, Marcia. Call Me Amy. (p. 254)
Stuart. Everywoman A Goddess: Everyman a Hero in her Service. (p. 546)
Stuart & McArthur, Amanda. Humphry & the Tree. (p. 827)
Stuart, B. S., illus. see Gates, Josephine Scribner.
Stuart, Carrie. Chinese New Year. (p. 307)
—How Flowers Grow. (p. 809)
—Kinds of Coins: Learning the Values of Pennies, Nickels, Dimes & Quarters. (p. 957)
—Lenore's Chores. (p. 991)
Stuart, Duncan. Whole of the Moon. (p. 1920)
Stuart, Janet. Something New in Cloverville? (p. 1610)
—What? No Easter Eggs? (p. 1878)
Stuart, Jon, illus. see Sage, Alison.
Stuart, Jon, illus. see Shipton, Paul.
Stuart, Kelly. Cancion de Cuna de la Virgen de Guadalupe. Caban, Carlos, tr. from ENG. (p. 261)
Stuart, Liam. Parade: Understand Place Value. (p. 1323)
Stuart, Lisa Marie. Little Cat, the Wonderful Witch, & the Clever Mouse. Potter, Lori, illus. (p. 1025)
Stuart, Matt. Who Can Run Fast? (p. 1914)
Stuart, Mitchell, illus. see Stewart, Angela.
Stuart, Natalie. Monster Alphabet. (p. 1166)
Stuart, P. Stage Fright. (p. 1638)
Stuart, Pamela Haught. Just like my Papa. (p. 939)
Stuart, Phillip. Stage Fright. (p. 1638)
Stuart, Raff. Roman Odyssey: Book One of the chronicles of Adam Black the Teenage Time Traveller. (p. 1486)
Stuart, Robert C., jt. auth. see Gregory, Paul R.
Stuart, Ron. Day Jack Frost Stole the Rainbow: A Buck, Tim & Bright Eyes Story. (p. 413)
Stuart, Ruth Mcenery. Christmas Guest. (p. 314)
Stuart, Sam. Stuart & Sami Go Bowling: Stuart's Special Friend Sami. (p. 1668)
Stuart, Sorais. Nutrition for Your Body Mind & Spirit - Unveiling health Improvement Strategies & Successful Weight Loss. (p. 1274)
Stuart, Tara. Tara's Tales: Lake. (p. 1706)
—Tara's Tales: Dream. (p. 1706)
—Tara's Tales: Trees. (p. 1706)
—Tara's Tales: Mountain. (p. 1706)
—Trees: A Tara's Tale about Being Yourself. (p. 1784)
Stuart, W. Howard. Astonishing Adventures of Miss Courtney & Little Cloud. (p. 108)
Stuart, Walter, illus. see Young, Carol.
Stuart, Wrigley. Once upon a Time in Elmore: When Gumball Met Penny. Johnson, Shane L., illus. (p. 1293)
—Who'd Have Thunk It? (p. 1919)
Stuart-Clark, Christopher, jt. auth. see Harrison, Michael.
Stuart-Russell, C. Playtime with the Animals. (p. 1373)
Stubben, Michael. Clark vs. the Rainforest. (p. 327)
Stubbing, Lori, illus. see Rjk.
Stubblefield, Karen. Anna & Chen. (p. 85)
Stubblefield, Linda, ed. see Hammah, Aisha.
Stubbs, Dave. Our Game: The History of Hockey in Canada. (p. 1308)
Stubbs, Lori. Fearfully & Wonderfully Made: A Christian Health & Puberty Guide for Preteen Boys & Girls. Stubbs, Robert Earl, illus. (p. 579)
Stubbs, Robert Earl, illus. see Stubbs, Lori.
Stubbs, Tommy. Crack in the Track. (p. 375)
—Fearsome Footprints/Thomas the Brave Pictureback. (p. 579)
—Thomas & Friends Little Golden Book Library (Thomas & Friends) (p. 1738)
Stubbs, Tommy, illus. see Awdry, W.
Stubbs, Tommy, illus. see Awdry, Wilbert V.
Stubbs, Tommy, illus. see Awdry, Wilbert V. & Awdry, W.
Stubbs, Tommy, illus. see Awdry, Wilbert V. & Terrill, Elizabeth.
Stubbs, Tommy, illus. see Awdry, Wilbert Were.
Stubbs, Tommy, illus. see Golden Books Staff.
Stubbs, Tommy, illus. see Hit Entertainment.
Stubbs, Tommy, illus. see Hooke, R. Schuyler.
Stubbs, Tommy, illus. see Neusner, Dena.
Stubbs, Tommy, illus. see Random House.
Stuber, Barbara. Crossing the Tracks. (p. 385)
—Girl in Reverse. (p. 678)
Stuby, Tim, illus. see Bataille Lange, Nikki.
Stuchin, Mallory. We're in This Together: 15 Teens Reveal How They Get along with Their Parents (And Other Sanity-Saving Insights) (p. 1875)
Stuchner, Joan Betty. Bagels Come Home Whamond, Dave, illus. (p. 132)
—Bagels the Brave Whamond, Dave, illus. (p. 132)
—Can Hens Give Milk? Weissmann, Joe, illus. (p. 258)
—Kugel Valley Klezmer Band. Row, Richard, illus. (p. 968)
—Time to Be Brave. Nugent, Cynthia, illus. (p. 1753)
Stuckenschneider, Chris. Twist of Fate: The Miracle Colt & His Friends. (p. 1802)
Stuckey. Call to Freedom: 1865 to Present (p. 254)
—Call to Freedom: 1877-Present: Online Edition Plus. (p. 254)
—Call to Freedom: Beginning-1877: Online Edition Plus. (p. 254)
Stuckey, Denise. Jesus, I Feel Close to You. Saroff, Phyllis, illus. (p. 915)
Stuckey, Gary & Siddall, Ann. Tending the Seed: Nurture Your God-Given Potential. (p. 1719)
Stuckey, Kevin, jt. auth. see Snyders, Natalie.
Stuckey, Rachel. African Americans in the West. (p. 27)
—Digital Dangers. (p. 439)
—Energy from Living Things: Biomass Energy. (p. 528)
—Explore with Lewis & Clark. (p. 550)
—Full Court Press: Basketball Skills & Drills. (p. 646)
—Lebron James. (p. 987)
—Play Ball! Baseball Tips & Tricks. (p. 1371)
—Ride It Bmx. (p. 1471)
—Sexual Orientation & Gender Identity. (p. 1556)
—Up Your Game on & off the Ice. (p. 1824)
—Wagon Trains Heading West. (p. 1852)
—Women in the West. (p. 1946)
Stuckey, Rachel, jt. auth. see Crabtree Editors.
Stuckey, Rachel, jt. auth. see Crabtree Publishing Company Staff.
Stuckey, Rachel, jt. auth. see Crabtree Staff.
Stucki, Jacob C. Remembering the Indian School. (p. 1460)
Stucki, Ron, illus. see Adams, Jennifer.
Stucky, Mark D. Gospel in Greasepaint: Creative Biblical Skits for Clowns, Mimes & Other Fools for Christ. (p. 703)
Studebaker, Richard F. Mystery of the Manse. (p. 1225)
Studelska, Jana Voelke. Archery for Fun! (p. 95)
—Skateboarding for Fun! (p. 1583)
—Yoga for Fun! (p. 1972)
Student Horizons Inc Staff. Colleges of Distinction. (p. 340)
Student Life Staff. 31 Verses - Following: Every Teenager Should Know. (p. 1996)
—31 Verses - Love: Every Teenager Should Know. (p. 1996)
—31 Versus - Inhabit: Every Teenager Should Know. (p. 1996)
Student Life Staff, jt. auth. see Hooten, Emily.
Student Life Staff & Navigators Staff, The. 31 Verses - Community: Every Teenager Should Know. (p. 1996)
—31 Verses - Reverb: Every Teenager Should Know. (p. 1996)
Students & Teachers at Christian Academy. Cutting Class: The St. Baldrick's Story of Christian Academy of Louisville Rock Creek. (p. 396)
Students, Blue Ridge. Blue Ridge Writes! Black Mesa Publishing. (p. 203)
Students, Liberty Elementary School. Patriot Pages, Liberty Elementary School. (p. 1329)
Students of Animo Inglewood Charter High School Staff. Rhythm of the Chain: Young Writers Explore Teamwork. (p. 1468)
Students of Dorsey High School Staff. From the Couch to the Kitchen: A Book to Indulge In. (p. 644)
Students of Fletcher Hills Elementary School. Many Voices: Where Dreams Take Flight II. (p. 1089)
Students of Galileo Academy of Science and Technology Staff. Home Wasn't Built in a Day: Constructing the Stories of Our Families. (p. 793)
Students of the Los Angeles School of Global Studies Staff. Elotes Man Will Soon Be Gone. (p. 516)
Students of Wallenberg Traditional High School Staff. Exactly: Ten Beavers, Nine Fairies, Eight Dreams, Seven Knights, Six Princesses, Five Dogs, Four Otters, Three Old Men, Two Robots, One Traveling Shoe & Everything Else It Takes to Make a Great Children's Story Book. San Francisco Bay Area Staff, illus. (p. 547)
Students, Shelton Intermediate School Art, illus. see Gelderman, Robert G.
Studer, Diana. Tabby's Gift. (p. 1694)
Studies and Research Unit of Wamy Staff. Principles of Dialogue. (p. 1406)
Studio, Gau Family, illus. see Jusino, Cindy M.
Studio IBOIX, illus. see Bazaldua, Barbara & Bergen, Lara.
Studio IBOIX, illus. see Loggia, Wendy.
Studio IBOIX, illus. see Nathan, Sarah.
Studio IBOIX, illus. see Perelman, Helen.
Studio Iboix Staff, illus. see Disney Book Group Staff & Richards, Kitty.
Studio Iboix Staff, illus. see Disney Princess Staff & Disney Book Group Staff.
Studio IBOIX Staff, illus. see Posner-Sanchez, Andrea.
Studio Iboix Staff, illus. see Random House Editors & RH Disney Staff.
Studio Iboix Staff, illus. see RH Disney Staff & Knowles, Heather.
Studio Mouse. Chicken Little Pack. (p. 300)
—Happy Endings: Ariel, Snow White. (p. 745)
—Nursery Rhymes. (p. 1273)
—Piglet's 123s. (p. 1358)
—Pooh & Friends Seasons Pack. (p. 1383)
—Pooh's ABCs. (p. 1383)
—Princess 1 to 10. (p. 1402)
—Princess Colors & Shapes Pack. (p. 1403)
—Princess Language Pack. (p. 1404)
—Princess Meals Pack. (p. 1404)
—Sesame Street Abby Cadabby's Nursery Rhymes. (p. 1553)
—Sesame Street Celebrates School: Learn & Carry 4 Books with CD. (p. 1553)
—Sesame Street: Counting All Around: Zip & Carry Book & CD. (p. 1553)
Studio Mouse, jt. auth. see Studio Mouse.
Studio Mouse & Studio Mouse. My First Sleepover. (p. 1208)
Studio Mouse, creator. Explore with Little Einsteins. (p. 550)
—Get Your Grouchies Out! A Vocabulary of Feelings. (p. 668)
—Kindness Counts. (p. 957)
—Let's Listen: Nursery Rhymes for Listening & Learning. (p. 998)
—Let's Move: Nursery Rhymes for Moving & Learning. (p. 999)
—Let's Play: Nursery Rhymes for Playing & Learning. (p. 999)
—Let's Sing: Nursery Rhymes for Singing & Learning. (p. 1000)
—Mother Goose Counting Rhymes. (p. 1178)
—My Clubhouse Alphabet. (p. 1200)
—Princess Shapes. (p. 1405)
—Rhymes on the Go! (p. 1468)
—Tracing ABCs. (p. 1775)
—Tracing Punctuation! (p. 1775)
Studio Mouse, ed. Disney Preincess Best Friends: Flat Learn & Carry 4 Board Books & CD. (p. 452)
—Disney Time to Learn with Pooh: Flat Learn & Carry 4 Board Books & CD. (p. 453)
—Jojo's Circus Get up & Move! Flat Learn & Carry 4 Board Books & CD. (p. 924)
Studio Mouse Editorial. Ariel: The Brave Little Mermaid. (p. 98)
—Belle: The Power of Love. (p. 162)
—Happy Endings: Belle, Cinderella. (p. 745)
Studio Mouse Editorial, jt. auth. see Galvin, Laura Gates.
Studio Mouse Editorial, jt. auth. see Nussbaum, Ben.
Studio Mouse Staff. Captain Jack Sparrow's Secret Journal. (p. 264)
—Cars on the Road to Learning: Flat Learn & Carry 4 Board Books & CD. (p. 272)
—Disney Princess - Happy Endings. (p. 452)
—First Concepts. (p. 593)
—Five Little Monkeys: And Other Counting Rhymes. Elliott, Rebecca et al, illus. (p. 600)
—Friends Collection: Pooh & Piglet, Pooh & Roo. (p. 638)
—Friends Collection: Pooh & Eeyore, Pooh & Piglet, Pooh & Tigger. Soundprints Staff, ed. (p. 638)
—Kindness Counts. (p. 957)
—Learn about Five Senses with JoJo! - My Five Senses. (p. 982)
—Let's Listen: Nursery Rhymes for Listening & Learning. (p. 998)
—Let's Move: Nursery Rhymes for Moving & Learning. (p. 999)
—Let's Play: Nursery Rhymes for Playing & Learning. (p. 999)
—Mickey Mouse Clubhouse Count Along. (p. 1136)
—Mother Goose Lullabies. de La Cour, Gary et al, illus. (p. 1178)
—Musical Fun: Colors & Patterns. (p. 1194)
—Pet Friends. (p. 1345)
—Pooh & Eeyore. (p. 1383)
—Pooh & Eeyore, Pooh & Tigger. (p. 1383)
—Pooh & Friends ABCs & 123s: First Concepts. (p. 1383)
—Pooh & Piglet. (p. 1383)
—Pooh & Roo. (p. 1383)
—Pooh & Tigger. (p. 1383)
—Princess Rhyme Time. (p. 1405)
—Puppy Dog Tails. (p. 1418)
—Sesame Street Bert & Ernie Work Together. (p. 1553)
—Sesame Street Colors & Shapes. (p. 1553)
—Sesame Street My First Instrument. (p. 1553)
—Sesame Street Rosita Reads a Recipe. (p. 1553)
—Sesame Street Share & Care, It's Only Fair. (p. 1553)
—Space Adventure. (p. 1618)
—Spelling Fun. (p. 1625)
—Take-with-Me Counting. (p. 1697)
—Take-with-Me-Alphabet. (p. 1697)
—Tesoro de los Amigos: Puffy Book & CD. (p. 1722)
—Time to Learn! (p. 1753)
—Tinkerbell's Magic Story Writer. (p. 1756)
—Walt Disney Bambi Learning Library. (p. 1855)
—Wedding Countdown. (p. 1870)
—Winnie Pooh y sus amigos Ejercicios: Puffy Book with CD. (p. 1937)
Studio Mouse Staff, ed. see Nussbaum, Ben.
Studio Mouse Staff, jt. auth. see Bentley, Dawn.
Studio Mouse Staff, jt. auth. see Galvin, Laura Gates.
Studio Mouse Staff, jt. auth. see Mother Goose Staff.
Studio Mouse Staff, jt. auth. see Sesame Street Staff.
Studio Mouse Staff, jt. auth. see Soundprints Staff.
Studio Mouse Staff, creator. Write-with-Me Numbers. (p. 1964)
Studio Redstone, jt. auth. see Seock Seo, Hong.
Studio Redstone, jt. auth. see Studio Redstone.
Studio Redstone & Studio Redstone. Dragon Hunter. Im, Hye-Young, tr. from KOR. (p. 477)
Studio Stalio, illus. see Houghton, Gillian.
Studio, Xian Nu, illus. see Robbins, Trina.
Studiomouse Staff, jt. auth. see Disney Publishing Staff.
Studiomouse Staff, jt. auth. see Disney.
Studiomouse Staff, jt. auth. see Galvin, Laura Gates.
Studiomouse Staff, jt. auth. see Mother Goose Staff.
Studios, A&J, illus. see Ricci, Christine.
Studios, Arcana, illus. see Calkhoven, Laurie.
Studios, Arcana, illus. see Falligant, Erin.
Studios, Arcana, illus. see Hart, Alison.
Studios, P. c., jt. auth. see Carman, Patrick.
Studley, Wanda Jean. Shorty Stories: A Story about a Dog & Her Famous Wheels. (p. 1569)
Stuefloten, Helen. There's A Giant in the Garden. Janguay, Patricia, illus. (p. 1730)
Stuermer, Christoph B. & Rosengarten, Philipp G. Premium Power: The Secret of Success of Mercedes-Benz, BMW, Porsche & Audi. (p. 1395)
Stuhmer, Bob, illus. see Mauzy, Barbara E.
Stuhr, Carri. Arctic Foxes. (p. 96)
Stukey, Beth. Power Poems for Kids. (p. 1390)
Stuksrud, Anne Connie, tr. see Mankell, Henning.
Stulginsky, Maryfran. Going for the Christmas Tree: A True Story. (p. 692)
Stull, Judy. From Darkness to Color: A Trilogy. (p. 642)
—Gray World. (p. 713)
—Great Connection. (p. 715)
—Secret Mission. (p. 1542)
Stultz, Janice. Harry Turnaround. (p. 751)

Stultz, Marie. Innocent Sounds: Building Choral Tone & Artistry with the Beginning Treble Voice. (p. 875)
—Innocent Sounds, Book II: Building Choral Tone & Artistry in Your Children's Choir. (p. 875)
Stumme, Nathan C. Life Without Mosquitoes. (p. 1013)
Stump, Chuck & Strawn, Jim. Another Sad Mad Glad Book: The Anatomy of Your Attitude. (p. 88)
Stump, Linda. Empty Manger. (p. 521)
Stumpe, Jennifer. Aunt Jo Jo's Magical Gifts: Amazing Underwater Adventure. (p. 115)
—Aunt Jo Jo's Magical Gifts: Ethan's Great African Journey. (p. 115)
Stumpf, Dawn Schaefer, jt. auth. see Stumpf, Tobias.
Stumpf, Tobias & Stumpf, Dawn Schaefer. Journal of an ADHD Kid: The Good, the Bad, & the Useful. (p. 927)
Stumpff, April D. & Johnston, Cassandra. Frontier Fun. (p. 644)
Stumpff, April D. & Messersmith, Patrick. Ann Richards: A Woman's Place Is in the Dome. (p. 85)
Stunkard, Geoff. Rail Mail: A Century of American Railroading on Picture Postcards. (p. 1433)
Stupniker, Yehudit. Remarkable Invention That Saves Zion: A Tale of Triz. (p. 1458)
Stupp, Robert Dock. Fable of Freddy & the Frockett. (p. 559)
Sturcke, Otto, illus. see List, Gloria A.
Sturdevant, Lori, ed. see Davis, W. Harry.
Sturdevant, Lynda. Amazing Adventures of Superfeet: The Awesome Book. (p. 52)
Sturdivant, Brad, jt. auth. see Blake, Kevin.
Sturdy, Sandy. Bird Who Wouldn't Sing (p. 190)
Sturey, James D. and His Perfect Son, Justus: In the Land of Fell. (p. 71)
Sturgen, Bobbi, illus. see Johnson, Sandi.
Sturgeon, Bobbi, illus. see Johnson, Sandi.
Sturgeon, Brad, illus. see Cruz-Martinez, George.
Sturgeon, Kristi. Freckle Juice: An Instructional Guide for Literature (p. 632)
Sturgeon, Lisa Marie. Shape up with Jeremiah. (p. 1560)
Sturges, Judy Sue Goodwin. Construction Kitties. Halpern, Shari, illus. (p. 359)
Sturges, Philemon. How Do You Make a Baby Smile? Strevens-Marzo, Bridget, illus. (p. 808)
—I Love Bugs! Halpern, Shari, illus. (p. 842)
—I Love Cranes! Halpern, Shari, illus. (p. 842)
—I Love Planes! Halpern, Shari, illus. (p. 842)
—I Love School! Halpern, Shari, illus. (p. 843)
—I Love Tools! Halpern, Shari, illus. (p. 843)
—I Love Trains! Halpern, Shari, illus. (p. 843)
—I Love Trucks! Halpern, Shari, illus. (p. 843)
Sturgill, Jean A. Bouncing Beaver Discovers God: A Drew's Animals Book. (p. 216)
Sturgill, Ruthy. Christmas Tree Advent Calendar: A Country Quilted & Appliquéd Project. (p. 316)
Sturgis, Anne. When Pigs Fly & the King of Zar: Two Books in One. (p. 1904)
Sturgis, Brenda Reeves. 10 Turkeys in the Road Slonim, David, illus. (p. 1994)
Sturgis, James. Adam Beck (p. 11)
Sturhan, Nicole. Twilight Travels 2011: Book-Series Locations. (p. 1801)
Sturk, Karl. Movie Star Mystery. (p. 1183)
Sturkie, Joan & Cassady, Marsh. Acting It Out: 74 Short Plays for Starting Discussions with Teenagers. (p. 10)
—Acting It Out - Junior. (p. 10)
Sturm, Ellen. New York. (p. 1247)
—Ohio. (p. 1281)
Sturm, Ellen, illus. see Niz, Ellen S.
Sturm, Ilana. 13th Moon. (p. 1995)
Sturm, James. Fantastic Four: Unstable Molecules. Davis, Guy & Sikoryak, Bob, illus. (p. 571)
Sturm, James & Arnold, Andrew. Adventures in Cartooning: Characters in Action. (p. 15)
—Adventures in Cartooning Christmas Special. (p. 15)
Sturm, James, et al. Adventures in Cartooning Activity Book. (p. 15)
—Characters in Action! Sturm, James, illus. (p. 291)
—Christmas Special! Sturm, James, illus. (p. 315)
—Sleepless Knight. (p. 1589)
Sturm, Jeanne. American Flag. (p. 60)
—Comprension de los Modelos. (p. 354)
—Filling the Earth with Trash. (p. 586)
—Growing up Green. (p. 726)
—Inventors & Discoveries. (p. 884)
—Marsupials. (p. 1097)
—MP3 Players. (p. 1184)
—Nuestra Huella en la Tierra. (p. 1270)
—Our Footprint on Earth. (p. 1308)
—Restoring Wetlands. (p. 1464)
—Scavengers. (p. 1521)
—Understanding Biomes. (p. 1815)
—Understanding Models. (p. 1816)
—Video Games. (p. 1841)
Sturm, Jeanne, jt. auth. see Greve, Meg.
Sturm, M., jt. auth. see Sturm, Matthew.
Sturm, Matthew & Sturm, M. Apun: The Arctic Snow. (p. 93)
Sturman, Jennifer. And Then Everything Unraveled. (p. 71)
—And Then I Found Out the Truth. (p. 71)
Sturman, Veronica. Isabella & the Mystery of the Hatchling Alligators. (p. 891)
Sturrup Rosado, Alfredia, jt. auth. see Sturrup Rosado, Alfredia.
Sturrup Rosado, Alfredia & Sturrup Rosado, Alfredia. SHOO MOOT (the Featherweight) The Feather Weight. (p. 1568)
Sturt, M. Canterbury Pilgrims. (p. 262)
Sturtevant, Karen. Adventures of Gert & Stu & Zippy Too. (p. 18)
Sturtz, Maria. Coloring Book in the Bible. (p. 344)
—Coloring Book Living for Jesus. (p. 344)
—God Gave Me. (p. 688)
—God Gave Me Spanish. (p. 688)
—God Is. (p. 689)
—God Is Spanish. (p. 689)
—Spanish Coloring in the Bible. (p. 1621)
—Spanish Coloring Living for Je. (p. 1621)
Sturtz, Maria Ester H. Vida de Jesus. (p. 1840)
Sturup, Signe. Circles of Round. Ma, Winnie, illus. (p. 321)
Stuska, Susan J. Horsemanship Handbook. (p. 800)
Stussy, Virginia. Wishes & Wonder. (p. 1940)
Stute, Lela LaBree. Big Bad Blonde (p. 177)
—New Guy (p. 1244)
—When Pugs Fly! (p. 1904)
Stute, Lela LaBree, jt. auth. see Stute, Lela Labree.
Stute, Lela Labree & Stute, Lela LaBree. Three Pugs & a Canadian Spy. (p. 1743)
Stutley, D. J. It Doesn't Matter / No Importa. (p. 894)
Stutley, Dj. It Doesn't Matter. (p. 894)
Stutman, Suzanne. All the Power Rests with You. (p. 46)
Stutson, Caroline. By the Light of the Halloween Moon Hawkes, Kevin, illus. (p. 249)
—Cats' Night Out. Klassen, Jon, illus. (p. 281)
—Prairie Primer: A to Z. Lamb, Susan Condie, illus. (p. 1392)
Stutt, Ryan. Skateboarding Field Manual. (p. 1583)
Stuttering Foundation, The. Trouble at Recess (p. 1789)
Stutz, Chris, illus. see Barr, Barbara Jean.
Stutz, Chris, illus. see Depucci, Diana M.
Stutz, Chris, illus. see McArthur, Cathy E.
Stutz, Chris, illus. see Pam, Miss.
Stutz, David. Hydraulics on My Stroller! (p. 831)
Stutzman, D. J. Promise Ring. (p. 1411)
Stutzman, Laura, illus. see Menendez, Shirley.
Stutzman, Laura, illus. see Wilde, Oscar & Grodin, Elissa.
Stuve-Bodeen, Stephanie. Babu's Song. Boyd, Aaron, illus. (p. 124)
—Escuela de Elizabeti. Sarfatti, Esther, tr. from ENG. (p. 535)
—Muneca de Elizabeti. Sarfatti, Esther, tr. (p. 1191)
Stuve-Bodeen, Stephanie & Hale, Christy. Elizabeti's Doll. (p. 513)
—Mama Elizabeti. (p. 1084)
Stux, Erica. Achievers: Great Women in the Biological Sciences. (p. 9)
—Enrico Fermi: Trailblazer in Nuclear Physics. (p. 531)
Stycznski, Gary. Animals of Greenback Valley: The Magic Card. (p. 83)
Style Guide, jt. illus. see Style Guide Staff.
Style Guide Staff. Everyone Is Different: Why Being Different Is Great! (p. 544)
—Feel Better, Toodee! (p. 580)
—Gift of the Night Fury. (p. 675)
—Good Po, Bad Po. (p. 700)
—Home: The Chapter Book. (p. 791)
—I'm Thankful for You! (p. 860)
—Kung Fu to the Rescue! (p. 968)
—Missing Apple Mystery. (p. 1152)
—Po's Secret Move. (p. 1387)
—SpongeBob's Backpack Book. (p. 1630)
—Two to Kung Fu. (p. 1804)
Style Guide Staff, illus. see Evans, Cordelia.
Style Guide Staff, illus. see Friedman, Becky.
Style Guide Staff, illus. see Gallo, Tina.
Style Guide Staff, illus. see Jameson, Louise.
Style Guide Staff, illus. see Katschke, Judy.
Style Guide Staff, illus. see Lewman, David.
Style Guide Staff, illus. see McMahon, Kara.
Style Guide Staff, illus. see Santomero, Angela C.
Style Guide Staff, illus. see Shaw, Natalie.
Style Guide Staff, illus. see Silverhardt, Lauryn.
Style Guide Staff, illus. see Testa, Maggie.
Style Guide Staff & Fruchter, Jason. Daniel Goes to School. (p. 405)
Style Guide Staff & Garwood, Gord. Thank You Day. (p. 1725)
Style Guide Staff & Style Guide. Patricks Backpack Book. (p. 1329)
Style Guide, Style. Furry & the Furious. (p. 650)
—Knightly Campout. (p. 964)
—Lovely, Love My Family. (p. 1061)
—School Is Awesome! (p. 1523)
Style Guide, Style, illus. see Pendergrass, Daphne.
Style Guide, Style, illus. see Testa, Maggie.
Style Guide, Style, jt. illus. see Schwarz, Thies.
Style Guide, Style & Schwarz, Thies. Tip's Tips on Friendship. (p. 1757)
Styles, Cyndie M. Crossing Burning Bridges: One Woman's Amazing Journey. (p. 385)
Styles, Emily, illus. see Johnson, Julia.
Styles, Howard. Technician Certification for Refrigerants: Text. (p. 1711)
—Technician Certification for Refrigerants: Answer Key. (p. 1711)
Styles, Showell. Flying Ensign: Greencoats Against Napoleon. (p. 610)
Stylou, Georgia, illus. see Spergel, Heather.
Su, Keren, photos by see Global Fund for Children Staff.
Su, Keren, photos by see Stone, Lynn M.
Su, Lucy. Children of Lir Jigsaw Book. (p. 302)
—Make a Picnic. Su, Lucy, illus. (p. 1078)
—Make Cards. Su, Lucy, illus. (p. 1079)
—Play Dressing Up. Su, Lucy, illus. (p. 1371)
—Play Hide & Seek. Su, Lucy, illus. (p. 1371)
—Say Good Morning. Su, Lucy, illus. (p. 1518)
—Say Good Night. Su, Lucy, illus. (p. 1518)
Su, Lucy, illus. see Carroll, Yvonne.
Su, Qin, illus. see MacLeod, Jean.
Su, Tami. Sword to Words. Hills, Laila, illus. (p. 1692)
Su'a, Melissa L. What Animals Eat Can Be My Healthy Treat. (p. 1879)
Suad, Laura, illus. see Dolan, Penny.
Suarez, Carlos Ruiz. Hormiga de Sayil. Ugalde, Felipe, illus. (p. 798)
Suarez de la Prida, Isabel. Diminutos. Bouchain, Nava, illus. (p. 440)
Suarez, Linda. Wicked Watermelon. (p. 1927)
Suárez, Ma. Luisa. Eranse Una Vez Los Dioses: La Mitología Para Todos. (p. 533)
Suarez, Maria. Mr Giggles. (p. 1185)
Suarez, Maribel. Ramon & His Mouse. (p. 1438)
—Rebecca. (p. 1450)
Suarez, Maribel, illus. see Mora, Pat.
Suarez, Maribel, illus. see Namm, Diane.
Suarez, Maribel, illus. see Robleda, Margarita.
Suarez, Maribel, illus. see Santillana USA.
Suarez, Maribel, tr. see Namm, Diane.
Suarez, Nora, illus. see Peirce-Bale, Mary.
Suarez, Nora & Gertz, Mercedes, concepts. When Words Dream, Cuando las Palabras Sueñan: Children's Poetry, Poesia Infantil. (p. 1905)
Suarez, Rosa Virginia Urdaneta, photos by see Pantin, Yolanda.
Suarez, Sergio Lopez. Huakala! a los Miedos. Suarez, Sergio Lopez, illus. (p. 824)
Suart, Peter. Secret of the Universe. (p. 1543)
—Sirens. (p. 1580)
Subanthore, Aswin, jt. auth. see Harper, Robert Alexander.
Suben, Eric. Spanish Missions of Florida. (p. 1621)
Suber, Melissa, illus. see Krensky, Stephen.
Suber, Melissa, jt. auth. see Meng, Cece.
Subi, illus. see Obiols, Anna.
Subi, illus. see Palacio, Carla, tr.
Subirana, Joan, illus. see Bailer, Darice, et al.
Sublett, Kit. After Camp: Beginning the Christian Adventure. (p. 28)
Sublette, Guen. Here's Lookin' at Lizzie. (p. 771)
Subramaniam, Manasi. Dancing Bear. Gwangjo & Park, Jung-a, illus. (p. 402)
—Story & the Song. Sankaranarayanan, Ayswarya, illus. (p. 1656)
Subramanian, Mathangi. Bullying: The Ultimate Teen Guide. (p. 241)
Subrina. Jacko the Monkey. (p. 904)
Suchanek, David. 10 Most Inspiring Speeches. (p. 1994)
Suchecki, Carol. My Dream with Grandp. (p. 1202)
Suchowacki, William. Adventures of Maggie & Mikey. (p. 20)
Suchy, Julianne. Eek! Me Alone. (p. 982)
Suda, Shiho Kemp, tr. see Yoshinaga, Masayuki & Ishikawa, Katsuhiko.
Sudbury, Dave & Saefkow, Hans. King of Rome. (p. 959)
Suddard, Lisa. Money Grows with Bees. Cabrillo, Cinthya, illus. (p. 1164)
Sudderth, Jean. Incredible Edible Girl & Friends. (p. 869)
Sudduth, Brent. I Am Superman! Edwards, Tommy Lee, illus. (p. 834)
Sudduth, Brent & Meredith Books Staff. Doom in a Box. Panosian, Dan, illus. (p. 470)
—Heads or Tails. Mada Design Staff, illus. (p. 757)
Sudduth, Brent H. Buster. Spengler, Kenneth J., illus. (p. 245)
Sudeith, Alaina. Superman Classic: The Superman Reusable Sticker Book. (p. 1683)
Suderman, Colleen C. Norgee & the Christmas Tree: A Norgee Story. (p. 1264)
—Norgee Does the Laundry (p. 1264)
Sudjic, Deyan. Future Systems. Scaro, Diego, ed. (p. 651)
—John Pawson Works. Codell, Esmé Raji, illus. (p. 922)
Sudo, Kumiko. Coco-Chan's Kimono. Sudo, Kumiko, illus. (p. 337)
Sudyka, Diana, illus. see Stewart, Trenton Lee.
Sudzuka, Goran, jt. auth. see Vaughan, Brian K.
Sue. Whinermans. (p. 1911)
Sue, Bright-Moore, jt. auth. see Miller, Reagan.
Sue, David, et al. Essentials of Understanding Abnormal Behavior. (p. 537)
Sue, Eugene. Godolphin Arabian. De Jonge, Alex, tr. from FRE. (p. 690)
Sue, Grandma. Best Book in the Library. Cherry, Gale, illus. (p. 168)
—Zibbins: The Golden Necklace. (p. 1986)
Sue-A-Quan, Goomatie. Seal Fascination at Sea: A Fascinating Seal. (p. 1536)
Suedkamp, Shirley M. Cat Who Lost His Meow. (p. 278)
Suekane, Kumiko. Afterschool Charisma. Suekane, Kumiko, illus. (p. 29)
Suen, Anastasia. Air Show. Mariniello, Cecco, illus. (p. 31)
—Alternate Reality Game Designer Jane Mcgonigal. (p. 50)
—Asociacion Para la Prevencion de la Crueldad de los Animales, (ASPCA) (p. 106)
—Asociación para la prevención de la crueldad de los animales, ASPCA (the Association for the Prevention of Cruelty to Animals) (p. 106)
—Association for the Prevention of Cruelty to Animals. (p. 107)
—At the Aquarium. Allen, Marie, illus. (p. 110)
—Aviones supersónicos (Supersonic Jets) (p. 120)
—Big Catch: A Robot & Rico Story Laughead, Mike, illus. (p. 180)
—Career Building Through Using Search Engine Optimization Techniques. (p. 266)
—Careers with Swat Teams. (p. 268)
—Clubhouse. Eitzen, Allan, illus. (p. 335)
—Cruz Roja. (p. 387)
—Cruz Roja (the Red Cross) (p. 387)
—Cuerpo de Paz. (p. 390)
—Cuerpo de Paz (the Peace Corps) (p. 390)
—Cutting in Line Isn't Fair! Ebbeler, Jeffrey, illus. (p. 396)
—Dino Hunt: A Robot & Rico Story. Laughead, Mike, illus. (p. 441)
—Doctors Without Borders. (p. 459)
—Don't Forget! A Responsibility Story. Ebbeler, Jeff, illus. (p. 467)
—Downloading & Online Shopping Safety & Privacy. (p. 474)
—Elephant Grows Up Huiett, William J. & Denman, Michael L., illus. (p. 511)
—Envelopes Everywhere! Allen, Marie, illus. (p. 531)
—Finding a Way: Six Historic U.S. Routes. (p. 587)
—Fly, Emma, Fly. Mitchell, Hazel, illus. (p. 609)
—Fossil Hunt. Allen, Marie, illus. (p. 623)
—From Accident to Hospital. (p. 641)
—From Factory to Store. (p. 642)
—Game Over: Dealing with Bullies. Ebbeler, Jeff, illus. (p. 654)
—Getting a Job in Child Care. (p. 668)
—Girls Can, Too! A Tolerence Story. Ebbeler, Jeff, illus. (p. 680)
—Girl's Guide to Volleyball (p. 680)
—Good Team: A Cooperation Story. Ebbeler, Jeffrey, illus. (p. 700)
—Great Idea? An Up2U Character Education Adventure. Dippold, Jane, illus. (p. 716)
—Great Plains Region. (p. 717)
—Gulf Coast Region. (p. 731)
—Habitat for Humanity. (p. 734)
—Habitat Para la Humanidad. (p. 734)
—Hábitat para la Humanidad (Habitat for Humanity) (p. 734)
—Helping Sophia. Ebbeler, Jeffrey, illus. (p. 766)
—Historia Del Baloncesto. (p. 782)
—historia del baloncesto (the Story of Basketball) (p. 782)
—Historia del Beisbol. Spanish Educational Publishers Staff, tr. (p. 782)
—historia del béisbol (the Story of Baseball) (p. 782)
—Historia del Futbol. Spanish Educational Publishers Staff, tr. (p. 782)
—Historia Del Futbol Americano. (p. 782)
—historia del fútbol americano (the Story of Football) (p. 782)
—historia del fútbol (the Story of Soccer) (p. 782)
—Historia del Hockey. Spanish Educational Publishers Staff, tr. (p. 782)
—historia del hockey (the Story of Hockey) (p. 782)
—Historia Del Patinaje Artistico. (p. 782)
—historia del patinaje artístico (the Story of Figure Skating) (p. 782)
—Hollywood Here We Come! Allen, Marie, illus. (p. 789)
—In the Big City. Myer, Ed, illus. (p. 865)
—Instrument Petting Zoo. Allen, Marie, illus. (p. 879)
—Ipod & Electronics Visionary Tony Fadell. (p. 886)
—Johnny Appleseed. Myer, Ed, illus. (p. 923)
—Loose Tooth. Eitzen, Allan, illus. (p. 1052)
—Main Street School ~Kids with Character Set 2 - 6 Titles (p. 1077)
—Medicos Sin Fronteras. (p. 1119)
—Médicos sin Fronteras (Doctors Without Borders) (p. 1119)
—Mountain Region. (p. 1181)
—New Girl: An Up2U Character Education Adventure. Dippold, Jane, illus. (p. 1244)
—Noche de Terror. Heck, Claudia M., tr. from ENG. (p. 1262)
—Peace Corps. (p. 1331)
—Pirate Map: A Robot & Rico Story. Laughead, Mike, illus. (p. 1362)
—Premio Adentro. Heck, Claudia M., tr. from ENG. (p. 1395)
—Prize Inside: A Robot & Rico Story Laughead, Mike, illus. (p. 1408)
—Raising the Flag. Ebbeler, Jeffrey, illus. (p. 1437)
—Read & Write Sports: Readers Theatre & Writing Activities for Grades 3-8 (p. 1443)
—Red Cross. (p. 1453)
—Save the Best for Last, Abby: All-Star Cheerleaders. Mitchell, Hazel, illus. (p. 1516)
—Scary Night: A Robot & Rico Story Laughead, Mike, illus. (p. 1520)
—Scissors, Paper & Sharing. Ebbeler, Jeffrey, illus. (p. 1529)
—Show Some Respect. Ebbeler, Jeffrey, illus. (p. 1571)
—Skate Trick: A Robot & Rico Story Laughead, Mike, illus. (p. 1583)
—Snow Games: A Robot & Rico Story. Laughead, Mike, illus. (p. 1599)
—Story of Baseball. (p. 1657)
—Story of Basketball. (p. 1657)
—Story of Soccer. (p. 1660)
—Subway. Katz, Karen, illus. (p. 1671)
—Test Drive: A Robot & Rico Story. Laughead, Mike, illus. (p. 1723)
—Tick Tock, Taylor! All-Star Cheerleaders. Mitchell, Hazel, illus. (p. 1747)
—Times Tables Cheat. Ebbeler, Jeffrey, illus. (p. 1754)
—Toco Toucans: Bright Enough to Disappear. (p. 1760)
—Tooth Fairy. Myer, Ed, illus. (p. 1768)
—Top STEM Careers in Science. (p. 1769)
—Trucos en la Patineta. Heck, Claudia M., tr. from ENG. (p. 1791)
—Trust Me: A Loyalty Story. Ebbeler, Jeff, illus. (p. 1793)
—Tyrannasaurus Rex. (p. 1805)
—Tyrannosaurus. (p. 1805)
—U. S. Supreme Court Skeens, Matthew, illus. (p. 1807)
—UNICEF. (p. 1818)
—Unicef. (p. 1818)
—Unicef (unicef) (p. 1818)
—Vote for Isaiah! A Citizenship Story. Ebbeler, Jeff, illus. (p. 1850)
—We're Going on a Dinosaur Dig. Myer, Ed, illus. (p. 1875)
—Wired. Carrick, Paul, illus. (p. 1939)
Suen, Anastasia & Heck, Claudia M. Gran Pesca. Laughead, Mike, illus. (p. 707)
Suen, Anastasia & Maddox, Jake. BMX Bully Tiffany, Sean, illus. (p. 204)
Suen, Anastasia & Mitchell, Hazel. Just So, Brianna: All-Star Cheerleaders. (p. 939)
Suenobu, Keiko. Life Suenobu, Keiko, illus. (p. 1007)
Suetonius. Twelve Caesars. Graves, Robert, tr. from LAT. (p. 1800)
Sugamoto, Junichi. Creating Stories. Kawanishi, Mikio, illus. (p. 379)
Sugano, Douglas & Pickering, Kenneth. Midlands Mysteries. (p. 1138)
SUGAR. Sugar Story. (p. 1673)
Sugarek, Trisha. Exciting Exploits of an Effervescent Elf. (p. 547)
Sugarman, Allan S., jt. auth. see Greenberg, Sidney.
Sugarman, Brynn Olenberg. Rebecca's Journey Home. Shapiro, Michelle, illus. (p. 1450)
Sugarman, Dorothy, jt. auth. see Herwick Rice, Dona.
Sugarman, Dorothy, jt. auth. see Rice, Dona Herwick.
Sugarman, S. Allan, illus. see Rosenfield, Geraldine.
Sugaya, Atsuo. Leonardo Da Vinci: The Life of a Genius. Kobayashi, Tatsuyoshi, illus. (p. 992)
Sugden, Madeleine. Frog in the Bog. (p. 640)
Sugg, Nan. Erin & Katrina. Huber, Becca & Pope, Lauren, illus. (p. 533)
Sugg, Zoe "Zoella". Girl Online. (p. 678)
Suggs, Aisha, illus. see Williams, Tova.
Suggs, Dona. Adventures of Ms Dee & Misti the Kitten. (p. 21)
Suggs, Margaret, illus. see Magee, Wes.
Suggs, Rob. Comic Book Bible. (p. 348)
Suggs, Robb, jt. auth. see Wilkinson, Bruce.
Sugimoto, Nao. 100 Shapes. (p. 1999)
Sugisaki, Yukiru. Candidate for Goddess (p. 261)

Full bibliographic information is available on the Title Index page number referenced in parentheses at the end of each entry

—D. N. Angel (p. 398)
—D. N. Angel Nibley, Alethea & Nibley, Athena, trs. from JPN. (p. 398)
—D. N. Angel. (p. 398)
—D. N. Angel. Sugisaki, Yukiru, illus. (p. 398)
—D. N. Angel. Nibley, Alethea & Nibley, Athena, trs. from JPN. (p. 398)
—Lagoon Engine. (p. 971)
—Rizelmine Sugisaki, Yukiru, illus. (p. 1476)
Sugisaki, Yukiru, illus. see Tomino, Yoshiyuki.
Sugisaki, Yukiru, jt. auth. see Clamp Staff.
Sugisaki, Yukiru, creator. Candidate for Goddess (p. 261)
—D. N. Angel (p. 398)
—Lagoon Engine (p. 971)
Sugita, Yataka, illus. see Beach, Stewart.
Sugita, Yutaka. Goodnight, One, Two, Three. Sugita, Yutaka, illus. (p. 701)
Sugiyama, Yoshishige, jt. ed. see Hironaka, Heisuke.
Sugiyama, Yoshishige, ed. Tokyo Shoseki's Mathematics for Elementary School (Grades 1 - 6 set, 11 vol. Set) (p. 1762)
Sugobono, Nahuel. Leyendas, Mitos, Cuentos y Otros Relatos de las Praderas Norteamericanas. Huadi, illus. (p. 1004)
—Leyendas, Mitos, Cuentos y Otros Relatos Tobas. Huadi, illus. (p. 1004)
Suguitan, Jazel A. We're Moving?! Shari Tucker's Wacky World #1. (p. 1875)
Suhajcik, Andrea. Mommy, I Did Nothing Wrong! (p. 1162)
Suhay, Lisa. Haddy the Doorstopasaurus: North America's First Dinosaur. (p. 735)
—Our Fantasy Island: An Interactive Book. Hundley, Sam, illus. (p. 1308)
—Pardon Me, It's Ham, Not Turkey. Barcita, Pamela, illus. (p. 1324)
—There Goes a Mermaid - A NorFolktale. Sam, Hundley, illus. (p. 1729)
Suhr, James W., illus. see Donlon, Diane Youngblood.
Suhr, Joanne, jt. auth. see Blanchard, Patricia.
Suib, Stella. Inside Russia's SVR: The Federal Security Service. (p. 877)
—Inside Russia's SVR: The Foreign Intelligence Service. (p. 877)
Suits, Barbara Bradford. Hidden Treasure. (p. 776)
Suits, Patti J. Topa & the Path of the Pum. (p. 1769)
Suits, Rosella, illus. see Ostrom, Gladys.
Sukanada, I. Gusti Made, illus. see Bowler, Ann Martin & Bowler, Anna.
Suker, Ashlee, illus. see Bullard, Lisa.
Sukhin, Igor. Gary's Adventures in Chess Country. (p. 657)
Sukhram-Harris, Karen. Saturdays with Mom. (p. 1515)
SukWon, Sa, illus. see SungJa, Cho.
Sulborski, Christine. Alex's Winter Adventure. (p. 37)
Suleman, Shilo Shiv, illus. see R. N., Lavanya.
Suleman, Shilo Shiv, illus. see Ranade, Soumitra.
Suleyman, R. H. Tales Within. (p. 1703)
Sulgit, Nicole. Caillou Leads the Parade. Poupart, Jean-Sébastien, illus. (p. 251)
Sulkowski, Jennifer Suzanne. Pony Named Napoleon. (p. 1382)
Sulley, Robert. First Aid in Mathematics. (p. 592)
Sulllivan, Erin. Matemáticas en la Luna. Hanner, Albert, illus. (p. 1104)
Sullivan. Brief Calculus Instructor's Solution Manual. (p. 227)
—Computerized Test Bank to Accompany Brief Calculus. (p. 355)
—Computerized Test Bank to Accompany Finite Mathema Tics: An Applied Approach. (p. 355)
—Instructor's Solutions Manual to Accompany Finite Mathematics: An Applied Approach. (p. 878)
—Test Bank to Accompany Brief Calculus: An Applied Approach, First Edition. (p. 1723)
—Test Bank to Accompany Finite Mathematics: An Appl led Approach, Ninth Edition. (p. 1723)
Sullivan, jt. auth. see Buchanan.
Sullivan, A. E. Truly Terrible C Word. (p. 1793)
Sullivan, Abigail, jt. auth. see Epstein, Diane.
Sullivan & Buchanan. Programmed Reading 1. (p. 1410)
—Programmed Reading 2. (p. 1410)
—Programmed Reading 3. (p. 1410)
—Programmed Reading 4. (p. 1410)
—Programmed Reading 5. (p. 1410)
—Programmed Reading 6. (p. 1410)
—Programmed Reading 7. (p. 1410)
—Programmed Reading: Achievement Tests. (p. 1410)
—Programmed Reading: Blackline Masters. (p. 1410)
—Programmed Reading: For Placement of Corrective or Remedial Pupils Placement Exams. Bks. 1-23 (p. 1410)
—Programmed Reading. (p. 1410)
Sullivan, Ann. Florida. (p. 606)
Sullivan, Anne Marie. Albert Einstein: Great Scientist. (p. 34)
—Dalai Lama: Spiritual Leader. (p. 401)
—Dalai Lama: Spiritual Leader of Tibet. (p. 401)
—Franklin D. Roosevelt. (p. 630)
—Mother Teresa: Religious Humanitarian. (p. 1178)
—Mother Theresa: Religious Humanitarian. (p. 1178)
—Sir Isaac Newton: Famous English Scientist. (p. 1580)
—Syria (p. 1693)
—Syria. (p. 1693)
Sullivan Associates Staff. Programmed Math for Adults: Multiplication & Division of Fractions (Job Corps) (p. 1410)
Sullivan Associates Staff & Buchanan. Emergent Reading: Sounds & Letters. 3 (p. 518)
—Emergent Reading: Sounds & Letters. 4 (p. 518)
—Emergent Reading: Letters of the Alphabet. 1 (p. 518)
—Emergent Reading: Letters of the Alphabet. 2 (p. 518)
—Emergent Reading. (p. 518)
Sullivan, Ayn Cates. Sparkle & the Light. duCray, Belle Crow, illus. (p. 1622)
Sullivan, Bryan & French, Jackie. To the Moon & Back: The Amazing Australians at the Forefront of Space Travel. Gordon, Gus, illus. (p. 1759)
Sullivan, Candida. Zippy & the Stripes of Courage. (p. 1987)
—Zippy y Las Rayas de Valor. Foster, Jack, illus. (p. 1987)
Sullivan, Carolyn. Cutter the Crab: Spring Break. (p. 396)
Sullivan, Carolyn Rose. Music Box: Songs, Rhymes, & Games for Young Children (p. 1193)
Sullivan, Cheryl. New Nursery Rhymes. (p. 1246)
Sullivan, Chris Mann. Oh No, Not the Shot! (p. 1281)
Sullivan, Courtney. Reptiles at the Zoo: Divide Within 100 (p. 1461)
Sullivan, Dana. Ozzie & the Art Contest. Sullivan, Dana, illus. (p. 1316)
Sullivan, Dana, illus. see Kertell, Lynn Maslen.
Sullivan, Dana, illus. see Young, Judy.
Sullivan, Dana, jt. auth. see Young, Judy.
Sullivan, Davina & Smith, Rebekah. Day Roo Flew. (p. 414)
Sullivan, Derek, illus. see MacDonald, Margaret Read.
Sullivan, Derek E. Biggie. (p. 185)
Sullivan, Don, illus. see Boniface, William.
Sullivan, Don, illus. see Forbes, Chris.
Sullivan, E. J. Bubba the Redneck Reindeer. Eldredge, Ernie, illus. (p. 233)
—F Is for Florida. Eldredge, Ernie, illus. (p. 559)
—G Is for Georgia. Cross, Neal, illus. (p. 651)
—How Santa Got His Elves. Eldredge, Ernie, illus. (p. 812)
—Is for Alabama. Eldredge, Ernie, illus. (p. 889)
—N Is for North Carolina. Eldredge, Ernie illus. (p. 1227)
Sullivan, E J. Redneck Christmas Carol. (p. 1456)
Sullivan, E. J. S Is for South Carolina. Eldredge, Ernie, illus. (p. 1499)
—T Is for Tennessee. Cross, Neal, illus. (p. 1694)
—Tennessee Night Before Christmas. Eldredge, Larry, illus. (p. 1720)
—V Is for Virginia. Eldredge, Ernie, illus. (p. 1829)
Sullivan, Edward T. Ultimate Weapon: The Race to Develop the Atomic Bomb. (p. 1810)
Sullivan, Elizabeth, illus. see Schiller Brenz, Jeanne.
Sullivan, Ellen. North Carolina Night Before Christmas. Eldredge, Ernie, illus. (p. 1265)
Sullivan, Ellen & Moore, Clement C. Virginia Night Before Christmas. Franks, C. J., illus. (p. 1844)
Sullivan, Erin. Baseball Math. (p. 141)
—Baseball Math & el juego de Béisbol: 6 English, 6 Spanish Adaptations (p. 141)
—Cookie Count! (p. 361)
—Cookie Count! & la venta de Galletas: 6 English, 6 Spanish Adaptations (p. 361)
—Juego de Béisbol: Set Of 6. (p. 931)
—Los Matemáticos. (p. 1054)
—Matemáticas en los Deportes: Set Of 6. (p. 1104)
—Math on the Moon & Matemáticas en la Luna: 6 English, 6 Spanish Adaptations Hanner, Albert, illus. (p. 1106)
—Mathematical Thinkers & Los Matemáticos: 6 English, 6 Spanish Adaptations (p. 1107)
—Probabilidad: Set Of 6. (p. 1408)
—Probability. (p. 1408)
—Sports Math & Matemáticas en los Deportes: 6 English, 6 Spanish Adaptations (p. 1633)
—Tesoro: Set Of 6. (p. 1722)
—Treasure Hunt & el Tesoro: 6 English, 6 Spanish Adaptations (p. 1781)
—Venta de Galletas: Set Of 6. (p. 1836)
Sullivan, Erin Ash. Ancient Rome: Set Of 6. (p. 70)
—Ancient Rome: Text Pairs. (p. 70)
—Class Election: Set Of 6. (p. 327)
—Communities Helping Communities: Set Of 6. (p. 349)
—Communities Helping Communities: Text Pairs. (p. 349)
—Counting Clues: Set Of 6. (p. 371)
—Counting Clues. (p. 371)
—Holidays Around the World: Set Of 6. (p. 788)
—Holidays Around the World: Text Pairs. (p. 788)
—Human Body Math: Set Of 6. (p. 825)
—Human Body Math & Matemáticas del cuerpo Humano: 6 English, 6 Spanish Adaptations. (p. 825)
—Liquids & Gases: Set Of 6. (p. 1021)
—Liquids & Gases: Text Pairs. (p. 1021)
—Math Around the Globe: Set Of 6. (p. 1105)
—Math Around the Globe & Matemáticas alrededor del Mundo: 6 English, 6 Spanish Adaptations. (p. 1105)
—Math at the Olympics: Set Of 6. (p. 1105)
—Math at the Olympics & Matemáticas en las Olimpiadas: 6 English, 6 Spanish Adaptations. (p. 1105)
—Math in a Democracy: Set Of 6. (p. 1106)
—Math in a Democracy & Matemáticas en una Democracia: 6 English, 6 Spanish Adaptations. (p. 1106)
—Measuring Matter: Set Of 6. (p. 1117)
—Measuring Matter: Text Pairs. (p. 1117)
—Metric Math: Set Of 6. (p. 1130)
—Metric Math & Matemáticas Métricas: 6 English, 6 Spanish Adaptations. (p. 1130)
—Music Counts: Set Of 6. (p. 1193)
—Music Counts & Cálculos Musicales: 6 English, 6 Spanish Adaptations. (p. 1193)
—Patterns in Nature: Set Of 6. (p. 1329)
—Pyramids: Set Of 6. (p. 1421)
—Pyramids. (p. 1421)
—Seven Wonders of the Ancient World. (p. 1555)
—Seven Wonders of the Ancient World & Las siete maravillas del mundo Antiguo: 6 English, 6 Spanish Adaptations. (p. 1555)
Sullivan, George. All about Soccer. (p. 43)
—Click! Click! Click! Photography for Children. (p. 331)
—Geronimo: Apache Renegade. (p. 667)
—Helen Keller: Her Life in Pictures. (p. 763)
—Journalists at Risk: Reporting America's Wars. (p. 927)
—Knockout! A Photobiography of Boxer Joe Louis. (p. 965)
—Tom Thumb: The Remarkable True Story of a Man in Miniature. (p. 1764)
Sullivan, Herman. Adventures of Stinky Poo the Little Skunk. (p. 23)
Sullivan, J. Courtney. Dating Up: Dump the Schlump & Find a Quality Man. (p. 409)
Sullivan, Jaclyn. What's in Your Chicken Nugget? (p. 1898)
—What's in Your Hamburger? (p. 1898)
—What's in Your Hot Dog? (p. 1898)
—What's in Your Pizza? (p. 1898)
—What's in Your Soda? (p. 1898)
Sullivan, Jacqueline Levering. Annie's War. (p. 87)
Sullivan, James Kevin. What Went Right Today? Journal: WWRT Journal. (p. 1895)
Sullivan, Janet O'Neill, jt. auth. see O'Neill, David.
Sullivan, Jean. Blakely Field Stories. (p. 198)
Sullivan, Jenny. Great Cake Bake. (p. 714)
—Magic Apostrophe. (p. 1071)
—Nowhere Again. (p. 1269)
Sullivan, Jessie. My Little Hand in His Big One. (p. 1212)
Sullivan, Jody. Crabs [Scholastic]. (p. 375)
—Georgia. (p. 665)
—Hawaii. (p. 755)
—Parrotfish (p. 1325)
—Sea Anemones (p. 1534)
—Sea Stars (p. 1535)
—Sea Stars [Scholastic]. (p. 1535)
Sullivan, Jody, jt. auth. see Lindeen, Carol K.
Sullivan, Jody & Capstone Press Staff. Crabs (p. 375)
—Sea Stars (p. 1535)
Sullivan, John Jeremiah & Johnson, Jeremiah Sullivan. Blood Horses: Notes of a Sportswriter's Son. (p. 200)
Sullivan, K. Osborn. Graveyard Kids. (p. 712)
Sullivan, Kate. On Linden Square. Sullivan, Kate, illus. (p. 1289)
Sullivan, Kathryn. Michael & the Elf. Dunningham, Jo, illus. (p. 1134)
Sullivan, Kevin. Best Hawaiian Style Mother Goose Ever. Aoki, Deb, illus. (p. 170)
—New Beginning. (p. 1243)
Sullivan, Kevin & Goldman, Leslie. Anne & the Bully. (p. 85)
—Anne's Babysitting Blues. (p. 86)
—Anne's Red Hair. (p. 86)
Sullivan, Kevin & Morgan, Elizabeth. Anne's New Home. (p. 86)
Sullivan, Kiki. Dolls. (p. 464)
—Midnight Dolls. (p. 1138)
Sullivan, Kim. Mr. Lewis Finds a Home. (p. 1185)
Sullivan, Kimberly L. Muammar Al-Qaddafi's Libya. (p. 1188)
—Slobodan Milosevic's Yugoslavia. (p. 1591)
Sullivan, Laura. Colonial Cook. (p. 341)
Sullivan, Laura L. Black Bart Roberts. (p. 195)
—Blackbeard. (p. 197)
—Colonial Dressmaker. (p. 341)
—Colonial Minuteman. (p. 341)
—Colonial Slave Family. (p. 341)
—Colonial Wigmaker. (p. 342)
—Colonial Woodworker. (p. 342)
—Delusion. (p. 425)
—Gail Carson Levine. (p. 652)
—Jacqueline Woodson. (p. 905)
—Ladies in Waiting. (p. 970)
—Life As a Cowboy in the American West. (p. 1008)
—Life As a Spy in the American Revolution. (p. 1008)
—Life As an Explorer with Lewis & Clark. (p. 1008)
—Love by the Morning Star. (p. 1059)
—Pros & Cons of Solar Power. (p. 1412)
—Sir Henry Morgan. (p. 1580)
—Under the Green Hill. (p. 1813)
—What Is Gravity? (p. 1889)
—What Is Heat? (p. 1889)
—What Is Motion? (p. 1890)
Sullivan, Laura L., et al. Georgia. (p. 665)
—Tennessee. (p. 1720)
—Virginia. (p. 1844)
Sullivan, Lauren M. & Lewis, Samantha. Chipwrecked. (p. 308)
Sullivan, Leo. Life. (p. 1007)
Sullivan, Licsw. Mindfully Me! (p. 1145)
Sullivan, Lisa, compiled by. Happy Days. (p. 745)
Sullivan, Lori Lynn. Our Sunny Day Ride. (p. 1310)
Sullivan, Marija. Mermaid's Dream, Internationally Illustrated Picture Book: This Is a Unique & Beautiful Fairy Tale That Resolves the Mermaid's Age-Old Dilemma of Where to Live - On the Sea or on the Land. Colley, Abdoulie et al, illus. (p. 1128)
Sullivan, Martha. Around My City: Describe & Compare Measurable Attributes. (p. 100)
—If You Love Honey. Morrison, Cathy, illus. (p. 854)
—Pitter & Patter. Morrison, Cathy, illus. (p. 1364)
Sullivan, Mary. Ball. (p. 134)
—Dear Blue Sky. (p. 418)
—Lessons for Guided Writing: Whole-Class Lessons & Dozens of Student Samples with Teacher Comments to Effectively Scaffold the Writing Process. (p. 993)
Sullivan, Mary, illus. see Brown, Susan Taylor.
Sullivan, Mary, illus. see Connolly, Timothy.
Sullivan, Mary, illus. see Gaydos, Nora.
Sullivan, Mary, illus. see Jones, Christianne C.
Sullivan, Mary, illus. see Meyer, Joyce.
Sullivan, Mary, illus. see Mortensen, Lori.
Sullivan, Mary, illus. see Sateren, Shelley Swanson.
Sullivan, Mary, illus. see School Zone Interactive Staff.
Sullivan, Mary, illus. see Wax, Wendy.
Sullivan, Mary C. Bugs! a Counting Book. Sullivan, Mary C., illus. (p. 237)
Sullivan, Mary Jo. Wonder of Us (p. 1947)
Sullivan, Mary M. If I Had a Daddy. Jane, Nance', illus. (p. 853)
Sullivan, Maureen. Cabbages & Queens. Ferrando, Carol, illus. (p. 250)
—Custard & Mustard: Carlos in Coney Island. Josephs, Alison, illus. (p. 395)
Sullivan, Maureen & Josephs, Alison. Ankle Soup: A Thanksgiving Story. Josephs, Alison, illus. (p. 84)
Sullivan, Melody. Lillibit's Dream. Grof, Stanislav, illus. (p. 1017)
Sullivan, Michael. Brief Calculus: An Applied Approach. (p. 227)
—Escapade Johnson & Mayhem at Mount Moosilauke. Kolitsky, Joy, illus. (p. 534)
—Escapade Johnson & the Witches of Belknap County. Kolitsky, Joy, illus. (p. 534)
Sullivan, Michael John & Petrone, Susan. Sockkids Meet Lincoln. (p. 1605)
Sullivan, Michael P., jt. auth. see O'Brien, Tony.
Sullivan, Mike & Joynt, Amanda. Fish of Alberta. (p. 598)
Sullivan, Myra L., ed. see Sullivan, R. J.
Sullivan, Navin. Area, Distance, & Volume. (p. 97)
—Measure Up! (p. 1117)
—Speed. (p. 1624)
—Temperature. (p. 1717)
—Time. (p. 1750)
—Weight. (p. 1872)
Sullivan, Otha Richard. African American Inventors. Haskins, Jim, ed. (p. 27)
Sullivan, Paul. Breaker at Dawn. (p. 224)
Sullivan, Paula. Todd's Box. Westcott, Nadine Bernard, illus. (p. 1761)
Sullivan, Paula, jt. auth. see Moran, Alex.
Sullivan, R. J. Tales of a Florida Boyhood. Voldseth, Beverly & Sullivan, Myra L., eds. (p. 1702)
Sullivan Rake, Jody & Rake, Jody Sullivan. Airedale Terriers (p. 31)
—Boxers (p. 217)
—Bulldogs (p. 240)
—Collies (p. 340)
—English Springer Spaniels Saunders-Smith, Gail, ed. (p. 530)
—Mutts (p. 1195)
Sullivan Rake, Jody, et al. Manatees Saunders-Smith, Gail, ed. (p. 1086)
—Sea Snakes Saunders-Smith, Gail, ed. (p. 1535)
Sullivan, Sarah. All That's Missing. (p. 45)
—Dear Baby: Letters from Your Big Brother. Meisel, Paul, illus. (p. 418)
—Once upon a Baby Brother. Sullivan, Sarah & Tusa, Tricia, illus. (p. 1292)
—Passing the Music Down. Root, Barry, illus. (p. 1326)
Sullivan, Silvia. Hip Hip Hurray We Found Teddy: A Book Series to Teach Children Practical Life Skills & Eco-Friendly Skills. (p. 780)
Sullivan, Simon, illus. see Lakin, Patricia.
Sullivan, Simon, illus. see Redmond, Shirley Raye & Redmond, Shirley Raye.
Sullivan, Sonja. I Am A Kumeyaay. Stanley, Barbara, ed. (p. 832)
Sullivan, Stephen D. Fantastic Four: The Junior Novel. (p. 571)
Sullivan, Tara. Golden Boy. (p. 694)
Sullivan, Therese M. & Bitner, Pamela. Gift from Valentine. (p. 675)
Sullivan, told to. Adventures of the Pink Shovel & the Red Pail. (p. 23)
Sullivan, Troy, illus. see Giuffre, Mary & Clark, Paul L.
Sullivan, William J. About Black Bat. (p. 5)
—About Black Head. (p. 5)
—About Blue Boo. (p. 5)
Sullivan-Fraser, Deannie. Johnny & the Gypsy Moth Rose, Hilda, illus. (p. 923)
Sullivan-Ringe, Laurie. Noise in the Night. Matiuzzo, Nick, illus. (p. 1262)
Sullivant, Holly. Ferrets. (p. 582)
—Hamsters. (p. 740)
Sullivant, Holly J. Ferrets. (p. 582)
—Hamsters. (p. 740)
Sully, Katherine. Baby Goldstars Rainbow Peekaboo! (p. 126)
—Where, Oh Where Is Huggle Buggle Bear? Samuel, Janet, illus. (p. 1909)
Sultan, Larry & Mandel, Mike, selected by. Larry Sultan & Mike Mandel: Evidence (p. 976)
Sulurayok, Matilda. Kamik's First Sled Leng, Qin, illus. (p. 942)
Suma, Nova Ren. Dani Noir. (p. 404)
—Fade Out. (p. 562)
—Imaginary Girls. (p. 860)
—Walls Around Us. (p. 1855)
Suman, Michelle, ed. see Ireland, Barb.
Suman, Surendra, illus. see Menon, Geeta.
Sumberac, Manuel, illus. see Andersen, Hans Christian.
Sumberac, Manuel, illus. see Woodward, Kay & Andersen, Hans Christian.
Sumberac, Manuel, jt. illus. see Basic, Zdenko.
Sume, Lori Anne. Sorry, Sorry, Sorry: Learning to Choose the Right. (p. 1614)
Sumerak, Marc. All-Ghoul School. (p. 44)
—Big Trouble at the Big Top! Gurihiru Staff, illus. (p. 184)
—Costumes On! Gurihiru Staff, illus. (p. 369)
—Machine Teen. (p. 1068)
—Mind over Matter. Gurihiru Staff, illus. (p. 1145)
—Ororo: Before the Storm. Barberi, Carlo, illus. (p. 1304)
—Wolverine Comic Reader 2. Di Vito, Andrea & Gurihiru Staff, illus. (p. 1944)
Sumerak, Marc, jt. text see Eliopoulis, Chris.
Sumerton, Amy, ed. Tall Tales & True Stories. (p. 1704)
Sumichrast, Jozef, illus. see Hillert, Margaret.
Summa, Pam. Groping for Luna. (p. 725)
Summer, Angel, ed. see Turner, Dale.
Summer, Deborah & Doyle, Winifred. Andi's Antics: A Girl's Adventures with ADD. (p. 72)
Summer, Joan. Dark on the Outside Bright on the Inside. (p. 408)
Summer, L. S. Rosa Parks. (p. 1488)
Summer, Laura LeClair. Mommy will always come Home. White, Kathy, illus. (p. 1162)
Summer, Mary Elizabeth. Trust Me, I'm Lying. (p. 1793)
Summer Rogers Martin. Kaylea Grows Up: Mommy & Me Days. Debi Rogers, illus. (p. 946)
Summerer, Eric. Wolfgang Amadeus Mozart. (p. 1944)
Summerer, Eric Michael. Franz Joseph Haydn. (p. 631)
—Franz Peter Schubert. (p. 631)
—Frederic Chopin. (p. 633)
—Frédéric Chopin. (p. 633)
—Johann Sebastian Bach. (p. 920)
—Ludwig van Beethoven. (p. 1064)
—Wolfgang Amadeus Mozart. (p. 1944)
Summerer, Marilyn. First Christmas Present. van der Sterre, Johanna, illus. (p. 593)
Summerhayes, Roger, photos by see Ruffner, Melissa.
Summers, Alex. Rescue & Shelter Cats. (p. 1462)
—Rescue & Shelter Dogs. (p. 1462)
Summers, Amy T. Vbs 04 Adult Leader Pack. (p. 1833)
—Vbs 04 Adult Learner Guide. (p. 1833)

Summers, Barbara, ed. Open the Unusual Door: True Life Stories of Challenge, Adventure, & Success by Black Americans. (p. 1299)
Summers, Courtney. All the Rage. (p. 46)
—Cracked up to Be. (p. 375)
—Fall for Anything. (p. 566)
—Some Girls Are. (p. 1609)
—This Is Not a Test. (p. 1736)
—What Goes Around: Two Books in One: Cracked up to Be & Some Girls Are. (p. 1884)
Summers, Dana, illus. see Higdon, Hal.
Summers, Darien. Mischievous Hare. (p. 1150)
Summers, David. Real Spaces: World Art History & the Rise of Western Modernism. (p. 1449)
Summers, Elizabeth. Tools of War. (p. 1767)
—Weapons & Vehicles of the Iraq War. (p. 1869)
—Weapons & Vehicles of the Vietnam War. (p. 1869)
—Weapons & Vehicles of World War I. (p. 1869)
Summers, Everette. Grandaddy's Short Stories. (p. 707)
Summers, Gillian. Goblin's Curse: The Scions of Shadow Trilogy, Book 3. (p. 688)
—Into the Wildewood. (p. 881)
—Quicksilver Faire: The Scions of Shadow Trilogy, Book 2. (p. 1427)
—Secret of the Dread Forest: The Faire Folk Trilogy. (p. 1542)
—Shadows of the Redwood Bk. 1 (p. 1558)
—Tree Shepherd's Daughter. (p. 1783)
Summers, Jean. Kids' Guide to Writing Great Thank-You Notes. (p. 954)
Summers, Jodi. Making & Marketing Music: The Musician's Guide to Financing, Distributing & Promoting Albums. (p. 1080)
Summers, Katani. Style in with Katani. (p. 1670)
Summers, Kathryn & Summers, Michael. Creating Websites That Work. (p. 379)
Summers, Kim. Senor Mundo & Me: A Happy Birthday Story. Mariscal, Javier, illus. (p. 1550)
Summers, Kimberly Dillon. Miley Cyrus: A Biography (p. 1142)
—United Kingdom. (p. 1819)
Summers, Marilee. C Is for Carbon. Wojtko, Kimberlee, illus. (p. 249)
Summers, Mark, illus. see Frisch, Aaron.
Summers, Michael, jt. auth. see Summers, Kathryn.
Summers, Natalie. Noweos: Neighbors One with Each Other. (p. 1269)
Summers, Rowan, jt. auth. see Bryant, Nick.
Summers, Sherri Pankratz. Humpty Dumpty, Back Together Again? Pankratz, Justin, illus. (p. 827)
Summers, Sherry, jt. auth. see Holyoak, Kathleen.
Summers, Sue L. Eye Spy Program: Early Youth Education Program. (p. 558)
—Media Alert! 200 Activities to Create Media-Savvy Kids. (p. 1118)
—Programa Espio Con los Ojos: Programa de Educacion para Jovenes. (p. 1410)
Summers, Susan. Greatest Gift: The Story of the Other Wise Man. Morris, Jackie, illus. (p. 720)
Summers, Tamara. Never Bite a Boy on the First Date. (p. 1242)
Summers, Terry. Peter Wanted a Pet. Kai, illus. (p. 1347)
Summerville, Justin. Forgetful Freddie. (p. 619)
Summit, Clark. I Want a Hero: A Young Adult Adventure Novel. (p. 847)
Summitt, April R. Sequoyah & the Invention of the Cherokee Alphabet (p. 1552)
Summy, Barrie. Disappearance of Emily H. (p. 446)
—I So Don't Do Famous. (p. 846)
—I So Don't Do Makeup. (p. 846)
—I So Don't Do Mysteries. (p. 846)
—I So Don't Do Spooky. (p. 846)
Summy, Margaret A. Imagine Me... Love My Body. (p. 861)
Summy, Rachel C. Good Night Sweet Home. (p. 700)
Sumner, Bea. Sisters Three: Scary's Not a Part of Me. (p. 1581)
Sumner, Christine. I Can Be: A Child's Whimsical Introduction to Yoga. Salopek, Kirk, illus. (p. 834)
Sumner, M. C. Common Enemy. (p. 349)
—Deadly Secrets. (p. 418)
—Inhuman Fury. (p. 874)
—Lost Soul. (p. 1056)
—Night Terrors. (p. 1254)
—Unseen Powers. (p. 1822)
Sumner, Ray, ed. World Geography (p. 1955)
Sumner, Tracy M. Kids' Guide to the 50 States: History, Geography, Fun Facts, & More—All from a Christian Perspective. (p. 954)
Sumner, Tracy M. & Landreth, Jane. Big Bible Guide: Kids' Guide to Creation & Bible Animals: Fun & Fascinating Bible Reference for Kids Ages 8-12. (p. 178)
Sumner, William, jt. auth. see Halls, Kelly Milner.
Sumner, William Graham. Challenge of Facts & Other Essays. (p. 289)
—Folkways. (p. 611)
—Forgotten Man & Other Essays. (p. 620)
Sumners, Carolyn T. & Handron, Kerry. Earthling's Guide to Mars: Travel to Mars with Pathfinder. (p. 497)
Sumpolec, Sarah Anne. Alliance. (p. 47)
—Encore. (p. 524)
—Masquerade. (p. 1102)
—Passage. (p. 1326)
Sumpter, Rachell, illus. see Baum, L. Frank.
Sumpter, Rachell, illus. see Tung, Jennifer.
Sun, Amanda. Ink. (p. 874)
—Rain. (p. 1434)
—Storm. (p. 1655)
Sun, Antuanette, illus. see Dellas, Melanie & Woodworth, John.
Sun Edit and Book Design, ed. Abraham Lincoln & the Forest of Little Pigeon Creek. (p. 6)
Sun, Jennie. Doodle Design & Draw ROCK STAR FASHIONS. (p. 469)
—Fashion. (p. 575)
Sun, Jennie & Kraft, Ellen Christiansen. Doodle Design & Draw GIRL STYLE. (p. 469)
Sun, Jun, illus. see Chen, Bill.
Sun, Michelle, jt. auth. see Chen, D. M.
Sun, Ming-Ju. Creative Haven Japanese Kimono Designs Coloring Book. (p. 379)
—Cut & Color Paper Dolls: Alice & Anna. (p. 395)
—Flower Fashion Fantasies Paper Dolls. (p. 607)
—Godey's Fashions. (p. 690)
—Godey's Fashions Paper Dolls 1860-1879. (p. 690)
—Old-Time Children's Fashions Coloring Book. (p. 1285)
—Traditional Japanese Fashions Paper Dolls. (p. 1776)
—Women in Japanese Art: Ukiyo-E Woodblock Prints. (p. 1945)
Sun, Ming-Ju & Creative Haven Staff. Creative Haven Art Nouveau Fashions Coloring Book. (p. 379)
—Flower Fashion Fantasies. (p. 607)
Sun Rise Illustration and Computer Animation Staff, illus. see Esmaili, Roza.
Sun, Ru, illus. see Ziefert, Harriet.
Sun Star, Elan, illus. see Chauvin, Belinda N.
Sun, Steve. Story of Robot Rob: New Beginning. (p. 1659)
—Story of Robot Rob: Troubles Ahead. (p. 1659)
—Story of Robot Rob: Teacher Appreciation Day. (p. 1659)
Sunami, Christopher, jt. auth. see Sunami, Kitoba.
Sunami, Kitoba & Sunami, Christopher. How the Fisherman Tricked the Genie. Hirao, Amiko, illus. (p. 813)
Sunantha Phusomsai, jt. auth. see Hawker, Frances.
Sunao, Yoshida. Trinity Blood - Reborn on the Mars: The Star of Sorrow. (p. 1786)
Sund, Mike. My Family Vacation! A Book about Me! Peterson, Stacy, illus. (p. 1203)
Sundance, Kyra. 101 Dog Tricks, Kids Edition: Fun & Easy Activities, Games, & Crafts. (p. 1999)
Sundance/Newbridge LLC Staff. Abominable Snowman. (p. 5)
—Amazing Water. (p. 56)
—America Is Voting. (p. 59)
—Animal Life Cycles. (p. 78)
—Animals & Their Babies. (p. 82)
—Animals in Hiding. (p. 83)
—Apple a Day. (p. 92)
—Being a Good Citizen. (p. 160)
—Being Human. (p. 161)
—Big Bears. (p. 178)
—Birds, Birds, Birds. (p. 191)
—Bubbles, Bubbles Everywhere. (p. 233)
—Busy As a Bee. (p. 245)
—Butterfly Is Born. (p. 248)
—Charts & Graphs. (p. 294)
—Circling the Sun. (p. 321)
—Design It! Build It! (p. 430)
—Dollars & Cents. (p. 463)
—Earth's Changing Surface. (p. 498)
—Energy. (p. 528)
—Energy from the Sun. (p. 528)
—Exploring Our Oceans. (p. 553)
—Fact Families. (p. 561)
—Follow the River. (p. 612)
—For Your Information. (p. 616)
—Four Seasons. (p. 625)
—From Circles to Cubes. (p. 642)
—From Peanuts to Peanut Butter. (p. 643)
—Gravity. (p. 712)
—Growing Pumpkins. (p. 726)
—How Animals Survive. (p. 805)
—How Life Changed. (p. 810)
—How We Use Electricity. (p. 823)
—Human Body. (p. 825)
—Inventions. (p. 884)
—Is It Alive? (p. 889)
—It's on the Map. (p. 898)
—Kids for the Earth. (p. 953)
—Leaping Frogs. (p. 982)
—Let's Measure It! (p. 999)
—Life in a Pond. (p. 1010)
—Life in a Tree. (p. 1010)
—Life in the Sea. (p. 1011)
—Light. (p. 1014)
—Lost Jewels of Nafouti. (p. 1056)
—Make a Good Guess. (p. 1078)
—Make Mine Ice Cream. (p. 1079)
—Maps & Globes. (p. 1090)
—Matter Is Everything. (p. 1109)
—Mystery of Magnets. (p. 1224)
—Mystery of the Maya. (p. 1225)
—On the Move! (p. 1291)
—One World, Many Cultures. (p. 1297)
—Our American Folklore. (p. 1307)
—Our Natural Resources. (p. 1309)
—Our Sun, Our Weather. (p. 1310)
—Out in Space. (p. 1311)
—Parts of a Whole. (p. 1325)
—Pasta, Please! (p. 1327)
—People & Technology. (p. 1339)
—Predators & Prey. (p. 1394)
—Predicting the Weather. (p. 1395)
—Properties of Materials. (p. 1411)
—Push & Pull. (p. 1420)
—Rain Forest. (p. 1434)
—Rocks & Soil. (p. 1483)
—See, Hear, Touch, Taste, Smell. (p. 1546)
—Seeds Get Around. (p. 1547)
—Simple Machines. (p. 1577)
—Sink or Float? (p. 1579)
—Six Simple Machines. (p. 1582)
—Sound. (p. 1615)
—Spinning a Web. (p. 1628)
—Squirrels All Year Long. (p. 1637)
—Symbols of America. (p. 1693)
—Time & Temperature. (p. 1751)
—Vegetable Garden. (p. 1834)
—Wants & Needs. (p. 1857)
—Wetlands. (p. 1877)
—What Is a Cycle? (p. 1888)
—What Is Matter? (p. 1889)
—What Is Technology? (p. 1890)
—What's That Sound? (p. 1899)
—Where Do Animals Live? (p. 1906)
—Where Does All the Garbage Go? (p. 1907)
—Where Plants Live. (p. 1909)
—Who Cares about the Weather? (p. 1914)
—Why Cities Grow. (p. 1923)
—World of Ants. (p. 1956)
—World of Dinosaurs. (p. 1956)
—World of Tools. (p. 1957)
—World of Work. (p. 1958)
—You Are What You Eat. (p. 1973)
Sundaram, Renuka. Sammy, the Galapagos Sea Lion. (p. 1508)
Sundaram, Siddhartha & Raghuraman, Renuka S. Horace Leclaire & His Bottles of Air. Raghuraman, Savitri, illus. (p. 797)
Sundaravej, Sittisan, illus. see Wallace, Jim.
Sundaravej, Sittisan & Thongmoon, Kriangsak. House of Danger. (p. 803)
—Race Forever. (p. 1431)
—Return to Atlantis. (p. 1465)
Sunday, Bonnie. Sparkles, Dragons, & Dragonfly Land. (p. 1622)
Sunday, Ian. Space Ace & the Flying Ace. (p. 1618)
Sundberg, Angela M., et al. Pottamus Family & the Unhappy Pottamus. Sundberg, Angela M. et al, illus. (p. 1388)
Sundberg, Mary Rose, tr. see Blondin, John & Blondin, George.
Sundberg, Mary Rose, tr. see Blondin, John.
Sundberg, Norma J. Odd Fable. Leiper, Esther M., illus. (p. 1278)
Sundberg, Peggy. Isabelle Lives a Dream. Wiles, Pat, illus. (p. 891)
—Jazmine's Incredible Story. Wiles, Pat, illus. (p. 910)
—Okey-Dokey Oakie. Wiles, Pat, illus. (p. 1282)
—Shortstuff Bucks! (p. 1569)
Sundberg, Wayne C. & Hoskinson, Susan. Fort Collins' First Water Works: Again a Work in Progress. (p. 623)
Sundblom, Haddon H. Night Before Christmas: A Family Treasury of Songs, Poems, & Stories. (p. 1252)
Sundell, Joanne. Arctic Shadow. (p. 96)
Sundell, Todd Andrew. Tales from the Valley of Shadows. (p. 1702)
Sundem, Garth. Real Kids, Real Stories, Real Change: Courageous Actions Around the World. (p. 1448)
Sunderland, Alan. Octavius O'Malley & the Mystery of the Criminal Cats. (p. 1277)
—Octavius O'Malley & the Mystery of the Exploding Cheese. Redlich, Ben, illus. (p. 1277)
—Octavius O'Malley & the Mystery of the Missing Mouse. Redlich, Ben, illus. (p. 1277)
Sunderland, Margot. Helping Children Pursue Their Hopes & Dreams - A Pea Called Mildred Armstrong, Nicky, tr. (p. 766)
—Helping Children Who Bottle up Their Feelings: A Niffenoo Called Nevermind. Armstrong, Nicky, illus. (p. 766)
—Helping Children Who Have Hardened Their Hearts or Become Bullies Armstrong, Nicky, illus. (p. 766)
—Helping Children Who Have Hardened Their Hearts or Become Bullies - A Wibble Called Bipley (p. 766)
—Science of Parenting. (p. 1527)
Sunderland, Margot, jt. auth. see Armstrong, Nicky.
Sunderland, Margot, jt. auth. see Hancock, Nicky.
Sunderland, Margot & Armstrong, Nicky. Helping Children Locked in Rage or Hate: A Guidebook. (p. 766)
Sunderland, Margot & Hancock, Nicky. Day the Sea Went Out & Never Came Back Armstrong, Nicky, tr. (p. 414)
—Frog Who Longed for the Moon to Smile Armstrong, Nicky, tr. (p. 640)
—Helping Children Pursue Their Hopes & Dreams. Armstrong, Nicky, illus. (p. 766)
—Helping Children Who Are Anxious or Obsessional - Willy & the Wobbly House Armstrong, Nicky, tr. (p. 766)
—Helping Children Who Bottle up Their Feelings & a Niffenoo Called Nevermind Armstrong, Nicky, tr. (p. 766)
—Helping Children Who Yearn for Someone They Love: The Frog Who Longed for the Moon to Smile Armstrong, Nicky, illus. (p. 766)
—Helping Children Who Yearn for Someone They Love & the Frog Who Longed for the Moon to Smile Armstrong, Nicky, tr. (p. 766)
—Helping Children with Fear: A Guidebook Armstrong, Nicky, tr. (p. 766)
—Helping Children with Loss: A Guidebook. Armstrong, Nicky, tr. (p. 766)
—How Hattie Hated Kindness. Armstrong, Nicky, tr. (p. 809)
—Niffenoo Called Nevermind. Armstrong, Nicky, tr. (p. 1252)
—Pea Called Mildred. Armstrong, Nicky, tr. (p. 1331)
—Ruby & the Rubbish Bin. Armstrong, Nicky, tr. (p. 1493)
—Teenie Weenie in a Too Big World Armstrong, Nicky, tr. (p. 1714)
—Wibble Called Bipley (And a Few Honks) Armstrong, Nicky, tr. (p. 1927)
—Willy & the Wobbly House. Armstrong, Nicky, tr. (p. 1934)
Sunderland, Margot & Pickering, Ken. Choreographing the Stage Musical. Engleheart, Phil, illus. (p. 310)
Sunderland, Margot, et al. Helping Children Who Think They Are Worthless. (p. 766)
Sunderman, Savannah. A-b-c. (p. 1)
Sundermann, Dan & Sundermann, Sally. Childhood Memories: Grandma & Grandpa's Earliest Recollections. (p. 302)
Sundermann, Elke. Look! Ancient Asia! (p. 1048)
—Look! Ancient China! (p. 1048)
—Look! Ancient India! (p. 1048)
—Look! Ancient Mound-Builders! (p. 1048)
—Look! Cherokee! (p. 1049)
—Look! Iroquois! (p. 1049)
—Look! Lakota! (p. 1049)
—Look! Native Americans! (p. 1049)
—Look! Navajo! (p. 1049)
—Look! Nez Perce! (p. 1049)
—Wow! Ancient Asia! Sundermann, Elke, illus. (p. 1962)
—Wow! Ancient Mound-Builders! (p. 1962)
—Wow! Cherokee! (p. 1962)
—Wow! Iroquois! (p. 1962)
—Wow! Lakota! (p. 1962)
—Wow! Native Americans! (p. 1962)
Sundermann, Sally, jt. auth. see Sundermann, Dan.
Sundgaard, Arnold. Lamb & the Butterfly. Carle, Eric, illus. (p. 972)
Sundquist, Josh. We Should Hang Out Sometime: Embarrassingly, a True Story. (p. 1868)
Sundram, Steve, illus. see Kita, Suzanne.
Sundstrom, Dainel H. Return of Oz. (p. 1464)
Sundstrom, Mary, illus. see Hunter, Skillman
Sundy, Jonathan, illus. see Benoist, Cathy & Gilmore, Cathy.
Sundy, Jonathan, illus. see Gilmore, Cathy & Benoist, Carol.
Suneby, Elizabeth. Razia's Ray of Hope: One Girl's Dream of an Education. Verelst, Suana, illus. (p. 1441)
Suneby, Elizabeth, jt. auth. see Heiman, Diane.
Suneby, Liz, jt. auth. see Heiman, Diane.
Suneby, Liz & Heiman, Diane. It's a ... It's a ... It's a Mitzvah. Molk, Laurel, illus. (p. 895)
—Mitzvah Project Book: Making Mitzvah Part of Your Bar/Bat Mitzvah & Your Life. (p. 1156)
Sunflower Education Staff. Golden Thread. (p. 695)
SungJa, Cho. Bubbly & Grumpy. SukWon, Sa, illus. (p. 233)
Sunita, Sunita. Gobble You Up! (p. 688)
Sunkara, Naveena, jt. auth. see Kong, Anja.
Sunkuli, O. Hero & the Dream. (p. 772)
Sunn, Dionny. Betty Duck's Adventures in Paradise. Sunn, Dionny, illus. (p. 172)
Sunnex, Hayley. Grandma's Hugs. (p. 708)
Sunni Brannan, illus. see Sally Spencer.
Sunny. Mona Lisa Awakening. (p. 1163)
Sunseri, Heather. Mindsiege. (p. 1145)
Sunseri, Sophia Natasha. Working As a Teacher in Your Community. (p. 1952)
Sunset Books Staff, jt. auth. see Barnes, Christine E.
Sunset Books Staff, et al. Kids Parties: Creative Ideas & Recipes for Making Celebrations Special. (p. 954)
Sunset Producciones, illus. see Cordero, Silvia Jaeger & Cordero, Silvia Jaegar.
Sunshine, Grammy. Father Tavish's Ten Timeless Truths. (p. 577)
Sunshine, Mary Lou, illus. see Orth, Jack.
Sun-Tzu. Arte de la Guerra. Griffith, Samuel B. & Parra, Jaime Barrera, trs. (p. 103)
Sun-Tzu & Gagliardi, Gary. Strategy for Sales Managers: Sun Tzu's the Art of War Plus Book Series. (p. 1666)
Sunwall, James. Postman Roulin. (p. 1388)
Suomalainen, Sami, illus. see Munsch, Robert.
Suorsa, Michael, illus. see Gregory, Caroline.
Supeene, Shelagh Lynne. My Name Is Mitch (p. 1215)
Super Achievement. Math Magic Workbook. (p. 1106)
Super Achievement, creator. Multimagic Table. (p. 1190)
Super Duper Inc. Staff, photos by. Artic Photos Fun Deck S Blends: Ap04. (p. 104)
Super Duper Publications Staff. Electronic Spinner 1-6: Spin267. (p. 509)
Super, John C., ed. see Salem Press Staff.
Super Kids Nutrition, creator. Super Baby Abigail's Lunch Time Advenutre. (p. 1679)
Super Why Staff. Ghost Who Was Afraid of Halloween. (p. 672)
Superle, Michelle. Black Dog Dream Dog Balance, Millie, illus. (p. 196)
Superstars!. Editors. Superstars! One Direction. (p. 1684)
Superstars! Editors. Superstars! One Direction: Inside Their World. Superstars! Editors, ed. (p. 1684)
—Superstars! - The Stars of the Hunger Games. (p. 1684)
Suphandagi, Lale. Dream Bird. (p. 483)
Suplicki, Mark J. Mirthburdz: The Discovery. (p. 1149)
Supplee, Audra. I Almost Love You, Eddie Clegg (p. 831)
Supplee, Kathryn. Choose Happy. (p. 310)
Supplee, Suzanne. Artichoke's Heart. (p. 104)
—Somebody Everybody Listens To. (p. 1609)
—When Irish Guys Are Smiling. (p. 1903)
Supples, Kevin. Speaking Out: The Civil Rights Movement 1950-1964. (p. 1623)
Supples, Kevin & National Geographic Learning Staff, Mali. (p. 1083)
Supples, Kevin, et al. Civil Rights Movement. (p. 325)
Supples, Lottie K. Happy, the Red Duck. (p. 747)
Sur La Table Staff & Mushet, Cindy. Baking Kids Love. (p. 133)
Surace, Joan. Story of Lucia. Rockford, Nancy, illus. (p. 1659)
Surber, Mary Brigid. Last Stork Summer. (p. 978)
Surber, Shawn-Michelle. Hope Surber, Shawn-Michelle, illus. (p. 796)
Surdu, John R. "Buck". Wellington Rules: Tactical Rules for the Napoleonic Wars. (p. 1874)
Suresh, Shreyas. Joy! a Book of Poems. (p. 929)
—Magic Lighthouse & other Stories. (p. 1072)
Surette, Janet H. Prince & the Gift: A Tale of True Beauty. (p. 1401)
Surf Lifesaving Australia Staff. First Aid & Emergency Care. (p. 592)
Surface, Mary Hall. More Short Scenes & Monologues for Middle School Students: Inspired by Literature, Social Studies, & Real Life. (p. 1174)
—Spirit Shall Fly: (play Script) (p. 1628)
Surfer Magazine Staff. Guide to Northern & Central California Surf Spots. (p. 730)
Surgal, Jon. Have You Seen My Dinosaur? Mathieu, Joe, illus. (p. 754)
Surges, James, tr. see Grimm, Jacob & Grimm, Wilhelm K.
Surget, Alain. Ghost Ship. (p. 671)
—Tirya y el Complot del Nilo. (p. 1757)
Surget, Alain & Hirsinger, Julien. Half & Half-People of the Caves. Avril, Francois & Duffour, Jean-Pierre, illus. (p. 736)
Surget, Alain & Yeardley, Glynne. Caesar, Who's He? Parme, Fabrice, illus. (p. 250)
—Cleopatra Must Be Saved! Parme, Fabrice, illus. (p. 331)
—Danger at the Circus! Parme, Fabrice, illus. (p. 403)
—Prisoners in the Pyramid. Parme, Fabrice, illus. (p. 1407)

S

Surhone, Lambert M., et al, eds. Adventures of Tintin: Secret of the Unicorn. (p. 24)
—Walter the Farting Dog. (p. 1856)
Suri, Jane Fulton & IDEO Staff. Thoughtless Acts? Observations on Intuitive Design. (p. 1740)
Suriano, Andy, illus. see Torres, J.
Suriano, Andy, illus. see Wayne, Matt.
Suritsch, Gina. Magical Tales from India: The Secret of the White Elephant & Mukti the Lion Finds Himself. (p. 1075)
Surman, Susan. Max & Friends. Owings, Rae, illus. (p. 1110)
Surman-Hobbs, Debbi. Little Brown Moth (p. 1025)
Surojegin, Pirkko-Liisa, illus. see Mäkinen, Kirsti.
Surovec, Yasmine. Bed for Kitty. Surovec, Yasmine, illus. (p. 156)
—I See Kitty. Surovec, Yasmine, illus. (p. 845)
—My Pet Human. (p. 1217)
Surplice, Holly. About a Bear. (p. 5)
—Guinea Pig Party. Surplice, Holly, illus. (p. 731)
—Peek-a-Boo Bunny. Surplice, Holly, illus. (p. 1334)
Surratt, Christopher. My Dad Is a Vampire. Boyles, Jolene, ed. (p. 1201)
Surratt, Denise. Cows at Honey Hill: Friends for Life. Haith, Sera, illus. (p. 374)
Surrey, Michael, illus. see Harner, Ron.
Surridge, Gerry, jt. auth. see Murphy, Bernadette.
Surridge, Malcolm, et al. Applied Business. (p. 93)
Susaeta, Equipo. Bella Durmiente -Sleeping Beauty. Susaeta Publishing, Inc., Staff, ed. (p. 162)
—Blancanieves / Snow White. Susaeta Publishing, Inc., Staff, ed. (p. 198)
Susaeta, Equipo, jt. auth. see Busquets, Jordi.
Susaeta, Equipo, jt. auth. see Martin, Manuela.
Susaeta Publishing, Inc., Staff. Los Reyes Magos y la Navidad. (p. 1054)
Susaeta Publishing, Inc., Staff, ed. see Martin, Manuela & Socolovsky, Gisela.
Susaeta Publishing, Inc., Staff, ed. see Martin, Manuela & Susaeta, Equipo.
Susaeta Publishing, Inc., Staff, ed. see Martin, Manuela.
Susaeta Publishing, Inc., Staff, ed. see Susaeta, Equipo.
Susaeta Publishing, Inc., Staff, ed. see Vara, Ana Serna, et al.
Susaeta Publishing, Inc., Staff, ed. Cocina para Niños. (p. 337)
Susan A. McCoy. Christmas That Saved Pie Town. (p. 316)
Susan, Hammond. Lord Calls Samuel. Swisher, Elizabeth, illus. (p. 1052)
Susan, Lisbin, illus. see Soloway, Cindy.
Susan, Paradis. Edna. Susan, Paradis, illus. (p. 504)
Susan, Turnbull, illus. see Eastman, Charles A. & Eastman, Elaine Goodale.
Suseata Publishing, Inc. Circulación Vial: Un Juego de Niños. (p. 321)
Susedik, Tina. Hat Peddler. Comstock, Chris, illus. (p. 752)
Susedik, Tina & Heers, Alli. Uncle Bills Farm: True Stories of His Crazy Farm Animals. Sutula, Hollie, illus. (p. 1811)
Susi, Geraldine Lee. For My People: The Jennie Dean Story (p. 616)
Süskind, Patrick, jt. auth. see Süskind, Patrick.
Süskind, Patrick & Süskind, Patrick. Taube. (p. 1707)
Susko, Mark D. Sally Sassafras, the Girl with Monster Hair. (p. 1505)
Sussex, Lucy. Revognase. (p. 1466)
Sussman, Elissa. Stray. (p. 1666)
Sussman, Ellen, ed. see Etringer, Kathy.
Sussman, Joni. My First Yiddish Word Book. Marzel, Pepi, illus. (p. 1208)
Sutanto, Tommy, illus. see Gopinath, Karin Ursula.
Sutcliff, Rosemary. Black Ships Before Troy: The Story of the Iliad. (p. 196)
—Dawn Wind. (p. 412)
—Eagle. (p. 492)
—Eagle of the Ninth. (p. 492)
—Iliad. Lee, Alan, illus. (p. 856)
—Knight's Fee. (p. 964)
—Lantern Bearers. (p. 975)
—Mark of the Horse Lord. (p. 1095)
—Odyssey. Lee, Alan & Sutcliff, Rosemary, illus. (p. 1279)
—Silver Branch. (p. 1576)
—Sword Song. (p. 1692)
—Wanderings of Odysseus: The Story of the Odyssey. (p. 1856)
Sutcliffe, Jane. Abigail Adams. (p. 5)
—Attack on Pearl Harbor Lentz, Bob, illus. (p. 114)
—Barack Obama. (p. 137)
—Chester Nimitz & the Sea Kodera, Craig, illus. (p. 298)
—Jesse Owens. Porter, Janice Lee, illus. (p. 914)
—John Adams. (p. 921)
—Leonardo's Monster Leonhard, Herb & Leonard, Herb, illus. (p. 992)
—Marian Anderson. (p. 1093)
—Milton Hershey. Parlin, Tim, illus. (p. 1144)
—Ronald Reagan. (p. 1486)
—Sacagawea. (p. 1500)
—Stone Giant: Michelangelo's David & How He Came to Be. (p. 1652)
—Stone Giant: Michelangelo's David & How He Came to Be. Shelley, John, illus. (p. 1652)
—White House Is Burning: August 24 1814. Farquharson, Alexander, illus. (p. 1913)
Sutcliffe, Kathy. When Romeo Kissed Mercutio. (p. 1904)
Sutcliffe, Kristen. Fabric Paper Thread: 26 Projects to Stitch with Friends. (p. 559)
Sutcliffe, William. Bad Influence. Anderson, Laura Ellen & Busby, Ailie, illus. (p. 131)
—Wall. (p. 1854)
Suter, Janine. Day the World Went Wacky. Gunther, Richard, illus. (p. 414)
—Noah's Floating Animal Park. Gunther, Richard, illus. (p. 1262)
—Not So Super Skyscraper! Gunther, Richard, illus. (p. 1267)
Suter, Joanne. Beginning Writing 1 Laurel Associates Inc. Staff, ed. (p. 160)
—Beginning Writing 2 Laurel Associates Inc. Staff, ed. (p. 160)
—Building Vocabulary Skills & Strategies Level 4 Laurel Associates Inc. Staff, ed. (p. 239)
—Community Resources. (p. 350)
—Good Grammar Laurel Associates Inc, ed. (p. 698)
—Health & Safety. (p. 757)
—Public Transportation & Travel. (p. 1414)
—Read Reflect Respond (p. 1443)
—Reading Comprehension Nonfiction 1 Reproducible Book with CD Saddleback Educational Publishing Staff, ed. (p. 1445)
Suter, Joanne & Greene, Janice. Read Reflect Respond 1 (p. 1443)
Suter, Lorenzo. TrYouth Truth Knowledge Apprehension Cog. (p. 1795)
Suteski, Monika, illus. see O'Brien, Cormac.
Sutherland, Adam. Armed Services. (p. 99)
—Being a Formula One Driver. (p. 160)
—Being a Model. (p. 160)
—Body Decoration. (p. 207)
—Police Forensics. (p. 1380)
—Political Leaders. (p. 1380)
—Soccer Stars. (p. 1603)
—Special Forces. (p. 1623)
—Story of Google. (p. 1658)
—Street Art. (p. 1666)
—Undercover Operations. (p. 1814)
Sutherland, David. Samantha Cardigan & the Genie's Revenge. Roberts, David, illus. (p. 1507)
—Samantha Cardigan & the Ghastly Twirling Sickness. Roberts, David, illus. (p. 1507)
Sutherland, David & Roberts, David. Samantha Cardigan & the Genie's Revenge. (p. 1507)
—Samantha Cardigan & the Ghastly Twirling Sickness. (p. 1507)
Sutherland, David, et al. Siriol Llywelyn a Dial y Bwgan. (p. 1581)
—Siriol Llywelyn A'R Salwch Chwyrlio Erchyll. Roberts, David, illus. (p. 1581)
Sutherland, Dianne. Rashiecoat: A Story in Scots for Young Readers. (p. 1439)
Sutherland, E. B. Tallie's in a Sea of Trouble. (p. 1704)
Sutherland, Eileen. Mom & the Polka-Dot Boo-Boo: A Gentle Story Explaining Breast Cancer to a Young Child. Sutherland, Eileen & Sutherland, Maggie, illus. (p. 1161)
Sutherland, Harry A. Dad's Car Wash. (p. 399)
Sutherland, James. Tale of the Miserous Mip. Sutherland, James, illus. (p. 1700)
Sutherland, James B. Ronald Reagan: Political Star. (p. 1486)
Sutherland, Joe. Broken Egg: A story to help children cope with the loss of a younger Sibling. (p. 230)
Sutherland, John. Victorian Fiction: Writers, Publishers, Readers. (p. 1840)
Sutherland, John, jt. auth. see Canwell, Diane.
Sutherland, John, et al. Aircraft Carriers. (p. 31)
Sutherland, Johnathan, jt. auth. see Canwell, Diane.
Sutherland, Jon & Canwell, Diane. Poisonings. (p. 1377)
Sutherland, Jon & Chalk, Gary. Avon United - Diamond. (p. 120)
—Bridgewater FC - 5-3-2. (p. 227)
—Football Fantasy Clyde Rovers. (p. 614)
—Medway United - 4-5-1. (p. 1120)
—Mersey City - 4-4-2. (p. 1129)
—Thames United. (p. 1725)
—Trent Albion. (p. 1784)
—Tyne Athletic - 4-3-3. (p. 1805)
Sutherland, Jon, et al. Emerald Pirate. (p. 517)
—Spy Master. (p. 1636)
Sutherland, Jonathan, jt. auth. see Canwell, Diane.
Sutherland, Jonathan, jt. auth. see McNab, Chris.
Sutherland, Jonathan & Canwell, Diane. African Americans in the Vietnam War. (p. 27)
—American Women in the Vietnam War. (p. 64)
—Container Ships & Oil Tankers. (p. 360)
—Violent Crimes. (p. 1843)
Sutherland, Jonathan & McNab, Chris. Flying Insects. (p. 610)
—Social Insects. (p. 1604)
Sutherland, Karl, jt. auth. see Sutherland, Tui T.
Sutherland, Karl H., jt. auth. see Sutherland, Tui T.
Sutherland, Kate. All in Together Girls. (p. 44)
Sutherland, Keith. Two Tubby Teddies Have a Very Busy Week. (p. 1804)
Sutherland, Keston & Dart, Lisa. Linguistics of Light. (p. 1019)
Sutherland, Leah, illus. see Larsen, Carolyn.
Sutherland, Lin. Terremotos y Volcanes. Lopez-Izquierdo, Nieves, tr. (p. 1721)
Sutherland, Lucille, jt. auth. see Ware, Kay.
Sutherland, Maggie, illus. see Sutherland, Eileen.
Sutherland, Marc. Waiting Place. Sutherland, Marc, illus. (p. 1853)
Sutherland, Margaret. Valentines Are for Saying I Love You. Wummer, Amy, illus. (p. 1830)
Sutherland, Margaret Bradt. Life of Mary Jemison, Indian Captive. (p. 1012)
Sutherland, Nicholas, illus. see Shumate, Robert O.
Sutherland, Paul H. Finding Utopia. Gibbons, Timothy M., illus. (p. 588)
—Mani & Pitouee: The True Legend of Sleeping Bear Dunes. Gibbons, Timothy M., illus. (p. 1087)
Sutherland, Robert. Son of the Hounds (p. 1611)
—Survivor's Leave. (p. 1687)
Sutherland, Rowan. Talitha & the Gnome: The Warg. Gross, Maia, illus. (p. 1703)
Sutherland, Steve. Courage to Win. (p. 372)
Sutherland, Suzanne. Something Wiki. (p. 1610)
—When We Were Good (p. 1905)
Sutherland, T. T. Bulldog Won't Budge. (p. 240)
Sutherland, Tui. Brightest Night. (p. 228)
Sutherland, Tui T. Against the Tide. (p. 29)
—Brightest Night. (p. 228)
—Dark Secret. (p. 408)
—Dragonet Prophecy. (p. 478)
—Hidden Kingdom. (p. 775)
—Lost Heir. (p. 1055)
—Moon Rising. (p. 1172)
—Shadow Falling. (p. 1557)
—So This Is How It Ends. (p. 1602)
—This Must Be Love. (p. 1737)
—Winter Turning. (p. 1938)
Sutherland, Tui T. & Sutherland, Karl. Dragon on Trial. (p. 477)
Sutherland, Tui T. & Sutherland, Karl H. Menagerie. (p. 1126)
—Menagerie Krakens & Lies. (p. 1126)
Sutinis, Beth. Crime Scene Techs! (p. 382)
Sutliff, Jamie. Elves of Owl's Head Mountain. Blumberg, Christine A., ed. (p. 517)
—Land of Nen-Us-Yok. Blumberg, Christine A., ed. (p. 973)
Sutliff Sanders, Joe, tr. see Shakespeare, William.
Sutliff Sanders, Joe, tr. see Shelley, Mary & Shelley, Mary.
Sutnick, Barbara, ed. see Wigoder, Geoffrey, et al.
Sutoski, Jennifer. Barbara Reid. (p. 137)
—Canadian Biographies Set 2. (p. 260)
—Carey Price. (p. 268)
—Hedley. (p. 762)
—Patrick Chan. (p. 1329)
—Stephen Harper. (p. 1648)
—Terry Fox. (p. 1722)
Sutoski, Jennifer & Donaldson, Chelsea. Canadian Biographies: Set 1-2. (p. 260)
—Canadian Biographies Set 1-2. (p. 260)
Sutphin, Joe, illus. see Guar, Sheila.
Sutryn, Barbara M. Heartstrings: A Biography of Wilmos Csehy. (p. 760)
Sutter, Daniel R. Is a Tattoo Right for You? (p. 889)
Sutter, Debra, et al. Moons of Jupiter. Klofkorn, Lisa, illus. (p. 1173)
Suttie, Alan, illus. see Bramwell, Martyn.
Suttle, Darlene. On that Mountain So Hilly! (p. 1289)
Suttles, B. Mr Frog. (p. 1185)
Suttles, Teresa. Little Gray Box. (p. 1028)
Suttom, jt. auth. see Prenzlau.
Sutton, A. Trevor. Dr. Bessie Rehwinkel. Pierce, Linda, illus. (p. 475)
Sutton, Adam J. What Happened at the Boston Tea Party? (p. 1885)
Sutton, Anna Michelle. Peas on My Feet. (p. 1333)
Sutton, Anthony, et al. Motocross: How to Be an Awesome Motocross Rider (p. 1179)
Sutton, Benn. Hedgehug's Halloween. Pinto, Dan, illus. (p. 762)
Sutton, Benn, jt. auth. see Pinto, Dan.
Sutton, Emily, illus. see Davies, Nicola.
Sutton, Felix. We Were There at the First Airplane Flight. Matulay, Laszlo, illus. (p. 1868)
Sutton, Felix & Loening, Grover. We Were There at the First Airplane Flight. Matulay, Laszlo, illus. (p. 1868)
Sutton, Garrett & Kiyosaki, Robert T. How to Buy & Sell a Business: How You Can Win in the Business Quadrant. (p. 815)
Sutton, George Miksch, illus. see Burgess, Thornton W.
Sutton, Jane. Esther's Hanukkah Disaster. Rowland, Andy, illus. (p. 538)
—What's up with This Chicken? Welling, Peter, illus. (p. 1900)
Sutton, Jennifer. Little Dude's Big Day. (p. 1027)
Sutton, Joe. Wanda & the Oblahlahs. (p. 1856)
Sutton, Katisha Barner. Caring & Sharing. (p. 269)
Sutton, Kay. Nan & Grandad's Book of Short Stories. (p. 1228)
Sutton, Kelsey. Some Quiet Place. (p. 1609)
—Where Silence Gathers. (p. 1909)
Sutton, Kyle, jt. auth. see Harte, Lawrence.
Sutton, Laurie. Joker's Dozen. Beavers, Ethen, illus. (p. 924)
Sutton, Laurie S. Batman vs. the Penguin. Vecchio, Luciano, illus. (p. 144)
—Cheetah & the Purrfect Crime Vecchio, Luciano, illus. (p. 296)
—Curse of Atlantis. Neely, Scott, illus. (p. 394)
—Dark Knight: the Penguin's Crime Wave. Vecchio, Luciano, illus. (p. 407)
—Dark Side of the Apokolips. Vecchio, Luciano, illus. (p. 408)
—Demons of Deep Space. Vecchio, Luciano, illus. (p. 426)
—Fear the Shark Schoening, Dan, illus. (p. 579)
—Fright at Zombie Farm. Neely, Scott, illus. (p. 639)
—Ghost of the Bermuda Triangle Neely, Scott, illus. (p. 671)
—Going Ape. (p. 692)
—Going Ape. Gordon, Eric A. & Gordon, Steven E., illus. (p. 692)
—House on Spooky Street. Neely, Scott, illus. (p. 803)
—Killer Croc of Doom! Vecchio, Luciano, illus. (p. 956)
—Light King Strikes! Schoening, Dan, illus. (p. 1015)
—Mystery of the Aztec Tomb Neely, Scott, illus. (p. 1225)
—Night of a Thousand Doomsdays Vecchio, Luciano, illus. (p. 1253)
—Night of a Thousand Doomsdays. Vecchio, Luciano, illus. (p. 1253)
—Penguin's Crime Wave Vecchio, Luciano, illus. (p. 1337)
—Planet Collector Vecchio, Luciano, illus. (p. 1367)
—Real Man of Steel Vecchio, Luciano, illus. (p. 1448)
—Secret of the Flying Saucer. Neely, Scott, illus. (p. 1542)
—Secret of the Sea Creature Neely, Scott, illus. (p. 1543)
—Sinestro & the Ring of Fear McManus, Shawn, illus. (p. 1578)
—Sword of the Dragon Schoening, Dan, illus. (p. 1692)
—Terrible Trio. Beavers, Ethen, illus. (p. 1721)
—Terror of the Bigfoot Beast Neely, Scott, illus. (p. 1722)
—The History of the Maze Monster. (p. 1728)
—You Choose: Scooby-Doo. (p. 1975)
Sutton, Laurie S., jt. auth. see Bright, J. E.
Sutton, Laurie S., jt. auth. see Simonson, Louise.
Sutton, Laurie S., jt. auth. see Stone Arch Books Staff.
Sutton, Laurie S. & Loughridge, Lee. Sinestro & the Ring of Fear McManus, Shawn, illus. (p. 1578)
Sutton, Laurie S. & Sazaklis, John. You Choose Stories: Batman (p. 1975)
Sutton, Laurie S., et al. Dark Knight. (p. 407)
—Gorilla Warfare Doescher, Erik, illus. (p. 703)
—Master of Mirrors! (p. 1103)
Sutton, Margaret. Discovery at the Dragon's Mouth: A Judy Bolton Mystery. (p. 450)
—Haunted Fountain: A Judy Bolton Mystery. (p. 753)
—Palace Wagon Family: A True Story of the Donner Party. Stevens, Mary, illus. (p. 1319)
—Phantom Friend Doane, Pelagie, illus. (p. 1349)
—Secret Quest: Judy Bolton. (p. 1543)
—Trail of the Green Doll: A Judy Bolton Mystery. (p. 1776)
—Unfinished House Doane, Pelagie, illus. (p. 1817)
—Yellow Phantom: A Judy Bolton Mystery. Doane, Pelagie, illus. (p. 1970)
Sutton, MaryBeth. Adventure of Blondie & Oreo. (p. 14)
Sutton, Michelle. It's Not about Him. (p. 897)
—It's Not about Me. (p. 897)
Sutton, Nicky C. Blake's Oddity. (p. 198)
Sutton, Pam. Apologia Exploring Creation with Biology 2nd Ed INTERACTIVE Lapbook Journal. Kinney, Cyndi, ed. (p. 92)
Sutton, Pamelina Jean'e. Bill Bill the Burger Boy. (p. 186)
Sutton, Richard, et al. Car. (p. 265)
Sutton, Rosalind, et al. Robin Hood. Rowe, Eric F., tr. (p. 1480)
Sutton, S. A. Hero for Quale. (p. 772)
Sutton, Sally. Construction. Lovelock, Brian, illus. (p. 359)
—Construir una Carretera (Roadwork) Lovelock, Brian, illus. (p. 360)
—Demolicion. Lovelock, Brian, illus. (p. 426)
—Demolition. Lovelock, Brian, illus. (p. 426)
—Farmer John's Tractor. Belton, Robyn, illus. (p. 574)
—Roadwork. Lovelock, Brian, illus. (p. 1477)
Sutton, Toby & Carson-Dellosa Publishing Staff. Beyond the Gym, Grade 3: Physical Activity Lessons for the Non-Gym Teacher. Thompson, Karen, ed. (p. 174)
Sutula, Hollie, illus. see Susedik, Tina & Heers, Alli.
Suwannakit, Tul, illus. see Vries, Lizzette de & Vries, Cecile de.
Suyenaga, Joan. Indonesian Children's Favorite Stories. Martowiredjo, Salim, illus. (p. 872)
Suyenaga, Ruth. Korean Children's Day. Kyong-Nan, Nani, illus. (p. 967)
Suyenaga, Ruth, et al. Korean Children's Day. Kyong-Nan, Nani, illus. (p. 967)
Suzan, Gerardo, illus. see Bracho, Coral.
Suzan, Gerardo, illus. see Hall, Kirsten.
Suzanne, Jamie, jt. auth. see Pascal, Francine.
Suzanne, Rentz. Daughters of Heaven Devotional. (p. 410)
Suzanne, Walker. Treasure Chest Blueprint Adventures of Mark & James Coloring Book. (p. 1781)
Suzhen, Fang. Grandma Lives in a Perfume Village. Danowski, Sonja, illus. (p. 708)
Suzukaze, Ryo. Attack on Titan: Before the Fall (Novel) Kyklo. Shibamoto, Thores, illus. (p. 114)
Suzuki, David. From Naked Ape to Superspecies. (p. 643)
—There's a Barnyard in My Bedroom. Fernandes, Eugenie, illus. (p. 1730)
Suzuki, David, jt. auth. see Ellis, Sarah.
Suzuki, David & Vanderlinden, Kathy. Eco-Fun: Projects, Experiments & Games for a Greener Earth. Kurisu, Jane, illus. (p. 502)
—You Are the Earth: Know Your World So You Can Help Make It Better. Edwards, Wallace, illus. (p. 1973)
Suzuki, David T. & Hehner, Barbara. Descubre el Cuerpo Humano. (p. 428)
—Descubre los Insectos. (p. 428)
Suzuki, David T. & Heimer, Barbara. Descubre las Plantas. (p. 428)
Suzuki, David T., et al. Descubre el Medio Ambiente. (p. 428)
Suzuki, Genevieve A. Original Poi Cats on Oahu. (p. 1304)
Suzuki, Genevieve A. & Murakami, Jon J. Original Poi Cats on Oahu. (p. 1304)
Suzuki, Ichiro, jt. auth. see Komatsu, Narumi.
Suzuki, Koji. Dark Water. Walley, Glynne, tr. from JPN. (p. 408)
—Ring. Rohmer, Robert B. & Walley, Glynne, trs. (p. 1473)
Suzuki, Koji & Walley, Glynne. Loop. (p. 1052)
Suzuki, Mary, illus. see Meyer, Carolyn.
Suzuki, Nakaba. Seven Deadly Sins (p. 1554)
Suzuki, Shinichi. Suzuki Cello School: Piano Accompaniment (p. 1688)
Suzuki, Shinichi & Alfred Publishing Staff. Suzuki Cello School (p. 1688)
Suzuma, Tabitha. Forbidden. (p. 616)
Suzy. Game Day Youth: Learning Baseball's Lingo. (p. 654)
Suzy, Kline. Horrible Harry in Room 2B. (p. 798)
Svagerko, Keith & Svagerko, Sydney. Sydney Travels to Rome: A Guide for Kids - Let's Go to Italy Series! (p. 1692)
Svagerko, Sydney, jt. auth. see Svagerko, Keith.
Svarney, Thomas E., jt. auth. see Barnes-Svarney, Patricia.
Svendsen, Mark. To Die For. (p. 1758)
Svendson, Elisabeth D. Tale of Naughty Mac & Other Donkey Stories. (p. 1699)
Svenson, Niki. I Can Series: Mime for Michael. (p. 836)
Svensson, Richard, illus. see Killam, Catherine D.
Svensson, Schery Kay, jt. ed. see Lewallen, Shirley Ann.
Svetlin, illus. see de Cervantes, Miguel.
Svistunova, Natalia, ed. see AZ Books Staff.
Svitil, Torene & Dunkleburger, Amy. So You Want to Work in Set Design, Costuming, or Make-Up? (p. 1602)
Svoboda, David. Angel Frequency 775 Mn (p. 73)
Svoboda, Linda Sue. Little Brown Bird That Could. (p. 1025)
—Loving Times with Grandma. (p. 1061)
Svoboda, Megan. Esther Katz a Girl of Hope. (p. 538)
Swaab, Neil. Secrets to Ruling School (p. 1546)
Swaab, Neil, illus. see Patterson, James & Papademetriou, Lisa.
Swaab, Neil, illus. see Patterson, James, et al.
Swaab, Neil, illus. see Ursu, Anne.
Swaby, Barbara. When Will Daddy Be Home? (p. 1905)
Swad, Libby White. Christmas Tree. (p. 316)
Swaim, illus. see Crichton, Julie.
Swaim, Colleen. Lleven Su Fuego Al Mundo: Jóvenes Que Alcanzaron la Santidad. (p. 1043)
—Radiate: More Stories of Daring Teen Saints. (p. 1432)
Swaim, Jessica. Scarum Fair. Ashley, Carol, illus. (p. 1520)

Swaim, Keshia. Blood Bound. (p. 200)
Swaim, Michael, illus. see Britland, Jan.
Swaim, Michael, illus. see Repp, Gloria.
Swaim, Mike, illus. see Britland, Jan.
Swaim, Mike, illus. see Clish, Marian L.
Swaim, Mike, illus. see MacDonald, Alysha.
Swaim, Ramon, illus. see Crichton, Julie.
Swain. Calling You (p. 254)
Swain, Alison Campbell, illus. see Baker, Kane.
Swain, Cameron, jt. auth. see Smith, Carrie.
Swain, Claudia. What's a Girl to Do? (p. 1896)
Swain, Cynthia. Bill's First Day. (p. 187)
—Birthday Flowers. (p. 192)
—Can We Have a Pet? (p. 258)
—Families Have Rules. (p. 567)
—I Have a Coin. (p. 839)
—No, Tim! (p. 1260)
—Plant Has Parts. (p. 1369)
—Sorting at the Nature Center. (p. 1614)
—Sorting at the Park. (p. 1614)
—What Do You Think? (p. 1883)
—Wishing with Pennies. (p. 1941)
Swain, Cynthia & Benchmark Education Co., LLC. Opinions about Odysseus: A Greek Hero. Ramos, José, illus. (p. 1300)
Swain, Cynthia & Benchmark Education Co. Staff. Folksongs: The Music of My Life. (p. 611)
Swain, Gwenyth. Bedtime! (p. 156)
—Celebrating. (p. 284)
—Declaring Freedom: A Look at the Declaration of Independence, the Bill of Rights, & the Constitution. (p. 422)
—Documents of Freedom: A Look at the Declaration of Independence, the Bill of Rights, & the U.S. Constitution. (p. 460)
—Documents of Freedom: A Look at the Declaration of Independence, the Bill of Rights, & the U. S. Constitution. (p. 460)
—Dred & Harriet Scott: A Family's Struggle for Freedom. (p. 484)
—Freedom Seeker: A Story about William Penn. Harvey, Lisa, illus. (p. 635)
—Get Dressed! (p. 667)
—Hope & Tears: Ellis Island Voices. (p. 796)
—Hunger for Learning: A Story about Booker T. Washington. Johnson, Larry, illus. (p. 827)
—I Wonder As I Wander. Himler, Ronald, illus. (p. 849)
—I Wonder as I Wander. Himler, Ronald, illus. (p. 849)
—Little Crow: Leader of the Dakota. (p. 1026)
—Riding to Washington. Geister, David, illus. (p. 1471)
—Theodore Roosevelt. (p. 1729)
—Tidy Up! (p. 1747)
—Voices for Freedom. Frankenhuyzen, Gijsbert van et al, illus. (p. 1848)
—Wanda Ga'g: Storybook Artist. (p. 1856)
—World War I: An Interactive History Adventure (p. 1958)
Swain, Gwenyth, jt. auth. see Milet Limited Publishing Staff.
Swain, Gwenyth & Gitlin, Martin. You Choose: History. (p. 1975)
Swain, H. A. Hungry. (p. 828)
Swain, Heather. Me, My Elf & I. (p. 1116)
—Play These Games: 101 Delightful Diversions Using Everyday Items. (p. 1371)
—Selfish Elf Wish. (p. 1549)
Swain, Holly, illus. see Bradman, Tony.
Swain, Holly, illus. see Puttock, Simon.
Swain, Holly, illus. see Singleton, Debbie.
Swain, Ruth Freeman. Underwear: What We Wear under There. O'Brien, John A., illus. (p. 1817)
Swain, Wilson, illus. see Covert, Ralph & Mills, G. Riley.
Swain, Wilson, illus. see MacDonald, Kimber.
Swaine, Meg. Career Building Through Alternate Reality Gaming. (p. 266)
Swainson, Esme. Adventures of Rex & Zendah in the Zodiac. (p. 22)
Swainson, Jess, jt. auth. see Compton, Zella.
Swainston, Jeani. Grandma Stuff: ... it's what love is made Of. (p. 708)
Swajeski, Donna M. Revolution Machine: Playscript. (p. 1466)
Swalin, Benjamin. Hard Circus Road: The Odyssey of the North Carolina Symphony. McVaugh, Julia A., ed. (p. 748)
Swallow. Penrose The Private (Spangles L,1) (p. 1338)
Swallow, Pamela. It Only Looks Easy. (p. 894)
Swallow, Pamela C. Melvil & Dewey Teach Literacy Eliasen, Lorena & Schroeder, Judith, eds. (p. 1125)
Swallow, Pamela C., jt. auth. see Swallow, Pamela Curtis.
Swallow, Pamela Curtis. Melvil & Dewey Gone Fishing. Eliasen, Lorena, ed. (p. 1125)
—Melvil & Dewey in the Chips Schroeder, Judith, ed. (p. 1125)
—Melvil & Dewey in the Fast Lane Schroeder, Judith, ed. (p. 1125)
Swallow, Pamela Curtis & Swallow, Pamela C. Groundhog Gets a Say. Bunkus, Denise, illus. (p. 725)
Swamp, Jake. Giving Thanks: A Native American Good Morning Message. (p. 681)
Swan. Rumpelstiltskin. (p. 1495)
—Sleeping Beauty. (p. 1589)
Swan, Angela, illus. see Bentley, Sue.
Swan, Bill. Corner Kick (p. 367)
—Deflection! (p. 424)
—Enforcer (p. 529)
—Fourteen & Sentenced to Death: The Story of Steven Truscott (p. 625)
—Man-to-Man (p. 1085)
—Mud Happens (p. 1188)
—Mud Run (p. 1188)
—Off Track (p. 1279)
—Real Justice: Jailed for Life for Being Black: The Story of Rubin Hurricane Carter (p. 1448)
—Road Rage (p. 1477)
Swan, Carroll Judson. My Company. (p. 1200)
Swan, Curt, illus. see Coleman, Jerry, et al.
Swan, Curt, illus. see Maggin, Elliot, et al.
Swan, Erin Pembrey. Pelicans, Cormorants, & Their Kin. (p. 1336)
—Penguins: From Emperors to Macaronis. (p. 1337)
Swan, Gloria, illus. see Finke, Margot.
Swan, Henry, jt. auth. see Mills, Nathan.
Swan, Jonathan, Sr., jt. auth. see Swan, Talbert, 2nd.
Swan, Kenneth. Pigboy: The Legend of a Wildchild. Swan, Shawn, illus. (p. 1357)
Swan, Kenneth D. Pigboy: The Legend of a Wildchild, New Edition. (p. 1357)
Swan Publishing Inc. Brave Little Bee. (p. 223)
Swan, Richard. Listeners. (p. 1022)
—Pardoner's Prologue & Tale. (p. 1324)
Swan, Shawn, illus. see Swan, Kenneth.
Swan, Susan, illus. see Chernesky, Felicia Sanzari.
Swan, Susan, illus. see Glaser, Linda.
Swan, Susan, illus. see Nidey, Kelli.
Swan, Susan, illus. see Profiri, Charline.
Swan, Susan, illus. see Slade, Suzanne.
Swan, Susan, jt. auth. see Rusch, Elizabeth.
Swan, Talbert, 2nd & Swan, Jonathan, Sr. Standing on Broad Shoulders: A Genealogical Study of an African American Family. (p. 1639)
Swan, Talbert W., II. Exploring Ephesians: An Expository Commentary. (p. 552)
Swanberg, Arvon & Spicer, Carolyn. Big, Blue, Overstuffed Chair. (p. 178)
Swanepoel, Rudi. Mountains of God: Exploring the Significance of High Places. (p. 1181)
Swanepoel, Sharon. Adventures of Seek & Save Volume 3: The Village. Locsinto, Lucas, illus. (p. 22)
Swaney, Kathleen M. William's in a Wheelchair. Wysong, Ryan, illus. (p. 1934)
Swango, Lynn. No Baseball in Fairview. (p. 1257)
Swank-Gattuso, Jill. Gabrielle Rae: Who Do You Want to Be Today? (p. 652)
Swann, Elaine. Girls Have Style... at School! A Glam Girl's Guide to Taking on the Day with Grace & Style. (p. 680)
Swann, Jill, ed. see Onish, Liane.
Swann, Joyce. McAloons: A Horse Called Lightning, a House of Clowns. (p. 1114)
—Tales of Pig Isle. Swann, Stefan, illus. (p. 1702)
Swann, Kristina. Meaningful Math. (p. 1117)
—US Law - Student Text. (p. 1826)
Swann, Linda. Land of Watermelon Mountains: Destinations Thru Imaginations. (p. 973)
Swann, Mary. Fearsome Day. Swann, Mary, illus. (p. 579)
Swann, Michelle. Angels Watching over Me. (p. 75)
Swann, S. Andrew. Hostile Takeover. (p. 801)
Swann, Sandy, jt. auth. see McKain, Susan.
Swann, Sandy & McKain, Susan. Tugger: The Pretzel Pup. (p. 1796)
Swann, Stefan, illus. see Swann, Joyce.
Swann, Stephen. Blooter Boys. (p. 202)
—Magical TV. (p. 1075)
—Where's Our Submarine. (p. 1910)
Swann, Susan. Cakes & Cookies Recipes for Children on Restricted Diets. (p. 252)
Swann, Tammy & Benchmark Education Co., LLC Staff. Roy Makes a Choice. (p. 1492)
—Stop! It's a Frog! (p. 1653)
Swanscombe, Wendy. Prize of Pain. (p. 1408)
—Sexual Heeling. (p. 1556)
Swanson, A. M. Momma's Biscuits. (p. 1162)
Swanson, Bill, jt. auth. see Swanson, Bruce.
Swanson, Bruce & Swanson, Bill. Gray Wolf's Search Peterson, Gary, illus. (p. 713)
Swanson, Christopher, jt. auth. see Ganzer, Diane.
Swanson, David. Tube World. Burke, Shane, illus. (p. 1795)
Swanson, David C. N. Tube World. Burke, Shane, illus. (p. 1795)
Swanson, Denise. Murder of a Chocolate-Covered Cherry. (p. 1192)
Swanson, Diane. Alligators & Crocodiles (p. 47)
—Animals Can Be So Playful (p. 82)
—Animals Can Be So Sleepy (p. 82)
—Animals Can Be So Speedy (p. 82)
—Bats (p. 144)
—Bugs up Close. Davidson, Paul, illus. (p. 237)
—Cheetah Cubs & Beetle Grubs: The Wacky Ways We Name Young Animals. Spencer, Mariko Ando, illus. (p. 296)
—Coyotes (p. 375)
—Eagles (p. 492)
—Elephants (p. 511)
—Elephants. (p. 511)
—Foxes (p. 626)
—Frogs & Toads (p. 641)
—Frogs & Toads. (p. 641)
—Hummingbirds (p. 826)
—Kangaroos (p. 942)
—Moose (p. 1173)
—Nibbling on Einstein's Brain: The Good, the Bad & the Bogus in Science. Blake, Francis, illus. (p. 1250)
—Octopuses (p. 1278)
—Orangutans (p. 1302)
—Otters (p. 1307)
—Penguins (p. 1337)
—Penguins. (p. 1337)
—Porcupines (p. 1386)
—Raccoons (p. 1430)
—Safari Beneath the Sea: The Wonder World of the North Pacific Coast. Royal British Columbia Museum Staff, photos by. (p. 1501)
—Sharks (p. 1562)
—Snakes (p. 1596)
—Spirit Bears (p. 1628)
—Turn It Loose: The Scientist in Absolutely Everybody. Clark, Warren, illus. (p. 1797)
—Welcome to the World of Animals (p. 1874)
—Welcome to the World of Bears. (p. 1874)
—Welcome to the World of Rabbits & Hares (p. 1874)
—Why Seals Blow Their Noses: Canadian Wildlife in Fact & Fiction Penhale, Douglas, illus. (p. 1925)
—Wild Cats (p. 1929)
—Wild Horses (p. 1929)
—Wild Horses. (p. 1929)
—Wolverines (p. 1944)
—Wonder in Water. (p. 1947)
—You Are Weird: Your Body's Peculiar Parts & Funny Functions. Boake, Kathy, illus. (p. 1973)
Swanson, Diane, jt. auth. see Haynes, Diane.
Swanson, Diane & Wood, Daniel. Welcome to the World of Wolves (p. 1874)
Swanson, Gary B. Click Here: Interactive Devotionals for Teens. (p. 332)
Swanson, James L. Bloody Times: The Funeral of Abraham Lincoln & the Manhunt for Jefferson Davis. (p. 201)
—Chasing Lincoln's Killer: The Search for John Wikes Booth. (p. 294)
—President Has Been Shot! The Assassination of John F. Kennedy. (p. 1397)
Swanson, Jennifer. Amazing Feats of Electrical Engineering. (p. 54)
—Attractive Truth about Magnetism Lum, Bernice, illus. (p. 114)
—Body Bugs: Invisible Creatures Lurking Inside You (p. 207)
—How Electricity Works. Mullaly, Glen, illus. (p. 809)
—How Submarines Work. Mullaly, Glen, illus. (p. 812)
—Metamorphic Rocks. (p. 1130)
—Shocking Truth about Electricity. Lum, Bernice, illus. (p. 1568)
—Top Secret Science: Projects You Aren't Supposed to Know About (p. 1769)
—Tsunamis. (p. 1795)
—Uninvited Guests: Invisible Creatures Lurking in Your Home (p. 1818)
Swanson, Jennifer A. How Have Animals Evolved & Adapted? (p. 809)
—Smart Strategies for Turning an Idea into a Product or Service. (p. 1593)
—Top 10 Secrets for Saving Successfully. (p. 1768)
—Wonderful World of Wearable Devices (p. 1948)
Swanson, Jennifer & Leet, Karen M. Tiny Creepy Creatures. (p. 1756)
Swanson, Jennifer Ann. Shocking Truth about Electricity Lum, Bernice, illus. (p. 1568)
Swanson, Jennifer, et al. LOL Physical Science. Lum, Bernice, illus. (p. 1045)
Swanson, Jessica, jt. auth. see Jessi Swanson And Jessica Swanson.
Swanson, Jill K., tr. see Shakespeare, William, et al.
Swanson, Julie A. Going for the Record. (p. 692)
Swanson, Karl, illus. see Koehler-Pentacoff, Elizabeth.
Swanson, Katharine, jt. auth. see Delacre, Lulu.
Swanson, Kerry. Bacteria, Fungi, Lichens & Plants. (p. 131)
Swanson, Linnea C., jt. auth. see Gritzner, Charles F.
Swanson, Maggie. Best-Loved Aesop's Fables Coloring Book. (p. 170)
—Easy Christmas Crafts: 12 Holiday Cut & Make Decorations. (p. 500)
—Easy Easter Tabletop Crafts. (p. 500)
—Floral Fantasies Stained Glass Coloring Book. (p. 606)
—Goldilocks & the Three Bears: A Tale about Respecting Others. (p. 696)
—Kitten's Christmas Lullaby. (p. 963)
—Let's Color Together — Sun, Moon & Stars. (p. 995)
—My First Christmas. Swanson, Maggie, illus. (p. 1206)
—My Storybook Paper Dolls. (p. 1219)
—SPARK - Sun, Moon & Stars Coloring Book. (p. 1622)
—Sun, Moon & Stars Designs to Color. (p. 1676)
—Tale of Two Bad Mice. (p. 1700)
—Zany Zoo Stained Glass Jr. Coloring Book. (p. 1985)
Swanson, Maggie, illus. see Albee, Sarah, et al.
Swanson, Maggie, illus. see Albee, Sarah.
Swanson, Maggie, illus. see Allen, Constance & Albee, Sarah.
Swanson, Maggie, illus. see Allen, Constance.
Swanson, Maggie, illus. see Davidson, Alice Joyce.
Swanson, Maggie, illus. see Dreyer, Ellen.
Swanson, Maggie, illus. see Muldrow, Diane.
Swanson, Maggie, illus. see Muntean, Michaela.
Swanson, Maggie, tr. see Dreyer, Ellen.
Swanson, Maggie & Paper Dolls. Lucky Cats Paper Dolls: Maneki Neko. (p. 1062)
Swanson, Peter Joseph, illus. see Bond, Alan.
Swanson Sateren, Shelley. Adventures of Hound Hotel. Melmon, Deborah, illus. (p. 18)
Swanson Sateren, Shelley, jt. auth. see Sateren, Shelley Swanson.
Swanson, Stan. Misadventures of Hobart Hucklebuck. (p. 1150)
Swanson, Susan Marie. House in the Night. Krommes, Beth, illus. (p. 803)
Swanson, Tina M. Silly Sierra & the Mysterious Mushroom. (p. 1576)
Swanson, Tom. Twas the Night Before Christmas. (p. 1799)
Swanson, Wayne. Why the West Was Wild. (p. 1926)
Swanson, Weldon, illus. see Scholastic, Inc. Staff.
Swanson, Weldon, illus. see Zuravicky, Orli & Scholastic Canada Ltd. Staff.
Swanton, John R. Indian Tribes of Mexico, Central America & the West Indies. (p. 871)
Swarabi, Fatma Abdulla & El Amin, Khalid Hamid. Marim & Her Grandmother. (p. 1094)
Swarbrick, David E. Peggy's Play House. (p. 1335)
—Twenty Goofy Gumballs: Counting Made Fun. (p. 1801)
Sward, Adam, illus. see Cook, Gary.
Sward, Robert. God Is in the Cracks: A Narrative in Voices (p. 689)
Swarner, Kristina. Bedtime Sh'ma: A Good Night Book. (p. 157)
—BEDTIME SH'MA, Book & CD Set. (p. 157)
—Modeh Ani: A Good Morning Book. (p. 1157)
Swarner, Kristina, illus. see Gayzagian, Doris K.
Swarner, Kristina, illus. see Gillen, Lynea.
Swarner, Kristina, illus. see McCaughrean, Geraldine & Hoffmann, E. T. A.
Swarner, Kristina, illus. see Schwartz, Howard.
Swart, Sharon. Adventures of Matthew the Monkey. (p. 20)
—Matthew the Monkey Goes Bananas for Fire Safety. (p. 1109)
Swarte, Joost, illus. see Lewis, Catherine.
Swartley, Ron. Quirky Kactus: Why the Giant Saguaro Gets Away with Being so Different & Quirky. (p. 1428)
Swarts, Katherine. Genetic Disorders. (p. 660)
—Welfare. (p. 1874)
Swartz, Daniel J. Bim & Bom: A Shabbat Tale. Iwai, Melissa, illus. (p. 188)
Swartz, Ellen. Reconstruction: Moving Toward Democracy: People of African Descent Define Freedom after the Civil War. (p. 1452)
Swartz, Larry & Margolin, Indrani. 10 Coolest Dance Crazes. (p. 1993)
Swartz, Michael. Bikes & Bullies: A Neil Everheart Mystery. (p. 185)
Swartz, Nancy Sohn. How Did the Animals Help God? Hall, Melanie, illus. (p. 806)
Swartz, Neva. Tommy the Timid Turtle. Steinbauer, Larry, illus. (p. 1765)
Swartz, Patricia. Pig-A-Poo Moves to the Zoo. (p. 1357)
Swartz Pepper, Kenda. Well Earth Well Me! (p. 1874)
Swartz, Tracy. Blue for Me! (p. 202)
Swatman, Simon. Plants vs. Zombies: Official Guide to Protecting Your Brains. Howling, Adam, illus. (p. 1370)
Swayne Tidwell, Deborah. Magic Eraser & Camp Real. (p. 1072)
Swayze, Alan. End of World War I: The Treaty of Versailles & Its Tragic Legacy. (p. 526)
Swazinski, Ed. At the Carnival: Understand & Apply Properties of Operations. (p. 111)
Swearingen, Greg, illus. see Donaldson, Julia.
Swearingen, Greg, illus. see Easton, Kelly.
Swearingen, Greg, illus. see Niner, Holly L.
Swearingen, Greg, illus. see Schanen, Adriana Brad.
Swearingen, Greg, illus. see Strasser, Todd.
Swearingen, Greg, illus. see Williams, Tad & Beale, Deborah.
Sweat, Anthony, jt. auth. see Hilton, John.
Sweat, Lynn, illus. see Parish, Herman.
Sweat, Lynn, illus. see Parish, Peggy & Parish, Herman.
Sweat, Lynn, illus. see Parish, Peggy.
Swecker, Susan J. Who's Looking for Cheese! (p. 1920)
Swedeen, Staci. Como la ardilla listada obtuvo sus marcas & How the Chipmunk Got Its Stripes. (p. 351)
—How the Chipmunk Got It's Stripes. (p. 813)
—Phoebe & the Flame-Bellied Toad: An Original Fairy Tale. (p. 1351)
—Rumor Report, the Big Jump. (p. 1495)
—Toad Bridegroom: A Fairy Tale from Korea. (p. 1759)
—Tombi-Ende & the Frog: A Fairy Tale from Southern Africa. (p. 1764)
Swedroe, Larry E. Successful Investor Today: 14 Simple Truths You Must Know When You Invest. (p. 1672)
Sweeden, Rachael. Pickleberry Bloat. (p. 1354)
Sweeney, Alyse. Canyons (p. 262)
—Cheeky Chiller. (p. 295)
—Easy Reader Biographies: Johnny Appleseed: An American Who Made a Difference. (p. 500)
—Easy Reader Biographies: Martin Luther King, Jr: A Man with a Dream. (p. 500)
—Fluency Lessons for the Overhead: 15 Passages & Lessons for Teaching Phrasing, Rate, & Expression to Build Fluency for Better Comprehension. (p. 608)
—Frogs (p. 641)
—High-Rise Thriller. (p. 778)
—Mudpuppies (p. 1189)
—Rivers (p. 1476)
—Toads (p. 1760)
Sweeney, Alyse & Rustad, Martha E. H. Masked Mob Mystery: A Zoo Animal Mystery (p. 1102)
Sweeney, Bernadette. Monster Machines. (p. 1167)
Sweeney, Jacqueline. Perfect Poetry Playlets: Read-Aloud Reproducible Mini Plays That Boost All-Important Speaking & Fluency Skills to Meet the Common Core. (p. 1342)
Sweeney, Joyce. Players (p. 1372)
—Waiting for June (p. 1852)
Sweeney, Kathleen. Matty Monster Truck. (p. 1110)
Sweeney, Kathleen L. Dream of a Little Farmer Girl. (p. 483)
Sweeney, Kevin, jt. auth. see Carroll, Lewis, pseud.
Sweeney, Kimberly A. Tippy Meets the Easter Bunny! (p. 1757)
Sweeney, Leann. Pushing up Bluebonnets. (p. 1420)
Sweeney, Linda Booth. When the Wind Blows. Christy, Jana, illus. (p. 1905)
Sweeney, Monica, jt. auth. see Brothers Grimm, Becky.
Sweeney, Tass. Funny Friends & Faces of Henry P. Gruber. (p. 650)
Sweeny, Elizabeth Mifflin, illus. see Sweeny, Vell.
Sweeny, Sheila. Wacky Basketball Facts to Bounce Around. Wolf, Cathrine, ed. (p. 1852)
—Wacky Football Facts to Kick Around. Safro, Jill, ed. (p. 1852)
Sweeny, Vell. Second Hand Cat. Sweeny, Elizabeth Mifflin, illus. (p. 1539)
Sweet Briar School, illus. see Wolf, Penny, et al.
Sweet, Caitlin. Door in the Mountain. (p. 470)
Sweet, Darrell, illus. see Mathewson, Robert F.
Sweet, George M. Old Alligator & the Young Bird. (p. 1283)
Sweet, Glenn. Fuzzy. Sweet, Glenn, illus. (p. 651)
Sweet, J. H. Foo & Friends Storybook. (p. 612)
Sweet, J. H., et al. Cinabrio y la Isla de las Sombras Rabascall, Iolanda, tr. (p. 319)
Sweet, M. Anne. Nailed to the Sky. (p. 1227)
Sweet, Melissa. Balloons over Broadway: The True Story of the Puppeteer of Macy's Parade. (p. 135)
—Carmine: A Little More Red. (p. 270)
—Some Writer! The Story of E. B. White. (p. 1609)
Sweet, Melissa, illus. see Appelt, Kathi.
Sweet, Melissa, illus. see Bauer, Marion Dane.
Sweet, Melissa, illus. see Berger, Samantha & Chanko, Pamela.
Sweet, Melissa, illus. see Bryant, Jen.
Sweet, Melissa, illus. see Bryant, Jennifer.
Sweet, Melissa, illus. see Choldenko, Gennifer.
Sweet, Melissa, illus. see Davies, Jacqueline.

S

Sweet, Melissa, illus. see Holub, Joan.
Sweet, Melissa, illus. see Hood, Susan.
Sweet, Melissa, illus. see Johnston, Tony.
Sweet, Melissa, illus. see Knight, Joan MacPhail.
Sweet, Melissa, illus. see Markel, Michelle.
Sweet, Melissa, illus. see Martin, David Lozell.
Sweet, Melissa, illus. see Martin, David.
Sweet, Melissa, illus. see Potter, Alicia.
Sweet, Melissa, illus. see Rupp, Rebecca.
Sweet, Melissa, illus. see Ryder, Joanne.
Sweet, Melissa, illus. see Rylant, Cynthia.
Sweet, Melissa, illus. see Sierra, Judy.
Sweet, Melissa, illus. see Thimmesh, Catherine.
Sweet, Melissa, illus. see Wilson, Sarah.
Sweet, Melissa, illus. see Yarrow, Peter.
Sweet, Melissa, illus. see Yolen, Jane & Stemple, Heidi.
Sweet, Muriel. Common Edible & Useful Plants of the West. (p. 349)
Sweet, Stephen, illus. see Parker, Steve.
Sweet, Susan D. & Miles, Brenda. Princess Penelopea Hates Peas: A Tale of Picky Eating & Avoiding Catastropeas. (p. 1405)
Sweeten, Sami, illus. see Blackman, Malorie.
Sweetland, Nancy & Sweetland, Robert. If I Could/Si Yo Pudiera. (p. 853)
Sweetland, Robert, illus. see Bertrand, Diane Gonzales.
Sweetland, Robert, jt. auth. see Sweetland, Nancy.
Sweetman, Bill. Combat Rescue Helicopters: The MH-53 Pave Lows. (p. 346)
—High-Altitude Spy Planes: The U-2s. (p. 777)
—Strike Fighters: The F/A - 18E/F Super Hornets. (p. 1667)
—Supersonic Fighters: The F-16 Fighting Falcons. (p. 1684)
Sweetman, Gary W., photos by see Deveny, Mary Alice.
Sweetser, Kate Dickinson. Boys & girls from Thackeray. (p. 220)
—Ten Boys from Dickens. (p. 1718)
—Ten Girls from Dickens. (p. 1718)
—Ten Girls from Dickens. Williams, George Alfred, illus. (p. 1718)
Sweetwater Press Staff, jt. contrib. by see Cliff Road Books Staff.
Swegles, Maryanne. Digging for Bottles. (p. 439)
Sweitzer, James, jt. auth. see Gendell, Megan.
Swender, Jennifer, jt. auth. see Jacobs, Paul DuBois.
Swendson, Shanna. Rebel Mechanics: All Is Fair in Love & Revolution. (p. 1450)
Swensen, Karen & Ronquillo, Karen. Catherine the Great & Her Teatime Tagalongs Kirkman, Kelly, illus. (p. 280)
Swensen, Rigmor, jt. auth. see Capriola, Arlene.
Swenson, Brenda. Steps to Success in Watercolor. (p. 1648)
Swenson, Dianne. Ended Friendship: And Other Short Stories. (p. 527)
Swenson, Jamie A. Big Rig. Young, Ned, illus. (p. 183)
—Boom! Boom! Boom! Walker, David, illus. (p. 213)
—If You Were a Dog. Raschka, Chris, illus. (p. 854)
Swenson, Julie. High-Speed Trains: Use Place Value Understanding & Properties of Operations to Add & Subtract. (p. 778)
Swenson, Lynn. Rollie & Mollie: Disappearing Act. Baker, David, illus. (p. 1485)
Swenson, Rigmor, jt. auth. see Capriola, Arlene.
Swenson, S. Don. HVAC-Heating, Ventilating, & Air Conditioning: Answer Key. (p. 830)
—HVAC-Heating, Ventilating, & Air Conditioning: Text. (p. 831)
—HVAC-Heating, Ventilating, & Air Conditioning: Workbook. (p. 831)
—HVAC-Heating, Ventilating, & Air Conditioning: Resource Guide. (p. 831)
Swenson, Suzanna. All Good Things. (p. 44)
—Love in Many Faces. (p. 1059)
—Whirlwind Days. (p. 1912)
Swerling, Lisa & Lazar, Ralph. Dogs Going Places. (p. 463)
—Flying Memos & Other Office Antics. (p. 610)
—We Without You. (p. 1868)
Swerts, An. Get Well Soon, Grandpa. Bakker, Jenny, illus. (p. 668)
Swiatek, Robert S. Don't Bet on It. (p. 467)
Swiatkowska, Gabi. Queen on Wednesday. Swiatkowska, Gabi, illus. (p. 1425)
Swiatkowska, Gabi, illus. see Banks, Kate.
Swiatkowska, Gabi, illus. see Cooper, Ilene.
Swiatkowska, Gabi, illus. see Holt, Kimberly Willis.
Swiatkowska, Gabi, illus. see Hosford, Kate.
Swiatkowska, Gabi, illus. see Recorvits, Helen & Recorvits, H.
Swiatkowska, Gabi, illus. see Recorvits, Helen.
Swiatkowska, Gabi, illus. see Schaefer, Lola M.
Swiatoviak, Jeri, illus. see Gissing, Kathleen.
Swiatowska, Gabi, illus. see Cooper, Ilene.
Swick, Carmen D. Patch Land Adventures Book 2 Camping at Mimi's Ranch. Lambert, Page, ed. (p. 1328)
Swickle, Dvora. Legend of Santa Owl. (p. 988)
Swiderska, Barbara. Fisherman's Bride. Swiderska, Barbara, illus. (p. 599)
Swierczynski, Duane. Godzilla: History's Greatest Monster: History's Greatest Monster. (p. 692)
Swierczynski, Duane, jt. auth. see Spurrier, Simon.
Swift, Amanda. Big Bones. (p. 178)
Swift, Amanda, jt. auth. see Gray, Jennifer.
Swift, Austin Christopher. Mako Meets a Puffer: A Reel Fish Story. Breeden, Don, illus. (p. 1082)
Swift, Carolyn. Robbers in the House. (p. 1478)
Swift, Casey Anne, jt. auth. see Swift, Gayle H.
Swift, Christine. Croak, Frog! (p. 384)
—Splash, Dolphin! (p. 1629)
Swift, Donna, jt. auth. see Mihalko, Ross.
Swift, Frank. Planet Gazimbo in Galaxy Zamz. (p. 1367)
Swift, Gary, illus. see Aboff, Marcie & Lee, Sally.
Swift, Gary, illus. see Aboff, Marcie.
Swift, Gary, illus. see Fleming, Maria.
Swift, Gary, illus. see Lee, Sally.
Swift, Gayle H. & Swift, Casey Anne. Abc, Adoption & Me. Griffin, Paul, illus. (p. 3)
Swift, Hildegarde H. Little Red Lighthouse & the Great Gray Bridge: Restored Edition. Ward, Lynd, illus. (p. 1035)
Swift, Jessica, ed. see Manley, Heather.
Swift, John. Tea with a Vampire. (p. 1708)
Swift, Jonathan. Gulliver's Travels Martin, Cynthia, illus. (p. 731)
—Gulliver's Travels: And A Discussion of Tolerance. Clift, Eva, illus. (p. 731)
—Gulliver's Travels. (p. 731)
—Gulliver's Travels. Akib, Jamel, illus. (p. 731)
—Gulliver's Travels. Walker, John, illus. (p. 731)
—Gulliver's Travels - Literary Touchstone Edition. (p. 731)
—Jonathan Swift's Gulliver: Candlewick Illustrated Classic. Riddell, Chris, illus. (p. 925)
—Viajes de Gulliver. (p. 1839)
Swift, Jonathan, jt. auth. see Crocker, Carter.
Swift, Jonathan, jt. auth. see Findlay, Lisa.
Swift, Jonathan, jt. auth. see Swift, Jonathan.
Swift, Jonathan & Priory Books Staff. Gulliver's Travels. (p. 731)
Swift, Jonathan & Swift, Jonathan. Viajes de Gulliver. (p. 1839)
Swift, Jonathan, et al. Adventure Collection: Treasure Island, the Jungle Book, Gulliver's Travels, White Fang, the Merry Adventures of Robin Hood Macdonald, Ross, illus. (p. 14)
Swift, Julian. Merlin & His Teapot Eagles. (p. 1128)
Swift, K. Marie. Adventures of Jake & George: Jake Gets a New Brother. Paul, Kate, illus. (p. 19)
Swift, Kathy, et al. Homes. (p. 793)
Swift, Melanie. Rioc & Elber's Arctic Adventure. (p. 1473)
Swift, Richard. Gangs (p. 655)
Swift, Teresa. Alligator with One Shoe. (p. 47)
—JC's Cooking Class. (p. 911)
—Ladybug & the Bird. (p. 971)
Swift, Thomas. Ted Tumble: So Cuddly. (p. 1712)
Swigelson, Kayce M. Grand Adventures of Petit Louis. Swigelson, Kayce M., illus. (p. 707)
Swiger, Lenora. Colt under the Wire. (p. 346)
Swigert, Nancy. Source for Children's Voice Disorders. (p. 1616)
Swigert, Nancy B. Early Intervention Kit Activities Book. (p. 493)
—Early Intervention Kit Therapy Guide. (p. 493)
Swigget, Chelsea. Rae: My True Story of Fear, Anxiety, & Social Phobia. (p. 1433)
Swigut, Bernadetta. First Star: Vigilja- First Star. (p. 597)
Swim, Luann. Cracking the System. (p. 375)
Swinburne, Minnie. Laz's Perfect State Machine. (p. 981)
Swinburne, Stephen R. Black Bear: North America's Bear. (p. 195)
—Butterfly Grows. (p. 248)
—Lots & Lots of Zebra Stripes. (p. 1057)
—Moon in Bear's Eyes. Forest, Crista, illus. (p. 1172)
—Muchas, Muchisimas Rayas de Cebra: Lots & Lots of Zebra Stripes. (p. 1188)
—Ocean Soup: Tide-Pool Poems. Peterson, Mary, illus. (p. 1276)
—Ocean Soup. Peterson, Mary, illus. (p. 1276)
—Safe in a Storm. Bell, Jennifer, illus. (p. 1502)
—Saving Manatees. (p. 1517)
—Sea Turtle Scientist. (p. 1535)
—Turtle Tide: The Ways of Sea Turtles. Hiscock, Bruce, illus. (p. 1798)
—Whose Shoes? A Shoe for Every Job. (p. 1922)
Swinburne, Stephen R. & Hiscock, Bruce. Armadillo Trail: The Northward Journey of the Armadillo. Hiscock, Bruce, illus. (p. 99)
Swindells, Pat. Junk Food Hero. (p. 936)
Swindells, Robert. Abomination. (p. 5)
—Blackout. (p. 197)
—Blitzed. (p. 199)
—Doodlebug Alley. (p. 469)
—Ghosts of Givenham Keep. (p. 672)
—In the Nick of Time. (p. 867)
—Kidnap at Denton Farm. (p. 952)
—Nightmare Stairs. (p. 1255)
—Peril in the Mist. (p. 1343)
—Room 13 & Inside the Worm. Riley, Jon, illus. (p. 1488)
—Ruby Tanya. (p. 1493)
—Secret of Weeping Wood. (p. 1543)
—Skull in Shadows Lane. (p. 1586)
—Strange Tale of Ragger Bill. (p. 1665)
—Timesnatch. Riley, Jon, illus. (p. 1754)
—Trick or Treat. (p. 1786)
—We Didn't Mean to, Honest! (p. 1867)
Swindells, Robert & Swindells, Robert E. Shrapnel. (p. 1571)
Swindells, Robert E., jt. auth. see Swindells, Robert.
Swindells, Robert, et al. Cuentos de Terror. (p. 390)
Swindle, David. Christmas Gift. (p. 314)
Swindle, James L. If I Had a Purple Horse: Poems Mostly for Fun. (p. 853)
Swindle, Stephanie. Pumpkin Pants. (p. 1416)
Swiney, Wendy D. Harvey's First Halloween. (p. 752)
—Harvey's Very Favorite Place. (p. 752)
Swinford, Betty. Cry of the Wild. (p. 387)
—Missionary Stories from Around the World. (p. 1153)
—Rocky Mountain Adventures. (p. 1484)
—Sandstone Tower. (p. 1511)
—Secrets. (p. 1544)
—Woman of the Forest. (p. 1945)
Swinford, Charles, illus. see Cotter, Amelia.
Swing, Michael, illus. see Johnson, Russell W. & Johnson, Annie P.
Swinger-Ellbogen, Sue. Campfire Kids (p. 257)
Swingle, Digna. Night Before Christmas. (p. 1252)
Swingler, Simon, illus. see Badger, M. C.
Swingler, Simon, illus. see Fraillon, Z.
Swingler, Simon, jt. auth. see Badger, M. C.
Swiniarski, Louise, jt. auth. see Breitborde, Mary-Lou.
Swinks, Judi, photos by see Goldstein, Joyce Esersky.
Swinney, Geoff & Mason, Janeen. Fish Facts (p. 598)
Swinney, Kay. Marty Moose & the Mystical Reunion (p. 1098)
Swinney, Nicola Jane. I Love Horses & Ponies. (p. 842)
Swinson, Joyce Ann. Noah's Boat. Clark, Casey, illus. (p. 1262)
Swire, Otta. Skye: The Island & Its Legends. Black, Ronald, ed. (p. 1587)
Swirnow, Linda. Take on Alaska! a Photophonics Reader. (p. 1697)
—Take on Yellowstone! (p. 1697)
—What's New at the Zoo? A PhotoPhOnics (c)Reader. (p. 1898)
Swisher, Clarice. Women of the Roaring Twenties. (p. 1946)
—Women of Victorian England. (p. 1946)
Swisher, Dianne. To Save a Mockingbird. (p. 1759)
Swisher, Elizabeth, illus. see Larkin, Jean, ed.
Swisher, Elizabeth, illus. see Sanders, Nancy I.
Swisher, Elizabeth, illus. see Susan, Hammond.
Swisher, Elizabeth, illus. see Ward, Hadley & Castano, Marie.
Swisher, Michael-Che, illus. see Troeger, Virginia B.
Swisher, Michael-Che, tr. see Troeger, Virginia B.
Swiss, Harold F. Rabbi. Ebb & the Flow. (p. 501)
Switek, Brian. Prehistoric Predators. Csotonyl, Julius, illus. (p. 1395)
Switzer, Bobbi, illus. see Barreto, Sonia.
Switzer, Bobbi, illus. see Elliott, Linda.
Switzer, Bobbi, illus. see Menge, Dawn.
Switzer, Bobbi, illus. see Moore, S. D.
Switzer, Bobbi, illus. see Sampson, Brent.
Switzer, Bobby, illus. see Rhoton, Lesa.
Switzer, Chris. Projects for Alpaca & Llama. (p. 1410)
—Spinning Llama & Alpaca. (p. 1628)
Switzer, Holly. Attitude of Gratitude. (p. 114)
Switzer Hutson, Betty. History of the Christian Methodist Episcopal Church for Children. (p. 784)
Switzer, Vern. Hard Heads Make Soft Bottoms. Connally, Perry L., Sr., illus. (p. 748)
—Lucy the Cantaloupe. Connally, Perry L., Sr., illus. (p. 1063)
—Puffy the Watermelon. Listokin, David & Connally, Perry L., Sr., illus. (p. 1415)
Swoboda, Lois. Old Neb & the Lighthouse Treasure. Wallace, Leslie, illus. (p. 1284)
Swogger, John-Gordon, illus. see Evans, Kirsti.
Swope, Bob. Teach'n Beginning Defensive Basketball Drills, Plays, & Games Free Flow Handbook. (p. 1710)
—Teach'n Beginning Defensive Football Drills, Plays, & Games Free Flow Handbook. (p. 1710)
—Teach'n Beginning Hunting & Hunter Safety Free Flow Handbook. (p. 1710)
—Teach'n Beginning Offensive Basketball Drills, Plays, & Games Free Flow Handbook. (p. 1710)
—Teach'n Beginning Offensive Soccer Drills, Plays, Strategies, & Games Free Flow Handbook. (p. 1710)
Swope, Brenda, illus. see Blace, Maria.
Swope, Brenda, illus. see Calabrese, Diane Marie.
Swope, Brenda, illus. see Cardona, Nancy.
Swope, Brenda, illus. see Dornan, Dave.
Swope, Brenda, illus. see Dubrule, Jackie.
Swope, Brenda, illus. see Emanuel, Lora.
Swope, Brenda, illus. see Fass, Amanda L.
Swope, Brenda, illus. see Ferry, Ann.
Swope, Brenda, illus. see Hart-Plaugher, Teresa.
Swope, Brenda, illus. see Joseph, Beverly L.
Swope, Brenda, illus. see Kelty, Colleen Alyce.
Swope, Brenda, illus. see Kirkland, Kim M.
Swope, Brenda, illus. see Lawson, Barbara.
Swope, Brenda, illus. see Mattingly, Robin.
Swope, Brenda, illus. see McDade Jr, Bert M.
Swope, Brenda, illus. see Murray, Rosalie.
Swope, Brenda, illus. see Ramirez, Iz.
Swope, Brenda, illus. see Robinson Ed. D., Shannon R.
Swope, Brenda, illus. see Seaman, Lucy.
Swope, Brenda, illus. see Stewart, Mark R.
Swope, Brenda, illus. see Trimoglie, Mario.
Swope, Brenda, illus. see V.
Swope, Brenda, illus. see Wade, Joan.
Swope, Gretchen, jt. auth. see Intravia, Emily.
Swope, Gretchen, jt. auth. see Renick, Ricki.
Swope, Sam. Gotta Go! Gotta Go! Riddle, Sue, illus. (p. 704)
—I Am a Pencil: A Teacher, His Kids, & Their World of Stories. (p. 832)
—Krazees. (p. 967)
Sword, Elizabeth H., jt. auth. see Sword, Elizabeth Hauge.
Sword, Elizabeth Hauge & Sword, Elizabeth H. Child's Anthology of Poetry. (p. 304)
Sycamore, Hilary, illus. see Abadzis, Nick.
Sycamore, Hilary, illus. see Bogaert, Harmen Meyndertsz van den & O'Connor, George.
Sycolin Creek Elementary School (Leesburg, Va.) Staff, contrib. by. Greatest Homework Excuse Book Ever. (p. 720)
Syddall, Susan. It's a Bad Day to Be a Fly! (p. 895)
Sydney, Pamela. Mikey the Chicken Turtle. (p. 1141)
Sydor, Colleen. McGuillicuddy Book of Personal Records (p. 1114)
—My Mother Is a French Fry & Further Proof of My Fuzzed-Up Life. (p. 1214)
—Raising a Little Stink. Constantin, Pascale, illus. (p. 1437)
—Smarty pants. Langlois, Suzane, illus. (p. 1593)
—Timmerman Was Here. Debon, Nicolas, illus. (p. 1754)
Sydor, Colleen & Constantin, Pascale. Camilla Chameleon. Constantin, Pascale, illus. (p. 256)
Syed, E. A. Jerry Cleans up His Act. (p. 913)
Syed, Hafsa N. Piggy Wanted to Learn. (p. 1358)
Syed, Ibrahim. Quranic Inspirations. (p. 1429)
Syed, Jaweria T. Enchantment Realm's First Adventure. (p. 523)
Syers, Rita Hsu. Mystery of the Crying Ghost. (p. 1225)
Sykes, Andy. Hexjibber Colouring & Activity Book. (p. 774)
Sykes, Harold S. Beacon of Airport Seven. (p. 149)
Sykes, John. Modular Maths for Edexcel A2 Pure Mathematics. (p. 1159)
Sykes, Julie. Beware the Werepup. Reed, Nathan, illus. (p. 173)
—Bless You, Santa! Warnes, Tim, illus. (p. 199)
—Dora's Chicks. Chapman, Jane, illus. (p. 471)
—Dora's Eggs. Chapman, Jane, illus. (p. 471)
—I Don't Want to Go to Bed! Warnes, Tim, illus. (p. 838)
—Shhh! Warnes, Tim, illus. (p. 1566)
—That Pesky Dragon. Williamson, Melanie, illus. (p. 1726)
Sykes, Julie, jt. auth. see Warnes, Tim.
Sykes, Shannon, illus. see Love, Pamela.
Sykes, Shelley & Szymanski, Lois. Soldier in the Cellar. (p. 1607)
—Whisper of War. (p. 1912)
Sykes, Tina . Elliot Makes a Friend. (p. 514)
Sylliboy, Helen, tr. see Trottier, Maxine.
Sylvada, Peter, illus. see Bunting, Eve.
Sylvada, Peter, illus. see Thomas, Patricia.
Sylvada, Peter, illus. see Whelan, Gloria.
Sylvaine, Jenny, illus. see Malaspina, Ann.
Sylvan, Jade. Kissing Oscar Wilde: A Love Story in the City of Lights. (p. 962)
Sylvan Learning. First Grade Super Games & Puzzles (Sylvan Super Workbooks) (p. 595)
—Kindergarten Super Games & Puzzles (Sylvan Super Workbook) (p. 957)
—Second Grade Super Games & Puzzles (Sylvan Super Workbooks) (p. 1539)
—Sylvan Kick Start for First Grade. (p. 1692)
—Sylvan Kick Start for Kindergarten. (p. 1692)
Sylvan Learning Staff. First Grade Basic Math Success (Sylvan Workbooks) (p. 595)
—First Grade Fun with Numbers (Sylvan Fun on the Run Series) (p. 595)
—First Grade Language Arts Success (Sylvan Super Workbooks) (p. 595)
—First Grade Math Games & Puzzles. (p. 595)
—First Grade Spelling Games & Activities (Sylvan Workbooks) (p. 595)
—First Grade Super Math Success (Sylvan Super Workbooks) (p. 595)
—First Grade Vocabulary Puzzles (Sylvan Workbooks) (p. 595)
—First Grade Word Puzzles. (p. 595)
—Kindergarten Alphabet Activities (Sylvan Workbooks) (p. 957)
—Kindergarten Basic Math Success (Sylvan Workbooks) (p. 957)
—Kindergarten Math Games & Puzzles. (p. 957)
—Kindergarten Numbers & Counting (Sylvan Workbooks) (p. 957)
—Kindergarten Page per Day: Math Skills. (p. 957)
—Kindergarten Page per Day: Reading Skills. (p. 957)
—Kindergarten Reading Readiness (Sylvan Workbooks) (p. 957)
—Kindergarten Super Math Success (Sylvan Super Workbooks) (p. 957)
—Kindergarten Word Games (Sylvan Fun on the Run Series) (p. 957)
—Pre-K Beginning Numbers (Sylvan Workbooks) (p. 1394)
—Pre-K Letters, Numbers & Shapes Super Workbook (Sylvan Super Workbooks) (p. 1394)
—Pre-K Page per Day: Letters. (p. 1394)
—Second Grade Language Arts Success (Sylvan Super Workbooks) (p. 1539)
—Second Grade Spelling Games & Activities (Sylvan Workbooks) (p. 1539)
—Second Grade Vocabulary Puzzles (Sylvan Workbooks) (p. 1539)
Sylvan Learning Staff, jt. auth. see Gogol, Nikolai.
Sylvan, Lu. Vladimir Putin: Russian Leader. (p. 1846)
Sylver, Adrienne. Hot Diggity Dog: The History of the Hot Dog. Smith, Elwood H., illus. (p. 801)
Sylvester, Alden W. Five Minutes in America a Voyage in Life. (p. 601)
Sylvester, Diane. Ancient China. Hillam, Corbin, illus. (p. 68)
—Ancient Greece. VanBlaricum, Pam, ed. (p. 69)
—Ancient Rome. Hillam, Corbin, illus. (p. 70)
—Current Events: Looking at Current Issues from Different Perspectives. Larson, Eric, ed. (p. 394)
Sylvester, Kevin. Baseballogy: Tons of Things You Never Knew. (p. 141)
—Game Day: Meet the People Who Make It Happen. (p. 654)
—Gold Medal for Weird. Sylvester, Kevin, illus. (p. 693)
—Miners. (p. 1146)
—MiNRS. (p. 1148)
—Neil Flambé & the Aztec Abduction. Sylvester, Kevin, illus. (p. 1240)
—Neil Flambé & the Bard's Banquet. Sylvester, Kevin, illus. (p. 1240)
—Neil Flambé & the Crusader's Curse. Sylvester, Kevin, illus. (p. 1240)
—Neil Flambé & the Marco Polo Murders. Sylvester, Kevin, illus. (p. 1240)
—Neil Flambé & the Tokyo Treasure. Sylvester, Kevin, illus. (p. 1240)
—Neil Flambé Capers Collection: Neil Flambé & the Marco Polo Murders; Neil Flambé & the Aztec Abduction; Neil Flambé & the Crusader's Curse; Neil Flambé & the Tokyo Treasure. Sylvester, Kevin, illus. (p. 1240)
—Showtime: Meet the People Behind the Scenes. (p. 1571)
—Splinters. (p. 1630)
—Sports Hall of Weird. Sylvester, Kevin, illus. (p. 1632)
Sylvester, Kevin, illus. see Hoyte, Carol-Ann.
Sylvester, Kevin, illus. see Rondina, Catherine.
Sylvester, Kevin & Hlinka, Michael. Follow Your Money: Who Gets It, Who Spends It, Where Does It Go? Sylvester, Kevin, illus. (p. 612)
Sylvester, Merrill. Ho-Ho Where Did All My Reindeer Go? The Chicken Leg Detective Service. (p. 786)
Sylvester, Oscar. Life on a Commercial Fishing Boat. (p. 1012)
Sylvester, Sr. Land of the Angels Morrison, Nancy, illus. (p. 973)
—Talking Memories. Morrison, Nancy, illus. (p. 1703)
Sylvester Sr, John S. Our Day on the Farm (p. 1308)
Sylvester, Suzanne, photos by see Stoltz, Susan.
Sylvestre, Daniel, illus. see Desrosiers, Sylvie.
Sylvestre, Daniel, illus. see Duggan, Paul.
Sylvestre, Daniel, tr. see Audet, Martine.
Sylvestre, Gibson. Life on Purpose: Allow God to Ignite His Passion & Purpose in You! (p. 1012)
Sylvia, Davison. Jack's Cap: More Short Vowel Stories. Holly, Davison, illus. (p. 904)

—Noses & Roses: More Long Vowel Stories. Holly, Davison, illus. (p. 1266)
Symank, Cara, jt. auth. see Lewis, Carole.
Syme, Daniel B., jt. auth. see Sonsino, Rifat.
Symes, R. F. Crystal & Gem. (p. 387)
—DK Eyewitness Books: Rocks & Minerals: Rocks & Minerals. (p. 456)
Symes, R. F. & Harding, Robert. Crystal & Gem: Eyewitness Books. Keates, Colin, photos by. (p. 387)
Symes, Ruth Louise. Floppy Ears. Kenyon, Tony, illus. (p. 606)
—Mondays at Monster School. Reeve, Rosie, illus. (p. 1163)
Symes, Sally. Funny Face, Sunny Face. Beardshaw, Rosalind, illus. (p. 649)
—Whose Toes Are Those? Sharratt, Nick, illus. (p. 1922)
—Yawn. Sharratt, Nick, illus. (p. 1968)
Symington, Lindsay, illus. see McNabb, Vincent.
Symington, Martha M. Emily: Dream Believe Achieve. Nolan, Amanda M., illus. (p. 518)
—Global Heart Warming: Dream Believe Achieve Series. Sanderson, Jessica B., illus. (p. 684)
Symmons, Sheeres, illus. see Leslie, Emma.
Symonds, Doris. How I Saved $10,500 with Only 4 Quarters a Day. (p. 810)
Symons, Anna Jane. Nanna & Me. (p. 1229)
Symons, Brandy. Lemonade Kisses. (p. 991)
—Peek A Boo, I See You. (p. 1334)
Symons, J. B. Turms of Peace. (p. 1797)
Symons, Mitchell. Don't Wipe Your Bum with a Hedgehog. (p. 469)
—Why Don't You Smell When You're Sleeping? (p. 1924)
—Why Spacemen Can't Burp. (p. 1926)
Synarski, Susan, illus. see Gordon, Lynn & Chronicle Books Staff.
Synarski, Susan, illus. see Gordon, Lynn.
Synder, Bernadette. 131 Fun-Damental Facts for Catholic Kids: Liturgy, Litanies, Rituals, Rosaries, Symbols, Sacraments & Sacred Scripture. Sharp, Chris, illus. (p. 2000)
Synder, Gail. Teens & Smoking. (p. 1715)
Synepolsky, I., illus. see Slupskiy, Leon.
Synge, E. M., illus. see Synge, M. B.
Synge, John M. Playboy of the Western World. Landes, William-Alan, ed. (p. 1372)
—Playboy of the Western World & Riders to the Sea. Hart, William E., ed. (p. 1372)
—Riders to the Sea. Landes, William-Allan, ed. (p. 1471)
Synge, M. B. Awakening of Europe (Yesterday's Classics) Synge, E. M., illus. (p. 120)
—Discovery of New Worlds, Book II of the Story of the World. (p. 450)
—Discovery of New Worlds (Yesterday's Classics) Synge, E. M., illus. (p. 450)
—Growth of the British Empire (Yesterday's Classics) Synge, E. M., illus. (p. 727)
—On the Shores of the Great Sea, Book I of the Story of the World. (p. 1291)
—On the Shores of the Great Sea (Yesterday's Classics) Synge, E. M., illus. (p. 1291)
—Struggle for Sea Power. (p. 1668)
—Struggle for Sea Power, Book Iv of the Story of the World. (p. 1668)
—Struggle for Sea Power (Yesterday's Classics) Synge, E. M., illus. (p. 1668)
Synopsis, Q. Johnny Werd: The Fire Continues. (p. 923)
Synoracki, Amy R. Don't They Know I'm a Kid? (p. 468)
Sypolt, Carl W. Adventures of David the Honeybee. (p. 17)
—Fibber Lygood at Christmas, Easter, & St. Patrick's Day. (p. 583)
Syrewicz, Connor. Arts: Dance, Music, Theater, & Fine Art. (p. 104)
—Energizing Energy Markets: Clean Coal, Shale, Oil, Wind, & Solar. (p. 528)
—Farming, Ranching, & Agriculture. (p. 574)
—Masseur & Massage Therapist. (p. 1102)
—Personal Assistant. (p. 1344)
—Truck Driver. (p. 1791)
Syrstad, Suzi. Timmy the Tiny Troubled Turtle Maki, Tab, illus. (p. 1755)
Sytsma, Mary, jt. auth. see Vogel, Jane.
Syverson, Carolyn. Community Helpers. (p. 350)
—Places to Go! (p. 1366)
Szabo, Erika. Our Summer Guests. (p. 1310)
Szabo, Grable. Holy Donuts: Impacting Schools for Christ. (p. 791)
Szafranski, Keith. Barrington Bear Visits the Emperor - the Emperor Penguin That Is. Szafranski, Keith, illus. (p. 140)
Szaky, Tom. Revolution in a Bottle: How Terracycle Is Redefining Green Business. (p. 1466)
Szanto, Hubert, tr. see Hünermann, Wilhelm.
Szarka, Balazs. European Folk Tales. (p. 540)
Szcsesniak, Janet. Frog Who Made Friends. (p. 640)
Szczurek, Gregory. U. S. Coast Guard Licenses & Certificates: How to qualify, apply, Prepare. (p. 1806)
Szegedi, Katalin, illus. see Nobisso, Josephine.
Szegedi, Katalin, illus. see Sorenson, Margo.
Szegedy, Esther, illus. see Polette, Keith.
Szejko, Allyn, jt. auth. see Aronson, Virginia.
Szekeres, Cyndy. Buenas Noches, Rapo. (p. 235)
—Comer! (p. 348)
—Cuentas Osito. (p. 389)
—Dia Muy Especial. (p. 433)
—Juego de Las Escondidas. (p. 931)
—Mudanza de la Ratita. (p. 1188)
—Nada Que Hacer. (p. 1227)
—Perrito Perdido. (p. 1343)
—Small Child's Book of Prayers. Szekeres, Cyndy, illus. (p. 1592)
Szekeres, Cyndy, illus. see Appelt, Kathi.
Szekeres, Vivienne, jt. auth. see Zera, Annette.
Szeps-Fralin, Christiane. Drole de Mission. (p. 485)
—Poursuite Inattendue. (p. 1389)
Szeps-Fralin, Christiane, jt. auth. see Fralin, Alfred G.
Szewczyk, Manda, illus. see Weber, Roopa.
Szijgyarto, Cynthia, illus. see Nagy, Jennifer.
Szilagyi, Mary, illus. see Krauss, Ruth.
Szilagyi, Mary, illus. see Rylant, Cynthia.
Szirtes, Helen, jt. auth. see Horne, Richard.
Szish, Jill Henry. TJ & the Good Luck Cricket. Perry, Jennifer A., illus. (p. 1758)
Szitas, Kathie, ed. see Santora, L. Steven.
Szkop, Catherine. Adventures of Arathmatar. (p. 16)
Szollosi, Nick. Escape: One Refugee's Journey. (p. 534)
Szpirglas, Jeff. Evil Eye. (p. 546)
—Fear This Book: Your Guide to Fright, Horror, & Things That Go Bump in the Night. Pérez, Ramón & Owlkids Books Inc. Staff, illus. (p. 579)
—Gross Universe: Your Guide to All Disgusting Things under the Sun. Cho, Michael & Owlkids Books Inc. Staff, illus. (p. 725)
—You Just Can't Help It! Your Guide to the Wild & Wacky World of Human Behavior. Holinaty, Josh, illus. (p. 1975)
Szpirglas, Jeff & Saint-Onge, Danielle. Messy Miranda Whamond, Dave, illus. (p. 1130)
Szuc, Jeff, illus. see Kaner, Etta.
Szucs, Sandor, jt. auth. see Anderson, Lil.
Szulhan, Rebecca. Contemporary Achievements. (p. 360)
Szumski, Bonnie. Angelina Jolie. Greenhaven Press Staff, ed. (p. 74)
—Careers in Biotechnology. (p. 267)
—Careers in Fashion. (p. 267)
—Cheating. (p. 295)
Szumski, Bonnie, ed. see Ruggiero, Adriane.
Szumski, Bonnie, ed. see Young, Mitchell.
Szumski, Bonnie, jt. auth. see Greenhaven Press Editors.
Szumski, Bonnie & Karson, Jill. Careers in Engineering. (p. 267)
Szymanski, Lois. Chincoteague Pony Identification Cards Kantjas, Linda, photos by. (p. 307)
—Out of the Sea: Today's Chincoteague Pony (p. 1311)
—True Story of Miracle Man. (p. 1793)
—True Story of Quintilius. (p. 1793)
—Wild Colt Kantjas, Linda, illus. (p. 1929)
Szymanski, Lois, jt. auth. see Sykes, Shelley.
Szymanski, Lois K. Grandfather's Secret (p. 707)
—Pony in Need. (p. 1382)
—Pony to the Rescue. (p. 1383)
—True Story of Sea Feather (p. 1793)
Szymanski, Therese. When It's All Relative. (p. 1903)
Szymona, Marlene L. My Sister Beth's Pink Birthday. Battuz, Christine, illus. (p. 1218)

T

T. Adventures of Sugar the Pup. Baker, David, illus. (p. 23)
.T. Ozzie the Spider. (p. 1316)
T., Bobby. Chicalafur. (p. 299)
T. M. K. Dewey Does Exercise. (p. 432)
—Dewey Does for President. (p. 432)
—Doctor, Lawyer, Indian Chief. (p. 459)
—New Kid in the Neighborhood. (p. 1245)
—One Busy Day. (p. 1294)
T. N., illus. see Tinti, Natalie.
T R Thomas & Thomas, T. R. Celebrity Cases: True Crime (p. 285)
—Cold Cases (p. 338)
—DNA Evidence (p. 456)
—Forensics: True Crime (p. 617)
—Serial Killers (p. 1552)
T. W. Zimmerman, illus. see Dodgson, Y. K.
Taaffe, Gary. Bullies: Billy's Gotta Survive the City. (p. 240)
Taback, Simms. 1, 2, 3. (p. 1990)
—Colors. Taback, Simms, illus. (p. 345)
—Coupons for Readers (p. 372)
—Dinosaurs: A Giant Fold-Out Book. (p. 444)
—Do You Have a Tail? (p. 457)
—Joseph Had a Little Overcoat. Taback, Simms, illus. (p. 926)
—Moo Baby Gift Set. (p. 1171)
—Peek-A-Boo Who? Taback, Simms, illus. (p. 1335)
—Postcards from Camp. Taback, Simms, illus. (p. 1388)
—Safari Animals. Taback, Simms, illus. (p. 1501)
—Simms Taback's City Animals. (p. 1577)
—Simms Taback's Farm Animals. (p. 1577)
—This Is the House That Jack Built. Taback, Simms, illus. (p. 1736)
Taback, Simms, illus. see Blue Apple Staff.
Taback, Simms, illus. see LePan, Don.
Taback, Simms, illus. see Ziefert, Harriet.
Taback, Simms, jt. auth. see Blue Apple Staff.
Taback, Simms, jt. auth. see Ziefert, Harriet.
Taback, Simms & Ziefert, Harriet. Quack Like a Duck! (p. 1422)
Tabak, John. Biofuels. (p. 188)
—Coal & Oil. (p. 336)
—Natural Gas & Hydrogen. (p. 1235)
—Nuclear Energy. (p. 1269)
—Solar & Geothermal Energy. (p. 1606)
—Wind & Water. (p. 1935)
Tabak, John, jt. auth. see Billings, Charlene W.
Tabak, John, jt. auth. see Grady, Sean M.
Tabak, Lawrence. In Real Life. (p. 864)
Tabares, Bridgitt, illus. see Tabares, Veronica.
Tabares, Veronica. Monkeys on an Island. Tabares, Bridgitt, illus. (p. 1166)
Tabary, illus. see Goscinny, René.
Tabary, Armelle, illus. see Goscinny, René.
Tabary, Jean, illus. see Goscinny, René.
Tabary, Jean, jt. auth. see Goscinny, René.
Tabatabaei, Maryam, illus. see Glaser, Linda.
Tabb, Mark, jt. auth. see Baldwin, Stephen.
Tabbutt, Steven, illus. see Gates Galvin, Laura.
Tabby, Abigail. Hokey Pokey Elmo. Brannon, Tom, illus. (p. 787)
—KnitWits Make a Move! Wildish, Lee, illus. (p. 965)
—Monsters Munch Lunch! (p. 1169)
—Monsters Munch Lunch! (Sesame Street) Womble, Louis, illus. (p. 1169)
Taber, Chera. Muddle Creek Zoo. (p. 1188)
Taber, Kristen. Ærenden - the Child Returns. (p. 1460)
Taber-Montgomery, Kathy. We Live in a Zoo. (p. 1867)
Tabernik, John. Ricky the Picky Koala. Wise, Catin, illus. (p. 1470)
Tabibi, Alexis Deeba. Unusual World. (p. 1823)
Tabibzadeh, M. R. Angels' Whisper. Sholevar, Bahman, ed. (p. 75)
Tablason, Jamie, illus. see Barchers, Suzanne.
Tabler, Judith. Rat Terrier (p. 1440)
Tabler, Marie, jt. auth. see Meyer, Julia.
Tabor, Nancy Maria Grande. Celebraciones: Dias Feriados de los Estados Unidos y Mexico. Tabor, Nancy Maria Grande, illus. (p. 283)
—Somos un Arco Iris (We Are a Rainbow) Tabor, Nancy Maria Grande, illus. (p. 1611)
Tabor, Nathan, illus. see Sims, Nat.
Tabor, Stephen A. When I Wished ... Shamp, Danielle, illus. (p. 1903)
Tabori, Lena, jt. ed. see Wong, Alice.
Taborn, Debbie. When a Feather Fell. (p. 1901)
Taborn, Deborah V. Donia & Her Marvelous Bag of Cents. (p. 466)
Tabs, Judy & Steinberg, Barbara. Matzah Meals: A Passover Cookbook for Kids. Hauser, Bill, illus. (p. 1110)
Tacang, Brian. Bully-Be-Gone: The Misadventures of Millicent Madding #1. (p. 241)
Tachell, Judy, jt. auth. see Smith, Alastair.
Tachibana, Yutaka, jt. auth. see Tachibana, Yutaka.
Tachibana, Yutaka & Beck, Adrienne. Gatcha Gacha (p. 658)
Tachibana, Yutaka & Tachibana, Yutaka. Gatcha Gacha Tachibana, Yutaka, illus. (p. 657)
Tachikawa, Carter. Half-Baked Kate. (p. 736)
Tackach, James. Civil War. (p. 325)
Tackett, Mike. Holoholo I Hawaii. (p. 789)
Tackett, Mike, illus. see Mora, Ebie.
Tackett, Wendy. Jefferson Wish. (p. 912)
—Snow Wish. (p. 1600)
Tada, Hiroshi. Who's There. Perry, Mia, tr. (p. 1921)
Tadano, Kazuko. Kazuko Tadano Portfolio. (p. 946)
Taddeo, John, illus. see Chilman-Blair, Kim.
Taddeo, John, jt. auth. see Chilman-Blair, Kim.
Tadder, Karen Mc. Donald. Picture Your Invisible Self: A Universal Lesson Plan for Learning Intrapersonal Skills. (p. 1356)
Taddonio, Susan A., jt. auth. see Moss, Wendy L.
Tademy, Lalita. Red River. (p. 1455)
Tadgell, Nicole, illus. see Birtha, Becky.
Tadgell, Nicole, illus. see Derby, Sally.
Tadgell, Nicole, illus. see Elster, Jean Alicia.
Tadgell, Nicole, illus. see Elvgren, Jennifer.
Tadgell, Nicole, illus. see Grigsby, Susan.
Tadgell, Nicole, illus. see Scholastic, Inc. Staff & Grimes, Nikki.
Tadgell, Nicole, illus. see Slade, Suzanne.
Tadiello, Ed, illus. see Wiggin, Kate Douglas Smith.
Tadjo, Veronique. Mamy Wata & the Monster (p. 1085)
Taeckens, Geri. Walking along with My Dog. Carney, Deborah, illus. (p. 1854)
Taeger, Oonagh, tr. see Desnos, Robert.
Tae-Hyung, Kim. Planet Blood Tae-Hyung, Kim, illus. (p. 1367)
Tae-Hyung Kim, creator. Planet Blood (p. 1367)
Tae-Jun, Lee, et al. Waiting for Mama. Dong-Seong, Kim & Kim, Tong-Song, illus. (p. 1852)
Taeryn, M. S. Chosen Four: The Faelan Prophecies, Book One. (p. 310)
Taeschner, Jacquelin. Boss. (p. 215)
Tafalla, Ortiz, illus. see Kelly, Jack.
Tafolla, Carmen. Fiesta Babies. Córdova, Amy, illus. (p. 584)
—What Can You Do with a Paleta? Morales, Magaly, illus. (p. 1881)
—What Can You Do with a Paleta? (¿Que Puede Hacer con una Paleta?) Morales, Magaly, illus. (p. 1881)
—What Can You Do with a Rebozo? Córdova, Amy, illus. (p. 1881)
—What Can You Do with a Rebozo? ?Qu? Puedes Hacer con un Rebozo? Córdova, Amy & Cordova, Amy, illus. (p. 1881)
—What Can You Do with a Rebozo? (¿Qué Puedes Hacer Con un Rebozo?) Córdova, Amy & Córdova, Amy, illus. (p. 1881)
Tafolla, Carmen & Teneyuca, Sharyll. That's Not Fair! - ¡No es Justo! Emma Tenayuca's Struggle for Justice - La Lucha de Emma Tenayuca Por la Justicia. Ybáñez, Terry, illus. (p. 1727)
Tafoya, Jody. Sammy: A Day in the Life of a Snail. (p. 1507)
Tafoya, Nathan & Nash, Kevin. University of Arizona College Prowler off the Record. (p. 1820)
Taft, Christopher C. Witch of Green Spring. (p. 1941)
Taft, Rick. Shorty the Dreamer. (p. 1569)
Tafuri, Nancy. All Kinds of Kisses. (p. 45)
—Big Storm: A Very Soggy Counting Book. Tafuri, Nancy, illus. (p. 184)
—Blue Goose. Tafuri, Nancy, illus. (p. 203)
—Busy Little Squirrel. Tafuri, Nancy, illus. (p. 246)
—Daddy Hugs. (p. 398)
—Five Little Chicks. Tafuri, Nancy, illus. (p. 600)
—Have You Seen My Duckling? Tafuri, Nancy, illus. (p. 754)
—Mama's Little Bears. (p. 1084)
—Silly Little Goose. Tafuri, Nancy, illus. (p. 1576)
—Whose Chick Are You? Tafuri, Nancy, illus. (p. 1921)
Tageau, Jerry, illus. see Edgers, Geoff.
Tagel, Peggy. Animal Safari. (p. 79)
—Color My World Blue. (p. 343)
—Dinosaurs. (p. 444)
—On the Go. (p. 1290)
Tagel, Peggy, illus. see McGrath, Barbara Barbieri.
Tager, Gavriella, jt. auth. see Fuks, Menuhah.
Tagert-Paul, Kimberley. God's Ten Promises: Helping Children Understand the Ten Commandments. (p. 692)
Tagg, Christine. Cinderlily: A Floral Fairy Tale. Ellwand, David, ed. (p. 321)
—Who Will You Meet on Scary Street? Nine Pop-up Nightmares! Fuge, Charles, illus. (p. 1919)
Taggar, Sam & Williamson, Susan. Great Games! Old & New, Indoor-Outdoor, Board, Card, Ball, & Word. (p. 716)
Taggart, B., ed. see Cruse, Howard.
Taggart, Katy, et al. Workin' on the Railroad: And Other Favorite Rhymes. (p. 1952)
Tagge, Mark. Coma & Convulsion Club: The Retreat. (p. 346)
Tagholm, Sally. Complete Book of the Night. (p. 352)
—Rabbit. (p. 1429)
Tagle, illus. see Abodehman, Ahmed.
Tagle, illus. see Soci Et E de La Faune Et Des Parcs Du Qu Ebec.
Tagliaferri, Sarla & Spada, Alberto. My Baby Teeth (p. 1196)
—Why That Face (p. 1926)
Tagliaferro, Linda. Animals Babies Pack [Scholastic]. (p. 82)
—Ants & Their Nests (p. 90)
—Bears & Their Cubs. (p. 151)
—Bears & Their Cubs [Scholastic]. (p. 151)
—Bears & Their Dens (p. 151)
—Bears & Their Dens [Scholastic]. (p. 151)
—Bees & Their Hives (p. 158)
—Bees & Their Hives [Scholastic]. (p. 158)
—Birds & Their Nests (p. 191)
—Birds & Their Nests [Scholastic]. (p. 191)
—Dogs & Their Puppies (p. 462)
—Dogs & Their Puppies [Scholastic]. (p. 462)
—Explore the Deciduous Forest (p. 550)
—Explore the Tropical Rain Forest (p. 550)
—Explore the Tundra (p. 550)
—How Does a Volcano Become an Island? (p. 808)
—How Does an Earthquake Become a Tsunami? (p. 808)
—Palace of Versailles: France's Royal Jewel. (p. 1319)
—Puerto Rico in Pictures. (p. 1415)
—Rabbits & Their Burrows. (p. 1430)
—Rabbits & Their Burrows [Scholastic]. (p. 1430)
—Robins & Their Chicks (p. 1480)
—Service Dogs. (p. 1553)
—Spiders & Their Webs. (p. 1627)
—Taj Mahal: India's Majestic Tomb. (p. 1696)
—Therapy Dogs. (p. 1729)
—Thomas Edison: Inventor of the Age of Electricity. (p. 1738)
—Who Lands Planes on a Ship? Working on an Aircraft Carrier. (p. 1916)
—Who Walks in Space? Working in Space. (p. 1918)
—World's Smartest Machines (p. 1961)
Tagliaferro, Linda & Capstone Press Staff. Life Cycle of a Bean Saunders-Smith, Gail, ed. (p. 1008)
—Life Cycle of a Carrot Saunders-Smith, Gail, ed. (p. 1009)
—Life Cycle of a Pine Tree Saunders-Smith, Gail, ed. (p. 1009)
—Life Cycle of a Sunflower Saunders-Smith, Gail, ed. (p. 1009)
—Life Cycle of an Apple Tree Saunders-Smith, Gail, ed. (p. 1009)
—Life Cycle of an Oak Tree Saunders-Smith, Gail, ed. (p. 1009)
Tagliaferro, Linda & Heinemann Library Staff. How Does a Volcano Become an Island? (p. 808)
—How Does an Earthquake Become a Tsunami? (p. 808)
Taglietti, Emanuele, illus. see Carr, Simonetta.
Tagnetti, Stefano & Watt, Fiona. Busy Car. (p. 246)
Tago, Anita. Traditional Stories from Binandere in Oro Province, Papua New Guinea. (p. 1776)
Tagore, Rabindranath. Crescent Moon - Child Poems. (p. 381)
—Gitanjali - Song Offerings. (p. 681)
Tagore, Rabindranath & Ray, Sukhendu. Chirakumar Sabha: The Bachelor's Club: a Comedy in Five Acts. (p. 308)
Taguchi, Masayuki, illus. see Takami, Koushun.
Taguchi, Randy. Outlet. Walley, Glynne, tr. from JPN. (p. 1313)
Tague, James E. Krankel Family. (p. 967)
Tagyos, Paul Rátz de, illus. see Speck, Katie.
Taher, Amr. Jimmy the Squirrel. Taher, Layal, ed. (p. 918)
Taher, Layal, ed. see Taher, Amr.
Tahir, Sabaa. Ember in the Ashes. (p. 517)
Tahir "Z", Zarghuna. Lazy Froggies. (p. 981)
Tahleh, Eleykaa, illus. see Westerman, Rob.
Tahmaseb, Charity & Vance, Darcy. Geek Girl's Guide to Cheerleading. (p. 659)
Tahrike Tarsile Qur'an Editors. Glorious Qur'an: A Simplified Translation for the Young People. Ahamed, S. V., tr. (p. 685)
Tahta, Sophie. What's under the Sea? Trotter, Stuart, illus. (p. 1900)
Tai, Elise See. Farm Animal Counting. (p. 573)
—Wild Animal Alphabet. (p. 1928)
—Write & Draw Dinosaurs. (p. 1963)
—Write & Draw Wild Animals. (p. 1963)
Tai, Elise See & Cole, Linda. Creative Card Making Pack: Blank Cards, Decoupage, Stencils, Stickers. (p. 379)
Taibah, Nadia Jameel, jt. auth. see MacDonald, Margaret Read.
Taifeather, Speck Lee, jt. auth. see Gurney, Stella.
Taimy Studios, illus. see Turnbull, Betty Turnbull.
Tainsh, Robert & Priddy, Roger. Zoo's Who? (p. 1990)
Tainsh, Robert, et al. I Love Animals: Wild, Scary, Cute or Cuddly, We Love them All! (p. 841)
Tait, Barbara. Timothy Toot... Finds A Hat. Margolis, Al, illus. (p. 1755)
—Timothy Toot... Goes Fishing. Margolis, Al, illus. (p. 1755)
—Timothy Toot... Goes to the Zoo. (p. 1755)
Tait, Chris. Dr. Knucklehead's Knock-Knocks. Lekander, Lance, illus. (p. 475)
—Ridiculous Knock-Knocks. Zahnd, Mark, illus. (p. 1471)
—Ridiculous Riddles. Zahnd, Mark, illus. (p. 1471)
—Ridiculous Tongue Twisters. Jones, Buck, illus. (p. 1471)
Tait, Chris & Horsfall, Jacqueline. Super Colossal Knock-Knocks. (p. 1679)
Tait, Chris & Wyss, Johann David. Swiss Family Robinson. Akib, Jamel, illus. (p. 1691)
Tait, Chris, et al. Super Silliest Riddles. (p. 1681)

Tait, Elena. Day My Peanut Butter Lost Its Stick. Lee, Joe, illus. (p. 413)
—Mommy Why Wasn't I at Your Wedding? (p. 1162)
—Twisted Fairy Tale. (p. 1802)
Tait, Lela. Avi. (p. 119)
—Birds. (p. 191)
—Caring for Your Potbellied Pig. (p. 269)
—Cinco de Mayo. (p. 319)
—Emi the Sumatran Rhino. (p. 518)
—Flowers. (p. 608)
—Little Draggin' Bear. (p. 1027)
—Mice. (p. 1134)
—Pecorino. (p. 1334)
—Primary Sources. (p. 1400)
—Queen Rania Al-Abdullah. (p. 1425)
Tait, Lela, jt. auth. see Wiseman, Blaine.
Tait, Noel. Insects & Spiders. (p. 876)
Tait, Noel, ed. Bugs. (p. 237)
Taitano, Janice G. Legend of Lutung. (p. 988)
Taitz, Emily. Judaism (p. 930)
Taixi, Su, illus. see Ma, Zheng & Li, Zheng.
Tajadod, Nahal. Rumi: The Fire of Love. Bononno, Robert, tr. from FRE. (p. 1495)
Tak, Bibi Dumon. Mikis & the Donkey. Hopman, Philip, illus. (p. 1141)
Tak, Bibi Dumon & Dumon Tak, Bibi. Soldier Bear. Hopman, Philip, illus. (p. 1607)
Takabatake, Jun, illus. see Takeshita, Fumiko.
Takabayashi, Mari. I Live in Brooklyn. (p. 841)
—I Live in Tokyo. (p. 841)
Takac, Esther. Genesis-the Book with Seventy Faces: A Guide for the Family. Pignataro, Anna, illus. (p. 660)
Takach, Jessica. Wheaton College Massachusetts College Prowler off the Record. (p. 1900)
Takacs, Sarolta A., ed. see Cline, Eric H.
Takacs, Stefanie. Iroquois. (p. 888)
—Seminole. (p. 1550)
Takacs-Moore, Mary, jt. auth. see Reilly, Kathleen M.
Takada, Eriko, illus. see Naasel, Kenrya R. & Rankin, Kenrya.
Takada, Rie. Gaba Kawa Takada, Rie, illus. (p. 652)
—Happy Hustle High Takada, Rie, illus. (p. 746)
Takagi, Satoshi. Origami for Playtime (p. 1304)
Takagi, Shigeyoshi. Flower in a Storm. Takagi, Shigeyoshi, illus. (p. 607)
Takahashi, Genichiro. Sayonara, Gangsters. Emmerich, Michael, tr. from JPN. (p. 1519)
Takahashi, Hideko. Hello, New Baby. (p. 764)
Takahashi, Hideko, illus. see Balsley, Tilda.
Takahashi, Kazuki. Duelist. Wall, Frances, ed. (p. 489)
—Millenium Puzzle. Sengupta, Anita, tr. (p. 1143)
—Millennium World. Takahashi, Kazuki, illus. (p. 1143)
—Movie Ani-Manga. Takahashi, Kazuki, illus. (p. 1183)
—Yu-Gi-Oh! Takahashi, Kazuki, illus. (p. 1983)
—Yu-Gi-Oh! Sengupta, Anita, tr. from JPN. (p. 1983)
—Yu-Gi-Oh! Duelist. Takahashi, Kazuki, illus. (p. 1983)
—Yu-Gi-Oh!: Duelist. Vol. 2 Takahashi, Kazuki, illus. (p. 1983)
—Yu-Gi-Oh!: Duelist. Vol. 4 Takahashi, Kazuki, illus. (p. 1983)
—Yu-Gi-Oh!: Duelist. Vol. 6 Takahashi, Kazuki, illus. (p. 1983)
—Yu-Gi-Oh!: Capsule Monster Chess. Vol. 3 Sengupta, Anita, tr. (p. 1983)
—Yu-Gi-Oh! - Duelist. (p. 1983)
—Yu-Gi-Oh! - Duelist! Takahashi, Kazuki, illus. (p. 1983)
—Yu-Gi-Oh! - Duelist. Takahashi, Kazuki, illus. (p. 1983)
—Yu-Gi-Oh! Duelist 3. Takahashi, Kazuki, illus. (p. 1983)
—Yu-Gi-Oh! - Millennium World. Wall, Frances, ed. (p. 1983)
—Yu-Gi-Oh! the Duelist. Takahashi, Kazuki, illus. (p. 1983)
Takahashi, Kazuki, jt. auth. see Ito, Akira.
Takahashi, Kazuki, jt. auth. see Kageyama, Naoyuki.
Takahashi, Kazuki & Ito, Akira. Yu-Gi-Oh! R. Ito, Akira, illus. (p. 1983)
Takahashi, Kazuki & Kageyama, Naoyuki. Yu-Gi-Oh! GX Kageyama, Naoyuki, illus. (p. 1983)
Takahashi, Peter X. Jimi's Book of Japanese: A Motivating Method to Learn Japanese (Kanji) Moto, Mikki, ed. (p. 918)
—Jimi's Book of Japanese: A Motivating Method to Learn Japanese (Katakana) Moto, Mikki, ed. (p. 918)
—Jimi's Book of Japanese: A Motivating Method to Learn Japanese (Hiragana) Toka, Yumie, illus. (p. 918)
—Jimi's Book of Japanese: A Motivating Method to Learn Japanese (Extra Spicy Super Crunchy Edition) Toka, Yumie, illus. (p. 918)
—Jimi's Book of Japanese: A Motivating Method to Learn Japanese (Some of My Best Friends Are Monkeys Edition) Moto, Mikki, ed. (p. 918)
—Jimi's Sumo Stack: A Motivating Method to Memorize Japanese. Toka, Yumie, illus. (p. 918)
Takahashi, Rumiko. Intensive Care Takahashi, Rumiko, illus. (p. 879)
—Inu Yasha Ani-Manga Takahashi, Rumiko, illus. (p. 883)
—Inuyasha: Demon Box Set. Vol. 19 (p. 883)
—Inuyasha Takahashi, Rumiko, illus. (p. 883)
—Inuyasha: Ani-Manga. Vol. 7 Takahashi, Rumiko, illus. (p. 883)
—Inuyasha Ani-Manga. (p. 883)
—Inuyasha Ani-Manga. Takahashi, Rumiko, illus. (p. 883)
—Inu-Yasha Ani-Manga: Volume 5. Takahashi, Rumiko, illus. (p. 883)
—Inuyasha the Movie Ani-Manga: Affections Touching Across Time. Takahashi, Rumiko, illus. (p. 883)
—Maison Ikkoku. Takahashi, Rumiko, illus. (p. 1077)
—Mermaid Saga (p. 1128)
—Mermaid Saga Takahashi, Rumiko, illus. (p. 1128)
—Ranma 1/2 (p. 1438)
—Rin-Ne (p. 1473)
—Rin-Ne Takahashi, Rumiko, illus. (p. 1473)
Takahashi, Shin. Saikano: The Last Love Song on This Little Planet. Takahashi, Shin, illus. (p. 1503)
—Saikano. Takahashi, Shin, illus. (p. 1503)
Takaki, Ronald. Different Mirror for Young People: A History of Multicultural America. (p. 438)
Takamado, Hisako de. Luli, el Iceberg. Aska, Warabe, illus. (p. 1064)
Takami, Koushun. Battle Royale Taguchi, Masayuki, illus. (p. 147)
Takamisaki, Ryo. Megaman NT Warrior Takamisaki, Ryo, illus. (p. 1124)
—Megaman Nt Warrior Takamisaki, Ryo, illus. (p. 1124)
—Megaman NT Warrior W/Trading Card (no foil Wrap) Takamisaki, Ryo, illus. (p. 1124)
Takamisaki, Ryo, jt. auth. see Viz Media Staff.
Takamiya, Satoru. Heaven's Will. Takamiya, Satoru, illus. (p. 761)
Takanaga, Hinako. Challengers: Volume 4 (p. 289)
—Challengers: Boys Love. (p. 289)
—Love Round!! (p. 1060)
Takanashi, Mitsuba. Crimson Hero. Takanashi, Mitsuba, illus. (p. 383)
Takano, Tsuneo & Obata, Takeshi. Ral Grad. (p. 1437)
Takara, Kathryn Waddell. Timmy Turtle Teaches. Driver, Audrey, illus. (p. 1755)
Takara, Marcio, illus. see Waid, Mark & Walker, Landry.
Takara, Marcio, illus. see Waid, Mark.
Takara, Marcio, illus. see Walker, Landry.
Takarai, Saori. Manga Moods: 40 Faces + 80 Phrases. (p. 1087)
Takase, Naoko. Helen Keller: From Darkness to Light. (p. 763)
Takashima, Kazusa. Man's Best Friend - Inu Mo Aruke Ba Fall in Love (p. 1088)
—Wild Rock. (p. 1930)
Takaya, Natsuki. Fruits Basket (p. 645)
—Fruits Basket Nibley, Athena, tr. from JPN. (p. 645)
—Fruits Basket Nibley, Alethea & Nibley, Athena, trs. from JPN. (p. 645)
—Fruits Basket. (p. 645)
—Fruits Basket (p. 646)
—Fruits Basket Takaya, Natsuki, illus. (p. 646)
—Fruits Basket, Volume 1. (p. 646)
—Fruits Basket, Volume 3. Aoki, Yuya, illus. (p. 646)
—Official Fruits Basket Journal. (p. 1280)
Takaya, Natsuki, creator. Fruits Basket (p. 645)
Takayama, Sandi. Musubi Baby. Hall, Pat, illus. (p. 1194)
Takei, Hiroyuki. Shaman King Vol. 6. Takei, Hiroyuki, illus. (p. 1559)
—Shaman King. Takei, Hiroyuki, illus. (p. 1559)
—Ultimo. Takei, Hiroyuki, illus. (p. 1810)
Takei, Hiroyuki, et al. Kung-Fu Master. Olsen, Lillian, tr. (p. 968)
—Shaman in Tokyo. Caselman, Lillian, tr. (p. 1559)
—Shaman King. Takei, Hiroyuki, illus. (p. 1559)
Takemiya, Masaki. Imagination of a Go Master: Logic-Shattering Cosmic Style. Bianchi, Leslie, ed. (p. 860)
Takemori, Ginny Tapley, tr. see Nosaka, Akiyuki.
Takemori, Lianne K. Four Dog Blues Band, or How Chester Boy, Dog in the Fog, & Diva Took the Big City by Storm. Dietrick, Robin C. & Klein, Bradley S., eds. (p. 624)
Takemoto, Novala. Kamikaze Girls Wegmuller, Akemi, tr. from JPN. (p. 942)
—Kamikaze Girls. Kanesata, Yukio, illus. (p. 942)
Takenaga, Francis. Wicked (p. 1927)
Takenashi, Eri. Kannagi Volume 2. (p. 942)
Takes, Deb, jt. auth. see Bush, Suzanne.
Takeshi, Obata, jt. auth. see Ohba, Tsugumi.
Takeshita, Fumiko. Hello, Hello. Takabatake, Jun, illus. (p. 764)
Takeshita, Gene, illus. see Block, Cheryl.
Takeuchi, Kana. Death Trance (p. 420)
—Death Trance Takeuchi, Kana, illus. (p. 420)
Takeuchi, Naoko. Sailor Moon. (p. 1503)
—Sailor Moon 9. (p. 1503)
Takhar, Jodi. Four Seasons of Fun. Takhar, Jodi & Jones, Paul, illus. (p. 625)
—What Can I Do Today? Takhar, Jodi & Jones, Paul, illus. (p. 1880)
Takhar, Jodi, jt. auth. see Tisdell, Wendy.
Taki, Emiko, photos by see Jamison, Heather & Meckenstock, Shay.
Takidaira, Jiro, jt. auth. see Saito, Ryusuke.
Takita, Yoshihiro. Biographical Comics: Mother Teresa: Modern Saint of the Poor. Abe, Sayori, illus. (p. 188)
Takita, Yoshihiro, jt. auth. see Takita, Yoshihiro.
Takita, Yoshihiro & Takita, Yoshihiro. Biographical Comics: Mother Teresa: Modern Saint of the Poor. Abe, Sayori, illus. (p. 188)
Takitin, Sarah, jt. auth. see Cole, Steve.
Takken, Sylvia. Aquarius: January 21-February 19. (p. 94)
—Aries: March 21-April 20. (p. 98)
—Cancer. (p. 260)
—Capricorn: December 22-January 20. (p. 263)
—Gemini: May 22-June 21. (p. 659)
—Leo: July 23-August 23. (p. 991)
—Libra: September 24-October 23. (p. 1005)
—Pisces: February 20-March 20. (p. 1364)
—Sagittarius: November 23-December 21. (p. 1503)
—Scorpio: October 24-November 22. (p. 1530)
—Taurus: April 21-May 21. (p. 1707)
—Virgo: August 24-September 23. (p. 1844)
Taks, Melvin. Daisy Duck Teaches School. (p. 400)
—Do You Know Us? Guess Who Rhymes about North American Animals. (p. 458)
Takvorian, Nadine. Jason & the Argonauts (p. 910)
—Odysseus & the Cyclops (p. 1278)
Takvorian, Nadine, illus. see Bullard, Lisa.
Takvorian, Nadine, illus. see Koontz, Robin Michal.
Takvorian, Nadine, illus. see Koontz, Robin.
Takvorian, Nadine, illus. see Muehlenhardt, Amy Bailey.
Tal, Eve. Cursing Columbus. (p. 395)
—Double Crossing: A Jewish Immigration Story. (p. 472)
—Double Crossing. (p. 472)
Talarico Briffitt, Lauren. Teatime with Tigers: A Book of Children's Poetry. (p. 1711)
Talarico Msn, Karen M. My Hands. (p. 1210)
—My New Brother: A Counting Book. (p. 1216)
Talaris Institute. Baby Feelings. (p. 126)
Talaris Research Institute Staff, ed. see Gottman, John.
Talaro, Theresa. Mommy Teach Us to Pray. (p. 1162)
—Mother's Prayer: A Life Changing Prayer for Children. Castulo Aten, Vicky Talaro & Ikaia Aten, Dayle Marc, illus. (p. 1179)
Talbert, Barbara. Where Can We Live? (p. 1906)
Talbert, Marc. Ahold of the Reins. (p. 30)
—Doble o Nada. (p. 459)
—Holding the Reins: A Ride Through Cowgirl Life. Van Cleve, Barbara, photos by. (p. 788)
Talbot, Amy. Deer & His Dear Friends: A Tale from India. (p. 423)
Talbot, Ethel. Natural History Story Book. Noble, Edwin & Grieve, Walter G., illus. (p. 1235)
Talbot Healy, John Adrian. Flea & the Cauliflower. (p. 603)
Talbot, Ian & Tatla, Darshan Singh, eds. Amritsar: Voices from Between India & Pakistan. (p. 66)
Talbot, Jeffrey, jt. auth. see Miller, Dean.
Talbot, Jim, illus. see Lerangis, Peter.
Talbot, Kathy. Camille's Rainy Day Adventure. (p. 256)
—My Magic Swing. (p. 1213)
Talbot, Laura, illus. see Talbot, Sharon.
Talbot, Marilyn. Roland, el Vergonzoso. (p. 1485)
Talbot, Ret, jt. auth. see Martin, Mark W.
Talbot, Rose. Adventures of Peanut, the Sugar Glider: Holiday Celebrations & Outings. (p. 21)
—Adventures of Peanut, the Sugar Glider. (p. 21)
Talbot, Sharon. If I Were a French Quarter Rat. Talbot, Laura, illus. (p. 853)
Talbot, Sophie. Chloe. (p. 308)
—Fabulous Terrible: The Adventures of You. (p. 560)
Talbott, Hudson. It's All about Me-Ow. Talbott, Hudson, illus. (p. 896)
—River of Dreams: The Story of the Hudson River. Talbott, Hudson, illus. (p. 1476)
—Safari Journal. (p. 1502)
—United Tweets of America: 50 State Birds Their Stories, Their Glories. Talbott, Hudson, illus. (p. 1820)
Talbott, Hudson, illus. see Fritz, Jean.
Talbott, Hudson, illus. see Woodson, Jacqueline.
Talbott, Hudson & Lapine, James. Into the Woods. Talbott, Hudson, ed. (p. 881)
Talbott, Kerry, illus. see Gutman, Dan.
Talbott, Kerry, illus. see Trounstine, Connie / Remlinger.
Talbott, Shawn M. Springtime Robins. (p. 1635)
Talbott, Sherri, illus. see Rose, Sandra.
Talburt, Tony. History on the Page: Adventures in Black British History. (p. 785)
Tale, . Palace of Poems: Blue Princess. (p. 1319)
Talen, Hunter. Xander Nash Kleid, Neil, illus. (p. 1967)
Talhah, Abu & Books, Greenbird. My Sister Saarah. Fowler, Claire, illus. (p. 1218)
Talhamy, Sarah. Children's Workbook. (p. 304)
Taliadoros, Jenny, ed. see Byj, Charlot.
Taliadoros, Jenny, ed. see Mingo, Norman.
Taliadoros, Jenny, ed. Doris Day Paper Dolls. (p. 471)
—Lollypop Crowd Stand-up Paper Dolls. (p. 1046)
Taliaferro, Margaret. Real Reason for Christmas: Letters to Children for the Twelve Nights of Christmas. (p. 1448)
Talib, Binny, illus. see Chandab, Taghred.
Talic, Serkan, photos by see Sullivan, Marija.
Talkington, Amy. Liv, Forever. (p. 1039)
Talkowski, Steve, illus. see Tillworth, Mary & Random House Children's Books Staff.
Tallardy, Laura, illus. see Bergen, Lara.
Tallardy, Laura, illus. see Dunham, Kelli.
Tallardy, Laura, illus. see Speregen, Devra Newberger.
Tallarico, Tony. Find & Color Activity Book. (p. 587)
—How Fire Came to the Indians. (p. 809)
—Hunt for Hector. (p. 828)
—Nature Trivia Mazes. (p. 1236)
—Sports Spot-the-Differences. (p. 1633)
—Things That Go. (p. 1733)
—Ultimate Hidden Pictures Across America. (p. 1809)
—Under the Sea. (p. 1814)
Tallarico, Tony & Drawing Staff. Quick Draw Animals. (p. 1427)
Tallarico, Tony & Tallarigo, Tony. License Plates Across the States: Travel Puzzles & Games. Tallarico, Tony & Eagle, Cameron, illus. (p. 1007)
Tallarico, Tony J., Jr. Baseball Activity Book. (p. 141)
—Bugs! Bugs! Bugs! (p. 237)
—Eco-Logical Brain Games. (p. 502)
—English - Spanish Word Search: Sopa de Letras (p. 529)
—English-Spanish Word Search. (p. 530)
—Famous Firsts Activity Book. (p. 569)
—Frightfully Fun Halloween Activity Book. (p. 639)
—Presidents Activity Book. (p. 1397)
—Spot-the-Differences Across the USA. (p. 1633)
—Spot-the-Differences Around the World. (p. 1633)
—U. S. A. Secret Code Puzzles for Kids. (p. 1806)
Tallarico, Tony J., Jr., jt. auth. see Tallarico, Tony, Sr.
Tallarico, Tony, Sr. Little Hidden Pictures. (p. 1029)
Tallarico, Tony, Sr. & Activity Books Staff. More Little Hidden Pictures. (p. 1174)
Tallarico, Tony, Sr. & Drawing Staff. Drawing & Cartooning Monsters: A Step-by-Step Guide for the Aspiring Monster-Maker. (p. 481)
Tallarico, Tony, Sr. & Tallarico, Tony J., Jr. Cars & Trucks Mazes. (p. 272)
Tallarigo, Tony, jt. auth. see Tallarico, Tony.
Tallec, Olivier, illus. see Babin, Claire.
Tallec, Olivier, illus. see Brun-Cosme, Nadine.
Tallec, Olivier, illus. see Moundlic, Charlotte.
Tallec, Olivier, illus. see Picouly, Daniel.
Tallec, Olivier, creator. Waterloo & Trafalgar. (p. 1863)
Tallent, Alyssa, illus. see Bolger, Z. C.
Talley, Gigi T. Fairest Florabell. (p. 562)
Talley, Leslie. Thought Is Just a Thought: A Story of Living with OCD. (p. 1740)
Talley, Linda. Aloha Potter! - hardcover Book. Chase, Andra, illus. (p. 48)
—Ludmila's Way. Chase, Andra, illus. (p. 1064)
Talley, Pam, illus. see Bevis, Brittany.
Talley, Rebecca Cornish. Heaven Scent. (p. 761)
Talley, Robin. Lies We Tell Ourselves. (p. 1007)
Tallinda, Theodore. Math at Henry Ford's Factory: Identify & Explain Patterns in Arithmetic (p. 1105)
Tallman, Cheryl, jt. auth. see Ahlers, Joan.
Tallman, Dylan. Blessing in Disguise. (p. 199)
Talmadge, Joyce. Alpacas All the Way (A Slightly True Story) Mostow, Sarah, illus. (p. 48)
Talmadge Salle, Katherine. Daily Life Around the World: Set Of 6. (p. 399)
Talmage, Frank, jt. ed. see Dan, Joseph.
Talmi, Mary, ed. see Uralskaia, Valeria, et al.
Talty, Caryn. Cilie Yack Is under Attack: This Is the story of how one boy turned his problems into a Triumph (p. 319)
Talvacchia, Bette & Raphael. Raphael. (p. 1439)
Talwar, Abhinav, jt. auth. see Talwar, Ankoor.
Talwar, Ankoor & Talwar, Abhinav. Children's Garden. Chatterjee, Susnata, illus. (p. 303)
Talwar, Robert B., jt. auth. see Peto, Judith E.
Tama. Black Cow. (p. 195)
Tamaja Press & Tillman, Gloria J. Teeth for Thanksgiving. (p. 1715)
Tamaki, Chihiro. Walkin' Butterfly (p. 1854)
Tamaki, Chihiro, Jr. Walkin' Butterfly (p. 1854)
Tamaki, Jillian, illus. see Tamaki, Mariko.
Tamaki, Mariko. Emiko Superstar. (p. 518)
—This One Summer. Tamaki, Jillian, illus. (p. 1737)
Tamaki, Nozomu. Dance in the Vampire Bund. Tamaki, Nozomu, illus. (p. 402)
Tamambang, Andrew Tangang, et al. Mastering Mathematics Form 3 Student's Book: Volume 0, Part 0. (p. 1103)
Tamang, Mayan. Captain Remarkable; Girls can be Superheroes Too! (p. 264)
Tamang, Mayan, illus. see O'Neal-Thorpe, Rochelle.
Tamanini, Kara T. I Promised Not to Tell. (p. 844)
Tamar, Erika, jt. auth. see Kinkade, Thomas.
Tamar, Hela. Wrong Fairy Tale. (p. 1965)
Tamara, Chamberlain. If I Could Dance Around the World. (p. 852)
Tamara, Popa. Boy & His Pets. (p. 217)
Tamara, Visco, illus. see Colon De Mejias, Leticia.
Tamarin, Nicole, illus. see Yumel, Demain.
Tamaro, Susanna. Anima Mundi. Blum, Cinzia Sartini & Valentino, Russell Scott, trs. from ITA. (p. 76)
—Castello Dei Sogni Storie Che. (p. 276)
—Gran Arbol. (p. 706)
Tamayo, Alex. Horizons Set 1 Shea, Steve, ed. (p. 798)
Tamayo, José Luis & Martín, Inés, trs. Hombre y Sus Descubrimientos. (p. 791)
—Naturaleza y el Universo. (p. 1236)
Tamayo, Natalia, illus. see Vasco, Irene.
Tambellini, Stefano, illus. see Kimmelman, Leslie.
Tamblyn, Amber. Free Stallion: Poems. (p. 634)
Tamblyn, Catherine. 40 Fabulous Social Studies Activities: Easy Projects That Work with the Topics You Teach & Help Build Reading, Writing, & Research Skills. (p. 1997)
—Neighborhoods & Communities: 10 Color Transparencies, Mini-Lessons, & Activities That Teach Essential Map Skills. (p. 1240)
Tamburri, Pasqualino. Alex & the Trampoline. (p. 35)
Tameka Trask. Thank You Jesus: A Child's Everyday Book of Praise, & Song!!! (p. 1725)
Tames, Richard. 1920s. (p. 2002)
—Ancient Greece. (p. 69)
—Engineers. (p. 529)
—Hands-On History! Ancient Greece: Step into the World of the Classical Greeks, with 15 Step-by-Step Projects & 350 Exciting Pictures. (p. 741)
—Step Into: Ancient Greece. (p. 1648)
—Tell Me Why Didn't Mummies Have Brains? And More about History. (p. 1717)
Tames, Richard, jt. auth. see Kelly, Nigel.
Tames, Richard, et al. Ancient World, the Illus Children. (p. 71)
Tamez, Juliza. Trixie & Dixie: The Mystery of the Missing Cape. Almanza, Roberto, illus. (p. 1788)
Tamiel. I'm Special. (p. 860)
—Two Lives. (p. 1804)
Tamkin, Cynthia. Beulah's Rainbow. (p. 173)
Tamla, Berthe Kamga, ed. see Nama, Michael D., et al.
Tam-McMillan, Gianni. Your Journey Through the Airport. (p. 1981)
Tammen, Christina. C h u m P. (p. 249)
—Chump Ii Every Team Has an Undiscovered Secret Weapon! (p. 318)
Tammi Reichel, tr. see Schrocke, Kathrin.
Tamura, Mitsuhisa. Bakegyamon. Tamura, Mitsuhisa, illus. (p. 133)
—BakéGyamon. Tamura, Mitsuhisa, illus. (p. 133)
Tamura, Mitsuhisa & Fujita, Kazuhiro. Bakégyamon. (p. 133)
Tamura, Yumi. Basara (p. 140)
—Basara Tamura, Yumi, illus. (p. 140)
—Basara Olsen, Lillian, tr. from JPN. (p. 140)
—Basara. Olsen, Lillian, tr. (p. 140)
—Basara. Tamura, Yumi, illus. (p. 140)
—Book of Justice. Tamura, Yumi, illus. (p. 211)
—Wild Com. Tamura, Yumi, illus. (p. 1929)
Tamura, Yumi, illus. see Yuki, Kaori, et al.
Tan, Anthony, illus. see Christine, Peymani.
Tan, Billy, et al. Thor by Kieron Gillen Ultimate Collection. (p. 1739)
Tan, Chung Lee. Finland. (p. 589)
Tan, Huay Peng. Fun with Chinese Characters 1: The Straits Times Collection (p. 648)
—Fun with Chinese Characters 2: The Straits Times Collection Vol. 2 (p. 648)
—Fun with Chinese Characters 3: The Straits Times Collection Vol. 3 (p. 648)
Tan, Joyce. Finding the Lord's ELect: How Missionaries can Tract Fruitfully. (p. 588)
Tan, Li. Paradox of Catching Up: Rethinking of State-Led Economic Development. (p. 1323)
Tan, Ming, et al. Getting Ready. (p. 669)
Tan, Richard. Bridges & Tunnels of New York City. (p. 227)
—Dutch New Amsterdam & English New York. (p. 490)

T

For book reviews, descriptive annotations, tables of contents, cover images, author biographies & additional information, updated daily, subscribe to **www.booksinprint2.com**

—Famous Explorers of New York City. (p. 569)
—Native American Peoples of New York City. (p. 1234)
—New York City's Neighborhoods. (p. 1248)
Tan, Ruth. Darling, Honey Is Good for You! A Little Honey Book for Your Little One. (p. 409)
Tan, Shaun. Arbol Rojo. (p. 94)
—Arrival. (p. 101)
—Arrival. Tan, Shaun, illus. (p. 101)
—Bird King: An Artist's Notebook. (p. 190)
—Lost & Found. Tan, Shaun, illus. (p. 1054)
—Lost Thing. (p. 1056)
—Rules of Summer. (p. 1495)
—Tales from Outer Suburbia. (p. 1701)
—Tales from Outer Suburbia. Tan, Shaun, illus. (p. 1701)
Tan, Shaun, illus. see Crew, Gary.
Tan, Shaun, illus. see Marsden, John.
Tan, Sheri. Handshake in Space: The Apollo-Soyuz Test Project. Bond, Higgins, illus. (p. 741)
Tan, Valerie Genevivie. Hello! I'm Sha Sha: Join Sha Sha in Her New School. (p. 764)
Tana, Hoban. I Read Signs. (p. 844)
Tanabe, Yellow. Kekkaishi. (p. 948)
—Kekkaishi. Tanabe, Yellow, illus. (p. 948)
—Kekkaishi 24. Tanabe, Yellow, illus. (p. 948)
Tanaka, Kazumi. Kazumi Tanaka: Words & Works. (p. 946)
Tanaka, Masashi. Gon 1. (p. 697)
—Gon 2. (p. 697)
—Gon 3. (p. 697)
Tanaka, Rin. Motorcycle Jackets: Ultimate Biker's Fashions (p. 1179)
—Sounds of Love. (p. 1615)
Tanaka, Shelley. Alamo: Surrounded & Outnumbered, They Chose to Make a Defiant Last Stand. Craig, David, illus. (p. 33)
—Amelia Earhart: The Legend of the Lost Aviator. Craig, David, illus. (p. 58)
—Buried City of Pompeii: What It Was Like When Vesuvius Exploded. Ruhl, Greg, illus. (p. 243)
—Day That Changed America - The Alamo: Surrounded & Outnumbered,They Chose to Make a Defiant Last Stand. Craig, David, illus. (p. 414)
—D-Day: They Fought to Free Europe from Hitler's Tyranny. Craig, David, illus. (p. 397)
—Earthquake! A Day That Changed America. Craig, David, illus. (p. 497)
—Earthquake! On a Peaceful Spring Morning, Disaster Strikes San Francisco. Craig, David, illus. (p. 497)
—Gettysburg: The Legendary Battle & the Address That Inspired a Nation. Craig, David, illus. (p. 670)
—Graveyards of the Dinosaurs: What It's Like to Discover Prehistoric Creatures. Barnard, Alan, illus. (p. 712)
—Lost Temple of the Aztecs: What It Was Like When the Spaniards Invaded Mexico. Ruhl, Greg, illus. (p. 1056)
—New Dinos: The Latest Finds! the Coolest Dinosaur Discoveries! Barnard, Alan, illus. (p. 1244)
—Nobody Knows (p. 1262)
—On Board the Titanic: What It Was Like When the Great Liner Sank. Marschall, Ken, illus. (p. 1288)
Tanaka, Shelley, jt. auth. see Combres, Élisabeth.
Tanaka, Shelley, tr. see Bach, Tamara.
Tanaka, Shelley, tr. see Berner, Rotraut Susanne.
Tanaka, Shelley, tr. see de Moüy, Iris.
Tanaka, Shelley, tr. see Noel, Michel.
Tanaka, Shinsuke. Wings. (p. 1936)
Tanaka, Suzuki. Menkui! Tanaka, Suzuki, illus. (p. 1126)
Tanaka, Usa. Give Me That! Tanaka, Usa, illus. (p. 681)
Tanaka, Yoko, illus. see DiCamillo, Kate.
Tanaka, Yoko, illus. see Godwin, Laura.
Tanaka, Yoko, illus. see Kelly, L. J. R.
Tanaka, Yoko, illus. see LaFevers, R. L.
Tanaka, Yoko, illus. see McGowan, Keith.
Tanaka, Yoko, illus. see Pennypacker, Sara.
Tanakura, Jessi. Down in the 5th Grade Hallway. (p. 474)
Tanami, Roy. Angling the World: Ten Spectacular Adventures in Fly Fishing. (p. 75)
Tanchak, Diane, illus. see Beckenstein, Cara.
Tanchez, Plinio, illus. see Garcia, Elizabeth.
Tanco, Miguel, illus. see Kim, YeShil.
Tancre, Bonnie. BOUGH That Will Not Break: An Allegorical Novel in Three Parts. (p. 216)
Tancredi, Sharon, illus. see Nagaraja, Dharmachari.
Tandoc, Melissa, illus. see Durham, Roy.
Tandy, Clive. Quarry Grove. (p. 1422)
Tandy, Russell H., illus. see Keene, Carolyn.
Taneda, Naoyuki & Taneda, Ruth. Education for Absolute Pitch: A New Way to Learn Piano. Aruffo, Christopher, tr. (p. 505)
Taneda, Ruth, jt. auth. see Taneda, Naoyuki.
Taneja, Sweta. Krishna - Defender of Dharma. Nagulakonda, Rajesh, illus. (p. 967)
Tanem, Bob & Williamson, Don. Gardening Month by Month in Northern California (p. 656)
—Tree & Shrub Gardening for Northern California. (p. 1783)
Tanemura, Arina. Gentlemen's Alliance Tanemura, Arina, illus. (p. 661)
—Gentlemen's Alliance + Tanemura, Arina, illus. (p. 661)
—Gentlemen's Alliance Cross. Tanemura, Arina, illus. (p. 661)
—Mistress Fortune. Tanemura, Arina, illus. (p. 1155)
—O Sagashite Tanemura, Arina, illus. (p. 1274)
—O Sagashite Vol. 6 Tanemura, Arina, illus. (p. 1274)
—Sagashite Tanemura, Arina, illus. (p. 1502)
Tanemura, Arina & Kimura, Tomo. Sagashite Tanemura, Arina, illus. (p. 1502)
Tanen, Sloane. Appetite for Detention. Hagen, Stefan, illus. (p. 92)
—Are You Going to Kiss Me Now? (p. 97)
—Coco All Year Round. Hagen, Stefan, illus. (p. 337)
Tanenbaum, Teri, jt. auth. see Schwartz, Julie.
Tang, Charles. Mystery in New York. (p. 1224)
Tang, Eric M., jt. auth. see Ifkovic, Ed.
Tang, Greg. Grapes of Math: Mind-Stretching Math Riddles. Briggs, Harry, illus. (p. 710)
—Grapes of Math. Briggs, Harry, illus. (p. 710)
—Math Appeal. Briggs, Harry, illus. (p. 1105)
—Math Fables. Cahoon, Heather, illus. (p. 1106)
—Math for All Seasons. Briggs, Harry, illus. (p. 1106)
—Math Potatoes: Mind-Stretching Brain Food. Briggs, Harry, illus. (p. 1107)
—Math-Terpieces: The Art of Problem-Solving. Paprocki, Greg, illus. (p. 1107)
Tang, Greg & Greg, Tang. Come una y Cuenta Veinte. Briggs, Harry, illus. (p. 347)
—Un, Dos, Tres, el Ano Se Fue. Briggs, Harry, illus. (p. 1811)
Tang, Li Chu, illus. see Pitman, Norman Hinsdale.
Tang, Sandara, illus. see Duey, Kathleen.
Tang, Sanmu. Celebrating Chinese Festivals: A Collection of Holiday Tales, Poems & Activities. (p. 284)
—Celebrating the Chinese New Year. Ying, Wu, tr. from CHI. (p. 285)
—Celebrating the Dragon Boat Festival. Tenison, Mina, tr. from CHI. (p. 285)
—Celebrating the Mid-Autumn Festival. Tenison, Mina, tr. from CHI. (p. 285)
—Chinese Zodiac Animals. Jingwen, Zhu, tr. (p. 308)
Tang, Sanmu, jt. auth. see Shanghai Animation Studio Staff.
Tang, Youshan. Magical Monkey King: Mischief in Heaven. (p. 1075)
Tang, Youshan, illus. see de la Paz, Myrna J.
Tang, Youshan, illus. see De La Paz, Myrna J.
Tang, Youshan, illus. see Mehta, Lila.
Tang, You-shan, illus. see Yamada, Debbie Leung.
Tangang Tamambang, Andrew, et al. Mastering Mathematics Form 1 Student's Book. (p. 1103)
Tangen, Nick, illus. see Trombello, William.
Tangerine Designs Ltd. Bobby Bunny. (p. 206)
—Casey Chick. (p. 275)
—Cuddle up Teddy: A Soft & Snuggly Pillow Book. (p. 389)
—Katie Kitten. (p. 945)
—Lucy Lamb. (p. 1063)
—Sleep Tight Bunny: A Soft & Snuggly Pillow Book. (p. 1588)
—Who Am I? Moo, I Am a Cow! Peep Through the Eyes. Who Are You Today? (p. 1914)
—Who Am I? Roar, I Am a Tiger! Peep Through the Eyes. Who Are You Today? (p. 1914)
Tangerine Press Staff & Scholastic, Inc. Staff, contrib. by. Kid Biz. (p. 951)
Tangerine Press Staff, contrib. by. LOL! Laugh Out Loud Joke Book! (p. 1045)
Tangerine, Tracey. Buddy Zooka: In the French Quarter & Beyond. (p. 235)
Tango Books. Book of Greek Gods Pop-Up Board Games. Maddison, Kevin, illus. (p. 211)
—Mini Trucks: Crane: A Lift-the-Flap & Stand Up. Burton, Terry, illus. (p. 1146)
—Tractor: A Lift-the-Flap & Stand-Up. Burton, Terry, illus, (p. 1775)
Tango Books Staff. Armour. Moulder, Bob, illus. (p. 100)
—Book of Dragon Myths. Wade, Gini, illus. (p. 211)
—Car. Abbott, Simon, illus. (p. 265)
—Count! Baruzzi, Agnese, illus. (p. 369)
—Digger: A Lift-the-Flap & Stand Up. Burton, Terry, illus. (p. 438)
—Fire Engine. Burton, Terry, illus. (p. 590)
—Life in a Castle. Hutchinson, Tim, illus. (p. 1010)
—Meow! Abbott, Simon, illus. (p. 1127)
—Noisy Pops - Fire Engine. Abbott, Simon, illus. (p. 1263)
—Subtraction. Abbott, Simon, illus. (p. 1671)
Tango Books Staff, jt. auth. see Beeson, Samantha.
Tango Books Staff, jt. auth. see Cheshire, Gerard.
Tango Books Staff, jt. auth. see Fields, Sadie.
Tango-Hampton, Doreen. I Like Gum. Pfleegor, Gina, illus. (p. 841)
Tango-Schurmann, Ann, illus. see Mariotti, Celine Rose.
Tanguay, Dave. Come Together! Vaughns, Byron, illus. (p. 347)
—Deception Reception! Vaughns, Byron, illus. (p. 421)
—Fire Fire Everywhere! Vaughns, Byron, illus. (p. 590)
—Legacy of Mr. Banjo! Vaughns, Byron, illus. (p. 987)
—To Be King! DeStefano, Stephen, illus. (p. 1758)
Tanguay, Dave, jt. auth. see Branch, Ken.
Tanguay, David D., illus. see Wrecks, Billy.
Tanguy, Elara, illus. see Brunelle, Lynn.
Tangvald, Christine, jt. auth. see Cook, David C. Publishing Staff.
Tangvald, Christine Harder. Best Thing about Christmas. Nobens, C. A., illus. (p. 171)
—Playtime Devotions: Sharing Bible Moments with Your Baby or Toddler. Schmitz, Tamara, illus. (p. 1373)
Tani, Branca. New York in The 1700s. (p. 1248)
—New York in The 1800s. (p. 1248)
—New York in The 1900s. (p. 1248)
—Sam the Cat. (p. 1507)
Tani, Mizue, jt. auth. see Ayuko.
Tani, Mizue & Ayuko. Earl & the Fairy. (p. 492)
Tani, Toshihiko, illus. see Yamanushi, Toshiko.
Tanigawa, Nagaru. Boredom of Haruhi Suzumiya. (p. 214)
—Disappearance of Haruhi Suzumiya. (p. 446)
—Dissociation of Haruhi Suzumiya. (p. 453)
—Indignation of Haruhi Suzumiya. (p. 872)
—Intrigues of Haruhi Suzumiya. (p. 882)
—Melancholy of Haruhi Suzumiya. Pai, Chris, tr. from JPN. (p. 1125)
—Melancholy of Suzumiya Haruhi-Chan (p. 1125)
—Rampage of Haruhi Suzumiya. (p. 1438)
—Sigh of Haruhi Suzumiya (p. 1573)
—Sigh of Haruhi Suzumiya. (p. 1573)
—Surprise of Haruhi Suzumiya. (p. 1686)
—Wavering of Haruhi Suzumiya. (p. 1864)
Taniguchi, Jiro, jt. auth. see Furuyama, Kan.
Taniguchi, Tomoko. Aquarium Taniguchi, Tomoko, illus. (p. 94)
—Call Me Princess. Taniguchi, Tomoko, illus. (p. 254)
—Just a Girl Pannone, Frank, ed. (p. 937)
—Just a Girl 2 Pannone, Frank, ed. (p. 937)
—Let's Stay Together Forever. Pannone, Frank, ed. (p. 1000)
—Miss Me? Pannone, Frank, ed. (p. 1151)
—Popcorn Romance. Taniguchi, Tomoko, illus. (p. 1384)
—Princess Prince. Taniguchi, Tomoko, illus. (p. 1405)
Tanious, Karen Wagdy Aldy. My Life, My Favorites, My Dreams. (p. 1212)
Tanis, Joel, illus. see Zondervan Publishing Staff.
Tanis, Joel E., illus. see Klein, Pamela.
Tank, Daniel, illus. see Brand, Ruth R.
Tank, Daniel, illus. see Brand, Ruth Redding.
Tank, Daniel, illus. see Brand, Ruth.
Tank, Daniel, jt. illus. see Pennington, Jack.
Tank, Daniel, jt. illus. see Vitale, Raoul.
Tank, Daniel, jt. illus. see White, John, Jr.
Tankard, Jeremy. Boo Hoo Bird. Tankard, Jeremy, illus. (p. 209)
—Grumpy Bird. Tankard, Jeremy, illus. (p. 727)
—Me Hungry! Tankard, Jeremy, illus. (p. 1116)
Tankard, Jeremy, illus. see LaRochelle, David.
Tankard, Jeremy, illus. see Peters, Diane.
Tankard, Jeremy, illus. see Reynolds, Aaron.
Tankard, Jeremy, illus. see Vail, Rachel.
Tanksley, Ann, illus. see Hurston, Zora Neale & Thomas, Joyce Carol.
Tanksley, Ann, illus. see Hurston, Zora Neale.
Tanksley, David. Michael Waylon & His Dinosaur Crew. (p. 1135)
Tannehill, Mary Jo, illus. see Kauble, Christa.
Tannenbaum, Alison, jt. auth. see Imholtz, August.
Tannenbaum, Judith, ed. see Bush, Valerie Chow, et al.
Tannenbaum, Rose, illus. see Sireau, Christine.
Tanner, Dave. Collectible Soda Cans 2005 Zip Codes: Comprehensive soda can identification & price guide for cans with zip Codes 1964-1980 (p. 339)
Tanner, Dawn Leasman. Kitty Named Indra/Una Gata Llamada Indra. Leasman, Nancy Packard, illus. (p. 963)
Tanner, Dean, photos by see Burton, Martin Nelson.
Tanner, Earnest D., Jr. Creation the Sixth Day. (p. 379)
Tanner, Henry Samuel. Pre-historic Man; The First Settlers on the Western Continent Oriental Free Masons. (p. 1394)
Tanner, Jennifer. Robin Hood. (p. 1480)
Tanner, Jennifer, illus. see Stone Arch Books Staff.
Tanner, Jerome E. Myeloma. (p. 1222)
Tanner, Lian. City of Lies. (p. 324)
—Icebreaker. (p. 851)
—Museum of Thieves. (p. 1193)
—Path of Beasts. (p. 1328)
Tanner, Martha. And God Said. (p. 71)
Tanner, Matthew J. Winds of Aragon. (p. 1936)
Tanner, Mike. Resurrection Blues. (p. 1464)
Tanner, Miriam. Rose after Midnight. (p. 1489)
Tanner, S. Clouds: Learning the CL Sound. (p. 335)
—Wild Wolf: Learning the W Sound. (p. 1930)
Tanner, Sally Thompson. God Shoes. (p. 690)
Tanner, Stephanie, illus. see Brown, Gary.
Tanner, Suzan. Most Unusual Adventures of Black Shadow Smokey & the Blue Streak. (p. 1177)
Tanner, Suzy-Jane. Nursery Rhymes. (p. 1273)
Tanner Voyles, illus. see Jean Emily Myers, Emily Myers & Jean Emily Myers.
Tanner-Moore, Margie. What Noah Knows. (p. 1892)
Tanos, Elaine. Anadarko & Pugwash: The Delbert Adventures. (p. 66)
Tans, Adrian, illus. see Bannatyne, Lesley Pratt.
Tans, Adrian, illus. see Gribnau, Joe.
Tans, Adrian, illus. see Knowlton, Laurie.
Tans, Adrian, illus. see Peck, Jan.
Tans, Adrian, illus. see Pilegard, Virginia.
Tanselle, Eve, illus. see Ruurs, Margriet.
Tansil-Mitchell, Angela. Kimmie C Sunshine: When Mommy & Daddy Loses Their Jobs. (p. 957)
Tansley, Eric, illus. see Patchett, Mary Elwyn.
Tansman, Alexandre. Alexandre Tansman: Je Joue Pour Papa: Douze Morceaux Tres Faciles et en Grosses Notes. (p. 37)
Tanton, James Stuart. Encyclopedia of Mathematics. (p. 525)
Tanwar, Rajesh. Goldilocks & the Three Bears. (p. 696)
Tao, Ming, tr. see Bobrick, Julie, ed.
Tao, Ted. Monkey King & the Book of Death. (p. 1165)
Tao, Teri. Bird that Played Old. (p. 190)
—Butterfly Lovers. (p. 248)
—Carpet that Disappeared. (p. 271)
—Cowherd Boy & Weaver Girl. (p. 374)
—Dragon Pearl. (p. 477)
—Gold Scissors. (p. 694)
—Legend of the White Snake. (p. 989)
—Lotus Lantern. (p. 1057)
—Mouse Wedding (I) Finding a Groom. (p. 1182)
—Mouse Wedding (II) Groom Found! (p. 1182)
—Princess Pearl: The Dragon Arch. Bk. 1 Teague, Yanhua & Teague, Lauren, trs. (p. 1405)
Taor, Adam. There's a Worm on My Eyeball: The Alien Zoo of Germs, Worms & Lurgies That Could Be Living Inside You. Holgate, Douglas, illus. (p. 1731)
Tapeworm Staff. 1337 H4x0r H4ndb00k. (p. 2002)
Tapia, Alfredo, illus. see Wynne-Jones, Tim.
Tapia, Alfredo, jt. auth. see Wynne-Jones, Tim.
Tapia, Jeff. Hippomobile! (p. 781)
Tapia, Rayner. Adventures of Tom Mcguire: Morkann's Revenge. (p. 24)
—Adventures of Tom Mcguire: The Bard of Typheousina. (p. 24)
Tapia, Sonia, tr. see Bach, Richard & Gardner, Sally.
Tapia, Sonia, tr. see Cabot, Meg.
Tapia, Sonia, tr. see Gardner, Sally.
Tapler, Judy. Santa Horse. Kohler, Michelle, illus. (p. 1512)
Tapley, Scott, jt. auth. see Dharkar, Anuja.
Tapley-Milton, Katherine. Adventures of Sir Lancelot the Cat. (p. 23)
Taplin, Sam. 50 Optical Illusions. Seckel, Al, illus. (p. 1997)
—Animal. (p. 76)
—Baby Animals. (p. 124)
—Baby's Bedtime Storybook CV. (p. 128)
—Christmas Poems. Luraschi, Anna, illus. (p. 315)
—Diggers Sticker Book. (p. 439)
—Dinosaurs. Lamb, Stacey, illus. (p. 444)
—Easter Bunny Flap Book. (p. 499)
—Farm Sticker Book. (p. 574)
—First Encyclopedia of Dinosaurs & Prehistoric Life: Internet-Linked. Hancock, David, illus. (p. 594)
—First Encyclopedia of Dinosaurs II. (p. 594)
—First Encyclopedia of Dinosaurs - Internet Linked. Hancock, David, illus. (p. 594)
—First Picture Dinosaurs. Van Wyk, Hanri, illus. (p. 596)
—First Sticker Book Santa. (p. 597)
—First Sticker Book Trains. (p. 597)
—Listen & Learn First English Words. (p. 1022)
—Little Encyclopedia of Dinosaurs. (p. 1027)
—Little Red Riding Hood. (p. 1035)
—Little Stories for Bedtime. Chiara, Francesca De, illus. (p. 1037)
—Little Stories for Christmas. (p. 1037)
—Mummies & Pyramids. (p. 1191)
—My First Christmas Keyboard Book. (p. 1206)
—Night-Night Stories. (p. 1253)
—Noisy Building Site Board Book. (p. 1263)
—Noisy Diggers. (p. 1263)
—Noisy Orchestra. (p. 1263)
—Noisy Pirates. Chambers, Mark, illus. (p. 1263)
—Noisy Spooky Book. (p. 1263)
—Noisy Zoo. Wildish, Lee, illus. (p. 1263)
—Optical Illusions Tin. (p. 1301)
—Pirates First Coloring Book. (p. 1363)
—Pop-Up Haunted House. (p. 1384)
—Sleeping Beauty. (p. 1589)
—Sleepytime Stories. Chaira, Francesca di, illus. (p. 1590)
—This Is My Dinosaur. (p. 1736)
—This Is My Monster. Furukawa, Masumi, illus. (p. 1736)
—Trucks Sticker Book. (p. 1791)
—Usborne Book of Bedtime Rhymes. Luraschi, Anna, illus. (p. 1827)
—Usborne Book of Poems for Little Children. Furukawa, Masumi, illus. (p. 1827)
—Usborne Official Pirate's Handbook. McNee, Ian, illus. (p. 1827)
—Zoo (First Sticker Book) Johansson, Cecilia, illus. (p. 1989)
Taplin, Sam, jt. auth. see Greenwell, Jessica.
Taplin, Sam, compiled by. Poems for Young Children. (p. 1376)
Taplinger, Lee, photos by see Florian, Douglas.
Tapp, Karen J. Molly the Mallard Duck: The True Story of Kathy & the Mallard Duck She Named Molly. (p. 1161)
Tappan, Eva March. Children's Hour: Stories from Seven Old Favorites (p. 303)
—Children's Hour, Volume 4. Stories of Legendary Heroes. (p. 303)
—Children's Hour, Volume V: Stories from Seven Old Favorites. (p. 303)
—Heroes of Progress: Stories of Successful Americans. (p. 773)
—In the Days of Queen Victori. (p. 865)
—When Knights Were Bold (Yesterday's Classics) (p. 1903)
Tapper, Suzanne Cloud. Voices from Slavery's Past: Yearning to Be Heard. (p. 1848)
Tapper, Suzanne Cloud, jt. auth. see Cloud Tapper, Suzanne.
Tappin, Christine, illus. see Viswanath, Shobha.
Taptich, J. E. Tana Ray, & Its No Time to Play. Townsend, Leah, illus. (p. 1705)
Taql, Allage Monique. Why Wait? I Want It Now! (p. 1926)
Tara. Knot Today. (p. 965)
Tara, Stephanie. I'll Follow the Moon. Fodi, Lee Edward, illus. (p. 856)
Tara, Stephanie L. Gwynne, Fair & Shining. Fodi, Lee Edward, illus. (p. 733)
Tara, Stephanie Lisa. Eliza's Forever Trees. Walton, Alex, illus. (p. 513)
—I'll Follow the Moon. Fodi, Lee Edward, illus. (p. 856)
—Little Library Mouse. Walton, Alex, illus. (p. 1030)
—Snowy White World to Save. Walton, Alex, illus. (p. 1601)
Taraborrelli, J. Randy. Once upon a Time: Behind the Fairy Tale of Princess Grace & Prince Rainier. (p. 1293)
Tarantino, Mardijah Aldrich. Marvellous Stories from the Life of Muhammad. Murad, Khurram, ed. (p. 1099)
Tarantino, Scott & Ruggiero, David. High Sticking: Xylophone & Marimba Pieces for Grades 4 - 8. (p. 778)
Taraschi-Carr, Gola, jt. auth. see Hickman, Pamela.
Tarasova, Julia. Daniel's Travels. (p. 405)
Taravant, Jacques. Little Wing Giver. Ignatowicz, Nina, tr. from FRE. (p. 1037)
Tarazona, Oscar. Volando con Alas Propias. (p. 1848)
Tarbell, Ida M. Boy Scouts' Life of Lincoln. (p. 218)
—Father Abraham. Campbell, Blendon, illus. (p. 577)
Tarbett, Debbie. Ten Wriggly Wiggly Caterpillars. (p. 1719)
Tarbett, Debbie, illus. see Brooks, Susie.
Tarbett, Debbie, illus. see Rivers-Moore, Debbie.
Tarbox, A. D. Arctic Tundra Food Chain: Nature's Bounty. (p. 96)
—Arctic Tundra Food Chain. (p. 96)
—Desert. (p. 428)
—Desert Food Chain: Nature's Bounty. (p. 429)
—Desert Food Chain. (p. 429)
—Mountain Food Chain: Nature's Bounty. (p. 1180)
—Mountain Food Chain. (p. 1180)
—Nature's Bounty: A Mountain Food Chain. (p. 1237)
—Nature's Bounty: Ocean. (p. 1237)
—Nature's Bounty: Rainforest. (p. 1237)
—Ocean Food Chain: Nature's Bounty. (p. 1276)
—Ocean Food Chain. (p. 1276)
—Pairie Food Chain. (p. 1318)
—Prairie Food Chain: Nature's Bounty. (p. 1392)
—Prairie Food Chain. (p. 1392)
—Rain Forest Food Chain. (p. 1434)
—Rainforest Food Chain: Nature's Bounty. (p. 1436)
Tarbox, Charlene. Creative Haven Beautiful Flower Arrangements Coloring Book. (p. 379)
—Floral Beauty Coloring Book. (p. 606)
—Glitter Flowers Stickers. (p. 684)
—Glow-in-the-Dark Tattoos Flowers. (p. 685)
Tarbox, Jonathan, jt. auth. see Yagi, Norihiro.
Tarchon The Etruscan. Nubian Gold: A Conspiracy of Jewish Proportions. (p. 1269)
Tardieu, Carine, jt. auth. see Xerri-L., Nadia.

Tardif, Elizabeth. Bunny Named Apple. Buehrle, Jacquelyn, illus. (p. 242)
Tardif, Mandy, illus. see Perez, Claudia.
Tardiff, Carol Ann. Windmill Gardens. (p. 1936)
Tardiff, Joe. Congressional Ethics. Greenhaven Press Editors & Zott, Lynn, eds. (p. 357)
Tardiff, Joseph. Consumer Debt. (p. 360)
Tardiff, Joseph C., ed. Marijuana. (p. 1094)
Taree, Aerle. Molly's Mental Health: Love Me Too. (p. 1161)
Tarendash, Albert S. Chemistry: The Physical Setting. (p. 297)
—Physics: The Physical Setting. (p. 1353)
Tarentino, Kathy, jt. auth. see Leahy, Sandy.
Tarico, Valerie. Deas & Other Imaginings: Ten Spiritual Folktales for Children. Troy, Tony, illus. (p. 419)
Taris, James Robert & Taris, Louis James. Hands-On Science Mysteries, Grades 3-6: Standards-Based Inquiry Investigations. (p. 741)
Taris, Louis James, jt. auth. see Taris, James Robert.
Tarkington, Booth. Beasley's Christmas Party. (p. 152)
—Beasley's Christmas Party. Clements, Ruth Sypherd, illus. (p. 152)
—Ramsey Milholland. (p. 1438)
Tarlow, Ellen. Mole Catches the Sky. Bogacki, Tomek, illus. (p. 1160)
—Pinwheel Days Parker, Gretel, illus. (p. 1361)
Tarman, Mel. Judah: The Story of Judah P. Benjamin, Confederate Statesman. (p. 930)
Tarman, Mel, jt. auth. see Pushker, Gloria Teles.
Tarn, Nathaniel. Recollections of Being. (p. 1452)
Tarnow, Barbara. My Friend Noah. (p. 1209)
Tarnow, Georgette H. Special Secret Hearts: A Child's Introduction to Dementia & Pink Curls - a Santa Claus Story. (p. 1623)
Tarnowska, Wafa'. Arabian Nights. Henaff, Carole, illus. (p. 94)
—Arabian Nights Chapter. Hénaff, Carole, illus. (p. 94)
—Seven Wise Princesses: A Medieval Persian Epic. Nilesh, Misty, illus. (p. 1555)
Tarnowski, Mark, illus. see Treanor, H. T.
Tarore, Martha. Runaway Bubble. (p. 1496)
Tarpley, Natasha Anastasia. Bippity Bop Barbershop. Lewis, E. B., illus. (p. 190)
—I Love My Hair! Lewis, E. B., illus. (p. 842)
Tarpley, Todd. Beep! Beep! Go to Sleep! Rocco, John, illus. (p. 157)
—My Grandma's a Ninja. Chatzikonstantinou, Danny, illus. (p. 1210)
—Ten Tiny Toes. (p. 1719)
Tarr, Judith, jt. auth. see Bryan, Kathleen.
Tarr, Lisa M., illus. see Perry, Phyllis J.
Tarr, Rebecca M. My Cricket & Me. (p. 1200)
Tarrant, Percy, illus. see Vaizey, George de Horne.
Tarrant-Reid, Linda. Discovering Black America: From the Age of Exploration to the Twenty-First Century. (p. 449)
Tarshis, Lauren. Attacks of September 11, 2001. (p. 114)
—Bombing of Pearl Harbor 1941. (p. 208)
—Emma-Jean Lazarus Fell in Love. (p. 519)
—Emma-Jean Lazarus Fell Out of a Tree. (p. 519)
—Great Chicago Fire 1871. (p. 714)
—I Survived: True Stories, Five Epic Disasters. (p. 846)
—I Survived Hurricane Katrina 2005. (p. 846)
—I Survived - Hurricane Katrina 2005. (p. 846)
—I Survived the Attacks of September 11, 2001. (p. 846)
—I Survived the Battle of Gettysburg 1863. (p. 846)
—I Survived the Bombing of Pearl Harbor 1941. (p. 846)
—I Survived the Destruction of Pompeii, 79 A. D. (p. 846)
—I Survived the Japanese Tsunami 2011. (p. 846)
—I Survived the Japanese Tsunami 2011. Dawson, Scott, illus. (p. 846)
—I Survived the Nazi Invasion 1944. (p. 846)
—I Survived the San Francisco Earthquake 1906. (p. 846)
—I Survived the Shark Attacks of 1916. (p. 846)
—I Survived the Sinking of the Titanic 1912. (p. 846)
—Nazi Invasion 1944. (p. 1238)
Tarshis, Thomas Paul. Living with Peer Pressure & Bullying. (p. 1042)
Tarsy, Jean. Just Molly & Me & Nikki Make Three. LaGrange, Tiffany, illus. (p. 939)
Tartakoff, Katy. Burned & Beautiful. Shields, Laurie, illus. (p. 244)
—Let Me Show You My World. Shields, Laurie, illus. (p. 994)
Tarter, Mildred. Alexis Sets up Search Groups. (p. 37)
—Alexis Uses the Elements of Nature. (p. 37)
—Rexis! Where Are You! (p. 1467)
Tarver, H. Micheal, jt. auth. see Frederick, Julia C.
Tarver, Kevin L. Genesis Project. (p. 660)
Tarver, Monroe S. Little Light Shine Bright. Tarver, Monroe S., illus. (p. 1030)
—Nubia Web: Legend of the Stone (p. 1269)
—Tales from the Mapmaker: Imagia & the Magic Pearls. (p. 1702)
Tarver, S., 1st. Imaga & the Magic Pearls (p. 860)
Tarver, Whitney B. Best Day Ever! (p. 168)
—When Mommy Went Back to Work. (p. 1903)
Tarzia, Antonio, jt. auth. see Forte, Bruno.
Taschek, Karen. Civil War. (p. 325)
—Death Stars, Weird Galaxies, & a Quasar-Spangled Universe: The Discoveries of the Very Large Array Telescope. (p. 420)
—Hanging with Bats: Ecobats, Vampires, & Movie Stars. (p. 742)
—Horse of Seven Moons. (p. 800)
—Risen Horse. (p. 1475)
Tash, Sarvenaz. Mapmaker & the Ghost. (p. 1090)
—Three Day Summer. (p. 1742)
Tashiro, Chisato. Chameleon's Colors. (p. 289)
—Chameleon's Colors. Martens, Marianne, tr. from JPN. (p. 289)
—Colores del Camaleon. Zatz, Asa, tr. from GER. (p. 344)
Tashjian, Jake, illus. see Tashjian, Janet.
Tashjian, Janet. Einstein the Class Hamster. Tashjian, Jake, illus. (p. 507)
—Einstein the Class Hamster & the Very Real Game Show. Tashjian, Jake, illus. (p. 507)
—Einstein the Class Hamster Saves the Library. Tashjian, Jake, illus. (p. 507)
—Fault Line. (p. 577)
—For What It's Worth. (p. 616)
—Gospel According to Larry. (p. 703)
—Larry & the Meaning of Life. (p. 976)
—My Life As a Book. Tashjian, Jake, illus. (p. 1211)
—My Life As a Cartoonist. Tashjian, Jake, illus. (p. 1211)
—My Life As a Gamer. Tashjian, Jake, illus. (p. 1212)
—My Life As a Joke. Tashjian, Jake, illus. (p. 1212)
—My Life as a Stuntboy. Tashjian, Jake, illus. (p. 1212)
—Tru Confessions. (p. 1791)
—Vote for Larry. (p. 1850)
Tashlikowich, Natasha. Secret of the Seven Stones. (p. 1543)
Tashlin, Frank. Bear That Wasn't. (p. 151)
Tashlin, Frank, jt. auth. see Minarik, Else Holmelund.
Taso, Alex, illus. see Grahame, Kenneth.
Taste of Home Editorial Staff. Cake Mix Creations: 216 Easy Desserts That Start with a Mix. (p. 252)
—Casseroles, Slow Cooker & Soups: 536 Family Pleasing Recipes. (p. 276)
Tata. I Smile. (p. 845)
Tata, Cb. Ernie the Eagle Goes to Maine. Hanley, Zachary, illus. (p. 534)
Tatam, Michelle. Chameleon. (p. 289)
—Midnight Running. (p. 1139)
Tatar, Maria, ed. see Andersen, Hans Christian.
Tatarnikau, Pavel, illus. see Matthews, John & Matthe, John.
Tatarnikov, Pavel, illus. see Andersen, Hans Christian.
Tataryn, Myroslaw. How to Pray with Icons: An Introduction for Children. (p. 821)
Tatchell, J., jt. auth. see Smith, A.
Tatchell, Judy. Animal Homes. (p. 78)
—Bugs & Slugs. (p. 237)
—Bugs & Slugs Lift-the-Flap. (p. 237)
—Dragons. Scott, Peter David & Furnival, Keith, illus. (p. 478)
—Dragons Lift-the-flap. Scott, Peter, illus. (p. 479)
—How Do Your Senses Work? Wheatley, Maria, illus. (p. 808)
—How to Draw Cartoons & Caricatures. Bave, Terry et al, illus. (p. 817)
—How to Draw Cartoons & Caricatures. Round, Graham et al, illus. (p. 817)
—On the Farm. Smith, Alastair, illus. (p. 1290)
—Pocket Artist. (p. 1375)
—Science Encyclopedia. (p. 1525)
—World of Ballet: Internet-Linked. Miles, Lisa, ed. (p. 1956)
—World of Ballet. (p. 1956)
—World of Ballet. Miles, Lisa, ed. (p. 1956)
Tatchell, Judy, ed. see Beasant, Pam.
Tatchell, Judy, ed. see Claridge, Marit.
Tatchell, Judy, ed. see Cook, Janet.
Tatchell, Judy, ed. see Dalby, Elizabeth.
Tatchell, Judy, jt. auth. see Smith, Alastair.
Tatchell, Judy & Rogers, Kirsteen. Dragons Jigsaw Book. Scott, Peter, illus. (p. 479)
Tatchell, Judy & Varley, Carol. How to Draw Lettering. Brown, Fiona, illus. (p. 818)
Tatcheva, Eva. Witch Zelda's Birthday Cake: A Wild & Wicked Pop-up, Pull-the-Tab Book. Tatcheva, Eva, illus. (p. 1941)
Tate, Andrew, jt. auth. see Tate, Bernice.
Tate, Andy. I Love My Church. Tate, Lizzy, illus. (p. 842)
Tate, Barbara. Little Mouse & Sister Mouse: A Surprise in the Night. (p. 1032)
—Little Mouse, Sister Mouse: A Great Lunch. (p. 1032)
Tate, Bernice & Andy. Funspell. (p. 650)
Tate, Bernice & Tate, Andrew. Zanzy's Purple Cheese & Orange Peas. (p. 1985)
Tate, Brucetta McClue. Jolly Meets Cyber Air Bully. (p. 924)
Tate, Cynthia Wagoner. Gordy's Grimy but Groovy Adventure. (p. 702)
Tate, Don, illus. see Barton, Chris.
Tate, Don, illus. see Blue, Rose, et al.
Tate, Don, illus. see Bunting, Eve.
Tate, Don, illus. see Celenza, Anna Harwell.
Tate, Don, illus. see Christie, R. Gregory.
Tate, Don, illus. see Hamilton, Martha & Weiss, Mitch.
Tate, Don, illus. see Hubbell, Patricia.
Tate, Don, illus. see Lyons, Kelly Starling.
Tate, Don, illus. see Mandel, Peter.
Tate, Don, illus. see Vernick, Audrey.
Tate, Don, illus. see Wangerin, Walter, Jr.
Tate, Don, jt. auth. see Hubbell, Patricia.
Tate, Eleanora E. Blessing in Disguise. (p. 199)
—Celeste's Harlem Renaissance. (p. 285)
—Minstrel's Melody. (p. 1148)
Tate, Elizabeth Dawn. On My Front Porch Swing. (p. 1289)
—There's a Storm Brewing Outside. (p. 1731)
Tate, Fleeta Loudermilk. Ollie's Adventures with Nana Kate. (p. 1287)
Tate, J. Pops. (p. 1385)
Tate, Kelly. Selling Popcorn: Understand Place Value. (p. 1550)
Tate Kuelling, Judy. Hitchhiker. (p. 786)
Tate, Lizzy, illus. see Tate, Andy.
Tate, Lori A. Helpful Henry: Adventures in the Big Woods. (p. 766)
Tate, M. My Little Life: A Cancer Survivor's Story As Told by Nature. Tate, M., photos by. (p. 1212)
Tate, Mary Jo. Critical Companion to F. Scott Fitzgerald: A Literary Reference to His Life & Times. (p. 383)
Tate, Micheal R. Adventures of Sugarcube. (p. 23)
Tate, N. F. Witch of Hambone: Books 1 And 2. (p. 1941)
Tate, Nancy. Grandmother Ellie's Attic. (p. 709)
Tate, Nikki. Battle for Camillo Williams, E. Colin, illus. (p. 145)
—Behind the Scenes: The Racehorse (p. 160)
—Double Take: Karen Brain's Olympic Journey (p. 473)
—Down to Earth: How Kids Help Feed the World (p. 474)
—Fallout (p. 567)
—Razor's Edge (p. 1441)
—Trouble on Tarragon Island (p. 1790)
—Venom (p. 1835)
Tate, Nikki & Tate-Stratton, Dani. Take Shelter: At Home Around the World (p. 1697)
Tate Publishing, creator. Land of Ahppiness: The Adventures of Ish & Parr. (p. 973)
Tate, Singleton M. Laugh a Little. Vorella2000, illus. (p. 980)
Tate, Suzanne. Color with the Wright Brothers: See How They Made History. Melvin, James, illus. (p. 343)
—Danny & Daisy: A Tale of a Dolphin Duo. Melvin, James, illus. (p. 405)
—Flyer: A Tale of the Wright Dog. Melvin, James, illus. (p. 609)
—Great Sharky Shark: A Tale of a Big Hunter. Melvin, James, illus. (p. 718)
—Johnny Longlegs: A Tale of Big Birds. Melvin, James, illus. (p. 923)
—Katie K. Whale: A Whale of a Tale. Melvin, James, illus. (p. 945)
—Rosie Ray: A Tale of Watery Wings. Melvin, James, illus. (p. 1490)
—Sandy Seal: A Tale of Sea Dogs. Melvin, James, illus. (p. 1511)
—Skippy Scallop: A Tale of Bright Blue Eyes. Melvin, James, illus. (p. 1586)
—Tammy Turtle: A Tale of Saving Sea Turtles. Melvin, James, illus. (p. 1704)
—Teena Tortoise: A Tale of a Little Giant. Melvin, James, illus. (p. 1714)
Tate, Sylvia, jt. auth. see Wadsworth, Pamela.
Tate, Zachary. No Way Out. (p. 1261)
Tate-Stratton, Dani, jt. auth. see Tate, Nikki.
Tatge, Cathy. Airplanes. (p. 32)
—Boats. (p. 205)
—Cars. (p. 272)
—Trucks. (p. 1791)
Tatham, Betty. How Animals Play. (p. 804)
Tatla, Darshan Singh, jt. ed. see Talbot, Ian.
Tatro, John L. Bugs Bugs Bugs. (p. 237)
Tatro, MaryAnn. Milton the Square Shell Turtle. Lucas, Diane, illus. (p. 1144)
Tatsi, Andreanna, tr. see Downie, David.
Tatsuya, Hamazaki, jt. auth. see Hamazaki, Tatsuya.
Tatsuyama, Sayuri. Happy Happy Clover. Tatsuyama, Sayuri, illus. (p. 745)
Tattam, Mark. Pets. (p. 1348)
Tattam, Mark, jt. auth. see Phillips, Sarah.
Tattersall, Clare, jt. auth. see Wallach, Jonah M.
Tattersall, Ian. Monkey in the Mirror: Essays on the Science of What Makes Us Human. (p. 1165)
Tattersfield, Jane, illus. see Francis, Pauline.
Tattoos, jt. auth. see Dover.
Tattum, Stephan. Bad Ram. (p. 132)
—Bear Cub. (p. 150)
—Bus. (p. 244)
—Dad. (p. 398)
—Fun Pup. (p. 648)
—Hip Kid. (p. 780)
—Hot Sun. (p. 802)
—Mad Cat. (p. 1068)
—Mom. (p. 1161)
—Wet Fun. (p. 1877)
Tatulli, Mark. Desmond Pucket & the Mountain Full of Monsters. (p. 430)
—Desmond Pucket Makes Monster Magic. (p. 430)
—Lio: Making Friends. (p. 1019)
Tatulli, Mark, et al. Lio: Making Friends. (p. 1019)
—Lio: There's a Monster in My Socks. (p. 1019)
Tatum, Doug. No Man's Land: Where Growing Companies Fail. (p. 1259)
Tau, Beckie. Little Can'telope: Animals with Attitude: Animals with Attitude. (p. 1025)
—Little Ele-Funny: Animals with Attitude. (p. 1027)
Taub, Daniel, jt. auth. see Hawker, Frances.
Taub, Melinda. Still Star-Crossed. (p. 1650)
Taub, Udi, illus. see Davis, Linda.
Tauber, Sabine. Architecture: Create Your Own City!—Sticker Book. (p. 95)
—Hieronymus Bosch: Coloring Book. (p. 777)
Taubman, Bruce. Why Is My Baby Crying? The 7-Minute Program for Soothing the Fussy Baby. (p. 1925)
Tauger, Eliyahu, tr. see Rabbi Schneur Zalman of Liadi.
Tauiliili, Pemerika L. Rat & the Bat: And Other Short Stories. (p. 1440)
Taulo, Tuija, illus. see Steinberg, Sari.
Taus-Bolstad, Stacy. From Clay to Bricks. Richter, Cheryl R., photos by. (p. 642)
—From Grass to Milk. (p. 642)
—From Milk to Ice Cream. (p. 643)
—From Shoot to Apple. (p. 643)
—From Wheat to Bread. (p. 644)
—Iran in Pictures. (p. 886)
—Iraq in Pictures. (p. 887)
—Koreans in America. (p. 967)
—Pakistanis in America. (p. 1319)
—Spain in Pictures. (p. 1620)
—Thailand in Pictures. (p. 1724)
Taus-Bolstad, Stacy & Goldstein, Margaret J. Cambodia in Pictures. (p. 255)
Tausig, Ben. Mad Tausig vs the Interplanetary Puzzling Peace Patrol. Goopymart, illus. (p. 1069)
Tauss, Marc, illus. see Ehrmann, Max.
Tavaci, Elspeth & Quarto Generic Staff. Stone of Destiny: Tales from Turkey. Hess, Paul, illus. (p. 1652)
Tavadze, Olesya. Bursunsul & Paskualina. Ivanov, Evgueni, illus. (p. 244)
Tavakkoli, Aryan. Abc Animals Are My Friends. (p. 3)
Tavano, Joe. Dachshund's Wish. Yu, Ji, illus. (p. 398)
Tavares, Gary Gene. Inspirational & Educational Poems. (p. 878)
Tavares, Matt. Becoming Babe Ruth. Tavares, Matt, illus. (p. 156)
—Growing up Pedro: How the Martinez Brothers Made It from the Dominican Republic All the Way to the Major Leagues. Tavares, Matt, illus. (p. 727)
—Henry Aaron's Dream. Tavares, Matt, illus. (p. 767)
—Iron Hans. (p. 888)
—Mudball. Tavares, Matt, illus. (p. 1188)
—Oliver's Game. Tavares, Matt, illus. (p. 1286)
—There Goes Ted Williams: The Greatest Hitter Who Ever Lived. Tavares, Matt, illus. (p. 1729)
—Zachary's Ball. Tavares, Matt, illus. (p. 1984)
Tavares, Matt, illus. see Anonymus.
Tavares, Matt, illus. see Child, L. Maria.
Tavares, Matt, illus. see Kladstrup, Kristin.
Tavares, Matt, illus. see Nesbit, E.
Tavares, Matt, illus. see Rappaport, Doreen.
Tavares, Victor. Beauty & the Beast. (p. 154)
Tavares, Victor, illus. see Sims, Lesley.
Tavares, Victor, illus. see Williams, Brenda.
Tavares, Victor, jt. auth. see Heine, Theresa.
Tavares, Victore, illus. see Levene, Rebecca, ed.
Tavener, Carys. Adventures of T. C & Friends. (p. 23)
Tavicat Staff. Reality Check (p. 1449)
Tavicat Staff, creator. Reality Check (p. 1449)
Tavner, Gill, jt. auth. see Moore, Alan.
Tavner, Gill & Dickens, Charles. David Copperfield. Donnelly, Karen, illus. (p. 410)
—Hard Times. Donnelly, Karen, illus. (p. 748)
Tavolacci, Joyce. Teen Wise Guide to Relationships. (p. 1714)
Tavoularis, Alex, illus. see Mitchell, Barbara.
Tawa, Renee. Tink's Magical Day. (p. 1756)
Taxali, Gary. This Is Silly! (p. 1736)
Taxali, Gary, illus. see DePrisco, Dorothea.
Tay, Kalyee, illus. see Willetts, Lucy & Waite, Polly.
Tayac, Gabrielle. Meet Naiche: A Native Boy from the Chesapeake Bay Area. Harrington, John, photos by. (p. 1121)
Tayal, Amit, illus. see Dumas, Alexandre.
Tayal, Amit, illus. see Gunderson, Jessica & Loewen, Nancy.
Tayal, Amit, illus. see Helfand, Lewis.
Tayal, Amit, illus. see Hoena, B. A.
Tayal, Amit, illus. see Loewen, Nancy.
Tayal, Amit, illus. see Shaskan, Trisha Speed & Loewen, Nancy.
Tayal, Amit, illus. see Shaskan, Trisha Speed.
Tayal, Amit, illus. see Wyss, Johann David.
Tayama, Thomas, illus. see Jackson, Marilyn Malloy, ed.
Tay-Audouard, L. K., jt. auth. see Taylor, Diane.
Tay-Audouard, Lak-Khee, jt. auth. see Bowler, Ann Martin.
Tay-Audouard, Lak-Khee, jt. auth. see Nunes, Shiho S.
Taybert, Efim. I Kedriy Tojze Plachyt. (p. 840)
Taycop, Faith. Progressive Era. (p. 1410)
Taykutgul, Selcuk & Akin, Ferruh. Uthman: Bearer of Two Pure Lights. (p. 1829)
Tayler, Amber. What Do Monsters Look Like? Birth, Ryan, illus. (p. 1882)
Tayler, Kassy. Ashes of Twilight. (p. 105)
—Remnants of Tomorrow. (p. 1460)
—Shadows of Glass. (p. 1558)
Tayler, Sandra. Hold on to Your Horses. Call, Angela, illus. (p. 788)
Tayleur, Karen. Excuses! Survive & Succeed with David Mortimore Baxter. Garvey, Brann, illus. (p. 548)
—Famous (Scholastic) The Awesome Life of David Mortimore Baxter. Garvey, Brann, illus. (p. 569)
—Forgetting to Remember. Gamble, Penel, illus. (p. 619)
—Liar! The True Story of David Mortimore Baxter. Garvey, Brann, illus. (p. 1005)
—Manners! Staying Out of Trouble with David Mortimore Baxter. Garvey, Brann, illus. (p. 1088)
—Promises! Vote for David Mortimore Baxter. Garvey, Brann, illus. (p. 1411)
—Secrets! The Secret Life of David Mortimore Baxter Garvey, Brann, illus. (p. 1544)
—Truth! David Mortimore Baxter Comes Clean Garvey, Brann, illus. (p. 1793)
Tayloe, McConnell Dubay, ed. see Muller, Seth.
Taylor, Adam. George in the UK: The Unknown Kingdom. Taylor, Adam & West, Jeannette, eds. (p. 663)
Taylor, Adam, illus. see Heidari, Mahdi.
Taylor, Adam, illus. see Hickman, Debbie.
Taylor, Adam, illus. see Le Verrier, Renee & Frank, Samuel.
Taylor, Adam, illus. see Murphy, T. M.
Taylor, Alastair. Mr. Blewitt's Nose. (p. 1184)
Taylor, Ali. Cotton Wool. (p. 369)
Taylor, Alice. Secrets of the Oak. Barnett, Russell, illus. (p. 1545)
Taylor, Allan, jt. auth. see Parish, James Robert.
Taylor, Allan & Parish, James Robert. Career Opportunities in Writing. (p. 267)
—Library & Information Science. (p. 1005)
Taylor, Allison Wagner, jt. auth. see Hurst, Donna L.
Taylor, Amber, illus. see Reyes, S. L.
Taylor, Amber L., illus. see Reyes, Shawntie L.
Taylor, Andrew. Stain on the Silence. (p. 1638)
Taylor, Andrew, jt. ed. see Stolcheff, Peter.
Taylor, Andrew, Jr. Collected Poems. (p. 339)
Taylor, Ann Creal, jt. auth. see Creal, Nancy.
Taylor, Anna. Sophia's Favorite Squirrel Browny. (p. 1613)
Taylor, Arthur Charles. Bears Like Us. (p. 152)
Taylor, B. F. Miss Shoog's Spirit. (p. 1152)
Taylor, B. J. Ella Mae & the Great Depression. (p. 514)
Taylor, Barbara. 3-D Explorer: Predators. Veres, Laszlo, illus. (p. 1991)
—Amazing World Of: Castles. (p. 56)
—Arctic & Antarctic. (p. 96)
—Atlas Visual de los Animales. Lilly, Kenneth, illus. (p. 113)
—Bug Athletes. (p. 236)
—Bug Hunters. (p. 236)
—Bugs That Swim. (p. 237)
—Build the Shark. Ruffle, Mark & Bernstein, Galia, illus. (p. 238)
—Coastal Habitats. (p. 336)
—Dinosaurs: A Journey Through the Prehistoric World. (p. 444)
—Discover Science: Apes & Monkeys. (p. 448)
—Elephants. (p. 511)
—Exploring Nature: Fantastic Penguins. (p. 552)
—Exploring Nature: Incredible Crocodiles. (p. 552)

T

—Exploring Nature: A Fascinating Guide to the Gentle Giants That Dominate Africa & Asia, Shown in More Than 190 Pictures: Incredible Elephants. (p. 552)
—Exploring Nature - Amazing Snakes: An Exciting Insight into the Weird & Wonderful World of Snakes & How They Live, with 190 Pictures. (p. 552)
—Exploring Nature - Sensational Spiders: A Comprehensive Guide to Some of the Most Intriguing Creatures in the Animal Kingdom, with over 220 Pictures. (p. 552)
—Hidden in the Grass. (p. 775)
—Hidden in the Sand. (p. 775)
—Hidden in the Snow. (p. 775)
—I Wonder Why Soap Makes Bubbles: And Other Questions about Science. (p. 849)
—I Wonder Why Zippers Have Teeth. (p. 849)
—Inland Water Habitats. (p. 874)
—Inside Plants. (p. 877)
—Inventions. (p. 884)
—Looking at Maps. (p. 1051)
—My Big Animal World: Essential Facts from the Amazing World of Animals. (p. 1197)
—Oceans. (p. 1277)
—Poisonous Bugs. (p. 1377)
—Polar Habitats. (p. 1379)
—Rivers. (p. 1476)
—Safari Animals: A Journey Through the African Wilderness. (p. 1501)
—Slide & Discover: Animal Atlas. (p. 1590)
—Slide & Discover: Human Body. (p. 1590)
—Slimy Spawn & Other Gruesome Life Cycles. (p. 1590)
—Snakes. (p. 1596)
—Stinky Skunks & Other Animal Adaptations. (p. 1651)
—Temperate Forest Habitats. (p. 1717)
—Trees. (p. 1784)
—Tropical Rain Forest Habitats. (p. 1789)
—Understanding Landforms. (p. 1815)
—Urban Wildlife Habitats. (p. 1825)
—Water Bugs. (p. 1862)
Taylor, Barbara & Chancellor, Deborah. Discover Science: Planet Earth. (p. 448)
Taylor, Barbara & Green, Jen. Explore the Deadly World of Bugs, Snakes, Spiders, Crocodiles: The Dramatic Lives & Conflicts of the World's Strangest Creatures Shown in 1500 Amazing Close-Up Photographs. (p. 550)
Taylor, Barbara & Griffiths, Richard A. Nature Watch: Crocodiles. Taylor, Barbara, ed. (p. 1236)
Taylor, Barbara & O'Shea, Mark. Ultimate Book of Snakes & Reptiles: Discover the Amazing World of Snakes, Crocodiles, Lizards & Turtles. (p. 1809)
Taylor, Barbara & Parker, Steve. Animals. (p. 81)
Taylor, Barbara, et al. Deadly World of Bugs, Snakes, Spiders, Crocodiles: And Hundreds of Other Amazing Reptiles & Insects. (p. 418)
—Illustrated Wildlife Encyclopedia: Bugs & Minibeasts. (p. 858)
—Wild Animals the Best-Ever Box of Books: A Fabulous Collection of Eight Wildlife Books with Fascinating Facts & over 1600 Amazing Photographs (p. 1928)
Taylor, Bayard. Unpublished Letters. (p. 1822)
Taylor, Beth. Tina's Toys. (p. 1755)
Taylor, Betty Ann. Mari's Miracle. (p. 1094)
Taylor, Beverley, et al. Teaching Physics with TOYS, EASYGuide Edition. Sarquis, Mickey, ed. (p. 1710)
Taylor, Beverly. Elusive Puffin. (p. 516)
Taylor, Bonnie Highsmith. Simon Can't Say Hippopotamus. Hornung, Phyllis, tr. (p. 1577)
Taylor, Bridget Starr, illus. see Edwards, Pamela Duncan.
Taylor, Bridget Starr, illus. see Troupe, Thomas Kingsley.
Taylor, Brigid. How I Turn My Mom into a Monster! (p. 810)
Taylor, Brooke. Undone. (p. 1817)
Taylor, Byron, illus. see McNeil, W. K., ed.
Taylor, C. Brian. Atop the Tree Top: A Christmas Story. Butler, Sharon, illus. (p. 113)
Taylor, C. J. Peace Walker: The Legend of Hiawatha & Tekanawita. (p. 1331)
—Spirits, Fairies, & Merpeople: Native Stories of Other Worlds. (p. 1629)
Taylor, Carol, illus. see Watts, Ana Dearborn & Dearborn, Dorothy.
Taylor, Carol & Taylor, Winford. Take Time to Know & Love Them. (p. 1697)
Taylor, Carol K. Behind the Fence. (p. 160)
Taylor, Caroline. All Things Bright & Beautiful. Longfoot, Stephanie, illus. (p. 46)
—All Things Wise & Wonderful. Longfoot, Stephanie, illus. (p. 46)
—Lord God Made Us All. Longfoot, Stephanie, illus. (p. 1052)
Taylor, Carolyn, illus. see Johnson, Esther A.
Taylor, Catherine. Thirst (p. 1734)
Taylor, Catherine, illus. see Taylor, Douglas.
Taylor, Celestine. Just Another Life. (p. 937)
Taylor, Centrella P. Little Miss Sunshine (p. 1032)
Taylor, Chandra. Greatest Gift of All. (p. 720)
Taylor, Chandra Sparks, ed. see Preston, Frederick James.
Taylor, Charles. Kingfisher Science Encyclopedia. Kingfisher Publications, Inc. Staff, ed. (p. 960)
Taylor, Charles & Kingfisher Editors. Kingfisher Science Encyclopedia. (p. 960)
Taylor, Charlotte. Crispus Attucks: A Hero of the American Revolution. (p. 383)
—Get to Know Andy Warhol. (p. 668)
—Get to Know Edward Hopper. (p. 668)
—Get to Know Georgia O'Keeffe. (p. 668)
—Sojourner Truth: Abolitionist & Activist. (p. 1606)
Taylor, Charlotte & Feinstein, Stephen. Barack Obama: First African-American President. (p. 137)
—Harriet Tubman: Hero of the Underground Railroad. (p. 750)
—LeBron James: Basketball Champion. (p. 987)
—Lebron James: Basketball Champion. (p. 987)
—Mae Jemison: First African-American Woman in Space. (p. 1070)
Taylor, Charlotte & Kent, Deborah. Internment of Japanese Americans. (p. 880)
Taylor, Charlotte & Miller, Mara. Little Rock Nine & School Desegregation. (p. 1036)
Taylor, Charlotte & Stein, R. Conrad. Underground Railroad. (p. 1814)
Taylor, Chet. Last, but Not Least. (p. 977)
—Last, but Not Least. Taylor, Chet, illus. (p. 977)
Taylor, Chet, illus. see Branson, Terri.
Taylor, Chet, illus. see Goodspeed, Judy.
Taylor, Chet, illus. see Gorgas, Paula Blais.
Taylor, Chloë. Cute As a Button. Zhang, Nancy, illus. (p. 396)
—Knot Too Shabby! Zhang, Nancy, illus. (p. 965)
Taylor, Chloe. Lights, Camera, Fashion! Zhang, Nancy, illus. (p. 1016)
—On Pins & Needles. Christy, Jana & Zhang, Nancy, illus. (p. 1289)
—Ready to Wear. Christy, Jana & Zhang, Nancy, illus. (p. 1448)
—Stitches & Stones. Zhang, Nancy, illus. (p. 1651)
Taylor, Chloë. Swatch Out! Zhang, Nancy, illus. (p. 1689)
—Tangled Thread. Zhang, Nancy, illus. (p. 1705)
Taylor, Chris, jt. auth. see Greenwood, Carmel.
Taylor, Christine. Red Riding Hood & the Toad. (p. 1454)
Taylor, Christy Lee, jt. auth. see Bowman, Crystal.
Taylor, Clif. Snowflake. Whitmire, Anna, illus. (p. 1600)
Taylor, Clifford. Taylor's Tales. (p. 1708)
Taylor, Clive, illus. see Eggleton, Jill.
Taylor, Colin, et al. Plains Indians. (p. 1366)
Taylor, Cora. Champlain & Cartier (p. 289)
—Finding Melissa (p. 588)
—Matthew (p. 1109)
—On Wings of Evil (p. 1292)
Taylor, Corey. House of Gold & Bones. Hahn, Sierra, ed. (p. 803)
Taylor, Dahl. Legend of the Three Trees (p. 989)
Taylor, Dale B. Biomedical Foundations of Music as Therapy. (p. 189)
Taylor, Damon J. Aprende de las Emociones con la Biblia. (p. 93)
Taylor, Dan, illus. see Shields, Gillian.
Taylor, Dan, jt. auth. see Harper, E. T.
Taylor, Darlene. Thank You Notes from Grandma. (p. 1725)
Taylor, David. Sony A77: The Expanded Guide. (p. 1613)
Taylor, David A. Eternal Vision: Seeing Life from Heaven's Perspective. (p. 539)
Taylor, David A., illus. see McCorkle, Barbara.
Taylor, David W., illus. see Redmond, Stephanie L.
Taylor, Debbie A. Sweet Music in Harlem. Morrison, Frank, illus. (p. 1690)
Taylor, Debbie & Morrison, Frank. Sweet Music in Harlem (p. 1690)
Taylor, Dereen. Alien Adventure: Peek Inside the Pop-Up Windows! Hutchinson, Tim, illus. (p. 40)
—Celts. (p. 286)
—Dragon's Magic Wish. Hutchinson, Tim, illus. (p. 479)
—Fairy Midnight Surprise Party. Stone, Lyn, illus. (p. 563)
—Journey to the World of the Dinosaurs: Peek Inside the Pop-Up Windows! Kavanagh, Peter, illus. (p. 929)
—Knight's First Tournament. Kavanagh, Peter, illus. (p. 964)
—Lost Treasure of the Jungle Temple: Peek Inside the 3D Windows! Hutchinson, Tim, illus. (p. 1057)
—Mermaid's Treasure Hunt. East, Jacqueline, illus. (p. 1128)
—Mystery of the Vampire Boy: Dare You Peek Through the Pop-Up Windows? Spoor, Mike, illus. (p. 1226)
—Nigeria. (p. 1252)
—Paulo & the Football Thieves: Peek Inside the Pop-Up Windows! Hutchinson, Tim, illus. (p. 1331)
—Robo-Pup to the Rescue! Hutchinson, Tim, illus. (p. 1480)
—Rosie Rides to the Rescue: Peek Inside the Pop-Up Windows! Stone, Lyn, illus. (p. 1490)
—Trapped in the Witch's Lair: Peek Inside the Pop-Up Windows! Catchpole, Diana, illus. (p. 1779)
—Vikings. (p. 1842)
Taylor, Derrick & Garnett, Kaila. Jessica & Madison: Being Beautiful. Peters, Rob, illus. (p. 914)
Taylor, Des. Cartoons & Manga. (p. 273)
Taylor, Di. Lost Kitten. Wright, Craig, ed. (p. 1056)
—Moving House. Wright, Craig, ed. (p. 1183)
Taylor, Diane & Tay-Audouard, L. K. Singapore Children's Favorite Stories. (p. 1579)
Taylor, Donna. Riley to the Rescue on the Hudson River. (p. 1472)
Taylor, Dorothy L. Abigail's New Home. Schimmel, Beth, illus. (p. 5)
Taylor, Douglas. Downtown Ducks. Taylor, Catherine, illus. (p. 474)
Taylor, Drew. Night Wanderer: A Graphic Novel. Wyatt, Michael, illus. (p. 1254)
Taylor, Drew Hayden. Night Wanderer: A Native Gothic Novel. (p. 1254)
Taylor, Ed. Dirty Bombers: Terrorism with a Twist. (p. 446)
Taylor, Edgar, tr. see Grimm, Jacob & Grimm, Wilhelm.
Taylor, Edward C. Ted Strong's Motor Car or Fast & Furio. (p. 1712)
Taylor, Eileen. Adventures of Betty Bunratty McNamara, Lisa, illus. (p. 16)
—Adventures of Eddy Moneypenny. McNamara, Lisa, illus. (p. 17)
Taylor, Elaine Kaufman. Taylor's Educational Internet Connections: Webquest Directory for Teachers, Parents, & Students. (p. 1708)
—Taylor's Educational Internet Connections: Webquest Interactive Educational Internet Site Directory. (p. 1708)
—Taylor's Educational Internet Connections Interactive Media Set: Webquest Interactive Educational Directory. (p. 1708)
Taylor, Eleanor, illus. see Almond, David.
Taylor, Eleanor, illus. see Durango, Julia.
Taylor, Eleanor, illus. see Nichols, Grace.
Taylor, Eleanor, illus. see Thompson, Emma.
Taylor, Eleonor, illus. see Thompson, Emma, et al.
Taylor, Emma. Adventures of Bunting, the Turtle. (p. 17)
Taylor, Erin, illus. see Evans, Rosemary R.
Taylor, Erin, illus. see Lee, Bonnie.
Taylor, G. P. First Escape. (p. 594)
—Great Mogul Diamond. (p. 717)
—Hechicero de las Sombras. Attrache, Ismael, tr. (p. 761)
—Secret of Indigo Moon. (p. 1542)
—Shadowmancer: What Can Stand Against an Ancient Evil... (p. 1558)
—Shadowmancer Returns: The Curse of Salamander Street. (p. 1558)
—Tizzle Sisters & Erik. (p. 1758)
—Wormwood. (p. 1961)
Taylor, Gaylia. George Crum & the Saratoga Chip Morrison, Frank, illus. (p. 663)
Taylor, Gaylia & Morrison, Frank. George Crum & the Saratoga Chip. (p. 663)
Taylor, Geoff, illus. see Paver, Michelle & Paver, Michelle.
Taylor, Geoff, illus. see Paver, Michelle.
Taylor, Gerad, illus. see Maier, Paul L.
Taylor, "Grandma" Mary. Randy Grows a Garden for Julia. Lawson, Keri, photos by. (p. 1438)
Taylor, Greg. Killer Pizza. (p. 956)
—Killer Pizza: the Slice. (p. 956)
Taylor, Gregg. Red Panda: Mask of the Red Panda: Mask of the Red Panda. (p. 1454)
Taylor, Gwen. Exploring Idaho from A to Z. Harvey, Robin, illus. (p. 552)
Taylor, Gypsy, illus. see Harmer, Wendy.
Taylor Harris Photography, photos by see Harris, Patricia Taylor.
Taylor, Heather. Love Is a Circle. (p. 1060)
Taylor, Helen. Emu Can't Fly. Gilles-Gray, Carolyn, illus. (p. 522)
Taylor, Helen & Harris, Andrew J. R., eds. Learning & Teaching Mathematics 0-8. (p. 985)
Taylor, Helen L. Little Pilgrim's Progress: From John Bunyan's Classic. (p. 1033)
Taylor, Ina. Respect: Citizenship Through RE & PSE. (p. 1463)
Taylor, Ina, ed. Christianity. (p. 312)
Taylor, Isaac. Scenes in America, for the Amusement & Instruction of Little Tarry-at-Home Travellers by the Rev Isaac Taylor. (p. 1521)
Taylor, Jaclyn. When Jesus Sneezes. (p. 1903)
Taylor, Jacqui. African ABC. (p. 26)
—Baobab Is Big: And Other Verses from Africa. (p. 137)
Taylor, Jacqui, illus. see Clanahan, Mary.
Taylor, Jane. Imperial Istanbul: A Traveller's Guide - Includes Iznik, Bursa & Edirne. (p. 862)
—Twinkle, Twinkle, Little Star. Holm, Sharon Lane, illus. (p. 1802)
Taylor, Jane, jt. auth. see Reasoner, Charles.
Taylor, Jane & MacKenzie, Carine. Jesus: The Promised Child. (p. 914)
—Saul: The Miracle on the Road. Apps, Fred, illus. (p. 1516)
Taylor, Jane & Macleod, Una. God Made Animals. Matthews, Derek, illus. (p. 689)
—God Made Me. Matthews, Derek, illus. (p. 689)
Taylor, Jane, et al. God Made Colours. (p. 689)
—God Made the World. (p. 690)
Taylor, Janelle. How the Zebra Got Its Stripes. Avrett, Judy, illus. (p. 813)
Taylor, Janet. Timmy's Trip to Yellowstone. (p. 1755)
Taylor, Janet B. Dim. (p. 440)
Taylor, Janet E. Sleeping with the Enemy. (p. 1589)
Taylor, Je'. Animal Dance. (p. 77)
Taylor, Jeannie. You Wouldnt Love Me If You Kne. (p. 1976)
Taylor, Jeannie St. John, illus. see Mehl, Ron, et al.
Taylor, Jeannie St. John & St. John Taylor, Jeannie. Out at Home: A Novel. (p. 1310)
Taylor, Jeff. Friendlationships: From Like, to Like Like, to Love in Your Twenties. (p. 637)
Taylor, Jennifer. Dragon Sitter. (p. 478)
Taylor, Jennifer, ed. see Abrams, Majella.
Taylor, Jennifer, ed. see Allen, Margaret.
Taylor, Jennifer, ed. see Allen, Molly.
Taylor, Jennifer, ed. see Callella, Trisha.
Taylor, Jennifer, illus. see Akerson, Julie Chicos.
Taylor, Jennifer, illus. see Appelbaum, Susannah.
Taylor, Jennifer, illus. see Clark, Abbie.
Taylor, Jennifer, illus. see Peters, Lisa Westberg.
Taylor, Jennifer, illus. see Rickman, Jeanie Parker.
Taylor, Jennifer Louise, illus. see Johnson, Doris M.
Taylor, Jenny, illus. see McDougall, Jill.
Taylor, Jeremy. Strength of Love. (p. 1667)
Taylor, Jill, illus. see Hopkins, Suzette.
Taylor, Jo. Back to School Sticker Paper Dolls. (p. 130)
Taylor, Jo-Ann. Alchemist's Secret. (p. 35)
Taylor, Joanne. Making Room. Rankin, Peter, illus. (p. 1082)
—There You Are. (p. 1730)
Taylor, Jody. Hidden Pictures 2008. (p. 776)
Taylor, John. Greek to GCSE (p. 721)
Taylor, John B. Study Guide: Used with ... Taylor-Economics. (p. 1670)
Taylor, Jon. Tower of Babel. (p. 1773)
Taylor, Jonathan, illus. see Ham, Ken.
Taylor, Joseph. Allison Investigates. (p. 47)
Taylor, Josephine, illus. see Marks, William C.
Taylor, Josh, illus. see Blocker, Adam P.
Taylor, Judy. Hidden Pictures 2005. (p. 776)
Taylor, Julia V. Body Image Workbook for Teens: Activities to Help Girls Develop a Healthy Body Image in an Image-Obsessed World. (p. 207)
Taylor, Julia V., jt. auth. see Lohmann, Raychelle Cassada.
Taylor, Julianne. Girl Called Ugly. (p. 678)
Taylor, Julie & Brown, Marion, eds. Bratz. (p. 223)
Taylor, Julie & Mayer, Kirsten, eds. Open Season. (p. 1299)
Taylor, K. C. Any Possible Outcome: A Book of Urban Tales. (p. 90)
—Easier Without. (p. 498)
Taylor, K. L. Poetry for Children: Poems Too Make You Smile. (p. 1376)
Taylor, Kara. Deadly Little Sins. (p. 417)
—Prep School Confidential. (p. 1395)
—Wicked Little Secrets. (p. 1927)
Taylor, Kathleen. Eddie & Bingo: A Friendship Tale. Taylor, Kathleen, illus. (p. 503)
Taylor, Kay Lovelace. Princess Aisha & the Cave of Judgment. Rhine, Karen C., illus. (p. 1402)
Taylor, Keary. Bane. (p. 136)
Taylor, Kelda. Look at My Feet Feet Go! (p. 1048)
Taylor, Kenneth N. Classic Bible Storybook. (p. 327)
—Family-Time Bible in Pictures. (p. 569)
—Historias de la Biblia Al Dia. (p. 782)
—Jesus in Pictures for Little Eyes. Spenceley, Annabel, illus. (p. 915)
—New Bible in Pictures for Little Eyes. Spenceley, Annabel, illus. (p. 1243)
—Nueva Biblia en Cuadros para Niños (p. 1270)
—Picture Bible for Little People. (p. 1355)
—Vida de Jesus para Ninos Pequenos (p. 1840)
Taylor Kent, Derek. Perro en Sombrero: A Bilingual Doggy Tale. Henry, Jed, illus. (p. 1344)
Taylor, Keren. Nothing Held Back: Truth & Fiction from WriteGirl. (p. 1268)
Taylor, Keren, jt. ed. see Reber, Deborah.
Taylor, Keren, ed. Pieces of Me: The Voices of WriteGirl. (p. 1356)
Taylor, Keren, Sr. Listen to Me: Shared Secrets from WriteGirl. (p. 1022)
Taylor, Kim. Accion. (p. 8)
—Action. (p. 10)
—Cissy Funk. (p. 322)
—Cold. (p. 338)
—Demasiado Pequeno para Verlo. (p. 425)
—Flight. (p. 604)
—Heat. (p. 760)
—Light. (p. 1014)
—Pattern. (p. 1329)
—Structure. (p. 1668)
—Water. (p. 1862)
Taylor, Kristen Fitz & McDonald, Cheryl. Danceland: Fun Songs & Activities to Improve Sensory Skills. (p. 402)
Taylor, Kristen Michelle, illus. see Mbonu, Ngozi Elizabeth.
Taylor, Kyle. Friends That Care Always Share. (p. 639)
Taylor, L. D. Motive Games. (p. 1179)
Taylor, Lacy. Public Speaking Student Activity Book. Matthews, Douglas L., ed. (p. 1414)
Taylor, Laini. Blackbringer. (p. 197)
—Daughter of Smoke & Bone. (p. 409)
—Daughter of Smoke & Bone Trilogy Hardcover Gift Set. (p. 409)
—Days of Blood & Starlight. (p. 415)
—Lips Touch: Three Times. Di Bartolo, Jim, illus. (p. 1021)
Taylor, Lauren. My Busy Stomach. (p. 1200)
—My Clever Brain. (p. 1200)
—My Lively Heart & Lungs. (p. 1213)
—My Strong Bones. (p. 1219)
Taylor, Lauren, ed. see Head, Honor.
Taylor, Lauren, ed. see Mist, Rosalind.
Taylor, Lauren, ed. see Rooney, Anne.
Taylor, LaVonne, ed. see Chambers, Vickie.
Taylor, Lawrie, illus. see Andrews, Jackie.
Taylor, Leatrice. Thank God for Daddy! (p. 1725)
Taylor, Leighton. Anemone Fish. (p. 73)
—Great White Sharks. (p. 719)
Taylor, Lenette. Brutus the French Mastiff: The Case of the Missing Sock. (p. 233)
Taylor, Lillian Webb. Santa's Musical Elves. (p. 1513)
Taylor, Linda. My Dog Is Barking: A Story from Nigeria. (p. 1202)
—My Dog Is Barking. (p. 1202)
Taylor, Linda, illus. see Johnson, Jann A.
Taylor, Linda Colquitt. LSU Alphabet Book. (p. 1061)
—New Orleans Saints Alphabet Book. (p. 1246)
Taylor, Lisa. Face to Face in the Mirror. (p. 560)
Taylor, Lori. Squirrelly Celebration. (p. 1637)
—Squirrelly Tale. (p. 1637)
—What to Do When Your Hoof Turns Blue!!! Taylor, Lori, illus. (p. 1894)
Taylor, Margaret. Christmas Card Angel. (p. 313)
Taylor, Mari Jo. Not One of the Robot Children. (p. 1267)
Taylor, Maria, illus. see Pipe, Jim.
Taylor, Marian. Harriet Tubman. (p. 750)
Taylor, Marianne. What If... Humans Were Like Animals? Moran, Paul, illus. (p. 1887)
—What If Humans Were Like Animals? The Amazing & Disgusting Life You'd Lead As a Snake, Bird, Fish, or Worm! (p. 1887)
Taylor, Marilyn. 17 Martin Street. (p. 1995)
Taylor, Marjorie, illus. see Bankier, William.
Taylor, Marjorie, illus. see Bricker, Sandra D.
Taylor, Marjorie, illus. see Cruise, Robin.
Taylor, Marjorie, illus. see Skip Press Staff.
Taylor, Mark. Henry Explores the Jungle. Booth, Graham, illus. (p. 768)
—Henry the Castaway. Booth, Graham, illus. (p. 768)
—Henry the Explorer. Booth, Graham, illus. (p. 768)
Taylor, Mark, illus. see Younge, Cathy.
Taylor, Mark A. Breakfast with Jesus. (p. 225)
—One Tiny Baby. Burroughs, Scott, illus. (p. 1297)
Taylor, Mark D. Complete Book of Bible Basics. (p. 352)
Taylor, Martin. Lost Treasure of the Sunken City. Catling, Andy, illus. (p. 1057)
Taylor, Mary, jt. auth. see Ginsburg, Lynn.
Taylor, Mary Ann. Spies: A Gander's Cove Mystery. Casteel, Kay, illus. (p. 1627)
—Traitors: A Gander's Cove Mystery. Casteel, Kay, illus. (p. 1777)
Taylor, Mary Ellen. Maniac Magee: An Instructional Guide for Literature (p. 1087)
Taylor, Mary J. God's Miracle Process: Trauma Transformed into Treasures (p. 691)
Taylor, Maurie. French Word Games: 24 Word Games & Puzzles for Beginning & Intermediate Students. (p. 636)
Taylor, Maxwell. Fun with Letters. Mshindu, illus. (p. 648)
Taylor, Melissa Utz. Sneaky Snake. (p. 1597)
Taylor, Michael. Devil's Hideaway. (p. 432)
Taylor, Michael, tr. see Jonquet, Francois.
Taylor, Michael W. Tar Heels: How North Carolinians Got Their Nickname. (p. 1706)
Taylor, Michaelle. Singing Across the Old North State: Story-Songs of North Carolina. (p. 1579)
Taylor, Michelle A. If Bees Rode Shiny Bicycles. (p. 852)
Taylor, Michelle M. What's Happily Ever after, Anyway? (p. 1897)

Taylor, Mike, illus. see Binns, Tristan Boyer.
Taylor, Mike, illus. see West, David.
Taylor, Mike, photos by see Hodgkins, Fran.
Taylor, Mildred D. Friendship. (p. 639)
—Land. (p. 973)
—Lloro por la Tierra. (p. 1043)
—Roll of Thunder, Hear My Cry. (p. 1485)
—Roll of Thunder, Hear My Cry (Puffin Modern Classics) (p. 1485)
—Song of the Trees. (p. 1611)
—Song of the Trees. Pinkney, Jerry, illus. (p. 1611)
Taylor, Minnie, ed. see Wright, Chris.
Taylor, Mitch. Camburin Seed. (p. 256)
Taylor, Molly. Crazy Cool Windows. (p. 377)
—Special Shoes. (p. 1623)
Taylor, Myonna. Show & Tell. Phillips, Hope Ann, illus. (p. 1570)
Taylor, Nate, illus. see Rothfuss, Patrick.
Taylor, Nicole, illus. see Church, Anna.
Taylor, Nicole, jt. auth. see Ma, Karin.
Taylor, Non, illus. see Gilpin, Rebecca & Atkinson, Catherine.
Taylor, O. H. Judge Not? Am I My Brother's Keeper? (p. 930)
—One Flock: Who Is the Church? (p. 1295)
Taylor, Pat, jt. auth. see Shuter, Jane.
Taylor, Pat Eytcheson. Scamper Tangles with Christmas. (p. 1519)
Taylor, Paul. Fossil. Dorling Kindersley Publishing Staff, ed. (p. 623)
Taylor, Paul S. Great Dinosaur Mystery & the Bible. (p. 715)
Taylor, Paula. Mother's Secrets. (p. 1179)
—Run Farrah Run: Detecting, Ditching & Dealing with Dating Dopes. von Seeburg, Kate, ed. (p. 1496)
Taylor, Pearl Fleming. Snowbird Weenie (p. 1600)
Taylor, Peter Lane & Nicola, Christos. Secret of Priest's Grotto: A Holocaust Survival Story. (p. 1542)
Taylor, Phillip J. Brian, His Granddad & the Cup of Ages. (p. 226)
Taylor, Qiana. Jordyen & Lionnel the Seal. (p. 925)
Taylor, R., illus. see Leslie, Emma.
Taylor, R. W. Curiosity of Sadie: A Collection of 35 Individual Stories about an Individual Little Girl & Her Puppy. (p. 392)
Taylor, Richard A. Ships of Children. (p. 1567)
Taylor, Richard B. Chispita Service Dog Extraordinaire: Volume 2. the Pack Trip. (p. 308)
—Chispita Service Dog Extraordinaire: Volume 3. Alaskan Cruise. (p. 308)
—Chispita Service Dog Extraordinaire: Volume 5. Indian Country. (p. 308)
—Chispita Service Dog Extraordinaire: Volume 4. Alaskan Land Cruise. (p. 308)
—Chispita Service Dog Extraordinaire Volume 1: Introduction. (p. 308)
Taylor, Richard Dean. Gonna Sing My Song. (p. 697)
Taylor, Robert. Adventures of BooBear the Bountiful: A Honeyfly's Won-Dream. (p. 16)
—Strokes. (p. 1668)
Taylor, Robert & Kling, Andrew A. Ballistics. (p. 135)
Taylor, Robert & MacKay, Jennifer. Profiling. (p. 1410)
Taylor, Robert J., jt. auth. see Taylor, Roger.
Taylor, Robin. Shy Jenny & Her Special Ears. (p. 1572)
Taylor, Rodney L. & Choy, Howard. Illustrated Encyclopedia of Confucianism (p. 857)
Taylor, Roger. Atlas Visual de las Aves. (p. 113)
—Seven Silly Stories. (p. 1554)
Taylor, Roger, illus. see MacKenzie, Carine.
Taylor, Roger & Taylor, Robert J. Move on Maths Ages 9-11: 50+ Flexible Maths Activities (p. 1183)
Taylor, Ronald J. Desert Wildflowers of North America. Ort, Kathleen, ed. (p. 429)
—Sagebrush Country: A Wildflower Sanctuary. Ort, Kathleen, ed. (p. 1502)
Taylor, Ronald J. & Douglas, George. Mountain Plants of the Pacific Northwest: A Field Guide to Washington, Western British Columbia, & Southeastern Alaska. Ort, Kathleen, ed. (p. 1181)
Taylor, Rose. Johnny's Great Adventure (p. 924)
Taylor, Rosemary. Eddie's Rocket Adventure. (p. 504)
Taylor, Roy. Matilda's Magic Wand: Dreamland Adventure. (p. 1109)
Taylor, Ruby. Priceless Project Presents Confidence to Greatness for Teenage Girls. (p. 1398)
Taylor, S. S. Expeditioners & the Secret of King Triton's Lair. Roy, Katherine, illus. (p. 548)
—Expeditioners & the Treasure of Drowned Man's Canyon. Roy, Katherine, illus. (p. 548)
Taylor, Sally. Money Talks: The Ultimate Crash Course on Money for Young Adults. (p. 1164)
—On My Own: The Ultimate How-to Guide for Young Adults. (p. 1289)
Taylor, Sally, illus. see Gregory, Philippa.
Taylor, Sarah. Alison Learns to Deal with Her Dad's Ptsd. (p. 41)
—Howie the Wonder Pug. (p. 823)
—Howie the Wonder Pug Learns the Importance of Sharing. (p. 823)
Taylor, Saranne. Ancient Homes. Chiacchiera, Moreno & Todd, Michelle, illus. (p. 69)
—Animal Homes. Chiacchiera, Moreno & Todd, Michelle, illus. (p. 78)
—Futuristic Homes. Chiacchiera, Moreno & Todd, Michelle, illus. (p. 651)
—Green Homes. Chiacchiera, Moreno & Todd, Michelle, illus. (p. 722)
Taylor, Scott L. Opportunity in Every Problem. (p. 1300)
Taylor, Sean. Crocodiles Are the Best Animals of All! Shaw, Hannah, illus. (p. 384)
—Goal! Vilela, Caio, photos by. (p. 687)
—Hoot Owl, Master of Disguise. Jullien, Jean, illus. (p. 796)
—Huck Runs Amuck! Reynolds, Peter, illus. (p. 824)
—Mojo & Weeza & the New Hat: Band 04/Blue. Mosedale, Julian, illus. (p. 1160)
—Small Bad Wolf. Lewis, Jan, illus. (p. 1591)
—That's What Makes a Hippopotamus Smile. Cardon, Laurent, illus. (p. 1727)
—When a Monster Is Born. Sharratt, Nick, illus. (p. 1901)
—World Champion of Staying Awake. Liao, Jimmy, illus. (p. 1954)
Taylor, Sean, tr. see Vilela, Caio.
Taylor, Sean & Quarto Generic Staff. Grizzly Bear with the Frizzly Hair. Shaw, Hannah, illus. (p. 724)
—Waste of Good Paper. (p. 1860)
—We Have Lift-Off! Shaw, Hannah, illus. (p. 1867)
Taylor, Sean & Shaw, Hannah. Who Ate Auntie Iris. (p. 1914)
Taylor, Sean, et al. Grizzly Bear with the Frizzly Hair. Shaw, Hannah, illus. (p. 724)
—We Have Lift-Off! Shaw, Hannah, illus. (p. 1867)
—Who Ate Auntie Iris? Shaw, Hannah, illus. (p. 1914)
Taylor, Shane. Magic of Mortals. (p. 1073)
Taylor, Shirley A. Stable Boy. Hall, Wendell E., illus. (p. 1638)
Taylor Sr., Anthony. I Pray. (p. 844)
Taylor, Stephen, illus. see Aubin, Henry T.
Taylor, Stephen, illus. see Helmso, Candy Grant.
Taylor, Stephen, illus. see Morgan, Cliff.
Taylor, Stephen, illus. see Winters, Karl-Lynn.
Taylor, Steve. Fruit Facts. (p. 645)
Taylor, Stuart. Austin & the Lost Kingdom of Atlantis: The Austin Chronicles Volume Iii. (p. 116)
Taylor, Sue, illus. see Olofson, Darrell.
Taylor, Sue, jt. auth. see Green, Teri.
Taylor, Susan. Blast Off! (p. 198)
Taylor, Sydney. All-Of-a-Kind Family Uptown. (p. 45)
—Ella of All-Of-a-Kind Family. (p. 514)
Taylor, T. M. Players: The Novel (p. 1372)
Taylor, Terry. Clay Play! (p. 330)
—Sand Play! 20+ SANDsational Ideas. (p. 1510)
—Tim the Young Magician: Tim Discovers Magic. (p. 1750)
Taylor, Theodore. Boy Who Could Fly Without a Motor. (p. 219)
—Cay. (p. 282)
—Maldonado Miracle. (p. 1083)
—Odyssey of Ben O'Neal. (p. 1279)
—Teetoncey. (p. 1715)
—Teetoncey & Ben O'Neal. (p. 1715)
—Timothy of the Cay. (p. 1755)
—Weirdo. (p. 1873)
Taylor, Theodore, jt. auth. see Taylor, Theodore.
Taylor, Theodore & Taylor, Theodore. Billy the Kid: A Novel. (p. 187)
—Bomb. (p. 208)
—Cay. (p. 282)
—cayo. (p. 282)
—Ice Drift. (p. 850)
—Sniper. (p. 1598)
—Weirdo. (p. 1873)
Taylor, Theodore, III, illus. see Hill, Laban Carrick.
Taylor, Thomas. Haunters. (p. 754)
—Jack's Tractor. Kelly, John, illus. (p. 904)
—Loudest Roar. (p. 1057)
—Pets You Get. Reynolds, Adrian, illus. (p. 1348)
—Superstar Coach. (p. 1684)
Taylor, Thomas, illus. see Cleary, Beverly.
Taylor, Thomas, illus. see d'Lacey, Chris.
Taylor, Thomas, illus. see Reader's Digest Editors, ed.
Taylor, Thomas, illus. see Stewart, Dorothy M.
Taylor, Thomas W. Monhegan Island & Its Lighthouse. (p. 1164)
Taylor, Tijuana. Adventures of Buddy Blue Bug & the Critters of the Gospel. (p. 17)
Taylor, Tom. Deep: The Vanishing Island Edwards, Gary, ed. (p. 422)
Taylor, Tom, jt. auth. see Zimmerman, Tom and Kat.
Taylor, Trace. Afghanistan. (p. 26)
—African Lions. (p. 27)
—Antarctic Penguins. (p. 88)
—Ants. (p. 90)
—Asian Elephants. (p. 106)
—B. (p. 122)
—Baseball. Taylor, Trace, illus. (p. 140)
—Basketball. Taylor, Trace, illus. (p. 143)
—Beetles. (p. 158)
—Bikes. Taylor, Trace, illus. (p. 185)
—C. (p. 249)
—Camels of Asia. (p. 256)
—Cats. (p. 280)
—China. (p. 306)
—D. (p. 397)
—Dogs. (p. 462)
—Dogtown #4. (p. 463)
—Dogtown #5. (p. 463)
—Dogtown #6. (p. 463)
—Dogtown Diner. (p. 463)
—Dogtown Diner. Taylor, Trace, illus. (p. 463)
—Dogtown's Got Talent. (p. 463)
—Earth Movers. Taylor, Trace, illus. (p. 496)
—F. (p. 559)
—Flying over Dogtown. (p. 610)
—G. (p. 651)
—H. (p. 734)
—Hair Day in Dogtown. (p. 736)
—Happy Birthday Dogtown. (p. 744)
—India. (p. 870)
—J. (p. 901)
—Jumping Spiders. Taylor, Trace, illus. (p. 934)
—K. (p. 941)
—Kenya. (p. 949)
—Komodo Dragons. (p. 966)
—L. (p. 969)
—Lions of Africa. Taylor, Trace, illus. (p. 1021)
—M. (p. 1067)
—Mexico. (p. 1131)
—N. (p. 1227)
—Nile Crocodiles. Taylor, Trace, illus. (p. 1255)
—One World Single Copy Set. (p. 1297)
—Orangutan. (p. 1302)
—P. (p. 1316)
—R. (p. 1429)
—S. (p. 1499)
—Soccer. Taylor, Trace, illus. (p. 1603)
—South Africa. (p. 1616)
—T. (p. 1693)
—Tigers of Asia. (p. 1749)
—Tree Truck. Taylor, Trace, illus. (p. 1784)
—Vietnam. (p. 1841)
—Wasps. (p. 1860)
—Wedding Day in Dogtown. (p. 1870)
—Wheels. Taylor, Trace, illus. (p. 1900)
—Who Took That Dog? Taylor, Trace, illus. (p. 1917)
—Work Trucks. (p. 1952)
—You Think You Know Giraffes. Taylor, Trace, illus. (p. 1976)
—You Think You Know Hippos. Taylor, Trace, illus. (p. 1976)
—You Think You Know Zebras. (p. 1976)
Taylor, Trace, illus. see Pitt, Marilyn, et al.
Taylor, Trace, illus. see Sánchez, Lucía M.
Taylor, Trace, jt. auth. see Lynch, Michelle.
Taylor, Trace, jt. auth. see Sánchez, Lucía M.
Taylor, Trace & Lynch, Michelle. Cobras. (p. 337)
Taylor, Trace & Rupp, Kristina. Tarantulas (English) (p. 1706)
Taylor, Trace & SáNchez, LucíA M. Afghanistan. (p. 26)
Taylor, Trace & Sánchez, Lucía M. Águilas Calvas. (p. 30)
—Avispas. (p. 120)
Taylor, Trace & Sanchez, Lucia M. Avispas (Wasps) (p. 120)
Taylor, Trace & Sánchez, Lucía M. Ballenas: Whales. (p. 134)
Taylor, Trace & Sanchez, Lucia M. Ballenas (Whales) (p. 134)
Taylor, Trace & SáNchez, LucíA M. BáSquetbol (Basketball) (p. 143)
—Bélsbol (Baseball) (p. 161)
—China. (p. 306)
Taylor, Trace & Sánchez, Lucía M. Delfines: Dolphins. (p. 424)
Taylor, Trace & Sanchez, Lucia M. Delfines (Dolphins) (p. 424)
—En el bosque (in the Woods) (p. 522)
—En el Parque: At the Park. (p. 522)
—En el parque (at the Park) (p. 522)
—En el zoológico (at the Zoo) (p. 522)
Taylor, Trace & Sánchez, Lucía M. Escarabajos: Beetles. (p. 535)
Taylor, Trace & Sanchez, Lucia M. Escarabajos (Beetles) (p. 535)
—Focas (Seals) (p. 610)
—Hormigas (Ants) (p. 798)
Taylor, Trace & SáNchez, LucíA M. India. (p. 870)
—Kenya. (p. 949)
—Leones Africanos (African Lions) (p. 992)
Taylor, Trace & Sanchez, Lucia M. Mantis religiosa (Praying Mantis) (p. 1088)
Taylor, Trace & SáNchez, LucíA M. Mexico. (p. 1131)
Taylor, Trace & Sánchez, Lucía M. Osos Pardos. (p. 1306)
—PingüInos de la AntáRtida: Antarctic Penguins. (p. 1359)
—Pumas. (p. 1416)
Taylor, Trace & SáNchez, LucíA M. South Africa. (p. 1616)
Taylor, Trace & Sanchez, Lucia M. Tarántulas (Tarantulas) (p. 1706)
—Tiburones (Sharks) (p. 1747)
—Vamos de acampada (Let's Go Camping) (p. 1831)
Taylor, Trace & SáNchez, LucíA M. Viet Nam. (p. 1841)
Taylor, Trace & Sánchez, Lucía M. Vietnam. (p. 1841)
Taylor, Trace & Zorzi, Gina. This Is a Desert. (p. 1735)
—This Is a Forest. (p. 1735)
—This Is a Prairie. (p. 1735)
—This Is a Rainforest. (p. 1735)
—This Is a Wetland. (p. 1735)
—This Is an Ocean. (p. 1735)
Taylor, Trace, et al. En el Bosque. (p. 522)
—En el Lago. (p. 522)
—In the Ocean. Reese, Jonathan, illus. (p. 867)
—This Is a Prairie. (p. 1735)
—This Is a Savannah. Washington, Joi, illus. (p. 1735)
—This Is an Ocean. Washington, Joi, illus. (p. 1735)
—Vamos de Acampada: Let's Go Camping. (p. 1831)
Taylor, Tracie. Find Your Shoes, John Blane. (p. 587)
Taylor, Tracy Carol. Tale of Two Teeth. (p. 1701)
Taylor, Troy. Creepy Libraries. (p. 381)
Taylor, Troy, jt. auth. see Lunis, Natalie.
Taylor, Vacen. Starchild: The City of Souls. (p. 1642)
Taylor, Val Paul, illus. see Gourley, Catherine.
Taylor, Vernon T. Why Do Dogs Bark? (p. 1923)
Taylor, Victoria. Caitlin's Wish. (p. 252)
Taylor, Victoria, jt. auth. see Dorling Kindersley Publishing Staff.
Taylor, Victoria & Dolan, Hannah. LEGO Kingdoms: Defend the Castle. (p. 990)
Taylor, Victoria & Dorling Kindersley Publishing Staff. Defend the Castle. (p. 423)
Taylor, Victoria, et al. Brickbeard's Treasure. (p. 227)
Taylor, Vincent. Cornbread Has a Bad Habit. (p. 367)
—Cornbread Runs for Class President Griffin, Kasana & Griggs, Charles, eds. (p. 367)
Taylor, W. Y. Baby Goes to Market. (p. 126)
—I'm Not too Little to Help the Earth. (p. 859)
—This Little Piggy Goes Green. (p. 1737)
Taylor, Wanda. Birchtown & the Black Loyalists (p. 190)
Taylor, William. At the Big Red Rooster. (p. 110)
—Land of Milk & Honey. (p. 973)
—Scarface & the Angel. (p. 1520)
Taylor, Winford, jt. auth. see Taylor, Carol.
Taylor, Yuval, ed. Growing up in Slavery: Stories of Young Slaves as Told by Themselves. (p. 726)
—Growing up in Slavery: Stories of Young Slaves as Told by Themselves. Judge, Kathleen, illus. (p. 726)
Taylor, Yvonne. Hartlie: The Streak. Taylor, Yvonne, ed. (p. 751)
Taylor, Zachary. David. (p. 410)
Taylor-Bonds, Darlena. I Am Not Chocolate, It Melt's. (p. 833)
Taylor-Butler, Christine. Ah-Choo. Koeller, Carol, illus. (p. 30)
—Amphibians. (p. 65)
—Bill of Rights: American History. (p. 186)
—Bill of Rights. (p. 186)
—Circulatory System. (p. 322)
—Congress of the United States. (p. 357)
—Constitution. (p. 359)
—Constitution of the United States. (p. 359)
—Digestive System. (p. 438)
—Earth. (p. 495)
—Experiment with Magnets. (p. 549)
—Experiment with Solar Energy. (p. 549)
—Experiments with Liquids (p. 549)
—Experiments with Magnets & Metals (p. 549)
—Experiments with Plants (p. 549)
—Experiments with Plants. (p. 549)
—Experiments with Rocks (p. 549)
—Experiments with Soil (p. 549)
—Experiments with Solids, Liquids, & Gases. (p. 549)
—Explorers of North America. (p. 551)
—Fish. (p. 598)
—Food Safety. (p. 614)
—Hawaii. (p. 755)
—Hydrology: The Study of Water. (p. 831)
—I Am Smart. Borlasca, Hector, illus. (p. 833)
—Insects & Spiders. (p. 876)
—Jupiter. (p. 937)
—Kansas. (p. 943)
—Mercury. (p. 1127)
—Meteorology: The Study of Weather. (p. 1130)
—Michelle Obama. (p. 1135)
—Missouri. (p. 1154)
—Missouri River. (p. 1154)
—Moon. (p. 1171)
—My Science Investigations (p. 1218)
—Nervous System. (p. 1241)
—Ohio. (p. 1281)
—Planet Earth. (p. 1367)
—Planet Uranus. (p. 1368)
—Planet Venus. (p. 1368)
—Pluto: Dwarf Planet. (p. 1374)
—Presidency. (p. 1396)
—Respiratory System. (p. 1463)
—Respitory System. (p. 1463)
—Rosa Parks. (p. 1488)
—Sacred Mountain: Everest. (p. 1500)
—Saturn. (p. 1515)
—Step-by-Step. Miller, Susan, illus. (p. 1647)
—Sun. (p. 1675)
—Super Cool Science Experiments: Sound. (p. 1679)
—Super Cool Science Experiments: Magnets. (p. 1679)
—Super Cool Science Experiments: Solar Energy. (p. 1679)
—Supreme Court. (p. 1684)
—Think Like a Scientist in the Gym. (p. 1734)
—Thurgood Marshall. (p. 1746)
—Tiny Life in the Air. (p. 1756)
—Tiny Life on Your Body. (p. 1756)
—True Book: Health & the Human Body (p. 1792)
—Understanding Charts & Graphs. (p. 1815)
—Understanding Diagrams. (p. 1815)
—Uranus. (p. 1825)
—Vermont. (p. 1837)
—Water Everywhere! Manning, Maurie, illus. (p. 1862)
—Water Everywhere! Manning, Maurie J., illus. (p. 1862)
—Who Needs Friends? Havice, Susan, illus. (p. 1917)
Taylor-Butler, Christine, jt. auth. see Scholastic, Inc. Staff.
Taylor-Chiarello, Robin. Blue Lobster. Bohart, Lisa, illus. (p. 203)
Taylor-Dill, Judith Nell. I Can Fly! (p. 835)
Taylor-Eades, Elizabeth. McDuffie Gets into Trouble. (p. 1114)
Taylor-Gaines, Lonnetta. Fia & the Butterfly: 7 Stories for Character Education. (p. 583)
Taylor-Gooby, Peter, ed. Ideas & Welfare State Reform in Western Europe. (p. 852)
Taylor-Kielty, Simon, illus. see Walters, Catherine.
Tayts, Alexandra, illus. see Typaldos, Melanie.
Tazewell, Charles. Littlest Angel. (p. 1038)
—Littlest Angel. Micich, Paul, illus. (p. 1038)
—Littlest Angel. Porfirio, Guy, illus. (p. 1038)
Tazewell, Lora A. Jelly Bread & Water Juice. (p. 912)
Tazzyman, David, illus. see Stanton, Andy.
tbd. Disney Palace Pets: Adventure Tales. (p. 452)
Tbd Staff, jt. auth. see Davis, Mo'ne.
Tcachenco, Natalya. Best on the East Mystery & Adventures (p. 171)
Tchana, Katrin Hyman. Changing Woman & Her Sisters: Stories of Goddesses from Around the World. Hyman, Trina Schart, illus. (p. 290)
Tcherevkoff, Michel, illus. see Quinton, Sasha.
Te Loo, Sanne. Pescadito. Te Loo, Sanne, illus. (p. 1345)
Te Papa Press Staff, et al. My New Zealand 123 Book: Learn Counting with Art & Objects from Te Papa. (p. 1216)
—My New Zealand ABC Book: Learn the Alphabet with Art & Objects from Te Papa. (p. 1216)
—My New Zealand Colours Book: Learn Colours with Art & Objects from Te Papa. (p. 1216)
Te Selle, Davis, illus. see Berry, Wendell & Rorer, Abigail.
Te Selle, Davis, illus. see Berry, Wendell.
Tea, Michelle. Girl at the Bottom of the Sea. Verwey, Amanda, illus. (p. 678)
—Mermaid in Chelsea Creek. Polan, Jason, illus. (p. 1128)
Teach, William, retold by. Blackbeard's Pirateworld: Cut-Throats of the Caribbean. (p. 197)
Teacher Created Materials. Early America (p. 493)
—Time for Kids(r) Nonfiction Readers Challenging (p. 1751)
Teacher Created Materials Staff, jt. auth. see Barchers, Suzanne I.
Teacher Created Materials Staff, ed. 20th Century Add-on Pack: Primary Source Readers. (p. 1996)
—Biographies II U. S. & World Leaders: Themed Classroom Readers- (p. 188)
—Biographies III Science Pioneers: Themed Classroom Readers- (p. 188)
—Crash Course: Guide: Active Algebra. (p. 376)
—Earth & Space Science: Add-on Pack. (p. 495)
—Kids Learn! Grade PreK-K. (p. 954)
—Life Science: Themed Classroom Reader Set. (p. 1013)
—Physical Science: Add-on Pack. (p. 1353)
—Physical Science: Themed Classroom Reader Set. (p. 1353)
Teacher Created Resources Staff. America: Come on a Journey of Discovery. (p. 58)

T

—France: Come on a Journey of Discovery. (p. 627)
—India: Come on a Journey of Discovery. (p. 870)
—Japan: Come on a Journey of Discovery. (p. 909)
—Learning to Print Grd K-2. (p. 986)
—Mastering Fifth Grade Skills. (p. 1103)
—Reading Comprehension, Grade 5. (p. 1445)
—Space Guides: Discovering the Solar System. (p. 1619)
—Space Guides - Discovering the Universe: A Galaxy of Mind-Expanding Information! (p. 1619)
—Travel Through - China: Come on a Journey of Discovery. (p. 1780)
—Travel Through - Spain: Come on a Journey of Discovery. (p. 1780)
Teacher Created Resources Staff, jt. auth. see Guckian, Mara Ellen.
Teacher Created Resources Staff, jt. auth. see Morgan, Sally.
Teacher Created Resources Staff, jt. auth. see Petersen, Casey Null.
Teacher Created Resources Staff, jt. auth. see Peterson, Casey Null.
Teacher Created Resources Staff & Collins, Susan. Guide for Using Time Soldiers in the Classroom. (p. 730)
Teacher's Friend Publications Staff, creator. Color & Shape Puzzles. (p. 342)
Teachers Writers Collaborative, ed. Poem As Big As New York City: Little Kids Write about the Big Apple. D'Yans, Masha, illus. (p. 1375)
Teaching Resources Corporation Staff, creator. Number Puzzles. (p. 1271)
Teaching Resources Staff. AlphaTales Interactive E-Storybooks: 26 e-Books with Engaging Interactive Whiteboard Activities for Systematic Alphabet Instruction. (p. 50)
—Phonics Tales! Interactive E-Storybooks: 25 e-Books with Engaging Interactive Whiteboard Activities That Teach Key Phonics Skills. (p. 1352)
—Reading & Math. Cooper, Terry, ed. (p. 1445)
—Summer Express PreK-K. (p. 1674)
—Vocabulary, Grammar, Writing, Reading, Math. (p. 1847)
—Vocabulary - Grammar - Writing - Reading - Math. (p. 1847)
—Vocabulary - Grammer - Writing - Reading - Math. (p. 1847)
Teaching Resources Staff, jt. auth. see Dooley, Virginia.
Teagarden, Janine. Dog Named Opposite. Kennedy, Kelly, illus. (p. 461)
Teagle, Caitlyn, illus. see Spalding, Brenda M.
Teague, David. Henry Cicada's Extraordinary Elktonium Escapade. (p. 767)
Teague, David, jt. auth. see de los Santos, Marisa.
Teague, Deborah Coxwell, jt. auth. see Bishop, Wendy.
Teague, Lauren, tr. see Tao, Teri.
Teague, Mark. Dear Mrs. LaRue: Letters from Obedience School. Teague, Mark, illus. (p. 419)
—Detective LaRue: Letters from the Investigation. Teague, Mark, illus. (p. 431)
—Firehouse! Teague, Mark, illus. (p. 592)
—Funny Farm. Teague, Mark, illus. (p. 649)
—Pigsty. (p. 1358)
—Secret Shortcut. (p. 1543)
—Sky Is Falling! (p. 1586)
—Three Little Pigs & the Somewhat Bad Wolf. (p. 1743)
Teague, Mark, illus. see Rylant, Cynthia.
Teague, Mark, illus. see Verburg, Bonnie.
Teague, Mark, illus. see Yolen, Jane.
Teague, Mark & Scholastic, Inc. Staff. Doom Machine. Teague, Mark, illus. (p. 470)
Teague Meyer, Terry. Optimism. (p. 1301)
—Vo-Tech Track to Success in Information Technology. (p. 1847)
Teague, Monica. Diary of a Teenager in Junior High. (p. 435)
Teague, Patricia. Gilda the Gluten Free Mouse: A Story about Living Gloriously with Celiac Sprue Disease. (p. 676)
Teague Sr., Charles R. Right Way Family Meets Popper (p. 1472)
Teague, Victoria. Dragons, Demons, & Feathers. (p. 479)
Teague, Yanhua, tr. see Tao, Teri.
Teal, Joyce Willard. Clifford's War & A. E. P. (p. 332)
—Learning A, B, C's with Seth. (p. 984)
Teal, Marion. I Like Me. (p. 841)
Teal, Sean F., Sr. Kingdom Foundations. (p. 959)
Teal, Val. Little Woman Wanted Noise. Lawson, Robert, illus. (p. 1038)
Teall, Wayne. Bong the Bouncing Elephant & His Fantastic Friends. (p. 209)
Teare, Nellie. Celia & the Witches. Senkel, Nicholas, illus. (p. 286)
Tearne, Roma. Mosquito. (p. 1176)
Teasdale, J. R. Immediacy. (p. 861)
Teasdale, Nancy, ed. see Carlson, Dale.
Teaster, Gerald Fred. Confederate Steam Torpedo Boat CSS DAVID. (p. 356)
—Spirit up the People: Four Days to the Cowpens. (p. 1629)
Tebalan, Helman, illus. see Menchú, Rigoberta & Liano, Dante.
Tebbetts, Chris, jt. auth. see Papademetriou, Lisa.
Tebbetts, Chris, jt. auth. see Patterson, James.
Tebbetts, Chris, jt. auth. see Probst, Jeff.
Tebbetts, Christopher, jt. auth. see Patterson, James.
Tebbetts, Christopher, jt. auth. see Probst, Jeff.
Tebbit, Jake, illus. see MacKey, Cindy.
Tebbit, Jake, illus. see Odom, Rebecca.
Tebbs, Victoria. Christmas Story. Mitchell, Melanie, illus. (p. 315)
—What Can You See? On Christmas Night. Julian, Russell, illus. (p. 1881)
Tebo, Mary Elizabeth. Angel of God, My Guardian Dear. Slade, Christian, illus. (p. 74)
—Feast Days & Holy Days: Dias Festivos de la Iglesia. Richards, Virginia Helen, illus. (p. 579)
—My First Book about Jesus. Peterson, Mary Joseph, illus. (p. 1205)
Tebow, Tim. Through My Eyes: A Quarterback's Journey (p. 1745)
Tecco, Betsy Dru. Food for Fuel: The Connection Between Food & Physical Activity. (p. 613)
—How to Draw France's Sights & Symbols. (p. 817)
—How to Draw Germany's Sights & Symbols. (p. 817)
—How to Draw Hungary's Sights & Symbols. (p. 817)
—How to Draw Italy's Sights & Symbols. (p. 817)
—How to Draw Japan's Sights & Symbols. (p. 817)
—How to Draw Thailand's Sights & Symbols. (p. 818)
—How to Draw the Life & Times of Grover Cleveland. (p. 819)
—How to Draw the Life & Times of John Quincy Adams. (p. 819)
—How to Draw the United Kingdom's Sights & Symbols. (p. 819)
—Kid's Guide to Drawing the Countries of the World: Set 1 (p. 953)
Techau, Ashlyn, illus. see Midden, Maribeth Grubb.
Technology Education Design Forum Staff, jt. auth. see Stewart, Rhea A.
Teckentrup, Britta. Animal 123. Anderson, Amelia, illus. (p. 76)
—Animal Spots & Stripes. Anderson, Amelia, illus. (p. 79)
—Big & Small. (p. 177)
—Busy Bunny Days: In the Town, on the Farm & at the Port. (p. 246)
—Fast & Slow. (p. 576)
—Fast & Slow Spanish. (p. 576)
—Grande y Pequeno. (p. 707)
—Grumpy Cat. (p. 727)
—Memory Tree. (p. 1126)
—Odd One Out. Teckentrup, Britta, illus. (p. 1278)
—Sleep Tight, Little Bear. (p. 1588)
—Up & Down. Teckentrup, Britta, illus. (p. 1824)
—Where's the Pair? Teckentrup, Britta, illus. (p. 1911)
Teckentrup, Britta, illus. see Fletcher, Corina.
Teckentrup, Britta, illus. see McKinlay, Penny.
Teckentrup, Britta, illus. see Nosy Crow.
Tectum, compiled by. Our Amazing World: Discover cultural sites 1, from the Unesco World Heritage (p. 1307)
Tectum Publishers Staff, compiled by. Our Amazing World: Discover cultural sites 2, from the Unesco World Heritage (p. 1307)
Ted, Hood, Jr., photos by see Dealia, Yancey.
Tedder, Elizabeth. Alphabet & Numbers in a New Way. (p. 49)
—Three Bears. (p. 1741)
Tedder, Kacy Allen. Fly, Sally, Fly: A True Story of Sally's Flight to Freedom. (p. 609)
Tedesco, Ann, jt. auth. see Alimonti, Frederick.
Tedesco, Ann & Alimonti, Frederick. Not Everyone Is Nice: Helping Children Learn Caution with Strangers. DePrince, Erik & Volinski, Jessica, illus. (p. 1267)
Tedesco, Leah/Hollis. Junior Showmanship How to get started in One of the Best Family Sports. (p. 936)
Tedesco, Tina. Stork Dropped Your Here for a Reason. (p. 1655)
Tee, Willie. Winds of Destiny: The Keepers of the Secret. (p. 1936)
Tee, Willie, mem. Winds of Destiny - the Keepers of the Secret. (p. 1936)
Teel, Gina & Mott, A. S. Ghost Stories of Wisconsin (p. 671)
Teel, Julie. Biggest Bear in the World: As Told by Grandpa Kingsford. (p. 185)
Teel, Karen. Robot Rhymes. Teets, Ashley, illus. (p. 1480)
Teel, Linda. Priceless Cup. (p. 1398)
Teen People Magazine Editors. Celebrity Style Guide. (p. 285)
Teen Vogue Staff. Teen Vogue Handbook: An Insider's Guide to Careers in Fashion. (p. 1714)
Teenage Mutant Ninja Turtles, Teenage Mutant. Teenage Mutant Ninja Turtles - Battle Ready! (p. 1714)
—Teenage Mutant Ninja Turtles Green Team. (p. 1714)
Teeple, Jackie, illus. see Hensley, Sarah M.
Teeple, Jackie, illus. see Howard-Parham, Pam.
Teeple, Jackie, illus. see Jarrell, Pamela R.
Teeple, Jackie, illus. see Muench-Williams, Heather.
Teeple, Jackie, illus. see Vonthron, Satanta C.
Teer, Robert & Demartino, Damian. Gloom & Dread. (p. 685)
Teer, Samuel. Veda: Assembly Required. Park, Hyeondo, illus. (p. 1834)
Teets, Ashley, illus. see Benedetti, Debra.
Teets, Ashley, illus. see Teel, Karen.
Teets, Ashley, illus. see Wilson, Angie.
Teets, Ashley, jt. illus. see McNeal, Drema.
Teevee, Ningeokuluk. Alego Manning-Toonoo, Nina, tr. (p. 35)
Tegan-Olsen, Sandra. Joey's adventures by the Sea: Jellyfish Everywhere! (p. 920)
Tegen, Katherine. Dracula & Frankenstein Are Friends. Cushman, Doug, illus. (p. 476)
—Pink Cupcake Magic. Varner, Kristin, illus. (p. 1359)
—Story of the Easter Bunny. Lambert, Sally Anne, illus. (p. 1660)
Tegen, Katherine Brown. Snowman Magic. Dorman, Brandon, illus. (p. 1601)
—Story of the Jack O'Lantern. Dorman, Brandon, illus. (p. 1661)
—Story of the Leprechaun. Lambert, Sally Anne, illus. (p. 1661)
Tegnér, Esaias. Fritiofs Saga. ANDREW A. STOMBERG, ed. (p. 639)
Teich, Melle, illus. see Harter, Gage.
Teichert, Herman U. & Teichert, Lovette. Allerlei Zum Lesen. (p. 46)
Teichert, Lovette, jt. auth. see Teichert, Herman U.
Teichman, Diane E., tr. see Van Scoyoc, Pam.
Teichmann, Iris. China. (p. 306)
—Globalization. (p. 685)
—Immigration & Asylum. (p. 861)
—Life as an Immigrant. (p. 1008)
—Multicultural World. (p. 1190)
Teis, Kyra. Look! (p. 1047)
Teis, Kyra, illus. see Baer, Edith.
Teis, Kyra, illus. see Mathers, Beth.
Teis, Kyra, illus. see Morellion, Judi.
Teis, Kyra, adapted by. Magic Flute: An Opera by Mozart (p. 1072)
Teis, Sean P. After the Ark: Eli & Ella the Little Elephants - Children of the King! Boutheyette, Valerie, illus. (p. 28)
Teitel, Linda & Teitel, Linda Phillips. Angus MacMouse Brings down the House. Francis, Guy, illus. (p. 75)
Teitel, Linda Phillips. Angus MacMouse Brings down the House. Francis, Guy, illus. (p. 75)
Teitel, Linda Phillips, jt. auth. see Teitel, Linda.
Teitelbaum, Michael. Baseball. (p. 140)
—Batman: Meet the Super Heroes. Gordon, Steven E., illus. (p. 144)
—Bigfoot Caught on Film: And Other Monster Sightings! (p. 185)
—Cave of No Return. (p. 282)
—Cine en casa: Heroes de Cine: Movie Theater: Marvel Heroes. (p. 321)
—Curse of the Haunted House. (p. 395)
—Disney Princess Little Golden Book Favorites Williams, Don et al, illus. (p. 452)
—Electrician. (p. 509)
—Garfield & the Santa Spy. Fentz, Mike, illus. (p. 656)
—Ghastly Ghost Town. (p. 670)
—Ghost at the Grand Inn. (p. 670)
—Ghosts: And Real-Life Ghost Hunters. (p. 672)
—Halloween Howlers: Frightfully Funny Knock-Knock Jokes. Ho, Jannie, illus. (p. 737)
—Humvees: High Mobility in the Field. Nelson, Scott, photos by. (p. 827)
—I Am Superman. (p. 834)
—I Am Superman. Farley, Rick, illus. (p. 834)
—Invincible Iron Man. (p. 885)
—Jackie Robinson: Champion for Equality. (p. 904)
—Jigsaw Journey: the 50 States. Allen, Jessica, illus. (p. 917)
—Little Mermaid. DiCicco, Sue, illus. (p. 1031)
—Mars & Venus Space Exploration: Set Of 6. (p. 1096)
—Mars & Venus: Space Exploration: Text Pairs. (p. 1096)
—Marvel Heroes Mix & Match. Almeida, Michelangelo, illus. (p. 1098)
—Meet the Super Heroes. (p. 1123)
—Mountain Biking. (p. 1180)
—Mutant Origin: Leonardo/Donatello (Teenage Mutant Ninja Turtles) Random House Staff, illus. (p. 1194)
—Mutant Origin: Michelangelo/Raphael (Teenage Mutant Ninja Turtles) Random House Staff, illus. (p. 1194)
—Mysterious Creatures. (p. 1223)
—NFC North. (p. 1249)
—Night of the Gravedigger. (p. 1254)
—Phantom Pharaoh. (p. 1349)
—Pirate Life. (p. 1362)
—Rock Climbing. (p. 1482)
—Sailing. (p. 1503)
—Scary States of America. (p. 1520)
—Scuba Diving. (p. 1533)
—Secret Life of Black Cat. Sazaklis, John, illus. (p. 1541)
—Secret of the Tragic Theater. (p. 1543)
—Skiing. (p. 1584)
—Sports Broadcasting. (p. 1632)
—Steer the Wheel! Shannon, David et al, illus. (p. 1646)
—Submarines: Underwater Stealth. (p. 1671)
—Superman Versus Mongul. Mada Design Staff, illus. (p. 1684)
—Tale of Zuko. Spaziante, Patrick, illus. (p. 1701)
—Teenage Mutant Ninja Turtles Wall Clings. (p. 1714)
—Teenage Mutant Ninja Turtles Wheel Power Book & Skateboard. (p. 1714)
—Television. (p. 1716)
—Texas, 1527-1836. (p. 1724)
—Tony Stewart. (p. 1766)
—Transformers Armada Official Guidebook. (p. 1778)
—Wild Man of the Woods! Following in the Footsteps of Bigfoot. (p. 1929)
Teitelbaum, Michael, jt. auth. see Helfand, Lewis.
Teitelbaum, Michael, jt. auth. see Kiland, Taylor Baldwin.
Teitelbaum, Michael, jt. auth. see Reader's Digest Staff.
Teitelbaum, Michael, jt. auth. see RH Disney Staff.
Teitelbaum, Michael, adapted by. Skateboard Adventures. (p. 1583)
Teitelbaum, Michael & Golden Books Staff. Sleeping Beauty. DiCicco, Sue & Dias, Ron, illus. (p. 1589)
Teitelbaum, Michael & Marvel Spider-Man Staff. Amazing Spider-Man. (p. 55)
Teitelbaum, Michael & Scieszka, Jon. On the Move! Shannon, David et al, illus. (p. 1291)
Teitelbaum, Michael, et al. DC Comics Encyclopedia. (p. 415)
—Disney Princess Little Golden Book Favorites. (p. 452)
Teitlebaum, Michael. Chinese Immigrants. (p. 307)
Teixeira, Brenda Lopez, ed. see Webb, Joseph A.
Teixeira, Brenda Lopez, tr. see Webb, Joseph A.
Teixeira, Doug, illus. see Teixeira, G. Ann.
Teixeira, G. Ann. Mystery at the O'Reilly Farm. Teixeira, Doug, illus. (p. 1224)
Teixeira, Lucas. Mi Pequeña Biblia Hispana. (p. 1133)
Teixeira, Thiago Jorge. Neymar. (p. 1249)
Tejada, Marguerita, jt. auth. see Smith, Emilie.
Tejado, Irene, illus. see Ibarrola, Begonia.
Tejpar, Iman, illus. see Abdullah, Shaila.
Tekavec, Heather. Cost of Passage. (p. 368)
—Storm Is Coming! Spengler, Margaret, illus. (p. 1656)
Tekenteam. My Favorite Safari. (p. 1203)
Tekiela, Stan. Floppers & Loppers (p. 606)
—Paws & Claws (p. 1331)
—Peepers & Peekers (p. 1335)
—Snouts & Sniffers (p. 1598)
—Whose Butt? (p. 1921)
Tekiela, Stan, photos by see Bauer, Marion Dane.
Tela, Carl M. Squnky's Big Awakening. Tela, Donna L., illus. (p. 1637)
Tela, Donna L., illus. see Tela, Carl M.
Telchin, Eric. See a Heart, Share a Heart. (p. 1546)
Telep, Trisha, ed. Kiss Me Deadly: 13 Tales of Paranormal Love. (p. 961)
Telford, Carole & Theodorou, Rod. Up a Rainforest Tree (p. 1824)
Telford, Jane, illus. see Welton, Jude.
Telford, Jeremy. Balloonology: 32 Fun Projects to Take You from Beginner to Expert. (p. 135)
Telgemeier, Raina. Drama. (p. 480)
—Sisters. (p. 1581)
—Smile. (p. 1593)
—Smile. (p. 1594)
Telgemeier, Raina, illus. see Martin, Ann M.
Telgemeier, Raina, jt. auth. see Martin, Ann M.
Telgen, Diane. Brown V. Board of Education. (p. 232)
—Gilded Age. (p. 676)
Telgmaa, Aksel, jt. auth. see Nurk, Enn.
Telias, Ari. Tales of the Chocolate River: How to Make Your Dreams Come True. (p. 1702)
Telleiska, M. Magdalena, illus. see Doolittle, Eva M.
Telle, Anita. Always Time for Kindness. (p. 51)
—Little Different All Perfect. (p. 1026)
Telle, Nils. Magical Forest. (p. 1074)
Tellechea Idígoras, José Ignacio & Tellechea, José Ignacio. Ignacio de Loyola: Solo y a Pie. (p. 856)
Tellechea, José Ignacio, jt. auth. see Tellechea Idígoras, José Ignacio.
Tellegen, Toon. Far Away Across the Sea. Ahlberg, Jessica, illus. (p. 572)
—Letters to Anyone & Everyone. Ahlberg, Jessica, illus. (p. 1002)
—Squirrel's Birthday & Other Parties. Ahlberg, Jessica, illus. (p. 1637)
Tellekamp, Lynda, illus. see McKnight, Alex.
Teller, Jackson. Free Running. (p. 634)
—Skateboarding: How to Be an Awesome Skateboarder (p. 1583)
—Skateboarding. (p. 1583)
Teller, Janne. Nothing. Aitken, Martin, tr. (p. 1268)
Telles, Cecilia R. & Heinerke, Kristina. Soar with the Angels. (p. 1603)
Tello, Antonio & Alvarez Boccardo, Johanna. Me Llamo Leonardo Da Vinci. (p. 1116)
Tello, Jorge. Here Come the Blobbies. Tello, Jorge, illus. (p. 770)
—Pookie & Tushka Find a Little Piano. Tello, Jorge, illus. (p. 1383)
Telly, J. J. Schismarch: Book II of the Aerolith Adventures. (p. 1521)
Telma, Tante. Telma's Day at Magens Bay. (p. 1717)
Telmosse, Gerard. Curse of the Sourlands. (p. 395)
Tel-Or, Nava. Tristan & the Magical Vegetable Stew. (p. 1787)
Tel-Oren, Sharona, tr. see Regelson, Abraham.
Temairik, Jaime. Alice & Lucy Will Work for Bunk Beds. (p. 39)
Temairik, Jaime, illus. see Smallman, Steve.
Temairik, Jaime, illus. see Spellman, David & Lutz, Lisa.
Tembo, Wilson. Creative & Technology Studies for Zambia Basic Education Grade 2. (p. 379)
—Creative Technology Studies for Zambia Basic Education Grade 1 Pupil's Book. (p. 380)
Temerson, Catherine, tr. see Stolz, Joelle.
Temko, Florence. Cut & Color My Fun Furniture. (p. 395)
—Cut & Color Things That Go. (p. 395)
Temperley, Alan. Murdo's War (p. 1192)
Temperley, Howard. In the Days of Dinosaurs: A Rhyming Romp Through Dino History. Kline, Michael P., illus. (p. 865)
—In The Days of the Dinosaurs. Kline, Michael P., illus. (p. 865)
Tempesta, Franco, illus. see Hughes, Catherine D.
Tempesta, Franco, illus. see Lessem, Don.
Tempesta, Franco, illus. see Milton, Joyce.
Tempesta, Franco, illus. see National Geographic Editors & Esbaum, Jill.
Temple, Bob. Arlington National Cemetery. (p. 99)
—Day Mom Finally Snapped Harpster, Steve, illus. (p. 413)
—Dominican Republic Henderson, James D., ed. (p. 465)
—Dominican Republic. (p. 465)
—E-Baseball: Mining the Internet for History, Stats, Fantasy Leagues, & Memorabilia. (p. 492)
—Ellis Island. (p. 515)
—Ghost of J. Stokely. Nitzsche, Shane, illus. (p. 671)
—Golden Age of Pirates: An Interactive History Adventure (p. 694)
—Guyana Henderson, James D., ed. (p. 733)
—Guyana. (p. 733)
—Haiti Henderson, James D., ed. (p. 736)
—Haiti. (p. 736)
—Ice Storm! The 1998 Freeze. (p. 850)
—Nose for Danger. Harpster, Steve, illus. (p. 1266)
—Protecting the Prairie Horrocks, Savannah, illus. (p. 1412)
—Science Tales Horrocks, Savannah, illus. (p. 1528)
—Summer of Sabotage. Martin, Cynthia, illus. (p. 1674)
—Taking Back the Tundra Horrocks, Savannah, illus. (p. 1698)
—Titanic: An Interactive History Adventure (p. 1757)
—Titanic [Scholastic]: An Interactive History Adventure. (p. 1758)
—War over the Wetlands Horrocks, Savannah, illus. (p. 1858)
Temple, Bob, illus. see Moreno, Barry.
Temple, Bob, jt. auth. see Temple, Teri.
Temple, Chuck, illus. see Shaw, Mary.
Temple, Deanne. Petes Surprise. (p. 1348)
Temple, Emily, jt. auth. see Temple, Teri.
Temple, Frances. Taste of Salt: A Story of Modern Haiti. (p. 1707)
Temple, John. Collected Poems. (p. 339)
Temple, Kathryn. Art for Kids: Drawing: The Only Drawing Book You'll Ever Need to Be the Artist You've Always Wanted to Be. (p. 102)
—Drawing in Color - Art for Kids. (p. 482)
Temple, Mary V. How Jedaiah Changed Junk-Food-Nation-Land. (p. 810)
Temple, Ramey. New York Jets. (p. 1248)
—Tampa Bay Buccaneers. (p. 1704)
—Washington Redskins. (p. 1860)
Temple, Teri. Aphrodite: Goddess of Love & Beauty. Squier, Robert, illus. (p. 91)
—Apollo: God of the Sun, Healing, Music, & Poetry. Squier, Robert, illus. (p. 91)
—Ares: God of War. Squier, Robert, illus. (p. 97)
—Artemis: Goddess of Hunting & Protector of Animals. Squier, Robert, illus. (p. 103)
—Athena: Goddess of Wisdom, War, & Crafts. Squier, Robert, illus. (p. 112)
—Eros: God of Love. Squier, Robert, illus. (p. 534)

—Hades: God of the Underworld. Squier, Robert, illus. (p. 735)
—Hephaestus: God of Fire, Metalwork, & Building. Squier, Robert, illus. (p. 769)
—Hera: Queen of the Gods, Goddess of Marriage. Squier, Robert, illus. (p. 769)
—Hermes: God of Travels & Trade. Squier, Robert, illus. (p. 771)
—Poseidon: God of the Sea & Earthquakes. Squier, Robert, illus. (p. 1387)
—Zeus: King of the Gods, God of Sky & Storms. Squier, Robert, illus. (p. 1986)
Temple, Teri & Temple, Bob. Remember the Alamo. (p. 1459)
—Welcome to Grand Canyon National Park. (p. 1873)
—Welcome to Hawai'i Volcanoes National Park. (p. 1873)
Temple, Teri & Temple, Emily. Cupid: God of Love. Young, Eric, illus. (p. 392)
—Diana: Goddess of Hunting & Protector of Animals. Young, Eric, illus. (p. 434)
—Juno: Queen of the Gods, Goddess of Marriage. Young, Eric, illus. (p. 936)
—Jupiter: King of the Gods, God of Sky & Storms. Young, Eric, illus. (p. 937)
—Mars: God of War. Young, Eric, illus. (p. 1096)
—Mercury: God of Travels & Trade. Young, Eric, illus. (p. 1127)
—Minerva: Goddess of Wisdom, War, & Crafts. Young, Eric, illus. (p. 1146)
—Neptune: God of the Sea & Earthquakes. Young, Eric, illus. (p. 1241)
—Pluto: God of the Underworld. Young, Eric, illus. (p. 1374)
—Saturn: God of Sowing & Seeds. Young, Eric, illus. (p. 1515)
—Venus: Goddess of Love & Beauty. Young, Eric, illus. (p. 1836)
Temple University Graduate English Staff. Schuylkill Fall 2002. (p. 1524)
Temple, Valerie. Mud Witch Boy of Ghost Canyon. (p. 1188)
Templeman, McCormick. Glass Casket. (p. 682)
Templeton, Donna L. Mother's Surprise. Berlinger, Nancy A., illus. (p. 1179)
Templeton Elementary Students. Tales from Templeton III. (p. 1701)
Templeton, Julia. Return to Me. (p. 1465)
Templeton, Robyn & Jackson, Sarah. Tell Me Why. Templeton, Robyn, illus. (p. 1717)
Templeton, Ty, illus. see Nobleman, Marc Tyler.
Templeton, Ty, illus. see Slott, Dan, et al.
Templeton, Ty, jt. auth. see Slott, Dan.
Templeton, Ty & Slott, Dan. Free Man Templeton, Ty, illus. (p. 634)
—Need to Know Templeton, Ty, illus. (p. 1239)
—No Asylum Templeton, Ty, illus. (p. 1257)
Templeton-Spears, Shawn. Eugene the Duck. (p. 540)
Templin, Stephen, jt. auth. see Wasdin, Howard E.
Temporin, Elena. Gingerbread Man. (p. 677)
—Usborne Book of Christmas Lullabies. (p. 1827)
Temporin, Elena, illus. see Denham, Joyce.
Temporin, Elena, illus. see Fearn, Laura.
Temporin, Elena, illus. see Joslin, Mary.
Temporin, Elena, illus. see Milbourne, Anna.
Temporin, Elena, jt. auth. see Amery, Heather.
Ten Cate, Marijke. God's Word for Me: Favorite Bible Stories from the International Children's Bible. (p. 692)
ten Cate, Marijke. Who Has the Biggest Bottom. (p. 1915)
ten Cate, Marijke, illus. see Van Der Heide, Iris.
Ten Hagen, Evelyn. Malcolm Dooswaddles Good Day. Hutchinson, Michelle, illus. (p. 1083)
Tenaglia-Webster, Maria. Drugs. (p. 487)
Tenah, Ann. Brainiac's Bug Book: Creepy Crawly Activities. McGuinness, Tracy, illus. (p. 222)
Tenascon, Patrick, jt. auth. see Odjick, Jay.
Tenbeth, Kate. Burly & Grum & the Birthday Surprise. Jones, Rob, illus. (p. 243)
—Burly & Grum & the Secret City. Jones, Rob, illus. (p. 243)
—Burly & Grum & the Tiger's Tale. Jones, Rob, illus. (p. 243)
Tench, D. A., jt. auth. see Tench, U. M.
Tench, U. M. & Tench, D. A. Cranberry & Friends. (p. 376)
Tenenbaum, Frances & Peterson, Roger Tory. Wildflowers. Peterson, Roger Tory, ed. (p. 1931)
Teneyuca, Sharyll, jt. auth. see Tafolla, Carmen.
Tengan, G. Shay. Marching Dinosaur Parade. (p. 1092)
Tenggren, Gustaf, illus. see Jackson, Kathryn & Jackson, B.
Tenggren, Gustaf, illus. see Jackson, Kathryn.
Tenggren, Gustaf, illus. see Lowery, Janette Sebring.
Tenggren, Gustaf, illus. see Lowrey, Janette Sebring.
Tenggren, Gustaf, illus. see Schurr, Cathleen.
Tenggren, Gustaf, illus. see Sebring Lowrey, Janette.
Tenison, Mina, tr. see Tang, Sanmu.
Tennant Iain Staff. Alby's Letters to Henry: Written from Isle of Mull. Smith, William, illus. (p. 35)
Tennant, Jon. Excavate! Dinosaurs. (p. 547)
Tennant, Kim. Thin Club. (p. 1732)
Tennant, Linda. Polly & Meril & the Wicked Spell. (p. 1381)
TenNapel, Doug. Bad Island. (p. 131)
Tennapel, Doug. Cardboard. (p. 265)
—Creature Tech. (p. 380)
TenNapel, Doug. Escape from the Lizzarks. (p. 535)
—Ghostopolis. (p. 672)
Tennapel, Doug. Ghostopolis. (p. 672)
—Monster Zoo. (p. 1168)
TenNapel, Doug. Tommysaurus Rex. (p. 1765)
Tennapel, Doug. Tommysaurus Rex. (p. 1765)
Tenney, Bob & Choice Technologies. Choice Accounting Handbook + Software. (p. 309)
Tenney, Richard L. Conflict & Calling. (p. 357)
Tenney, Shawna J. C., illus. see Braun, Eric.
Tenney, Shawna J. C., illus. see Gudmundson, C. J.
Tenney, Tommy. Finding Your Way:... to Things That Really Matter. (p. 588)
—God Chasers for Kids. (p. 688)
Tenney, Tommy & Dockery, Amie. On Daddy's Shoulders: Leaving & Receiving a Spiritual Legacy. (p. 1288)
Tenney, Yevet. I Never Got to Say Goodbye. (p. 844)
Tenniel, John, illus. see Carroll, Lewis, pseud & Frith, Barbara.
Tenniel, John, illus. see Carroll, Lewis, pseud.
Tenniel, Sir John, illus. see Carroll, Lewis, pseud.
Tennslwood, Mark. Thank You God for Onions. Motz, Mike, illus. (p. 1725)
Tennyson, Patrick & Bickford, Nicole. Tarantula Tracks: Rosie's Wild Adventure. (p. 1706)
Tenorio, Miguel A., ed. see Alexander, Martha, et al.
Tenorio-Gavin, Lucero, tr. see Sample, Jewel.
Tenpas, Steve. Job Coaching Strategies: A Handbook for Supported Employment. Smith, Barb & Kinney, Tom, eds. (p. 919)
Tent, M. B. W. Emmy Noether: The Mother of Modern Algebra. (p. 520)
Tent, M. B. W., ed. Gottfried Wilhelm Leibniz: The Polymath Who Brought Us Calculus. (p. 704)
Teo, Ali, illus. see Gabel, Ngareta.
Teo, Ali, illus. see Mewburn, Kyle.
Teo, Ali, illus. see Rainforth, Hannah.
Teodora, Mona. Max & the Missing Puzzle Piece. (p. 1110)
Teora. Addition Scratch & Learn. (p. 12)
Teora, creator. 400 Funny Games for Smart Kids. (p. 2001)
—500 Games for Smart Kids. (p. 2001)
—Dinosaurs. (p. 444)
—Dogs. (p. 462)
—Dolphins. (p. 464)
—Farm Animals. (p. 573)
—Insects. (p. 875)
—Let's Get to Know the Animals! (p. 997)
—My First Sticker Activity Book: Basic Skills for 3-5 Year Olds. (p. 1208)
—Picture Sudoku. (p. 1356)
—Sea Animals. (p. 1534)
—Sudoku 1: 42 Puzzles for Kids. (p. 1672)
—Sudoku 2: 42 Puzzles for Kids. (p. 1672)
—Wild Animals. (p. 1928)
Teora, ed. Activity & Game BK. (p. 10)
—Amazing Games. (p. 54)
—Hi Read Stick & Learn about Farm Animals. (p. 775)
Teora Staff. Baby Animals. (p. 124)
Tepfer, Joyce. Big Book of Volunteer Appreciation Ideas: Features 100 Great Ways to Thank Volunteers. (p. 179)
Teplin, Scott, illus. see Barnett, Mac, et al.
Tepper, Yona. Passing By. Guthman, Deborah, tr. from HEB. (p. 1326)
Ter Haar, Carol. Chris T. Saves the Wetlands. (p. 311)
Ter Haar, Jaap. Ice Road. Mearns, Martha, tr. from DUT. (p. 850)
Terada, Junzo. Good Home for Max. (p. 698)
Terango, Christine. Teddy's Surprise Adventure. (p. 1713)
Teraoka, Masami, jt. auth. see Hoffman, Kathryn A.
Terasaki, Stanley Todd. Ghosts for Breakfast. Shinjo, Shelly, illus. (p. 672)
Terban, Marvin. Dove Dove: Funny Homograph Riddles. Huffman, Tom, illus. (p. 473)
—Eight Ate: A Feast of Homonym Riddles. Maestro, Giulio, illus. (p. 507)
—Guppies in Tuxedos: Funny Eponyms. Maestro, Giulio, illus. (p. 732)
—In a Pickle: And Other Funny Idioms. Maestro, Giulio, illus. (p. 863)
—Mad As a Wet Hen! And Other Funny Idioms. Maestro, Giulio, illus. (p. 1068)
—Marvin Terban's Guide to Grammar: Parts of Speech - A Mini-Curriculum with Engaging Lessons, Fun Videos, Interactive Whiteboard Activities, & Reproducible Practice Pages for Teaching the Parts of Speech. (p. 1100)
—Scholastic Dictionary of Idioms. (p. 1521)
—Too Hot to Hoot: Funny Palindrome Riddles. Maestro, Giulio, illus. (p. 1766)
—Your Foot's on My Feet! And Other Tricky Nouns. Maestro, Giulio, illus. (p. 1980)
Terbay, Susan Handle. Jeremiah & the Man Mariants, tr. (p. 913)
Terborg-Hershman, Donna M. Why Sheep Don't Shrink. (p. 1926)
Tercio, Ricardo. Jack & the Beanstalk: The Graphic Novel. (p. 902)
Tercio, Ricardo, illus. see Andersen, Hans Christian & Capstone Press Staff.
Tercio, Ricardo, illus. see Andersen, Hans Christian & Stone Arch Books Staff.
Tercio, Ricardo, illus. see McGovern, Ann.
Tercio, Ricardo, illus. see Stone Arch Books Staff.
Terena Luvica Taff. Rising Sun. (p. 1475)
Terence. Phormio. Landes, William-Alan, ed. (p. 1352)
—Terence - Phormio. Maltby, Robert, ed. (p. 1721)
Teresa of Avila. Teresa of Avila: The Way of Prayer. Kavanaugh, Kieran, ed. (p. 1721)
Teresa, Olive. Story of the Good Samaritan. (p. 1661)
Terhaar, April. Through the Eyes of Snowball. (p. 1745)
Terheyden, Jerry, reader. Crow Boy. (p. 385)
Terhume, Albert Pays. Further Adventures of Lad. (p. 650)
—His Dog. (p. 781)
Terhune, Albert Payson. Buff, a Collie & Other Dog Stories. (p. 235)
—Caleb Conover: Railroader. (p. 252)
—Grey Dawn. (p. 723)
—His Dog. (p. 781)
—Lad: A Dog. (p. 970)
—Lad of Sunnybank. (p. 970)
—Lochinvar Luck. (p. 1045)
Terhune, Charlotte. There's a Possum in the Pillows. (p. 1731)
TerKeurst, Lysa. It Will Be Okay: Trusting God Through Fear & Change (p. 894)
—Sweetest Story Ever Told: A New Christmas Tradition for Families. Sparks, Michal, illus. (p. 1690)
—Sweetest Story Ever Told Activity Kit. Sparks, Michal, illus. (p. 1690)
Terlouw, Jan. Winter in Wartime. (p. 1938)
Terman Cohen, Sheila. Sterling North & the Story of Rascal. (p. 1649)
Terman Cohen, Sheila, jt. auth. see Cohen, Sheila.
Terman, Douglas. By Balloon to the Sahara. (p. 249)
Ternay, Andrew. Language of Nightmares. (p. 975)
Ternes, Caroline. Will You Be My Friend? The Prancer & Button Story. (p. 1932)
Ternier Gordon, Irene. Grey Owl (Junior Edition) (p. 723)
Terpening, Lori. Hey! You Bug Me. (p. 775)
Terpinski, Anna Simone. Will There Be Ladybugs in Heaven? (p. 1932)
Terpstra, Marcia J. Splinters from My Rocking Chair: A Journey Through Incest Survival. (p. 1630)
Terrazzini, Daniela Jaglenka, illus. see Dahl, Roald.
Terrazzini, Daniela Jaglenka, illus. see Green, Roger Lancelyn & Green, Richard.
Terrazzini, Daniela Jaglenka, illus. see Jackson, John.
Terrazzini, Daniela Jaglenka, illus. see London, Jack.
Terrazzini, Daniela Jaglenka, illus. see Yolen, Jane.
Terrell, Amber. Surprised by Grace: A Search for Inner Peace & How that Search Came to an End. (p. 1686)
Terrell, Andrea M. Adventures of Sammy the Squirrel: Buying Shoes. Mitchell, Anthony W., illus. (p. 22)
Terrell, Brandon. 8-Bit Baseball Ferrara, Eduardo, illus. (p. 1993)
—Above Cano, Fernando, illus. (p. 6)
—Fearless Cano, Fernando, illus. (p. 579)
—Flipside Majado, Caio, illus. (p. 605)
—Flipside: Volume Eleven Majado, Caio, illus. (p. 605)
—Greek Mythology's Twelve Labors of Hercules (p. 720)
—High Drama. (p. 777)
—Horizon Dal Bello, Thiago & Tortosa, Wilson, illus. (p. 797)
—Mars for Humanity. Foti, Anthony J., illus. (p. 1096)
—Recharged Tortosa, Wilson, illus. (p. 1451)
—Recharged: Volume Twelve Tortosa, Wilson, illus. (p. 1451)
—Solo (p. 1608)
—Sports Illustrated Kids Graphic Novels Ferrara, Eduardo, illus. (p. 1632)
—Summer Freeze! Beavers, Ethen, illus. (p. 1674)
—Take Away. (p. 1696)
—Unearthed Tortosa, Wilson, illus. (p. 1817)
—Unearthed: Volume Ten Tortosa, Wilson, illus. (p. 1817)
Terrell, Brandon, jt. auth. see Hoena, Blake A.
Terrell, Brandon & Fuentes, Benny. Quarterback Scramble Sandoval, Gerardo, illus. (p. 1423)
Terrell, Brandon & Majado, Caio. Tunnel Vision Ito, Leonardo, illus. (p. 1797)
Terrell, Brandon & Tortosa, Wilson. Exiled Ito, Leonardo, illus. (p. 548)
Terrell, Brandon, et al. Riptide Pride (p. 1474)
Terrell, Caitlyn, jt. auth. see Powers, Nelda Means.
Terrell, Charles. Hey, God, Let's Talk! Teaching Children about Prayer. (p. 774)
—Hey, God, Let's Talk! Teaching Children about Prayer: Keepsake Prayer Journal. (p. 774)
Terrell, Cheryl. Beginning of a Good Friendship. (p. 159)
Terrell, Heather. Boundary. (p. 216)
—Eternity. (p. 539)
—Fallen Angel. (p. 566)
—Relic: the Books of Eva 1. (p. 1458)
—Relic (the Books of Eva I) Cortes, Ricardo, illus. (p. 1458)
Terrell, Stuart. Geography of Sport & Leisure. (p. 662)
Terri, Branson. Brother Dragon. (p. 231)
Terri, Janke, jt. auth. see Pitt, Tamina.
Terri, Johnson, jt. auth. see Cook, Sherry.
Terrian, Michael W. Chalie's Brand New Coat. (p. 288)
Terrill, Cristin. All Our Yesterdays. (p. 45)
Terrill, Elizabeth, jt. auth. see Awdry, Wilbert V.
Terrill Holdman, Shirley. Adventures of Giggles & Owen: Adventure Two - Pawsistance Pays Off. Wright, Wendy L., illus. (p. 18)
—Adventures of Giggles & Owen: Adventure Three - Unlimited Pawsibilities. Leeds, Marjorie M., illus. (p. 18)
Terris, Susan, jt. ed. see Follett, C. B.
Terronez, Azul. Adventures of the 7th Grade Mind: I am an Author. (p. 23)
Terry, Alana. What Hurricane? My Solar-Powered History on a Supply Ship to the Jamestown Colony. Steffen, Jeremy, illus. (p. 1886)
—What, No Sushi? Steffen, Jeremy, illus. (p. 1892)
Terry, Alice. Classroom Management/I Love Lists 2 Set (p. 329)
Terry, Anne. Honest Bob, the Dog, Has a Tea Party. (p. 794)
Terry Anne. Honest Bob, the Dog, Plays Ball. (p. 794)
—Honest Bob, the Dog, Tells the Truth. (p. 794)
Terry, Barb, jt. auth. see Burkhardt, Mary Sue.
Terry, Brian, illus. see Hafer, Tom.
Terry, Charles L. Sing Mama's Boy Sing. (p. 1579)
Terry, Chris, photos by see Oliver, Jamie.
Terry, Donna. Whose Toes Are Those? (p. 1922)
Terry, Frederick H. Gingerbread for All Seasons. (p. 677)
Terry, Gail Contreina. Twins. (p. 1802)
Terry, Janice J., et al, eds. Encyclopedia of World History (p. 526)
Terry, Jeff. Aerial Hunters: Red-Tailed Hawk. (p. 25)
Terry, Jill. Jack & a Worm (p. 902)
Terry, Judith A. Why Bully Me? (p. 1923)
Terry Lowey's Children's Stories Staff. Secret of the Wizard's Wand. (p. 1543)
Terry, Michael. Captain Wag & the Big Blue Whale. Terry, Michael, illus. (p. 264)
—Rhinos Horns. (p. 1467)
—Who Lives Here? (p. 1916)
Terry, Michael, illus. see Blight, Peter.
Terry, Michael, illus. see Charles, Faustin & Beynon-Davies, Paul.
Terry, Michael, illus. see Charles, Faustin.
Terry, Michael, illus. see Reader's Digest Editors & Zobel-Nolan, Allia.
Terry, Michael, illus. see Roddie, Shen.
Terry, Michael, jt. auth. see Charles, Faustin.
Terry, Michael, jt. auth. see French, Vivian.
Terry, Michael, tr. see Roddie, Shen.
Terry, Nicolas. Origami Adventures: Oceans. Quigley, Sebastian, illus. (p. 1303)
Terry, Paul. Top 10 for Kids Deadly Animals. (p. 1768)
—Top 10 for Kids Gaming. (p. 1768)
—Top 10 for Kids Nature. (p. 1768)
—Top 10 for Kids Pets. (p. 1768)
—Top 10 of Everything 2015. (p. 1768)
Terry, Paul, jt. auth. see Ash, Russell.
Terry, Robert J., tr. see Takemiya, Masaki.
Terry, Rod. Kwanzaa: The Seven Principles. Williams, Angela, illus. (p. 969)
Terry, Roger. God's Executioner: The Prosecution Is about to Put God on Trial. (p. 691)
Terry, Roger, illus. see Miceli, Mary Anne.
Terry, Sonya. L Is for Library. Wong, Nicole, illus. (p. 969)
Terry, Teri. Fractured. (p. 627)
—Shattered. (p. 1563)
—Slated. (p. 1588)
Terry, Trueman & Trueman. Stuck in Neutral. (p. 1668)
Terry, Will. Frog with the Big Mouth (p. 640)
—Frog with the Big Mouth. (p. 640)
—Little Rooster's Diamond Button. (p. 1036)
Terry, Will, illus. see Corey, Shana.
Terry, Will, illus. see Cuyler, Margery.
Terry, Will, illus. see Holub, Joan.
Terry, Will, illus. see Hopkins, Lee Bennett.
Terry, Will, illus. see Ketteman, Helen.
Terry, Will, illus. see Kimmelman, Leslie.
Terry, Will, illus. see MacDonald, Margaret Read.
Terry, Will, illus. see Peterson, Eugene H.
Terry, Will, illus. see Vaughan, Marcia.
Terry-Bryant, Wincey. Bullying Is Wrong. (p. 241)
Terry-Todd, Terlene. Sweetie's Healthy Start. (p. 1690)
Tervo, Regina. Emmie Rue's Adventures. (p. 520)
Terwilliger, Kelly. Barnyard Purim. Newman, Barbara Johansen, illus. (p. 140)
Terwilliger, Robert. Betrayed: Murder in the Bahamas. (p. 172)
Terzi, Marinella, tr. see Rius, Roser, et al.
Terzian, Alexandria M. Kids Multicultural Art Book. Terzian, Alexandria M., illus. (p. 954)
Tesar, Jenny E., jt. auth. see Bunch, Bryan H.
Tesch, Lisa. Little Princess. (p. 1033)
Tesh, Jane & Klein-Higger, Joni. Land of Lost Socks: A Children's Musical. (p. 973)
Teske, Steven. Natural State Notables: Twenty-One Famous People from Arkansas. (p. 1236)
Teskey, Donald, illus. see Conlon-McKenna, Marita.
Teskey, Donald, illus. see Mac Uistin, Liam.
Tesler, Ellen. Maggie Adopts a Rescue Dog. (p. 1071)
—Zeke in Central Park. (p. 1985)
Tesler Stein, Mara, jt. auth. see Davis, Deborah L.
Tess, Jennifer. Dream Runner. Redd, Michael, ed. (p. 483)
Tessama, C., illus. see Johannes, Avril & Branham, Jan.
Tessen, Daryl D., jt. auth. see Janssen, Robert B.
Tessie & Devore, David. Happy Birthday to Me. (p. 745)
Tessier, Beth Marie, photos by see Barry, Debra R.
Tessin, Kit Elaine. My Little Pinto Bates, Brenda J. et al, illus. (p. 1212)
—Never Enough Frogs Whitman, Jennifer, illus. (p. 1242)
Tessitore, John. Extraordinary American Writers. (p. 555)
Tessler, Daria, illus. see Kaufman, Jeanne.
Testa, Dom. Cassini Code: A Galahad Book. (p. 276)
—Comet's Curse: A Galahad Book. (p. 348)
—Comet's Curse. (p. 348)
—Dark Zone. (p. 408)
—Galahad 1: The Comet's Curse. (p. 652)
—Galahad 2: The Web of Titan. (p. 652)
—Galahad 3: The Cassini Code. (p. 652)
—Web of Titan. (p. 1870)
Testa, Fulvio. Es Hora de Salir. (p. 534)
Testa, Fulvio, illus. see Collodi, Carlo.
Testa, Fulvio, illus. see Waters, Fiona.
Testa, Fulvio & Aesop Enterprise Inc. Staff. Aesop's Fables. Testa, Fulvio, illus. (p. 25)
Testa, Fulvio, et al. Aesop's Fables. Testa, Fulvio, illus. (p. 25)
Testa, Joseph Anthony. Are Cat Ears Made of Chocolate? A Children's Rhyme. (p. 96)
Testa, Maggie. Daniel Plays Ball. (p. 405)
—Evie the Knight. (p. 546)
—Friends Are the Best! Style Guide, Style & Fruchter, Jason, illus. (p. 638)
—Gift of the Night Fury. (p. 675)
—Guide to the Dragons. Style Guide, Style, illus. (p. 730)
—Happy Halloween, Brobee! (p. 745)
—Legendary Legends. Style Guide Staff, illus. (p. 989)
—Max's Big Show. Shannon, David et al, illus. (p. 1112)
—Mike & Trollee in Trouble. (p. 1141)
—Olivia & Her Alien Brother. (p. 1286)
—OLIVIA & Her Favorite Things. Spaziante, Patrick, illus. (p. 1286)
—Olivia & the Rain Dance. (p. 1286)
—Olivia Builds a House. (p. 1286)
—OLIVIA Counts down to Christmas. Johnson, Shane L., illus. (p. 1286)
—OLIVIA Loves Halloween. Osterhold, Jared, illus. (p. 1286)
—Olivia Measures Up. (p. 1287)
—Play with Plex. Zdanowicz, Paul, illus. (p. 1371)
—Ride Through the Neighborhood. Style Guide Staff, illus. (p. 1471)
—Tricky Trail. (p. 1786)
—Welcome to Glendragon Castle. (p. 1873)
Testa, Maggie, jt. auth. see Ciminera, Siobhan.
Testa, Maggie, adapted by. Galahad the Great. (p. 653)
—Mike & the Scary Noise. (p. 1141)
—Mike & Trollee in Trouble. (p. 1141)
Testa, Maria. Becoming Joe Dimaggio. Hunt, Scott, illus. (p. 156)
—Something about America. (p. 1609)
Testa, Susan L. Myra the House Cat & the Garbage Can Monster. (p. 1222)
Testar, Sue, illus. see Glover, Harry.
Testino, Mario, photos by see Farina von Buchwald, Martin & Prado Farina, Gabriela.
Testino, Mario & Kinmonth, Patrick. Any Objections? (p. 90)
Tetirck, Jack E. Joey the Motor Home Mouse. (p. 920)
Tetlow, Adam, illus. see Lundy, Miranda & Mcnaughton, Phoebe.
Tetlow, Karin. Harry Goes Rowing. Guze, Tessa, illus. (p. 750)
—Harry the Carousel Horse. Guze, Tessa, illus. (p. 751)
Tetrick, Byron. Choosing a Career as a Pilot. (p. 310)

T

Tetrick, Chase. Hot Dog Who Wanted to Play Basketball. (p. 801)
Tetro, Marc. I Can Skate. (p. 836)
—My Favourite Hat. (p. 1203)
—No Rest for Edwin. (p. 1260)
—One, Two, Three. (p. 1297)
—Where Are You from Little Goose? (p. 1906)
Tettmar, Jacqueline, illus. see Dann, Colin.
Tetz, RosAnne C., told to. God's Big Idea. (p. 691)
Tetzlaff, Wendy Jo. Girl Named Frannie. (p. 678)
—Summertime: A Girl Named Frannie (p. 1675)
Tetzner, Annika. Lullabies for Annik. (p. 1064)
Teulade, Pascale. Mas Bonito de Todos los Regalos del Mundo. Sarrazin, Jean-charles, illus. (p. 1101)
Teulade, Pascale, jt. auth. see Sarrazin, Jean-charles.
Teves, Miles. Dragon Hunter's Handbook. (p. 477)
Tewa, Rev. Bagan. Man at the Cross. (p. 1085)
Tewee, Laqaixit. Winterbloom & the Magical Swan: Book 1 Discovery of the Moon Treasure. (p. 1938)
Tewkesbury, Alexa. Benny's Barmy Bits. (p. 165)
—Camel Who Found Christmas. (p. 256)
—Danny's Daring Days (p. 406)
—John's Jam-Packed Jottings (p. 924)
—Josie's Jazzy Journal. (p. 927)
—Paul's Potty Pages. (p. 1331)
—Perfect Christmas Present. (p. 1341)
—Sarah's Secret Scribblings. (p. 1514)
Texas Golden Retriever, Casanova & Jason, Daniel. I Can't Do That I Have Paws. (p. 837)
Texas Tenors Staff, jt. auth. see Ziefert, Harriet.
Texidor, Dee, jt. auth. see Millett, Peter.
Texier, Jean, illus. see O'Brien, Joe.
Texier, Ophélie. Baby Animals. (p. 124)
Texier, Ophelie. Papa Lobo. (p. 1322)
Texier, Ophélie & Baumann, Anne-Sophie. Colors. (p. 345)
—Numbers. (p. 1272)
Texier, Ophélie & Guidoux, Valerie. Wild Animals. (p. 1928)
Teys, Jo-Anne. I Wish I Was... Lahdensuo, Debbie, illus. (p. 849)
Tezuka, Osamu. Astro Boy. (p. 109)
—Atomcat. (p. 113)
—Buddha: Prince Ajatasattu Vol. 7 Rosewood, Maya, tr. (p. 234)
—Civil War Tezuka, Osamu, illus. (p. 325)
—Civil War. (p. 325)
—Dawn. Tezuka, Osamu, illus. (p. 411)
—Devadatta (p. 431)
—Forest of Uruvela (p. 618)
—Forest of Uruvela. Vertical Inc. Staff, ed. (p. 618)
—Four Encounters. Vertical Inc. Staff, ed. (p. 624)
—Jetavana Vol. 8 Rosewood, Maya, tr. (p. 916)
—Kapilavastu. Vertical Inc. Staff, ed. (p. 943)
—Karma. Tezuka, Osamu, illus. (p. 944)
—Nextworld. Tezuka, Osamu, illus. (p. 1249)
—Nostalgia (p. 1266)
—Princess Knight. (p. 1404)
—Resurrection. Tezuka, Osamu, illus. (p. 1464)
—Yamato/Space Tezuka, Osamu, illus. (p. 1968)
Thach, Charles C., Jr. Creation of the Presidency, 1775-1789: A Study in Constitutional History. (p. 379)
Thach, James Otis. Child's Guide to Common Household Monsters. Udovic, David, illus. (p. 305)
—Seal Pup. Cutler, Warren, illus. (p. 1536)
Thacker, Becky. Chorus Kids' Memorial Day Parade. Thacker, Becky, illus. (p. 310)
Thacker, Nola. My Big Feet Out for a Walk. (p. 1197)
Thacker, Nola, jt. auth. see Strasser, Todd.
Thackeray, Frank W., ed. see ABC-CLIO Inc. Staff, Inc.
Thackham, R. P. Company House: Love, Laughter & Rigor Mortis. (p. 351)
Thackston, David. Loose Ends. (p. 1052)
Thaddeus, Eva. Powering the Future: New Energy Technologies. (p. 1391)
Thain, Gerald J., jt. auth. see Lusted, Marcia Amidon.
Thakkar, Ravina. Adventure of a Lifetime. (p. 14)
Thakkar, Vatsal. Depression & Bipolar Disorder. Collins, Christine, ed. (p. 427)
Thal, Karuna, jt. auth. see Kalman, Bobbie.
Thal, Lilli. Mimus. Brownjohn, John, tr. from GER. (p. 1145)
Thalacker, Karen & Dwyer, Mindy. Knitting with Gigi: Includes Step-By-Step Instructions & 8 Patterns. (p. 965)
Thalamus, illus. see Donahue, Shari Faden.
Thalcker, Karen. Knitting with Gigi. Dwyer, Mindy, illus. (p. 965)
Thaler, Mike. 100th Day of School from the Black Lagoon. Lee, Jared, illus. (p. 1999)
—Amusement Park from the Black Lagoon. Lee, Jared D., illus. (p. 66)
—April Fools' Day from the Black Lagoon. Lee, Jared, illus. (p. 93)
—Art Teacher from the Black Lagoon. Lee, Jared, illus. (p. 103)
—Bible Knock Knock Jokes from the Back Pew Lee, Jared, illus. (p. 175)
—Big Game from the Black Lagoon. Lee, Jared D., illus. (p. 181)
—Black Lagoon Lee, Jared, illus. (p. 196)
—Book Fair from the Black Lagoon. Lee, Jared, illus. (p. 210)
—Bully from the Black Lagoon. Lee, Jared, illus. (p. 241)
—Cafeteria Lady from the Black Lagoon. Lee, Jared, illus. (p. 251)
—Christmas Party from the Black Lagoon. Lee, Jared, illus. (p. 315)
—Church Harvest Mess-Tivall Lee, Jared, illus. (p. 318)
—Church Summer Cramp Lee, Jared, illus. (p. 318)
—Class Election from the Black Lagoon. Lee, Jared, illus. (p. 327)
—Class Pet from the Black Lagoon. Lee, Jared, illus. (p. 327)
—Class Picture Day from the Black Lagoon. Lee, Jared D., illus. (p. 327)
—Class Trip from the Black Lagoon. Lee, Jared, illus. (p. 327)
—Computer Teacher from the Black Lagoon. Lee, Jared, illus. (p. 355)
—Custodian from the Black Lagoon. (p. 395)
—Earth Day from the Black Lagoon. Lee, Jared D., illus. (p. 495)
—Easter Egg Haunt Lee, Jared, illus. (p. 499)
—Field Day from the Black Lagoon. Lee, Jared, illus. (p. 583)
—Groundhog Day from the Black Lagoon. Lee, Jared, illus. (p. 725)
—Gym Teacher from the Black Lagoon. Lee, Jared, illus. (p. 733)
—In the Big Inning Bible Riddles from the Back Pew. Lee, Jared, illus. (p. 865)
—Librarian from the Black Lagoon. Lee, Jared, illus. (p. 1005)
—Little League Team from the Black Lagoon. (p. 1030)
—Little League Team from the Black Lagoon. Lee, Jared D., illus. (p. 1030)
—Meatloaf Monster from the School Cafeteria. Lee, Jared D., illus. (p. 1118)
—Music Teacher from the Black Lagoon. Lee, Jared, illus. (p. 1193)
—New Kid from the Black Lagoon. (p. 1245)
—New Kid from the Black Lagoon. Lee, Jared, illus. (p. 1245)
—New Year's Eve Sleepover from the Black Lagoon. (p. 1247)
—Oinkers Away. (p. 1282)
—Preacher Creature Strikes on Sunday Lee, Jared, illus. (p. 1394)
—Principal from the Black Lagoon. (p. 1406)
—Principal from the Black Lagoon. Lee, Jared, illus. (p. 1406)
—Reading Challenge from the Black Lagoon. Lee, Jared D., illus. (p. 1445)
—School Bus Driver from the Black Lagoon. Lee, Jared, illus. (p. 1522)
—School Carnival from the Black Lagoon. Lee, Jared, illus. (p. 1522)
—School Nurse from the Black Lagoon. Lee, Jared, illus. (p. 1523)
—School Play from the Black Lagoon. (p. 1523)
—School Riddles from the Black Lagoon. Lee, Jared, illus. (p. 1523)
—School Secretary from the Black Lagoon. Lee, Jared, illus. (p. 1523)
—Science Fair from the Black Lagoon. Lee, Jared, illus. (p. 1526)
—Secret Santa from the Black Lagoon. Lee, Jared D., illus. (p. 1543)
—Seven Little Hippos. Smath, Jerry, illus. (p. 1554)
—Snow Day from the Black Lagoon. Lee, Jared, illus. (p. 1598)
—Spring Dance from the Black Lagoon. Lee, Jared, illus. (p. 1635)
—St. Patrick's Day from the Black Lagoon. Lee, Jared, illus. (p. 1638)
—Summer Vacation from the Black Lagoon. Lee, Jared D., illus. (p. 1675)
—Talent Show from the Black Lagoon. Lee, Jared, illus. (p. 1701)
—Teacher from the Black Lagoon. (p. 1709)
—Teacher from the Black Lagoon. Lee, Jared, illus. (p. 1709)
—Teacher from the Black Lagoon. Lee, Jared D., illus. (p. 1709)
—Thanksgiving Day from the Black Lagoon. Lee, Jared, illus. (p. 1726)
—Three Wise Guys Lee, Jared, illus. (p. 1744)
—Vacation Bible Snooze Lee, Jared, illus. (p. 1829)
—Valentine's Day from the Black Lagoon. (p. 1830)
—Vice Principal from the Black Lagoon. Lee, Jared, illus. (p. 1840)
—Walking the Plank to the Baptism Tank Lee, Jared, illus. (p. 1854)
Thaler, Mike, text. Substitute Teacher from the Black Lagoon. (p. 1671)
Thaler, Richard. Catzilla: Cat Riddles, Cat Jokes, & Cartoons. (p. 281)
Thaler, Shmuel, photos by see Gifford, Scott.
Thaler, Shmuel, photos by see Levenson, George.
Thales, Sharon. Wheels & Axles to the Rescue (p. 1901)
Thales, Sharon & Capstone Press Staff. Levers to the Rescue (p. 1004)
—Pulleys to the Rescue (p. 1416)
—Screws to the Rescue (p. 1533)
—Wedges to the Rescue (p. 1871)
Thalhamer, Ellen Viola. I'm a Daddy: I Love to Pretend! (p. 858)
—Let's Play Cashier: I Love to Pretend! (p. 1000)
—Let's Play Doctor: I Love to Pretend! (p. 1000)
Thalheimer, Ellee. Cycling Sojourner: A Guide to the Best Multi-Day Bicycle Tours in Oregon. (p. 397)
Thalia. Chupi: El Binky Que Regresó a Su Hogar. Larranaga, Ana Martin, illus. (p. 318)
—Chupie: The Binky That Returned Home. Larranaga, Ana Martin, illus. (p. 318)
Thame, Val. Witches in Deed. (p. 1941)
—Witches in Secret. (p. 1941)
—Witches in Trouble. (p. 1941)
Thames, Bob. Hermy the Hermit Crab Goes Shrimping. (p. 771)
Thames, Fiona. Dog's Mad Dash for Home. (p. 463)
Thames, Susan. Our American Symbols. (p. 1307)
—Our Digestion System. (p. 1308)
—Our Immune System. (p. 1309)
—Our Muscles. (p. 1309)
—Our Senses. (p. 1310)
—Our Skeleton. (p. 1310)
—Our Skin. (p. 1310)
Thamm, Shane. My Private Pectus. (p. 1217)
Thammavongsa, Christine, jt. illus. see Disney Storybook Artists Staff.
Than, Ker. Black Holes. (p. 196)
—Earthquakes. (p. 497)
—Stars. (p. 1643)
Thanet, Octave, pseud. Rowdy. (p. 1492)
Thanhha, Lai. Inside Out & Back Again. (p. 877)
Thaniel, Sharon Dolores. When God Made Me. (p. 1902)
Thanner, Eric. Leaping Lengths! Relate Addition & Subtraction to Length (p. 982)
Thanos, Jerald. Princess Christmas. (p. 1403)
Thapaliya, Bishnu Prasad & Karki, Ajay. Distribution & Status of Gharials. (p. 454)
Thapar, Bindia, illus. see Dharmarajan, Geeta.
Tharlet, Eve. Happy Birthday, Davy Tuff Book. (p. 744)
Tharlet, Eve, illus. see Loupy, Christophe.
Tharlet, Eve, illus. see Luciani, Brigitte.
Tharlet, Eve, illus. see Weninger, Brigitte.
Tharlet, Eve, jt. auth. see Loupy, Christophe.
Tharlet, Eve, jt. auth. see Luciani, Brigitte.
Tharlet, Eve, jt. auth. see Weninger, Brigitte.
Tharp, Barbara, et al. Tillena Lou's Day in the Sun. Denk, James, ed. (p. 1750)
Tharp, Jason, illus. see Bowman, Bianca.
Tharp, Jason, illus. see Musgrave, Ruth.
Tharp, Lauren R., illus. see Barlow, C. E.
Tharp, Tim. Badd. (p. 132)
—Knights of the Hill Country. (p. 964)
—Mojo. (p. 1160)
—Spectacular Now. (p. 1624)
Tharp, Tricia, illus. see Lee, Calee M.
Thatch, Nancy, ed. see Miller, Jayna.
Thatcher, Allison, ed. see Munaka, Marie, et al.
Thatcher Murcia, Rebecca. Thomas Edison: Great Inventor. (p. 1738)
—We Visit Colombia. (p. 1868)
—What Its Like to Be Marta Vieira. de la Vega, Eida, tr. (p. 1891)
—What It's Like to Be Shakira. de la Vega, Eida, tr. from SPA. (p. 1891)
Thausing, Julius E., et al. Theory & Practice of the Preparation of Malt & the Fabrication of Beer. (p. 1729)
Thaxter, Celia. Poems for Children, by Celia Thaxter; with Illustrations by Miss a G Plymptom. (p. 1376)
Thaxton, Brittney. Triple Warriors. (p. 1787)
Thay, Edrick. Ghost Stories of London (p. 671)
—Ghost Stories of North Carolina (p. 671)
—Ghost Stories of the Old South (p. 671)
—Haunted Cemeteries (p. 753)
—Haunted Houses French, Diana, ed. (p. 753)
—Premonitions & Psychic Warnings: Real Stories of Haunting Predictions (p. 1395)
—Weird Canadian Words: How to Speak Canadian. (p. 1872)
Thay, Edrick, jt. auth. see Asfar, Dan.
Thay, Edrick, jt. auth. see McFay, Edgar.
Thayer, Elizabeth, illus. see Harrar, George.
Thayer, Ernest L. Casey at the Bat: A Ballad of the Republic Sung in the Year 1888. Payne, C. F., illus. (p. 275)
—Casey at the Bat. Morse, Joe, illus. (p. 275)
Thayer, Ernest L. & Gardner, Martin. Casey at the Bat. Hull, Jim, illus. (p. 275)
Thayer, Ernest Lawrence. Casey at the Bat: A Ballad of the Republic, Sung in the Year 1888. (p. 275)
Thayer, Jane. Part-Time Dog. Barasch, Lynne & McCue, Lisa, illus. (p. 1325)
—Puppy Who Wanted a Boy. McCue, Lisa, illus. (p. 1418)
Thayer, Kristi. Life of Pajamas. (p. 1012)
—Pajama Knights. Willis, Caleb, illus. (p. 1319)
Thayer, Robert Scott. Kobee Manatee: Heading Home to Florida. Korman, Susan, ed. (p. 966)
Thayer, Tanya. Invierno. Translations.com Staff, tr. (p. 885)
—Otoño. Translations.com Staff, tr. (p. 1307)
—Primavera. Translations.com Staff, tr. (p. 1400)
—Verano. Translations.com Staff, tr. (p. 1836)
Thayer, William Makepeace. Bobbin Boy: Or, How Nat Got His Learning. (p. 206)
—From Boyhood to Manhood: Life of Benjamin Franklin. (p. 642)
Thayne, Tamira Ci, illus. see Estep, Lorena.
The 2nd & 7 Foundation. Hog Mollies & the Camp Carmen Campfire. (p. 787)
The Administrator. Holes in the Eagles Wing: Churches are Marxism holes per Separation of Church & State. (p. 788)
The Artifact Group, illus. see Banks, Steven.
The Artist, Eleven. Spirit Comes to Earth: Fearless Love. The Artist, Eleven, illus. (p. 1628)
—Spirit Comes to Earth: Renewing Your Heart's Mission. The Artist, Eleven, illus. (p. 1628)
The Association of Jewish Libraries Staff, jt. auth. see Kamin, Rachel.
The Beatles Staff. Yellow Submarine: Midi Edition. (p. 1970)
The Bee Guru, Gregg McMahan. Christmas Honey. (p. 314)
The Book Company, ed. Home. (p. 791)
—Park. (p. 1324)
—School. (p. 1522)
—Store. (p. 1654)
The Born Storytellers. Eye of the Tiger: A Born Storyteller Collection of Fantasy & Horror Stories. Price, Kevin, ed. (p. 558)
The Box Girls Staff, creator. Christmas Box of Questions: Cards to Create Great Conversatons. (p. 313)
The Calaiacovo Family. Amazing Adventures of Ruby & Rubette: San Francisco. (p. 52)
the Cat, Pete, jt. auth. see Kehret, Peg.
The Celebrities Arts Center. Beyonce Knowles, the Marvelous Queen. (p. 173)
The Choices Program - Brown University Staff. More Perfect Union: Shaping American Government (p. 1174)
The Ciletti Publishing Group. Story Time Cafe Maisy's Blue Bath Set. The Ciletti Publishing Group, illus. (p. 1663)
The Concerned Group, prod. See Baby Jesus. (p. 1546)
The Creators of Glee & Lowell, Sophia. Glee: Foreign Exchange: An Original Novel. (p. 682)
The Crip, Godfather. Hooked: On Satan's Stone. (p. 795)
The de Villiers Family Staff. Long Shortcut. The de Villiers Family Staff, illus. (p. 1047)
The Duda Family. Adventures of Newo: Newo & Emma Visit Their Furry Friends. (p. 21)
The Editors of Field & Stream, ed. see Bestful, Scott & Hurteau, Dave.
The Editors of Field & Stream, ed. see Cermele, Joe.
The Equality Of Genders Project. Billy Conquers the Bully. (p. 187)
The Fairy, Thimble. Thimble the Fairy's Acorns & Tea. Patch, Sebastion, illus. (p. 1732)
The Giving Tree. Expressions of Charity. (p. 555)
The Guide Dog, Thelma. For the Love of My Pet. Hartley, Joshua, illus. (p. 616)
The Jim Henson Company. Ride with Buddy. (p. 1471)
the lavanga group. Law of Sevens: For a Balanced & Inspired Life. (p. 981)
The Learning Company, The Learning. Achieve! Grade 1: Think. Play. Achieve! (p. 9)
—Achieve! Grade 2: Think. Play. Achieve! (p. 9)
—Achieve! Grade 3: Think. Play. Achieve! (p. 9)
—Curious George Adventures in Learning, Grade 1: Story-Based Learning. (p. 393)
—Curious George Adventures in Learning, Kindergarten: Story-Based Learning. (p. 393)
—Curious George Adventures in Learning, Pre-K: Story-Based Learning. (p. 393)
The Library Fairy. Magical Tree & Musical Wind. Faust, Laurie A., illus. (p. 1075)
The Literary Arts Forum. Passages: Collected Works from the Literary Arts Forum of Sulphur, Oklahoma 2003. (p. 1326)
The Mailbox Books Staff. Totally for Twos: Art Age 2. (p. 1771)
The Mamas. Meet the Yids: Mr. Mentch. (p. 1123)
The Man From A.N.K.L.E. Myles a Hedd. (p. 1222)
The Math Forum & Math Forum Staff. Dr. Math Introduces Geometry: Learning Geometry Is Easy! Just Ask Dr. Math! (p. 475)
The Metropolitan Museum of Art, The Metropolitan, jt. auth. see Falken, Linda.
The Mousekins Staff, illus. see Knaus, Patricia.
The Museum of Modern Art, contrib. by. MoMA Art While You Eat Place Mats. (p. 1161)
The Poet 174. Ways of Life. (p. 1865)
The Pope Twins, illus. see Kim, YeShil.
The Prayer Children. Whispers in God's Ears. (p. 1912)
The Series, Superdaddies. Superdaddies; the Series, Presents: Daddy, I Broke My Snowball! (p. 1683)
The Society For The Study Of Manga Techniques, jt. auth. see Society for the Study of Manga Techniques Staff.
The Storybook Art Group, illus. see Thomas, Rich.
The Strode Family. Magical Land of Far, Far Away. (p. 1074)
The, Tienny, illus. see Lee, Karen.
The Toy Box, illus. see Wolfe, Jane.
The West Milwaukee Historical Society. West Milwaukee. (p. 1876)
Thebeau, Anthony W. On the Way to Grandpa's (p. 1292)
Thebo, Mimi. Dibujemos Juntos. Meserve, Jessica, illus. (p. 435)
Thebo, Patricia J. Uncle Looker & the Hurricane. (p. 1812)
Thecla, Abbiati. Lineus Longissimus. (p. 1019)
Theer, Justine M. Backwards Town (p. 130)
The\Georgia Shorthand Reporters Association, compiled by. What's Cooking in the Courtroom. (p. 1896)
Theis, Matthew, jt. auth. see Theis, Patricia.
Theis, Patricia & Theis, Matthew. Clarabelle the Cat Loses Her Hair. Norheim, Karen, illus. (p. 326)
Theisen, Manfred. Ohne Fehl und Makel: Ein Junge im Lebensborn-Heim. (p. 1282)
Theisen, Patricia. Enchanting Song of the Human: Composed of Thoughts Generated by Ancient Eastern Tradition & Modern Western Science. (p. 523)
—Magical Mystery Tour of hte Senses: What Does it Mean to be a Human? All about Your Body & You Theisen, Patricia, illus. (p. 1075)
Theisen, Paul. Bigfoot. (p. 184)
Theisen, Sue. My Angel in a Doggy Suit. Dorman, Daniel, illus. (p. 1196)
Theiss, Lewis E. Secret Wireless: Or the Spy Hunt of the Camp Brady Patrol. (p. 1544)
—Young Wireless Operator -As a Fire. (p. 1979)
—Young Wireless Operator-As a Fire Patrol: The Story of a Young Wireless Amateur Who Made Goo. (p. 1979)
Theisz, R. D. Sharing the Gift of Lakota Song (p. 1561)
Thelan, Mary, illus. see Williams, Rozanne Lanczak.
Thelen, Bob. Adventures with Grandpa: The Fishing Trip. (p. 25)
Thelen, Mary, illus. see Shahan, Sherry.
Thelen, Mary, illus. see Williams, Rozanne Lanczak.
Them, Albert. Ghost Stories & Other Tales of Lansdowne. (p. 671)
Themerson, Franciszka, illus. see Themerson, Stefan.
Themerson, Franciszka, jt. auth. see Themerson, Franciszka.
Themerson, Franciszka & Themerson, Franciszka. My First Nursery Book. (p. 1207)
Themerson, Stefan. Table That Ran Away to the Woods. Themerson, Franciszka, illus. (p. 1694)
Thenen, Peter Von & Creative Haven Staff. Creative Haven Prismatic Designs Coloring Book. (p. 379)
Theo. Oscar & Hoo. Dudok de Wit, Michael, illus. (p. 1305)
Theobald, Denise, illus. see Hein, Connie L.
Theobald, Denise, illus. see Webb, Willyn.
Theobald, Joseph. Collins Big Cat - When Arthur Wouldn't Sleep: Band 06/Orange. Theobald, Joseph, illus. (p. 340)
—Marvin Gets Mad! (p. 1099)
—Marvin Wanted More! (p. 1100)
—Marvin Wanted More! Theobald, Joseph, illus. (p. 1100)
Theodore, Berlin J. Historical Perspective on Liberty in Haiti. (p. 783)
Theodore, Elizabeth. Lily's Lollipop Moments. (p. 1018)
Theodoridou, Despoina. Lola, the Lonely Doctor. (p. 1046)
Theodorou, Rod. Anfibios (p. 73)
—Aves (p. 119)
—I Wonder Why - Triceratops Had Horns: And Other Questions about Dinosaurs. (p. 849)
—Insectos (p. 875)
—Mamíferos (p. 1084)
—Peces (p. 1334)
—Reptiles (p. 1461)
Theodorou, Rod, jt. auth. see Telford, Carole.
Theophile, Conneau. Captain Canot; or Twenty Years of an African Slaver. (p. 263)
Theophilopoulos, Andrew, illus. see Panayotis.
Theresa, Myers. Inspirations for the Heart. (p. 878)
Theresa, Nina. Allosaurus. (p. 47)
Theresa Speight, L.L.C. Staff, ed. see Beshears, Linda Gills.

Theresine, Mary. Challenge to Freedom. O'Leary, Timothy F. & Veronica, M., eds. (p. 289)

Therian, Francis Patrick. Tommy Too. Therian, Francis Patrick & Bruha, Victor, illus. (p. 1765)

Theriault, Francis. Just Another Ghost Story: A critical thinking Novel. (p. 937)

Theriault, Sherrie. Peep Eye Coloring Book. (p. 1335)

Thermes, Jennifer, illus. see Barry, Holly M.

Thermes, Jennifer, illus. see Calmenson, Stephanie.

Thermes, Jennifer, illus. see Hobbs, Valerie.

Thermes, Jennifer, illus. see Kule, Elaine A.

Thermes, Jennifer, illus. see McDonough, Yona Zeldis.

Thermes, Jennifer, illus. see Rule, Rebecca.

Thermes, Jennifer, illus. see Skofield, James.

Theroux, Phyllis. Serefina under the Circumstances. Priceman, Marjorie, illus. (p. 1552)

Therrian, John, illus. see Kimani, Kamande.

Therriault - Bruder, Dovie G. Life on the Farm: Story One Adventure with the Chickens. (p. 1012)

—Life on the Farm - Adventure with the Dogs: Story Ten. (p. 1012)

Therriault, Teresa, jt. auth. see Hoyt, Linda.

Therrien, Patricia. Amish & Mennonite Cooking. (p. 65)

—Enemy Within: Overcoming Cancer & Other Life-Threatening Diseases. (p. 527)

—Hawaiian. (p. 755)

The\September 11 Generation. Freedom's Answer: When the Twin Towers Fell, the Next Generation Rose! (p. 635)

Theule, Larissa. Fat & Bones. Doyle, Adam, illus. (p. 576)

Theunissen, Steve. Battle of the Little Bighorn. (p. 146)

Theurer, Harold, Jr. Hey Dad, Let's Have a Catch! (p. 774)

Theurer, Heather. Thaddeus Macdonald III: Aka the Boss. (p. 1724)

Theval, Lio. Angela's Lost Turtle. (p. 74)

Thewes Nicolai, Susan. Thirteenth Butterfly: A Lizzie's Life Novel. (p. 1735)

Theys, Erchen. Birdie Hop: The True Story. (p. 191)

Thibault, Dominique, illus. see Grimm, Jacob, et al.

Thibault, Terri, jt. auth. see Blanchette, Peg.

Thibaut, Francois. Professor Toto Multi-Media Language Education Kit - Chinese. (p. 1409)

—Unassigned. (p. 1811)

Thibert, Art, illus. see Bendis, Brian Michael.

Thibodeaux, Frances, illus. see Moffett, Elzater.

Thiebaux-Heikalo, Tamara, illus. see Grant, Shauntay.

Thiel, Annie. Chloe Loses Her Pet. Edwards, W M, illus. (p. 308)

—Chloe's New Baby Brother. Marjoribanks, Karen & Edwards, William M., illus. (p. 308)

—Cosmos' Blended Family. Edwards, William M., illus. (p. 368)

—Cosmos' Mom & Dad Are Moving Apart. Edwards, William M. & Marjoribanks, Karen, illus. (p. 368)

—Dakota's Mom Goes to the Hospital. Edwards, William M. & Marjoribanks, Karen, illus. (p. 401)

—Danny Is Moving. Edwards, William M., illus. (p. 405)

—Danny's Secret. Edwards, W M, illus. (p. 406)

Thiel Annie. Playdate Kids Chloe Loses Her Pet. (p. 1372)

—Playdate Kids Chloe's New Baby Brother 2ED 2007. (p. 1372)

—Playdate Kids Cosmos' Blended Family. (p. 1372)

—Playdate Kids Cosmos' Mom & Dad are Moving Apart 2ED 2007. (p. 1372)

—Playdate Kids Dakota Gets Lost. (p. 1372)

—Playdate Kids Dakota's Mom Goes to the Hospital 2ED 2007. (p. 1372)

Thiel, Annie & Fanning, Tena. Dakota Gets Lost. Edwards, William M., illus. (p. 401)

Thiel, Hans Peter. Meyers Grosses Indianlexikon. (p. 1131)

Thielbar, Melinda. #5 the Ancient Formula: A Mystery with Fractions. Pantoja, Tintin, illus. (p. 1992)

—#6 the Fishy Fountain: A Mystery with Multiplication & Division. Lin, Yali, illus. (p. 1992)

—#7 the Book Bandit: A Mystery with Geometry. Lee, Jenn Manley & Chow, Candice, illus. (p. 1993)

—Ancient Formula: A Mystery with Fractions. Pantoja, Tintin, illus. (p. 69)

—Ancient Formula: A Mystery with Fractions. No. 5 Pantoja, Tintin, illus. (p. 69)

—Book Bandit: A Mystery with Geometry. Grandt, Eve et al, illus. (p. 210)

—Book Bandit: A Mystery with Geometry. No. 7 Lee, Jenn Manley & Chow, Candice, illus. (p. 210)

—Fishy Fountain: A Mystery with Multiplication & Division. Lin, Yali, illus. (p. 599)

—Fishy Fountain. Lin, Yali, illus. (p. 599)

—Hundred-Dollar Robber: A Mystery with Money. Pantoja, Tintin, illus. (p. 827)

—Hundred-Dollar Robber: A Mystery with Money. Pantoja, Maria Kristina, illus. (p. 827)

—Hundred-Dollar Robber. (p. 827)

—Kung Fu Puzzle: A Mystery with Time & Temperature. Helmer, De-Shing, illus. (p. 968)

—Kung Fu Puzzle. (p. 968)

—Lost Key: A Mystery with Whole Numbers. Pantoja, Tintin, illus. (p. 1056)

—Lost Key: A Mystery with Whole Numbers. Pantoja, Maria Kristina, illus. (p. 1056)

—Lost Key. (p. 1056)

—Secret Ghost: A Mystery with Distance & Measurement. Ota, Yuko, illus. (p. 1541)

—Secret Ghost. (p. 1541)

Thiele, Bob & Weiss, George David. What a Wonderful World. Hopgood, Tim, illus. (p. 1878)

Thiele, Christine. What Catholic Teens Should Know about Suicide. Larkin, Jean K., ed. (p. 1881)

Thiele, Colin. Brahminy: The Story of a Boy & a Sea Eagle. (p. 221)

—Cave & the Glory of Galumph. (p. 282)

—Danny's Egg. (p. 406)

—Hammerhead Light. (p. 739)

—River Murray Mary. (p. 1476)

—Speedy. (p. 1624)

—Storm Boy. Ingpen, Robert R., illus. (p. 1655)

Thieman, Linda. Katie & Kimble: A Ghost Story. (p. 944)

—Katie & Kimble: The Magic Wish. (p. 944)

Thieme-Baeseman, Rebecca. Miller: The Mostly Misunderstood Mischief-Maker Who Went Missing. Konecny, John, illus. (p. 1143)

Thien, Madeleine. Certainty. (p. 287)

Thienes-Schunemann, Mary. Lavender's Blue Dilly Dilly (p. 981)

—Sing a Song with Baby Smith. Lurs Schwarz, illus. (p. 1578)

Thierry, Raphael. Green Butterfly. (p. 721)

Thiessen, Andrea G. Little Kite & the Big Wind. (p. 1030)

Thiessen, Carolyn, tr. see Baker, Sandy.

Thiessen, Gordon, et al. Team Studies on Character: Inspiration for Life & Sports. Vol 2 (p. 1710)

Thiessen, Karen J. World Landmark Books, A Homeschoolers' Guide: Select, Find, & Use World Landmarks in Homeschool Curriculum. (p. 1956)

Thigpen, Meredith. Saving Nidia. Pruitt, Jason, illus. (p. 1517)

Thill, Mary Kay. Wablenica: The Tale of a Lakotah Orphan. (p. 1852)

Thimmesh, Catherine. Friends: True Stories of Extraordinary Animal Friendships. (p. 638)

—Madam President: The Extraordinary, True (and Evolving) Story of Women in Politics. Jones, Douglas B., illus. (p. 1069)

—Scaly Spotted Feathered Frilled: How Do We Know What Dinosaurs Really Looked Like? (p. 1519)

—Sky's the Limit: Stories of Discovery by Women & Girls. Sweet, Melissa, illus. (p. 1587)

—Team Moon: How 400,000 People Landed Apollo 11 on the Moon. (p. 1710)

Thirault, Philippe. Miss: Better Living Through Crime. (p. 1151)

Thirkell-White, Ben. IMF & the Politics of Financial Globalization: From the Asian Crisis to a New International Financial Architecture? (p. 861)

Thiruppathi, Shanthi. Tales of Tiggy & Tobias: Brotherly Love. (p. 1703)

Thiruvalluvar. Tirukkural Manthiram Coloring Book with Meditation. (p. 1757)

Thiry, Joan. We'll Ring in God's Name. Titra, Stephen, illus. (p. 1874)

Thisdale, Francois. Nini. Thisdale, Francois, illus. (p. 1256)

Thisdale, Francois, illus. see Forler, Nan.

Thisdale, Francois, illus. see Lanthier, Jennifer.

Thistle, Louise. Dramatizando la Gallinita Roja: Un Cuento para Contar y Actuar. Packer, Emily, illus. (p. 480)

—Dramatizing the Little Red Hen. Landes, William-Alan, ed. (p. 480)

—Little Red Snares the Wolf. (p. 1035)

Thiveos, Maria, tr. Planet Splooch. Woodward, Sarah, illus. (p. 1368)

Thivierge, Claude. BOOST The World of Turtles Coloring Book. (p. 213)

—World of Turtles. (p. 1957)

Thivierge, Claude, illus. see Giancamilli, Vanessa.

Thoburn, Michelle, illus. see Noe, David C.

Thoene, Bodie & Thoene, Brock. Second Touch. (p. 1539)

Thoene, Brock, jt. auth. see Thoene, Bodie.

Thoene, Rachel. Vase of Many Colors. (p. 1833)

Thoenig, Donald. Double Image Magic Artwork & Cards: Christmas. (p. 473)

Tholen, Shane, illus. see Haynes, Cate.

Thom, jt. auth. see Holmes.

Thom, Kara Douglass. See Mom Run. Golden, Lilly, illus. (p. 1546)

Thomalla, Deborah Ann. Bumblebee Cousins: Wyatt & Nolan Search for the Truth. (p. 241)

Thomas, A. M. Splinter Sprite. (p. 1630)

Thomas, Aaron. Logs & Lumber: From the Forest to Your Home. (p. 1045)

Thomas, Abraham, jt. ed. see Robinson, Malcolm K.

Thomas, Alease Allen. Bobby Jones of Beardsley Terrace. (p. 206)

Thomas, Amy A. Abominog. Williams, Gail, illus. (p. 5)

Thomas, Amy Maude. Stories in My Bag. (p. 1654)

Thomas, Amy N. Burning Money: The Cost of Smoking. (p. 244)

Thomas, Amy T. Story of Rocco on Satterwhite Ridge: Spring Surprises. Lester, Roseanna, illus. (p. 1659)

Thomas & Friends, Thomas & ; Thomas & Friends; Thomas Speeds Along. (p. 1738)

Thomas, Andy, jt. ed. see Thomas, Dina M.

Thomas, Ann. Food Series (p. 614)

Thomas, AnnMarie P., jt. auth. see Fontichiaro, Kristin.

Thomas, Anoine. Praying in the Presence of Our Lord for Children. (p. 1393)

Thomas, Antoine. Flower's Bed. (p. 608)

—No Regrets. (p. 1260)

—That Gangsta Sh!t. (p. 1726)

—Unwilling to Suffer. (p. 1823)

Thomas, B. K. Logs. Thomas, B. K., illus. (p. 1045)

Thomas, Beth. Jack & the Richmond Bubble. (p. 902)

Thomas, Bette. Herman's Adventures: Book 1. (p. 771)

Thomas, Bill, illus. see Bokram, Karen, ed.

Thomas, Bill, illus. see Cole, Joanna.

Thomas, Bill, illus. see Scholastic, Inc. Staff.

Thomas, Bill, jt. auth. see Thomas, William David.

Thomas, Blair L. Sabatini Prophecy. (p. 1499)

Thomas, Bob. Old Man & the Sea: Golf's Gift. (p. 1284)

—Why Bobby Jones Quit: A Literary Portrait. (p. 1922)

Thomas, Brandis. Cancer: Where Is the Real Cure? (p. 260)

Thomas, Brandon. Voltron - Year One. (p. 1850)

Thomas, Brenda. Feelings from Autumn. (p. 580)

Thomas, Brian. Stegosaurus. (p. 1646)

Thomas, Brook. SNU & the Greed Seed. (p. 1601)

Thomas, Bruce. Unto Us a Child Is Born. (p. 1823)

Thomas, C. Gordon. Adventures of Jack & Jim. (p. 19)

Thomas, Cameron. Mystery of the Lake. Krystoforski, Andrej, illus. (p. 1225)

—Shipwrecked on the Island of Skree. Krystoforski, Andrej, illus. (p. 1567)

—Utt Jungle Airline: The Jungle of Utt. Krystoforski, Andrej, illus. (p. 1829)

Thomas, Carroll. Town on Rambling Creek: A Matty Trescott Novel. (p. 1773)

Thomas, Carroll, creator. Under the Open Sky: A Matty Trescott Novel. (p. 1814)

Thomas, Cassia, illus. see Bergman, Mara.

Thomas, Cassia, illus. see Simons, Paullina.

Thomas, Cathlyn & Littlejohn, Carol. Still Talking That Book!, Grades 3-12: Booktalks to Promote Reading Vol.4 (p. 1650)

Thomas, Catori Hope. Bakota & Rudy; (p. 133)

Thomas, Chad, illus. see Schweizer, Chris.

Thomas, Chandler Turner. Fundays Food Dilemm. (p. 649)

—Fundays with the Crime Fighters for Justice. (p. 649)

Thomas, Charlene. Dog Named Munson Finds the Missing Game Ball. Repetto, Laurie, illus. (p. 461)

Thomas, Charlie. I Need Glasses. Goldfinger, Jennifer P., illus. (p. 844)

Thomas, Chericia. Buffy the Football Player. (p. 236)

Thomas, Cheryl Ann, jt. auth. see Cozens, Gaynor.

Thomas, Christina L. Dear Little One. (p. 419)

—Lizzie Thompson: My Dog Knows Kung Fu! (p. 1043)

Thomas, Christine. Language Development Inquiry Research. (p. 975)

—Language Development Variety Text. (p. 975)

Thomas, Cici. Give Me Some Sugar! (p. 681)

Thomas, Colleen. No Monster Here. (p. 1259)

Thomas, Cristine. Can I Catch Cancer? Explaing cancer to Children. Thomas, Cristine, illus. (p. 258)

Thomas, Cristine Leeann. I Can Too! Cancer Kids Can Too African American Series. Thomas, Cristine Leeann, illus. (p. 836)

Thomas, Cynthia. Little Mountain Princess. (p. 1032)

—Promise Ring: The Promise. (p. 1411)

Thomas, Dagny. Courageous Hearts. (p. 373)

Thomas, Dalandra. Noonimals. (p. 1264)

Thomas, Dale. Soot & Frogskin. (p. 1613)

Thomas, Daniel D. Prophecies of Fire. (p. 1411)

Thomas, Daniel Paul. Essays from the Ten. (p. 536)

Thomas, Danita, jt. auth. see Thomas, John E.

Thomas, Danita & Thomas, John E. Inventos de Dimensiones Biblicas para Ninos. (p. 884)

—Inventos y Experimentos para Ninos: Una Nueva Coleccion de Inventos y Experimentos un Poco Locos y Chiflados. (p. 884)

—Kid Concoctions of Biblical Proportions. (p. 951)

—Ultimate Book of Holiday Kid Concoctions: More Than 50 Wacky, Wild, & Crazy Concoctions for All Occasions. (p. 1809)

—Ultimate Book of Kid Concoctions. (p. 1809)

Thomas, David, ed. Animal Stories: Young Readers. Osborne, Richard, illus. (p. 79)

—Teenage Horse Stories. Osborne, Richard, illus. (p. 1714)

—Teenage Sea Stories. (p. 1714)

Thomas, Debbie. Dead Hairy. MacDonald, Stella, illus. (p. 416)

—Jungle Tangle. MacDonald, Stella, illus. (p. 935)

—Monkie Business. (p. 1166)

Thomas, Deborah E. Bramble Thicket. (p. 222)

Thomas, Dee. Silly, Silly, Eggleton Egg: Meet the Egg's of Eggville. (p. 1576)

Thomas, Denis. Newly Wed & Newly Cooking. (p. 1249)

Thomas, Dina M. & Thomas, Andy, eds. Artful Journey: The Artwork of Andy Thomas. Thomas, Tria M., photos by. (p. 103)

Thomas, Doni Zasloff, jt. auth. see Harkham, Rachel.

Thomas, Doni Zasloff & Lindberg, Eric. Sing-Along Alef Bet. Gilboa, Rinat, illus. (p. 1578)

Thomas, Doris. Through the Eyes of the Orcas. (p. 1745)

Thomas, Dylan. Child's Christmas in Wales. Raskin, Ellen, illus. (p. 304)

—Iona'r Iâr. (p. 886)

Thomas, Dylan, illus. see Thomas-Christensen, Sheelagh.

Thomas, Dylan, jt. auth. see Gwilym, Mari.

Thomas, E. J. Brooster Rooster: King of the Farmyard (p. 231)

Thomas, E. L. Draco's Fire. (p. 476)

Thomas, Edwin J., ed. Behavior Modification Procedure: A Sourcebook. (p. 160)

Thomas, Elizabeth. Bottlenose Dolphins. (p. 215)

—Clean Air. (p. 330)

—Clean Water. (p. 330)

—Conserving Energy. (p. 359)

—Desert Tortoises. (p. 429)

—Eastern Box Turtles. (p. 499)

—Goblin Sharks. (p. 688)

—Great White Sharks. (p. 719)

—Octopuses. (p. 1278)

—Reduce, Reuse, Recycle. (p. 1456)

—Snapping Turtles. (p. 1597)

Thomas, Emma. Inca Tomb. (p. 868)

Thomas, Eric. Community Workers. (p. 350)

Thomas, Eric, illus. see Brown, Laaren & Dorling Kindersley Publishing Staff.

Thomas, Eric, illus. see Hastings, Selina.

Thomas, Eric, illus. see Owen, Ann & Picture Window Books Staff.

Thomas, Eric, illus. see Owen, Ann.

Thomas, Eric, illus. see Wohlrabe, Sarah C.

Thomas, Erika & Treg, Mccoy. Petey Yikes! A very, very true story about a homeless little blue bird in New York City. (p. 1348)

Thomas, Erin. Boarder Patrol (p. 205)

—Haze. (p. 756)

Thomas, Evan, jt. auth. see Bryan, Sean.

Thomas, Frances. Polly's Absolutely Worst Birthday Ever. Gardner, Sally, illus. (p. 1381)

—Polly's Running Away Book. Gardner, Sally, illus. (p. 1381)

Thomas, Frances, jt. auth. see Carradice, Phil.

Thomas, Franselica, illus. see Isabel, Michelle.

Thomas, G. D. Keep Your Head Down. (p. 947)

Thomas, Gary & Vaughan, Mark. Inclusive Education: A Reader. (p. 869)

—Inclusive Education: Readings & Reflections. (p. 869)

Thomas, Gene. Tales from the Tree House. (p. 1702)

Thomas, Geraint. Agent Mouse: Snowdon Adventure. (p. 29)

Thomas, Gerry. Umbrella Race. (p. 1810)

Thomas, Gina. Mr Taxi Man Meets Irene. (p. 1186)

Thomas, Glenn. Little Flowers Can't Talk. (p. 1027)

Thomas, Glenn, illus. see Trevayne, Emma.

Thomas, Gould H. American in China, 1936-1939: A Memoir. (p. 61)

Thomas, Gwyn. King Arthur. Jones, Margaret, illus. (p. 958)

—Story of Dafydd AP Gwilym. Jones, Margaret, illus. (p. 1658)

Thomas, Helen. Caryl Phillips. (p. 273)

Thomas, Ian. Where's My Shoggoth? Bolton, Adam, illus. (p. 1910)

Thomas, Isabel. Alligator vs. Crocodile (p. 47)

—Alphabet Fun: Making Letters with Your Body (p. 49)

—Beaky's Guide to Caring for Your Bird Peterson, Rick, illus. (p. 150)

—Being a Fashion Stylist. (p. 160)

—Being a Photographer. (p. 160)

—Being a Stunt Performer. (p. 160)

—Board Sports. (p. 205)

—Brilliant Birds. (p. 228)

—Cindy-Ella & the Incredible Techno-Slippers. (p. 321)

—City Safari (p. 324)

—Collages (p. 339)

—Cool Cat Projects. (p. 363)

—Crazy Creepy Crawlies (p. 377)

—Dealing with Feeling... (p. 418)

—Dealing with Feeling... Angry. (p. 418)

—Dealing with Feeling... Caring. (p. 418)

—Dealing with Feeling Happy (p. 418)

—Dealing with Feeling... Jealous. (p. 418)

—Dealing with Feeling... Sad. (p. 418)

—Designer Dog Projects. (p. 430)

—Drawing (p. 481)

—Experiments with Electricity. (p. 549)

—Experiments with Forces. (p. 549)

—Experiments with Heating & Cooling. (p. 549)

—Experiments with Light. (p. 549)

—Experiments with Magnets. (p. 549)

—Experiments with Materials. (p. 549)

—Experiments with Plants. (p. 549)

—Experiments with Sound. (p. 549)

—Fantastic Fish (p. 571)

—Fox: City Safari (p. 626)

—Freestyle BMX. (p. 635)

—Giggle's Guide to Caring for Your Gerbils Peterson, Rick, illus. (p. 676)

—Gordon's Guide to Caring for Your Guinea Pigs Peterson, Rick, illus. (p. 702)

—Graphing Food & Nutrition. (p. 711)

—Graphing Population. (p. 711)

—Handy Horse Projects. (p. 742)

—Harry, Greta & the Dastardly Dinner Lady. (p. 750)

—Henrietta's Guide to Caring for Your Chickens Peterson, Rick, illus. (p. 767)

—Hip Hamster Projects. (p. 780)

—Latin Dance. (p. 979)

—Lion vs. Tiger (p. 1020)

—Marvelous Mammals (p. 1099)

—Masks & Face Painting (p. 1102)

—Mercury & Venus (p. 1127)

—Number Fun: Making Numbers with Your Body (p. 1271)

—Painting (p. 1318)

—Pet Projects. (p. 1345)

—Pets' Guides (p. 1348)

—Photographs (p. 1353)

—Pigeon: City Safari (p. 1357)

—Prints (p. 1407)

—Pros & Cons of Biomass Power. (p. 1412)

—Pros & Cons of Solar Power. (p. 1412)

—Raccoon: City Safari (p. 1430)

—Rat: City Safari (p. 1440)

—Read & Experiment. (p. 1442)

—Remarkable Reptiles (p. 1459)

—Sculptures (p. 1534)

—Seagull: City Safari (p. 1536)

—Search & Rescue: Heat & Energy Transfer (p. 1537)

—Shark vs. Killer Whale (p. 1562)

—Should Scientists Pursue Cloning? (p. 1570)

—Slinky's Guide to Caring for Your Snake Peterson, Rick, illus. (p. 1590)

—Squeak's Guide to Caring for Your Pet Rats or Mice Peterson, Rick, illus. (p. 1636)

—Squirrel: City Safari (p. 1637)

—Stars & Galaxies (p. 1643)

—Textiles (p. 1724)

—What Is the Controversy over Stem Cell Research? (p. 1890)

—Why Do I Burp? Digestion & Diet (p. 1923)

—Why Do I Have Periods? Menstruation & Puberty (p. 1923)

Thomas, Isabel & Thomas, Marilyn. Stargazing from Nowhere. (p. 1642)

Thomas, Isaiah, creator. Curious Hieroglyphick Bible. (p. 394)

Thomas, J. L. Die Golden Goose. (p. 437)

Thomas, Jack. Eliminate Stress Forever with Psychoharmonics: A Revolutionary System for Understanding & Mastering Your Emotions Inspired by the Aramaic Teachings of Jesus of Nazareth (p. 512)

Thomas, Jacquelin. Divine Confidential. (p. 454)

—Divine Match-Up. (p. 454)

—It's a Curl Thing. (p. 895)

—Simply Divine. (p. 1578)

—Split Ends. (p. 1630)

Thomas, Jacqui, illus. see Jeffs, Stephanie.

Thomas, Jacqui, illus. see Williams, Derek.

Thomas, James. Investigator. (p. 885)

Thomas, James, illus. see Kesecker, Jennifer.

Thomas, James, illus. see Traywick-Jones, Andrea.

Thomas, James, jt. auth. see James, Thomas.

Thomas, Jan. Birthday for Cow! (p. 192)

—Can You Make a Scary Face? Thomas, Jan, illus. (p. 259)

—Doghouse. (p. 462)

—Easter Bunny's Assistant. Thomas, Jan, illus. (p. 499)

—Here Comes the Big, Mean Dust Bunny! Thomas, Jan, illus. (p. 770)

—Is Everyone Ready for Fun? Thomas, Jan, illus. (p. 889)

—Let's Sing a Lullaby with the Brave Cowboy. Thomas, Jan, illus. (p. 1000)

—Pumpkin Trouble. Thomas, Jan, illus. (p. 1416)
—Rhyming Dust Bunnies. Thomas, Jan, illus. (p. 1468)
—What Will Fat Cat Sit On? (p. 1895)
Thomas, Jan, illus. see Fox, Mem.
Thomas, Jane. Zioc Saves His Planet. (p. 1987)
Thomas, Jane Resh. Counterfeit Princess. (p. 370)
Thomas, Janet. Can I Play? Bartlett, Alison, illus. (p. 258)
Thomas, Jared. Sweet Guy. (p. 1689)
Thomas, Jason. Adventures of Bird & Gator: Best Friends. (p. 16)
Thomas, Jatavius. Weird Things Happening at Southside Middle School: And Other Stories. (p. 1872)
Thomas, Jean, illus. see Lynn, Auntie.
Thomas, Jean Monrad. How Many Kisses Good Night? Bryant, Laura J., illus. (p. 811)
Thomas, Jeanne Taylor. Kerry Mcdaniels & the Cave. (p. 949)
Thomas, Jeannine. Little Girl & the Fish. (p. 1028)
—Nutter the Survivor. (p. 1274)
Thomas, Jenni, jt. auth. see Jay, Caroline.
Thomas, Jerry D. Shoebox Kids Bible Stories Justinen, Kim, illus. (p. 1568)
—What We Believe: Helping Children Understand the Beliefs of the Seventh-Day Adventist Church. (p. 1895)
Thomas, Jerry D. & Thomas, Kitty. Step by Step: Helping Children Understand the Principles of Steps to Christ. (p. 1647)
Thomas, Jesse & Keller, Carolyn. University of Oregon College Prowler off the Record. (p. 1821)
Thomas, Jesse Lee. Ghost House. Daily, Rick, illus. (p. 670)
Thomas, Jill. Start to Bead. (p. 1643)
Thomas, Jim. Comic Book Heroes. Ruiz, Aristides & Giles, Mike, illus. (p. 348)
—Fame & Glory. (p. 567)
—Super Slam Turtles! Spaziante, Patrick, illus. (p. 1681)
Thomas, Joan G. If Jesus Came to My House. McElrath-Eslick, Lori, illus. (p. 853)
Thomas, John & Rowe, Susan. Mynydd y Brain. (p. 1222)
Thomas, John E., jt. auth. see Thomas, Danita.
Thomas, John E. & Thomas, Danita. Kid Concoctions & Contraptions. (p. 951)
—Ultimate Book of Kid Concoctions 2. (p. 1809)
Thomas, John Ira. Zoo Force: Dear Eniko. Smith, Jeremy, illus. (p. 1989)
Thomas, John, Jr., illus. see Bullard, Lisa.
Thomas, Joyce Carol. Blacker the Berry. Cooper, Floyd, illus. (p. 197)
—Christmas & the Magic Pie Pan. (p. 312)
—Gospel Cinderella. Diaz, David, illus. (p. 703)
—Linda Brown, You Are Not Alone: The Brown V. Board of Education Decision. (p. 1019)
—Singing Mama's Songs. (p. 1579)
Thomas, Joyce Carol, jt. auth. see Hurston, Zora Neale.
Thomas, Joyce Carol, jt. auth. see Thomas, Kenneth W.
Thomas, K. Clyde the Long Fingered Lemur. (p. 336)
Thomas, K. A. Ravenheart. (p. 1441)
Thomas, Kate. Mother Duck Knows the Way. Larkins, Mona, illus. (p. 1177)
Thomas, Keith A. Cross-Lengua Coloring Book for Kids. Thomas, Keith A., illus. (p. 385)
—Idioms. Thomas, Keith A., illus. (p. 852)
—Walk of the Giraffes. (p. 1853)
Thomas, Keltie. Animals That Changed the World. (p. 84)
—Bear Rescue: Changing the Future for Endangered Wildlife. (p. 151)
—How Baseball Works. Hall, Greg, illus. (p. 805)
—How Basketball Works. Hall, Greg & Owlkids Books Inc. Staff, illus. (p. 805)
—How Football Works. MacEachern, Stephen, illus. (p. 809)
—How Hockey Works. Hall, Greg & Owlkids Books Inc. Staff, illus. (p. 809)
—How Soccer Works. MacEachern, Stephen & Owlkids Books Inc. Staff, illus. (p. 812)
—Inside Hockey! The Legends, Facts, & Feats That Made the Game. Kicksee, John & Owlkids Books Inc. Staff, illus. (p. 876)
—Kids Guide to Money Cent$ MacEachern, Stephen, tr. (p. 953)
Thomas, Kenneth W. & Thomas, Joyce Carol. In the Land of Milk & Honey. Cooper, Floyd, illus. (p. 866)
Thomas, Kerrie Annette. Jinja of the Munjyburr. Jacobs, D. K., illus. (p. 919)
Thomas, Kimberly. Greatest Flag in the World: The Universal Family Flag. (p. 719)
Thomas, Kitty, jt. auth. see Thomas, Jerry D.
Thomas, Kristina. Where Is God? A book for Toddlers. (p. 1908)
Thomas, Laura. Welcome to Berry Bitty City. (p. 1873)
Thomas, Laura, illus. see Ackelsberg, Amy.
Thomas, Laura, illus. see Brooke, Samantha.
Thomas, Laura, illus. see Gallo, Lisa.
Thomas, Laura, illus. see Heller, Alyson.
Thomas, Laura, illus. see Matheis, Mickie.
Thomas, Laura, illus. see Pinehurst, Bonnie.
Thomas, Laura, illus. see Unknown.
Thomas, Laura Michelle. Polly Wants to Be a Writer - the Junior Authors Guide to Writing & Getting Published. (p. 1381)
Thomas, Leah. Because You'll Never Meet Me. (p. 155)
Thomas, Leanne & Schlebold, Olivia. Puppylicious. (p. 1418)
Thomas, LeSean, illus. see David, Peter.
Thomas, Lillie Michelle, illus. see Q., Bev.
Thomas, Linda. Cats of Dogwood Lane: Daisy Finds a Home. (p. 281)
Thomas, Lindy. Redemption of Nick Howard. (p. 1455)
Thomas, Lisa E. Friends of the Heart. (p. 638)
—Puppy. (p. 1418)
Thomas, Lloyd. Black Sheep That Earned Respect. (p. 196)
Thomas, Lois Jean. Me & You—We Are Who? (p. 1115)
Thomas, Lori. Daisy Family. (p. 400)
Thomas, Lyn. 100% Pure Fake: Gross Out Your Friends & Family with 25 Great Special Effects! (p. 1998)

—Ha! Ha! Ha! & Much More: The Ultimate Round-Up of Jokes, Riddles, Facts, & Puzzles. Eastman, Dianne & Owlkids Books Inc. Staff, illus. (p. 734)
Thomas, M. I Jog Around: Learning the J Sound. (p. 839)
—Summer at the Beach: Learning the EA Sound. (p. 1673)
Thomas, M. L. Brut Mccloud & His Friends. (p. 233)
Thomas, Mack. What Would Jesus Pray? A Story to Change the World. (p. 1895)
Thomas, Mack, jt. auth. see Wilkinson, Bruce.
Thomas, Mar Andres. Mi Primer Libro Bilingue: la Comida/My First Bilingual Book: Food. (p. 1133)
Thomas, Marc, illus. see Elder, Jennifer.
Thomas, Margaret. Algebra II, Grades 5 - 8. (p. 38)
Thomas, Margaret, jt. auth. see Vivian, Mary Lee.
Thomas, Maria José, jt. auth. see Thomas, Maria Jose.
Thomas, Maria Jose & Thomas, María José. !Bravo, Rosina! Muñoz, Claudio, illus. (p. 224)
Thomas, Marian. Adventure Writer. (p. 15)
—Comedy Writer. (p. 348)
—Fantasy Writer. (p. 572)
—Mystery Writer. (p. 1226)
Thomas, Maribel. Party in the Sky. (p. 1326)
Thomas, Marilyn, jt. auth. see Thomas, Isabel.
Thomas, Marjorie & Raffenach, Jessie. What Does 'died' Mean? Halíshá óolyé Daaztsâa? Begay, Patrick, illus. (p. 1884)
Thomas, Mark. Akashi-Kaikyo Bridge: World's Longest Bridge. (p. 32)
—Discoverer Enterprise: World's Largest Offshore Drilling Rig. (p. 448)
—Discoverer Enterprise: La Plataforma de Perforacion Mas Grande Del Mundo. (p. 448)
—Discoverer Enterprise: La plataforma de perforación más grande del mundo (the Discoverer Enterprise: World's Largest Offshore Drilling Rig) (p. 448)
—Itaipu Dam: World's Biggest Dam. (p. 894)
—Las Torres Gemelas Petronas. (p. 977)
—Maracana: World's Largest Soccer Stadium. (p. 1091)
—Maracana: El Estadio de Futbol Mas Grande del Mundo. (p. 1091)
—Maracaná: El estadio de fútbol más grande del mundo (the Maracaná: World's Largest Soccer Stadium) (p. 1091)
—Petronas Twin Towers: World's Tallest Buildings. (p. 1348)
—Puente Akashi Kaikyo: El Puente Mas Largo Del Mundo. (p. 1414)
—puente Akashi Kaikyo: El puente más largo del mundo (the Akashi-Kaikyo Bridge: World's Longest Bridge) (p. 1414)
—Represa de Itaipu: La Represa Mas Grande Del Mundo. (p. 1461)
—represa de Itaipú: La represa más grande del mundo (the Itaipu Dam: World's Biggest Dam) (p. 1461)
—Seikan Railroad Tunnel: World's Longest Tunnel. (p. 1548)
—Torres Gemelas Petronas: Los Edificios Más Altos del Mundo (The Petronas Twin Towers: World'S Tallest Building) (p. 1770)
—Tunel Ferroviario Seikan: El Tunel Mas Largo Del Mundo. (p. 1796)
—túnel ferroviario Seikan: El túnel más largo del mundo (the Seikan Railroad Tunnel: World's Longest Tunnel) (p. 1796)
Thomas, Mark Lawton. My Lemonade Stand Can't Stand Me. Hoke, Jeenhyun, illus. (p. 1211)
Thomas, Mario, et al, eds. Thanks & Giving: All Year Long. (p. 1725)
Thomas, Mary Ann. Bonnie's Bakery. (p. 209)
—New Neighbors. (p. 1246)
—Our Train Trip: Learning to Add Times by the Half Hour. (p. 1310)
—Trip to the Post Office. (p. 1787)
Thomas, Meredith, illus. see Kettle, Shey.
Thomas, Micahla F. Anna & Jasmine & the Tale of the Gateway Castle. (p. 85)
Thomas, Michael, illus. see Grube, George.
Thomas, Michael Lee, illus. see James-Carde, Genice.
Thomas, Michele. Oxygen. (p. 1316)
—Sodium. (p. 1605)
Thomas, Michelle. Bubble World & the Enchanted Garden. (p. 233)
—Bubble World & the Olympics. (p. 233)
—Sodium. (p. 1605)
Thomas, Middy, illus. see Lowry, Lois.
Thomas, Mike. Mysterious Treasure of Jerry Lee Thorton. (p. 1223)
Thomas, Mikey. Mouse & the House. (p. 1181)
Thomas, Morgan. Saturday Shot. (p. 1515)
Thomas, Nancy S. William the Winter Warbler. (p. 1933)
Thomas, Natasha. Mommy & Daddy Is There Really Greatness in Me? (p. 1162)
Thomas, Nayomi. Thankables: Three Little Creatures with Very Large Features. (p. 1725)
Thomas Nelson. My Pretty Pink Bible Purse. (p. 1217)
—My Pretty Pink Prayer Purse. (p. 1217)
Thomas Nelson & Sons Staff, jt. auth. see Peretti, Frank E.
Thomas Nelson & Sons Staff, jt. auth. see Stortz, Diane.
Thomas Nelson Community College Staff. God's Love in My Heart. (p. 691)
Thomas Nelson Publishing Staff. Adventures in Odyssey & the Great Escape: The Ultimate Test of Time Awaits You Inside! (p. 15)
—Adventures in Odyssey & the Treasure of the Incas: The Chase Is on. Discover the Treasure. Reveal the Truth. (p. 15)
—Brave Girls - Better Than Perfect: A 90-Day Devotional for Brave Girls Like You! (p. 223)
—Brave Girls Bible Stories. (p. 223)
—Camping the Bug-A-Boo Way: Go for the Gold Against Camp Hot Foot! (p. 257)
—Daddy Loves You So Much Parry, Jo, illus. (p. 398)
—Dance Praise Expansion Pack Vol 2: Hip-Hop/Rap. (p. 402)
—Faith Journal. (p. 565)
—Grandma Kisses (p. 708)
—Holy Bible (p. 791)
—Joy Journal (p. 929)
—Just for Me Bible (p. 938)

—Light Rangers: Mending the Maniac Madness: Protect the Children of Angeltown. (p. 1015)
—Mommy Loves You So Much Parry, Jo, illus. (p. 1162)
—My Big Book of Catholic Bible Stories (p. 1197)
—My Rainbow Promise Bible (p. 1217)
—My Very First Bible Stories. (p. 1221)
—Original Dance Praise: Game Only (p. 1304)
—Pirates Who Don't Do Anything: A VeggieTales Movie: Discovery Bay. (p. 1364)
—Pirates Who Don't Do Anything: A VeggieTales Movie: Clapping Rocks Crafts. (p. 1364)
—Pirates Who Don't Do Anything: A VeggieTales Movie: Rowboat Bible Stories. (p. 1364)
—Pirates Who Don't Do Anything: A VeggieTales Movie: Whiprack Island Games. (p. 1364)
—Pirates Who Don't Do Anything: A VeggieTales Movie: Rock Monster Science Lab. (p. 1364)
—Pirates Who Don't Do Anything: A VeggieTales Movie: Preschool Director's Guide. (p. 1364)
—Pirates Who Don't Do Anything: A VeggieTales Movie: Elementary Director's Guide. (p. 1364)
—Pirates Who Don't Do Anything: A VeggieTales Movie: Spyglass Bible Theater Guide. (p. 1364)
—Pirates Who Don't Do Anything: A VeggieTales Movie: Yo-Ho-Ho Opening & Closing Show. (p. 1364)
—Pirates Who Don't Do Anything: A VeggieTales Movie: Cheesecurl Cave Snacks & Science. (p. 1364)
—Pirates Who Don't Do Anything - Veggietales Movie: Squawk-Along Songs & Games. (p. 1364)
—Read Me a Bible Story 365 (p. 1443)
—Solomon Says Bible Trivia: Anything Goes: Test Your Bible Knowledge in this Wacky Game Show! (p. 1608)
—Solomon Says Bible Trivia for Kids: Amazing Animals: Learn about Animals of the Bible. (p. 1608)
—Story of Christmas (p. 1657)
Thomas Nelson Publishing Staff, jt. auth. see Fischer, Jean.
Thomas Nelson Publishing Staff, jt. auth. see Spady, Angela.
Thomas Nelson Publishing Staff & Hall, Hannah. God Bless You & Good Night (p. 688)
Thomas Nelson Publishing Staff & Nelson Bibles Staff. Baby's First Bible (p. 129)
Thomas Nelson Publishing Staff, creator. Compact Kids Bible: Glitter Wings (p. 351)
—Holy Bible (p. 791)
Thomas Nelson Publishing Staff, ed. Refuel: Mark (p. 1456)
Thomas, Nigel. Tom Travis: The Lost People of Orion. (p. 1764)
Thomas, Novene. Enchanted Opera: Supernaturally Enchanting & Spiritually Enlightening. (p. 523)
Thomas, P. J. Cloud & the Cat. (p. 334)
Thomas, Pam. Mamarswpial. (p. 1084)
Thomas, Pamela L., illus. see Rome, Jacqueline Thomas.
Thomas, Pat. Come Home Soon: A First Look at When a Parent Goes to War. Harker, Lesley, illus. (p. 347)
—Do I Have to Go to the Hospital? A First Look at Going to the Hospital. Harker, Lesley, illus. (p. 457)
—Don't Call Me Fat! A First Look at Being Overweight. (p. 467)
—Everyone Matters: A First Look at Respect for Others. Harker, Lesley, illus. (p. 544)
—I Can Be Safe: A First Look at Safety. Harker, Lesley, illus. (p. 835)
—I Can Do It! A First Look at Not Giving Up. Harker, Lesley, illus. (p. 835)
—I Can Make a Difference: A First Look at Setting a Good Example. Harker, Lesley, illus. (p. 836)
—I Miss My Pet: A First Look at When a Pet Dies. Harker, Lesley, illus. (p. 844)
—I See Things Differently: A First Look at Autism. (p. 845)
—I'm Feeling Bashful: A First Look at Shyness. (p. 858)
—Is It Right to Fight? A First Look at Anger. Harker, Lesley, illus. (p. 889)
—My Manners Matter: A First Look at Being Polite. Harker, Lesley, illus. (p. 1214)
—My New Family: A First Look at Adoption. Harker, Lesley, illus. (p. 1216)
—Skin I'm In: A First Look at Racism. Harker, Lesley, illus. (p. 1585)
—This Is My Family: A First Look at Same-Sex Parents. Harker, Lesley, illus. (p. 1736)
—Why Do I Feel Scared? A First Look at Being Brave. Harker, Lesley, illus. (p. 1923)
Thomas, Patricia. Firefly Mountain Sylvada, Peter, illus. (p. 592)
—Green Bean! Green Bean! Hunner, Trina L., illus. (p. 721)
—Mouse's Christmas Cookie Nez, Jon, illus. (p. 1182)
—Nature's Paintbox: A Seasonal Gallery of Art & Verse. Orback, Craig, illus. (p. 1237)
—Red Sled. Demarest, Chris L., illus. (p. 1455)
Thomas, Patsy E. Camp Carrot Cheer for Good Nutrition. (p. 257)
—My Favorite Dog. (p. 1203)
—Why Not Me? (p. 1925)
Thomas, Paul. Olaudah Equiano: From Slavery to Freedom. Ambrus, Victor, illus. (p. 1283)
—Revolutionaries. (p. 1466)
Thomas, Paul R., reader. Reeve's Tale. (p. 1456)
Thomas, Peggy. Farmer George Plants a Nation. Johnson, Layne, illus. (p. 574)
—For the Birds: The Life of Roger Tory Peterson. Jacques, Laura, illus. (p. 616)
—Joshua the Giant Frog Smith, Cat Bowman, illus. (p. 927)
—Post-Traumatic Stress Disorder. (p. 1387)
—Snow Dance Facklam, Paul, illus. (p. 1598)
Thomas, Peggy, jt. auth. see Facklam, Margery.
Thomas, Penny. Powwow Counting in Cree. Josie, Melinda, illus. (p. 1391)
Thomas, Peter. Sweet Robert's Serenade. (p. 1690)
Thomas, Peter, jt. auth. see Cornell, Karl.
Thomas, Peter, jt. auth. see Winkelman, Barbara Gaines.
Thomas, Peter, tr. see Blue, Martha.
Thomas, Peter, tr. see John, Roberta.
Thomas, Peter, tr. see Powell, Patricia Hruby.
Thomas, Peter, tr. see Ruffenach, Jessie, ed.

Thomas, Peter A., tr. see John, Roberta.
Thomas, Peter A., tr. see Powell, Patricia Hruby.
Thomas, Peter A., tr. see Tsinajinnie, Veronica.
Thomas, Peter A., tr. see Yazzie, Seraphine G.
Thomas, Peter, Jr. & Denby, Neil. GCSE Business Studies - The Essentials. (p. 659)
Thomas, R. Kayeen. Light: Stories of Urban Resurrection. (p. 1014)
Thomas, Ray aka The Bull Cutter. What's Wrong in America. (p. 1900)
Thomas, Rebecca. Adventures of Jade & Izzy: Jade & the Doctor. (p. 19)
Thomas, Rebecca L., jt. auth. see East, Kathy.
Thomas, Rhianedd, jt. auth. see Hallam, Gwion.
Thomas, Rhianedd, jt. auth. see Lewis, Siân.
Thomas, Rhiannon. Wicked Thing. (p. 1927)
Thomas, Rich. Amazing Spider-Man: An Origin Story. Clark, Jeff, illus. (p. 55)
—Captain America: The Tomorrow Army. (p. 263)
—Courageous Captain America: An Origin Story. Semeiks, Val, illus. (p. 372)
—Incredible Hulk: An Origin Story. Semeiks, Val, illus. (p. 869)
—Invincible Iron Man: An Origin Story. Rousseau, Craig, illus. (p. 885)
—Mighty Avengers: An Origin Story. Olliffe, Pat, illus. (p. 1139)
—Mighty Thor: An Origin Story. (p. 1140)
—Mighty Thor: An Origin Story. Clark, Jeff, illus. (p. 1140)
—Spider-Man: Attack of the Heroes. (p. 1626)
—Spider-Man: Attack of the Heroes: A Marvel Chapter Book. Disney Book Group Staff, illus. (p. 1626)
—Thor: An Origin Story. Olliffe, Pat, illus. (p. 1739)
—Uncanny X-Men: An Origin Story. The Storybook Art Group, illus. (p. 1811)
Thomas, Rich, jt. auth. see Disney Book Group Staff.
Thomas, Rich, Jr. Avengers: An Origin Story. Olliffe, Pat, illus. (p. 118)
—Iron Man: An Origin Story. Grummett, Tom & Disney Storybook Artists Staff, illus. (p. 888)
—Spider-Man: An Origin Story. Olliffe, Pat et al, illus. (p. 1626)
Thomas, Rich, Jr. & Siglain, Michael. Captain America: The Tomorrow Army. Disney Book Group Staff et al, illus. (p. 263)
Thomas, Richard. Avengers Assemble. (p. 118)
Thomas, Richard A., illus. see Lamuth, Nancy.
Thomas, Rick. Twisters: A Book about Tornadoes Shea, Denise, illus. (p. 1803)
Thomas, Rick & Picture Window Books Staff. Eye of the Storm: A Book about Hurricanes Shea, Denise, illus. (p. 557)
—Ojo de la Tormenta: Un Libro Sobre Huracanes Robledo, Sol, tr. from ENG. (p. 1282)
—¡Juush! ¡Ruum! Un Libro Sobre Tornados. Robledo, Sol, tr. from ENG. (p. 941)
—¡Rambum! ¡Pum! Un Libro Sobre Tormentas. Robledo, Sol, tr. from ENG. (p. 1437)
Thomas, Rob. Boom! Boom! Boom! There's a Dinosaur in My Room! (p. 213)
—Rats Saw God. (p. 1440)
Thomas, Robyn, illus. see Holman, Felice.
Thomas, Rockwell. How to Eat Fried Worms. (p. 819)
Thomas, Roger B. Accidental Marriage. (p. 8)
Thomas, Ron & Herran, Joe. Getting into Sports. (p. 669)
Thomas, Rosemary. Kiwi Kingdom. (p. 963)
Thomas, Ross, jt. auth. see Thomas, Ross.
Thomas, Ross & Thomas, Ross. Chinaman's Chance. (p. 307)
Thomas, Roy. Monster of the Monoliths & Other Stories (p. 1168)
—Shadow in the Tomb & Other Stories. (p. 1557)
—Stoker's Dracula. Beazley, Mark D., ed. (p. 1651)
Thomas, Roy & Buscema, Sal. Essential Avengers Adams, Neal, illus. (p. 536)
Thomas, Roy & Howard, Robert E. Tower of the Elephant & Other Stories. Windsor-Smith, Barry, illus. (p. 1773)
Thomas, Roy, et al. All Star Comics Kahan, Bob, ed. (p. 45)
—War of the Worlds (p. 1858)
Thomas, Ruth. Emma: Insight Text Guide (Large Print 16pt) (p. 519)
—Superstar Creativity Book. (p. 1684)
Thomas, Sara. McCoy & the Pond. (p. 1114)
Thomas, Schmitt, compiled by. Portraits of Nebraska: Pride in Our Hometowns. (p. 1387)
Thomas, Scott. Angry Aardvark to Zealous Zebra-Curious Creatures ABC. (p. 75)
—Prayers & Pledges. (p. 1393)
Thomas, Scott, jt. auth. see Janic, Susan.
Thomas, Sean Michael. Sedikit-Sedikit Menjadi Bukit: Little by Little We Climb the Mountain. (p. 1546)
Thomas, Sheeba P. Fun with Numbers. (p. 648)
Thomas, Shelley Moore. Get Well, Good Knight. (p. 668)
—Get Well, Good Knight. Plecas, Jennifer, illus. (p. 668)
—Happy Birthday, Good Knight. (p. 744)
—Happy Birthday, Good Knight. Plecas, Jennifer, illus. (p. 744)
—No, No, Kitten! Nichols, Lori, illus. (p. 1259)
—Secrets of Selkie Bay. (p. 1545)
—Seven Tales of Trinket. (p. 1555)
—Somewhere Today: A Book of Peace. Futran, Eric, photos by. (p. 1610)
—Take Care, Good Knight. Meisel, Paul, illus. (p. 1696)
Thomas, Shelley Moore, jt. auth. see Moore Thomas, Shelley.
Thomas, Sherry. Burning Sky. (p. 244)
—Immortal Heights. (p. 861)
—Perilous Sea. (p. 1343)
Thomas, Sonya, illus. see Magee, Kanika A. M.
Thomas, Sonya, illus. see Magee, Kanika.
Thomas, Stephen, ed. Hot Summer Fun, Cool Summer Stars. Staake, Bob et al, illus. (p. 802)
Thomas, Susan. Beyond the Mist: Sequel to Mist on the Window. (p. 174)
Thomas, Susan & Hughes, Annie. Mini Flashcards Language Games. (p. 1146)
Thomas, Susanna. Akhenaten & Tutankhamen: The Religious Revolution. (p. 32)
—Snefru: The Pyramid Builder. (p. 1597)

Thomas, Sylvia. Jesus, My Lord. (p. 916)
Thomas, Sylvia A. Disciples of Jesus. (p. 447)
—Moses & the Exodus from Egypt. (p. 1176)
Thomas, T. R., jt. auth. see T R Thomas.
Thomas, Taffy, jt. auth. see Watts, Helen.
Thomas, Tamara. ABC Poem Book. Thomas, Tamara, illus. (p. 3)
Thomas, Tavy, ed. see DeLong, Ron & Brown-McCracken, Janet.
Thomas, Teri. Barge Ghost. (p. 139)
—Bus 99. (p. 244)
—Dimes to Dollars. (p. 440)
Thomas, Terri. Barge Ghost (p. 139)
—Bus 99 (p. 244)
—J Mac Is the Freestyle King! Sefcik, Wendy, illus. (p. 901)
Thomas, Terri, jt. auth. see Greene, Janice.
Thomas, Terri & Greene, Janice. Dimes to Dollars (p. 440)
Thomas The Tank Engine & Egmont Staff. Thomas & Friends. (p. 1737)
Thomas The Toad. Willie the Frog Learns to Fly. (p. 1934)
Thomas, Tim. Fruitman. (p. 645)
Thomas, Tim, illus. see Dixon, Virginia.
Thomas, Tim, illus. see Lowery, Paul.
Thomas, Tina, illus. see Moore, Clement C.
Thomas, Titus V., illus. see Azima, Cricket.
Thomas, Tom, ed. see Naomi, Aunt & Landa, Gertrude.
Thomas, Tom, ed. see Winter, John.
Thomas, Tracy. Family Comes First. (p. 568)
—Hustler's Handbook. (p. 830)
—Sasha's Story. (p. 1515)
—Track. (p. 1775)
Thomas, Tria M., photos by see Thomas, Dina M. & Thomas, Andy, eds.
Thomas, Valerie, jt. auth. see Kramer, Stacy.
Thomas, Velma Maia. No Man Can Hinder Me: The Journey from Slavery to Emancipation Through Song. (p. 1258)
Thomas, Vernada. Butterflies & Balloons: A Coloring Book for All Ages. (p. 247)
—Pre-Handwriting Book. (p. 1394)
—Pre-K Math. (p. 1394)
Thomas, W. Laverne, jt. auth. see Holt, Rinehart and Winston Staff.
Thomas, Warren. Adventures of Mu-Mu Lost in the Outback. (p. 21)
Thomas, Wendy Russell & Ruchman, Laura. Bliss Live It! Bliss Give It! Starmer, Anika & Wertz, Michael, illus. (p. 199)
Thomas, Wes. Down the Crawfish Hole Thomas, Wes, illus. (p. 474)
Thomas, Wes, illus. see Blazek, Frank.
Thomas, Wes, illus. see Bullard, Lisa.
Thomas, William. Deep Sea Fisher. (p. 423)
—District of Columbia. (p. 454)
—Movie Stunt Worker. (p. 1183)
—Oil Rig Worker. (p. 1282)
—Wilderness Rescue Pilot. (p. 1931)
Thomas, William David. Alaska. (p. 33)
—Como Elegimos a Nuestros Lideres? (p. 350)
—Deep-Sea Fishing. (p. 423)
—Flight Attendant. (p. 604)
—Forest Firefighter. (p. 618)
—Hawaii. (p. 755)
—Home Front in the Vietnam War. (p. 792)
—How Do We Elect Our Leaders? (p. 807)
—How to Become an FBI Agent. (p. 815)
—Johnny Depp. (p. 923)
—Journalist. (p. 927)
—Kansas. (p. 943)
—Kenny Chesney. (p. 949)
—Korean Americans. (p. 967)
—Marine Biologist. (p. 1094)
—Mountain Rescuer. (p. 1181)
—New Hampshire. (p. 1244)
—Pete Thompson & the Long Road Home. (p. 1346)
—Truck Driver. (p. 1791)
—Veterinarian. (p. 1839)
—What Are Citizens' Basic Rights? (p. 1879)
—What Are the Parts of Government? (p. 1880)
—What Is a Constitution? (p. 1888)
—Wildlife Photographer. (p. 1931)
—William Lloyd Garrison: A Radical Voice Against Slavery. (p. 1933)
—Wyoming. (p. 1966)
—¿Cómo Elegimos a Nuestros Líderes? (p. 350)
—¿Cuáles son las partes del gobierno? (p. 388)
—¿Cuáles son las partes del gobierno? (What Are the Parts of Government?) (p. 388)
—¿Cuáles Son Los Derechos Básicos de Los Ciudadanos? (p. 388)
—¿Cuáles son los derechos básicos de los ciudadanos? (p. 388)
—¿Qué Es Una Constitucion? (p. 1423)
—¿Qué Es una Constitución? (p. 1423)
Thomas, William David, jt. auth. see RJF Publishing Staff.
Thomas, William David, jt. auth. see Thomas, William David.
Thomas, William David & Nations, Susan. Archaeologist. (p. 95)
Thomas, William David & Thomas, Bill. Kansas. (p. 943)
Thomas, William David & Thomas, William David. Working in Law Enforcement. (p. 1953)
Thomas, Zachary & Wilson, Natashya. Melting Pot: The People & Cultures of New York. (p. 1125)
Thomas-Bakker, Oslyn. Poetry for Children. (p. 1376)
Thomas-Brown, Cauline, ed. see Whitaker, Sue.
Thomas-Christensen, Sheelagh. Morus Yr Ystlum. Thomas, Dylan, illus. (p. 1176)
Thomasian, Sara. Charlie's Magical Night. Harrington, David, illus. (p. 293)
Thomas-Logan, Sharon. Miracles of Jesus Christ. (p. 1149)
Thomasma, Eric. Billy's Family. Thomasma, Lanin, illus. (p. 187)
Thomasma, Lanin, illus. see Thomasma, Eric.
Thomas-Ngabe, T-Imani. Once upon a Frog: From the Chronicles Of. (p. 1292)
—Who Stole the Nutz? From the Chronicles of Poems & Stories Mother Goose Forgot. (p. 1917)
Thomason, Cathy, jt. auth. see Main, Mary.
Thomason, Tom. Tara the Tuna. (p. 1706)
Thomason-Carroll, Kristi L. Young Adult's Guide to Business Communications. (p. 1978)
Thomas-Roots, Pamela. FACTS & MEMOIRS of BABY DIARY: A Diary to Record & Save Valuable Information on Facts & Memoirs of Your Pregnancy & Baby from Birth to Age 18. (p. 561)
Thomassen, Hellen, illus. see Nunez, Marisa.
Thomassie, Tynia. Feliciana Feydra Leroux: A Cajun Tall Tale Smith, Cat Bowman, illus. (p. 581)
—Feliciana Meets d'Loup Garou: A Cajun Tall Tale Smith, Cat Bowman, illus. (p. 581)
Thomasson, Daniel E. Lion & the Egg. (p. 1019)
Thomasson, Merry F. Hey, Look at Me! Baby Days. Kopald, Sue-Anne, illus. (p. 774)
Thomburgh, Rebecca, illus. see Connelly, Neil O.
Thomes, William Henry. Bushrangers a Yankee's Adventures During His Second Visit to Australia by William H Thomes. (p. 244)
Thomey, Zedar. Red Star Red Tar. (p. 1455)
Thompson, Adria. Droves Cove. (p. 486)
Thompson, Aiyana M. Miranda Fishhook: Makes a New Friend. (p. 1149)
Thompson, Alan, jt. auth. see Mahmout, Ulfet.
Thompson, Alicia. Psych Major Syndrome. (p. 1413)
Thompson, Alicia, jt. auth. see Moceanu, Dominique.
Thompson, Allister, ed. see Emery, Joanna.
Thompson, Allister, jt. auth. see Janveau, Teri-Lynn.
Thompson, Alyce C. Watching over Us. (p. 1861)
Thompson, Angie, illus. see April, Elyse.
Thompson, Anne. Arrow Sparrow. (p. 101)
Thompson, Aron. Biography of a Grizzly. (p. 189)
—Grammy & Me: The Family Tree. (p. 706)
Thompson, Bailey, jt. auth. see Thompson, Kim Mitzo.
Thompson, Barbara C. Famine at the Feast. (p. 569)
Thompson, Becki & Reinke, Missy. Building Math Vocabulary: 70 Engaging Reproducible Activities That Go Beyond the Textbook to Help Students Practice & Really Learn the Math Terms They Need to Know. (p. 239)
Thompson, Ben. Guts & Glory: World War II. Butzer, C. M., illus. (p. 733)
—Guts & Glory: the American Civil War. Butzer, C. M., illus. (p. 733)
—Guts & Glory: the Vikings. (p. 733)
Thompson, Berine. Tedi the Bear & His Pals Adventure at the Zoo! (p. 1713)
Thompson, Betsy, illus. see Halfmann, Janet.
Thompson, Bill. Legend of Gunners Cove. (p. 988)
Thompson, Bill, III. Young Birder's Guide to Birds of Eastern North America. (p. 1978)
Thompson, Brian. Reject High. (p. 1457)
Thompson, Brian, illus. see Kozlowsky, M. P.
Thompson Bros., jt. auth. see Willson, Sarah.
Thompson Brothers Staff, illus. see Tomaselli, Doris.
Thompson Brothers Studio Staff, illus. see Willson, Sarah & Thompson Bros.
Thompson, Bruce E. R. Capital Punishment. Poole, Mary Jo, ed. (p. 262)
Thompson, Bruce R. If I Made a Hat. (p. 853)
Thompson, Bryon, illus. see Higgins, Nadia.
Thompson, C. Michael. Twinsational. (p. 1802)
Thompson, Camille & Gohari, Omid. College of William & Mary College Prowler off the Record. (p. 340)
Thompson, Carol. Climb! Thompson, Carol, illus. (p. 332)
—Crawl! Thompson, Carol, illus. (p. 376)
—I Like You the Best. Thompson, Carol, illus. (p. 841)
—Jump! Thompson, Carol, illus. (p. 933)
—Mockingbird Song. (p. 1157)
—My Squashy Pumpkin! (p. 1219)
—Noo-Noos. (p. 1263)
—Rain! (p. 1434)
—Run! Thompson, Carol, illus. (p. 1496)
—Snow! (p. 1598)
—Snug! (p. 1601)
—Sun! (p. 1675)
—Wind! (p. 1935)
Thompson, Carol, illus. see Bernstein, Owen.
Thompson, Carol, illus. see Crum, Shutta.
Thompson, Carol, illus. see Hamm, Mia.
Thompson, Carol, illus. see Ormerod, Jan.
Thompson, Carol, illus. see Zolotow, Charlotte.
Thompson, Carol, jt. auth. see Thompson, Carol.
Thompson, Carol & Newman, Lesléa. Daddy, Papa, & Me. Thompson, Carol, illus. (p. 398)
—Mommy, Mama, & Me. Thompson, Carol, illus. (p. 1162)
Thompson, Carol & Thompson, Carol. America the Good: Stories of Goodwill by Good Americans. (p. 59)
Thompson, Carolyn. BJ S Bean Patch. (p. 194)
Thompson, Celia. Academic Word Power 2. (p. 7)
Thompson, Chad. If You're Happy & You Know It. (p. 855)
—Itsy Bitsy Spider (p. 900)
—Itsy Bitsy Spider. (p. 900)
—Old Mother Hubbard. (p. 1284)
—Viera Madre Hubbard. (p. 1841)
—Yankee Doodle. (p. 1968)
Thompson, Chad, illus. see Birky, Joy.
Thompson, Chad, illus. see Bykowski, Christy.
Thompson, Chad, illus. see Crow, Melinda Melton.
Thompson, Chad, illus. see Houghton, Jill Zieréis.
Thompson, Chad, illus. see Umina, Lisa.
Thompson, Chad, jt. auth. see Rice, Dona Herweck.
Thompson, Chad, jt. auth. see Smith, Jodene Lynn.
Thompson, Chantal, jt. auth. see Hirsch, Bette.
Thompson, Cheryl. Skeeter's Tomorrow. (p. 1584)
Thompson, Clifford. Archaeologists! (p. 95)
—Climatologists! (p. 332)
Thompson, Colin. Amazing Illustrated Floodsopedia. Thompson, Colin, illus. (p. 54)
—Barry. Thompson, Colin, illus. (p. 140)
—Better Homes & Gardens. Thompson, Colin, illus. (p. 172)
—Bewitched. (p. 173)
—Big Little Book of Happy Sadness. Thompson, Colin, illus. (p. 182)
—Camelot. Thompson, Colin, illus. (p. 256)
—Castles. (p. 277)
—Castles. Thompson, Colin, illus. (p. 277)
—Disasterchef. Thompson, Colin, illus. (p. 447)
—Excalibur. Thompson, Colin, illus. (p. 547)
—Floods #2: School Plot. Scrambly, Crab, illus. (p. 605)
—Floods Family Files. Thompson, Colin, illus. (p. 605)
—Free to a Good Home. Thompson, Colin, illus. (p. 634)
—Good Neighbors. Scrambly, Crab, illus. (p. 698)
—Great Montefiasco. Redlich, Ben, illus. (p. 717)
—Great Outdoors. (p. 717)
—Home & Away. Thompson, Colin, illus. (p. 791)
—How to Live Forever. (p. 820)
—Last Alchemist. Thompson, Colin, illus. (p. 977)
—Lost. (p. 1054)
—Mordred. (p. 1173)
—Pictures of Home. Thompson, Colin, illus. (p. 1356)
—Playschool. Thompson, Colin, illus. (p. 1373)
—Prime Suspect. (p. 1400)
—Royal Family. (p. 1492)
—Ruby. Thompson, Colin, illus. (p. 1493)
—Second Forever. (p. 1539)
—Short & Incredibly Happy Life of Riley. Lissiat, Amy, illus. (p. 1569)
—Survivor. Thompson, Colin, illus. (p. 1687)
—Top Gear. Thompson, Colin, illus. (p. 1769)
—Who Wants to Be a Billionaire? Thompson, Colin, illus. (p. 1918)
Thompson, Colin & Lissiat, Amy. Norman & Brenda. (p. 1264)
Thompson, Colin W., illus. see Kerns, Ann.
Thompson, Colleen. Claudine & Claudette: A Bug Story. (p. 329)
—Claudine & Claudette a Bug Story. (p. 329)
Thompson, Craig. ABC's of Black Inventors: A Children's Guide. (p. 4)
Thompson, Cynthia. Princess Esmeralda of the Land of Ur: The Sharing of Gifts Book Two. (p. 1403)
Thompson, David. Nine Clues of Christmas (p. 1256)
—Poems & Illustrations for Preschool Children. (p. 1376)
—Processes That Shape the Earth. (p. 1408)
Thompson, Deanna. 100 Years Old with Baby Teeth: Will Caroline Ever Lose Her Tooth? Wolf, Claudia, illus. (p. 1999)
Thompson, Deanna T. What's So Great about Silent E? The Thoughts of Sunnie Rae. Thompson, Sunnie R., illus. (p. 1899)
Thompson, Debra. Crumb Snatchers. Dennis, Tammy D., illus. (p. 386)
Thompson, Deirdre. Nana, Dey, & Peanut's Adventures. (p. 1228)
Thompson, Del, illus. see Salerno, Tony, et al.
Thompson, Dennis & Watt, W. Bryce. Watt Pottery: A Collector's Reference with Price Guide (p. 1864)
Thompson, Don. Bunny World: Kindness Is the Key to Happiness. (p. 242)
Thompson, Dorcas, jt. auth. see Bill.
Thompson, Dorcas, jt. auth. see Thompson, William.
Thompson, Dorothy. Dewey Does Adding & Subtractions: Activity Sports Book. Bk. 2 (p. 432)
Thompson, E. L. Cesar Chavez, with Profiles of Terence V. Powderly & Dolores Huerta. (p. 288)
Thompson, Egil, illus. see Lane, Alison Hoffman.
Thompson, Elaine. Touch, Trace & Write Uppercase. (p. 1772)
Thompson, Elissa. Tryin' Ryan. (p. 1795)
Thompson, Elizabeth, illus. see Trollinger, Patsi B.
Thompson, Emma. Christmas Tale of Peter Rabbit. Taylor, Eleanor, illus. (p. 316)
—Further Tale of Peter Rabbit. Taylor, Eleanor, illus. (p. 650)
—Nanny Mcphee Returns (p. 1229)
—Spectacular Tale of Peter Rabbit. Taylor, Eleanor, illus. (p. 1624)
Thompson, Emma, et al. Sgeulachd Eile Mu Pheader Rabaid. Taylor, Eleonor, illus. (p. 1556)
Thompson, Frances McBroom. Math Essentials, High School Level: Lessons & Activities for Test Preparation. (p. 1106)
—Math Essentials, Middle School Level: Lessons & Activities for Test Preparation. (p. 1106)
Thompson, Frank. King Arthur. (p. 958)
Thompson, Freida. Believe. (p. 161)
Thompson, G. R., jt. auth. see Poe, Edgar Allen.
Thompson, Gabrielle. ABCs of Childhood Cancer. (p. 4)
Thompson, Gare. Amazon Journey: Cruising the Rain Forest. (p. 56)
—Civil War Battleship: The Monitor. Day, Larry, illus. (p. 325)
—Lever, Screw, & Inclined Plane: The Power of Simple Machines. (p. 1003)
—Main Idea & Details/Determine Importance - Forward, March! (p. 1077)
—Motorcycles. (p. 1179)
—My Balloon Ride. (p. 1196)
—Our Journey West: An Adventure on the Oregon Trail. (p. 1309)
—Riding with the Mail: The Story of the Pony Express. (p. 1471)
—Roald Amundsen & Robert Scott Race to the South Pole. (p. 1477)
—Roaring 20s: Voices from America's Past. (p. 1478)
—Serengeti Journey: On Safari in Africa. (p. 1552)
—Shaping the Constitution: Set Of 6. (p. 1561)
—Shaping the Constitution: Text Pairs. (p. 1561)
—Southeast: Its History & People. (p. 1617)
—Suburban Community of the 1950s. (p. 1671)
—We Came Through Ellis Island: The Immigrant Adventures of Emma Markowitz. (p. 1866)
—Whales. (p. 1878)
—Whaling Community: Set of 6: New Bedford, Mass. (p. 1878)
—Whaling Community: New Bedford, Mass: Text Pairs. (p. 1878)
—When the Mission Padre Came to the Rancho: The Early California Adventures of Rosalinda & Simon Delgado. (p. 1904)
—Who Was Eleanor Roosevelt? (p. 1918)
—Who Was Eleanor Roosevelt? Wolf, Elizabeth, tr. (p. 1918)
—Who Was Eleanor Roosevelt? Wolf, Elizabeth, illus. (p. 1918)
—Who Was Helen Keller? O'Brien, John A. & Harrison, Nancy, illus. (p. 1918)
Thompson, Gare, jt. auth. see Andrews, Carolyn.
Thompson, Gare, jt. auth. see O'Brien, John A.
Thompson, Gare & National Geographic Learning Staff. Kids Care for the Earth. (p. 953)
—Missions & Ranchos. (p. 1153)
—Northeast: Its History & People. (p. 1265)
—West: Its History & People. (p. 1876)
Thompson, Gare & Peratt, Karen. Seeking the American Revolution - History Comes Alive! (p. 1548)
Thompson, Gare & West, Elizabeth. Main Idea & Details/Determine Importance: Symbols of Freedom. (p. 1077)
Thompson, Gare, et al. Our New Life in America: The Marks Family Lives the American Dream. (p. 1309)
Thompson, Gareth. Anarchist's Angel. (p. 67)
—Sunshine to the Sunless. (p. 1679)
Thompson, Gary. Digital Photography & Your PC: A Guide to Using Your PC to Create Your Own Personalized Photo Albums. (p. 440)
—What Every Teen Should Know Before Getting Behind the Wheel Alone: A Guide to Increasing Your Child's Safety While Reducing Your Auto Repair Expenses. (p. 1884)
Thompson, Gene. Kitchen Science. (p. 962)
Thompson, George, illus. see Jungman, Ann.
Thompson, Graham. Physical Education: Anatomy & Exercise Physiology. (p. 1353)
Thompson, Gwendolyn. Hayride to Heaven. (p. 755)
—Tiniest Angel with the Strongest Weapons. (p. 1755)
Thompson, Heather M. If the World Were Made of Chocolate (p. 854)
Thompson, Helen. Banking Math. (p. 136)
—Business & the Government: Law & Taxes. Madrian, Brigitte, ed. (p. 244)
—Cookies or Carrots? You Are What You Eat. (p. 361)
—Cost of Living. (p. 368)
—Culinary Math. (p. 390)
—Investing Money. (p. 885)
—Managing Employees. Madrian, Brigitte, ed. (p. 1086)
—Shopping Math. (p. 1569)
—Travel Math. (p. 1780)
—Understanding Business Math & Budgets. Madrian, Brigitte, ed. (p. 1815)
—Understanding Credit. (p. 1815)
—Understanding the Stock Market. (p. 1816)
—Weighted Down: When Being Overweight makes You Sick. (p. 1872)
Thompson, Holland. Age of Invention: A Chronicle of Mechanical Conquest. (p. 29)
Thompson, Holly. Language Inside. (p. 975)
—Orchards. (p. 1302)
—Wakame Gatherers. Wilds, Kazumi, illus. (p. 1853)
Thompson, Holly Sue. Molly, the Good Furry Friend. Thompson, Kristi June, illus. (p. 1161)
—Molly's Muffins. (p. 1161)
Thompson, Homer A. Athenian Agora, a Short Guide. (p. 112)
Thompson, Ian, illus. see Richards, Jon.
Thompson, Ian, jt. auth. see Bewes, Richard.
Thompson II, Roger E. Sister's Love: A Novel. (p. 1581)
Thompson III, Bill. Young Birder's Guide to Birds of North America. (p. 1978)
Thompson, J. E. Disappearance at Hangman's Bluff. (p. 446)
—Girl from Felony Bay. (p. 678)
Thompson, James A., Jr. Amarna Experiment. (p. 52)
Thompson, Jan. Islam (p. 891)
—Islam. (p. 891)
Thompson, Jan & Sharpe, Jaime. Amara's Magical Playhouse: The Adventure Begins. (p. 52)
Thompson, Janet M., illus. see Hierl, Christine Gormican.
Thompson, Janice, jt. auth. see Hanna, Janice.
Thompson, Jean M. Water Wonders Every Child Should Know: L. (p. 1863)
Thompson, Jeffrey, illus. see Doering Tourville, Amanda.
Thompson, Jeffrey, illus. see Mortensen, Lori & Picture Window Books Staff.
Thompson, Jeffrey, illus. see Mortensen, Lori.
Thompson, Jeffrey, illus. see Slade, Suzanne.
Thompson, Jeffrey, illus. see Tourville, Amanda Doering.
Thompson, Jeffrey, illus. see Wohlrabe, Sarah C.
Thompson, Jenean. All in a Day's Play. Thompson, Jenean, illus. (p. 44)
Thompson, Jerry D., contrib. by. Symbols of American Freedom Set, 10-Volumes. (p. 1693)
Thompson, Jessica, illus. see Burt, Vickie.
Thompson, Jill. Dead Boy Detectives. (p. 416)
—Death at Death's Door (p. 420)
—Little Endless Storybook. (p. 1027)
—Magic Trixie. Thompson, Jill, illus. (p. 1074)
—Magic Trixie & the Dragon. Thompson, Jill, illus. (p. 1074)
—Revenge of Jimmy. (p. 1465)
—Scary Godmother. (p. 1520)
—Scary Godmother Comic Book Stories. (p. 1520)
Thompson, Jill, illus. see Hawthorne, Nathaniel.
Thompson, Jill, illus. see Stine, R. L.
Thompson, Jill, creator. Scary Godmother: The Mystery Date. (p. 1520)
Thompson, Joan. Lucy Russell: Lucy in the Wings. (p. 1063)
—Lucy Russell: Stardom & Stinkwater. (p. 1063)
—Lucy Russell: The Starstruck Summer. (p. 1063)
—Mudpack & Melt Isnt Easy Getting Gorge. (p. 1189)
Thompson, Joan R. Terrible Tumoff & Me. (p. 1721)
Thompson, Joel. Critter Sitters: And Other Stories That Teach Christian Values. (p. 384)
Thompson, John. Daniel & the Amazing Tickling Keefro. (p. 404)
Thompson, John, illus. see Chall, Marsha Wilson.

T

Thompson, John, illus. see Clark, Clara Gillow.
Thompson, John, jt. auth. see Lewis, J. Patrick.
Thompson, John & Thompson, Susan. Lilychild. (p. 1018)
Thompson, John M. & Schultz, George M. Just Imagine. Wodin, illus. (p. 938)
Thompson, Josephine, illus. see Gilpin, Rebecca & Pratt, Leonie.
Thompson, Josephine, illus. see Watt, Fiona.
Thompson, Josephine Et Al, illus. see Pratt, Leonie.
Thompson, Judith Davis. Bagpiper. (p. 132)
Thompson, Julee Dickerson. Dance of the Rain Gods. (p. 402)
Thompson, Julian. Grounding of Group 6. (p. 725)
Thompson, Julie Y. Wendy & Nora's Little Farm Adventure. (p. 1875)
Thompson, Karen. Preschool. (p. 1396)
Thompson, Karen, ed. see Carson-Dellosa Publishing Staff & Spectrum Staff.
Thompson, Karen, ed. see Sutton, Toby & Carson-Dellosa Publishing Staff.
Thompson, Karin, illus. see Lord, Pia.
Thompson, Kate. Beguilers. (p. 160)
—Highway Robbery. Dress, Robert & Duddle, Johnny, illus. (p. 779)
—I'm Just a Little Pig. Reasoner, Charles, illus. (p. 859)
—Last of the High Kings. (p. 978)
—Midnight's Choice. (p. 1139)
—Most Wanted. (p. 1177)
—Musica del Tiempo. Delgado, Diana, tr. (p. 1193)
—New Policeman. (p. 1246)
—Salteador de Caminos/Highway Robbery. Acevedo, Adriana, tr. (p. 1505)
—Sneaky Snappy Mr Croc. Green, Barry, illus. (p. 1597)
—Sneezy Wheezy Mr Shark. Green, Barry, illus. (p. 1597)
—Switchers. (p. 1692)
—White Horse Trick. (p. 1913)
Thompson, Kathy. Lessons from the Vine Second Grade Spring Quarter. Fahringer, Sarah, illus. (p. 993)
Thompson, Kay. Eloise at the Wedding. Lyon, Tammie Speer, illus. (p. 516)
—Eloise's What I Absolutely Love Love Love. (p. 516)
Thompson, Kay, jt. auth. see McClatchy, Lisa.
Thompson, Kay, jt. auth. see McNamara, Margaret.
Thompson, Kay & Brenner, Marie. Kay Thompson's Eloise: The Absolutely Essential 50th Anniversary Edition: A Book for Precocious Grown-Ups. Knight, Hilary, illus. (p. 946)
Thompson, Kay & Knight, Hilary. Eloise Ready-To-Read Value Pack #2: Eloise Breaks Some Eggs; Eloise & the Dinosaurs; Eloise at the Ball Game; Eloise Has a Lesson; Eloise Skates!; Eloise's New Bonnet. (p. 516)
—Eloise's Christmas Trinkles. (p. 516)
Thompson, Kay & McClatchy, Lisa. Eloise Visits the Zoo. Lyon, Tammie, illus. (p. 516)
Thompson, Keith. Bells Lake Treasure. (p. 163)
Thompson, Keith, illus. see Oppel, Kenneth.
Thompson, Keith, illus. see Skye, Obert.
Thompson, Keith, illus. see Westerfeld, Scott.
Thompson, Kel, et al. Should, Could, & Would. (p. 1569)
Thompson, Kelly. Lasting. (p. 979)
Thompson, Kelvin. Stop & Think about It: Ten Tips to Take Teens Higher. (p. 1653)
Thompson, Kim. Eldritch Manor. (p. 508)
Thompson, Kim, ed. see Bagge, Peter.
Thompson, Kim, illus. see Regan, Lisa.
Thompson, Kim & Carder, Ken. Phonics. Billman, Dave et al, illus. (p. 1351)
Thompson, Kim Mitzo. Bible Songs. (p. 176)
—Bible Stories. (p. 176)
—Birthday Party. (p. 193)
—Easter Story. (p. 499)
—Five Little Monkeys Jumping on the Bed. Girouard, Patrick, illus. (p. 600)
—Old MacDonald Had a Farm. Girouard, Patrick, illus. (p. 1284)
—Wheels on the Bus. Holm, Sharon Lane, illus. (p. 1901)
Thompson, Kim Mitzo, jt. auth. see Hilderbrand, Karen Mitzo.
Thompson, Kim Mitzo, jt. auth. see Twin Sisters(r) Staff.
Thompson, Kim Mitzo & Hilderbrand, Karen Mitzo. Alphabet. (p. 49)
—Counting. (p. 370)
—Deluxe Phonics Kit (p. 425)
—Farm Animals. (p. 573)
Thompson, Kim Mitzo & Hilderbrand, Karen Mitzo, adapted by. Multiplication. (p. 1190)
Thompson, Kim Mitzo & Hilderbrand, Karen Mitzo. Multiplication Rap. (p. 1190)
—Wild Animals. (p. 1928)
Thompson, Kim Mitzo & Thompson, Bailey. I Love You More. (p. 843)
Thompson, Kim Mitzo, et al. My First Bible Color & Trace Book. (p. 1204)
—My First Bible Cut & Glue Book. (p. 1204)
—Trace & Learn Sticker Fun: Numbers & Counting. (p. 1774)
Thompson, Kimberly. Toulouse Tangled up in Lights. Easey, Chris, illus. (p. 1773)
Thompson, Kirk Robert. Paradise Lost: Earth First. (p. 1323)
Thompson, Kristi June, illus. see Thompson, Holly Sue.
Thompson, Kristin, jt. auth. see Bordwell, David.
Thompson, Kristin & Grigsby, Ann, creators. Creating a Legacy: Leave More Than Money. (p. 378)
Thompson, L. J. Nick & Thomas: The Watering Hole. (p. 1251)
Thompson, Landy. Altamaha River. (p. 50)
Thompson, Larry Clinton. William Scott Ament & the Boxer Rebellion: Heroism, Hubris & the Ideal Missionary. (p. 1933)
Thompson, Lauren. Apple Pie That Papa Baked. Bean, Jonathan, illus. (p. 92)
—Chew, Chew, Gulp! Krosoczka, Jarrett J., illus. (p. 299)
—Christmas Gift for Mama. Burke, Jim, illus. (p. 314)
—Christmas Magic. Muth, Jon J., illus. (p. 314)
—Cuaquito (Little Quack) Anderson, Derek, illus. (p. 388)
—Forgiveness Garden. Hale, Christy & Apostolou, Christine Hale, illus. (p. 619)
—Hop, Hop, Jump! Krosoczka, Jarrett J., illus. (p. 796)
—Leap Back Home to Me. Cordell, Matthew, illus. (p. 982)
—Little Bunny. Butler, John, illus. (p. 1025)
—Little Chick. Butler, John, illus. (p. 1026)
—Little Chick/Little Bunny Vertical 2-Pack. Butler, John, illus. (p. 1026)
—Little Lamb. Butler, John, illus. (p. 1030)
—Little Quack. Anderson, Derek, illus. (p. 1034)
—Little Quack Counts. Anderson, Derek, illus. (p. 1034)
—Little Quack Loves Colors. Anderson, Derek, illus. (p. 1034)
—Little Quack's ABC's. Anderson, Derek, illus. (p. 1034)
—Little Quack's Bath Book. Anderson, Derek, illus. (p. 1034)
—Little Quack's Bedtime. Anderson, Derek, illus. (p. 1034)
—Little Quack's New Friend. Anderson, Derek, illus. (p. 1034)
—Little Quack's Opposites. Anderson, Derek, illus. (p. 1034)
—Mouse Loves School. Erdogan, Buket, illus. (p. 1182)
—Mouse's First Christmas. Erdogan, Buket, illus. (p. 1182)
—Mouse's First Day of School. Erdogan, Buket, illus. (p. 1182)
—Mouse's First Fall. Erdogan, Buket, illus. (p. 1182)
—Mouse's First Halloween. Erdogan, Buket, illus. (p. 1182)
—Mouse's First Snow. Erdogan, Buket, illus. (p. 1182)
—Mouse's First Spring. Erdogan, Buket, illus. (p. 1182)
—Mouse's First Summer. Erdogan, Buket, illus. (p. 1182)
—Mouse's First Valentine. Erdogan, Buket, illus. (p. 1182)
—One Starry Night. Bean, Jonathan, illus. (p. 1297)
—Polar Bear Morning. Savage, Stephen, illus. (p. 1378)
—Polar Bear Night. Savage, Stephen, illus. (p. 1378)
—Wee Little Bunny. Butler, John, illus. (p. 1871)
—Wee Little Chick. Butler, John, illus. (p. 1871)
—Wee Little Lamb. Butler, John, illus. (p. 1871)
Thompson, Lauren & Anderson, Derek. Little Quack's Bedtime. (p. 1034)
—Little Quack's Hide & Seek. (p. 1034)
Thompson, Lauren & Ferrara, Joanne. Ballerina Dreams. Estrin, James, photos by. (p. 134)
Thompson, Lauren & Jackson, Livia. Mouse's First Day of School. Erdogan, Buket, illus. (p. 1182)
Thompson, Laurie. Be Gentle with Baby (p. 148)
Thompson, Laurie Ann. Emmanuel's Dream: The True Story of Emmanuel Ofosu Yeboah. Qualls, Sean, illus. (p. 520)
—My Dog Is the Best. Schmid, Paul, illus. (p. 1202)
Thompson, Lesley. Zombie Attack! (p. 1988)
Thompson, Linda. California Gold Rush. (p. 253)
—Grandes Lagos. (p. 707)
—Santa Fe Trail. (p. 1511)
—Spanish in America. (p. 1621)
—Territorios de Estados Unidos. (p. 1722)
Thompson, Linda C. I Am My Own Dragon: A Metaphysical Novel Offering Transformation & Hope While Engrossing, Entertaining, & Enlightening. (p. 833)
Thompson, Lisa. Art in Action: Have You Got What It Takes to Be an Animator? (p. 102)
—Battling Blazes: Have You Got What It Takes to Be a Firefighter? (p. 147)
—Behind Every Step: Have You Got What It Takes to Be a Choreographer? (p. 160)
—Creating Cuisine: Have You Got What It Takes to Be a Chef? (p. 378)
—Creatures of the Deep. (p. 380)
—Digging for Buried Treasure. Cantell, Brenda, illus. (p. 439)
—Game On: Have You Got What It Takes to Be a Video Game Developer? (p. 654)
—Hard Hat Area: Have You Got What It Takes to Be a Contractor? (p. 748)
—Head of the Class: Have You Got What It Takes to Be an Early Childhood Teacher? (p. 756)
—In Search of the Egyptian Queen. Cantell, Brenda, illus. (p. 864)
—Inventing the Future. (p. 883)
—Lookout London Jurevicius, Nathan, illus. (p. 1051)
—New York City Thompson, Lisa, illus. (p. 1248)
—Objection! Have You Got What It Takes to Be a Lawyer? (p. 1275)
—On the Job (p. 1290)
—Pop the Hood: Have You Got What It Takes to Be an Auto Technician? (p. 1384)
—Quest for El Dorado. (p. 1426)
—Sea Life Scientist: Have You Got What It Takes to Be a Marine Biologist? (p. 1534)
—Search for the Lost Cavern. (p. 1537)
—Sent to Sydney Squire, Stan, illus. (p. 1551)
—Spectacular Spain Jones, Helen, illus. (p. 1624)
—Tokyo Techno Chan, Jimmy, illus. (p. 1762)
—Wild about Wildlife: Have You Got What It Takes to Be a Zookeeper? (p. 1928)
—Wild Waves. (p. 1930)
—Wreck of the Atocha. (p. 1962)
Thompson, Lisa, jt. auth. see O'Neill, Katrina.
Thompson, Louise. Cold Weather Readers. (p. 339)
Thompson, Love. Lineage. (p. 1019)
Thompson, Luke. Earth. (p. 495)
—Neptune. (p. 1241)
Thompson, Lydia, illus. see Hunter, Lee Hargus.
Thompson, Maeva. How Shall They Hear? (p. 812)
Thompson, Margaret. Fox Winter. Akin, Galan, tr. (p. 626)
Thompson, Margot, illus. see Cumbaa, Stephen.
Thompson, Margot, illus. see Lee, Dora & Palmer, Dora.
Thompson, Margot, illus. see Mason, Adrienne.
Thompson, Margot, illus. see Strauss, Rochelle.
Thompson, Maria, illus. see Russell, Margaret.
Thompson, Marilyn. Adopting Liberty the Mustang. (p. 13)
Thompson, Marjorie J., jt. auth. see Job, Rueben P.
Thompson, Mary G. Escape from the Pipe Men! (p. 535)
—Wuftoom. (p. 1966)
Thompson, Mel. Buddhism (p. 234)
Thompson, Michael. Los Otros Osos Thompson, Michael, illus. (p. 1054)
—Los Otros Osos / the Other Bears. Thompson, Michael, illus. (p. 1054)
—Other Bears Thompson, Michael, illus. (p. 1306)
Thompson, Michael J. Lenny the Leaf Has a Wonderful Day. (p. 991)
Thompson, Michelle. Taming the Wind. (p. 1704)
Thompson, Michelle Gormican, illus. see Hierl, Christine Gormican.
Thompson, Mike. Chicken Boy & the Wrath of Dr. Dimwad. Thompson, Mike, illus. (p. 300)
Thompson, Neil. People Problems. Campling, Jo, ed. (p. 1340)
Thompson, Nina C. Puzzle King. (p. 1421)
Thompson, Ofa, jt. auth. see Thompson, Richard.
Thompson, Patricia. Psalms 23: A Child's Story. (p. 1413)
Thompson, Patricia Parrott. Chocolate & Her Meow. (p. 309)
Thompson, Patti. Just Like Jesus. (p. 939)
—Just Like My Dad. (p. 939)
—Shepherd vs the World: A Middle Child's Boo-Boo Book. (p. 1565)
Thompson, Paul B. Battle for the Brightstone: Book III of the Brightstone Saga. (p. 145)
—Billy the Kid: It Was a Game of Two & I Got There First. (p. 187)
—Brightworking (p. 228)
—Brightworking: Book I of the Brightstone Saga. (p. 228)
—Devil's Door: A Salem Witchcraft Story. (p. 432)
—Fortune-Teller: Book II of the Brightstone Saga. (p. 623)
—Joan of Arc: Warrior Saint of France. (p. 919)
—Liberty's Son: A Spy Story of the American Revolution. (p. 1005)
—Lost Republic. (p. 1056)
Thompson, Richard. Mighty Alice Goes Round & Round: A Cul de Sac Book. (p. 1139)
Thompson, Richard, illus. see Shields, Carol Diggory.
Thompson, Richard, jt. auth. see Thompson, Springett.
Thompson, Richard & Spicer, Maggee. We'll All Go Exploring LaFave, Kim, illus. (p. 1874)
—When They Are Up... Wakelin, Kirsti Anne, illus. (p. 1905)
Thompson, Richard & Thompson, Ofa. Ko 'Eku Tohi Lau Maau. Slutz, Stephani, illus. (p. 966)
—Ko 'Eku Tohi 'oe Fanga Manu. Slutz, Stephani, illus. (p. 966)
—Ko'eku Tohi Lau Fika. Lee, Bill, illus. (p. 966)
Thompson, Richard, et al. Ko 'Eku Tohi Lau Mata'itohi. (p. 966)
Thompson, Richard, Jr. Ice Cream Bucket Effect. (p. 850)
Thompson, Ricki. City of Cannibals. (p. 323)
Thompson, Robb. Excellence in the Workplace. (p. 547)
Thompson, Robert B. Heaven-God's Wonderful World. (p. 761)
Thompson, Robert W., jt. auth. see Bardakigian, K. D.
Thompson, Ruth. What Are Textiles? (p. 1879)
Thompson, Ruth Plumly. Enchanted Island of Oz. (p. 523)
—Royal Book of Oz. (p. 1492)
—Sissajig & Other Surprises. (p. 1581)
—Wonder Book. (p. 1947)
—Yankee in Oz. (p. 1968)
Thompson, Ruth Plumly, jt. auth. see Baum, L. Frank.
Thompson, Ruth Plumly & Baum, L. Frank. Silver Princess in Oz. Neill, John R., illus. (p. 1576)
Thompson, Ruth-Ann. Connections in the Open Field. (p. 358)
Thompson, Samantha, illus. see Goodall, Lian.
Thompson, Samantha, illus. see Janveau, Teri-Lynn & Thompson, Allister.
Thompson, Sandra S. Numbers & Me. (p. 1272)
Thompson, Scott M., illus. see Lilly, Melinda.
Thompson, Scott M., photos by see Lilly, Melinda.
Thompson, Shannon Raines. Mad about Miller. Stone, Kathrine Thompson, ed. (p. 1068)
—Nuts about Neal. Stone, Kathrine Thompson, ed. (p. 1274)
Thompson, Sharon. Bible Story Puppets & Poems. (p. 176)
—Map Skills: Grade 1. Poitras, Tara & Brooks, Whitney, eds. (p. 1090)
—Map Skills: Grade 3. Poitras, Tara & Brooks, Whitney, eds. (p. 1090)
—Map Skills: Grade 5. Poitras, Tara & Brooks, Whitney, eds. (p. 1090)
Thompson, Sharon, illus. see Broome, Errol.
Thompson, Sharon, illus. see Forrestal, Elaine.
Thompson, Sharon, illus. see Wolfer, Dianne.
Thompson, Sharon & Booth, Vanessa. Christian Crafts for Gift-Giving. Seltzer, Erin, ed. (p. 311)
Thompson, Springett & Thompson, Richard. Follower Springett, Martin, illus. (p. 612)
Thompson, Stephen, ed. Teens at Risk. (p. 1715)
Thompson, Sunnie R., illus. see Thompson, Deanna T.
Thompson, Susan, jt. auth. see Helms, Selah.
Thompson, Susan, jt. auth. see Thompson, John.
Thompson, Susan A. Katie the Christian Caterpillar: The Loss of a Loved One. (p. 945)
Thompson, Susan C. Elephants Are Wrinkly: Integrated Science Activities for Young Children. (p. 512)
Thompson, Susan Conklin, et al, eds. Mayan Folktales: Cuentos Folklóricos Mayas (p. 1113)
Thompson, Tamara. Abortion. Greenhaven Press Staff, ed. (p. 5)
—Before You Were Born. (p. 159)
—Expanding the Human Lifespan. Greenhaven Press Editors, ed. (p. 548)
—Fast Food. Greenhaven Press Staff, ed. (p. 576)
—Homelessness. Greenhaven Press Editors, ed. (p. 793)
—Oil Spills. Greenhaven Press Editors & Gale, A. G., eds. (p. 1282)
—Oil Spills. Greenhaven Press Editors & Gale Editors, eds. (p. 1282)
—Rap & Hip-Hop. (p. 1438)
—Right to Die. Gale, G., ed. (p. 1472)
—Self-Defense Laws. Greenhaven Press Editors, ed. (p. 1549)
—Self-Defense Laws. Greenhaven Press Editors & Gale, A. G., eds. (p. 1549)
—Solar Storms. (p. 1607)
—Transgender People. (p. 1778)
Thompson, Tamara, ed. Ethics of Medical Testing. (p. 539)
—Solar Storms. (p. 1607)
Thompson, Tate. Senioritis. (p. 1550)
Thompson, Tavia. Made by God Wonderfully. (p. 1070)
Thompson, Ted, ed. see McSweeney's Books Staff.
Thompson, Teresa. Adventures of Shasta & Nikki: A True Friendship. (p. 22)
Thompson, Terri. Journey to Thelo. (p. 929)
Thompson, Timothy. Adam & Eve. (p. 11)
Thompson, Tolya L. Catchin' Cooties Consuelo. Harrold, Brian, illus. (p. 279)
—Ingrown Tyrone. Brian, Harrold, illus. (p. 874)
Thompson, Tracey, jt. auth. see Rolle, Joan.
Thompson, Traci Shirley, jt. auth. see Davis, Catherine Jennings.
Thompson, Troy, Jr. Bayou Duprey. (p. 147)
Thompson, Tyler. Sneaker Freak (p. 1597)
Thompson, Ursula. Nobody Owes Me Anything: A Child's Guide to Self-Responsibility. (p. 1262)
Thompson, Vicki Lewis. Wild & Hexy. (p. 1928)
Thompson, Vinny. Vinny & Bud. (p. 1843)
—Vinny & Bud Comix Book II. (p. 1843)
Thompson, Vivian L. Neat! Said Jeremy. (p. 1239)
Thompson, Wendy. Claude Debussy: Composer's World. (p. 329)
—Pyotr Ilyich Tchaikovsky: Composer's World. (p. 1421)
Thompson, William & Thompson, Dorcas. George W. Bush. (p. 664)
—Iraq. (p. 887)
Thompson, Yvonne. Miss Tilly's Marching Band. Hardy, Chris, illus. (p. 1152)
—Miss Tilly's Party. Krecskay, Stephen, illus. (p. 1152)
Thompson-Bass, Hester, jt. auth. see Bass, Hester Thompson.
Thompson-Swift, Joseph. Adventures of Primrose Perfect. (p. 21)
Thoms, Annie. With Their Eyes: September 11th - The View from a High School at Ground Zero. (p. 1942)
Thoms, Scott, illus. see Niz, Ellen S.
Thoms, Susan Collins. Twelve Days of Christmas in Michigan. Pilutti, Deb, illus. (p. 1800)
Thomsen, Brian M., ed. see Roosevelt, Theodore, IV.
Thomsen, Natasha. Women's Rights. (p. 1946)
Thomsen, Ruth. Ghastly & Gruesome. (p. 670)
—Myths & Legends. (p. 1227)
—Out & About. (p. 1310)
—Saints. (p. 1504)
Thomson, Andrew, illus. see Anastasio, Dina & Brown, Dinah.
Thomson, Andrew, illus. see Frith, Margaret.
Thomson, Andrew, illus. see Herman, Gail.
Thomson, Andrew, illus. see Medina, Nico.
Thomson, Arthur. Handbook of Anatomy for Art Students. (p. 740)
Thomson, Bill. Chalk Thomson, Bill, illus. (p. 288)
—Fossil Thomson, Bill, illus. (p. 623)
Thomson, Bill, illus. see Nevius, Carol & Nevius, Thomson.
Thomson, Bill, illus. see Nevius, Carol.
Thomson, Carly. Truth Seekers. (p. 1794)
Thomson, Celia. Fallen. (p. 566)
—Stolen. (p. 1652)
Thomson, Celia & Braswell, Liz. Nine Lives of Chloe King: The Fallen; the Stolen; the Chosen. (p. 1256)
Thomson, Cindy. Kenny Chesney. (p. 949)
Thomson, E. Gertrude, illus. see Carroll, Lewis, pseud.
Thomson, Elizabeth & Albert, Sarah. Andros: the Last Villager. (p. 72)
Thomson, Emma. Birthday Ball. Thomson, Emma, illus. (p. 192)
—Fashion Fairytale. Thomson, Emma, illus. (p. 575)
—Friend to Treasure. Thomson, Emma, illus. (p. 637)
—Lili's Fairytale. (p. 1017)
—Princess Pearl & the Underwater Kingdom. Thomson, Emma, illus. (p. 1405)
—Royal Ballet. Thomson, Emma, illus. (p. 1492)
Thomson Gale Staff. Colonial Period: 1607-1750. (p. 341)
—Prejudice in the Modern World. Hanes, Sharon M., ed. (p. 1395)
—Prejudice in the Modern World - Almanac Hanes, Richard C. et al, eds. (p. 1395)
—Reptiles - Grzimek's Student Animal Life (p. 1461)
Thomson Gale Staff & Hermsen, Sarah. Prejudice in the Modern World: Cumulative Index. (p. 1395)
—Prejudice in the Modern World: Biographies. Hanes, Richard C. & Rudd, Kelly, eds. (p. 1395)
Thomson, Jamie. Dark Lord: The Early Years. (p. 407)
—School's Out. (p. 1524)
Thomson, Jane. Jenny Wants to Talk to Jesus-V. 1. 2 Sm. (p. 913)
Thomson, Jeanette. Hurry up Joey: It's Time to Go! (p. 830)
Thomson, Jimmy. Koala Bounces Back. Lobbecke, Eric, illus. (p. 966)
—Koala Bounces Back. Löbbecke, Eric, illus. (p. 966)
—Koala Who Bounced. Löbbecke, Eric, illus. (p. 966)
Thomson, John. Small Boat at the Bottom of the Sea. (p. 1591)
Thomson, Kate. Wild Blood. (p. 1929)
Thomson, Leo. Sense of Place: Landscapes. (p. 1551)
Thomson, Linda. Harry the Hypno-potamus: Metaphorical Tales for the Treatment of Children. (p. 751)
Thomson, Malcolm. Let's Go Nuts. (p. 997)
—Saga of the Vegvisir. (p. 1502)
Thomson, Maria, ed. see Yorke, Jane & Dorling Kindersley Publishing Staff.
Thomson, Melissa. Keena Ford & the Field Trip Mix-Up. (p. 946)
—Keena Ford & the Second-Grade Mix-Up. Morrison, Frank, illus. (p. 946)
—Keena Ford & the Secret Journal Mix-Up. Morrison, Frank, illus. (p. 946)
Thomson, Melissa & Dean, Ruth. Women of the Renaissance. (p. 1946)
Thomson, Pat. It's So Unfair! Allen, Jonathan, illus. (p. 899)
Thomson, Rachel Starr. Theodore Pharris Saves the Universe. (p. 1729)
Thomson, Rachel Starr & Currey, Carolyn Joy. Tales of the Heartily Homeschooled. (p. 1702)
Thomson, Regan, illus. see Kootstra, Kara.
Thomson, Roger, jt. auth. see Shock, Tanya.
Thomson, Russell, jt. auth. see Harris, Dave.
Thomson, Ruth. 1, 2, 3. (p. 1990)
—Adventure Stories: Writing Activities to Brong Out Your Senses of Adventure! (p. 14)

—Amazing Stories. (p. 56)
—Art Creativity Book. (p. 101)
—Art Pocket Activity Fun & Games: Games & Puzzles, Fold-Out Scenes, Patterned Paper, Stickers! (p. 103)
—Bee's Life Cycle. (p. 158)
—Celebrations. (p. 285)
—Chicken's Life Cycle. (p. 300)
—Coasts. (p. 336)
—Countries (p. 372)
—Creatures. (p. 380)
—Dinosaur's Day. (p. 444)
—Fairy Tales: Writing Activities with Your Favorite Fairy Tale Characters. (p. 564)
—Families: Relationships in Art. (p. 567)
—Families. (p. 567)
—First Look At. (p. 596)
—Four Freckled Frogs. (p. 625)
—France. (p. 627)
—Frog's Life Cycle. (p. 641)
—India. (p. 870)
—Journeys. (p. 929)
—Leaves. (p. 986)
—Let's Look at Life Cycles (p. 999)
—Life Cycle of a Bean. (p. 1008)
—Life Cycle of a Cat. (p. 1009)
—Life Cycle of a Chicken. (p. 1009)
—Life Cycle of a Crab. (p. 1009)
—Life Cycle of a Frog. (p. 1009)
—Life Cycle of a Honeybee. (p. 1009)
—Life Cycle of a Ladybug. (p. 1009)
—Life Cycle of a Rose. (p. 1009)
—Life Cycle of a Salmon. (p. 1009)
—Life Cycle of an Apple. (p. 1009)
—Life Cycle of an Oak Tree. (p. 1009)
—Life Cycle of an Owl. (p. 1009)
—Living in Bangladesh. Matthews, Jenny, photos by. (p. 1041)
—Living in India. Hampton, David, illus. (p. 1041)
—Living in Kenya. Hampton, David, photos by. (p. 1041)
—Mountains. (p. 1181)
—Myths. (p. 1227)
—Photos Framed: A Fresh Look at the World's Most Memorable Photographs. (p. 1353)
—Places. (p. 1366)
—Poland. (p. 1378)
—Portraits. (p. 1387)
—Rain Forests. (p. 1434)
—Rivers. (p. 1476)
—Ruidos. (p. 1494)
—Science & Inventions Creativity Book: Games, Models to Make, High-Tech Craft Paper, Stickers, & Stencils. (p. 1525)
—Science & Inventions Pocket Activity Fun & Games: Games & Puzzles, Fold-Out Scenes, Patterned Paper, Stickers! (p. 1525)
—Sixteen Fleecy Sheep. (p. 1583)
—Spain. (p. 1620)
—Sunflower's Life Cycle. (p. 1676)
—Terezin: Voices from the Holocaust. (p. 1721)
—Two Blue Cockatoos. (p. 1803)
—Weather. (p. 1869)
Thomson, Ruth, jt. auth. see Langmuir, Erika.
Thomson, Ruth & Corbett, Pie. Chatting Cheetahs & Jumping Jacks. (p. 295)
Thomson, Ryan J. Captain Fiddle's Tunes & Variations (p. 264)
—Left Handed Fiddling for Beginners: A Teach Yourself Method (p. 987)
Thomson, Sarah, jt. auth. see Ford, Gabrielle.
Thomson, Sarah L. Amazing Dolphins! Wildlife Conservation Society, photos by. (p. 54)
—Amazing Gorillas! Wildlife Conservation Society, photos by. (p. 54)
—Amazing Sharks! (p. 55)
—Amazing Sharks! Wildlife Conservation Society, photos by. (p. 55)
—Amazing Snakes! Wildlife Conservation Society, photos by. (p. 55)
—Amazing Tigers! (p. 56)
—Amazing Whales! (p. 56)
—Amazing Whales! Wildlife Conservation Society, photos by. (p. 56)
—American Flag Q & A. Collins Staff, illus. (p. 60)
—Ancient Animals: Saber-Toothed Cat. Plant, Andrew, illus. (p. 67)
—Around the Neighborhood: A Counting Lullaby Christy, Jana, illus. (p. 100)
—Cinderella Ceccoli, Nicoletta, illus. (p. 320)
—Cub's Big World. Cepeda, Joe, illus. (p. 389)
—Dragon's Egg. (p. 479)
—Extreme Dinosaurs! Q & A. (p. 556)
—Extreme Stars! Q&A. (p. 557)
—Feel the Summer. Yamada, Kana, illus. (p. 580)
—Imagine a Day. Gonsalves, Robert & Gonsalves, Rob, illus. (p. 860)
—Imagine a Night. Gonsalves, Rob, illus. (p. 860)
—Imagine a Place. Gonsalves, Rob, illus. (p. 860)
—Mercy: The Last New England Vampire (p. 1127)
—Pirates, Ho! Gilpin, Stephen, illus. (p. 1363)
—Stars & Stripes: The Story of the American Flag. Dacey, Bob & Bandelin, Debra, illus. (p. 1643)
—What Lincoln Said. Ransome, James E., illus. (p. 1891)
—Where Do Polar Bears Live? Chin, Jason, illus. (p. 1907)
Thomson, Sarah L., jt. auth. see McGuinness, Denis E.
Thomson, Sarah L., jt. auth. see Mendell, David.
Thomson, Sarah L., jt. auth. see Piven, Hanoch.
Thomson, Sarah L. & Plant, Andrew. Ancient Animals: Terror Bird. (p. 67)
—Ancient Animals: Terror Birds. (p. 68)
Thomson, Tom, jt. auth. see Newlands, Anne.
Thomson, Tracy, illus. see Watson, Patrick.
Thomson-Swift, Joe. Monkeyboy & the Gruffits. (p. 1165)
—Twig People of Mossdown Woods. (p. 1801)
Thomson-Swift, Joe, jt. auth. see Thomson-Swift, Joseph.
Thomson-Swift, Joseph & Thomson-Swift, Joe. Giant, the Antman & the Mermaid. (p. 674)
Thong, Roseanne. Cuddly Bear Cubs Carnival. (p. 389)
—Fly Free! Neilan, Eujin Kim, illus. (p. 609)
—Gai See: What You Can See in Chinatown. Choi, Yangsook, illus. (p. 652)
—Red Is a Dragon: A Book of Colors. Lin, Grace, illus. (p. 1454)
—Red Is a Dragon. Lin, Grace, illus. (p. 1454)
—Round Is a Mooncake: A Book of Shapes. Lin, Grace, illus. (p. 1491)
—Round Is a Mooncake. (p. 1491)
—Round Is a Tortilla. Parra, John, illus. (p. 1491)
—Wishing Tree. McLennan, Connie, illus. (p. 1940)
Thong, Roseanne, jt. auth. see Chronicle Books Staff.
Thong, Roseanne Greenfield. Green Is a Chile Pepper: A Book of Colors. (p. 722)
—Green Is a Chile Pepper: A Book of Colors. Parra, John, illus. (p. 722)
—Noodle Magic. So, Meilo, illus. (p. 1264)
—Round Is a Tortilla: A Book of Shapes. (p. 1491)
—Round Is a Tortilla: A Book of Shapes. Parra, John, illus. (p. 1491)
Thongmoon, Kriangsak, illus. see Montgomery, R. A.
Thongmoon, Kriangsak, jt. illus. see Sundaravej, Sittisan.
Thonissen, Uta, jt. auth. see Cratzius, Barbara.
Thor, Annika. Faraway Island. Schenck, Linda, tr. (p. 573)
—Lily Pond. Schenck, Linda, tr. (p. 1018)
Thor, Annika & Schenck, Linda. Deep Sea. (p. 423)
Thor, Cook Jean. Jesus Calms the Storm. (p. 915)
Thoraval, Carly, illus. see Belanger, Madeleine.
Thorburn, Mark. Executive Branch: Leading the Nation. (p. 548)
—President & the Executive Branch: How Our Nation Is Governed. (p. 1396)
Thordsen, Isabella, jt. auth. see Busath, Isabelle.
Thoreau, Henry. Thoreau: A Book of Quotations. Blaisdell, Bob, ed. (p. 1740)
—Walking. Clifton Johnson, illus. (p. 1854)
Thoresen, Susan Werner. Yoyo & the Piggy Bank. Eveland, Keith & Eveland, Keith, illus. (p. 1982)
Thoreson-Snipes, Nanette. Elijah Helps the Widow. Morris, Susan, illus. (p. 512)
Thorhauer, Laura L. Molly's Wings. (p. 1161)
Thorn, Aramis. Foster Father of God. (p. 624)
Thorn, Pepper. Princess Rose & the Crystal Castle. (p. 1405)
Thorn, Randall. Through the Valley of Bones. (p. 1745)
Thornborough, Kathy. Animals. Petelinsek, Kathleen, illus. (p. 81)
—Colors & Shapes. Petelinsek, Kathleen, illus. (p. 345)
—Days & Times. Petelinsek, Kathleen, illus. (p. 415)
—Family & Friends. Petelinsek, Kathleen, illus. (p. 568)
—Feelings & Emotions. Petelinsek, Kathleen, illus. (p. 580)
—Food. Petelinsek, Kathleen, illus. (p. 612)
—Greetings & Phrases. Petelinsek, Kathleen, illus. (p. 723)
—Questions & Answers. Petelinsek, Kathleen, illus. (p. 1426)
—School. Petelinsek, Kathleen, illus. (p. 1522)
—Seasons. Petelinsek, Kathleen, illus. (p. 1538)
—Weather. Petelinsek, Kathleen, illus. (p. 1869)
—Work. Petelinsek, Kathleen, illus. (p. 1952)
Thornborough, Tim. Fright of Your Life (p. 639)
Thornborrow, Nick, illus. see Walker, Persephone.
Thornburg, Linda. Cool Careers for Girls in Cybersecurity & National Safety. (p. 362)
Thornburg, Michael. Monster Kids' Adventures: The Retur. (p. 1167)
Thornburgh, Gail, jt. auth. see Donahue, Mary R.
Thornburgh, Rebecca. Cars, Trucks & Things That Go. (p. 272)
Thornburgh, Rebecca, illus. see Bostrom, Kathleen Long.
Thornburgh, Rebecca, illus. see DeRubertis, Barbara.
Thornburgh, Rebecca, illus. see Dussling, Jennifer.
Thornburgh, Rebecca, illus. see Hopkins, Jackie Mims.
Thornburgh, Rebecca, illus. see Moncure, Jane Belk.
Thornburgh, Rebecca, illus. see Pingry, Patricia A.
Thornburgh, Rebecca, illus. see Ritchie, Joseph R.
Thornburgh, Rebecca, illus. see Rollins, Jack & Nelson, Steve.
Thornburgh, Rebecca, illus. see Trueit, Trudi Strain.
Thornburgh, Rebecca McKillip. Rufus & Ryan Give Thanks. (p. 1494)
Thornburgh, Rebecca McKillip, illus. see Driscoll, Laura.
Thornburgh, Rebecca McKillip, illus. see Dussling, Jennifer.
Thornburgh, Rebecca McKillip, illus. see Hopkins, Jackie Mims.
Thornburgh, Rebecca McKillip, illus. see Pingry, Patricia A.
Thornburgh, Rebecca McKillip, illus. see Ritchie, Joseph R.
Thornburgh, Rebecca McKillip, illus. see Rollins, Jack & Nelson, Steve.
Thornburgh, Rebecca McKillip, illus. see Stevenson, Robert Louis.
Thorne, B. Michael & Henley, Tracy. Connections in the History & Systems of Psychology. (p. 358)
Thorne, Bella. Autumn Falls. (p. 118)
Thorne, Frank. Prodigal: Egg of First Light: Egg of First Light. (p. 1409)
Thorne, Hayden. Icarus in Flight. (p. 850)
—Masks: Evolution. (p. 1102)
—Renfred's Masquerade. (p. 1460)
Thorne, Jenn Marie. Wrong Side of Right. (p. 1965)
Thorne, Jenny, illus. see Adair, Gilbert.
Thorne, Jenny, illus. see Baxter, Nicola, ed.
Thorne, Jenny, illus. see Baxter, Nicola.
Thorne, Jenny, illus. see Dickens, Charles.
Thorne, Jenny, illus. see Kipling, Rudyard.
Thorne, Jenny, illus. see Wilde, Oscar.
Thorne, Justin. In the Shadows: An Anthology of the Curious. (p. 867)
Thorne, K. C. Troll of MacKinac. Johnson, Vickie, illus. (p. 1788)
Thorne, Lawrence R., jt. creator see Seltzer, Donna Lee.
Thorne MBE, Tony. junior philosophical Society. (p. 936)
Thorne, Pat. My First Word Book. (p. 1208)
Thorne, Paul & Johnson, Michael. Workaholism: Getting a Life in the Killing Fields of Work. Johnson, Michael, illus. (p. 1952)
Thorne, Randy. Quick & Short Book Reports. (p. 1427)
Thorne, Rick. Hidden Secrets of Jesus & Other Revelations. (p. 776)
Thorne, Sean, illus. see Captain, Tamira.
Thorne, Sydney, jt. auth. see Berwick, Gwen.
Thorne, Troy. Getting Started in Pinewood Derby: Step-by-Step Workbook to Building Your First Car. (p. 669)
Thorne-Thomsen, Gudrun. East O' the Sun & West O' the Moon: With Other Norwegian Folk Tales. (p. 498)
—East O' the Sun & West O' the Moon. Richardson, Frederick, illus. (p. 498)
Thorne-Thomsen, Kathleen. Frank Lloyd Wright for Kids: His Life & Ideas. (p. 628)
—Huntington for Kids: A Kaleidoscope of Books, Art, & Nature. (p. 829)
—Shaker's Dozen: Counting Book. Thorne-Thomsen, Kathleen, illus. (p. 1559)
Thornewell, Danielle. Mems. (p. 1126)
Thorneycroft, Berni. Nap Sack Cat Tales. (p. 1229)
Thornhill, Chris, jt. auth. see King, Michael.
Thornhill, Gail. Secret Life of Truly Jones. (p. 1541)
Thornhill, Jan. Is This Panama? A Migration Story. Kim, Soyeon & Owlkids Books Inc. Staff, illus. (p. 890)
—Kyle Goes Alone. Barron, Ashley, illus. (p. 969)
—Over in the Meadow. (p. 1313)
—Over in the Meadow. Thornhill, Jan, illus. (p. 1313)
—Who Wants Pizza? The Kids' Guide to the History, Science & Culture of Food. (p. 1918)
—Wildlife 123: A Nature Counting Book. (p. 1931)
—Wildlife ABC: A Nature Alphabet Book. Thornhill, Jan, illus. (p. 1931)
—Winter's Coming: A Story of Seasonal Change. Bisaillon, Josée, illus. (p. 1938)
Thornhill, Jan & Owlkids Books Inc. Staff. This Is My Planet: The Kids' Guide to Global Warming. (p. 1736)
Thornhill, Robert. Christmas Crooks of Rainbow Road. (p. 313)
—Ghosts & Goblins of Rainbow Road. (p. 672)
—Sports Heroes of Rainbow Road. (p. 1632)
Thornhill, Ron. Ronnie the Rambunctious Rhino. (p. 1487)
Thornhorn. Kestrel Waters: A Tale of Love & Devil. (p. 949)
Thornley, John, tr. see Zei, Alki.
Thornley, Rebecca Gundersen. I Know He Is There: A Lift-A-Flap Book about Faith. Dorman, Brandon, illus. (p. 840)
Thornley, Stew. Derek Jeter: Daring to Dream. (p. 427)
—Kevin Garnett: Champion Basketball Star. (p. 950)
—Roberto Clemente. (p. 1479)
—Sports Jokes to Tickle Your Funny Bone. (p. 1633)
—Super Sports Star Barry Bonds. (p. 1682)
—Super Sports Star Brett Favre. (p. 1682)
—Super Sports Star Chipper Jones. (p. 1682)
—Super Sports Star Daunte Culpepper. (p. 1682)
—Super Sports Star Eddie George. (p. 1682)
—Super Sports Star Ken Griffey, Jr. (p. 1682)
—Super Sports Star Randy Moss. (p. 1682)
Thornton, Amy. Meet Sambam. (p. 1122)
Thornton, Barbara, illus. see Stolz, Donald R.
Thornton, Brian. Everything Kids' Presidents Book: Puzzles, Games, & Trivia - For Hours of Presidential Fun! (p. 545)
—States Book: Wind Your Way Across Our Great Nation. (p. 1644)
Thornton, Catherine. Why Mum? A Small Child Dealing with a Big Problem. (p. 1925)
Thornton, Christine, illus. see Shacter, Sara F.
Thornton, D. S. Scrap City. Bowater, Charlie, illus. (p. 1532)
Thornton, Denise. Living with Cancer: The Ultimate Teen Guide. (p. 1042)
—Physical Disabilities: The Ultimate Teen Guide. (p. 1353)
Thornton, E. J. I Have a Secret: Do I Keep It? (p. 839)
Thornton, Fleur, jt. auth. see Edwards, Andrew.
Thornton, Geoffrey. Illustrated Wynken, Blynken, & Nod. (p. 858)
—What's Wrong? Visual Adventures in Critical Thinking. (p. 1900)
Thornton, J. D. How to Make Money. (p. 820)
Thornton, Jan. Haunted Fairy Tales - Volume 1. Thornton, Jan, illus. (p. 753)
—Spooky Halloween Stories Volume 1. Thornton, Jan, illus. (p. 1631)
—Spooky Haunted Castle. (p. 1631)
—Spooky Haunted Forest. (p. 1631)
—Spooky Haunted Graveyard. (p. 1631)
—Spooky Haunted Halloween House. (p. 1631)
—Spooky Haunted Hollow. (p. 1631)
—Spooky Haunted House. (p. 1631)
—Spooky Haunted Stories Part 1. Thornton, Jan, illus. (p. 1631)
Thornton, Jeremy. Birth of the American Navy. (p. 192)
—Famous Women of the American Revolution. (p. 570)
—Foreign-Born Champions of the American Revolution. (p. 617)
—French & Indian War. (p. 635)
—Gold Rush: Chinese Immigrants Come to America (1848-1882) (p. 694)
—Hard Times in Ireland: The Scotch-Irish Come to America (1603-1775) (p. 748)
—History of Early New York. (p. 784)
—Immigration & the Slave Trade: Africans Come to America, 1607-1830. (p. 861)
—Irish Potato Famine: Irish Immigrants Come to America, 1845-1850. (p. 888)
—New Industries, New Jobs: British Immigrants Come to America(1830s-1890s) (p. 1245)
—New Industries, New Jobs: British Immigrants Come to America (1830s-1890s) (p. 1245)
—Religious Intolerance: Jewish Immigrants Come to America (1881-1914) (p. 1458)
—Tories & Patriots: Neighbors at War. (p. 1769)
Thornton, Kim. Safety. (p. 1502)
Thornton, Kristen. God Cares for Little Birdies Too. (p. 688)
Thornton, Laura. Name of an Angel. (p. 1228)
Thornton, M. H. Kylee & Lexie: Mystery of the Gholdees. (p. 969)
Thornton, MaryAnne. Fiona Fabulous O'Malley: One of a Kind. (p. 589)
—Penelope the Princess. (p. 1336)
Thornton, Peter J., illus. see Dooley, Norah.
Thornton, Randy, jt. auth. see Disney Book Group Staff.
Thornton, Susan, jt. auth. see Steffen, Tim.
Thornton, Susan Ann, jt. auth. see Steffen, Tim.
Thornton, Vera E. Useless Donkey. (p. 1828)
Thornycroft, Rosalind, illus. see Farjeon, Eleanor & Farjeon, Herbert.
Thorogood, Keith. Milli Meets the Tooth Fairies. (p. 1143)
Thorold, David & Barber, Jill. Roman Invaders & Settlers. (p. 1485)
Thorold, Jade Melissa. Dirty Dinosaur. (p. 446)
Thoron, Joe. Earthquakes. (p. 497)
—Hurricanes. (p. 830)
—Kaleidoscope Natural Disasters Group 1 (p. 942)
—Tornadoes. (p. 1770)
—Volcanoes. (p. 1849)
Thorp, Cameron, illus. see Miller, Ray, et al.
Thorp, Cameron, illus. see Ritsi, Renee.
Thorp, Gloria J. & Ruotsala, Charity Ali. Anna's Hats: Anna has a hat for every Adventure. (p. 85)
Thorp, Michael. Legend of the Abominable Huckleberry: (or) the Practically True Story of How the Huckleberry Railroad Got its Name. (p. 989)
Thorp, Michael C. Ben Brown & the Return of the Nephilim. Mazumdar, Sintu, illus. (p. 163)
Thorpe, Dan K., ed. see Ricketts, Mark.
Thorpe, Kiki. Before the Bell. (p. 158)
—Before the Bell. RH Disney Staff, illus. (p. 158)
—Dandelion Wish. Christy, Jana, illus. (p. 403)
—Disney's Kim Possible: Chapter Book (p. 453)
—Dónde Está Boots? - Cuento para Levantar la Tapita. Savitsky, Steven, illus. (p. 466)
—Dora's Chilly Day. Savitsky, Steven, illus. (p. 471)
—Fairy's Gift (Disney: the Never Girls) RH Disney Staff, illus. (p. 565)
—Far from Shore. (p. 572)
—Far from Shore. RH Disney Staff, illus. (p. 572)
—From the Mist. Christy, Jana, illus. (p. 644)
—In a Blink. Christy, Jana, illus. (p. 862)
—In a Blink. Christy, Jana & RH Disney Staff, illus. (p. 862)
—Never Girls Collection Christy, Jana & RH Disney Staff, illus. (p. 1243)
—On the Trail. Christy, Jana, illus. (p. 1291)
—Pinch of Magic. (p. 1359)
—Pinch of Magic. Christy, Jana, illus. (p. 1359)
—Space Between. Christy, Jana, illus. (p. 1618)
—Space Between. Christy, Jana & RH Disney Staff, illus. (p. 1618)
—Three's a Krowd. (p. 1744)
—Wedding Wings. (p. 1871)
—Wedding Wings. Christy, Jana, illus. (p. 1871)
—Woods Beyond. Christy, Jana, illus. (p. 1949)
—Woods Beyond. Christy, Jana, illus. (p. 1950)
Thorpe, Kiki, see McCoy, Mimi, pseud.
Thorpe, Kiki, adapted by. Broken Hearts. (p. 230)
Thorpe, Kiki & RH Disney Staff. From the Mist. Christy, Jana & RH Disney Staff, illus. (p. 644)
Thorpe, Leonie Jayne. Archie's Adventures. (p. 95)
Thorpe, Linda W. Teeny-Weeny's Two Front Teeth. (p. 1715)
Thorpe, Patrick, ed. see Himekawa, Akira, et al.
Thorpe, Patrick, ed. see Lenkov, Peter.
Thorpe, Patrick, ed. see Norton, Mike & Hopeless, Dennis.
Thorpe, Patrick, ed. see Powell, Martin.
Thorpe, Patrick, ed. see Remender, Rick.
Thorpe, Peter, illus. see Osterweil, Adam.
Thorpe, Rochelle O'Neal. Gabe's Nantucket Adventure: Daffodils, Dogs, & Cars. Nakell, Eugenie, ed. (p. 652)
Thorpe, Roslyn C. Danny the New Kid in School. (p. 406)
—Rayray's Amazing Dream: An Adventurous Week. (p. 1441)
Thorpe, Sandy. Sand in Their Shoes. (p. 1510)
Thorpe, Tony & Citizenship Foundation Staff. Understanding Citizenship (p. 1815)
Thorpe, Tony & Marsh, David. Citizenship Studies for OCR GCSE Short Course. (p. 323)
Thorpe, Yvonne. Snowboarding. (p. 1600)
Thorpe, Yvonne, jt. auth. see Downing, David.
Thorpe, Yvonne & Mason, Paul. Graphing Buildings & Structures (p. 711)
Thorsen, Jody & Gates, Jeremy S. Boy Who Cried Dinosaur. (p. 219)
Thorsland, Dan, ed. see Starlin, Jim, et al.
Thorson, Kristine, jt. auth. see Thorson, Robert.
Thorson, Kristine, et al. Stone Wall Secrets Moore, Gustav, illus. (p. 1653)
Thorson, Robert & Thorson, Kristine. Stone Wall Secrets. Moore, Gustav, illus. (p. 1653)
Thorup, Bryce. Doctor Matthews' Family Christmas. Muller, Ruth, illus. (p. 459)
—Two Birthdays. Muller, Daniel, illus. (p. 1803)
Thottam, Meena. Do or Die Caterpillar. (p. 457)
—Last Dancer. (p. 977)
Thottam, Meena, adapted by. Brothers of the Jungle. (p. 231)
—Chameli's Choice. (p. 289)
—Death, Where are You? (p. 420)
—Maybe I am, Maybe I am Not. (p. 1113)
—Monkey Do as Monkey Does. (p. 1165)
—Pretender. (p. 1398)
—Road to Riches. (p. 1477)
—Sage's Daughter. (p. 1503)
Thoughts Staff. Bugsy Rabbit: Furry Tales (p. 237)
—Lucky Clayman's Story. (p. 1062)
—PNUT BUDDY & JUDDY (the adventures Of) #1. (p. 1374)
—Police Stories: the fight Call. (p. 1380)
Thouin, Juanita. Get Your Wallet On: The Money Quiz for High School Grads. (p. 668)
Thouw, Jennifer. Under the Rainbow. (p. 1814)
Thrall, Gordon & Heflin, Jenifer. Puertas Abiertas Student Workbook: Open Doors to Spanish. Level 1 (p. 1414)
Thran, Nick. Halifax Hal. Foreman, Gabe, illus. (p. 737)

T

Thrash, Maggie. Honor Girl: A Graphic Memoir. Thrash, Maggie, illus. (p. 795)
Thrasher, Amanda M. Fairy Match in the Mushroom Patch. (p. 563)
—Ghost of Whispering Willow. (p. 671)
—Ghost of Whispering Willow. Dunigan, Anne, ed. (p. 671)
—Mischief in the Mushroom Patch. (p. 1150)
Thrasher, Brian, illus. see Bowlin, Serina.
Thrasher, Crystal. Dark Didn't Catch Me. (p. 407)
Thrasher, Grady. Tim & Sally's Beach Adventure. Rabon, Elaine Hearn, illus. (p. 1750)
—Tim & Sally's Vegetable Garden. Rabon, Elaine Hearn, illus. (p. 1750)
—Tim & Sally's Year in Poems. Rabon, Elaine Hearn, illus. (p. 1750)
Thrasher, Jenny & Thrasher, Phil. Golden Egg: A Story about Adoption. Enroc Illustrations, illus. (p. 694)
Thrasher, Phil, jt. auth. see Thrasher, Jenny.
Thrasher, Travis. Wonder. (p. 1947)
Threadgould, Tiffany. ReMake It! Recycling Projects from the Stuff You Usually Scrap. (p. 1458)
Threatt, Cedric Lanier, Sr. Different, but the Same. (p. 438)
Threatt, Cedric, Sr. Boy Called Short Rock: The Early Years. (p. 217)
Threw, Debra. Pirate Appeared at My Party. (p. 1362)
Throckmorton, Sylvestra. Annie Cabannie's Star Baby. (p. 86)
—Star Baby. Throckmorton, Sylvestra et al, illus. (p. 1640)
Thronson, Lloyd. Gomer the Goat & His New Home. (p. 697)
—White Rockets with Four Hooves. (p. 1913)
Throp, Claire. All about Flowers (p. 42)
—All about Leaves (p. 42)
—All about Plants (p. 43)
—All about Roots (p. 43)
—All about Seeds (p. 43)
—All about Stems (p. 43)
—Angela Merkel (p. 74)
—Curling (p. 394)
—Day Inside the Human Body: Fantasy Science Field Trips (p. 413)
—England (p. 529)
—Exploring Other Worlds: What Is Science Fiction? (p. 553)
—Fantasy Science Field Trips (p. 572)
—Figure Skating (p. 586)
—Heroes of World War Two. (p. 773)
—Israel (p. 893)
—Italy (p. 894)
—Journey to the Center of the Earth: Fantasy Science Field Trips (p. 929)
—Latvia (p. 980)
—Lemurs (p. 991)
—Leopards (p. 993)
—Lions (p. 1021)
—Look It Up: Finding Information (p. 1049)
—Malala Yousafzai. (p. 1083)
—Marie Curie. (p. 1093)
—Monkeys (p. 1165)
—Nile River (p. 1255)
—Orcas (p. 1302)
—Put It Together: Using Information (p. 1420)
—Resisting the Nazis. (p. 1463)
—Seals (p. 1536)
—Sort It Out: Choosing Information (p. 1614)
—South Africa (p. 1616)
—Spies & Codebreakers. (p. 1627)
—Visit to a Space Station: Fantasy Science Field Trips (p. 1845)
—Weekend with Dinosaurs: Fantasy Science Field Trips (p. 1872)
—What's It About? Information Around Us (p. 1898)
—What's Next? Instructions & Directions (p. 1898)
Throp, Claire, jt. auth. see Colson, Mary.
Throp, Claire, jt. auth. see Senker, Cath.
Throp, Claire, et al. Winter Sports. (p. 1938)
Thrum, Thomas G., compiled by. Hawaiian Folk Tales. (p. 755)
Thryce, Marc & Robinson, Tim. Look at the Pictures. (p. 1049)
Thucydides. Thucydides Cress, J. H. E. & Wordsworth, J. C., eds. (p. 1745)
Thug, Slim. How to Survive: In a Recession. (p. 821)
Thuillier, Eleonore. Wolf, Are You There? Learn How to Get Dressed with the Little Wolf. (p. 1943)
Thuillier, Eleonore, illus. see Lallemand, Orianne.
Thuma, Chris. Cigarette Sue. (p. 319)
Thuma, Cynthia & Lower, Catherine. Creepy Colleges & Haunted Universities: True Ghost Stories (p. 381)
Thumann, Robin K. Peaceful Thoughts: An Interactive Journey in Positive Thinking for Children & Their Parents. Thumann, Robin K., illus. (p. 1332)
Thumser, Judith. Grady & Gus Go to Grandmas. (p. 705)
Thung, Diana. August Moon. (p. 115)
—Captain Long Ears. (p. 264)
Thurber, Ginny. My Nanny Comes Today. (p. 1215)
Thurber, James. 13 Clocks. Simont, Marc, illus. (p. 1994)
—Wonderful O. Simont, Marc, illus. (p. 1948)
Thurlby, Paul. Paul Thurlby's Alphabet. Thurlby, Paul, illus. (p. 1330)
—Paul Thurlby's Wildlife. Thurlby, Paul, illus. (p. 1330)
Thurman, Carol. Molly's Field of Dreams. (p. 1161)
Thurman, Debbie. Hold My Heart: A Teen's Journal for Healing & Personal Growth. (p. 787)
—Sheer Faith: A Teen's Journey to Godly Growth. (p. 1564)
—Teen's Guide to Christian Living: Practical Answers to Tough Questions about God & Faith. (p. 1715)
Thurman, Joann M., ed. see Cheng, Haw.
Thurman, Kathryn. Garden for Pig. Ward, Lindsay M., illus. (p. 656)
Thurman, Mark, illus. see Choyce, Lesley.
Thurman, Mark, illus. see Drake, Jane & Love, Ann.
Thurman, Mark, illus. see Hearn, Emily.
Thurman, Rob. Madhouse (p. 1070)
Thurmond, Cindy. What If There Were No Colors? (p. 1887)
Thurmond, Joey. Nojoe Makes New Friends. (p. 1263)
Thurmond, Michael. 6-Day Body Makeover: Drop One Whole Dress or Pant Size in Just 6 Days - And Keep It Off. (p. 1992)
Thurn, David Ryan, illus. see Crotty, Martha.
Thurn, Gwen, illus. see Crotty, Martha.
Thurner, Zoe. Dress Rehearsal. (p. 485)
Thurnherr, Paige. Hunting with Bald Eagles. (p. 829)
Thurston, Alecia Frances. Shumalady's Butterfly Tree. (p. 1571)
Thurston, Cheryl M. Frog King's Daughter Is Nothing to Sneeze At: Playscript. (p. 640)
Thurston, Cheryl Miller & DiPrince, Dawn. Unjournaling: Daily Writing Exercises That Are Not Personal, Not Introspective, Not Boring! (p. 1821)
Thurston, Cheryl Miller & Etzel, Laurie Hopkins. Live! From the Classroom! It's Mythology! Five Read-Aloud Plays Based on Hero Myths from Around the World. Howard, Patricia, illus. (p. 1040)
Thurston, Cheryl Miller, et al. Attitude! Helping Students Want to Succeed & Then Setting Them up for Success. (p. 114)
Thurston, Sandie. Annalee's Family Tree. (p. 85)
Thurston, Scott, ed. Salt Companion to Geraldine Monk. (p. 1505)
Thury, Fredrick H. Hoshmakaka. van Kampen, Vlasta, illus. (p. 801)
Thwin, Soe Soe. Story of Inle in the Galapagos. (p. 1658)
Thyberg, Kathleen. Pianomouse's Musical Circus: Lesson Book 1 (p. 1354)
Thydell, Johanna & Martens, Helle. There's a Pig in My Class! Ramel, Charlotte, illus. (p. 1731)
Thygerson, Alton L. Blast! Babysitter Lessons & Safety Training. (p. 198)
Thyrion, Marie-Noelle, photos by see Alvarez, Michel J.
Thyroff, Brad. Albert & Freddie. Gillen, Rosemarie, illus. (p. 34)
Tia, Rocio. Maire & the Monster (p. 1077)
Tian, Elli. Silly nursery Rhymes. Tian, Elli, illus. (p. 1576)
Tiano, Danielle. Tillie Is Terrific. (p. 1750)
Tibballs, Geoff. Sports: Fun, Facts, & Action... (p. 1632)
—Sports. (p. 1632)
Tibballs, Geoff & Ripley's Believe It or Not Editors. Expect... the Unexpected. (p. 548)
Tibbets, Albert B. Youth, Youth, Youth: Stories of Challenge, Confidence & Comradeship. Tibbets, Albert B., ed. (p. 1982)
Tibbets, Mike. Murdering Mum. Landes, William-Alan, ed. (p. 1192)
Tibbett, Teri. Listen to Learn: Using American Music to Teach Language Arts & Social Studies (Grades 5-8) (p. 1022)
Tibbetts, John C. & Welsh, James M. Encyclopedia of Novels into Film. (p. 525)
Tibbetts, John C. & Welsh, James Michael. Encyclopedia of Novels into Film. (p. 525)
Tibbetts, Peggy. Road to Weird. (p. 1477)
Tibbetts, Stacy Glen. Reading Roll of Thunder, Hear My Cry. (p. 1446)
Tibbitts, Alison Davis. Henry Clay: From War Hawk to the Great Compromiser. (p. 767)
Tibbles, Jean-Paul, illus. see Buckey, Sarah Masters.
Tibbles, JeanPaul, illus. see Buckey, Sarah Masters.
Tibbles, Jean-Paul, illus. see Coleman, Evelyn.
Tibbles, Jean-Paul, illus. see Ernst, Kathleen.
Tibbles, JeanPaul, illus. see Ernst, Kathleen.
Tibbles, JeanPaul, illus. see Greene, Jacqueline.
Tibbles, JeanPaul, illus. see Hart, Alison.
Tibbles, JeanPaul, illus. see Jones, Elizabeth McDavid.
Tibbles, Jean-Paul, illus. see Reiss, Kathryn.
Tibbles, JeanPaul, illus. see Reiss, Kathryn.
Tibbles, JeanPaul, illus. see Steiner, Barbara.
Tibbles, Jean-Paul, illus. see Tripp, Valerie.
Tibbott, Julie. Members Only: Secret Societies, Sects, & Cults-Exposed! (p. 1125)
Tibbs, Ely. Mouse under My House - Ingle & the Cats Meow. (p. 1182)
Tibbs, Janet. Being A Leader (p. 160)
Tibensky, Arlaina. And Then Things Fall Apart. (p. 71)
Tibi, Bassam. Islam Between Culture & Politics. (p. 891)
Tibke, Terry. Upgrader: Re-Engineered. (p. 1824)
Tibo, Gilles. Au Boulot les Animaux. (p. 114)
—Corre, Nicolas, Corre! Rioja, Alberto Jiménez, tr. from FRE. (p. 368)
—Gardien du Sommeil. Jorisch, Stéphane, illus. (p. 656)
—Grand Voyage de Monsieur. (p. 707)
—Noches de Papel. (p. 1262)
—Quatre Saisons de Simon. (p. 1423)
—Simon et la Musique. (p. 1577)
—Simon et le Petit Cirque. (p. 1577)
—Simon et les Deguisements. (p. 1577)
—Simon Makes Music. (p. 1577)
—Simon's Disguise. (p. 1577)
—Voyage du Funambule. (p. 1850)
Tibo, Gilles, illus. see Fillion, Pierre.
Tibo, Gilles & Bisaillon, Josée. My Diary: The Totally True Story of ME! (p. 1201)
Tibo, Gilles & Vaillancourt, François. Senor Patapum. (p. 1550)
Ticall, Antoinette. Invisible Dinosaur. (p. 885)
Tichelaar, Tyler, ed. see Mills, Arthur.
Tichenor, Austin, jt. auth. see Martin, Reed.
Tick, David, ed. see Cecca, John.
Tick Tock. 500 Ways to Make Me Laugh until I Cry. (p. 2001)
—500 Ways to Make Me Laugh until I Explode. (p. 2001)
Tick Tock Musical Staff & Morton, Sasha. Super Sleepover Secrets. (p. 1681)
Tick Tock Staff & Gifford, Clive. Monster Trucks. (p. 1168)
Tickle, Jack. Look Out, Ladybug. (p. 1050)
Tickle, Jack, illus. see Cain, Sheridan.
Tickle, Jack, illus. see Chapman, Keith.
Tickle, Jack, illus. see Finn, Isobel.
Tickle, Jack, illus. see Lloyd, Sam R.
Tickle, Jack, illus. see Murray, Andrew.
Tickle, Jack, jt. auth. see Finn, Isobel.
Tickle, Jack, tr. see Murray, Andrew.
Tickoo, Sham & McLees, David. Learning Autodesk VIZ: A Tutorial Approach Release 4. (p. 985)
Ticktock. Adine's Igloo. (p. 12)
—Bad Rat! (p. 132)
—Bad Zombie Movie. (p. 132)
—Bart's Go-Cart. (p. 140)
—Best Gift. (p. 170)
—Beth & the Bugs. (p. 171)
—Big Book of Dinosaurs. (p. 179)
—Bret & Grandma's Trip! (p. 226)
—Budge Troll, Budge! (p. 235)
—Busy Lunch. (p. 246)
—Celebrity Celia! (p. 285)
—Cemetery Dance. (p. 286)
—Chuck & Duck. (p. 318)
—Circus Mice. (p. 322)
—Clint & Grant Play I-Spy. (p. 333)
—Clumsy Eagle. (p. 336)
—Cowboy's Star. (p. 374)
—Daniel in the Lions Den. (p. 405)
—David & Goliath. (p. 410)
—Deadly Animals. (p. 417)
—Dina the Rapper. (p. 440)
—Dragon in the Sandbox. (p. 477)
—Duck in Luck! (p. 488)
—Ernie & Hermie Visit Earth. (p. 534)
—Eve the Knight. (p. 541)
—Fairy Fay's Bad Day. (p. 563)
—Fast & Furious. (p. 576)
—George the Genius Gerbil. (p. 663)
—Gigantic Bear. (p. 676)
—Goat in a Boat. (p. 687)
—Goose Flight. (p. 702)
—Hugh Is New. (p. 825)
—I Am a Princess: My Little Book of Secrets. (p. 832)
—If Dinosaurs Were Alive Today: New Edition. (p. 852)
—Jemima the Spy. (p. 912)
—King Arthur & the Knights of the Round Table. (p. 958)
—Kyle in Trouble. (p. 969)
—Let's Go to the Swings. (p. 998)
—Little Princess. (p. 1033)
—Make Me a Princess. (p. 1079)
—Max's Trip. (p. 1112)
—Maze. (p. 1113)
—Monster's Night. (p. 1169)
—Mummy Code. (p. 1191)
—My Big Animal Book. (p. 1197)
—My Big Dinosaur Book. (p. 1197)
—My Big Fast Car Book. (p. 1197)
—My Big Truck Book. (p. 1197)
—My First 100 Animals. (p. 1203)
—My First 100 Machines. (p. 1203)
—My First 100 Numbers. (p. 1203)
—My First 100 Words. (p. 1203)
—My First Book of Animal Babies. (p. 1205)
—My First Book of Farm Animals. (p. 1205)
—Nativity Story. (p. 1235)
—Noah's Ark. (p. 1261)
—Owen the Astronaut. (p. 1314)
—Pink Bunny. (p. 1359)
—Pirate School. (p. 1363)
—Pop Duet. (p. 1384)
—Puff Flies. (p. 1415)
—Queen Ella's Feet. (p. 1424)
—Robot Bop. (p. 1480)
—Secret Garden. (p. 1541)
—Snail Trail. (p. 1596)
—Snapped by Sam! (p. 1597)
—Superhero Ed! (p. 1683)
—That Dog! (p. 1726)
—Top Dog. (p. 1769)
—Treasure Island. (p. 1782)
—What Wally Wanted. (p. 1894)
—Wish Fish. (p. 1940)
—Zoom In: An Extraordinary Look at Ordinary Stuff. (p. 1989)
Ticktock & Pipe, Jim. Dirty Rotten Rulers: History's Villains & Their Dastardly Deeds. Mazzara, Mauro, illus. (p. 446)
Ticktock & Ziliz, Anna. Fairies. (p. 562)
—Fashion. (p. 575)
TickTock Books Ltd. Amazing Inventions. (p. 54)
—Cold Book. (p. 338)
—Fierce Predators. (p. 584)
Ticktock Media, Ltd. Staff. Amazing Dinosaurs. (p. 54)
—At the Beach with the Snappy Little Crab. (p. 110)
—Birthday Party. (p. 193)
—Civilizations: The History of the Ancient World. (p. 326)
—Deadly Animals. (p. 417)
—Deadly Creatures. (p. 417)
—Dinosaurs. (p. 444)
—Extreme Machines. (p. 556)
—Farm. (p. 573)
—Favorite Foods: Colors & Shapes. (p. 578)
—Friendly Dinosaurs. (p. 637)
—Guess What? Everyday Things. (p. 729)
—Guess What? Things That Go. (p. 729)
—Hungry Dinosaurs. (p. 828)
—In the Garden with the Hungry Little Snail. (p. 866)
—Itsy Bitsy Spider. (p. 900)
—Jungle. (p. 934)
—Kittens & Puppies: Counting. (p. 963)
—Little Helper. (p. 1029)
—Living Planet: Uncovering the Wonders of the Natural World. (p. 1041)
—My Fairy Garden. (p. 1202)
—My First Book of Bugs & Spiders. (p. 1205)
—My First Book of Dinosaurs. (p. 1205)
—My First Book of Machines. (p. 1205)
—My First Book of Mammals. (p. 1205)
—My First Book of Ocean Life. (p. 1205)
—My First Book of Reptiles & Amphibians. (p. 1205)
—My Night-Time Animals. (p. 1216)
—My Ocean Creatures. (p. 1216)
—My Space Adventure. (p. 1219)
—My World: Opposites. (p. 1221)
—Ocean. (p. 1276)
—Old McDonald Had a Farm. (p. 1284)
—Scary Dinosaurs. (p. 1520)
—Shopping Day. (p. 1569)
—Summer Vacation. (p. 1675)
—Undead: Zombies, Vampires, Werewolves. (p. 1813)
—Under the Ocean with the Little Yellow Submarine. (p. 1814)
—Unexplained: Encounters with Ghosts, Monsters, & Aliens. (p. 1817)
—Violent Planet. (p. 1843)
—What Am I? Animal Moms & Babies. (p. 1879)
—What Do Cows Do? (p. 1882)
—What Do Hippos Do? (p. 1882)
—What Do Penguins Do? (p. 1882)
—What Do Sheep Do? (p. 1882)
—What Do Tigers Do? (p. 1882)
—What Do Zebras Do? (p. 1883)
—Wheels on the Bus. (p. 1901)
—Who Am I? Wild Animal Babies. (p. 1914)
—Zoom into Space with the Shiny Red Rocket. (p. 1989)
Ticktock Media, Ltd. Staff, ed. see Dixon, Dougal.
Ticktock Media, Ltd. Staff, jt. auth. see Parker, Steve.
Ticktock Media, Ltd. Staff, jt. auth. see Phillips, Dee.
Ticktock Media, Ltd. Staff, jt. auth. see Spence, David.
Ticktock Media, Ltd. Staff & Parker, Steve. Bug Wars: Deadly Insects & Spiders Go Head to Head. Mendez, Simon, illus. (p. 236)
TickTock Staff & Ziliz, Anna. Ballerinas. (p. 134)
—Ponies & Unicorns. (p. 1382)
—Princesses. (p. 1406)
tictock Media, Ltd. Ultimate Guide to Dinosaurs. (p. 1809)
Ticulous, Maurice. Herbert the Turbot. (p. 769)
Tidball, Derek. Wisdom from Heaven: The Message of the Letter of James for Today. (p. 1939)
Tidball, Lee. Windfork Secrets. (p. 1936)
Tidd, Louise Vitellaro. Can a Hippo Hop? Brown, Kevin, illus. (p. 258)
—Lo Haré Después. Translations.com Staff, tr. from ENG. (p. 1044)
Tiddle, Deanna Hessedal. Apartment Horse & Friends. (p. 91)
Tidey, Jackie, jt. auth. see Tidey, John.
Tidey, John & Tidey, Jackie. Arts & Culture. (p. 105)
—China: Land, Life, & Culture (p. 306)
—History & Government. (p. 783)
—Land & Climate. (p. 973)
—People & Cities. (p. 1339)
—Plants. (p. 1369)
—Wildlife. (p. 1931)
Tidgwell, R. Harry Bones & the Treasure of Raiders Cove. (p. 750)
Tidholm, Anna-Clara. Knock! Knock! Bradley, MaryChris, tr. (p. 965)
Tidmarsh, Celia. Focus on France. (p. 610)
—Focus on Japan. (p. 610)
—Focus on Mexico. (p. 611)
Tidwell, Deborah Swayne. Magic Eraser: And the Substitute Teacher. (p. 1072)
Tidwell, Emmy. Superanimals. (p. 1682)
Tidwell, Jeral, illus. see Baldwin, Stephen & Rosato, Bruno.
Tidwell, Mae B. & Hancock, Vicki. Kyle Wants to Be a Monkey (p. 969)
Tidwell, Marina Curtis. Beyond the Beach Blanket: A Field Guide to Southern California Coastal Wildlife. (p. 174)
Tidwell, Susan. Little Lotus & the Loving-Kindness Cup. Lee, Wei-Chun, illus. (p. 1031)
—Three Virtuous Brothers: A Story of the Three Acts of Goodness. Tidwell, Susan, illus. (p. 1744)
Tieck, Sarah. Abigail Breslin: Famous Actress. (p. 5)
—Adam Levine: Famous Singer & Songwriter. (p. 11)
—Adele: Singing Sensation. (p. 12)
—Alabama. (p. 33)
—Alaska. (p. 33)
—Algonquin. (p. 38)
—Aliens. (p. 41)
—American Idol Host & Judges. (p. 61)
—Apache. (p. 91)
—Ariana Grande: Famous Actress & Singer. (p. 98)
—Arizona. (p. 98)
—Arkansas. (p. 99)
—Astronauts. (p. 109)
—ATVs. (p. 114)
—Australia. (p. 116)
—Aztec. (p. 122)
—Barack Obama. (p. 137)
—Be Safe. (p. 149)
—Beyonce: Famous Singer/Actress. (p. 173)
—Big Buddy Biographies (p. 180)
—Big Buddy Biographies Set 2 (p. 180)
—Big Time Rush: Popular Boy Band. (p. 184)
—Bigfoot. (p. 184)
—Biking. (p. 186)
—Bindi Irwin: Star of Bindi the Jungle Girl. (p. 188)
—Blackfoot. (p. 197)
—Blake Shelton: Country Music Star. (p. 198)
—Body Systems (p. 207)
—Brazil. (p. 224)
—Brooklyn Bridge. (p. 231)
—Bruno Mars: Popular Singer & Songwriter. (p. 232)
—California. (p. 253)
—Carly Rae Jepsen: Pop Star. (p. 270)
—Carrie Underwood: American Idol Winner. (p. 271)
—Cherokee. (p. 298)
—Choppers. (p. 310)
—Chris Colfer: Star of Glee. (p. 311)
—Chumash. (p. 318)
—Circulatory System. (p. 322)
—Colorado. (p. 343)
—Commercial Fishermen. (p. 349)
—Connecticut. (p. 357)
—Creek. (p. 380)
—Daft Punk: Electronic Music Duo. (p. 399)
—Dakota Fanning: Talented Actress. (p. 401)
—Dancing. (p. 402)
—Daniel Radcliffe: Harry Potter Star. (p. 405)
—David Beckham: Soccer Superstar. (p. 410)

—Debby Ryan: Disney TV Star. (p. 421)
—Delaware. (p. 424)
—Demi Lovato: Talented Actress & Singer. (p. 425)
—Derek Jeter: Baseball Superstar. (p. 427)
—Diego Rivera. (p. 437)
—Digestive System. (p. 438)
—Dirt Bikes. (p. 446)
—Dragsters. (p. 479)
—Drake Bell & Josh Peck: Famous Actors. (p. 480)
—Dune Buggies. (p. 490)
—Earthmovers. (p. 497)
—Eat Well. (p. 501)
—Eleanor Roosevelt. (p. 508)
—Eli Manning: Football Star. (p. 512)
—Eli Manning CD & Book. (p. 512)
—Eli Manning Site CD & Book. (p. 512)
—Emma Stone: Talented Actress. (p. 520)
—Emma Watson: Harry Potter Star. (p. 520)
—Empire State Building. (p. 521)
—Farm Tractors. (p. 574)
—Fire Trucks. (p. 591)
—First Biographies. (p. 593)
—Florence Nightingale. (p. 606)
—Florida. (p. 606)
—France. (p. 627)
—Gabby Douglas: Historic Olympic Champion. (p. 652)
—Georgia. (p. 665)
—Germany. (p. 666)
—Get Rest. (p. 668)
—Ghosts. (p. 672)
—Hawaii. (p. 755)
—Helicopters. (p. 763)
—Hiking. (p. 779)
—Hillary Rodham Clinton. (p. 779)
—Hopi. (p. 797)
—Hovercraft. (p. 804)
—Idaho. (p. 852)
—Inclined Planes. (p. 869)
—Indy Cars. (p. 873)
—Iroquois. (p. 888)
—Italy. (p. 894)
—J. K. Rowling. (p. 901)
—Jaden Smith: Talented Actor. (p. 905)
—Jamestown. (p. 907)
—Jennifer Lawrence: Star of the Hunger Games. (p. 913)
—Jennifer Lopez: Famous Entertainer. (p. 913)
—Jets. (p. 916)
—Jimmie Johnson: NASCAR Champion. (p. 918)
—Joe Mauer: Baseball Superstar. (p. 920)
—Johnny Depp: Famous Actor. (p. 923)
—Jonas Brothers: Singing Sensations. (p. 925)
—Jonas Brothers CD & Book. (p. 925)
—Jonas Brothers Site CD & Book. (p. 925)
—Justin Bieber: Singing Sensation. (p. 940)
—Justin Bieber: Pop Music Superstar. (p. 940)
—Justin Timberlake: Famous Entertainer. (p. 940)
—Kacey Musgraves: Country Music Star. (p. 941)
—Kate Middleton: Real-Life Princess. (p. 944)
—Katy Perry: Singing Sensation. (p. 946)
—Keep Clean. (p. 946)
—Kelly Clarkson: Original American Idol. (p. 948)
—Kristen Stewart: Twilight Star. (p. 967)
—Kyle Massey: Talented Entertainer. (p. 969)
—Lady Gaga: Famous Singing Sensation. (p. 970)
—Laura Marano: Famous Actress & Singer. (p. 980)
—Lea Michele: Star of Glee. (p. 981)
—LeBron James: Basketball Superstar. (p. 987)
—LEGO Build-It Book: Amazing Vehicles. (p. 990)
—Levers. (p. 1003)
—Liam Hemsworth: Star of the Hunger Games. (p. 1004)
—Lindsey Vonn: Olympic Champion. (p. 1019)
—Lorde: Singing Sensation. (p. 1052)
—Manage Feelings. (p. 1086)
—Mark Twain. (p. 1095)
—Maya. (p. 1112)
—Mexico. (p. 1131)
—Michael Jackson: Music Legend. (p. 1134)
—Michael Phelps: Olympic Champion. (p. 1134)
—Michael Phelps: The Greatest Olympian. (p. 1134)
—Miley Cyrus: Singer/Actress/ Star of Hannah Montana. (p. 1142)
—Miley Cyrus CD & Book. (p. 1142)
—Miley Cyrus Site CD & Book. (p. 1142)
—Miners. (p. 1146)
—Miranda Cosgrove: Famous Actress & Singer. (p. 1149)
—Miranda Lambert: Country Music Star. (p. 1149)
—Monticello. (p. 1170)
—Mummies. (p. 1190)
—Muscular System. (p. 1192)
—Nat & Alex Wolff: Stars of Nickelodeon's the Naked Brothers Band. (p. 1230)
—Navajo. (p. 1237)
—Nervous System. (p. 1241)
—Nez Perce. (p. 1249)
—Niagara Falls. (p. 1250)
—One Direction: Popular Boy Band. (p. 1294)
—Oregon. (p. 1302)
—Oregon Trail. (p. 1303)
—Paul Revere. (p. 1330)
—Pennsylvania. (p. 1337)
—Peyton Manning: Famous Quarterback. (p. 1349)
—Prince William: Real-Life Prince. (p. 1401)
—Psy: Gangnam Style Rapper. (p. 1413)
—Puerto Rico. (p. 1415)
—Pulleys. (p. 1416)
—Respiratory System. (p. 1463)
—Rhode Island. (p. 1468)
—Rihanna: Singing Sensation. (p. 1472)
—Robert Downey Jr. Star of Iron Man. (p. 1479)
—Robert Pattinson: Twilight Star. (p. 1479)
—Rosa Parks. (p. 1488)
—Russell Wilson: Super Bowl Champion. (p. 1498)
—Sacagawea. (p. 1500)
—Sasha & Malia Obama: Historic First Kids. (p. 1515)

—Sasha & Malia Obama: Historic First Kids CD & Book. (p. 1515)
—Sasha & Malia Obama: Historic First Kids Site CD & Book. (p. 1515)
—Scotty Mccreery: American Idol Winner. (p. 1532)
—Screws. (p. 1533)
—Selena Gomez: Star of Wizards of Waverly Place. (p. 1549)
—Seminole. (p. 1550)
—Shakira: International Music Star. (p. 1559)
—Shaun White: Olympic Champion. (p. 1563)
—Shawnee. (p. 1563)
—Shia Labeouf: Movie Star. (p. 1566)
—Sidney Crosby: Hockey Champion. (p. 1573)
—Simple Machines. (p. 1578)
—Sioux. (p. 1580)
—Skateboarding. (p. 1583)
—Skeletal System. (p. 1584)
—Smoke Jumpers. (p. 1594)
—Snowmobiles. (p. 1601)
—South Carolina. (p. 1616)
—South Dakota. (p. 1617)
—Spain. (p. 1620)
—Speedboats. (p. 1624)
—Stay Fit. (p. 1645)
—Storm Chasers. (p. 1655)
—Superbikes. (p. 1682)
—Swimming. (p. 1691)
—Taylor Lautner: Star of Twilight. (p. 1708)
—Taylor Swift: Country Music Star. (p. 1708)
—Taylor Swift: Country Music Star CD & Book. (p. 1708)
—Taylor Swift: Country Music Star Site CD & Book. (p. 1708)
—Tennessee. (p. 1720)
—Texas. (p. 1724)
—Tiger Woods: Famous Golfer. (p. 1749)
—Tom Brady: Famous Quarterback. (p. 1762)
—United Kingdom. (p. 1819)
—Usher: Famous Singer. (p. 1828)
—Utah. (p. 1829)
—Vampires. (p. 1832)
—Vanessa Hudgens: High School Musical Star. (p. 1833)
—Vermont. (p. 1837)
—Victoria Justice: Famous Actress & Singer. (p. 1840)
—Virginia. (p. 1844)
—Walt Disney. (p. 1855)
—Washington. (p. 1859)
—Washington DC. (p. 1860)
—Wedges. (p. 1871)
—Werewolves. (p. 1875)
—West Virginia. (p. 1876)
—Wheels & Axles. (p. 1900)
—Wisconsin. (p. 1939)
—Witches. (p. 1941)
—Wright Brothers. (p. 1963)
—Wyoming. (p. 1966)
—Yoga. (p. 1972)
—Zac Efron: High School Musical Star. (p. 1984)
—Zac Efron CD & Book. (p. 1984)
—Zac Efron Site CD & Book. (p. 1984)
—Zombies. (p. 1988)
—Zookeepers. (p. 1989)
Tiede, Dirk, illus. see Mayhall, Robin.
Tiede, Karen. Carve Smart. (p. 273)
Tiegreen, Alan, illus. see Cleary, Beverly.
Tiegreen, Alan, illus. see Cole, Joanna & Calmenson, Stephanie.
Tiegreen, Alan, illus. see Delton, Judy & Pee Wee Scouts Staff.
Tiegren, Alan, illus. see Cole, Joanna & Calmenson, Stephanie, eds.
Tieman, Ruth Anne. Elmo & Dorothy: Friends Forever! Brannon, Tom, illus. (p. 515)
Tiemann, Amy. High Water. (p. 778)
Tiemens, Toni. Teddy & Me (p. 1712)
Tien, Wai, illus. see Robertson, David.
Tieri, Frank. Weapon X: Defection Youngquist, Jeff, ed. (p. 1869)
—Weapon X: The Underground Youngquist, Jeff, ed. (p. 1869)
Tieri, Frank, jt. auth. see Brubaker, Ed.
Tieri, Frank, jt. auth. see Quesada, Joe.
Tiernan, Cate. Awakening. (p. 120)
—Balefire: A Chalice of Wind - A Circle of Ashes - A Feather of Stone - A Necklace of Water. (p. 134)
—Book of Shadows (p. 211)
—Book of Shadows - The Coven - Blood Witch. (p. 211)
—Calling (p. 254)
—Changeling. (p. 290)
—Changeling. (p. 290)
—Dark Magick (p. 407)
—Dark Magick - Awakening - Spellbound. (p. 407)
—Darkest Fear. (p. 408)
—Darkness Falls. (p. 408)
—Eternally Yours. (p. 539)
—Immortal Beloved. (p. 861)
—Spellbound. (p. 1625)
—Sweep: The Calling - Changeling - Strife Vol. 3 (p. 1689)
—Sweep: Reckoning, Full Circle, & Night's Child. Vol. 5 (p. 1689)
Tierney, Fiona. Lion's Lunch? Chamberlain, Margaret, illus. (p. 1021)
Tierney, Jim, illus. see Oppel, Kenneth.
Tierney, John. Jack, Tommy & the Phoenix Street Firefighters. Algar, James, illus. (p. 903)
Tierney, Kathleen, jt. auth. see Kiernan, Caitlin R.
Tierney, Melissa. Elly's True Colors. (p. 515)
Tierney, Thomas, jt. auth. see Robinetie, Joseph.
Tierney, Tom. American Family of the 1980s Paper Dolls. (p. 60)
—American Fashion Designers Paper Dolls. (p. 60)
—Art Deco Fashions Paper Dolls. (p. 101)
—Best Actresses of the 1990s Paper Dolls. (p. 168)
—Betty Grable Paper Dolls. (p. 172)
—Brides from Around the World Paper Dolls. (p. 227)
—Byzantine Fashions. (p. 249)
—Cavalier & Puritan Fashions. (p. 282)
—Dalai Lama Paper Doll. (p. 401)

—Elegant Debutante Gowns of the 1800s Paper Dolls. (p. 510)
—Famous African-American Actresses Paper Dolls. (p. 569)
—Famous Movie Dance Stars Paper Dolls. (p. 569)
—Famous Torch Singers Paper Dolls. (p. 570)
—Fashions from India. (p. 576)
—Fashions of the First Ladies Paper Dolls. (p. 576)
—Fashions of the Old South Coloring Book. (p. 576)
—Fashions of the Roaring Twenties Coloring Book. (p. 576)
—Ferdinand & Isabella Paper Dolls. (p. 581)
—French Film Stars Paper Dolls. (p. 635)
—Givenchy Paper Dolls. (p. 681)
—Glamorous Television Stars Paper Dolls. (p. 682)
—Great Costumes from Classic Movies Paper Dolls: 30 Fashions by Adrian, Edith Head, Walter Plunkett & Others. (p. 715)
—Greek & Roman Fashions. (p. 720)
—Italian & Spanish Fashion Designers Paper Dolls. (p. 894)
—Late Victorian & Edwardian Fashions. (p. 979)
—Legendary Baseball Stars. (p. 989)
—Life's a Drag! Paper Dolls. (p. 1013)
—Mae West Paper Doll. (p. 1070)
—Mexican Folk Dance Paper Dolls. (p. 1131)
—Michelle Obama Paper Dolls. (p. 1135)
—Mikado Paper Dolls. (p. 1141)
—Movie Mobsters Paper Dolls. (p. 1183)
—Napoleon & Josephine Paper Dolls. (p. 1229)
—Nelson Mandela Paper Dolls. (p. 1241)
—Newport Fashions of the Gilded Age Paper Dolls. (p. 1249)
—Pin-Up Girls of World War II. (p. 1359)
—Rock & Roll Legends of the 1950s Paper Dolls. (p. 1481)
—Soap Opera Divas Paper Dolls. (p. 1603)
—Southern Belle Ball Gowns Paper Dolls. (p. 1617)
—Woodstock Paper Dolls: 40th Anniversary Flashback Edition. (p. 1950)
—Ziegfeld Girls Paper Dolls. (p. 1986)
Tierney, Tom, et al. Award-Winning Fashions of Edith Head Paper Dolls. (p. 642)
Tierra, Lesley. Kid's Herb Book: For Children of All Ages. Wilson, Susie, illus. (p. 954)
Tietjen, Amy. Birds I've Met Through the Alphabet. Fitts, Seth, illus. (p. 191)
Tietz, Heather. Rockabye Baby Jesus. Miller, Nancy, illus. (p. 1482)
—Yes, Jesus Loves You. Miller, Nancy, illus. (p. 1970)
Tiffany, Grace. Ariel. (p. 98)
Tiffany, Sean. Hockey. (p. 786)
Tiffany, Sean, illus. see Maddox, Jake.
Tiffany, Sean, illus. see Stevens, Eric & Maddox, Jake.
Tiffany, Sean, illus. see Suen, Anastasia & Maddox, Jake.
Tiffany, Sean & Maddox, Jake. Mr. Strike Out Tiffany, Sean, illus. (p. 1186)
Tiger, Caroline. Isamu Noguchi. (p. 891)
Tiger Tales, ed. Baby Animals. (p. 124)
—Christmas Holiday Fun. (p. 314)
—Christmas Prayer. Rescek, Sanja, illus. (p. 315)
—Christmas Sticker Activities. (p. 315)
—Christmas Surprise. (p. 315)
—First Words. (p. 597)
—Five Minute Bedtime Stories. (p. 601)
—Five Minute Christmas Stories. (p. 601)
—Funny Faces (Boys) (p. 649)
—Funny Faces (Girls) (p. 649)
—Halloween Sticker Activities. (p. 738)
—Halloween Surprise. (p. 739)
—Jingle Bells: A Collection of Songs & Carols. Kolvanovic, Dubravka, illus. (p. 918)
—Kittens. (p. 963)
—Puppies. (p. 1417)
—This Little Light of Mine. Kolvanovic, Dubravka, illus. (p. 1737)
Tiger Tales Staff. 5 Minute Nursery Rhymes. (p. 1992)
—First ABC. (p. 592)
—Five Little Pumpkins. Tiger Tales Staff, ed. (p. 600)
—Hug! Mantle, Ben, illus. (p. 824)
—Lift & See Animals. (p. 1014)
—My First Book of Things to See. (p. 1205)
—Peek-A-Boo! Mantle, Ben, illus. (p. 1334)
—Things to Learn. (p. 1733)
Tiger Tales Staff, ed. see Kanzler, John.
Tiger Tales Staff, creator. 100 First Animals. (p. 1998)
—100 First Words. (p. 1998)
—123 Counting Fun. (p. 2000)
—5 Minute Farm Tales. (p. 1992)
—Animal Antics. (p. 76)
—Busy Bugs. (p. 246)
—Count 123. (p. 369)
—Farm. (p. 573)
—Farm Puzzle + Book. (p. 574)
—First Colors. (p. 593)
—First Numbers. (p. 596)
—Lift & See Farm. (p. 1014)
—My Busy Day. (p. 1199)
—Pets. (p. 1348)
—Savanna Animals: Fun Facts & Stuff to Do. (p. 1516)
—Things That Go. (p. 1733)
Tiger Tales Staff, ed. 1 2 3 Count With Me. Birkett, Georgie, illus. (p. 1990)
—Animals Go. Emily, Bolam, illus. (p. 82)
—Animals Talk. Emily, Bolam, illus. (p. 84)
—Deck Halls. Vasylenko, Veronica, illus. (p. 421)
—Easter Surprise: My First Lift & Learn. (p. 499)
—Hickory, Dickory, Dock: And Other Favorite Nursury Rhymes. Rescek, Sanja, illus. (p. 775)
—is for Apple. Birkett, Georgie, illus. (p. 889)
—Jingle Bells. Vasylenko, Veronica, illus. (p. 918)
—This Little Piggy. Mannum, Carol, illus. (p. 1737)
—Twinkle, Twinkle Little Star: And Other Favorite Bedtime Rhymes. Rescek, Sanja, illus. (p. 1808)
Tiger Woods Foundation Staff, jt. auth. see Woods, Earl.
Tighe, Elizabeth, jt. auth. see Corrigan, Delia Stubbs.
Tigue, Terry, illus. see Mundy, Dawn.
Tihe Bookazines Staff. Sports Illustrated: Brett Favre: The Tribute. (p. 1632)
Tiitinen, Esko-Pekka. Drops of Life. (p. 486)
Tijerina, Arnold G., III, ed. see Schlaht, Kim.

Tika. Baby Love. Standish, Joyce, ed. (p. 127)
Tiki Machine, LLC Staff, creator. Deus Libris: An Illustrated Collection. (p. 431)
Tilak, Brian, illus. see Elliott, Sherria L.
Tilbury, Shannon. Lost Tribe. (p. 1057)
Tilby, Ginny. You Should, You Should. (p. 1976)
Tilde, photos by see Kim, Sue.
Tilde, photos by see McElroy, Jean.
Tilden, Paul. Stones, Swords & Dragons: Alluthian Chronicles Trilogy Book One (p. 1653)
Tilden, Thomasine E. Lewis. Flesh Wound: A Minor Injury Takes a Deadly Turn. (p. 630)
—Mind Games! Can a Psychic Tell What You're Thinking? (p. 1145)
—Worms! Parasites Plague a Village. (p. 1961)
Tilden, Thomasine E. Lewis & Lewis-Tilden, Thomasine E. Belly-Busting Worm Invasions! Parasites That Love Your Insides! (p. 163)
—Help! Whats Eating My Flesh? Runaway Staph & Strep Infections! (p. 766)
—Mind Readers: Science Examines ESP. (p. 1145)
Tildes, Phyllis L. Garden Wall. Tildes, Phyllis L., illus. (p. 656)
Tildes, Phyllis Limbacher. Baby Animals Spots & Stripes. Tildes, Phyllis Limbacher, illus. (p. 125)
—Eye Guess: A Foldout Guessing Game. Tildes, Phyllis Limbacher, illus. (p. 557)
—Magic Babushka. Tildes, Phyllis Limbacher, illus. (p. 1071)
—Will You Be Mine? A Nursery Rhyme Romance. Tildes, Phyllis Limbacher, illus. (p. 1932)
Tildes, Phyllis Limbacher, illus. see Farmer, Jacqueline.
Tildes, Phyllis Limbacher, illus. see Goodman, Emily.
Tilert, Heather R. Ming-Ming Saves the Day: Follow the Reader Level 1. (p. 1146)
Tilford, Gregory L. Edible & Medicinal Plants of the West. (p. 504)
—From Earth to Herbalist: An Earth-Conscious Guide to Medicinal Plants. (p. 642)
Tilford, Gregory L., jt. auth. see Wulff, Mary L.
Tilford, Michael. Reemie the Preemie. (p. 1456)
Tilghman, Natalie, jt. auth. see Sommer, Bill.
Till, Danelle. Max's Moving Adventure: A Coloring Book for Kids on the Move. Spooner, Joe, illus. (p. 1112)
Till, Nan. Solomon Finds His Spots. (p. 1608)
Till, Tom. Photographing the World: A Guide to Photographing 201 of the Most Beautiful Places on Earth. Martres, Laurent, ed. (p. 1353)
Tillamook County Creamery Association & Holstad, Kathy. Tillamook Cheese Cookbook: Celebrating 100 Years of Excellence. Holstad, Kathy, photos by. (p. 1750)
Tillema, Juliana O., jt. auth. see Turner, Donald R.
Tillen, James. Close Look at Soil. (p. 333)
Tiller, Amy. My Sister Is Like a Baby Bird. Tiller, Amy, illus. (p. 1218)
Tiller, Jerome. Sammy's Day at the Fair: The Digestive System Featuring Gut Feelings & Reactions. (p. 1508)
Tiller, Steve. Colonia de Arco Iris. Cremeans, Robert, illus. (p. 341)
—Connectada al Corazon. Cremeans, Robert, illus. (p. 357)
Tiller, Sue. Breastfeeding 101: A Step-by-Step Guide to Successfully Nursing Your Baby. (p. 225)
Tillery, Brad, jt. auth. see LaFleur, Richard.
Tilley. Damaged. (p. 401)
Tilley, Adrian. Spider's Web. (p. 1627)
Tilley, Debbie, illus. see Burns, Marilyn.
Tilley, Debbie, illus. see Danzig, Dianne.
Tilley, Debbie, illus. see Gilson, Jamie.
Tilley, Debbie, illus. see Hoose, Phillip & Hoose, Hannah.
Tilley, Debbie, illus. see Hurwitz, Johanna.
Tilley, Debbie, illus. see Jane, Pamela.
Tilley, Laura. Magic of the Morning. (p. 1073)
Tilley, Lawrence. Animal Retreat. (p. 79)
Tilley, R. Sudgen, ed. see Salten, Felix.
Tilley, Scott, illus. see Herman, Gail.
Tilley, Scott, illus. see Posner-Sanchez, Andrea.
Tilley, Scott, illus. see RH Disney Staff.
Tilley, Scott, illus. see Saxon, Victoria & RH Disney Staff.
Tilley, Scott, illus. see Uyeda, Laura.
Tilley, Scott, jt. illus. see Orpinas, Jean-Paul.
Tilley, Sophie. Sparkly Shoes & Picnic Parties. (p. 1622)
Tilley, Steve, et al. Airlock: Arrival. (p. 31)
—Airlock: Becoming. (p. 31)
—Airlock. (p. 31)
Tilli, Jess, jt. auth. see Tilli, Laura.
Tilli, Laura & Tilli, Jess. Baking. (p. 133)
—Cakes. (p. 252)
Tillis, Carrie, illus. see Tillis, Doris.
Tillis, Dionne. Willameana Whitney White & the Magical Butterfly. (p. 1933)
Tillis, Doris. Rudy the Rabbit. Tillis, Carrie, illus. (p. 1494)
Tillit, L. B. 2 Days. (p. 1991)
—Edge of Ready. (p. 504)
—Unchained. (p. 1811)
Tillman, CeCe, jt. auth. see Hall, Dorothy P.
Tillman, Gloria J., jt. auth. see Tamaja Press.
Tillman, Nancy. Crown on Your Head. Tillman, Nancy, illus. (p. 386)
—Heaven of Animals. Tillman, Nancy, illus. (p. 761)
—I'd Know You Anywhere, My Love. Tillman, Nancy, illus. (p. 851)
—On the Night You Were Born. (p. 1291)
—On the Night You Were Born. (p. 1291)
—On the Night You Were Born. Tillman, Nancy, illus. (p. 1291)
—Spirit of Christmas. Tillman, Nancy, illus. (p. 1628)
—Tumford the Terrible. Tillman, Nancy, illus. (p. 1796)
—Tumford's Rude Noises. Tillman, Nancy, illus. (p. 1796)
—Wherever You Are: My Love Will Find You. Tillman, Nancy, illus. (p. 1911)
—Wonder of You: A Book for Celebrating Baby's First Year. Tillman, Nancy, illus. (p. 1947)
—You're Here for a Reason. (p. 1982)
Tillman, Nancy, illus. see Tutu, Desmond.
Tillman, Nancy & Metaxas, Eric. It's Time to Sleep, My Love. Tillman, Nancy, illus. (p. 899)
Tillotson, Katherine, illus. see Jackson, Richard.
Tillotson, Katherine, illus. see Lyon, George Ella.

T

For book reviews, descriptive annotations, tables of contents, cover images, author biographies & additional information, updated daily, subscribe to www.booksinprint2.com

2761

Tillotson, Katherine, illus. see McDonald, Megan.
Tillotson, Katherine, illus. see Olson, Mary W.
Tillotson, Katherine, tr. see McDonald, Megan.
Tillotson, Ted. Magic Meadow. (p. 1072)
Tillson, Linda L., illus. see Ryan, Christopher.
Tillson, M C. Secret of Bete Gris Bay. (p. 1542)
Tillworth, Mary. All of My Friends! (Dora & Friends) Random House, illus. (p. 45)
—Barbie in Princess Power. (p. 138)
—Barbie in the Pink Shoes. Golden Books, illus. (p. 138)
—Barbie - The Pearl Princess. (p. 138)
—Big Monster, Little Monster. (p. 182)
—Bubble Ball Game! (Bubble Guppies) MJ Illustrations, illus. (p. 233)
—Busy as a Bee! (Seuss/Cat in the Hat) Moroney, Christopher, illus. (p. 245)
—Crayon Craze! (Julius Jr.) Random House & Song, Jennifer, illus. (p. 377)
—Cupcake Challenge! (p. 392)
—Cupcake Challenge! (Barbie: Life in the Dreamhouse) (p. 392)
—Dora in Wonderland. (p. 470)
—Dora in Wonderland (Dora the Explorer) Miller, Victoria, illus. (p. 470)
—Dora's Christmas Star (Dora the Explorer) Miller, Victoria, illus. (p. 471)
—Dragon in the School (Dora & Friends) Goddard, Brenda & Haskett, Dan, illus. (p. 477)
—Dragon Quest (Winx Club) Cartobaleno, illus. (p. 478)
—Dump Truck Trouble/Let's Build a Doghouse! (Bubble Guppies) Random House Beginners Books Staff & MJ Illustrations Staff, illus. (p. 489)
—Fairytale Adventure. (p. 565)
—Fairytale Adventure (Dora the Explorer) Jackson, Mike, illus. (p. 565)
—Firefighter Gil! (Bubble Guppies) Nunn, Paul, illus. (p. 591)
—Friend at the Zoo/un Amigo en el Zoologico (Bubble Guppies) Gomez, Yuliana, tr. (p. 637)
—Happy Birthday, Chelsea! (p. 744)
—Happy Holidays, Bubble Guppies! (Bubble Guppies) Jackson, Mike, illus. (p. 746)
—Here Come the Bubble Guppies! (Bubble Guppies) Random House Staff, illus. (p. 770)
—Howdy-Doodle-Doo! Random House & Song, Jennifer, illus. (p. 823)
—It's Time for Ballet! (Bubble Guppies) MJ Illustrations, illus. (p. 899)
—Legend of Pinkfoot (Bubble Guppies) MJ Illustrations, illus. (p. 988)
—Licensed to Drive. (p. 1007)
—Licensed to Drive (Barbie Life in the Dream House) (p. 1007)
—Meet My Friends! (Dora & Friends) Aikins, David, illus. (p. 1121)
—Mermaid Treasure Hunt. (p. 1128)
—Mermaid Treasure Hunt (Dora & Friends) Aikins, David, illus. (p. 1128)
—My Favorite Explorers (Dora the Explorer) Random House Staff, illus. (p. 1203)
—Princess & the Ring (Dora & Friends) Perilli, Marilena & Miller, Victoria, illus. (p. 1403)
—Puppy & the Ring (Bubble Guppies) Random House Staff & MJ Illustrations Staff, illus. (p. 1418)
—Rock & Rule. Golden Books, illus. (p. 1481)
—Too Many Puppies! (p. 1767)
—Triple-Track Train Race! (Bubble Guppies) Unten, Eren, illus. (p. 1787)
—Welcome to Fairy World! (Dora & Friends) Aikins, David, illus. (p. 1873)
Tillworth, Mary, jt. auth. see Hashimoto, Meika.
Tillworth, Mary, jt. auth. see Man-Kong, Mary.
Tillworth, Mary, jt. auth. see Random House Staff.
Tillworth, Mary, jt. auth. see RH Disney Staff.
Tillworth, Mary & Random House Children's Books Staff. Fin-Tastic Friends! Talkowski, Steve & MJ Illustrations Staff, illus. (p. 586)
Tilly, Meg. First Time (p. 597)
Tilmont, Amy. Man vs. Animal: Species at Risk. (p. 1086)
—Trash Talk: What You Throw Away. (p. 1780)
Tilson, Gina L. Patches: Adventures of a Country Cavalier. (p. 1328)
Tilthem, Sam. Pete Plan Pup. (p. 1346)
Tilton, David, jt. auth. see Smith, Matt.
Tilton, Patricia. Reproducible Little Books for Sight Words. (p. 1461)
Tilton, Rafael. Rulers of the Middle Ages. (p. 1495)
Tim, Fireball. Big Book of Wacky Rides! by Fireball Tim. (p. 179)
Tim Todd. Town of Ill. (p. 1773)
Tim, Tornado. Tornado Chaser: Life on the Edge. (p. 1770)
Timbaland & Myers, Christopher. Nighttime Symphony. Myers, Christopher, illus. (p. 1255)
Timberlake, Amy. Dirty Cowboy. Rex, Adam, illus. (p. 446)
—One Came Home. (p. 1294)
Timberlake, Gail. Rescue of the Lady's Slipper. (p. 1462)
Timbers, James. Salmon & Fuzz in Helping a Friend. (p. 1505)
Timblin, Stephen. Kitesurfing. (p. 962)
—Muhammad Ali: King of the Ring. (p. 1189)
—MX Champions: The Stars of the Show - Past & Present. (p. 1195)
—Race Week: Seven Crazy Days. (p. 1431)
—Spy Technology. (p. 1636)
—Swimming. (p. 1691)
Time for Kids Editors. Abigail Adams: Eyewitness to America's Birth. (p. 5)
—Alexander Graham Bell: Inventor of the Telephone. (p. 36)
—Ants! (p. 90)
—Bats! (p. 144)
—Bees! (p. 158)
—Benjamin Franklin - A Man of Many Talents. (p. 165)
—Butterflies! (p. 247)
—Clara Barton: Angel of the Battlefield. (p. 326)
—Dinosaurs 3D: An Incredible Journey Through Time. (p. 444)
—Earthquakes! (p. 497)
—Frogs! (p. 641)
—Jesse Owens: Running into History. (p. 914)
—Planets! Discover Our Solar System! (p. 1368)
—Presidents of the United States. (p. 1397)
—Rosa Parks: Civil Rights Pioneer. (p. 1489)
—Snakes! (p. 1596)
—Time for Kids Big Book of How. (p. 1751)
—Time for Kids Big Book of Science Experiments: A Step-by-Step Guide. (p. 1751)
—TIME for Kids Big Book of What. (p. 1751)
—Time for Kids - Planets! (p. 1751)
—Time for Kids: Ronald Reagan: From Silver Screen to Oval Office. (p. 1751)
—Time for Kids - Thomas Edison: A Brilliant Inventor. (p. 1751)
—Time for Kids Top 5 of Everything. (p. 1751)
—TIME for Kids Weather Kit. (p. 1751)
—Why, How, & What? (p. 1925)
Time for Kids Editors, ed. see El Nabli, Dina.
Time for Kids Editors, jt. auth. see Betz, Adrienne.
Time for Kids Editors, jt. auth. see DeMauro, Lisa.
Time for Kids Editors, jt. auth. see Iorio, Nicole.
Time for Kids Editors, jt. auth. see Patrick, Denise Lewis.
Time for Kids Editors, jt. auth. see Skelton, Renee.
Time for Kids Editors, jt. auth. see Upadhyay, Ritu.
Time for Kids Editors & Dickstein, Leslie. Storms! (p. 1656)
Time for Kids Editors & Iasevoli, Brenda. Plants! (p. 1369)
Time for Kids Editors & Iorio, Nicole. Time for Kids - Bears! (p. 1751)
Time for Kids Editors & Time Inc. Home Entertainment Staff. Big Book of Why: 1,001 Facts Kids Want to Know. (p. 179)
Time for Kids Magazine Editors. Big Book of Why Crazy, Cool, & Outrageous. (p. 179)
—Really Cool People & Places - Time for Kids Book of Why. (p. 1449)
—Stellar Space - Time for Kids Book of Why. (p. 1647)
—Top 5 of Everything: Tallest, Tastiest, Fastest! (p. 1768)
Time for Kids Magazine Editors, ed. TIME for Kids Big Book of Where. (p. 1751)
Time for Kids Magazine Staff. Almanac 2006. Rowen, Beth & Slepian, Curtis, eds. (p. 48)
—Amazing Sports & Science - Time for Kids Book of Why. (p. 56)
—Earthquakes! (p. 497)
—Franklin D. Roosevelt - A Leader in Troubled Times. (p. 630)
—Grammar Rules! (p. 706)
—Middle East: The History, the Cultures, the Conflicts, the Faiths. Knauer, Kelly, ed. (p. 1137)
—Presidents of the United States. (p. 1397)
—Time for Kids Big Book of How: 501 Facts Kids Want to Know. (p. 1751)
—TIME for Kids Big Book of What. (p. 1751)
—Time for Kids: Eleanor Roosevelt: First Lady of the World. (p. 1751)
—TIME for Kids That's Strange but True! The World's Most Astonishing Facts & Records. (p. 1751)
—Time for Kids X-Why-Z: Kids Ask - We Answer. (p. 1751)
Time for Kids Magazine Staff, jt. auth. see Capstone Press Staff.
Time for Kids Magazine Staff & Satterfield, Kathryn Hoffman. Frogs! (p. 641)
Time for Kids Magazine Staff, ed. Bats! (p. 144)
—Butterflies! (p. 247)
—Plants! (p. 1369)
—Storms! (p. 1656)
—Volcanoes! (p. 1849)
Time Inc. Home Entertainment Staff, jt. auth. see Time for Kids Editors.
Time Magazine Editors. 21 Days to Baghdad: The Inside Story of How America Won the War Against Iraq. (p. 1996)
Time Magazine Editors, creator. What to Eat Now: Your Guide to Good, Healthy Food. (p. 1894)
Time Magazine Staff, creator. Unexplained: The World's Greatest Marvels, Mysteries & Myths. (p. 1817)
Time Out Guides Ltd Staff. Time Out London for Children. (p. 1752)
Time to Sign. Time to Sign with Children: Toddler/Preschool. (p. 1753)
—Time to Sign with Children Infant/Toddler: Time to Sign with Music Infant/Toddler. (p. 1753)
—Time to Sign with Children Preschool/School Age. (p. 1753)
Time-Life Audiobooks Staff, contrib. by. Egypt. (p. 506)
Time-Life Books Editors. Art of the Essay: Questions in Time. (p. 102)
—Fall of Camelot (Part of the "Enchanted World" Series) (p. 566)
—Famous Faces of the 20th Century: What Makes a Leader? (p. 569)
—Presidential Decisions: The Burden of Leadership in the Twentieth Century. (p. 1397)
—U. S. in World Affairs: The American Century. (p. 1806)
—Wild Discovery: Natures Pageant of Life. (p. 1929)
—Women in the 20th Century: The Pursuit of Equality. (p. 1946)
Time-Life Books Staff, contrib. by. Spells & Bindings. (p. 1625)
Timmerman, Charles. Large-Print Travel Word Search Book: Find Your Way Through 150 Easy-to-Read Puzzles. (p. 975)
Timmerman, Gayla. Charlie & the Mystery in the Box. (p. 292)
Timmermeyer, Stephanie R. Savannah Finds a Lovey. (p. 1516)
Timmers, Leo. Bang. Timmers, Leo, illus. (p. 136)
—Crow. Timmers, Leo, illus. (p. 385)
—I Am the King. Timmers, Leo, illus. (p. 834)
—Magical Life of Mr. Renny. Nagelkerke, Bill, tr. from DUT. (p. 1074)
—Oops! Timmers, Leo, illus. (p. 1299)
—Toot! (p. 1767)
—Who Is Driving? Timmers, Leo, illus. (p. 1915)
Timmers, Leo, illus. see Reidy, Jean.
Timmins, Jeffrey Stewart. Cinderella: The Graphic Novel (p. 320)
Timmins, Jeffrey Stewart, illus. see Andersen, Hans Christian & Capstone Press Staff.
Timmins, Jeffrey Stewart, illus. see Andersen, Hans Christian & Stone Arch Books Staff.
Timmins, Jeffrey Stewart, illus. see Andersen, Hans Christian.
Timmins, Jeffrey Stewart, illus. see Capstone Press Staff.
Timmins, Jeffrey Stewart, illus. see Lewis, J. Patrick & Yolen, Jane.
Timmins, Jeffrey Stewart, illus. see Soup, Cuthbert.
Timmins, Jeffrey Stewart, illus. see Stone Arch Books Staff.
Timmins, William, illus. see Stone, Ethel B.
Timmis, Jeff. Arlo's Job Hunt. (p. 99)
—You'd Have Wings If You'd Just Said No. (p. 1977)
Timmo. Magic Christmas Fairy. (p. 1072)
Timmons, Anne, illus. see Biskup, Agnieszka.
Timmons, Anne, illus. see Clay, Kathryn.
Timmons, Anne, illus. see Engfer, Lee.
Timmons, Anne, illus. see Jolley, Dan.
Timmons, Anne, illus. see Krohn, Katherine.
Timmons, Anne, illus. see Robbins, Trina & Capstone Press Staff.
Timmons, Anne, illus. see Robbins, Trina.
Timmons, Anne, illus. see Sohn, Emily, et al.
Timmons, Anne, jt. auth. see Sohn, Emily.
Timmons, Bonnie, illus. see Settel, Joanne.
Timmons, Bonnie, illus. see Truss, Lynne.
Timmons, Gayle, illus. see Schad, Kristine.
Timmons, Jasmine, jt. auth. see Grimes, Terri.
Timmons, Jonathan, illus. see Brown, Jonatha A. & Goff, Elizabeth Hudson.
Timmons, Jonathan, illus. see Mayo, Gretchen Will & O'Hern, Kerri.
Timmons, Nick, jt. auth. see Harland, Joan.
Timmons, Robbie. Twoey & the Goat. (p. 1804)
Timmons, Tim. Coaching Success: Creating Champions for the Business World. (p. 336)
Timms, Diann. Hare & Bear Draw (p. 748)
Timms, E. H. Ring of Nine. (p. 1473)
Timothy Batt, Jennifer. I Hope You Dream. (p. 839)
Timothy E. Dillinger. Pick Pocket Pirate: An Original Pirate Tale. (p. 1354)
Timothy, Ering. Frog Belly Rat F & G. (p. 640)
Timothy, Hamilton Baird, illus. see Stevenson, Robert Louis.
Timothy Nixon. Henry to the Rescue. (p. 768)
Timroth, Stephen. Dreamhawk. (p. 484)
Tina, Dunnier, illus. see Kneisley, Amy.
Tina, Schwartzenberger. Substance Use & Abuse. (p. 1671)
Tincknell, Cathy. Amazing Things for Boys to Make & Do. Kelly, John, illus. (p. 56)
—Amazing Things for Girls to Make & Do. Kelly, John, illus. (p. 56)
Tindyebwa, Lillian. Recipe for Disaster. (p. 1451)
Tineo, Suzanne Nicoll. Danny the Damsel: Sharing. (p. 406)
Tiner, John. Exploring the World of Mathematics: From the Checker Board to the Super Computer. (p. 554)
—Story of in God We Trust: Discovering Our Nations Heritage. (p. 1658)
—Story of the Pledge of Allegiance: Discovering Our Nations Heritage. (p. 1662)
Tiner, John Hudson. Airplanes. (p. 32)
—Cars. (p. 272)
—Cloth. (p. 334)
—Coal Makes Electric Power. (p. 336)
—Levers. (p. 1003)
—Motorcycles. (p. 1179)
—Pulleys. (p. 1416)
—Ships & Boats. (p. 1567)
—Trains. (p. 1777)
—Trucks. (p. 1791)
—Uranium & Plutonium Make Nuclear Power. (p. 1825)
—Water, Acid, & a Metal Make Battery Power. (p. 1862)
—Wood. (p. 1949)
Tinerella, Paul P. & Gundersen, Ralph. Water Boatmen (Insecta: Heteroptera: Corixidae) of Minnesota. (p. 1862)
Tinetti, Elizabeth Ordaz. Love Is Patient. (p. 1060)
Ting, Mary. Three Best Friends: Fabulous Day (p. 1741)
Ting, Renee. Chinese History Stories: Stories from the Zhou Dynasty. Vol. 1 (p. 307)
—Chinese History Stories: Stories from the Imperial Era. Vol. 2 (p. 307)
—Prince's Diary. Dulemba, Elizabeth O., illus. (p. 1402)
Tingay, Graham, jt. auth. see Marks, Anthony.
Tingle, Rebecca. Edge on the Sword. (p. 504)
Tingle, Tim. Crossing Bok Chitto: A Choctaw Tale of Friendship & Freedom. Bridges, Jeanne Rorex, illus. (p. 385)
—Danny Blackgoat, Navajo Prisoner. (p. 405)
—How I Became a Ghost: A Choctaw Trail of Tears Story (p. 810)
—Saltypie: A Choctaw Journey from Darkness into Light. Clarkson, Karen, illus. (p. 1506)
—Walking the Choctaw Road: Stories from Red People Memory. Howard, Norma, illus. (p. 1854)
Tingle, Tim & Moore, James W. Spooky Texas Tales. Miller, Gina, illus. (p. 1631)
Tingley, Megan, ed. see Stewart, Trenton Lee.
Tingwald, Jady Ann. Adventures of Rady Red Comb. Powell, James, illus. (p. 22)
Tingwald, July Ann. Orrie's Christmas. Powell, James, illus. (p. 1305)
Tinkelman, Murray, illus. see Stolz, Mary.
Tinker, Jason, illus. see Martin, Tamra.
Tinkler, David. Revenge of the Dinner Ladies. (p. 1465)
Tinling, Christine I. Heroes of the Cross, All for Jesus (p. 773)
Tinling, Marion. Sacagawea's Son: The Life of Jean Baptiste Charbonneau. (p. 1500)
Tinling, Molly, illus. see Wand, Dana.
Tinnell, Robert. Faceless: A Terry Sharp Story. (p. 561)
Tinnell, Robert, jt. auth. see Livingston, Todd.
Tinnemeyer, Andrea. Student's Encyclopedia of Great American Writers (p. 1669)
Tino, illus. see Agustin, Jose.
Tino, illus. see Spinelli, Jerry.
Tinsley, Helen. Me & My Grandma: A Story for Children about AIDS. (p. 1115)
Tinsley, Jillian. Wally the Warthog. Wood, Douglas, illus. (p. 1855)
Tinsley, P. S. House with No Mouse. Deans, Nora L., ed. (p. 804)
Tinsley, Sarah V. Instant Bible Plays, Just Add Kids! (p. 878)
Tinstman, Gretchen. Meet the Silly Sisters. (p. 1123)
Tintera, Amy. Rebel. (p. 1450)
—Reboot. (p. 1451)
Tinti, Natalie. Magic in Us. the Healing Circle Tinti, Natalie, illus. (p. 1072)
—Magic in Us. the Healing Circle: The Healing Circle Tinti, Natalie, illus. (p. 1072)
—Magic in Us. the Power of Imagination Tinti, Natalie, illus. (p. 1072)
—Magic in Us. the Power of Imagination: The Power of Imagination T, N., illus. (p. 1072)
—Sewing a Friendship. Tinti, Natalie, illus. (p. 1556)
Tintjer, Birgit, illus. see Wilson, Jessica.
Tiong Yau, Toh. Perform! the illustrated Thoughts: Pictures that unleash your imagination to redefine your Performance. (p. 1342)
Tipene, Tim. Bullies & Warriors. (p. 240)
—Haere: Farewell, Jack, Farewell. Smith, Huhana, illus. (p. 735)
—Patu. (p. 1330)
Tipeo, illus. see Savary, Fabien & Vadeboncoeur, Isabelle.
Tipeo, illus. see Savary, Fabien.
Tipper, Sarah. Eviscerated Panda: Back in Bamboo. (p. 546)
Tippets, Lynn M. Nature at My Doorstep. (p. 1236)
Tippett, Amey. Spilled Ink. (p. 1627)
Tipping, Naomi, illus. see Safran, Sheri.
Tippit-Young (Watson), Amy. Makin' Memories. (p. 1080)
Tipton, Angela, jt. auth. see Grateful Steps Publishing.
Tipton, Annie. Diary of a Real Payne Book 2: Church Camp Chaos. (p. 435)
—Diary of a Real Payne Book 3: Oh Baby! (p. 435)
Tipton, Denton J. Dorothy of Oz Prequel. (p. 472)
—Legends of Oz: Dorothy's Return. (p. 990)
Tipton, Michelle. Mommy See Me. (p. 1162)
Tipton, R. Kent. Kid Posse & the Phantom Robber. (p. 951)
Tipton, Scott, et al. Star Trek: Best of Klingons TP: Best of Klingons TP. (p. 1641)
Tipton, Stacey. Complete Musical Spanish: With New Bonus Verbs Learning CD (p. 353)
Tirabassi, Maren C. Footlights & Fairy Dust: Matt & Maria Go to the Theatre. Kramer, Brandie, illus. (p. 615)
Tirabosco, Tom, illus. see Wazem, Pierre.
Tirado, Margot A. New Friends. (p. 1244)
Tirado, Raquel. That Sticky Cat. (p. 1726)
Tirey, Rodney. Coppershoo Saves the Sarge's Saddle! Tirey, Rodney, illus. (p. 366)
Tirgari, Simin. Color of the Heart. (p. 343)
Tirion, Wil, illus. see Ridpath, Ian.
Tirion, Wil, illus. see Storm, Dunlop.
Tiritilli, Robert, illus. see Hellman, Charles.
Tiritilli, Robert, jt. auth. see Hellman, Charles.
Tiritilli, Robert A., illus. see Hellman, Charles S.
Tiritilli, Robert A., jt. auth. see Hellman, Charles S.
TIRONE, Lisa, jt. auth. see Tirone, Lisa.
Tirone, Lisa & TIRONE, Lisa. Chef It Up! (p. 297)
Tischler, Faye, jt. auth. see Gordon, Fran.
Tischler, Tracey. Heroes in the Sandbox. (p. 773)
Tischner, Lukasz. Milosz & the Problem of Evil. Bill, Stanley, tr. from POL. (p. 1144)
Tisdale, Rachel, jt. auth. see Loveless, Antony.
Tisdale, Towanda. Wallace Mack Has a Bug Attack! (p. 1855)
Tisdale, Towanda L. Kelcey Reed Loves to Read. (p. 948)
Tisdall, Sarah, illus. see Rosen, Michael.
Tisdel, L. L, illus. see Bryson, Karen Mueller.
Tisdell, Wendy & Takhar, Jodi. Angela Goes to Daycare. (p. 74)
Tish, Aunty. Kiddiwink Kingdom. (p. 952)
Tisha Admire Duncan. My Dirty Cat Mutt. (p. 1202)
Tisserand, Jean-Louis. That Easter Morn. (p. 1726)
Tissot, Bob & Rahill, Alex. Purity & Holiness: A Biblical Perspective on Sexuality & Relationships. (p. 1419)
Tissot, Caperton. History between the Lines: Women's Lives & Saranac Lake Customs. (p. 783)
Tissot Lcsw, Jennifer. Grateful Gracie: A Story about Gratitude. Washburn, Cecilia, illus. (p. 712)
Titan Books Staff & Korman, Susan. Noah - Ila's Story. (p. 1261)
Titan Books Staff, et al. Monsters vs. Aliens: the M Files. Dalton, Alex & Laguna, Fabio, illus. (p. 1169)
Titan Comics Staff, jt. auth. see Furman, Simon.
Titan Comics Staff & Furman, Simon. DreamWorks' Dragons: Dangers of the Deep. Vol.2 Max, Iman, illus. (p. 484)
—DreamWorks' Dragons: Dragon Down (How to Train Your Dragon TV) Vol. 1 Nazif, Iwan, illus. (p. 484)
Titan Comics, Titan. Ice Castle. Lawrence, Jack, illus. (p. 850)
Titan Comics, Titan, et al. Minions (p. 1147)
Titchenell, Elsa-Brita. Once Round the Sun. Gruelle, Justin C., illus. (p. 1292)
Titchenell, F. J. R. & Carter, Matt. Shards. (p. 1561)
—Splinters. (p. 1630)
Titcomb, Gordon. Last Train. Minor, Wendell, illus. (p. 979)
Titcomb, Timothy. Lessons in Life: a Series of Familiar Essays. (p. 993)
Titelman, Becky. Wonky Witch & the Witching Well. (p. 1949)
Titherington, Jeanne. Pumpkin Pumpkin. (p. 1416)
Titherington, Karen M. Gavin Goes to Kindergarten! Prepare Your Child for the First Day of School. (p. 658)
Titlebaum, Ellen, jt. auth. see Hapka, Cathy, pseud.
Titley, Alan, jt. auth. see Tolkien, J. R. R.
Titonis, George. Gift of the Giggles. (p. 675)
Titra, Stephen, illus. see Thiry, Joan.
Tittnich, Emie. Starting Young: Supporting Parents for Peaceful Lifestyles 2004. (p. 1644)
Titus, David. Native Alaskan String Figures. (p. 1234)
Titus, Eve. Anatole. (p. 67)
—Anatole. Galdone, Paul, illus. (p. 67)
—Anatole & the Cat. (p. 67)

Full bibliographic information is available on the Title Index page number referenced in parentheses at the end of each entry

T

Titus, Gregory, illus. see Jolley, Dan.
Titus, Julia. Claudia's Pink Piggy Bank: Saving. (p. 329)
Titzer, Robert C. Book Your Baby Can Read! Dozier, Brendan et al, photos by. (p. 212)
—Book Your Baby Can Read! Early Language Development Series. Dozier, Lisa et al, photos by. (p. 212)
—Book Your Baby Can Read! 5 Book Set: Early Language Development Series (p. 212)
—Book Your Baby Can Read! Review: Early Language Development Series. Dozier, Brendan et al, photos by. (p. 212)
—Book Your Baby Can Read! Starter: Early Language Development Series Dozier, Lisa et al, photos by. (p. 212)
Tiwari, Saral. Abraham Lincoln: The Civil War President (p. 6)
—Abraham Lincoln: The Civil War President. Turner, Ginger, illus. (p. 6)
Tiwari, Saral, illus. see Pettinato, Laura.
Tize W. Clark. Street Jokes: 1st Edition. (p. 1666)
—Twin Poems. (p. 1802)
Tjernagel, Kelsi Turner. Animals That Live in Groups. (p. 84)
—Gross Recipes (p. 725)
Tjernagel, Shirley. Obee & the Great Bank Heist. (p. 1275)
Tjia, Sherwin, illus. see Lawson, Jon Arno.
Tjia, Sherwin, illus. see Lawson, JonArno.
Tjong-Khing, Thé. Birthday Cake Mystery. (p. 192)
Tju, Lim Cheng, ed. see Liew, Sonny.
T.K. Wheels on the Bus. (p. 1901)
Tk, illus. see Riordan, Rick.
Tkach, Glenn. Gwyneth Paltrow: Grace & the Girl Next Door. (p. 733)
Tlali, Miriam. Between Two Worlds. (p. 173)
Tnt. Gospel Parables, the Easter Story & Parables on the Second Coming. (p. 703)
—Samson, Ruth, Samuel & Saul Christian Focus Publications (CFP) Staff, ed. (p. 1509)
Tnt, jt. auth. see Christian Focus Publications (CFP) Staff.
TNT Ministries Staff. Game Is Up (p. 654)
—God's Miracle Maker: Elisha. (p. 691)
Tnt Ministries Staff. On the Way 11 - 14's (p. 1291)
TNT Ministries Staff, jt. auth. see Blundell, T.
Tnt Ministries Staff, jt. auth. see Christian, Focus.
TNT Resource Material Staff. Beginning with the Bible: A Class above - A Child's Further Lessons in Knowing God. (p. 159)
—Beginning with the Bible. (p. 159)
—Game Is Up. (p. 654)
—On the Way, 11-14yr (p. 1291)
—On the Way 3-9's (p. 1291)
—On the Way for 11 - 14's (p. 1291)
—On the Way for 3 - 9's (p. 1291)
—On the Way for 3 - 9's: Kings, Daniel, Esther, Nehemiah. Vol. 14 (p. 1291)
TNT Resource Material Staff, jt. auth. see Blundell, T.
To, Vivienne, illus. see Enderle, Dotti.
To, Vivienne, illus. see Fiedler, Lisa.
To, Vivienne, illus. see Fields, Jan.
To, Vivienne, illus. see Rhodes, O. K. & Spencer, Octavia.
Toader, Alex. Max's Journal: The Adventures of Shark Boy & Lava Girl. Rodriguez, Robert, illus. (p. 1112)
Toader, Alex, illus. see Rodriguez, Robert & Roberson, Chris.
Toader, Alex, illus. see Rodriguez, Robert, et al.
Tobar, Jorge, illus. see Tobar, Malena & Oyola, Milta, eds.
Tobar, Malena, illus. see Brannan, Dara, ed.
Tobar, Malena, illus. see Jingling, Kathy, ed.
Tobar, Malena & Oyola, Milta, eds. Cuaderno de la Margarita Tomo 2 (p. 387)
—Cuaderno de la Rosa Tomo 4 Tobar, Jorge, illus. (p. 387)
Tobar, Norma. Heather's Feathers. (p. 760)
Tobel, Susan Von. Mei-Ling's Forever Mommy. (p. 1124)
Tobella, Montse, illus. see Albanell, Pep.
Tobella, Montse, illus. see Navarro, Carlos.
Tobey, Carole. If Frogs Could Talk. (p. 852)
Tobey, Carole A. Frog Olympics. (p. 640)
Tobey, Cheryl. Choosing a Career as a Model. (p. 310)
Tobia, Lauren, illus. see Atinuke.
Tobia, Lauren, illus. see Manushkin, Fran.
Tobia, Lauren, illus. see Robinson, Michelle.
Tobia, Lauren, illus. see Shields, Carol Diggory.
Tobias, Anne B. Harry Meets a Bully. Tobias, Tom, illus. (p. 750)
—Harry's Problem First Loose Tooth. Tobias, Tom, illus. (p. 751)
Tobias, Jack. New Home for Mopgolly Mole. (p. 1245)
Tobias, Jerry E. There's No Better Place Than the U. S. of A. (p. 1731)
Tobias, Jerry J. Imma Toy. (p. 861)
Tobias, Tobi. Wishes for You. Sorensen, Henri, illus. (p. 1940)
Tobias, Tom, illus. see Tobias, Anne B.
Tobin, Adriana, jt. auth. see Tobin, Jennifer.
Tobin, Deborah. Tangled in the Bay: The Story of a Baby Right Whale Domm, Jeffrey, illus. (p. 1705)
Tobin, Irene. Tidy Bunch. (p. 1747)
Tobin, Jason. Algebra (p. 38)
Tobin, Jennifer & Tobin, Adriana. ABCs of the BWCAW: A Fun Guide to the Boundary Waters Canoe Area Wilderness. Tobin, Jennifer, photos by. (p. 4)
Tobin, Jim. Sue MacDonald Had a Book. (p. 1672)
—Very Inappropriate Word. Coverly, Dave, illus. (p. 1838)
Tobin, John, ed. see Herbert, George.
Tobin, Marc, illus. see Woik, Julie.
Tobin, Nancy, illus. see Seuling, Barbara.
Tobin, Paul. Colder Allie, Scott & Chabon, Daniel, eds. (p. 339)
—Marvel Adventures Spider-Man: Sensational. Vol. 3 Camagni, Jacopo, illus. (p. 1098)
—Marvel Adventures Spider-Man - Friendly Neighborhood. Di Salvo, Roberto, illus. (p. 1098)
—Plants vs. Zombies: Lawnmageddon: Lawnmageddon. Simon, Philip, ed. (p. 1370)
—Spider-Man & the Secret Wars GN. (p. 1626)
—Spider-Man: the Extremist. Clayton, Henry et al, illus. (p. 1626)
Tobin, Paul, jt. auth. see Coover, Colleen.
Tobin, Richard K. Skating on Thick Ice. LeBlanc, Rebecca, ed. (p. 1584)
Tobon, Sara, tr. see Irving, Washington & Gutierrez, Dave.
Tobon, Sara, tr. see Stone Arch Books Staff.
Tobon, Sara, tr. see Verne, Jules.
Toby Forward Staff. Doubleborn. (p. 473)
—Fireborn. (p. 591)
Tocchini, Greg, illus. see Ciencin, Scott.
Tocci, Salvatore. Chaparral: Life on the Scrubby Coast. (p. 291)
—Chlorine. (p. 309)
—Experiments with Colors. (p. 549)
—Experiments with Soap. (p. 549)
—Holt Chemistry: Visualizing Matter Technology Edition. (p. 789)
—Jonas Salk: Creator of the Polio Vaccine. (p. 925)
—Lead. (p. 981)
—Life in the Temperate Forests. (p. 1011)
—Marine Habitats: Life in Saltwater. (p. 1094)
—Mercury. (p. 1127)
—More Simple Science Fair Projects: Grades 3-5. Wiacek, Bob, illus. (p. 1175)
—Oxygen. (p. 1316)
—Science Fair Projects with Everyday Stuff. (p. 1526)
—Silicon. (p. 1575)
—Sodium. (p. 1605)
—Zinc. (p. 1987)
Tocci, Salvatore, jt. auth. see Friedhoffer, Bob.
Tocci, Salvatore, jt. auth. see Gardner, Robert.
Tocco, Douglas, illus. see Tocco, John V.
Tocco, Heather L. Addisyn's Bedtime Grace. (p. 12)
Tocco, John V. Meet the Gizmos: The First Kids on the International Space Station. Tocco, Douglas, illus. (p. 1122)
Tocher, Timothy. Bill Pennant, Babe Ruth, & Me. (p. 186)
—Chief Sunrise, John McGraw, & Me. (p. 301)
—Odd Ball: Hilarious, Unusual, & Bizarre Baseball Moments Curtis, Stacy, illus. (p. 1278)
Tocquigny, Rick. Life Lessons from Family Vacations. (p. 1011)
Toda, Yasunari, illus. see Chiba, Tomohiro.
Toda, Yasunari, illus. see Kuroda, Yosuke.
Todaro, Dianne. How to Talk to Boys. (p. 822)
Todd, Anne. Teddy Powers: The Stone Keepers. (p. 1712)
Todd, Anne M. Chris Rock: Comedian & Actor. (p. 311)
—Jamie Foxx. (p. 907)
—Mohandas Gandhi. (p. 1160)
—Roger Maris. (p. 1484)
—Susan B. Anthony: Activist. (p. 1688)
—Tyra Banks. (p. 1805)
—Venus & Serena Williams. (p. 1836)
—Will Smith: Actor. (p. 1932)
Todd, Anne M. & Bankston, John. Jacqueline Wilson. (p. 905)
Todd, Barbara. Edward & the Eureka Lucky Wish Company. Storms, Patricia, illus. (p. 505)
—Roger Gets Carried Away. Rogé, illus. (p. 1484)
Todd, Burt Kerr. Bun Bun & Other Tales. (p. 241)
Todd, Chelva E. Up from the Barber's Chair. (p. 1824)
Todd, Chuck, illus. see Bogue, Gary.
Todd, Danielle & Keller, Carolyn. University of Delaware College Prowler off the Record. (p. 1820)
Todd, Deborah. Facts on File Algebra Handbook. (p. 561)
Todd, Diana. Carrotsville. (p. 271)
Todd, Francine E. Todds in America: 1741-2005: An American History/Genealogy Curriculum for Grades 3-5. (p. 1761)
Todd, Heather. Tapping Away My Worries: A Book for Children, Parents, & Teachers. (p. 1706)
Todd, Ilima. Remake. (p. 1458)
Todd, John. Nuts for Boys to Crack: Earthly Stories with a Heavenly Meaning. (p. 1274)
Todd, John S. Goodfellow Boys & the Talking Dinosaur. (p. 701)
Todd, Justin, illus. see Stevenson, Robert Louis.
Todd, Justin, jt. auth. see Grahame, Kenneth.
Todd Kaplan, Delia Angelescu, tr. see Creanga, Ion.
Todd, Kim D. Jean Jennings Bartik: Computer Pioneer. (p. 911)
Todd, Margaret. Explorers. (p. 551)
Todd, Mark. Food Trucks! (p. 614)
Todd, Mark, illus. see Harris, John.
Todd, Mark, illus. see Watson, Esther Pearl.
Todd, Michelle, illus. see Taylor, Saranne.
Todd, Mort, illus. see Van Lente, Fred, et al.
Todd, Pamela. Blind Faith Hotel. (p. 199)
Todd, Penelope. Dark. (p. 407)
Todd, Richard E. Baptism: A Bible Study Wordbook for Kids. (p. 137)
—Church: A Bible Study Wordbook for Kids. (p. 318)
—Communion: A Bible Study Wordbook for Kids. (p. 349)
—Giving: A Bible Study Wordbook for Kids. (p. 681)
—Salvation: A Bible Study Wordbook for Kids. (p. 1506)
Todd, Ruthven. Space Cat. (p. 1618)
Todd, Sheri, illus. see Speed, Bryan W.
Todd, Strasser. Give a Boy a Gun. (p. 681)
Todd, Sue. One Last Wish: A Tale from India. (p. 1295)
Todd, Sue, illus. see Alary, Laura.
Todd, Sue, illus. see Barchers, Suzanne I.
Todd, Sue, illus. see Coleman, Wim & Perrin, Pat.
Todd, Sue, illus. see StJohn, Amanda.
Todd, Traci N. Drum Circle. Reisch, Jesse, illus. (p. 487)
—Wiggle, Waggle, Loop-De-Loo! Barner, Bob, illus. (p. 1927)
Toddy, Irving, illus. see Gowan, Barbara.
Toddy, Irving, illus. see Parsons Yazzie, Evangeline.
Toddy, Irving, illus. see Shoulders, Michael & Shoulders, Debbie.
Toddy, Irving, illus. see Trotter, Deborah W.
Todeschi, Kevin J. Edgar Cayce's ESP: Who He Was, What He Said, & How It Came True. (p. 504)
Todesco, Angelique. Way of the Pendant. (p. 1864)
Todino, Grace. Tina the Turtle. Keeble, Susan, illus. (p. 1755)
Todo Color, illus. see Winkler, Jude.
Todolibro, Equipo, jt. auth. see Todolibro, equipo.
Todolibro, equipo & Todolibro, Equipo. Fabulas Doradas. (p. 559)
—Historias Doradas. (p. 782)
Todoro, Carlie. Is It Rough? Is It Smooth? (p. 889)
—Let's Draw! (p. 995)
—Our Earth. (p. 1308)
Todorov, Boriana & Todorov, Vladimir. Moon Rock. (p. 1172)
—Oliver's Tantrums. (p. 1286)
Todorov, Vladimir, jt. auth. see Todorov, Boriana.
Todras, Ellen & Bjorklund, Ruth. New Mexico. (p. 1246)
Todras, Ellen H. Explorers, Trappers, & Pioneers. (p. 551)
—Wagon Trains & Settlers. (p. 1852)
Todras, Ellen H., jt. auth. see Bjorklund, Ruth.
Todras, Ellen H., jt. auth. see RJF Publishing Staff.
Toenes, Claudia. Very Special Penguin. (p. 1838)
Toenjes. Residential Printreading. (p. 1463)
Toenjes, Annette. What If Grandma Didn't Have a Nose? (p. 1887)
Toenjes, Leonard P. Building Trades Dictionary: Text. (p. 239)
—Building Trades Estimating. (p. 239)
—Printreading for Heavy Commercial Construction: Text. (p. 1407)
Toenjes, Leonard P., jt. auth. see Proctor, Thomas E.
Toepperwein, Emilie & Toepperwein, Fritz A. Chinto, the Chaparral Cock. (p. 308)
Toepperwein, Fritz A., jt. auth. see Toepperwein, Emilie.
Toer, Pramoedya Ananta. Girl from the Coast. (p. 678)
Toews, Marj. Black & White Blanche Bonder, Dianna, illus. (p. 195)
Toews, Rita. Bully: A Discussion & Activity Story. Ljungberg, Jon, illus. (p. 241)
Toews, Rita Y. Bully: A Discussion & Activity Story. Ljungberg, Jon, illus. (p. 241)
Toews, Sheena. Beary Fun! (p. 152)
—Beary Snowy. (p. 152)
Toffler-Corrie, Laura. My Totally Awkward Supernatural Crush. (p. 1220)
Toffolo, Cris E. Arab League. (p. 94)
Toft, Barbara. Complete Guides Animals. (p. 353)
Toft, Di. Twilight Circus. (p. 1801)
—Wolven. (p. 1944)
Toft, Julie. Blot on the Landscape. (p. 202)
Toft, Kim Michelle. World That We Want. (p. 1958)
—World That We Want. Toft, Kim Michelle, illus. (p. 1958)
Tofte, Mavis. Doogie Dork & Marta. (p. 470)
—Doogie Dork & the Storm. Tofte, Mavis, illus. (p. 470)
—Doogie Dork Meets Trouble. (p. 470)
—Doogie Dork's Wish. Tofte, Mavis, illus. (p. 470)
—Franny Frumpel's Secret. (p. 631)
Tofts, Hannah. Collage. (p. 339)
—One Cool Watermelon. (p. 1294)
—One Cool Watermelon. Tofts, Hannah, illus. (p. 1294)
—Sandia Bien Fria. (p. 1511)
Togashi, Yoshihiro. Hunter X Hunter (p. 828)
—Hunter X Hunter Togashi, Yoshihiro, illus. (p. 828)
—Hunter X Hunter. Togashi, Yoshihiro, illus. (p. 828)
—Hunter X Hunter. Olsen, Lillian, tr. from JPN. (p. 828)
—Yu Yu Hakusho: Lonesome Ghosts Olsen, Lillian, tr. (p. 1983)
—Yu Yu Hakusho. Togashi, Yoshihiro, illus. (p. 1983)
—YuYu Hakusho. Togashi, Yoshihiro, illus. (p. 1983)
—Yuyu Hakusho. Togashi, Yoshihiro, illus. (p. 1983)
Togden, Ra Chel. Legendary Rabbit of Death - Volume One [Paperback]. (p. 989)
Togel, Peggy, jt. auth. see McGrath, Barbara Barbieri.
Together!. Come & See - Leader's Manual. (p. 347)
Tognozzi, Elissa. Student Lab Audio CDs: Used with ... Tognozzi-Ponti: Italiano Terzo Millennio. (p. 1669)
—Workbook/Lab Manual: Used with ... Tognozzi-Ponti: Italiano Terzo Millennio. (p. 1952)
Toh, Irene. Kumi the Bear. Hagan, Stacy, illus. (p. 968)
Tok, Stephanie, jt. auth. see Eng, Paul.
Tok, Stephanie, jt. auth. see Park, Y. H.
Tok, Stephanie, jt. auth. see Rielly, Robin L.
Toka, Yumie, illus. see Takahashi, Peter X.
Tokarjewa, Viktorija. Pianist: Erzaehlungen. (p. 1354)
Tokarz, Brenda. Curious Jane's: A Balloon Adventure. (p. 394)
Toki, Sela Tuita. Pati Loves to Walk Barefoot to School. (p. 1328)
Toki, Wilfred. Grandpa, What's a Humuhumu? Toki, Wilfred, illus. (p. 709)
—Hana & the Honu. Toki, Wilfred, illus. (p. 740)
—Moku & the Heoe of Waimea. Toki, Wilfred, illus. (p. 1160)
Tokidoki. Tokidoki Cactus Pups. (p. 1762)
Tokio, Marnelle. More Than You Can Chew. (p. 1175)
—Room 207. Hendry, Linda, illus. (p. 1488)
Tokoro, Juzo. Shadows of Spawn (p. 1558)
—Spawn Manga!!! (p. 1622)
Tokuda, Wendy. Samson the Hot Tub Bear: A True Story. (p. 1509)
Tokunaga, Wendy. Niagara Falls. (p. 1250)
Tokunbo, Dimitrea, illus. see Johnson, G. Francis.
Tokunbo, Dimitrea, illus. see Saint-Lot, Katia Novet.
Tokyopop and Art Impression Staff & Peymani, Christine. Skelanimals: It's a Wonderful Afterlife. Vol. 1 (p. 1584)
Tokyopop, creator. Lady & the Tramp. (p. 970)
Tokyopop Staff. Passion Fruit: Sweat & Honey Tokyopop Staff, illus. (p. 1327)
—Rave Master: The Sound of Thunder (p. 1441)
Tokyopop Staff, ed. see Wizards of the Coast Team.
Tokyopop Staff, creator. Contents under Pressure (p. 360)
—Dino Thunder Vol. 1. (p. 441)
—Donut Worry, Be Happy! (p. 469)
—Jesse McCartney (p. 914)
—Power Rangers 'Ninja Storm' Dark Sky Overhead (p. 1390)
—Rave Master: The Quest Begins Vol. 1 (p. 1441)
Tokyopop Staff, ed. Jackie Chan Adventures (p. 903)
—Jackie Chan Adventures: Enter the Dark Hand (p. 903)
—Jackie Chan Adventures: Jackie & Jade Save the Day Vol. 3 (p. 903)
Tokyopop Staff, et al. King of Hell (p. 958)
Tokyopop Staff, prod. Psychic Academy Bundle (p. 1413)
Tol, Alex Van. Dolores Huerta: Voice for the Working Poor. (p. 464)
—Sonia Sotomayor: U.S. Supreme Court Justice. (p. 1612)
Tolan, Sandy. Children of the Stone: The Power of Music in a Hard Land. (p. 302)
Tolan, Stephanie S. Applewhites at Wit's End. (p. 93)
—Bartholomew's Blessing. Moore, Margie, illus. (p. 140)
—Surviving the Applewhites. (p. 1687)
—Wishworks, Inc. Bates, Amy June, illus. (p. 1941)
Toland, Darrell, illus. see Holechek, Max.
Toland, Mischa P., creator. She Ain't Angry for Nothin' Intervention & Behavior Modification Curriculum. (p. 1564)
Tolar, Bill. Hope When Believers Struggle: Studies in Mark's Gospel. (p. 797)
Tolar, Kathy. I Must Be from Another Planet. (p. 844)
Tolbert-Klein, Wa-Landa. Paladin: A Different Type of Werewolf Story. (p. 1319)
Toledano, Connie. Mardi Gras Abcs. Toledano, Connie, illus. (p. 1092)
Toledo, Francisco, illus. see Toledo, Natalia.
Toledo, Leila J. Little Peter & Sela. Davis, Chad L., illus. (p. 1033)
Toledo, Natalia. Light Foot (Pies Ligeros) Amado, Elisa, tr. from CAI. (p. 1015)
Toledo, Salvador de & de, Toledo Salvador. Zoologico. (p. 1989)
Toler, Pamela. War Of 1812 Musteen, Jason R., ed. (p. 1857)
Toler, Pamela D. Causes of the War of 1812. (p. 282)
—Matt Damon. (p. 1109)
Toler, Violet M. Churchmouse Tales: Puppet Book Koefler, Leatha, illus. (p. 318)
—Churchmouse Tales: Puppet Plays Koefler, Leatha, illus. (p. 318)
Toles-Stotts, LaShunda. When I Learned to Read. Stotts, Jasmyn & Jayda, illus. (p. 1903)
Tolford, Joshua, illus. see Beatty, Hetty Burlingame.
Tolhurst, Deirdre. Christmas I Remember. (p. 314)
Tolhurst, Marilyn. Lights & Candles. (p. 1016)
Toliver, Gwen. Seed Sowers: Gospel-Planting Adventures. (p. 1547)
Toliver, K. S. Pam Brown Is Picture Perfect!! (p. 1320)
Toliver, Marilyn. Marcellus Alphabet Book: One, Two, Three What a Words Do You See? (p. 1091)
—Marcellus Really Wants a Pet. (p. 1091)
Toliver, Wendy. Lifted. (p. 1014)
—Miss Match. (p. 1151)
—Secret Life of a Teenage Siren. (p. 1541)
Tolkien, Baillie, ed. see Tolkien, J. R. R.
Tolkien, J. R. R. Bilbo's Last Song. Baynes, Pauline, illus. (p. 186)
—Como Se Hizo el Senor de los Anillos. (p. 351)
—Comunidad de los Anillos (p. 355)
—Fellowship of the Ring: Being the First Part of the Lord of the Rings. (p. 581)
—Guia de Fotos. (p. 729)
—Hobbit. (p. 786)
—Hobbit. Tolkien, J. R. R., illus. (p. 786)
—Kleine Hobbit. (p. 963)
—Las Aventuras de Tom Bombadil/the Adventures of Tom Bombadil: Y Otros Poemas de el Libro Rojo/and Other Verses from the Red Book. Baynes, Pauline, illus. (p. 976)
—Letters from Father Christmas. Tolkien, Baillie, ed. (p. 1002)
—Retorno del Rey. (p. 1464)
—Senhor dos Aneis. (p. 1550)
Tolkien, J. R. R. & Titley, Alan. Hobad: Nó Anonn Agus Ar Ais Arís. (p. 786)
Tolkien, J. R. R., et al. Hobad: Nó Anonn Agus Ar Ais Arís. (p. 786)
—Hobbit. Diaz, Lorenzo, tr. from ENG. (p. 786)
Tolkien, Michael. Woodsy. (p. 1950)
Tolkien, Michael G. R. Wish. (p. 1940)
Toll, Damien. Drawing Is Awesome! (p. 482)
Toll, Nelly S. Behind the Secret Window: A Memoir of a Hidden Childhood During World War II. (p. 160)
Tolle, Eckhart. Quietud Habla. (p. 1428)
Tolle, Eckhart & Friedman, Robert S. Milton's Secret: An Adventure of Discovery Through Then, When & the Power of Now. Riccio, Frank, illus. (p. 1144)
Tolleson, Rose. Jaycee & the Magic Scissors. (p. 910)
Tolley, Diane Stringam. Kris Kringle's Magic. (p. 967)
Tolley, Diane Stringam, jt. auth. see Tolley, Diane Stringham.
Tolley, Diane Stringham & Tolley, Diane Stringam. Carving Angels. (p. 273)
Tolley, Kristy. Mommy Interviews. (p. 1162)
Tollison, Hal. Cartooning. (p. 273)
Tolliver, Julia. Distinguishable Gentleman & the Presidential Race Of '08. (p. 454)
Tolman, Marije. Tree House. Tolman, Marije & Tolman, Ronald, illus. (p. 1783)
Tolman, Marije, illus. see Heide, Iris van der.
Tolman, Marije, illus. see Langen, Annette.
Tolman, Marije, illus. see Vanden Heede, Sylvia.
Tolman, Marije & Tolman, Ronald. Island. (p. 892)
—Tree House. (p. 1783)
Tolman, Marvin N. Hands-On Physical Science Activities for Grades K-6. (p. 741)
Tolman, Ronald, illus. see Tolman, Marije.
Tolman, Ronald, jt. auth. see Tolman, Marije.
Tolman, Tom, illus. see Reid, Pamela Carrington.
Tolmans, Tristan, ed. see Wardwell, Stacey DeMille.
Tolomeo, Concettina (Tina). Medication Inhalation Therapy: A Comprehensive Guide for Asthma Educators. (p. 1119)
Tolpen, Stanley. Crosscurrents. Hauser, Sheri, photos by. (p. 385)
Tolson, Aaron J. Washington Putter. (p. 1860)
Tolson, Scott, illus. see Owens, L. L.
Tolstikova, Dasha. Year Without Mom (p. 1969)
Tolstikova, Dasha, illus. see Hall, Kirsten.
Tolstoy, Aleksei. Gigantic Turnip. Sharkey, Niamh, illus. (p. 676)
Tolstoy, Aleksei & Sharkey, Niamh. Gigantic Turnip. (p. 676)
Tolstoy, Aleksei, et al. Gigantic Turnip. (p. 676)
Tolstoy, Alexei. Enormous Turnip. (p. 531)
—Enormous Turnip. Goto, Scott, illus. (p. 531)

Tolstoy, Leo. Anna Karenina (p. 85)
—Czar & the Shirt. Leal, Mireya Fonseca, ed. (p. 397)
—Leon y el Perrito: Y Otros Cuentos. Montana, Francisco, tr. (p. 992)
—Muerte de Ivan Ilich. (p. 1189)
—Ratoncita Nina y Otros Cuentos. (p. 1440)
Tolstoy, Leo & Riordan, James. Lion & the Puppy: And Other Stories for Children. Riordan, James, tr. from RUS. (p. 1020)
Tolstoy, Leo, et al. Prisonero del Caucaso. (p. 1407)
Tom, Darcy, ed. see Phillips, Heather.
Tom, Darcy, illus. see Callella, Kim.
Tom, Darcy, illus. see Cernak, Kim.
Tom, Darcy, illus. see Cernek, Kim & Williams, Rozanne Lanczak.
Tom, Darcy, illus. see Cernek, Kim, et al.
Tom, Darcy, illus. see Cernek, Kim.
Tom, Darcy, illus. see Eagan, Robynne.
Tom, Darcy, illus. see Hults, Alaska.
Tom, Darcy, illus. see Jennett, Pamela.
Tom, Darcy, illus. see Jordano, Kimberly & Adsit, Kim.
Tom, Darcy, illus. see Jordano, Kimberly & Corcoran, Tebra.
Tom, Darcy, illus. see Lubben, Amy & Williams, Rozanne Lanczak.
Tom, Darcy, illus. see Morss, Martha.
Tom, Darcy, illus. see Phillips, Heather.
Tom, Darcy, illus. see Shiotsu, Vicky.
Tom, Darcy, illus. see Williams, Rozanne Lanczak.
Tom Head, jt. auth. see Head, Carol Carwile.
Tom, Kelley. Missing the Moon. (p. 1153)
Tom, LaBaff, illus. see Gardner, Robert.
Tom, LaBaff, illus. see Wingard-Nelson, Rebecca.
Toma, Al. Rainbow on the Tree of Life. (p. 1435)
Tomasek, Dean, illus. see Marshall, Jane Garrett.
Tomaselli, Anthony. Play Guitar 1. (p. 1371)
Tomaselli, Doris. My Little People Farm (Mi Pequena Granja) Thompson Brothers Staff, illus. (p. 1212)
Tomaselli, Doris, jt. auth. see Reader's Digest Staff.
Tomaselli, Mela. Magic Pot: Folk Tales & Legends of the Giriama of Kenya. (p. 1073)
Tomasello, Heather. Hello, Florida! Walker, David, illus. (p. 763)
Tomasello, Sam, illus. see Hanneman, Monika, et al.
Tomasi, Joseph. Miss Wheezer Comes to Stay. (p. 1152)
Tomasi, Peter, ed. see Goyer, David S. & Johns, Geoff.
Tomasi, Peter J. Light Brigade. Hansen, Bjarne, illus. (p. 1015)
Tomasi, Peter J., et al. Jsa Classified - Honor among Thieves. (p. 930)
Tomasi-Dubois, Mary. Danger in the Jeweled City: A Matt & Heather Thriller. (p. 404)
Tomasso, Phillip. King Gauthier & the Little Dragon Slayer. (p. 958)
Tomaszewski, Suzanne Lyon. Samuel's Exeter Walkabout. Dionne, Nina, illus. (p. 1509)
Tomberg, Andrea. Teddie's Tales: A Very Busy Day. (p. 1712)
Tombers, Monica, ed. see Mitchell, Shirley Lipscomb.
Tomblin, Marian Strong. Mystery at Hotel Ormond (p. 1223)
—Where's Capone's Cash? (p. 1910)
Tomblin, Mark. Itchy-Scratchy Caterpillar. Jones, Doug, illus. (p. 895)
Tombo. Magic Nickel: A Fable about an Unhappy Salesman, a Sad Retired Person, & an Invisible Monster. (p. 1072)
Tomczyk, Mary. Early Learning Skill-Builders: Colors, Shapes, Numbers & Letters. (p. 493)
Tomczyk, Tara & Smith, Terry L. Nutrition & Food Safety. (p. 1274)
Tome. Adventure down Under Saincantin, Jerome, tr. from FRE. (p. 14)
—Spirou & Fantasio in New York. Janry, illus. (p. 1629)
Tomecek, Stephen M. Animal Communication. (p. 77)
—Art & Architecture. (p. 101)
—Electromagnetism, & How It Works. (p. 509)
—Food. (p. 612)
—Man-Made Materials. (p. 1085)
—Music. (p. 1193)
—Plate Tectonics. (p. 1370)
—Sports. (p. 1632)
—Tools & Machines. (p. 1767)
Tomecek, Stephen M. & West, Krista. Animal Courtship. (p. 77)
Tomecek, Steve. Coffee Can Science: 25 Easy, Hands-On Activities That Teach Key Concepts in Physical, Earth, & Life Sciences - And Meet the Science Standards. (p. 338)
—Dirt. (p. 446)
—Dirt. Woodman, Nancy, illus. (p. 446)
—Dirtmeister's Nitty Gritty Planet Earth: All about Rocks, Minerals, Fossils, Earthquakes, Volcanoes, & Even Dirt! Harper, Fred, illus. (p. 446)
—Moon. Guida, Liisa C., illus. (p. 1171)
—Moon. Guida, Liisa Chauncy, illus. (p. 1171)
—National Geographic Kids Everything Rocks & Minerals: Dazzling Gems of Photos & Info That Will Rock Your World. (p. 1232)
—Rocks & Minerals. Poling, Kyle, illus. (p. 1483)
—Stars. (p. 1643)
—Stars. Guida, Liisa C., illus. (p. 1643)
—Stars. Yoshikawa, Sachiko, illus. (p. 1643)
—Sun. Golembe, Carla, illus. (p. 1675)
Tomecek, Steve the Dirtmeister. Rocks & Minerals: Dazzling Gems of Photos & Info That Will Rock Your World. (p. 1483)
Tomedi, John. Dublin. (p. 487)
—Kurt Vonnegut. (p. 968)
Tomes, Margot, illus. see De Regniers, Beatrice Schenk.
Tomes, Margot, illus. see Fritz, Jean.
Tomes, Margot, illus. see Goudge, Elizabeth.
Tometich, Annabelle. Fruits Group. (p. 646)
—I Know Basketball. (p. 840)
—I Know Gymnastics. (p. 840)
—Judo. (p. 931)
—Lacrosse. (p. 970)
—Mixed Martial Arts. (p. 1156)
—Superstars of the New York Yankees. (p. 1684)
—Superstars of the Philadelphia Phillies. (p. 1684)
—Superstars of the San Francisco Giants. (p. 1684)
—Superstars of the St. Louis Cardinals. (p. 1684)
—Vegetables Group. (p. 1834)
Tomey, Ingrid. Queen of Dreamland. (p. 1425)
Tomic, Tomislav, illus. see Hamilton, Libby.
Tomino, Yoshiyuki. Brain Powered Sugisaki, Yukiru, illus. (p. 221)
—Brain Powered Matsunaga, Aya, tr. from JPN. (p. 221)
Tomita, Kuni, illus. see Buckley, MacKenzie.
Tomita, Sukehiro. Baby Birth (p. 125)
—Wedding Peach Tomita, Sukehiro & Yazawa, Nao, illus. (p. 1871)
—Wedding Peach. Yazawa, Nao, illus. (p. 1871)
—Young Love Yazawa, Nao, illus. (p. 1979)
Tomizawa, Hitoshi. Alien Nine: Emulators. Pannone, Frank, ed. (p. 41)
—Alien Nine 1 Pannone, Frank, ed. (p. 41)
—Alien Nine 2 Pannone, Frank, ed. (p. 41)
—Treasure Hunter 1: Eternal Youth Pannone, Frank, ed. (p. 1781)
—Treasure Hunter 2: Figurehead of Souls Pannone, Frank, ed. (p. 1781)
—Treasure Hunter 3: The Last Crusade Pannone, Frank, ed. (p. 1781)
Tomkies, Kelly Kagamas. Food Services. (p. 614)
Tomkins, D. Michael. World Below. (p. 1954)
Tomkins, Jasper. Nimby: An Extraordinary Cloud Who Meets a Remarkable Friend. (p. 1256)
Tomkinson, Tim, illus. see Demuth, Patricia Brennan.
Tomkinson, Tim, illus. see Holub, Joan.
Tomkinson, Tim, illus. see Krull, Kathleen.
Tomko, Karen, jt. auth. see Heine, Laura.
Tomlin, James C. Adventures of I Am, I Can & I Feel: A Journey into Positive. (p. 18)
Tomlin, S. E. Children of Bairnbough Forest. (p. 302)
Tomlins, Karen, illus. see Daynes, Katie.
Tomlinson, Andrew, jt. auth. see Bonaddio, T. L.
Tomlinson, Carol Ann & Cooper, James M. Educator's Guide to Differentiating Instruction. (p. 505)
Tomlinson, Carol Ann & Imbeau, Marcia B. Managing a Differentiated Classroom: A Practical Guide. (p. 1086)
Tomlinson, Elisa. True Reflection: A Girls' Guide to Identity in Christ. (p. 1792)
Tomlinson, Everett T. War of 1812. (p. 1857)
—Winning His W. (p. 1937)
Tomlinson, Harry. Bonsai. (p. 209)
Tomlinson, Heather. Aurelie: A Faerie Tale. (p. 116)
—Swan Maiden. (p. 1688)
Tomlinson, Jill. Cat Who Wanted to Go Home. Howard, Paul, illus. (p. 278)
—Gorilla Who Wanted to Grow Up. Howard, Paul, illus. (p. 703)
—Hen Who Wouldn't Give Up. Howard, Paul, illus. (p. 767)
—Otter Who Wanted to Know. Howard, Paul, illus. (p. 1307)
—Owl Who Was Afraid of the Dark Howard, Paul, illus. (p. 1315)
—Owl Who Was Afraid of the Dark. (p. 1315)
—Owl Who Was Afraid of the Dark. Howard, Paul, illus. (p. 1315)
—Penguin Who Wanted to Find Out. Howard, Paul, illus. (p. 1337)
—Three Favourite Animal Stories. Howard, Paul, illus. (p. 1742)
Tomlinson, Mark K. Share the Grain. (p. 1561)
Tomlinson, Michael, jt. auth. see Nixon, Caroline.
tomlinson, rick. Adventures of Bob & Mr. Ant the MAZE. (p. 16)
Tomlinson, Suzy. Teddy Meets a Bully & Finds a Friend. (p. 1712)
Tomlinson, Theresa. Ironstone Valley: A Story of Family Life in the 19th Century. (p. 888)
—Voyage of the Snake Lady. (p. 1850)
Tomljanovic, Tatiana. Bison. (p. 193)
—Bluenose: Canadian Icons. (p. 204)
—Borrowing. (p. 214)
—Camping. (p. 257)
—Caring for Your Salamander. (p. 269)
—Cornelia Funke: My Favorite Writer. (p. 367)
—Cornelia Funke. (p. 367)
—Cougars. (p. 369)
—Megan McDonald. (p. 1124)
—Rallying. (p. 1437)
—Ramadan. (p. 1437)
—Ramadan with Code. (p. 1437)
—Rock Climbing. (p. 1482)
—Skiing: X Games. (p. 1584)
—Skiing. (p. 1584)
—Wedges. (p. 1871)
Tommalieh, Fakhri & Hujeer, Majeda. 1st Grade Learning Arabic Language Step - by - Step Approach Workbook Part 2,Third Edition: Learn Arabic Language. Al-Ghussinu, Wa'ad Diab, illus. (p. 1991)
Tommasi, Michael Richard. Stinky Mcgee. (p. 1651)
Tommer, Sarah, illus. see Penn, M. W.
Tommer, Sarah, illus. see Penn, Mw.
Tommy. Bubba & Cecil. (p. 233)
Tomnay, Susan & Australian Women's Weekly Staff. Kids in the Kitchen: More Than 90 Fabulous Recipes for Kids to Make. (p. 954)
Tomonari, Itsuko. Adventures of Meow Meow & Friends. (p. 20)
Tomori, Miyoshi. Devil & Her Love Song (p. 432)
Tomories, K. G. Someone Special for You to Know. (p. 1609)
Tomorrow, Tom. Very Silly Mayor. (p. 1838)
Tomos, Angharad. Ceridwen. (p. 287)
—Cosyn. (p. 369)
—Diffodd Yr Haul. (p. 438)
—Diwrnod Golchi. (p. 455)
—Jam Poeth. (p. 906)
—Mali Meipen. (p. 1083)
—Rala Rwdins. Tomos, Angharad, illus. (p. 1437)
—Strempan. (p. 1667)
—Y Dewin Dwl. (p. 1968)
—Y Llipryn Llwyd. (p. 1968)
Tomos, Morgan, illus. see Edwards, Meinir Wyn.
Tompert, Ann. Errant Knight. Keith, Doug, illus. (p. 534)
—Grandfather Tang's Story. Parker, Robert A., illus. (p. 707)
—Harry's Hats. Elizalde, Marcelo, illus. (p. 751)
—Joan of Arc: Heroine of France. Garland, Michael, illus. (p. 919)
—Saint Nicholas. Garland, Michael, illus. (p. 1504)
Tompert, Ann & Lister, Ralph. Little Fox Goes to the End of the World Bryant, Laura J., illus. (p. 1028)
Tompkins, Bill. Keep-It-Cheap: Financially Surviving the Honey-Do List. Carson, Shawn, illus. (p. 946)
Tompkins, Janice M. Prayer: The First Line of Defense. (p. 1393)
Tompkins, Lisa. Why Are You Looking at Me? I Just Have down Syndrome. (p. 1922)
Tompkins, Michael A. & Martinez, Katherine A. My Anxious Mind: A Teen's Guide to Managing Anxiety & Panic. Sloan, Michael, illus. (p. 1196)
Tompkins, Michelle & Rahimi, Joey. Columbia University College Prowler off the Record. (p. 346)
Tompkins, Robyn & Moser, Franz. Cool Songs for Cool Kids... in the Classroom: Fun & Interactive Music & Activities for Early Childhood. Bk. 1 (p. 364)
Tompkins, Robyn Lee. Miss Molly's Adventure at the Beach: Another Great Adventure Brought to You by Miss Molly & Her Dog Reyburn Kantz, Bill, illus. (p. 1151)
—Miss Molly's Adventure in the Park: Another Great Adventure Brought to You by Miss Molly & Her Dog Reyburn Carson, Shawn K., illus. (p. 1151)
—Miss Molly's Adventure on the Farm: Another great adventure brought to you by Miss Molly & her dog Reyburn. Carson, Shawn, illus. (p. 1151)
Tompsett, Norm, jt. auth. see Barlas, Robert.
Toms, K. 10 Little Penguins. (p. 1993)
—10 Little Penguins Mini Book & Plush. (p. 1993)
Toms, Kate. Animal Tails. (p. 80)
—Bear Who Dares. (p. 151)
—Bear Who Dares Book & Plush. (p. 151)
—Dinosaur Tails. (p. 443)
—Duckie Duck. (p. 488)
—Duckie Duck Boxed Set. (p. 488)
—Funny Faces Cloth Book Jogger Dog. (p. 649)
—Funny Faces Moo-Riel Cow. (p. 649)
—God Knows All about Me. (p. 689)
—I Udderly Love You! (p. 847)
—I Udderly Love You. (p. 847)
—Sticky Little Fingers Rainy Day Activity Book. (p. 1650)
—Twinkle Twinkle Box Set. (p. 1802)
—Twinkle, Twinkle, Little Star. (p. 1802)
Toms, Kate & Funny Faces Staff. Jogger Dog. (p. 920)
Toms, Kate & Make Believe Ideas Staff. Itsy Bitsy Spider. (p. 900)
Toms, Kate, et al. God Knows All about Me. (p. 689)
Tomsu, Doug & Tomsu, Melodee. Smiling Places: Two Bumbling Idiots Hit the Road (p. 1594)
Tomsu, Melodee, jt. auth. see Tomsu, Doug.
Tonaki, Nicole. You Don't Eat, You Don't Grow. (p. 1975)
Tonatiuh, Duncan. Dear Primo: A Letter to My Cousin. (p. 419)
—Diego Rivera: His World & Ours. (p. 437)
—Funny Bones: Posada & His Day of the Dead Calaveras. (p. 649)
—Pancho Rabbit & the Coyote: A Migrant's Tale. (p. 1320)
—Separate Is Never Equal: Sylvia Mendez & Her Family's Fight for Desegregation. (p. 1551)
Tonatiuh, Duncan, illus. see Argueta, Jorge.
Tonderum, Angela. Kaycee Kangaroo Lost in Alphabet Forest: Adventures of Kaycee Kangaroo. Carlson, Christine, illus. (p. 946)
Tondino-Gonguet, Grace. Halimah & the Snake & Other Omani Folktales. Keeble, Susan, illus. (p. 737)
Tone. Stop Picking on Me! (p. 1653)
Tone, Satoe. Very Big Carrot. (p. 1837)
Tonei, illus. see Dole, Mayra L.
Toner, Gerald R. Lipstick Like Lindsay's & Other Christmas Stories Haynes, Joyce, illus. (p. 1021)
Toner, Jacqueline B., jt. auth. see Freeland, Claire A.B.
Toner, Jacqueline B. & Freeland, Claire A.B. What to Do When It's Not Fair: A Kid's Guide to Handling Envy & Jealousy. (p. 1894)
Tong, Andie, illus. see Huelin, Jodi.
Tong, Andie, illus. see Lee, Stan & Moore, Stuart.
Tong, Andie, illus. see Lemke, Donald.
Tong, Andie, illus. see Rosen, Lucy.
Tong, Andie, illus. see Sazaklis, John & Merkel, Joe F.
Tong, Andie, illus. see Sazaklis, John.
Tong, Kevin. Earth Machine. Tong, Kevin, illus. (p. 496)
Tong, Paul, illus. see Adler, David A.
Tong, Paul, illus. see Carlstrom, Nancy White.
Tong, Paul, illus. see Krensky, Stephen.
Tong, Paul, illus. see Ransom, Candice.
Tong, Rela D. Lonely Gourmet: Juan the Vegetarian Wolf. (p. 1046)
Tonge, Neil. Banished, Beheaded, or Boiled in Oil: A Hair-Raising History of Crime & Punishment Throughout the Ages! (p. 136)
Tonges Wilshire, et al. Slurping Soup & Other Confusions. (p. 1591)
Tong-Li, Candace. Tales of Titans: Timeless Dinosaur Stories. Tong-Li, Candace, illus. (p. 1703)
Toni, Alessandra, illus. see Hao, K. T.
Toni Eubanks. Journey Home. (p. 928)
Tonk, Ernest, illus. see McCracken, Harold.
TONKA. TONKA Busy Trucks: A Lift-The-Flap Book. (p. 1765)
Tonkin, Rachael & Hachette Children's Books Staff. Alien Hunter's Guide. (p. 40)
Tonkin, Rachel. Leaf Litter: Exploring the Mysteries of a Hidden World. (p. 982)
Tonn, Mary Jane. Jolly Old Santa Claus. (p. 924)
Tonner, Leslie, jt. auth. see Turecki, Stanley.
Tono, Lucia, tr. see Ferrin, Wendy Wakefield.
Too, Lillian. Total Feng Shui: Bring Health, Wealth, & Happiness into Your Life. Pilston, Jim, illus. (p. 1771)
Toohey, Cathy, jt. auth. see Mattern, Joanne.
Toohey, Eileen N., illus. see Myers, Robert.
Tooke, Susan. B Is for Bluenose: A Nova Scotia Alphabet. Tooke, Susan, illus. (p. 122)
Tooke, Susan, illus. see Bastedo, Jamie.
Tooke, Susan, illus. see Clarke, George Elliott.
Tooke, Susan, illus. see Grant, Shauntay.
Tooke, Susan, illus. see Grassby, Donna.
Tooke, Susan, illus. see Lohnes, Marilyn.
Tooke, Susan, illus. see McNaughton, Janet.
Tooke, Susan, illus. see Wilson, Budge.
Tooke, Wes. King of the Mound: My Summer with Satchel Paige. (p. 959)
—Lucky: Maris, Mantle, & My Best Summer Ever. (p. 1062)
Tooker, Richard N. Business of Database Marketing. (p. 245)
Tookes, Edward. Future Rebuke: Hip hop meets science fiction, & science fiction meets Morality. (p. 651)
Tool Kits for Kids LLC Staff, creator. Build up Your Resilience - Tool Kit for Kids: Elementary School Edition. (p. 238)
—Build up Your Resilience - Tool Kit for Kids: High School / Middle School Edition. (p. 238)
—Charge up Your Confidence - Tool Kit for Kids: Elementary School Edition. (p. 291)
—Charge up Your Confidence - Tool Kit for Kids: High School / Middle School Edition. (p. 291)
—Outsmart Your Worry - Tool Kit for Kids: Elementary School Edition. (p. 1313)
—Outsmart Your Worry - Tool Kit for Kids: High School / Middle School Edition. (p. 1313)
Toole, Darlene. Cajun's Song. (p. 252)
Toole, Glenn & Toole, Susan. Essential AS Biology for OCR. (p. 536)
Toole, Susan, jt. auth. see Toole, Glenn.
Tooley, Mike. Engineering a Level. (p. 529)
—Engineering GCSE. (p. 529)
Tooley, S. D. Skull. (p. 1586)
Toombs, Robert. Dottie the Bus Driver in Bicycle Safety. Barnett, Linda, illus. (p. 472)
Toombs, Tom. Big Camping Adventure: Little Tommy Learns Lessons from the Great Outdoors. Wells-Smith, Abby, illus. (p. 180)
—Mysterious Money Tree: Little Tommy Learns a Lesson in Giving. Smith, Abby, illus. (p. 1223)
—Way to Be a Winner: Little Tommy Learns a Lesson in Working Together. Wells Smith, Abby, illus. (p. 1864)
Toonkel, Jessica, jt. auth. see Baylies, Peter.
Toonz Animation, ed. see Olsen, Lauri.
Toor, Rachel. On the Road to Find Out. (p. 1291)
Tooth, Lucy. Star the Tooth Fairy from Treasure Cloud Shares Secrets with You! (p. 1641)
—Star the Tooth Fairy Haunted by Mr. Jack-O-Lantern in Pumpkinland! (p. 1641)
—Star the Tooth Fairy Is Checking on You! (p. 1641)
—Star the Tooth Fairy Takes A Holiday to Visit Santa at the North Pole! (p. 1641)
—Star the Tooth Fairy Wants to Know If You Need Braces? (p. 1641)
—Tooth Fairy Loose & Lost Baby Tooth Coloring Log. (p. 1768)
—Tooth Fairy Loose & Lost Tooth Coloring Log. (p. 1768)
Toothman, Lindsey, illus. see Toothman, Sherry.
Toothman, Sherry. I'm Okay, Mommy. Toothman, Lindsey, illus. (p. 859)
Tooty. Patches in Winter. (p. 1328)
Top That!. Alphabet Farm (large Version) Parry, Jo, illus. (p. 49)
—Color Safari (large Version) Parry, Jo, illus. (p. 343)
Top That. Fun Kits Amazing Magic. (p. 648)
—Fun Kits Cool Cat's Face Painting. (p. 648)
—Fun Kits Play the REC. (p. 648)
Top That!. Jungle Numbers (large Version) Parry, Jo, illus. (p. 935)
Top That. Let's Stencil Animals. (p. 1000)
—Let's Stencil Things That Go. (p. 1000)
Top That!. Playtime Shapes (large Version) Parry, Jo, illus. (p. 1373)
Top That. Press Out & Play Magic Castle. (p. 1397)
—Press Out & Play Princess Castle. (p. 1397)
Top That!, creator. 123 Train. (p. 2000)
—ABC Train. (p. 3)
—Animals with Martha the Monkey. (p. 84)
—Counting with Billy the Bear. (p. 372)
—Dressing-up Fun: Learn to Lace. (p. 485)
—Flags Sticker Book. (p. 602)
—How to Draw Managa Fantasy Fighters. (p. 818)
—How to Draw Manga Ninja Warriors. (p. 818)
—How to Draw Manga Transforming Robots. (p. 818)
—Journey to the Bottom of the Sea. (p. 929)
—Old MacDonald's Farm. (p. 1284)
—Roald Dahl Build Your Own Willy Wonka's Chocolate Factory. (p. 1478)
—Shapes with Penny the Penguin. (p. 1561)
—Wild Animals. (p. 1928)
Top That, ed. Cock a Doodle Boo. (p. 337)
Top That!, ed. How to Draw 101 Super Heroes. Griffin, Hedley, illus. (p. 816)
Top That, ed. Let's Play Magnetic Play Scene Diggers. (p. 1000)
—Let's Play Magnetic Play Scene Trains. (p. 1000)
—Night Light Sleepy Bear. (p. 1253)
—Revolving Nursery Rhymes. (p. 1467)
—Sammy the Snake. (p. 1508)
Top That! Kids, creator. Brilliant Beads & Bracelets. (p. 228)
—Fabulous Footware. (p. 560)
—Let's Build. (p. 994)
—Magnetic Play + Learn Shapes. (p. 1075)
—Magnetic Silly Animals. (p. 1075)
—Magnetic Silly Faces. (p. 1075)
—Make Your Own Pencil Toppers. (p. 1080)
—Things That Go. (p. 1733)
Top That Publishing. Writing My First Sums. (p. 1965)
Top That Publishing, creator. Writing My First Words: Early Days Magic Writing Book. (p. 1965)
Top That Publishing, ed. Mixed up Animals. (p. 1156)
—Mixed up Monsters. (p. 1156)
Top That Publishing Editors, ed. Beastly Ballons. Dahl, Roald, illus. (p. 152)

—Fiendish Faces. Dahl, Roald, illus. (p. 584)
—Ghastly Grub. Dahl, Roald, illus. (p. 670)
—Magical Mischief. Dahl, Roald, illus. (p. 1075)
—Silly Scribbles. Dahl, Roald, illus. (p. 1576)
—Stupendous Stampers. Dahl, Roald, illus. (p. 1670)
Top That Publishing Staff. Extreme Sports. (p. 557)
—How Many. (p. 810)
—Today's Technology. (p. 1761)
—What Am I. (p. 1879)
Top That Publishing Staff, ed. see Cabral, Jeane.
Top That Publishing Staff, ed. see Conchie, Kathryn.
Top That Publishing Staff, ed. see Munton, Gill.
Top That Publishing Staff, ed. see Ranson, Erin.
Top That Publishing Staff, ed. see Trowell, Michelle.
Top That Publishing Staff, ed. 101 Brainbender Puzzles. (p. 1999)
—101 Crossword Search Puzzles. (p. 1999)
—101 Picture Puzzles. (p. 1999)
—101 Wordsearch Puzzles. (p. 2000)
—7 Wonders of World. (p. 1993)
—Aircraft. (p. 31)
—Alphabet Farm. Parry, Jo, illus. (p. 49)
—Animal Fun. (p. 78)
—Animals. (p. 81)
—Arctic Animals. (p. 96)
—Aztec Madness. (p. 122)
—Birds of Paradise. (p. 191)
—Birds of World. (p. 192)
—Bobby Badgers Box of Books. (p. 206)
—Boob Juggling. (p. 210)
—Brain Workout. (p. 222)
—Brilliant Balloon Modeling. (p. 228)
—Calligraphy Skills. (p. 254)
—Cartoon Sculpture. (p. 273)
—Celtic Double Cross. (p. 286)
—Chinese Myst. (p. 307)
—Colors. (p. 345)
—Counting. (p. 370)
—Counting on the Farm. Sapp, Karen, illus. (p. 371)
—Create Your Own Lettering. (p. 378)
—Creepy Crawlies. (p. 381)
—Dinosaurs. (p. 444)
—Drawing with Pastels. (p. 482)
—Electric Science. (p. 508)
—Fabulous Facials. (p. 560)
—Fairy Princess Letter Writing. (p. 563)
—Fast Cars. (p. 576)
—Favorite Recipes. (p. 578)
—First Words. (p. 597)
—Flight. (p. 604)
—Freaky Fredas Ghost. (p. 632)
—Funky Fabrics. (p. 649)
—Funny Monsters. (p. 650)
—Glass Painting. (p. 682)
—Goldilocks & Three Bears. (p. 696)
—Halfpipe Heroes. (p. 737)
—How to Draw Monster Reptiles. (p. 818)
—Human Body. (p. 825)
—In My Little Blue Bed. Henley, Claire, illus. (p. 864)
—In My Little Pink Bed: A Counting Book. Henley, Claire, illus. (p. 864)
—Incredible Insects. (p. 869)
—Inventions. (p. 884)
—Jungle Numbers. Parry, Jo, illus. (p. 935)
—Kittens & Cats. (p. 963)
—Lets Explore Space. (p. 996)
—Lets Explore Time. (p. 996)
—Lets Go Bubbletastic. (p. 997)
—Lets Learn about Energy. (p. 998)
—Lets Learn Dinosaurs. (p. 998)
—Light Science. (p. 1015)
—Magical Horses Letter Writing. (p. 1074)
—Magnet Science. (p. 1075)
—Magnetic Play & Learn ABC. (p. 1075)
—Make it Grow. (p. 1079)
—Midnight Fairies. Atkins, Alison, illus. (p. 1138)
—Millie the Millipede: Collects Colors as She Munches Her Way Through the Pages. Elliott, Rebecca, illus. (p. 1144)
—Mini Monsters. (p. 1146)
—Mirror Science. (p. 1149)
—Monster Plants. (p. 1168)
—Mr. Mouse Needs House. (p. 1185)
—My First Library. (p. 1207)
—My School Days Yearbook. (p. 1218)
—Ocean Predators. (p. 1276)
—One Little Penguin & His Friends: A Pushing, Turning, Counting Book. Gévry, Claudine, illus. (p. 1295)
—Our Planet. (p. 1309)
—Party Tattoos. (p. 1326)
—Practical Jokes. (p. 1392)
—Princess Letter Writing. (p. 1404)
—Puppies & Dogs. (p. 1418)
—Real Spies. (p. 1449)
—Rescue Helicopter. Dronsfield, Paul, illus. (p. 1462)
—Rude Cocktails. (p. 1494)
—Safe & Simple Science Tricks. (p. 1502)
—Shadow on Wall. (p. 1557)
—Sharks. (p. 1562)
—Sketching with Pencils. (p. 1584)
—Sketching with Watercolor Pencils. (p. 1584)
—Space. (p. 1618)
—Strip Poker. (p. 1667)
—Survival. (p. 1686)
—There Were Ten Bears in a Bed: A Count-and-Feel Book. Atkins, Alison, illus. (p. 1730)
—Ultimate Micro Fliers. (p. 1809)
—Wacky Bull. (p. 1852)
—Wacky Cow. (p. 1852)
—Wacky Duck. (p. 1852)
—Wacky Goat. (p. 1852)
—Wacky Hen. (p. 1852)
—Wacky Pig. (p. 1852)
—Wacky Pony. (p. 1852)
—Wacky Sheep. (p. 1852)
—Watercolor Painting. (p. 1863)
—Weather Watch. (p. 1870)
—What's My Job. (p. 1898)
—Who's My Mommy. (p. 1920)
Top That! Staff, ed. see Ranson, Erin.
Top That! Team Staff. Mini Temporary Tattoos. Stillview, photos by. (p. 1146)
Top That! Team Staff, contrib. by. Design & Fly Paper Airplanes. (p. 429)
Topakian, Patricia E. Mystery of the Old Brown Suitcase. (p. 1225)
Topaz, Ksenia, illus. see Lehman-Wilzig, Tami.
Topaz, Ksenia, illus. see Levine, Anna.
Topek, Susan Remick. Ten Good Rules: A Counting Book. Cohen, Tod, photos by. (p. 1718)
—Ten Good Rules: A Ten Commandments Counting Book. Cohen, Tod, photos by. (p. 1718)
Topia, Beegee, illus. see Myracle, Lauren.
Topliff, Delores. Whoosh. (p. 1920)
Toporoff, Debi. Boogie. (p. 210)
—Boogie 3D. (p. 210)
—Herbie the Dung Beetle. (p. 769)
—Here Fishy Fishy. (p. 770)
—Katherine. (p. 944)
—Little David & the Big One. (p. 1026)
—Roscoe Gets a Haircut. (p. 1489)
—Roscoe Goes to the Gym. Butler, Gregory J., illus. (p. 1489)
—Roscoe Meets Gramps the Catfish 3D. (p. 1489)
—Roscoe Meets Gramps the Catfish (softcover) (p. 1489)
—Roscoe Meets Nurse Quacker. (p. 1489)
—Roscoe Meets Nurse Quacker 3D. (p. 1489)
—Roscoe's Deep Sea Adventure. (p. 1489)
—Roscoe's Deep Sea Adventure 3D. (p. 1489)
—Roscoe's Deep Sea Adventure (softcover) (p. 1489)
—Sniffles Possum Looks for Bad Boy: Mocosito Zarigeya Busca a Chico Malo. (p. 1597)
—When God Came Down. (p. 1902)
—Who Parked the Ark? (p. 1917)
—Yammi Finds a Friend. (p. 1968)
Topp, Elizabeth, jt. auth. see Livoti, Carol.
Topp, Patricia. This Strange Quantum World & You. (p. 1737)
Toppenberg, Lily, illus. see Cruz, Stefanie.
Topper, Wendy. Where's the Pacifier? (p. 1911)
Toppi, Sergio, illus. see Pagotto, Toni.
Toppin, Olivier, photos by see Coxe, Molly.
Topping, Jay, jt. auth. see van Dam, M. Nicole.
Topsell, John. How to Raise & Keep a Dragon. Nigg, Jospeh, ed. (p. 821)
Tor, Regina, et al. Growing Toward Peace. (p. 726)
Tor, Seidler, jt. auth. see Seidler, Tor.
Toral, Miguel A. Babu Goes Back to the Zoo. (p. 124)
Torbert, Wayne E. Twelve for Thebes, a Tale of Ancient Greece. Torbert, Wayne E., illus. (p. 1800)
Torchinsky, Oleg, et al. Russia. (p. 1498)
Torcida, María Luisa, illus. see Herrera, J. Ignacio.
Torcida, María Luisa, jt. auth. see Fuertes, Gloria.
Torckler, Darryl, jt. auth. see Torckler, Gillian.
Torckler, Gillian & Torckler, Darryl. Life-Size Guide to New Zealand Fish. (p. 1013)
Torday, Piers. Dark Wild. (p. 408)
—Last Wild. (p. 979)
Tordella, Frederic. Yachting in the Sahara. (p. 1968)
Toreeva, Natalia G. Battle on the Kalinov-Bridge: A Russian Fairy Tale. (p. 147)
—Greg & the Sea Monster. (p. 723)
Toresen, Eli B. Summer with Prince. (p. 1675)
—Yearbook Trouble at the Riding Camp. (p. 1969)
Toretto, Jordana. Runaway Children. (p. 1496)
Torey Fuller, illus. see Fuller, Taneka.
Torgan, Keith & Siesel, Barbara. Green Golly & Her Golden Flute. Langelier-Lebeda, Suzanne, illus. (p. 722)
Torgerson, Scotty Delray. Jacob Goes to the Moon. (p. 904)
Torgeson, Sarah, illus. see Delashmutt, Amy.
Torgrimsen, Reidun. Timmy's Christmas, a Very Special Pig from Sugar Valley & His Best Friend. (p. 1755)
Tori. Be the Truth. (p. 149)
—Heal the Separation. (p. 757)
Torices, Jose Gonzalez, et al. Cuatro Estaciones: Teatro para Ninos. (p. 388)
—Poemas para la Paz. Noriega, Fernando, illus. (p. 1376)
Toriello, James. Human Genome Project. (p. 826)
—Stomach: Learning How We Digest. (p. 1652)
Toriello, James, jt. auth. see Bayden, Maya.
Toriyama, Akira. Cowa! Toriyama, Akira, illus. (p. 373)
—Dr. Slump (p. 475)
—Dr. Slump Toriyama, Akira, illus. (p. 475)
—Dr. Slump. Toriyama, Akira, illus. (p. 475)
—Dragon Ball (p. 476)
—Dragon Ball Morimoto, Mari, tr. (p. 476)
—Dragon Ball Morimoto, Mari, tr. from JPN. (p. 476)
—Dragon Ball. Toriyama, Akira, illus. (p. 476)
—Dragon Ball. Morimoto, Mari, tr. from JPN. (p. 476)
—Dragon Ball Full Color. (p. 476)
—Dragon Ball Z Toriyama, Akira, illus. (p. 476)
—Dragon Ball Z. Toriyama, Akira, illus. (p. 476)
—Dragon Ball Z, Vol. 8 (VIZBIG Edition) Toriyama, Akira, illus. (p. 476)
—Fight to the Finish! Toriyama, Akira, illus. (p. 585)
—Is This the End? Vol. 9. Toriyama, Akira, illus. (p. 890)
—Let the Tournament Begin! Toriyama, Akira, illus. (p. 994)
—One Enemy, One Goal. Toriyama, Akira, illus. (p. 1294)
—Sand Land. Toriyama, Akira, illus. (p. 1510)
—Strongest under the Heavens. Toriyama, Akira, illus. (p. 1668)
—Yami No Matsuei Toriyama, Akira, illus. (p. 1968)
Toriyama, Akira, jt. auth. see Akira, Shouko.
Toriyama, Akira, jt. auth. see Inagaki, Riichiro.
Toriyama, Akira & Akira, Shouko. Dr. Slump Toriyama, Akira, illus. (p. 475)
Toriyama, Akira & Jones, Gerard. Dragon Ball (p. 476)
—Dragon Ball in Danger! (p. 476)
—Dragon Ball Z Olsen, Lillian, tr. from JPN. (p. 476)
—Dragon Ball Z. Toriyama, Akira, illus. (p. 476)
—Dragon Ball Z. Olsen, Lillian, tr. from JPN. (p. 476)
Torke, Kyle, ed. see Phillips, Louis.
Torma, Patrick. Alphabet for American Children Coloring Book. (p. 49)
Torme, Mel. Christmas Song: Chestnuts Roasting on an Open Fire. Barrette, Doris, illus. (p. 315)
Tormé, Mel. Christmas Song: Chestnuts Roasting on an Open Fire. Barrette, Doris, illus. (p. 315)
Tormey, Carlotta, illus. see McDonnell, Peter.
Tormont Publications Inc., des. Perfect Presents (p. 1342)
Tornatore, Carol, illus. see Salisbury, Linda G.
Tornatore, Carol, illus. see Salisbury, Linda.
Tornatore, Carol, jt. auth. see Ryan, Susan Jane.
Tornio, Stacy. Cathy's Animal Garden: Enter at Your Own Risk. Bell, Samantha, illus. (p. 280)
Tornio, Stacy & Keffer, Ken. Kids' Outdoor Adventure Book: 448 Great Things to Do in Nature Before You Grow Up. (p. 954)
—Truth about Nature: A Family's Guide to 144 Common Myths about the Great Outdoors. (p. 1794)
Tornquist, Carol. Creativity - Level 5: Music in Me - A Piano Method for Young Christian Students. (p. 380)
—Hymns & Holidays - Solos to Play, Level 4: Music in Me - A Piano Method for Young Christian Students. (p. 831)
—Keys for God's Kids! Big-Note Piano. (p. 950)
—Lesson - Level 4: Reading Music: Music in Me - A Piano Method for Young Christian Students. (p. 993)
—Music in Me: A Piano Method for Young Christian Students. (p. 1193)
—Music in Me - A Piano Method for Young Christian Students: Lesson (Reading Music) Level 5. (p. 1193)
—Theory & Technique - Level 4: Music in Me - A Piano Method for Young Christian Students. (p. 1729)
Tornqvist, Carl-Erik. Plant Genetics. Hopkins, William G., ed. (p. 1369)
Tornqvist, Marit, illus. see Lindgren, Astrid & Crampton, Patricia.
Törnqvist, Marit, illus. see Lindgren, Astrid.
Toro, et al. Gandhi Me Llamo Conmigo Nacio el Pacifismo. (p. 655)
Toro, Jorge, tr. see Hoffmann, E. T. A.
Torode, Justine, illus. see Smith, Alastair.
Torode, Sam, illus. see Santorum, Karen.
Toron, Eli, illus. see Greenberger, Tehilla.
Toron, Eli, illus. see Juravel, Rabbi.
Toron, Eli, illus. see Mindel, Nissan.
Toronto Child Abuse Centre Staff, jt. auth. see Grossman, Linda Sky.
Toronto Public Library. Research Ate My Brain: The Panic-Proof Guide to Surviving Homework. Newbigging, Martha, illus. (p. 1462)
Toronto Public Library, jt. auth. see Toronto Public Library.
Toronto Public Library & Toronto Public Library. Research Ate My Brain: The Panic-Proof Guide to Surviving Homework. Newbigging, Martha, illus. (p. 1462)
Toropov, Brandon, jt. auth. see Woodger, Elin.
Torowski, Dave, jt. auth. see Roach, Sandra.
Torphy, William & Gowack, Paul. Snakebite. (p. 1596)
Torpie, Kate. Cinco de Mayo. (p. 319)
—Diwali. (p. 455)
—Drawing Maps. (p. 482)
—Knights & Castles. Denmark, Thomas, illus. (p. 964)
—Magical Creatures. Shroades, John, illus. (p. 1074)
—Map Parts. (p. 1090)
Torpie, Kate & Becker, Ann. Map Types. (p. 1090)
Torpie, Kate & Sandvold, Rolf. Reading Maps. (p. 1446)
Torr, James D. Civil Rights. (p. 324)
—Responding to Attack: Firefighters & Police. (p. 1463)
Torr, James D. & Cothran, Helen, eds. Abortion. (p. 5)
Torr, James D., ed. Abortion. (p. 5)
—Internet. (p. 880)
—Westward Expansion. (p. 1876)
Torrance-Matthews, Armer, et al. Miss Bertha, the Talking Tree: A Delightful Story of a Talking Tree. (p. 1151)
Torras, Meri. Mi Hermana Aixa. Valverde, Mikel, illus. (p. 1132)
Torre, Attilio, illus. see Patrick, B.
Torre, Cristina de la. About Mammals: A Guide for Children = Sobre Los Mamíferos: Una Guía para Niños. Sill, Cathryn P. & Sill, John, illus. (p. 6)
Torrecilla, Pablo, illus. see Figueredo, D. H.
Torrecilla, Pablo, illus. see Whitehead, Kathy.
Torrecilla, Pablo, illus. see Zepeda, Gwendolyn.
Torrecilla, Pablo, jt. auth. see Benatar, Raquel.
Torrecilla, Pablo, jt. auth. see Caraballo, Samuel.
Torregrosa, Jose Canas, et al. Cara de la Inocencia. (p. 265)
Torrel, Wendy. GUARDIAN of DREAMS (1st Edition) Klingbeil, Kendall, illus. (p. 728)
Torrence, Jack. Light Show: Reflection & Absorption. (p. 1015)
Torres, Alfredo. My Sick Teacher. (p. 1218)
Torres Batista, Nellíud. Prende y aprende con tu PC: Aplicaciones Office XP. Diaz Caballero, Jose Juan, ed. (p. 1395)
Torres, Christopher S. Salma & the Christmas Star. Hildebrandt, Lowell, illus. (p. 1505)
Torres, Daniel. arte de Daniel Torres. (p. 103)
—Jovenes Dibujantes. (p. 929)
—Las Aventuras de Tom Tu Gran Amigo. (p. 976)
—Tom: Tom en Nueva York. Vol. 2 (p. 1762)
—Tom: Tom en Los Ángeles. Vol. 3 (p. 1762)
—Tom: Las Aventuras de Tom. Vol. 1 (p. 1762)
—Tom Tu Gran Amigo: Juega al Fútbol (p. 1764)
—Tom Tu Gran Amigo: Descubre el Carnaval. Vol. 6 (p. 1764)
—Tom Tu Gran Amigo en Paris (p. 1764)
Torres, Diana, illus. see Bronstein, Arlene.
Torres, Dottie, illus. see Sobel, Gerrie.
Torres, Elena, illus. see Montes, Graciela.
Torres, Eliseo & Sawyer, Timothy L. Stories of Mexico's Independence Days & Other Bilingual Children's Fables. Ramirez, Herman, illus. (p. 1655)
Torres, Elliott. Undaunted. (p. 1813)
Torres, Estela Gutierrez, tr. see Fisher, Jude.
Torres, German, illus. see Beauregard, Lynda.
Torres, German, illus. see Tsang, Evonne & Jimenez, Adan.
Torres, Irving, illus. see Liberto, Lorenzo, et al.
Torres, Irving, illus. see Liberto, Lorenzo.
Torres, J. Batman: the Brave & the Bold. Beatty, Terry et al, illus. (p. 144)
—Batman Versus the Yeti! Barberi, Carlo & Beatty, Terry, illus. (p. 144)
—Birthquake. (p. 193)
—Case of the Fractured Fairy Tale Barberi, Carlo & Beatty, Terry, illus. (p. 274)
—Charge of the Army Eternal Davis, Dan & Suriano, Andy, illus. (p. 291)
—Checkers & Dot at the Beach. Lum, J., illus. (p. 295)
—Checkers & Dot at the Zoo. Lum, J., illus. (p. 295)
—Checkers & Dot on the Farm. Lum, J., illus. (p. 295)
—Christmas Eve. Harpster, Steve, illus. (p. 313)
—Collected Alison Dare Little Miss Adventures. Bone, J., illus. (p. 339)
—Degrassi the Next Generation Extra Credit Suddenly, Last Summer. Northcott, Ed, illus. (p. 424)
—Degrassi The Next Generation Extra Credit Turning Japanese. (p. 424)
—In My House. Rolston, Steve, illus. (p. 864)
—Into the Woods. Hicks, Faith Erin, illus. (p. 881)
—Jinx: Little Miss Steps. Burchett, Rick & Austin, Terry, illus. (p. 919)
—Lola. (p. 1045)
—Love as a Foreign Language (p. 1059)
—Machina Ex Deus. (p. 1068)
—Power Lunch Book 1: First Course: First Course. (p. 1389)
—Power Lunch Book 2: Seconds. (p. 1389)
—Secret of the Doomsday Design! Bone, J., illus. (p. 1542)
—Transfer Student - Sidekicks. (p. 1778)
—Unkindness of Ravens. Hicks, Faith Erin, illus. (p. 1821)
—Yo Gabba Gabba: Good Night, Gabbaland: Good Night, Gabbaland. (p. 1971)
Torres, J., jt. auth. see Wayne, Matt.
Torres, J., jt. auth. see Wheeler, Shannon.
Torres, J., jt. ed. see Jones, James Lucas.
Torres, J. & Kim, Eric. Extra Credit No. 3. (p. 555)
—Missing You. (p. 1153)
Torres, J. & Norton, Mike. Teen Titans Go!: Titans Together. (p. 1714)
Torres, J. & Rolston, Steve. Safety Dance (p. 1502)
Torres, J., et al. Beast Boy Who Cried Wolf (p. 152)
—Blackfire's Back! (p. 197)
—Demo (p. 425)
—Lame (p. 972)
—Legion of Super-Heroes in the 31st Century: Tomorrow's Heroes. Greene, Sanford & Serra, Alexander, illus. (p. 990)
—Monster Zit! (p. 1168)
—My Crummy Valentine (p. 1200)
—Teen Titans GO! (p. 1714)
—Thunder & Lightning Strike! (p. 1746)
Torres, Jennifer. Alan Jackson. (p. 33)
—Ashanti. (p. 105)
—Ashton Kutcher. (p. 106)
—Battle: The Briny Deep Mysteries Book 3. (p. 145)
—Disappearing: The Briny Deep Mysteries Book 1. (p. 446)
—Eve. (p. 541)
—Finding the Music Alarcão, Renato, illus. (p. 588)
—Kate Hudson. (p. 944)
—Mary J. Blige. (p. 1100)
—Paris Hilton. (p. 1324)
—Return: The Briny Deep Mysteries Book 2. (p. 1464)
—Selena Gomez: Pop Singer & Actress. (p. 1549)
Torres, Jickie. Learn to Draw Farm Animals: Step-by-Step Instructions for 21 Favorite Subjects, Including a Horse, Cow & Pig! Cuddy, Robbin, illus. (p. 983)
—Watch Me Draw - Robots: A Step-by-Step Drawing & Story Book. Berry, Bob, illus. (p. 1861)
Torres, Jickie, illus. see Walter Foster Publishing & Berry, Bob.
Torres, John. Carmelo Anthony. (p. 270)
—Hurricane Katrina 2005. (p. 830)
—Sonia Sotomayor: First Latina Supreme Court Justice. (p. 1612)
—Threat to the Giant Panda. (p. 1741)
—Tim Tebow. (p. 1750)
—Usher. (p. 1828)
—We Visit Puerto Rico. (p. 1868)
—We Visit the Dominican Republic. (p. 1868)
Torres, John A. Ancient Mystery of Easter Island. (p. 70)
—Lil Wayne. (p. 1017)
—Meet Our New Student from Haiti. (p. 1121)
—Timbaland. (p. 1750)
Torres, John Albert. African Elephant: A MyReportLinks. com Book. (p. 27)
—Allen Iverson: Never Give Up. (p. 46)
—Cherokee Trail of Tears & the Forced March of a People. (p. 298)
—Clay Aiken. (p. 330)
—Derek Jeter. (p. 427)
—Disaster in the Indian Ocean, Tsunami 2004. (p. 446)
—Dwight Howard: A Basketball Star Who Cares. (p. 491)
—Hong Kong. (p. 795)
—Hurricane Katrina & the Devastation of New Orleans 2005. (p. 830)
—Jay-Z: Hip-Hop Mogul. (p. 910)
—Ludacris: Hip-Hop Mogul. (p. 1064)
—Manatee: A MyReportLinks. com Book. (p. 1086)
—Meet Our New Student from Nicaragua. (p. 1122)
—Meet Our New Student from Zambia. (p. 1122)
—P. Diddy. (p. 1316)
—Shaquille O'Neal: Gentle Giant. (p. 1561)
—Shaun White: A Snowboarder & Skateboarder Who Cares. (p. 1563)
—Soccer Star Cristiano Ronaldo. (p. 1603)
—Soccer Star Lionel Messi. (p. 1603)
—Soccer Star Ronaldinho. (p. 1603)
—Sports Great Sammy Sosa. (p. 1632)
—Texas Fight for Independence: From the Alamo to San Jacinto. (p. 1724)
—Threat to Haiti. (p. 1741)
—Top 25 Basketball Skills, Tips, & Tricks. (p. 1768)
—Top 25 Football Skills, Tips, & Tricks. (p. 1768)
—Tsunami Disaster in Indonesia 2004. (p. 1795)

T

—Vince Carter: Slam Dunk Artist. (p. 1842)
Torres, Jos A. & Torres, Jose A. Joey Kanga Roo: Plays the Trumpet. (p. 920)
Torres, Jose A. Joey Kanga Roo: First Day of School. (p. 920)
Torres, Jose A., jt. auth. see Torres, Jos A.
Torres, Jotam D. Weagol's Big Mess. Gomez, Sergio, illus. (p. 1869)
Torres, Laura. Brazaletes de la Amistad. (p. 224)
—Formas Fantasticas. (p. 620)
—Rocas Pintadas. (p. 1481)
—Rock Your Party. (p. 1482)
—Rock Your Room. (p. 1482)
—Rock Your School Stuff. (p. 1482)
—Rock Your Wardrobe. (p. 1482)
Torres, Laura & Sherman, Michael. Limpiapipas de Locura. (p. 1018)
Torres, Leyla. Untitled Picture Book. (p. 1823)
Torres, Marcela H., tr. see Scalzo, Linda V.
Torres, Marina, illus. see Fernandez, Cesar.
Torres, Mario. My Fun Wonderworld: Children's Stories Book (p. 1209)
Torres, Mario J. Incredible Adventures of Kaplan & Dylan: Book One: Present (p. 869)
Torres Moliner, Isabel & Puche, Lola Soriano. Espacio Espacial. (p. 536)
Torres Moliner, Isabel & Soriano Puche, Lola. Domino Domino. (p. 465)
Torres, Nora Estela, illus. see Caballero, Eduardo.
Torres, Nora Estela, illus. see Calderon, Eduardo Caballero.
Torres, Nora Estela, illus. see Espriella, Leopoldo Berdella De La.
Torres, Raul Vazquez, illus. see Ordonez, Paulino.
Torres, Rosa, tr. see Clarke, Denise B.
Torres, Veronica Hilda. My Mommy's Sweater. Rottinger, Amy, illus. (p. 1214)
Torres, Walter, illus. see De Matos, Isabel Freire.
Torres, Walter, illus. see Flor Ada, Alma.
Torres, Walter, illus. see León, Georgina Lázaro.
Torres, Walter, illus. see Montero, Mayra.
Torres, Zoe. At the Block Sale: Add & Subtract Within 20. (p. 110)
Torres-Vidal, Nina, tr. see Santiago, Esmeralda.
Torrey Balsara, Andrea, illus. see Roy, Philip.
Torrey, Bradford. Clerk of the Woods. (p. 331)
—Everyday Birds. (p. 543)
—Footing It in Franconia. (p. 615)
—Friends on the Shelf. (p. 638)
—Nature's Invitation. (p. 1237)
Torrey, Jesse, photos by see Mordhorst, Heidi.
Torrey, Michele. Case of the Barfy Birthday. Newman, Barbara Johansen, illus. (p. 273)
—Case of the Crooked Carnival. Newman, Barbara Johansen, illus. (p. 274)
—Case of the Gasping Garbage. Torrey, Michele & Newman, Barbara Johansen, illus. (p. 274)
—Case of the Graveyard Ghost. Newman, Barbara Johansen, illus. (p. 274)
—Case of the Mossy Lake Monster. Torrey, Michele & Newman, Barbara Johansen, illus. (p. 274)
—Case of the Terrible T. Rex. Newman, Barbara Johansen, illus. (p. 275)
Torrey, Rich, illus. see Pérez-Mercado, Mary Margaret.
Torrey, Rich, illus. see Stiles, Amanda.
Torrey, Rich, jt. auth. see Pérez-Mercado, Mary Margaret.
Torrey, Richard. Ally-Saurus & the First Day of School. (p. 48)
—Almost. Torrey, Richard, illus. (p. 48)
—Baseball Story. Torrey, Richard, illus. (p. 141)
—Basketball Story. Torrey, Richard, illus. (p. 143)
—Because. Torrey, Richard, illus. (p. 155)
—Football Story. Torrey, Richard, illus. (p. 615)
—Hockey Story. Torrey, Richard, illus. (p. 787)
—Moe Is Best. Torrey, Richard, illus. (p. 1160)
—My Dog, Bob. (p. 1202)
—Why? Torrey, Richard, illus. (p. 1922)
Torrey, Richard L. Beans Baker's Best Shot. Torrey, Richard L., illus. (p. 150)
Torrey, Richard L., illus. see Pérez-Mercado, Mary Margaret.
Torribio, Penelope. Magic in You: From vacant lot to community Garden. (p. 1072)
—Never Get Too Close to a Fish. (p. 1243)
Torricelli, Dr Richard & Torricelli, Richard. Tale of a Schnauzer. (p. 1699)
Torricelli, Richard, jt. auth. see Torricelli, Dr Richard.
Torrijos, Eduardo & Garcia, Gretel. Papalotes: Tecnicas de Armado y Vuelo. Torrijos, Eduardo, illus. (p. 1322)
Torrington, Emma. Street Dance. (p. 1666)
Torrisi, Cathy. Eat All Your Colors. (p. 501)
—Get up & Go! (p. 668)
—Healthy Day. (p. 758)
—I Know First Aid. (p. 840)
—Take a Stand. (p. 1696)
—Tell Someone You Trust. (p. 1717)
Torseter, Oyvind, illus. see Lunde, Stein Erik.
Torseter, Oyvind & Steven, Kenneth. Why Dogs Have Wet Noses. (p. 1924)
Torseter, Oyvind, creator. Hole. (p. 788)
Torsiello, David P. Michael Phelps: Swimming for Olympic Gold. (p. 1134)
—Read about Alex Rodriguez. (p. 1442)
—Read about Carmelo Anthony. (p. 1442)
—Read about Derek Jeter. (p. 1442)
—Read about Drew Brees. (p. 1442)
—Read about Eli Manning. (p. 1442)
—Read about Kobe Bryant. (p. 1442)
Tort, Pep & Josep, Tort. Rey Ignacio. Duran, Teresa, illus. (p. 1467)
Tortop, Anil, illus. see Hogan, Tamara Anne.
Tortora, Gerard J. Computerized Test Bank to Accompany Introduction to the Human Body. (p. 355)
—Computerized Test Bank to Accompany Principles of Anatomy & Physiology. (p. 355)
—Introduction to the Human Body, Instructor's Resource. (p. 882)
—Photographic Atlas of the Human Body: With Selected Cat, Sheep, & Cow Dissections (p. 1353)
—Powerpoint Slides for Anatomy & Physiology. (p. 1391)
—Principles of Anatomy & Physiology, Instructor's Resource. (p. 1406)
—Principles of Human Anatomy: Test Bank. (p. 1406)
—Principles of Human Anatomy: Computerized Test Bank for Mac & Windows. (p. 1406)
—Test Bank to Accompany Introduction to the Human B Ody. (p. 1723)
—Test Bank to Accompany Principles of Anatomy & Physiology. (p. 1723)
Tortorella, Jackie. Our Father: Living the Lord's Prayer (p. 1308)
Tortorello, Lisa A. Mark the Missing Moose. (p. 1095)
—Moose at the Manger. (p. 1173)
Tortorich, Vinnie. Monty: A Friendship Can Lead to a Miracle (p. 1170)
Tortosa, Wilson, illus. see Bowen, Carl & Fuentes, Benny.
Tortosa, Wilson, illus. see Bowen, Carl.
Tortosa, Wilson, illus. see Terrell, Brandon.
Tortosa, Wilson, jt. auth. see Hoena, Blake A.
Tortosa, Wilson, jt. auth. see Terrell, Brandon.
Toscani, Oliviero, des. Prayer. (p. 1393)
Toscano, Charles. Papa's Pastries Lamut, Sonja, illus. (p. 1322)
Toscano, Leesa. Eat Your Vegetables. Bodoff, Janet, illus. (p. 501)
Tosches, Nick. In the Hand of Dante: A Novel. (p. 866)
Toselli, Leigh. Pro Nail Care: Salon Secrets of the Professionals. (p. 1408)
Toshiley. Sponge & the River of Sleepiness. (p. 1630)
Toska, Mary Lou. Ernest's Dream: A Young Boy Wanting to Spend the Summer in the High Alps. (p. 534)
—Shepherd Boy. (p. 1565)
Tossell, David H. Charlie & Chippo Meet a Ghost. Pritchard, Louise, illus. (p. 292)
Tossuon, Nevin, et al. T Is for Turkey. Das, Prodeepta, photos by. (p. 1694)
Tosten, S. Kennedy. Troy's Amazing Universe: T for Toy. Bk. 2 (p. 1790)
—Troy's Amazing Universe: M for Mall. Bk. 1 (p. 1790)
Tosten, Sharon. Troy's Amazing Universe: K for Karate. (p. 1790)
Tosto, Salvatore, Jr. Kid Power: A Simple Guide to a Lean, Healthy & Happy Child. (p. 951)
Totaro, Roberto & Guidobaldi, Serena. Jungle Journal. (p. 935)
Tötemeyer, Andree-Jeanne. Under the Story Tree: Readathon Stories. (p. 1814)
Toten, Teresa. Bright Red Kisses. Betteridge, Deirdre, illus. (p. 228)
—Unlikely Hero of Room 13B. (p. 1821)
Toth, Carolyn. Where Is Baby? (p. 1908)
Toth, Henrietta. Career As a Heavy Equipment Operator. (p. 266)
Toth, J. A. Those Fabulous 50 States (Esos 50 Estados Fabulosos) (p. 1740)
Toth, M., jt. auth. see Rieder, E.
Toth, Nina Vincent. Living Proof of Natural Cures. (p. 1041)
Toth, Shannon, illus. see Wittrock, Jeni.
Toth-Chernin, Jan. E-Textiles. (p. 492)
Tóth-Jones, Dee S. Street Cats of Marrakech. Stevenson, Seline, illus. (p. 1666)
Totilo, Rebecca Park. Christian Girl's Guide to Money. Heiser, Aline & DuFalla, Anita, illus. (p. 311)
—Christian Kids' Gardening Guide: Cool Stuff for You to Make & Grow. (p. 312)
Totire, Valerie, illus. see Coulton, Mia.
Totire, Valerie, illus. see Ketch, Ann.
Totire, Valerie, illus. see Worthington, Lisa & Moon, Susan.
Totter, Donald. Architectural Presentation with DataCad 10. (p. 95)
Totton, Nick. Press When Illuminated: New & Selected Poems 1968-2003. (p. 1397)
Touchstones Discussion Project, prod. Touchpebbles Volume A - Student's Guide (p. 1772)
Toufexis, Donna & Hammack, Sayamwong E. Anti-Anxiety Drugs. Triggle, David J., ed. (p. 89)
Toufexis, George. At the Zoo Stickers. (p. 111)
—Extreme Lions & Tigers Tattoos. (p. 556)
—Glitter Tattoos Day of the Dead. (p. 684)
—Glitter Tattoos Mermaids. (p. 684)
—Great Explorers Activity Book. (p. 715)
—Halloween Super Sticker Book. (p. 739)
—History's Mysteries! Animals: Activity Book. (p. 785)
—History's Mysteries! Dinosaurs: Activity Book. (p. 785)
—Monster Mall Activity Book. (p. 1167)
—MONSTER MASH-Up—Aliens Meet Their Match. (p. 1167)
—MONSTER MASH-Up—Dinosaurs Face Destruction. (p. 1167)
—MONSTER MASH-Up—Rise of the Predators. (p. 1167)
—MONSTER MASH-Up—Robots' Revenge. (p. 1167)
—Monster Matrix Activity Book. (p. 1167)
—Nelson Mandela Coloring Book. (p. 1241)
—Outrageous Human Body Activity Book. (p. 1313)
—River Monsters of the World. (p. 1476)
—Sharks! Stained Glass Coloring Book. (p. 1563)
—Ultimate Horse-Athon Facts & Activity Book. (p. 1809)
—Ultimate Shark-Athon Facts & Activity Book. (p. 1810)
—Unbelievable Cryptozoology Coloring Book. (p. 1811)
—World Atlas Activity & Coloring Book. (p. 1954)
Toufexis, George & Coloring Books Staff. Sharks! Coloring Book. (p. 1563)
Toufexis, George, et al. 3-D Coloring Book—Sharks. (p. 1991)
Tougas, Chris. Dojo Daycare. (p. 463)
—Mechanimals. (p. 1118)
Tougas, Joe. Beatles: Defining Rock 'n' Roll. (p. 153)
—Mind-Blowing Movie Stunts. (p. 1145)
—New York. (p. 1247)
—Virginia. (p. 1844)
Tougas, Joe, et al. Wild Stunts. (p. 1930)
Tougas, Shelley. Birmingham 1963: How a Photograph Rallied Civil Rights Support. (p. 192)
—Finders Keepers. (p. 587)
—Girls Rock! Amazing Tales of Women in Music (p. 680)
—Girls Rule! Amazing Tales of Female Leaders (p. 680)
—Girls Star! Amazing Tales of Hollywood's Leading Ladies (p. 681)
—Graham Cracker Plot. (p. 705)
—Little Rock Girl 1957: How a Photograph Changed the Fight for Integration (p. 1036)
—Science of Weapons (p. 1527)
—Weapons, Gear, & Uniforms of the Iraq War (p. 1869)
—Weapons, Gear, & Uniforms of the Vietnam War (p. 1869)
—What Makes a Terrorist? (p. 1892)
Tougas, Shelley & Phillips, Jennifer. Girls Rock! (p. 680)
Tougas, Shelley, et al. Captured History. (p. 265)
Touger, Malka. Door That's Never Locked. (p. 470)
—Just My Style - A Tznius Reader. (p. 939)
Tougias, Michael, et al. Good Night Vermont. Kelly, Cooper, illus. (p. 700)
Tougias, Michael J. & Sherman, Casey. Finest Hours: The True Story of a Heroic Sea Rescue. (p. 589)
Toullatou, Sophia, illus. see Poitier, Anton.
Toulmin & Piper, Sophie. How to Be Good. Birkett, Georgie, illus. (p. 815)
Toulmin, Sarah. Baby Prayers Stephenson, Kristina, illus. (p. 127)
—Baby's Little Bible. Stephenson, Kristina, illus. (p. 129)
—Baby's Tiny Bible & Prayers Stephenson, Kristina, illus. (p. 129)
Toulmin, Sarah & Stephenson, Kristina. Baby's Little Bible & Prayers (p. 129)
Toulmin-Rothe, Ann, illus. see Sabin, Francene & Macken, JoAnn Early.
Toulon, Juliette Bellot. Amazing Friendship. (p. 54)
Touma, Patricia. Happy Times, Book: Ish & Mish Go to the Carnival. (p. 747)
—Happy Times, the Adventures of Ish & Mish: Ish & Mish Go to the Circus. Vol. 1 (p. 747)
Toume, Kei. Lament of the Lamb (p. 972)
Toupin, Laurie. Freshwater Habitats: Life in Freshwater Ecosystems. (p. 637)
Toupin, Laurie Peach. Taiga: Life in the Boreal Forest. (p. 1695)
Tourenne, Virginie. Snow White & the Seven Dwarfs. (p. 1600)
Tourlonias, Joëlle, illus. see Engler, Michael.
Tournemille, Harry. Attention Deficit Hyperactivity Disorder. (p. 114)
Tourneville, Harry. Attention-Deficit Hyperactivity Disorder. (p. 114)
Tourville, Amanda Doering. Alimenta Tu Cuerpo. Rooney, Ronnie, illus. (p. 41)
—Animal Invaders. (p. 78)
—Brush, Floss, & Rinse: Caring for Your Teeth & Gums Rooney, Ronnie, illus. (p. 232)
—Bulldozers. Trover, Zachary, illus. (p. 240)
—Buzzing Bees: Discovering Odd Numbers. Holm, Sharon Lane, illus. (p. 249)
—Cepíllate, Usa Hilo Dental y Enjuágate. Rooney, Ronnie, illus. (p. 287)
—Comportamiento Con Libros de la Biblioteca. Lensch, Chris, illus. (p. 354)
—Comportamiento y Modales en la Cafetería. Lensch, Chris, illus. (p. 354)
—Count the Critters: 6 Titles Holm, Sharon Lane, illus. (p. 370)
—Cranes. Trover, Zachary, illus. (p. 376)
—Dump Trucks. Trover, Zachary, illus. (p. 489)
—Exploring the Solar System. (p. 554)
—Fire Trucks. Trover, Zachary, illus. (p. 591)
—Flutter & Float: Bringing Home Goldfish Carter, Andi, illus. (p. 608)
—Friends with Disabilities Sorra, Kristin, illus. (p. 639)
—Fuel the Body: Eating Well Rooney, Ronnie, illus. (p. 646)
—Garbage Trucks. Trover, Zachary, illus. (p. 655)
—Get up & Go: Being Active Rooney, Ronnie, illus. (p. 668)
—Go Wash Up: Keeping Clean Rooney, Ronnie, illus. (p. 687)
—Helen Keller: Courageous Learner & Leader. (p. 763)
—Hiding Hippos: Counting from 1 To 10. Holm, Sharon Lane, illus. (p. 777)
—Kangaroo Grows Up Huiett, William J. & Denman, Michael L., illus. (p. 942)
—King Tut's Tomb (p. 959)
—Lávate. Rooney, Ronnie, illus. (p. 981)
—Lions Leaving: Counting from 10 To 1. Holm, Sharon Lane, illus. (p. 1021)
—Manners at a Friend's House Lensch, Chris, illus. (p. 1088)
—Manners on the School Bus Lensch, Chris, illus. (p. 1088)
—Manners on the School Bus (Comportamiento y Modales en el Autobús Escolar) Lensch, Chris, illus. (p. 1088)
—Manners with a Library Book Lensch, Chris, illus. (p. 1088)
—Mi Amiga Tiene Dislexia. Translations.com Staff, tr. (p. 1132)
—Muévete. Rooney, Ronnie, illus. (p. 1189)
—My Friend Has ADHD Sorra, Kristin, illus. (p. 1209)
—My Friend Has Autism Sorra, Kristin, illus. (p. 1209)
—My Friend Has down Syndrome Sorra, Kristin, illus. (p. 1209)
—My Friend Has Dyslexia Sorra, Kristin, illus. (p. 1209)
—Out of the Dark: Coping with Emotional Challenges. (p. 1311)
—Penguin Pairs: Counting By 2s. Holm, Sharon Lane, illus. (p. 1337)
—Prairie Dogs Perching: Counting By 3s. Holm, Sharon Lane, illus. (p. 1392)
—Purr & Pounce: Bringing Home a Cat Carter, Andi, illus. (p. 1419)
—Scurry & Squeak: Bringing Home a Guinea Pig Carter, Andi, illus. (p. 1534)
—Skitter & Scoot: Bringing Home a Hamster Carter, Andi, illus. (p. 1586)
—Sunning Sea Lions: Discovering Even Numbers. Holm, Sharon Lane, illus. (p. 1677)
—Tractors. Trover, Zachary, illus. (p. 1775)
—Transportation in the City Thompson, Jeffrey, illus. (p. 1779)
—Twitter & Tweet: Bringing Home a Bird Carter, Andi, illus. (p. 1803)
—Veteran's Day. Ouren, Todd, illus. (p. 1839)
—Whose Equipment Is This? (p. 1921)
—Whose Gadgets Are These? (p. 1921)
—Whose Gear Is This? (p. 1921)
—Whose Tools Are These? (p. 1922)
Tourville, Amanda Doering & Sorra, Kristin. Mi Amiga Tiene Sindrome de Down. Translations.com Staff, tr. from ENG. (p. 1132)
—Mi Amigo Tiene ADHD. Translations.com Staff, tr. from ENG. (p. 1132)
—Mi Amigo Tiene Autismo. Translations.com Staff, tr. (p. 1132)
Tourville, Jacqueline. Albie's First Word: A Tale Inspired by Albert Einstein's Childhood. Evans, Wynne, illus. (p. 35)
Tousey, Ben. Acting Your Dreams: Using Acting Techniques to Interpret Your Dreams (p. 10)
Tousey, Sanford. Indians & Cowboys: A One Volume Edition of Indians of the Plains & Cowboys of America. (p. 871)
—Jack Finds Gold. (p. 903)
Toussaint, Jonathan. How to Talk to Girls. (p. 822)
Toussaint, Simone. Sharing My Shoes. (p. 1561)
Toutz-Hager, Tanya. Goddesses of Legend & Myth: A Coloring Book Celebrating the Heroines of Ancient Europe. Stockton, Greta & Philbrick, Katie, illus. (p. 690)
Touvay, Monique, jt. auth. see Chic, Suzy.
Tov, Basia, illus. see Bennett, Larry.
Tovar, Alicia. Boston Tea Party: No Taxation Without Representation. (p. 215)
Tovar Cross, Juan Elias, tr. see Howker, Janni.
Tovar, Laura. Autumn Colors. (p. 118)
—Months Fly By. (p. 1170)
Tovey, Imogen. Maddy's Dolphin. (p. 1070)
Tovey, Peter. Chester the Crab. Hinkler Books Staff, ed. (p. 298)
Tow, Jack. Up All Night with Howie. Tow, Jack, illus. (p. 1824)
—Who's Afraid of Howie? (p. 1920)
Towbin, Meredith. Straightjacket. (p. 1664)
Towe, H.P. Mr. Monkey Sees & Mr. Monkey Do. (p. 1185)
Towe, Randall. End of Time. (p. 526)
Towell, Ann. Grease Town. (p. 713)
Towell, Katy. Charlie & the Grandmothers. (p. 292)
—Skary Childrin & the Carousel of Sorrow. (p. 1583)
Tower, Cory L. Adventures of Courtney, Morgan & the Magic Toy Bears Book 2: In the Beginning. (p. 17)
Towle, Barbara E. How Timbo & Trevor Got Together. Spellman, Susan, illus. (p. 814)
Towle, Mike. Walter Payton: Football's Sweetest Superstar. (p. 1856)
Town, Florida Ann. With a Silent Companion. (p. 1942)
Town, Nathan. Ned Stapleton & the Wrath of the Death Gods. (p. 1239)
Town, Vicky. Mayhem in the Museum. (p. 1113)
—Runaway Pumpkin Pie Man Baird, Roberta, illus. (p. 1496)
Towne, C. Ross. Old Jack: The very smart Dog. (p. 1284)
Towne, Isobel & MacAdam, Lea. Dealing with Family Rules. (p. 418)
Towne, Isobel & Porterfield, Jason. Strategic Searches Using Digital Tools. (p. 1666)
Towne, Isobel & Viegas, Jennifer. Mouth & Nose in 3D. (p. 1182)
Townes-Richards, Carolyn. Nothing Like Christine: Living Through Literature with Aunt Curly's Collection. (p. 1268)
Townley, Alvin. Legacy of Honor: The Values & Influence of America's Eagle Scouts. (p. 987)
Townley, Alvin, III. Legacy of Honor: The Values & Influence of America's Eagle Scouts. (p. 987)
Townley, Roderick. Door in the Forest. (p. 470)
—Great Good Thing. (p. 716)
—Red Thread: A Novel in Three Incarnations. (p. 1455)
—Sky. (p. 1586)
Towns, Elmer & Porter, Douglas. Ten Greatest Revivals Ever. (p. 1718)
Townsan, Judy. Story Lady. (p. 1657)
—Wishing Flower Rosado, Michael, illus. (p. 1940)
Townsel, Kim. Teen 101: Questions & Advice from Real Teens. (p. 1713)
Townsend, Amber C. Hungry Chickens. (p. 828)
—Once upon a Time. (p. 1293)
Townsend, Beth. Publishing. (p. 1414)
Townsend, Brenda. Toad S Trilogy. (p. 1760)
Townsend, Charlene. Trap & the Trip. (p. 1779)
Townsend, Chris. Francesca Woodman. Woodman, ed. (p. 627)
Townsend, Dana E. Ellis Island. (p. 515)
—Sequoyah & the Cherokee Alphabet. Gabriel, Andrea, illus. (p. 1552)
Townsend, Daniel. Trumpet. (p. 1793)
Townsend, Diana. He Saw Their Faith. (p. 756)
Townsend, Donna. Apple Fractions. (p. 92)
Townsend, E. J., tr. see Hilbert, David.
Townsend, Emily Rose. Arctic Foxes (p. 96)
—Armadillos Saunders-Smith, Gail, ed. (p. 99)
—Deer (p. 423)
—Deer Saunders-Smith, Gail, ed. (p. 423)
—Lizards Saunders-Smith, Gail, ed. (p. 1043)
—Penguins Saunders-Smith, Gail, ed. (p. 1337)
—Polar Animals (p. 1378)
—Polar Bears Saunders-Smith, Gail, ed. (p. 1379)
—Seals (p. 1536)
—Squirrels Saunders-Smith, Gail, ed. (p. 1637)
—Woodland Animals Saunders-Smith, Gail, ed. (p. 1949)
Townsend, Ernest N., jt. auth. see Sherman, Harold Morrow.
Townsend, F. H., illus. see Dickens, Charles.
Townsend, George Fyler, tr. see Aesop.
Townsend, Harry R. Bull & Bluster: Volume #2. (p. 240)
Townsend, John. 101 Things You Didn't Know about Your Body (p. 2000)
—Amazing Animal Communicators (p. 53)
—Amazing Animal Movers (p. 53)
—Amazing Animal Senses (p. 53)
—Amazing Animal Survivors (p. 53)
—Amazing Predators (p. 55)
—Anfibios Increíbles (p. 73)
—Arácnidos Increíbles (p. 94)
—Aves Increíbles (p. 119)
—Big Book of Baddies. Lewis, Simon, illus. (p. 178)
—Bone Dectectives. (p. 208)

—Cars & Motorcycles (p. 272)
—Crime Lab Technician. (p. 382)
—Earthquakes & Volcanoes: A Survival Guide - Earth's Physical Processes. (p. 497)
—Famous Forensic Cases. (p. 569)
—Forensic Evidence: Prints. (p. 617)
—Gone Missing. (p. 697)
—Hunter's Moon. (p. 828)
—Insectos Increíbles (p. 875)
—Is Our Weather Getting Worse? (p. 889)
—Mamíferos Increíbles (p. 1084)
—Messenger. (p. 1129)
—Omen & the Ghost Cunningham, Kelley, illus. (p. 1288)
—Peces Increíbles (p. 1334)
—Reptiles Increíbles (p. 1461)
—Robberies & Heists. (p. 1478)
—Rotters! Decomposition (p. 1491)
—Strange Creatures. (p. 1665)
—Travel Tips (p. 1780)
—Unsolved Crimes. (p. 1822)
—Using Nuclear Energy (p. 1828)
—Werewolf Attack. (p. 1875)
—World War II. (p. 1959)
—Would You Survive? Animal & Plant Adaptation (p. 1962)
Townsend, Karl. Fused. (p. 650)
Townsend, Laura, jt. auth. see Sohn, Emily.
Townsend, Leah, illus. see Taptich, J. E.
Townsend, Lois Ritter. Our Journey Through Breast Cancer: -a story based on a teacher's journey through breast cancer with her kindergarten Class. (p. 1309)
Townsend, Marjorie. Wee's Moving Day. (p. 1872)
Townsend, Michael. Cute & Cuter. (p. 396)
—Mr. Ball: An Egg-Cellent Adventure. (p. 1184)
—Mr. Ball Makes a to-Do List. Townsend, Michael, illus. (p. 1184)
—On the Move. (p. 1291)
—Ugly Necklace. (p. 1808)
—Where Do Presidents Come From? And Other Presidential Stuff of Super Great Importance. (p. 1907)
Townsend, Mike. Amazing Greek Myths of Wonder & Blunders. (p. 54)
Townsend, Peter. Shelly & Muffin's Big Lesson Learned. (p. 1565)
Townsend, Peter, illus. see Turner, Jill.
Townsend, Peter, illus. see Whiting, Sue.
Townsend, S. P. Star of Persia. (p. 1640)
Townsend, Shannon, illus. see Gunderson, J.
Townsend, Sierra A. Dad & Me. (p. 398)
Townsend, Stephanie Z. Not Too Small at All: A Mouse Tale. Looney, Bill, illus. (p. 1267)
Townsend, Sue. France (p. 627)
—Secret Diary of Adrian Mole, Aged 13 3/4. (p. 1540)
Townsend, Sue & Young, Caroline. Vegetarian Foods (p. 1834)
Townsend, Tamela Ann. Finding Pumpkin (p. 588)
Townsend, Tom. Ballad of Ol' Hook. (p. 134)
—Powderhorn Passage. (p. 1389)
Townsend, Una Belle. Grady's in the Silo Artley, Bob, illus. (p. 705)
—Great Elephant Escape Hechter, Janice, illus. (p. 715)
—Oklahoma Land Run Henriquez, Emile, illus. (p. 1283)
—Racecar Driver's Night Before Christmas Anderson, Rick, illus. (p. 1431)
Townsend, Vanessa. What's in Molly's.... Bedroom? (p. 1897)
Townsend, Vanessa Jane. What's in Molly's... Garden? (p. 1897)
Townsend, Wendy. Blue Iguana. (p. 203)
—Lizard Love. (p. 1042)
—Sundown Rule. (p. 1676)
Townshend, Dominique. Shantideva: How to Wake up a Hero. Norbu, Tenzing, illus. (p. 1559)
Townshend, Katie, illus. see Rath, Tom H.
Townsley, Janet Howe. Dakota Dreams: Fannie Sabra Howe's Own Story, 1881-1884. (p. 401)
Townson, Duncan, jt. auth. see Rees, Dylan.
Townson, H., jt. auth. see Peschke, Marci.
Townson, Hazel. Dark Deeds at Deathwood. (p. 407)
—Deathwood Damian Strikes Again. Ross, Tony, illus. (p. 420)
—Vanishing Village. (p. 1833)
Towsend, Dana. Lonely Orphan Girl: The Story of Nellie Bly. (p. 1046)
Towsley, Nanette. Little Birds of a Feather: The Fantastic Adventures of Steve & Timmy. (p. 1024)
Towson, Robert. Wrong Bus (p. 1965)
Toy Box Innovations, creator. Disney/Pixar: Volume 2. (p. 453)
Toy Box Staff, illus. see Wolfe, Jane.
Toy, J. Watch Me Shine. (p. 1861)
Toybox Innovations, jt. creator see Toybox Innovations Staff.
Toybox Innovations, jt. creator see Toybox Innovations.
Toybox Innovations & Toybox Innovations, creators. At Worlds End. (p. 111)
ToyBox Innovations & Walt Disney Records Staff, creators. Disney's Lilo & Stitch: Read-along. (p. 453)
ToyBox Innovations, creator. Curse of the Black Pearl. (p. 394)
—Dead Man's Chest. (p. 417)
—Deep in the Jungle. (p. 423)
—Disney Pixar's Toy Story: Read-along. (p. 452)
—Disney Princess: Cinderella/Snow White/Sleeping Beauty. (p. 452)
—Disney's Chicken Little Read-along. (p. 453)
—Disney's Cinderella Read-along. (p. 453)
Toybox Innovations, creator. Disney's Enchanted. (p. 453)
ToyBox Innovations, creator. Disney's Finding Nemo Read-along. (p. 453)
—Disney's Instant Classics: Chicken Little/Lilo & Stitch/Brother Bear. (p. 453)
—Disney's Monsters, Inc. Read-along. (p. 453)
—Disney's the Little Mermaid: Read-along. (p. 453)
—Disney's the Little Mermaid. (p. 453)
—Disney's Winnie the Pooh: Winnie the Pooh Springtime with Roo/Pooh's Heffalump Movie/Piglet's Big Movie. (p. 453)
Toybox Innovations, creator. Meet the Robinson's. (p. 1123)
—Pirates of the Caribbean: the Complete Collection: The Curse of the Black Pearl/Dead Man's Chest/at World's End. (p. 1364)
—Pixar's Ratatouille. (p. 1365)
Toybox Innovations Staff & Toybox Innovations, creators. Disney Read along Little Mermaid Collection (p. 453)
Toybox Innovations Staff, creator. School Day Memories Album. (p. 1522)
Toye, Clive. Toby & the Greatest Game. (p. 1760)
Toye, Derek, illus. see Siegel, Elizabeth.
Toye, Derek, illus. see Troupe, Thomas Kingsley.
Toyne, Jessica. Dali (p. 401)
—Justin Bieber. (p. 940)
Toynton, Ian. Hooligan Bear Home. Dietrich, Andrea, illus. (p. 795)
—Hooligan Bear New Friends. Dietrich, Andrea, illus. (p. 795)
Toz, Karen Pokras. Millicent Marie Is Not My Name. (p. 1143)
—Nate Rocks the World. (p. 1230)
Tozer, S. J. MI29 - Mouseweb International to the Rescue! (p. 1133)
Tozier, Christopher. Olivia Brophie & the Pearl of Tagelus. (p. 1286)
—Olivia Brophie & the Sky Island. (p. 1286)
Tra, Frank. Spy School. O'Reilly, Sean Patrick, ed. (p. 1636)
Trabalka, Pegy, illus. see Rudner, Barry.
Trabbold, Andrew, illus. see Qitsualik-Tinsley, Rachel & Qitsualik-Tinsley, Sean.
Trabel, Diana & Hoggatt, Jack. Learning with Computers. (p. 986)
Trabert, John. Gnome Chronicles. (p. 685)
Tracey, Alice. Animal Friends. (p. 77)
Tracey, Andrée. Storyland: Poppy & Her Magic Hat: A Story Coloring Book. (p. 1663)
Tracey, Grant Annis George. Parallel Lines & the Hockey Universe. (p. 1324)
Tracey, Rhian. Isla & Luke: Make or Break? (p. 891)
—True Colours. (p. 1792)
—When Isla Meets Luke Meets Isla. (p. 1903)
Tracey, Scott. Darkbound. (p. 408)
—Phantom Eyes. (p. 1349)
—Witch Eyes. (p. 1941)
Trachock, Cathy, illus. see Luther, Jacqueline & Lind, Alan.
Trachock, Cathy, illus. see Luther, Jacqueline.
Trachok, Cathy, illus. see Otto, Carolyn B.
Trachtenberg, Martha P. Bono: Rock Star Activist. (p. 209)
Trachtenberg, Stanley. Elevator Man. Cox, Paul, illus. (p. 512)
Trachtman, Joseph. Kosher Tales: Not So Grim Stories for Children. (p. 967)
Tracqui, Valérie. Face-to-Face with the Dog: Loyal Companion. Laird, Lisa, tr. from FRE. (p. 560)
—Face-to-Face with the Horse: Faster Than the Wind. Delaborde, Gilles, photos by. (p. 560)
—Face-to-Face with the Ladybug: Little Garden Monster. Lorne, Patrick, photos by. (p. 560)
—Whale. (p. 1877)
Tracy, Blaise. Inside Out & Upside Town. (p. 877)
Tracy, Jean. Character Building on BackTalk Street. (p. 291)
Tracy, Joe. Arnie the Imagination Boy. (p. 100)
Tracy, Judith. Wildsidhe Chronicles: Dark Proposal. Bk. 3 (p. 1931)
Tracy, Kathleen. Aly & AJ. (p. 51)
—Ancient Assyria. (p. 68)
—Avril Lavigne. (p. 120)
—Bessie Smith. (p. 168)
—Beyonce. (p. 173)
—Carrie Underwood. (p. 271)
—Cerberus. (p. 287)
—Chris Brown. (p. 311)
—Chris Daughtry. (p. 311)
—Clay Aiken: From Second Place to the Top of the Charts. (p. 330)
—Day by Day with Eli Manning. (p. 412)
—Demi Lovato. (p. 425)
—Edouard Manet. (p. 504)
—Emma Watson. (p. 520)
—Evolution of Government & Politics in Iraq. (p. 547)
—Fall of the Berlin Wall. (p. 566)
—Friedrich Miescher & the Story of Nucleic Acid. (p. 637)
—Frog in Our Class. (p. 640)
—Gwen Stefani. (p. 733)
—Hamster in Our Class. (p. 739)
—Henry Bessemer: Making Steel from Iron. (p. 767)
—Historic Fight for the 2008 Democratic Presidential Nomination: The Clinton View. (p. 782)
—John Steinbeck. (p. 922)
—Johnny Depp. (p. 923)
—Justin Berfield. (p. 940)
—Justin Bieber. (p. 940)
—Justin Timberlake. (p. 940)
—Kelly Clarkson. (p. 948)
—Leonardo Da Vinci. (p. 992)
—Life & Times of Cicero. (p. 1008)
—Life & Times of Confucius. (p. 1008)
—Life & Times of Constantine. (p. 1008)
—Life & Times of Homer. (p. 1008)
—Life & Times of Rosa Parks. (p. 1008)
—Lindsay Lohan. (p. 1019)
—Mariah Carey. (p. 1093)
—Mario. (p. 1094)
—Mary-Kate & Ashley Olsen. (p. 1100)
—Matt Christopher. (p. 1109)
—McCarthy Era. (p. 1114)
—Medusa. (p. 1120)
—Megan Fox. (p. 1124)
—Nathan Hale. (p. 1231)
—Odysseus. (p. 1278)
—Orianthi. (p. 1303)
—Paul Cezanne. (p. 1330)
—Pierre & Marie Curie & the Discovery of Radium. (p. 1357)
—Plymouth Colony: The Pilgrims Settle in New England. (p. 1374)
—Prince William of Wales. (p. 1401)
—Queen Latifah. (p. 1425)
—Railroad Grows into an Industry (1840-1850) (p. 1434)
—Robert Koch & the Study of Anthrax. (p. 1479)
—San Diego. (p. 1510)
—Seattle. (p. 1539)
—Story of September 11, 2001. (p. 1660)
—Tennessee Williams. (p. 1720)
—Theseus. (p. 1732)
—Top Secret: The Story of the Manhattan Project. (p. 1769)
—Troy Polamalu. (p. 1790)
—Turtle in Our Class. (p. 1798)
—Watergate Scandal. (p. 1863)
—We Visit Brazil. (p. 1868)
—We Visit Cuba. (p. 1868)
—We Visit Kuwait. (p. 1868)
—We Visit Saudi Arabia. (p. 1868)
—What It's Like to Be Mark Sanchez. de la Vega, Eida, tr. from ENG. (p. 1891)
—Zac Efron. (p. 1984)
Tracy, Kristen. Bessica Lefter Bites Back. (p. 168)
—Camille McPhee Fell under the Bus. (p. 256)
—Crimes of the Sarahs. (p. 382)
—Hung Up. (p. 827)
—Reinvention of Bessica Lefter. (p. 1457)
—Too Cool for This School. (p. 1766)
Tracy, Kristina, jt. auth. see Dyer, Wayne W.
Tracy, Kristina, jt. auth. see Hay, Louise L.
Tracy, Kristina, jt. auth. see Lucero, Len.
Tracy, Kristina, et al. Chris P. Bacon: My Life So Far... (p. 311)
Tracy, Libba, illus. see Buchanan, Ken.
Tracy, Louis. Black Cat. (p. 195)
Tracy, Mary Lee & McCabe, Ginny. Living the Gold-Medal Life: Inspirations from Female Athletes. (p. 1041)
Tracy, Roseann. Do You Love Me When I Am Upside Down? (p. 458)
—Whose Toes Are Those? (p. 1922)
Tracy, Sophia Okun. Woman Ahead of Her Time: Christine de Pizan, Defender of Womankind. (p. 1945)
Tracy, Stephen V., jt. auth. see Neils, Jenifer.
Traditional. Away in a Manger. Reed, Lisa & Bennett, Randle Paul, illus. (p. 120)
—Jesus Loves the Little Children. Gulliver, Amanda, illus. (p. 916)
—Jolly Old Santa's Workshop Activity Book. Pulley, Kelly & Reed, Lisa, illus. (p. 924)
—O Little Town of Bethlehem. Beauvois, Nathalie, illus. (p. 1274)
—Silent Night. Pulley, Kelly & Reed, Lisa, illus. (p. 1575)
Traditional & Cloke, Rene. My Book of Favourite Tales & Rhymes. (p. 1199)
Traditional Staff. Dayenu! A Favorite Passover Song. Latimer, Miriam, illus. (p. 415)
Traeger, Heather. Rabbiting on Nowingi - A Coloring Book: A Bush Kid Loving the Red Soil, Australian Bush Animals & Starry Nights! (p. 1429)
Trafford, Adrienne. Cat & Dog See the World Coloring Book. (p. 277)
—Journey Coloring Book (p. 928)
—Tarot Designs Coloring Book. (p. 1706)
Trafton, Jennifer. Rise & Fall of Mount Majestic. Helquist, Brett, illus. (p. 1474)
Trahan, Kendra. Disneyland Detective: An Independent Guide to Discovering Disney's Legend, Lore, & Magic. McKim, Brian & Yamauchi, Karl, illus. (p. 453)
Trahan, Kendra Swain. Following Jesus: Obeying His Commandments (Children's Version) (p. 612)
Trail, George. Moby & Family. (p. 1157)
Trail, Sara. Sew with Sara: Fun Stuff to Keep, Give, Sell! (p. 1555)
Train, Alan Mark. Strawberry Fairchild & the Green Flame: A Fable by Alan Mark Train. (p. 1666)
Train, Mary. Time for the Fair. Hayes, Karel, illus. (p. 1752)
Trainer, Chaim. Shalom Secrets: How to Live in Peace with Friends & Family, A Children's Guide. (p. 1559)
Trainer, Maria T. Kids Are Gifts from Heaven (p. 952)
Traini, Agostino. Chef Foody's Field Trip. (p. 297)
—Christmas Find & Color. (p. 314)
—Springtime Find & Color. (p. 1635)
Tramer, Ava, jt. auth. see Sones, Sonya.
Trammel, Howard K. Galaxies. (p. 653)
—Solar System. (p. 1607)
—Wildfires. (p. 1931)
Trammell, Brandon, illus. see Birt, Michael.
Trammell, Fredi. Journey Through the Bible for Kids. (p. 928)
Trammell, Jack, jt. auth. see Gorman, Joe.
Trammell, Jeremiah, illus. see Stihler, Cherie B.
Trammell, Jeremiah, illus. see Stihler, Cherie.
Trammell, Jeremiah, illus. see Vanasse, Deb.
Trammell, Jeremiah, illus. see Vaughan, Richard Lee & Vaughan, Marcia.
Trammell, Menlia Moss. Rob & Rex Prevent a Poaching. (p. 1478)
Tramonte, Katherine H., illus. see Cander, Chris.
Tran, Christine & Nash, Kevin. Scripps College College Prowler off the Record. (p. 1533)
Tran, Dao X., jt. ed. see Bollinger, Michele.
Tran, Hensley. Agatha's Stolen Curve. (p. 29)
Tran, Kim-Lan & Millar, Louise. Tet: The New Year. Vo-Dinh, Mai, illus. (p. 1723)
Tran, Quoc. Tet Pole/Su Tich Cay Neu Ngay Tet: The Story of Tet Festival. Smith, William, tr. from VIE. (p. 1723)
Tran, Tien Cong. Buddha & the Way to Happiness. (p. 234)
Tran, Tommy. Forever & a Day. (p. 619)
Tran, Truong. Going Home, Coming Home. Phong, Ann, illus. (p. 692)
Tran-Davies, N. Daddy Is a Conundrum! (p. 398)
Transchel, Kate. Breakup of Yugoslavia: Conflict in the Balkans. (p. 225)
Translation Services Staff, tr. see Clay, Kathryn.
Translation Services Staff, tr. see Lindeen, Carol K.
Translation Services Staff, tr. see Schuh, Mari C.
Translations.com Staff, jt. auth. see Kudela, Katy R.
Translations.com Staff, tr. see Arnold, Caroline.
Translations.com Staff, tr. see Boothroyd, Jennifer.
Translations.com Staff, tr. see Braithwaite, Jill.
Translations.com Staff, tr. see Brill, Marlene Targ.
Translations.com Staff, tr. see Carlson, Nancy.
Translations.com Staff, tr. see Clay, Kathryn.
Translations.com Staff, tr. see Dahl, Michael & Jensen, Brian.
Translations.com Staff, tr. see Eaton, Deborah.
Translations.com Staff, tr. see Hill, Lee Sullivan.
Translations.com Staff, tr. see Jango-Cohen, Judith.
Translations.com Staff, tr. see Johnson, Rebecca L.
Translations.com Staff, tr. see Kalz, Jill.
Translations.com Staff, tr. see Kelley, Emily.
Translations.com Staff, tr. see Kessel, Joyce K.
Translations.com Staff, tr. see Kishel, Ann-Marie.
Translations.com Staff, tr. see Kudela, Katy R.
Translations.com Staff, tr. see Leonard, Marcia.
Translations.com Staff, tr. see Lessem, Don.
Translations.com Staff, tr. see Limke, Jeff.
Translations.com Staff, tr. see Lindeen, Carol K.
Translations.com Staff, tr. see Lowery, Linda.
Translations.com Staff, tr. see Markle, Sandra.
Translations.com Staff, tr. see Marshall, Pam.
Translations.com Staff, tr. see Mayesky & Kalz, Jill.
Translations.com Staff, tr. see Nelson, Kristin L.
Translations.com Staff, tr. see Nelson, Kristin.
Translations.com Staff, tr. see Nelson, Robin.
Translations.com Staff, tr. see Patrick, Jean L. S.
Translations.com Staff, tr. see Portnoy, Mindy Avra.
Translations.com Staff, tr. see Ransom, Candice.
Translations.com Staff, tr. see Riley, Joelle.
Translations.com Staff, tr. see Rivera, Sheila.
Translations.com Staff, tr. see Schuh, Mari C.
Translations.com Staff, tr. see Schulz, Walter A.
Translations.com Staff, tr. see Sherrow, Victoria.
Translations.com Staff, tr. see Shores, Lori.
Translations.com Staff, tr. see Simon, Charnan.
Translations.com Staff, tr. see Storad, Conrad J.
Translations.com Staff, tr. see Thayer, Tanya.
Translations.com Staff, tr. see Tidd, Louise Vitellaro.
Translations.com Staff, tr. see Tourville, Amanda Doering & Sorra, Kristin.
Translations.com Staff, tr. see Tourville, Amanda Doering.
Translations.com Staff, tr. see Walker, Sally M.
Translations.com Staff, tr. see Welch, Catherine A.
Translations.com Staff, tr. see Wetterer, Margaret K.
Translations.com Staff, tr. see Zemlicka, Shannon.
Translations.com Staff, tr. see Zuehlke, Jeffrey.
TransPerfect Translations Staff, tr. see Kalz, Jill.
Transue, Emily R. On Call: A Doctor's Days & Nights in Residency. (p. 1288)
Transworld Publishing Staff, jt. auth. see Red Fox Picture Books Staff.
Tranter, John. Studio Moon. (p. 1670)
—Trio. (p. 1787)
Tranter, Nigel. Folly of Princes. (p. 612)
—Unicorn Rampant. (p. 1818)
Trantham, Cary. Monster of Lake Champlain. (p. 1168)
Trantham, Cary Gordon. Saving of Sophi: El Rescate de Sofia. (p. 1517)
Trap, Paul, jt. ed. see Wagenaar, Larry J.
Trapani, Iza. Bear Went over the Mountain. Trapani, Iza, illus. (p. 151)
—Froggie Went A-Courtin' Trapani, Iza, illus. (p. 640)
—Gabe & Goon. (p. 652)
—Haunted Party. Trapani, Iza, illus. (p. 753)
—Here We Go 'Round the Mulberry Bush. Trapani, Iza, illus. (p. 771)
—Jingle Bells. Trapani, Iza, illus. (p. 918)
—Little Miss Muffet. Trapani, Iza, illus. (p. 1031)
—Mary Had a Little Lamb. Trapani, Iza, illus. (p. 1100)
—Oh Where, Oh Where Has My Little Dog Gone? Trapani, Iza, illus. (p. 1281)
—Old King Cole. Trapani, Iza, illus. (p. 1284)
—Rufus & Friends: Rhyme Time. Trapani, Iza, illus. (p. 1494)
—Rufus & Friends: School Days. Trapani, Iza, illus. (p. 1494)
—Shoo Fly! Trapani, Iza, illus. (p. 1568)
—Sing along with Iza & Friends: Row Row Row Your Boat. Trapani, Iza, illus. (p. 1579)
—Sing along with Iza & Friends: The Itsy Bitsy Spider. Trapani, Iza, illus. (p. 1579)
—Sing along with Iza & Friends: Twinkle, Twinkle Little Star. Trapani, Iza, illus. (p. 1579)
—Twinkle, Twinkle, Little Star. Trapani, Iza, illus. (p. 1802)
Trapani, Iza, illus. see Bunting, Eve.
Trapani, Iza, illus. see Merrill, Bob.
Trapani, Margi. Working Together Against Gang Violence. (p. 1953)
Trapero, Florentino, tr. see Kahn, Michàele.
Trapolsi, Audrey. Teaching Struggling Readers to Tackle Math Word Problems: Effective Strategies & Practice Pages That Help Kids Develop the Skills They Need to Read & Solve Math Word Problems. (p. 1710)
Trapp, Karla, illus. see Wiemeler, Aaron.
Trapp, Kyrima. Que? Como? Por Que?: Los Colores. (p. 1423)
Trasacco, Christina. Indigo. (p. 872)
Trasler, Janee. Bathtime for Chickies. Trasler, Janee, illus. (p. 144)
—Bedtime for Chickies. Trasler, Janee, illus. (p. 156)
—Benny's Chocolate Bunny. Trasler, Janee, illus. (p. 165)
—Dinnertime for Chickies. Trasler, Janee, illus. (p. 441)
—Mimi & Bear in the Snow. Trasler, Janee, illus. (p. 1145)
—New Chick for Chickies. Trasler, Janee, illus. (p. 1244)
—Pottytime for Chickies. Trasler, Janee, illus. (p. 1389)
Trasler, Janee, illus. see Feldman, Thea.
Trasler, Janee, illus. see Zondervan Publishing Staff.
Traudel, Hartel, jt. auth. see Hartel, Traudel.
Traugh, Steven & Traugh, Susan. Mother Goose Brain Boost: Using Music & Movement to Teach Cognitive Skills. (p. 1178)
Traugh, Susan. Sean Combs. (p. 1536)
Traugh, Susan, jt. auth. see Traugh, Steven.
Traugh, Susan M. Sex Smarts: You & Your Sexuality (p. 1556)
Traugh, Susan M., ed. Vegetarianism. (p. 1834)
Traupman, John C. Latin Dictionary. (p. 979)
—New College Latin & English Dictionary. (p. 1244)

T

Trautmann, Nancy M. Decay & Renewal. (p. 421)
Traver, N. K., jt. auth. see Traver., N. K.
Traver., N. K. & Traver, N. K. Duplicity. (p. 490)
Travers, Georgia. Wily Woodchucks. Gag, Flavia, illus. (p. 1935)
Travers, James A. Kitten & the Barn. (p. 962)
Travers, Jasmine, jt. auth. see Rhodes, Genee M.
Travers, P. L. Mary Poppins. (p. 1101)
—Mary Poppins. Shepard, Mary, illus. (p. 1101)
—Mary Poppins: 80th Anniversary Collection. Shepard, Mary, illus. (p. 1101)
—Mary Poppins & Mary Poppins Comes Back. Shepard, Mary, illus. (p. 1101)
—Mary Poppins Comes Back. Shepard, Mary, illus. (p. 1101)
—Mary Poppins from A to Z. Shepard, Mary, illus. (p. 1101)
—Mary Poppins in the Kitchen: A Cookery Book with a Story. Shepard, Mary, illus. (p. 1101)
—Mary Poppins in the Park. Shepard, Mary, illus. (p. 1101)
—Mary Poppins Opens the Door. Shepard, Mary & Sims, Agnes, illus. (p. 1101)
—Mary Poppins Opens the Door. Sims, Agnes & Shepard, Mary, illus. (p. 1101)
—Mary Poppins Vintage Boxed Set: Three Enchanting Classics: Mary Poppins, Mary Poppins Comes Back, & Mary Poppins Opens the Door. (p. 1101)
Travesty, Shrill. Taking Tree: A Selfish Parody. Cummins, Lucy Ruth, illus. (p. 1698)
Travis, Allison J. Bundy. One More Wake Up: With Faith All Things Are Possible-Even Surviving the Loss of a Loved One. (p. 1296)
Travis, Alva. Secret of the Hidden Chamber. (p. 1542)
Travis, Caroline, illus. see Black, Cary & Schott, Gretchen Victoria.
Travis, Cathy. Constitution Translated for Kids. (p. 359)
—Constitution Translated for Kids / la Constitución traducida para Niños. (p. 359)
Travis, Cindie, jt. auth. see Travis, Tim.
Travis, Joelle & Figueras, Ligaya, eds. Animaux et les Verbes. Hazan, Maurice, illus. (p. 84)
—Chiffres, Couleurs, Verbes et Phrases. Hazan, Maurice, illus. (p. 301)
—Francais en Images Hazan, Maurice, illus. (p. 627)
—Français en Images Hazan, Maurice, illus. (p. 627)
—French Gerard et Ses Copains Hazan, Maurice, illus. (p. 635)
—French Gérard et Ses Copains Hazan, Maurice, illus. (p. 635)
—French Gérard et ses Copains. Hazan, Maurice, illus. (p. 635)
—French Junior Book Gérard et ses Copains. Hazan, Maurice, illus. (p. 635)
—French Junior Book Gérard et ses Copains Teacher's Guide. Hazan, Maurice, illus. (p. 635)
—Los Animales y los Verbos. Hazan, Maurice, illus. (p. 1053)
—Numeros, Colores, Verbos y Frases. Hazan, Maurice, illus. (p. 1273)
—Spanish Espanol en Imagenes Hazan, Maurice, illus. (p. 1621)
—Spanish Junior Book Pablo y sus Amigos. Hazan, Maurice, illus. (p. 1621)
—Spanish Junior Book Pablo y sus amigos Teacher's Guide. Hazan, Maurice, illus. (p. 1621)
—Spanish Level 1 Assessment. Hazan, Maurice, illus. (p. 1621)
—Spanish Pablo y sus amigos Hazan, Maurice, illus. (p. 1621)
—Spanish Pablo y sus Amigos. Hazan, Maurice, illus. (p. 1621)
Travis, Joelle, ed. French Level 1 Assessment with Stickers. Hazan, Maurice, illus. (p. 636)
Travis, Lucille. Far Journey. (p. 572)
—Timna. (p. 1755)
—Tirzah. Garber, S. David, ed. (p. 1757)
Travis, Stephanie, illus. see Bowman, Andy.
Travis, Tim & Travis, Cindie. Road That Has No End: How We Traded in Our Ordinary Lives for an Around the World Bicycle Adventure. (p. 1477)
Travis, Yolanda Rene'. Waam: The Family. (p. 1851)
Travitzky, Brianna Marie, jt. auth. see Travitzky, Paul Joseph.
Travitzky, Paul Joseph & Travitzky, Brianna Marie. Brianna Marie Wants to Be: A Cowgirl. (p. 227)
—Brianna Marie Wants to Be... A Veterinarian. (p. 227)
Trawick, Gary E. Born in Reconstruction: The Story of Pender County, 1524-2010. (p. 214)
Trawick, Renee. Mrs. T's Day of Numbers (p. 1187)
Trawick, Ruth. Jeremy Bird. (p. 913)
Trayer, Edward. Struggles of Felicity Brady. (p. 1668)
Trayer, Edward H. Struggles of Felicity Brady: Articulus Quest. (p. 1668)
Traylor, Javier. Day at School with Sally Sue. (p. 412)
Traylor, Marci. What Will I Be? (p. 1895)
Traylor, Margaret, ed. see Traylor, Waverley.
Traylor, Waverley. Indian Legends of the Great Dismal Swamp. Traylor, Margaret, ed. (p. 871)
Traylor, Waverley, ed. see Roberts, Curt.
Traylor, Waverley, illus. see Roberts, Curt.
Traynor, Elizabeth, illus. see Crane, Carol.
Traynor, Elizabeth, illus. see Gagliano, Eugene.
Traynor, Tracy. American English with Abby & Zak. Hambleton, Laura, illus. (p. 60)
—Cheese Please, Chimpanzees: Fun with Spelling. Bronfeyn, Lily, illus. (p. 296)
Traynor, Tracy & Pérez, Maria. Spanish with Abby & Zak. Hambleton, Laura, illus. (p. 1621)
Traywick-Jones, Andrea. God Loves Me! Thomas, James, illus. (p. 689)
Treadway, Clifton. Benny & Bugsy. (p. 165)
Treadway, Kathryn & Seaman, Jim. Providence College College Prowler off the Record. (p. 1413)
Treadwell, Harriette Taylor & Free, Margaret. Furst Readin Book in Ulster Scot. (p. 650)
—Primer. (p. 1400)
—Reading-Literature: First Reader. Carroll, Sheila, ed. (p. 1446)
—Reading-Literature Second Reader. Richardson, Frederick, illus. (p. 1446)
—Reading-Literature the Primer (Yesterday's Classics) Richardson, Frederick, illus. (p. 1446)
—Reading-Literature Third Reader. Richardson, Frederick, illus. (p. 1446)
Treadwell, James, Jr. Revelation of Faith: Another Perspective. (p. 1465)
Treanor, H. T. Sun Stone. Tarnowski, Mark, illus. (p. 1676)
Treanor, Nick. Animal Rights. (p. 79)
Trease, Geoffrey, text. Word to Caesar. (p. 1951)
Treasure, Kevin A. Decisions Determine Destiny: Stories & Scenarios. (p. 421)
Treasuree Cash. Tyler Learns to Do Tricks! (p. 1805)
Treat, Thomas M. Adventures of Shrimely. (p. 23)
Treatner, Meryl, illus. see Carson, Jana.
Treatner, Meryle, illus. see Goldish, Meish.
Treays, R. Understanding Your Brain. (p. 1816)
Treays, R., jt. auth. see Claybourne, A.
Treays, Rebecca. Understanding Your Body: Internet Linked (Combined Volume) (p. 1816)
—Understanding Your Brain. (p. 1816)
—Understanding Your Brain - Internet Linked. Fox, Christyan, illus. (p. 1816)
—Understanding Your Muscles & Bones: Internet-Linked. Fox, Christyan, illus. (p. 1816)
—Understanding Your Senses. (p. 1816)
—Understanding Your Senses - Internet Linked. Fox, Christyan, illus. (p. 1816)
Treays, Rebecca, ed. see Litchfield, Jo.
Trebes, Stacie A. Hurry! Hurry! Rush! Rush! (p. 830)
Trebi-Ollennu, Flora. My Daily Walk: Discover the Life of Jesus. Barker, Peter, ed. (p. 1201)
Trechsel, Keili. Whale Set Sail. Renfroe, Leisa, illus. (p. 1877)
Tredell, Nicholas, ed. see Childs, Peter.
Treder-Wolff, Jude. Possible Futures: Creative Thinking for the Speed of Life. (p. 1387)
Tree, Marcie M., as told by. Marcie the Marvelous Tree: An Autobiography. (p. 1092)
Trees, Annie Mae. Last Days of Summer: A Mystery of Two Children & Their Grandma Set Out on an Adventure. (p. 977)
—Mystery of the Big Bone. (p. 1225)
—Old Apartment Building: A Tale from the Trees. (p. 1283)
Treffeisen, Brian, photos by see Bird, Janie.
Treffry, Teresa, illus. see Stagnitti, Karen.
Trefil. Liberal Arts Physics: Includes Instructor's Solutions Manual. (p. 1005)
Trefil, James. (WCS)Sciences: With eGrade Set. (p. 1865)
—(WCS)Sciences. (p. 1865)
Trefil, James & Hazen, Robert M. Physics Matters: An Introduction to Conceptual Physics. (p. 1353)
—Physics Matters. (p. 1353)
—Physics Matters, Activity Book: An Introduction to Conceptual Physics. (p. 1353)
Trefil, James, et al. Cells & Heredity. (p. 286)
—Ecology. (p. 502)
—Life Science 2005. (p. 1013)
Trefry, Deana. Even When. (p. 541)
Treg, Mccoy, jt. illus. see Thomas, Erika.
Tregay, Sarah. Fan Art. DeJesus, Melissa, illus. (p. 570)
—Love & Leftovers. (p. 1059)
Treggiari, Jo. Ashes, Ashes. (p. 105)
Trehearne, Miriam P. Comprehensive Literacy Resource for Kindergarten Teachers. (p. 354)
Treiber, Jutta & Antoni, Birgit. Porque Siempre Va a Ser Asi. (p. 1386)
Treigle, Jimmy, jt. auth. see Gaskins, Terry.
Treis, Connie. Bartrob. (p. 140)
Treister, Neil W. Heartfulness: A Guide to Heart Health & Life Balance. (p. 760)
Trelease, Jim. Read Aloud Handbook. (p. 1442)
Treloar, Debi, photos by see Wilson, Judith.
Trelogan, Stephanie. Mask Parade: Forest Animals. Armstrong, Katharine, illus. (p. 1102)
Tremaine, John, jt. auth. see Fullman, Joe.
Tremaine, Jon. Magic Handbook - Paper Tricks. (p. 1072)
—Magic with Numbers. (p. 1074)
—Magical Illusions. (p. 1074)
—Origami: Papiroflexia para Principiantes. (p. 1303)
—Paper Tricks. (p. 1323)
—Pocket Tricks. (p. 1375)
—Tangrams: Magnéticos. (p. 1705)
Tremaine, Michele, illus. see Wick, Elaine.
Tremayne, Peter, pseud. Ensuing Evil & Others. (p. 531)
Trembath, Brent. Scruggy Puppies Book. (p. 1533)
Trembath, Don. Emville Confidential (p. 522)
—Hypnotized (p. 831)
—Rooster (p. 1488)
Trembinski, Donna. Famous People of the Middle Ages. (p. 569)
—Medieval Law & Punishment. (p. 1119)
—Medieval Laws & Punishment. (p. 1119)
—Medieval Myths, Legends & Songs. (p. 1119)
—Medieval Myths, Legends, & Songs. (p. 1119)
Trembinsky, Laverne Gray. Friend Sent from Heaven for Andrew: A Little Boy Finds His Self Experiencing Loneliness Because His Family Had to Move Because of Financial Hardsh. (p. 637)
Tremblay, Alain Ulysse. Don de Jonathan. Malepart, Celine, tr. (p. 465)
—Héritage de Julien. Malépart, Céline, illus. (p. 771)
—Jeanne la Terrienne. Malepart, Celine, tr. (p. 911)
Tremblay, Amanda. Tornado Trial. (p. 1770)
Tremblay, Carl, photos by see Sampson, Sally.
Tremblay, Carole. Floop Does the Laundry. Beshwaty, Steve, illus. (p. 606)
—Floop in the Dark. Beshwaty, Steve, illus. (p. 606)
—Floop's Flowers. Beshwaty, Steve, illus. (p. 606)
—Floop's New Umbrella. Beshwaty, Steve, illus. (p. 606)
—Romeo, le Rat Romantique. (p. 1486)
Tremblay, E. A. Rachel Carson. (p. 1431)
Tremblay, Marc. Petit Frere du Chaperon Rouge. Fil et al, illus. (p. 1348)
Tremblay, Patrick. Poor, Poor Jack. (p. 1383)
Trembley, Becky A. Nimbus Numbers. (p. 1256)
Trembley, Skip & Ochs, Susan A. You'll See, Little Tree. Hollis, Michael, illus. (p. 1978)
Treml, Renee. Colour for Curlews. Treml, Renee, illus. (p. 346)
—One Very Tired Wombat. Treml, Renee, illus. (p. 1297)
Tremlin, Nathan, illus. see Werner, Teresa O.
Tremlin, Nathan, illus. see Werner, Teresa Orem.
Tremlin, Nathan, et al. Mookie: A Girl in Maximsubomia. Tremlin, Nathan & Chomiak, Joseph, illus. (p. 1171)
Trenard Sayago, Mauricio, illus. see Hayes, Joe.
Trenc, Milan. Another Night at the Museum. Trenc, Milan, illus. (p. 88)
—Night at the Museum. (p. 1252)
Trenc, Milan, jt. auth. see Goldman, Leslie.
Trenchard, Robert. Famous Frog Fiasco. (p. 569)
Trends Magazine Editors, ed. Trends Very Best Kitchens & Bathrooms. (p. 1784)
Trenga, Bonnie. Off-the-Wall, Skits with Phrasal Verbs. (p. 1279)
Trenowden, Mark. Miracle of Bean's Bullion. (p. 1148)
Trent, John. Superhero Swamp: A Slimy, Smelly Way to Find the Superhero God Placed in You! Finger, Matthew, illus. (p. 1683)
Trent, John, illus. see Menzies, Britt.
Trent, Rodney. Sadie Mae's Big Adventure. (p. 1501)
Trent, Sandy Chase. Tommy's Amazing Journey: The Cat that Could Fly. (p. 1765)
Trent, Shanda. Farmers' Market Day. Dippold, Jane, illus. (p. 574)
Trent, Tiffany. Tinker King. (p. 1755)
—Unnaturalists. (p. 1822)
Trenton, Russell. Russian Revolution: The Fall of the Tsars & the Rise of Communism. (p. 1498)
Trenton, Russell, ed. Russian Revolution: The Fall of the Tsars & the Rise of Communism. (p. 1498)
Trenton, Trisha. Trisha Trenton: Dance Diva Dance! (p. 1787)
Tresco, Betsy Dru. How to Draw Hungary's Sights & Symbols. (p. 817)
Tresselt, Alvin & Ewing, Carolyn. Rabbit Story. (p. 1429)
Tresh, Doreene. Elephants, Aren't They Great? (p. 512)
Tresidder, Megan. Secret Language of Love: A Visual Treasury of Love Through the Ages. (p. 1541)
Tresilian, S., illus. see Reynolds, E. E.
Tresilian, Stuart, illus. see Blyton, Enid.
Treske, D. B. Safety Witch. (p. 1502)
Treskillard, Robert. Merlin's Nightmare (p. 1128)
Tresniowski, Alex, jt. auth. see Schroff, Laura.
Tress, Arthur, photos by. Facing Up: Tress: Facing Up. (p. 561)
Tressler, Jill. Papaw, Read to Me. (p. 1322)
Trest, Candace D. Zack & Tripp & the Indian Village. (p. 1984)
Tretter, Cydnie Jo. Sarah's Special Wish. (p. 1514)
—Timothy & Wallie. (p. 1755)
Trevas, Chris, illus. see Wallace, Daniel.
Trevathan, Melissa, jt. auth. see Goff, Sissy.
Trevayne, Emma. Accidental Afterlife of Thomas Marsden. (p. 8)
—Chorus. (p. 310)
—Coda. (p. 338)
—Flights & Chimes & Mysterious Times. (p. 604)
—Flights & Chimes & Mysterious Times. Thomas, Glenn, illus. (p. 604)
Trevelyan, R. C., tr. see Sophocles, et al.
Trevethan, Glenn A. Adventures of Sammi Snake: Sammi's Coat. (p. 22)
Trevia, Rick & Benchmark Education Co., LLC Staff. City Lights. (p. 323)
—Squid Twins. (p. 1637)
Trevinio, Juan, illus. see Johnson, Sandi.
Trevino, Carlos Juan Ramirez. Strike Zone Paipa. (p. 1667)
Trevino, David. Colorful Carnival of Kids in the Kingdom of Marbles: Mission #2. (p. 344)
—Colorful Carnival of Kids in the Kingdom of Marbles: Mission #3. (p. 344)
—Colorful Carnival of Kids in the Kingdom of Marbles: Mission #1 the Cemetery Ghost. (p. 344)
Trevino, Elizabeth Borton de, see de Trevino, Elizabeth Borton.
Trevino, Esther, jt. auth. see Corman, Clifford L.
Trevino, Frank. Haley Is Waiting for You. (p. 736)
—Haley Wants to Color Out Side the Lines. (p. 736)
Treviño, Hilda L. Ladybugs on a Mission. (p. 971)
Trevino, Juan, illus. see Johnson, Sandi.
Trevino, Ruby. Chocolate Feet (p. 309)
Trevisan, Marco, illus. see Belloni, Giulia.
Trevitt, Roger & Lewis, Roger. Vocational Business Financial Accounting. (p. 1847)
Trévol, S. A., jt. auth. see Produccions Editorials, Trèvol.
Trévol, S. A. & Produccions Editorials, Trèvol. ¡No Quiero Dormir! Rius, Roser, illus. (p. 1260)
Trevor, Meriol. Sun Slower Sun Faster. Ardizzone, Edward, illus. (p. 1676)
Trevor, Simeon. I'm Going to Fly SomeDay. (p. 859)
Trevor, William. Fools of Fortune. (p. 614)
Treweek, Cherie, illus. see Scholtz, Pieter.
Trewin, Trudie. I Lost My Kisses. Bland, Nick, illus. (p. 841)
Trexler, Jennifer Suther, illus. see Ritch, Catherine.
Treyes, Jill. Brooke & Brandon Welcome Brandon. (p. 230)
Trezzo-Braren, Loretta, jt. auth. see Press, Judy.
Triana, Gaby. Cubanita. (p. 388)
—Riding the Universe. (p. 1471)
—Summer of Yesterday. (p. 1674)
—Temptress Four. (p. 1718)
Triana, Gaby, jt. auth. see Gonzalez, Gabriela.
Triano, Jay. Basketball Basics: How to Play Like the Pros (p. 143)
Tribble. Word for Word. (p. 1950)
Tribble, Derrick. Servants & Thieves: Wanderers in Time, Book One. (p. 1552)
Tribolet, Leslie L. Danny's Tale: Adventures of an Arabian Horse in his Own Words. (p. 406)
Tribuzi, Luke. What's the Difference Between Forests & Prairies? (p. 1899)
Tricarico, Mark. Zoe Pope: Unlicensed Lawyer. (p. 1987)
Tricchinelli, Rob. Arizona Diamondbacks. (p. 98)
—Golden State Warriors. (p. 695)
Trice, Lenora. Somewhere in Here There's You. (p. 1610)
Trice, Linda. Kenya's Song. Johnson, Pamela, illus. (p. 949)
Tricia Lowenfield design. S Is for Shepherd. (p. 1499)
Trier, George. Music of Heartohopia. (p. 1193)
Trier, Walter, illus. see Kästner, Erich.
Trier, Walter, jt. auth. see Rowohlt, Harry.
Triffo, Kahini H. Relentless Tears. (p. 1458)
Trifunov, David. Ice Time (p. 851)
Trigg, Michael J. Greanwold & the Mystery Cave: Greanwold & the Minosaurs Story Books. (p. 713)
Trigg, Roberta. Haworth Idyll: A Fantasy. Dashiell, Margaret, illus. (p. 755)
Triggle, David J., ed. see Busse, Gregory D.
Triggle, David J., ed. see Olive, M. Foster.
Triggle, David J., ed. see Santella, Tom.
Triggle, David J., ed. see Toufexis, Donna & Hammack, Sayamwong E.
Triggle, David J., jt. auth. see Adamec, Christine.
Triggle, David J., jt. auth. see May, Suellen.
Triggle, David J., jt. auth. see Santella, Thomas.
Triggle, David J., ed. Drugs: The Straight Facts. (p. 487)
—Straight Facts. (p. 1664)
Triggs, Pat, jt. auth. see O'Riordan, Aileen.
Trigiani, Adriana. Viola in Reel Life. (p. 1843)
—Viola in the Spotlight. (p. 1843)
Trigueros, Nury. I Don't Like to Be Afraid. (p. 838)
Trilling, Richard J. More Stories of Stephanie & Friends: Volume 2 in the Stephanie Stories. (p. 1175)
—Still More Stories of Stephanie & Friends: Volume 3 in the Stephanie Series. (p. 1650)
—Stories of Stephanie & Friends. (p. 1655)
Trillo, Carlos. Bird. Bobillo, Juan, illus. (p. 190)
Trillo, Carlos, jt. auth. see Risso, Eduardo.
Trim, John & Kohl, Katrin M. Deutsch Direkt! (p. 431)
—Deutsch Direkt. (p. 431)
—Deutsch Direkt! Textbook. (p. 431)
—Deutsch Direkt! Answer Key. (p. 431)
Trim, Laura A. N. Grandma's Treasury of Inspirational Poems. (p. 709)
Trimble, Aidan, contrib. by. Martial & Fighting Arts (p. 1097)
Trimble, Anne M., illus. see Jeswald, Mary J.
Trimble, Gina. Little Tiny Mouse (p. 1037)
Trimble, Irene. Barbie - Princess & the Popstar. Random House Staff, illus. (p. 138)
—Brave. (p. 223)
—Snow Princesses (Disney Princess) RH Disney Staff, illus. (p. 1599)
—Tangled. Walt Disney Animation Studios (Firm) Staff, illus. (p. 1705)
Trimble, Irene, jt. auth. see RH Disney Staff.
Trimble, Marcia. Adventure of Pushy Octopus & His Friends. Sprague, Dean, illus. (p. 14)
—Liberty Cafe Is Open. Hayden, Jennifer, illus. (p. 1005)
—Peppy's Shadow. Pellegrini, Will, illus. (p. 1340)
Trimble, Marcia J. Marsby & the Martian Detectives. Hayden, Jennifer H., illus. (p. 1096)
Trimble, Mary E. McClellan's Bluff. (p. 1114)
Trimble, Patti. What Day Is It? Moreton, Daniel, illus. (p. 1881)
Trimble, Patti, jt. auth. see Moran, Alex.
Trimble, Patti & Moran, Alex. Lost! Moreton, Daniel, illus. (p. 1054)
Trimble, Tonya. Curiosity, with a Capital S. Enik, Ted, illus. (p. 392)
Trimmer, Christian, jt. auth. see Jin, Chris.
Trimmer, Joseph F. Writing Without a Purpose: AP Version. (p. 1965)
Trimmer, Tony, illus. see Kingfisher Editors.
Trimmer, Tony, illus. see Place, John.
Trimmer, Tony, illus. see Rooke, Thom.
Trimmer, Tony, illus. see Slade, Suzanne.
Trimoglie, Mario. Rivers. Swope, Brenda, illus. (p. 1476)
—Story of Ocos: King of the Sky, Master of the Water. Buehrle, Jacquelyn, illus. (p. 1659)
—Thom. (p. 1740)
Trimper, Marty. Hermione: Shipwrecked! in Ocean City, Maryland. Amy, Holloway, illus. (p. 771)
Trinco, Trish. Leaf That Wouldn't Leave. Langdo, Bryan, illus. (p. 982)
Trine, Greg. Attack of the Valley Girls. Montijo, Rhode, illus. (p. 114)
—Brotherhood of the Traveling Underpants. (p. 231)
—Brotherhood of the Traveling Underpants. Montijo, Rhode, illus. (p. 231)
—Curse of the Bologna Sandwich. Montijo, Rhode, illus. (p. 394)
—Dinos Are Forever. Dormer, Frank W., illus. (p. 441)
—Fake Cape Caper. Montijo, Rhode, illus. (p. 565)
—Grateful Fred. Montijo, Rhode, illus. (p. 712)
—Invasion from Planet Dork. Montijo, Rhode, illus. (p. 883)
—Pinkbeard's Revenge. Dormer, Frank W., illus. (p. 1360)
—Revenge of the McNasty Brothers. Montijo, Rhode, illus. (p. 1466)
—Shifty Business. Dormer, Frank W., illus. (p. 1566)
—Terror in Tights. Montijo, Rhode, illus. (p. 1722)
—Willy Maykit in Space. Burks, James, illus. (p. 1934)
—Wyatt Burp Rides Again. Dormer, Frank W., illus. (p. 1966)
Trini Torres Carrion. Magic of a Strawberry Lollipop. (p. 1072)
Trinidad Joe. Santa's Key West Vacation. (p. 1513)
Trinity University Press Staff. 123 Sí! An Artistic Counting Book in English & Spanish. (p. 2000)
Triplett, Annette. From the Farm to You Coloring Book. Vale, Joe, ed. (p. 644)
Triplett, Chris Harper, illus. see Kreitz, Tina.
Triplett, Donald & Eiland, Marie. Castle Club Leader Manual: ... Children walking in the way of the Lord Rdm, tr. from SPA. (p. 276)
—Castle Club - Student Guide: Children Walking in the Way of the Lord Rdm, tr. (p. 276)
—Club castillo Manual del Alumno: ... ninos marchando en el camino del Senor Jacobo, Daysi, ed. (p. 335)
Triplett, Gina, illus. see Malone, Marianne.
Triplett, Ginger. Stringed Princess. (p. 1667)
Triplett, Ginger, illus. see Roark, Algernon Michael.

Tripp, Ben. Accidental Highwayman: Being the Tale of Kit Bristol, His Horse Midnight, a Mysterious Princess, & Sundry Magical Persons Besides. (p. 8)
Tripp, Christine, illus. see Brimner, Larry Dane.
Tripp, Christine, illus. see Kripke, Dorothy Karp.
Tripp, Christine, tr. see Kripke, Dorothy Karp.
Tripp, Jenny. Fais Do-Do. (p. 565)
—Pete & Fremont. Manders, John, illus. (p. 1346)
Tripp, Kanila, illus. see Vivinetto, Gina.
Tripp, Melinda Reynolds. What Should You Do? Helping Children Protect Themselves in the Twenty-first Century. (p. 1893)
Tripp, Natalie. We Care! Making Care Packages: Understand the Relationship Between Multiplication & Division. (p. 1866)
Tripp, Patricia. Bears That Lived in Evergreen Forest. (p. 152)
Tripp, Paul. Tubby the Tuba. Cole, Henry, illus. (p. 1795)
Tripp, Penny. Animal Rights. (p. 79)
Tripp, Terry. Growing in God's Word. (p. 726)
Tripp, Valerie. Brave Emily. England, Tamara, ed. (p. 223)
—Felicity Story Collection. Andreasen, Dan, illus. (p. 581)
—Josefina Story Collection. Tibbles, Jean-Paul, illus. (p. 926)
—Kit's Surprise. Rane, Walter & McAliley, Susan, illus. (p. 962)
—Molly Story Collection. Backes, Nick, illus. (p. 1161)
—Nellie's Promise. England, Tamara, ed. (p. 1240)
—Very Funny, Elizabeth! England, Tamara, ed. (p. 1838)
Tripp, Valerie, jt. auth. see Jazynka, Kitson.
Tripp, Wallace, illus. see Brock, Betty & Brock.
Tripp, Will. Water Adventures. (p. 1862)
Trippe, Dean, jt. auth. see Wilson, Daniel H.
Trippi, Peter. J. W. Waterhouse. (p. 902)
Trish, jt. auth. see Joe.
Trish Lynch Marquis. Pesty Neighbor. (p. 1345)
Trissel, SallyAnne. Nosey Rosie: Sharing Kindness Through Life Adventures. (p. 1266)
Trissler, Rebecca Johns. Vinny's Secret. (p. 1843)
Trissler, Rebecca Johns, ed. see Bonk, John J.
Trissler, Rebecca Johns, ed. see Butler, Dori Hillestad.
Tristan, Sarah. Cheat Codes. (p. 295)
Tristen And Tahleez. Bubba & Tata the Hermit Crabs: New Shells. (p. 233)
—Bubba & Tata the Hermit Crabs. (p. 233)
Trites, Judy. Charlie's Challenge. (p. 293)
Tritle, Lawrence A. Peloponnesian War. (p. 1336)
Triton, Mathias & Martinez, Alitha. Rise of el Diablo. (p. 1474)
—WWE Slam City: Finished. (p. 1966)
Tritt, Adam Byrn. Bud the Spud. Goldacker, "Java John", illus. (p. 234)
Trittin, Paul S., illus. see Baker, Marvin G.
Triumph Books Staff. 5 Seconds of Summer: She Looks So Perfect. (p. 1992)
—Austin Mahone: Startin' Something Spectacular. (p. 116)
—Baseball All-Stars. (p. 141)
—Believe. (p. 161)
—Big Book of One Direction. (p. 179)
—Hilary Duff: Total Hilary, Metamorphosis, Lizzie McGuire. . . & More. (p. 779)
—Jennifer Lawrence: Burning Bright. (p. 913)
—Lindsay Lohan: Rising Star. (p. 1019)
—One Direction: Where We Are. (p. 1294)
—One Direction: What Makes You Beautiful. (p. 1294)
—Rev-O-LOOM-tion: A Modern Kids' Guide to Rocking Rubber Bands. (p. 1465)
Triumph Books Staff, ed. see Kidder, Lisa & Kidder, Lisa Damian.
Trivas, Tracy. Wish Stealers. (p. 1940)
Trivedi, Harish, ed. see Kipling, Rudyard.
Trivelli, John. I Wanna Play Golf. (p. 847)
—Qbee Wants to Bee a Dolphin Trainer. Snyder, Anthony, illus. (p. 1422)
—Qbee Wants to Bee a Figherfighter. Snyder, Anthony, illus. (p. 1422)
—Qbee Wants to Bee a Homebuilder. Snyder, Anthony, illus. (p. 1422)
—Qbee Wants to Bee a Pilot. Snyder, Anthony, illus. (p. 1422)
—Qbee Wants to Bee a Racecar Driver. (p. 1422)
—Qbee Wants to Bee a Racecar Driver. Snyder, Anthony, illus. (p. 1422)
—Qbee Wants to Bee a Rock Star. Snyder, Anthony, illus. (p. 1422)
—Qbee Wants to Bee a Soldier. Snyder, Anthony, illus. (p. 1422)
—Qbee Wants to Bee an Author. Snyder, Anthony, illus. (p. 1422)
Trivette, Donna K. Friend for Ringo & Girl. (p. 637)
—One Special Christmas. (p. 1297)
—Ringo & Girl. (p. 1473)
Trivizas, Eugene. Three Little Wolves & the Big Bad Pig: A Pop-up Storybook. Oxenbury, Helen, illus. (p. 1743)
—Three Little Wolves & the Big Bad Pig. Oxenbury, Helen, illus. (p. 1743)
—Tres Lobitos y el Cochino Feroz. Oxenbury, Helen, illus. (p. 1784)
Trobaugh, Scott, illus. see Bersson, Robert & Shoup, Dolores.
Trobisch, Ingrid & Trobisch, Walter A. My Beautiful Feeling. (p. 1196)
Trobisch, Walter A., jt. auth. see Trobisch, Ingrid.
Trock, Kathleen. Hiding Places. (p. 777)
Trock, Kitty. Cricket Story. (p. 382)
Trocki, Phillip. Spelling Workout. (p. 1625)
Trockstad, Marcy, illus. see Unger-Pengilly, Elaine.
Trod, Mariano, et al. Brilliant Dr. Wogan. (p. 228)
Trodd, Mark. Hippo in the Stable. (p. 781)
Troeger, Virginia B. Berkeley Heights Revisited. (p. 167)
—Secret along the St. Mary's. Swisher, Michael-Che, tr. (p. 1540)
Trogdon, Kathryn, illus. see DeVogt, Rindia M.
Trogdon, Wendell. Incredible Indiana: Scenic Splendor/Awesome Wonders. (p. 869)
—Who Killed Hoosier Hysteria? Sport Survives amid Fading Fervor. (p. 1916)
Troia, Gary A. Instruction & Assessment for Struggling Writers: Evidence-Based Practices. Troia, Gary A., ed. (p. 878)
Troisi-Paton, Kimberly. Property Rights. (p. 1411)
Troisi-Paton, Kimberly, jt. auth. see Tubb, Kristin O'Donnell.
Troisi-Paton, Kimberly, ed. Right to Due Process. (p. 1472)
Trolenberg, Karl, illus. see Kula, Cheryl.
Trollinger, Patsi B. Thrill in The 'Ville. Thompson, Elizabeth, illus. (p. 1744)
Trollinger, Valerie L., jt. auth. see Flohr, John W.
Trollope, Anthony. Autobiography: And Other Writings. Shrimpton, Nicholas, ed. (p. 117)
Trollope, Joanna. Girl from the South. (p. 678)
Trombello, William. Trains & Tow Boats. Tangen, Nick, illus. (p. 1777)
Trombley, Carl L. Animals, Questions, & One Big Tale. (p. 83)
Trombley, Cyndi. According to Abbey. (p. 8)
Tromly, Stephanie. Trouble Is a Friend of Mine. (p. 1790)
Troncale, Steven L. Yankee Boys of War. (p. 1968)
Trondheim, Lewis. Kaput & Zosky. Gauvin, Edward, tr. from FRE. (p. 943)
—Mister O. Trondheim, Lewis, illus. (p. 1155)
—Monster Dinosaur. Trondheim, Lewis, illus. (p. 1167)
—Monster Graphic Novels: Monster Christmas. Trondheim, Lewis, illus. (p. 1167)
—Monster Graphic Novels: Monster Turkey. (p. 1167)
Trondheim, Lewis, jt. auth. see Sfar, Joann.
Trondheim, Lewis & Parme, Fabrice. Rey Catastrofe: Vaya Cara Tiene Adalberto. (p. 1467)
Trondheim, Lewis & Robin, Theirry. Happy Halloween, Li'l Santa. Robin, Thierry, illus. (p. 745)
Trone, Jo, illus. see Glass, Graeme.
Trone, Melody Karns, illus. see Davis, Lynda S. & Weisel, Kaitlyn E.
Tronheim, Lewis. Monster Graphic Novels: Monster Mess. (p. 1167)
Tronslin, Andrea, ed. see Nelson, Ray & Nelson, Douglas.
Trooboff, Rhoda. Ben, the Bells & the Peacocks. Bucher, Cecile, illus. (p. 163)
—Book for Elie. Radjou, Anna Nazaretz, illus. (p. 210)
—Punkinhead's Veggie Adventure: And the Strange Contraption in the Kitchen. Easton, Susan, illus. (p. 1417)
Troop 70239, Girl Scout, et al. I Don't Want to Be Your Friend Anymore. (p. 838)
Troop, Judson. Gatekeeper: Day of the Dinosaurs. (p. 658)
Trosper, Chad. Apples in a Pail. (p. 93)
Trost, Shannon, jt. auth. see Lewandowski, Lisa.
Trotman, Althea. How the East Pond Got Its Flowers. Sasso, illus. (p. 813)
Trotman, Felicity. Exploration of Space. (p. 550)
Trotman, Phd Gloria, et al. Fun Time with Jesus. (p. 648)
Trotta-Gilbert, Susan. What Ever Happened to Puppy? (p. 1884)
Trotter, Bob. Curious Tale of Marmalade Tuttle. (p. 394)
—Curious Tale of Marmalade Tuttle - Book Two Marmalade Tuttle & the Battle of Caldor. (p. 394)
—Up the Wooden Hill: Bedtime Stories for Little Ones. Edgar, Barrie, illus. (p. 1824)
Trotter, Deborah W. Summer's Trade/Shiigo Na'iini' Toddy, Irving, illus. (p. 1675)
Trotter, Jim. Junior Seau: Overcoming the Odds. (p. 936)
Trotter, Pamela D., III. Lantern on a Hitching Post: African-American Heritage Quiz Book. (p. 975)
Trotter, Stuart, illus. see Larkin, Susan.
Trotter, Stuart, illus. see Martin, Jane.
Trotter, Stuart, illus. see Mayes, Susan.
Trotter, Stuart, illus. see Smith, Lucy.
Trotter, Stuart, illus. see Tahta, Sophie.
Trotter, Stuart, illus. see Williams, Sam.
Trottier, Doug. Crow & His Boy. (p. 385)
Trottier, Maxine. Death of My Country: The Plains of Abraham Diary of Geneviève Aubuchon. (p. 420)
—Forget-Me-Not Keating, Nancy, illus. (p. 619)
—Little Dog Moon Fernandez, Laura & Jacobson, Rick, illus. (p. 1027)
—Long White Scarf. Craig, David, illus. (p. 1047)
—Loon Rock. Sylliboy, Helen, tr. (p. 1052)
—Migrant Arsenault, Isabelle, illus. (p. 1140)
—Mr. Hiroshi's Garden Morin, Paul, illus. (p. 1185)
—One Is Canada. (p. 1295)
—Paint Box East, Stella, illus. (p. 1318)
—Three Songs for Courage. (p. 1744)
—Walking Stick Galouchko, Annouchka, illus. (p. 1854)
Trottot, Tammy. Little Judy Talks to God. (p. 1029)
Trought, Susan. Harbour Cafe. (p. 747)
—Jimmy Miller. (p. 918)
Troughton, Guy, illus. see Evans, Lynette.
Troughton, Joanna. Animal Wrestlers. (p. 80)
—Tiger Child: A Folk Tale from India. Troughton, Joanna, illus. (p. 1748)
Troughton, Ruth. Invisible Ones. (p. 886)
Trouillot, Virgile, jt. auth. see Sarn, Amélie.
Troulis, Jennifer. Penelope & Priscilla: And the Enchanted House of Whispers. (p. 1336)
—Penelope & Priscilla & the City of the Banished. (p. 1336)
—Penelope & Prisilla & the Enchanted House of Whispers (p. 1336)
Troum, Carole. Sharing Chair: Tell about your holiday In... (p. 1561)
Trounce, Charlotte. San Francisco: A 3D Keepsake Cityscape. Trounce, Charlotte, illus. (p. 1510)
Trounce, Charlotte, illus. see Candlewick Press, Candlewick.
Trounstine, Connie / Remlinger. Fingerprints on the Table: The Story of the White House Treaty Table. Talbott, Kerry, illus. (p. 589)
Troupe, Thomas Kingsley. Are Bowling Balls Bullies? Learning about Forces & Motion with the Garbage Gang. Toye, Derek, illus. (p. 96)
—Big Hairy Secret Gilpin, Stephen, illus. (p. 181)
—Blow It Up! (p. 202)
—Crush It! (p. 386)
—Destruction. (p. 431)
—Diggin' Dirt: Science Adventures with Kitanai the Origami Dog Christoph, Jamey, illus. (p. 439)
—Do Ants Get Lost? Learning about Animal Communication with the Garbage Gang Toye, Derek, illus. (p. 456)
—Do Bees Poop? Learning about Living & Nonliving Things with the Garbage Gang Toye, Derek, illus. (p. 456)
—Do Plants Have Heads? Learning about Plant Parts with the Garbage Gang. Toye, Derek, illus. (p. 457)
—Fighting a Fire, Step by Step (p. 585)
—Furry & Flo (p. 650)
—Garbage Gang's Super Science Questions Toye, Derek, illus. (p. 655)
—Glowing with Electricity: Science Adventures with Glenda the Origami Firefly Christoph, Jamey, illus. (p. 685)
—I Want to Be... Rodriguez, Christina Ann et al, illus. (p. 847)
—I Want to Be a Bald Eagle. Rodriguez, Christina Ann, illus. (p. 847)
—I Want to Be a Crocodile. Wald, Christina, illus. (p. 847)
—I Want to Be a Great White Shark. Boey, Stephanie, illus. (p. 847)
—I Want to Be a Lion. Beavers, Melinda, illus. (p. 847)
—If I Were a Ballerina Heyworth, Heather, illus. (p. 853)
—If I Were a Firefighter Reid, Mick, illus. (p. 853)
—If I Were the President Heyworth, Heather, illus. (p. 853)
—If I Were the President [Scholastic]. Heyworth, Heather, illus. (p. 853)
—Kitanai & Cavity Croc Brush Their Teeth. Christoph, Jamey, illus. (p. 962)
—Kitanai & Filthy Flamingo Wash Up. Christoph, Jamey, illus. (p. 962)
—Kitanai & Hungry Hare Eat Healthfully. Christoph, Jamey, illus. (p. 962)
—Kitanai & Lazy Lizard Get Fit. (p. 962)
—Kitanai & Lazy Lizard Get Fit. Christoph, Jamey, illus. (p. 962)
—Kitanai's Healthy Habits. Christoph, Jamey, illus. (p. 962)
—Knock It Down! (p. 965)
—Legend of Atlantis Cressy, Mike, illus. (p. 988)
—Legend of Bigfoot Dumm, Brian Caleb, illus. (p. 988)
—Legend of the Bermuda Triangle Aon, Carlos & Aón, Carlos, illus. (p. 989)
—Legend of the Loch Ness Monster Ice, D. C., illus. (p. 989)
—Legend of the Vampire Kemarskaya, Oksana, illus. (p. 989)
—Legend of the Werewolf Ice, D. C., illus. (p. 989)
—Legend of UFOs Vignaga, Francesca Dafne, illus. (p. 989)
—Magnet Power! Science Adventures with MAG-3000 the Origami Robot Christoph, Jamey, illus. (p. 1075)
—Margo & Marky's Adventures in Reading Vasquez, Natalia, illus. (p. 1092)
—Misplaced Mummy Gilpin, Stephen, illus. (p. 1151)
—Mount Rushmore Skeens, Matthew, illus. (p. 1180)
—Problems with Goblins Gilpin, Stephen, illus. (p. 1408)
—Quinn & Penny Investigate How to Research Otero, Sole, illus. (p. 1428)
—Shred It! (p. 1571)
—Skeletons in City Park Gilpin, Stephen, illus. (p. 1584)
—Solemn Golem. Gilpin, Stephen, illus. (p. 1607)
—Truth about Elves Squier, Robert, illus. (p. 1794)
—Truth about Trolls Taylor, Bridget Starr, illus. (p. 1794)
—Voiceless Vampire. Gilpin, Stephen, illus. (p. 1848)
—What's with the Long Naps, Bears? Learning about Hibernation with the Garbage Gang. Toye, Derek, illus. (p. 1900)
—Why Do Dead Fish Float? Learning about Matter with the Garbage Gang Toye, Derek, illus. (p. 1923)
—Why Does My Body Make Bubbles? Learning about the Digestive System with the Garbage Gang. Toye, Derek, illus. (p. 1924)
—Wild Weather: Science Adventures with Sonny the Origami Bird Christoph, Jamey, illus. (p. 1930)
—You Call That a Nose? Learning about Human Senses with the Garbage Gang. Toye, Derek, illus. (p. 1973)
—Your Life as a Settler in Colonial America. Canga, C. B., illus. (p. 1981)
—Your Life As an Explorer on a Viking Ship. Ebbeler, Jeffrey, illus. (p. 1981)
Troupe, Thomas Kingsley, jt. auth. see Braun, Eric.
Troupe, Thomas Kingsley & Braun, Eric. Origami Science Adventures. Christoph, Jamey, illus. (p. 1304)
Troupe, Thomas Kingsley & Ebbeler, Jeffrey. Truth about Dragons Troupe, Thomas Kingsley & Ebbeler, Jeffrey, illus. (p. 1794)
Troupe, Thomas Kingsley, et al. Making a Jack-O'-Lantern. (p. 1080)
Trousdale, Jonathan & Skindzier, Jon. Georgia Tech College Prowler off the Record: Inside Georgia Institute of Technology. (p. 665)
Trousdale, Taryn, illus. see Pelz, Ramona.
Trout Fishing in America Staff & Jorisch, Stéphane. Chicken Joe Forgets Something Important. (p. 300)
Trout Fishing in America Staff, et al. My Name Is Chicken Joe. Jorisch, Stéphane, illus. (p. 1215)
Trout, Holly Christian. Firefly Who Lost Her Way. (p. 592)
Trout, Jenny. Such Sweet Sorrow. (p. 1672)
Trout, John, Jr. Hunting Rutting Bucks: Secrets for Tagging the Biggest Buck of Your Life! (p. 829)
Trout, Judy, jt. auth. see Kinney, Cyndi.
Trout, Laura. POGIL Activities for High School Biology. (p. 1376)
—POGIL Activities for High School Chemistry. (p. 1376)
Trout, Lisa, jt. auth. see Wells, Elizabeth.
Trout, Richard. Czar of Alaska: The Cross of Charlemagne (p. 397)
—Devil's Breath Volcano (p. 432)
—Eclipse of the Jaguar (p. 502)
—Elephant Tears: Mask of the Elephant (p. 511)
—Sign of the Dragon (p. 1574)
Trout, Richard E. Cayman Gold: Lost Treasure of Devils Grotto (p. 282)
—Falcon of Abydos: Oracle of the Nile (p. 565)
Trout, Robert J. Drumbeat: The Story of a Civil War Drummer Boy. (p. 487)
—Two-Bits: A Horse Tale of Courage & Devotion - Based on a True Story. (p. 1803)
Troutman, Kathryn K. Creating Your High School Resume, Second Edition: A Step-by-Step Guide to Preparing an Effective Resume for Jobs, College & Training Programs. (p. 379)
Troutman, Naamah M. Sheer Luck. (p. 1564)
Troutman, Pamela. Deadly Diamonds. (p. 417)
Troutt, Susan. Math Problem. (p. 1107)
—Not As It Seems. (p. 1267)
Trouvé, Marianne Lorraine. Saint Catherine Labouré: And Our Lady of the Miraculous Medal. (p. 1503)
Trouve, Marianne Lorraine. Saint Clare of Assisi: A Light for the World. Peterson, Mary Joseph, illus. (p. 1503)
Trouvé, Marianne Lorraine. Saint Thomas Aquinas: Missionary of Truth. Morrison, Cathy, illus. (p. 1504)
Trouve, Marianne Lorraine, tr. see Selucky, Oldrich.
Trover, Zachary. Spring Chicken! (p. 1635)
Trover, Zachary, illus. see Aboff, Marcie.
Trover, Zachary, illus. see Attebury, Nancy Garhan.
Trover, Zachary, illus. see Brill, Marlene Targ.
Trover, Zachary, illus. see Dahl, Michael.
Trover, Zachary, illus. see Emerson, Carl.
Trover, Zachary, illus. see Jones, Christianne C.
Trover, Zachary, illus. see Kemper, Bitsy.
Trover, Zachary, illus. see Littlefield, Holly.
Trover, Zachary, illus. see Patrick, Jean L. S.
Trover, Zachary, illus. see Random House Staff.
Trover, Zachary, illus. see Ransom, Candice.
Trover, Zachary, illus. see Roop, Peter & Roop, Connie.
Trover, Zachary, illus. see Shea, Kitty.
Trover, Zachary, illus. see Slater, David Michael.
Trover, Zachary, illus. see Tourville, Amanda Doering.
Trover, Zachary, illus. see Wetterer, Margaret K.
Trover, Zachary, illus. see Wetterer, Margaret K. & Wetterer, Charles M.
Trow, M. J. Lestrade & the Ripper. (p. 994)
—Lestrade & the Sawdust Ring. (p. 994)
—Lestrade & the Sign of Nine. (p. 994)
Trowbridge, J. T. Lawrence's Adventures among the Ice-Cutters, Glass-Makers, Coal-Miners, Iron-Men, & Ship-Builders by J T Trowbridge. (p. 981)
Trowbridge, John Townsend. My Own Story. (p. 1216)
—Pair of Madcaps. (p. 1318)
—Poetical Works. (p. 1376)
Trowbridge, Terri. Tulowly the Possum. McConkey, Barbara, illus. (p. 1796)
Trowell, Cynthia. Out of the Mist: A Survival Guide for Young Adults. (p. 1311)
Trowell, Michelle. Magical Mermaids. Top That Publishing Staff, ed. (p. 1075)
—Magnetic My First Words Day's Out. (p. 1075)
—Magnetic My First Words School Days. (p. 1075)
—Pilot Your Own Deep-Sea Submarine. Dronsfield, Paul, illus. (p. 1359)
Troxell, Melanie. David Asks Why: Ellen G. White's Classic Steps to Christ Adapted to Children. (p. 410)
Troy, Andy, illus. see Wyatt, Chris.
Troy, Don. Booker T. Washington. (p. 212)
—W. E. B. du Bois. (p. 1851)
Troy, Ellen. Mr. Beasley Takes a Chance. (p. 1184)
Troy, Michael, illus. see Morris, Elizabeth.
Troy, Tony, illus. see Tarico, Valerie.
Troyan, Slava & Katya. Brave Little Girl, Scary Chuchurella & a Christmas Tree. Chikvaidze, Yuriy, illus. (p. 223)
Troyer, Gloria Irene. Beatrice & the Snow People. (p. 153)
Truax, Lois. Grandmothers Are Magic. (p. 709)
Truchses, Susan Ruth. Time to Be. (p. 1753)
Truckey, Don. Adventures of Caraway Kim... Right Wing. (p. 17)
—Adventures of Caraway Kim... Southpaw. Macintyre, R P, ed. (p. 17)
Trudeau, Lawrence J., jt. ed. see Schoenberg, Thomas J.
Trudeau, Paul. Where Did We Come From? (p. 1906)
Trudeau, Scott & Holzbauer, David. Treasure to Share: Adventures in Social Skills. Trudeau, Scott, illus. (p. 1782)
Trudel, Jean-Louis. Princesse de Tianjin. (p. 1406)
Trudel, Marcel. Jumonville Affair: The French Perspective of the Jumonville Skirmish & the Prelude to the Battle of Fort Necessity. Kent, Donald H., tr. (p. 933)
Trudel, Robin Edward. Carving for Kids: An Introduction to Woodcarving. (p. 273)
Trudel, Sylvain & Langlois, Suzane. Pourquoi le Monde Est Comme il Est? (p. 1389)
Trudell, Devin. 3 Stories. (p. 1991)
Trudgian, Sherri. Psalm 1 for Kidz: I'm So Happy I Want to Shout! Moreland Krass, Melanie, illus. (p. 1413)
Trudi, Strain Trueit. ADHD. (p. 12)
True, J. J. Billy Brite: Africa & Beyond. (p. 187)
True, John Preston. Iron Star. (p. 888)
Trueba, Jose Luis. Descubre... La Tierra y el Cosmos. Cortes, Osvaldo, illus. (p. 428)
—Descubre... Las Raices de Mexico. Cortes, Osvaldo, illus. (p. 428)
—Descubre... Los Animales. Cortes, Osvaldo, illus. (p. 428)
Trueblood, Dawn. Bethlehem Star. (p. 171)
Trueblood, Valerie. Seven Loves. (p. 1554)
Trueit, Trudi. Mom, There's a Dinosaur in Beeson's Lake. Paillot, Jim, illus. (p. 1161)
—No Girls Allowed (Dogs Okay) Paillot, Jim, illus. (p. 1258)
—Scab for Treasurer? Paillot, Jim, illus. (p. 1519)
—Stealing Popular. (p. 1646)
—What Is Poetry? (p. 1890)
Trueit, Trudi Strain. Animal Physical Therapist. (p. 79)
—Animal Trainer. (p. 80)
—Animation. (p. 84)
—Ants. (p. 90)
—Beetles. (p. 158)
—Birds. (p. 191)
—Boston Tea Party. (p. 215)
—Camera. (p. 256)
—Caterpillars. (p. 279)
—Caterpillars & Butterflies. (p. 280)
—Christmas. (p. 312)
—Christmas. Bryan-Hunt, Jan, illus. (p. 312)
—Cloudy Days. (p. 335)
—Dragonflies. (p. 478)
—Easter. Huang, Benrei, illus. (p. 499)
—Eating Disorders. (p. 501)
—Frogs & Toads. (p. 641)
—Giant Pandas. (p. 674)
—Grasshoppers. (p. 711)

T

—Grizzly Bears. (p. 724)
—Gunpowder. (p. 732)
—Halloween. (p. 737)
—Hanukkah. (p. 744)
—Hanukkah. Thornburgh, Rebecca, illus. (p. 744)
—Horse Care. (p. 799)
—Jellyfish. (p. 912)
—Keeping a Journal. (p. 947)
—Lizards. (p. 1043)
—Martin Luther King Jr. Day. (p. 1098)
—Martin Luther King, Jr. Day. Snyder, Joel, illus. (p. 1098)
—Massachusetts. (p. 1102)
—Mississippi. (p. 1154)
—Mom, There's a Dinosaur in Beeson's Lake. Paillot, Jim, illus. (p. 1161)
—Octopuses. (p. 1278)
—Polar Bears. (p. 1379)
—Rainy Days. (p. 1436)
—Rocks, Gems, & Minerals. (p. 1484)
—Sharks. (p. 1562)
—Slugs, Snails & Worms. (p. 1591)
—Slugs, Snails, & Worms. (p. 1591)
—Snowy Days. (p. 1601)
—Spiders. (p. 1627)
—Squirrels. (p. 1637)
—Starfish. (p. 1642)
—Stormy Days. (p. 1656)
—Sunny Days. (p. 1677)
—Thanksgiving. (p. 1725)
—Thomas Jefferson. (p. 1739)
—Utah. (p. 1829)
—Valentine's Day. (p. 1830)
—Veterinarian. (p. 1839)
—Video Gaming. (p. 1841)
—Vikings. (p. 1842)
—What Is Poetry? (p. 1890)
—Wildlife Conservationist. (p. 1931)
—Windy Days. (p. 1936)
—Worms. (p. 1961)
Trueit, Trudi Strain, jt. auth. see Bjorklund, Ruth.
Trueit, Trudi Strain & Strain-Trueit, Trudi. Diwali. (p. 455)
—Earth Day. (p. 495)
—Independence Day. (p. 870)
Trueman, jt. auth. see Terry, Trueman.
Trueman, jt. auth. see Trueman, Terry.
Trueman, Matthew, illus. see Lasky, Kathryn.
Trueman, Matthew, illus. see London, Jonathan.
Trueman, Matthew, illus. see Rockwell, Anne F.
Trueman, Matthew, jt. auth. see Kimmel, Eric A.
Trueman, Terry. 7 Days at the Hot Corner. (p. 1992)
—Cruise Control. (p. 386)
—Hurricane. (p. 829)
—Inside Out. (p. 877)
—Life Happens Next. (p. 1010)
—No Right Turn. (p. 1260)
Trueman, Terry & Trueman. Stuck in Neutral. (p. 1668)
Truesdell, Ann. Being Respectful Online. Petelinsek, Kathleen, illus. (p. 161)
—Find New Words with Dictionaries. (p. 587)
—Find the Facts with Encyclopedias. (p. 587)
—Fire Away: Asking Great Interview Questions. (p. 590)
—Get to the Right Site. (p. 668)
—How to Handle Cyberbullies. Petelinsek, Kathleen, illus. (p. 820)
—Make Your Point: Creating Powerful Presentations. (p. 1080)
—Present It! Creating & Sharing a Slide Show. (p. 1396)
—Super Smart Information Strategies: Find the Right Site. (p. 1681)
—Wonderful Wikis. (p. 1948)
Truesdell, Ann, jt. auth. see Fontichiaro, Kristin.
Truesdell, Ann & Fontichiaro, Kristin. Starting Your Own Blog. Petelinsek, Kathleen, illus. (p. 1644)
Truesdell, Charlotte White. Steinway Kitty. (p. 1646)
Truesdell, Sue, illus. see Byars, Betsy.
Truesdell, Sue, illus. see George, Jean Craighead.
Truesdell, Sue, illus. see Grant, Judyann Ackerman.
Truesdell, Sue, illus. see Grant, Judyann.
Truesdell, Sue, illus. see Hamburg, Jennifer.
Truesdell, Sue, illus. see Little, Jean.
Truesdell, Sue, illus. see Stainton, Sue.
Truet, Turin & Gilman, Laura Anne. Searching for Yeti: The Abominable Snowman. (p. 1538)
Truette, Charlotte. Adam's Adventure: Walking in the Footsteps of History in His Hometown. (p. 11)
Trufant, Robert & Mullins, Tinnesha. Angel Fingers Series: Na'dyd Goes to School. (p. 73)
Truillo, Francisco. Conquista para Ninos. (p. 358)
Truitt, Gloria. Jesus bendice a los ninos (Jesus Blesses the Children)- Bilingual. Fernández, Cecilia, ed. (p. 915)
Truitt, Tiffany. Naturals. (p. 1236)
Trujillo, Rafael E. Mira: La Granja. Liu, Kimi, illus. (p. 1148)
—Mira. Liu, Kimi, illus. (p. 1148)
—ultima ola de Marianela. Liu, Kimi, illus. (p. 1809)
Trujillo, Robert, illus. see Bertrand, Diane Gonzales & Ventura, Gabriela Baeza.
Trujillo, Ron. Bird & the Butterfly. (p. 190)
Trukhan, Ekaterina. Five Little Ducks. (p. 600)
—Me & My Cat. (p. 1115)
—Patrick Wants a Dog! (p. 1329)
Trukhan, Ekaterina, illus. see Ziefert, Harriet.
Trulock, Alison. Build Your Own Snow Globe. (p. 238)
Truly Blessed Ink. I Know You Won't Forget. Jordan, Carol, illus. (p. 840)
Truman, Dennay H. Happy Endings. (p. 745)
Truman, Margaret. President's House: 1800 to the Present - The Secrets & History of the World's Most Famous Home. (p. 1397)
Truman, Timothy & Dixon, Chuck. Airboy (p. 31)
Trumbauer, Lisa. Abraham Lincoln & the Civil War (p. 6)
—Abraham Lincoln y la Guerra Civil (p. 7)
—All about Light. (p. 42)
—All about Sound. (p. 43)
—Animal Giants. (p. 78)
—Aztec World. (p. 122)
—Brain Quest Workbook: A Whole Year of Curriculum-Based Exercises & Activities in One Fun Book! Rogers, Betsy, ed. (p. 222)
—Brain Quest Workbook: Kindergarten - A Whole Year of Curriculum-Based Exercises & Activities in One Fun Book! Oliver, Kimberly, ed. (p. 222)
—Corn. (p. 367)
—Dachshunds Saunders-Smith, Gail, ed. (p. 398)
—Diente esta Flojo: A Tooth Is Loose. Gray, Steve, illus. (p. 437)
—Discover the Rain Forest. (p. 448)
—Double the Animals. (p. 473)
—Earthquake! (p. 497)
—Eating Well. (p. 501)
—Eleanor Roosevelt Saunders-Smith, Gail, ed. (p. 508)
—First Americans (p. 593)
—George Washington & the Revolutionary War (p. 664)
—George Washington y la Guerra Revolucionaria (p. 665)
—German Immigrants. (p. 666)
—Glaciers. (p. 682)
—Golden Retrievers Saunders-Smith, Gail, ed. (p. 695)
—Golden Retrievers/Golden Retrievers. (p. 695)
—Great Reindeer Rebellion. Ho, Jannie, illus. (p. 718)
—Hopes Fulfilled: The Irish Immigrants in Boston. (p. 797)
—Inca World. (p. 868)
—King Ludwig's Castle: Germany's Neuschwanstein. (p. 958)
—Let's Graph. (p. 998)
—Life Cycle of a Butterfly (p. 1009)
—Life Cycle of a Cat (p. 1009)
—Life Cycle of a Chicken (p. 1009)
—Life Cycle of a Dog (p. 1009)
—Life Cycle of a Frog (p. 1009)
—Life Cycle of a Grasshopper (p. 1009)
—Life Cycle of a Kangaroo (p. 1009)
—Life Cycle of a Penguin (p. 1009)
—Life Cycle of a Salmon (p. 1009)
—Life Cycle of a Turtle (p. 1009)
—Life Cycle of a Whale (p. 1009)
—Lighthouses of North America! Exploring Their History, Lore & Science. Kline, Michael, illus. (p. 1015)
—Living in a City (p. 1041)
—Living in a Rural Area (p. 1041)
—Living in a Suburb (p. 1041)
—Lo Que Hacen los Carteros. (p. 1044)
—Maya World. (p. 1113)
—Mountain Manor Mystery. Hawkes, Kevin, illus. (p. 1181)
—National Parks. (p. 1233)
—Paul Revere (p. 1330)
—Paul Revere. Saunders-Smith, Gail, ed. (p. 1330)
—Pennsylvania, 1643-1776. (p. 1338)
—Pocahontas & the Early Colonies (p. 1375)
—Pocahontas y las Primeras Colonias. (p. 1375)
—Poodles/Poodles. (p. 1383)
—Primeros Norteamericanos. (p. 1401)
—Russian Immigrants. (p. 1498)
—Salchichas. (p. 1504)
—Sam Houston. Saunders-Smith, Gail, ed. (p. 1506)
—Set in Stone. (p. 1553)
—Sitting Bull (p. 1582)
—Sitting Bull. Saunders-Smith, Gail, ed. (p. 1582)
—Standoff: Remembering the Alamo Schoonover, Brent, illus. (p. 1639)
—Story of Orange Juice. (p. 1659)
—Tiny Life in Your Home. (p. 1756)
—To the Core... Earth's Structure. (p. 1759)
—Tooth Is Loose. Gray, Steve, illus. (p. 1768)
—Trees Are Terrific! (p. 1784)
—Water (p. 1862)
—We Need Construction Workers Saunders-Smith, Gail, ed. (p. 1867)
—Weathering & Erosion. (p. 1870)
—What Are Atoms. (p. 1879)
—What Does a Mail Carrier Do? (p. 1883)
—What Does a Nurse Do? (p. 1883)
—What Does a Truck Driver Do? (p. 1884)
—What Is an Insect? (p. 1888)
—What Is Electricity? (p. 1889)
—What Is Friction? (p. 1889)
—What Is Gravity? (p. 1889)
—What Is Volume? (p. 1891)
—Wisconsin. (p. 1939)
—Year in the Desert. (p. 1969)
Trumbauer, Lisa, jt. auth. see Catala, Ellen.
Trumbauer, Lisa, jt. auth. see Cipriano, Jeri.
Trumbauer, Lisa & Gray, Steve. Diente Está Flojo. Gray, Steve, illus. (p. 437)
Trumbauer, Lisa & Martin, Elena. ¿Caliente o Frío? (p. 253)
Trumbauer, Lisa & Reed, Janet. Partes de un Entero. (p. 1325)
Trumbauer, Lisa, et al. Fire Trucks (p. 591)
Trumbo, Stephen. Dreamers, Fantasies & Thrill Seekers. (p. 484)
—Friends of the Forest. (p. 638)
Trumbore, Cindy. Genie in the Book. Alley, R. W., illus. (p. 661)
—New Year's Around the World. (p. 1247)
—Prairie Dog Song: How One Small Animal Helps North America's Grasslands. Roth, Susan L., illus. (p. 1392)
Trumbore, Cindy, jt. auth. see Roth, Susan L.
Trumbull, Jamie. Barney Ford: Pioneer Businessman. (p. 139)
Trummel, D. Pauline. Reformed Baptist Sunday School Curriculum: New Testament Survey, year 2 Semester 1. Nichols, Gregory G., ed. (p. 1456)
Trump, D. I'm Dougal Trump... - Where's My Tarantula? (p. 858)
Trump, D. & Marchant, Jackie. I'm Dougal Trump... & It's Not My Fault! (p. 858)
Trump, Nicole. Infected. (p. 873)
Trumpet Club, Inc Staff, contrib. by. Young Authors of America. (p. 1978)
Trumpet Of God Ministries. E I I Children's Prayers from the Heart. (p. 492)
Trumpold, Brenda Lee. Mouse Tales: The Magic Begins. (p. 1182)
Trunick, Kimberley Olney. Paw Paw Duck Defeats Darkness. (p. 1331)
Trunkhill, Brenda. Christmas Around the World. Carnehl, Jeff, illus. (p. 312)
Truog, Chas, illus. see Morrison, Grant.
Truong, Anh Thuy. Chuyen Mua. (p. 318)
Truong, Marcelino, illus. see Marchon, Benoit & Rosa, Jean-Pierre.
Trupiano, Katie Belle, jt. auth. see Durango, Julia.
Truran, Stacy. Troy's Tree Fort: Measure Lengths in Standard Units. (p. 1790)
Truscelli, John J. Can P B Find the Jelly? (p. 258)
Truscott, Julia. Your Safari: In Search of the Real Komodo Dragon. White, Daniel, photos by. (p. 1981)
Trusdell, Brian. Great Moments in Olympic Skiing. (p. 717)
—Miracle on Ice. (p. 1148)
—Pel: Soccer Star & Ambassador. (p. 1335)
—US Women Win the World Cup. (p. 1826)
Trusler, Heidi Jo. Firecracker the Miniature Donkey: Makes A Marvelous Choice! (p. 591)
Truss, Jan. Red. (p. 1453)
Truss, Lynne. Eats, Shoots & Leaves: Why, Commas Really Do Make a Difference! Timmons, Bonnie, illus. (p. 501)
—Girl's Like Spaghetti: Why, You Can't Manage Without Apostrophes! Timmons, Bonnie, illus. (p. 680)
—Twenty-Odd Ducks: Why, Every Punctuation Mark Counts! Timmons, Bonnie, illus. (p. 1801)
Trussell-Cullen, Alan. African Grasslands (p. 27)
—American Civics Teacher's Guide. (p. 60)
—American Revolution Teacher's Guide. (p. 63)
—Animal Disguises (p. 77)
—Animal Groups (p. 78)
—Animal Travellers (p. 80)
—Animals II Teacher's Guide. (p. 83)
—Animals Teacher's Guide. (p. 84)
—Antarctic Animals. (p. 88)
—Biographies Teacher's Guide. (p. 188)
—Character Education Teacher's Guide. (p. 291)
—Civil War Teacher's Guide. (p. 326)
—Colonial America Teacher's Guide. (p. 341)
—Community Helpers Teacher's Guide. (p. 350)
—Countries of the World Teacher's Guide. (p. 372)
—Early Civilizations Teacher's Guide. (p. 493)
—Earth & Space Teacher's Guide. (p. 495)
—Ecosystems Teacher's Guide. (p. 503)
—Edmund Hillary. (p. 504)
—Everyday Animals Teacher's Guide. (p. 543)
—Explore Space! II Teacher's Guide. (p. 550)
—Explore Space! Teacher's Guide. (p. 550)
—Exploring the West Teacher's Guide. (p. 554)
—Extreme Sports Teacher's Guide. (p. 557)
—Family Relationships Teacher's Guide. (p. 568)
—Galaxy Teacher's Guide. (p. 653)
—Great Inventions Teacher's Guide. (p. 716)
—Health & the Human Body II Teacher's Guide. (p. 757)
—Health & the Human Body Teacher's Guide. (p. 757)
—Heating Up (p. 761)
—Holidays Teacher's Guide. (p. 788)
—Insect Sounds. (p. 875)
—Insects Teacher's Guide. (p. 876)
—Insects Teacher's Guide, Grade 5. (p. 876)
—Jackie Robinson. (p. 903)
—Lonely Penguin's Blog. (p. 1046)
—Mahatma Gandhi. (p. 1076)
—Maui Tames the Sun: Band 15/Emerald. Vol. 7 Grimwood, Tracie, illus. (p. 1110)
—Mother Teresa. (p. 1178)
—Move It! (p. 1183)
—Native People Teacher's Guide. (p. 1235)
—Natural Partners (p. 1235)
—Nelson Mandela. (p. 1240)
—Photo-Illustrated Biographies II Teacher's Guide. (p. 1352)
—Photo-Illustrated Biographies Teacher's Guide. (p. 1352)
—Plant Life Teacher's Guide. (p. 1369)
—Plastic World. (p. 1370)
—Princess Diana. (p. 1403)
—Rigby PM Math Readers. (p. 1472)
—Sam the Incredible Inventor. (p. 1507)
—Transportation Teacher's Guide. (p. 1779)
—Twin Competition. Hurst, Elise, illus. (p. 1801)
—Weather & Seasons Teacher's Guide. (p. 1870)
—Wild Rides! Teacher's Guide. (p. 1930)
—Wildlife of North America Teacher's Guide. (p. 1931)
—Winston Churchill. (p. 1937)
—World Cultures Teacher's Guide. (p. 1954)
Trussoni, Danielle. Falling Through the Earth: A Memoir. (p. 567)
Trust, Richard. Baseball Pictionary. (p. 141)
Trusty, Brad & Trusty, Cindy. Kids' Guide to Balloon Twisting (p. 953)
Trusty, Cindy, jt. auth. see Trusty, Brad.
Truswell, P. Diane. Star Climber. (p. 1640)
Tryon, Leslie, illus. see Chocolate, Debbi.
Tryon, Leslie, illus. see Flor Ada, Alma.
Trzasko, Cheryl. Around the World in a Cement Boat: A Young Girl's True Adventure. (p. 101)
Tsahiridis, Van. Peree' & the Magic Fish: Fairy Tale from Pontos. (p. 1341)
Tsai, Dora, illus. see Young, Lena.
Tsaioun, Katya & Kates, Steven A., eds. ADMET for Medicinal Chemists: A Practical Guide. (p. 13)
Tsairis, Jeannie Brett, illus. see Crane, Carol.
Tsakiridis, Dimitra. Art & Culture of Ancient Greece. (p. 101)
Tsakiridis, Dimitra & Bardi, Matilde. Art & Culture of Ancient Greece. (p. 101)
Tsaliovich, Anatoly. Of Wolves & Lambs & Others. Burke, Daniel, illus. (p. 1279)
Tsang, Evonne. #01 I Love Him to Pieces. Görrissen, Janina, illus. (p. 1991)
—I Love Him to Pieces. Görrissen, Janina, illus. (p. 842)
—Kung Fu Masters. Martinez, Alitha E., illus. (p. 968)
Tsang, Evonne & Jimenez, Adan. Hero City. BaróN, Lara & Torres, German, illus. (p. 772)
—Hero City. Barón, Lara & Torres, German, illus. (p. 772)
Tsang, Nina, jt. auth. see Sohn, Emily.
Tsang, Sonic. Little Cog. (p. 1026)
Tsao, Don. Anna Gets Her Vaccination. (p. 85)
Tsao, Jessica. Peacebringers. (p. 1332)
Tsavalas, Helena Macree. Dazzling Beast. (p. 415)
Tschanz, Mary K. & Myers, Theresa F., texts. Jesus Walks with Us. (p. 916)
Tschirky, Hugo, jt. auth. see Sauber, Tim.
Tschudi, Bob & Tschudi, Marilyn Howard. Club4Girls: #1: the Girls with Boys' Names. (p. 335)
Tschudi, Marilyn Howard, jt. auth. see Tschudi, Bob.
Tse, Brian. This Is the Greatest Place! A Palace Inspired by the World of Small Animals. Steinhardt, Nancy S., ed. (p. 1736)
Tse, Glenda, illus. see Paleja, S. N.
Tseng, Jean, illus. see Park, Linda Sue.
Tseng, Mou-Sien, illus. see Park, Linda Sue.
Tshekeche. Old Order Changes. Curtis King, Anna, illus. (p. 1284)
—Tsuro to the Rescue. Curtis King, Anna, illus. (p. 1795)
Tshekeche, Anna. Old Order Changes. (p. 1284)
Tshekeche, Anna & Curtis King. Tsuro to the Rescue. (p. 1795)
Tshionyi, Muabilai. Reach from Within, Dreams Never Die. (p. 1442)
Tsiang, Sarah. Flock of Shoes. Leng, Qin, illus. (p. 605)
—Warriors & Wailers: One Hundred Ancient Chinese Jobs You Might Have Relished or Reviled. Newbigging, Martha, illus. (p. 1859)
Tsibana, Rosana, tr. see Close, Rosa.
Tsien, Billie, jt. auth. see Williams, Tod.
Tsilis, Thanos, illus. see Homer.
Tsin, Justin. What Would You Imagine? (p. 1895)
Tsinajinnie, Veronica. Johonaa'éi: Bringer of Dawn. Thomas, Peter A., tr. from NAV. (p. 924)
Tsintziras, Aya. Pretty Bones (p. 1398)
Tsitoukis, Kristen L. Tooth Song. (p. 1768)
Tsogyal, Yeshe. Lotus-Born: The Life Story of Padmasambhava. Kunsang, Erik Pema, tr. from TIB. (p. 1057)
Tsong, Jing Jing. Aloha Zoo. (p. 48)
—Counting Birds. (p. 370)
—Sam Surfs. (p. 1507)
Tsong, Jing Jing, illus. see Hyde, Heidi Smith.
Tsong, Jing Jing, illus. see Melmed, Laura Krauss.
Tsong, Jing Jing, illus. see Sehgal, Kabir & Sehgal, Surishtha.
Tsosie, Dennison, illus. see Alexander, Carmen.
Tsoukanelis, Erika Alexia. Latin Music Scene: The Stars, the Fans, the Music. (p. 979)
Tsoukas, Mary Esworthy. Santa Pledge. (p. 1513)
Tsubaki, Izumi. Magic Touch. Tsubaki, Izumi, illus. (p. 1074)
Tsuchiya, Fujio, illus. see Yoshiike, Yoshitaka.
Tsuda, Efrain Rodriguez, illus. see Dubuvoy, Silvia, et al.
Tsuda, Masami. Kare Kano (p. 943)
—Kare Kano: His & Her Circumstances Vols. 1-3 (p. 943)
—Kare Kano: His & Her Circumstances Vols. 1-3 Tsuda, Masami, illus. (p. 943)
—Kare Kano: His & Her Circumstances. Vols. 1-3 Tsuda, Masami, illus. (p. 943)
—Kare Kano: His & Her Circumstances Vols. 1-3 Niida, Jack, tr. from JPN. (p. 943)
—Kare Kano: His & Her Circumstances Vols. 1-3 Forsyth, Amy, tr. from JPN. (p. 943)
—Kare Kano: His & Her Circumstances Vols. 1-3 Kobayashi, Michelle, tr. from JPN. (p. 943)
—Kare Kano. (p. 943)
—Kare Kano - His & Her Circumstances Vol. 18 (p. 943)
Tsuda, Masami, illus. see Kobayashi, Michelle, tr.
Tsuda, Masami, creator. Kare Kano: His & Her Circumstances Vols. 1-3 (p. 943)
Tsuda, Mikiyo. Family Complex. (p. 568)
Tsukamoto, Allen. Somethin Fishy for the Small Fry. (p. 1609)
Tsukiyama, Gail. Dreaming Water. (p. 484)
Tsunetomo, Yamamoto & Wilson, William Scott. Hagakure: The Code of the Samurai. Kutsuwada, Chie, illus. (p. 735)
Tu, Alice. Fair Is Fun (p. 562)
—Fair Is Fun. (p. 562)
Tu, Alice & Capstone Press Staff. Fair Is Fun (p. 562)
Tu, Stella. Follow your Dream: Asian American Essay. (p. 612)
Tu, Tzu Hui. Traveling Tree. (p. 1780)
Tuason, Scott, illus. see Turner, Pamela S.
Tuason, Scott, photos by see Turner, Pamela S.
Tubb, Kristin O' Donnell. 13th Sign. (p. 1995)
—Selling Hope. (p. 1550)
Tubb, Kristin O'Donnell. Freedom from Cruel & Unusual Punishment. (p. 634)
Tubb, Kristin O'Donnell & Troisi-Paton, Kimberly. Freedom from Unfair Searches & Seizures. (p. 634)
Tubbs, Stephen Philip. PSpice Power Electronic & Power Circuit Simulation: Practical Examples Using the PSpice a/d Demo to Simulate Power Electronic & Electrical Power Circuits. (p. 1413)
Tuber, Douglas & Maile, Tim. Lizzie's Nightmare; Sibling Bonds (p. 1043)
Tucci, Al, illus. see Kivel, Lee.
Tucci, Billy. Shi: Ju-Nen. (p. 1566)
Tucci, Paul A. & Rosenberg, Mathew T. Handy Geography Answer Book. (p. 741)
Tuccy, Alycia, illus. see Tuccy, Angel.
Tuccy, Angel. Mommy Has Lots to Do. Tuccy, Alycia, illus. (p. 1162)
Tuch, Hans N. Arias, Cabalettas, & Foreign Affairs: A Public Diplomat's Quasi-Musical Memoir. (p. 98)
Tuchman, Gail. Race Day! (p. 1430)
—Race Day. (p. 1430)
—Safari. (p. 1501)
—Scholastic Discover More Reader Level 1: Busy Butterflies. (p. 1521)
Tuchman, Gail, jt. auth. see Arlon, Penelope.
Tuchman, Gail & Buckley, James, Jr. Dolphin Dive. (p. 464)
Tuchman, Gail & Gray, Margaret. AddUps Fun for All Seasons! Griego, Tony, illus. (p. 12)
—AddUps Going Places! Griego, Tony, illus. (p. 12)
—AddUps My Day! Griego, Tony, illus. (p. 12)
—AddUps Things That Go! Griego, Tony, illus. (p. 12)

T

Tuchman, Laura. Welcome to the Daisy Flower Garden. Kalis, Jennifer, illus. (p. 1874)
Tuchman, Laura, jt. auth. see Welsh, Anne Marie.
Tuchman, Lauryn & Silverhardt, Lauryn. Visit to the Firehouse. Craig, Karen, illus. (p. 1845)
Tucholke, April Genevieve. Between the Devil & the Deep Blue Sea. (p. 173)
—Between the Spark & the Burn. (p. 173)
—Slasher Girls & Monster Boys. (p. 1588)
Tuck, Beverly, illus. see Webb, Mack Henry, Jr.
Tuck, Helen. House at the Bend of Contently Creek. Melton, Eric, illus. (p. 803)
Tuck, Justin. Home-Field Advantage. Rodriguez, Leonardo, illus. (p. 792)
Tuck, Mildred. Child's Book of Miracles & Wonders. Moroney, Tracey, illus. (p. 304)
Tuck, Pamela M. As Fast As Words Could Fly Velasquez, Eric, illus. (p. 105)
Tuck-Bernstein, Cheryl, illus. see Rosen, Wendy & End, Jackie.
Tucker, Amanda, illus. see Valentine, Victoria.
Tucker and Hossler Staff, photos by see Croce, Julia Della & Williams-Sonoma Staff.
Tucker, Angel. Four Pals on a Field Trip: An Adventure with Friends Who Are Different. Pileggi, Steve, illus. (p. 625)
Tucker, Barclay, illus. see Holzer, Angela.
Tucker, Charlotte Maria. Driven into Exile: A Story of the Huguenots. (p. 485)
Tucker, Clementine & Sakany, Lois. How Cell Processes Are Regulated (p. 805)
Tucker, Daniel. Buzzy the Bee-Ginning. (p. 249)
Tucker, Daniel Deon. Littlest Pumpkin (p. 1039)
Tucker, David J. Fourth Gift. (p. 625)
—Stickman World. (p. 1650)
—Stickman World Larry & George have a Merry Christmas. (p. 1650)
Tucker, Diane, ed. see Spence, Craig.
Tucker, Diane, illus. see Edelson, Madelyn.
Tucker, Diane, jt. auth. see Tucker, Diane L.
Tucker, Diane L. & Tucker, Diane. His Sweet Favour. (p. 781)
Tucker, E., illus. see Hazlett, V.
Tucker, Ellen. Cats in the Belfry. (p. 281)
Tucker, Eric, illus. see Wundram, Bill.
Tucker, Ezra, illus. see Blade, Adam.
Tucker, Ezra, illus. see Scholastic, Inc. Staff & Blade, Adam.
Tucker, Jasmin. Robot School. (p. 1480)
Tucker, Jasmine. Robbie the Robot. (p. 1478)
Tucker, Jason. Ferdinand Uses the Potty. West, D. E., illus. (p. 582)
Tucker, Jill C. Dylan Rides the Sleepy Town Express (p. 491)
Tucker, Joe & Tucker, Kathryn. Destiny Journal. (p. 431)
Tucker, Julie, illus. see Zajac, Kristen.
Tucker, Kathryn, jt. auth. see Tucker, Joe.
Tucker, Kathy. Do Pirates Take Baths? (p. 457)
—Leprechaun in the Basement. Sandford, John, illus. (p. 993)
—Seven Chinese Sisters. Lin, Grace, illus. (p. 1554)
Tucker, Kathy & Hong, Lily Toy. Seven Chinese Sisters Hong, Lily Toy & Lin, Grace, illus. (p. 1554)
Tucker, Keith, illus. see Fandel, Jennifer.
Tucker, Keith, illus. see Lemke, Donald & Lemke, Donald B.
Tucker, Keith, illus. see Niz, Ellen Sturm.
Tucker, Keith, illus. see Olson, Nathan.
Tucker, Lewis R., illus. see Gelber, Peter Frost.
Tucker, Lindy. Oddvark & the Yellow Kazoo. (p. 1278)
Tucker, Louise, ed. Visual Dictionary of Military Uniforms: Eyewitness Visual Dictionaries. (p. 1846)
Tucker, Margaret E. Biography of Richard Bullard: From Shoe Cobbler in England to Minister for Jesus Christ in America. (p. 189)
Tucker, Marianne, jt. illus. see Mosqueda, Olga T.
Tucker, Marianne & Gilbert, Elizabeth T. Watch Me Draw Cinderella's Enchanted World. (p. 1861)
Tucker, Marianne & Phillipson, Andy. Learn to Draw Plus Disney Pixar Cars. (p. 983)
Tucker, Mark. Super Phil. Petete, Christine, illus. (p. 1680)
—Super Phil & the Missing Mom. Patete, Christine, illus. (p. 1680)
—Super Phil & the Sphiddle of the Rinks. Patete, Christine, illus. (p. 1680)
Tucker, Mary. Christian Bulletin Board Ideas & Patterns: Holidays & Seasons. (p. 311)
—Cut & Create! Ocean Life. Mitchell, Judy & Lindeen, Mary, eds. (p. 395)
—Cut & Create! Spring & Summer. Mitchell, Judy & Lindeen, Mary, eds. (p. 395)
Tucker, Patricia Wright. Princess Who Couldn't Laugh. (p. 1406)
Tucker, Peter. Pumpkin Bunch. (p. 1416)
Tucker, Peter E. Pumpkin Bunch. (p. 1416)
Tucker, Regina E. Legend of the Lost Dutchman's Gold Mine. (p. 989)
—When History Sings, the Heart Listens: From Tales of Our Fathers, Songs of Our Mothers Poetry Series (p. 1902)
Tucker, Rosalyn. Famous Pirates. (p. 569)
—Pirate Gear. (p. 1362)
—Pirate Ships. (p. 1363)
—Pirate Treasure. (p. 1363)
—Pirates Ahoy! (p. 1363)
—Ronald Reagan (p. 1486)
Tucker, Rosalyn, jt. auth. see Hasselius, Michelle M.
Tucker, S. J. & Herring, Trudy. Rabbit's Song. Martin, W. Lyon, illus. (p. 1430)
Tucker, Sally A. Leo & Apollo: The Forbidden Land. (p. 992)
Tucker, Seletha Marie Head. Hat for Melinda: Fighting Leukemia Together. Lee, Anais, illus. (p. 752)
Tucker, Shannon. Hamsters in the House are No Better than a Mouse. (p. 740)
Tucker, Shelley. Painting the Sky. (p. 1318)
Tucker, Sian. My Book of First Numbers. Tucker, Sian, illus. (p. 1199)
—My Book of First Words. Tucker, Sian, illus. (p. 1199)
Tucker, Sian, illus. see Young, Jay.
Tucker Slingsby Ltd., Staff. My Big Book of Fairy Tales in Rhyme! Lewis, Jan, illus. (p. 1197)
Tucker, Spencer C. & Roberts, Priscilla Mary, eds. World War II: A Student Encyclopedia (p. 1959)
Tucker, Stephen, jt. auth. see Sharratt, Nick.
Tucker, Susan K. Ridiculously Ridiculous. Foster, Jack, illus. (p. 1471)
—Tucker's Chocolate Covered Bump! (p. 1795)
Tucker, Terra. Daughter of the King: Daughter of the King: Book with Audio CD. Marsee, Kimberly, illus. (p. 409)
Tucker, Tom. Bolt of Fate: Benjamin Franklin & His Electric Kite Hoax. (p. 208)
Tucker, Tracey, illus. see Black, Cassandra.
Tucker, Valerie Nell. Hermit's Box. (p. 771)
Tucker, Zekita. Don't Call Me N!gga. (p. 467)
Tudge, Colin. Alimentos para el Futuro. Barois, Lorena Stoopen, tr. (p. 41)
Tudhope, Simon. Build Your Own Cars Sticker Book. Shirley, John, illus. (p. 238)
—Build Your Own Motorcycles Sticker Book. (p. 238)
—Pencil & Paper Games. (p. 1336)
Tudhope, Simon, jt. ed. see Clarke, Phillip.
Tudhope, Simon & Cox, Phil Roxbee. Slot-Together Castle with an Usborne Book. (p. 1591)
Tudor, Andy. 200 Paper Planes. (p. 2001)
Tudor, Andy, illus. see Pearcey, Alice.
Tudor, Andy, illus. see Pratt, Leonie.
Tudor, Andy, illus. see Stowell, Louie & Pearcey, Alice.
Tudor, Andy, illus. see Turnbull, Stephanie.
Tudor, Tasha. A Is for Annabelle: A Doll's Alphabet. Tudor, Tasha, illus. (p. 1)
—Around the Year. Tudor, Tasha, illus. (p. 101)
—Corgiville Christmas. (p. 367)
—Tale for Easter. (p. 1699)
—Tale for Easter. Tudor, Tasha, illus. (p. 1699)
Tudor, Tasha, illus. see Burnett, Frances Hodgson.
Tudor, Tasha, illus. see Collins, Carolyn Strom & Eriksson, Christina Wyss.
Tudor, Tasha, illus. see Moore, Clement C.
Tudosa, Lucia, jt. auth. see Creanga, Emil.
Tudosa-Fundureanu, Lucia. Coloring Book Happy Vegetables. Chabvepi-Tudosa, Patricia, tr. (p. 344)
Tudyk, Adeline. Mystery of the Lost Fish. (p. 1225)
Tuel, Patricia, jt. auth. see Smart, Margaret.
Tuell, Julia E., photos by see Aadland, Dan & Michaelides, Marina.
Tuell, Todd. Ninja, Ninja, Never Stop! Carpenter, Tad, illus. (p. 1256)
Tueller, Joe R. Teacher & Puddin' Head. (p. 1709)
Tuey. Doug E Do. Martin, Susan, illus. (p. 473)
Tuffen, Hugh & Waldron, Melanie. Volcanologist: The Coolest Jobs on the Planet HL Studios Staff, illus. (p. 1849)
Tufts, Brianne. Princess Zoey & Moonbeam. (p. 1406)
Tufts, N. Jo, illus. see Wake, Shelley.
Tugeau, Jeremy. Animal Tales from Mother Goose. (p. 80)
—Cars, Trucks, & Planes. (p. 272)
—Count along with Mother Goose. (p. 369)
—Making Friends with Mother Goose. (p. 1081)
—Mother Goose Nursery Rhymes (p. 1178)
—Seeing Colors with Mother Goose. (p. 1548)
—Weather Fun with Mother Goose. (p. 1870)
Tugeau, Jeremy, illus. see Adams, Michelle M.
Tugeau, Jeremy, illus. see Butler, Dori Hillestad.
Tugeau, Jeremy, illus. see Edgers, Geoff.
Tugeau, Jeremy, illus. see Hedlund, Stephanie.
Tugeau, Jeremy, illus. see Herron, Caroliva.
Tugeau, Jeremy, illus. see Krensky, Stephen.
Tugeau, Jeremy, illus. see Lehman-Wilzig, Tami & Katzman, Nicole.
Tugeau, Jeremy, illus. see Rosa-Mendoza, Gladys.
Tuggle, Jeremy M. Rooted in Shasta County. (p. 1488)
Tuggle, Le Ann S. Let's Go Fishing. (p. 997)
Tugman, Etta. Smokey Mountain Bears. (p. 1594)
Tuitel, J. Adventure in Bear Tooth Mountains. (p. 14)
Tuitel, Johnnie & Lamson, Sharon. Light in Bradford Manor. (p. 1015)
Tujner-Marko, B., jt. auth. see Madl-Palfi, L.
Tukan, Jaytoe Anthony, Sr. John Reid Edwards: The People's Senator. (p. 922)
—Kitty cat had a Dream: Kingdom without a King. (p. 963)
—United States Senators from North Carolina 1954 - 2008. (p. 1820)
Tukel, Onur. Little Friends (p. 1028)
—Rainstack! (p. 1436)
Tukey, Paul & Rowell, Victoria. Tag, Toss & Run: 40 Classic Lawn Games. (p. 1695)
Tulani, K. Todd & Ricca: The Pepperoni Pizza. (p. 1761)
Tulien, Sean. Black Masquerade. Vecchio, Luciano, illus. (p. 196)
—Super Billy Goats Gruff. Cano, Fernando, illus. (p. 1679)
Tulien, Sean & Maese, Fares. Paintball Punk Aburto, Jesus & Esparza, Andres, illus. (p. 1318)
Tulien, Sean & Poe, Edgar Allen. Pit & the Pendulum Fabul, J. C. & Calero, Dennis, illus. (p. 1364)
Tulien, Sean, et al. Clock King's Time Bomb Schoening, Dan, illus. (p. 333)
—Shadow of the Sun (p. 1557)
Tulik, Alice, et al. Fishing Adventures. Tulik, Alice et al, illus. (p. 599)
Tulip, Jenny. My First Book of Numbers. (p. 1205)
—My First French Word Book. (p. 1206)
—My First Spanish Word Book. (p. 1208)
—Who Lives Here? (p. 1916)
—Who's Hiding in the Garden? (p. 1920)
—Who's Hiding in the Jungle? A Mystery Touch-and-Feel Flap Book! (p. 1920)
Tulip, Jenny, illus. see Clark, Isobel.
Tulip, Jenny, illus. see Clarke, Isabel.
Tulip, Jenny, illus. see Jeffs, Stephanie.
Tulip, Jenny, illus. see Somerville, Louisa & Smith, David.
Tulip, Jenny, illus. see Vaamonde, Conchita, tr.
Tulip, Jenny, illus. see Wotton, Joy.
Tulip, Jenny, jt. auth. see Jeffs, Stephanie.
Tull, Linda Handy. Fofo's Journey. (p. 611)
Tull, Mary. Deserts. (p. 429)
—Mountains. (p. 1181)
—Plains. (p. 1366)
—Rivers & Lakes. (p. 1476)
Tull, Mary & National Geographic Learning Staff. Coasts. (p. 336)
Tullet, Hervé. 10 Times 10. (p. 1994)
—Ball Game. (p. 134)
—Big Book of Art. (p. 178)
—Book with a Hole. (p. 212)
—Coloring Book. (p. 344)
—Countryside Game. (p. 372)
—Doodle Cook. Barbour, Susan, tr. from FRE. (p. 469)
—Eyes Game. (p. 558)
—Finger Circus Game. Oceano Editorial Staff, ed. (p. 589)
—Five Senses. (p. 601)
—Game in the Dark. (p. 654)
—Game of Finger Worms. (p. 654)
—Game of Let's Go! Edicare Staff, ed. (p. 654)
—Game of Light. (p. 654)
—Game of Lines. (p. 654)
—Game of Mirrors. (p. 654)
—Game of Mix & Match. Edicare, ed. (p. 654)
—Game of Mix-Up Art. (p. 654)
—Game of Patterns. (p. 654)
—Game of Red, Yellow & Blue. (p. 654)
—Game of Sculpture. (p. 654)
—Game of Shadows. (p. 654)
—Game of Tops & Tails. (p. 654)
—Giant Game of Sculpture. (p. 673)
—Good Morning Game. (p. 698)
—Help! We Need a Title! Tullet, Hervé, illus. (p. 766)
—I Am Blop! Stetter, tr. (p. 832)
—Mix It Up! (p. 1156)
—Press Here. (p. 1397)
—Press Here Game. (p. 1397)
—Scribble Book. (p. 1533)
—Trail Game. (p. 1776)
Tullet, Hervé & Perez, Peter L. Presiona Aqui. Perez, Peter L., illus. (p. 1397)
Tulley, Tara. Dancing Waters. Clark, K. C., illus. (p. 403)
Tullgren, Terrence. Donnie Makes New Friends: A Lesson in Eye-to-Eye Contact. Gibson, Charles, illus. (p. 466)
Tullgren, Tom. Journey to Imagiland. (p. 928)
Tullis, Jamie. Rudolph, I Think You Need Glasses! (p. 1494)
Tullis, Shaquiya, jt. auth. see Wimbush, Jalen.
Tulloch, Coral. Antarctica: The Heart of the World. (p. 88)
Tulloch, Coral, jt. auth. see Turnbull, Stephen.
Tulloch, Fiona, ed. Children's Bible: Illustrated Stories from the Old & New Testament. (p. 303)
Tulloch, Richard. Beastly Tales: Six Crazy Creature Capers. Denton, Terry, illus. (p. 152)
Tulloch, S. A. Night Prayers. (p. 1254)
Tulloch, Scott. Willy's Dad. Tulloch, Scott, illus. (p. 1934)
—Willy's Mum. (p. 1934)
Tulloch, Scott, jt. auth. see Jones, V. M.
Tullos, Matt. Vital Skills: How to Develop Communication Skills. (p. 1846)
Tullson, Diane. Blue Highway. (p. 203)
—Darwin Expedition (p. 409)
—Edge (p. 504)
—Lockdown (p. 1045)
—Red Sea (p. 1455)
—Riley Park (p. 1472)
—Riot Act (p. 1473)
—Sea Change (p. 1534)
—Zero. (p. 1986)
Tully, Justin. Lost from the Christmas Mansion. (p. 1055)
Tully, Lisa, jt. auth. see McLaughlin, Diane.
Tully, Sandra M. Cherry Pie Charlie & More Poems for Children. Sadowski, Jeff, illus. (p. 298)
Tulsidas. Sundarkaand: Triumph of Hanuman. Nagar, Sachin, illus. (p. 1676)
Tulup, Natalia, ed. see AZ Books Staff.
Tulup, Natasha, ed. see AZ Books Staff.
Tuma, Tomas. Gladiators. (p. 682)
Tuma, Tomas, illus. see Dusek, Jiri & Pisala, Jan.
Tumas, Grace, jt. auth. see Boyer, Marilyn.
Tumbrello, Shannon. Freedom Forest. (p. 634)
Tuminelly, Nancy. Cool Meat-Free Recipes: Delicious & Fun Foods Without Meat. (p. 363)
—Cool Nut-Free Recipes: Delicious & Fun Foods Without Nuts. (p. 364)
—Cool Raw Food Recipes: Delicious & Fun Foods Without Cooking. (p. 364)
—Cool Sugar-Free Recipes: Delicious & Fun Foods Without Refined Sugar. (p. 364)
—Cool Wheat-Free Recipes: Delicious & Fun Foods Without Gluten. (p. 364)
—Dixie's Big Heart: A Story about Alabama. Doucet, Bob, illus. (p. 455)
—Est As in Nest. (p. 537)
—Horse Shoes. Nobens, C. A., illus. (p. 800)
—Horse Shoes. Nobens, Cheryl A., illus. (p. 800)
—Let's Cook with Apples! Delicious & Fun Apple Dishes Kids Can Make. (p. 995)
—Let's Cook with Cereal! Delicious & Fun Cereal Dishes Kids Can Make. (p. 995)
—Let's Cook with Cheese! Delicious & Fun Cheese Dishes Kids Can Make. (p. 995)
—Let's Cook with Eggs! Delicious & Fun Egg Dishes Kids Can Make. (p. 995)
—Let's Cook with Noodles! Delicious & Fun Noodle Dishes Kids Can Make. (p. 995)
—Let's Cook with Popcorn! Delicious & Fun Popcorn Dishes Kids Can Make. (p. 995)
—Missy the Show-Me Mule: A Story about Missouri. Doucet, Bob, illus. (p. 1155)
—Ook As in Hook. (p. 1298)
—Super Simple Bend & Stretch: Healthy & Fun Activities to Move Your Body. (p. 1681)
—Super Simple Breakfasts: Easy No-Bake Recipes for Kids. (p. 1681)
—Super Simple Cooking (p. 1681)
—Super Simple Desserts: Easy No-Bake Recipes for Kids. (p. 1681)
—Super Simple Dinners: Easy No-Bake Recipes for Kids. (p. 1681)
—Super Simple Holiday Treats: Easy No-Bake Recipes for Kids. (p. 1681)
—Super Simple Hop & Jump: Healthy & Fun Activities to Move Your Body. (p. 1681)
—Super Simple Lunches: Easy No-Bake Recipes for Kids. (p. 1681)
—Super Simple Move & Shake: Healthy & Fun Activities to Move Your Body. (p. 1681)
—Super Simple Punch & Kick: Healthy & Fun Activities to Move Your Body. (p. 1681)
—Super Simple Snacks: Easy No-Bake Recipes for Kids. (p. 1681)
—Super Simple Throw & Catch: Healthy & Fun Activities to Move Your Body. (p. 1681)
—Super Simple Walk & Run: Healthy & Fun Activities to Move Your Body. (p. 1681)
—Ub As in Tub. (p. 1807)
—Uck As in Duck. (p. 1807)
—Uff As in Cuff. (p. 1807)
—Ug As in Bug. (p. 1808)
—Um As in Drum. Marx, Monica, ed. (p. 1810)
—Ump As in Jump. (p. 1810)
—Zapatos de la Potranca. Nobens, C. A., illus. (p. 1985)
Tumminello, Giovanna, illus. see Isler, Linda Germano.
Tumwesigye, Elioda. Fountain Youth Survival Kit for Schools. a Teacher' Handbook on Hiv/Aids Prevention in Schools: Pupil's Resource Book. Student's Resource Book. (p. 624)
Tunberg, Jennifer Morrish, tr. see Seuss, Dr.
Tunberg, Terence O., jt. auth. see Minkova, Milena.
Tunberg, Terence O., tr. see Seuss, Dr.
Tunbridge, J. L. Jellybean Tree. (p. 912)
Tunceren, Li-Lee & Cavusgil, Sharon. College Writing (p. 340)
Tunell, Ken, illus. see Goss, Leon, 3rd.
Tunell, Ken, illus. see Goss, Leon.
Tunell, Ken, illus. see Shiotsu, Vicky.
Tung, Jennifer. InStyle Getting Gorgeous: The Step-by-Step Guide to Your Best Hair, Makeup & Skin. Sumpter, Rachell, illus. (p. 879)
Tung, Kadhima Ren, illus. see Currim, Nazli.
Tung, King. King of Fighters 2003 (p. 958)
Tung, King, jt. auth. see Yan, Wing.
Tunick, I. Walter. Spiritual Journey: The Bahandaacute;andiacute; Faith. (p. 1629)
Tunis, John R., jt. auth. see Tunis, John Roberts.
Tunis, John Roberts. Keystone Kids. (p. 951)
—Kid from Tomkinsville. (p. 951)
—Rookie of the Year. (p. 1487)
Tunis, John Roberts & Tunis, John R. Kid from Tomkinsville. (p. 951)
—Rookie of the Year. (p. 1487)
—World Series. (p. 1958)
Tunkin, David & National Geographic Learning Staff. New Clothes. (p. 1244)
Tunks, Karyn. Jubilee! Buckner, Julie, illus. (p. 930)
Tunnell, Amber. Night Sky: Stories of the Stars (Bedtime Shadow Book) Zschock, Martha Day, illus. (p. 1254)
Tunnell, Michael. Moon Without Magic. (p. 1172)
—Wishing Moon. (p. 1940)
Tunnell, Michael & Chilcoat, George. Children of Topaz: The Story of a Japanese-American Internment Camp Based on a Classroom Diary. (p. 303)
Tunnell, Michael O. Brothers in Valor: A Story of Resistance. (p. 231)
—Candy Bomber: The Story of the Berlin Airlift's Chocolate Pilot. (p. 261)
—Mailing May. Rand, Ted, illus. (p. 1077)
Tunnicliff, H. G. Story of the Pilgrim Fathers. (p. 1662)
Tunnicliffe, C. F., illus. see Darling, F. Fraser.
Tunstall, Tiki. Will You Be My Friend? (p. 1932)
Tunstall, Tricia. Note by Note: A Celebration of the Piano Lesson. (p. 1267)
Tunstel Jr., Robert L., illus. see Griffin, Ramona Rorie.
Tuohy, Hannah, illus. see Crawford, Jennifer.
Tuorto, Diana. Janie's New Legs. (p. 908)
Tupera, Tupera. Make More Faces: Doodle & Sticker Book with 52 Faces + 6 Sticker Sheets. (p. 1079)
—Polar Bear's Underwear. (p. 1379)
Tupper Ling, Nancy. My Sister, Alicia May. Bersani, Shennen, illus. (p. 1218)
Tupper, Mark, jt. auth. see Cook, Brian.
Turakhia, Smita, illus. see Arnett, Robert.
Turan, Kemal. Essence of Wisdom: Parables from Prophet Muhammad. (p. 536)
Turchan, Monique. Mydoit. Turchan, Monique, illus. (p. 1222)
Turchan, Monique, illus. see Demonia, Lori.
Turchan, Monique, illus. see Nero, Molly.
Turchan, Monique, illus. see Roth, Irene.
Turchan, Monique, illus. see Wamsley, Jody.
Turchyn, Sandie, illus. see Collier-Thompson, Kristi.
Turcios, Guadalupe Vanessa, tr. see Villaseñor, Victor.
Turcios, Omar. David, Fish & Penguins... (p. 411)
—David, Peces, Pinguinos ... (p. 411)
Turck, Mary C. Freedom Song: Young Voices & the Struggle for Civil Rights. (p. 635)
—Mexico & Central America: A Fiesta of Cultures, Crafts, & Activities for Ages 8-12. (p. 1131)
Turco, Laura Lo, illus. see Mann, Elizabeth.
Turconi, Stefano, illus. see Secchi, Richard & Salati, Giorgio.
Turconi, Stefano, illus. see Stevenson, Steve.
Turcotte, Carolyn E. Little Drip Drop's Big Rainy Day. (p. 1027)
Turcotte, Danielle. My Brother's Keeper. (p. 1199)
Turcotte, Derek, illus. see Turcotte, Michael.
Turcotte, Michael. Colours Made in Heaven Turcotte, Derek, illus. (p. 346)
Turecki, Stanley & Tonner, Leslie. Nino Dificil: Como Entenderlo y Desarrollar sus Cualidades. (p. 1257)

Turetsky, Bianca. Time-Traveling Fashionista & Cleopatra, Queen of the Nile. (p. 1753)
—Time-Traveling Fashionista at the Palace of Marie Antoinette. (p. 1753)
—Time-Traveling Fashionista on Board the Titanic. (p. 1753)
Turgeon, Carolyn, jt. auth. see Downtown Bookworks Inc. Staff.
Turgeon, Stephane. Noah's Ark. (p. 1261)
Turhan, Sedat. Milet Flashwords English. Hagin, Sally, illus. (p. 1142)
—Milet Picture Dictionary. (p. 1142)
Turhan, Sedat, jt. auth. see Hambleton, Laura.
Turhan, Sedat & Hagin, Sally. Milet Flashwords. (p. 1142)
—Milet Flashwords English-Turkish. (p. 1142)
—Milet Mini Picture Dictionary. (p. 1142)
—Milet Picture Dictionary. (p. 1142)
—Milet Picture Dictionary. Hagin, Sally, illus. (p. 1142)
Turhan-Kayaalp, Banu. Jeff, Bethesda'nın, Pizza Yiyen, Limonata İçen Rakunu. (p. 911)
Turiel, Isaac. How Do We Know the Size of the Solar System? (p. 808)
Turin, Adela. Arturo y Clementina. Bosnia, Nella, illus. (p. 105)
—Herencia del Hada. Bosnia, Nella, illus. (p. 771)
—Rosa Caramelo. Bosnia, Nella, illus. (p. 1488)
Turk, Caron, illus. see Elwell, Ellen Banks.
Turk, Caron, illus. see Larsen, Carolyn.
Turk, Caron, jt. illus. see Elwell, Ellen Banks.
Turk, Cheri. Stone Between Kings. Turk, Cheri, illus. (p. 1652)
Turk, Cynthia. My Daddy Stays at Home with Me. (p. 1201)
Turk, et al. 7 Days to Die. (p. 1992)
Turk, Evan. Storyteller. (p. 1663)
Turk, Evan, illus. see Gandhi, Arun & Hegedus, Bethany.
Turk, Hanne, illus. see Landa, Norbert.
Turk, Judy Vanslyke, et al. Laughing Thief. (p. 980)
—My Dear Wilkinson. (p. 1201)
Turkienicz, Rachael, jt. auth. see Morgan, Anna.
Turkington, Carol. Encyclopedia of Children's Health & Wellness (p. 525)
Turkington, Carol, jt. auth. see Devantier, Alecia T.
Turkington, Carol A., jt. auth. see Devantier, Alecia T.
Turkington, Carol A. & Ashby, Bonnie Lee. A to Z of Infectious Diseases. (p. 2)
Turkington, Carol A. & Devantier, Alecia T. Extraordinary Jobs for Adventurers. (p. 555)
—Extraordinary Jobs for Creative People. (p. 555)
—Extraordinary Jobs in Agriculture & Nature. (p. 555)
Turkington, Carol A. & Harris, Joseph R. Encyclopedia of Learning Disabilities. (p. 525)
Turkington, Carol & Ashby, Bonnie Lee. Encyclopedia of Infectious Diseases. (p. 525)
Turkington, Carol & Dover, Jeffrey S. Encyclopedia of Skin & Skin Disorders. Cox, Birck, illus. (p. 525)
Turkington, Carol & Straus, Marc J. Encyclopedia of Cancer. (p. 525)
Turkle, Brinton. Obadiah the Bold. (p. 1275)
—Rachel & Obadiah. (p. 1431)
Turkoglu, Nurcay, jt. auth. see Cornell, Kari.
Turkovitz, Karen. Not Again, Frannie! A Frannie Flotnick Adventure. Ryan, Linda et al, eds. (p. 1266)
Turley, Joyce M., illus. see Winfrey, Michelle Whitaker.
Turley, Joyce Mihran, illus. see Larsen, Laurel.
Turley, Joyce Mihran, illus. see Love, Donna.
Turley, Joyce Mihran, tr. see Love, Donna.
Turley, LuAnn & Whiteman, Rita. View, a Clue, & You: Poetry & American Art at the Museum of Fine Arts, Houston. (p. 1841)
Turley, Meredith & Burns, Adam. New York University College Prowler off the Record: Inside NYU. (p. 1248)
Turley, Richard & Littke, Lael. Stories from the Life of Joseph Smith. (p. 1654)
Turley, Richard E. & Littke, Lael. Stories from the Life of Joseph Smith. (p. 1654)
Turley, Sandy. Clock & the Mouse: A Teaching Rhyme about Time. Peterson, Sara & Lindstrom, Brita, illus. (p. 333)
Turley/Alber. And the Tide Comes In. (p. 71)
Turman, Adam, illus. see Turman, Evelyn.
Turman, Evelyn. J. B.'s Christmas Presents. Turman, Adam, illus. (p. 901)
Turman, Joe Garner. Sling Creek. (p. 1590)
Turnage, Cyndy. Trip to Washington, D. C. A Capital Idea. Fagan, Martin, illus. (p. 1787)
Turnage, Sheila. Ghosts of Tupelo Landing. (p. 672)
—Ghosts of Tupelo Landing. (p. 673)
—Three Times Lucky. (p. 1744)
Turnbaugh, Kay. Mountain Pine Beetle. Brooks, David, illus. (p. 1181)
Turnblacer, Margaret, jt. auth. see Rosson, Denise.
Turnbloom, Lucas, illus. see Allabach, P. R.
Turnbull, Ann. Caballo de Arena. Foreman, Michael, illus. (p. 250)
—Deep Water. (p. 423)
—Forged in the Fire. (p. 619)
—Greek Myths. Young, Sarah, illus. (p. 720)
—Josie under Fire. (p. 927)
—Maroo of the Winter Caves. (p. 1096)
—Mary Ann & Miss Mozart. (p. 1100)
—No Shame, No Fear. (p. 1260)
Turnbull, Betty. Sergeant in the House. Senning, Susan, illus. (p. 1552)
Turnbull, Betty J. Sergeant in the House. Senning, Susan, illus. (p. 1552)
Turnbull, Betty Turnbull. Isobel's New World. Taimy Studios, illus. (p. 893)
Turnbull, Brian, illus. see Maclean, Fiona.
Turnbull, David. Cuba Travels in the West; with Notices of Porto Rico, & the Slave Trade. (p. 388)
Turnbull, Elizabeth. Bonnwit Kabrit. Vaganos, Erin, illus. (p. 209)
—Janjak & Freda Go to the Iron Market. Turnbull, Wally, tr. (p. 908)
Turnbull, Elizabeth, ed. Music from the Romantic Era: Violin & Piano. (p. 1193)
Turnbull, Elizabeth J. Janjak & Freda Go to the Iron Market. Turnbull, Wally R., tr. (p. 908)
Turnbull, George. Principles of Moral & Christian Philosophy (p. 1406)
Turnbull, Jackie, jt. auth. see Stewart, Trudy.
Turnbull, Jesse, illus. see Aryal, Aimee.
Turnbull, Kathie. Because Everyone Needs a Friend. (p. 155)
Turnbull, Peter. Aftermath. (p. 28)
Turnbull, S. Castles. (p. 277)
—Caterpillars & Butterflies. (p. 280)
—Dino Kit (Box) (p. 441)
—Dinosaur Jigsaw Book. (p. 442)
—Trains. (p. 1777)
—Trenes. (p. 1784)
Turnbull, S., jt. auth. see Sheikh-Miller, J.
Turnbull, Stephanie. Accessories: Style Secrets for Girls. (p. 8)
—Acting Skills. (p. 10)
—Alligator. (p. 47)
—Art Skills. (p. 103)
—Camel. (p. 256)
—Cards & Gifts: Style Secrets for Girls. (p. 266)
—Castles: Information for Young Readers - Level 1. King, Colin, illus. (p. 277)
—Castles IR (Rev Cover) (p. 277)
—Caterpillars & Butterflies. Guille, Rosanne & Mayer, Uwe, illus. (p. 280)
—Cold! (p. 338)
—Cooking Skills. (p. 362)
—Cool Stuff to Bake. (p. 364)
—Cool Stuff to Collect. (p. 364)
—Cool Stuff to Grow. (p. 364)
—Cool Stuff to Make with Paper. (p. 364)
—Cool Stuff to Photograph. (p. 364)
—Cool Stuff to Sew. (p. 364)
—Craft Skills. (p. 375)
—Diaries & Keepsakes: Style Secrets for Girls. (p. 434)
—Dinosaurios Con Cuatro Puzzles Sencillos. Scott, Peter, illus. (p. 443)
—Dinosaurs. (p. 444)
—Dinosaurs. Kushii, Tetsuo, illus. (p. 444)
—Dinosaurs. Wray, Zoe & Kushii, Tetsuo, illus. (p. 444)
—Do You Really Want to Visit Neptune? (p. 458)
—Do You Really Want to Visit Uranus? (p. 458)
—Dolphin. (p. 464)
—Dolphins. (p. 464)
—Eagle. (p. 492)
—Easy Coin Tricks. (p. 500)
—Easy Scarf & Rope Tricks. (p. 500)
—Egyptians. (p. 507)
—Egyptians. King, Colin, illus. (p. 507)
—Egyptians Kid Kit. (p. 507)
—Egyptians Kid Kit. King, Colin, illus. (p. 507)
—Elephant. (p. 511)
—Elizabeth I Internet Referenced. King, Colin, illus. (p. 513)
—Emergency! (p. 518)
—Essential Atlas of the World. (p. 536)
—Fall. (p. 566)
—Fun with Friends: Style Secrets for Girls. (p. 648)
—Giraffe. (p. 677)
—Gorilla. (p. 703)
—Health & Fitness: Style Secrets for Girls. (p. 757)
—Hippo. (p. 781)
—Hungry! (p. 828)
—Kangaroo. (p. 942)
—Komodo Dragon. (p. 966)
—Lion. (p. 1019)
—Looking Good: Style Secrets for Girls. (p. 1051)
—Lost! (p. 1054)
—Magic Skills. (p. 1073)
—Panda. (p. 1320)
—Polar Bear. (p. 1378)
—Ponies. (p. 1382)
—Racehorses. (p. 1431)
—Shark. (p. 1561)
—Show Horses. (p. 1570)
—Snake. (p. 1596)
—Sports Horses. (p. 1632)
—Spring. (p. 1634)
—Stranded! (p. 1664)
—Summer. (p. 1673)
—Sun, Moon & Stars. Chen, Kuo Kang & Mayer, Uwe, illus. (p. 1676)
—Thirsty! (p. 1734)
—Tiger. (p. 1748)
—Trains. (p. 1777)
—Transformation & Vanishing Tricks. (p. 1778)
—Trash & Recycling. (p. 1779)
—Trash & Recycling. Fox, Christyan, illus. (p. 1779)
—Vikings. Larkum, Adam, illus. (p. 1842)
—Volcanoes. Tudor, Andy, illus. (p. 1849)
—Whale. (p. 1877)
—Why Do We Eat? Haggerty, Tim, illus. (p. 1924)
—Why Do We Eat? (Lematha Na'Kol) Ibrahim, Nouran, tr. (p. 1924)
—Wild Horses. (p. 1929)
—Winter. (p. 1937)
—Working Horses. (p. 1952)
—Your Body. (p. 1980)
—Your Body (Jismok) Ibrahim, Nouran, tr. (p. 1980)
Turnbull, Stephanie, ed. see Brocklehurst, Ruth.
Turnbull, Stephanie, ed. see Davidson, Susannah.
Turnbull, Stephanie, jt. auth. see Gulliver, Amanda.
Turnbull, Stephanie, jt. auth. see Morgan, Philip.
Turnbull, Stephanie & Helbrough, Emma. Children's World Atlas. (p. 304)
—Usborne Internet-Linked Children's World Atlas. (p. 1827)
Turnbull, Stephen. Real Samurai: Over 20 True Stories about the Knights of Old Japan! Field, James, illus. (p. 1449)
Turnbull, Stephen & Tulloch, Coral. Real Ninja: Over 20 Stories of Japan's Secret Assassins. Field, James, illus. (p. 1448)
Turnbull, Stephen R. Most Daring Raid of the Samurai. (p. 1177)
Turnbull, Susan, illus. see Meierhenry, Mark & Volk, David.
Turnbull, Wally, tr. see Turnbull, Elizabeth.
Turnbull, Wally R., tr. see Turnbull, Elizabeth J.
Turnbull-Kennedy, Tiffany. No School for Evil Eraser! (p. 1260)
Turndorf, Genene Levy, jt. auth. see Rouss, Sylvia A.
Turner, Adam, illus. see Diller, Janelle.
Turner, Alan. National Geographic Prehistoric Mammals. Anton, Mauricio, illus. (p. 1233)
Turner, Alan H. Dinosaurios. (p. 443)
Turner, Amber McRee. Circa Now. (p. 321)
Turner, Angie Avard. U R my BFF. (p. 1805)
Turner, Ann. My Name Is Truth: The Life of Sojourner Truth. Ransome, James, illus. (p. 1215)
—Pumpkin Cat. Bates, Amy, illus. (p. 1416)
—Sewing Quilts. Allen, Thomas B., illus. (p. 1556)
—Shaker Hearts. Minor, Wendell, illus. (p. 1558)
Turner, Ann, jt. auth. see Turner, Ann Warren.
Turner, Ann Warren. Abe Lincoln Remembers. Minor, Wendell, illus. (p. 4)
—Hard Hit. (p. 748)
—When Mr. Jefferson Came to Philadelphia: What I Learned of Freedom 1776. Hess, Mark, illus. (p. 1904)
Turner, Ann Warren & Turner, Ann. Sitting Bull Remembers. Minor, Wendell, illus. (p. 1582)
Turner, Aubrey, illus. see Crawford, Deborah Kay.
Turner Banks, Jacqueline, jt. auth. see Banks, Jacqueline Turner.
Turner, Barbara. Day in San Francisco (p. 413)
Turner, Barrie Carson. Bach. (p. 130)
—Beethoven. (p. 158)
—Mozart. (p. 1184)
Turner, Bernard. Our Chicago—People & Places. (p. 1308)
Turner, Blaine. Beastmasters. (p. 152)
Turner, Brenda. Cimarron Sunrise: Teacher's Guide. (p. 319)
—Cimarron Sunrise. (p. 319)
Turner, Carolyn. Sam Houston. (p. 1506)
Turner, Carolyn S., jt. auth. see Lewis, Evelyn L.
Turner, Cecilia, illus. see Wood, Cary D.
Turner, Cherie. Adventure Tour Guides: Life on Extreme Outdoor Adventures. (p. 15)
—Everything You Need to Know about the Riot Grrrl Movement: The Feminism of a New Generation. (p. 546)
—Marathon Cycling. (p. 1091)
—Stunt Performers: Life Before the Camera. (p. 1670)
Turner, Cherie, illus. see Jay, Gina & Beattie, Julie.
Turner, Chris. Key Facts: Contract Law. (p. 950)
—Key Facts: Employment Law. (p. 950)
Turner, Christina. Hello Santa! Turner, Christina, illus. (p. 765)
Turner, Christina S. Chip Tees Off! (p. 308)
Turner Classic Movies Staff & Chronicle Books Staff. Hollywood Kisses. (p. 789)
Turner, Corey W. Little Benjamin & the Red Fire Ants. (p. 1024)
—Little Benjamin, the Bugs, & the Holy Spirit. (p. 1024)
Turner, Dale. Free to Be. Summer, Angel, ed. (p. 634)
Turner, Daniel. Cinnamon the Adventurous Guinea Pig Goes to Devil's Island. Skinner, Gayle, illus. (p. 321)
Turner, Dannie E. You Don't Know Beans: the Great Frog Adventure. (p. 1975)
Turner, Darlene. Tommy Gets Lost! Rottinger, Amy, illus. (p. 1765)
Turner, Deborah & Mohler, Diana. How Willy Got His Wings: The Continuing Adventures of Wheely Willy. Ahrends, Susan, illus. (p. 823)
Turner, Deirdre. Lilac Sky. (p. 1017)
Turner, Diane. Tangle-Leina? I'll Tangle-Leina Them. Mason, Roberta Black, illus. (p. 1705)
Turner, Diane, illus. see Mundy, Dawn.
Turner, Diane D. My Name Is Oney Judge. Massey, Cal, illus. (p. 1215)
—My Name Is Oney Judge. Massey, Call, illus. (p. 1215)
Turner, Dona. Ella Minnow Pea. Turner, Dona, illus. (p. 514)
Turner, Dona, illus. see Duksta, Laura.
Turner, Dona, illus. see Schwartz, Betty Ann.
Turner, Dona & Dunn, Mark. Ella Minnow Pea. Turner, Dona & Brennan, Tim, illus. (p. 514)
Turner, Donald R. & Tillema, Juliana O. Production of Goods & Services. (p. 1409)
Turner, Ethel. Seven Little Australians. (p. 1554)
Turner, F. Bernadette. Faith of Little Creatures. (p. 565)
Turner, Gary. Guitar Method for Young Beginners, Book 1. Stewart, James, illus. (p. 731)
—Keyboard Method for Young Beginners, Book 1. Stewart, James, illus. (p. 950)
—Piano Method for Young Beginners, Book 1. Stewart, James, illus. (p. 1354)
—Recorder Method for Young Beginners, Book 1. Stewart, James, illus. (p. 1452)
Turner, Gary, jt. auth. see McNamara, Pat.
Turner, Gil, illus. see Connell, Del, et al.
Turner, Ginger. Gold Mine! The California Gold Rush Story. (p. 693)
Turner, Ginger, illus. see Tiwari, Saral.
Turner, Ginger & Shimpi, Shekhar. Gold Mine! The California Gold Rush Story. (p. 693)
Turner, Glennette Tilley. Apple for Harriet Tubman. Keeter, Susan, illus. (p. 92)
—Fort Mosé: And the Story of the Man Who Built the First Free Black Settlement in Colonial America. (p. 623)
—Running for Our Lives. (p. 1497)
Turner, Helen. Knock, Knock, It's Easter! (p. 965)
Turner, Helen, illus. see Moss, Olivia.
Turner, Helen, illus. see Shields, Gillian.
Turner, Helen, jt. auth. see Bingham, Jane.
Turner, Henry. Ask the Dark. (p. 106)
Turner, J. Joseph's New Camera: The Joseph Land Series. (p. 926)
Turner, J. Hale. I Love to Sing & Dance. (p. 843)
Turner, J. R. School's Out 4-Ever. (p. 1524)
Turner, James. Enchanted Monlongo, Jorge, illus. (p. 523)
—Mameshiba: We Could Be Heroes. Monlongo, Jorge, illus. (p. 1084)
—Nil: A World Beyond Belief. (p. 1255)
—On the Loose! Monlongo, Jorge & Correll, Gemma, illus. (p. 1290)
Turner, Jane, jt. auth. see Bage, Grant.
Turner, Jason. World War I. (p. 1958)
Turner, Jennifer. My Name Is Jake. Bell, Susan, illus. (p. 1215)
Turner, Jill. Percival's Party. Townsend, Peter, illus. (p. 1341)
Turner, Jill & Cassettari, Noeline. Happy Helicopters. (p. 746)
Turner, Judy. English 9 Student Activity Book: Student Activities Book. (p. 529)
Turner, Julie Anne. Tale of Summerland. (p. 1700)
Turner, Juliette. Our Constitution Rocks! (p. 1308)
—Our Presidents Rock! Oesch, Brian, illus. (p. 1309)
Turner, Kara, ed. see Craats, Rennay.
Turner, Kara, ed. see Weigl Publishers Staff & Craats, Rennay.
Turner, Kate. Australia. (p. 116)
Turner, Katharine. Decepticon in Disguise. (p. 421)
—Reptile Rampage. (p. 1461)
—Reptile Rampage. Gordon, Eric A. & Gordon, Steven E., illus. (p. 1461)
Turner, Katharine, jt. text see Mayer, Kirsten.
Turner, Kathy. Bobby Magilacahde's Trip to the Hospital. (p. 206)
Turner, Keith. H Is for Healthy Diet: H Is for Hope Book Series (p. 734)
Turner, Lee. Who Ate My French Fries. (p. 1914)
Turner, Lorraine. Calico Horses & the Patchwork Trail. (p. 253)
Turner, Margaret, jt. auth. see Kunoth, Mark.
Turner, Margaret Petyerr, tr. see Kunoth, Mark & Turner, Margaret.
Turner, Marianne, tr. see Lindgren, Astrid.
Turner, Mark. Winter Tale: How Raven Gave Light to the World. Graves, Emily, illus. (p. 1938)
Turner, Mary. Colored Balloons & Clowns. (p. 343)
Turner & Still Owl. (p. 1428)
Turner, Max. End of Days. (p. 526)
—Night Runner: A Novel. (p. 1254)
Turner, Megan Whalen. Conspiracy of Kings: The Queen's Thief No. 4 (p. 359)
—Conspiracy of Kings: The Queen's Thief. No. 4 (p. 359)
—Instead of Three Wishes: Magical Short Stories. (p. 878)
—King of Attolia. (p. 958)
—Queen of Attolia. (p. 1425)
—Thief. (p. 1732)
Turner, Michael. Michael Turner's Soulfire Definitive Edition Volume 1 TP. (p. 1135)
Turner, Michael, jt. auth. see Kelly, Joe.
Turner, Michael W., illus. see Goodnight, Rosemary.
Turner, Morrie. Super Sistahs: Featuring the Accomplishments of African-American Women. (p. 1681)
Turner, Nancy J., jt. auth. see Halter, Reese.
Turner, Nathan Paul, jt. auth. see Shackleton, Caroline.
Turner, Nicci. Milky's Story (p. 1143)
Turner, Pamela S. Crow Smarts. (p. 386)
—Dolphins of Shark Bay. Tuason, Scott, photos by. (p. 465)
—Frog Scientist. Comins, Andy, illus. (p. 640)
—Gorilla Doctors: Saving Endangered Great Apes. (p. 703)
—Life in the Wild: George Schaller's Struggle to Save the Last Great Beasts. (p. 1011)
—Life on Earth - And Beyond: An Astrobiologist's Quest. (p. 1012)
—Project Seahorse. Tuason, Scott, illus. (p. 1410)
—Prowling the Seas: Exploring the Hidden World of Ocean Predators. (p. 1413)
Turner, Paul. ULYSSES: the Pegasi Incident. (p. 1810)
Turner, Phil, Jr. Credit Bible: Everything You Ever Want to Know about Credit. (p. 380)
Turner, Queen of England Patrenia. Queen Patrenialla The Story Poem. (p. 1425)
Turner, Queen Patrenia. Barbie In The Queen Patrenialla Fairy - Tale. (p. 138)
Turner, Rich, photos by. Delta Skies Fine Art Folio (p. 425)
Turner, Rosebud Alford. Through Talen's Eyes: A Visit to Grandma's House. (p. 1745)
Turner, Sandra, jt. auth. see Johnson, D. C.
Turner, Sandy, illus. see Steig, Jeanne.
Turner, Sarah Elizabeth. Littlest Monkey (p. 1039)
—Ribbon's Way (p. 1469)
Turner, Shelley A. Dae Dae & Dirky. (p. 399)
Turner, Stephanie. Dirty the Dog & the King of Mud Puddles. (p. 446)
Turner, Steve, jt. auth. see Ziegesar, Cecily von.
Turner, Steve & Mostyn, David. Don't Take Your Elephant to School: An Alphabet of Poems. (p. 468)
Turner, Suzette, illus. see Semple, Veronique & Semple, J. J.
Turner, Suzy. Ghost of Josiah Grimshaw: A Morgan Sisters Novel. (p. 671)
—Temporal Stone: A Morgan Sisters Novel. (p. 1718)
Turner, Taquila Lanina. New Friends. (p. 1244)
Turner, Thomas N. Country Music Night Before Christmas Rice, James, illus. (p. 372)
Turner, Tom. Sign of the Sandman. (p. 1574)
Turner, Tracey. Daring, Deadly, Brilliant, Brave: History's Toughest People. Lenman, Jamie, illus. (p. 407)
—Deadly Perils: And How to Avoid Them. Hasler, Ben & Horne, Richard, illus. (p. 417)
—Disgusting Dictionary. (p. 450)
—Dreadful Fates: What a Shocking Way to Go! Kindberg, Sally, illus. (p. 482)
—Hard As Nails in Ancient Egypt. Lenman, Jamie, illus. (p. 748)
—Hard As Nails in Ancient Greece. Lenman, Jamie, illus. (p. 748)
—Hard As Nails in Ancient Rome. Lenman, Jamie, illus. (p. 748)
—Hard As Nails in Myths & Legends. (p. 748)
—Hard As Nails in Wars & Battles. Lenman, Jamie, illus. (p. 748)
—Hard As Nails Kings & Queens. (p. 748)
—Hard As Nails Travelers & Explorers. (p. 748)
—Hard as Nails Warriors. Lenman, Jamie, illus. (p. 748)
—Lost in the Desert of Dread. (p. 1055)
—Lost in the Jungle of Doom. (p. 1055)
—Lost in the Mountains of Death. (p. 1055)
—Lost in the Sea of Despair. (p. 1056)

—Who's Who of Horrors: An A to Z of Loathsome Lives. (p. 1921)
—Wimp-O-Meter's Guide to Extreme Sports. (p. 1935)
—Wimp-O-Meter's Guide to Jungle Survival. (p. 1935)
—Wimp-O-Meter's Guide to the Supernatural. (p. 1935)
—World of the Weird. (p. 1957)
Turner, Tracey & Foster, Jo. How Can a Pigeon Be a War Hero? Questions & Answers about the First World War. (p. 805)
Turner, Tracey & Kindberg, Sally. Comic Strip Big Fat Book of Knowledge. (p. 348)
Turner, Tracie & Dyson, Kyree. Adventures of Kyree the Chocolate Moose. (p. 19)
Turner, Tracy. Yuk Factor. (p. 1983)
Turner, Wilson G. Aztec Designs. (p. 122)
Turner, Yahmanali. Bugs on a Trip. (p. 237)
Turner-Barnes, Sandra. Beyond the Back of the Bus. Collins, Bernard, Jr., illus. (p. 174)
Turner-Deckert, Dianne, illus. see John Knapp, II.
Turner-Rahman, Gregory. Ellabug. (p. 514)
Turney, Chris. Bones, Rocks & Stars: The Science of When Things Happened. (p. 209)
Turney, Jon. Technology: Ethical Debates about the Application of Science. (p. 1711)
Turney, Maria, jt. auth. see Mosher, Nancy.
Turnipseed, Susan. South Dakota: A Journey Through Time Student Workbook. Heers, Matt & Heers, Nate, illus. (p. 1617)
—South Dakota: A Journey Through Time Student Workbook Answer Key. Heers, Matt & Heers, Nate, illus. (p. 1617)
Turnmyre, Dustin, illus. see McClean, Will.
Turnquist, C. H., jt. auth. see Althouse, A. D.
Turnquist, Myrtle Moose. How Do Dandelions Grow. (p. 806)
Turpin, Dominic. Mathsheets: A Collection of 32 Useful Worksheets on a Variety of Mathematical Topics. (p. 1108)
Turpin, Nick. Molly Is New. Raga, Silvia, illus. (p. 1160)
Turpin, Tom. What's Buggin' You Now? Bee's Knees, Bug Lites & Beetles. (p. 1896)
Turquoise Class. George's Dragon Adventure. (p. 665)
Turrell, Linda. Complete Library Skills, Grade 5. (p. 353)
—Everyday Writing - How to Master Basic Writing Skills Student Activities Book. Matthews, Douglas L., ed. (p. 544)
—Mastering Prepositions, Conjunctions, Phrases & Clauses Student Activities Book: Mastering Language Arts Series. Matthews, Douglas L., ed. (p. 1103)
—Synonyms, Antonyms, & Homonyms Student Activities Book: Mastering Language Arts Series. Matthews, Douglas L., ed. (p. 1693)
Turrill, Tiffany, illus. see Errico, Daniel.
Turrion, Celia, tr. see Scuderi, Lucia.
Turrion, Celia, tr. see Slegers, Liesbet.
Turton, Karalynn Teresa. Passion for Children: Bilingual (English & Spanish) Guide to the Passion of Christ Ruiz, Jeanette, tr. (p. 1327)
Turvey, Raymond, illus. see Morris, Ting & Morris, Neil.
Turvey, Roger. Henry VII. (p. 768)
Tusa, Tricia. Follow Me. (p. 612)
Tusa, Tricia, illus. see Ashman, Linda.
Tusa, Tricia, illus. see Averbeck, Jim.
Tusa, Tricia, illus. see Avi.
Tusa, Tricia, illus. see Coffelt, Nancy.
Tusa, Tricia, illus. see Earl, Janice.
Tusa, Tricia, illus. see Feiffer, Kate.
Tusa, Tricia, illus. see Fox, Mem.
Tusa, Tricia, illus. see Hanson, Warren.
Tusa, Tricia, illus. see Lynch, Jane, et al.
Tusa, Tricia, illus. see Mitchard, Jacquelyn.
Tusa, Tricia, illus. see Murphy, Stuart J. & Murphy.
Tusa, Tricia, illus. see Pattou, Edith.
Tusa, Tricia, illus. see Queen Rania of Jordan Al Abdullah Staff, et al.
Tusa, Tricia, illus. see Ray, Mary Lyn.
Tusa, Tricia, illus. see Sullivan, Sarah.
Tusan, Stan, illus. see Knowlton, Laurie Lazzaro.
Tuschman, Richard, illus. see Gordon, Amy.
Tuska, George, illus. see Friedrich, Mike, et al.
Tuska, George & Pollard, Keith. Avengers: The Coming of the Beast. (p. 118)
Tusman, Jordana. Hoops & Yoyo: Friends Rock! Running Press Staff, ed. (p. 795)
Tusón, Vicente, ed. see varios & Varios.
Tusón, Vicente, ed. see Vega, Garcilaso de la.
Tusón, Vicente, tr. see varios & Varios.
Tusón, Vicente, tr. see Vega, Garcilaso de la.
Tusquets, Eugenia, tr. see Rey, H. A. & Rey, Margret.
Tussman, Jordana. Purple Doodle Book. (p. 1419)
Tussman, Jordana, jt. auth. see Running Press Staff.
Tust, Dorothea, illus. see Van Saan, Anita.
Tustison, Matt. Detroit Lions. (p. 431)
—Jacksonville Jaguars. (p. 904)
—Sacramento Kings. (p. 1500)
Tuszynski, Kathy & Yarber, Angela. Discovering Differentiation: Strategies for Success in the Language Arts Classroom. Mitchell, Judy, ed. (p. 449)
Tuszynski, Kathy Cromwell & Yarber, Angela. Write Answer. (p. 1963)
Tuthill, Louisa C. Hurrah for New England! or the Virginia Boy's Vacation. (p. 829)
Tutino, Stefania, ed. see Bellarmine, Robert.
Tutor, Margaret. Make-Do Christmas. (p. 1079)
Tutos, Joanna, ed. see Wright, Joe.
Tutos, Joanna, ed. see Wright, Joseph B.
Tutt, Candy Taylor. Ten Dragon Tails. (p. 1718)
Tuttle, Beth. Manna from Mama. (p. 1087)
Tuttle, Brad. Kevin & the Magic Skateboard. Hollis, Tyler, illus. (p. 949)
Tuttle, Brenda L. Chef Joey's Cupcake Creation. (p. 297)
Tuttle, Cheryl Gerson. Medications: The Ultimate Teen Guide. (p. 1119)
Tuttle, Cheryl Gerson, jt. auth. see Paquette, Penny Hutchins.
Tuttle, Justin J. If My Toes Could Talk. (p. 853)
Tuttle, Lucia. There's a Mouse in the House. (p. 1731)
Tuttle, Mark. Lexi's Tea Party. Combs, Bradley, illus. (p. 1004)
Tuttle, Merlin D., photos by see Irbinskas, Heather.
Tuttle Publishing Staff. More Chinese for Kids: Traditional Character. (p. 1174)
—More Chinese for Kids. (p. 1174)
Tuttle, Todd. Spot. Tuttle, Todd, illus. (p. 1633)
Tutu, Desmond. Children of God Storybook Bible (p. 302)
—Desmond & the Very Mean Word. Ford, A. G., illus. (p. 430)
—Let There Be Light Tillman, Nancy, illus. (p. 994)
Tutu, Desmond, jt. auth. see Abrams, Douglas Carlton.
Tutu, Desmond & Abrams, Douglas Carlton. God's Dream. Pham, LeUyen, illus. (p. 691)
Tuvu. Tiny & Flat: Two Bestfriends. (p. 1756)
Tuxbury, Larry, jt. auth. see McElligott, Matthew.
Tuxbury, Larry, jt. auth. see Mcelligott, Matthew.
Tuxbury, Larry David, jt. auth. see McElligott, Matthew.
Tuxford, Jenny & Brazier, Jenny. Fred Boggitt & the Great Garden Centre Plot. (p. 632)
—Fredd Boggitt & the Loch Ness Monster. (p. 632)
Tuxworth, Nicola. Colors. (p. 345)
—Colours: Learn-A-Word Book. (p. 346)
—Diggers & Dumpers. (p. 439)
—Farm Animals. (p. 573)
—Hop, Skip & Jump. (p. 796)
—Learn-A-Word Book: Clothes. (p. 982)
—Messy. (p. 1130)
—Numbers. (p. 1272)
—Puppies. (p. 1417)
—Splish Splash. (p. 1630)
—Teddy Bears. (p. 1712)
Tuya, Jez, illus. see Gibson, Douglas.
Tuyl, Christine Van & Merino, Noël. Media Violence. (p. 1118)
Tuymans, Luc, et al. Luc Tuymans. (p. 1062)
Tuzee, Diane, jt. auth. see Tuzee, John.
Tuzee, John & Tuzee, Diane. Charlie Canoe & Other Boats, Too. Kasun, Mike, illus. (p. 293)
Tuzee, John, creator. What A Grape Can Be. (p. 1878)
Tuzee, John, text. Puffy: La Nube Que No Podia Llover. (p. 1415)
Tveite, William P. Adventures of Maximillian P. Dogg - Rescue Dog: Max Finds a New Home. Steele, Gregory D., illus. (p. 20)
Twain, Mark, jt. auth. see Imbernón, Teresa.
Twain, Mark, jt. auth. see Lawson, Jessica.
Twain, Mark, pseud. Adventures of Huckleberry Finn: With a Discussion of Friendship. Lauter, Richard, tr. (p. 18)
—Adventures of Huckleberry Finn. (p. 18)
—Adventures of Huckleberry Finn. Andreasen, Dan, illus. (p. 18)
—Adventures of Huckleberry Finn. McKowen, Scott, illus. (p. 18)
—Adventures of Tom Sawyer: A Song for Aunt Polly. Bates, Amy, illus. (p. 24)
—Adventures of Tom Sawyer: With a Discussion of Imagination. Butterfield, Ned, illus. (p. 24)
—Adventures of Tom Sawyer. Reed, Neil, illus. (p. 24)
—Adventures of Tom Sawyer. Corvino, Lucy, illus. (p. 24)
—Adventures of Tom Sawyer. McKowen, Scott, illus. (p. 24)
—Adventures of Tom Sawyer. Ingpen, Robert R., illus. (p. 24)
—Adventures of Tom Sawyer, Complete. (p. 24)
—Adventures of Tom Sawyer - Literary Touchstone Edition. (p. 24)
—Advice to Little Girls. Radunsky, Vladimir, illus. (p. 25)
—Alonzo Fitz & Other Stories. (p. 48)
—Aventuras de Huckleberry Finn. de Atauri, Ines & de Atauri, Juan Diaz, eds. (p. 119)
—Aventuras de Tom Sawyer. (p. 119)
—Avventure di Tom Sawyer. (p. 120)
—Birthday Boy. Bates, Amy June, illus. (p. 192)
—Connecticut Yankee in King Arthur's Court. (p. 358)
—Huckleberry Finn. (p. 824)
—Mark Twain/the Adventures of Huckleberry Finn. Redondo, Frank, illus. (p. 1095)
—Mark Twain/the Adventures of Tom Sawyer. Cruz, E. R., illus. (p. 1095)
—Mysterious Stranger. (p. 1223)
—Prince & the Pauper: Response Journal. (p. 1401)
—Prince & the Pauper: With a Discussion of Respect. (p. 1401)
—Prince & the Pauper. (p. 1401)
—Prince & the Pauper. Akib, Jamel, illus. (p. 1401)
—Prince & the Pauper. Pamment, Katie, illus. (p. 1401)
—Principe y el Mendigo. (p. 1406)
—Principe y el Mendigo. Castro, Patricia & Avila, Jorge, illus. (p. 1406)
—Song for Aunt Polly. Bates, Amy, illus. (p. 1611)
—Song for Aunt Polly. Bates, Amy & Bates, Amy June, illus. (p. 1611)
—Spelling Bee. Bates, Amy, illus. (p. 1625)
—The Adventures of Tom Sawyer. Corvino, Lucy, illus. (p. 1728)
—Tom Sawyer. (p. 1763)
—Tom Sawyer. Le Fevebvre, Severine, illus. (p. 1763)
—Tom Sawyer, Detective. (p. 1763)
Twain, Mark, pseud & Clemens, Samuel L. Prince & the Pauper. (p. 1401)
Twain, Mark, pseud, et al. Prince & the Pauper. Kliros, Thea, illus. (p. 1401)
Twain, Mark, pseud, tr. from GER. Slovenly Peter. Kredel, Fritz, illus. (p. 1591)
Twamley, Erin, jt. auth. see Sneideman, Joshua.
Twead, Victoria. Morgan & the Martians. (p. 1175)
Tweddle, Beth. Becoming an Olympic Gymnast. (p. 156)
Tweed, Anne, jt. auth. see Koba, Susan.
Tweed, Matt. Compact Cosmos: A Journey Through Space & Time. (p. 351)
Tweed, Sean, jt. illus. see Henkel, Vernon.
Tweed, Sean, jt. illus. see McInturff, Linda.
Tweed, Susan Larned. Sailor's Adventure: Sailing Stormy Seas. (p. 1503)
Tweedy, Bonnie. Grandma Bonnie's Cats: A Happy Place. (p. 708)
—Grandma Bonnie's Cats: In Love Again. (p. 708)
Tweh, Steven R. Traveling Abroad: How to Proceed & Succeed. (p. 1780)
Twelsiek, Monika, ed. Animals: 30 Easy Piano Pieces for Children. (p. 81)
Twemlow, Nick. Josh Gibson. (p. 926)
Twenstrup, Norm. Surprise for Santa. DHP, Inc. Staff, ed. (p. 1686)
Twentieth Century Fox Home Entertainment Staff & Anderson, Wes. Making of Fantastic Mr. Fox. (p. 1082)
Twenty-Third Publications, creator. Celebrating Eucharist: A Mass Book for Children. (p. 284)
Tweti, Mira. Here, There, & Everywhere: The Story of Sreeeeeeeet the Lorikeett. Brady, Lisa, illus. (p. 770)
Twichell, David E. Global Implications of the UFO Reality. (p. 684)
Twiford, Jerod. Kisho. (p. 961)
Twigg, Aeres. Green Hawk. (p. 722)
Twigg, Craig, illus. see Rogers, Bryar Elizabeth.
Twigg, Julia. Body in Health & Social Care. (p. 207)
Twigg, Natalie, jt. auth. see Wheeler, David.
Twigger, J. Nicci & Her Amazing Adventure. (p. 1250)
Twiggs, Ruth, jt. auth. see Cormack, Malcolm.
Twin Sister Produtions. Sesame Street What Did Elmo Say? (p. 1553)
Twin Sister Produtions & Galvin, Laura Gates. Sesame Street Abby Cadabby's Nursery Rhymes. (p. 1553)
—Sesame Street What Did Elmo Say? (p. 1553)
Twin Sister Produtions & Shepherd, Jodie. Sesame Street Big Red Riding Hood. (p. 1553)
—Sesame Street Rosita & the Beanstalk. (p. 1553)
Twin Sister Produtions Staff & Galvin, Laura Gates. Sesame Street What Did Elmo Say? (p. 1553)
Twin Sister Produtions Staff & Shepherd, Jodie. Sesame Street Big Red Riding Hood. (p. 1553)
—Sesame Street Rosita & the Beanstalk. (p. 1553)
Twin Sisters(r) Staff. 12 Days of Christmas. (p. 1994)
—120 Kids' Songs 4CD Digipack. (p. 2000)
—30 Nursery Rhymes Songs CD. (p. 1996)
—Abc Nursery Rhymes. (p. 3)
—Bible Songs Workbook/CD Set. (p. 176)
—B-I-N-G-O. (p. 122)
—B-i-n-g-o. (p. 122)
—Christmas Songs 4 Kids 3. (p. 315)
—Christmas Story. (p. 315)
—Down by the Bay. (p. 474)
—Down Through the Chimney. (p. 474)
—Farmer in the Dell. (p. 574)
—Five Little Monkeys Jumping on the Bed. (p. 600)
—Five Little Skunks. (p. 601)
—Five Trick or Treaters. (p. 601)
—Gruesome Grub. (p. 727)
—Humpty Dumpty & More. (p. 827)
—Jesus Loves the Little Children. (p. 916)
—Jolly Old St.Nicholas. (p. 924)
—Kids' Favorite Songs & Stories- 4books. (p. 953)
—Kids' Halloween Party. (p. 954)
—Kids Learn Spanish Handlebox- 4 books. (p. 954)
—Learning with Elmo: Animals. (p. 986)
—Lord Is My Shepherd. (p. 1052)
—Multiplication Workbook & Music CD. (p. 1190)
—Old MacDonald Had a Farm. (p. 1284)
—Old Testament Handlebox-4 books. (p. 1284)
—Rise & Shine. (p. 1474)
—Santa Songs & More Boxed Set- 2 books. (p. 1513)
—Six Little Ducks. (p. 1582)
—Spanish Workbook. (p. 1622)
—Story of Jesus Handlebox-4books. (p. 1658)
—Ten in the Bed. (p. 1718)
—Twelve Days of Christmas. (p. 1800)
—Up on the Housetop. (p. 1824)
—Wheels on the Bus. (p. 1901)
—When I Go Trick or Treating. (p. 1902)
Twin Sisters(r) Staff & Hilderbrand, Karen Mitzo, adapted by. Subtraction. (p. 1671)
—Ten in the Bed. (p. 1718)
Twin Sisters(r) Staff & Thompson, Kim Mitzo. My First Old Testament Bible Stories. (p. 1207)
—Night-Night Song. (p. 1253)
—Subtraction. (p. 1671)
Twin Sisters(r) Staff, creator. Gross & Annoying Songs. (p. 725)
Twin Sisters(r) Staff, et al. David & Goliath Padded Board Book & CD (p. 410)
—Five Little Bunnies. (p. 600)
—I Thank God for You. (p. 846)
—It's Silly Time. (p. 898)
—Jonah & the Whale Padded Board Book & CD (p. 925)
—My First Bible Promises with CD. (p. 1204)
—My First Bible Songs Book with CD. (p. 1204)
—My First New Testament Bible Stories. (p. 1207)
—My First Old Testament Bible Stories. (p. 1207)
—Noah & the Ark Padded Board Book & CD (p. 1261)
—Play & Learn Bible Stories: God Made Everything: Wipe-Clean Storybook. (p. 1371)
—Play & Learn Bible Stories: Noah's Ark: Wipe-Clean Storybook. (p. 1371)
—Trace & Learn Sticker Fun: ABCs. (p. 1774)
Twin Sisters(r) Staff, et al, adapted by. B-i-n-g-o. (p. 122)
—Six Little Ducks. (p. 1582)
Twin Sisters(r) Staff, prod. Alphabet & Counting: Songs That Teach. (p. 49)
—Bible Stories: Songs That Teach. (p. 176)
—Preschool: Songs That Teach. (p. 1396)
Twine, Alice. Alligators. (p. 47)
—Alligators/Caimanes. (p. 47)
—Alligators/Caimanes. Obregon, Jose Maria, tr. from ENG. (p. 47)
—Baby Animals (p. 124)
—Baby Animals/Bebe Animales (p. 125)
—Baby Elephants. (p. 126)
—Baby Elephants/Elefantes Bebe. Obregon, Jose Maria, tr. from ENG. (p. 126)
—Bears. (p. 151)
—Bears/Osos. (p. 152)
—Bears/Osos. Obregon, Jose Maria, tr. (p. 152)
—Cats of the Wild. (p. 281)
—Cats of the Wild/Gatos Salvajes. (p. 281)
—Cats of the Wild/Gatos Salvajes. Obregon, Jose Maria, tr. (p. 281)
—Ducks. (p. 488)
—Ducks/Patos. (p. 488)
—Ducks/Patos. Obregon, Jose Maria, tr. (p. 488)
—Elephants/Elefantes Bebé. (p. 512)
—Horses. (p. 800)
—Horses/Caballos. (p. 800)
—Horses/Caballos. Obregon, Jose Maria, tr. (p. 800)
—Kangaroos. (p. 942)
—Kangaroos/Canguros. (p. 942)
—Kangaroos/Canguros. Obregon, Jose Maria, tr. from ENG. (p. 942)
—Kittens. (p. 963)
—Kittens/Gatitos. (p. 963)
—Kittens/Gatitos. Obregon, Jose Maria, tr. from ENG. (p. 963)
—Monkeys. (p. 1165)
—Monkeys/Monos. (p. 1166)
—Monkeys/Monos. Obregon, Jose Maria, tr. (p. 1166)
—My Favorite Book of Colors. (p. 1203)
—My Favorite Book of Numbers. (p. 1203)
—My Favorite Book of Opposites. (p. 1203)
—Penguins. (p. 1337)
—Penguins/Pinguinos. (p. 1337)
—Penguins/Pinguinos. Obregon, Jose Maria, tr. from ENG. (p. 1337)
—Puppies. (p. 1417)
—Puppies/Cachorros. (p. 1418)
—Puppies/Cachorros. Obregon, Jose Maria, tr. from ENG. (p. 1418)
—Seals. (p. 1536)
—Seals/Focas. (p. 1536)
—Seals/Focas. Obregon, Jose Maria, tr. (p. 1536)
Twinem, Neecy. Baby Coyote Counts. (p. 125)
—Baby Snake's Shapes. (p. 128)
—Noisy Beasties. Twinem, Neecy, illus. (p. 1262)
Twinem, Neecy, illus. see Bentley, Dawn.
Twinem, Neecy, illus. see James, Helen Foster.
Twinem, Neecy, illus. see Williams, Rozanne Lanczak.
Twinkle Books. Terrible Tommy. (p. 1721)
Twinn, A. Down by the Station. Stockham, Jess, illus. (p. 474)
—Ten Little Monkeys: Jumping on the Bed. Freeman, Tina, illus. (p. 1719)
Twinn, M. Metamorphoses: Butterfly. (p. 1130)
—Metamorphoses: Egg, Tadpole, Frog. (p. 1130)
—Old MacDonald Had a Farm. Adams, Pam, illus. (p. 1284)
—There Was an Old Lady Who Swallowed a Fly. Adams, Pam, illus. (p. 1730)
Twinney, Dick, illus. see Davies, Gill.
Twins, Pope. Poke-A-Dot!: Who's in the Ocean? (30 Poke-able Poppin' Dots) (p. 1377)
Twisdale, Monica. Old Man Goes to Show & Tell. (p. 1284)
Twist, Clint. 1000 Things You Should Know about Oceans. (p. 2001)
—Cleopatra: Queen of Egypt. Andrew, Ian, illus. (p. 331)
—Electricity: The Best Start in Science. (p. 509)
—Electricity. (p. 509)
—Endangered Animals Dictionary: An a to Z of Threatened Species. (p. 526)
—Extreme Earth. (p. 556)
—Forces & Motion: The Best Start in Science. (p. 617)
—Life Cycle of Army Ants. (p. 1009)
—Life Cycle of Cockroaches. (p. 1009)
—Life Cycle of Dung Beetles. (p. 1009)
—Life Cycle of Fleas. (p. 1009)
—Life Cycle of Honey Bees. (p. 1009)
—Life Cycle of Tarantulas. (p. 1009)
—Light & Sound: The Best Start in Science. (p. 1014)
—Light & Sound. (p. 1014)
—Little Book of Slime: Everything That Oozes, from Killer Slime to Living Mold. (p. 1025)
—Marco Polo: History's Great Adventurer. (p. 1092)
—Reptiles & Amphibians Dictionary. (p. 1461)
Twist, Clint, ed. see Aronnax, Pierre.
Twist, Clint, ed. see Calhoun, Marmaduke Randolph.
Twist, Clint, ed. see Lubber, William.
Twist, Clint, jt. auth. see Parker, Steve.
Twist, Clint & Fitzgibbon, Monty. Tyrannosaur. Wallis, Diz & Nicholls, Emma, illus. (p. 1805)
Twist, Clint & Orme, Helen. What Things Are Made Of: The Best Start in Science. (p. 1894)
Twist, Clint & Wells-Cole, Catherine. Charles Dickens: England's Most Captivating Storyteller. (p. 292)
Twist, Clint & Wood, A. J. Charles Darwin & the Beagle Adventure. Wallis, Diz, illus. (p. 292)
Twist, Clint, et al. Extreme Earth. (p. 556)
Twist, Sean, jt. auth. see Southwell, David.
Twitchell, Kim. Dare to Be Different. (p. 406)
Twitchell, Paul. Eckankar: The Key to Secret Worlds. (p. 502)
—Stranger by the River. (p. 1665)
—Talons of Time Graphic Novel. (p. 1704)
—Tiger's Fang. (p. 1749)
Twitty, Mary F. Ashley Visits Urchin Village. (p. 106)
Two Bulls, Marty Grant, illus. see Meierhenry, Mark V. & Volk, David.
Two Little Hands, creator. Everyday Signs Board Book. (p. 544)
—My First Signs Board Book. (p. 1208)
—Playtime Signs Board Book. (p. 1373)
Two Sisters Circle. Lady of the Lane. (p. 971)
Two-Can Publishing Ltd, creator. Hearts & Stars. (p. 760)
—Spots & Dots. (p. 1634)
Two-Can Publishing Ltd. Staff, contrib. by. My First Trip Around the World: A Picture Atlas Adventure. (p. 1208)
—Planet Earth. (p. 1367)
—Stand up for Your Rights. (p. 1639)
Twofeathers, Manny. My Road to the Sundance: My Vision Continues. (p. 1217)
Twohy, Mike. Outfoxed. Twohy, Mike, illus. (p. 1312)
—Poindexter Makes a Friend. Twohy, Mike, illus. (p. 1377)
—Wake up, Rupert! Twohy, Mike, illus. (p. 1853)
Twomey, Cathleen. Beachmont Letters. (p. 149)

Twomey, Emily Golden. Buster's Brilliant Dot to Dot. Twomey, Emily Golden, illus. (p. 245)
—Dot to Dot. Twomey, Emily Golden, illus. (p. 472)
Twomey, Lisa A., tr. see Comella, Angels.
Twomey-Lange, Marianna, photos by see Halstead, Jayce N.
Twork, Amanda J. O., photos by see Twork, Carol Camp.
Twork, Carol Camp. "I Want to Be Jesus" Over 150 Easy-to-Use Gospel Plays for Children. (p. 848)
—Rock! Answers to Questions of Faith. Twork, Amanda J. O. & Twork, R. Cody, photos by. (p. 1481)
Twork, Carol Camp, des. Scripture Notebook. (p. 1533)
Twork, R. Cody, photos by see Twork, Carol Camp.
Tyburski, Kimberly. Pesty Boy. (p. 1345)
Tydings, Faith H. Little Yellow Star. (p. 1038)
Tye, Laurie. Animal in Me: Is Very Plain to See. Mangelsen, Thomas D., photos by. (p. 78)
Tye, Peter. Crocodile Tours. Howe, Norma, illus. (p. 384)
Tyger, Rory, illus. see Faulkner, Keith.
Tyger, Rory, illus. see Freedman, Claire, et al.
Tyger, Rory, illus. see Freedman, Claire.
Tyger, Rory, jt. auth. see Faulkner, Keith.
Tyldesley, Joyce A. Egypt. (p. 506)
Tyle, Laura B. Making the Grade: Everything Your 1st Grader Needs to Know. (p. 1082)
Tyle, Shirley. Where Is Time (p. 1909)
Tyler, Alison. Rumors. (p. 1495)
—Something about Workmen. (p. 1609)
—Sticky Fingers. (p. 1650)
Tyler, Alyson. Don't Say Preschool! (p. 468)
Tyler, Amy J. & RH Disney Staff. Best Dad in the Sea. RH Disney Staff, illus. (p. 168)
Tyler, Barbara A. Picture Yourself Writing Drama: Using Photos to Inspire Writing (p. 1356)
Tyler, Braxton. Chains of Whispers. (p. 288)
Tyler, Brenda. Tomtes of Hilltop Wood. (p. 1765)
Tyler, Craig. Fine Kettle of Fish. (p. 589)
Tyler, Gemma. Crocodile. (p. 384)
Tyler, Gillian, illus. see Chaconas, Dori.
Tyler, Gillian, illus. see Rosen, Michael.
Tyler, Jenny. Animal Stories for Little Children. (p. 79)
—Baby's Very First Getting Dressed. (p. 129)
—Baby's Very First Mealtime Book. (p. 129)
—Big Pig on a Dig. Cartwright, Stephen, illus. (p. 183)
—Dot-to-Dot on the Farm. (p. 472)
—Duck's Bathtime. Cartwright, Stephen, illus. (p. 488)
—Jugamos Al Escondite? (p. 931)
Tyler, Jenny, ed. see Amery, Heather.
Tyler, Jenny, ed. see Bryant-Mole, Karen.
Tyler, Jenny, ed. see Cox, Phil Roxbee.
Tyler, Jenny, ed. see Dowswell, Paul.
Tyler, Jenny, ed. see Hawthorn, Phillip.
Tyler, Jenny, ed. see Leigh, Susannah.
Tyler, Jenny, ed. see Marks, Anthony.
Tyler, Jenny, ed. see O'Brien, Eileen.
Tyler, Jenny, ed. see Roxbee Cox, Phil.
Tyler, Jenny, jt. auth. see Blundell, Kim.
Tyler, Jenny, jt. auth. see Brooks, Felicity.
Tyler, Jenny, jt. auth. see Bryant-Mole, Karen.
Tyler, Jenny, jt. auth. see Hawthorn, Philip.
Tyler, Jenny, jt. auth. see Hawthorn, Phillip.
Tyler, Jenny, jt. auth. see Hawthorne, Philip.
Tyler, Jenny & Blundell, Kim. Animal Mazes. (p. 78)
—Monster Mazes. (p. 1167)
Tyler, Jenny & Cartwright, S. Animal Hide-and-Seek. (p. 78)
Tyler, Jenny & Cartwright, S. Duck by the Sea. (p. 488)
Tyler, Jenny & Doherty, Gillian, eds. Usborne Stories for Little Boys. (p. 1827)
—Usborne Stories for Little Girls. (p. 1827)
Tyler, Jenny & Gee, R. Counting up to Ten. (p. 371)
—Odd One Out. (p. 1278)
—Ready for Reading. (p. 1447)
—Ready for Writing. (p. 1447)
—Time. Bryant-Mole, K., ed. (p. 1750)
Tyler, Jenny & Hawthorn, P. There's a Monster in My House. (p. 1731)
—Who's Making That Mess? (p. 1920)
—Who's Making That Smell? (p. 1920)
Tyler, Jenny & Hawthorn, Phillip. Who's Making That Noise? (p. 1920)
—Who's Making That Smell? Cartwright, Stephen, illus. (p. 1920)
Tyler, Kate, ed. see Scales, Peter C. & Leffert, Nancy.
Tyler, Kip, jt. auth. see Tyler, Marya Washington.
Tyler, M. Ramifications in Genesis 1-3. (p. 1438)
Tyler, Maggie Ann. Fantasy on 4th Street. (p. 572)
Tyler, Marya Washington & Tyler, Kip. Extreme Math: Real Math, Real People, Real Sports. (p. 556)
Tyler, Michael. Skin You Live In. Csicsko, David Lee, illus. (p. 1585)
Tyler, Royall. Island of Barrataria; Tantalization: The Govenor of a Day (unpublished plaus) (p. 892)
Tyler, Sandy. Herkimer's Big Day: Herkimer the Police Horse Meets a Young Girl Named Sammy. Williams, Brian, illus. (p. 771)
Tyler, Sean P. Grassroots. (p. 712)
Tyler, Shirley. Nite Nite Bedtime (p. 1257)
Tyler, Tanith. Aegis Rising. (p. 25)
Tyler, Tim, illus. see Mazur, Cathy May.
Tyler, William H. Little Wolf Cubs' Christmas Gift. (p. 1038)
—Who Let the Mongoose Loose? (p. 1916)
Tylers, Michael. Predators of North America. (p. 1395)
—Predators of South America & Antarctica. (p. 1395)
Tyler-Vaughn, Savanna. Flour Sack Wear. (p. 607)
Tylevich, Katherine & Skindzier, Jon. Macalester College College Prowler off the Record. (p. 1067)
Tylicki, Gene J. & Tylicki, Jo. Lonesome George: The First Three Weeks (p. 1046)
—More Cat Tails As Told by George to Guy: A Lonesome George Work. (p. 1174)
—Saga Continues As Told by George to Guy: A Lonesome George Work. (p. 1502)
Tylicki, Jo, jt. auth. see Tylicki, Gene J.
Tym, Kate. Be Nice. (p. 148)
—Say Please. (p. 1518)
—Tell the Truth. (p. 1717)
—Time to Share. (p. 1753)
Tym, Kate, illus. see Williams, Sophy.
Tyminski, Lori, illus. see Driscoll, Laura & Disney Book Group Staff.
Tyminski, Lori, illus. see Driscoll, Laura.
Tyminski, Lori, illus. see Redbank, Tennant, et al.
Tyminski, Lori, illus. see RH Disney Staff & Glum, Felicity.
Tyminski, Lori, illus. see Richards, Kitty & Disney Book Group Staff.
Tymony, Cy. Sneaky Book for Boys: How to Perfom Sneaky Magic Tricks, Escape a Grasp, Craft a Compass, Walk Through a Postcard, Survive in the Wilderness, & Learn about Sneaky Animals & Insects, Sneaky Escapes & Sneaky Human Feats. (p. 1597)
Tyndale House Publishers Staff, jt. contrib. by see Group Publishing Staff.
Tyndale House Publishers Staff & Livingstone Corporation Staff, prods. Girls Life Application Study Bible NLT. (p. 680)
Tyndale House Publishers Staff, ed. One Year Bible for Kids. (p. 1297)
Tyndale, prod. Armor of God. (p. 99)
—Big Bible Fun Color & Learn (p. 178)
—Christmas Story. (p. 315)
—Count My Blessings. (p. 369)
—Favorite Bible Stories from the Old Testament. (p. 578)
—Gigantic Coloring Book of Bible Stories. (p. 676)
—Gigantic Coloring Book of God's World. (p. 676)
—God Always Cares. (p. 688)
—In the Beginning. (p. 865)
—Jesus Is Born. (p. 915)
—Jesus Teaches Me. (p. 916)
—My Bible. (p. 1197)
—My Church. (p. 1200)
Tyner, Christopher. I'll Do It Tommarra Laura. (p. 856)
Tyner, Stuart. Meanest Man in the Army: And Other Stories of Grace. (p. 1116)
Tyo, Courtney. Holiday Puzzles. (p. 788)
Typaldos, Melanie. Celeste & the Adorable Kitten. Tayts, Alexandra, illus. (p. 285)
Typaldos, Sylvia. Don't Call Me Lassie! The Fascinating Lives of Seven Family Dogs. (p. 467)
Tyre, Greg R. Fun with Sockie. (p. 649)
Tyree, Debi. Jessica's Little Sister: A Story about Autism. (p. 914)
Tyree, Debra, ed. see Stafford, Lonnie.
Tyree, Omar R. 12 Brown Boys. (p. 1994)
Tyrell, Melissa. Hurray for Snow! Patrick, Tom, illus. (p. 829)
—Little Reindeer. Brooks, Nan, illus. (p. 1035)
Tyrer, Robert. Ralphie the Polar Bear. (p. 1437)
Tyrol, Adelaide, illus. see Caduto, Michael J.
Tyrrell, Frances. Huron Carol. (p. 829)
Tyrrell, George Augustus. Book of Thomas the Doubter: Unovering the Hidden Teachings. (p. 212)
Tyrrell, Helen. Nora & the Dancing Horse. (p. 1264)
Tyrrell, Karen. Bailey Beats the Blah. Pocock, Aaron, illus. (p. 133)
Tyrrell, Kayla, illus. see Tyrrell, Kevin.
Tyrrell, Kevin. Froggy Kisses. Tyrrell, Kayla, illus. (p. 641)
Tyrrell, Melissa. Beauty & the Beast. McMullen, Nigel, illus. (p. 154)
—Gingerbread Man. McMullen, Nigel, illus. (p. 677)
—Hansel & Gretel. McMullen, Nigel, illus. (p. 743)
—Pinocchio. McMullen, Nigel, illus. (p. 1360)
Tyrtania, Joachim & Hemrich-Skomer, Denise. Together Time: Cycle A. (p. 1762)
Tysinger, Dona. Cheyenne Dragon & the Dragonfly. (p. 299)
Tyson, Carolee. Factory Ride. (p. 561)
Tyson, Delilah Cottingham. Color Us Rainbow. (p. 343)
Tyson, Ian. Primera: The Story of Wild Mustangs. Halvorson, Adeline, illus. (p. 1400)
Tyson, Leigh Ann. Good Night, Little Dragons. (p. 699)
—Interview with Harry the Tarantula. Drescher, Henrik, illus. (p. 881)
Tyson, Liz, illus. see Hevesi, Rachel.
Tyson, Neil deGrasse, jt. auth. see Graubart, Norman D.
Tyson, Peter K. Winning Touch: A story about football for teenage boys (and maybe a few Girls) (p. 1937)
Tysseland, Elsie. Hershel the Dog. Fitch, Rik, illus. (p. 774)
Tzekov, Jack, illus. see Soares, Valérie I. O.
Tzingoker, Lilach. Sonny's Adventure in Mystery Park. (p. 1612)
Tzvi, G. J. Great Adventure of la Gang du Sept. (p. 713)
Tzvieli, Neta. Private Eyes & the Mysterious Submarine. (p. 1407)

U

U. S. A. Global Investment Center Staff. Morocco Customs, Trade Regulations & Procedures Handbook. (p. 1176)
U. S. Bureau of American Anthology Staff. Articles on Archeological Subjects Reprinted from the Handbook of American Indians. (p. 104)
U. S. Congress House Committee. Hearings Before the Committee on the Public Lands, January 11, 1905, for Preservation of Prehistoric Ruins on the Public Lands. (p. 759)
U S Games Systems, Inc., creator. Guardian Angel Cards. (p. 728)
U. S. Kids Editorial Staff. Best Adventure of the Puzzle Squad. (p. 168)
U. S. National Geographic Society Staff. Animal Pop! With 5 Incredible, Life Size Fold-Outs. (p. 79)
—Anybody Home? (p. 91)
—Awesome Animals: With Games, Facts, & 10 Pull-Out Posters! (p. 120)
—Baby Animal Pop! With 5 Incredible, Life-Size Fold-Outs. (p. 124)
—Beginner's United States: It's Your Country. Be a Part of It! (p. 159)
—Beginner's United States Atlas. (p. 159)
—Beginner's World Atlas. (p. 159)
—Count! No. 1,2,3. (p. 369)
—Dinosaur Museum: An Unforgettable, Interactive Virtual Tour Through Dinosaur History. Quigley, Sebastian, illus. (p. 442)
—Get with the Beat! (p. 668)
—Great Cheese Chase. (p. 714)
—Halloween Book of Fun! (p. 737)
—Hide & Seek. (p. 776)
—How Does Your Garden Grow? (p. 809)
—Monsters of the Deep. (p. 1169)
—Mystery of the Disappearing Swing. (p. 1225)
—Nat Geo Wild Animal Atlas: Earth's Astonishing Animals & Where They Live. (p. 1230)
—National Geographic Kids Almanac 2011. (p. 1231)
—National Geographic Kids Beginner's World Atlas. (p. 1231)
—National Geographic Kids United States Atlas. (p. 1232)
—National Geographic Little Kids Word Book: Learning the Words in Your World. (p. 1233)
—National Geographic World Atlas for Young Explorers. (p. 1233)
—NG Kids Big Book of Fun. (p. 1250)
—Our World: A Child's First Picture Atlas. (p. 1310)
—Student Atlas of the World. (p. 1669)
—True or False Animal Cards. (p. 1792)
—Ultimate Weird but True: 1,000 Wild & Wacky Facts & Photos. (p. 1810)
—United States Atlas for Young Explorers. Lamichhane, Priyanka, ed. (p. 1819)
—Weird but True! 3: 300 Outrageous Facts. (p. 1872)
—Weird but True: Stupid Criminals: 100 Brainless Baddies Busted, Plus Wacky Facts. Cocotos, Tom Nick, illus. (p. 1872)
—What Is It? (p. 1889)
—World Atlas. (p. 1954)
—Xtreme Illusions. (p. 1967)
—You Are the World! (p. 1973)
—You are the World! (p. 1973)
U. S. National Geographic Society Staff, jt. auth. see Gray, Leon.
U. S. National Geographic Society Staff, jt. auth. see Heiligman, Deborah.
U. S. National Geographic Society Staff, jt. auth. see Hossell, Karen.
U. S. National Geographic Society Staff, jt. auth. see Richards, Mose.
U. S. National Geographic Society Staff, jt. auth. see Zoehfeld, Kathleen Weidner.
U. S. National Geographic Society Staff, photos by see Stewart, Melissa.
U. S. National Geographic Society Staff & Dalal, A. Kamala. National Geographic Countries of the World - Laos. (p. 1231)
U. S. National Geographic Society Staff & Deckker, Zilah Quezado. Portugal. (p. 1387)
U. S. National Geographic Society Staff & Delano, Marfe Ferguson. Earth in the Hot Seat: Bulletins from a Warming World. (p. 496)
U. S. National Geographic Society Staff & Furgang, Kathy. National Geographic Kids Everything Volcanoes & Earthquakes: Earthshaking Photos, Facts, & Fun! (p. 1232)
U. S. National Geographic Society Staff & Harness, Cheryl. Ye Olde Weird but True: 300 Outrageous Facts from History. (p. 1969)
U. S. National Geographic Society Staff & Marsh, Laura. National Geographic Readers: Weird Sea Creatures. (p. 1233)
U. S. National Geographic Society Staff & National Geographic Kids Staff. Weird but True: 300 Outrageous Facts. Halling, Jonathan, illus. (p. 1872)
U. S. National Geographic Society Staff & Phillips, Charles. Sweden. (p. 1689)
U. S. National Geographic Society Staff & Shields, Sarah D. Turkey. (p. 1797)
U. S. National Geographic Society Staff & Spelman, Lucy H. Animal Encyclopedia: 2,500 Animals with Photos, Maps, & More! (p. 77)
U. S. National Geographic Society Staff & Spears, James. National Geographic Kids Everything Pets: Furry Facts, Photos, & Fun-Unleashed! (p. 1232)
U. S. National Geographic Society Staff & Stewart, Melissa. Deadliest Animals. (p. 417)
U. S. National Geographic Society Staff, contrib. by. Midwest Today. (p. 1139)
—Northeast Today. (p. 1265)
—Southeast Today. (p. 1617)
—Southwest Today. (p. 1618)
—West Today. (p. 1876)
U. S. National Geographic Society Staff, creator. National Geographic Atlas of the Middle East. (p. 1231)
—National Geographic Beginner's World Atlas. (p. 1231)
U. S. National Geographic Society Staff, ed. Books for Young Explorers (p. 212)
U. S. National Geographic Society Staff, et al. Bizarre Dinosaurs: Some Very Strange Creatures & Why We Think They Got That Way. U. S. National Geographic Society Staff, illus. (p. 194)
U X L, ed. UXL Encyclopedia of Science (p. 1829)
—UXL Man-Made Disasters (p. 1829)
Uahc, Ecarg. Adventures of I. Firebrace: The Battle in the Underground. (p. 18)
Ubberball, R. Wham-O Superball. Copeland, Cynthia L., illus. (p. 1878)
Uberoi, Meera. Myths & Legends: From Around the World. (p. 1227)
Uboh, Victoria. Let's Clean My Room !! (p. 995)
UC Publishing Staff & Murphy, Sally. Action Numeracy: Who Wants to be a Millionaire? (p. 10)
Uccellini, Louis W., jt. auth. see Kocin, Paul J.
Uchida, Kazuna. I Shall Never Return (p. 845)
Uchida, Kazuna, jt. auth. see Uchida, Kazuna.
Uchida, Kazuna & Uchida, Kazuna. I Shall Never Return (p. 845)
Uchida, Yoshiko. Desert Exile: The Uprooting of a Japanese-American Family. (p. 429)
—Journey to Topaz. (p. 929)
—Samurai of Gold Hill. Forberg, Ati, illus. (p. 1510)
Uchilla, Canchi. 1532: A Test of Courage. (p. 2002)
Uchiyama, Akira & Kodaira, Hiromi. Yubisashi Yubinazori Aiueo. (p. 1983)
Udagawa, Avery Fischer, tr. see Oketani, Shogo.
Udall, Anne J., jt. auth. see Mandel, Scott.
Udelhoven, Hermann-Josef, jt. auth. see Hattstein, Markus.
Udelhoven, Hermann-Josef, jt. auth. see Knebel, Arthur.
Uderzo, jt. auth. see Goscinny, René.
Uderzo, A., illus. see Goscinny, R.
Uderzo, A., illus. see Goscinny, René & Livre, Hachette.
Uderzo, A., jt. auth. see Goscinny, R.
Uderzo, A., jt. auth. see Goscinny, René.
Uderzo, A. & Goscinny, R. Asterix Omnibus 4: Includes Asterix the Legionary #10, Asterix & the Chieftain's Shield #11, & Asterix at the Olympic Games #12. (p. 108)
Uderzo, Albert, illus. see Goscinny, R.
Uderzo, Albert, illus. see Goscinny, René, et al.
Uderzo, Albert, jt. auth. see Goscinny, R.
Uderzo, Albert, jt. auth. see Goscinny, Rene.
Uderzo, Albert, jt. auth. see Goscinny, René.
Uderzo, Albert, jt. auth. see Goscinny, René.
Uderzo, Albert, jt. auth. see Uderzo, Albert.
Uderzo, Albert & Goscinny, René. Asterix & the Black Gold. Bell, Anthea & Hockbridge, Derek, trs. from FRE. (p. 107)
—Asterix & the Falling Sky. Bell, Anthea & Hockridge, Derek, trs. from FRE. (p. 107)
Uderzo, Albert & Goscinny, Rene. Asterix & the Vikings: The Book of the Film. (p. 108)
Uderzo, Albert & Goscinny, René. Asterix & the Vikings: The Book of the Film. Bell, Anthea, tr. (p. 108)
Uderzo, Albert & Goscinny, Rene. Asterix at the Olympic Games. Uderzo, Albert, illus. (p. 108)
Uderzo, Albert & Uderzo, Albert. Astérix en América: El álbum de la Película. (p. 108)
—Astérix y Latraviata. (p. 108)
—Golpe de Menhir: El álbum de la Película. (p. 697)
—Gran Zanja. (p. 707)
—Mal Trago de Obélix. (p. 1083)
—Odisea de Astérix. (p. 1278)
Uderzo, Albert, et al. Asterix & the Falling Sky. Bell, Anthea & Hockridge, Derek, trs. from FRE. (p. 107)
Uderzo, M., illus. see Lefèvre-Garros, J. P.
Uderzo, M., illus. see Rideau, J. & Asso, B.
Uderzo, M., jt. auth. see Goscinny, René.
Uderzo, Marcel, illus. see Asso, Bernard & Rideau, Joel.
Udo, Victoria. Children & the Yard Animals: Children of an African Village Volume 1. (p. 302)
UDON. VENT Volume 1. (p. 1836)
Udon, illus. see Jerwa, Brandon.
Udon Entertainment Corp Staff, illus. see Reader's Digest Staff & Teitelbaum, Michael.
Udon Kids Staff & Hakamada, Mera. Fairy Idol Kanon (p. 563)
Udon Kids Staff & Mizuna, Tomomi. Big Adventures of Majoko (p. 177)
Udovic, David, illus. see Cleary, Brian P.
Udovic, David, illus. see Thach, James Otis.
Udry, Janice M., jt. auth. see Udry, Janice May.
Udry, Janice May. Moon Jumpers. Sendak, Maurice, illus. (p. 1172)
Udry, Janice May & Udry, Janice M. Arbol es Hermoso. Fiol, Maria A., tr. (p. 94)
Udvari, Joseph G. Courage. (p. 372)
Ueda, Kumiko, illus. see Nelson, Brett Alan.
Ueda, Miwa. Change of Heart (p. 290)
—Peach Girl: Change of Heart. Vol. 11 Ueda, Miwa, illus. (p. 1332)
Ueda, Rinko. Tail of the Moon (p. 1695)
—Tail of the Moon Ueda, Rinko, illus. (p. 1695)
Uegaki, Chieri. Rosie & Buttercup. Jorisch, Stéphane, illus. (p. 1490)
—Suki's Kimono. Jorisch, Stephane, illus. (p. 1673)
Uehashi, Nahoko. Guardian of the Darkness. Hirano, Cathy, tr. (p. 728)
—Guardian of the Spirit. Hirano, Cathy, tr. (p. 728)
Uehashi, Nahoko & Hirano, Cathy. Guardian of the Darkness. Shimizu, Yuko, illus. (p. 728)
Ueyama, Michiro. Chaotic Century. Ueyama, Michiro, illus. (p. 291)
UFA National Team. Let's Learn How to Learn: Workshops for Key Stage 2. Beckman, Rosalind & Martin, Lily, eds. (p. 998)
Ufer, David A. Giraffe Who Was Afraid of Heights Carlson, Kirsten, illus. (p. 677)
Uff, Caroline, illus. see Doyle, Malachy & Black, Jeremy.
Uff, Caroline, illus. see Doyle, Malachy.
Uff, Caroline, illus. see Nimmo, Jenny.
Uff, Caroline, reader. Dia con Lulu. (p. 433)
—Feliz Cumpleanos, Lulu. (p. 581)
UFlipp. You & Your Military Hero: Building Positive Thinking Skills During Your Hero's Deployment. (p. 1973)
UG, Philippe. Funny Birds. (p. 649)
—In the Butterfly Garden. (p. 865)
—Robots: Watch Out, Water About! (p. 1481)
Ugaki, Matome. Fading Victory: The Diary of Admiral Matome Ugaki, 1941-1945. Dillon, Katherine V. & Goldstein, Donald M., eds. (p. 562)
Ugalde Alcantara, Felipe, illus. see Villaseñor, Victor.
Ugalde, Felipe, illus. see Gazquez, Juan Pablo Hernandez, et al.
Ugalde, Felipe, illus. see Suarez, Carlos Ruiz.
Ugalde, Raquel, tr. see Harter, Debbie.
Ugarte, Ane Miren De Rotaeche. Very Special Tea Party. (p. 1838)
Ugarte, Julia & Jendrey, Julie. Seattle University College Prowler off the Record. (p. 1539)
Ugawa, Hiroki. Shrine of the Morning Mist Ugawa, Hiroki, illus. (p. 1571)
Ugezene, Esther I. KiKi, the School Truant. (p. 955)

Ugliano, Natascia, illus. see Gellman, Ellie B.
Ugliano, Natascia, illus. see Jules, Jacqueline & Hechtkopf, Jacqueline.
Ugliano, Natascia, illus. see Jules, Jacqueline.
Uglow, Lorna. Fairy in the Potting Shed. (p. 563)
Uglow, Loyd. Abraham Lincoln: Will You Ever Give Up? James, Kennon, illus. (p. 6)
—Benjamin Franklin: You Know What to Say. Budwine, Greg, illus. (p. 165)
Ugochuku, Ike. Christ My Life: Foundation. (p. 311)
Ugon, Gabriela Armand. Secreto de la Casa Gris. (p. 1544)
Uher, Brett. Dark Moon Diary (p. 407)
Uher, John, photos by see Fishbein, Susie.
Uhía, Manuel, illus. see Casalderrey, Fina & Casalderrey Fraga, Xosefa.
Uhía, Manuel, tr. see Casalderrey, Fina & Casalderrey Fraga, Xosefa.
Uhlberg, Myron. Dad, Jackie, & Me Bootman, Colin, illus. (p. 398)
—Flying over Brooklyn Fitzgerald, Gerald, illus. (p. 610)
—Printer Sorensen, Henri, tr. (p. 1407)
—Printer Sørensen, Henri, illus. (p. 1407)
—Storm Called Katrina Bootman, Colin, illus. (p. 1655)
Uhles, Mary, illus. see Enderle, Dotti.
Uhles, Mary, illus. see Riehle, Mary Ann McCabe.
Uhlig, Elizabeth. Children Just Like You. Uhlig, Elizabeth, illus. (p. 302)
—I See America! Uhlig, Elizabeth, illus. (p. 845)
—I Want to Be. Uhlig, Elizabeth, illus. (p. 847)
—Memoir Writing & Illustrating for Children. (p. 1125)
Uhlig, Elizabeth, illus. see Anderson, Lillian.
Uhlig, Elizabeth, illus. see Laub, Frima.
Uhlig, Elizabeth, illus. see Rothstein, Evelyn.
Uhlig, Elizabeth, tr. see Ledu-Frattini, Stephanie.
Uhlman, Tom, illus. see Rusch, Elizabeth.
Uhlman, Tom, photos by see Carson, Mary Kay.
Uhlmann, Chris, jt. auth. see Lee, Cathy.
Uhouse, Debra, illus. see Moss, Lucille.
Uihlein, Mary. Hello Little Owl. Uihlein, Mary, illus. (p. 764)
—Hello Little Owl, I Am Hermit Crab! Uihlein, Mary, illus. (p. 764)
U-Inspire Inc, ed. see Jefferson, Thomas.
U-Inspire Inc, ed. see Washington, George.
Uitgeverij, Clavis, illus. see De Smet, Marian & Meijer, Marja.
Uitti, Dan. Keep Your Computer Alive - Coloring Book. Hudson, Ted, illus. (p. 947)
Ukoha, Ndubuisi. Dear England. (p. 419)
Ukrainian Orthodox League Staff, prod. Andrew's First Holy Confession: The ABC's of My Church. (p. 72)
—Anne Learns about Holy Communion: The ABC's of My Church. (p. 86)
Ulasevich, Olga, ed. see AZ Books Staff.
Ulasi, Zekeriya, et al. Ali Ibn Abi Talib. (p. 39)
—Umar Ibn Al-Khattab. (p. 1810)
Ulasowski, Muza, illus. see Poulter, J. R.
Ulasowski, Muza, illus. see Rausin, K. D.
Ulasowski, Muza, jt. auth. see Horn, Sandra.
Ulbrich, Jasper. Little Owl. (p. 1032)
Ulch, Virginia. I Love You Anyway. (p. 843)
—Love, Bandit - a Tail of Foster Care. (p. 1059)
—Love You, Teddy - a Tail of Loss & Hope. Burkert, Howard, photos by. (p. 1061)
Ulene, Nancy, illus. see Peterson, Scott.
Ulerio, Michelle. Lily Finds Her Way Home. (p. 1018)
Uletilovic, Patricia. Merlin's Return. (p. 1128)
Ulick, Michael Ackerman. Romeo the Rhino's Rocky Romance: A Cautionary Tale about Differences. Guy, Will, illus. (p. 1486)
Ulinski, Michael. Why Do Animals Hibernate? (p. 1923)
Ulker, Munise. Little Batul's Eid Celebration: The Most Pleasant Festival of Sacrifice. (p. 1023)
Ulkutay & Co Ltd, illus. see Gerlings, Rebecca, ed.
Ulkutay Design Group, illus. see Fontes, Justine.
Ulkutay Design Group, illus. see Landolf, Diane Wright.
Ulkutay Design Group Staff. Barbie Princess Charm School. (p. 138)
Ulkutay Design Group Staff, illus. see Fontes, Justine.
Ulkutay Design Group Staff, illus. see Gerlings, Rebecca, ed.
Ulkutay Design Group Staff, illus. see Reader's Digest Staff.
Ullman, Barb Bentler. Whistle Bright Magic: A Nutfolk Tale. (p. 1912)
Ullmann, Carol. Copyright Infringmnt. Greenhaven Press Editors, ed. (p. 366)
—Copyright Infringmnt. Greenhaven Press Editors & Gale Editors, eds. (p. 366)
Ullmann, Carol & Zott, Lynn M. Religious Liberty. (p. 1458)
Ulloa, Justo & Ulloa, Leonor. Graded Spanish Reader: Primera Etapa. (p. 705)
Ulloa, Leanor Alvarez De, see Ulloa, Justo.
Ulloa, Leonor, jt. auth. see Ulloa, Justo.
Ullrich, Hortense. Aventura de Lorenzo. (p. 119)
—Prueba de Valor de Lorenzo. (p. 1413)
Ullrich, Jan F. Lakhotiya Woglaka Po! - Speak Lakota! Level 1. (p. 972)
Ullrich, Nal D. Octo-Annie: Home-Help Super Star. (p. 1277)
Ulmer, D. M. Silent Battleground. (p. 1575)
Ulmer, Dwayne, compiled by. Basic Student Ministry in the Kingdom-Focused Church. (p. 142)
Ulmer, Louise. Bible That Wouldn't Burn: William Tyndale's New Testament. Ulmer, Louise, illus. (p. 176)
—Bible That Wouldn't Burn: How the Tyndale English Version of the Bible Came About. (p. 176)
—Good Friday. Sandland, Reg, illus. (p. 698)
Ulmer, Michael. H Is for Horse: An Equestrian Alphabet. vanFrankenhuyze, Gijsbert, illus. (p. 734)
—J Is for Jump Shot: A Basketball Alphabet. Braught, Mark, illus. (p. 901)
—M Is for Maple Leafs. Rose, Melanie, illus. (p. 1067)
Ulmer, Michael, jt. auth. see Ulmer, Mike.
Ulmer, Mike. Gift of the Inuksuk. Rose, Melanie, illus. (p. 675)
—J Is for Jump Shot: A Basketball Alphabet. Braught, Mark, illus. (p. 901)
—Loonies & Toonies: A Canadian Number Book. Rose, Melanie, illus. (p. 1052)
—M Is for Maple: A Canadian Alphabet. Rose-Popp, Melanie, illus. (p. 1067)
Ulmer, Mike & Ulmer, Michael. M Is for Maple: A Canadian Alphabet. Rose, Melanie, illus. (p. 1067)
Ulmer, Wendy. A Isn't for Fox: An Isn't Alphabet. Knorr, Laura, illus. (p. 1)
Ulmer, Wendy K. Campfire for Cowboy Billy. Spengler, Kenneth J., illus. (p. 257)
—Zero, Zilch, Nada: Counting to None. Knorr, Laura, illus. (p. 1986)
Ulrich, Ann Carol. Light Being. (p. 1015)
—Mystery at Hickory Hill: Annette Vetter Adventure #1. (p. 1223)
Ulrich, George. Mrs. Picasso's Polliwog: A Mystery. Ulrich, George, illus. (p. 1187)
Ulrich, George, illus. see Christopher, Matt.
Ulrich, George, illus. see Gikow, Louise.
Ulrich, George, illus. see Kramer, Sydelle.
Ulrich, George, illus. see Willson, Sarah.
Ulrich, Kelly, illus. see Griffiths, Allen & Godinez, Mary.
Ulrich, Kelly, illus. see Yrjana, Colleen.
Ulrich, Maureen. Breakaway (p. 224)
—Face Off (p. 560)
—Power Plays (p. 1390)
Ulrich, Paulina. Flightless Bird. (p. 604)
Ulrich, Tom J. Birds of the Northern Rockies. (p. 192)
Ultimate Sports Force Staff. Super Squad: Basketball's Superstars. (p. 1682)
Uluadluak, Donald. Kamik: An Inuit Puppy Story Leng, Qin, illus. (p. 942)
Ulve, Kirsten. Kook Book. (p. 967)
Ulz, Ivan. Fire Truck! Kaida, Garrett, illus. (p. 591)
Uman, Jennifer, jt. auth. see Vidali, Valerio.
Umana, Maria Gomez, illus. see Archer, Colleen Rutherford.
Umansky, jt. auth. see Umansky, Kaye.
Umansky, Kaye. Cinderella: Photocopiable Plays. (p. 320)
—Cinderella. Crossland, Caroline, illus. (p. 320)
—Clover Twig & the Perilous Path. Wright, Johanna, illus. (p. 335)
—Emperor's New Clothes. (p. 521)
—Emperor's New Clothes. Crossland, Caroline, illus. (p. 521)
—Jealous Giant. Weir, Doffy, illus. (p. 911)
—Noah's Ark (p. 1261)
—Noah's Ark. Richardson-Jones, Tessa, illus. (p. 1261)
—Pongwiffy. Smedley, Chris, illus. (p. 1382)
—Sleeping Beauty. Crossland, Caroline, illus. (p. 1589)
—Solomon Snow & the Silver Spoon. Nash, Scott, illus. (p. 1608)
—Sophie & Abigail Currey, Anna, illus. (p. 1613)
—Sophie & the Mother's Day Card. Currey, Anna, illus. (p. 1613)
—Sophie & the Wonderful Picture. Currey, Anna, illus. (p. 1613)
—Sophie in Charge. Currey, Anna, illus. (p. 1613)
Umansky, Kaye, jt. auth. see Umansky, Kaye.
Umansky, Kaye & Currey, Anna. Sophie & Abigail. (p. 1613)
Umansky, Kaye & Umansky. Sophie & the Mother's Day Card Currey, Anna, illus. (p. 1613)
—Sophie & the Wonderful Picture Currey, Anna, illus. (p. 1613)
Umansky, Kaye & Umansky, Kaye. Romantic Giant. Weir, Doffy, illus. (p. 1486)
Umbach, Andrea. Conquer Your Fears & Phobias for Teens: How to Overcome Scary Situations & Increase Your Freedom. (p. 358)
Umbreit, Wayne. Ah!I Remember it Well. (p. 30)
Umezawa, Rui. Strange Light Afar: Tales of the Supernatural from Old Japan Fujita, Mikiko, illus. (p. 1665)
Umezu, Kazuo. Drifting Classroom Umezu, Kazuo, illus. (p. 485)
—Drifting Classroom. Roman, Annette, ed. (p. 485)
Umicini, Roberta, tr. see McKee, David.
Umicini, Roberta, tr. see Mycek-Wodecki, Anna.
Umina, Lisa. Milo & the Green Wagon. (p. 1144)
—Milo Finds His Best Friend. Thompson, Chad, illus. (p. 1144)
Umina, Lisa M. Milo with a Halo. (p. 1144)
Umpierre, Migdalia, illus. see Iturrondo, Angeles Molina.
Umscheid, Kit, illus. see Wigington, Patti.
Umstattd, William D. & Davis, Charles W. Modern Cabinetmaking. (p. 1158)
—Modern Cabinetmaking Instructor's Manual. (p. 1158)
Umstatter, Jack. Words, Words, Words! Ready-to-Use Games & Activities for Vocabulary Building, Grades 7-12. (p. 1952)
Unalp, Janet, illus. see Banks, Celia.
Unamuno, Miguel de. San Manuel Bueno Martir y Tres Historias Mas. (p. 1510)
Unamuno, Miguel de, jt. auth. see Unamuno, Miguel de.
Unamuno, Miguel de & Unamuno, Miguel de. San Manuel Bueno Martir. (p. 1510)
—San Manuel Bueno, Mártir. Cabrales Arteaga, José Manuel, ed. (p. 1510)
Uncle Bernie. Michaels Adventures in the Land of Nod Book: Michaels Trip to Orange County. (p. 1135)
Uncle Bob. Tobi the Little Puppy Dog. Arnold, Stephen, illus. (p. 1760)
Uncle Bobby. Herman & Hariett. (p. 771)
Uncle Chuck. Monkey Puzzle Tree. (p. 1165)
Uncle E. ADVENTURES of Diggle, Boogie & Lolo: Boogie & the Bubbles (p. 17)
Uncle Henry. Biode. Uncle Henry, illus. (p. 188)
—How the Tooth Fairy, of All People, Saved the Day Uncle Henry, illus. (p. 813)
—Vileburgers: With Friends Like This Who Needs Halloween? Uncle Henry, illus. (p. 1842)
Uncle, J. & Mom. Sean Learns the Tummy Town Way. (p. 1537)
Uncle Markie. Piglettè & Bobo Christmas in Palm Springs. (p. 1358)
—Piglettè & Bobo Have Visitors. (p. 1358)
—Piglettè & Bobo in Berkeley. (p. 1358)
—Piglettè & Bobo in Estonia. (p. 1358)
—Piglettè & Bobo in Kansas City. (p. 1358)
—Piglettè & Bobo in Sud Africa. (p. 1358)
—Piglettè & Bobo in the New Territories. (p. 1358)
—Piglettè & Bobo in the United Kingdom. (p. 1358)
—Piglettè & Bobo Join the Manscouts. (p. 1358)
—Piglettè & Bobo on Safari. (p. 1358)
—Piglettè & Bobo Winter in Zagreb. (p. 1358)
—Piglettè & BoBoTrash Orange County. (p. 1358)
Undercuffler, Gary. Boy Who Cried Wolf: A Tale about Telling the Truth. (p. 219)
Undercuffler, Gary, illus. see Allen, Nancy Kelly.
Undercuffler, Gary, illus. see Gulla, Rosemarie.
Undercuffler, Gary, illus. see Klepeis, Alicia & Ventura, Gabriela Baeza.
Underdown, Harold D., ed. see Dunham, Montrew.
Underdown, Harold D., ed. see Higgins, Helen Boyd.
Underdown, Harold D., ed. see Sisson, Kathryn Cleven.
Underhill, Alecia, illus. see Wilsdon, Christina.
Underhill, Alice Mertie. Dookie, Sookie, & Big Mo. (p. 470)
Underhill, Marjorie Fay. Jeremiah. Garrett, Caroline S., tr. (p. 913)
Understein, Adam L. Learn2study Student Pocket Guide. (p. 984)
Underton, Wysteria. Simple Scripts: Pedro's Research Project. (p. 1578)
Underwood, Dale, jt. contrib. by see Aho, Kirsti.
Underwood, Dale & Aho, Kirsti. Town Website Project for Macromedia Dreamweaver MX 2004: Communicating Information & Ideas on the Web Dharkar, Anuja & McCain, Malinda, eds. (p. 1773)
Underwood, Deborah. 101 Ways to Organize Your Life (p. 2000)
—101 Ways to Save the Planet (p. 2000)
—Africa. (p. 26)
—Animal Secrets: Animal Life Processes (p. 79)
—Bad Bye, Good Bye. Bean, Jonathan, illus. (p. 131)
—Balloon for Isabel. Rankin, Laura, illus. (p. 135)
—Ballroom Dancing (p. 135)
—Christmas Quiet Book. Liwska, Renata, illus. (p. 315)
—Colorful Peacocks. (p. 344)
—Creature Camouflage (p. 380)
—Graphing Transportation. (p. 711)
—Has a Cow Saved Your Life? The Scientific Method (p. 752)
—Here Comes Santa Cat. Rueda, Claudia, illus. (p. 770)
—Here Comes the Easter Cat. Rueda, Claudia, illus. (p. 770)
—Hiding in Deserts (p. 777)
—Hiding in Forests (p. 777)
—Hiding in Grasslands (p. 777)
—Hiding in Mountains (p. 777)
—Hiding in Oceans (p. 777)
—Hiding in Rain Forests (p. 777)
—Hiding in the Polar Regions (p. 777)
—Hiding in Wetlands (p. 777)
—Loud Book! Liwska, Renata, illus. (p. 1057)
—Loud Book! Padded Board Book. Liwska, Renata, illus. (p. 1057)
—Mexico or Bust! Migration Patterns (p. 1131)
—Nat Love. (p. 1230)
—Part-Time Mermaid. Evans, Cambria, illus. (p. 1325)
—Part-Time Princess. Evans, Cambria, illus. (p. 1325)
—Pirate Mom. Gilpin, Stephen, illus. (p. 1362)
—Quiet Book. Liwska, Renata, illus. (p. 1428)
—Staging a Play (p. 1638)
Underwood, Deborah, jt. auth. see Goldberg, Whoopi.
Underwood, Deborah & Rueda, Claudia. Here Comes the Tooth Fairy Cat. (p. 770)
Underwood, Gary. Frogs. (p. 641)
—Reptiles. (p. 1461)
Underwood, Jamilah. Today's Rain, Tomorrow's Sunshine. (p. 1761)
Underwood, Kathie L. Sarah & the Sand Dollar. (p. 1514)
Underwood, Kay Povelite, illus. see Feeney, Kathy.
Underwood, Kay Povelite, illus. see Fleming, Sally.
Underwood, Kim. Wonderful World of Sparkle Girl & Doobins. Goldman, Garnet, illus. (p. 1948)
Underwood, Ralph Kim. His Dogness Finds a Blue Heart. Goldman, Garnet, illus. (p. 781)
Underwood, Shelley. Insects. (p. 875)
—Minibeasts. (p. 1146)
Underwood, Trudy. Hippity Hop .... My Cat. (p. 780)
Undset, Sigrid. Happy Times in Norway. (p. 747)
—Sigurd & His Brave Companions: A Tale of Medieval Norway. Bull Teilman, Gunvor, illus. (p. 1574)
Undset, Sigrid, ed. True & Untrue & Other Norse Tales. Chapman, Frederick T., illus. (p. 1791)
Ung, Bunheang, jt. auth. see Bednark, Sara.
Ungar, Richard. Rachel's Gift. (p. 1432)
—Rachel's Library. (p. 1432)
Ungaro, Ellen. Diamonds: Set Of 6. (p. 434)
—Diamonds: Text Pairs. (p. 434)
Ungaro, Marley. Darling Dozen of the Deep. (p. 409)
Unger, David, tr. see Liano, Dante, et al.
Unger, David, tr. see Machado, Ana Maria.
Unger, David, tr. see Martinez, Rueben.
Unger, David, tr. see Menchú, Rigoberta & Liano, Dante.
Unger, David, tr. see Montejo, Victor.
Unger, Erin, illus. see Gragg, Karla.
Unger, Karen. Don't Go There! Staying Safe for Girls Ages 6-8. (p. 467)
—I Don't Think So! A Book about Staying Safe for Girls Ages 8-11. (p. 838)
Unger, Kathryn. When Will My Mommy Pick Me Up? (p. 1905)
Unger, Pam. Fly, Greyhound Racer: A Special Dog's Tale. (p. 609)
Ungerer, Tomi. Adelaide: The Flying Kangaroo. (p. 12)
—Beast of Monsieur Racine. (p. 152)
—Christmas Eve at the Mellops' (p. 313)
—Crictor. (p. 382)
—Emile. (p. 518)
—Fog Island. (p. 611)
—Hombre de la Luna. (p. 791)
—Hombre de la Luna. Ungerer, Tomi, illus. (p. 791)
—Mellops Go Diving for Treasure. (p. 1125)
—Mellops Strike Oil. (p. 1125)
—Moon Man. (p. 1172)
—No Kiss for Mother. (p. 1258)
—One, Two, Where's My Shoe? (p. 1297)
—Otto: The Autobiography of a Teddy Bear. (p. 1307)
—Rufus. Ungerer, Tomi, illus. (p. 1494)
—Snail, Where Are You? (p. 1596)
—Sombrero. (p. 1608)
—Three Robbers. (p. 1743)
Ungermann Marshall, Yana. Gilda Gets Wise. Ungermann Marshall, Yana, illus. (p. 676)
Unger-Pengilly, Elaine. Rat. Trockstad, Marcy, illus. (p. 1440)
Ungor, Rita. No Nana's for Hannah. (p. 1259)
Ungs, Tim. Paul McCartney & Stella McCartney. (p. 1330)
—Paul Mccartney & Stella Mccartney. (p. 1330)
Ungureanu, Dan Paul, illus. see DeLong, Lucianne.
Uni Photo Picture Agency Staff, photos by see Campodonica, Carol A.
Unicef, India Country Office, jt. auth. see Dorling Kindersley Publishing Staff.
U'Nique, Mystique Ann. Reg, Dave & Zach. (p. 1457)
Unisystem Staff. Eden Studios Presents (p. 504)
United Educators Staff. My Book House (p. 1198)
United Nations Development Program Staff, ed. Human Development Report 2006: Beyond Scarcity - Power, Poverty & the Global Water Crisis. (p. 826)
United Nations Environment Programme Staff. Pachamama: Nuestra Tierra, Nuestro Futuro. (p. 1317)
United States Air Force Staff, creator. B-1 Lancer Bomber Pilot's Flight Operating Instructions. (p. 122)
—B-29 Airplane Commander Training Manual. (p. 122)
—B-29 Airplane Commander Training Manual in Color. (p. 122)
—Bell P-39 Airacobra Pilot's Flight Operating Instructions. (p. 162)
—Douglas A-20 Havoc Pilot's Flight Operating Instructions. (p. 473)
—Douglas Skystreak & Skyrocket Flight Operating Manual. (p. 473)
—F-82 Twin Mustang Pilot's Flight Operating Instructions. (p. 559)
—Lockheed T-33 Thunderbird / Shooting Star Pilot's Flight Operating Manual. (p. 1045)
—Northrop F-89 Scorpion Pilot's Flight Operating Manual. (p. 1266)
United States Navy, creator. A-7 Corsair Pilot's Flight Operating Manual. (p. 1)
—Chance Vought F7U Cutlass Pilot's Flight Operating Instructions. (p. 289)
—Douglas A-1H Skyraider Pilot's Flight Operating Instructions. (p. 473)
—Douglas F4D Skyray Pilot's Flight Operating Instructions. (p. 473)
—Grumman / G. M. F4F Wildcat Fighter Pilot's Flight Operating Manual. (p. 727)
—Grumman F11F Tiger Pilot's Flight Operating Instructions. (p. 727)
—Grumman F6F Hellcat Pilot's Flight Operating Instructions. (p. 727)
—Grumman F7F Tigercat Pilot's Flight Operating Instructions. (p. 727)
—Grumman F8F-2 Bearcat Fighter Aircraft Pilot's Flight Manual. (p. 727)
—North American FJ-3 Fury Pilot's Flight Operating Instructions. (p. 1264)
—Standard Submarine Phraseology. (p. 1639)
—Submarine: Basic Enlisted Submarine Text. (p. 1671)
—Submarine Electrical Installations. (p. 1671)
—Submarine Trim & Drain Systems. (p. 1671)
Universal. Minions: the Movie Poster Book. (p. 1147)
Universal & King, Trey. Minions: The Road to Villain-Con - Reusable Sticker Book. (p. 1147)
Universal & Rosen, Lucy. Minions: Long Live King Bob! (p. 1147)
Universal Books (Panama) Staff & King, Trey. Minions: Seek & Find. Fractured Pixels Staff, illus. (p. 1147)
Universal Dreamworks Pictures Staff & Greenberg, James. Cat in the Hat. (p. 278)
Universal Marketing Media, ed. see Gibson, Chris.
Universal Studios Staff, jt. auth. see Chesterfield, Sadie.
University Games Staff. Crosswords for Kids. (p. 385)
—I Have. (p. 839)
—More 30 Second Mysteries for Kids. (p. 1173)
—Very Hungrey Caterpillar. (p. 1838)
—Word Searches for Kids. (p. 1951)
University Games Staff, compiled by. i-Ballers: University Games. (p. 834)
—I-Ballers: Little Books for Big Minds. (p. 834)
—Made You Laugh for Kids! Books So Fun You'll Pee Your Pants! (p. 1070)
University of Alabama Staff, jt. auth. see Gibler, Douglas M.
University of Cambridge Local Examinations Syndication Staff. HIGCSE First Language Zulu. (p. 777)
University of Cape Town Staff & Press, Karen. Cambridge Mathematics Dictionary for Schools. (p. 255)
University of Wales, Aberystwyth, Centre for Educational Studies Staff, contrib. by. Arch Noa: Casgliad o Sbardunau Ac Ymarferion Ar Thema Creaduriaid. (p. 95)
Unknown. Amazing World of Gumball Mad Libs. (p. 56)
—Baby Loves Shapes. Aikins, Dave, illus. (p. 127)
—Baby's Day. Aikins, Dave, illus. (p. 129)
—Battle for Skylands. (p. 145)
—Big! Little! A Book of Opposites. Aikins, Dave, illus. (p. 182)
—C. L. O. N. C. Sticker Activity Book. (p. 250)
—Christmas Is Here! (p. 314)
—Doctor Who Mad Libs. (p. 459)
—Doctor Who - Official Annual 2013. (p. 459)
—Flip, Sip, or Mad Libs. (p. 605)
—Fun at the Fair. (p. 647)
—Fun with Our Family. (p. 649)
—I Am Peter. (p. 833)
—Let's Count! A First Book of Numbers. Aikins, Dave, illus. (p. 995)
—Mad about Mad Libs. (p. 1068)
—Mad Scientist Mad Libs. (p. 1069)
—Max & Ruby's Winter Adventure. (p. 1110)
—Max & the Easter Egg Hunt. (p. 1110)

—More Little Peppers. (p. 1174)
—Moshi Monsters Doodle Book. (p. 1176)
—Moshi Monsters Mad Libs. (p. 1176)
—Moshi-Tastic Things to Make & Do. (p. 1176)
—Moshlings Official Sticker Book. (p. 1176)
—Mr. Men Little Miss Christmas Mad Libs. (p. 1185)
—Nutkin on the Run! (p. 1274)
—Peter's Favorite Places (Sticker Stories) (p. 1347)
—Ruby's Beauty Day. (p. 1493)
—Spooky Sticker Activity Book. (p. 1631)
—Springtime Fun with Max & Ruby. (p. 1635)
—Strawberry Shortcake's Easter Egg Hunt. Thomas, Laura, illus. (p. 1666)
—Tag This! (p. 1695)
—Teenage Mutant Ninja Turtles Mad Libs. (p. 1714)
—Totally Rad Book of Secrets. (p. 1771)
—Ultimate Search-and-Find. (p. 1810)
—Valentine's Day Fun! (p. 1830)
—Villains on the Loose. (p. 1842)
—We Play & Pretend. (p. 1868)
—Where in Tinga Tinga Is Tickbird? (p. 1908)
—Where's Ruby? (p. 1910)
Unknown, Unknown. Dick & Jane Fun Wherever We Are. (p. 435)
—My Colours Sticker Activity Book. (p. 1200)
—My Pretty Pink Ballet Activity & Sticker Book. (p. 1217)
—My Space Activity & Sticker Book. (p. 1219)
Unkovic, Rachel & Burns, Adam. Trinity College Connecticut College Prowler off the Record. (p. 1786)
Unlocking the Truth Staff & Jones, Charisse. Unlocking the Truth: Three Brooklyn Teens on Life, Friendship & Making the Band. (p. 1821)
Ünlükoç, Müge. Real Race. (p. 1448)
Unobagha, Uzo. Grandma, How Do You Say I Love You? Krassa, Victoria, illus. (p. 708)
UNOS (Organization) Staff, contrib. by. Organ Transplants: What Every Kid Needs to Know. (p. 1303)
Unrau, Adela. Big Change Friesen, Anni, illus. (p. 180)
—That Was a Nice Surprise Friesen, Anni, illus. (p. 1726)
Unrau, Bernie. Alligator Alley. (p. 47)
—Big B. (p. 177)
—Board. (p. 205)
—Confusion. (p. 357)
—Deadly Implant. (p. 417)
—Dentinator. (p. 426)
—Enlightened. (p. 530)
—Glazers. (p. 682)
—God Almighty. (p. 688)
—Golden Mask. (p. 695)
—Hooked. (p. 795)
—Meltdown. (p. 1125)
—New Millenium. (p. 1246)
—Not a Drop. (p. 1266)
—Pulling Strings. (p. 1416)
—Pulpit Fiction. (p. 1416)
—Questa. (p. 1426)
—Reflections. (p. 1456)
—Rom. (p. 1485)
—Rook. (p. 1487)
—Sabotage. (p. 1500)
—Scrying. (p. 1533)
—Stemwinder. (p. 1647)
—Submarine Slide. (p. 1671)
—Terra Vista. (p. 1721)
—Ubar. (p. 1807)
Unruh, Cindy. Sierra, the Black Lab Who Loved to Eat: (a True Story) Krehbiel, Angie, illus. (p. 1573)
—What to Expect When Your Family Becomes a Foster Family. (p. 1894)
Unser, Virginia. Night Before Cat-Mas. Anagost, Karen, illus. (p. 1252)
Unstead, Sue. DK Readers L1: a Year on the Farm: A Year on the Farm. (p. 456)
—Mysterious Case of Pirates & Buccaneers: Seafaring Skills & Pirate Tales. (p. 1222)
—Say Hello. (p. 1518)
—Seashore. (p. 1538)
Unstead, Sue, jt. auth. see Patenaude, Jeremy.
Unswood, Cassie. Exploring Plane Figures: Understand Concepts of Area (p. 553)
Unsworth, Anne. Danny Is Dyslexic. (p. 405)
—Just Be, Little Bee. (p. 938)
Unsworth, Tania. One Safe Place. (p. 1296)
Unten, Eren, illus. see Golden Books.
Unten, Eren, illus. see Man-Kong, Mary.
Unten, Eren, illus. see Posner-Sanchez, Andrea.
Unten, Eren, illus. see Tillworth, Mary.
Unten, Eren Blanquet, illus. see Golden Books Staff.
Unwin, M. Science Activities. (p. 1524)
Unwin, Mike. Where Did Dinosaurs Go? Evans, Cheryl, ed. (p. 1906)
—Where Did Dinosaurs Go? Robinson, Andrew et al, illus. (p. 1906)
—Why Do Tigers Have Stripes? Morton, Robert, illus. (p. 1924)
—Why Do Tigers Have Stripes? Morton, Robert et al, illus. (p. 1924)
Unwin, Mike, illus. see Davidson, Susanna.
Unwin, Mike, jt. auth. see Davidson, Susanna.
Unwin, Mike & Woodward, Kate. What Makes You Ill? Meredith, Susan, ed. (p. 1892)
Unzner, Christa, illus. see Dickins, Rosie & Ball, Karen.
Unzner, Christa, illus. see Paquette, Ammi-Joan.
Unzner, Christa, illus. see Wilson, Karma.
Unzner, Christa, jt. auth. see Fackelmayer, Regina.
Unzner, Christa, jt. auth. see Paquette, Ammi-Joan.
Uon, Taraku, illus. see Zappa, Go.
Uonca Staff, jt. auth. see Okawa, Junko.
Upadhyay, Ritu. John F Kennedy the Making of a Leader. (p. 921)
Upadhyay, Ritu & Time for Kids Editors. Making of a Leader. (p. 1082)
Upadhye, Nitin, photos by see Heydlauff, Lisa.
Upchurch, Sandra June. Pathways to Adventure. (p. 1328)
Updale, Eleanor. Johnny Swanson. (p. 923)
—Montmorency's Revenge. (p. 1170)
—Thief, Liar, Gentleman? (p. 1732)
Updike, John. Child's Calendar Hyman, Trina Schart, illus. (p. 304)
—Child's Calendar. Updike, John & Hyman, Trina Schart, illus. (p. 304)
Updike, Lisa. Shorty, the Ugly Dog. (p. 1569)
Upenieks, Valda V. Percy. (p. 1341)
Upham, Linda. Divided Loyalties. Littlejohn, Anna, illus. (p. 454)
Uphoff, Pam, jt. auth. see Ivers, Zoey.
Upitis, Alvis, photos by see Peterson, Cris.
Upjohn, Rebecca. Last Loon (p. 978)
—Lily & the Paper Man Benoit, Renne & Second Story Press Staff, illus. (p. 1018)
—Secret of the Village Fool Benoit, Renné, illus. (p. 1543)
Upjohn, Rebecca, et al. Patrick's Wish (p. 1329)
Upkins, Dennis. Hollowstone. (p. 789)
Upper Room Books, creator. Courageous Spirit: Voices from Women in Ministry. (p. 373)
—Way of the Child: Resource Booklet: Reproducible Pages for the Way of the Child Sessions. (p. 1864)
Upthegrove, C. S. Wait... the Power... the Evidence... Miracles That Followed the Angelic Visit (p. 1852)
Upton, George, tr. see Muller, Max.
Upton, Lawrence, et al, eds. Salt Companion to Maggie O'Sullivan. (p. 1505)
Upton, Rachael, jt. auth. see Feldman, Thea.
Ural, Serpil. Folktales of Anatolia: From Agri to Zelve. Arin, Dilara, illus. (p. 611)
Uralskaia, Valeria, et al. Tales of Classical Ballet Talmi, Mary, ed. (p. 1702)
Uram, Maggie. Good Night Good Knight. (p. 699)
Urasawa, Naoki. 20th Century Boys. Urasawa, Naoki, illus. (p. 1996)
—Herr Dr Tenma. Urasawa, Naoki, illus. (p. 774)
—Urasawa X Tezuka. (p. 1825)
—Urasawa X Tezuka. Urasawa, Naoki, illus. (p. 1825)
Urbach, Jourdan. Inside the Music. (p. 877)
—Leaving Jeremiah. (p. 986)
Urbain, Catherine. Manuel & the Lobsterman. (p. 1089)
Urbain, Christophe, photos by. Emma in Paris. (p. 519)
Urban, Brian. Tale of the Howling Dog. (p. 1700)
Urban, Chieu Anh. Away We Go! A Shape & Seek Book. Urban, Chieu Anh, illus. (p. 120)
Urban Donahue, Jill. Play It Smart: Playground Safety Masheris, Bob, illus. (p. 1371)
—Say No & Go: Stranger Safety Masheris, Bob, illus. (p. 1518)
Urban, Erin & Romano, Alexis, eds. Sailors' Snug Harbor Coloring Book. (p. 1503)
Urban, Helle, illus. see Brennan-Nelson, Denise.
Urban, Helle, illus. see Brooks, Robert.
Urban, Helle, illus. see Crane, Carol.
Urban, Helle, illus. see Gagliano, Eugene M.
Urban, Helle, illus. see James, Helen Foster & Wilbur, Helen L.
Urban, Helle, illus. see Wargin, Kathy-jo.
Urban, Helle, illus. see Young, Judy & Wargin, Kathy-jo.
Urban, Joyce. Teeny Tiny Tulula. Urban, Keith, illus. (p. 1715)
Urban, Keith, illus. see Urban, Joyce.
Urban, Linda. Center of Everything. (p. 287)
—Crooked Kind of Perfect. (p. 384)
—Hound Dog True. (p. 802)
—Little Red Henry. Valentine, Madeline, illus. (p. 1035)
—Milo Speck, Accidental Agent. (p. 1144)
—Mouse Was Mad. (p. 1182)
—Mouse Was Mad. Cole, Henry, illus. (p. 1182)
—Mouse Was Mad Big Book. Cole, Henry, illus. (p. 1182)
Urban, Suzanne, illus. see Gold-Vukson, Marji.
Urban, William. Wyatt Earp: The OK Corral & the Law of the American West. (p. 1966)
—Wyatt Earp: The O. K. Corral & the Law of the American West. (p. 1966)
Urbanek, Mae. Wyoming Place Names. (p. 1966)
Urbanek Reese, Dorothy. When Mice Sing—the Story of Mei & Yu. (p. 1903)
Urbanik, Karen L. Words with Wings: Poetic Words of Inspiration & Healing. (p. 1952)
Urbano, Aide, jt. auth. see Pingry, Patricia A.
Urbano, Emilio, illus. see Gianatti, Silvia, et al.
Urbano, Emilio, illus. see Machetto, Augusto, et al.
Urbano, Emilio, illus. see Mulazzi, Paola, et al.
Urbanovic, Jackie. Duck & Cover. Urbanovic, Jackie, illus. (p. 488)
—Duck at the Door. Urbanovic, Jackie, illus. (p. 488)
—Duck Soup. Urbanovic, Jackie, illus. (p. 488)
—Ducks in a Row. Urbanovic, Jackie & Mathieu, Joe, illus. (p. 488)
—Happy Go Ducky. (p. 745)
—Happy Go Ducky. Urbanovic, Jackie & Mathieu, Joe, illus. (p. 745)
—Prince of a Frog. (p. 1401)
—Sitting Duck. Urbanovic, Jackie, illus. (p. 1582)
Urbanovic, Jackie, illus. see Bateman, Teresa.
Urbanovic, Jackie, illus. see Beaumont, Karen.
Urbanovic, Jackie, illus. see Hester, Denia Lewis.
Urbanovic, Jackie, illus. see Koller, Jackie French & Koller.
Urbanovic, Jackie, illus. see Peri, Erica S.
Urbanovic, Jackie, illus. see Prelutsky, Jack.
Urbanovic, Jackie, illus. see Ransom, Jeanie Franz.
Urbanovic, Jackie, illus. see Sayre, April Pulley.
Urbansky, Edward. Caroline Counting. (p. 270)
Urberuaga, Emilio, illus. see Alonso, Fernando.
Urberuaga, Emilio, illus. see Ganges, Montse.
Urberuaga, Emilio, illus. see Garcia Dominguez, Ramon.
Urberuaga, Emilio, illus. see Guerrero, Pablo.
Urberuaga, Emilio, illus. see Lindo, Elvira.
Urberuaga, Emilio, illus. see Liébana, Luisa Villar.
Urberuaga, Emilio, jt. auth. see Ganges, Montse.
Urbigkit, Cat. Brave Dogs, Gentle Dogs: How They Guard Sheep. (p. 223)
—Cattle Kids: A Year on the Western Range. (p. 281)
—Guardian Team: On the Job with Rena & Roo. Urbigkit, Cat, photos by. (p. 728)
—Path of the Pronghorn. Goeke, Mark, photos by. (p. 1328)
—Puppies, Puppies Everywhere! (p. 1418)
—Shepherd's Trail. (p. 1565)
—Young Shepherd. (p. 1979)
—Young Shepherd. Urbigkit, Cat, photos by. (p. 1979)
Urbina, Manuel Iván. Sören Kierkegaard -la conciencia de un Desesperado. (p. 1614)
Urdahl, Catherine. Emma's Question. Dawson, Janine, illus. (p. 520)
—Polka-Dot Fixes Kindergarten. Kemble, Mai S., illus. (p. 1381)
Ure, Daylene Mary. Today I'm Going to be a Hedgehog. (p. 1760)
Ure, Jean. Babycakes. (p. 128)
—Bad Alice. (p. 131)
—Boys Beware. (p. 220)
—Boys Will Be Boys. (p. 220)
—Family Fan Club. (p. 568)
—Flower Power Collection: Passion Flower, Shrinking Violet & Pumpkin Pie. (p. 607)
—Fortune Cookie. (p. 623)
—Friends Forever Collection. (p. 638)
—Gone Missing. (p. 697)
—Here Comes Ellen. (p. 770)
—Ice Lolly. (p. 850)
—Is Anybody There? Seeing Is Believing... Donnelly, Karen, illus. (p. 889)
—Jelly Baby. (p. 912)
—Kissing Game. (p. 962)
—Love & Kisses. (p. 1059)
—Meet the Radish. (p. 1123)
—My Sister Sam. (p. 1218)
—Over the Moon. Donnelly, Karen, illus. (p. 1314)
—Passion Flower. (p. 1327)
—Secret Meeting. (p. 1542)
—Star Crazy Me! (p. 1640)
Ureel, Jessica & Jacobs, Jessica. Peanut Pickle: A Story about Peanut Allergy. Roslyn, Jacquelyn, illus. (p. 1332)
Ureel, Jessica Mary. Allergy Express: Food Allergy Coloring & Activity Book. (p. 46)
U'Ren, Andrea, illus. see DeFelice, Cynthia C.
U'Ren, Andrea, illus. see Moss, Marissa.
U'Ren, Andrea, illus. see Schubert, Leda.
Urey, Gary. Super Schnoz & the Gates of Smell. Long, Ethan, illus. (p. 1680)
—Super Schnoz & the Invasion of the Snore Snatchers. Frawley, Keith, illus. (p. 1680)
Uribe, Denise. My Best Friend Sarah. (p. 1196)
—Queen MacHine. (p. 1425)
Uribe, Veronica & Espopo. Libro de Oro de las Fabulas. Bravo, Constanza, illus. (p. 1006)
Urick, Jane. Timothy Turtle. (p. 1755)
Urick, Jane A. Hooked Not Cooked. (p. 795)
—Nicky the Little Nail. (p. 1251)
Urish, J. D. Adventures of Rex Bolton Volume 1. (p. 22)
Uriss, Mike. Critteriddles: Funny Rhymes, Riddles & Pictures. (p. 384)
Uriz, Francisco J. & Harling, Birgit. En el Mundo Hispanico. (p. 522)
Urmston, Grant, jt. auth. see Urmston, Kathleen.
Urmston, Kathleen. Sammy. Gedeon, Gloria, illus. (p. 1507)
Urmston, Kathleen, jt. auth. see Evans, Karen.
Urmston, Kathleen & Evans, Karen. Snowflakes. Kaeden Corp. Staff, ed. (p. 1600)
Urmston, Kathleen & Urmston, Grant. Rainy Day for Sammy. Gedeon, Gloria, illus. (p. 1436)
Urmy, Deanne, ed. Merry Christmas: Best - Loved Stories & Carols. Green, Donna, illus. (p. 1128)
Urne, Anne. Spiritual Trilogy. Hudson, David W., photos by. (p. 1629)
Urofsky, Melvin. 100 Americans Making Constitutional History: A Biographical History (p. 1998)
Urofsky, Melvin I. Public Debate over Controversial Supreme Court Decisions (p. 1414)
Urquhart, Diane. Ladies of Londonderry: Women & Political Patronage. (p. 970)
Urrea, Enrique Hubbard, tr. see Urrea, Luis Alberto.
Urrea, Lourdes. Athon Labar. (p. 112)
—Calle Secreto Numero 31. (p. 254)
—Circo. (p. 321)
—Huellas en la Escalera. (p. 824)
—Juego de Ajedrez. (p. 931)
—Mago. (p. 1076)
—Nina del Cuadro. (p. 1256)
—Nino de la Ventana. (p. 1257)
—No Juegues de Noche! (p. 1258)
—Vacaciones Mortales. (p. 1829)
Urrea, Lourdes, jt. auth. see Urrea, Luis Alberto.
Urrea, Lourdes, et al. Dragon Jines. (p. 477)
—En Busca de Dracu. (p. 522)
—Piel de Gallina. (p. 1357)
—Secreto Gitano. (p. 1544)
—Si Juegas Con Fuego. (p. 1572)
—Tenebroso. (p. 1720)
Urrea, Luis. Fuera de Este Mundo. (p. 646)
—Gatos Muertos. (p. 658)
—Gruta Encantada. (p. 728)
Urrea, Luis Alberto. Hija de la Chuparrosa. Urrea, Enrique Hubbard, tr. (p. 779)
Urrea, Luis Alberto & Urrea, Lourdes. Silencio en el Castillo. (p. 1575)
Urru, Franco, illus. see Lynch, Brian.
Uruela, Maria Cristina, tr. see McCalla Njee, Lena.
Urrutia, Cristina. Who Will Save My Planet? (p. 1919)
Urrutia, Maria Christina & Libura, Krystyna. Ecos de la Conquista. (p. 503)
—Estampas de la Colonia. (p. 538)
Urrutia, Maria Cristina & Orozco, Rebeca. Cinco de Mayo: Yesterday & Today. (p. 319)
Urrutia, Maria Cristina, et al. Cinco de Mayo. (p. 319)
Urwin-Camara, Nancy, tr. see Messick, Maxine.
Urs, Fischer. Fractured Figure, Volume I (p. 627)
Ursell, Martin. You Can Draw Cartoons: A Step-By-Step Guide to Drawing Great Cartoons. (p. 1974)
—You Can Draw Horses. (p. 1974)
—You Can Draw Monsters. (p. 1974)
Ursell, Martin, illus. see Benton, Lynne.
Ursell, Martin, illus. see Bushell, Nick & Martineau, Susan.
Ursell, Martin, illus. see Donaldson, Julia.
Ursell, Martin, illus. see Goodhart, Pippa.
Ursell, Martin, illus. see Lister, Adrian.
Ursell, Martin, illus. see Martineau, Susan.
Ursell, Martin, illus. see Martinneau, Susan.
Ursell, Martin, illus. see Rabley, Stephen.
Ursell, Martin, illus. see Roberts, Sheena.
Ursell, Martin, illus. see Vincent, Jenny & Laird, Elizabeth.
Ursell, Martin, tr. see Martinneau, Susan.
Ursone, Adele, jt. auth. see Matteson, George.
Ursu, Anne. Breadcrumbs. (p. 224)
—Breadcrumbs. McGuire, Erin, illus. (p. 224)
—Immortal Fire. Swaab, Neil, illus. (p. 861)
—Immortal Fire. Fortune, Eric & Swaab, Neil, illus. (p. 861)
—Real Boy. McGuire, Erin, illus. (p. 1448)
—Shadow Thieves. Fortune, Eric, illus. (p. 1558)
—Siren Song. Fortune, Eric, illus. (p. 1580)
—Spilling Clarence. (p. 1627)
Uruno, Munetsugu, jt. auth. see Rost, Michael.
Urushibara, Yuki. Mushishi, Volume 2. Flanagan, William, tr. (p. 1193)
Urwin, Kirsten. Betsy Ross & the Creation of the American Flag. (p. 172)
Ury, David, tr. see Akamatsu, Ken.
Ury, David, tr. see Matsushita, Yoko.
Ury, Laura, illus. see Redmond, Mark L.
U.S. Defense Dept. & Defense Department Staff, eds. Julie & the Atom. (p. 932)
USA Today Staff, contrib. by. USA Today Weather Wonders: Discover What's up & What's Coming Down. (p. 1826)
Usak, Donald. Beyond the Next Ridge: A Quest for Adventure in the Hunting Fields of the World (p. 174)
Usatschow, Andre. Giant Wheel. (p. 674)
Usborne Books. Going to School Kid Kit. (p. 693)
Usborne Books, creator. 100 Dinosaurs to Spot. (p. 1998)
—100 Things to Spot in the Night Sky. (p. 1999)
—50 Fairy Things to Make & Do. (p. 1997)
—50 Travel Games & Activities. (p. 1997)
—Dinosaur Excavation Kid Kit. (p. 442)
—How to Draw Horses Kid Kit. (p. 817)
—Pirate Treasure Kid Kit. (p. 1363)
—Starting Cooking Kid Kit. (p. 1644)
—Usborne Big Book of Christmas Things to Make & Do. (p. 1827)
—Volcanoes Kid Kit. (p. 1849)
—Young Naturalist Kid Kit. (p. 1979)
Usborne Books Staff & Doherty, Gillian. 1001 Cosas Que Buscar en el Pasado. (p. 2002)
Usborne Books Staff, ed. Illustrated Dictionary of Chemistry. (p. 857)
—Illustrated Dictionary of Physics. (p. 857)
Usborne Publishing Ltd, creator. Usborne Doodle Pad for Boys. (p. 1827)
—Usborne Doodle Pad for Girls. (p. 1827)
Usborne Publishing Staff, ed. Animales del Mundo. (p. 81)
—Pintar Personajes. (p. 1361)
USCCB Department of Justice, Peace, and Human Development. Drop by Drop. (p. 485)
—Green Street Park. (p. 722)
Uschan, Michael V. 50 Cent. (p. 1997)
—Alex Rodriguez. (p. 36)
—Apolo Ohno. (p. 92)
—Beslan School Siege & Separatist Terrorism. (p. 168)
—Blacks in Political Office. (p. 197)
—Blues. (p. 204)
—Bombing of Pearl Harbor. (p. 208)
—Brian Urlacher. (p. 226)
—California Gold Rush. (p. 253)
—Chinese Mythology. (p. 307)
—Civil Rights Movement. (p. 325)
—Comic Art. (p. 348)
—David Beckham. (p. 410)
—Fidel Castro. (p. 583)
—Fort Sumter: The Civil War Begins. (p. 623)
—German Americans. (p. 666)
—Golf. Greenhaven Press Editors, ed. (p. 696)
—Graffiti. (p. 705)
—Halle Berry. (p. 737)
—Hate Crimes. (p. 752)
—Holocaust. (p. 789)
—Irish Americans. (p. 887)
—James Foreman & SNCC. Greenhaven Press Staff, ed. (p. 907)
—Jet Li. (p. 916)
—Joe Biden. (p. 920)
—Lexington & Concord. (p. 1004)
—Matt Dalio: China Care Founder. (p. 1109)
—Michelle Obama. (p. 1135)
—Oregon Trail. (p. 1303)
—Reconstruction. (p. 1452)
—Salem Witch Trials. (p. 1504)
—Scopes "Monkey" Trial. (p. 1530)
—Scottsboro Case. (p. 1532)
—Serena Williams. (p. 1552)
—Suicide Bombings in Israel & Palestinian Terrorism. (p. 1673)
—Transcontinental Railroad. (p. 1778)
—Tupac Shakur. (p. 1797)
—Watergate. (p. 1863)
—Wisconsin. (p. 1939)
Uschan, Michael V., jt. auth. see Crewe, Sabrina.
Uschan, Michael V., jt. auth. see Goff, Elizabeth Hudson.
Uschan, Michael V., jt. auth. see Hudson Goff, Elizabeth.
Uschan, Michael V. & Crewe, Sabrina. Transcontinental Railroad. (p. 1778)
Uschan, Michael V. & Goff, Elizabeth Hudson. Bombing of Pearl Harbor. Floor, Guus, illus. (p. 208)
Uschan, Michael V. & Juettner, Bonnie. Will Smith. (p. 1932)
Uschan, Michael V., ed. Tyler Perry. (p. 1805)
Usera, Abe. Pigs & Friends. (p. 1358)
Usera, Christian. Ones. (p. 1298)
Usher, Angie. Freddie's Adventures: Firefly Tails, Bright Trails, & Fishy Tales. (p. 633)
Usher, Carolyn. Chip Takes Off. (p. 308)

Usher, M. D. Golden Ass of Lucius Apuleius. Motley, T., illus. (p. 694)
Usher, Sam, illus. see Houran, Lori Haskins.
Ushler, John, illus. see Snow, Dorothea J.
Usilton, Terry. Color Guard Competition. (p. 342)
Usilton, Theresa A. Let's Go team: Cheer, Dance, & March (p. 997)
Uslan, Michael E. Chatterbox: The Bird Who Wore Glasses. Gurney, John Steven, illus. (p. 295)
Uslander, Arlene S., ed. When Cotton Was King: Memoirs of a Boy's Summer. (p. 1901)
Uss, John & Benchmark Education Co., LLC Staff. Dan & Ed. (p. 401)
Ustinov, Pavla. Peggy Pots. (p. 1335)
Ustinov, Peter. Orchestra. (p. 1302)
Usual Gang of Idiots Staff. Mad about the Fifties. (p. 1068)
—Totally Useless MAD. (p. 1771)
Usui, Kanako. Fantastic Mr Wani. Usui, Kanako, illus. (p. 572)
Usui, Kanako, illus. see Cleary, Daniel.
Utarid, Anjana. Count Me In. (p. 369)
Uting, Justin, illus. see Kidpressions!.
Utley, David, illus. see Ross, Kathryn & Pruitt, Kimberly.
Utley, J. Stacy, illus. see Harvey Mph, Janera P.
Utomo, Gabhor, illus. see Jordan, Christina.
Utomo, Gabhor, illus. see Kalomas, Alice & Kerr, Lenora.
Utomo, Gabhor, illus. see Ruiz-Flores, Lupe.
Utomo, Gabhor, illus. see Simpson, C. E. & Smith, C. E.
Utomo, Gabhor, illus. see Windover, Liz.
Utopia, illus. see Shears, William.
Uto-Uko, Iniobong, illus. see Butler, Darnell.
Utsler, Elaine. Black Cherry Forest: Storybook 1. Wendle, Stan, ed. (p. 195)
Utt, Mary Ann, illus. see Pingry, Patricia A.
Utt, Mary Ann, jt. illus. see Rader, Laura.
Uttendorfsky, Irene. Punkeyville Girl: A Tale of Old Forestport & the Canals. (p. 1417)
Utter, Mark, jt. auth. see Rustad, Mark.
Utterly Global Youth Empowerment. Anti-Bullying Club/Project Manual. (p. 89)
Uttley, Alison & Singh, Mahendra. Traveller in Time. Bray, Phyllis, illus. (p. 1780)
Uttley, Colin. Experiments with Force & Motion. (p. 549)
Uttley, Tracy. Molly Mcsholly Conquers Kindergarten. (p. 1160)
Utton, Peter, illus. see Anderson, Jill, ed.
Utton, Peter, illus. see Grindley, Sally.
Utton, Peter, jt. auth. see Adams, Georgia.
Utton, Peter, jt. auth. see Adams, Georgie.
Uttridge, Sarah. Dinosaurs Around the World. (p. 444)
—Horses Around the World. (p. 800)
—Jungle Animals Around the World. (p. 935)
—Mammals Around the World. (p. 1085)
—Ocean Animals Around the World. (p. 1276)
—Sharks & Sea Creatures Around the World. (p. 1563)
—Snakes & Reptiles Around the World. (p. 1596)
—Spiders & Bugs Around the World. (p. 1627)
Uvezian, Verne. Day Benny Stuck His Neck Out. (p. 412)
Uwe, Timm. Rennschwein Rudi Rüssel. (p. 1460)
Uwuigiaren, Omoruyi. Adventures of Nihu. Ayalomeh, Shedrach, illus. (p. 21)
Uxó, Carlos, tr. see O'Reilly, Bill.
Uy, Katherine Nepomuceno. Adventures of Tess: Tessa & the Secret Tunnel. (p. 23)
—Teeny Tiny People & Pets. (p. 1715)
Uy, Meqan Black, jt. auth. see Clifford, Kathleen.
Uy, Steve, jt. auth. see Austen, Chuck.
Uyeda, Laura. Bing Bong Book. Tilley, Scott, illus. (p. 188)
Uzon, Jorge. Go, Baby, Go! (p. 686)
—Hello, Baby! (p. 763)
—Look Around, Baby! (p. 1048)
—Not a Baby Anymore! (p. 1266)

V

V. Isabelle's Star. (p. 891)
—Nine & a Half Dozen Swope, Brenda, illus. (p. 1256)
V, Larry. Larry Bendeco Johannes Von Sloop. K, Mark, illus. (p. 976)
V., Patti. My Na Na Stories. (p. 1215)
V, Vasanthi. Toy-Gobbling Monster. Lee, Anais, illus. (p. 1774)
Vaage, Carol. Bibi & the Bull Graham, Georgia, illus. (p. 175)
Vaamonde, Conchita, tr. My First Spanish Words. Tulip, Jenny, illus. (p. 1208)
Vaca, Sally, illus. see Darden, Hunter.
Vacca, John, et al. Identity Theft. (p. 852)
Vacca, Richard T., jt. auth. see Marrow, Lesley Mandel.
Vacco, Corina. My Chemical Mountain. (p. 1200)
Vachon, Jennifer & Vachon, Lance. Bread over Heels. (p. 224)
Vachon, Lance, jt. auth. see Vachon, Jennifer.
Vachon, Mary Beth. Mac s Mackinac Island Adventure. Rusky, Ann G., illus. (p. 1067)
Vachss, Andrew. Heart Transplant. Caruso, Frank, illus. (p. 760)
Vachula, Monica, illus. see Longfello, Henry Wadsworth.
Vachula, Monica, illus. see Shea, Pegi Deitz.
Vachuska, Kameron. My Grandma Dances with Angels. (p. 1210)
Vadalia, Hemali, illus. see Graham, Rita Z.
Vadasy, Patricia, jt. auth. see Meyer, Donald J.
Vadeboncoeur, Isabelle, jt. auth. see Savary, Fabien.
Vadeboncoeur, Jim, Jr. & Kinstler, Everett Raymond. Everett Raymond Kinstler: 1942-1962: the Artist's Journey Through Popular Culture. (p. 542)
Vadeboncoeur, Jim, Jr., prod. Black & White Images: 2004. (p. 195)
Vadney, Jackie. Pokey's Promise: A Charming Tale of Telling Time. Balogh, Jared, illus. (p. 1378)
Vado, Dan, ed. see Weisman, Greg.
Vadon, Catherine. Meet the Shark. (p. 1123)
Vaello, Elda G. Magical Goat. (p. 1074)
Vaganos, Erin, illus. see Turnbull, Elizabeth.
Vaggi, Gianni & Groenewegen, Peter. Concise History of Economic Thought: From Mercantilism to Monetarism. (p. 355)
Vagharshyan, Lilit, illus. see Liliom, Laura.
Vagin, Vladimir, illus. see Asch, Frank.
Vagin, Vladimir, illus. see Paterson, Katherine.
Vagin, Vladimir, illus. see Yolen, Jane.
Vagner, Bohdanka. Bullying, Change, Friendship & Trust. Montgomerie, Genevieve, illus. (p. 241)
Vagnozzi, Barbara. Jack & the Beanstalk. (p. 902)
—Musicians of Bremen: Flip up Fairy Tales. (p. 1194)
—Musicians of Bremen. (p. 1194)
—Sleeping Beauty. (p. 1589)
Vagnozzi, Barbara, illus. see Adeney, Anne.
Vagnozzi, Barbara, illus. see Cunningham, Anna.
Vagnozzi, Barbara, illus. see Morgan, Ruth.
Vagnozzi, Barbara, illus. see Pasquali, Elena.
Vagnozzi, Barbara, illus. see Rock, Lois.
Vagnozzi, Barbara, jt. auth. see Pasquali, Elena.
Vagreti, Eva, illus. see Holloway, Kari.
Vagts, Carolyn, ed. I Can Quilt. (p. 836)
Vague, David. Knightmare. (p. 964)
Vahidi, Mohd, tr. see King, Dedie.
Vahle, Neal. Spiritual Journey of Charles Fillmore: Discovering the Power Within. (p. 1629)
Vaid, Raj. Case of Cold Feet: The Super Sleuth - Mystery #2. (p. 273)
—Case of the Holi Chocolate: The Super Sleuth - Mystery #1. (p. 274)
Vaid, Stephen. Moo's Walk. (p. 1173)
Vail, Emily Blake. Carla & the Con Men. (p. 269)
—Grey Ghost of the Pharaoh. Barbra K. Mudd, illus. (p. 723)
—Search for Ole Ben's Treasure. (p. 1537)
Vail, Grace. Death Valley. (p. 420)
—Dolphin Doubles. (p. 464)
—Earthquakes: Energy in Motion. (p. 497)
—Hunting with Hawks (p. 829)
—Jaguars. (p. 905)
—Motors & Generators. (p. 1180)
Vail, Martha, jt. auth. see Anderson, Harry S.
Vail, Rachel. Brilliant. (p. 228)
—Flabbersmashed about You. Heo, Yumi, illus. (p. 601)
—Gorgeous. (p. 702)
—If We Kiss. (p. 854)
—If You Only Knew. (p. 854)
—Justin Case: School, Drool, & Other Daily Disasters. Cordell, Matthew, illus. (p. 940)
—Justin Case: Rules, Tools, & Maybe a Bully. Cordell, Matthew, illus. (p. 940)
—Kiss Me Again. (p. 961)
—Lucky. (p. 1062)
—Me Gustas Tu... Recasens, Elena, tr. (p. 1116)
—Not That I Care. (p. 1267)
—Piggy Bunny. Tankard, Jeremy, illus. (p. 1358)
—Please, Please, Please. (p. 1373)
—Prefiero Perder! Recasens, Elena, tr. (p. 1395)
—Rules, Tools, & Maybe a Bully. (p. 1495)
—School, Drool, & Other Daily Disasters. Cordell, Matthew, illus. (p. 1522)
—Shells, Smells, & the Horrible Flip-Flops of Doom. Cordell, Matthew, illus. (p. 1565)
—Sometimes I'm Bombaloo. Heo, Yumi, illus. (p. 1610)
—Unfriended. (p. 1817)
—What Are Friends For? (p. 1879)
—You, Maybe: The Profound Asymmetry of Love in High School. (p. 1976)
Vail, Rachel, jt. auth. see Avi.
Vail, Rachel & Avi. Never Mind! (p. 1243)
Vail, Rochelle Kelly. Critters: A Dog's Tale. (p. 384)
Vail, Sue, tr. see Powers, David M. F.
Vaillancourt, François, jt. auth. see Tibo, Gilles.
Vaillant, George E. Aging Well: Surprising Guideposts to a Happier Life from the Landmark Study of Adult Development. (p. 29)
Vaillard, Fabiola. Tongo: The Wish Train. (p. 1765)
Vaincourt, A. Lawrence. Just a Common Soldier (a Soldier Died Today) & Other Poems. (p. 937)
Vaing, Jocelang, illus. see Diep, Bridgette.
Vainio, Pirkko. Little Bunny Finds Christmas. Vainio, Pirkko, illus. (p. 1025)
—Nightingale. (p. 1255)
—Tom the Christmas Elf. (p. 1764)
—Who Hid the Easter Egg? (p. 1915)
Vainio, Pirkko, illus. see Lukkarinen, Ritva.
Vair, Hayley, illus. see Shapiro, David R.
Vaisey, Gill & Lewis, Siân. William Booth: Cristion Arbennig lawn. (p. 1933)
Vaishali. You Are What You Love. (p. 1973)
Vaizey, George de Horne. Etheldreda the Ready. Horrell, Charles, illus. (p. 539)
—Tom & Some Other Girls. Tarrant, Percy, illus. (p. 1762)
Vajda, Tibor Timothy. End of the World. (p. 526)
Vakker, Hans Alric. Riddle of the Jade Collar: A Twelve Cousins Book. (p. 1470)
Valas, Claudia, jt. auth. see Resnikoff, Irene.
Valat, Pierre Marie & Valat, Pierre-Marie. Navidad. (p. 1237)
Valat, Pierre-Marie. Animal Faces: 15 Punch-Out Masks. (p. 77)
—Deporte. (p. 427)
—Fruit. (p. 645)
—Manzana y Otras Frutas. (p. 1089)
—Pirates. Valat, Pierre-Marie, illus. (p. 1363)
—Water. Valat, Pierre-Marie, illus. (p. 1862)
Valat, Pierre-Marie, illus. see Grant, Donald & Vallon, Jacqueline.
Valat, Pierre-Marie, jt. auth. see Delafosse, Claude.
Valat, Pierre-Marie, jt. auth. see Valat, Pierre Marie.
Valat, Pierre-Marie & Houbre, Gilbert. Inside the Body. Valat, Pierre-Marie, illus. (p. 877)
Valat, Pierre-Marie, et al. Color. (p. 342)
Valay, Ana Patricia & Sandoval, Ana Valay. Arnoldo Iguaran. (p. 100)
Valdenebro, Eladio De, see De Valdenebro, Eladio.
Valder, Justin, illus. see Valder, Margret.
Valder, Margret. Henry the Honey Bee. Valder, Justin, illus. (p. 768)
Valderrama, Linda N. Brush Barry Brush. Memarzadeh, Sudabeh, illus. (p. 232)
Valderrama, Rosario, illus. see Pettersson, Aline.
Valdes, Alisa. Perdition: A Kindred Novel. (p. 1341)
—Temptation. (p. 1718)
Valdes, et al. Composicion: Proceso y Sintesis: Sin Falta Spanish Writing. (p. 354)
Valdes, Leslie. At the Carnival. (p. 111)
—At the Carnival. Roper, Robert, illus. (p. 111)
—Dora Goes to School. Roper, Robert, illus. (p. 470)
—Meet Diego! Hall, Susan, illus. (p. 1120)
Valdés, M. Isabel. Hispanic Customers for Life: A Fresh Look at Acculturation. (p. 781)
Valdes-Rodriguez, Alisa. Haters. (p. 752)
—Make Him Look Good. (p. 1079)
Valdez, Jannay. Bonnie & Clyde - Villains or Victims? (p. 209)
Valdez, Joseph G. Lean on Me, Lee. Martinez, Gayle Denise, illus. (p. 982)
Valdez, Luis. Zoot Suit: A Bilingual Edition. Ochoa, Edna, tr. (p. 1990)
Valdez Y Alanis, Erik. Rumpelstiltskin: The Graphic Novel. (p. 1495)
Valdez Y Alanis, Erik, illus. see Andersen, Hans Christian & Capstone Press Staff.
Valdez Y Alanis, Erik, illus. see Capstone Press Staff.
Valdez-Moore, Pura J. Tippy the Special Star. (p. 1757)
Valdivia, Benjamin. Cage of the Different People: A Story of Brotherly Love. (p. 251)
Valdivia, Paloma. Up above & down Below. (p. 1824)
Vale, A. M. & Melton, H. Keith. Spy's Guide to Disguise. (p. 1636)
Vale, David. Picture Grammar for Children 1: Topic-Based Grammar Practice. (p. 1355)
—Picture Grammar for Children 1: Topic-Based Grammar Practice, Answer Key. (p. 1355)
Vale, Janice. Going Fast. (p. 692)
—True Life Survival. Wademan, Spike, illus. (p. 1792)
—Where Do You Live? Band 15. (p. 1907)
Vale, Joe, ed. see Triplett, Annette.
Vale, Mitch, et al. Trauma Shift: Have You Got What It Takes to Be an ER Nurse? (p. 1780)
Valelly, Richard M. Voting Rights Act: Securing the Ballot CQ Press Staff, ed. (p. 1850)
Valencia, Esau Andrade, illus. see Sáenz, Benjamin Alire.
Valencia, O. R. Savior in the Blue Mermaid. (p. 1518)
Valencia, Vanessa. Mamma's Planet Earth. (p. 1085)
Valens, Victor Manuel, jt. auth. see Behnke, Alison.
Valent, Fred. Tiniest Raindrop (p. 1755)
Valent, Lee Ann. Nest of Color. (p. 1242)
Valente, Catherynne M. Boy Who Lost Fairyland. Juan, Ana, illus. (p. 219)
—Girl Who Circumnavigated Fairyland in a Ship of Her Own Making. Juan, Ana, illus. (p. 679)
—Girl Who Fell Beneath Fairyland & Led the Revels There. Juan, Ana, illus. (p. 679)
—Girl Who Soared over Fairyland & Cut the Moon in Two. Juan, Ana, illus. (p. 679)
—Smoky & the Feast of Mabon: A Magical Child Story. (p. 1595)
Valente, Christa, illus. see Gray, Elizabeth.
Valente, Shannon. Puddle That Ate My Boot! (p. 1414)
—Trucks, Trains & Worm Brains. (p. 1791)
—Why Baby Toes Aren't Big! (p. 1922)
Valenti, Joseph. NERO Rule Book: 8th Edition. (p. 1241)
Valentin, Jean. Bravery of Amelia Earhart. (p. 223)
Valentin, Jeannette, illus. see Guardado, Maria.
Valentin, Karen. Allie's World: Abuela & Abuelo Move: Abuela & Abuelo Move. (p. 47)
—Block Party. (p. 200)
—What Did Abuela Say? (p. 1882)
—When Are We Going to the Beach? (p. 1901)
Valentina, Marina. Lost in the Roses. (p. 1056)
—Lost in the Roses. Valentina, Marina, illus. (p. 1056)
Valentina, Serena, jt. auth. see Gray, Amy.
Valentine, illus. see Addabbo, Carole.
Valentine, Allison, illus. see Cook, Julia & Jana, Laura.
Valentine, Allison, illus. see Cook, Julia.
Valentine, Allyson. How (Not) to Find a Boyfriend. (p. 811)
Valentine, Amanda, ed. see Harris, Carrie.
Valentine, Billy. Trust Love: A Tale of Angels. (p. 1793)
Valentine, Billy, compiled by. Dear Smarty: A Collection of Letters Written to Smarty Jones by Children, Families & Other Animals from Across America. (p. 419)
Valentine, Bridget. Building with Shapes: Analyze, Compare, Create, & Compose Shapes. (p. 239)
Valentine, Christopher & Von Lahr, Christian. Seeing & Sensing Gnomes... Hey Looky Hea'h: A Direct Approach to Seeing the Gnomes, Elves, Leprechauns & Fairies Around You & Learning How to Sense Their Presence & Influence in Your Life. (p. 1548)
Valentine, Emily. Mother Teresa: With a Discussion of Compassion. (p. 1178)
—Steven Spielberg: With a Discussion of Imagination. (p. 1649)
Valentine, James. Future Is Unknown. (p. 651)
—Past Is Gone. (p. 1327)
—Present Never Happens. (p. 1396)
Valentine, Jenny. Broken Soup. (p. 230)
—Double. (p. 472)
—Me, the Missing, & the Dead. (p. 1116)
Valentine, M. K., illus. see Fantastik, B.
Valentine, Madeline. Bad Birthday Idea. (p. 131)
—George in the Dark. (p. 663)
Valentine, Madeline, illus. see Best, Cari.
Valentine, Madeline, illus. see Urban, Linda.
Valentine, Nancy. I Heart My Dentist. (p. 839)
Valentine, Peggy. Katie's Christmas. (p. 945)
Valentine, Rebecca & Baker, Lawrence W. Gilded Age & Progressive Era (p. 676)
Valentine, Sally. Ghost of the Charlotte Lighthouse. (p. 671)
Valentine, Sophie. Zoo Hullabaloo. (p. 1989)
Valentine, Stephen J. Lazarus Game. (p. 981)
Valentine, Teresa, ed. see Marsh, Carole.
Valentine, Victoria. Cutest Little Duckie. Tucker, Amanda, illus. (p. 396)
Valentino, Amanda & Bell, Cathleen Davitt. Unraveled (p. 1822)
Valentino, Amanda & Stolarz, Laurie Faria. Shattered (p. 1563)
Valentino, Carla. When Can We Run, Play & Dance Again? An Enchanting Story about Family, Learning & Imagination. (p. 1901)
Valentino, Catherine. Blue Ribbon Spelling & Vocabulary (p. 203)
Valentino, Jim, text. Guardians of the Galaxy (p. 728)
Valentino, Russell Scott, tr. see Tamaro, Susanna.
Valentino, Serena. How to Be a Werewolf: The Claws-On Guide for the Modern Lycanthrope. (p. 815)
Valentino, Serena, jt. auth. see Calle, Juan.
Valentino, Serena & Disney Book Group Staff. Beast Within: A Tale of Beauty's Prince. Disney Storybook Artists Staff & Disney Storybook Art Team, illus. (p. 152)
—Fairest of All: A Tale of the Wicked Queen. Disney Storybook Artists Staff, illus. (p. 562)
Valenza, Christine, jt. auth. see Margulies, Nancy.
Valenzuela, Anabelle. Day an Angel Ran into My Room. Latham, Sarah, illus. (p. 412)
Valenzuela, José Ignacio. De Que Color Es Tu Sombra? (p. 416)
Valenzuela, Kristine. Secret Sydney. Green, Matthew, illus. (p. 1544)
Valenzuela, Liliana, tr. see Alvarez, Julia.
Valenzuela, Liliana, tr. see O'Connor, Jane.
Valenzuela, Raquel, tr. see Valenzuela, Roger.
Valenzuela, Roger. Paulie Pick Finds Studioland. Valenzuela, Raquel, tr. from ENG. (p. 1331)
Valenzuela, S. Silesia: the Outworlder. (p. 1575)
Valer, Frantisek. Buffalo & the Boat: Thathánka na Wáta. (p. 235)
—Pispiza WAN Wayawa Iyaye/Prairie Dog Goes to School. (p. 1364)
Valera, Sinead De, see De Valera, Sinead.
Valeri, Jennifer. God from A-Z: A Child's Guide to Learning about God. (p. 688)
Valeri, Jim, illus. see Golden Books Staff.
Valeri, Jim, illus. see Golden Books.
Valeri, Maria Eulàlia & Fontaine, La. Leon y el Raton. (p. 992)
Valerio, Geraldo. Go to Sleep, Gecko! A Balinese Folktale. (p. 687)
Valério, Geraldo. Go to Sleep, Gecko! A Balinese Folktale. (p. 687)
Valerio, Geraldo, illus. see Harby, Melanie.
Valério, Geraldo, illus. see Heneghan, James & McBay, Bruce.
Valerio, Geraldo, illus. see Hickman, Pamela.
Valério, Geraldo, illus. see MacDonald, Margaret Read.
Valério, Geraldo, illus. see Spinelli, Eileen.
Vales, Chrissie, illus. see Paticoff, Melanie.
Valeska, John & Fripp, Jean. Secret of the Sand. Fripp, Jean, ed. (p. 1543)
Valeska, Jon & Fripp, Jean. Thunder & the Pirates. Fripp, Jean, ed. (p. 1746)
Valette, Jean-Paul & Valette, Rebecca M. Discovering French: Nouveau! 1B, Bleu, Deuxieme Partie. (p. 449)
—Discovering French Blanc, Euro Edition. (p. 449)
—Discovering French Bleu, Euro Edition. (p. 449)
Valette, Rebecca M., jt. auth. see Valette, Jean-Paul.
Valhouli, Alex & Skindzier, Jon. University of Southern California College Prowler off the Record. (p. 1821)
Vali, Ali. Blue Skies. (p. 203)
Valiant, Kristi, illus. see Accord Publishing Staff & Hannigan, Paula.
Valiant, Kristi, illus. see Accord Publishing Staff.
Valiant, Kristi, illus. see Galante, Cecilia.
Valiant, Kristi, illus. see Lazo Gilmore, Dorina K.
Valiant, Kristi, illus. see Matthies, Jana.
Valiant, Kristi, illus. see Ohrt, Kate.
Valiant, Kristi, illus. see Steel, Danielle.
Valientes, Corazones, illus. see Reiser, Lynn.
Valk, Laurens. LEGO MINDSTORMS NXT 2. 0 Discovery Book: A Beginner's Guide to Building & Programming Robots. (p. 990)
Valkenburgh. Electricidad Basica. (p. 509)
Valkenburgh, Van & Nooger & Neville. Electricidad Basica, Volume 4 (p. 509)
Valko, Danna. Dee & Maya Are Best Friends. (p. 422)
Valko, Diane, illus. see Geiser, Traci Ferguson & Boylan, Maureen McCourt.
Valko, Diane, illus. see Kupperstein, Joel.
Valko, Diane, illus. see McFarren, Kathleen & Graf, Mike.
Valkov, Julian. Fork & the Spoon. Valkov, Julian, illus. (p. 620)
Valladares, Ellen Wolfson. Jonathan's Journey to Mount Miapu. (p. 925)
Vallaly, Barbara Dean, compiled by. Life on East 76th Street: Stories of an American Family (p. 1012)
Vallat, Christelle. Celia. Augusseau, Stphanie, illus. (p. 286)
Vallbona, et al. Tommy, the Amazing Cat: Troubles in Paradise. (p. 1770)
Valldejuly, Frances Bragan. Keka en el Museo de Arte de Ponce. Rabenau, Francesca von, illus. (p. 948)
Valle, Anita. Best Princess Coloring Book. (p. 171)
Valle, Jo Anne. Sweet Dreams: El Yunque Dreams. Valle, Jo Anne, photos by. (p. 1689)
—Taina Wants to Salsa. Valle, Jo Anne, photos by. (p. 1696)
Valle, José A. Ira de los Cascabeles. (p. 886)
Valleau, Gailon, illus. see Hearn, Emily.
Vallecchi, Alessandro, photos by see Williams, Megan K.
Vallejo, Esperanza, illus. see Arciniega, Triunfo.
Vallejo, Esperanza, illus. see Arciniegas, Triunfo.
Vallejo, Esperanza, illus. see Gomez, Luis Marcelino.
Vallejo, Esperanza, illus. see Quiroga, Horacio.
Vallejo, Fabio Silva. Cuentos para Leer Antes de Dormir. (p. 390)
Vallejo, Fernando. Desbarrancadero. (p. 428)
Vallejo, Harry. Dropping Clues from the Sky. (p. 486)
Vallejo-Nagera, Alejandra. Bigotes de Chocolate. (p. 185)

V

—Cazadores de Monstruos. (p. 283)
—Cazadores de Monstruos. Guerrero, Andrés, illus. (p. 283)
—Cuando Llegara Mi Cumpleanos? Guerrero, Andrés, illus. (p. 388)
—Cuanto me Quieren! Guerrero, Andrés, illus. (p. 388)
—Mira como He Crecido. (p. 1148)
—Mira Como He Crecido. Guerrero, Andrés, illus. (p. 1148)
—No Tengo Sueno! Guerrero, Andrés, illus. (p. 1260)
Vallencourt, Margaret. History of Photography. (p. 784)
—Technology of the Industrial Revolution. (p. 1712)
Valles, Lizette. Land of the Lost Socks: La Tierra de Los Calcetines Perdidos. (p. 973)
Valliant, Doris. Bangladesh. (p. 136)
—History of Cheerleading. (p. 783)
Valliant, Kristi, illus. see Cunningham, Elaine.
Valliant, Regina. Judy Garland Cut-Out Dolls. Valliant, Regina & Lunzer, Lee, illus. (p. 931)
Vallier, Jean, tr. see Seuss, Dr.
Vallon, Jacqueline, jt. auth. see Grant, Donald.
Vallorani, Giorgio, illus. see Driscoll, Laura & Disney Book Group Staff.
Valmiki, jt. auth. see Arni, Samhita.
Valmiki, jt. auth. see Doherty, Vrinda.
Valois, Rob. Intergalactic Adventure. (p. 879)
Valois, Rob, jt. auth. see Star Wars Staff.
Valois, Rob & Caravan Studios Staff. Spyro & the Giants. (p. 1636)
Valois, Rob & Penguin Young Readers Group. Spyro & the Giants. (p. 1636)
Valois, Rob, ed. Rising Stars of Manga (p. 1475)
Valor, De. Pirate Adventures of Sea Worthy: Featuring: the Treasure of Captain Blue Beard & the Return of Captain Blue Beard. (p. 1362)
Valuel. Star Wars Episode 3: Revenge of the Sith. Vol. 1 (p. 1641)
Valverde, Carlos. Sorpresa en la Granja. (p. 1614)
Valverde, Carlos M. Grumpy Frog. (p. 727)
—Surprise at the Farm. (p. 1685)
Valverde, Mariana. Force of Law (p. 616)
Valverde, Mikel. Paula en Nueva York. (p. 1330)
Valverde, Mikel, illus. see Atxaga, Bernardo & Costa, Margaret Jull.
Valverde, Mikel, illus. see MacHado, Ana Maria & Machado, Ana Maria.
Valverde, Mikel, illus. see Torras, Meri.
Valzania, Kimberly. Great Lakes. (p. 716)
—Kentucky. (p. 949)
—Tennessee. (p. 1720)
Vamos, Lesley, illus. see Brown, Ruby.
Vamos, Samantha R. Alphabet Trains. O'Rourke, Ryan, illus. (p. 50)
—Cazuela That the Farm Maiden Stirred. López, Rafael, illus. (p. 283)
Vamosh, Miriam F. Vida Diaria en Tiempos de Jesús. (p. 1840)
Van Ackeren, Elaine. Grandma's Pretend Teeth. (p. 709)
Van Ackooy, Maureen, jt. auth. see Pickles, Jonathan.
Van Allsburg, Chris. Jumanji. (p. 933)
—Just a Dream. (p. 937)
—Just a Dream. Van Allsburg, Chris, illus. (p. 937)
—Just a Dream 25th Anniversary Edition. (p. 937)
—Misadventures of Sweetie Pie. (p. 1150)
—Polar Express: Sam's Edition. (p. 1379)
—Polar Express Big Book. (p. 1379)
—Probuditi! (p. 1408)
—Queen of the Falls. (p. 1425)
—Sweetest Fig. (p. 1690)
—Wreck of the Zephyr. (p. 1962)
Van Allsburg, Chris, illus. see Lewis, C. S.
Van Allsburg, Chris, illus. see Zemeckis, Robert, et al.
Van Allsburg, Chris, et al. Chronicles of Harris Burdick: Fourteen Amazing Authors Tell the Tales. Van Allsburg, Chris, illus. (p. 317)
van Amelsfort, Barbara, illus. see Purperhart, Helen.
Van Ark, Katie. Boy Next Door. (p. 218)
van Beirs, Pat, jt. auth. see van Rijckeghem, Jean-Claude.
Van Biesen, Koen, illus. see Watkinson, Laura.
Van Binsbergen-Pritchard, Marion, tr. see Slier, Deborah & Shine, Ian, eds.
Van Buren, David. I Love You As Big As the World. Warnes, Tim, illus. (p. 843)
Van Buskirk, Steve. Dinosaurs. Van Buskirk, Steve, illus. (p. 444)
Van Camp, Diana. Jumbo Human Body Yearbook: Grade 5. (p. 933)
—Jumbo Human Body Yearbook: Grade 6. (p. 933)
—Jumbo Human Body Yearbook: Grade 7. (p. 933)
—Jumbo Human Body Yearbook: Grade 8. (p. 933)
Van Camp, Katie. Cookiebot! A Harry & Horsie Adventure. Agnew, Lincoln, illus. (p. 361)
—Harry & Horsie. Agnew, Lincoln, illus. (p. 750)
Van Camp, Richard. Little You Flett, Julie, illus. (p. 1038)
—Welcome Song for Baby: A Lullaby for Newborns (p. 1873)
—What's the Most Beautiful Thing You Know about Horses? Littlechild, George, illus. (p. 1899)
Van Cleave, Ryan G. Unlocked. (p. 1821)
Van Cleve, Barbara, photos by see Talbert, Marc.
Van Cleve, Kathleen. Drizzle. (p. 485)
Van Cleve, Kathleen & DeMarco, Kathleen. Drizzle. (p. 485)
van Dam, M. Nicole. Background Story of Inca Dink, the Great Houndini (Magician in Training) (p. 130)
van Dam, M. Nicole & Topping, Jay. This Little Puppy. van Dam, M. Nicole, illus. (p. 1737)
van de Liejgraaf, Deborah, illus. see Wehrmeijer, Annelien.
van de Liejgraaf, Deborah, illus. see Wejrmeijer, Annelien.
Van De Luecht, Susan. Children's Poetry - Dreams & Visions. (p. 304)
van de Ruit, John. Spud. (p. 1635)
Van De Ruit, John. Spud-the Madness Continues. (p. 1635)
Van de Vendel, Edward. Dog That Nino Didn't Have. Van Hertbruggen, Anton, illus. (p. 461)
Van de Vendel, Edward & van der Linden, Martijn. For You & No One Else. (p. 616)
van Deelen, Fred, illus. see Gregory, Philippa.
Van Den Abeele, Veronique. Still My Grandma. DuBois, Claude, illus. (p. 1650)
Van den Abeele-Kinget, Inge, tr. see Amant, Kathleen.
Van Den Berg, Helen, illus. see Veldkamp, Debby.
Van den Dries, Sidonie, jt. auth. see Moncomble, Gerard.
Van der Flier-Keller, Eileen. Field Guide to the Identification of Pebbles. (p. 584)
Van Der Gaag, Nikki, jt. auth. see Arbuthnot, Felicity.
Van Der Heide, Iris. Red Chalk. (p. 1453)
—Strange Day. ten Cate, Marijke, illus. (p. 1665)
van der Heide, William. Bollywood Babylon: Interviews with Shyam Benegal. (p. 208)
Van der Linde, Polly & Van der Linde, Tasha. Around the World in Eighty Dishes. Lemke, Horst, illus. (p. 101)
Van der Linde, Tasha, jt. auth. see Van der Linde, Polly.
Van Der Linden, Elly. Little Hamster. Lavreys, Debbie, illus. (p. 1028)
—Prickly Hedgehog. Lavreys, Debbie, illus. (p. 1398)
—Woolly Sheep. Lavreys, Debbie, illus. (p. 1950)
Van Der Linden, Gerdien, illus. see Stein, Mathilde.
Van Der Linden, Martijn, illus. see Rinck, Maranke.
van der Linden, Martijn, jt. auth. see Rinck, Maranke.
van der Linden, Martijn, jt. auth. see Van de Vendel, Edward.
van der Lith, Daan. Study & Master Accounting Grade 12 Workbook Afrikaans Translation. (p. 1670)
Van der Meer, Ron. How Many? (p. 810)
van der Meer, Ron & Whitford, Frank. Interactive Art Book. (p. 879)
Van Der Merwe, Stefan. ABC of All the Questions We Never Dare to Ask. (p. 3)
Van Der Merwe, Steve. Policeman Bobby. (p. 1380)
Van Der Paardt, Melissa, illus. see Jin, Chris & Trimmer, Christian.
van der Put, Klaartje, illus. see Chronicle Books Staff & ImageBooks Staff.
van der Put, Klaartje, illus. see Image Books Staff & Chronicle Books Staff.
van der Put, Klaartje, illus. see ImageBooks Staff & Chronicle Books Staff.
van der Put, Klaartje, et al. Little Duck: Finger Puppet. (p. 1027)
—Little Lamb. (p. 1030)
Van Der Put, Klaatje, illus. see ImageBooks Staff & Chronicle Books Staff.
van der Rol, Ruud, jt. auth. see Metselaar, Menno.
van der Smissen, Betty, et al. Nature-Oriented Activities. (p. 1236)
van der Sterre, Johanna, illus. see Hinkle, Cynthia.
van der Sterre, Johanna, illus. see Hyde, Heidi Smith.
van der Sterre, Johanna, illus. see Miller, Claire.
van der Sterre, Johanna, illus. see Summerer, Marilyn.
van der Sterre, Johanna, illus. see Van Slyke, Marge.
van der Sterre, Johnanna, illus. see Bradford, Wade.
Van Der Veer, Andrew. Bible Lessons for Juniors, Book 1: Creation Through Moses. (p. 175)
—Bible Lessons for Juniors, Book 2: Kings & Prophets. (p. 175)
Van der Veer, Andrew. Bible Lessons for Juniors, Book 3: The Life of Christ. (p. 175)
Van Der Veer, Andrew. Bible Lessons for Juniors, Book 4: The Early Church. (p. 175)
Van Der Watt, Tony. Balthazar, the Wolf Who Reformed. (p. 135)
Van der Westhuizen, Kevin. Inside the Minds of the Tsunami Children. (p. 877)
van der Zande, Irene. Kidpower Book for Caring Adults. (p. 952)
—Kidpower Safety Comics: An Introduction to "People Safety" for Young Children Ages 3 to 10 & Their Adults. Golert, Amanda, illus. (p. 952)
van Dernoot, Peter R., jt. auth. see Van Dernoot, Peter R.
Van Dernoot, Peter R. & van Dernoot, Peter R. Talking with My Treehouse Friends about Cancer: An Activity Book for Children of Parents with Cancer. Opsahl, Gail Kohler, illus. (p. 1704)
Van Diepen, Allison. Light of Day. (p. 1015)
Van Diepen, Allison. On the Edge. (p. 1290)
—Oracle of Dating. (p. 1301)
—Raven. (p. 1441)
—Snitch. (p. 1598)
—Street Pharm. (p. 1666)
—Takedown. (p. 1697)
—Vampire Stalker. (p. 1832)
Van Dijk, Jerianne, illus. see Alt, Susan.
Van Dijk, Jerianne, illus. see Danforth, Suzanne.
Van Dijk, Jerianne, illus. see Donaldson, Babette.
Van Dijk, Sheri. Don't Let Your Emotions Run Your Life for Teens: Dialectical Behavior Therapy Skills for Helping You Manage Mood Swings, Control Angry Outbursts, & Get along with Others. (p. 468)
—Relationship Skills 101 for Teens: Your Guide to Dealing with Daily Drama, Stress & Difficult Emotions Using Dbt. (p. 1457)
Van Diver, Bradford B. Roadside Geology of Vermont & New Hampshire. Alt, David & Hyndman, Donald W., eds. (p. 1477)
Van Dixhorn, Brenda. Pigeon Books: An Instructional Guide for Literature (p. 1357)
Van Dolzer, Krista. Don't Vote for Me. (p. 469)
—Sound of Life & Everything. (p. 1615)
Van Doninck, Sebastiaan, illus. see Goebel, Jenny.
Van Doorn, Sandra. Paper Hearts. (p. 1322)
Van Draanen, Wendelin. Attack of the Tagger. Biggs, Brian, illus. (p. 114)
—Confessions of a Serial Kisser. (p. 356)
—Enemy Spy. Biggs, Brian, illus. (p. 527)
—Flipped. (p. 605)
—Gecko & Sticky: the Power Potion. Gilpin, Stephen, illus. (p. 659)
—Greatest Power. Gilpin, Stephen, illus. (p. 720)
—Meet the Gecko. Biggs, Brian, illus. (p. 1122)
—Runaway. (p. 1496)
—Running Dream. (p. 1497)
—Sammy Keyes & the Art of Deception. (p. 1508)
—Sammy Keyes & the Art of Deception. Van Draanen, Wendelin, illus. (p. 1508)
—Sammy Keyes & the Cold Hard Cash. (p. 1508)
—Sammy Keyes & the Curse of Moustache Mary. (p. 1508)
—Sammy Keyes & the Dead Giveaway. (p. 1508)
—Sammy Keyes & the Hollywood Mummy. (p. 1508)
—Sammy Keyes & the Hotel Thief. (p. 1508)
—Sammy Keyes & the Killer Cruise. (p. 1508)
—Sammy Keyes & the Kiss Goodbye. (p. 1508)
—Sammy Keyes & the Night of Skulls. (p. 1508)
—Sammy Keyes & the Power of Justice Jack. (p. 1508)
—Sammy Keyes & the Psycho Kitty Queen. (p. 1508)
—Sammy Keyes & the Runaway Elf. (p. 1508)
—Sammy Keyes & the Search for Snake Eyes. (p. 1508)
—Sammy Keyes & the Search for Snake Eyes. Van Draanen, Wendelin, illus. (p. 1508)
—Sammy Keyes & the Showdown in Sin City. (p. 1508)
—Sammy Keyes & the Sisters of Mercy. (p. 1508)
—Sammy Keyes & the Wedding Crasher. (p. 1508)
—Sammy Keyes & the Wild Things. Biggs, Brian, illus. (p. 1508)
—Shredderman: Secret Identity. (p. 1571)
—Shredderman: Secret Identity. Biggs, Brian, illus. (p. 1571)
—Sinister Substitute. Gilpin, Stephen, illus. (p. 1579)
—Swear to Howdy. (p. 1689)
Van Draanen, Wendelin, jt. auth. see Stafford, Jean.
Van Dusen, Chris. Camping Spree with Mr. Magee. (p. 257)
—Circus Ship. Van Dusen, Chris, illus. (p. 322)
—Circus Ship Big Book. (p. 322)
—Down to the Sea with Mr. Magee. (p. 474)
—If I Built a Car. Van Dusen, Chris, illus. (p. 852)
—If I Built a House. (p. 852)
—King Hugo's Huge Ego. (p. 958)
—Learning to Ski with Mr. Magee. (p. 986)
—Randy Riley's Really Big Hit. Van Dusen, Chris, illus. (p. 1438)
Van Dusen, Chris, illus. see DiCamillo, Kate.
Van Dusen, Chris, jt. auth. see DiCamillo, Kate.
Van Dusen, Ross. Crocka Dog in the Evil Forest. (p. 384)
—How Crocka Dog Came to Be. (p. 806)
—What Makes a Rainbow? (p. 1892)
—What Makes a Snowflake? (p. 1892)
Van Duyne, Sara. Stress & Anxiety-Related Disorders. (p. 1667)
Van Duyne, Sara, jt. auth. see Way, Jennifer.
Van Duzen, Fisher. Searching for Sand Dollars. (p. 1537)
Van Dyck, Sara. Bumblebees. (p. 241)
—Electric Eels. (p. 508)
Van Dyke, Edith. Mary Louise. (p. 1100)
Van Dyke, Henry. Mansion: 100th Anniversary Edition. (p. 1088)
—Other Wise Man. (p. 1306)
—Other Wise Man. Barrett, Robert, illus. (p. 1306)
—Sad Shepherd: A Christmas Story, & the Unruly Sprite. (p. 1501)
—Story of the Other Wise Man. (p. 1662)
Van Dyke, Henry, et al. Greatest Christian Stories Ever Written. (p. 719)
Van Dyke, Jan. Living Like a King's Kid. Van Order, Laura & VonSeggen, Jon, illus. (p. 1041)
Van Dyke, Sissy. Adventures of Sissy Van Dyke: It's Not Just a Name, It's a Lifestyle. (p. 23)
Van Dyke, Tony & Van Dyke, Tracey. Ricky & Friends Go to Africa. Perry, Craig Rex & Preston, Felicia, illus. (p. 1470)
Van Dyke, Tracey, jt. auth. see Van Dyke, Tony.
Van Dyne, Edith. Aunt Jane's Nieces. (p. 115)
—Aunt Jane's Nieces Abroad. (p. 115)
—Aunt Jane's Nieces & Uncle John. (p. 115)
—Aunt Jane's Nieces at Millville. (p. 115)
—Aunt Jane's Nieces at Work. (p. 115)
—Aunt Jane's Nieces in Society. (p. 115)
—Aunt Jane's Nieces in the Red Cross. (p. 115)
—Aunt Jane's Nieces on Vacation. (p. 115)
—Aunt Jane's Nieces Out West. (p. 115)
—Aunt Jane's Nieces out West. (p. 115)
—Mary Louise. (p. 1100)
van Dyne, Edith, jt. auth. see Baum, L. Frank.
Van Eeden, Estelle. Lost Things. (p. 1056)
Van Eekhout, Greg. Boy at the End of the World. (p. 217)
—Kid vs. Squid. (p. 951)
Van Eerbeek, Ton. World of Wild Animals: An Early Encyclopedia for Beginning Readers. Balloon Books Staff, ed. (p. 1957)
Van Etten, Chris. Wickedpedia. (p. 1927)
Van Eyck, Laura, jt. auth. see Modica, Cathy.
Van Fleet, Mara. Little Color Fairies. Van Fleet, Mara, illus. (p. 1026)
—Night-Night, Princess. Van Fleet, Mara, illus. (p. 1253)
—Three Little Mermaids. Van Fleet, Mara, illus. (p. 1742)
Van Fleet, Mara & Wade, Sarah. Very Mixed-Up Princess. (p. 1838)
Van Fleet, Matthew. Alphabet. Skwarek, Skip, ed. (p. 49)
—Cat. Stanton, Brian, photos by. (p. 277)
—Color Dog. Stanton, Brian, illus. (p. 342)
—Dog. Stanton, Brian, photos by. (p. 460)
—Heads. Van Fleet, Matthew, illus. (p. 757)
—Lick! Van Fleet, Matthew, illus. (p. 1007)
—Monday the Bullfrog. Van Fleet, Matthew, illus. (p. 1163)
—Moo. Stanton, Brian, photos by. (p. 1171)
—Munch! Van Fleet, Matthew, illus. (p. 1191)
—Sniff! Van Fleet, Matthew, illus. (p. 1597)
—Tails. Van Fleet, Matthew, illus. (p. 1695)
—Van Fleet Alphabet Heads: Alphabet; Heads. Van Fleet, Matthew, illus. (p. 1832)
—Van Fleet Animal Trio: Moo; Cat; Dog. Stanton, Brian, photos by. (p. 1832)
—Van Fleet Sniff! Lick! Munch! Van Fleet, Matthew, illus. (p. 1832)
Van Frankenhuyzen, Gijsbert, illus. see Noble, Trinka Hakes.
van Frankenhuyzen, Gijsbert, illus. see Salten, Felix.
van Frankenhuyzen, Gijsbert, illus. see Shoulders, Debbie & Shoulders, Michael.
van Frankenhuyzen, Gijsbert, illus. see Smith van Frankenhuyzen, Robbyn.
van Frankenhuyzen, Gijsbert, illus. see Strother, Ruth.
van Frankenhuyzen, Gijsbert, illus. see Van Frankenhuyzen, Robbyn Smith.
van Frankenhuyzen, Gijsbert, illus. see Wargin, Kathy-jo.
van Frankenhuyzen, Gijsbert, illus. see Whelan, Gloria.
Van Frankenhuyzen, Robbyn Smith. Itsy Bitsy & Teeny Weeny. van Frankenhuyzen, Gijsbert, illus. (p. 900)
—Kelly of Hazel Ridge. van Frankenhuyzen, Gijsbert, illus. (p. 948)
van Galen, Maggie. Adventures of Keeno & Ernest: The Diamond Mine. (p. 19)
van Garderen, Ilse, illus. see Pearce, Margaret.
van Genechten, Guido. Because You Are My Friend. (p. 155)
—Big & Small. (p. 177)
—Big Baby Book. (p. 177)
—Big Eating Book. (p. 181)
—Big Sleep Book. (p. 183)
—Big Woods Orchestra. (p. 184)
—Can't We Share? (p. 262)
—Circus 123. (p. 322)
—Crinkle Animals - Garden. (p. 383)
—Crinkle Animals - Jungle. (p. 383)
—Daddies & Their Babies. (p. 398)
Van Genechten, Guido. Floppy. (p. 606)
—Floppy's Friends. (p. 606)
van Genechten, Guido. Floppy's Friends. van Genechten, Guido, illus. (p. 606)
—Guess What? (p. 729)
—Guess Where? (p. 729)
—Guess Who? van Genechten, Guido, illus. (p. 729)
—Guido's Great Coloring & Drawing Book. (p. 730)
—Knight Ricky. van Genechten, Guido, illus. (p. 964)
Van Genechten, Guido. Little Snowman Stan. (p. 1036)
—Look at That! Farm Animals. (p. 1049)
van Genechten, Guido. Look at That! Wild Animals. (p. 1049)
—Mommies & Their Babies. (p. 1162)
—Moon Is Sad. (p. 1172)
—My Daddy. (p. 1201)
—No Ghost under My Bed. (p. 1258)
—Piggy Goes to the Beach. (p. 1358)
—Ricky & Annie. van Genechten, Guido, illus. (p. 1470)
—Ricky & the Squirrel. van Genechten, Guido, illus. (p. 1470)
—Ricky Is Brave. van Genechten, Guido, illus. (p. 1470)
—Ricky's Birthday. (p. 1470)
Van Genechten, Guido. Ricky's Christmas Tree. (p. 1470)
van Genechten, Guido. Super Ladybug to the Rescue! (p. 1680)
—Water - Crinkle Animals. (p. 1862)
van Genechten, Guido & Fripplat, Stéphanie. In, Out & All Around. (p. 864)
—Kai-Mook. van Genechten, Guido, illus. (p. 941)
van Genechten, Guido & Mann, Holly. Farm - Crinkle Animals. (p. 573)
Van Gessel, Chad. Demons: The Titan Clash. (p. 426)
van Gogh, Vincent. Make a Masterpiece — Van Gogh's Starry Night. (p. 1078)
—Vincent's Colors. (p. 1843)
van Gogh, Vincent, jt. auth. see Bassil, Andrea.
van Gogh, Vincent, jt. auth. see Lossani, Chiara.
van Gogh, Vincent & Lach, William. Vincent's Colors: Words & Pictures by Van Gogh. (p. 1843)
van Gogh, Vincent & Noble, Marty. Van Gogh Stained Glass Coloring Book. (p. 1833)
Van Gool, A, et al. Mis Primeras Palabras Inglés-Español: Más de 500 Palabras. Edimat Libros, ed. (p. 1150)
Van Gorder, Vivian Ezelfe. Master Kofi & Friskey the Dog. (p. 1103)
Van Gorp, Lynn. Antoine Lavoisier: Founder of Modern Chemistry. (p. 89)
—Antoine Lavoisier: And His Impact on Modern Chemistry (p. 89)
—Earth Scientists: From Mercator to Evans (p. 497)
—Elements (p. 510)
—Genetics (p. 661)
—Gregor Mendel: Genetics Pioneer (p. 723)
—Gregor Mendel: Genetics Pioneer. (p. 723)
—Investigating Landforms. (p. 884)
—Landforms (p. 974)
—Pioneers of Earth Science. (p. 1361)
—World of Elements & Their Properties. (p. 1956)
Van Gorp, Lynn, jt. auth. see Science Readers Staff.
van Gosen, Ryan O'Dell, IV. Ray Conka & the Sortian Jewell. Maximilian Staff, ed. (p. 1441)
Van Gruisen, Janette van de Geest, et al. Redwood Review Summer 2003 Ellis, Melissa Martin, photos by. (p. 1456)
van Gurp, Peggy. Lucky's Little Feather. van Gurp, Peggy, illus. (p. 1063)
Van Haeringen, Annemarie. Princesa de Largos Cabellos. De Sterck, Goedele, tr. (p. 1402)
Van Haeringen, Annemarie, illus. see Kromhout, Rindert.
Van Halsema, Thea B. This Was John Calvin. (p. 1737)
van Hamersveld, Madeleine. Good Luck, Tiny Chuck: A Book for Big Brothers & Sisters of Very Small Babies. van Hamersveld, Madeleine, illus. (p. 698)
Van Hamme, Jean. Beyond the Shadows. Rosinski, Grzegorz, illus. (p. 174)
—Brand of the Exiles. Rosinski, Grzegorz, illus. (p. 222)
—Curse of the 30 Pieces of Silver Shreder, Etienne & Aubin, Antoine, illus. (p. 394)
—Curse of the 30 Pieces of Silver Sterne, René & De Spiegeleer, Chantal, illus. (p. 394)
—Guardian of the Keys. Rosinski, Grzegorz, illus. (p. 728)
—Heir. Francq, Philippe, illus. (p. 762)
—Invisible Fortress. Rosinski, Grzegorz, illus. (p. 885)
—Mas alla de las Sombras Rosinski, Grzegorz, illus. (p. 1101)
—Strange Encounter (p. 1665)
—Thorgal: La Maga Traicionada. Rosinski, Grzegorz, illus. (p. 1740)
—Thorgal: La Galera Negra Vol. 4 Rosinski, Grzegorz, illus. (p. 1740)
—Thorgal: La Isla de los Mares Helados Rosinski, Grzegorz, illus. (p. 1740)
van Hamme, Jean. Thorgal - City of the Lost God. Rosinski, Grzegorz, illus. (p. 1740)

Van Hamme, Jean. Thorgal Vol. 13: Ogotai's Crown. Rosinski, Grzegorz, illus. (p. 1740)
—Three Elders of Aran. Rosinski, illus. (p. 1742)
—Tres Ancianos del pais de Aran Roskinski, Grzegorz, illus. (p. 1784)
Van Hamme, Jean, jt. auth. see Rosinski.
Van Hauten, Jacques. Llega el Zorro. (p. 1043)
van Heerden, Marjorie, illus. see Luckett, Kathy.
Van Hemeldonck, Tineke, illus. see De Kockere, Geert & Dom, An.
Van Hemeldonck, Tineke, illus. see De Kockere, Geert.
Van Hertbruggen, Anton, illus. see Van de Vendel, Edward.
Van Herwerden, Julie. Kids Love Cooking. (p. 954)
—Kids Luv Healthy Cooking. (p. 954)
Van Hoorn, Aurea, illus. see Hirabayashi, Suzanne.
Van Horn, Patricia, jt. auth. see Lieberman, Alicia F.
Van Horn, Stephanie. Math Rapmatics: Mathematical Rhymes Right on Time. Daniel, Rick, illus. (p. 1107)
Van Horn, William. Walt Disney's Comics Clark, John, ed. (p. 1855)
Van Horn, William, jt. auth. see Cole, Joanna.
Van Horn, William, jt. auth. see Rawson, Dave.
Van Horn, William & Block, Shelly. Uncle Scrooge #343 Clark, John, ed. (p. 1812)
Van Horn, William & Gilbert, Janet. Uncle Scrooge Clark, John, ed. (p. 1812)
Van Horn, William & Rawson, Dave. Walt Disney's Comics Clark, John, ed. (p. 1855)
Van Horn, William & Rosa, Don. Walt Disney's Comics Clark, John, ed. (p. 1855)
Van Horn, William, et al. Walt Disney's Comics Clark, John, ed. (p. 1855)
—Walt Disney's Comics. Clark, John, ed. (p. 1855)
Van Hout, Mies. Friends. (p. 638)
—Happy. (p. 744)
Van Hout, Mies, illus. see Stein, Mathilde.
Van Hout, Mies, illus. see Van Lieshout, Elle & Van Os, Erik.
Van Houten, Elizabeth. Women in the World of Japan. (p. 1946)
Van Hoven, Constance. Twelve Days of Christmas in Minnesota. Wohnoutka, Mike, illus. (p. 1800)
Van Hoven, Constance & Walker, David. Hello, Minnesota! (p. 764)
Van Kampen, Megan, illus. see Hancock, Rusty.
Van Kampen, Megan, illus. see Wells, Sherry A.
van Kampen, Vlasta, illus. see Silsbe, Brenda.
van Kampen, Vlasta, illus. see Thury, Fredrick H.
Van Kersen, Elizabeth. Who's Riley. (p. 1921)
—Whos' Riley? Stevens, Debra, illus. (p. 1921)
van Keuren, Luise. Raven, Stay by Me. (p. 1441)
Van King, L. Dwarf in the Drawer: A Mischievous Parody. Gonzales, Chuck, illus. (p. 491)
Van Klompenburg, Carol. King Who Wouldn't Stop Dancing: The Story of David. (p. 959)
Van Laan, Nancy. Forget Me Not. Graegin, Stephanie, illus. (p. 619)
—Nit-Pickin' Booth, George, illus. (p. 1257)
—Scrubba Dub. Pons, Bernadette, illus. (p. 1533)
—Teeny Tiny Tingly Tales. Chess, Victoria, illus. (p. 1715)
van Leer, Jake, et al. Over the Moon: A Musical Play. (p. 1314)
van Leer, Samantha, jt. auth. see Picoult, Jodi.
Van Leeuwed, Wendy. Agents of God Activity Book. (p. 29)
Van Leeuwen, Jean. Amanda Pig & Her Big Brother Oliver. Schweninger, Ann, illus. (p. 52)
—Amanda Pig & the Awful, Scary Monster. Schweninger, Ann, illus. (p. 52)
—Amanda Pig & the Really Hot Day. Schweninger, Ann, illus. (p. 52)
—Amanda Pig & the Wiggly Tooth. Schweninger, Ann, illus. (p. 52)
—Amanda Pig, First Grader. Schweninger, Ann, illus. (p. 52)
—Cabin on Trouble Creek. (p. 250)
—Chicken Soup. Gavril, David, illus. (p. 300)
—Five Funny Bunnies: Three Bouncing Tales Wilsdorf, Anne, illus. (p. 600)
—Great Cheese Conspiracy (p. 714)
—Missing Pieces of Me (p. 1152)
—Tales of Oliver Pig. Schweninger, Ann, illus. (p. 1702)
van Leeuwen, Joke. Day My Father Became a Bush. (p. 413)
Van Leeuwen, Michele D., creator. Summer Bridge Activities: Grades PK to K. (p. 1674)
Van Leeuwen, Wendy. Itty-bitty Bible Activity Book, God's Big Christmas Plan. (p. 900)
—Miracle Man Activity Book. (p. 1148)
—Ten Commandments Activity Book. (p. 1718)
Van Lemon, M. Champions of the Garden Games: Winter Fun for Everyone. (p. 289)
Van Lente, Fred. Hercules (p. 769)
—Marvel Universe Iron Man - Comic Reader 1. (p. 1099)
Van Lente, Fred, et al. Crypt-Keeping It Real. Zanier, Christian et al, illus. (p. 387)
—Tales from the Crypt. Todd, Mort et al, illus. (p. 1701)
—Yabba Dabba Voodoo. Mannion, Steve et al, illus. (p. 1968)
Van Lente, Fred, et al, texts. Marvel Zombies Return. (p. 1099)
Van Lieshout, Elle, jt. auth. see Van Os, Erik.
Van Lieshout, Elle & Van Os, Erik. Lovey & Dovey. Van Hout, Mies, illus. (p. 1061)
—Nothing King. Gerritsen, Paula, illus. (p. 1268)
—Wish. (p. 1940)
van Lieshout, Maria. Backseat A-B-See. (p. 130)
—Flight 1-2-3. (p. 604)
—Flight 1-2-3. van Lieshout, Maria, illus. (p. 604)
—Hopper & Wilson. van Lieshout, Maria, illus. (p. 797)
—Traffic Jam Matching Game. (p. 1776)
van Lieshout, Maria, illus. see Gibson, Amy.
van Lieshout, Maria, illus. see Love, Maryann Cusimano.
van Lieshout, Ted. Uncle Gus's Magic Box. Sideri, Simona, tr. from DUT. (p. 1811)
Van Liew Cassels, Rosemary. Santa's Dilemm. (p. 1513)
Van Liew, Denisha. Johnson Family & Friends Picnic: An Alphabet Book. (p. 924)
van Lindehuizen, Eline, illus. see Nijssen, Elfi.
van Lindenhuizen, Eline, illus. see Koppens, Judith.
Van Loon, Hendrik, illus. see Mitchell, Lucy Sprague.
Van Loon, Hendrik Willem. Ancient Man: The Beginning of Civilizations. (p. 69)
—Ancient Man. (p. 69)
—Short History of Discovery: From the Earliest Times to the Founding of Colonies in the American Continent. (p. 1569)
—Story of Mankind. (p. 1659)
van Loon, Hendrik Willem, et al. Story of Mankind. (p. 1659)
Van Maarsen, Jacqueline. Friend Called Anne: One Girl's Story of War, Peace, & a Unique Friendship with Anne Frank. (p. 637)
Van Maarsen, Jacqueline & Lee, Carol Ann. Friend Called Anne. (p. 637)
Van Manen, Dave. Plants of the Pueblo Mountain Park. (p. 1370)
Van Manen, Max. Tone of Teaching. (p. 1765)
Van Meter, Larry A. Miranda V. Arizona: The Rights of the Accused. (p. 1149)
—United States V. Nixon: The Question of Executive Privilege. (p. 1820)
—Women Win the Vote: The Hard-Fought Battle for Women's Suffrage. (p. 1946)
—Yerba Buena. (p. 1970)
Van Middeldyk, R. A. History of Puerto Rico from Spanish Discovery to American Occupation. (p. 784)
Van Munching, Philip. Boys Will Put You on a Pedestal (So They Can Look up Your Skirt) A Dad's Advice for Daughters. (p. 220)
Van, Muon. In a Village by the Sea. Chu, April, illus. (p. 863)
Van Niekerk, Clarabelle, jt. auth. see Venter, Liezl.
Van Norstrand, Kain, illus. see Bonasia, Steve.
Van Nostrand, Michele. Little Witch. (p. 1038)
Van Nutt, Robert. Ugly Duckling. Van Nutt, Robert & Bogdanovic, Toma, illus. (p. 1808)
Van Nutt, Robert, illus. see Andersen, Hans Christian.
Van Nutt, Robert, illus. see Irving, Washington.
Van Nutt, Robert, illus. see Kessler, Brad.
van Oirschot, Allene. Daddy's Little Girl. (p. 399)
Van Ommen, Sylvia, illus. see Westera, Marleen.
Van Order, Bill. Wondrous Sky. (p. 1949)
Van Order, Laura, illus. see Van Dyke, Jan.
Van Os, Erik, jt. auth. see Van Lieshout, Elle.
Van Os, Erik & Van Lieshout, Elle. How Much Does the Gray in an Elephant Weigh? Hoogstad, Alice, illus. (p. 811)
Van Os, Joanne. Castaway. (p. 276)
—Secret of the Lonely Isles. (p. 1542)
Van Oss, Laura. Indigo's Gift: Does Indigo Have a Secret Gift? Wolf, Claudia, illus. (p. 872)
Van Osten, Carson, jt. auth. see Keely, Jack.
Van Patten, Barbara. Whoo Saves the Symphony: A Shenandoah Music Festival Adventure. (p. 1920)
Van Patten, Bill, et al. Sabías Que... ? (p. 1500)
—Sabías Que... ? With Online Learning Center Bind-In Card. (p. 1500)
Van Patten, Bruce, illus. see Miller, William.
Van Patter, Bruce. Farley Found It! (p. 573)
—Tucker Took It! (p. 1795)
Van Patter, Bruce, illus. see Meade, Starr.
Van Patter, Bruce, illus. see Spyri, Johanna.
Van Pelt, Don & Wingate, Brian. Insider's Guide to Football. (p. 878)
Van Pelt, Jason. Color Wheel. (p. 343)
Van Pelt, Peggy. Imagineering Workout: Exercises to Shape Your Creative Muscles. (p. 861)
Van Pelt, Todd, jt. auth. see Matthews, Rupert.
Van Ravenswaay, Susan. Reading Is So Easy. (p. 1446)
van Reek, Wouter. Coppernickel: The Invention. (p. 366)
van Reek, Wouter, creator. Coppernickel Goes Mondrian. (p. 366)
van Rheenen, Barbara, illus. see Douglas, Jozua.
van Rijckeghem, Jean-Claude & van Beirs, Pat. Sword in Her Hand. Nieuwenhuizen, John, tr. from DUT. (p. 1692)
van Rijswijk, Cor. David & Goliath. Visser, Rino, illus. (p. 410)
—Gideon Blows the Trumpet. Visser, Rino, illus. (p. 674)
Van Riper, Guernsey, Jr. Babe Ruth. Fleishman, Seymour, illus. (p. 123)
—Will Rogers, Young Cowboy. (p. 1932)
Van Rose, S. Atlas Visual de la Tierra. (p. 113)
van Rose, Susanna. DK Eyewitness Books: Earth: Earth. (p. 456)
Van Rose, Susanna. Eyewitness Books - Volcano & Earthquake. (p. 558)
van Rose, Susanna & Dorling Kindersley Publishing Staff. Earth. (p. 495)
Van Ryk, Laverne. Garland of Emeralds. (p. 657)
Van Rynbach, Iris. Pilgrim House Sticker Activity Book. (p. 1358)
Van Rynbach, Iris & Shea, Pegi Deitz. Taxing Case of the Cows: A True Story about Suffrage. McCully, Emily Arnold, illus. (p. 1707)
Van Rys, John, et al. Business Writer. (p. 245)
Van Saan, Anita. Experimentos para Cada Dia del Otono. Bravo, J. A., tr. (p. 549)
Van Sant, Barb. Kid Sense! Good Answers to Your Child's Tough Questions about Personal Safety. (p. 951)
Van Schoyk. Burn Rate Diet: The New Mind-Body Treatment for Permanent Weight Control. (p. 243)
Van Scott, Miriam. Candy Canes in Bethlehem. Van Wagoner, Traci, illus. (p. 261)
Van Scoyoc, Pam. Ballerina with Webbed Feet/la Bailarina Palmipeda. Teichman, Diane E., tr. from ENG. (p. 134)
—I Could Catch a Whale/ Yo Podria Pescar una Ballena. Santillan-Cruz, Sylvia R., tr. (p. 837)
Van Severen, Joe, illus. see Sanders, Nancy I.
Van Sicklen, Margaret. Origami on the Go! 40 Paper-Folding Projects for Kids Who Love to Travel. (p. 1304)
Van Sise, George W. Wonderfultales from the Land of the Seven Kingdoms. (p. 1948)
Van Sluys, Katie, contrib. by. Global Connections (p. 684)
Van Slyke, Lucille. Little Miss by-the-Day. (p. 1031)
van Slyke, Lucille. Little Miss By-the-Day. (p. 1031)
Van Slyke, Marge. Furniture Refinishing in A Class by Yourself. Lambert, Barbara, ed. (p. 650)
Van Slyke, Rebecca. Mom School. Burris, Priscilla, illus. (p. 1161)
Van Slyke, Rebecca, illus. see Kohl, MaryAnn F. & Potter, Jean.
Van Steenwyk, Elizabeth. First Dog Fala Montgomery, Michael G., illus. (p. 594)
—One Fine Day: A Radio Play. Farnsworth, Bill, illus. (p. 1295)
—Prairie Christmas. Himler, Ronald, illus. (p. 1392)
—When Abraham Talked to the Trees. Farnsworth, Bill, illus. (p. 1901)
Van Stockum, Hilda. Day on Skates: The Story of a Dutch Picnic. Van Stockum, Hilda, illus. (p. 414)
—King Oberon's Forest. (p. 958)
Van Stokkum, Colombe Marie. Potency Matters. (p. 1388)
Van Straaten, Harmen. Little trunk Late. (p. 1037)
—Snowman's Wish. (p. 1601)
—TIM & the FLYING MACHINE. (p. 1750)
—Tough guy Tim. (p. 1772)
Van Straaten, Harmen & Straaten, Harmen Van. For Me? Bradley, MaryChris, tr. from DUT. (p. 616)
Van Stralen, Dirk, illus. see Wakeman, Daniel.
van Swol-Ulbrich, Hilly, jt. auth. see Kaltenhauser, Bettina.
Van Syckle, A. & Schwartz, Josh. OC: 'twas the Night Before Chrismukkah. (p. 1275)
Van Tassel, Mary. Beach Ball's Journey (p. 149)
Van Tassel, Mary A. Beach Ball's Discovery. (p. 149)
—Beach Ball's Return. DeBroech, Sarah, illus. (p. 149)
Van Til, Meaghan. Mysteries. (p. 1222)
Van Til, Meaghan, jt. auth. see Harris, Dave.
Van Tine, Laura, illus. see Sharp, Michael.
Van Tol, Alex. Dolores Huerta: Voice for the Working Poor. (p. 464)
—Gravity Check (p. 712)
—Knifepoint (p. 964)
—Oracle (p. 1301)
—Punta de Cuchillo (p. 1417)
—Redline (p. 1455)
—Shallow Grave (p. 1559)
—Sonia Sotomayor: U. S. Supreme Court Justice. (p. 1612)
—Viral (p. 1844)
Van Turennout, Paola, jt. auth. see Winters, Kari-Lynn.
Van Valkenburgh, Blaire, jt. auth. see Strother, Ruth.
Van Valkenburgh, Norman J. America's First Wilderness: New York State's Forest Preserves. (p. 64)
Van Veldhoven, Marijke, illus. see Blackford, Andy.
Van Vleet, Carmella. Amazing Ben Franklin Inventions: You Can Build Yourself. (p. 54)
—Amazing Ben Franklin Inventions. (p. 54)
—Eliza Bing Is (Not) a Big, Fat Quitter. Donnelly, Karen, illus. (p. 513)
—Explore Ancient Egypt! 25 Great Projects, Activities, Experiments. Kim, Alex, illus. (p. 550)
—Explore Ancient Greece! 25 Great Projects, Activities, Experiments. Shedd, Blair & Kim, Alex, illus. (p. 550)
—Explore Ancient Rome! 25 Great Projects, Activities, Experiments. Kim, Alex, illus. (p. 550)
—Explore Electricity! With 25 Great Projects. Stone, Bryan, illus. (p. 550)
—Great Ancient Egypt Projects. (p. 713)
—Seven Wonders of the World: Discover Amazing Monuments to Civilization with 20 Projects. Rizvi, Farah, illus. (p. 1555)
—Writing Club: A Year of Writing Workshops for Grades 2-5 (p. 1964)
Van Vleet, Jessica. 202 Good Clean Jokes for Kids. (p. 2001)
Van Volkinburg, Becky. Linc Adams & the Freddie Fantastic Summer. (p. 1018)
Van Vynckt, Virginia, photos by see Grunes, Barbara.
Van Wagenen, Maya. Popular: Vintage Wisdom for a Modern Geek. (p. 1385)
Van Wagenen, Maya, jt. auth. see Cornell, Betty.
Van Wagoner, Traci, illus. see Van Scott, Miriam.
Van Walsum-Quispel, J. M. Tina's Island Home. Leeflang-Oudenarden, C., illus. (p. 1755)
Van Wassenhove, Sue. Seldom-Ever-Shady Glades. (p. 1549)
Van Wemmer, Deby. Wishes & Walnuts. (p. 1940)
Van Winkle, Amy. Flower Fairy (p. 607)
Van Wright, Cornelius. When an Alien Meets a Swamp Monster. (p. 1901)
Van Wright, Cornelius, illus. see Black, Sonia W.
Van Wright, Cornelius, illus. see Bridges, Ruby & Maccarone, Grace.
Van Wright, Cornelius, illus. see Chinn, Karen.
Van Wright, Cornelius, illus. see da Costa, Deborah.
Van Wright, Cornelius, illus. see Glass, Susan.
Van Wright, Cornelius, illus. see Grubman, Bonnie.
Van Wright, Cornelius, illus. see Hoffman, Mary.
Van Wright, Cornelius, illus. see Levinson, Lara.
Van Wright, Cornelius, illus. see Medearis, Angela Shelf.
Van Wright, Cornelius, illus. see Pringle, Laurence.
Van Wright, Cornelius, illus. see Rappaport, Doreen.
Van Wright, Cornelius, illus. see Scholastic, Inc. Staff & Black, Sonia.
Van Wright, Cornelius, illus. see Scholastic, Inc. Staff & Medearis, Angela Shelf.
Van Wright, Cornelius, illus. see Schroeder, Alan.
Van Wright, Cornelius, illus. see Shahan, Sherry.
Van Wright, Cornelius, illus. see Starr, Meg.
Van Wright, Cornelius, illus. see Stewig, John Warren.
Van Wright, Cornelius, tr. see Shahan, Sherry.
Van Wright, Cornelius & Hu, Ying-Hwa. I Told You I Can Play! (p. 846)
Van Wyk, Hanri, illus. see Brooks, Felicity & Litchfield, Jo.
Van Wyk, Hanri, illus. see Brooks, Felicity.
Van Wyk, Hanri, illus. see Helbrough, Emma & Brooks, Felicity.
Van Wyk, Hanri, illus. see Taplin, Sam.
Van Wyk, Rupert, illus. see Cuillain, Adam & Cuillain, Charlotte.
Van Wyk, Rupert, illus. see Guillain, Adam & Guillain, Charlotte.
van Wyk, Rupert, illus. see Platt, Richard.
Van Wyk, Tasja. Twins: Meet the Doctor. (p. 1802)
Van Young, Sayre. Unofficial Harry Potter Vocabulary Builder: Learn the 3,000 Hardest Words from All Seven Books & Enjoy the Series More. (p. 1822)
Van Zandt, Steve. River Song: With the Banana Slug String Band. Zecca, Katherine, illus. (p. 1476)
—River Song: With the Banana Slug String Band (Includes Music CD) Zecca, Katherine, illus. (p. 1476)
Van Zant, Dawn. Bradford & the Journey to the Desert of Lop. (p. 221)
—No More Night Mares: A Dream of Freedom. McElroy, Kim, illus. (p. 1259)
van Zante, Janis, et al. Audio Cd: Used with ... van Zante-Grammar Links 3: A Theme-Based Course for Reference & Practice. (p. 114)
—Grammar Links 3 (p. 706)
—Grammar Links 3: A Theme-Based Course for Reference & Practice. (p. 706)
Van Zee, Amy. How to Analyze the Works of C. S. Lewis. (p. 814)
Van Zeyl, Marjan, illus. see Grimm, Wilhelm K. & Grimm, Jacob.
Van Zile, Susan, jt. auth. see Longhi, Sarah.
Van Zyle, Daniel, illus. see Miller, Debbie S.
Van Zyle, Jon, illus. see Carlstrom, Nancy White.
Van Zyle, Jon, illus. see Flowers, Pam.
Van Zyle, Jon, illus. see Heinz, Brian J.
Van Zyle, Jon, illus. see Levine, Ellen & Megarry, Tim.
Van Zyle, Jon, illus. see London, Jonathan.
Van Zyle, Jon, illus. see McDaniel, Jequita Potts.
Van Zyle, Jon, illus. see Miller, Debbie S.
Van Zyle, Jon, illus. see Miller, Debbie S. & Eller, John H.
Van Zyle, Jon, illus. see Shields, Mary & Grace, Susan.
Van Zyle, Jon, jt. auth. see McDaniel, Jequite Po.
Vana, Dan. Joey & the Magic Dream Pillow. Ware, Quinton, illus. (p. 920)
VanAllen, Cindy. Animal ABC's: A little book to make you glad, Hot off the press, from Nana¿s Pad. (p. 76)
Vanalstine, Carrie. Frizzy Izzy Yelp! (p. 639)
Vanarsdale, Anthony, illus. see Norwich, Grace.
VanArsdale, Anthony, illus. see Warner, Gertrude Chandler.
Vanasse, André. Gabrielle Roy: A Passion for Writing. (p. 652)
Vanasse, Deb. Alaska Animal Babies. Jecan, Gavriel, photos by. (p. 34)
—Cold Spell. (p. 338)
—Lucy's Dance. (p. 1063)
—Totem Tale: A Tall Story from Alaska. Brooks, Erik, illus. (p. 1772)
—Under Alaska's Midnight Sun. Trammell, Jeremiah, illus. (p. 1813)
Vanasse, Patricia. Resilient. Shalaby, Asharaf, illus. (p. 1463)
VanBibber, Jodi. Bible Story Concepts for Fours & Fives: A Unique Blend of Bible Concepts & Preschool Skills. VanBibber, Jodi, ed. (p. 176)
—CD: An Early Childhood Learning Program designed especially for One-Year-Olds. (p. 283)
—CD: An Early Childhood Learning Program designed especially for two & three year olds. It's educational & easy to do. but best of all, it's fun!: Bible Story Concepts for 2s And 3s. (p. 283)
—CD-Bible Story Concepts for 4s And 5s: An Early Childhood Learning Program designed especially for four & five year olds. It's educational & easy to do. but best of all, it's Fun! (p. 283)
VanBlaricum, Pam, ed. see Klawitter, Pamela Amick.
VanBlaricum, Pam, ed. see Schwartz, Linda.
VanBlaricum, Pam, ed. see Sylvester, Diane.
VanBrandwijk, Clare. Called to Covenant: Living Your Response to God's Love. (p. 254)
VanBrugge, Jeanne, tr. see Vogelaar, Alie.
VanBuskirk, Alan, illus. see VanBuskirk, Gary.
VanBuskirk, Gary. Scott & Jake. VanBuskirk, Alan, illus. (p. 1530)
VanBuskirk, Luegenia. God Loves Me. (p. 689)
VanCamp, Marilyn. Jumbo Nutrition Yearbook: Grade 3. (p. 933)
Vancata, Brad, illus. see Mayer, Kirsten.
Vancata, Brad, illus. see Sazaklis, John.
Vancata, Brad, illus. see Sonneborn, Scott.
Vancata, Brad, jt. auth. see Sazaklis, John.
Vance, Alexander. Heartbreak Messenger. (p. 760)
Vance, Ashley & Gohari, Omid. Brigham Young University College Prowler off the Record: Inside BYU. (p. 228)
Vance Barnum. Frank & Andy Afloat. (p. 628)
—Joe Strong the Boy Fire-Eater. (p. 920)
Vance, Colleen. Flip Flop Family. Kinra, Richa, illus. (p. 605)
Vance, Cynthia. Red, Yellow, Blue & You. Whitman, Candace, illus. (p. 1455)
Vance, Darcy, jt. auth. see Tahmaseb, Charity.
Vance, Elsbet, ed. Mistletoe Madness: A Short Story Collection. (p. 1155)
Vance, Jack. Lurulu. (p. 1066)
Vance, Jennifer. Solomon. (p. 1608)
Vance, L. K. Jennadi. (p. 912)
VanCe, Lilo. Once upon a Time & Other Stories. (p. 1293)
Vance, Mimi Brian. Baby & Bunny: Sharing Sign Language with Your Child Gillen, Rosemarie, illus. (p. 124)
—Boat & Bath: Sharing Sign Language with Your Child Gillen, Rosemarie, illus. (p. 205)
—Book & Bed Gillen, Rosemarie, illus. (p. 210)
—Milk & More: Sharing Sign Language with Your Child Gillen, Rosemarie, illus. (p. 1143)
—Words by the Handful: Sharing Sign Language with Your Child - Four Stories to Help You & Your Baby Communicate Set Gillen, Rosemarie, illus. (p. 1951)
Vance, Rodney. De'Monte Love. (p. 426)
Vance, Talia. Silver. (p. 1576)
Vance, Vince. Vince Vance Rock & Roll Reader: Bedtime Stories, Poems, Songs, Jokes, Pictures & Other Real Cool Stuff for Kids of All Ages. Pennington, Carole, ed. (p. 1842)
Vancil, Mark. NBA Basketball Offense Basics. (p. 1238)
Vancil, Marybelle. Adventures with Macy & the Sneezy, Sneezy Dog: First Adventure: We Visit Indians. (p. 25)

V

VanCil, Marybelle. Sadie Fourpaws & the Magic Rocking Chair. (p. 1501)
VanCleave, Janice. Step-by-Step Science Experiments in Astronomy. (p. 1647)
—Step-by-Step Science Experiments in Biology. (p. 1647)
—Step-by-Step Science Experiments in Earth Science. (p. 1647)
—Step-by-Step Science Experiments in Energy. (p. 1647)
—Super Science Challenges: Hands-On Inquiry Projects for Schools, Science Fairs, or Just Plain Fun! (p. 1680)
VanCleave, Janice Pratt. A+ Projects in Physics: Winning Experiments for Science Fairs & Extra Credit. (p. 1)
—A+ Science Fair Projects. (p. 1)
—A+ Science Fair Workbook & Project Journal, Grades 7-12. (p. 1)
—Engineering for Every Kid: Easy Activities That Make Learning Science Fun. (p. 529)
—Janice VanCleave's Big Book of Play & Find Out Science Projects. (p. 908)
—Janice VanCleave's Energy for Every Kid: Easy Activities That Make Learning Science Fun. (p. 908)
—Janice VanCleave's Great Science Project Ideas from Real Kids. (p. 908)
—Janice VanCleave's Science Around the World: Activities on Biomes from Pole to Pole. (p. 908)
—Scientists Through the Ages. (p. 1529)
Vandalay, Martha. Pittsburgh a to Z. (p. 1364)
Vandawalker, Marianne. Conquering Bullies: 27 Game-Oriented Guidance Lessons for Grades 2-5 & 12 Story-Based Guidance Lessons for Grades K-12. (p. 358)
Vande Velde, Vivian. 8 Class Pets + 1 Squirrel ÷ 1 Dog = Chaos. Björkman, Steve, illus. (p. 1993)
—All Hallow's Eve: 13 Stories. (p. 44)
—Being Dead. (p. 161)
—Book of Mordred. (p. 211)
—Curses, Inc. & Other Stories. (p. 395)
—Deadly Pink. (p. 417)
—Dragon's Bait. (p. 479)
—Frogged. (p. 640)
—Ghost of a Hanged Man (p. 671)
—Heir Apparent. (p. 762)
—Hidden Magic. (p. 776)
—Magic Can Be Murder. (p. 1072)
—Never Trust a Dead Man. (p. 1243)
—Now You See It ... (p. 1269)
—Rumpelstiltskin Problem. (p. 1495)
—Smart Dog. (p. 1592)
—Stolen (p. 1652)
—Tales from the Brothers Grimm & the Sisters Weird. Weinman, Brad, illus. (p. 1701)
—There's a Dead Person Following My Sister Around. (p. 1730)
—Three Good Deeds. (p. 1742)
—User Unfriendly. (p. 1828)
—Well-Timed Enchantment. (p. 1874)
—Witch Dreams (p. 1941)
—Wizard at Work. (p. 1942)
Vandegrift, Tom. 24 New Moons. (p. 1996)
Vanden Berg, Myra, illus. see Kreder Sr., Edward G. & Kreder, Mary Ellen DeLuca.
Vanden Broeck, Fabricio, illus. see Markle, Sandra.
Vanden Heede, Sylvia. Wolf & Dog. Nagelkerke, Bill, tr. from DUT. (p. 1943)
Vandenberg, Maritz. Farnsworth House. Cook, Peter, photos by. (p. 575)
Vandenberg, Michael, photos by see Jacob, Ellen, et al.
VanDenberg, Saidat. Tadias & the Pitbully Tree. (p. 1695)
VandenBroeck, Fabricio, illus. see Durango, Julia.
VandenBroeck, Fabricio, illus. see Johnston, Tony.
VandenBroeck, Fabricio, illus. see Romeu, Emma.
VanDenhoven, Godelieve. Louis in Kindergarten. (p. 1058)
Vandepeer, Helen. Gifts. (p. 675)
Vander Giessen, Mark D. My Daddy Is Ten Feet Tall. (p. 1201)
—Princess & the Prince. (p. 1403)
Vander Hook, Sue. Adolf Hitler: German Dictator. (p. 13)
—Building the Panama Canal. (p. 239)
—Civil War Spy: Elizabeth Van Lew (p. 325)
—Colin Powell: General & Statesman. (p. 339)
—Communism. (p. 349)
—Democracy. (p. 425)
—Dust Bowl. (p. 490)
—Franklin D. Roosevelt: 32nd U. S. President. (p. 630)
—Frederick Douglass: Fugitive Slave & Abolitionist. (p. 633)
—Hip-Hop Fashion (p. 780)
—How to Analyze the Roles of Paul Newman. (p. 814)
—Johannes Gutenberg: Printing Press Innovator. (p. 920)
—Louis Pasteur: Groundbreaking Chemist & Biologist. (p. 1058)
—Mahatma Gandhi: Proponent of Peace. (p. 1076)
—Rupert Murdoch: News Corporation Magnate. (p. 1497)
—Southern Atlantic Coast Region. (p. 1617)
—Steven Spielberg: Groundbreaking Director. (p. 1649)
—Titanic. (p. 1757)
—Trail of Tears. (p. 1776)
—United States Enters World War I. (p. 1819)
—West Coast Region. (p. 1876)
—Winston Churchill: British Prime Minister & Statesman. (p. 1937)
Vander Hook, Sue, jt. auth. see Englar, Mary.
Vander Klipp, Michael. God Made Animals (p. 689)
—God Made Food (p. 689)
—God Made My Body (p. 690)
—God Made the World (p. 690)
Vander May, Jim. Borderline. (p. 214)
Vander Pluym, Andrea. Mission: Sisterhood. Waters, Susy Pilgrim, illus. (p. 1153)
Vander Pol, Matt, illus. see Crouch, Cheryl.
Vander Pol, Matt, jt. auth. see Crouch, Cheryl.
Vander Zee, Ruth. Always with You. Himler, Ronald, illus. (p. 51)
—Erika's Story. Innocenti, Roberto, illus. (p. 533)
—Mississippi Morning. Cooper, Floyd, illus. (p. 1154)
Vander Zee, Ruth & Sneider, Marian. Eli Remembers. Farnsworth, Bill, illus. (p. 512)
Vanderbeek, Don, illus. see Metaxas, Eric.
Vanderberg, Hope, ed. see Youth Communication.
Vanderbilt, Amy & Vanderbilt, Sabrina. Negative Nine: Book 1 of the Early Math Series. Vanderbilt, Amy, illus. (p. 1240)
Vanderbilt, David. Up & down on the Elevator: Add & Subtract Within 20. (p. 1824)
VanDerbilt, Deanna. Dog with a Thousand Names. (p. 462)
Vanderbilt, Sabrina, jt. auth. see Vanderbilt, Amy.
VanDerBrink, Yvette. My Mom Looks Like a Turtle. (p. 1214)
Vandercook, Margaret. Camp Fire Girls at Sunrise Hill. (p. 257)
—Camp Fire Girls at Sunrise Hill, the (Fi. (p. 257)
—Red Cross Girls with the Russian Army. (p. 1453)
Vandereyken, Leen. Loulou in Love. (p. 1059)
Vanderhoof, Gabrielle. Air Force. (p. 31)
—Basketball. (p. 143)
—Cheerleading. (p. 296)
—Hockey. (p. 786)
—Lacrosse. (p. 970)
—Track & Field. (p. 1775)
—Volleyball. (p. 1849)
Vanderhoof, Gabrielle, jt. auth. see Earl, C. F.
Vanderhoop, Jannette. Legend of Katama: The Creation Story of Dolphins, A Wampanoag Legend of Martha's Vineyard. (p. 988)
Vanderlaan, Karen. Special Friends. (p. 1623)
VanDerlinden, Jean A. Family Tree: The Secret Door. (p. 569)
Vanderlinden, Kathy, jt. auth. see Suzuki, David.
Vanderpool, Clare. Moon over Manifest. (p. 1172)
—Navigating Early. (p. 1238)
VanDerpool, Jessie. Little Rose Becomes a Hunter. (p. 1036)
VanDerTuuk-Perkins, Jennifer E. Life with Gabriel. VanDerTuuk-Perkins, Jennifer E. & Perkins, Rodney R., illus. (p. 1013)
Vandervelde, Beatrice. Home Ice (p. 792)
Vandervelde, Mark. Pizza for Everyone. (p. 1365)
VanDervleuten, Robin M. Keepers of the Fairy Moon. (p. 947)
Vanderwal, Andrew H. Battle for Duncragglin. (p. 145)
Vanderwerf, Rob. Craftsman. (p. 376)
VanDerwest, Steven M. Reuben's First Christmas Crow. (p. 1465)
VandeVoorde, Jay. Muskegon Lumberjacks-the Life of a Hockey Puck! (p. 1194)
Vandewalker, Pamela. King David & the National Treasure: An Easy Kids Musical about Worshiping God. (p. 958)
Vandewater, Rena, illus. see Sharp, Rhonda Winchell.
VanDeWeghe, Lindsay, illus. see Fitzsimmons, Kakie.
VanDeWeghe, Lindsay, illus. see Pastel, JoAnne & Fitzsimmons, Kakie.
Vandewiele, Agnes. Monster Machines! on the Farm. Lepretre, Jean-Marc, illus. (p. 1167)
vanDommelen, Deborah & Porter, Patricia. Read, Write, Edit: Grammar for College Writers. (p. 1444)
VanDusen, Sarah. Hail, Brave Friend. (p. 735)
VanDycke, Lilian Claudine. Mystery Fire. (p. 1224)
Vandygrift, Wendy. Lilly Lamoo & the Stray Gray Hair: A Book about Bad Hair, Bullies & Being Your Best. (p. 1017)
Vane, Mitch. Princess & the Pea. (p. 1402)
Vane, Mitch, illus. see Arena, Felice & Kettle, Phil.
Vane, Mitch, illus. see Arena, Felice, et al.
Vane, Mitch, illus. see Bursztynski, Sue.
Vane, Mitch, illus. see French, Jackie.
Vane, Mitch, illus. see Green, Jessica.
Vane, Mitch, illus. see Headley, Justina Chen.
Vane, Mitch, illus. see Katz, Danny.
Vane, Mitch, illus. see Lasky, Kathryn.
Vane, Mitch, illus. see Plourde, Lynn.
Vaneck Holub, Helen. Beloved Companion. (p. 163)
Vanek, Karen & Schmidt, Sharon Vanek. Santa Claus Meets the Tooth Fairy. (p. 1511)
Vanengen, Susan. 100th Day Surprise! (p. 1999)
Vanerio, Carrie. Jack & Al. (p. 902)
vanFrankenhuyze, Gijsbert, illus. see Ulmer, Michael.
Vang Nyman, Ingrid, illus. see Lindgren, Astrid.
Vang Nyman, Ingrid, jt. auth. see Lindgren, Astrid.
Vang, Richard. My Dad Is a Freemason. Vang, Richard, illus. (p. 1200)
Vangsgard, Amy, illus. see Allen, Margaret.
Vangsgard, Amy, illus. see Ellermeyer, Deborah & Rowell, Judy.
Vangsgard, Amy, illus. see Hults, Alaska, ed.
Vangsgard, Amy, illus. see Jennett, Pamela.
Vangsgard, Amy, illus. see Williams, Rozanne Lanczak.
VanHecke, Susan. Raggin', Jazzin', Rockin' A History of American Musical Instrument Makers. (p. 1433)
—Under the Freedom Tree. Ladd, London, illus. (p. 1813)
Vanhecke, Susan. Under the Freedom Tree. Ladd, London, illus. (p. 1813)
VanHecke, Susan, jt. auth. see Kohler, Dean Ellis.
Vanhee, Jason. Engines of the Broken World. (p. 529)
Vanholme, Virginie. Malevolence & Mandrake. (p. 1083)
—Vampire from the Marshes. Mauricet, illus. (p. 1832)
Vania, Tatio, illus. see Hall, Mark & West, Matthew.
Vanier, Jolie. Puwaii Adventures with Joliea & Friends. (p. 1420)
Vaniko, K. L. Why the Dog Chases the Cat & the Cat Chases the Mouse. (p. 1926)
Vanissery, Matthew. Awesome Homilies: The Power of His Word. (p. 121)
VanLeeuwen. Phonics Connection Grade 3. (p. 1352)
—Reading Connection Grade 4. (p. 1445)
—Summer Brains! Summer Travel Cards. (p. 1674)
VanLeeuwen & Rainbow Bridge Publishing Staff. Math Connection, Grade 6. (p. 1105)
—Phonics Connection(tm), Grade 1. (p. 1352)
Vanmechelen, Koen, jt. auth. see de Maeyer, Gregie.
Vann, Donna. Corin's Quest. (p. 367)
—King Arthur's Ransom. (p. 958)
—Which Way You Gonna Jump? (p. 1911)
—Wild West Adventures. (p. 1930)
Vann, Lula Renee. Children Won Their Souls. (p. 303)
Vann, Robert Winter Owl. Bull & the Peacock: And Other Animal Stories. (p. 240)
Vanneman, Alan. Sherlock Holmes & the Giant Rat of Sumatra. (p. 1565)
VanNuys, Elroy. Mysterious Cave. (p. 1223)
Vanoosting, James. Walking Mary. (p. 1854)
Vanorny-Barcus, LaVina. I Get a Baby Brother Instead. Mac, Sami, illus. (p. 838)
—Perfect in Mother Nature's Eyes. Mac, Sami, illus. (p. 1342)
—Perfecto en Los Ojos de la Madre Naturaleza: A Spanish/English Children's Book. Mac, Sami, illus. (p. 1342)
—Perfektni V Prirode Matky Oci: Perfect in Mother Nature's Eyes. Mac, Sami, illus. (p. 1342)
Vanover, Howard, jt. auth. see Sheets, Scott.
Vanover, Rita. Yellow Head the Cockatiel. (p. 1970)
VanRiper, Gary, jt. auth. see VanRiper, Justin.
VanRiper, Gary & VanRiper, Justin. Escape from Black Bear Mountain. (p. 534)
—Final Daze of Summer. (p. 586)
—Great Train Robbery. (p. 719)
—Islands in the Sky. (p. 892)
—Legend of the Lake Monster. (p. 989)
—Mystery of the Missing Moose. (p. 1225)
—Secret of the Skeleton Key. (p. 1543)
VanRiper, Justin, jt. auth. see VanRiper, Gary.
VanRiper, Justin & VanRiper, Gary. Fall of Fort Ticonderoga. (p. 566)
—Lost Lighthouse. Gary, Glenn, illus. (p. 1056)
—Pond Hockey Challenge. (p. 1382)
Vansant, Wayne. Battle of the Bulge: A Graphic History of Allied Victory in the Ardennes 1944-1945. Vansant, Wayne, illus. (p. 146)
—Grant vs. Lee: The Graphic History of the Civil War's Greatest Rivals During the Last Year of the War. (p. 710)
—Grant vs. Lee: The Graphic History of the Civil War's Greatest Rivals During the Last Year of the War. Vansant, Wayne, illus. (p. 710)
—Red Baron: The Graphic History of Richthofen's Flying Circus & the Air War in WWI. Vansant, Wayne, illus. (p. 1453)
Vansant, Wayne, jt. illus. see Golden, Mike.
Vanslette, Roxy, illus. see Devereux, Jan.
Vanston, Vincent J. Jeremiah, My Servant. (p. 913)
Vant, Jeanie. Witch's Cat. Vant, Tim, illus. (p. 1941)
Vant, Tim, illus. see Vant, Jeanie.
VanTassell - Luto, Ceneca. Other White House. (p. 1306)
VanTine, Karl. Sweet Dreams: A Lullaby. (p. 1689)
Vantrease, Brenda Rickman. Illuminator. (p. 857)
Vantrease, Norma. Ants in My Pants. Cox, Steve, illus. (p. 90)
VanTseva-Fornshell, Ekaterina. Morgan & His Dino Friends. (p. 1175)
VanTuyle, David, illus. see Golden Books Staff.
VanTuyle, David, illus. see Liberts, Jennifer.
VanTuyle, David, illus. see Webster, Christy.
VanVoorst, Jennifer. Can You Guess? (p. 259)
—Letter Zz: How Things Move. (p. 1002)
—Make It Move! (p. 1079)
—Making Shapes (p. 1082)
—Things That Are Cold (p. 1733)
—Who Builds? (p. 1914)
—Working (p. 1952)
VanVoorst, Jennifer, jt. auth. see VanVoorst, Jennifer Fretland.
VanVoorst, Jennifer & Capstone Press Staff. Letter Ii: Things That Are Cold (p. 1002)
VanVoorst, Jennifer Fretland. Ancient Maya (p. 70)
—Byzantine Empire (p. 249)
—Can You Guess? (p. 259)
—Make It Move! (p. 1079)
—Making Shapes. (p. 1082)
—Rise of the Thinking Machines: The Science of Robots (p. 1475)
—Who Builds? (p. 1914)
—Working. (p. 1952)
VanVoorst, Jennifer Fretland & Ring, Susan. Mamíferos. (p. 1084)
—Océano. (p. 1277)
VanVoorst, Jennifer Fretland & VanVoorst, Jennifer. Make It Move! (p. 1079)
VanVoorst, Jenny. What's Great about New Mexico? (p. 1897)
—What's Great about Tennessee? (p. 1897)
VanVoorst, Jenny Fretland. Fossils. (p. 624)
—Gems. (p. 660)
—Take a Closer Look at Your Ears. (p. 1696)
—Take a Closer Look at Your Teeth. (p. 1696)
—What's Great about New Mexico? (p. 1897)
—What's Great about Tennessee? (p. 1897)
Vanwye, Karissa. 1 2 3 Count with Me (p. 1990)
Vanzet, Gaston, illus. see Dale, Jay.
Vanzet, Gaston, illus. see Giulieri, Anne.
Vanzet, Gaston, jt. auth. see Wagner, Michael.
Vara, Ana Serna, et al. Nuestro Bebé. Susaeta Publishing, Inc., Staff, ed. (p. 1270)
Varacalli, Lauren, jt. auth. see Clapp, Sarah.
Varacalli, Lauren, jt. auth. see Core, Sarah.
Varacalli, Lauren, jt. auth. see Davis, Lauren.
Varacalli, Lauren, jt. auth. see Dutt, Arjun.
Varacalli, Lauren, jt. auth. see Eagan, Colin.
Varacalli, Lauren, jt. auth. see Gatker, Anna.
Varacalli, Lauren, jt. auth. see Klein, Nadav.
Varacalli, Lauren, jt. auth. see Leitikow, Greg.
Varacalli, Lauren, jt. auth. see Lewis, Brooke.
Varacalli, Lauren, jt. auth. see Mitchell, Kyra.
Varacalli, Lauren, jt. auth. see Murphy, Ryan.
Varacalli, Lauren, jt. auth. see Murray, Melanie.
Varacalli, Lauren, jt. auth. see Nolan, Lindsey.
Varacalli, Lauren, jt. auth. see S. Wong, Derrick.
Varacalli, Lauren, jt. auth. see Sheik, Mayra.
Varacalli, Lauren, jt. auth. see Striker, Oliver.
Varacalli, Lauren, jt. auth. see Walker, Caren.
Varacalli, Lauren, jt. auth. see Zang, Adam.
Varacchi, Barbara. Desiree & Daisy Mae & All That Love. (p. 430)
—Desiree's Adventures with Her Friends. (p. 430)
Varble, Rachel McBrayer. Beth & Seth. Reynolds, Doris, illus. (p. 171)
Vardamaskos, Angela. Everlasting Truth. Boumakis, Maria, illus. (p. 542)
Vardeman, Robert E. Stories from Desert Bob's Reptile Rahcn. (p. 1654)
Vareberg, Gladys, illus. see Burns, Helen Marie.
Varekamp, Marjolein. Wonderful Week. Varekamp, Marjolein, illus. (p. 1948)
Varela, Alejandra López, tr. see Bourgeois, Paulette.
Varela, Barry. Young Patriots' Guide to Colonial Williamsburg's Historic Area. (p. 1979)
Varela, Barry, et al. Arctic Tale: A Companion to the Major Motion Picture. (p. 96)
—Arctic Tale. (p. 96)
Varela, Carmen, tr. see Gummelt, Donna & Melchiorre, Dondino.
Varela, Cecilia, illus. see Gerhard, Ana.
Varela, John Owen, jt. auth. see Robinson, Jimmy D.
Varela, Juan D., illus. see Gummelt, Donna & Melchiorre, Dondino.
Varela, Juan D., illus. see Sinclair, Nicholas, et al.
Varela, Juan D., tr. see Gummelt, Donna & Melchiorre, Dondino.
Varela, Juan D., tr. see Sinclair, Nicholas, et al.
Varela, Sandra Lopez, tr. see Wells, Rosemary & Rosemary, Wells.
Varez, Dietrich. Legend of La'ieikawai. (p. 988)
Vargas, Constanza Orozco. Coco Chanel: Una Mujer Salida del Molde. (p. 337)
Vargas, Daraciela. HyperStudio: Para Maestros y Estudiantes: 20 Ejercicios de Practica. (p. 831)
Vargas, Daraciela, adapted by. Refranero Popular de Puerto Rico. (p. 1456)
Vargas, Daraciela, des. Internet en la Escuela y el Hogar. (p. 880)
Vargas, Emmanuel, jt. auth. see Augustine, Peg.
Vargas, Emmanuel, tr. see Augustine, Peg.
Vargas, Fredrico, jt. auth. see Vazquez, Gustavo.
Vargas, George. Prophecy of the Ages: Of War & Choices. (p. 1411)
Vargas Llosa, Mario. Historia de Mayta. (p. 782)
—Letters to a Young Novelist. Wimmer, Natasha, tr. from SPA. (p. 1002)
Vargas, Luis Alberto & Long-Solis, Janet. Food Culture in Mexico (p. 613)
Vargas, Robert, illus. see Grannis, Greg.
Vargas Tejada, Luis. Las Convulsiones. (p. 976)
Vargo, Joseph. Born of the Night: The Gothic Fantasy Artwork of Joseph Vargo. (p. 214)
Vargo, Joseph, jt. illus. see Filipak, Christine.
Vargo, Kurt, illus. see Gleeson, Brian.
Vargo, Sharon. Sugar & Shadow. (p. 1672)
Vargo, Sharon, illus. see Geiger, Lorraine Lynch.
Vargo, Tim. Unbound: A Tale of Temptation & Terror. (p. 1811)
Vargus, Nanci, ed. see Wax, Wendy & Weiss, Bobbi.
Vargus, Nanci R. Flying. (p. 609)
—On the Move (p. 1291)
—Volar! (p. 1848)
Vargus, Nanci R., ed. see Meachen Rau, Dana.
Vargus, Nanci Reginelli, jt. auth. see Alexander, Carol.
Vargus, Nanci Reginelli, jt. auth. see Bennett, Kelly.
Vargus, Nanci Reginelli, jt. auth. see Evento, Susan.
Vargus, Nanci Reginelli, jt. auth. see Sapre, Reshma.
Vargus, Nanci Reginelli, jt. auth. see Walker, Cynthia.
Varian, George, illus. see Stockton, Frank R.
Varian, George, illus. see Stockton, Frank Richard.
Varicak, Rebecca. Journey of a Toys for Tots Toy! (p. 928)
Varikyan, Arpine & Wallace, Dejuanna. From the Inside Out. (p. 644)
Varini, Felice. Bellinzona 2001. Bernado, Jordi et al, photos by. (p. 163)
Varin-Mignano, Regina, Lcsw. Autism: A Holistic View, Hard Cover Edition. (p. 117)
Varios, jt. auth. see varios.
varios & Varios. Antologia de la Generacion del 27. Ortega, Esperanza, ed. (p. 89)
—Antologia de la Poesia Barroca. Tusón, Vicente, ed. (p. 89)
—Por Caminos Azules... De Horna, Luis, illus. (p. 1385)
Varios Autores. Dedos en la Nuca. Balzola, Asun, tr. (p. 422)
Varios Autores, jt. auth. see Doherty, Berlie.
Various. 5-Minute Batman Stories. (p. 1992)
—Alvin & the Chipmunks Storybook Collection. (p. 51)
—Childhood of Famous Americans Ready-To-Read Value Pack: Abe Lincoln & the Muddy Pig; Albert Einstein; John Adams Speaks for Freedom; George Washington's First Victory; Ben Franklin & His First Kite; Thomas Jefferson & the Ghostriders. (p. 302)
—Donald Duck Adventures. (p. 465)
—Dora's 10 Best Adventures. (p. 471)
—Graphic Survival Stories (p. 711)
—HarperCollins Treasury of Picture Book Classics: A Child's First Collection. (p. 749)
—How to Draw Super-Powered Heroes. (p. 818)
—I Can Read (p. 836)
—Justice League Reading Collection. (p. 940)
—Let's Read with Dora! (p. 1000)
—Magic Begins (p. 1071)
—Mickey Mouse Adventures (p. 1136)
—OLIVIA Loves to Read: Olivia Trains Her Cat; Olivia & Her Ducklings; Olivia Takes a Trip; Olivia & the Snow Day; Olivia Plants a Garden; Olivia Goes Camping. (p. 1286)
—Olivia Ready-To-Read Value Pack #2: Olivia & the Kite Party; Olivia & the Rain Dance; Olivia Becomes a Vet; Olivia Builds a House; Olivia Measures up; Olivia Trains Her Cat. (p. 1287)
—Shrek TP Volume 1 Limited Edition Collection. (p. 1571)
—Story Time with Princess OLIVIA: Olivia the Princess; Olivia & the Puppy Wedding; Olivia Sells Cookies; Olivia & the Best Teacher Ever; Olivia Meets Olivia; Olivia & Grandma's Visit. (p. 1663)
—Teenage Mutant Ninja Turtles Animated Volume 3: the Showdown: The Showdown. (p. 1714)
—Turbo Prequel GN. (p. 1797)
—Uncle Scrooge #331. (p. 1812)
—Uncle Scrooge #333. (p. 1812)
—Uncle Scrooge #334. (p. 1812)

—Uncle Scrooge #335. (p. 1812)
—Uncle Scrooge #336. (p. 1812)
—Walt Disney's Christmas Parade #2. (p. 1855)
—Walt Disney's Comics & Stories #645. (p. 1855)
—When Cutie Calls. (p. 1901)
Various, illus. see Aladdin Books.
Various, illus. see Paiva, Johannah Gilman, ed.
Various Artists, illus. see Adams, John Joseph, ed.
Various Artists, illus. see Modern Painters Staff & Quarto Generic Staff.
Various Authors. Dora's Bedtime Adventures. (p. 471)
—Fairy Tale Comics: Classic Tales Told by Extraordinary Cartoonists. Duffy, Chris, ed. (p. 564)
—OLIVIA on the Go: Dinner with OLIVIA; OLIVIA & the Babies; OLIVIA & the School Carnival; OLIVIA Opens a Lemonade Stand; OLIVIA Cooks up a Surprise; OLIVIA Leads a Parade. (p. 1287)
Various Authors, Disney Publishing. Walt Disney's Classic Storybook. (p. 1855)
Various Experts, compiled by. Draw It! Learn to Draw from Real Life with This Exciting Step-By-Step Guide. (p. 480)
—Very Merry Christmas Activity Pad: Festive Puzzles, Amazing Mazes, Cool Doodles, Fantastic Fun! (p. 1838)
Various writers. Rise of the Turtles (p. 1475)
Vark, Anna. Adventures of Otis & Peck. (p. 21)
Varkarotas, Heather, illus. see Morris, Ann.
Varley, Carol, jt. auth. see Tatchell, Judy.
Varley, Susan. Badger's Parting Gifts. (p. 132)
Varley, Susan, illus. see Dunbar, Joyce.
Varley, Susan, illus. see Graham, Richard.
Varley, Susan, illus. see Jarman, Julia.
Varley, Susan, illus. see Waddell, Martin.
Varley, Susan, illus. see Willis, Jeanne.
Varley, Susan & Grindley, Sally. Why Is the Sky Blue? (p. 1925)
Varma, Eric. Orphaned Knight. (p. 1305)
Varma, Ishan, illus. see Stamper, Judith Bauer.
Varnadeau, Jeni. Chikchat(r) Workshop Manual. (p. 301)
Varnedoe, Catharine E., illus. see Lee, Betsy B.
Varner, Carla. Theodore Gets Salty. (p. 1729)
—Theodore Goes Fishing. (p. 1729)
—Worrisome Worm. (p. 1961)
Varner, Kristin, illus. see Tegen, Katherine.
Varner, Marcus, et al, eds. True Secrets of Key West Revealed! (p. 1792)
Varod, Gil, et al. Oedipus for Kids. (p. 1279)
Varon, Sara. Bake Sale. Varon, Sara, illus. (p. 133)
—Robot Dreams. Varon, Sara, illus. (p. 1480)
Varonka, Steve. Hard Coal Times: Pennsylvania Anthracite Stories (p. 748)
—Hard Coal Times: Early Coal Transportation. Vol. 3 (p. 748)
Varrato, Tony. Outrage. Doherty, Catherine, illus. (p. 1313)
Varricchio, Carmen. Haute Couture Doll Fashions, 1970s (p. 754)
Vars, Elle Márjá. Most Beautiful Dawn. Janda, Laura A., tr. (p. 1177)
Varsell, Linda. Ends of Rainbow. Curtis, E., illus. (p. 527)
—Humane Touch. Curtis, E., illus. (p. 826)
—Journey for Rainbows. Curtis, E., illus. (p. 928)
—Rainbow Breakers. Curtis, E., illus. (p. 1435)
—Rainbow Circle. Curtis, E., illus. (p. 1435)
—Rainbow Dreamers. Curtis, E., illus. (p. 1435)
—Rainbow Makers. Curtis, E., illus. (p. 1435)
—Rainbow Planet. Curtis, E., illus. (p. 1435)
—Rainbow Remnants. Curtis, E., illus. (p. 1435)
—Rainbow Rescue. Curtis, E., illus. (p. 1435)
—With a Human Touch. Curtis, E., illus. (p. 1942)
Vartanian, Ivan, ed. see Vartanian, Nara, et al.
Vartanian, Nara, et al. Drop Dead Cute. Vartanian, Ivan, ed. (p. 485)
Varvaris, Cathy. Jesus, Can I Talk with You? A Prayer Journal for Teens. (p. 915)
Varvaris, Cathy, jt. auth. see Fryar, Jane L.
Varveris, Ariana Eleni. Adventures of Magic Island: Book I-Welcome to Magic Island. (p. 20)
Vasan, Gandee, jt. auth. see Andrews McMeel Publishing Staff.
Vasan, Mildred, ed. see Hastedt, Glenn.
Vasan, Mildred, ed. see Stewart, Chuck.
Vasari, Giorgio. Life of Michelangelo. Sadowski, Frank, ed. (p. 1012)
Vasco, Irene. Conjuros y Sortilegios. Isaza, Juanita, illus. (p. 357)
—Dedo de Estefanía y Otros Cuentos. (p. 422)
—Don Salomon y la Peluquera. (p. 465)
—Paso A Paso. Tamayo, Natalia, illus. (p. 1326)
Vasconcellos, Daniel, illus. see Christopher, Matt.
Vasconcellos, Daniel, illus. see Cohn, Arlen.
Vasconcellos, Daniel, illus. see Post, Jim.
vasey, john. Amazing Adventure of Thomas & Erin with Grandad - the Zoo. (p. 52)
—Amazing Adventures of Thomas & Erin with Grandad - Market Day. (p. 52)
Vasil, Bob. Adventures of Benny, Lenny, & Al: Three Boy Chickens. (p. 16)
Vasilevsky, Marina, illus. see Dube, Tory.
Vasiliou, Fotini. Lies Are Trouble in a Bubble. (p. 1007)
Vasiliu, Michelle & Orsini, Cheryl. Fire Ready. (p. 590)
Vasiliu, Mircea. Day at the Beach. (p. 412)
Vasilkova, Elena, ed. see AZ Books Staff.
Vasillu, Michelle. Future of Forests. (p. 651)
Vasilovich, Guy. 13 Nights of Halloween. Vasilovich, Guy, illus. (p. 1995)
Vasquez, Cherrye S. Clique, Clique, Stop. (p. 333)
—No Tildes on Tuesday. (p. 1260)
Vasquez, Elisa Irene. My Little Piggy: A Bilingual English-Spanish Children's Book. (p. 1212)
Vasquez, Gloria, jt. auth. see Mills, Nathan.
Vasquez, Hugh, et al. Making Allies, Making Friends: A Curriculum for Making the Peace in Middle School. (p. 1080)
Vasquez, Ivan, illus. see Figueroa, Acton.
Vasquez, John A. War Puzzle Revisited. (p. 1858)
Vasquez, Juan Jose, illus. see Warren, Sandra J.
Vásquez, Juan José, illus. see Warren, Sandra Jane.
Vasquez, Lidia. Damaged Friends: Sad but true stories about damaged Books. (p. 401)
Vasquez, Natalia. Pied Piper of Hamelin. (p. 1356)
Vasquez, Natalia, illus. see Fox, Tamar.
Vasquez, Natalia, illus. see Troupe, Thomas Kingsley.
Vasquez, Vivian Maria. Literacy As Social Practice: Primary Voices K-6. (p. 1022)
Vass, Selynda. Camilla Chinchilla & the Heroes of the Tornado. (p. 256)
Vassallo, Rebecca. Listen to Luther. (p. 1022)
Vassallo, Theresa. Day at the Zoo Sing-along. (p. 412)
Vassallo, Virginia. Unsung Patriot: How the Stars & Stripes Began: Guy T. Visknisski. (p. 1823)
Vassar, Michael. Learning the Alphabet Can Be Easy A-Z. (p. 986)
Vastola, P. Huge Animals: Learning the Long U Sound. (p. 824)
—Rain: Learning the Al Sound. (p. 1434)
—What I Think: Learning the TH Sound. (p. 1887)
Vasudevan, Vidya, illus. see Free, Zaccai.
Vasudevan, Vidya, illus. see Lizzy Anne's Adventures Staff & Zarrella, Sharon.
Vasudevan, Vidya, illus. see Ringgold, Robyn.
Vaswani, Navina. Where's Moni. (p. 1910)
—Wonderful Christmas. (p. 1948)
Vaswani, Neela, jt. auth. see House, Silas.
Vasylenko, Veronica. Jingle Bells. (p. 918)
Vasylenko, Veronica, illus. see Fortner, Tama.
Vasylenko, Veronica, illus. see Platt, Cynthia.
Vasylenko, Veronica, illus. see Stahl, Stephanie.
Vasylenko, Veronica, illus. see Tiger Tales Staff, ed.
Vatcher-Martin M.A., Cheryl. Haiku for You: With Some One Room School House History. (p. 735)
Vatcher-Martin M.A., Cheryl A. Cornstalks Are Whispering. (p. 367)
Vattel, Emmeich de, et al. Law of Nations. (p. 981)
Vaugelade, Anais. Lorenzo Esta Solo. (p. 1053)
—Sopa de Piedra. (p. 1613)
Vaugelade, Anaïs. War. Vaugelade, Anaïs, illus. (p. 1857)
Vaughan, Brenna, illus. see Hayes, Kate.
Vaughan, Brian K. Fact V. Fiction Feister, Tom, illus. (p. 561)
—Girl on Girl Guerra, Pia et al, illus. (p. 678)
—Kimono Dragons. Guerra, Pia & Marzan, Jose, Jr., illus. (p. 957)
—Last Man - Ring of Truth Guerra, Pia & Marzan, Jose, illus. (p. 978)
—One Small Step. Guerra, Pia & Marzan, Jose, Jr., illus. (p. 1297)
—Runaways: The Good Die Young. Vol. 3 Alphona, Adrian, illus. (p. 1497)
Vaughan, Brian K. & Kubert, Andy. Cry Wolf (p. 387)
Vaughan, Brian K. & Marzon, Jose. Last Man: Safeword Vol. 4 Guerra, Pia, illus. (p. 978)
Vaughan, Brian K. & Sudzuka, Goran. Y - The Last Man: Paper Dolls. Marzan, Jose, Jr. & Guerra, Pia, illus. (p. 1968)
Vaughan, Brian K., et al. Y: The Last Man: Motherland. (p. 1968)
Vaughan, Carolyn. First Ladies. Fandex Family Field Guides Staff, ed. (p. 595)
—Invitation to Ballet: A Celebration of Dance & Degas. Isadora, Rachel, illus. (p. 886)
—New York City. (p. 1248)
Vaughan, Christina. Artie Goes to Hollywood. (p. 104)
Vaughan, Dai. Germs. (p. 667)
Vaughan, Garth. Tommy's New Block Skates Smith, David Preston, illus. (p. 1765)
Vaughan, Grace. Annie & the Magic Book. (p. 86)
Vaughan, Jack, illus. see Parks, Amy.
Vaughan, Jack, jt. illus. see Golliher, Bill.
Vaughan, Jenny. Causes & Campaigns. (p. 282)
—Genetics. (p. 661)
—Making New Life. (p. 1082)
—Minibeasts. (p. 1146)
—Politics. (p. 1380)
—Selena Gomez - Teen Stars. (p. 1549)
—Who Discovered DNA? (p. 1915)
Vaughan, Jenny, jt. auth. see Anderson, Judith.
Vaughan, Jenny & Beauchamp, Penny. Christmas Foods (p. 314)
—Festival Foods (p. 582)
Vaughan, Jeremy, illus. see Coy, Steven.
Vaughan, Kathryn Mademann. Little One... Good Night: A Lullaby from Vermont. Edson, Anharad, illus. (p. 1032)
—What's under the Sea? (p. 1900)
Vaughan, M. M. Ability. Bruno, Iacopo, illus. (p. 5)
—Mindscape. Bruno, Iacopo, illus. (p. 1145)
—Six. (p. 1582)
Vaughan, Marcia. Irena's Jars of Secrets Mazellan, Ron, illus. (p. 887)
—Story Teller Quilts: Level S (p. 1663)
—Treasure of Ghostwood Gully: A Southwest Mystery. Terry, Will, illus. (p. 1782)
Vaughan, Marcia, jt. auth. see Vaughan, Richard Lee.
Vaughan, Mark, jt. auth. see Connely, Chris L.
Vaughan, Mark, jt. auth. see Thomas, Gary.
Vaughan, Rhonda Green. Three Little Pigs & the Rock. (p. 1743)
Vaughan, Richard. Levantemos el Cielo (p. 1003)
—Universo (p. 1821)
Vaughan, Richard Lee. Eagle Boy: A Pacific Northwest Native Tale. Christiansen, Lee, illus. (p. 492)
Vaughan, Richard Lee & Vaughan, Marcia. Three Bears of the Pacific Northwest. Trammell, Jeremiah, illus. (p. 1741)
Vaughan, Rob, jt. auth. see Mark, Rebecca.
Vaughan, Rober, ed. see Vaughan, Robert.
Vaughan, Robert. South Mark, Rebecca & Vaughan, Rober, eds. (p. 1616)
Vaughan, Susan. Let's Eat Lunch: Learning about Picture Graphs. (p. 996)
—Making Muffins: Learning the Fractions 1/2, 1/3 & 1/4. (p. 1081)
Vaughan, William, et al. Friedrich. (p. 637)
Vaughn, Brian K. Runaways: Pride & Joy. Alphona, Adrian, illus. (p. 1497)
Vaughn, Brian K., text. Escape to New York. (p. 535)
Vaughn, C. L. I See Aliens. (p. 845)
Vaughn, Carrie. Dreams of the Golden Age. (p. 484)
—Kitty Goes to Washington. (p. 963)
—Steel. (p. 1646)
—Voices of Dragons. (p. 1848)
Vaughn, Deborah. Sneaky Secret Steff & Her Problem Solving Adventure. (p. 1597)
Vaughn, Inés. Chiles. (p. 305)
—Chocolate. (p. 309)
—Potatoes: Papas. (p. 1388)
—Potatoes/Papas. (p. 1388)
—Squash/Calabazas. (p. 1636)
—Tomatoes/Tomates. (p. 1764)
Vaughn, Inés & Sanz, Ma Pilar. Squash: Calabazas. (p. 1636)
—Tomatoes: Tomates. (p. 1764)
Vaughn, J. D. Paula & the Parrot. Brislane, Niche, illus. (p. 1330)
—Second Guard. (p. 1539)
Vaughn, James, jt. auth. see Kent, V. E.
Vaughn, Jen, illus. see Latham, Donna.
Vaughn, Jenn, illus. see Mooney, Carla.
Vaughn, Jerry T. Spiritually Speaking to Find our Way Home. (p. 1629)
Vaughn, Jim. Jumbo Math Yearbook: Grade 5. (p. 933)
—Jumbo Math Yearbook: Grade 8. (p. 933)
—Jumbo Vocabulary Development Yearbook: Grade 7. (p. 933)
—Jumbo Vocabulary Development Yearbook: Grade 10. (p. 933)
Vaughn, Lauren Roedy. OCD, the Dude, & Me. (p. 1275)
Vaughn Loeffler. Love Makes the Green Grass Grow. (p. 1060)
Vaughn, Marcia. I Howl, I Growl: Southwest Animal Antics. Powell, Polly, illus. (p. 839)
Vaughn, Richard. Rowena & the Magic Hawk, the First Adventure. (p. 1492)
Vaughn, Royce. Seymour Bluffs & Robert Wadlow, the Tallest Man in the World: A Story about Diversity & Tolerance. (p. 1556)
—Seymour Bluffs & the Legend of the Piasa Bird. (p. 1556)
Vaughn, Sydney. At the Track Meet: Understand Place Value. (p. 111)
Vaughn, Trudy D. Bugs Beware My Mom Doesn't Care! (p. 237)
Vaughn, Wally G. & Davis, Mattie Campbell, eds. Selma Campaign, 1963-1965: The Decisive Battle of the Civil Rights Movement. (p. 1550)
Vaughn, Wendy. For Children of the World with Love. (p. 615)
Vaughn Zimmer, Tracie, jt. auth. see Zimmer, Tracie Vaughn.
Vaughns, Byron, illus. see Tanguay, Dave.
Vaught, S. R. & Redmond, J. B. Prince among Killers (p. 1401)
Vaught, Susan. Fat Tuesday. Hamilton, Dianne, ed. (p. 577)
—Footer Davis Probably Is Crazy. Reinhardt, Jennifer Black, illus. (p. 615)
—Freaks Like Us. (p. 631)
—Going Underground. (p. 693)
—Insanity. (p. 875)
—Trigger. (p. 1786)
Vaupel, Robin. My Contract with Henry. (p. 1200)
—Rules of the Universe. (p. 1495)
Vaux, F. B. Domestic Pleasures or the Happy Fire Side Illustrated by Interesting Conversations. (p. 465)
Vaux, Patricia, illus. see Andrews McMeel Publishing Staff & Wang, Dorthea Deprisco.
Vaux, Patricia, illus. see Wang, Dorthea Deprisco.
Vavak, S. Dean, illus. see Arroyo, Madeline.
Vaval, Fisepe. Blueprint. Bubsy, Nancy, ed. (p. 204)
Vawter, Vince. Paperboy. (p. 1323)
Vawter, Will, illus. see Riley, James Whitcomb.
Vayenas, Christina. Snozo, the Polar Bear. (p. 1601)
Vayssiere, Frederique, illus. see Hooper, Mary.
Vaz de Carvalho, Joao, illus. see Carvalho, Adelia.
Vaz, Mark Cotta. Art of Finding Nemo. (p. 102)
—Art of the Incredibles. (p. 102)
—Twilight Saga Breaking Dawn: The Official Illustrated Movie Companion. Pt. 1 (p. 1801)
Vaz, Mark Cotta, ed. see Macauley, Michael.
Vaz, Megan X. Melody of Short Stories. (p. 1125)
Vazov, George D. Other Side of the Mushroom. (p. 1306)
Vazquez, Ana Maria & Dean, Jennings. Blessed Pier Giorgio Frassati: Journey to the Summit. Stewart, Don, illus. (p. 199)
Vazquez, Gustavo & Vargas, Fredrico. Chicharito Hernndez. (p. 299)
Vazquez, Itos, compiled by. Cocina Del Caribe y de Centro America. (p. 337)
—Helados. (p. 762)
—Huevos. (p. 824)
—Internacional. (p. 880)
—Microondas 1. (p. 1136)
—Microondas 2. (p. 1136)
—Pizzas, Sandwiches. (p. 1365)
—Postres. (p. 1388)
—Regalos. (p. 1457)
—Reposteria. (p. 1461)
—Salsas. (p. 1505)
—Sobrantes. (p. 1603)
—Vegetariana. (p. 1834)
Vazquez, Tiziana & Llano, Gabriella. In My World: Down Syndrome. (p. 864)
Vázquez-Figueroa, Alberto. Anaconda. (p. 66)
—Montenegro. (p. 1170)
Vazquez-Lozano, Gustavo. Ivan Cordoba. (p. 900)
Vazquez-Lozano, Gustavo & Benard, Federico Vargas. Luis Suarez. (p. 1064)
Vázquez-Vigo, Carmen, jt. auth. see Vazquez-Vigo, Carmen.
Vazquez-Vigo, Carmen & Vázquez-Vigo, Carmen. Caramelos de Menta. (p. 265)
—Fuerza de la Gacela. (p. 646)
—Gafitas. (p. 652)
Veague, Heather Barnett. Schizophrenia. (p. 1521)
Veague, Heather Barnett & Collins, Christine. Cutting & Self-Harm. (p. 396)
Veague, Heather Barnett, et al. Autism. (p. 117)
Veasey, Michele, illus. see Bohlken, Robert L.
Veasey, Nick. X-Treme X-Ray: See the World Inside Out! (p. 1967)
Vecchini, Silvia. 10 Commandments Explained. Vincenti, Antonio, illus. (p. 1993)
Vecchini, Silvia & Daughters of St. Paul Staff. Creed Explained. Vincenti, Antonio, illus. (p. 380)
Vecchio, Luciano, illus. see Beatty, Scott, et al.
Vecchio, Luciano, illus. see Beatty, Scott.
Vecchio, Luciano, illus. see Black, Jake.
Vecchio, Luciano, illus. see Bright, J. E.
Vecchio, Luciano, illus. see Bright, J. E. & Sutton, Laurie S.
Vecchio, Luciano, illus. see Cohen, Ivan & Eltaeb, Gabe.
Vecchio, Luciano, illus. see Cohen, Ivan, et al.
Vecchio, Luciano, illus. see Cohen, Ivan.
Vecchio, Luciano, illus. see Hult, Gene & Bright, J. E.
Vecchio, Luciano, illus. see Manning, Matthew K.
Vecchio, Luciano, illus. see Manning, Matthew K. & Sazaklis, John.
Vecchio, Luciano, illus. see Mason, Jane B.
Vecchio, Luciano, illus. see Sazaklis, John.
Vecchio, Luciano, illus. see Simonson, Louise & Sutton, Laurie S.
Vecchio, Luciano, illus. see Simonson, Louise.
Vecchio, Luciano, illus. see Sonneborn, Scott.
Vecchio, Luciano, illus. see Stone Arch Books Staff & Sutton, Laurie S.
Vecchio, Luciano, illus. see Stone Arch Books Staff, et al.
Vecchio, Luciano, illus. see Sutton, Laurie S.
Vecchio, Luciano, illus. see Tulien, Sean.
Vecchione, Glen. Experimentos Sencillos con la Luz y el Sonido. Elena, Horacio, tr. (p. 549)
—Kids' Games. (p. 953)
—Science Facts. Harris, Joel & Harris, Sharon, illus. (p. 1526)
Veceric, Danica. Slovenia. (p. 1591)
Veciana-Suarez, Ana. Vuelo a la Libertad. (p. 1851)
Vedder, Erik, illus. see Beechen, Adam & Age, Heroic.
Veenendall, Jennifer. Arnie & His School Tools: Simple Sensory Solutions That Build Success. (p. 100)
—Why Does Izzy Cover Her Ears? Dealing with Sensory Overload. (p. 1924)
Veerkamp, Misty J. Oh What I Could Do with a Neck Like a Giraffe. (p. 1281)
Veerman, David. Ready for Life. (p. 1447)
Vega, Alison, illus. see Foster, Marilyn.
Vega, Danielle. Merciless. (p. 1127)
—Survive the Night. (p. 1687)
Vega, Denise. Click Here: (To Find Out How I Survived Seventh Grade) (p. 332)
—Rock On: A Story of Guitars, Gigs, Girls, & a Brother (Not Necessarily in That Order) (p. 1482)
Vega, Diego. Iron Brand. (p. 888)
Vega, Elda de la, see de la Vega, Elda, tr.
Vega, Elda de la, tr. see Kondrchek, Jamie & Rasemas, Joe.
Vega, Elda de la, tr. see Kondrchek, Jamie.
Vega, Elda de la, tr. see Leavitt, Amie Jane.
Vega, Elda de la, tr. see Sherman, Patrice.
Vega, Garcilaso de la. Antologia Poetica de los Siglos XV y XVI. Tusón, Vicente, ed. (p. 89)
Vega, Lope de. Caballero de Olmedo. (p. 250)
—Fuente Ovejuna. (p. 646)
—Mejor Alcalde, el Rey Fuenteovejuna. (p. 1124)
—Mejor Alcalde, el Rey/Fuente Ovejuna. (p. 1124)
Vega, Lope de, et al. Fuenteovejuna. (p. 646)
Vega, Victoria. It's Nice to be Nice. (p. 897)
Vegetarians of Washington Staff. Vegetarian Pacific Northwest: A Guide to Restaurants & Shopping. (p. 1834)
Veggie Tales Cast. Veggietales Lots of Fun Color. (p. 1834)
Veggie Tales, Veggie. Little Lessons from God. (p. 1030)
—VeggieTales: Bob Is a Buddy! A Story about Friends. (p. 1834)
VeggieTales, contrib. by. Pirates Who Don't Do Anything. (p. 1364)
Vehlmann, Fabien. Green Manor: Assassins & Gentleman. Pt. 1 Bodart, Denis, illus. (p. 722)
—Green Manor: The Inconvenience of Being Dead. Bodart, Denis, illus. (p. 722)
Veigas, Jennifer, ed. Critical Perspectives on Natural Disasters. (p. 383)
Veglie, William J. Sea Bag of Memories: Images, Poems, Thoughts, & Crafts of the small Ship Sailors of World War II. (p. 1534)
Veil, Karney. Sun & Moon Play Hide & Seek: A Children's Story. (p. 1676)
Veillette, Sally M. Coming to Your Senses: Soaring with Your Soul. (p. 348)
Veillon, A. M. Shelby & the Shifting Rings: Defender of Time Series. Bk. 1 (p. 1564)
—Shelby & the Shifting Rings: Book One—Defender of Time Series (p. 1564)
Veinje, Marie. Manuscript Writing. Boyer, Robin, illus. (p. 1089)
Veinshtein, Debbie, illus. see Daleski, Gil.
Veit, Kimberly Michelle. To Be Thirteen. (p. 1758)
Veitch, Catherine. Amphibian Babies (p. 65)
—Animal Babies (p. 76)
—Bailar (p. 132)
—Big Machines (p. 182)
—Big Machines Build! (p. 182)
—Big Machines Drive! (p. 182)
—Big Machines Float! (p. 182)
—Big Machines Fly! (p. 182)
—Big Machines Rescue! (p. 182)
—Big Machines Ride Rails! (p. 182)
—Bird Babies (p. 190)
—Bug Babies (p. 236)
—Changing Designs. (p. 290)
—Dancing (p. 402)
—Farms Around the World (p. 575)
—Fish Babies (p. 598)
—Gimnasia (p. 676)

V

—Gymnastics (p. 734)
—Learning about Animals (p. 984)
—Learning about Insects (p. 984)
—Learning about Plants (p. 984)
—Learning about Trees (p. 985)
—Mammal Babies (p. 1084)
—Natural World. (p. 1236)
—Reptile Babies. (p. 1461)
—Sea Monsters (p. 1535)
Veitch, Sarah. Serving Time. (p. 1553)
VeJauan, Sherea. Realistically Speaking: Speaking What's Real... Keeping What's Holy. (p. 1449)
Vekaria, Alka, jt. auth. see Dicker, Katie.
Vela, Eugenio H. Twinkle, Twinkle Little Harold. (p. 1802)
Velarde, Chase, illus. see Etherly, L. D.
Velarde, Chase, illus. see Frantz, Kevin.
Velasco, Agustin. Agustin's Linux Manual (p. 30)
Velasco, Francisco Ruiz, illus. see Kennedy, Mike.
Velasco, George. Coconut Named Jose. (p. 337)
Velasquez, Crystal. Hunters of Chaos. (p. 828)
Velasquez, Elisa. Peaches in Heaven. (p. 1332)
Velasquez, Eric. Grandma's Gift. (p. 708)
—Grandma's Gift. Velasquez, Eric, illus. (p. 708)
—Grandma's Records. (p. 709)
—Grandma's Records. Velasquez, Eric, illus. (p. 709)
Velasquez, Eric, illus. see Bolden, Tonya.
Velasquez, Eric, illus. see Boswell, Addie & Addie, Boswell.
Velasquez, Eric, illus. see Brigham, Marilyn.
Velasquez, Eric, illus. see Fradin, Dennis Brindell & Fradin, Judith Bloom.
Velasquez, Eric, illus. see Gayle, Sharon Shavers.
Velasquez, Eric, illus. see Grimes, Nikki.
Velasquez, Eric, illus. see Hudson, Cheryl Willis.
Velasquez, Eric, illus. see Ieronimo, Christine.
Velasquez, Eric, illus. see Johnson, Angela.
Velasquez, Eric, illus. see Krull, Kathleen.
Velasquez, Eric, illus. see Malaspina, Ann.
Velasquez, Eric, illus. see McKissack, Patricia C.
Velasquez, Eric, illus. see Meyer, Susan Lynn.
Velasquez, Eric, illus. see Tuck, Pamela M.
Velasquez, Eric, illus. see Walvoord, Linda & Walvoord.
Velasquez, Eric, illus. see Watkins, Angela Farris.
Velasquez, Eric, illus. see Weatherford, Carole Boston.
Velásquez, Gloria. Rudy's Memory Walk. (p. 1494)
Velasquez, Gloria. Teen Angel. (p. 1713)
—Tyrone's Betrayal. (p. 1805)
Velasquez, Leonor Bravo. ¡Quiero Chocolate! Ruiz, Jorge, illus. (p. 1428)
Velasquez, Maria. Pet Parade. Mooney, Alyssa, illus. (p. 1345)
Velasquez, Nicole, illus. see Winner, Ramona Moreno.
Velástegui, Cecilia. Olinguito Speaks Up. (p. 1285)
Velazquez, Anna. Stewart's Airplane Adventure. (p. 1649)
Velazquez, Catherine. Dirty Birdie. (p. 446)
Velázquez de León, Mauricio. 20 Soccer Legends. (p. 1995)
—20 Soccer Superstars. (p. 1995)
—Top Soccer Tournaments Around the World. (p. 1769)
Velazquez De Leon, Mauricio, tr. see Adams, Lisa K.
Velazquez De Leon, Mauricio, tr. see Chouette Publishing Staff.
Velazquez De Leon, Mauricio, tr. see Croft, Priscilla.
Velazquez De Leon, Mauricio, tr. see Houghton, Gillian.
Velazquez De Leon, Mauricio, tr. see Johnston, Marianne.
Velazquez, Diego. Velazquez: 16 Art Stickers. (p. 1835)
Velazquez, Jose Luis Reye, illus. see Cohen, Milly.
Velazquez, Jose Luis Reyes, illus. see Cohen, Milly.
Velazquez, Loreta Janeta, jt. auth. see Velazquez, Loreta Janeta.
Velazquez, Loreta Janeta & Velazquez, Loreta Janeta. Woman in Battle, a Narrative of the Exploits, Adventures, & Travels of Madame Loreta Janeta Velazquez. (p. 1945)
Veld, Valorie. I Am a Montessori Kid. (p. 832)
Velde, Henry. Night I Became... (p. 1253)
Velde, Marie. Laundry Day. (p. 980)
Veldhoven, Marijke, illus. see Eason, Sarah.
Veldkamp, Debby. Quake! Six Point Five: The Cat Survived. Van Den Berg, Helen, illus. (p. 1422)
Veldkamp, Tjibbe. Tom the Tree. Hopman, Philip, illus. (p. 1764)
Veldmeyer, Michele E. Francine's Freckles. (p. 627)
Veleno, Cynthia M. All God's Creatures Great & Very Small. (p. 44)
Velert, Miriam, illus. see Garrido, Pedro Gelabert.
Velez, Edia L. Jessica's Summer Vacation - Las Vacaciones de Verano de Jéssic. (p. 914)
Vélez, Elizabeth Ash, jt. auth. see Esselman, Mary D.
Vélez, Gabriel J., illus. see alurista, et al.
Velez, Ivan, Jr. Tales of the Closet: The Collected Series (p. 1702)
Velez, Jill Ondercin, illus. see Goss, Leon.
Vélez, Manuel J., ed. see alurista, et al.
Velez, Stacey, ed. see Plaut, Thomas F.
Velez, Walter. Little Red Riding Hood: A Tale about Staying Safe. (p. 1035)
Velez, Walter, illus. see Albee, Sarah.
Velez, Walter, illus. see Dingles, Molly.
Velhuijs, Max. Kind-Hearted Monster. (p. 957)
Velica, Teodora, illus. see Myers, Janice Limb.
Velichko, Vera. best on the east, volume 4, the shadow of the USSR: Volume 4, the shadow of the USSR Velichko, Vera, ed. (p. 171)
Velie, Alan, jt. auth. see McClinton-Temple, Jennifer.
Velikan, Phil, illus. see Doyle, Mary K.
Velikanje, Kathryn. B Is for Boys & Bees. Wilson, Lynda Farrington, illus. (p. 123)
—Bike of Bees. Hovhannisyan, Nune, illus. (p. 185)
—C Is for Crazy Cats. Wilson, Lynda Farrington, illus. (p. 250)
—D Is for Dragon. Wilson, Lynda Farrington, illus. (p. 397)
—E Is for Elephant. Wilson, Lynda Farrington, illus. (p. 492)
—F Is for Face. Wilson, Lynda Farrington, illus. (p. 559)
—G Is for Girly Girls. Wilson, Lynda Farrington, illus. (p. 651)
—H Is for Horse. Wilson, Lynda Farrington, illus. (p. 734)
—I Is for Ice Cream. Wilson, Lynda Farrington, illus. (p. 839)
—Is for Alligator. Wilson, Lynda Farrington, illus. (p. 889)
—Zebras Paint Themselves Rainbow. Hovhannisyan, Nune, illus. (p. 1985)
Velitchenko, Olga, illus. see Holman, Nedra.
Vella, Sheldon, jt. auth. see Way, Daniel.
Vella, Sylvia. It's Okay to Tell. (p. 898)
Velle, Tori. Jake the Snake. (p. 906)
Velmans, Hester. Isabel of the Whales. (p. 890)
Velthaus, Sally. Geckos Rasch, Patricia, illus. (p. 659)
Velthuijs, Max. Frog & Hare. (p. 640)
—Frog & the Stranger. (p. 640)
—Frog Is Frog. (p. 640)
VeLure Roholt, Christine. Foods of Brazil. (p. 614)
—Foods of China. (p. 614)
—Foods of France. (p. 614)
—Foods of India. (p. 614)
—Foods of Italy. (p. 614)
—Foods of Japan. (p. 614)
—Foods of Mexico. (p. 614)
—Foods of Thailand. (p. 614)
Velvet. Black Door. (p. 196)
Velvet, Black. Adventures of Sam in Space: Planet of the Sweets. (p. 22)
Velvin, Ellen. Rataplan. (p. 1440)
—Rataplan, a Rogue Elephant & Other Stories. (p. 1440)
Venable, Alan. Man in the Iron Mask. (p. 1085)
—Take Me with You When You Go. Marshall, Laurie, illus. (p. 1696)
Venable, Alan, jt. auth. see Stevenson, Robert Louis.
Venable, Colleen A. F. And Then There Were Gnomes. Yue, Stephanie, illus. (p. 71)
—Ferret's a Foot Yue, Stephanie, illus. (p. 582)
—Fish You Were Here Yue, Stephanie, illus. (p. 598)
—Going, Going, Dragon! (p. 692)
—Going, Going, Dragon! Yue, Stephanie, illus. (p. 692)
—Hamster & Cheese. Yue, Stephanie, illus. (p. 739)
—Raining Cats & Detectives. Yue, Stephanie, illus. (p. 1436)
Venable, James, illus. see Chandler, Ann.
Venable Jr, Al B. Captain Tom, the Sea Adventurer. (p. 264)
Venables, Julie. Day I Carried the King. (p. 413)
Venables, Julie, illus. see Pearson, Georgene.
Vendera, Jaime & McGee, Anne Loader. Sing Out Loud Book I: Discovering Your Voice. Bastien, Valerie & Bingham, Jerry, illus. (p. 1579)
—Sing Out Loud Book II: Developing Your Voice. Bastien, Valerie, illus. (p. 1579)
—Sing Out Loud Book III: Owning Your Voice. Bastien, Valerie, illus. (p. 1579)
—Sing Out Loud Book IV: Owning the Stage. Bingham, Jerry, illus. (p. 1579)
Vendittelli, Marie & Griotto, Sophie. Fashion Book. (p. 575)
Venditti, Robert. Attack of the Alien Horde. Higgins, Dusty, illus. (p. 113)
Venditti, Robert, jt. auth. see Cornell, Paul.
Venditti, Robert, jt. auth. see Riordan, Rick.
Venditti, Robert & Riordan, Rick. Sea of Monsters. (p. 1535)
—Titan's Curse. Futaki, Attila & Guilhaumond, Gregory, illus. (p. 1758)
Venditti, Stacey Marie. Stashi the Rainbow Star: Her Journey Home. Provenzano, Jeannine, illus. (p. 1644)
Vendlinger, Joan. Littlest Chair. (p. 1039)
Vendrell, Maria Martinez, jt. auth. see Capdevila, Roser.
Vendrell, Maria Martinez & Capdevila, Roser. Noche. (p. 1262)
Vene, Alessandro, illus. see Cervone, Shannon.
Vene, Alessandro, illus. see Schleuning, Todd & Schleuning, Cheryl.
Vene, Alessandro, illus. see Spergel, Heather.
Venema, Lisa J., illus. see Coppage, Merry Ann.
Veness, Coleen Degnan & Pearson Education Staff. King Kong. (p. 958)
Venezia, Mike. Albert Einstein: Universal Genius. Venezia, Mike, illus. (p. 34)
—Alexander Graham Bell: Setting the Tone for Communication. Venezia, Mike, illus. (p. 36)
—Andrew Jackson: Seventh President, 1829-1837. Venezia, Mike, illus. (p. 72)
—Andrew Jackson. Venezia, Mike, illus. (p. 72)
—Andrew Johnson: Seventeenth President. Venezia, Mike, illus. (p. 72)
—Benjamin Franklin: Electrified the World with New Ideas. Venezia, Mike, illus. (p. 165)
—Benjamin Harrison. Venezia, Mike, illus. (p. 165)
—Bill Clinton: Forty-Second President, 1993-2001. Venezia, Mike, illus. (p. 186)
—Camille Pissarro. (p. 256)
—Camille Pissarro. Venezia, Mike, illus. (p. 256)
—Charles Drew: Doctor Who Got the World Pumped up to Donate Blood. Venezia, Mike, illus. (p. 292)
—Chester A. Arthur: Twenty-First President, 1881-1885. Venezia, Mike, illus. (p. 298)
—Chester A. Arthur. Venezia, Mike, illus. (p. 298)
—Claude Monet. Venezia, Mike, illus. (p. 329)
—Claude Monet (Revised Edition) (p. 329)
—Daniel Hale Williams: Surgeon Who Opened Hearts & Minds. (p. 405)
—Diego Rivera. Venezia, Mike, illus. (p. 437)
—Diego Velázquez. Venezia, Mike, illus. (p. 437)
—Dwight D. Eisenhower: Thirty-Fourth President 1953-1961. Venezia, Mike, illus. (p. 491)
—Eugene Delacroix. Venezia, Mike, illus. (p. 540)
—Eugène Delacroix. Venezia, Mike, illus. (p. 540)
—Faith Ringgold. Venezia, Mike, illus. (p. 565)
—Franklin Pierce: Fourteenth President. Venezia, Mike, illus. (p. 630)
—Frederic Remington. Venezia, Mike, illus. (p. 633)
—Frida Kahlo. Venezia, Mike, illus. (p. 637)
—George Bush. Venezia, Mike, illus. (p. 663)
—George Washington. Venezia, Mike, illus. (p. 664)
—Georgia O'Keefe. Venezia, Mike, illus. (p. 665)
—Gerald R. Ford: Thirty-Eighth President, 1974-1977. Venezia, Mike, illus. (p. 666)
—Getting to Know the U. S. Presidents Venezia, Mike, illus. (p. 669)
—Getting to Know the World's Greatest Artists - Titian. Venezia, Mike, illus. (p. 670)
—Getting to Know the World's Greatest Inventors & Scientists Venezia, Mike, illus. (p. 670)
—Grandma Moses. Venezia, Mike, illus. (p. 708)
—Grover Cleveland: Twenty-Second & Twenty-Fourth President, 1885-1889, 1893-1897. Venezia, Mike, illus. (p. 725)
—Harry S. Truman: Thirty-Third President. Venezia, Mike, illus. (p. 751)
—Henry Ford: Big Wheel in the Auto Industry. Venezia, Mike, illus. (p. 768)
—Horace Pippin. Venezia, Mike, illus. (p. 797)
—James A. Garfield. Venezia, Mike, illus. (p. 906)
—James Buchanan: Fifteenth President. Venezia, Mike, illus. (p. 907)
—James K. Polk: Eleventh President, 1845-1849. Venezia, Mike, illus. (p. 907)
—James McNeill Whistler. Venezia, Mike, illus. (p. 907)
—James Monroe. Venezia, Mike, illus. (p. 907)
—Jane Goodall: Researcher Who Champions Chimps. (p. 908)
—Jane Goodall: Researcher Who Champions Chimps. Venezia, Mike, illus. (p. 908)
—Jimmy Carter: Thirty-Ninth President 1977-1981. Venezia, Mike, illus. (p. 918)
—John Quincy Adams: Sixth President, 1825-1829. Venezia, Mike, illus. (p. 922)
—John Tyler: Tenth President, 1841-1845. Venezia, Mike, illus. (p. 923)
—Leonardo Davinci. Venezia, Mike, illus. (p. 992)
—Lise Meitner: Had the Right Vision about Nuclear Fission. Venezia, Mike, illus. (p. 1022)
—Luis Alvarez: Wild Idea Man. Venezia, Mike, illus. (p. 1064)
—Lyndon B. Johnson: Thirty-Sixth President, 1963-1969. Venezia, Mike, illus. (p. 1066)
—Marie Curie: Scientist Who Made Glowing Discoveries. Venezia, Mike, illus. (p. 1093)
—Martin Van Buren. Venezia, Mike, illus. (p. 1098)
—Mary Cassatt. Venezia, Mike, illus. (p. 1100)
—Mary Leakey - Archaeologist Who Really Dug Her Work. Venezia, Mike, illus. (p. 1100)
—Michelangelo. Venezia, Mike, illus. (p. 1135)
—Michelangelo (Revised Edition) (p. 1135)
—Millard Fillmore: Thirteenth President. Venezia, Mike, illus. (p. 1143)
—Millard Fillmore: Thirteenth President, 1850-1853. Venezia, Mike, illus. (p. 1143)
—Pablo Picasso. Venezia, Mike, illus. (p. 1316)
—Rachel Carson: Clearing the Way for Environmental Protection. Venezia, Mike, illus. (p. 1431)
—Rembrandt. Venezia, Mike, illus. (p. 1459)
—Richard M. Nixon: Thirty-Seventh President, 1969-1974. Venezia, Mike, illus. (p. 1469)
—Ronald Reagan: Fortieth President, 1981-1989. Venezia, Mike, illus. (p. 1486)
—Rutherford B. Hayes: Nineteenth President, 1877-1881. Venezia, Mike, illus. (p. 1499)
—Salvador Dali. Venezia, Mike, illus. (p. 1506)
—Stephen Hawking: Cosmologist Who Gets a Big Bang Out of the Universe. Venezia, Mike, illus. (p. 1648)
—Steve Jobs & Steve Wozniak: Geek Heroes Who Put the Personal in Computers. (p. 1649)
—Thomas Edison: Inventor with a Lot of Bright Ideas. Venezia, Mike, illus. (p. 1738)
—Thomas Jefferson: Third President, 1801-1809. Venezia, Mike, illus. (p. 1739)
—Titian. Venezia, Mike, illus. (p. 1758)
—Ulysses S. Grant. Venezia, Mike, illus. (p. 1810)
—Vincent Van Gogh. Venezia, Mike, illus. (p. 1843)
—Vincent Van Gogh (Revised Edition) (p. 1843)
—Warren G. Harding: Twenty-Ninth President, 1921-1923. Venezia, Mike, illus. (p. 1858)
—William Henry Harrison: Ninth President 1841. Venezia, Mike, illus. (p. 1933)
—William Henry Harrison. Venezia, Mike, illus. (p. 1933)
—William Howard Taft: Twenty-Seventh President. Venezia, Mike, illus. (p. 1933)
—William McKinley. Venezia, Mike, illus. (p. 1933)
—Winslow Homer. Venezia, Mike, illus. (p. 1937)
—Woodrow Wilson: Twenty-Eighth President. Venezia, Mike, illus. (p. 1949)
—Wright Brothers: Inventors Whose Ideas Really Took Flight. (p. 1963)
—Wright Brothers: Inventors Whose Ideas Really Took Flight. Venezia, Mike, illus. (p. 1963)
—Zachary Taylor: Twelfth President, 1849-1850. Venezia, Mike, illus. (p. 1984)
Venezia, Mike, illus. see Snow, Pegeen.
Venezia, Mike & Magritte, Rene. René Magritte. Venezia, Mike, illus. (p. 1460)
Venezia, Mike & Seurat, Georges. Georges Seurat. Venezia, Mike, illus. (p. 665)
Veneziano, Chuckie. My Time on Nantucket. (p. 1220)
Venkatakrishnan, Rames, illus. see Frye, Keith.
Venkatesh, Katherine, jt. auth. see Firth, Charlotte.
Venkatraman, Padma. Climbing the Stairs. (p. 333)
—Double Stars: The Story of Caroline Herschel. (p. 473)
—Island's End. (p. 892)
—Time to Dance. (p. 1753)
—Women Mathematicians. (p. 1946)
Venne, Matt. Beyond the Wall. (p. 174)
Venning, Barry. Turner. (p. 1798)
Venning, Edward W. Story of Pete & Ralph. (p. 1659)
—Truck & a Boy: The Truck with a big Heart. (p. 1791)
Venning, Timothy & Harris, Jonathan. Chronology of the Byzantine Empire. (p. 317)
Veno, Joe, illus. see Adams, David J.
Veno, Joe, illus. see Bouse, Susan & Gamble, Adam.
Veno, Joe, illus. see Gamble, Adam & Clark, Dennis.
Veno, Joe, illus. see Gamble, Adam & Jasper, Mark.
Veno, Joe, illus. see Gamble, Adam.
Veno, Joe, illus. see Hirschfield, Beth.
Veno, Joe, illus. see Jasper, Mark & Kelly, Cooper.
Veno, Joe, illus. see McCarthy, Dan & Rosen, Anne.
Veno, Joe, illus. see Steere, Jay & Gamble, Adam.
Vens, William D. Alias Pecos Bill. (p. 39)
Vent des Hove, Yael, jt. auth. see Vent des Hove, Yaël.
Vent des Hove, Yaël & Vent des Hove, Yael. Mama, Me Cuentas un Cuento? Vent des Hove, Yaël, illus. (p. 1084)
Venter, Liezl & Van Niekerk, Clarabelle. Understanding Sam & Asperger Syndrome. (p. 1816)
Venter, Sahm. Freedom Day: 27 April. (p. 634)
—Human Rights Day March 21. (p. 826)
—Youth Day June 16. (p. 1982)
Venti, Debra, jt. auth. see Fisher, BreeAnn.
Ventimilia, Jeffrey, jt. auth. see Sternin, Joshua.
Ventline, D. Min. Tale So True of My Christmas Tree: Everything Belongs in Our World. (p. 1701)
Ventling, Elisabeth, illus. see Cook, Julia.
Vento, Anthony. Holes Are Us: A Worm's Tale about Friendship & Trust. (p. 788)
Ventresca, Yvonne. Pandemic. (p. 1321)
Ventrillo, James & Ventrillo, Nick. Rick & Bobo: Two Brothers. One a Genius. One Not Kunardi, Marco, illus. (p. 1470)
Ventrillo, Nick, jt. auth. see Ventrillo, James.
Ventura, Antonio. Lucas y el Ruisenor. Angela-Lago, illus. (p. 1062)
Ventura, Charles. Paper Dolls in the Style of Mucha. (p. 1322)
Ventura, Gabriela Baeza, jt. auth. see Bertrand, Diane Gonzales.
Ventura, Gabriela Baeza, jt. auth. see Brown, Monica.
Ventura, Gabriela Baeza, jt. auth. see Klepeis, Alicia.
Ventura, Gabriela Baeza, jt. auth. see Mora, Pat.
Ventura, Gabriela Baeza, jt. auth. see Ortiz, Raquel M.
Ventura, Gabriela Baeza, jt. auth. see Price, Mara.
Ventura, Gabriela Baeza, jt. auth. see Zepeda, Gwendolyn.
Ventura, Gabriela Baeza, tr. see Armas, Teresa.
Ventura, Gabriela Baeza, tr. see Bertrand, Diane Gonzales.
Ventura, Gabriela Baeza, tr. see De Anda, Diane.
Ventura, Gabriela Baeza, tr. see Garza, Xavier.
Ventura, Gabriela Baeza, tr. see Gonzalez Bertrand, Diane.
Ventura, Gabriela Baeza, tr. see Jaffe, Nina.
Ventura, Gabriela Baeza, tr. see Lachtman, Ofelia Dumas.
Ventura, Gabriela Baeza, tr. see Ruiz-Flores, Lupe.
Ventura, Gabriela Baeza, tr. see Villasenor, Victor.
Ventura, Gabriela Baeza, tr. see Zepeda, Gwendolyn.
Ventura, Marco, illus. see Grodin, Elissa D., et al.
Ventura, Marne. 12 Biggest Breakthroughs in Computer Technology. (p. 1994)
—12 Biggest Breakthroughs in Food Technology. (p. 1994)
—12 Biggest Breakthroughs in Robot Technology. (p. 1994)
—Amazing Recycled Projects You Can Create. (p. 55)
—Astrophysicist & Space Advocate Neil Degrasse Tyson. (p. 109)
—Awesome Paper Projects You Can Create. (p. 121)
—Big Book of Building: Duct Tape, Paper, Cardboard, & Recycled Projects to Blast Away Boredom. (p. 179)
—Cool Cardboard Projects You Can Create. (p. 362)
—Fun Things to Do with Cardboard Tubes (p. 648)
—Fun Things to Do with Milk Jugs (p. 648)
—Google Glass & Robotics Innovator Sebastian Thrun. (p. 702)
—Gross Brain Teasers (p. 725)
—How to Survive a Flood. (p. 821)
—How to Survive a Tornado. (p. 821)
—How to Survive a Tsunami. (p. 821)
—How to Survive an Animal Attack. (p. 821)
—Imagine It, Build It. (p. 861)
—Incredible Duct Tape Projects You Can Create. (p. 869)
—Take a Closer Look at Your Bladder. (p. 1696)
Ventura, Marne & Laughlin, Kara L. 10 Things to Do (p. 1994)
Ventura, Marne & Peschke, Marci. Kylie Jean Party Craft Queen Mourning, Tuesday, illus. (p. 969)
—Kylie Jean Summer Camp Craft Queen Mourning, Tuesday, illus. (p. 969)
Ventura, Marne, et al. Gross Guides. (p. 725)
—Kylie Jean Craft Queen Mourning, Tuesday, illus. (p. 969)
Ventura, Paola Fratalocchi, jt. auth. see Hoffmann, E. T. A.
Ventura, Piero. Book of Cities. (p. 211)
Ventura, Piero & Piero, Ventura. Historia Ilustrada de la Humanidad: La Comunicación. Ventura, Piero, illus. (p. 782)
Venturini, Claudia. Ali Baba & the Forty Thieves. (p. 39)
—Tom Thumb: Flip up Fairy Tales. (p. 1764)
—Tom Thumb. (p. 1764)
Venturini, Claudia, illus. see Foster, Evelyn.
Venturi-Pickett, Stacy. Halloween. (p. 737)
Venturi-Pickett, Stacy, illus. see Pingry, Patricia A.
Venturi-Pickett, Stacy, illus. see Skarmeas, Nancy J.
Venturi-Pickett, Stacy, jt. auth. see Ruff, Kimberly.
Venturi-Pickett, Stacy, jt. tr. see Pingry, Patricia A.
Venus, Joanna, illus. see Patchett, Fiona.
Vera, Andrew, illus. see Guettler, Nancy.
Vera, J. Mustard Seed Prayer. Brown, Kevin Christian, illus. (p. 1194)
Vera, Luisa. Ali Baba & the Forty Thieves. (p. 39)
Veranda, Molly. Molly & Tucker get Shanghaied. (p. 1160)
Verano, M. Diary of a Haunting. (p. 434)
Verano, Vladimir. Prince, the Demon King, & the Monkey Warrior. (p. 1401)
Verano, Vladimir, illus. see Xu, Lei.
Veranos, Sandi. Gabriel's Visit. (p. 652)
Verba, Joan Marie. Action Alert. (p. 10)
—North Dakota. (p. 1265)
Verbeck, Frank, illus. see MacManus, Seumas.
Verbrugge, Allen. Muslims in America. (p. 1194)
Verburg, Bonnie. Kiss Box. Cole, Henry, illus. (p. 961)
—Tree House That Jack Built. Teague, Mark, illus. (p. 1783)
Vercesi, Anthony, illus. see Milgrim, Sally-Anne.
Vercoe, Elizabeth & Abramowski, Kerry. Grief Book: Strategies for Young People. (p. 723)
Vercz, Carol A. Magic of Hildie. (p. 1073)
Verday, Jessica. Beautiful & the Damned. (p. 153)
—Haunted. (p. 753)
—Hidden. (p. 775)
—Hollow. (p. 789)
Verde, Susan. I Am Yoga. Reynolds, Peter H., illus. (p. 834)
—Museum. Reynolds, Peter H., illus. (p. 1192)
—You & Me. Reynolds, Peter H., illus. (p. 1973)

Verderosa, Laura. At Grandma's House. (p. 110)
—At My School. (p. 110)
—Dad Likes New Clothes. (p. 398)
—In Our Town. (p. 864)
—In the Band. (p. 865)
—My Favorite Places. (p. 1203)
—When I Grow Up. (p. 1902)
—With My Friends. (p. 1942)
Verdet, Jean-Pierre. Weltall. (p. 1875)
Verdi, Jessica. My Life after Now. (p. 1211)
—Summer I Wasn't Me. (p. 1674)
—What You Left Behind. (p. 1896)
Verdick, Elizabeth. Bedtime. Heinlen, Marieka, illus. (p. 156)
—Bye-Bye Time. Heinlen, Marieka, illus. (p. 249)
—Calm-Down Time. Heinlen, Marieka, illus. (p. 254)
—Clean-Up Time. Heinlen, Marieka, illus. (p. 330)
—Diapers Are Not Forever. Heinlen, Marieka, illus. (p. 434)
—Don't Behave Like You Live in a Cave. Mark, Steve, illus. (p. 467)
—Feet Are Not for Kicking. Heinlen, Marieka, illus. (p. 580)
—Germs Are Not for Sharing. Heinlen, Marieka, illus. (p. 667)
—Listening Time. Heinlen, Marieka, illus. (p. 1022)
—Manners Time. Heinlen, Marieka, illus. (p. 1088)
—Mealtime. Heinlen, Marieka, illus. (p. 1116)
—Naptime. Heinlen, Marieka, illus. (p. 1229)
—Noses Are Not for Picking. Heinlen, Marieka, illus. (p. 1266)
—On-the-Go Time. Heinlen, Marieka, illus. (p. 1290)
—Pacifiers Are Not Forever. Heinlen, Marieka, illus. (p. 1317)
—Peep Leap Bendall-Brunello, John, illus. (p. 1335)
—Sharing Time. Heinlen, Marieka, illus. (p. 1561)
—Tails Are Not for Pulling. Heinlen, Marieka, illus. (p. 1695)
—Teeth Are Not for Biting. Heinlen, Marieka, illus. (p. 1715)
—Voices Are Not for Yelling. Heinlen, Marieka, illus. (p. 1848)
—Words Are Not for Hurting. Heinlen, Marieka, illus. (p. 1951)
Verdick, Elizabeth, ed. see Romain, Trevor.
Verdick, Elizabeth, jt. auth. see Agassi, Martine.
Verdick, Elizabeth, jt. auth. see Crist, James J.
Verdick, Elizabeth, jt. auth. see Espeland, Pamela.
Verdick, Elizabeth, jt. auth. see Kaufman Goodstein, Phyllis.
Verdick, Elizabeth & Agassi, Martine. Words Are Not for Hurting (Las Palabras No Son para Lastimar) Heinlen, Marieka, illus. (p. 1951)
Verdick, Elizabeth & Heinlen, Marieka. Germs Are Not for Sharing. (p. 667)
—Germs Are Not for Sharing/Los Gérmenes No Son Para Compartir. (p. 667)
Verdick, Elizabeth & Lisovskis, Marjorie. Cuddle. (p. 389)
—How to Take the Grrrr Out of Anger. (p. 822)
—Move. (p. 1183)
—Play. (p. 1370)
—Reach. (p. 1442)
—Rest. (p. 1464)
Verdick, Elizabeth & Reeve, Elizabeth. Survival Guide for Kids with Autism Spectrum Disorders (and Their Parents) (p. 1686)
Verdick, Elizabeth & Romain, Trevor. Stress Can Really Get on Your Nerves! Romain, Trevor, illus. (p. 1667)
Verdoux, Aurélia, illus. see Crupi, Jaclyn.
Verdu, Jeanyves, jt. auth. see Niepold, Mil.
Vere, Ed. Banana! Vere, Ed, illus. (p. 135)
—Bedtime for Monsters. Vere, Ed, illus. (p. 157)
—Dormir, Monstruos! (p. 471)
—Everyone's Hungry. (p. 544)
—Everyone's Little. (p. 544)
—Everyone's Noisy. (p. 544)
—Everyone's Sleepy. (p. 544)
—Max el Valiente- Max the Brave. (p. 1111)
—Max the Brave. (p. 1111)
Vere, Ed, illus. see DOYLE, Malachy.
Verelst, Suana, illus. see Guggenheim, Jaenet.
Verelst, Suana, illus. see Suneby, Elizabeth.
Veremiah, Omari. Paper Boy Two: Over Whelming 0005. Rolling, Beanic, illus. (p. 1322)
Veres, Laszlo, illus. see Green, Jen.
Veres, Laszlo, illus. see Taylor, Barbara.
Veres, Laszlo, illus. see Waddell, Martin.
Vergo, Franny. Jonathan Ray & His Superhero Pack: Respect. (p. 925)
—Jonathan Ray & His Superhero Pack: Be Bully-Free. (p. 925)
—Mathapalooza: A Collection of Math Poetry for Primary & Intermediate Students. (p. 1107)
—Sciencepalooza: A Collection of Science Poetry for Primary & Intermediate Students. (p. 1528)
Vergo, Peter. That Divine Order. Davies, Beulah, ed. (p. 1726)
Verhaagen, David Allan, jt. auth. see Borum, Randy.
Verheiden, Mark & Simone, Gail. Journey. (p. 927)
Verheijen, Jan, illus. see Sehlin, Gunhild.
Verhoef, Sharon, illus. see Roland-James, Patricia & James, Robert L.
Verhoeff, Carolyn. All about Johnnie Jones. (p. 42)
Verhoosky, Michele. Molly Marie & the Amazing Jimmy. Verhoosky, Michele, illus. (p. 1160)
Verhoosky, Michele, illus. see Fonte, Mary Roessler & Hoppe, Jessica.
Verhoye, Annabelle, illus. see Asai, Carrie & Gray, Mitchel.
Verhoye, Annabelle, illus. see Asai, Carrie.
Verileah, Teets. Rain Storm. (p. 1435)
Veritas. Children's Everyday Prayer Book. (p. 303)
—Children's Everyday Prayerbook: For four to seven year Olds. (p. 303)
Verkruysse, Toni, illus. see Gould, Susan Lynn.
Verlag, Arena. Kids' Magical Mandalas. (p. 954)
Verlag, Arena, jt. auth. see Sterling Publishing Co., Inc.
Verlag, Don Bosco Medien, jt. auth. see Portmann, Rosemarie.
Verloren, Ada, jt. auth. see Bookmiller, Kirsten N.
Verma, Dheeraj, illus. see Abnett, Dan.
Verma, Dheeraj, illus. see Jeffrey, Gary.
Verma, Dinesh. Indian Festivals Activity Workbook. (p. 871)
Verma, Dinesh, et al. Hindi Alphabet Activity Book International Edition. (p. 780)
Verma, Jatinder. Story of Divaali. Mistry, Nilesh, illus. (p. 1658)
Verma, Monika. My Storyland Animals. (p. 1219)
Verma, Riya. Hindi Children's Book Level 1 Easy Reader Aamoo the Mango. (p. 780)
Vermazen, Eve. Dog Tales: Sam, the Tree & the Crystal. (p. 461)
—Dogtales: Sebastian & the Destiny Stone. (p. 463)
Vermeer, Jan, illus. see Voigt, Cynthia.
Vermeer, Johannes, jt. auth. see Raczka, Bob.
Vermes, Geza. Authentic Gospel of Jesus. (p. 117)
Vermeulen, Thomas. Gabangani Guinea Fowl & Huzu the Bird Eating Spider. (p. 652)
Vermillion, Danny, illus. see McGhee, Patti Gray.
Vermillion, Patricia. Hound Dawg. Pilgrim, Cheryl, illus. (p. 802)
—Texas Chili? Oh My! Smith, Kuleigh, illus. (p. 1724)
—¿Chili Texano? ¡Ay Dios! Guadalupe, Jezabel, tr. from ENG. (p. 305)
Vermond, Kira. Growing Up. Chin, Carl & Owlkids Books Inc. Staff, illus. (p. 726)
—Growing Up, Inside & Out. (p. 726)
—Why We Live Where We Live. McLaughlin, Julie, illus. (p. 1926)
Vern, Alex. Where Do Frogs Come From? (p. 1907)
Verne, Jules. 20,000 Leagues under the Sea: Retold from the Jules Verne Original. Andreasen, Dan, illus. (p. 2003)
—20,000 Leagues under the Sea. (p. 2003)
—20,000 Leguas de Viaje Submarino. (p. 2003)
—Adventures of a Special Correspondent. (p. 16)
—Around the World in 80 Days. (p. 100)
—Around the World in 80 Days. Akib, Jamel, illus. (p. 100)
—Around the World in 80 Days. McKowen, Scott, illus. (p. 100)
—Around the World in 80 Days. Soleilhac, Aude, illus. (p. 100)
—Around the World in Eighty Days. Ingpen, Robert R., illus. (p. 101)
—Capitan de Quince Anos. (p. 262)
—De la Tierra a la Luna. (p. 416)
—Dick Sand. Munro, George, tr. (p. 436)
—Dick Sands: The Boy Captain. ELLEN E. FREWER, tr. (p. 436)
—Dick Sands: The Boy Captain. Frewer, Ellen E., tr. (p. 436)
—English at the North Pole. (p. 529)
—Field of Ice: Part II of the Adventures of Captain Hatteras. (p. 584)
—From the Earth to the Moon. (p. 644)
—Hijos del Capitan Grant (Captain Grant's Children) (p. 779)
—Isla Misteriosa. (p. 891)
—Journey to the Center of the Earth Rebis, Greg, illus. (p. 929)
—Journey to the Center of the Earth. (p. 929)
—Journey to the Center of the Earth. Kumar, Vinod, illus. (p. 929)
—Journey to the Center of the Earth. Freeberg, Eric, illus. (p. 929)
—Journey to the Center of the Earth. McKowen, Scott, illus. (p. 929)
—Journey to the Centre of the Earth. (p. 929)
—Journey to the Centre of the Earth. Baldick, Robert, tr. from FRE. (p. 929)
—Journey to the Interior of the Earth. (p. 929)
—Jules Verne/Journey to the Center of the Earth. (p. 932)
—Michael Strogoff. (p. 1135)
—Miguel Strogoff. (p. 1141)
—Mysterious Island Laurel Associates Inc. Staff & Saddleback Educational Publishing Staff, eds. (p. 1223)
—Mysterious Island. (p. 1223)
—Secret of the Island. Kingston, W. H. G., tr. (p. 1542)
—Topsy-Turvy. Ogilvie, J. G., tr. (p. 1769)
—Tour du Monde en 80 Jours. (p. 1773)
—Twenty Thousand Leagues under the Sea. (p. 1801)
—Veinte Mil Leguas de Viaje Submarino. (p. 1834)
—Viaje Al Centro de la Tierra Tobon, Sara, tr. from ENG. (p. 1839)
—Viaje al Centro de la Tierra. (p. 1839)
—Voyage au Centre de la Terre. (p. 1850)
—Vuelta Al Mundo en 80 Dias. (p. 1851)
—Vuelta al Mundo en 80 Dias. (p. 1851)
Verne, Jules, jt. auth. see Francis, Pauline.
Verne, Jules & Fuentes, Benny. 20,000 Leguas de Viaje Submarino Smith, Tod, illus. (p. 2003)
Verne, Jules & Lokus, Rex. Around the World in 80 Days. Smith, Tod G., illus. (p. 100)
Verne, Jules & Verne, Julio. 20,000 Leguas de Viaje Submarino. (p. 2003)
—Hijos del Capitan Grant. (p. 779)
—Miguel Strogoff. (p. 1141)
Verne, Jules, ed. Cinco Semanas en Globo. (p. 319)
Verne, Julio, jt. auth. see Verne, Jules.
Vernescu, Maritza, tr. see Pan, Hui-Mei.
Verney, Jeff. Christmas Book of Hope. (p. 313)
Vernick, Audrey. Bogart & Vinnie: A Completely Made-Up Story of True Friendship. Cole, Henry, illus. (p. 207)
—Brothers at Bat: The True Story of an Amazing All-Brother Baseball Team. Salerno, Steven, illus. (p. 231)
—Edgar's Second Word. Burris, Priscilla, illus. (p. 504)
—First Grade Dropout. Cordell, Matthew, illus. (p. 595)
—Is Your Buffalo Ready for Kindergarten? Jennewein, Daniel, illus. (p. 890)
—Screaming at the Ump. (p. 1533)
—She Loved Baseball: The Effa Manley Story. Vernick, Audrey & Tate, Don, illus. (p. 1564)
—So You Want to Be a Rock Star. Edmunds, Kirstie, illus. (p. 1602)
—Teach Your Buffalo to Play Drums. Jennewein, Daniel, illus. (p. 1709)
—Unlike Other Monsters. Jack, Colin, illus. (p. 1821)
—Water Balloon. (p. 1862)
Vernick, Audrey Glassman & Gidaro, Ellen Glassman. Bark & Tim: A True Story of Friendship. Brown, Tim, illus. (p. 139)
Vernick, Shirley Reva. Black Butterfly. (p. 195)
—Blood Lie. (p. 200)
—Remember Dippy. (p. 1459)
Verniero, Joan C., jt. auth. see Rappaport, Doreen.
Vernon, Caitlyn. Nowhere Else on Earth: Standing Tall for the Great Bear Rainforest (p. 1269)
Vernon, Elisient Maeve. Ava's Bad Day. (p. 118)
Vernon, Jeff, illus. see Boritzer, Etan.
Vernon, Louise A. Key to the Prison. Eitzen, Allan, illus. (p. 950)
Vernon, Magan. How to Date an Alien: My Alien Romance. (p. 816)
Vernon, Rion, illus. see Langteau, Scott.
Vernon, Roland. Introducing Composers. (p. 882)
Vernon, Steve. Maritime Monsters Solway, Jeff, illus. (p. 1094)
Vernon, Ursula. Attack of the Ninja Frogs. (p. 114)
—Case of the Toxic Mutants. (p. 275)
—Castle Hangnail. (p. 276)
—Curse of the Were-Wiener. (p. 395)
—Dani Bocafuego. la Cueva Del Murcielago Gigante. (p. 404)
—Dani Bocafuego. la Salchicha Maldita. (p. 404)
—Dragonbreath. (p. 478)
—Dragonbreath. Vernon, Ursula, illus. (p. 478)
—Harriet the Invincible. (p. 749)
—Knight-Napped! (p. 964)
—Lair of the Bat Monster. (p. 972)
—Nightmare of the Iguana. (p. 1255)
—No Such Thing as Ghosts. (p. 1260)
—Nurk: The Strange, Surprising Adventures of a (Somewhat) Brave Shrew. (p. 1273)
—Revenge of the Horned Bunnies (p. 1466)
—When Fairies Go Bad (p. 1902)
Vernon-Jackson, Hugh. West African Folk Tales. Wright, Patricia, illus. (p. 1876)
Verona Publishing, illus. see DeRosa, Nancy.
Veronica Dauber. Mudslide. (p. 1189)
Veronica, M., ed. see Theresine, Mary.
Veronique, Catel. Bluesy Lucy - the Existential Chronicles of a Thirtysomething. (p. 204)
Verral, Charles Spain. Annie Oakley, Sharpshooter. Dreany, E. Joseph, illus. (p. 87)
—Rin Tin Tin & the Outlaw. Crawford, Mel, illus. (p. 1473)
Verrall, Lisa, illus. see Litton, Jonathan.
Verrecas, Charlotte. Big Book of Face Painting. (p. 179)
Verrept, Paul. Pequeno Soldado. Bourgeois, Elodie, tr. (p. 1341)
Verrett, Michael. Cozmo the Elf. (p. 375)
—Galid's Christmas Wish. (p. 653)
—It Followed Me Home Can I Keep It? (p. 894)
—It Followed Me Home Can I Keep It? (full Color) (p. 894)
—Rhymes of the Gray Beard Tree. (p. 1468)
—White Alligator Crown Quatro. (p. 1912)
—White Alligator (paper Back) (p. 1912)
—White Alligator (paperback full Color) (p. 1912)
Verrett, Michael, illus. see Wilson, Janet.
Verrico, Susan. Privateer's Apprentice (p. 1408)
Verrier, Steven. Don't Needle Me: A Ten-Minute Comedy Duet. (p. 468)
—Few Tiles Short: A Comedy Skit (p. 583)
—Golf Doctor: A Ten-Minute Comedy Duet. (p. 696)
Verrier, Suzy. Titus Tidewater. (p. 1758)
Verrill, Alpheus Hyatt. American Indian, North, South & Central America. (p. 62)
—Old Civilizations of the New World. (p. 1283)
Verrill, William, illus. see Puppel, Douglas.
Verrillo, Erica, jt. auth. see Verrillo, Erica F.
Verrillo, Erica F. & Verrillo, Erica. Elissa's Quest. (p. 513)
Verroken, Sarah, illus. see Derom, Dirk.
Verrone, Patric C. W. Sharktooth. (p. 1563)
Versace, Matthew, jt. auth. see Wright, Lisa.
Verstegen, Jeska, illus. see Wilkeshuis, Cornelius.
Verstegen, Mark & Williams, Pete. Core Performance: The Revolutionary Workout Program to Transform Your Body & Your Life. (p. 367)
—Core Performance Essentials: The Revolutionary Nutrition & Exercise Plan Adapted for Everyday Use. (p. 367)
Verster, Sean, jt. auth. see Grobbelaar, Pieter W.
Verstraete, Christine. Searching for a Starry Night: A Miniature Art Mystery. (p. 1537)
Verstraete, Elaine, illus. see Alphin, Elaine Marie.
Verstraete, Elaine, illus. see Pfeffer, Wendy.
Verstraete, Elaine, illus. see Walker, Sally M.
Verstraete, Elaine S., illus. see DiVencenzo, Maria T.
Verstraete, Larry. G Is for Golden Boy: A Manitoba Alphabet. Lund, Brian, illus. (p. 651)
—S Is for Scientists: A Discovery Alphabet. Geister, David, illus. (p. 1499)
—Surviving the Hindenburg. (p. 1687)
Verstraete, Majanka. Doll Maker: Weirdville. (p. 463)
—Fright Train: Weirdville. (p. 639)
—House of Horrors: Weirdville. (p. 803)
—Valentina & the Haunted Mansion (Valentina's Spooky Adventures - 1) Giffin, Noelle, illus. (p. 1830)
—Valentina & the Whackadoodle Witch: Valentina's Spooky Adventures. Giffin, Noelle, illus. (p. 1830)
Vertical Inc. Staff, ed. see Tezuka, Osamu.
Vertley, Barbara. Back in the Day. (p. 130)
Verville, Claudia. Piggy with the Curly Tail. (p. 1358)
Verville, Claudia J. Little Duckie Doodle. (p. 1027)
Verville, Kathleen. Testicular Cancer. (p. 1723)
Vervoort, Sarah, illus. see Collar, Bill.
Verwey, Amanda, illus. see Tea, Michelle.
Very, Lydia L. Little Red Riding Hood: Treasures from the Library of Congress. (p. 1035)
Verzov, Ella & Olrechman, Chana. Moshe of Japan. (p. 1176)
—Tamar of Venice. (p. 1704)
Vesazquez, Gloria, tr. see Liccioni, Tina.
Vescera, Dean & Yager, A. J. One: A Revolutionary Self-Empowerment Book Based on the Matrix. (p. 1293)
Vescia, Monique. Battle Reenactments. (p. 147)
—David Karp & Tumblr. (p. 411)
—Fashion. (p. 575)
—Markus Zusak (p. 1095)
—What Is Animal Behavior? (p. 1889)
—Zachary Quinto (p. 1984)
Vescia, Monique, jt. auth. see DonRauf.
Vescia, Monique, jt. auth. see Rauf, Don.
Vescia, Monique, et al. What You Can Do about ADHD. (p. 1895)
—What You Can Do about Sickle Cell Disease. (p. 1896)
Vescia, Peter. Pikes Peak Gold Rush. (p. 1358)
Vescio & LohnRiver, Jenna. Rainbow Journey Screen Play (with Pictures) (p. 1435)
Vescio, Robert. Ganz Gleich Mit Wem Wir Zusammen Sind. Beer, Michele, tr. from ENG. (p. 655)
—No Matter Who We're With. Scholten, Cheri, illus. (p. 1259)
Vescovi, Laura A. Good Morning Sleepyhead. (p. 698)
Vess, Charles, illus. see Alexander, Lloyd, et al.
Vess, Charles, illus. see de Lint, Charles.
Vess, Charles, illus. see Gaiman, Neil.
Vess, Charles, illus. see Myers, Anna.
Vess, Charles, illus. see Smith, Jeff.
Vest, Bonnie A. Tuxedo, Oreo, & Socks. (p. 1799)
Vest, Dale G., jt. auth. see Overstreet, Tommy.
Vest, Dianne, illus. see Lewis, Orane.
Vestal, Julie Cheek. Gracie's Lullaby Land. (p. 705)
Vestergaard, Hope. Digger, Dozer, Dumper. Slonim, David, illus. (p. 438)
—Potty Animals: What to Know When You've Gotta Go! Petrone, Valeria, illus. (p. 1388)
Vestry, Annabelle. Carlyles (p. 270)
Vetleseter, Tonje, tr. see Bringsvaerd, Tor Age.
Vetleseter, Tonje, tr. see Sande, Hans.
Vetleseter, Tonje, tr. see Sandemose, Iben.
Vetro, Daniela, illus. see Radice, Teresa, et al.
Vetsch, Rita Kaye. Many Colors of Friendship. (p. 1089)
Vetta, Pierpaolo, jt. auth. see Polano, Sergio.
Vetter, Darren. I Want to Go to the Lake with My Dog! (p. 848)
Vetter Squires, Diane. Basil's New Home: The Garden Rabbit Series - Part One. McAteer, Thomas, illus. (p. 142)
Vevaina, Coomi S. Bernice Banan. (p. 167)
Vevers, Rachel. Quest for the Unicorn. (p. 1426)
Veyret, Yvette, jt. auth. see Husson, Severin.
Vezeau, Sheila. Sky, the Blue Bunny. Ostrowski, Justin, illus. (p. 1587)
Vezo, Tom, photos by see Choiniere, Joseph & Golding, Claire Mowbray.
Via, Jennifer Welsh. Foggy Meadow Discovery. (p. 611)
Viall, Pauline, illus. see Richards, Sonja.
Vian, Boris. Ecume des Jours (p. 503)
Viana, Luis Diaz, see Diaz Viana, Luis.
Vianney, M. John, illus. see Dominic, Sister M.
Viano, Hannah. Arrow to Alaska: A Pacific Northwest Adventure. (p. 101)
—S Is for Salmon: A Pacific Northwest Alphabet. Viano, Hannah, illus. (p. 1499)
Viard, Michel, illus. see Eid, Alain.
Viau, Nancy. City Street Beat. (p. 324)
—City Street Beat. Bakos, Barbara, illus. (p. 324)
—Samantha Hansen Has Rocks in Her Head. Pham, LeUyen, illus. (p. 1507)
—Storm Song. Gynux, illus. (p. 1656)
Viau, Nancy & Bolinao, Mela. Storm Song Gynux, illus. (p. 1656)
Viau, Nancy & Vojtech, Anna. Look What I Can Do! Vojtech, Anna, illus. (p. 1050)
Vicario, Arantxa Sanchez, see Sanchez Vicario, Arantxa.
Vicario, Evelyn. Mathematics for Life - Moses Meets the Triangles. Vicario, Evelyn, illus. (p. 1108)
—Mathematics for Life - Moses Teaches Properties of Addition. (p. 1108)
—Mathematics for Life Practice Workbook - Kindergarten. (p. 1108)
Vicario, Miguel Medina & Miguel, Medina Vicario. Quico: El Nino Que Quiso Ser Comico. (p. 1427)
Vicary, Tim. Elephant Man, Level 1. (p. 511)
—Grace Darling. Oxford University Press Staff & Bassett, Jennifer, eds. (p. 704)
—Hitchhiker. (p. 786)
Vicens, Paula, tr. see Jacobs, Nadine.
Vicens, Paula, tr. see Pennart, Geoggroy, et al.
Vicens, Paula, tr. see Solotareff, Gregoire.
Vicente, Alidis. Missing Chancleta & Other Top-Secret Cases / la Chancleta Perdida y Otros Casos Secretos. (p. 1152)
Vicente, Fernando, illus. see Barrie, J. M.
Vicente, Luis San. Festival de las Calaveras. (p. 582)
Vicente, Luise San, illus. see Aguirre, Sonia Montecino.
Vicente, Marta. Cajita. (p. 252)
Vick, Jacqueline. Logical Larry. (p. 1045)
Vick, Mamie Farrar. Someone's Near. (p. 1609)
Vick-E & RH Disney Staff. Wall-E. Orpinas, Jean-Paul et al, illus. (p. 1854)
Vickers, Rebecca. 101 Ways to Be Smart about Money. (p. 2000)
—Asa Candler: The Founder of Coca-Cola. (p. 105)
—Every Person Has a History (p. 543)
—Every Possession Has a History (p. 543)
—Industrial Age Medicine (p. 872)
—J. L. Kraft. (p. 901)
—Making Better Sentences: The Power of Structure & Meaning (p. 1080)
—Medicine (p. 1119)
—Punctuation & Spelling: Rules That Make Things Clear (p. 1417)
—Types of Words: Unleashing Powerful Parts of Speech (p. 1805)
Vickers, Rebecca & Langley, Andrew. Everything Has a History (p. 545)
Vickers, Rebecca & Miles, Liz. Find Your Way with Words. (p. 587)
Vickers, Roy Henry, illus. see Bouchard, David.
Vickers, Sheree. Drama Scripts for People with Special Needs. (p. 480)
Vickers, Stormi. My Beautiful Alone. Vickers, Stormi, illus. (p. 1196)
Vickers, Tamara. Mr. Green & the Animal Kingdom: (Imagine That!) You Draw the Picture! (p. 1185)
Vickery, Anne. Stressing the Modern: Cultural Politics in Australian Women's Poetry. (p. 1667)
Vickery, Kenneth V. In Honor of People Like Us. (p. 863)
Vickery-Bharadwaj, Janice. Valentino & His Friends: It's Magic! (p. 1830)
Vicki, Jones, ed. see Jones, Carl L.
Vickie A. Soman. Sahara Desert Angel: Education & Nature Folktales 2. (p. 1503)
Vickie Washington and Carla Watts, ed. see Young, T. M.

V

Victor, Appleton. Tom Swift among the Fire Fighters: Or Battling with Flames from the Air. (p. 1763)
—Tom Swift & His Aerial Warship: Or the Naval Terror of the Seas. (p. 1763)
—Tom Swift & His Air Scout: Or Uncle Sam's Mastery of the Sky. (p. 1763)
—Tom Swift & His Undersea Search: Or the Treasure on the Floor of the Atlantic. (p. 1763)
—Tom Swift & His Wizard Camera: Or Thrilling Adventures While Taking Moving Pictu. (p. 1763)
Victor, Archimede J. In the Name of Liberty: A History of Haiti (Pre-1492-1806) (p. 866)
Victor, Pamela. Baj & the Word Launcher: Space Age Asperger Adventures in Communication. (p. 133)
Victor, Rae Anna. George Washington's Revolutionary Marshals. (p. 665)
Victor, Ralph. Boy Scouts Patrol. (p. 219)
Victoria, Kirton, illus. see Redmond, Valerie.
Victoria, Lisa. Clara's Gift from the Heart. (p. 326)
Victoria, Lisa, illus. see Davis, L. J.
Victoria, Marie Alexandra. Christmas Tale. (p. 316)
Victoria, Roberts. Best Pet Ever. Deborah, Allwright, illus. (p. 171)
Victoria Washington and Carla Watts, ed. see Young, T. M.
Victory Productions, Inc. Staff, tr. see Gordon, Sharon.
Victory Productions, Inc. Staff, tr. see Rau, Dana Meachen.
Vicuna, Claudio Orrego. Surprising Adventures of Balthazar. (p. 1686)
Vic-Vincent, Victor Neil, creator. Inventors Guidebook: Patent, Protect, Produce & Profit from Your Ideas & Inventions Yourself! (p. 884)
Vidal, Beatriz Martin. Bird. (p. 190)
Vidal de Albó, Gloria. Lucita la Luciernaga. (p. 1062)
Vidal, Jordi, tr. see Hulme, John & Wexler, Michael.
Vidal, Oriol. Build a Picture Monsters Sticker Book. (p. 237)
Vidal, Oriol, illus. see Bailey, Catherine.
Vidal, Oriol, illus. see Dahl, Michael.
Vidal, Séverine. Mega Bunny. Barroux, Stephane, illus. (p. 1124)
—Mega Mouse. Barroux, Stephane, illus. (p. 1124)
—Mega Pig. Barroux, Stephane, illus. (p. 1124)
—Mega Wolf. Barroux, Stephane, illus. (p. 1124)
Vidal-Badalamenti, Nellian. Daddy's Little Girl: A Lullaby for Little Girls & Their Daddy. (p. 399)
Vidali, Valerio & Uman, Jennifer. Jemmy Button. Vidali, Valerio & Uman, Jennifer, illus. (p. 912)
Vidov, Oleg, jt. ed. see Borsten, Joan.
Vidrine, Beverly Barras. Easter Day Alphabet Lyne, Alison Davis, illus. (p. 499)
—Halloween Alphabet Lyne, Alison Davis, illus. (p. 737)
—Thanksgiving Day Alphabet Lyne, Alison D., illus. (p. 1726)
Vidro, Kenn. Square Pears Three: Hey Diddle Riddle. (p. 1636)
—Square Pears Two: The Equal Sequel. Vidro, Kenn, illus. (p. 1636)
Vidro, Kenn G. Square Pears. (p. 1636)
Vieceli, Emma, illus. see Mead, Richelle.
Vieceli, Emma, illus. see Shakespeare, William & Appignanesi, Richard.
Vieceli, Emma, illus. see Shakespeare, William.
Viegas, Jennifer. Beethoven's World. (p. 158)
—Eye: Learning How We See. (p. 557)
—Fungi & Molds. (p. 649)
—Kinetic & Potential Energy: Understanding Changes Within Physical Systems. (p. 958)
—Parasites. (p. 1324)
—Pierre Omidyar: The Founder of Ebay. (p. 1357)
—Revolution in Healing the Brain. (p. 1466)
—Uranus. (p. 1825)
—William James: American Philosopher, Psychologist, & Theologian. (p. 1933)
Viegas, Jennifer, jt. auth. see Coots, Catherine.
Viegas, Jennifer, jt. auth. see Gill, Monica.
Viegas, Jennifer, jt. auth. see Huddle, Rusty.
Viegas, Jennifer, jt. auth. see Kingston, Anna.
Viegas, Jennifer, jt. auth. see Towne, Isobel.
Viegas, Jennifer, jt. auth. see Wolfe, James.
Viegas, Jennifer, ed. Critical Perspectives on Natural Disasters. (p. 383)
—Critical Perspectives on Planet Earth. (p. 383)
—Laws of Thermodynamics: An Anthology of Current Thought. (p. 981)
—Role of the Sun in Our Solar System: An Anthology of Current Thought. (p. 1485)
Viegas, Marneta. Magic Box. (p. 1071)
—Relax Kids: The Wishing Star. (p. 1458)
—Relax Kids: Little Book of Stars. (p. 1458)
—Relax Kids - Aladdin's Magic Carpet: Let Snow White, the Wizard of Oz & Other Fairytale Characters Show You & Your Child How to Meditate & Relax. (p. 1458)
Viegas-Barros, Rocio, tr. see Bertrand, Diane Gonzales.
Viehl, Lynn. Dead of Night. (p. 417)
—Evermore (p. 542)
Vieira, Andrei, illus. see Gibbs, Noni & Kahrs, Christina.
Vieira, Linda. Mighty Mississippi: The Life & Times of America's Greatest River. Bond, Higgins, illus. (p. 1140)
Vieira, Sueli, illus. see Dahlgren, Leta.
Vierow, Wendy. 1864 Presidential Election: A War-Weary Nation Reelects President Abraham Lincoln. (p. 2002)
—Africa. (p. 26)
—Antarctica. (p. 88)
—Asia. (p. 106)
—Assault on Fort Wagner: Black Union Soldiers Make a Stand in South Carolina Battle. (p. 107)
—Australia. (p. 116)
—Battle of Bull Run: Confederate Forces Overwhelm Union Troops. (p. 146)
—Battle of Bull Run. (p. 146)
—Battle of Gettysburg: The Civil War's Biggest Battle. (p. 146)
—Battle of Saratoga. (p. 146)
—Battle of Trenton. (p. 147)
—Battle of Yorktown. (p. 147)
—Capture of New Orleans: Union Fleet Takes Control of the Lower Mississippi. (p. 265)
—Capture of New Orleans: Union Fleet Takes Control of the Lower Mississippi River. (p. 265)
—Europe. (p. 540)
—North America. (p. 1264)
—Shots Fired at Fort Sumter: Civil War Breaks Out! (p. 1569)
—Shots Fired at Fort Sumter. (p. 1569)
—South America. (p. 1616)
Viescas, John L., et al. Microsoft(r) Office Access(tm) 2007 (p. 1136)
Vietch, Catherine. Sound & Hearing. (p. 1615)
Vigen, Arno. 2MPower Decision Matrix Writing. (p. 1991)
Viggers, Katie. 1 to 20 Animals Aplenty. (p. 1991)
—Almost an Animal Alphabet. (p. 48)
Vigil, Angel. Papi, How Many Stars Are in the Sky? Ahmad, Aadil & James, Martin, illus. (p. 1323)
Vigil, Cristina, illus. see Fairchild-Lenyo, Mary.
Vigil, Florida. Child's Imagination: Childhood Poems. (p. 305)
Vigil, Linda Nova. Sacred Promises. (p. 1500)
Vigil, Luis Gerardo Sanchez, illus. see Romeu, Emma.
Vigil, Sabrina, ed. see Irvin, Feliza & Irvin, Feliza.
Vigilante, Danette. Saving Baby Doe. (p. 1517)
—Trouble with Half a Moon. (p. 1790)
Vigilante, Sylvester, jt. auth. see Meadowcroft, Enid Lamonte.
Vigla, Vincent. My Magnetic Word Puzzles: Let's Make Words. (p. 1214)
Vigla, Vincent, illus. see Broski, Julie.
Vigla, Vincent, illus. see Little, Penny.
Vigliano, Adrian. Being a Good Citizen. (p. 160)
—Shipwrecks (p. 1567)
Vigliano, Adrian, jt. auth. see Rissman, Rebecca.
Viglione, Steve. I AM! Affirmation Book: Discovering the Value of Who You Are, English~French: Discovering the Value of Who You Are. (p. 832)
—I AM! Affirmation Book (English-Spanish Edition) Discovering the Value of Who You Are. (p. 832)
Vigna, Judith. When Eric's Mom Fought Cancer. (p. 1902)
Vignaga, Francesca Dafne, illus. see Magni, Aurora.
Vignaga, Francesca Dafne, illus. see Troupe, Thomas Kingsley.
Vignazia, Franco, illus. see Biffi, Inos, ed.
Vignazia, Franco, illus. see Biffi, Inos.
Vigneault, Gilles. Cadeau Pour Sophie: Conte et Chansons. Jorisch, Stéphane, illus. (p. 250)
—Gift for Sophie. Jorisch, Stéphane, illus. (p. 675)
—Treasure in My Garden. Jorisch, Stéphane, illus. (p. 1781)
Vignoli, Daniella, illus. see Visconti, Guido.
Vignolo, Enrique, illus. see McMillan, Dawn.
Vignolo, Enrique, illus. see Sommer, Carl.
Vigue, Jim, ed. Peak Power Baseball: How to Turn Your Little League Dream into Major League Reality. (p. 1332)
Vigue, Kris, Sr. How to Achieve Your Million-Dollar Dreams at Any Age. (p. 814)
Viguié, Debbie. Fall of Candy Corn (p. 566)
—Midnight Pearls: A Retelling of the Little Mermaid. (p. 1139)
—Scarlet Moon. (p. 1520)
—Spring of Candy Apples (p. 1635)
—Summer of Cotton Candy (p. 1674)
—Violet Eyes. (p. 1843)
Viguié, Debbie, jt. auth. see Burge, Constance M.
Viguié, Debbie, jt. auth. see Holder, Nancy.
Viguié, Debbie & Elmer, Robert. Owling (p. 1315)
Viguie, Debbie & Holder, Nancy. Unleashed. (p. 1821)
Vigus, Rebecka. Only a Start & Beyond. (p. 1298)
Vihlstrand, George. Tanya, the Black Jaguar. (p. 1705)
ViiiZ. Photo Doodles: 200 Photos for You to Complete. (p. 1352)
Viknesh, R. My Fantasy Your Treat. (p. 1203)
Vil, Steve. Arvid & Hornschwatz Go Skunk Scoffing. Witt, Eddie, illus. (p. 105)
Vila, Alvaro F., illus. see Capstone Press Staff.
Vila, Carmen. Tracy Knows Picasso: Children's Art History Read-Along Book. (p. 1776)
Vila Delclòs, Jordi, illus. see Bailer, Darice & Dominguez, Madelca.
Vila, Laura. Building Manhattan. (p. 239)
Vilagut & Anton. Regalo Del Pescador. (p. 1457)
Vilarino, Andres Garcia. Cocodrilo en Mi Habitacion. (p. 337)
Vilarrubias Codina, Pia, jt. auth. see Vilarrubias, Pia.
Vilarrubias, Pia & Vilarrubias Codina, Pia. Cua, el Amigo de Tona. (p. 387)
Vilarrubias, Pia, et al. Juguemos a Volar! (p. 932)
—Kiko Sale Del Libro. (p. 956)
—Lina Tambien Juega. (p. 1018)
—Que Juegan Nico y Max? (p. 1424)
Vilchez, Deann. Boy Who Loved His Dad. (p. 219)
Vilcoq, Marianne. Espero un Hermanito. (p. 536)
Vilela, Caio. Goal! Taylor, Sean, tr. from POR. (p. 687)
Vilela, Caio, photos by see Taylor, Sean.
Vilela, Fernando, illus. see Argueta, Jorge.
Vilela, Luiz, illus. see Golden Books.
Vilela, Luiz, illus. see Osborne, Mary Pope & Boyce, Natalie Pope.
Viles, Anne. Passages Through the Desolate Soul. (p. 1326)
Vili, Fane. Mano: The Awakening. Frakes, Clint, ed. (p. 1088)
Villa, Alvaro F. Flood. (p. 605)
—Flood. (p. 605)
Villa, Elisabeth. My Massachusetts. Fazio, Nicole, illus. (p. 1214)
Villa, Jaime Valencia. Akhenatón. (p. 32)
Villa, Leesan. Angel on Top of the Tree. (p. 74)
Villa, Maria, tr. Quien Es la Senora Garcia? (p. 1427)
Villa, Ruben. Granola Farm. (p. 710)
Villa, Victor Rivas, illus. see Marcionette, Jake.
Villacis, Alexandra. Bombón la Chihuahua Extraviada. Molinari, Fernando, illus. (p. 208)
Villacis, Alexandra. Bombón the Lost Chihuahua. Molinari, Fernando, illus. (p. 208)
Villafane-Leon, Ines. Story for All Seasons: Un Cuento Para Cada Estacion: Immigration of One. (p. 1657)
Villagomez, Raul, illus. see Santirso, Liliana.
Villagran, Ricardo, illus. see London, Jack.
Villalba Casas, Consuelo. Insomnios. Scarrone, Gustavo, illus. (p. 878)
Villalobos, Ethel M., illus. see Pierce, Terry.
Villalobos, Serenity. Yasso's Adventure: Written by Serenity M. Villalobos Illustrated & Designed by Alisha & Kristen Villalobos & Yes Even Dad AKA Jody Villalobos Helped! (p. 1968)
Villaloz, ChiChi & Etheridge, Katy. Do Dogs Dream? Villaloz, ChiChi & Etheridge, Katy, illus. (p. 456)
—Do Dogs Vote? Villaloz, ChiChi & Etheridge, Katy, illus. (p. 456)
Villalpando, Jose Manuel. Diario de Clara Eugenia (1864-67) (p. 434)
Villalta, Ingrid, illus. see Lin, Chris.
Villamuza Manso, Noemí, jt. auth. see Villamuza, Noemí.
Villamuza, Noemí, illus. see Keselman, Gabriela.
Villamuza, Noemí, illus. see Plaza, José María & María, Plaza José.
Villamuza, Noemí, illus. see Puelles, Vicente Munoz & Muñoz Puelles, Vicente.
Villamuza, Noemí, illus. see Sobrino, Javier.
Villamuza, Noemí, tr. see Sobrino, Javier.
Villamuza, Noemí & Villamuza Manso, Noemí. Lola Trae Regalos. (p. 1046)
—Merienda de Micaela. (p. 1127)
Villan, Oscar, illus. see Nunez, Marisa.
Villanes Cairo, Carlos, jt. auth. see Cairo, Carlos Villanes.
Villanes, Carlos, et al. Cesar Vallejo para Ninos. (p. 288)
Villani, Agostino. Pain Is Not A Disease: Solving America's Growing Epidemic of Chronic Pain May Be as Simple as Recognizing That.... (p. 1318)
Villani, Donna. Capture of Art. (p. 265)
Villanueva, David. Caleb's Birthday Wish. Sanchez, Edmundo, illus. (p. 252)
Villanueva Leonard. Hungry Puaa. (p. 828)
Villanueva, Leonard. Kaipo & the Mighty Ahi. Villanueva, Leonard, illus. (p. 941)
Villar Liébana, Luisa. Misterio de la Gata Maga. (p. 1155)
Villar Liébana, Luisa, jt. auth. see Villar Liebana, Luisa.
Villar Liebana, Luisa & Villar Liébana, Luisa. Ladron de Salchichon. (p. 970)
—Ladron Sin Huellas. (p. 970)
—Misterio en el Campo de Golf. (p. 1155)
Villar, Rose, jt. auth. see Rice, Ruth Mason.
Villard, Ray. Supertelescopios: Por dentro y por fuera (Large Telescopes: Inside & Out) (p. 1684)
Villard, Ray, ed. Changes Within Physical Systems and/or Conservation of Energy & Momentum: An Anthology of Current Thought. (p. 290)
Villard, Raymond. Large Telescopes: Inside & Out. (p. 975)
Villareal, Ray. Alamo Wars. (p. 33)
—Body Slammed! (p. 207)
—Don't Call Me Hero. (p. 467)
—On the Other Side of the Bridge. (p. 1291)
—Who's Buried in the Garden? (p. 1920)
Villarreal, Carlos C. Light Beneath the Shadow: Sharing God's Love with Your Child as You Read Together: A Bedtime Story Intended to Awaken Your Parental Christian Spirit. (p. 1015)
Villarreal, Francisco, photos by see Villalba Casas, Consuelo.
Villarreal, Jennifer. Monster under My Bed. (p. 1168)
Villarreal, Rosa Martha. Stillness of Love & Exile. (p. 1650)
Villarreal, Tanya E. Izzie's First Christmas Villarreal, Tanya E., illus. (p. 901)
Villarroel, Carolina, jt. auth. see Garza, Xavier.
Villarroel, Carolina, jt. auth. see Luna, James.
Villarroel, Carolina, tr. see Baca, Ana.
Villarroel, Carolina, tr. see Saldana, Rene.
Villarroel, Carolina, tr. see Saldaña, René.
Villarroel, Carolina, tr. see Villasenor, Victor.
Villarrubia, Jose, illus. see Carey, Mike & Fern, Jim.
Villarrubia, Jose, illus. see Riordan, Rick & Venditti, Robert.
Villarrubia, Jose, jt. auth. see Niles, Steve.
Villaseñor, Victor. Frog & His Friends Save Humanity/la Rana y Sus Amigos Salvan ALA Humanidad. Ochoa, Edna, tr. (p. 640)
Villasenor, Victor. Goodnight, Papito Dios/Buenos Noches, Papito Dios. Villarroel, Carolina, tr. (p. 701)
—Little Crow to the Rescue/el Cuervito al Rescate. Munoz, Elizabeth Cummins, tr. (p. 1026)
Villaseñor, Victor. Mother Fox & Mr. Coyote / Mamá Zorra y Don Coyote. Turcios, Guadalupe Vanessa, tr. (p. 1177)
Villasenor, Victor. Stranger & the Red Rooster: El Forastero y el Gallo Rojo. Ventura, Gabriela Baeza, tr. (p. 1665)
—Walking Stars: Stories of Magic & Power. (p. 1854)
Villaseñor, Victor. Walking Stars. (p. 1854)
Villata, Diane A. Louie the Lizard. (p. 1058)
Villavert, Armand, Jr., illus. see Beedle, Tim.
Villegas, Aline Guevara. Dentro del Cubo. Alvarez, Diego, illus. (p. 427)
Villegas, Eduardo. Baul de los Cuentos. (p. 147)
Villegas, Mercedes, tr. see Ahlberg, Allan.
Villegas, Teresa, illus. see Stavans, Ilan.
Villegas Viera, Ana A. Mundicuentos. (p. 1191)
Villella, Jessica, illus. see Branda, Barnabus.
Villeneuve, Anne. Loula Is Leaving for Africa. Villeneuve, Anne, illus. (p. 1059)
Villeneuve, Anne-Louise. Red Scarf. (p. 1455)
Villeneuve, Kevin J. Adventures of Nick the Ecologist & His Robot O-Zone: The Mystery of the Missing Trees. (p. 21)
Villeneuve, Marie-Paule & Audet, Patrice. Qui a Enleve Polka? (p. 1427)
Villet, Olivia, illus. see McLaren, Thando.
Villet, Olivia, illus. see Pym, Tasha.
Villiers, Alan. Joey Goes to Sea. Dowling, Victor J., illus. (p. 920)
Villiers, Les de, see de Villiers, Les.
Villim, Jim, illus. see Heitritter, Laura.
Villines, Carol. Clean Your Room. Villines, Leo, illus. (p. 330)
Villines, Leo, illus. see Villines, Carol.
Villing, Alexandra. Ancient Greeks: Their Lives & Their World. (p. 69)
Villnave, Erica. Sophie's Lovely Locks Villnave, Erica, illus. (p. 1613)
Villnave, Erica Pelton, illus. see Burns, Ellen Flanagan.
Villnave, Erica Pelton, illus. see Galvin, Laura Gates.
Villnave, Erica Pelton, illus. see Galvin, Laura.
Villnave, Erica Pelton, illus. see Wallingford, Stephanie & Rynders, Dawn.
Villnerve, Janice C. Mama Cat's Adventures in Child Training Presents No Whining! (p. 1084)
Villoldo, Alberto. Skeleton Woman. (p. 1584)
Villoldo, Alberto, jt. auth. see Jendresen, Erik.
Villoro, Carmen & Perez, Federico. Amarina y el Viejo Pesadilla y Otros Cuentos. (p. 52)
Villoro, Juan. Profesor Ziper y la Fabulosa Guitarra Electrica. El Fisgsn, illus. (p. 1409)
Vilma Muises, ed. see Marcamo, Thais.
Vilsaint, Fequiere. Children Songs from Haiti: Chante Timoun Ayiti. (p. 303)
—Jokes, Riddles & Proverbs: In Haitian Creole. (p. 924)
—Map Skills Bilingual English, Haitian Creole: Ladres nan Jeyografi. (p. 1090)
—Writing about the History of Haiti. (p. 1964)
Vilsaint, Fequiere, ed. see Heurtelou, Maude.
Vilsaint, Fequiere, ed. see Paul, Cauvin.
Vilsaint, Henock. Math Pack Bilingual English, Haitian Creole: PakMat. (p. 1106)
Vimislik, Matthew, illus. see Bean, Raymond.
Vin, Lee. Crazy Love Story (p. 377)
—Crazy Love Story. (p. 377)
—One (p. 1293)
—One Vin, Lee, illus. (p. 1293)
Vin, Lee, creator. One (p. 1293)
Viñals, Noemi, illus. see Alkonada, Jesus Muñoz.
Vinberger, Naftali Yehiel ben Shelomoh Avraham, et al. Story of Rebbetzin Kanievsky: A Biography for Young Readers. (p. 1659)
Vince Crandall, Vince. Village Baker. (p. 1842)
Vince, Dawn, illus. see Langford, Jane.
Vince, Dawn, illus. see McAllister, Margaret.
Vince, Paula. Picking up the Pieces. (p. 1354)
Vincent, Allison, illus. see Cuthbert, R M.
Vincent, Andrew M., illus. see Fox, Frances Margaret.
Vincent, Annick & Guerard, Mathieu. My Brain Needs Glasses: Living with Hyperactivity. (p. 1199)
Vincent, Benjamin, illus. see Abercrombie, Josephine.
Vincent, Benjamin, illus. see Agarwal, Nikita & Agarwal, Chitra.
Vincent, Benjamin, illus. see Casad, Mary Brooke & Brooke Casad, Mary.
Vincent, Benjamin, illus. see Casad, Mary Brooke.
Vincent, Benjamin, illus. see Speregen, Devra Newberger & Running Press Staff.
Vincent, Beverly & Greenberger, Robert. Frequently Asked Questions about Birth Control. (p. 636)
Vincent, Cindy. Mystery of the Missing Ming: A Daisy Diamond Detective Novel. (p. 1225)
Vincent, Eric. Aesop's Fables. (p. 25)
Vincent, Eric, illus. see Wells, H. G., et al.
Vincent, Erin. Grief Girl. (p. 724)
Vincent, Harris T. & Brewer, Mary. When Grandmother Was A Little Girl. (p. 1902)
Vincent, Jenny & Laird, Elizabeth. Where's Toto?/Ou est Toto? Bougard, Marie-Terese, tr. (p. 1911)
Vincent, Jim. Wizzikids! (p. 1943)
Vincent, Karen. Robbie Learns a Lesson on Truth. (p. 1478)
Vincent, Lynn, jt. auth. see Burpo, Todd.
Vincent, Mary. Cultural Atlas of Spain & Portugal. (p. 391)
Vincent, Monica-Marie. Roses are Red...Violet Is Dead. (p. 1489)
Vincent, Patti. Village Heroes Meet the Dragon. (p. 1842)
Vincent, Rachel. Flame Never Dies. (p. 602)
—My Soul to Save. (p. 1219)
—My Soul to Steal. (p. 1219)
—My Soul to Take. (p. 1219)
—Soul Screamers: If I Die; Never to Sleep; Before I Wake Vol. 3 (p. 1614)
—Soul Screamers Volume Two: My Soul to Keep My Soul to Steal Reaper. (p. 1614)
—Stars Never Rise. (p. 1643)
—With All My Soul. (p. 1942)
Vincent, Seth, jt. auth. see Daniels, Susan.
Vincent, Victoria. City of Kind Words: A Story by Tory. (p. 324)
Vincent, Zu. Catherine the Great: Empress of Russia. (p. 280)
—Lucky Place. (p. 1063)
Vincenti, Antonio, illus. see Vecchini, Silvia & Daughters of St. Paul Staff.
Vincenti, Antonio, illus. see Vecchini, Silvia.
Vincenti, Catherine, ed. Pet Pals Grades 3-4: A Spanish-English Workbook. (p. 1345)
—Pet Pals Grades 5-6: A Spanish-English Workbook. (p. 1345)
—Pet Pals Grades K-2: A Spanish-English Workbook. (p. 1345)
Vincent-Whitmer, Tara. My Momma's Heartbeat: The Loving Rhythm of Adoption. (p. 1214)
Vincenza. My Name Is Mollie. (p. 1215)
Vincenzi, Penny. Dilemma. (p. 440)
Vincer, Carole, illus. see Watson, Mary Gordon.
Vincer, Carole, illus. see Webber, Toni.
Vinci, Daniela V. Hi, My Name Is Daniela & I Want to Be a Great Woman: How I Found Me. (p. 775)
Vinci, Leonardo da, see da Vinci, Leonardo.
Vincolisi, Marnie. House Who Found Its Home. Clarke, Benjamin S., illus. (p. 804)
Vinden, David, jt. auth. see Rowsell, Cyrilla.
Vine, Deryth. Fiskers Meets Santa Claus. (p. 599)
Vine, Joshua M. Gnomey & Froggie. (p. 685)
Vine, Rachel Shana, illus. see Sherman, Paulette Kouffman.
Vinent, Julia, tr. see Dufresne, Didier, et al.
Viner, Callie Lee. Pebbles Loves Counting. Viner, Callie Lee, photos by. (p. 1333)
Vines, Audrey. Miranda. (p. 1149)
Vines, Connie. Murmullo Sobre el Agua. Perez, Laura C., tr. (p. 1192)
Viney, Brigit & Pearson Education Staff. Kim's Choice. (p. 957)
Viney, Peter. Case of the Dead Batsman. (p. 274)
—Casualty! (p. 277)

—Collector. (p. 340)
—Space Romance. (p. 1619)
—Strawberry & the Sensations. (p. 1666)
—Sunnyvista City. (p. 1677)
—Tidy Ghost. (p. 1747)
—Underground. (p. 1814)
Vineyard Church of Columbus. Great Big Holy Bible: Fall Quarter, Year One. Campbell, Karen, illus. (p. 714)
—Little Son Catchers Leader's Guide: Pre-school curriculum Fall Quarter, Year One. (p. 1036)
Vinge, Vernor. Peace War. (p. 1332)
Vining, Alex, illus. see Potter, Beatrix.
Vining, Diana. Flower Friends Paper Dolls. (p. 607)
Vining, Kathryn. You've Been Touched by the F. O. G. (Fingerprints of God) (p. 1982)
Vinopol, Corinne. Con-SIGN-tration 3: Computer Software Game in American Sign Language. (p. 355)
—Con-SIGN-tration 4: Computer Software Game in American Sign Language. (p. 355)
—Spell Well: CD-ROM American Sign Language Spelling Game. (p. 1625)
Vinopol, Corinne & Bednarczyk, Angela. American Sign Language Clip & Create: Clip Art Software. (p. 63)
—ASL Tales & Games for Kids - Biscuit Blvd: Computer Software in American Sign Language. (p. 106)
Vinopol, Corinne K. American Sign Language Clip & Create 2. (p. 63)
Vinopoll, Dianne. Poco uno & the Magical Kingdom. (p. 1375)
Vinos, Maria, tr. see Burks, Brian.
Vinsh, Aara J. Ben, the Miracle Horse (p. 163)
—Playtime Adventures. Leijs, Tommie, illus. (p. 1373)
Vinson, Haley. Horizons Set 2 Shea, Steve, ed. (p. 798)
Viola, Herman, jt. auth. see Crow, Joseph Medicine.
Viola, Herman, jt. auth. see Lekuton, Joseph Lemasolai.
Viola, Herman J. & Layson, Annelex Hofstra. Lost Childhood: My Life in a Japanese Prison Camp During World War II. (p. 1055)
Viola, Karen. Good Night Sun, Hello Moon. Chung, Chi, illus. (p. 700)
Violeta, Monreal, jt. auth. see Monreal, Violeta.
Violi, Daniela, illus. see Arciniegas, Triunfo.
Violi, Daniela, illus. see Horvath, Polly.
Violo, Linda. Don't Talka Me! (p. 468)
Viorst, Judith. Alexander & the Terrible, Horrible, No Good, Very Bad Day: Lap Edition. Cruz, Ray, illus. (p. 36)
—Alexander & the Terrible, Horrible, No Good, Very Bad Day. Cruz, Ray, illus. (p. 36)
—Alexander, Who's Not (Do You Hear Me? I Mean It!) Going to Move. Glasser, Robin Preiss, illus. (p. 37)
—Alexander, Who's Trying His Best to Be the Best Boy Ever. (p. 37)
—And Two Boys Booed. Blackall, Sophie, illus. (p. 71)
—Earrings! (p. 494)
—Earrings! Malone, Nola Langner, illus. (p. 494)
—Just in Case. Bluthenthal, Diana Cain, illus. (p. 938)
—Lulu & the Brontosaurus. (p. 1064)
—Lulu & the Brontosaurus. Smith, Lane, illus. (p. 1064)
—Lulu Walks the Dogs. (p. 1065)
—Lulu Walks the Dogs. Smith, Lane, illus. (p. 1065)
—Lulu's Mysterious Mission. Smith, Lane, illus. (p. 1065)
—Super-Completely & Totally the Messiest. Glasser, Robin Preiss, illus. (p. 1679)
Vipah Interactive, illus. see Rey, Margret.
Vipah Interactive Staff, illus. see Rey, Margret & Rey, H. A.
Vipont, Elfrida. Lark in the Morn. Freeman, T. R., illus. (p. 975)
—Lark on the Wing. Freeman, T. R., illus. (p. 975)
Virant, Janice. T-Bone the Flying Horse. (p. 1693)
Viray, Sherwin, illus. see Lee, Laura.
Virden, Carole, jt. auth. see Kinder, Connie.
Virden, William & Borg, Mary. My Colorado Teacher Guide. (p. 1200)
Virges, Audrey M. Day in Kindergarten. (p. 413)
Virgil. Eneida. (p. 527)
—Vergil's Aeneid: Books I-VI. (p. 1837)
Virgillo, Carmelo, et al. Aproximaciones al Estudio de la Literatura Hispánica. (p. 93)
Virginia H. Lasher. Secret of Crooked Creek. (p. 1542)
Virgo, Seán. Shadow Mother. Pérez, Javier Serrano, illus. (p. 1557)
Virján, Emma J. What This Story Needs Is a Pig in a Wig. Virján, Emma J., illus. (p. 1894)
Virr, Paul. Dragon Tattoo Book: With 24 Fabulous Temporary Tattoos! Mitchell, Joanne & Hurst, Ceri, illus. (p. 478)
—Fashion & Friendship Tattoo Book: With 24 Stylish Play Tattoos to Wear & Share! Mitchell, Joanne & Hurst, Ceri, illus. (p. 575)
Virtue, Doreen. Thank You, Angels! Keeler, Patricia, illus. (p. 1725)
Virtue, Queen Petals De. Princess & the Rain. (p. 1403)
Virzi, Frank. Hidden Animals Alphabet Sudoku for Kids: Ages 9-99. (p. 775)
Vis, Gracy & Vis, Nancy. Guide to College in Canada for American Students, 2007-2008. (p. 730)
Vis, Jan & Boyds Mills Press Staff. For You. (p. 616)
Vis, Leendert Jan & Boyds Mills Press Staff. For You. (p. 616)
Vis, Nancy, jt. auth. see Vis, Gracy.
Visaya, Artemio, illus. see Schliewen, Richard.
Visca, Curt. How to Draw Cartoon Careers. (p. 817)
—How to Draw Cartoon Fish. (p. 817)
—How to Draw Cartoon Holiday Symbols. (p. 817)
—How to Draw Cartoon Spacecraft & Astronauts in Action. (p. 817)
—How to Draw Cartoon Symbols of the United States. (p. 817)
—How to Draw Cartoon Symbols of the Wild West. (p. 817)
Visca, Curt, jt. auth. see Visca, Kelley.
Visca, Curt & Visca, Kelley. How to Draw Cartoon Careers. (p. 817)
—How to Draw Cartoon Crustaceans. (p. 817)
—How to Draw Cartoon Holiday Symbols. (p. 817)
—How to Draw Cartoon Spacecraft & Astronauts in Action. (p. 817)
—How to Draw Cartoon Symbols of the United States. (p. 817)
—How to Draw Cartoon Symbols of the Wild West. (p. 817)
Visca, Kelley, jt. auth. see Visca, Curt.
Visca, Kelley & Visca, Curt. How to Draw Cartoon Birds. (p. 817)
Visca, Kelly. How to Draw Cartoon Birds. (p. 817)
—How to Draw Cartoon Crustaceans. (p. 817)
—How to Draw Cartoon Fish. (p. 817)
—How to Draw Cartoon Rodents. (p. 817)
Viscardi, Chris, jt. auth. see McRobb, Will.
Viscardi, Dolly. All Around Cats Brooks, David, illus. (p. 43)
Vischer, Frans. Fuddles. Vischer, Frans, illus. (p. 646)
—Very Fuddles Christmas. Vischer, Frans, illus. (p. 1838)
Vischer, Lisa. Three Pirates & You! (p. 1743)
Vischer, Phil. God Is Bigger Than the Boogie Man. Pulley, Kelly & Reed, Lisa, illus. (p. 689)
Visco, Tamara, illus. see Yao, Tao-chung & McGinnis, Scott.
Visconti, Guido. Clare & Francis. Landmann, Bimba, illus. (p. 326)
—One Night in a Stable. Cimatoribus, Alessandra, illus. (p. 1296)
—Wolf on a Leash. Vignoli, Daniella, illus. (p. 1944)
Viselman, Kenn. I Love You Bunches. (p. 843)
—Li'l Pet Hospital: The Great Race. (p. 1017)
—Surprise. (p. 1685)
Vishpriya. Tales from Indi: Character Counts! RESPECT. Ruble, Eugene, illus. (p. 1701)
Visibooks. Word 2002 for Visual Learners. (p. 1950)
Vision, David. Who's That Crying! Alcantara, Ignacio, illus. (p. 1921)
Vision, David, jt. auth. see Vision, Mutiya.
Vision, David & Vision, Mutiya. What Makes Me Beautiful? ¿Qué Es lo Que Me Hace Hermoso? (p. 1892)
Vision, David & Vision, Mutiya Sahar. Daddy Loves His Baby Girl. Vision, Mutiya Sahar, illus. (p. 398)
—If Only I Could! Alcantara, Ignacio, illus. (p. 853)
—Missing You. Alcantara, Ignacio, illus. (p. 1153)
—What Makes Me Beautiful? Alcantara, Ignacio, illus. (p. 1892)
Vision, David, et al. My Very Breast Friend. Alcantara, Ignacio, illus. (p. 1221)
Vision, Mutiya, jt. auth. see Vision, David.
Vision, Mutiya & Vision, David. Land of Expression. Alcantara, Ignacio, illus. (p. 973)
—My Choices Make Me Who I Am. Alcantara, Ignacio, illus. (p. 1200)
Vision, Mutiya Sahar. Disabilities. Alcantara, Ignacio, illus. (p. 446)
Vision, Mutiya Sahar, jt. auth. see Vision, David.
Visscher, Marjoke, jt. auth. see Bersma, Danielle.
Visser, Joan. Angel Messages: Stories of Inspiration & Healing for Children. (p. 73)
Visser, Rino, illus. see van Rijswijk, Cor.
Visto, Joy. How Much Is Infinity? (p. 811)
—What Are the Chances? (p. 1880)
—When Does a Line Become a Shape? (p. 1902)
—Where Does a Graph Go? (p. 1907)
—Whose Foot Is a Foot? (p. 1921)
—Why Do Math with Letters? (p. 1923)
Viswanath, Shobha. Elephant in My Backyard. Jawa, Sadhvi, illus. (p. 511)
—When the Earth Lost Its Shapes. Kastl, Christine, illus. (p. 1904)
—Whose Lovely Child Can You Be? Tappin, Christine, illus. (p. 1921)
Vita. Head in the Clouds. (p. 756)
Vita, Ariela, illus. see Kay, Sjoukje & Kay, Sjoukje.
Vitale, Ann. Drug Therapy & Sexual Disorders. (p. 487)
—Manager. Riggs, Ernestine G. & Gholar, Cheryl, eds. (p. 1086)
—Sexual Disorders. McDonnell, Mary Ann & Esherick, Donald, eds. (p. 1556)
Vitale, Ann E. Drug Therapy & Sexual Disorders. (p. 487)
—Regional Folklore. (p. 1457)
Vitale, Jill. Freddie: The Free-Range Chicken. (p. 632)
—Freddie the Free-Range Chicken. (p. 632)
Vitale, Mary Ann. Water Lily Fairy. (p. 1863)
Vitale, Raoul, illus. see Brand, Ruth R.
Vitale, Raoul, illus. see Coatsworth, Elizabeth.
Vitale, Raoul, illus. see Rodda, Emily.
Vitale, Raoul & Tank, Daniel. Adam & Eve. (p. 11)
Vitale, Samantha. Wasted Time. (p. 1860)
Vitale, Stefano, illus. see Franco, Betsy.
Vitale, Stefano, illus. see Sloat, Teri.
Vitale, Stefano, illus. see Walker, Alice.
Vitali, Daniela. Play with My Animals ABCs. (p. 1371)
Vitaliev, Vitali. Granny Yaga. (p. 710)
Vitek, John, ed. see John Paul II, pseud.
Vitello, Kathy, jt. auth. see Fey, Sid.
Vitello, Suzy. Moment Before. (p. 1161)
Vitez, Imre, et al. Our Favorite Time of the Year. (p. 1308)
Vitsky, Sally, illus. see Schwaeber, Barbie Heit.
Vitsky, Sally, illus. see Schwaeber, Barbie.
Vitt, Dale H., et al. Mosses Lichens & Ferns of Northwest North America. (p. 1177)
Vitt, Karren, illus. see Kerr, Mike.
Vittachi, Nury & Ros, Laura, contrib. by. Thomas Beckham Wang & Other Stories. (p. 1738)
Vitterito, Joseph A., 2nd. My Sister Is a Preemie: A Children's Guide to the NICU Experience. Chuzzlewit, Abraham R., illus. (p. 1218)
Vitti, Alessandro. Secret Warriors: Wheels Within Wheels. (p. 1544)
Vittorini, Candace & Boyer-Quick, Sara. Joey Goes to the Dentist. (p. 920)
Vitzthum, Virginia. I Love You, Let's Meet: Adventures in Online Dating. (p. 843)
Viva, Frank. Along a Long Road. (p. 48)
—Long Way Away. (p. 1047)
—Outstanding in the Rain. (p. 1313)
—Trip to the Bottom of the World with Mouse. (p. 1787)
—Young Frank, Architect. (p. 1978)
Vivanco, Kelly, illus. see Andersen, Hans Christian.
Vivanco, Kelly, illus. see Brothers Grimm.
Vivas, Julie. Nativity. (p. 1235)
Vivas, Julie, illus. see Fox, Mem.
Vivas, Julie, illus. see Manos, Helen.
Vivas, Julie, illus. see Wild, Margaret.
Vivas, Julie, illus. see Williams, Sue.
Viverito, Philip J. & Flemins, Allan D. Classical Hack Scenarios Macedonia. (p. 328)
Vivès, Bastien, et al. Royal Cup. (p. 1492)
Vivian, Bart. Imagine. Vivian, Bart, illus. (p. 860)
Vivian Levinge, Suzanne, jt. auth. see Corley.
Vivian, Mary Lee & Thomas, Margaret. Algebra, Grades 5-8. (p. 38)
—Pre-Algebra, Grades 5-8. (p. 1394)
Vivian May Edwards. Creation's Praise: For little Ones. (p. 379)
Vivian, Siobhan. List. (p. 1022)
—Little Friendly Advice. (p. 1028)
—Not That Kind of Girl. (p. 1267)
—Same Difference. (p. 1507)
Vivian, Siobhan, illus. see Chronicle Books Staff.
Vivian, Siobhan, jt. auth. see Han, Jenny.
Viviani, Luisa. There Is Something Special Inside of Me. (p. 1730)
Vivinetto, Gina. Batman: With Superman & Wonder Woman. Farley, Rick & Tripp, Kanila, illus. (p. 144)
Viz Media. Adventures Away. (p. 15)
—Fairy Dreams. (p. 563)
—Time for Magic. (p. 1751)
VIZ Media, jt. auth. see Viz Media Staff.
VIZ Media, . & Straffi, Iginio. Winx Club. (p. 1939)
—WINX Club, Vol. 7. (p. 1939)
Viz Media Staff. Bloom's Discovery Vol. 1. (p. 201)
VIZ Media Staff. Complete Pokémon (p. 353)
—Complete Pokémon Pocket Guide Jungle Factor Staff, illus. (p. 353)
—Mameshiba: How to Be the Best Friend Ever. (p. 1084)
—Mameshiba Love Winter. Flintham, Thomas, illus. (p. 1084)
Viz Media Staff. Meet Mameshiba! (p. 1121)
—Secrets of Alfea Vol. 2. (p. 1545)
VIZ Media Staff. WINX Club, Vol. 1. (p. 1939)
—WINX Club, Vol. 3. (p. 1939)
Viz Media Staff & Mizobuchi, Makoto. Ranger & the Temple of the Sea. Mizobuchi, Makoto, illus. (p. 1438)
Viz Media Staff & Smith, Brian. Parasites. Wijngaard, Jan, illus. (p. 1324)
VIZ Media Staff & Straffi, Iginio. WINX Club, Vol. 5. (p. 1939)
VIZ Media Staff & Straffi, Iginio. WINX Club, Vol. 2. (p. 1939)
—WINX Club, Vol. 4. (p. 1939)
—WINX Club, Vol. 6. (p. 1939)
Viz Media Staff & Takamisaki, Ryo. Rise of Darkrai. Takamisaki, Ryo, illus. (p. 1474)
Viz Media Staff & VIZ Media. Year's Best Articles 2003. (p. 1969)
Viza, Monserrat & Lavarello, Jose Mo. Viajo En: Viajo en Barco (I Travel by Boat) (p. 1839)
Viza, Monserrat & Rius, Maria. Cuatro Partes del Dia: La Noche (Night) (p. 388)
—Cuatro Partes del Dia: La Manana (Morning) (p. 388)
—Cuatro Partes del Dia: La Tarde (Afternoon) (p. 388)
—Cuatro Partes del Dia: El Anochecer (Evening) (p. 388)
Viza, Monserrat & Rovira, Francesc. Viajo En: Viajo en Carro (I Travel by Car) (p. 1839)
—Viajo En: Viajo en Tren (I Travel by Train) (p. 1839)
—Viajo En: Viajo en Avion (I Travel by Plane) (p. 1839)
Vize, Bonnie. Mystery of the Park Pavilion. (p. 1226)
Vize, Dania. Fruity Fun. (p. 646)
—High Chair Buddy Silly Snacks. (p. 777)
—Lift, Stick & Learn Baby Animals. (p. 1014)
—My Dress up Book. (p. 1202)
—My Princess Dress up Storybook. (p. 1217)
Vizi, Henry. 21st Century American Bible. (p. 1996)
—God & Satan Are Aliens! (p. 688)
Vizoso Veiga, Xoán Antón. READING LESSON: Adventures of Huckleberry Finn. (p. 1446)
Vizquel, Omar & Dyer, Bob. Omar! My Life on & off the Field. (p. 1288)
Vizzi, Maria. Morely: The Mouse in the Bakery. (p. 1175)
Vizzini, Med. Be More Chill. (p. 148)
Vizzini, Ned. Be More Chill. (p. 148)
—It's Kind of a Funny Story. (p. 897)
—Other Normals. (p. 1306)
—Teen Angst? Naaah... A Quasi-Autobiography. (p. 1713)
—Teen Angst? Naaah... A Quasi-Autobiography. Schons, Chris, illus. (p. 1713)
Vizzini, Ned, jt. auth. see Columbus, Chris.
Vlahakis, Andrea. Christmas Eve Blizzard Schongut, Emanuel, illus. (p. 313)
Vlahov, Edward. Fighting the Man. (p. 586)
Vlahutin, Peter, jt. auth. see Gallagher, Heather Marie.
Vlashka, Vania. Versaggi Brothers: Indigo Children are Here. (p. 1837)
VN Industries, Inc. Editorial Staff, ed. 5 Angels - A Jigsaw Puzzle Book: With Inspirational Messages from the Bible. (p. 1992)
Vo, Dzung X. Mindful Teen: Powerful Skills to Help You Handle Stress One Moment at a Time. (p. 1145)
Voake, Charlotte. Johann Sebastian Bach. (p. 920)
—Little Guide to Wild Flowers. (p. 1028)
—Melissa's Octopus & Other Unsuitable Pets. Voake, Charlotte, illus. (p. 1125)
—Tweedle Dee Dee. Voake, Charlotte, illus. (p. 1799)
Voake, Charlotte, illus. see Babin, Pierre.
Voake, Charlotte, illus. see Baumont, Olivier.
Voake, Charlotte, illus. see Du Bouchet, Paule & Khoury, Marielle D.
Voake, Charlotte, illus. see Du Bouchet, Paule.
Voake, Charlotte, illus. see French, Vivian.
Voake, Charlotte, illus. see Khoury, Marielle D. & du Bouchet, Paule.
Voake, Charlotte, illus. see Ollivier, Stephane.
Voake, Charlotte, illus. see Voake, Steve.
Voake, Charlotte, illus. see Walcker, Yann.
Voake, Charlotte, illus. see Weill, Catherine.
Voake, Charlotte, illus. see Zolotow, Charlotte.
Voake, Charlotte, et al. Little Guide to Trees. (p. 1028)
Voake, Steve. Daisy Dawson & the Big Freeze. Meserve, Jessica, illus. (p. 400)
—Daisy Dawson & the Secret Pond. Meserve, Jessica, illus. (p. 400)
—Daisy Dawson at the Beach. Meserve, Jessica, illus. (p. 400)
—Daisy Dawson Is on Her Way! Meserve, Jessica, illus. (p. 400)
—Daisy Dawson on the Farm. Meserve, Jessica, illus. (p. 400)
—Hooey Higgins & the Shark. Dodson, Emma, illus. (p. 795)
—Hooey Higgins & the Tremendous Trousers. Dodson, Emma, illus. (p. 795)
—Insect Detective. (p. 875)
—Insect Detective. Voake, Charlotte, illus. (p. 875)
Voboril, Evan T. Poems about the Natural World (p. 1376)
Vodicka-Paredes, Lenka & Curte, Asia. Forest Fairy Crafts: Enchanting Fairies & Felt Friends from Simple Supplies. (p. 618)
Vo-Dinh, Mai, illus. see Tran, Kim-Lan & Millar, Louise.
VOE. Tale of Two Kitty's: The Secret World of Kitty Cats. (p. 1700)
Voege, Debra, jt. auth. see Herman, Gail.
Voege, Debra, jt. auth. see Prokos, Anna.
Voege, Debra, jt. auth. see Ruscoe, Michael.
Voege, Debra, jt. auth. see Science.
Voege, Debra & Science Applications, Inc Staff. Science in the Real World Set, 10-Volumes. (p. 1526)
Voegeli, Deanna. Grieving for Grandma: Singh Hai Purrrrrs His Support. (p. 724)
Voelkel, Jon & Voelkel, Pamela. Middleworld. (p. 1138)
Voelkel, Pamela, jt. auth. see Voelkel, Jon.
Voerg, Kathy, illus. see Jett, Cindy.
Voerg, Kathy, illus. see Martin, Don, et al.
Voerg, Kathy, illus. see Pando, Nancy J.
Voerg, Kathy, illus. see Smith-Mansell, Dana.
Voet. Instructor's Cd-Rom to Accompany Biochemistry, Thi Rd Edition. (p. 878)
—Molecular Movies Cd to Accompany Biochemistry. (p. 1160)
Vogel, Cara Lynn. Lottie & Annie Upside-down Book. Adkins, Loretta B., illus. (p. 1057)
Vogel, Carole G. Dangerous Crossings. (p. 404)
—Human Impact. (p. 826)
—Savage Waters. (p. 1516)
—Shifting Shores. (p. 1566)
—Underwater Exploration. (p. 1817)
Vogel, Carole Garbuny. Savage Waters. (p. 1516)
—Underwater Exploration. (p. 1817)
Vogel, Carole Garbuny & Leshem, Yossi. Man Who Flies with Birds. (p. 1086)
Vogel, Elizabeth. Al Agua Patos. (p. 32)
—Big Cats (p. 180)
—Cheetahs. (p. 296)
—Comer Sanamente! (p. 348)
—Conflict Resolution Library: Set 4: Facing Changes (p. 357)
—Cuidado de Tu Cabello. (p. 390)
—Eating Right. (p. 501)
—Hacer Ejercicio! (p. 735)
—Jaguars. (p. 905)
—Lavarse Las Manos! (p. 980)
—Lavarse Los Dientes! (p. 981)
—Leopards. (p. 993)
—Let's Exercise / ¡A hacer Ejercicio! (p. 996)
—Let's Exercise = a Hacer Ejercicio. (p. 996)
—Lions. (p. 1021)
—Meet My Teacher. (p. 1121)
—Meet the Cafeteria Workers. (p. 1122)
—Meet the Librarian. (p. 1123)
—Meet the Principal. (p. 1123)
—Meet the School Nurse. (p. 1123)
—My School (p. 1218)
—Pumas. (p. 1416)
—Taking Care of My Hair: El Cuidado de Tu Cabello. (p. 1698)
—Taking Care of My Hair. (p. 1698)
—Taking Care of My Hair / ¡el cuidado de Tu Cabello! (p. 1698)
—Taking My Bath: Al Agua Patos. (p. 1698)
—Taking My Bath. (p. 1698)
—Taking My Bath / ¡Al agua Patos! (p. 1698)
—Tigers. (p. 1749)
—¡A comer sanamente! (Eating Right) (p. 1)
—¡A hacer ejercicio! (Let's Exercise) (p. 1)
—¡A lavarse las manos! (Washing My Hands) (p. 1)
—¡A lavarse los dientes! (Brushing My Teeth) (p. 1)
—¡Al agua patos! (Taking My Bath) (p. 32)
—¡el cuidado de tu cabello! (Taking Care of My Hair) (p. 507)
Vogel, Jane & Sytsma, Mary. Questions Worth Asking: A Study of the Heidelberg Catechism, Year 2. (p. 1426)
Vogel, Jennifer. Library Story: Building a New Central Library. (p. 1006)
Vogel, Julia. Are You My Fish? Williams, Matthew, illus. (p. 97)
—Are You My Rabbit? Williams, Matthew, illus. (p. 97)
—Bats. Recher, Andrew, illus. (p. 144)
—City Food Chains. Adams, Hazel, illus. (p. 323)
—Coyotes. Recher, Andrew, illus. (p. 375)
—Crescents. Holm, Sharon, illus. (p. 381)
—Deciduous Forest Food Chains. Adams, Hazel, illus. (p. 421)
—Desert Food Chains. Adams, Hazel, illus. (p. 429)
—Discover Air. Yamada, Jane, illus. (p. 447)
—Discover Electricity. Yamada, Jane, illus. (p. 447)
—Discover Energy. Yamada, Jane, illus. (p. 447)
—Discover Magnets. Yamada, Jane, illus. (p. 447)
—Measuring Length. Marten, Luanne, illus. (p. 1117)
—Measuring Temperature. Marten, Luanne, illus. (p. 1117)
—Measuring Time: the Calendar. Marten, Luanne, illus. (p. 1117)
—Measuring Time: the Clock. Marten, Luanne, illus. (p. 1117)
—Measuring Volume. Marten, Luanne, illus. (p. 1117)
—Measuring Weight. Marten, Luanne, illus. (p. 1117)
—Ovals. Holm, Sharon, illus. (p. 1313)
—Save the Planet: Local Farms & Sustainable Foods. (p. 1516)
—Solar Power. (p. 1606)
—Tigers: Built for the Hunt. (p. 1749)
—What Are Food Chains & Food Webs? Adams, Hazel, illus. (p. 1879)
—Wild Horses. (p. 1929)
—Your Sensational Sense of Hearing. Squier, Robert, illus. (p. 1981)
Vogel, Julia, jt. auth. see Vogel, Julie.
Vogel, Julie. Your Sensational Sense of Sight. Squier, Robert, illus. (p. 1981)

V

Vogel, Julie & Vogel, Julia. Your Sensational Sense of Smell. Squier, Robert, illus. (p. 1981)
Vogel, Kimberly. Sticks & Stones. (p. 1650)
Vogel, Leland G. Huffin & Puffin. (p. 824)
Vogel, Malvina G., ed. see Doyle, Arthur.
Vogel, Mark A. Adventures of Professor Poodle & Auggie: Let's Collect the Alphabet. (p. 22)
—This Fun Family Has Fun with Numbers. (p. 1735)
Vogel, Michelle. Three Twisted Tales. (p. 1744)
Vogel, Peter C. Mike Duffy & His Adventure Witht the World's Smallest Person. (p. 1141)
Vogel, Rob & Azarov, Max. Garry the Groundhog (p. 657)
Vogel, Sean. Celtic Run. (p. 286)
Vogel, Vin, illus. see Brandt, Lois.
Vogel, Vin, illus. see Weinstone, David.
Vogelaar, Alie. One Day at a Time, Margreet. VanBrugge, Jeanne, tr. from DUT. (p. 1294)
Vogel-Placides, Joan Katherine. Safe Place. Placides, Del S., illus. (p. 1502)
Voght, Victor A. Fun with Huff & Puff (p. 648)
Vogiel, Eva. Facing the Music. (p. 561)
Vogiel, Eva & Steinberg, Ruth. Light for Greytowers. (p. 1015)
Vogl, Mark. Confederate Night Before Christmas Ford, Stephanie, illus. (p. 356)
Vogl, Nancy, jt. auth. see Cole, Heidi.
Vogl, Nancy & Strange, David. Grandma Loves Her Harley Too. Gibson, Nichoel, illus. (p. 708)
Vogler, Sara, jt. auth. see Burchett, Jan.
Vogler, Sara, jt. auth. see Burchett, Janet.
Vogt, Denis, jt. auth. see Barrett, Audrey.
Vogt, Gregory. Atmosphere: Planetary Heat Engine. (p. 113)
—Biosphere: Realm of Life. (p. 190)
—Dwarf Planet Pluto. (p. 491)
—Hydrosphere: Agent of Change. (p. 831)
—Mercury. (p. 1127)
—Meteors & Comets. (p. 1130)
—Milky Way. (p. 1143)
—Pluto: A Dwarf Planet. (p. 1374)
—Solar System. (p. 1607)
—Stars. (p. 1643)
—Uranus. (p. 1825)
Vogt, Gregory & Waxman, Laura. Sun. (p. 1675)
Vogt, Gregory L. Constellations (p. 359)
—Landscapes of Mars: A Visual Tour (p. 974)
—Lithosphere: Earth's Crust. (p. 1023)
—Solar System (p. 1607)
Vogt, Janet. Music Brain Teasers. (p. 1193)
Vogt, Janet, jt. creator see Lorenz, Geoff.
Vogt, Peter. Career Wisdom for College Students: Insights You Won't Get in Class, on the Internet, or from Your Parents. (p. 267)
Vogt, Richard C. Rain Forests. (p. 1434)
Vohra, Sibi, illus. see Asbjornsen, Peter Christen.
Vohra, Subhash. Little Red Hen. (p. 1034)
Vohwinkel, Astrid, illus. see Holtei, Christa.
Voice, Jeff. Kirstie & the Hawaiian Sea Turtles. (p. 961)
Voight, Joseph. My Grandma Has Alzheimer's Too. (p. 1210)
Voight, Lisa, illus. see Drez, Jennifer & Bumstead, Robin.
Voigt, Brian Jeffrey. Guardian of the Zercons. (p. 728)
Voigt, Cynthia. Angus & Sadie. Leigh, Tom, illus. (p. 75)
—Book of Lost Things. Bruno, Iacopo, illus. (p. 211)
—Come a Stranger. (p. 347)
—Dicey's Song. (p. 435)
—Elske: A Novel of the Kingdom. Vermeer, Jan, illus. (p. 516)
—Izzy, Willy-Nilly. (p. 901)
—Jackaroo. (p. 903)
—Mister Max: the Book of Lost Things: Mister Max 1. Bruno, Iacopo, illus. (p. 1155)
—Mister Max: the Book of Secrets: Mister Max 2. Bruno, Iacopo, illus. (p. 1155)
—Mister Max: the Book of Secrets. Bruno, Iacopo, illus. (p. 1155)
—Orfe. (p. 1303)
—Rosie Stories. Smith, Cat Bowman, illus. (p. 1490)
—Runner. (p. 1497)
—Solitary Blue. (p. 1608)
—Sons from Afar. (p. 1613)
—Tale of Birle. (p. 1699)
—Tale of Elske. (p. 1699)
—Tale of Oriel. (p. 1700)
—The Book of Kings. Bruno, Iacopo, illus. (p. 1728)
—Tillerman Encuentran Hogar. (p. 1750)
—Young Fredle. Yates, Louise, illus. (p. 1978)
Voigt, Cynthia & Marcus, Barry David. Bad Girls in Love. (p. 131)
Voigt, David & Voigt, Grady. Socky, the Soft-Hearted Soccer Ball. Wagner, Steve, illus. (p. 1605)
Voigt, Grady, jt. auth. see Voigt, David.
Voigt, William. Common Denominator. (p. 349)
Voigts, Ron. Penelope & the Ghost's Treasure. (p. 1336)
Voigtsberger, Sandra A. Jack's Pockets. (p. 904)
Voiles, Alison. My Family Forest. Mikle, Toby, illus. (p. 1202)
Voisin, Mandy Madson. Star of Deliverance. (p. 1640)
Vojta, Pat Stemper. Mr. Groundhog Wants the Day Off/El Senor Marmota Quiere el Dia Libre. Leviskiy, Olga, illus. (p. 1185)
Vojtech, Anna, illus. see Alexander, Cecil Frances.
Vojtech, Anna, illus. see Mackall, Dandi Daley.
Vojtech, Anna, illus. see St. James, Rebecca.
Vojtech, Anna, illus. see Wadsworth, Olive A.
Vojtech, Anna, jt. auth. see Viau, Nancy.
Vokes, Neil, et al. From the Marvel Vault. (p. 644)
Vokey, Jessica. Chester the Easter Chicken. (p. 298)
Vol, Vera, ed. see AZ Books Staff.
Voland, Wanda. Ivan Icicle's Wedding. Giovannucci, Sharon, illus. (p. 900)
Volchko, Kristy Jo. Frogs Can Fly. (p. 641)
Voldseth, Beverly, ed. see Sullivan, R. J.
Volinski, Jessica, illus. see Tedesco, Ann & Alimonti, Frederick.
Volk, David, jt. auth. see Meierhenry, Mark V.
Volk, David, jt. auth. see Meierhenry, Mark.
Volk, Gretchen. Amazing Adventures of Tristy Ruth, Raisin Girl. (p. 52)
Volke, Gordon. Big Posh Yacht. Bowler, Colin, illus. (p. 183)
—Big World Activity Sticker Book (p. 184)
—Little Lost Whale. Bowler, Colin, illus. (p. 1031)
—Louis the Lifeboat Activity Sticker Book. Bowler, Colin, illus. (p. 1058)
—Nasty Black Stuff. Bowler, Colin, illus. (p. 1230)
—Old Grumpus & Other Stories. (p. 1284)
—Our Planet. (p. 1309)
—Pirate's Gold. Bowler, Colin, illus. (p. 1363)
—Spider for Tea & Other Stories. (p. 1626)
Volke, Gordon, jt. auth. see Popper, Garry.
Volke, Gordon & Book Company Staff. Disco Fish. (p. 447)
Volke, Gordon, et al. Panda Patrol Big Activity Book. (p. 1320)
—Panda Patrol Sticker, Story & Activity Book (p. 1320)
—Panda Patrol Sticker, Story & Activity Book. (p. 1320)
—Panda Patrol Travel Games with Stickers. (p. 1320)
Volker, Kerstin. Emma Goes Shopping. (p. 519)
—Henry Builds a Tree House. (p. 767)
—Lilly's Birthday Party. (p. 1017)
—Suzie Goes to Sleep. (p. 1688)
Volkman, John D. Collaborative Library Research Projects: Inquiry That Stimulates the Senses (p. 339)
Volkmer, Todd. Stacey Mcduver's House. (p. 1638)
Volkov, Alexander. Tales of Magic Land 1. (p. 1702)
Vollbracht, James. Mishan's Garden. Brooke, Janet, illus. (p. 1150)
Volley, Will, illus. see Shakespeare, William.
Vollmar, Rob. Inanna's Tears. MpMann, illus. (p. 868)
Vollmer, Cheryl. Hungry Lion in My Tummy. Dimitriadis, Nick, illus. (p. 828)
Vollmer, Chuck, illus. see McCorkle, Brent & Parker, Amy.
Vollmer, Howard R. Adventures of the Chipmunks Three. (p. 23)
Vollstedt, Maryana. Big Book of Easy Suppers: 270 Delicious Recipes for Casual Everyday Cooking. (p. 179)
—Big Book of Potluck. (p. 179)
Volovar, Vivian. Lobster Lady. (p. 1044)
Volp, Denise. Gregory the Greedy Duck. (p. 723)
Volpari, Daniela, illus. see Dickens, Charles.
Volpari, Daniela, jt. auth. see Premonville, Marie de.
Volpe, Karen. Get to Know Levers. (p. 668)
—Get to Know Pulleys. (p. 668)
Volpe, L. Carl. Battered Women. (p. 145)
Volpe, Theresa. All about Continents. (p. 42)
—King's Mapmaker. (p. 960)
Volpi, Sophia. White Fawn. (p. 1913)
Volponi, Paul. Black & White. (p. 195)
—Crossing Lines. (p. 385)
—Final Four. (p. 586)
—Game Seven. (p. 654)
—Hand You're Dealt. (p. 740)
—Homestretch. (p. 794)
—Hurricane Song. (p. 830)
—Response. (p. 1463)
—Rikers High. (p. 1472)
—Rooftop. (p. 1487)
—Rucker Park Setup. (p. 1494)
Volta, A. Patulous, the Different Caterpillar. (p. 1330)
Voltaggio, Nicholas, illus. see Hippocrene Books Staff.
Voltaggio, Nicholas, illus. see Martin, Robert, Jr.
Voltaire, Aurelio. Call of the Jersey Devil. (p. 254)
Voltz, Ralph, illus. see Holmes, Andy.
Voltz, Ralph, illus. see Perrenot, Christine.
Voltz, Ralph, jt. auth. see Holmes, Andy.
Volunteers of the Colorado Historical Society Staff, contrib. by. More Across Colorado. (p. 1174)
Volz, Carole A. Tiggy Finds a Home. Volz, Katie, illus. (p. 1749)
Volz, Katie, illus. see Volz, Carole A.
von Allmen, Tania, illus. see Weckworth, Rodney R.
Von Amelsfort, Barbara, illus. see Purperhart, Helen.
von Bassewitz, Gerdt. Peter & Anneli's Journey to the Moon. Baluschek, Hans, illus. (p. 1346)
Von Bergen, Ingri. Friend to Friend. (p. 637)
Von Bidder, Alex, jt. auth. see McGuirk, Leslie.
Von Bissing, R. Land of the Burning Gold. (p. 973)
Von Bissing, Ronimund. Tierra del Oro Ardiente. (p. 1748)
Von Borstel, Marc. Eleven: The Eleven Principal Dancers of Pacific Northwest Ballet. (p. 512)
von Botefuhr, Andrea & Russel, Angela. Land of Smaerd. (p. 973)
Von Buhler, Cynthia. But Who Will Bell the Cats? Von Buhler, Cynthia, illus. (p. 246)
von Buhler, Cynthia, illus. see Fradin, Dennis Brindell.
von Buhler, Cynthia, illus. see Rockwell, Anne F.
von Buhler, Cynthia, tr. see Fradin, Dennis Brindell.
Von Chamisso, Adelbert. Peter Schlemihl. Bowring, John, tr. (p. 1347)
Von, Cristina. Diego y el Monstruo. (p. 437)
von der Sterre, Johanna, illus. see Bader, Joanne.
Von Dornheim, Curt H. Children's Angel Clock. (p. 303)
—Little Baron's Christmas Angel. (p. 1023)
Von Eggers, J., et al. Times Tales Deluxe with Division: A Trigger Memory System. (p. 1754)
von Eggers, Jennie, et al, creators. Times Tales. (p. 1754)
Von Finn, Denny. 4x4 Trucks. (p. 1992)
—Abrams Tanks. (p. 7)
—AH-1W Super Cobras. (p. 30)
—Apache Helicopters. (p. 91)
—B-2 Stealth Bombers. (p. 122)
—Bullet Trains. (p. 240)
—Concept Cars. (p. 355)
—Drag Racing Motorcycles. (p. 476)
—F/A-18E/F Super Hornets. (p. 559)
—F-14 Tomcats. (p. 559)
—F-15 Eagles. (p. 559)
—F-16 Fighting Falcons. (p. 559)
—F-22 Raptors. (p. 559)
—F-35 Lightning IIs. (p. 559)
—Formula 1 Cars. (p. 620)
—Funny Cars. (p. 649)
—Humvees. (p. 827)
—Indy Cars. (p. 873)
—Jet Fighters. (p. 916)
—M109A6 Paladins. (p. 1067)
—M-ATVs. (p. 1067)
—Military Helicopters. (p. 1143)
—Muscle Cars. (p. 1192)
—Nimitz Aircraft Carriers. (p. 1256)
—Powerboats. (p. 1390)
—Predator Drones. (p. 1394)
—Racing Motorcycles. (p. 1432)
—Roller Coasters. (p. 1485)
—Snowmobiles. (p. 1601)
—Sports Cars. (p. 1632)
—Sprint Cars. (p. 1635)
—Stanley Hotel. (p. 1640)
—Stock Cars. (p. 1651)
—Super Cars. (p. 1679)
—Top Fuel Dragsters. (p. 1769)
—Torque: 4X4 Trucks. (p. 1770)
—Torque: Funny Cars. (p. 1770)
—Torque - Cool Rides (p. 1770)
—U-2 Planes. (p. 1805)
—UH-60 Black Hawks. (p. 1808)
Von Finn, Denny, jt. auth. see Alvarez, Carlos.
Von Finn, Denny, jt. auth. see McClellan, Ray.
Von Hagen, Victor Wolfgang. Incas: People of the Sun. (p. 868)
Von Harbou, Thea, jt. auth. see von Harbou, Thea.
von Harbou, Thea & Von Harbou, Thea. Metropolis. (p. 1130)
von Holleben, Jan & Helms, Antje. Does This Happen to Everyone? A Budding Adult's Guide to Puberty. (p. 460)
Von Kanel, Liz. Search for Cuddles & Jonathan's Dream. (p. 1537)
von Kessel, Carola. Understanding Horses with Caddie. Guhe, Irmtraud, illus. (p. 1815)
Von Kitzing, Constanze. Pearls of Wisdom. (p. 1333)
Von Klan, Stella and Laurene. Beauty & the Boy. (p. 154)
von Königslöw, Andrea Wayne. How Do You Read to a Rabbit? von Königslöw, Andrea Wayne, illus. (p. 808)
—Toilet Tales. von Königslöw, Andrea Wayne, illus. (p. 1762)
von Königslöw, Andrea Wayne, illus. see Parkinson, Curtis.
Von La Valette, Desiree, ed. Cool Shops New York. (p. 364)
Von Lahr, Christian, jt. auth. see Valentine, Christopher.
von Mackensen, Manfred, et al. Uprightness, Weight, & Balance: Human Biology in Grade Eight. Mitchell, David S., ed. (p. 1825)
Von Meck. My Name Is Vaselinetjie. (p. 1215)
Von Michaelis, Carol. Magpie Grows Up. (p. 1076)
von Mises, Ludwig. Planning for Freedom: Let the Market System Work - A Collection of Essays & Addresses. Greaves, Bettina Bien, ed. (p. 1368)
von Olfers, Sibylle. Mother Earth & Her Children: A Quilted Fairy Tale. Zipes, Jack, tr. from GER. (p. 1177)
—Story of the Snow Children (p. 1662)
von Rosenberg, Byron. Dale the Uniclyde: An adventure in Friendship. Parrott, Heather, illus. (p. 401)
—O Christmas Treed. (p. 1274)
Von Rosenburg, Marjorie. Artists Who Painted Texas. (p. 104)
Von Schiller, Friedrich. Maid of Orleans. (p. 1076)
Von Schlichten, David. H-E-Double Hockey Stick. (p. 734)
Von Schmid. Stolen Child. (p. 1652)
von Seeburg, Kate, ed. see Taylor, Paula.
Von Sneidern, Maja-Lisa, jt. auth. see Canfield, J. Douglas.
Von Wielligh, G. R. Animal Tales Bankenaar, Dale, illus. (p. 80)
von Ziegesar, Cecily, jt. auth. see Ziegesar, Cecily von.
Von Zumbusch, Amelie. Ancient Roman Culture. (p. 70)
—Ancient Roman Daily Life. (p. 70)
—Cheetahs: World's Fastest Cats. (p. 296)
von Zumbusch, Amelie. Cheetahs: World's Fastest Cats. (p. 296)
Von Zumbusch, Amelie. Cheetahs. (p. 296)
von Zumbusch, Amelie. Cheetahs. (p. 296)
—Cheetahs/Guepardos. (p. 296)
Von Zumbusch, Amelie. Cheetahs/Guepardos. Sanz, Pilar, tr. from ENG. (p. 296)
—Dangerous Cats (p. 404)
—Elephants. (p. 511)
von Zumbusch, Amelie. Elephants. (p. 511)
—Elephants/Elefantes. (p. 512)
Von Zumbusch, Amelie. Elephants/Elefantes. Sanz, Pilar, tr. (p. 512)
—Giraffes. (p. 677)
von Zumbusch, Amelie. Giraffes. (p. 677)
—Giraffes/Jirafas. (p. 678)
Von Zumbusch, Amelie. Giraffes/Jirafas. Sanz, Pilar, tr. from ENG. (p. 678)
—Hippos. (p. 781)
von Zumbusch, Amelie. Hippos. (p. 781)
Von Zumbusch, Amelie. Hippos/Hipopotamos. (p. 781)
von Zumbusch, Amelie. Hippos/Hipopótamos. (p. 781)
Von Zumbusch, Amelie. Jaguars: World's Strongest Cats. (p. 905)
von Zumbusch, Amelie. Jaguars: World's Strongest Cats. (p. 905)
Von Zumbusch, Amelie. Leopards: Silent Stalkers. (p. 993)
von Zumbusch, Amelie. Leopards: Silent Stalkers. (p. 993)
Von Zumbusch, Amelie. Lions: King of the Beasts. (p. 1021)
von Zumbusch, Amelie. Lions: King of the Beasts. (p. 1021)
Von Zumbusch, Amelie. Lions. (p. 1021)
von Zumbusch, Amelie. Lions. (p. 1021)
Von Zumbusch, Amelie. Lions/Leones. (p. 1021)
von Zumbusch, Amelie. Lions/Leones. (p. 1021)
—Pumas: Lone Hunters. (p. 1416)
Von Zumbusch, Amelie. Safari Animals (p. 1501)
—Tigers: World's Largest Cats. (p. 1749)
von Zumbusch, Amelie. Tigers: World's Largest Cats. (p. 1749)
—True Story of the American Flag. (p. 1793)
Von Zumbusch, Amelie. True Story of the Battle of Lexington & Concord. (p. 1793)
von Zumbusch, Amelie. True Story of the Battle of Lexington & Concord. (p. 1793)
Von Zumbusch, Amelie. True Story of the Salem Witch Hunts. (p. 1793)
von Zumbusch, Amelie. True Story of the Salem Witch Hunts. (p. 1793)
Von Zumbusch, Amelie. Zebras. (p. 1985)
von Zumbusch, Amelie. Zebras. (p. 1985)
Von Zumbusch, Amelie. Zebras/Cebras. (p. 1985)
von Zumbusch, Amelie. Zebras/Cebras. (p. 1985)
Von Zumbusch, Amelie, jt. auth. see Zumbusch, Amelie Von.
VonBokel, Jan, illus. see Fonner, Deborah K.
vonderLuft, Lydia, illus. see Gowing, Pattie.
Vong, Yumi. Aloha Sun. (p. 48)
Vongraprachanh, Somchith, illus. see Chrisp, Peter.
VonRecht, Ellie, illus. see Kay, Susan.
VonSeggen, Jon, illus. see Van Dyke, Jan.
VonSeggen, Liz. King's Commandments: Teaching Unit. (p. 960)
—Travel God's Way. Albright, Tawnya, illus. (p. 1780)
VonSeggen, Liz, jt. auth. see Liebenow, Todd.
Vonthron, Satanta C. Caillou's Community. Storch, Ellen N., illus. (p. 251)
—Caillou's Dinosaur Day. Neveu, Fred, illus. (p. 251)
—Caillou Visits the Farmer's Market. Meier, Kerry L., illus. (p. 252)
—Down at the Shore. Storch, Ellen N., illus. (p. 474)
—In the Kitchen. Storch, Ellen N., illus. (p. 866)
—Marsy's Perfect Eyesight. Teeple, Jackie, illus. (p. 1097)
Vonthron-Laver, Sarah, illus. see Mueller, Kirk Jay.
Voorhees, Coert. In Too Deep. (p. 868)
—Storm Wrangler. (p. 1656)
Voorhees, Don. Disgusting Things: A Miscellany. (p. 451)
Voorhees, Sue. I'm Your Very Own Flag. (p. 860)
Voorheis, Tracy. Nibbles... a strawberry Tale. Voorheis, Tracy, illus. (p. 1250)
Voorhoere, Anne G. & Voorhoeve, Anne C. My Family for the War. (p. 1202)
Voorhoeve, Anne C. My Family for the War. Reichel, Tammi, tr. from GER. (p. 1202)
Voorhoeve, Anne C., jt. auth. see Voorhoere, Anne G.
Voranin, Supissara, jt. auth. see Wastvedt, Bjorn.
Vorderman, Carol, jt. auth. see Dorling Kindersley Publishing Staff.
Vorella2000, illus. see Tate, Singleton M.
Voremberg, Linda. Robbie: A Journey of Hope (p. 1478)
Vorgan, Gigi, jt. auth. see Small, Gary.
Vorhees, D. Lawrey. Doorways of New Mexico. (p. 470)
Vorm, Dan, ed. see Keels, Steve.
Vorndran, Judith Clay. Mr. Bear Lives There. (p. 1184)
Vornholt, John. Troll Treasure. (p. 1788)
Voronina, Natasha, illus. see Buyske, Gail.
Vorster, Nicola. Monkeys' Wedding. (p. 1166)
Vos MacDonald, Joan. J. K. Rowling: Banned, Challenged, & Censored. (p. 901)
Vos, Sharon. Neddy the Nutty Acorn. Rosenfelder, Cheryl, illus. (p. 1239)
Vosailagi, Jo. Pentapus. (p. 1338)
Vosburg, L., illus. see Latham, Frank Brown.
Vosburg, M., illus. see Schauer, M.
Vosburg, Mike, jt. auth. see Stevenson, Robert Louis.
Vosburgh, Leonard, illus. see De Leeuw, Cateau.
Vosburgh, Leonard, illus. see Ford, Anne.
Vosburgh, Leonard, illus. see Lane, Frederick A.
Vosburgh, Leonard, illus. see Malkus, Alida Sims.
Vosburgh, Leonard, illus. see Webb, Robert N.
Vosjoli, Philippe De, see de Vosjoli, Philippe.
Vosk, Fred. Bikesters: An Adventure in Racing & Technology. (p. 185)
Voskamp, Sarah. Filly Girls: Chasing the Dream. (p. 586)
Voskoboinikov, Valery & Linnamagi, Anne. Icicle. (p. 851)
Vosloo, Isak. Kemeelsie Droom Groot. (p. 949)
—Rooster Lost His Crow: Vossie's Children Book Series. (p. 1488)
—Rooster Verloor Sy Kraai: 'Oom Vossie Vertel ...' Kinderboekreeks. (p. 1488)
Voss, Dawn. Avenging Aja. (p. 119)
Voss, Deanna. Secrets. (p. 1544)
Voss, Fonda. Bossy Girl. (p. 215)
Voss, Jonathan D., illus. see Walker, Sally M.
Voss, Judy, compiled by. Compasion y Alegria: Al fianl de la Vida. (p. 352)
Voss, Leann. Finance Matters! Exploring Your Assets & Securing Your Future. (p. 587)
Vossmeyer, Gabriele, jt. auth. see Fuller, Barbara.
Votaw, Carol. Waking up down Under. Banta, Susan, illus. (p. 1853)
Votaw, Carol J. Good Morning, Little Polar Bear. Banta, Susan, illus. (p. 698)
Vote, Steven, photos by see Shapiro, Ouisie.
Votruba, Erik C. Cowboy Mile. (p. 374)
Votry, Kim & Waller, Curt. Book of Colors. (p. 211)
—Out for a Walk. (p. 1310)
Voudrie, Krista. Sisters of Destiny. (p. 1581)
Voute, Kathleen, illus. see Biemiller, Carl L.
Voutila, Ritva, illus. see Hathorn, Libby.
Voutila, Ritva, illus. see Wild, Margaret.
Voyager, Beatrice Nambouy. Mama Minko: A Survival Quest. (p. 1084)
Voyer, Dorothy May. Henry Hedgehog's Holiday. (p. 768)
Voynick, Stephen M. Colorado Rockhounding: A Guide to Minerals, Gemstones, & Fossils. (p. 343)
—New Mexico Rockhounding: A Guide to Minerals, Gemstones, & Fossils. (p. 1246)
—Yogo: The Great American Sapphire. (p. 1972)
Voysest, Oswaldo, ed. see Cabello de Carbonera, Mercedes.
Voz, Samuel. Exploring the Great Basin. (p. 553)
Vrabel, Beth. Pack of Dorks. (p. 1317)
Vranich, Belisa & Eagleson, Holly. Boys Lie: How Not to Get Played. (p. 220)
Vrba, Christina. Good Night Connecticut. Rosen, Anne, illus. (p. 699)
Vrettos, Adrienne Maria. Burnout. (p. 244)
—Exile of Gigi Lane. (p. 548)
—Sight. (p. 1574)
—Skin. (p. 1585)
Vries, Anne De, see De Vries, Anne.

Vries, Cecile de, jt. auth. see Vries, Lizzette de.
Vries, Lizzette de & Vries, Cecile de. How the Tooth Mouse Met the Tooth Fairy. Suwannakit, Tul, illus. (p. 813)
Vries, Maggie De, see De Vries, Maggie.
Vroman, Dave, illus. see Irwin, Esther.
Vrombaut, An. Georgina the Giraffe. (p. 665)
—Henrietta the Hairy Hippo. Vrombaut, An, illus. (p. 767)
—Kevin the Crocodile. (p. 950)
—Zed the Zebra. Vrombaut, An, illus. (p. 1985)
Vroom, Angela. Airplane Letters to God. (p. 32)
Vrtis, Nikola, ed. D6 Adventure. Bridges, John et al, illus. (p. 398)
Vry, Silke. 13 Art Illusions Children Should Know. (p. 1994)
—Trick of the Eye: Art & Illusion. (p. 1786)
Vry, Silke & Klee, Paul. Paul Klee for Children. (p. 1330)
Vu, Thi, illus. see Johnson, Sandi.
Vuchic-Radovich, Sladjana, tr. see Lukic, Dragan.
Vue, Jeng Tong & Vue, See. Baby Chick & the Fox. (p. 125)
Vue, See, jt. auth. see Vue, Jeng Tong.
Vue, Tou, illus. see Brezenoff, Steve.
Vue, Tou, illus. see Dahl, Michael.
Vuillamy, Clara. Bear with Sticky Paws Won't Go to Bed. Vuillamy, Clara, illus. (p. 151)
Vujadinovic, Nenad. Ronny. Fur, Emil, illus. (p. 1487)
Vujovich, Dian. Grace, the Other Christmas Angel. (p. 705)
Vukelic, Deneen. Soaring - a Teen's Guide to Spirit & Spirituality. (p. 1603)
Vukelich, Carol, jt. ed. see Justice, Laura M.
Vulliamy, Claire. Bear with Sticky Paws. (p. 151)
Vulliamy, Clara. Bear with Sticky Paws Goes to School. Vulliamy, Clara, illus. (p. 151)
—Bedtime Cuddles. (p. 156)
—Martha Bunny Loves School. Vulliamy, Clara, illus. (p. 1097)
—Muffin & the Expedition. Vulliamy, Clara, illus. (p. 1189)
Vulliamy, Clara, illus. see Andreae, Giles.
Vulliamy, Clara, illus. see Hughes, Shirley.
Vulliamy, Clara, illus. see Mayhew, James.
V.V.A.A., et al. Enciclopedia "Me Pregunto Por Que" (p. 524)
Vyas, Bhavana, illus. see Padma, T. V.
Vyff, Shannon. 21st Century Kids. (p. 1996)
Vyn, Gerrit. Wildlife Photographer: The Coolest Jobs on the Planet (p. 1931)
Vyner, Tim, illus. see Stewart, Paul.
Vyvyan, Taylor. Beyond the Waterfall. (p. 174)
—Dragon's Odyssey. (p. 479)

W

W. Parents Are Lucky: They Don't Have to Do Chores. (p. 1324)
W., E., illus. see Leslie, Emma.
W, Farnsworth, illus. see Cussler, Clive.
W, J., illus. see Ward, J.
W, Maurice. No One Told Me I Could Be Presient. Samuels, Ryan, illus. (p. 1259)
W. Weston, Chris. Baseball Man. (p. 141)
—Hawgeye. (p. 755)
Waananen, Lisa, illus. see Higgins, Nadia.
Waard, Nancy De, see De Waard, Nancy.
Waas, Uli, illus. see Hanel, Wolfram & Hänel, Wolfram.
Waber, Bernard. Ask Me. Lee, Suzy, illus. (p. 106)
—Betty's Day Off. (p. 172)
—Ira Sleeps Over (p. 886)
—Lyle, Lyle Crocodile (p. 1066)
—Lyle, Lyle, Crocodile Storybook Treasury. (p. 1066)
—Lyle Walks the Dogs. Waber, Paulis, illus. (p. 1066)
—Quique Duerme Fuera de Casa. Mlawer, Teresa, tr. (p. 1428)
Waber, Paulis, illus. see Waber, Bernard.
Wach, Delia Bowman, jt. auth. see Cloyd, Nancy J.
Wach, Martin. Adventure in Writing. (p. 14)
—Great West Virginia Snow Adventure: Teddy Bear Guardians of the Rain Forest. (p. 719)
Wach, Randy-Lynne. Child's Collection of Parables. Harston, Jerry, illus. (p. 304)
Wachal, Barbara S. American Encounter with Islam. (p. 60)
Wachob, Chuck. Why Ducks Waddle & Geese Don't. Zembrowski, Sunni, illus. (p. 1924)
Wacholtz, Anthony. Can You Survive a Zombie Apocalypse? Nathan, James, illus. (p. 259)
—Drawing with Sports Illustrated Kids Haya, Erwin & Ray, Mike, illus. (p. 482)
—Drawing with Sports Illustrated Kids. Ray, Mike & Haya, Erwin, illus. (p. 482)
—Joe Mauer: Baseball Superstar (p. 920)
—Mummies & Sound Mallea, Cristian, illus. (p. 1191)
—Picture a Home Run: A Baseball Drawing Book Haya, Erwin, illus. (p. 1355)
—Picture a Slam Dunk: A Basketball Drawing Book Haya, Erwin, illus. (p. 1355)
—Picture a Slap Shot: A Hockey Drawing Book Ray, Mike, illus. (p. 1355)
—Picture a Touchdown: A Football Drawing Book Ray, Mike, illus. (p. 1355) Ray, Mike, illus. (p. 1355)
—Ultimate Collection of Pro Baseball Records (p. 1809)
Wacholtz, Anthony, jt. auth. see Adamson, Thomas K.
Wacholtz, Anthony, jt. auth. see Doeden, Matt.
Wacholtz, Anthony, jt. auth. see Dougherty, Terri.
Wacholtz, Anthony, jt. auth. see Frederick, Shane.
Wacholtz, Anthony & Doeden, Matt. Superstar Athletes. (p. 1684)
Wachtel, Alan. FBI's Most Wanted. (p. 578)
—Investigative Techniques of the FBI. (p. 885)
—Southeast Asian Americans. (p. 1617)
Wachtel, Alan, et al. Geothermal Energy. (p. 665)
Wachtel, Aleina, jt. ed. see Johnson, Miri.
Wachtel, Roger. Old Ironsides. (p. 1284)
—Tomb of the Unknown Soldier. (p. 1764)
Wachtel, Shirley Russak. Brad Sureshot—Coach-Detective: The Baffling Case of the Disappearing Dribbler. (p. 221)
Wachter, Dave, illus. see Niles, Steve & Santoro, Matt.
Wachter, Joanne. Boston Tea Party. (p. 215)
—George Washington & the American Revolution. (p. 664)
—Thirteen Colonies. (p. 1734)
Wack, Nancy. Puddle Pirate. (p. 1414)
Wacker, Eileen. Black Tortoise & the Dynasty Dragon. Low, Alan M., illus. (p. 197)
—Fujimini Adventure Series Box Set. (p. 646)
—Rainbow Panda & the Firecracker Fiasco. (p. 1435)
Wacker, Ranae, illus. see Comley, Kathryn.
Wada, Stephanie. Momotaro & the Island of Ogres. (p. 1163)
Waddell, Barbara. Hooray, Hooray, Today's the Day. (p. 796)
—If I Could Catch a Train. (p. 852)
Waddell, Dan. How to Be a Detective. Smith, Jim, illus. (p. 814)
—Who Do You Think You Are? Be a Family Tree Detective. (p. 1915)
Waddell, James M. Puppy Dog Tails. (p. 1418)
Waddell, John. John & Jeanie Fly: Living the Law of Attraction. (p. 921)
Waddell, Martin. Bears, Bears, Bears! Wildish, Lee, illus. (p. 151)
—Can't You Sleep, Little Bear? (p. 262)
—Can't You Sleep, Little Bear? Firth, Barbara, illus. (p. 262)
—Can't You Sleep, Little Bear?: Candlewick Storybook Animations. Firth, Barbara, illus. (p. 262)
—Captain Small Pig Varley, Susan, illus. (p. 264)
—Class Six & the Very Big Rabbit. Ross, Tony, illus. (p. 327)
—Farmer Duck. Oxenbury, Helen, illus. (p. 574)
—Football Spy. Keylock, Andy & Veres, Laszlo, illus. (p. 615)
—It's Quacking Time! Barton, Jill, illus. (p. 898)
—Let's Go Home, Little Bear. (p. 997)
—Muy Bien, Osito. (p. 1195)
—Non Dormi Piccolo Orso. (p. 1263)
—Orchard Book of Goblins Ghouls & Ghosts & Other Magical Stories. Ross, Tony, illus. (p. 1302)
—Owl Babies: Book & Toy Gift Set. Benson, Patrick, illus. (p. 1315)
—Owl Babies. (p. 1315)
—Owl Babies. Benson, Patrick, illus. (p. 1315)
—Owl Babies: Candlewick Storybook Animations. Benson, Patrick, illus. (p. 1315)
—Room for a Little One: A Christmas Tale. Cockcroft, Jason, illus. (p. 1488)
—Something So Big. Canty, Charlotte, illus. (p. 1610)
—Super Hungry Dinosaur. Lord, Leonie, illus. (p. 1680)
—Super Swooper Dinosaur. Lord, Leonie, illus. (p. 1682)
—Tiny's Big Adventure. Lawrence, John, illus. (p. 1757)
—Webster J. Duck. Parkins, David & Firth, Barbara, illus. (p. 1870)
—You & Me, Little Bear. (p. 1973)
Waddilove, Guy. Dancing with the Dragleon. (p. 403)
Waddington, Nicole, illus. see Moore, Shahari.
Waddle, Ray. Against the Grain: Unconventional Wisdom from Ecclesiastes. (p. 29)
Waddy, F., illus. see Nesbitt, M. L.
Waddy, Lawrence H. Florence Nightingale. (p. 606)
—Jonah. (p. 924)
—Shakespeare Remembers. (p. 1559)
Wade, A. Edward. Remiinds Me of the Time: Vietnam 1968. (p. 1460)
Wade, Alison. Female Distance Runner's Training Log. (p. 581)
Wade, Angela. New York City. (p. 1248)
Wade, Barbara. Smokey Gets His Christmas Wish. (p. 1594)
Wade, Chad A. Cracking the Producers Code. (p. 375)
Wade, Connie Morgan. Bible Songs & Action Rhymes, Ages 3-6. (p. 176)
Wade, Ey. In My Sister's World. (p. 864)
Wade, Gini, illus. see Edwards, Meinir Wyn.
Wade, Gini, illus. see Peters, Andrew Fusek.
Wade, Gini, illus. see Tango Books Staff.
Wade, Gloria. Hurting & Healing: How to Overcome the Trauma of Sexual Abuse & Rape. (p. 830)
Wade, Jan, jt. auth. see Bruce, Jill B.
Wade, Jerry, illus. see Sargent, Alan E.
Wade, Joan. Zoey Finds a New Home. Swope, Brenda, illus. (p. 1987)
Wade, Judith. Faelen, the Horse from the Sea. (p. 562)
—Mermaid Dreams. (p. 1128)
—Mermaid's Gift. (p. 1128)
—Secret of Mermaid Island. (p. 1542)
Wade, Kerry. Page Turns Twelve & Comes of Age. (p. 1318)
Wade, Laura. Sea & Sealife. (p. 1534)
Wade, Linda R. Condoleezza Rice. (p. 356)
—Everglades National Park. (p. 542)
—Yosemite National Park. (p. 1972)
Wade, Linda R. & Hamilton, John. Glacier National Park. (p. 682)
—Grand Canyon National Park. (p. 707)
—Yellowstone National Park. (p. 1970)
Wade, M. J. Lucy Finds Her Moo. (p. 1063)
Wade, Mary D., jt. auth. see Wade, Mary Dodson.
Wade, Mary Dodson. Amazing Arctic Explorer Matthew Henson. (p. 53)
—Amazing Champion of the Earth Rachel Carson. (p. 54)
—Amazing Cherokee Writer Sequoyah. (p. 54)
—Amazing Civil War Nurse Clara Barton. (p. 54)
—Amazing Olympic Athlete Wilma Rudolph. (p. 55)
—Amazing President Theodore Roosevelt. (p. 55)
—C. S. Lewis: The Chronicler of Narnia. (p. 250)
—Christopher Columbus: Famous Explorer Whigham, Rod & Barnett, Charles, III, illus. (p. 316)
—Christopher Columbus. (p. 316)
—Cinco de Mayo. (p. 319)
—Condoleezza Rice. (p. 356)
—David Crockett: Creating a Legend. Hein, Joy Fisher, illus. (p. 411)
—Deadly Waves: Tsunamis. (p. 418)
—Flowers Bloom! (p. 608)
—Henrietta King: La Patrona. Farnsworth, Bill, illus. (p. 767)
—Henrietta King: Loving the Land. Farnsworth, Bill, illus. (p. 767)
—Jane Long: Texas Journey. Roeder, Virginia, illus. (p. 908)
—Jane Long: Choosing Texas. Roeder, Virginia Marsh, illus. (p. 908)
—Joan Lowery Nixon: Masterful Mystery Writer. (p. 919)
—Map Scales. (p. 1090)
—No Year of the Cat. (p. 1261)
—People Need Plants! (p. 1339)
—Plants Grow! (p. 1370)
—Plants Live Everywhere! (p. 1370)
—Presidents' Day: Honoring the Birthdays of Washington & Lincoln. (p. 1397)
—Sam Houston: Standing Firm. Fisher Hein, Joy, illus. (p. 1506)
—Seeds Sprout! (p. 1548)
—Stephen F. Austin: Keeping Promises. (p. 1648)
—Texas History. (p. 1724)
—Texas Native Peoples. (p. 1724)
—Texas Plants & Animals. (p. 1724)
—Tiny Life on the Ground. (p. 1756)
—Tipos de Mapas. DelRisco, Eida, tr. from ENG. (p. 1757)
—Trees, Weeds, & Vegetables- So Many Kinds of Plants! (p. 1784)
—Trees, Weeds, & Vegetables-So Many Kinds of Plants! (p. 1784)
—Types of Maps. (p. 1805)
—Uniquely Texas. (p. 1818)
Wade, Mary Dodson, jt. auth. see Stewart, Mark.
Wade, Mary Dodson & Capstone Press Staff. Christopher Columbus: Famous Explorer Whigham, Rod & Barnett, Charles, III, illus. (p. 316)
Wade, Mary Dodson & Collins, Don. David Crockett: Hero & Legend. Collins, Don, illus. (p. 411)
Wade, Mary Dodson & Finney, Pat. Sam Houston: I Am Houston. Finney, Pat, illus. (p. 1506)
—Stephen F. Austin: The Son Becomes Father of Texas. Finney, Pat, illus. (p. 1648)
Wade, Mary Dodson & Wade, Mary D. Indonesia: A Question & Answer Book (p. 872)
Wade, Mary H. Light-Bringers. (p. 1015)
—Swift Fawn the Little Foundling. Betts, Louis, illus. (p. 1690)
Wade, Mary Hazelton. Indian Fairy Tales As Told to Little Chi. (p. 871)
Wade, Maryam. Bently & the Crooked Carrot. (p. 166)
—Bently & the Silver Wings. (p. 166)
Wade McCormick, Lisa. Albert Einstein. (p. 34)
—Rick Yancey. (p. 1470)
—Ucla Basketball. (p. 1807)
Wade, Mervin. Prime Time Dimes in the Feds. Wade, Mervin, ed. (p. 1400)
Wade, Natalie. Trials of Otto. (p. 1785)
Wade, Rebecca. Theft & the Miracle. (p. 1728)
—Whispering House. (p. 1912)
Wade, Rex A., ed. Revolutionary Russia: New Approaches to the Russian Revolution Of 1917. (p. 1466)
Wade, Rosalyn. Polar Worlds. (p. 1379)
Wade, Sarah, jt. auth. see Van Fleet, Mara.
Wade, Stephen. War Poets: The Secrets of Poems from the Great War. (p. 1858)
Wade, Taylor. Magical Well. (p. 1075)
Wade, Winnie, jt. auth. see Hughes, Colin.
Wademan, Spike, illus. see Vale, Janice.
Wadeson, Jacki. Brilliant Braids, Beads & Bows: 25 Fantastic Hairstyles That You Can Create Yourself! (p. 228)
Wadham, Anna, illus. see Latham, Irene.
Wadham, Anna, illus. see Peters, Andrew Fusek.
Wadham, Anna, illus. see Peters, Andrew.
Wadham, Tim. Queen of France. Denton, Kady MacDonald, illus. (p. 1425)
Wadhams, Doyle, jt. auth. see Altobello, Albert.
Wadhwa, Vick. New Take on ABCs - S Is for Smiling Sunrise: An Alphabet Book of Goodness, Beauty, & Wonder [Free Audio-Book Download Included]. Artists, Various, illus. (p. 1247)
Wadkins, Fran, illus. see Bradford, Amy L. & Larmoyeux, Mary.
Wadkovsky, Alex. Forces of Mother Nature. (p. 617)
Wadsworth, Ginger. Benjamin Banneker: Pioneering Scientist. Orback, Craig, illus. (p. 164)
—Camping with the President. Dugan, Karen, illus. (p. 258)
—Cesar Chavez. Schroder, Mark, illus. (p. 288)
—César Chávez. Fitzpatrick, Julia, tr. from ENG. (p. 288)
—Survival in the Snow. Orback, Craig, illus. (p. 1686)
—Woolly Mammoths. Zalewski, Todd, illus. (p. 1950)
—Yosemite's Songster: One Coyote's Story. San Souci, Daniel, illus. (p. 1972)
Wadsworth, Kay. Daisy Moon & the Worm Armies. (p. 400)
Wadsworth, Olive A. Over in the Meadow: A Counting Rhyme. Vojtech, Anna, illus. (p. 1313)
Wadsworth, Pamela. Amser a Gofod. (p. 66)
—Creigiau, Pridd a Thywydd. (p. 381)
—Cynefinoedd. (p. 397)
—Defnyddio Egni. (p. 424)
—Golwg Gyntaf Ar Amser a Gofod. (p. 697)
—Golwg Gyntaf Ar Bethau Byw. Owen, Ken & Owen, Siân, illus. (p. 697)
—Golwg Gyntaf Ar Bethau'n Symud. (p. 697)
—Golwg Gyntaf Ar Ble Mae Pethau'n Byw. (p. 697)
—Golwg Gyntaf Ar Ddefnyddiau. (p. 697)
—Golwg Gyntaf Ar Drydan a Magnetau. (p. 697)
—Golwg Gyntaf Ar Egni. (p. 697)
—Golwg Gyntaf Ar Olau. (p. 697)
—Golwg Gyntaf Ar Sain a Cherddoriaeth. (p. 697)
—Golwg Gyntaf Ar Wahanol Blanhigion Ac Anifeiliaid. (p. 697)
—Grymoedd a Symud. (p. 728)
—Gwahanol Blanhigion Ac Anifeiliaid. Owen, Ken & Owen, Siân, illus. (p. 733)
—Pethau Byw Ar Waith. (p. 1348)
—Rhagor Am Amser a Gofod. (p. 1467)
—Rhagor Am Bethau Byw Ar Waith. (p. 1467)
—Rhagor Am Ddefnyddio Egni. (p. 1467)
—Rhagor Am Gynefinoedd. (p. 1467)
—Rhagor Am Rymoedd a Symud. (p. 1467)
—Rhagor Am Wahanol Blanhigion Ac Anifeiliaid. (p. 1467)
Wadsworth, Pamela, jt. auth. see Barlex, David.
Wadsworth, Pamela, jt. auth. see Boulter, Carol.
Wadsworth, Pamela, jt. auth. see Newson, Lesley.
Wadsworth, Pamela & Tate, Sylvia. Golwg Gyntaf Ar Greigiau, Pridd a Thywydd. (p. 697)
Wadsworth, Peter. Wicked Witch of the Woods. (p. 1927)
Wadsworth, Wallace. Modern Story Book. Eger, Caroline Ruth, illus. (p. 1159)
Wadsworth, Wallace C., jt. auth. see Price, Margaret Evans.
Waechter, Philip, illus. see Port, Moni.
Waerea, James. Pukunui. FireHydrant Creative Studios, ed. (p. 1415)
Waerea, Mitch, illus. see Waerea, James.
Wafer, C. K. Adventures of Brady Bean: Operation: Canine Caper. Myers, Alishea, illus. (p. 16)
Wafer, C. K., jt. auth. see Wafer, C. K.
Wafer, C. K. & Wafer, C. K. Adventures of Brady Bean: Operation: Georgie Porgie. Myers, Alishea, illus. (p. 17)
Wagele, Elizabeth. Finding the Birthday Cake: Helping Children Raise Their Self-Esteem. Wagele, Elizabeth, illus. (p. 588)
Wagenaar, Larry J. & Trap, Paul, eds. Michigan History Directory of Historical Societies, Museums, Archives, Agencies & Commissions. (p. 1135)
Wagenbach, Debbie. Grouchies. Mack, Steve, illus. (p. 725)
Wagener, Wolfgang, jt. auth. see Buckner, Cory.
Waggaman, Mary T. Con of Misty Mountain. (p. 355)
Waggener, Anna. Grim. (p. 724)
Waggoner, Brittany. Prayer for When You're Mad, Sad or Just Totally Confused. (p. 1393)
Waggoner, Sandra. Maggie's Treasure (p. 1071)
—Son of an Honest Man. (p. 1611)
Waggoner, Susan. Neptune's Tears. (p. 1241)
—Starlight's Edge. (p. 1642)
Waggoner, Tom. Danger in the Hills. (p. 404)
Wagle, Gina, ed. see Ibbetson, Paul.
Wagler, Elizabeth. Sojourn in Africa. (p. 1606)
Wagner, Amy, ed. see Warner, Penny.
Wagner, Amy, photos by see Warner, Penny.
Wagner, Andy, illus. see Wood, Douglas.
Wagner, Anke. Help, I Don't Want a Babysitter! Behl, Anne-Kathrin, illus. (p. 765)
—Tim's Big Move. Eriksson, Eva, illus. (p. 1755)
Wagner, Aubrey, jt. auth. see Wagner, Kathi.
Wagner, Aureen Pinto. Up & down the Worry Hill: A Children's Book about Obsessive-Compulsive Disorder & Its Treatment. (p. 1824)
Wagner, B. J. & WrightGroup/McGraw-Hill Staff. Language Roundup. (p. 975)
Wagner, B. J., et al. Language Roundup. (p. 975)
Wagner, B.J. & WrightGroup/McGraw-Hill Staff. Language Roundup. (p. 975)
—Language Roundup Level 4. (p. 975)
—Language Roundup, Level 5. (p. 975)
Wagner, Brian. 10 Things Not to Do with Your Eyeball. (p. 1994)
Wagner, C. Peter. Second Apostolic Age: How God Is Leading His Church into the Future. (p. 1539)
Wagner, Connie, illus. see Wagner-Robertson, Garry.
Wagner, Craig R. When You're Feeling Spiritually Empty. (p. 1906)
Wagner, Danielle. Cubbie Tails: Nice to Meet You. (p. 388)
Wagner, Dennis. Grampa Chair. (p. 706)
—Have You Seen God Today? (p. 754)
Wagner, Douglas, et al. Stepping into Natural Science & Technology Matters Grade 4 Learner's Book. (p. 1648)
—Stepping into Natural Science & Technology Matters Grade 5 Facilitators Guide. (p. 1648)
—Stepping into Natural Science & Technology Matters Grade 4 Facilitator's Guide. (p. 1648)
—Stepping into Natural Science & Technology Matters Grade 5 Learner's Book Afrikaans Translation. (p. 1648)
—Stepping into Natural Science & Technology Matters Grade 4 Learner's Book (Afrikaans Translation) (p. 1648)
—Stepping into Natural Science & Technology Matters Grade 5 Facilitator's Guide Afrikaans Translation. (p. 1648)
Wagner, Elaine. Racin' Jason. Kaszonyi, Janet, illus. (p. 1432)
Wagner, Elaine, jt. auth. see Wagner, Elaine J.
Wagner, Elaine J. & Wagner, Elaine. Meshom & the Little One. Hamelin, Marie-Micheline et al, illus. (p. 1129)
Wagner, Emily. Asleep under the Moon. (p. 106)
Wagner, Fiona. Little Cat. (p. 1025)
Wagner, Gavin, illus. see Cerpok, M. L.
Wagner, Gerard, illus. see Steiner, Rudolf.
Wagner, Heather Lehr. Alcohol. (p. 35)
—Algerian War. (p. 38)
—Anwar Sadat & Menachem Begin: Negotiating Peace in the Middle East. (p. 90)
—Aretha Franklin: Singer. (p. 97)
—Arrival of the Mayflower: Pilgrims Sail to the New World. (p. 101)
—Barack Obama: Politician. (p. 137)
—Barack Obama. (p. 137)
—Benjamin Banneker. (p. 164)
—Central Intelligence Agency. (p. 287)
—Cuban Missile Crisis: Cold War Confrontation. (p. 388)
—Division of the Middle East: The Treaty of Sevres. (p. 455)
—Elie Wiesel: Messenger of Peace. (p. 512)
—Federal Bureau of Investigation. (p. 580)
—Henry Kissinger: Ending the Vietnam War. (p. 768)
—Hernan Cortes. (p. 771)
—How the President Is Elected. (p. 813)
—Iran. (p. 886)
—Iranian Revolution. (p. 887)
—Jane Austen. (p. 908)
—King Abdullah II: King of Jordan. Schlesinger, Arthur M., Jr., ed. (p. 958)
—Machiavelli: Renaissance Political Analyst & Author. (p. 1068)
—Medicis: A Ruling Dynasty. (p. 1119)
—Outbreak of the Civil War. (p. 1312)
—Paul Revere: Messenger for Freedom. (p. 1330)
—Pompeii. (p. 1382)
—Presidency. (p. 1396)
—Rigoberta Menchu Tum: Activist for Indigenous Rights in Guatemala. (p. 1472)
—Saudi Arabia. (p. 1516)
—Supreme Court. (p. 1684)
—Watergate Scandal. (p. 1863)

W

—William Bradford. (p. 1933)
Wagner, Heather Lehr, ed. see Lawler, Mary.
Wagner, Heather Lehr, jt. auth. see Rummel, Jack.
Wagner, Heather Lehr, jt. auth. see Schroeder, Alan.
Wagner, Heather Lehr, et al. Organization of the Petroleum Exporting Countries. (p. 1303)
Wagner, Hilary. Lords of Trillium: Book III of the Nightshade Chronicles. Rayyan, Omar, illus. (p. 1053)
—Lords of Trillium: Book Iii of the Nightshade Chronicles. Rayyan, Omar, illus. (p. 1053)
—Nightshade City. Rayyan, Omar, illus. (p. 1255)
—White Assassin. (p. 1912)
—White Assassin. Rayyan, Omar, illus. (p. 1912)
Wagner, Jane. J. T. (p. 902)
Wagner, Jay. H Is for Hawkeye. Potts Dawson, Eileen, illus. (p. 734)
Wagner, Jeff. My Day... at the Zoo. Alvarado, Paulo, illus. (p. 1201)
Wagner, Jenny. High Hopes on Sea. Rogers, Gregory, illus. (p. 777)
Wagner, John. Banzai Battalion: Just Another Bug Hunt. Bolland, Brian et al, illus. (p. 137)
Wagner, Jordan. Nightmare Awakened. (p. 1255)
Wagner, Josh. Sky Pirates of Neo Terra. (p. 1587)
Wagner, Julie. Watch Out Pool. (p. 1861)
Wagner, Julie G. Watch Out: Stove. (p. 1861)
—Watch Out: Dangerous People (p. 1861)
Wagner, Karen. Mosasaurus: Mighty Ruler of the Sea. (p. 1176)
—Mosasaurus: Mighty Ruler of the Sea. Carr, Karen, illus. (p. 1176)
Wagner, Kathi & Racine, Sheryl. Kids' Astronomy Book: Blast into Outer Space with Steller Facts, Intergalatic Trivia, & Out-of-This-World Puzzles. (p. 952)
Wagner, Kathi & Wagner, Aubrey. Kids' Bible Trivia Book: Stump Your Friends & Family with Your Bible Knowledge! (p. 952)
—Riddles & Brain Teasers Book: Hours of Challenging Fun. (p. 1471)
Wagner, Kelsey. Rumble with Grumble: The Epic Adventures of a Turtle... & Some Bees. (p. 1495)
Wagner, Larry. Adventures of Sally Sunflower. (p. 22)
Wagner, Laura Rose. Hold Tight, Don't Let Go. (p. 788)
Wagner, Linda. Lady Flatterley. (p. 970)
Wagner, Lisa. Cool African Cooking: Fun & Tasty Recipes for Kids. (p. 362)
—Cool Chinese & Japanese Cooking: Fun & Tasty Recipes for Kids. (p. 363)
—Cool French Cooking: Fun & Tasty Recipes for Kids. (p. 363)
—Cool Italian Cooking: Fun & Tasty Recipes for Kids. (p. 363)
—Cool Mexican Cooking: Fun & Tasty Recipes for Kids. (p. 364)
—Cool Middle Eastern Cooking: Fun & Tasty Recipes for Kids. (p. 364)
—Cool World Cooking: Fun & Tasty Recipes for Kids! (p. 364)
Wagner, Lloyd S. Ghosts at Gettysburg: An Oliver Family Adventure. (p. 672)
Wagner, Lori. Gateway of the Sun. (p. 658)
Wagner, Martin. Little Driver. (p. 1027)
Wagner, Matt. Batman & the Monster Men. Research & Education Association Editors & Leigh, Rob, illus. (p. 144)
—Batman/Superman/Wonder Woman: Trinity. (p. 144)
—Demon - From the Darkness. (p. 426)
—Devil Inside. (p. 432)
—Hero Defined (p. 772)
Wagner, Matt & Mahfood, Jim. Further Adventures of One-Page Filler Man (p. 650)
Wagner, Matt & Seagle, Steven. Tarantula. Kahan, Bob, ed. (p. 1706)
Wagner, Matt, et al. Dr. Death & the Night of the Butcher (p. 475)
Wagner, Mckenzie. Casters of Doovik. (p. 276)
—Keys to the Dream World. (p. 951)
—Rescue. (p. 1462)
Wagner, Michael & Vanzet, Gaston. Mess. (p. 1129)
Wagner (minor), McKenzie. Magic Meadow & the Golden Locket: Blue Lagoon & the Magic Coin. (p. 1072)
Wagner, Paul. Jock Jokes: And Other Stories. (p. 919)
—Just One Mo. (p. 939)
Wagner, Rachel A. Bogie the Boxer: Gardens. (p. 207)
Wagner, Sally R. Grandmother Who Climbed to the Top of the World. (p. 709)
Wagner, Sandra Glahn. Ants Have Dyed. Wagner, Sandra Glahn, illus. (p. 90)
Wagner, Stefani. School Is Hard for Me. (p. 1523)
Wagner, Steve, illus. see Voigt, David & Voigt, Grady.
Wagner, Sy. Brownie Math. (p. 232)
—I Write for the Newspaper. (p. 849)
Wagner, Veronica. Disney Mickey Mouse Clubhouse: 3 Book Play-A-Sound Set (p. 451)
Wagner, Viqi. Eating Disorders. (p. 501)
—Endangered Species. (p. 527)
—Labor Unions. (p. 969)
—Military Draft. (p. 1143)
Wagner, Viqi, ed. Endangered Species. (p. 527)
Wagner, Willis H. & Kicklighter, Clois E. Modern Woodworking: Tools, Materials, & Processes. (p. 1159)
—Modern Woodworking: Teaching Package Instructor's Guide. (p. 1159)
Wagner, Willis H. & Smith, Howard Bud. Modern Carpentry: Teaching Package Teacher's Resource Binder. (p. 1158)
—Modern Carpentry: Building Construction Details in Easy-to-Understand Form. (p. 1158)
—Modern Carpentry. (p. 1158)
Wagner, Wolfgang & Hayes, Nicky. Everyday Discourse & Common Sense: The Theory of Social Representations. (p. 543)
Wagner, Yulia. Flying-Fur Bus. (p. 610)
Wagner-Martin, Linda. Barbara Kingsolver. (p. 137)
—Sylvia Plath: A Literary Life. (p. 1693)
Wagner-Robertson, Garry. Evil Mailbox & the Super Burrito Wagner, Connie, illus. (p. 546)
Wagoner, Jay J. Arizona Civics & Government. (p. 98)
Wagoner, Kim, illus. see Medler, John, Jr.
Wagoner, Timothy Allen. Adventures of Jacque & Wanderwan: Naoo. Bk. 1 (p. 19)
Wagschal, Shaul. Pleasant Ways of the Jewish Daughter. (p. 1373)
Wagstaff, Brenda L. Runtly's Unforgettable Adventure. (p. 1497)
Wagstaff, Janiel. Stella & Class: Information Experts. (p. 1646)
—Stella Tells Her Story. (p. 1647)
—Stella Writes an Opinion. (p. 1647)
Waguespack, Michael. Deer Hunting Book. (p. 423)
Wahab, Shaista & Youngerman, Barry. Afghanistan. (p. 26)
Wahid, Kelli. As Children Grow: Poetry for Children. (p. 105)
Wahl, Charis. Rosario's Fig Tree Melanson, Luc, illus. (p. 1489)
Wahl, Charis, jt. auth. see Falcone, L. M.
Wahl, Charis, jt. auth. see MacDonald, Anne Louise.
Wahl, Jan. Art Collector. Bonnet, Rosalinde, illus. (p. 101)
—Bear Dance. Felix, Monique, illus. (p. 150)
—Candy Shop. Wong, Nicole, illus. (p. 261)
—Candy Shop. Wong, Nicole E., illus. (p. 261)
—Cobweb Castle. (p. 337)
—Golden Christmas Tree. Weisgard, Leonard, illus. (p. 694)
—How the Children Stopped the Wars. (p. 813)
—I Met a Dinosaur. Sheban, Chris, illus. (p. 844)
—Little Johnny Buttermilk: After an Old English Folktale. Mazzucco, Jennifer, illus. (p. 1029)
—Long Tall Journey. Gapaillard, Laurent, illus. (p. 1047)
—Pleasant Fieldmouse. Sendak, Maurice, illus. (p. 1373)
Wahl, Leslea. Perfect Blindside. (p. 1341)
Wahl, Phoebe. Sonya's Chickens. (p. 1613)
Wahl, Valerie, illus. see Conover, Sarah.
Wahman, Joe. Snowboy 1, 2, 3. Wahman, Wendy, illus. (p. 1600)
Wahman, Wendy. Cat Like That. Wahman, Wendy, illus. (p. 278)
—Don't Lick the Dog: Making Friends with Dogs. Wahman, Wendy, illus. (p. 468)
Wahman, Wendy, illus. see Wahman, Joe.
Wahn, Udo. Cabo & Coral Go Surfing! Lyn, Jami, illus. (p. 250)
Wai, Joan. 100+ Baby Shower Games. (p. 1998)
Waibel, Stacy Raye. Rudy's Incredible Kidney Machine. Gruebele, Michelle, illus. (p. 1494)
Waid, Antoinette M., illus. see Murphy, Breena.
Waid, Casey. Adventures of Adam the Atom. (p. 16)
Waid, Mark. Authoritative Action (p. 117)
—Birthright - The Origin of the Man of Steel. (p. 193)
—Captain America: To Serve & Protect. Ramos, Humberto et al, illus. (p. 263)
—Captain America: Man Out of Time. Molina, Jorge & Kirby, Jack, illus. (p. 263)
—City of Incredibles Takara, Marcio, illus. (p. 324)
—Death of a Dream (p. 420)
—Enter the Detective. Guice, Butch & Perkins, Mike, illus. (p. 531)
—Family Matters. Takara, Marcio, illus. (p. 568)
—Fantastic Four Wieringo, Mike, illus. (p. 571)
—Fantastic Four by Waid & Wieringo Ultimate Collection Book 2. Wieringo, Mike & Jones, Casey, illus. (p. 571)
—Imaginauts. Wieringo, Mike, illus. (p. 860)
—Incorruptible. Takara, Marcio, illus. (p. 869)
—Incredibles: City of Incredibles Takara, Marcio, illus. (p. 870)
—Kingdom. (p. 959)
—Silent Partner (p. 1575)
—Strange Visitor from Another Century. (p. 1665)
—Teenage Revolution (p. 1714)
—Unthinkable Wieringo, Mike, illus. (p. 1823)
Waid, Mark, jt. auth. see DC Comics Staff.
Waid, Mark, jt. auth. see Slott, Dan.
Waid, Mark & Beatty, Scott. Silent Partner Guice, Butch et al, illus. (p. 1575)
Waid, Mark & Chinsang, Wayne. Bad Ideas Collected!!! Silvestri, Marc et al, illus. (p. 131)
Waid, Mark & Haspiel, Dean. Fox - Freak Magnet. Haspiel, Dean, illus. (p. 626)
Waid, Mark & Johns, Geoff. Future Is Now. (p. 651)
Waid, Mark & Lee, Stan. Origin of the Species. Azaceta, Paul & Martin, Marcos, illus. (p. 1304)
Waid, Mark & Porter, Howard. Fantastic Four by Waid & Wieringo Ultimate Collection Book 3. Wieringo, Mike & Smith, Paul, illus. (p. 571)
Waid, Mark & Walker, Landry. Revenge from Below. Takara, Marcio, illus. (p. 1465)
Waid, Mark, et al. Sigil: Out of Time. Lai, Ben et al, illus. (p. 1574)
—Supergirl & the Legion of Super-Heroes (p. 1683)
—Tower of Babel Geraci, Drew, illus. (p. 1773)
Waid, Sara J., illus. see Murphy, Breena.
Waid, Sara Joyce, illus. see Murphy, Breena.
Wain, Doug. War Against Violence Everywhere. (p. 1857)
Waines, Frances Drummond. Humpi, the Orphan Camel (p. 827)
Wainscott, Bud. Candy Well. (p. 261)
—Wounded Hawk. (p. 1962)
Wainwright, Debra. That Kind of Dog. (p. 1726)
Wainwright, Jen. Bedtime Story Book: Classic Tales from Childhood. Dominguez, Angel, illus. (p. 157)
—There's Only One Direction (p. 1731)
Wainwright, Jen, jt. auth. see McMillan, Sue.
Wainwright, Jen, ed. Winter Wonderland Doodles: Festive Full-Color Pictures to Complete & Create. (p. 1938)
Wainwright, Joann M. Winston, the Polite St Bernard. Ross, Adam, illus. (p. 1937)
Wainwright, Tabitha. You & an Illness in Your Family. (p. 1972)
Wainwright, Tabitha, jt. auth. see Jones, Viola.
Wainwright, W. O. O' Mista' Whadda' Wata' Bug! (p. 1274)
Waisanen, Emily. Book Monster. Konecny, John, illus. (p. 210)
Wait, Colleen. Lessons Learned at Summer Camp. (p. 994)
Wait, Lea. Finest Kind. (p. 589)
—Seaward Born. (p. 1539)
—Stopping to Home. (p. 1654)
—Wintering Well. (p. 1938)
Waite, Judy. Digging for Dinosaurs. Parsons, Garry, illus. (p. 439)
—Game Girls. (p. 654)
Waite, Judy, tr. see Baumgart, Klaus.
Waite, Lana. Madd Mountain Murders. (p. 1069)
Waite, Lance. Day with Dad at the Beach. (p. 415)
—Day with My Dad. Pentangelo, Manuela, illus. (p. 415)
Waite, Polly, jt. auth. see Willetts, Lucy.
Waites, Joan, illus. see Butler, Dori Hillestad.
Waites, Joan, illus. see Slade, Suzanne.
Waites, Joan, illus. see St. Romain, Rose Anne.
Waites, Joan, illus. see Wallace, Susan Helen.
Waites, Joan, jt. auth. see Slade, Suzanne.
Waites, Joan C. How-to Cowboy: 22 Secret, Magic How-to Fun Tricks. (p. 816)
Waites, Joan C., illus. see Allen, Nancy Kelly.
Waites, Joan C., illus. see Butler, Dori Hillestad.
Waites, Joan C., illus. see Nicholas, J. B.
Waites, Joan C., illus. see St. Romain, Rose Anne.
Waites, Matthew. Age of Consent: Young People, Sexuality & Citizenship. (p. 29)
Waits, Kristine. Sweet Sam Shares. (p. 1690)
Wakabi, Wairagala. Tanzania. (p. 1705)
Wakageryu, et al. Ryu-Ki System: Sunserra. (p. 1499)
Wake, Iam & Carr, Bret. Ricky Remington Dolphin Dreamer: A Story. (p. 1470)
Wake, Katherine, illus. see Steven, Kenneth.
Wake, Rich, illus. see Murphy, Angela.
Wake, Shelley. Wrinkly Socks Make Me Giggle. Tufts, N. Jo, illus. (p. 1963)
Wakefield, Beth. Cleaner. (p. 330)
Wakefield, Chris. Dad Did It! (p. 398)
Wakefield, Chris, jt. auth. see Johnstone, Drummond.
Wakefield, Mike. Jbs 2004 Dispatched to Serve: Studies from 1 & 2 Timothy. (p. 911)
—Jbs 2004 Student Leader Guide. (p. 911)
Wakefield, Nelida. Little Flathead & the Black Pearl. Smith, Nathan, illus. (p. 1027)
Wakefield, Scott, illus. see Namm, Diane.
Wakefield, Scott, illus. see Olmstead, Kathleen.
Wakefield, Scott J., illus. see McFadden, Deanna.
Wakefield, Scott J., illus. see Namm, Diane.
Wakefield, Vikki. Friday Never Leaving. (p. 637)
Wakelin, Bob, illus. see Running Press Staff & Speregen, Devra Newberger.
Wakelin, Kirsti Anne, illus. see Bar-el, Dan.
Wakelin, Kirsti Anne, illus. see Gilmore, Rachna.
Wakelin, Kirsti Anne, illus. see LaRochelle, David.
Wakelin, Kirsti Anne, illus. see McFarlane, Sheryl.
Wakelin, Kirsti Anne, illus. see Thompson, Richard & Spicer, Maggee.
Wakelin, Kirsti Anne, jt. auth. see Lloyd, Jennifer.
Wakem, Samantha. Milly's Magic Play House: The Hospital Herridge, Debbie, illus. (p. 1144)
Wakeman, Bill, illus. see Ferguson, Don.
Wakeman, Daniel. Ben's Big Dig Van Stralen, Dirk, illus. (p. 165)
—Ben's Bunny Trouble Van Stralen, Dirk, illus. (p. 165)
Wakeman, Lars. Prince Harry the Hairy Prince: A hairy fairy Tale. (p. 1401)
Wakeman, Peter, photos by see Pohlman, Jennifer & Searle, Rodney.
Wakiyama, Hanako, illus. see Archer, Peggy.
Wakiyama, Hanako, illus. see Dealey, Erin.
Wakiyama, Hanako, illus. see LaRochelle, David.
Wakiyama, Hanako, illus. see Novesky, Amy.
Wakumelo, Mubiana. Creative & Technology Studies for Zambia Basic Education Grade 6. (p. 379)
Walberg, Anders. Sport Fishermen's Cookbook. (p. 1631)
Walbesser, Henry H. Imagination. (p. 860)
Walbruck, Rita M. Auf Heiber Spur, Erlebnisse in Deutschland: Das Ratsel vom Waldsee (p. 115)
Walburg, Lori. Legend of the Candy Cane: The Inspirational Story of Our Favorite Christmas Candy Bernardin, James & Cowdrey, Richard, illus. (p. 989)
Walburg, Lori, jt. auth. see Zondervan.
Walch, Michelle E. & Maddin, John. Letters of the West. Maddin, John, illus. (p. 1002)
Walch Publishing Staff. Assessment Strategies for Math. (p. 107)
—Assessment Strategies for Reading. (p. 107)
—Daily Warm-Ups: Analogies. (p. 400)
—Humanities. (p. 826)
Walch Publishing Staff, creator. Math & Science. (p. 1105)
Walchle, Donna Douglas. There's an Owl in the Closet. Galeano, Jose Daniel Oviedo, illus. (p. 1731)
Walcker, Yann. Ludwig Van Beethoven Voake, Charlotte, illus. (p. 1064)
—Ludwig Van Beethoven. (p. 1064)
—Wolfgang Amadeus Mozart Voake, Charlotte, illus. (p. 1944)
—Wolfgang Amadeus Mozart. (p. 1944)
Wald, Christina. Barnyard. (p. 139)
—Johnny Tractor's Animal Opposites. Running Press Staff, ed. (p. 923)
Wald, Christina, illus. see Bowman, Donna H.
Wald, Christina, illus. see Claybourne, Anna.
Wald, Christina, illus. see Cooper, Sharon Katz.
Wald, Christina, illus. see Downing, Johnette.
Wald, Christina, illus. see Driscoll, Laura.
Wald, Christina, illus. see East, Cathy.
Wald, Christina, illus. see Gerber, Carole.
Wald, Christina, illus. see Kieber-King, Cynthia.
Wald, Christina, illus. see Lay, Kathryn.
Wald, Christina, illus. see Love, Donna.
Wald, Christina, illus. see Pearson, Carrie A.
Wald, Christina, illus. see Pearson, Carrie.
Wald, Christina, illus. see Robinson, Tom.
Wald, Christina, illus. see Spangler, Lois.
Wald, Christina, illus. see Troupe, Thomas Kingsley.
Wald, Christina, jt. auth. see Pearson, Carrie A.
Wald, Heywood. Spanish Is Fun Book 2 Audio Program: Lively Lessons for Advancing Students. Bk. 2 (p. 1621)
Wald, Susana, tr. see Comino, Sandra.
Walde, Christine. Candy Darlings. (p. 261)
Waldeck, Aaron. Space Rocks: A Look at Asteroids & Comets. (p. 1619)
—Space Rocks: A Look at Asteroids & Comets. (p. 1619)
Waldek, Kelly, illus. see Richemont, Enid.
Walden, Katherine. Baboons. (p. 124)
—Leopards of the African Plains. (p. 993)
—Meerkats. (p. 1120)
—Rhinoceroses. (p. 1467)
—Warthogs. (p. 1859)
—Wildebeests. (p. 1931)
Walden, Katherine & Watson, Stephanie. Conquering Anorexia. (p. 358)
Walden, Mark. Aftershock. (p. 29)
—Deadlock. (p. 417)
—Dreadnought. (p. 482)
—Earthfall. (p. 497)
—Escape Velocity. (p. 535)
—H. I. V. E. Higher Institute of Villainous Education. (p. 734)
—Higher Institute of Villainous Education. (p. 779)
—Overlord Protocol. (p. 1314)
—Retribution. (p. 1464)
—Rogue. (p. 1485)
—Zero Hour. (p. 1986)
Walden, Pamela Charlene. Puff Bear Goes to the Hospital. (p. 1415)
Walden, Walter. Boy Scouts Afloat. (p. 218)
Walder, Chaim. Kids Speak (p. 955)
Walder, Chaim, jt. auth. see Raanan, Ahuva.
Walder, Lysa. Katie the Paramedic. (p. 945)
Waldherr, Kris, illus. see Cotner, June, ed.
Waldman, Alan/A. Erica from America & the Start of the Gang of Four. Scobie, Andrea, illus. (p. 533)
Waldman, Bruce, illus. see Peter Pauper Press Staff, et al.
Waldman, Carl. Encyclopedia of Native American Tribes. (p. 525)
Waldman, Carl & Mason, Catherine. Encyclopedia of European Peoples (p. 525)
Waldman, David K. How Teddy Bears Find Their Homes. Danner, Maggie, illus. (p. 812)
Waldman, Debby. Addy's Race (p. 12)
—Sack Full of Feathers Revell, Cindy, illus. (p. 1500)
Waldman, Debby & Feutl, Rita. Room Enough for Daisy Revell, Cindy, illus. (p. 1488)
Waldman, Maya. To-Do List. (p. 1758)
Waldman, Neil. Al & Teddy. (p. 32)
—Land of Big Dreamers: Voices of Courage in America. Waldman, Neil, illus. (p. 973)
—Out of the Shadows: An Artist's Journey. (p. 1311)
—Say-Hey & the Babe: Two Mostly True Baseball Stories. Waldman, Neil, illus. (p. 1518)
—Snowflake: A Water Cycle Story. Waldman, Neil, illus. (p. 1600)
—Starry Night. (p. 1642)
—Voyages: Reminiscences of Young Abe Lincoln. (p. 1850)
Waldman, Neil, illus. see Brimner, Larry Dane.
Waldman, Neil, illus. see Oberman, Sheldon.
Waldman, Nomi J. Deadwood, South Dakota A Frontier Community: Set Of 6. (p. 418)
—Deadwood, South Dakota: A Frontier Community: Text Pairs. (p. 418)
Waldman, Scott. Gunfight at the O. K. Corral: Wyatt Earp Upholds the Law. (p. 732)
—Victory at Sea: John Paul Jones & the Continental Navy. (p. 1840)
Waldman, Scott P. Battle of Bunker Hill. (p. 146)
—Battle of Lexington & Concord. (p. 146)
—Battle of Monmouth. (p. 146)
—Battle of Trenton. (p. 147)
—Battle of Yorktown. (p. 147)
Waldman, Stuart. Last River: John Wesley Powell & the Colorado River Exploring Expedition. Manchess, Gregory, illus. (p. 978)
—Magellan's World. Manchess, Gregory, illus. (p. 1071)
—We Asked for Nothing. McNally, Tom, illus. (p. 1866)
Waldman, Thomas. 1 ! 2 ! 3 ! 4 ! Saisons. (p. 1990)
Waldo, Dixie. Persuasive Speaking. (p. 1344)
Waldock, Sarah. Tabitha Tabs the Farm Kitten. Waldock, Sarah, illus. (p. 1694)
Waldorf, Heather. Grist (p. 724)
—Leftovers (p. 987)
—Tripping (p. 1787)
Waldrep, Adriane. Izora the Magical Horse. (p. 901)
Waldrep, Evelyn L., ed. see Lundy, Charlotte.
Waldrep, Susan. Papa Ant's Picnic. (p. 1321)
Waldrip, Gayle, jt. auth. see Bauld, Jane Scoggins.
Waldrod, Amy, illus. see Howe, James.
Waldron, Ann. Who Was Claude Monet? (p. 1918)
—Who Was Claude Monet? Harrison, Nancy & Marchesi, Stephen, illus. (p. 1918)
Waldron, Douglas E. Cody Sackett of Montana: Tales of Adventure. (p. 338)
Waldron, Douglas Edward. Pathway to Montan: The Settlers Rest (p. 1328)
Waldron, Hannah. Pirate Adventure Dice. (p. 1362)
Waldron, Kathleen Cook. Five Stars for Emily (p. 601)
—Roundup at the Palace Daniel, Alan & Daniel, Lea, illus. (p. 1491)
Waldron, Kathleen Cook, jt. auth. see Walsh, Ann.
Waldron, Kevin. Mr. Peek & the Misunderstanding at the Zoo. Waldron, Kevin, illus. (p. 1186)
—Panda-Monium at Peek Zoo. Waldron, Kevin, illus. (p. 1320)
Waldron, Kevin, illus. see Rosen, Michael.
Waldron, Melanie. Adaptation (p. 11)
—Coasts (p. 336)
—Deserts (p. 429)
—Flowers (p. 608)
—Geography Matters in Ancient Civilizations. (p. 662)
—Geography Matters in Ancient Egypt. (p. 662)
—Geography Matters in Ancient Greece. (p. 662)
—Geography Matters in Ancient Rome. (p. 662)
—Geography Matters in the Inca Empire. (p. 662)
—Human Body. (p. 825)
—Iceland (p. 851)
—Ireland (p. 887)
—Leaves (p. 986)
—Let's Get Mapping! (p. 997)
—Lithuania (p. 1023)
—Mapping Communities (p. 1090)
—Mapping Information (p. 1090)

—Mapping the Land & Weather (p. 1090)
—Mapping the World (p. 1090)
—Mountains (p. 1181)
—Plant Parts (p. 1369)
—Plants (p. 1369)
—Polar Regions (p. 1379)
—Rivers (p. 1476)
—Roots (p. 1488)
—Scotland (p. 1530)
—Seeds & Fruits (p. 1547)
—Stems & Trunks (p. 1647)
—Types of Maps (p. 1805)
—Variation & Classification (p. 1833)
—Your Body by Numbers (p. 1980)
—Your Brain: Understand It with Numbers (p. 1980)
—Your Digestive System: Understand It with Numbers (p. 1980)
—Your Respiration & Circulation: Understand Them with Numbers (p. 1981)
—Your Skin & Bones: Understand Them with Numbers (p. 1981)
Waldron, Melanie, jt. auth. see Tuffen, Hugh.
Waldron, Melanie, et al. Essential Life Science (p. 537)
Waldron, Stephanie. Hannah Learns about Prayer. (p. 742)
Waldroop, Wista, ed. see Deffenbaugh, David & McFarland, Bill.
Waldrop, Dave & Pannell, Lillie Clayton. Am I. (p. 51)
Waldvogel, Merikay. Childhood Treasures: Doll Quilts by & for Children. (p. 302)
Wales, Amy S. Fiona & the Fiddle Tree. (p. 589)
Wales, Dirk. Further Adventures of a Lucky Dog: Owney, U. S. Rail Mail Mascot. DeJong Artman, Catherine & Artman, Townsend, illus. (p. 650)
—Jack London's Dog. Moser, Barry, illus. (p. 903)
—Lucky Dog: Owney, U.S. Rail Mail Mascot. Kenna, Diane, illus. (p. 1062)
—Penny House. Kenna, Diane, illus. (p. 1338)
—Twice a Hero: Polish American Heroes of the American Revolutuion. Peterson, Lynn Ihsen, illus. (p. 1801)
Wales, Sid. Freddie & Mee. Bryant, Kerry, illus. (p. 632)
Waley, Safiya & Woodcock, Victoria. Making Stuff for Kids. Smith, Raven, photos by. (p. 1082)
Walfish, Miriam. Jewel & the Journey. (p. 916)
Walford, N. E. Island Hunters Bk. 1. (p. 892)
—Island Hunters: The Legend of Brown Eyed James. (p. 892)
—Island Hunters - Book I: The Backyard Pirate Adventure. (p. 892)
—Island Hunters - Book II: Trail of the Tomb Robbers. (p. 892)
—Island Hunters - Book III: The Legend of Brown Eyed James. N Gallerie Studios, illus. (p. 892)
Walford, Rod. Chronicles of Sir Hifford Wilkingford-Bisset: Part 1 ~ in the Beginning. Mcleod, Rebecca, illus. (p. 317)
Walk, John. Fenton Glass Compendium: 1985-2001 (p. 581)
—Fenton Special Orders: 1980-Present: QVC; Mary Walrath; Martha Stewart; Cracker Barrel; JC Penney; National Fenton Glass Society; & Fenton Art Glass Club of America (p. 581)
—Fenton Special Orders, 1940-1980: 1940-1980. L. G. Wright; Abels, Wasserberg & Company; Devilbiss; Sears, Roebuck & Company; Macy's; & Levay (p. 581)
Walke, Ted. Boating Safety Sidekicks Color a Fish: Freshwater Fish Coloring Book. (p. 205)
Walker. Be a Sport. (p. 148)
Walker, Alcee Howard. Substitute #8. (p. 1671)
Walker, Alice. There Is a Flower at the Tip of My Nose Smelling Me. Vitale, Stefano, illus. (p. 1729)
—Why War Is Never a Good Idea. Vitale, Stefano, illus. (p. 1926)
Walker, Andrew D., jt. auth. see Martin, Ashley P.
Walker, Andrew D. & Brown, Heather E. How to Improve at Gymnastics. (p. 820)
Walker, Anna. Goldilocks & the Three Bears. (p. 696)
—I Love Birthdays. Walker, Anna, illus. (p. 841)
—I Love Christmas. Walker, Anna, illus. (p. 842)
—I Love My Dad. Walker, Anna, illus. (p. 842)
—I Love My Mom. Walker, Anna, illus. (p. 842)
—I Love to Dance. Walker, Anna, illus. (p. 843)
—I Love to Sing. Walker, Anna, illus. (p. 843)
—I Love Vacations. Walker, Anna, illus. (p. 843)
—Peggy: A Brave Chicken on a Big Adventure. (p. 1335)
—Twelve Dancing Princesses. (p. 1800)
Walker, Anna, illus. see Mitchell, Ainslie.
Walker, Anna, illus. see Quay, Emma.
Walker, B. Girls' Guide to Ad/Hd. (p. 680)
—Mr Peeze, Say Something Else Please! (p. 1186)
Walker, Bobbie H., illus. see Pace, Betty.
Walker, Brad. Thanos Imperative. (p. 1726)
Walker, Bradley, illus. see Schuette, Leslie Elaine.
Walker, Brian F. Black Boy White School. (p. 195)
Walker, Caren & Varacalli, Lauren. Boston University College Prowler off the Record. (p. 215)
Walker, Charmaine. Jon & Alex: Goes to School. (p. 924)
—Our Voices Through Writing. (p. 1310)
Walker, Cheryl. Black Snake, King Snake. (p. 197)
—Little Black & White Pony. (p. 1024)
Walker, Chris, creator. Collision Course Goad by Zombienose. (p. 341)
Walker, Christine, jt. auth. see Hysom, Dennis Joe.
Walker, Cindy. Serenade of the Cricket. (p. 1552)
Walker, Claudette. To Love the Rose: (Is Washington Stoned?) (p. 1759)
Walker, Colin. Plants Grow Almost Anywhere. Simons, Sally, illus. (p. 1370)
Walker, Colin, et al. Differentes Cosas Que Vienende las Plantas. (p. 438)
—Explorando el Espacio. (p. 550)
—Pajaros Son Animales. (p. 1319)
—Peces Son Animales. (p. 1334)
—Seres Vivos. (p. 1552)
—Superficie de la Tierra. (p. 1683)
—Tierra Cambia. (p. 1748)
Walker, Cory, illus. see Kirkman, Robert.
Walker, Crystal. Do Angels Like Chocolate? (p. 456)
—Maceys Magic Tree. (p. 1068)
Walker, Cynthia. Colorado. (p. 343)
—Colorado. Hamilton, Harriet, tr. (p. 343)
—Maine. (p. 1077)
—Nuevo Mexico. (p. 1270)
Walker, Cynthia & Vargus, Nanci Reginelli. New Mexico. (p. 1246)
Walker, David. Hello, New York City! (p. 764)
Walker, David, illus. see Bennett, Kelly.
Walker, David, illus. see Berne, Jennifer.
Walker, David, illus. see Boelts, Maribeth.
Walker, David, illus. see Dombey, Elizabeth & Muldrow, Diane.
Walker, David, illus. see Engle, Margarita.
Walker, David, illus. see Gershator, Phillis & Green, Mim.
Walker, David, illus. see Gibby, Bayne.
Walker, David, illus. see Jennings, Christopher S.
Walker, David, illus. see Johnston, Tony.
Walker, David, illus. see Knapman, Timothy.
Walker, David, illus. see Macken, JoAnn Early.
Walker, David, illus. see Martin, David.
Walker, David, illus. see Muldrow, Diane.
Walker, David, illus. see Parenteau, Shirley.
Walker, David, illus. see Paul, Ann Whitford.
Walker, David, illus. see Root, Phyllis.
Walker, David, illus. see Roscoe, Lily.
Walker, David, illus. see Swenson, Jamie A.
Walker, David, illus. see Tomasello, Heather.
Walker, David, jt. auth. see Gershator, Phillis.
Walker, David, jt. auth. see Gordon, George W.
Walker, David, jt. auth. see Ransom, Candice.
Walker, David, jt. auth. see Van Hoven, Constance.
Walker, David H. Rocky Mountain Spotted Fever. Alcamo, I. Edward, ed. (p. 1484)
Walker, Deborah L. Beauty of His Hands. (p. 154)
Walker, Denise. Cells & Life Processes. (p. 286)
—Materials. (p. 1104)
Walker, Doris D. Lucky, the Little Talking Puppy! (p. 1063)
Walker, D.S. Delightfully Different. (p. 425)
Walker, Dwight. Walking in Grace: Dwayne's Disobedience. (p. 1854)
Walker, E. G. Boys' Club. Graffam, Merle, illus. (p. 220)
Walker, Elizabeth, jt. auth. see Waterman, Jill.
Walker, Fay Alice. In Search of My Brotha, My Lover, My Man. (p. 864)
Walker, Frank S., Jr. Remembering: A History of Orange County, Virginia. (p. 1459)
Walker, G. L. Good Morning Baby. (p. 698)
Walker, Gary C. Confederate Coloring & Learning Book. Breaux, Joe Ann, illus. (p. 356)
Walker, Geof. William Shakespeare's 'A Midsummer Night's Dream' - a playscript for younger Students. (p. 1933)
—William Shakespeare's 'the Tempest' - a playscript for younger Students. (p. 1933)
—William Shakespeare's 'Twelfth Night' - a playscript for younger Students. (p. 1933)
Walker, George, illus. see Raab, Evelyn.
Walker, Gloria. Stop & Go Safety. (p. 1653)
Walker, Ida. Addiction in America: Society, Psychology & Heredity. (p. 11)
—Addiction in America: Society, Psychology, & Heredity. (p. 11)
—Addiction in America: Society, Psychology & Heredity. Henningfield, Jack E., ed. (p. 11)
—Addiction Treatment: Escaping the Trap. (p. 11)
—Around the World. (p. 100)
—Assassination of Dr. Martin Luther King Jr. (p. 107)
—Belgium. (p. 161)
—Boston Tea Party. (p. 215)
—France. (p. 627)
—Germany. (p. 666)
—Homelessness. (p. 793)
—Ireland. (p. 887)
—Lynyrd Skynyrd. (p. 1066)
—Lynyrd Skynyrd. (p. 1066)
—Natural & Everyday Drugs: A False Sense of Security. (p. 1235)
—Natural & Everyday Drugs: A False Sense of Security. Henningfield, Jack E., ed. (p. 1235)
—Nigeria. (p. 1252)
—Nigeria. Rotberg, Robert I., ed. (p. 1252)
—Painkillers: Prescription Dependency. (p. 1318)
—Painkillers: Prescription Dependency. Henningfield, Jack E., ed. (p. 1318)
—Sedatives & Hypnotics: Deadly Downers. (p. 1546)
—Sedatives & Hypnotics: Deadly Downers. Henningfield, Jack E., ed. (p. 1546)
—un Security Council & the Center of Power Russett, Bruce, ed. (p. 1811)
Walker, Ida, jt. auth. see McIntosh, Kenneth.
Walker, Ida, jt. auth. see Nelson, Sheila.
Walker, Ida & Indovino, Shaina C. Belgium. Bruton, John, ed. (p. 161)
—Germany. Bruton, John, ed. (p. 666)
Walker, Ida & Indovino, Shaina Carmel. Belgium. (p. 161)
—Germany. (p. 666)
—Ireland. (p. 887)
—Ireland. Bruton, John, ed. (p. 887)
Walker, Ida J. Alcohol Addiction: Not Worth the Buzz. (p. 35)
—Sedatives & Hypnotics: Deadly Downers. (p. 1546)
Walker, Jack, illus. see Kelly, Diana.
Walker, Jane. 100 Things You Should Know about Knights & Castles. (p. 1999)
—Ancient Egypt. (p. 68)
—Knights & Castles. (p. 964)
Walker, Jeff, jt. auth. see Dixon, Franklin W.
Walker, Joe. Belief & Science: Intermediate & Higher RMPS. (p. 161)
Walker, John. Pioneer Parables. (p. 1361)
—Story of Christmas: The Birth of Jesus. (p. 1657)
Walker, John, illus. see Ashley, Jane, IV.
Walker, John, illus. see Mackall, Dandi Daley.
Walker, John, illus. see Rainey, Barbara.
Walker, John, illus. see Swift, Jonathan.
Walker, John, photos by see van Gosen, Ryan O'Dell, IV.
Walker, John, tr. see Hichs, Donald E. & Demers, Aimee.
Walker, John Anthony. Frel. (p. 635)
Walker, John R. Exploring Metalworking: Teaching Package. (p. 552)
—Exploring Metalworking. (p. 552)
—Machining Fundamentals: Teaching Package Instructor's Resource Binder. (p. 1068)
—Machining Fundamentals. (p. 1068)
—Machining Fundamentals Instructor's Manual. (p. 1068)
—Modern Metalworking. (p. 1158)
—Modern Metalworking Instructor's Manual. (p. 1158)
Walker, John R. & Mathis, Bernard D. Exploring Drafting: Teaching Package Worksheets. (p. 552)
—Exploring Drafting: Fundamentals of Drafting Technology. (p. 552)
—Exploring Drafting. (p. 552)
Walker, John R. & Polanin, W. Richard. Arc Welding: Answer Key. (p. 95)
Walker, Johnny. Planet Blue: The Adventures of Harry Lee & Bingo. (p. 1367)
Walker, Joni. Apostles Creed. Walker, Joni, illus. (p. 92)
—Confession. (p. 356)
—Follow & Do Books: The Lord's Prayer. Walker, Joni, illus. (p. 612)
—Gods Ten Commandments. (p. 692)
—Holy Baptism. Walker, Joni, illus. (p. 791)
—Jesus Hears Me. (p. 915)
—Jesus Is with Me. Walker, Joni, illus. (p. 915)
—Jesus Knows Me. Walker, Joni, illus. (p. 915)
—Jesus Rose on Easter Morn Span. (p. 916)
—Lords Supper. Walker, Joni, illus. (p. 1053)
—Tell Me the Christmas Story. Walker, Joni, illus. (p. 1716)
—Tell Me the Easter Story. (p. 1716)
—Tell Me What God Made. Walker, Joni, illus. (p. 1716)
Walker, Jorge. Little Winston's Desire. (p. 1038)
Walker, Joyce MacKichan. Faithful Questions Student Book. (p. 565)
Walker, Joyce MacKichan & Freeman, Deborah. Questions & Beliefs. (p. 1426)
Walker, Judy. Carrying the Cross. (p. 271)
Walker, Kagon. Amber Wings. (p. 57)
Walker, Karen, illus. see London, Jack.
Walker, Kate. Air. (p. 31)
—Clothing. (p. 334)
—Food & Garden Waste. (p. 613)
—Glass. (p. 682)
—I Hate Books! Cox, David, illus. (p. 838)
—Metal Cans. (p. 1130)
—Paper. (p. 1322)
—Plants. (p. 1369)
—Plastic Bottles & Bags. (p. 1370)
—Rocks. (p. 1483)
—Soil. (p. 1606)
—Water. (p. 1862)
—Weather. (p. 1869)
Walker, Katherine, illus. see Cottringer, Anne.
Walker, Kathryn. Mysteries of Alien Visitors & Abductions. (p. 1222)
—Mysteries of Giant Humanlike Creatures. (p. 1222)
—Mysteries of the Ancients. (p. 1222)
—Mysteries of the Bermuda Triangle. (p. 1222)
—Mysteries of the Cosmic Joker. (p. 1222)
—Mysteries of the Mind. (p. 1222)
—Mysteries of Water Monsters. (p. 1222)
—Mysterious Healing. (p. 1223)
—Mysterious Predictions. (p. 1223)
—Mystery of Atlantis. (p. 1224)
—Mystery of the Ghosts of Flight 401. (p. 1225)
—See How Cats Grow. (p. 1546)
—See How Dogs Grow. (p. 1546)
—See How Horses & Ponies Grow. (p. 1546)
—See How Rabbits Grow. (p. 1546)
—Unsolved! (p. 1822)
Walker, Kathryn, jt. auth. see Hunter, Rebecca.
Walker, Keegan Holmes. Sebastianus: The War Begins. (p. 1539)
Walker, Kennesha M. Word in Due Season. (p. 1950)
Walker, Kev, illus. see Lente, Fred Van.
Walker, Kev, jt. illus. see Shalvey, Declan.
Walker, Kev & Shalvey, Declan. Thunderbolts: Violent Rejection. (p. 1746)
Walker, Kristin. Match Made in High School. (p. 1104)
Walker, Landry. Little Gloomy Super Scary Monster Show Volume 1. (p. 1028)
—Secrets & Lies. Takara, Marcio, illus. (p. 1544)
Walker, Landry, jt. auth. see Waid, Mark.
Walker, Landry Q. Danger Club (p. 403)
—Secret Entity! #4 Jones, Eric, illus. (p. 1540)
—Super Hero School: #3 Jones, Eric, illus. (p. 1680)
—Supergirl: Cosmic Adventures in the 8th Grade. Jones, Eric, illus. (p. 1683)
Walker, Landry Q. & Mason, Joey. Evil in a Skirt! #5 Jones, Eric, illus. (p. 546)
—Her First Extra-Ordinary Adventure! #1 Jones, Eric, illus. (p. 769)
—My Own Best Frenemy: #2 Jones, Eric, illus. (p. 1216)
—Off to Save the Day... Jones, Eric, illus. (p. 1279)
Walker, Lane. Boss on Redemption Road. (p. 215)
—Day It Rained Ducks. (p. 413)
—Hunt for Scarface. (p. 828)
—Legend of the Ghost Buck. (p. 989)
—Terror at Deadwood Lake. (p. 1722)
Walker, Lindsey. You Be Me, I Will Be You. (p. 1973)
Walker, Lisa & Coyne, Adrian. Boy Who Brought Thunder. (p. 219)
Walker, Lois. Crazy Critters. Boyer, Susy, illus. (p. 377)
—Gigantic Turnip Tug. Guthridge, Bettina, illus. (p. 676)
Walker, Lovoni. Essential Canadian Christmas Cookbook. Prosofsky, Merle, photos by. (p. 536)
—Essential Christmas Cookbook Prosofsky, Merle, photos by. (p. 536)
Walker, Mark Evan, illus. see Lorenzo, Amanda.
Walker, Mary. Flower Tree. (p. 607)
Walker, Maryalice. Development of Antidepressants: The Chemistry of Depression. (p. 432)
—Entomology & Palynology. Noziglia, Carla Miller & Siegel, Jay A., eds. (p. 531)
—Pathology. (p. 1328)
—Pathology. Noziglia, Carla Miller & Siegel, Jay A., eds. (p. 1328)
Walker, Melissa. Ashes to Ashes. (p. 106)
—Dust to Dust. (p. 490)
—Lovestruck Summer. (p. 1061)
—Small Town Sinners. (p. 1592)
—Unbreak My Heart. (p. 1811)
Walker, Melissa & Walker, Richard. Place for Delta. (p. 1365)
Walker, Melzina. Little Melvin's Blue Coat. (p. 1031)
Walker, Michael & Walker, Michael J. Field Guide: The Layout & Dimensions of Sports Fields. (p. 583)
Walker, Michael J., jt. auth. see Walker, Michael.
Walker, Nan. Bay School Blogger. Wummer, Amy, illus. (p. 147)
—Check It Out! Sims, Blanche, illus. (p. 295)
—Day Camp. (p. 412)
—Follow That Clue! Palmisciano, Diane, illus. (p. 612)
—Midnight Kid. Gott, Barry, illus. (p. 1139)
—Spork Out of Orbit. Warrick, Jessica, illus. (p. 1631)
—Stressbusters. Wummer, Amy, illus. (p. 1667)
—Thanksgiving Then & Now. (p. 1726)
—Weather. (p. 1869)
—Yum-Yum House. Pilz, M. H., illus. (p. 1983)
Walker, Nan, jt. auth. see Kulling, Monica.
Walker, Nan & Kulling, Monica. Messiest Room on the Planet. (p. 1130)
Walker, Nicole. Gingersnap. (p. 677)
Walker, Niki. Biomass: Fueling Change. (p. 189)
—Generating Wind Power. (p. 660)
—Harnessing Power from the Sun. (p. 749)
—Hydrogen: Running on Water. (p. 831)
—Transportation Disaster Alert! (p. 1779)
—Tsunami Alert! (p. 1795)
Walker, Niki, jt. auth. see Kalman, Bobbie.
Walker, Niki & Dann, Sarah. Badminton in Action. (p. 132)
—Bowling in Action. (p. 216)
—Fútbol en Acción. (p. 650)
—Fútbol en Accion. (p. 651)
—Hockey. (p. 786)
—Soccer. Briere, Marie-Josee, tr. from ENG. (p. 1603)
Walker, Niki & Kalman, Bobbie. Animaux en Mouvement. (p. 84)
—Dinosaurs. Mondor, Lyne, tr. from ENG. (p. 444)
—Gatitos. Crabtree, Marc, photos by. (p. 658)
—Kittens. (p. 963)
—Native North American Wisdom & Gifts. (p. 1235)
—¿Qué Es un Dinosaurio? (p. 1423)
Walker, Niki & Owlkids Books Inc. Staff. Why Do We Fight? Conflict, War, & Peace. (p. 1924)
Walker, Niki, et al. Badminton. (p. 132)
—Chatons. (p. 295)
Walker, Pam & Wood, Elaine. Continental Shelf. (p. 360)
—Ecosystem Science Fair Projects, Revised & Expanded Using the Scientific Method. (p. 503)
—Ecosystem Science Fair Projects Using Worms, Leaves, Crickets, & Other Stuff. (p. 503)
—Life in the Sea Set (p. 1011)
—Open Ocean. (p. 1299)
—People & the Sea. (p. 1339)
—Saltwater Wetland. (p. 1506)
—Science Experiments on File (p. 1525)
—Stimulants. (p. 1651)
Walker, Pamela, jt. auth. see Coster, Patience.
Walker, Pamela & Wood, Elaine. Chemistry Experiments. (p. 297)
—Computer Science Experiments. (p. 355)
—Earth Science Experiments. (p. 496)
—Ecology Experiments. (p. 502)
—Environmental Science Experiments. (p. 532)
—Forensic Science Experiments. (p. 617)
—Genetics Experiments. (p. 661)
—Human Body Experiments. (p. 825)
—Marine Science Experiments. (p. 1094)
—Physical Science Experiments. (p. 1353)
—Space & Astronomy Experiments. (p. 1618)
Walker, Patricia. Tommy's New Barn Mates. (p. 1765)
Walker, Patricia M., illus. see Goguen, Martha M.
Walker, Paul Robert. American Indians. (p. 62)
—Remember Little Bighorn: Indians, Soldiers, & Scouts Tell Their Stories. (p. 1459)
—Remember Little Rock: The Time, the People, the Stories. (p. 1459)
—Remember the Alamo: Texians, Tejanos, & Mexicans Tell Their Stories. (p. 1459)
Walker, Peggy. My First Book of Buddhist Treasures. (p. 1205)
Walker Perry, Kelley. Joy in the Darkness. (p. 929)
Walker, Persephone. Brain Quest Workbook: Grade 6. Thornborrow, Nick, illus. (p. 222)
Walker, Peter. Gimnasia Divertida para Niños: Estimula a Tu Hijo Mediante Ejercicios y Juegos con Movimiento. (p. 676)
—Magic Airplane. (p. 1071)
Walker, Peter Lancaster. Space Travelers Land at Buckingham Palace. Dixit, Rama, illus. (p. 1620)
Walker, Rachael. Angel Starlight & the Wish Book. (p. 74)
Walker, Raven. Dragalleon. (p. 476)
—Feather Giant. (p. 579)
Walker, Raynn. Toadina: The Story of a Lady Toad. (p. 1760)
Walker, Rebecca, frwd. It's up to Me: Stories of Choices, Predicaments & Decisions by San Francisco Youth. (p. 899)
Walker, Rhonda. Willie Out West. (p. 1934)
Walker, Richard. Barefoot Book of Pirates. Whelan, Olwyn, illus. (p. 139)
—Build the Human Body. Bernstein, Galia & Ruffle, Mark, illus. (p. 238)
—Epidemics & Plagues. (p. 532)
—Human Body. (p. 825)
—Human Body in 360°: Explored in 5 Virtual Journeys. (p. 825)
—Jack & the Beanstalk. (p. 902)
—Juan y los Frijoles Magicos. (p. 930)
—KFK Epidemics & Plagues. (p. 951)

W

—Your Amazing Body. (p. 1979)
Walker, Richard, jt. auth. see Clark, John.
Walker, Richard, jt. auth. see Dorling Kindersley Publishing Staff.
Walker, Richard, jt. auth. see Knight, Richard John.
Walker, Richard, jt. auth. see Sharkey, Niamh.
Walker, Richard, jt. auth. see Walker, Melissa.
Walker, Rob. Baby Animals. (p. 124)
—Farm Animals. (p. 573)
—Mapping Towns & Cities. (p. 1090)
—Pet Animals. (p. 1345)
—Wild Animals. (p. 1928)
Walker, Robert. Bar & Bat Mitzvahs. (p. 137)
—Eid Al-Adha. (p. 507)
—Flag Day. (p. 602)
—Happy Birthday! (p. 744)
—Labor Day. (p. 969)
—Live It: Optimism. (p. 1040)
—Live It: Integrity. (p. 1040)
—Live It: Initiative. (p. 1040)
—Maserati. (p. 1102)
—Porsche. Crabtree, ed. (p. 1386)
—Pushes & Pulls: Why Do People Migrate? (p. 1420)
—Sheamus. (p. 1564)
—Transportation Inventions: Moving Our World Forward. (p. 1779)
—Transportation Inventions. (p. 1779)
—Veterans Day. (p. 1839)
—What Is the Theory of Evolution? (p. 1890)
—World War I: 1917-1918 — the Turning of the Tide. (p. 1958)
Walker, Robert, jt. auth. see Miller, Reagan.
Walker, Robin & Harding, Keith. Tourism 2. (p. 1773)
Walker, Robyn. Sergeant Gander: A Canadian Hero. (p. 1552)
Walker, Rory, illus. see Graham, Ian.
Walker, Rory, illus. see Pipe, Jim.
Walker, Rowe Jl, jt. auth. see Walker Rowe, Jl.
Walker Rowe, Jl & Walker, Rowe Jl. Andys Family Secret: Brave Little Boy BK One. (p. 73)
Walker, Russell D. Michelle & the Magic Timepiece. (p. 1135)
Walker, Rysa. Timebound (p. 1753)
Walker, Sally. Ghost Walls: The Story of a 17th-Century Colonial Homestead. (p. 672)
Walker, Sally J. Letting Go of Sacred Things. (p. 1003)
Walker, Sally M. American Chestnut: The Comeback Tale of a Champion Tree. (p. 60)
—Bessie Coleman: Daring to Fly. Porter, Janice Lee, illus. (p. 168)
—Blizzard of Glass: The Halifax Explosion Of 1917. (p. 200)
—Calor. Translations.com Staff, tr. from ENG. (p. 255)
—Caves. (p. 282)
—Crocodiles. (p. 384)
—Dolphins. (p. 464)
—Druscilla's Halloween. White, Lee, illus. (p. 487)
—Earthquakes. (p. 497)
—Electricity. King, Andy, photos by. (p. 509)
—Figuring Out Fossils. (p. 586)
—Fossils. (p. 624)
—Freedom Song: The Story of Henry "Box" Brown. Qualls, Sean, illus. (p. 635)
—Frozen Secrets: Antarctica Revealed. (p. 645)
—Glaciers. (p. 682)
—Heat. King, Andy, photos by. (p. 760)
—Hippos. (p. 781)
—Investigating Electricity. (p. 884)
—Investigating Heat. (p. 884)
—Investigating Light. (p. 884)
—Investigating Magnetism. (p. 885)
—Investigating Matter. (p. 885)
—Investigating Sound. (p. 885)
—Jackie Robinson. Translations.com Staff, tr. (p. 903)
—Jaguars. (p. 905)
—Libros de Energía para Madrugadores; Early Bird Energy: Complete Set. (p. 1007)
—Libros de Energía para Madrugadores; Early Bird Energy: Classroom Set. (p. 1007)
—Libros de Energía para Madrugadores (Early Bird Energy) Translations.com Staff, tr. (p. 1007)
—Light. King, Andy, photos by. (p. 1014)
—Luz. Translations.com Staff, tr. from ENG. (p. 1066)
—Magnetism. King, Andy, photos by. (p. 1076)
—Magnetismo. Translations.com Staff, tr. from ENG. (p. 1076)
—Marveling at Minerals. (p. 1099)
—Materia. Translations.com Staff, tr. from ENG. (p. 1104)
—Materia; Matter. (p. 1104)
—Opossum at Sycamore Road. Snyder, Joel, illus. (p. 1300)
—Opossums. (p. 1300)
—Reefs. (p. 1456)
—Researching Rocks. (p. 1463)
—Rhinos. (p. 1467)
—Rocks. (p. 1483)
—Seahorse Reef: A Story of the South Pacific. Petruccio, Steven James, illus. (p. 1536)
—Search for Antarctic Dinosaurs. Bindon, John, illus. (p. 1537)
—Secrets of a Civil War Submarine: Solving the Mysteries of the H. L. Hunley. (p. 1545)
—Shipwreck Search: Discovery of the H. L. Hunley. Verstraete, Elaine, illus. (p. 1567)
—Sonido. Translations.com Staff, tr. from ENG. (p. 1612)
—Studying Soil. (p. 1670)
—Volcanoes. (p. 1849)
—Vowel Family: A Tale of Lost Letters. Luthardt, Kevin, illus. (p. 1850)
—Winnie: The True Story of the Bear Who Inspired Winnie-the-Pooh. Voss, Jonathan D., illus. (p. 1937)
—Written in Bone: Buried Lives of Jamestown & Colonial Maryland. (p. 1965)
Walker, Sally M., jt. auth. see Feldman, Roseann.
Walker, Sally M. & Feldmann, Roseann. Planos Inclinados. King, Andy, photos by. (p. 1368)
—Poleas. King, Andy, photos by. (p. 1379)
—Put Inclined Planes to the Test. (p. 1420)
—Put Levers to the Test. (p. 1420)
—Put Pulleys to the Test. (p. 1420)
—Put Screws to the Test. (p. 1420)
—Put Wedges to the Test. (p. 1420)
—Put Wheels & Axles to the Test. (p. 1420)
—Ruedas y Ejes. King, Andy, photos by. (p. 1494)
—Tornillos. King, Andy, photos by. (p. 1770)
—Trabajo. King, Andy, photos by. (p. 1774)
Walker, Saskia, et al. Secrets Volume 19 Timeless Passions - the Secrets Collection: The Best in Women's Erotic Romance: Timeless Passions (p. 1546)
Walker, Sharon. Little Rose Grows. (p. 1036)
Walker, Sholto, illus. see Fuerst, Jeffrey B.
Walker, Sholto, illus. see Kozlowski, Michal.
Walker, Sholto, jt. auth. see Donaldson, Julia.
Walker, Sholto, jt. auth. see Durant, Alan.
Walker, Simion. Milburn the Macaroni Penguin. (p. 1142)
Walker, Steve, illus. see Lagos, Alexander & Lagos, Joseph.
Walker, Steve, illus. see Lagos, Joseph & Lagos, Alexander.
Walker, Steve, illus. see Nunn, Daniel.
Walker, Steven, illus. see Kittinger, Jo S.
Walker, Steven, illus. see Pingry, Patricia A.
Walker, Steven, illus. see Zimmermann, Karl.
Walker, Susan Eileen. I Know the Quigglebush Heroes. (p. 840)
—Not Enough Time (p. 1267)
—Secret of the Dance. (p. 1542)
Walker, Suzanne. Treasure Chest Blueprint Adventures of Mark & James: Fun Stories for Young Children to Learn Solving Daily Problems Using Scripture... FORGIVENESS (Which Is What the Story Is About) (p. 1781)
Walker, Sylvia. Art Museum: A Sticker Story Coloring Book. (p. 102)
—At the Wedding. (p. 111)
—Halloween ABC Coloring Book. (p. 737)
—Happy New Year Around the World. (p. 746)
—Let's Color Together — My Sleepover. (p. 995)
—Little Musicians Stickers. (p. 1032)
—My Sleepover Coloring Book. (p. 1219)
—Our New Baby Coloring Book. (p. 1309)
—Storyland: We're Moving! A Story Coloring Book. (p. 1663)
Walker, Sylvia, illus. see Hooks, Gwendolyn.
Walker, Sylvia, illus. see Parker, David.
Walker, Sylvia, illus. see Scholastic, Inc. Staff & Hooks, Gwendolyn.
Walker, Sylvia, illus. see Scholastic, Inc. Staff & Hudson, Cheryl Willis.
Walker, Sylvia & Coloring Books Staff. Easter Egg Hunt Coloring Book. (p. 499)
Walker, Tanisha. Rainbow Tots- 10-28. (p. 1436)
Walker, Terrence E. World of Hartz. (p. 1956)
Walker, Theo. City Experiment: Rebuilding Greensburg, Kansas. (p. 323)
—Eat Up! (p. 501)
—Sugar: Our Guilty Pleasure Low Intermediate Book with Online Access. (p. 1673)
—Swing, Slither, Swim Low Intermediate Book with Online Access. (p. 1691)
Walker, Tom, photos by see Jones, Tim.
Walker, Victoria. Winter of Enchantment. (p. 1938)
Walker, Wendy & Maidment, Stella. Draw It! (p. 480)
Walker, Whitney. Doubting Destiny. (p. 473)
Walker, William. Pen to the Page. (p. 1336)
Walker, Willie. Walker's Method: A Recipe for Mental Math. (p. 1854)
Walker, Yonette. Soul Soup Sunday. (p. 1614)
Walker-Cox, Krysten. Amber's Metal Singlet. (p. 57)
Walker-Hirsch, Leslie & Champagne, Marklyn. Circles I, Level 1: Intimacy & Relationships. Stanfield, James, ed. (p. 321)
Walker-Jones, Alexandra & Herrera, Hanna. Adventures of Hobnob & Raisin - Paris Airport. (p. 18)
Walker-Renner, Christa. Santa's Magic. (p. 1513)
Walking Bull, Gilbert & Moore, Sally. Rocks Not Happy in Sack. (p. 1484)
Walkinshaw, Jean, jt. ed. see James, Gregory.
Walkinshaw, Jean, ed. Model & Talent 2003 Directory: The International Directory of Model & Talent Agencies & Schools. (p. 1157)
Walkley, Andrew & Dellar, Hugh. Innovations Elementary. (p. 875)
Walko. Amigos: Friends Forever. (p. 65)
Walkowski, A. J. Reflections of the Savior. (p. 1456)
Walkup, Jennifer. Second Verse. (p. 1539)
Walkush, Donna, ed. see Wallaker, Jillayne Prince.
Wall, Anne. Librarius Quest. (p. 1005)
Wall, Billy James. Mystery of Marcy & the Stony Squirrel. (p. 1224)
Wall, Charles H., tr. see Molière.
Wall Darby, Colleen, illus. see Exelby, Kathy.
Wall, Dorothy. Complete Adventures of Blinky Bill. (p. 352)
Wall, Frances, ed. see Kishimoto, Masashi.
Wall, Frances, ed. see Kubo, Tite.
Wall, Frances, ed. see Takahashi, Kazuki.
Wall, Frances, jt. auth. see Watsuki, Nobuhiro.
Wall, Jean Jones. I Can Stand by a Rase. (p. 836)
Wall, Joanne. Anna of Allegheny. Wall, Joanne, ed. (p. 85)
Wall, Julia. Discovering 2-D Shapes in Art (p. 448)
—Finding 3-D Shapes in New York City (p. 587)
—Mapping Shipwrecks with Coordinate Planes (p. 1090)
—Marty & the Magazine. (p. 1098)
—Nico's List. (p. 1251)
Wall, Julia & McKenzie, Heather. Nico's List. (p. 1251)
Wall, Julia & Nickel, Adam. Bruno's Tea. (p. 232)
Wall, Karen, illus. see Helmore Wall Staff & Helmore, Jim.
Wall, Karen, illus. see Helmore, Jim.
Wall, Karen, illus. see Singh, Lee.
Wall, Karen, jt. auth. see Helmore, Jim.
Wall, Laura. Goose. (p. 702)
—Goose Goes to School. Wall, Laura, illus. (p. 702)
—Goose Goes to the Zoo. Wall, Laura, illus. (p. 702)
Wall, Layton E. Rat Fishin' with Ralphie Rat: A Bully Learns a Lesson. (p. 1440)
Wall, Mike, illus. see Posner-Sanchez, Andrea.
Wall, Patricia Q. Child Out of Place: A Story for New England. Ronnquist, Debby, illus. (p. 301)
Wall, Pauline & Smith, Shelley. What the Mouse Saw: An Easter Story. (p. 1893)
Wall, Randy Hugh, ed. see Gummelt, Donna & Melchiorre, Dondino.
Wall, Randy Hugh, ed. see Sinclair, Nicholas, et al.
Wall, Suzy. Dodo's Last Stand. (p. 460)
—Earth Day Garden. (p. 495)
—Hurricanes. (p. 830)
—Our New Home. Leon, Karen, illus. (p. 1309)
Wall, Terry & Pimental, Ric. Checkpoint Mathematics. (p. 295)
Wall, Terry & Pimentel, Ric. Checkpoint Maths (p. 295)
Wallace. Morgan the Magnificent. (p. 1175)
Wallace, Adam. Dawn of the Zombie Knights. (p. 412)
—Incredible Journey of Pete McGee. (p. 869)
—Mac O'Beasty McKenzie, Heath, illus. (p. 1067)
—Rhymes with Art: Learn Cartooning the Fun Way! Wallace, Adam, illus. (p. 1468)
Wallace, Alfred Russel, jt. auth. see Berry, Andrew.
Wallace, Amanda D., jt. auth. see Wallace II, James C.
Wallace, Amy & Henkin, Bill. Psychic Healing Book. (p. 1413)
Wallace, Andrea, illus. see Fox, Nita.
Wallace, Ann Hamilton. Messenger: Revelations from an Unlikely Prophet. (p. 1129)
Wallace, Archer. Men Who Played the Game. (p. 1126)
Wallace, B. My Books of Colors Slipcase. (p. 1199)
Wallace, Barbara Brooks. Argyle. Sandford, John, illus. (p. 98)
—Interesting Thing That Happened at Perfect Acres, Inc. (p. 879)
—Miss Switch Online. (p. 1152)
—Peppermints in the Parlor. (p. 1340)
—Perils of Peppermints. (p. 1343)
—Secret in St. Something. (p. 1541)
Wallace, Becky. Skylighter. (p. 1587)
—Storyspinner. (p. 1663)
Wallace, Bill. Beauty. (p. 154)
—Danger on Panther Peak. (p. 404)
—Dog Called Kitty. (p. 461)
—Dog Who Thought He Was Santa. (p. 462)
—Final Freedom. (p. 586)
—Goosed! Rogers, Jacqueline, illus. (p. 702)
—Legend of Thunderfoot. (p. 989)
—No Dogs Allowed! (p. 1258)
—Pick of the Litter. (p. 1354)
—Skinny-Dipping at Monster Lake. (p. 1585)
—Snot Stew. McCue, Lisa, illus. (p. 1598)
—That Doggone Calf. Wallace, Carol, illus. (p. 1726)
—Totally Disgusting! Morrill, Leslie, illus. (p. 1771)
Wallace, Bill, jt. auth. see Wallace, Carol.
Wallace, Bill & Wallace, Carol. That Doggone Calf. (p. 1726)
Wallace, Bonny. Raymond Wikins' Adventures, Children of Straw. (p. 1441)
Wallace, Brandon. Wilder Boys. (p. 1931)
Wallace, Bruce. Wild Animals. (p. 1928)
Wallace, Bruce, jt. auth. see Phillips, Sarah.
Wallace, Bruce & Make Believe Ideas Staff. Pets. (p. 1348)
Wallace, Carey. Ghost in the Glass House. (p. 670)
Wallace, Carol. Easter Bunny Blues. Björkman, Steve, illus. (p. 499)
—One Nosy Pup. Björkman, Steve, illus. (p. 1296)
—Pumpkin Mystery. Björkman, Steve, illus. (p. 1416)
—Santa Secret. Björkman, Steve, illus. (p. 1513)
—Turkeys Together. Rogers, Jaqueline & Rogers, Jacqueline, illus. (p. 1797)
Wallace, Carol, illus. see Wallace, Bill.
Wallace, Carol, jt. auth. see Wallace, Bill.
Wallace, Carol & Wallace, Bill. Bub, Snow, & the Burly Bear Scare. Gurney, John Steven, illus. (p. 233)
—Meanest Hound Around. Gurney, John Steven, illus. (p. 1116)
Wallace, Chad. Mouse & the Meadow. Wallace, Chad, illus. (p. 1181)
Wallace, Chad, illus. see Bowen, Sherry.
Wallace, Chad, illus. see Curtis, Jennifer Keats.
Wallace, Chad, illus. see Gulberson, Brenda Z.
Wallace, Chad, illus. see Mason, Chad.
Wallace, Chad, illus. see McKinney, Barbara Shaw.
Wallace, Chad, illus. see Quattlebaum, Mary.
Wallace, Chad, illus. see Schnetzler, Pattie.
Wallace, Chad, illus. see Schoonmaker, Frances, ed.
Wallace, Clinton. H. Adventures of Roger Eldemire. (p. 22)
Wallace, Daggi, illus. see Petrick, Neila S.
Wallace, Daniel. Cat's Pajamas. (p. 281)
—Darth Vader: A 3-D Reconstruction Log. Reiff, Chris & Trevas, Chris, illus. (p. 409)
—Star Wars Rebels - Ezra's Journal. Barthelmes, Andrew, illus. (p. 1641)
—Star Wars Rebels - Find It Solve It Match It. Froeb, Lori & Nathanson, Amy, eds. (p. 1641)
—Star Wars Rebels: Sabine My Rebel Sketchbook. Stoll, Annie, illus. (p. 1642)
Wallace, Daniel, jt. auth. see Dorling Kindersley Publishing Staff.
Wallace, Daniel & Dorling Kindersley Publishing Staff. Batman - The World of the Dark Knight. (p. 144)
—Superman - The Ultimate Guide to the Man of Steel. (p. 1683)
Wallace, Daniel B., et al. Workbook for New Testament Syntax: Companion to Basics of New Testament Syntax & Greek Grammar Beyond the Basics (p. 1952)
Wallace, Dejuanna, jt. auth. see Varikyan, Arpine.
Wallace, Dianne. Jungle in the Sky. (p. 935)
Wallace, Dillon. Troop One of the Labrador. (p. 1788)
—Ungava Bob. (p. 1817)
Wallace, Dora J. Twas the Night Before Jesus Was Born. (p. 1799)
Wallace, G. G. Illustrate It Yourself Book. (p. 857)
Wallace, G. Ira. Bunny Tales: The Journey Begins. (p. 242)
Wallace, Holly. Buddhism: Yuranan's Story. (p. 234)
—Cells & Systems. (p. 286)
—Christianity: Herbert's Story. (p. 312)
—Food Chains & Webs. (p. 613)
—Glass. (p. 682)
—Hinduism: Babu's Story. (p. 780)
—Islam: Hambali's Story. (p. 891)
—Judaism: Yoni's Story. (p. 930)
—Life Cycles. (p. 1009)
—Paper. (p. 1322)
—Plastic. (p. 1370)
—This Is My Faith: Judaism. (p. 1736)
—Wood. (p. 1949)
Wallace Hunchak, Lisa. It Could Happen. (p. 893)
Wallace, Ian. Boy of the Deeps (p. 218)
—Huron Carol (p. 829)
—Man Who Walked the Earth (p. 1086)
—Mavis & Merna (p. 1110)
—Morgan the Magnificent. (p. 1175)
—Mr. Kneebone's New Digs. Wallace, Ian, illus. (p. 1185)
—Sleeping Porch. (p. 1589)
—Slippers' Keeper (p. 1590)
—True Story of Trapper Jack's Left Big Toe. (p. 1793)
Wallace, Ian, illus. see Andrews, Jan.
Wallace, Ian, illus. see Davidge, Bud.
Wallace, Ian, illus. see Kipling, Rudyard.
Wallace, Ian, illus. see Lightfoot, Gordon.
Wallace II, James C. & Wallace, Amanda D. Emerald Slippers of Oz. (p. 517)
Wallace, James. Tsunami: Ghost Eagle 1. (p. 1795)
Wallace, James, jt. auth. see Baxley, Ron.
Wallace, Jason. Out of Shadows. (p. 1311)
Wallace, Jazey. Smile Bright. Fraser, Sigmund, illus. (p. 1594)
Wallace, Jessica. Present KinderConcepts. 6 Packs. Gardner, Marjory, illus. (p. 1396)
—Weather: KinderConcepts Individual Title Six-Packs. Ross, Christine, illus. (p. 1869)
Wallace, Jessica K., jt. auth. see McBride, Maurice.
Wallace, Jim. Search for the Mountain Gorillas. Nugent, Suzanne & Donploypetch, Jintanan, illus. (p. 1537)
—Terror on the Titanic. Sundaravej, Sittisan & Barchus, Nathan, illus. (p. 1722)
Wallace, John, illus. see Bauer, Dane.
Wallace, John, illus. see Bauer, Marion Dane.
Wallace, John, illus. see Evans, Kristina.
Wallace, John, illus. see Fox, Kathleen.
Wallace, John, illus. see Knudsen, Michelle.
Wallace, John, jt. auth. see Bauer, Marion Dane.
Wallace, Joshua, illus. see Riley, Lehman & Austin, Megan.
Wallace, Kali. Shallow Graves. (p. 1559)
Wallace, Karen. ABCs of What Children Need from their Parents: ABCs You Can Learn Throughout Your Lives. (p. 4)
—Bears in the Forest: Read & Wonder. Firth, Barbara, illus. (p. 152)
—Born to Be a Butterfly. (p. 214)
—Case of the Howling Armor. (p. 274)
—Connection Between Object Relations & Health. (p. 358)
—Creepy-Crawlies. Humphries, Tudor, illus. (p. 381)
—Crias del Mundo Animal. (p. 382)
—Detective Derek. Blake, Beccy, illus. (p. 431)
—Diamond Takers. (p. 434)
—DK Readers L1: Diving Dolphin: Diving Dolphin. (p. 456)
—Dragon Hunt Baines, Nigel, illus. (p. 477)
—Flash Harriet & the Loch Ness Monster. Nayler, Sarah, illus. (p. 602)
—Flash Harriet & the Outrageous Ostrich Egg Mystery. (p. 602)
—Flip the Flaps: Farm Animals. Palin, Nicki, illus. (p. 605)
—Footprints in the Snow Harland, Jackie, illus. (p. 615)
—Gentle Giant Octopus: Read, Listen & Wonder. Bostock, Mike, illus. (p. 661)
—Ghost Mouse. Blake, Beccy, illus. (p. 671)
—I Wonder Why Flip the Flaps Farm Animals. (p. 849)
—Lost Kittens. Harland, Jackie, illus. (p. 1056)
—Minestrone Mob. Brown, Judy, illus. (p. 1146)
—Mirror, Mirror Brett, Cathy, illus. (p. 1149)
—Quirky Times at Quagmire Castle Flook, Helen, illus. (p. 1428)
—Raspberries on the Yangtze. (p. 1439)
—Rockets & Spaceships. (p. 1483)
—Rockets & Spaceships, Level 1. (p. 1483)
—Snow White Sees the Light. Rowland, Andrew, illus. (p. 1600)
—Stinky Giant. Brett, Cathy, illus. (p. 1651)
—Stolen Egg. Harland, Jackie, illus. (p. 1652)
—Think of an Eel: Read, Listen & Wonder. Bostock, Mike, illus. (p. 1734)
—Think of an Eel Big Book. Bostock, Mike, illus. (p. 1734)
—Think of an Eel with Audio, Peggable: Read, Listen & Wonder. Bostock, Mike, illus. (p. 1734)
—Thunderbelle's Song. Parker-Rees, Guy, illus. (p. 1746)
—Treasure Trail Harland, Jackie, illus. (p. 1782)
—Trip to the Zoo. (p. 1787)
—Wendy. (p. 1875)
—Where Are My Shoes? Allwright, Deborah, illus. (p. 1906)
—Wild Baby Animals. (p. 1928)
—Wild Baby Animals, Level 1. (p. 1929)
—Wolves. (p. 1945)
Wallace, Karen & Bostock, Mike. Imagine You Are a Dolphin. (p. 861)
Wallace, Karen & Chapman, Neil. Arthur the King. (p. 104)
—Round Table. (p. 1491)
—Sir Lancelot & the Ice Castle. (p. 1580)
Wallace, Karen & Mackey, James. Queen Carrion's Big Bear Hug Flook, Helen, illus. (p. 1424)
Wallace, Karen & Parker-Rees, Guy. Thunderbelle's Beauty Parlour. (p. 1746)
Wallace, Karen & Platt, Richard. D-Day Landings, Level 4: The Story of the Allied Invasion. (p. 397)
Wallace, Karen & Willey. Blue Eyes. (p. 202)
Wallace, Kim. Erik & Isabelle Freshman Year at Foresthill High. (p. 533)
—Erik & Isabelle Junior Year at Foresthill High. (p. 533)
—Erik & Isabelle Senior Year at Foresthill High. (p. 533)
—Erik & Isabelle Sophomore Year at Foresthill High. (p. 533)
Wallace, Leslie, illus. see Swoboda, Lois.
Wallace, Lew. Autobiography. (p. 117)
—Ben-Hur. (p. 163)

Wallace, Lizzie. My Sister's Turning into a Monster. (p. 1218)
—Sam the Baker & the Buns of Courage. (p. 1507)
Wallace, Loston, illus. see Black, Jake & Meredith Books Staff.
Wallace, Loston, illus. see Eliopulos, Nick & Random House Staff.
Wallace, Lynn. Do Kangaroos Carry Platypuses? (p. 457)
Wallace, Marianne D. America's Forests: Guide to Plants & Animals. (p. 64)
—America's Seashores: Guide to Plants & Animals. (p. 64)
—America's Wetlands: Guide to Plants & Animals. (p. 64)
Wallace, Marianne D., illus. see Spickert, Diane Nelson.
Wallace, Mary. Inuksuk Book. Wallace, Mary & Owlkids Books Inc. Staff, illus. (p. 883)
—Inuksuk Means Welcome. (p. 883)
Wallace, Mary & Owlkids Books Inc. Staff. I Can Make That! Fantastic Crafts for Kids (p. 836)
—Make Your Own Inuksuk. (p. 1080)
Wallace, MaryAlice & Lindstrom, Charlotte. Scripture Puzzlers: Crosswords, Word Searches, & Other Brain Teasers. (p. 1533)
Wallace, Maurice O. Langston Hughes: The Harlem Renaissance. (p. 974)
Wallace, Michael. You, Mommy & Me. (p. 1976)
Wallace, Mike, jt. auth. see Mikaelian, Allen.
Wallace, Nancy. Alphabet House (p. 49)
—Christmas Cats Housley, Cathren, illus. (p. 313)
—Fly, Monarch! Fly! (p. 609)
—Shells! Shells! Shells! (p. 1565)
—Valentine Express (p. 1830)
—Water! Water! Water! (p. 1863)
Wallace, Nancy Elizabeth. Apples, Apples, Apples (p. 92)
—Kindness Quilt (p. 957)
—Leaves! Leaves! Leaves! (p. 986)
—Look! Look! Look! Wallace, Nancy Elizabeth, illus. (p. 1049)
—Planting Seeds (p. 1369)
—Pumpkin Day Wallace, Nancy Elizabeth, illus. (p. 1416)
—Ready, Set, 100th Day! (p. 1447)
—Recycle Every Day! Wallace, Nancy Elizabeth, illus. (p. 1452)
—Rocks! Rocks! Rocks! (p. 1484)
—Seeds! Seeds! Seeds! Wallace, Nancy Elizabeth, illus. (p. 1548)
—Stars! Stars! Stars! Wallace, Nancy Elizabeth, illus. (p. 1643)
—Tell-A-Bunny Wallace, Nancy Elizabeth, illus. (p. 1716)
Wallace, Nancy Elizabeth & Friedlaender, Linda. Look! Look! Look! at Sculpture (p. 1049)
Wallace, Nancy K. Claim to Fame. Chronister, Amanda, illus. (p. 326)
—Farmyard Security: A Readers' Theater Script & Guide. (p. 575)
—Fettuccine & Four-Leaf Clovers: A Readers' Theater Script & Guide. Mata, Nina, illus. (p. 583)
—Ghosts & Gummy Worms: A Readers' Theater Script & Guide. Fleming, Lucy, illus. (p. 672)
—Groundhogs & Guinea Pigs: A Readers' Theater Script & Guide. Fleming, Lucy, illus. (p. 725)
—Hair Today, Gone Tomorrow: A Readers' Theater Script & Guide. (p. 736)
—Haunted Sleepover. Chronister, Amanda, illus. (p. 753)
—Medals & Memorials: A Readers' Theater Script & Guide. Mata, Nina, illus. (p. 1118)
—Movie Mishaps. Chronister, Amanda, illus. (p. 1183)
—Mystery of the Golden Key. Chronister, Amanda, illus. (p. 1225)
—Out to Lunch. Chronister, Amanda, illus. (p. 1311)
—Pickles & Parks: A Readers' Theater Script & Guide. Fleming, Lucy, illus. (p. 1354)
—Presumed Missing. Chronister, Amanda, illus. (p. 1398)
—Pricked Pinkies: A Readers' Theater Script & Guide. (p. 1398)
—Princedom of Pea: A Readers' Theater Script & Guide. Mata, Nina, illus. (p. 1401)
—Princess & the Frog: A Readers' Theater Script & Guide. Henninger, Michelle, illus. (p. 1402)
—Snow White & the Seven Dorks: A Readers' Theater Script & Guide. Mata, Nina, illus. (p. 1599)
—Turkey & Take-Out: A Readers' Theater Script & Guide. Fleming, Lucy, illus. (p. 1797)
Wallace, Patrick. Jared: Boy from the Bottom. Boller, David, illus. (p. 909)
Wallace, Paula S. Rick & Rocky. Fruisen, Catherine Myler, illus. (p. 1470)
Wallace, R. Mike. Saunter. (p. 1516)
Wallace, Rich. Ball Hogs Holder, Jimmy, illus. (p. 134)
—Benched. Holder, Jimmy, illus. (p. 164)
—Between the Sticks. Heitz, Tim, illus. (p. 173)
—Chasing the Baton. Heitz, Tim, illus. (p. 294)
—Curveball (p. 395)
—Double-Crossed at Cactus Flats: An Up2 U Western Adventure. Mitchell, Hazel, illus. (p. 472)
—Dunk under Pressure (p. 490)
—Emergency Quarterback. (p. 518)
—Fake Out. Holder, Jimmy, illus. (p. 565)
—Fast Company. (p. 576)
—Game-Day Jitters. Holder, Jimmy, illus. (p. 654)
—Kickers #3: Benched. Holder, Jimmy, illus. (p. 951)
—No Relief. Heitz, Tim, illus. (p. 1260)
—Pressure Point. Heitz, Tim, illus. (p. 1397)
—Roar of the Crowd. (p. 1478)
—Room of Woe: An Up2U Horror Adventure. Emroca Flores, Jose, illus. (p. 1488)
—Second-String Center. (p. 1539)
—Shots on Goal. (p. 1569)
—Southpaw. (p. 1617)
—Sports Camp. (p. 1632)
—Takedown. (p. 1697)
—Technical Foul. (p. 1711)
—War & Watermelon. (p. 1857)
—Wicked Cruel. (p. 1927)
Wallace, Rich & Warner, Sally. Not-So-Weird Emma. Harper, Jamie, illus. (p. 1267)
Wallace, Robert. Phantom Detective, The - 06/34. (p. 1349)
Wallace, Robert E. Adventures of Ichi, the Baby Deer: The Rescue. Bk. 1 Wallace, Robert E., photos by. (p. 18)
Wallace, Sally. Big Secret: A Nativity Story. (p. 183)
—Peter's Puzzling Purple Easter Egg. (p. 1347)
—Three Parables & A Pickle. (p. 1743)
Wallace, Sam Amber, illus. see Miller, Dennis.
Wallace, Sandra Neil. Little Joe. Elliott, Mark, illus. (p. 1029)
Wallace, Sharolyn. Adventures of Bruce, Ben & Gerry: The Surprise. (p. 17)
—Adventures of Bruce, Ben & Gerry: Training Day. (p. 17)
—Adventures of Bruce, Ben & Gerry: Bruce's Dream. (p. 17)
Wallace, Sheila Ryan. Diving for the Gold. (p. 455)
—Miss Abigail's Antique Treasures. (p. 1151)
—Missing Heir. (p. 1152)
Wallace, Stone. Famous Canadian Actors: The Stories Behind Today's Popular Hollywood Celebrities (p. 569)
—Johnny Depp: The Passionate Rebel. (p. 923)
—Pioneer Canadian Actors: The Stories of Early Hollywood Celebrities (p. 1361)
Wallace, Stone & Carrière, Nicole. Russell Crowe: Maverick with a Heart. Vol. 1 (p. 1498)
Wallace, Susan F. S. P. & Wright, Melissa. Saints for Young Readers for Every Day Aven, Jamie H., illus. (p. 1504)
Wallace, Susan Helen. Blessed John Paul II: Be Not Afraid. Craig, Charles, illus. (p. 199)
—Little Book of Saints: Volume 4 Kinarney, Tom, illus. (p. 1025)
—Little Book of Saints. Kinarney, Tom, illus. (p. 1025)
—Saint Bakhita of Sudan: Forever Free. Alfano, Wayne, illus. (p. 1503)
—Saint Faustina Kowalska: Messenger of Mercy. Waites, Joan, illus. (p. 1503)
—Saint Gianna Beretta Molla: The Gift of Life. (p. 1503)
—Saint Katharine Drexel: The Total Gift. Kiwak, Barbara, illus. (p. 1503)
—Saint Teresa of Avila: Joyful in the Lord. Kiwak, Barbara, illus. (p. 1504)
Wallace, Susan Helen, jt. auth. see Muldoon, Kathleen M.
Wallace, Susan Helen & Jablonski, Patricia E. Saint Thomas More: Courage, Conscience, & the King. Lachuk, Dani, illus. (p. 1504)
Wallace, Susan Helen & Wright, Melissa. Saints for Young Readers for Every Day Aven, Jamie H., illus. (p. 1504)
Wallace, Suzanne. Man Who Loved Violins. (p. 1086)
—When I Was a Baby, What Did I Do? What Did I Do? (p. 1903)
Wallace, T. M. Under a Fairy Moon. (p. 1813)
Wallace, Tig, ed. see Cope, Andrew.
Wallace, Wade. Escape from Lego City! (p. 535)
Wallace, William H. Santa's Magic Key. (p. 1513)
Wallace, William K. Kuleana. (p. 968)
Wallace-Brodeur, Ruth. Home by Five. (p. 792)
—Stories from the Big Chair. (p. 1654)
Wallace-Crabbe, Chris. Read It Again. (p. 1443)
Wallace-Frimpong, A. Loving Your Vegetable Friends the Alphabet Way. (p. 1061)
Wallacel, Karen. Bad Rat. O'Neill, Rachael, illus. (p. 132)
Wallace-Lang, Maxine Lois. Sheldon's Adventures in Heaven. Porfirio, Guy, illus. (p. 1564)
Wallace-Mitchell, Jane, jt. auth. see Millett, Peter.
Wallace-Mitchell, Jane, jt. auth. see Reilly, Carmel.
Wallace-Smith, Susan. Chipmunk Adventure. (p. 308)
Wallace-Williams, Twila. Donovan the Dragon. (p. 466)
Wallach, Anya, jt. auth. see Fiedler, Lisa.
Wallach, Joel Dennis & Ma, Ian. Hell's Kitchen. (p. 765)
Wallach, Jonah M. & Tattersall, Clare. Money & Banking. (p. 1163)
Wallach, Marlene. Official Book of Me: Tips for a Lifestyle of Health, Happiness & Wellness. Roe, Monika, illus. (p. 1280)
Wallach, Michelle. Hanna & the Pajama Girls: The Case of the Sandy Keys. Mattheson, Jenny, illus. (p. 742)
Wallach, Paul Ross. Chief Architect 9. 5 tutorials Workbook. (p. 301)
Wallach, Tommy. We All Looked up. (p. 1865)
Wallach, Van. Black Mambas (p. 196)
—Cobra Al Descubierto. (p. 336)
—Cobras (p. 337)
—Corn Snakes (p. 367)
—Garter Snakes (p. 657)
Wallaker, Jillayne Prince. Grammar Rules! High-Interest Activities for Practice & Mastery of Basic Grammar Skills. Walkush, Donna, ed. (p. 706)
—Grammar Rules!, Grades 3-4: High-Interest Activities for Practice & Mastery of Basic Grammar Skills. Walkush, Donna, ed. (p. 706)
—Grammer Rules! High-Interest Activities for Practice & Mastery of Basic Grammar Skills. Walkush, Donna, ed. (p. 706)
Wallaker, Jillayne Prince & Prince Wallaker, Jillayne. Mastering Math Facts: Multiplication & Division. (p. 1103)
Wallas Reidy, Sarah, jt. auth. see Rodhe, Paul.
Wallechinsky, David, et al. Book of Lists: The Original Compendium of Curious Information. (p. 211)
Wallen, Virginia. Amanda: Duck or Chicken? (p. 52)
—Boo Boo Bear. (p. 209)
—Sonny & Sammy. (p. 1612)
Wallenfeldt, Jeff. United Kingdom: Northern Ireland, Scotland, & Wales. Wallenfeldt, Jeff, ed. (p. 1819)
Wallenfeldt, Jeff, ed. Birth of Rock & Roll: Music in the 1950s Through the 1960s. (p. 192)
—Black American Biographies: The Journey of Achievement. (p. 194)
—Ireland. (p. 887)
—New World Power: America from 1920 to 1945. (p. 1247)
—United Kingdom: England. (p. 1819)
Wallenfeldt, Jeffrey H. American Revolutionary War & the War of 1812: People, Politics, & Power. (p. 63)
—New World Power: America from 1920 to 1945. (p. 1247)
Wallenfeldt, Jeffrey H., ed. Africa to America: From the Middle Passage Through the 1930s. (p. 26)
—African American History & Culture (p. 27)
—American Civil War & Reconstruction: People, Politics, & Power. (p. 60)
—Black American Biographies: The Journey of Achievement. (p. 194)
—Black Experience in America: From Civil Rights to the Present. (p. 196)
Wallenfels, Linda, jt. auth. see Buxton, Karen.
Wallenfels, Stephen. Pod. (p. 1375)
Wallen-Nichols, Missy. Be Good Fairy Journal. Ballard, Ben, illus. (p. 148)
—Be Good Fairy Journal. (p. 148)
Wallenta, Adam, jt. auth. see Lee, Kanani K. M.
Waller, Alesha. Spotted Zebr. (p. 1634)
Waller, Barrett. New Feet for Old. (p. 1244)
Waller, C. L. Lady Sun & the Man in the Moon. (p. 971)
Waller, Curt, jt. auth. see Votry, Kim.
Waller, Diane Hardy, photos by see Gold, August.
Waller, Joan Sodaro. Picture It Yourself: Little Red Bird's Bright Idea & Seven Other Stories. (p. 1355)
Waller, Joyce, illus. see Nelson, Connie.
Waller, Linda. Hard Road to Manhood: I Ain't No Snitch. (p. 748)
Waller, Robert James. Thousand Country Roads: An Epilogue to the Bridges of Madison County. (p. 1740)
Waller, Sharon Biggs. Mad, Wicked Folly. (p. 1069)
Waller, Stephen & Pearson Education Staff. Run for Your Life. (p. 1496)
Waller, Steven H. My Child: Boy. Fincher, Kathy, illus. (p. 1200)
—My Child: Girl. Fincher, Kathy, illus. (p. 1200)
Wallerstein, Judith S. & Blakeslee, Sandra. What about the Kids? Raising Your Children Before, During, & after Divorce. (p. 1879)
Walles, Dwight, illus. see Coleman, William L.
Walles, Dwight, illus. see Nystrom, Carolyn, et al.
Walley, Diane D. Codger & Baggs. (p. 338)
Walley, Glynne, jt. auth. see Suzuki, Koji.
Walley, Glynne, tr. see Suzuki, Koji.
Walley, Glynne, tr. see Taguchi, Randy.
Walley, Judith L. & Faith, Virginia T. Faerywood. Spohn, Onna J., illus. (p. 562)
Walley, Keith. Angel to Guide Me. (p. 74)
Walley, Nathan R. Treasure of Frank & Jesse James. (p. 1782)
Walliman, Dominic. Professor Astro Cat's Frontiers of Space. Newman, Ben, illus. (p. 1409)
Wallin, Betsy. My First Farm Friends (p. 1206)
Walling, Lani. Clyde-Fred & the Color of Friendship. (p. 336)
Walling, Sandy Seeley. ABC's at the Zoo! The Fun Way to Teach Your Child the Relationship between Upper Case & Lower Case Letters (p. 4)
—Day at the Beach: A Seaside Counting Book from One to Ten. Walling, Sandy Seeley, illus. (p. 412)
Walling, Sandy Seeley, illus. see Shimberg, Elaine Fantle.
Wallingford, Stephanie & Rynders, Dawn. Day at the Lake. Villnave, Erica Pelton, illus. (p. 412)
Wallis, Angie, illus. see Gallardo-Walker, Gloria.
Wallis, Becky, illus. see Bentley, Dawn.
Wallis, Diz, illus. see Calhoun, Marmaduke Randolph.
Wallis, Diz, illus. see Twist, Clint & Fitzgibbon, Monty.
Wallis, Diz, illus. see Twist, Clint & Wood, A. J.
Wallis, Ginger. Finch Discoveries: An Inspiring Tale of Adaptation to a Changing Environment. Dodson, Bert, illus. (p. 587)
Wallis, Jeffrey. Trials in Salem. (p. 1785)
Wallis, Karen, jt. auth. see Domiteaux, Diane.
Wallis, Mary Alice & Lindstrom, C. G. Prophets & Apostles. (p. 1411)
Wallis, Michael. Art of Cars. (p. 102)
Wallis, Michelle. Settling Your Child in School: A Parent's Guide. (p. 1554)
Wallis, Paul. Landlubbers Logbook. (p. 974)
Wallis, Ralph. Memoirs of a Rambling Mind. (p. 1125)
Wallis, Rebbeca, illus. see Zocchi, Judy.
Wallis, Rebecca. Number 1 What Grows in the Sun? (p. 1271)
—Number 1 What Grows in the Sun?/Número 1 Qué crece en el Sol? (p. 1271)
—Number 10 Where Is the Hen? (p. 1271)
—Number 10 Where Is the Hen?/Número 10 en dónde está la Gallina? (p. 1271)
Wallis, Rebecca, illus. see Dingles, Molly.
Wallis, Rebecca, illus. see Ganeri, Anita.
Wallis, Rebecca, illus. see Zocchi, Judy.
Wallis, Rebecca, intro. Number 1 What Grows in the Sun? (p. 1271)
—Number 2 Let's Go to the Zoo! (p. 1271)
Wallmark, Laurie. Ada Byron Lovelace & the Thinking Machine. Chu, April, illus. (p. 10)
Wallner, Alexandra. Abigail Adams. (p. 5)
—Lucy Maud Montgomery. Wallner, Alexandra, illus. (p. 1063)
—Sergio & the Hurricane. (p. 1552)
—Susan B. Anthony. (p. 1687)
Wallner, Alexandra, illus. see Adler, David A.
Wallner, Alexandra, illus. see Woelfle, Gretchen.
Wallner, Alexandra & Wallner, John C. J. R. R. Tolkien. (p. 902)
Wallner, Alexandra, tr. Grandma Moses. (p. 708)
Wallner, John, illus. see Adler, David A.
Wallner, John C., illus. see Adler, David A.
Wallner, John C., jt. auth. see Wallner, Alexandra.
Wallner, S. J. Hans & the Golden Stirrup. (p. 743)
Walls, P. Abby: En busca del Tesoro. (p. 2)
—Abby: El oro de California. (p. 2)
Walls, Pamela June. Sp Abby Lost at Sea. (p. 1618)
—Sp Abby Secret at Cutter Grove. (p. 1618)
Walls, Robert D. Tiny's Second-Grade Field Trip. (p. 1757)
Walls, Sarah. Christmas Kitten: Special Delivery. (p. 314)
Walls, Steven. Ark Endeavor. (p. 99)
Walls, Suzanne L. Insects & Spiders. Maiden, D. W. & Govoni, Dennis, photos by. (p. 876)
Walls, Ty, illus. see Sawler, Kimberly.
Walluk, Wilbur. Alaskan Ten-Footed Bear & Other Legends. (p. 34)
Wallwork, Adrian. Business Vision. (p. 245)
Wally, Walter. What Daddy Did Today: A Father's Bedtime Story. Bicking, Judith, illus. (p. 1881)
Walmsley, Jane, illus. see Dahl, Roald.
Walmsley, Tom. Kid Stuff: A Novel. (p. 951)
Walpole, Brenda. I Wonder Why the Sun Rises: And Other Questions about Time & Seasons. (p. 849)
—I Wonder Why the Sun Rises & Other Questions about Time & Seasons. (p. 849)
Walpole, Sharon, jt. auth. see McKenna, Michael C.
Walrath, Steve. Divorced Dad's Guide to Seeing Your Kids: What Judges, Attorneys, & Your Ex Have Not Told You. (p. 455)
Walrod, Amy, illus. see Howe, James.
Walrod, Amy, jt. auth. see Howe, James.
Walrus Books. Children's Treasure Chest: Fairy Tales, Nursery Rhymes, & Nonsense Verse. (p. 304)
—Kids' Canadian Atlas. (p. 953)
Walsch, Neale Donald. Conversations with God for Teens. (p. 361)
—Little Soul & the Earth: A Children's Parable Adapted from Conversations with God. Riccio, Frank, illus. (p. 1036)
—Santa's God: A Children's Fable about the Biggest Question Ever. (p. 1513)
Walser, David. Thousand Nights & One Night. Pienkowski, Jan, illus. (p. 1740)
Walser, David, jt. auth. see Pienkowski, Jan.
Walser, Jo. Chasing the Rising Moon. (p. 294)
Walser, Richard & Street, Julia Montgomery. North Carolina Parade: Stories of History & People. Browning, Dixie Burrus, illus. (p. 1265)
Walsh, Alice. Buried Truth (p. 243)
—Gift of Music: Emile Benoit & His Fiddle Butler, Geoff, illus. (p. 675)
—Heroes of Isle aux Morts. (p. 773)
—Long Way from Home (p. 1047)
—Pomiuk, Prince of the North. Whitehead, Jerry, illus. (p. 1382)
—Sky Black with Crows (p. 1586)
—Uncle Farley's False Teeth. (p. 1811)
Walsh, Alison. Hugh O'Flaherty: His Wartime Adventures. (p. 825)
Walsh, Aly. My Mum Says Blah Blah Blah. Walsh, Marilyn, illus. (p. 1215)
Walsh, Ann. By the Skin of His Teeth: A Barkerville Mystery. (p. 249)
—By the Skin of His Teeth. (p. 249)
—Doctor's Apprentice: A Barkerville Mystery. (p. 459)
—Doctor's Apprentice. (p. 459)
—Flower Power (p. 607)
—Flower Power. (p. 607)
—Ghost of Soda Creek. (p. 671)
—Horse Power (p. 800)
—Moses, Me, & Murder: A Barkerville Mystery. (p. 1176)
—Shabash! (p. 1556)
—Whatever. (p. 1896)
Walsh, Ann & Waldron, Kathleen Cook. Forestry A-Z Warick, Bob, illus. (p. 618)
Walsh, Ann, ed. Beginnings: Stories of Canada's Past. (p. 160)
—Winds Through Time: An Anthology of Canadian Historical Young Adult Fiction. (p. 1936)
Walsh, Barbara. Poppy Lady: Moina Belle Michael & Her Tribute to Veterans. Johnson, Layne, illus. (p. 1385)
—Sammy in the Sky. Wyeth, Jamie, illus. (p. 1508)
Walsh Bellville, Cheryl, photos by see Rendon, Marcie R.
Walsh, Ben. GCSE Modern World History. (p. 659)
Walsh, Ben, jt. auth. see Dawson, Ian.
Walsh, Ben & Birks, Wayne. Modern World History. (p. 1159)
Walsh, Ben, et al. Modern World History. (p. 1159)
Walsh, Bill. Dog Show. (p. 461)
Walsh, Bill, et al. Walt Disney's Comics Clark, John, ed. (p. 1855)
Walsh, Brenda, ed. see Sanner, Catie.
Walsh, Brendan & Benchmark Education Co., LLC. Greek & Roman Gods & Goddesses. (p. 720)
—Hats off to the President: A White House Mystery. McEvenue, Tim, illus. (p. 752)
Walsh, Brendan, et al. Opinions about Three Victorian Era Poets: Christina Rossetti, Robert Louis Stevenson, Emily Dickinson. (p. 1300)
Walsh, Brian Everard. Thinking, Reading, Remembering: Brain-Friendly Tips & Techniques for a Student's Enriched Learning. (p. 1734)
Walsh, Christopher. Tucker's Tale. Lavar, Vanda, illus. (p. 1796)
Walsh, Christopher J. Cowboys Trivology: Fascinating Facts from the Sidelines. (p. 374)
—Packers Trivology: Fascinating Facts from the Sidelines. (p. 1317)
Walsh, D. T., illus. see Smith, Sherri Graves.
Walsh, D. T., illus. see Smith, Sherri.
Walsh, David. British Redcoats. (p. 230)
Walsh, David, jt. auth. see Winn, Christine M.
Walsh, Doug. Viewtiful Joe 2 Official Strategy Guide. (p. 1842)
Walsh, Ellen Stoll. Balancing Act. Walsh, Ellen Stoll, illus. (p. 133)
—Mouse Count / Cuenta de Ratón. Campoy, F. Isabel, tr. (p. 1182)
—Mouse Paint: Lap-Sized Board Book. (p. 1182)
—Mouse Paint - Pintura de Ratón. (p. 1182)
—Mouse Shapes. (p. 1182)
Walsh, Enda. Chatroom: A Play. (p. 295)
Walsh, Francis. Daring Women of the American Revolution. (p. 407)
Walsh, Frank. Montgomery Bus Boycott. (p. 1170)
—New York City. (p. 1248)
Walsh, Frank, jt. auth. see O'Hern, Kerri.
Walsh, Frank & O'Hern, Kerri. Montgomery Bus Boycott. McHargue, D., illus. (p. 1170)
Walsh, Franny. Who Cat: A Louisiana Tale. (p. 1915)
Walsh, Jean. Gaffer Samson's Luck. (p. 652)
Walsh, Jennifer, illus. see Rafael, Janis.
Walsh, Jennifer, illus. see Yager, Karen & Williams, Kiersten.
Walsh, Jill Paton. Emperor's Winding Sheet. (p. 521)
—Green Book. Bloom, Lloyd, illus. (p. 721)
—Pepi & the Secret Names: Help Pepi Crack the Hieroglyphic Code. French, Fiona, illus. (p. 1340)
Walsh, Joanna. Biggest Kiss. Abbot, Judi, illus. (p. 185)
—I Love Mom. Abbot, Judi, illus. (p. 842)
—Perfect Hug. Abbot, Judi, illus. (p. 1342)
Walsh, Joseph, text. Gambler on the Loose. (p. 654)

Walsh, Judith E. India. (p. 870)
Walsh, Karen E. College Writing (p. 340)
Walsh, Kay. Amy Carmichael - Rescuer by Night. (p. 66)
—John Paton - South Sea Island Rescue. (p. 922)
Walsh, Kenneth. Our Earth (p. 1308)
—Our Earth. (p. 1308)
—Outer Space. (p. 1312)
—Solar System (p. 1607)
—Solar System. (p. 1607)
Walsh, Kent D. Babydoll's Honor: A Boy & His Horse of Valor. (p. 128)
Walsh, Kent D. "Uncle Kent". In Search of the Pink Seagull. (p. 865)
Walsh, Kieran. Animal Math. (p. 78)
—Construction Math. (p. 359)
—Iraq. (p. 887)
—Saudi Arabia. (p. 1516)
—Space Math. (p. 1619)
—Sports Math. (p. 1633)
Walsh, Kim Carmen. Safari Finn. (p. 1502)
Walsh, Laura, jt. auth. see Seymour, Sharon.
Walsh, Laurence & Walsh, Suella. In the Middle of the Night. (p. 866)
Walsh, Liza Gardner. Muddy Boots: Outdoor Activities for Children. (p. 1188)
—Treasure Hunters Handbook. (p. 1781)
Walsh, Maria Elena. Chaucha y Palito. Ink, Lancman, illus. (p. 295)
—Cuentopos de Gulubu. Lavandeira, Sandra, illus. (p. 389)
—Dailan Kifki. Lavandeira, Sandra, illus. (p. 399)
—Nube Traicionera. Fiorini, Nancy, illus. (p. 1269)
Walsh, Marilyn, illus. see Walsh, Aly.
Walsh, Mark, et al. Health & Social Care. (p. 757)
Walsh, Meg. Mama, Won't You Play with Me? (p. 1084)
Walsh, Melanie. 10 Things I Can Do to Help My World. Walsh, Melanie, illus. (p. 1994)
—Living with Mom & Living with Dad. Walsh, Melanie, illus. (p. 1042)
—Trick or Treat? Walsh, Melanie, illus. (p. 1786)
Walsh, Mike, illus. see Jackaman, Philippa.
Walsh, Pat. Crowfield Curse. (p. 386)
—Crowfield Demon. (p. 386)
Walsh, Patricia, jt. auth. see Fridell, Ron.
Walsh, Patrick M., Jr. Derby: A Timmy Wallings Story. McGriff, Aaron C., ed. (p. 427)
—Who Says Timmy Can't Play: The Derby: A Timmy Wallings Story. McGriff, Aaron, ed. (p. 1917)
Walsh, Rebecca, illus. see Ehrlich, Amy.
Walsh, Roger L. When Dandelions Fly. (p. 1901)
Walsh, Roger M. Tommy-Aquinas in San Francisco. (p. 1764)
Walsh, Russ. Snack Attack & Other Poems for Developing Fluency in Beginning Readers. (p. 1595)
Walsh, Sara. Dark Light. (p. 407)
Walsh, Sheila. Gigi, God's Little Princess (p. 676)
—Gigi, God's Little Princess Johnson, Meredith, illus. (p. 676)
—God's Little Princess Treasury Johnson, Meredith, illus. (p. 691)
—Goodnight Warrior: Bedtime Bible Stories, Devotions, & Prayers (p. 701)
—I Am Loved (p. 833)
—I'M Not Wonder Woman: But God Made Me Wonderful! (p. 859)
—Perfect Christmas Gift Johnson, Meredith, illus. (p. 1341)
—Sweet Dreams Princess: God's Little Princess Bedtime Bible Stories, Devotions, & Prayers (p. 1689)
—Will, God's Mighty Warrior Johnson, Meredith, illus. (p. 1932)
Walsh Shepherd, Donna. New Zealand. (p. 1249)
Walsh, Steve. Chief Ouray: Ute Chief & Man of Peace. (p. 301)
—Zebulon Montgomery Pike: Explorer & Military Officer. (p. 1985)
Walsh, Suella. Case of Erica's Weird Behavior. (p. 273)
Walsh, Suella, jt. auth. see Walsh, Laurence.
Walsh, Susanne. My Very Favorite Time of Year: Featuring the Whimsy Kids. (p. 1221)
Walsh, T. B. R., illus. see Pinder, Eric.
Walsh, Tina, illus. see Guettier, Nancy.
Walsh, Vivian. June & August. McCauley, Adam, illus. (p. 934)
Walsh, William, illus. see Zahn, Muriel.
Walsh, William S. Story of Santa Klaus: Told for Children of All Ages from Six To. (p. 1659)
Walshaw, Rodney, jt. auth. see Farndon, John.
Walshaw, Sam. Lulu Ladybug. (p. 1065)
Walshe, Dermot, illus. see Helmer, Marilyn.
Walshe, Elizabeth Hely. Under the Inquisition: A Story of the Reformation in Italy. (p. 1813)
Walshon, Jay. Eye See You Africa. (p. 558)
Walske, Christine Zuchora. Pythons. (p. 1422)
Walsleben, Edda Brigitte. Little Bee Who Would Be Queen. (p. 1024)
—Scotty the Little Westie Dog & His Diary. (p. 1532)
Walstead, Curt, illus. see Knopf, Susan.
Walstead, Curt, illus. see Ormond, Jennifer.
Walston, Dave, illus. see Golden Books Staff.
Walt & Wells. Este No Es Mi Dinosaurio. (p. 538)
Walt Disney Animation Studios (Firm) Staff, illus. see Trimble, Irene.
Walt Disney Company Staff. Pocahontas. (p. 1375)
—Walt Disney's Mickey Mouse Tales: Classic Stories. (p. 1855)
Walt Disney Company Staff, illus. see Bedford, Annie North & Golden Books Staff.
Walt Disney Company Staff, illus. see Golden Books Staff.
Walt Disney Company Staff, illus. see RH Disney Staff.
Walt Disney Company Staff & Phidal Publishing Staff, contrib. by. Cars. (p. 272)
Walt Disney Company Staff & Pixar Animation Studios Staff, contrib. by. Finding Nemo: Fish in a Box. (p. 588)
Walt Disney Productions Staff, contrib. by. Three Musketeers. (p. 1743)
Walt Disney Records Staff, jt. creator see ToyBox Innovations.
Walt Disney Studios Staff, illus. see Barrie, J. M. & RH Disney Staff.
Walt Disney Studios Staff, illus. see RH Disney Staff.
Walt Disney Studios Staff, illus. see Werner, Janet & Golden Books Staff.
Walt, G. L. Heroes All Around. (p. 772)
Walter, Aaron T. Mr Lincoln's Hat. (p. 1185)
Walter, C. Lyn. Five Dollar Christmas Tree. (p. 600)
Walter, Chris. Tell Your Dreams to Me. (p. 1717)
Walter, Dan. Hello, Willie! (p. 765)
Walter, Debbie. Introducing Russell. Walter, Debbie, illus. (p. 882)
Walter, Deborah, illus. see Rigg, Diana.
Walter Foster Creative Team. Animals: Step-by-Step Instructions for 26 Captivating Creatures. Fisher, Diana, illus. (p. 81)
—Chalkboard 123: Learn Your Numbers with Reusable Chalkboard Pages! Barker, Stephen, illus. (p. 288)
—Dogs & Puppies: Step-by-Step Insructions for 25 Different Breeds. Fisher, Diana, illus. (p. 462)
—Frozen: Featuring Anna, Elsa, Olaf, & All Your Favorite Characters! (p. 645)
—I Love Sweet Treats! A Yummy Assortment of Stickers, Games, Recipes, Step-by-Step Drawing Projects, & More to Satisfy Your Sweet Tooth! (p. 843)
—Learn to Draw Almost Naked Animals: Learn to Draw Howie, Octo, Narwhal, Bunny, & Other Favorite Characters from the Hit T. V. Show! (p. 983)
—Learn to Draw Angry Birds Space: Learn to Draw All Your Favorite Angry Birds & Those Bad Piggies-In Space! (p. 983)
—Learn to Draw Archie & Friends: Featuring Betty, Veronica, Sabrina the Teenage Witch, Josie & the Pussycats, & More! (p. 983)
—Learn to Draw Cars, Planes & Moving Machines: Step-By-Step Instructions for More Than 25 High-Powered Vehicles. LaPadula, Tom & Shelly, Jeff, illus. (p. 983)
—Learn to Draw Cats & Kittens: Step-By-Step Instructions for More Than 25 Favorite Feline Friends. Cuddy, Robbin, illus. (p. 983)
—Learn to Draw Dinosaurs: Step-By-Step Instructions for More Than 25 Prehistoric Creatures. Cuddy, Robbin, illus. (p. 983)
—Learn to Draw Disney Minnie & Daisy Best Friends Forever Fabulous Fashions. Disney Storybook Artists Staff, illus. (p. 983)
—Learn to Draw Forest Animals: Step-By-Step Instructions for More Than 25 Woodland Creatures. Cuddy, Robbin, illus. (p. 983)
—Learn to Draw Horses & Ponies: Step-By-Step Instructions for More Than 25 Different Breeds. Cuddy, Robbin, illus. (p. 983)
—Learn to Draw Safari Animals: Step-By-Step Instructions for More Than 25 Exotic Animals. Cuddy, Robbin, illus. (p. 983)
—Learn to Draw the Best of Nickelodeon: Featuring Characters from Your Favorite TV Shows, Including SpongeBob SquarePants, the Teenage Mutant Ninja Turtles, the Fairly OddParents, & More! (p. 983)
—Madagascar. (p. 1069)
—My Learning Adventures: 123. (p. 1211)
—Palace Pets: Featuring Pumpkin, Beauty, Treasure, Blondie & All of Your Favorite Princesses' Pets! (p. 1319)
—Pets: Step-by-Step Insructions for 23 Favorite Animals. Mueller, Peter, illus. (p. 1348)
—Sea Creatures: Step-by-Step Insructions for 25 Ocean Animals. Farrell, Russell, illus. (p. 1534)
Walter Foster Creative Team & Legendre, Philippe. Animals Around the World: Learn to Draw More Than 25 Exotic Animals Step by Step! (p. 82)
—Dinosaurs, Dragons & Prehistoric Creatures: Learn to Draw More Than 25 Reptilian Beasts & Fantasy Characters Step by Step! (p. 444)
—Planes, Trains & Moving Machines: Learn to Draw More Than 25 Flying, Locomotive, & Heavy-Duty Machines Step by Step! (p. 1367)
Walter Foster Creative Team, creator. Learn to Draw Angry Birds. (p. 983)
—Learn to Draw Disney/Pixar's Toy Story. (p. 983)
—Learn to Draw Disney's Enchanted Princesses. (p. 983)
—Learn to Draw Disney's Favorite Fairies. (p. 983)
—Learn to Draw Mickey & His Friends. (p. 983)
—Learn to Draw Phineas & Ferb. (p. 983)
—Learn to Draw the Best of Nickelodeon Collection. (p. 984)
—Learn to Draw Winnie the Pooh. (p. 984)
Walter Foster Creative Team, ed. All about Drawing Dinosaurs & Reptiles. (p. 42)
—All about Drawing Horses & Pets. (p. 42)
—All about Drawing Sea Creatures & Animals. (p. 42)
—How to Draw Transformers. (p. 819)
Walter Foster Creative Team Staff & Legendre, Philippe. Favorite Pets: Learn to Draw More Than 25 Furry Friends & Cute Companions Step by Step. (p. 578)
—Princesses, Fairies & Fairy Tales: Learn to Draw More Than 25 Pretty Princesses & Fairy Tale Characters Step by Step! (p. 1406)
—Sea Creatures & Other Favorite Animals: Learn to Draw More Than 25 Land & Sea Animals Step by Step! (p. 1534)
Walter Foster Creative Team Staff, et al. Big Book of Art - Draw! Paint! Create! An Adventurous Journey into the Wild & Wonderful World of Art! (p. 178)
—Big Book of Color: An Adventurous Journey into the Magical & Marvelous World of Color! (p. 179)
Walter Foster Custom Creative Team. Chalkboard ABC: Learn the Alphabet with Reusable Chalkboard Pages! Barker, Stephen, illus. (p. 288)
—Chalkboard Shapes: Learn Your Shapes with Reusable Chalkboard Pages! Barker, Stephen, illus. (p. 288)
—Construction: Interactive Fun with Fold-Out Play Scene, Reusable Stickers, & Punch-out, Stand-up Figures! Cerato, Mattia, illus. (p. 359)
—Fairies: Interactive Fun with Fold-Out Play Scene, Reusable Stickers, & Punch-out, Stand-up Figures! Renn, Chantal, illus. (p. 562)
—Jungle Animals: Interactive Fun with Fold-Out Play Scene, Reusable Stickers, & Punch-out, Stand-up Figures! Basaluzzo, Constanza, illus. (p. 935)
—On the Farm: Interactive Fun with Fold-Out Play Scene, Reusable Stickers, & Punch-out, Stand-up Figures! Luthringer, Melisande, illus. (p. 1290)
Walter Foster (Firm) Staff, contrib. by. Learn to Draw Walt Disney's Mickey Mouse. (p. 984)
Walter Foster Jr. Creative Team. 150 Fun Holiday Things to Doodle: An Interactive Adventure in Drawing Holiday Fun! (p. 2000)
—Dinosaurs: Interactive Fun with Reusable Stickers, Fold-Out Play Scene, & Punch-out, Stand-up Figures! Cerato, Mattia, illus. (p. 444)
—Learn to Draw Angry Birds: Bad Piggies: Featuring All Your Favorite Crafty, Crazy Pigs, Including King Pig, Foreman Pig, Corporal Pig, & More! (p. 983)
—My Big, Crazy Drawing & Doodle Book: An Interactive Adventure with More Than 100 Creative Ideas for Tons of Doodling Fun. (p. 1197)
—Under the Sea: Interactive Fun with Reusable Stickers, Fold-Out Play Scene, & Punch-out, Stand-up Figures! Cis, Valeria, illus. (p. 1814)
Walter Foster Jr. Creative Team & DreamWorks Animation Creative Team. Learn to Draw Dreamworks' Madagascar: Featuring the Penguins of Madagascar & Other Favorite Characters! (p. 983)
Walter Foster Publishing & Berry, Bob. Watch Me Draw Robots. Torres, Jickie, illus. (p. 1861)
Walter, J., illus. see Frederick, Susan.
Walter, Jon. Close to the Wind. (p. 334)
Walter, Judy S. Grey & White Stranger. (p. 723)
Walter, Kristin. Elves & the Shoemaker. (p. 517)
—Hansel & Gretel. (p. 743)
—Last of the Dragons: Based on the sotry by Edith Nesbit. (p. 978)
—Selfish Giant. (p. 1549)
Walter, LaDawn, ed. see Allen, Margaret.
Walter, Lee. Gifts That Are Forgotten. (p. 676)
Walter, Lorin, illus. see Rauen, Amy & Ayers, Amy.
Walter, Lorin, illus. see Rauen, Amy.
Walter, Lorin, illus. see Sharp, Jean.
Walter, Lorin, photos by see Rauen, Amy & Ayers, Amy.
Walter, Mildred Pitts. Alec's Primer. Johnson, Larry, illus. (p. 35)
—Justin & the Best Biscuits in the World. (p. 940)
—Justin & the Best Biscuits in the World. Stock, Catherine, illus. (p. 940)
Walter, Nancy. Bumpsie's Colorful Garden. (p. 241)
Walter, Virginia A. War & Peace: A Guide to Literature & New Media, Grades 4-8 (p. 1857)
Walter, Wendy D., jt. auth. see Walter, Wendy D.
Walter, Wendy D. & Walter, Wendy D. Return of the Dullaith: Ambri's Tale. (p. 1464)
Walter-Goodspeed, Dee Dee. Friends Will Be There Forever. Jones, Ayanna, illus. (p. 639)
Walters, Adam. Little Red Riding Hood. (p. 1035)
Walters, Anne S., ed. see Poole, H. W.
Walters, Bob, illus. see Dodson, Peter & Library Association Staff.
Walters, Catherine. Special Christmas Tree. Taylor-Kielty, Simon, illus. (p. 1623)
Walters, Celeste. Certain Music. Spudvilas, Anne, illus. (p. 287)
—Deception. (p. 421)
—Glass Mountain. (p. 682)
—Puppy Playtime 1, 2, 3. Jaunn, Adele, illus. (p. 1418)
—Treading the Boards. (p. 1781)
Walters, Celeste & Spudvilas, Anne. Certain Music. (p. 287)
Walters, Christina, jt. auth. see Walters, Eric.
Walters, Clare, jt. auth. see Kemp, Jane.
Walters, Clare & Kemp, Jane. I Very Really Miss You. Langley, Jonathan, illus. (p. 847)
Walters, Cloe. Get Quilting with Angela & Cloe: 14 Projects for Kids to Sew. (p. 668)
Walters, Danna J. Every Good Princess Marries a Prince. (p. 542)
Walters, David. Gifts of the Spirit Ellis, Jessica, illus. (p. 675)
Walters, Ednah. Awakened: Book One of the Guardian Legacy. (p. 120)
Walters, Eric. Al Límite (p. 32)
—Alexandria of Africa. (p. 37)
—Au Pas, Camarade (p. 114)
—Between Heaven & Earth (p. 172)
—Branded (p. 222)
—Camp 30. (p. 257)
—Diamonds in the Rough (p. 434)
—Ed Spécial (p. 503)
—Elixir. (p. 513)
—Fight for Power. (p. 585)
—Fond la Planche! (p. 612)
—Grind (p. 724)
—Home Team (p. 793)
—Hope Springs. Fernandes, Eugenie, illus. (p. 796)
—House Party (p. 803)
—Hunter (p. 828)
—In a Flash (p. 863)
—I've Got an Idea. (p. 900)
—Juice (p. 932)
—Laggan Lard Butts (p. 971)
—Matatu Campbell, Eva, illus. (p. 1104)
—Money Pit Mystery. (p. 1164)
—My Name Is Blessing. Fernandes, Eugenie, illus. (p. 1215)
—Northern Exposures (p. 1265)
—Off Season (p. 1279)
—Overdrive (p. 1314)
—Overdrive. (p. 1314)
—Pole. (p. 1379)
—Prince for a Princess Parkins, David, illus. (p. 1401)
—Rebound (p. 1451)
—Reventar. (Stuffed) (p. 1466)
—Ricky. (p. 1470)
—Rule of Three. (p. 1495)
—Run. (p. 1496)
—Saving Sammy Meissner, Amy, illus. (p. 1517)
—Skye Above Parkins, David, illus. (p. 1587)
—Sleeper (p. 1588)
—Special Edward (p. 1623)
—Splat! (p. 1629)
—Stand Your Ground (p. 1639)
—Stranded. (p. 1664)
—Stuffed (p. 1670)
—Tagged (p. 1695)
—Tiger by the Tail. (p. 1748)
—Toda Velocidad (p. 1760)
—Underdog (p. 1814)
—United We Stand. (p. 1820)
—Visions. (p. 1845)
—Walking Home. (p. 1854)
—We All Fall Down. (p. 1865)
Walters, Eric, jt. auth. see Ellis, Deborah.
Walters, Eric & Spreekmeester, Kevin. Death by Exposure. (p. 420)
Walters, Eric & Walters, Christina. True Story of Santa Claus. Gooderham, Andrew, illus. (p. 1793)
Walters, Eric & Williams, Jerome. Triple Threat (p. 1787)
Walters, Gregory. Fouling Out (p. 624)
Walters, Heidi. Hospitals Aren't So Scary. (p. 801)
Walters, Helen B. When John Wesley Was a Boy. (p. 1903)
Walters Iii, Harry C. Little Sam's Secret Place. Nicol, Brock, illus. (p. 1036)
Walters, Jack C. Bird Stories & Sightings in Nevada: Loons to Nighthawks Vol. 1 (p. 190)
Walters, Janis. Adventures of Libby & Sophie: Sometimes Our Friends Can Get Us into Trouble. (p. 19)
Walters, Jennipher, jt. auth. see Whitehead, Erin.
Walters, Jim. 50 Book Report Ideas. (p. 1997)
Walters, John. Sports Broadcasting Ferrer, Al, ed. (p. 1632)
—Sportswriting & Sports Photography Ferrer, Al, ed. (p. 1633)
Walters, John, jt. auth. see Gigliotti, Jim.
Walters, Julie & Walters, Stuart. Julie Walters Is an Alien. (p. 932)
Walters, Kathy. Circles into Another World, the Amazing World of Coloring: Prelude. (p. 321)
Walters, Kurt K. C., illus. see Wetterer, Charles M. & Wetterer, Margaret K.
Walters, Martin & Johnson, Jinny. World of Animals. (p. 1956)
Walters, Nicole Y. Charis: Journey to Pandora's Jar. (p. 291)
—Charis: A Journey to Pandora's Jar. Conard, Vincent, illus. (p. 291)
Walters, Percy. Scott's Ark. (p. 1532)
Walters, Peter. Hungriest Mouth in the Sea (p. 828)
Walters, Robert, illus. see Brett-Surman, Michael K. & Holtz, Thomas R.
Walters, Robert, illus. see McKay, Sindy.
Walters, Robert, et al. Discovering Dinosaurs. (p. 449)
Walters Schermerhorn, Lilly. Face Painting Tips & Designs: A Face Painters Guide to Go from Amateur to Professional. (p. 560)
Walters, Scott. Woman Too Young of Panther Cave. (p. 1945)
Walters, Steve, ed. see Scretching, Dorothy/Janis.
Walters, Stuart, jt. auth. see Walters, Julie.
Walters, Tara. Brazil. (p. 224)
—North Korea. (p. 1265)
—South Korea. (p. 1617)
Walters, Tracey. Zadie Smith. (p. 1984)
Walters, Tracey Lorraine. Zadie Smith. (p. 1984)
Walters, Virginia. Are We There Yet, Daddy? Schindler, S. D., illus. (p. 96)
Walter-Sereg, D. Bonnie Catches Lights in the Night Sky. (p. 209)
—Bonnie, the Trapeze Artist. (p. 209)
—Bonnie Tracks a Jungle Animal. (p. 209)
Walthall, Anne. Japan: A Cultural, Social, & Political History. (p. 909)
Walther, William. Collection of Fairy Tales: Volume One. (p. 340)
Walthers, Don, illus. see Walthers, Joanie.
Walthers, Joanie. Fish Smuggler. Walthers, Don, illus. (p. 598)
Waltman, Kevin. Next. (p. 1249)
—Slump. (p. 1591)
Waltner, Elma. Carving Animal Caricatures. (p. 273)
Walton, A. E. What Should I Do with My Love for You? (p. 1893)
Walton, Adrienne. Food. (p. 612)
Walton, Alex, illus. see Fraser, Theresa.
Walton, Alex, illus. see Tara, Stephanie Lisa.
Walton, Alex, jt. auth. see Preece, Bronwyn.
Walton, Amy Catherine. Susan: A Story for Children. (p. 1687)
Walton, Ann. Something to Do. Hinrichsen, Natalie, illus. (p. 1610)
—Tale of Sun & Moon. Hinrichsen, Tamsin, illus. (p. 1700)
Walton, Bedelia C., ed. see O'Neill, Joe.
Walton, Dana E. Bo John's Train. (p. 205)
Walton, Emmitt. Adventures of Mr. Hensworth: Hibernate. (p. 20)
Walton, Eugene, jt. auth. see Lapham, Steven Sellers.
Walton, Evangeline. Misadventures of Rufus & Misha: Two Dogs Who Are Smart Enough to Go to School. (p. 1150)
Walton Hamilton, Emma, jt. auth. see Andrews, Julie.
Walton, J. Ambrose, illus. see Eustace, Robert & Meade, L. T.
Walton, K. M. Cracked. (p. 375)
—Empty. (p. 521)
Walton, Leslye. Strange & Beautiful Sorrows of Ava Lavender. (p. 1664)
Walton, Mildred D. Spring Reborn. (p. 1635)
Walton, O. F. Christie's Old Organ: A Little Boy's Journey to Find a Home of His Own. (p. 312)
—Christie's Old Organ or Home, Sweet Home. (p. 312)
—Peep Behind the Scenes: A Little Girl's Journey of Discovery. (p. 1335)
—Saved at Sea: A Young Boy in a Dramatic Rescue. (p. 1517)
—Saved at Sea A Lighthouse Story. (p. 1517)
Walton, Phillip. Auto-B-Good - Citizen Miles: A Lesson in Citizenship. Rising Star Studios, illus. (p. 117)
Walton, Rick. Bullfrog Pops! McAllister, Chris, illus. (p. 240)

—Bullfrog Pops! Adventures in Verbs & Objects McAllister, Chris, illus. (p. 240)
—Bunny Christmas: A Family Celebration. Miglio, Paige, illus. (p. 242)
—Frankenstein. Hale, Nathan, illus. (p. 629)
—Frankenstein's Fright Before Christmas. Hale, Nathan, illus. (p. 629)
—Girl & Gorilla. Berger, Joe, illus. (p. 678)
—Herd of Cows! Flock of Sheep! Olson, Julie, illus. (p. 769)
—I Need My Own Country! Hargis, Wes, illus. (p. 844)
—Just Me & 6,000 Rats: A Tale of Conjunctions Gordon, Carl & Gordon, Mike, illus. (p. 939)
—Just Me & 6,000 Rats: A Tale of Conjunctions Gordon, Mike & Gordon, Carl, illus. (p. 939)
—Mini Mysteries: 20 Tricky Tales to Untangle. American Girl Editorial Staff & Magruder, Trula, eds. (p. 1146)
—Mini Mysteries 2: 20 More Tricky Tales to Untangle. Scheuer, Lauren, illus. (p. 1146)
—Mini Mysteries 3: 20 More Tricky Tales to Untangle. Scheuer, Lauren, illus. (p. 1146)
—Mr. President Goes to School Sneed, Brad, illus. (p. 1186)
—Pig Pigger Piggest. Holder, Jimmy, illus. (p. 1357)
—Suddenly Alligator: Adventures in Adverbs Bradshaw, Jim, illus. (p. 1672)
—What Do We Do with the Baby? Miglio, Paige, illus. (p. 1882)
Walton, Rick & Earl, Cheri. Psst... Secret Instructions Every Girl Should Know. (p. 1413)
Walton, Rick & Kraus, Franz. I Need My Own Country! Hargis, Wes, illus. (p. 844)
Walton, Ruth. Let's Bake a Cake. (p. 994)
—Let's Drink Some Water. (p. 996)
—Let's Get Dressed: Find Out about Clothes & Fabric. (p. 997)
—Let's Read a Book: Find Out about Books & How They Are Made. (p. 1000)
—Let's Ride a Bike. (p. 1000)
Walton, Sally. Show Me How: I Can Do Crafts. (p. 1570)
Walton, Sally, jt. auth. see Walton, Stewart.
Walton, Sally & Donaldson, Stephanie. Show Me How: I Can Grow Things. (p. 1570)
Walton, Sally & Painter, Lucy. 100 Fantastic Things to Make, Do & Play: Simple, Fun Projects That Use Easy Everyday Materials. (p. 1998)
Walton, Sally, et al. Fun Projects & Amazing Things to Make, Do, Play & Give: Two Fantastic Books in a Box - the Ultimate Rainy-Day Collection with 220 Exciting Step-By-Step Projects Shown in over 3000 Photographs (p. 648)
Walton, Stewart & Walton, Sally. Stamp Decorating: A Step-by-Step Guidebook & Inspirational Sourcebook, with over 80 Projects & Techniques. (p. 1639)
Walton, Tony, illus. see Andrews, Julie & Hamilton, Emma Walton.
Walton, Tony, illus. see Andrews, Julie.
Walton, Will. Anything Could Happen. (p. 91)
Walton, William J. Polly. Walton, William J., illus. (p. 1381)
Waltrip, Mildred, illus. see Morris, Richard B.
Walty, Margaret T. Rock-a-Bye Baby: Lullabies for Bedtime. (p. 1481)
Waltz, Dan. Dragon Fly: A Gnome's Great Adventure. Waltz, Dan, illus. (p. 477)
—Kornstalkers: Corn Maze Massacre. Waltz, Dan, illus. (p. 967)
Waltz, Dan, illus. see Loper, Kathleen.
Waltz, Dan Hall. Freckles the Frog: A Read-a-Long/Sing-a-Long Story Book. Waltz, Dan Hall, illus. (p. 632)
Waltz, Michael. Hen & I. (p. 767)
Waltz, Tom. Little Jackie Lantern. (p. 1029)
Waltz, Tom, jt. auth. see Eastman, Kevin B.
Waltz, Tom, jt. auth. see Lynch, Brian.
Waltz, Tom, jt. auth. see Ryall, Chris.
Waltz, Tom & Eastman, Kevin B. Teenage Mutant Ninja Turtles Volume 1: Change Is Constant Deluxe Edition: Change Is Constant Deluxe Edition. (p. 1714)
—Teenage Mutant Ninja Turtles Volume 10: New Mutant Order: New Mutant Order. (p. 1714)
—Teenage Mutant Ninja Turtles Volume 3: Shadows of the Past: Shadows of the Past. (p. 1714)
—Teenage Mutant Ninja Turtles Volume 5: Krang War: Krang War. (p. 1714)
Walvoord, jt. auth. see Walvoord, Linda.
Walvoord, Linda. Razzamadaddy Yoshikawa, Sachiko, tr. (p. 1441)
Walvoord, Linda & Walvoord. Rosetta, Rosetta, Sit by Me! Velasquez, Eric, illus. (p. 1490)
Walz, Joel & Piriou, Jean Pierre. Rapports: An Introduction to French Language & Francophone Culture. (p. 1439)
Walz, Richard, illus. see Kulling, Monica.
Walz, Richard, illus. see Murphy, Frank & Brenner, Martha.
Walz, Richard, illus. see Murphy, Frank.
Walz, Richard, illus. see Wooldridge, Connie Nordhielm.
Walz, Susan. Balloons to the Moon. (p. 135)
Wampol, Pam & Woodard, Heather. Oscar's Dreamzz: The Story of Santa's First Elf. (p. 1305)
Wamsley, Jody. What Am I Gonna Do? Turchan, Monique, illus. (p. 1879)
Wan Aisyah, jt. auth. see Wan Aisyah, Aisyah.
Wan Aisyah, Aisyah & Wan Aisyah. Potty Monster. (p. 1388)
Wan, Guofang & Capstone Press Editors. Virtually True: Questioning Online Media (p. 1844)
Wan, Guofang & Capstone Press Staff. TV Takeover: Questioning TV (p. 1799)
Wan, Guofang & Cheng, Hong. Media-Savvy Student: Teaching Media Literacy Skills. (p. 1118)
Wan, Jian Q. Meditating into Wellness with San He Qigong. (p. 1120)
Wan, Joyce. Are You My Mommy? (p. 97)
—Frog & Friends. Wan, Joyce, illus. (p. 639)
—Hug You, Kiss You, Love You. Wan, Joyce, illus. (p. 824)
—My Lucky Little Dragon. Wan, Joyce, illus. (p. 1213)
—Owl & Friends. Wan, Joyce, illus. (p. 1314)
—Peek-A-Boo Zoo. (p. 1335)
—We Belong Together. Wan, Joyce, illus. (p. 1866)
—Whale in My Swimming Pool. (p. 1877)
—You Are My Cupcake. Wan, Joyce, illus. (p. 1973)
Wan, Joyce, illus. see Howatt, Sandra J.
Wan, Vanessa. Welcome to Taiwan. (p. 1873)
Wanardi, Jennifer, illus. see Iyengar, Malathi Michelle.
Wanasejla, Patricia, illus. see Steel, Joleen.
Wanat, John A., et al. Learning for Earning: Wraparound Edition. (p. 985)
—Learning for Earning: Your Route to Success. (p. 985)
—Learning for Earning: Teaching Package Teacher's Resource Guide. (p. 985)
—Learning for Earning. (p. 985)
Wand, Dana. Shanie June Jumped over the Moon. Tinling, Molly, illus. (p. 1559)
Wand, Kelly. Astrology. (p. 109)
Wand, Kelly, ed. Animal Rights Movement. (p. 79)
—Voodoo. (p. 1850)
Wanda, Wingler. Acts of Christmas: Playing with Angels. (p. 10)
Wandelmaier, Michael, illus. see Hughes, Susan.
Wandelmaier, Michael, jt. auth. see Hughes, Susan.
Wandersman, Aldo. Ronaldinho. (p. 1487)
—Ronaldo. (p. 1487)
Wandless, David. Natural Magic. (p. 1235)
—Natural Magic Book 3 - the Milk Stone & the Tauren. (p. 1235)
Wanecski, Erica Joan, illus. see Stafford, Gerry.
Waner, Stefan & Costenoble, Steven R. Student Solutions Manual for Applied Calculus. (p. 1669)
Wanert, Amandine, illus. see Davidson, Susanna.
Wang, Adria. My World: My Family. Nicholls, Paul, illus. (p. 1221)
—My World: My Busy Day. Nicholls, Paul, illus. (p. 1221)
—My World: My Outdoors. Nicholls, Paul, illus. (p. 1221)
—My World: My Playtimes Toys. Nicholls, Paul, illus. (p. 1221)
Wang, An. Anywhere but Here. (p. 91)
Wang, Andrea. How Can We Reduce Fossil Fuel Pollution? (p. 805)
—Learning about Asia. (p. 984)
—Malala Yousafzai: Nobel Peace Prize Winner & Education Activist. (p. 1083)
—What's Great about Georgia? (p. 1897)
—What's Great about Maine? (p. 1897)
Wang, Ben, tr. see Kwong-Chiu, Chiu.
Wang, Ben, tr. see Tse, Brian.
Wang, Connie, jt. auth. see Hudnall, Ken.
Wang, Dorothea DePrisco & Imperato, Teresa. All the Ways I Love You. Downing, Julie, illus. (p. 46)
Wang, Dorthea Deprisco. Five Minutes until Bed. Vaux, Patricia, illus. (p. 601)
Wang, Dorthea Deprisco, jt. auth. see Andrews McMeel Publishing Staff.
Wang, Emily, jt. auth. see Smith, Michael.
Wang, Eric. Engineering with LEGO Bricks & ROBOLAB: 2nd Edition. (p. 529)
Wang, Eva. Auntie Tigress & Other Favorite Chinese Folk Tales. (p. 115)
Wang, Eva, illus. see Kung, Annie, tr.
Wang, Gabrielle. Garden of Empress Cassia. (p. 656)
—Jardin de la Emperatriz Casia. Holguin, Magdalena, tr. (p. 909)
—Race for the Chinese Zodiac. Rippin, Sally & Abos, Regine, illus. (p. 1431)
—Wishbird. (p. 1940)
Wang, Holman, jt. auth. see Wang, Jack.
Wang, Holman & Wang, Jack. Epic Yarns - The Empire Strikes Back. (p. 532)
—Star Wars - Return of the Jedi. (p. 1641)
—Star Wars Short & Sweet - A New Hope. (p. 1642)
Wang, Jack, jt. auth. see Wang, Holman.
Wang, Jack & Wang, Holman. Adventures of Huckleberry Finn. (p. 18)
—Cozy Classics - Les Miserables. (p. 375)
—Cozy Classics: the Adventures of Tom Sawyer. (p. 375)
—Emma. (p. 519)
—Herman Melville's Moby Dick. (p. 771)
—Oliver Twist. (p. 1286)
—Pride & Prejudice. (p. 1399)
—War & Peace. (p. 1857)
Wang, Jack, et al. Jane Eyre. (p. 908)
Wang, Jacqueline, illus. see O'Loughlin, Chloe & Borrowman, Mary.
Wang, Jen, illus. see Doctorow, Cory.
Wang, Jianwei, ed. see Bo, Zhiyue.
Wang, Jianwei, ed. see Hollihan-Elliot, Sheila.
Wang, Jianwei, ed. see Liao, Yan.
Wang, Jianwei, ed. see Lin, Zhimin.
Wang, Jianwei, ed. see Lu, Jia.
Wang, Jianwei, ed. see Luh, Shu Shin.
Wang, Jianwei, ed. see Yu, Bin.
Wang, Jianwei, ed. China (p. 306)
Wang, Jue, illus. see Cook, Gerri.
Wang, Kateri. Wang Ming: The Greatest of the Great Pandas. (p. 1856)
Wang, Lin, illus. see Branscombe, Allison.
Wang, Lin, illus. see Konrad, Marla Stewart.
Wang, Lin, illus. see Qu, Zhi.
Wang, Lin, jt. auth. see Yoo, Paula.
Wang, Lucy. Art of Chinese Brush Painting. (p. 102)
Wang, Margaret. Baby Mine Touch & Feel Flashcards. (p. 127)
—Easter Egg Hunt. Johnson, Richard, illus. (p. 499)
—Eency Weency Spider. Rueda, Claudia, illus. (p. 505)
—Five Little Puppies. Haines, Genny, illus. (p. 600)
—I Love You, Every Little Bit. Butler, John, illus. (p. 843)
—Monkey Tumbles. Elliott, Rebecca, illus. (p. 1165)
—Postcards from Kitty. Silver-Thompson, Pattie, illus. (p. 1388)
—Right Shoes for Me! Kightly, Rosalinda, illus. (p. 1472)
—Turtles Take Their Time. (p. 1799)
—Who Do You Love? A Touch & Feel Book. Mitchell, Melanie, illus. (p. 1915)
—Who Stole the Cookie from the Cookie Jar? Schneider, Christine, illus. (p. 1917)
Wang, Margaret C. When I Grow Up: A Touch & Feel Book. Gévry, Claudine, illus. (p. 1903)
Wang, Michael. Blizzard. (p. 199)
Wang, Qi, illus. see Schwaeber, Barbie H.
Wang, Qi, illus. see Schwaeber, Barbie.
Wang, Qi Z., illus. see Aller, Susan Bivin.
Wang, Qi Z., illus. see Brill, Marlene Targ.
Wang, Qi Z., illus. see Falk, Elizabeth Sullivan.
Wang, Qijun, illus. see Sadler, Rosemary.
Wang, Ruowen. To Share One Moon. Xu, Wei & Zheng, Xiaoyan, illus. (p. 1759)
Wang, Sarah. My Quilt. (p. 1217)
Wang, Sean. Runners: Volume 1: Bad Goods. (p. 1497)
Wang, Sean, illus. see King, Trey.
Wang, Sean, illus. see Steele, Michael Anthony.
Wang, Shaoli. Chinese Fairy Tale Feasts: A Literary Cookbook. (p. 307)
Wang, Shaoli, illus. see Yee, Paul.
Wang, Suling, illus. see Bauer, Marion Dane.
Wang, Suling, illus. see Yep, Laurence.
Wang, Sylvia. Guardians. (p. 728)
Wang, Xiaohong. One Year in Beijing. Lin, Grace, illus. (p. 1298)
Wang, Zong, illus. see Crane, Carol.
Wang, Zong-Zhou, illus. see Crane, Carol.
Wangerin, Walter, Jr. Bedtime Rhyme. Huang, Benrei, illus. (p. 157)
—I Am My Grandpa's Enkelin. Tate, Don, illus. (p. 833)
—Probity Jones & the Fear Not Angel. Ladwig, Tim, illus. (p. 1408)
Wangerin, Walter, Jr., et al. Little Ones Talk with God: A Book of Prayers. Rama, Sue, illus. (p. 1032)
Wangler, Chris. Famous People of the Paranormal: Psychics, Clairvoyants & Charlatans. Vol. 1 (p. 569)
—Ghost Stories of Georgia: True Tales of Ghostly Hauntings (p. 671)
Wangler, Chris, ed. see Burtinshaw, Julie.
Wangler, Chris, ed. see Smitten, Susan.
Wanha lidih, illus. see Menase Debora.
Wanjie, Anne, ed. Basics of Animal Systems. (p. 142)
—Basics of Biochemistry. (p. 142)
—Basics of Biology. (p. 142)
—Basics of Ecology. (p. 142)
—Basics of Evolution. (p. 142)
—Basics of Genetics. (p. 142)
—Basics of Microbes. (p. 142)
—Basics of Plant Structures. (p. 142)
—Basics of Reproduction. (p. 142)
—Basics of the Human Body. (p. 142)
Wanless, Harold R. Book of Aerial Stereo Photographs (p. 210)
Wann. 100% Perfect Girl (p. 1998)
WannaBees Media LLC, creator. HoniBee Loses Her Voice (paperback) The Do'Bees. (p. 795)
Wannamaker, Joni Gruelle, illus. see Hall, Patricia.
Wanniarachchi, Ruwan. Early Childhood Computer Learning Workbook - Level 1. (p. 493)
Wapahi, Robert, illus. see Hay, John & Harwich, Mary Belle.
Warabe, Kimika, illus. see Ebina, Hiro.
Warbelow, Willy L. Guffinys' Chimney. (p. 729)
Warbrick, Caroline. Taking Action Against Eating Disorders. (p. 1698)
Warburton, Carol. Edge of Night: A Novel. (p. 504)
Warburton, Dustin, jt. auth. see Rodman, Dennis.
Warburton, Fiona, jt. auth. see Smith, John D.
Warburton, Lianne & Callfas, Diana. Amphetamines & Other Stimulants. (p. 65)
Warburton, Olivia. I Love You This Much. Wright Sisters Staff, illus. (p. 844)
—Thank You. Wright Sisters Staff, illus. (p. 1725)
Warburton, Ruth. Witch Alone. (p. 1941)
—Witch Finder. (p. 1941)
—Witch Hunt. (p. 1941)
Warburton, Sarah, illus. see Bradman, Tony.
Warburton, Sarah, illus. see Hart, Caryl.
Warburton, Sarah, illus. see Holabird, Katherine.
Warburton, Sarah, illus. see Magee, Wes.
Warburton, Sarah, illus. see Oram, Hiawyn.
Warburton, Sarah, illus. see Sperring, Mark.
Warburton, Thomas, tr. see Jansson, Tove.
Warburton, Tom. 1000 Times No. Warburton, Tom, illus. (p. 2001)
Warchocki, Tim. Have Your Cake & Eat It Too: The Family Plan for Lifelong Health & Fitness. (p. 754)
—My Fit Family. . . a Quick Start. (p. 1208)
Ward, Adam. Motson's National Obsession: The Greatest Football Trivia Book Ever. (p. 1180)
Ward, Adam, jt. auth. see Sterling Publishing Company Staff.
Ward, Adam, jt. contrib. by see Sterling Publishing Company Staff.
Ward, Anna, jt. auth. see Burton, Terry.
Ward, April, illus. see Brown, Monica.
Ward, April, illus. see Feldman, Thea.
Ward, April, illus. see Garza, Xavier.
Ward, April, illus. see Zepeda, Gwendolyn & Ventura, Gabriela Baeza.
Ward, Arthur Henry Sarsfield, see Rohmer, Sax, pseud.
Ward, B. J. Farty Marty. Kellogg, Steven, illus. (p. 575)
Ward, Barnaby, jt. auth. see Burgis, Stephanie.
Ward, Brian R. Story of Medicine. (p. 1659)
—Tunas. (p. 1796)
Ward, Brian R., et al. History Encyclopedia: Follow the Development of Human Civilization Around the World. (p. 783)
Ward, C. L. Portia the Porcupine Visits the Doctor. (p. 1386)
Ward, Caias. Only Brother. (p. 1298)
Ward, Candace, ed. Children's Christmas Stories & Poems. (p. 303)
Ward, Carla. Emily Finds a Dog. Ward, Megan, illus. (p. 518)
Ward, Charlotte, ed. Gem Care. Ward, Fred, photos by. (p. 659)
Ward, Cherise, illus. see Mitchell, Carol.
Ward, Cherise, illus. see Picayo, Mario, et al.
Ward, Chris. Adventures of Seabome Morse. (p. 22)
—Discover Australia. (p. 447)
—Discover Kenya. (p. 447)
—Discover South Africa. (p. 448)
Ward, Chris, jt. auth. see Wilson, Rosie.
Ward, Christopher. Mac in the City of Light. (p. 1067)
—Mac on the Road to Marseille. (p. 1067)
Ward, Cindi. Back Yard Capers: The Secret Club. (p. 130)
Ward, Cindy. Cookie's Week. dePaola, Tomie, illus. (p. 361)
Ward, D. J. Exploring Mars. (p. 552)
—Materials Science. (p. 1104)
—Seven Wonders of Space Phenomena. (p. 1555)
—Simple Machines. Lowery, Mike, illus. (p. 1578)
—What Happens to Our Trash? Meisel, Paul, illus. (p. 1886)
Ward, Damian. Everyone Has Feelings (p. 544)
Ward, Damian, illus. see Aboff, Marcie.
Ward, Damian, illus. see Coleman, Wim & Perrin, Pat.
Ward, Damian, illus. see Higgins, Nadia.
Ward, Damian, illus. see Meister, Cari.
Ward, Damian, illus. see Schwaeber, Barbie Heit.
Ward, Dan. Meet the Boomer Sisters. (p. 1122)
Ward, David. Archipelago (p. 95)
—Beneath the Mask (p. 164)
—Between Two Ends. (p. 173)
—Beyond the Mask. (p. 174)
Ward, David Wood. Next Crisis: Direct & Equity Investment in Developing Countries. (p. 1249)
Ward, Dorothy. Miracle in the Barrel: A Story of Faith. (p. 1148)
Ward, Duren J. H. Problem of the Mounds. (p. 1408)
—Some Iowa Mounds, an Anthropological Survey. (p. 1609)
Ward, E. F., illus. see Webb, Robert N.
Ward, Elaine M. Old Testament Women. (p. 1285)
Ward, Eva D. Calvin C. Waxwing. York, Deborah Ward, illus. (p. 255)
Ward, Finn. Avestruces / Ostriches at the Zoo. (p. 119)
—Elefantes / Elephants at the Zoo. (p. 510)
—Elephants at the Zoo. (p. 512)
—Giraffes at the Zoo. (p. 678)
—Gorilas / Gorillas at the Zoo. (p. 702)
—Gorillas at the Zoo. (p. 703)
—Jirafas / Giraffes at the Zoo. (p. 919)
—Osos Polares / Polar Bears at the Zoo. (p. 1306)
—Ostriches at the Zoo. (p. 1306)
—Penguins at the Zoo. (p. 1337)
—Pingüinos / Penguins at the Zoo. (p. 1359)
—Polar Bears at the Zoo. (p. 1379)
Ward, Fred. Pearls. (p. 1333)
Ward, Fred, photos by see Ward, Charlotte, ed.
Ward, Geoff, illus. see Green, Jen.
Ward, Geoffrey C., et al. Who Invented the Game? Baseball: the American Epic. (p. 1915)
Ward, Greta. Pinkie the Cat Gets a Baby Sister. (p. 1360)
Ward, Hadley & Castano, Marie. Days of Faith: Student Planner & Assignment Book/Primary Grades 2005-2006. Cannizzo, Karen, ed. (p. 415)
Ward, Heather P. I Promise I'll Find You. McGraw, Sheila, illus. (p. 844)
Ward, Helen. Hare & Tortoise. (p. 748)
—Moon Dog. (p. 1172)
—Snutt the Ift: A Small but Significant Chapter in the Life of the Universe. O'Malley, Judy, ed. (p. 1601)
—Spots in a Box. Ward, Helen, illus. (p. 1634)
—Tin Forest. Anderson, Wayne, illus. (p. 1755)
—Town Mouse & the Country Mouse. Ward, Helen, illus. (p. 1773)
—Twenty-five December Lane. Anderson, Wayne, illus. (p. 1801)
Ward, Helen & Aesop. Hare & Tortoise. (p. 748)
Ward, Ian. Bobby Blah Blah & the Mystery of the U F O in Sniggery Woods. (p. 206)
—Cars & How They Work. (p. 272)
—Magic of the Matrix: Making Arithmetic Practice Fun. (p. 1073)
Ward, J. Three Monsters. W, J., illus. (p. 1743)
Ward, J. R., pseud. Lover Unbound (p. 1061)
Ward, James. Asylum Light: Stories from the George A. Zeller Era & Beyond, Peoria State Hospital, Galesburg Mental Health Center, & George A. Zeller Mental Health Center. (p. 109)
Ward, James M. Time Curse. (p. 1751)
Ward, Jan Price. Smokey & the Great Escape. (p. 1594)
—Smokey, the Gentle Guardian. (p. 1594)
Ward, Jason E. First Love. (p. 596)
Ward, Jason E., creator. First Love. (p. 596)
Ward, Jay Bryant, illus. see Nunes, Rachel Ann.
Ward, Jean Elizabeth. Barbara Anne Bushy Tale: Book #2 in a Series. (p. 137)
—Rabbits Too. (p. 1430)
Ward, Jean Elizabeth, Poet Laureate. BARBARA ANNE BUSHY TALE: Book I. (p. 137)
—BARBARA ANNE BUSHY TALE Book III. (p. 137)
Ward, Jennifer. Because You Are My Baby. Long, Sylvia, illus. (p. 155)
—Busy Tree Falkenstern, Lisa, illus. (p. 246)
—Forest Bright, Forest Night. Henterly, Jamichael, illus. (p. 618)
—Let's Go Outside! Outdoor Activities & Projects to Get You & Your Kids Closer to Nature. (p. 997)
—Little Creek. Scott, Julie, illus. (p. 1026)
—Mama Built a Little Nest. Jenkins, Steve, illus. (p. 1084)
—Seed & the Giant Saguaro. Rangner, Mike K., illus. (p. 1547)
—Sunhat. Sisson, Stéphanie Roth, illus. (p. 1677)
—There Was an Odd Princess Who Swallowed a Pea Calderon, Lee, illus. (p. 1730)
—There Was an Old Monkey Who Swallowed a Frog Gray, Steve, illus. (p. 1730)
—Way up in the Arctic. Spengler, Kenneth J., illus. (p. 1864)
—What Will Hatch? Ghahremani, Susie, illus. (p. 1895)
Ward, Jessica, jt. auth. see Disney Book Group Staff.
Ward, Jill. Cherokees. (p. 298)
—Creeks. (p. 380)
—Creeks & Cherokees Today. (p. 380)
—Georgia's First People. (p. 665)
—Martin Luther King, Jr. (p. 1098)
—Mississippian Indians. (p. 1154)
—Oconee River. (p. 1277)
—Shell Mound Builders. (p. 1564)
—St. Marys River. (p. 1638)

—Woodland Indians. (p. 1949)
Ward, John. Secret de l'Alchimiste. Guitard, Agnes & Pineau, Severine, trs. from ENG. (p. 1540)
—Stone of Sorrow: The Revealer of Wonders. (p. 1652)
Ward, John, illus. see Miller, William.
Ward, John H. West Point Mutiny of 1818 & its Aftermath: Five West Point Cadets & Their Quixotic Crusade Against West Point, the Commandant, the Superintendent, the Army, the Secretary of War, & the President of the United States. (p. 1876)
Ward, Jonathan, jt. auth. see Hughes, Mair Wynn.
Ward, Joshua. Eric the Dragon: Gr... Atchoooo!! Dragon Flu! (p. 533)
Ward, Joyce Claudine. Nanny the Goat. (p. 1229)
Ward, Juliana, illus. see Ward, Teresa.
Ward, Karen. Fun with Mexican Cooking. (p. 648)
Ward, Kari. Marley & Maverick & the Haunted Maze. (p. 1095)
—Marley & Maverick Go Fishing. (p. 1095)
Ward, Keith, illus. see Farley, Walter.
Ward, Kelly, illus. see Kelly, Thomas E.
Ward, Kris A. Tony's Day in the Park. (p. 1766)
Ward, Krista, jt. auth. see Kelly, Bernadette.
Ward, Kristin, ed. see Dorling Kindersley Publishing Staff.
Ward, Kyla, jt. auth. see Marrion, Thom.
Ward, L. B. B. Professor Angelicus Visits the Big Blue Ball. Watt, Coulter, illus. (p. 1409)
Ward, Lesley. Jumping for Kids. (p. 934)
—Your Healthy & Happy Horse: How to Care for Your Horse & Have Fun Too! (p. 1980)
Ward, Lester Frank. Glimpses of the Cosmos. (p. 683)
—Pure, Sociology. (p. 1419)
Ward, Lindsay. Henry Finds His Word. (p. 768)
—Pelly & Mr. Harrison Visit the Moon. Ward, Lindsay, illus. (p. 1336)
—Please Bring Balloons. (p. 1373)
—Rosco vs. the Baby. (p. 1489)
—When Blue Met Egg. (p. 1901)
Ward, Lindsay, illus. see Gill, Mehrnaz S.
Ward, Lindsay M., illus. see Thurman, Kathryn.
Ward, Lynd, illus. see Henry, Marguerite.
Ward, Lynd, illus. see Hewes, Agnes Danforth.
Ward, Lynd, illus. see Robinson, Mabel L.
Ward, Lynd, illus. see Swift, Hildegarde H.
Ward, M. P. Sam & the Sea Witch. (p. 1506)
Ward, Marcia. Girl Who Found Her Voice. (p. 679)
Ward, Matt, illus. see Collins Educational Staff & Harvey, Damian.
Ward, Matt, illus. see Harvey, Damien.
Ward, Matthew. Fantastic Family Whipple. (p. 571)
—War of the World Records. (p. 1857)
Ward, Matthew, photos by see Khan, Jahangir & Pratt, Kevin.
Ward, Mayan. First Time I Saw the Ocean. (p. 597)
Ward, Megan, illus. see Ward, Carla.
Ward, Michael. Mike & the Bike. (p. 1141)
Ward, Mike. Scratch & Solve Hangman (p. 1532)
—Scratch & Solve Hangman #1 (p. 1532)
Ward, Nancy. Sir Walter Raleigh: Founding the Virginia Colony. (p. 1580)
Ward, Nathan. Salida Singletrack: Mountain Biking in Colorado's Upper Arkansas Valley. (p. 1504)
Ward, Nick. Come on, Baby Duck! (p. 347)
—I Wish ... Ward, Nick, illus. (p. 848)
—Ice Child. Bailey, Peter, tr. (p. 850)
—Ice Child. Bailey, Peter, illus. (p. 850)
—Naughty Fairy's Naughty Surprise! (p. 1237)
—Nicest Naughty Fairy. (p. 1250)
—Rumpus in the Night. (p. 1495)
—Tadpole Prince. (p. 1695)
—Tinyrannosaurus. (p. 1757)
Ward, Nick, illus. see Dealey, Erin.
Ward, Nick, illus. see Fischel, Emma.
Ward, P. Contract of Terror: An Essay Regarding the Intellectual Origins of Modern Terrorism. (p. 361)
Ward, Pat Mays. Big Mama's Storm Cellar. (p. 182)
Ward, Patricia R., illus. see Sharpe, Paula A.
Ward, Rachel. Chaos. (p. 291)
—Drowning. (p. 486)
—Infinity. (p. 873)
—Infinity. (p. 873)
—Numbers. (p. 1272)
Ward, Rachel, tr. see Blobel, Brigitte.
Ward, Rachel, tr. see Grossmann-Hensel, Katharina.
Ward, Ray. Those Brave Crews: The Epic Raid to Destroy Hitler's Ploesti Oil Fields. (p. 1740)
Ward, Ruth. Adventures of Bloor Bone. (p. 16)
Ward, S. Meet A. A. Milne. (p. 1120)
—Meet E. B. White. (p. 1121)
—Meet J. K. Rowling. (p. 1121)
Ward, Sarah, illus. see Macmillan, Sue.
Ward, Sarah E. Electricity in the Real World. (p. 509)
Ward, Sarah G., illus. see Scholastic, Inc. Staff.
Ward, Scott, illus. see Reynolds, D. G.
Ward, Shirley. Preventing the Heartaches. (p. 1398)
Ward, Stephen J. GREATEST Togger Story Ever Told - Part 1: Thrifty's Stand. (p. 720)
—GREATEST Togger Story Ever Told - Part 2: the Boot of All Evil. (p. 720)
—GREATEST Togger Story Ever Told - Part 3: Far from the Screaming Crowd. (p. 720)
—GREATEST Togger Story Ever Told - Part 4: the Raiders of Leaf. (p. 720)
Ward, Stuart. Body Freedom Day. (p. 207)
Ward, Sue. One Gal's Army. (p. 1295)
Ward, Sue Marshall, illus. see Davis, David.
Ward, Sue Marshall, illus. see Simmons, Lynn Sheffield.
Ward, Susan. Red Crayon. (p. 1453)
Ward, Sylvia, illus. see David, Juliet.
Ward, Teresa. Blackie's Day Out. Ward, Juliana, illus. (p. 197)
Ward, Terri & Ward, Tom. Aunt Tami's Strawberry Farm. Kindt, Rita, illus. (p. 115)
Ward, Terry. Major Decisions: A Guide to College Majors. (p. 1078)
Ward, Tom, jt. auth. see Ward, Terri.
Ward, Tony. Whacker McCracker's Vineyard: The Story of Waiheke Island's Infamous Vineyeard. (p. 1877)
Ward, VanCe. What If. (p. 1887)
Ward, Wendy. My One-of-a-Kind Fashion Design. Neild, Robyn, illus. (p. 1216)
Ward (Willard), Bernice. God Says, Momma Says, & Children Says. (p. 690)
Wardale, David. Psico. (p. 1413)
Wardell, Joe. Doodey the Combat Camel. Bane, T. Glenn, illus. (p. 469)
Warden, Andrew J. Grecko the Gecko Starts School. (p. 720)
Warden, Evelyn. Oh, Please, Cricket. (p. 1281)
Warden, Gillian, illus. see Crew, Gary.
Warden, John. Chronicles of Zabaduk. (p. 317)
Warden, Kristina. Sparkle: A Star's Story. (p. 1622)
Warden, Margrethe. Lory Owner's Survival Guide. (p. 1053)
Warder, Aaron, illus. see Moore, J. S.
Ward-Johnson, Chris. Computers: A Magic Mouse Guide. Laughing Gravy Design Staff, illus. (p. 355)
—E-Mail: A Magic Mouse Guide. Laughing Gravy Design Staff, illus. (p. 492)
—Internet: A Magic Mouse Guide. Laughing Gravy Design Staff, illus. (p. 880)
—World Wide Web: A Magic Mouse Guide. Laughing Gravy Design Staff, illus. (p. 1959)
Ward-Johnson, Chris & Gould, William. Magic Mouse Dictionary of Computers & Information Technology. Laughing Gravy Design Staff, illus. (p. 1072)
Wardlaw, Lee. 101 Ways to Bug Your Friends & Enemies. (p. 2000)
—101 Ways to Bug Your Parents. (p. 2000)
—Coreys Fire. (p. 367)
—Red, White, & Boom! Lee, Huy Voun, illus. (p. 1455)
—Won Ton: A Cat Tale Told in Haiku. Yelchin, Eugene, illus. (p. 1947)
—Won Ton & Chopstick. Yelchin, Eugene, illus. (p. 1947)
Wardle, Sue & Porter, Eleanor H. Kites Funstation. (p. 962)
Wardley, R. & Bingham, J. First Dictionary. (p. 594)
WARDLEY, RACHEL, jt. auth. see Equipo Staff.
Wardlow, Lynn. Friends with My Brother. (p. 639)
Wardrope, William. Venezuela. (p. 1835)
Ward-Showers, Latanya. Could It Be a Monster in the Attic? (p. 369)
Ward-Singer, Tonya & Singer, Bill. Scholastic Teacher Plan Book. (p. 1522)
Wardup, Shirley, ed. see Campodonica, Carol A.
Wardwell, Stacey DeMille. Be Not Afraid: A Young Woman's Guide to Personal Defense. Tolmans, Tristan, ed. (p. 149)
Ware, Claudia. Day the Alphabet Rebelled. (p. 414)
Ware, Fletcher K. Empress Conspiracy. (p. 521)
Ware, Kay & Sutherland, Lucille. Greek & Roman Myths. Kottmeyer, William, ed. (p. 720)
Ware, Lesley. Sew Fab: Sewing & Style for Young Fashionistas. (p. 1555)
Ware, Patricia M. Morning Moon. (p. 1175)
Ware, Quinton, illus. see Vana, Dan.
Ware, Richard. I'm Glad God Made Me... Me. McQuitty, LaVonia Corbin, illus. (p. 859)
Ware, Shirley. Just Kids. (p. 939)
Wareh, Denny T. Nee Nee the Woodpecker. (p. 1239)
—School Bound Nee Nee the Woodpecker. (p. 1522)
Warf, Gracie, illus. see Pangan, Catherine Hagerman.
Warfield, D. L., illus. see LeFlore, Lyah B.
Warfield, Laura Castillo. Daisy's Faith. (p. 401)
Warfield, O. Omar Blue & K-9 Town, USA. (p. 1288)
Warga, Jasmine. My Heart & Other Black Holes. (p. 1210)
Wargin, Ed, photos by see Wargin, Kathy-jo.
Wargin, Kathy-jo. Alfred Nobel: The Man Behind the Peace Prize. Pullen, Zachary, illus. (p. 37)
—American Reader. Darnell, K. L., illus. (p. 63)
—B Is for Badger: A Wisconsin Alphabet. Graef, Renee, illus. (p. 122)
—D Is for Dala Horse: A Nordic Countries Alphabet. Graef, Renée, illus. (p. 397)
—Edmund Fitzgerald: The Song of the Bell. van Frankenhuyzen, Gijsbert, illus. (p. 504)
—F Is for Fireflies: God's Summertime Alphabet Bronson, Linda, illus. (p. 559)
—Frank & Beans Lewis, Anthony, illus. (p. 628)
—Frank & Beans & the Grouchy Neighbor Lewis, Anthony, illus. (p. 628)
—Frank & Beans & the Scary Campout Lewis, Anthony, illus. (p. 628)
—I Spy with My Little Eye: Minnesota. Wargin, Ed, photos by. (p. 846)
—K Is for Kite: God's Springtime Alphabet Gatto, Kim, illus. (p. 941)
—L Is for Lincoln: An Illinois Alphabet. van Frankenhuyzen, Gijsbert, illus. (p. 969)
—Legend of Leelanau. van Frankenhuyzen, Gijsbert, illus. (p. 988)
—Legend of Minnesota. Geister, David, illus. (p. 988)
—Legend of Old Abe: A Civil War Eagle. Caple, Laurie, illus. (p. 988)
—Legend of the Petoskey Stone. van Frankenhuyzen, Gijsbert, illus. (p. 989)
—Little Minnesota. Urban, Helle, illus. (p. 1031)
—Little Wisconsin. (p. 1038)
—M Is for Melody: A Music Alphabet. Larson, Katherine, illus. (p. 1067)
—Michigan Counting Book. Monroe, Michael Glenn, illus. (p. 1135)
—Minn from Minnesota. Holman, Karen Busch, illus. (p. 1147)
—Mitt & Minn at the Wisconsin Cheese Jamboree. Holman, Karen Busch, illus. (p. 1156)
—Mitt & Minn's Illinois Adventure. Holman, Karen Busch, illus. (p. 1156)
—Moose on the Loose. Bendall-Brunello, John, illus. (p. 1173)
—North Star Numbers: A Minnesota Number Book. Caple, Laurie, illus. (p. 1265)
—P Is for Pumpkin: God's Harvest Alphabet Pang, YaWen Ariel, illus. (p. 1316)
—Prairie Numbers: An Illinois Number Book. O'Malley, Kathy, illus. (p. 1392)
—S Is for Sleeping Bear Dunes: A National Lakeshore Alphabet. Frankenhuyzen, Gijsbert van, illus. (p. 1499)
—S Is for Snowman Johnson, Richard G., illus. (p. 1499)
—V Is for Viking: A Minnesota Alphabet. Latham, Karen & Latham, Rebecca, illus. (p. 1829)
—Voyageur's Paddle. Geister, David & Van Frankenhuyzen, Gijsbert, illus. (p. 1851)
—Win One for the Gipper: America's Football Hero. Langton, Bruce, illus. (p. 1935)
Wargin, Kathy-jo, jt. auth. see Young, Judy.
Wargin, Kathy-jo & Bendall-Brunello, John. Scare a Bear. (p. 1519)
Warhol, Andy, jt. auth. see Willett, Edward.
Warhol, Tom. Aptera. (p. 93)
—Chaparral & Scrub. (p. 291)
—Desert. (p. 428)
—Earth's Biomes (p. 498)
—Forest. (p. 618)
—Grassland. (p. 712)
—Hawks. (p. 755)
—Owls. (p. 1315)
—Smart Car. (p. 1592)
—Tundra. (p. 1796)
—Water. (p. 1862)
Warhola, James. If You're Happy & You Know It. (p. 855)
—Uncle Andy's: A Faabbbulous Visit with Andy Warhol. Warhola, James, illus. (p. 1811)
—Uncle Andy's. Warhola, James, illus. (p. 1811)
—Uncle Andy's Cats. Warhola, James, illus. (p. 1811)
WARHOLA, JAMES, jt. auth. see Warhola, James.
Warhola, James & Scholastic, Inc. Staff. If You're Happy & You Know It. Geist, Ken, ed. (p. 855)
Warhola, James & WARHOLA, JAMES. Mi Tío Andy. (p. 1133)
Warick, Bob, illus. see Walsh, Ann & Waldron, Kathleen Cook.
Waring, Geoff. Oscar & the Bat: A Book about Sound. Waring, Geoff, illus. (p. 1305)
—Oscar & the Bird: A Book about Electricity. Waring, Geoff, illus. (p. 1305)
—Oscar & the Cricket: A Book about Moving & Rolling. Waring, Geoff, illus. (p. 1305)
—Oscar & the Frog: A Book about Growing. Waring, Geoff, illus. (p. 1305)
—Oscar & the Moth: A Book about Light & Dark. Waring, Geoff, illus. (p. 1305)
—Oscar & the Snail: A Book about Things That We Use. Waring, Geoff, illus. (p. 1305)
Waring, Geoff, illus. see Fontes, Justine.
Waring, Kerry Jones, jt. auth. see Gaines, Ann.
Waring, Kerry Jones, et al. Arizona. (p. 98)
—New Hampshire. (p. 1245)
—Pennsylvania. (p. 1338)
Waring, Richard & Jayne, Waring -. Gallina Hambrienta. Church, Caroline Jayne, illus. (p. 653)
Waring, Rob. Cupid the Dolphin (US) (p. 392)
Waring, Scott C. West's Time MacHine. (p. 1876)
Wark, Jasmine. Bee Happy. (p. 157)
Wark, L. A. Tuffy Tufferson Is a Bully. (p. 1796)
Wark, Laurie & Ritchie, Scot. Baseball. (p. 140)
Warlick, Sonya. King's Love for His Daughter. (p. 960)
Warm Day, Jonathan. Painted Stories from Taos Pueblo. (p. 1318)
Warm Day, Jonathan, illus. see Orona-Ramirez, Kristy.
Warman, Jessica. Beautiful Lies. (p. 153)
—Between. (p. 172)
—Breathless. (p. 226)
—Last Good Day of the Year. (p. 978)
—Where the Truth Lies. (p. 1909)
Warmus, Paul J. Sue's Zoo & the Magic Garden. (p. 1672)
Warmuth, Donna Akers. Plumb Full of History: A Story of Abingdon, Virginia. Gobble, DeAnna Akers, illus. (p. 1374)
Warn, Sue & Holmes, David. Fieldwork Investigations: A Self Study Guide. (p. 584)
Warnack, Rhonda. Kelsey's Candy World Adventure. (p. 948)
Warnasuriya, Chandrani. Children's Stories of Wit & Humor: Stories from Sri Lanka (The Grand-Old-Man & The Big Five) (p. 304)
—Favorite Folktales of Sri Lank. (p. 578)
—Spooky Tales from the Orient: Tales of Ogres, Demons, Ghosts, Spells, Charms & the Enchanted (p. 1631)
Warnau, Genevieve. Encyclopedia of Animals. (p. 524)
Warne. Hop to It! Sticker Activity Book. (p. 796)
—My Father's Flying Machine. (p. 1203)
—Present for Mom. (p. 1396)
Warne, jt. auth. see Barker, Cicely Mary.
Warne, Frederick. Giant Pumpkin. (p. 674)
Warne, Frederick & Barker, Cicely Mary. Flower Fairies Art Activity Book. (p. 607)
Warne, Frederick & Potter, Beatrix. Complete Adventures of Peter Rabbit. (p. 352)
Warner. Ask Quinney. (p. 106)
Warner, Allison H., jt. auth. see Johnson, Alice W.
Warner, Anna Bartlett. Yes Jesus Loves Me. (p. 1970)
Warner, Barbara. ABC's of Dollhouse Finishing. (p. 4)
Warner Bros. Entertainment Staff. Harry Potter Poster Book: Inside the Magical World. (p. 751)
—Harry Potter Poster Collection: The Quintessential Images. (p. 751)
—Harry Potter Poster Collection: The Definitive Movie Posters. (p. 751)
—Officially Awesome Scooby-Doo! Spooky Puzzles, Scary Mazes, & Much, Much More! (p. 1280)
Warner, Carl. World of Food: Discover Magical Lands Made of Things You Can Eat! (p. 1956)
Warner, Charles Dudley. Being A Boy. (p. 160)
—Fashions in Literature. (p. 576)
Warner, Cheryl Ware. Chunkerella. (p. 318)
Warner, Chris, ed. see Baron, Mike.
Warner, Chris, ed. see Horton, Steve.
Warner, Chris, ed. see Lorimer, Colin.
Warner, Christopher, ed. see Roybal, Laura.
Warner, Christopher S., jt. ed. see Dark Horse Comics Staff.
Warner, Danielle, illus. see Warner, Jeremy.
Warner, Darrell, illus. see Brontë, Emily.
Warner, Dave. Friend in Need. (p. 637)
—Hilarious Misadventures of an Outback Girl & a Hollywood Horse. (p. 779)
Warner, Deborah. Phineas Willerbee - in the Code of the Realm: The Chosen One Revealed. (p. 1351)
Warner, Dennis. Beads on One String. (p. 149)
Warner, Emilia & Garland, Peter. Micia. (p. 1135)
Warner, Emily B. Dottie Lamm: A Friend to Families. (p. 472)
Warner, Etta Miller. Fish Named Max. (p. 598)
—Max Has the Hiccups. (p. 1111)
Warner, Gertrude Chandler. Bicycle Mystery Dunn, Joeming W. & Dunn, Ben, illus. (p. 177)
—Blue Bay Mystery Dubisch, Michael, illus. (p. 202)
—Blue Bay Mystery. Gringhuis, Dirk, illus. (p. 202)
—Boxcar Children. (p. 216)
—Boxcar Children Graphic Novels Dubisch, Mike, illus. (p. 216)
—Boxcar Children Graphic Novels Dunn, Ben, illus. (p. 217)
—Boxcar Children Graphic Novels - 6 Titles Dubisch, Michael, illus. (p. 217)
—Boxcar Children Guide to Adventure: A How-To for Mystery Solving, Make-It-Yourself Projects, & More. (p. 217)
—Clue in the Corn Maze. (p. 335)
—Dog-Gone Mystery. (p. 461)
—Haunted Cabin Mystery Bloodworth, Mark, illus. (p. 753)
—Houseboat Mystery Dunn, Joeming W. & Dunn, Ben, illus. (p. 804)
—Lighthouse Mystery. (p. 1015)
—Mike's Mystery Dubisch, Michael, illus. (p. 1141)
—Mike's Mystery. (p. 1141)
—Mike's Mystery. Gringhuis, Dirk, illus. (p. 1141)
—Mystery of the Grinning Gargoyle. VanArsdale, Anthony, illus. (p. 1225)
—Mystery of the Runaway Ghost. Soileau, Hodges, illus. (p. 1226)
—Mystery of the Soccer Snitch. VanArsdale, Anthony, illus. (p. 1226)
—Mystery Ranch Dubisch, Michael, illus. (p. 1226)
—Mystery Ranch. (p. 1226)
—Mystery Ranch. Gringhuis, Dirk, illus. (p. 1226)
—Snowbound Mystery Dubisch, Mike, illus. (p. 1600)
—Snowbound Mystery. Dubisch, Mike, illus. (p. 1600)
—Star Stories for Little Folks. (p. 1641)
—Yellow House Mystery Dubisch, Mike, illus. (p. 1970)
—Yellow House Mystery Dubisch, Michael, illus. (p. 1970)
—Yellow House Mystery. (p. 1970)
—Yellow House Mystery. Gehr, Mary, illus. (p. 1970)
Warner, Gertrude Chandler, jt. auth. see Denton, Shannon Eric.
Warner, Gertrude Chandler, jt. auth. see Dunn, Joeming.
Warner, Gertrude Chandler, jt. auth. see Long, Christopher E.
Warner, Gertrude Chandler, jt. auth. see Worley, Rob M.
Warner, Gertrude Chandler, creator. Black Widow Spider Mystery. (p. 197)
—Bookshelf (p. 212)
—Boxcar Children Halloween Special. (p. 217)
—Clue in the Corn Maze. (p. 335)
—Comic Book Mystery. (p. 348)
—Creature in Ogopogo Lake. (p. 380)
—Finders Keepers Mystery. (p. 587)
—Garden Thief (the Boxcar Children Mysteries #130) The Boxcar Children Mysteries #130. (p. 656)
—Ghost at the Drive-in Movie. (p. 670)
—Ice Cream Mystery. (p. 850)
—Midnight Mystery. (p. 1139)
—Mystery in the Mall. (p. 1224)
—Mystery of the Haunted Boxcar. (p. 1225)
—Mystery of the Missing Pop Idol. (p. 1225)
—Mystery of the Stolen Dinosaur Bones. (p. 1226)
—Mystery of the Traveling Tomatoes. (p. 1226)
—Radio Mystery. (p. 1433)
—Tattletale Mystery. (p. 1707)
—Vanishing Passenger. (p. 1833)
Warner, Iris M. World of Maggie-Mae. (p. 1957)
Warner, J. C., jt. auth. see Brandt, Daniel A.
Warner, Jeremy. Hidden Mickeys: A Mouse in the Land. Warner, Danielle, illus. (p. 776)
Warner, Joan E. African American Poetry. (p. 27)
Warner, Jodi. Shia's Tail. (p. 1566)
—Shia's Tail 2. (p. 1566)
Warner, Jody Nyasha. Viola Desmond Won't Be Budged Rudnicki, Richard & Junaid, Bushra, illus. (p. 1843)
Warner, John Harley, et al. Major Problems in the History of American Medicine & Public Health. (p. 1078)
Warner, Joie. Joie Warner's Fresh from the Garden Cookbook. (p. 924)
Warner, Larry. Chocolate Island (p. 309)
Warner, Linda, illus. see Love, Pamela.
Warner, Liz. Conejito Grande. (p. 356)
Warner, Margaret. Just for Kids Interactive Concept Pictures Manual. (p. 938)
Warner, Margaret & Brown, Susie. Lone Pine: First World War Centenary Edition. Ciaffaglione, Sebastian, illus. (p. 1046)
—Lone Pine. Ciaffaglione, Sebastian, illus. (p. 1046)
Warner, Marty, et al. Little Girl in the Yellow Dress. (p. 1028)
Warner, Michael, illus. see King, J. Eric & Graham, Greg.
Warner, Michael N. Tales to Make You Scream for Your Momma. Warner, Robert, illus. (p. 1703)
—Titanic Game. Ordaz, Frank, illus. (p. 1758)
Warner, Nathan. Knight Before Christmas. (p. 964)
Warner, Patricia T. God's Business Plan: 12 Keys to Experience Success As You Glorify Almighty God in Your Business. (p. 691)
Warner, Penny. Fiestas de Cumpleaños Infantiles: Divertidas Sugerencias para los Primeros Cumpleaños de Tus Hijos. Guix, Joan Carles, tr. (p. 584)
—Mystery of the Missing Mustangs. (p. 1225)
—Project Book: Ideas, Tips & Techniques for School Projects. Wagner, Amy, ed. (p. 1410)
—Signing Fun: American Sign Language Vocabulary, Phrases, Games, & Activities. Gray, Paula, illus. (p. 1574)
Warner, Penny, jt. auth. see Hodges, Diane.

Warner Press, creator. Best Christmas Gift Ever: Coloring & Activity Book. (p. 168)
—Bible Sports Heroes: Great Lessons You Can Learn from God's Favorite Athletes Activity Book. (p. 176)
—Don't You Wonder about This World? (p. 469)
—Itty-Bitty Bible Activity Book: The First Collection. (p. 900)
—Itty-Bitty Bible Activity Book, Easter Edition. (p. 900)
—Itty-Bitty Bible Activity Book of Trivia & Cartoons! (p. 900)
—Learning the Lord's Prayer: Coloring & Activity Book. (p. 985)
—My Favorite Bible Stories Coloring Book. (p. 1203)
—Ten Commandments Coloring Book. (p. 1718)
—Zacchaeus Climbs a Tree Coloring Book. (p. 1984)
Warner Press Kids, creator. First Christmas. (p. 593)
—Jelly Bean Prayer Coloring & Activity Book. (p. 912)
—Jelly Bean Witness. (p. 912)
—Jesus Is Born: Coloring Book. (p. 915)
—Paul, a Servant of Jesus: Activity Book. (p. 1330)
—Queen Esther. (p. 1424)
Warner Press Staff. Divorce Comes to Our House. (p. 455)
—Jesus in My Heart Coloring Books Intermediate. (p. 915)
—Jesus Loves Me Coloring Book Pre-K. (p. 915)
Warner, Rex. Men & Gods: Myths & Legends of the Ancient Greeks. Gorey, Edward, illus. (p. 1126)
Warner, Robert, illus. see Warner, Michael N.
Warner, Sally. Best Friend Emma. Harper, Jamie, illus. (p. 169)
—Como ser una Persona de Verdad. (p. 351)
—Dragon Slayer! Biggs, Brian, illus. (p. 478)
—EllRay Jakes & the Beanstalk. (p. 515)
—EllRay Jakes & the Beanstalk. Biggs, Brian, illus. (p. 515)
—EllRay Jakes Is a Rock Star Harper, Jamie, illus. (p. 515)
—Ellray Jakes Is a Rock Star. (p. 515)
—Ellray Jakes Is Magic. (p. 515)
—EllRay Jakes Is Magic. Biggs, Brian, illus. (p. 515)
—EllRay Jakes Is Not a Chicken Harper, Jamie, illus. (p. 515)
—EllRay Jakes Is Not a Chicken! (p. 515)
—Ellray Jakes Rocks the Holidays! (p. 515)
—Ellray Jakes Rocks the Holidays! Biggs, Brian, illus. (p. 515)
—Ellray Jakes the Dragon Slayer Biggs, Brian, illus. (p. 515)
—EllRay Jakes the Dragon Slayer. (p. 515)
—Ellray Jakes the Recess King! (p. 515)
—EllRay Jakes the Recess King! Biggs, Brian, illus. (p. 515)
—EllRay Jakes Walks the Plank! (p. 515)
—Excellent Emma. Harper, Jamie, illus. (p. 547)
—Hattie's Year. (p. 753)
—Not-So-Weird Emma. Harper, Jamie, illus. (p. 1267)
—Only Emma. Harper, Jamie, illus. (p. 1298)
—Quinney Novel (p. 1428)
—Super Emma. Harper, Jamie, illus. (p. 1680)
—Walks the Plank! Harper, Jamie, illus. (p. 1854)
Warner, Sally, jt. auth. see Buller, Jon.
Warner, Sally, jt. auth. see Wallace, Rich.
Warner, Sally & Harper, Jamie. Excellent Emma. Harper, Jamie, illus. (p. 547)
—Only Emma. (p. 1298)
Warner, Susan. Daisy. (p. 400)
Warner, Susan & Wetherell, Elizabeth. Daisy in the Field. (p. 400)
—Queechy. (p. 1424)
Warner, Timothy M., jt. auth. see Anderson, Neil T.
Warner, Tucker. Breakthrough & Funeral of a Grandfather (p. 225)
Warnes, Tim. Can't You Sleep, Dotty? Warnes, Tim, illus. (p. 262)
—Can't You Sleep, Little Puppy? Warnes, Tim, illus. (p. 262)
—Chalk & Cheese. Warnes, Tim, illus. (p. 288)
—Daddy Hug. Chapman, Jane, illus. (p. 398)
—Happy Birthday, Dotty. Warnes, Tim, illus. (p. 744)
—Jesus Loves Me! (p. 915)
—Jesus Loves Me! Warnes, Tim, illus. (p. 915)
—No! Warnes, Tim, illus. (p. 1257)
—Sweet Dreams, Little Bear. (p. 1689)
Warnes, Tim, illus. see Bedford, David.
Warnes, Tim, illus. see Chapman, Jane.
Warnes, Tim, illus. see Freedman, Claire, et al.
Warnes, Tim, illus. see Grant, Nicola.
Warnes, Tim, illus. see Jennings, Linda.
Warnes, Tim, illus. see Lobel, Gillian.
Warnes, Tim, illus. see MacDonald, Alan.
Warnes, Tim, illus. see Oram, Hiawyn.
Warnes, Tim, illus. see Public Domain Staff.
Warnes, Tim, illus. see Smallman, Steve.
Warnes, Tim, illus. see Sykes, Julie.
Warnes, Tim, illus. see Van Buren, David.
Warnes, Tim, illus. see West, Judy.
Warnes, Tim, illus. see Whybrow, Ian.
Warnes, Tim, jt. auth. see Rawlinson, Julia.
Warnes, Tim, jt. auth. see Whybrow, Ian.
Warnes, Tim, tr. see Jennings, Linda.
Warnes, Tim & Sykes, Julie. Bathtime, Little Tiger! Warnes, Tim, illus. (p. 144)
—Hide & Seek, Little Tiger. Warnes, Tim, illus. (p. 776)
Warnes, Tim, et al. My Little Box of Bedtime Stories: Can't You Sleep, Puppy?/Time to Sleep, Little Bear!/What Are You Doing in My Bed?/Sleep Tight, Giner Kitten/Good Night, Emily!/Don't Be Afraid, Little Ones. Pedler, Caroline & Massey, Jane, illus. (p. 1212)
Warnick, Elsa, illus. see Spinelli, Eileen.
Warnick, Ryan. Gracie. (p. 705)
Warnock, Chris. Toys Overboard! (p. 1774)
Warr, Peter. Kung Fu Handbook. (p. 968)
Warren, Adam. Clockwork Thugs, Yo Digest. (p. 333)
Warren, Andrea. Charles Dickens & the Street Children of London. (p. 292)
—Escape from Saigon: How a Vietnam War Orphan Became an American Boy. (p. 535)
—Pioneer Girl: A True Story of Growing up on the Prairie. (p. 1361)
—Under Siege! Three Children at the Civil War Battle for Vicksburg. (p. 1813)
—We Rode the Orphan Trains. (p. 1868)
Warren, Bernie. Drama Games. (p. 480)
Warren, Bertie. Sammie's Journey to Freedom. (p. 1507)
Warren, Beverly, illus. see Moore, Beth.
Warren, Beverly, illus. see Simon, Mary Manz.
Warren, Cathy. Saturday Belongs to Sara. (p. 1515)
Warren, Celia. Big Surprise (p. 184)
—Bouncing with the Birdie (p. 216)
—Lenny's Lost Spots. (p. 991)
—Ready for a Picnic. (p. 1447)
Warren, Celia, illus. see Crebbin, June, et al.
Warren, Cindy. Unicorn's Horn. (p. 1818)
Warren, Cynthia Marie. Crazy Untamable, Tamable Tongue: Love with Your Words. (p. 378)
Warren, Dianne, jt. auth. see Jones, Susan Smith.
Warren, Donna E. Colors of the Rainbow. (p. 345)
Warren, Dotti M. Dreama Lynn & the Magic Tu Tu. (p. 484)
Warren, Eliza, ed. see Burnett, Frances Hodgson.
Warren, Eliza Gatewood, ed. see Wiggin, Kate Douglas Smith.
Warren, Elizabeth V., jt. auth. see Coleman, Janet Wyman.
Warren, Emily, illus. see Brallier, Max.
Warren, Emily Laber & Goldman, Laurie. Walk on the Beach: Into the Field Guide. (p. 1853)
Warren, F., illus. see Martinek, Frank V.
Warren, F., illus. see Martinek, Frank Victor.
Warren, G. A. Starr Light & the Christmas Story. Ciesinska, Izabela, illus. (p. 1642)
Warren, George A. Banner Boy Scouts: Or the Struggle for Leadership. (p. 136)
—Banner Boy Scouts on a Tour. (p. 136)
—Banner Boy Scouts or the Struggle for le. (p. 136)
—Bob Chase after Grizzly Bears. (p. 205)
Warren George A. Staff. Banner Boy Scouts. (p. 136)
Warren, Heather, jt. auth. see Byerly, Robbie.
Warren, Heather & Byerly, Robbie. Brown Bear or Black Bear. (p. 231)
Warren, Howard. Life Cycle of Plants: Set Of 6. (p. 1009)
—Life Cycle of Plants: Text Pairs. (p. 1009)
Warren, Jessica. Prime-Time Kid. (p. 1400)
Warren, Jill. Abe's Lucky Day: Second Edition. (p. 5)
—Bizzy Bee & the Flowers. (p. 194)
Warren, Johnette. Princess Joy. Whitsett, Darron, illus. (p. 1404)
Warren, Johnny, jt. auth. see Abela, Deborah.
Warren, Johnny & Abela, Deborah. Finals. (p. 587)
—Game of Life. (p. 654)
—Striker. (p. 1667)
Warren, Jordan L. Jo's Rainy Sad Day. (p. 926)
Warren, Joyce, illus. see Broughton, Theresa.
Warren, Leonard, illus. see Colby, Carolyn.
Warren, Marie. Frog That Never Smiled. (p. 640)
Warren, Marion E., photos by see Carr, Stephen.
Warren, Maude Radford. King Arthur & His Knights (Yesterday's Classics) Enright, Walter J., illus. (p. 958)
Warren, Mnetha, illus. see Riley, Christine.
Warren, Nagueyalti. Grandfather of Black Studies: W.E.B. du Bois. (p. 707)
Warren, Nikola. What Happened to Junior? A Child & Bear Memoir. (p. 1885)
Warren, Pamela, ed. see Session, Garry.
Warren Photographic Staff, photos by see Calver, Paul & Gunzi, Christiane.
Warren, Rebecca. Rebecca Warren Ruf, Beatrix, ed. (p. 1450)
Warren, Rebecca, ed. see Carson-Dellosa Publishing Staff.
Warren, Rick, jt. auth. see Zondervan Publishing Staff.
Warren, Rick H. Quinn at School: Relating, Connecting & Responding at School. (p. 1428)
Warren, Samuel. Spectre Smitten. (p. 1624)
Warren, Sandra J. Times to Remember, the Fun & Easy Way to Memorize the Multiplication Tables: Home & Classroom Resources. Vasquez, Juan Jose, illus. (p. 1754)
Warren, Sandra Jane. Times to Remember, the Fun & Easy Way to Memorize the Multiplication Tables. Vásquez, Juan José, illus. (p. 1754)
Warren, Sarah E. Dolores Huerta: A Hero to Migrant Workers Casilla, Robert, illus. (p. 464)
Warren, Shari, illus. see Bader, Bonnie.
Warren, Shari, illus. see Kittinger, Jo S.
Warren, Shari, illus. see Miller, Pam, et al.
Warren, Shari, illus. see Omartian, Stormie.
Warren, Steph & Harcourt, Mike. Tomorrow's Geography for Edexcel Specification A: Revision Guide. (p. 1765)
Warren, Steven Mathew, illus. see Warren, Tania Catherine.
Warren, Tania Catherine. All about Charlie Horse: Charlie Horse & His Adventures. Warren, Steven Mathew, illus. (p. 42)
Warren, Ty. Princess & the Ugly Mirror. (p. 1403)
Warren, Vince H. Adventures of Meka & Her Two Cubs. (p. 20)
Warren, Wendy Ann. Potato Chip, an Irish Tale. (p. 1388)
Warren, Wilda. Tejan: A Story of Life with the Comanche Indians. (p. 1715)
Warrick, Jessica, illus. see Houran, Lori Haskins.
Warrick, Jessica, illus. see Landgraf, James, Jr.
Warrick, Jessica, illus. see McMahon, Jeff.
Warrick, Jessica, illus. see Paniagua, Kelly.
Warrick, Jessica, illus. see Rosenthal, Cathy M.
Warrick, Jessica, illus. see Walker, Nan.
Warrick, Karen Clemens. Alamo: Victory or Death on the Texas Frontier. (p. 33)
—Benjamin Franklin: Creating a Nation. (p. 164)
—Gettysburg National Military Park: A MyReportLinks.com Book. (p. 670)
—Hannibal: Great General of the Ancient World. (p. 743)
—Independence National Historical Park: A MyReportLinks.com Book. (p. 870)
—Perilous Search for the Fabled Northwest Passage in American History. (p. 1343)
—Race for the North Pole & Robert Peary in World History. (p. 1431)
—Sandra Cisneros: Inspiring Latina Author. (p. 1511)
—Who Needs That Nose? Neidigh, Sherry, tr. (p. 1917)
Warrick, Leanne. Hair Trix for Cool Chix: The Real Girl's Guide to Great Hair. (p. 736)
Warrick, Natalie. Mighty Warrior Is the Ant. (p. 1140)
Warring, Molly-Ann. Paradise Acres. (p. 1323)
Warrington, Dean Grey. Perfection. (p. 1342)
Warshaw, Shirley Anne. Clinton Years. (p. 333)
Warstler, Mary Lu. Michael's Angel (p. 1135)
Warstler, Pasqua Cekola, jt. auth. see Donohoe, Kitty.
Warter, Fred, illus. see Kunstler, James Howard.
Wartik, David J. VonNesta Project: Camp Fingerlake. (p. 1850)
—Vonnesta Project. (p. 1850)
Wartko, Karen J. I Know My Daddy Works on the Moon. (p. 840)
Warwaruk, Larry. Andrei & the Snow Walker. (p. 72)
—Brovko's Amazing Journey (p. 231)
Warwaruk, Larry & Coteau Books Staff. Sundog Highway: Writing from Saskatchewan. (p. 1676)
Warwick, Andrew. Scary Stories: A Cryptic Collection of 28 Twisted Tales. (p. 1520)
Warwick, Andrew & Mott, A. S. Campfire Ghost Stories (p. 257)
Warwick, Carrie, illus. see Welch, Catherine A.
Warwick, Carrie H., illus. see Welch, Catherine A.
Warwick, Ellen. Everywear. Lum, Bernice, illus. (p. 546)
—Fully Woolly. Lum, Bernice, illus. (p. 647)
—Injeanuity. Lum, Bernice, illus. (p. 874)
—Stuff for Your Space. Lum, Bernice, tr. (p. 1670)
—Stuff to Hold Your Stuff. Lum, Bernice, illus. (p. 1670)
Warwick, Ellen, jt. auth. see Roderick, Stacey.
Warwick, Ellen & Di Salle, Rachel. Junk Drawer Jewelry. Kurisu, Jane, illus. (p. 936)
Warwick, J. M. Open Vein. (p. 1299)
Warwick, Richard, illus. see Cox, Lisa.
Warwillow, Lucas D. Marick's Cross (p. 1093)
Waryanto, Ian, illus. see Sanchez, Ricardo.
Waryncia, Lou. Abraham Lincoln: Defender of the Union. Hale, Sarah Elder, ed. (p. 6)
—Antietam: Day of Courage & Sacrifice. Hale, Sarah Elder, ed. (p. 89)
—Gettysburg: Bold Battle in the North. Hale, Sarah Elder, ed. (p. 670)
—Nation at War: Soldiers, Saints, & Spies. Hale, Sarah Elder, ed. (p. 1231)
—Young Heroes of the North & South. Hale, Sarah Elder, ed. (p. 1978)
Waryncia, Lou, et al. If I Were a Kid in Ancient China: Children of the Ancient World. (p. 853)
Waschak, Jay, et al. Wars of the Boltians & Kuissians. Watson, Travis & Lohr, Tyrel, illus. (p. 1859)
Wasco, Cindy, illus. see Mahany, Patricia Shely.
Wasden, Kevin, illus. see Wright, Julie.
Wasdin, Howard E. & Templin, Stephen. I Am a Seal Team Six Warrior: Memoirs of an American Soldier. (p. 832)
—I Am a Seal Team Six Warrior. (p. 832)
Wasenius, Richard. Friends. (p. 638)
Wash, Melissa. My Beautiful Girl Close Your Eyes. (p. 1196)
Washakie, John. Yuse: The Bully & the Bear. Cox, Jon, illus. (p. 1983)
Washam, Christie, illus. see Ruff, Carolyn.
Washburn, Cecilia, illus. see Tissot Lcsw, Jennifer.
Washburn, Chris, photos by see Slade, Suzanne Buckingham.
Washburn, Gabe. Easter Frog. (p. 499)
Washburn, Kim. Beyond the Music: The Bono Story. (p. 174)
—Breaking Through by Grace: The Bono Story (p. 225)
—Defender of Faith: The Mike Fisher Story (p. 423)
Washburn, Lucia, illus. see Clarke, Ginjer L.
Washburn, Lucia, illus. see Ostby, Kristin.
Washburn, Lucia, illus. see Zoehfeld, Kathleen Weidner.
Washburn, Patrik. Punchkinhead, the Never-Give-Up Boy. J.A.M.A.D., illus. (p. 1416)
Washburn, Sandi. Good Night, Grandma. Roehler, Yvonne Fetig, illus. (p. 699)
Washburn, Sue, ed. see Liebenow, Todd.
Washer, Mark Gregory. Blue Bonnie Butterfly: Tale of Two Tails. (p. 202)
Washer, S. N. Wingate Adventures: Our New Friends. (p. 1936)
Washington. Jack the Boogey Is My Real Name: The Truth about the Boogeyman. (p. 903)
Washington, Aimee, jt. auth. see Grimes, Craig.
Washington, AlTonya. Expectation of Beauty. (p. 548)
Washington, Angel D. Always Remember You Are Loved: When a Child Seeks Guidance on Cyber & Peer Bullying. Perry, Curtis, illus. (p. 51)
Washington, Balondo. Kayla's First Day of School. (p. 946)
Washington, C. E., illus. see Washington, Ida H.
Washington, Curtis. Story of Sue. (p. 1660)
Washington, De'borah L. Fairytale Holiday 1 And. (p. 565)
Washington, Donna, jt. auth. see Washington, Donna L.
Washington, Donna L. Li'l Rabbit's Kwanzaa. Evans, Shane W., illus. (p. 1017)
Washington, Donna L. & Washington, Donna. Big Spooky House: Picture Book. Rogers, Jacqueline, illus. (p. 184)
Washington, Edwina D. Baby Heaven. (p. 126)
Washington Elementary School. Principal Dusanek. (p. 1406)
Washington, George. George Washington's Rules to Live By: How to Sit, Stand, Smile, & Be Cool! a Good Manners Guide from the Father of Our Country. Harper, Fred, illus. (p. 665)
—Quotations of George Washington. U-Inspire Inc, ed. (p. 1429)
Washington, George, jt. auth. see Shearer, Cynthia.
Washington, Ida H. Brave Enough: The Story of Rob Sanford, Vermont Pioneer Boy. Smoak, I. W. & Washington, C. E., illus. (p. 223)
Washington, Joi. Ant. (p. 88)
—Ants. (p. 90)
—Baseball (2Y) (p. 141)
—Dragonflies. (p. 478)
—Dragonfly. (p. 478)
—Jumping Spiders. (p. 934)
—Mantises. (p. 1088)
—Pink Book. (p. 1359)
—Pink Book. Washington, Joi, illus. (p. 1359)
—Robber Flies. (p. 1478)
—Wasp. (p. 1860)
—Wasps. (p. 1860)
—Wolf Spider. (p. 1944)
Washington, Joi, illus. see Fleischer, Jayson.
Washington, Joi, illus. see Lynch, Michelle.
Washington, Joi, illus. see Taylor, Trace, et al.
Washington, Joi, jt. auth. see Brown, Penny.
Washington, Joi, jt. auth. see Dibble, Traci.
Washington, Joi & Byerly, Robbie. Ants. Byerly, Robbie, illus. (p. 90)
Washington, Joi & Dibble, Traci. Robber Flies. Dibble, Traci, illus. (p. 1478)
Washington, Joi & Fleischer, Jayson. These Are Wolves. (p. 1731)
Washington, Joi & Sanchez, Lucia M. ArañAs Saltadoras: Jumping Spiders. (p. 94)
—Avispas: Wasps. (p. 120)
Washington, Joi & Sánchez, Lucía M. Las Mantis: Mantises. (p. 976)
Washington, Joi & Sanchez, Lucia M. Las Mantis (Mantises) (p. 976)
Washington, Joi, et al. Hormigas: Ants. (p. 798)
—Moscas Predadoras. (p. 1176)
Washington, Joy Louise. Gingerbread House. (p. 677)
Washington, Kathleen. School Bully. (p. 1522)
Washington, Kathy. Three Colors of Katie. Farina, Kathy, illus. (p. 1741)
Washington, L. Manners First - G I F T S. (p. 1088)
Washington, LaShawn, jt. auth. see Washington, LaVonne.
Washington, LaShawn & Washington, LaVonne. Cartoon Bible: Featuring Crafty the Serpent. (p. 272)
Washington, LaVonne, jt. auth. see Washington, LaShawn.
Washington, LaVonne & Washington, LaShawn. How the Grinch Hare Became a Christian. (p. 813)
—Parables of Humpty Dumpty: Volume 1. (p. 1323)
Washington, Linda. Home & Back. (p. 791)
Washington, Linda, jt. auth. see Alcorn, Randy.
Washington, Linda, jt. auth. see Dall, Jeanette.
Washington, Linda, jt. auth. see Pyykkonen, Carrie.
Washington, Linda & Dall, Jeanette. Favorite Bible Children: Ages 2 & 3. (p. 578)
—Favorite Bible Children: Ages 4 & 5. (p. 578)
—Home & Back: Bible Activities. (p. 791)
Washington, Lorna. How Wonderful Are the Works of Your Hands. (p. 823)
Washington, Peter, ed. Eat, Drink, & Be Merry: Poems about Food & Drink. (p. 501)
Washington, Ronald. Sleepy Time Space Tales: Fairy Tales for Our Future. (p. 1590)
Washington, Sharalee Marie Shepherd. Little Bear Rabbit Goes to London. (p. 1024)
Washington, Shirley. Gift for Girls: Words of Wisdom from Successful Women. (p. 675)
Washington Sr., Terence B. Terry, Bear & Duck (p. 1722)
Washington Sr., Von H. Journey Begins: Seven Stops to Freedom & Contact in Harmonia. (p. 928)
Washington, Tiana. Shanna's Lost Ribbon. (p. 1559)
Washington, Victoria, ed. see Du Lac, Leo J.
Washington, Victoria, ed. see Young, T. M.
Washington, William W., Jr. His Grace Is Sufficient: An Autobiography. (p. 781)
Washington-Gaines, Carolyn. Blues!. . Why Blues & Latin Music? Bluesman, Bluesman, Bluesman. (p. 204)
Washington-Gattis, Ishia L. Meet Camden: Living with Sickle Cell Anemia. (p. 1120)
Washinton, LaShon & Washinton, LaVan. Picture It: Shabbat 104A for Kids. (p. 1355)
Washinton, LaVan, jt. auth. see Washinton, LaShon.
Wasielewski, Margaret, illus. see Markarian, Marianne.
Wasielewski, Margaret M., illus. see Markarian, Marianne.
Wasik, Barbara A., jt. auth. see Byrnes, James P.
Wasikhongo, Odalo Magruder. My First Book of Numbers. Wasikhongo, Odalo Magruder, illus. (p. 1205)
Wasniewski, Matthew, ed. see Dodge, Andrew.
Wasniowski, Miroslaw. ATM Basics: High-Speed Packet Network Operation & Services. (p. 113)
Wass, Chip, illus. see Capote, Lori.
Wassel, Linda. Turtlebee. (p. 1798)
Wasser, Barbara, jt. auth. see Routenburg, Rise'.
Wasserman, Curt, jt. auth. see Wasserman, Shannon.
Wasserman, Fran. Miracle Kitten. (p. 1148)
Wasserman, Gary. Politics in Action: Cases from the Frontlines of American Government. (p. 1381)
Wasserman, Mira. Too Much of a Good Thing. Carolan, Christine, illus. (p. 1767)
Wasserman, Robin. Book of Blood & Shadow. (p. 211)
—Crashed. (p. 376)
—Envy. (p. 532)
—Frozen. (p. 645)
—Gluttony. (p. 685)
—Greed. (p. 720)
—Hacking Harvard. (p. 735)
—Life, Starring Me! (p. 1013)
—Lust. (p. 1066)
—Lust; Envy. (p. 1066)
—Oops! I Did It (Again)! Martini, Angela, illus. (p. 1299)
—Pride. (p. 1398)
—Pride - Wrath Vol. 2. (p. 1398)
—Search for Scooby Snacks. (p. 1537)
—Seven Deadly Sins: Sloth; Gluttony; Greed. Vol. 3 (p. 1554)
—Shattered. (p. 1563)
—Skinned. (p. 1585)
—Sloth. (p. 1591)
—Torn. (p. 1770)
—Waking Dark. (p. 1853)
—Wired. (p. 1939)
—Wrath. (p. 1962)
Wasserman, Robin, jt. auth. see Soderberg, Erin.
Wasserman, Robin & Soderberg, Erin. Puppy Pirates #2: X Marks the Spot. (p. 1418)
Wasserman, Sand. Sun's Special Blessing: Happens Only Once in 28 Years - HC. Koffsky, Ann, illus. (p. 1677)
—Sun's Special Blessing: Happens Only Once in 28 Years - French Flap. Koffsky, Ann, illus. (p. 1677)
Wasserman, Shannon & Wasserman, Curt. Adventures of Ruff-N-Rescue: Adventures with the Heroes of New Barker Island. Wasserman, Curt et al, illus. (p. 22)

W

Wassillie, Eliza, et al. Four Legged Adventures. Wassillie, Eliza et al, illus. (p. 625)
Wassman, Paul A., jt. illus. see Wassmann, Marilyn B.
Wassmann, Marilyn B. & Wassman, Paul A. What the Wind Blew In: 6 Stories to Read with Children. (p. 1894)
Wassner, Gary. Mystery of the Jubilee Emerald. (p. 1225)
Wassner, Sarah & Furgang, Kathy. National Geographic Kids Animal Records: The Biggest, Fastest, Weirdest, Tiniest, Slowest, & Deadliest Creatures on the Planet. (p. 1231)
—National Geographic Kids Animal Records: The Biggest, Weirdest, Fastest, Tiniest, Slowest, & Deadliest Creatures on the Planet. (p. 1231)
Wasson, Christopher. Quest for Adlaremzee Molair Nopeeoh. (p. 1426)
Wasson, Dave. Big Ideas of Buster Bickles. Wasson, Dave, illus. (p. 182)
Wasson, Dawn K. T. Kuu Tutu. (p. 968)
Wasson, Dawn Kahalaomapuana Tautafa. Keana. (p. 946)
—Kilia & Wahiopua the Reefs of Hauula. (p. 956)
Wasson, E. & Strausser, A. Mommies & Daddies Are Nurses. Ebert, Roey, illus. (p. 1162)
Wasson, Ellis. Aristocracy & the Modern World. (p. 98)
Wasson, Ellis A. Multiple Choice & Free Response Questions in Preparation for the AP European History Examination 5th Edition. (p. 1190)
—Teacher's Manual to Accompany Multiple-Choice & Free-Response Questions with DBQ in Preparation for the AP European History Examination 5th Edition. (p. 1709)
Wastvedt, Bjorn & Voranin, Supissara. Call from Paradise: In search for my true Love. (p. 254)
Wasvary, Marcia, illus. see George, Francis.
Wasylyk, Thomas M. Second Edition Handwriting: Manuscript Writing. (p. 1539)
—Second Edition Handwriting: Writing in Cursive. (p. 1539)
—Second Edition Handwriting: Writing for Learning. (p. 1539)
—Second Edition Handwriting: Introduction to Cursive. (p. 1539)
—Second Edition Handwriting: Beginning Cursive Writing. (p. 1539)
—Second Edition Handwriting: Improving Cursive Writing. (p. 1539)
—Second Edition Handwriting: A Self-Improvement Workbook. (p. 1539)
—Second Edition Handwriting: Manuscript Review & Enrichment. (p. 1539)
—Second Edition Handwriting: Writing the Manuscript Letters. (p. 1539)
—Second Edition Handwriting: Reading & Writing Readiness Skills. (p. 1539)
Wasz, Bill. We Only Kill Our Friends: An Ex-con's Memoir on Crime, Punishment & Rehabilitation. (p. 1868)
Waszak, Madonna. Mason's Mashed Potato Tree. Johnston, Lisa Harp, illus. (p. 1102)
Watanabe, Akira, tr. see Miyasaka, Kaho.
Watanabe, Etsuko. My Japan. Watanabe, Etsuko, illus. (p. 1211)
Watanabe, Kaori. Sweet Dreams. (p. 1689)
Watanabe, Kaori, illus. see Grace, Will.
Watanabe, Kaori, illus. see Hudson, Sue.
Watanabe, Kaori, illus. see Michalak, Jamie.
Watanabe, Shigeo. Jeeper the Fire Engine. Yamamoto, Tadayoshi, illus. (p. 911)
Watanabe, Yoshitomo, et al. Beyond the Beyond (p. 174)
Watanai, Nozomi. Brigadoon (p. 228)
Watase, Yû. Bandit Watase, Yû, illus. (p. 136)
—Ceres: Celestial Legend Vol. 6 (p. 287)
—Ceres - Celestial Legend Watase, Yû, illus. (p. 287)
—Ceres - Celestial Legend Olsen, Lillian, tr. from JPN. (p. 287)
—Disciple (p. 447)
—Enemy: Vol. 10 Watase, Yû, illus. (p. 527)
—Fushigi Yûgi Watase, Yû, illus. (p. 650)
—Girlfriend. Watase, Yû, illus. (p. 679)
—Imadoki: Nowadays Vol. 4 Watase, Yû, illus. (p. 860)
—Lover (p. 1061)
—Maya. Watase, Yû, illus. (p. 1112)
—Mikage Watase, Yû, illus. (p. 1141)
—Oracle: Vol. 2. Watase, Yû, illus. (p. 1301)
Watase, Yû, jt. auth. see Watase, Yuu.
Watase, Yû & Watase, Yuu. Aya Watase, Yuu, illus. (p. 121)
—Fushigi Yugi: Genbu Kaiden. Vol. 3 Watase, Yû, illus. (p. 650)
—Toya Watase, Yû & Watase, Yuu, illus. (p. 1774)
Watase, Yuu. Absolute Boyfriend (p. 7)
—Absolute Boyfriend Watase, Yuu, illus. (p. 7)
—Alice 19th: Blindness Vol. 6 Watase, Yuu, illus. (p. 39)
—Arata: The Legend. Watase, Yuu, illus. (p. 94)
—Arata: The Legend. Vol. 5 Watase, Yuu, illus. (p. 94)
—Arata: The Legend. Vol. 6 Watase, Yuu, illus. (p. 94)
—Castaway Watase, Yuu, illus. (p. 276)
—Ceres Olsen, Lillian, tr. from JPN. (p. 287)
—Ceres: Celestial Legend Vol. 10 Watase, Yuu, illus. (p. 287)
—Ceres, Celestial Legend Watase, Yuu, illus. (p. 287)
—Ceres - Celestial Legend. Watase, Yuu, illus. (p. 287)
—Chidori Watase, Yuu, illus. (p. 301)
—Dandelion Vol. 1 Watase, Yuu, illus. (p. 403)
—Fushigi Ygi Watase, Yuu, illus. (p. 650)
—Fushigi Yûgi - Assassin Watase, Yuu, illus. (p. 650)
—Fushigi Yugi Genbu Kaiden Watase, Yuu, illus. (p. 650)
—Fushigi Yûgi - Genbu Kaiden. Watase, Yuu, illus. (p. 650)
—Genbu Kaiden. Watase, Yuu, illus. (p. 660)
—Goddess. Watase, Yuu, illus. (p. 690)
—Hagoromo (p. 735)
—Legend Vol. 2 Watase, Yuu, illus. (p. 988)
—Legend. Watase, Yuu, illus. (p. 988)
—Maiden Watase, Yuu, illus. (p. 1077)
—Miori Watase, Yuu, illus. (p. 1148)
—Mysterious Play. Watase, Yuu, illus. (p. 1223)
—Mysterious Play - Guardian Watase, Yuu, illus. (p. 1223)
—Nowadays Watase, Yuu, illus. (p. 1269)
—Priestess Watase, Yuu, illus. (p. 1399)
—The Mysterious Play Watase, Yuu, illus. (p. 1728)
Watase, Yuu, jt. auth. see Watase, Yû.
Watase, Yuu & Caselman, Lance. Alice 19th - Chained Vol. 3 Watase, Yuu, illus. (p. 39)
—Inner Heart Vol. 2 JN Productions Staff, tr. from JPN. (p. 875)
—Lost Word Watase, Yuu, illus. (p. 1057)
—Lotis Master Vol. 1 Watase, Yuu, illus. (p. 1057)
Watase, Yuu & Watase, Yû. Fushigi Yugi Watase, Yuu & Watase, Yû, illus. (p. 650)
—Mysterious Play Watase, Yuu & Watase, Yû, illus. (p. 1223)
Watcher, Jill, illus. see Ius, Dawn.
Watcyn-Jones, Peter. Fun Class Activities. (p. 647)
Water, Charles. Road to Iadorre. (p. 1477)
Water, Mark. Pilgrim Book of Bible Stories. Shimon, Diana, illus. (p. 1358)
Waterbury, Matthew. Little Pig. Muro, Jenny, illus. (p. 1033)
Waterby, Ralph. Muscogee (Creek) (p. 1192)
Waterfield, Gail L. Iron Boy. (p. 888)
Waterfield, Susan. Spunkie's Magical Garden. (p. 1635)
Waterhouse, Raymond & Lawrie, Gabrielle. Yoppi A Bear Story. (p. 1972)
Waterhouse, Stephen, illus. see Ganeri, Anita.
Waterhouse, Stephen, illus. see Goodwin, John.
Waterhouse, Stephen, illus. see Mitchell, Pratima.
Waterman, Diana. Don't Bite, Dwight. (p. 467)
—In a While, Kyle. (p. 863)
Waterman, Jill & Walker, Elizabeth. Helping At-Risk Students: A Group Counselling Approach for Grades 6-9. (p. 766)
Waterman, Russell, jt. auth. see Jarvis, James.
Waters, Alice & Duane, Daniel. Edible Schoolyard: A Universal Idea. Liittschwager, David, photos by. (p. 504)
Waters, Bella. Kazakhstan in Pictures. (p. 946)
—Uzbekistan in Pictures. (p. 1829)
—Zambia in Pictures. (p. 1984)
Waters, Carrie. Look Back in Time: A Content Area Reader-Social Studies. (p. 1049)
Waters, Cassie. Cool Down. (p. 363)
—Dive In! (p. 454)
—Heat Wave. (p. 760)
Waters, Daniel. Break My Heart 1,000 Times. (p. 224)
Waters, Erica-Jane. Mr. Pepper's Perfect Pet Shop. (p. 1186)
Waters, Erica-Jane, illus. see Jakubowski, Michele.
Waters, Erica-Jane, illus. see Jarman, Julia.
Waters, Erica-Jane, illus. see Karr, Lily.
Waters, Erica-Jane, illus. see Lewis, Jill & Blue Bananas.
Waters, Erica-Jane, illus. see Meister, Cari.
Waters, Erica-Jane, illus. see Milbourne, Anna.
Waters, Erica-Jane, illus. see Perelman, Helen.
Waters, Fiona. Aesop's Forgotten Fables. Testa, Fulvio, illus. (p. 26)
—Fire & Stone, Wind & Tide: Poems About the Elements. Corfield, Robin Bell, illus. (p. 590)
—Great Irish Heroes. Marklew, Gilly, illus. (p. 716)
Waters, Fiona, illus. see Hall, Amanda.
Waters, Fiona, illus. see Negrin, Fabian.
Waters, Fiona, jt. as told by see Carroll, Yvonne.
Waters, Fiona, retold by. Faithful Sister. (p. 565)
Waters, Gaby, ed. see Leigh, Susannah.
Waters, Galadriel & Mithrandir, Astre. New Clues to Harry Potter: Hints from the Ultimate Unofficial Guide to the Mysteries of Harry Potter Waters, Galadriel, illus. (p. 1244)
Waters, Galadriel, ed. Plot Thickens... Harry Potter Investigated by Fans for Fans. Rogers, Melissa & Heran, Michelle, illus. (p. 1374)
Waters, George T. Perfect Little Pumpkin. Duquet, Guy J., illus. (p. 1342)
Waters, Ginny B. Miracle House. (p. 1148)
Waters, Grace, jt. auth. see Mills, Nathan.
Waters, Graham. Raindrops & the Wrong Cloud. (p. 1436)
Waters, Jeff. Adventures of Cover Girl Katie: A Tale of Canine Magic. (p. 17)
Waters, Jennifer. All Kinds of Motion (p. 45)
—Todo Tipo de Movimiento. (p. 1761)
Waters, John F. Sharks Have Six Senses. Barner, Bob, illus. (p. 1563)
Waters, Kate. Day in the Life of a Pilgrim Girl. Kendall, Russell, illus. (p. 413)
—Monarch Butterflies. (p. 1163)
—Ocean Giants. (p. 1276)
—Penguins. (p. 1337)
Waters, Kim, photos by see Mandala Publishing Staff.
Waters, Linda. Case of the Missing Chick. (p. 274)
—Scout Hatches a Plan. (p. 1532)
—Those Batty Bats of Bainesville. (p. 1740)
Waters, Liz, tr. see Meijer, Fik.
Waters, Michael. Dumdickle & Tweedy: A Tail of Two Cats. (p. 489)
—Tommy & his Flying Saucer of Milk. (p. 1764)
Waters, Michael, jt. auth. see Poulin, A.
Waters, Rachel. Wanamea: A Choctaw Princess. (p. 1856)
Waters, Rod. Eric's Big Day: A Bicycle Race Unlike Any Other. (p. 533)
Waters, Rosa. Anger. Croft, Cindy, ed. (p. 75)
—Ashanti. (p. 105)
—Bob Marley & the Wailers. (p. 205)
—Emotional Self-Awareness. (p. 520)
—Empathy & Compassion. Croft, Cindy, ed. (p. 520)
—Instagram: How Kevin Systrom & Mike Krieger Changed the Way We Take & Share Photos. (p. 878)
—Legal & Developmental Consequences. Borus, Joshua, ed. (p. 987)
—Marijuana: Legal & Developmental Consequences. Borus, Joshua, ed. (p. 1094)
—Methamphetamine & Other Amphetamines. Borus, Joshua, ed. (p. 1130)
—My Daily Diet: Dairy. (p. 1201)
—My Daily Diet: Fruits. Prock, Lisa Albers, ed. (p. 1201)
—My Daily Diet: Grains. Prock, Lisa Albers, ed. (p. 1201)
—Over-The-Counter Medications. Borus, Joshua, ed. (p. 1314)
—Oxycontin(r), Percocet(r), Vicodin(r), & Other Addictive Analgesics. Borus, Joshua, ed. (p. 1316)
—Pinterest(r): How Ben Silbermann & Evan Sharp Changed the Way We Share What We Love. (p. 1361)
—Ritalin(r), Adderall(r), & Other Addictive Stimulants. Borus, Joshua, ed. (p. 1475)
—Stress & Tension. Croft, Cindy, ed. (p. 1667)
—Surprise & Flexibility. Croft, Cindy, ed. (p. 1685)
—Yung Joc. (p. 1983)
Waters, Sophie. Dealing with PMS. (p. 418)
—Female Reproductive System. (p. 581)
—Seeing the Gynecologist. (p. 1548)
Waters, Summer. High Tide. (p. 778)
—Rising Star. (p. 1475)
—River Rescue. (p. 1476)
Waters, Susy Pilgrim, illus. see Divakaruni, Chitra Banerjee.
Waters, Susy Pilgrim, illus. see Vander Pluym, Andrea.
Waters, Tawni. Beauty of the Broken. (p. 154)
Waters, Terrance D. I f I Y: A Novel Based on a True Story. (p. 838)
Waters, Tony. Cinnamon's Busy Year. Guevara, Linda L. & Merrill, Libby, eds. (p. 321)
Waters, Tony, illus. see Solesbee, Mary Ann.
Waters, Wylla. Bebek of the Bosphorus. (p. 155)
Waters, Zack C. Blood Moon Rider. (p. 200)
Waters-Porter, Amber Rae. Rachael's Auntie Is Bald-Headed. (p. 1431)
Waterston, Elizabeth, ed. see Montgomery, L. M.
Waterton, Betty. Bumblebee Sweater LaFave, Kim, illus. (p. 241)
—Pettranella. Waterton, Betty & Blades, Ann, illus. (p. 1349)
—Plain Noodles. (p. 1366)
Watier, Matt. Ants. (p. 90)
Watjen, Laureen, illus. see Davidson, Michele R.
Watkins, Abbey, illus. see Hurley, Tonya.
Watkins, Adam, illus. see Loewen, Nancy.
Watkins, Adam F. R Is for Robot: A Noisy Alphabet. Watkins, Adam F., illus. (p. 1429)
Watkins, Adam F., illus. see Winters, Ben H.
Watkins, Albert. Brothers Three. (p. 231)
Watkins, Angela Farris. Love Will See You Through: Martin Luther King Jr.'s Six Guiding Beliefs. Comport, Sally Wern, illus. (p. 1060)
—My Uncle Martin's Big Heart. Velasquez, Eric, illus. (p. 1220)
—My Uncle Martin's Words for America: Martin Luther King Jr.'s Niece Tells How He Made a Difference. Velasquez, Eric, illus. (p. 1220)
Watkins, Bessie. Presidents in Profile: Three Views of One Face. (p. 1397)
Watkins, Bessie Ann. Among the Unsung Segments: Celebrating African-American Heros & Icons. (p. 65)
Watkins, Boyce. Everything You Ever Wanted to Know about College: A Guide for Minority Students. (p. 545)
Watkins, Christi, ed. How Can Gang Violence Be Prevented? (p. 805)
Watkins, Christine. Age of Consent. Greenhaven Press Editors, ed. (p. 29)
—Are Adoption Policies Fair? (p. 96)
—Biological Warfare. (p. 189)
—Can Diets Be Harmful? (p. 258)
—Ethics of Capital Punishment. (p. 539)
—How Can Gang Violence Be Prevented? (p. 805)
—Is Selling Body Parts Ethical? (p. 890)
—Sports & Athletes (p. 1632)
—Teens at Risk. (p. 1715)
Watkins, Christine & Haugen, David. Do Children Have Rights? (p. 456)
Watkins, Christine & Haugen, David M. Do Children Have Rights? (p. 456)
Watkins, Christine, ed. Alcohol Abuse. (p. 35)
—Are Adoption Policies Fair? (p. 96)
—Can Diets Be Harmful? (p. 258)
—Is Selling Body Parts Ethical? (p. 890)
Watkins, Christopher. Exposure. (p. 554)
Watkins, Christopher, illus. see Watkins, Patricia.
Watkins, Constance L. Happy Was His Name. (p. 747)
—That Was, the Kitten, That Was. (p. 1726)
Watkins, Courtney, illus. see MacCoon, Nancy.
Watkins, Dawn L. Shield. (p. 1566)
—Zoli's Legacy (Christian Fiction) (p. 1987)
Watkins, Dewhite. Quick & Dirty Secrets of College Success: A Professor Tells It All. (p. 1427)
Watkins, Elaine. Billy Bobbin at Mystery Farm. (p. 187)
Watkins, Fred L. Sue, Mary & Charles (p. 1672)
Watkins, Graham, jt. auth. see Breman, Billy.
Watkins, Greg. Big Beaked, Big Bellied Bird Named Bill Watkins, Greg, illus. (p. 178)
—Big Beaked, Big Bellied Bird Named Bill. Watkins, Greg, illus. (p. 178)
—Brendon Mouse's Big Idea to Save the Bad Bird Bunch Watkins, Greg, illus. (p. 226)
—Brendon Mouse's Big Idea to Save the Bad Bird Bunch. (p. 226)
Watkins, Heidi. Dropping Out of School. (p. 486)
—Homeschooling. (p. 793)
—Social Networking. Friedman, Lauri S., ed. (p. 1604)
—Teens & Employment. (p. 1714)
Watkins, Kathryn Blystone. Log Cabin Stories: Pixie. (p. 1045)
—Log Cabin Stories: Angel Baby. (p. 1045)
—Log Cabin Stories: Baby the Goat. (p. 1045)
—Log Cabin Stories: Muffin the Cat. (p. 1045)
—Log Cabin Stories: Angel Baby: Book 6. (p. 1045)
—Log Cabin Stories: Baby the Goat: Book 5. (p. 1045)
—Log Cabin Stories: Bill the Bull: Book 4. (p. 1045)
—Log Cabin Stories: Falicity the Quarter Horse: Book 3. (p. 1045)
—Log Cabin Stories: Muffin the Cat: Book 2. (p. 1045)
—Log Cabin Stories: Pixie: Book 1. (p. 1045)
Watkins, Laura, illus. see Shaw, Stephanie.
Watkins, Laura, tr. see Stoffels, Karlijn.
Watkins, Linda. Althea. (p. 50)
Watkins, Liselotte, illus. see Fredericks, Mariah.
Watkins, Michelle, ed. see Holyoke, Nancy.
Watkins, Michelle, illus. see Criswell, Patti Kelley.
Watkins, Patricia. Boyd-Friend: His Yippie-Skippie Journey to a Forever Home. Watkins, Christopher, illus. (p. 220)
Watkins, Paul. Fellowship of Ghosts: Travels in the Land of Midnight Sun. (p. 581)
Watkins, Richard. Slavery: Bondage throughout History. Watkins, Richard, photos by. (p. 1588)
Watkins, Rowboat. Rude Cakes. (p. 1494)
Watkins, Samuel R. Ant-Bee Kingdom. (p. 88)
—Precious Palm Tree. (p. 1394)
Watkins, Steve. Down Sand Mountain. (p. 474)
—Ghosts of War #2: Lost at Khe Sanh. (p. 673)
—Juvie. (p. 941)
—Secret of Midway. (p. 1542)
—What Comes After. (p. 1881)
Watkins, Sue. Getting Involved! A Guide to Hunting & Conservation for Kids. (p. 669)
Watkins, T. a. Joey & the Ancient Horn: A Mystery Revealed. Davis, Marcus, illus. (p. 920)
Watkins, Tammy, illus. see Franklin, Cathy.
Watkins, Yoko K., jt. auth. see Watkins, Yoko Kawashima.
Watkins, Yoko Kawashima & Watkins, Yoko K. So Far from the Bamboo Grove. (p. 1602)
Watkinson, Laura. Roger Is Reading a Book. Van Biesen, Koen, illus. (p. 1484)
Watkinson, Laura, illus. see Prins, Marcel & Steenhuis, Peter Henk.
Watkinson, Laura, jt. auth. see Zoboli, Giovanna.
Watkinson, Laura, tr. see Schutten, Jan Paul.
Watkinson, Laura, tr. see Schwartz, Simon.
Watkins-Pitchford, Denys, illus. see Andrews, Julie.
Watley, Deborah, jt. auth. see Burch, Sharon.
Watley, Mitchell, illus. see Asper-Smith, Sarah.
Watling, James. Jehoshaphat: 2 Chronicles 20:1-30. (p. 912)
Watling, James, illus. see Banks, Lynne Reid.
Watling, James, illus. see Berleth, Richard.
Watling, James, illus. see Karwoski, Gail Langer.
Watlington, Elizabeth. Binky's Big Adventure. (p. 188)
Watley, Maylin. Malachi Goes Fishing with His Pap. (p. 1083)
Watsky, Paul. Telling the Difference. (p. 1717)
Watson, Andi. Clubbing. (p. 335)
—Glister #3. (p. 683)
—Princess at Midnight. (p. 1403)
—Princess Decomposia & Count Spatula. (p. 1403)
—Quest. Yuji, Iwahara, illus. (p. 1426)
Watson, Andi, jt. auth. see Jemas, Bill.
Watson, Anne-Marie. Old Lady in the Woods. (p. 1284)
Watson Bain, E., ed. Poetry Book for Boys & Girls. (p. 1376)
Watson, Ben, illus. see Bush, Randall.
Watson, Brenda C. Betwixt: The mystery of talon Mountain. (p. 173)
Watson, Carol. Christian. (p. 311)
—My First Book of Facts. (p. 1205)
Watson, Carol & Moyle, Philippa. Let's Learn French. Foster, Teresa, illus. (p. 998)
Watson, Carol, et al. Let's Learn Spanish. (p. 998)
Watson, Carrie Gordon. Ascending the Boneyard. (p. 105)
Watson, Casey. Dirty Heart Clean Heart. (p. 446)
Watson, Charles D. Christianity for Fools: A Simple Understanding of the Christian Faith. (p. 312)
Watson, Chris, illus. see Price, Robin.
Watson, Cindy. Out of Darkness: The Jeff Healey Story. (p. 1311)
—Unloved & Endangered Animals: What You Can Do. (p. 1821)
Watson, Clyde. Midnight Moon. Natti, Susanna, illus. (p. 1139)
Watson, Craig. Maddie Counts Marbles: Number Names & Count Sequence. (p. 1069)
Watson, Cristy. Benched (p. 164)
—Living Rough (p. 1041)
Watson, Don. Amazing Graci & River Bottom Goats. (p. 54)
—Legend of Red Leaf. Robbins, Ashley, illus. (p. 988)
Watson, Donn, ed. Growing up in Wisdom: A Story of Jesus as a Baby & a Young Boy. Reller, Marcia Mattingly, illus. (p. 726)
Watson, Donna. Houses: Past & Present. (p. 804)
Watson Dubisch, Carolyn. Horribles. (p. 798)
Watson, Emily G. Prophecy's Heirs. (p. 1411)
Watson, Emma, et al. Religions to Inspire for KS3: Judaism Pupil's Book. (p. 1458)
Watson, Esther Pearl. Whatcha Mean, What's a Zine? The Art of Making Zines & Mini-Comics. Todd, Mark, illus. (p. 1896)
Watson, Esther Pearl, illus. see McArthur, Meher.
Watson, Galadriel. Angel Falls. (p. 73)
—Bushmen of Southern Africa with Code. (p. 244)
—David Beckham. (p. 410)
Watson, Galadriel Findlay. Amazon Rain Forest: The Largest Rain Forest in the World. (p. 56)
—Amazon Rain Forest. (p. 56)
—Angel Falls: The Largest Waterfall in the World. (p. 73)
—Angel Falls. (p. 73)
—Bushmen of South Africa. (p. 244)
—Bushmen of Southern Africa. (p. 244)
—David Beckham. (p. 410)
—Europe. (p. 540)
—Mongols. (p. 1164)
—Mount Kilimanjaro. (p. 1180)
—North Dakota. (p. 1265)
—Tigers. (p. 1749)
—Toni Morrison. (p. 1765)
—Trees. (p. 1784)
—Venus & Serena Williams. (p. 1836)
—Wetlands. (p. 1877)
Watson, Garry. Church Meeting. (p. 318)
Watson, Gayle. Catie Corn & the Corn Cops. Fautsch, Jackie, illus. (p. 280)
Watson, George. 190 Ready-to-Use Activities That Make Math Fun! Anthony, Alan, illus. (p. 2000)
Watson, H. B. Marriott. Stone Chamber. (p. 1652)
Watson, Heather M. J. L. Thistle Lodge: The Legendary Sidhe Saga. (p. 1737)
Watson, J. D. My Socks Don't Match. (p. 1219)
Watson, J. R. Wizard down Under. (p. 1942)
Watson, Jacqueline. Mattie-Jo-Calico. (p. 1110)
—Six Frogs on a Log! (p. 1582)
Watson, James. Collins Drama - Gotcha. (p. 340)
Watson, Jane Werner. Fuzzy Duckling. Provensen, Martin & Provensen, Alice, illus. (p. 651)
—Story of Jesus. Smath, Jerry, illus. (p. 1658)
—Wonders of Nature. Wilkin, Eloise, illus. (p. 1948)
Watson, Jane Werner, jt. auth. see Broughton, Pamela.

Watson, Jean. Corrie Ten Boom: The Watchmaker's Daughter. (p. 368)
—Onyx the Butterfly. (p. 1298)
Watson, Jean & Bunyan, John. Family Pilgrim's Progress: Adapted from John Bunyan's Classic. (p. 568)
Watson, Jesse Joshua, illus. see Bildner, Phil.
Watson, Jesse Joshua, illus. see Draper, Sharon M.
Watson, Jesse Joshua, illus. see Medina, Tony.
Watson, Jesse Joshua, illus. see Neri, G.
Watson, Jesse Joshua, illus. see Winkler, Henry & Oliver, Lin.
Watson, Jesse Joshua, jt. auth. see Medina, Tony.
Watson, Joan. Jacob's Fishing Day. (p. 904)
Watson, Joe. Las Zapatillas Del Abuelo. (p. 977)
Watson, John & Burgess, Graham. Chess Openings for Kids. (p. 298)
Watson, Joy. Birthday Flood: Level O (p. 192)
Watson, Jude. 39 Clues # 6: En Las Profundidades. (p. 1996)
—Beyond the Grave. (p. 174)
—Death on Naboo. (p. 420)
—Desperate Mission. (p. 430)
—In Too Deep. (p. 868)
—King's Ransom. (p. 961)
—Loot. (p. 1052)
—Mission Titanic. (p. 1153)
—Nowhere to Run. (p. 1269)
—Premonitions. (p. 1395)
—Underworld. (p. 1817)
Watson, Jude, jt. auth. see Scholastic, Inc. Staff.
Watson, Jude & Scholastic, Inc. Staff. Beyond the Grave. (p. 174)
Watson, Jude, et al. Vespers Rising. (p. 1839)
Watson, Judy, illus. see Bedford, David.
Watson, Judy, illus. see Watts, Fraces.
Watson, Judy, illus. see Watts, Frances.
Watson, Judy, jt. auth. see Allum, Margaret.
Watson, K. R. Little Gabby Meets Her New Family. (p. 1028)
Watson, Kenneth C. Big Yellow Butterfly. (p. 184)
Watson, Kit. Day the Birds Sang. Watson, Kit, illus. (p. 414)
Watson, Krista M. Pépère's Fiddle. (p. 1340)
Watson, Laura, illus. see Crozier, Lorna.
Watson, Laura, illus. see Fitch, Sheree.
Watson, Laura, illus. see Ghigna, Charles.
Watson, Laura, illus. see Hallinan, P. K.
Watson, Laura, illus. see Profiri, Charline.
Watson, Lauren, ed. Little Doctor. (p. 1026)
Watson, Lena. Noise in My Room: The Adventure of Jane Barnette, the Problem Solver. (p. 1262)
Watson, Lori Ann. Beginnings. Bersani, Shennen, illus. (p. 160)
Watson, Louise. Mouse in Our House. (p. 1182)
Watson, Lucy, jt. auth. see Lask, Bryan.
Watson, M. Desmond & the Challenge on Mudwig Mountain. (p. 430)
—Veg Patch Gang. (p. 1834)
Watson, M. C. V. Fairy Tales & Pixie Trails: From the Series. (p. 564)
Watson Manhardt, Laurie. In the Beginning: Catholic Bible Study for Children. Alleen Co & Dayton, Melissa, illus. (p. 865)
Watson, Margery. Ruffles & Danny or the Responsibility. (p. 1494)
Watson, Marilyn Myrick. Barry Goldwater: State Greats Arizona. (p. 140)
—Bary Goldwater: State Greats Arizona. (p. 140)
—Frank Luke, the Arizona Balloon Buster. (p. 628)
—Raul Castro: Arizona's First Hispanic Governor. (p. 1440)
—Rose Mofford: State Greats Arizona. (p. 1489)
Watson, Mary. More Merrier: A Craft Book for Groups. (p. 1174)
—Paper Dragonfly. Watson, Mary, illus. (p. 1322)
Watson, Mary, illus. see Watson, Peter.
Watson, Mary Gordon. Beds & Bedding. Vincer, Carole, illus. (p. 156)
Watson, Michael. Search, Secrets, & Spies. (p. 1537)
—Treasure, Trash, & Turtles. (p. 1782)
Watson, Michael C., frwd. Why Mom Deserves a Diamond(r) -Twelve Years of Love: Twelve Years of Love. (p. 1925)
Watson, Moray, tr. see Carroll, Lewis, pseud.
Watson, Myrtle. Kite Flying in the Village: A Guyanese Girl's Story. (p. 962)
Watson, Nathan, illus. see Snider, Jesse Blaze.
Watson, Patrick. Ahmek. Thomson, Tracy, illus. (p. 30)
—Wittgenstein & the Goshawk: A Fable. (p. 1942)
Watson, Paul. Robot. (p. 1480)
Watson, Peter. Heart of the Lion. Watson, Mary, illus. (p. 759)
Watson, Philip & Oflesh, Nicole. Treasure Chest. (p. 1781)
Watson, Regal. Ant That Can't (p. 88)
Watson, Renée. Harlem's Little Blackbird. Robinson, Christian, illus. (p. 749)
—Place Where Hurricanes Happen. Stickland, Shadra, illus. (p. 1366)
—Place Where Hurricanes Happen. Strickland, Shadra, illus. (p. 1366)
—This Side of Home. (p. 1737)
—What Momma Left Me. (p. 1892)
Watson, Rhonda. Becoming God's Friend. Hedstrom, Leigh, illus. (p. 156)
Watson, Richard, illus. see Bone, Emily.
Watson, Richard, illus. see Bracken, Beth.
Watson, Richard, illus. see Doyle, Malachy.
Watson, Richard, illus. see Gassman, Julie A.
Watson, Richard, illus. see Gassman, Julie.
Watson, Richard, illus. see Goldsmith, Mike.
Watson, Richard, illus. see Jones, Christianne C.
Watson, Richard A. In the Dark Cave Norman, Dean, illus. (p. 865)
Watson, Richard J., illus. see Hodges, Margaret.
Watson, Richard Jesse. Magic Rabbit. Watson, Richard Jesse, illus. (p. 1073)
—Psalm 23 (p. 1413)
Watson, Richard Jesse, illus. see Hodges, Margaret.
Watson, Richard Jesse, illus. see Moore, Clement C.
Watson, Richard Jesse, illus. see Ryder, Joanne.
Watson, Richard Jesse, illus. see Zondervan Publishing Staff & Warren, Rick.
Watson, Robert P., jt. auth. see Lansford, Tom.
Watson, S. B., jt. auth. see Child's World Staff, The.
Watson, S. B., jt. auth. see Child's World Staff.
Watson, Sally. Linnet. (p. 1019)
—Witch of the Glens. (p. 1941)
Watson, Sasha, tr. see Guibert, Emmanuel & Sfar, Joann.
Watson, Sharon. Jump in, A Workbook for Reluctant Writers: 2-book Set. Wile, Kathleen J., ed. (p. 934)
—Jump in, A Workbook for Reluctant Writers: Student Text. Wile, Kathleen J., ed. (p. 934)
Watson, Sherri & Abney, Paula. Faith in Fay: The Lost Child. (p. 565)
Watson, Stephanie. Amy Poehler. Greenhaven Press Editors, ed. (p. 66)
—Animal Testing: Issues & Ethics. (p. 80)
—Anorexia. (p. 87)
—Binge Drinking. (p. 188)
—Binge Eating. (p. 188)
—Brain Injuries in Football. (p. 221)
—Bulimia. (p. 240)
—Career as a Police Officer. (p. 266)
—Cee lo Green: Rapper, Singer, & Record Producer. (p. 283)
—Club. (p. 335)
—Daniel Radcliffe: Film & Stage Star. (p. 405)
—Earnhardt NASCAR Dynasty: The Legacy of Dale Sr. & Dale Jr. (p. 494)
—Elvis & Olive. (p. 517)
—Elvis Presley: Rock & Roll's King. (p. 517)
—Endometriosis. (p. 527)
—Escape from Alcatraz. (p. 534)
—Gay Rights Movement. (p. 659)
—Georgia: Past & Present. (p. 665)
—Heath Ledger: Talented Actor. (p. 760)
—Jamie Oliver. Greenhaven Press Editors, ed. (p. 907)
—Keith Urban: Award-Winning Country Star. (p. 948)
—Making Good Choices about Recycling & Reuse. (p. 1081)
—Messages from Beyond. (p. 1129)
—Mystery Meat: Hot Dogs, Sausages, & Lunch Meats. (p. 1224)
—Plan a Birthday Party. (p. 1366)
—Plan a Sleepover Party. (p. 1366)
—Pope Francis: First Pope from the Americas. (p. 1384)
—Robert Downey Jr: Blockbuster Movie Star. (p. 1479)
—Streetwear Fashion. Kubley, Ashley Newsome, illus. (p. 1667)
—Superbugs: The Rise of Drug-Resistant Germs. (p. 1682)
—Timeline History of the California Gold Rush. (p. 1754)
—Tundra. (p. 1796)
—Urinary System (p. 1825)
—Vitamins & Minerals: Getting the Nutrients Your Body Needs. (p. 1846)
—What's in Your Food? Processed Food. (p. 1898)
Watson, Stephanie, jt. auth. see Drew, Ursula.
Watson, Stephanie, jt. auth. see Earl, Sari.
Watson, Stephanie, jt. auth. see Laser, Tammy.
Watson, Stephanie, jt. auth. see Mallick, Nita.
Watson, Stephanie, jt. auth. see Walden, Katherine.
Watson, Stephanie & Miller, Kelli. Endocrine System (p. 527)
Watson, Stephanie, ed. Critical Perspectives on Pollution. (p. 383)
—Mechanisms of Genetics: An Anthology of Current Thought. (p. 1118)
Watson, Stephanie Elaine. Behold! a Baby. Ang, Joy, illus. (p. 160)
—Elvis & Olive: Super Detectives. (p. 517)
Watson, T. Steuart, jt. auth. see Steege, Mark W.
Watson, Tom. Stick Dog. Long, Ethan, illus. (p. 1649)
—Stick Dog Chases a Pizza. (p. 1649)
—Stick Dog Dreams of Ice Cream. (p. 1649)
—Stick Dog Wants a Hot Dog. Long, Ethan, illus. (p. 1649)
Watson, Tracy S. David the Daring & His Fantastic Journey: Cherokee Grotto. (p. 411)
Watson, Travis, illus. see Waschak, Jay, et al.
Watson, Vicki. Bob & the Alien Escapade. (p. 205)
Watson, Viola. Selection of Children's Short Stories. (p. 1549)
Watson, W. Hamp, Jr. Frederick Wilson Still Speaks - Big Words for Our Time. Watson, W. Hamp, Jr., ed. (p. 633)
Watson, Wendy, illus. see Hesse, Karen.
Watson, Yolanda. Which Holiday Is It? (p. 1911)
Watson, Yolanda & Capstone Press Staff. Which Holiday Is It? (p. 1911)
Watson-Brugess, Linda. Parade Is Always Good Fun, Isn't It? (p. 1323)
—Readers Theatre. (p. 1444)
Watson-Doost, Valeria. Issa. (p. 893)
—Phillis Wheatley. (p. 1350)
Watson-Dubisch, Carolyn. Andy! & the Magician's Horn (p. 73)
—Bug-a-boo (p. 236)
—Night of the Armadillos Watson-Dubisch, Carolyn, illus. (p. 1253)
Watson-Kell, Katy. Mama's Trippin' (p. 1084)
Watsuki, Nobuhiro. Busou Renkin: Fade to Black. Vol. 2 (p. 245)
—Busou Renkin. (p. 245)
—Overture to Destruction Watsuki, Nobuhiro, illus. (p. 1314)
—Rurouni Kenshin: On the East Sea Road. Vol. 8 Watsuki, Nobuhiro, illus. (p. 1497)
—Rurouni Kenshin. Watsuki, Nobuhiro, illus. (p. 1497)
—Rurouni Kenshin. Yagi, Kenichiro, tr. from JPN. (p. 1497)
Watsuki, Nobuhiro, jt. auth. see Miyazaki, Hayao.
Watsuki, Nobuhiro & Wall, Frances. Buso Renkin Watsuki, Nobuhiro, illus. (p. 245)
Watt, Cliff. Jenny Brown & the Search for Eusebio's Star. (p. 913)
Watt, Coulter, illus. see Ward, L. B. B.
Watt, D. Alison. Hurricane Dancing: Glimpses of Life with an Autistic Child. Fields, Carole Ruth, photos by. (p. 829)
Watt, E. Planeta Tierra: Ciencia y Experimentos. (p. 1368)
Watt, E. Melanie. Leatherback Turtles, with Code. (p. 986)
—Tigers. (p. 1749)
Watt, F. Al Agua Patos! (p. 32)
—Art Ideas Pack. (p. 102)
—Art Skills. (p. 103)
—Felices Suenos! (p. 581)
—Halloween Activities. (p. 737)
—Vamos a Comer! (p. 1831)
Watt, F., jt. auth. see Gibson, R.
Watt, F., jt. auth. see Watt, Fiona.
Watt, F. & Wells, R. Farm Animals. (p. 573)
—Pets. (p. 1348)
—That's Not My Dinosaur... It's Body Is Too Squashy. (p. 1727)
—That's Not My Dolly. (p. 1727)
—That's Not My Lion. (p. 1727)
—Things That Go. (p. 1733)
Watt, Fiona. 123 Touchy Feely (Farmyard Tales) (p. 2000)
—365 Things to Draw & Paint. (p. 2001)
—365 Things to Make & Do. Harrison, Erica, illus. (p. 2001)
—50 Christmas Things to Make & Do. (p. 1997)
—50 Things to Draw & Paint. (p. 1997)
—ABC. Elkerton, Andy, illus. (p. 3)
—Animal Fun. (p. 78)
—Animales de la Granja. Wells, Rachel, illus. (p. 80)
—Animals. Wells, Rachel, illus. (p. 81)
—Art Ideas Drawing Pack: Internet-Linked. (p. 102)
—Art Projects. (p. 103)
—Art Projects. Miller, Antonia et al, illus. (p. 103)
—Art Projects. Miller, Antonia & Figg, Non, illus. (p. 103)
—Art Skills. (p. 103)
—Art Skills. Miller, Antonia, illus. (p. 103)
—Baby Dinosaur Cloth Bk. Wells, Rachel, illus. (p. 125)
—Baby Monster Cloth Book. Wells, Rachel, illus. (p. 127)
—Baby's First Christmas. (p. 129)
—Baby's Very First Book of Little Babies. (p. 129)
—Baby's Very First Little Touchy-Feely Play Book. (p. 129)
—Baby's Very First Slide & See Animals. (p. 129)
—Baby's Very First Slide & See under the Sea. (p. 129)
—Baby's Very First Word Book. (p. 129)
—Bats: Internet- Referenced. (p. 145)
—Beep Beep. (p. 157)
—Big Book of Sticker Math. Wells, Rachel, illus. (p. 179)
—Big Dinosaur Sticker Book. (p. 181)
—Big Doodling Book. (p. 181)
—Big Drawing Book. Thompson, Josephine & Day, Caroline, illus. (p. 181)
—Busy Bug Book. Mantle, Ben, illus. (p. 246)
—Busy Helicopter Book. (p. 246)
—Busy Santa Book. (p. 246)
—Cars. (p. 272)
—Children's Cookbook. Cartwright, Stephen & Sage, Molly, illus. (p. 303)
—Children's World Cookbook. (p. 304)
—Choo Choo. (p. 310)
—Christmas Art Ideas. (p. 312)
—Christmas Baby. (p. 312)
—Christmas Baby Jigsaw Book. Wells, Rachel, illus. (p. 312)
—Christmas decorations & Cards. (p. 313)
—Christmas Decorations to Cut, Fold & Stick. (p. 313)
—Christmas Doodles. (p. 313)
—Christmas Eve. Wells, Rachel, illus. (p. 313)
—Christmas Magic Painting Book. (p. 314)
—Christmas Mice. (p. 314)
—Christmas Things to Draw. (p. 316)
—Complete Book of Art Ideas. (p. 352)
—Complete Book of Chess. (p. 352)
—Complete Book of First Experiences. (p. 352)
—Cuddly Baby: Snuggletime. MacKinnon, Catherine-Anne, illus. (p. 389)
—Dibujos Paso A Paso Dinosaurios. Figg, Non et al, illus. (p. 435)
—Dinosaur Fun. Lovell, Katie, illus. (p. 442)
—Drawing, Doodling & Coloring Fashion. Miller, Antonia, illus. (p. 481)
—Earthquakes & Volcanoes. Stockley, Corinne & Brooks, Felicity, eds. (p. 497)
—Easter Activities. (p. 499)
—Easter Fun. (p. 499)
—Esta No Es Mi Muneca. Wells, Rachel, illus. (p. 538)
—Este No Es Mi Osito. (p. 538)
—Este No Es Mi Perrito. (p. 538)
—Este No es Mi Sirenita. (p. 538)
—Este No Es Mi Tren. (p. 538)
—Fairies. Cartwright, Stephen & Bird, Glen, illus. (p. 562)
—Fairies Jigsaw Book. Cartwright, Stephen & Bird, Glen, illus. (p. 563)
—Fairy Things to Stitch & Sew. Fearn, Katrina & Hussain, Nelupa, illus. (p. 564)
—Farm. Wells, Rachel, illus. (p. 573)
—Farm Fun. (p. 574)
—Farm Stroller Book. Baggott, Stella, illus. (p. 574)
—Fashion Designer Summer Collection. Baggott, Stella & Miller, Antonia, illus. (p. 575)
—Fingerprint Activities. (p. 589)
—Go to Sleep Little Baby. Watt, Fiona, illus. (p. 687)
—Hide-and-seek baby board Book. (p. 776)
—Hide-and-Seek Bunnies. Danson, Lesley, illus. (p. 776)
—Hide-and-Seek Dragons. Fiorin, Fabiano, illus. (p. 776)
—Hide-and-Seek Penguins. (p. 777)
—How to Draw Ballerinas & Princesses. (p. 817)
—How to Draw Dinosaurs. Figg, Non et al, illus. (p. 817)
—How to Draw Fairies & Mermaids. (p. 817)
—How to Knit. Baggott, Stella, illus. (p. 820)
—I Love You, Baby. MacKinnon, Catherine-Anne, illus. (p. 843)
—Jungle. Elkerton, Andy, illus. (p. 934)
—Little Ballerina Dancing Book. Cascio, Maria Cristina Lo & McNicholas, Shelagh, illus. (p. 1023)
—Little Children's Christmas Music Book. (p. 1026)
—Little Children's Music Book. (p. 1026)
—Lots of Things to Find & Color. (p. 1057)
—Making Cards. Figg, Non Et Al, illus. (p. 1080)
—Mascotas. Wells, Rachel, illus. (p. 1102)
—Mermaids. Cartwright, Stephen, illus. (p. 1128)
—Mermaids Jigsaw Book. Cartwright, Stephen & Bird, Glen, illus. (p. 1128)
—Mini Art Ideas. Barlow, Amanda, illus. (p. 1146)
—Monster Doodles. (p. 1167)
—My Scrapbook. (p. 1218)
—Nativity. Wells, Rachel, illus. (p. 1235)
—Nursery Rhymes Touchy-Feely Board Book. Meyer, Kerry, illus. (p. 1273)
—Pasta & Pizza: For Beginners. Lane, Kim, illus. (p. 1327)
—Penguins Luxury Touchy-Feely Board Book. (p. 1337)
—Pirate Sticker Book. Nichols, Paul, illus. (p. 1363)
—Planes: Internet-Referenced. (p. 1367)
—Polar Bears. Chiara, Francesca De, illus. (p. 1379)
—Pull-Back Busy Train. Field, Jim, illus. (p. 1415)
—Puppies. (p. 1418)
—Quack, Quack, Quack. (p. 1422)
—Rainy Day Stroller Book. Baggott, Stella, illus. (p. 1436)
—Santa Claus. (p. 1511)
—Seaside Stroller Book. Baggott, Stella, illus. (p. 1538)
—Sing-Along Christmas Carols. Bonnet, Rosalinde, illus. (p. 1578)
—Sing-along Nursery Rhymes. Bordoni, Chiara, illus. (p. 1578)
—Sleepy Baby. MacKinnon, Catherine-Anne, illus. (p. 1589)
—Snuggletime Busy Baby. MacKinnon, Catherine-Anne, illus. (p. 1601)
—Space Sticker Book. (p. 1620)
—Sparkly Christmas Angel. Kightley, Rosalinda, illus. (p. 1622)
—Spooky Sticker Book. (p. 1631)
—Spooky Things to Make & Do. (p. 1631)
—Sports Sticker Book. (p. 1633)
—Sticker Dolly Dressing Back to School. (p. 1650)
—Sticker Dolly Dressing Ballerinas & Dolls (Combined Volume) (p. 1650)
—Sticker Dolly Dressing Costumes Around the World. (p. 1650)
—Sticker Dolly Dressing Dancers. Baggott, Stella, illus. (p. 1650)
—Sticker Dolly Dressing Dolls. Leyhane, Vici & Baggott, Stella, illus. (p. 1650)
—Sticker Dolly Dressing Fashion Designer Home Designer. (p. 1650)
—Sticker Dolly Dressing Parties. Moore, Jo, illus. (p. 1650)
—Sticker Dolly Dressing Princesses. Leyhane, Vici & Baggott, Stella, illus. (p. 1650)
—Sticker Dolly Dressing Princesses & Fairies (Combined Volume) (p. 1650)
—Sticker Dolly Dressing Sportsgirls. (p. 1650)
—Sticker Dolly Dressing Travel. (p. 1650)
—Sticker Dolly Dressing Weddings. Baggott, Stella, illus. (p. 1650)
—Sticker Dressing Explorers. (p. 1650)
—That's Not My Angel. (p. 1727)
—That's Not My Baby (Boy) (p. 1727)
—That's Not My Baby (Girl) (p. 1727)
—That's Not My Bunny. Wells, Rachel, illus. (p. 1727)
—That's Not My Car. Wells, Rachel, illus. (p. 1727)
—That's Not My Cow. (p. 1727)
—That's Not My Dolly. (p. 1727)
—That's Not My Donkey. Wells, Rachel, illus. (p. 1727)
—That's Not My Dragon. (p. 1727)
—That's Not My Dragon... Wells, Rachel, illus. (p. 1727)
—That's Not My Duck... Wells, Rachel, illus. (p. 1727)
—That's Not My Elephant. Wells, Rachel, illus. (p. 1727)
—That's Not My Fairy. Wells, Rachel, illus. (p. 1727)
—That's Not My Frog. Wells, Rachel, illus. (p. 1727)
—That's Not My Hamster. (p. 1727)
—That's Not My Kitten. Wells, Rachel, illus. (p. 1727)
—That's Not My Meerkat. (p. 1727)
—That's Not My Mermaid: Her Hair Is Too Fluffy. Wells, Rachel, illus. (p. 1727)
—That's Not My Mermaid. (p. 1727)
—That's Not My Monkey. (p. 1727)
—That's Not My Monster. Wells, Rachel, illus. (p. 1727)
—That's Not My Panda. (p. 1727)
—That's Not My Penguin. Wells, Rachel, illus. (p. 1727)
—That's Not My Pig... Its Nose Is Too Fuzzy. Wells, Rachel, illus. (p. 1727)
—That's Not My Pirate. Wells, Rachel, illus. (p. 1727)
—That's Not My Plane. (p. 1727)
—That's Not My Polar Bear. (p. 1727)
—That's Not My Pony... Its Mane Is Too Fluffy. Wells, Rachel, illus. (p. 1727)
—That's Not My Prince. Wells, Rachel, illus. (p. 1727)
—That's Not My Princess. Wells, Rachel, illus. (p. 1727)
—That's Not My Reindeer: Its Body Is Too Furry. Wells, Rachel, illus. (p. 1727)
—That's Not My Reindeer... Wells, Rachel, illus. (p. 1727)
—That's Not My Robot... Wells, Rachel, illus. (p. 1727)
—That's Not My Santa. (p. 1727)
—That's Not My Snowman. (p. 1727)
—That's Not My Snowman. Wells, Rachel, illus. (p. 1727)
—That's Not My Teddy... Wells, Rachel, illus. (p. 1727)
—That's Not My Tiger. Wells, Rachel, illus. (p. 1727)
—That's Not My Train. (p. 1727)
—That's Not My Truck. (p. 1727)
—Tie-a-Bow Book. (p. 1747)
—Tractors. King, Sue, illus. (p. 1775)
—Tweet Tweet. (p. 1800)
—Under the Sea Baby Jigsaw Book. (p. 1814)
—Understanding Your Brain Kid Kit. (p. 1816)
—Usborne Book of Art Ideas. Barlow, Amanda, illus. (p. 1827)
—Usborne Book of Drawing, Doodling & Coloring Book. Harrison, Erica & Lovell, Katie, illus. (p. 1827)
—Usborne Book of Drawing, Doodling & Coloring for Christmas. Harrison, Erica, illus. (p. 1827)
—Usborne Color by Numbers Book. Harrison, Erica, illus. (p. 1827)
—Usborne Complete Book of Art Ideas. Miller, Antonia et al, illus. (p. 1827)
—Water Baby. (p. 1862)
—Winter Wonderland Sticker Book. (p. 1938)
—Ya Se Hacer Lazos. Cartwright, Stephen, illus. (p. 1968)
Watt, Fiona, ed. see Bowman, Lucy & MacLaine, James.
Watt, Fiona, ed. see Civardi, Anne.
Watt, Fiona, ed. see Gibson, Ray.
Watt, Fiona, ed. see MacLaine, James & Bowman, Lucy.
Watt, Fiona, ed. see MacLaine, James.
Watt, Fiona, ed. see Starke, Katherine.
Watt, Fiona, jt. auth. see Bone, Emily.
Watt, Fiona, jt. auth. see Denny, Roz.
Watt, Fiona, jt. auth. see Starke, Katherine.

W

Watt, Fiona, jt. auth. see Tagnetti, Stefano.
Watt, Fiona, jt. auth. see Wilkes, Angela.
Watt, Fiona, jt. ed. see Daynes, Katie.
Watt, Fiona & Cartwright, Stephen. Children's Cookbook. (p. 303)
—Tie-a-Bow Book. (p. 1747)
Watt, Fiona & Gilpin, Rebecca. Big Bk of Fairy Things to Make & Do. (p. 178)
—Usborne Big Book of Christmas Things to Make & Do. Fearn, Katrina, illus. (p. 1827)
Watt, Fiona & Watt, F. Baby's Mealtime. (p. 129)
Watt, Fiona & Wells, R. That's Not My Bear. (p. 1727)
Watt, Fiona & Wells, Rachel. Adding II. (p. 11)
—Anifeiliaid y Fferm. (p. 76)
—Baby's Bedtime. (p. 128)
—Christmas. (p. 312)
—Diggers. (p. 439)
—Gatitos. (p. 658)
—Hen. (p. 767)
—Numbers. (p. 1272)
—Starting Times Tables. (p. 1644)
—Sticker Maths: Adding. (p. 1650)
—Sticker Maths: Taking Away. (p. 1650)
—That's Not My Puppy... Its Coat Is Too Hairy. (p. 1727)
—That's Not My Tractor. (p. 1727)
—That's Not My Train: Its Wheels Are Too Slippery. (p. 1727)
—Trucks. (p. 1791)
Watt, Fiona & Wells, Rachel, eds. Potty Time. (p. 1388)
—That's Not My Teddy: Its Paws Are Too Woolly. (p. 1727)
Watt, Fiona & Wilkes, Angela. Children's World Cookbook. (p. 304)
Watt, Fiona, des. Sticker Dolly Dressing Princess Kit. (p. 1650)
Watt, Fiona, et al. Big Book of Things to Draw. Figg, Non et al, illus. (p. 179)
—Usborne Big Book of Vacation Things to Make & Do. Baggott, Stella, illus. (p. 1827)
Watt, J. S. Hall of Sorrows. (p. 737)
Watt, Jeffrey. Long Reformation. (p. 1047)
Watt, Marg. Tales from Hallowed Hollow: Karma. Finn, Jenny, illus. (p. 1701)
Watt, Mélanie. Alphabet. Watt, Mélanie, illus. (p. 49)
—Augustine. Watt, Mélanie, illus. (p. 115)
—Bug in a Vacuum. (p. 236)
—Chester. Watt, Mélanie, illus. (p. 298)
—Chester's Back! Watt, Mélanie, illus. (p. 298)
—Chester's Masterpiece. Watt, Mélanie, illus. (p. 298)
—Colors. Watt, Mélanie, illus. (p. 345)
—Have I Got a Book for You! Watt, Mélanie, illus. (p. 754)
—Leatherback Turtles. (p. 986)
—Leon the Chameleon. (p. 992)
—Leon the Chameleon. Watt, Mélanie, illus. (p. 992)
—Numbers. Watt, Mélanie, illus. (p. 1272)
—Opposites. Watt, Mélanie, illus. (p. 1300)
—Scaredy Squirrel. Watt, Mélanie, illus. (p. 1519)
—Scaredy Squirrel. (p. 1520)
—Scaredy Squirrel at Night. Watt, Mélanie, illus. (p. 1520)
—Scaredy Squirrel at the Beach. (p. 1520)
—Scaredy Squirrel Goes Camping. Watt, Mélanie, illus. (p. 1520)
—Scaredy Squirrel Has a Birthday Party Watt, Mélanie, illus. (p. 1520)
—Scaredy Squirrel Makes a Friend. Watt, Mélanie, illus. (p. 1520)
—Scaredy Squirrel Prepares for Christmas. Watt, Mélanie, illus. (p. 1520)
—Scaredy Squirrel Prepares for Halloween. (p. 1520)
—Shapes. Watt, Mélanie, illus. (p. 1560)
—You're Finally Here! Watt, Mélanie, illus. (p. 1982)
Watt, Mélanie, illus. see Jennings, Sharon.
Watt, Mike. Sponged Stone: Or the Hunt for Christmas Yet-to-Come. England, Donald, illus. (p. 1631)
Watt, Nigel, jt. auth. see Martin, Dave.
Watt, R. J. C. Shakespeare's History Plays. (p. 1559)
Watt, Stephen, et al, eds. Ian Fleming & James Bond: The Cultural Politics Of 007. (p. 849)
Watt, Susan. Cobalt. (p. 336)
—Zirconium. (p. 1987)
Watt, W. Bryce, jt. auth. see Thompson, Dennis.
Wattenberg, Jane. Mrs. Mustard's Baby Faces. (p. 1187)
Wattenberg, Jane, illus. see Lear, Edward.
Wattenberg, Jane, jt. auth. see Cohn, Rachel.
Watters, Debbie, et al. Where's Mom's Hair? A Family's Journey Through Cancer Hogan, Sophie, photos by. (p. 1910)
Watters, Donna. Mystery of the Flaming Sword. (p. 1225)
Watters, Mark. Bedtime Snories for Children, Volume One. (p. 157)
Watters, Sandy. Love, Hope & Faith Play Seek & Find! A Positive Word, Horse in the House Series Book. (p. 1059)
Watters, Shannon, ed. Adventure Time - Cover Gallery (p. 14)
Watterson, Bill. Achtung, Fertig, Los! Goetting, Waltraud, tr. from ENG. (p. 9)
—Alles unter Kontrolle. Goetting, Waltraud, tr. from ENG. (p. 47)
—Auf dem Sprung. Goetting, Waltraud, tr. from ENG. (p. 115)
—Bloss nicht Aergern. Goetting, Waltraud, tr. from ENG. (p. 202)
—Calvin & Hobbes: Das Jubilaumsalbum Bartoszko, Alexandra, tr. from ENG. (p. 255)
—Einfach Umwerfend. Goetting, Waltraud, tr. from ENG. (p. 507)
—Enorm in Form. Goetting, Waltraud, tr. from ENG. (p. 530)
—Feine Freunde. Goetting, Waltraud, tr. from ENG. (p. 581)
—Fix & Fertig. Goetting, Waltraud, tr. from ENG. (p. 601)
—Ganz schoen Daneben. Goetting, Waltraud, tr. from ENG. (p. 655)
—Immer mit der Ruhe. Goetting, Waltraud, tr. from ENG. (p. 861)
—Immer Voll Drauf. Goetting, Waltraud, tr. from ENG. (p. 861)
—Jetzt Erst Recht. Goetting, Waltraud, tr. from ENG. (p. 916)
—Jetzt geht's Rund. Goetting, Waltraud, tr. from ENG. (p. 916)
—Mach mir den Tiger. Goetting, Waltraud, tr. from ENG. (p. 1068)
—Phantastischen Zwei. Goetting, Waltraud, tr. from ENG. (p. 1349)
—Steil nach Oben. Goetting, Waltraud, tr. from ENG. (p. 1646)
—Tierisch Lyrisch. Goetting, Waltraud, tr. from ENG. (p. 1748)
—Welt der Wunder. Bartoszko, Alexandra, tr. from ENG. (p. 1875)
Watterson, Carol. Edible Alphabet: 26 Reasons to Love the Farm. Sorrentino, Michela, illus. (p. 504)
Watterson, Michelle. My Pet Dinosaur. (p. 1217)
Watterson, Steve, jt. auth. see Hill, Bert.
Wattley, Jason J. Anthology of Chaconia Creations. (p. 89)
Wattley, Maylin. Malachi's Pap: The Book of Malachi Book 1. (p. 1083)
Watton, Ross, illus. see Petty, Kate.
Watton, Ross, illus. see West, David.
Watts, Ana Dearborn & Dearborn, Dorothy. Pony Princess. Taylor, Carol, illus. (p. 1382)
Watts, Andrew. Carnival of Carols. (p. 270)
Watts, Barrie. Bean. (p. 150)
—Bee. (p. 157)
—Beetles. (p. 158)
—Butterfly. (p. 247)
—Butterfly & Caterpillar. (p. 247)
—Earthworms. (p. 498)
—Frog. (p. 639)
—Hamster. (p. 739)
—Mouse. (p. 1181)
—Sunflower. (p. 1676)
Watts, Bernadette. Bernadette Watts Collection: Stories & Fairy Tales. (p. 167)
—Golden Plate. (p. 695)
—Smallest Snowflake. Watts, Bernadette, illus. (p. 1592)
—Will You Be My Friend? (p. 1932)
Watts, Bernadette, illus. see Aesop Enterprise Inc. Staff.
Watts, Bernadette, illus. see Andersen, Hans Christian & Kurt, Robert.
Watts, Bernadette, illus. see Grimm, Jacob & Grimm, Wilhelm K.
Watts, Bernadette, illus. see Grimm, Jacob, et al.
Watts, Bernadette, et al. Little Red Riding Hood. Watts, Edith M B., illus. (p. 1035)
Watts, Claire. Rescue: Eyewitness Books. Rayner, Amanda, ed. (p. 1462)
—White-Out: Blizzards (p. 1913)
Watts, Debbie. Long Shot: Louie: the Adventures of a Wondering Wiener Dog. (p. 1047)
Watts, Debra G. Carter Car & His Wild & Carazy Birthday. (p. 272)
Watts, Edith, illus. see Grimm, Jacob & Grimm, Wilhelm K.
Watts, Edith M B., illus. see Watts, Bernadette, et al.
Watts, Edith M B. B., Bernadette, illus. see Grimm, J. & W.
Watts, Eleanor. Storytelling. (p. 1664)
Watts, Fraces. Middle Sheep. Watson, Judy, illus. (p. 1138)
Watts, Frances. Extraordinary Ernie & Marvelous Maud. Watson, Judy, illus. (p. 555)
—Greatest Sheep in History. (p. 720)
—Heroes of the Year. Watson, Judy, illus. (p. 773)
—Kisses for Daddy. Legge, David, illus. (p. 962)
—Kisses for Daddy Gift Pack: Book & Soft Toy. Legge, David, illus. (p. 962)
—Pigeon Problems. Rogers, Gregory, illus. (p. 1357)
—Poison Plot. Rogers, Gregory, illus. (p. 1377)
—Secret of the Ginger Mice. Francis, David, illus. (p. 1542)
—Secret of the Swords. Rogers, Gregory, illus. (p. 1543)
—Secrets of Flamant Castle: The Complete Adventures of Sword Girl & Friends. Rogers, Gregory, illus. (p. 1545)
—Song of the Winns: the Spies of Gerander. (p. 1611)
—Terrible Trickster. Rogers, Gregory, illus. (p. 1721)
Watts, Franklin. Beating Odds. (p. 152)
—Fifth Harmony - The Dream Begins ...Now! (p. 584)
Watts, Gail. Kevin Thinks: ...About Outer Space, Confusing Expressions & the Perfectly Logical World of Asperger Syndrome. (p. 950)
Watts, Gillian. Hear My Roar: A Story of Family Violence. Hodson, Ben, illus. (p. 759)
Watts, Helen & Thomas, Taffy. Ghost of the Trenches & Other Stories. (p. 671)
Watts., I. Divine Songs. (p. 454)
Watts, Irene N. Escape from Berlin. (p. 534)
—Flower. (p. 607)
—Good-Bye Marianne: A Story of Growing up in Nazi Germany. Shoemaker, Kathryn E., illus. (p. 697)
—Munsch at Play: Eight Stage Adaptations for Young Performers. (p. 1191)
—No Moon. (p. 1259)
—Telling Time Shoemaker, Kathryn E., illus. (p. 1717)
—Touched by Fire. (p. 1772)
—When the Bough Breaks. (p. 1904)
Watts, Irene N & Boraks-Nemetz, Lillian, compiled by. Tapestry of Hope: Halocaust Writing for Young People. (p. 1705)
Watts, James. Quest Begins: Magic Bag Trilogy Book One. Leonhard, Herb, illus. (p. 1426)
Watts, James, illus. see Curry, Jane Louise.
Watts, James, illus. see Mozelle, Shirley.
Watts, Jan. CAKE! A comedy script for young People. (p. 252)
—Zipline. (p. 1987)
Watts, Jane & Nobel, DeAnna. Adventures of Alligator Tater. (p. 16)
Watts, Jeri. Kizzy Ann Stamps. (p. 963)
Watts, Jeri Hanel. Keepers. Marshall, Felicia, illus. (p. 947)
Watts, John, illus. see Parr, Letitia.
Watts, Julia. Free Spirits. (p. 634)
—Kindred Spirits. (p. 957)
—Revived Spirits. (p. 1466)
—Secret City. (p. 1540)
Watts, Julia, et al, eds. Women. Period. (p. 1946)
Watts, Juliette, illus. see Burzynski, Roberta.
Watts, Katherine. Tiger Tails. (p. 1748)
Watts, Kevin. Snowman Capers of Finneus Bleek. (p. 1601)
Watts, Kevin Bradley. Ben & the Mysterious Sound: Series: the Adventures of Tug Boat Ben. (p. 163)
Watts, Leander. Beautiful City of the Dead. (p. 153)
Watts, Leslie. Just Leah. (p. 939)
Watts, Leslie Elizabeth. Baabaasheep Quartet Watts, Leslie Elizabeth, illus. (p. 123)
Watts, Leslie Elizabeth, illus. see Gilmore, Rachna.
Watts, Leslie Elizabeth, illus. see Spalding, Andrea.
Watts, Murray. The Bible for Children. Cann, Helen, illus. (p. 1728)
Watts, Robin Queen. Adventures of Beauty & Sam. (p. 16)
Watts, Sarah, illus. see Jinks, Catherine.
Watts, Sarah, illus. see Legrand, Claire.
Watts, Sarah, illus. see Samoun, Abigail.
Watts, Sharon, illus. see Phillips, Betty Lou.
Watts, Sharon, illus. see Post, Peggy & Senning, Cindy Post.
Watts, Suzanne, illus. see Williams, Suzanne.
Watts, Suzanne, illus. see Wilson, Karma.
Watts, Tammy E. From Libya to Namibi. (p. 643)
Watts, Tom. Pacific Coast Tree Finder: A Pocket Manual for Identifying Pacific Coast Trees. (p. 1317)
Waugh, David. New Wider World. (p. 1247)
Waugh, Ethan & Waugh, Geoff. My First Stories (in Colour) (p. 1208)
Waugh, Geoff, jt. auth. see Waugh, Ethan.
Waugh, John C. On the Brink of Civil War: The Compromise of 1850 & How It Changed the Course of American History. (p. 1290)
Waugh, Leslie, ed. see Eisenstein, Ann.
Waugh, Peter. Cannon Beach Mouse Caper. (p. 261)
Waugh, Sandra. Lark Rising. (p. 975)
—Silver Eve. (p. 1576)
Waugh, Steven, jt. auth. see Wright, John.
Waugh, Sylvia. Carrera Espacial. (p. 271)
Waunsch, John. My Very, Very First Weather Book. (p. 1221)
Wauters, Julia. One Night, Far from Here. (p. 1296)
Wax, Naomi, jt. auth. see Wax, Wendy A.
Wax, Naomi, jt. auth. see Wax, Wendy.
Wax, Wendy. Animal Family Christmas. (p. 77)
—Baby Genius Storybook (p. 126)
—City Witch, Country Switch Gibala-Broxholm, Scott, illus. (p. 324)
—Diego & Papi to the Rescue. Hom, John, illus. (p. 437)
—Diego y Papi al Rescate. Ziegler, Argentina Palacios, tr. (p. 437)
—Easter Bunny on the Loose! Garbot, Dave, illus. (p. 499)
—Look Who's Buzzing. (p. 1050)
—Meet Leatherhead. Spaziante, Patrick, illus. (p. 1121)
—Phonics Comics: Clara the Klutz - Level 2. Sullivan, Mary, illus. (p. 1352)
—Picnic Day! Artful Doodlers, illus. (p. 1355)
—Renoir & the Boy with Long Hair: A Story about Pierre-Auguste Renoir. Lane, Nancy, illus. (p. 1460)
—Sugar & Spice. Perrett, Lisa, illus. (p. 1672)
—Valentine for Tommy. (p. 1830)
—What Do You Say? Please & Thank You. Dillard, Sarah, illus. (p. 1883)
Wax, Wendy A. Musica en Casa: Libro de Cuentos. de Alba, Arlette, tr. (p. 1194)
Wax, Wendy A. & Wax, Naomi. Even Princesses Go to the Potty. Carabelli, Francesca, illus. (p. 541)
Wax, Wendy & A and J Studios Staff. Dora's Camping Trip. (p. 471)
Wax, Wendy & Kwiat, Ernie. Guess Who, Elmo! (p. 729)
Wax, Wendy & Wax, Naomi. Even Firefighters Go to the Potty: A Potty Training Lift-the-Flap Story. Sisk, Clay & Gilpin, Stephen, illus. (p. 541)
Wax, Wendy & Weiss, Bobbi. Tale of Too Many Cities - Egypt. Vargus, Nanci, ed. (p. 1700)
Waxman, Laura, jt. auth. see Hamilton Waxman, Laura.
Waxman, Laura, jt. auth. see Levine, Michelle.
Waxman, Laura, jt. auth. see Vogt, Gregory.
Waxman, Laura Hamilton. Aerospace Engineer Aprille Ericsson. (p. 25)
—Ambulances on the Move. (p. 57)
—Anne Frank. (p. 85)
—Bald Eagles: Prey-Snatching Birds. (p. 134)
—Colin Powell. (p. 339)
—Computer Engineer Ruchi Sanghvi. (p. 354)
—Coretta Scott King. (p. 367)
—Dr. Seuss. (p. 475)
—Emperor Penguins: Antarctic Diving Birds. (p. 521)
—Exploring Black Holes. (p. 551)
—Exploring Space Travel. (p. 553)
—Exploring the International Space Station. (p. 554)
—Genetics Expert Joanna L. Kelley. (p. 661)
—Gerald R. Ford. (p. 666)
—How Did Slaves Find a Route to Freedom? And Other Questions about the Underground Railroad. (p. 806)
—Jane Goodall. Butler, Tad, illus. (p. 908)
—Jimmy Carter. (p. 918)
—Let's Look at Monarch Butterflies. (p. 999)
—Let's Look at Snails. (p. 999)
—Marie Curie. (p. 1093)
—Moon. (p. 1171)
—Ostriches: Fast Flightless Birds. (p. 1306)
—Pileated Woodpeckers. (p. 1358)
—Saturn. (p. 1515)
—Sequoyah. (p. 1552)
—Sojourner Truth. (p. 1606)
—Solar System. (p. 1607)
—Sun. (p. 1675)
—Terrific Transportation Inventions. (p. 1721)
—Toco Toucans: Big-Billed Tropical Birds. (p. 1760)
—Uncommon Revolutionary: A Story about Thomas Paine. Orback, Craig, illus. (p. 1812)
—What Are the Articles of Confederation? And Other Questions about the Birth of the United States. (p. 1879)
—Why Did the Pilgrims Come to the New World? And Other Questions about the Plymouth Colony. (p. 1923)
—Woodrow Wilson. (p. 1949)
Waxman, Laura Hamilton, jt. auth. see Levine, Michelle.
Waxman, Laura Hamilton, see Hamilton Waxman, Laura.
Waxman, Malcolm & Porter, Malcolm. Atlas of South America & Antarctica. (p. 113)
Waxman, Melanie Brown. Little Carrot Friend, Bonnie, illus. (p. 1025)
Way, Charles. Classic Fairytales: Retold for the Stage. Vol. 2 (p. 328)
—Classic Fairytales. (p. 328)
—Dutiful Daughter. Lijun, Yang, tr. (p. 491)
—New Plays for Young People. (p. 1246)
Way, Daniel. Sabretooth: Open Season. Sears, Bart, illus. (p. 1500)
Way, Daniel & Medina, Paco. Venom by Daniel Way Ultimate Collection. Herrera, Francisco et al, illus. (p. 1836)
Way, Daniel & Vella, Sheldon. Operation Annihilation (p. 1300)
Way, Daniel, et al. Wolverine. Coipel, Olivier, illus. (p. 1944)
Way, Jennife. Hopping Book / Brincar en un Pie. (p. 797)
Way, Jennifer. Exploring Comets. (p. 551)
—Hopping Book. (p. 797)
—Hopping Book/Brincar en un Pie. Brusca, Maria Cristina, tr. from ENG. (p. 797)
—New Hampshire. (p. 1245)
—New Hampshire/Nuevo Hampshire. Brusca, Maria Cristina, tr. from ENG. (p. 1245)
—Ohio. (p. 1281)
—Ohio. Brusca, Maria Cristina, tr. from ENG. (p. 1281)
—Oregon. Brusca, Maria Cristina, tr. from ENG. (p. 1302)
—Pennsylvania. (p. 1338)
—Pennsylvania/Pensilvania. Brusca, Maria Cristina, tr. from ENG. (p. 1338)
—Rhode Island. (p. 1468)
—Rhode Island. Brusca, Maria Cristina, tr. from ENG. (p. 1468)
—Running Book: Correr. (p. 1497)
—Running Book. (p. 1497)
—South Carolina. (p. 1616)
—South Carolina/Carolina del Sur. Brusca, Maria Cristina, tr. (p. 1616)
—Vermont. (p. 1837)
—Vermont. Brusca, Maria Cristina, tr. from ENG. (p. 1837)
—Virginia. (p. 1844)
—Virginia. Brusca, Maria Cristina, tr. from ENG. (p. 1844)
—Washington. (p. 1859)
—Washington. Brusca, Maria Cristina, tr. from ENG. (p. 1859)
—West Virginia. (p. 1876)
—West Virginia/Virginia Occidental. Brusca, Maria Cristina, tr. from ENG. (p. 1876)
—What Is the Constitution? (p. 1890)
Way, Jennifer & Van Duyne, Sara. What You Can Do about Stress & Anxiety. (p. 1896)
Way, Jennifer L. & Gaffney, Timothy R. Severe-Storm Scientists: Chasing Tornadoes & Hurricanes. (p. 1555)
Way, Jennifer L. & Monroe, Judy. Are You Afraid? (p. 97)
Way, Jennnifer. Oregon. (p. 1302)
Way, MaryFaye, illus. see Anton, Amy Way.
Way, Steve. Fighting Disease. (p. 585)
—Materials. (p. 1104)
Way, Steve, jt. auth. see Bailey, Gerry.
Way, Steve, jt. auth. see Law, Felicia.
Way, Steve & Bailey, Gerry. Energy. (p. 528)
—Land Transportation. (p. 974)
—Light & Color. (p. 1014)
—Simple Machines. (p. 1578)
—Space. (p. 1618)
—Structures. (p. 1668)
Wayans, Jacqueline. Ambrose. (p. 57)
Wayland, April Halprin. New Year at the Pier: A Rosh Hashanah Story. Jorisch, Stéphane, illus. (p. 1247)
Wayne, Matt. Attack of the Virtual Villains. Moy, Philip, illus. (p. 114)
—Menace of the Time Thief Suriano, Andy & Davis, Dan W., illus. (p. 1126)
—Panic of the Composite Creatures. Suriano, Andy & Davis, Dan W., illus. (p. 1321)
—President Batman Suriano, Andy & Davis, Dan W., illus. (p. 1396)
Wayne, Matt & Torres, J. Batman - The Brave & the Bold. (p. 144)
Wayne, Melody & Hayhurst, Chris. Bike Trekking. (p. 185)
Wayne, Tiffany K. Encyclopedia of Transcendentalism. (p. 525)
Wayne, Viv. Bloom Where You Are Planted: A garden story about overcoming your Challenges. (p. 201)
Waysman, Dvora. Jewish Detective Stories for Kids. (p. 917)
Waytula, Brian, illus. see Zachary, Ken.
Waywell, Valerie J., illus. see Jorden, Edwin W.
Wazem, Pierre. Like a River. Wazem, Pierre, illus. (p. 1017)
—Weekend with Purpose. Tirabosco, Tom, illus. (p. 1872)
We are Photogirls Staff. DIY Fashion Shoot Book. (p. 455)
We are What We Do Staff. 31 Ways to Change the World. (p. 1996)
Weagly, John. Undertow of Small Town Dreams: Stories of Currie Valley. (p. 1817)
Weakland, Mark. Bubbles Float, Bubbles Pop. (p. 233)
—Captain Kidd's Crew Experiments with Sinking & Floating Cummings, Troy, illus. (p. 264)
—Comienza la Ciencia. (p. 348)
—Do-4U the Robot Experiences Forces & Motion. Moran, Mike, illus. (p. 456)
—Do-4U the Robot Experiences Forces & Motion. Moran, Michael & Moran, Mike, illus. (p. 456)
—Engranajes Trabajan, los Ruedas Ruedan. (p. 530)
—Fast, Strong, Fearless: Football Adjectives. (p. 576)
—Football ABC (p. 615)
—Football Colors (p. 615)
—Football Opposites (p. 615)
—Football Words. (p. 615)
—Gears Go, Wheels Roll (p. 659)
—Gut Bugs, Dust Mites, & Other Microorganisms You Can't Live Without. (p. 733)
—Hockey Counting (p. 786)
—Hockey Patterns (p. 786)
—Hockey Shapes (p. 787)
—How Heavy? Wacky Ways to Compare Weight Bolton, Bill, illus. (p. 809)
—How Tall? Wacky Ways to Compare Height Sinkovec, Igor, illus. (p. 812)
—Imanes Atraen, los Imanes Repelen. (p. 861)
—Las Burbujas Flotan, Las Burbujas Explotan/Bubbles Float, Bubbles Pop. (p. 976)
—Lonely Existence of Asteroids & Comets Lazzati, Laura & Aón, Carlos, illus. (p. 1046)
—Lonely Existence of Asteroids & Comets. Aón, Carlos & Lazzati, Laura, illus. (p. 1046)

—Magnets Push, Magnets Pull (p. 1076)
—Onion Juice, Poop, & Other Surprising Sources of Alternative Energy (p. 1298)
—Pass, Catch, Tackle: Football Verbs. (p. 1326)
—Science Starts (p. 1528)
—Science Starts. (p. 1528)
—Scooby-Doo! a Number Comparisons Mystery: The Case of the Lunchroom Gobbler Gross, Scott, illus. (p. 1529)
—Scooby-Doo! a Subtraction Mystery: The Case of the Disappearing Doughnuts Gross, Scott, illus. (p. 1529)
—Scooby-Doo! an Addition Mystery: The Case of the Angry Adder Gross, Scott, illus. (p. 1529)
—Scooby-Doo! an Even or Odd Mystery: The Case of the Oddzilla Gross, Scott, illus. (p. 1529)
—Seeds Go, Seeds Grow (p. 1547)
—Semillas Se Plantan, las Semillas Crecen. (p. 1550)
—SI Kids Rookie Books. (p. 1572)
—SI Kids Rookie Books: Football. (p. 1572)
—SI Kids Rookie Books: Football & Hockey. (p. 1572)
—SI Kids Rookie Books: Hockey. (p. 1572)
—Smash! Wile E. Coyote Experiments with Simple Machines Cornia, Christian, illus. (p. 1593)
—Solid Truth about Matter. Lum, Bernice, illus. (p. 1607)
—Solve It with Scooby-Doo!: Math: Math Gross, Scott, illus. (p. 1608)
—Stadium, Jersey, Player: Football Nouns. (p. 1638)
—Thud! Wile E. Coyote Experiments with Forces & Motion Cornia, Christian, illus. (p. 1745)
—Yogi Bear's Guide to Animal Tracks. Cornia, Christian, illus. (p. 1972)
—Yogi Bear's Guide to Bugs. Beach, Bryan, illus. (p. 1972)
—Yogi Bear's Guide to Plants. Cornia, Christian, illus. (p. 1972)
—Yogi Bear's Guide to Rocks. Beach, Bryan, illus. (p. 1972)
—Yogi Bear's Guide to the Great Outdoors. Beach, Bryan & Cornia, Christian, illus. (p. 1972)
—Zombies & Electricity Jok, illus. (p. 1988)
—Zombies & Electricity Jok, Diego, illus. (p. 1988)
—Zombies & Forces & Motion Gervasio, illus. (p. 1988)
Weakland, Mark, jt. auth. see Collins, Terry.
Weakland, Mark, jt. auth. see Gunderson, Jessica.
Weakland, Mark, jt. auth. see Salas, Laura Purdie.
Weakland, Mark & Collins, Terry. Scooby-Doo! Unmasks Monsters: The Truth Behind Zombies, Werewolves, & Other Spooky Creatures. Cornia, Christian et al, illus. (p. 1529)
Weakland, Mark & Jensen Shaffer, Jody. Monster Science. Gervasio et al, illus. (p. 1168)
Weakland, Mark & Slade, Suzanne. Wile E. Coyote, Physical Science Genius Cornia, Christian & Ricci, Andrés Martínez, illus. (p. 1932)
Weakland, Mark Andrew. Solid Truth about Matter Lum, Bernice, illus. (p. 1607)
Weakland, Mark Andrew, jt. auth. see Collins, Terry Lee.
Weakland, Mark Andrew & Collins, Terry Lee. Scooby Doo Unmasks the Truth behind Mummies. (p. 1529)
—Scooby Doo Unmasks the Truth behind Vampires. (p. 1529)
—Scooby Doo Unmasks the Truth behind Werewolves. (p. 1529)
Weakland, Mark, et al. Monster Science. Gervasio & Aón, Carlos, illus. (p. 1168)
Weakland, Mark, retold by. Adventures of Perseus: A Graphic Retelling. (p. 21)
Weakley, David. Rowley to the Rescue. (p. 1492)
Weakly, Chris A. Toby the Little Switch Engine. (p. 1760)
Weaks, Peri. Murphy Five & the Guardian in the Woods. (p. 1192)
Wealden House Staff. Soul-Fire. (p. 1614)
Weale, Andrew. Dinosaur Doo. (p. 442)
—Nora: The Girl Who Ate & Ate & Ate. Cort, Ben, illus. (p. 1264)
—Nora: The Girl Who Ate & Ate & Ate ... Cort, Ben, illus. (p. 1264)
Weale, Andrew, illus. see Kuenzler, Lou.
Weale, David. Doors in the Air Pratt, Pierre, illus. (p. 470)
—Everything That Shines. McNevin, Dale, illus. (p. 545)
—Three Tall Trees. McNevin, Dale, illus. (p. 1744)
Wealer, Sara Bennett. Rival. (p. 1475)
Wealth, Viktoria. Aadorn Kingdom of the Dragons' Light: Book-I. (p. 2)
Wean, Sarah. Teach Them to Your Children: An Alphabet of Biblical Poems, Verses, & Stories. Sanford, Lori Hood, illus. (p. 1708)
Weare, Tim. I'm a Little Frog. (p. 858)
Wearing, Judy. Abraham Lincoln: My Life. (p. 6)
—Abraham Lincoln. (p. 6)
—Amelia Earhart. (p. 58)
—Bacteria: Staph, Strep, Clostridium, & Other Bacteria. (p. 131)
—Chickens. (p. 300)
—Fall: WOW Study of Day & Seasons. (p. 566)
—Fall. (p. 566)
—Fungi: Classifying Mushrooms, Toadstools, Molds, Yeasts, & Other Fungi. (p. 649)
—Golden Gate Bridge. (p. 694)
—Jellyfish: World of Wonder: Underwater Life. (p. 912)
—Jellyfish. (p. 912)
—Manta Rays: World of Wonder: Underwater Life. (p. 1088)
—Manta Rays. (p. 1088)
—Octopuses. (p. 1278)
—Roberta Bondar: Canada's First Woman in Space. (p. 1479)
—Sea Turtle: World of Wonder: Underwater Life. (p. 1535)
—Sea Turtles. (p. 1536)
—Seahorses: World of Wonder: Underwater Life. (p. 1536)
—Seahorses. (p. 1536)
—Smell. (p. 1593)
—Taste. (p. 1707)
—Winter: WOW Study of Day & Seasons. (p. 1937)
—World of Wonder: Underwater Life (p. 1957)
Wearing, Judy, jt. auth. see Riddolls, Tom.
Wearing, Judy & Diemer, Lauren. Winter. (p. 1937)
Wearing, Judy & Riddolls, Tom. Golden Gate Bridge. (p. 694)
Wearing, Judy & Yasuda, Anita. Lebron James. (p. 987)
Weatherall, Barry. Jay & the Worm Save the Day. (p. 910)
Weatherall, Donald M. & Quinn. Addition & Subtraction Learning Module. (p. 12)
Weatherbee, Tabatha. Dream Sharers: Love/Hate. (p. 483)
—Shasta (p. 1563)
Weatherby, W. J. Chariots of Fire. Morris, Margery, ed. (p. 291)
Weatherford, Carole Boston. Beatitudes: From Slavery to Civil Rights. Ladwig, Tim, illus. (p. 152)
—Becoming Billie Holiday. Cooper, Floyd, illus. (p. 156)
—Before John Was a Jazz Giant: A Song of John Coltrane. Qualls, Sean, illus. (p. 158)
—Birmingham 1963. (p. 192)
—Celebremos Juneteenth! de La Vega, Eida, tr. from ENG. (p. 285)
—First Pooch: The Obamas Pick a Pet Bates, Amy, illus. (p. 596)
—Freedom on the Menu: The Greensboro Sit-Ins. Lagarrigue, Jerome, illus. (p. 634)
—Freedom on the Menu: The Greensboro Sit-Ins. Lagarrigue, Jerome Lagarrigue, illus. (p. 634)
—Gordon Parks: How the Photographer Captured Black & White America. Christoph, Jamey, illus. (p. 702)
—Great African-American Lawyers: Raising the Bar of Freedom. (p. 713)
—I, Matthew Henson: Polar Explorer. Velasquez, Eric, illus. (p. 844)
—Jesse Owens: Fastest Man Alive. Velasquez, Eric, illus. (p. 914)
—Leontyne Price: Voice of a Century. Colón, Raúl, illus. (p. 992)
—Library Ghost. White, Lee, illus. (p. 1006)
—Michelle Obama: First Lady Barrett, Robert, illus. (p. 1135)
—Moses: When Harriet Tubman Led Her People to Freedom. Nelson, Kadir, illus. (p. 1176)
—Negro League Scrapbook. (p. 1240)
—Racing Against the Odds: The Story of Wendell Scott, Stock Car Racing's African-American Champion (p. 1432)
—Sound That Jazz Makes Velasquez, Eric, illus. (p. 1615)
—Sugar Hill: Harlem's Historic Neighborhood. Christie, R. Gregory, illus. (p. 1673)
—Voice of Freedom - Fannie Lou Hamer: The Spirit of the Civil Rights Movement. Holmes, Ekua, illus. (p. 1848)
Weatherford, Carole Boston & Weatherford, Jeffery Boston. You Can Fly: The Tuskegee Airmen. (p. 1974)
Weatherford, Jeffery Boston, jt. auth. see Weatherford, Carole Boston.
Weatherford, Robert, illus. see Johnston, Tony.
Weatherhead, Yvonne. Enriching Circle Time: Dream Journeys & Positive Thoughts. Drakeford, Philippa, illus. (p. 531)
Weatherill, Stephen, jt. auth. see Weatherill, Sue.
Weatherill, Steve, illus. see Frances Lincoln Staff, ed.
Weatherill, Sue & Weatherill, Stephen. Romans. (p. 1486)
Weatherly. Working with Numbers. (p. 1953)
Weatherly, L. A. Angel Burn. (p. 73)
—Angel Fever. (p. 73)
—Angel Fire. (p. 73)
—Them. (p. 1728)
—Watcher. (p. 1861)
Weatherly, Lee. Child X. (p. 302)
—Pigwitchery. Reed, Nathan, illus. (p. 1358)
Weatherly, Myra. Dolley Madison: America's First Lady. (p. 464)
—Elizabeth I: Queen of Tudor England (p. 513)
—Living in Elizabethan England. (p. 1041)
—Lure of Mountain Peaks. (p. 1066)
—Nebraska. (p. 1239)
—Ralph Lauren. (p. 1437)
—William Marshal: Medieval England's Greatest Knight. (p. 1933)
Weatherly, Myra S. Nebraska. (p. 1239)
—South Carolina. (p. 1616)
—Tennessee. (p. 1720)
Weathers, Andrea. Hermy the Hermit Crab: The Adventure Begins. (p. 771)
Weathers, Marion. Henry Baldpate & His Treetop Friends. (p. 767)
Weathers, R. F. Jill's Joyful Surprise. (p. 917)
Weathers, Regina Lorick. Safety Sam, I Am: How to Avoid A Sticky Jelly Jam. Short, Gregory T., illus. (p. 1502)
Weatherstone, Hollie. When the Pandas Came to Scotland. (p. 1905)
Weatherwalk, Wendy. Ants Don't Eat That. (p. 90)
Weatherwax, Barbara. Gaited Games: Activities for the Young Gaited Horse Fancier. Weatherwax, Barbara, illus. (p. 652)
Weatheryly, Myra & Cothran, Helen, eds. Living in 1920s America. (p. 1041)
Weaver, A. J. Big Cats, Little Cats. Budgen, Tim, illus. (p. 180)
Weaver, Allie, jt. auth. see Weaver, Greg.
Weaver, Amy Garrett. Zoe the Zebra. Schneider, Robin, illus. (p. 1987)
Weaver, Anna E. Birds at My Window. (p. 191)
—Stories From Grandma's Day. (p. 1654)
Weaver, Anne H. Children of Time: Evolution & the Human Story. Celeskey, Matt, illus. (p. 303)
—Voyage of the Beetle: A Journey Around the World with Charles Darwin & the Search for the Solution to the Mystery of Mysteries, as Narrated by Rosie, an Articulate Beetle. Lawrence, George, illus. (p. 1850)
Weaver, Brandon, illus. see Mally, Sarah.
Weaver, Brian M., illus. see Numberman, Neil.
Weaver, Brian M., illus. see Reynolds, Aaron.
Weaver, Brynda Mason. Goose Bumps. (p. 702)
Weaver, C. Kay, jt. auth. see Carter, Cynthia.
Weaver, Clare, jt. auth. see MacDonald, Fiona.
Weaver, David J. Only Mortals Can Be Heroes: A True Story about Drug Addiction. (p. 1298)
Weaver, Debra Stephens. Fuzzy & Magpie: A Tale of True Friendship. (p. 651)
Weaver, Greg & Weaver, Allie. Mickey the Monkey Makes a Friend. (p. 1136)
Weaver, Griz. Along Came Lizzie. (p. 48)
—Day in the Rain. (p. 413)
—How It Came to Be Seven Cats, A Woman, A Man & Me. (p. 810)
Weaver, Harriett E. There Stand the Giants: The Story of the Redwood Trees. (p. 1730)
Weaver, Jack. Uga Hunkers down in Athens Town. Ingram, Glenda Brown, illus. (p. 1808)
Weaver, Jack, jt. auth. see Gaspar, Joe.
Weaver, Jack W. Cat & Dog Breath Meet the Last Pirates: How to Fly a Basset Hound. (p. 277)
Weaver, Janice. A to Z of Everyday Things. Blake, Francis, illus. (p. 2)
—From Head to Toe: Bound Feet, Bathing Suits, & Other Bizarre & Beautiful Things. Blake, Francis, illus. (p. 642)
—Harry Houdini: The Legend of the World's Greatest Escape Artist. Lane, Chris, illus. (p. 750)
—Hudson. Craig, David, illus. (p. 824)
—Mirror with a Memory: A Nation's Story in Photographs. (p. 1149)
Weaver, Janice & Wishinsky, Frieda. It's Your Room: A Decorating Guide for Real Kids. Dávila, Claudia, illus. (p. 899)
Weaver, Jeanne. Wetlands Journey. (p. 1877)
Weaver, Jenny. Following the Raven. (p. 612)
Weaver, Jo. Paul Bunyan: A Very Tall Tale (p. 1330)
Weaver, Joyce A. Mckissick. Adventures of Mopey Bear & His Two Brothers (p. 20)
—Chubby Bear & His Two Brothers. (p. 317)
Weaver, Joyce Mckissick. Little Rhymes for Little Minds (p. 1035)
Weaver, Kimberley & Murphy, Allyson. Pack Your Bags... . Go U. S. A. Holdren, Maria K., illus. (p. 1317)
Weaver, Lisa, illus. see Martin, Rebecca.
Weaver, Lisa D. Praying with Our Feet. Hess, Ingrid, illus. (p. 1393)
Weaver, Madeline. Near & Far at the Park: Describe & Compare Measurable Attributes. (p. 1238)
Weaver, Margo. Mitch with an Itch. (p. 1155)
Weaver, Nancy. In Her Presence: A Husband's Dirty Secret. (p. 863)
Weaver, Nicole. Beauty & Other Traps. (p. 154)
—My Birthday Is September Eleven & Other Short Stories. (p. 1198)
Weaver, Roger. Holy Eucharist for the Children of God. (p. 791)
Weaver, Ruth. Magical Labyrinth. Lloyd, Anna, illus. (p. 1074)
Weaver, Steve, illus. see Cussen, Sarah R.
Weaver, Steve, illus. see Cussen, Sarah.
Weaver, Steve, illus. see Feeney, Kathy.
Weaver, Steve, illus. see Magellan, Marta.
Weaver, Steve, illus. see Nickel, Bonnie.
Weaver, Steve, illus. see Wicker, Jan L.
Weaver, Steve, illus. see Wicker, Jan Lee.
Weaver, Steve, illus. see Wyatt, Laura.
Weaver, Sue. Llamas & Alpacas: Small-Scale Herding for Pleasure & Profit. (p. 1043)
Weaver, Susan. My Goofy Girls. (p. 1210)
Weaver, Will. Checkered Flag Cheater. (p. 295)
—Clay. (p. 330)
—Memory Boy. (p. 1126)
—Saturday Night Dirt. (p. 1515)
—Survivors. (p. 1687)
Webb, Anne Aldridge. Appalachian State, A to Z. Bostian, Laurie, illus. (p. 92)
Webb, Arch, illus. see Brereton, F. S.
Webb, Arthur, jt. auth. see Webb, Derek.
Webb, Barb. Endangered! (p. 526)
—Helping Habitats. (p. 766)
—What Does Green Mean? (p. 1884)
Webb, Barbara & Webb, Barbara L. Trees: Earth's Lungs. (p. 1784)
Webb, Barbara L. Graph It! (p. 710)
—Hot or Cold? (p. 802)
—Order of Things. (p. 1302)
—Play with Counting! (p. 1371)
—Recycling Earth's Resources. (p. 1453)
Webb, Barbara L., jt. auth. see Webb, Barbara.
Webb, Beth. Fleabag Trilogy. (p. 603)
Webb, Carla. Magic in Believing: The Tooth Fairies. Lee, Kim, illus. (p. 1072)
Webb, Catherine. Doomsday Machine: Another Astounding Adventure of Horatio Lyle. (p. 470)
—Extraordinary & Unusual Adventures of Horatio Lyle. (p. 555)
—Mirror Wakes. (p. 1149)
—Obsidian Dagger: Being the Further Extraordinary Adventures of Horatio Lyle. (p. 1275)
—Timekeepers. (p. 1754)
Webb, Celia, illus. see Webb, Mack H., Jr.
Webb, Celia, illus. see Webb, Mack Henry, Jr.
Webb, Cheryl Renee. Do Pets & Other Animals Go to Heaven? How to Recover from the Loss of an Animal Friend. (p. 457)
Webb, Christine. Elsie Files: A Mostly True Story of a Cat on a Mission. (p. 516)
Webb, Dave. Barkley Rules. (p. 139)
—Middle School Mania. (p. 1137)
Webb, David A. Alaskan Holiday. (p. 34)
—Rock Star. (p. 1482)
Webb, Derek & Webb, Arthur. Is. (p. 888)
Webb, Dirk. Amazing City of Arbella Lamore. School, Liberty, illus. (p. 54)
—Warm Summer's Day. (p. 1858)
Webb, Dirk & School, Liberty. Warm Summer's Day. (p. 1858)
Webb, Ernie. Joshua Freeman. (p. 927)
Webb, Eugene Lawrance. Arlen the Elf: The Gathering. (p. 99)
Webb, Heather. Frog & the Fly. Sanderson, Constance, illus. (p. 640)
Webb, Holly. Case of the Feathered Mask. Lindsay, Marion, illus. (p. 274)
—Case of the Phantom Cat. Lindsay, Marion, illus. (p. 274)
—Lily. (p. 1017)
—Lily & the Prisoner of Magic. (p. 1018)
—Lily & the Shining Dragons. (p. 1018)
—Lost in the Snow. Williams, Sophy, illus. (p. 1056)
—Rabbit Magic. (p. 1429)
—Rose. (p. 1489)
—Rose & the Lost Princess. (p. 1489)
—Rose & the Magician's Mask. (p. 1489)
—Rose & the Silver Ghost. (p. 1489)
Webb, Holly & Lindsay, Marion. Case of the Stolen Sixpence. Lindsay, Marion, illus. (p. 275)
Webb, Jack B. & Webb, Susan Hankey. True North in Alaska: Memories of Indians, Eskimos, Bush Pilots & Us. (p. 1792)
Webb, James, Jr. They Call Me Giz. (p. 1732)
Webb, Jane K. My Super Stupendous Day at the Beach. Cupolo, Eileen, illus. (p. 1219)
Webb, Janeen. Silken Road to Samarkand. (p. 1575)
—Tales from Beyond. (p. 1701)
Webb, Jessica. Simple Wish. (p. 1578)
Webb, Joseph A. Hasta Que la Muerte nos Separe? Lo Que la Biblia Verdaderamente Dice Sobre el Divorcio y el Matrimonio. Teixeira, Brenda Lopez, ed. (p. 752)
Webb, Josh. Dudley's Muddley Day. Antonini, Gabriele, illus. (p. 489)
Webb, Kate R. God Made Katie, & He Made You Too. (p. 689)
Webb, Lexy, jt. auth. see Webb, Melissa.
Webb, Lois. Tall Tales. (p. 1704)
Webb, Lois Sinaiko, jt. auth. see Roten, Lindsay Grace.
Webb, Lois Sinaiko & Roten, Lindsay Grace. Holidays of the World Cookbook for Students: Updated & Revised (p. 788)
Webb, M. St. John. Knock Three Times! (p. 965)
Webb, Mack H., Jr. Danny & the Detention Demons. Espinola, Nicole & Nealon, Eve, illus. (p. 405)
—Webb's Wondrous Tales Book 2. Webb, Celia, illus. (p. 1870)
Webb, Mack Henry, Jr. Little Bianca. Tuck, Beverly, illus. (p. 1024)
—Webb's Wondrous Tales Book 1. Webb, Celia, illus. (p. 1870)
Webb, Margaret. Pump It up Cheerleading. (p. 1416)
Webb, Margaret, jt. auth. see Crabtree Editors.
Webb, Margaret, jt. auth. see Crabtree Publishing Company Staff.
Webb, Margaret, jt. auth. see Crabtree Staff.
Webb, Margot. Too Young to Die: The Story of José. (p. 1767)
Webb, Margot & Chorpash, Marci. My Grandmommy Is Shrinking. (p. 1210)
Webb, Mary, et al. My Ireland Counting Book. (p. 1211)
Webb, Melissa, illus. see Farrer, Vashti.
Webb, Melissa, jt. auth. see Brasch, Nicolas.
Webb, Melissa & Webb, Lexy. Zoe the Earless Kitten: Zoe Meets the Family. (p. 1987)
Webb, Mick. Book of Languages: Talk Your Way Around the World. (p. 211)
Webb, Philip. Six Days. (p. 1582)
—Where the Rock Splits the Sky. (p. 1909)
Webb, Philip, illus. see Burslem, Diana & Freeman, Diana.
Webb, Philip, illus. see Dale, Jay.
Webb, Philip, illus. see Eggleton, Jill.
Webb, Philip, illus. see Holden, Pam.
Webb, Philip, illus. see Punter, Russell.
Webb, Philip, illus. see Windsor, Jo.
Webb Quest, By Sara. Aydil Vice, Author of Kiski the Cat. (p. 121)
Webb Quest, Sara. Angel's Shore. (p. 75)
—Aydil Vice & Her Disgustin' Hair Knots. (p. 121)
Webb, Ramona. Tee & Tye Learn to Fly. Webb, Terris, illus. (p. 1713)
Webb, Richard. Secret Magic Rocks: In the Land of Miracles. (p. 1542)
Webb, Rita. Tears. (p. 1711)
Webb, Robert N. How & Why Wonder Book of Florence Nightingale. Vosburgh, Leonard, illus. (p. 804)
—We Were There at the Boston Tea Party. Ward, E. F., illus. (p. 1868)
Webb, Ryan. Buddy: Dog of the Smoky Mountains. (p. 234)
Webb, Sarah. Ask Amy Green: Boy Trouble. (p. 106)
—Ask Amy Green: Love & Other Drama-Ramas! (p. 106)
—Ask Amy Green: Dancing Daze. (p. 106)
—Ask Amy Green: Wedding Belles. (p. 106)
—Boy Trouble. (p. 219)
—Bridesmaid Blitz. (p. 227)
—Summer Secrets. (p. 1675)
Webb, Sarah, illus. see Claus, Fred J.
Webb, Sarah & Ranson, Claire. Sally Go Round the Stars: Favourite Rhymes for an Irish Childhood. McCarthy, Steven, illus. (p. 1505)
Webb, Sarah Powers. Marie Antoinette: Fashionable Queen or Greedy Royal? (p. 1093)
—Perspectives on History. (p. 1344)
Webb, Shamore, illus. see Nicholson, Wanda.
Webb, Shirley G. Tales from the Keeper of the Myths: Cherokee Stories for Children. (p. 1701)
Webb, Shirley G., jt. auth. see Moreland, Janet.
Webb, Sophie. Far from Shore: Chronicles of an Open Ocean Voyage. (p. 572)
Webb, Stephen, jt. auth. see Runkle, Toni.
Webb, Steve. City Kitty Cat. Le Huche, Magali, illus. (p. 323)
—Happy Zappa Cat. Le Huche, Magali, illus. (p. 747)
—Rocket Racers. Mantle, Ben, illus. (p. 1483)
—Tigerbear. McEwen, Katharine, illus. (p. 1749)
Webb, Stuart. UFOs. (p. 1808)
Webb, Susan. Glory's Tale: A Tale of Three Donkeys. (p. 685)
—Tale of Two Brothers. (p. 1700)
Webb, Susan Hankey, jt. auth. see Webb, Jack B.
Webb, Terris, illus. see Webb, Ramona.
Webb, Willyn. Baby, the Poodle Cow Dog. Theobald, Denise, illus. (p. 128)
Webber, Andrew Lloyd, jt. auth. see Rice, Tim.
Webber, Barbara. Feeling Loved: A Ted E. Bear Story. (p. 580)
Webber, Berryl & Barnes, Terry. How to Dazzle at Algebra. (p. 816)
Webber, Beryl & Haigh, Jean. How to Dazzle at Oral & Mental Starters. (p. 816)
—How to Dazzle at Written Calculations. (p. 816)
—How to Sparkle at Number Bonds. (p. 821)
Webber, Carol, illus. see Polinski, Jo.

W

Webber, Christopher L. Shout for Joy & Sing! Psalm 65 for Children. McDaniels, Preston, illus. (p. 1570)
Webber, Desiree Morrison. Bone Head: Story of the Longhorn. Shropshire, Sandy, illus. (p. 209)
Webber, Diane. Celebrity's Son Snatched: Can Handwriting Help Nab the Perp? (p. 285)
—Do You Read Me? Famous Cases Solved by Handwriting Analysis! (p. 458)
—Shot & Framed: Photographers at the Crime Scene. (p. 1569)
—Skin You're In: Staying Healthy Inside & Out. (p. 1585)
—Your Space: Dealing with Friends & Peers. (p. 1981)
Webber, Diane & Mandel, Laurie. Totally Tolerant: Spotting & Stopping Prejudice. (p. 1771)
Webber, Gail. Time of the Cats. (p. 1752)
Webber, Helen. Webber Quartet (p. 1870)
Webber, Helen, illus. see Meislin, Barbara.
Webber, Jake. Lafitte's Black Box: Boit Noir. (p. 971)
Webber, Jennifer Wynne. Defying Gravity. Coteau Books Staff, ed. (p. 424)
Webber, Jerry. Game: None. (p. 654)
Webber, John, illus. see Drake, Tim.
Webber, John, et al. Childhood of Jesus / la niñez de Jesús. (p. 302)
Webber, Mike, illus. see Wozniak, Paul.
Webber, Penny, illus. see Njenga, Wamoro P.
Webber, Sharon. Changing Statements to Questions Fun Deck: Fd55. Schwartz, Marty, illus. (p. 290)
Webber, Sharon & Bradburn, Ryan, concepts. Holiday & Seasonal Chipper Chat: Cc99. (p. 788)
Webber, Sharon, creator. Around the Home & Food Lotto Game: Lot100. (p. 100)
—Webber Photo Lotto Games Things to Wear & Animals: Lot222. (p. 1870)
Webber, Sharon, et al. Party Pups: The Game of Prepositional Fun! Ink, Bruce, illus. (p. 1326)
Webber, Thomas. Using I & Me Fun Deck: Fd61. Bradburn, Ryan, illus. (p. 1828)
Webber, Thomas, ed. see Larson, Jennifer.
Webber, Toni. Mounted Games. Vincer, Carole, illus. (p. 1181)
Webb-King, Marian. Sweet Dreams Bear Cub: My Life As a Cricket. (p. 1689)
Weber, Amy, ed. see Rosa-Mendoza, Gladys.
Weber, Amy & Creative Haven Staff. Creative Haven Curious Creatures Coloring Book. (p. 379)
Weber, Andra, illus. see Sirotzky, Sara.
Weber, Belinda. Discover Science: Animal Disguises. (p. 448)
—Discover Science: Reptiles. (p. 448)
—I Wonder Why Animals Are Amazing Sticker Activity Book. (p. 849)
—I Wonder Why Caterpillars Eat So Much: And Other Questions about Life Cycles. (p. 849)
—I Wonder Why Dinosaurs Ruled Sticker Acitivity Book. (p. 849)
—Kingfisher Young Knowledge - Reptiles. (p. 960)
Weber, Belinda & Butterfield, Moira. I Wonder Why Cars Go Fast. (p. 849)
Weber, Belinda & Jewitt, Kathryn. I Wonder Why Astronauts Wear Spacesuits. (p. 849)
Weber, Bob. Go Fun! Slylock Fox Mystery Puzzles. (p. 686)
—Go Fun! Spot Six Differences. (p. 686)
Weber, Caressa, illus. see Carithers, Rochelle.
Weber, D. G. Downthelane Bears. (p. 474)
Weber, David. Beautiful Friendship. (p. 153)
Weber, David & Lindskold, Jane. Fire Season. (p. 590)
Weber, Dennis, illus. see Bouchard, David.
Weber, Elka. One Little Chicken. Kleven, Elisa, illus. (p. 1295)
—Yankee at the Seder. Gustavson, Adam, illus. (p. 1968)
Weber, Erec-Michael Ollier. Bryce & the Blood Ninjas. Harvey II, Alvin, illus. (p. 233)
Weber Feeney, Siri, illus. see Coleman, Wim & Perrin, Pat.
Weber, Francis J., ed. see Campodonica, Carol A.
Weber, Ilse. Mendel Rosenbusch: Tales for Jewish Children. Fisher, Hans, tr. from GER. (p. 1126)
—Mendel Rosenbusch: Tales for Jewish Children Fisher, Hans & Fisher, Ruth, trs. from GER. (p. 1126)
Weber, Jen Funk. Thimbletack's Activity Book. (p. 1732)
Weber, Jennifer. Summer's Bloodiest Days: The Battle of Gettysburg as Told from All Sides. (p. 1675)
Weber, Jennifer L. Key Concepts in American History (p. 950)
Weber, Jill, illus. see Adler, David A.
Weber, Jill, illus. see Buller, Jon, et al.
Weber, Jill, illus. see Delton, Judy.
Weber, Jill, illus. see Driscoll, Laura.
Weber, Jill, illus. see Judy Delton Family Trust Staff & Delton, Judy.
Weber, Jill, illus. see Kimmel, Eric A.
Weber, Jill, illus. see McDonough, Yona Zeldis.
Weber, Jill, illus. see Peretz, I. L.
Weber, Jill, illus. see Purnell, Ann.
Weber, Jill, illus. see Salamon, Julie.
Weber, Joanne M. Flabby Rabbit. (p. 601)
Weber, John. Orphan. (p. 1304)
Weber, Judith Eichler. Seeking Safety. Martin, John F., illus. (p. 1548)
Weber, K. E. Cake on a Plate. Baldassi, Deborah, illus. (p. 252)
Weber, Ken. Five-Minute Halloween Mysteries. De la Hoz, Cindy, ed. (p. 601)
—Five-Minute Mysteries (p. 601)
Weber, Kristin, jt. auth. see Shellenberger, Susie.
Weber, Levi B. Possum Hollow (p. 1387)
Weber, Lisa K., illus. see Baratz-Logsted, Lauren, et al.
Weber, Lisa K., illus. see Baratz-Logsted, Lauren.
Weber, Lisa K., illus. see Braun, Eric & Bowman, James Cloyd.
Weber, Lisa K., illus. see Brezenoff, Steve.
Weber, Lisa K., illus. see Brezenoff, Steven.
Weber, Lisa K., illus. see Capstone Press Staff.
Weber, Lisa K., illus. see Dahl, Michael.
Weber, Lisa K., illus. see Grimm, Jacob, et al.
Weber, Lisa K., illus. see Hirschfeld, Leila & Hirschfeld, Tom.
Weber, Lisa K., illus. see Stone Arch Books Staff.
Weber, Lori. Klepto (p. 963)
—My Granny Loves Hockey. Liska, Eliska, illus. (p. 1210)
—Picture Me (p. 1355)
—Split (p. 1630)
—Strange Beauty (p. 1664)
—Tattoo Heaven (p. 1707)
—Yellow Mini (p. 1970)
Weber, M. S., illus. see Bennett, Howard J.
Weber, Mark M., illus. see Philip, Neil & Naohman.
Weber, Matt. California's Missions: From A to Z. (p. 253)
Weber, Michael, jt. auth. see Hicks, Kelli L.
Weber, Paige. Early Amer. (p. 493)
Weber, Penny. Ava's Adventure (p. 118)
—On My Way to School. (p. 1289)
Weber, Penny, illus. see Hohmeier, Marla.
Weber, Penny, illus. see Kline, Tom.
Weber, Penny, illus. see McCloud, Carol & Wells, Karen.
Weber, Penny, illus. see McCloud, Carol.
Weber, Penny, illus. see Moss, Peggy.
Weber, Penny, illus. see Pedersen, Laura.
Weber, Penny, illus. see Rowland, Joanna.
Weber, Philip A., Jr., illus. see Gerald, Tom.
Weber, Philip A., Jr., illus. see Gunn, Barbara, et al.
Weber, Phillip A., Jr., illus. see Sprick, Marilyn, et al.
Weber, R. David & Schlachter, Gail Ann. Money for Christian College Students 2005-2007. (p. 1164)
Weber, Rebecca. Ciclo de Tu Vida/the Cycle of Your Life (p. 318)
—Cómo Funciona Tu Cuerpo. (p. 351)
—Cycle of Your Life (p. 396)
—Ellen Ochoa. (p. 514)
—First Aid Basics. (p. 592)
—Hábitos Saludables. (p. 735)
—Health & Your Body. (p. 757)
—Healthy Habits (p. 758)
—How Many Legs? (p. 811)
—How Your Body Works (p. 823)
—Lost Cities: Set Of 6. (p. 1055)
—Making a House. (p. 1080)
—My Grandma. (p. 1210)
—Party for Rabbit: Set Of 6. (p. 1326)
—Poder de la Energía. (p. 1375)
—Safety Basics (p. 1502)
—Salud y Tu Cuerpo. (p. 1506)
—Science & Your Health (p. 1525)
—Telling Time Through the Ages: Set Of 6. (p. 1717)
—Time to Recycle (p. 1753)
Weber, Rebecca, et al. Health & Your Body. (p. 757)
Weber, Rich, illus. see Mott, Professor.
Weber, Richard D. Elvis & Me. (p. 517)
Weber, Rita J. Standing at the Edge. (p. 1639)
Weber, Rivka Doba. Dear Tree. Rosenfeld, D. L., ed. (p. 419)
Weber, Roopa. Messy Penny. Szewczyk, Manda, illus. (p. 1130)
Weber, Sandra. Internet. (p. 880)
—Personal Computer. (p. 1344)
—Two in the Wilderness. Hellman, Carl, II, illus. (p. 1803)
Weber, Saul. Lesson My Cat Taught Me. Lepri, Nancy, illus. (p. 993)
Weber, Seth. It Is I. Weber, Seth, illus. (p. 894)
Weber, Terri. Alicia Keys. (p. 40)
—Oscar de la Hoya. (p. 1305)
—Ricky Williams. (p. 1470)
Weber, Terri Smith. Alex Rodrigues: Improving His Game. (p. 36)
—Alex Rodriguez: Improving His Game. (p. 36)
—Alex Rodriguez: Mejorando Su Juego. (p. 36)
—Beyonce Knowles: Seeking the Spotlight. (p. 173)
—Bios for Kids: Series Set 1. (p. 190)
—Bios for Kids: Series Set, Series 1. (p. 190)
—Bios for Kids: Library Set, Series 1. (p. 190)
—Dixie Chicks. (p. 455)
—Frankie Muniz: Enjoying His Success. (p. 629)
—Halle Berry: Fighting for First. (p. 737)
—Hilary Duff: Branching Out. (p. 779)
—Jeff Gordon: Racing to Win. (p. 911)
—Jennifer Lopez: Living the Dream. (p. 913)
—Jennifer Lopez: Realizando Los Suenos. (p. 913)
—Jessica Simpson. (p. 914)
—Lebron James: Rising Star. (p. 987)
—Shakira: Following Her Heart. (p. 1559)
—Tony Hawk: Flying High. (p. 1766)
Weber, Valerie J. Anglerfish. (p. 75)
—Coelacanth: The Living Fossil. (p. 338)
—Dolphins. (p. 464)
—Dolphins (Delfines) (p. 465)
—Dolphins/Delfines. (p. 465)
—Giant Tubeworms. (p. 674)
—I Come from Afghanistan. (p. 837)
—I Come from Chile. (p. 837)
—I Come from India. (p. 837)
—I Come from Ivory Coast. (p. 837)
—I Come from South Korea. (p. 837)
—I Come from Ukraine. (p. 837)
—Manatees. (p. 1086)
—Manatees/Manatíes. (p. 1086)
—Octopuses & Squids. (p. 1278)
—Octopuses & Squids/Pulpos y Calamares. (p. 1278)
—Por Qué Algunos Animales Tejen Telarañas. (p. 1385)
—Por Qué Algunos Animales Tienen Caparazón. (p. 1385)
—Por qué algunos animales tienen caparazón (Why Animals Live in Shells) (p. 1385)
—Por Que Algunos Animales Viven en Colmenas. (p. 1385)
—Por Qué Algunos Animales Viven en Colmenas. (p. 1385)
—Por Qué Algunos Animales Viven en Madrigueras. (p. 1385)
—Por qué algunos animales viven en madrigueras (Why Animals Live in Burrows) (p. 1385)
—Por Que Algunos Animales Viven en Nidos. (p. 1385)
—Por Qué Algunos Animales Viven en Nidos. (p. 1385)
—Sea Horses. (p. 1534)
—Sea Horses/Caballitos de Mar. (p. 1534)
—Sea Slugs. (p. 1535)
—Sea Turtles. (p. 1536)
—Sea Turtles/Tortugas Marinas. (p. 1536)
—Sharks. (p. 1562)
—Sharks/Tiburones. (p. 1563)
—Squids. (p. 1637)
—Walruses. (p. 1855)
—Walruses/Morsas. (p. 1855)
—Whale Sharks. (p. 1877)
—Whales/Ballenas. (p. 1878)
—Why Animals Live in Burrows. (p. 1922)
—Why Animals Live in Caves. (p. 1922)
—Why Animals Live in Shells. (p. 1922)
—Why Animals Live in Webs. (p. 1922)
Weber, Valerie J., jt. auth. see Weber, Valerie J.
Weber, Valerie J. & Weber, Valerie J. I Come from South Korea. (p. 837)
—Sea Horses: Caballitos de Mar. (p. 1534)
—Sea Horses. (p. 1534)
—Whales. (p. 1878)
—Why Animals Live in Shells. (p. 1922)
Weber, Vicky. Animal Babies on the Farm. Kingfisher Editors, ed. (p. 76)
Webley, Ann. Collins Primary Literacy (p. 341)
—Homework (p. 794)
Webley, Nicholas. Taste of Wartime Britain. (p. 1707)
Webre, Mary M. Just a Little Hugo. (p. 937)
Webster, Amye. Shell's Journey. (p. 1565)
Webster, Andrea K. Pigeon in the Park. (p. 1357)
Webster, Belinda. Magic Times Tables. (p. 1074)
Webster, Carroll, illus. see Baldner, Jean V.
Webster, Christine. Beyonce Knowles. (p. 173)
—Canyons McMullen, Anne, illus. (p. 262)
—Clouds. (p. 335)
—Clouds with Code. (p. 335)
—Condylures étoilés: Les Animaux du Canada. Karvonen, Tanjah, tr. from ENG. (p. 356)
—Connecticut. (p. 357)
—Coyotes. (p. 375)
—Coyotes. Hudak, Heather C., ed. (p. 375)
—Deer. (p. 423)
—Glaciers. (p. 682)
—Great Wall of China. (p. 719)
—How to Draw Christmas Symbols. (p. 817)
—How to Draw Easter Symbols. (p. 817)
—How to Draw Hanukkah Symbols. (p. 817)
—How to Draw Kwanzaa Symbols. (p. 818)
—How to Draw Passover Symbols. (p. 818)
—How to Draw Thanksgiving Symbols. (p. 818)
—Jeff Kinney. (p. 912)
—Jonas Brothers. (p. 925)
—K2. (p. 941)
—Maine. (p. 1077)
—Masters. (p. 1103)
—Masters Golf Tournament. (p. 1103)
—Matter (p. 1109)
—Mauna Loa: The Largest Volcano in the United States. (p. 1110)
—Mauna Loa. (p. 1110)
—Mi'kmaq: Les Autochtones du Canada. Karvonen, Tanjah, tr. from ENG. (p. 1141)
—Mosquitoes. (p. 1177)
—Opossums. (p. 1300)
—Opossums. Hudak, Heather C., ed. (p. 1300)
—Otter Everywhere: Brand New Readers. Nihoff, Tim, illus. (p. 1307)
—Plains (p. 1366)
—Pledge of Allegiance. (p. 1374)
—Polynesians. (p. 1381)
—Porcupines. (p. 1386)
—Ravens. (p. 1441)
—Sandra Cisneros: My Favorite Writer. (p. 1511)
—Sparrows. (p. 1622)
—Sparrows. Hudak, Heather C., ed. (p. 1622)
—Star-Nosed Mole. (p. 1640)
—Storms. (p. 1656)
—Taj Mahal. (p. 1696)
—Water Power. (p. 1863)
—Who on Earth Is Archie Carr? Protector of Sea Turtles. (p. 1917)
—Yanomami. (p. 1968)
Webster, Christine, jt. auth. see Strudwick, Leslie.
Webster, Christine & Kissock, Heather. Great Wall of China. (p. 719)
—Salish. (p. 1505)
Webster, Christy. Anna's Best Friends. (p. 85)
—Barbie: A Fairy Secret. Random House Staff, illus. (p. 138)
—Barbie in a Mermaid Tale. (p. 138)
—Barbie in a Mermaid Tale. Random House Editors, illus. (p. 138)
—Bath Party! Random House Editors & VanTuyle, David, illus. (p. 144)
—Double-Team! (Teenage Mutant Ninja Turtles) Spaziante, Patrick, illus. (p. 473)
—Green Team! (p. 722)
—Green Team! (Teenage Mutant Ninja Turtles) Spaziante, Patrick, illus. (p. 722)
—I Can Be a Ballerina. Random House Staff & Riley, Kellee, illus. (p. 835)
—I Can Be President. Riley, Kellee, illus. (p. 835)
—Perfect Christmas. Random House Staff, illus. (p. 1341)
—Robot Rampage! (p. 1480)
—Scooter Trouble (Pocoyo) Random House Staff, illus. (p. 1529)
—Surprise for Pocoyo (Pocoyo) Random House Staff, illus. (p. 1685)
—Teenage Mutant Ninga Turtles: Double-Team! (p. 1714)
—Toy Box Heroes! RH Disney Staff, illus. (p. 1774)
—What Shape Is a Grape? Moroney, Christopher, illus. (p. 1893)
Webster, Christy, jt. auth. see Random House Staff.
Webster, Clare L., retold by. Elf (p. 512)
Webster, Daniel. Letters. (p. 1002)
—Works & Speeches (p. 1953)
Webster, David. Book Two of the Naxos Island Mages: The War of the Dark Mages. (p. 212)
Webster, David Scott. Book One of the Naxos Island Mages: The Grand Adventure. (p. 212)
Webster, Dennis & Cunningham, Kim Webster. Absolutely Wild. (p. 7)
Webster, Frank V. Bob Chester's Grit: From Ranch to Riches. (p. 205)
—Bob Chester's Grit. (p. 205)
—Boy from the Ranch: Or; Roy Bradner's City Experiences. (p. 218)
—Boy Scouts of Lenox: Or the Hike over Big Bear Mountain. (p. 218)
—Boys of Bellwood School. (p. 220)
—Comrades of the Saddle. (p. 355)
—Comrades of the Saddle or the Young Rough Riders of the Plains. (p. 355)
—Cowboy Dave. (p. 374)
—Dick the Bank Boy: Or A Missing Fortune. (p. 436)
—Dick the Bank Boy. (p. 436)
—Jack of the Pony Express. (p. 903)
Webster, Fred S. Riddle at Lost Acres. (p. 1470)
Webster, Gayle. I Can Still Remember ... (p. 836)
Webster, Genevieve & de Souza, Michael. Rastamouse & the Micespace Mystery. (p. 1440)
Webster, Grace & Golden, Emily. Elephant's Ears. (p. 512)
Webster, Helen & Jackson, Helen. It's a Princess! (p. 896)
Webster, Jean. Daddy-Long-Legs. (p. 398)
—Daddy-Long-Legs. Webster, Jean, illus. (p. 398)
—Dear Enemy. (p. 419)
—Jerry. (p. 913)
—Jerry Junior. (p. 913)
—Just Patty. (p. 939)
—Papaito-Piernas-Largas. (p. 1322)
Webster, Jeanne. If You Could Be Anything What Would You Be? A Teen's Guide to Mapping Out the Future. Nelson, Dianne, ed. (p. 854)
Webster, Jess. Secret Stealer. (p. 1544)
Webster, John, jt. auth. see Webster, John.
Webster, John & Webster, John. Duchess of Malfi. Millet, Fred B., ed. (p. 487)
Webster, Keith. Why Can't My Turtle Be a Ninja? (p. 1923)
Webster, Kyle T. Please Say Please. (p. 1373)
Webster, Kyle T., illus. see Keenan-Bolger, Andrew & Wetherhead, Kate.
Webster, Lance. Media Training for Executives & Professionals: A Media Training Seminar Companion Workbook (p. 1118)
Webster, Matt. Inside Israel's Mossad: The Institute for Intelligence & Special Tasks. (p. 876)
Webster, Michelle B. Christmas of Miracles. (p. 315)
Webster, Penny. Allergy Free for All Ages: Milk-Free, Egg-Free, Nut-Free Recipes. (p. 46)
Webster, Raelyn & Rasmussen, Kenneth L. My Grandma Mary. Johnson, Kimberli Anne, illus. (p. 1210)
Webster, Rob, photos by see Rooyackers, Paul.
Webster, S. My Best Friend Fred. Fuller, E., illus. (p. 1196)
Webster, Sarah, illus. see Gil, Carmen.
Webster, Travis. Sally Forth, Vile Curmudgeon! (p. 1505)
Webster, W. Russell, jt. auth. see Barbo, Theresa Mitchell.
Webster, Wendy. Magicus Perfecticum. (p. 1075)
Webster-Smith, Angela. In the Presence of a King. (p. 867)
Webster-Tyson, Paulette L. I Gotta Get a Nickname! (p. 838)
Wechsler, Doug. Bald Eagles. (p. 133)
—Bizarre Birds. (p. 194)
—Bizarre Bugs. (p. 194)
—Bullfrogs. (p. 240)
—Garter Snakes. (p. 657)
—Glass Frogs. (p. 682)
—Great Horned Owls. (p. 716)
—Leopard Frogs. (p. 992)
—Marvels in the Muck: Life in the Salt Marshes. (p. 1099)
—Ospreys. (p. 1306)
—Peregrine Falcons. (p. 1341)
—Rattlesnakes. (p. 1440)
—Really Wild Life of Birds of Prey (p. 1450)
—Really Wild Life of Frogs (p. 1450)
—Really Wild Life of Snakes (p. 1450)
—Red- Tailed Hawks. (p. 1453)
—Vultures. (p. 1851)
—Wood Frogs. (p. 1949)
Wechsler, Kimberly. 303 Kid-Approved Exercises & Active Games. Sleva, Michael, illus. (p. 2001)
—303 Preschooler-Approved Exercises & Active Games. Sleva, Michael, illus. (p. 2001)
—303 Tween-Approved Exercises & Active Games. Sleva, Michael, illus. (p. 2001)
Wechsler, Nathalie. Once upon A Fly: The Adventures of Lamouche. Wechsler, Nathalie, illus. (p. 1292)
—Once upon A Fly - Hardcover: The Adventures of Lamouche. Wechsler, Nathalie, illus. (p. 1292)
Weck, Claudia de, illus. see Rechels, Kèathe, et al.
Weck, Claudia de, tr. see Rechels, Kèathe, et al.
Weck, Peter. Labyrinth. DiSalvo, Len, illus. (p. 970)
—Lima Bear's Halloween. DiSalvo, Len, illus. (p. 1018)
Weck, Peter, jt. auth. see Weck, Thomas.
Weck, Thomas & Weck, Peter. Bully Bean. DiSalvo, Len, illus. (p. 241)
Weckmann, Anke, illus. see Peters, Polly & Fusek Peters, Andrew.
Weckworth, Rodney R. Ponders, Proverbs & Principles. von Allmen, Tania, illus. (p. 1382)
Wedding, Linda. Blue-Eyed, Tri-Colored American Paint: A Lesson in Trust for Baby. (p. 202)
Weddington, Carole. D+Anger I'm Mad! Anger Management Teen Style. (p. 403)
Weddle, Nikki, jt. auth. see Weddle, Steve.
Weddle, Steve & Weddle, Nikki. Can Hedgehogs Jump? (p. 258)
Wedekind, Annie. Horse of Her Own. (p. 800)
—Samirah's Ride: The Story of an Arabian Filly. (p. 1507)
Wedekind, Annie, jt. auth. see Haas, Jessie.
Wedekind, Annie & Haas, Jessie. Little Prince: The Story of a Shetland Pony. (p. 1033)
—Wild Blue: The Story of a Mustang Appaloosa. Wedekind, Annie, illus. (p. 1929)
Wedeven, Carol. arca de Noé (Noah's 2-by-2 Adventure) - Bilingual. (p. 95)
—Easter Cave. (p. 499)
—Easter Cave. Ebert, Len, illus. (p. 499)

Wedge, Chris. Bunny: A Picture Book Adapted from the Animated Film. Wedge, Chris, illus. (p. 242)
Wedge, Hayden. Examining Shipwrecks. (p. 547)
Wedgeworth, Anthony G. Nums of Shoreview: Baka's Curse. (p. 1273)
—Nums of Shoreview: Unfair Trade. (p. 1273)
Wedgwood, Pam. More Up-Grade Piano. (p. 1175)
—Up-Grade Piano. (p. 1824)
Wedgwood, Pamela. Up-Grade Flute: Light Relief Between Grades. (p. 1824)
—Up-Grade! Piano. (p. 1824)
Wedman, Belgin K., illus. see Novesky, Amy.
Wedman, Belgin K., jt. auth. see Novesky, Amy.
Wedman, Paige Renee. Once upon a Whimsical Tale. (p. 1293)
Wedwick, Daryl M., jt. auth. see Lee, Briant H.
Wedzin, James, illus. see Football, Virginia & Mantia, Rosa.
Wedzin, James, illus. see Football, Virginia.
Wee Sing Staff. Games, Games, Games. (p. 655)
Weeber, Stephanie B., jt. auth. see Beach, Kathleen H.
Weed, Thurlow R. Camel Fables from the Sailors of the Sudan. (p. 256)
Weeder, H. Leonard. Architecture for Survival: In Our Nuclear World of the 21st Century. (p. 95)
Weedin, Chris. Horror Worlds. (p. 799)
Weedn, Flavia, illus. see York Lumbard, Alexis.
Week, Jason, illus. see Meyerhoff, Jenny.
Weekley, Randy J. Strangers, Bullies, Safety & More (Spanish Version) A How to Guide to Child Safety. (p. 1665)
Weekley, Randy/ J. Strangers Bullies Safety & More... A How to Guide to Child Safety. (p. 1665)
Weekly, Ellen M. Do Pigfish Really Oink? (p. 457)
Weekly Reader Early Learning Library Staff. Cosas con las Que Juego. (p. 368)
—Things I Play With. (p. 1733)
Weekly Reader Early Learning Library Staff, contrib. by. I Know Numbers/Los Números. (p. 840)
Weekly Reader Editorial Staff. Cosas Que Como. (p. 368)
—I Know Big & Small: Grande y Pequeño. (p. 840)
—I Know Numbers. (p. 840)
—I Know Same & Different. (p. 840)
—I Know Shapes: Las Figuras. (p. 840)
—I Know Shapes (Las Figuras) (p. 840)
—Numeros. (p. 1273)
—Things at Home (Las Cosas de Mi Casa) (p. 1733)
—Things at School (Las Cosas de la Escuela) (p. 1733)
—Things at School/Las Cosas de la Escuela. (p. 1733)
—Things at the Park. (p. 1733)
—Things at the Park (Las Cosas Del Parque) (p. 1733)
—Things at the Park/Las Cosas del Parque. (p. 1733)
—Things I Eat. (p. 1733)
—Things I Play With/Las Cosas con las Que Juego. (p. 1733)
—Things I Wear. (p. 1733)
—Things I Wear (Las cosas que me Pongo) (p. 1733)
Weekly Reader Editorial Staff, jt. auth. see Nations, Susan.
Weekly Reader Editorial Staff, contrib. by. I Know Big & Small. (p. 840)
—I Know Numbers. (p. 840)
—I Know Same & Different (Igual y Diferente) (p. 840)
—I Know Shapes. (p. 840)
—Things at Home (Las Cosas De Mi Casa) (p. 1733)
—Things at School. (p. 1733)
—Things at the Park. (p. 1733)
—Things I Eat/las Cosas Que Como. (p. 1733)
—Things I Wear. (p. 1733)
Weeks, jt. auth. see Weeks, Sarah.
Weeks, G. Brian. Adventures of Ricky Raccoon: Volume One. (p. 22)
—Adventures of Ricky Raccoon. (p. 22)
Weeks, Jeanne G., illus. see Weeks, Timothy A.
Weeks, Kermit. All of Life Is a School. Project Firefly, illus. (p. 45)
—Spirit of Lindy. Premise Entertainment, illus. (p. 1628)
Weeks, Lee, illus. see Casey, Joe & Reed, Brian.
Weeks, Marcus. Mozart: The Boy Who Changed the World with His Music. (p. 1184)
—World History Biographies: Mozart: The Boy Who Changed the World with His Music. (p. 1955)
Weeks, Marcus & Dorling Kindersley Publishing Staff. Heads up Psychology. (p. 757)
Weeks, Mary, illus. see Schneider, Judy.
Weeks, Sarah. Angel Face. Diaz, David, illus. (p. 73)
—As Simple as It Seems. (p. 105)
—Be Mine, Be Mine, Sweet Valentine. Kosaka, Fumi, illus. (p. 148)
—Cake Lady. (p. 252)
—Catfish Kate & the Sweet Swamp Band. Smith, Elwood H., illus. (p. 280)
—Counting Ovejas. Diaz, David, illus. (p. 371)
—Don't Discover Me. (p. 467)
—Ella, of Course! Cushman, Doug, illus. (p. 514)
—Follow the Moon. Duranceau, Suzanne, illus. (p. 612)
—Glamourpuss. Small, David, illus. (p. 682)
—Honey. (p. 794)
—If I Were a Lion. Solomon, Heather M., illus. (p. 853)
—I'm a Pig. Berry, Holly, illus. (p. 858)
—Jumping the Scratch. (p. 934)
—Little Farmer. (p. 1027)
—Mac & Cheese. Manning, Jane K., illus. (p. 1067)
—Mac & Cheese & the Perfect Plan. Manning, Jane, illus. (p. 1067)
—Michael. (p. 1134)
—Oggie Cooder. (p. 1280)
—Oggie Cooder - Party Animal! (p. 1280)
—Pie. (p. 1356)
—Pip Squeak. Manning, Jane K., illus. (p. 1361)
—Sophie Peterman Tells the Truth! Neubecker, Robert, illus. (p. 1613)
—Two Eggs, Please. Lewin, Betsy, illus. (p. 1803)
—What Is a Kiss? (p. 1888)
—Who's under That Hat? A Lift-the-Flap Pop-up Adventure. Carter, David A., illus. (p. 1921)
—Without You. Duranceau, Suzanne, illus. (p. 1942)
—Woof. Berry, Holly, illus. (p. 1950)
—Z Is for Zoe. (p. 1984)
Weeks, Sarah & Lewin, Betsy. Two Eggs, Please. (p. 1803)
Weeks, Sarah & Weeks. Baa-Choo! Manning, Jane K., illus. (p. 123)
—So B. It. (p. 1601)
Weeks, Sophie. Soured Earth. (p. 1616)
Weeks, Stephanie. Triplex Coniunctio: The Witch War Histories (p. 1787)
Weeks, Timothy. Wise Mullet of Cook Bayou. Jeanne, Miss, illus. (p. 1940)
Weeks, Timothy A. Goldie's Search for Silver: The Wise Mullet Finale! Weeks, Timothy A. & Weeks, Jeanne G., illus. (p. 696)
—Ol' Middler Saves the Day: A Mullet Buddy Homecoming. (p. 1283)
—Wise Mullet of Cook Bayou (p. 1940)
Weel, Rosalinda. Dream Clouds: Float Away with Seven Enchanting Children's Stories for Relaxation & Bedtime. (p. 483)
Weeldreyer, Laura. Everything You Need to Know about Volunteering. (p. 546)
Weems, Renita J. What Matters Most: Ten Lessons in Living Passionately from the Song of Solomon. (p. 1892)
Weerstand, R. Quintus: A Story about the Persecution of Christians at the Time of Emperor Nero. (p. 1428)
Weerts, Christine. Hero of Faith - Rosa Young. (p. 772)
Wegener, Bill. Bible Game - New Testament: The Bible Game - New Testament. (p. 175)
—Bible Game - Old Testament: The Bible Game - Old Testament. (p. 175)
Wegener, Scott, illus. see Marvel Comics Staff.
Wegener, Scott, illus. see Yost, Christopher.
Wegener, Scott & Scherberger, Patrick. Avengers: Earth's Mightiest Heroes. (p. 118)
Wegerif, Gay. Up Close. (p. 1824)
Weglarz, Lynn. I Can Sew. Frank, Sharon, ed. (p. 836)
Wegman, Marcia. Lula Belle. Wegman, Marcia, illus. (p. 1064)
Wegman, William. 3... 2... 1... Circus! (p. 1991)
—Chip Wants a Dog. (p. 308)
—Dress up Batty. Wegman, William, illus. (p. 485)
—Early Rider. (p. 494)
—Farm Days. Wegman, William, illus. (p. 573)
—Flo & Wendell. (p. 605)
—Hardly Boys. (p. 748)
Wegmuller, Akemi, tr. see Takemoto, Novala.
Wegner, Fritz, illus. see Winterfeld, Henry.
Wegner, Jennifer Houser, jt. auth. see Forest, Christopher.
Wegwerth, A. L. Stegosaurus (p. 1646)
—Tyrannosaurus Rex (p. 1805)
Wehmeyer, Michael L. Promoting Self-Determination in Students with Developmental Disabilities. (p. 1411)
Wehner, Adrienna. Elephants & Roses. (p. 511)
Wehr, Julian. Snow White. (p. 1599)
Wehr, Julian, illus. see Wehr, Paul.
Wehr, Paul. Animated Bunny's Tail. Wehr, Julian, illus. (p. 84)
Wehrheim, Carol. Friends & Family in Faith: Faith for Life2 Course One Teacher Guide. Janssen, Patricia E., ed. (p. 638)
—My Friendship Album: Faith for Life2 Course One Student Book. Janssen, Patricia E., ed. (p. 1209)
—My Research Notes Student Book. (p. 1217)
—Time for Jesus. (p. 1751)
Wehrheim, Carol A. Word & Picture Books: For Year C/A Set 2 (p. 1950)
—Word & Picture Books: For Year A/B Set 3 (p. 1950)
Wehrley, Susan K. Secret to I Am: A True Story - Discover Courage, Truth, Purpose, & Peace in Difficult Times. (p. 1544)
Wehrman, Richard, illus. see Martin, Rafe.
Wehrman, Tom. Grandpa's a Martian. Dunnier, Tina, illus. (p. 709)
Wehrman, Vicki, illus. see Ehrmantraut, Brenda.
Wehrman, Vicki, illus. see Lehman-Wilzig, Tami.
Wehrmeijer, Annelien. Anik & Yukon. van de Liejgraaf, Deborah, illus. (p. 76)
—Jacob & Rex. van de Liejgraaf, Deborah, illus. (p. 904)
—Kato & Simba. van de Liejgraaf, Deborah, illus. (p. 945)
—Mimi & Ling. van de Liejgraaf, Deborah, illus. (p. 1145)
—Noah & Dexter. van de Liejgraaf, Deborah, illus. (p. 1261)
—Ruby & Molly. van de Liejgraaf, Deborah, illus. (p. 1493)
—Sophie & Daisy. van de Liejgraaf, Deborah, illus. (p. 1613)
—Tariq & Mika. van de Liejgraaf, Deborah, illus. (p. 1706)
Wei, Deborah, ed. see Cheung, Shu Pui, et al.
Wei, Miao, illus. see Ma, Zheng & Li, Zheng.
Weibel, Suzy, jt. auth. see Gresh, Dannah K.
Weicker, Gretchen. Kanye West: Hip-Hop Star. (p. 943)
Weidemann, Christiane. Year in Art: The Activity Book. (p. 1969)
Weidemann, Linda, illus. see Christian, David.
Weidensee, Ralph. Cry'N Lion. (p. 387)
Weider, Nicole. Project Inspired: Tips & Tricks for Staying True to Who You Are (p. 1410)
Weidknecht, Lisa. E Is for Emotions. (p. 492)
Weidman, James, illus. see Schombs, James.
Weidman, Meg, jt. auth. see Hays, K. D.
Weidner, Teri. Always Twins. Weidner, Teri, illus. (p. 51)
—Five Little Ducks. (p. 600)
—Sleep, Baby, Sleep. (p. 1588)
—Three Little Kittens. Weidner, Teri, illus. (p. 1742)
Weidner, Teri, illus. see Brown, Margaret Wise.
Weidner, Teri, illus. see Heinrichs, Ann.
Weidner, Teri, illus. see Hueston, M. P.
Weidner, Teri, illus. see Shoulders, Michael.
Weidner, Teri, illus. see Spelman, Cornelia Maude.
Weidner, Teri, illus. see York, J.
Weidner, Teri, illus. see Zimmerman, Brooke.
Weidt, Maryann N. Daddy Played Music for the Cows. Sorensen, Henri, illus. (p. 398)
—Fighting for Equal Rights: A Story about Susan B. Anthony. Sartor, Amanda, tr. (p. 585)
Weierbach, Jane & Phillips-Hershey, Elizabeth. Mind over Basketball: Coach Yourself to Handle Stress. Beyl, Charles, illus. (p. 1145)
Weigand, Edith S. If Mandy Ruled the World. (p. 853)
Weigand, Jessica. I Have a Monster under My Bed. (p. 839)
Weigand, John, photos by see Dyan, Penelope.
Weigand, John, photos by see Hillan, Pamela & Dyan, Penelope.
Weigand, John D. Wonderful, Wonderful Copenhagen! a Kid's Guide to Copenhagen, Denmark. Dyan, Penelope, photos by. (p. 1948)
Weigand, John D., illus. see Dyan, Penelope.
Weigand, John D., photos by see Dyan, Penelope.
Weigand, John D., photos by see Hillan, Pamela & Dyan, Penelope.
Weigant, Chris. Choosing a Career in Computers. (p. 310)
Weigel, Hans, ed. see Schnitzler, Arthur.
Weigel, Jeff. Atomic Ace & the Robot Rampage. Weigel, Jeff, illus. (p. 113)
—Dragon Girl: the Secret Valley. (p. 477)
Weigel, Jeff, illus. see Spradlin, Michael P.
Weigel, Marlene. U-X-L Encyclopedia of Biomes. (p. 1807)
Weigelt, Udo. Becky the Borrower. Weigelt, Udo & Henn, Astrid, illus. (p. 156)
—Hide Easter Bunny Hide. Kadmon, Christina, illus. (p. 777)
Weight, Jay. She's an Angel. (p. 1566)
Weightman, Amelia. Piggy Tales: Escape to the Orchard. (p. 1358)
Weightman, Bud & Williams, Amelia. Peeper the Duck. (p. 1335)
Weigl Publishers, creator. Crab & Its Mother: What Is the Best Way to Teach Others? (p. 375)
—Crow & the Raven: Why Should You Be Yourself? (p. 385)
—Farmer & His Sons: Why Should You Work Hard? (p. 574)
—Goose & the Golden Egg: What Happens When You Are Greedy? (p. 702)
—Lion & the Mouse: Can Little Friends Be Great Friends? (p. 1020)
—Milk Woman & Her Pail: What Happens If You Count on Getting Something Before You Have It? (p. 1143)
—Shoemaker & His Medicine: Why Should You Tell the Truth? (p. 1568)
—Snake & His Tail: How Can You Support Your Team? (p. 1596)
—Wild Donkey & the Tame Donkey: Why Should You Not Judge Others by Their Appearance? (p. 1929)
Weigl Publishers Staff & Craats, Rennay. For the Love of Skateboarding. Nault, Jennifer & Turner, Kara, eds. (p. 616)
Weigman, Matthew. Liberty's Journey: The Story of Our Freedom. Eve, Lealand, illus. (p. 1005)
Weihrich, Carroll. In the Meantime. (p. 866)
—On Jim Street. (p. 1289)
—Out on Windfern. (p. 1311)
Weihs, Erika, illus. see Chaikin, Miriam.
Weihs, Erika, illus. see Kimmel, Eric A.
Weihs, Sally. Big Blue Goes Green. (p. 178)
Weikart, Cindy. Ohio Graduation Test: Science Study Guide. (p. 1281)
Weikart, Phyllis S. Movement in Steady Beat: Learning on the Move, Ages 3-7. (p. 1183)
Weikert, Dana, jt. illus. see O'Kane, George.
Weikert Stelmach, Katherine, jt. auth. see Amdahl Elco, Anita.
Weil, Ann. Australia. (p. 116)
—Betsy Ross: Creator of Our Flag. Fiorentino, Al, illus. (p. 172)
—BMX Racing (p. 204)
—Bomb-Sniffing Dogs. (p. 208)
—British Redcoats (p. 230)
—Deadly Storms (p. 418)
—Earthquakes (p. 497)
—Ecological Disasters (p. 502)
—Fire Disasters (p. 590)
—Geronimo (p. 667)
—Ice Skating. Fletcher, Rusty, illus. (p. 850)
—Italy in Our World. (p. 895)
—Medgar Evers (p. 1118)
—Medgar Evers Oxford Bible Staff, illus. (p. 1118)
—Meet Our New Student from Australia. (p. 1121)
—Meet Our New Student from Malaysia. (p. 1122)
—Meet Our New Student from New Zealand. (p. 1122)
—Meet Our New Student from Quebec. (p. 1122)
—Mountain Disasters (p. 1180)
—Pro Wrestling Greats (p. 1408)
—Sea Disasters (p. 1534)
—Sitting Bull (p. 1582)
—Space Disasters (p. 1619)
—Story Behind Silk (p. 1656)
—Terrorism (p. 1722)
—Volcanoes (p. 1849)
—World's Most Amazing Castles (p. 1960)
—World's Most Amazing Dams (p. 1960)
—World's Most Amazing Lost Cities (p. 1960)
—World's Most Amazing Monuments (p. 1960)
—World's Most Amazing National Parks (p. 1960)
—World's Most Amazing Pyramids (p. 1960)
Weil, Ann, jt. auth. see Weil, Anne.
Weil, Ann & Guillain, Charlotte. American Indian Cultures (p. 62)
Weil, Anne & Weil, Ann. Matter of Survival: Properties of Matter (p. 1109)
Weil, Bonnie Eaker, see Eaker Weil, Bonnie.
Weil, Cynthia. I'm Glad I Did. (p. 859)
Weil, Elizabeth, jt. auth. see Maniatis, Amy.
Weil, Jamie. Jeff Bezos: Founder of Amazon. com. (p. 911)
—Mark Zuckerberg: Creator of Facebook. (p. 1095)
Weil, Jennifer. Marvin's Lump. (p. 1100)
Weil, Sylvie. Elvina's Mirror. (p. 517)
—My Guardian Angel. Rosner, Gillian, tr. from FRE. (p. 1210)
Weil, Zoe. Claude & Medea: The Hellburn Dogs. (p. 329)
Weiland, Carla, et al. Truth about Illness & Disease. (p. 1794)
Weiland, Peter. So Big yet So Small. Coffey, Kevin, illus. (p. 1601)
Weilerstein, Sadie Rose. Jewish Heroes Cassel, Lili, illus. (p. 917)
Weill, Catherine. Frédéric Chopin. Voake, Charlotte, illus. (p. 633)
—Fryderyk Choppin. Voake, Charlotte, illus. (p. 646)
Weill, Cynthia. ABeCedarios: Mexican Folk Art ABCs in English & Spanish. Basseches, K. B., photos by. (p. 4)
—Count Me In: A Parade of Mexican Folk Art Numbers in English & Spanish. Aguilar Sisters Staff, illus. (p. 369)
—My Skeleton Family. de Oaxaco, Jesus & Zarate, Jesus, illus. (p. 1219)
—Opuestos: Mexican Folk Art Opposites in English & Spanish. (p. 1301)
Weill, Cynthia & Cinco Puntos Press Staff. Colores de la Vida: Mexican Folk Art Colors in English & Spanish. (p. 344)
Weiman, Jon, illus. see Hollenbeck, Kathleen M.
Weiman, Jon, illus. see Lingemann, Linda.
Weimer, Heidi. I Love You More Than.... (p. 843)
—You're My Little Love Bug! (p. 1982)
—You're My Little Love Bug. Sharp, Chris, illus. (p. 1982)
Weimer, Heidi R. Happy Birthday to You! (p. 745)
—How Do I Kiss You? Sharp, Chris, illus. (p. 807)
—Love from My Heart: To a Snuggly Cuddly Little Boy. (p. 1059)
—Love from My Heart: To a Precious Sweet Little Girl. (p. 1059)
Wein, Berel & Mahr, Aryeh. Of Heaven & Earth: Stories of the Chassidic Masters. (p. 1279)
Wein, Elizabeth. Black Dove, White Raven. (p. 196)
—Coalition of Lions. (p. 336)
—Code Name Verity. (p. 338)
—Rose under Fire. (p. 1489)
Wein, Len. Secret of the Swamp Thing. Wrightson, Berni, illus. (p. 1543)
Wein, Len, jt. auth. see Conway, Gerry.
Wein, Len & Wolfman, Marv. Fantastic Four: The Overthrow of Doom. Perez, George & Pollard, Keith, illus. (p. 571)
Wein, Len, et al. House of Mystery (p. 803)
Weinand, Margaret & Johnson, Thomas M. Tommy's Treasured Christmas Tree. (p. 1765)
Weinbach, Shaindel. Cartons in the Air & Other Stories. Dershowitz, Yosef, illus. (p. 272)
—Friendly Persuader & Other Stories. Dershowitz, Yosef, illus. (p. 638)
—Shimmee & the Taste-Me Tree. Backman, Aidel, illus. (p. 1566)
Weinbach, Shaindel, tr. see Matov, G.
Weinberg, Devorah, illus. see Yerushalmi, Miriam.
Weinberg, James, illus. see Nayeri, Daniel.
Weinberg, Jennifer. Happy Birthday, Princess! (Disney Princess) Marrucchi, Elisa, illus. (p. 745)
—Surprise for a Princess. (p. 1685)
Weinberg, Jennifer & RH Disney Staff. Surprise for a Princess. Emslie, Peter & Marrucchi, Elisa, illus. (p. 1685)
Weinberg, Jennifer Liberts. Christmas Toys. (p. 316)
—Christmas Toys (Disney/Pixar Toy Story) RH Disney Staff, illus. (p. 316)
—Doc Mcstuffins: Blame It on the Rain. (p. 459)
—Fly, Dumbo, Fly! Kurtz, John & Lo Raso, Carlo, illus. (p. 609)
—Happy Birthday, Mike! (p. 745)
—Happy Birthday, Mike! (Disney/Pixar Monsters, Inc.) RH Disney Staff, illus. (p. 745)
—Happy Birthday, Princess! (p. 745)
—Pretty Pearl Mermaid. (p. 1398)
—Princess Hearts. (p. 1404)
—Princess Hearts (Disney Princess) RH Disney Staff & Legramandi, Francesco, illus. (p. 1404)
—Princesses & Puppies. (p. 1406)
—Princesses & Puppies (Disney Princess) Legramandi, Francesco & Matta, Gabriella, illus. (p. 1406)
—This Little Piggy (Disney Junior: Minnie's Bow-Toons) RH Disney Staff, illus. (p. 1737)
Weinberg, Jennifer Liberts, jt. auth. see Disney Book Group Staff.
Weinberg, Jennifer Liberts, jt. auth. see Posner-Sanchez, Andrea.
Weinberg, Jennifer Liberts & RH Disney Staff. What Is a Princess? Harchy, Atelier Philippe, illus. (p. 1888)
Weinberg, Leonard & Eubank, William L. What Is Terrorism? (p. 1890)
Weinberg, Moshe. Unforgettable Journey. (p. 1817)
Weinberg, Steven. Rex Finds an Egg! Egg! Egg! Weinberg, Steven, illus. (p. 1467)
Weinberg, Steven, illus. see Kramer, Lance.
Weinberg, Steven, illus. see Scieszka, Casey.
Weinberger, David J. Answers to a Christmas Question. (p. 88)
—Answers to a Christmas Question Coloring Book. (p. 88)
Weinberger, Kimberly. Dolphin's Big Leap. Ziss, Debra, illus. (p. 465)
—Let's Read About— Pocahontas. Marchesi, Stephen, illus. (p. 1000)
Weinbrecht, William. Stories for Amand. (p. 1654)
Weinbrenner, Darlene. Hannah, Mable, & the Moving Van. (p. 742)
—My Silly Willy Loose Tooth. Weinbrenner, Jacquelyn, illus. (p. 1218)
Weinbrenner, Jacquelyn, illus. see Weinbrenner, Darlene.
Weindorf, William J., jt. auth. see Mazur, Glen A.
Weiner, Brian. Toad Catchers' Creek. Weintraub, Claudia & Frederick, Robin, eds. (p. 1759)
Weiner, Devora. White Ice. (p. 1913)
Weiner, Ellis. Make a Scene Holmes, Jeremy, illus. (p. 1078)
—Templeton Twins Have an Idea: Book 1. Holmes, Jeremy, illus. (p. 1718)
—Templeton Twins Have an Idea. Holmes, Jeremy, illus. (p. 1718)
—Templeton Twins Make a Scene: Book 2. Holmes, Jeremy, illus. (p. 1718)
Weiner, Eric, jt. auth. see Inches, Alison.
Weiner, Eric & Golden Books Staff. Trick or Treat! (p. 1786)
Weiner, Eric J. What Goes Up: The Uncensored History of Modern Wall Street as Told by the Bankers, Brokers, Ceos, & Scoundrels Who Made It Happen. (p. 1885)
Weiner, Joan. Frege Explained. (p. 635)
Weiner, Jonathan, illus. see English, Karen.
Weiner, Kimberly. Not My Reality. (p. 1267)
Weiner, Lawrence. Lawrence Weiner. (p. 981)
Weiner, Linda, ed. see Monnar, Alberto.
Weiner, Marcella Bakur, jt. auth. see Neimark, Jill.

W

Weiner, Marcella Bakur & Neimark, Jill. I Want Your Moo: A Story for Children about Self-Esteem. Adinolfi, JoAnn, illus. (p. 848)
Weiner, Miriam. Shakespeare's Seasons. Whitt, Shannon, illus. (p. 1559)
Weiner, Rex. American Photo Mission to India: Portrait of a Volunteer Surgical Team in Action. Schoenfeld, Wayne, photos by. (p. 62)
Weiner, Roberta, jt. auth. see Arnold, James R.
Weiner, Stephen, jt. auth. see Couch, N. C. Christopher.
Weiner, Vicki. Brooklyn Bridge: New York City's Graceful Connection. (p. 231)
Weiner-Booth, Patsy. Day Santa Met Jesus: A Christmas story & Play. (p. 414)
Weinert, Matthias. No Bath, No Cake! Polly's Pirate Party. (p. 1257)
Weinert, Stella, compiled by. Come on Clouds, Fly Away! (p. 347)
Weinfeld, Chaya Baila. Unexpected Detour: And Other Stories. (p. 1817)
Weing, Drew, jt. auth. see Davis, Eleanor.
Weingart, Sharlene. Grandpa's Proud Loud. (p. 710)
Weingarten, A. J. Rock Climbing. (p. 1482)
Weingarten, E. T. Fishing. (p. 599)
Weingarten, E. T., jt. auth. see Weingarten, Ethan.
Weingarten, Ethan. Graphs with Giraffes. (p. 711)
—Transylvania. (p. 1779)
—What Is a Circuit? (p. 1888)
Weingarten, Ethan & Weingarten, E. T. Graphs with Giraffes. (p. 711)
Weingarten, Lynn. Book of Love. (p. 211)
—Secret Sisterhood of Heartbreakers. (p. 1543)
—Suicide Notes from Beautiful Girls. (p. 1673)
—Wherever Nina Lies. (p. 1911)
Weingarth, Poss. Gurgle, Gurgle Splash: I'm Always in a Hurry. (p. 732)
Weingartner, Amy, jt. auth. see RH Disney Staff.
Weingärtner, Jörn. Arts as a Weapon of War: Britain & the Shaping of National Morale in the Second World War. (p. 105)
Weingast, Susana. Percepcion simbolica en el Arte. Weingast, Susana, illus. (p. 1341)
Weinhaus, Anthony J., jt. auth. see Korb, Rena B.
Weinheimer, Kim. Bear Song. (p. 151)
Weinhold, Angela. Bosque. (p. 214)
Weinick, Suzanne. How Do I Use an Encyclopedia? (p. 807)
—Professional Connections: Learning How to Network. (p. 1409)
Weinman, Brad, illus. see Holm, Jennifer L. & Hamel, Jonathan.
Weinman, Brad, illus. see Neimark, Anne E.
Weinman, Brad, illus. see Vande Velde, Vivian.
Weinman, Logan & Bennett, Jeffrey. Max's Ice Age Adventure. (p. 1112)
Weinmann, Julianne. Mis-Adventures of Frissue the Tissue. (p. 1149)
Weinmeister, Cleo. Time to Go. (p. 1753)
Weinreb, Matthew, photos by see Meek, H. A.
Weinsberg, Edgar. Conquer Prostate Cancer: How Medicine, Faith, Love & Sex Can Renew Your Life. (p. 358)
Weinshall Liberman, Judith. Ice Cream Snow. (p. 850)
—Little Fairy. (p. 1027)
Weinstein, Anna. Kevin Jones: Snowboarding Superstar. (p. 950)
—Kevin Jones, Snowboarding Superstar. (p. 950)
Weinstein Books Staff, jt. auth. see Hunt, Elizabeth Singer.
Weinstein, Bruce D. Is It Still Cheating If I Don't Get Caught? Russell, Harriet, illus. (p. 889)
Weinstein, Grit. Tale of the Little Duckling: Who Am I & Where Do I Belong? O'Shea, Miranda, illus. (p. 1700)
Weinstein, Holly, illus. see Shear, Dani.
Weinstein, Howard. Mickey Mantle. (p. 1136)
Weinstein, Muriel Harris. Play, Louis, Play! The True Story of a Boy & His Horn. Morrison, Frank, illus. (p. 1371)
Weinstein, Natalie. Katrina's New Room. Pluum, Ave, illus. (p. 945)
Weinstein, Robert A., jt. auth. see Greenfeld, Barbara.
Weinstein, Stephen. Final Solution. (p. 586)
Weinstein, Susan. Tales of the Mer Family Onyx: Mermaid Stories on Land & under the Sea. (p. 1702)
Weinstock, Tony, illus. see Ferreri, Della Ross.
Weinstone, David. Music Class Today! Vogel, Vin, illus. (p. 1193)
Weintraub, A. How to Draw District of Columbia's Sights & Symbols. (p. 817)
—How to Draw Nebraska's Sights & Symbols. (p. 818)
—How to Draw New Mexico's Sights & Symbols. (p. 818)
—How to Draw Ohio's Sights & Symbols. (p. 818)
—How to Draw Rhode Island's Sights & Symbols. (p. 818)
—How to Draw South Carolina's Sights & Symbols. (p. 818)
—How to Draw Texas's Sights & Symbols. (p. 818)
—How to Draw Washington's Sights & Symbols. (p. 819)
Weintraub, Aileen. Alcatraz Island Light: The West Coast's First Lighthouse. (p. 35)
—Barbarossa Brothers: 16th-Century Pirates of the Barbary Coast. (p. 137)
—Boston Light: The First Lighthouse in North America. (p. 215)
—Bowhunting. (p. 216)
—Cape Disappointment Light: The First Lighthouse in the Pacific Northwest. (p. 262)
—Cape Hatteras Light: The Tallest Lighthouse in the United States. (p. 262)
—Captain Kidd: 17th-Century Pirate of the Indian Ocean & African Coast. (p. 264)
—Choosing a Career in Child Care. (p. 310)
—Discovering Africa's Land, People, & Wildlife: A MyReportLinks. com Book. (p. 448)
—Discovering Europe's Land, People, & Wildlife: A MyReportLinks. com Book. (p. 449)
—Everything You Need to Know about Being a Babysitter: A Teen's Guide to Responsible Child Care. (p. 545)
—Everything You Need to Know about Being a Baby-sitter: A Teen's Guide to Responsible Child Care. (p. 545)
—Everything You Need to Know about Eating Smart. (p. 545)
—First Response by Sea. (p. 596)
—Grand Canyon: The Widest Canyon. (p. 707)
—Henry Morgan: 17th-Century Buccaneer. (p. 768)
—Heroin: A MyReportLinks. com Book. (p. 773)
—Jean Lafitte: Pirate Hero of the War Of 1812. (p. 911)
—Kiss: I Wanna Rock & Roll All Night. (p. 961)
—Knock Knock Book: Jokes Guaranteed to Leave Your Friends in Stitches. (p. 965)
—Lee Sobre George Washington/Read about George Washington. (p. 987)
—Library of Pirates (p. 1006)
—Mount Everest: The Highest Mountain. (p. 1180)
—Navesink Twin Lights: The First U. S. Lighthouse to Use a Fresnel Lens. (p. 1237)
—Nile: The Longest River. (p. 1255)
—Pacific Ocean: The Largest Ocean. (p. 1317)
—Point Pinos Light: The West Coast's Oldest Continuously Active Lighthouse. (p. 1377)
—Read about George Washington. (p. 1442)
—Rock Climbing. (p. 1482)
—Sahara Desert: The Biggest Desert. (p. 1503)
Weintraub, Aileen, tr. Cape Hatteras Light: The Tallest Lighthouse in the United States. (p. 262)
Weintraub, Claudia, ed. see Weiner, Brian.
Weintraub, David, jt. auth. see Harris, Rae Ann.
Weir, Arabella. Does My Bum Look Big in This? (p. 460)
—Does My Bum Look Big in This? The Diary of an Insecure Woman. (p. 460)
Weir, Ben. Maggie's Money: Understanding Addition & Subtraction. (p. 1071)
Weir, Carrie, illus. see Ferguson, Gloria.
Weir, Christina, jt. auth. see DeFilippis, Nunzio.
Weir, Christina, jt. auth. see Defilippis, Nunzio.
Weir, Christina & Defilippis, Nunzio. Maria's Wedding. (p. 1093)
Weir, Cyril, jt. auth. see Weir, Cyril J.
Weir, Cyril J. & Weir, Cyril. Language Testing & Validation: An Evidence-Based Approach. (p. 975)
Weir, Doffy, illus. see Umansky, Kaye & Umansky, Kaye.
Weir, Doffy, illus. see Umansky, Kaye.
Weir, Jaime L. Out of Bed. (p. 1311)
Weir, Jane. Forces & Motion (p. 617)
—Inside the World of Matter. (p. 878)
—Investigating Forces & Motion. (p. 884)
—Isaac Newton: Groundbreaking Physicist & Mathematician (p. 890)
—Isaac Newton & the Laws of the Universe. (p. 890)
—Matter (p. 1109)
—Max Planck: Revolutionary Physicist (p. 1111)
—Max Planck: Uncovering the World of Matter. (p. 1111)
Weir, Kirsten. Bugs That Help. (p. 237)
—Bugs That Live on Animals. (p. 237)
Weir, Kirsten & Brent, Lynnette. Elements & Compounds. (p. 510)
—States of Matter. (p. 1644)
Weir, Liz. Boom Chicka Boom. Lizatovic, Josip, illus. (p. 213)
—Here, There & Everywhere: Stories from Many Lands. (p. 770)
Weir, Marjorie Van Winkle. Book of Treasured Words. (p. 212)
Weir, Nolet, illus. see Ferguson, Gloria.
Weir, Patricia. My Kitty & Me. (p. 1211)
Weir, Susan, illus. see Gelderman, Robert G.
Weir, Theresa, see Frasier, Anne, pseud.
Weir, Thurlow. Young Man's Journey Through World War II. (p. 1979)
Weir, William. Border Patrol. (p. 214)
—Wright Brothers: The First to Fly. (p. 1963)
Weir, William, jt. auth. see Mills, Nathan.
Weis, Carol. When the Cows Got Loose. Hoyt, Ard, illus. (p. 1904)
Weis, Claudia Brigitte. B R A H A M: Bist du neugierig? (p. 123)
Weis, Lyle Percy. Let's Wrestle. (p. 1001)
Weis, Margaret, et al. Towers of High Sorcery. (p. 1773)
Weis, Michael David. Diamond & the Fosters. Avant, Matthew, illus. (p. 434)
Weis, Ms. Jane. Silas the Special Swan. (p. 1575)
Weisbarth, Bracha. To Live & Fight Another Day: The Story of a Jewish Partisan Boy. (p. 1759)
Weisberg, Barbara & Haley, Alex. Coronado's Golden Quest. Eagle, Mike, illus. (p. 368)
Weisberg, E. Gathering Roses. (p. 658)
Weisberg, Ellen & Yoffe, Ken. All Across Chin. (p. 43)
Weisblatt, Jayne & Perez, Orlando J., eds. World Encyclopedia of Political Systems & Parties, 3-Volume Set (p. 1955)
Weisbrod, Aaron. Nightmare World: Knee Deep in the Dead & Other Tales of Terror. (p. 1255)
—Nightmare World: The Same Deep Water as You & Other Stories of Suspense. (p. 1255)
Weisbrod, Eva. Student's Guide to F. Scott Fitzgerald. (p. 1669)
Weisburd, Claudia & Sniad, Tamara. Afterschool Style Guide: Graffitiwall. (p. 29)
—Global GraffitiWall. (p. 684)
Weisburd, Claudia, et al. Afterschool Style in Practice: 25 Skill-Building Meetngs for Staff. (p. 29)
Weisburd, Stefi. Barefoot: Poems for Naked Feet. McElrath-Eslick, Lori, illus. (p. 139)
Weise, Mutch, jt. auth. see Hamilton, Martha.
Weisel, Kaitlyn E., jt. auth. see Davis, Lynda S.
Weisell, Sandra Rabey, ed. Great Playwrights. (p. 718)
Weisenfeld, Aron, jt. auth. see Kelly, Joe.
Weisenfluh, C. C. In the Garden with the LittleWeeds: A Counting Book for Little Ones. Freeman, Julie, illus. (p. 866)
Weisenfluh, Craig. ABC's in the Trees, a LittleWeeds Adventure: A book for Little Ones. (p. 4)
Weiser, Joey. Mermin. (p. 1128)
—Mermin Volume 2: the Big Catch: The Big Catch. (p. 1128)
—Ride Home. (p. 1471)
Weiser, Robert, ed. see Lee, Julia Elizabeth.
Weisgard, Leonard, illus. see Brown, Margaret Wise.
Weisgard, Leonard, illus. see Wahl, Jan.
Weisgerber, Amy, jt. auth. see Bender, Abby.
Weisgerber, Amy, jt. auth. see Rosenbaum, Jason.
Weishaar, Mary Konya & Scott, Victoria Joan Groves. Practical Cases in Special Education for All Educators. (p. 1392)
Weishampel, W. A. Mystery of the Green Stone (p. 1225)
Weishampel, Winifred Ann, illus. see Gibson, Steve.
Weisheit, Eldon. 150 Psalms for Teens. (p. 2000)
Weiskal, N. J. C Is for the Christ Child. (p. 250)
Weiskal, N. J., jt. auth. see Weiskal, N. J.
Weiskal, N. J. & Weiskal, N. J. Skittery Kitten & the Scaredy Cat. Weiskal, N. J., illus. (p. 1586)
Weiskel, Portia Williams. Moliere. (p. 1160)
Weisleder, Stanley. Wings of the Panther. (p. 1936)
Weisman, Alan. Countdown: Our Last, Best Hope for a Future on Earth? (p. 370)
Weisman, Greg. Clan Building Vado, Dan & de Guzman, Jennifer, eds. (p. 326)
—Gargoyles #1. (p. 657)
—Rain of the Ghosts. (p. 1435)
—Spirits of Ash & Foam. (p. 1629)
—The Amazing Spider-Man. Quinones, Joe et al, illus. (p. 1724)
Weisman, Greg, et al. Rabbit Holes Davis, Dan, illus. (p. 1429)
—Wonderland Jones, Christopher, illus. (p. 1948)
Weisman, Jordan, jt. auth. see Stewart, Sean.
Weisman, Linda Klein. Yes, I Can Read! (p. 1970)
Weisner, Candace. Let's Get Going! The Step-by-Step Guide to Successful Outings with Children Leonard, Terry, illus. (p. 997)
Weisner, David. Mr. Wuffles! Weisner, David, illus. (p. 1187)
Weisner, Jane Lee. Who Am I? Yoga for Children of All Ages. White, Annie, illus. (p. 1914)
Weiss, Bernard P. I Am Jewish. (p. 833)
Weiss, Bobbi, jt. auth. see Wax, Wendy.
Weiss, Bobbi & Weiss, David. Hiro Dragon Warrior: Battle at Mount Kamado. Short, Robbie, illus. (p. 781)
—Hiro: Dragon Warrior: Level 2. Short, Robbie, illus. (p. 781)
—Monsters: The Hunt & the Capture. Deen, David, illus. (p. 1169)
—Twisted Tales II (p. 1802)
Weiss, Bobbi Jg & Weiss, David Cody. Phonic Comics - Hiro Dragon Warrior: Fight or Flight Level 2, Issue 3. (p. 1351)
Weiss, Carrie & Lukes, Jessica. Step into the Courtroom: An Overview of Laws, Courts & Jury Trials. (p. 1648)
Weiss, D. A. Parker & Phoebe & the Penguin Tour Guide. (p. 1324)
—Parker & Phoebe in the Wondrous Garden. (p. 1324)
—Parker & Phoebe K9 Time Travelers. (p. 1324)
Weiss, David. Carl the Frog. (p. 269)
Weiss, David, jt. auth. see Weiss, Bobbi.
Weiss, David Cody, jt. auth. see Weiss, Bobbi Jg.
Weiss, Douglas. Ten-Minute Marriage Principle: Quick, Daily Steps for Refreshing Your Relationship. (p. 1719)
Weiss, Ellen. African Elephant: American Museum of Natural History Book & Diorama. Popeson, Pamela, illus. (p. 27)
—Babar: Four Stories to Read & Share. Gibert, Jean Claude & Gray, J. M. L., illus. (p. 123)
—Bathtime for Twins. Williams, Sam, illus. (p. 144)
—Christmastime Is Here! SI Artists Staff, illus. (p. 316)
—Eloise & the Very Secret Room. Lyon, Tammie Speer & Lyon, Tammie, illus. (p. 516)
—Feeling Happy: A Turn-and-Learn Emotions Book. Bennett, Andy, illus. (p. 580)
—From Bulb to Daffodil. (p. 642)
—From Eye to Potato. (p. 642)
—From Kernel to Corncob. (p. 643)
—From Pinecone to Pine Tree. (p. 643)
—From Pit to Peach Tree. (p. 643)
—From Seed to Dandelion. (p. 643)
—Fruit Salad: A Touch-and-Learn Book. Bennett, Andy, illus. (p. 645)
—I Don't Want to Go to School! A Fold-Out Surprise Book. Bennett, Andy, illus. (p. 838)
—I Love You, Little Monster. Arnold, Alli, illus. (p. 843)
—Let's Go to the Zoo! SI Artists Staff, illus. (p. 998)
—Lucky Duck. Lies, Brian, illus. (p. 1062)
—Math in the Backyard. (p. 1106)
—Math in the Car. (p. 1106)
—Math in the Kitchen. (p. 1106)
—Math in the Neighborhood. (p. 1106)
—Math on the Playground. (p. 1106)
—Mystery of Microsneezia: A ClueFinders Mystery Adventure. (p. 1224)
—Odd Jobs: The Wackiest Jobs You've Never Heard Of. Ross, Damon, photos by. (p. 1278)
—Playtime for Twins. Williams, Sam, illus. (p. 1373)
—Sense of Sight. (p. 1551)
—Sense of Smell. (p. 1551)
—Sense of Taste. (p. 1551)
—Simba's Moon. Cuddy, Robin, illus. (p. 1577)
—Taming of Lola: A Shrew Story. Smath, Jerry, illus. (p. 1704)
—Twins in the Park. Williams, Sam, illus. (p. 1802)
—Whatever You Do, I Love You. Williams, Sam, illus. (p. 1896)
—Winter Spring Summer Fall: A Touch-and-Feel Seasons Book. Bennett, Andy, illus. (p. 1938)
Weiss, Ellen, jt. auth. see Froeb, Lori C.
Weiss, Ellen & Friedman, Mel. Jimmy Carter: Champion of Peace. (p. 918)
—Porky & Bess. Winborn, Marsha, illus. (p. 1386)
—Stinky Giant. Girasole, Alessia, illus. (p. 1651)
Weiss, Ellen & Gormley, Beatrice. President George W. Bush: Our Forty-Third President. (p. 1397)
Weiss, Ellen & Nelson, Marybeth. Dinosaur Rescue. Weiss, Ellen & Nelson, Marybeth, illus. (p. 442)
—Elmo's Beautiful Day. Weiss, Ellen & Nelson, Marybeth, illus. (p. 515)
Weiss, Esti, jt. auth. see Rosenberg, Faigy.
Weiss, Flo. Little Bit Is Big Enough. (p. 1024)
Weiss, Fred G. Mag-Nan-I-Mous Monkey & Gerald Giraffe. (p. 1071)
Weiss, George David, jt. auth. see Thiele, Bob.
Weiss, Harvey, illus. see Simon, Norma.
Weiss, Jennifer, ed. see Sanchez, Alex.
Weiss, Jim, jt. auth. see Phillips, Robin.
Weiss, Lynne. Crispus Attucks & the Boston Massacre. (p. 383)
—Frederick Douglass & the Abolitionist Movement. (p. 633)
Weiss, Lynne, jt. auth. see Crabtree Publishing Company Staff.
Weiss, Mitch, jt. auth. see Hamilton, Martha.
Weiss, Mitch, jt. auth. see Sallah, Michael.
Weiss, Mitch, jt. retold by see Hamilton, Martha.
Weiss, Mitch & Hamilton, Martha. Rooster's Night Out. Hoffmire, Baird, illus. (p. 1488)
Weiss, Monica, illus. see Flor Ada, Alma.
Weiss, Mónica, jt. auth. see Flor Ada, Alma.
Weiss, N. E. According to Plan. (p. 8)
Weiss, Nicki. Where Does the Brown Bear Go. (p. 1907)
Weiss, Rebecca J. Grandpa & Me Love Hotdogs! (p. 709)
Weiss, S. I. Coping with the Beauty Myth: A Guide for Real Girls. (p. 365)
Weiss, Sam. Jesus Plays the Catskills. (p. 916)
Weiss, Shelly. Dillin the Dolphin. (p. 440)
Weiss, Stacy, jt. auth. see Charlton, Dan.
Weiss, Stefanie Iris. Coping with the Beauty Myth: A Guide for Real Girls. (p. 365)
Weiss, Thomas G., et al. Voices: The Struggle for Development & Social Justice. (p. 1848)
Weiss, Tracy, illus. see Mors, Peter D. & Mors, Terry M.
Weissberger, Ela, jt. auth. see Rubin, Susan Goldman.
Weissburg, Paul. Batman Undercover Levins, Tim & DC Comics Staff, illus. (p. 144)
—Batman Undercover. Levins, Tim, illus. (p. 144)
—Man of Gold Cavallaro, Mike & Levins, Tim, illus. (p. 1085)
Weiss-Malik, Linda S. New Mexico. (p. 1246)
Weissman, Annie. Expand & Enrich Reading, Grades 3-6: Reading & Writing Activities (p. 548)
Weissman, Bari, illus. see Gross, Judith, et al.
Weissman, Bari, illus. see Heiligman, Deborah.
Weissman, Elissa Brent. Nerd Camp. (p. 1241)
—Nerd Camp 2. 0. Willis, Drew, illus. (p. 1241)
—Nerd Camp 2.0. Willis, Drew, illus. (p. 1241)
—Short Seller. (p. 1569)
—Standing for Socks. Sonkin, Jessica, illus. (p. 1639)
Weissman, Steven. Chocolate Cheeks. (p. 309)
—Kid Firechief. (p. 951)
—White Flower Day. (p. 1913)
Weissmann, Joe. Gingerbread Man. (p. 677)
Weissmann, Joe, illus. see Centre for Addiction and Mental Health Staff.
Weissmann, Joe, illus. see Fromer, Liza & Francine, Gerstein.
Weissmann, Joe, illus. see Fromer, Liza & Gerstein, Francine.
Weissmann, Joe, illus. see Stuchner, Joan Betty.
Weitekamp, Margaret. Pluto's Secret: An Icy World's Tale of Discovery. Kidd, Diane, illus. (p. 1374)
Weitekamp, Margaret A. & DeVorkin, David. Pluto's Secret: An Icy World's Tale of Discovery. Kidd, Diane, illus. (p. 1374)
Weitl, Joe. My Book of Poems to Enjoy: Volume 1 (p. 1199)
Weitz, Chris. New Order. (p. 1246)
—Young World. (p. 1979)
Weitzel, Erica, illus. see LaFer, Jenni.
Weitzel, Karen E. John & Betty Stam: Missionary Martyrs to China. Ober, Jonathan & Willoughby, Yuko, illus. (p. 921)
Weitzman, David. Jenny: The Airplane That Taught America to Fly. Weitzman, David, illus. (p. 913)
—Pharaoh's Boat. Weitzman, David, illus. (p. 1349)
—Skywalkers: Mohawks Ironworkers Build the City. (p. 1587)
Weitzman, Elizabeth. Brazil. (p. 224)
—Let's Talk about Living in a Blended Family. (p. 1001)
—Let's Talk about Staying in a Shelter. (p. 1001)
—Let's Talk about When Someone You Love Has Alzheimer's Disease. (p. 1001)
—Living in a Blended Family. (p. 1041)
Weitzman, Gary, jt. auth. see Newman, Aline Alexander.
Weitzman, Jacqueline Preiss. Superhero Joe. Barrett, Ron, illus. (p. 1683)
—Superhero Joe & the Creature Next Door. Barrett, Ron, illus. (p. 1683)
Weitzman, Stanley. Terrorism (p. 1722)
Weitzman, Stanley H. Terrorism. (p. 1722)
Wejrmeijer, Annelien. Dan & Max. van de Liejgraaf, Deborah, illus. (p. 401)
—Emma & Bo. van de Liejgraaf, Deborah, illus. (p. 519)
—Lily & Dolly. van de Liejgraaf, Deborah, illus. (p. 1017)
—Mason & Buddy. van de Liejgraaf, Deborah, illus. (p. 1102)
Wekelo, Kerry. Audrey's Journey: Round & Round Yoga. (p. 115)
Wekelo, Kerry Alison. Audrey's Coloring & Activity Book: Let's Do Yoga. (p. 115)
—Audrey's Journey: Playful Namaste. (p. 115)
Welborn, Amy. Adventures in Assisi: on the Path with St. Francis: On the Path with St. Francis. Engelhart, Ann Kissane, illus. (p. 15)
—Bambinelli Sunday: A Christmas Blessing. Engelhart, Ann, illus. (p. 135)
—Loyola Kids Book of Heroes: Stories of Catholic Heroes & Saints Throughout History. Konstantinov, Vitali, illus. (p. 1061)
Welborn, Amy, ed. Prove It! The Catholic Teen Bible. (p. 1413)
Welborn, Kathleen. Cacklebeans (p. 250)
Welbourne, Dave, jt. auth. see Evers, Charlotte.
Welch, Ariel & Welch, Ashley. Waiting. (p. 1852)
Welch, Ashley, jt. auth. see Welch, Ariel.
Welch, Barbara Kathleen. Bello Yellow's Amazing Surprise. (p. 163)
—Habit the Rabbit. (p. 734)
—My Wonderful Hands. (p. 1221)
—Paddle B. Daddle & Splasher. (p. 1317)
Welch, Brian Scott, jt. auth. see Moreau, Maryellen Rooney.
Welch, Brian Scott, jt. auth. see Rooney Moreau, Maryellen.
Welch, Catherine A. Bandera de Estrellas Centelleantes: El Himno Nacional. Translations.com Staff, tr. from ENG. (p. 136)

—Farmland Innovator: A Story about Cyrus Mccormick. Jones, Jan Naimo, illus. (p. 574)
—Forces & Motion: A Question & Answer Book (p. 617)
—George H. W. Bush. (p. 663)
—Geronimo. (p. 667)
—Star-Spangled Banner. Warwick, Carrie, illus. (p. 1641)
Welch, Chad, illus. see James, Richard E., III.
Welch, Christopher Shiveley. Christopher Bullfrog Catcher. (p. 316)
Welch, Deborah. Economic Issues & Development. (p. 502)
Welch, Debra Shiveley & Greene, Linda Lee. Jesus Gandhi Oma Mae Adams. (p. 915)
Welch, Eric. Jimmy the Gnome Won't Leave His Home Natelli, Kenny, illus. (p. 918)
Welch, Fay. Magic Swap Shop. (p. 1073)
Welch, Fred. Little Duck Who Lost His Quack. (p. 1027)
Welch, Gerry F., jt. auth. see Welch, Patrick J.
Welch, Ginger. Dream Reader. (p. 483)
Welch, Gracie, illus. see Wolfe, Susan Markle.
Welch, Holly, illus. see Mason, Margaret.
Welch, Holly Felsen, ed. see Felsen, Henry Gregor.
Welch, Holly Felsen, illus. see Felsen, Henry Gregor.
Welch, Jack & Byrne, John A. Jack: Straight from the Gut. (p. 902)
Welch, Jaime. Runes from the Woodpile: Runic Knowledge Revealed. (p. 1497)
Welch, Jim. Steven Stevens' Killer App. (p. 1649)
Welch, Julie. Happy Hearts (p. 746)
Welch, Kelly, illus. see Collins, David R., et al.
Welch, Lance. Counting with the Fairies of Willow Garden. Welch, Mark, illus. (p. 372)
Welch, Laura. Dragons at Play. (p. 479)
Welch, Laura, et al, eds. Big Book of History: A 15' fold-out time-line from Creation to Modern Computers. (p. 179)
Welch, Leah. Pretty on the Inside. (p. 1398)
Welch, Lester. Last Summer. (p. 979)
Welch, Mark. Tales of the Little Lagoon: Kiwa's Story. (p. 1702)
Welch, Mark, illus. see Welch, Lance.
Welch, Martha Mckeen. Close Looks in a Spring Woods. (p. 333)
Welch, Michael Eric, Sr. What the Devil Do Not Want You to Know... (p. 1893)
Welch, Michael, Sr. Why You Can Do God's Will. Butler, Latrica, ed. (p. 1927)
Welch, Michelle Rose. Country Hands. Harris, Patrick O'Neil, illus. (p. 372)
Welch, Pastor Clarence. My Friend the Lizzard. (p. 1209)
Welch, Patrick J. & Welch, Gerry F. Economics: Theory & Practice: Test Bank. (p. 503)
—Economics: Theory & Practice: Instructor's Manual. (p. 503)
Welch, Sheila. Waiting to Forget. (p. 1853)
Welch, Sheila Kelly. Shadowed Unicorn. (p. 1558)
—Waiting to Forget. (p. 1853)
Welch, Sheila Kelly, illus. see Anderson, Leone Castell.
Welch, Sheila Kelly, illus. see Jones, Molly.
Welch, Teri. My New Dance. (p. 1216)
Welch, Vala Jeanne, jt. auth. see Fancy, Robin Lyn.
Welch, Willy. Grumbly Bunnies. Lyon, Tammie Speer, illus. (p. 727)
Welchlin, Jewell. Babysitting Grandmama. (p. 129)
Welchman, Galina. Amy 's Treasure. (p. 66)
—King's Treasure. (p. 961)
Welchman-Tischler, Rosamond. Teaching with Manipulatives: Middle School Investigations. (p. 1710)
Welch-Stamos, Lisbeth. Jeremy Bixtu & the Hillman Husky. (p. 913)
Weld, Bill. Easy & Durwood's Country Life. (p. 500)
Weld, Larry. Counting with Silly Critters. (p. 372)
Welden, Amelie, jt. auth. see McCann, Michelle Roehm.
Welden, Amelie, jt. auth. see Mccann, Michelle Roehm.
Weldin, Frauke, illus. see Kempter, Christa.
Weldin, Frauke, illus. see Kruss, James.
Weldin, Frauke, illus. see Stalder, Päivi.
Weldin, Frauke, jt. auth. see Kempter, Christa.
Weldon, Andrew, illus. see Jennings, Paul.
Weldon, Andrew, illus. see MacDonald, Beverley.
Weldon, Andrew, jt. auth. see Jordan, Mary Ellen.
Weldon, Beth. What Does Luke Do in Heaven All Day? (p. 1884)
Weldon, George. It Could Only Happen at Christmas. (p. 894)
Weldon, Louise B., jt. auth. see Mather, Anne D.
Weldon, Stayton. Whitey on the Ranch. Anderson-Shorter, Susan, illus. (p. 1914)
Weldon-Owe. Grassland Safari. (p. 712)
—Shifting Sands. (p. 1566)
Weldon-Veitch, Jan. Maggie O'Riley. (p. 1071)
Welfing, Melanie Rook. Sing for Joy. (p. 1579)
Welford, Sue. Devoted Dogs: True Animal Stories. (p. 432)
—Nowhere to Run. (p. 1269)
—Secret Love. (p. 1542)
Welin, Raquel, illus. see Ortega, Ingrid.
Welker, Matthew S., illus. see Buckner, Andrew.
Welldon, Christine. Children of the Titanic (p. 302)
—Pier 21 - Listen to My Story (p. 1357)
—Reporter in Disguise: The Intrepid Vic Steinberg (p. 1461)
Weller, Alan. Celtic Clip Art for Machine Embroidery. (p. 286)
—Chinese Butterfly Clip Art for Machine Embroidery. (p. 307)
—Chinese Vector Motifs. (p. 308)
Weller, Alan & Dover Publications Inc. Staff. Spot the Differences (p. 1633)
—Spot the Differences Bk. 2 (p. 1633)
Weller, Andrew, tr. see Saumande, Juliette.
Weller, Frances Ward. Day the Animals Came: A Story of Saint Francis Day. Long, Loren, illus. (p. 414)
Weller, George. Story of Submarines. (p. 1660)
Weller, Kathleen & Beadles, Barbara. See Eye A: Case of the Blue Cast. (p. 1546)
—See Eye a - Case of the Freaky Flu. (p. 1546)
—See Eye A - Case of the Terrible Tremors. (p. 1546)
Weller, Linda, illus. see Jennett, Pamela.
Weller, Linda, illus. see Johnson, Virginia.
Weller, Linda, illus. see Jordano, Kimberly & Adsit, Kim.
Weller, Sadie Bedoka. Tsa Ch'ayah/How the Turtle Got Its Squares: A Traditional Caddo Indian Children's Story. Chafe, Wallace, tr. (p. 1795)
Weller, Shane. Beckett, Literature & the Ethics of Alterity. (p. 156)
Weller, Ursula, illus. see Caballero, D., tr.
Welles, Caryn. Baby the Freeway Bird. (p. 128)
Welles, Lee. Enter the Earth. Hameister, Ann, illus. (p. 531)
—Gaia Girls: Way of Water. Coogan, Carol, illus. (p. 652)
—Way of Water. Coogan, Carol, illus. (p. 1864)
Wellesley, Rosie. Moonlight Bear. Wellesley, Rosie, illus. (p. 1172)
—Very Helpful Hedgehog. Wellesley, Rosie, illus. (p. 1838)
Wellesley, Rosie, illus. see Grylls, Pinny.
Welling, Martin. Eston Discovers Home: A Dog Discovers Freedom, Fear and, Finally, Family. (p. 538)
—Guardian of the Stones: Nat & Mateo Discover the Two Forces of Magic Stones. (p. 728)
Welling, Peter. Joe Van der Katt & the Great Picket Fence Welling, Peter, illus. (p. 920)
Welling, Peter, illus. see Berlin, Bill & Berlin, Susan.
Welling, Peter, illus. see Brokamp, Elizabeth.
Welling, Peter, illus. see Sutton, Jane.
Welling, Peter J. Darlene Halloween & the Great Chicago Fire Welling, Peter J., illus. (p. 409)
—Justin Potemkin & the 500-Mile Race Welling, Peter J., illus. (p. 940)
—Michael le Soufflé & the April Fool Welling, Peter J., illus. (p. 1134)
Wellings, Chris. Sparkles Visits the Farm. Paluseka, Julia, illus. (p. 1622)
Wellings, Chris R. How Sparkles Came About: The Adventures of Sparkles. Nunnally, Carson, illus. (p. 812)
—Sparkles Goes Home for the Holidays. Kennell, Julie, illus. (p. 1622)
—Sparkles Meets the Easter Bunny: The Adventures of Sparkles. Hammersley, Karen, illus. (p. 1622)
Wellington, George. People, the World & I. (p. 1340)
Wellington, Monica. Apple Farmer Annie. Wellington, Monica, illus. (p. 92)
—Apple Farmer Annie Board Book. Wellington, Monica, illus. (p. 92)
—Apple Farmer Annie/ Anna Cultiva Manzanas. Del Risco, Eida & del Risco, Eida, trs. from ENG. (p. 92)
—Color & Cook BREAKFAST. (p. 342)
—Color & Cook CHRISTMAS COOKIES. (p. 342)
—Color & Cook CUPCAKES. (p. 342)
—Color & Cook HALLOWEEN. (p. 342)
—Color & Cook HEALTHY SNACKS. (p. 342)
—Color & Cook PIZZA. (p. 342)
—Color & Cook Story Coloring Book. (p. 342)
—Color & Cook TEA PARTY! (p. 342)
—Color & Garden FLOWERS. (p. 342)
—Color & Garden VEGETABLES. (p. 342)
—Colors for Zena. (p. 345)
—Firefighter Frank. (p. 591)
—Gabby & Grandma Go Green. (p. 652)
—Little Gardener's Stickers. (p. 1028)
—Mr. Cookie Baker. Wellington, Monica, illus. (p. 1184)
—Mr. Cookie Baker (Board Book Edition) (p. 1184)
—My Garden Stickers. (p. 1209)
—My Garden Super Sticker Book. (p. 1209)
—My Leaf Book. (p. 1211)
—Night House Bright House Find & Color. (p. 1253)
—Pizza at Sally's. Wellington, Monica, illus. (p. 1365)
—Riki's Birdhouse. Wellington, Monica, illus. (p. 1472)
—Truck Driver Tom. (p. 1791)
—Zinnia's Flower Garden. (p. 1987)
—Zinnia's Flower Garden. Wellington, Monica, illus. (p. 1987)
Wellington, Monica, illus. see Metzger, Steve.
Wellington, Monica & Activity Books. What's Cooking? Stickers. (p. 1896)
Wellington, Stanley. Where Monsters Hide. (p. 1909)
Wellington-Johnson, Sharon. Mouse in My House. (p. 1182)
Wellman, Doug, et al. Service Living: Building Community through Public Parks & Recreation. (p. 1553)
Wellman, Kathleen, jt. auth. see Goodman, Dena.
Wellman, Megan, illus. see Zuzo, Cheryl.
Wellman, Megan D., illus. see Graham, Patti.
Wellman, Mike, ed. see Patton, Chris.
Wells, jt. auth. see Walt.
Wells, Aja, illus. see Carr, Bernie.
Wells, Aja, illus. see Mogk, Matt.
Wells, Alexis, jt. auth. see Wells, Bridget.
Wells, Angela. Tales of Albie the Talking Dog. (p. 1702)
Wells, Anita. Nephi, Nephi, the Scriptures Are True. Anderson, Neal, illus. (p. 1241)
Wells, Aurora. Prayers That Bring Deliverance for Teens. (p. 1393)
Wells, Betty. Aardvark on the Ark. (p. 2)
—Gawky the Awkward Donkey. (p. 658)
—How the Goldfish Became Gold. (p. 813)
Wells, Bridget & Wells, Alexis. Mason & Molly: Picnic. (p. 1102)
Wells, C. Jumper: A Very Strange Tail. (p. 934)
Wells, Carolyn. Marjorie at Seacote. (p. 1094)
—Marjorie's Maytime. (p. 1094)
—Patty at Home. (p. 1329)
—Patty Fairfield. (p. 1330)
—Patty in Paris. (p. 1330)
—Patty's Butterfly Days. (p. 1330)
—Sherlock Holmes & the Adventure of the Clothes-Line. (p. 1565)
—Two Little Women on a Holiday. (p. 1804)
Wells, Carolyn & E. C. CASWELL. Two Little Women on a Holiday. (p. 1804)
Wells, Catherine. Hillary Clinton. (p. 779)
—John McCain. (p. 922)
—Strange Creatures: The Story of Mary Shelley. (p. 1665)
Wells, Charity. Trouble with the Supernatural (p. 1790)
Wells, Charles Knox Polk. Life & Adventures of Polk Wells (Charles Knox Polk Wells) the Notorious Outlaw... (p. 1007)
Wells, Craig. Fangs for God: A Vampire Satire. (p. 571)
Wells, Dan. Fragments. (p. 627)
—Partials. (p. 1325)
—Ruins. (p. 1494)
Wells, Daryl, illus. see Igus, Toyomi.
Wells, David M. & Faires, J. Douglas, eds. Contest Problem Book IX: American Mathematics Competitions (AMC 12) 2001-2007. (p. 360)
Wells, Don. Cheerleading. (p. 296)
—For the Love of Golf. (p. 616)
—For the Love of Tennis. (p. 616)
—Golf. (p. 696)
—Lacrosse. (p. 970)
—Tennis. (p. 1720)
Wells, Donald. Golf. (p. 696)
—Silk Road. (p. 1575)
—Spice Trade. (p. 1626)
—Tennis. (p. 1720)
Wells, Donald, ed. Terrorism. (p. 1722)
Wells, Donna. You & Me Brother. (p. 1973)
Wells, E. A. Butterfly Weed Patch. (p. 248)
Wells, Elizabeth & Trout, Lisa. All Is Gift: Catholic Stewardship / Intermediates Grades. (p. 44)
Wells, Erica. Diamonds in the Snow: A Story about the Magic of Snow. (p. 434)
Wells, Eva. Wishing I Was Fishing. (p. 1940)
Wells, Garrison. Amateur Wrestling: Combat on the Mat. (p. 52)
—Brazilian Jiujitsu: Ground-Fighting Combat. (p. 224)
—Mixed Martial Arts: Ultimate Fighting Combinations. (p. 1156)
—Muay Thai: Kickboxing Combat. (p. 1188)
—Tae Kwon Do: Korean Foot & Fist Combat. (p. 1695)
Wells, H. G. Invisible Man Calero, Dennis, illus. (p. 885)
—Invisible Man. (p. 885)
—Invisible Man. Calero, Dennis, illus. (p. 885)
—Island of Doctor Moreau. (p. 892)
—Little Wars & Floor Games (A companion piece to Little Wars) (p. 1037)
—Lost World. (p. 1057)
—Maquina del Tiempo. Smith, Tod, illus. (p. 1091)
—Three Prophetic Science Fiction Novels. Bleiler, Everett F., ed. (p. 1743)
—Time Machine (p. 1752)
—Time Machine. (p. 1752)
—Time Machine. Dunn, Ben, illus. (p. 1752)
—Time Machine. Howell, Troy, illus. (p. 1752)
—War in the Air. Parrinder, Patric, ed. (p. 1857)
—War of the Worlds. (p. 1857)
—War of the Worlds. Gorey, Edward, illus. (p. 1857)
—War of the Worlds. Simmans, Sean, illus. (p. 1857)
—War of the Worlds. Bennett, Felix, illus. (p. 1857)
—War of the Worlds. Akib, Jamel, illus. (p. 1858)
—War of the Worlds Study Guide. (p. 1858)
—Wheels of Chance: a Bicycling Idyll. (p. 1901)
Wells, H. G., jt. auth. see Protobunker Studio Staff.
Wells, H. G., jt. auth. see Sasaki, Chris.
Wells, H. G. & Geary, Rick. Invisible Man. (p. 885)
Wells, H. G., et al. Island of Doctor Moreau Vincent, Eric, illus. (p. 892)
—Island of Doctor Moreau. (p. 892)
Wells, Helen. Cherry Ames, Army Nurse. (p. 298)
—Cherry Ames at Hilton Hospital: Book 13. (p. 298)
—Cherry Ames, Boarding School Nurse. (p. 298)
—Cherry Ames Boxed Set: Volumes 17-20. (p. 298)
—Cherry Ames, Camp Nurse. (p. 298)
—Cherry Ames, Chief Nurse. (p. 298)
—Cherry Ames, Companion Nurse. (p. 298)
—Cherry Ames, Cruise Nurse. (p. 298)
—Cherry Ames, Department Store Nurse. (p. 298)
—Cherry Ames, Flight Nurse. (p. 298)
—Cherry Ames, Island Nurse. (p. 298)
—Cherry Ames Jungle Nurse. (p. 298)
—Cherry Ames, Private Duty Nurse. (p. 298)
—Cherry Ames, Rural Nurse. (p. 298)
—Cherry Ames, Senior Nurse. (p. 298)
—Cherry Ames, Ski Nurse Mystery. (p. 298)
—Cherry Ames, Staff Nurse. (p. 298)
—Cherry Ames, Student Nurse. (p. 298)
—Cherry Ames, the Mystery in the Doctor's Office. (p. 298)
—Cherry Ames Veteran's Nurse. (p. 298)
—Cherry Ames, Visiting Nurse. (p. 298)
—Silver Ring Mystery: The Vicki Barr Flight Stewardess Series. (p. 1576)
Wells, J. & L. Antares & the Zodiac. (p. 88)
Wells, Jack, jt. auth. see Irwin, Robert.
Wells, Jack & Irwin, Robert. Robert Irwin, Dinosaur Hunter: The Discovery Collection (p. 1479)
Wells, Jack J., illus. see Shaw, Bill.
Wells, James. Stuffy, the Short-Neck Giraffe Who Liked Peanut Butter. (p. 1670)
Wells, Jan. Philemon - an Inductive Bible Study. (p. 1350)
Wells, Jane. Bird on Fire. (p. 190)
Wells, Janet F. For Petey's Sake! (p. 616)
Wells, Jason. Why Children Should Listen to Their Mothers. (p. 1923)
Wells, Jason & Wells, Jeff. Albert Is Our Mascot. Carlson, Patrick, illus. (p. 34)
—Aubie Is Our Mascot. Carlson, Patrick, illus. (p. 114)
—Big Al Is Our Mascot. Carlson, Patrick, illus. (p. 177)
—Big Red Is Our Mascot. Carlson, Patrick, illus. (p. 183)
—Bully Is Our Mascot. Carlson, Patrick, illus. (p. 241)
—Cocky Is Our Mascot. Carlson, Patrick, illus. (p. 337)
—Hairy Dawg Is Our Mascot. Carlson, Patrick, illus. (p. 736)
—Mike the Tiger Is Our Mascot. Carlson, Patrick, illus. (p. 1141)
—Rebel Is Our Mascot. (p. 1450)
—Reveille Is Our Mascot. Carlson, Patrick, illus. (p. 1465)
—Scratch Is Our Mascot. Carlson, Patrick, illus. (p. 1532)
—Smokey Is Our Mascot. Carlson, Patrick, illus. (p. 1594)
—Truman Is Our Mascot. Carlson, Patrick, illus. (p. 1793)
Wells, Jeff, jt. auth. see Wells, Jason.
Wells, Joe. Touch & Go Joe: An Adolescent's Experience of OCD. Wells, Joe, illus. (p. 1772)
Wells, Karen, jt. auth. see McCloud, Carol.
Wells, Kitty. Paw Power. Harrison, Joanna, illus. (p. 1331)
Wells, Leah, jt. see Beausoliel, Loyan.
Wells, Lorraine, illus. see Pingry, Patricia A.
Wells, Marcia. Mystery in Mayan Mexico. Calo, Marcos, illus. (p. 1224)
—Mystery on Museum Mile. Calo, Marcos, illus. (p. 1226)
Wells, Marcus. Lifestyles for the 21st Century: Sole Food for Life. (p. 1014)
Wells, Mark. Renée Zellweger: From Small Town Girl to Superstar. (p. 1460)
Wells, Mark & Wells, Meagan. Tommy's Lost Tooth. Wells, Mark, illus. (p. 1765)
Wells, Martha. Emilie & the Hollow World. (p. 518)
—Emilie & the Sky World. (p. 518)
Wells, Meagan, jt. auth. see Wells, Mark.
Wells, Melisa. Remembering Ruby: For Families Living Beyond the Loss of a Pet. (p. 1459)
Wells, Misty. Hank the Horse. (p. 742)
Wells, Pamela. Crushes. (p. 387)
—Heartbreakers. (p. 760)
Wells, Peggy Sue. Fergie. (p. 582)
—Kanye West. (p. 943)
—Soulja Boy Tell 'Em. (p. 1614)
Wells, Philip. Alien Guide from Inner Space: And Other Poems. (p. 40)
—Daddy Island. Daly, Niki, illus. (p. 398)
Wells, Phillip. Where's Charlie. (p. 1910)
Wells, Polly. Freaking Out: Real-Life Stories about Anxiety. Mitchell, Peter, illus. (p. 631)
Wells, Q. B. Blackface: A Novel. (p. 197)
Wells, Quierra LaQuelle, illus. see Wells-Sanders, Glenora.
Wells, R. Legend of the Wampus: Smoky Mountain Bedtime Tales. (p. 989)
Wells, R., jt. auth. see Milbourne, A.
Wells, R., jt. auth. see Watt, F.
Wells, R., jt. auth. see Watt, Fiona.
Wells, R. W. Black Mountain Express: A Smoky Mountain Bedtime Tale. (p. 196)
Wells, Rachel. Farm. (p. 573)
—That's Not My Christmas Coloring Book. (p. 1727)
—That's Not My Sticker Book Christmas. (p. 1727)
—That's Not My Sticker Book Farm. (p. 1727)
Wells, Rachel, illus. see Brooks, Felicity & Allen, Francesca.
Wells, Rachel, illus. see Cartwright, Mary.
Wells, Rachel, illus. see Durber, Matt & Brooks, Felicity.
Wells, Rachel, illus. see Watt, Fiona.
Wells, Rachel, jt. auth. see Watt, Fiona.
Wells, Rachel, jt. ed. see Watt, Fiona.
Wells, Rebekah. What Does Mommy Do All Day? (p. 1884)
Wells, Riki. Sarah's Special Christmas Day. (p. 1514)
Wells, Rita. Janie Plants a Tree. (p. 908)
Wells, Robert. ¿Sabes Contar Hasta un Googol? (p. 1500)
Wells, Robert, jt. auth. see Wells, Robert E.
Wells, Robert E. Can We Share the World with Tigers? Wells, Robert E., illus. (p. 258)
—Can You Count to a Googol? (p. 258)
—Did a Dinosaur Drink This Water? (p. 436)
—Did a Dinosaur Drink This Water? Wells, Robert E., illus. (p. 436)
—How Do You Lift a Lion? (p. 808)
—Is a Blue Whale the Biggest Thing There Is? (p. 888)
—Polar Bear, Why Is Your World Melting? Wells, Robert E., illus. (p. 1379)
—What's Faster Than a Speeding Cheetah? (p. 1897)
—What's Older Than a Giant Tortoise? Wells, Robert E., illus. (p. 1898)
—What's Smaller Than a Pygmy Shrew? (p. 1899)
—What's So Special about Planet Earth? (p. 1899)
—What's So Special about Planet Earth? Wells, Robert E., illus. (p. 1899)
—Why Do Elephants Need the Sun? (p. 1923)
—Why Do Elephants Need the Sun? Wells, Robert E., illus. (p. 1923)
Wells, Robert E. & Wells, Robert. Como Se Mide el Tiempo? (p. 351)
—Hay Algo Mas Grande Que una Ballena Azul? (p. 755)
—Hay Algo Mas Pequeno Que Una Musarana? (p. 755)
Wells, Robison. Blackout. (p. 197)
—Dead Zone. (p. 417)
—Feedback. (p. 580)
—Variant. (p. 1833)
Wells, Rosemary. Bunny Cakes. Wells, Rosemary, illus. (p. 242)
—Bunny Mail. Wells, Rosemary, illus. (p. 242)
—Bunny Party. (p. 242)
—Christmas Tree for Ruby. (p. 316)
—Eduardo: Cumpleanos en la Piscina. (p. 505)
—Eduardo: El Primer Dia de Colegio. (p. 505)
—Emily's First 100 Days of School. (p. 519)
—Emily's First 100 Days of School. Wells, Rosemary, illus. (p. 519)
—Estupenda Mama de Roberta. (p. 539)
—Felix Stands Tall. Wells, Rosemary, illus. (p. 581)
—Following Grandfather. Denise, Christopher, illus. (p. 612)
—Hands Off, Harry! Wells, Rosemary, illus. (p. 741)
—Hungry Bunny Tales. (p. 828)
—Ivy Takes Care. LaMarche, Jim, illus. (p. 901)
—Julieta, Estate Quieta! (p. 932)
—Julieta, Estate Quieta! Wells, Rosemary, illus. (p. 932)
—Lincoln & His Boys. Lynch, P. J., illus. (p. 1018)
—Love Waves: Midi Edition. Wells, Rosemary, illus. (p. 1060)
—Love Waves. Wells, Rosemary, illus. (p. 1060)
—Max & Ruby at the Warthogs' Wedding. Wells, Rosemary, illus. (p. 1110)
—Max & Ruby Play School. (p. 1110)
—Max & Ruby Play School. Wells, Rosemary, illus. (p. 1110)
—Max & Ruby's Bedtime Book. (p. 1110)
—Max & Ruby's Show-and-Tell. (p. 1110)
—Max & Ruby's Snowy Day. (p. 1110)
—Max & Ruby's Treasure Hunt. (p. 1110)
—Max & the Fall Parade. (p. 1110)
—Max Counts His Chickens. (p. 1111)
—Max Drives Away. (p. 1111)
—Max to the Rescue. (p. 1111)
—Max's ABC. (p. 1112)
—Max's Bedtime. (p. 1112)
—Max's Birthday. (p. 1112)
—Max's Breakfast. (p. 1112)
—Max's Bunny Business. (p. 1112)
—Max's Christmas. (p. 1112)

W

—Max's First Word. (p. 1112)
—Max's Halloween. Wells, Rosemary, illus. (p. 1112)
—Max's New Suit. (p. 1112)
—Max's Special Spring. (p. 1112)
—Max's Toys: A Counting Book. (p. 1112)
—Max's Valentine. (p. 1112)
—McDuff Comes Home. Jeffers, Susan, illus. (p. 1114)
—McDuff's New Friend with Plush Box Set. (p. 1114)
—Miracle Melts Down. Wells, Rosemary, illus. (p. 1148)
—Noisy Nora. Wells, Rosemary, illus. (p. 1263)
—On the Blue Comet. Ibatoulline, Bagram, illus. (p. 1289)
—Otto Runs for President. Wells, Rosemary, illus. (p. 1307)
—Read to Your Bunny. Wells, Rosemary, illus. (p. 1443)
—Red Boots (p. 1453)
—Red Moon at Sharpsburg. (p. 1454)
—Ruby Gets Crafty. (p. 1493)
—Ruby's Beauty Shop. Wells, Rosemary, illus. (p. 1493)
—Ruby's Falling Leaves. (p. 1493)
—Ruby's Party. (p. 1493)
—Ruby's Rainbow. (p. 1493)
—Ruby's Rainy Day. Wells, Rosemary, illus. (p. 1494)
—Sandbox. (p. 1511)
—Shopping. (p. 1569)
—Sophie's Terrible Twos. Wells, Rosemary, illus. (p. 1613)
—Sporty Bunny Tales. (p. 1633)
—Stella's Starliner. Wells, Rosemary, illus. (p. 1647)
—Time-Out for Sophie. Wells, Rosemary, illus. (p. 1752)
—Use Your Words, Sophie! (p. 1827)
—Visit to Dr. Duck. Wells, Rosemary, illus. (p. 1845)
—Voyage to the Bunny Planet. (p. 1850)
—Yoko. Wells, Rosemary, illus. (p. 1972)
—Yoko Finds Her Way. (p. 1972)
—Yoko Learns to Read. (p. 1972)
Wells, Rosemary, illus. see Gaarder, Jostein.
Wells, Rosemary, illus. see Loesser, Frank.
Wells, Rosemary, illus. see Opie, Ian, ed.
Wells, Rosemary, illus. see Opie, Iona, ed.
Wells, Rosemary, illus. see Opie, Iona.
Wells, Rosemary, illus. see White, E. B.
Wells, Rosemary, jt. auth. see Kisseloff, Jeff.
Wells, Rosemary & Grosset and Dunlap Staff. Happy Halloween! (p. 745)
—Max's Easter Surprise. (p. 1112)
—Max's Worm Cake. (p. 1112)
—Snow Bunny Tales. (p. 1598)
—Sunny Bunny Tales. (p. 1677)
Wells, Rosemary & Jeffers, Susan. McDuff Moves In. (p. 1114)
Wells, Rosemary & Rosemary, Wells. Listos para Leer. Fernandez, Leire Amigo, tr. (p. 1022)
—Mundo Que Nos Rodea. Fernandez, Leire Amigo, tr. (p. 1191)
—Yoko. (p. 1972)
—Yoko. Varela, Sandra Lopez, tr. (p. 1972)
Wells, Rosemary, et al. Hide-and-Seek. (p. 776)
—My Havana: Memories of a Cuban Boyhood. Ferguson, Peter, illus. (p. 1210)
Wells, Roth. Big Book of Dinosaurs. (p. 179)
Wells, Ruth. Farmer & the Poor God. (p. 574)
Wells, S. G. 1,000 Days: The Beginning, a Novel. (p. 2001)
Wells, Shan, illus. see Mills, Nancy Libbey.
Wells, Shannon Nicole. Gold! A Tall Tale. (p. 693)
Wells, Sharon D. God Made Us Special. Wright, Alson, illus. (p. 690)
Wells, Sheila Rae. Waiting for a Letter. (p. 1852)
Wells, Sherry A. Father, Ford, $5 a Day: The Mullers from Missouri. Bulla, Randy, illus. (p. 577)
—Warm & Wonderful Stepmothers of Famous People. Van Kampen, Megan, illus. (p. 1858)
Wells Smith, Abby, illus. see Toombs, Tom.
Wells, Steve, illus. see Cookson, Paul.
Wells, Susan. Rainbow Dragon/ the Sorcerer's Race. (p. 1435)
—Rock Parables. (p. 1482)
Wells, Tina. Friends Forever? (p. 638)
—Mackenzie Blue: Friends Forever? (p. 1068)
—Mackenzie Blue: Double Trouble. Vol. 5 Segawa, Michael, illus. (p. 1068)
—Mackenzie Blue. (p. 1068)
—Mackenzie Blue. Segawa, Michael, illus. (p. 1068)
—Mixed Messages. (p. 1156)
—Secret Crush. (p. 1540)
—Secret Crush. Segawa, Michael, illus. (p. 1540)
Wells, Tom. Strange Seasons: Summer. (p. 1665)
Wells, Valori. Boho Designs Coloring Book. (p. 207)
Wells, Vivi. Whispers: The Cat with Nine Lives. (p. 1912)
Wells, Zachariah, et al. Anything but Hank! Orchard, Eric, illus. (p. 91)
Wells, Zeb. Carnage: Family Feud. Crain, Clayton, illus. (p. 270)
Wells-Cole, Catherine. Slavery & the Forging of Early America. (p. 1588)
Wells-Cole, Catherine, jt. auth. see Twist, Clint.
Wells-Dunn, Mildred. Tid Bit the Teddy Bear. (p. 1747)
Wells-Sanders, Glenora. Trinny Bear & Dallas. Wells, Quierra LaQuelle, illus. (p. 1787)
Welply, Michael, illus. see Osborne, Mary Pope & Boyce, Natalie Pope.
Wels, Susan. Pearl Harbor: America's Darkest Day. (p. 1333)
Welsbacher, Anne. Delaware. (p. 424)
—Earth-Friendly Design. (p. 496)
—Life in a Rain Forest: The Hawaiian Islands. (p. 1010)
—Protecting Earth's Rain Forests. (p. 1412)
Welsch, Camille-Yvette. Meg Cabot. (p. 1124)
Welsch, Gabe. Philip Roth. (p. 1350)
—Wallace Stevens. Bloom, Harold, ed. (p. 1855)
Welsh, Anne Marie & Fenly, Leigh. Wow! Wonders of Water. Garcia, Helena, illus. (p. 1962)
Welsh, Anne Marie & Tuchman, Laura. World of Girls. Garcia, Helena, illus. (p. 1956)
Welsh Books Staff. Llyfr Lliwio Sali Mali. (p. 1044)
Welsh, C. E. L. Space Race. Jones, K. L., illus. (p. 1619)
Welsh, Carol M. Stop when You See Red. (p. 1654)
Welsh, Charles. Goody Two Shoes. (p. 702)
Welsh, Charles, ed. Stories Children Love: a Collection of Stories Arranged for Children. Grimball, Meta, illus. (p. 1654)
Welsh, Frank. Battle for Christendom: The Council of Constance & the Dawn of Modern Europe. (p. 145)
Welsh, Hayley, illus. see Bennett, Sandra.
Welsh, James M., jt. auth. see Tibbetts, John C.
Welsh, James Michael, jt. auth. see Tibbetts, John C.
Welsh, Joey. Gekkleberry Tree: A Humorous Tail about the Gekkards & One Legendary Tree. Welsh, Joey, illus. (p. 659)
Welsh, Karen Leis. Eh, Spaghetti You Say? (p. 507)
—Frolicking Friends. (p. 641)
—Gingerbread Class. (p. 677)
Welsh, Kariamu. African Dance. (p. 27)
Welsh, Kenneth Wilbur. Magic Chalk. (p. 1072)
—Oak Brothers. (p. 1274)
Welsh, Lisa. Sammy Swan: The Big Storm. (p. 1508)
Welsh, M. Mistress of the Storm. (p. 1155)
Welsh, M. L. Heart of Stone. (p. 759)
Welsh, Mary Reddick. Sammy, the Little Green Snake Who Wanted to Fly. Welsh, Mary Reddick, illus. (p. 1508)
Welsh, Phoebe. Wonder What Do First Day Heaven. (p. 1947)
Welsh-Howard, Paula, jt. auth. see Howard, Jim.
Welshman, Kate. Anais Butt & the Hairy-Handed Gent. (p. 66)
—Posse. (p. 1387)
Welter, Anni. Child of War: How We Lived & Survived under the Third Reich. (p. 301)
Welter, Victor D. Fishers of Men. (p. 599)
Welters, M. Andrine. My Confession Book: A Child's Preparation for the Sacrament of Penance. (p. 1200)
Weltevrede, Pieter, illus. see Johari, Harish & Sperling, Vatsala.
Weltevrede, Pieter, illus. see Sperling, Vatsala.
Weltig, Matthew Scott. Aftermath of the Anglo-Zulu War. (p. 28)
Weltman, June. Mystery of the Missing Candlestick. (p. 1225)
Weltner, Dave, illus. see Chamberlain, Lyn.
Weltner, Dave, illus. see DuVall, Nell.
Weltner, Dave, illus. see Hanna, Margaret Leis.
Welton, David. Children & Their World: Strategies for Teaching Social Studies. (p. 302)
Welton, Jude. Adam's Alternative Sports Day: An Asperger Story. (p. 11)
—Marc Chagall. (p. 1091)
—Tomas Loves... A Rhyming Book about Fun, Friendship - & Autism. Telford, Jane, illus. (p. 1764)
—Water Supplies. (p. 1863)
Welty, Carolyn. Look at Little Lucy Pratt, Susan, illus. (p. 1048)
Welty, Charles R. Ludington's Ride. (p. 1064)
Welty, Lauresta. Best Place in the World (p. 171)
Welty, Tara. Jane Goodall. (p. 908)
Welty, Tara & Banas, Sharon L. Handling Teamwork & Respect for Others. (p. 741)
Welty, Tony. Ricardo the Fierce. (p. 1469)
Welvaert, Scott R. Bear in Its Den. (p. 151)
—Curse of the Wendigo: An Agate & Buck Adventure Garvey, Brann, illus. (p. 395)
—Follow That Crop: From the Farmer's Field to Our Grocery Store. (p. 612)
—Gorillas Lentz, Bob, illus. (p. 703)
—Lions Lentz, Bob, illus. (p. 1021)
—Mosquito King: An Agate & Buck Adventure Garvey, Brann, illus. (p. 1176)
—Thomas Edison & the Lightbulb Miller, Phil et al, illus. (p. 1738)
—Whales (p. 1878)
Welvaert, Scott R., jt. auth. see Welveart, Scott R.
Welvaert, Scott R. & Jungman, Ann. Curse of the Wendigo: An Agate & Buck Adventure Garvey, Brann, illus. (p. 395)
Welveart, Scott R. & Welvaert, Scott R. Donner Party Frenz, Ron et al, illus. (p. 466)
Welykochy, Dawn. C Is for Chinook: An Alberta Alphabet. Bennett, Lorna, illus. (p. 249)
Welzen, Joe. Gutsy Stomach Walker. (p. 733)
Wemmer, Constance. My Sweet Tangerine. (p. 1219)
Wemmlinger, Raymond. Booth's Daughter. (p. 213)
Wemple, Sabrina. Gumby & Beanie. (p. 731)
Wen, Dref. Fy Llyfr Geiriau Croes Cyntaf. (p. 651)
—Fy Llyfr Rhifau Cyntaf. (p. 651)
—Traeth Prysur. (p. 1776)
Wen, Dref, jt. auth. see Cambell, Rod.
Wen, Dref, jt. auth. see Eynon, Bob.
Wen, Dref, jt. auth. see Haf, Eurgain.
Wen, Dref, jt. auth. see Maddox, Tony.
Wenatchee High School Staff. W Is for Washington. (p. 1851)
Wenberg, Michael. Seattle Blues. (p. 1539)
—Stringz. (p. 1667)
Wencel, Dave. UFOs. (p. 1808)
Wenckebach, L. W. R., illus. see Hoffmann, E. T. A.
Wend, Arran. King & the Fire Chanter. (p. 958)
Wendel, Carie, illus. see Everett, Melissa.
Wendel, Carrie, illus. see Everett, Melissa.
Wendel, Gretchen Schomel, et al. All Around Town. Renthrope, Damon, illus. (p. 44)
—Becka Goes to India. Renthrope, Damon, illus. (p. 155)
—Becka Goes to San Francisco. Renthrope, Damon, illus. (p. 156)
—Becka Goes to the North Pole. Renthrope, Damon, illus. (p. 156)
Wendel, Gretchen Schomer & Schomer, Adam Anthony. All Around Town. Renthrope, Damon, illus. (p. 44)
—Becka Goes to Chicago. Renthrope, Damon, illus. (p. 155)
—Becka Goes to India. Renthrope, Damon, illus. (p. 155)
Wendel, Gretchen Schomer & Schomer, Adam Anthony. Becka Goes to San Diego. Renthrope, Damon, illus. (p. 155)
Wendel, Gretchen Schomer & Schomer, Adam Anthony. Becka Goes to the North Pole. Renthrope, Damon, illus. (p. 156)
Wendel, Kelley. Birds of a Different Feather. (p. 191)
Wendel, Tim. My Man Stan. (p. 1214)
Wendell, Jeremy, illus. see Lieberman, Sylvia.
Wendell, Ulises, illus. see Alonso, Fernando.
WendellDowling, illus. see Atkinson, Janet I.
Wendig, Chuck. Under the Empyrean Sky (p. 1813)
Wendinger, Jennifer. Unusual & Awesome Jobs Using Science: Hollywood Animal Trainer, Cave Diver, & More. (p. 1823)
Wendland, Paula, illus. see Malaspina, Ann.
Wendland, Zachary, illus. see Peters, Dylan.
Wendle, Stan, ed. see Utsler, Elaine.
Wendling, Nathalie & Glatzmayer, Thomas. Melanie & Tommy Have Two Pet Rats & One Syndrome. (p. 1125)
Wendling, Patricia A. Adventures in Video: A Guide to the Best Instructional Videos for Children. (p. 16)
Wendling, Peter. Caterpillars Never Lie (p. 280)
—Magic of the Dark Ravine. Durie, Sally, illus. (p. 1073)
—Matthew Leads the Animal Parade (p. 1109)
Wendorf, Sarah. Is for Appaloosa! (p. 889)
Wendorff, Anne. Bear Cubs. (p. 150)
—Blastoff! Readers - Watch Animals Grow (p. 198)
—Droughts. (p. 486)
—Eaglets. (p. 492)
—Fawns. (p. 578)
—Gymnastics. (p. 734)
—Ice Storms. (p. 851)
—Lambs. (p. 972)
—Orcas. (p. 1302)
—Paintball. (p. 1318)
—Penguins. (p. 1337)
—Pugs. (p. 1415)
—Saint Bernards. (p. 1503)
—Sea Otters. (p. 1535)
—Shetland Sheepdogs. (p. 1566)
—Siberian Huskies. (p. 1572)
—Soccer. (p. 1603)
—Swimming. (p. 1691)
—Tennis. (p. 1720)
—Tornadoes. (p. 1770)
—Tsunamis. (p. 1795)
Wendt, Harry. Divine Drama - Our Narrative. (p. 454)
—Divine Drama - the Biblical Narrative. (p. 454)
Wendt, Matt, illus. see Croall, Marie P. & Jolley, Dan.
Wendt, Matt, illus. see Jolley, Dan & Croall, Marie P.
Wendt, Matt, illus. see Jolley, Dan.
Wendt, Yohanna, illus. see Saint, Mimi.
Wendy Bissinger, jt. auth. see Bissinger, Wendy.
Wendy Lee Jungling; Illustrated By My Fa. Who Do You Want to Be? (p. 1915)
Wendy, Watson, illus. see Keen, Marian.
Wenger, Brahm. Dewey Doo-It at the Jingle Jangle Jamboree: A Musical Storybook Inspired by Arnold Schwarzenegger to Benefit Inner-City Games. (p. 432)
—Dewey's Helping Heart: To Beneift the Larry King Cardiac Foundation. (p. 432)
—Dewey's Magical Sleigh. (p. 432)
—Dewey's Magical Sleigh, from the Dewey Doo-it Series. (p. 432)
Wenger, Brahm & Green, Alan. Dewey Doo-It Builds a House: A Children's Story about Habitat for Humanity. (p. 432)
—Dewey Doo-It Feeds a Friend. Gillmore, Jean, illus. (p. 432)
Wenger, Jennifer, et al. Teen Knitting Club: Chill Out & Knit. (p. 1713)
Wenger, Shaunda. Caterpillar Can't Wait! (p. 279)
—Farm Stand Mystery. (p. 574)
—How Many Muffins? (p. 811)
—Little Red Riding Hood. into the Forest Again. (p. 1035)
—Watch a Butterfly Grow. (p. 1860)
Wenger, Shaunda Kennedy. Ghost in Me. (p. 670)
—Reality Bites: Tales of a Half-Vampire. (p. 1449)
Weninger, Brigitte. Child Is a Child. Tharlet, Eve, illus. (p. 301)
—Davy in the Middle. Tharlet, Eve, illus. (p. 411)
—Davy Loves the Baby. Tharlet, Eve, illus. (p. 411)
—Davy, Soccer Star! Tharlet, Eve, illus. (p. 411)
—Happy Easter, Davy! Tharlet, Eve, illus. (p. 745)
—Merry Christmas Davy. Tharlet, Eve, illus. (p. 1128)
Weninger, Brigitte & Tharlet, Eve. Davy Loves His Mommy. (p. 411)
Wenisch, Tanja. Friends Always. (p. 638)
Wenke, Christine. Willa's Secret. (p. 1933)
Wenman, Alexandra. Ariel. (p. 98)
Wennekes, Ron, illus. see Stanley, Jan.
Wennick, Elizabeth. Whatever Doesn't Kill You (p. 1896)
Wenning, Jeremy. Coco & Pebbles: Bath Night. Barrett, Casey, illus. (p. 337)
—Coco & Pebbles: That's My Duck! Barrett, Casey, illus. (p. 337)
—Roscoe the Volunteer Emt. Burns, Sandra, illus. (p. 1489)
Wensell, Paloma. Christmas Star. Maloney, Linda M., tr. from GER. (p. 315)
Wensell, Ulises, illus. see Flor Ada, Alma & Campoy, F. Isabel.
Wensell, Ulises, illus. see Kunzler-Behncke, Rosemarie.
Wensell, Ulises, illus. see Linke, Uwe.
Wensell, Ulises, illus. see Lopez, Susana.
Wensell, Ulises, illus. see Reviejo Hernandez, Carlos.
Wensell, Ulises, illus. see Roncagliolo, Santiago.
Wensell, Ulises, illus. see Wensell, Paloma.
Wensley, Walter F. Yorkie. (p. 1972)
Went, Jannetje Van. Wishing Bear: The Impossible Wish. (p. 1940)
Wentworth, Marjory. Shackles. Pratt-Thomas, Leslie, illus. (p. 1556)
Wentz, Lorraine. Who Has Barney. (p. 1915)
Wentz, Tim. Dark Secret at Twenty-Five Feet. (p. 408)
Wentzel, Jim. Beatles. (p. 153)
Wentzel, Jim, jt. auth. see Glass, Sherri.
Wenz, Graham D. Day a Cockroach Crawled under My Door: This Book Won't Be a Bore! (p. 412)
Wenzel, Angela. 13 Art Mysteries Children Should Know. (p. 1994)
—13 Art Techniques Children Should Know. (p. 1994)
—13 Artists Children Should Know. (p. 1994)
—13 Paintings Children Should Know. (p. 1995)
—13 Sculptures Children Should Know. (p. 1995)
—Mad, Mad, Mad World of Salvador Dali. (p. 1069)
—Paul Cezanne: How He Amazed the World. (p. 1330)
Wenzel, Angela & Schuelmann, Bettina. 13 Women Artists Children Should Know. (p. 1995)
Wenzel, Brendan, illus. see DiTerlizzi, Angela.
Wenzel, Brendan, illus. see Jackson, Ellen.
Wenzel, David, illus. see Cricket Books Staff.
Wenzel, David, illus. see Deutsch, Stacia & Cohon, Rhody.
Wenzel, David, illus. see Deutsch/Cohon.
Wenzel, David, illus. see Lucado, Max, et al.
Wenzel, David, illus. see Lucado, Max.
Wenzel, David, illus. see Ross, Dev.
Wenzel, David, illus. see Spinelli, Eileen.
Wenzel, David, illus. see StJohn, Amanda.
Wenzel, David T., illus. see Capucilli, Alyssa Satin.
Wenzel, David T., illus. see Deutsch, Stacia & Cohon, Rhody.
Wenzel, David T., illus. see Kennedy, Pamela.
Wenzel, David T., illus. see Lepp, Bil.
Wenzel, David T., illus. see Lucado, Max, et al.
Wenzel, David T., illus. see Murphy, Stuart J.
Wenzel, David T., illus. see Rothenberg, Annye.
Wenzel, Dominique, tr. see Lomba, Ana.
Wenzel, Gregory. Feathered Dinosaurs of China. Wenzel, Gregory, illus. (p. 579)
Wenzel, Gregory, illus. see Collard, Sneed B., III.
Wenzel, Gregory, illus. see Nussbaum, Ben.
Wenzel, Jan-Udo. Ginter. (p. 677)
Wenzel, Kurt. Exposure. (p. 554)
Wenzel, Terri. Dragon Called Leona. (p. 476)
Wenzell, Gregory, jt. auth. see Nussbaum, Ben.
Wenz-Vietor, Else, illus. see Bauer, Sepp.
Werden's class. Nunamiut ABC: A Child's View of Life in an Alaska Village. Written & Illustrated by the 4th & 5th Graders of Anaktuvuk Pass, Alaska. Werden's class, illus. (p. 1273)
Wergeland, Oystein. Celina Louise Feeds the Ducks: A Winter Day in Norway. (p. 286)
—Celina Louise, the Flower Girl: The Wedding. (p. 286)
Werkema, Mark A. Flight Before Christmas. (p. 604)
Werker, Kim, jt. auth. see Werker, Kim Piper.
Werker, Kim Piper & Werker, Kim. Get Hooked Again: Simple Steps to Crochet More Cool Stuff. Frenette, Cynthia, illus. (p. 667)
Werle, Simone. 13 Fashion Styles Children Should Know. (p. 1995)
Werlin, Nancy. Are You Alone on Purpose? (p. 97)
—Black Mirror. (p. 196)
—Double Helix. (p. 473)
—Extraordinary. (p. 555)
—Impossible. (p. 862)
—Killer's Cousin. (p. 956)
—Rules of Survival. (p. 1495)
—Unthinkable. (p. 1823)
WERLIN, NANCY, jt. auth. see Werlin, Nancy.
Werlin, Nancy & WERLIN, NANCY. Reglas de Supervivencia de Matt. D'Omellas, Veronica, tr. (p. 1457)
Werlock, Abby H. P. Facts on File Companion to the American Novel (p. 561)
Wermund, Jerry. Earthscapes: Landforms Sculpted by Water, Wind, & Ice. (p. 498)
—Soil: More Than Just Dirt. (p. 1606)
—World According to Rock. Sansevero, Tony, illus. (p. 1953)
Werner, Aviva. Experience Modern Israel: Explore, Discover, Connect. (p. 548)
Werner, Cherie. New Life in Jesus! (p. 1246)
Werner, Doug & Badillo, Steve. Skateboarder's Start-Up: A Beginner's Guide to Skateboarding. (p. 1583)
Werner, James R. Dave's Christmas Surprise & a Puppy Named Oxley. (p. 410)
Werner, Jane. Mr. Noah & His Family. (p. 1185)
—Twelve Dancing Princesses. (p. 1800)
Werner, Janet. Giant Golden Book of Elves & Fairies. Williams, Garth, illus. (p. 673)
Werner, Janet & Golden Books Staff. Grandpa Bunny. Walt Disney Studios Staff, illus. (p. 709)
Werner, Joe, jt. auth. see Lowenthal, Ambur.
Werner, Justine, tr. see Leblanc, André.
Werner, Michael. Aspey's Adventures with Asperger's. (p. 107)
Werner, Nate. ABC Maze Book: The Unique Way to Discover Your ABC. (p. 3)
Werner, Sharon, jt. auth. see Forss, Sarah.
Werner, Sharon & Forss, Sarah. Alphabeasties Amazing Activities. (p. 48)
—Alphasaurs & Other Prehistoric Types. (p. 50)
—Bugs by the Numbers Counting Cards. (p. 237)
Werner, Sharon, et al. Alphabeasties. Nelson, Sarah, illus. (p. 48)
Werner, Teresa O. Quilt of Wishes. Tremlin, Nathan, illus. (p. 1428)
Werner, Teresa Orem. Quilt of Wishes. Tremlin, Nathan, illus. (p. 1428)
Werner Watson, Jane. Fuzzy Duckling. Provensen, Alice & Provensen, Martin, illus. (p. 651)
Wernham, Sara. Jolly Readers Level 2 Complete Set: Pack of 18 Books Stephen, Lib, illus. (p. 924)
—Jolly Readers Level 2 Inky & Friends: Pack of 6 Books Level 2 Stephen, Lib, illus. (p. 924)
—Jolly Readers Level 3 Inky & Friends: Pack Of 6 Stephen, Lib, illus. (p. 924)
—Jolly Readers Level 4 - General Fiction: Pack of 6 Books Stephen, Lib, illus. (p. 924)
—Jolly Readers Level 4 - Inky & Friends: Pack Of 6 (p. 924)
—Jolly Readers Level 4 - Non-Fiction: Set of 6 Books Stephen, Lib, illus. (p. 924)
Wernham, Sara, jt. auth. see Lloyd, Sue.
Wernham, Sara & Lloyd, Sue. Jolly Dictionary (US Print Letters) North American English Edition. (p. 924)
—Jolly Phonics Activity Book 4: Ai, J, Oa, Ie, Ee, Or Stephen, Lib, illus. (p. 924)
Wernicke, Maria, illus. see Baranda, Maria.
Wernicke, Maria, illus. see Galmez, Griselda.
Wernicke, Maria, illus. see White, Amy.
Werntz, Terry. Grace the Church Mouse. (p. 705)

Werrun, Anna, illus. see Pulchinski, Erin.
Wersba, Barbara. Dream Watcher. (p. 484)
—Walter: The Story of a Rat. Diamond, Donna, illus. (p. 1856)
Wert, Michael, tr. see Ozaki, Kaori.
Wert, Richard. Boxer's Backyard. (p. 217)
Wert, Yijin, tr. see Jian, Li.
Wert, Yijin, tr. Little Monkey King's Journey: Retold in English & Chinese. Jian, Li, illus. (p. 1032)
Werth, Kurt, illus. see Mincieli, Rose Laura & Ross, Rose Laura.
Werth, Kurt, illus. see Pedersen, Elsa.
Wertheim, Anne, illus. see Amstutz, Lisa J.
Wertheim, Anne, illus. see Halfmann, Janet.
Wertheim, Anne, illus. see Sherrow, Victoria.
Wertheim, Anne, illus. see Slade, Suzanne.
Wertheim, Arthur Frank. Vaudeville Wars: How the Keith-Albee & Orpheum Circuits Controlled the Big-Time & Its Performers. (p. 1833)
Wertheim, Jane, et al. Illustrated Dictionary of Chemistry. Rogers, Kirsteen, ed. (p. 857)
Wertheim, L. Jon & Moskowitz, Tobias J. Rookie Bookie. (p. 1487)
Wertheimer, Beverly, ed. see Quest, Stacy.
Werther, Mark & Mott, Lorenzo. Linen Postcards, Images of the American Dream, PRICE GUIDE 2004. (p. 1019)
Werther, Scott P. Alive! Airplane Crash in the Andes Mountains. (p. 41)
—Long Limosines: Limosinas Largas. (p. 1047)
—Long Limosines / Limosinas Largas. (p. 1047)
—Powerboats: Lanchas Motorizadas. (p. 1390)
—Powerboats / Lanchas Motorizadas. (p. 1390)
Werthiemer, Beverly, ed. see Bee, Granny.
Werthwein, Bruce. Papa Bear Goes Everywhere from His Living Room Chair: London England. (p. 1321)
Wertlake, Paul. Jules: Desert Adventure & Found Treasure: Explore with Jules, Discover Sky Art in the Anza-Borrego Desert. (p. 932)
Wertsch, Mary Edwards. Military Brats: Legacies of Childhood inside the Fortress. (p. 1142)
Wertz, Michael, illus. see Franco, Betsy.
Wertz, Michael, illus. see Moss, Samantha.
Wertz, Michael, illus. see Thomas, Wendy Russell & Ruchman, Laura.
Wesbrooks, Linda. New You: Lessons for Teenage Girls. (p. 1249)
Weschler, Toni. Cycle Savvy: The Smart Teen's Guide to the Mysteries of Her Body. (p. 397)
Wescott, Derek. Terry & Thomas the Tandem Twins. (p. 1722)
Wescott, Kelley. Street Face: Public Persona Private Pain. (p. 1666)
Wescott, Shelbi. Virulent: The Release. (p. 1844)
Wescott, Shelbi D. System (Virulent: Book Two) (p. 1693)
Wesemann, Tim. It's Your Birthday . . . Let's Celebrate! (p. 899)
—Lights! Camera! Boomer: A Bible Memory Buddy Book about Being God's Special Creation. Harrington, David, illus. (p. 1016)
—Tassel-Free Living for Grads: God's Grace for Grads. (p. 1707)
Wesley, Ann, jt. auth. see McIntyre, Abigael.
Wesley, Ann, jt. auth. see Stanley, Glen F.
Wesley, Jack, jt. auth. see Campbell, Jon.
Wesley, John. John Wesley's A Plain Account of Christian Perfection. Olson, Mark K., ed. (p. 923)
Wesley, Mary. Haphazard House. (p. 744)
Wesley, Milliana, ed. see Rosa-Mendoza, Gladys.
Wesley, Milliana, ed. My Week. Grosshauser, Peter, illus. (p. 1221)
Wesley, Misty Lynn. Dancing Easter Lilies. (p. 402)
Wesley, Omarr, illus. see Sherman, Josepha & Picture Window Books Staff.
Wesley, Omarr, illus. see Sherman, Josepha.
Wesley, Valerie Wilson. How to Almost Ruin Your School Play. (p. 814)
—How to Fish for Trouble. Roos, Maryn, illus. (p. 819)
—Willimena & Mrs. Sweetly's Guinea Pig. (p. 1934)
Wesleyan Publishing House, creator. Growing Like Jesus. (p. 726)
—Knowing God's Truth: 52 Reproducible in-Class Activities & Family Devotionals. (p. 965)
—Learning about God Student Activity Book: 52 Reproducible in-Class Activities & Family Devotionals. (p. 984)
Wesolick, Trenton. Why the Life of a Dinosaur Is Hard. (p. 1926)
Wesolowski, Harriet. Songs We Sing: Honoring Our Country. (p. 1612)
Wesolowski, Harriet, jt. auth. see Mills, Nathan.
Wesolowski, Janice. Day at the Beach: Represent & Solve Addition Problems. (p. 412)
Wess, Robert. Friends at Work & Play. Bunnett, Rochelle, photos by. (p. 638)
Wessel, Nancy Davis. People of Friendlyville. (p. 1339)
Wesseldyke, Joel. Daily Youth Devotions: Helping Teens Grow Closer to God One Day at A Time. (p. 400)
Wessel-Estes, Pam. Quilt & a Home. (p. 1428)
Wesselhoeft, Conrad. Dirt Bikes, Drones, & Other Ways to Fly. (p. 446)
Wessels, Marcie. Pirate's Lullaby. Bowers, Tim, illus. (p. 1363)
Wessling, Katherine. Backstage at a Movie Set. (p. 130)
Wessman, Bo. Building Your Own Rod. (p. 239)
Wessman, Susan C., ed. Deny Them the Night Sky: A History of the 548th Night Fighter Squadron (p. 427)
Wesson, André. Mrs. Applebee & the Sunshine Band, Book 1: Meet the Class! (p. 1187)
Wesson, Andrea, illus. see Elliott, David.
Wesson, Andrea, illus. see Knudsen, Michelle.
Wesson, Andrea, illus. see Nolan, Lucy & Nolan.
Wesson, Andrea, illus. see Young, Judy.
Wesson, Andrea, illus. see Ziefert, Harriet.
Wesson, Kevin, et al. Sport & PE: A Complete Guide to Advanced Level Study. (p. 1631)
Wesson, Seb. Guitar. (p. 731)
Wesson, Tim, illus. see Catlow, Nikalas.
Wesson, Tim, jt. auth. see Catlow, Nikalas.
Wesson, Tim & Catlow, Nikalas. Pirates v. Ancient Egyptians in a Haunted Museum. Catlow, Nikalas, illus. (p. 1364)
West, Abby. Adventures of Penny Ann & Alexa Jane. (p. 21)
West, Alex, jt. auth. see Hughes, Mair Wynn.
West, Alma Brown. Princess Logan & the Shy Spell. (p. 1404)
West, Barbara A. Encyclopedia of the Peoples of Asia & Oceania (p. 525)
West, C. Adventures of Ice Cream & Honey Buns: It's a Party. (p. 18)
—Adventures of Ice Cream & Honey Buns: Ready to Learn. (p. 18)
—Adventures of Ice Cream & Honey Buns: What Time Is It? (p. 18)
—Adventures of Ice Cream & Honey Buns: A Day in the Park. (p. 18)
West, Carly Anne. Bargaining. (p. 139)
—Murmurings. (p. 1192)
West, Casey. To Nicole with Love. Miller, Fujiko, illus. (p. 1759)
West, Cj. Taking Stock. (p. 1698)
West, Clare. Recycling Advanced English Student's Book. (p. 1453)
West, Clare, ed. see Escott, John & Henry, O.
West, Colin. Grandpa's Boneshaker Bicycle. West, Colin, illus. (p. 709)
—Have You Seen the Crocodile? Read & Share. West, Colin, illus. (p. 754)
—Helicopter Hare. (p. 763)
—Marmaduke the Magic Cat 1. (p. 1096)
—Uncle Pat & Auntie Pat. West, Colin, illus. (p. 1812)
West, Cyndi. Do I Really Want to be a Princess? (p. 457)
West, D. E., illus. see Tucker, Jason.
West, David. Allosaurus & Other Dinosaurs & Reptiles from the Upper Jurassic. (p. 47)
—Animals in the Home. (p. 83)
—Ankylosaurus: The Armored Dinosaur. West, David & Spender, Nik, illus. (p. 84)
—Ankylosaurus & Other Armored & Plated Herbivores. (p. 84)
—Astronauts. (p. 109)
—Astronauts. Robins, Jim, illus. (p. 109)
—Bermuda Triangle: Strange Happenings at Sea. (p. 167)
—Bermuda Triangle: Strange Happenings at Sea. Lacey, Mike, illus. (p. 167)
—Brachiosaurus & Other Long-Necked Herbivores. (p. 221)
—Cetiosaurus & Other Dinosaurs & Reptiles from the Middle Jurassic. (p. 288)
—Christopher Columbus: The Life of a Master Navigator & Explorer. (p. 316)
—Coelophysis & Other Dinosaurs & Reptiles from the Upper Triassic. West, David, illus. (p. 338)
—Dinosaurs on My Street. (p. 445)
—Farm Animals. (p. 573)
—Fighter Pilots. (p. 585)
—Fighter Pilots. Field, James, illus. (p. 585)
—Garden Animals. (p. 656)
—George Washington: The Life of an American Patriot. (p. 664)
—Ghosts & Poltergeists: Stories of the Supernatural. (p. 672)
—Ghosts & Poltergeists: Stories of the Supernatural. Riley, Terry, illus. (p. 672)
—Hernán Cortés: The Life of a Spanish Conquistador. (p. 771)
—Iguanodon. (p. 856)
—Illustrated Guide to Mythical Creatures. (p. 857)
—Lesothosaurus & Other Dinosaurs & Reptiles from the Lower Jurassic. West, David, illus. (p. 993)
—Lots of Things You Want to Know about Astronauts ...and Some You Don't! (p. 1057)
—Lots of Things You Want to Know about Cowboys: ... & Some You Don't! (p. 1057)
—Lots of Things You Want to Know about Gladiators: ... & Some You Don't! (p. 1057)
—Lots of Things You Want to Know about Pirates... & Some You Don't! (p. 1057)
—Lots of Things You Want to Know about Plains Indians... & Some You Don't! (p. 1057)
—Mesoamerican Myths. Taylor, Mike, illus. (p. 1129)
—Mini Beasts. (p. 1146)
—Object Thinking. (p. 1275)
—Parasaurolophus & Other Duck-Billed & Beaked Herbivores. (p. 1324)
—Pets in the Home. West, David, illus. (p. 1348)
—Pond Life. (p. 1382)
—Pteranodon: Giant of the Sky. (p. 1413)
—Pteranodon: Giant of the Sky. Riley, Terry & Ball, Geoff, illus. (p. 1413)
—Race Car Drivers. (p. 1430)
—Richard the Lionheart: The Life of a King & Crusader. (p. 1470)
—Rise of Humans. (p. 1474)
—Rockpool Animals. (p. 1483)
—Roman Myths. Watton, Ross, illus. (p. 1486)
—Spinosaurus. (p. 1628)
—Spinosaurus & Other Dinosaurs & Reptiles from the Upper Cretaceous. (p. 1628)
—Ten of the Best Adventures in Frozen Landscapes. (p. 1719)
—Ten of the Best Adventures in New Worlds. (p. 1719)
—Ten of the Best Adventures in Space. (p. 1719)
—Ten of the Best Adventures in the Sky. (p. 1719)
—Ten of the Best Adventures on the Seas. (p. 1719)
—Ten of the Best Animal Myths. (p. 1719)
—Ten of the Best Ghost Stories. (p. 1719)
—Ten of the Best Giant Stories. (p. 1719)
—Ten of the Best God & Goddess Stories. (p. 1719)
—Ten of the Best Monster Stories. (p. 1719)
—Ten of the Best Mythical Hero Stories. (p. 1719)
—Ten of the Best Prince & Princess Stories. (p. 1719)
—Ten of the Best Witch & Sorcerer Stories. (p. 1719)
—Tide Pool Animals. (p. 1747)
—Trains. (p. 1777)
—Triceratops & Other Horned Herbivores. (p. 1785)
—Tyrannosaurus Rex & Other Giant Carnivores. (p. 1805)
—Utahraptor & Other Dinosaurs & Reptiles from the Lower Cretaceous. (p. 1829)
—Velociraptor: The Speedy Thief. (p. 1835)
—Velociraptor: The Speedy Thief. Field, James, illus. (p. 1835)
—Velociraptor & Other Raptors & Small Carnivores. (p. 1835)
West, David, illus. see Ganeri, Anita.
West, David, jt. auth. see Corporate Contibutor Staff.
West, David, jt. auth. see Ganeri, Anita.
West, David, jt. auth. see Oxlade, Chris.
West, David & Gaff, Jackie. Christopher Columbus: The Life of a Master Navigator & Explorer. (p. 316)
—Richard the Lionheart: The Life of a King & Crusader. (p. 1470)
West, David & Ganeri, Anita. Giants & Ogres. West, David & Ganeri, Anita, illus. (p. 674)
—Vampires & the Undead. West, David & Ganeri, Anita, illus. (p. 1832)
—Werewolves & Other Shape-Shifters. West, David & Ganeri, Anita, illus. (p. 1875)
—Witches & Warlocks. West, David & Ganeri, Anita, illus. (p. 1941)
West, David & Parker, Steve. Ecological Disasters. (p. 502)
—Human-Made Disasters. (p. 826)
—Natural Disasters. (p. 1235)
West, David Anthony. Baseball: Secrets of the Know 'n Go Game. (p. 140)
West, Denis. Sam of the Forest Railway. (p. 1507)
West, Dorothy F. Nutrition & Fitness: Lifestyle Choices for Wellness. (p. 1274)
—Nutrition Food & Fitness. (p. 1274)
—Nutrition, Food, & Fitness: Teaching Package Teacher's Wraparound Edition. (p. 1274)
—Nutrition, Food, & Fitness. (p. 1274)
West, Edith. World Just for Me. (p. 1956)
West, Elizabeth, jt. auth. see Thompson, Gare.
West, Gina. Pookie's New Faith (p. 1383)
West, Gordon. General Class Book & Software Package: FCC Element 3 Amateur Radio License Preparation. (p. 660)
West, Hadley. Doggie Daycare. (p. 462)
West, Herbert. Forms of Energy. (p. 620)
West, Hilary. Secret Kingdom. (p. 1541)
West, Jacqueline. Second Spy Bernatene, Poly, illus. (p. 1539)
—Second Spy. (p. 1539)
—Second Spy. Bernatene, Poly, illus. (p. 1539)
—Shadows. (p. 1558)
—Shadows. Bernatene, Poly, illus. (p. 1558)
—Spellbound (p. 1625)
—Spellbound. (p. 1625)
—Still Life: The Books of Elsewhere: Volume 5. Bernatene, Poly, illus. (p. 1650)
—Still Life. (p. 1650)
—Still Life. Bernatene, Poly, illus. (p. 1650)
—Strangers. (p. 1665)
—Strangers. Bernatene, Poly, illus. (p. 1665)
West, Jeannette, ed. see Taylor, Adam.
West, Jeff, illus. see Bauer, Susan Wise.
West, Jeff, illus. see Crandell, Joyce & Bauer, Susan Wise.
West, Jeff, illus. see Phillips, Robin.
West, Jennifer, illus. see Boritzer, Etan.
West, Jeremy, illus. see Conquistadore, H.
West, Jerry. Happy Hollisters & the Haunted House Mystery. (p. 746)
—Happy Hollisters & the Indian Treasure. Hamilton, Helen, illus. (p. 746)
—Happy Hollisters at Mystery Mountain. Hamilton, Helen, illus. (p. 746)
—Happy Hollisters at Sea Gull Beach. Hamilton, Helen, illus. (p. 746)
—Happy Hollisters at Snowflake Camp. (p. 746)
—Happy Hollisters on a River Trip. Hamilton, Helen, illus. (p. 746)
West, John O. Mexican-American Folklore. (p. 1130)
West, Jonathan, jt. auth. see West, Keith R.
West, Joseph, Jr. Watching the Hokies with Daddy. (p. 1861)
West, Joyce. Drovers Road Collection: Three New Zealand Adventures West, Joyce, illus. (p. 486)
West, Judy. Do You Have My Purr? Warnes, Tim, illus. (p. 457)
West, Judy & Westerink, Gerda. Christmas Owls. (p. 315)
West, June, illus. see West, Lily June Wolford.
West, Karen L. Tommy the Squirrel Wants to Be Human. (p. 1765)
West, Kasie. Distance Between Us. (p. 453)
—On the Fence. (p. 1290)
—Pivot Point. (p. 1365)
—Split Second. (p. 1630)
West, Kathleen R. Relic. (p. 1458)
West, Kathryn E. Garden of Roses. (p. 656)
West, Keith. Parliamentary Debate. (p. 1325)
West, Keith R. & West, Jonathan. Birds. (p. 191)
West, Krista. Ansel Adams. (p. 88)
—Basics of Metals & Metalloids. (p. 142)
—Biofeedback. (p. 188)
—Carbon Chemistry. (p. 265)
—Carl Friedrich Gauss. (p. 269)
—Cocaine & Crack. (p. 337)
—Critical Perspectives on Environmental Protection. (p. 383)
—Echinoderms: Sea Stars, Sea Urchins, Sea Cucumbers, & Their Relatives. (p. 502)
—Hands-on Projects about Changes in the Earth. (p. 741)
—Hands-on Projects about Oceans. (p. 741)
—Layers of the Earth. (p. 981)
—States of Matter: Gases, Liquids, & Solids. (p. 1644)
—Underwater Warfare of the Future. (p. 1817)
—Urinary Tract Infections. (p. 1825)
West, Krista, jt. auth. see Tomecek, Stephen M.
West, Krista, ed. Critical Perspectives on Environmental Protection. (p. 383)
—Critical Perspectives on the Oceans. (p. 383)
West, Krista, et al. Steroids & Other Performance-Enhancing Drugs. (p. 1649)
West, L. J. Mr. Blacky & His Palace. (p. 1184)
West Lewis, Amanda. September 17: A Novel (p. 1551)
West, Lily June Wolford. Trip to the Cellar. West, June & Wright, Shannon, illus. (p. 1787)
West, Linzi, illus. see Kemp, Jane & Walters, Clare.
West, Linzi, illus. see Simpson-Enock, Sarah & Quarto Generic Staff.
West, Lois, jt. auth. see Snyder, Vicki.
West, Lorraine. I Like You but I Love Me. (p. 841)
—Mirror & Me. (p. 1149)
West, Maddie, ed. see Quinn, K. A. S.
West, Martha. Run, Run As Fast As You Can! (p. 1496)
West, Mary. He Called, I Answered. (p. 756)
West, Matthew, jt. auth. see Hall, Mark.
West, Meg. Bumper. (p. 241)
West, Melissa. Gravity (p. 712)
—Hover. (p. 804)
West, Mira. If Beaumont Could Speak. (p. 852)
West, Nancy. Chips - the War Dog: Based on the True-Life Adventures of the World War II K-9 Hero. (p. 308)
West, Nancy, jt. auth. see Shields, Scott.
West, Nancy H., jt. auth. see Williams, Joyce Hall.
West, Patricia. East Meets West: Japan & America. (p. 498)
West, Patty Old. Wizard of Wozzle: The Twith Logue Chronicles: Adventures with the Little People. (p. 1943)
West, Patty Old, jt. auth. see Old, Kenneth G.
West, Patty Old, jt. auth. see Old, Kennth G.
West, Patty Old & Kenneth, G. Wizard of Wozzle. (p. 1943)
West, Patty Old & Old, Kenneth G. Squidgy on the Brook: The Twith Logue Chronicles Adventures with the Little People. (p. 1637)
West, Paul & Denslow, W. W. Pearl & the Pumpkin: A Classic Halloween Tale. Denslow, W. W., illus. (p. 1333)
West, Penelope Pelham. Once upon a Time Nobody Could Read. (p. 1293)
West, Richard A. & Shortt, Yvonne M. Spell of the Iris. (p. 1625)
West, Robert. Attack of the Spider Bots (p. 114)
—Escape from the Drooling Octopod! (p. 535)
—There's a Spaceship in My Tree! (p. 1731)
West, Sara. Critters in Rainbow Forest. (p. 384)
West, Shawna Makala. Is There an Alligator at Kaipapau? (p. 890)
West, Shelia. Porky Porcupine Tackles Football. Written by Shelia West; Illustrated by D, illus. (p. 1386)
West, Simon, ed. see West, Tracey.
West, Stan, ed. see Robinson, Dino.
West, Stephen Earl. My Grandfather's Farm. Eller, Jerod R., illus. (p. 1210)
West, Steve, reader. Island of Legends. (p. 892)
West, Temple. Velvet. (p. 1835)
West, Tracey. 365 Silly Jokes for Kids. West, Simon, ed. (p. 2001)
—Attack of the Nindroids. (p. 114)
—Audio Files. Harrington, Rich, illus. (p. 115)
—Battle Match Up. (p. 146)
—Beyblade - Official Handbook: Metal Fusion & Metal Masters. (p. 173)
—Birthday Surprise. (p. 193)
—Chronicles of Ninjago: An Official Handbook. (p. 317)
—Clothing Capers. Harrington, Rich, illus. (p. 334)
—Costa Rica. (p. 368)
—Dragon Masters #1: Rise of the Earth Dragon (a Branches Book) Howells, Graham, illus. (p. 477)
—Dragon Masters #1: Rise of the Earth Dragon (a Branches Book) - Library Edition. Howells, Graham, illus. (p. 477)
—Dragon Masters #2: Saving the Sun Dragon (a Branches Book) Howells, Graham, illus. (p. 477)
—Dragon's Lair. Phillips, Craig, illus. (p. 479)
—Enemy Rising. Phillips, Craig, illus. (p. 527)
—Fingerprint Files. Harrington, Rich, illus. (p. 589)
—Free Realms: The Official Handbook & Strategy Guide. (p. 634)
—Golden Weapons. (p. 695)
—Green Ninja. (p. 722)
—Grodd's Army. Panosian, Dan, illus. (p. 725)
—Haunted Gym. (p. 753)
—How to Draw Pokemon. (p. 818)
—Lego Legends of Chima: Official Guide. (p. 990)
—Lego Ninjago: Breakout. (p. 990)
—Lego Ninjago: Chronicles of Ninjago: an Official Handbook. (p. 990)
—Lego Ninjago Reader. (p. 990)
—Mario & the Incredible Rescue. (p. 1094)
—Masters of Spinjitzu. (p. 1103)
—Me & My Robot: The Show-and-Tell Show-Off. No.2 (p. 1115)
—Me & My Robot. Revell, Cindy, illus. (p. 1115)
—Muscle Man's Guide to Life. (p. 1192)
—Night of the Mummy. Panosian, Dan, illus. (p. 1254)
—Ninja's Path. (p. 1257)
—No Way ... Way!: Road Trip. (p. 1261)
—Normal Pokédex. (p. 1264)
—Origins: A Starter Handbook. (p. 1304)
—Pirates vs. Ninja. (p. 1364)
—Plant Your Path. (p. 1369)
—Power of the Fire Dragon. Howells, Graham, illus. (p. 1389)
—Rabbit Hood: Stealing Laughs in Sherwood Forest. (p. 1429)
—Rise of the Earth Dragon. (p. 1474)
—Rise of the Snakes. (p. 1475)
—Saving the Sun Dragon. (p. 1517)
—Saving the Sun Dragon. Howells, Graham, illus. (p. 1517)
—Secret Cipher Cases. Harrington, Rich, illus. (p. 1540)
—Secret of the Water Dragon. Howells, Graham, illus. (p. 1543)
—Snake Attack! (p. 1596)
—Team Divided (p. 1710)
—Team Divided. (p. 1710)
—Teeny Tiny Cases. Harrington, Rich, illus. (p. 1715)
—Temple Run: Race Through Time to Unlock Secrets of Ancient Worlds. (p. 1718)
—Which Way, Dude?: Lumpy Space Princess Saves the World. No. 3 McGinty, Ian, illus. (p. 1911)
West, Tracey, jt. auth. see Noll, Katherine.
West, Tracey, jt. auth. see Scholastic, Inc. Staff.
West, Tracey, adapted by. Bagon Can Fly! (p. 132)
—Jack in! MegaMan! (p. 903)
—New Hero. (p. 1245)
—Penguins of Madagascar Movie Novelization. (p. 1337)
—Phantom Unmasked. (p. 1349)
—Pokémon: I Feel Skitty. (p. 1377)
—Robotic Fish Gone Wild! (p. 1480)

W

West, Tracey & Howard, Kate. Attack of the Nindroids. (p. 114)
—Techno Strike! (p. 1711)
—Titanium Ninja. (p. 1758)
West, Tracey & Noll, Katherine. Psychic Pokédex. (p. 1413)
—Top 10 Handbook. (p. 1768)
West, Tracey & Nolls, Katherine. Challenge. (p. 288)
—Ice & Fighting Pokédex. (p. 850)
—Official Pokémon Pokédex. (p. 1280)
West, Walter. When Your Success in on the Line. (p. 1906)
West, William. All about Ants. (p. 42)
—Gardener: The Tale of Toby the Tumbleweed. (p. 656)
Westall, Robert. Cielo Negro Sobre Kuwait. (p. 319)
—David & the Kittens. Geldart, William, illus. (p. 410)
—Ghost Stories. (p. 671)
—Machine Gunners. (p. 1068)
—Scarecrows. (p. 1519)
—Voces en el Viento. (p. 1847)
Westbeld, Kristine, illus. see Bert, Ruth J.
Westberg, Hannah. Hannah: My True Story of Drugs, Cutting, & Mental Illness. (p. 742)
Westberg, Jan. Athlete with Big Feet. (p. 112)
—Bale of Mail. (p. 134)
—Bo Loves to Row. (p. 205)
—Curious Miss Muss. (p. 394)
—Cute Boot. (p. 396)
—Door to the Shore. (p. 470)
—Guy the Shy Fly. (p. 733)
—Polite Knight. (p. 1380)
Westberg, Jan, illus. see Freese, Susan M.
Westbrook, Charles. Kabalyon Key. (p. 941)
Westbrook, Dick, illus. see Sommer, Carl.
Westbrook, Joe, jt. auth. see Chaffey, Tim.
Westcott, Jim. Gift. (p. 675)
—Upper Plains: Montana, North Dakota, South Dakota (p. 1825)
Westcott, Nadine Bernard. I Know an Old Lady Who Swallowed a Fly (p. 840)
Westcott, Nadine Bernard, illus. see Ayres, Katherine.
Westcott, Nadine Bernard, illus. see Bateman, Teresa.
Westcott, Nadine Bernard, illus. see Buzzeo, Toni.
Westcott, Nadine Bernard, illus. see Greenberg, David.
Westcott, Nadine Bernard, illus. see Harris, Robie H.
Westcott, Nadine Bernard, illus. see Hoberman, Mary Ann.
Westcott, Nadine Bernard, illus. see Lewison, Wendy Cheyette.
Westcott, Nadine Bernard, illus. see London, Jonathan.
Westcott, Nadine Bernard, illus. see Moran, Alex & Sullivan, Paula.
Westcott, Nadine Bernard, illus. see Pirner, Connie White.
Westcott, Nadine Bernard, illus. see Sullivan, Paula.
Westen, Leah. Jack the Tooth Rat. (p. 903)
Westen, Robin. Oprah Winfrey: I Don't Believe in Failure. (p. 1301)
—Oprah Winfrey: A Biography of a Billionaire Talk Show Host. (p. 1301)
Westenbroek, Ken, illus. see Krueger, Diane.
Westendorf, Sandra. World According to August: One Good Friend. Rand, Tracy, illus. (p. 1953)
Westera, Marleen. Sheep & Goat. Forest-Flier, Nancy, tr. from DUT. (p. 1564)
Westerfeld, Scott. Afterworlds. (p. 29)
—Behemoth. (p. 160)
—Behemoth. Thompson, Keith, illus. (p. 160)
—Blue Noon. (p. 203)
—Bogus to Bubbly: An Insider's Guide to the World of Uglies. Phillips, Craig, illus. (p. 207)
—Extras. (p. 555)
—Goliath. (p. 696)
—Goliath. Thompson, Keith, illus. (p. 696)
—Last Days. (p. 977)
—Leviathan: Leviathan; Behemoth; Goliath. Thompson, Keith, illus. (p. 1004)
—Leviathan. (p. 1004)
—Leviathan. Thompson, Keith, illus. (p. 1004)
—Manual of Aeronautics: An Illustrated Guide to the Leviathan Series. Thompson, Keith, illus. (p. 1089)
—Peeps. (p. 1335)
—Pretties (p. 1398)
—Pretties. (p. 1398)
—Secret Hour. (p. 1541)
—So Yesterday. (p. 1602)
—Specials. (p. 1623)
—Touching Darkness. (p. 1772)
—Uglies: Uglies; Pretties; Specials; Extras. (p. 1808)
—Uglies. (p. 1808)
—Uglies. Fournier, Guillaume, tr. (p. 1808)
Westerfeld, Scott & Castro, Adam-Troy. Mind-Rain: Your Favorite Authors on Scott Westerfeld's Uglies Series. Westerfeld, Scott, ed. (p. 1145)
Westerfeld, Scott & Grayson, Devin. Uglies: Cutters. (p. 1808)
—Uglies: Shay's Story. (p. 1808)
—Uglies-Cutters. Cummings, Steven, illus. (p. 1808)
Westerfield, David, illus. see Peterson, Tiffany.
Westerfield, William Stephen, illus. see Mears, Richard Chase.
Westergard, Jim, illus. see Page, P. K.
Westergard, Tim. Jesus Box (p. 915)
—Penny for Your Thoughts. (p. 1338)
Westerhout, Lynn. Making It Home: The Story of Catharine Parr Traill. (p. 1081)
Westerink, Gerda, jt. auth. see West, Judy.
Westerman, Johanna, illus. see Carson, Jana.
Westerman, Johanna, illus. see Cuyler, Margery.
Westerman, Johanna, illus. see Edwards, Julie Andrews.
Westerman, Rob. Legend of Kalikimaka: Alohalani, Kalikimaka Auntie. Tahleh, Eleykaa, illus. (p. 988)
Westerman, Robert. Alohalani Kalikimaka Auntie: Sheet Music & Lyrics. (p. 48)
—Santa We've Been Good: Sheet Music & Lyrics. (p. 1513)
Western, Colleen. Why Elephants Don't Ride School Buses. (p. 1924)
Western, David. Booms, Bubbles & Busts in the US Stock Market. (p. 213)
Western, Foley. To Be Young: Alex, 75 Lilymeg Lane, Billy Goat & Bassey. (p. 1758)
Western National Parks Association Staff, jt. contrib. by see Chaco Culture National Historical Park (N.M.) Staff.
Westerskov, Kim, photos by. Albatrosses. (p. 34)
—Diving in Antarctica. (p. 455)
—Dolphins. (p. 464)
—Forests in the Sea. (p. 618)
—Friends in the Sea. (p. 638)
—Life in a Frozen Sea. (p. 1010)
—Ocean Travelers. (p. 1277)
—Penguins. (p. 1337)
—Whales. (p. 1878)
Westfall, Douglas. History of Corona del Mar: Centennial Issue (p. 783)
Westfeldt, Linda M. Buttons' Big Ears. (p. 248)
Westfield, Patricia & Soper, Nan. Exploring the Great Lakes: A Logbook of Adventures. (p. 554)
Westheimer, Ruth K. Leopold. (p. 993)
Westhuizen, Kevin Van der, see Van der Westhuizen, Kevin.
Westine, Katherine & Craig, Phebe, texts. Dance at a Glance: Being a Quick Musical Guide. (p. 402)
Westlake, Courtney. That's How You Know. (p. 1727)
Westlake, Donald E. Risk Profession. (p. 1475)
Westley, Joan. Readers' Theater the Emperor's New Clothes: Scripts for Young Readers: (p. 1444)
Westley, Joan, retold by. Readers' Theater the Ugly Duckling: Scripts for Young Readers: the Ugly Duckling. (p. 1444)
Westley, Susan. Only Losers Cry. (p. 1298)
Westley, William. Charlie & Crow. (p. 292)
Westling, Vicki Diane. Cats Keep Out: Sam & Friends. (p. 281)
—Finders Keepers: Sam & Friends. (p. 587)
—Hannibal Breaks His Promise: Sam & Friends. (p. 743)
—Hannibal Goes to the Hospital: A Sam & Friends Book. (p. 743)
—Rudie & the Blue Van: Sam & Friends. (p. 1494)
Westlund, Emmaline. Fatim. (p. 577)
Westlund, Laura, illus. see Kenney, Karen Latchana.
Westlund, Laura, illus. see Kenney, Karen.
Westney, D. Eleanor, jt. ed. see Ghoshal, Sumantra.
Westoby, Grant. New Connections: Thinking & Learning Skills. (p. 1244)
—New Foundations: Thinking & Learning Skills. (p. 1244)
—Thinking & Learning Skills: Interactions. (p. 1734)
Weston, Alan & Gempko, Gloria. Girl from Keelonia. (p. 678)
Weston, Anne. My Brother Needs a Boa Nathan, Cheryl, illus. (p. 1199)
Weston, Avalon. All the Sky. (p. 46)
Weston, Carol. Ava & Pip. (p. 118)
—Ava & Taco Cat. (p. 118)
—Girls' Life Awesome Advice Guide to Everything. (p. 680)
—Girltalk: All the Stuff Your Sister Never Told You. (p. 681)
Weston, Carrie. If a Chicken Stayed for Supper. Fatus, Sophie, illus. (p. 852)
—Queen, the Mice & the Cheese. (p. 1425)
—What Noise Does a Rabbit Make? Byme, Richard, illus. (p. 1892)
Weston, Chris, illus. see Morrison, Grant.
Weston, Chris W. Hawgeye. (p. 755)
Weston, Elise. Coastwatcher. (p. 336)
Weston, Eunice Guy, ed. see Barrett, Anna Pearl.
Weston, Greg. Charlie Cornwall & the Historymakers. (p. 293)
—Inventors. (p. 884)
—Man Upstairs. (p. 1086)
—Ocean View Terrace & the Blue Pirate Eater. (p. 1277)
Weston, M. R. Dawn of the Shadowcasters. (p. 412)
Weston, Mark & Yamasaki, Katie. Honda: The Boy Who Dreamed of Cars. (p. 794)
Weston, Martha. Cats Are Like That. Weston, Martha, illus. (p. 281)
—Dr. Clock-Sicle: A Holiday House Reader, Level 1. (p. 475)
—Takes a Train. (p. 1697)
Weston, Martha, illus. see Cushman, Jean.
Weston, Martha, illus. see Greene, Stephanie.
Weston, Martha, illus. see Rey, H. A. & Rey, Margret.
Weston, Martha, illus. see Sharmat, Marjorie Weinman & Sharmat, Mitchell.
Weston, Martha, illus. see Sharmat, Marjorie Weinman.
Weston, Martha, illus. see Winters, Kay.
Weston, Michael R. Jerry Yang & David Filo: The Founders of Yahoo! (p. 914)
Weston, Paul, illus. see Bone, Emily.
Weston, Paula. Shadows. (p. 1558)
Weston, Rhonda. Playing to Distraction. (p. 1372)
Weston, Robert Paul. Blues for Zoey. (p. 204)
—Creature Department. Framestore, illus. (p. 380)
—Dust City. (p. 490)
—Gobbled by Ghorks. Framestore, illus. (p. 688)
—Prince Puggly of Spud & the Kingdom of Spiff. (p. 1401)
—Zorgamazoo. (p. 1990)
—Zorgamazoo. Rivas, Victor, illus. (p. 1990)
Weston, Simon. Nod from Nelson. Jones, Jac, illus. (p. 1262)
Weston, Steve, illus. see Dixon, Dougal & Picture Window Books Staff.
Weston, Steve, illus. see Dixon, Dougal.
Weston, Steve, illus. see Graf, Mike & Kaske, Anne.
Weston, Steve, jt. auth. see Barnes, Kate.
Weston, Steve, jt. auth. see Legg, Gerald.
Weston, Steve, jt. illus. see Field, James.
Weston, Steve & Field, James. Mahakala & Other Insect-Eating Dinosaurs (p. 1076)
—Masiakasaurus & Other Fish-Eating Dinosaurs (p. 1102)
—Saurophaganax & Other Meat-Eating Dinosaurs (p. 1516)
Weston Woods Staff, creator. All the Colors of the Earth. (p. 45)
—Anansi the Spider. (p. 67)
—And Then What Happened, Paul Revere? (p. 71)
—Angus & the Ducks. (p. 75)
—Antarctic Antics. (p. 88)
—Arrow to the Sun. (p. 101)
—Biggest Bear. (p. 185)
—Brave Irene. (p. 223)
—Burt Dow: Deep Water Man. (p. 244)
—Can't You Make Them Behave, King George? (p. 262)
—Caps for Sale. (p. 263)
—Casi. (p. 276)
—Caterpillar & the Polliwog. (p. 279)
—Charlie Needs a Cloak. (p. 293)
—Chato & the Party Animals. (p. 295)
—Chato's Kitchen. (p. 295)
—Chicken Little. (p. 300)
—Chicken Soup with Rice. (p. 300)
—Children Make Terrible Pets. (p. 302)
—Chrysanthemum. (p. 317)
—Clown of God. (p. 335)
—Corduroy. (p. 367)
—Crazy Hair Day. (p. 377)
—Crictor. (p. 382)
—Crow Boy. (p. 385)
—Crow Call. (p. 385)
—Curious George Rides a Bike. (p. 393)
—Dark, Dark Tale. (p. 407)
—Day of the Dead / el Día de Los Muertos. (p. 414)
—Dem Bones. (p. 425)
—Doctor de Soto. (p. 459)
—Doctor Desoto. (p. 459)
—Dot the Fire Dog. (p. 472)
—Drummer Hoff. (p. 487)
—Duck for President. (p. 488)
—Duck on a Bike. (p. 488)
—Duke Ellington. (p. 489)
—Each Peach Pear Plum. (p. 492)
—Elizabeti's Doll. (p. 513)
—Ella Fitzgerald. (p. 514)
—Elves & the Shoemaker. (p. 517)
—Emily's First 100 Days of School. (p. 519)
—Five Creatures. (p. 600)
—Fletcher & the Falling Leaves. (p. 603)
—Fletcher & the Snowflake Christmas. (p. 603)
—Frog Went A-Courtin' (p. 640)
—Funny Little Woman. (p. 650)
—George Washington's Mother. (p. 665)
—Giggle, Giggle Quack. (p. 676)
—Giving Thanks. (p. 681)
—Goggles! (p. 692)
—Goldilocks & the Three Bears. (p. 696)
—Goodnight Moon. (p. 701)
—Grandfather's Journey. (p. 707)
—Gym Teacher from the Black Lagoon. (p. 733)
—Hansel & Gretel. (p. 743)
—Happy Birthday Moon. (p. 745)
—Harold & the Purple Crayon. (p. 749)
—Harold's Fairy Tale. (p. 749)
—Henry Hikes to Fitchburg. (p. 768)
—Henry's Freedom Box. (p. 769)
—Hiawatha. (p. 775)
—Hiawatha Weston Woods. (p. 775)
—Hondo & Fabian. (p. 794)
—How Do Dinosaurs Eat Their Food? (p. 806)
—How Do Dinosaurs Get Well Soon? (p. 807)
—How Do Dinosaurs Go to School? (p. 807)
—How Much Is a Million? (p. 811)
—I Like Me! (p. 841)
—I Lost My Bear. (p. 841)
—I Stink! (p. 846)
—If You Made a Million. (p. 854)
—In the Night Kitchen. (p. 867)
—In the Small, Small Pond. (p. 867)
—Inch by Inch. (p. 868)
—Island of the Skog. (p. 892)
—James Marshall's Cinderella. (p. 907)
—Johnny Appleseed. (p. 923)
—Joseph Had a Little Overcoat. (p. 926)
—Kiss for Little Bear. (p. 961)
—Kitten's First Full Moon. (p. 963)
—Little Bear's Visit. (p. 1024)
—Little Drummer Boy. (p. 1027)
—Little House. (p. 1029)
—Little Old Lady Who Was Not Afraid of Anything. (p. 1032)
—Little Red Hen. (p. 1034)
—Little Red Lighthouse & the Great Gray Bridge. (p. 1035)
—Lon Po Po. (p. 1046)
—Madeline's Rescue. (p. 1070)
—Make Way for Ducklings. (p. 1079)
—Man Who Walked Between the Towers. (p. 1086)
—March on! the Day My Brother Martin Changed the World. (p. 1091)
—Martin's Big Words. (p. 1098)
—May I Bring a Friend? (p. 1112)
—Mike Mulligan & His Steam Shovel. (p. 1141)
—Millions of Cats Weston Woods. (p. 1144)
—Miss Nelson Is Missing. (p. 1151)
—Morris's Disappearing. (p. 1176)
—Morris's Disappearing Bag. (p. 1176)
—Mr Rabbit & the Lovely Present. (p. 1186)
—Mr. Rabbit & the Lovely Present. (p. 1186)
—Mufaro's Beautiful Daughters. (p. 1189)
—Napping House. (p. 1229)
—Norman the Doorman. (p. 1264)
—North Star. (p. 1265)
—One Fine Day. (p. 1295)
—Open Wide- Tooth School Inside. (p. 1299)
—Otto Runs for President. (p. 1307)
—Over in the Meadow. (p. 1313)
—Owen. (p. 1314)
—Pet Show! (p. 1345)
—Peter's Chair. (p. 1347)
—Pete's a Pizza. (p. 1348)
—Petunia. (p. 1349)
—Picture for Harold's Room. (p. 1355)
—Pigeon Finds a Hot Dog. (p. 1357)
—Pinkerton, Behave! (p. 1360)
—Planting a Rainbow. (p. 1369)
—Players in Pigtails. (p. 1372)
—Possum Magic. (p. 1387)
—Rainbabies. (p. 1435)
—Rapunzel. (p. 1439)
—Ready, Freddy! #1: Tooth Trouble. (p. 1447)
—Ready, Freddy! #3: Homework Hassles. (p. 1447)
—Ready, Freddy! #4: Don't Sit on My Lunch! (p. 1447)
—Red Riding Hood. (p. 1454)
—Rikki-Tikki-Tavi. (p. 1472)
—Roberto the Insect Architect. (p. 1479)
—Rosa. (p. 1488)
—Scrambled States of America Talent Show. (p. 1532)
—Seven Blind Mice. (p. 1554)
—Shh! We're Writing the Constitution. (p. 1566)
—Snowflake Bentley. (p. 1600)
—Snowy Day. (p. 1601)
—Star Spangled Banner. (p. 1641)
—Stone Soup. (p. 1652)
—Story about Ping. (p. 1656)
—Story-A Story. (p. 1656)
—Story-Astory. (p. 1656)
—Sylvester & the Magic Pebble. (p. 1692)
—T Is for Terrible. (p. 1694)
—Tale of the Mandarin Ducks. (p. 1700)
—There Was an Old Lady Who Swallowed a Fly. (p. 1730)
—This Is the House That Jack Built. (p. 1736)
—Three Cheers for Catherine the Great. (p. 1741)
—Three Little Pigs. (p. 1743)
—Tikki Tikki Tembo. (p. 1750)
—Time of Wonder. (p. 1752)
—Too Many Tamales. (p. 1767)
—Too Many Toys! (p. 1767)
—True Story of the 3 Little Pigs. (p. 1793)
—Ugly Duckling. (p. 1808)
—Waiting for Wings. (p. 1853)
—Weeekend with Wendell. (p. 1871)
—Weekend with Wendell. (p. 1872)
—What to Do about Alice? (p. 1894)
—Where Was Patrick Henry on the 29th of May? (p. 1910)
—Whistle for Willie. (p. 1912)
—Wild about Books. (p. 1928)
—Wilfrid Gordon Mcdonald Partridge. (p. 1932)
—Will I Have a Friend? (p. 1932)
—Will You Sign Here, John Hancock? (p. 1932)
—Wings: A Tale of Two Chickens. (p. 1936)
Weston Woods Studios Inc. Staff, creator. Good Night, Gorilla. (p. 699)
Westover, Alli. My Daddy Works at NASA. (p. 1201)
Westover, G. R. Fireplace: Where Usual & Unusual Things Happen. (p. 592)
Westover, Gail. Mrs Mouse's Garden Party in Giggleswick Village. Daly, Karen Anne, illus. (p. 1187)
Westover, Steve. Crater Lake: Battle for Wizard Island. (p. 376)
—Nothing Named Silas. (p. 1268)
—Return of the Mystic Gray. (p. 1464)
Westphal, Jeremy. Mummy's Curse. (p. 1191)
Westphal, Laurie E. Science Dictionary for Kids: The Essential Guide to Science Terms, Concepts, & Strategies. (p. 1525)
Westphal, Michael, jt. auth. see Sequeira, Michele.
West-Pratt, Judy Lea. Just Like Me! (p. 939)
Westra, Elizabeth. Alexander & the Stallion. Ampel, Kenneth Robert, illus. (p. 36)
Westrick, A. B. Brotherhood. (p. 231)
Westrup, Hugh. Electricity. (p. 509)
—Mixtures & Solutions. (p. 1156)
West-Smith, Sandy. Who Will Teach Johnny: The Difference Between Good Touches & Bad Touches? (p. 1919)
Westwell, Ian. Civil War. (p. 325)
—Vietnam War. (p. 1841)
—World War I. (p. 1958)
Westwood, Chris. Graveyard Shift. (p. 712)
Wetherby, Mark. Tales of Mossy Dell. (p. 1702)
Wetherell, Elizabeth, jt. auth. see Warner, Susan.
Wetherhead, Kate, jt. auth. see Keenan-Bolger, Andrew.
Wethington, Constance. Adventures of One-Eyed Jack. (p. 21)
Wethington, Constance. Butterfly's Ball. (p. 248)
Wethington, Constance. Mystic Imaginations. (p. 1226)
Wethington, Julie & Wethington, Lang. Yes I Can! Have My Cake & Food Allergies Too. Wethington, Julie & Wethington, Lang, illus. (p. 1970)
Wethington, Lang, jt. auth. see Wethington, Julie.
Wetmore, Barry, illus. see Frankel, Fred.
Wetmore, Barry, illus. see Whitham, Cynthia.
Wetterau, John Moncure. Joe Burke's Last Stand: Every Story Is a Love Story. (p. 920)
Wetterer, Charles M. When Grandad Babysat. (p. 1902)
Wetterer, Charles M., jt. auth. see Wetterer, Margaret K.
Wetterer, Charles M. & Wetterer, Margaret K. Chief Justice. Walters, Kurt K. C., illus. (p. 301)
Wetterer, Margaret K. Kate Shelley y el Tren de Medianoche. Translations.com Staff, tr. (p. 944)
—Midnight Adventure of Kate Shelley, Train Rescuer. (p. 1138)
—Midnight Adventure of Kate Shelley, Train Rescuer. Trover, Zachary, illus. (p. 1138)
Wetterer, Margaret K., jt. auth. see Wetterer, Charles M.
Wetterer, Margaret K. & Wetterer, Charles M. Caminando Bajo la Nieve. Young, Mary, illus. (p. 256)
—Snow Walker. Young, Mary O'Keefe, illus. (p. 1599)
—Snowshoeing Adventure of Milton Daub, Blizzard Trekker. (p. 1601)
—Snowshoeing Adventure of Milton Daub, Blizzard Trekker. Trover, Zachary, illus. (p. 1601)
Wettersten, Laura. My Fair Lady. (p. 1202)
Wetzel, Kurt, ed. Labour Relations & Health Reform: A Comparative Study of Five Jurisdictions. (p. 970)
Weulersse, Odile & Merz, Kathleen. Nasreddine. Dautremer, Rebecca, illus. (p. 1230)
Weverka, Peter. Office 2003 All-in-One Desk Reference for Dummies(r). (p. 1280)
Wevers, Lydia. Reading on the Farm: Victorian Fiction & the Colonial World. (p. 1446)
Wewer, Iris. My Wild Sister & Me. (p. 1221)
Wewers, Jason. Candy Bar Adventures: March of the Evil Mard. (p. 261)
Wexler, Django. Forbidden Library. (p. 616)

—Mad Apprentice. Jansson, Alexander, illus. (p. 1068)
Wexler, Michael, jt. auth. see Hulme, John.
Wexo, John Bonnett. Alligators & Crocodiles. (p. 47)
—Bears. (p. 151)
—Big Cats. (p. 180)
—Dinosaurs. (p. 444)
—Eagles. (p. 492)
—Elefantes. Rountree, Monica, tr. (p. 510)
—Elephants. (p. 511)
—Focas y Leones Marinos. Rountree, Monica, tr. (p. 610)
—Giraffes. (p. 677)
—Gorilas. Rountree, Monica, tr. (p. 702)
—Gorillas. (p. 703)
—Jirafas. Rountree, Monica, tr. (p. 919)
—Osos. Rountree, Monica, tr. (p. 1306)
—Panteras. Rountree, Monica, tr. (p. 1321)
—Seals & Sea Lions. (p. 1536)
—Serpientes. Rountree, Monica, tr. (p. 1552)
—Sharks. (p. 1562)
—Snakes. (p. 1596)
—Whales. (p. 1878)
—Wolves. (p. 1945)
Weyland, Jack. As Always, Dave. (p. 105)
—Brianna, My Brother, & the Blog. (p. 227)
Weymouth Seguin, Marilyn. Freedom Stairs: The Story of Adam Lowry Rankin, Underground Railroad Conductor. (p. 635)
Weyn, Suzanne. Bar Code Prophecy. (p. 137)
—Bar Code Rebellion. (p. 137)
—Bar Code Tattoo. (p. 137)
—Beaten. (p. 152)
—Crimson Thread: A Retelling of Rumpelstiltskin. (p. 383)
—Cursed Scarab. (p. 395)
—Daring to Dream. (p. 407)
—Dr. Frankenstein's Daughters. (p. 475)
—Empty. (p. 521)
—Faces of the Dead. (p. 561)
—Full Impact. (p. 646)
—Haunted Museum #2: the Phantom Music Box: (a Hauntings Novel) (p. 753)
—Haunted Museum #3: the Pearl Earring: (a Hauntings Novel) (p. 753)
—Haunted Museum - The Cursed Scarab. (p. 753)
—Invisible World. (p. 886)
—Learning to Fly. (p. 985)
—Night Dance: A Retelling of the Twelve Dancing Princesses. (p. 1253)
—Pearl Earring. (p. 1333)
—Phantom Music Box. (p. 1349)
—Recruited. (p. 1452)
—Reincarnation. (p. 1457)
—Renaissance Kids. Graves, Linda Dockey, illus. (p. 1460)
—Titanic Locket. (p. 1758)
—Water Song: A Retelling of the Frog Prince. (p. 1863)
Weyn, Suzanne, jt. auth. see Windham, Ryder.
Weyn, Suzanne, adapted by. Ice Princess. (p. 850)
Weyn, Suzanne & Gonzalez, Diana. South Beach Sizzle. (p. 1616)
Weyn, Suzanne, et al. Gracie. (p. 705)
Wezeman, Phyllis Vos & Liechty, Anna L. Hymn Stories for Children: Spirituals. (p. 831)
—Tell Me a Story: 30 Children's Sermons Based on Best-Loved Books. (p. 1716)
Wezeman, Phyllis Vos, et al. Guiding Young Teens Through Life's Losses. (p. 730)
—Wipe the Tears: 30 Children's Sermons on Death. (p. 1939)
Wezeman, Phylllis Vos & Liechty, Anna L. Hymn Stories for Children: The Apostles' Creed. (p. 831)
WFM Services, illus. see Walsh, Patrick M., Jr.
WGBH, illus. see Candlewick Press, Candlewick.
WGBH Educational Foundation Staff, illus. see Candlewick Press Staff.
Whalen, Diane. Tales of the Christmas Store. (p. 1702)
Whalen, Erin T. Charlie Gets Spooked (p. 293)
Whaley, John Corey. Noggin. (p. 1262)
—Where Things Come Back. (p. 1910)
Whaley, Michelle Marie. Does It Really Rain Cats & Dogs? Ortiz, Ada, illus. (p. 460)
Whaley, Stacey Lynn, jt. auth. see Faye, Joanne.
Whallett, Liz, illus. see Chowdhury, Uttom & Robertson, Mary.
Whalon, Pete. Saigon Zoo: Vietnam's Other War:Sex, Drugs, Rock n' Roll. (p. 1503)
Whamhower, Shogun. Nerdy Ninjas vs the Really Really Bad Guys. McKenzie, Heath, illus. (p. 1241)
Whamond, Dave. My Think-a-Ma-Jink. Whamond, Dave & Owlkids Books Inc. Staff, illus. (p. 1220)
—Oddrey. (p. 1278)
—Superbrain: The Insider's Guide to Getting Smart. (p. 1682)
Whamond, Dave, illus. see Becker, Helaine.
Whamond, Dave, illus. see Brouwer, Sigmund.
Whamond, Dave, illus. see Rovetch, L. Bob.
Whamond, Dave, illus. see Stuchner, Joan Betty.
Whamond, Dave, illus. see Szpirglas, Jeff & Saint-Onge, Danielle.
Whamond, Dave, illus. see Wyatt, Valerie.
Whamond, Dave & Owlkids Books Inc. Staff. Oddrey. (p. 1278)
—Oddrey & the New Kid. (p. 1278)
Whamond, O. T. Wiffin & Wussell Go Digging. (p. 1927)
Wharnsby, Dawud. Picnic of Poems: In Allah's Green Garden. (p. 1355)
Wharry, David, tr. see Durand, Stephane & Poyet, Guillaume.
Wharton, Edith. Edith Wharton. McConnell, James, illus. (p. 504)
—Ethan Frome - Literary Touchstone. (p. 539)
Wharton, Ellie. Fairy Magic! Lee, Maxine & Enright, Amanda, illus. (p. 563)
—Preschool Pirates. Enright, Amanda & Lee, Maxine, illus. (p. 1396)
Wharton, Jennifer Heyd, illus. see Martelli, Dawn.
Wharton, Kate. What Does Mrs. Claus Do? Slade, Christian, illus. (p. 1884)
Wharton, Laura Spanton, et al. Mystery at the Phoenix Festival. (p. 1224)
Whatley, jt. auth. see Whatley, Bruce.
Whatley, Ben Smith, illus. see Whatley, Bruce.
Whatley, Bruce. Clinton Gregory's Secret. (p. 333)
—Little Drummer Boy. Whatley, Bruce, illus. (p. 1027)
—Tin Toys. Whatley, Ben Smith, illus. (p. 1755)
—Watchmaker Who Saved Christmas: A Christmas Classic. (p. 1861)
Whatley, Bruce, illus. see Autry, Gene & Haldeman, Dakley.
Whatley, Bruce, illus. see Berger, Samantha.
Whatley, Bruce, illus. see Brenner, Emily.
Whatley, Bruce, illus. see Crew, Gary.
Whatley, Bruce, illus. see French, Jackie.
Whatley, Bruce, illus. see Gwynne, Phillip.
Whatley, Bruce, illus. see Kimmel, Eric A. & Korelitz, Jean Hanff.
Whatley, Bruce, illus. see Moore, Clement C.
Whatley, Bruce, illus. see Palatini, Margie.
Whatley, Bruce, illus. see Rox, John.
Whatley, Bruce, illus. see Smith, Rosie.
Whatley, Bruce, jt. auth. see French, Jackie.
Whatley, Bruce & Beatrice, Chris. Aesop's Fables: A Pop-Up Book of Classic Tales. (p. 26)
Whatley, Bruce & Smith Whatley, Ben. Tin Toys. (p. 1755)
Whatley, Bruce & Whatley. Wait! No Paint! Whatley, Bruce, illus. (p. 1852)
Whatley, Charlotte. Peter Pan Paper Dolls. (p. 1347)
Whatley, Roger Vaughn. Lost Friends. (p. 1055)
Whatmore, Candace. Monsters Coloring Book. (p. 1169)
Whatmore, Candice. 25 Postcards to Color. (p. 1996)
Whatmore, Candice, illus. see Dalby, Elizabeth.
Whatmore, Candice, illus. see Khan, Sarah.
Whatmore, Candice, illus. see Marks, Anthony.
Whatmore, Candice, jt. illus. see Barrance, Reuben.
Whatmore, George B. De-Contaminating the New Testament Based on Lessons Learned from the Galileo School. (p. 416)
Whatmore, Richard & Young, Brian, eds. Palgrave Advances in Intellectual History. (p. 1320)
Wheadon, Bill, jt. auth. see Wheadon, Bill(Beepa).
Wheadon, Bill(Beepa) & Wheadon, Bill. Josie's Very Unhappy Hair: Up North at Nana's. Clay, Josh, illus. (p. 927)
Wheat, Charlotte. That Bodacious, God-Trustin' Prophet, Elijah! From the down-home Bible Stories Series. (p. 1726)
Wheat, Tiffany. There's a Gopher in My Garden! (p. 1731)
Wheat, Valerie A. Kid Who Loved Mac & Cheese. (p. 952)
Wheatley, A. Greeks. (p. 721)
Wheatley, Abigail. Children's Cupcake Kit. (p. 303)
—Story of Painting. Riley, Janis, ed. (p. 1659)
Wheatley, Abigail, ed. see Hindley, Judy.
Wheatley, Maria, illus. see Smith, Alastair.
Wheatley, Maria, illus. see Tatchell, Judy.
Wheatley, Nadia. Australians All: A History of Growing up from the Ice Age to the Apology. Searle, Ken, illus. (p. 116)
—Listening to Mondrian. (p. 1022)
—Playground: Listening to Stories from Country & from Inside the Heart. Searle, Ken, illus. (p. 1372)
Wheatley, Sandra. Marmaduke the Mighty. (p. 1096)
Wheatley, Steven. Jack's Little Angel. (p. 904)
Wheaton, David. University of Destruction: Your Game Plan for Spiritual Victory on Campus. (p. 1820)
Wheaton, Elizabeth. Ms. The Story of Gloria Steinem. (p. 1188)
Wheatonnovember. Little Hermit Ant. (p. 1029)
Whedon, Joss. Fray: Future Slayer: Future Slayer. (p. 631)
—Gift. (p. 675)
Whedon, Joss, et al. MySpace Dark Horse Presents Allie, Scott & Hahn, Sierra, eds. (p. 1222)
Whedon, Zack. Shepherd's Tale. (p. 1565)
Whedon, Zack, illus. see Rugg, Jim.
Wheeler, Alex, jt. auth. see Scholastic, Inc. Staff.
Wheeler, Alyssa. Tilley Tally's Adventures: Book One. (p. 1750)
Wheeler, Amanda, jt. auth. see Culham, Ruth.
Wheeler, Annie. Painting on a Canvas: Art Adventures for Kids Dixon, Debra Spina & Spina Dixon, Debra, illus. (p. 1318)
Wheeler, Arville. White Squaw: The True Story of Jennie Wiley. Bengtz, Ture, illus. (p. 1913)
Wheeler, Barbara-Ann. In My Own Words: Genesis & Exodus. (p. 864)
Wheeler, Billy E., jt. auth. see Jones, Loyal.
Wheeler, Billy Edd. Star of Appalachia. (p. 1640)
Wheeler, Billy Edd, jt. auth. see Jones, Loyal.
Wheeler, Billy Edd & Jones, Loyal, eds. Laughter in Appalachia: A Festival of Southern Mountain Humor. (p. 980)
Wheeler, Camaryn. Talking Dolls. (p. 1703)
Wheeler, Christine. Bella's Marigold Cake. (p. 162)
Wheeler, Darcy. Lydia the Lazy Ladybug. (p. 1066)
Wheeler, David & Twigg, Natalie. My Pirate Grandad. (p. 1217)
Wheeler, David Cole, illus. see Nemmers, Lee.
Wheeler, E. B. Haunting of Springett Hall. (p. 754)
Wheeler, Eliza. Miss Maple's Seeds. Wheeler, Eliza, illus. (p. 1151)
Wheeler, Eliza, illus. see Black, Holly.
Wheeler, Eliza, illus. see Rockliff, Mara.
Wheeler, Eliza, illus. see Springstubb, Tricia.
Wheeler, Eliza, illus. see Wood, Maryrose.
Wheeler, Elizabeth. Asher's Fault. (p. 105)
—Asher's Shot. (p. 105)
Wheeler, Esther. Loner. (p. 1046)
Wheeler, Irvin. Justina's Dream. (p. 940)
Wheeler, Isabelle. Many a Mickle: Little Things Not to Be Forgotten. (p. 1089)
Wheeler, J. D. Gummery & Lubber. (p. 731)
Wheeler, Jacque & Hartsfield, Mariella G. Tall Betsy & the Crackerbarrel Tales. (p. 1704)
Wheeler, Jacque & Laughlin, Haller. Assignments in Musical Theatre: Acting & Directing. Landes, William-Alan, ed. (p. 107)
Wheeler, Janet D. Billie Bradley & Her Inheritance or the Queer Homestead at Cherry Corners. (p. 187)
Wheeler, Jennifer Lynn. Can't Kill This Love. (p. 262)
Wheeler, Jenny Lee. Weird Is Normal When Teenagers Grieve. (p. 1872)
Wheeler, Jenny Lee, illus. see Wheeler, Karla.
Wheeler, Jill C. Alvin Schwartz. (p. 51)
—Antonia Novello: Fantastic Physician. (p. 90)
—Beetle. (p. 158)
—Brad Pitt. (p. 221)
—Breaking Barriers Set 3. (p. 225)
—Camaro. (p. 255)
—Cesar Chavez. (p. 288)
—Chien-Shiung Wu: Phenomenal Physicist. (p. 301)
—Coalition Leaders. (p. 336)
—Cynthia Kadohata. (p. 397)
—Dav Pilkey. (p. 410)
—Denzel Washington. (p. 427)
—E. B. White. (p. 491)
—Faith Hill. (p. 565)
—Gandhi. (p. 655)
—Gary Paulsen. (p. 657)
—George Washington Carver. (p. 664)
—Harriet Tubman. (p. 750)
—Hayat Sindi: Brilliant Biochemist. (p. 755)
—Hillary Rodham Clinton. (p. 779)
—Iowa. (p. 886)
—Jackie Robinson. (p. 904)
—Jennifer Lopez. (p. 913)
—Joanne Simpson: Magnificent Meteorologist. (p. 919)
—Kansas. (p. 943)
—Kelly Clarkson. (p. 948)
—L. Frank Baum. (p. 969)
—Laura Bush. (p. 980)
—Madonna. (p. 1070)
—Mae Jemison: Awesome Astronaut. (p. 1070)
—Martin Luther King, Jr. (p. 1098)
—Maserati. (p. 1102)
—Mel Gibson. (p. 1125)
—Mercedes-Benz. (p. 1127)
—Michael Vick. (p. 1135)
—New Jersey. (p. 1245)
—New Mexico. (p. 1246)
—Pennsylvania. (p. 1338)
—Pioneer Practices with Ree Drummond. (p. 1361)
—Pope John Paul II. (p. 1384)
—Rachel Carson: Extraordinary Environmentalist. (p. 1431)
—Rick Riordan. (p. 1470)
—Rolls Royce. (p. 1485)
—Rosa Parks (p. 1488)
—Saddam Hussein. (p. 1501)
—Scott O'Dell. (p. 1531)
—Sharon Creech. (p. 1563)
—Simple Solutions with Rachael Ray. (p. 1578)
—Susan B. Anthony. (p. 1687)
—Suzanne Collins. (p. 1688)
—Thurgood Marshall. (p. 1746)
—Walter Dean Myers. (p. 1856)
—Yuyi Morales. (p. 1983)
Wheeler, Jill C., jt. auth. see ABDO Publishing Company Staff.
Wheeler, Jody. First Noel. (p. 596)
Wheeler, Jody, illus. see Alcott, Louisa May.
Wheeler, Jody, illus. see Freeman, Don & Hennessy, B. G.
Wheeler, Jody, illus. see Lindemann, Lindy.
Wheeler, Jody, illus. see Sharmat, Marjorie Weinman & Sharmat, Mitchell.
Wheeler, Jody, illus. see Sharmat, Mitchell.
Wheeler, Jody, illus. see Wilder, Laura Ingalls.
Wheeler, Jordan. Chuck in the City. Auchter, Christopher, illus. (p. 318)
—Just a Walk. (p. 937)
Wheeler, Jordan, ed. see Smith, M. Jane.
Wheeler, Jordan & Jackson, Dennis. Christmas at Wapos Bay (p. 312)
Wheeler, Joyce. Countries of Whine & Roses. (p. 372)
Wheeler, Karla. Heart-Shaped Pickles: Gentle Grief Support for Kids & Grownups. Wheeler, Jenny Lee, illus. (p. 760)
Wheeler, Kathryn. Act It Out with Readers' Theater, Grades 4 - 5: Build Fluency with Multi-Level Plays! (p. 9)
Wheeler, Kim. Adventures of Jonny Plumb. (p. 19)
—Even More Adventures of Jonny Plumb. (p. 541)
—Jonny Plumb's New Adventures... (p. 925)
Wheeler, Kimberly. Emma's Extravagant Expedition. (p. 520)
Wheeler, Lance. Kula & the Old Ukulele. (p. 968)
Wheeler, Laura C. I'll Kiss You A Promise. (p. 856)
Wheeler, Lee Alden. Bucking the Odds (p. 234)
Wheeler, Leslie. Dolly's Day in the Garden. (p. 464)
Wheeler, Lisa. Boogie Knights. Siegel, Mark, illus. (p. 210)
—Bubble Gum, Bubble Gum. Huliska-Beith, Laura & Harriet Kasak Portfolio Staff, illus. (p. 233)
—Castaway Cats. Goembel, Ponder, illus. (p. 276)
—Dino-Baseball. Gott, Barry, illus. (p. 441)
—Dino-Basketball. Gott, Barry, illus. (p. 441)
—Dino-Boarding. Gott, Barry, illus. (p. 441)
—Dino-Football. Gott, Barry, illus. (p. 441)
—Dino-Hockey. Gott, Barry, illus. (p. 441)
—Dino-Soccer. Gott, Barry, illus. (p. 441)
—Dino-Swimming. Gott, Barry, illus. (p. 441)
—Dino-Wrestling. Gott, Barry, illus. (p. 441)
—Farmer Dale's Red Pickup Truck. Bates, Ivan, illus. (p. 574)
—Invasion of the Pig Sisters. Ansley, Frank, illus. (p. 883)
—Jazz Baby. Christie, R. Gregory, illus. (p. 911)
—Mammoths on the Move. Cyrus, Kurt, illus. (p. 1085)
—New Pig in Town. Ansley, Frank, illus. (p. 1246)
—Old Cricket. Goembel, Ponder, illus. (p. 1283)
—One Dark Night. Bates, Ivan, illus. (p. 1294)
—Pet Project: Cute & Cuddly Vicious Verses. OHora, Zachariah, illus. (p. 1345)
—Seadogs: An Epic Ocean Operetta. Siegel, Mark, illus. (p. 1536)
—Sixteen Cows. Cyrus, Kurt, illus. (p. 1583)
—Spinster Goose: Twisted Rhymes for Naughty Children. Blackall, Sophie, illus. (p. 1628)
—Turk & Runt: A Thanksgiving Comedy. Ansley, Frank, illus. (p. 1797)
—Ugly Pie. Solomon, Heather, illus. (p. 1808)
—Uncles & Antlers. Floca, Brian, illus. (p. 1812)
—When Pigs Fly. Ansley, Frank, illus. (p. 1904)
—Where, Oh Where, Is Santa Claus? Bates, Ivan, illus. (p. 1909)
—Who's Afraid of Granny Wolf? Ansley, Frank, illus. (p. 1920)
Wheeler, Lisa, jt. auth. see Ansley, Frank.
Wheeler, Mary A. Over the Edge. (p. 1314)
—Secret Stone: Book One. (p. 1544)
Wheeler, Opal. Frederic Chopin, Son of Poland Later Years. Price, Christine, illus. (p. 633)
—Handel: at the Court of Kings. Greenwalt, Mary, illus. (p. 740)
—Ludwig Beethoven & the Chiming Tower Bells. Greenwalt, Mary, illus. (p. 1064)
Wheeler, Opal & Deucher, Sybil. Franz Schubert & his Merry Friends. Greenwalt, Mary, illus. (p. 631)
—Joseph Haydn: the Merry Little Peasant. Greenwalt, Mary, illus. (p. 926)
—Mozart the Wonder Boy. Greenwalt, Mary, illus. (p. 1184)
—Sebastian Bach: the Boy from Thuringia. Greenwalt, Mary, illus. (p. 1539)
Wheeler, Patti & Hemstreet, Keith. Travels with Gannon & Wyatt: Botswana. (p. 1780)
—Travels with Gannon & Wyatt - Botswana. (p. 1780)
—Travels with Gannon & Wyatt - Egypt. (p. 1780)
—Travels with Gannon & Wyatt - Great Bear Rainforest. (p. 1780)
Wheeler, Ron. Stinky Stevens: The Missing Soggy Soccer Shoe (Book 3) (p. 1651)
—Stinky Stevens: Escape from Aunt Smoochie-Kiss (Book 4) (p. 1651)
Wheeler, Ron, illus. see Davis, Brian.
Wheeler, Ron, illus. see Gould, Judith S. & Burke, Mary F.
Wheeler, Ron, illus. see Gould, Judith S. & Gould, Evan Jay.
Wheeler, Ron, illus. see Hein, Marilyn B.
Wheeler, Ron, illus. see Shevick, Ed.
Wheeler, Ron, illus. see Woodman, Ros.
Wheeler, Sara. Evia: Travels on an Undiscovered Greek Island. (p. 546)
Wheeler, Shannon & Torres, J. Wall E: Recharge. Vol. 1 Luthi, Morgan, illus. (p. 1854)
Wheeler, Shannon, et al. Wall-E: Recharge. Vol. 1 Luthi, Morgan & Barks, Carl, illus. (p. 1854)
Wheeler, Sherrie Leigh. Defending Americ: A Children's Guide to Understanding the Circumstances & Sacrifices of War. (p. 423)
Wheeler, Sr, CR. Timmy the Lonely Ghost: Case of the Missing Parents. (p. 1755)
Wheeler, T. Runaway River: Two Boys, a Raft, a Dog, & an Eagle. (p. 1496)
Wheeler, Tonika Yvonne. Damaged Goods. Attaway, Anelda, ed. (p. 401)
Wheeler, William Bruce, et al. Discovering the Ancient Past: A Look at the Evidence. (p. 449)
—Discovering the Twentieth-Century World: A Look at the Evidence. (p. 450)
Wheeler-Cribb, Peggy. Madeline Becomes a Star. Bensch, April, illus. (p. 1070)
Wheeler-Gibb, Madelon, tr. from CHI. Star & Cloud: Venerable Master Hsing Yun. Zheng, Wen, illus. (p. 1640)
Wheeler-Toppen, Jodi. Cool Chemistry Activities for Girls (p. 363)
—Ghosts & Atoms Haus, Estudio, illus. (p. 672)
—Human Muscles (p. 826)
—Orchid Mantises & Other Extreme Insect Adaptations (p. 1302)
—Science Experiments That Explode & Implode: Fun Projects for Curious Kids (p. 1525)
—Science Experiments That Fizz & Bubble: Fun Projects for Curious Kids (p. 1525)
Wheeler-Toppen, Jodi, et al. Extreme Adaptations (p. 556)
—Girls Science Club. (p. 680)
Wheeler-Toppen, Jodi Lyn. Gross Science Projects (p. 725)
Wheelhouse, M. V., illus. see Ewing, Juliana Horatia.
Wheelie, P. Fishing Trip: The tales of Tommy the tortoise & Friends. (p. 599)
—Tommy's Triumph: The tales of Tommy the tortoise & Friends. (p. 1765)
Wheelwright, Ryan. Olivar & the Forbidden Plum Patch. (p. 1285)
Wheen, A. W., tr. see Remarque, Erich-Maria.
Wheiler, Robert. Herphus & the importance of Aroooo. (p. 774)
—Snowflake a Christmas Gift. (p. 1600)
—Wink's , Boo, & Who! (p. 1936)
Whelahan, Marlene. Once upon a Peanut: A true Story... Killian, Sue, illus. (p. 1293)
Whelahan, Marlene Verno. My Best Friend's Sister... A True Story. (p. 1197)
Whelan. Princesses Diamond Gift Wrap ((p. 1406)
Whelan, Denise. In the Land of Six & Seven. (p. 866)
Whelan, Elaine P., narrated by. My Mom's Making History: The Story of Computer Software, Copyrights & Creativity (p. 1214)
Whelan, Gloria. After the Train. (p. 28)
—All My Noble Dreams & Then What Happens. (p. 45)
—Angel on the Square. (p. 74)
—Boy Who Wanted to Cook. Adams, Steve, illus. (p. 219)
—Burying the Sun. (p. 244)
—Chu Ju's House. (p. 317)
—Disappeared. (p. 446)
—Farewell to the Island. (p. 573)
—Forgive the River, Forgive the Sky. (p. 619)
—Friend on Freedom River. van Frankenhuyzen, Gijsbert, illus. (p. 637)
—Fruitlands: Louisa May Alcott Made Perfect. (p. 645)
—Homeless Bird. (p. 793)
—Listeners. Benny, Mike, illus. (p. 1022)
—Listening for Lions. (p. 1022)

—Mackinac Bridge: The Story of the Five-Mile Poem. van Frankenhuyzen, Gijsbert, illus. (p. 1068)
—Megan's Year: An Irish Traveler's Story. Peck, Beth, illus. (p. 1124)
—Parade of Shadows. (p. 1323)
—Silver. Marchesi, Stephen, illus. (p. 1576)
—Small Acts of Amazing Courage. (p. 1591)
—Summer of the War. (p. 1674)
—Time to Keep Silent. (p. 1753)
—Waiting for the Owl's Call. Milelli, Pascal, illus. (p. 1853)
—Yatandou. Sylvada, Peter, illus. (p. 1968)
—Yuki & the One Thousand Carriers. Nascimbene, Yan, illus. (p. 1983)
Whelan, Gloria & Nolan, Jenny. K Is for Kabuki: A Japan Alphabet. Han, Oki S., illus. (p. 941)
Whelan, Kat, illus. see Moore, Clement C.
Whelan, Kat, illus. see Salzano, Tammi.
Whelan, Kevin, illus. see Cook, Peter.
Whelan, Kevin, jt. auth. see Cook, Peter.
Whelan, Michael, illus. see King, Stephen.
Whelan, Olwyn. Pirates Artist Card Portfolio. (p. 1363)
—Pirates Invitations. (p. 1363)
—Princesses Artist Card Portfolio. (p. 1406)
—Princesses Invitations. (p. 1406)
—Star Child. Maidment, Stella, illus. (p. 1640)
Whelan, Olwyn, illus. see Dearborn, Sabrina.
Whelan, Olwyn, illus. see House, Catherine.
Whelan, Olwyn, illus. see Maidment, Stella & Wilde, Oscar.
Whelan, Olwyn, illus. see Matthews, Caitlin, et al.
Whelan, Olwyn, illus. see Matthews, Caitlin.
Whelan, Olwyn, illus. see Parkinson, Siobhan.
Whelan, Olwyn, illus. see Walker, Richard.
Whelan, Olwyn, tr. see Maidment, Stella & Wilde, Oscar.
Whelan, Patrick, jt. auth. see Keene, Carolyn.
Whelan, Richard. Robert Capa: The Definitive Collection. Capa, Robert, photos by. (p. 1478)
Wheldon, Nicole. 1, 2, 3 Bees: A Counting Book. Zourelias-Noro, Diane, illus. (p. 1990)
Whelehan, Imelda, ed. Feminist Bestseller: From Sex & the Single Girl to Sex & the City. (p. 581)
Whelen-Banks, Jane. Liam Goes Poo in the Toilet: A Story about Trouble with Toilet Training. (p. 1004)
Whelen-Banks, Jane, jt. auth. see Banks, Jane Whelen.
Wheller, Opal. Frederic Chopin, Son of Poland, Early Years. Price, Christine, illus. (p. 633)
Whelon, Chuck. 3-D Mazes—Treasure Hunters. (p. 1991)
—Alien Invasion! Mazes. (p. 41)
—Alien Invasion! Stickers. (p. 41)
—Create Your Own Monsters Sticker Activity Book. (p. 378)
—Dinoscenes. (p. 445)
—FLIP OUTS — Dinosaurs: Color Your Own Cartoon! (p. 605)
—Sea Animals Finger Tattoos. (p. 1534)
—Smiley Things That Go Sticker Activity Book. (p. 1594)
—Treasure Hunter Activity Book. (p. 1781)
—What to Doodle? Adventure Stories! Pirates, Robots & More. (p. 1894)
—What to Doodle? Adventure Stories! Princesses, Fairies & More. (p. 1894)
—What to Doodle? All Sorts of Sports! (p. 1894)
—What to Doodle? Amazing Animals! (p. 1894)
—What to Doodle? Best Friends Forever! (p. 1894)
—What to Doodle? Christmas Creations! (p. 1894)
—What to Doodle? Dinosaurs! (p. 1894)
—What to Doodle? Fantastic Fantasy! (p. 1894)
—What to Doodle? Happy Halloween! (p. 1894)
—What to Doodle? in the Garden! (p. 1894)
—What to Doodle? Things That Go! (p. 1894)
—Word Play: Write Your Own Crazy Comics (p. 1951)
—Word Play - Write Your Own Crazy Comics (p. 1951)
—Word Play! - Write Your Own Crazy Comics (p. 1951)
—Zoo Animals Finger Tattoos. (p. 1988)
Whelon, Chuck & Dinosaurs. Dinosaur Rampage Activity Book. (p. 442)
Wherry, Alwyn. Hungry Little Mouse. (p. 828)
Whetung, James. Vision Seeker Morin, Paul, illus. (p. 1845)
Whicheloe, Paul, photos by see Brown, Katie.
Whidbee, Evelyn, told to. It's Called Blame. (p. 896)
Whigham, Rod, illus. see Anderson, Jameson.
Whigham, Rod, illus. see Fandel, Jennifer.
Whigham, Rod, illus. see Sautter, Aaron.
Whigham, Rod, illus. see Seidman, David & Williams, Keith.
Whigham, Rod, illus. see Seidman, David, et al.
Whigham, Rod, illus. see Wade, Mary Dodson & Capstone Press Staff.
Whigham, Rod, illus. see Wade, Mary Dodson.
Whild, Katharine. Marlowe the Great Detective. Whild, Katharine, illus. (p. 1096)
Whilldin, Sunny. Alex P. Maxwell's Rainy Day Adventure. (p. 36)
Whimp, Pauline, illus. see Holden, Pam.
Whimsy. Benny's Pets. Meadow, Amy, illus. (p. 165)
Whint, Ana Lee. Espalemit. (p. 536)
Whipp, Jo. Otis & Baby Jean. Whipp, Katie, illus. (p. 1307)
Whipp, Katie, illus. see Whipp, Jo.
Whipple, Cynthia, jt. auth. see Cashman, Mary.
Whipple, Heather. Hillary & Norgay: To the Top of Mount Everest. (p. 779)
Whipple, Jennifer. Hidden Treasure. (p. 776)
—Mrs. Korinek's Class. (p. 1187)
Whipple, Laura. Snowflake Fell: Poems about Winter. Hori, Hatsuki, illus. (p. 1600)
Whipple, Natalie. House of Ivy & Sorrow. (p. 803)
—Transparent. (p. 1779)
Whipple, Rick, illus. see Drummond, Ree.
Whipple, Rick, illus. see Grogan, John.
Whipple, Vicky. Little Weed Flower. Barcita, Pamela, illus. (p. 1037)
—Little Weed Flower/La Florecita de la Maleza. Barcita, Pamela, illus. (p. 1037)
Whipple, Wayne. Radio Boys Cronies. (p. 1432)
Whirlwhim. Baffelgagging Blundernagging Brothers: In Curse of the Bog Frog. (p. 132)
Whisenant, Jessica Manney. Day of Value. (p. 414)
Whiskeyman, Lauri, et al. Spotlight on Articulation Set (6) (p. 1634)
Whisler, Barbara. Shag Finds a Home. Jackson, Kay, illus. (p. 1558)
Whisp, Kennilworthy, pseud. Quidditch Through the Ages. (p. 1427)
Whispering Pine Press International, ed. see Hood, James G.
Whispering Pine Press International, ed. see Hood, Kared Jean Matsko.
Whispering Pine Press International, ed. see Hood, Karen Jean Matsko.
Whispering Pine Press International, ed. Petting Farm Fun, Translated Amharic Artistic Design Service Staff, illus. (p. 1348)
Whispering Pine Press International, Inc. Staff, ed. see Hilderbrandt, Sandra June.
Whispering Pine Press International, Inc. Staff, ed. see Hood, Karen Jean Matsko.
Whispering Pine Press International, Inc. Staff, ed. see O'Coyne, James.
Whispering Pine Press International Staff, ed. see Hood, Karen Jean Matsko.
Whispering Wind, jt. auth. see Flying Eagle.
Whistler, Charles W. Havelok the Dane: A Legend of Old Grimsby & Lincoln. (p. 754)
—King Alfred's Vikings, a Story of the First English Fleet. (p. 958)
—Sea-Queen's Sailing. Groome, W. H. C., illus. (p. 1535)
—Wulfric the Weapon Thane. (p. 1966)
Whit, Kelly. Solar System Forecast Klein, Laurie Allen, illus. (p. 1607)
Whitacre, Nicole Mahaney, jt. auth. see Mahaney, Carolyn.
Whitaker, Alecia. Queen of Kentucky. (p. 1425)
—Road to You. (p. 1477)
—Wildflower. (p. 1931)
Whitaker, Ginger. Teen Etiquette: Lessons in Grooming a Gentleman. (p. 1713)
—Teen Etiquette. (p. 1713)
Whitaker, Jimmy. Lilly & Twinkle Eyes (p. 1017)
Whitaker, Joan. Cartwheeling. Cusack, Elizabeth, illus. (p. 273)
Whitaker, Julian M. & Dace, Peggy. Reversing Diabetes Cookbook: More Than 200 Delicious, Healthy Recipes. (p. 1466)
Whitaker, Kenneth. Hood-Hearted Child, Life as a Nobody: Based on a True Story (p. 795)
Whitaker, Kent. Big Mo's Tennis Ball Hunt. (p. 182)
Whitaker, Margaret. Stacie's Geese at Goose Lake. Whitaker, Margaret, illus. (p. 1638)
Whitaker, Nathan. Snap Decision (p. 1597)
Whitaker, Sue. And Jake Makes Three. Ludlam, Jamie, illus. (p. 71)
—And Jake Makes Three & the Secret of Badlands. Ludlam, Jamie, illus. (p. 71)
—And Jake Makes Three in the Snow. Ludlam, Jamie, illus. (p. 71)
—And Jake Makes Three in the Vampires Den. Thomas-Brown, Cauline, ed. (p. 71)
Whitaker, Suzanne, illus. see Stamm, Linda J.
Whitaker, Suzanne George. Daring Miss Quimby. Stock, Catherine, illus. (p. 407)
Whitaker, Tu-Shonda L., jt. auth. see Santiago, Danielle.
Whitaker, Zai. Kali & the Rat Snake. Natarajan, Srividya, illus. (p. 942)
Whitaker-Taylor, Kandice. Child Is Born. (p. 301)
Whitbread, Henry. Lives of the Great Spiritual Leaders: 20 Inspirational Tales. (p. 1040)
Whitby, Adele. Beth's Story 1914. (p. 171)
—Kate's Story 1914. (p. 944)
—Kay's Story 1934. (p. 946)
Whitby, Charlotte, illus. see Black, Jess.
Whitby, Charlotte, illus. see Harding, David.
Whitby, Charlotte, illus. see Kelly, Helen.
Whitby, Charlotte, illus. see Kunz, Chris.
Whitby, Michael. All or Nothing. (p. 45)
Whitby, Rozene. Luke & Nana Fowler, Elizabeth, illus. (p. 1064)
Whitchurch III, D. E. Pied Piper Project Russia's Child. (p. 1356)
Whitcomb, Laura. Certain Slant of Light. (p. 287)
—Fetch. (p. 582)
—Under the Light. (p. 1813)
Whitcombe, Renee Raab. Look Who's Going to Be a Big Brother. (p. 1050)
—Look Who's Going to Be a Big Sister. (p. 1050)
Whitcraft, Melissa. Mayflower Compact. (p. 1113)
White. Naja Learns to Ride. Hyatt, Sean & McGrath, Michael, illus. (p. 1228)
—Naja Plays Hide-Go-Seek Hyatt, Sean, illus. (p. 1228)
—Tela di Carlotta. (p. 1716)
White, A. Rose. Just the Way I Am. (p. 940)
White, Aaron D. Creek Babies. (p. 380)
White, Alexina B. Frisky Brisky Hippity Hop. Head, Murray, illus. (p. 639)
White, Alexis. Three Peas in a Pod. (p. 1743)
White, Amanda. Sand Sister. Morales, Yuyi, illus. (p. 1510)
White, Amy. Dia Sin Tele. Kratky, Lada J., tr. (p. 433)
—Estoy Orgullosa de Mi Pasado. Kratky, Lada J., tr. (p. 538)
—Fiesta Saludable. Kratky, Lada J., tr. (p. 584)
—No Necesito Paraguas. Kratky, Lada J., tr. (p. 1259)
—Te Presento a Jacobo. Kratky, Lada J., tr. (p. 1708)
—¡A la Busqueda del Tesoro! Kratky, Lada J., tr. (p. 1)
White, Amy Brecount. Forget-Her-Nots. (p. 619)
White, Anaarista, jt. auth. see White, Joseph.
White & Hyatt, Sean. Naja vs P3OPLES Water Fight (p. 1228)
White, Andre'. Bird Is a Bird (p. 190)
White, Andrea. Radiant Girl. (p. 1432)
—Surviving Antarctica: Reality TV 2083. (p. 1687)
—Window Boy. (p. 1936)
—Windows on the World. (p. 1936)
White, Andrea & Mimi, Vance. Tummies on the Run. Shepperson, Rob, illus. (p. 1796)
White, Andrew Dickson. Autobiography of Andrew Dickson White. (p. 117)
—Fiat Money in France. (p. 583)
White, Angel. Seed in My Pocket. (p. 1547)
White, Anne. Lessons in Responsibility for Girls: Level Two (p. 994)
—Lessons in Responsibility for Girls: Level One. (p. 994)
—Lessons in Responsibility for Girls: Level Three (p. 994)
White, Annie, illus. see Weisner, Jane Lee.
White, Ayoola. When I Came to Imagice. (p. 1902)
White, Becky. Betsy Ross. Lloyd, Megan, illus. (p. 172)
—PawPrints on Your Heart. Cranford, Darren, illus. (p. 1331)
White, Bender Richardson. Daoism. (p. 406)
—Hinduism. (p. 780)
—Judaism. (p. 930)
—Shinto. (p. 1567)
White, Bender Richardson, et al. African Traditional Religion. (p. 28)
—Baha'i Faith. (p. 132)
—Buddhism. (p. 234)
—Catholicism & Orthodox Christianity. (p. 280)
—Confucianism. (p. 357)
—Islam. (p. 891)
—Native American Religions. (p. 1234)
—Protestantism. (p. 1412)
—Sikhism. (p. 1575)
—Zoroastrianism. (p. 1990)
White, Betty. Touring Polka-Dot Village. (p. 1773)
White, Billy. Kids & Money. (p. 952)
White, Cal. Apple Tree. Boyne, Linda, illus. (p. 92)
White, Carolyn. Snowff & the Rowdy-Cloudy Bunch. (p. 1600)
—Snowff Visits Razorteeth Village. (p. 1600)
—Snowff's MIST.erious Journey (Snowff the Snowflake Kid Adventure, 1) (p. 1600)
—Standing in the Shoes of a Member of the House of Representatives. (p. 1639)
White, Casey. John Jay: Diplomat of the American Experiment. (p. 922)
—Sergey Brin & Larry Page: The Founders of Google. (p. 1552)
White, Cathy. Duck Named Dean. (p. 488)
—Maury the Mouse. (p. 1110)
White, Cathy Finch. Anna Learns to Play the Violin. (p. 85)
—Scary Bully. (p. 1520)
White, Charlotte, illus. see Krasner, Nick.
White, Charlotte L., illus. see Smith, Maggie Caldwell.
White, Chris. Great Jammy Adventures: The Flying Cowboy. (p. 716)
—Vital Skills: How to Have Accountable Relationships. (p. 1846)
—Vital Truth Christian Citizenship Is in God We Trust More Than. (p. 1846)
White, Claudia. Aesop's Secret. (p. 26)
White, Clyde, 1st. Garbage Angel: Sarah's Story (p. 655)
White, Connor, jt. auth. see Bondor-Stone, Annabeth.
White, Daniel, photos by see Truscott, Julia.
White, Danny. One Direction: La Historia. (p. 1294)
White, Darrell. Red Silk Thread. (p. 1455)
White, Dave, illus. see Harper, Benjamin.
White, Dave, illus. see Landers, Ace.
White, David. Bad Luck Gang & the Ghost That Wasn't. (p. 132)
White, David, illus. see Barna, Beverly.
White, David, illus. see Guess, Alison.
White, David, illus. see Leipold, Judith.
White, David, illus. see Lindemann, Lindy.
White, David, illus. see Rotner, Shelley.
White, David A., illus. see Cohen, Alana.
White, David A., illus. see Landers, Ace.
White, David A., illus. see Rotner, Shelley.
White, Deborah, illus. see Jahsmann, Allan Hart & Simon, Martin P.
White, Deborah, illus. see Zirin, David.
White, Deborah J., illus. see Grube, Edward C.
White, Denise A. Goose & the Crone. (p. 702)
White, Dianne. Blue on Blue. Krommes, Beth, illus. (p. 203)
White, Dorine. Emerald Ring (Cleopatra's Legacy) (p. 517)
White, Doug. Gift: A Supernatural Hint to What Peter Is... (p. 675)
White Driscoll, Heather. He Calls Me Harp. (p. 756)
White, E. B. Avventure di Stuart Little. (p. 120)
—Charlotte's Web. (p. 294)
—Charlotte's Web. Williams, Garth, illus. (p. 294)
—E. B. White: Charlotte's Web, Stuart Little, & the Trumpet of the Swan (p. 491)
—Stuart Little. (p. 1668)
—Stuart Little. Williams, Garth, illus. (p. 1668)
—Stuart Little. Williams, Garth & Wells, Rosemary, illus. (p. 1668)
—Stuart Little Book & Charm. Williams, Garth, illus. (p. 1668)
—Telarana de Carlota. Williams, Garth, illus. (p. 1716)
—Telarana de Carlota (La Telarana de Carlota) Williams, Garth, illus. (p. 1716)
—Telarana de Carlota (LaTelarana de Carlota) Williams, Garth, illus. (p. 1716)
—Trumpet of the Swan. (p. 1793)
—Wilbur's Adventure: A Charlotte's Web Picture Book. Kneen, Maggie, illus. (p. 1928)
White, E. B., jt. auth. see Strunk, William, Jr.
White, E. B. & DiCamillo, Kate. Charlotte's Web. Williams, Garth, illus. (p. 294)
White, Ed. African Treasure: A True Story from the Horn of Africa (p. 28)
White, Eleanor Dantzler. Sincere Sentiments. (p. 1578)
White, Elga Haymon. Children's Adventure Duo: Thad the Sailor & Little Miss Lavendar. Freudiger, Victoria, ed. (p. 303)
White, Ella. I Can Write Numbers! Number Names & Count Sequence. (p. 837)
White, Ella, jt. auth. see Mills, Nathan.
White, Ella & White, Emma. I Can Write Numbers! Number Names & Count Sequence. (p. 837)
White, Ellen, jt. auth. see Holmes, Ellen.
White, Ellen Emerson. Long Live the Queen. (p. 1047)
—Long May She Reign. (p. 1047)
—President's Daughter. (p. 1397)
—Voyage on the Great Titanic. (p. 1850)
—White House Autumn. (p. 1913)
White, Ellen Emerson, jt. auth. see Edwards, Nicholas.
White, Ellen G. Amazing Love (p. 55)
—Ministry of Healing. (p. 1147)
—Story of Jesus. (p. 1658)
—Tempesta Perfetta Viene! (p. 1717)
White, Emily, jt. auth. see Henderson, Susan.
White, Emma, jt. auth. see White, Ella.
White Fox. Boy's Book of Signs & Symbols. (p. 220)
White, Frances, illus. see Judson, Clara Ingram.
White, Gene. Billy's Big Tomato. Davis, Shelley & Davis, Betsy, illus. (p. 187)
White, George. Halloween at the Zoo: A Pop-up Trick of Treat Experience. (p. 737)
—Kirby the Easter Dog: A Pop-up Easter Egg Hunt. (p. 961)
—Kirby's Derby: Pop-Up Animals on Wheels. O'Malley, Jason, illus. (p. 961)
White, Gloria. Something More Important. (p. 1610)
White, Graham. Maze Adventure: Search for Pirate Treasure. (p. 1113)
White, Gregory. Little House Search: A Puzzle Book & Tour of the Works of Laura Ingalls Wilder. (p. 1029)
White, Herman H. Valley of the Flames. (p. 1831)
White, Howard. Airplane Ride. Guzek, Greta, illus. (p. 32)
White, Howard Ray, Jr., ed. see White, Martha Frances Bell.
White, Ian, illus. see Clark, Karen.
White, Ian, jt. illus. see Clark, Karen.
White, Ian J. Keren! The Complete Indonesian Package. (p. 949)
White, Iris Weddell, illus. see Radford, Ruby Lorraine.
White, J. Scratch & Sniff: The Case of the Stuck Seagull. (p. 1532)
White, J. A. Path Begins. Offermann, Andrea, illus. (p. 1328)
—Whispering Trees. Offermann, Andrea, illus. (p. 1912)
White, James C. David Goes Fishing. Chapin, Patrick, illus. (p. 411)
White, Jamie Nicole. How I Wish I Could Share My Nice Words. (p. 810)
White, Jan. Mystery of Mingus Mountain. (p. 1224)
White, Janet. Tales of Leafy Lane. White, Lee et al, illus. (p. 1702)
White, Jennifer. Survival Strategies of the Almost Brave. (p. 1687)
White, Jenny. Surprise for Junior. (p. 1685)
White, Jill & White, Robbin. Can Starfish Make A Wish. (p. 258)
White, Jo Ella. Jincey's Rock: Lettie's Journey. (p. 918)
White, John, Jr., illus. see Brand, Ruth Redding.
White, John, Jr. & Tank, Daniel. Abraham. (p. 6)
White, John S. Boys' & Girls' Plutarch. (p. 220)
White, Joseph & White, Anaarista. Catholic Parent Know How: Forming Your Childs Faith-gr. 6. (p. 280)
—Catholic Parent Know How: Forming Your Child's Faith-gr. 3. (p. 280)
—Catholic Parent Know How: Forming Your Child's Faith- Gr. 8. (p. 280)
—Catholic Parent Know How: Forming Your Child's Faith-Grade 1. (p. 280)
—Catholic Prent Know How: Forming Your Child's Faith Gr. 4. (p. 280)
White, Joseph C. Forged in a Country Crucible. (p. 619)
White, Julie. High Fences (p. 777)
—Secret Pony (p. 1543)
White, June. Amazing Adventure of Tiptoe & the Yellow Balloon. Starkey, Fiona, illus. (p. 52)
White, K. B. Adrianna Angelica Andrea Mystery Stories: The Case of the Missing Bath Towel. (p. 13)
—Adrianna*Angelica*Andrea Mystery Stories: The Case of the Missing Dog. (p. 13)
White, Kate. Cooking in a Can: More Campfire Recipes for Kids Dixon, Debra, illus. (p. 362)
—Over Her Dead Body. (p. 1313)
White, Katherine. 2000-2002 Forest Fires in the Western United States. (p. 2003)
—Elton John. (p. 516)
—Little Girls & Their Ponytails. (p. 1028)
—Sylvia Earle: Deep Sea Explorer & Ocean Activist. (p. 1692)
—Wayans Brothers. (p. 1864)
White, Katherine, jt. auth. see White, Linda.
White, Kathryn. Emily Green & Me. (p. 519)
—Hermanito de Ruby. Latimer, Miriam, illus. (p. 771)
—Nutty Nut Chase. Cabban, Vanessa, illus. (p. 1274)
—Ruby's Baby Brother. Latimer, Miriam, illus. (p. 1493)
—Ruby's School Walk. Latimer, Miriam, illus. (p. 1494)
—Ruby's Sleepover. Latimer, Miriam, illus. (p. 1494)
—Snowshoe the Hare. Rivers, Ruth, illus. (p. 1601)
White, Kathy. Little Green Riding Hood. (p. 1028)
White, Kathy, illus. see Summer, Laura LeClair.
White, Kelly. Girls' Life Guide to Being the Best You! Parett, Lisa, illus. (p. 680)
White, Kelly & Stacy, Lori. Ask Lucky! The Girls'life Guide to Dealing with Dilemmas. (p. 106)
White, Kenna. Comfortable Distance. (p. 348)
White, Kiersten. Chaos of Stars. (p. 291)
—Endlessly. (p. 527)
—Illusions of Fate. (p. 857)
—Mind Games. (p. 1145)
—Paranormalcy. (p. 1324)
—Perfect Lies. (p. 1342)
—Supernaturally. (p. 1684)
White, Kiersten & Di Bartolo, Jim. In the Shadows. Di Bartolo, Jim, illus. (p. 867)
White, Kimberly. Mood Music: Musical Colors Series Axford, Elizabeth C., ed. (p. 1171)
White, Kittie. Magic Butterfly: And Other Tales. (p. 1072)
White, Larisa. Teacup Rhymes for Teacup Humans. (p. 1710)
White, LaToya, jt. auth. see Bailey, LaNiyah.
White, Lee, illus. see Agosin, Marjorie.
White, Lee, illus. see Britt, Paige.
White, Lee, illus. see Cannon, A. E.
White, Lee, illus. see Levine, Martha Peaslee.
White, Lee, illus. see Odanaka, Barbara.
White, Lee, illus. see Ribke, Simone T.
White, Lee, illus. see Rosen, Michael J.

White, Lee, illus. see Scillian, Devin.
White, Lee, illus. see Walker, Sally M.
White, Lee, illus. see Weatherford, Carole Boston.
White, Lee, illus. see White, Janet.
White, Leslie, illus. see Hitchcock, S. C. & Flynn, Tom.
White, Lia. Alkis. (p. 41)
White, Linda. Too Many Turkeys. Lloyd, Megan, illus. (p. 1767)
White, Linda & White, Katherine. Pocket Guide to Camping (p. 1375)
White, Linda Arms. I Could Do That! Esther Morris Gets Women the Vote. (p. 837)
—I Could Do That! Esther Morris Gets Women the Vote. Carpenter, Nancy, illus. (p. 837)
—Too Many Turkeys. Lloyd, Megan, illus. (p. 1767)
White, Loricia. Little Tail's Rhyming Roots. (p. 1037)
White, Mack, illus. see Kearby, Mike.
White, Mandy. Imagine with Me. (p. 861)
White, Marcia. Adventures of Ragpatch: Love Lost & Found. (p. 22)
White, Marco. Freddy's Fishbowl. (p. 633)
White, Margaret (Kintner). 18 Lives: The Adventures of Sam & Emil. (p. 1995)
White, Marian Frances, jt. auth. see Malone, Beni.
White, Mark. Ant & the Grasshopper: A Retelling of Aesop's Fable Pérez, Sara Rojo, illus. (p. 88)
—Cigarra y la Hormiga: Versión de la Fábula de Esopo Abello, Patricia, tr. (p. 319)
—Fox & the Grapes: A Retelling of Aesop's Fable Pérez, Sara Rojo, illus. (p. 626)
—Leon y el Raton: Versión de la Fábula de Esopo. Abello, Patricia, tr. from ENG. (p. 992)
—Lion & the Mouse: A Retelling of Aesop's Fable Pérez, Sara Rojo, illus. (p. 1020)
—Wolf in Sheep's Clothing: A Retelling of Aesop's Fable Pérez, Sara Rojo, illus. (p. 1943)
—Zorra y Las Uvas. Abello, Patricia, tr. (p. 1990)
White, Mark & Aesop Enterprise Inc. Staff. Ant & the Grasshopper: A Retelling of Aesop's Fable Pérez, Sara Rojo, illus. (p. 88)
—Fox & the Grapes: A Retelling of Aesop's Fable Pérez, Sara Rojo, illus. (p. 626)
—Lion & the Mouse: A Retelling of Aesop's Fable Pérez, Sara Rojo, illus. (p. 1020)
—Wolf in Sheep's Clothing: A Retelling of Aesop's Fable Pérez, Sara Rojo, illus. (p. 1944)
White Marklin, Mary M. I Was Beautiful Once. (p. 848)
White, Marquis. O. B. E. Out-of-Body Experience. (p. 1274)
White, Marsha. Bear's New Classes. White, Marsha, illus. (p. 152)
White, Martha Frances Bell. Springfield Girl, a Memoir. (p. 1635)
—Springfield Girl, a Memoir. White, Howard Ray, Jr., ed. (p. 1635)
White, Mary. Jack the Rat & His Funny Little Hat. (p. 903)
White, Mel. National Geographic Guide to Birding Hot Spots of the United States. Alderfer, Jonathan, ed. (p. 1231)
White, Melissa. Purple Frogs, Imagine High. (p. 1419)
White, Mia. CAREFUL, YOU Could HURT the DOLPHINS - Zoe's World Dr. Mia White. White, Mia, illus. (p. 268)
—Careful- Not to HURT MY BABY, LOVE. White, Mia, illus. (p. 268)
—Femme FATALE - When Good Girls Are Caught in BAD Situations they become Femme Fatales: Vamp. White, Mia, illus. (p. 581)
—On the day you were Born Everything that has Breath: Dr. Mia White. (p. 1290)
—VAMP -Chronicles - Pin up Heros don't become BaD: Vamp Series 2 the Golden Vessel. White, Mia, illus. (p. 1831)
—VAMP Courtesan - Beauties in Tough Spots an Historic Graphic Novel: Vamp's Adventures Time Travel Chronicles. White, Mia, illus. (p. 1831)
White, Michael, illus. see Shope, Ray & Shope, Lois.
White, Michael P., illus. see Deedy, Carmen Agra.
White, Michaela. His Servant: Kain's Song. (p. 781)
White, Michelle. George Washington America's Bulletproof Hero! (p. 664)
White, Michelle, illus. see Ellsworth, Nick.
White, Michelle A. Anthony with an A. (p. 89)
White, Mike, jt. auth. see Hynes, Margaret.
White, Mus, jt. auth. see Andersen, Hans Christian.
White, Mus, tr. see Andersen, Hans Christian.
White, N. M. & White, N.m. Unlock Level 1 Listening & Speaking Skills Student's Book & Online Workbook. (p. 1821)
White, Nancy. Aviation Firefighters. (p. 119)
—Black Mambas: Sudden Death! (p. 196)
—Coral Snakes: Beware the Colors! (p. 366)
—Crafty Garden Spiders. (p. 376)
—Creeping Land Snails. (p. 381)
—Death Adders: Super Deadly! (p. 420)
—Diamondback Rattlers: America's Most Venomous Snakes! (p. 434)
—Fer-de-Lance: Master Killer! (p. 581)
—Giant-O-Saurs. (p. 673)
—King Cobras: The Biggest Venomous Snakes of All! (p. 958)
—Maine Coons: Super Big. (p. 1077)
—Make a Pattern: A Content Area Reader-math. (p. 1078)
—Paramedics to the Rescue. (p. 1324)
—Police Officers to the Rescue. (p. 1380)
—Por qué hay osos polares en la nieve ... y no hay Flamencos. (p. 1385)
—President's Challenge: A Content Area Reader-health. (p. 1397)
—Push, Pull, Play the Game: A Content Area Reader-science. (p. 1420)
—Siamese: Talk to Me! (p. 1572)
—Using Earth's Underground Heat. (p. 1828)
—Why Polar Bears Like Snow... & Flamingos Don't & Por qué hay osos polares en la nieve ... y no hay Flamencos: 6 English, 6 Spanish Adaptations (p. 1925)
White, Nancy, jt. auth. see Lunis, Natalie.
White, N.m., jt. auth. see White, N. M.
White, Nonie H. D. Woodpecker Who Suffered from Headaches. White, Nonie H. D., illus. (p. 1949)
White, Pam. Buddy Goes to the Beach. (p. 235)
—Buddy's First White Christmas. (p. 235)
—Buddy's Trip to the Blueberry Farm. (p. 235)
White, Pamela. Magic Number 5. (p. 1072)
—Poppa Full of Pictures. (p. 1384)
White, Pari. Never Enough! (p. 1242)
White, Paul. Jungle Doctor & the Whirlwind. (p. 935)
—Jungle Doctor in Slippery Places. (p. 935)
—Jungle Doctor Looks for Trouble. (p. 935)
—Jungle Doctor Meets a Lion. (p. 935)
—Jungle Doctor on Safari. (p. 935)
—Jungle Doctor on the Hop. (p. 935)
—Jungle Doctor Operates. (p. 935)
—Jungle Doctor Pulls a Leg. (p. 935)
—Jungle Doctor Spots a Leopard. (p. 935)
—Jungle Doctor Stings a Scorpion. (p. 935)
—Jungle Doctor to the Rescue. (p. 935)
—Jungle Doctor's Africa. (p. 935)
—Jungle Doctor's Crooked Dealings. (p. 935)
—Jungle Doctor's Enemies. (p. 935)
White, Pauline. Jewel Baxter & Friends (p. 916)
White, Prentice L. Christmas at Mimi's. (p. 312)
White, Rachael, jt. auth. see White, Stanley I.
White, Rachel, illus. see Huppert, Susan.
White, Ramy Allison. Sunny Boy & His Playmates. (p. 1677)
—Sunny Boy in the Far West. Hastings, Howard L., illus. (p. 1677)
White, Randy Wayne, jt. auth. see Striker, Randy, pseud.
White, Randy Wayne, see Striker, Randy, pseud.
White, Rebecca. Holly's Not So Plain & Ordinary Day. (p. 789)
White, Rebecca, jt. auth. see Whiting, Karen.
White, Robb. Lion's Paw. Ray, Ralph, illus. (p. 1021)
White, Robbin, jt. auth. see White, Jill.
White, Rowland. Cleared for Takeoff! The Ultimate Book of Flight. (p. 330)
White, Russ. Cat Got Your Tongue? A Book of Idioms. Cornelison, Reuel, illus. (p. 278)
White, Ruth. Belle Prater's Boy. (p. 163)
—Buttermilk Hill. (p. 248)
—Month of Sundays. (p. 1170)
—Search for Belle Prater. (p. 1537)
—Treasure of Way down Deep. (p. 1782)
—Way down Deep. (p. 1864)
—You'll Like It Here (Everybody Does) (p. 1977)
White, Sandi. Playing with Rain. (p. 1372)
White, S.D. Sing along with the Santa Claus That Never Saw a Child. (p. 1579)
White, Shawna, jt. auth. see Falconer, Shelley.
White, Sheri. Box: A Christmas Story. (p. 216)
White, Sherrie, jt. auth. see Bama.
White, Siobhán, illus. see Rankin, H. L.
White, Stanley I. & White, Rachael. Absence Abbey (p. 7)
White, Stephanie. Ludwig Van Beethoven: Famous Composer. (p. 1064)
White, Stephen. Dry Ice. (p. 487)
White, Steve. Battle of Midway: The Destruction of the Japanese Fleet. (p. 146)
—Cleo the Curious Cat. (p. 331)
—Combat Fighter F-22 Raptor. (p. 346)
—Day of Infamy: Attack on Pearl Harbor. Spahn, Jerrold & Erskine, Gary, illus. (p. 414)
—Modern Bombs. (p. 1158)
—Naval Warship: FSF-1 Sea Fighter. (p. 1237)
—Naval Warship FSF-1 Sea Fighter. (p. 1237)
—Pearl Harbor: A Day of Infamy. (p. 1333)
White, Steve D. Military Robots. (p. 1143)
—Modern Bombs. (p. 1158)
—Pearl Harbor: A Day of Infamy. Spahn, Jerrold, illus. (p. 1333)
White Stone Books (Firm) Staff, contrib. by. Scriptural Prayers for the Praying Teen. (p. 1533)
White Stone Books Staff. Bible Almanac for Kids: A Journey of Discovery into the Wild, Incredible, & Mysterious Facts & Trivia of the Bible! (p. 175)
White, Susan K. Jesus Does Good Things. McQuitty, LaVonia Corbin, illus. (p. 915)
—Mickey's Wish. (p. 1136)
White, T. Diogenes in a Barrel of Fun. (p. 445)
White, T. H. Mistress Masham's Repose. Eichenberg, Fritz, illus. (p. 1155)
—Sword in the Stone. (p. 1692)
White, Tara. I Like Who I Am (p. 841)
—Where I Belong (p. 1908)
White, Tara B., illus. see Hughes, John P.
White, Teagan. Adventures with Barefoot Critters. (p. 25)
White, Teagan, illus. see DeStefano, Lauren.
White, Teagan, illus. see Johnson, Hal.
White, Teagan, illus. see Marr, Melissa.
White, Ted. My Ride to Daycare. (p. 1217)
White, Tekla. San Francisco Bay Area Missions. (p. 1510)
White, Terry, jt. auth. see Maynard, Christopher.
White, Terry L. Linda's Crystal Garden. (p. 1019)
White, Tim. Single Heart. (p. 1579)
White, Timothy. Catch a Fire: The Life of Bob Marley. (p. 279)
White, Timothy, illus. see Millman, Lawrence.
White, Tina Jorgenson, illus. see Briceno, Carole.
White, Tom. Lost in the Texas Desert. (p. 1056)
White, Toni. Ridge Street Prom. (p. 1471)
White, Tracy. How I Made It to Eighteen: A Mostly True Story. White, Tracy, illus. (p. 810)
White, Trudy. Could You? Would You? White, Trudy, illus. (p. 369)
White, Vernon. Birdhouse. (p. 190)
White, Vicky, illus. see Jenkins, Martin.
White, Virginia K. Warren the Honking Cat & the Exciting Winter Recital. (p. 1858)
—Warren the Honking Cat Saves the Day. (p. 1858)
White, Wendy. Welsh Cakes & Custard. Flook, Helen, illus. (p. 1874)
White, Whitney Yarber. Don't Swallow the Baby Jesus! (p. 468)
—Who Left Jesus in the Box? (p. 1916)
White-Adams, Beverly. Adventures of Rusty: Rusty Goes to Maine Vol. 3. (p. 22)
—Adventures of Rusty: Rusty Goes to Tennessee the Adventures Continue Vol. 4. (p. 22)
White-Adams, Beverly & Adams, Rusty. Adventures of Rusty: Rusty Goes to Virginia Vol. 1. (p. 22)
Whitebread, David, jt. auth. see Siraj-Blatchford, John.
Whitecap Books Staff. Ants Lewis, Kimberly & Stead, Kevin, illus. (p. 90)
—Dinosaurs (p. 444)
Whitecap Books Staff, jt. auth. see McLeish, Ewan.
Whitecap Books Staff & Simpson, Judith. North America (p. 1264)
Whitecap Books Staff, ed. Best of Children's Arts & Crafts. (p. 170)
Whitecap Books Staff, et al. Spiders (p. 1627)
Whited, Melissa F. Bear Brothers' Big Adventure (p. 150)
Whited, Wayne & Burns, Robert David. Adventures of Orie Alexander - the Story Thief (Paperback Edition) (p. 21)
Whited, Zillah. Flower Fables. (p. 607)
Whitedove, Michelle. My Invisible Friends. Poynter, Linda, illus. (p. 1211)
Whitefield, Gary T. China. Gritzner, Charles F., ed. (p. 306)
Whiteford & Fitzs. Better Handwriting. (p. 172)
Whiteford, Gary T., jt. auth. see Salter, Christopher L.
Whiteford, Rhona. Complete English (p. 352)
—Grammar & Punctuation. (p. 706)
Whiteford, Rhona, jt. auth. see Fitzsimmons, Jim.
Whiteford, Rhona & Fitzsimmons, Jim. Complete English (p. 352)
—Complete Math (p. 353)
—English for the Brighter Child. (p. 530)
—Maths for the Brighter Child. (p. 1108)
Whiteford, Rhona & Hodder Children's Books Staff. Spelling: Helping You Support Your Child in Year 6. (p. 1625)
Whitehead, Bert "Tiger". Spirit of the Tithe. (p. 1628)
Whitehead, Erin & Walters, Jennipher. Girl's Guide to Fitting in Fitness. (p. 680)
Whitehead, Jackie. Lindsey Lauren's Adventure Diaries. (p. 1019)
Whitehead, Jenny. You're a Crab! A Moody Day Book. Whitehead, Jenny, illus. (p. 1982)
Whitehead, Jenny, illus. see Bruno, Elsa Knight.
Whitehead, Jerry, illus. see Walsh, Alice.
whitehead, judith, ed. Tales & Tribulations of This Baby Boomer. (p. 1701)
Whitehead, Kathy. Art from Her Heart: Folk Artist Clementine Hunter. Evans, Shane W., illus. (p. 102)
—Looking for Uncle Louie on the Fourth of July. Torrecilla, Pablo, illus. (p. 1051)
Whitehead, Kim. Afghanistan (p. 26)
—Afghanistan. (p. 26)
Whitehead, Paul, illus. see Auerbach, Annie.
Whitehead, Pete. Mostly Ink & Wink. (p. 1177)
—Scooters. (p. 1529)
Whitehead, Pete, illus. see Inches, Alison.
Whitehead, Pete, illus. see Moore, Tim.
Whitehead, S. B., illus. see Leno, Jay.
Whitehead, Sarah. How to Speak Cat! (p. 821)
Whitehead, Sarah, jt. auth. see Bailey, Gwen.
Whitehead, William. Family Money. Beech, Mark, illus. (p. 568)
Whitehead, William, et al. Country Money. Beech, Mark, illus. (p. 372)
White-Hill, Carol. Dreams Do Come True. (p. 484)
Whitehill, Simcha. Chikorita & Chums. (p. 301)
—Meet Buizel & Friends. (p. 1120)
—Now You See It! Watch Pokémon Evolve— Right Before Your Eyes! (p. 1269)
—Pikachu & Pals. (p. 1358)
—Pokemon: Super Showdowns. (p. 1378)
—Pokemon: Unova Reader #3. (p. 1378)
—World of Sinnoh. (p. 1957)
Whitehill, Simcha, jt. auth. see Scholastic, Inc. Staff.
Whitehill, Simcha & Scholastic, Inc. Staff. Kalos Beginner's Handbook. (p. 942)
Whitehill, Simcha, et al. Pokemon Visual Companion. (p. 1378)
Whitehouse, Anna. Last Sant. (p. 978)
Whitehouse, Ben, illus. see Meister, Cari.
Whitehouse, Elizabeth. Bag Babies & the Secret of Civilization: A Jensen Family Story. (p. 132)
—Black Boys. (p. 195)
—Bones in Bonnieux. (p. 209)
—Ogham in Orkney: A Jensen Family Story. (p. 1280)
—Sushi for Lunch. (p. 1688)
Whitehouse, Howard. Faceless Fiend: Being the Tale of a Criminal Mastermind, His Masked Minions & a Princess with a Butter Knife, Involving Explosives & a Certain Amount of Pushing & Shoving. Slavin, Bill, illus. (p. 561)
—Island of Mad Scientists: Being an Excursion to the Wilds of Scotland, Involving Many Marvels of Experimental Invention, Pirates, a Heroic Cat, a Mechanical Man & a Monkey. Slavin, Bill, illus. (p. 892)
—Strictest School in the World: Being the Tale of a Clever Girl, a Rubber Boy & a Collection of Flying Machines, Mostly Broken. Slavin, Bill, illus. (p. 1667)
Whitehouse, Patricia. Barn Owls (p. 139)
—Coyote (p. 374)
—Coyotes (p. 375)
—Flowers (p. 608)
—Hiding in a Desert. (p. 777)
—Las Flores (p. 976)
—Las Hojas (p. 976)
—Leaves (p. 986)
—Lechuza (p. 987)
—Mapache (p. 1090)
—Murciélago (p. 1192)
—Opossums (p. 1300)
—Raccoons (p. 1430)
—Raíces. (p. 1433)
—Rata (p. 1440)
—Rats (p. 1440)
—Roots (p. 1488)
—Seeds (p. 1547)
—Semillas. (p. 1550)
—Skunks (p. 1586)
—Stars. (p. 1643)
—Zarigüeya (p. 1985)
—Zorrillo (p. 1990)
Whitehouse, Patricia & Heinemann Library Staff. Bats (p. 145)
—Opossums (p. 1300)
—Raccoons (p. 1430)
—Skunks (p. 1586)
Whitehouse, Patricia & Spilsbury, Louise. Zorro (p. 1990)
Whitehouse, Patty. Energia Por Dondequiera / Energy Everywhere. (p. 528)
—Energy Everywhere. (p. 528)
—Moving Machines. (p. 1183)
—Pushes & Pulls. (p. 1420)
Whitehurst, Debbie. Humphrey's Flight. (p. 827)
Whitehurst, John, illus. see Knapp, Susan.
Whitehurst, Susan. Mayflower. (p. 1113)
—Pilgrims Before the Mayflower. (p. 1358)
—Plymouth Partnership: Pilgrims & Native Americans. (p. 1374)
—William Bradford & Plymouth: A Colony Grows. (p. 1933)
White-Johnson, Adair F. Get over It! How to Bounce Back after Hitting Rock Bottom for Teens. (p. 668)
Whiteknact, Sandra. Primary Source History of the Colony of Virginia. (p. 1400)
Whitelaw, Ian & Dorling Kindersley Publishing Staff. Snow Dogs! Racers of the North Level 4. (p. 1599)
Whitelaw, Nancy. Andrew Jackson: Frontier President. (p. 72)
—Bram Stoker: Author of Dracula. (p. 222)
—Catherine de Medici & the Protestant Reformation. (p. 280)
—Dark Dreams: The Story of Stephen King. (p. 407)
—Homestead Steel Strike Of 1892. (p. 794)
—Jimmy Carter: President & Peacemaker. (p. 918)
—Joseph Pulitzer: And the New York World. (p. 926)
—Joseph Pulitzer & the New York World. (p. 926)
—Let's Go! Let's Publish! Katharine Graham & the Washington Post. (p. 997)
—More Perfect Union: The Story of Alexander Hamilton. (p. 1174)
—Mr. Civil Rights: The Story of Thurgood Marshall. (p. 1184)
—Nathaniel Hawthorne: American Storyteller. (p. 1231)
—Queen Isabella & the Unification of Spain. (p. 1424)
—Queen Victoria & the British Empire. (p. 1425)
—Rebels & Revolutionaries: Voices of American Labor. (p. 1451)
—Shot Heard Round the World: The Battles of Lexington & Concord. (p. 1569)
—Thomas Jefferson: Philospher & President. (p. 1739)
—Thurgood Marshall. (p. 1746)
—William Randolph Hearst: And the American Century. (p. 1933)
—William Randolph Hearst & the American Century. (p. 1933)
—William Tecumseh Sherman: Defender & Destroyer. (p. 1933)
Whiteley, Jason. Tales from the Tacklebox: Escape from the Crooked Tree. (p. 1702)
Whiteley, Peter & Bassarath, Haydn. CXC Revision Guide for Physics. (p. 396)
Whitely, Heather. Line. (p. 1019)
Whitely, Heather, jt. auth. see May, Susie.
Whiteman, Dorit Bader. Lonek's Journey: The True Story of a Boy's Escape to Freedom (p. 1046)
Whiteman, Rita, jt. auth. see Turley, LuAnn.
Whiteman, Sarah Helen. Last Letters of Edgar Allan Poe to Sarah Helen Whitman. (p. 978)
Whiten, Jan. Chooky-Doodle-Doo. Hanley, Sinéad, illus. (p. 310)
Whitenburg, Shelly Morrow. Angels Are God's Helpers. (p. 75)
White-Petaway, Davida, jt. auth. see Woodard, April.
Whiteside, Alan, jt. auth. see Barnett, Tony.
Whiteside, Andy. Valentino Finds a Home Hnatov, Catherine, illus. (p. 1830)
Whiteside, Doug. Thank You... No, Thank You! (p. 1725)
Whiteside, Randy. Travis & the Courageous Path: [Black & White Edition]. Whiteside, Randy, illus. (p. 1781)
Whiteside, S. K. Inheritance. (p. 874)
Whiteside, Shaun, tr. see Dufosse, Christophe.
Whitesides, Tyler. Curse of the Broomstaff. (p. 394)
—Heroes of the Dustbin. (p. 773)
—Janitors. (p. 908)
—Secrets of New Forest Academy. (p. 1545)
—Strike of the Sweepers. (p. 1667)
Whitethorne, Bahe, Jr., illus. see Flood, Nancy Bo.
Whitethorne, Bahe, Jr., illus. see Muller, Seth.
Whitethorne, Bahe, Jr., illus. see Ruffenach, Jessie E., et al.
Whitethorne, Baje, illus. see Farley, Walter.
Whitethorne, Baje, Sr., illus. see Yazzie, Seraphine G.
Whitethorne, Billy, illus. see Flood, Nancy Bo.
Whitfield, Andrea Billingsley. Felicia Fights Fat with Phone Fitness. (p. 581)
Whitfield, Cathy. History Odyssey, Ancients (level One) (p. 783)
—History Odyssey, Early Modern - Level One. (p. 783)
—History Odyssey, Middle Ages - Level One. (p. 783)
Whitfield, David. Northern Lights. (p. 1266)
—Penguins. (p. 1337)
—Rainbows. (p. 1436)
—World Cup. (p. 1954)
Whitfield, Eric, illus. see Harrold, Kimberly.
Whitfield, Eric T., illus. see Banister, Katie Rodriguez & Banister, Steve.
Whitfield, Kate. Empowered Gal's 9 Life Lessons: Keys, Tips, Strategies, Advice & Everything You Need to Know to be a Confident, Successful, in Control Gal. (p. 521)
Whitfield, Laurie A. & Cammarata, Robert P. Taking Care of God's Gifts Stewardship: A Way of Life Grades 3-5. (p. 1698)
Whitfield, Mary. Mrs. Adams Teaches a Lesson for a Lifetime. (p. 1187)
Whitfield, Peter. Bruno Dreams of Ice Cream. Bevington, Nancy, illus. (p. 232)
—No Presents Please. Bevington, Nancy, illus. (p. 1260)
—Up & Down. Bevington, Nancy, illus. (p. 1824)
Whitfield, Philip. Firefly Encyclopedia of Animals. (p. 592)

W

—Scholastic's Children's Guide to Dinosaurs. (p. 1522)
Whitfield, Simon & Dheensaw, Cleve. Simon Says Gold: Simon Whitfield's Pursuit of Athletic Excellence (p. 1577)
Whitfield, Susan. Afghanistan. (p. 26)
—Philosophy & Writing. (p. 1351)
Whitfield, Willie. Big Pigpen Willie's Inheritance. (p. 183)
Whitfirld, Eric, illus. see Showstack, Richard.
Whitford, Frank, jt. auth. see van der Meer, Ron.
Whitford Paul, Ann. Fiesta Fiasco. (p. 584)
Whitford, Rebecca. Little Yoga: A Toddler's First Book of Yoga. Selway, Martina, illus. (p. 1038)
—Sleepy Little Yoga. Selway, Martina, illus. (p. 1590)
Whitham, Cynthia. Answer Is NO: Saying It & Sticking to It. Wetmore, Barry, illus. (p. 88)
—Gana la Guerra de los Berrinches y Otras Contiendas: Un Plan de Paz Familiar. (p. 655)
—Win the Whining War & Other Skirmishes: A Family Peace Plan. Wetmore, Barry, illus. (p. 1935)
Whiting, Chuck, jt. auth. see Roberg, Robert.
Whiting, Jim. Air Force Special Operations Command. (p. 31)
—American Idol Judges. (p. 61)
—America's Got Talent. (p. 64)
—Anne Frank. (p. 85)
—Annie Oakley. (p. 87)
—Auguste & Louis Lumiere: And the Rise of Motion Pictures. (p. 115)
—Bayern Munich. (p. 147)
—Benjamin Franklin. (p. 164)
—Bermuda Triangle. (p. 167)
—Black Holes. (p. 196)
—Blood & Guts: The Basics of Mixed Martial Arts (p. 200)
—Blue Banner Biographies-Pop Entertainers III. (p. 202)
—Booker T. Washington. (p. 212)
—Bubonic Plague. (p. 234)
—Care for a Pet Chameleon. (p. 266)
—Care for a Pet Snake. (p. 266)
—Charles Darwin & the Origin of the Species. (p. 292)
—Claude Monet. (p. 329)
—Creation of Isreal. (p. 379)
—Cuban Missile Crisis: The Cold War Goes Hot. (p. 388)
—David Beckham. (p. 410)
—Delta Force. (p. 425)
—Edgar Allan Poe. (p. 504)
—Edvard Munch. (p. 505)
—Election Firsts. (p. 508)
—Energy. (p. 528)
—Ernest Hemingway. (p. 533)
—FBI Hostage Rescue & Swat Teams. (p. 578)
—FC Barcelona. (p. 578)
—Ferdinand Magellan. (p. 581)
—Frederick Douglass. (p. 633)
—Frogs in Danger. (p. 641)
—Galileo. (p. 653)
—Gravity. (p. 712)
—Green Berets. (p. 721)
—Hercules. (p. 769)
—Hilary Duff. (p. 779)
whiting, jim. Identity Theft. (p. 852)
Whiting, Jim. Inside the Cage: The Greatest Fights of Mixed Martial Arts (p. 877)
—James Watt & the Steam Engine. (p. 907)
—Jason. (p. 910)
—Jim Beckwourth: The Man Who Opened the West. (p. 917)
—John R. Pierce: Pioneer in Satellite Communication. (p. 922)
—Life & Times of Abigail Adams. (p. 1007)
—Life & Times of Antonio Lucio Vivaldi. (p. 1007)
—Life & Times of Aristotle. (p. 1007)
—Life & Times of Augustus Caesar. (p. 1008)
—Life & Times of Charlemagne. (p. 1008)
—Life & Times of Franz Liszt. (p. 1008)
—Life & Times of Frederic Chopin. (p. 1008)
—Life & Times of Genghis Khan. (p. 1008)
—Life & Times of George Gershwin. (p. 1008)
—Life & Times of Gilbert & Sullivan. (p. 1008)
—Life & Times of Guiseppe Verdi. (p. 1008)
—Life & Times of Hector Berlioz. (p. 1008)
—Life & Times of Hernando Cortes. (p. 1008)
—Life & Times of Herodotus. (p. 1008)
—Life & Times of Hippocrates. (p. 1008)
—Life & Times of Igor Stravinsky. (p. 1008)
—Life & Times of Joan of Arc. (p. 1008)
—Life & Times of John Adams. (p. 1008)
—Life & Times of Julius Caesar. (p. 1008)
—Life & Times of Moses. (p. 1008)
—Life & Times of Nero. (p. 1008)
—Life & Times of Paul Revere. (p. 1008)
—Life & Times of Pericles. (p. 1008)
—Life & Times of Plato. (p. 1008)
—Life & Times of Rameses the Great. (p. 1008)
—Life & Times of Richard Wagner. (p. 1008)
—Life & Times of Samuel de Champlain. (p. 1008)
—Life & Times of Thucydides. (p. 1008)
—Light. (p. 1014)
—Liverpool FC. (p. 1040)
—Manchester United. (p. 1086)
—Mandy Moore. (p. 1087)
—Marine Corps Forces Special Operations Command. (p. 1094)
—Maryland Colony: Lord Baltimore. (p. 1101)
—Mass & Matter. (p. 1102)
—Medieval Arms & Armor (p. 1119)
—Medieval Castles (p. 1119)
—Medieval Knights (p. 1119)
—Michelangelo. (p. 1135)
—Miserable Life of Medieval Peasants (p. 1150)
—Mysteries of the Universe: Black Holes. (p. 1222)
—Mysteries of the Universe: Energy. (p. 1222)
—Mysteries of the Universe: Gravity. (p. 1222)
—Mysteries of the Universe: Light. (p. 1222)
—Mysteries of the Universe: Mass & Matter. (p. 1222)
—Mysteries of the Universe: Space & Time. (p. 1222)
—Navy SEALs. (p. 1238)
—NBA: a History of Hoops: the Story of the Atlanta Hawks. (p. 1238)
—NBA: a History of Hoops: the Story of the Boston Celtics. (p. 1238)
—NBA: a History of Hoops: the Story of the Detroit Pistons. (p. 1238)
—NBA: a History of Hoops: the Story of the Los Angeles Clippers. (p. 1238)
—NBA: a History of Hoops: the Story of the Philadelphia 76ers. (p. 1238)
—NBA: a History of Hoops: the Story of the Sacramento Kings. (p. 1238)
—New Generation of Warriors: The History of Mixed Martial Arts (p. 1244)
—NFL Today: Arizona Cardinals. (p. 1249)
—NFL Today: Chicago Bears. (p. 1249)
—NFL Today: Miami Dolphins. (p. 1250)
—NFL Today: New England Patriots. (p. 1250)
—NFL Today: New Orleans Saints. (p. 1250)
—NFL Today: New York Giants. (p. 1250)
—NFL Today: New York Jets. (p. 1250)
—NFL Today: Pittsburgh Steelers. (p. 1250)
—NFL Today: San Diego Chargers. (p. 1250)
—NFL Today: San Francisco 49ers. (p. 1250)
—NFL Today: Seattle Seahawks. (p. 1250)
—No Perfect People, Please! Poems & audio cd By. (p. 1259)
whiting, jim. Online Communication & Social Networking. (p. 1298)
Whiting, Jim. Otto Hahn & the Story of Nuclear Fission. (p. 1307)
—Overview of World War I. (p. 1314)
—Peter Stuyvesant. (p. 1347)
—Real Madrid. (p. 1448)
—Really Scary Stuff (p. 1450)
—Robert Fulton. (p. 1479)
—Rosa Parks. (p. 1488)
—Russian Revolution 1917. (p. 1498)
—Scary Ghosts. (p. 1520)
—Scary Monsters. (p. 1520)
—Scary Places. (p. 1520)
—Scary Stories. (p. 1520)
—Science of Hitting a Home Run: Forces & Motion in Action. (p. 1527)
—Science of Lighting a City: Electricity in Action. (p. 1527)
—Scopes Monkey Trial. (p. 1530)
—Sinking of the Titanic. (p. 1580)
—Space & Time. (p. 1618)
—Stars. (p. 1643)
—Story of No Limit Records. (p. 1659)
—Story of the Arizona Cardinals. (p. 1660)
—Story of the Atlanta Hawks. (p. 1660)
—Story of the Attack on Pearl Harbor. (p. 1660)
—Story of the Boston Celtics. (p. 1660)
—Story of the Charlotte Hornets. (p. 1660)
—Story of the Chicago Bears. (p. 1660)
—Story of the Detroit Pistons. (p. 1660)
—Story of the Holocaust. (p. 1661)
—Story of the Los Angeles Clippers. (p. 1661)
—Story of the Miami Dolphins. (p. 1661)
—Story of the New England Patriots. (p. 1661)
—Story of the New Orleans Saints. (p. 1661)
—Story of the New York Giants. (p. 1661)
—Story of the New York Jets. (p. 1661)
—Story of the Orlando Magic. (p. 1662)
—Story of the Pittsburgh Steelers. (p. 1662)
—Story of the Pphiladelphia 76ers. (p. 1662)
—Story of the Sacramento Kings. (p. 1662)
—Story of the San Diego Chargers. (p. 1662)
—Story of the San Francisco 49ers. (p. 1662)
—Story of the Seattle Seahawks. (p. 1662)
—Story of the Washington Wizards. (p. 1662)
—Striking, Grappling, & Ground Fighting: The Skills Behind Mixed Martial Arts (p. 1667)
—Threat to Ancient Egyptian Treasures. (p. 1741)
—Troy Polamalu. (p. 1790)
—U. S. Special Forces: Air Force Special Operations Command. (p. 1807)
—U. S. Special Forces: Delta Force. (p. 1807)
—U. S. Special Forces: Green Berets. (p. 1807)
—U. S. Special Forces: Marine Corps Forces Special Operations Command. (p. 1807)
—U. S. Special Forces: Navy SEALs. (p. 1807)
—Ultra Running with Scott Jurek. (p. 1810)
—Vincent Van Gogh. (p. 1843)
—Volcanic Eruption on Santorini, 1650 BCE. (p. 1848)
—W. E. B. du Bois: Civil Rights Activist, Author, Historian. (p. 1851)
—William Shakespeare. (p. 1933)
—World of Mixed Martial Arts (p. 1957)
Whiting, Jim, jt. auth. see Eugster, Rachel.
Whiting, Jim, jt. auth. see LeVert, Suzanne.
Whiting, Jim & Loewen, Nancy. Voices in Poetry: Walt Whitman. Day, Rob, illus. (p. 1848)
Whiting, Karen, jt. auth. see Florea, Jesse.
Whiting, Karen & White, Rebecca. Nature Girl: A Guide to Caring for God's Creation (p. 1236)
Whiting, Sandra, illus. see Shoemaker, Sharon.
Whiting, Sue. All about Ants. (p. 42)
—Ancient Orbiters: A Guide to the Planets. (p. 70)
—Machine Mates. Townsend, Peter, illus. (p. 1068)
—Portraits of Celina. (p. 1387)
Whiting, Sue & Martin, Stuart. That's Funny! (p. 1726)
Whitis, Cindy. Flower Child from Fish Village. (p. 607)
Whitlatch, Jessica A., illus. see Dalton, Sherry A.
Whitler, Candra. Mama, How Will I Know? (p. 1084)
Whitler, Celia. On the Way to Somewhere: Stories & Songs for the Journey. (p. 1292)
Whitler, Larry. Oreo & Braun XOB the Full Circle Quest. (p. 1303)
Whitley, David. Canticle of Whispers. (p. 262)
—Midnight Charter. (p. 1138)
Whitley, David S. Guide to Rock Art Sites: Southern California & Southern Nevada. (p. 730)
Whitley, Jared & Mandelbaum, Jolie. University of Utah College Prowler off the Record. (p. 1821)
Whitley, Jeremy. Get over Yourself. (p. 668)
Whitley, Peggy, et al. 99 Jumpstarts for Kids: Getting Started in Research (p. 1998)
Whitley, Peggy J. & Goodwin, Susan Williams. 99 Jumpstarts for Kids' Science Research (p. 1998)
Whitley-Kinzett, Sara. Grumpy Ted: The Teds Volume One. Ellams, Victoria, illus. (p. 727)
Whitlock, Bonnie. Momma Yeti & the Terribly Tiresome Goodnight. (p. 1162)
Whitlock, Jill, jt. auth. see Gerwitz, Felice.
Whitlock, Matt. Punk 'n Patch. Whitlock, Matt, illus. (p. 1417)
—Punk's Christmas Carol: A Punk 'n Patch Book. Whitlock, Matt, illus. (p. 1417)
Whitlock, Matt, illus. see Cider Mill Press, Cider Mill & Abramson, Andra.
Whitlock, Matt, illus. see Sanzo, Stephen.
Whitlock, Val, jt. see Court, Shirley.
Whitlow, Crystal K. Charles Gordon Willingham. Fisher, Bonnie & Wolski, Bobbi, illus. (p. 292)
Whitlow, Steve, illus. see Dowley, Tim & David, Juliet.
Whitlow, Steve, illus. see Hall, Hannah C.
Whitman Blair, Margaret. Liberty or Death: The Surprising Story of Runaway Slaves Who Sided with the British During the American Revolution (Large Print 16pt) (p. 1005)
Whitman, Candace. Lines That Wiggle. Wilson, Steve, illus. (p. 1019)
Whitman, Candace, illus. see Vance, Cynthia.
Whitman, David L. Friends. (p. 638)
Whitman, Diana McManus, illus. see Guilmette, Patty.
Whitman, Emily. Radiant Darkness. (p. 1432)
—Wildwing. (p. 1931)
Whitman, Emily, jt. auth. see Rovetch, L. Bob.
Whitman Guszcza, Helen Suzanne. Little Lilli & Willy Live Here. (p. 1030)
Whitman, Jennifer, illus. see Tessin, Kit Elaine.
Whitman, Jim, ed. see Lu, Catherine.
Whitman, John. Extinction. (p. 555)
Whitman, Jonathan, ed. see Cook, Esky.
Whitman, Jonathan, ed. Jewish Artwork by Esky: Shabbat & Jewish Holidays. (p. 917)
Whitman, Lynn. Forever Home: Tales of Four Lucky Dogs. Hoeffner, Deb, illus. (p. 619)
Whitman, Nancy C. Counting Petals: Using Flowers of Hawaii. Chong, Luther, photos by. (p. 371)
—Counting Petals. (p. 371)
Whitman Publishing, creator. Discover the American Revolution: History Project Toolkit. (p. 448)
—Discover the Civil War: History Project Toolkit. (p. 448)
—Discover Westward Expansion History Project Toolkit. (p. 448)
—Discover World War II: History Project Toolkit. (p. 448)
Whitman Publishing, ed. Adventure Across the States: Collecting State Quarters & Other Coins. (p. 14)
Whitman, Stacy, ed. see Hess, Nina.
Whitman, Sylvia. Milk of Birds. (p. 1143)
—Under the Ramadan Moon Williams, Sue, illus. (p. 1814)
—Under the Ramadan Moon. Williams, Sue, illus. (p. 1814)
—World Poverty. (p. 1958)
Whitman, Theresa M., illus. see Tulik, Alice, et al.
Whitman, Walt. American Primer. (p. 62)
—Criticism: An Essay. (p. 383)
—Gathering of the Forces (p. 658)
—I Hear America Singing. Sabuda, Robert, illus. (p. 839)
—I Sit & Look Out. (p. 845)
—Letters of Anne Gilchrist & Walt Whitman. (p. 1002)
—Nothing but Miracles. Roth, Susan L., illus. (p. 1268)
—Uncollected Poetry & Prose. (p. 1812)
—Walt Whitman & the Civil War. (p. 1856)
—Walt Whitman's Diary in Canada. (p. 1856)
Whitman, Walt & Long, Loren. When I Heard the Learn'd Astronomer. Long, Loren, illus. (p. 1903)
Whitmire, Anna, illus. see Taylor, Clif.
Whitmire, Warren. Juan & the Little Red Boat. (p. 930)
Whitmore, Andre. FunnyFruit. (p. 650)
—Math Lingo Homework Helper. (p. 1106)
Whitmore, Andrew. Beast of the Jungle. (p. 152)
—How to Build a Monster. (p. 815)
—How to Survive Asteroids & Other Disasters. (p. 821)
Whitmore, Arvella. Bread Winner. (p. 224)
Whitmore, G. A. Place to Call Home: Toby's Tale. (p. 1365)
Whitmore, Gary. Prince Luna & the Space Dreamers. (p. 1401)
Whitmore, Hugh. Three Madelines. Wilson, Raylene Jenee & Gibbons, Deanna, illus. (p. 1743)
Whitmore, Patrick Charles. Cookie & the Golden Quill. (p. 361)
Whitmore, Rubin. Arrow to the Moon. (p. 101)
Whitmore, Yvette, illus. see Alexander, Florence.
Whitney, A. D. T. Other Girls. (p. 1306)
—Patience Strong's Outings by Mrs a D T Whitney. (p. 1328)
—Sights & Insights: Patience Strong's Story of over the Way. Vol. 1. (p. 1574)
Whitney, Barbara I. Barbara's Quest to Find a Messenger: Journeys I & II. (p. 137)
Whitney, Brooks. How to Master the School Universe: Homework, Teachers, Tests, Bullies, & Other Ways to Survive the Classroom. Kennedy, Kelly, illus. (p. 820)
—How to Survive Almost Anything. (p. 821)
Whitney, Caffy, illus. see Helms, Selah & Thompson, Susan.
Whitney, Caffy, illus. see Helms, Selah, et al.
Whitney, Daisy. Fire Artist. (p. 590)
—Mockingbirds. (p. 1157)
—Rivals. (p. 1475)
—Starry Nights. (p. 1642)
—When You Were Here. (p. 1905)
Whitney, Elliott. Blind Lion of the Congo. (p. 199)
Whitney, Gleaves & Whitney, Louise. B Is for Buckaroo: A Cowboy Alphabet. Guy, Sue & Guy, Susan, illus. (p. 123)
Whitney, Gleaves & Whitney, Louise Doak. B Is for Buckaroo: A Cowboy Alphabet. Guy, Susan, illus. (p. 123)
Whitney, J. D. Grandmother Says. (p. 709)
Whitney, Kim Ablon. Other Half of Life. (p. 1306)
Whitney, Leah, ed. see Gray, Erick S.
Whitney, Louise, jt. auth. see Whitney, Gleaves.
Whitney, Louise Doak, jt. auth. see Whitney, Gleaves.
Whitsett, Darron, illus. see Warren, Johnette.
Whitt, Carlynn, illus. see Mackall, Dandi Daley.
Whitt, Carlynn, illus. see Snyder, Laurel.
Whitt, Kelly Kizer. Pronóstico Del Sistema Solar Klein, Laurie Allen, illus. (p. 1411)
—Solar System Forecast Klein, Laurie Allen, illus. (p. 1607)
Whitt, Shannon, illus. see Weiner, Miriam.
Whitt, Shannon, jt. auth. see Ross, Timothy.
Whitt, Stephen. Turtle & the Universe. Hernandez, Stephanie, illus. (p. 1798)
Whittaker, Andrea. All-Star Animals: Pets who'd rather play than Stay. (p. 45)
Whittaker, Brian. Quest for the Kangoalaplatybat. (p. 1426)
Whittaker, Heather. Different Little Doggy. Alberts, Scott, illus. (p. 438)
Whittaker, Helen. Clothing. (p. 334)
—Energy. (p. 528)
—Food. (p. 612)
—How Toys Fly. (p. 823)
—How Toys Roll. (p. 823)
—How Toys Slide. (p. 823)
—How Toys Spin. (p. 823)
—Leisure. (p. 991)
—Living & Working in Space. (p. 1040)
—Our Solar System. (p. 1310)
—Space Missions. (p. 1619)
—Space Science. (p. 1619)
—Space Technology. (p. 1620)
—Universe. (p. 1820)
—Waste. (p. 1860)
—Water. (p. 1862)
Whittaker, Kay, illus. see Ashe, Gregory.
Whittaker, Liz. Fizzing Stone. (p. 601)
—Manawl's Treasure. (p. 1086)
—Shapeshifters at Cilgerran. (p. 1561)
Whittaker, Stephen, illus. see Blevins, James.
Whittemore, Constance, illus. see Hudson, Arthur K.
Whittemore, Jo. Colonial Madness. (p. 341)
—D Is for Drama. (p. 397)
—Front Page Face-Off. (p. 644)
—Odd Girl In. (p. 1278)
Whittemore, Susan. Circulatory System. (p. 322)
—Respiratory System. (p. 1463)
Whitten, A. J. Cellar. (p. 286)
—Well. (p. 1874)
Whitten, Bill, text. Like Riding a Bike in the Sand: The Great Depression in Small Town Texas. (p. 1017)
Whitten, Kyle. Mr. Makerkus' Magical Flying Circus. (p. 1185)
Whitten, Mindy J. B. Alpaca in My Pocket. (p. 48)
Whitten, Samantha & Lee, Jeannie. How to Draw Manga Chibis & Cute Critters. (p. 818)
Whittenberg, Allison. Tutored. (p. 1799)
Whittier, Mary Ann. Tales from 1492. (p. 1701)
Whittingham, Kim, illus. see Brynie, Faith Hickman.
Whittingham, Stephen. Best Summer Holiday. (p. 171)
Whittingham, Wendy, illus. see Sherrard, Valerie.
Whittington, Amanda. Satin 'n' Steel. (p. 1515)
Whittington, Belle. Cicada Vol.1. (p. 318)
Whittington, Joseph. Hippopotamus Who Didn't Like Himself. (p. 781)
Whittington, M. & Pinnington, Andrea. Mi Gran Libro del Cuerpo. (p. 1132)
Whittington, Melanie & Holtz, Lara Tankel, eds. Counting Book. King, Dave, photos by. (p. 370)
Whittington, Phillip. What a Hullabaloo! (p. 1878)
Whittington, Thea. Dragon's Back. (p. 479)
Whittington, Vi, illus. see Brand, Joe.
Whittle, J. Robert. Lizzie's Secret Angels (p. 1043)
Whittle, J. Robert & Sandilands, Joyce. Leprechaun Magic. Galego, Ane M., illus. (p. 993)
Whittlesey, Charles. Great Mound on the Etowah River, Georgia. (p. 717)
Whittlesey, Lisa & Seagraves, Randy. Junior Master Gardener Level One Teacher Leader Guide. (p. 936)
Whittley, Sarah & Showler, Dave. Frogs & Toads. Croucher, Barry, illus. (p. 641)
Whittock, Martyn J. Medieval Britain, 1066-1500. (p. 1119)
Whitty, Hannah. Woodland Christmas Tale: Lift the Flap for Every Day of Advent. (p. 1949)
Whitty, Hannah, illus. see Platt, Cynthia.
Whitwell, Stephen. Battles of Lexington & Concord: First Shots of the American Revolution. (p. 147)
Whitworth, Christy. Come Back, o Tiger! A Jataka Tale. (p. 347)
Who, Carrie Lou, illus. see Klitzner, Irene.
WHS Staff, contrib. by. Vocabulary Workshop, Level Green: Answers to Tests (Cycles One & Two) (p. 1847)
—Vocabulary Workshop, Level Green, Test Booklets Cycle One. (p. 1847)
Whybrow, Ian. Ella the Superstar. McCullen, Sam, illus. (p. 514)
—Faraway Farm. Ayliffe, Alex, illus. (p. 573)
—Harry & the Bucketful of Dinosaurs. Reynolds, Adrian, illus. (p. 750)
—Harry & the Dinosaurs Go to School. Reynolds, Adrian, illus. (p. 750)
—Harry & the Dinosaurs - The Flying Save! (p. 750)
—Hello! Is This Grandma? Allwright, Deborah, illus. (p. 764)
—Little Wolf, Terror of the Shivery Sea. Ross, Tony, illus. (p. 1038)
—Lobito Aprende a Ser Malo. Azaola, Miguel, tr. from ENG. (p. 1044)
—Malicia para Principiantes: Una Aventura de Lobito y Apestosito. Quintana, Joela, tr. (p. 1083)
—Meerkat Madness. (p. 1120)
—Merry Meerkat Madness. (p. 1129)
—Miss Wire's Christmas Surprise. Chichester Clark, Emma, illus. (p. 1152)
—More Meerkat Madness. (p. 1174)
—Noisy Way to Bed. Beeke, Tiphanie, tr. (p. 1263)
—Say Boo to the Animals! Warnes, Tim, illus. (p. 1518)
—Say Goodnight to the Sleepy Animals! Eaves, Ed, illus. (p. 1518)
—Say Hello to the Snowy Animals! Eaves, Ed, illus. (p. 1518)

—Say Hello to the Snowy Animals! Eaves, Edward, illus. (p. 1518)
—Tim, Ted & the Pirates. Ayto, Russell, illus. (p. 1750)
—Unvisibles. (p. 1823)
—Where's Tim's Ted? It's Time for Bed! Ayto, Russell, illus. (p. 1911)
Whybrow, Ian, jt. auth. see Clark, Anthony.
Whybrow, Ian, jt. auth. see Melling, David.
Whybrow, Ian & Ayto, Russell. Tim, Ted & the Pirates. (p. 1750)
Whybrow, Ian & Warnes, Tim. Say Hello to the Animals (p. 1518)
Whybrow, Ian, et al. Owain A'r Cloc. (p. 1314)
Whykes, Susan. Let's Practise: Be a Better Musician. (p. 1000)
Whyman, Jennifer E., text. Heavenly Blessings: Baby's Book of Bible Blessing/Baby's Book of Bible Promises. (p. 761)
Whyman, Matt. Boy Kills Man. (p. 218)
—Goldstrike: A Thriller. (p. 696)
—Icecore: A Thriller. (p. 851)
—Icecore: A Carl Hobbes Thriller. (p. 851)
—Savages. (p. 1516)
—Street Runners. (p. 1666)
Whyman, Matthew. Turn in Two. (p. 1797)
Whyte, Alice, illus. see Oren, Miriam & Schram, Peninnah.
Whyte, Daniel, III. Money under the Car Seat: And Other Things to Thank God For. (p. 1164)
Whyte, Donna. What Makes a Good Teacher? Here's What the Kids Say! Garamella, Joyce Orchard, illus. (p. 1892)
Whyte, Elana. My Gift: A Book about a Child Who Sees Spirit. (p. 1209)
Whyte, Elizabeth. Making Tally Charts. (p. 1082)
—Tigers. (p. 1749)
Whyte, Harlinah. England. (p. 529)
Whyte, Harlinah & Frank, Nicole. Japan. (p. 909)
Whyte, Hugh. Rock Steady: A Story of Noah's Ark. (p. 1482)
Whyte, Janet M. Rescue Rider (p. 1462)
Whyte, June. Murder Sucks. (p. 1192)
Whyte, Mariam & Yong, Jui Lin. Bangladesh. (p. 136)
Whyte, Mary, illus. see McGeorge, Constance W.
Whyte, S. L. Stelladaur: Finding Tir Na Nog. (p. 1647)
Whytock, Cherry. My Cup Runneth Over: The Life of Angelica Cookson Potts. Whytock, Cherry, illus. (p. 1200)
—My Scrumptious Scottish Dumplings: The Life of Angelica Cookson Potts. Whytock, Cherry, illus. (p. 1218)
Wiacek, Bob, illus. see Burgan, Michael & Hoena, Blake A.
Wiacek, Bob, illus. see Tocci, Salvatore.
Wiater, Stanley, et al. Complete Stephen King Universe: A Guide to the Worlds of Stephen King. (p. 353)
Wibberley, Leonard. John Treegate's Musket. (p. 923)
—Peter Treegate's War. (p. 1347)
—Treegate's Raiders. (p. 1784)
Wiberg, Harald, jt. auth. see Lindgren, Astrid.
Wichman, David, jt. auth. see Evans, Michael.
Wick. Elfish Fantasy: The Great Chocolate Caper. (p. 512)
Wick, Elaine. It's MY Future: Should I Be a Nurse Practitioner? Tremaine, Michele, illus. (p. 897)
Wick, Jacque. Colorful Cooking. (p. 344)
—to Z Cookbook. (p. 1759)
Wick, Kimberly. Katie's First Day of School: The Adventures of Mrs. Swirlie. (p. 945)
—Reaching for Heaven. (p. 1442)
Wick, Lori. Just above a Whisper. (p. 937)
—Moonlight on the Millpond. (p. 1173)
Wick, Michael J. I Love You All the Time. (p. 843)
Wick, Walter. Can You See What I See? Animals. Wick, Walter, illus. (p. 259)
—Can You See What I See? Dream Machine. Wick, Walter, illus. (p. 259)
—Can You See What I See? Night Before Christmas. Wick, Walter, photos by. (p. 259)
—Can You See What I See? - 100 Fun Finds Read-and-Seek. Wick, Walter, photos by. (p. 259)
—Can You See What I See? - Christmas Read-and-Seek. Wick, Walter, illus. (p. 259)
—Can You See What I See? Games. Wick, Walter, photos by. (p. 259)
—Dinosaurs. Wick, Walter, photos by. (p. 444)
—On a Scary Scary Night: Picture Puzzles to Search & Solve. Wick, Walter, illus. (p. 1288)
—Once upon a Time: Picture Puzzles to Search & Solve. Wick, Walter, photos by. (p. 1293)
—Optical Tricks. Wick, Walter, illus. (p. 1301)
—Out of This World: Picture Puzzles to Search & Solve. Wick, Walter, photos by. (p. 1311)
—Picture Puzzles to Search & Solve. Wick, Walter, illus. (p. 1356)
—Seymour & the Juice Box Boat. Wick, Walter, illus. (p. 1556)
—Seymour Makes New Friends. Wick, Walter, illus. (p. 1556)
—Toyland Express: Picture Puzzles to Search & Solve. Wick, Walter, photos by. (p. 1774)
—Toys - Read-and-Seek. Wick, Walter, photos by. (p. 1774)
—Treasure Ship: Picture Puzzles to Search & Solve. Wick, Walter, illus. (p. 1782)
—Trucks & Cars. Wick, Walter, photos by. (p. 1791)
Wick, Walter, illus. see Marzollo, Jean & Scholastic / LeapFrog.
Wick, Walter, illus. see Marzollo, Jean.
Wick, Walter, jt. auth. see Marzollo, Jean.
Wick, Walter, photos by see Marzollo, Jean.
Wick, Walter, photos by. I Spy: Interactive Sound Book of Picture Riddles. (p. 846)
Wicke, Ed. Akayzia Adams & the Masterdragon's Secret. (p. 32)
—Akayzia Adams & the Mirrors of Darkness. (p. 32)
—Bullies. (p. 240)
—Mattie & the Highwaymen. (p. 1110)
—Muselings. Douglas, Janine, illus. (p. 1192)
—Nicklus. (p. 1251)
—Wicked Tales. (p. 1927)
Wickenden, Nadine. Story of Jonah. (p. 1658)
Wickenden, Nadine, illus. see Ryton, Charlotte.
Wickenden, Nadine, illus. see Slade, Suzanne.
Wickenden, Nadine, jt. auth. see Boon, Fiona.
Wicker, Jan L. Those Excellent Eagles. Weaver, Steve, illus. (p. 1740)
—Those Funny Flamingos. Weaver, Steve, illus. (p. 1740)
—Those Magical Manatees. Weaver, Steve, illus. (p. 1740)
Wicker, Jan Lee. Those Big Bears. (p. 1740)
—Those Delightful Dolphins. Weaver, Steve, illus. (p. 1740)
—Those Excellent Eagles. Weaver, Steve, illus. (p. 1740)
—Those Funny Flamingos. Weaver, Steve, illus. (p. 1740)
—Those Giant Giraffes. Weaver, Steve, illus. (p. 1740)
—Those Magical Manatees. Weaver, Steve, illus. (p. 1740)
Wicker, R. Doug. Bombing of Pan Am Flight 103. (p. 208)
Wickes, Frances, jt. auth. see Skinner, Ada.
Wickett, Maryann & Burns, Marilyn. Lessons for Extending Place Value, Grade 3. (p. 993)
Wickham, Geoffrey. Rapid Perspective. (p. 1439)
Wickham, Kimberly. Angels & Horses. (p. 75)
—Summer of Magic Horses. (p. 1674)
Wickham, Madeleine, see Kinsella, Sophie, pseud.
Wickham, Martha. Mysterious Journey. (p. 1223)
Wickings, Ruth. Pop-Up: Everything You Need to Create Your Own Pop-up Book. Castle, Frances, illus. (p. 1384)
Wickline, Dan. 1001 Arabian Nights: The Adventures of Sinbad. Vol. 2 (p. 2001)
Wicklund, Bruce. Boat, Dive & Fish Catalina Island. (p. 205)
Wickman, Allen, ed. Forest Management Digest. (p. 618)
Wickman, Don. We Are Coming Father Abra'am: The History of the 9th Vermont Volunteer Infantry, 1862-1865 Schroeder, Patrick & Maria, ed. (p. 1865)
Wicks, Alan. Mathematics Standard Level for the International Baccalaureate: A Text for the new Syllabus. (p. 1108)
—Teacher's Supplement Mathematics Standard Level for the International Baccalaureate: A Rest for the New Syllabus. (p. 1709)
Wicks, J. G. On Being Ninety. (p. 1288)
Wicks, Krista. Mazie Moo & Her Clever Clouds, Wonderful Water & Silly Sunshine. (p. 1113)
Wicks, Malcolm. Plaidosoar. (p. 1366)
Wicks, Maris, illus. see Longstreth, Galen Goodwin.
Wicks, Maris, illus. see Ottaviani, Jim.
Wicks, Ruth. It's What Counts That Matters. (p. 899)
—Our World As Told by Baggy Pants & Elsa Belle. (p. 1310)
—Rhyming Gone Wild. (p. 1468)
Wicks, Valerie. Seven Spectral: The Orange World Outlaw. Lang, Leslie, ed. (p. 1555)
Wickstrom, Lois June & Darling, Lucrecia. Orange Forest Rabbit Mysteries: Book One. (p. 1301)
Wickstrom, Sylvie, illus. see Hays, Anna Jane.
Wickstrom, Sylvie K. I Love You, Mister Bear. (p. 843)
Wickstrom, Sylvie K., illus. see Hautzig, Deborah.
Wickstrom, Sylvie K., illus. see Schaefer, Lola M.
Wickstrom, Sylvie K., tr. see Schaefer, Lola M.
Wickstrom, Sylvie Kantorovitz, illus. see Schaefer, Lola M.
Wickstrom, Thor, illus. see Plourde, Lynn.
Widdemer, Mabel Cleland. James Monroe, Good Neighbor Boy: Childhood of Famous Americans Series. Rawson, Maurice, illus. (p. 907)
Widdows, Nancy, jt. auth. see Cooper, Barbara.
Widdowson, John. Geography for Common Entrance. (p. 662)
—Map Skills for Common Entrance Geography & Key Stage 3. (p. 1090)
—This Is Geography (p. 1735)
—This Is Geography Book (p. 1735)
—This Is Geography Book 3 Pupil's (p. 1735)
Widdowson, Kay. Clap Your Hands. (p. 326)
—Give a Little Clap. (p. 681)
—Please, Mr. Crocodile. (p. 1373)
Widdowson, Kay, illus. see Brooks, Felicity.
Widdowson, Kay, illus. see Capucilli, Alyssa Satin.
Widdowson, Kay, illus. see Piper, Sophie & Rock, Lois.
Widdowson, Kay, illus. see Rock, Lois.
Widdowson, Kay, illus. see Segal, Douglas.
Widdowson, Peter. Thomas Hardy. (p. 1738)
Widener, Leslie Stall. Chukfi Rabbit's Big, Bad Bellyache: A Trickster Tale. (p. 318)
Widener, Terry, illus. see Adler, David A.
Widener, Terry, illus. see Hopkinson, Deborah.
Widener, Terry, illus. see Lyons, Mary E.
Widener, Terry, illus. see Rosenstock, Barb.
Widener, Terry, illus. see San Souci, Robert D.
Widener, Terry, illus. see Winter, Jonah.
Widener, Terry, illus. see Yarrow, Peter.
Widenhouse, Kathy. Christian Girl's Guide to Friendship. (p. 311)
—Un-Bunny Book. (p. 1810)
Widermann, Eva, illus. see Christopher, Neil.
Widermann, Eva, illus. see Qaunaq, Sakiasi.
Widgen, Susan. Caring Deed for Becky. Novak, Steven, illus. (p. 269)
Widger, Caeli Wolfson. Real Happy Family: A Novel. (p. 1448)
Widmark, Martin. Cafe Mystery. Willis, Helena, illus. (p. 251)
—Circus Mystery Willis, Helena, illus. (p. 322)
—Diamond Mystery Willis, Helena, illus. (p. 434)
—Hotel Mystery Willis, Helena, illus. (p. 802)
—Mummy Mystery. Willis, Helena, illus. (p. 1191)
—Mummy Mystery #5. Willis, Helena, illus. (p. 1191)
Widmayer, Paul. Jake & the Cowboy Hat. (p. 905)
Widmayer, Paul E. Bessie & Bo: The Story of a Mother's Love. (p. 168)
Widmer, Becky. Bible Awareness Series Christian, Heather, illus. (p. 175)
Widmer, Kirsten & Buxton, Sarah. Workshops That Work! 30 Days of Mini-Lessons That Help Launch & Establish All-Important Routines for an Effective Reading & Writing Workshop. (p. 1953)
Widner, Jan. Then Came the Rains. (p. 1729)
Widowati, Marini, illus. see Norman, Donna Marie.
Wiebe, Joanna. Unseemly Education of Anne Merchant. (p. 1822)
—Wicked Awakening of Anne Merchant. (p. 1927)
Wiebe, Kathleen. Willow Creek Summer. (p. 1934)
Wiebe, Kurtis J. Peter Panzerfaust Deluxe Edition Volume 1 HC. (p. 1347)
Wiebe, Rudy. Hidden Buffalo Lonechild, Michael, illus. (p. 775)
—Mad Trapper (p. 1069)
Wiebe, Ruth Lent. African Americans. (p. 27)
Wiebe, Trina. Lizards Don't Wear Lip Gloss. Sarrazin, Marisol, illus. (p. 1043)
Wiecek, William, jt. auth. see Littlefield, Sophie W.
Wiechman, Kathy Canon. Like a River: A Civil War Novel. (p. 1017)
Wiechmann, Angela, jt. ed. see Lansky, Bruce.
Wiede, Matt. Star, Circle, Baylor: A Little Bear Shapes Book (p. 1640)
Wiede, Matt, illus. see Big Bear Books Staff.
Wiedeman, Connie. Grandma, Do Angels Have Wings? Gaston, Sierra, illus. (p. 708)
Wiedemer & Steel, Abigail. Africa. (p. 26)
Wiedemer, Leah, illus. see Scimone, Diana.
Wiedenhoeft, Alex C. Plant Nutrition. Hopkins, William G., ed. (p. 1369)
Wieder, Joy Nelkin. Secret Tunnel: Israel in the Days of King Chizkiyohu. (p. 1544)
Wiederblank. Save Our School. (p. 1516)
Wiederhold, Kathryn. Ravenwhale. (p. 1441)
Wiedmer, Caroline, jt. auth. see Parker, Michael.
Wiedmer, Caroline & Hardy, Sarah, eds. Motherhood & Space: Configurations of the Maternal Through Politics, Home, & the Body. (p. 1178)
Wiedrich, Merrick & Scheff, William. University of Alabama College Prowler off the Record. (p. 1820)
Wiegers, Karl E. More about Software Requirements: Thorny Issues & Practical Advice. (p. 1173)
Wiegle, Matt, illus. see SparkNotes Staff.
Wielkiewicz, Richard M. Okay, Riders, Set 'Em Up: A Nate Walker BMX Adventure. Dwyer, Corinne et al, illus. (p. 1282)
Wiemeler, Aaron. My Feelings Workbook. Trapp, Karla, illus. (p. 1203)
Wiener. 13 Colonies (p. 1995)
Wiener, Gary. Child Labor. (p. 301)
—Gender in Lorraine Hansberry's a Raisin in the Sun. (p. 660)
—Internet. (p. 880)
—War in Ernest Hemingway's for Whom the Bell Tolls. (p. 1857)
—Women's Issues in Amy Tan's The Joy Luck Club. (p. 1946)
—Worker's Rights in Upton Sinclair's The Jungle. (p. 1952)
Wiener, Gary, ed. Environment in Rachel Carson's Silent Spring. (p. 532)
—War in Ernest Hemingway's for Whom the Bell Tolls. (p. 1857)
Wiener, Leo. Africa & the Discovery of America. (p. 26)
Wiener, Roberta, jt. auth. see Arnold, James R.
Wiener, Roberta, et al. Pennsylvania (p. 1338)
Wiens, Patti. Child's ABCs of Praise Spieler, Leah, ed. (p. 304)
Wierenga, Emily Theresa. Save My Children: The Story of a Father's Love. (p. 1516)
Wieringo, Mike, illus. see Waid, Mark & Porter, Howard.
Wieringo, Mike, illus. see Waid, Mark.
Wieringo, Mike & Buckingham, Mike. Fantastic Four by Waid & Wieringo Ultimate Collection Book 1. (p. 571)
Wiersbitzky, Shannon. Summer of Hammers & Angels. (p. 1674)
Wiersum, Gale. Animals' Christmas Eve. (p. 82)
Wiese, Erika J., jt. auth. see Wiese, Fritz H.
Wiese, Fritz H. & Wiese, Erika J. Erika & the Mermaids. (p. 533)
Wiese, Jim. Ancient Science: 40 Time-Traveling, World-Exploring, History-Making Activities for Kids. Shems, Ed, illus. (p. 70)
Wiese, Jim & Melton, H. Keith. Spy's Guide to Counterintelligence. (p. 1636)
—Spy's Guide to Scouting & Reconnaissance. (p. 1636)
—Spy's Guide to Security. (p. 1636)
Wiese, Jim & Shems, Ed. Weird Science: 40 Strange-Acting, Bizarre-Looking, & Barely Believable Activities for Kids. Shems, Ed, illus. (p. 1872)
Wiese, Kurt, illus. see Brooks, Walter R.
Wiese, Kurt, illus. see Brooks, Walter R. & Slayton-Mitchell, Joyce.
Wiese, Kurt, illus. see O'Brien, Jack.
Wiese, Kurt, illus. see Reely, Mary Katharine.
Wiese, Kurt, illus. see Smither, Ethel L.
Wiesenfeld, Lori P., jt. auth. see Hess, Debra.
Wiesner, Al, illus. see Stoltz, Donald R.
Wiesner, David. Art & Max. (p. 101)
—Flotsam. (p. 607)
—Free Fall. Wiesner, David, illus. (p. 634)
—Hurricane Wiesner, David, illus. (p. 829)
—Mr. Wuffles! (p. 1187)
—Tres Cerditos. (p. 1784)
—Tuesday. (p. 1796)
Wiesner, David, illus. see Bunting, Eve.
Wiesner, David, illus. see Leiber, Fritz.
Wiesner, David, adapted by. Gonna Roll the Bones. (p. 697)
Wiesner, Karen Sue. Cody Knows. Hardy, Candace J., illus. (p. 338)
Wiesner, Leesa. Last Stand of the Fire Dragons. (p. 978)
Wiesner, Leona Shew. Lundy: Adventures of A Little Boy in Early America. (p. 1065)
Wiesner, Merry E. Age of Voyages, 1450-1600. (p. 29)
Wiesner-Hanks, Merry E. Age of Voyages, 1350-1600. (p. 29)
Wiess, Laura. Leftovers. (p. 987)
Wiewandt, Thomas A. Hidden Life of the Desert. (p. 776)
Wigal, Mike, illus. see Escott, Maria.
Wigand, Molly. Being Mad: A Book about Anger... Just for Me! Fitzgerald, Anne, illus. (p. 161)
—How to Be a Friend: A Book about Friendship... Just for Me! Fitzgerald, Anne, illus. (p. 814)
Wigden, Susan. I Want to Learn to Dance. Franzese, Nora Tapp, illus. (p. 848)
—Silly Rhymes for Fun Times. Columbin, Corey, illus. (p. 1576)
Wigden, Susan & Salem, I. Mitzva for Zelda. (p. 1156)
Wigens, Lynne, jt. auth. see Russell, Julia.
Wiggan, Desmond, illus. see Roberts, Pauline.
Wigger, J. Bradley. Thank You, God. Jago, illus. (p. 1725)
Wigger, Sherry. Scary Stories for Brave Kids (p. 1521)
Wiggers, jt. auth. see Hogan.
Wiggers, Raymond. Geology Underfoot in Illinois (p. 662)
Wiggin, Kate Douglas. Bird's Christmas Carol. (p. 191)
—Birds' Christmas Carol. (p. 191)
—Birds' Christmas Carol. Wireman, Katharine R., illus. (p. 191)
—Diary of a Goose Girl. (p. 434)
—Diary of a Goose Girl. Shepperson, Claude A., illus. (p. 434)
—Girl & the Kingdom. (p. 678)
—Homespun Tales. (p. 793)
—Marm Lisa. (p. 1096)
—New Chronicles of Rebecc. (p. 1244)
—New Chronicles of Rebecca. (p. 1244)
—Old Peabody Pew. (p. 1284)
—Penelope Travels Abroad. (p. 1336)
—Penelope's English Experiences. (p. 1336)
—Penelope's Experiences in Scotland. (p. 1336)
—Penelope's Irish Experiences. (p. 1336)
—Penelope's Postscripts. (p. 1336)
—Polly Oliver's Problem. (p. 1381)
—Rebecca of Sunnybrook Farm. Akib, Jamel, illus. (p. 1450)
—Rose O' the River. (p. 1489)
—Story of Patsy. (p. 1659)
—Summer in a Canyon. (p. 1674)
—Susanna & Sue. (p. 1688)
—Village Stradivarius. (p. 1842)
—Village Watchtower. (p. 1842)
Wiggin, Kate Douglas & Smith, Archibald Nora. Tales of Wonder Every Child Should Know. (p. 1703)
Wiggin, Kate Douglas & Smith, Nora Archibald. Fairy Ring. MacKinstry, Elizabeth, illus. (p. 564)
Wiggin, Kate Douglas Smith. Rebecca of Sunnybrook Farm. (p. 1450)
—Rebecca of Sunnybrook Farm. Warren, Eliza Gatewood, ed. (p. 1450)
Wiggins, Bethany. Cured. (p. 392)
—Shifting. (p. 1566)
—Stung. (p. 1670)
Wiggins, D. L. Where Dreams Are Born. Carter, Kelly, illus. (p. 1907)
Wiggins, L. J., ed. see Evans, Laneta Fullenwiley.
Wiggins, Leah Holder. My Neighbor Is Gone. Wiggins, Margaret W., illus. (p. 1215)
Wiggins, Margaret W., illus. see Hopkins, Nicolla.
Wiggins, Margaret W., illus. see Wiggins, Leah Holder.
Wiggins, Mick, illus. see Lyon, George Ella & Lyon, Benn.
Wiggins, Mick, illus. see Lyon, George Ella.
Wiggins, Rosie. Adventures at a Ray of Hope Preschool. (p. 15)
Wiggins-Edwards, Linda. I Am Beautiful! (p. 832)
Wiggins-James, Nesta. Physical Education: Historical Factors & Contemporary Issues. (p. 1353)
Wigglesworth, Gayle. Malice in Mexico: A Claire Gulliver Mystery. (p. 1083)
Wigglesworth, Penny. Penny Bear's Gift of Love: A Story of Friendship Between a Grieving Young Boy & a Magical Little Bear. Eager, Michiko, illus. (p. 1338)
Wiggs, Lance Claiborne. Frog's Surprise. (p. 641)
Wiggs, Sue, illus. see Lester, Vivian.
Wight, Al, jt. auth. see Clarke, Roger.
Wight, Eric. Frankie Pickle & the Closet of Doom. Wight, Eric, illus. (p. 630)
—Frankie Pickle & the Mathematical Menace. Wight, Eric, illus. (p. 630)
—Frankie Pickle & the Pine Run 3000. Wight, Eric, illus. (p. 630)
—My Dead Girlfriend: A Tryst of Fate Vol. 1 (p. 1201)
Wight, Eric, illus. see DiPucchio, Kelly.
Wight, Eric, illus. see Egan, Kate & Lane, Mike.
Wight, Eric, illus. see Scaletta, Kurtis.
Wight, Joe, jt. auth. see Bozanich, Tony L.
Wight, Joseph. Storm (p. 1655)
—Storm Vol. 2, No. 2. (p. 1655)
—Twilight X (p. 1801)
Wight, Joseph, illus. see Dunn, Joe.
Wight, Karol. Paperweight Pals. (p. 1323)
Wight, Milan E. & Bratton, Chris. Chickens Are Our Friends. (p. 300)
Wight, Tamra. Mystery on Pine Lake (p. 1226)
—Mystery on Pine Lake: A Cooper & Packrat Mystery. (p. 1226)
Wightman, Gregory J. Origins of Religion in the Paleolithic. (p. 1304)
Wightman, Jillian C. Adventures of Erin Mctavitt. (p. 18)
Wightwick, Jane. Spanish on the Move: The Lively Audio Language Program for Busy People. (p. 1621)
—Way Cool French Phrasebook. (p. 1864)
—Way Cool Italian Phrasebook. (p. 1864)
—Way Cool Spanish Phrasebook. (p. 1864)
Wigington, Patti. Pirate's Alphabet. Umscheid, Kit, illus. (p. 1363)
—Summer's Ashes. (p. 1675)
Wigley, Audrey Watson, illus. see Ignerl, David S.
Wignall, K. J. Death. (p. 420)
Wignell, Edel. Bendelomena. Goss, Mini, illus. (p. 164)
—Bilby: Secrets of an Australian Marsupial. Jackson, Mark, illus. (p. 186)
Wignell, Edel & Argent, Leanne. I Wonder Who Lives Upstairs. (p. 849)
Wigoder, Geoffrey, et al. Student's Encyclopedia of Judaism. Sutnick, Barbara, ed. (p. 1669)
Wigsby, Nick, illus. see Peacock, L. A.
Wigu Publishing. When I Grow Up I Want to Be... a Teacher! Carlee Learns a Surprising Lesson! (p. 1903)
Wilson, Gabriella S. Anything on Earth Poems: Children's Poetry. (p. 91)
Wijesinha, Rajiva. Foundations of Modern Society. (p. 624)
Wijngaard, Jan, illus. see Pinchuk, Tom.
Wijngaard, Jan, illus. see Viz Media Staff & Smith, Brian.
Wijngaard, Juan, illus. see Peet, Mal & Graham, Elspeth.
Wik, Jenny, illus. see Reuterstrand, Siri.
Wik, John. Visual Chaos Stained Glass Coloring Book. (p. 1846)
Wik, John & Coloring Books for Adults. Deco Tech: Geometric Coloring Book. (p. 422)
Wik, John & Creative Haven Staff. Creative Haven Tessellation Patterns Coloring Book. (p. 379)
Wike, Dorothy. Eternal Spring. (p. 539)

W

Wiker, Benjamin. Mystery of the Periodic Table. Bendick, Jeanne, illus. (p. 1226)
Wikland, Ilon, illus. see Lagerlöf, Selma.
Wikland, Ilon, illus. see Lindgren, Astrid.
Wikler, Madeline, jt. auth. see Groner, Judye.
Wikler, Madeline, jt. auth. see Groner, Judyth Saypol.
Wikler, Madeline, jt. auth. see Groner, Judyth.
Wiklund, Alison, jt. auth. see Ringbom, Antonia.
Wiklund, Alison & Ringbom, Antonia. Hiding Hyena. (p. 777)
Wilber, Peggy M., ed. see Gemmen, Heather.
Wilberforce, Bertram. Why We Need Laws. (p. 1926)
Wilberforce, Samuel. Agathos the Rocky Island & Other Sunday Stories & Parables. (p. 29)
Wilbur, Claire & Wilbur, Steve. Southeast Asian Textiles. (p. 1617)
Wilbur, Eleanor. Bump Thump! (p. 241)
Wilbur, Helen. Lily's Victory Garden. Steele, Robert, illus. (p. 1018)
—Little New York. Brett, Jeannie, illus. (p. 1032)
Wilbur, Helen L. D Is for Derby: A Kentucy Derby Alphabet. Corum, Jaime, illus. (p. 397)
—E Is for Eiffel Tower: A France Alphabet. Nascimbene, Yan, illus. (p. 492)
—Finnegan & Fox: The Ten-Foot Cop. Manders, John, illus. (p. 589)
—M Is for Meow: A Cat Alphabet. Papp, Robert, illus. (p. 1067)
—Z Is for Zeus: A Greek Mythology Alphabet. Juhasz, Victor, illus. (p. 1984)
Wilbur, Helen L., jt. auth. see James, Helen Foster.
Wilbur, Regina, ed. Keys to Success: Getting Control of Mr. & Mrs. Attitude & Temper (A. T.) Student Workbook Grades 6-12. (p. 951)
—Keys to Success: Getting Control of Mr. & Mrs Attitude & Temper (A. T.) Teacher's Guide/Students Assignments Grades 6-12. (p. 951)
Wilbur, Richard. Loudmouse. (p. 1057)
—Pig in the Spigot. Siebold, J. Otto, illus. (p. 1357)
Wilbur, Steve, jt. auth. see Wilbur, Claire.
Wilburg, Dale, jt. auth. see Evans, Richard.
Wilburn, Kathy, illus. see Hall, Kirsten.
Wilburn, Mary Lynne. Sam's Toy Museum. (p. 1509)
Wilce, Colin. Rain & Blossom (Rabbit Brook Tales Volume 2) (p. 1434)
—Valley & Daffodils (Rabbit Brook T. (p. 1830)
—Youngsters' Adventure & Thanksgiving (Rabbit Brook Tales Volume 4) (p. 1979)
Wilce, Ysabeau S. Flora's Dare: How a Girl of Spirit Gambles All to Expand Her Vocabulary, Confront a Bouncing Boy Terror, & Try to Save Califa from a Shaky Doom (Despite Being Confined to Her Room) (p. 606)
—Flora's Fury: How a Girl of Spirit & a Red Dog Confound Their Friends, Astound Their Enemies, & Learn the Importance of Packing Light. (p. 606)
Wilcock, Lizzie. Give Me Four Reasons. (p. 681)
Wilcockson, Michael. Access to Religion & Philosophy: Medical Ethics. (p. 8)
Wilcox. Hidden Men. (p. 776)
Wilcox, Alison. Descriptosaurus: Supporting Creative Writing for Ages 8-14. (p. 428)
Wilcox, Brian & David, Lawrence. Full Moon. Wilcox, Brian, illus. (p. 646)
Wilcox, Cathy, illus. see Gervay, Susanne.
Wilcox, Cathy, jt. auth. see Gervay, Susanne.
Wilcox, Charlotte. All about Dogs. (p. 42)
—Chow Chows. (p. 311)
—Earth-Friendly Waste Management. (p. 496)
—Greyhounds. (p. 723)
—Iroquois. (p. 888)
—Newfoundlands. (p. 1249)
—Recycling. (p. 1453)
—Weimaraners. (p. 1872)
Wilcox, Christine. Careers in Information Technology. (p. 268)
—Cell Phones & Teens. (p. 286)
—Gambling Addiction. (p. 654)
—How Is Online Pornography Affecting Society? (p. 810)
—Justin Bieber. Greenhaven Press Staff, ed. (p. 940)
—Oscar Pistorius. (p. 1305)
—Shaun White. Greenhaven Press Editors, ed. (p. 1563)
—Teens & Body Image. (p. 1714)
—Teens, Nutrition, & Dieting. (p. 1715)
—Thinking Critically: Online Privacy. (p. 1734)
Wilcox, Clifford, ed. see Redfield, Robert.
Wilcox, Dominic. Variations on Normal. (p. 1833)
Wilcox, Edee. Saved Times Three. (p. 1517)
Wilcox, Ella Wheeler. Historical Mother Goose: A Jingle Book O. (p. 783)
Wilcox, Jean A. Diary of Sir Winston Loki (p. 435)
—Winston's New Camelot. (p. 1937)
Wilcox, Jean K. & Cameron, E. Jane. AbuLLard's ABC's of Branding: 26 Concepts That Capture the Essence of Good Brand Management Kopervas, Gary & Hanes, Don, illus. (p. 7)
Wilcox, JoAnn Pinkney. My Sister the Sociopath. (p. 1218)
—Why Do Men Love Bitches? & the Women Who Love Them: A Fresh Perspective: for the Women who are Not Bitches, & for the Men who need to Appreciate Them. (p. 1923)
Wilcox, Jonathan & Latif, Zawiah Abdul. Iceland. (p. 851)
Wilcox, Judy. Ferderic Chopin, Son of Poland, Early & Later Years Study Guide. (p. 581)
Wilcox, Katherine A. Let Me Be Myself. (p. 994)
Wilcox, Leah. Falling for Rapunzel. Monks, Lydia, illus. (p. 566)
—Waking Beauty. Monks, Lydia, illus. (p. 1853)
Wilcox, Leigh Attaway. All Better: A Touch-and-Heal Book. Wildish, Lee, illus. (p. 44)
Wilcox, Lucy. Eva the Diva's Fashion Fun Shop: The Birthday Surprise. (p. 540)
Wilcox, Marelene. Dixie Street Boys: The Promise. (p. 455)
Wilcox, Mary, ed. see Dunrea, Olivier.
Wilcox, Mary, ed. see Rey, H. A.
Wilcox, Merrie-Ellen. What's the Buzz? Keeping Bees in Flight (p. 1899)
Wilcox, Michael. Colors Around Us. Barber, Julia, illus. (p. 345)
—What Is Color. (p. 1889)
Wilcox, R. B. Karma on Tap: The Online Buddhist Revolution. (p. 944)
Wilcox, S. Michael, jt. auth. see Gibbons, Ted.
Wilcoxson, Billy. CB Cowboys: The Saga of the Legendary Christensen Family. (p. 283)
Wilcut-Bledsoe, Robin. Imagination of Hollie Mason. (p. 860)
Wild, Anne. Christmas Carousel: The Story of the Nativity in Five Scenes to Cut Out & Make. (p. 313)
Wild, Anne S. Wildlife Pop-Ups: A Collection of 3-D Greetings Cards on Wildlife Themes to Cut Out & Make. (p. 1931)
Wild, Cynthia & Nash, Kevin. UC Riverside College Prowler off the Record: Inside University of California Riverside. (p. 1807)
Wild, Gill, illus. see Childress, Gavin & Dooley, Audrey.
Wild, Kate. Fight Game (p. 585)
—Firefight. (p. 591)
Wild, Margaret. Dream of the Thylacine. Brooks, Ron, illus. (p. 483)
—Fox. Brooks, Ron, illus. (p. 626)
—Harry & Hopper. Blackwood, Freya, illus. (p. 750)
—Hop, Little Hare! Shaw, Peter, illus. (p. 796)
—Hush, Hush! Strevens-Marzo, Bridget, illus. (p. 830)
—Itsy-Bitsy Animals. Ormerod, Jan, illus. (p. 900)
—Itsy-Bitsy Babies. Ormerod, Jan, illus. (p. 900)
—Jinx. Gould, Jason, photos by. (p. 919)
—Kiss Kiss! Strevens-Marzo, Bridget, illus. (p. 961)
—Kiss, Kiss! Strevens-Marzo, Bridget, illus. (p. 961)
—Let the Celebrations Begin. Vivas, Julie, illus. (p. 994)
—Lucy Goosey. James, Ann, illus. (p. 1063)
—No More Kisses! Rycroft, Nina, illus. (p. 1259)
—No More Kisses. Rycroft, Nina, illus. (p. 1259)
—On the Day You Were Born. Brooks, Ron, illus. (p. 1290)
—Piglet & Granny. King, Stephen Michael, illus. (p. 1358)
—Piglet & Mama. King, Stephen Michael, illus. (p. 1358)
—Ruby Roars. Argent, Kerry, illus. (p. 1493)
—Seven More Sleeps. Rawlins, Donna, illus. (p. 1554)
—Stone Lion. Voutila, Ritva, illus. (p. 1652)
—This Little Piggy Went Dancing. Niland, Deborah, illus. (p. 1737)
—Vanishing Moment. (p. 1833)
Wild, Margaret & Rawlins, Donna. Seven More Sleeps. (p. 1554)
Wild, Margaret & Strevens-Marzo, Bridget. Kiss, Kiss Box Set. (p. 961)
Wildavsky, Rachel. Secret of Rover. Caparo, Antonio, illus. (p. 1542)
Wilde, Carol, illus. see Butters, Dorothy Gilman, pseud.
Wilde, Cindy. Beautiful Copycat Coloring Book: Pretty Pictures to Copy & Complete. (p. 153)
Wilde, David, jt. auth. see Cox, Kimberley.
Wilde, George, illus. see Christie, Caroline.
Wilde, George, illus. see Wilde, Irma.
Wilde, Gloria. Lucifer: Good Angel Gone Bad. Bauer, John, illus. (p. 1062)
Wilde, Irma. Mr. Wishing Went Fishing. Wilde, George, illus. (p. 1187)
Wilde, Irma, illus. see Hillert, Margaret.
Wilde, Jeanne Wilkins. Two Dogs Long & Half a Dog High. (p. 1803)
Wilde, Jerry. Hot Stuff to Help Kids Cheer Up: The Depression & Self-Esteem Workbook. (p. 802)
—Peace in the Halls: Stories & Activities to Manage Anger & Prevent School Violence. (p. 1331)
Wilde, Kim. Harry's Garden. (p. 751)
—How to Make a Scarecrow: Band 00/Lilac. (p. 820)
Wilde, Lori. License to Thrill. (p. 1007)
Wilde, Oscar. Ballad of Reading Gaol & Other Poems. (p. 134)
—Canterville Ghost: Complete & Unabridged with Extensive Notes. (p. 262)
—Canterville Ghost. (p. 262)
—Canterville Ghost. Marks, Alan, illus. (p. 262)
—Classic Tales of Oscar Wilde. Robinson, Charles, illus. (p. 328)
—Complete Fairy Tales of Oscar Wilde. (p. 352)
—Cuentos. Cherician, David, tr. (p. 389)
—Cuentos de Oscar Wilde. (p. 390)
—Fairy Tales of Oscar Wilde: The Devoted Friend, The Nightengale, & the Rose Vol. 4 Russell, P. Craig, illus. (p. 564)
—Fairy Tales of Oscar Wilde: the Complete Hardcover Set 1-5. Russell, P. Craig, illus. (p. 564)
—Fairy Tales of Oscar Wilde: the Happy Prince Signed & Numbered. Russell, P. Craig, illus. (p. 564)
—Fantasma de Canterville: Y otros Cuentos. (p. 571)
—Fantasma de Canterville. (p. 571)
—Fantasma de Canterville y Otros Cuentos. (p. 571)
—Happy Prince. (p. 746)
—Happy Prince. Delessert, Etienne, illus. (p. 746)
—Happy Prince & Other Stories. (p. 746)
—Happy Prince & Other Stories. Bo, Lars, illus. (p. 746)
—Happy Prince & Other Tales. (p. 746)
—House of Pomegranates. (p. 803)
—House of Pomegranates. King, Jessie Marion, illus. (p. 803)
—Importance of Being Earnest: Prestwick House Literary Touchstone Edition. (p. 862)
—Importance of Being Earnest. Bryant, Clive, ed. (p. 862)
—Importance of Being Earnest the Graphic Novel Quick Text: (American English) Stokes, John, illus. (p. 862)
—Lady Windermere's Fan. Landes, William-Alan, ed. (p. 971)
—Picture of Dorian Gray (p. 1355)
—Prince Hereux. (p. 1401)
—Retrato de Dorian Gray. (p. 1464)
—Salomé. (p. 1505)
—Selfish Giant: A Tale about Being Unselfish. Eberl, Len, illus. (p. 1549)
—Selfish Giant. (p. 1549)
—Selfish Giant & Other Classic Tales. Thorne, Jenny, illus. (p. 1549)
Wilde, Oscar, jt. auth. see Clark, Phil.
Wilde, Oscar, jt. auth. see Maidment, Stella.
Wilde, Oscar, jt. auth. see Piumini, Roberto.
Wilde, Oscar, jt. auth. see Russell, P. Craig.
Wilde, Oscar & Grodin, Elissa. Happy Prince. Stutzman, Laura, illus. (p. 746)
Wilde, Oscar & Hollingsworth, Mary. Selfish Giant. Bell, Bill, illus. (p. 1549)
Wilde, Oscar & Lynch, P. J. Oscar Wilde Stories for Children. (p. 1305)
Wilde, Oscar & O'Flahertie Wills Wilde, Oscar Fingal. Fantasma de Canterville y Otros Cuentos. Ballesteros, Antonio, tr. (p. 571)
Wilde, Oscar & Oscar, Wilde. Famoso Cohete. Zwerger, Lisbeth, illus. (p. 569)
—Gigante Egoista. Zwerger, Lisbeth, illus. (p. 676)
—Principe Feliz y Otros Cuentos. (p. 1406)
Wilde, Oscar & SparkNotes Staff. Importance of Being Earnest. Kestler, Justin & Florman, Ben, eds. (p. 862)
Wilde, Oscar, contrib. by. Canterville Ghost. (p. 262)
Wilde, Oscar, et al. Oscar Wilde Pomplun, Tom, ed. (p. 1305)
Wilde, Raymond. Under a Stern Reign. (p. 1813)
Wilde, Terry Lee. Ghostly Liaisons. (p. 672)
—Vampire... in My Dreams. (p. 1832)
Wilden, Beverley. Who Said Monsters Don't Exist? (p. 1917)
Wilder, Adrienne. Dragon Unlikely. (p. 478)
Wilder, Beth. Bugs in Shoes (p. 237)
Wilder, Brenda. Grand Adventures of Sadie Mae Fuller. (p. 707)
—Sadie in St. Louis: The Grand Adventures of Sadie Mae Fuller. (p. 1501)
Wilder, John Watson. His Name Is Jesus. (p. 781)
Wilder, K. C. Tour de You: Swirling Circles of Freedom. (p. 1773)
Wilder, Laura Ingalls. By the Shores of Silver Lake. (p. 249)
—By the Shores of Silver Lake. Williams, Garth, illus. (p. 249)
—County Fair. Wheeler, Jody, illus. (p. 372)
—Farmer Boy. (p. 574)
—Farmer Boy. Williams, Garth, illus. (p. 574)
—First Four Years. Williams, Garth, illus. (p. 595)
—Little House Williams, Garth, illus. (p. 1029)
—Little House 02: Little House on the Prairie. (p. 1029)
—Little House Christmas Treasury: Festive Holiday Stories. Williams, Garth, illus. (p. 1029)
—Little House Collection Williams, Garth, illus. (p. 1029)
—Little House in the Big Woods. (p. 1029)
—Little House in the Big Woods. Williams, Garth, illus. (p. 1029)
—Little House on the Prairie. (p. 1029)
—Little House on the Prairie. Williams, Garth, illus. (p. 1029)
—Little House Traveler: Writings from Laura Ingalls Wilder's Journeys Across America. (p. 1029)
—Little Town on the Prairie. (p. 1037)
—Little Town on the Prairie. Williams, Garth, illus. (p. 1037)
—Long Winter. Williams, Garth, illus. (p. 1047)
—On the Banks of Plum Creek. (p. 1289)
—On the Banks of Plum Creek. Williams, Garth, illus. (p. 1289)
—These Happy Golden Years. (p. 1731)
—These Happy Golden Years. Williams, Garth, illus. (p. 1731)
Wilder, Laura Ingalls & Ingalls, Laura. Aquellos Anos Dorado. Williams, Garth, illus. (p. 94)
—Cuatro Primeros Anos. Williams, Garth, illus. (p. 388)
Wilder, M. L. Missionary Annuls: Memoir of Robert Moffat. (p. 1153)
Wilder, Nellie. Changing Weather. (p. 290)
—On Land. (p. 1289)
—On Water. (p. 1292)
—What Is the Weather? (p. 1890)
Wilder, Stephanie. Legends of the Blues. (p. 990)
Wilder, Vickie. Umbrella. (p. 1810)
Wilderness, Dale. Drift in Your Pillow's Eyes. (p. 485)
Wildes, Emma. Mr. Poot's Christmas [a Scary Baby Adventure]. (p. 1186)
Wildfong, Tonya. Bee in the Barn. Cichos, Tomek, illus. (p. 157)
Wilding, Diane, ed. see Bercik, Mark.
Wilding, Val. Dodging the Donkey Doo. Broad, Michael, illus. (p. 460)
Wilding, Valerie. Diggers & Dumpers. Maddocks, Maria, illus. (p. 439)
—Grumpy Queen. Sanfilippo, Simona, illus. (p. 727)
Wildish, Lee. Boy Who Cried Wolf. (p. 219)
Wildish, Lee, illus. see Clarke, Jane.
Wildish, Lee, illus. see Crum, Shutta.
Wildish, Lee, illus. see Gray, Kes.
Wildish, Lee, illus. see Greenwell, Jessica.
Wildish, Lee, illus. see Guillain, Adam & Guillain, Charlotte.
Wildish, Lee, illus. see Guillain, Adam.
Wildish, Lee, illus. see Guillain, Charlotte & Guillain, Adam.
Wildish, Lee, illus. see Hendra, Sue.
Wildish, Lee, illus. see Reagan, Jean.
Wildish, Lee, illus. see Scholastic, Inc. Staff & Ackerman, Jill.
Wildish, Lee, illus. see Singer, Marilyn.
Wildish, Lee, illus. see Tabby, Abigail.
Wildish, Lee, illus. see Taplin, Sam.
Wildish, Lee, illus. see Waddell, Martin.
Wildish, Lee, illus. see Wilcox, Leigh Attaway.
Wildlife Conservation Society, photos by see Thomson, Sarah L.
Wildlife Education. Elephants. (p. 511)
—Giraffes. (p. 677)
—Penguins. (p. 1337)
—Polar Bears. (p. 1379)
—Sharks. (p. 1562)
Wildlife Education. Tigers. (p. 1749)
Wildlife Education. Wolves. (p. 1945)
Wildlife Education, compiled by. Alligators. (p. 47)
—Frogs. (p. 641)
—Great Apes. (p. 713)
—Seals. (p. 1536)
—Turtles. (p. 1799)
Wildlife Education, contrib. by. Tigers. (p. 1749)
Wildlife Education, Ltd. Staff. Animal Babies 1. (p. 76)
Wildlife Education, Ltd Staff, contrib. by. Butterflies. (p. 247)
—Dolphins. (p. 464)
—Monkeys. (p. 1165)
Wildlife Education, Ltd. Staff, contrib. by. Spanish Hardcover Set (p. 1621)
Wildlife Education, Ltd Staff, contrib. by. Whales. (p. 1878)
Wildman, Dale. Big Rig Daddy: A Ride in the Truck of All Trucks. Dickson, Bill, illus. (p. 183)
—Do You Know the Way to Find an A? A Rhyming ABC Book. Sisung, Peter, illus. (p. 458)
—Nicholas Knows: Big Brother Nicholas Knows It All! Sisung, Peter, illus. (p. 1251)
Wildot Press. Amanda Patricia's Kitchen. (p. 52)
—David's Garage. (p. 411)
—Jacob's Back Yard. (p. 904)
—Jacob's Front Yard. (p. 904)
Wilds, Kazumi, illus. see Moore, Sandra.
Wilds, Kazumi, illus. see Thompson, Holly.
Wilds, Kazumi, jt. auth. see Moore, Willamarie.
Wilds, Mary. I Dare Not Fail: Notable African American Women Educators. (p. 837)
Wildsmith, Brian. Animal Colors (Arabic/English) wintranslation.com, tr. (p. 77)
—Animal Colors (Bengali/English) (p. 77)
—Animal Colors (Farsi) Wildsmith, Brian, illus. (p. 77)
—Animals to Count (Farsi) Wildsmith, Brian, illus. (p. 84)
—Animals to Count (Simplified Mandarin) Wildsmith, Brian, illus. (p. 84)
—Animaux de la Ferme. (p. 84)
—Brian Wildsmith's Amazing Animal Alphabet (p. 226)
—Brian Wildsmith's Amazing Animal Alphabet Book (p. 226)
—Brian Wildsmith's Amazing Animal Alphabet Book. Wildsmith, Brian, illus. (p. 226)
—Brian Wildsmith's Animal Colors (p. 226)
—Brian Wildsmith's Animal Colors (Arabic) (p. 226)
—Brian Wildsmith's Animal Colors (Korean) Wildsmith, Brian, illus. (p. 226)
—Brian Wildsmith's Animal Colors (Portugese) (p. 226)
—Brian Wildsmith's Animal Colors (Simplified Mandarin) Wildsmith, Brian, illus. (p. 226)
—Brian Wildsmith's Animal Colors (Tagalog) Wildsmith, Brian, illus. (p. 226)
—Brian Wildsmith's Animal Colors (Traditional Cantonese) Wildsmith, Brian, illus. (p. 226)
—Brian Wildsmith's Animal Colors (Vietnamese) (p. 226)
—Brian Wildsmith's Animals to Count Wildsmith, Brian, illus. (p. 226)
—Brian Wildsmith's Animals to Count (Korean) Wildsmith, Brian, illus. (p. 226)
—Brian Wildsmith's Animals to Count (Portugese) Wildsmith, Brian, illus. (p. 226)
—Brian Wildsmith's Animals to Count (Tagalog) Wildsmith, Brian, illus. (p. 226)
—Brian Wildsmith's Animals to Count (Traditional Cantonese) (p. 226)
—Brian Wildsmith's Animals to Count (Vietnamese) (p. 226)
—Brian Wildsmith's Farm Animals (p. 226)
—Brian Wildsmith's Farm Animals (Korean) Wildsmith, Brian, illus. (p. 226)
—Brian Wildsmith's Farm Animals (Navajo) (p. 226)
—Brian Wildsmith's Farm Animals (Portugese) (p. 226)
—Brian Wildsmith's Farm Animals (Tagalog) Wildsmith, Brian, illus. (p. 226)
—Brian Wildsmith's Farm Animals (Vietnamese) (p. 226)
—Brian Wildsmith's Opposites (p. 226)
—Colores de los Animales/Animal Colors. (p. 344)
—Couleurs des Animaux. (p. 369)
—Easter Story. Wildsmith, Brian, illus. (p. 499)
—Farm Animals (Simplified Mandarin) Wildsmith, Brian, illus. (p. 573)
—Farm Animals (Traditional Cantonese) Wildsmith, Brian, illus. (p. 573)
—Hunter & His Dog Wildsmith, Brian, illus. (p. 828)
—Jesus. Wildsmith, Brian, illus. (p. 914)
—Jungle Party (p. 935)
—Jungle Party Wildsmith, Brian, illus. (p. 935)
—Little Wood Duck (p. 1038)
—Little Wood Duck Wildsmith, Brian, illus. (p. 1038)
—Owl & the Woodpecker Wildsmith, Brian, illus. (p. 1315)
—Professor Noah's Spaceship Wildsmith, Brian, illus. (p. 1409)
Wildsmith, Brian, illus. see Ikeda, Daisaku.
Wildsmith, Brian, illus. see Stevenson, Robert Louis.
Wildsmith, Sarah. Princess Charming. Paramonova, Lea, illus. (p. 1403)
Wildt, Bill. My Love for the Game. (p. 1213)
Wildwood, Gretchen. Ancient Mesopotamian Civilization. Cantucci, Alessandro & Morandi, Andrea, illus. (p. 70)
Wile, Jay L. Exploring Creation with Physical Science: Student Text. (p. 552)
Wile, Jay L., ed. see Fulbright, Jeannie.
Wile, Jay L., ed. see Seligson, Sherri.
Wile, Jay L. & Durnell, Marilyn F. Exploring Creation with Biology (p. 552)
Wile, Jay L. & Shannon, Marilyn. Companion CD-ROM for the Human Body: Fearfully & Wonderfully Made! on CD-ROM. (p. 351)
Wile, Kathleen J., ed. see Watson, Sharon.
Wile, Mary Lee. Season of Angels. Stossel, Sage, illus. (p. 1538)
Wilensky, Alexander. Splendid Spotted Snake: A Magic Ribbon Book. (p. 1630)
Wiles, Andrew, et al. Fermat's Last Theorem: The Theorem & Its Proof: An Exploration of Issues & Ideas. (p. 582)
Wiles, Deborah. Aurora County All-Stars. (p. 116)
—Countdown. (p. 370)
—Each Little Bird That Sings. (p. 492)
—Freedom Summer. Lagarrigue, Jerome, illus. (p. 635)
—Hang the Moon. (p. 742)
—Love, Ruby Lavender. (p. 1060)
—Revolution. (p. 1466)
Wiles, Faith R. Pumpkin who couldn't say BOO! (p. 1416)
Wiles, Frank, illus. see Smith, Evelyn.
Wiles, Jon. Landon's Local Government. (p. 974)
Wiles, Lynn. Nathaniel's Gift. (p. 1231)
Wiles, Pat, illus. see Nawashani.
Wiles, Pat, illus. see Sundberg, Peggy.
Wiles, Patricia. Early-Morning Cemetery: A Novel. (p. 494)
—Final Farewell: A Novel. (p. 586)
—My Mom's a Mortician: A Novel. (p. 1214)
Wiley, Billy. Extraordinary Adventures of Ordinary Basil: Island of the Volcano Monkeys. (p. 555)

Wiley, Amanda. Mommy Thinks I'm Pretty. (p. 1162)
Wiley, Bee, illus. see Aiken, Joan.
Wiley, Brandie. Why Won't He Look at Me? A Book for Children Struggling to Understand Autism. (p. 1927)
Wiley, Debra D. Peanut Butter Boogers. (p. 1332)
Wiley, Elizabeth. Carousel Horse: Keiry. (p. 271)
Wiley, G. D. Tropical Rain Forests. (p. 1789)
Wiley, Gordon. Journey Finds Family. (p. 928)
—Through the Eyes of Imagination. (p. 1745)
Wiley, Jean. Sweet Dreams for Sydney: A Book to Help Dissipate Nightmares Green, Burt, illus. (p. 1689)
Wiley, Judeanne Winter, illus. see Jackson, Ellen B.
Wiley, Judith Gupton. Something More Special. (p. 1610)
Wiley, Kim Wright. Fodor's Walt Disney World with Kids 2016: With Universal Orlando, SeaWorld & Aquatica. (p. 611)
Wiley, Lori. Character Education Activities. (p. 291)
Wiley, Melissa. Across the Puddingstone Dam. Andreasen, Dan, illus. (p. 9)
—Beyond the Heather Hills. Graef, Renee, illus. (p. 174)
—Fox & Crow Are Not Friends. (p. 626)
—Fox & Crow Are Not Friends. Braun, Sebastien, illus. (p. 626)
—Inch & Roly & the Sunny Day Scare. Jatkowska, Ag, illus. (p. 868)
—Inch & Roly & the Very Small Hiding Place. (p. 868)
—Inch & Roly & the Very Small Hiding Place. Jatkowska, Ag, illus. (p. 868)
—Inch & Roly Make a Wish. (p. 868)
—Inch & Roly Make a Wish. Jatkowska, Ag, illus. (p. 868)
—Little House by Boston Bay. (p. 1029)
—Little House in the Highlands. (p. 1029)
—Prairie Thief. Madrid, Erwin, illus. (p. 1392)
Wiley, Nancy, illus. see Carroll, Lewis, pseud.
Wiley, Patricia Ann, creator. Time to Change: A Daily Devotinoal. (p. 1753)
Wiley, Paula. Groove with the Animals. (p. 725)
Wiley, Ralph, jt. auth. see King, Dexter Scott.
Wiley, Thom. Big Earth, Little Me. Endle, Kate, illus. (p. 181)
—Leaves on the Trees. Day, Andrew, illus. (p. 986)
—One Sheep, Blue Sheep. Mantle, Ben, illus. (p. 1296)
Wiley, Thomas L. Angels of Lockhart. (p. 75)
Wilger, Jennifer Root. Wiggle Worms Learn the Psalms. (p. 1928)
Wilharm, Sabine, illus. see Ludwig, Sabine.
Wilhelm, Doris L., illus. see Rogers, Leslie E.
Wilhelm, Doug. Alexander the Great: Master of the Ancient World. (p. 36)
—Alexander the Great. (p. 36)
—Curse of the Pirate Mist. (p. 395)
—Revealers. (p. 1465)
—True Shoes. (p. 1792)
Wilhelm, Hans. All for the Best! The Secret to Happiness. (p. 44)
—Best Friends Stickers. (p. 169)
—Bunny Trouble Treasury. (p. 242)
—Chico Valiente Como Yo. (p. 301)
—Hole in the Wall. (p. 788)
—I Love Rainy Days! Wilhelm, Hans, illus. (p. 842)
—I Love School! Wilhelm, Hans, illus. (p. 843)
—I Love Valentine's Day! (p. 843)
—I Won't Share! Wilhelm, Hans, illus. (p. 849)
—No Kisses, Please! (p. 1258)
—Noodles & the Bully. (p. 1264)
—Ouch! It Hurts! (p. 1307)
—Pelican & Pelican't. (p. 1335)
—Seamos Amigos Otra Vez. (p. 1536)
—Tyrone the Double Dirty Rotten Cheater. (p. 1805)
—Yo Siempre te Quierre. (p. 1971)
Wilhelm, Hans, illus. see Harrison, David L.
Wilhelm, Hans, jt. auth. see Katie, Byron.
Wilhelm, Hans, retold by. Musicos de Bremen. (p. 1194)
Wilhelm, James J., ed. see Schachner, Judy.
Wilhelm, Jeffrey D. Reading Is Seeing: Learning to Visualize Scenes, Characters, Ideas & Text Worlds to Improve Comprehension & Reflective Reading. (p. 1446)
Wilhelm, Kj. Grandma Coocoonutts Goes to Boston. (p. 708)
Wilhelm, Lauren, illus. see Merker, Patricia D.
Wilhelm, Peggy Jo. 10 Most Innovative Bands. (p. 1994)
Wilhelm, Richard, ed. Chinese Fairy Book. Martens, Frederick H., tr. from CHI. (p. 307)
Wilhite, Becca. Bright Blue Miracle. (p. 228)
Wilhite, Cindy. Santa He Sees You When. (p. 1512)
Wilhite, Kenneth. Little Black Bear's Lunch. (p. 1024)
Wilhite, Susan L., jt. auth. see Lewis, Calvin, Jr.
Wiliams, Cornelius, jt. auth. see Melvin E., Meggan.
Wiliamson, Nancy. 52 Ideas for Special Days. (p. 1997)
Wilke, Daria & Schwartz, Marian. Playing a Part. (p. 1372)
Wilkens, Karen & Benchmark Education Co., LLC Staff. ABC. (p. 3)
—I Like. (p. 841)
Wilkens, Steven A. Tattooed Angels. (p. 1707)
Wilkenstanley, Ellen. Berryville Bully. (p. 168)
Wilker, Ian, jt. auth. see Kelly, Evelyn B.
Wilker, Josh & Prentzas, G. S., texts. A. J. Foyt. (p. 1)
Wilkerson, Alison. Adventures of Tabby Cat. (p. 23)
Wilkerson, Dawn. Katie & Katoa Travel down the River. (p. 944)
Wilkerson, Grandma. Mac the Stray Dog. (p. 1067)
Wilkerson, J. L. Sad-Face Clown: Emmett Kelly. (p. 1501)
—Story of Pride, Power & Uplift: Annie T. Malone. (p. 1659)
Wilkerson, Karen. Mommy, I Know the F-Word! (p. 1162)
Wilkerson, L. Kobie, 3rd, reader. Fred & Mary. (p. 632)
Wilkerson, Teresa, illus. see Major, Wayne A. & Major, Ralphine.
Wilkerson, W. R., III. Monk's Son. (p. 1166)
Wilkes, Angela. Activities for All Year Round. (p. 10)
—Big Book of Dinosaurs. (p. 179)
—Child Magazine's Book of Children's Parties. (p. 301)
—Children's Quick & Easy Cookbook. (p. 304)
—Discover Science: Animal Homes. (p. 448)
—Mi Primer Libro de Cocina. (p. 1133)
—Science Encyclopedia. Bhachu, Verindr, illus. (p. 1525)
—Wild Places: Combined Volume. (p. 1930)
Wilkes, Angela, jt. auth. see Watt, Fiona.
Wilkes, Angela & Cartwright, Stephen. Usborne First Cookbook. Gilpin, Rebecca, ed. (p. 1827)
Wilkes, Angela & Rawson, Christopher. Robinson Crusoe. (p. 1480)
Wilkes, Angela & Watt, Fiona. Little Round World Cookbook Internet Linked. (p. 1036)
Wilkes, Angela, contrib. by. Bajo el Mar: Under the Sea. (p. 133)
—Mi Cuerpo y Yo: Me & My Body. (p. 1132)
Wilkes, Angela, et al. Rain Forest Animals. Holmes, Steve, illus. (p. 1434)
Wilkes, C. Gene. Paul on Leadership. (p. 1330)
Wilkes, Donald & Hamilton-Wilkes, Viola. Teen Guide Job Search: 10 Easy Steps to Your Future. (p. 1713)
Wilkes, George. Angry Trout Cafe Notebook: Friends, Recipes, & the Culture of Sustainability. (p. 75)
Wilkes, Ian. London Rabbit: A Guide to Cockney Rhyming Slang. (p. 1046)
Wilkes, Ian, ed. see Crancher, Steve.
Wilkes, Ian, ed. see James, David.
Wilkes, Irene. Elvie Saves Christmas. Montgomery, Jason, illus. (p. 517)
Wilkes, Lucy. Cackle, Packle, & Friends. (p. 250)
Wilkes, Maria D. Little House in Brookfield. (p. 1029)
—Little Town at the Crossroads. (p. 1037)
Wilkes, Nita. Stalking Bailey. (p. 1639)
Wilkes, Rebecca. King Mertagon's Box. (p. 958)
Wilkes, Ruth. Dancing Fruit Put on a Show! Cross, James, illus. (p. 403)
Wilkes, Sarah. Amphibians. (p. 65)
Wilkeshuis, Cornelius. Gift for the Child. Verstegen, Jeska, illus. (p. 675)
Wilkey, David. Through the Black Hole: The Incredible Adventures of Justin Hart. (p. 1745)
Wilkie, E. m. Garden of Eden Adventure. Wilkie, E. m., illus. (p. 656)
—Noah's Ark Adventure. (p. 1261)
Wilkie, Katharine E. George Rogers Clark: Boy of the Northwest Frontier Morrison, Cathy, illus. (p. 663)
Wilkie, Sara. Super Smart Information Strategies: Social Studies Projects That Shine. (p. 1682)
Wilkie, Sara, jt. auth. see Pascaretti, Vicki.
Wilkin, Eloise, illus. see Cushman, Jean, et al.
Wilkin, Eloise, illus. see Golden Books Staff, et al.
Wilkin, Eloise, illus. see Golden Books Staff.
Wilkin, Eloise, illus. see Johnson, Florence.
Wilkin, Eloise, illus. see Watson, Jane Werner.
Wilkin, Eloise, illus. see Wilkin, Esther.
Wilkin, Esther. Baby Listens. Wilkin, Eloise, illus. (p. 127)
—Baby's Christmas. Wilkin, Eloise, illus. (p. 128)
Wilkin, Wendy. Bible Stories for Children. Cloke, Rene, illus. (p. 176)
Wilkins, Amy, ed. Dogs on Rocks. (p. 463)
Wilkins, Ebony Joy. Sellout. (p. 1550)
Wilkins, James Francis. Queen & Mr Brown: A Day for Dinosaurs. (p. 1424)
—Queen & Mr Brown - A Day for Dinosaurs. (p. 1424)
Wilkins, Jessica. Date Rape. (p. 409)
—Street Pharma. (p. 1666)
Wilkins, John-Paul. What Can Live at the Beach? (p. 1880)
—What Can Live in the Garden? (p. 1880)
—What Can Live in the River? (p. 1880)
—What Can Live in the Snow? (p. 1880)
—What Can Live There? (p. 1880)
Wilkins, Kevan, ed. see Rowe, Papa.
Wilkins, LaTanya. Adventures of Dedan & Dylan Jackson: The Second Day of School. (p. 17)
Wilkins, Lisa. Key Seekers. (p. 950)
Wilkins, Nalini. Doby's First Christmas. Robb, Jonathan, illus. (p. 459)
Wilkins, Phil Cole. Dragog & the Seven Weeks of Summer. (p. 476)
Wilkins, Rose. So Super-Starry. (p. 1602)
Wilkins, Sarah, illus. see Bornholdt, Jenny.
Wilkins, Verna. Children Around the World. (p. 302)
—Dave & the Tooth Fairy. (p. 410)
Wilkins, Wendy H., illus. see Frederick, H. J.
Wilkinson, jt. auth. see Price.
Wilkinson, Annie, illus. see Cooke, Brandy.
Wilkinson, Aubrey Corrine. Fading Stripes: Saving a Species. (p. 562)
Wilkinson, Brenda. Ludell. (p. 1064)
Wilkinson Brown, Valerie. Me & My Faith. (p. 1115)
Wilkinson, Bruce. Life God Rewards for Teens. (p. 1010)
—My 100 Best-Loved Bible Stories. (p. 1195)
Wilkinson, Bruce & Suggs, Robb. Prayer of Jabez for Young Hearts. Martinez, Sergio, illus. (p. 1393)
Wilkinson, Bruce & Thomas, Mack. Life God Rewards: Guys Only. (p. 1010)
Wilkinson, Carole. Buried at Sea. (p. 243)
—How to Live in the Dark Ages. (p. 820)
—How to Wreck a Ship. (p. 822)
Wilkinson, Colin. Gaming: Playing Safe & Playing Smart. (p. 655)
—Mobile Platforms: Getting Information on the Go. (p. 1157)
—Twitter & Microblogging: Instant Communication with 140 Characters or Less. (p. 1803)
Wilkinson, J. M. Secret Within. (p. 1544)
Wilkinson, James. Gypsy Dolls. (p. 734)
Wilkinson, James H. Yang the Dragon Tells His Story, Halloween Train. Blake, Carol, illus. (p. 1968)
Wilkinson, Jody, jt. auth. see Wilson, Scott.
Wilkinson, John. Contrivances. (p. 361)
—Proud Flesh. (p. 1412)
Wilkinson, Kerry. Reckoning. (p. 1452)
—Renegade. (p. 1460)
Wilkinson, Lili. Not Quite Perfect Boyfriend. (p. 1267)
—Pink. (p. 1359)
—Pocketful of Eyes. (p. 1375)
—Zigzag Effect. (p. 1986)
Wilkinson, Lisa. Prickle Says I'm Sorry. McCord, Kathi, illus. (p. 1398)
Wilkinson, Louise C., jt. ed. see Silliman, Elaine R.
Wilkinson, Philip. Chinese Myth: A Treasury of Legends, Art, & History. (p. 307)
—Explorers. (p. 551)
—Gandhi: The Young Protester Who Founded a Nation. (p. 655)
—Joan of Arc: The Teenager Who Saved Her Nation. (p. 919)
—Michelangelo: The Young Artist Who Dreamed of Perfection. (p. 1135)
—Spacebusters: Race to the Moon. (p. 1620)
—Spacebusters. (p. 1620)
—Titanic: Disaster at Sea (p. 1757)
Wilkinson, Philip, jt. auth. see Dorling Kindersley Publishing Staff.
Wilkinson, Philip & Donati, Paolo. Amazing Buildings. (p. 54)
Wilkinson, Phillip. Science Museum Series: Speed, Time, Space, & Flight (p. 1526)
Wilkinson, Richard. Wilkinson Tales: A Collection of Holiday Short Stories for Young People. (p. 1932)
Wilkinson, Richard, illus. see Nelson, Jo.
Wilkinson, Richard Fergus. Wilkinson Tales: A Collection of Adventure Short Stories for Young People. Murphy, Andrea, illus. (p. 1932)
Wilkinson, Sheena. Taking Flight (p. 1698)
Wilkinson, Simon. Noah's Ark Black & White Visual Development Book for Babies. (p. 1261)
Wilkinson, Steve, jt. auth. see Knudson, Mike.
Wilkinson, Thomas M. Forest Through the Trees. (p. 618)
—Willie-off-the-Pickleboat. (p. 1934)
Wilkinson, Todd. Watching Yellowstone & Grand Teton Wildlife. Francis, Michael Harlowe, photos by. (p. 1861)
Wilkinson, William L. Glorious Praise. Blackmon, Kim, illus. (p. 685)
Wilkinson-Latham, Christopher. Boer War. Roffe, Michael, illus. (p. 207)
Wilkon, Jozef, illus. see Friesel, Uwe.
Wilkon, Jozef, illus. see Schnell, Robert W.
Wilks, Eileen. Night Season: Moon Children Vol. 4 (p. 1254)
Wilks, Jackie, jt. auth. see Branson, Terri.
Wilks, Madeline Joan. Yellow Dot Red Dot. (p. 1970)
Wilks, Peter. Foragers. (p. 616)
Wilks, Peter, illus. see Leaney, Cindy.
Wilks, Peter, tr. see Leaney, Cindy.
Wilks, Tom. Texas Roadkill. (p. 1724)
Will, Clark Moor, illus. see Kopp, J. J.
Will, Heidi. Ghillie Girls: Irish Dance Pals. Will, Heidi, illus. (p. 670)
Will, Julianne, jt. auth. see Ball, Ann.
Will, Julianne, ed. Catholic Prayer Book for Children. (p. 280)
Will, Julianne M. Stations of the Cross for Children. Mattozzi, Patricia, illus. (p. 1644)
Will, Julianne M., jt. auth. see Ball, Ann.
Will Mayo, Gretchen, jt. auth. see O'Hern, Kerri.
Will Mcallister. Sam Rivers & the Night Rustlers. (p. 1507)
Will, R. K. Harry's Flowers. (p. 751)
Will, Rebel. Who Lives/Twgn/C. (p. 1916)
Will, Sandra. Baseball for Fun! (p. 141)
—Golf for Fun! (p. 696)
—Lacrosse for Fun! Will, Sandra, illus. (p. 970)
—Transportation Inventions: From Subways to Submarines. (p. 1779)
Will, Sheri Sue. Butterfly Babies for Boys. (p. 247)
—Butterfly Babies for Girls. (p. 247)
Willams, Brian, tr. see Perelman, Yakov.
Willan, Anne. Country Cooking of France. Ruffenach, France, photos by. (p. 372)
Willard, Baron And Mary. Hugs Are for Every One... Willard, Mary, illus. (p. 825)
Willard, Carolyn, jt. auth. see Erickson, John.
Willard, Christopher. Mindfulness for Teen Anxiety: A Workbook for Overcoming Anxiety at Home, at School, & Everywhere Else. (p. 1145)
Willard, Claudette. Chloe & Banana Island. (p. 308)
Willard Crompton, Samuel. Discovering Ancient Rome (p. 448)
Willard, Dallas & Frazee, Randy. Renovation of the Heart: Putting on the Character of Christ. (p. 1460)
Willard, Eliza, et al. Love Is in the Air. (p. 1060)
Willard, Elizabeth Kimmel. Mary Ingalls on Her Own. (p. 1100)
Willard F. Baker. Boy Ranchers among the Indians. (p. 218)
Willard, Gerald. Amy Firefly. (p. 66)
Willard, Hugh. Goodwill Vultures Club: No Time for Play. Holjes, Kerry, ed. (p. 701)
—Goodwill Vultures Club: The Gift of the Vulture. Dozier, Dolly, ed. (p. 701)
—Goodwill Vultures Club. Holjes, Kerry, ed. (p. 701)
Willard, J. H., jt. auth. see De Segur, Comtesse.
Willard, Mary, illus. see Willard, Baron And Mary.
Willard, Nancy. Cracked Corn & Snow Ice Cream: A Family Almanac. Dyer, Jane, illus. (p. 375)
—Starlit Snowfall. Pinkney, Jerry, illus. (p. 1642)
—Three Mouths of Little Tom Drum. Hawkes, Kevin, illus. (p. 1743)
Willard, Renee. Mama Who Didn't Work. (p. 1084)
—Memommy's Miracles. (p. 1125)
Willardson, David, illus. see Geiser, Traci Ferguson & Boylan, Maureen McCourt.
Willebrandt, Avery. Spitting Cobra / Cobra Escupidora. (p. 1629)
—Spitting Cobras. (p. 1629)
Willebrant, Avery. Meat-Eating Plants. (p. 1118)
Willeford, Tammy Jean. Alphabear. Hopkins, Emily, illus. (p. 48)
Willemin, Veronique, illus. see Orliac, Catherine.
Willems, Ashley. Boy & the Wind. (p. 217)
Willems, Mo. Are You Ready to Play Outside? Willems, Mo, illus. (p. 97)
—Big Guy Took My Ball! Willems, Mo, illus. (p. 181)
—Can I Play Too? Willems, Mo, illus. (p. 258)
—Cat the Cat Who Is That? Willems, Mo, illus. (p. 278)
—Cautionary Tale. Willems, Mo, illus. (p. 282)
—City Dog, Country Frog. Muth, Jon J., illus. (p. 323)
—Conejito Knuffle: Un Cuento Aleccionador. Willems, Mo, illus. (p. 356)
—Don't Let the Pigeon Drive the Bus! (p. 468)
—Don't Let the Pigeon Drive the Bus! Willems, Mo, illus. (p. 468)
—Don't Let the Pigeon Finish This Activity Book! Willems, Mo, illus. (p. 468)
—Don't Let the Pigeon Stay Up Late! (p. 468)
—Don't Let the Pigeon Stay Up Late! Willems, Mo, illus. (p. 468)
—Duckling Gets a Cookie!? Willems, Mo, illus. (p. 488)
—Edwina, the Dinosaur Who Didn't Know She Was Extinct. Willems, Mo, illus. (p. 505)
—Elephants Cannot Dance! Willems, Mo, illus. (p. 512)
—Goldilocks & the Three Dinosaurs. Willems, Mo, illus. (p. 696)
—Happy Pig Day! Willems, Mo, illus. (p. 746)
—Hooray for Amanda & Her Alligator! Willems, Mo, illus. (p. 795)
—I Am Going! Willems, Mo, illus. (p. 833)
—I Am Invited to a Party! Willems, Mo, illus. (p. 833)
—I Broke My Trunk! Willems, Mo, illus. (p. 834)
—I Love My New Toy! Willems, Mo, illus. (p. 842)
—I Will Surprise My Friend! Willems, Mo, illus. (p. 848)
—I Will Take a Nap! Willems, Mo, illus. (p. 848)
—I'm a Frog! Willems, Mo, illus. (p. 858)
—It's a Busload of Pigeon Books! Willems, Mo, illus. (p. 895)
—Knuffle Bunny: A Cautionary Tale. Willems, Mo, illus. (p. 965)
—Knuffle Bunny. (p. 965)
—Knuffle Bunny Free: An Unexpected Diversion. Willems, Mo, illus. (p. 965)
—Knuffle Bunny Free: An Unexpected Diversion. (p. 966)
—Knuffle Bunny Too: A Case of Mistaken Identity. Willems, Mo, illus. (p. 966)
—Leonardo, the Terrible Monster. Willems, Mo, illus. (p. 992)
—Let's Go for a Drive! Willems, Mo, illus. (p. 997)
—Let's Say Hi to Friends Who Fly! Willems, Mo, illus. (p. 1000)
—Listen to My Trumpet! Willems, Mo, illus. (p. 1022)
—My Friend Is Sad. Willems, Mo, illus. (p. 1209)
—My New Friend Is So Fun! Willems, Mo, illus. (p. 1216)
—Naked Mole Rat Gets Dressed. Willems, Mo, illus. (p. 1228)
—Pigeon Finds a Hot Dog! Willems, Mo, illus. (p. 1357)
—Pigeon Has Feelings, Too! Willems, Mo, illus. (p. 1357)
—Pigeon Loves Things That Go! Willems, Mo, illus. (p. 1357)
—Pigeon Needs a Bath! Willems, Mo, illus. (p. 1357)
—Pigeon Wants a Puppy! Willems, Mo, illus. (p. 1357)
—Pigs Make Me Sneeze! Willems, Mo, illus. (p. 1358)
—Should I Share My Ice Cream? Willems, Mo, illus. (p. 1569)
—That Is Not a Good Idea! Willems, Mo, illus. (p. 1726)
—There Is a Bird on Your Head! Willems, Mo, illus. (p. 1729)
—Time to Pee! Willems, Mo, illus. (p. 1753)
—Time to Say Please! Willems, Mo, illus. (p. 1753)
—Time to Sleep, Sheep the Sheep! Willems, Mo, illus. (p. 1753)
—Today I Will Fly! Willems, Mo, illus. (p. 1760)
—Waiting Is Not Easy! (an Elephant & Piggie Book) Willems, Mo, illus. (p. 1853)
—Watch Me Throw the Ball! Willems, Mo, illus. (p. 1861)
—We Are in a Book! Willems, Mo, illus. (p. 1865)
—What's Your Sound Hound the Hound? Willems, Mo, illus. (p. 1900)
—What's Your Sound, Hound the Hound? Willems, Mo, illus. (p. 1900)
—Who Flies, Cat the Cat? Willems, Mo, illus. (p. 1915)
—Who Is That, Cat the Cat? Willems, Mo, illus. (p. 1916)
—Who Says That, Cat the Cat? Willems, Mo, illus. (p. 1917)
—Who Sleeps, Cat the Cat? Willems, Mo, illus. (p. 1917)
—You Can Never Find a Rickshaw When It Monsoons: The World on One Cartoon a Day. Willems, Mo, illus. (p. 1974)
—¡No Dejes Que la Paloma Conduzca el Autobús! Willems, Mo, illus. (p. 1258)
Willems, Mo & Campoy, F. Isabel. !Estamos en un Libro! Willems, Mo, illus. (p. 538)
—Paloma Encuentra un Perro Caliente! Willems, Mo, illus. (p. 1320)
—¿Debo Compartir Mi Helado? Willems, Mo, illus. (p. 421)
Willems, Mo & Scieszka, Jon, narrated by. Don't Let the Pigeon Drive the Bus! (p. 468)
Willems, Mo & Willems, Trixie, narrated by. Knuffle Bunny Too: A Case of Mistaken Identity. (p. 966)
—Pigeon Finds a Hot Dog! (p. 1357)
Willems, Mo, et al, narrated by. Naked Mole Rat Gets Dressed. (p. 1228)
Willems, Mo, narrated by. Leonardo, the Terrible Monster. (p. 992)
Willems, Trixie, jt. narrated by see Willems, Mo.
Willen, Janet, jt. auth. see Gann, Marjorie.
Willen, Janet & Gann, Marjorie. Speak a Word for Freedom: Women Against Slavery. (p. 1622)
Willerth, Cynthia. Knife of Truth, A Matter of Honor (p. 964)
Willet, Edward. Rock Sport Climbing: Techniques & Tricks. (p. 1482)
—Skateboarding: Techniques & Tricks. (p. 1583)
Willett, Andrew, jt. auth. see Willett, Andy.
Willett, Andy & Willett, Andrew. Swimming for Fun! (p. 1691)
Willett, Christie. Isabella. (p. 890)
Willett, Edward. Ayatollah Khomeini. (p. 121)
—Basics of Quantum Physics: Understanding the Photoelectric Effect & Line Spectra. (p. 142)
—Bounty Mutiny: From the Court Case to the Movie. (p. 216)
—Career As a Mason. (p. 266)
—Career Building Through Using Digital Design Tools. (p. 266)
—Careers in Outer Space: New Business Opportunities. (p. 268)
—Disease-Hunting Scientist: Careers Hunting Deadly Diseases. (p. 450)
—Ebola Virus. (p. 502)
—Fires & Wildfires: A Practical Survival Guide. (p. 592)
—Frequently Asked Questions about Exercise Addiction. (p. 636)
—Infectious Disease Specialists: Hunting down Disease. (p. 873)
—Iran-Iraq War. (p. 886)
—J. R. R. Tolkien: Master of Imaginary Worlds. (p. 902)
—Janis Joplin: Take Another Little Piece of My Heart. (p. 908)
—Jimi Hendrix: Kiss the Sky. (p. 918)
—Johnny Cash: "The Man in Black" (p. 923)
—Kiera Cass (p. 955)
—Magnesium. (p. 1075)
—Negative Body Image. (p. 1240)

W

—Neon. (p. 1241)
—Orson Scott Card: Architect of Alternate Worlds. (p. 1305)
—Rock Sport Climbing. (p. 1482)
—Skateboarding: Techniques & Tricks. (p. 1583)
—Space. (p. 1618)
—Space Q&a. (p. 1619)
—Speed. (p. 1624)
—Twist of the Blade (p. 1802)
—What Is the Milky Way? (p. 1890)
—What You Can Do about Ebola. (p. 1896)
Willett, Edward, jt. auth. see Jones, Viola.
Willett, Edward & Warhol, Andy. Andy Warhol: "Everyone Will Be Famous for 15 Minutes" (p. 73)
Willett, Frances. Trooper's Tale. (p. 1789)
Willett, Marcia. First Friends. (p. 595)
—Friend of the Family. (p. 637)
Willett, Mindy, jt. auth. see Jumbo, Sheyenne.
Willett, Mindy, jt. auth. see McLeod, Tom.
Willett, Mindy & Enyagotailak, Darla. No Borders Macintosh, Tessa, photos by. (p. 1257)
Willett, Mindy & Enzoe, Pete. Caribou Feed My Soul Macintosh, Tessa, photos by. (p. 269)
Willett, Mindy & Pokiak, James. Proud to Be Inuvialuit: Quviahuktunga Inuvialuugama (p. 1413)
Willett, Walter, jt. auth. see Katzen, Mollie.
Willetts, Lucy & Waite, Polly. Can I Tell You about Anxiety? A Guide for Friends, Family & Professionals. Tay, Kaiyee, illus. (p. 258)
Willever, Lisa. Exciting Writing. (p. 547)
Willever, Lisa & Funari-Willever, Lisa. Nicky Fifth's Garden State Adventure. (p. 1251)
Willever, Lisa Funari, see Funari Willever, Lisa.
Willey, jt. auth. see Wallace, Karen.
Willey, Bee, illus. see Alrawi, Karim.
Willey, Bee, illus. see Gavin, Jamila & Quarto Generic Staff.
Willey, Bee, illus. see Hooper, Meredith.
Willey, Bee, illus. see Husain, Shahrukh.
Willey, Bee, illus. see Matthews, Andrew.
Willey, Bee, illus. see Matthews, Caitlin.
Willey, Bee, illus. see McCaughrean, Geraldine.
Willey, Bee, illus. see Page, Nick & Page, Claire.
Willey, Bee, jt. auth. see McCaughrean, Geraldine.
Willey, Bee, jt. auth. see Shahrukh Husain.
Willey, Margaret. 3 Bears & Goldilocks. Solomon, Heather M., illus. (p. 1991)
—Beetle Boy. (p. 158)
—Clever Beatrice. Solomon, Heather M., illus. (p. 331)
—Clever Beatrice & the Best Little Pony. Solomon, Heather M., illus. (p. 331)
—Clever Beatrice Christmas. Solomon, Heather M., illus. (p. 331)
—Four Secrets. Hauser, Bill, illus. (p. 625)
—Summer of Silk Moths. (p. 1674)
Willey, Rich. I'd Rather Be Boppin' ¿ 24 Bop Duets for C Treble Clef Instruments. (p. 851)
Willey, Sarah Jo. Lullaby for Birds. (p. 1064)
Willhite, Dana. Dyslexic Dalmatian. (p. 491)
William Elliot, Griffis. Dutch Fairy Tales for Young Folks. (p. 490)
William, Graf, illus. see Sparks, Candi.
William H. Sadlier, Inc Staff, contrib. by. We Believe & Pray: Prayers & Practices for Young Catholics. (p. 1866)
William H. Sadlier Staff. Ah-choo! (p. 30)
—Alexander Ant Cools Off. (p. 36)
—All Mixed Up. (p. 45)
—Amazing Blue Animals (p. 54)
—At Space Camp (p. 110)
—Basket Full of Surprises. (p. 142)
—Best Place. (p. 171)
—Best Ride: Big Book (p. 171)
—Brush, Brush, Brush! (p. 232)
—Buggy Riddles (p. 236)
—Building an Enriched Vocabulary: Student Text. (p. 238)
—Building an Enriched Vocabulary: (with Answers to Testing Program) (p. 238)
—Building an Enriched Vocabulary: Supplementary Exercise & Testing Program (p. 238)
—Bye-bye, Katy (p. 249)
—Cats! Cats! Cats! (p. 281)
—Cheerful King (p. 296)
—Colors at the Zoo. (p. 345)
—Come Meet Some Seals (p. 347)
—Composition Workshop: Level Blue. (p. 354)
—Composition Workshop: Level Green. (p. 354)
—Composition Workshop: Student Text. (p. 354)
—Composition Workshop. (p. 354)
—Content Area Readers Library: Early (K-2) (p. 360)
—Content Area Readers Library: Emergent (PreK-1) (p. 360)
—Count with Me. (p. 370)
—Counting Sheep. (p. 371)
—Did You Know? (p. 437)
—Dinosaur Dance. (p. 441)
—Discovering Dinosaurs (p. 449)
—Do You See a Dozen? Big Book (p. 458)
—Don't Tell! (p. 468)
—Emergent Library (p. 518)
—Emergent Library. (p. 518)
—Emergent Library I Big Book Package. (p. 518)
—Emergent Library I Little Book. (p. 518)
—Emergent Super Libraries (p. 518)
—Family Fun. (p. 568)
—Felix, the Very Hungry Fish. (p. 581)
—Float or Sink? (p. 605)
—From Head to Toes. (p. 642)
—Funny Bugs. (p. 649)
—Getting to Know Sharks. (p. 669)
—Goldilocks & the Three Bears. (p. 696)
—Good Food. (p. 698)
—Good Pets: Big Book (p. 700)
—Harry's Hat. (p. 751)
—Here Comes the Rain! (p. 770)
—Hippo in June's Tub (p. 781)
—How Many Are Here? Big Book. (p. 811)
—How to Make a Crocodile. (p. 820)
—I Have a Question: Big Book. Vol. 4 (p. 839)
—I Love to Read (p. 843)
—In January & June (p. 864)
—J My Name Is Jess. (p. 901)
—Joey's Rowboat (p. 920)
—Keeping Baby Animals Safe. (p. 947)
—Lion & the Mouse (p. 1020)
—Look at the Pictures. (p. 1049)
—Looking at Lizards: Big Book (p. 1051)
—Messy Moose. (p. 1130)
—My Favorite Things. (p. 1203)
—New Progress in Mathematics. (p. 1246)
—Nice Vine, Quite Fine (p. 1250)
—Niles Likes to Smile (p. 1255)
—Nora Plays All Day. (p. 1264)
—Over, under, Left, Right. (p. 1314)
—Party for Nine: Big Book (p. 1326)
—Patty & Pop's Picnic. (p. 1329)
—Peach Tree Street (p. 1332)
—Play it Safe! (p. 1371)
—Progress in Mathematics. (p. 1410)
—Pumpkin Days (p. 1416)
—Show & Tell. (p. 1570)
—Splish, Splash! (p. 1630)
—Stop by a Pond. (p. 1653)
—Stop Germs. (p. 1653)
—Tina's Toys: Big Book. (p. 1755)
—Tongue Twister Prize. (p. 1765)
—Too Small Jill (p. 1767)
—Trash Can Band. (p. 1780)
—Ultra-Saver Library Emergent, Early, & Fluent. (p. 1810)
—Valentine's Checkup. (p. 1830)
—Violets & Vegetables: Big Book. Vol. 4 (p. 1843)
—Vocabulary Vocabulary Test Booklets, Level C, Form A. (p. 1847)
—Vocabulary Workshop: Test Booklet Form A; Level Purple. (p. 1847)
—Vocabulary Workshop: (with Answer Key to Tests, Forms A & B); Level Purple. (p. 1847)
—Vocabulary Workshop Test Booklets. (p. 1847)
—Vocabulary Workshop, Test Booklets, Cycle 1, Level Blue. (p. 1847)
—Vocabulary Workshop Test Booklets, Level A, Form A: 2002. (p. 1847)
—Vocabulary Workshop Test Booklets, Level B, Form A. (p. 1847)
—Vocabulary Workshop, Test Booklets Level Orange, Cycle 2. (p. 1847)
—Vocabulary Workshop TEST PREP Blackline Masters, Level B. (p. 1847)
—Vocabulary Workshop, TEST PREP Blackline Masters, Level A. (p. 1847)
—Vocabulary Workswhop Test Booklets, Level D, Form B. (p. 1847)
—Wait for Me. (p. 1852)
—Wake up, Sleepyheads! (p. 1853)
—Weather Wise (p. 1870)
—What Bear Cubs Like to Do. (p. 1880)
—What Do You See by the Sea? (p. 1883)
—What Does Lucy Like? (p. 1884)
—What Does Sam Sell? (p. 1884)
—What Is the Weather Today? (p. 1890)
—When Mr Quinn Snored. (p. 1904)
—Who Can Run Fast? (p. 1914)
—Who Has Four Feet? Big Book. (p. 1915)
—Who Is My Mom? (p. 1916)
—Who Works Here? (p. 1919)
—Why Coyote Howls at Night. (p. 1923)
—Writing a Research Paper: A Student Guide to Writing a Research Paper. (p. 1964)
—Writing a Research Paper. (p. 1964)
—Writing for Standardized Tests. (p. 1964)
—Yellow Yarn Mystery. (p. 1970)
—Yes, You Can. (p. 1971)
—You Can Sort. (p. 1974)
—Zack Can Fix It!: Big Book. Vol. 4 (p. 1984)
William, Harper, illus. see Elliott, Craig.
William, Icebergg Dunbar, illus. see Williams, Guana Dunbar.
William MacLeod Raine. Gunsight Pass. (p. 732)
William Miles, jt. auth. see Myers, Walter Dean.
William Murray Hogben. Johnny & Mr Reb: A Civil War Tale. (p. 923)
Williamgoldenpen. Quacker's Bedtime Stories. (p. 1422)
—Quacker's Bedtime Stories... Continued. (p. 1422)
Williams Aber, Linda. Quien Tiene Manchas? Fiammenghi, Gioia, illus. (p. 1427)
Williams, Adele Knight. What's in a Smile. (p. 1897)
Williams, Alan. Archy the Flying Dolphin: & the Vampire's Curse. (p. 95)
—Archy the Flying Dolphin & the Vampire's Curse. (p. 95)
Williams, Albert E. Black Warriors: The Korean War. (p. 197)
Williams, Alex. Deep Freeze of Bartholomew Tullock. (p. 423)
—Holy Spy: Student Ministry in Eastern Europe. (p. 791)
Williams, Alexandra & Williams, David. Fairy Nyumbani. (p. 563)
Williams, Alison. Pink Cat Blue Cat. (p. 1359)
Williams, Allen. Claude the Backward Jumping Bullfrog. (p. 329)
—Claude the Backward Jumping Bullfrog - Firefighter: Buster's Great Adventure. (p. 329)
—Claude the Backward-Jumping Bullfrog: Space Shuttle Commander. (p. 329)
Williams, Allix Elise. Adventures of Prince Thaddeus: The Glamorous Guest. (p. 22)
Williams, Alwena & Drake, Gwasg Addysgol. Morfilod. (p. 1175)
Williams, Amanda Schaefer. Sadie in Heaven. (p. 1501)
Williams, Amelia. Piggy Tales: Try a New Food. (p. 1358)
—Piggy Tales: Meet A New Friend. (p. 1358)
—Piggy Tales: The Terrible Scary Storm: the Terrible Scary Storm. (p. 1358)
—Piggy Tales: Gladys' First Adventure - Going to a New Farm: Gladys' First Adventure - Going to a New Farm. (p. 1358)
Williams, Amelia, jt. auth. see Weightman, Bud.
Williams, Amy. Gertrude the Silly Puppy. (p. 667)
Williams, Andrew. Biblical Responses to Some of the Most Asked Questions about Life. (p. 177)
Williams, Angela, illus. see Terry, Rod.
Williams, Angela Claudette. Wonderful Things about a Flower. (p. 1948)
Williams, Angie, photos by see Martin, Paige.
Williams, Ann. Multifarious Adventures of Fred the Raindrop. (p. 1190)
Williams, Ann M., ed. see Daniels, Kathryn.
Williams, Ann Marie, illus. see Carney-Nunes, Charisse.
Williams, Ann Marie, illus. see Carney-Nunes, Charisse.
Williams, Ann Marie, jt. auth. see Carney-Nunes, Charisse.
Williams, Anna Graf, et al. Family Guide to the American Workplace. Williams, Anna Graf, ed. (p. 568)
Williams, Annie Morris. Marianne's Secret Cousins. Oldham, Cindi, illus. (p. 1093)
Williams, Annik. Mr. Mole's Day Off: With Goodnight Little Birdie. (p. 1185)
Williams, Ann-Marie. Learn to Speak Dance: A Guide to Creating, Performing & Promoting Your Moves. Kulak, Jeff & Owlkids Books Inc. Staff, illus. (p. 984)
Williams, Anthony. Creating Superhero Comics (p. 379)
—Dracula: A Classic Pop-Up Tale. (p. 476)
—Hound of the Baskervilles. (p. 802)
Williams, Anthony, illus. see Abnett, Dan.
Williams, Anthony, illus. see Hama, Larry.
Williams, Anthony, illus. see Shelley, Mary.
Williams, Anthony, illus. see Stoker, Bram.
Williams, Antonio. Day in the World of Todd the Squirrel. (p. 413)
Williams, Armstrong. Reawakening Virtues: Restoring What Makes America Great. (p. 1450)
Williams, Avery. Alchemy of Forever. (p. 35)
—Impossibility of Tomorrow: An Incarnation Novel. (p. 862)
—Impossibility of Tomorrow. (p. 862)
Williams, Avery, jt. auth. see Childrens Books Staff.
Williams, Barbara, jt. auth. see Marsh, Jennifer.
Williams, Barbara A. Tilli's Tale. Lewis, Rebecca, illus. (p. 1750)
Williams, Barbara Foster. Please Get off the Tilt-a-Whirl. (p. 1373)
Williams, Becky. Good Night Little Piggy. Howarth, Daniel, illus. (p. 699)
—Ten Little Mermaids. East, Jacqueline, illus. (p. 1719)
Williams, Ben. Look Inside: Your Brain (p. 1049)
—Look Inside: Your Heart & Lungs (p. 1049)
—Look Inside: Your Skeleton & Muscles (p. 1049)
—Look Inside - Your Brain (p. 1049)
—Your Skeleton & Muscles. (p. 1981)
Williams, Benjamin, creator. Behind the Blackberry Bush. (p. 160)
Williams, Betsy, ed. UU & Me Collected Stories. (p. 1829)
Williams, Bill, illus. see Lytle, Robert A.
Williams, Billie. Angela's Bedtime Adventures (p. 74)
Williams, Billie A. Fourteen Is Too Many: The Survivors. (p. 625)
—Haying Time: Fire. (p. 755)
—Watch for the Raven. (p. 1860)
Williams, Bobbie. Pieces from the Heart. (p. 1356)
Williams, Bonnie. Meet Teddy Rex! Gordon, John, illus. (p. 1122)
—Pete Can Fly! Gordon, John, illus. (p. 1346)
—Scoop on Ice Cream! Burroughs, Scott, illus. (p. 1529)
Williams, Brenda. Amazing Birds. (p. 54)
—Birds. (p. 191)
—Fun with Action Rhymes & Poems. Jolliffe, Angela, illus. (p. 648)
—Home for a Tiger, Home for a Bear. Fowler, Rosamund, illus. (p. 792)
—Lin Yi's Lantern: A Moon Festival Tale. Tavares, Victor, illus. (p. 1018)
—Lin Yi's Lantern: A Moon Festival Tale. Lacombe, Benjamin, illus. (p. 1018)
—Millie's Chickens. Cis, Valeria, illus. (p. 1144)
—Outdoor Opposites. Oldfield, Rachel, illus. (p. 1312)
—Real Princess. Fatus, Sophie, illus. (p. 1448)
Williams, Brenda, jt. auth. see Foster, John.
Williams, Brenda, jt. selected by see Foster, John.
Williams, Brenda & Barefoot Books Staff. Princesa Real: Un Cuento Matemagico. Fatus, Sophie, illus. (p. 1402)
Williams, Brenda & Fatus, Sophie. Real Princess. Fatus, Sophie, illus. (p. 1448)
Williams, Brenda & Fowler, Rosamund. Home for a Tiger, Home for a Bear. (p. 792)
Williams, Brenda & Lacombe, Benjamin. Lin Yi's Lantern. Lacombe, Benjamin, illus. (p. 1018)
Williams, Brenda & Mayo, Diana. House That Jack Built. (p. 804)
Williams, Brenda & Williams, Brian. Reach for the Stars: Ancient Egyptian Pyramids (p. 1442)
—Saving the Persecuted. (p. 1517)
—Staying Alive in Ancient Rome: Life in Ancient Rome (p. 1645)
—Trading Up: Indus Valley Trade (p. 1776)
Williams, Brenda Gail. Little Mo Weep. (p. 1032)
Williams, Brenda May. Unusual Pet Shop. Williams, Raymond, illus. (p. 1823)
Williams, Brian. Amazing Reptiles & Amphibians. (p. 55)
—America under Attack. (p. 59)
—Canada. (p. 260)
—Daily Life in the Indus Valley Civilization. (p. 400)
—Fall of the Berlin Wall. (p. 566)
—Heroes of the Battlefield. (p. 773)
—History: Biggest & Best. (p. 783)
—History. (p. 783)
—How We Live. (p. 823)
—Natural World: Biggest & Best. (p. 1236)
—Natural World. (p. 1236)
—Normandy Beaches. (p. 1264)
—People & Places. (p. 1339)
—Pilots in Peril (p. 1359)
—Pirates. (p. 1363)
—Planet Earth: Biggest & Best. (p. 1367)
—Planet Earth. (p. 1367)
—Reptiles & Amphibians. (p. 1461)
—Sailors under Fire (p. 1503)
—Science Across Cultures (p. 1524)
—Science & Technology: Biggest & Best. Gallagher, Belinda, ed. (p. 1525)
—Science of a Pair of Glasses: The Science of Light. (p. 1527)
—Special Forces (p. 1623)
—Sport & Entertainment: Biggest & Best. (p. 1631)
—Transport Technology. (p. 1779)
—Transportation Technology. (p. 1779)
—Understanding Norse Myths. (p. 1816)
—Universe: Biggest & Best. (p. 1820)
—Universe. (p. 1820)
—War in Afghanistan. (p. 1857)
—War on Terror. (p. 1858)
—Way We Live: Biggest & Best. (p. 1864)
—What about HIST. (p. 1878)
—What about How We Live. (p. 1878)
—What about People & Places. (p. 1879)
—What about Planet Earth. (p. 1879)
—What about the Natural World. (p. 1879)
—What about the Universe. (p. 1879)
—What about World Wonders. (p. 1879)
—Who Invented the Automobile? (p. 1915)
—Wonders of the World: Biggest & Best. (p. 1949)
—World Wonders. (p. 1960)
Williams, Brian, illus. see Hunt, Elizabeth Singer.
Williams, Brian, illus. see Tyler, Sandy.
Williams, Brian, jt. auth. see Crabtree Staff.
Williams, Brian, jt. auth. see Gordon, Roderick.
Williams, Brian, jt. auth. see Williams, Brenda.
Williams, Brian & Brian, Williams. Ciencia y Tecnologia. (p. 319)
Williams, Brian & Egan, Vicky. Solar System. Dogi, Flammetta, illus. (p. 1607)
Williams, Brian & Heinemann Library Staff. Science Across Cultures (p. 1524)
Williams, Brian James, jt. auth. see Gordon, Roderick.
Williams, Brittney, illus. see Bodden, Michelle.
Williams, C. B. Walkers. (p. 1854)
Williams, C. E. Cj's World: My First Day of Second Grade. (p. 326)
Williams, C. G. Incredibly Helpful Helper. (p. 870)
Williams, Carla. Big Puzzles for Little Hands: Children of the Bible. (p. 183)
—Big Puzzles for Little Hands: Jesus' Life & Lessons. (p. 183)
—Big Puzzles for Little Hands: People Who Obeyed God. (p. 183)
—Big Puzzles for Little Hands: The Bible Tells Me So. (p. 183)
—Fold & Do. (p. 611)
—Little Hands Fold & Do. (p. 1029)
Williams, Carlene H., illus. see Basore, Polly M.
Williams, Carol. Beth Yw'r Gair Am... (p. 171)
Williams, Carol J. Dickey: Second Edition. (p. 436)
Williams, Carol Lynch. Chosen One. (p. 310)
—Glimpse. (p. 683)
—Haven: A Novel. (p. 754)
—Pretty Like Us (p. 1398)
—Signed, Skye Harper. (p. 1574)
—Waiting. (p. 1852)
Williams, Carol Lynch, jt. auth. see Earl, Cheri Pray.
Williams, Carol Lynch & Earl, Cheri Pray. Sweet Secrets in Pennsylvania. Oliphant, Manelle, illus. (p. 1690)
Williams, Carol Lynch & Gregg, L. B. Glimpse. Gregg, Anna, photos by. (p. 683)
Williams, Carolea, ed. see Callella, Trisha.
Williams, Carolea, ed. Beginning Consonants Instant Learning Centers (p. 159)
—Ending Consonants Instant Learning Centers (p. 527)
—Long & Short Vowels Instant Learning Centers (p. 1047)
—Phonemic Awareness Instant Learning Centers (p. 1351)
—Word Families Instant Learning Centers (p. 1950)
Williams, Caroline. Twinkle, Twinkle Time for Bed. (p. 1802)
Williams, Caroline, illus. see Pfeiffer, Sophie.
Williams, Caroline Randall, jt. auth. see Randall, Alice.
Williams, Caspar, illus. see Egginton, Jane.
Williams, Caspar, illus. see Kirkby, Mandy.
Williams, Caspar, illus. see O'Neill, Mary.
Williams, Caspar, illus. see Sanderson, Caroline.
Williams, Chase. Tale of the Beaver. (p. 1700)
Williams, Cheryl & Williams, Sheila. People of Colour Illustrations: Klip-Klik Art (p. 1339)
Williams, China. City Walks: Boston: 50 Adventures on Foot. (p. 324)
—Washington, D.C. 50 Adventures on Foot. (p. 1860)
Williams, Christine M. Building a Sight Vocabulary with Comprehension: The It Family. (p. 238)
Williams, Christopher. One Incredible Dog! Boone. Friedman, Judith, illus. (p. 1295)
—One Incredible Dog! Lady. Friedman, Judith, illus. (p. 1295)
Williams, Christopher, illus. see Esdaille-Richardson, Eudora.
Williams, Christopher D. Fastest Way to Get Pregnant Naturally: The Latest Information on Conceiving a Healthy Baby on Your Timetable. (p. 576)
Williams, Christy Jo, jt. auth. see Peacock-Williams, Carol A.
Williams, Chuck, ed. see Croce, Julia Della & Williams-Sonoma Staff.
Williams, Chuck, ed. see Rosenbaum, Stephanie.
Williams, Cinthia Louise. Flippin' Soccer Guide. (p. 605)
Williams, Claudette, jt. auth. see Evans, David.
Williams, Colleen. Homes of the Native Americans. Johnson, Troy, ed. (p. 793)
—Native American Family Life. Johnson, Troy, ed. (p. 1234)
Williams, Colleen Madonna Flood. Bahamas. (p. 132)
—Chuck Yeager. (p. 318)
—Ecuador. (p. 503)
—Geography of Mexico. (p. 662)
—Homes of the Native Americans. (p. 793)
—Jamaica. (p. 906)
—My Adventure at the Amusement Park. (p. 1195)
—My Adventure at the Safari Park. (p. 1195)
—My Adventure at the Sea Life Park. (p. 1195)
—My Adventure at the Water Park. (p. 1195)

—My Adventure in Ancient Egypt: Advanced My Adventure. (p. 1195)
—My Adventure in the Mesozoic Period: Advanced My Adventure. (p. 1195)
—My Adventure in the Wild West. (p. 1195)
—My Adventure on April Fool's Day. (p. 1195)
—My Adventure on Christmas. (p. 1195)
—My Adventure on Easter. (p. 1195)
—My Adventure on Father's Day. (p. 1195)
—My Adventure on Groundhog Day. (p. 1195)
—My Adventure on Halloween. (p. 1195)
—My Adventure on Martin Luther King Jr. Day. (p. 1195)
—My Adventure on Mother's Day. (p. 1195)
—My Adventure on My Birthday. (p. 1195)
—My Adventure on New Year's Day. (p. 1195)
—My Adventure on President's Day. (p. 1195)
—My Adventure on St. Patrick's Day. (p. 1195)
—My Adventure on Thanksgiving Day. (p. 1195)
—My Adventure on the Fourth of July. (p. 1195)
—My Adventure on Valentine's Day. (p. 1195)
—My Adventure on Veteran's Day. (p. 1195)
—My Adventure with Knights. (p. 1195)
—My Adventure with Leonardo da Vinci. (p. 1195)
—My Adventure with Shakespeare. (p. 1195)
—My Adventure with Vikings. (p. 1195)
—People of Mexico. (p. 1339)
—Schooling Day-by-day in May. (p. 1524)
—What the Native Americans Wore. (p. 1893)
—What the Native Americans Wore. Johnson, Troy, ed. (p. 1893)
Williams, Colleen Madonna Flood & Flood Williams, Colleen Madonna. Suriname. (p. 1685)
Williams, Dan. Duck That Lost His Waddle. (p. 488)
Williams, Darlene. Where the Angry Grass Grows. (p. 1909)
Williams, Darnell Denzel. One in a Million. (p. 1295)
Williams, Darnell L. Building Wealth with Corporate Bonds. (p. 239)
Williams, Dave. Windgalore Farm. (p. 1936)
Williams, David, jt. auth. see Williams, David K.
Williams, David, jt. illus. see Williams, Alexandra.
Williams, David G. Chemistry of Essential Oils (p. 297)
Williams, David K. Picnic. Ovresat, Laura, illus. (p. 1355)
Williams, David K. & Williams, David. Picnic. Ovresat, Laura, illus. (p. 1355)
—Tick Tock. Ovresat, Laura, illus. (p. 1747)
Williams, David Morgan. Dragonrise. (p. 478)
—Ebony & Ivory. (p. 502)
—Xcalibur, Merlin & the Teeth of the Dragon. (p. 1967)
Williams, Dawn. Betsy B's Big Blue Bouncing Bubble. Chou, Joey, illus. (p. 172)
—Cyril T. Centipede Looks for New Shoes Chou, Joey, illus. (p. 397)
—How Hooper the Hyaena Lost His Laugh. Chou, Joey, illus. (p. 809)
—Very Little Venus & the Very Friendly Fly. Chou, Joey, illus. (p. 1838)
—Winston J. Worm Hunts for a New Name. Chou, Joey, illus. (p. 1937)
Williams, Deb. Ryan Newman: From Purdue to Penske. (p. 1499)
Williams, Deborah. I Have a Watch. Graves, Dennis, illus. (p. 839)
—Little Rabbit Is Sad. Gedeon, Gloria, illus. (p. 1034)
—Nickels & Pennies. Gedeon, Gloria, illus. (p. 1251)
Williams, Debra R. Conoce la Familia Clock. (p. 358)
—Meet the Clock Family. (p. 1122)
Williams, Delphine. Freckles with All the Speckles. (p. 632)
Williams, Denny, illus. see Prater, Cindy.
Williams, Derek. Bible from Beginning to End. Thomas, Jacqui, illus. (p. 175)
—What's What in the Bible. Thomas, Jacqui, illus. (p. 1900)
Williams, Deshantren, illus. see Sherry, Raymond.
Williams, Diana. Early Listening Skills. (p. 493)
—Early Visual Skills. (p. 494)
Williams, Diana, jt. auth. see Cooke, Jackie.
Williams, Dinah. Abandoned Amusement Parks. (p. 2)
—Abandoned Insane Asylums. (p. 2)
—Creepy Islands. (p. 381)
—Creepy Stations. (p. 381)
—Dark Mansions. (p. 407)
—Haunted Hollywood. (p. 753)
—Haunted Houses. (p. 753)
—I Can Be Kind Lap Book. Mones, Marc, illus. (p. 835)
—I Can Follow the Rules. Patton, Julia, illus. (p. 835)
—I Can Follow the Rules Lap Book. Patton, Julia, illus. (p. 835)
—Monstrous Morgues of the Past. (p. 1169)
—Secrets of Disneyland: Weird & Wonderful Facts about the Happiest Place on Earth. (p. 1545)
—Secrets of Walt Disney World: Weird & Wonderful Facts about the Most Magical Place on Earth. (p. 1546)
—Shocking Seafood. (p. 1568)
—Shuttered Horror Hospitals. (p. 1572)
—Slithery, Slimy, Scaly Treats. (p. 1591)
—Spooky Cemeteries. (p. 1631)
—UFO Crash Sites. (p. 1807)
Williams, Don, illus. see Poindexter, Katherine & RH Disney Staff.
Williams, Don, illus. see Teitelbaum, Michael.
Williams, Donald & Williams, Ronald. Adventures of Wacko Rabbit. (p. 24)
Williams, Dontez D. Finding True Love... God's Way! (p. 588)
Williams, Dorinda J., creator. Teaching the Difficult Sounds & Words of First Grade. (p. 1710)
Williams, Doug. Girls' Basketball. (p. 679)
—Great Moments in Olympic Basketball. (p. 717)
—Oregon Ducks. (p. 1303)
—Tiger Woods Makes Masters History. (p. 1749)
Williams, Douglas. Guide to Our Nation's Capital. (p. 730)
Williams, Dylan, jt. auth. see Coplans, Peta.
Williams, Dylan, tr. see Cooper, Helen & Butterworth, Ian.
Williams, Dylan, tr. see Gates, Susan & Ceredigion, Cymdeithas Lyfrau.
Williams, Dylan, tr. see McAllister, Angela.
Williams, Dylan, tr. see McNaughton, Colin.
Williams, Dylan, tr. see Rix, Jamie.
Williams, Dylan, et al. Pawb Yn Cuddio. (p. 1331)
Williams, E. Colin, illus. see Tate, Nikki.
Williams, Eli & Jensen, Donald D. Decoy. Huddleston, Courtney, illus. (p. 422)
Williams, Emma. Adventures of Emma & Scruffy. (p. 18)
—Story of Hurry. Quraishi, Ibrahim, illus. (p. 1658)
Williams, Emma Louise. 30 Sheep & One Cow. Williams, Emma Louise, illus. (p. 1996)
—Daddy Loves You This Much. (p. 398)
—Harry the Hedgehog Loses His Favorite Sock. (p. 751)
—What's That Smell Monkey? williams, Emma Louise, illus. (p. 1899)
williams, Emma Louise, illus. see Williams, Emma Louise.
Williams, Emmy. Prestina Quacks: Emmy Williams. Williams, Emmy, illus. (p. 1397)
Williams, Eric, illus. see Kirov, Erica.
Williams, Eric L., illus. see Drago, Ty.
Williams, Erika. Through the Shattered Glass (p. 1745)
Williams, Eula. Loving Danger. Branch Jr., Robert F., illus. (p. 1061)
Williams Evans, Freddi & Evans, Freddi Williams. Battle of New Orleans: The Drummer's Story Henriquez, Emile, illus. (p. 146)
Williams, Fawn. Adventures of Jj the Amazon Parrot. (p. 19)
Williams, Felicie, jt. auth. see Chronic, Halka.
Williams, Felisha. Allison's Rainbow. (p. 47)
—I'm No Bully, Am I? (p. 859)
—Milk Chocolate Kid. (p. 1143)
Williams, Flood, jt. auth. see Madonna, Colleen.
Williams, Freddie, jt. auth. see Beechen, Adam.
Williams, Frederick C., jt. auth. see Chappell, Billie-Jean.
Williams, G. L., illus. see Evans, Carol Wolfe.
Williams, Gail, illus. see Thomas, Amy A.
Williams, Gareth, illus. see Evans, Michael & Wichman, David.
Williams, Gareth, illus. see Scandiffio, Laura.
Williams, Gareth, et al. New Physics for You. (p. 1246)
Williams, Gareth Glyn, illus. see Butts, Edward.
Williams, Garth. Baby Animals. Williams, Garth, illus. (p. 124)
—Baby Farm Animals. Williams, Garth, illus. (p. 126)
—Baby's First Book. Williams, Garth, illus. (p. 129)
—Benjamin's Treasure. (p. 165)
Williams, Garth, illus. see Brown, Margaret Wise.
Williams, Garth, illus. see Collins, Carolyn Strom & Eriksson, Christina Wyss.
Williams, Garth, illus. see Golden Books Staff.
Williams, Garth, illus. see Golden Books.
Williams, Garth, illus. see Jarrell, Randall.
Williams, Garth, illus. see Lindquist, Jennie D.
Williams, Garth, illus. see Moore, Lilian.
Williams, Garth, illus. see Norton, Miriam.
Williams, Garth, illus. see Selden, George.
Williams, Garth, illus. see Sharp, Margery.
Williams, Garth, illus. see Werner, Janet.
Williams, Garth, illus. see White, E. B.
Williams, Garth, illus. see White, E. B. & DiCamillo, Kate.
Williams, Garth, illus. see Wilder, Laura Ingalls & Ingalls, Laura.
Williams, Garth, illus. see Wilder, Laura Ingalls.
Williams, Gaylyn & Williams, Ken. Keys to Joy: How to Unlock God's Secrets of Lasting Happiness. (p. 950)
Williams, Geoffrey T. Devil Fish. Artful Doodlers, illus. (p. 432)
—Great White Red Alert. Artful Doodlers, illus. (p. 719)
—Hammerheads of Treasure Island. (p. 739)
—Manatees & Mermaids. (p. 1086)
Williams, George Alfred, illus. see Sweetser, Kate Dickinson.
Williams, Gerald W. Sins of Salome. (p. 1580)
Williams, Gianna & Riehecky, Janet. Colonia de Plymouth. (p. 341)
Williams, Gilda, et al. Art Book: Children's Edition. Ace, Jane, ed. (p. 101)
Williams, Gladys. What Do Apples Have? Special Steven Series. (p. 1882)
Williams, Glenn, illus. see Lapsley, Sarah.
Williams, Glenn, photos by see Lapsley, Sarah.
Williams, Greg. Airmont the Flying Squirrel. (p. 31)
—Albert the Ant. (p. 34)
—Cuddie the Cut Throat Trout. (p. 389)
—Dudley the Duck. (p. 489)
—Puggley Wuggley & the Three-Legged Chicken. (p. 1415)
—Salty the Sea Gull. (p. 1506)
—Townsworth the Turkey. (p. 1774)
—Wilberton the Worm. (p. 1928)
—Yarborrow. (p. 1968)
Williams, Guana Dunbar. Wacky Winter Witch. William, Icebergg Dunbar, illus. (p. 1852)
Williams, Guy. Billy Budd. (p. 187)
—Burning Fiery Furnace: Shadrach, Meshach, & Abednego. (p. 244)
—Choosing & Staging a Play. (p. 310)
—David & Goliath. (p. 410)
—Joseph & His Brothers. (p. 926)
—Nicholas Nickleby: Playscript. (p. 1251)
Williams, Hal G. Qudola's Quest. (p. 1423)
Williams Hall, Kathy. Kay Kay's Adventures on Ojo Caliente: The Old Aspen Tree & the Posi Ouinge. (p. 946)
Williams, Hap. Henry the Elf. Graves, Michelle, illus. (p. 768)
Williams, Harland. Kid with Too Many Nightmares. (p. 952)
Williams, Hays. Tangled Web: A Mother's Secret - a Jenny & Pete Mystery. (p. 1705)
Williams, Heather. Farmer Boy Goes West. (p. 574)
—Nellie Oleson Meets Laura Ingalls. (p. 1240)
Williams, Heather L. Andy & Jerome. Crowell, Knox, illus. (p. 72)
—Brians Garden. Gillen, Lisa P., illus. (p. 227)
—Caillou's Castle. Meier, Kerry L., illus. (p. 251)
Williams, Heather L., jt. auth. see Mullican, Judy.
Williams, Heather L. & Muench-Williams, Heather. Caillou Learns about Space. Storch, Ellen N., illus. (p. 252)
Williams, Heidi. Child Abuse (p. 301)
—Obsessive-Compulsive Disorder. (p. 1275)
—Teen Pregnancy. (p. 1713)
Williams, Heidi, jt. auth. see Merino, Noël.
Williams, Holly J. Cowgirl Ballerina. (p. 374)
—Waffles at Grandma's: A Sweet Story Plus Delicious Recipes Too! (p. 1852)
Williams, Howard. Salmon Sam's Great Salmon Run. (p. 1505)
Williams, Ike, jt. auth. see Stout, Glenn.
Williams, Imogen, jt. auth. see Bailey, Ellen.
Williams, J. H., III, illus. see Morrison, Grant.
Williams, Jack. Magic of Gracie Bear. (p. 1073)
—Miwok of California. (p. 1156)
—Modoc of California. (p. 1159)
—Mojave of California. (p. 1160)
—Mono of California. (p. 1166)
—Shasta of California. (p. 1563)
Williams, Jack R. Be Brave, Tah-Hy! The Journey of Chief Joseph's Daughter. Proferes, Jo, illus. (p. 148)
Williams, Jack S. Chumash of California. (p. 318)
—Craftsmen & Craftswomen. (p. 376)
—Craftsmen & Craftswomen of the California Mission Frontier. (p. 376)
—Esselen of California. (p. 536)
—Indians of the California Mission Frontier. (p. 872)
—Luiseano of California. (p. 1064)
—Luiseno of California. (p. 1064)
—Miwok of California. (p. 1156)
—Modoc of California. (p. 1159)
—Mojavo of California. (p. 1160)
—Mono of California. (p. 1166)
—Ohlone of California. (p. 1282)
—Padres of the California Mission Frontier. (p. 1317)
—Pomo of California. (p. 1382)
—Sailors, Merchants, & Muleteers of the California Mission Frontier. (p. 1503)
—Shasta of California. (p. 1563)
—Shoshone of California. (p. 1569)
—Soldiers & Their Families of the California Mission Frontier. (p. 1607)
—Tongva of California. (p. 1765)
—Townspeople & Ranchers of the California Mission Frontier. (p. 1773)
Williams, Jack S. & Davis, Thomas L. Indians of the California Mission Frontier. (p. 872)
—Padres of the California Mission Frontier. (p. 1317)
—Sailors, Merchants, & Muleteers. (p. 1503)
—Soldiers & Their Families of the California Mission Frontier. (p. 1607)
—Townspeople & Ranchers of the California Mission Frontier. (p. 1773)
Williams, Jackie. Liam & Storm's Alien Adventure. (p. 1004)
—Tori-Jean's Clever Ideas. (p. 1769)
Williams, Jacklyn. Feliz Cumpleanos, Gus! Abello, Patricia, tr. from ENG. (p. 581)
—Feliz Dia de Gracias, Gus! Abello, Patricia, tr. from ENG. (p. 581)
—Let's Go Fishing, Gus! Cushman, Doug, illus. (p. 997)
—Merry Christmas, Gus! Cushman, Doug, illus. (p. 1128)
Williams, Jacob & Burns, Adam. University of Tennessee College Prowler off the Record. (p. 1821)
Williams, James. Edna's Creek. (p. 504)
Williams, James D., et al. Writing & Language Arts: Writer's Workbook. (p. 1964)
Williams, James E. Accessory after the Fact. (p. 8)
Williams, James Glassco, Jr. Turning Your Defeat into Victory: It's Praying Time. (p. 1798)
Williams, Jamie L. Mommy's Little Helper (p. 1163)
Williams, Jan. Amazing Storytelling Cat. Peecock, Simon & McKissock, Charmaine, illus. (p. 56)
Williams, Jane. Days Like These: New & Selected Poems 1998-2013. (p. 415)
—Heeey Ma. (p. 762)
Williams, Jane A. Bluestocking Guide - Ancient Rome: Companion Workbook for Richard J. Maybury's Ancient Rome: How it Affects You Today. Daniels, Kathryn, ed. (p. 204)
—Bluestocking Guide - Building a Personal Model for Success: Companion Workbook to Richard J. Maybury's Uncle Eric Talks about Personal, Career, & Financial Security. Daniels, Kathryn, ed. (p. 204)
—Bluestocking Guide - Political Philosophies: Companion Workbook to Richard J. Maybury's Are You Liberal? Conservative? or Confused? Daniels, Kathryn, ed. (p. 204)
—Bluestocking Guide - the Thousand Year War in the Mideast: Based on Richard J. Maybury's book the Thousand Year War in the Mideast. (p. 204)
—Bluestocking Guide - World War I: Based on Richard J. Maybury's Book World War I. (p. 204)
—Bluestocking Guide - World War II: Based on Richard J. Maybury's book World War II. (p. 204)
Williams, Jane A., ed. see Daniels, Kathryn.
Williams, Jane A., ed. see Hess, Karl.
Williams, Jane A., ed. see Maybury, Richard J.
Williams, Jane A. & Daniels, Kathryn, eds. Economics - A Free Market Reader. (p. 502)
Williams, Jane & Cohen. Graphing Across the Curriculum. (p. 711)
Williams, Jared T., illus. see Kovacs, Deborah.
Williams, Jasmine. Daddy, Who Am I? (p. 399)
Williams, Jason & Felt, Jeremy. Adventures of Sam & Rowdy: Two Best Friends. (p. 22)
Williams, Jayne, illus. see Cutrer, Elisabeth.
Williams, Jean, illus. see Payne, Jackson.
Williams, Jean Kinney. Bridget Biddy Mason: From Slave to Businesswoman (p. 227)
—Cook: James Cook Charts the Pacific Ocean (p. 361)
—Empire of Ancient Greece, Revised Edition. (p. 521)
—U. S. Constitution. (p. 1806)
Williams, Jeffrey Lewis. Cheek Family Chronicles: Of America, England & Australia, a 700 Year History. (p. 295)
Williams, Jennifer. Oobleck, Slime & Dancing Spaghetti: Twenty Terrific at Home Science Experiments Inspired by Favorite Children's Books. (p. 1298)
Williams, Jenny, illus. see Birch, Beverley & Shakespeare, William.
Williams, Jenny, illus. see Kanyer, Laurie A.
Williams, Jenny, illus. see Larrison, Joanne.
Williams, Jenny, illus. see Riley, Kana.
Williams, Jenny, illus. see Young, Lesley.
Williams, Jerome, jt. auth. see Walters, Eric.
Williams, Jill Ann. Listen to the Flowers: Ten Flower Stories for Children. (p. 1022)
Williams, Jo. Golden Dolphin. (p. 694)
Williams, John. Harry Potter & the Chamber of Secrets: Sheet Music for Flute with C. D. (p. 750)
—Smokie Forever. (p. 1594)
Williams, John, illus. see Layburn, Joe.
Williams, John Joseph. Frightened Garden. (p. 639)
—Vak's War. (p. 1830)
Williams, Jonnie. Harry the Hopetown Hermit Crab. Kanitsch, Christine, illus. (p. 751)
Williams, Josh, jt. auth. see O'Neill, Terence.
Williams, Josie. Hoppy Finds Friends. (p. 797)
Williams, Joyce. Daddy's Love Through a Girl's Eye. Petroff, Kathryn, illus. (p. 399)
Williams, Joyce Hall & West, Nancy H. Ruffitt versus Do-Well: Let's Play Ball at the Taj Mahal. (p. 1494)
Williams Jr., Anthony, illus. see Williams-Ashe, Marcella Norton.
Williams Jr., Floyd. Lenney the Lightning Bug. Roberts, Joel, illus. (p. 991)
Williams, Judith. Descubriendo Dinosaurios con un Cazador de Fsiles. Skrepnick, Michael W., illus. (p. 428)
—Discovering Dinosaurs with a Fossil Hunter. Skrepnick, Michael William, illus. (p. 449)
—Discovery & Mystery of a Dinosaur Named Jane. (p. 450)
—Does the Sun Make Weather? (p. 460)
—En Busca de Tormentas con un Cientifico/Searching for Storms with a Scientist. (p. 522)
—Explorando la Selva Tropical con una Cientifica. (p. 550)
—Exploring the Rain Forest Treetops with a Scientist. (p. 554)
—Forensic Scientist: Careers Solving Crimes & Scientific Mysteries. (p. 617)
—How Come It's Raining? (p. 806)
—How Come It's Snowing? (p. 806)
—How Come It's Windy? (p. 806)
—How Does the Sun Make Weather? (p. 809)
—Saving Endangered Animals with a Scientist. (p. 1517)
—Searching for Stormy Weather with a Scientist. (p. 1537)
—Why Is It Raining? (p. 1925)
—Why Is It Snowing? (p. 1925)
—Why Is It Windy? (p. 1925)
Williams, Judith, jt. auth. see Rauf, Don.
Williams, Judith M. Montana. (p. 1170)
Williams, Judy. 50 Recipes for Kids to Cook: Tasty Food to Make Yourself Shown in Step-By-Step Pictures. (p. 1997)
Williams, Julie. Drama Queens in the House. (p. 480)
—Escaping Tornado Season: A Story in Poems. (p. 535)
—Islam: Understanding the History, Beliefs, & Culture. (p. 891)
Williams, Julie-Anne. Bully Me Not. (p. 241)
Williams, Justine. Nobody Likes Me: What Am I Doing Wrong? Martinez, Michael, illus. (p. 1262)
Williams, K. R. Natural Calculator: Using the Natural Processes of the Mind for Mental Calculation. (p. 1235)
Williams, Kara. Diet Drugs. (p. 437)
—Fertility Technology: The Baby Debate. (p. 582)
—Frequently Asked Questions about My Pyramid: Eating Right. (p. 636)
—Mypyramid: Eating Right. (p. 1222)
Williams, Kara, jt. auth. see Faulkner, Nicholas.
Williams, Karen Lynn. Beach Tail. Cooper, Floyd, illus. (p. 149)
—Beatrice's Dream: Life in an African Slum. Stone, Wendy, illus. (p. 153)
—Circles of Hope. (p. 321)
—Circles of Hope. Saport, Linda, illus. (p. 321)
—Galimoto. Stock, Catherine, illus. (p. 653)
—Lubuto Means Light. Grifalconi, Ann, illus. (p. 1062)
—One Thing I'm Good At. (p. 1297)
Williams, Karen Lynn, jt. auth. see Mohammed, Khadra.
Williams, Karen Lynn & Mohammad, Khadra. Four Feet, Two Sandals. Chayka, Doug, illus. (p. 625)
Williams, Kashamba, jt. auth. see Precious, Precious.
Williams, Kate, tr. see de Bie, Ceciel.
Williams, Kathleen. Jetway Geographer - Helena, Montana, to Salt Lake City, Utah. (p. 916)
Williams, Kathryn. Pizza, Love, & Other Stuff That Made Me Famous. (p. 1365)
Williams, Kathy, jt. auth. see Williams, Vicki.
Williams, Katie. Absent. (p. 7)
—Space Between Trees. (p. 1618)
Williams, Katie & Chronicle Books Staff. Space Between Trees. (p. 1618)
Williams, Katina T. Jeremiah Pie. (p. 913)
Williams, Katy. Barn Cat in the Christmas Tree. (p. 139)
—Where's My Cowboy Hat? (p. 1910)
Williams, Keith, illus. see Krohn, Katherine.
Williams, Keith, jt. auth. see Seidman, David.
Williams, Kelly Ann. Pye. (p. 1421)
Williams, Ken, jt. auth. see Williams, Gaylyn.
Williams, Kenneth. Triples: Applications of Pythagorean Triples. (p. 1787)
Williams, Kethette. Ghosts on the Hill. (p. 673)
Williams, Kiersten, jt. auth. see Yager, Karen.
Williams, Kimone. Reflection: This Is my voice. These are my Words. (p. 1456)
Williams, Kristen. Sheepy Sue & the Bedtime Blues. (p. 1564)
Williams, Larry. League of Clique. Williams, Larry, illus. (p. 982)
Williams, Laura E. Behind the Bedroom Wall. Goldstein, A. Nancy, illus. (p. 160)
—Best Winds. Neilan, Eujin Kim, illus. (p. 171)
—Executioner's Daughter. (p. 548)
—Father Damien. Kofsky, Kristen, illus. (p. 577)
—Slant. (p. 1587)
Williams, Laura E. & Orback, Craig. Can Man. (p. 258)
Williams, Laura M. Why Was Jesus Born. (p. 1926)
Williams, Lee. Seaweed, the Purrfect Cat. Johnson, Tamaris, illus. (p. 1539)
—Twin Dragons. Johnson, Tamaris, illus. (p. 1801)

W

Williams, Levester. Adventures od Crunchy & Munchy Squirrel: Field Nuts. (p. 16)
Williams, Linda D. Backhoes (p. 130)
—Bulldozers (p. 240)
—Camiones de Volteo/Dump Trucks. (p. 256)
—Careers in Forensics. (p. 268)
—Concrete Mixers (p. 355)
—Cranes (p. 376)
—Cranes (Grúas) Ferrer, Martin Luis Guzman, tr. (p. 376)
—Dump Trucks (p. 489)
—Earthmovers (p. 497)
—Earthmovers (Removedoras de Tierra) Ferrer, Martin Luis Guzman, tr. (p. 497)
—Forensics & Medicine. (p. 617)
—Navigational Aids. (p. 1238)
Williams, Linda Nugent. God Works Through You. (p. 690)
Williams, Lisa, illus. see French, Vivian.
Williams, Lisa, illus. see Graves, Sue.
Williams, Lisa, illus. see Hughes, Mónica.
Williams, Lisa E. Christmas Hippo. (p. 314)
Williams, Loeb Lee & Loeb, Jeph. Hush. (p. 830)
Williams, Lori. Being Me. (p. 161)
—Henrietta Peddles Her Eggs. (p. 767)
Williams, Lori Aurelia. Broken China. (p. 230)
—Shayla's Double Brown Baby Blues. (p. 1563)
—When Kambia Elaine Flew in from Neptune. (p. 1903)
Williams, Lorraine. Poor Dan. Felton, Richard, illus. (p. 1383)
Williams, Lorraine, illus. see Reid, Rob.
Williams, Lynda Anne. This Is Why I Talk to Jesus. (p. 1737)
Williams, Lyndsay. NonSense! It's Banana Cheese! (p. 1263)
Williams, Lynette Gain. Handwriting Begins with Art: The Partner Book to ArbeZ ZebrA Teaches A to Z. (p. 741)
Williams, M. C. No where to be Found: Time Is Short. (p. 1261)
Williams, M. Ed. Friends in the Meadow - Squirrels the Frolics of Scamp & Scooter. (p. 638)
Williams, M. J. Alora & the Howling Guff. (p. 48)
Williams, Mabel, jt. as told by see Williams, Robert F.
Williams, Maiya. Fizzy Whiz Kid. (p. 601)
—Golden Hour. (p. 695)
—Hour of the Outlaw. (p. 802)
—Middle-School Cool. (p. 1137)
Williams, Mandi. Mortimer's Book of What-Ifs (A Children's Rhyming Picture Book of Poetry) Williams, Mandi, illus. (p. 1176)
Williams, Mandi Tillotson. Many Adventures of Mortimer Crump: Mortimer's Sweet Retreat. (p. 1089)
Williams, Marcia. Elephant's Friend & Other Tales from Ancient India. Williams, Marcia, illus. (p. 512)
—Greek Myths. Williams, Marcia, illus. (p. 720)
—Hooray for Inventors! Williams, Marcia, illus. (p. 796)
—Lizzy Bennet's Diary: Inspired by Jane Austen's Pride & Prejudice. Williams, Marcia, illus. (p. 1043)
—More Tales from Shakespeare. Williams, Marcia, illus. (p. 1175)
—Romans: Gods, Emperors, & Dormice. (p. 1486)
Williams, Marcia, jt. auth. see Yang, Belle.
Williams, Marcia & Shakespeare, William. Tales from Shakespeare. Williams, Marcia, illus. (p. 1701)
Williams, Margery. Little Wooden Doll. (p. 1038)
—Velveteen Rabbit Spirin, Gennady, illus. (p. 1835)
—Velveteen Rabbit: Or, How Toys Become Real. Encarnacion, Liz, ed. (p. 1835)
—Velveteen Rabbit: Or How Toys Become Real. Santore, Charles, illus. (p. 1835)
—Velveteen Rabbit. (p. 1835)
—Velveteen Rabbit. Daily, Don, illus. (p. 1835)
—Velveteen Rabbit. Kliros, Thea, illus. (p. 1835)
—Velveteen Rabbit. Felix, Monique, illus. (p. 1835)
—Velveteen Rabbit. Hague, Michael, illus. (p. 1835)
—Velveteen Rabbit. Jorgensen, David, illus. (p. 1835)
—Velveteen Rabbit. Miles, Elizabeth, illus. (p. 1835)
—Velveteen Rabbit. Wilson, Katherine, illus. (p. 1835)
—Velveteen Rabbit. Nicholson, William, illus. (p. 1835)
—Velveteen Rabbit & Other Stories Book & Charm. (p. 1835)
—Velveteen Rabbit Book & Charm. Nicholson, William, illus. (p. 1835)
—Velveteen Rabbit Coloring Book. Kliros, Thea, illus. (p. 1835)
Williams, Margery, jt. auth. see Charles Santore.
Williams, Margery & Blanco, Margery Williams. Velveteen Rabbit. Felix, Monique, illus. (p. 1835)
Williams, Margery & Daily, Don. Velveteen Rabbit: Or, How Toys Become Real. (p. 1835)
Williams, Margery & Raiten-D'Antonio, Toni. Velveteen Collection: The Velveteen Principles & the Velveteen Rabbit Set Nicholson, William, illus. (p. 1835)
Williams, Marian. Bigdaddy: A Grand-daughter's Love Story. (p. 184)
Williams, Marie Sheppard. Magic Stories. (p. 1073)
Williams, Marilyn & Caspersen, Barbara. Peggy & Barbie on the Farm. (p. 1335)
Williams, Mark. Hooty & Pig: The Missing Christmas Pudding. Garrett, Keith, illus. (p. 796)
Williams, Mark, jt. auth. see Salariya, David.
Williams, Mary. Brothers in Hope: The Story of the Lost Boys of Sudan Christie, R. Gregory, illus. (p. 231)
Williams, Mary E. Antibiotics. Greenhaven Press Editors, ed. (p. 89)
—Growth Disorders. (p. 727)
—Mark Zuckerberg. Greenhaven Press Staff, ed. (p. 1095)
—Media Bias. (p. 1118)
—Self-Injury. (p. 1549)
—Self-Mutilation. (p. 1549)
—Synthetic Drugs. Gale, G., ed. (p. 1693)
—Tourette Syndrome. (p. 1773)
Williams, Mary E., ed. see Greenhaven Press Editors.
Williams, Mary E., ed. Is It Unpatriotic to Criticize One's Country? (p. 889)
—Lyme Disease. (p. 1066)
—Self-Mutilation. (p. 1549)
Williams, Matthew. Are You My Pet? Set of 6 (p. 97)
Williams, Matthew, illus. see Mataya, Marybeth.
Williams, Matthew, illus. see Vogel, Julia.
Williams, Mavis E. Cricket. (p. 382)
Williams, May Brenda. Shop of Magical Things. (p. 1568)
Williams, Megan K. Maddy's Amazing African Birthday Vallecchi, Alessandro et al, photos by. (p. 1070)
Williams, Mel. Robert Pattinson: Fated for Fame. (p. 1479)
—Stars in the Arena: Meet the Hotties of the Hunger Games. (p. 1643)
—Taylor Lautner: Overnight Sizzlin' Sensation. (p. 1708)
Williams, Melanie, jt. auth. see Frino, Lucy.
Williams, Mercedes. Little Tree. (p. 1037)
Williams, Michael. Diamond Boy. (p. 434)
—Now Is the Time for Running. (p. 1269)
—Power Tractors. (p. 1390)
Williams, Michael, contrib. by. Secret Song. (p. 1544)
Williams, Nadia, jt. auth. see Davis, Sheila.
Williams, Nancy. More Paperwork. (p. 1174)
Williams, Nancy E., ed. see Barnes, Brenda J.
Williams, Nancy E., ed. see Carty, Amy.
Williams, Nancy E., ed. see Dixon, Dallas L.
Williams, Nancy E., ed. see Ghani, Samna.
Williams, Nancy Noel. Don't Lose It, Reuse It. (p. 468)
—Have a Ball. (p. 754)
—Rice Is Nice. (p. 1469)
Williams, Nanon McKewn, jt. auth. see Short, Robyn.
Williams, Naomi. Jacob's Daughter. (p. 904)
Williams, Nate, illus. see Bodden, Valerie.
Williams, Nate, illus. see Riggs, Kate.
Williams, Nate, jt. auth. see Gibbs Smith.
Williams, Nate & Smith, Gibbs. Hank & Snoliver in What Can I Be? Williams, Nate, illus. (p. 742)
Williams, Nate & Snow, Virginia Brimhall. Spring Walk (p. 1635)
Williams, Nicholas, jt. auth. see Carroll, Lewis, pseud.
Williams, Nicholas, jt. auth. see Grahame, Kenneth.
Williams, Nicholas, tr. see Nesbit, Edith.
Williams, Nicole. Clash. (p. 327)
—Crash. (p. 376)
—Crush. (p. 386)
Williams, Noele. Little Red Frog. Kern, Debb, illus. (p. 1034)
Williams, Oleta Darlene. God Shines Brighter: A Use-Your-Imagination Book. (p. 690)
Williams, Pat. Souls of Steel: How to Build Character in Ourselves & Our Kids. (p. 1614)
Williams, Pat & Wimbish, David. Play to Win (For Girls) Strategies for Success in the Game of Life. (p. 1371)
Williams, Patricia de Belloy. Pioneers-1937. (p. 1361)
Williams, Paul. How the Bat Got Its Wings & Young Bear's Lesson: Two Cherokee Stories. (p. 812)
Williams, Paula. Tom's Wish. Graham, Carl, illus. (p. 1765)
Williams, Pete. Draft: A Year Inside the NFL's Search for Talent. (p. 476)
Williams, Pete, jt. auth. see Verstegen, Mark.
Williams, Quatessa. Little Fritter Counters. (p. 1028)
Williams, Rachel. Alex & the Archangel. Konopka, Jan, illus. (p. 35)
—Alex & the Bully. (p. 35)
—Little Pear Tree. Bowers, Jenny, illus. (p. 1033)
Williams, Randy. Hero Named Herman. (p. 772)
Williams, Raymond. House of Useful Things. (p. 803)
—Tales from the Willow Tree. (p. 1702)
Williams, Raymond, illus. see Williams, Brenda May.
Williams, Renee Pierce. Buck the Good Doog. (p. 234)
Williams, Rhonda, photos by. Mommy, Daddy, Where Do Babies Come From? Activity Book. (p. 1162)
Williams, Ricardo. Monstruos. Sozapato, illus. (p. 1170)
—Verde Manzana. Cornejo, Eulalia, illus. (p. 1836)
Williams, Richie. There's a Bear with a Pear! (p. 1730)
Williams, Rob. Indiana Jones & the Tomb of the Gods Scott, Steve, illus. (p. 871)
—Skaar: King of the Savage Land. Ching, Brian, illus. (p. 1583)
Williams, Rob, illus. see Eldridge, Sherrie.
Williams, Rob, illus. see Kitze, Carrie A.
Williams, Rob, et al. Amazing Spider-Man: The Fantastic Spider-Man. (p. 55)
Williams, Robert, illus. see Doering, Amanda.
Williams, Robert & Wood, Robert. Stacked Deck: A Program to Prevent Problem Gambling: Facilitator's Guide. (p. 1638)
Williams, Robert F. & Williams, Mabel, as told by. Robert & Mabel Williams Resource Guide. (p. 1478)
Williams, Robert L., jt. auth. see Long, James D.
Williams, Roberta C. Lonely Little Puppy. (p. 1046)
Williams, Ron, illus. see Smith, Jennifer Crown.
Williams, Ronald, jt. auth. see Williams, Donald.
Williams, Rose. Labors of Aeneas: What a Pain It Was to Found the Roman Race. (p. 970)
—Tres Porculi. L and L Enterprises, ed. (p. 1784)
—Young Romans. (p. 1979)
—Young Romans. Bennington, Mark, illus. (p. 1979)
Williams, Rozalia. College FAQ Book: Over 5,000 Not Frequently Asked Questions about College! (p. 340)
Williams, Rozanne Lanczak. Adding. Jarrett, Michael, illus. (p. 11)
—All about Real Bears. Christensen, David, illus. (p. 43)
—All about Real Bears. Maio, Barbara & Faulkner, Stacey, eds. (p. 43)
—All Week at School. Hamaguchi, Carla, ed. (p. 46)
—Ants & the Grasshopper Adnet, Bernard, illus. (p. 90)
—Are We There Yet? Leary, Catherine, illus. (p. 96)
—Author with the Fancy Purple Pen. Richard, Ilene, illus. (p. 117)
—Big Hungry Bear. Hockerman, Dennis, illus. (p. 181)
—Bugs in Your Backyard. Hamaguchi, Carla, ed. (p. 237)
—Build-a-Skill Instant Books Sight Words, Part 1. Faulkner, Stacey, ed. (p. 238)
—Captain Jack's Journal. Maio, Barbara, ed. (p. 264)
—Captain Jack's Journal. Grayson, Rick, illus. (p. 264)
—Cat Can't Write: A Cat & Dog Story. Leary, Catherine, illus. (p. 277)
—Cat's Fairy Tale: A Cat & Dog Story. Maio, Barbara, ed. (p. 281)
—Cat's Fairy Tale: A Cat & Dog Story. Leary, Catherine, illus. (p. 281)
—Crayola Counting. Jarrett, Michael, illus. (p. 377)
—Creepy, Crawly Bugs. Harris, Jennifer Beck, illus. (p. 381)
—Emily Santos, Star of the Week. Maio, Barbara, ed. (p. 519)
—Emily Santos, Star of the Week. Burris, Priscilla, illus. (p. 519)
—Fairy Tale Mail. Allen, Joy, illus. (p. 564)
—Fairy Tale Rock. Christensen, David & Leary, Catherine, illus. (p. 564)
—Fluency Readers: 144 Reader Books, 2 Resource Guides, 2 Read-Along. Box Set (p. 608)
—Grandma's Lists. Briles, Patty, illus. (p. 709)
—Grandma's Lists. Maio, Barbara & Faulkner, Stacey, eds. (p. 709)
—Here Comes Coco. Banta, Susan, illus. (p. 770)
—Hide & Seek Monsters. Dunne, Kathleen, illus. (p. 776)
—How Can I Get a Pet? Reid, Mick, illus. (p. 805)
—How Can I Get a Pet? Maio, Barbara & Faulkner, Stacey, eds. (p. 805)
—How to Make a Friend. Nobens, Cheryl, illus. (p. 820)
—I Love Mud! Twinem, Neecy, illus. (p. 842)
—I Love to Write! Schuett, Stacey, illus. (p. 843)
—I Love to Write! Maio, Barbara & Faulkner, Stacey, eds. (p. 843)
—Learning about Coins. Jarrett, Michael, photos by. (p. 984)
—Little Cookie Girl. Hamaguchi, Carla, ed. (p. 1026)
—Little Monster Becomes an Author. Maio, Barbara, ed. (p. 1032)
—Little Monster Becomes an Author. Hefferan, Rob, illus. (p. 1032)
—Little Red Hen Makes Soup. Hamaguchi, Carla, ed. (p. 1035)
—Look Closer. Vangsgard, Amy, illus. (p. 1049)
—Lost Puppy, Found Puppy. Maio, Barbara, ed. (p. 1056)
—Lost Puppy, Found Puppy. Motoyama, Keiko, illus. (p. 1056)
—Mice Are Nice. Moore, Margie, illus. (p. 1134)
—Monkey in the Story Tree. Hanke, Karen, illus. (p. 1165)
—Monkey in the Story Tree. Maio, Barbara & Faulkner, Stacey, eds. (p. 1165)
—Mouse Who Cried Cat Mahan, Benton, illus. (p. 1182)
—My Favorites, Your Favorites. Hamaguchi, Carla, ed. (p. 1203)
—My Friends. Hamaguchi, Carla, ed. (p. 1209)
—My Loose Tooth. Hamaguchi, Carla, ed. (p. 1213)
—My Picture Story. Mahan, Benton, illus. (p. 1217)
—My Picture Story. Maio, Barbara & Faulkner, Stacey, eds. (p. 1217)
—My Pink Piggy Bank. Fletcher, Rusty, illus. (p. 1217)
—Old MacDonald's Funny Farm Starr Taylor, Bridget, illus. (p. 1284)
—Pirates Coming Through Pamintuan, Macky, illus. (p. 1363)
—Postcards from Barney Bear. Maio, Barbara & Faulkner, Stacey, eds. (p. 1388)
—Purple Snerd. (p. 1419)
—Purple Snerd. GrandPré, Mary, illus. (p. 1419)
—Room 9 Writes a Report. Maio, Barbara, ed. (p. 1488)
—Room 9 Writes a Report. Lucas, Margeaux, illus. (p. 1488)
—Seasons. Maio, Barbara & Faulkner, Stacey, eds. (p. 1538)
—Sight Word Poetry Pages: 100 Fill-in-the-Blank Practice Pages That Help Kids Really Learn the Top High-Frequency Words. (p. 1574)
—Sight Word Readers Collection Box Set. (p. 1574)
—Slow & Steady Wins the Race Edwards, Karl, illus. (p. 1591)
—Space Trip. Burnett, Lindy, illus. (p. 1620)
—Special Memories. (p. 1623)
—Special Memories. Maio, Barbara, ed. (p. 1623)
—Subtracting. Jarrett, Michael, photos by. (p. 1671)
—Swim Lesson. Burris, Priscilla, illus. (p. 1690)
—Teacher with the Alligator Purse Richard, Ilene, illus. (p. 1709)
—Tess Builds a Snowman. Harris, Jenny B., illus. (p. 1722)
—Tess Builds a Snowman. Maio, Barbara & Faulkner, Stacey, eds. (p. 1722)
—This Is My Story. Burris, Priscilla, illus. (p. 1736)
—This Is My Story. Maio, Barbara & Faulkner, Stacey, eds. (p. 1736)
—Today Is Somebody's Birthday. Mahan, Benton, illus. (p. 1760)
—Two Stories, Two Friends. Allen, Joy, illus. (p. 1804)
—Two Stories, Two Friends. Maio, Barbara, ed. (p. 1804)
—We Are the Monsters! Hamaguchi, Carla, ed. (p. 1866)
—What Is the Best Pet? Briles, Patty, illus. (p. 1890)
—What Is This? Hamaguchi, Carla, ed. (p. 1890)
—What's So Bad about the Big Bad Wolf? Catalano, Dominic, illus. (p. 1899)
—When You Go Walking. Maio, Barbara, ed. (p. 1905)
—When You Go Walking. Briles, Patty, illus. (p. 1905)
—Where Have You Been? Hamaguchi, Carla, ed. (p. 1907)
—Which Way Did They Go? Hamaguchi, Carla, ed. (p. 1911)
—Writing about Books. Schneider, Christine, illus. (p. 1964)
—Writing about Books. Maio, Barbara & Faulkner, Stacey, eds. (p. 1964)
—Writing Dino-Mite Poems. Adnet, Bernard, illus. (p. 1964)
—You Can't Catch Me. Edwards, Karl, illus. (p. 1974)
Williams, Rozanne Lanczak, jt. auth. see Callella, Kim.
Williams, Rozanne Lanczak, jt. auth. see Cernak, Kim.
Williams, Rozanne Lanczak, jt. auth. see Cernek, Kim.
Williams, Rozanne Lanczak, jt. auth. see Lubben, Amy.
Williams, Rozanne Lanczak & Connelly, Luella. Best of Learn to Read, Set 1 Box Set. (p. 170)
Williams, Rozanne Lanczak & Faulkner, Stacey. Learn to Write Resource Guide: Grades K-2. (p. 984)
Williams, Rufus. Frog & the Butterfly. (p. 640)
Williams, S. L. Polka-Dot Maddy's Birthday Fun: Colors of the Rainbow. (p. 1381)
Williams, Sam. Are You a Bully? (p. 96)
—Bunny & Bee Can't Sleep. (p. 242)
—Bunny & Bee Play Days. (p. 242)
—I'm the Boss. Dufalla, Anita, illus. (p. 860)
—It's My Turn. Dufalla, Anita, illus. (p. 897)
—Santa's Toys. Gill, Tim, illus. (p. 1513)
—School Bus Bunny Bus. Trotter, Stuart, illus. (p. 1522)
—Sharing. (p. 1561)
—Talk Peace. Moriuchi, Mique, illus. (p. 1703)
—That's Love. Moriuchi, Mique, illus. (p. 1727)
Williams, Sam, illus. see Ferguson, Sarah & Duchess of York Staff.
Williams, Sam, illus. see Ford, Bernette G.
Williams, Sam, illus. see Ford, Bernette.
Williams, Sam, illus. see Higginson, Sheila Sweeny.
Williams, Sam, illus. see Hyperion Staff.
Williams, Sam, illus. see Rollins, Walter & Nelson, Steve.
Williams, Sam, illus. see Weiss, Ellen.
Williams, Sam, illus. see Wilson, Karma.
Williams, Sam, illus. see Yolen, Jane & Stemple, Heidi E. Y.
Williams, Sam, jt. auth. see Beake, Lesley.
Williams, Samantha. Big Like Me. (p. 182)
Williams, Sandra. God Knows Me: Pslam 139 for Little Hearts. Williams, Sandra, illus. (p. 689)
—Look with Me. (p. 1050)
Williams, Sarah A. President. (p. 1396)
Williams, Sarah DeFord. Palace Beautiful. (p. 1319)
Williams, Sarajane. Dreamtime: Lullabies for Lever & Pedal Harp (p. 484)
Williams, Scott, illus. see Azzarello, Brian & Loeb, Jeph.
Williams, Sean. Changeling. (p. 290)
—Hollowgirl: A Twinmaker Novel. (p. 789)
—Twinmaker. (p. 1802)
Williams, Sean, jt. auth. see Nix, Garth.
Williams, Sean J. Fashion Fairies. (p. 575)
Williams, Serena, jt. auth. see Williams, Venus.
Williams, Shan, illus. see Shelton, Ricky V.
Williams, Shane, ed. see Gotthardt, Katherine.
Williams, Shanica. Amy Goes Shopping for School. (p. 66)
Williams, Shannon. School Rules! Nelson, Anndria, illus. (p. 1523)
—Songs of Science: Physics in the Car. (p. 1612)
—Songs of Science: Physics in the Bathtub. (p. 1612)
—Where Does Money Come From? Book One of Money Matters for Children. (p. 1907)
Williams, Shaun. Sea Beds. (p. 1534)
Williams, Sheila, jt. auth. see Williams, Cheryl.
Williams, Shelton L. Washed in the Blood. (p. 1859)
Williams, Sherri. Adventures of Little Mouse: (Life Outside the Mouse Hole) (p. 19)
—My Daddy Is in the Army. (p. 1201)
Williams, Shirley. Zipper - the Mischievous Kid. (p. 1987)
Williams, Simon. Kite Who Was Scared of Heights. Papaleo, Antonio, illus. (p. 962)
Williams, Simon, jt. auth. see Cullen, Dave.
Williams, Sophy. Princess Stories from Around the World. Tym, Kate, illus. (p. 1405)
Williams, Sophy, illus. see Catchpool, Michael.
Williams, Sophy, illus. see Hartman, Bob.
Williams, Sophy, illus. see McCaughrean, Geraldine & Dubravka, Kolanovic.
Williams, Sophy, illus. see Webb, Holly.
Williams, Sophy, jt. auth. see Matthews, Caitlin.
Williams, Stanley. Willie's Dad. (p. 1934)
Williams, Stanley R. Not Me. (p. 1267)
Williams, Steve, illus. see Krakow, Amy.
Williams, Steve, jt. auth. see Barr, Catherine.
Williams, Sue. I Went Walking: Lap-Sized Board Book. Vivas, Julie, illus. (p. 848)
—I Went Walking. Vivas, Julie, illus. (p. 848)
—Let's Go Visiting. Vivas, Julie, illus. (p. 998)
Williams, Sue, illus. see Albee, Sarah.
Williams, Sue, illus. see Whitman, Sylvia.
Williams, Susan. Wind Rider. (p. 1935)
Williams, Suzanna. Ninety-Five Percent Human. (p. 1256)
Williams, Suzanne. China's Daughters. MacLean, Amber, illus. (p. 307)
—Daisy & the First Wish. Sansom, Fiona, illus. (p. 400)
—Fairy Blossoms: Daisy & the Magic Lesson. Sansom, Fiona, illus. (p. 563)
—Gigantic, Genuine Genie. Gonzales, Chuck, illus. (p. 676)
—Human or Alien? Carter, Abby, illus. (p. 826)
—Kentucky. (p. 949)
—Leo School Trio: Here Comes Hilary. No. 1 (p. 992)
—Lucky Penny? Carter, Abby, illus. (p. 1063)
—Master of Minds? Carter, Abby, illus. (p. 1103)
—Mysterious, Mournful Maiden. Gonzales, Chuck, illus. (p. 1223)
—Nevada. (p. 1242)
—Ten Naughty Little Monkeys. Watts, Suzanne, illus. (p. 1719)
Williams, Suzanne, jt. auth. see Holub, Joan.
Williams, Suzanne Morgan. Bull Rider. (p. 240)
—Inuit. (p. 883)
—Ojibwe Indians. (p. 1282)
—Powhatan Indians. (p. 1391)
—Tlingit Indians. (p. 1758)
Williams, T. Puddin the Pudgy Panda Makes A New Friend. (p. 1414)
Williams, T. D. Happy Village. (p. 747)
Williams, T. E. Fluffy!! (p. 608)
Williams, T. H. Jo's Bright New Day. (p. 926)
Williams, Tad & Beale, Deborah. Dragons of Ordinary Farm. Swearingen, Greg, illus. (p. 479)
Williams, Tara. Angel Friends. (p. 73)
—Ben & Berttie & Fried Pizza. (p. 163)
Williams, Ted, illus. see Alexander, Heather.
Williams, Ted, illus. see Bayrock, Fiona.
Williams, Ted, illus. see Douglas, Babette.
Williams, Ted, illus. see Miller, Susan A.
Williams, Ted, illus. see Ollen, Rebecca.
Williams, Ted, illus. see Sievert, Terri & Dougherty, Terri.
Williams, Ted & Kaminski, Karol. My First English-Spanish Picture Dictionary. (p. 1206)
Williams, Ted & Katschke, Judy. Johnny Tractor & the Big Surprise. (p. 923)
Williams, Tennessee, jt. auth. see Onyett, Nicola.
Williams, Teresa Ann. Friends of Wildwood (p. 638)
Williams, Teri. I Got Bank! What My Granddad Taught Me about Money. (p. 838)
Williams, Terri. R. E. A. L. Science- Life (level One) Read, Explore, Absorb & Learn Science. (p. 1429)
Williams, Thomas. Christmas Chair. (p. 313)
Williams, Thomas D. Spiritual Progress: Becoming the Christian You Want to Be. (p. 1629)
Williams, Thomas L. Learning How to Learn: A Complete Summary of the Tools, Tips, & Techniques for Becoming an Effective, Efficient, & Successful Student: the Secrets of Becoming A Successful Student. (p. 985)
Williams, Tim. New School University College Prowler off the Record. (p. 1247)
Williams, Tim, illus. see Altman, Joel.

Williams, Tim, illus. see Callahan, Lauren & Callahan, Michael T.
Williams, Tim, illus. see Zangas, Sherri.
Williams, Tim, jt. auth. see Knight, Russell.
Williams, Tim, jt. auth. see Lewis, Jennifer.
Williams, Tim, jt. auth. see Lynn Sauthoff, Taryn.
Williams, Tim, jt. auth. see Rosario, Nicole.
Williams, Tim, jt. auth. see Roth, Pam.
Williams, Tim, jt. auth. see Salaver, Jillianne.
Williams, Tim & Williams, Tony. Timmy's Bedtime: A Monster Bear Tale. (p. 1755)
Williams, Toby, illus. see Martin, Tyler.
Williams, Tod & Tsien, Billie. Architecture of the Barnes Foundation: Gallery in a Garden, Garden in a Gallery. (p. 95)
Williams, Tony, jt. auth. see Williams, Tim.
Williams, Tova. Boy Who Did Not Want to Read Suggs, Aisha, illus. (p. 219)
Williams, Tracee, ed. see Bentley, Dawn, et al.
Williams, Tracee, ed. see Galvin, Laura Gates & Soundprints Editorial Staff.
Williams, Tracee, ed. see Galvin, Laura Gates & Studio Mouse Editorial.
Williams, Tracee, ed. see Galvin, Laura Gates.
Williams, Tracee, ed. see Soundprints Staff.
Williams, Tracee, ed. Dinosaurs Write-with-Me Alphabet. (p. 445)
Williams, Tracy. Mini Adventures of Lally Lola. (p. 1146)
Williams, Ursula Moray. Adventures of the Little Wooden Horse. Brisley, Joyce Lankester, illus. (p. 23)
—Gobbolino, the Witch's Cat. Rayner, Catherine, illus. (p. 688)
Williams, Val. Martin Parr. Parr, Martin, photos by. (p. 1098)
Williams, Valerie. Funny Dreams of Dennis the Dartmoor Pony. (p. 649)
Williams, Vanessa. Did You See That? The Bug & Itself. (p. 437)
Williams, Vanessa A. Missing Penny. (p. 1152)
Williams, Venus & Williams, Serena. SisterTales 2. (p. 1581)
Williams, Vera B. Amber Was Brave, Essie Was Smart. (p. 57)
—Amber Was Brave, Essie Was Smart. Williams, Vera B., illus. (p. 57)
—Chair for Always. Williams, Vera B., illus. (p. 288)
—Chair for My Mother. (p. 288)
—Chair for My Mother. Williams, Vera B., illus. (p. 288)
—Cherries & Cherry Pits. (p. 298)
—Sillón para Mi Mamá. Marcuse, Aida E., tr. from ENG. (p. 1575)
—Sillón para Siempre. Williams, Vera B., illus. (p. 1575)
Williams, Versey. My Grandma's Dog. (p. 1210)
Williams, Vicki & Williams, Kathy. Everybody Has a Daddy. Wood, Joe, illus. (p. 543)
Williams, Virginia, jt. auth. see Potter, Alan Mitchell.
Williams, Vivienne. Mummy's Gorgeous Hair. Neogi, Joyeeta, illus. (p. 1191)
—Rosie & Her Formidable Bark, Indomitable Nose & Rambunctioustail. Wotton, Jon, illus. (p. 1490)
Williams, Walter. Bicycle Garden. (p. 177)
—Monster for Tea. Williams, Walter, illus. (p. 1167)
Williams, Wendy. Hold Me in Contempt: A Romance. (p. 787)
Williams, William J. Ask Alice & Other Stories. (p. 106)
Williams, Wish, illus. see Christian, Cheryl.
Williams, Wish, illus. see Halfmann, Janet.
Williams, Zac. Little Aliens Cookbook (p. 1023)
Williams, Zac, jt. auth. see Anderson, Lisa.
Williams, Zac, photos by see Anderson, Lisa Turner & Barlow, Melissa.
Williams, Zac, photos by see Beery, Barbara.
Williams, Zachary. Cleaning up the Park: Learning to Count by Fives. (p. 330)
—How Do Airplanes Fly? (p. 806)
—Lions at the Library? (p. 1021)
—Lost Nickel. (p. 1056)
—What Will It Be? (p. 1895)
Williams, Zella. America Ferrera: Award-Winning Actress. (p. 59)
—America Ferrera: Award-Winning Actress = Estrella de la Pantalla. (p. 59)
—Coqui Frogs & Other Latin American Frogs. (p. 366)
—Coqui Frogs & Other Latin American Frogs/Coquies y Otras Ranas de Latinoamerica. (p. 366)
—Do-It-Yourself Science (p. 457)
—Experiments about Planet Earth. (p. 549)
—Experiments about the Natural World. (p. 549)
—Experiments on Rocks & the Rock Cycle. (p. 549)
—Experiments on the Weather. (p. 549)
—Experiments with Physical Science. (p. 549)
—Experiments with Solids, Liquids, & Gases. (p. 549)
—Howler Monkeys & Other Latin America Monkeys: Monos Aulladores y Otros Monos de Latino América. (p. 824)
—Jaguars & Other Latin American Wild Cats: Jaguares y Otros Felinos de Latino América. (p. 905)
—Llamas & Other Latin American Camels: Llamas y Otros Camélidos de Latinoamérica. (p. 1043)
—Mark Sanchez: Quarterback on the Rise. (p. 1095)
—Mark Sanchez: Quarterback on the Rise - Mariscal de Campo en Ascenso. (p. 1095)
—Piranhas & Other Creatures of the Amazon: Pirañas y Otros Animales de la Selva Amazónica. (p. 1362)
—Quetzals & Other Latin American Birds: Quetzales y Otras Aves de Latino América. (p. 1427)
—Selena Gomez: Actress & Singer. (p. 1549)
—Selena Gomez: Actress & Singer - Actriz y Cantante. (p. 1549)
—Shakira: Star Singer. (p. 1559)
—Shakira: Star Singer - Estrella de la Canción. (p. 1559)
—Sonia Sotomayor: Supreme Court Justice. (p. 1612)
—Sonia Sotomayor: Supreme Court Justice - Sonia Sotomayor: Jueza de la Corte Suprema. (p. 1612)
—Tony Romo: Star Quarterback. (p. 1766)
—Tony Romo: Star Quarterback - Tony Romo - Mariscal de Campo Estrella. (p. 1766)
Williams-Ashe, Marcella Norton. Granny Says. Williams Jr., Anthony, illus. (p. 710)
Williams-El, Belinda Irene, illus. see Singh, Rajinder.
Williams-Garcia, Rita. Bottle Cap Boys on Royal Street. (p. 215)
—Catching the Wild Waiyuuzee. Reed, Mike, illus. (p. 279)
—Gone Crazy in Alabama. (p. 697)
—One Crazy Summer. (p. 1294)
—P. S. Be Eleven. (p. 1316)
Williams-Hines, Jacqueline. Joshua, That's Sooo Slimming! (p. 927)
Williamson, A. M. Castle of the Shadows. (p. 277)
Williamson, Ada C., illus. see Fisher, Dorothy Canfield.
Williamson, Ada Clendenin, illus. see Hopkins, William J.
Williamson, Al, illus. see Simon, Joe.
Williamson, Alan, 8th, illus. see Williamson, Jennifer.
Williamson, Barbara. Wishbone. (p. 1940)
Williamson, Brian. Comic Maths: Sue. (p. 348)
Williamson, Brian, illus. see Hunt, Elizabeth Singer & Weinstein Books Staff.
Williamson, Brian, illus. see Hunt, Elizabeth Singer.
Williamson, Brian, illus. see Rimmer, Ian.
Williamson, Chet. Pennsylvania Dutch Alphabet Stacy, Alan, illus. (p. 1338)
Williamson, David. War & Peace: International Relations, 1919-1939. (p. 1857)
Williamson, Denise J. Forbidden Gates. (p. 616)
—River of Danger. (p. 1476)
—Silent Road to Rescue. (p. 1575)
Williamson, Don. Lawns Natural & Organic. (p. 981)
—Organic Lawns in Canada (p. 1303)
Williamson, Don, jt. auth. see Aldrich, William.
Williamson, Don, jt. auth. see Dillard, Tara.
Williamson, Don, jt. auth. see Engebretson, Don.
Williamson, Don, jt. auth. see Joggerst, Anita.
Williamson, Don, jt. auth. see Tanem, Bob.
Williamson, Don & Binetti, Marianne. Best Garden Plants for Washington & Oregon (p. 169)
Williamson, Don & Dilliard, Tara. Perennials for Georgia. (p. 1341)
Williamson, Duncan, jt. auth. see Maddern, Eric.
Williamson, Froser. My Clothes: Individual Title Six-Packs. (p. 1200)
Williamson, Greg. How Do I Cure This Cold? Popko, Wendy, illus. (p. 807)
—Why Do I Have to Wear Glasses? Popko, Wendy, illus. (p. 1923)
—Why Do I Have to Wear Glasses? Popkp, Wendy, illus. (p. 1923)
Williamson, Hilary & Adams, Lynne. Magic Pumpkin. (p. 1073)
Williamson, James, illus. see Hall, Pamela.
Williamson, Jan. Special Day in May. (p. 1623)
Williamson, Jennifer. Timmy the Tow Truck Williamson, Alan, 8th, illus. (p. 1755)
Williamson, Jill. Project Gemini. (p. 1410)
—Rebels (p. 1451)
Williamson, Josh E. & Williamson, Joshua. Dear Dracula. (p. 418)
Williamson, Joshua. Sketch Monsters Book 1: Escape of the Scribbles: Escape of the Scribbles. (p. 1584)
Williamson, Joshua, jt. auth. see Williamson, Josh E.
Williamson, Joshua & Navarrete, Vinny. New Kid (p. 1245)
Williamson, Judithe Anne. Princess Kara in Her Village (p. 1404)
—Tiny with a Twist: Book 3 of the Tiny Village Series (p. 1757)
Williamson, K. E. Kayla & the Christmas Monkey. (p. 946)
Williamson, Karen. Daniel & the Lions Connor, Sarah, illus. (p. 404)
—David & Goliath Connor, Sarah, illus. (p. 410)
—Easter Embleton-Hall, Chris, illus. (p. 499)
—Lift the Flap Bible Anglicas, Louise, illus. (p. 1014)
—My First Bible Stories Allen, Marie, illus. (p. 1204)
—My Little Life of Jesus Enright, Amanda, illus. (p. 1212)
—Noah Embleton-Hall, Chris, illus. (p. 1261)
—Noah & the Animals Hanton, Sophie, illus. (p. 1261)
—Play-Time Noah Anglicas, Louise, illus. (p. 1371)
Williamson, Karen & David, Juliet. Build Your Own Noah's Ark Bolton, Bill, illus. (p. 238)
Williamson, Kate T. Hello Kitty Through the Seasons! Butefish, Jennifer & Soares, Maria Fernanda, photos by. (p. 764)
Williamson, Kenneth L. Organic Experiments. (p. 1303)
Williamson, Kevin, jt. auth. see Smith, L. J.
Williamson, Linda. Groundhog Breakfast, Soft Petals, & a Roof That Don't Leak Too Much Mollett, Irene, illus. (p. 725)
Williamson, Linda K., illus. see Birkholz, Gay Lyn.
Williamson, Liza. Emily to the Rescue. Keddy, Brian, illus. (p. 519)
Williamson, Margaret. First Book of Bugs. (p. 593)
Williamson, Mary. Life of George Washington. (p. 1012)
Williamson, Melanie. Cactus Annie. Williamson, Melanie, illus. (p. 250)
—Drift upon a Dream: Poems for Sleepy Babies. (p. 485)
—magnifico plan de Lobo/ Wolf's Magnificent Plan. Williamson, Melanie, illus. (p. 1076)
Williamson, Melanie, illus. see Amador Family Staff & Barefoot Books Staff.
Williamson, Melanie, illus. see Barefoot Books Staff & Amador Family Staff.
Williamson, Melanie, illus. see Bedford, David.
Williamson, Melanie, illus. see Conway, David.
Williamson, Melanie, illus. see Don, Lari.
Williamson, Melanie, illus. see Kerven, Rosalind.
Williamson, Melanie, illus. see Sykes, Julie.
Williamson, Nancy. 52 Bible Drills & Quizzes. (p. 1997)
—52 Games That Teach the Bible. (p. 1997)
—52 Ways to Teach Bible Reading. (p. 1997)
—52 Ways to Teach Children to Pray. (p. 1997)
—52 Ways to Teach Memory Verses. (p. 1997)
—52 Ways to Teach Missions. (p. 1997)
—52 Ways to Teach Stewardship. (p. 1997)
Williamson, Pam. Sweet & Sour Milk. (p. 1689)
Williamson, Peggy. Beth's Journey. (p. 171)
—Who Was Here First? (p. 1918)
Williamson, Penelope. Mortal Sins. (p. 1176)
Williamson, Pete, illus. see Bass, Guy.
Williamson, Ray A. & Monroe, Jean Guard. They Dance in the Sky: Native American Star Myths. Stewart, Edgar, illus. (p. 1732)
Williamson, Rebekah. But God's Word Says: Book 1. (p. 246)
Williamson, Robert C. Latin America: Cultures in Conflict. (p. 979)
Williamson, Rose. Look at Me! Look at Me! Marts, Doreen, illus. (p. 1048)
Williamson, Sharon. Grandma Says, Don't Climb the Peach Tree. (p. 708)
Williamson, Stafford. Puppy Goes to Lambergarten. (p. 1418)
—Puppyfish. (p. 1418)
Williamson, Susan, jt. auth. see Taggar, Sam.
Williamson, Walter. Theater for Young Actors: The Definitive Teen Guide. (p. 1728)
Williamson, Wendy. Christian Martial Arts 101. (p. 312)
—Christian Martial Arts 101 (Instructor's Edition) (p. 312)
Williams-Reyes, Inez. Kimani's Visit to the Dentist. (p. 957)
Williams-Sonoma Staff, jt. auth. see Croce, Julia Della.
Williams-Wheeler, Dorrie. Unplanned Pregnancy Book for Teens & College Students. (p. 1822)
Willian, Michael. Essential It's a Wonderful Life Film Guidebook: A scene by scene look at a holiday Classic. (p. 537)
Willians, Rozanne Lanczak. Sing & Read with Greg & Steve All-in-One Pack. (p. 1579)
Willie, Kirsten, ed. see Dankberg, Tracy & Graham, Leland.
Willie, Kirsten, ed. see Ledbetter, Darril & Graham, Leland.
Willie, Kirsten, ed. see Moore, Jennifer, et al.
Willie, Kirsten, ed. see Moore, Jennifer.
Willier, Shelley, jt. auth. see Bouchard, David.
Williford, Barbara. Child's Prayer. (p. 305)
Willingham, Bill. 1,001 Nights of Snowfall. Bolton, John et al, illus. (p. 2002)
—Animal Farm. (p. 77)
—Arabian Nights (And Days) Buckingham, Mark et al, illus. (p. 94)
—Fables: Homelands Leialoha, Steve, illus. (p. 559)
—March of the Wooden Soldiers. Buckingham, Mark, illus. (p. 1091)
—Mean Seasons. Buckingham, Mark, illus. (p. 1116)
—Proposition Player. Guinan, Paul & Randall, Ron, illus. (p. 1412)
—Storybook Love. Buckingham, Mark, illus. (p. 1663)
—To Kill a Bird. (p. 1759)
—Warriors Three: Dog Day Afternoon. (p. 1859)
Willingham, Bill, jt. auth. see Buckhingham, Mark.
Willingham, Bill & Jean, James. Sons of Empire. Leialoha, Steve et al, illus. (p. 1613)
Willingham, Bill, et al. Infinite Crisis Companion. Didio, Dan, ed. (p. 873)
—(Nearly) Great Escape (p. 1239)
—Vertigo First Offenses. (p. 1837)
—War Games. (p. 1857)
Willingham, Bob, jt. auth. see Chesterman, Barnaby.
Willingham, Elizabeth. Teens in England (p. 1715)
Willingham, Ellie. Wildwood. Willingham, Ellie, illus. (p. 1932)
Willingham, Fred, illus. see Bowie, C. W.
Willis & Ross, Melanie H. Dr Xargle's Book of Earth Hounds. (p. 475)
Willis, Ben. Ben's Flight South. (p. 165)
Willis, Caleb, illus. see Thayer, Kristi.
Willis, Carrie (Hunter) & Saunders, Lucy S. Those Who Dared: Stories of Early Days in Our Country. (p. 1740)
Willis, Chris. Dutch Clark: The Life of an NFL Legend & the Birth of the Detroit Lions. (p. 490)
Willis, Chris, ed. see Richardson, Angelique.
Willis, Cynthia Chapman. Dog Gone. (p. 461)
Willis, Dan, jt. auth. see Paquette, Lenny.
Willis, Danny. Why Pigeons? a Young Boy Discovers Gods Masterpieces. (p. 1925)
Willis, Drew, illus. see Bell, Hilari.
Willis, Drew, illus. see Freeman, Philip.
Willis, Drew, illus. see Packard, Edward.
Willis, Drew, illus. see Paulsen, Gary.
Willis, Drew, illus. see Weissman, Elissa Brent.
Willis, H. Thomas. 69 Reasons in Plain English Why Marriages Fail & a Smidgen of other Groovy Stuff. (p. 1998)
Willis, Helena, illus. see Widmark, Martin.
Willis Hudson, Cheryl. From Where I Stand. (p. 644)
—Hands Can. Bourke, John-Francis, illus. (p. 741)
—Sights I Love to See. (p. 1574)
—Sounds I Love to Hear. (p. 1615)
Willis, Janet. Dad's Delight. (p. 399)
Willis, Jaymie Janaye. Deal. (p. 418)
Willis, Jeanne. Boa's Bad Birthday. Ross, Tony, illus. (p. 205)
—Bog Baby. Millward, Gwen, illus. (p. 207)
—Caterpillar Dreams. Ross, Tony, illus. (p. 279)
—Cottonball Colin. Ross, Tony, illus. (p. 369)
—Cow Tripped over the Moon: a Nursery Rhyme Emergency. Stewart, Joel, illus. (p. 373)
—Daft Bat. Ross, Tony, illus. (p. 399)
—Dr Xargle's Book of Earth Hounds. Ross, Tony, illus. (p. 475)
—Dr Xargle's Book of Earth Relations. Ross, Tony, illus. (p. 475)
—Dr Xargle's Book of Earth Tiggers. Ross, Tony, illus. (p. 475)
—Dr Xargle's Book of Earthlets. Ross, Tony, illus. (p. 476)
—Elephants Can't Jump. Reynolds, Adrian, illus. (p. 512)
—Flabby Cat & Slobby Dog. Ross, Tony, illus. (p. 601)
—Fly, Chick, Fly! Ross, Tony, illus. (p. 609)
—Grill Pan Eddy. Ross, Tony, illus. (p. 724)
—Hippospotamus. Ross, Tony, illus. (p. 781)
—I'M Sure I Saw a Dinosaur. Reynolds, Adrian, illus. (p. 860)
—Mammoth Pie. Ross, Tony, illus. (p. 1085)
—Monster Bed. Varley, Susan, illus. (p. 1166)
—Never Too Little to Love. Fearnley, Jan, illus. (p. 1243)
—Nino Que Perdio el Ombligo. Ross, Tony, illus. (p. 1257)
—Nino y los Osos de Pelucke. (p. 1257)
—Old Dog. Ross, Tony, illus. (p. 1283)
—Penguin Pandemonium. (p. 1337)
—Penguin Pandemonium: the Rescue. (p. 1337)
—Prince Charmless. Ross, Tony, illus. (p. 1401)
—Really Rude Rhino. Ross, Tony, illus. (p. 1450)
—Shamanka. (p. 1559)
—Slug Needs a Hug! Ross, Tony, illus. (p. 1591)
—Stomp! Howard, Paul, illus. (p. 1652)
—Supercat vs. the Fry Thief. (p. 1682)
—Supercat vs the Party Pooper (Supercat, Book 2) (p. 1682)
—Tadpole's Promise. Ross, Tony, illus. (p. 1695)
—Tale of Georgie Grub. Chamberlain, Margaret, illus. (p. 1699)
—That's Not Funny! Reynolds, Adrian, illus. (p. 1727)
—Tormenta Monstruosa. (p. 1770)
—Upside down Babies. Reynolds, Adrian, illus. (p. 1825)
—Who's in the Loo? Reynolds, Adrian, illus. (p. 1920)
—Wind in the Wallows. Ross, Tony, illus. (p. 1935)
Willis, Jeanne, jt. auth. see Paul, Jeanne WI.
Willis, Jeanne, jt. auth. see Ross, Melanie H.
Willis, Jeanne, jt. auth. see Ross, Tony.
Willis, Jeanne & Jossen, Penelope. When Stephanie Smiled... (p. 1904)
Willis, Jeanne & Ross, Tony. Como Era Yo Cuando Era un Bebe? (p. 350)
—We're Going to a Party! (p. 1875)
Willis Jr., Joseph H. Silly the Scarecrow. (p. 1576)
Willis, Judith, tr. see Farre, Lluis.
Willis, Kristen. Honey's Big Adventure. (p. 795)
Willis, Laurie. Culture of Beauty. (p. 391)
—Divorce. (p. 455)
—Electronic Devices in Schools. (p. 509)
—Exercise & Fitness. (p. 548)
—Extremism. (p. 557)
—Gangs. (p. 655)
—Holocaust. (p. 789)
Willis, Laurie, ed. Teen Parenting. (p. 1713)
Willis, Lisa M. Bug's Picnic. (p. 237)
Willis, Mariaemma & Kindle Hodson, Victoria. Mid-life Crisis Begins in Kindergarten: How we learn the habit of settling for Less. (p. 1137)
Willis, McKenzie. Tales of the Rainbow Forest. Holland, Rick, illus. (p. 1702)
Willis, Meredith. City Built of Starships. (p. 323)
Willis, Meredith Sue. Billie of Fish House Lane. (p. 187)
—Blazing Pencils. (p. 199)
—Meli's Way. (p. 1125)
Willis, Michelle "Osawazhinkwaa-Ikwe. Kwezenhs Bimose. Willis, Michelle "Osawazhinkwaa-Ikwe, illus. (p. 969)
Willis, Nancy Carol. Red Knot: A Shorebird's Incredible Journey. (p. 1454)
Willis, Nancy Carol, illus. see Graham-Barber, Lynda.
Willis, Ninfas. PPO of Marriage. (p. 1391)
Willis, S. J. Wishwasher. (p. 1941)
Willis, Sherry. Cowboy Tad, the Triangle Man. (p. 374)
Willis, Sherry Galloway. Rex the Mighty Rectangle. (p. 1467)
Willis, Tacey Lynn. Ellie, Tellie & Mellie: Best Jungle Friends Forever. (p. 514)
Willis, Tania, illus. see Debram, Mio.
Willis, Terri. Afghanistan. (p. 26)
—Lebanon. (p. 986)
—Libya. (p. 1007)
—Venezuela. (p. 1835)
—Vietnam. (p. 1841)
Willis, Wren. Flower I Met in My Garden. (p. 607)
—Why Is My Name September? (p. 1925)
Willis-Crowley, Kate. Jack & Jill. (p. 902)
Willis-Crowley, Kate, illus. see McNiff, Dawn.
Willis-Gould, Glennis. Dad's New Shed. (p. 399)
Williston, Teresa Peirce. Hindu Stories. Squire, Maud Hunt, illus. (p. 780)
—Hindu Tales. Squire, Maud Hunt, illus. (p. 780)
Willker, Joshua D. G. Everything You Need to Know about Sports Gambling. (p. 546)
Willmott, H. P., et al. World War II. (p. 1959)
Willner, Judy. How My Sun Got Its Smile: The Story of Deana Vega. (p. 811)
Willner-Pardo, Gina. Hard Kind of Promise. (p. 748)
—Prettiest Doll. (p. 1398)
Willocks, Tim. Doglands. (p. 462)
Willoughby, Alana. Real Math Fourth Grade. (p. 1448)
Willoughby, Bebe. Saving Emma. Dacus, Bobbie, illus. (p. 1517)
Willoughby, Nick. Digital Filmmaking for Kids for Dummies. (p. 439)
Willoughby, R. Peter Goes Feet First! Buckley, Joel, illus. (p. 1346)
—Peter Puts His Foot in It! Buckley, Joel, illus. (p. 1347)
—Peter Strides Out. Buckley, Joel, illus. (p. 1347)
Willoughby, R. A. Guia de la Biblia para Ninos. (p. 729)
Willoughby, Robert. Children's Guide to the Bible. Morris, Tony, illus. (p. 303)
—Three Christmas Journeys. Miller, David, illus. (p. 1741)
—Three Easter Journeys. (p. 1742)
Willoughby, Stephen S., et al. Math Explorations & Applications: Practice Workbook. (p. 1106)
—Math Explorations & Applications: Practice Workbook Level 5. (p. 1106)
—Math Explorations & Applications: Enrichment Blackline Masters. (p. 1106)
—Math Explorations & Applications. (p. 1106)
—Real Math. (p. 1448)
Willoughby, Susan. Art, Music, & Writings from the Holocaust. (p. 102)
Willoughby, Yuko, illus. see Carvin, Rose-Mae.
Willoughby, Yuko, illus. see Hershey, Katherine.
Willoughby, Yuko, illus. see Lyster, R. Iona.
Willoughby, Yuko, illus. see Piepgrass, Arlene & Hershey, Katherine.
Willoughby, Yuko, illus. see Weitzel, Karen E.
Willow. Tirissa & the Necklace of Nulldor. (p. 1757)
Willow, Blm. I-Can't & I-Can! Morales, Jose, illus. (p. 837)
Willow Creek Press, creator. Secret of the Pasture. (p. 1542)
—What Camping Can Teach Us: Life's Lessons Learned from the Great Outdoors. (p. 1880)
Willowbough, W. K. Day at the Old Man's Garden. (p. 412)
WillowRaven, Aidana, illus. see Laughter, Jim.
WillowRaven, Aidana, illus. see Sansone, V. K.
Willows, Jennifer. Chess Master's Violin. (p. 298)
Willows, Vicky, jt. auth. see Stamper, Judith Bauer.
Wills, Adele. Texts Through History. (p. 1724)
Wills, Charles. America in The 1940s. (p. 59)

Wills, Charles A. America in The 1950s. (p. 59)
Wills, Chuck. Annie Oakley. (p. 87)
Wills, Henrietta. Wind Twins & the Oracle of Secrets. (p. 1935)
Wills, Joseph. World. (p. 1953)
Wills, Morgan B. Mulright Island. (p. 1189)
Wills, Ora, ed. Images in Black: A Pictorial History of Black Pensacola. (p. 860)
Wills, Steven R., jt. auth. see Wills, Susan.
Wills, Susan & Wills, Steven R. Meteorology: Predicting the Weather. (p. 1130)
Willsea, Hedley. Heath of the Graves. (p. 760)
Willson, Daria K. High Lee Land of Parnadia. (p. 778)
Willson, Sarah. Behold, No Cavities! A Visit to the Dentist. Moore, Harry, illus. (p. 160)
—Class Confusion. Dress, Robert, illus. (p. 327)
—Cookie Crisis! Ross, Sharon & Bergman, Shannon, illus. (p. 361)
—Do Not Wake Jake. Johnson, Meredith, illus. (p. 457)
—Dora's Halloween Adventure. Savitsky, Steven, illus. (p. 471)
—Just Say Please! Moore, Harry, illus. (p. 939)
—Mochila de Dora. Roper, Robert, illus. (p. 1157)
—Mother Knows Best. Dress, Robert, illus. (p. 1178)
—Pet Peeves! Nez, John A., illus. (p. 1345)
—Simon Says. Ulrich, George, illus. (p. 1577)
Willson, Sarah & Thompson Bros. Estrellita. Thompson Brothers Studio Staff, illus. (p. 538)
Willy, April, illus. see McClaine, Jamie.
Willy, April, illus. see St. Germain, Mark.
Willy, Romont, illus. see Canetti, Yanitzia.
Wilmes, Dick, jt. auth. see Wilmes, Liz.
Wilmes, Liz. Parachute Play: For Indoor/Outdoor Fun. (p. 1323)
Wilmes, Liz & Wilmes, Dick. 2's Experience - Stories. (p. 1991)
—Easel Art. Koeller, Carol, illus. (p. 498)
—Exploring Art: Create It - Display It. Healy, Jeane, illus. (p. 551)
—Felt Board Fun: For Everyday & Holidays. Dane, Donna, illus. (p. 581)
Wilmes, Liz, et al. Circle Time Book: For Holiday & Seasons. Dane, Donna, illus. (p. 321)
Wilmore, Kathy. Jackie Robinson: With a Discussion of Respect. (p. 904)
—Muhammad Ali: With a Discussion of Honesty. (p. 1189)
Wilmot, Anita, illus. see Neyer, Daniel.
Wilmot, Patti M. Forget-Me-Nots. (p. 619)
Wilmot, Rod. Meal of Magic Cards (p. 1116)
Wilmot-Buxton, E. M. Viking Gods & Heroes. (p. 1842)
Wilner, Barry. Basketball's Top 10 Scorers. (p. 143)
—Best Auto Racers of All Time. (p. 168)
—Best NBA Dunkers of All Time. (p. 170)
—Best NBA Shooters of All Time. (p. 170)
—Best NFL Defensive Players of All Time. (p. 170)
—Best NFL Receivers of All Time. (p. 170)
—Buffalo Bills. (p. 235)
—Dallas Cowboys. (p. 401)
—Eli Manning: A Football Star Who Cares. (p. 512)
—Football's Top 10 Quarterbacks. (p. 615)
—Football's Top 10 Running Backs. (p. 615)
—Miami Dolphins. (p. 1133)
—New England Patriots. (p. 1244)
—New York Giants. (p. 1248)
—New York Jets. (p. 1248)
—Peyton Manning: A Football Star Who Cares. (p. 1349)
—Philadelphia Eagles. (p. 1350)
—Sports Great Peyton Manning. (p. 1632)
—Super Bowl. (p. 1679)
—Tennessee Volunteers. (p. 1720)
—Tom Brady: A Football Star Who Cares. (p. 1762)
—USC Trojans. (p. 1827)
—Washington Redskins. (p. 1860)
Wilner, Barry, jt. auth. see Gregory, Josh.
Wilsdon, Christina. Alligator Adventure in Florida. Mayo, Frank, illus. (p. 47)
—Amusement Park Mystery in Ohio. Ebert, Len, illus. (p. 66)
—Animal Defenses. (p. 77)
—Arthropods on Land. (p. 103)
—Baboons. (p. 124)
—Cats. (p. 280)
—Dogs. (p. 462)
—Ducks. (p. 488)
—For Horse-Crazy Girls Only: Everything You Want to Know about Horses. Underhill, Alecia, illus. (p. 615)
—Hippopotamus. (p. 781)
—Hippopotamuses. (p. 781)
—Horses. (p. 800)
—Kangaroos. (p. 942)
—Lights! Action! California! Hockerman, Dennis, illus. (p. 1016)
—Monkeys. (p. 1166)
—New York Sailing Adventure. Hockerman, Dennis, illus. (p. 1248)
—On the Trail of Bigfoot in Washington. McCreary, Jane, illus. (p. 1291)
—Otters. (p. 1307)
—Pigs. (p. 1358)
—Polar Bears. (p. 1379)
—Seals. (p. 1536)
—Sharks. (p. 1562)
—Sheep. (p. 1564)
—Snakes. (p. 1596)
—Tigers. (p. 1749)
—Turtles. (p. 1799)
—White-Tailed Deer. (p. 1913)
—Wild Ride in Texas. Jaekel, Susan, illus. (p. 1930)
—Wolves. (p. 1945)
—Zebras. (p. 1985)
Wilsdon, Christina, jt. auth. see Barnard, Edward S.
Wilsdon, Christina, jt. auth. see Disney Book Group Staff.
Wilsdon, Christina, jt. auth. see Greenberg, Daniel A.
Wilsdon, Christina, jt. auth. see Wilson, Christina.
Wilsdorf, Anne, illus. see Bluemle, Elizabeth.
Wilsdorf, Anne, illus. see Lindbergh, Reeve.
Wilsdorf, Anne, illus. see Look, Lenore.
Wilsdorf, Anne, illus. see Miller, Pat Zietlow.
Wilsdorf, Anne, illus. see Protopopescu, Orel Odinov.
Wilsdorf, Anne, illus. see Spinelli, Eileen.
Wilsdorf, Anne, illus. see Van Leeuwen, Jean.
Wilsdorf, Anne, jt. auth. see Look, Lenore.
Wilshire, Florence. All from the Skies. (p. 44)
Wilshire, Florence A. Messages from the Skies. (p. 1129)
—They're all from the Skies. (p. 1732)
Wilson. Keely, Ivy, & Me. (p. 946)
Wilson, A. C., jt. auth. see Wilson, A. c.
Wilson, A. c. & Wilson, A. C. Ambersil - the Legacy of Mr Harrison. (p. 57)
Wilson, Abby. What Makes Rain? (p. 1892)
Wilson, Adele Tolley. Plum Gum & Other Chunk Poems: Teacher Tested Kid Approved Poems for Building Fluency Through Phonics. (p. 1374)
Wilson, Agy. From Heaven to Earth - Angel on My Shoulder. Wilson, Agy, illus. (p. 642)
Wilson, Alex, illus. see Hill, Douglas.
Wilson, Alexandria M. Happy Birthday Gideon. (p. 744)
Wilson, Alisha, illus. see Edman Lamote, Lisa.
Wilson, Alison, ed. see Gioffre, Rosalba, et al.
Wilson, Alonzo S., illus. see Renfroe, Ann.
Wilson, A'ndrea J. Ready & ABLE Teens: Ebony's Bad Habit. (p. 1447)
Wilson, Angela. Frog Makes a Friend. Wilson, Whiteigh & Wilson, John, illus. (p. 640)
—Grandma's Traditions. Basta, Stormie, illus. (p. 709)
—My Aunt & Me. Basta, Stormie, illus. (p. 1196)
—Tara the Terrified Turtle. Basta, Stormie, illus. (p. 1706)
Wilson, Angie. Dori's Gift. Teets, Ashley, illus. (p. 471)
Wilson, Ann, illus. see Casey, Dawn.
Wilson, Anna. Dotty Dalmatian (p. 472)
—Kitten Smitten (p. 962)
—Monkey Business (p. 1165)
—Monkey Madness: The Only Way Is Africa! (p. 1165)
—Poodle Problem (p. 1383)
—Puppy Party (p. 1418)
—Smug Pug (p. 1595)
—Summer's Shadow (p. 1675)
Wilson, Anne. Lord Is My Shepherd. Wilson, Anne, illus. (p. 1052)
Wilson, Anne, illus. see Bateson Hill, Margaret.
Wilson, Anne, illus. see Blackstone, Stella & Broadbent, Jim.
Wilson, Anne, illus. see Blackstone, Stella.
Wilson, Anne, illus. see Casey, Dawn, et al.
Wilson, Anne, illus. see Casey, Dawn.
Wilson, Anne, illus. see Krebs, Laurie.
Wilson, Anne, illus. see Morpurgo, Michael.
Wilson, Anne, illus. see Piper, Sophie.
Wilson, Anne, illus. see Schlafer, Linda.
Wilson, Annemarie. What Could Have Happened to Max? (p. 1881)
Wilson, Annette. K'Nyah's Big Celebration. (p. 966)
Wilson, Anthony. Science Museum Book of Amazing Facts: Energy. (p. 1526)
Wilson, Antoine. Assassination of William McKinley. (p. 107)
—S. E. Hinton. (p. 1499)
Wilson, Antoine, jt. auth. see Franklin, Joseph.
Wilson, Antoine, jt. auth. see Kidde, Rita.
Wilson, Antoine, jt. auth. see Murley, Leon.
Wilson, Audrey. Dante Goes to the Circus. (p. 406)
Wilson, Barbara. Bud the Pup. Caracino, Leah, illus. (p. 234)
—City & Guilds: Information Technology. (p. 323)
—Jack & His Pal Max. Caracino, Leah, illus. (p. 902)
—Milly & Her Kittens. Fine, Aron, illus. (p. 1144)
—Mrs. Hen & Her Six Chicks. Fine, Aron, illus. (p. 1187)
—Mrs. Piglin Visits Sick Mr. Fox. Caracino, Leah, illus. (p. 1187)
—Ted & Matt. Caracino, Leah, illus. (p. 1712)
Wilson, Barbara E. Small Enough Tall Enough. Gospodinov, George, illus. (p. 1592)
Wilson, Barbara K. Day of the Elephant. Lessac, Frané, illus. (p. 414)
Wilson, Barbara Ker & So, Meilo. Wishbones: A Folk Tale from China. (p. 1940)
Wilson, Barbara Rogers. Deva & the Soul Snatcher an Environmental Fantasy. (p. 431)
Wilson, Barbara-Ann. Faerie Hill. (p. 562)
Wilson, Bernie. Los Angeles Angels. (p. 1053)
—Los Angeles Clippers. (p. 1053)
—San Diego Chargers. (p. 1510)
—San Diego Padres. (p. 1510)
Wilson, Betsy, jt. auth. see Wilson, John.
Wilson, Betty. Printed & Lace Handkerchiefs: Interpreting a Popular 20th Century Collectible. (p. 1407)
Wilson, Betty, jt. auth. see Wilson, Elizabeth.
Wilson, Bill. Dorf's Art Lesson. Wilson, Bill, illus. (p. 471)
Wilson, Bob. Football Fred (p. 615)
—Stanley Bagshaw & the Fourteen-Foot Wheel. (p. 1639)
—Stanley Bagshaw & the Mafeking Square Cheese Robbery. (p. 1639)
—Stanley Bagshaw & the Twenty Two Ton Whale. (p. 1639)
Wilson, Bonnita, illus. see Patterson, Trina Dawkins.
Wilson, Brenda. Totally Amazing Careers in Environmental Sciences. (p. 1771)
Wilson, Bruce A. Design Dimension & Tolerancing. (p. 429)
—Design Dimensioning & Tolerancing. (p. 429)
Wilson, Bryan M. Benjamin's Report Card Blues. (p. 165)
Wilson, Budge. Courtship (p. 373)
—Fear of Angelina Domino. (p. 579)
—Fiddle for Angus. (p. 583)
—Fiddle for Angus. Tooke, Susan, illus. (p. 583)
—Leaving (p. 986)
—Lorinda's Diary (p. 1053)
Wilson, Budge & Roscoe, Terry. Imperfect Perfect Christmas. (p. 862)
Wilson, Camilla. Civil War Spies: Behind Enemy Lines. (p. 325)
—Frederick Douglass: A Voice for Freedom in the 1800s. (p. 633)
Wilson, CeCe. Bees, Bees, Bees. (p. 158)
—Lily's Tomato. (p. 1018)
—Thunder Cloud Cookies. (p. 1746)
Wilson, Charles, jt. auth. see Schlosser, Eric.
Wilson, Charles Banks, illus. see Kjelgaard, Jim.
Wilson, Charles Banks, illus. see Reeder, Red.
Wilson, Christina & Wilsdon, Christina. Deer. (p. 423)
Wilson, Christopher. Understanding A/S Level Government Politics. (p. 1815)
Wilson, Claire, jt. auth. see Kelly, Evelyn B.
Wilson, Cristi. Just Because. Wilson, Cristi, illus. (p. 938)
Wilson, D. Arthur. Little Red Rhupert. (p. 1035)
Wilson, Daniel. Huxtabook: Recipes from Sea, Land & Earth. (p. 830)
Wilson, Daniel H. Boy & His Bot. (p. 217)
Wilson, Daniel H. & Trippe, Dean. Bro-Jitsu: The Martial Art of Sibling Smackdown. McClaine, Les, illus. (p. 230)
Wilson, Daniel J. Polio (p. 1380)
Wilson, Danny. Lots & Lots of Orange: A Trip to Neyland Stadium. Wilson, Danny, illus. (p. 1057)
Wilson, Dave. Rock Formations: Categorical Answers to How Band Names Were Formed. (p. 1482)
Wilson, David. Adventures of Jack Bennett James Bay or Bust. (p. 19)
—Adventures of Jack Bennett Winter Rescue. (p. 19)
—Ciudad en Ruinas (The Ruined City) (p. 324)
—Strategies for Application: Applying Information for Classroom, Homework, & Test Success. (p. 1666)
Wilson, David Cramb. Day that the Fairies stole Badger! (p. 414)
Wilson, David Henry, jt. auth. see Bloom, Steve.
Wilson, David Henry, tr. see Boie, Kirsten.
Wilson, David Henry, tr. see Kruss, James.
Wilson, David Henry, tr. see Reh, Rusalka.
Wilson, David Lloyd. Some Dogs Fly (p. 1609)
Wilson, Db. Teale Tales: Wyv Land of Magik. (p. 1710)
Wilson, Deborah A. What's Your Number? 3 Digit Lottery Tracker. (p. 1900)
Wilson, Debra. 65 Mustang: A Novel. (p. 1997)
Wilson, Diane Lee. Black Storm Comin' (p. 197)
—Firehorse. (p. 592)
—I Rode a Horse of Milk White Jade. (p. 844)
—Raven Speak. (p. 1441)
—To Ride the Gods' Own Stallion. (p. 1759)
—Tracks. (p. 1775)
Wilson, Donna. Creative Creatures: A Step-by-Step Guide to Making Your Own Creations. Wilson, Donna, illus. (p. 379)
Wilson, Douglas. Blackthorn Winter. Bently, Peter, illus. (p. 198)
—Maude, the Flop-Eared Mule. Fore, Elizabeth, illus. (p. 1110)
Wilson, Douglas J., jt. auth. see Nance, James B.
Wilson, Douglas, reader. What I Learned in Narnia. (p. 1886)
Wilson, Edwin Graves, ed. Poetry for Young People: Maya Angelou. Lagarrigue, Jerome, illus. (p. 1376)
Wilson, Elaine. Fisherman Jack's Secret. (p. 599)
Wilson, Elaine Moody. Fisherman Jack Meets the River Creatures Ducker Signs Plus, illus. (p. 599)
Wilson, Elizabeth, jt. auth. see De Los Heros, Luis.
Wilson, Elizabeth & de los Heros, Luis. Chifa Chi's Little Adventure in Cuzco & MacHu Picchu. (p. 301)
Wilson, Elizabeth & Wilson, Betty. Song Dogs. (p. 1611)
Wilson, Ellen Judy & Reill, Peter Hanns. Encyclopedia of the Enlightenment. (p. 525)
Wilson, Emily. Inside Beaver Lodges. (p. 876)
—Madrigueras de Castores (Inside Beaver Lodges) (p. 1070)
Wilson, Emily, jt. auth. see Mills, Nathan.
Wilson, Essdale. Growing up on the cul de Sac. (p. 727)
—Horses, Tigers & Neighbors. (p. 800)
Wilson, Etta, jt. auth. see Kennedy, Dana.
Wilson, Eva Adriana. My Power Ball. (p. 1217)
Wilson, F. Paul. Infernal. (p. 873)
—Jack: Secret Histories. (p. 902)
Wilson, F. Paul & Brackett, Leigh. Hounds of Skaith Mona, Erik et al, eds. (p. 802)
Wilson, Gahan, illus. see Bierce, Ambrose.
Wilson, Gahan, illus. see Poe, Edgar Allen.
Wilson, Gahan, illus. see Roy, Keri Anne & Holt, K. A.
Wilson, Gahan, jt. auth. see Poe, Edgar Allen.
Wilson, George. Arron the Royal Archer. (p. 101)
Wilson, George H. Arrival of Grand Princess Leandra. (p. 101)
—Legend of Thompson the Gazelle. (p. 989)
—Message of the Writing Spider. (p. 1129)
—Path of the Little Porcupine. (p. 1328)
—Perils of Cory the Caterpillar. (p. 1343)
Wilson, Geraline. Billy & Willy Learn to Share. (p. 187)
Wilson, Gerrard. Alice on Top of the World. (p. 39)
Wilson, Grant, jt. auth. see Hawes, Jason.
Wilson, Hannah. Flip the Flaps: Baby Animals. Palin, Nicki, illus. (p. 605)
—Flip the Flaps: Jungle Animals. Palin, Nicki, illus. (p. 605)
—Flip the Flaps: Pets. Butler, John, illus. (p. 605)
—Kingfisher Readers L2: Combine Harvesters. (p. 960)
—Kingfisher Readers L2: Sun, Moon, & Stars. Feldman, Thea, ed. (p. 960)
—Life-Size Reptiles. (p. 1013)
—Swimming the Bosphorus. (p. 1691)
Wilson, Hannah, ed. see Dorling Kindersley Publishing Staff.
Wilson, Hannah & Mendez, Simon. Flip the Flaps: Seashore. (p. 605)
Wilson, Hannah & Parrish, Emma. Hoppity Frog: A Hide-and-Seek Book. (p. 797)
Wilson, Heather Gemmen. Lydia Barnes & the Blood Diamond Treasure. (p. 1066)
—Lydia Barnes & the Escape from Shark Bay. (p. 1066)
—Lydia Barnes & the Mystery of the Broken Cross. (p. 1066)
Wilson, Helen Hughes, illus. see Phelps, Netta Sheldon.
Wilson, Henrike, illus. see Stohner, Anu.
Wilson, Henrike, jt. auth. see Stohner, Anu.
Wilson Hills, Atheen. Little Crane: A Fairy Tale for All Ages. (p. 1026)
Wilson, Hoyt R. Joe Louis: The Brown Bomber. (p. 920)
—They Never Gave Up. (p. 1732)
Wilson, Hugh T. Annual Editions: Drugs, Society, & Behavior 04/05. (p. 87)
Wilson, Ian. Murder at Golgotha: Revisiting the Most Famous Crime Scene in History. (p. 1192)
Wilson, Iris. Boys Dance Too! (p. 220)
Wilson, J. H. Bright Sunset. (p. 228)
Wilson, J. M. & Zolkowski, Cathy A. Blue: Adventures of a Gymnast. (p. 202)
Wilson, Jacqueline. Beauty & the Beast. (p. 154)
—Beauty & the Beast. Kavanagh, Peter, illus. (p. 154)
—Best Friends. Sharratt, Nick, illus. (p. 169)
—Candyfloss. Sharratt, Nick, illus. (p. 261)
—Cookie. Sharratt, Nick, illus. (p. 361)
—Double Act. Sharratt, Nick & Heap, Sue, illus. (p. 472)
—Kiss. (p. 961)
—Story of Tracy Beaker. Sharratt, Nick, illus. (p. 1662)
Wilson, Jacqueline & Carey, Joanna. Interview with Jacqueline Wilson. (p. 881)
Wilson, Jacqueline & Jacqueline, Wilson. Doble Funcion. (p. 459)
Wilson, Jacqui. Little Johnny's Faith Adventures: Our Beginnings. (p. 1029)
—Little Johnny's Faith Adventures: Creation Curiosity! (p. 1029)
Wilson, James. Collected Works of James Wilson (p. 339)
Wilson, James, ed. Rhode Island Treasures. (p. 1468)
Wilson, James Q. & Dilulio, John J., Jr. American Governement. (p. 61)
—American Government: Institutions & Policies. (p. 61)
Wilson, Janet. LSU Night Before Christmas. Verrett, Michael, illus. (p. 1061)
—One Peace: True Stories of Young Activists (p. 1296)
—Our Heroes: How Kids Are Making a Difference (p. 1309)
—Our Rights: How Kids Are Changing the World (p. 1309)
—Severn & the Day She Silenced the World (p. 1555)
—Shannen & the Dream for a School (p. 1559)
Wilson, Janet, illus. see Granfield, Linda.
Wilson, Janet, illus. see Parker, Marjorie Blain.
Wilson, Janet, illus. see Quinlan, Patricia.
Wilson, Janet, illus. see Spalding, Andrea.
Wilson, Janet & Second Story Press Staff. Our Earth: How Kids Are Saving the Planet (p. 1308)
Wilson, Janet & Wilson, Michael. Battle for the Book of Good Deeds. (p. 145)
Wilson, Jef. Hiking for Fun! Wilson, Jef, illus. (p. 779)
Wilson, Jenine. My Familiar. (p. 1202)
Wilson, Jerry S. & Blumenthal, Ira. Managing Brand You: Seven Steps to Creating Your Most Successful Self (p. 1086)
Wilson, Jesse. Night the Moon Ate My Room! (p. 1254)
Wilson, Jessica. Stary's Secret. Tintjer, Birgit, illus. (p. 1644)
Wilson, Jim. Uma Thurman. (p. 1810)
Wilson, Jodi L. When I Grow Up. Anderson, Kari A., illus. (p. 1902)
Wilson, John. Across Frozen Seas. (p. 9)
—Adrift in Time. (p. 13)
—Battle Scars. (p. 147)
—Bitter Ashes: The Story of WW II. (p. 194)
—Bones (p. 209)
—Broken Arrow (p. 230)
—Death on the River (p. 420)
—Desperate Glory: The Story of WWI. (p. 430)
—Discovering the Arctic: The Story of John Rae. (p. 449)
—Failed Hope: The Story of the Lost Peace. (p. 562)
—Failed Hope: The Story of the Lost Peace (Large Print 16pt) (p. 562)
—Flags of War. (p. 602)
—Flames of the Tiger. (p. 602)
—Four Steps to Death. (p. 625)
—Ghost Moon (p. 671)
—Ghosts of James Bay. (p. 672)
—Lost Cause (p. 1055)
—Porcupine's Quills. (p. 1386)
—Red Goodwin. (p. 1454)
—Stolen (p. 1652)
—Victorio's War (p. 1840)
—Written in Blood (p. 1965)
Wilson, John, illus. see Wilson, Angela.
Wilson, John & Wilson, Betsy. Followers of Jesus. Powell, Kara Eckmann, ed. (p. 612)
Wilson, Jon. Statue of Liberty. (p. 1645)
—White House. (p. 1913)
Wilson, Judith. Childrens Spaces: From Zero to Ten. Treloar, Debi, photos by. (p. 304)
Wilson, Julius & Benchmark Education Co. Staff. I Was a 21st Century Civil War Reporter. (p. 848)
Wilson, K. C. Where's Daddy? The Mythologies Behind Custody-Access-Support. (p. 1910)
Wilson, Karen Collett. Autumn Rescue. Zerga, Susan A., photos by. (p. 118)
Wilson, Karma. Animal Strike at the Zoo - It's True! Spengler, Margaret, illus. (p. 80)
—Baby Cakes. Williams, Sam, illus. (p. 125)
—Baby, I Love You. Williams, Sam, illus. (p. 126)
—Bear Counts. Chapman, Jane, illus. (p. 150)
—Bear Feels Scared. Chapman, Jane, illus. (p. 150)
—Bear Feels Sick. Chapman, Jane, illus. (p. 150)
—Bear Hugs: Romantically Ridiculous Animal Rhymes. Watts, Suzanne, illus. (p. 150)
—Bear Says Thanks. Chapman, Jane, illus. (p. 151)
—Bear Sees Colors. Chapman, Jane, illus. (p. 151)
—Bear Snores On. Chapman, Jane, illus. (p. 151)
—Bear Stays up for Christmas. Chapman, Jane, illus. (p. 151)
—Bear Wants More. Chapman, Jane, illus. (p. 151)
—Bear's Loose Tooth. Chapman, Jane, illus. (p. 152)
—Bear's New Friend. Chapman, Jane, illus. (p. 152)
—Beautiful Babies. Wilson, Karma, photos by. (p. 153)
—Cow Loves Cookies. Hall, Marcellus, illus. (p. 373)
—Don't Be Afraid, Little Pip. Chapman, Jane, illus. (p. 466)
—Duddle Puck: The Puddle Duck. Hall, Marcellus, illus. (p. 489)
—Frog in the Bog. Rankin, Joan, illus. (p. 640)
—Hello, Calico! Erdogan, Buket, illus. (p. 763)
—Hilda Must Be Dancing. Watts, Suzanne, illus. (p. 779)
—Hogwash! McMullan, Jim, illus. (p. 787)
—Horseplay! McMullan, Jim, illus. (p. 800)
—How to Bake an American Pie. Colón, Raúl, illus. (p. 814)
—I Will Rejoice: Celebrating Psalm 118. Bates, Amy June, illus. (p. 848)
—Mama Always Comes Home. Dyer, Brooke, illus. (p. 1084)
—Mama, Why? Mendez, Simon, illus. (p. 1084)

—Moose Tracks! Davis, Jack E., illus. (p. 1173)
—Mortimer's Christmas Manger. Chapman, Jane, illus. (p. 1176)
—Mortimer's First Garden. Andreasen, Dan, illus. (p. 1176)
—Never, Ever Shout in a Zoo. Cushman, Douglas, illus. (p. 1242)
—Princess Me. Unzner, Christa, illus. (p. 1404)
—Sleepyhead. Segal, John, illus. (p. 1590)
—Trick or Treat, Calico! Erdogan, Buket, illus. (p. 1786)
—What's in the Egg, Little Pip? Chapman, Jane, illus. (p. 1898)
—What's the Weather Inside? Blitt, Barry, illus. (p. 1900)
—Where Is Home, Little Pip? Chapman, Jane, illus. (p. 1908)
—Who Goes There? Currey, Anna, illus. (p. 1915)
—Whopper Cake. Hillenbrand, Will, illus. (p. 1920)
Wilson, Karma & Chapman, Jane. Bear Snores On. (p. 151)
Wilson, Katherine, illus. see Williams, Margery.
Wilson, Kay, illus. see Mika, Sharon Ann.
Wilson, Keith, illus. see Fandel, Jennifer, et al.
Wilson, Keith, ed. Aircraft. (p. 31)
Wilson, Kevin. Brown Spot. (p. 232)
Wilson, Kris E. & Maurer, Toby. How Putter Learned His ABC's: An alphabet Book for Your Littlest Golfer. (p. 812)
Wilson, Kyla. Stretch It Yoga. (p. 1667)
Wilson, Kyla, jt. auth. see Crabtree Editors.
Wilson, Land. Sofia's Dream. O'Malley, Judy, ed. (p. 1605)
Wilson, Laura. How I Survived the Oregon Trail: The Journal of Jesse Adams. (p. 810)
Wilson, Laurie Harman. Treasures of Destiny. (p. 1782)
Wilson, Leonard W. Realms of Flimenia Jeremyes Journey. (p. 1450)
Wilson, Leslie & Wilson, Leslie Erika. Saving Rafael. (p. 1517)
Wilson, Leslie Erika, jt. auth. see Wilson, Leslie.
Wilson, Lia. Class Treats: Take-To-School Goodies for Every Occasion: All Nut-Free Recipes. (p. 327)
Wilson, Liesl-Yvette. Balloon & a Bear. (p. 135)
Wilson, Lois Miriam & Fox, Matthew. Miriam, Mary & Me. (p. 1149)
Wilson, Lorna, illus. see Leighton, Noreen.
Wilson, Lynda Farrington, illus. see Shan Shan, Kathryn Velikanje.
Wilson, Lynda Farrington, illus. see Shan Shan, Kathryn.
Wilson, Lynda Farrington, illus. see Velikanje, Kathryn.
Wilson, Lynn. Ava & Drew Join the Cheese Heroin Patrol (p. 118)
Wilson, M. Leonora. Karol from Poland: The Life of Pope John Paul II for Children. Koch, Carla, illus. (p. 944)
Wilson, Maggie, jt. auth. see Dawson, Ian.
Wilson, Mark. Mark Wilson's Complete Course in Magic. (p. 1095)
Wilson, Mark, illus. see Duder, Tessa.
Wilson, Mark, illus. see McLaughlin, Richard.
Wilson, Mark A. Amazing Gift from the Woods. (p. 54)
—Legend of Crawley Creek. (p. 988)
—Old Man's Secret Friend (p. 1284)
Wilson, Marlys, jt. auth. see Henne, R. J.
Wilson, Marshall, jt. auth. see Wilson, Robert.
Wilson, Martha. Latin Primer II - Student. (p. 979)
Wilson, Martin. Uniquely Mississippi (p. 1818)
—What They Always Tell Us. (p. 1894)
Wilson, Martin, jt. auth. see McClellan, Adam.
Wilson, Mary. Kopper "K" Kidds & Corky. (p. 967)
—Mark & the Mega Buffet. (p. 1095)
Wilson, Mary & Berrios, Frank. Disney Tales of Magic (p. 453)
Wilson, Mary Ann, illus. see Cunningham, Kay.
Wilson, Mary Ellen. Cutie Patootie & Grandpa Grouchy Pants. (p. 396)
Wilson, Matt, jt. creator see Snoddy, Brian.
Wilson, Matthew. Scrooge & Santa GN. (p. 1533)
Wilson, Melissa Anne. Nalyn & the Indigo Pearl. (p. 1228)
Wilson, Michael. Storytelling & Theatre: Contemporary Professional Storytellers & Their Art. (p. 1664)
Wilson, Michael, jt. auth. see Wilson, Janet.
Wilson, Michael R. Endocrine System: Hormones, Growth, & Development. (p. 527)
—Frequently Asked Questions about How the Teen Brain Works. (p. 636)
—Hunger: Food Insecurity in America. (p. 827)
—Hunger: Food Insecurity in the United States. (p. 827)
—Living a Heart-Healthy Life. (p. 1040)
Wilson, Michelle L. Nash Happy from Cloud 9: The Unassigned Mission. (p. 1230)
Wilson, Mike. Britney Spears. (p. 230)
—Civil Liberties. (p. 324)
—Destiny's Child. (p. 431)
—Divorce. (p. 455)
—Domestic Violence. (p. 465)
—Election Process. (p. 508)
—Eminem. (p. 519)
—Lennox Lewis. (p. 991)
—Mahatma Gandhi (p. 1076)
—Poverty. (p. 1389)
—Terrorism. (p. 1722)
—Williams Sisters: Venus & Serena. (p. 1934)
Wilson, Mimi & Lagerborg, Mary Beth. Once-a-Month Cooking: A Proven System for Spending Less Time in the Kitchen & Enjoying Delicious, Homemade Meals Every Day. (p. 1292)
Wilson, Moira. How to Sparkle at Counting to 10. (p. 821)
Wilson, Mollie. Duck Tape 2. (p. 488)
Wilson, Mollie, jt. auth. see Lucht, Susan.
Wilson, Murray. Goofus & Other Silly Poems Morrison, Tyler, illus. (p. 702)
Wilson, N. D. 100 Cupboards. (p. 1998)
—Boys of Blur. (p. 220)
—Chestnut King. (p. 298)
—Dragon & the Garden. (p. 476)
—Dragon's Tooth. (p. 479)
—Drowned Vault. (p. 486)
—Empire of Bones. (p. 521)
—Empire of Bones (Ashtown Burials #3) (p. 521)
—In the Time of Noah. (p. 867)
—Leepike Ridge. (p. 987)
—Ninja Boy Goes to School. (p. 1256)
Wilson, N. D. & Wilson, Nathan D. Dandelion Fire. (p. 403)
Wilson, Nancy. Our Mother Tongue: A Guide to English Grammar. (p. 1309)
—Our Mother Tongue - Answer Key. (p. 1309)
Wilson, Natashya. Bats. (p. 145)
—Bears: Osos. Beullens, Nathalie, tr. (p. 151)
—Bears. (p. 151)
—Bears / Osos. (p. 151)
—Census & America's People: Analyzing Data Using Line Graphs & Tables. (p. 287)
—How to Draw the Life & Times of Herbert Hoover. (p. 819)
—How to Draw the Life & Times of William Howard Taft. (p. 819)
Wilson, Natashya, jt. auth. see Thomas, Zachary.
Wilson, Natashya & Natashya, Wilson. How to Draw the Life & Times of James Earl Carter Jr. (p. 819)
Wilson, Nathan D., jt. auth. see Wilson, N. D.
Wilson, Nathaniel. Jessie's Big Move. Shoopik, Marina, illus. (p. 914)
Wilson, Nicola. B. B. & the New Student. (p. 122)
Wilson, Nicole. Callie Gang: Who Said Cats Don't Talk? (p. 254)
Wilson, Nolan. Teen's Guide to Getting Ahead: How to Succeed in High School & Beyond. (p. 1715)
Wilson, Norah & Doherty, Heather. Embrace the Night. (p. 517)
Wilson, P. G. Big Move: Fear vs Communication. (p. 182)
Wilson, P. M., ed. see Ferguson, R. L.
Wilson, P. R. Readle the Reading Beetle: The Journey to Love Read Land. (p. 1447)
Wilson, Pamela J. Tales from Tubblewood Too: Miss Duck to the Rescue. (p. 1702)
—Tales from Tubblewood Too. (p. 1702)
Wilson, Patricia. Rocking Horse & the Fighting Fish. (p. 1483)
Wilson, Patricia P. Rocking Horse & the Fighting Fish. (p. 1483)
Wilson, Patrick. Navigation & Signaling. (p. 1238)
—Ropes & Knots for Survival. Carney, John, ed. (p. 1488)
—Survival Equipment. (p. 1686)
—Survival Equipment. Carney, John, ed. (p. 1686)
—Survival First Aid. (p. 1686)
—Survival First Aid. Carney, John, ed. (p. 1686)
—Surviving by Trapping, Fishing, & Eating Plants. Carney, John, ed. (p. 1687)
—Surviving Natural Disasters. (p. 1687)
—Surviving Natural Disasters. Carney, John, ed. (p. 1687)
—Surviving with Navigation & Signaling. Carney, John, ed. (p. 1687)
—Trapping, Fishing, & Plant Food. (p. 1779)
—Urban Survival Techniques. (p. 1825)
Wilson, Patty Ann. Where Do I Belong? (p. 1907)
Wilson, Pauline. Animal & Other Antics. (p. 76)
Wilson, Peter L., jt. ed. see Mandl, Dave.
Wilson, Phil. Medieval Castle: A Three Dimensional. (p. 1119)
Wilson, Phil, illus. see Brown, Charlotte Lewis & Brown, Charlotte L.
Wilson, Phil, illus. see Brown, Charlotte Lewis.
Wilson, Phil, illus. see DeLand, M. Maitland.
Wilson, Phil, illus. see Horner, Jack.
Wilson, Phil, illus. see Livshits, Larisa.
Wilson, Phyllis M. My Two Friends. (p. 1220)
Wilson, Porcia D. My Pink Friend: A Rhyming Love Story. (p. 1217)
Wilson, R. Dean. Boiler Operator's Workbook: Text. (p. 207)
—Boiler Operator's Workbook: Answer Key. (p. 207)
Wilson, Rachel M. Don't Touch. (p. 469)
Wilson, Randall W. Group 72. (p. 725)
Wilson, Ray. Kelsey's Lessons on Africa Vol 2. (p. 948)
Wilson, Raylene Jenee, illus. see Whitmore, Hugh.
Wilson, Rebekah. Grandmother's Hope Chest: Lucie's Snowflakes. (p. 709)
—Grandmother's Hope Chest: The Running Rooster. (p. 709)
—Hope Chest: A Legacy of Love (p. 796)
Wilson, Rene. Kenny Chesney. (p. 949)
Wilson, Ricky Derail. Mirror of Hope Mirror of Fame. (p. 1149)
Wilson, Robert. Estudiante's Planificador - La Escuela a la Casa Heramienta de Communicacion. (p. 538)
—Pippy: The Miracle of A Dream. (p. 1362)
Wilson, Robert & Wilson, Marshall. Liberta Desarrollo (IEP) (p. 1005)
Wilson, Robert B. Learn it Fast! NJ ASK4 Math. (p. 983)
Wilson, Roberta, illus. see Jacobson, John.
Wilson, Robin, jt. auth. see Flood, Raymond.
Wilson, Robin M., ed. see Dell, Jacob J. & Dell, Rachel E.
Wilson, Rock. If I Had My Way—/By Rock S. Wilson ; Illustrated by Carol Dixon. Dixon, Carol, illus. (p. 853)
Wilson, Roger, jt. auth. see Davidson, Margaret.
Wilson, Roman. How Does a Battery Work? (p. 808)
Wilson, Ron, et al. Captain America: Scourge of the Underworld. (p. 263)
Wilson, Ronald. Call Waiting: Hearing & Answering God's Call on Your Life. Keels, Steve, ed. (p. 254)
Wilson, Rosalee. Elijah the Penguin. (p. 512)
—Mushy Mouse Tale. (p. 1193)
Wilson, Rosie. Discover Iran. (p. 447)
—Discover Poland. (p. 448)
—Fashion Industry. (p. 575)
—Media & Communications Industry. (p. 1118)
Wilson, Rosie, jt. auth. see Bowden, Rob.
Wilson, Rosie & Bowden, Rob. Modern Africa (p. 1158)
Wilson, Rosie & Ward, Chris. Discover Poland. (p. 448)
—Discover South Africa. (p. 448)
Wilson, Rosie, et al. Modern Africa (p. 1158)
Wilson Sanger, Amy, jt. auth. see Sanger, Amy Wilson.
Wilson, Sarah. Hocus Focus. Wummer, Amy, tr. (p. 787)
—Love & Kisses. Sweet, Melissa, illus. (p. 1059)
—Moms Are the Best! (p. 1163)
Wilson, Sarah, jt. auth. see Random House Staff.
Wilson, Sarah, jt. auth. see Random House.
Wilson, Scott. Embracing Bureaucracy. (p. 517)
Wilson, Scott & Wilkinson, Jody. Eating Healthy, Eating Right. (p. 501)
Wilson, Sean Michael. Lafcadio Hearn's Japanese Ghost Stories. Miyabi, Haruka, illus. (p. 971)
Wilson, Sean Michael, jt. auth. see Gale Editors.
Wilson, Sean Michael & Dickson, Benjamin. Fight the Power! A Visual History of Protest among the English Speaking Peoples. Emerson, Hunt et al, illus. (p. 585)
Wilson, Shannan. Littlest Peanut: A Baby Book for the Teeny Tiny Ones. Cuniff, Joe, illus. (p. 1039)
Wilson, Shawn V., jt. auth. see Mallonee, Dennis.
Wilson, Sheba. Down & Out in Halfville. (p. 474)
Wilson, Shellah. Samuel's Little Brother. (p. 1509)
Wilson, Steve. California Gold Rush: Chinese Laborers in America (1848-1882) (p. 253)
—Snakes, Lizards, Crocs & Turtles of Australia. (p. 1597)
Wilson, Steve, ed. see Hooker, Forrestine Cooper.
Wilson, Steve, illus. see Nagel, Karen.
Wilson, Steve, illus. see Whitman, Candace.
Wilson, Steve, jt. auth. see Smith, Pohla.
Wilson, Susie, illus. see Tierra, Lesley.
Wilson, Teddy, illus. see Brown, Ivorine.
Wilson, Thomas M. & Donnan, Hastings. Anthropology of Ireland. (p. 89)
Wilson, Todd. American Government AP Version. (p. 61)
—Investigating Childhood in Tudor England. (p. 884)
—Southwest Desert Animal Coloring Book. (p. 1617)
Wilson, Tony. Princess & the Packet of Frozen Peas deGennaro, Sue, illus. (p. 1402)
—Thirsty Flowers. Knoblock, Julie, illus. (p. 1734)
Wilson, Troy. Perfect Man Griffiths, Dean, illus. (p. 1342)
Wilson, Tyrone L. Spectacle of Lights. (p. 1624)
Wilson, Veronica B. Aswald's ABC Adventure. (p. 109)
Wilson, Vicky, ed. Touch Wood. (p. 1772)
Wilson, W. Shane. Gavin the Gnome. (p. 658)
—Little Monsters. (p. 1032)
—Ryan of the Wildfire. (p. 1499)
—sprite Adventure. (p. 1635)
—War for Ice. (p. 1857)
—world of Ice. (p. 1956)
Wilson, Walt. Jimmie Johnson. (p. 918)
Wilson, Wayne. Allen Iverson. (p. 46)
Wilson, Wayne L. Kate, the Ghost Dog: Coping with the Death of a Pet. Soud, illus. (p. 944)
Wilson, Wayne L., jt. auth. see Bernard, Teko.
Wilson, Wendy. First Book of Red. (p. 593)
—Just Desserts. (p. 938)
Wilson, Whitleigh, illus. see Wilson, Angela.
Wilson, William Scott, jt. auth. see Tsunetomo, Yamamoto.
Wilson Young, Elaine. Butch, the Cape Cod Dog. (p. 246)
Wilson, Zachary. Circle in the Sky. Adinolfi, JoAnn, illus. (p. 321)
—Circulo en el Cielo. Adinolfi, JoAnn, illus. (p. 322)
—Number One Puppy. Pertile, Paula, illus. (p. 1271)
Wilson, Zachary & Adinolfi, JoAnn. Circulo en el Cielo. Adinolfi, JoAnn, illus. (p. 322)
Wilson-Max, Ken. Big Red Fire Engine. (p. 183)
—Happy Cat, Me! A Slide-the-Spot Book of Animals. Stojic, Manya & Hamilton, Allen, illus. (p. 745)
—Lenny Has Lunch. (p. 991)
—Lenny in the Garden. (p. 991)
Wilson-Max, Ken, illus. see Baicker, Karen & Chronicle Books Staff.
Wilson-Max, Ken, illus. see Marzollo, Jean.
Wilson-Max, Ken, illus. see O'Connell, Rebecca.
Wilson-Max, Ken, illus. see Scholastic, Inc. Staff & Bermiss, Aamir Lee.
Wilson-Max, Ken, illus. see Stanley, Malaika Rose.
Wilson-Max, Ken & Quarto Generic Staff. Lenny Goes to Nursery School. (p. 991)
—Where's Lenny? (p. 1910)
Wilson-Timmons, Karen & Dubois, Marie Thérèse. Agha the Eight-Mile Monster. (p. 29)
Wilt, Gerri Ann, et al. My Little One: A Mother's Lullaby. Sargent, Shannon Marie, illus. (p. 1212)
Wilt, Lisa Marie, jt. auth. see Wilt, Lisa Marie.
Wilt, Lisa Marie & Wilt, Lisa Marie. Thank You Notes - A Young Person's Guide. (p. 1725)
Wiltbank, Ryan. Land of Bland: Illustrations by Dan Cooper on the Title Page. (p. 973)
Wilton, Jene, Jr. Little Blue Blessings. (p. 1024)
Wiltse, Kris, illus. see Newman, Lesléa.
Wiltshire, Alan. Creativity Through Design: Challenges in Art & Mathematics Using the Anglemaster. (p. 380)
Wiltshire, Alex, jt. auth. see Scholastic Editors.
Wim, Coleman. Classroom Plays by Wim Coleman. (p. 329)
Wimberley, Daniel. Flowers on Golgotha. (p. 608)
Wimberley, John. Life in the Republic of Texas. (p. 1011)
Wimberley, Judy. Jack Book: Who Can Help Him on Sunny Days & on Stormy Days? (p. 903)
Wimberly, Nikisha. Hair Like That. Drewes, Dan, illus. (p. 736)
Wimbiscus, Robin. Somewhere in the Garden. (p. 1610)
Wimbish, David, jt. auth. see Williams, Pat.
Wimbrey, Crystal M. Alphascripts: The ABC's of the Bible. Mozley, Peggy, illus. (p. 50)
Wimbush, Jalen & Tullis, Shaquiya. Growing Adventures of Jalen: Dream. (p. 726)
Wimbush, Jeff. Stars. (p. 1643)
Wimbush, Jeff, jt. auth. see Crabtree Editors.
Wimmer, Mary. Reaching Shore. (p. 1442)
Wimmer, Michael, illus. see Smith, Doris Buchanan & Smith.
Wimmer, Mike, illus. see Burleigh, Robert.
Wimmer, Mike, illus. see Coville, Bruce.
Wimmer, Mike, illus. see Keating, Frank.
Wimmer, Mike, illus. see Smith, Doris Buchanan.
Wimmer, Natasha, tr. see Vargas Llosa, Mario.
Wimmer, Sonja. Word Collector. (p. 1950)
Wimmer, Teresa. Ants. (p. 90)
—Beatles' Sgt. Pepper's Lonely Hearts Club Band. (p. 153)
—Bees. (p. 158)
—Butterflies. (p. 247)
—Causes. (p. 282)
—Cloning: Dolly the Sheep. (p. 333)
—Controversies. (p. 361)
—Delaware. (p. 424)
—Earth. (p. 495)
—Environmental Protection Agency. (p. 532)
—Florida. (p. 606)
—Ideology & Information. (p. 852)
—Important Figures. (p. 862)
—Jupiter. (p. 937)
—Mars. (p. 1096)
—Maryland. (p. 1101)
—Massachusetts. (p. 1102)
—Mercury. (p. 1127)
—Missouri. (p. 1154)
—National Aeronautics & Space Administration. (p. 1231)
—Neptune. (p. 1241)
—New Hampshire. (p. 1245)
—New Jersey. (p. 1245)
—North Carolina. (p. 1264)
—Rhode Island. (p. 1468)
—Saturn. (p. 1515)
—Snakes. (p. 1596)
—Spiders. (p. 1627)
—Uranus. (p. 1825)
—Venus. (p. 1836)
—Wolves. (p. 1945)
Wimperis, Sarah, illus. see Remarque, Erich Maria.
Wimsatt, William Upski, ed. see De Leon, Aya, et al.
Winans, Carvin. Conrad Saves Pinger Park. Harrington, Leslie, illus. (p. 358)
Winans, Jay D. Delaware. (p. 424)
—Iowa. (p. 886)
—Oregon. (p. 1302)
—Rhode Island. (p. 1468)
Winans, Vickie & Rush, Rickie. May I Have Your Order Please: How to Get What You Want from God. (p. 1112)
Winbolt-Lewis, Martin. Never Rely on a Lion. (p. 1243)
—Owliviah. Cressey, Roger, illus. (p. 1315)
—Soggy Saga of Samuel Sprat. Mason, Abi, illus. (p. 1606)
Winborn, Marsha, illus. see Baker, Barbara.
Winborn, Marsha, illus. see Bunting, Eve.
Winborn, Marsha, illus. see Daniel, Claire.
Winborn, Marsha, illus. see Powell, Alma.
Winborn, Marsha, illus. see Weiss, Ellen & Friedman, Mel.
Winborne, Mamie Pearl. Sweet Sugar I Got Your Back. (p. 1690)
Winborne, Stephanie. Peace of Heaven on Earth. (p. 1331)
Winburn, William B. Hide-And-Peek. (p. 776)
—Knees & Toes. (p. 964)
Winch, John. Run, Hare, Run: The Story of a Drawing. (p. 1496)
—Run, Hare, Run. (p. 1496)
—Two by Two. (p. 1803)
Winch, John, illus. see Kimmel, Eric A.
Winchel, Heidi, illus. see Romano, Elaine.
Winchell, Cory W. Supper of the Great God, Armageddon or the Battle of Gog & Magog. (p. 1684)
Winchell, Donna. North Ducky Passage. (p. 1265)
Winchester, Elizabeth Siris & Siris-Winchester, Elizabeth. Right Bite: Dentists As Detectives. (p. 1472)
—Sisters & Brothers: The Ultimate Guide to Understanding Your Siblings & Yourself. (p. 1581)
Winchester, Jim. Civil Aircraft. (p. 324)
—Jet Fighters: Inside & Out. (p. 916)
—Record Breakers. (p. 1452)
—Soldier. (p. 1607)
—World's Worst Aircraft. (p. 1961)
Winchester, Simon. Day the World Exploded: The Earthshaking Catastrophe at Krakatoa. Chin, Jason, illus. (p. 414)
—When the Earth Shakes: Earthquakes, Volcanoes, & Tsunamis. (p. 1904)
Winclk, Stephanie. Journey: A Northern Lights Adventure. (p. 927)
Winckelmann, Thom. Genocide. (p. 661)
Winckelmann, Thom & Abushanab, Lynn. Bono: Rock Star & Humanitarian. (p. 209)
Winckler, Alette-Johanni. My LullaBible. (p. 1213)
Wind, Chuck T. Test of Love. (p. 1723)
Windeatt, Mary F. Pauline Jaricot: Foundress of the Living Rosary & the Society for the Propagation of the Faith. Grout, Paul A., illus. (p. 1331)
—Saint Anthony of Padua. Harmon, Gedge, illus. (p. 1503)
—Saint Catherine of Siena: The Story of the Girl Who Saw Saints in the Sky. Beccard, Helen L., illus. (p. 1503)
—Saint Francis of Assisi. Harmon, Gedge, illus. (p. 1503)
—Saint Hyacinth of Poland: The Story of the Apostle of the North. Mary Jean, illus. (p. 1503)
—Saint John Masias: Marvelous Dominican Gatekeeper of Lima, Peru. Sister Mary of the Compassion, illus. (p. 1503)
—Saint Louis de Montfort: The Story of Our Lady's Slave. Grout, Paul A., illus. (p. 1503)
—Saint Maria Goretti. Harmon, Gedge, illus. (p. 1503)
—Saint Teresa of Avila. Harmon, Gedge, illus. (p. 1504)
Windeatt, Mary Fabyan & Ignatz, Marie. Vocabulary Quiz Workbook: Based on 6 Great Saints' Lives by Mary Fabyan Windeatt. Lester, Mary Frances, ed. (p. 1847)
Windelspecht, Michael. Digestive System (p. 438)
Windelspecht, Michael, jt. auth. see McDowell, Julie.
Windelspecht, Michael, ed. Human Body Systems (p. 825)
Winderman, Jay B. Thunder on the Desert. Becker, LuAnne E. & Becker, Lisa E., illus. (p. 1746)
—Thunder on the Reservation. Becker, LuAnne E., illus. (p. 1746)
Winders, Gertrude Hecker. Jeb Stuart: Boy in the Saddle. Doremus, Robert, illus. (p. 911)
Winders, Richard Bruce. Davy Crockett: The Legend of the Wild Frontier. (p. 411)
Windett, Dave, illus. see Gatehouse, John.
Windham, Kathryn Tucker. 13 Georgia Ghosts & Jeffrey. (p. 1995)
—Ernest's Gift. Hardy, Frank, illus. (p. 534)
—Jeffrey Introduces 13 More Southern Ghosts: Commemorative Edition. (p. 912)
Windham, Roy, jt. auth. see Roy Windham, Windham.
Windham, Ryder. DK Readers L2: Star Wars: Journey Through Space: Star Wars: Journey Through Space. (p. 456)
—Empire Strikes Back. (p. 521)
—Galactic Crisis! (p. 652)
—Journey Through Space. (p. 928)

W

—Luke Skywalker. (p. 1064)
—Millennium Falcon. (p. 1143)
—New Hope: The Life of Luke Skywalker. (p. 1245)
—New Hope. (p. 1245)
—Shape-Shifter Strikes. (p. 1560)
—Star Wars Rebels. (p. 1641)
—Wrath of Darth Maul. (p. 1962)
Windham, Ryder, jt. auth. see Beecroft, Simon.
Windham, Ryder, jt. auth. see Disney Book Group Staff.
Windham, Ryder, jt. auth. see Dorling Kindersley Publishing Staff.
Windham, Ryder, jt. auth. see Fry, Jason.
Windham, Ryder, jt. auth. see Scholastic, Inc. Staff.
Windham, Ryder & Fry, Jason. Battle Mountain. (p. 146)
—Transformers Classified: Battle Mountain. (p. 1778)
—Transformers Classified: Satellite of Doom. (p. 1778)
—Transformers Classified: the Complete Mission. (p. 1778)
Windham, Ryder & Stine, R. L. Rise & Fall of Darth Vader. (p. 1474)
Windham, Ryder & Weyn, Suzanne. Indiana Jones Collector's Edition. (p. 871)
Windham, Sophie, illus. see French, Vivian.
Windhorst, Brenda. Do You Want a Henry Story? (p. 458)
Windle, Jeanette & Clements, Jan. Yandicu: Ein Medizinmann Wird Evangelist. (p. 1968)
Windle, Margaret. Assorted Saints & the Virtues. (p. 107)
—St Catherine Laboure. (p. 1637)
Windler-Cheren, Victoria, tr. see Duey, Kathleen & Gould, Robert.
Windling, Terri. Midsummer Night's Faery Tale. Froud, Wendy, illus. (p. 1139)
Windling, Terri, ed. see Datlow, Ellen.
Windling, Terri, jt. auth. see Datlow, Ellen.
Windling, Terri, jt. ed. see Datlow, Ellen.
Windling, Terri & Datlow, Ellen, eds. Troll's-Eye View: A Book of Villainous Tales. (p. 1788)
Windmill Books, jt. auth. see Windmill Books.
Windmill Books & Windmill Books. Let's Look at Trains. (p. 999)
Windolph, Marla Theresa. Sugar Bear. (p. 1672)
Windover, Liz. Blood Island. Utomo, Gabhor, illus. (p. 200)
Windsor. Sail Main4 Comets Nf. (p. 1503)
Windsor, Herbert C. Colour Monster. (p. 346)
Windsor, Jo. Animal Lights: Early Level Satellite Individual Title Six-Packs. (p. 78)
—Bats in Blankets: Early Level Satellite Individual Title Six-Packs. (p. 145)
—Foxes: Early Level Satellite Individual Title Six-Packs. (p. 626)
—Lazy Duck: 3-in-1 Package. Webb, Philip, illus. (p. 981)
—Lazy Duck. Webb, Philip, illus. (p. 981)
—Long Time Ago: Early Level Satellite Individual Title Six-Packs. (p. 1047)
—Upside down Life: Early Level Satellite Individual Title Six-Packs. (p. 1825)
Windsor, Lucinda. Grammar in Story: The Transparencies Vol. 2 (p. 706)
Windsor, Wesley. American Wilderness: Alaska & the National Parks, 1865-1890. (p. 64)
—American Wilderness: Alaska & the National Parks (1865-1890) Rakove, Jack N., ed. (p. 64)
—Civil War: America Torn Apart, 1860-1865. (p. 325)
—Civil War: America Torn Apart, 1860-1865. Rakove, Jack N., ed. (p. 325)
Windsor-Smith, Barry. X-Men - Lifedeath. (p. 1967)
Windsor-Smith, Barry, illus. see Thomas, Roy & Howard, Robert E.
Windsor-Smith, Barry, jt. illus. see Romita, John.
Windsor-Smith, Barry, et al. Avengers (p. 118)
Windt, Zelna Banks. Blow, Wind, Blow! (p. 202)
Windwalker, Stephen. 100 Greatest Baseball Games of All Time: Box Scores & Game Stories of Baseball's Unforgettable Moments. (p. 1998)
Wine, Bill. Johnny Depp. (p. 923)
—Salma Hayek. (p. 1505)
Wine, Mary. Lady Can Never Be Too Curious. (p. 970)
Winegar, Angela. Adventures of Grinn & Barrett. (p. 18)
—Missy's Memoirs: The Life & Times of One Domesticated Dog. (p. 1155)
—Music Man's Guitar Superstar. (p. 1193)
—Music Man's Little Cellist. (p. 1193)
—Music Man's Little Drummer Girl. (p. 1193)
—Music Man's Piano Prodigy. (p. 1193)
—My Magic Violin & Me. (p. 1213)
—Very Backwards ~What If~ Book. (p. 1837)
Winegar, Tracy. Keeping Keller. (p. 947)
Winegarten, Debra L. Katherine Stinson: The Flying Schoolgirl. (p. 944)
Wineinger, Cherylann. Corgy & His Friends: A Trip to the Unknown. (p. 367)
Winer, Yvonne. Frogs Sing Songs. Oliver, Tony, illus. (p. 641)
Winerip, Michael. Adam Canfield of the Slash. (p. 11)
—Adam Canfield the Last Reporter. (p. 11)
—Adam Canfield Watch Your Back! (p. 11)
Wines, Jacquie. You Can Save the Planet: 50 Ways You Can Make a Difference. Horne, Sarah, illus. (p. 1974)
Wines, Michael P. Stupid Alabama: A Laugh-So-Hard-You-Will-Snot about Growing up to Discover Not All Things Are Stupid but a Lot of Them Are. Gierhart, Steve, ed. (p. 1670)
Wines, Richard. Five Stones. (p. 601)
Wines, Shawn & Pecsenye, Jessica. University of Miami College Prowler off the Record. (p. 1820)
Winfield, A. C. Star Pirate. (p. 1641)
Winfield, Alison, illus. see Hall, Patricia.
Winfield, Amy, illus. see Harvey, Natalie.
Winfield, Amy, illus. see Jackson, Kristina.
Winfield, Arthur M. Mystery at Putnam Hall. (p. 1223)
—Putnam Hall Champions or Bound to Win Ou. (p. 1420)
—Putnam Hall Rivals. (p. 1420)
—Rover Boys at College. (p. 1491)
—Rover Boys at College or the Right Road. (p. 1491)
—Rover Boys at School. (p. 1491)
—Rover Boys down East or the Struggle for the Stanhope Fortune. (p. 1491)
—Rover Boys in Alaska or Lost in the Fiel. (p. 1491)
—Rover Boys in Business or the Search for the Missing Bonds. (p. 1491)
—Rover Boys in New York. (p. 1491)
—Rover Boys in New York or Saving the. (p. 1491)
—Rover Boys in New York or Saving Their Father's Honor. (p. 1491)
—Rover Boys in the Air. (p. 1491)
—Rover Boys in the Air or from College Campus to the Clouds. (p. 1491)
—Rover Boys in the Jungle. (p. 1491)
—Rover Boys in the Land of Luck or Stirri. (p. 1491)
—Rover Boys in the Mountains: Or, A Hunt for Fun & Fortune. (p. 1491)
—Rover Boys in the Mountains. (p. 1491)
—Rover Boys in the Mountains or a Hunt for Fun & Fortune. (p. 1491)
—Rover Boys on A Tour or Last Days at Bri. (p. 1491)
—Rover Boys on Land & Sea. (p. 1491)
—Rover Boys on Land & Sea or the Crusoes of Seven Islands. (p. 1491)
—Rover Boys on Snowshoe Island or the Old Lumberman's. (p. 1491)
—Rover Boys on the Farm. (p. 1491)
—Rover Boys on the Great Lakes. (p. 1491)
—Rover Boys on the Ocean. (p. 1491)
—Rover Boys on the Plains or the Mystery of Red Rock Ranch. (p. 1491)
—Rover Boys on the River. (p. 1491)
—Rover Boys on the River or the Search for the Missing. (p. 1491)
—Rover Boys on Treasure Isle or the Stran. (p. 1491)
—Rover Boys Out West. (p. 1491)
Winfield, Cynthia L. Gender Identity: The Ultimate Teen Guide. (p. 660)
Winfrey, Michelle Whitaker. It's My Birthday. . . Finally! A Leap Year Story. Turley, Joyce M., illus. (p. 897)
Winfrey, Michelle/w. It's My Birthday.. Finally! A Leap Year Story. (p. 897)
Winfrey, Shakeeta & Winfrey, Shakeeta Ann. Other Winfrey: Life in the Shadow of O. (p. 1306)
Winfrey, Shakeeta Ann, jt. auth. see Winfrey, Shakeeta.
Wing, Avra. After Isaac. (p. 28)
Wing, Carol. Lio the Carousel Horse. Moen, Ruth, illus. (p. 1019)
Wing, Laura A. Gun Is Not a Toy: Gun Safety for Children. (p. 732)
Wing, Lorna, ed. see Yoshida, Yuko.
Wing, Natasha. Eye for Color: The Story of Josef Albers. Breckenreid, Julia, illus. (p. 557)
—Night Before Father's Day. (p. 1253)
—Night Before Father's Day. Wummer, Amy, illus. (p. 1253)
—Night Before First Grade. Zemke, Deborah, illus. (p. 1253)
—Night Before Hanukkah. (p. 1253)
—Night Before Hanukkah. Wummer, Amy, illus. (p. 1253)
—Night Before Kindergarten. Durrell, Julie, illus. (p. 1253)
—Night Before Mother's Day. Wummer, Amy, illus. (p. 1253)
—Night Before My Birthday. (p. 1253)
—Night Before My Birthday. Wummer, Amy, illus. (p. 1253)
—Night Before My Birthday Gift Set. Wummer, Amy, illus. (p. 1253)
—Night Before New Year's. Wummer, Amy, illus. (p. 1253)
—Night Before Preschool. Wummer, Amy, illus. (p. 1253)
—Night Before St. Patrick's Day. Wummer, Amy, illus. (p. 1253)
—Night Before Summer Camp. Pierce, Mindy & M, Pierce, illus. (p. 1253)
—Night Before the 100th Day of School. Pierce, Mindy, illus. (p. 1253)
—Night Before the Fourth of July. (p. 1253)
—Night Before the Fourth of July. Wummer, Amy, illus. (p. 1253)
—Night Before the Tooth Fairy. Newman, Barbara Johansen, illus. (p. 1253)
Wingard, Lucinda. Turn-Around Bird. (p. 1797)
Wingard-Nelson, Rebecca. Addition & Subtraction: Ace Your Math Test. (p. 12)
—Addition & Subtraction. (p. 12)
—Addition Made Easy. LaBaff, Tom, illus. (p. 12)
—Algebra & Pre-Algebra: It's Easy. (p. 38)
—Algebra & Pre-Algebra. (p. 38)
—Algebra I & Algebra II. (p. 38)
—Algebra I & Algebra II Smarts! (p. 38)
—Algebra Word Problems: No Problem! (p. 38)
—Amusement Park Word Problems Starring Pre-Algebra: Math Word Problems Solved. (p. 66)
—Animal Word Problems Starring Addition & Subtraction. LaBaff, Tom, illus. (p. 80)
—Big Truck & Car Word Problems Starring Multiplication & Division. (p. 184)
—Data, Graphing, & Statistics. (p. 409)
—Data, Graphing, & Statistics Smarts! (p. 409)
—Decimals & Fractions: It's Easy. (p. 421)
—Decimals & Fractions. (p. 421)
—Division & Multiplication: It's Easy. (p. 455)
—Division & Multiplication. (p. 455)
—Division Made Easy. LaBaff, Tom, illus. (p. 455)
—Figuring Out Geometry. (p. 586)
—Fraction & Decimal Word Problems: No Problem! (p. 626)
—Fractions & Decimals. (p. 626)
—Fractions & Decimals: Ace Your Math Test. (p. 627)
—Fractions & Decimals Made Easy. Tom, LaBaff, illus. (p. 627)
—Fun Food Word Problems Starring Fractions: Math Word Problems Solved. (p. 647)
—Geometry: It's Easy. (p. 662)
—Geometry: Ace Your Math Test. (p. 662)
—Geometry. (p. 662)
—Geometry, It's Easy. (p. 662)
—How Many Pennies Make a Dollar? (p. 811)
—I Can Add Bills & Coins. (p. 834)
—I Can Count Money. (p. 835)
—I Can Do Money Word Problems. (p. 835)
—I Can Name Bills & Coins. (p. 836)
—I Can Subtract Bills & Coins. (p. 836)
—Multiplication & Division: Ace Your Math Test. (p. 1190)
—Multiplication & Division. (p. 1190)
—Multiplication & Division Word Problems: No Problem! (p. 1190)
—Multiplication Made Easy. LaBaff, Tom, illus. (p. 1190)
—Percents & Ratios: Ace Your Math Test. (p. 1341)
—Percents & Ratios. (p. 1341)
—Pre-Algebra & Algebra: Ace Your Math Test. (p. 1394)
—Pre-Algebra & Algebra. (p. 1394)
—Problem Solving & Word Problem Smarts! (p. 1408)
—Problem Solving & Word Problems. (p. 1408)
—Ratios & Percents: It's Easy. (p. 1440)
—Ratios & Percents. (p. 1440)
—Ready for Addition. (p. 1447)
—Ready for Addition. LaBaff, Tom, illus. (p. 1447)
—Ready for Division. LaBaff, Tom, illus. (p. 1447)
—Ready for Fractions & Decimals. LaBaff, Tom, illus. (p. 1447)
—Ready for Multiplication. LaBaff, Tom, illus. (p. 1447)
—Ready for Subtraction. LaBaff, Tom, illus. (p. 1447)
—Ready for Word Problems & Problem Solving. LaBaff, Tom, illus. (p. 1447)
—Space Word Problems Starring Ratios & Proportions: Math Word Problems Solved. (p. 1620)
—Sports Word Problems Starring Decimals & Percents. (p. 1633)
—Subtraction & Addition: It's Easy. (p. 1671)
—Subtraction & Addition. (p. 1671)
—Subtraction Made Easy. LaBaff, Tom, illus. (p. 1671)
—Trigonometry. (p. 1786)
—Word Problems Made Easy. LaBaff, Tom, illus. (p. 1951)
Wingard-Nelson, Rebecca & Library. Geometry Word Problems: No Problem! (p. 663)
—Graphing & Probability Word Problems: No Problem! (p. 711)
—Math Measurement Word Problems: No Problem! (p. 1106)
Wingart, Ramona A. Where Is Brother Beaver? (p. 1908)
Wingate, Barbara. Petey the One Lopped Eared Dog Mignano, Daniel, illus. (p. 1348)
Wingate, Brian. BMX Bicycle Racing: Techniques & Tricks. (p. 204)
—BMX Bicycle Racing. (p. 204)
—Football: Rules, Tips, Strategy, & Safety. (p. 615)
—Saddam Hussein: The Rise & Fall of a Dictator. (p. 1501)
—Saddam Hussein. (p. 1501)
—Soccer: Rules, Tips, Strategy, & Safety. (p. 1603)
—Tony Hawk: Skateboarding Champion. (p. 1766)
—Violence at Sports Events. (p. 1843)
Wingate, Brian, jt. auth. see Van Pelt, Don.
Wingate, Frank. Herman the Hedgehog: Bedtime Tales from the Woodland. (p. 771)
Wingate, Kate. Political Reforms: American Citizens Gain More Control over Their Government. (p. 1380)
Wingate, Katherine. Intifadas. (p. 881)
—Political Reforms: American Citizens Gain More Control over Their Government. (p. 1380)
Wingate, Lisa. Tending Roses. (p. 1719)
Wingate, Philippa. Dinosaurs. (p. 444)
Wingate, Philippa, ed. see Enright, Dominique, et al.
Wingate, Philippa, ed. see Foster, Juliana.
Wingate, Philippa, ed. see Heywood, Rosie.
Wingate, Philippa & Millard, Anne. Viking World. Wood, Gerald, illus. (p. 1842)
Wingate, Philippa & Reid, Struan. Who Were the First North Americans? (p. 1919)
Wingert, H. C. Bucket Full of Love. (p. 234)
Wingert, Sheryl. Osborne & Grandpa. (p. 1305)
—Osborne & the Smells of Christmas. (p. 1305)
Wingerter, Linda. Home on the Range. (p. 792)
Wingerter, Linda, illus. see Seeger, Pete.
Wingerter, Linda, illus. see Sherman, Josepha.
Winget, Dianna Dorisi. Million Ways Home. (p. 1144)
—Smidgen of Sky. (p. 1593)
Winget, Kerry. Differential Processing Training Program Acoustic Tasks. (p. 438)
—Differential Processing Training Program Acoustic Linguistic Tasks. (p. 438)
—Differential Processing Training Program Linguistic Tasks. (p. 438)
Winget, Mary. Cooking the North African Way. (p. 362)
—Floods. (p. 605)
—Subways. (p. 1671)
—Taxis. (p. 1707)
Winget, Mary & Winget, W. Bryan. Tow Trucks. (p. 1773)
Winget, Susan. Tucker's Apple-Dandy Day. Winget, Susan, illus. (p. 1795)
—Tucker's Four-Carrot School Day. Winget, Susan, illus. (p. 1796)
Winget, Susan, illus. see Moore, Clement C., ed.
Winget, Susan, illus. see Moulton, Mark K.
Winget, Susan, illus. see Moulton, Mark Kimball.
Winget, Susan, tr. see Moulton, Mark Kimball.
Winget, W. Bryan, jt. auth. see Winget, Mary.
Wingfield, Eileen Wani & Austin, Emily Munyungka. Living Alongside the Animals - Anangu Way. McKenna, Brenton, illus. (p. 1040)
Wingfield, George. Belgium. (p. 161)
Wingfield, George & Gritzner, Charles F. Belgium. (p. 161)
Wingfield, Hayley. Little Johnny's Book of Wild & Crazy Friends. (p. 1029)
Wingham, Peter, illus. see Somper, Justin.
Wingo, W. Bruce. There Grows a Crooked Tree. (p. 1729)
Wings, Tanina. Little Seagull. (p. 1036)
Winick, Judd. Boy Who Crashed to Earth. (p. 219)
—Good Fight Vol. 5. (p. 698)
—Green Arrow: City Walls. (p. 721)
—Legacy Calafiore, Jim & Holdredge, Jon, illus. (p. 987)
—Outsiders: Wanted. Vol. 3 (p. 1313)
—Passing the Torch. (p. 1326)
—Pay As You Go. (p. 1331)
—Pedro & Me: Friendship, Loss, & What I Learned. (p. 1334)
—Sum of All Evil (p. 1673)
—Trials of Shazam (p. 1785)
Winick, Judd, jt. auth. see Jimenez, Phil.
Winick, Judd, jt. auth. see Middleton, Josh.
Winick, Judd & Owens, Andy. Crawling Through the Wreckage. (p. 377)
Winick, Judd, et al. Crisis Intervention. Smith, Dietrich, illus. (p. 383)
Winik, Edward. Horse's Tale. (p. 800)
Wininger, Stephen T. Adventure of Pirate Pete Moss. (p. 14)
—It Had to Be Done. (p. 894)
Winitz, Harris, et al. Gombinski's Colors in Spanish, French, & German. Baker, Syd & Gombinski, Rita, illus. (p. 697)
Winkel, Andrew. Raceboy & Super Qwok Adventures. Brault, Christopher, illus. (p. 1431)
Winkelman, Barbara Gaines. Pinocchio's Nose Grows. Lopez, Paul et al, illus. (p. 1361)
—Puffer's Surprise. Petruccio, Steven James, illus. (p. 1415)
—Sockeye's Journey Home: The Story of a Pacific Salmon. Popeo, Joanie, illus. (p. 1605)
Winkelman, Barbara Gaines, jt. auth. see RH Disney Staff.
Winkelman, Barbara Gaines & Thomas, Peter. Sockeye's Journey Home: The Story of a Pacific Salmon. Popeo, Joanie, illus. (p. 1605)
Winkelmann, Mary. Wheels. (p. 1900)
Winkelmann, Rachele, jt. auth. see Smyth, Bethinna.
Winkk. Misleading. (p. 1151)
Winkleby, Marilyn A. & Steele, Julia P. Healing Journeys: Teaching Medicine, Nuturing Hope. (p. 757)
—Healing Journeys: Teaching Medicine, Nurturing Hope. (p. 757)
Winkler, Ashley & Winkler, Michael. One Good Quest Deserves Another: A Crown of Amaranth Story. (p. 1295)
Winkler, Henry, jt. auth. see Oliver, Lin.
Winkler, Henry & Oliver, Lin. Always Dance with a Hairy Buffalo. (p. 51)
—Barfing in the Backseat: How I Survived My Family Road Trip Watson, Jesse Joshua, illus. (p. 139)
—Barfing in the Backseat: How I Survived My Family Road Trip. Watson, Jesse Joshua, illus. (p. 139)
—Bookmarks Are People Too! (p. 212)
—Bookmarks Are People Too! Garrett, Scott, illus. (p. 212)
—Brand-New Me! Watson, Jesse Joshua, illus. (p. 222)
—Brand-New Me! Watson, Jesse Joshua & Heitz, Tim, illus. (p. 222)
—Curtain Went Up, My Pants Fell Down Watson, Jesse Joshua, illus. (p. 395)
—Day of the Iguana Heyer, Carol, illus. (p. 414)
—Day of the Iguana. (p. 414)
—Dump Trucks & Dogsleds Watson, Jesse Joshua, illus. (p. 489)
—Dump Trucks & Dogsleds - I'm on My Way, Mom! Watson, Jesse Joshua, illus. (p. 489)
—Fake Snakes & Weird Wizards. Garrett, Scott, illus. (p. 565)
—Ghost Buddy: Always Dance with a Hairy Buffalo. (p. 670)
—Help! Somebody Get Me Out of Fourth Grade! Watson, Jesse Joshua & Heitz, Tim, illus. (p. 766)
—Holy Enchilada! Heyer, Carol et al, illus. (p. 791)
—How to Scare the Pants off Your Pets. (p. 821)
—I Got a D in Salami Watson, Jesse Joshua et al, illus. (p. 838)
—I Got a D in Salami. (p. 838)
—Life of Me: Enter at Your Own Risk. Watson, Jesse Joshua, illus. (p. 1012)
—Life of Me (Enter at Your Own Risk) (p. 1012)
—Mind If I Read Your Mind? (p. 1145)
—My Dog's a Scaredy-Cat Watson, Jesse Joshua, illus. (p. 1202)
—My Secret Life as a Ping-Pong Wizard (p. 1218)
—My Secret Life as a Ping-Pong Wizard Heyer, Carol & Watson, Jesse Joshua, illus. (p. 1218)
—Never Feed a Hairy Buffalo! (p. 1242)
—Niagara Falls, or Does It? (p. 1250)
—Niagara Falls, or Does It? Watson, Jesse Joshua et al, illus. (p. 1250)
—Short Tale about a Long Dog. (p. 1569)
—Short Tale about a Long Dog. Garrett, Scott, illus. (p. 1569)
—Stop That Frog! (p. 1653)
—Stop That Frog! Garrett, Scott, illus. (p. 1653)
—Summer School! What Genius Thought That Up? (p. 1675)
—Summer School! What Genius Thought That Up? Heyer, Carol, illus. (p. 1675)
—Summer School! What Genius Thought That Up? Heyer, Carol et al, illus. (p. 1675)
—Tale of Two Tails Watson, Jesse Joshua, illus. (p. 1701)
—Who Ordered This Baby? Definitely Not Me! (p. 1917)
—Who Ordered This Baby? Definitely Not Me! Watson, Jesse Joshua & Heitz, Tim, illus. (p. 1917)
—Zero to Hero. (p. 1986)
—Zippity Zinger Heitz, Tim, illus. (p. 1987)
—Zippity Zinger. (p. 1987)
Winkler, J., jt. auth. see Lovasik, Lawrence G.
Winkler, Jude. Biblia Ilustrada para Ninos. Todo Color, illus. (p. 176)
—Noah & the Flood. (p. 1261)
—Scriptural Rosary for Children. (p. 1533)
Winkler, Kathleen. Are You Being Bullied? How to Deal with Taunting, Teasing, & Tormenting. (p. 97)
—Bullying: How to Deal with Taunting, Teasing, & Tormenting. (p. 241)
—Cosmetic Surgery for Teens: Choices & Consequences. (p. 368)
—Cutting & Self-Mutilation: When Teens Injure Themselves. (p. 396)
—High-Tech Babies: The Debate over Assisted Reproductive Technology. (p. 778)
Winkler, Michael, jt. auth. see Winkler, Ashley.
Winkler, Peter & National Geographic Learning Staff. Animal Adaptations. (p. 76)
Winkler, Peter, et al. Keeping Fit. (p. 947)
Winkler, Scott A. Wide Turn Toward Home. (p. 1927)
Winkler, Susan Elliott. Haylee & the Mud Puddle. (p. 755)
Winkler, Ziporah, jt. creator see Koenigsberg, Phyllis.
Winkowski, Jackie. Miki's Challenge: One sled dog's Story. Winkowski, Jackie, photos by. (p. 1141)
Winks, P. M. Romany Gnomanies in the Emerald Isle. (p. 1486)
Winmilawe. Shango's Son. Melchishua, Tewodross, illus. (p. 1559)
Winn, Chris, illus. see Davis, Mary.
Winn, Christine M. & Walsh, David. Clover's Secret. Winn, Christine M., illus. (p. 335)
Winn, Christopher, illus. see Winn, Sheridan.
Winn, Don M. Chipper the Clown. (p. 308)

Full bibliographic information is available on the Title Index page number referenced in parentheses at the end of each entry

—Tortoise & the Hairpiece. Hefflin, Toby, illus. (p. 1771)
Winn, L. B. Butterpod Jerome & the Planet of Gabool. Winn, L. B., illus. (p. 248)
Winn, Michael. Shape People. (p. 1560)
Winn, Sheridan. Sprite Sisters: Magic at Drysdale's School (Vol 7) Winn, Christopher, illus. (p. 1635)
Winnacker, Susanne. Other Life (p. 1306)
Winnard, Linda, jt. auth. see Winnard, Rebecca Victoria.
Winnard, Rebecca Victoria & Winnard, Linda. Giraffe Liberation: An Act of Freedom. (p. 677)
Winne, Tina M. So Many Puppies. (p. 1602)
Winner, Cherie. Animal Minis! What Kids Really Want to Know about Tiny Animals. (p. 78)
—Camels. (p. 256)
—Circulating Life: Blood Transfusion from Ancient Superstition to Modern Medicine. (p. 321)
—Cryobiology. (p. 387)
—Everything Bird: What Kids Really Want to Know about Birds. (p. 544)
—Everything Bug. (p. 544)
—Everything Reptile: What Kids Really Want to Know about Reptiles. (p. 545)
—Everything Reptile. (p. 545)
—Life in the Tundra. (p. 1011)
—Life on the Edge. (p. 1012)
—Little Book of Dinosaurs. (p. 1025)
—Little Book of Dinosaurs. Chesterman, Al, illus. (p. 1025)
Winner, Ramana Moreno. Freaky Foods from Around the World: Platillos Sorprendentes de todo el Mundo. Haake, Susana, tr. (p. 632)
Winner, Ramona Moreno. It's Okay to Be Different! (Esta Bien Ser Diferente!) Velasquez, Nicole, illus. (p. 898)
Winnick, Judd. Pedro & Me. (p. 1334)
Winnick, Karen B. Cassie's Sweet Berry Pie: A Civil War Story. (p. 276)
—Lucy's Cave: A Story of Vicksburg 1863. (p. 1063)
—Sybil's Night Ride. (p. 1692)
Winnick, Neil. Hearing. (p. 759)
Winnick, Nick. Build Green. (p. 238)
—Butterflies. (p. 247)
—Green Power. (p. 722)
—Moose. (p. 1173)
—Owls. (p. 1315)
—Reduce Waste. (p. 1456)
—Salamanders. (p. 1504)
—Summer: Wow Study of Day & Seasons. (p. 1673)
—Summer. (p. 1673)
Winnie, Joanne M. Alphabet Safari of East Africa. (p. 50)
Winnie the Pooh. Close-up Day. (p. 334)
—Goodbye, Honeypot! (p. 701)
—Spring Cleaning. (p. 1635)
—Winnie the Pooh Nature's True Colors. (p. 1937)
Winningham, Barbara. Turtle Pit. (p. 1798)
Winpenny, Patricia, et al. Teaching Russian Studies. (p. 1710)
Winrich, Ralph. Moon. (p. 1171)
—Neptune. (p. 1241)
—Sun (p. 1675)
Winrich, Ralph & Adamson, Thomas K. Pluto: A Dwarf Planet (p. 1374)
Winseman, Albert L., et al. Living Your Strengths: Discover Your God-Given Talents & Inspire Your Community. (p. 1042)
Winship, Daniel. Tortoise & the Hare: The Tortoise & the Hare. (p. 1771)
Winskill, John. Jungle Friends. Disney Global Artists Staff & RH Disney Staff, illus. (p. 935)
Winslade, Jayn E. Emily & Jen Dance for Deeron. (p. 518)
Winslow, Barbara. Dance on a Sealskin. Sloat, Teri, illus. (p. 402)
—Fancy & Francis. (p. 570)
Winslow, Jeremy. Hours of Coloring Fun with Shapes & Patterns. (p. 802)
Winslow, Justin. Perro y el Gato. (p. 1344)
Winslow, Justin, illus. see Hines, Chrissie & Ferreras, Alberto.
Winslow, Marjorie. Mud Pies & Other Recipes: A Cookbook for Dolls. Blegvad, Erik, illus. (p. 1188)
Winslow, Theresa. Katie the Bear & Her Adventure for Honey (p. 945)
Winslow, Tim. Kingdom of Avalon. (p. 959)
Winsor, Justin. Memorial History of Boston (p. 1126)
Winsor, Kathy, jt. auth. see Lane, Lori.
Winsor, Michael & Daidoji, Yoko. Going Somewhere. (p. 693)
Winstanley, Liz. Adventures of Abra & His Magic Carpet. (p. 16)
Winstanley, Nicola. Cinnamon Baby. Nadeau, Janice, illus. (p. 321)
—Pirate's Bed. (p. 1363)
Winstead, Amy. Star-Spangled Banner. Dacey, Bob & Bandelin, Debra, illus. (p. 1641)
Winstead, Leo, illus. see Jackson, Mary Helene.
Winstead, Rosie. Sprout Helps Out. (p. 1635)
Winstead, Rosie, illus. see Spinelli, Eileen.
Winstead, V. L. Wings. (p. 1936)
Winsten, Martha Raleigh. Awesome Elijah. (p. 121)
Winstock, April. Eating & Drinking Difficulties in Children: A Guide for Practitioners. (p. 501)
—Practical Management of Eating & Drinking Difficulties in Children. (p. 1392)
Winston, David Lorenz, illus. see Wolfman, Judy.
Winston, David Lorenz, photos by see Wolfman, Judy.
Winston, Dennis, illus. see Wooden, Thomas James, Jr.
Winston, Jeannie. Head, Shoulders, Knees, & Toes. (p. 756)
Winston, Jeannie, illus. see Imperato, Teresa.
Winston, Jeannie, illus. see Winters, Kay.
Winston, Robert. Science Rocks! (p. 1527)
Winston, Robert, jt. auth. see Dorling Kindersley Publishing Staff.
Winston, Robert P., jt. auth. see Romer, John.
Winston, Sherri. President of the Whole Fifth Grade. (p. 1397)
Wint, Eleanor. Marcus Teaches Us. (p. 1092)
Wint, Florence, illus. see Grossman, Bill.
Winter, Ariel S. One of a Kind. Hitch, David, illus. (p. 1296)
Winter, Barbara. 10 Most Endangered Animals. (p. 1993)
—Chameleon Capers. (p. 289)
—Fight for Rights. Kostic, Dimitri, illus. (p. 585)
—Golden Scarab. (p. 695)
—Spider Saga. (p. 1626)
—Trapped in Gallipoli. (p. 1779)
Winter, Bruce. Texas Hold'em No-Limit Poker ... the Next Level. (p. 1724)
Winter, Christopher. Henrietta the Farmer & the Long, Long, Long, Long Vacation! O'Shea, Bonnie, illus. (p. 767)
Winter, Dave, illus. see Keller, Charles.
Winter, David. Espresso Prayers: Perfect Shots for Any Time of Day. (p. 536)
Winter, Isobelle. Weather. Odgers, Sally, ed. (p. 1869)
Winter, James de. Discovering Lost Cities & Pirate Gold (p. 449)
Winter, Jane Kohen. Italy. (p. 894)
Winter, Janet, illus. see Brandon, Wendy.
Winter, Janet, illus. see O'Brien, Kristen.
Winter, Jeanette. Biblioburro: A True Story from Colombia. Winter, Jeanette, illus. (p. 177)
—Follow the Drinking Gourd. Winter, Jeanette, illus. (p. 612)
—Henri's Scissors. Winter, Jeanette, illus. (p. 767)
—Kali's Song. Winter, Jeanette, illus. (p. 942)
—Librarian of Basra: A True Story from Iraq. Winter, Jeanette, illus. (p. 1005)
—Mr. Cornell's Dream Boxes. Winter, Jeanette, illus. (p. 1184)
—My Name Is Georgia. (p. 1215)
—Nasreen's Secret School: A True Story from Afghanistan. Winter, Jeanette, illus. (p. 1230)
—Wangari's Trees of Peace: A True Story from Africa. Winter, Jeanette, illus. (p. 1856)
—Watcher: Jane Goodall's Life with the Chimps. Winter, Jeanette, illus. (p. 1861)
Winter, Jeanette, illus. see Winter, Jonah.
Winter, John. Christmas Fairy. Thomas, Tom, ed. (p. 313)
Winter, Jonah. Amnesia. (p. 65)
—Barack (p. 137)
—Barack. Ford, A. G., illus. (p. 137)
—Born & Bred in the Great Depression. Root, Kimberly Bulcken, illus. (p. 214)
—Dizzy. Qualls, Sean, illus. (p. 455)
—Fabulous Feud of Gilbert & Sullivan. Egielski, Richard, illus. (p. 560)
—Founding Fathers! Those Horse-Ridin', Fiddle-Playin', Book-Readin', Gun-Totin' Gentlemen Who Started America. Blitt, Barry, illus. (p. 624)
—Gertrude Is Gertrude Is Gertrude Is Gertrude. Brown, Calef, illus. (p. 667)
—How Jelly Roll Morton Invented Jazz. Mallett, Keith, illus. (p. 810)
—Jazz Age Josephine: Dancer, Singer- Who's That, Who? Why That's Miss Josephine Baker, to You! Priceman, Marjorie, illus. (p. 911)
—JFK. Ford, A. G., illus. (p. 917)
—Just Behave, Pablo Picasso! Hawkes, Kevin, illus. (p. 938)
—Lillian's Right to Vote: A Celebration of the Voting Rights Act of 1965. Evans, Shane W., illus. (p. 1017)
—Paul Revere & the Bell Ringers. Dodson, Bert, illus. (p. 1330)
—Peaceful Heroes. Addy, Sean, illus. (p. 1332)
—Roberto Clemente: Pride of the Pittsburgh Pirates. Colón, Raúl, illus. (p. 1479)
—Secret World of Hildegard. Winter, Jeanette, illus. (p. 1544)
—Sonia Sotomayor: A Judge Grows in the Bronx. Ziegler, Argentina Palacios, tr. from SPA. (p. 1612)
—Sonia Sotomayor. Rodriguez, Edel, illus. (p. 1612)
—Steel Town. Widener, Terry, illus. (p. 1646)
—Wild Women of the Wild West. Morgan, Mary & Guevara, Susan, illus. (p. 1930)
—You Never Heard of Sandy Koufax?! Carrilho, Andre, illus. (p. 1976)
—You Never Heard of Willie Mays?! Widener, Terry, illus. (p. 1976)
—¡Compórtate, Pablo Picasso! Hawkes, Kevin, illus. (p. 354)
Winter, Jonah & Addy, Sean. Peaceful Heroes. (p. 1332)
Winter, Judy A. Joke Books (p. 924)
—Jokes about Animals (p. 924)
—Jokes about Bugs (p. 924)
—Jokes about Food (p. 924)
—Jokes about Monsters (p. 924)
—Jokes about School (p. 924)
—Jokes about Sports (p. 924)
—Knock-Knock Jokes (p. 965)
—Really Funny Riddles (p. 1449)
Winter, Judy A. & Shores, Erika L. Joke Books. (p. 924)
Winter, Laurel. Growing Wings. (p. 727)
Winter, Max. Afghanistan War. (p. 26)
—Civil Rights Movement. (p. 325)
—Did You Know? Rechin, Kevin, illus. (p. 437)
—Japan. (p. 909)
—Powering up a Career in Artificial Intelligence. (p. 1391)
—Vietnam. (p. 1841)
Winter, Melissa Ann. Butterfly Dreams. (p. 247)
—Dream Come True. (p. 483)
—When Teddy Bears Cry. (p. 1904)
Winter, Milo. Aesop's Fables. (p. 25)
—Aesops Fables for Children. (p. 26)
—Aesop's Fables for Children. (p. 26)
—Greek Myths. (p. 720)
—Three Little Pigs. (p. 1743)
Winter, Milo, illus. see Aesop.
Winter, Milo, illus. see Faulkner, Georgene.
Winter, Milo, illus. see Loveland, Seymour.
Winter, Milo, illus. see Mother Goose.
Winter, Nilo, illus. see Handford, S. A.
Winter, Nix. Tokala. (p. 1762)
Winter, P. K. Back at Eagle Lake: More Eagle Lake Giant Stories. Winter, P. K., illus. (p. 130)
Winter, Rosalind. Mice of St Goran. (p. 1134)
Winter, Susan, illus. see Anastas, Margaret.
Winter, Susan, illus. see Ashman, Linda.
Winter, Susan, illus. see Bedford, David.
Winter, Susan, photos by see Anastas, Margaret.
Winter, William. Life & Art of Richard Mansfield. (p. 1007)
—Life of David Belasco. (p. 1011)
—Old Friends: Being Recollections of Other Days. (p. 1283)
—Other Days: Being Chronicles & Memories of the Stage. (p. 1306)
—Over the Border. (p. 1314)
—Shakespeare on the Stage. (p. 1559)
—Tyrone Power. (p. 1805)
—Vagrant Memories. (p. 1830)
Winterberg, Jenna. Balanced & Unbalanced Forces. (p. 133)
—Chemical Reactions. (p. 297)
—Conservation of Mass. (p. 359)
—Dinosaurs. Fisher, Diana, illus. (p. 444)
—Dolphins, Whales, Fish & More. Fisher, Diana, illus. (p. 465)
—Electromagnetism. (p. 509)
—Favorite Pets: A Step-By-step Drawing & Story Book for Preschoolers. Fisher, Diana, illus. (p. 578)
—Light & Its Effects. (p. 1014)
—Outer Space: A Step-by-Step Drawing & Story Book. Fisher, Diana, illus. (p. 1312)
—Sound Waves & Communication. (p. 1615)
—Things Girls Love. Fisher, Diana, illus. (p. 1733)
—Zoo: A Step-by-Step Drawing & Story Book. Fisher, Diana, illus. (p. 1988)
Winterbotham, R. R. Convoy Patrol: A Thrilling Story of the U. S. Navy. Hess, Erwin L., illus. (p. 361)
Winterbottom, Julie. Pranklopedia: The Funniest, Grossest, Craziest, Not-Mean Pranks on the Planet! (p. 1393)
Winterburn, Emily. Astronomers Royal. (p. 109)
Winterfeld, Henry. Star Girl. Schabert, Kyrill, tr. from GER. (p. 1640)
Winterhager, Randerath -, jt. auth. see Randerath, Jeanette.
Winterhalt, Tara, illus. see Dias, Denise.
Winterhaven Elementary Staff. O Is for Oregon. (p. 1274)
Winters, Adam. Choosing a Career in the Fishing Industry. (p. 310)
—Destruction of Earth's Resources: The Need for Sustainable Development. (p. 431)
—Everything You Need to Know about Being a Teen Driver. (p. 545)
—Everything You Need to Know about Lupus. (p. 545)
—Syphilis. (p. 1693)
Winters, Adam & Sommers, Michael A. Tobacco & Your Mouth: The Incredibly Disgusting Story. (p. 1760)
Winters, Ashleigh. Never-Ending Adventures of Zing. (p. 1242)
Winters, Ben H. Literally Disturbed: More Tales to Keep You up at Night. Watkins, Adam F., illus. (p. 1022)
—Literally Disturbed: Tales to Keep You up at Night. No. 1 Watkins, Adam F., illus. (p. 1022)
—Mystery of the Missing Everything. (p. 1225)
—Secret Life of Ms. Finkleman. (p. 1541)
Winters, Cat. Cure for Dreaming. (p. 392)
—In the Shadow of Blackbirds. (p. 867)
Winters, Eleanor. Calligraphy for Kids. (p. 254)
Winters, Jaime. Breakaway! The History of Hockey. (p. 224)
—Carve It Snowboarding. (p. 273)
—Center Court: The History of Basketball. (p. 287)
—Center Field: The History of Baseball. (p. 287)
—Center Ice: The Stanley Cup. (p. 287)
—For the Win: The World Series. (p. 616)
—Ruling the Court: Basketball's Biggest Wins. (p. 1495)
—Shred It Skateboarding. (p. 1571)
Winters, Jaime, jt. auth. see Crabtree Editors.
Winters, Jeffrey. Mystic Uncle & the Magical Bridge. (p. 1226)
Winters, John. Gramps' Children's Stories. (p. 706)
Winters, Karl, told to. Princess Fiona: My Purrsonal Story. (p. 1403)
Winters, Kari-Lynn. Buzz about Bees (p. 248)
—Gift Days Taylor, Stephen, illus. (p. 675)
—Jeffrey & Sloth Hodson, Ben, illus. (p. 912)
—No-Matter-What Friend Pratt, Pierre, illus. (p. 1259)
—On My Walk Leist, Christina, illus. (p. 1289)
—Runaway Alphabet. Frey, Ben, illus. (p. 1496)
Winters, Kari-Lynn & Sherritt-Fleming, Lori. Hungry for Math: Poems to Munch On Collins, Peggy, illus. (p. 828)
Winters, Kari-Lynn & Van Turennout, Paola. Stinky Skunk Mel. George, Kallie, ed. (p. 1651)
Winters, Kay. Abe Lincoln: The Boy Who Loved Books. Carpenter, Nancy, illus. (p. 4)
—Bears Go to School. Kirkland, Katherine, illus. (p. 152)
—Colonial Voices: Hear Them Speak. Day, Larry, illus. (p. 341)
—Colonial Voices - Hear Them Speak. Day, Larry, illus. (p. 341)
—Did You See What I Saw? Weston, Martha, illus. (p. 437)
—John Appleseed: A Trail of Trees. Pullen, Zachary, illus. (p. 921)
—My Teacher for President. Brunkus, Denise, illus. (p. 1219)
—My Teacher for President. Brunkus, Denise, illus. (p. 1220)
—Teeny Tiny Ghost & the Monster Munsinger, Lynn, illus. (p. 1715)
—This School Year Will Be the Best! Andriani, Renee, illus. (p. 1737)
—Voices from the Oregon Trail. Day, Larry, illus. (p. 1848)
—Voices of Ancient Egypt. (p. 1848)
—Voices of Ancient Egypt. Moser, Barry, illus. (p. 1848)
—Whooo's That? Winston, Jeannie, illus. (p. 1920)
Winters, Kay & Carpenter, Nancy. Abe Lincoln: The Boy Who Loved Books. (p. 4)
Winters, Linda. My Trip to Chattanooga: A Child's Perspective. (p. 1220)
Winters, Nicole. TT: Full Throttle (p. 1795)
Winters, Pierre. Thankyouplease. Ortelli, Barbara, illus. (p. 1726)
—Traveling by Airplane. Meirink, Tineke, illus. (p. 1780)
Winters, Robert. Freedom of Assembly & Petition. (p. 634)
—What Is a Hate Crime? (p. 1888)
Winters, Robert, ed. Right to a Trial by Jury. (p. 1472)
—Right to Bear Arms. (p. 1472)
—What Is a Hate Crime? (p. 1888)
Winters, Tom, jt. auth. see Bordon, David.
Winters-Johnson, Diane. View from under the Pew. Freed, Margaret, illus. (p. 1842)
Winterson, Jeanette. Battle of the Sun. (p. 147)
—Tanglewreck. (p. 1705)
Winterton, Kathleen. Star Light, Star Bright. (p. 1640)
Wintgens, Alison, jt. auth. see Johnson, Maggie.
Winther, Barbara. India, Burma/Thailand, Vietnam. (p. 871)
—India, Indonesia/Malaysia, China. (p. 871)
—Japan & Korea. (p. 909)
Winthrop, jt. auth. see Winthrop, Elizabeth.
Winthrop, Elizabeth. Battle for the Castle. (p. 145)
—Counting on Grace. (p. 371)
—Dumpy la Rue. Lewin, Betsy, illus. (p. 490)
—Franklin Delano Roosevelt: Letters from a Mill Town Girl. Winthrop, Elizabeth, illus. (p. 630)
—Maia & the Monster Baby. Haley, Amanda, illus. (p. 1076)
—Red-Hot Rattoons. Lewin, Betsy, illus. (p. 1454)
—Squashed in the Middle. Cummins, Pat, illus. (p. 1636)
Winthrop, Elizabeth & Winthrop. Dancing Granny Murdocca, Sal, illus. (p. 403)
Winthrop, John. Miscellany - A Journal of the Transcactions & Occurrences in the Settlement of Massachusetts & Other New England Colonies. (p. 1150)
Winton, Andrea Evans, illus. see Gleasner, Diana C.
Winton, Byron, illus. see Droney, Susan K.
Winton, Tim. Deep. Louise, Karen, illus. (p. 422)
Wintour, Riwa. Scripture Chorus Plays. (p. 1533)
wintranslation.com, tr. see Wildsmith, Brian.
wintranslation.com, tr. Carry Me (French/English) (p. 271)
—Eating the Rainbow (French/English) (p. 501)
Wintrob, Kitty. I'm Not Going Back: Wartime Memoir of a Child Evacuee. (p. 859)
Winward, Makenzie, illus. see Meyer, Lisa O.
Wipperfurth, Jenny. God Made You Special: A Celebration of Uniqueness. (p. 690)
Wire, Patrick, illus. see Greene, Joshua M.
Wireman, Katharine R., illus. see Wiggin, Kate Douglas.
Wireman, Peggy. Connecting the Dots: Government, Community, & Family. (p. 358)
Wirkala, Rita, tr. see Shah, Idries.
Wirkner, Linda. Learning about America's Colonial Period with Graphic Organizers. (p. 984)
—Learning about America's Industrial Growth & Expansion with Graphic Organizers. (p. 984)
—Learning about America's Industrial Growth with Graphic Organizers. (p. 984)
—Learning about Life in the New American Nation with Graphic Organizers. (p. 984)
—Learning about the American Revolution with Graphic Organizers. (p. 984)
—Learning about the American Revolutionary War with Graphic Organizers. (p. 984)
—Learning about the Settlement of the Americas with Graphic Organizers. (p. 985)
—Learning about Urban Growth in America with Graphic Organizers. (p. 985)
Wirrenga, Shannon, illus. see Ficocelli, Elizabeth.
Wirt, Mildred A. Brownie Scouts at Silver Beach. (p. 232)
—Guilt of the Brass Thieves. (p. 730)
—Saboteurs on the River. (p. 1500)
—Signal in the Dark. (p. 1574)
—Swamp Island. (p. 1688)
—Voice from the Cave. (p. 1848)
—Whispering Walls. (p. 1912)
Wirth, Beverly. Flowers from Seeds: A Garden Parable. (p. 608)
Wirth, Margie & Sherfinski, Julie. BF: the Carrot Monster. (p. 174)
Wirth, Petra, tr. see Burke, David.
Wirths, Claudine G. Choosing a Career in Law Enforcement. (p. 310)
Wirths, Claudine G., jt. auth. see Bowman-Kruhm, Mary.
Wirtzfeld, Beverly. Bear's Designs Unlimited (p. 151)
Wisa, Louis, illus. see Garis, Howard R.
Wisa, Louis, illus. see Garis, Howard.
Wisbauer, Cortney. Rodney, the Ice Dragon. Wisbauer, Cortney, illus. (p. 1484)
Wisbey, David. Magical Circles: A Children's Coloring & Activity Book. (p. 1074)
Wisch, Robin. Clear Margins. (p. 330)
Wisdom, Eileen Mary. Harry Meets Mathilda Saunders, M. D., illus. (p. 750)
Wisdom, Gail Ann. Trouble with Bullies. (p. 1790)
Wisdom, Linda. Demon Does It Better. (p. 426)
Wisdom, Liz. There's No Such Thing As a No Good Man. (p. 1731)
—Too Many Lonely Nights. (p. 1766)
Wise, Alicia. Myrtle's True Friend. Wise, Jesse D., illus. (p. 1222)
Wise, Anna. Vala of Trinity: Book One Norse Series (p. 1830)
Wise Baxter, Danielle. Corkie the Cajun Puppy: Black Lake Friends. (p. 367)
Wise, Bill. Louis Sockalexis: Native American Baseball Pioneer Farnsworth, Bill, illus. (p. 1058)
Wise, Catlin, illus. see Tabernik, John.
Wise, D. Rudd & Wise, Rachel. Three Little Orphan Kittens. Gottschalk, Deana, illus. (p. 1742)
Wise, Derba. Great Big Book of Children's Games. (p. 714)
Wise, Ella, jt. auth. see Bailey, Viola.
Wise, Erin, jt. auth. see Montague, Gay.
Wise, Gary, jt. auth. see Andrews McMeel Publishing, LLC Staff.
Wise, Jesse D., illus. see Wise, Alicia.
Wise, Keith. Isabella's Playmate. (p. 891)
Wise, Linda. Pearl's Gems. (p. 1333)
Wise, Noreen, ed. see Balawajder, Thomas, et al.
Wise, Noreen, ed. see Isom, Lori Boyd.
Wise Owl Printing Plus Inc, creator. I Can Write Streetland, PreK-2: Integrated learning Workbook. (p. 837)
Wise, Rachel. Black & White & Gray All Over. (p. 195)
—Breaking News. (p. 225)
—Cast Your Ballot! (p. 276)
—Digital Disaster! (p. 439)
—Everyone's a Critic. (p. 544)
—Late Edition. (p. 979)
—Level Playing Field. (p. 1003)
—Old Story, New Twist. (p. 1284)
—Read All about It! (p. 1442)
—Set the Record Straight! (p. 1554)
—Stop the Presses! (p. 1654)
—Texting 1, 2, 3. (p. 1724)

Wise, Rachel, jt. auth. see Wise, D. Rudd.
Wise, Robert L. Wired. (p. 1939)
Wise, Ronald L. Urban Griot Speaks. (p. 1825)
Wise, Sean. How to Be a Business Superhero: Prepare for Everything, Train with the Best, Make Your Own Destiny at Work. (p. 814)
Wise, Sue. Cómo se Dice... ? Coirault, Christine, illus. (p. 351)
—How Do I Say That? (¿Cómo se Dice?) Coirault, Christine, illus. (p. 807)
Wise, Tama. Street Dreams. (p. 1666)
Wise, William. Christopher Mouse: The Tale of a Small Traveler. Benson, Patrick, tr. (p. 317)
—Christopher Mouse: The Tale of a Small Traveler. Benson, Patrick, illus. (p. 317)
—Christopher Mouse. (p. 317)
—Ten Sly Piranhas: A Counting Story in Reverse (A Tale of Wickedness - And Worse!) Chess, Victoria, illus. (p. 1719)
—Zany Zoo. Munsinger, Lynn, illus. (p. 1985)
Wise-Douglas, Terri. Wonderful World of Cupcakes. Duckworth, Jeffrey, illus. (p. 1948)
Wisely, Deanna. Dear Santa, My Letter Is a Little Different this Year. (p. 419)
Wiseman, Ann Sayre. Best of Making Things: A Handbook of Creative Discovery. (p. 170)
Wiseman, Ann Sayre, jt. auth. see Langstaff, John.
Wiseman, Blaine. Argentina. (p. 97)
—Baseball. (p. 140)
—Basketball. (p. 143)
—Beavers. (p. 155)
—Blizzards. (p. 200)
—Budgeting. (p. 235)
—Bulldozers. (p. 240)
—Dump Trucks: WOW: Big Machines. (p. 489)
—Dump Trucks. (p. 489)
—Excavators. (p. 547)
—Extreme Excavators. (p. 556)
—Father's Day: Canadian Celebrations. (p. 577)
—Fête des Pères: Les Célébrations Canadiennes. Karvonen, Tanjah, tr. from ENG. (p. 583)
—Football. (p. 615)
—Jumbo Jets: WOW: Big Machines. (p. 933)
—Jumbo Jets. (p. 933)
—Lynxes. (p. 1066)
—Martial Arts. (p. 1097)
—Midwest. (p. 1139)
—Mighty Bulldozers. (p. 1140)
—Monster Trucks: WOW: Big Machines. (p. 1168)
—Monster Trucks. (p. 1168)
—MotoX. (p. 1180)
—Nigeria. (p. 1252)
—Northeast. (p. 1265)
—Record Breakers (p. 1452)
—Shaun White. (p. 1563)
—Skateboarding: X Games. (p. 1583)
—Skateboarding. (p. 1583)
—Snowboarding: X Games. (p. 1600)
—Snowboarding. (p. 1600)
—Snowmobiling. (p. 1601)
—Soccer. (p. 1603)
—Southeast. (p. 1617)
—Southwest. (p. 1617)
—Stanley Cup. (p. 1639)
—Surfing: X Games. (p. 1685)
—Surfing. (p. 1685)
—Tough Tractors. (p. 1773)
—Tractors: WOW: Big Machines. (p. 1775)
—UFC Championship: Sporting Championships. (p. 1807)
—UFC Championship. (p. 1807)
—Volcanoes. (p. 1849)
—West. (p. 1876)
—World of Wonder: Big Machines (p. 1957)
Wiseman, Blaine & Tait, Lela. Hockey Records. (p. 786)
Wiseman, David. Jeremy Visick. (p. 913)
Wiseman, Eva. Kanada. (p. 942)
—Last Song. (p. 978)
—No One Must Know. (p. 1259)
—Place Not Home (p. 1365)
—Puppet. (p. 1417)
—World Outside. (p. 1958)
Wiseman, Gale. How Mr. Branch Got A New Name. (p. 811)
Wiseman, Holly. Xavier & Lynx: And the Mean Trick. (p. 1967)
Wiseman, Howard W. Second Wiseman: A Quest for Liberty & Justice. (p. 1540)
Wiseman, Neil B. & London, H. B. For Kids' Sake: Winning the Tug-of-War for Future Generations. (p. 615)
Wiseman, Nicholas Patrick. Fabiola: Oder Die Kirche der Katakomben. (p. 559)
Wiseman, Rosalind. Boys, Girls & Other Hazardous Materials. (p. 220)
Wisenfeld, Alison, illus. see Joslin, Mary.
Wisenrich, Athena. Sitar: Legend of the Morning Star. (p. 1582)
Wish, Katia, illus. see Dixon, Amy.
Wish, Katia, illus. see Smith, Bryan.
Wisham Fenstermacher, Mary. Pablo Visits the Desert. (p. 1316)
Wishbone, jt. auth. see Smith, Cynthia.
Wisher, Mark. Don't kiss the Prince. (p. 467)
Wishinsky, Frieda. Arctic Storm Lewis-MacDougall, Patricia Ann & Owlkids Books Inc. Staff, illus. (p. 96)
—Avis Dolphin Dawson, Willow, illus. (p. 120)
—Bee in Your Ear Laliberté, Louise-Andrée, illus. (p. 157)
—Bee in Your Ear. Laliberte, Louise-Andree, illus. (p. 157)
—Beware, Pirates! Griffiths, Dean & Owlkids Books Inc. Staff, illus. (p. 173)
—Blob (p. 200)
—Could We Live on the Moon? (p. 369)
—Crazy for Gold. Griffiths, Dean & Owlkids Books Inc. Staff, illus. (p. 377)
—Danger, Dinosaurs! Griffiths, Dean & Owlkids Books Inc. Staff, illus. (p. 403)
—Dimples Delight Laliberté, Louise-Andrée, illus. (p. 440)
—Dimples Delight. Laliberte, Louise-Andree, illus. (p. 440)
—Each One Special. (p. 492)
—Flying High! Griffiths, Dean & Owlkids Books Inc. Staff, illus. (p. 610)
—Frog in My Throat Laliberté, Louise-Andrée, illus. (p. 640)
—Halifax Explodes! Lewis-MacDougall, Patricia Ann & Owlkids Books Inc. Staff, illus. (p. 737)
—Hurry, Freedom. Griffiths, Dean & Owlkids Books Inc. Staff, illus. (p. 830)
—Maggie Can't Wait Griffiths, Dean, illus. (p. 1071)
—Make It Fair! Lewis-MacDougall, Patricia Ann & Owlkids Books Inc. Staff, illus. (p. 1079)
—Man Who Made Parks: The Story of Parkbuilder Frederick Law Olmsted. Zhang, Song Nan, illus. (p. 1086)
—No Frogs for Dinner Hendry, Linda, illus. (p. 1258)
—Noodle up Your Nose Laliberté, Louise-Andrée, illus. (p. 1264)
—On the Case. Franson, Leanne et al, illus. (p. 1290)
—Pioneer Kids. Griffiths, Dean & Owlkids Books Inc. Staff, illus. (p. 1361)
—Please, Louise! Gay, Marie-Louise, illus. (p. 1373)
—Profiles #4: Freedom Heroines. (p. 1409)
—Queen of the Toilet Bowl (p. 1425)
—Remembering the Titanic. (p. 1460)
—SOS! Titanic! Eid, Jean-Paul & Owlkids Books Inc. Staff, illus. (p. 1614)
—Stop That Stagecoach! Eid, Jean-Paul & Owlkids Books Inc. Staff, illus. (p. 1653)
—Whale Tale. Griffiths, Dean & Owlkids Books Inc. Staff, illus. (p. 1877)
—What's up, Bear? A Book about Opposites. Moore, Sean L., illus. (p. 1900)
—Where Are You, Bear? A Canadian Alphabet Adventure. Moore, Sean L. & Owlkids Books Inc. Staff, illus. (p. 1906)
—Yikes, Vikings! Griffiths, Dean & Owlkids Books Inc. Staff, illus. (p. 1971)
—You're Mean, Lily Jean! Denton, Kady MacDonald, illus. (p. 1982)
Wishinsky, Frieda, jt. auth. see Weaver, Janice.
Wishinsky, Frieda & Dorling Kindersley Publishing Staff. Albert Einstein - A Photographic Story of a Life. (p. 34)
Wishinsky, Frieda & Griffiths, Dean. Far from Home. Franson, Leanne & Owlkids Books Inc. Staff, illus. (p. 572)
—Give Maggie a Chance (p. 681)
—Lost in the Snow. Franson, Leanne & Owlkids Books Inc. Staff, illus. (p. 1056)
Wisinski, Ed, illus. see Harper, Benjamin.
Wisk, Dar. Grandma Always Says... (p. 707)
Wisler, G. Clifton. Caleb's Choice. (p. 252)
Wismer, C. L. Missing Chocolate Chip Oatmeal Peanut Butter Raisin Cookie. (p. 1152)
Wisner, Franz. Honeymoon with My Brother: A Memoir. (p. 795)
Wisner, Karen. Country Seasons (p. 372)
Wisner, Luke, illus. see Burciaga, David.
Wisnewski, Andrea. Little Red Riding Hood. (p. 1035)
Wisnewski, Andrea, illus. see Bennett, William J., ed.
Wisnewski, Andrea, illus. see Millen, C. M.
Wisnia, Chris. Doris Danger: Giant Monster Adventures. Vol. 1 (p. 471)
Wisnia, Saul. Miracle at Fenway: The Inside Story of the Boston Red Sox 2004 Championship Season. (p. 1148)
Wisniewski, David. Golem. Wisniewski, David, illus. (p. 696)
Wisniewski, David, illus. see Bunting, Eve.
Wisniewski, Lori. Importance of Being Uu. (p. 862)
Wissing, Caroline. Voiceless. (p. 1848)
Wissinger, Tamera Will. Gone Fishing: A Novel. Cordell, Matthew, illus. (p. 697)
—This Old Band. Loveridge, Matt, illus. (p. 1737)
Wissinger, Tamera Will & Long, Earlene R. Gone Fishing. Cordell, Matthew & Brown, Richard, illus. (p. 697)
Wissler, Clark. American Indian: An Introduction to the Anthropology of the New World. (p. 61)
Wissman, Celeste Farris. When I Teach My Monkey How to Dance. (p. 1903)
Wissolik, Richard David. Ice Cream Joe: The Valley Dairy Story—: & America's Love Affair with Ice Cream. Greubel, Joseph E., ed. (p. 850)
Wist, S. J. Whispering Stone. (p. 1912)
Wister, Sally. Diary of Sally Wister: A Colonial Quaker Girl (p. 435)
Wistow, David, et al. Meet the Group of Seven. (p. 1122)
Wistrand, Carolyn Nur. Beauty in Black Performance: Plays for African American Youth. (p. 154)
Wisuri, Marlene, jt. auth. see Peacock, Thomas Love.
Wiszowaty, Robin. My Maasai Life: From Suburbia to Savannah (p. 1213)
Witcher, Chanz'e. All I Want. (p. 44)
Witcher, John. 123 & Me. (p. 2000)
Witcher, Lillie. Ican & the Little Mermaid. (p. 850)
Witcher, Monte L. Cleared Hot: A Story of the Battle of Observation Post 4. (p. 330)
Witek, Jo. Brave as Can Be: A Book of Courage. Roussey, Christine, illus. (p. 223)
—Hello in There! A Big Sister's Book of Waiting. Roussey, Christine, illus. (p. 764)
—In My Heart: A Book of Feelings. Roussey, Christine, illus. (p. 864)
With, Barbara. Party of Twelve: Post 9/11. (p. 1326)
Withall, Stephen J. Software Requirement Patterns. (p. 1606)
Withaneye, Toni. Little Thunder's First Sound. (p. 1037)
Wither, George. Poetry (p. 1376)
Witherell, Nancy L., jt. auth. see McMackin, Mary C.
Witherick, M. E. Urban World. (p. 1825)
Witherow, Wendy. Bridget's Blog. Pulley, Kelly, illus. (p. 227)
—Miranda's Makeover. Pulley, Kelly, illus. (p. 1149)
Withers, Margaret. Welcome to the Lord's Table: A Practical Course for Preparing Children to Receive Holy Communion. (p. 1874)
Withers, Pam. Adrenalin Ride (p. 13)
—BMX Tunnel Run (p. 204)
—Breathless (p. 226)
—Camp Wild (p. 257)
—Camp Wild. (p. 257)
—Casse-Cous: (Daredevil Club) (p. 276)
—Daredevil Club (p. 406)
—Dirtbike Daredevils (p. 446)
—First Descent. (p. 594)
—Mountainboard Maniacs (p. 1181)
—Peak Survival (p. 1332)
—Respira (p. 1463)
—Skater Stuntboys (p. 1584)
—Surf Zone (p. 1685)
—Vertical Limits (p. 1837)
—Wake's Edge (p. 1853)
Withers, Wendy Marie. Adventures of My Brother's Keeper: Let Our Ball Go! (p. 21)
Witherspoon, Diane L. Madison's Adventures - Madison & the Family Tree. (p. 1070)
—Madison's Adventures - Madison & the Schoolyard Bully. (p. 1070)
Witherspoon Press Staff, contrib. by. Belonging to God: A First Catechism. (p. 163)
Withey, Gail. Give It Up. (p. 681)
Withrow, Brandon, jt. auth. see Withrow, Mindy.
Withrow, Brandon & Withrow, Mindy. Hearts & Hands: Chronicles of the Awakening Church. (p. 760)
—Monks & Mystics: Chronicles of the Medieval Church (p. 1166)
—Peril & Peace: Chronicles of the Ancient Church (p. 1343)
Withrow, Mindy, jt. auth. see Withrow, Brandon.
Withrow, Mindy & Withrow, Brandon. Courage & Conviction: Chronicles of the Reformation Church (p. 372)
—Rescue & Redeem: Chronicles of the Modern Church. Vol. 5 (p. 1462)
Withrow, Sarah. Black Sunshine of Goody Pryne (p. 197)
Witkin, Kim. Butterfly Blessings. (p. 247)
Witkowski, Teri. Bitty Bear & the Bugs. Ackley, Peggy Jo, illus. (p. 194)
—Bitty Bear, Flower Girl. Ackley, Peggy Jo, illus. (p. 194)
—Bitty Bear's Birthday Treats. Ackley, Peggy Jo, illus. (p. 194)
—Bitty Bear's New Friend. Ackley, Peggy Jo, illus. (p. 194)
—Bitty Bear's Snowflake Dreams. Ackley, Peggy Jo, illus. (p. 194)
—Bitty Bear's Valentines. Ackley, Peggy Jo, illus. (p. 194)
—Bitty Bear's Walk in the Woods. Ackley, Peggy Jo, illus. (p. 194)
—Bitty Bunch Bath Book. Ackley, Peggy Jo, illus. (p. 194)
—Bitty Bunny's Bedtime. Ackley, Peggy Jo, illus. (p. 194)
—Bitty Bunny's Slipper Search. Ackley, Peggy Jo, illus. (p. 194)
—Bunny & Piggy at the Beach. Ackley, Peggy Jo, illus. (p. 242)
—Happy Birthday, Bitty Bear! Ackley, Peggy Jo, illus. (p. 744)
—It's Spring, Bitty Bear! Ackley, Peggy Jo, illus. (p. 899)
—Time for Bed, Bitty Bunch. Ackley, Peggy Jo, illus. (p. 1751)
—Wait Your Turn, Bitty Froggy! Ackley, Peggy Jo, illus. (p. 1852)
Witkowski, Teri, ed. see Hirsch, Jennifer & Jones, Michelle.
Witmer, Edith. Dancing Buttercups: Poems for Little Children. (p. 402)
Witmer, Ruth, illus. see Martin, Mabel.
Witmer, Scott. Bookings & Gigs. (p. 212)
—Drums, Keyboards, & Other Instruments. (p. 487)
—Guitars & Bass. (p. 731)
—History of Rock Bands. (p. 784)
—Managing Your Band. (p. 1086)
—Political Systems (p. 1380)
—Recording. (p. 1452)
—Show. (p. 1570)
—Songwriting. (p. 1612)
—Sports & Society (p. 1632)
Witnes, Vitus, illus. see Baia, Edward.
Witowski, Teri, jt. auth. see Brown, Harriet.
Witrago, Jost. Wooden Dove. (p. 1949)
Witschen, Kay. Clinker's Christmas Star. Witschen, Kay, illus. (p. 333)
—Clinker's Dragon. (p. 333)
—Johnny Coalboy. Luckemeyer, Norma, illus. (p. 923)
Witschonke, Alan, illus. see Mann, Elizabeth.
Witschonke, Alan, illus. see Robb, Don.
Witschonke, Alan, jt. auth. see Mann, Elizabeth.
Witt, David, illus. see Fontes, Ron & Fontes, Justine.
Witt, David, illus. see Jolley, Dan.
Witt, David, illus. see Limke, Jeff.
Witt, David, illus. see Schweizer, Chris.
Witt, David, illus. see Storrie, Paul D.
Witt, Eddie, illus. see Vil, Steve.
Witt, Janice. Harold Discovers Santa's Secret: A Very Long Dog with a Very Big Heart. Reznicek, Curtis, illus. (p. 749)
Witt, Joe & Gallaway, Kate. Managing Your Mathematics Classroom. (p. 1086)
Witt, Marcos. Liderazgo al Extremo (p. 1007)
Witt, Mary Ann Frese, et al. Humanities (p. 826)
Witt, P. J. Early One Christmas Morning. (p. 494)
Witt, Patricia. When Grandpa & Grandma Visit. (p. 1902)
Witt, Rici, illus. see Rose, Alea.
Witte, Anna. Fandango de Lola. Archer, Micha, illus. (p. 570)
—Lola's Fandango. Archer, Micha, illus. (p. 1046)
—Lola's Fandango. Masse, Josée & Archer, Micha, illus. (p. 1046)
—Loro Tico Tango. Witte, Anna, illus. (p. 1053)
—Parrot Tico Tango. (p. 1325)
—Parrot Tico Tango. Witte, Anna, illus. (p. 1325)
Witte, Anna & Amador, Brian. Parrot Tico Tango. Witte, Anna, illus. (p. 1325)
Witte, Carol, ed. see Fisher, Nancy.
Witte, Jessica Pierce. Dexter the Duck Gets His Quack. York, Shane, illus. (p. 432)
Witte, Sam. Gamal Abdel Nasser. (p. 654)
Wittebrood, Menno, illus. see Coxall, Darcy.
Wittekind, Erika. Afghanistan. (p. 26)
—Amazon. com: The Company & Its Founder. (p. 56)
—Argentina. (p. 97)
—Big Push: How Popular Culture Is Always Selling (p. 183)
—Gloria Steinem: Women's Liberation Leader. (p. 685)
—James Madison's Presidency. (p. 907)
—Violence as Entertainment: Why Aggression Sells. (p. 1843)
—What's Great about Wisconsin? (p. 1897)
Wittekind, Erika & Gerhardt, Michael J. United States v. Nixon: The Watergate Scandal & Limits to US Presidential Power. (p. 1820)
Wittels, Harriet & Greisman, Joan. First Dictionary. Biggs, Gene, illus. (p. 594)
Witteman, Barbara. Leonardo Da Vinci (p. 992)
Wittenbach, Jennie. Little Stories for Little Folks. (p. 1037)
Wittenback, Janet. God Makes Me His Child in Baptism. McDonnell, Janet, illus. (p. 690)
Wittenberg, John C. Amazing Adventures of Spirit & Opportunity. (p. 52)
Wittenberg, Stella, illus. see Ende, Michael.
Wittenstein, Vicki O. Reproductive Rights: Who Decides? (p. 1461)
Wittenstein, Vicki Oransky. Planet Hunter: Geoff Marcy & the Search for Other Earths. (p. 1367)
Witter, Bret, jt. auth. see Myron, Vicki.
Witter, Pamela. Chuck & Spark Explore the Park. (p. 318)
Witter, Rahad, illus. see Moore, Clement C.
Witthaus, A. S. Princess Sach. (p. 1405)
Wittkamp, Frantz, illus. see Nöstlinger, Christine.
Wittkamp, Frantz, tr. see Nöstlinger, Christine.
Wittkopf, Eugene R., jt. auth. see Kegley, Charles W., Jr.
Wittlinger, Ellen. Blind Faith. (p. 199)
—Hard Love. (p. 748)
—Heart on My Sleeve. (p. 760)
—Lombardo's Law. (p. 1046)
—Love & Lies: Marisol's Story. (p. 1059)
—Parrotfish. (p. 1325)
—Razzle. (p. 1441)
—Sandpiper. (p. 1511)
—This Means War! (p. 1737)
—Zigzag. (p. 1986)
Wittlinger, Laurie A., photos by see Jin, Hong Gang, et al.
Wittman, Kathy A. Raina's Vision Quest (p. 1435)
Wittman, Kelly. Botswana. Rotberg, Robert I., ed. (p. 215)
Wittman, Patricia. Scrabble Creek. (p. 1532)
Wittman, Patricia, illus. see Murray, Marjorie Dennis.
Wittman, Susan S. Heroes of the Civil War (p. 773)
—Reconstruction: Outcomes of the Civil War (p. 1452)
Wittmann, Kelly. Botswana. (p. 215)
—Botswana. Rotberg, Robert I., ed. (p. 215)
—Sean Diddy Combs. (p. 1536)
Wittmer, Michael E. Heaven Is a Place on Earth: Why Everything You Do Matters to God (p. 761)
Wittner, David G. Commodore Matthew Perry & the Perry Expedition to Japan. (p. 349)
Wittner, Shirley. Kemira & the Ancient Book of Spells. (p. 948)
Wittreich, Yvonne M. B. True Story of Sasha, from Homelessness to Happiness. (p. 1793)
Wittrock, Jeni. ABCs. Banks, Timothy, illus. (p. 4)
—All about Pit Bulls (p. 43)
—Ancient Armadillos. (p. 68)
—Baby Rabbit Story (p. 127)
—Historia de un Conejo Bebé) Strictly Spanish Translation Services Staff, tr. (p. 127)
—How Honest Are You? (p. 809)
—Laika the Space Dog: First Hero in Outer Space Toth, Shannon, illus. (p. 972)
—Pet Hermit Crabs up Close. (p. 1345)
—Pet Rabbits up Close. (p. 1345)
—Pets up Close. (p. 1348)
—Tarantulas (p. 1706)
—W. E. B. du Bois. (p. 1851)
Wittrock, Jeni, jt. auth. see Jones, Jen.
Wittrock, Jeni, jt. auth. see Rustad, Martha E. H.
Wittrock, Jeni, jt. auth. see Shores, Erika L.
Wittrock, Jeni & Rustad, Martha E. H. Baby Animals. (p. 124)
Wittrock, Jeni, et al. Animal Heroes (p. 78)
—Great African-Americans (p. 713)
Wittry, John, jt. auth. see McGhee, Sally.
Wittwer, Hala, illus. see Loehr, Mallory.
Wittwer, Hala Swearingen, illus. see Hays, Anna Jane.
Witvliet, John D., jt. auth. see Steenwyk, Carrie.
Wiviott, Meg. Benno & the Night of Broken Glass. Bisaillon, Josée, illus. (p. 165)
Wixom, Jason Kay & Wixom, Tedi Tuttle. Cock-a-Doodle-Doo, I Love You. Lancaster, Derek, illus. (p. 337)
Wixom, Tedi Tuttle, jt. auth. see Wixom, Jason Kay.
Wiyd, Lewis. Dogs on the Porch: Dispelling the All Men are Dogs Myth. (p. 463)
Wizards of the Coast Team. Duel Masters: Enter the Battle Zone. Vol. 1 Tokyopop Staff, ed. (p. 489)
Wizkids, creator. Star War Pocketmodel TCG Trading Card Game: Imperial Power-up Pack. (p. 1641)
Wizner, Jake. Spanking Shakespeare. (p. 1622)
—Spanking Shakespeare. Ewing, Richard, illus. (p. 1622)
Wizner, Kira. John McCain: Profile of a Leading Republican. (p. 922)
WJW. Leroy & Cheryl's Adventure. (p. 993)
Wlodarski, Loran. Felina's New Home: A Florida Panther Story Clayton, Lew, illus. (p. 581)
—If a Dolphin Were a Fish Klein, Laurie Allen, illus. (p. 852)
Wlodarski, Robert James & Nathan-Wlodarski, Anne. Haunted Whaley House, Old Town, San Diego, California: A History & Guide to the Most Haunted House in America. (p. 754)
Wnuk, Wade J. Pink Slip Power. (p. 1360)
Wodarski, Bo. Caveboy Bob & the Hole of Doom. (p. 282)
Wodehouse, P. G. Mike at Wrykyn. (p. 1141)
—William Tell Told Again - Illustrated in Color. Philip Dadd, illus. (p. 1933)
Wodhull, Michael, tr. see Euripides.
Wodin, illus. see Thompson, John M. & Schultz, George M.
Woebkenberg, Valerie. Story the Little Christmas Tree Told. (p. 1663)
Woebkenberg, Valerie & Ingels, Diane. Story the Little Christmas Tree Told. (p. 1663)
Woehlke, Joshua. Shakespeare's Painless Romeo & Juliet. (p. 1559)
Woelfle, Gretchen. All the World's a Stage: A Novel in Five Acts. Cox, Thomas, illus. (p. 46)
—Animal Families, Animal Friends. Hynes, Robert, illus. (p. 77)
—Mumbet's Declaration of Independence. Delinois, Alix, illus. (p. 1190)
—Wind at Work: An Activity Guide to Windmills. (p. 1935)

—Write on, Mercy! The Secret Life of Mercy Otis Warren. Wallner, Alexandra, illus. (p. 1963)
Woell, J. Fred. Gloucester: College Life Between Classes. Woell, J. Fred, illus. (p. 685)
Woell, Tamara. A-Z Teacher Manual, Simon Peter School Scripture Study. (p. 2)
Woff, Richard. Pocket Dictionary of Ancient Greek Heroes & Heroines. (p. 1375)
—Pocket Dictionary of Greek & Roman Gods & Goddesses. (p. 1375)
Wofford, Delaney. For Courage. (p. 615)
Wofford, Sherry Lynn. Introducing the Adventures of Jerry Giraffe & Feather Bird. (p. 882)
Wohl, David, et al. Crossovers. (p. 385)
—Top Cow's Best of Michael Turner. (p. 1769)
Wohl, Lauren L. Eighth Menorah. Hughes, Laura, illus. (p. 507)
Wohlenhaus, Kim, ed. Suicide Information for Teens. (p. 1673)
Wohlers, Bob. Life on an Ocean Planet Student Text Book. (p. 1012)
Wohlers, Terry. Wohlers Report 2005. (p. 1943)
Wohlfahrt, Franz. Easiest Elementary Method for Violin: Op. 38. (p. 498)
Wohlford, Connie. Joy Comes to Bethlehem. (p. 929)
Wohlford, Martha Crikelair. Splash: The Staniel Cay Cat. (p. 1629)
Wohlrabe, Sarah C. Helping You Heal: A Book about Nurses. Thomas, Eric, illus. (p. 766)
—Helping You Learn: A Book about Teachers Thomas, Eric, illus. (p. 766)
—Visit to the Library Thompson, Jeffrey, illus. (p. 1845)
Wohlt, Julia. Naughty Eddie Larue. Brown, Clovis, illus. (p. 1237)
Wohnoutka, Mike. Dad's First Day. (p. 399)
—Head, Shoulders, Knees, & Toes. (p. 756)
—Little Puppy & the Big Green Monster. Wohnoutka, Mike, illus. (p. 1034)
—This Little Piggy. (p. 1737)
Wohnoutka, Mike, illus. see Beil, Karen Magnuson.
Wohnoutka, Mike, illus. see Buzzeo, Toni.
Wohnoutka, Mike, illus. see Hill, Susanna Leonard.
Wohnoutka, Mike, illus. see Kehoe, Tim.
Wohnoutka, Mike, illus. see Kimmel, Eric A.
Wohnoutka, Mike, illus. see LaRochelle, David.
Wohnoutka, Mike, illus. see Pace, Anne Marie.
Wohnoutka, Mike, illus. see Schotter, Roni.
Wohnoutka, Mike, illus. see Van Hoven, Constance.
Woik, Julie. Life & Times of Lilly the Lash: The Garden Gathering. Tobin, Marc, illus. (p. 1008)
Wojahn, Donald, jt. auth. see Wojahn, Rebecca Hogue.
Wojahn, Rebecca, jt. auth. see Wojahn, Rebecca Hogue.
Wojahn, Rebecca Hogue & Donald. Australian Outback Food Chain: A Who-Eats-What Adventure. (p. 116)
—Desert Food Chain: A Who-Eats-What Adventures in North America. (p. 429)
—Rain Forest Food Chain: A Who-Eats-What Adventures in South America. (p. 1434)
—Savanna Food Chain: A Who-Eats-What Adventure in Africa. (p. 1516)
—Tundra Food Chain: A Who-Eats-What in the Arctic. (p. 1796)
Wojahn, Rebecca Hogue & Wojahn, Donald. Australian Outback Food Chain: A Who-Eats-What Adventure. (p. 116)
—Cloud Forest Food Chain: A Who-Eats-What Adventure in Africa. (p. 334)
—Coral Reef Food Chain: A Who-Eats-What Adventure in the Caribbean Sea. (p. 366)
—Desert Food Chain: A Who-Eats-What Adventure in North America. (p. 429)
—Estuary Food Chain: A Who-Eats-What Adventure in North America. (p. 538)
—Galápagos Island Food Chain: A Who-Eats-What Adventure. (p. 653)
—Mangrove Forest Food Chain: A Who-Eats-What Adventure in Asia. (p. 1087)
—Nile River Food Chain: A Who-Eats-What Adventure. (p. 1255)
—Rain Forest Food Chain: A Who-Eats-What Adventure in South America. (p. 1434)
—Savanna Food Chain: A Who-Eats-What Adventure in Africa. (p. 1516)
—Temperate Forest Food Chain: A Who-Eats-What Adventure in North America. (p. 1717)
—Tundra Food Chain: A Who-Eats-What Adventure in the Arctic. (p. 1796)
Wojahn, Rebecca Hogue & Wojahn, Rebecca. Dr. Kate: Angel on Snowshoes. (p. 475)
Wojcicki, Ronda M. Speech Class Rules: An Introduction to Speech Therapy for Children. (p. 1624)
Wojciechowska, Maia. Dreams of the Super Bowl. Karsky, A. K., illus. (p. 484)
—Kingdom in a Horse. (p. 959)
—Shadow of a Bull. (p. 1557)
—Shadow of the Bull. (p. 1557)
Wojciechowska, Maia & Manna, Sal. Kingdom in a Horse. (p. 959)
Wojciechowski, Christine. Duck, Duck, Dive. (p. 488)
—When We Adopted You. (p. 1905)
Wojciechowski, Susan. Beany & the Dreaded Wedding. Natti, Susanna, illus. (p. 150)
—Beany & the Magic Crystal. Natti, Susanna, illus. (p. 150)
—Beany Goes to Camp. Natti, Susanna, illus. (p. 150)
—Beany (Not Beanhead) Natti, Susanna, illus. (p. 150)
—Best Halloween of All. (p. 170)
—Best Halloween of All. Meddaugh, Susan, illus. (p. 170)
—Christmas Miracle of Jonathan Toomey. Lynch, P. J., illus. (p. 314)
—Fine St. Patrick's Day. Curry, Tom, illus. (p. 589)
Wojcik, Joe. Call Me Yubbie. (p. 254)
Wojick, Luke. I Can Draw Shapes: Shapes & Their Attributes. (p. 835)
—I Can Draw Shapes. (p. 835)
Wojna, Lisa. Canadian Inventions: Fantastic Feats & Quirky Contraptions. (p. 260)
—Great Canadian Women: Portraits of Nineteen Extraordinary Women. (p. 714)
Wojna, Lisa, jt. auth. see Georgi, Tamela.
Wojtak, James, jt. auth. see Chachas, George.
Wojtanik, Andrew. Afghanistan to Zimbabwe: Country Facts That Helped Me Win the National Geographic Bee. (p. 26)
Wojtko, Kimberlee, illus. see Summers, Marilee.
Wojton, Roxane. My Mommy & Me & Baby Makes Three. (p. 1214)
Wojtowicz, Jen. Boy Who Grew Flowers. Adams, Steve, illus. (p. 219)
Wojtowicz, Jen & Wojzowitz, Jen. Boy Who Grew Flowers. Adams, Steve, illus. (p. 219)
Wojtowycz, David. Elephant Joe, Brave Firefighter! (p. 511)
—Fizz the Fire Engine! (p. 601)
—Let's Play, Dudley! Colors. (p. 1000)
—Nursery. (p. 1273)
—Playday. (p. 1372)
—Scoop, the Digger! (p. 1529)
—What Will You Wear, Claude? (p. 1895)
—Whatever the Weather, Clavde! (p. 1896)
Wojtowycz, David, illus. see Andreae, Giles.
Wojtusik, Elizabeth. Kitty Up! Yoshikawa, Sachiko, illus. (p. 963)
Wojtyla, Karol, see John Paul II, pseud.
Wojzowitz, Jen, jt. auth. see Wojtowicz, Jen.
Wolak, Camilla H. Squire Gullible & the Dragon. (p. 1637)
Wolberg, K. A. Beyond the Hedge. (p. 174)
Wolbert, Christine. History... Through the Eyes of a Child: Nathan Hale. (p. 785)
Wolbrueck, Cherri. Amy Finds a Home. (p. 66)
—Chippi's Adopted Dozen. (p. 308)
Wolchansky, Molly Kay. Cactus & the Balloon. (p. 250)
Wolcott, James. Attack Poodles & Other Media Mutants: The Looting of the News in a Time of Terror. (p. 114)
Wolcott, K. Hannah, ed. see Wolcott, P. A.
Wolcott, Karen, illus. see Gordh, Bill & Pugliano-Martin, Carol.
Wolcott, Karen, illus. see Jordan, Apple & RH Disney Staff.
Wolcott, Karen, illus. see Kilgras, Heidi & Parker, Jessie.
Wolcott, Karen, illus. see Landolf, Diane Wright.
Wolcott, Karen, illus. see Man-Kong, Mary & Roberts, Angela.
Wolcott, Karen, illus. see Roberts, Angela.
Wolcott, P. A. Fox, the Badger, & the Bunny: A Dales Tale. Wolcott, K. Hannah, ed. (p. 626)
Wolczuk, Alice. Discovering Sauerkraut. Hammond, Gaye, illus. (p. 449)
Wolczyk, Deborah R. Maisie - the Dress up Cat. (p. 1077)
Wold, Joyce. God's Creations. (p. 691)
—Grayson Gorilla Learns to Grin. (p. 713)
Wold, Justin And Janet. This Thing I Made Can Make Anything but Can't Make Friends & Family. (p. 1737)
Woldegiorgis, Abraham, jt. auth. see Parker, Ben.
Wolek, Guy. Dinner with OLIVIA. (p. 441)
—OLIVIA & the Rain Dance. (p. 1286)
—OLIVIA & the School Carnival. (p. 1286)
—OLIVIA Builds a Snowlady. (p. 1286)
Wolek, Guy, illus. see Donnelly, Shannon.
Wolek, Guy, illus. see Horender, Philip M.
Wolek, Guy, illus. see Huneke, Amanda.
Wolek, Guy, illus. see Silverhardt, Lauryn.
Wolf, Aaron D., ed. see Gressman, Carylee Anne.
Wolf, Allan. Blood-Hungry Spleen & Other Poems about Our Parts. Clarke, Greg, illus. (p. 200)
—New Found Land: Lewis & Clark's Voyage of Discovery. (p. 1244)
—Watch That Ends the Night: Voices from the Titanic. (p. 1861)
Wolf, Allan, jt. auth. see Holbrook, Sara.
Wolf, Alvin, et al. Social Work Skills for Beginning Direct Practice: Text, Workbook, & Interactive Web Based Case Studies. (p. 1605)
Wolf, Bob. Halo's Story: As told by the dog that walked with Jesus. (p. 739)
Wolf, Bruce, illus. see Abrams, Pam.
Wolf, Bruce, photos by see Rudy, Maggie & Abrams, Pam.
Wolf, Carla. Moving Towards a Dream. (p. 1184)
Wolf, Carol A. Foggy Dog. (p. 611)
—Foggy Dog Discovers Christmas. (p. 611)
Wolf, Cathrine, ed. see Sweeny, Sheila.
Wolf, Cathrine, ed. Inside Space Jam. (p. 877)
Wolf, Clarissa. Cat, Cat, Feral Cat. Messer, Corey, illus. (p. 277)
—Orange Fizz. Wolf, Myron, photos by. (p. 1301)
Wolf, Claudia. Grandma & Me. Wolf, Claudia, illus. (p. 708)
Wolf, Claudia, illus. see Blair, Eric.
Wolf, Claudia, illus. see Mackall, Dandi Daley.
Wolf, Claudia, illus. see Nicola, Robbin.
Wolf, Claudia, illus. see Schroeder, Holly.
Wolf, Claudia, illus. see Thompson, Deanna.
Wolf, Claudia, illus. see Van Oss, Laura.
Wolf, Edward, jt. auth. see Wolf, Edward C.
Wolf, Edward C. & Wolf, Edward. Klamath Heartlands: A Guide to the Klamath Reservation Forest Plan. (p. 963)
Wolf, Elaine. Camp. (p. 257)
Wolf, Elisabeth. Lulu in la la Land. (p. 1065)
Wolf, Elizabeth, illus. see Bader, Bonnie.
Wolf, Elizabeth, illus. see Falk, Elizabeth Sullivan.
Wolf, Elizabeth, illus. see Kramer, Sydelle.
Wolf, Elizabeth, illus. see Lehman-Wilzig, Tami.
Wolf, Elizabeth, illus. see Milton, Joyce.
Wolf, Elizabeth, illus. see Thompson, Gare.
Wolf, Elizabeth, tr. see Thompson, Gare.
Wolf, Ellen. Ballad of the Wild Bear: Teaching Guide. (p. 134)
Wolf, Ema. 18 Cuentos de amor. (p. 1995)
—Silencio, Ninos! Y Otros Cuentos. Pez, illus. (p. 1575)
Wolf, Fred Alan. Dr. Quantum in the Grandfather Paradox. (p. 475)
Wolf, Gita. Very Hungry Lion: A Folktale. Roy, Indrapramit, illus. (p. 1838)
Wolf, Gita, jt. auth. see Rao, Nikhil.
Wolf, Gita, adapted by. Enduring Ark. (p. 527)
Wolf, Gita & Anastasio, Andrea. Alone in the Forest. Shyam, Bhajju, illus. (p. 48)
Wolf, Gita & Ramanathan, Rathna. In the Land of Punctuation. Rao, Sirish, tr. from GER. (p. 866)
Wolf, Helmut, photos by. Flowers of India. (p. 608)
Wolf, J. M. Leveled Read-Aloud Plays: U.S. Civic Holidays: 5 Short Plays with Multi-Leveled Reading Parts to Build Fluency-and Engage All Students. (p. 1003)
Wolf, Jackie. My Baby Book. Roush, April, illus. (p. 1196)
—My Sparkle Present. (p. 1219)
—My Sparkle Pumpkin. (p. 1219)
—Night Night Sleep Tight. Garofoli, Viviana, illus. (p. 1253)
—Picture Me Easter Babies (large Egg) (p. 1355)
—Picture Me Easter Baby (mini Bunny) (p. 1355)
—Picture Me Peek-a-Boo! (p. 1355)
—Sparkle Basket. (p. 1622)
Wolf, Jackie, et al. My Sparkle Egg Book. (p. 1219)
Wolf, Jennifer Shaw. Breaking Beautiful. (p. 225)
—Dead Girls Don't Lie. (p. 416)
Wolf, Joan. That Summer. (p. 1726)
Wolf, Joan M. Someone Named Eva. (p. 1609)
Wolf Jump, Rebecca R. Home for A Husky: The Husky Tales - Book 1. (p. 792)
Wolf, Justin. Adventures of Silly Monkey & Jack. (p. 23)
Wolf, Karina & Hilts, Brothers. Insomniacs. (p. 878)
Wolf, Kathryn Nider & Robbins, Heather P. Make a Joyful Noise! Music, Movement, & Creative Play to Teach Bible Stories: Preschool - Grade 1. (p. 1078)
Wolf, Kirsten. Daily Life of the Vikings (p. 400)
Wolf, Laurie Goldrich. Crafty Princess: Green & Groovy. (p. 376)
—Do It Myself Kids' Cookbook: Nothing Hot, Nothing Sharp. (p. 457)
—Lonely Sock Club: One Sock, Tons of Cool Projects! (p. 1046)
Wolf, Laurie Goldrich, jt. auth. see Downtown Bookworks Inc. Staff.
Wolf, Laurie Goldrich & Abrams, Pam. Fairy Crafts: Green & Groovy. (p. 563)
Wolf, Linda. Cozy Kitty (p. 375)
Wolf, Linda Little. Great Spirit Horse (p. 718)
—Visions of the Buffalo People (p. 1845)
Wolf, Mari. Empty Bottle. (p. 521)
Wolf, Mária. Black Dog. (p. 196)
—Extraordinary Ordinary Day. (p. 555)
—Maggy Cans. (p. 1071)
Wolf, Marie. Ghb & Analogs: High-Risk Club Drugs. (p. 670)
Wolf, Marie E. GHB & Analogs: High-Risk Club Drugs. (p. 670)
Wolf, Matt, illus. see Stilton, Geronimo.
Wolf, Matt, jt. auth. see Stilton, Geronimo.
Wolf, Myron, photos by see Wolf, Clarissa.
Wolf, Penny, et al. Bea's Almost Bad Day. Sweet Briar School, illus. (p. 152)
Wolf, Sallie. Peter's Trucks. (p. 1347)
—Truck Stuck. Davies, Andy Robert, illus. (p. 1791)
Wolf, Sallie & Bornstein, Micah. Robin Makes a Laughing Sound: A Birder's Journal. (p. 1480)
Wolf, Shari. Ohio Graduation Test: Math. (p. 1281)
Wolfe, Allison, jt. auth. see Yazawa, Al.
Wolfe, Andrew, ed. see Young, Bruce & Young, Jennifer Law.
Wolfe, Art. 1, 2, 3 Moose: A Counting Book. (p. 1990)
Wolfe, Art, photos by see Helman, Andrea.
Wolfe, Bob, photos by see Anderson, Jenna.
Wolfe, Bob, photos by see Rocker, Megan.
Wolfe, Bob, photos by see Shofner, Shawndra.
Wolfe, Bradley W. Upside Downside Up. (p. 1825)
Wolfe, Brian & Wolfe, Nick. Fun Face Painting Ideas for Kids: 40 Step-By-Step Demos. (p. 647)
Wolfe, Carolyn. Bedtime of the Sky & Other Sleepy-Bye Stories. Mathis, Leslie, illus. (p. 157)
—Unhappy Little Dragon: Lessons Begin. Mathis, Leslie, illus. (p. 1817)
Wolfe, D. K. Flap Doodle & the Incredible Kibbil Caper (p. 602)
Wolfe, Diane, photos by see Anderson, Jenna.
Wolfe, Diane, photos by see Rocker, Megan.
Wolfe, Diane, photos by see Shofner, Shawndra.
Wolfe, Elisabeth, jt. auth. see Monaghan, Annabel.
Wolfe, Frances. Little Toy Shop. Wolfe, Frances, illus. (p. 1037)
Wolfe, Frances, et al. Deseo. (p. 428)
Wolfe, Gene. Knight. (p. 964)
—Wizard. (p. 1942)
Wolfe, Gillian. Look! Body Language in Art. (p. 1047)
—Look! Seeing the Light in Art. (p. 1050)
—Look! Zoom in on Art! (p. 1050)
Wolfe, Gillian & Quarto Generic Staff. Look! Really Smart Art. (p. 1050)
Wolfe, Helen. Terrific Women Teachers (p. 1721)
Wolfe, Hillary, jt. auth. see Rice, William B.
Wolfe, Hillary & Rice, William B. Blast off to Space Camp. (p. 198)
Wolfe, Jack & Wolfe, Jennifer. Tales of Spy Dogs Archie & Hazel. (p. 1702)
Wolfe, Jacqueline A. Megan Has to Move Kouse, Patrick, illus. (p. 1124)
Wolfe, James. Colonial Period. (p. 341)
—Genetic Testing & Gene Therapy. (p. 660)
—Industrial Revolution: Steam & Steel. (p. 872)
Wolfe, James & Callahan, Kerry P. Understanding the Articles of Confederation. (p. 1816)
Wolfe, James & Moe, Barbara A. Understanding the Charter of the Massachusetts Bay Colony. (p. 1816)
Wolfe, James & Stair, Nancy L. Understanding the Bill of Rights. (p. 1816)
Wolfe, James & Viegas, Jennifer. Understanding the Declaration of Independence. (p. 1816)
Wolfe, James, ed. Industrial Revolution. (p. 872)
Wolfe, James, et al. Understanding the Iroquois Constitution. (p. 1816)
Wolfe, Jane. Crazy Cow. Benham, Tors, illus. (p. 377)
—Messy Pig. Benham, Tors, illus. (p. 1130)
—Noisy Dog. Benham, Tors, illus. (p. 1263)
—Pull the Lever: Who Are You? The Toy Box, illus. (p. 1415)
—Pull the Lever: Who Does What? Benham, Tors, illus. (p. 1415)
—Pull the Lever: Who's in Here? Benham, Tors, illus. (p. 1415)
—Sleepy Sheep. Benham, Tors, illus. (p. 1590)
—Who Lives Here? Toy Box Staff, illus. (p. 1916)
—Who Says Moo? Toy Box Staff, illus. (p. 1917)
—Who's Hiding? Toy Box Staff, illus. (p. 1920)
Wolfe, Jane & Baxter, Nicola. Who's on the Farm? Lawson, Peter, illus. (p. 1921)
Wolfe, Jason & Wolfe, Stephanie. Autumn's Cathedrals: A Pictorial Tour of 117 Division 1-A College Football Stadiums (p. 118)
Wolfe, Jaymie Stuart. Adoring Jesus with the Holy Father. (p. 13)
—Family Matters: Thirteen Short Stories. (p. 568)
Wolfe, Jaymie Stuart, jt. auth. see Monge, Marlyn.
Wolfe, Jennifer, jt. auth. see Wolfe, Jack.
Wolfe, Linda. Across the Road. (p. 9)
Wolfe, Lynn. Viku & the Elephant: A story from the Forests of India. (p. 1842)
Wolfe, Mike & Sprengelmeyer, Lily. Kid Pickers: How to Turn Junk into Treasure. Right, Mike, illus. (p. 951)
Wolfe, Myra & Monescillo, Maria. Charlotte Jane Battles Bedtime. Monescillo, Maria, illus. (p. 293)
Wolfe, Nick, jt. auth. see Wolfe, Brian.
Wolfe, Richard. Short History of Sheep in New Zealand. (p. 1569)
Wolfe, Rita M., jt. auth. see Baldwin, Sage.
Wolfe, Sean Fay. Elementia Chronicles (p. 510)
—Quest for Justice. (p. 1426)
Wolfe, Stephanie, jt. auth. see Wolfe, Jason.
Wolfe, Sue. Lily Bouquet & a Special May Day. (p. 1018)
Wolfe, Susan Markle. Deer from Ponchatoula Welch, Gracie, illus. (p. 423)
Wolfe, Trisha. Fireblood. (p. 591)
Wolfel, Ursula. Abecedario Fantastico. (p. 4)
—Estrella Fugaz. (p. 538)
—Fliegender Stern. (p. 603)
Wolfelt, Alan D. & Maloney, Raelynn. Healing after Divorce: 100 Practical Ideas for Kids. (p. 757)
Wolfensberger Singer, Beth. Sweet & Simple Granny Squares: 8 Irresistible Crochet Projects. (p. 1689)
Wolfer, Dianne. Choices. (p. 309)
—Horse Mad. Thompson, Sharon, illus. (p. 799)
Wolfer, Dianne & Harrison-Lever, Brian. Photographs in the Mud. (p. 1353)
Wolferman, Iris, illus. see Hachler, Bruno.
Wolferman, Iris, illus. see Stalder, Pälvi.
Wolfermann, Iris, illus. see Hubner, Marie.
Wolff, Ariana. Khan Academy & Salman Khan (p. 951)
Wolff, Ariana, ed. see Barrington, Richard.
Wolff, Ashley. Baby Bear Counts One. Wolff, Ashley, illus. (p. 125)
—Baby Bear Sees Blue. Wolff, Ashley, illus. (p. 125)
—Baby Chicks Are Singing: Sing along in English & Spanish! Wolff, Ashley, illus. (p. 125)
—I Call My Grandpa Papa. Wolff, Ashley, illus. (p. 834)
—When Lucy Goes Out Walking: A Puppy's First Year. Wolff, Ashley, illus. (p. 1903)
Wolff, Ashley, illus. see Elsohn Ross, Michael.
Wolff, Ashley, illus. see Gaylord, Laurel Porter.
Wolff, Ashley, illus. see Porter-Gaylord, Laurel.
Wolff, Ashley, illus. see Ross, Michael Elsohn.
Wolff, Ashley, illus. see Scanlon, Liz Garton.
Wolff, Ashley, illus. see Shulman, Lisa.
Wolff, Ashley, illus. see Siddals, Mary McKenna.
Wolff, Ashley, illus. see Slate, Joseph.
Wolff, D. O. Precious Little. (p. 1394)
Wolff, Ferida. It Is the Wind. Ransome, James E., illus. (p. 894)
Wolff, Ferida & Savitz, Harriet May. Is a Worry Worrying You? LeTourneau, Marie, illus. (p. 889)
—Story Blanket Odriozola, Elena, illus. (p. 1656)
Wolff, Jason, illus. see Bardhan-Quallen, Sudipta.
Wolff, Jason, illus. see Gonzalez-Jensen, Margarita.
Wolff, Jason, illus. see Lenhard, Elizabeth.
Wolff, Jason, illus. see Rauchwerger, Diane Levin.
Wolff, Jason, illus. see Rosa-Mendoza, Gladys.
Wolff, Marcia. Frictions Becoming Pearl: A Slow Awakening. (p. 637)
Wolff, Marion. Shedding Skins. (p. 1564)
Wolff, Pat. Noah's Faith: A Children's Poem. (p. 1262)
Wolff, Susan. Quackers Wants to Fly. Currie, Justin, illus. (p. 1422)
Wolff, Veronica. Vampire's Kiss: The Watchers (p. 1832)
Wolff, Virginia Euwer. Bat 6. (p. 143)
—Make Lemonade. (p. 1079)
—Mozart Season. (p. 1184)
—This Full House. (p. 1735)
—True Believer. (p. 1791)
Wolfgang, Engel, ed. see St-Laurent, Sebastien.
Wolfgang, Jane. Art Today. (p. 103)
Wolfgarth-Simons, Tavisha. Shutterbox (p. 1572)
Wolfhard, Steve, illus. see Kloepfer, John.
Wolfhound Publishing Editors, ed. see Harrison, Cora.
Wolfhound Publishing Editors, ed. see Lysaght, Richard.
Wolfinger, Sheri. Has Anyone Seen Puff? A Billy & Jake Adventure. (p. 752)
Wolfman, Judy. Life on a Chicken Farm. Winston, David Lorenz, illus. (p. 1012)
—Life on a Dairy Farm. Winston, David Lorenz, illus. (p. 1012)
—Life on a Sheep Farm. Winston, David Lorenz, illus. (p. 1012)
—Life on an Apple Orchard. Winston, David Lorenz, illus. (p. 1012)
Wolfman, Marv. 10th Muse Omnibus. (p. 1994)
—Defex (p. 424)
—History of the DC Universe. Kesel, Karl, illus. (p. 785)
—Nova Classic Volume 3. Buscema, John et al, illus. (p. 1268)
Wolfman, Marv, jt. auth. see Byrne, John.
Wolfman, Marv, jt. auth. see Claremont, Chris.
Wolfman, Marv, jt. auth. see Perez, George.
Wolfman, Marv, jt. auth. see Shooter, Jim.
Wolfman, Marv, jt. auth. see Wein, Len.
Wolfman, Marv, jt. auth. see Yuki, Kaori.

W

Wolfman, Marv & Davis, Darren G. 10th Muse. (p. 1994)
Wolfman, Marv & Mantlo, Bill. Fantastic Four: Reunited They Stand. Pollard, Keith et al, illus. (p. 571)
Wolfman, Marv & Perez, George. Terror of Trigon. (p. 1722)
Wolfman, Marv, et al. Nova Classic - Volume 1. Buscema, John et al, illus. (p. 1268)
—Tomb of Dracula. (p. 1764)
Wolford, Margaret. Byte by Byte: An Alana Davis Journal. (p. 249)
—Love Our Lockwood: The Story of Belva Lockwood. (p. 1060)
—There's a Hair in My Lasagna. (p. 1731)
—Will Work for Food: An Alana Davis Journal. (p. 1932)
Wolford, Margo. Moinks Collection Presents: Sami's Big Day. (p. 1160)
Wolford, Merle & Harvey, Karen. Pau Pua & the Watering Hole. (p. 1330)
Wolfram, Amy, jt. auth. see Fisch, Sholly.
Wolfsgruber, Linda. Daisy Is a Daisy Is a Daisy (Except When It's Girl's Name) (p. 400)
Wolfsgruber, Linda, illus. see Lecis, Alessandro & Shirtliffe, Leanne.
Wolfsgruber, Linda, illus. see Lottridge, Celia Barker.
Wolfsgruber, Linda, illus. see Ondaatje, Griffin.
Wolfson, Evelyn. Mythology of King Arthur & His Knights. (p. 1227)
—Mythology of the American Indians. (p. 1227)
—Mythology of the Inuit. (p. 1227)
—Mythology of the Romans. (p. 1227)
—Native Americans. (p. 1234)
—Wayland A-Z: A Dictionary of Then & Now. Wolfson, Evelyn, ed. (p. 1865)
Wolfson, Jill. What I Call Life. (p. 1886)
Wolfson, Jonathan. Great Debate! Freedom to Communicate! A Handbook for Policy Debate. (p. 715)
Wolfson, Ron. Be Like God: God's To-Do List for Kids. (p. 148)
Wolfson, Ron, jt. auth. see Hoffman, Lawrence A.
Wolfson, Steve. Elephants at the Airport. Brulot, Heleen, illus. (p. 512)
—Monster Cheese. Johnson, Bill, illus. (p. 1166)
Wolfson, Tanya, tr. see Levin, Vadim.
Wolgemuth, Bobbie, jt. auth. see Eareckson Tada, Joni.
Woliczko, Wit. Secrets to the Universe. (p. 1546)
Wolif, T. Hal & His Pal Al: The Easter Bunny's Helpers. (p. 736)
Wolin, Steven. ELSB STUDENT ASSESSMENT Level 2&3. (p. 516)
Wolinsky, Art. Internet Power Research Using the Big6 Approach. (p. 880)
—Safe Surfing on the Internet. (p. 1502)
Wolitzer, Meg. Belzhar. (p. 163)
—Fingertips of Duncan Dorfman. (p. 589)
Wolkoff, Judie, jt. auth. see Murphy, Barbara Beasley.
Wolk-Stanley, Jessica, illus. see Geiger, Beth & Fuerst, Jeffrey B.
Wolkstein, Diane. Banza: A Haitian Story. Brown, Marc, illus. (p. 137)
—Fairy Tales from Estonia. (p. 564)
Woll, Kris. Nelson Mandela: South African President & Civil Rights Activist. (p. 1241)
—Pope Francis: Catholic Spiritual Leader. (p. 1384)
Wollard, K. & Wollard, Kathy. Porque de las Cosas. (p. 1386)
Wollard, Kathy. How Come? Every Kid's Science Questions Explained. Solomon, Debra, illus. (p. 806)
—How Come? in the Neighborhood. Solomon, Debra, illus. (p. 806)
—Libro de los Porques. (p. 1006)
Wollard, Kathy, jt. auth. see Wollard, K.
Wollard, Kathy & Solomon, Debra. Libro de Los Porqués 2: Las Preguntas Más Difíciles y Las Respuestas Más Fáciles Sobre Las Personas, Los Animales y Las Cosas. Solomon, Debra, tr. (p. 1006)
Wollering, Loretta. Tai Chi (p. 1695)
Wollman, Jessica. Chipster's Sister. MacNeil, Chris, illus. (p. 308)
—Meet the Phonees. MacNeil, Chris, illus. (p. 1123)
Wollman, Neil & Fuller, Abigail. What Animal Needs a Wig? Fuller Baldwin, Fran, illus. (p. 1879)
Wollstonecraft Shelley, Mary, see Reed, Gary & Shelley, Mary.
Wollstonecraft Shelley, Mary, see Shelley, Mary.
Wollstonecraft Shelley, Mary, see Sierra, Sergio A. & Shelley, Mary.
Wolnik, Charlotte. Chocolate Chip Ghost. (p. 309)
Wolny, Philip. Abusing Prescription Drugs. (p. 7)
—American Troops in Afghanistan: Building a New Nation. (p. 63)
—Avoiding Danger on the Hunt. (p. 120)
—Chemical Reactions. (p. 297)
—Constructing, Using, & Interpreting Spreadsheets. (p. 359)
—Creating Electronic Graphic Organizers. (p. 378)
—Defeating Gangs in Your Neighborhood & Online. (p. 423)
—Delaware: Past & Present. (p. 424)
—Discovering Dark Matter (p. 449)
—Discovering the Empire of Mali. (p. 449)
—Food Supply Collapse. (p. 614)
—Foursquare & Other Location-Based Services: Checking in, Staying Safe, & Being Savvy. (p. 625)
—Getting a Job in Building Maintenance. (p. 668)
—Google & You: Maximizing Your Google Experience. (p. 702)
—Gun Rights: Interpreting the Constitution. (p. 732)
—Hamid Karzai: President of Afghanistan. (p. 739)
—High Risk Construction Work: Life Building Skyscrapers, Bridges, & Tunnels. (p. 778)
—High-Risk Construction Work: Life Building Skyscrapers, Bridges, & Tunnels. (p. 778)
—Hurricane: True Stories of Survival. (p. 829)
—I Have an STD. Now What? (p. 839)
—Investigating Atlantis & Other Lost Cities (p. 884)
—Iran & Iraq: Religion, War, & Geopolitics. (p. 886)
—Isaac Asimov. (p. 890)
—James Dashner. (p. 907)
—Ludacris. (p. 1063)
—Money-Making Opportunities for Teens Who Are Handy. (p. 1164)
—Muslims Around the World Today. (p. 1194)
—Sean Combs. (p. 1536)
—Stephen Chbosky (p. 1648)
—Truth about Heroin. (p. 1794)
—Underground Railroad: A Primary Source History of the Journey to Freedom. (p. 1814)
—Understanding Financial Frauds & Scams. (p. 1815)
—Water Fowl. (p. 1862)
—Weapons Satellites. (p. 1869)
Wolny, Philip, jt. auth. see Jones, Viola.
Wolos-Fonteno, Mary, et al. Tales with Tails: Animal Stories for Young People. Salaam, Kiini Ibura, ed. (p. 1703)
Woloson, Eliza. My Friend Isabelle. Gough, Bryan, tr. (p. 1209)
Wolpe, Nina. Forest of Trees Does Not Grow There in Rows. Cable, Annette, illus. (p. 618)
Wolper, Joanna. Man Who Could Be Santa. (p. 1086)
Wolpert, David K. Scoliosis Surgery: The Definitive Patient's Reference (2nd Edition) (p. 1529)
Wolshon, Brian. Harry's Healthy Heart. (p. 751)
Wolski, Bobbi, illus. see Whitlow, Crystal K.
Wolstenholm, Jessica & Rupe, Heather. Pregnancy Companion: A Faith-Filled Guide for Your Journey to Motherhood. (p. 1395)
Wolstenholme, Susan, ed. see Baum, L. Frank.
Wolverton, Barry. Neversink. Nielson, Sam, illus. (p. 1243)
—Vanishing Island. Stevenson, Dave, illus. (p. 1833)
Wolverton, Terry. Embers. (p. 517)
Womack, Rowena. Popcorn. Archer, Angela, illus. (p. 1384)
—Yellowstone Moose. (p. 1970)
Womack, Vernesia. What If... (p. 1887)
Woman, Magpie Sleeping. Big Eyes: The Keeper of the Night. (p. 181)
Wombacher, Michael. There's a Puppy in the House: Surviving the First Five Months. (p. 1731)
Womble, Louis, illus. see Kleinberg, Naomi.
Womble, Louis, illus. see Tabby, Abigail.
Women, Warlpiri. Jaru-Kurlu: Warlpiri Stories & Songs from Wirliyajarrayi, Yurntumu, Lajamanu & Nyirrpi. (p. 909)
Won, Brian. Hooray for Hat! (p. 796)
Won, Brian, illus. see Nayeri, Daniel.
Won, Brian, illus. see Sanders, Robert L.
Won, Kim Kang. I. N. V. U. (p. 844)
—I. N. V. U. Na, Lauren, tr. from KOR. (p. 844)
—Queen's Knight Won, Kim Kang, illus. (p. 1425)
Won, Soo Yon. Full House 3: Discord Won, Soo Yon, illus. (p. 646)
Won, Sooyeon. Let Dai (p. 994)
Wonder Forge Staff, creator. Horton Hears a Who! - You to the Rescue! Game. (p. 801)
Wonderley, Stanley. Boy & His Horse. (p. 217)
—My Lamb. (p. 1211)
Wondra, Ashley E. Kelsey's Coat. (p. 948)
Wondriska, William. Puff. (p. 1415)
Wong, Alice & Tabori, Lena, eds. Big Book for Toddlers. (p. 178)
—Goodnight Book for Moms & Little Ones. (p. 701)
—Little Big Book for Boys. (p. 1024)
Wong, Angi Ma. Barack Obama: Historymaker. (p. 137)
—Meet President Obama: America's 44th President. (p. 1122)
—My Story: Reggie: The L.A. Gator. (p. 1219)
—Who Ate My Socks? (p. 1914)
Wong, Benedict Norbert. Lo & Behold: A Boy & His Dragon. (p. 1044)
—Lo & Behold: Words That Walk & Run. (p. 1044)
—Lo & Behold: The Millennia Just Roll By. (p. 1044)
—Lo & Behold: Good Enough to Eat. Wong, Benedict Norbert, illus. (p. 1044)
—Lo & Behold. Wong, Benedict Norbert, illus. (p. 1044)
Wong, Carmen L. F. Written By... (p. 1965)
Wong, Clarissa & Disney Book Group Staff. Amazing Spider-Man Storybook Collection. (p. 56)
Wong, Clarissa S. Story of the Guardians of the Galaxy. (p. 1661)
—World of Reading: Black Widow This Is Black Widow. Di Vito, Andrea, illus. (p. 1957)
Wong, Clarissa S., jt. auth. see Marvel Book Group.
Wong, Clarissa S., jt. auth. see Palacios, Tomas.
Wong, Cynthia F. Nhw:Ishiguro Kazuo 2e Pb. (p. 1250)
Wong, Gabriel. Patches the Beaver: Welcome to Harmony Woods. (p. 1328)
Wong, Janet G., jt. auth. see Wong, Janet S.
Wong, Janet S. Alex & the Wednesday Chess Club. Schuett, Stacey, illus. (p. 35)
—Apple Pie Fourth of July. Chodos-Irvine, Margaret, illus. (p. 92)
—Before It Wriggles Away. Lindsay, Anne, photos by. (p. 158)
—Dumpster Diver. Roberts, David, illus. (p. 490)
—Homegrown House. Lewis, E. B., illus. (p. 793)
—Me & Rolly Maloo. Buttler, Elizabeth, illus. (p. 1115)
—Minn & Jake's Almost Terrible Summer. Côté, Geneviève, illus. (p. 1147)
—Twist: Yoga Poems. Paschkis, Julie, illus. (p. 1802)
Wong, Janet S. & Paschkis, Julie. Knock on Wood: Poems about Superstitions. Paschkis, Julie, illus. (p. 965)
Wong, Janet S. & Wong, Janet G. Minn & Jake. Cote, Genevieve, illus. (p. 1147)
Wong, Joanne. Do Polar Bears Wear Pearls? (p. 457)
Wong, Joyce Lee. Seeing Emily. (p. 1548)
Wong, JoyLynn Charity. Carried Away: A Collection of Wrapscapes & Nursery Rhymes. (p. 271)
Wong, Karine. Don't Sit on Her! (p. 468)
Wong, Li Keng. Good Fortune: My Journey to Gold Mountain (p. 698)
Wong, Liz, illus. see Mahle, Melissa & Dennis, Kathryn.
Wong, Melissa Oliaivar, illus. see Ito, Jerilyn.
Wong, Nichole, illus. see Manalang, Dan.
Wong, Nicole, illus. see Butler, Dori Hillestad.
Wong, Nicole, illus. see Buzzeo, Toni.
Wong, Nicole, illus. see Cheng, Andrea.
Wong, Nicole, illus. see Churchill, Ginger.
Wong, Nicole, illus. see Kenah, Katharine.
Wong, Nicole, illus. see Nelmark, Jill.
Wong, Nicole, illus. see Scacco, Linda.
Wong, Nicole, illus. see Stewart, Melissa & Young, Allen M.
Wong, Nicole, illus. see Stiegemeyer, Julie.
Wong, Nicole, illus. see Terry, Sonya.
Wong, Nicole, illus. see Wahl, Jan.
Wong, Nicole E., illus. see Wahl, Jan.
Wong, Pindy Y. & Luk, Hoenie W. Your Body Is Not A Car: The Secrets for Good Health Based on Traditional Chinese Medicine. (p. 1980)
Wong, Priscilla, illus. see Griesmer, Russell.
Wong, Richard. Modern Asian Flavors: A Taste of Shanghai. Barnhurst, Noel, photos by. (p. 1158)
Wong, Scott, illus. see Avery, Ben & Zondervan Publishing Staff.
Wong, Scott, illus. see Rogers, Bud & Avery, Ben.
Wong, Scott, illus. see Rogers, Buddy & Avery, Ben.
Wong, Stanley, illus. see Hathorn, Libby.
Wong, Stephen. Baseball Treasures. Einstein, Susan, illus. (p. 141)
Wong, Tony, illus. see Cha, Louis.
Wong, Walden, illus. see Beechen, Adam.
Wong, Walden, illus. see Roman, Annette.
Wong, Walden, jt. auth. see Beechen, Adam.
Wong, Winnie, jt. auth. see Barlas, Robert.
Wong, Winnie, jt. auth. see Heale, Jay.
Wong, Winnie, jt. auth. see Holmes, Timothy.
Wong, Winnie, jt. auth. see Jermyn, Leslie.
Wong, Winnie, jt. auth. see Levy, Patricia.
Wong, Winnie, jt. auth. see Spilling, Michael.
Wong-Avery, Sally. Chinese Manners. (p. 307)
Wonlah, Ivis. King Ola's Pepper Jar. (p. 959)
Woo. Rebirth (p. 1451)
—Rebirth Woo, illus. (p. 1451)
—RebirthTM Hahm, Jennifer, tr. from KOR. (p. 1451)
Woo, illus. see Lee, Kang-Woo.
WOO, illus. see Yi, Kang-u.
Woo, Alison, jt. auth. see Claxton, Lena.
Woo, et al. Rebirth Lee, Kang-Woo, illus. (p. 1451)
Woo, Howie, illus. see Wyatt, Valerie.
Woo, Howie, illus. see Yes Magazine Editors, ed.
Woo, Howie, illus. see Yes Magazine Editors.
Woo Kim, Jin, illus. see McFadden, Deanna.
Woo, Melissa. Cooper's Big Bear Hug. Couch, Crista, illus. (p. 365)
Woo, SooJung, jt. auth. see Kara.
Woo, Yen Yen, jt. auth. see Goh, Colin.
Wood, A. J. Christmas Hat. Kneen, Maggie, illus. (p. 314)
—Christmas Is Coming! Lambert, Stephen, illus. (p. 314)
Wood, A. J., jt. auth. see Twist, Clint.
Wood, Aimee, jt. auth. see Wood, David.
Wood, Alberta Auringer, ed. see Atwal, Jeet, et al.
Wood, Alexander. Our Jobs. (p. 1309)
—Visit Independence Hall. (p. 1845)
Wood, Alissa. Vicki Silver Mysteries: Hoofbeats. (p. 1840)
—Vicki Silver Mysteries: Cruise Control. (p. 1840)
—Vicki Silver Mysteries: The Stolen Gem. (p. 1840)
Wood, Alix. Aikido. (p. 30)
—Amazing Animal Homes. (p. 53)
—Amazing Animal Journeys. (p. 53)
—Amazing Animal Life Cycles. (p. 53)
—Amazing Animals at Night. (p. 53)
—Animal Camouflage. (p. 77)
—Anthony Van Dyck (p. 89)
—Artists Through the Ages: Set 2 (p. 104)
—Body Art. (p. 207)
—Body Bugs. (p. 207)
—Body Snatching. (p. 207)
—Body Snatching. Wood, Alix, illus. (p. 207)
—Claude Monet. (p. 329)
—Dinosaurs on the Map. (p. 445)
—Disasters on the Map. (p. 447)
—Dueling. (p. 489)
—Dueling. Wood, Alix, illus. (p. 489)
—Edgar Degas (p. 504)
—Francisco Goya. (p. 628)
—Freaky Flying Animals. (p. 632)
—Georgia O'Keeffe. (p. 665)
—Gladiators: Fighting to the Death. Wood, Alix, illus. (p. 682)
—Gruesome Animals in the Ground. (p. 727)
—Human Sacrifice. (p. 826)
—Human Sacrifice. Wood, Alix, illus. (p. 826)
—Hunting on the Map. (p. 829)
—Johannes Vermeer. (p. 921)
—Judo. (p. 931)
—Jujitsu. (p. 932)
—Karate. (p. 943)
—Kung Fu. (p. 968)
—Leonardo Da Vinci. (p. 992)
—Military on the Map. (p. 1143)
—Mummification. Wood, Alix, illus. (p. 1191)
—Paul Cézanne. (p. 1330)
—Paul Gauguin (p. 1330)
—Pirates on the Map. (p. 1364)
—Serving in the Air Force. (p. 1553)
—Serving in the Army. (p. 1553)
—Serving in the Coast Guard. (p. 1553)
—Serving in the Marine Corps. (p. 1553)
—Serving in the Navy. (p. 1553)
—Sports on the Map. (p. 1633)
—Tae Kwon Do. (p. 1695)
—Ugly Creatures under Water. (p. 1808)
—Vincent Van Gogh. (p. 1843)
—Wacky & Dangerous. (p. 1852)
—Wacky in the Water. (p. 1852)
—Wacky Moments in Sports. (p. 1852)
—Wacky Races. (p. 1852)
—Wacky Team Sports. (p. 1852)
—Wacky Throwing Sports. (p. 1852)
—Weird Animals in the Wild. (p. 1872)
—Witch Trials. Wood, Alix, illus. (p. 1941)
—Yucky Animals in the Yard. (p. 1983)
Wood, Amanda. Amazing Baby Look & Play! (p. 53)
—Amazing Baby Touch & Play! (p. 53)
—Rainbow. (p. 1435)
Wood, Amanda & Kneen, Maggie. Christmas in the Mouse House. Kneen, Maggie, illus. (p. 314)
Wood, Angela Gluck. Judaism. (p. 930)
Wood, Anita. BFF Journal Kalis, Jennifer, illus. (p. 174)
—City Doodles San Francisco (p. 323)
—Cowboy Doodles. (p. 374)
—Doodle Your Day Kalis, Jennifer, illus. (p. 469)
—Fairy Doodles Kalis, Jennifer, illus. (p. 563)
—Fashion Doodles Kalis, Jennifer, illus. (p. 575)
—Pocketdoodles for Christmas Brockschmidt, Kev, illus. (p. 1375)
—Pocketdoodles for Girls Kalis, Jennifer, illus. (p. 1375)
—Pocketdoodles for Princesses Kalis, Jennifer, illus. (p. 1375)
—Travel Doodles for Kids (p. 1780)
Wood, Anita & Sabatino, Chris. Camping Doodles (p. 257)
Wood, Ashley. Complete World War Robot. (p. 353)
Wood, Audrey. Alphabet Mystery. Wood, Bruce, illus. (p. 49)
—Alphabet Rescue. Wood, Bruce, illus. (p. 50)
—Balloonia. Wood, Audrey, illus. (p. 135)
—Balloonia & Magic Shoelaces. (p. 135)
—Birthday Queen. Wood, Don, illus. (p. 193)
—Bunyans. (p. 243)
—Bunyans. Shannon, David, illus. (p. 243)
—Dog Needs a Bone! (p. 461)
—Full Moon at the Napping House. Wood, Don, illus. (p. 646)
—King Bidgood's in the Bathtub. Wood, Don, illus. (p. 958)
—Little Mouse, the Red Ripe Strawberry & the Big Hungry Bear. Wood, Don, illus. (p. 1032)
—Magic Shoelaces. Wood, Audrey, illus. (p. 1073)
—Napping House. Wood, Don, illus. (p. 1229)
—Napping House. Wood, Audrey & Wood, Don, illus. (p. 1229)
—Napping House / La Casa Adormecida. Wood, Don, illus. (p. 1229)
—Piggy Pie Po. Wood, Don, illus. (p. 1358)
—Presto Change-O. Wood, Audrey, illus. (p. 1397)
—Presto Change-O & Tooth Fairy. (p. 1397)
—Princess & the Dragon. (p. 1402)
—Princess, the Dragon & Scaredy Cats. (p. 1406)
—Scaredy Cats. Wood, Audrey, illus. (p. 1519)
—Silly Sally: Lap-Sized Board Book. (p. 1576)
—Silly Sally. (p. 1576)
—Ten Little Fish. Wood, Bruce, illus. (p. 1719)
—Tooth Fairy. (p. 1768)
—Twenty-Four Robbers. (p. 1801)
Wood, Audrey & Wood, Bruce Robert. Alphabet Rescue. (p. 50)
Wood, Audrey & Wood, Don. It's Duffy Time! (p. 896)
Wood, Barbie. Adventure of Mookin Munchkin. Klick, Gloria, illus. (p. 14)
Wood, Beatrice. I Shock Myself: The Autobiography of Beatrice Wood. Smith, Lindsay, ed. (p. 845)
Wood, Beverley & Wood, Chris. DogStar. (p. 463)
Wood, Brian. Couriers (p. 373)
—Couriers: The Ballad of Johnny Funwrecker. Vol. 3 (p. 373)
—Cramp Twins: Lucien's Little. (p. 376)
—Dmz - On the Ground. (p. 456)
—Mara TP. (p. 1091)
—New York Four. (p. 1248)
—Star Wars. D'Anda, Carlos, illus. (p. 1641)
Wood, Brian, jt. auth. see ABDO Publishing Company Staff.
Wood, Brian & Burchielli, Riccardo. Body of a Journalist (p. 207)
Wood, Bruce, illus. see Wood, Audrey.
Wood, Bruce Robert, jt. illus. see Wood, Audrey.
Wood, Carol. Grandma Carol's Book of Stories in Rhyme. (p. 708)
Wood, Cary D. Davis & Pop Go Hiking. Turner, Cecilia, illus. (p. 411)
Wood, Charles M., II. Living the Good Life: Surviving in the 21st Century. (p. 1041)
Wood, Chaz, illus. see Auty, Rob.
Wood, Chris, jt. auth. see Wood, Beverley.
Wood, Christine, ed. see Wood, Francis Eusene.
Wood, Christine, photos by see Wood, Francis Eusene.
Wood, Cindi. Frazzled Female Bible Study. (p. 631)
Wood, Colleen, illus. see McLeod, Elaine.
Wood, Courtney. Just the Way It Was. (p. 940)
Wood, D. K. Nightmare at Indian Cave. (p. 1255)
Wood, Damian, illus. see Galvin, Laura Gates.
Wood, Damian, illus. see Schwaeber, Barbie Heit.
Wood, Daniel, jt. auth. see Swanson, Diane.
Wood, Dave, jt. auth. see Kirby, Jack.
Wood, David. Christmas Story. (p. 315)
—Little House on Buchanan Street. (p. 1029)
—Present for Santa Claus. Kubick, Dana, illus. (p. 1396)
—There's a World in My House. Dissler, Erica, illus. (p. 1731)
—Toy Cupboard. Fowler, Richard, illus. (p. 1774)
—Twits. (p. 1803)
—Year in the Life of the Kingwood Bunnies. Floeter, Nell, illus. (p. 1969)
—Zombie-Driven Life: What in the Apocalypse Am I Here For? (p. 1988)
Wood, David & Dahl, Roald. Danny the Champion of the World. (p. 406)
Wood, David & Wood, Aimee. Beautiful Swan. (p. 154)
Wood, David, et al. Challenges of the Unknown (p. 289)
Wood, Deanna Plummer. Whenever Monkeys Move Next Door (p. 1906)
Wood, Debra. Just A Little Child. Blake, Joshua Aaron, illus. (p. 937)
—William Warrior Bear. Blake, Joshua Aaron, illus. (p. 1933)
Wood, Dick. Boris Karloff Tales of Mystery Archives Volume 5. (p. 214)
Wood, Dominic, jt. auth. see McCourt, Richard.
Wood, Don. Into the Volcano. (p. 881)
—Into the Volcano. Wood, Don, illus. (p. 881)
—Joyeux Noel, Ours Affamé! (p. 930)
Wood, Don, illus. see Wood, Audrey.
Wood, Don, jt. auth. see Wood, Audrey.
Wood, Dorreya. Pick-a-WooWoo - Bliss: A breathtaking story of transformation that reveals 'we are never Alone' Wood, Dorreya, illus. (p. 1354)
—Planet Cannibal. (p. 1367)

Wood, Douglas. Aunt Mary's Rose. Shed, Greg & Pham, LeUyen, illus. (p. 115)
—Franklin & Winston: A Christmas That Changed the World. Moser, Barry, illus. (p. 630)
—Grandad's Prayers of the Earth. Lynch, P. J., illus. (p. 707)
—Making the World. Yoshi, illus. (p. 1082)
—No One but You. Lynch, P. J., illus. (p. 1259)
—Nothing to Do. Halperin, Wendy Anderson, illus. (p. 1268)
—Old Turtle & the Broken Truth. Muth, Jon J., illus. (p. 1285)
—Quiet Place. Andreasen, Dan, illus. (p. 1428)
—Secret of Saying Thanks. Shed, Greg, illus. (p. 1542)
—What Dads Can't Do. (p. 1881)
—What Grandmas Can't Do. Cushman, Doug, illus. (p. 1885)
—What Santa Can't Do. Cushman, Doug, illus. (p. 1893)
—When a Dad Says "I Love You" Bell, Jennifer A., illus. (p. 1901)
—When a Grandpa Says I Love You. Bell, Jennifer A., illus. (p. 1901)
—When Mama Mirabelle Comes Home. Wagner, Andy, illus. (p. 1903)
—Where the Sunrise Begins. Popp, K. Wendy, illus. (p. 1909)
Wood, Douglas, illus. see Tinsley, Jillian.
Wood, Elaine, jt. auth. see Sherman, Patrice.
Wood, Elaine, jt. auth. see Walker, Pam.
Wood, Elaine, jt. auth. see Walker, Pamela.
Wood, Elizabeth Lamb. There Go the Apaches. (p. 1729)
Wood, Ethel, compiled by. Presidency. (p. 1396)
wood, fern. Blank, the Dog with No Name. (p. 198)
Wood, Fiona. Six Impossible Things. (p. 1582)
—Wildlife. (p. 1931)
Wood, Francis. SnowPeople. Larsen, Dan, illus. (p. 1601)
Wood, Francis Eugene. Autumn's Reunion: A Story of Thanksgiving. Dean, Tina & Marken, Jon, eds. (p. 118)
—Return to Winterville. Pickett, Elizabeth & Dean, Tina, eds. (p. 1465)
Wood, Francis Eugene & McDermott, Robert. Nipkins (p. 1257)
Wood, Francis Eusene. Christmas Letter. Wood, Christine & Marken, Jon, eds. (p. 314)
Wood, Frank. Little Ray's Trip to the Doctor. (p. 1034)
Wood, Frank & Sangster, Alan. Frank Wood's A-Level Accounting. (p. 629)
Wood, Frank K. & FC and A Publishing Staff. 405 Woodworking Patterns. (p. 2001)
Wood, Franklin. Teddy the Cat That Barks. (p. 1712)
Wood, Gail. Lizzie & the Big Lake Mystery. (p. 1043)
—Lizzie, Light Feather & the Quarry Bluff Storm. (p. 1043)
Wood, Gail Ann. Lizzie & the Prairie Fire: Girl Pioneer in the American Midwest. (p. 1043)
Wood, Gardner. Newspaper King. (p. 1249)
Wood, Gary. Bertrand - The Story of a Cat. (p. 168)
Wood, Gerald, illus. see Cox, Phil Roxbee & Reid, Struan.
Wood, Gerald, illus. see Danes, Emma.
Wood, Gerald, illus. see Marks, Anthony & Tingay, Graham.
Wood, Gerald, illus. see Wingate, Philippa & Millard, Anne.
Wood, Gillian W. Bumbles Barely a Bear & His 4000 Mile Journey. (p. 241)
Wood, Gillian Wheeler. Bumble an Interesting Bear. (p. 241)
Wood, Greg V. & Benchmark Education Co., LLC. Opinions about Themes in Science Fiction: Two Stories about Veronica Logan, Interstellar Troubleshooter. Retwick, Roy, illus. (p. 1300)
Wood, Hannah. Dino Pop-up Faces: A Let's Pretend Pop-up Book. (p. 441)
—Hey, Diddle, Diddle & More Favorite Nursery Rhymes. (p. 774)
—Old MacDonald Had a Farm: And Other Favorite Songs. (p. 1284)
Wood, Hannah, illus. see David, Juliet.
Wood, Hannah, illus. see Hodgman, Ann.
Wood, Hannah, illus. see Hopgood, Sally & Graham, Oakley.
Wood, Hannah, illus. see Junor, Amy.
Wood, Hannah, illus. see Ranson, Erin.
Wood, Hannah, illus. see Salzano, Tammi J.
Wood, Hannah, illus. see Salzano, Tammi.
Wood, Hannah, illus. see Scott, Janine.
Wood, Hannah, jt. auth. see Reasoner, Charles.
Wood, Heather & Wood, Heather J. Fortune Cookie. (p. 623)
Wood, Heather J., jt. auth. see Wood, Heather.
Wood, Helen, jt. des. see Leschnikoff, Nancy.
Wood, Holly J. Invaluable. (p. 883)
Wood, I. Sharks: Learning the SH Sound. (p. 1563)
Wood, Ian. Hudson River. (p. 824)
Wood, Ian S. Churchill. (p. 318)
Wood, Ira. Fort Sumter: Where the Civil War Began. (p. 623)
—Fourth of July. (p. 625)
—How to Stay Safe at Home & On-line. (p. 821)
—Let's Wash Up. (p. 1001)
—Mexican Feast: The Foods & Recipes of Mexico. (p. 1131)
—Sandcastle. (p. 1511)
—Water, Ice, & Steam. (p. 1862)
Wood, J. G. Illustrated Natural History: Arranged Fo. (p. 857)
Wood, Jacqueline & Wood, Jakki. Baby Parade. (p. 127)
Wood, Jakki. Hole in the Road. (p. 788)
—March of the Dinosaurs: A Dinosaur Counting Book. (p. 1091)
—Moo Moo, Brown Cow. (p. 1171)
Wood, Jakki, jt. auth. see Wood, Jacqueline.
Wood, James. Irresponsible Self: On Laughter & the Novel. (p. 888)
Wood, James Playsted. Queen's Most Honorable Pirate. Fisher, Leonard Everett, illus. (p. 1425)
Wood, Jamie Robyn. Bearskin. (p. 152)
Wood, Jane R. Adventures on Amelia Island: A Pirate, a Princess, & Buried Treasure. Blacker, Elizabeth A., illus. (p. 24)
Wood, Jennifer, illus. see Chin, Oliver, ed.
Wood, Jennifer, illus. see Chin, Oliver.
Wood, Jenny. Desiertos. (p. 429)
—I Wonder Why Kangaroos Have Pouches. (p. 849)
Wood, Jill G. Florence Nightingale: Called to Serve with Buffalo Biff & Farley's Raiders. Cox, Brian T., illus. (p. 606)
Wood, Joe, illus. see Williams, Vicki & Williams, Kathy.
Wood Jr, Richard L. Stick Family. (p. 1649)
Wood, Julie M. Learn to Read with Tug the Pup & Friends! Braun, Sebastien, illus. (p. 984)
Wood, June Rae. Man Who Loved Clowns. (p. 1086)
Wood, Karen. Diamond Spirit. (p. 434)
—Golden Stranger. (p. 695)
—Moonstone Promise. (p. 1173)
Wood, Karen D. & Mraz, Maryann. Teaching Literacy in Sixth Grade. (p. 1710)
Wood, Kate. Twinkle. (p. 1802)
Wood, Kathryn J. Morty Mouse: I Wish I Could Fly. (p. 1176)
Wood, Katie, illus. see Gurtler, Janet.
Wood, Katie, illus. see Maddox, Jake & Berne, Emma Carlson.
Wood, Katie, illus. see Maddox, Jake.
Wood, Kerry & Muskat, Carrie. All You Can Be: Learning & Growing Through Sports. (p. 46)
Wood, Kristen. Find Albert Alberta Too. (p. 587)
—Find Big Al. (p. 587)
—Find Masked Rider. (p. 587)
—Find Reveille. (p. 587)
—Find Uga Hairy Dawg Too. (p. 587)
Wood Lake Books Staff & Novalis Staff. Your Child's Baptism: Roman Catholic. (p. 1980)
Wood, Laura, illus. see Dillemuth, Julie.
Wood, Laura, illus. see Fischer, Ellen.
Wood, Lee. Wonderful Day. (p. 1948)
Wood, Lena. Elijah Creek & the Armor of Gift Set. (p. 512)
Wood, Leslie, illus. see Ross, Diana.
Wood, Lily. Skeletons. (p. 1584)
Wood, Lisa. Human Hotel. (p. 826)
—Marine Science (p. 1094)
—Okay with Me. (p. 1282)
Wood, Madeline, illus. see Schmidt, Mollie.
Wood, Mandy. My First Kitty. (p. 1207)
—My First Puppy. (p. 1207)
Wood, Mark. Beyond Classroom Enrichment: Creative Units for Gifted Students. (p. 173)
Wood, Mary, jt. auth. see Low, Emma.
Wood, Maryrose. Hidden Gallery. (p. 775)
—Hidden Gallery. Klassen, Jon, illus. (p. 775)
—How I Found the Perfect Dress. (p. 810)
—Incorrigible Children of Ashton Place: The Unmapped Sea. Bk. 5 Wheeler, Eliza, illus. (p. 869)
—Incorrigible Children of Ashton Place: The Interrupted Tale. Bk. 4 Wheeler, Eliza, illus. (p. 869)
—Incorrigible Children of Ashton Place: The Interrupted Tale. Bk. IV Wheeler, Eliza, illus. (p. 869)
—Mysterious Howling. Klassen, Jon, illus. (p. 1223)
—Unseen Guest. (p. 1822)
—Unseen Guest. Klassen, Jon, illus. (p. 1822)
—What I Wore to Save the World. (p. 1887)
—Why I Let My Hair Grow Out. (p. 1925)
Wood, Maryrose & Duchess of Northumberland Staff. Poison Diaries. (p. 1377)
Wood, Matthew. One Pole, Two Pole: Poems of Daily Bipolar Life. (p. 1296)
Wood, Michael. Road to Delphi: The Life & Afterlife of Oracles. (p. 1477)
—Villains in Virginia Beach. (p. 1842)
Wood, Michele, illus. see Grady, Cynthia.
Wood, Michele, illus. see Grimes, Nikki.
Wood, Michele, illus. see Igus, Toyomi.
Wood, Minister Dorothy F. Samuel's New Suit. (p. 1509)
Wood, Morgan, illus. see Sackanay, Kathleen.
Wood, Muriel, illus. see Fitz-Gibbon, Sally.
Wood, Muriel, illus. see Laurence, Margaret.
Wood, Muriel, illus. see Lowery, Lawrence F.
Wood, Muriel, illus. see Morck, Irene.
Wood, Muriel, illus. see Skrypuch, Marsha Forchuk.
Wood, Muriel, illus. see Skrypuch, Marsha.
Wood, Nancy. Mr. & Mrs. God in the Creation Kitchen. Ering, Timothy Basil, illus. (p. 1184)
Wood, Nathaniel. Play Me Backwards. (p. 1371)
Wood, Nick. Warrior Square. (p. 1859)
Wood, Nicki Pendleton. London Shopping Companion: A Personal Guide to Shopping in London for Every Pocketbook. (p. 1046)
Wood, Patricia. Lottery. (p. 1057)
Wood, Peter H. Strange New Land: Africans in Colonial America. (p. 1665)
Wood, Ramona. Goat Woman of Smackover: An Arkansas Legend. (p. 687)
—Now Caitlin Can: A Donated Organ Helps a Child Get Well. (p. 1269)
Wood, Rob. Kingfish Way: One Man's Escape from Mediocrity. (p. 960)
Wood, Robert, jt. auth. see Williams, Robert.
Wood, Robert Muir. Discovering Prehistory. (p. 449)
Wood, Robert Williams. How to Tell the Birds from the Flowers. (p. 822)
Wood, Roberta. There's a Mouse in the House That Grandpa Built. (p. 1731)
Wood, Ruth, illus. see Conkling, Fleur.
Wood, Ryan, illus. see Bardhan-Quallen, Sudipta.
Wood, Selina. Dog. (p. 460)
—Egypt. (p. 506)
—Fish. (p. 598)
—Hamster. (p. 739)
—Snakes. (p. 1596)
—Spiders. (p. 1627)
Wood, Steve, illus. see Hillyer, Rhonda.
Wood, Steve & Fox, Woody. Courageous Cats Compete. (p. 372)
Wood, Steven, illus. see Shaw, Gina.
Wood, Steven, jt. auth. see Reasoner, Charles.
Wood, T. L. Eldohr Adventures: Quest for Windsoar (Book 2) (p. 508)
Wood, Teri Sue. Wandering Star (p. 1856)
Wood, Tim, jt. auth. see Beck, Alison.
Wood, Tim & Beck, Alison. Best Garden Plants for Michigan (p. 169)
Wood, Timothy D. & Beck, Alison. Tree & Shrub Gardening for Michigan. (p. 1783)
Wood, Tracey, illus. see Heiman, Diane & Suneby, Liz.
Wood, Tracey, illus. see Magruder, Trula.
Wood, Trish. 80hd: A Child's Perspective on ADHD. (p. 1998)
—What Was Asked of Us: An Oral History of the Iraq War by the Soldiers Who Fought It. (p. 1894)
Wood, Vanessa, ed. Antique Names: Tried & True & Truly Rare Historical Names. (p. 89)
Woodall, Karen. Listen to the Stars. (p. 1022)
Woodard, Amy. Day the Teacher Rode a Horse to School. (p. 414)
Woodard, April & White-Petaway, Davida. Adventures of Frankie & Lucy. (p. 18)
Woodard, Cheryl. Storm. (p. 1655)
Woodard, Dana, illus. see Galloway, Shannon.
Woodard, Heather, jt. auth. see Wampol, Pam.
Woodard, Loretta Gilchrist, ed. see Samuels, Wilfred D.
Woodard, Sorah Junkin, illus. see Murdock, Bob E.
Woodard-Lynk, Cher Rhonda. Between Secrets. (p. 173)
Woodberry, Gareth. Gakeva Gluntok's New School. (p. 652)
Woodbridge, Nancy Garfield. Bouquet of Fairy Tales. (p. 216)
Woodbridge, Robyn. Fabulous Beastes. (p. 559)
Wood-Bryce, Ellen, ed. Once upon a Holy Night. (p. 1293)
Woodbury et al, Charles H., illus. see Burroughs, John.
Woodbury, Karl. England Is Truly a Magical Place. (p. 529)
Woodbury, Mary. Flight of the Tiger Moth (p. 604)
—Ghost in the Machine. (p. 671)
—Innocent Polly McDoodle. (p. 875)
Woodcock, George. Gabriel Dumont (p. 652)
Woodcock, John. Color & Doodle Your Way Across the USA. (p. 342)
Woodcock, John, illus. see Bates, Michelle.
Woodcock, John, illus. see Chandler, Fiona.
Woodcock, John, illus. see Davidson, Susannah, et al.
Woodcock, John, illus. see Dowswell, Paul.
Woodcock, John, illus. see Harvey, Gill.
Woodcock, Marcy, illus. see Bloom, Janice Stitziel.
Woodcock, Paul, jt. auth. see Gelder, Darren.
Woodcock, Sandra. Livewire Chillers Black Spot. (p. 1040)
—Livewire Chillers Mind Games. (p. 1040)
—Volcanoes. (p. 1849)
Woodcock, Sandra, jt. auth. see Holt, Julia.
Woodcock, Sandra, et al. Being a Model. (p. 160)
Woodcock, Victoria, jt. auth. see Waley, Safiya.
Woodell, Dolly M. Little Old Woman with a Wart on Her Nose. (p. 1032)
Woodell, Rejoice. Kohara, the White Veiled City. (p. 966)
Wooden, Itanza L. Chill Street Gang Spring Break Vacation. (p. 305)
Wooden, John. Fiesta. Cornelison, Susan F., illus. (p. 584)
Wooden, John, et al. Inch & Miles: The Journey to Success. Cornelison, Sue, illus. (p. 868)
—Inch & Miles: The Journey to Success. Cornelison, Sue F., illus. (p. 868)
Wooden, Lenny, illus. see Kudlinski, Kathleen.
Wooden, Thomas James, Jr. Four-Hundred Meter Champion. Winston, Dennis, illus. (p. 625)
Wooden, Walter. Little Bear's Journey. (p. 1024)
Woodend, Rosetta. Sammy Salmon's Big Adventure: The lifecycle of a Salmon (p. 1508)
Wooderson, Philip. Arf & the Happy Campers. (p. 97)
—Arf & the Tarantula. (p. 97)
Woodfield, Elaine. Stories of the Saints V1 Staggenborg, Kim, illus. (p. 1655)
Woodfield, Gary. Time Thief. (p. 1753)
Woodford, jt. auth. see Schmitt, Conrad J.
Woodford, Chris. Arctic Tundra & Polar Deserts (p. 96)
—Area. (p. 97)
—Distance. (p. 453)
—Electricity: Investigating the Presence & Flow of Electric Charge. (p. 509)
—Experiments with Electricity & Magnetism. (p. 549)
—Experiments with Sound & Hearing. (p. 549)
—Gravity: Investigating the Force, Mass, & Attraction of Physical Bodies. (p. 712)
—Height. (p. 762)
—Light: Investigating Visible & Invisible Electromagnetic Radiation. (p. 1014)
—Light & Radiation. (p. 1014)
—Speed. (p. 1624)
—Temperature. (p. 1717)
—Time. (p. 1750)
—Volume. (p. 1850)
—Weight. (p. 1872)
Woodford, Chris & Clowes, Martin. Atoms & Molecules: Investigating the Building Blocks of Matter. (p. 113)
Woodford, Pamela. King Giggle. (p. 958)
—Lilly & Harry. (p. 1017)
—Ning. (p. 1256)
—Sid, Spark & the Signal Man. (p. 1572)
—Sortof the Snail. (p. 1614)
—Watching Raindrops. (p. 1861)
Woodforde, John. Truth about Cottages: A History & an Illustrated Guide to 50 Types of English Cottage. (p. 1794)
Woodger, Elin, jt. auth. see Burg, David F.
Woodger, Elin & Toropov, Brandon. Encyclopedia of the Lewis & Clark Expedition. (p. 525)
Woodhouse, Cynthia. Lincoln-Douglas Debate. (p. 1018)
Woodhouse, John. 1 Samuel (Redesign) Looking for a Leader. (p. 1991)
Woodhull, Anne Love, jt. auth. see Rotner, Shelley.
Wooding, Chris. Havoc. (p. 755)
—Malice Chernett, Dan, illus. (p. 1083)
—Malice #2: Havoc. (p. 1083)
—Pale. (p. 1319)
—Pandemonium. Diaz, Cassandra, illus. (p. 1321)
—Poison. (p. 1377)
—Silver. (p. 1576)
Wooding, Sharon. Mark Twain in Nevada, a History Coloring Book for Children. (p. 1095)
Woodington, Artie. Elroy, the Big Bad Wolf: The product of his Environment. (p. 516)
Woodlan Jr. Sr. High Students. Devon Makes a Promise. (p. 432)
Woodland, Bette, illus. see Hochman, Marisa.
Woodman, ed. see Townsend, Chris.
Woodman, Melissa. Lessons with Our Jungle Friends. (p. 994)
Woodman, Nancy, illus. see Prager, Ellen J.
Woodman, Nancy, illus. see Tomecek, Steve.
Woodman, Ned, illus. see Gunderson, J.
Woodman, Ned, illus. see Zucker, Jonny.
Woodman, Ros. Beautiful Bride: A Puzzle Book about Rebecca. (p. 153)
—Bible Detectives Puzzle Book. (p. 175)
—Bible Detectives Quiz Book: Noughts & Crosses. (p. 175)
—Exodus: Fun Bible Studies Using Puzzles & Stories. Wheeler, Ron, illus. (p. 548)
—Fun Bible Studies Using Puzzles & Stories. Wheeler, Ron, illus. (p. 647)
—Genesis: Fun Bible Studies Using Puzzles & Stories. Wheeler, Ron, illus. (p. 660)
—Great Celebration: A Puzzle Book about Hezekiah. (p. 714)
—Master Puzzles. (p. 1103)
—Matthew - Bible Detectives. (p. 1109)
—Wise King: A Puzzle Book about Solomon. (p. 1940)
Woodman, Rosalind. Thank You God: God Is Good. (p. 1725)
Woodman, Rosalind & Scrimshire, Hazel. God Loves Me: A Colouring Book. (p. 689)
Woodrell, Daniel. Winter's Bone. (p. 1938)
Woodrich, Erin. Andrew & the Chipmunk: A Lesson in Forgiveness. (p. 72)
Woodroffe, David. Making Paper Airplanes: Make Your Own Aircraft & Watch Them Fly! (p. 1082)
Woodroffe, David, illus. see Gribble, John.
Woodroffe, David, illus. see Maloney, Alison.
Woodrow, Allan. Pet War. (p. 1346)
Woodruff, Ellen Larkin. Tale of Jacob's Journey. Samuel, Dot, illus. (p. 1699)
Woodruff, Elvira. Fearless. (p. 579)
—George Washington's Spy. (p. 665)
—Ravenmaster's Secret. (p. 1441)
Woodruff, Joe. My Too Blue Shoes: A Parable about Wearing Your Convictions. Gates, Phyllis, illus. (p. 1220)
Woodruff, Lisa. ABC's of the Bible: A Companion to My First Study Bible. (p. 4)
Woodruff, Liza. Mary Had a Little Lamb. Woodruff, Liza, illus. (p. 1100)
—What Time Is It? (p. 1894)
Woodruff, Liza, illus. see Brenner, Martha F.
Woodruff, Liza, illus. see Cirrone, Dorian & Cirrone.
Woodruff, Liza, illus. see Cirrone, Dorian.
Woodruff, Liza, illus. see Greenberg, David.
Woodruff, Liza, illus. see Harrod-Eagles, Cynthia.
Woodruff, Liza, illus. see Norman, Kim.
Woodruff, Liza, illus. see Norman, Kimberly.
Woodruff, Liza, illus. see Pitino, Donna Marie.
Woodruff, Liza & Demar, Regier. What Time Is It? Woodruff, Liza, illus. (p. 1894)
Woodruff, M. C. Woods of Arreth. (p. 1950)
Woodruff, Paul. M. Monsters, Myths, & Mysteries: A Tangled Tour Maze Book. Woodruff, Paul. M, illus. (p. 1169)
Woodruff, Rosalind D. Big Surprise! (p. 184)
Woodruff, Stephen B. Esther. (p. 538)
—Noah. (p. 1261)
Woodruff, Tania, jt. auth. see Oppong, Joseph R.
Woodrum, Larry, illus. see Woodrum, Margaret.
Woodrum, Margaret. Christmas Tree Fort. Woodrum, Larry, illus. (p. 316)
Woods, Barbara. Understanding Psychology. (p. 1816)
Woods, Bob. Day with a Pilot. (p. 414)
—Hottest Motorcycles. (p. 802)
—Hottest Muscle Cars. (p. 802)
—Hottest Sports Cars. (p. 802)
—In-Line Skating. (p. 864)
—Massive Machines. (p. 1103)
—Motocross History: From Local Scrambling to World Championship MX to Freestyle. (p. 1179)
—NASCAR Tech. (p. 1230)
—Racer Girls. (p. 1431)
—Shark Attack! (p. 1562)
—Smokin' Motorcycles. (p. 1594)
—Smokin' Muscle Cars. (p. 1594)
—Smokin' Sports Cars. (p. 1594)
—Snowboarding. (p. 1600)
—Snowmobile Racers. (p. 1601)
—Sports in America, 1990-1999. (p. 1632)
—Talkin' NASCAR. (p. 1703)
—Want to Be a NASCAR Driver? (p. 1856)
—Water Sports. (p. 1863)
—Wild Racers. (p. 1930)
Woods, Brenda. Blossoming Universe of Violet Diamond. (p. 202)
—Emako Blue. (p. 517)
—My Name Is Sally Little Song. (p. 1215)
—Red Rose Box. Woods, Brenda, illus. (p. 1455)
—Saint Louis Armstrong Beach. (p. 1503)
Woods, Bridget. Life Drawing: A Journey to Self-Expression. (p. 1010)
Woods, Bronagh. London 2012 Games Activity Book. (p. 1046)
Woods, Candy Godwin. Shimmer Finds Her Gift. (p. 1566)
Woods, Carol, ed. see Hernandez, Regina.
Woods, Caroline. Quick Revision KS3 French. (p. 1427)
Woods, Christopher & McClintic, Ben. Where's Hanuman? (p. 1910)
Woods, Cindy Smith. Happy, Happy Christmas Book. (p. 745)
—Once Inside A Storybook... Good Morals in Short Stories to Encourage Correct Behavior in the Little Ones in Your Life. (p. 1292)
Woods, Dave, jt. auth. see Inns, Chris.
Woods, Dave & Inns, Chris. Junior Caesar. (p. 936)
—Robin Hoodie. (p. 1480)
—Short John Silver. (p. 1569)
—Sir Lance-a-Little. (p. 1580)
Woods, Dawn. Best Day Ever! (p. 168)
Woods, Denise M. & McKelvain, Dana. Legend of the Donkey's Cross. (p. 989)
Woods, Earl & Tiger Woods Foundation Staff. Start Something: You Can Make a Difference. (p. 1643)

W

Woods, Elizabeth. Choker. (p. 309)
Woods, Emily. Thingamafig B Quaxindehouse: Best Friends. (p. 1733)
Woods, Emmett L. Black Frog. (p. 196)
Woods, Gemal. From the Limbs of My Poetree: Selected Poems by Omekongo Dibinga. (p. 644)
Woods, Jeanne & Lugo, Patricia. Bonita Bones & the Halloween Surprise. (p. 209)
Woods, Jessica I. Iowa. (p. 886)
Woods, Karen. Creative Textiles Projects for Children. (p. 380)
Woods, Lin. Kenny Can: "Don't Judge Me" (p. 949)
Woods, Linda. Mystery of the Missing Season. (p. 1225)
Woods, Linda J. Dino-Alphabet Book. (p. 441)
—Gift of the Jumping Goldfish (A True Story) (p. 675)
Woods, Margaret, tr. see Burloux, Gabriel.
Woods, Mark. Xtreme! Owen, Ruth, illus. (p. 1967)
Woods, Mark & Gifford, Clive. Basketball Legends. (p. 143)
Woods, Mark & Owen, Ruth. Ace! (p. 8)
—Ace! Tennis Facts & Stats. (p. 8)
—Goal! (p. 687)
—Goal! Soccer Facts & Stats. (p. 687)
—Scrum! (p. 1533)
—Slam Dunk! (p. 1587)
—Xtreme! Extreme Sports Facts & Stats. (p. 1967)
Woods, Marlene. Rudolph Has the Flu. (p. 1494)
—Rudolph Has the Flu, Second Edition. (p. 1494)
Woods, Mary B., jt. auth. see Woods, Michael.
Woods, Mary B. & Woods, Michael. Ancient Warfare Technology: From Javelins to Chariots. (p. 71)
—Seven Wonders of Ancient North America. (p. 1555)
Woods, Michael. Factoring. (p. 561)
Woods, Michael, illus. see Johnson, Jinny.
Woods, Michael, jt. auth. see Johnson, Jinny.
Woods, Michael, jt. auth. see Woods, Mary B.
Woods, Michael & Woods, Mary B. Air Disasters. (p. 31)
—Ancient Agricultural Technology: From Sickles to Plows. (p. 67)
—Ancient Communication Technology: From Hieroglyphics to Scrolls. (p. 68)
—Ancient Computing Technology: From Abacuses to Water Clocks. (p. 68)
—Ancient Construction Technology: From Pyramids to Fortresses. (p. 68)
—Ancient Machine Technology: From Wheels to Forges. (p. 69)
—Ancient Medical Technology: From Herbs to Scalpels. (p. 70)
—Ancient Transportation Technology: From Oars to Elephants. (p. 71)
—Avalanches. (p. 118)
—Blizzards. (p. 200)
—Disasters at Sea. (p. 447)
—Earthquakes. (p. 497)
—Environmental Disasters. (p. 532)
—Fires. (p. 592)
—Floods. (p. 605)
—History of Medicine. (p. 784)
—Mudflows & Landslides. (p. 1189)
—Seven Natural Wonders of Africa. (p. 1554)
—Seven Natural Wonders of Asia & the Middle East. (p. 1554)
—Seven Natural Wonders of Australia & Oceania. (p. 1554)
—Seven Natural Wonders of Central & South America. (p. 1554)
—Seven Natural Wonders of North America. (p. 1554)
—Seven Natural Wonders of the Arctic, Antarctica, & the Oceans. (p. 1554)
—Seven Wonders (p. 1555)
—Seven Wonders of Ancient Africa. (p. 1555)
—Seven Wonders of Ancient Asia. (p. 1555)
—Seven Wonders of Ancient Central & South America. (p. 1555)
—Seven Wonders of the Ancient Middle East. (p. 1555)
—Seven Wonders of the Ancient World. (p. 1555)
—Space Disasters. (p. 1619)
—Technology in Ancient Cultures (p. 1711)
—Tomb of King Tutankhamen. (p. 1764)
—Volcanoes. (p. 1849)
Woods, Michele, illus. see Fotso, Serge.
Woods, Muriel, illus. see Woods, Shirley E.
Woods, P. Improve Your Soccer Skills. (p. 862)
Woods, Pete, illus. see Grayson, Devin, et al.
Woods, Pete, photos by see Busiek, Kurt, et al.
Woods, Rebecca. Rising Winds of Silver Falls. (p. 1475)
Woods, Rosemary, illus. see Strauss, Rochelle.
Woods, Samuel G., jt. auth. see Collins, Nicholas.
Woods, Shirley. Planet of Success: An Inspirational Book about Attitude Adn Character. Lee, Haylen, illus. (p. 1367)
Woods, Shirley E. Amber: The Story of a Fox Godkin, Celia, tr. (p. 56)
—Jack: The Story of a Beaver Godkin, Celia, illus. (p. 902)
—Tooga: The Story of a Polar Bear Woods, Muriel, illus. (p. 1767)
Woods, Stuart. Iron Orchid. (p. 888)
—Shoot Him If He Runs (p. 1568)
Woods, Tara Denise. Maze. (p. 1113)
Woods, Theresa. Jaguars. (p. 905)
Woods, Thomas E., Jr., jt. auth. see Lansford, Tom.
Woods, Titania. Fairy Dust. (p. 563)
—Friends Forever. (p. 638)
—Midnight Feast. (p. 1138)
Woods, Valerie. Princess Portia's Enchanted Journey (p. 1405)
Woods, Vanessa, illus. see Atkins, Ben.
Woods, Wendy. Welcome Home, Indigeaux: A Louisiana Adventure. Martin, Sherry, illus. (p. 1873)
Woodside, Martin. Thomas Edison: The Man Who Lit up the World. (p. 1738)
Woodside, Martin & Grahame, Kenneth. Wind in the Willows. Akib, Jamel, illus. (p. 1935)
Woodsmall, Marilyne. On the Wings of Angels: Inspirational Verses for Everyday Living. Davidson, Jamie, illus. (p. 1292)
Woodson, Elijah. Fish & Spider: English. (p. 598)
Woodson, J. L. Superwoman's Child: Son of a Single Mother. Malone, Susan Mary, ed. (p. 1684)
—Things I Could Tell You! Malone, Susan Mary et al, eds. (p. 1733)
—Things I Could Tell You! Malone, Susan Mary & Meister, Christine, eds. (p. 1733)
Woodson, Jacqueline. After Tupac & d Foster. (p. 28)
—Behind You. (p. 160)
—Beneath a Meth Moon: An Elegy. (p. 164)
—Brown Girl Dreaming. (p. 232)
—Coming on Home Soon. Lewis, Earl & Lewis, E. B., illus. (p. 348)
—Dear One. (p. 419)
—Each Kindness. Lewis, E. B., illus. (p. 492)
—Feathers. (p. 579)
—From the Notebooks of Melanin Sun. (p. 644)
—House You Pass on the Way. (p. 804)
—Hush. (p. 830)
—I Hadn't Meant to Tell You This. (p. 838)
—If You Come Softly. (p. 854)
—If You Come Softly & Behind You. (p. 854)
—Locomotion. (p. 1045)
—Miracle's Boys. (p. 1148)
—Miracle's Boys. (p. 1149)
—Peace, Locomotion. (p. 1331)
—Pecan Pie Baby. Blackall, Sophie, illus. (p. 1333)
—Show Way. Talbott, Hudson, illus. (p. 1571)
—This Is the Rope: A Story from the Great Migration. Ransome, James, illus. (p. 1736)
—Visiting Day. Ransome, James, illus. (p. 1845)
Woodson, Lissa, ed. see Morton Cuthrell, Kimberly.
Woodson, Marion. Charlotte's Vow. (p. 294)
—Dinosaur Fever. (p. 442)
Woodson, Rick. Poodles & Thunderchicken. (p. 1383)
Woodson, Vera. Lady Bug, Beetle Boy, & Friends: Bullies Be Gone! (p. 970)
Woodsonrick. Poodles in Space. (p. 1383)
Woods-Whitaker, Kim. Elijah's Big Imagination: A Ball of an Adventure. (p. 512)
Woodward, Alice B., illus. see Barrie, J. M.
Woodward, Alice B., illus. see O'Connor, Daniel & Barrie, J. M.
Woodward, Caroline. Singing Away the Dark. Morstad, Julie, illus. (p. 1579)
Woodward, Christopher. Electricity. (p. 509)
Woodward, David R. World War I Almanac. (p. 1959)
Woodward, Elaine, illus. see Sargent, Dave & Sargent, Pat.
Woodward, Horace B. History of Geology. (p. 784)
Woodward II, Ed, illus. see Francis, JennaKay.
Woodward, J. Howland. Moment in Time. (p. 1161)
Woodward, Joanie. Seven Little Monkeys. Woodward, Joanie, illus. (p. 1554)
Woodward, Joe, jt. auth. see Ross, Stewart.
Woodward, John. Along the Shore. (p. 48)
—Ant. (p. 88)
—Bee. (p. 157)
—Beetle. (p. 158)
—Butterfly. (p. 247)
—Cricket. (p. 382)
—Deep, Deep Ocean. (p. 422)
—Dragonfly. (p. 478)
—Ethics of Human Cloning. (p. 539)
—Garden Minibeasts up Close (p. 656)
—Grizzly Bears. (p. 724)
—Loons. (p. 1052)
—Oceans. (p. 1277)
—On the Seabed. (p. 1291)
—Right to Die. (p. 1472)
—Salamanders. (p. 1504)
—Snail. (p. 1595)
—Spider. (p. 1626)
—Swarms. (p. 1689)
—Temperate Forests (p. 1717)
—Under the Waves. (p. 1814)
—What Lives in the Garden? (p. 1891)
—What Lives on Other Animals? (p. 1892)
—What Lives on Your Body? (p. 1892)
—What Lives under the Carpet? (p. 1892)
Woodward, John, jt. auth. see Dodson, Emma.
Woodward, John, jt. auth. see Dorling Kindersley Publishing Staff.
Woodward, John & Dorling Kindersley Publishing Staff. Horses: The Ultimate Treasury. (p. 800)
Woodward, John & Gray, Leon. Backyard. (p. 130)
—Insects. (p. 875)
—Our Bodies. (p. 1307)
Woodward, John & Skancke, Jennifer. Conserving the Environment. (p. 359)
Woodward, John & Stroh, Mary. Fact Fluency & More (Addition) (p. 561)
Woodward, Jonathan, illus. see Deutch, Yvonne.
Woodward, Kate, jt. auth. see Unwin, Mike.
Woodward, Kay. Sleeping Handsome & the Princess Engineer. (p. 1589)
Woodward, Kay & Andersen, Hans Christian. Snow Queen: The Hans Christian Andersen Classic Story. Sumberac, Manuel, illus. (p. 1599)
Woodward, Mac. Sam Houston: For Texas & the Union. (p. 1506)
Woodward, Molly, jt. auth. see Schindel, John.
Woodward, Ryan. Invincible Ed. (p. 885)
Woodward, Sarah, illus. see Thiveos, Maria, tr.
Woodward, Simon. Brave Dave: Book III - the Caribbean Conspiracy. (p. 223)
Woodward, Walter M. Sam Houston: For Texas & the Union. (p. 1506)
Woodword, Elaine, illus. see Sargent, Dave & Sargent, Pat.
Woodworth, Adam. Monsters under My Bed. (p. 1169)
Woodworth, Bradley & Richards, Constance E., eds. St. Petersburg. (p. 1638)
Woodworth, John, jt. auth. see Dellas, Melanie.
Woodworth, Ralph, ed. see Laubach, Frank.
Woodworth, Viki. 3-D Mazes—Maze Mania. (p. 1991)
—50 States: Facts & Fun. (p. 1997)
—A-B-C Mazes. (p. 1)
—Birthday Party. (p. 193)
—Daisy the Dancing Cow. Woodworth, Viki, illus. (p. 400)
—Insects A-B-C. (p. 876)
—Little Monster Mazes. (p. 1032)
—Maze Mania. (p. 1113)
—Princess Mazes. (p. 1404)
—United States Maze Craze. (p. 1819)
—World of Mazes. (p. 1957)
Woody, illus. see Howell, Gill.
Woody, D. L. Town Center Mansion Halloween Gala. (p. 1773)
Woody, John. Ernie Tales. Byars, Bob M., illus. (p. 534)
Woody, Velma B. Branscum. Bandits, Bears & Backaches: A Collection of Short Stories Based on Arkansas History. (p. 136)
Woody, Winfree. I Am Beautiful - Teen: Attitudes, Advice, & Affirmations from & for Today's Girl. (p. 832)
Woodyard, Chris. Haunted Ohio V: 200 Years of Ghosts. (p. 753)
Woodyard, Janelle Valido. Girl's Guide to Softball (p. 680)
Woodyard, Sandy Lilly, illus. see Young, Norene.
Woofter, Susi, jt. auth. see Holtel, Christa.
Woog, Adam. Bigfoot. (p. 184)
—Billy the Kid. (p. 187)
—Bionic Hand. (p. 190)
—Blake Shelton. (p. 198)
—Careers in Forensic Science. (p. 268)
—Careers in Homeland Security. (p. 268)
—Careers in State, County, & City Police Forces. (p. 268)
—Careers in the ATF. (p. 268)
—Careers in the FBI. (p. 268)
—Careers in the Secret Service. (p. 268)
—Derrick Rose. (p. 427)
—Early Middle Ages. (p. 494)
—Emancipation Proclamation: Ending Slavery in America. (p. 517)
—Fight Renewed: The Civil Rights Movement. (p. 585)
—Giants. (p. 674)
—History of Gospel Music. (p. 784)
—History of Gospel Music. Greenhaven Press Editors, ed. (p. 784)
—Jacques Cartier. (p. 905)
—Jennifer Lopez. (p. 913)
—Jesse James: The Wild West for Kids. (p. 914)
—Jesse James. (p. 914)
—Joe Montana. (p. 920)
—John Lasseter: Pixar Animator. (p. 922)
—Jyotirmayee Mohapatra, Advocate for India's Young Women. (p. 941)
—LaDainian Tomlinson. (p. 970)
—Life During the Spanish Inquisition. (p. 1010)
—Matt Damon. (p. 1109)
—Medieval Knight. (p. 1119)
—Military Might & Global Intervention. (p. 1143)
—Mummies. (p. 1190)
—Oprah Winfrey. (p. 1301)
—Palestinian National Authority. (p. 1320)
—Pearl Harbor. (p. 1333)
—Pierre M. Omidyar: Creator of Ebay. (p. 1357)
—Reality TV. (p. 1449)
—Reggie Bush. (p. 1457)
—Robert Kirkman. (p. 1479)
—Samurai Warrior. (p. 1510)
—SCRATCHbot. (p. 1532)
—Trey Parker, Matt Stone, & South Park: South Park. (p. 1785)
—Vampires in the Movies. (p. 1832)
—Walter Payton. (p. 1856)
—What Makes Me a Quaker? (p. 1892)
—Wyatt Earp. (p. 1966)
—YouTube. (p. 1982)
—Zuckerberg. (p. 1990)
Woog, Adam, jt. auth. see Koestler-Grack, Rachel A.
Woog, Adam, jt. auth. see Malaspina, Ann.
Woog, Adam & Hirschmann, Kris. Mirror Image: How Guys See Themselves (p. 1149)
Woog, Dan. Jesse Jackson. (p. 914)
Wool, Daniel. Judaism. (p. 930)
Wool, Danny & Yudin, Yefim (Chaim). Animated Jewish Year. Portnoi, Jeremy, illus. (p. 84)
Wooldridge, Connie N. & Wooldridge, Connie Nordhielm. Thank You Very Much, Captain Ericsson! Glass, Andrew, photos by. (p. 1725)
Wooldridge, Connie Nordhielm. Brave Escape of Edith Wharton. (p. 223)
—Just Fine the Way They Are: From Dirt Roads to Rail Roads to Interstates. Walz, Richard, illus. (p. 938)
Wooldridge, Connie Nordhielm, jt. auth. see Wooldridge, Connie N.
Wooldridge, Susan. Bathing with Ants. (p. 144)
Wooley, John & Price, Michael H. Big Book of Biker Flicks: 40 of the Best Motorcycle Movies of All Times (p. 179)
Woolf, Alex. Arab-Israeli War Since 1948 (p. 94)
—Asteroid Strike. (p. 108)
—Buildings (p. 239)
—Chemical Accident. (p. 297)
—Children of the Holocaust. (p. 302)
—Democracy. (p. 425)
—Encounters with the Past. (p. 524)
—Euthanasia. (p. 540)
—Expedition to the Arctic. (p. 548)
—Focus on Israel. (p. 610)
—Focus on the United Kingdom. (p. 611)
—Genocide. (p. 661)
—Impact of Technology in Art. (p. 862)
—Impact of Technology in History & Archaeology. (p. 862)
—Journey along the Amazon. (p. 927)
—Killer Bears. (p. 956)
—Killer Cats. (p. 956)
—Killer Sharks. (p. 956)
—Killer Snakes. (p. 956)
—Killer Spiders. (p. 956)
—Let's Think about the Internet & Social Media (p. 1001)
—Meet the Ancient Romans. (p. 1122)
—Meet the Tudors. (p. 1123)
—Meet the Vikings. (p. 1123)
—Meteor: Perspectives on Asteroid Strikes (p. 1130)
—My Life in India. (p. 1212)
—My Life in Indonesia. (p. 1212)
—My Life in Kenya. (p. 1212)
—Mystery of Maddie Musgrove. (p. 1224)
—Rise of Nazi Germany. (p. 1474)
—Sailing the Great Barrier Reef. (p. 1503)
—Terrorism. (p. 1722)
—Trekking in the Congo Rainforest. (p. 1784)
—You Wouldn't Want to Live Without Books! Antram, David, illus. (p. 1977)
—You Wouldn't Want to Live Without Fire! (p. 1977)
—You Wouldn't Want to Live Without Soap! Bergin, Mark, illus. (p. 1977)
Woolf, Alex, ed. see Elgin, Kathy.
Woolf, Alex, ed. see Hibbert, Clare & Hibbert, Adam.
Woolf, Alex, ed. see Rooney, Anne.
Woolf, Alex, ed. see Steele, Philip.
Woolf, Alex, jt. auth. see Farndon, John.
Woolf, Alex & Anniss, Matthew. Impact of Technology. (p. 862)
Woolf, Alex, et al. Design & Engineering for STEM. (p. 429)
—World After. (p. 1953)
Woolf, Catherine Maria. My First Hike. Woolf, Catherine Maria, illus. (p. 1206)
Woolf, Julia. Gingerbread Joy. (p. 677)
—Jack's Room. (p. 904)
—Reindeer Run. (p. 1457)
—Snowman Surprise. (p. 1601)
—Special Star. (p. 1623)
Woolf, Julia, illus. see Albee, Sarah.
Woolf, Julia, illus. see Ghigna, Charles.
Woolf, Julia, illus. see Hegarty, Patricia.
Woolf, Julia, illus. see North, Merry.
Woolf, Julia, illus. see Plourde, Lynn.
Woolf, Julia, illus. see Stockland, Patricia M.
Woolf, Virginia. Jacob's Room. (p. 904)
Woolfe, Angela. Avril Crump. (p. 120)
Woolfson, Richard. Bebe Genial. (p. 155)
Woolf-Wade, Sarah J. Nightsong. (p. 1255)
Woollacott, Angela. Gender & Empire. (p. 660)
Woollard, Mary. Illustrated Guide to Staging History. (p. 857)
Woollatt, Margaret. Twelve Days of Christmas in New Jersey. Rossi, Richard, illus. (p. 1800)
Woollatt, Sue, illus. see Farrington, Karen.
Woollett, Laura A. Big Top Burning: The Story of an Arsonist, a Missing Girl, & the Greatest Show on Earth. (p. 184)
Woolley, A. Rocks & Minerals. (p. 1483)
Woolley, Alan. Rocks & Minerals Spotter's Guide: With Internet Links. Freeman, Mike, photos by. (p. 1483)
Woolley, Barbara B. Freedom West. (p. 635)
Woolley, Bryan. Mr. Green's Magnificent Machine. Arbuckle, Scott, illus. (p. 1185)
Woolley, John. I Am with You: For Young People & for Those Young at Heart. (p. 834)
Woolley, Kim, illus. see Sansone, Emma.
Woolley, Patricia, illus. see Evans, Olive.
Woolley, Sara, illus. see Sosin, Deborah.
Woolley, Steph. Where's Sonic? A Search-and-Find Adventure. (p. 1910)
Woolley, Steph & MacMillan Art Publishing Staff. Bin Weevils. (p. 188)
Woolley, Steph & Macmillan Audio Staff. Where's Octeelia? A Search-and-Find Adventure. (p. 1910)
Woolmer, Nancy, illus. see Gregory, Larry.
Woolsey, Matthew & Keller, Carolyn. Vanderbilt University College Prowler off the Record. (p. 1833)
Woolson, Constance Fenimore. Old Stone House. (p. 1284)
Woolson, Constance Fenimore (A. K. A. Anne March). Old Stone House. (p. 1284)
Woolston, Blythe. Black Helicopters. (p. 196)
—Freak Observer. (p. 631)
—Troutzilla. (p. 1790)
Woolway, Colin. Drumsense: The First Steps Towards Co-Ordination, Style & Technique Vol. 1 (p. 487)
Woolwine, Dale. Fighter, Fighter, Firefighter. (p. 585)
Woomer, Lisa. Cookie. (p. 361)
Woon, Yvonne. Life Eternal (a Dead Beautiful Novel) (p. 1010)
—Love Reborn. (p. 1060)
Woop Studios Staff. Zeal of Zebras: An Alphabet of Collective Nouns. (p. 1985)
Wooster, Devin Ann. Sing It Out. (p. 1579)
Wooster, Devin Ann, jt. auth. see RH Disney Staff.
Wooster, Patricia. Fashion Designer. (p. 575)
—Flickr Cofounder & Web Community Creator Caterina Fake. (p. 603)
—Illustrated Timeline of Dinosaurs Epstein, Len, illus. (p. 858)
—Illustrated Timeline of Space Exploration Doty, Eldon, illus. (p. 858)
—Illustrated Timeline of U. S. States Morgan, Rick, illus. (p. 858)
—Music Producer. (p. 1193)
—Show Me Rocks & Minerals: My First Picture Encyclopedia (p. 1570)
—Show Me Rocks & Minerals. (p. 1570)
—Show Me the United States: My First Picture Encyclopedia (p. 1570)
—Youtube Founders Steve Chen, Chad Hurley, & Jawed Karim. (p. 1982)
Wooster, Patricia & Dell, Pamela. My First Picture Encyclopedias. (p. 1207)
Wooster, Robert, jt. ed. see Kessel, William B.
Wooten, Arthur. Wise Bear William: A New Beginning. Santora, Bud, illus. (p. 1940)
Wooten, Deborah, jt. ed. see Cullinan, Bernice E.
Wooten, Joyce Honeycutt, jt. auth. see Parnell, Frances Baynor.
Wooten, Laura. With My Little Box of Crayons. Pennington, Kelly, illus. (p. 1942)
Wooten, Neal, illus. see Austin, Antoinette & Austin, John.
Wooten, Neal, illus. see McKelvey, Lonnie.
Wooten, Neal, illus. see Mitchell, Malinda.
Wooten, Neal, illus. see Skerwarski, N. D.
Wooten, Sara McIntosh. Denzel Washington: Academy Award-Winning Actor. (p. 427)
—Donald Trump: From Real Estate to Reality TV. (p. 466)
—Frida Kahlo: Her Life in Paintings. (p. 637)

—Robert Frost: The Life of America's Poet. (p. 1479)
—Tim McGraw: Celebrity with Heart. (p. 1750)
—Tim McGraw. (p. 1750)
Wooten, Sara McIntosh, jt. auth. see Medina, Mariana.
Wooten, Sherry. Cowboy Connor. (p. 373)
Wooten, Terry. When the Bear Came Back: The Whole Story. Lechler, Louan, illus. (p. 1904)
Wooten, Vernon Lee, illus. see Briggs-Anderson, Naomi.
Wooters, Duane. Unnamed Manuscript. (p. 1822)
Woram, Catherine. Christmas Crafting with Kids: 35 Projects for the Festive Season. (p. 313)
—Christmas Crafting with Kids. Wreford, Polly, photos by. (p. 313)
—Crafting with Kids: Creative Fun for Children Aged 3-10. Davies, Vanessa, photos by. (p. 375)
Woram, Catherine, jt. auth. see Cox, Martyn.
Woram, Catherine, jt. auth. see Rigg, Annie.
Woram, Catherine & Youngs, Clare. Rainy Day Book of Things to Make & Do. (p. 1436)
Worcester, Daryl D. Story of the Famous Traves Travislot. (p. 1661)
—Traves Travislot: The North American Adventure (p. 1781)
—Traves Travislot's Going South for the Winter. (p. 1781)
Worcester, Heidi P., jt. auth. see Stern, Ricki.
Worcester, Joseph E. (Joseph Emerson). Elementary Dictionary of the English Language by Joseph E Worcester, Ll D. (p. 510)
Worcester, Sue. Ernesto Nia Lakeru. (p. 534)
Word Among Us Editorial Staff. 42 Bible Stories for Little Ones: From Creation to Pentecost. Round, Graham, illus. (p. 1997)
Word, Brian H. Jenks Jupiter. (p. 912)
Word, Miriam F. Moki & the Cherry Pie. (p. 1160)
Word of Life Fellowship Inc, creator. Quiet Time: One Year Daily Devotional for Children in Grades 3-4 (p. 1428)
—Quiet Time: 1 Year Daily Devotional: Grades 1-2. (p. 1428)
—Quiet Time Daily Devotional for Early Learners Ages 4-6 (p. 1428)
Word of Life Fellowship Staff. Quiet Time Daily Devotional for Early Learners. (p. 1428)
Word of Life Press, creator. Manga Bible Story. (p. 1087)
Word, Sharon. Word Is Alphabet Poems. (p. 1950)
Wordsworth, J. C., ed. see Thucydides.
Wordwindow. Shakespeare for Children Picture Book. (p. 1559)
Worek, Michael. Nobel Prize: The Story of Alfred Nobel & the Most Famous Prize in the World. (p. 1262)
—What's on My Farm? (p. 1899)
Worek, Michael, jt. auth. see Firefly Books Staff.
Worek, Michael, jt. auth. see Marshall, Stephen A.
Worek, Michael & Marshall, Stephen A. Weird Insects. (p. 1872)
Work, Rhoda O. Mr Dawson Had an Elephant. Maas, Dorothy, illus. (p. 1184)
Workinger, Shelley. Settling: Solid. Bk. 2 (p. 1554)
Workman, Dan, illus. see Rondina, Catherine.
Workman, James G. Water. (p. 1862)
Workman, Joan. Scavenger Hunt: The Twokay Kids at the Mall. (p. 1521)
Workman, Lisa, illus. see Bellen-Berthézène, Cyndie.
Workman, Lisa, illus. see Harlmann, Sierra.
Workman, Paula J., illus. see Stamps, Sarah.
Workman Publishing Company Staff. Horse Farm. Graham, Lindsay, illus. (p. 799)
—Space. (p. 1618)
—Wild Animals. (p. 1928)
Workman Publishing, Workman. Eyelike Stickers: Christmas. (p. 558)
Workman, Ross, jt. auth. see Myers, Walter Dean.
Workman, Terry, illus. see Bellen-Berthézène, Cyndie.
Workman, Terry, illus. see Cecil, Lauren.
Workman, Terry, illus. see Fuerst, Jeffrey B.
Worland, Sally T. Mom, Why Can't We Just Be a Normal Family? The adventures of a mom, a dad, 4 kids, an RV, 6 bicycles - & 50 states - in 12 Months. (p. 1161)
World Almanac Editors. Great Stories of Courage: The Call of the Wild; the Red Badge of Courage; Treasure Island. (p. 718)
—Murder & Mystery: The Hound of the Baskervilles; Macbeth; the Legend of Sleepy Hollow. (p. 1192)
—Travel & Adventure. (p. 1780)
—World Almanac(r) 2013 Trivia Game. (p. 1953)
—World Almanac(r) for Kids 2012. Janssen, Sarah, ed. (p. 1953)
—World Almanac(r) for Kids 2013. (p. 1953)
—World Almanac(r) for Kids 2013 Trivia Game. (p. 1953)
World Almanac Editors, creator. Great Stories of Courage: The Call of the Wild, the Red Badge of Courage, Treasure Island. (p. 718)
World Almanac Editors, et al. Historical Adventure: A Connecticut Yankee in King Arthur's Court/ Around the World in 80 Days/the Prisoner of Zenda. (p. 782)
World Almanac Staff. World Almanac for Kids 2014. Janssen, Sarah, ed. (p. 1953)
World Bank Staff & Roman, Annette. 1 World Manga: Passage 6: Corruption. (p. 1991)
World Book, contrib. by. Earth & Earth's Moon. (p. 495)
—Galaxies & the Universe. (p. 653)
—Human Space Exploration. (p. 826)
—Jupiter, Ceres & the Asteroids. (p. 937)
—Mars. (p. 1096)
—Mercury & Venus. (p. 1127)
—Neptune & the Distant Dwarf Planets. (p. 1241)
—Saturn & Uranus. (p. 1515)
—Sun & Other Stars. (p. 1676)
World Book, Inc. Box Turtles & Other Pond & Marsh Turtles. (p. 216)
World Book, Inc. Staff. Atlas of the World. (p. 113)
—Christmas Around the World (p. 312)
—Christmas in Russia. (p. 314)
—Documenting History (p. 460)
—Explore the Solar System (p. 550)
—Explore the Universe (p. 550)
—Learning Ladders (p. 985)
—Living Green (p. 1041)
—Wonderful World of English. (p. 1948)
—World Adventure. (p. 1953)
—World Book's Young Scientist (p. 1954)
World Book, Inc Staff, contrib. by. Aboriginal Rights Movement. (p. 5)
—African American Civil Rights Movement. (p. 26)
—Age of Knights & Castles. (p. 29)
—Alien Planets. (p. 41)
World Book, Inc. Staff, contrib. by. All about Birds: A Supplement to Childcraft—The How & Why Library. (p. 42)
World Book, Inc Staff, contrib. by. Amphibians. (p. 65)
World Book, Inc. Staff, contrib. by. Amphibians & Reptiles of the United States & Canada. (p. 66)
World Book, Inc. Staff, contrib. by. Ancient Egyptians. (p. 69)
—Ancient Greeks. (p. 69)
—Animal Babies. (p. 76)
—Animal Behavior. (p. 76)
—Animal Homes. (p. 78)
—Animal Life Cycles. (p. 78)
—Animal Structure & Classification. (p. 80)
—Arabians & Other Horses. (p. 94)
—Architecture & Engineering. (p. 95)
—Armored & Duckbilled Dinosaurs: The Ornithischians. (p. 99)
—Armored Dinosaurs! The Ornithischians. (p. 100)
—Arts. (p. 104)
—Astronomy. (p. 109)
—Australian Aborigines. (p. 116)
—Aztec. (p. 122)
World Book, Inc. Staff, contrib. by. Baby's First Book: A Book of Learning: Featuring Selections from Childcraft—the How & Why Library. (p. 129)
World Book, Inc. Staff, contrib. by. Beagles & Other Hounds. (p. 150)
—Bermuda Triangle & Other Mysteries of the Deep. (p. 167)
—Birdlike Dinosaurs: Small Theropods & Prehistoric Birds. (p. 191)
—Birds. (p. 191)
—Birth & Growing up Celebrations. (p. 192)
—Blizzards. (p. 200)
World Book, Inc. Staff, contrib. by. Blue Whales & Other Baleen Whales. (p. 203)
World Book, Inc Staff, contrib. by. Bulldogs & Other Nonsporting Dogs. (p. 240)
—Bullied by Boys. (p. 240)
—Bullied by Friends. (p. 240)
—Bullied by Girls. (p. 240)
—Bullied by Groups. (p. 240)
—Bullied in Cyberspace. (p. 240)
—Bullied to Belong. (p. 240)
World Book, Inc. Staff, contrib. by. Butterflies of the United States & Canada. (p. 247)
World Book, Inc Staff, contrib. by. Canadian Independence. (p. 260)
—Cell Cycle. (p. 286)
—Childcraft: The How & Why Library (p. 302)
World Book, Inc. Staff, contrib. by. Childcraft: The How & Why Library (p. 302)
—Childcraft - the How & Why Library. (p. 302)
World Book, Inc. Staff, contrib. by. Chinese of the Shang, Zhou, & Qin Dynasties. (p. 307)
—Chinese Revolution. (p. 307)
—Christmas in America in the 1700's & 1800's. (p. 314)
World Book, Inc. Staff, contrib. by. Christmas in Belgium. (p. 314)
World Book, Inc Staff, contrib. by. Christmas Train Across Canada. (p. 316)
—Circulatory System. (p. 322)
—Code Red: Animals in Peril: A Supplement to Childcraft-The How & Why Library. (p. 338)
—Community Helpers. (p. 350)
—Consumable Goods. (p. 360)
—Cumulative Glossary & Index. (p. 392)
—Deserts & Scrublands. (p. 429)
—Digestive & Urinary Systems. (p. 438)
—Digestive System/The Urinary System. (p. 438)
—Dogs, from Woofs to Wags. (p. 463)
—Dream Takes Flight: A Supplement to Childcraft, the How & Why Library. (p. 484)
—Droughts. (p. 486)
—Durable Goods. (p. 490)
—Earth. (p. 495)
—Earth & Earth's Moon. (p. 495)
—Earth & Space. (p. 495)
—Earthquakes. (p. 497)
—Earth's Features. (p. 498)
—Economics. (p. 502)
—Electricity. (p. 509)
—Encyclopedia of Animals. (p. 524)
—Encyclopedia of Human Beings (p. 525)
—Encyclopedia of Matter & Energy. (p. 525)
—Encyclopedia of Plants. (p. 525)
—Encyclopedia of Space. (p. 525)
—Endangered & Threatened Species of Africa. (p. 526)
—Endangered Animals of Australia, New Zealand, & Pacific Islands. (p. 526)
World Book, Inc. Staff, contrib. by. Endangered Animals of Europe. (p. 526)
World Book, Inc Staff, contrib. by. Endangered Animals of North America. (p. 526)
—Endangered Animals of the Oceans. (p. 526)
—Endangered Animals of the World. (p. 526)
—Endocrine & Reproductive Systems. (p. 527)
—End-Of-Life Rituals. (p. 526)
World Book, Inc. Staff, contrib. by. End-of-Life Rituals. (p. 526)
World Book, Inc Staff, contrib. by. Enduring Mystery of Machu Picchu. (p. 527)
—Everyday Celebrations & Rituals. (p. 543)
World Book, Inc. Staff, contrib. by. Everyday Celebrations & Rituals. (p. 543)
World Book, Inc Staff, contrib. by. Explore & Learn—Atlas of the World. (p. 550)
—Explore & Learn-Me & My Body. (p. 550)
—Explore & Learn—People in Place & Time. (p. 550)
—Explore & Learn—The Natural World. (p. 550)
World Book, Inc Staff, contrib. by. Extinct! (p. 555)
World Book, Inc. Staff, contrib. by. Federation of Australia. (p. 580)
—¡Feliz Navidad¡: Celebrating a Mexican Christmas. (p. 581)
—Fierce Dinosaurs: The Large Theropods. (p. 584)
—Fighting Sickness. (p. 586)
—Fish. (p. 598)
—Floods. (p. 605)
World Book, Inc. Staff, contrib. by. Flying Foxes & Other Bats. (p. 610)
World Book, Inc Staff, contrib. by. Forces of Nature. (p. 617)
—Forests & Wetlands. (p. 618)
—Fractions. (p. 626)
World Book, Inc. Staff, contrib. by. Freshwater Life of the United States & Canada. (p. 637)
—Frogs & Other Amphibians. (p. 641)
World Book, Inc Staff, contrib. by. Fun with Cultural Crafts & Performing Arts. (p. 648)
—Fun with Numbers. (p. 648)
—Fun with Painting & Sculpture. (p. 649)
—Fun with Shapes. (p. 649)
—Galaxies. (p. 653)
—Galaxies & the Universe. (p. 653)
—German Shepherds & Other Herding Dogs. (p. 666)
—Giant Dinosaurs: The Sauropods. (p. 673)
—Golda Meir: With Profiles of David Ben-Gurion & Yitzhak Rabin. (p. 694)
—Golden Retrievers & Other Sporting Dogs. (p. 695)
—Goldfish & Other Carp. (p. 695)
—Good Food for You. (p. 698)
World Book, Inc. Staff, contrib. by. Gorillas & Other Apes. (p. 703)
World Book, Inc Staff, contrib. by. Grasslands. (p. 712)
—Gravity. (p. 712)
—Great Depression. (p. 715)
—Green Anoles & Other Pet Lizards. (p. 721)
—Green Buildings. (p. 721)
—Green Transportation. (p. 722)
—Hamsters & Other Pet Rodents. (p. 740)
—Harvest Celebrations. (p. 751)
—Heat. (p. 760)
—Heat Waves. (p. 760)
World Book, Inc. Staff, contrib. by. Heroes & Helpers: A Supplement to Childcraft: The How & Why Library. (p. 772)
World Book, Inc Staff, contrib. by. Holland Lops & Other Rabbits. (p. 789)
—Human Space Exploration. (p. 826)
—Hurricanes, Typhoons, & Other Tropical Cyclones. (p. 830)
—Ice Storms. (p. 851)
—Icy Worlds. (p. 851)
World Book, Inc. Staff, contrib. by. Iguanas & Other Lizards. (p. 856)
World Book, Inc. Staff, contrib. by. Inca. (p. 868)
—Independence of India & Pakistan. (p. 870)
—Indians of Eastern Canada & the United States. (p. 871)
—Indians of the Great Plains & Great Basin. (p. 872)
—Indians of the Northwest Coast & Plateau. (p. 872)
—Indians of the Southwest. (p. 872)
—Industry & Manufacturing. (p. 873)
—Insects & Spiders. (p. 876)
World Book, Inc. Staff, contrib. by. Insects of the United States & Canada. (p. 876)
World Book, Inc. Staff, contrib. by. Insects, Spiders, & Creepy Crawlers: A Supplement to Childcraft, the How & Why Library. (p. 876)
—Inventions & Discoveries. (p. 884)
—Jupiter. (p. 937)
—Jupiter & the Asteroids. (p. 937)
—Learning about Animals. (p. 984)
—Learning about Energy, Forces, & Motion. (p. 984)
—Learning about Matter. (p. 984)
—Learning about Plants. (p. 984)
—Learning about the Sun, Moon, Planets, & Stars. (p. 985)
—Learning about Weather. (p. 985)
—Legend of King Arthur. (p. 988)
—Letters to Words: A Supplement to Childcraft—The How & Why Library. (p. 1003)
—Library of Natural Disasters (p. 1006)
—Light. (p. 1014)
World Book, Inc. Staff, contrib. by. Lobsters & Other Crustaceans. (p. 1044)
World Book, Inc. Staff, contrib. by. Magnetism. (p. 1076)
—Mammals. (p. 1085)
World Book, Inc. Staff, contrib. by. Mammals of the United States & Canada. (p. 1085)
World Book, Inc Staff, contrib. by. Maori. (p. 1089)
—Marriage Celebrations. (p. 1096)
World Book, Inc. Staff, contrib. by. Marriage Celebrations. (p. 1096)
World Book, Inc Staff, contrib. by. Mars. (p. 1096)
World Book, Inc. Staff, contrib. by. Mars. (p. 1096)
World Book, Inc. Staff, contrib. by. Matter & How It Changes. (p. 1109)
—Matter & Its Properties. (p. 1109)
—Maya. (p. 1112)
—Medicine. (p. 1119)
—Mercury & Venus. (p. 1127)
World Book, Inc. Staff, contrib. by. Mercury & Venus. (p. 1127)
World Book, Inc Staff, contrib. by. Milky Way. (p. 1143)
—Miniature Schnauzers & Other Terriers. (p. 1146)
—Mollusks & Similar Sea Creatures. (p. 1160)
World Book, Inc. Staff, contrib. by. Monarchs & Other Butterflies. (p. 1163)
World Book, Inc Staff, contrib. by. Mountains & Polar Regions. (p. 1181)
—Mountains, Deserts, & Grasslands. (p. 1181)
—My Body. (p. 1198)
—Mysteries in the Nazca Desert. (p. 1222)
—Mysteries of Easter Island. (p. 1222)
—Mysteries of Egypt's Pyramids: The Secrets of the Pharaoh. (p. 1222)
—Mysteries of Stonehenge. (p. 1222)
—Mysteries of the Amazon Rain Forest. (p. 1222)
—Mysteries of the Maya. (p. 1222)
—Mysteries of the Trojan War. (p. 1222)
—Mystery of Tutankhamun. (p. 1226)
—Myths & Legends of Africa. (p. 1227)
—Myths & Legends of Ancient Egypt. (p. 1227)
—Myths & Legends of North America: The Southwestern United States & Mexico. (p. 1227)
—National Celebrations. (p. 1231)
—Nature's Patterns. (p. 1237)
—Nature's Places. (p. 1237)
—Neptune & Pluto. (p. 1241)
—Neptune, Comets, & Dwarf Planets. (p. 1241)
—Nervous System. (p. 1241)
—New Year's Celebrations. (p. 1247)
—Numbers. (p. 1272)
—Observatories in Space. (p. 1275)
—Observatories on Earth. (p. 1275)
—Oceans. (p. 1277)
—Oceans, Islands, & Polar Regions. (p. 1277)
—On the Move. (p. 1291)
—Pandemics. (p. 1321)
World Book, Inc Staff, contrib. by. Party Animal (p. 1326)
World Book, Inc. Staff, contrib. by. Peoples of the Arctic & Subarctic. (p. 1340)
World Book, Inc. Staff, contrib. by. Persians & Other Long-Haired Cats. (p. 1344)
World Book, Inc Staff, contrib. by. Pinktoes & Other Tarantulas. (p. 1360)
—Plant & Animal Adaptations. (p. 1368)
—Plants Around the World. (p. 1370)
—Pollution. (p. 1381)
—Polynesians. (p. 1381)
—Portuguese Water Dogs & Other Working Dogs. (p. 1387)
—Producing & Obtaining Food. (p. 1409)
—Purple Pinchers & Other Hermit Crabs. (p. 1419)
World Book, Inc. Staff, contrib. by. Quail & Other Galliforms. (p. 1422)
World Book, Inc Staff, contrib. by. Quasars & Black Holes. (p. 1423)
—Rain Forest Animals. (p. 1434)
—Religious Celebrations. (p. 1458)
World Book, Inc. Staff, contrib. by. Religious Celebrations. (p. 1458)
World Book, Inc Staff, contrib. by. Reptiles. (p. 1461)
—Resources & Cumulative Index. (p. 1463)
—Respiratory System. (p. 1463)
—Revealing the Secrets of Dinosaurs. (p. 1465)
—Rivers, Lakes, & Wetlands. (p. 1476)
—Saturn & Uranus. (p. 1515)
World Book, Inc. Staff, contrib. by. Saturn & Uranus. (p. 1515)
World Book, Inc Staff, contrib. by. Savannas. (p. 1516)
—Science & Technology. (p. 1525)
—Sea & Its Marvels. (p. 1534)
—Searching for Atlantis. (p. 1537)
—Searching for the Real Dracula. (p. 1538)
—Seasonal Forests. (p. 1538)
—Secrets of Ancient Tombs. (p. 1545)
—Secrets of the Pharaohs. (p. 1545)
—Shih Tzu & Other Toy Dogs. (p. 1566)
—Siamese & Other Short-Haired Cats. (p. 1572)
—Skeletal System/The Muscular System. (p. 1584)
—Sound. (p. 1615)
—South Africa's Anti-Apartheid Movement. (p. 1616)
—Space Exploration. (p. 1619)
—Spring Celebrations. (p. 1635)
—Stars— Birth & Death. (p. 1643)
—Stars— the Inside Story. (p. 1643)
World Book, Inc Staff, contrib. by. Storks & Other Large Wading Birds. (p. 1655)
World Book, Inc Staff, contrib. by. Subtraction. (p. 1671)
—Sun & Other Stars. (p. 1676)
—Tales of Mystery & the Unknown: A Supplement to Childcraft— the How & Why Library. (p. 1702)
—Tales Through Time: A Supplement to Childcraft-The How & Why Library. (p. 1703)
—Technology. (p. 1711)
—Telescopes & Space Probes. (p. 1716)
—Things I Like. (p. 1733)
—Thunderstorms. (p. 1746)
—Tornadoes. (p. 1770)
—Tough Trucks. (p. 1773)
—Traits & Heredity. (p. 1777)
—Transportation. (p. 1779)
World Book, Inc. Staff, contrib. by. Trees of the United States & Canada. (p. 1784)
World Book, Inc Staff, contrib. by. Tropical Regions & Rain Forests. (p. 1789)
—Tsunamis & Seiches. (p. 1795)
—Under the Sea. (p. 1814)
—Universe—A Cosmic Tour. (p. 1820)
—Universe— Mysteries & Marvels. (p. 1820)
—Volcanoes. (p. 1849)
—Voyages of Exploration. (p. 1851)
—Warfare. (p. 1858)
—Weather. (p. 1869)
—Wild Animals. (p. 1928)
—Wildfires. (p. 1931)
—Winter Celebrations. (p. 1938)
World Book, Inc. Staff, contrib. by. Winter Celebrations. (p. 1938)
World Book, Inc Staff, contrib. by. Wonders of the World. (p. 1949)
World Book, Inc. Staff, contrib. by. World Book Encyclopedia (p. 1954)
World Book, Inc Staff, contrib. by. World Book Encyclopedia 2013. (p. 1954)
World Book, Inc. Staff, contrib. by. World Book Encyclopedia of People & Places (p. 1954)
—World Book of America's Multicultural Heritage (p. 1954)
—World Book of America's Presidents (p. 1954)
—World Book Student Discovery Encyclopedia (p. 1954)
—World Book's Animals of the World Set 4. (p. 1954)
—World Book's Science & Nature Guides (p. 1954)

W

World Book, Inc Staff, contrib. by. World of Dinosaurs. (p. 1956)
—World of Insects. (p. 1956)
—World of Pets. (p. 1957)
—World War II in Europe. (p. 1959)
—World War II in the Pacific. (p. 1959)
World Book Staff. Cells to Organ Systems. (p. 286)
—Circulatory System. (p. 322)
World Book-Childcraft International Staff, contrib. by. Brain Games: A Supplement to Childcraft—The How & Why Library. (p. 221)
World Health Organization, Regional Office for the Western Pacific Staff. Responding to Questions about the 100% Condom Use Programme: A Job Aid for Programme Staff. (p. 1463)
World Health Organization Staff. Quality Assessment Guidebook: A Guide to Assessing Health Services for Adolescent Clients. (p. 1422)
World Library Publications, creator. Catholic Corner Puzzles & Activities: Year C. (p. 280)
World Myths Staff. Europe. (p. 540)
—India. (p. 870)
—Russia. (p. 1498)
—Southeast Asia. (p. 1617)
World Of Happy Staff, jt. auth. see Andreae, Giles.
World Peace, Metta & McBride, Heddrick. Metta's Bedtime Stories. Pax, H. H. -, illus. (p. 1130)
World Syndicate Publishing. Fairy Tales & Other Stories. (p. 564)
World-Famous San Diego Zoo Staff, photos by see Ryder, Joanne.
Worley, Brandi. Crumb Snatchers, Part I. (p. 386)
Worley, Carla. Freedom Choice: A Book that Allows You to Consider Your Options. (p. 634)
Worley, Karen E., jt. auth. see Pearce, Claudia.
Worley, Michelle. Buster Goes to the White House (p. 245)
Worley, Rob M. Pet Project (p. 1345)
Worley, Rob M. & Warner, Gertrude Chandler. Pizza Mystery Dubisch, Mike, illus. (p. 1365)
—Surprise Island Dubisch, Michael, illus. (p. 1686)
Worley, Roger. Wishbone Journal. (p. 1940)
Worley, Roger A. 14 Wishes (p. 1995)
Worm, Piet. Three Little Horses. (p. 1742)
Wormell, Chris. Eric!... the Hero? Wormell, Chris, illus. (p. 533)
—Molly & the Night Monster. Wormell, Chris, illus. (p. 1160)
—Number of Animals. (p. 1271)
—Sea Monster. Wormell, Chris, illus. (p. 1535)
—Wild Girl. Wormell, Chris, illus. (p. 1929)
—Wings, Horns, & Claws: A Dinosaur Book of Epic Proportions. (p. 1936)
Wormell, Chris, illus. see Lewis, J. Patrick.
Wormell, Chris, et al. Dos Ranas. Bourgeois, Elodie, tr. (p. 472)
Wormell, Christopher. Mice, Morals, & Monkey Business: Lively Lessons from Aesop's Fables. (p. 1134)
—Scruffy Bear & the Lost Ball. (p. 1533)
—Teeth, Tails & Tentacles: An Animal Counting Book. (p. 1715)
—Teeth, Tails & Tentacles. (p. 1715)
Wormell, Christopher, illus. see Green, Kate.
Wormell, Christopher, illus. see Lewis, J. Patrick.
Wormell, Christopher, illus. see Moore, Clement C.
Wormell, Christopher, jt. auth. see Reasoner, Charles.
Worms, Penny. Dinosaurs: Over 1000 Reusable Stickers! (p. 444)
—Dinosaurs. (p. 444)
—Snow White Creativity Book: Games, Cut-Outs, Art Paper, Stickers, & Stencils. Basic, Zdenko et al, illus. (p. 1600)
Wornell, Rick. Two-Toed Toad on the Road. (p. 1804)
Worrall, Linda. Snow White & the Seven Dwarfs: A Story about Vanity. (p. 1600)
Worre, John Arthur. Gospel According to Scrooge: A Dickens of A Tale. (p. 703)
Worrell, Maryellen. Accidental Hero. (p. 8)
Worrell, Nicole, illus. see Fraley, Patty.
Worsham, Adria F. Max Celebrates Cinco de Mayo Gallagher-Cole, Mernie, illus. (p. 1111)
—Max Celebrates Groundhog Day Gallagher-Cole, Mernie, illus. (p. 1111)
—Max Celebrates Martin Luther King Jr. Day Gallagher-Cole, Mernie, illus. (p. 1111)
—Max Celebrates Ramadan Gallagher-Cole, Mernie, illus. (p. 1111)
Worsham, Brown LaWanda. Angel on Duty. (p. 74)
Worsley, Arlene. Bald Eagles. (p. 134)
—For the Love of Gymnastics. (p. 616)
—Gymnastics. (p. 734)
—Veterans Day. (p. 1839)
Worsley, Belinda, illus. see Graves, Sue.
Worsley, Belinda, illus. see Gurney, Stella.
Worsley, Belinda, illus. see Harrison, Paul.
Worsley, Belinda, illus. see Powell, Jillian.
Worsley, John, ill. Painkillers: Book One. (p. 1318)
Worsley, Norman H., jt. auth. see Bumstead, Pat.
Worstine, Wanetta Cotner. Grandma's Yarn. (p. 709)
Worthe, Allison. Rosie Sprout's Time to Shine. Barton, Patrice, illus. (p. 1490)
Worth, Bonnie. Cat in the Hat - Cooking with the Cat. Moroney, Christopher, illus. (p. 278)
—Hark! a Shark! All about Sharks. Ruiz, Aristides & Mathieu, Joe, illus. (p. 748)
—I Can Name 50 Trees Today! All about Trees. Ruiz, Aristides & Mathieu, Joe, illus. (p. 836)
—Ice Is Nice! All about the North & South Poles. Ruiz, Aristides & Mathieu, Joe, illus. (p. 850)
—If I Ran the Horse Show: All about Horses. Ruiz, Aristides & Mathieu, Joe, illus. (p. 853)
—If I Ran the Rain Forest: All about Tropical Rain Forests. Ruiz, Aristides, illus. (p. 853)
—Looking for Bigfoot. Nelson, Jim, illus. (p. 1051)
—Oh, the Places on Earth! A Cat in the Hat's Learning Library Collection (p. 1281)
—Oh, the Things They Invented! All about Great Inventors. (p. 1281)
—Oh, the Things They Invented! All about Great Inventors. Ruiz, Aristides & Mathieu, Joe, illus. (p. 1281)
—Once upon a Mastodon: All about Prehistoric Mammals. (p. 1293)
—One Cent, Two Cents, Old Cent, New Cent: All about Money. Ruiz, Aristides & Mathieu, Joseph, illus. (p. 1294)
—Safari, So Good! All about African Wildlife. Ruiz, Aristides & Mathieu, Joe, illus. (p. 1502)
—Way to Go, Chipmunk Cheeks. (p. 1864)
—Whale of a Tale! All about Porpoises, Dolphins, & Whales. Ruiz, Aristides & Mathieu, Joe, illus. (p. 1877)
—Would You Rather Be a Pollywog? All about Pond Life. Ruiz, Aristides & Mathieu, Joseph, illus. (p. 1962)
Worth, Bonnie & Klimo, Kate. Ginger. Jessell, Tim, illus. (p. 676)
Worth, Douglas. Thumpy the Christmas Hound. (p. 1746)
Worth, Richard. 1950s to 1960s. (p. 2002)
—1970s to the 1980s. (p. 2002)
—African Americans During Reconstruction. Schwarz, Philip, ed. (p. 27)
—Africans in America. (p. 28)
—America in World War I. (p. 59)
—Apache: A Proud People. (p. 91)
—Arab-Israeli Conflict. (p. 94)
—Cleopatra: Queen of Ancient Egypt. (p. 331)
—Colonial America: Building Toward Independence. (p. 341)
—Elisabeth Kubler-Ross: Encountering Death & Dying. (p. 513)
—Eva Longoria: Actress, Activist, & Entrepreneur. (p. 540)
—Gambling: Winner or Loser? (p. 654)
—George Catlin: Painter of Indian Life. (p. 663)
—Great Empire of China & Marco Polo in World History. (p. 715)
—Gunpowder. (p. 732)
—Harlem Renaissance: An Explosion of African-American Culture. (p. 749)
—Heinrich Himmler: Murderous Architect of the Holocaust. (p. 762)
—Illegal Drugs: Condone or Incarcerate? (p. 856)
—Independence for Latino America. (p. 870)
—Jack Kerouac: The Road Is Life. (p. 903)
—Johnny Appleseed: Select Good Seeds & Plant Them in Good Ground. (p. 923)
—Lewis Hine: Photographer of Americans at Work. (p. 1004)
—Life at School & in the Community. (p. 1008)
—Los Angeles Police Department. (p. 1053)
—Louisiana, 1682-1803. (p. 1058)
—Massacre at Virginia Tech: Disaster & Survival. (p. 1102)
—Mexican Immigrants. (p. 1131)
—New France, 1534-1763. (p. 1244)
—Pervez Musharraf. (p. 1345)
—Ponce de Leon & the Age of Spanish Exploration in World History. (p. 1382)
—Pope Francis: The People's Pope. (p. 1384)
—Puerto Rico: From Colony to Commonwealth. (p. 1415)
—Puerto Rico in American History. (p. 1415)
—Saladin: Sultan of Egypt & Syria. (p. 1504)
—San Francisco Earthquake. (p. 1510)
—Sherman Antitrust ACT. (p. 1566)
—Slave Life on the Plantation: Prisons Beneath the Sun. (p. 1588)
—Slave Trade in America: Cruel Commerce. (p. 1588)
—Social Security ACT. (p. 1604)
—Teetotalers & Saloon Smashers: The Temperance Movement & Prohibition. (p. 1715)
—Telegraph & Telephone. (p. 1716)
—Texas War of Independence. (p. 1724)
—Vasco da Gama. (p. 1833)
—Weight Control Drugs. (p. 1872)
—Workers' Rights. (p. 1952)
—Yo-Yo Ma. (p. 1972)
Worth, Richard, jt. auth. see Hasday, Judy L.
Worth, Richard & Asher, Robert. Jewish Immigrants. (p. 917)
Worth, Richard & Benchmark Education Co., LLC. Adaptation & Biodiversity. (p. 11)
Worth, Sharon. Jacob's Garden (p. 904)
Worth, Valerie. Animal Poems. Jenkins, Steve, illus. (p. 79)
—Pug: And Other Animal Poems. Jenkins, Steve, illus. (p. 1415)
Wortham, Caledra. Way up High in the Sky. (p. 1864)
Worth-Baker, Marcia. Greek Mythology Activities: Activities to Help Students Build Background Knowledge about Ancient Greece, Explore the Genre of Myths, & Learn Important Vocabulary. (p. 720)
Worthen, Bonnie, jt. auth. see Loulan, Joann.
Worthen, Diane. Oliver's Wish: A Tale from the Garden. (p. 1286)
Worthen, Johnny. Celeste. (p. 285)
Worthington, Heather. Rise of the Detective in Early Nineteenth-Century Popular Fiction. (p. 1474)
Worthington, Heather Hill. Miles of Smiles: The Story of Roxey, the Long Island Rail Road Dog. Farnsworth, Bill, illus. (p. 1142)
Worthington, Jennifer & Shoals, Melinda. Gift That Saved Christmas. (p. 675)
Worthington, Joe. Mannings: Football's Famous Family. (p. 1088)
Worthington, Leonie, illus. see Bedford, David.
Worthington, Leonie, illus. see Bowring, Jane.
Worthington, Leonie, illus. see McLean, Wendy & Book Company Staff.
Worthington, Leonie, illus. see Munro, Maisie.
Worthington, Leonie, jt. auth. see Bedford, David.
Worthington, Leonie & Bedford, David. Bums. (p. 241)
Worthington, Lisa & Moon, Susan. My Magic Bike. Harston, Jerry, illus. (p. 1213)
—People Do Silly Things. Totire, Valerie, illus. (p. 1339)
Worthington, Michelle. Noah Chases the Wind. Cowman, Joseph, illus. (p. 1261)
—Start of the Ocean. Finn, Ann-Marie, illus. (p. 1643)
Worthington, Niles. Chef's Job. (p. 297)
—Plumber's Job. (p. 1374)
—Vet's Job. (p. 1839)
Worthington, Sandi. Adventure with Rainy Twostep. (p. 15)
Worthy, Jo. Readers Theater for Building Fluency: Strategies & Scripts for Making the Most of This Highly Effective, Motivating, & Research-Based Approach to Oral Reading. (p. 1444)
Worthy Kids, creator. My Great Big Veggie Storybook: With Lessons from God's Word. (p. 1210)
Worthy, Kimberly. Poetry Is Not Just Rhyming: An Innovative Learning Tool & Coloring Book for Kids. (p. 1376)
Worthy, Shanya. LeBron James: Basketball Legend. (p. 987)
—Taipan. (p. 1696)
—Taipan / Taipán. (p. 1696)
Worthy, Shanya, jt. auth. see Mills, Nathan.
Wortman, Barbara. Key in the Candle. (p. 950)
Worton, Sylvia Wells. Sylvias World & the Spirit of Tree. (p. 1693)
Wortzman, Ricki, jt. auth. see Nyman, Debbie.
Wortzman, Rickie, jt. auth. see Harcourt, Lalie.
Woszczylo, Noushka. Escape. (p. 534)
Wotherspoon, John, jt. auth. see Park, Barbara.
Wotton, Jon, illus. see Williams, Vivienne.
Wotton, Joy. My First Word Book: Pictures & Words to Start Toddlers Reading & to Help Pre-Schoolers Develop Vocabulary Skills. Tulip, Jenny, illus. (p. 1208)
Wouk, Henry. Hearing Disorders. (p. 759)
—Organ Transplants. (p. 1303)
—Tuberculosis. (p. 1795)
Wouk, Henry & Colligan, Douglas. Kung Fu. (p. 968)
Woulf, David. Southern Complexion. (p. 1617)
Woupio, Amy, illus. see Woupio, Isaac Jay.
Woupio, Isaac Jay. Making Faces. Woupio, Amy, illus. (p. 1081)
Woywada, Allison. Little Fir Tree: A Musical for Primary Children Based on a Story by Hans Christian Andersen. (p. 1027)
—Sunnyside Junior High. (p. 1677)
Wozniak, Patricia. McGooster & Mcgyman Begin Their Adventures. (p. 1114)
Wozniak, Patricia A., illus. see Rochkind, Pat.
Wozniak, Paul. Stranded in a Snowstorm! Webber, Mike, illus. (p. 1664)
Wragg, Nate, illus. see Schwartz, Corey Rosen & Coulton, Beth.
Wraight, Colin. Poppy Darke & the Cauldron of Fear. (p. 1385)
Wranovics, John. Chaplin & Agee: The Untold Story of the Tramp, the Writer, & the Lost Screenplay. (p. 291)
Wrate, Richard. Din-o-mite in Aarons Closet. (p. 440)
Wray, Anna. This Belongs to Me: Cool Ways to Personalize Your Stuff. (p. 1735)
Wray, Charles. Spell of Cold Weather. (p. 1625)
Wray, Melissa. Destiny Road. (p. 431)
Wray, Patricia. Sasha, the Dreamer (p. 1515)
Wray, Ramona. Women Writers of the Seventeenth Century. (p. 1946)
Wray, Zoe, illus. see Daynes, Katie.
Wray, Zoe, illus. see Milbourne, Anna.
Wray, Zoe, illus. see Patchett, Fiona.
Wray, Zoe, illus. see Turnbull, Stephanie.
Wray, Zoe, jt. auth. see Daynes, Katie.
Wray, Zoe, contrib. by. Usborne Illustrated Stories for Girls. (p. 1827)
Wrazen, Nicholas. Don't Talk to Strangers. (p. 468)
Wrecks, Billy. Batman! (DC Super Friends) Schoening, Dan & Beavers, Ethen, illus. (p. 144)
—Batman's Hero Files. (p. 144)
—Batman's Hero Files (DC Super Friends) Random House Editors et al, illus. (p. 144)
—Battle in Space! (DC Super Friends) Doescher, Erik & Marrucchi, Elisa, illus. (p. 146)
—Big Heroes! (DC Super Friends) Golden Books Staff, illus. (p. 181)
—Bizarro Day! (p. 194)
—Bizarro Day! (DC Super Friends) Legramandi, Francesco, illus. (p. 194)
—Catch Catwoman! (p. 279)
—Catch Catwoman! DeCarlo, Mike & Tanguay, David D., illus. (p. 279)
—Cosmic Legends (DC Super Friends) Golden Books Staff, illus. (p. 368)
—Crime Wave! (p. 382)
—Crime Wave! (DC Super Friends) Schoening, Dan, illus. (p. 382)
—Green Lantern vs. the Meteor Monster! Random House Staff, illus. (p. 722)
—Here Come the Heroes! Golden Books, illus. (p. 770)
—Heroes! Golden Books Staff, illus. (p. 772)
—Heroes vs. Villains/Space Chase! (p. 773)
—Heroes vs. Villains/Space Chase! (DC Super Friends) Doescher, Erik et al, illus. (p. 773)
—In the Lead! (Disney Planes) RH Disney Staff, illus. (p. 866)
—Jailbreak! (p. 905)
—Jailbreak! (DC Super Friends) Legramandi, Francesco, illus. (p. 905)
—Mighty & Amazing (DC Super Friends) Golden Books Staff, illus. (p. 1139)
—Mighty Mazes (DC Super Friends) Doescher, Erik & DeCarlo, Mike, illus. (p. 1140)
—Monster Madness! (DC Super Friends) Random House Staff, illus. (p. 1167)
—Reptile Rumble! (p. 1461)
—Reptile Rumble! Doescher, Erik, illus. (p. 1461)
—Reptile Rumble! (DC Super Friends) Doescher, Erik, illus. (p. 1461)
—Skyscraper Showdown. Schoening, Dan, illus. (p. 1587)
—Super Friends Save Christmas/Race to the North Pole! Random House Staff, illus. (p. 1680)
—Superman! (DC Super Friends) Beavers, Ethen, illus. (p. 1683)
—T. Rex Trouble! Random House Staff, illus. (p. 1694)
—Time-Travel Trouble! (p. 1753)
—To the Rescue! (DC Super Friends) Golden Books, illus. (p. 1759)
—Unstoppable! (DC Super Friends) Golden Books, illus. (p. 1823)
—X-Ray Vision! (DC Super Friends) Borkowski, Michael, illus. (p. 1967)
Wrecks, Billy, jt. auth. see Awdry, Wilbert V.
Wrede, Patricia, jt. auth. see Wrede, Patricia C.
Wrede, Patricia C. Across the Great Barrier. (p. 9)
—Book of Enchantments. (p. 211)
—Calling on Dragons. (p. 254)
—Far West. (p. 572)
—Revenge of the Sith. (p. 1466)
—Searching for Dragons. (p. 1537)
—Snow White & Rose Red. (p. 1599)
—Talking to Dragons. (p. 1703)
—Thirteenth Child. (p. 1735)
Wrede, Patricia C., jt. auth. see Stevermer, Caroline.
Wrede, Patricia C. & Stevermer, Caroline. Mislaid Magician or Ten Years After: Being the Private Correspondence Between Two Prominent Families Regarding a Scandal Touching the Highest Levels of Government & Thesecurity of the Realm. (p. 1151)
Wrede, Patricia C. & Wrede, Patricia. Calling on Dragons. (p. 254)
Wreford, Polly, photos by see Collister, Linda.
Wreford, Polly, photos by see Cox, Martyn & Woram, Catherine.
Wreford, Polly, photos by see Woram, Catherine.
Wreggelsworth, Irene. Funny, Naughty Bunny: A Bilingual Book in English & German. Piccione, Dana, illus. (p. 650)
—Help, Children! - The Monsters Kidnapped Santa Claus: Bilingual Book in English & Spanish. Piccione, Dana, illus. (p. 765)
—Liv's Search for the Last Unicorn. Anderson, Anya, illus. (p. 1042)
Wren, Coretta. Counting on God. (p. 371)
Wren, Laura Lee. Pirates & Privateers of the High Seas. (p. 1363)
Wren, Wendy. Nelson Comprehension Pupil Book 2 Jackman, John, ed. (p. 1240)
Wrench, Peter. Night of the Round Stable. Holland, Ruth, illus. (p. 1254)
—Web She Wove. (p. 1870)
Wrenn, Charles, illus. see Altsheler, Joseph A.
Wrenn, Charles L., illus. see Altsheler, Joseph A.
Wrenn, Luanne, jt. auth. see Bartlett, Susan.
Wrenn, Tom. Clever Monkey Rides Again. (p. 331)
Wrenn, Tom, illus. see Acevedo, Ari.
Wrenn, Tom, illus. see Cleveland, Rob.
Wrenn, Tom, illus. see DeSpain, Pleasant.
Wrenn, Tom, illus. see Hamilton, Martha & Weiss, Mitch.
Wrenn, Tom, jt. auth. see Padma, T. V.
Wright, A. Gilbert. In the Steps of the Great American Herpetologist. Kalmenoff, Matthew, illus. (p. 867)
Wright, Alex, illus. see Lefkon, Wendy, et al, eds.
Wright, Alex, illus. see Safro, Jill, ed.
Wright, Alex, jt. auth. see Imagineers Staff.
Wright, Alice & Bridges, LaVon. Alaska Animals We Love You: Chants & Poems for Children. (p. 34)
Wright, Alson, illus. see Wells, Sharon D.
Wright, Amber. Celebrate! Your Inner Star. (p. 284)
Wright, Annabel, illus. see Davies, Nicola.
Wright, Anne. City States (p. 324)
—City States. (p. 324)
—Mythology. (p. 1227)
—Philosophy & Writing. (p. 1351)
—War & Warfare. (p. 1857)
Wright, Anne & Croy, Anita. Art & Architecture. (p. 101)
Wright, Anne Margaret, jt. auth. see Croy, Anita.
Wright, Barbara. Crow. (p. 385)
Wright, Ben. Top Priority: Manna 2. (p. 1769)
Wright, Ben, ed. see Hamrick, Frank, et al.
Wright, Benjamin, ed. see Hamrick, Frank, et al.
Wright, Betty Ren. Blizzard. Himler, Ronald, illus. (p. 199)
—Christina's Ghost. (p. 312)
—Crandalls' Castle. (p. 376)
—Dollhouse Murders. (p. 464)
—Princess for a Week. Rogers, Jacqueline, illus. (p. 1403)
Wright, Bil. Putting Makeup on the Fat Boy. (p. 1420)
—Sunday You Learn How to Box. (p. 1676)
Wright, Bil, jt. auth. see Wright, Bill.
Wright, Bill, illus. see De Maris, Merrill, et al.
Wright, Bill & Wright, Bil. When the Black Girl Sings. (p. 1904)
Wright, Bill, Sr. Gleedus the Happy Grasshopper. Fraser, Jess, illus. (p. 683)
Wright, Blanche Fisher. Mother Goose Nursery Rhymes. (p. 1178)
—Real Mother Goose Clock Book. (p. 1448)
Wright, Blanche Fisher, illus. see Gache, Stephen Vance.
Wright, Blanche Fisher, illus. see Scholastic, Inc. Staff.
Wright, Blanche Fisher, jt. auth. see Donahue, Peter.
Wright, Boyd. Donkey Tales. (p. 466)
Wright, Brendan, ed. see Baron, Mike.
Wright, Brendan, ed. see Gill, Joe.
Wright, Brendan, ed. see Hicks, Faith Erin & Druckmann, Neil.
Wright, Brendan, ed. see Sakai, Stan.
Wright, Brendan, ed. Archie Archives Volume 7. (p. 95)
Wright, Brent A., illus. see Keith, Patty J.
Wright, Bud. My Momma Raised Ugly Children Not Stupid Ones: The Ruminations & Reminiscences of a Gentle Southern Man. (p. 1214)
Wright, Caleb E. Marcus Blair A Story of Provincial Times. (p. 1092)
Wright, Carol, ed. see Boyd, Roland.
Wright, Carol, illus. see Bradman, Tony.
Wright, Carolyn. In the Beginning. (p. 865)
Wright, Cavin. Bedtime Tales. (p. 157)
Wright, Chantal, jt. auth. see Steinhöfel, Andreas.
Wright, Chris. Incubating Miracle Taylor, Minnie, ed. (p. 870)
Wright, Chris, illus. see Patterson, Eric.
Wright, Christine. My Little Green Book: First Steps in Bible Reading. (p. 1212)
Wright, Christopher, illus. see Brock, Justin.
Wright, Christopher, illus. see Patterson, Eric.
Wright, Cindy, ed. see Brundige, Patricia.
Wright, Cori. Courtesy. (p. 373)
Wright, Cornelius Van, see Chin, Karen.
Wright, Cornelius Van, see Van Wright, Cornelius.
Wright, Craig. Dolphin Readers. (p. 464)

—Double Trouble. (p. 473)
—Matt's Mistake. (p. 1110)
—Meet Molly, Level 1. (p. 1121)
—Silly Squirrel. (p. 1576)
—Uncle Jerry's Great Idea, Level 3. (p. 1811)
Wright, Craig, ed. see Kenshole, Fiona.
Wright, Craig, ed. see Lindop, Christine.
Wright, Craig, ed. see Northcott, Richard.
Wright, Craig, ed. see Rose, Mary.
Wright, Craig, ed. see Taylor, Di.
Wright, Craig, ed. City Girl, Country Boy. (p. 323)
—In the Ocean, Level 4. (p. 867)
—Just Like Mine. (p. 939)
—Let's Go to the Rainforest. (p. 997)
—My Family. (p. 1202)
—New Girl in School, Level 3. (p. 1244)
—Students in Space, Level 3. (p. 1669)
—Things That Fly. (p. 1733)
—Tough Task. (p. 1773)
—What Did You Do Yesterday? (p. 1882)
—Where People Live, Level 4. (p. 1909)
—Wonderful Wild Animals, Level 3. (p. 1948)
—Yesterday, Today, & Tomorrow, Level 4. (p. 1971)
Wright, Cynthia. Everything You Need to Know about Dealing with Stalking. (p. 545)
Wright, Danielle. Japanese Nursery Rhymes: Carp Streamers, Falling Rain & Other Traditional Favorites. Acraman, Helen, illus. (p. 909)
—Korean Nursery Rhymes: Wild Geese, Land of Goblins & Other Favorite Songs & Rhymes. Acraman, Helen, illus. (p. 967)
Wright, Dare. Edith & Little Bear Lend a Hand. (p. 504)
—Holiday for Edith & the Bears. (p. 788)
—Lonely Doll Learns a Lesson. (p. 1046)
Wright, David. Unexpected Event That Took Place at the Lake. (p. 1817)
Wright, David, illus. see Gilpin, Rebecca.
Wright, David F., et al. Wright Balance Focus for Success Series - Relaxation: A Guide to Your Best Golf. (p. 1963)
Wright, David K. Cuba. (p. 388)
—Life of Arthur Ashe: Smashing the Color Barrier in Tennis. (p. 1011)
—Life of Paul Robeson: Actor, Singer, Political Activist. (p. 1012)
Wright, Deana. Playground. (p. 1372)
Wright, Dee. Peanut Butter Finger Mystery. (p. 1332)
Wright, Diane Beem, illus. see Camden, Marian Louise.
Wright, Dixie Lee. Job Smarts: 12 Steps to Job Success. (p. 919)
—Job Smarts Instructor's Manual: 12 Steps to Job Success for Students with Special Needs. (p. 919)
Wright, Donald R. African-Americans in the Early Republic, 1789-1831. Eisenstadt, Abraham S. & Franklin, John Hope, eds. (p. 27)
Wright, Douglas, illus. see Lopez, Horacio.
Wright, Edgar, jt. auth. see Palacios, Tomas.
Wright, Elsie. Patty & Jo, Detectives. (p. 1329)
Wright, Evan. Generation Kill: Devil Dogs, Iceman, Captain America, & the New Face of American War. (p. 660)
Wright, Frank E. Bad Adam Stories. (p. 131)
Wright, Gail. Adventures of Alfred in Mom, I'm Growing up Now: Decision Making. (p. 16)
Wright, Gail R. Adventures of Alfred in the Greatest Fruit of All: Conflicts & Resolutions. (p. 16)
Wright, Gary Thorup. Jaguar: A Tale of the Christ in Ancient America. Part 1 (p. 905)
Wright, Genevieve, tr. see Daigle, Evelyne.
Wright, Gina. My Mommy Has Breast Cancer. (p. 1214)
Wright, Greg. Peter Jackson in Perspective: The Power Behind Cinema's the Lord of the Rings: A Look at Hollywood's Take on Tolkien's Epic Tale. (p. 1346)
Wright Group. Early Emergent Guided Reading. (p. 493)
—Ssn/Ef/Grk 1/Comp. (p. 1637)
Wright Group, Incorporated Staff. Brice & the Whale: Decodable Books (p. 227)
Wright, H. Norman, jt. auth. see Oliver, Gary J.
Wright, Hawley, illus. see Andrews, Beth.
Wright, Heather. Writing Fiction: A Hands-on Guide for Teens. (p. 1964)
Wright, Herbert Francis. Origin of American Aborigines: A Famous Controversy. (p. 1304)
Wright, Holly. River. (p. 1475)
—Sky. (p. 1586)
—Star. (p. 1640)
—Sunflower. (p. 1676)
—Wave. (p. 1864)
Wright, I. B. Wife Training! A Pig's Guide to Love & Marriage. (p. 1927)
Wright, Jason F. Penny's Christmas Jar Party. Sowards, Ben, illus. (p. 1338)
Wright, Jay, illus. see Anorak Press Staff.
Wright, Jessica Noelani. Exploring Modern Art. (p. 552)
Wright, Joan M. Flo: A Very Special Budgie. (p. 605)
Wright, Joe. Math's Mate Orange: Student Pad. Tutos, Joanna, ed. (p. 1108)
Wright, Johanna. Bunnies on Ice. Wright, Johanna, illus. (p. 242)
—Orchestra Pit. Wright, Johanna, illus. (p. 1302)
Wright, Johanna, illus. see Sternberg, Julie.
Wright, Johanna, illus. see Umansky, Kaye.
Wright, John. Baseball. (p. 140)
—Basketball. (p. 143)
—Equestrian Sport. (p. 533)
—Hockey. (p. 786)
—U. S. Transportation Security Administration. (p. 1807)
Wright, John & Waugh, Steven. USA 1929-1980. (p. 1826)
Wright, John D. Counterterrorist Forces with the CIA. (p. 370)
—Football. (p. 615)
—Race & Crime. (p. 1430)
—Sports Injuries: How to Prevent, Diagnose & Treat (p. 1632)
Wright, John D. & Singer, Jane. Fire & Explosives. (p. 590)
—Hair & Fibers. (p. 736)
Wright, John R., illus. see Marsh, Laura F.
Wright Johnson, Shelli. Falcon in the Nest: A Story of Bes Adventure. (p. 565)
Wright, Joseph B. Math's Mate Rose: Student Pad. Tutos, Joanna, ed. (p. 1108)
Wright, Joshua. Hapless, Hopeless, Horrible. (p. 744)
—Plotless, Pointless, Pathetic. (p. 1374)
Wright, Julie. Hazzardous Universe. Wasden, Kevin, illus. (p. 756)
—My Not-So-Fairytale Life. (p. 1216)
Wright, K. Paige. Steven & Huggey: The story of a boy & his Blankey. (p. 1649)
Wright, Karen. Adventures of Martha & Sully. Paneva, Valya, illus. (p. 20)
Wright, Kathryn, illus. see Bates, Dianne.
Wright, Kirby. Punahou Blues: A Hawaiian Novel. (p. 1416)
Wright, Kit. Magic Box: Poems for Children. Bailey, Peter, illus. (p. 1071)
Wright, Kiyah. Joshua's Surprise. (p. 927)
—Vacation Fun. (p. 1830)
Wright, Lacie. Covenant for Kids! Student Workbook. (p. 373)
Wright, Lanikka. Fab Four 2: Eva's Obsession. (p. 559)
Wright, Lisa & Versace, Matthew. Adventures of Sam & Doodle: Escape from Robot Island. Wright, Lisa, illus. (p. 22)
Wright, Lloyd. Gramp's Variety of Stories. (p. 706)
—More Stories for Gramp's Little Friends. (p. 1175)
—Stories for Gramp's Little Friends. (p. 1654)
Wright, Lucy, illus. see Carter, R J.
Wright, Lucy, illus. see Carter, R. J.
Wright, Lynda. Flowers for Addison. (p. 608)
Wright, Mabel Osgood. Citizen Bird. (p. 322)
—Citizen Bird Scenes from Bird-Life in Plain English for Beginners. (p. 323)
—Garden You & I. (p. 656)
Wright, Mabel Osgood, jt. auth. see Coues, Elliott.
Wright, Mabel Osgood & Coues, Elliott. Citizen Bird: Scenes from bird-life in plain English for Beginners. (p. 322)
—Citizen Bird: Scenes from Bird Life in Plain English for Beginners. Fuertes, Louis Agassiz, illus. (p. 322)
—Citizen Bird: Scenes from Bird Life in Plain English for Beginners (1897) Fuertes, Louis Agassiz, illus. (p. 322)
—Citizen Bird Scenes from Bird-Life in Plain English for Beginners. (p. 323)
Wright, Mabel Osgood, creator. Citizen Bird: Scenes from Bird-Life in Plain English for Beginners. (p. 322)
Wright, Mabel Osgood, et al. Citizen Bird: Scenes from bird-life in plain English for Beginners. (p. 322)
Wright, Marcus. Raincloud. (p. 1436)
Wright, Marcy. Juan Pablo Montoya. (p. 930)
Wright, Marsha. Sentences & Vowel Pairs - Digraphs (p. 1551)
—Sentences for Consonant Blends - Digraphs (p. 1551)
—Sentences for R-Controlled Vowels - Diphthongs (p. 1551)
—Sentences for Short - Long Vowels (p. 1551)
—Stories for Consonant Blends - Digraphs (p. 1654)
—Stories for R-Controlled Vowels - Diphthongs (p. 1654)
—Stories for Short - Long Vowels (p. 1654)
—Stories for Vowel Pairs - Digraphs (p. 1654)
Wright, Mary. Co-Man & Poppa Meet Kanka. Dewitt, Levi, illus. (p. 336)
—Justice for All. (p. 940)
Wright, Mary F. Co-Man the Dolphin. (p. 336)
Wright, Mary H. Grandma Spoils Me. Megenhardt, Bill, illus. (p. 708)
Wright, Maureen. Barnyard Fun De Tagyos, Paul Ratz, illus. (p. 140)
—Earth Day, Birthday! Kim, Violet, illus. (p. 495)
—Sleep, Big Bear, Sleep! Hillenbrand, Will, illus. (p. 1588)
—Sneeze, Big Bear, Sneeze! Hillenbrand, Will, illus. (p. 1597)
Wright, Melissa, jt. auth. see Wallace, Susan F. S. P.
Wright, Melissa, jt. auth. see Wallace, Susan Helen.
Wright, Melissa & Curelli, Augusta. My Bible: The Story of God's Love. Curelli, Augusta, illus. (p. 1197)
Wright, Michael. Jake Goes Peanuts. Wright, Michael, illus. (p. 906)
—Jake Starts School. Wright, Michael, illus. (p. 906)
Wright, Mike. Li'l Book O' Big Laughs. (p. 1017)
—When the Music Stopped. (p. 1905)
Wright, Neville. Cop Car: And the Phantom Street Gang. (p. 365)
Wright, Nicola. Diggers. (p. 439)
—Ships. (p. 1567)
Wright, Olivia. Malarie Jane Learns to Help. (p. 1083)
Wright, Pam, jt. auth. see Sohn, Emily.
Wright, Pamela. Rant Room. (p. 1438)
Wright, Pamela, jt. auth. see Bair, Diane.
Wright, Patricia, illus. see Vernon-Jackson, Hugh.
Wright, Pauline. Why Did My Dad Go to War? (p. 1923)
Wright, Peter M. Stone Prince (p. 1652)
Wright, Petrina, illus. see Pickering, Jill.
Wright, Philip Lee & Foster, John. Mail Pilot's Hunch: Or A Crash in Death Valley. (p. 1077)
Wright, R. Thomas. Exploring Manufacturing. (p. 552)
—Manufacturing & Automation Technology. (p. 1089)
—Processes of Manufacturing. (p. 1408)
—Processes of Manufacturing Instructor's Guide. (p. 1408)
—Technology: Wraparound Edition. (p. 1711)
—Technology. (p. 1711)
Wright, R. Thomas & Brown, Ryan A. Technology: Design & Applications. (p. 1711)
—Technology: Design & Applications, Wraparound Edition. (p. 1711)
Wright, Ralph. Wild. (p. 1928)
Wright, Randall, jt. auth. see Deedy, Carmen Agra.
Wright, Rebecca Hu-Van & Asbjornsen, Peter Christen. Three Billy Goats Gruff Hu, Ying-Hwa, illus. (p. 1741)
Wright, Richard, illus. see George, Erin.
Wright, Richard C. Wagon Tracks on the Masa. (p. 1852)
Wright, Robert, jt. auth. see Collette, Paul.
Wright, Robin & Costello, Dee. Doodle Bug: Catch the Doodle Bug! Corke, Estelle, illus. (p. 469)
Wright, Roosevelt, jt. auth. see Wright, Roosevelt, Jr.
Wright, Roosevelt, Jr. And I Said to Myself. (p. 71)
—Choir Rehearsal. (p. 309)
—Deacon Willie's Last Will & Testament. (p. 416)
—For Such a Time As This. (p. 616)
—Shoe Shine. (p. 1568)
—We Three Kings. (p. 1868)
Wright, Roosevelt, Jr. & Wright, Roosevelt. Honey Babe's Treasure: A Black Heritage Drama in Two Acts. (p. 794)
Wright, Roosevelt, Sr. Prodigals. (p. 1409)
Wright, Russell G. Asteroid! Investigations in Astronomy. (p. 108)
—Blackout! Investigations in Electricity. (p. 197)
—Blight! Investigations in Plant Diseases. (p. 199)
—Fire! Investigations in the Nature of Fire. (p. 590)
—First Flight! Investigations in the Physics of Flight. (p. 595)
—Survive? Investigations in Animal Diversity. (p. 1687)
Wright, S. B. Lissa Discovers the Secrets of the Castle (p. 1022)
Wright, Sabrina L. & Griffin, Dexter. Kalilah: the Whispered Promise. (p. 942)
Wright, Sally Ann. Bible Adventures & Activities. Maclean, Moira, illus. (p. 175)
—Biblia para Niños. Ayres, Honor, illus. (p. 176)
—Big Book of Bible Questions. Grudina, Paola Bertolini, illus. (p. 178)
—Child's Book of Prayers. Ayres, Honor, illus. (p. 304)
—Christmas Activity Book. Grudina, Paola Bertolini, illus. (p. 312)
—Christmas Baby. (p. 312)
—Look & See Bible. MacLean, Moira, illus. (p. 1048)
—Mix & Match Bible. (p. 1156)
—My First Christmas Sticker Book. MacLean, Moira, illus. (p. 1206)
—What Did the Fishermen Catch? And Other Questions. Grudina, Paola Bertolini, illus. (p. 1882)
—Where Do Babies Come From? Ayres, Honor, illus. (p. 1906)
—Who Built the Ark? And Other Questions. Grudina, Paola Bertolini, illus. (p. 1914)
Wright, Sara Ann, illus. see Morimoto, Diana.
Wright, Sarah Bird. Nathaniel Hawthorne: A Literary Reference to His Life & Work. (p. 1231)
Wright, Sarah Jane, illus. see Beha, Eileen.
Wright, Sarah Jane, illus. see Godwin, Laura & Buck, Nola.
Wright, Shamekia. Mr. Fatty Mcfatterton. (p. 1185)
Wright, Shannon. Children's Secret Diary: Kid's Diary. (p. 304)
—Dinosaurs & Monsters Coloring Book. (p. 444)
—Wild Wild Animals Coloring Book. (p. 1930)
Wright, Shannon, illus. see West, Lily June Wolford.
Wright, Sharrie. Wee Friends. (p. 1871)
Wright, Simeon & Boyd, Herb. Simeon's Story: An Eyewitness Account of the Kidnapping of Emmett Till. (p. 1577)
Wright Sisters Staff, illus. see Warburton, Olivia.
Wright, Sky'asia. Big, Blue Raspberry. (p. 178)
Wright, Spencer, illus. see Sanborn, Perry F.
Wright, Sue, ed. Doghouse Dreamhouse. (p. 462)
Wright, Susan. Civil Rights Act Of 1964: Landmark Antidiscrimination Legislation. (p. 324)
—Civil Rights Act Of 1964: Landmark Anti-Discrimination Legislation. (p. 324)
—Grandma's Haunted House. (p. 708)
—Weapons of Mass Destruction: Illicit Trade & Trafficking. (p. 1869)
Wright, Terry. One-Eyed Monster. (p. 1294)
Wright, Tish. Boy & the Blue Painted Pony. (p. 217)
Wright, Tony. Classroom Management in Language Education. (p. 329)
—Collins Picture Dictionary for Young Learners. (p. 341)
Wright, Unasue Sellers. Dr. Chubby. (p. 475)
Wright, Velma. Fuzz, an Impatient Chick. (p. 651)
Wright, W. Ivan. Black People: For Entertainment Purposes Only. (p. 196)
—Indentured Scholars: The Inner City Scandal. (p. 870)
Wright, Wendy L., illus. see Terrill Holdman, Shirley.
Wright, Wendy M. Exploring Spiritual Guidance. (p. 553)
WrightGroup/McGraw-Hill. Foro abierto para la Lectura: Classroom Set. (p. 620)
—Foro abierto para la Lectura: Big Book Package. (p. 620)
—Foro abierto para la Lectura: Classroom Core Set. (p. 620)
—Foro Abierto Para la Lectura: Classroom Set, Grade 2. (p. 620)
—Foro abierto para la Lectura: Classroom Practice Set. (p. 620)
—Foro abierto para la Lectura: Annabelle Swift, Parvula. (p. 620)
—Foro Abierto Para la Lectura: Big Book Package, Grade K. (p. 620)
—Foro abierto para la Lectura: Assessment Workbook - Unit 7. (p. 620)
—Foro Abierto Para la Lectura: 4-Color (Pkg. of 25), Grade 2. (p. 620)
—Foro abierto para la Lectura: Assessment Workbook - Unit 10. (p. 620)
—Foro abierto para la Lectura: Assessment Workbook - Units 1-6. (p. 620)
—Foro abierto para la Lectura: Assessment Workbook Pkg. - Unit 4. (p. 620)
—Foro abierto para la Lectura: Assessment Teacher Edition - Unit 7. (p. 620)
—Foro abierto para la Lectura: Assessment Teacher Edition - Unit 10. (p. 620)
—Foro abierto para la Lectura: Assessment Blackline Masters - Unit 1. (p. 620)
—Foro abierto para la Lectura: Assessment Teacher's Edition - Unit 1. (p. 620)
—Foro abierto para la Lectura: Assessment Blackline Masters - Unit 10. (p. 620)
—Foro abierto para la Lectura: Assessment Teacher Edition - Units 1-6. (p. 620)
—Foro abierto para la Lectura: Assessment Blackline Masters - Units 1-6. (p. 620)
—Foro abierto para la Lectura: Comprehension & Language Arts Skills Workbook. (p. 620)
—Foro abierto para la Lectura: Abecedario de los animales (Animals of the Alphabet) (p. 620)
—Foro abierto para la Lectura: Comprehension & Language Arts Skills Teacher Edition. (p. 620)
—Foro Abierto Para la Lectura: Comprehension & Language Arts Skills Workbook, Grade 1. (p. 620)
—Foro abierto para la Lectura: Comprehension & Language Arts Skills Teacher's Edition. (p. 620)
—Foro Abierto Para la Lectura: Comprehension & Language Arts Skills Teachers Edition, Grade 4. (p. 620)
—Foro Abierto Para la Lectura: Comprehension & Language Arts Skills Blackline Masters, Grade 2. (p. 620)
—Foro abierto para la Lectura: First Reader. (p. 621)
—Foro abierto para la Lectura: Hola, Oceano. (p. 621)
—Foro abierto para la Lectura: Second Reader. (p. 621)
—Foro abierto para la Lectura: Individual Set. (p. 621)
—Foro abierto para la Lectura: El regalo de Li. (p. 621)
—Foro abierto para la Lectura: Inquiry Journal. (p. 621)
—Foro abierto para la Lectura: Takehome, Color. (p. 621)
—Foro abierto para la Lectura: La gallinita Roja. (p. 621)
—Foro abierto para la Lectura: Student Anthology. (p. 621)
—Foro abierto para la Lectura: Las rosas de Wanda. (p. 621)
—Foro abierto para la Lectura: No necesito Amigos. (p. 621)
—Foro abierto para la Lectura: Individual Core Set. (p. 621)
—Foro abierto para la Lectura: Little Book Package. (p. 621)
—Foro abierto para la Lectura: Language Arts Big Book. (p. 621)
—Foro abierto para la Lectura: Takehome Core 1, Color. (p. 621)
—Foro abierto para la Lectura: Takehome Core 2, Color. (p. 621)
—Foro Abierto Para la Lectura: Individual Set, Grade 2. (p. 621)
—Foro abierto para la Lectura: Individual Practice Set. (p. 621)
—Foro abierto para la Lectura: Phonics Skills Workbook. (p. 621)
—Foro Abierto Para la Lectura: Inquiry Journal, Grade 2. (p. 621)
—Foro abierto para la Lectura: Teacher Edition - Unit 1. (p. 621)
—Foro Abierto Para la Lectura: Takehome 4-Color, Grade K. (p. 621)
—Foro abierto para la Lectura: Diagnostic Assessment K-3. (p. 621)
—Foro abierto para la Lectura: Reading & Phonics Package. (p. 621)
—Foro abierto para la Lectura: Teacher Edition - Unit 10. (p. 621)
—Foro Abierto Para la Lectura: Student Anthology, Grade 5. (p. 621)
—Foro abierto para la Lectura: Sombras (Shadows) - Unit 2. (p. 621)
—Foro abierto para la Lectura: Takehome Blackline Masters. (p. 621)
—Foro abierto para la Lectura: Takehome Practice 1, Color. (p. 621)
—Foro Abierto Para la Lectura: Little Book Package, Grade 1. (p. 621)
—Foro abierto para la Lectura: La escuela (School) - Unit 1. (p. 621)
—Foro abierto para la Lectura: Nada se pega como una Sombra. (p. 621)
—Foro abierto para la Lectura: El viento (the Wind) - Unit 4. (p. 621)
—Foro abierto para la Lectura: En equipo (Teamwork) - Unit 7. (p. 621)
—Foro abierto para la Lectura: First Reader (Getting Started) (p. 621)
—Foro abierto para la Lectura: Language Arts Skills Workbook. (p. 621)
—Foro abierto para la Lectura: Story Time Selections Package. (p. 621)
—Foro abierto para la Lectura: El viento da las buenas Noches. (p. 621)
—Foro abierto para la Lectura: Phonics Skills Teacher Edition. (p. 621)
—Foro Abierto Para la Lectura: Language Arts Big Book, Grade K. (p. 621)
—Foro Abierto Para la Lectura: Language Arts Handbook, Grade 2. (p. 621)
—Foro abierto para la Lectura: En el mar (by the Sea) - Unit 8. (p. 621)
—Foro abierto para la Lectura: Inquiry Journal Teacher Edition. (p. 621)
—Foro Abierto Para la Lectura: Overhead Transparencies, Grade 1. (p. 621)
—Foro abierto para la Lectura: Persevera (Stick to It) - Unit 5. (p. 621)
—Foro abierto para la Lectura: Phonics Skills Blackline Masters. (p. 621)
—Foro abierto para la Lectura: Sounds & Letters Skills Workbook. (p. 621)
—Foro Abierto Para la Lectura: Student Anthology Book 1, Grade 2. (p. 621)
—Foro abierto para la Lectura: Takehome Core 1 Blackline Masters. (p. 621)
—Foro abierto para la Lectura: Takehome Core 2 Blackline Masters. (p. 621)
—Foro Abierto Para la Lectura: Reading & Phonics Package, Grade 1. (p. 621)
—Foro Abierto Para la Lectura: Student Anthology, Vol. 4, Grade 4. (p. 621)
—Foro abierto para la Lectura: Program Assessment Teacher Edition. (p. 621)
—Foro Abierto Para la Lectura: Takehome Blackline Masters, Grade 2. (p. 621)
—Foro Abierto Para la Lectura: Program Assessment Workbook, Grade 2. (p. 621)
—Foro abierto para la Lectura: Language Arts Skills Teacher Edition. (p. 621)
—Foro Abierto Para la Lectura: Takehome 4-Color (Pkg of 25), Grade K. (p. 621)
—Foro abierto para la Lectura: Spelling & Vocabulary Skills Workbook. (p. 621)
—Foro abierto para la Lectura: Takehome Practice 1 Blackline Masters. (p. 621)
—Foro Abierto Para la Lectura: Takehome 4-Color (Pkg. of 25), Grade 3. (p. 621)
—Foro abierto para la Lectura: Language Arts Skills Blackline Masters. (p. 621)

—Foro abierto para la Lectura: Sounds & Letters Skills Teacher Edition. (p. 621)
—Foro Abierto Para la Lectura: Inquiry Journal Blackline Msters, Grade 2. (p. 621)
—Foro Abierto Para la Lectura: Student Anthology Vol. 1, Book 1, Grade 1. (p. 621)
—Foro abierto para la Lectura: Pinas y elefantes (Pineapples & Elephants) (p. 621)
—Foro Abierto Para la Lectura: Sounds & Letters Skills Blackline Masters. (p. 621)
—Foro Abierto Para la Lectura: Inquiry Journal Blackline Masters, Grade 3. (p. 621)
—Foro Abierto Para la Lectura: Program Assessment Teacher Edition, Grade K. (p. 621)
—Foro Abierto Para la Lectura: Program Assessment Teachers Edition, Grade 3. (p. 621)
—Foro abierto para la Lectura: Spelling & Vocabulary Skills Teacher Edition. (p. 621)
—Foro Abierto Para la Lectura: Program Assessment Blackline Masters, Grade 1. (p. 621)
—Foro Abierto Para la Lectura: Takehome Core 1 4-Color (Pkg. of 25), Grade 1. (p. 621)
—Foro Abierto Para la Lectura: Takehome Core 2 4-Color (Pkg. of 25), Grade 1. (p. 621)
—Foro abierto para la Lectura: En busca de amigos (Finding Friends) - Unit 3. (p. 621)
—Foro abierto para la Lectura: Reading, Phonics & Phonemic Awareness Package. (p. 621)
—Foro Abierto Para la Lectura: Spelling & Vocabulary Skills Workbook, Grade 1. (p. 621)
—Foro abierto para la Lectura: Spelling & Vocabulary Skills Blackline Masters. (p. 621)
—Foro abierto para la Lectura: Rojo, blanco y azul (Red, White & Blue) - Unit 6. (p. 621)
—Foro Abierto Para la Lectura: Takehome Practice 1 4-Color (Pkg. of 25), Grade 1. (p. 621)
—Foro Abierto Para la Lectura: Comprehension & Language Arts Skills Workbook, Grade 5. (p. 621)
—Foro Abierto Para la Lectura: Spelling & Vocabulary Skills Teachers Edition, Grade 4. (p. 621)
—Foro abierto para la Lectura: Los cuadros nos cuentan cuentos (Pictures Tell Stories) (p. 621)
—Foro Abierto Para la Lectura: Spelling & Vocabulary Skills Blackline Masters, Grade 1. (p. 621)
—Foro abierto para la Lectura: Writer's Workbook. (p. 622)
—Foro abierto para la Lectura: Teacher Read Alouds. (p. 622)
—Foro abierto para la Lectura: Student Anthology. 1 (p. 622)
—Foro abierto para la Lectura: Student Anthology. 2 (p. 622)
—Foro abierto para la Lectura: Teacher Edition - Unit 6. (p. 622)
—Foro abierto para la Lectura: Unit Assessment Workbook. (p. 622)
—Foro Abierto Para la Lectura: Writer's Workbook, Grade 1. (p. 622)
—Foro abierto para la Lectura: Teacher's Edition - Unit 2. (p. 622)
—Foro abierto para la Lectura: Big Book 2: Sombras (Shadows) 2 (p. 622)
—Foro abierto para la Lectura: Big Book 1: la Escuela (School) 1 (p. 622)
—Foro abierto para la Lectura: Big Book: 5 el Tiempo (Weather) 5 (p. 622)
—Foro abierto para la Lectura: Writer's Workbook Teacher Edition. (p. 622)
—Foro abierto para la Lectura: Big Book 4: el viento (the Wind) 4 (p. 622)
—Foro abierto para la Lectura: Big Book 7: en Equipo (Teamwork) 7 (p. 622)
—Foro abierto para la Lectura: Big Book: 6 Los Viajes (Journeys) 6 (p. 622)
—Foro Abierto Para la Lectura: Unit 1 Assessment Workbook, Grade 2. (p. 622)
—Foro Abierto Para la Lectura: Unit 2 Assessment Workbook, Grade 2. (p. 622)
—Foro Abierto Para la Lectura: Unit 3 Assessment Workbook, Grade 2. (p. 622)
—Foro Abierto Para la Lectura: Unit 4 Assessment Workbook, Grade 2. (p. 622)
—Foro Abierto Para la Lectura: Unit 5 Assessment Workbook, Grade 2. (p. 622)
—Foro Abierto Para la Lectura: Unit 6 Assessment Workbook, Grade 2. (p. 622)
—Foro abierto para la Lectura: Big Book: 2 Los Animales (Animals) 2 (p. 622)
—Foro abierto para la Lectura: Little Book 5: el Tiempo (Weather) 5 (p. 622)
—Foro abierto para la Lectura: Big Book 8: en el mar (by the Sea) 8 (p. 622)
—Foro abierto para la Lectura: Big Book 5: Persevera (Stick to It) 5 (p. 622)
—Foro abierto para la Lectura: Little Book 6: Los Viajes (Journeys) 6 (p. 622)
—Foro Abierto Para la Lectura: Unit 1 Assessment Workbook Pkg. , Grade 4. (p. 622)
—Foro abierto para la Lectura: Big Book: 1 Vamos a leer! (Let's Read!) 1 (p. 622)
—Foro Abierto Para la Lectura: Unit 2 Assessment Workbook Pkg. , Grade 5. (p. 622)
—Foro Abierto Para la Lectura: Unit 3 Assessment Workbook Pkg. , Grade 4. (p. 622)
—Foro Abierto Para la Lectura: Unit 4 Assessment Workbook Pkg. , Grade 4. (p. 622)
—Foro Abierto Para la Lectura: Unit 5 Assessment Workbook Pkg. , Grade 4. (p. 622)
—Foro Abierto Para la Lectura: Unit 6 Assessment Workbook Pkg. , Grade 4. (p. 622)
—Foro Abierto Para la Lectura: Writer's Workbook Teacher Edition, Grade K. (p. 622)
—Foro Abierto Para la Lectura: Writer's Workbook Teachers Edition, Grade 4. (p. 622)
—Foro abierto para la Lectura: Little Book 1: Vamos a leer! (Let's Read!) 1 (p. 622)
—Foro Abierto Para la Lectura: Unit 1 Assessment Blackline Masters, Grade 2. (p. 622)
—Foro Abierto Para la Lectura: Unit 2 Assessment Blackline Masters, Grade 2. (p. 622)
—Foro Abierto Para la Lectura: Unit 3 Assessment Blackline Masters, Grade 3. (p. 622)
—Foro Abierto Para la Lectura: Unit 4 Assessment Blackline Masters, Grade 2. (p. 622)
—Foro Abierto Para la Lectura: Unit 5 Assessment Blackline Masters, Grade 2. (p. 622)
—Foro Abierto Para la Lectura: Unit 6 Assessment Blackline Masters, Grade 2. (p. 622)
—Foro Abierto Para la Lectura: Writer's Workbook Blackline Masters, Grade 1. (p. 622)
—Foro Abierto Para la Lectura: Unit 1 Assessment Teacher Edition Pkg. , Grade 3. (p. 622)
—Foro Abierto Para la Lectura: Unit 2 Assessment Teacher Edition Pkg. , Grade 3. (p. 622)
—Foro Abierto Para la Lectura: Unit 3 Assessment Teacher Edition Pkg. , Grade 3. (p. 622)
—Foro Abierto Para la Lectura: Unit 4 Assessment Teacher Edition Pkg. , Grade 3. (p. 622)
—Foro Abierto Para la Lectura: Unit 5 Assessment Teacher Edition Pkg. , Grade 3. (p. 622)
—Foro Abierto Para la Lectura: Unit 6 Assessment Teacher Edition Pkg. , Grade 3. (p. 622)
—Foro abierto para la Lectura: Big Book: 3 de un lugar a otro (Things That Go) 3 (p. 622)
—Foro Abierto Para la Lectura: Unit 1 Assessment Teachers Edition Pkg. , Grade 4. (p. 622)
—Foro Abierto Para la Lectura: Unit 2 Assessment Teachers Edition Pkg. , Grade 4. (p. 622)
—Foro Abierto Para la Lectura: Unit 3 Assessment Teachers Edition Pkg. , Grade 4. (p. 622)
—Foro Abierto Para la Lectura: Unit 4 Assessment Teachers Edition Pkg. , Grade 4. (p. 622)
—Foro Abierto Para la Lectura: Unit 5 Assessment Teachers Edition Pkg. , Grade 4. (p. 622)
—Foro Abierto Para la Lectura: Unit 6 Assessment Teachers Edition Pkg. , Grade 4. (p. 622)
—Foro abierto para la Lectura: Big Book 3: en busca de amigos (Finding Friends) 3 (p. 622)
—Foro Abierto Para la Lectura: Unit 1 Assessment Teacher's Edition Pkg. , Grade 2. (p. 622)
—Foro Abierto Para la Lectura: Unit 2 Assessment Teacher's Edition Pkg. , Grade 2. (p. 622)
—Foro Abierto Para la Lectura: Unit 4 Assessment Teacher's Edition Pkg. , Grade 2. (p. 622)
—Foro Abierto Para la Lectura: Unit 5 Assessment Teacher's Edition Pkg. , Grade 2. (p. 622)
—Foro Abierto Para la Lectura: Unit 6 Assessment Teacher's Edition Pkg. , Grade 2. (p. 622)
—Foro abierto para la Lectura: Little Book 3: de un lugar a otro (Things That Go) 3 (p. 622)
—Foro abierto para la Lectura: Big Book 6: Rojo, blanco y azul (Red, White & Blue) 6 (p. 622)
—Foro abierto para la Lectura: Big Book 10: Pinas y elefantes (Pineapples & Elephants) 10 (p. 622)
—Foro abierto para la Lectura: Big Book 9: Abecedario de los animales (Alphabet of the Animals) 9 (p. 622)
—Foro abierto para la Lectura: Big Book: 4 Nuestro vecindario en accion (Our Neighborhood at Work) 4 (p. 622)
—Foro abierto para la Lectura: Big Book 11: Los cuadros nos cuentan cuentos (Pictures Tell Stories) 11 (p. 622)
—Foro abierto para la Lectura: Little Book 4: Nuestro vecindario en accion (Our Neighborhood at Work) 4 (p. 622)
—Foro Abierto Para la Lectura: Takehome: 4-Color, Grade 2. (p. 622)
—Foro Abierto Para la Lectura: Teacher Edition: Unit 1, Grade 1. (p. 622)
—Foro Abierto Para la Lectura: Teacher Edition: Unit 1, Grade 2. (p. 622)
—Foro Abierto Para la Lectura: Teacher Edition: Unit 1, Grade 3. (p. 622)
—Foro Abierto Para la Lectura: Teacher Edition: Unit 1, Grade 4. (p. 622)
—Foro Abierto Para la Lectura: Teacher Edition: Unit 1, Grade K. (p. 622)
—Foro Abierto Para la Lectura: Teacher Edition: Unit 2, Grade 1. (p. 622)
—Foro Abierto Para la Lectura: Teacher Edition: Unit 2, Grade 2. (p. 622)
—Foro Abierto Para la Lectura: Teacher Edition: Unit 2, Grade 3. (p. 622)
—Foro Abierto Para la Lectura: Teacher Edition: Unit 2, Grade 4. (p. 622)
—Foro Abierto Para la Lectura: Teacher Edition: Unit 2, Grade K. (p. 622)
—Foro Abierto Para la Lectura: Teacher Edition: Unit 3, Grade 1. (p. 622)
—Foro Abierto Para la Lectura: Teacher Edition: Unit 3, Grade 3. (p. 622)
—Foro Abierto Para la Lectura: Teacher Edition: Unit 3, Grade 4. (p. 622)
—Foro Abierto Para la Lectura: Teacher Edition: Unit 3, Grade K. (p. 622)
—Foro Abierto Para la Lectura: Teacher Edition: Unit 4, Grade 1. (p. 622)
—Foro Abierto Para la Lectura: Teacher Edition: Unit 4, Grade 2. (p. 622)
—Foro Abierto Para la Lectura: Teacher Edition: Unit 4, Grade 3. (p. 622)
—Foro Abierto Para la Lectura: Teacher Edition: Unit 4, Grade 4. (p. 622)
—Foro Abierto Para la Lectura: Teacher Edition: Unit 4, Grade K. (p. 622)
—Foro Abierto Para la Lectura: Teacher Edition: Unit 5, Grade 1. (p. 622)
—Foro Abierto Para la Lectura: Teacher Edition: Unit 5, Grade 2. (p. 623)
—Foro Abierto Para la Lectura: Teacher Edition: Unit 5, Grade 3. (p. 623)
—Foro Abierto Para la Lectura: Teacher Edition: Unit 5, Grade 4. (p. 623)
—Foro Abierto Para la Lectura: Teacher Edition: Unit 5, Grade K. (p. 623)
—Foro Abierto Para la Lectura: Teacher Edition: Unit 6, Grade 1. (p. 623)
—Foro Abierto Para la Lectura: Teacher Edition: Unit 6, Grade 2. (p. 623)
—Foro Abierto Para la Lectura: Teacher Edition: Unit 6, Grade 4. (p. 623)
—Foro Abierto Para la Lectura: Teacher Edition: Unit 6, Grade K. (p. 623)
—Foro Abierto Para la Lectura: Teacher Edition: Unit 7, Grade K. (p. 623)
—Foro Abierto Para la Lectura: Teacher Edition: Unit 8, Grade K. (p. 623)
—Fourth Grade Mathematics. (p. 625)
—German. (p. 666)
—Open Court Reading: Listening Library CDs. (p. 1299)
—Open Court Reading: Teacher's Edition - Unit 9. (p. 1299)
—Open Court Reading: Over in the Meadow Big Book. (p. 1299)
—Open Court Reading: Teacher's Edition - Unit 10. (p. 1299)
—Open Court Reading: Trade Book Package - Unit 1. (p. 1299)
—Open Court Reading: Listening Library Audiocassettes. (p. 1299)
—Open Court Reading: Teacher's Edition - Units 1 And 2. (p. 1299)
—Open Court Reading: Exploring Sounds & Letters Package. (p. 1299)
—Open Court Reading: Complete Trade Book Set - Units 1-8. (p. 1299)
—Open Court Reading Spanish: Unit 3 Assessment Ate Level 2. (p. 1299)
—Open Court Reading Spanish: Decodable Takehome Blm Level K. (p. 1299)
—Photo Library: Collection A. (p. 1352)
—SRA Spelling: Grade 4. (p. 1637)
Wrightgroup/Mcgraw-Hill. Third Grade Mathematics. (p. 1734)
WrightGroup/McGraw-Hill & WrightGroup/McGraw-Hill Staff. Kaleidoscope: Leveled Library Level C (p. 941)
WrightGroup/McGraw-Hill Staff. Breaking the Code: Teacher Resource Package. (p. 225)
—Cumulative Folder. (p. 392)
—Decodable Stories & Comprehension Skills. (p. 422)
—Fifth Grade Mathematics. (p. 584)
—Kaleidoscope (p. 941)
—Kaleidoscope: Placement Guide. (p. 941)
—Kaleidoscope: Reader, Level D. (p. 941)
—Kaleidoscope: Reader, Level E. (p. 941)
—Kaleidoscope: Intervention Package. (p. 941)
—Kaleidoscope: Leveled Library Level B (p. 941)
—Kaleidoscope: Assessment Guide Workbook, Level A. (p. 941)
—Kaleidoscope: Placement/Exit Assessmentate Level A-E. (p. 941)
—Kaleidoscope: Listening Library Audiocassettes LEVEL B. (p. 941)
—Kaleidoscope: Kaleidoscope Intervention Package, Level D. (p. 941)
—Kaleidoscope: Kaleidoscope Intervention Package, Level C LEVEL C. (p. 941)
—Kaleidoscope: Decodable Stories & Comprehension Skills Workbook Level E. (p. 941)
—Kaleidoscope. (p. 941)
—Kaleidoscope Assessment Guide. (p. 941)
—Language Arts Workbook, Level D. (p. 974)
—Language Arts Workbook Level E. (p. 974)
—Language Roundup: Level 5. (p. 975)
—Leap into Phonics: Teacher's Edition. (p. 982)
—Leap into Phonics. (p. 982)
—Open Court Reading: Story Lines. (p. 1299)
—Open Court Reading: Power Vocabulary. (p. 1299)
—Open Court Reading: VHS Lesson Models. (p. 1299)
—Open Court Reading: Assessment - Units 1-8. (p. 1299)
—Open Court Reading: Alphabet Sound Wall Cards. (p. 1299)
—Open Court Reading: Power Vocabulary - Level 4. (p. 1299)
—Open Court Reading: Kindergarten Blackline Masters. (p. 1299)
—Open Court Reading: Alphabet Sound Individual Cards. (p. 1299)
—Open Court Reading: Home Connection Blackline Masters. (p. 1299)
—Open Court Reading: Getting Started Read Aloud Package. (p. 1299)
—Open Court Reading: Willy the Wisher & Other Thinking Stories. (p. 1299)
—Open Court Reading 2002: Power Vocabulary - Level 3. (p. 1299)
—Open Court Reading 2002: Sound/Spelling Individual Cards - Levels 1-3, Additional Resources, Grade 3. (p. 1299)
—Power Vocabulary. (p. 1390)
—Pre-Decodable Takehome Books. (p. 1394)
—Pre-Decodable Takehome Books. (p. 1394)
—Sound Spelling Cards, Levels 1-3. (p. 1615)
—Teacher's Resource Book. (p. 1709)
—Vhs Lesson Models. (p. 1839)
WrightGroup/McGraw-Hill Staff, jt. auth. see McGraw-Hill Staff.
WrightGroup/McGraw-Hill Staff, jt. auth. see Wagner, B. J.
WrightGroup/McGraw-Hill Staff, jt. auth. see Wagner, B.J.
WrightGroup/McGraw-Hill Staff, jt. auth. see WrightGroup/McGraw-Hill.
Wright-Mcadoo, Joyce, jt. auth. see Wright-McAdoo, Joyce.
Wright-McAdoo, Joyce & Wright-Mcadoo, Joyce. Zimb: Believe. (p. 1986)
Wrighton, Charlene. Using the Wild to Teach the Child K-2 Lesson Guide. (p. 1828)
Wrighton, Charlene, jt. auth. see Bradshaw, Georgine.
Wrighton, Charlene & Bradshaw, Georgine. Basic Kit - Preschool. Clark, Irene, illus. (p. 142)
Wrightson, Berni, illus. see Wein, Len.
Wrightson, Patricia. I Own the Racecourse! (p. 844)
Wrigley, Annabel. We Love to Craft—Christmas: Fun Stuff for Kids * 17 Handmade Fabric & Paper Projects. (p. 1867)
—We Love to Sew: 28 Pretty Things to Make. (p. 1867)
—We Love to Sew—Bedrooms: 23 Projects, Cool Stuff for Your Space. (p. 1867)
—We Love to Sew—Gifts: Fun Stuff for Kids to Stitch & Share. (p. 1867)
Wrigley, Karen D. Town Named Hopeville. (p. 1773)
Wrigley-Field, Elizabeth, ed. see IraqiGirl.
Writing Club, Dancing Pencils, compiled by. Budding Words: An Anthology. (p. 234)
Written By Dana Wright; Illustrated By S. Crazy Pants. (p. 378)
Written By Doretta Elaine Wilson; Illust. Ultimate Heart. Baker, Jonathan, illus. (p. 1809)
Written by Elli Matthews; Illustrated by, illus. see Matthews, Elli.
Written By Kimberly M Sosnowski; Illustr. Ace's Wish for a Forever Home. Sosnowski, Tiffany, illus. (p. 8)
Written By Pamela McFarland; Illustrated. Guide Me Home, Sunny. Bates, Bill, illus. (p. 730)
Written by Shelia West; Illustrated by D, illus. see West, Shelia.
Written By Susan J. Perry; Illustrated B. Snuckle-Bee & Snuckle-Bun: The Bee-Attitudes. Dedering, Victoria, illus. (p. 1601)
Written By Tori Velle; Illustrated By Al. Tia Tot Rules! Aguila, Alicia del, illus. (p. 1746)
Wrobel, C. J., ed. see Beddor, Frank & Cavalier, Liz.
Wroble, Lisa A. Dealing with Stress. (p. 418)
—Kids in Ancient Egypt. (p. 954)
—Kids in the Middle Ages. (p. 954)
—Right to Counsel: From Gideon V. Wainwright to Gideon's Trumpet. (p. 1472)
Wroble, Lisa A. & Library. Food for a Greener Planet: What You Can Do. (p. 613)
Wroe, Dameon K., ed. see Banks, Kimberly E.
Wroth, Dean, illus. see Castro, Anita.
Wroth, Dean, illus. see Chamberlin, Kate.
Wroth, Dean, illus. see Feuerbach, Jennifer.
Wrucke, Mary. Timmy the Tadpole Cooke, Bev, illus. (p. 1755)
Wshington, Ned, jt. auth. see Harline, Leigh.
Wu, Donald, illus. see Boelts, Maribeth.
Wu, Donald, illus. see Brennan-Nelson, Denise.
Wu, Donald, illus. see Crimi, Carolyn.
Wu, Donald, illus. see Hubbell, Patricia.
Wu, Donald, illus. see Loewen, Nancy.
Wu, Donald, illus. see Sherman, Caroline.
Wu, Faye-Lynn. Chinese & English Nursery Rhymes: Share & Sing in Two Languages. Dutcher, Kieren, illus. (p. 307)
—My First Book of Chinese Words: An ABC Rhyming Book. Padron, Aya, illus. (p. 1205)
Wu, Janice, jt. auth. see Moiz, Azra.
Wu, Julie, illus. see Crowe, Ellie.
Wu, Leslie, illus. see Bauer, Marion Dane.
Wu, Leslie, illus. see Markle, Sandra.
Wu, Mike. Ellie. Wu, Mike, illus. (p. 514)
Wu, Miriam, et al. Scaling the Tenor Clef Dragon: A Tenor Clef Workbook for Cellists. (p. 1519)
Wu, Nicholas. Bears' Story by Baldwin B. Bear. (p. 152)
—Princess & the Pea: A Retelling of Hans Christian Andersen's Story. (p. 1402)
—Princess & the Pea. (p. 1402)
—Tiddalick, the Greedy Frog: An Aboriginal Dreamtime Story (p. 1747)
Wu, Ronald W. Carbon. (p. 265)
WU, Stacie, illus. see Anderson, Pamela Dell.
Wu, Stacie, illus. see Anderson, Pamela.
Wu, Yoken, illus. see Yu, Jennifer.
Wuehr, Tina L. Field Dance. Brown, Mari, illus. (p. 583)
—Neela Potts Has Lots of Knots. Brown, Mari, illus. (p. 1240)
—Why Can't I Have Glue? Brown, Mari, illus. (p. 1923)
Wuest, Marcia. Twelve Things to Do at Age 12. (p. 1800)
Wukovits, John, ed. see Hay, Jeff.
Wukovits, John, ed. George Clooney. (p. 663)
Wukovits, John F. Bombing of Pearl Harbor. (p. 208)
—Booker T. Washington & Entrepreneurship. (p. 212)
—Ellen Ochoa, First Female Hispanic Astronaut. (p. 514)
—George W Bush: People in the News. (p. 664)
—Jackie Robinson & the Integration of Baseball. (p. 904)
—Manhattan Project. Greenhaven Press Editors, ed. (p. 1087)
—Robin Williams. (p. 1480)
—Victorian Era. Greenhaven Press Editors, ed. (p. 1840)
—World War II in Europe. (p. 1959)
Wulf, Linda Press. Night of the Burning. (p. 1254)
Wulff, Alana. Love You, Mum. (p. 1061)
Wulff, Mary L. & Tilford, Gregory L. Herbs for Pets: The Natural Way to Enhance Your Pet's Life. (p. 769)
Wulffson, Don. Toys! Keller, Laurie, illus. (p. 1774)
Wulffson, Don, jt. auth. see Wulffson, Don L.
Wulffson, Don L. Before Columbus: Early Voyages to the Americas. (p. 158)
—Upside-Down Voyage. Lyall, Dennis, illus. (p. 1825)
Wulffson, Don L. & Wulffson, Don. Soldier X. (p. 1607)
Wulfing, Amy J., illus. see Baretz, Susie.
Wulfing, Amy J., illus. see Shortle, Stacy & Mooney, Dean J. M.
Wulfing, Sulamith. Fairy Tales. (p. 564)
Wulfsohn, Gisèle & Quarto Generic Staff. Bongani's Day: From Dawn to Dusk in a South African City. (p. 209)
Wullert, Mark. Quest for Curtana: The Quest for Curtana. (p. 1426)
Wullschleger Daldini, Elena. Ma tu, che Babbo Natale Sei? Caccia, Christiane, illus. (p. 1067)
Wummer, Amy, illus. see Adams, Michelle Medlock.
Wummer, Amy, illus. see Bishop, Jennie.
Wummer, Amy, illus. see Buzzeo, Toni.
Wummer, Amy, illus. see Clarke, Ginjer L.
Wummer, Amy, illus. see Driscoll, Laura.
Wummer, Amy, illus. see Dussling, Jennifer.
Wummer, Amy, illus. see Harkrader, Lisa.
Wummer, Amy, illus. see Hepker, Sue.
Wummer, Amy, illus. see Jordan, Taylor.
Wummer, Amy, illus. see Kennedy, Pamela & Brady, Anne Kennedy.
Wummer, Amy, illus. see Kennedy, Pamela & Kennedy, Douglas.
Wummer, Amy, illus. see Kennedy, Pamela.

Wummer, Amy, illus. see Kline, Suzy.
Wummer, Amy, illus. see Knudsen, Michelle.
Wummer, Amy, illus. see Knudson, Michelle.
Wummer, Amy, illus. see Lansky, Bruce.
Wummer, Amy, illus. see Lord, Jill Roman.
Wummer, Amy, illus. see May, Eleanor.
Wummer, Amy, illus. see Montgomery, Lewis B.
Wummer, Amy, illus. see Moore, Karen.
Wummer, Amy, illus. see Sutherland, Margaret.
Wummer, Amy, illus. see Walker, Nan.
Wummer, Amy, illus. see Wilson, Sarah.
Wummer, Amy, illus. see Wing, Natasha.
Wummer, Amy, tr. see Wilson, Sarah.
Wunder, Wendy. Museum of Intangible Things. (p. 1193)
—Probability of Miracles. (p. 1408)
Wunderli, Stephen. Little Boo. Zeltner, Tim, illus. (p. 1025)
Wundram, Bill. Finnius: The Tale of a Lost Little Elephant. Tucker, Eric, illus. (p. 589)
Wunsch, Andrew. Let's Play Cricket! (p. 1000)
Wunsch, Marjory, jt. auth. see Lang, Glenna W.
Wunsch, Marjory, jt. auth. see Lang, Glenna.
Wunungmurra, Helen, jt. auth. see Wunungmurra, Johnny.
Wunungmurra, Johnny & Wunungmurra, Helen. Djet & Nak Nak. (p. 455)
Wurdinger, Scott, jt. auth. see Rapparlie, Leslie.
Wurge, B. B. Billy & the Birdfrogs. (p. 187)
—Last Notebook of Leonardo. (p. 978)
—Squiggle. (p. 1637)
Wurm, Kristine. Truman's Loose Tooth Chesworth, Michael D., illus. (p. 1793)
Wurst, Thomas Scott. Pearl's Christmas Present. Wurst, Thomas Scott, illus. (p. 1333)
Wurster, Laurie, illus. see Roman, Stacey.
Wurzburg, Robert. Where Are the Dogsharks? (p. 1906)
—Who Took the Cake? (p. 1917)
Wusinich, Bill, jt. auth. see Callanan, Michael I.
Wyant, J. Anamnesis: The Further Adventures of Struth Digger. (p. 67)
Wyant, Sharon Kay. Adventures of Brody. (p. 17)
Wyatt, Cherokee. Adventures of Margaret Mouse: The Magic Star. (p. 20)
—Adventures of Margaret Mouse: Harvest Carnival. (p. 20)
—Adventures of Margaret Mouse: The Picnic. Redmon, Angela M., illus. (p. 20)
—Adventures of Margaret Mouse: School Days. Redmon, Angela M., illus. (p. 20)
—Adventures of Margaret Mouse: Hide 'n Seek. Redmon, Angela M., illus. (p. 20)
Wyatt, Chris. Falcon: Fight or Flight. (p. 565)
—Falcon: Fight or Flight: A Mighty Marvel Chapter Book. Grummett, Tom, illus. (p. 565)
—Meet the Marvel Super Heroes. Lim, Ron, illus. (p. 1123)
—Star-Lord: Knowhere to Run. (p. 1640)
—Star-Lord - Knowhere to Run. Lim, Ron & Troy, Andy, illus. (p. 1640)
—This Is Ant-Man. (p. 1735)
—World of Reading: Ant-Man This Is Ant-Man: Level 1. Lim, Ron & Rosenberg, Rachelle, illus. (p. 1957)
Wyatt, Chris, jt. auth. see Marvel Book Group.
Wyatt, Chris, jt. auth. see Marvel Books Staff.
Wyatt, Chris, jt. auth. see Marvel.
Wyatt, Chris "Doc". Great Core Caper. Howell, Corin, illus. (p. 715)
Wyatt, David, illus. see Alexander, Lloyd.
Wyatt, David, illus. see Baldry, Cherith.
Wyatt, David, illus. see Butler, Charles, Jr. & Butler, Charles.
Wyatt, David, illus. see Langrish, Katherine.
Wyatt, David, illus. see Lennon, Joan.
Wyatt, David, illus. see McCaughrean, Geraldine.
Wyatt, David, illus. see Peyton, K. M.
Wyatt, David, illus. see Reeve, Philip.
Wyatt, David, illus. see Schafer, Albert.
Wyatt, Ellen. Sheriff Buzzy Bullet & the Bank Robbers. (p. 1565)
Wyatt, James. Basketball. (p. 143)
—Football. (p. 615)
Wyatt, Katherine. Science of Light & Color. (p. 1527)
Wyatt, Laura. Those Outrageous Owls. Weaver, Steve, illus. (p. 1740)
Wyatt, Leslie. Noah Learns His Numbers: Number Names & Count Sequence. (p. 1261)
Wyatt, Leslie J. Poor Is Just a Starting Place. (p. 1383)
Wyatt, Melissa. Funny How Things Change. (p. 650)
Wyatt, Michael, illus. see Taylor, Drew.
Wyatt, Sue, illus. see O'Brien, May L.
Wyatt, Thomas. Love for Love: Selected Poems. (p. 1059)
Wyatt, Tona. Booger under My Bed. (p. 210)
Wyatt, Trina. Magical Mrs Mable Comes to Green Hills. (p. 1075)
Wyatt, Valerie. Boy Meets Dog: A Word Game Adventure. Whamond, Dave, illus. (p. 218)
—How to Build Your Own Country. Fredericks, Karen & Rix, Fred, illus. (p. 815)
—Inventions. Fernandes, Matthew, illus. (p. 884)
—Welcome to the World. Newell, Lennette, illus. (p. 1874)
—Who Discovered America? Woo, Howie, illus. (p. 1915)
Wyatt, Winnie Dowden. Travis' Ladder. (p. 1781)
Wyborney, Steve. Week-By-Week Math Review for the Digital Classroom: Grade 1: Ready-To-Use, Animated PowerPoint(r) Slideshows with Practice Pages That Help Students Master Key Math Skills & Concepts. (p. 1871)
Wyborny, Sheila. Alcoholism. (p. 35)
—Anxiety Disorders. (p. 90)
—Connecticut. (p. 357)
—Dwayne Johnson. (p. 491)
—Electricity. (p. 509)
—Hodgkin's Disease. (p. 787)
—Kim Jong Il. (p. 956)
—New Hampshire. (p. 1245)
—Nikola Tesla. (p. 1255)
Wybomy, Shelia. Frederick W. Smith: Founder of FedEx. (p. 633)
Wyche, Wofford, Jane. Adventures at Hi-Lonesome Ranch: The Magic Cabin, Book Two. (p. 15)
Wyckoff, Edwin Brit. African-American Heart Surgery Pioneer: The Genius of Vivien Thomas. (p. 27)
—Electric Guitar Man: The Genius of les Paul. (p. 508)
—Guy Who Invented Home Video Games: Ralph Baer & His Awesome Invention. (p. 733)
—Hair-Care Millionaire: Madam C.J. Walker & Her Amazing Business. (p. 736)
—Heart Man: Vivien Thomas, African-American Heart Surgery Pioneer. (p. 759)
—Helicopter Man: Igor Sikorsky & His Amazing Invention. (p. 763)
—Laser Man: Theodore H. Maiman & His Brilliant Invention. (p. 977)
—Man Behind the Gun: Samuel Colt & His Revolver. (p. 1085)
—Man Who Invented Basketball: The Genius of James Naismith. (p. 1086)
—Man Who Invented Basketball: James Naismith & His Amazing Game. (p. 1086)
—Man Who Invented Television: The Genius of Philo T. Farnsworth. (p. 1086)
—Man Who Invented the Electric Guitar: The Genius of les Paul. (p. 1086)
—Man Who Invented the Game of Basketball: The Genius of James Naismith. (p. 1086)
—Man Who Invented the Laser: The Genius of Theodore H. Maiman. (p. 1086)
—Stopping Bullets with a Thread: Stephanie Kwolek & Her Incredible Invention. (p. 1654)
—Teen Who Invented Television: Philo T. Farnsworth & His Awesome Invention. (p. 1714)
—Woman Who Invented the Thread That Stops Bullets: The Genius of Stephanie Kwolek. (p. 1945)
Wyckoff, Edwin Brit & Library. Sign Language Man: Thomas H. Gallaudet & His Incredible Work. (p. 1574)
Wyckoff, Joanne Francis. Wally the Spelling Whiz. (p. 1855)
Wyeth, Andrew N., illus. see McLellan, Richard A.
Wyeth, Jamie, illus. see Walsh, Barbara.
Wyeth, N. C., illus. see Cooper, James Fenimore.
Wyeth, N. C., illus. see Lanier, Sidney.
Wyeth, N. C., illus. see Rawlings, Marjorie Kinnan.
Wyeth, N. C., jt. auth. see Creswick, Paul.
Wyeth, N. C., jt. auth. see Stevenson, Robert Louis.
Wyeth, Sharon Dennis. Granddaughter Necklace. Ibatoulline, Bagram, illus. (p. 707)
—Message in the Sky: Corey's Underground Railroad Diary. Bk. 3 (p. 1129)
Wygand, Melissa. Sponge Who Saved Christmas (SpongeBob SquarePants) Petrossi, Fabrizio, illus. (p. 1630)
—Where the Pirates Arrgh! (SpongeBob SquarePants) Martinez, Heather, illus. (p. 1909)
Wyk, Hanri van, jt. illus. see Meredith, Samantha.
Wyke-Smith, E. A. Marvellous Land of Snergs. Morrow, George, illus. (p. 1099)
Wyland Studios Staff. Wyland's Spouty And Friends. (p. 1966)
Wyldeck, Kathi. English for Everyone - Book. (p. 530)
—English for Everyone - Book 1. (p. 530)
—Grammar & Vocabulary Games for Children. (p. 706)
Wyler, Melissa. Adventures of Henry the Sports Bug: Book 1. (p. 18)
Wyler, Rose & McSpadden, Warren W. Oil Comes to Us. Luykx, Th. D., illus. (p. 1282)
Wyles, Betty, illus. see Eichler, Darlene.
Wyley, Enda. Boo & Bear. Massardier, Greg, tr. (p. 209)
—Silver Notebook. (p. 1576)
Wylie, Peter. Chem Cloud. (p. 297)
Wylie, Sarah. All These Lives. (p. 46)
Wylie, T. J., illus. see Kranowitz, Carol Stock.
Wyllie, Jim & Wyllie, Miggie. Cedric's Day at the Castle. (p. 283)
Wyllie, Miggie, jt. auth. see Wyllie, Jim.
Wyllie, Ruth G. Adventures of George the Turtle. (p. 18)
Wyman, Bruce C., jt. auth. see Stevenson, L. Harold.
Wyman, Dorothy. Kaysell the Dragon Pup. (p. 946)
Wyman, M. C., illus. see Harris, Kandi.
Wyman, Susan. Pipsqueak's Puny Peepholes. (p. 1362)
Wymarra, Elizabeth & Wymarra, Wandihnu. Wandihnu & the Old Dugong. Hodges, Benjamin, illus. (p. 1856)
Wymarra, Wandihnu, jt. auth. see Wymarra, Elizabeth.
Wyn, Dafydd. Hunting the Man in the Moon. (p. 829)
Wyn, Delyth, tr. see Howie, Vicky & MacLean, Moira.
Wyn, Delyth, tr. see Stowell, Gordon.
Wynbrandt, James, jt. auth. see Ludman, Mark D.
Wyndham, jt. auth. see Eastaway, Rob.
Wyndham, John. Midwich Cuckoos. (p. 1139)
Wyndham, John, jt. auth. see Francis, Pauline.
Wyndham, Lee, ed. Acting, Acting, Acting: Stories of Stardust & Grease Paint, of Amateur Striving & Professional Polish. (p. 9)
Wyneken, Cherise. Spaceship Lands in Africa (p. 1620)
Wyner, Zach. Arizona Cardinals. (p. 98)
—Atlanta Falcons. (p. 112)
—Atlanta Hawks. (p. 112)
—Baltimore Ravens. (p. 135)
—Brooklyn Nets. (p. 231)
—Buffalo Bills. (p. 235)
—Carolina Panthers. (p. 270)
—Cincinnati Bengals. (p. 319)
—Cleveland Browns. (p. 331)
—Dallas Cowboys. (p. 401)
—Denver Broncos. (p. 427)
—Denver Nuggets. (p. 427)
—Detroit Pistons. (p. 431)
—Golden State Warriors. (p. 695)
—Green Bay Packers. (p. 721)
—Houston Texans. (p. 804)
—Indiana Pacers. (p. 871)
—Indianapolis Colts. (p. 871)
—Jacksonville Jaguars. (p. 904)
—Kansas City Chiefs. (p. 943)
—Miami Dolphins. (p. 1133)
—Minnesota Vikings. (p. 1147)
—Music. (p. 1193)
—New England Patriots. (p. 1244)
—New Orleans Saints. (p. 1246)
—New York Giants. (p. 1248)
—New York Jets. (p. 1248)
—Oakland Raiders. (p. 1275)
—Philadelphia 76ers. (p. 1350)
—Philadelphia Eagles. (p. 1350)
—Phoenix Suns. (p. 1351)
—Pittsburgh Steelers. (p. 1365)
—San Diego Chargers. (p. 1510)
—Seattle Seahawks. (p. 1539)
—St. Louis Rams. (p. 1638)
—Tennessee Titans. (p. 1720)
—TennesseeTitans. (p. 1720)
Wyngarden, Rod Van. Case of the St. Patrick's Day Mystery Trip: A Lake Alamo Mystery - March 1967. (p. 275)
—Hidden Relic: A Lake Alamo Mystery January 1973. (p. 776)
—Stranger Comes to Town: A Lake Alamo Mystery January 1967. (p. 1665)
Wynn, Juliette, jt. auth. see Wynn, Thad.
Wynn, Linda T., jt. auth. see Smith, Jessie Carney.
Wynn, Mychal. High School Plan for Students with College-Bound Dreams. Bassett, Melvyn & Bascome, Glenn, eds. (p. 778)
—Middle School Plan for Bermudian Students with College-Bound Dreams. (p. 1138)
Wynn, Raquel. Stretch Your Dog Healthy: A Hands-on Approach to Natural Canine Care. (p. 1667)
Wynn, Robbin. Final Showdown under the Sun: You vs. Adversary. (p. 586)
Wynn, Thad & Wynn, Juliette. Tale of a Dragon. (p. 1699)
Wynne, Christopher, ed. see Anton, Ferdinand.
Wynne, Dudley, jt. auth. see Blyton, Enid.
Wynne, Jessica, et al. Meditations for Kids by Kids. (p. 1120)
Wynne, Nick. Florida Tales. (p. 607)
Wynne, Patricia, illus. see Chaikin, Andrew.
Wynne, Patricia, illus. see DeSalle, Rob.
Wynne, Patricia J. 3-D Mazes—Dinosaurs. (p. 1991)
—BOOST Seashore Activity Book. (p. 213)
—Butterfly Activity Book. (p. 247)
—Creative Haven NatureScapes Coloring Book. (p. 379)
—Creative Haven SeaScapes Coloring Book. (p. 379)
—Easy Dinosaur Mazes. (p. 500)
—Evolution of the Horse. (p. 547)
—Exploring the American Museum of Natural History: A Children's Guide with Pictures to Color. (p. 553)
—Extreme Mammals. (p. 556)
—Feathered Dinosaurs Stickers. (p. 579)
—Feathered Dinosaurs Tattoos. (p. 579)
—Glow-in-the-Dark Frogs. (p. 685)
—Glow-in-the-Dark Skeleton Stickers. (p. 685)
—King Tut Coloring Book. (p. 959)
—New York for Kids: 25 Big Apple Sites to Color. (p. 1248)
—Seashore Activity Book. (p. 1538)
—Shiny King Tut Treasure Stickers. (p. 1567)
—Travel Fun Stickers. (p. 1780)
—Wild Animals Activity Book. (p. 1928)
Wynne, Patricia J., illus. see Arnold, Caroline.
Wynne, Patricia J., illus. see Lincoln, Nan.
Wynne, Patricia J., illus. see Lunde, Darrin P.
Wynne, Patricia J., illus. see Lunde, Darrin P. & Stock, Catherine.
Wynne, Patricia J., illus. see Lunde, Darrin.
Wynne, Patricia J., illus. see Sayre, April Pulley.
Wynne, Patricia J., jt. auth. see Silver, Donald M.
Wynne, Patricia J., jt. auth. see Silver, Donald.
Wynne, Patricia J. & MacPhee, Ross. Race to the South Pole Coloring Book. (p. 1431)
Wynne, Patricia J. & Silver, Donald. My First Book about the Brain. (p. 1205)
Wynne, Patricia J. & Silver, Donald M. BOOST My First Human Body Coloring Book. (p. 213)
—My First Book about Outer Space. (p. 1205)
—My First Human Body Book. (p. 1206)
Wynne Pechter, Lesley. Alligator, Bear, Crab: A Baby's ABC (p. 47)
Wynne, Rhys. Magic Pencil (p. 1073)
Wynne, Sarah & Clark, Katie. River Royals: Master the Mississippi. (p. 1476)
Wynne-Jones, Diana. Hour of the Frog. (p. 802)
Wynne-Jones, Tim. Blink & Caution. (p. 199)
—Boat in the Tree. Shelley, John, illus. (p. 205)
—Boy in the Burning House (p. 218)
—Boy in the Burning House. (p. 218)
—I'll Make You Small. (p. 856)
—Last Piece of Sky. (p. 978)
—Lord of the Fries. (p. 1052)
—Lord of the Fries & Other Stories: Other Stories. (p. 1052)
—Maestro (p. 1070)
—Maestro. (p. 1070)
—Mischief City. (p. 1150)
—Ned Mouse Breaks Away Petricic, Dusan, illus. (p. 1239)
—On Tumbledown Hill Petricic, Dusan, illus. (p. 1292)
—Pounce de Leon Tapia, Alfredo, illus. (p. 1389)
—Rex Zero & the End of the World. (p. 1467)
—Rex Zero, King of Nothing. (p. 1467)
—Stephen Fair. (p. 1648)
—Uninvited. (p. 1818)
—Zoom Beddows, Eric, illus. (p. 1989)
—Zoom at Sea Beddows, Eric, illus. (p. 1989)
—Zoom Upstream. (p. 1989)
Wynne-Jones, Tim & Tapia, Alfredo. Pounce de Leon (p. 1389)
Wyont, Wanda. Sunbeam. Huskins, Suzanne Hallier, illus. (p. 1676)
Wyre, Yvonne. Adventures of Cuthbert the Coal Lorry. (p. 17)
—Further Adventures of Cuthbert the Coal Lorry & all His Friends. (p. 650)
Wyrick, June Gray & Jones, Kristen Wyrick. Mommy, What Is Salvation? (p. 1162)
Wyrick, Monica, illus. see Crane, Carol.
Wyrick, Monica, illus. see Penn, Audrey.
Wyrick, Monica Dunsky, illus. see Penn, Audrey.
Wyroski, Kim. Big Blue Chair. (p. 178)
Wyrwas, Kim. Lonely Cat. (p. 1046)
Wyse, Liz & Barnes, Jon. Insects. (p. 875)
Wysocki, Michelle Lee. My First Baby Bible. (p. 1204)
Wysong, Ryan, illus. see Swaney, Kathleen M.
Wysotski, Chrissie, illus. see Emery, Joanna.
Wysotski, Chrissie, illus. see Konieczny, Vladimir.
Wysotski, Chrissie, illus. see McFarlane, Sheryl.
Wysotski, Chrissie, jt. auth. see Shardlow, Tom.
Wyss, J. D. Swiss Family Robinson. (p. 1691)
Wyss, Johann. Swiss Family Robinson (p. 1691)
—Swiss Family Robinson. (p. 1691)
—Swiss Family Robinson Study Guide. (p. 1691)
Wyss, Johann D. & Fuentes, Benny. Swiss Family Robinson. Sandoval, Gerardo, illus. (p. 1691)
Wyss, Johann David. Swiss Family Robinson: Critical Reading Series. (p. 1691)
—Swiss Family Robinson: A Classic Story about Initiative. (p. 1691)
—Swiss Family Robinson: Or Adventures in a Desert Island. (p. 1691)
—Swiss Family Robinson: With a Discussion of Teamwork. Butterfield, Ned, illus. (p. 1691)
—Swiss Family Robinson. (p. 1691)
—Swiss Family Robinson. Akib, Jamel, illus. (p. 1691)
—Swiss Family Robinson. Tayal, Amit, illus. (p. 1691)
—Swiss Family Robinson. Hunt, Robert, illus. (p. 1691)
—Swiss Family Robinson. McKowen, Scott, illus. (p. 1691)
Wyss, Johann David, illus. see Kingston, William Henry Giles, tr.
Wyss, Johann David, jt. auth. see Tait, Chris.
Wyss, Manspeter, illus. see Brenner, Peter.
Wyss, Thelma Hatch. Bear Dancer: The Story of a Ute Girl. (p. 150)
Wyss, Tyan. African Dream. Immelman, Sarita, illus. (p. 27)
—Night Flyer. Immelman, Sarita, illus. (p. 1253)
—Solitaire Prince. (p. 1608)
Wyttenbach, Bigna A. Francis-von. Coronets, Butterflies & Roses. (p. 368)
Wyvill, Grace. Charlie Basset: A Hound's Tail. (p. 292)

X

X. Before You Were Born - Our Wish for A Baby - Donor Sperm/IVF: Version 8: Donor Sperm (IVF) (p. 159)
—Before You Were Born - Our Wish for A Baby - Donor Insemination: Version 2: Donor Insemination. (p. 159)
—Before You Were Born - Our Wish for A Baby - Embryo Donation: Version 7: Embryo Donation. (p. 159)
—Before You Were Born - Our Wish for A Baby - Female Partners: Version 9: Female Partners. (p. 159)
—Before You Were Born - Our Wish for A Baby - Frozen Embryo: Version 6: Frozen Embryo. (p. 159)
—Before You Were Born - Our Wish for A Baby - Gestational Carrier: Version 5: Gestational Carrier. (p. 159)
—Before You Were Born - Our Wish for A Baby - IVF: Version 1: in Vitro Fertilization. (p. 159)
—Before You Were Born - Our Wish for A Baby - Male Partners: Version 10: Male Partners. (p. 159)
—Before You Were Born - Our Wish for A Baby - Traditional Surrogate: Version 4: Traditional Surrogate. (p. 159)
Xanthos, Carol, illus. see Carnesecca, Michele.
Xavier, Imbeus & Sanders, Martin B. Super Dentist Guy: Attack of the Yukkies. Sanders, Martin B., illus. (p. 1679)
—Super Dentist Guy: Attack of the Yukkies. Sanders, Martin B, et al, illus. (p. 1679)
Xavier, John. Darfur: African Genocide. (p. 406)
Xavier V, Sajjad. Baboonia. (p. 124)
Xebec & Akizuki, Ryo. Stellvia Volume 1 (p. 1647)
Xenophon. Xenophon's Cyrus the Great: The Arts of Leadership & War. Hedrick, Larry, ed. (p. 1967)
Xerri-L., Nadia & Tardieu, Carine. Just Julie & I Am Not Emmanuelle. (p. 938)
Xian Nu Studio, illus. see Marr, Melissa.
Xian Nu Studio, illus. see Schreiber, Ellen.
Xian Nu Studio Staff, illus. see Marr, Melissa.
Xian Nu Studio Staff, illus. see Robbins, Trina.
Xianoqing, Pan, illus. see Ma, Zheng & Li, Zheng.
Xiaofang, Ding, illus. see Ma, Zheng & Li, Zheng.
Xiaoming, Wang, illus. see Ma, Zheng & Li, Zheng.
Xiaoqing, Pan, illus. see Ma, Zheng & Li, Zheng.
Xiaozhen, Wu, tr. see Shanghai Animation Studio Staff & Tang, Sanmu.
Xie, Feng, ed. Works by Young Artists. (p. 1953)
Xin, Xiao, illus. see Bullard, Lisa.
Xin, Xiao, illus. see Harris, Brooke.
Xinran, Xinran & Mother's Bridge of Love Staff. Motherbridge of Love. Masse, Josee, illus. (p. 1178)
Xinran, Xinran, et al. Motherbridge of Love. Masse, José, illus. (p. 1178)
Xinying, L., jt. auth. see Yamin, M.
Xiong, Kim. Clay General. (p. 330)
—Dragon Tribe. (p. 478)
—Kitchen God. (p. 962)
—Little Stone Lion. Xiong, Kim, illus. (p. 1037)
—Paper Horse. (p. 1322)
Xirinacs, Olga. Arbol de Mi Patio. Balzola, Asun, illus. (p. 94)
Xocuasvili, Cico, jt. auth. see Rowling, J. K.
Xoul, illus. see Grant, Joan.
Xu, Cui, jt. auth. see Ji, Zhaohua.
Xu, Lei. Angry Sea, Hidden Sands. Mok, Kathy, tr. (p. 75)
—Cavern of the Blood Zombies. Mok, Kathy, tr. (p. 282)
—Graveyard of a Queen. Mok, Kathy, tr. (p. 712)
Xu, Wei, illus. see Wang, Ruowen.
Xuan, YongSheng, illus. see Compestine, Ying Chang.
Xueqin, Cao. Dream of the Red Chamber. Chiang, Shirley, illus. (p. 483)

X

Y

Yaakol, Shirim. How We Returned to Egypt: From Communist Russia to Fundamentalist Israel. (p. 823)
Yaakov, Juliette, ed. Senior High School Library Catalog. (p. 1550)
Yaber, Armando. Mariana Sale el Sol. (p. 1093)
Yablonski, Judy, jt. auth. see Kaspar, Anna.
Yabuki, Go. Scrapped Princess (p. 1532)
Yabuki, Go, illus. see Yubuki, Go & Azumi, Yukinobu.
Yabuki, Kentaro. Black Cat. (p. 195)
—Black Cat. Yabuki, Kentaro, illus. (p. 195)
Yaccarino, Dan. All the Way to America: The Story of a Big Italian Family & a Little Shovel. (p. 46)
—Billy & Goat at the State Fair. (p. 187)
—Cuatro Vientos. (p. 388)
—Dan Yaccarino's Mother Goose. Yaccarino, Dan, illus. (p. 402)
—Doug Unplugged. (p. 473)
—Doug Unplugs on the Farm. (p. 473)
—Every Friday. (p. 542)
—Every Friday. Yaccarino, Dan, illus. (p. 542)
—Fantastic Undersea Life of Jacques Cousteau. (p. 572)
—Lawn to Lawn. (p. 981)
—New Pet. Yaccarino, Dan, illus. (p. 1246)
—Unlovable. Yaccarino, Dan, illus. (p. 1821)
—Where the Four Winds Blow. Yaccarino, Dan, illus. (p. 1909)
Yaccarino, Dan, illus. see Burleigh, Robert.
Yaccarino, Dan, illus. see Churchill, Jill.
Yaccarino, Dan, illus. see Dyckman, Ame.
Yaccarino, Dan, illus. see Egan, Kate.
Yaccarino, Dan, illus. see Jacobs, Paul DuBois & Swender, Jennifer.
Yaccarino, Dan, illus. see Palatini, Margie.
Yaccarino, Dan, illus. see Parkhurst, Carolyn.
Yaccarino, Dan, illus. see Public Domain Staff.
Yackle, Deanne. Jenny & Me. (p. 913)
Yacobi, Diana, jt. auth. see Yacobi, Lily.
Yacobi, Diana, et al. Sarah, David & YOU Read Hebrew: Book 1. (p. 1514)
Yacobi, Lily & Yacobi, Diana. Aleph Bet Story: Featuring Sarah & David & Friends. (p. 35)
Yaconelli, Mark. Wonder, Fear, & Longing: A Book of Prayers (p. 1947)
Yaconelli, Mike. Devotion: A Raw-Truth Journal on Following Jesus (p. 432)
Yacoubou, Jeanne. I Am a Rainbow Child Coloring-Story Book. Stebakova, Elena, illus. (p. 832)
—Wanna Play? Coloring-Story Book. Stebakova, Elena, illus. (p. 1856)
—What's My Heritage? Coloring-Story Book. Stebakova, Elena, illus. (p. 1898)
Yacowitz, Caryn. I Know an Old Lady Who Swallowed a Dreidel. Slonim, David, illus. (p. 840)
—Inuit Indians. (p. 883)
—Iroquois Indians. (p. 888)
—Navajo Indians. (p. 1237)
—Seminole Indians (p. 1550)
—South Dakota. (p. 1617)
Yadate, Hajime. Cowboy Bebop Kuga, Cain, illus. (p. 373)
Yadav, S. S. Chickpea Breeding & Management. Chen, W. et al, eds. (p. 301)
Yadu, narrated by. Casey at the Bat. (p. 275)
Yaeger, Mark, illus. see Kelby, Tom.
Yagami, Yu & Yugami, Yu. Those Who Hunt Elves (p. 1740)
Yager, A. J., jt. auth. see Vescera, Dean.
Yager, Fred. Cybersona. (p. 396)
—Sound from a Star: A Novel. (p. 1615)
Yager, Jan. Reading Rabbit. Lyman, Mitzi, illus. (p. 1446)
Yager, Jeff. Atom & Eve. (p. 113)
Yager, Karen & Williams, Kiersten. Krickle Forest Adventures, Wizbet's Notebook. Walsh, Jennifer, illus. (p. 967)
Yagi, Kenichiro, tr. see Watsuki, Nobuhiro.
Yagi, Norihiro. Claymore Yagi, Norihiro, illus. (p. 330)
—Claymore. (p. 330)
Yagi, Norihiro & Tarbox, Jonathan. Claymore Yagi, Norihiro, illus. (p. 330)
—Claymore. Yagi, Norihiro, illus. (p. 330)
Yagi, Norihiro & Yago, Norihiro. Claymore. (p. 330)
Yagielo, Rosie. City Kitties. (p. 323)
Yagmin, Daniel, Jr. Norton B. Nice. (p. 1266)
Yago, Norihiro, jt. auth. see Yagi, Norihiro.
Yagyu, Genichiro. Breasts. (p. 225)
Yagyu, Geniehiro & Stinchecum, Amanda Mayer. All about Scabs. Yagyu, Genichiro, illus. (p. 43)
Yahgulanaas, Michael. Little Hummingbird. (p. 1029)
Yaiza, Alicia, jt. auth. see Patterson, Michael.
Yak, Rivais, jt. auth. see Rivais, Yak.
Yakin, Boaz. Marathon. Infurnari, Joe, illus. (p. 1091)
Yakola, Carrie. Full Moon Maxi. (p. 646)
Yakola, Carrie C. Clayton & the Planets. (p. 330)
Yakowicz, Susie. Fire Runner. (p. 590)
Yalata and Oak Valley Communities & Mattingley, Christobel. Maralinga: The Anangu Story. Yalata and Oak Valley Communities, illus. (p. 1091)
Yalata Communities, et al. Maralinga: The Anangu Story. (p. 1091)
Yaldezian, Lisa M. 500 Presents for Penelope Potts. Seltzer, Jerry, illus. (p. 2001)
Yale, Dallas. Colony of New Hampshire. (p. 342)
—Searching for Shapes in Art: Reason with Shapes & Their Attributes (p. 1537)
Yalmeh, Jacklin. Scruffy & the Blue Hazelnut Tree. (p. 1533)
—Scruffy & the Walnuts. (p. 1533)
Yalowitz, Paul, illus. see Spinelli, Eileen.
Yamada, Debbie Leung. Striking It Rich: Treasures from Gold Mountain. Tang, You-shan, illus. (p. 1667)
Yamada, Futaro. Kouga Ninja Scrolls. Sant, Geoff, tr. from JPN. (p. 967)
Yamada, Jane, illus. see Burch, Regina G.
Yamada, Jane, illus. see Callella, Trisha.
Yamada, Jane, illus. see Groeneweg, Nicole.
Yamada, Jane, illus. see Hall, Pamela.
Yamada, Jane, illus. see Higgins, Nadia.
Yamada, Jane, illus. see Vogel, Julia.
Yamada, Kana, illus. see Thomson, Sarah L.
Yamada, Kobi. What Do You Do with an Idea? Besom, Mae, illus. (p. 1883)
Yamada, Masaki. Innocence: After the Long Goodbye. Oniki, Yuji & Horn, Carl Gustav, trs. from JPN. (p. 875)
Yamada, Miho. Miyako from Tokyo. Camcam, Princesse, illus. (p. 1156)
Yamada, Rikako. Unordinary Elephant. States, Anna, illus. (p. 1822)
Yamada, Shale. Rainbow Kitty Saves the Day. Riedler, Amelia, ed. (p. 1435)
Yamada, Utako. Story of Cherry the Pig. Yamada, Utako, illus. (p. 1657)
Yamaguchi, Heidi, tr. see Shiozu, Shuri.
Yamaguchi, Keika, illus. see Norman, Kim.
Yamaguchi, Keika, illus. see Schwartz, Corey Rosen & Gomez, Rebecca J.
Yamaguchi, Kristi. Dream Big, Little Pig! Bowers, Tim, illus. (p. 483)
—It's a Big World, Little Pig! Bowers, Tim, illus. (p. 895)
Yamaguchi, Masakazu. Arm of Kannon (p. 99)
Yamaguchi, Yumi, tr. see Yasuda, Yuri & Yasuda, Yuri Old tales of Japan.
Yamamoto, Lani. Albert. Yamamoto, Lani, illus. (p. 34)
—Albert 2. Yamamoto, Lani, illus. (p. 34)
Yamamoto, Lun Lun. Swan in Space (p. 1688)
—Swans in Space. (p. 1689)
Yamamoto, Makoto. O Holy Night: The First Christmas. Moritsu, Wakako, illus. (p. 1274)
Yamamoto, Matsuko, illus. see Shimizu, Michio.
Yamamoto, Satoshi, illus. see Kusaka, Hidenori.
Yamamoto, Tadayoshi, illus. see Watanabe, Shigeo.
Yamamura, Hajime. Rebirth of the Demonslayer. Yamamura, Hajime, illus. (p. 1451)
Yamanaka, Lois-Ann. Behold the Many: A Novel. (p. 160)
Yamanushi, Toshiko. Deer King. Tani, Toshihiko, illus. (p. 423)
Yamasaki, James, illus. see Compestine, Ying Chang.
Yamasaki, James, illus. see Kalz, Jill.
Yamasaki, Katie. Fish for Jimmy. Yamasaki, Katie, illus. (p. 598)
—When the Cousins Came. (p. 1904)
Yamasaki, Katie, illus. see Lynch, Joseph.
Yamasaki, Katie, jt. auth. see Weston, Mark.
Yamashita, Haruo, jt. auth. see Iwamura, Kazuo.
Yamate, Sandra S. & Yao, Carolina. Char Siu Bao Boy. (p. 291)
Yamato, Nase. Take Me to Heaven. (p. 1696)
Yamauchi, Karl, illus. see Trahan, Kendra.
Yamawaki, Yuriko, illus. see Nakagawa, Masafumi.
Yamazaki, Joe, tr. see Aoyama, Gôshô.
Yamazaki, Joe, tr. see Konomi, Takeshi.
Yamazaki, Joe, tr. see Nishimori, Hiroyuki.
Yamazaki, Joe, tr. see Shinjo, Mayu.
Yamazaki, Joe, tr. see Yudetamago.
Yamazaki, Kore. Ancient Magus' Bride Vol. 2. DeAngelis, Jason, ed. (p. 69)
Yambar, Chris, ed. Edison's Frankenstein 1910. Bihun, Robb, illus. (p. 504)
Yamin, M. & Xinying, L. Chinese Made Easy: Characters & Roman. Bk. 1 (p. 307)
Yan, Geling. Banquet Bug. (p. 136)
Yan, Ma. Diary of Ma Yan: The Life of a Chinese School Girl. Haski, Pierre, ed. (p. 435)
Yan, Ma & Haski, Pierre. Diary of Ma Yan: The Struggles & Hopes of a Chinese Schoolgirl. (p. 435)
Yan, Martin. Martin Yan Quick & Easy. Jan, Stephanie Liu, photos by. (p. 1098)
Yan, Stan, illus. see Carew, Kieran.
Yan, Wing. King of Fighters 2003. (p. 958)
Yan, Wing & Tung, King. King of Fighters 2003 (p. 958)
Yanagisawa, Kazuaki, illus. see Kurimoto, Kaoru.
Yanai, Tal. Life Is Not a Candy Store It's the Way to the Candy Store: A Spiritual Guide to the Road of Life for Teens. (p. 1011)
Yanai, Tetsuo, tr. see Hara, Masahiro.
yancey, diane. Abolition of Slavery. (p. 5)
Yancey, Diane. Al Capone's Chicago. (p. 32)
—Ancient Greek Art & Architecture. Nardo, Don, ed. (p. 69)
—Basketball. (p. 143)
—Case of the Green River Killer. (p. 274)
—Forensic Anthropologist. (p. 617)
—Forensic Entomologist. (p. 617)
—Murder. (p. 1192)
—Piracy on the High Seas. (p. 1362)
—STDs. (p. 1645)
—Tracking Serial Killers. (p. 1775)
—Zodiac Killer. (p. 1987)
Yancey, Rick. 5th Wave. (p. 1992)
—Curse of the Wendigo. (p. 395)
—Final Descent. (p. 586)
—Infinite Sea. (p. 873)
—Isle of Blood. (p. 893)
—Monstrumologist. (p. 1169)
—Monstrumologist Collection: Monstrumologist; Curse of the Wendigo; Isle of Blood; Final Descent. (p. 1169)
—Thirteenth Skull. (p. 1735)
Yanez, Alberto. Ekg Rhythms Made Easy. (p. 507)
Yanez, Anthony & Guillory, Mike. Wild Ride on the Water Cycle. (p. 1930)
Yanez, Cecilia, tr. see Cherfas, Jeremy.
Yanez-Arellano, Katherine. Gunny Wolf Story. (p. 732)
Yang, A., illus. see Yang-Huan & Yang-Huan.
Yang, Angela. Out of the Dark. (p. 1311)
—Within the Mist. (p. 1942)
Yang, Belle. Always Come Home to Me. Yang, Belle, illus. (p. 51)
—Foo, the Flying Frog of Washtub Pond. Yang, Belle, illus. (p. 612)
—Hannah Is My Name: A Young Immigrant's Story. Yang, Belle, illus. (p. 742)
—Hannah Is My Name. Yang, Belle, illus. (p. 742)
—Nest in Springtime: A Bilingual Book of Numbers. Yang, Belle, illus. (p. 1242)
—Summertime Rainbow: A Mandarin Chinese-English Bilingual Book of Colors. Yang, Belle, illus. (p. 1675)
Yang, Belle & Williams, Marcia. Archie's War: My Scrapbook of the First World War. Williams, Marcia, illus. (p. 95)
Yang, Gene Luen. American Born Chinese. (p. 60)
—American Born Chinese. Yang, Gene Luen, illus. (p. 60)
—American Born Chinese. Yang, Gene Luen & Pien, Lark, illus. (p. 60)
—Animal Crackers: A Gene Luen Yang Collection. (p. 77)
—Boxers. (p. 217)
—Eternal Smile. Kim, Derek Kirk, illus. (p. 539)
—Level Up. Pham, Thien, illus. (p. 1003)
—Saints. (p. 1504)
—Secret Coders. Holmes, Mike, illus. (p. 1540)
—Shadow Hero. Liew, Sonny, illus. (p. 1557)
Yang, Gene Luen, illus. see Pien, Lark.
Yang, Gene Luen & DiMartino, Michael Dante. Avatar: the Last Airbender: the Rift Part 2. Gurihiru Staff, illus. (p. 118)
Yang, Gene Luen & Pien, Lark. Boxers. Yang, Gene Luen, illus. (p. 217)
—Saints. Yang, Gene Luen, illus. (p. 1504)
Yang, Gene Luen, et al. Avatar - The Last Airbender: The Rift. Pt. 1 Marshall, Dave, ed. (p. 118)
—Avatar - The Last Airbender. Marshall, Dave, ed. (p. 118)
Yang, Gladys. Frog Rider & Other Folktales from Chin. (p. 640)
Yang, Gladys, tr. see Shoushen, Jin.
Yang, Hae-won, illus. see Yoon, Ae-hae.
Yang, HyeWon, illus. see Lee, WonKyeong.
Yang, James. Joey & Jet: Book 1 of Their Adventures. Yang, James, illus. (p. 920)
—Joey & Jet in Space. Yang, James, illus. (p. 920)
Yang, John, Sr. You Can Eat Cheese but Don't Be Cheesy. (p. 1974)
Yang, Kyung-Il. Blade of Heaven (p. 198)
Yang, Kyung-Il, jt. auth. see Hwang, Yong-Su.
Yang, Robin. Enchanted Collar #5: Bandits & Robbers. (p. 523)
—Enchanted Collar(tm) #1: A Strange Gift. (p. 523)
—Enchanted Collar(tm) #2: Dog Fight. (p. 523)
—Enchanted Collar(tm) #3: Paradise Lost. (p. 523)
—Enchanted Collar(tm) #4: Squirrel Pot Pie. (p. 523)
Yang, Stella. My Family: Individual Title Six-Packs. (p. 1202)
—Snowman (p. 1601)
Yang, Sue, ed. see Ma, Wing Shing & Lau, Ding Kin.
Yang, Yi, illus. see Peterson, M. E.
Yangas, Angela Marie. Buggzzz: Let There Be Light. (p. 236)
Yang-Huan, jt. auth. see Yang-Huan.
Yang-Huan & Yang-Huan. Where Is Spring? Yang, A. & Huang, H Y, illus. (p. 1909)
Yangsook, Choi. Name Jar. (p. 1228)
Yanique, Tiphanie & Djeli, Moses. I Am the Virgin Islands. (p. 834)
Yanisko, Thomas. What You Eat It's up to You. Hoyes, Kerry, illus. (p. 1896)
Yanitzia, Canetti, jt. auth. see Canetti, Yanitzia.
Yankee, Kris. Saving Redwind: A Wallpaper Adventure. Covieo, Jeff, illus. (p. 1517)
Yankee, Kris & Nelson, Marian. Are You Confident Today? (p. 97)
—Are You Grateful Today? (p. 97)
—Are You Respectful Today? Becoming a Better You! (p. 97)
Yankee Magazine Editors. Panty Hose, Hot Peppers, Tea Bags, & More—For the Garden: 1,001 Ingenious Ways to Use Common Household Items to Control Weeds, Beat Pests, Cook Compost, Solve Problems, Make Tricky Jobs Easy, & Save Time. (p. 1321)
Yankey, Lindsey. Bluebird. (p. 204)
—Sun & Moon. (p. 1676)
Yankoglu, Berrin A. & Berkner, Kathrin. Document Recognition & Retrieval XV: 29-31 January 2008, San Jose, California, USA. (p. 459)
Yankoski, Mike. My 30 Days under the Overpass: Not Your Ordinary Devotional. (p. 1195)
Yankovic, Al, pseud. My New Teacher & Me! Hargis, Wes, illus. (p. 1216)
—When I Grow Up. Hargis, Wes, illus. (p. 1903)
Yankovic, Weird Al, see Yankovic, Al, pseud.
Yankus, Marc, jt. auth. see Hearn, Julie.
Yannayon, Kim. Lucy & the New Baby. (p. 1063)
—Lucy's Big Mess. (p. 1063)
Yannielli, Len, jt. auth. see Hecht, Alan.
Yannone, Deborah. Fun. Kaeden Corp. Staff, ed. (p. 647)
Yannuzzi, Della A. Life of Zora Neale Hurston: Author & Folklorist. (p. 1012)
Yannuzzi, Frank M. Magic Lacrosse Stick. (p. 1072)
Yano, Yuriko. Manga Doodles. Yano, Yuriko, illus. (p. 1087)
Yanofsky, Tsivia. Take Me to Europe: Jewish Life in England, Spain, France, & Italy. (p. 1696)
—Take Me to the Zoo: Lions, elephants & snakes in the Midrash & Nature. (p. 1696)
Yanow-Schwartz, Jo, ed. see Evers, Alf.
Yansky, Brian. Alien Invasion & Other Inconveniences. (p. 41)
—Homicidal Aliens & Other Disappointments. (p. 794)
—My Road Trip to the Pretty Girl Capital of the World. (p. 1217)
—Utopia, Iowa. (p. 1829)
Yant, Daisy M. Yellow Pages: A Directory from God. (p. 1970)
Yanuchi, Jeff, jt. auth. see Yanuchi, Lori.
Yanuchi, Lori & Yanuchi, Jeff. Ranger Trails: Jobs of Adventure in America's Parks. Morris, James R., illus. (p. 1438)
Yanuck, Debbie L. American Flag. (p. 60)
—American Symbols (p. 63)
—Bald Eagle. (p. 133)
—Liberty Bell. (p. 1005)
—Uncle Sam. (p. 1812)
—White House. (p. 1913)
Yanuck, Debbie L., jt. auth. see Nobleman, Marc Tyler.
Yao, Carolina, jt. illus. see Yamate, Sandra S.
Yao, Tao-chung & McGinnis, Scott. Let's Play Games in Chinese. Visco, Tamara, illus. (p. 1000)
Yao, Tao-chung, et al. Integrated Chinese: Character. (p. 879)
—Integrated Chinese. (p. 879)
Yao, Yuan. America Dream. (p. 59)
—Floating Cloud. (p. 605)
—Live in USA. (p. 1040)
Yap, Weda, illus. see Larrick, Nancy.
Yapp, R. H. Botany: A Junior Book for Schools. (p. 215)
Yarber, Angela, jt. auth. see Tuszynski, Kathy.
Yarber, Angela, jt. auth. see Tuszynski, Kathy Cromwell.
Yarber, Peggy Sue. Rocketships to Heaven & the Sos Fuel Station. (p. 1483)
Yarbray Brucke, Candice & Moore, Dawnyelle. Wrappers Wanted: A Mathematical Adventure in Surface Area. (p. 1962)
Yarbro, Tony. Witchbird. (p. 1941)
Yarbrough, Camille. Tamika & the Wisdom Rings. (p. 1704)
Yarbrough, Mark, illus. see Gossett, Robert A.
Yarbrough, Tammy. What Happens When Someone Dies? (p. 1886)
Yarchi, Jacky, illus. see Petersell, Yaacov.
Yardi, Robin. Midnight War of Mateo Martinez. (p. 1139)
—They Just Know: Animal Instincts Klein, Laurie Allen, illus. (p. 1732)
—They Just Know - Animal Instincts. Klein, Laurie Allen, illus. (p. 1732)
Yardley Hastings Primary School. Tim & Holly's Olympic Adventure. (p. 1750)
Yardley, Joanna, illus. see Collard, Sneed B., III.
Yardley, Joanna, illus. see Salonen, Roxane B.
Yardley, Liz. Firefly Legacy - Book Vi. Yardley, Liz, illus. (p. 592)
—Firefly Legacy - Book Vii. Yardley, Liz, illus. (p. 592)
Yardman, Barbara M. Crawl, Fly or Run Book. (p. 377)
Yarlett, Emma. Sidney, Stella, & the Moon. Yarlett, Emma, illus. (p. 1573)
Yarlett, Emma, illus. see Smallman, Steve.
Yarmosky, Michael. Growing Season. (p. 726)
Yarnall, Karen Sturdy, illus. see Maxson, H. A. & Young, Claudia H.
Yarnell, Duane. Winning Basket. (p. 1937)
Yarnell, Linda. One Last Breath. (p. 1295)
Yarney, Susan. Can I Tell You about ADHD? A Guide for Friends, Family & Professionals. Martin, Chris, illus. (p. 258)
Yaroshevich, Angelica, ed. see AZ Books Staff.
Yaroslavskaya, Lyudmila. Great Lakes Legends & Fairy Tales. (p. 717)
Yarrow, Peter. Day Is Done. Sweet, Melissa, illus. (p. 413)
—Favorite Folk Songs. Widener, Terry, illus. (p. 578)
—Let's Sing Together! Widener, Terry, illus. (p. 1000)
—Peter Yarrow Songbook: Songs for Little Folks. Widener, Terry, illus. (p. 1347)
—Sleepytime Songs. Widener, Terry, illus. (p. 1590)
Yarrow, Peter & Lipton, Lenny. Puff, the Magic Dragon. Puybaret, Eric, illus. (p. 1415)
—Puff, the Magic Dragon Pop-Up. Puybaret, Eric, illus. (p. 1415)
Yasar, Kerim, tr. see Higashino, Keigo.
Yasar, Kerim, tr. see Shiono, Nanami.
Yasgur, Abigail, jt. auth. see Lipner, Joseph.
Yashar, Michael. Chickadee Story. (p. 299)
Yashima, Taro. Crow Boy. Yashima, Taro, illus. (p. 385)
—Umbrella. (p. 1810)
Yashinsky, Dan. Ghostwise: A Book of Midnight Stories. (p. 673)
Yasko, Carmen R. Buddy & His Buddies. (p. 234)
Yasso, C. D. Adventures of Penn & Penelope in Washington, Dc. (p. 21)
Yasuda, Anita. 12 Most Amazing American Battles. (p. 1994)
—12 Most Amazing American Monuments & Symbols. (p. 1994)
—A. A. Milne. (p. 1)
—Albert Einstein. (p. 34)
—Asia. (p. 106)
—Astronomy: Cool Women in Space. (p. 109)
—Avestruces. (p. 119)
—Beach Bandit Harpster, Steve, illus. (p. 149)
—Beach Volleyball Is No Joke Santillan, Jorge H., illus. (p. 149)
—Big City Sights Harpster, Steve, illus. (p. 180)
—Burros. (p. 244)
—Chinese New Year. (p. 307)
—Colors of a Sunset: An Algonquin Nature Myth. Estudio Haus, illus. (p. 345)
—Crazy Clues Harpster, Steve, illus. (p. 377)
—Crazy Clues. Harpster, Steve, illus. (p. 377)
—Dino Detectives. Cameron, Craig, illus. (p. 441)
—Dino Detectives. Harpster, Steve, illus. (p. 441)
—Donkeys. (p. 466)
—Dragon, the Phoenix, & the Beautiful Pearl: A Chinese Dragon Spirit Myth. (p. 478)
—Earthworms. (p. 498)
—Eat Green. (p. 501)
—Explore Flight! With 25 Great Projects. Stone, Bryan, illus. (p. 550)
—Explore Native American Cultures! With 25 Great Projects. Keller, Jennifer K., illus. (p. 550)
—Explore Simple Machines! With 25 Great Projects. (p. 550)
—Explore the Wild West! With 25 Great Projects. Kim, Alex & Stone, Bryan, illus. (p. 550)
—Explore Water! 25 Great Projects, Activities, Experiments. Stone, Bryan, illus. (p. 550)
—First Base Blues Harpster, Steve, illus. (p. 593)
—Foxes. (p. 626)
—Ghost Sounds Harpster, Steve, illus. (p. 671)
—Giant Moray Eel. (p. 673)
—Gibbons. (p. 674)
—Green Ideas. (p. 722)
—Gulf War. (p. 731)
—Hannah Taylor: Ma Vie. Karvonen, Tanjah, tr. from ENG. (p. 742)
—Hannah Taylor. (p. 742)
—Haunted House Harpster, Steve, illus. (p. 753)
—Haunted House. Harpster, Steve, illus. (p. 753)
—How the World Was Made: A Cherokee Creation Myth. Pennington, Mark, illus. (p. 813)
—Indiana: The Hoosier State. (p. 871)
—Iowa: The Hawkeye State. (p. 886)

—I've Got the No-Skateboard Blues Santillan, Jorge H., illus. (p. 901)
—Jade Emperor: A Chinese Zodiac Myth. (p. 905)
—James Cameron. (p. 907)
—Johnny Depp. (p. 923)
—Justin Bieber: Ma Vie. Karvonen, Tanjah, tr. from ENG. (p. 940)
—Justin Bieber. (p. 940)
—Kansas: The Sunflower State. (p. 943)
—Kentucky: The Bluegrass State. (p. 949)
—Kristen Stewart. (p. 967)
—Lady Bird Johnson: My Life. (p. 970)
—Lady Bird Johnson. (p. 970)
—Lady Gaga. (p. 970)
—Louisiana: The Pelican State. (p. 1058)
—Maine: The Pine Tree State. (p. 1077)
—Mike Meyers. (p. 1141)
—Miranda Cosgrove. (p. 1149)
—Missing Trumpet Harpster, Steve, illus. (p. 1153)
—Monkey King: A Chinese Monkey Spirit Myth. (p. 1165)
—Mystery Coins Harpster, Steve, illus. (p. 1224)
—Mystery Coins. Harpster, Steve, illus. (p. 1224)
—N Gua Mends the Sky: A Chinese Flood Myth. (p. 1227)
—Native Nations of the Northwest Coast. (p. 1235)
—Native Nations of the Plains. (p. 1235)
—Neil Armstrong. (p. 1240)
—Nikki Yanofsky: Ma Vie. Karvonen, Tanjah, tr. from ENG. (p. 1255)
—Nikki Yanofsky. (p. 1255)
—Ostriches. (p. 1306)
—Pangu Separates the Sky from the Earth: A Chinese Creation Myth. (p. 1321)
—Political Leaders. (p. 1380)
—Provincial & Territorial Governments. (p. 1413)
—Rick Riordan. (p. 1470)
—Robert Pattinson. (p. 1479)
—Sinking of the Titanic. (p. 1580)
—Sinking of the Titanic Paperback. (p. 1580)
—Sky Woman & the Big Turtle: An Iroquois Creation Myth. Pennington, Mark, illus. (p. 1587)
—Slime Attack Harpster, Steve, illus. (p. 1590)
—South Carolina: The Palmetto State. (p. 1616)
—South Korea. (p. 1617)
—Stolen Fire: A Seminole Trickster Myth. Estudio Haus, illus. (p. 1652)
—Surprise Prize Harpster, Steve, illus. (p. 1686)
—Surprise Prize. Harpster, Steve, illus. (p. 1686)
—Swim Race Harpster, Steve, illus. (p. 1691)
—Taylor Lautner. (p. 1708)
—Taylor Swift. (p. 1708)
—There's No Crying in Baseball Santillan, Jorge H., illus. (p. 1731)
—Valentine's Day. (p. 1830)
—Warrior Twins: A Navajo Hero Myth. Pennington, Mark, illus. (p. 1859)
—What's Great about California? (p. 1897)
—What's Great about Maryland? (p. 1897)
—What's Great about Mississippi? (p. 1897)
—What's Great about North Carolina? (p. 1897)
—What's Great about Puerto Rico? (p. 1897)
—Yu the Great Conquers the Flood: A Chinese Nature Myth. (p. 1983)
Yasuda, Anita, jt. auth. see Wearing, Judy.
Yasuda, Anita & Goldsworthy, Kaite. Art. (p. 101)
Yasuda, Anita & Harpster, Steve. Crazy Clues. (p. 377)
—Haunted House. (p. 753)
—Mystery Coins. (p. 1224)
—Surprise Prize. (p. 1686)
Yasuda, Anita & Stone, Bryan. Explore the Solar System! 25 Great Projects, Activities, Experiments. Stone, Bryan, illus. (p. 550)
Yasuda, Yuri & Yasuda, Yuri Old tales of Japan. Treasury of Japanese Folktales. Matsunari, Yumi & Yamaguchi, Yumi, trs. (p. 1783)
Yasuda, Yuri Old tales of Japan, jt. auth. see Yasuda, Yuri.
Yasui, Koji, illus. see Kato, Etsuo.
Yasunari, Toda, illus. see Kuroda, Yosuke.
Yasunari, Toda, illus. see Yosuke, Kuroda.
Yatate, Hajime. Mobile Suit Gundam Seed (Novel) (p. 1157)
Yatate, Hajime, jt. auth. see Goto, Liu.
Yates, Alma J. Sammy's Song: A Novel. (p. 1508)
Yates, David, jt. auth. see Hatkoff, Craig.
Yates, David & Hatkoff, Craig. Hope for Winter - The True Story of Two Dolphins' Remarkable Friendship. (p. 796)
Yates, Donnalyn. Let's Memorize States & Capitals Using Pictures & Stories. (p. 999)
Yates, Elizabeth. Seventh One. (p. 1555)
Yates, Gene. Chameleon Colors Book. (p. 289)
—Dragon Opposites Book. (p. 477)
—Elephant Alphabet Book. (p. 511)
—Giraffe Numbers Book. (p. 677)
—Snake Shapes Book. (p. 1596)
—What Can Simon Be? (p. 1880)
Yates, Gene & Frank, Thomas. What Can Simon Be? Yates, Gene, illus. (p. 1880)
Yates, Irene. Birth to Death. (p. 192)
—Christmas Activities for ks1 Maths. (p. 312)
—Christmas Activities for Language & L. (p. 312)
—Colour. (p. 346)
—How to Be a Wizard at Grammer. Ford, Kate, illus. (p. 815)
—How to Be a Wizard at Reading. (p. 815)
—How to Be a Wizard at Spelling. (p. 815)
—How to Be a Wizard at Writing Stories. (p. 815)
—How to Dazzle at Grammar. (p. 816)
—How to Dazzle at Reading. (p. 816)
—How to Dazzle at Writing. (p. 816)
—Water. (p. 1862)
—Word Level Work - Vocabulary. (p. 1950)
Yates, Irene & Ladybird Books Staff. Three Billy Goats Gruff. (p. 1741)
Yates, Irene Dorothy. How to Be Brilliant at Writing Poetry. Ford, Kate, illus. (p. 815)
Yates, Irene Dorothy & Ford, Kate. How to Be Brilliant at Writing Stories. (p. 815)
Yates, Jolyon, illus. see Farshtey, Greg & Lee, Paul.
Yates, Jolyon, illus. see Farshtey, Greg.
Yates, Jolyon, jt. auth. see Farshtey, Greg.
Yates, Kelly, illus. see Krovatin, Christopher.
Yates, Louise. Dog Loves Books. (p. 461)
—Dog Loves Counting. (p. 461)
—Dog Loves Drawing. (p. 461)
—Dog Loves Fairy Tales. (p. 461)
—Kalb Yoheb Al Kotob (Dog Loves Books- Arabic Edition) (p. 941)
Yates, Louise, illus. see Voigt, Cynthia.
Yates, Marie. Reggie & Me: The First Book in the Dani Moore Trilogy. (p. 1457)
Yates, Martha, jt. auth. see Blake, Kevin.
Yates, Patty Fee, told to. Friends. (p. 638)
Yates, Philip. Pirate's Night Before Christmas. Serra, Sebastià, illus. (p. 1363)
—Pirate's Twelve Days of Christmas. Serra, Sebastià, illus. (p. 1364)
Yates, Philip & Rissinger, Matt. Laughs - Little Giant(r) Book. (p. 980)
—Silly Jokes & Giggles. Shems, Ed, illus. (p. 1576)
Yates, Vicki. Buildings (p. 239)
—Communication (p. 349)
—Having Fun (p. 755)
—Life at Home (p. 1008)
—Life at School (p. 1008)
—Life at Work (p. 1008)
—Travel (p. 1780)
Yates-Velez, C. My Baby Brother & Me. (p. 1196)
Yatscoff, Edward R. Archie's Gold. (p. 95)
Yaun, Ellen R. Christmas Problem for Samuel James. Murphy, Betsy, illus. (p. 315)
Yavari, Neguin, jt. auth. see Heiligman, Deborah.
Yaw, Valerie. Color-Changing Animals. (p. 342)
Yaweera, Sasipapa, illus. see Donploypetch, Jintanan.
Yawtsong, Lee, tr. see Shanghai Animation Studio Staff & Tang, Sanmu.
Yaxley, Trevor, jt. auth. see Killian, Rick.
Yaya, Grandma. Ali's Miracle: A Little Child Shall Lead Them. (p. 41)
Yayo. Tales of Pop & Grace: The Burglar. (p. 1702)
—Tales of Pop & Grace: Pop's Lucky Token. (p. 1702)
Yayo, illus. see Bateman, Teresa.
Yayo, illus. see Fitch, Sheree.
Yayo, illus. see Hopkins, Lee Bennett.
Yayo, illus. see Jones, Charlotte Foltz.
Yayo, illus. see New, William.
Yayo, illus. see Simpson, Lesley.
Yazawa, Ai. Nana. Bates, Megan, ed. (p. 1228)
—Nana. Yazawa, Ai, illus. (p. 1228)
—Paradise Kiss (p. 1323)
—Paradise Kiss Kubo, Shirley, tr. from JPN. (p. 1323)
Yazawa, Ai & Wolfe, Allison. Nana. Yazawa, Ai, illus. (p. 1228)
Yazawa, Nao. Moon & Blood (p. 1171)
—Wedding Peach. (p. 1871)
Yazawa, Nao, illus. see Tomita, Sukehiro.
Yazbeck, Peter & Castano, Clara. Learning Cards(tm) Scales in Q&A Form, All Levels (p. 985)
—Learning Cards(tm) Intervals in Q&A Form - All Levels (p. 985)
—Learning Cards(tm) Triad Inversions in Q&A Form - All Levels (p. 985)
—Learning Cards(tm) Musical Symbols in Q&A Form, Secondary Level (p. 985)
—Learning Cards(tm) Root Position Triads in Q&A Form - All Levels (p. 985)
—Learning Cards(tm) Fundamentals of Music in Q&A Form, Part 1, Secondary Level (p. 985)
—Learning Cards(tm) Fundamentals of Music in Q&A Form, Part 2 - Secondary Level (p. 985)
Yazdanfar, Farzin, tr. see Khanlari, Parviz-Natel.
Yazdani, Aliza. Protection: How far Would you go to Save a Brother? (p. 1412)
Yazdi, Ayatullah Agha H. M. M. Pooya & Ali, S. V. Mir Ahmed. Holy Qur'an. (p. 791)
Yazzie, Benton, illus. see Dewey, Jennifer Owings.
Yazzie, Johnson, illus. see Browne, Vee.
Yazzie, Peterson, illus. see Flood, Nancy Bo.
Yazzie, Seraphine G. Beauty Beside Me: Stories of My Grandmother's Skirts. Ruffenach, Jessie Eve, ed. (p. 154)
—Three Little Sheep/Dibe Yazhi Taa'go Baa Hane' Thomas, Peter A., tr. (p. 1743)
Yazzie, Serphine G. Beauty Beside Me: Stories of My Grandmother's Skirts. (p. 154)
Ybanez, Adelita. Heavenly Seed. (p. 761)
Ybáñez, Terry, illus. see Tafolla, Carmen & Teneyuca, Sharyll.
Ybarra, Andres. Phoenix Suns. (p. 1351)
Ycaza, Roger. Emocionante Historia de un Valiente Gato Que Subio a la Rama Más Alta de un Arbol... y Luego no Pudo Bajar. (p. 520)
—Suenos. (p. 1672)
Ye, Ting-Xing. Chinese Thought of It: Amazing Inventions & Innovations. (p. 308)
—My Name Is Number 4: A True Story from the Cultural Revolution. (p. 1215)
—Throwaway Daughter. (p. 1745)
—White Lily. (p. 1913)
Yeager, Alice. George C. Wallace: Alabama Political Power. (p. 663)
—Lurleen B. Wallace: Alabama's First Woman Governor. (p. 1066)
Yeager, Alice, jt. auth. see Autrey, Jacquelyn.
Yeager, Allison Blair. If I Could Change the World. Mesch, Kate, ed. (p. 852)
Yeager, C. R. Breakfast at Noon: Backwards in The 'Burbs. (p. 224)
Yeager, Graham. Diablo: The Third Millersburg Novel. (p. 433)
—Lake Haven: A Millersburg Novel. (p. 972)
—Stone Hedge: The Fourth Millersburg Novel. (p. 1652)
Yeager, Jamie. Going Home. (p. 692)
Yeager, Paugh Paugh Tom. 26th of June. (p. 1996)
Yeagle, Dean, illus. see Frost, Robert.
Yeagle, Gary. Angels Footprints. (p. 75)
Yeahpau, Thomas. X-Indian Chronicles: The Book of Mausape. (p. 1967)
Yealland, Jane, jt. auth. see Owens, Ann-Maureen.
Yeamans Simrell, Elizabeth. Only Mr. Bromley Will Do. (p. 1298)
Yeardley, Glynne, jt. auth. see Surget, Alain.
Yearling, A. K. My Little Pony: The Daring Do Adventure Collection. Set (p. 1213)
Yearling, Tricia. How Do I Find Information Online? (p. 807)
—How Do I Keep My Privacy Online? (p. 807)
—How Do I Play Games Online? (p. 807)
—How Do I Stay Safe from Cyberbullies? (p. 807)
—How Do I Stay Safe from Online Predators? (p. 807)
—How Do I Use Social Networking? (p. 807)
Yearwood, Owen. Gingerbread Girl. (p. 677)
Yeates, J. Lanier. Bay of One Hundred Fires. (p. 147)
Yeates, Thomas, illus. see Fontes, Justine & Fontes, Ron.
Yeates, Thomas, illus. see Jolley, Dan.
Yeates, Thomas, illus. see Limke, Jeff.
Yeates, Thomas, illus. see Storrie, Paul D.
Yeates, Thomas, illus. see Storrie, Paul.
Yeates, Thomas, et al. Hidden Lands. (p. 776)
Yeates, Tom, illus. see Moore, Alan, et al.
Yeatts, Karol, et al. Navigating through problem Solving & Reasoning in Grade 3. House, Peggy A. & Litwiller, Bonnie H., eds. (p. 1238)
Yeatts, Karol L. Mega-Fun Card-Game Math: 25 Games & Activities That Help Kids Practice Multiplication, Fractions, Decimals & More-All with Just a Deck of Cards! (p. 1124)
Yeatts, Tabatha. Albert Einstein: The Miracle Mind. (p. 34)
—Joan of Arc: Heavenly Warrior. (p. 919)
—Weisel, Wiesenthal, Klarsfeld: The Holocaust Survivors. (p. 1873)
—Wiesel, Wiesenthal, Klarsfeld: The Holocaust Survivors. (p. 1927)
Yebra, Antonio Gomez, et al. Adivina, Adivinanzas. (p. 12)
Yedwab, Paul. God Book: A Necessarily Incomplete Look at the Essence of God. (p. 688)
Yedwab, Paul Michael. Sex in the Texts. Schwartz, Katherine, ed. (p. 1556)
Yee, Jeanne, illus. see Oshiro, Kimberley.
Yee, Josie, illus. see Awdry, W.
Yee, Josie, illus. see Higginson, Sheila Sweeny.
Yee, Josie, illus. see Silverhardt, Lauryn.
Yee, Lauren D. How to Be the Perfect Parent: A Comedy Monologue. (p. 815)
—My Mother's Touch: A Dramatic Monologue. (p. 1215)
Yee, Linda L. Big Red Things. (p. 183)
Yee, Lisa. Absolutely Maybe. (p. 7)
—Bobby the Brave (Sometimes) (p. 206)
—Bobby the Brave (Sometimes) Santat, Dan, illus. (p. 206)
—Bobby vs. Girls (Accidentally) Santat, Dan, illus. (p. 206)
—Kidney Hypothetical. (p. 952)
—Millicent Min, Girl Genius. (p. 1143)
—Millicent Min, Girl Genius. (p. 1144)
—Stanford Wong Flunks Big-Time. (p. 1639)
—Warp Speed. (p. 1858)
Yee, Patrick, illus. see Fu, Shelley.
Yee, Patrick, illus. see Lyons, Kay, et al.
Yee, Paul. Bone Collector's Son (p. 208)
—Dead Man's Gold & Other Stories Chan, Harvey, illus. (p. 417)
—Ghost Train. Chan, Harvey, illus. (p. 672)
—Jade Necklace. Lin, Grace, illus. (p. 905)
—Learning to Fly (p. 986)
—Money Boy. (p. 1164)
—Roses Sing on New Snow: A Delicious Tale. Chan, Harvey, illus. (p. 1490)
—Shu-Li & Diego Wang, Shaoli, illus. (p. 1571)
—Shu-Li & Tamara Wang, Shaoli, illus. (p. 1571)
—Tales from Gold Mountain Ng, Simon, illus. (p. 1701)
—What Happened This Summer (p. 1885)
Yee, Rodney. Yoga the Poetry of the Body: 50 Card Practice Deck. (p. 1972)
Yee, Tammy. Easy Butterfly Origami. (p. 500)
Yee, Tammy, illus. see Fredericks, Anthony D.
Yee, Tammy, illus. see Goldsberry, U'ilani.
Yee, Tammy, illus. see Hirschi, Ron.
Yee, Wong Herbert. Abracadabra! Magic with Mouse & Mole. (p. 6)
—Brand-New Day with Mouse & Mole. (p. 222)
—Did You See Chip? (p. 437)
—Did You See Chip? Ovresat, Laura, illus. (p. 437)
—Eek! There's a Mouse in the House (p. 505)
—Fine Feathered Friends. Yee, Wong Herbert, illus. (p. 589)
—Hamburger Heaven. (p. 739)
—Mouse & Mole: A Perfect Halloween. (p. 1181)
—Mouse & Mole, a Perfect Halloween. (p. 1181)
—Mouse & Mole, a Winter Wonderland. Yee, Wong Herbert, illus. (p. 1181)
—Mouse & Mole, Fine Feathered Friends. Yee, Wong Herbert, illus. (p. 1181)
—Mouse & Mole, Secret Valentine. Yee, Wong Herbert, illus. (p. 1181)
—My Autumn Book. Yee, Wong Herbert, illus. (p. 1196)
—Summer Days & Nights. Yee, Wong Herbert, illus. (p. 1674)
—Tracks in the Snow. Yee, Wong Herbert, illus. (p. 1775)
—Upstairs Mouse, Downstairs Mole. (p. 1825)
Yee, Wong Herbert, illus. see Brandon, Anthony G.
Yee, Wong Herbert, illus. see Douglas, Erin.
Yee, Wong Herbert, illus. see Friend, Catherine.
Yee, Wong Herbert, jt. auth. see Douglas, Erin.
Yegoryan, Kristina & Yegoryan, Rubik. I Know Digits & Shapes. (p. 840)
Yegoryan, Rubik, jt. auth. see Yegoryan, Kristina.
Yeh, Alicia, illus. see Hsuan Hua.
Yeh, Julie. Poppie's Adventures: Serpents in Paradise. Hsu, Jack, illus. (p. 1384)
Yeh, Kat. Friend Ship. Groenink, Chuck, illus. (p. 637)
—Truth about Twinkie Pie. (p. 1794)
—You're Lovable to Me. Gioulis, Sue & Anderson, Sue, illus. (p. 1982)
Yeh, Kat & Lee, Huy Voun. Magic Brush: A Story of Love, Family, & Chinese Characters. (p. 1072)
Yeh, Phil. Dinosaurs Across America. Yeh, Phil, illus. (p. 444)
Yeh, Phil, jt. auth. see Murakami, Jon.
Yeh, Shao-Min. What Do You See? (p. 1883)
Yekutiel, Lea. Making the Breast of It. (p. 1082)
Yelagalawadi, Jyoti. Deep Sea Creatures. Nagaraju, Harsha, illus. (p. 423)
—Laugh with Dinosaurs. Nagaraju, Harsha, illus. (p. 980)
Yelavich, Susan. Contemporary World Interiors. (p. 360)
Yelchin, Eugene. Arcady's Goal. Yelchin, Eugene, illus. (p. 95)
—Breaking Stalin's Nose. (p. 225)
—Breaking Stalin's Nose. Yelchin, Eugene, illus. (p. 225)
Yelchin, Eugene, illus. see Beaumont, Karen.
Yelchin, Eugene, illus. see Fleming, Candace.
Yelchin, Eugene, illus. see Gerber, Carole.
Yelchin, Eugene, illus. see Wardlaw, Lee.
Yelchin, Eugene & Kuryla, Mary. Heart of a Snowman. Yelchin, Eugene & Kuryla, Mary, illus. (p. 759)
—Next Door Bear. Yelchin, Eugene & Kuryla, Mary, illus. (p. 1249)
Yelenak, Andy, illus. see Blackett, Dulcibella.
Yelle, Richard. International Glass Art (p. 880)
Yellowknife, Jessica. Spring Break Adventure. (p. 1635)
Yemm, Caterhine. Maths Problem Solving: Year 1 Endersby, Frank, illus. (p. 1108)
—Maths Problem Solving: Year 2 Endersby, Frank, illus. (p. 1108)
—Maths Problem Solving: Year 3 Endersby, Frank, illus. (p. 1108)
—Maths Problem Solving: Year 4 Endersby, Frank, illus. (p. 1108)
—Maths Problem Solving: Year 5 Endersby, Frank, illus. (p. 1108)
—Maths Problem Solving: Year 6 Endersby, Frank, illus. (p. 1108)
Yen Mah, Adeline. Chinese Cinderella Boy Knight (p. 307)
—Chinese Cinderella: True Story of an Unwanted Daughter. (p. 307)
Yenawine, Philip. Colors (p. 345)
—Lines (p. 1019)
—People (p. 1339)
—Places (p. 1366)
—Places. (p. 1366)
—Shapes (p. 1560)
—Stories (p. 1654)
Yenika-Agbaw, Vivian. Christmas Counting Book. (p. 313)
Yenne, Bill, jt. auth. see Johnson, Michael.
Yeo, Beop-Ryong. Chronicles of the Cursed Sword Hui-Jin, Park, illus. (p. 317)
Yeo, Ho-Khung. Honey Mustard (p. 794)
Yeo, Ho-Kyung. Honey Mustard. (p. 794)
Yeoman, John. Bear's Water Picnic. Blake, Quentin, illus. (p. 152)
—Bear's Winter House. Blake, Quentin, illus. (p. 152)
—Beatrice & Vanessa. Blake, Quentin, illus. (p. 153)
—Fabulous Foskett Family Circus. Blake, Quentin, illus. (p. 560)
—Heron & the Crane. Blake, Quentin, illus. (p. 773)
—Mouse Trouble. Blake, Quentin, illus. (p. 1182)
—Quentin Blake's Amazing Animal Stories. Blake, Quentin, illus. (p. 1425)
—Quentin Blake's Magical Tales. Blake, Quentin, illus. (p. 1425)
—Rumbelow's Dance. Blake, Quentin, illus. (p. 1495)
—Seven Voyages of Sinbad the Sailor. Blake, Quentin, illus. (p. 1555)
—Sixes & Sevens. Blake, Quentin, illus. (p. 1583)
—Up with Birds! (p. 1824)
—Wild Washerwomen. Blake, Quentin, illus. (p. 1930)
Yeoman, John, tr. see Luzzati, Emanuele.
Yeoman, R. S. Official Blue Book(r) Handbook of United States CoinsTM: With Premium List. Bressett, Ken, ed. (p. 1280)
Yep, Kathleen S., jt. auth. see Yep, Laurence.
Yep, Laurence. Bravo, Mia! England, Tamara, ed. (p. 224)
—Child of the Owl. (p. 301)
—City of Death. (p. 323)
—City of Fire. (p. 323)
—Dragon Prince: A Chinese Beauty & the Beast Tale. (p. 477)
—Dragons of Silk. (p. 479)
—Earth Dragon Awakes: The San Francisco Earthquake of 1906. (p. 495)
—Magic Paintbrush. Wang, Suling, illus. (p. 1073)
—Mia England, Tamara, ed. (p. 1133)
—Skunk Scout. (p. 1586)
—Staking a Claim: The Journal of Wong Ming-Chung, a Chinese Miner, California 1852. (p. 1638)
—Staking a Claim, the Journal of Wong Ming-Chung, a Chinese Miner, California 1852. (p. 1638)
—Star Maker. (p. 1640)
—Sweetwater. Noonan, Julia, illus. (p. 1690)
—Tigers Apprentice (p. 1749)
—Tiger's Apprentice. (p. 1749)
—Tiger's Blood. (p. 1749)
—Traitor. (p. 1777)
—Weaving Maid. (p. 1870)
—When the Circus Came to Town. Wang, Suling, illus. (p. 1904)
Yep, Laurence & Ryder, Joanne. Dragon's Guide to Making Your Human Smarter. GrandPré, Mary, illus. (p. 479)
—Dragon's Guide to the Care & Feeding of Humans. GrandPré, Mary, illus. (p. 479)
Yep, Laurence & Yep, Kathleen S. Dragon's Child: A Story of Angel Island. (p. 479)
Yepes, Rebecca. It Might Be A Crow. (p. 894)
Yerbey, Lindsey Blake, illus. see Peters, Elizabeth Anne.
Yeretskaya, Yevgeniya. Snow Queen: A Pop-Up Adaption of a Classic Fairytale. (p. 1599)
—Woodland Christmas: A Festive Wintertime Pop-Up Book. Ng, Neiko, illus. (p. 1949)
Yeretskaya, Yevgeniya, illus. see Preston Chushcoff, Jennifer.
Yerger, Susan M. Mighty Little Samuel Seagull. (p. 1140)
Yerges, Karen. Adventures of Scooper the Beagle Dog: Las aventuras de Scooper el perrito Beagle. (p. 22)
Yerkes, Jennifer. Funny Little Bird. (p. 650)
Yerkes, Lane, illus. see Casterline, L. C.

Yerkes, Lane, illus. see Rose, Shirley.
Yerkes, Lane, illus. see Slater, Teddy.
Yero, Judith Lloyd. Bill of Rights. (p. 186)
—Declaration of Independence. (p. 422)
—Mayflower Compact. (p. 1113)
Yero, Judith Lloyd & National Geographic Learning Staff. Bill of Rights. (p. 186)
—Mayflower Compact. (p. 1113)
Yerrid, Gable. Marley's Treasure. Fitzgerald, Jennifer, illus. (p. 1095)
Yerrill, Gail. Starry Night, Sleep Tight. (p. 1642)
Yerrill, Gail, illus. see Freedman, Claire.
Yerushalmi, Miriam. Feivel the Falafel Ball Who Wanted to Do a Mitzvah. Ginsberg, Dvora, illus. (p. 581)
—Gedalia the Goldfish Who Wanted Be Just Like the King. Weinberg, Devorah, illus. (p. 659)
—Let's Go Camping & Discover Our Nature. Perez, Esther Ido, illus. (p. 997)
Yerushalmi, Motty, et al. Buki the Flying Dog. (p. 240)
Yerxa, Leo. Ancient Thunder (p. 70)
—Last Leaf First Snowflake to Fall. Yerxa, Leo, illus. (p. 978)
Yes I Can Staff. Mariachi I'll Be. (p. 1093)
—Words Are Everywhere. (p. 1951)
Yes Magazine Editors. Amazing International Space Station. Cowles, Rose, illus. (p. 54)
—Fantastic Feats & Failures. Kurisu, Jane, illus. (p. 571)
—Hoaxed! Fakes & Mistakes in the World of Science. Woo, Howie, illus. (p. 786)
—Hoaxed! Fakes & Mistakes in the World of Science. Yes Magazine Editors, ed. (p. 786)
—Robots: From Everyday to Out of This World. (p. 1481)
—Science Detectives: How Scientists Solved Six Real-Life Mysteries. Cowles, Rose, illus. (p. 1525)
Yes Magazine Editors, ed. Robots: From Everyday to Out of This World. Woo, Howie, illus. (p. 1481)
Yesh, Jeff, illus. see Dahl, Michael.
Yesh, Jeff, illus. see Gregoire, Maryellen.
Yesh, Jeff, illus. see Loewen, Nancy.
Yesh, Jeff, illus. see Meachen Rau, Dana.
Yesh, Jeff, illus. see Nettleton, Pamela Hill.
Yesh, Jeff, illus. see Salas, Laura Purdie.
Yesh, Jeff, illus. see Schroeder, Holly.
Yesh, Jeff, illus. see Sherman, Josepha.
Yesh, Jeff, illus. see Slade, Suzanne.
Yesh, Jeff, illus. see Zurakowski, Michele.
Yespolov, Johnson & Kalna-Dubinyuk, Arynova. Extension in Kazakhstan & the Experience of the Us: Lessons from a Working National Model. (p. 555)
Yevtushenko, Yevgeny. Yevtushenko: Selected Poems. Milner-Gulland, Robin et al, trs. (p. 1971)
Yezerski, Thomas F. Meadowlands: A Wetlands Survival Story. Yezerski, Thomas F., illus. (p. 1116)
Yezerski, Thomas F., illus. see Daley, Michael J.
Yezerski, Thomas F., illus. see Nielsen, Laura F. & Nielsen, Laura.
Yhard, Jo Ann. Fossil Hunter of Sydney Mines (p. 623)
Yi, Hye Won, illus. see Jones, Christianne C.
Yi, J., illus. see Harvey, Jacqueline.
Yi, Kang-u. Rebirth WOO, illus. (p. 1451)
Yi, Liu, illus. see Sloan, Christopher.
Yi, Myong-Jin & Choi, Ellen. Lights Out (p. 1016)
Yi-Cline, Nancy, jt. auth. see Cline, Mike.
Yildirim, Rabia. Wind, Rain & Snow. (p. 1935)
Yilmaz, Necdet, illus. see Blaisdell, Molly.
Yilmaz, Necdet, illus. see Hardy, Lorién Trover.
Yilmaz, Necdet, illus. see Myers, Tim J.
Yilmaz, Necdet, illus. see Picture Window Books Staff.
Yim Bridges, Shirin, jt. auth. see Bridges, Shirin Yim.
Yim, Natasha. Goldy Luck & the Three Pandas. Zong, Grace, illus. (p. 696)
—Sacajawea of the Shoshone. Nguyen, Albert, illus. (p. 1500)
Yiming, Ji, et al. Short Stories for Kids & Teens. (p. 1569)
Yin. Coolies. Soentpiet, Chris K., illus. (p. 364)
Yin, Aidi. Emily & Her Dolls. (p. 518)
Yin, Leah. Zona & the Big Buzzzy Secret. Yin, Leah, illus. (p. 1988)
Yin, Saw Myat & Elias, Josie. Myanmar. (p. 1222)
Ying, Victoria, illus. see Burkhart, Jessica.
Ying, Victoria, illus. see Redbank, Tennant, et al.
Ying, Victoria, illus. see RH Disney Staff & Smiley, Ben.
Ying, Victoria, illus. see Stout, Shawn K.
Ying, Wu, tr. see Shanghai Animation Studio Staff & Tang, Sanmu.
Ying, Wu, tr. see Tang, Sanmu.
Yip, Mingmei. Chinese Children's Favorite Stories. (p. 307)
—Grandma Panda's China Storybook: Legends, Traditions & Fun. (p. 708)
Yisrael, A'mon. Mr. Jerry's Nap. (p. 1185)
YKids Staff. Curie. (p. 392)
—Einstein. (p. 507)
—Leonardo da Vinci. (p. 992)
—Mother Teresa. (p. 1178)
—Nelson Mandela. (p. 1240)
YKids Staff, jt. auth. see Gandhi, Mohandas.
Ylitalo, Becky Jean. Gretchen & the Grumpybugs. (p. 723)
Ylvis & Lochstoer, Christian. What Does the Fox Say? Nyhus, Svein, illus. (p. 1884)
Ylvisake, Anne. Land & Water: World Rivers. (p. 973)
Ylvisaker, Anne. Button Down. (p. 248)
—Curse of the Buttons. (p. 394)
—Dear Papa. (p. 419)
—Little Klein. (p. 1030)
—Luck of the Buttons. (p. 1062)
—Your Lungs. (p. 1981)
—Your Muscles. (p. 1981)
—Your Stomach. (p. 1981)
Yo, Yuen Wong. Digimon: Digital Monsters (p. 439)
Yoakem, Kevin. Wooly & Fuzzy. (p. 1950)
Yobe, Marjorie. Adventures of Little Tyke: A Loveab. (p. 20)
Yochum, Nikki. Shy Cheyenne & the Substitute Teacher. (p. 1572)
Yockteng, Rafael, illus. see Argueta, Jorge.
Yockteng, Rafael, illus. see Montejo, Victor.
Yockteng, Rafael, jt. auth. see Lázaro León, Georgina.
Yocum, Randi. Cowpie Corgi: A Dog's Tale. Yocum, Sam, 2nd, photos by. (p. 374)
Yocum, Sam, 2nd, photos by see Yocum, Randi.
Yoda, Hiroko, tr. see Sasaki, Joh.
Yoda, Obi-Wan. BICs 4 Derivatives: Theory (p. 177)
Yoder, Carolyn. Filipino Americans. (p. 586)
—Italian Americans. (p. 894)
Yoder, Carolyn P., compiled by. George Washington - The Writer: A Treasury of Letters, Diaries, & Public Documents. (p. 664)
Yoder, Elwood E. Margaret's Print Shop: A Novel of the Anabaptist Reformation. (p. 1092)
Yoder, Eric & Yoder, Natalie. 65 Short Mysteries You Solve with Science! (p. 1997)
—One Minute Mysteries: 65 Short Mysteries You Solve with Math! (p. 1296)
Yoder, Greg. Swing: A Storybook to Color. (p. 1691)
Yoder, James D. Echoes along the Sweetbriar. (p. 502)
Yoder, Laura, illus. see Martin, Rebecca.
Yoder, Lisa. One Spider's Web. (p. 1297)
Yoder, Natalie, jt. auth. see Yoder, Eric.
Yoder, Suzana E. Sensing Peace. (p. 1551)
Yoe, Craig, ed. see Lee, Stan, et al.
Yoe, Craig, jt. auth. see Herriman, George.
Yoe, Craig, et al. Felix the Cat Paintings. Ollerenshaw, Rod, ed. (p. 581)
Yoe! Studio Staff, illus. see Ciminera, Siobhan & Rao, Lisa.
Yoe! Studio Staff, illus. see Ciminera, Siobhan & Testa, Maggie.
Yoe! Studio Staff, illus. see Rao, Lisa.
Yoerg, Sharon, jt. auth. see Campbell, Maureen.
Yoffe, Ken, jt. auth. see Weisberg, Ellen.
Yogananda, Paramahansa. Due Rane Nei Guai. (p. 489)
Yogananda, Paramhansa. Two Frogs in Trouble: Based on a Fable Told by Paramahansa Yogananda. (p. 1803)
Yogis, John A. Canadian Law Dictionary. (p. 260)
Yohalem, Eve. Cast Off. (p. 276)
—Escape under the Forever Sky. (p. 535)
Yohn-Rhodes, Phyllis. Abbey & Jakey - Jakey's Happy Tale. (p. 2)
—Monster. (p. 1166)
—Wagon. (p. 1852)
Yokococo. Matilda & Hans. Yokococo, illus. (p. 1109)
Yokota, Hiromitsu. Tale of the Oki Islands: A Tale from Japan. (p. 1700)
Yokota, Hiromitsu, illus. see Barchers, Suzanne I.
Yolanda And Reese. Boy Who Loved to Be Like Michael Jackson. Harrell, Maurice, illus. (p. 219)
Yolen, Jane. All Star! Honus Wagner & the Most Famous Baseball Card Ever. Burke, James, illus. (p. 45)
—Animal Stories: Heartwarming True Tales from the Animal Kingdom. Ishida, Jui, illus. (p. 79)
—Baba Yaga. (p. 123)
—Ballad of the Pirate Queens. (p. 134)
—Birds of a Feather. Stemple, Jason, photos by. (p. 191)
—Bug Off! Creepy, Crawly Poems. Stemple, Jason, photos by. (p. 236)
—Centaur Rising. (p. 287)
—Color Me a Rhyme: Nature Poems for Young People. Stemple, Jason, photos by. (p. 342)
—Come to the Fairies' Ball. Lippincott, Gary, illus. (p. 347)
—Como Dicen Estoy Enojado los Dinosaurios? Teague, Mark, illus. (p. 350)
—Count Me a Rhyme: Animal Poems by the Numbers. Stemple, Jason, illus. (p. 369)
—Count Me a Rhyme: Animal Poems by the Numbers. Stemple, Jason, photos by. (p. 369)
—Creepy Monsters, Sleepy Monsters. Murphy, Kelly, illus. (p. 381)
—Curse of the Thirteenth Fey: The True Tale of Sleeping Beauty. (p. 395)
—Curses! Foiled Again. Cavallaro, Mike, illus. (p. 395)
—Devil's Arithmetic. (p. 432)
—Dragon's Blood. (p. 479)
—Dragon's Heart Vol. 4. Schmidt, Jonathon, ed. (p. 479)
—Dragon's Heart. Schmidt, Jonathon, ed. (p. 479)
—Egret's Day. Stemple, Jason, illus. (p. 506)
—Elsie's Bird. Small, David, illus. (p. 516)
—Emperor & the Kite. Young, Ed, illus. (p. 520)
—Fairy Tale Breakfasts: A Cookbook for Young Readers & Eaters. Béha, Philippe, illus. (p. 564)
—Fairy Tale Desserts: A Cookbook for Young Readers & Eaters. Béha, Philippe, illus. (p. 564)
—Fairy Tale Dinners: A Cookbook for Young Readers & Eaters. Béha, Philippe, illus. (p. 564)
—Fairy Tale Lunches: A Cookbook for Young Readers & Eaters. Béha, Philippe, illus. (p. 564)
—Flying Witch. Vagin, Vladimir, illus. (p. 610)
—Foiled. (p. 611)
—Foiled. Cavallaro, Mike, illus. (p. 611)
—Friend: The Story of George Fox & the Quakers. (p. 637)
—Heart's Blood (p. 760)
—How Do Dinosaurs Clean Their Rooms? Teague, Mark, illus. (p. 806)
—How Do Dinosaurs Count to Ten? Teague, Mark, illus. (p. 806)
—How Do Dinosaurs Eat Cookies? Teague, Mark, illus. (p. 806)
—How Do Dinosaurs Eat Their Food? Teague, Mark, illus. (p. 806)
—How Do Dinosaurs Get Well Soon? Teague, Mark, illus. (p. 807)
—How Do Dinosaurs Go to School? Teague, Mark, illus. (p. 807)
—How Do Dinosaurs Laugh Out Loud? Teague, Mark, illus. (p. 807)
—How Do Dinosaurs Learn Their Colors? Teague, Mark, illus. (p. 807)
—How Do Dinosaurs Love Their Cats? Teague, Mark, illus. (p. 807)
—How Do Dinosaurs Play All Day? Teague, Mark, illus. (p. 807)
—How Do Dinosaurs Play with Their Friends? Teague, Mark, illus. (p. 807)
—How Do Dinosaurs Say Good Night? Teague, Mark, illus. (p. 807)
—How Do Dinosaurs Say Happy Birthday? Teague, Mark, illus. (p. 807)
—How Do Dinosaurs Say I'm Mad? Teague, Mark, illus. (p. 807)
—How Do Dinosaurs Say Merry Christmas? Teague, Mark, illus. (p. 807)
—How Do Dinosaurs Stay Safe? Teague, Mark, illus. (p. 807)
—Hush, Little Horsie. Sanderson, Ruth, illus. (p. 830)
—Johnny Appleseed: The Legend & the Truth. Burke, Jim, illus. (p. 923)
—Last Dragon. (p. 977)
—Lost Boy: The Story of the Man Who Created Peter Pan. Adams, Steve, illus. (p. 1055)
—Meow: Cat Stories from Around the World. (p. 1127)
—Mirror to Nature: Poems about Reflection. Stemple, Jason, photos by. (p. 1149)
—My Father Knows the Names of Things. Jorisch, Stéphane, illus. (p. 1203)
—Naming Liberty. Burke, Jim, illus. (p. 1228)
—On the Slant. Stemple, Jason, photos by. (p. 1291)
—Once upon Ice: And Other Frozen Poems. Stemple, Jason, photos by. (p. 1293)
—Owl Moon. (p. 1315)
—Plague of Unicorns. (p. 1366)
—Romping Monsters, Stomping Monsters. Murphy, Kelly, illus. (p. 1486)
—Scarecrow's Dance. Ibatoulline, Bagram, illus. (p. 1519)
—Sea Queens: Women Pirates Around the World. Pratt, Christine Joy, illus. (p. 1535)
—Seeing Stick. Terrazzini, Daniela Jaglenka, illus. (p. 1548)
—Self-Portrait with Seven Fingers. (p. 1549)
—Sending of Dragons Vol. 3. (p. 1550)
—Sing a Season Song. Ashlock, Lisel Jane, illus. (p. 1578)
—Sister Bear: A Norse Tale Linda, Graves & Graves, Linda, illus. (p. 1581)
—Snow in Summer. (p. 1599)
—Snow, Snow: Winter Poems for Children. Stemple, Jason, photos by. (p. 1599)
—Stone Angel. Green, Katie May, illus. (p. 1652)
—Stranded Whale. Cataldo, Melanie, illus. (p. 1664)
—Sword of the Rightful King: A Novel of King Arthur. (p. 1692)
—Touch Magic: Fantasy, Faerie & Folklore in the Literature of Childhood. (p. 1772)
—Trash Mountain. Monroe, Chris, illus. (p. 1780)
—Waking Dragons. Anderson, Derek, illus. (p. 1853)
—Water Music: Poems for Children. Stemple, Jason, photos by. (p. 1863)
—Wee Rhymes: Baby's First Poetry Book. Dyer, Jane, illus. (p. 1871)
—Where Have the Unicorns Gone? Sanderson, Ruth, illus. (p. 1907)
—Wizard's Hall. (p. 1943)
—Young Merlin Trilogy: Passager, Hobby, & Merlin. (p. 1979)
—¿Cómo Aprenden los Colores los Dinosaurios? Teague, Mark, illus. (p. 350)
—¿Cómo Comen los Dinosaurios? Teague, Mark, illus. (p. 350)
Yolen, Jane, jt. auth. see Harris, Robert.
Yolen, Jane, jt. auth. see Lewis, J. Patrick.
Yolen, Jane, jt. auth. see Stemple, Heidi E. Y.
Yolen, Jane & Dotlich, Rebecca Kai. Grumbles from the Forest: Fairy-Tale Voices with a Twist. Mahurin, Matt, illus. (p. 727)
Yolen, Jane & Harris, Robert J. Atalanta & the Arcadian Beast. (p. 111)
—Girl in a Cage. (p. 678)
Yolen, Jane & Hayden, Patrick Nielsen. Year's Best Science Fiction & Fantasy for Teens: First Annual Collection. (p. 1969)
Yolen, Jane & Scholastic, Inc. Staff. How Do Dinosaurs Say Good Night? (p. 807)
Yolen, Jane & Stemple, Adam. Hostage Prince. (p. 801)
—Last Changeling. (p. 977)
—Stone Cold. (p. 1652)
—Troll Bridge: A Rock 'n' Roll Fairy Tale. (p. 1788)
Yolen, Jane & Stemple, Heidi. You Nest Here with Me. Sweet, Melissa, illus. (p. 1976)
Yolen, Jane & Stemple, Heidi E. Y. Bad Girls: Sirens, Jezebels, Murderesses, Thieves & Other Female Villains. Guay, Rebecca, illus. (p. 131)
—Fairy Tale Feasts: A Literary Cookbook for Young Readers & Eaters. Beha, Philippe, illus. (p. 564)
—Jewish Fairy Tale Feasts: A Literary Cookbook. Shefrin, Sima Elizabeth, illus. (p. 917)
—Not All Princesses Dress in Pink. Lanquetin, Anne-Sophie, illus. (p. 1267)
—Pretty Princess Pig. Williams, Sam, illus. (p. 1398)
—Roanoke, the Lost Colony: An Unsolved Mystery from History. Roth, Roger, Sr., illus. (p. 1478)
—Salem Witch Trials: An Unsolved Mystery from History. Roth, Roger, Sr., illus. (p. 1504)
—Sleep, Black Bear, Sleep. Dyer, Brooke, illus. (p. 1588)
Yolen, Jane & Stemple, Heidi Elisabet Y. Sleep, Black Bear, Sleep. Dyer, Brooke, illus. (p. 1588)
Yolen, Jane & Stemple, Jason. Shape Me a Rhyme: Nature's Forms in Poetry. (p. 1560)
Yolen, Jane, ed. Xanadu. (p. 1967)
Yolen, Jane, et al. Barefoot Book Stories from the Ballet. Guay, Rebecca, illus. (p. 139)
Yolen, Jane, narrated by. How Do Dinosaurs Eat Their Food? (p. 807)
Yolleck, Joan. Paris in the Spring with Picasso. Priceman, Marjorie, illus. (p. 1324)
Yomtob, Andrea, illus. see Dunn-Dern, Lisa.
Yomtov, Nel. Adventures in Science. O'Neill, Sean et al, illus. (p. 15)
—Amelia Earhart Flies Across the Atlantic. (p. 58)
—Andrew Jackson: Heroic Leader or Cold-Hearted Ruler? (p. 72)
—Animal Traffickers. (p. 80)
—Apollo 11 Moon Landing: July 20 1969 (p. 91)
—Attack on Pearl Harbor: December 7 1941 (p. 114)
—Bambino: The Story of Babe Ruth's Legendary 1927 Season Foley, Tim, illus. (p. 135)
—Colin Kaepernick. (p. 339)
—Colombia. (p. 341)
—Costa Rica. (p. 368)
—Defend until Death! Nickolas Flux & the Battle of the Alamo Ginevra, Dante, illus. (p. 423)
—Edmund Hillary Reaches the Top of Everest. (p. 504)
—Epidemiologist. (p. 532)
—Ferdinand Magellan Sails Around the World. (p. 582)
—From African Plant to Vaccine Preservation. (p. 641)
—From Termite Den to Office Building. (p. 644)
—How to Write a Comic Book. Petelinsek, Kathleen, illus. (p. 822)
—How to Write a Fractured Fairy Tale. Petelinsek, Kathleen, illus. (p. 822)
—How to Write a Lab Report. Petelinsek, Kathleen, illus. (p. 822)
—How to Write a Memoir. Petelinsek, Kathleen, illus. (p. 822)
—John Brown: Defending the Innocent or Plotting Terror? (p. 921)
—Lewis & Clark Map the American West. (p. 1004)
—Navy Seals in Action. (p. 1238)
—Night of Rebellion! Nickolas Flux & the Boston Tea Party Ginevra, Dante, illus. (p. 1253)
—Revolutionary War Spies (p. 1467)
—Roald Amundsen Explores the South Pole. (p. 1477)
—Robert Griffin III. (p. 1479)
—Rocks & the People Who Love Them Foss, Timothy, illus. (p. 1483)
—Sarah Palin: Political Rebel D'Ottavi, Francesca, illus. (p. 1514)
—Starting Your Own Business. (p. 1644)
—Syria. (p. 1693)
—Transportation Planner. (p. 1779)
—True Stories of Survival. Chater, Mack et al, illus. (p. 1792)
—True Stories of the Civil War. Molinari, Carlo, illus. (p. 1793)
—True Stories of World War I. Proctor, Jon, illus. (p. 1793)
—When Volcanoes Erupt! O'Neill, Sean, illus. (p. 1905)
Yomtov, Nel, jt. auth. see McCollum, Sean.
Yomtov, Nel, jt. auth. see Pearl, Norman.
Yomtov, Nel & Biskup, Agnieszka. American Graphic Fall 2011. (p. 61)
Yomtov, Nel & Fuentes, Benny. Reality Check Sandoval, Gerardo, illus. (p. 1449)
Yomtov, Nel & Gunderson, Jessica. Perspectives on History. (p. 1344)
Yomtov, Nel, et al. 24-Hour History (p. 1996)
—Adventures in Science. O'Neill, Sean et al, illus. (p. 15)
—Classified. (p. 328)
—Jason & the Golden Fleece Sandoval, Gerardo, illus. (p. 910)
—Nickolas Flux History Chronicles Ginevra, Dante, illus. (p. 1251)
—Perspectives on History. (p. 1344)
—Stories of War. (p. 1655)
—Theseus & the Minotaur Smith, Tod G., illus. (p. 1732)
Yomtov, Nelson. Adrift & Alone: True Tales of Survival at Sea. (p. 13)
—Ancient Egypt. (p. 68)
—Bambino: The Story of Babe Ruth's Legendary 1927 Season Foley, Tim, illus. (p. 135)
—Courage on the Battlefield: True Tales of Survival in the Military. (p. 372)
—Grimy, Gross Unusual History of the Toilet (p. 724)
—Haiti. (p. 736)
—How to Write a Comic Book. Petelinsek, Kathleen, illus. (p. 822)
—Indonesia. (p. 872)
—Internet Inventors. (p. 880)
—Internet Security: From Concept to Consumer. (p. 880)
—Israel. (p. 893)
—Poachers. (p. 1374)
—Polar Ice Caps in Danger: Expedition to Antarctica. (p. 1379)
—Rocks & the People Who Love Them Foss, Timothy, illus. (p. 1483)
—Sarah Palin: Political Rebel D'Ottavi, Francesca, illus. (p. 1514)
—Scotland. (p. 1530)
—Secret American Treasures: From Hidden Vaults to Sunken Riches (p. 1540)
—Terrors from the Deep: True Tales of Surviving Shark Attacks. (p. 1722)
—Titanic Disaster! Nickolas Flux & the Sinking of the Great Ship. Simmons, Mark, illus. (p. 1758)
—Tracking an Assassin! Nickolas Flux & the Assassination of Abraham Lincoln Pinelli, Amerigo, illus. (p. 1775)
—Tracking Sea Monsters, Bigfoot, & Other Legendary Beasts (p. 1775)
—Trapped in Antarctica! Nickolas Flux & the Shackleton Expedition. Simmons, Mark, illus. (p. 1779)
—True Stories of the Civil War Molinari, Carlo, illus. (p. 1793)
—True Stories of World War I Proctor, Jon, illus. (p. 1793)
—United States & Mexico. (p. 1819)
—When Volcanoes Erupt! O'Neill, Sean, illus. (p. 1905)
Yomtov, Nelson & Rogers, Stillman. Russia. (p. 1498)
Yonavjak, Logan, jt. auth. see Schoch, Robert M.
Yonay, Rina, jt. auth. see Yonay, Shahar.
Yonay, Shahar & Yonay, Rina. Ha-Mikraah Sheli: Osef Kite Keriah Le-Talmidim Ba-Tefutsot: Kolel Targile Lashon U-Fituah Ha-Habah Ve-Havanat Ha-Nikra. (p. 734)
Yonce, Kelly. Good Grief Gumballs. (p. 698)
Yonck, Barbara. Candle Crafts. (p. 261)
Yonebayashi, Hiromasa & Miyazaki, Hayao. Secret World of Arrietty. (p. 1544)
—Secret World of Arrietty Picture Book. (p. 1544)
Yonetai, Takane. Make Love & Peace (p. 1079)
Yonetani, Takane. Make More Love & Peace (p. 1079)
Yonezu, Yusuke. We Love Each Other. (p. 1867)
Yong, Jui Lin, jt. auth. see Barlas, Robert.
Yong, Jui Lin, jt. auth. see Cooper, Robert.
Yong, Jui Lin, jt. auth. see Heale, Jay.
Yong, Jui Lin, jt. auth. see Jermyn, Leslie.
Yong, Jui Lin, jt. auth. see Sheehan, Sean.
Yong, Jui Lin, jt. auth. see Whyte, Mariam.
Yong, Tohmoh J., et al. Tune in CE2 Pupil's Book. (p. 1796)

—Tune in CE2 Pupil's Workbook. (p. 1796)
—Tune in CM1 Pupil's Book. (p. 1796)
—Tune in CM1 Pupil's Workbook. (p. 1796)
—Tune in CM2 Pupil's Book. (p. 1796)
—Tune in CM2 Pupil's Workbook. (p. 1796)
Yonge, Charles Duke, tr. see Judæus, Philo.
Yonge, Charlotte. Little Duke. (p. 1027)
Yonge, Charlotte M. Chosen People: A Compendium of Sacred & Church History for School-Children. (p. 311)
—Chosen People A Compendium of Sacred & Church History for School Children. (p. 311)
—Dove in the Eagle's Nest. (p. 473)
—Little Duke. (p. 1027)
—Little Lucy's Wonderful Globe. (p. 1031)
—Stokesley Secret. (p. 1651)
—Trial. (p. 1785)
—Young Folks' History of England. (p. 1978)
Yonge, Charlotte Mary. Aunt Charlotte's Roman History. (p. 115)
Yonikus, Sandi. Dominga's Wonderful Year/El Año Maravilloso del Domingo. Nelson, Annika, illus. (p. 465)
Yonts, Barbara, photos by see Hawkins, Linda J.
Yontz, Barbara J. Adventures of Baby Z & the Rabbit of Oz. (p. 16)
Yontz-Oetting, Carolyn. Black & White Animals Color the World. (p. 195)
—Black & White Animals Color the World. Scobie, Andrea, illus. (p. 195)
Yoo, David. Detention Club. (p. 431)
Yoo, Hajin. Totally Captivated (p. 1771)
Yoo, Jinha. Aegis (p. 25)
Yoo, Paula. Good Enough. (p. 698)
—Sixteen Years in Sixteen Seconds: The Sammy Lee Story Lee, Dom, illus. (p. 1583)
—Twenty-Two Cents: Muhammad Yunus & the Village Bank. Akib, Jamel, illus. (p. 1801)
Yoo, Paula & Wang, Lin. Shining Star: The Anna May Wong Story. (p. 1566)
Yoo, Tae-Eun. Little Red Fish. (p. 1034)
Yoo, Taeeun. You Are a Lion! & Other Fun Yoga Poses: And Other Fun Yoga Poses. Yoo, Taeeun, illus. (p. 1973)
Yoo, Taeeun, illus. see Bridges, Shirin Yim.
Yoo, Taeeun, illus. see Harris, R. P.
Yoo, Taeeun, illus. see Kanevsky, Polly.
Yoo, Taeeun, illus. see McGhee, Alison.
Yoo, Taeeun, illus. see Shannon, George.
Yoon, Ae-hae. Who Eats First? Cruise, ed. (p. 1915)
Yoon, Jae-Ho. In Dream World (p. 863)
—In Dream World Yoon, Jae-Ho, illus. (p. 863)
Yoon, Je Ho & Ghun, Oh Rhe Bar. Cafe Occult. (p. 251)
Yoon, JooHee. Beastly Verse. (p. 152)
Yoon, Jung-Huyn. Popposites: A Lift, Pull, & Pop Book of Opposites. (p. 1385)
Yoon, Nicola. Everything, Everything. (p. 544)
Yoon, Paul. At the Amusement Park: Everyday Science. (p. 110)
Yoon, Salina. At the Beach. (p. 110)
—At the Beach Mad Art. (p. 110)
—At the Park. (p. 111)
—Deep Sea Dive. (p. 423)
—Do Cows Meow? (p. 456)
—Do Crocs Kiss? (p. 456)
—Five Silly Turkeys. Yoon, Salina, illus. (p. 601)
—Five Trick-or-Treaters. (p. 601)
—Found. Yoon, Salina, illus. (p. 624)
—Humpty Dumpty. Yoon, Salina, illus. (p. 827)
—I Feel Happy. (p. 838)
—In the Ocean. (p. 867)
—It's Christmas Time! Yoon, Salina, illus. (p. 896)
—Jack & Jill: A Halloween Nursery Rhyme. Yoon, Salina, illus. (p. 902)
—Kaleidoscope. (p. 941)
—Monsters. (p. 1168)
—My Chanukah Playbook. Yoon, Salina, illus. (p. 1200)
—My First Menorah. Yoon, Salina, illus. (p. 1207)
—My Shimmery Christmas Book. (p. 1218)
—My Shining Star. (p. 1218)
—Old MacDonald Had a Farm. (p. 1284)
—One Halloween Night: A Spooky Seek-and-Count Book. (p. 1295)
—Opposnakes: A Lift-the-Flap Book about Opposites. Yoon, Salina, illus. (p. 1301)
—Peek-a-Boo Farm Animals. (p. 1334)
—Peek-a-Boo Wild Animals. (p. 1335)
—Penguin & Pinecone. (p. 1336)
—Penguin & Pinecone. Yoon, Salina, illus. (p. 1336)
—Penguin & Pumpkin. (p. 1336)
—Penguin Gets Dressed! Yoon, Salina, illus. (p. 1336)
—Penguin Gets Ready for Bed! Yoon, Salina, illus. (p. 1337)
—Penguin Goes to the Farm! Yoon, Salina, illus. (p. 1337)
—Penguin in Love. (p. 1337)
—Penguin in Love. Yoon, Salina, illus. (p. 1337)
—Penguin on Vacation. Yoon, Salina, illus. (p. 1337)
—Penguin's Big Adventure. (p. 1337)
—Pinwheel. (p. 1361)
—Pretend & Play: Firefighter. (p. 1398)
—Pretend & Play: on the Farm. (p. 1398)
—Pretend & Play: Toolbox. (p. 1398)
—Read & Play: in the Jungle. (p. 1442)
—Read & Play: on the Go. (p. 1442)
—Read & Play: under the Sea. (p. 1442)
—Space Walk. (p. 1620)
—Spring Things Mad Art. (p. 1635)
—Stacking Shapes. Yoon, Salina, illus. (p. 1638)
—Stormy Night. (p. 1656)
—Tap to Play! (p. 1705)
—Toys. Yoon, Salina, illus. (p. 1774)
—What Am I? Yoon, Salina, illus. (p. 1879)
—Where's Boo? (p. 1910)
—Where's Ellie? (p. 1910)
—Who Am I? Yoon, Salina, illus. (p. 1914)
—Who Do I See? (p. 1915)
—Wings: A Book to Touch & Feel. Yoon, Salina, illus. (p. 1936)
—Zoo. Yoon, Salina, illus. (p. 1988)
Yoon, Salina, illus. see Ellis, Libby.
Yoon, Salina, jt. auth. see Knudsen, Michelle.
Yoon, Salina, creator. Bug Buddies: A Sparkling Little Colors Book. (p. 236)
—Country Pals: A Sparkling Little Colors Book. (p. 372)
—Little Friends: A Sparkling Little Colors Book. (p. 1028)
—Sea Creatures: A Sparkling Little Colors Book. (p. 1534)
Yoon, Salina, ed. see Chan, Hingman.
Yoon, Seok, illus. see Han, Kakao.
Yoon, Seok, jt. auth. see Oh, Soo.
Yorinks, Adrienne. Quilt of States: Piecing Together America. Larson, Jeanette, ed. (p. 1428)
Yorinks, Adrienne, jt. auth. see Larson, Jeanette.
Yorinks, Arthur. Company's Going. (p. 351)
—Flappy & Scrappy. Ivanov, Aleksey & Ivanov, Olga, illus. (p. 602)
—Flappy & Scrappy. Ivanov, Olga & Ivanov, Aleksey, illus. (p. 602)
—Flying Latke. (p. 610)
—Harry & Lulu. (p. 750)
—Harry & Lulu. Matje, Martin, illus. (p. 750)
—Homework. Egielski, Richard, illus. (p. 794)
—Invisible Man. (p. 885)
—Invisible Man. Cushman, Doug, illus. (p. 885)
—Maurice Sendak's Seven Little Monsters: Hide & Seek. (p. 1110)
—Maurice Sendak's Seven Little Monsters: Take a Hike. (p. 1110)
—Mommy? Sendak, Maurice, illus. (p. 1162)
—Nose. (p. 1266)
—Witch's Child. Smith, Jos. A., illus. (p. 1941)
Yorinks, Arthur, et al. Company's Going. (p. 351)
York. Phonics (p. 1351)
York, Canaan A. Cement Sky. (p. 286)
—Denny Dares to Dream. (p. 426)
—Difference Is Jesus: A Transformational Tale. (p. 437)
York, Carol Beach. Takers & Returners: A Novel of Suspense. (p. 1697)
York, Christopher, jt. auth. see Blue Ox Technologies Ltd., Blue Ox.
York, Deborah Ward, illus. see Ward, Eva D.
York, J. Boy at the Dike: A Dutch Folktale. Freeman, Laura, illus. (p. 217)
—Camping. (p. 257)
—Canoeing. (p. 261)
—Casey Jones. Garland, Michael, illus. (p. 275)
—Chicken Little. Weidner, Teri, illus. (p. 300)
—Constellation Hercules: The Story of the Hero. Morrow, J. T., illus. (p. 359)
—Hiking. (p. 779)
—How Many Spots Does a Leopard Have? An African Folktale. Zunon, Elizabeth, illus. (p. 811)
—Johnny Appleseed. Garland, Michael, illus. (p. 923)
—Learn French Words. Petelinsek, Kathleen, illus. (p. 983)
—Learn German Words. Petelinsek, Kathleen, illus. (p. 983)
—Learn Japanese Words. Petelinsek, Kathleen, illus. (p. 983)
—Learn Mandarin Chinese Words. Petelinsek, Kathleen, illus. (p. 983)
—Learn Russian Words. Petelinsek, Kathleen, illus. (p. 983)
—Learn Spanish Words. Petelinsek, Kathleen, illus. (p. 983)
—Little Red Hen. Freeman, Laura, illus. (p. 1034)
—Pecos Bill. Garland, Michael, illus. (p. 1334)
—Rock Climbing. (p. 1482)
—Three Little Pigs. Close, Laura Ferraro, illus. (p. 1743)
York, Jamie. Making Math Meaningful: A 6th Grade. (p. 1081)
—Making Math Meaningful: A 7th Grade. (p. 1081)
—Making Math Meaningful: An 8th Grade. (p. 1081)
—Making Math Meaningful: A 7th Grade Student's Workbook. (p. 1081)
—Making Math Meaningful: An 8th Grade Student's Workbook. (p. 1081)
—Making Math Meaningful: A Middle School Math Curriculum for Teachers & Parents. (p. 1081)
York, John Randall. King Bronty in the Days of the Dinosaurs. (p. 958)
York Lumbard, Alexis. Angels. Weedn, Flavia, illus. (p. 75)
—Everyone Prays: Celebrating Faith Around the World. Sadeghian, Alireza, illus. (p. 544)
York, M. J. Henry Ford: Manufacturing Mogul. (p. 768)
—Montana. (p. 1170)
—Nebraska. (p. 1239)
—Nevada. (p. 1242)
—New Hampshire. (p. 1245)
—New Jersey. (p. 1245)
—North Dakota. (p. 1265)
—Oklahoma. (p. 1283)
—Oregon. (p. 1302)
York, Sadie. Sarena of Beca. (p. 1515)
York, Sarah, jt. auth. see Mountbatten-Windsor, Sarah.
York, Shane, illus. see Witte, Jessica Pierce.
York, Susanne, photos by see Kendall, Diane & Marsh, Merle.
Yorke, Francesca, jt. auth. see Grant, Amanda.
Yorke, Jane & Dorling Kindersley Publishing Staff. Colors & Shapes Touch & Feel Picture Cards. Thomson, Maria & Hester, Elizabeth, eds. (p. 345)
—First Words. Thomson, Maria & Hester, Elizabeth, eds. (p. 597)
—Letters. Harrison, Anna, ed. (p. 1002)
—My First Numbers & Counting: Touch & Feel Picture Cards. Thomson, Maria & Hester, Elizabeth, eds. (p. 1207)
Yorke, Malcolm. Casa de los Sustez. (p. 273)
Yorke, Peter & Batley, Alan. Tales from Fidgety Forest. (p. 1701)
Yorkey, Mike, jt. auth. see LeGrand, Eric.
Yorkey, Mike & Florea, Jesse. Linspired: The Jeremy Lin Story (p. 1019)
Yorks, Sharon Lene. Finals Bound. (p. 587)
Yoshi. Untitled Yoshi Picture Book. (p. 1823)
Yoshi, illus. see Clements, Andrew.
Yoshi, illus. see Jendresen, Erik & Villoldo, Alberto.
Yoshi, illus. see Wood, Douglas.
Yoshida, Agnes, tr. see Ohkami, Mineko.
Yoshida, Akimi. Banana Fish. Yoshida, Akimi, illus. (p. 135)
—Banana Fish (p. 136)
—Banana Fish. Yoshida, Akimi, illus. (p. 136)
Yoshida, Raiko, jt. auth. see Ikumi, Mia.
Yoshida, Reiko. Tokyo Mew Mew: Volume 3 (p. 1762)
—Tokyo Mew Mew Hiroe, Ikoi, tr. from JPN. (p. 1762)
Yoshida, Reiko, illus. see Ikumi, Mia.
Yoshida, Reiko, jt. auth. see Ikumi, Mia.
Yoshida, Reiko, jt. auth. see Ilkumi, Mia.
Yoshida, Sunao. Trinity Blood - Reborn on the Mars: The Iblis. Vol. 2 (p. 1786)
Yoshida, Tatsuo. Speed Racer: Mach Go Go Go Set (p. 1624)
Yoshida, Toshifumi, tr. see Akamatsu, Ken.
Yoshida, Yuko. How to Be Yourself in a World That's Different: An Asperger Syndrome Study Guide for Adolescents. Wing, Lorna, ed. (p. 815)
Yoshiike, Yoshitaka. Christmas Interview: Reporting Live from Bethlehem! Tsuchiya, Fujio, illus. (p. 314)
Yoshikawa, Eiji. Vagabond Yoshikawa, Eiji, illus. (p. 1830)
—Vagabond. Yoshikawa, Eiji, illus. (p. 1830)
Yoshikawa, Eiji & Inoue, Takehiko. Vagabond. Yoshikawa, Eiji & Inoue, Takehiko, illus. (p. 1830)
Yoshikawa, Sachiko. Boy from the Dragon Palace: A Folktale from Japan. (p. 218)
—Boy from the Dragon Palace. (p. 218)
Yoshikawa, Sachiko, illus. see Bagert, Brod.
Yoshikawa, Sachiko, illus. see Buzzeo, Toni.
Yoshikawa, Sachiko, illus. see Calmenson, Stephanie.
Yoshikawa, Sachiko, illus. see Cuyler, Margery.
Yoshikawa, Sachiko, illus. see Dotlich, Rebecca Kai.
Yoshikawa, Sachiko, illus. see Hopkins, Lee Bennett.
Yoshikawa, Sachiko, illus. see Loewen, Nancy.
Yoshikawa, Sachiko, illus. see Tomecek, Steve.
Yoshikawa, Sachiko, illus. see Walvoord, Linda.
Yoshikawa, Sachiko, illus. see Wojtusik, Elizabeth.
Yoshikawa, Sachiko, tr. see Walvoord, Linda.
Yoshikawa, Shizuko, jt. auth. see Purcell, Kerry William.
Yoshimoto, Ray, tr. see Murakami, Maki.
Yoshimoto, Ray, tr. from JPN. Gravitation Murakami, Maki, illus. (p. 712)
—One I Love: Watashi No Sukinahito. (p. 1295)
—Tokyo Babylon Clamp Staff, illus. (p. 1762)
Yoshimura, Takumi. Neon Genesis Evangelion: the Shinji Ikari Detective Diary Volume 1: The Shinji Ikari Detective Diary Volume 1. Horn, Carl Gustav, ed. (p. 1241)
Yoshinaga, Aya, jt. auth. see Monsho, Seikaino.
Yoshinaga, Fumi. Antique Bakery (p. 89)
Yoshinaga, Masayuki & Ishikawa, Katsuhiko. Gothic & Lolita. Suda, Shiho Kemp, tr. (p. 704)
Yoshinaka, Shoko, jt. auth. see Kanzaka, Hajime.
Yoshizaki, Mine. Sgt. Frog (p. 1556)
—Sgt. Frog Yoshizaki, Mine, illus. (p. 1556)
—Sgt. Frog Fukami, Yuko, tr. from JPN. (p. 1556)
—Sgt. Frog. (p. 1556)
—Sgt. Frog. Yoshizaki, Mine, illus. (p. 1556)
Yoshizaki, Mine, creator. Sgt. Frog (p. 1556)
Yoshizuma, Watara, jt. auth. see Yoshizumi, Wataru.
Yoshizumi, Carol, illus. see American Girl Editors.
Yoshizumi, Carol, illus. see Kauchak, Therese.
Yoshizumi, Wataru. Ultra Maniac Yoshizumi, Wataru, illus. (p. 1810)
—Ultra Maniac. Yoshizumi, Wataru, illus. (p. 1810)
Yoshizumi, Wataru & Yoshizuma, Watara. Ultra Maniac Yoshizumi, Wataru, illus. (p. 1810)
Yoskowitz, Lisa, ed. see Myracle, Lauren.
Yost, B. L. Have You Ever Seen a Wild Bird Dance? Perkins, Chelsea, illus. (p. 754)
Yost, Beth. Mysterious Sock Caper. (p. 1223)
Yost, Christopher. Marvel Universe Avengers Earth's Mightiest Comic Reader 4. Scherberger, Patrick & Wegener, Scott, illus. (p. 1099)
Yost-Filgate, Susan. Good Day for Abbey. Filgate, Leonard, illus. (p. 697)
—Jesse's Book of Colors. Filgate, Leonard, illus. (p. 914)
—Rip Squeak & Friends: the Adventure. Filgate, Leonard, illus. (p. 1473)
—Rip Squeak & His Friends. Filgate, Leonard, illus. (p. 1473)
—Rip Squeak's A to Z Book. Filgate, Leonard, illus. (p. 1473)
—Treasure: A Rip Squeak Book. Filgate, Leonard, illus. (p. 1781)
—Treasure. (p. 1781)
Yosuke, Kuroda. Scryed Yasunari, Toda, illus. (p. 1533)
You. My Biggest Secret. (p. 1197)
You, Lee Young. Kill Me, Kiss Me (p. 956)
Youcha, Geraldine. How Does an Elephant Say Hello? (p. 808)
Youd, Pauline. I Wonder . . . Books: Pack 1 Garvin, Elaine, illus. (p. 849)
—I Wonder . . . Books: Pack 2 Garvin, Elaine, illus. (p. 849)
Youd, Pauline, jt. auth. see Garwin, Elaine.
YouDae, Kim, illus. see InSeon, Chae.
Youell, Ray. Complete A-Z Travel & Leisure Handbook. (p. 352)
Youjun, Sun. Adventures of a Little Rag Doll. Shi, Lily L., tr. from CHI. (p. 16)
Younce, Eldon, jt. compiled by see Hayes, J. D.
Young, A. From Chicago to the Canyon (p. 642)
Young, Abby. Jupiter. (p. 937)
Young, Allen M., jt. auth. see Stewart, Melissa.
Young, Amy. Belinda, the Ballerina. (p. 162)
—Don't Eat the Baby! (p. 467)
—Mud Fairy. Young, Amy, illus. (p. 1188)
Young, Andrea. Finny & the Boy from Horse Mountain. (p. 589)
Young, Andrew. Giving Mother. (p. 681)
Young, Ann Eastman. Once Blue. (p. 1292)
Young, Annemarie. At the Park. Redshaw, Louise, illus. (p. 111)
—In the Garden. Redshaw, Louise, illus. (p. 866)
—Let's Go Out. Redshaw, Louise, illus. (p. 997)
—Our Castle Redshaw, Louise, illus. (p. 1308)
Young, Annemarie, jt. auth. see Robinson, Anthony.
Young, April. To Be a Warrior. (p. 1758)
Young, Aviance, illus. see Alexander, Sy.
Young, Ben & Adams, Samuel. 10 Commandments of Dating: Time-Tested Laws for Building Successful Relationships (p. 1993)
Young, Bennett H. Prehistoric Men of Kentucky a History of What is Known of Their Lives & Habits, Together with a Description of Their Implements & Other Relics. (p. 1395)
Young, Beryl. Follow the Elephant. (p. 612)
Young, Bev. Presidential Cookies. (p. 1397)
Young, Beverley, illus. see Dorion, Christiane.
Young, Bill, illus. see Paul, John.
Young, Bill, illus. see Rodhe, Paul & Wallas Reidy, Sarah.
Young, Billy. Teddy the Bear. (p. 1712)
Young, Blaike. Window of Opportunity. (p. 1936)
Young, Brett. Twontle. (p. 1804)
Young, Brian. Doubts about Creation? Not after This! (p. 473)
Young, Brian, jt. ed. see Whatmore, Richard.
Young, Bruce & Young, Jennifer Law. Rockbridge: A Photographic Essay. Wolfe, Andrew, ed. (p. 1482)
Young, Candace June. My Name Is Wes & My Mema Has Ms. (p. 1215)
Young, Carlton. From Home to Homeless to Success: Turning Hope into Possibilities. (p. 643)
Young, Carol. Animales del Mundo. (p. 81)
—Little Walrus Warning. Stuart, Walter, illus. (p. 1037)
Young, Caroline. Big Bug Search. (p. 180)
—Big Bug Search. Jackson, Ian, illus. (p. 180)
—Calligraphy: From Beginner to Expert. Lyon, Chris, illus. (p. 254)
—Diggers & Cranes. Lyon, Chris et al, illus. (p. 439)
—Great Animal Search. Jackson, Ian, illus. (p. 713)
—Grubby Finn Robinson. (p. 727)
—Guide to Potty Training Internet-Referenced. (p. 730)
—Tractors. Lyon, Chris & Gower, Teri, illus. (p. 1775)
Young, Caroline, jt. auth. see Townsend, Sue.
Young, Caroline & Brooks, Felicity. Usborne Very First Dictionary. Litchfield, Jo, illus. (p. 1827)
Young, Caroline & Castor, Harriet. Usborne Book of Machines That Work. Lyon, Chris, illus. (p. 1827)
Young, Caroline & Needham, Kate. Great Wildlife Search: Big Bug Search, Great Animal Search & Great Undersea Search. Jackson, Ian, illus. (p. 719)
Young, Caroline, et al, des. First Picture Word Book. (p. 596)
Young, Charles A. Tractors. (p. 1775)
Young, Charles A., jt. auth. see Claybourne, A.
Young, Chris. Boko & the Big Red Bag. (p. 208)
Young, Claiborne. Cruising Guide to Eastern Florida Nudelman, Edward, ed. (p. 386)
Young, Clare, jt. auth. see Youngs, Clare.
Young, Claudia H., jt. auth. see Maxson, H. A.
Young, Cleous. Magical Rug. (p. 1075)
—Prophetic Artist. (p. 1411)
Young, Clint, illus. see Kelly, Jacqueline & Grahame, Kenneth.
Young, Craig. Arrr Marks the Spot. (p. 101)
Young, Craig, illus. see Akinje, Wale.
Young, Cybèle. Few Bites (p. 583)
—Few Blocks. (p. 583)
—Nancy Knows. (p. 1229)
—Out the Window (p. 1311)
—Ten Birds. Young, Cybèle, illus. (p. 1718)
Young, Cybèle, illus. see Patton, Christopher.
Young, Cynthia Anne. Muddy Little Piggy's. (p. 1188)
Young, Dan. Life among the Inuit. (p. 1007)
Young, David, tr. see Montale, Eugenio.
Young, David E., et al. Cree Healer & His Medicine Bundle: Revelations of Indigenous Wisdom—Healing Plants, Practices, & Stories. (p. 380)
Young, Dawn. Abcs of Making Good Choices. Keaggy, Sarah, illus. (p. 4)
Young, Diana S. Daddy Doesn't Live with Me Anymore. (p. 398)
Young, Diane. See No Evil (p. 1546)
Young, Dot, illus. see Rives, J. G.
Young, Ed. House Baba Built: An Artist's Childhood in China. (p. 803)
—Know Fear: Facing Life's Six Most Common Phobias. (p. 965)
—Lon Po Po: A Red-Riding Hood Story from China. (p. 1046)
—Seven Blind Mice. Young, Ed, illus. (p. 1554)
—Should You Be a River: A Poem about Love. (p. 1570)
—Sons of the Dragon King: A Chinese Legend. Young, Ed, illus. (p. 1613)
—X-Trial: Akin' Life to the X-Treme, a Sudy of the Book of James. (p. 1967)
Young, Ed, illus. see Burleigh, Robert.
Young, Ed, illus. see Cheng, Andrea.
Young, Ed, illus. see Gollo, Gary.
Young, Ed, illus. see Grimes, Nikki.
Young, Ed, illus. see Gulberson, Brenda Z.
Young, Ed, illus. see Hillert, Margaret.
Young, Ed, illus. see Johnston, Tony.
Young, Ed, illus. see Kajikawa, Kimiko.
Young, Ed, illus. see Oppenheim, Shulamith.
Young, Ed, illus. see Ramsden, Ashley.
Young, Ed, illus. see Reibstein, Mark.
Young, Ed, illus. see Singer, Marilyn.
Young, Ed, illus. see Yolen, Jane.
Young, Ed & Adams, Tracey. Lost Horse: A Chinese Folktale. (p. 1055)
Young, Eileen Parrigin. Cousins & the Cave of Fire (p. 373)
Young, Eleanor Patmore, ed. Shakespeare for Young Actors. (p. 1559)
Young, Elizabeth. ed up Platypus. Seabrooks, Lydia, illus. (p. 503)
Young, Elizabeth L. Dozens & Dozens of Cousins & Cousins. Perkins, Ruth, illus. (p. 474)
Young, Ella. Celtic Wonder-Tales. Gonne, Maud, illus. (p. 286)
Young, Ellsworth, illus. see Babbitt, Ellen C.
Young, Ellsworth, jt. auth. see Babbitt, Ellen C.
Young, Emma. Israel. (p. 893)
Young, Emma, illus. see Morris, Ting.
Young, Eric, illus. see Bambara, Toni Cade.
Young, Eric, illus. see Temple, Teri & Temple, Emily.
Young, Eugene Randolph. Food Convention. (p. 613)
Young, Francis Kerr. Paperweight. Steele, Andrew & Clement, Devyn, illus. (p. 1323)
Young, Frank. Oregon Trail: The Road to Destiny. Lasky, David, illus. (p. 1303)

Young, Franklin. S P o T S. (p. 1499)
Young, Gary. More Than Two: Under the Sea. (p. 1175)
Young, Greg. Alfred Wegener: Pioneer of Plate Tectonics (p. 37)
—Alfred Wegener: Uncovering Plate Tectonics. (p. 37)
—Investigating Plate Tectonics. (p. 885)
—Plate Tectonics (p. 1370)
Young, Gregory P. What to Do If the Stork Didn't Leave Instructions. (p. 1894)
Young, H. M. (Hal). huskies & the christmas Fawn. (p. 830)
Young, Heather. Norman. (p. 1264)
Young, Helen Ann. Hellie & the Sensational Magic Carpet. Young, Tim, illus. (p. 763)
—Hello to Hellie's World. Young, Tim Blair, illus. (p. 765)
—Your World Discovery Scrapbook. Young, Tim Blair, illus. (p. 1981)
Young, Ian. Amazing Journeys: Following in History's Footsteps (p. 54)
—Lance Armstrong: Champion for Life! (p. 973)
—Lance Armstrong: Champion for Life! Set (p. 973)
Young, J. E. Horror in Space. Huddleston, Courtney, illus. (p. 799)
Young, Jackie, jt. auth. see Blakley Kinsler, Gwen.
Young, Jackie, jt. auth. see Young, Rachel.
Young, Jacob. Examining Earthquakes. (p. 547)
Young, James. Nico. (p. 1251)
Young, James, illus. see Salsi, Lynn.
Young, Jan. Starting the Colt. (p. 1644)
Young, Janet Ruth. Babysitter Murders. (p. 129)
—My Beautiful Failure. (p. 1196)
—Opposite of Music. (p. 1300)
—Things I Shouldn't Think. (p. 1733)
Young, Jay. Magic World of Learning. Tucker, Sian, illus. (p. 1074)
Young, Jay, creator. Amazing Magic Fact Machine. (p. 55)
—Secret Ziga Zaga. (p. 1544)
—Ziga Zaga. (p. 1986)
Young, Jeanna, jt. auth. see Johnson, Jacqueline Kinney.
Young, Jeanna & Johnson, Jacqueline. Princess Hope Sticker & Activity Book Aranda, Omar, illus. (p. 1404)
—Princess Joy Sticker & Activity Book Aranda, Omar, illus. (p. 1404)
Young, Jeanna & Johnson, Jacqueline Kinney. Princess Charity Sticker & Activity Book Aranda, Omar, illus. (p. 1403)
—Princess Faith Sticker & Activity Book Aranda, Omar, illus. (p. 1403)
—Princess Grace Sticker & Activity Book Aranda, Omar, illus. (p. 1404)
Young, Jeanna Stolle, jt. auth. see Johnson, Jacqueline.
Young, Jeanna Stolle & Johnson, Jacqueline. Princess Hope & the Hidden Treasure Aranda, Omar, illus. (p. 1404)
Young, Jeanna Stolle & Johnson, Jacqueline Kinney. Princess Grace & the Little Lost Kitten Aranda, Omar, illus. (p. 1404)
—Princess Joy's Birthday Blessing Aranda, Omar, illus. (p. 1404)
Young, Jeff. Shaun White. (p. 1563)
Young, Jeff C. Albert Pujols: A Baseball Star Who Cares. (p. 34)
—Amazing African-American Actors. (p. 52)
—Arnold Schwarzenegger. (p. 100)
—Belaying the Line: Mountain, Rock, & Ice Climbing. (p. 161)
—Bleeding Kansas & the Violent Clash over Slavery in the Heartland. (p. 199)
—Brilliant African-American Scientists: Nine Exceptional Lives. (p. 228)
—Burning up the Court - The Miami Heat. (p. 244)
—Cesar Chavez. (p. 288)
—Dropping the Flag: Auto Racing. (p. 486)
—Dwight D. Eisenhower: Soldier & President. (p. 491)
—Dwyane Wade. (p. 491)
—Great Communicator: The Story of Ronald Reagan. (p. 714)
—Grover Cleveland: A MyReportLinks. Com Book. (p. 725)
—Henry Ford: Genius Behind the Affordable Car. (p. 768)
—Henry Hudson: Discoverer of the Hudson River. (p. 768)
—Hernando de Soto: Spanish Conquistador in the Americas. (p. 772)
—Inspiring African-American Inventors: Nine Extraordinary Lives. (p. 878)
—James A. Garfield: A MyReportLinks.com Book. (p. 906)
—James Buchanan: A MyReportLinks.com Book. (p. 907)
—Joe Biden. (p. 920)
—Korean War: A MyReportLinks. Com Book. (p. 967)
—Leading the Pack: Dogsled Racing. (p. 982)
—Michelle Wie. (p. 1135)
—Motorcycles: The Ins & Outs of Superbikes, Choppers, & Other Motorcycles (p. 1180)
—Operation Iraqi Freedom: A MyReportLinks. Com Book. (p. 1300)
—Pheasant Hunting for Kids (p. 1350)
—Pony Express & Its Death-Defying Mail Carriers. (p. 1382)
—Pulling the Rip Cord: Skydiving. (p. 1416)
—Running the Rapids: White-Water Rafting, Canoeing, & Kayaking. (p. 1497)
—Shooting the Curl: Surfing. (p. 1568)
—Trucks: The Ins & Outs of Monster Trucks, Semis, Pickups, & Other Trucks (p. 1791)
—True Underground Rescue Stories. (p. 1793)
—Yao Ming: Basketball's Big Man. (p. 1968)
Young, Jeff C., et al. Into the Great Outdoors. (p. 881)
Young, Jennifer, jt. auth. see Akselrad, January.
Young, Jennifer Hayman. Aliens, Eh ! (p. 41)
Young, Jennifer Law, jt. auth. see Young, Bruce.
Young, Jessica. Art-Rageous. Secheret, Jessica, illus. (p. 103)
—Finley Flowers. (p. 589)
—My Blue Is Happy. Chien, Catia, illus. (p. 1198)
—Nature Calls. Secheret, Jessica, illus. (p. 1236)
—New & Improved. Secheret, Jessica, illus. (p. 1243)
—Original Recipe. Secheret, Jessica, illus. (p. 1304)
—Spy Guy: The Not-So-Secret Agent. Santoso, Charles, illus. (p. 1636)
Young, Jessie Johnson. Young at Heart - Poems & Stories. (p. 1978)
Young, Jim, jt. auth. see Hardy, Ed.
Young, Joyce L. Don't Step on the Gum. (p. 468)
Young, Judy. Book for Black-Eyed Susan. Ettlinger, Doris, illus. (p. 210)
—Digger & Daisy Go on a Picnic. Sullivan, Dana, illus. (p. 438)
—Digger & Daisy Go to the Doctor. Sullivan, Dana, illus. (p. 438)
—Digger & Daisy Go to the Zoo. (p. 438)
—H Is for Hook: A Fishing Alphabet. Palmer, Gary, illus. (p. 734)
—Hidden Bestiary of Marvelous, Mysterious, & (Maybe Even) Magical Creatures. Filippucci, Laura Francesca, illus. (p. 775)
—Lazy Days of Summer. O'Malley, Kathy, illus. (p. 981)
—Lucky Star. Ellison, Chris, illus. (p. 1063)
—Minnow & Rose: An Oregon Trail Story. Farnsworth, Bill, illus. (p. 1148)
—Pet for Miss Wright. Wesson, Andrea, illus. (p. 1345)
—R Is for Rhyme: A Poetry Alphabet. Juhasz, Victor, illus. (p. 1429)
—Show Me the Number: A Missouri Number Book. Young, Ross, illus. (p. 1570)
—Tuki & Moka: A Tale of Two Tamarins. Madsen, Jim, illus. (p. 1796)
Young, Judy, jt. auth. see Scillian, Devin.
Young, Judy & A12. R Is for Rhyme: A Poetry Alphabet. Juhasz, Victor, illus. (p. 1429)
Young, Judy & Sullivan, Dana. Digger & Daisy Go to the City. (p. 438)
Young, Judy & Wargin, Kathy-jo. Little Missouri. Urban, Helle, illus. (p. 1032)
Young, Judy D., jt. auth. see Young, Richard.
Young, Judy D. & Young, Richard, eds. Outlaw Tales: Legends, Myths, & Folklore from America's Middle Border. (p. 1312)
Young, Judy Dockrey. Missouri Reader. Darnell, Kate, illus. (p. 1154)
Young, Judy Dockrey, jt. auth. see Dockrey Young, Richard.
Young, Julie. Defeat of Gullveig: Dragon Cliff Trilogy, Book Three. (p. 423)
—Dragon Stone: Dragon Cliff Trilogy Book Two. (p. 478)
Young, June. Energy Is Everywhere. (p. 528)
—Look How It Changes! (p. 1049)
Young, Justin. Most Vivid Day! (p. 1177)
Young, Karen. Chimpanzee Tale. (p. 306)
Young, Karen, jt. auth. see Reilly, Carmel.
Young, Karen Romano. Across the Wide Ocean: The Why, How, & Where of Navigation for Humans & Animals at Sea. Young, Karen Romano, illus. (p. 9)
—Bug Science: 20 Projects & Experiments about Arthropods - Insects, Arachnids, Algae, Worms, & Other Small Creatures. Goldin, David, illus. (p. 236)
—Bug Science. Goldin, David, illus. (p. 236)
—Cobwebs. (p. 337)
—Crime Scene Science. Goldin, David, illus. (p. 382)
—Doodlebug: A Novel in Doodles. (p. 469)
—Experiments to Do on Your Family. Goldin, David, illus. (p. 549)
—Junkyard Science. Goldin, David, illus. (p. 936)
—National Geographic Kids Mission: Sea Turtle Rescue: All about Sea Turtles & How to Save Them. (p. 1232)
—Space Junk: The Dangers of Polluting Earth's Orbit. (p. 1619)
—Stuck in the Middle (of Middle School) A Novel in Doodles. (p. 1668)
—Try This! 50 Fun Experiments for the Mad Scientist in You. Rakola, Matthew, photos by. (p. 1794)
Young, Karen Romano & Morgan, Pau. Blast off! Doodle Book. Morgan, Pau, illus. (p. 198)
Young, Katharine Anne. Grandmother Moon & Roy G Biv: A Colorful Bedtime Story for All Ages. EXPLORE the AMAZING SECRETS of COLOR. (p. 709)
Young, Kathy Chase. Gift. (p. 675)
Young, Kimberly Rich. Horse Is a Horse. (p. 799)
Young, Kirk. Chronicles of His Excellency: Almost-an-Eighth-of-a-Memoir. (p. 317)
Young, Kristi. Secret Club - the Powder Puff Club Book 1. (p. 1540)
Young, Larry. Astronauts in Trouble. (p. 109)
—Master Flight Plan. (p. 1103)
—Planet of the Capes. (p. 1367)
—Proof of Concept. (p. 1411)
Young, Laura. We Honor America. (p. 1867)
Young, Lauren. Ally M. & Ally G. Rooney, Sandra, illus. (p. 48)
Young, Laurie. I See a Monster! Mahoney, Daniel J., illus. (p. 845)
—I See a Monster! Mahoney, Daniel J. & Mahoney, Daniel, illus. (p. 845)
Young, Lena. Karma: Reaping What We Sow. Tsai, Dora, illus. (p. 944)
—One World Healing. Tsai, Dora, illus. (p. 1297)
Young, Lesley. Storyteller Book - Red Riding Hood. Williams, Jenny, illus. (p. 1663)
—Storyteller Book Sleeping Beauty. Press, Jenny, illus. (p. 1663)
Young, Lesley, retold by. Children's Treasury of Tales. (p. 304)
Young, Leslie. Plaid: A Tale of Compassion. (p. 1366)
Young, Linda P. Adventures of Anna & Andy Hummingbird: Anna & Andy Meet the Grandchildren, Book 3 Stories 11, 12 And 13. (p. 16)
—Adventures of Anna & Andy Hummingbird. (p. 16)
Young, Louise. Penguin Comes Home. Elmore, Larry, illus. (p. 1336)
Young, Louise O. Penguin Comes Home. Elmore, Larry, illus. (p. 1336)
Young, Louise O. & Elmore, Larry. Penguin Comes Home. (p. 1336)
Young, Lucie. Eva Zeisel. Bartolucci, Marisa & Cabra, Raul, eds. (p. 540)
Young, Lynn. Adventures with Looka (p. 25)
Young, Margie. April & Beagle One Monday Morning. (p. 93)
Young, Mariabelle & Buchwald, Ann. White Gloves & Party Manners. Christiane, illus. (p. 1913)
Young, Marilyn B., et al. Vietnam War: A History in Documents. (p. 1841)
Young, Marlene Lauster. Before Summer's End. (p. 158)
Young, Martha & McQuilkin, John A. Legend of the Land of Caelumen (p. 989)
Young, Mary. Nos Gusta Vivir Verde= We Like to Live Green. Parker, Zachary, illus. (p. 1266)
—We Like to Live Green. Parker, Zachary, illus. (p. 1867)
—We Like to Nurse Too. Parker, Zac, illus. (p. 1867)
Young, Mary, illus. see Wetterer, Margaret K. & Wetterer, Charles M.
Young, Mary & Parker, Zac. Tambian a Nosotros Nos Gusta Amamantar: We Like to Nurse Too. (p. 1704)
Young, Mary Beth. Christ's Passion: The Way of the Cross; A Guide to Understanding Your Path. Barone, Mark, illus. (p. 317)
Young, Mary O'Keefe, illus. see Anderson, R. P., et al.
Young, Mary O'Keefe, illus. see Capucilli, Alyssa Satin.
Young, Mary O'Keefe, illus. see Fishman, Cathy Goldberg.
Young, Mary O'Keefe, illus. see Rey, H. A.
Young, Mary O'Keefe, illus. see Rey, H. A., et al.
Young, Mary O'Keefe, illus. see Wetterer, Margaret K. & Wetterer, Charles M.
Young, Melanie. Fearless Fabulous You! (p. 579)
Young, Michael. Portrait of a Mother. (p. 1386)
Young, Miriam. Miss Suzy. Lobel, Arnold, illus. (p. 1152)
Young, Mitch. Terrorist Leaders. (p. 1722)
Young, Mitch & Engdahl, Sylvia. Religious Liberty. (p. 1458)
Young, Mitchell. Culture Wars. (p. 391)
—For-Profit Education. (p. 616)
—Government Spending. (p. 704)
—Islam. Szumski, Bonnie & Cothran, Helen, eds. (p. 891)
—Political Corruption. (p. 1380)
Young, Mitchell, ed. For-Profit Education. (p. 616)
—Scientific Revolution. (p. 1528)
Young, Moira. Blood Red Road. (p. 200)
—Blood Red Road. (p. 200)
—Raging Star. (p. 1433)
—Rebel Heart. (p. 1450)
Young, Ned. Zoomer. Young, Ned, illus. (p. 1989)
—Zoomer's Out-of-This-World Christmas. Young, Ned, illus. (p. 1989)
—Zoomer's Summer Snowstorm. Young, Ned, illus. (p. 1989)
Young, Ned, illus. see Swenson, Jamie A.
Young Noh, Mi. Threads of Time (p. 1741)
Young Noh, Mi, illus. see Hong, Jihae, tr.
Young, Norene. Cathy, the Castaway Cat. Woodyard, Sandy Lilly, illus. (p. 280)
Young, Norman. Christmas Story. (p. 315)
—Story of Jesus for Young Children. (p. 1658)
Young, Norman, illus. see Amery, Heather.
Young, Norman, illus. see Castor, Harriet.
Young, Norman, illus. see Dickins, Rosie & Pratt, Leonie.
Young, Norman, illus. see Edom, Helen & Osborne, Mike.
Young, Owen. Our Camping Trip: Subtract Within 20. (p. 1308)
Young, Paige. Homework Dilemm. (p. 794)
Young, Patricia A. Holy Monks of Mt. Athos. Young, Patricia A., illus. (p. 791)
Young, Patrick. Old Abe, Eagle Hero: The Civil War's Most Famous Mascot. Lee, Anne, illus. (p. 1283)
Young, Patty. Playful Designs Coloring Book. (p. 1372)
Young, Paul, illus. see McQuinn, Anna.
Young, Pershail Catherine. Rusty & Mr. Earlie. (p. 1498)
Young, Phil. Best Book on Northern Brown Snakes. (p. 168)
Young, Pippa. On the Farm. (p. 1290)
Young, Polly G. Pokey Pig's Picnic. Raymond, Janet Y., illus. (p. 1378)
Young, Rachel & Young, Jackie. Tale of Squabbit. Lynch, Stephanie, illus. (p. 1700)
Young, Rae. Drawing Appaloosas & Other Handsome Horses Q2AMedia Services Private Ltd, Q2AMedia Services, illus. (p. 481)
—Drawing Arabians & Other Amazing Horses Q2AMedia Services Private Ltd, Q2AMedia Services, illus. (p. 481)
—Drawing Barrel Racers & Other Speedy Horses Q2AMedia Services Private Ltd, Q2AMedia Services, illus. (p. 481)
—Drawing Friesians & Other Beautiful Horses Q2AMedia Services Private Ltd, Q2AMedia Services, illus. (p. 481)
—Drawing Horses Q2AMedia Services Private Ltd, Q2AMedia Services, illus. (p. 482)
—Drawing Mustangs & Other Wild Horses Q2AMedia Services Private Ltd, Q2AMedia Services, illus. (p. 482)
—Drawing Thoroughbreds & Other Elegant Horses Q2AMedia Services Private Ltd, Q2AMedia Services, illus. (p. 482)
—Ultimate Guide to Drawing Horses Q2AMedia Services Private Ltd Staff, illus. (p. 1809)
Young, Rebecca. 100 Great Monologs: A Versatile Collection of Monologs, Duologs & Triologs for Student Actors (p. 1998)
—101 Monologues for Middle Grades: Including Duologues & Triologues (p. 1999)
—102 Great Monologues: A versatile collection of monologues & duologues for student Actors (p. 2000)
—Watch Me Go! 8 Amazing Moving Pictures! Glitschka, Von, illus. (p. 1861)
—Watch Me Hop! 8 Amazing Moving Pictures! Glitschka, Von, illus. (p. 1861)
Young, Rebecca & Accord Publishing Staff. Hop, Pop, & Play: A Mini Animotion Book. (p. 796)
Young, Richard, jt. ed. see Young, Judy D.
Young, Richard & Dockrey Young, Judy. Favorite Scary Stories of American Children. Bell, Don, illus. (p. 578)
Young, Richard & Young, Judy D. African-American Folktales. (p. 27)
—Scary Story Reader. (p. 1521)
Young, Robert. One Star Hotel: A Christmas Story. (p. 1297)
Young, Ronald L. Divorce & Remarriage: Light from the Word. (p. 455)
Young, Ross, illus. see Young, Judy.
Young, Ruth. Aunty Marmalade. (p. 116)
Young, Samantha. I Can't Wait. (p. 837)
Young, Sandra M. Daniel, the Little Red Squirrel: Learns His Lessons. (p. 405)
Young, Sarah. Gasparilla's Key & the Revenge of the Purple Mermaid. (p. 657)
—Jesus Calling: 365 Devotions for Kids. (p. 915)
—Jesus Calling - 365 Devotions for Kids (p. 915)
—Jesus Calling for Little Ones (p. 915)
Young, Sarah, illus. see Turnbull, Ann.
Young, Sarah & Candlewick Press Staff. Endangered Animals: a 3D Pocket Guide. Young, Sarah, illus. (p. 526)
—Ocean Creatures: a 3D Pocket Guide. Young, Sarah, illus. (p. 1276)
Young, Sayre Van, see Van Young, Sayre.
Young, Scott Alexander. Wild Cats of Piran. Christe, Moreno, illus. (p. 1929)
Young Scribes Staff. Unlock the Secrets of Exeter: The Young Scribes of Exeter, NH. (p. 1821)
Young, Selina, illus. see French, Vivian.
Young, Serinity. Buddhism. (p. 234)
—Hinduism. (p. 780)
—Richard Francis Burton: Explorer, Scholar, Spy. (p. 1469)
Young, Shane, photos by see Gardner, Carol.
Young, Shelley. Doc Broc's Cave Adventure. Young, Shelley, illus. (p. 459)
Young, Skott, illus. see Andrews, Kaare.
Young, Skottie. Oz: The Marvelous Land of Oz. (p. 1316)
—Oz: The Wonderful Wizard of Oz. (p. 1316)
—Ozma of Oz. (p. 1316)
Young, Skottie, illus. see Connolly, MarcyKate.
Young, Skottie, illus. see Gaiman, Neil.
Young, Skottie, illus. see Kesel, Karl.
Young, Skottie, illus. see Shanower, Eric & Baum, L. Frank.
Young, Steve. 15 Minutes. (p. 1995)
—Winchell Mink: The Misadventure Begins. (p. 1935)
Young, Steve, illus. see Karwowski, Chris & Serwacki, Anita.
Young, Steve, illus. see Karwowski, Chris, et al.
Young, Steve, illus. see Karwowski, Chris.
Young, Steve, jt. auth. see Gentner, Norma L.
Young, Steven H., jt. auth. see Parsons, Marcella.
Young, Steven Hayes, jt. auth. see Parsons, Marcella.
Young, Sue, illus. see Ayers, Sanda.
Young, Sunshine. Mother Earth's ABC. (p. 1177)
Young, Susan. Music 3-5. (p. 1193)
Young, Susan, illus. see Barton, Brittney B.
Young, Suzanne. Need So Beautiful. (p. 1239)
—Program. (p. 1410)
—Remedy. (p. 1459)
—So Many Boys. (p. 1602)
—Treatment. (p. 1783)
Young, Suzanne, jt. auth. see Patrick, Cat.
Young, Suzanne Marie. Dedication to Free Spirit. (p. 422)
Young, T. M. My Ten Cents. Victoria Washington and Carla Watts, ed. (p. 1220)
—Playing Church. Washington, Victoria, ed. (p. 1372)
—What's Love Got to Do with It. Vickie Washington and Carla Watts, ed. (p. 1898)
Young, Tim, illus. see Young, Helen Ann.
Young, Tim Blair, illus. see Young, Helen Ann.
Young, Timothy. Angry Little Puffin (p. 75)
—I Hate Picture Books! (p. 839)
—Shadows on My Wall (p. 1558)
—They're Coming! (p. 1732)
Young, Timothy & Gralla, Howard. Drawn to Enchant: Original Children's Book Art in the Betsy Beinecke Shirley Collection. (p. 482)
Young, Tonya. Here's to the Nights. (p. 771)
Young, Valerie. Adventures of Todd & Friends. (p. 24)
Young, Wanda. Joyous Poems for Children. (p. 930)
Young, Wendy. Amazing Miss Amanda. (p. 55)
Youngberg, Gail, ed. see Holmlund, Mona.
Youngberg, Norma, jt. auth. see Kreye, Eric.
Youngberg, Norma R. Jungle Thorn. (p. 935)
—Singer on the Sand: The True Story of an Occurance on the Island of Great Sangir, North of the Celebes, More Than a Hundred Years Ago. (p. 1579)
Youngberg, Yvette M. Tooting Squirrel. (p. 1768)
Youngblood, Carol, illus. see Payne, Helen.
Youngblood, David W., illus. see Nicol, Scott Thomas.
Youngblood, Wayne. Mark Twain along the Mississippi. (p. 1095)
Youngbluth, Chris, illus. see Reardon, John.
Younge, Cathy. Tale of Sidney Elderberry - an Ordinary Boy with Extraordinary Bowels. Taylor, Mark, illus. (p. 1700)
Younge, Jewel Sophia, creator. Pg-13. (p. 1349)
Younger, Barbara. Purple Mountain Majesties: The Story of Katharine Lee Bates & America the Beautiful. Schuett, Stacey, illus. (p. 1419)
Younger, Barbara, jt. auth. see Flinn, Lisa.
Younger, Barbara & Flinn, Lisa. Easter A to Z: Every Letter Tells a Story. (p. 499)
—Good News Travels Fast! (p. 699)
Younger, David. Mysterious Moat Maiden: A Wandering Firefly Fairy Adventure (p. 1223)
—Spanky, the Brave Space Mouse (p. 1622)
Younger, Marshal, jt. auth. see Hering, Marianne.
Younger, Mary. You're Not A Ladybird You've Got No Spots. (p. 1982)
Youngerman, Barry. Pandemics & Global Health. (p. 1321)
Youngerman, Barry, jt. auth. see Wahab, Shaista.
Youngling, Meagan. New Life, My Pet's Adoption. (p. 1246)
Youngman, Jenny. CIC for Older Youth & Young Adults: Prayer: the Heart of the Pilgrimage. (p. 318)
Youngquist, D. M. Ghosts of Interstate 80. (p. 672)
Youngquist, Jeff, ed. see Bendis, Brian Michael.
Youngquist, Jeff, ed. see Busiek, Kurt.
Youngquist, Jeff, ed. see David, Peter.
Youngquist, Jeff, ed. see Jones, Bruce.
Youngquist, Jeff, ed. see Lee, Stan, et al.
Youngquist, Jeff, ed. see Starlin, Jim.
Youngquist, Jeff, ed. see Straczynski, J. Michael.
Youngquist, Jeff, ed. see Tieri, Frank.
Youngquist, Jeff, ed. If Looks Could Kill Brooks, Mark & Zircher, Patrick, illus. (p. 853)

—New Mutants. Finch, David, illus. (p. 1246)
—Ultimate Fantastic Four - The Fantastic Kubert, Adam, illus. (p. 1809)
—Ultimate Six Bagley, Mark, illus. (p. 1810)
—Wolverine: The End Castellini, Claudio, illus. (p. 1944)
Young-Robinson, Christine. Chicken Wing (p. 300)
Youngs, Bettie B. Living the Ten Commandments in New Times: A Book for Teens. (p. 1041)
Youngs, Bettie B., et al. 365 Days of Taste-Berry Inspiration for Teens. (p. 2001)
—Taste Berries for Teens #4: Short Stories & Encouragement on Being Cool, Caring & Courageous. (p. 1707)
Youngs, C. R. David: Prince of Israel. (p. 410)
Youngs, Clare, jt. auth. see Woram, Catherine.
Youngs, Clare & Young, Clare. Explorar y Crear. (p. 550)
Youngs, Kendahl Brooke. Kendahl Gets a Puppy. (p. 948)
Youngs, Puma Wun. Dreamtime. (p. 484)
Young-You, Lee. Moon Boy Im, HyeYoung, tr. from KOR. (p. 1172)
Younie, Bradford. Now Playing: Roleplaying in Every TV Genre (p. 1269)
Yount, David, jt. auth. see DeKock, Paul.
Yount, Lisa. Animal Rights. (p. 79)
—Antoine Lavoisier: Genius of Modern Chemistry. (p. 89)
—Antoine Lavoisier: Founder of Modern Chemistry. (p. 89)
—Antoni Van Leeuwenhoek: First to See Microscopic Life. (p. 90)
—Antoni Van Leeuwenhoek: Genius Discoverer of Microscopic Life. (p. 90)
—Craig Venter. (p. 376)
—Edward Pickering & His Women Computers. (p. 505)
—Energy Supply. (p. 528)
—Father of Anatomy: Galen & His Dissections. (p. 577)
—Forensic Science: From Fibers to Fingerprints. (p. 617)
—How Can Domestic Violence Be Prevented? (p. 805)
—Luc Montagnier. (p. 1062)
—Modern Genetics: Engineering Life. (p. 1158)
—Modern Marine Science: Exploring the Deep. (p. 1158)
—Nikola Tesla. (p. 1255)
—Right to Die & Euthanasia. (p. 1472)
—Rosalind Franklin. (p. 1489)
—William Harvey: Discoverer of How Blood Circulates. (p. 1933)
—William Harvey: Genius Discoverer of Blood Circulation. (p. 1933)
Yount, Lisa, ed. Does the Internet Increase the Risk of Crime? (p. 460)
Youree, Barbara. Senegal Sleuths. (p. 1550)
Yourell, Pam, illus. see Jones, Sandy.
Yourgrau, Barry. Another Nastybook: The Curse of the Tweeties. DeJesus, Robert, illus. (p. 88)
—Nasty Book. (p. 1230)
—NASTYbook. (p. 1230)
—Nastybook. (p. 1230)
Yousafzai, Malala. I Am Malala: How One Girl Stood up for Education & Changed the World. (p. 833)
—Malala: Mi historia. (p. 1083)
Youso, Justin, illus. see McNutt, Nan.
Youssef, Jagger. Making Bar Graphs. (p. 1080)
Youth Communication. My Secret Addiction: Teens Write about Cutting. Desetta, Al, ed. (p. 1218)
—Out with It: Gay & Straight Teens Write about Homosexuality. Desetta, Al, ed. (p. 1312)
—Rage: True Stories by Teens about Anger. Longhine, Laura & Vanderberg, Hope, eds. (p. 1433)
—Sticks & Stones: Teens Write about Bullying. Vanderberg, Hope, ed. (p. 1650)
Youth of the Achuar Tribe of Ecuador, illus. see Mayaprua, Alejandro Taish.
Youth Specialties Staff. Biblia G3 de Crecimiento Juvenil NVI (p. 176)
Youtsey, Scott, illus. see Oguneye, Kunle.
Youzhi, He, illus. see Ma, Zheng & Li, Zheng.
Yovanoff, Brenna. Fiendish. (p. 584)
—Paper Valentine. (p. 1323)
—Replacement. (p. 1461)
—Space Between. (p. 1618)
Yovanoff, Brenna, et al. Curiosities: A Collection of Stories. (p. 392)
Yoxen, Jackie. Hannah's Sunday Hats. Francis, Lauren, illus. (p. 743)
YoYo. Forms, Colors, & Opposites. (p. 620)
Yoyo. Learning Words. (p. 986)
—Ready for School. (p. 1447)
—Toddler's First Puzzle Fun—Blue. (p. 1761)
—Toddler's First Puzzle Fun—Green. (p. 1761)
—Toddler's First Puzzle Fun—Red. (p. 1761)
—Toddler's First Puzzle Fun—Yellow. (p. 1761)
Yoyo Books, creator. Baby Animals. (p. 124)
—Farm Animals. (p. 573)
—Numbers. (p. 1272)
—Pets. (p. 1348)
—Vroom. (p. 1851)
—Wild Animals. (p. 1928)
Yoyo Books Staff. ABC: Mini Baby's First Library. (p. 3)
—Animals: Mini Baby's First Library. (p. 81)
—Animals Around Me: Animal Jigsaw Fun. (p. 82)
—At Home: One Minute Goodnight Stories. (p. 110)
—At School: One Minute Goodnight Stories. (p. 110)
—At the Circus: Learning Words Series. (p. 111)
—Baby Animals: Animal Jigsaw Fun. (p. 124)
—Bedtime: Learning Words Series. (p. 156)
—Exciting Day Trip: Princess Charlotte's Picture Puzzles. (p. 547)
—Fantasy Stories: One Minute Goodnight Stories. (p. 572)
—Farm Animals: Animal Jigsaw Fun. (p. 573)
—Food: Mini Baby's First Library. (p. 612)
—Magic Gift: Princess Charlotte's Picture Puzzles. (p. 1072)
—Numbers: Mini Baby's First Library. (p. 1272)
—On the Farm: Learning Words Series. (p. 1290)
—On the Farm: One Minute Goodnight Stories. (p. 1290)
—Princess Charlotte Becomes a Magician. (p. 1403)
—Princess Charlotte's Journey Through History. (p. 1403)
—We are Tigers. (p. 1866)
—Wild Animals: Animal Jigsaw Fun. (p. 1928)
—Words: Mini Baby's First Library. (p. 1951)
Yoyo Books Staff, creator. Maxi Peekaboo Learning to Count. (p. 1112)
Yo-Yo Books, Yo-Yo. Super Easy Coloring — Blue. (p. 1680)
—Super Easy Coloring — Yellow. (p. 1680)
Yrjana, Colleen. Carry Me to Kinshasa Our Adoption Journey. Ulrich, Kelly, illus. (p. 271)
Ysseldyke, Jim, jt. auth. see Algozzine, Bob.
Ytak, Cathy & Abier, Gilles. Nothing but Your Skin & the Pool Was Empty. (p. 1268)
Ytearie Milliona Devalt. Princess Million: All about Me & Activity Book. (p. 1404)
Ytreeide, Arnold. Amon's Adventure: A Family Story for Easter (p. 65)
—Bartholomew's Passage. (p. 140)
—Ishtar's Odyssey: A Storybook for Advent (p. 891)
—Jotham's Journey. (p. 927)
—Tabitha's Travels: A Family Story for Advent (p. 1694)
—Tabitha's Travels: A Family Story for Advent. (p. 1694)
Yu, Bin. Government of China. (p. 704)
—Government of China. Wang, Jianwei, ed. (p. 704)
Yu, Chao, illus. see Bennett, Lorna & Galat, Joan Marie.
Yu, Chao, illus. see Cook, Gerri.
Yu, Chao, illus. see Galat, Joan Marie.
Yu, Chun. Little Green: Growing up During the Chinese Cultural Revolution. (p. 1028)
Yu, Jennifer. Talking Flower Garden: A Series of Ricky's Secret Friends Wu, Yoken, illus. (p. 1703)
—Texas Animal Ranch: A Series of Ricky's Secret Friends (p. 1724)
Yu, Jennifer, jt. auth. see Boocock, Charles.
Yu, Ji, illus. see Tavano, Joe.
Yu, Li, et al. Holy Spark: Rogel & the Goddess of Liberty. (p. 791)
Yu, Melissa. Ever after High. (p. 541)
—Ever after High: Thronecoming Reusable Sticker Book. (p. 541)
Yu, Melissa, jt. auth. see Mayer, Kirsten.
Yu, Ouyang. New & Selected Poems. (p. 1243)
Yu, Sue Mi. Animal Paradise Yu, Sue Mi, illus. (p. 79)
Yu, Yuen Wong. Digimon (p. 439)
Yuan, Margaret Speaker. Beatrix Potter. (p. 153)
Yuan, Margaret Speaker, jt. auth. see Speaker-Yuan, Margaret.
Yuasa, Kumiko, tr. from JPN. Deus VitaeTM (p. 431)
Yubuki, Go & Azumi, Yukinobu. Scrapped Princess Yabuki, Go, illus. (p. 1532)
Yudcovitch, Lorne. Pixality. (p. 1365)
Yudetamago. Kinnikuman LegacyTM. Yamazaki, Joe, tr. (p. 961)
—Kinnikuman Legancy (p. 961)
—Ultimate Muscle: Battle 6. Vol. 6 Yudetamago, illus. (p. 1809)
—Ultimate Muscle. Yudetamago, illus. (p. 1809)
Yudin, Yefim (Chaim), jt. auth. see Wool, Danny.
Yue, Gui & Farrow, Clare. Little Leap Forward: A Boy in Beijing. Cann, Helen, illus. (p. 1030)
Yue, Guo & Farrow, Clare. Little Leap Forward: A Boy in Beijing. Cann, Helen, illus. (p. 1030)
Yue, Stephanie, illus. see Schertle, Alice.
Yue, Stephanie, illus. see Venable, Colleen A. F.
Yue, Stephanie, jt. auth. see Breitrose, Prudence.
Yuen, Charles, illus. see Lagasse, Emeril.
Yuen, Dan. Charlie the Chopper & the Greatest Toymaker. Davis, Tim, illus. (p. 293)
Yuen Jr., Sammy, illus. see Decter, Ed.
Yuen, Kevin. 10 Most Intense College Football Rivalries. (p. 1994)
Yuen, Sammy, illus. see Fisher, Catherine.
Yuen, Sammy, Jr., illus. see Decter, Ed.
Yuen Wong Yu, illus. see Hongo, Akiyoshi.
Yugami, Yu, jt. auth. see Yagami, Yu.
Yu-gi-oh. Yu-gi-oh Duelist Genesis Blister. (p. 1983)
—Yu-gi-oh Premium Pack 2. (p. 1983)
Yuichi, Kumakura. Jing: King of Bandits—Twilight Tales (p. 918)
Yuji, Iwahara, illus. see Watson, Andi.
Yuki, Kaori. Angel Sanctuary (p. 74)
—Angel Sanctuary. Roman, Annette, ed. (p. 74)
—Angel Sanctuary. Yuki, Kaori, illus. (p. 74)
—Godchild (p. 690)
—Godchild Bates, Megan, ed. (p. 690)
—Godchild. Yuki, Kaori, illus. (p. 690)
—Grand Guignol Orchestra. Yuki, Kaori, illus. (p. 707)
—Sound of a Boy Hatching. Yuki, Kaori, illus. (p. 1615)
Yuki, Kaori & Wolfman, Marv. Angel Sanctuary Yuki, Kaori, illus. (p. 74)
—Angel Sanctuary. Yuki, Kaori, illus. (p. 74)
Yuki, Kaori, et al. Angel Sanctuary Yuki, Kaori & Tamura, Yumi, illus. (p. 74)
Yukino, Sai. Story of Saiunkoku. Yura, Kairi, illus. (p. 1659)
Yukish, Joseph. Nick Goes Fishing: World of Discovery II. Palmer, Kate S., illus. (p. 1251)
Yukkie the Yorkie, A. K. A. Marilyn J. Sanders. Adventures of Yukkie the Yorkie: The Beginning. (p. 24)
Yule, Dorothy A. & Yule, Susan Hunt. Souvenir of New York. (p. 1618)
Yule, Susan Hunt, jt. auth. see Yule, Dorothy A.
Yulia, Lushnikova, illus. see Baghdasaryan, Rouzanna.
Yuly, Toni. Early Bird. Yuly, Toni, illus. (p. 493)
—Night Owl. Yuly, Toni, illus. (p. 1254)
Yum, Hyewon. Mom, It's My First Day of Kindergarten! Yum, Hyewon, illus. (p. 1161)
—This Is Our House. Yum, Hyewon, illus. (p. 1736)
—Twins' Blanket. Yum, Hyewon, illus. (p. 1802)
—Twins' Little Sister. Yum, Hyewon, illus. (p. 1802)
Yum, Hyewon, illus. see Jenkins, Emily.
Yumeka, Sumomo. Tengu-Jin. (p. 1720)
Yumei, Demain. Little Yellow Pear Tomatoes. Tamarin, Nicole, illus. (p. 1038)
Yumoto, Kazumi. Friends. Hirano, Cathy, tr. (p. 638)
—Letters. Hirano, Cathy, tr. (p. 1002)
Yun, Hsing, et al. Prescription for the Heart: Between Ignorance & Enlightenment II (p. 1396)
Yun, Jiun. Cynical Orange (p. 397)
Yun, JiUn, creator. Time & Again (p. 1751)
Yun, Mi-Kyung. Bride of the Water God Volume 13. Simon, Philip, ed. (p. 227)
—Bride of the Water God Volume 4. Yun, Mi-Kyung, illus. (p. 227)
—Bride of the Water God Volume 9. (p. 227)
Yun, Yeo-rim. Liang's Treasure: China. Cowley, Joy, ed. (p. 1004)
Yung Dong, Venerable & Jacobs, Marjorie. Short March to Wisdom. Martin, Peter, illus. (p. 1569)
Yung, Kao, jt. auth. see Liang, Kuan.
Yung, Kao & Liang, Kuan. Magic Lover's Tower (p. 1072)
Yung Yoo, Sun, illus. see Andersen, Hans Christian & Fowler, Gloria.
Yunger, Joshua. Hippo & Monkey. (p. 781)
Yunger, Joshua, illus. see Homeyer, Henry.
Yungul, Elizabeth. I'm Looking from My Window—I'm Looking from My Room. (p. 859)
Yunisa. Schoolaholic Princess 1: the Miracle Boys. (p. 1523)
—Schoolaholic Princess 2: Romansa Singapura. (p. 1523)
—Schoolaholic Princess 3: Simfoni Cinta. (p. 1523)
Yura, Kairi, illus. see Yukino, Sai.
Yurdakul, Gökçe & Bodemann, Y. Michal, eds. Migration, Citizenship, Ethnos. (p. 1141)
Yuricich, Jillian Grace. What did Grandma See? (p. 1882)
Yurksaitis, Anne. Genevieve the Singing Ladybug. Yurksaitis, Stephanie, illus. (p. 661)
—Ingle Bingle. Yurksaitis, Stephanie, illus. (p. 874)
Yurksaitis, Stephanie, illus. see Yurksaitis, Anne.
Yurksas, Bronislao. Dibujo Geomitrico y de Proyeccion. (p. 435)
Yusuf. Butterfly & Bumble Bee: Adventure in Yellow Stone National Park. (p. 247)
Yusuf, Hanna S. & Day, Cansarra. Katie Mcchoir. (p. 945)
Yutenji, Ako. Liling Po Yutenji, Ako, illus. (p. 1017)
—Liling-PO (p. 1017)
—Liling-Po Yutenji, Ako, illus. (p. 1017)
Yutkins, Ellen A. Jack's Big Surprise. (p. 904)
Yuu, Lee Young. Kill Me, Kiss Me (p. 956)
—Kill Me, Kiss Me Yuu, Lee Young, illus. (p. 956)
Yuwiler, Janice. Diabetes. (p. 433)
Yuy, Beub-Ryong. Chronicles of the Cursed Sword Park, Hye-Jin, illus. (p. 317)
Yuzuk, David. Legend of the Smiling Chihuahua. (p. 989)
Yuzuru, illus. see Horowitz, Anthony & Johnston, Antony.
Yuzuru, illus. see Horowitz, Anthony.
Yver, Camila, tr. see Butcher, A. J. & Butcher, Andrew J.
Yvette, Sylvia. My Silly Imagination. (p. 1218)
Yvonne, Symank, illus. see Isabel, Delgado Maria.
Yzaguirre, Ricky. Day I Turned into a Duck. (p. 413)
Yzermans, Vincent A. Wonderworker: The True Story of How St. Nicholas Became Santa Claus. (p. 1949)

Z

Z, Elena Dianna. 102 Awesome School Jokes. (p. 2000)
Z, Jennie. Journal of a Teenage Poet. (p. 927)
Z., Mickey. No Innocent Bystanders: Riding Shotgun in the Land of Denial. (p. 1258)
Z, Susan, jt. auth. see Briant, Monta Z.
Zabala, Javier, illus. see Maestro, Pepe.
Zabarylo-Duma, Ewa, illus. see deVet, L. J.
Zabel. Posadas a Christmas Musical for Children Based on a Mexican Celebration. (p. 1387)
Zabel, Alanna. Chair in the Air. (p. 288)
—Seven Doors. (p. 1554)
Zabel, Albert. Journeys to Bethlehem. (p. 929)
Zabel, Bryce, jt. auth. see Dolan, Richard M.
Zabel, Randy & Broesch, Valerie. Al-the-Gator & Freddy Frog. (p. 33)
Zabel, Vivian. I Like Pink. Nielson, Ginger, illus. (p. 841)
Zabini, Eleni, jt. auth. see Lütje, Susanne.
Zable, Stacey. City by the Lake. (p. 323)
—Our Families. (p. 1308)
Zable, Stacy. City by the Lake: Set Of 6. (p. 323)
—Four Faces in Rock: Set Of 6. (p. 625)
—Our Families: Set Of 6. (p. 1308)
Zabludoff, Marc. Basilosaurus. Bollinger, Peter, illus. (p. 142)
—Beetles. (p. 158)
—Dire Wolf. Bollinger, Peter, illus. (p. 445)
—Doedicurus. Bollinger, Peter, illus. (p. 460)
—Ebox. (p. 502)
—Gastornis. Bollinger, Peter, illus. (p. 657)
—Giant Ground Sloth. Bollinger, Peter, illus. (p. 673)
—Hyracotherium. Bollinger, Peter, illus. (p. 831)
—Insect Class. (p. 875)
—Kronosaurus. Bollinger, Peter, illus. (p. 968)
—Mastodon. Bollinger, Peter, illus. (p. 1104)
—Monkeys. (p. 1166)
—Protoctist Kingdom. (p. 1412)
—Reptile Class. (p. 1461)
—Saber-Toothed Cat. Bollinger, Peter, illus. (p. 1499)
—Spiders. (p. 1627)
—Woolly Mammoth. (p. 1950)
Zaboly, Gary. Barack Obama Coloring Book. (p. 137)
—Frederick Douglass Coloring Book. (p. 633)
—Story of World War I. (p. 1663)
Zaborowski, Barbara, jt. auth. see Kohl, MaryAnn F.
Zaboski, Dave, illus. see Chopra, Deepak.
Zaboski, Dave, illus. see Dychtwald, Ken, et al.
Zabriskie, Cindy. Daily Adventures of Ruckus & Otis. Benger, Chelsi L., illus. (p. 399)
Zabriskie, Judy Mehn, illus. see Howey, Paul M.
Zabrosky, Joseph. Herbie Hanson (p. 769)
—Rudy Cazootie (p. 1494)
—Sunny & Hunny (p. 1677)
Zabrosky, Joseph & Jacobs, Nathaniel. Christmas Tree (p. 316)
Zabrowski, Kira A. Tiger's Tale. (p. 1749)
Zacarias, Karen. Einstein Is a Dummy. (p. 507)
—Looking for Roberto Clemente. (p. 1051)
Zaccaro, Edward. Challenge Math for the Elementary & Middle School Student. (p. 289)
Zaccaro, Edward D. Primary Grade Challenge Math. (p. 1399)
Zacchi, Lucia, illus. see Cross, Elsa.
Zacharias, Gary. Bill of Rights. (p. 186)
—Christianity. (p. 312)
—Events That Changed the World - 1900-1920. (p. 541)
Zacharias, Gary, ed. Freedom of Religion. (p. 634)
Zacharias, Jared. Amendment XII: Presidential Election Process. (p. 58)
Zacharias, Ravi. Merchant & the Thief: A Folktale from India Fournier, Laure, illus. (p. 1127)
Zacharies, Mae. Farmer's Market: Use Place Value & Properties of Operations to Add. (p. 574)
Zachary, Alyson A. Earth Helpers: Count the Ways to Save Our Planet. (p. 496)
Zachary, Ken. Missions of Big Zach. Waytula, Brian, illus. (p. 1153)
Zachmeyer, Mary L. Star That Sparkled. Ruzicka, Delores F., illus. (p. 1641)
Zachry, Juanita Daniel. Katy O'Neil: She Found a Way or Made One. (p. 946)
Zacker, Sandi, illus. see Alvarado, I. J.
Zackery, Gary D. & Borgstedt, John. Stephen. (p. 1648)
Zaczek, Iain. Édouard Manet. (p. 504)
—Georges Seurat. (p. 665)
—Leonardo Da Vinci. (p. 992)
—Mary Cassatt. (p. 1100)
—Paul Cézanne. (p. 1330)
—Vincent Van Gogh. (p. 1843)
Zadoff, Allen. Boy Nobody. (p. 218)
—I Am the Mission. (p. 834)
—I Am the Traitor. (p. 834)
—I Am the Weapon. (p. 834)
—Lost Mission. (p. 1056)
Zadrozny, Alicia & Church, Caroline Jayne. Wild Little Jungle: A Mix-and-Match Flap Book. (p. 1929)
Zadunajsky, Donna M. Tayla Takes a Trip. Bicking, Judith, illus. (p. 1708)
—Tayla's Day at the Beach. Bicking, Judith, illus. (p. 1708)
—Tayla's First Day of School. Bicking, Judith, illus. (p. 1708)
Zafar, Anas. Leader of the Pack. (p. 981)
Zafar, Nuzhat. Free Like a Bird. (p. 634)
Zaffo, George J., illus. see Gulkin, Sidney & Notkin, Jerome J.
Zafón, Carlos Ruiz. Marina. (p. 1094)
—Midnight Palace. (p. 1139)
—Watcher in the Shadows. (p. 1861)
Zafra, Jose. Historias de Sergio. (p. 782)
Zafra, José. Palacio de Papel. (p. 1319)
Zafrilla, Marta. Grandpa Monty's Muddles. (p. 709)
—Little Chick & Mommy Cat. (p. 1026)
Zagarenski, Pamela. Whisper. (p. 1912)
Zagarenski, Pamela, illus. see American Heritage Dictionary Editors, ed.
Zagarenski, Pamela, illus. see American Heritage Dictionary Editors.
Zagarenski, Pamela, illus. see Logue, Mary.
Zagarenski, Pamela, illus. see Sidman, Joyce.
Zagat Survey Staff, creator. Zagat San Francisco Nightlife. (p. 1984)
Zagdanski, Doris. What's Dead Mean? How to Help Children Cope with Death. (p. 1897)
Zager, Jack. Where Do the Tigers Go? A Collection of Children's Poetry. (p. 1907)
Zaglada, Vladimir. Gymmy the Owl & His Friends: Tales in Rhyme about the Animal Kingdom's Natural Gymnasts. (p. 733)
—Gymmy the Owl & His Friends. (p. 733)
Zagnoli, Olimpia, illus. see Bozzi, Riccardo.
Zagnoli, Olimpia, illus. see Révah, Noémie.
Zagon, Laurie. Art for Healing: A Beginner's Workshop (p. 102)
Zagorski, Astrid, tr. see Seglie, Susan & Schiefelbein, Janis.
Zagorski, Steve. River of Wisdom. (p. 1476)
Zahares, Wade. Frosty the Snowman. (p. 645)
Zahares, Wade, illus. see Harshman, Marc & Ryan, Cheryl.
Zahares, Wade, illus. see Shea, Pegi Deitz.
Zahares, Wade, jt. auth. see Ransom, Candice F.
Zaharias, Terrilynn, illus. see Hoercher, Donald F.
Zahedi, Morteza, illus. see Akbarpour, Ahmad.
Zahensky, Barbara. Diet Fads. (p. 437)
Zahensky, Barbara A. Diet Fads. (p. 437)
Zahensky, Kenneth & Egan, Tracie. Insider's Guide to Water Polo (p. 878)
Zahensky, Kenneth & Sommers, Michael A. Snowmobiling. (p. 1601)
Zahler, Diane. Black Death. (p. 195)
—Princess of the Wild Swans. Gilbert, Yvonne, illus. (p. 1405)
—Sleeping Beauty's Daughters. (p. 1589)
—Than Shwe's Burma. (p. 1725)
—Thirteenth Princess. (p. 1735)
—Thirteenth Princess. Gilbert, Yvonne, illus. (p. 1735)
—True Princess. (p. 1792)
Zahler, Kathy A. Assads' Syria. (p. 107)
Zahler, Thom, et al. Pony Tales (p. 1383)
Zahler, Thomas. Raider: A Cold Day in Heaven. (p. 1433)
Zahler, Thomas F. Twilight Sparkle. (p. 1801)
Zahlingen, Bronja. Lifetime of Joy: A Collection of Circle Games, Finger Games, Songs, Verses & Plays for Puppets & Marionettes (p. 1014)
Zahn, Ellsworth E. Dudley. Zahn, Ellsworth E., illus. (p. 489)
Zahn, Muriel. Grimsel: The Story of A Valiant Saint Bernard & Three Boys in the Swiss Alps. Walsh, William, illus. (p. 724)
Zahn, Peter. Let's Recycle: Represent & Solve Addition Problems. (p. 1000)
—Let's Recycle. (p. 1000)
Zahnd, Mark, illus. see Tait, Chris.
Zahnow, Vicki. My Little Kitten, Patch. (p. 1212)
Zahorak, Sarah. Candyland Forest. (p. 261)
Zahorian, Ashley, jt. auth. see Pattyn, Denny.
Zahradka, Miroslav. Un-Terrible Tiger. Zahradka, Miroslav, illus. (p. 1811)

Z

Zahradnik, Kristen M., jt. auth. see Frie, Robert R.
Zaibak, Bushra. I am Not Afraid. (p. 833)
Zaidi, Ishan. Keep Counting. (p. 946)
Zaidi, Nadeem. Baby Mozart: Musica Por Todas Partes. (p. 127)
—Formas: Libro con Ventanas. (p. 620)
Zaidi, Nadeem, illus. see Aigner-Clark, Julie.
Zaidi, Nadeem, illus. see Del Moral, Susana.
Zaidi, Nadeem, illus. see Silver Dolphin en Espanol Editors.
Zaidi, Nadeem, illus. see Singer, Marilyn.
Zaidi, Nadeem, jt. auth. see del Moral Zavariz, Susana.
Zaidova, Hijran. Poor Mum & Her Three Sons. (p. 1383)
Zaikina, Maria, illus. see Kasbarian, Lucine.
Zaikine, Zak. Mother's Love. Zaikine, Zak & O'Keefe, Karin, eds. (p. 1179)
Zail, Suzy. Dependable Dan. Stewart, Chantal, illus. (p. 427)
—Lulu. Hill, Trish, illus. (p. 1064)
—Playing for the Commandant. (p. 1372)
Zaionz, Ruth. Morris the Friendly Dinosaur. (p. 1176)
Zajac, Kristen. Chasing the Spirit of Service. Tucker, Julie, illus. (p. 294)
Zajac, Kristen J. Ebeneezer's Cousin. Houdeshell, Jennifer T., illus. (p. 501)
Zajac, Kristen K. Ebeneezer's Cousin. Houdeshell, Jennifer Thomas, illus. (p. 501)
—Primo de Ebeneezer. Houdeshell, Jennifer Thomas, illus. (p. 1401)
Zajceva, Ira, ed. see AZ Books Staff.
Zak, Drahos, illus. see Holden, Robert.
Zak, Drahos, jt. auth. see Lamond, Margete.
Zak, Faith. Naptime Adventures: Train. (p. 1229)
—Naptime Adventures: Christmas Tree. (p. 1229)
Zak, Monica. Niña y la Anguila. Orea, Lucia, tr. (p. 1256)
—Salven Mi Selva. Runnerstrom, Bengt-Arne, illus. (p. 1506)
Zak, Murray, jt. auth. see Ames, Lee J.
Zak, Roderick. Winning Is Everything: Especially When It Comes to Winning Souls. (p. 1937)
Zakanitch, Robert Rahway, illus. see Gottfried, Maya.
Zakarin, Debra Mostow. First Fairytales. Fiore, Rob, illus. (p. 594)
—Who's Your Superstar BFF? (p. 1921)
—Who's Your Superstar Soul Mate? (p. 1921)
Zakatchenko, Lilian. Girls from Brazil (p. 680)
Zake, Daiga. Oranges for Everyone. Stojanova, Elena, illus. (p. 1302)
Zakiyyah, jt. auth. see Zakiyyah.
Zakiyyah & Zakiyyah. Chatterworld My Numbers in Spanish/My Numbers in French: MIS Numeros en Espanol/Mes Mombres en Francais. (p. 295)
Zakon, Miriam. Kids' Kosher Cookbook. (p. 954)
Zakon, Miriam, creator. Baker's Dozen: Three-in-One 1-3, 4-6, 7-9, 10-12, 13-15, 16-17 (p. 133)
Zakon, Miriam Stark, jt. auth. see Blitz, Shmuel.
Zakour, John. Baxter Moon Galactic Scout. (p. 147)
Zalben, Jane Breskin. Mousterpiece. Zalben, Jane Breskin, illus. (p. 1182)
—Papa's Latkes. Zalben, Jane Breskin, illus. (p. 1322)
—Paths to Peace: People Who Changed the World. (p. 1328)
—Pearl's Eight Days of Chanukah: With a Story & Activity for Each Night. Zalben, Jane Breskin, illus. (p. 1333)
—Pearl's Eight Days of Chanukah. Zalben, Jane Breskin, illus. (p. 1333)
—Pearl's Passover: A Family Celebration Through Stories, Recipes, Crafts, & Songs. (p. 1333)
—Saturday Night at the Beastro. (p. 1515)
—Saturday Night at the Beastro. Zalben, Jane Breskin, illus. (p. 1515)
Zales, S. R. Jenny & the Hummingbird Faeries. (p. 913)
Zalesny, Michele. Elves' Surprise. (p. 517)
Zalevskaya, Anastacia, illus. see Brereton, Erin.
Zalewski, Todd, illus. see Wadsworth, Ginger.
Zalme, Ron. How to Draw Johto Heroes. (p. 817)
—How to Draw Nintendo Greatest Heroes & Villains. (p. 818)
—How to Draw Sinnoh Superstars. (p. 818)
—Humpback Whale Tale. (p. 827)
—LEGO Legends of Chima: How to Draw: Heroes & Villains. (p. 990)
—Pokémon: How to Draw Unova Heroes. (p. 1377)
—Rainy Day Tales. (p. 1436)
—Sunny Day Tales. (p. 1677)
Zalme, Ron, illus. see Golden Books Staff.
Zalme, Ron, illus. see Inches, Alison.
Zalme, Ron, illus. see Larsen, Kirsten.
Zalme, Ron, jt. auth. see Scholastic, Inc. Staff.
Zaloga, Steven J. Most Daring Raid of World War II: D-Day—Pointe-Du-Hoc. (p. 1177)
Zalonis, C. B. Strangers in the Forest. (p. 1665)
Zaman, Farida, illus. see Beliveau, Kathy.
Zaman, Farida, illus. see Fitz-Gibbon, Sally.
Zaman, Farida, illus. see Savedoff, Barbara E. & Elissa, Barbara.
Zaman, Farida, illus. see Singh, Rina.
Zaman, Natalie, jt. auth. see Bennardo, Charlotte.
Zaman, Niaz, jt. ed. see Azim, Firdous.
Zamanian, Marjan, illus. see Jalali, Yassaman.
Zamazing, Cherie. ComicQuest Adventure Island. (p. 348)
Zamazing, Cherie, illus. see Dale, Jay.
Zambarano, Richard. Wilbur & Wilma's Colorful Campus Tour - University of Arizona A-Z. (p. 1928)
Zamboni, David, illus. see Alpert, Barbara.
Zamboni, David, illus. see Heller, Donna & Payne, James.
Zamboni, David, illus. see Howell, Julie Ann.
Zamboni, David, illus. see Marie, Jill Jana.
Zambrano, Alicia. Adivinario de Diccionanzas. Acosta, Patricia, illus. (p. 13)
Zameen, E S. No Rouz Our Persian New Year. (p. 1260)
Zameenzad, Adam. Pepsi & Maria. (p. 1340)
Zamek, Scott. One More Horizon: Ohio to Hong Kong the Long Way. (p. 1296)
Zamenhof, Robert. Adventures of Armadillo Baby & Annabelli. Baker, Sara, illus. (p. 16)
Zammarchi, Fabrice & Mas, Sylvie. Life in the Golden Age of Jazz: A Biography of Buddy Defranco. (p. 1011)
Zamor, Nehemie Djose. Adventures of Naoomi. (p. 21)
Zamora, Dulce. How to Draw the Life & Times of Franklin Pierce. (p. 818)
—How to Draw the Life & Times of John F. Kennedy. (p. 819)
—How to Draw the Life & Times of John Fitzgerald Kennedy. (p. 819)
—How to Draw the Life & Times of John Tyler. (p. 819)
Zamora, Nancy. Back in the Band. (p. 130)
Zamora, Peter. Story about Kandie Cole. (p. 1656)
Zamorsky, Tania & Burnett, Frances Hodgson. Little Princess. Corvino, Lucy, illus. (p. 1033)
Zamosky, Lisa. Farmers Then & Now. (p. 574)
—Fishers Then & Now. (p. 599)
—Government Leaders Then & Now. (p. 704)
—Greece (p. 720)
—India. (p. 870)
—Investigating Simple Organisms. (p. 885)
—Louis Pasteur: Founder of Microbiology (p. 1058)
—Louis Pasteur & the Fight Against Germs. (p. 1058)
—Mansa Musa: Leader of Mali (p. 1088)
—Sanitation Workers Then & Now. (p. 1511)
—Siddhartha Gautama: The Buddha (p. 1573)
—Simple Organisms (p. 1578)
—Socrates: Greek Philosopher (p. 1605)
—Sub-Saharan Africa. (p. 1671)
—Woodrow Wilson. (p. 1949)
—World War I. (p. 1958)
Zamosky, Lisa & Conklin, Wendy. World War II. (p. 1959)
Zampino, Phil. Brush Beats: Different Brush Beats Rhythms & Sounds on the Drum Set. Zampino, Phil, ed. (p. 232)
Zana, Brian. Maurice Tries New Foods. (p. 1110)
Zander, Alex. School Track Meet: Understand Place Value. (p. 1523)
—School Track Meet. (p. 1523)
Zander, Julie McDonald, ed. see Rieken, Ethel Plaep.
Zander, R. W. When the Zombies Come Marchin' Home. (p. 1905)
Zander, Ray. Life of Faith: A Collection of Poems & Outlines. (p. 1012)
Zandman, Herm. It's Not a Truck! It's a B-Double! (p. 897)
Zaner, Bill. Different Stuff. (p. 438)
Zaner-Bloser Staff, ed. Zaner-Bloser Handwriting 1999: A Way to Self-Expression, Grade 4. (p. 1985)
Zang, Adam & Varacalli, Lauren. Carleton College College Prowler off the Record. (p. 270)
Zangas, Sherri. Is for Alabama: Roll Tide Roll. Williams, Tim, illus. (p. 889)
Zangri, Brian. Millie Mcpree: The Athlete in Me. (p. 1144)
Zangrillo, Marguerite Rochelle. Bunny with the Polka Dot Nose. (p. 242)
—Calli the Cat. (p. 254)
Zanier, Christian, illus. see Van Lente, Fred, et al.
Zann, Paul. Aussie Six in Australia. (p. 116)
Zannes, Addie Mercer & Mercer, Bonnie Kyllo. Wheel Rainbow. (p. 1900)
Zannos, Susan. Dmitri Mendeleyev & the Periodic Table. (p. 456)
—Guglielmo Marconi & Radio Waves. (p. 729)
—Life & Times of Archimedes. (p. 1007)
—Life & Times of Marco Polo. (p. 1008)
—Life & Times of Socrates. (p. 1008)
—Linus Pauling & the Chemical Bond. (p. 1019)
—Michael Faraday & the Discovery of Electromagnetism. (p. 1134)
—Ron Howard. (p. 1486)
—Samuel Morse & the Telegraph. (p. 1509)
Zanobini Leoni, Maria Teresa. Leonardo Da Vinci. (p. 992)
Zanotta, Roberta, illus. see Hilgenberg, Bob & Muir, Roberto.
Zantay, Valerie, tr. see Macveety, Sue Maney.
Zanzig, Thomas. Coordinator's Manual. (p. 365)
Zanzonico, Gaetana. Magical Dream. (p. 1074)
Zapata, Elizabeth. Puerto Rico. (p. 1415)
Zapata, Miguel, tr. see Sargent, Dave.
Zapata, Regulo, Jr. Desperate Lands: The War on Terror Through the Eyes of a Special Forces Soldier. (p. 430)
Zapater Oliva, Carlos, illus. see Friden, Chris.
Zapf, Marlena. Underpants Dance. Avril, Lynne, illus. (p. 1815)
Zapp, et al. Baby Bear's Read-Along Goldilocks & the Three Bears. (p. 125)
Zappa, Ahmet. Because I'm Your Dad. Santat, Dan, illus. (p. 155)
Zappa, Ahmet & Muldoon Zappa, Shana. Star Darlings Arly's Adventure. Bonatakis, Shannon & Disney Storybook Art Team, illus. (p. 1640)
Zappa, Ahmet & Zappa, Shane Muldoon. Sage's Story. Bonatakis, Shannon & Disney Storybook Art Team, illus. (p. 1503)
Zappa, Go. Mizuho & Kei's Diary. Hosaka, Toshi, tr. from JPN. (p. 1157)
Zappa, Marcia. Black Holes. (p. 196)
—Caves. (p. 282)
—Chicago Bears. (p. 299)
—Coconut Crabs. (p. 337)
—Constellations. (p. 359)
—Dallas Cowboys. (p. 401)
—Denver Broncos. (p. 427)
—Echidnas. (p. 502)
—Eclipses. (p. 502)
—Elephant Shrews. (p. 511)
—Erosion. (p. 534)
—Flying Squirrels. (p. 610)
—Fossil Fuels. (p. 623)
—Galaxies. (p. 653)
—Glaciers. (p. 682)
—Green Bay Packers. (p. 721)
—Indianapolis Colts. (p. 871)
—Minnesota Vikings. (p. 1147)
—NASA. (p. 1230)
—New England Patriots. (p. 1244)
—New Orleans Saints. (p. 1246)
—New York Jets. (p. 1248)
—NFL's Greatest Teams Set 2. (p. 1250)
—Oakland Raiders. (p. 1275)
—Pittsburgh Steelers. (p. 1365)
—Rockets & Satellites. (p. 1483)
—Rocks. (p. 1483)
—San Francisco 49ers. (p. 1510)
—Seattle Seahawks. (p. 1539)
—Space Exploration. (p. 1619)
—Space Stations. (p. 1620)
—Universe (p. 1820)
—Washington Redskins. (p. 1860)
—Water Cycle. (p. 1862)
Zappa, Shane Muldoon, jt. auth. see Zappa, Ahmet.
Zappia, Francesca. Made You Up. (p. 1070)
Zappler, Georg. Texas Indians. Ivy, Elena T., illus. (p. 1724)
Zappone, Melanie Lippincott. Sounds of Summer Sank in the Sea. (p. 1615)
Zappy, Erica, ed. see Rey, H. A.
Zapruder, Alexandra, jt. auth. see Carney, Elizabeth.
Zarabouka, Sofia & Perantakou-Cook, Mary. Jason & the Golden Fleece: The Most Adventurous & Exciting Expedition of All the Ages. (p. 910)
Zaragoza, Cynthia. There Must Be Elephants in Heaven. (p. 1730)
Zaragoza, Gonzalo. America Latina: Epoca Colonial. (p. 59)
Zarampouka, Sophia. Saga of Alexander the Great. (p. 1502)
Zárate, Antonio, et al. Atlas Geografico (Geographical Atlas) (p. 112)
Zarate, Gustavo Azgad. Youth Law: A Practical Guide to Legal Issues That Affect Young Adults. (p. 1982)
Zarate, Jesus, illus. see Weill, Cynthia.
Zárate, Patricia, jt. auth. see Carrión, Julio.
Zarb, Mike, illus. see Gold, Robin.
Zarb, Mike, illus. see Harmer, Wendy.
Zarcinas, Scott. Golden Chalice: A Pilgrim's Chronicle. (p. 694)
—Golden Chalice: A Pilgrim's Chronicle (Large Print 16pt) (p. 694)
Zarco, Carmen Saucedo. Diario de Mariana (1695-95) (p. 434)
Zardes, Cassandra. Cherokee. (p. 298)
Zareba, Lukasz, illus. see Lee, Stephi.
Zaretsky, Evan. Ashley's Elephant: The Pond Hockey Challenge. Spurll, Barbara, illus. (p. 106)
Zarin, Cynthia. Albert, the Dog Who Liked to Ride in Taxis. Pratt, Pierre, illus. (p. 34)
—Saints among the Animals. Gore, Leonid, illus. (p. 1504)
Zaring, Laurie. Who Could You Be at the Zoo? Barlup, Jessica, illus. (p. 1915)
Zarins, Kim. Helpful Puppy. McCully, Emily Arnold, illus. (p. 766)
Zaroulis, Christina. Tackling Your High School Term Paper. (p. 1694)
Zarr, Sara. How to Save a Life. (p. 821)
—Lucy Variations. (p. 1063)
—Story of a Girl. (p. 1657)
—Sweethearts. (p. 1690)
—What We Lost. (p. 1895)
Zarr, Sara & Altebrando, Tara. Roomies. (p. 1488)
Zarraonandia, Thomas. Johnny Jingle. Zarraonandia, Thomas, illus. (p. 923)
Zarrella, Sharon, jt. auth. see Lizzy Anne's Adventures Staff.
Zarrinnaal, Laura Nienhaus, jt. auth. see Lay, Richard.
Zartman, Jennifer. Abednego. (p. 4)
Zarvatski, Derek, illus. see Boyd, Roland.
Zarzycki, Daryl Davis. Johnny Appleseed. (p. 923)
Zaslavsky, Claudia. More Math Games & Activities from Around the World. (p. 1174)
Zatz, Asa, tr. see Tashiro, Chisato.
Zaugg, Sandra L. Escape. (p. 534)
—Hidden Notes & High Seas. (p. 776)
—Man in the Blue Skirt. (p. 1085)
—Prayer for Mother. (p. 1393)
—Secret of the Desert Lights: A Story about Following God's Laws. (p. 1542)
—Secret of the Yellow Van: A Book about Dealing with Loss. (p. 1543)
Zaugg, Sandy. Murdock Mystery #1: A House Called Fernley Manor. (p. 1192)
—Murdock Mystery #2: The Cats of Rome. (p. 1192)
Zaunders, Bo. Crocodiles, Camels & Dugout Canoes: Eight Adventurous Episodes. Munro, Roxie, illus. (p. 384)
—Great Bridge-Building Contest. Munro, Roxie, illus. (p. 714)
Zavada, Mary. Lady Head Vases: A Collector's Guide with Prices (p. 970)
Zavlek, Steve. What Am I Poems: Nature Riddles. (p. 1879)
Zavrel, Stepan. Vodnik. Zavrel, Stepan, illus. (p. 1847)
Zavyalov, Diana. Little Humpy: Derivative Translation from Russian Fairy Tale by Ershov. (p. 1029)
Zawacki, Neil. How to Be a Villain: Evil Laughs, Secret Lairs, Master Plans, & More!!! Dignan, James, illus. (p. 815)
Zawel, Marc. Untangling the Ivy League. Burns, Adam, ed. (p. 1823)
Zawisa, Doug. Hawkman Companion. (p. 755)
Zayarny, Jack. Humpback Whales. (p. 827)
Zayauskas, Victoria. Tent. (p. 1720)
Zayceva, Irina, ed. see AZ Books Staff.
Zazzetta, K. Purple Haired Girl of Eea. (p. 1419)
Zbida, Rima. 12 O'Clock. (p. 1994)
Zborowski, Paul. Can You Find Me? Nature's Hidden Creatures. (p. 258)
Zdanowicz, Paul, illus. see McElroy, Jean.
Zdanowicz, Paul, illus. see Testa, Maggie.
Zdenek, Joseph. Heart of Courage: The Narscix War. (p. 759)
Zdrok, Jodie L. 1840-1860 (Events That Changed the World) (p. 2002)
—1880-1900 (Events That Changed the World) (p. 2002)
Zdrok, Victoria. Anatomy of Pleasure. (p. 67)
Zdunich, Terrance. Molting: Issue #1 Guilty Susie. (p. 1161)
Zea, Amilcar. Zico Perico. Santa, Carlos Piedra, illus. (p. 1986)
Zebrowski, Debra. World Literature Student Activity Book. Matthews, Douglas L., ed. (p. 1956)
Zecca, Katherine, illus. see Brainerd, Debbi.
Zecca, Katherine, illus. see Glogas, Valarie.
Zecca, Katherine, illus. see Van Zandt, Steve.
Zeck, Mike, illus. see Stern, Roger, et al.
Zeck, Mike, jt. auth. see Duffy, Joe.
Zeckhausen, Dina. Full Mouse, Empty Mouse: A Tale of Food & Feelings. Boyd, Brian, illus. (p. 646)
Zedeck, Beth E. & Zedeck, Morris S. Forensic Pharmacology. (p. 617)
Zedeck, Morris S., jt. auth. see Zedeck, Beth E.
Zediker, Rose Ross. Wealth in Biblical Times. (p. 1869)
Zee, Amy Van. Constellation Draco: The Story of the Dragon. Morrow, J. T., illus. (p. 359)
—Indiana. (p. 871)
—Iowa. (p. 886)
—Kansas. (p. 943)
—Maine. (p. 1077)
—Massachusetts. (p. 1102)
—Michigan. (p. 1135)
—Minnesota. (p. 1147)
—Mississippi. (p. 1154)
—Missouri. (p. 1154)
—Rev up Your Writing in Procedural Texts. Gallagher-Cole, Memie, illus. (p. 1465)
—War Of 1812: A History Perspectives Book. (p. 1857)
Zee, Ruth Vander, see Vander Zee, Ruth.
Zeeh, Shawn. Tucker Farm: Under the Big Top. (p. 1795)
Zeer, Darrin. Lovers' Massage: Soothing Touch for Two. Saidens, Amy, illus. (p. 1061)
Zegers, Charlie, jt. auth. see Sandler, Michael.
Zehnder, Christopher. History: Sea to Shining Sea. (p. 783)
Zehnwirth, Harry. Sounds for Silence: Baby Settling & Health Guide. (p. 1615)
Zehr, Howard & Amstutz, Lorraine Stutzman. "What Will Happen to Me?" Every Night, Approximately Three Million Children Go to Bed with a Parent in Prison or Jail. Here Are Their Thoughts & Stories. (p. 1895)
Zehring Fischer, Nancy. Children of the Mission. (p. 302)
Zei, Alki. Tina's Web. Thornley, John, tr. from GRE. (p. 1755)
Zeichner, Craig. Montreal Canadiens. (p. 1170)
Zeichner, Steven. Jinson Twins, Science Detectives, & the Mystery of Echo Lake. (p. 919)
Zeidman, Bob. Amazing Adventure of Edward & Dr. Sprechtmachen. (p. 52)
Zeiger, Genie. Atta Girl! (p. 113)
Zeiger, Jennifer. Animals Helping after Disasters. (p. 82)
—Barack Obama. (p. 137)
—Bats. (p. 145)
—Camels. (p. 256)
—Civil Rights Movement. (p. 325)
—Compsognathus. (p. 354)
—Coyotes. (p. 375)
—Lions. (p. 1021)
—Lions - Nature's Children. (p. 1021)
—Maiasaura. (p. 1076)
—Oviraptor. (p. 1314)
—Pandas. (p. 1321)
—Pandas - Nature's Children. (p. 1321)
—Queen Elizabeth II. (p. 1424)
—Snowy Owls. (p. 1601)
—Stingrays. (p. 1651)
—Triceratops. (p. 1785)
—War in Afghanistan. (p. 1857)
—What Do They Do? Firefighters. (p. 1882)
—What Do They Do? Nurses. (p. 1882)
—What Does It Do? Digger. (p. 1884)
—What Does It Do? Dump Truck. (p. 1884)
Zeigler, Alex, jt. auth. see Zeigler Dendy, Chris A.
Zeigler Dendy, Chris A. & Zeigler, Alex. Bird's-Eye View of Life: Advice from Young Survivors. (p. 191)
Zeigler, Donald J. Israel. (p. 893)
Zeigler, Robbie. Down by the Se. (p. 474)
Zeigler, Terra. Grumplestone & the Magic Forest: Secrets. (p. 727)
Zeiler, Freddi. Kids Guide to Giving. Schumaker, Ward, illus. (p. 953)
Zeinert, Karen. McCarthyism & the Communist Scare in United States History. (p. 1114)
Zeinert, Karen, jt. auth. see Hart, Joyce.
Zeinert, Karen & Miller, Mary. Brave Women of the Gulf Wars: Operation Desert Storm & Operation Iraqi Freedom. (p. 223)
Zeisler, Riley, jt. auth. see Oksanen, Sue.
Zeiss, Joyce Burns. Out of the Dragon's Mouth. (p. 1311)
Zeitlin, Meredith. Freshman Year & Other Unnatural Disasters. (p. 636)
—Sophomore Year Is Greek to Me. (p. 1614)
Zeitzoff, Helen. Using Context Clues to Help Kids Tackle Unfamiliar Words: Strategies & Practice Pages That Teach Students How to Use Context Clues to Build Vocabulary & Comprehension. (p. 1828)
Zekauskas, Felicia, jt. auth. see Maloney, Peter.
Zekauskas, Felicia, jt. auth. see Maloney, Peter.
Zekina, Daniela, jt. auth. see Savoie, Jacques.
Zelaya, Carol. Caring for Emily's Family. (p. 269)
—Emily Waits for Her Family. Metcalf, Kristin, illus. (p. 519)
—Emily's New Home: Emily the Chickadee. (p. 519)
Zelch, Patti R. Ready, Set ... Wait! What Animals Do Before a Hurricane McLennan, Connie, illus. (p. 1447)
Zeldin, Danny. Cholent Man. (p. 309)
Zelenka, Yvonne. Aprendamos con Tito sobre la Epilepsia. Zelenka, Yvonne, illus. (p. 93)
Zelenyj, Alexander & Zelenyj, Alexander. Marquette & Jolliet: Quest for the Mississippi. (p. 1096)
Zelenyj, Alexander. Marco Polo: Overland to China. (p. 1092)
Zelenyj, Alexander, jt. auth. see Zelenyj, Alexander.
Zeliff, Janet. Clicker the Tap Dancer. (p. 332)
Zeligs, Dorothy Freda. Child's History of the Hebrew People: From Nomadic Times to the Destruction of the Second Temple. (p. 305)
Zelinger, Jordan, jt. auth. see Zelinger, Laurie E.
Zelinger, Jordan, jt. auth. see Zelinger, Laurie.
Zelinger, Laurie & Zelinger, Jordan. Please Explain Anxiety to Me! Simple Biology & Solutions for Children & Parents. Sabella, Elisa, illus. (p. 1373)
Zelinger, Laurie E. & Zelinger, Jordan. Please Explain "Anxiety" to Me! Simple Biology & Solutions for Children & Parents. Sabella, Elisa, illus. (p. 1373)
Zelinski, E. J. Pensar a lo Grande: Ejercicios Simples y Divertidos para Potenciar la Creatividad. (p. 1338)

Zelinsky, Paul O., illus. see Bingham, Kelly.
Zelinsky, Paul O., illus. see Cleary, Beverly.
Zelinsky, Paul O., illus. see Isaacs, Anne.
Zelinsky, Paul O., illus. see Jenkins, Emily.
Zelinsky, Paul O., illus. see Jones, Diana Wynne.
Zelinsky, Paul O., illus. see Manushkin, Fran.
Zelinsky, Paul O., illus. see Prelutsky, Jack.
Zelinsky, Paul O., illus. see Segal, Lore.
Zelkowicz, Benny, jt. auth. see Baity, Cameron.
Zeller, Beatriz, tr. see Comino, Sandra.
Zeller, Bob, jt. auth. see Richter, John J.
Zeller, Penny. Hollyhocks. (p. 789)
Zellerhoff, Christi. Princesses Can Be Pirates Too! Davis, Amy, illus. (p. 1406)
Zellers, Carolyn M. Computer Activities: Teaching with Spreadsheets (p. 354)
—Computer Activities: Making Slide Shows & Simple Web Pages (p. 354)
—Computer Activities - Word Processing Projects, Grades 5-8 (p. 354)
Zellers, Michelle. Maya's Magic Carpet. (p. 1113)
Zellmann, Anton Josef. I Read Minds: And So Do You! (p. 844)
Zelman, Laurie, jt. auth. see Miller, Mark A.
Zelman, Nancy Ellen. Conversation Inspirations: Over 2400 Conversation Topics. (p. 361)
Zelon, Helen. Apollo 13 Mission: Surviving an Explosion in Space. (p. 91)
—Endeavor Mission STS-61: Fixing the Hubble Space Telescope. (p. 527)
—Endeavor SRTM: Mapping the Earth. (p. 527)
—Gemini IV Mission: The First American Space Walk. (p. 660)
—Mercury 6 Mission: The First American Astronaut to Orbit Earth. (p. 1127)
Zeltner, Tim, illus. see Staniszewski, Anna.
Zeltner, Tim, illus. see Wunderli, Stephen.
Zelver, Patricia. Wonderful Towers of Watts. Lessac, Frané, illus. (p. 1948)
Zemach, Dorothy E., jt. auth. see Barnard, Roger.
Zemach, Kaethe. Ms. McCaw Learns to Draw. (p. 1188)
Zemach, Kaethe, jt. illus. see Zemach, Margot.
Zemach, Margot & Zemach, Kaethe. Eating up Gladys. (p. 501)
Zeman, Anne & Kelly, Kate. Everything You Need to Know about American History Homework. (p. 545)
Zeman, Ludmila. Gilgamesh. (p. 676)
—Gilgamesh the King. (p. 676)
—Sindbad: From the Tales of the Thousand & One Nights. (p. 1578)
—Sindbad in the Land of Giants: From the Tales of the Thousand & One Nights. (p. 1578)
—Sindbad's Secret: From the Tales of the Thousand & One Nights. (p. 1578)
—Sindbad's Secret. (p. 1578)
Zemanick, Patty. Walk with Papa. Hammack, Sandra, illus. (p. 1854)
Zembrowski, Sunni, illus. see Wachob, Chuck.
Zemeckis, Robert, et al. Polar Express Movie Shadowbook: An Interactive Shadow-Casting Bedtime Story. Van Allsburg, Chris, illus. (p. 1379)
Zemke, Deborah. D Is 4 Doodles. (p. 397)
—Doodles at Dinner: 36 Tear-Off Placemats. (p. 469)
—Doodles at Lunch: 36 Tear-Off Placemats. (p. 469)
—Fairy Doodles - 36 Tear-Off Placemats. (p. 563)
—Green Boots, Blue Hair, Polka-Dot Underwear. Zemke, Deborah, illus. (p. 721)
—How to Win Friends & Influence Creatures. (p. 822)
—Please Pass the Doodles. (p. 1373)
—Pocket Packs - Alpha-Doodles. (p. 1375)
—Pocket Packs - Doodles 2 Do! (p. 1375)
—Sports Doodles: 36 Tear-Off Placemats. (p. 1632)
Zemke, Deborah, illus. see Blue Apple Staff.
Zemke, Deborah, illus. see Degman, Lori.
Zemke, Deborah, illus. see Galloway, Ginger.
Zemke, Deborah, illus. see Newman, Robin.
Zemke, Deborah, illus. see Shannon, George.
Zemke, Deborah, illus. see Wing, Natasha.
Zemke, Deborah, illus. see Ziefert, Harriet.
Zemko Tetro, Maria, tr. from UKR. How the Animals Built their House & Other Stories. (p. 812)
Zemlicka, Shannon. Del Huevo a la Mariposa. Translations.com Staff, tr. from ENG. (p. 424)
—Del Renacuajo a la Rana. Translations.com Staff, tr. from ENG. (p. 424)
—Florence Nightingale. Debon, Nicolas, illus. (p. 606)
—From Egg to Butterfly. (p. 642)
—From Iron to Car. (p. 643)
—From Oil to Gas. (p. 643)
—From Sand to Glass. (p. 643)
—From Tadpole to Frog. (p. 644)
—Quanah Parker. (p. 1422)
—Thomas Edison. (p. 1738)
Zempel, Ulirich, jt. tr. see Barth, Katrin.
Zemser, Amy Bronwen. Dear Julia. (p. 419)
Zemtsov, Ilya & Farrar, John. Gorbachev: The Man & the System. (p. 702)
Zenatti, Valerie. Bottle in the Gaza Sea. Hunter, Adriana, tr. from FRE. (p. 215)
Zenchenko Esser, Diane. Kids of Northgate: A Baby Boomers' Guide to Write Their Story. (p. 954)
Zendrera, Concepcion. Yaci y Su Muneca. (p. 1968)
Zenescope Entertainment Staff. Discovery Channel's Great White Sharks. (p. 450)
—Discovery Channel's Megalodon & Prehistoric Sharks. (p. 450)
—Discovery Channel's Sharks Boxed Set. (p. 450)
Zenescope Entertainment Staff & Brusha, Joe. Sci-Fi & Fantasy: The Perfect Mate. (p. 1524)
Zenescope Entertainment Staff & Kaye, Daniel. Never Underestimate a Hermit Crab. (p. 1243)
Zenescope Entertainment Staff, et al. Mankind: The Story of All of Us. Vol. 1 (p. 1087)
—Mankind: The Story of All of Us. Vol. 2 (p. 1087)
Zeng, Sunny. Ni Hao Little Friends: Learn Chinese. (p. 1250)
—Ni Hao Little Friends 2: Chinese with Chinasprout (p. 1250)
—Student Workbook: To Accompany Videos 1 & 2. (p. 1669)
Zengin-Karaian, Alex, ed. see Feigin, Misha.
Zengin-Karaian, Alex, illus. see Feigin, Misha.
Zengin-Karaian, Victoria, ed. see Feigin, Misha.
Zeni, Marco, tr. see Guerra, Elisa Puricelli.
Zeni, Marco, tr. see Pavanello, Roberto.
Zenk, Molly. Hyperion Keats. (p. 831)
Zenkel, Suzanne Siegel. Fashion Astrology. Bigda, Diane, illus. (p. 575)
Zenker, Marlene M. Empty Bowl. (p. 521)
Zenko, Darren. Ghost Stories of Pets & Animals (p. 671)
—Werewolves & Shapeshifters Norell, Aaron, illus. (p. 1875)
Zenko, Darren & Gideon, Amos. Native American Ghost Stories. (p. 1234)
Zenner, Dale M. 'Twas the Night Before Christmas: Yet Few People Knew. (p. 1799)
Zenon, Paul. Cool Card Tricks: Techniques for the Advanced Magician. (p. 362)
—Gimmicks & Card Tricks: Illusions for the Intermediate Magician. (p. 676)
—Magic of the Mind: Tricks for the Master Magician. (p. 1073)
—Simple Sleight-of-Hand: Card & Coin Tricks for the Beginning Magician. (p. 1578)
Zentall, Sydney & Goldstein, Sam. Seven Steps to Homework Success: A Family Guide for Solving Common Homework Problems. DiMatteo, Richard A., illus. (p. 1555)
Zenz, Aaron. Chimpansneeze. (p. 306)
—Chuckling Ducklings & Baby Animal Friends. Zenz, Aaron, illus. (p. 318)
—Hiccupotamus (p. 775)
—Hug a Bull: An Ode to Animal Dads. Zenz, Aaron, illus. (p. 824)
—I Love Ewe: An Ode to Animal Moms. Zenz, Aaron, illus. (p. 842)
Zenz, Aaron, illus. see Henderson, Sara.
Zenz, Aaron, illus. see Ingalls, Ann.
Zenz, Aaron, illus. see Karr, Lily.
Zenz, Aaron, illus. see Lewis, Anne Margaret.
Zenz, Aaron, illus. see Metzger, Steve.
Zenz, Aaron, illus. see Newman, Patricia.
Zenz, Aaron, illus. see Ripes, Laura.
Zenz, Aaron, jt. auth. see Henderson, Sara.
Zep. What's Going on down There? All the Stuff Your Body Won't Tell You about Sex. Zimmerman, Dwight Jon, ed. (p. 1897)
Zepeda, Frank. Wad of Gum. (p. 1852)
Zepeda, Gwendolyn. Growing up with Tamales/Los Tamales de Ana: Los tamales de Ana. (p. 727)
—I Kick the Ball: Pateo el Balón. Ventura, Gabriela Baeza, tr. (p. 840)
—Level up / Paso de Nivel. Baeza Ventura, Gabriela, tr. from ENG. (p. 1003)
Zepeda, Gwendolyn & Ventura, Gabriela Baeza. Growing up with Tamales: Los Tamales de Ana. Ward, April, illus. (p. 727)
—Sunflowers/Girasoles. Gambino, Alisha Ann Guadalupe, illus. (p. 1677)
Zepeda, Monique. Pinatas. Graullera, Fabiola, illus. (p. 1359)
Zephaniah, Benjamin. Being Cool. Bellemare, Paule Trudel, illus. (p. 161)
—Chambers Primary Rhyming Dictionary. (p. 289)
—Face. (p. 560)
—Funky Chickens. (p. 649)
—Gangsta Rap. (p. 655)
—Talking Turkeys. (p. 1704)
—We Are Britain! Das, Prodeepta, photos by. (p. 1865)
Zephaniah, Benjamin, et al. Theatre Centre - Plays for Young People: Celebrating 50 Years of Theatre Centre. Vol. 1 (p. 1728)
Zephyr, Jay, illus. see Aronson, Jeff & Aronson, Miriam.
Zepke, Terrance. Lighthouses of the Carolinas for Kids. (p. 1015)
—Pirates of the Carolinas for Kids. (p. 1364)
Zepp, Gene W. Return of the Pied Piper of Hamelin. (p. 1464)
Zeppa, Talaylin. Teddy the Tub. (p. 1713)
Zera, Annette & Szekeres, Vivienne. Grandma Gets a Fright. (p. 708)
—Grandma Gets a Visitor. (p. 708)
Zera, Beata. Little Puppy Swifty & Elle. (p. 1034)
Zéraoui, Zidane, jt. auth. see Marin-Guzman, Roberto.
Zerbe, J. S. Electricity for Boys. (p. 509)
Zerbe, Tim. King of Pumpkin Ridge. (p. 959)
Zerbetz, Evon, illus. see Ewing, Susan.
Zerbetz, Evon, illus. see Hesse, Karen.
Zerfing, Robert A. Silencer: A U. N. Conspiracy Novel. (p. 1575)
Zerga, Susan A., photos by see Wilson, Karen Collett.
Zerhusen, Margaret, jt. auth. see May, Marcie.
Zerick, Lura. Getting Older & Enjoying It! (p. 669)
Zeringue, Dona. I Am I. Zeringue, Dona, illus. (p. 833)
Zermeno C., Francisco. Caft Chronicles. (p. 251)
Zermeno, Mariana. Nuevo Peinado para Abuelitas. (p. 1270)
Zermeno, Rebeca M. Dinosaurios. (p. 443)
Zern, Linda L. Pocket Fairies of Middleburg. Day, Linda S., illus. (p. 1375)
Zerner, Sandra, jt. auth. see It's Good 2b Good Staff.
Zero to Ten Publication Staff, jt. auth. see Got, Yves.
Zerucha, Ted. Human Development. (p. 826)
Zeruneith, Keld. Wooden Horse: The Liberation of the Western Mind from Odysseus to Socrates. Jones, W. Glyn, ed. (p. 1949)
Zerza, Safoora Z. Sophia V. Is Flower Girl. (p. 1613)
Zettel, Sarah. Bad Luck Girl. (p. 132)
—Dust Girl (p. 490)
—Dust Girl: The American Fairy Trilogy Book 1. (p. 490)
—Golden Girl: The American Fairy Trilogy Book 2. (p. 694)
—Palace of Spies. (p. 1319)
Zettler, Andrew. Teeniest Tiniest Yawn. Zettler, Andrew, illus. (p. 1714)
Zev, Marc, et al. 101 Things Everyone Should Know about Math. (p. 2000)
Zeveren, Michel van. That's Mine! Zeveren, Michel van, illus. (p. 1727)
Zevgolis, Irene. Dreamer & the Moon: An Inspirational Story with a Ballet Theme. (p. 484)
Zevin, Gabrielle. All These Things I've Done. (p. 46)
—Because It Is My Blood (p. 155)
—Because It Is My Blood. (p. 155)
—Elsewhere. (p. 516)
—In the Age of Love & Chocolate. (p. 865)
—Memoirs of a Teenage Amnesiac. (p. 1125)
Zezelj, Danijel, illus. see Jones, Bruce & Austen, Chuck.
Zhang, Amy. Falling into Place. (p. 567)
Zhang, Ange. Red Land Yellow River: A Story from the Cultural Revolution. (p. 1454)
Zhang, Annie, illus. see Rankine-Van Wassenhoven, Jacqueline.
Zhang, Charles Yu. Adventure into Mediterranean Cultures: Lasting Memories of Our First European Adventure. (p. 14)
—China Perceptions: Views from an American Teenager. (p. 307)
Zhang, Christopher Zhong-Yuan, illus. see Russell, Ching Yeung & Boyds Mills Press Staff.
Zhang, Crystal. Lil' P & His Big Problem (p. 1017)
Zhang, Elizabeth Yuan. Middle Kingdom As We Saw: My Journey to China In 2004. (p. 1137)
Zhang, Gui Jie. Bamboo Forest: I Truly Love You, & God Loves You Too (p. 135)
Zhang, Hao Yu, jt. auth. see Zhang, Song Nan.
Zhang, Jianyi. Chickens First, Untangling Mystery of Specification. (p. 300)
Zhang, Kat. Echoes of Us: The Hybrid Chronicles, Book 3. (p. 502)
—Echoes of US. (p. 502)
—Once We Were: The Hybrid Chronicles, Book 2. (p. 1293)
—What's Left of Me. (p. 1898)
Zhang, Nancy, illus. see Taylor, Chloe.
Zhang, Nancy, illus. see Taylor, Chloe.
Zhang, Nancy, illus. see Taylor, Chloe.
Zhang, Nancy, illus. see Taylor, Chloe.
Zhang, Nancy, illus. see Taylor, Chloë.
Zhang, Nancy, illus. see Taylor, Chloë.
Zhang, Nancy, illus. see Taylor, Chloë.
Zhang, Song Nan. Time of Golden Dragons. (p. 1752)
Zhang, Song Nan, illus. see Bannatyne-Cugnet, Jo.
Zhang, Song Nan, illus. see Chan, Arlene.
Zhang, Song Nan, illus. see Hodge, Deborah.
Zhang, Song Nan, illus. see Wishinsky, Frieda.
Zhang, Song Nan & Zhang, Hao Yu. Great Voyages of Zheng He: English/Vietnamese. Do, Kim-Thu, tr. from ENG. (p. 719)
—Great Voyages of Zheng He. Zhang, Song Nan, illus. (p. 719)
—Time of Golden Dragons. Zhang, Song Nan, illus. (p. 1752)
Zhang, Zhibo. Origin of Intelligence: Past, Present & Future of Man. (p. 1304)
Zhao, Amei, illus. see Mallory, Carolyn.
Zhao, Yun, tr. see I-Haun.
Zhao, Yun, tr. see Jozev.
Zhao, Yun, tr. see Ma, Wing Shing & Lau, Ding Kin.
Zhao, Yun & I-Haun. Real Fake Princess (p. 1448)
Zheng, Wen, illus. see Wheeler-Gibb, Madelon, tr.
Zheng, Xiaoyan, illus. see Wang, Ruowen.
Zheng, Xin, illus. see Bullard, Lisa.
Zhihong, He, jt. auth. see Gower, Catherine.
Zhizhenko, V. A., jt. auth. see Burian, Boris.
Zhou, Carmen. Tree's Dream. (p. 1784)
Zi, Ying. Letters of Love. (p. 1002)
Zia, F. Hot, Hot Roti for Dada-Ji. Min, Ken, illus. (p. 801)
Zia, Farhana. Garden of My Imaan (p. 656)
Ziarnik, Natalie. Madeleine's Light: A Story of Camille Claudel. Dunn, Robert, illus. (p. 1070)
Ziborova, Dasha, illus. see Nobisso, Josephine.
Zick, Bruce, illus. see Nordling, Lee.
Zick, Bruce, et al. Thor: Blood & Thunder. (p. 1739)
Zidrou. Ducoboo: In the Corner! Godi, illus. (p. 488)
—Ducoboo: The Class Struggle. Spear, Luke, tr. from FRE. (p. 488)
—Ducoboo: Your Answers or Your Life! No. 3 Godi, illus. (p. 489)
Ziefert, Harriet. 10 Little Fish. Kreloff, Elliot, illus. (p. 1993)
—101 Ways to Be a Good Granny. Wesson, Andrea & Kath, Katie, illus. (p. 2000)
—40 Uses for a Grandpa. Haley, Amanda, illus. (p. 1997)
—41 Uses for a Grandma. Haley, Amanda, illus. (p. 1997)
—ABC Dentist: Healthy Teeth from A to Z. Murphy, Liz, illus. (p. 3)
—ABC Dentist. (p. 3)
—ABC Doctor: Staying Healthy from A to Z. Murphy, Liz, illus. (p. 3)
—ABC Doctor. (p. 3)
—Animals. Kreloff, Elliot & Lee, Huy Voun, illus. (p. 81)
—Are You My Brown Bear? O Donovan, Christina, illus. (p. 97)
—Banana Bunch & the Birthday Party! Blunt, Fred, illus. (p. 135)
—Banana Bunch & the Magic Show. Blunt, Fred, illus. (p. 135)
—Best Smelling Christmas Book Ever: 9 Scents to Scratch & Sniff! Rader, Laura, illus. (p. 171)
—Bunny's Lessons. Barroux, illus. (p. 243)
—Can You Whoo, Too? Fatus, Sophie, illus. (p. 260)
—Crab Cab: Flip-a-Word. Kido, Yukiko, illus. (p. 375)
—Dancing Class. Haley, Amanda, illus. (p. 402)
—Ding-Dong, Trick or Treat! Demarest, Chris L., illus. (p. 440)
—Does a Bear Wear Boots? Bolam, Emily, illus. (p. 460)
—Does a Beaver Sleep in a Bed? Bolam, Emily, illus. (p. 460)
—Does a Camel Cook Spaghetti? Think about... How Everyone Gets Food. Bolam, Emily, illus. (p. 460)
—Does a Hippo Go to the Doctor? Bolam, Emily, illus. (p. 460)
—Does a Panda Go to School? Think about... How Everyone Learns. Bolam, Emily, illus. (p. 460)
—Does a Seal Smile? Bolam, Emily, illus. (p. 460)
—Does a Tiger Go to the Dentist? Bolam, Emily, illus. (p. 460)
—Does a Woodpecker Use a Hammer? Bolam, Emily, illus. (p. 460)
—Does an Owl Wear Eyeglasses? Bolam, Emily, illus. (p. 460)
—Doodles at Breakfast. Zemke, Deborah, illus. (p. 469)
—Draw + Learn - Animals. Roitman, Tanya, illus. (p. 480)
—Draw + Learn - Faces. Roitman, Tanya, illus. (p. 480)
—Draw + Learn - Faces Everywhere! Kido, Yukiko, illus. (p. 480)
—Draw + Learn - People. Roitman, Tanya, illus. (p. 480)
—Draw + Learn - Places. Roitman, Tanya, illus. (p. 480)
—Frog Jog. Kido, Yukiko, illus. (p. 640)
—Fun Land Fun! Kido, Yukiko, illus. (p. 648)
—Goodnight Underwear. Doodler, Todd H., illus. (p. 701)
—Hey, Baby, It's Time to Come Out! Bolam, Emily, illus. (p. 774)
—I Say Yes! I Say No! Braun, Sebastian, illus. (p. 845)
—Ice Mice. Kido, Yukiko, illus. (p. 850)
—I'm Going to Washington to Visit the President. Roitman, Tanya, illus. (p. 859)
—It's Raining Cats & Frogs! Long, Ethan, illus. (p. 898)
—It's Time to Say Good Night. Barroux, illus. (p. 899)
—Long Vowels. Roitman, Tanya, illus. (p. 1047)
—Lower-Case Letters. Kido, Yukiko, illus. (p. 1061)
—Lucy Rescued. Barroux, illus. (p. 1063)
—Max & Sarah Build a Snowman. Trukhan, Ekaterina, illus. (p. 1110)
—Messy Bessie: Where's My Homework? De Muth, Roger, illus. (p. 1130)
—Monkey's Noisy Jungle. Newton, Jill, illus. (p. 1166)
—Monster Needs One More. Marshall, Natalie, illus. (p. 1168)
—My Dog Thinks I'm a Genius. Barroux, illus. (p. 1202)
—One Red Apple. Gudeon, Karla, illus. (p. 1296)
—Ouch! Rossi, Rich, illus. (p. 1307)
—Posey Paints Princess. Kido, Yukiko, illus. (p. 1387)
—Posey Plans a Party. Kido, Yukiko, illus. (p. 1387)
—Posey Prefers Pink. Kido, Yukiko, illus. (p. 1387)
—Princess and... The Peas & Carrots. Foster, Travis, illus. (p. 1403)
—Quack Shack. Kido, Yukiko, illus. (p. 1422)
—Read + Write - Rhyming Words. Kido, Yukiko, illus. (p. 1442)
—Rhyming Words. Kido, Yukiko, illus. (p. 1468)
—Short Vowels. Roitman, Tanya, illus. (p. 1569)
—Sight Words. Roitman, Tanya, illus. (p. 1574)
—Sleepy Dog, Wake Up! Gorbaty, Norman, illus. (p. 1589)
—Snow Bow: Flip-a-Word. Kido, Yukiko, illus. (p. 1598)
—Stop Pop. Kido, Yukiko, illus. (p. 1653)
—Surprise! Brown, Richard, illus. (p. 1685)
—Tic & Tac. Kreloff, Elliot, illus. (p. 1747)
—Two Little Witches: A Halloween Counting Story. Taback, Simms, illus. (p. 1804)
—Upper-Case Letters. Kido, Yukiko, illus. (p. 1825)
—Use Isbn 1593541627. (p. 1827)
—What Is Part This, Part That? Slaughter, Tom, illus. (p. 1890)
—What Ship Is Not a Ship? Masse, Josee, illus. (p. 1893)
—Where Does Kitty Go in the Rain? Barrager, Brigette, illus. (p. 1907)
—Where Is My Baby? Taback, Simms, illus. (p. 1908)
—Where Is the Rocket? Barroux, illus. (p. 1909)
—Who Said Moo? Taback, Simms, illus. (p. 1917)
—Wiggle! Like an Octopus. Taback, Simms, illus. (p. 1927)
—You & Me: We're Opposites. Sun, Ru & Long, Ethan, illus. (p. 1973)
—You Can't Buy a Dinosaur with a Dime. Haley, Amanda, illus. (p. 1974)
—You Can't Ride a Bicycle to the Moon! Haley, Amanda, illus. (p. 1975)
—You Can't See Your Bones with Binoculars! Haley, Amanda, illus. (p. 1975)
—You Can't Taste a Pickle with Your Ear. Haley, Amanda, illus. (p. 1975)
Ziefert, Harriet, jt. auth. see Murphy, Liz.
Ziefert, Harriet, jt. auth. see Taback, Simms.
Ziefert, Harriet & Davis, Samantha A. Bear in Love. Fatus, Sophie, illus. (p. 151)
Ziefert, Harriet & Ehrlich, Fred. You Can't Build a House If You're a Hippo! Haley, Amanda, illus. (p. 1974)
—You Can't Take Your Body to a Car Mechanic! Haley, Amanda, illus. (p. 1975)
—You Can't Use Your Brain If You're a Jellyfish! Haley, Amanda, illus. (p. 1975)
Ziefert, Harriet & Gott, Barry. Class Worms. (p. 327)
Ziefert, Harriet & Harriet, Ziefert. 31 Usos para Mama. Sarfatti, Esther, tr. (p. 1996)
Ziefert, Harriet & Johnston, Jan. Sleepy Barker. Kreloff, Elliot, illus. (p. 1589)
Ziefert, Harriet & Kreloff, Elliot. Found an Apple. (p. 624)
Ziefert, Harriet & Nagel, Karen. Lights on Broadway: A Theatrical Tour from A to Z. Kreloff, Elliot, illus. (p. 1016)
Ziefert, Harriet & SAMI Staff. Furry Friends: Same & Different. (p. 650)
Ziefert, Harriet & Taback, Simms. Listomania. Taback, Simms, illus. (p. 1022)
Ziefert, Harriet & Texas Tenors Staff. Ruckus on the Ranch. Fitzgerald, Brian, illus. (p. 1494)
Ziegesar, Cecily von. Adored. (p. 13)
—Devious. (p. 432)
—Gossip Girl, Psycho Killer. (p. 703)
—I Like It Like That. (p. 841)
—I Will Always Love You. (p. 848)
—It Had to Be You. (p. 894)
—Love the One You're With. (p. 1060)
—Nobody Does It Better. (p. 1262)
—Only in Your Dreams. (p. 1298)
—Would I Lie to You. (p. 1962)
—You're the One That I Want. (p. 1982)
Ziegesar, Cecily von & Turner, Steve. All I Want Is Everything. (p. 44)
Ziegesar, Cecily von & von Ziegesar, Cecily. Because I'm Worth It. (p. 155)
—Nothing Can Keep Us Together. (p. 1268)
Ziegesar, Cecily von, creator. Don't You Forget about Me. (p. 469)
—It Girl. (p. 894)
—Notorious. (p. 1268)
Ziegler, Anna, jt. auth. see Hainnu, Rebecca.
Ziegler, Argentina Palacios, tr. see Beinstein, Phoebe.
Ziegler, Argentina Palacios, tr. see Boynton, Sandra.
Ziegler, Argentina Palacios, tr. see Katz, Karen.
Ziegler, Argentina Palacios, tr. see Ricci, Christine.
Ziegler, Argentina Palacios, tr. see Silverhardt, Lauryn.

Ziegler, Argentina Palacios, tr. see Wax, Wendy.
Ziegler, Argentina Palacios, tr. see Winter, Jonah.
Ziegler, Argentina Palacios, tr. Dora y la Princesa de la Nieve (Dora Saves the Snow Princess) Aikins, Dave, illus. (p. 471)
Ziegler, Jennifer. How Not to Be Popular. (p. 811)
—Revenge of the Flower Girls. (p. 1466)
—Sass & Serendipity. (p. 1515)
Ziegler, Lori, jt. auth. see Ziegler, Tom.
Ziegler, Mark, jt. auth. see Dahl, Michael.
Ziegler, Mark & Dahl, Michael. Funny Farm: Jokes about Dogs, Cats, Ducks, Snakes, Bears, & Other Animals Haberstroh, Anne et al, illus. (p. 649)
Ziegler, Michael, illus. see Bramwell, Wendie, et al.
Ziegler, Michael, photos by see Bramwell, Wendie, et al.
Ziegler, Rini. Danielle & the Strawberry Fairies. (p. 405)
Ziegler, Tom & Ziegler, Lori. As for Me & My House: 50 Easy-to-Use Devotionals for Families. (p. 105)
Zielin, Lara. Donut Days. (p. 469)
Zielinski, Dave, photos by see Louck, Cheryl.
Zielinski, David. Misadventures of Fink the Mink: Playground Troubles. Ballou, Miss, ed. (p. 1150)
Zielinski, Valerie & Skaletski, Roslyn. Adventures of Bella. (p. 16)
Zielski, Julie A., jt. auth. see Ditchfield, Lily K.
Ziemann, Benjamin. War Experiences in Rural Germany: 1914-1923. (p. 1857)
Ziembo, Daniel, illus. see Bresloff, Robert.
Ziemer, Laura. Deena, My Best Friend. (p. 422)
Ziemian, Joseph. Cigarette Sellers of Three Crosses Square. (p. 319)
Zieroth, Emily, illus. see De Saulnier, Gia Volterra.
Ziersch, Nahum. Show & Go. (p. 1570)
Ziersch, Nahum, illus. see Loughlin, Patrick.
Ziesemer, Douglas A. Kenzie & the Dinosaurs. (p. 949)
—Kenzie's Big Question. (p. 949)
Ziff, John. American Revolution Musteen, Jason R., ed. (p. 63)
—Causes of World War I. (p. 282)
—Cold War Musteen, Jason R., ed. (p. 339)
—Gulf States: Alabama, Louisiana, Mississippi (p. 731)
—Gun Laws. (p. 732)
—Korean War Musteen, Jason R., ed. (p. 967)
—Northeast: New Jersey, New York, Pennsylvania (p. 1265)
—Northern New England: Maine, New Hampshire, Vermont (p. 1266)
—Northwest: Idaho, Oregon, Washington (p. 1266)
—Western Great Lakes: Illinois, Minnesota, Wisconsin (p. 1876)
—World War I Musteen, Jason R., ed. (p. 1958)
Ziff, Marsha. Reconstruction of the South after the Civil War in United States History. (p. 1452)
Ziglar, Christy. Can't-Wait Willow! Marten, Luanne Voltmer, illus. (p. 262)
—Must-Have Marvin! Martin, Luanne, illus. (p. 1194)
—Whatever Wanda. Billin-Frye, Paige, illus. (p. 1896)
Zijnen, Nicole. Cuentos para Contar a Tu Hijo Cuando Está Enfermo. (p. 390)
Zike, Dinah & McGraw-Hill Education Staff. Mathematics - Applications & Concepts: Interactive Study Notebook with Foldables. (p. 1108)
Zike, Dinah & McGraw-Hill-Glencoe Staff. Mathematics - Applications & Concepts. (p. 1108)
—Mathematics - Applications & Concepts, Course 1. (p. 1108)
Ziker, Andrew. Drumscapes: Instructional Guide for Beginning to Intermediate Drum Students. (p. 487)
Zilber, Denis, illus. see Hood, Ann & Altmann, Scott.
Zilber, Denis, illus. see Hood, Ann.
Zilber, Denis, illus. see Maddox, Jake & McMullan, Kate.
Zilber, Denis, illus. see McMullan, Kate.
Zilber, Denis, illus. see Namm, Diane & Andersen, Hans Christian.
Zilber, Denis, illus. see Namm, Diane.
Zilber, Denis, jt. auth. see Hood, Ann.
Zilber, Jeremy. Why Mommy Is a Democrat. Firsova, Yuliya, illus. (p. 1925)
Zile, Susan Van. Awesome Hands-On Activities for Teaching Grammar: Easy, Learning-Rich Activities That Tap into Students' Multiple Intelligences - And Bring Excitement & Fun to Your Grammar Lessons. (p. 121)
Zile, Susan Van, jt. auth. see Chang, Maria L.
Zilis, Tom. Little Red Hen: Read Well Level K Unit 20 Storybook. (p. 1034)
Zilis, Tom, illus. see Sprick, Marilyn, et al.
Ziliz, Anna. Weddings. (p. 1871)
Ziliz, Anna, jt. auth. see TickTock Staff.
Ziliz, Anna, jt. auth. see Ticktock.
Ziller, Amanda. Steve Jobs: American Genius. (p. 1649)
Zima, Gordon. Sunbirds & Evergreens. (p. 1676)
Zima, Gordon & Zima, Paula. Sun Birds & Evergreens: The Nuk-Chuk Stories. (p. 1676)
Zima, Marjorie H. Meghan's Military Family. (p. 1124)
Zima, Paula, jt. illus. see Zima, Gordon.
Zima, Siegfried, illus. see Benchimol, Brigitte.
Zimelman, Nathan. Evening Song. Morrison, Cathy, illus. (p. 541)
—Fishy Story. O'Malley, Kathleen, illus. (p. 599)
—Great Adventure of Wo Ti. (p. 713)
Zimet, Sara Goodman. Hannah & the Perfect Picture Pony: A Story of the Great Depression. Fuller, Sandy Ferguson, illus. (p. 742)
—Monster Solution. Parish, Shannon, illus. (p. 1168)
Zimic, Lesley, tr. see Nascimbeni, Barbara.
Zimic, Lesley, tr. from FRE. Picture My Day. (p. 1355)
Zimmer, Dirk, illus. see Aardvark, Esperanza.
Zimmer, Dirk, illus. see HarperCollins Publishers Ltd. Staff, et al.
Zimmer, Elizabeth. Turtle & the Deep Blue Sky. Zimmer, Eric, illus. (p. 1798)
Zimmer, Eric, illus. see Zimmer, Elizabeth.
Zimmer, Frank. Bird Singing Contest. (p. 190)
Zimmer, Glenn, illus. see Deutsch, Tehilla.
Zimmer, Gretchen. Stinkin' Thinkin' (p. 1651)
Zimmer, Joan, illus. see Helm, Charles & Owlkids Books Inc. Staff.
Zimmer, Kevin, illus. see Berneger, Marcia.
Zimmer, Kevin, illus. see Crouch, Cheryl.
Zimmer, Kyle, frwd. Jane Yolen. (p. 908)
—Who Wrote That? (p. 1919)
Zimmer, Tracie Vaughn. 42 Miles. Clayton, Elaine, illus. (p. 1997)
—Cousins of Clouds: Elephant Poems. Halsey, Megan & Addy, Sean, illus. (p. 373)
Zimmer, Tracie Vaughn & Vaughn Zimmer, Tracie. Floating Circus. (p. 605)
Zimmerle, Mick. Hound & the Basketballs. (p. 802)
Zimmerly, et al. Keyboarding Connections: Projects & Applications: Microsoft Office 2000 Student Guide. (p. 950)
Zimmerman, Amanda. Spring Snowman. (p. 1635)
Zimmerman, Andrea. Eliza's Cherry Trees: Japan's Gift to America Chen, Ju-Hong, illus. (p. 513)
Zimmerman, Andrea, jt. auth. see Clemesha, David.
Zimmerman, Andrea & Clemesha, David. Dig! Rosenthal, Marc, illus. (p. 438)
—Digger Man. Zimmerman, Andrea & Clemesha, David, illus. (p. 438)
—Train Man. Zimmerman, Andrea & Clemesha, David, illus. (p. 1777)
Zimmerman, Andrea Griffing & Clemesha, David. Dig! Rosenthal, Marc, tr. (p. 438)
—Digger Man. Zimmerman, Andrea Griffing & Clemesha, David, illus. (p. 438)
Zimmerman, Barb. Buttons on my Head. (p. 248)
Zimmerman, Beverly. Bridal Planner. (p. 227)
Zimmerman, Bill. City Doodles: Los Angles. (p. 323)
—City Doodles New York (p. 323)
—Pocketdoodles for Kids (p. 1375)
—Pocketdoodles for Young Artists Bloom, Tom, illus. (p. 1375)
Zimmerman, Bob. American Challenge: Twenty-One Winning Strategies for the 21st Century. (p. 60)
Zimmerman, Brandon. Societal Equilibrium: The First Iteration. (p. 1605)
Zimmerman, Brian. Story of Tweeker the Time Traveler. Foraker, Doreen, ed. (p. 1662)
Zimmerman, Brooke. Read Me a Story. Weidner, Teri, illus. (p. 1443)
Zimmerman, Carol. Charlie the Spider. (p. 293)
Zimmerman, Diana S. Kandide & the Secret of the Mists. Gadd, Maxine, illus. (p. 942)
Zimmerman, Dorothy. Why Am I Different? (p. 1922)
Zimmerman, Dwight Jon. First Command: Paths to Leadership. (p. 593)
Zimmerman, Dwight Jon, ed. see Zep.
Zimmerman, Dwight Jon, jt. auth. see O'Reilly, Bill.
Zimmerman, Edith Fay Martin, illus. see Stoltzfus, Sherman Matthew.
Zimmerman, Erik. Booga-Boo - Coloring Book. (p. 210)
Zimmerman, George G. Dougie & the Dane: Chelsea the Great Dane. (p. 473)
Zimmerman, Howard. Armored & Dangerous. (p. 99)
Zimmerman, James P. Marylanders: A Story of the Civil War. (p. 1101)
Zimmerman, Joelle, tr. see Hausfater, Rachel.
Zimmerman, Kadie, illus. see Budds, Laura.
Zimmerman, Karla, et al. Eastern USA. (p. 500)
Zimmerman, Kathleen. Oscar's First Flight. Feldmeier Sims, Julie & Hartman, John, illus. (p. 1305)
Zimmerman, Kurt. Super Kids! Code Green! Somebody Kidnapped Grandpa! (p. 1680)
Zimmerman, Kwanza A. What Day Is It? (p. 1881)
Zimmerman, Larry J. Exploring the Life, Myth, & Art of Native Americans. (p. 554)
Zimmerman, Leora. God Loves Me. (p. 689)
Zimmerman, Louis, illus. see Richards, Arlene.
Zimmerman, Mary. Secret in the Wings. (p. 1541)
Zimmerman, Mary Joyce. Good Morning Baby! Hartzler, Maria, illus. (p. 698)
—Just Four. (p. 938)
Zimmerman, Michael. Mouse & the Acorn. (p. 1181)
Zimmerman, Natalie, tr. see Kinney, Jeff.
Zimmerman, Noam. Yom Kippur Children's Machzor. (p. 1972)
Zimmerman, Robert. Switchfoot. (p. 1692)
Zimmerman, Robert, illus. see Lore, Mark & Lore, Matthew.
Zimmerman, Robert K. Switchfoot. (p. 1692)
Zimmerman, Ron. Ultimate Adventures: One Tin Soldier. Vol. 1 (p. 1809)
Zimmerman, Rusty, illus. see Biskup, Agnieszka.
Zimmerman, Suzanne, illus. see Mast, Dorcas R.
Zimmerman, Suzi. Introduction to Theatre Arts: A 36-Week Action Handbook. (p. 882)
—Introduction to Theatre Arts: An Action Handbook for Middle Grade & High School Students & Teachers. (p. 882)
Zimmerman, T. W., illus. see Dodgson, Y. K.
Zimmerman, Tom and Kat & Taylor, Tom. Fun with Fred. (p. 648)
Zimmerman, W. Our Colorful Moon: Beautiful Images to Energize & Delight. (p. 1308)
Zimmerman, W. Frederick. Cool Maps for Curious Kids #2: Afghanistan, an Unauthorized Tour of the Land of A THOUSAND SPLENDID SUNS & the KITE RUNNER. (p. 363)
—Cool Maps of Cub: An Atlas of History, Population, Resources Before & after Fidel Castro. (p. 363)
—Cool Maps of Iran: Persian History, Oil Wealth, Politics, Population, Religion, Satellite, WMD & More. (p. 363)
—Cool Maps of Iraq: History, Oil Wealth, Politics, Population, Religion, Satellite, & More. (p. 363)
—Cool Science Images for Curious Kids #1: Our Splendid Sun. (p. 364)
—Nine Current Supreme Court Justices: Colorful Info for Curious Minds #3. (p. 1256)
—Unauthorized Harry Potter & the Alchemist's Cell News: Half-Blood Prince Analysis & Speculation. (p. 1811)
—Unauthorized Harry Potter & the Chariots of Light News: Half-Blood Prince Analysis & Speculation. (p. 1811)
Zimmermann, Andreas. Shard. (p. 1561)
Zimmermann, Antonie, tr. see Carroll, Lewis, pseud.
Zimmermann, Kari, photos by see Zimmermann, Karl.
Zimmermann, Karl. All Aboard! Passenger Trains Around the World. Zimmermann, Kari, photos by. (p. 41)
—Ocean Liners: Crossing & Cruising the Seven Seas. (p. 1276)
—Steamboats: The Story of Lakers, Ferries, & Majestic Paddle-Wheelers. Zimmermann, Karl, photos by. (p. 1646)
—Stourbridge Lion: America's First Locomotive. Walker, Steven, illus. (p. 1664)
Zimmermann, Natalie. Principe para Lila. (p. 1406)
Zimmerschied, P. Grampa Paul's Adventure Stories for Children. (p. 706)
Zimny, Joanne. Using Picture Books to Teach Comprehension Strategies: 30 Lessons That Teach Students the Six Comprehension Strategies They Need to Actively Engage with Text & Read for Meaning. (p. 1828)
Zimny, Stan, photos by see Goble, Brant & Goble, Faith, eds.
Zinczenko, David & Spiker, Ted. Abs Diet Get Fit Stay Fit Plan: The Exercise Program to Flatten Your Belly, Reshape Your Body, & Give You Abs for Life! (p. 7)
—Men, Love & Sex: The Complete User's Guide for Women. (p. 1126)
Zindel, Paul. Effect of Gamma Rays on Man-in-the-Moon Marigolds. (p. 505)
—Egyptian Mystery. (p. 507)
—Loch. (p. 1044)
—Pigman. (p. 1358)
—Pigman's Legacy. (p. 1358)
Zindel, Paul, jt. auth. see Zindel, Paul.
Zindel, Paul & Zindel, Paul. Gadget. (p. 652)
—My Darling, My Hamburger. (p. 1201)
—Pigman's Legacy. (p. 1358)
Ziner, Amie, illus. see Crelin, Bob.
Ziniti, Mike. Annie Mcgwire & the Time Flyer. (p. 87)
Zinjiba-Nyakutya, Peshie. From Adam to Noah in Coloring Pages: Genesis 1 To 9. Chitombo, Patience, illus. (p. 641)
Zink, Michelle. Circle of Fire. (p. 321)
—Lies I Told. (p. 1007)
—Promises I Made. (p. 1411)
—Prophecy of the Sisters. (p. 1411)
—Temptation of Angels. (p. 1718)
Zink, Michelle, jt. auth. see Osbourne, Ozzy, pseud.
Zink, Rui. Boy Who Did Not Like Television. Dreher, Patrick, tr. from POR. (p. 219)
Zinke, William. Bugs: Big & Small, God Made Them All. (p. 237)
Zinn, Alarna, illus. see Bartholomew, Andrew & Bartholomew, Hailey.
Zinn, Bridget. Poison. (p. 1377)
Zinn, Howard. Young People's History of the United States: Class Struggle to the War on Terror. Vol. 2 (p. 1979)
—Young People's History of the United States: Columbus to the Spanish-American War. Vol. 1 (p. 1979)
Zinnen, Linda. What Next? (p. 1892)
Zinner, Gennieve. UFB's of Bugsville, Florida USA Ballinger, Carolyn, illus. (p. 1807)
Zinni, Tony & Koltz, Tony. Battle for Peace: A Frontline Vision of America's Power & Purpose. (p. 145)
Zins, Rebecca, ed. see Stolarz, Laurie Faria.
Zinsmeister, Elke. Ten Fat Sausages. (p. 1718)
Zinsser, Kam. Turbo Fires Up! (p. 1797)
Zintel, Kristian. Frank Flower & Willie Weed. (p. 628)
Zintoll, Gabreyhl, illus. see Hinton, Amber.
Ziolkowski, Ania, illus. see Collins, Yozette Yogi & Jennings, Marlis.
Zion, jt. auth. see Zion, Gene.
Zion, Gene. Harry & the Lady Next Door. (p. 750)
—Harry & the Lady Next Door. Graham, Margaret Bloy, illus. (p. 750)
—Harry, el Perrito Sucio. Fiol, María A., tr. (p. 750)
—Harry the Dirty Dog. (p. 751)
—Harry the Dirty Dog. Graham, Margaret Bloy, illus. (p. 751)
Zion, Gene & Zion. Harry the Dirty Dog. Graham, Margaret Bloy, illus. (p. 751)
Zion, Noam, et al. Different Light: The Big Book of Hanukkah. (p. 438)
—Different Light: The Hanukkah Book of Celebration. (p. 438)
Zipes, Jack, tr. see von Olfers, Sibylle.
Zipes, Jack D., tr. see Grimm, Jacob & Grimm, Wilhelm K.
Zipes, Jack, ed. Beauties, Beasts & Enchantment: Classic French Fairy Tales. (p. 153)
Zipf, Sean. What Color Is Spring? Antkowski, Marygrace, illus. (p. 1881)
Zipperer, Susan Johnson, illus. see Childress, Mildred Tickfer.
Zircher, Patrick, illus. see Youngquist, Jeff, ed.
Zircher, Patrick, et al. Captain America by Ed Brubaker - Volume 3. (p. 263)
Zirin, David. My Name Is Erica Montoya de la Cruz. White, Deborah, illus. (p. 1215)
Zirkel, Scott, jt. auth. see Huddleston, Courtney.
Zirkind, Chaya Sara. Bas Mitzvah X 3. (p. 140)
Zirlin, Sande H. Visits to Gradma's House. (p. 1846)
Ziskie, Adam, illus. see Cook, Jane Hampton.
Ziskind, Héllo & Duchesne, Christiane. Géant de la Forêt: Un Voyage Musical. Pratt, Pierre, illus. (p. 659)
Ziss, Debra, illus. see Jukes, Mavis, et al.
Ziss, Debra, illus. see Weinberger, Kimberly.
Zitkala-Sa. Dance in a Buffalo Skull. Nelson, S. D., illus. (p. 402)
Zitkus, K S. Krissi Swan: Cover-up Girl. (p. 967)
Zitnak, Allison Day, illus. see DuBois, Juli.
Zito, Ann R. Rock, Stream, Tree. Matheny, Melody, illus. (p. 1482)
Zittel, Michael, illus. see Mongillo, Michael.
Zittrauer, G. Alwyn. Beauty of Truth: An Epic of Metaphysical Existence. (p. 154)
Zivney, Missy Mullican, jt. auth. see Mullican, Norma Waldon.
Zivoin, Jennifer, illus. see James, Brian.
Zivoin, Jennifer, illus. see McKay, Sindy.
Zivoin, Jennifer, illus. see Rudolph, Shaina & Royer, Danielle.
Zizka, Theo, jt. auth. see Zizkaj, Theo.
Zizkaj, Theo & Zizka, Theo. 3D Modeling. (p. 1992)
Zlatic, Tomislav, illus. see Clarke, Jane.
Zlatic, Tomislav, illus. see Roberts, Victoria.
Zlatic, Tomislav, jt. auth. see Hughes, Mónica.
Zmich, Elizabeth & Adler, Penny. Check Yourself into College: A Quick & Easy Guide for High School Students. (p. 295)
Zmina, Stephen. Don't Let the Dead Bugs Bite! Zmina, Stephen, illus. (p. 468)
Zmora, Avram, illus. see Lieberman, Naomi.
Zobel, Derek. A-10 Thunderbolts. (p. 1)
—Alligators. (p. 47)
—Asteroids. (p. 108)
—Badgers. (p. 132)
—Blastoff! Readers - Mighty Machines (p. 198)
—Bucket Trucks. (p. 234)
—Caring for Your Cat. (p. 269)
—Caring for Your Dog. (p. 269)
—Caring for Your Hamster. (p. 269)
—Chimpanzees. (p. 306)
—Chipmunks. (p. 308)
—Deer. (p. 423)
—Denmark. (p. 426)
—Diggers. (p. 439)
—Ducks. (p. 488)
—Earth. (p. 495)
—Eels. (p. 505)
—F-117A Nighthawks. (p. 559)
—F-22 Raptors. (p. 559)
—Fishing. (p. 599)
—Gophers. (p. 702)
—Gorillas. (p. 703)
—Hubble Telescope. (p. 824)
—Jupiter. (p. 937)
—Lions. (p. 1021)
—Mars. (p. 1096)
—Mercury. (p. 1127)
—Monster Vehicles. (p. 1168)
—Motorcycles. (p. 1179)
—NASA. (p. 1230)
—Neptune. (p. 1241)
—Nimitz Aircraft Carriers. (p. 1256)
—Norway. (p. 1266)
—Philippines. (p. 1350)
—Pickup Trucks. (p. 1354)
—Rabbits. (p. 1430)
—Race Cars. (p. 1430)
—Road Rollers. (p. 1477)
—Saturn. (p. 1515)
—Scotland. (p. 1530)
—Scrapers. (p. 1532)
—South Korea. (p. 1617)
—Squirrels. (p. 1637)
—Switzerland. (p. 1692)
—Tigers. (p. 1749)
—United States Air Force. (p. 1819)
—Wheel Loaders. (p. 1900)
—Zebras. (p. 1985)
Zobel, Melissa Tantaquidgeon. Wakanabi Blues: The Wabanaki Trilogy. (p. 1853)
Zobel-Nolan, Allia. Amazing Life of Jesus. Cox, Steve, illus. (p. 55)
—Animal Parade. Maddocks, Maria, illus. (p. 79)
—Bunnies Are for Kissing. East, Jacqueline, illus. (p. 242)
—Catholic Baby's Bedtime Bible Stories. Stevenson, Peter, illus. (p. 280)
—Hugs for Baby! Mitchell, Susan, illus. (p. 825)
—Living It: Young Christian Girl's Scrapbook. (p. 1041)
—Mrs. McGee's Coconut. Cottrill, Peter, illus. (p. 1187)
—Ninos en la Biblia. (p. 1257)
—Peek & Find Bible Stories. Cox, Steve, illus. (p. 1335)
—Peek & Find Christmas Story. Cox, Steve, illus. (p. 1335)
—Primera Biblia del Bebe. (p. 1400)
—Smelly Feet Sandwich: And Other Silly Poems. Leake, Kate, illus. (p. 1593)
—What I Like about Me! Sakamoto, Miki, illus. (p. 1886)
Zobel-Nolan, Allia, jt. auth. see Reader's Digest Editors.
Zoboli, Giovanna. Big Book of Slumber. Mulazzani, Simona, illus. (p. 179)
Zoboli, Giovanna & Mathews, Leslie. I Wish I Had... Mulazzani, Simona, illus. (p. 848)
Zoboli, Giovanna & Watkinson, Laura. Animal Supermarket. Mulazzani, Simona, illus. (p. 80)
Zocchi, Judith Mazzeo. In South Africa. Brodie, Neale, illus. (p. 865)
—Uri's "U" Book. Revutsky, Helen Ross, illus. (p. 1825)
—What Has Three Horns & a Sharp Beak? Daff, Russ, illus. (p. 1886)
—Will's W Book: El Libro "W" de Will. (p. 1934)
—Yola's "Y" Book. Revutsky, Helen Ross, illus. (p. 1972)
Zocchi, Judith Mazzeo, et al. Aimee's a Book: El Libro a de Aimee. Revutsky, Helen Ross, illus. (p. 30)
—Bebe's "B" Book: El Libro "B" de Bibi. Revutsky, Helen Ross, illus. (p. 155)
—Delia's D Book: El Libro D de Delia. Revutsky, Helen Ross, illus. (p. 425)
—Tad's "T" Book: El Libro "T" de Tad. (p. 1695)
—Vera's "V" Book: El Libro "V" de Vera. (p. 1836)
—Xavia's "X" Book: El Libro "X" de Xavia. Revutsky, Helen Ross, illus. (p. 1967)
—Zach's "Z" Book: El Libro "Z" de Zach. Revutsky, Helen Ross, illus. (p. 1984)
Zocchi, Judy. Cassie's "C" Book: El Libro "C" de Cassie. (p. 276)
—Curtain Up: Application Software. (p. 395)
—Dear Principal Petunia: Word Processing. Bird, Nikolai, illus. (p. 419)
—In Canada. Brodie, Neale, illus. (p. 863)
—In Canada/en Canada. Brodie, Neale, illus. (p. 863)
—In Cuba. Brodie, Neale, illus. (p. 863)
—In Cuba/en Cuba. Brodie, Neale, illus. (p. 863)
—In Germany. Brodie, Neale, illus. (p. 863)
—In Germany/en Alemania. Brodie, Neale, illus. (p. 863)
—In Japan. Brodie, Neale, illus. (p. 864)

—In Japan/en Japón. Brodie, Neale, illus. (p. 864)
—In Mexico. Brodie, Neale, illus. (p. 864)
—In Mexico/en México. Brodie, Neale, illus. (p. 864)
—In Nigeria. Brodie, Neale, illus. (p. 864)
—In Nigeria/en Nigeria. Brodie, Neale, illus. (p. 864)
—In Scotland. Brodie, Neale, illus. (p. 864)
—In Scotland/en Escocia. Brodie, Neale, illus. (p. 864)
—In Sweden. Brodie, Neale, illus. (p. 865)
—In Sweden/en Suecia. Brodie, Neale, illus. (p. 865)
—In Switzerland. Brodie, Neale, illus. (p. 865)
—In Switzerland/en Suiza. Brodie, Neale, illus. (p. 865)
—In the United States. Brodie, Neale, illus. (p. 867)
—In the United States/en los Estados Unidos. Brodie, Neale, illus. (p. 867)
—In Turkey. Brodie, Neale, illus. (p. 868)
—In Turkey/en Turquía. Brodie, Neale, illus. (p. 868)
—In Vietnam. Brodie, Neale, illus. (p. 868)
—In Vietnam/en Vietnam. Brodie, Neale, illus. (p. 868)
—In Vietnam/en Vietnam. Brodie, N. eale, illus. (p. 868)
—Meet Click & Squeak: How Computers Work. (p. 1120)
—Number 1 What Grows in the Sun? Wallis, Rebecca, illus. (p. 1271)
—On Chinese New Year. Wallis, Rebecca, illus. (p. 1288)
—On Chinese New Year/el Año Nuevo Chino. Wallis, Rebecca, illus. (p. 1288)
—On Christmas Eve. Wallis, Rebecca, illus. (p. 1288)
—On Christmas Eve/la Nochebuena. Wallis, Rebecca, illus. (p. 1288)
—On Easter Morning. Wallis, Rebecca, illus. (p. 1288)
—On Easter Morning/la mañana de Pascua. Wallis, Rebecca, illus. (p. 1288)
—On Halloween Night. Wallis, Rebecca, illus. (p. 1289)
—On Halloween Night/la noche de Halloween. Wallis, Rebecca, illus. (p. 1289)
—On Hanukkah. Wallis, Rebecca, illus. (p. 1289)
—On Hanukkah/la Hanukkah. Wallis, Rebecca, illus. (p. 1289)
—On Independence Day. Wallis, Rebecca, illus. (p. 1289)
—On Independence Day/el día de la Independencia. Wallis, Rebecca, illus. (p. 1289)
—On Kwanzaa. Wallis, Rebecca, illus. (p. 1289)
—On Kwanzaa/la Kwanzaa. Wallis, Rebecca, illus. (p. 1289)
—On New Year's Eve. Wallis, Rebecca, illus. (p. 1289)
—On New Year's Eve/la Nochevieja. Wallis, Rebecca, illus. (p. 1289)
—On Saint Patrick's Day. Wallis, Rebecca, illus. (p. 1289)
—On Saint Patrick's Day/el día de San Patricio. Wallis, Rebecca, illus. (p. 1289)
—On Thanksgiving Day. Wallis, Rebbeca, illus. (p. 1289)
—On Thanksgiving Day. Wallis, Rebecca, illus. (p. 1289)
—On Thanksgiving Day/el Día de Acción de Gracias. Wallis, Rebecca, illus. (p. 1289)
—On Three Kings Day. Wallis, Rebecca, illus. (p. 1292)
—On Three Kings Day/el día de los tres Reyes Magos. Wallis, Rebecca, illus. (p. 1292)
—On Valentine's Day. Wallis, Rebecca, illus. (p. 1292)
—On Valentine's Day/el día de San Valentín. Wallis, Rebecca, illus. (p. 1292)
—Secret Diary: Saving Files. (p. 1540)
—Squeak for President: Printing Documents. (p. 1636)
Zockoll, Brad. Risking Daylight (p. 1475)
Zodl, Joseph A. Export Import: Everything You & Your Company Need to Know to Compete in World Markets. (p. 554)
Zoehfeld, Kathleen Weidner. Apollo 13. Lowe, Wesley, illus. (p. 91)
—Curse of King Tut's Mummy. Nelson, Jim, illus. (p. 394)
—Did Dinosaurs Have Feathers? Washburn, Lucia, illus. (p. 436)
—Dinosaur Tracks. Washburn, Lucia, illus. (p. 443)
—Dinosaurs. (p. 444)
—Dolphin's First Day: The Story of a Bottlenose Dolphin. Petruccio, Steven James, illus. (p. 465)
—Fawn at Woodland Way. Snyder, Joel, illus. (p. 578)
—Finding the First T. Rex. Nelson, Jim, illus. (p. 588)
—From Tadpole to Frog. (p. 644)
—Ghost Mysteries: Unraveling the World's Most Mysterious Hauntings. Hale, Nathan, illus. (p. 671)
—Great White Shark: Ruler of the Sea. (p. 719)
—Great White Shark: Ruler of the Sea. Petruccio, Steven James, illus. (p. 719)
—How Deep Is the Ocean? Puybaret, Eric, illus. (p. 806)
—How Mountains Are Made. Hale, James Graham, illus. (p. 811)
—Manatee Winter. Petruccio, Steven James, illus. (p. 1086)
—National Geographic Readers: Prehistoric Mammals. (p. 1233)
—National Geographic Readers: Rocks & Minerals. (p. 1233)
—Seal Pup Grows Up: The Story of a Harbor Seal. Bonforte, Lisa, illus. (p. 1536)
—Secrets of the Garden: Food Chains & the Food Web in Our Backyard. Lamont, Priscilla, illus. (p. 1545)
—Secrets of the Seasons: Orbiting the Sun in Our Backyard. (p. 1546)
—What Is the World Made Of? Meisel, Paul, illus. (p. 1890)
—What Lives in a Shell? Davie, Helen K., illus. (p. 1891)
—Where Did Dinosaurs Come From? (p. 1906)
—Where Did Dinosaurs Come From? Washburn, Lucia, illus. (p. 1906)
Zoehfeld, Kathleen Weidner, jt. auth. see Barr, Brady.
Zoehfeld, Kathleen Weidner, jt. auth. see Skerry, Brian.
Zoehfeld, Kathleen Weidner & Petruccio, Steven James. Dolphin's First Day: The Story of a Bottlenose Dolphin. (p. 465)
Zoehfeld, Kathleen Weidner & Rey, H. A. Curious You on Your Way! (p. 394)
Zoehfeld, Kathleen Weidner & Smithsonian Institution Staff. Ladybug at Orchard Avenue (Mariquite en la avenida Orchard) (p. 971)
—Primer Dia del Delfin: La Historia de un Delfin Nariz de Botella. (p. 1400)
Zoehfeld, Kathleen Weidner & U. S. National Geographic Society Staff. Dinosaurs. (p. 444)
Zoellick, Todd. Daniel Harrington Fairbanks the Third & a Day on the Farm. (p. 405)
—Daniel Harrington Fairbanks the Third & the Dog That Wouldn't Bark. (p. 405)
Zograf, Aleksandar. Regards from Serbia: A Cartoonist's Diary of War in Serbia. (p. 1457)
Zola, Émile. Trois Nouvelles (p. 1788)
Zola, Mequido, jt. auth. see Downie, Mary Alice.
Zolan, Donald. My Favorite Farm Animal Friends. (p. 1203)
Zoldak, Joyce. Danger in the Deep: Surviving Shark Attacks. (p. 403)
—Danger in the Deep: Survivors of Shark Attacks. (p. 403)
—When Danger Hits Home: Survivors of Domestic Violence. (p. 1901)
Zoldak, Joyce, jt. auth. see Nelson, Sheila.
Zoldan, Yael. We Can Do Mitzvos from Aleph to Tav. Allen, Shira, illus. (p. 1866)
Zolinsky, Daniel, tr. see Lenain, Thierry.
Zolkower, Edie Stoltz. It's Tu B'Shevat. Johnson, Richard, illus. (p. 899)
—When It's Purim. Bjornson, Barb, illus. (p. 1903)
Zolkowski, Cathy A., jt. auth. see Wilson, J. M.
Zollars, Jaime, illus. see Glaser, Linda.
Zollars, Jaime, illus. see Goldin, Barbara Diamond.
Zollars, Jaime, illus. see Kimmelman, Leslie.
Zollars, Jaime, illus. see Milford, Kate.
Zollars, Jaime, illus. see Riggs, Shannon.
Zoller, Arthur David. Fish Colors. (p. 598)
Zoller, Elisabeth & Kolloch, Brigitte. Antonia & the Big Competition: The Rosenburg Riding Stables, Volume 2. Gotzen-Beek, Betina, illus. (p. 90)
Zöller, Elisabeth & Kolloch, Brigitte. Antonia, the Horse Whisperer: The Rosenburg Riding Stables, Volume 1. Gotzen-Beek, Betina, illus. (p. 90)
Zoller, Jayson D. Laziest Duck. (p. 981)
Zoller, Jayson D., illus. see Seagreaves, Kelly E.
Zollitsch, Mike. Buffalo, Rochester, & Pittsburgh Railway: In Color. (p. 236)
Zollman, Pam. Animal Life Cycles. (p. 78)
—Cómo Crece un Pollito. (p. 350)
—George W. Bush: President in a Turbulent World. (p. 664)
—Idaho. (p. 852)
—Lake Tahoe. (p. 972)
—Nebraska. (p. 1239)
—North Dakota. (p. 1265)
Zolotow, Charlotte. Changes: A Child's First Poetry Collection. Beeke, Tiphanie, illus. (p. 290)
—Father Like That. Scribner, Joanne & Pham, LeUyen, illus. (p. 577)
—Growing up Stories for 5-6 Year Olds. (p. 727)
—Hold My Hand: Five Stories of Love & Family. Thompson, Carol, illus. (p. 787)
—If It Weren't for You. Karas, G. Brian, illus. (p. 853)
—Janey. Himler, Ronald, illus. (p. 908)
—Say It! Voake, Charlotte, illus. (p. 1518)
—Seashore Book. Minor, Wendell, illus. (p. 1538)
—Sleepy Book. (p. 1589)
—Three Funny Friends. Bronson, Linda, illus. (p. 1742)
—When the Wind Stops. (p. 1905)
Zolty, H. Calli the Bear: the Story of a Little Bear Who Explores California & Helps Children Learn about the Golden State. (p. 254)
—Calli the Bear: the Story of a Little Bear Who Teaches Children about the Power of Friendship. (p. 254)
Zolty, Howard. Mountain View A through Z. A Colorful Reader for Children of All Ages. (p. 1181)
—What Is Math? Answer: Math Is Everything. (p. 1889)
Zolty, Meredith. Ben Has Autism. Ben Is Awesome. Rebecca, Rivard, illus. (p. 163)
—Ben Has Autism. Ben Is Awesome. Rivard, Rebecca, illus. (p. 163)
Zomchek, Rebecca, illus. see Calkhoven, Laurie.
Zomerdyke, Joy. Polar & Grizzly Find Christmas. (p. 1378)
—Teddy B Is for Bear: Meets a Scary Monster. (p. 1712)
Zommer, Yuval. Big Blue Thing on the Hill. Zommer, Yuval, illus. (p. 178)
Zompetti, Joseph P., et al, eds. International Criminal Court: Global Politics & the Quest for Justice. (p. 880)
ZonderKidz Staff. Precious Princess Bible (p. 1394)
ZonderKidz Staff, jt. auth. see Zondervan Publishing Staff.
Zondervan. Beginner's Bible Curriculum Kit: 30 Timeless Lessons for Preschoolers (p. 159)
—Believe - Coloring Book: Think, Act, & Be Like Jesus Pamintuan, Macky, illus. (p. 161)
—Curious Creatures (p. 392)
—Father's Love Miles, David, illus. (p. 577)
—God's Great Creation Miles, David, illus. (p. 691)
—Kids' Devotional Bible (p. 953)
—Miracles of Jesus Miles, David, illus. (p. 1149)
—Moses Leads the People Miles, David, illus. (p. 1176)
—NIRV Backpack Bible (p. 1257)
—Nirv Precious Princess Bible (p. 1257)
—Ocean Adventures, Volume 1: Whales, Waves, & Ocean Wonders (p. 1276)
—Ocean Adventures, Volume 3: Winged Creatures, Waterfalls, & Wild Reptiles (p. 1276)
—Plush - Backpack Bible (p. 1374)
—Super Heroes Backpack Bible (p. 1680)
—Wacky Bible Blockheads (p. 1852)
—Wacky Bible Gross Outs (p. 1852)
—Weird & Wonderful Creations (p. 1872)
—Wilderness Discoveries, Volume 1: Sand, Snakes, & Screeching Birds (p. 1931)
—Wilderness Discoveries, Volume 2: Forest, Frogs, & Feisty Critters (p. 1931)
—Wilderness Discoveries, Volume 3: Bugs, Bogs, & Spiky Beasts (p. 1931)
Zondervan, A. First Christmas Ever Jones, Dennis, illus. (p. 593)
Zondervan & Lyons, P. J. Little Bunny's Bible Mitchell, Melanie, illus. (p. 1025)
—Little Chick's Bible Mitchell, Melanie, illus. (p. 1026)
Zondervan & Poth, Karen. Yuletide Ice Cube Fair (p. 1983)
Zondervan & Schriemer, Peter. Ocean Adventures, Volume 2: Fins, Foliage, & Shoreline Fun (p. 1276)
Zondervan & Walburg, Lori. Legend of the Candy Cane Cowdrey, Richard, illus. (p. 989)
Zondervan Bibles Staff. Beginner's Bible Come Celebrate Easter Pulley, Kelly, illus. (p. 159)
—Big Bugs, Little Bugs (p. 180)
—Jonah, God's Messenger Jones, Dennis, illus. (p. 925)
—Moses & the King Pulley, Kelly, illus. (p. 1176)
—Noah's Voyage Miles, David, illus. (p. 1262)
—Story Trading Cards - For Preschool: Pre-K Through Grade 2 (p. 1663)
Zondervan Bibles Staff, jt. auth. see Martin, Gary.
Zondervan Publishing Staff. 1001 Bible Questions (p. 2001)
—Adam & Eve, God's First People Jones, Dennis, illus. (p. 11)
—Adam & Eve in the Garden Pulley, Kelly, illus. (p. 11)
—Adventure Bible for Early Readers (p. 14)
—Armor of God Bible (p. 99)
—Baby Jesus Is Born Pulley, Kelly, illus. (p. 126)
—Baby Moses & the Princess Pulley, Kelly, illus. (p. 127)
—Beginner's Bible All about Jesus Sticker & Activity Book Pulley, Kelly, illus. (p. 159)
—Beginner's Bible Collector's Edition: Timeless Children's Stories Pulley, Kelly, illus. (p. 159)
—Beginner's Bible Stories about Jesus Pulley, Kelly, illus. (p. 159)
—Beginners Bible Super Duper Mighty Jumbo Coloring Book (p. 159)
—Beginner's Bible(r) (p. 159)
—Cats, Dogs, Hamsters, & Horses (p. 281)
—Curious Creatures down Under (p. 392)
—Daniel & the Lions Pulley, Kelly, illus. (p. 404)
—Daniel God's Faithful Follower Jones, Dennis, illus. (p. 405)
—David & God's Giant Victory: Biblical Values Jones, Dennis, illus. (p. 410)
—David & the Giant Pulley, Kelly, illus. (p. 410)
—Everyday with God Collection (p. 544)
—First Communion Bible (p. 593)
—First Easter Ever Jones, Dennis, illus. (p. 594)
—Forest Friends (p. 618)
—Godly Relationships. (p. 690)
—He's Got the Whole World in His Hands Idle, Molly, illus. (p. 774)
—Holy Bible (p. 791)
—If You're Happy & You Know It Haley, Amanda, illus. (p. 855)
—Jesus & His Friends Pulley, Kelly, illus. (p. 915)
—Jesus Feeds the People Pulley, Kelly, illus. (p. 915)
—Jesus God's Great Gift Jones, Dennis G., illus. (p. 915)
—Jesus God's Only Son Jones, Dennis, illus. (p. 915)
—Jesus Loves Me Borlasca, Hector, illus. (p. 915)
—Jesus Loves the Little Children Trasler, Janee, illus. (p. 916)
—Jesus Saves the World Pulley, Kelly, illus. (p. 916)
—Joseph & His Brothers Pulley, Kelly, illus. (p. 926)
—Jungle Beasts (p. 935)
—Kid's Study Bible Tanis, Joel, illus. (p. 955)
—King James Version Kids Study Bible. (p. 958)
—Lost Son: Based on Luke 15:11-32 Pulley, Kelly, illus. (p. 1056)
—Mi Primera Biblia de Mano: Historias Bíblicas para Niños Pequeños (p. 1133)
—Moses, God's Brave Servant Jones, Dennis G., illus. (p. 1176)
—New Women's Devotioanl Bible (p. 1247)
—NIrV Gift & Award Bible (p. 1257)
—Nirv Gift & Award Bible (p. 1257)
—NIV Backpack Bible (p. 1257)
—NIV Clearlyu Bible (p. 1257)
—NIV Student Bible (p. 1257)
—Noah & God's Great Promise Jones, Dennis, illus. (p. 1261)
—Our Feathered Friends (p. 1308)
—Poisonous, Smelly, & Amazing Plants (p. 1377)
—Precious Princess Bible (p. 1394)
—Queen Esther Helps God's People Pulley, Kelly, illus. (p. 1424)
—Queen Esther Helps God's People (La Reina Ester Ayuda Al Pueblo de Dios) (p. 1424)
—Rainforest Friends (p. 1436)
—Redo Your Room: 50 Bedroom DIYs You Can Do in a Weekend Faithgirlz! and Girls' Life Magazine Editors, ed. (p. 1456)
—Santa Biblia Palabritas de Vida: La Nueva Biblia de Estudio de los Niños de Hispanoamérica (p. 1511)
—Sea Creatures (p. 1534)
—Spiders, Snakes, Bees, & Bats (p. 1627)
—Story Early Elementary Curriculum: 31 Lessons (p. 1657)
—Story for Kids-Nirv: Discover the Bible from Beginning to End (p. 1657)
—Story Preschool Curriculum: 31 Lessons. (p. 1663)
—Student Bible (p. 1669)
—Timeless Children's Stories Pulley, Kelly, illus. (p. 1754)
—Veggie Values (p. 1834)
—Veggietales Bible (p. 1834)
—Very First Easter Pulley, Kelly, illus. (p. 1838)
—Wild about Horses Bible (p. 1928)
Zondervan Publishing Staff, jt. auth. see Avery, Ben.
Zondervan Publishing Staff, jt. auth. see DeVries, Catherine.
Zondervan Publishing Staff, jt. auth. see Kirgiss, Crystal.
Zondervan Publishing Staff, jt. auth. see Krueger, Jim.
Zondervan Publishing Staff, jt. auth. see LeSourd, Nancy.
Zondervan Publishing Staff, jt. auth. see Martin, Gary.
Zondervan Publishing Staff, jt. auth. see Mission City Press Inc. Staff.
Zondervan Publishing Staff, jt. auth. see Pulley, Kelly.
Zondervan Publishing Staff, jt. auth. see Richards, Lawrence O.
Zondervan Publishing Staff & Berenstain, Jan. Show God's Love (p. 1570)
Zondervan Publishing Staff & Gorey, Haller. Pups of the Spirit (p. 1418)
Zondervan Publishing Staff & Inspirio Staff. NIV Backpack Bible (p. 1257)
Zondervan Publishing Staff & Poth, Karen. Junior Comes Clean (p. 936)
Zondervan Publishing Staff & Warren, Rick. Lord's Prayer Watson, Richard Jesse, illus. (p. 1053)
Zondervan Publishing Staff & ZonderKidz Staff. Shepherds Watch (p. 1565)
—Story: The Bible as One Continuing Story of God & His People (p. 1656)
Zondervan Publishing Staff, creator. Kids' Devotional Bible (p. 953)
—Kids' Quest Study Bible: Answers to over 500 Questions about the Bible (p. 955)
—Revolution (p. 1466)
—Revolution: The Bible for Teen Guys (p. 1466)
Zondervan Publishing Staff, ed. Family Keepsake Bible (p. 568)
—Nirv Backpack Bible (p. 1257)
Zondervan Publishing Staff, et al. My Holy Bible for African-American Children (p. 1211)
—Princess Petunia's Sweet Apple Pie (p. 1405)
—What's up with Lyle? (p. 1900)
Zondervan Staff. Polar Pals (p. 1379)
—Story for Kids: Later Elementary Curriculum - 31 Lessons (p. 1657)
—Story Trading Cards: for Elementary: Grades 3 & Up (p. 1663)
Zondervan Staff & Poth, Karen. Case of the Couch Potato Caper (p. 273)
—Larryboy & the Mudslingers (p. 976)
Zong, Grace, illus. see Yim, Natasha.
Zong, Grace, jt. auth. see Lewis, Rose.
Zonjic, Tonci. Heralds. (p. 769)
Zonneveld, Famke. Waldorf Alphabet Book. (p. 1853)
Zonneveld, Famke, illus. see Margulies, Paul.
Zonta, Pat. Jessica's X-Ray. Dobson, Clive, illus. (p. 914)
Zonta, Rose, illus. see Awad, Shelley.
Zoo, Keith, illus. see Payne, M. D.
ZOO, La. Incredible Stickers! An Activity Book with Stickers. Miyakoshi, Junko, tr. (p. 869)
ZOO, La, jt. auth. see Lazoo Publishing Staff.
Zook, Melinda. L-E-t-t-e-r-s. (p. 969)
Zorka, Shawna. Carter Goes to a Funeral Reyes, Arlene, illus. (p. 272)
Zorn, Claire. Sky So Heavy. (p. 1587)
Zorn, Steven. Masterpieces: A Fact-Filled Coloring Book. (p. 1103)
Zornow, Jeff. Werewolf. Zornow, Jeff, illus. (p. 1875)
Zorrilla, José. Don Juan Tenorio. (p. 465)
Zortman, Bruce. Eight Little Candles Plus: A Hanukkah Tale. (p. 507)
Zorzi, Gina, jt. auth. see Johnson, Gee.
Zorzi, Gina, jt. auth. see Taylor, Trace.
Zorzi, Gina & Cline, Gina. Lion Pride. Dibble, Traci, illus. (p. 1020)
Zorzi, Gina & Dibble, Traci. Lion Pride. (p. 1020)
Zorzi, Gina & Sánchez, Lucía M. Bosques: This Is a Forest. (p. 215)
Zorzi, Gina & Sanchez, Lucia M. Bosques (This Is a Forest) (p. 215)
Zorzi, Gina & Sánchez, Lucía M. Desiertos: This Is a Desert. (p. 429)
Zorzi, Gina & Sanchez, Lucia M. Desiertos (This Is a Desert) (p. 429)
—OcéAnos: This Is an Ocean. (p. 1277)
—Praderas: This Is a Prairie. (p. 1392)
Zoss, Lori. Bed for Fred. (p. 156)
Zott, Lynn, ed. see Greenhaven Press Editors & Haugen, David M.
Zott, Lynn, ed. see Haerens, Margaret.
Zott, Lynn, ed. see Tardiff, Joe.
Zott, Lynn, jt. ed. see Greenhaven Press Editors.
Zott, Lynn, ed. US Airport Security. (p. 1826)
Zott, Lynn M., jt. auth. see Ullmann, Carol.
Zou, Xiang Dong, prod. Gingerbread Multiplication Table. (p. 677)
Zourelias, Diana. All Around Chicago Mini Coloring Book. (p. 43)
—Barrel of Monkeys & Other Animal Groups. (p. 140)
—Build a Giant Poster Coloring Book—United States Map. (p. 237)
—Celebrity Parents, Celebrity Kids Paper Dolls. (p. 285)
—Easter Bunny Stickers. (p. 499)
—Fairyland Hidden Pictures. (p. 564)
—First Ladies Fascinating Facts. (p. 595)
—Fun Facts about Everyday Inventions. (p. 647)
—Laugh Out Loud Letters for Boys: The Easy Way to Create Fast & Funny Notes! (p. 980)
—Laugh Out Loud Letters for Girls! The Easy Way to Create Fast & Funny Notes! (p. 980)
—Monster Bugs. (p. 1166)
—Monster Reptiles: A Close-Up Coloring Book. (p. 1168)
—Presidential Pets Coloring Book. (p. 1397)
—Weird & Wacky Jobs. (p. 1872)
Zourelias, Diana, illus. see Pazzelli, John.
Zourelias, Diana & Coloring Books Staff. Monster Sea Creatures. (p. 1168)
Zourelias, Diana, et al. Mix & Match PRINCESSES. (p. 1156)
Zourelias-Noro, Diane, illus. see Wheldon, Nicole.
Zoutewelle-Morris, Sarah, illus. see Cooper, Diana.
Zovi, Lonnie Dai, see Dai Zovi, Lonnie.
Zralck, Robert, illus. see Moor-Doucette, Saba.
Zronik, John, jt. auth. see Dunlop, Jenna.
Zronik, John, jt. auth. see Zronik, John Paul.
Zronik, John Paul. Sieur de la Salle: New World Adventurer. (p. 1573)
Zronik, John Paul & Zronik, John. Biography of Rice. (p. 189)
—Daniel Boone: Woodsman of Kentucky. (p. 405)
—Francisco Pizarro: Journeys Through Peru & South America. (p. 628)
—Hernando Cortés: Spanish Invader of Mexico. (p. 772)
—Jacques Cousteau: Conserving Underwater Worlds. (p. 905)
—Metals. (p. 1130)
—Metals - Shaping Our World. (p. 1130)
—Street Cred. (p. 1666)
Zryl, Laya, jt. auth. see Grinvald, Zeev.
Zschock, Heather. Under the Sea Scratch & Sketch: An Art Activity Book for Imaginative Artists of All Ages. (p. 1814)
—Who's There? A Bedtime Shadow Book. Zschock, Martha Day, illus. (p. 1920)

Z

—Wild Safari: An Art Activity Book for Imaginative Artists of All Ages. Barbas, Kerren, illus. (p. 1930)
Zschock, Heather, jt. auth. see Peter Pauper Press Staff.
Zschock, Martha, illus. see Conlon, Mara.
Zschock, Martha, illus. see Paulding, Barbara.
Zschock, Martha, jt. auth. see Zschock, Martha Day.
Zschock, Martha & Zschock, Martha Day. Spooky Scratch & Sketch: For Spooky Artists & Trick-or-Treaters of All Ages. (p. 1631)
Zschock, Martha Day. Hello, Adirondacks! (p. 763)
—Hello, America! (p. 763)
—Hello, Brooklyn! (p. 763)
—Hello, Chicago! (p. 763)
—Hello Congress! (p. 763)
—Hello, Florida! (p. 764)
—Hello, New Orleans! (p. 764)
—Hello, Philadelphia! (p. 764)
—Hello, Rhode Island! (p. 765)
—Hello, Rockies! (p. 765)
—Hello, San Francisco! (p. 765)
—Hello Williamsburg! (p. 765)
—Hello, Yellowstone! (p. 765)
—Journey Around Chicago from A to Z. (p. 927)
—Journey Around Maine from A to Z. (p. 927)
—Journey Around Nantucket from A to Z. Zschock, Martha Day, illus. (p. 927)
—Journey Around Philadelphia from A to Z. (p. 927)
—Journey Around San Francisco from A to Z. (p. 927)
—Journey Around Washington D. C. from A to Z. (p. 927)
—Super Sand Art. (p. 1680)
Zschock, Martha Day, illus. see Gandolfi, Claudine.
Zschock, Martha Day, illus. see Levy, Talia.
Zschock, Martha Day, illus. see Nemmers, Lee.
Zschock, Martha Day, illus. see Nemmers, Tom.
Zschock, Martha Day, illus. see Tunnell, Amber.
Zschock, Martha Day, illus. see Zschock, Heather.
Zschock, Martha Day, jt. illus. see Zschock, Martha.
Zschock, Martha Day & Zschock, Martha. Hello, Cape Cod! (p. 763)
Zsikai-Spiker, Lisa Marie. Buster & Snoopy. Schimmelman, Alex, illus. (p. 245)
Zub, Jim. Makeshift Miracle Book 2: the Boy Who Stole Everything: The Boy Who Stole Everything. (p. 1080)
Zuba, Jesse. Derek Walcott. Bloom, Harold, ed. (p. 427)
—Hermann Hesse. Bloom, Harold, ed. (p. 771)
—Thomas Pynchon. (p. 1739)
Zubal, Lynn. Sonoran Desert Frog. Zubal, Lynn, illus. (p. 1612)
Zubek, Adeline. Counting Lions. (p. 371)
—Foxes in the Dark. (p. 626)
Zuber, Diane. Broken Doll A Musical Play for Christmas. (p. 230)
Zuber, Diane C. Broken Doll. Firtl, Mary Meehan, illus. (p. 230)
Zubeyr Mohamed. Fox & the Hyen. (p. 626)
Zubiat, Gabriel, illus. see González Reyes, Amaury.
Zubizarreta, Gabriel M., jt. auth. see Flor Ada, Alma.
Zubizarreta, Patxi. Magali Por Fin lo Sabe. (p. 1071)
—Paloma, Llegaste Por el Aire. Balzola, Asun, illus. (p. 1320)
Zubizarreta, Paxti. Que Llueva, Que Llueva. Lavarello, Jose Maria, illus. (p. 1424)
Zubizarreta, Rosa, tr. see Flor Ada, Alma.
Zubizarreta, Rosalma, jt. tr. see Flor Ada, Alma.
Zubizarreta, Rosalma, tr. see Rohmer, Harriet.
Zubrin, Robert. Holy Land. (p. 791)
Zuchora-Walske, Christine. Andrew Jackson's Presidency. (p. 72)
—Antibiotics. (p. 89)
—Bermuda Triangle. (p. 167)
—Chad in Pictures. (p. 288)
—Dominican Republic in Pictures. (p. 465)
—Dust Bowl: A History Perspectives Book. (p. 490)
—Energy in the Real World. (p. 528)
—Honduras in Pictures. (p. 794)
—How Can I Be a Good Digital Citizen? (p. 805)
—Internet Censorship: Protecting Citizens or Trampling Freedom? (p. 880)
—Key Discoveries in Earth & Space Science. (p. 950)
—Key Discoveries in Engineering & Design. (p. 950)
—Key Discoveries in Life Science. (p. 950)
—Killer Whales: Built for the Hunt. (p. 956)
—Let's Look at Prairie Dogs. (p. 999)
—Let's Make Some Gold! Science's Biggest Mistakes about Geology & Ecology. (p. 999)
—Mountain Lions (p. 1181)
—Nepal in Pictures. (p. 1241)
—Poland. (p. 1378)
—Robots at Home. (p. 1481)
—Science Lab: The Transfer of Energy. (p. 1526)
—Setters: Loyal Hunting Companions (p. 1554)
—Solar Energy. (p. 1606)
—That Bull Is Seeing Red! Science's Biggest Mistakes about Animals & Plants. (p. 1726)
—Weather Robots. (p. 1870)
—We're the Center of the Universe! Science's Biggest Mistakes about Astronomy & Physics. (p. 1875)
—What's Inside My Computer? (p. 1898)
—Your Head Shape Reveals Your Personality! Science's Biggest Mistakes about the Human Body. (p. 1980)
—Your Mission to Mercury. (p. 1981)
—Your Mission to Uranus. (p. 1981)
—Your Mission to Venus. (p. 1981)
Zuchora-Walske, Christine & Burroughs, Scott. Your Mission on Earth. (p. 1981)
Zucker, Faye. Depression. (p. 427)
Zucker, Jonny. Four Special Questions: A Passover Story. Cohen, Jan Barger, illus. (p. 625)
—Lanterns & Firecrackers: A Chinese New Year Story. Cohen, Jan Barger, illus. (p. 975)
—Lighting a Lamp: A Diwali Story. Cohen, Jan Barger, illus. (p. 1015)
—Mission 1: Game On. Woodman, Ned, illus. (p. 1153)
—Mission 2: Supersonic. Woodman, Ned, illus. (p. 1153)
—Mission 3: In Deep. Woodman, Ned, illus. (p. 1153)
—Mission 4: Grave Danger. Woodman, Ned, illus. (p. 1153)
—Mission 5: Subzero. Woodman, Ned, illus. (p. 1153)
—Mission 6: Short Circuit. Woodman, Ned, illus. (p. 1153)
—Stunt Girl. (p. 1670)
Zucker, Pearl, jt. auth. see Lehmann, Marcus.
Zuckerberg, Randi. Dot. Berger, Joe, illus. (p. 472)
Zuckerman, Al, jt. auth. see Hall, C. Aubrey.
Zuckerman, Amy, jt. auth. see Daly, James.
Zuckerman, Andrew, photos by. Creature ABC. (p. 380)
—Creature ABC Flash Cards. (p. 380)
—Creature Baby Animals. (p. 380)
—Creature Colors. (p. 380)
—Creature Matching Game. (p. 380)
—Creature Numbers. (p. 380)
—Creature Sounds. (p. 380)
Zuckerman, Heather. Monster Named Criney Who Makes Kids Whiney. Delice, Shelly Meredith, illus. (p. 1168)
Zuckerman, Lilla & Zuckerman, Nora. Beauty Queen Blowout. (p. 154)
Zuckerman, Linda. Day Is Waiting Freeman, Don, illus. (p. 413)
—I Will Hold You 'Til You Sleep. Muth, Jon J., illus. (p. 848)
—Taste for Rabbit. (p. 1707)
Zuckerman, Nora, jt. auth. see Zuckerman, Lilla.
Zuckerman, Rory. Alphabetical Sleepy Sheep. Roos, Maryn, illus. (p. 50)
—Colorful Sleepy Sheep. Roos, Maryn, illus. (p. 344)
—Counting Sleepy Sheep. Roos, Maryn, illus. (p. 371)
—Shapely Sleepy Sheep. Roos, Maryn, illus. (p. 1560)
Zuehlke, Jeffrey. Alex Rodriguez. (p. 36)
—Alex Rodriguez (Revised Edition) (p. 36)
—Ben Roethlisberger. (p. 163)
—Buses. (p. 244)
—Camionetas. Translations.com Staff, tr. from ENG. (p. 256)
—Camionetas (Pickup Trucks) Translations.com Staff, tr. (p. 256)
—Concept Cars. (p. 355)
—Curt Schilling. (p. 395)
—Dirk Nowitzki. (p. 445)
—Dirk Nowitzki (Revised Edition) (p. 445)
—Drag Racers. (p. 476)
—Earth. (p. 495)
—Egypt in Pictures. (p. 506)
—Ethiopia in Pictures. (p. 539)
—Fighter Planes. (p. 585)
—Germany in Pictures. (p. 666)
—Golden Gate Bridge. (p. 694)
—Grand Canyon. (p. 707)
—Helicopters. (p. 763)
—Helicopters on the Move. (p. 763)
—Hoover Dam. (p. 796)
—Joe Mauer. (p. 920)
—Joe Mauer (Revised Edition) (p. 920)
—Johan Santana. (p. 920)
—Kevin Garnett. (p. 950)
—Kevin Garnett (Revised Edition) (p. 950)
—Landslides. (p. 974)
—Michael Phelps. (p. 1134)
—Michael Phelps (Revised Edition) (p. 1134)
—Pickup Trucks. Mueller, Mike, photos by. (p. 1354)
—Pickup Trucks. (p. 1355)
—Pickup Trucks on the Move. (p. 1355)
—Poland in Pictures. (p. 1378)
—Rally Cars. (p. 1437)
—Rocky Mountains. (p. 1484)
—Snowplows. (p. 1601)
—Space Shuttle. (p. 1619)
—Supercross. (p. 1683)
—Tanks. (p. 1705)
—Tugboats. (p. 1796)
—Ukraine in Pictures. (p. 1808)
—Warships. (p. 1859)
Zuehlke, Jeffrey, jt. auth. see Lerner Classroom Staff.
Zuehlke, Jeffrey, jt. auth. see Lerner Classroom.
Zufelt, Esther. Dark, I'm Not Scared of You. (p. 407)
Zuffi, Stefano. Art 123: Count from 1 to 12 with Great Works of Art. (p. 101)
—Cat in Art. Jones, Simon, tr. (p. 278)
Zug, Mark, illus. see Fan, Nancy Yi.
Zug, Mark, illus. see Sage, Angie.
Zug, Mark & Fan, Nancy Yi. Swordbird. Zug, Mark, illus. (p. 1692)
Zuggo, Jutka, jt. auth. see Zuggo, Violeta.
Zuggo, Violeta & Zuggo, Jutka. Story Time for Kids with Nlp by the English Sisters: The Little Grasshopper & the Big Ball of Dung. Kecskés, Anna, illus. (p. 1663)
Zuhdi, Darla. South Sea Adventure (p. 1617)
Zuill, Veronica M. E. Short Stories for Children Book. (p. 1569)
Zuk, Valentina, ed. see AZ Books Staff.
Zulewski, Timothy, illus. see Doyle, V. L. & Rohm, Robert.
Zuljevic, Vida. I Was Almost Five. (p. 848)
Zulkey, Claire. Off Year. (p. 1279)
Zulkey, Claire, jt. auth. see Simmons, Carl.
Zulkifli, Azhari, illus. see Dhar, Lisa Jane.
Zulkifli, Azhar, illus. see D'Oyen, Fatima.
Zulkifli, Azhari, illus. see Ghani, Aisha.
Zulkifli, Azhari, illus. see Ibrahim, Yasmin.
Zullo, Allan. 10 True Tales: Heroes Of 9/11. (p. 1994)
—10 True Tales: Young Civil Rights Heroes. (p. 1994)
—Bad Pets: On the Loose! (p. 132)
—Bad Pets Save Christmas! (p. 132)
—Battle Heroes. (p. 145)
—Christmas Miracle Pets: Animals Who Saved the Day. (p. 314)
—Crime Scene Investigators. (p. 382)
—Fact or Fake? Test Your Smarts! (p. 561)
—Haunted Shortstop: True Ghostly Sports Stories. (p. 753)
—Heroes of 9/11. (p. 773)
—Heroes of Hurricane Katrina. (p. 773)
—Kid Pirates: Their Battles, Shipwrecks, & Narrow Escapes. (p. 951)
—Miracle Pets: True Tales of Courage & Survival. (p. 1148)
—Rescuers: Kids Who Risked Everything to Save Others. (p. 1462)
—Secret Agent & Other Spy Kids. (p. 1540)
—Surviving Sharks. (p. 1687)
—Surviving Sharks & Other Dangerous Creatures. (p. 1687)
—Survivors: True Stories of Children in the Holocaust. (p. 1687)
—Ten True Stories - FBI Heroes. (p. 1719)
—Titanic Young Survivors. (p. 1758)
—War Heroes: Voices from Iraq. (p. 1857)
—Worlds Dumbest Crooks 2: True Tales of Goofs, Giggles & Gaffes. (p. 1960)
Zullo, Allan & Bovsun, Mara. Heroes of the Holocaust: True Stories of Rescues by Teens. (p. 773)
Zullo, Germano. At the Seaside. Albertine, illus. (p. 111)
—Jumping Jack. Albertine, illus. (p. 934)
—Line 135. Albertine, illus. (p. 1019)
—Little Bird. Albertine, illus. (p. 1024)
—Sky High. Albertine, illus. (p. 1586)
Zuluaga, Conrado. Gabriel Garcia Marquez: El Vicio Incurable de Contar. (p. 652)
Zuluaga, Conrado, ed. see Pushkin, Alexander, et al.
Zumbrock, Kristin. MEville to WEville Unit 2: Unit 2 MY FAMILY (p. 1130)
—MEville to WEville Unit 3: Unit 3 MY SCHOOL (p. 1130)
Zumbusch, Amelie von. Ancient Roman Culture. (p. 70)
—Ancient Roman Daily Life. (p. 70)
—Ancient Roman Economy. (p. 70)
—Ancient Roman Geography. (p. 70)
—Ancient Roman Government. (p. 70)
—Ancient Roman Technology. (p. 70)
—Barack Obama: Man of Destiny. (p. 137)
—Barack Obama's Family Tree: Roots of Achievement. (p. 137)
—First Family: The Obamas in the White House. (p. 595)
—Making History: The Obamas (p. 1081)
—Michelle Obama: Our First Lady. (p. 1135)
—True Story of the American Flag. (p. 1793)
Zumbusch, Amelie Von & Von Zumbusch, Amelie. Ancient Roman Geography. (p. 70)
—Ancient Roman Technology. (p. 70)
Zumdahl, Steven S. Basic Chemistry. (p. 141)
—Chemical Principles. (p. 297)
—Chemistry. (p. 297)
—Introductory Chemistry: A Foundation (Zumdahl); Instructor's Annotated Edition. (p. 883)
—Introductory Chemistry. (p. 883)
Zumdahl, Steven S., jt. auth. see Hall, James W.
Zumdahl, Steven S. & Zumdahl, Susan A. Chemistry. (p. 297)
Zumdahl, Susan A., jt. auth. see Zumdahl, Steven S.
ZumFelde, Brett. Top 5 Book. (p. 1768)
Zumo. Awesome Run: Selected Works, 1978-2008. (p. 121)
Zumwalt, Susan. Shine on Me. (p. 1566)
Zunon, Elizabeth, illus. see Carolan, Joanna & Carolan, Terry.
Zunon, Elizabeth, illus. see Grimes, Nikki.
Zunon, Elizabeth, illus. see Harvey, Jeanne Walker.
Zunon, Elizabeth, illus. see Kamkwamba, William & Mealer, Bryan.
Zunon, Elizabeth, illus. see MacLachlan, Patricia.
Zunon, Elizabeth, illus. see Nelson, Vaunda Micheaux.
Zunon, Elizabeth, illus. see Paul, Miranda.
Zunon, Elizabeth, illus. see York, J.
Zunshine, Tatiana. Little Story about a Big Turnip. Antonenkov, Evgeny, illus. (p. 1037)
Zunshine, Tatiana, tr. see Levin, Vadim.
Zuppardi, Sam. Nowhere Box. Zuppardi, Sam, illus. (p. 1269)
Zuppardi, Sam, illus. see Elliott, David.
Zuppardi, Sam, illus. see McAlpine, Gordon.
Zupsic, Kelly. Mrs. Sneeze & the Three Legged Goat. (p. 1187)
Zur Muehlen, Nersel. Monkey in the Mirror. Sanchez, Sara, illus. (p. 1165)
Zurakowski, Michele. Evening Meals Around the World Yesh, Jeff, illus. (p. 541)
—Midday Meals Around the World Yesh, Jeff, illus. (p. 1137)
Zuravicky, Orli. Amazing Animals: Multiplying Multidigit Numbers by a One-Digit Number with Regrouping. (p. 53)
—Amazon & the Sahara: Using Double Line Graphs & Double Bar Graphs. (p. 56)
—Baby Faces. (p. 126)
—C Is for City: An Alphabet Book. Castellano, Giuseppe, illus. (p. 250)
—Cartas de Bebe. (p. 269)
—Color for Sketch: A Book about Colors. Castellano, Giuseppe, illus. (p. 342)
—Dear Diary: Monster House. (p. 418)
—Exploring Pyramids Around the World: Making Models of Geometric Solids. (p. 553)
—Galloping Book. (p. 653)
—Galloping Book / Trotar. (p. 653)
—Galloping Book/Trotar. De Leon, Mauricio Velzaquez, tr. from ENG. (p. 653)
—Map Math: Learning about Latitude & Longitude Using Coordinate Systems. (p. 1090)
—Skipping Book: Avanzar a Saltitos. Brusca, Maria C., tr. from ENG. (p. 1586)
—Skipping Book. (p. 1586)
—Skipping Book / Avanzar a Saltitos. (p. 1586)
—Stock Market: Understanding & Applying Ratios, Decimals, Fractions, & Percentages. (p. 1651)
—When There Were Dinosaurs: Using Expanded Notation to Represent Numbers in the Millions. (p. 1905)
Zuravicky, Orli, jt. auth. see Schimel, Kate.
Zuravicky, Orli, adapted by. Fun with Plex. (p. 649)
Zuravicky, Orli & Scholastic Canada Ltd. Staff. Who's Hiding? Swanson, Weldon, illus. (p. 1920)
Zurcher, Corina. Growing up Claus. (p. 726)
Zurchin, Cynthia, et al. Whale Done School: Transforming a School's Culture by Catching Students Doing Things Right. (p. 1877)
Zurlis, Peter A., jt. auth. see Mazur, Glen A.
Zurlo, Tony. Legislative Branch: Creating America's Laws. (p. 990)
—Syria in the News: Past, Present, & Future. (p. 1693)
—United States Congress & the Legislative Branch: How the Senate & House of Representatives Create Our Laws. (p. 1819)
Zurn, Jon. Louisiana Purchase. (p. 1059)
Zusak, Markus. Book Thief. (p. 212)
—Cartas Cruzadas. (p. 272)
—Getting the Girl. (p. 669)
—I Am the Messenger. (p. 834)
—Ladrona de Libros. (p. 970)
—Underdogs. (p. 1814)
Zusman, Evelyn, jt. auth. see Chanover, Hyman.
Zutell, Jerry, jt. auth. see Rasinski, Timothy.
Zuzo, Cheryl. Being Bella. Wellman, Megan, illus. (p. 161)
Zvetkoff, Kathleen Charnes. Adventures of Willy the Monkey. (p. 24)
Zvonarova, Jenny Desneige, illus. see Carruthers, Deborah.
Zwald, John & DesRochers, Diane O. Mahmoud Meets Moses. Zwald, John, illus. (p. 1076)
Zwaniga, Jennifer. Someone Else's Life: Book Two: Missing Pieces. Hiriart, Sherry, ed. (p. 1609)
Zweber, Rhonda. Mommy's Hats. (p. 1162)
Zwebner, Janet, illus. see Desnick, Chaim.
Zwebner, Janet, illus. see Rossel, Seymour.
Zwebner, Janet, illus. see Rouss, Sylvia.
Zweibel, Alan. Our Tree Named Steve. (p. 1310)
—Our Tree Named Steve. Catrow, David, illus. (p. 1310)
—Our Tree Named Steve. Catrow, David & David, Catrow, illus. (p. 1310)
Zweibel, Alan, jt. auth. see Mansbach, Adam.
Zweifel, Frances, illus. see Fredericks, Anthony D.
Zweig, Eric. Crazy Canucks: The Uphill Battle of Canada's Downhill Ski Team (p. 377)
—Dominant Defensemen. (p. 465)
—Fever Season. (p. 583)
—Great Goalies. (p. 716)
—Long Shot: How the Winnipeg Falcons Won the First Olympic Hockey Gold (p. 1047)
—Star Power: The Legend & Lore of Cyclone Taylor (p. 1641)
—Super Scorers. (p. 1681)
—Tough Guys: Hockey Rivals in Times of War & Disaster (p. 1772)
Zweig, Eric, jt. auth. see McMurchy-Barber, Gina.
Zwemmer, Dominic. Sharks. (p. 1562)
—Wild Cats. (p. 1929)
Zwemmer, Dominic, ed. see Gunzi, Christane.
Zwemmer, Dominic, des. Farm. (p. 573)
Zwerger, Lisbeth. Wonderment: The Lisbeth Zwerger Collection. (p. 1948)
Zwerger, Lisbeth, illus. see Andersen, Hans Christian.
Zwerger, Lisbeth, illus. see Baum, L. Frank.
Zwerger, Lisbeth, illus. see Brothers Grimm, Becky & Brothers Grimm.
Zwerger, Lisbeth, illus. see Grimm, Wilhelm K. & Grimm, Jacob.
Zwerger, Lisbeth, illus. see Henry, O.
Zwerger, Lisbeth, illus. see Moore, Clement C.
Zwerger, Lisbeth, illus. see Nesbit, E. & Edith, Nesbit.
Zwerger, Lisbeth, illus. see Wilde, Oscar & Oscar, Wilde.
Zwerger, Lisbeth, jt. auth. see Baum, L. Frank.
Zwerger, Lisbeth & Aesop. Aesop's Fables. (p. 25)
Zwerger, Lisbeth, et al. Sandman. (p. 1511)
Zwier, Lawrence, jt. auth. see Cunningham, Mark E.
Zwier, Lawrence J., jt. auth. see Cunningham, Mark E.
Zwingelberg, Wc. Adventures of Will W. Wilson. (p. 24)
Zybert, Sally. Sunny Ella. (p. 1677)
Zydek, Heather. Basil's Search for Miracles. (p. 142)
Zyl, Olga, ed. see AZ Books Staff.
Zyle, Jon Van, illus. see Flowers, Pam.
Zyle, Jon Van, illus. see London, Jonathan.
Zyle, Jon Van, see Freedman, Lew.
Zyle, Jon Van, see McDaniel, Jequite Po & Van Zyle, Jon.
Zyp, Nicole, ed. see Burncrot, Curt & Dunlap, Shiree.
Zyp, Nicole, ed. see Burncrot, Curt.
Zyp, Nikki, ed. see Burncrot, Curt & Dunlap, Shiree.
Zyrro, Roggen. Goatino. Shields, Ruth, illus. (p. 687)

ILLUSTRATOR INDEX

A

A and J Studios Staff. Dora's Valentine Adventure. Ricci, Christine. 2006. (Dora the Explorer Ser.). (ENG.). 14p. (J). (gr. -1-k). bds. 6.99 *(978-1-4169-1754-0(3)*, Simon Spotlight/Nickelodeon) Simon Spotlight/Nickelodeon.

—Navidad Estelar de Dora. Ricci, Christine. Ziegler, Argentina Palacios, tr. 2005. (Dora the Explorer Ser.). (SPA.). 24p. (J). pap. 3.99 *(978-1-4169-1183-8(9)*, Libros Para Ninos) Libros Para Ninos.

A-Park, Gwangjo & A-Park, Jung. Dorje's Stripes. Ruddra, Anshumani. ed. 2011. (ENG.). 40p. (J). (gr. k-4). 9.99 *(978-1-935279-98-3(X))* Kane Miller.

A-Park, Jung, jt. illus. see A-Park, Gwangjo.

Aardema, John. The Blizzard Wizard. Plourde, Lynn. ed. 2010. (ENG.). 32p. (J). (gr. -1-3). 16.95 *(978-0-89272-789-6(6))* Down East Bks.

—Emma's Rainy Day. Gillespie, Jane. 2010. (J). 14.95 *(978-1-933067-36-0(5))* Beachhouse Publishing, LLC.

—Slippery Fish in Hawaii. Diamond, Charlotte. 2013. (ENG.). (gr. -1). bds. 7.95 *(978-1-933067-57-5(8))* Beachhouse Publishing, LLC.

—There Was an Old Auntie. Gillespie, Jane. 2009. (J). *(978-1-933067-28-5(4))* Beachhouse Publishing, LLC.

Aardman Animations Staff. Shaun the Sheep Movie - Shear Madness. Candlewick Press, Candlewick. 2015. (Tales from Mossy Bottom Farm Ser.). (ENG.). 48p. (J). (gr. k-3). pap. 3.99 *(978-0-7636-7737-4(X))* Candlewick Pr.

—Shaun the Sheep Movie - the Great Escape. Candlewick Press, Candlewick. 2015. (Tales from Mossy Bottom Farm Ser.). (ENG.). 48p. (J). (gr. k-3). pap. 3.99 *(978-0-7636-7738-1(8))* Candlewick Pr.

—Shaun the Sheep Movie - Timmy in the City. Candlewick Press, Candlewick. 2015. (Tales from Mossy Bottom Farm Ser.). (ENG.). 12p. (J). (-k). bds. 7.99 *(978-0-7636-7875-3(9)*, Candlewick Entertainment) Candlewick Pr.

Aardvark, D. The Congraduation Fish. Aardvark, D. l.t. ed. 2005. 48p. (J). per. 12.95 *(978-0-9755567-1-9(1))* Aardvark's Weedpatch Pr.

—Merry Kissmoose. Aardvark, D. l.t. ed. 2005. 48p. (J). per. 12.95 *(978-0-9755567-2-6(X))* Aardvark's Weedpatch Pr.

Aardvark, Nathan. Blackbeard & the Monster of the Deep. Murtagh, Ciaran. 2014. (Collins Big Cat Progress Ser.). (ENG.). 32p. (J). pap. 7.99 *(978-0-00-751931-6(1))* HarperCollins Pubs. Ltd. GBR. Dist: Independent Pubs. Group.

Aaron, Rich. Mice Don't Taste Like Chicken. Heydt, Scott. 2011. 188p. pap. 13.00 *(978-0-9830109-2-0(7))* Helm Publishing.

Aarvig, Cindy. Turkeys in Disguise. Honeycutt, Scarlet. 2007. 48p. per. 24.95 *(978-1-4137-4035-6(9))* America Star Bks.

Abadzis, Nick & Sycamore, Hilary. Laika. Abadzis, Nick. 2007. (ENG.). 208p. (YA). (gr. 5-12). pap. 18.99 *(978-1-59643-101-0(6)*, First Second Bks.) Roaring Brook Pr.

Abasta, Mary. Simply & the Shiny Quarter. Mendoza, Madeleine. 2011. 24p. pap. 24.95 *(978-1-4560-3792-5(7))* America Star Bks.

Abate, Betelhem, et al, photos by. E Is for Ethiopia. Quarto Generic Staff. 2011. (World Alphabets Ser.). (ENG., 32p. (J). (gr. -1-2). 17.95 *(978-1-84507-825-6(X)*, Frances Lincoln) Quarto Publishing Group UK GBR. Dist: Hachette Bk. Group.

Abay, Ismail. Darryl & the Mountain. Ozgur, Lynne Emily. 2009. (ENG.). 32p. (J). (gr. 2-4). pap. 9.95 *(978-1-59784-138-2(2))* Tughra Bks.

Abboreno, Joseph F. & Fu, Sherwin. Hoyi the Archer & other Classic Chinese Tales. Fu, Shelley. 2005. 144p. (J). (gr. 4-8). reprint ed. 22.00 *(978-0-7567-9713-3(6))* DIANE Publishing Co.

Abbot, Judi. The Biggest Kiss. Walsh, Joanna. 2011. (ENG.). 32p. (J). (gr. -1-3). 14.99 *(978-1-4424-2769-3(8)*, Simon & Schuster/Paula Wiseman Bks.) Simon & Schuster/Paula Wiseman Bks.

—I Love Mom. Walsh, Joanna. 2014. (ENG.). 32p. (J). (gr. -1-3). 16.99 *(978-1-4814-2808-8(X)*, Simon & Schuster/Paula Wiseman Bks.) Simon & Schuster/Paula Wiseman Bks.

—The Perfect Hug. Walsh, Joanna. 2012. (ENG.). 32p. (J). (gr. -1-3). 14.99 *(978-1-4424-6606-7(5)*, Simon & Schuster/Paula Wiseman Bks.) Simon & Schuster/Paula Wiseman Bks.

—Snug as a Bug. Murray, Tamsyn. 2013. (ENG.). 32p. (J). *(978-0-85707-108-8(4))* Barnes & Noble, Inc.

—Snug as a Bug. Murray, Tamsyn. 2014. (ENG.). 32p. (gr. -1). pap. 8.99 *(978-0-85707-109-5(2))* Simon & Schuster, Ltd. GBR. Dist: Simon & Schuster, Inc.

Abbot, Judi & Gaviraghi, Giuditta. Snug As a Bug. Murray, Tamsyn. 2013. 30p. (J). *(978-1-4351-4731-7(6))* Barnes & Noble, Inc.

Abbott, Jane. Over the Moon. Robinson, Hilary. 2009. (Tadpoles Ser.). (ENG.). 24p. (J). (gr. k-2). pap. *(978-0-7787-3899-2(X))*; lib. bdg. *(978-0-7787-3868-8(X))* Crabtree Publishing Co.

Abbott, Jason. Bethany Bubbles Makes a Mistake. Edwards, Wysteria. 2011. 34p. pap. 14.50 *(978-1-60911-353-7(5)*, Strategic Bk. Publishing) Strategic Book Publishing & Rights Agency (SBPRA).

—Hot Cross Buns for Everyone. Fuerst, Jeffrey B. 2009. (Reader's Theater Nursery Rhymes & Songs Set B Ser.). 48p. (J). pap. *(978-1-60859-153-4(0))* Benchmark Education Co.

—Little Bo Peep. Smith, Carrie. 2010. (Rising Readers Ser.). (J). 3.49 *(978-1-60719-700-3(6))* Newmark Learning LLC.

—Where Are Bo Peep's Sheep? Smith, Carrie. 2009. (Reader's Theater Nursery Rhymes & Songs Set B Ser.). 48p. (J). pap. *(978-1-60859-171-8(9))* Benchmark Education Co.

Abbott, Kristin. Angel Birthdays. Garay, Erin. ed. 2013. (ENG.). 32p. (J). (gr. 2-3). 16.95 *(978-1-938301-94-0(3))* Familius LLC.

—The Baseball Princess: Samantha's Summer & the Unicorn Flu. Hegerhorst, Bethany. 2012. 32p. (J). *(978-0-9871281-5-7(9))* Murray Bks.

—The Six Sisters & Their Flying Carpets. Ford, Adam B. 2012. 34p. (-18). 20.95 *(978-0-9794104-6-8(0))* H Bar Pr.

—The Soccer Princess: Josephina & the Gown Fashion Runway Show, 13 bks., bk. 1. Hegerhorst, Bethany. 2011. 32p. (J). 17.99 *(978-0-615-35488-0(2))* Leo Publishing Works, Inc.

—The Soccer Princess: Josephina & the Gown Fashion Runway Show, 12. Hegerhorst, Bethany. 2011. 32p. (J). *(978-0-9803829-6-9(3))* Murray Bks.

Abbott, Simon. Baaah! Beeson, Samantha & Tango Books Staff. 2003. (Noisy Pops! Ser.). (ENG.). 10p. (J). (gr. -1-k). 11.99 *(978-1-85707-573-1(0))* Tango Bks. GBR. Dist: Independent Pubs. Group.

—Bible Stories Painting Book, 1 vol., Bk. 3. David, Juliet. 2014. (ENG.). 24p. (J). 7.99 *(978-1-85985-995-7(X)*, Candle Bks.) Lion Hudson PLC GBR. Dist: Kregel Pubns.

Abbott, Simon. Cafe. 2015. (Happy Street Ser.). (ENG.). 10p. (J). (gr. -1-k). bds. 9.99 ***(978-1-4052-7057-1(8))*** Egmont Bks., Ltd. GBR. Dist: Independent Pubs. Group.

Abbott, Simon. Car. Tango Books Staff. 2012. (Noisy Pops! Ser.). (ENG.). 10p. (J). (gr. -1-k). 11.99 *(978-1-85707-802-2(0))* Tango Bks. GBR. Dist: Independent Pubs. Group.

—Dinosaurs. 2011. (Learn to Draw Ser.). (ENG.). 24p. (J). (gr. k-2). pap. 6.95 *(978-1-84898-202-4(X)*, TickTock Books) Octopus Publishing Group GBR. Dist: Independent Pubs. Group.

—Dinosaurs. Goldsmith, Mike. 2011. (Flip Flap Science Ser.). (ENG.). 10p. (J). (gr. -1-k). 9.95 *(978-1-84898-365-6(4)*, TickTock Books) Octopus Publishing Group GBR. Dist: Independent Pubs. Group.

—Happy Street: Pet Shop. 2014. (Happy Street Ser.). (ENG.). 10p. (J). (gr. -1-k). bds. 9.99 *(978-1-4052-6864-6(6))* Egmont Bks., Ltd. GBR. Dist: Independent Pubs. Group.

—Henry Goes Skating. Biggs, Brian. ed. 2012. (My First I Can Read Ser.). lib. bdg. 13.55 *(978-0-606-26852-3(9)*, Turtleback) Turtleback Bks.

—Learn to Draw: Dragons. 2011. (Learn to Draw Ser.). (ENG.). 24p. (J). (gr. k-2). pap. 6.95 *(978-1-84898-201-7(1)*, TickTock Books) Octopus Publishing Group GBR. Dist: Independent Pubs. Group.

—Learn to Draw: Fairies. 2011. (Learn to Draw Ser.). (ENG.). 24p. (J). (gr. k-2). pap. 6.95 *(978-1-84898-203-1(8)*, TickTock Books) Octopus Publishing Group GBR. Dist: Independent Pubs. Group.

—Learn to Draw: Monsters. 2011. (Learn to Draw Ser.). (ENG.). 24p. (J). (gr. k-2). pap. 6.95 *(978-1-84898-200-0(3)*, TickTock Books) Octopus Publishing Group GBR. Dist: Independent Pubs. Group.

—Meow! Tango Books Staff. 2004. (Noisy Pops! Ser.). (ENG.). 10p. (J). (gr. -1-k). 11.99 *(978-1-85707-647-9(8))* Tango Bks. GBR. Dist: Independent Pubs. Group.

—Noisy Pops - Fire Engine. Tango Books Staff. 2011. (Noisy Pops! Ser.). (ENG.). 10p. (J). (gr. -1-k). bds. 11.99 *(978-1-85707-710-0(5))* Tango Bks. GBR. Dist: Independent Pubs. Group.

Abbott, Simon. Read It Build It Space. Hayes, Susan. 2015. (Read It Build It Ser.). (ENG.). 16p. (J). (gr. -1-1). 15.99 ***(978-1-4052-7165-3(5))*** Egmont Bks., Ltd. GBR. Dist: Independent Pubs. Group.

Abbott, Simon. Space Adventure. Goldsmith, Mike. 2011. (Flip Flap Science Ser.). (ENG.). 10p. (J). (gr. -1-k). 9.95 *(978-1-84898-364-9(6)*, TickTock Books) Octopus Publishing Group GBR. Dist: Independent Pubs. Group.

—Subtraction. Tango Books Staff. 2012. (Number Pops Ser.). (ENG.). 12p. (J). (gr. -1-k). 10.99 *(978-1-85707-851-0(9))* Tango Bks. GBR. Dist: Independent Pubs. Group.

—Supermarket. 2014. (Happy Street Ser.). (ENG.). 10p. (J). (gr. -1-k). bds. 9.99 *(978-1-4052-6865-3(4))* Egmont Bks., Ltd. GBR. Dist: Independent Pubs. Group.

Abbott, Simon. Toy Shop: With a Pop-Out Shop & Play Places! 2015. (Happy Street Ser.). (ENG.). 10p. (J). (gr. -1-k). bds. 9.99 ***(978-1-4052-7056-4(X))*** Egmont Bks., Ltd. GBR. Dist: Independent Pubs. Group.

Abbott, Simon. Little Mouse Visits Grandma: Mouse on Ribbon, Flaps, Acetates. Abbott, Simon. 2006. (ENG.). 16p. (J). (gr. -1-k). 15.99 *(978-1-85707-668-4(0))* Tango Bks. GBR. Dist: Independent Pubs. Group.

Abbott, Simon, jt. illus. see Biggs, Brian.

Abbrederis, Christoph & McLellen, Christoph Elizabeth. Sleeping Beauty. 2003. (Bilingual Fairy Tales Ser.: BILI).Tr. of Bella Durmiente. (ENG & SPA.). 32p. (J). (gr. -1-7). pap. 6.99 *(978-0-8118-3913-6(3))* Chronicle Bks. LLC.

Abby, Mitchell. The Bear & the Price. Bradford, Wilson D. 2012. 48p. (-18). pap. 12.00 *(978-0-9848651-2-3(8))* True Path Pubs.

Abdullah, Tariq. Goodnight Joy! Brown, Mia. 2010. 20p. 12.49 *(978-1-4520-1492-0(2))* AuthorHouse.

Abe, Hiroshi. One Stormy Night. Kimura & North, Lucy. 2005. 48p. (J). (gr. 1-3). 16.00 *(978-4-7700-2970-6(5))* Kodansha International JPN. Dist: Cheng & Tsui Co.

—One Sunny Day, 2 vols., Vol. 2. Kimura & North, Lucy. 2005. 48p. (J). 16.00 *(978-4-7700-2971-3(3))* Kodansha International JPN. Dist: Cheng & Tsui Co.

Abe, Sayori. Biographical Comics: Mother Teresa: Modern Saint of the Poor. Takita, Yoshihiro & Takita, Yoshihiro. 2012. (Biographical Comic Ser.). (ENG.). 152p. (J). (gr. 3-6). 18.99 *(978-1-4215-4322-2(2))* Shogakukan JPN. Dist: Simon & Schuster, Inc.

—Biographical Comics: Mother Teresa: Modern Saint of the Poor. Takita, Yoshihiro. 2012. (Biographical Comic Ser.). (ENG.). 152p. (J). (gr. 3-6). pap. 9.99 *(978-1-4215-4323-9(0))* Shogakukan JPN. Dist: Simon & Schuster, Inc.

Abel, Simone. And Everyone Shouted, Pull! A First Look at Forces & Motion. Llewellyn, Claire. 2004. (First Look: Science Ser.). (ENG.). 32p. (gr. -1-2). 25.99 *(978-1-4048-0656-6(3)*, Nonfiction Picture Bks.) Picture Window Bks.

—The Case of the Missing Caterpillar: A First Look at the Life Cycle of a Butterfly, 1 vol. Godwin, Sam. 2004. (First Look: Science Ser.). (ENG.). 32p. (gr. -1-2). 25.99 *(978-1-4048-0655-9(5)*, Nonfiction Picture Bks.) Picture Window Bks.

—Cuddly Critters: Animal Nursery Rhymes, 1 vol. 2007. (Mother Goose Rhymes Ser.). (ENG.). 32p. (gr. -1-2). lib. bdg. 25.99 *(978-1-4048-2344-0(1)*, 1265749, Nonfiction Picture Bks.) Picture Window Bks.

—The Drop Goes Plop: A First Look at the Water Cycle, 1 vol. Godwin, Sam. 2004. (First Look: Science Ser.). (ENG.). 32p. (gr. -1-2). 25.99 *(978-1-4048-0657-3(1)*, Nonfiction Picture Bks.) Picture Window Bks.

—Easy Guitar Tunes Internet Referenced. Marks, Anthony. 2004. 32p. (J). pap. 8.95 *(978-0-7945-0775-6(1)*, Usborne) EDC Publishing.

—The Hen Can't Help It: A First Look at the Life Cycle of a Chicken. Godwin, Sam. 2004. (First Look: Science Ser.). (ENG.). 32p. (gr. -1-2). 25.99 *(978-1-4048-0653-5(9)*, Nonfiction Picture Bks.) Picture Window Bks.

—Rainbow Duck. Lodge, Yvette. 2006. 8p. (J). (gr. -1-k). bds. 9.99 *(978-1-57791-263-7(2))* Brighter Minds Children's Publishing.

—Science with Plants. Edom, Helen. rev. ed. 2007. (Science Activities Ser.). 24p. (J). (gr. 3-7). pap. 5.99 *(978-0-7945-1485-3(5)*, Usborne) EDC Publishing.

—A Seed in Need: A First Look at the Plant Cycle. Godwin, Sam. 2004. (First Look: Science Ser.). (ENG.). 32p. (gr. -1-2). 25.99 *(978-1-4048-0920-8(1)*, Nonfiction Picture Bks.) Picture Window Bks.

—The Trouble with Tadpoles: A First Look at the Life Cycle of a Frog. Godwin, Sam. 2004. (First Look: Science Ser.). (ENG.). 32p. (gr. -1-2). 25.99 *(978-1-4048-0654-2(7)*, Nonfiction Picture Bks.) Picture Window Bks.

—Where Is Caterpillar Look & Play. (Lamaze Ser.). bds. 8.99 *(978-1-58663-731-6(2))* Friedman, Michael Publishing Group, Inc.

Abercrombie, Bethaney. Garrett the Firefighter. Garces Iii, Joseph Louis. 2008. 24p. pap. 12.99 *(978-1-59858-716-6(1))* Dog Ear Publishing, LLC.

Aberle, Xylena Apotheloz. Kenzie's Key. Doerr, Bonnie J. 2003. 211p. (J). 16.95 *(978-0-9619155-6-8(0))* Laurel & Herbert, Inc.

Ablett, Barry. Great Expectations. 2008. (Usborne Young Reading: Series Three Ser.). 61p. (J). 8.99 *(978-0-7945-1944-5(X)*, Usborne) EDC Publishing.

—Illustrated Stories from Dickens. Dickens, Charles. 2010. (Illustrated Stories Ser.). 352p. (YA). (gr. 3-18). 19.99 *(978-0-7945-2628-3(4)*, Usborne) EDC Publishing.

—Oliver Twist. Dickens, Charles. 2007. (Young Reading Series 3 Gift Bks.). 63p. (J). (gr. 3). 8.99 *(978-0-7945-1459-4(6)*, Usborne) EDC Publishing.

—See Inside Famous Buildings. Jones, Rob Lloyd. 2009. (See Inside Board Bks). 16p. (J). (gr. 2). bds. 13.99 *(978-0-7945-2350-3(1)*, Usborne) EDC Publishing.

—Tale of Two Cities: Internet-Referenced. Sebag-Montefiore, Mary, ed. 2009. (Young Reading 3 Ser.). 64p. (J). 6.99 *(978-0-7945-2319-0(6)*, Usborne) EDC Publishing.

Ablett, Barry, jt. illus. see Young, Norman.

Abolafia, Yossi. Harry's Birthday. Porte, Barbara Ann. 2003. (I Can Read Bks.). 48p. (J). 15.99 *(978-0-06-050355-0(6))*; 16.89 *(978-0-06-050356-7(4))* HarperCollins Pubs.

—Harry's Birthday. Porte, Barbara Ann. 2003. (I Can Read Bks.). 48p. (J). (gr. -1-3). 11.80 *(978-0-613-68428-6(1)*, Turtleback) Turtleback Bks.

—Harry's Pony. Porte, Barbara Ann. 2003. (I Can Read Bks.). 64p. (J). 16.89 *(978-0-06-050658-2(X))* HarperCollins Pubs.

—It's Snowing! It's Snowing! Prelutsky, Jack. 2007. (I Can Read Bks.). 48p. (gr. -1-3). 14.00 *(978-0-7569-8057-3(7))* Perfection Learning Corp.

—It's Snowing! It's Snowing! Winter Poems. Prelutsky, Jack. 2006. (I Can Read Bks.). 48p. (J). (gr. -1-3). lib. bdg. 16.89 *(978-0-06-053716-6(7))* HarperCollins Pubs.

—My Parents Think I'm Sleeping. Prelutsky, Jack. (I Can Read Book 3 Ser.). (J). 2008. (ENG.). 48p. (gr. k-3). pap. 3.99 *(978-0-06-053722-7(1))*; 2007. 48p. lib. bdg. 16.89 *(978-0-06-053721-0(3))*; 2007. 46p. (gr. -1-3). 15.99 *(978-0-06-053720-3(5))* HarperCollins Pubs.

Abos, Regine, jt. illus. see Rippin, Sally.

Abou El Azm, Mohsen. Muhammad: The Life of the Prophet - Based on Original Sources. Kheneigar, Ahmed Abou. adapted ed. 2014. (Muhammad: the Life of the Prophet Ser.). (ENG.). 64p. pap. 6.95 *(978-1-906230-62-3(5))* Real Reads Ltd. GBR. Dist: International Publishers Marketing.

Abraham, Joe, et al. Planetary Brigade. Giffen, Keith & DeMatteis, J. M. 2007. (ENG.). 128p. per. 14.99 *(978-1-934506-10-3(9))* Boom! Studios.

Abramson, Cathy. Wild Washington: Animal Sculptures A to Z. Arbuthnoy, Nancy. 2005. pap. 18.00 *(978-1-884878-09-1(1))* Annapolis Publishing Co.

Abramson, Stephen, photos by. Coco. Abramson, Laurin. 2010. 28p. pap. 8.75 *(978-1-935125-95-2(8))* Robertson Publishing.

Abraxas, Matt. Athanasius. Carr, Simonetta. 2011. 64p. (J). 18.00 *(978-1-60178-151-2(2))* Reformation Heritage Bks.

—John Knox. Carr, Simonetta. 2014. (ENG.). 64p. (J). 18.00 *(978-1-60178-289-2(6))* Reformation Heritage Bks.

—John Owen. Carr, Simonetta. 2010. (ENG.). 62p. (J). 18.00 *(978-1-60178-088-1(5))* Reformation Heritage Bks.

Abremski, Kathy. An a-Bee-Sea Book. Burr, Holly. 2012. 28p. pap. 14.95 *(978-1-61493-040-2(6))* Peppertree Pr., The.

—If I Get to Be in Charge of Spelling. Burr, Holly. 2012. 16p. pap. 10.95 *(978-1-61493-039-6(2))* Peppertree Pr., The.

Abreu, Raquel. Little Ruth Reddingford (and the Wolf) An Old Tale retold by Hank Wesselman, PH. D. 2004. 32p. (J). per. 15.95 *(978-0-9740190-0-0(3))* Illumination Arts Publishing Co., Inc.

—Your Father Forever. Griffith, Travis. 2005. 32p. (J). (gr. -1-3). 15.95 *(978-0-9740190-3-1(8))* Illumination Arts Publishing Co., Inc.

Abs, Renata. Erase Una Vez Galileo Galilei. Foelker, Rita. 2004. 24p. pap. 2.95 *(978-85-7416-192-1(6))* Callis Editora Ltda BRA. Dist: Independent Pubs. Group.

Abts, Stacey. I'm Trying to Be Like Jesus. Perry, Janice Kapp. 2003. (J). *(978-1-57008-843-8(8),* Bookcraft, Inc.) Deseret Bk. Co.

Abulafia, Yossi. A Kiss for Lily. Nirgad, Lia. 2006. (ENG.). 24p. (J). (gr. -1-1). *(978-1-59692-163-4(3))* MacAdam/Cage Publishing, Inc.

Aburto, Jesus. Battle for Home Plate, 1 vol. Kreie, Chris et al. 2010. (Sports Illustrated Kids Graphic Novels Ser.). (ENG.). 56p. (gr. 2-3). 25.32 *(978-1-4342-1913-8(5))* Stone Arch Bks.

Aburto, Jesus. Hoop Hustle. Maddox, Jake. 2015. (Jake Maddox Sports Stories Ser.). (ENG.). 72p. (gr. 2-3). lib. bdg. 23.99 ***(978-1-4965-0494-4(1))*** Stone Arch Bks.

Aburto, Jesus. Point-Blank Paintball, 1 vol. Ciencin, Scott et al. 2010. (Sports Illustrated Kids Graphic Novels Ser.). (ENG.). 56p. (gr. 2-3). pap. 7.19 *(978-1-4342-2293-0(4));* 25.32 *(978-1-4342-1914-5(3))* Stone Arch Bks.

—Secret Weapons: A Tale of the Revolutionary War, 1 vol. Gunderson, Jessica. 2008. (Historical Fiction Ser.). (ENG.). 56p. (gr. 2-3). pap. 6.25 *(978-1-4342-0848-4(6),* Graphic Flash) Stone Arch Bks.

Aburto, Jesus, et al. Snowboard Standoff, 1 vol. Ciencin, Scott et al. 2011. (Sports Illustrated Kids Graphic Novels Ser.). (ENG.). 56p. (gr. 2-3). lib. bdg. 25.32 *(978-1-4342-2242-8(X))* Stone Arch Bks.

Aburto, Jesus. Soccer Shake-Up. Maddox, Jake. 2015. (Jake Maddox Sports Stories Ser.). (ENG.). 72p. (gr. 2-3). lib. bdg. 23.99 ***(978-1-4965-0495-1(X))*** Stone Arch Bks.

—Touchdown Triumph. Maddox, Jake. 2015. (Jake Maddox Sports Stories Ser.). (ENG.). 72p. (gr. 2-3). lib. bdg. 23.99 ***(978-1-4965-0492-0(5))*** Stone Arch Bks.

Aburto, Jesus, et al. Track Team Titans, 1 vol. Peters, Stephanie True & Cano, Fernando M. 2011. (Sports Illustrated Kids Graphic Novels Ser.). (ENG.). 56p. (gr. 2-3). pap. 7.19 *(978-1-4342-3072-0(4));* lib. bdg. 25.32 *(978-1-4342-2224-4(1))* Stone Arch Bks.

Aburto, Jesus & Cano, Fernando M. Hoop Rat, 1 vol. Ciencin, Scott et al. 2011. (Sports Illustrated Kids Graphic Novels Ser.). (ENG.). 56p. (gr. 2-3). pap. 7.19 *(978-1-4342-3069-0(4));* lib. bdg. 25.32 *(978-1-4342-2223-7(3))* Stone Arch Bks.

Aburto, Jesus & Esparza, Andres. Avalanche Freestyle, 1 vol. Ciencin, Scott & Maese, Fares. 2010. (Sports Illustrated Kids Graphic Novels Ser.). (ENG.). 56p. (gr. 2-3). 25.32 *(978-1-4342-2009-7(5));* pap. 7.19 *(978-1-4342-2783-6(9))* Stone Arch Bks.

—BMX Blitz, 1 vol. Ciencin, Scott & Maese, Fares. 2011. (Sports Illustrated Kids Graphic Novels Ser.). (ENG.). 56p. (gr. 2-3). pap. 7.19 *(978-1-4342-3071-3(6))* Stone Arch Bks.

—Paintball Punk, 1 vol. Tulien, Sean & Maese, Fares. 2010. (Sports Illustrated Kids Graphic Novels Ser.). (ENG.). 56p. (gr. 2-3). 25.32 *(978-1-4342-2219-0(5));* pap. 7.19 *(978-1-4342-2788-1(X))* Stone Arch Bks.

—Shot Clock Slam. Kreie, Chris & Maese, Fares. 2010. (Sports Illustrated Kids Graphic Novels Ser.). (ENG.). 56p. (gr. 2-3). pap. 7.19 *(978-1-4342-2786-7(3))* Stone Arch Bks.

Aburto, Jesus, jt. illus. see Esparza, Andres.

Aburto, Jesus, jt. illus. see Maese, Fares.

Aburtov. Beach Bully, 1 vol. Maddox, Jake. 2013. (Jake Maddox Sports Stories Ser.). (ENG.). 72p. (gr. 2-3). pap. 5.95 *(978-1-4342-6206-6(5))* Stone Arch Bks.

—Pete Bogg: King of the Frogs. Sonneborn, Scott. 2013. (Pete Bogg Ser.). (ENG.). 48p. (gr. 1-3). pap. 5.95 *(978-1-4342-3872-6(5));* lib. bdg. 22.65 *(978-1-4342-3284-7(0))* Stone Arch Bks.

—Point-Blank Paintball, 1 vol. Ciencin, Scott. 2010. (Sports Illustrated Kids Graphic Novels Ser.). (ENG.). 32p. pap. 1.00 *(978-1-4342-2137-7(7))* Stone Arch Bks.

Aburtov, Jesus. Beach Bully, 1 vol. Maddox, Jake. 2013. (Jake Maddox Sports Stories Ser.). (ENG.). 72p. (gr. 2-3). lib. bdg. 23.99 *(978-1-4342-5973-8(0))* Stone Arch Bks.

—Kart Competition, 1 vol. Maddox, Jake. 2013. (Jake Maddox Sports Stories Ser.). (ENG.). 72p. (gr. 2-3). lib. bdg. 23.99 *(978-1-4342-5976-9(5))* Stone Arch Bks.

Aburtov, Jesus Aburto. Battle for Home Plate, 1 vol. Kreie, Chris et al. 2010. (Sports Illustrated Kids Graphic Novels Ser.). (ENG.). 56p. (gr. 2-3). pap. 7.19 *(978-1-4342-2290-9(X))* Stone Arch Bks.

—Board Battle, 1 vol. Maddox, Jake. 2013. (Jake Maddox Sports Stories Ser.). (ENG.). 72p. (gr. 2-3). pap. 5.95 *(978-1-4342-6208-0(1));* lib. bdg. 23.99 *(978-1-4342-5975-2(7))* Stone Arch Bks.

Aburtov, Jesus Aburto. Caught Stealing. Maddox, Jake. 2015. (Jake Maddox Sports Stories Ser.). (ENG.). 72p. (gr. 2-3). lib. bdg. 23.99 ***(978-1-4965-0493-7(3))*** Stone Arch Bks.

Aburtov, Jesus Aburto. Kart Competition, 1 vol. Maddox, Jake. 2013. (Jake Maddox Sports Stories Ser.). (ENG.). 72p. (gr. 2-3). pap. 5.95 *(978-1-4342-6209-7(X))* Stone Arch Bks.

—Paintball Problems, 1 vol. Maddox, Jake. 2013. (Jake Maddox Sports Stories Ser.). (ENG.). 72p. (gr. 2-3). pap. 5.95 *(978-1-4342-6207-3(3));* lib. bdg. 23.99 *(978-1-4342-5974-5(9))* Stone Arch Bks.

Acar, Sinan. Pancakes on Sunday. Cox, Miss Karin & Cox, Karin. 2012. 26p. pap. *(978-0-9873602-2-9(1))* Indelible Ink Pr.

Acayen, Alex. Chrichi & the Little Blue Bird: A Lesson Learned Book. Starkey, Ines. 2011. (ENG.). 30p. pap. 9.95 *(978-1-4663-2387-2(6))* CreateSpace Independent Publishing Platform.

Accardo, Anthony. Benito's Sopaipillas/Las Sopaipillas de Benito. Baca, Ana. Villarroel, Carolina, tr. 2007. (ENG & SPA.). 32p. (J). (gr. -1-2). 16.95 *(978-1-55885-370-6(7),* Piñata Books) Arte Publico Pr.

—Cesar Chavez: The Struggle for Justice (La Lucha por la Justicia) Griswold del Castillo, Richard. Colin, Jose Juan, tr. 2010. (ENG & SPA.). (J). (gr. 1-3). pap. 18.95 incl. audio compact disk *(978-1-4301-0834-4(7))* Live Oak Media.

—Cesar Chavez: The Struggle for Justice/la Lucha Por la Justicia. Griswold del Castillo, Richard. Colin, Jose Juan, tr. 2008. (Hispanic Civil Rights Ser.). (SPA & ENG.). 32p. (J). (gr. -1-3). pap. 7.95 *(978-1-55885-424-6(X),* Piñata Books) Arte Publico Pr.

—Chiles for Benito (Chiles para Benito) Baca, Ana. Colin, Jose Juan, tr. (ENG & SPA.). 32p. (J). 16.95 *(978-1-55885-389-8(8),* Piñata Books) Arte Publico Pr.

—Ricardo's Race/la Carrera de Ricardo. Bertrand, Diane Gonzales. Viegas-Barros, Rocio, tr. from ENG. 2007. (SPA.). 32p. (J). (gr. -1-2). 16.95 *(978-1-55885-481-9(9))* Arte Publico Pr.

—Waiting for Papá/Esperando a Papá. Laínez, René Colato.Tr. of Esperando a Papa. (ENG & SPA.). 32p. (gr. 1-3). 16.95 *(978-1-55885-403-1(7),* Piñata Books) Arte Publico Pr.

Accrocco, Anthony. Stewie Meets New Friends. Seitz, Melissa. 2012. 26p. pap. 12.95 *(978-1-61244-079-8(7))* Halo Publishing International.

Acedera, Kei. How to Talk to Dads. Greven, Alec. 2009. (ENG.). 48p. (J). (gr. 1-5). 9.99 *(978-0-06-172930-0(2),* Collins) HarperCollins Pubs.

—How to Talk to Girls. Greven, Alec. 2008. (ENG.). 48p. (J). (gr. 1-5). 9.99 *(978-0-06-170999-9(9),* Collins) HarperCollins Pubs.

—How to Talk to Moms. Greven, Alec. 2009. (ENG.). 48p. (J). (gr. 1-5). 9.99 *(978-0-06-171001-8(6),* Collins) HarperCollins Pubs.

—How to Talk to Santa. Greven, Alec. 2009. (ENG.). 48p. (J). (gr. 1-5). 9.99 *(978-0-06-180207-2(7),* Collins) HarperCollins Pubs.

—Liesl & Po. Oliver, Lauren. (ENG.). (J). (gr. 3-7). 2012. 336p. pap. 6.99 *(978-0-06-201452-8(8));* 2011. 320p. 16.99 *(978-0-06-201451-1(X))* HarperCollins Pubs.

—Rules for School. Greven, Alec. 2010. (ENG.). 48p. (J). (gr. 1-5). 9.99 *(978-0-06-195170-1(6),* Collins) HarperCollins Pubs.

Acerno, Gerry, et al. Eli Whitney & the Cotton Gin, 1 vol. Gunderson, Jessica Sarah et al. 2007. (Inventions & Discovery Ser.). (ENG.). 32p. (gr. 3-4). 29.99 *(978-0-7368-6843-3(7),* Graphic Library) Capstone Pr., Inc.

Acerno, Gerry. Eli Whitney & the Cotton Gin, 1 vol. Gunderson, Jessica Sarah et al. 2007. (Inventions & Discovery Ser.). (ENG.). 32p. (gr. 3-4). per. 8.10 *(978-0-7368-7895-1(5),* Graphic Library) Capstone Pr., Inc.

AcesGraphics. Birds, Bikes, & Ice Cream: A Lesson in Overcoming Adversity. Pie, Corey. 2010. (ENG.). 40p. pap. 9.95 *(978-1-4528-4009-3(1))* CreateSpace Independent Publishing Platform.

Achdé. Lucky Luke Versus the Pinkertons. Pennac, Daniel & Benacquista, Tonino. 2012. (ENG.). 48p. pap. 11.95 *(978-1-84918-098-6(9))* CineBook GBR. Dist: National Bk. Network.

Achilles, Pat. The Adventures of the Poodle Posse: [happy Tales 1 & 2]. Smith, Chrysa. 2007. 26p. (J). *(978-1-4243-3335-6(0))* Independent Publisher Services.

—Mommy's High Heel Shoes. Finnan, Kristie. 2008. 32p. (J). 16.99 *(978-0-9817565-2-3(2))* Mommy Workshop Bks.

Ackerley, Sarah. Your Fantastic, Elastic Brain: Stretch It, Shape It. Deak, JoAnn. O'Malley, Judy, ed. 2010. (ENG.). 32p. (J). (gr. -1-3). 18.95 *(978-0-9829938-0-4(3))* Little Pickle Press LLC.

Ackerley, Sarah. Patrick the Somnambulist. Ackerley, Sarah. 2008. (ENG.). 32p. (J). (gr. -1 — 1). 14.95 *(978-1-933831-07-7(3))* Blooming Tree Pr.

Ackerman, Dena. Red Is My Rimon: A Jewish Child's Book of Colors. Glick, Dvorah. 2012. 32p. (J). 12.95 *(978-1-929628-71-1(4))* Hachai Publishing.

Ackerman, Michele L. Jack & the Beanstalk Story in a Box. James, Annabelle. 2003. (Story in a Box Ser.). 12p. (J). bds. 8.99 *(978-1-883043-42-1(5))* Straight Edge Pr., The.

Ackison, Wendy Wassink. Catfish Annie to the Rescue. Crowe, Duane E. 2004. (Back River Adventures of Catfish Annie Ser.). 48p. (J). (gr. k-5). *(978-0-9672882-0-8(7))* Back River Company, The, LLC.

—The Twelve Gifts of Birth. Reger, Jill, photos by. Costanzo, Charlene A. & Costanzo, Charlene. 2011. (Twelve Gifts Ser.: 1). (ENG.). 64p. 21.99 *(978-0-06-621104-6(2),* Morrow, William & Co.) HarperCollins Pubs.

Ackley, Peggy Jo. Bitty Bear & the Bugs. Witkowski, Teri. 2008. (J). *(978-1-59369-383-1(4),* American Girl) American Girl Publishing, Inc.

—Bitty Bear, Flower Girl. Witkowski, Teri. 2009. (J). *(978-1-59369-564-4(0),* American Girl) American Girl Publishing, Inc.

—Bitty Bear's Birthday Treats. Witkowski, Teri. 2008. (J). *(978-1-59369-384-8(2),* American Girl) American Girl Publishing, Inc.

—Bitty Bear's New Friend. Witkowski, Teri. 2005. (J). *(978-1-59369-021-2(5))* American Girl Publishing, Inc.

—Bitty Bear's Sleigh Ride. Child, Lydia Maria. 2006. (J). *(978-1-59369-157-8(2))* American Girl Publishing, Inc.

—Bitty Bear's Snowflake Dreams. Witkowski, Teri. 2006. (J). *(978-1-59369-166-0(1))* American Girl Publishing, Inc.

—Bitty Bear's Valentines. Witkowski, Teri. 2004. (J). *(978-1-58485-837-9(0))* American Girl Publishing, Inc.

—Bitty Bear's Walk in the Woods. Witkowski, Teri. 2006. (J). *(978-1-59369-156-1(4))* American Girl Publishing, Inc.

—The Bitty Bunch Bath Book. Witkowski, Teri. 2006. (J). *(978-1-59369-080-9(0))* American Girl Publishing, Inc.

—Bitty Bunny's Bedtime. Witkowski, Teri. 2004. (J). *(978-1-58485-921-5(0))* American Girl Publishing, Inc.

—Bitty Bunny's Slipper Search. Witkowski, Teri. 2009. (J). *(978-1-59369-586-6(1),* American Girl) American Girl Publishing, Inc.

—Bunny & Piggy at the Beach. Witkowski, Teri. 2005. (J). *(978-1-58485-961-1(X))* American Girl Publishing, Inc.

—Happy Birthday, Bitty Bear! Witkowski, Teri. 2005. (J). *(978-1-58485-959-8(8))* American Girl Publishing, Inc.

—It's Spring, Bitty Bear! Witkowski, Teri. 2007. (J). *(978-1-59369-242-1(0))* American Girl Publishing, Inc.

—Time for Bed, Bitty Bunch. Witkowski, Teri. 2008. (J). *(978-1-59369-380-0(X))* American Girl Publishing, Inc.

—Wait Your Turn, Bitty Froggy! Witkowski, Teri. 2008. (J). *(978-1-59369-285-8(4))* American Girl Publishing, Inc.

Acosta, Patricia. Adivinario de Diccionanzas. Zambrano, Alicia. 2008. (SPA.). 32p. (J). (gr. 2). 10.95 *(978-958-28-1298-0(2))* Intermedio Editores S.A. COL. Dist: Random Hse., Inc.

—La Alegria de Querer: Poemas de Amor para Ninos. Nino, Jairo Anibal. 2003. (Literatura Juvenil (Panamericana Editorial) Ser.). (SPA.). 70p. (J). (gr. -1-7). pap. *(978-958-30-0293-9(3),* PV30142) Centro de Informacion y Desarrollo de la Comunicacion y la Literatura MEX. Dist: Lectorum Pubns., Inc.

—Andres, Perro y Oso en el Pais de los Miedos. Ibanez, Francisco Montana. 2003. (SPA.). 84p. (J). (gr. -1-7). pap. *(978-958-30-0997-6(0))* Editorial Medica Panamerican.

—Cuentos, Pombo Rafael. Pombo, Rafael. (SPA.). 68p. (J). (gr. 2). pap. *(978-958-30-0355-4(7),* PV0862) Panamericana Editorial COL. Dist: Lectorum Pubns., Inc.

—Fiodor Mijailovich Dostoievsky. Dostoevsky, Fyodor. 2003. (Cajon de Cuentos Ser.). (SPA.). 223p. (J). (gr. 4-7). *(978-958-30-1027-9(8))* Panamericana Editorial.

—Relatos para Muchachos. Ramirez, Gonzalo Canal. 2003. (Literatura Juvenil (Panamericana Editorial) Ser.). (SPA.). 110p. (YA). (gr. 4-7). pap. *(978-958-30-0351-6(4))* Panamericana Editorial.

Acraman, Helen. Japanese Nursery Rhymes: Carp Streamers, Falling Rain & Other Traditional Favorites. Wright, Danielle. 2012. (ENG.). 32p. (J). (gr. -1-2). 16.95 *(978-4-8053-1188-2(6))* Tuttle Publishing.

—Korean Nursery Rhymes: Wild Geese, Land of Goblins & Other Favorite Songs & Rhymes. Wright, Danielle. 2013. (ENG & KOR.). 32p. (J). (gr. -1-2). 16.95 *(978-0-8048-4227-3(2))* Tuttle Publishing.

Acreman, Hayley. Tai & the Tremorfa Troll. Davies, Lewis. 2007. (ENG.). 20p. (J). pap. 7.95 *(978-1-905762-48-4(8))* Parthian Bks. GBR. Dist: Independent Pubs. Group.

Acreman, Hayley. Found You Rabbit! Acreman, Hayley. 2011. (ENG.). 34p. (J). (gr. k-2). pap. 9.95 *(978-1-905762-87-3(9))* Parthian Bks. GBR. Dist: Independent Pubs. Group.

Acton, Sara. Esther's Rainbow. Kane, Kim. 2015. (ENG.). 32p. (J). (gr. -1-k). 16.99 ***(978-1-925266-28-3(1))*** Allen & Unwin AUS. Dist: Independent Pubs. Group.

Acuña, Daniel. Black Widow: The Name of the Rose. Liu, Marjorie M. 2011. (ENG.). 144p. (YA). (gr. 8-17). pap. 16.99 *(978-0-7851-4700-8(4))* Marvel Worldwide, Inc.

—Captain America: The Trial of Captain America. Brubaker, Ed. 2011. (ENG.). 152p. (YA). (gr. 8-17). 24.99 *(978-0-7851-5119-7(2))* Marvel Worldwide, Inc.

Acuña, Daniel, jt. illus. see Guice, Butch.

Ada, Alma Flor, jt. illus. see López, Rafael.

Adachi, Mitsuri. Cross Game, Vol. 2. Adachi, Mitsuri. 2011. (Cross Game Ser.: 2). (ENG.). 376p. pap. 14.99 *(978-1-4215-3766-5(4))* Viz Media.

Adachi, Mitsuru. Cross Game, Vol. 4. Adachi, Mitsuru. 2011. (Cross Game Ser.: 4). (ENG.). 376p. pap. 14.99 *(978-1-4215-3768-9(0))* Viz Media.

Adam, Mccauley, jt. illus. see McCauley, Adam.

Adam, Sarah E. Abby in Vermont Coloring & Activity Book. 2008. 32p. (J). 4.95 *(978-0-9793790-1-7(6))* Howard Printing, Inc.

Adams, Allysa. Pine Needle Pedro. Megerdichian, Janet. 2010. 36p. pap. 16.99 *(978-1-4520-4422-4(8))* AuthorHouse.

Adams, Ansel, photos by. Sierra Nevada: The John Muir Trail. Adams, Ansel. 2006. (ENG., 128p. 50.00 *(978-0-8212-5717-3(X))* Little Brown & Co.

Adams, Arlene. Locket Out. Bennett, Leonie. 2004. (ENG.). 24p. (J). lib. bdg. 23.65 *(978-1-59646-688-3(X))* Dingles & Co.

Adams, Art & Bolton, John. Destiny Calling. Perez, George. rev. ed. 2006. (Wonder Woman Ser.). (ENG.). 176p. pap. 19.99 *(978-1-4012-0943-8(2))* DC Comics.

Adams, Arthur, et al. New Mutants Classic, Vol. 5. 2010. (ENG.). 280p. (J). (gr. 4-17). pap. 29.99 *(978-0-7851-4460-1(9))* Marvel Worldwide, Inc.

Adams, Ben. Animals. O'Toole, Janet & Anness Publishing Staff. 2013. (ENG.). 16p. bds. 6.99 *(978-1-84322-793-9(2),* Armadillo) Anness Publishing GBR. Dist: National Bk. Network.

—First Words. O'Toole, Janet & Anness Publishing Staff. 2013. (ENG.). 16p. bds. 6.99 *(978-1-84322-795-3(9),* Armadillo) Anness Publishing GBR. Dist: National Bk. Network.

—Lift-the-Flap Learning: Lift the flaps to find out about vehicles! O'Toole, Janet & Anness Publishing Staff. 2013. (ENG.). 16p. bds. 6.99 *(978-1-84322-728-1(2),* Armadillo) Anness Publishing GBR. Dist: National Bk. Network.

—On the Farm. O'Toole, Janet. 2013. (ENG.). 16p. bds. 6.99 *(978-1-84322-794-6(0),* Armadillo) Anness Publishing GBR. Dist: National Bk. Network.

Adams, Beth. Confessions of a Former Bully. Ludwig, Trudy. 2012. (ENG.). 48p. (J). (gr. 3-7). pap. 7.99 *(978-0-307-93113-9(7),* Dragonfly Bks.) Random Hse. Children's Bks.

—Confessions of a Former Bully. Ludwig, Trudy. 2010. (ENG.). 48p. (J). (gr. 1-4). 15.99 *(978-1-58246-309-4(3),* Tricycle Pr.) Ten Speed Pr.

Adams, Craig. Edward of Canterbury & the King of Red. Cash, M. A. 2003. (J). *(978-0-9772711-0-8(2))* Jama Kids.

Adams, Denise H. Annabelle's Angels. Adams, Denise H. 2007. 24p. (J). (gr. -1-3). 11.99 *(978-1-59879-386-4(1))* Lifevest Publishing, Inc.

—Itchy the Witch. Adams, Denise H. 2007. 32p. (J). (gr. -1-3). 13.99 *(978-1-59879-385-7(3))* Lifevest Publishing, Inc.

Adams, Frank & Lawrence, C. H. Puss in Boots. Perrault, Charles. 2009. (ENG.). 16p. (J). (gr. -1-3). pap. 9.95 *(978-1-59583-361-7(7),* 9781595833617) Laughing Elephant.

Adams, Gil & Jessell, Tim. In the Ice Caves of Krog. Abbott, Tony. 2003. (Secrets of Droon Ser.: No. 20). 114p. (J). (gr. 2-5). 12.65 *(978-0-7569-3940-3(2))* Perfection Learning Corp.

Adams, Hazel. City Food Chains. Vogel, Julia. 2010. (Fascinating Food Chains Ser.). 32p. 28.50 *(978-1-60270-791-7(X,* Looking Glass Library-Nonfiction) Magic Wagon.

—Deciduous Forest Food Chains. Vogel, Julia. 2010. (Fascinating Food Chains Ser.). 32p. 28.50 *(978-1-60270-792-4(8),* Looking Glass Library-Nonfiction) Magic Wagon.

—Deep Ocean Food Chains. Mataya, Marybeth. 2010. (Fascinating Food Chains Ser.). 32p. 28.50 *(978-1-60270-793-1(6),* Looking Glass Library-Nonfiction) Magic Wagon.

—Desert Food Chains. Vogel, Julia. 2010. (Fascinating Food Chains Ser.). 32p. 28.50 *(978-1-60270-794-8(4),* Looking Glass Library- Nonfiction) Magic Wagon.

—Grassland Food Chains. Mataya, Marybeth. 2010. (Fascinating Food Chains Ser.). 32p. 28.50 *(978-1-60270-795-5(2),* Looking Glass Library-Nonfiction) Magic Wagon.

—What Are Food Chains & Food Webs? Vogel, Julia. 2010. (Fascinating Food Chains Ser.). 32p. 28.50 *(978-1-60270-796-2(0),* Looking Glass Library-Nonfiction) Magic Wagon.

Adams, Jean Ekman. Clarence & the Purple Horse Bounce into Town. Adams, Jean Ekman. 2003. 32p. (J). (gr. -1-3). 15.95 *(978-0-87358-826-3(6),* Rising Moon Bks. for Young Readers) Northland Publishing.

Adams, Kathryn. Camp Fossil Eyes: Digging for the Origins of Words. Abley, Mark. 2009. (ENG.). 136p. (J). (gr. 4-6). 19.95 *(978-1-55451-181-5(X),* 9781554511815); pap. 12.95 *(978-1-55451-180-8(1),* 9781554511808) Annick Pr., Ltd. CAN. Dist: Firefly Bks., Ltd.

Adams, Kevin & Price, Michael. A Stegosaurus Named Sam. Adams, Kevin. 2004. (J). per. 12.50 *(978-0-9740683-4-3(9))* Authors & Artists Publishers of New York, Inc.

Adams, Lisa. The Twelve Days of Christmas in New York City. Adams, Lisa. 2009. (Twelve Days of Christmas in America Ser.). (ENG.). 32p. (J). (gr. k-3). 12.95 *(978-1-4027-6440-0(5))* Sterling Publishing Co., Inc.

Adams, Liz. Brooke's Big Decision, No. 8. Jones, Jen. 2012. (Team Cheer Ser.). (ENG.). 112p. (gr. 4-4). 23.99 *(978-1-4342-4036-1(3))* Stone Arch Bks.

—Faith & the Dance Drama, No. 5. Jones, Jen. 2012. (Team Cheer Ser.: No. 5). (ENG.). 112p. (gr. 4-4). lib. bdg. 23.99 *(978-1-4342-4033-0(9))* Stone Arch Bks.

—Lissa on the Sidelines, No. 6. Jones, Jen. 2012. (Team Cheer Ser.). (ENG.). 112p. (gr. 4-4). lib. bdg. 23.99 *(978-1-4342-4034-7(7))* Stone Arch Bks.

—Save Our Squad, Gaby, No. 7. Jones, Jen. 2012. (Team Cheer Ser.). (ENG.). 112p. (gr. 4-4). lib. bdg. 23.99 *(978-1-4342-4035-4(5))* Stone Arch Bks.

Adams, Lucas. Can a Toucan Hoot Too? A Phonemic Awareness Tale, 10 vols. Carlson, Lavelle. 2003. 32p. (J). (gr. -1-1). per. 16.95 *(978-0-9725803-0-4(1))* Children's Publishing.

—Rocks in My Socks & Rainbows Too, 10 vols. Carlson, Lavelle. 2003. 32p. (J). per. 16.95 *(978-0-9725803-2-8(8))* Children's Publishing.

Adams, Lynn. Bears on the Brain. Penner, Lucille Recht. 2003. (Science Solves It! Ser.). 32p. (J). pap. 5.95 *(978-1-57565-121-7(1))* Kane Pr., Inc.

—Gallinas de Aqui para Alla. Pollack, Pam & Belviso, Meg. 2008. (Math Matters en Espanol Ser.). (SPA.). 32p. (J). (gr. -1-3). pap. 5.95 *(978-1-57565-268-9(4))* Kane Pr., Inc.

—Osos en la Mente. Penner, Lucille Recht. 2008. (Science Solves It! en Espanol Ser.). (SPA.). 32p. (J). (gr. -1-3). pap. 5.95 *(978-1-57565-261-0(7))* Kane Pr., Inc.

—Que Es Ese Sonido? Lawrence, Mary. 2008. (Science Solves It! en Espanol Ser.). (SPA.). 32p. (J). (gr. -1-3). pap. 5.95 *(978-1-57565-266-5(8))* Kane Pr., Inc.

—¿Qué es Ese Sonido? (What's That Sound?) Lawrence, Mary. 2009. (Science Solves It! (r) en Espanol Ser.). (SPA.). (gr. k-2). pap. 33.92 *(978-0-7613-4801-6(8))* Lerner Publishing Group.

Adams, Lynn. Un Castillo para Gatitos. Adams, Lynn. Friedman, Mel et al. 2008. (SPA.). (J). *(978-1-57565-275-7(7))* Kane Pr., Inc.

Adams, Lynn. Picky Peggy. Adams, Lynn, tr. Dussling, Jennifer. 2004. (Science Solves It! Ser.). 32p. (J). pap. 5.95 *(978-1-57565-138-5(6))* Kane Pr., Inc.

Adams, Lynne. Donde esta ese Hueso? Math Matters en Espanol. Penner, Lucille Recht. 2005. 32p. (J). pap. 5.95 *(978-1-57565-156-9(4))* Kane Pr., Inc.

Adams, Marcella Ryan. Around the World with Rosalie. Redman-Waldeyer, Christine. 2003. pap. 9.00 *(978-0-8059-6185-0(2))* Dorrance Publishing Co., Inc.

Adams, Mark W. My Friendly Giant. Rubenstein, Lauri. 2012. (ENG.). 36p. (J). 16.95 *(978-0-9770391-6-6(1))* Growing Field Bks.

Adams, Mark Wayne. The Belly Button Fairy. Hinman, Bobbie. 2009. (ENG.). 32p. (J). (gr. -1-k). 15.95 *(978-0-9786791-3-2(X))* Best Fairy Bks.

—The Fart Fairy. Hinman, Bobbie. 2010. (ENG.). 32p. (J). (gr. k-2). 15.95 *(978-0-9786791-4-9(8))* Best Fairy Bks.

—Jadyn & the Magic Bubble: I Met Gandhi. Benchimol, Brigitte. 2008. (J). 24.95 *(978-0-9799339-7-4(8))* East West Discovery Pr.

Adams Marks, Elizabeth. Comprehension Crosswords Grade 5, 6 vols. Koumpouras, Sally. 2003. 32p. (J). 4.99 *(978-1-56472-189-1(2))* Edupress, Inc.

—Comprehension Crosswords Grade 6, 6 vols. Hemminger, Marcia. 2003. 32p. (J). 4.99 *(978-1-56472-190-7(6))* Edupress, Inc.

—Lewis & Clark Famous Faces. Meinke, Amanda & Stegmann, Lisa. 2003. 2p. (J). pap. 2.99 *(978-1-56472-289-8(9))* Edupress, Inc.

Adams, Matt. Meet Ned Kelly. Brian, Janeen. (Meet... Ser.). (ENG.). (J). 2014. 36p. (gr. k). 13.99 *(978-1-74275-719-3(7))*; 2013. 32p. (gr. -1). 18.99 *(978-1-74275-718-6(9))* Random Hse. Australia AUS. Dist: Independent Pubs. Group.

Adams, Michael. Turning the Page: Frederick Douglass Learns to Read. Roos, Am & Hamilton, A. 2014. (ENG.). 28p. (J). pap. 8.50 *(978-1-61406-683-5(3))* American Reading Co.

Adams, Neal. Essential Avengers, Vol. 4. Thomas, Roy & Buscema, Sal. rev. ed. 2010. (ENG.). 640p. (J). (gr. -1-17). pap. 19.99 *(978-0-7851-1485-7(8))* Marvel Worldwide, Inc.

—First X-Men. 2013. (ENG.). 112p. (YA). (gr. 8-17). pap. 19.99 *(978-0-7851-6496-8(0))* Marvel Worldwide, Inc.

Adams, Pam. Dolphin. 2004. (Pals Ser.). (ENG.). 12p. (J). bds. *(978-1-904550-11-2(8))* Child's Play International Ltd.

—The Farmer in the Dell. 2013. (Classic Books with Holes Ser.). (ENG.). 16p. (gr. -1). pap. incl. audio compact disk *(978-1-84643-624-6(9))* Child's Play International Ltd.

—The First Day. 2009. 10p. (J). bds. *(978-0-85953-149-8(X))* Child's Play International Ltd.

—Kitten. 2004. (Pals Ser.). (ENG.). 12p. (J). bds. *(978-1-904550-08-2(8))* Child's Play International Ltd.

—Old Macdonald. 2004. (Classic Books with Holes Board Book Ser.). (ENG.). 16p. (J). bds. *(978-0-85953-317-1(4))* Child's Play International Ltd.

—Old MacDonald Had a Farm. Twinn, M. 2007. (Classic Books with Holes 8x8 with CD Ser.). (ENG.). 16p. (J). (gr. -1-1). *(978-1-904550-64-8(9))* Child's Play International Ltd.

—Puppy. 2004. (Pals Ser.). (ENG.). 12p. (J). bds. *(978-1-904550-09-9(6))* Child's Play International Ltd.

—There Was an Old Lady Who Swallowed a Fly. 2005. (Classic Books with Holes Ser.). (ENG.). 20p. (J). (gr. -1-1). bds. *(978-0-85953-314-0(X))* Child's Play International Ltd.

—There Was an Old Lady Who Swallowed a Fly. Twinn, M. 2007. (Classic Books with Holes 8x8 with CD Ser.). (ENG.). 16p. (J). (gr. -1-1). *(978-1-904550-62-4(2))* Child's Play International Ltd.

—There Was an Old Lady Who Swallowed the Sea. (Classic Books with Holes 8x8 with CD Ser.). (ENG.). (J). 2010. 16p. *(978-1-84643-363-4(0))*; 2007. 16p. (gr. -1-1). *(978-1-84643-084-8(4))*; 2007. 14p. (gr. -1-k). bds. *(978-1-84643-073-2(9))*; 2006. 16p. (gr. -1-k). *(978-1-84643-035-0(6))* Child's Play International Ltd.

—This Is the House That Jack Built. 2007. (Classic Books with Holes 8x8 with CD Ser.). (ENG.). 16p. (J). (gr. -1-1). *(978-1-904550-65-5(7))* Child's Play International Ltd.

—This Old Man. 2007. (Classic Books with Holes 8x8 with CD Ser.). (ENG.). 16p. (J). (gr. -1-1). *(978-1-904550-63-1(0))* Child's Play International Ltd.

Adams, Pam. Old Macdonald Had a Farm. Adams, Pam, tr. 2003. (Classic Books with Holes 8x8 Ser.). (ENG.). 16p. (J). pap. *(978-0-85953-135-1(X))* Child's Play International Ltd.

—There Was an Old Lady Who Swallowed a Fly. Adams, Pam, tr. 2003. (Classic Books with Holes 8x8 Ser.). (ENG.). 16p. (J). pap. *(978-0-85953-134-4(1))* Child's Play International Ltd.

Adams, Renee. Can Thunder Hurt Me? Adams, Renee. 2012. 24p. pap. 17.99 *(978-1-4685-5852-4(8))* AuthorHouse.

Adams, Rich. Rupert & the Bag. Staman, A. Louise. 2006. (J). 11.99 *(978-0-9787263-0-0(8))* Tiger Iron Pr.

Adams, Ronald. The Adventures of Junior & Mousey in the Land of Puttin Pow: Don't Talk to Strangers. Adams, Jjt. 2013. 32p. pap. 24.95 *(978-1-63004-457-2(1))* America Star Bks.

Adams, Sarah. Gary & Ray. 2010. (ENG.). 36p. (J). (gr. -1-2). 17.95 *(978-1-84507-955-0(8))*, Frances Lincoln) Quarto Publishing Group UK GBR. Dist: Hachette Bk. Group.

Adams, Shireen. Colours of Islam. Mair, J. Samia. 2013. (ENG.). 40p. (J). (gr. k-2). 22.95 *(978-0-86037-591-3(9))* Kube Publishing Ltd. GBR. Dist: Consortium Bk. Sales & Distribution.

—Snow White: An Islamic Tale. Gilani, Fawzia. 2013. (Islamic Fairy Tales Ser.). (ENG.). 40p. (J). (gr. k-3). 14.00 *(978-0-86037-526-5(9))* Kube Publishing Ltd. GBR. Dist: Consortium Bk. Sales & Distribution.

Adams, Steve. Believe Storybook: Think, Act, Be Like Jesus, 1 vol. Frazee, Randy. 2015. (ENG.). 288p. (J). 19.99 *(978-0-310-74590-7(X))* Zonderkidz.

—The Boy Who Grew Flowers. Wojtowicz, Jen & Wojzowitz, Jen. 2005. (ENG.). 32p. (J). (gr. -1-3). 16.99 *(978-1-84148-686-4(8))* Barefoot Bks., Inc.

—The Boy Who Grew Flowers. Wojtowicz, Jen. 2012. (ENG.). 32p. (J). pap. 7.99 *(978-1-84686-749-1(5))* Barefoot Bks., Inc.

—The Boy Who Wanted to Cook. Whelan, Gloria. 2011. (Tales of the World Ser.). (ENG.). 40p. (gr. k-5). lib. bdg. 16.95 *(978-1-58536-534-0(3))* Sleeping Bear Pr.

—Lost Boy: The Story of the Man Who Created Peter Pan. Yolen, Jane. 2010. (ENG.). 40p. (J). (gr. 1-3). 17.99 *(978-0-525-47886-7(8)*, Dutton Juvenile) Penguin Publishing Group.

Adamson, Bonnie. Bedtime Monster. Brunell, Heather. 2010. (ENG.). 32p. (J). (gr. -1-12). lib. bdg. 16.95 *(978-1-934960-03-5(9)*, Raven Tree Pr.,Csi) Continental Sales, Inc.

—Bedtime Monster/A Dormir, Monstruito! Brunell, Heather. de la Vega, Eida, tr. 2010. (ENG & SPA.). 32p. (J). (gr. -1-3). lib. bdg. 16.95 *(978-1-932748-80-2(6)*, Raven Tree Pr.,Csi) Continental Sales, Inc.

—Feeling Better: A Kid's Book about Therapy. Rashkin, Rachel. 2005. 48p. (J). (gr. -1-7). pap. 9.95 *(978-1-59147-238-4(5)*, Magination Pr.) American Psychological Assn.

—Feeling Better: A Kid's Books about Therapy. Rashkin, Rachel. 2005. 48p. (J). 14.95 *(978-1-59147-237-7(7)*, Magination Pr.) American Psychological Assn.

—I Wish I Had Freckles Like Abby. Heling, Kathryn & Hembrook, Deborah. (I Wish Ser.). (ENG.). 32p. (J). 2010. (gr. 4-7). pap. 7.95 *(978-1-934960-47-9(0))*; 2009. (gr. -1-3). 16.95 *(978-1-934960-46-2(2))* Continental Sales, Inc. (Raven Tree Pr.,Csi).

—I Wish I Had Freckles Like Abby/Quisiera Tener Pecas Como Abby. Heling, Kathryn & Hembrook, Deborah. 2007. (SPA & ENG.). 32p. (J). (gr. -1-3). pap. 7.95 *(978-0-9770906-6-2(3)*, Raven Tree Pr.,Csi) Continental Sales, Inc.

—I Wish I Had Freckles Like Abby/Quisiera Tener Pecas Como Abby. Heling, Kathryn et al. de La Vega, Eida, tr. 2007. (I Wish Ser.). (SPA & ENG.). 32p. (J). (gr. -1-3). 16.95 *(978-0-9724973-8-1(2)*, 626999, Raven Tree Pr.,Csi) Continental Sales, Inc.

—I Wish I Had Glasses Like Rosa. Heling, Kathryn & Hembrook, Deborah. (I Wish Ser.). (ENG.). 32p. (J). (gr. 4-7). 2010. pap. 7.95 *(978-1-934960-49-3(7))*; 2009. 16.95 *(978-1-934960-48-6(9))* Continental Sales, Inc. (Raven Tree Pr.,Csi).

—I Wish I Had Glasses Like Rosa/Quisiera Tener Lentes Como Rosa. Heling, Kathryn & Hembrook, Deborah. de La Vega, Eida, tr. 2007. (I Wish Ser.). (SPA & ENG.). 32p. (J). (gr. 4-7). 16.95 *(978-0-9724973-7-4(4)*, 626999, Raven Tree Pr.,Csi) Continental Sales, Inc.

—I Wish I Was Strong Like Manuel. Heling, Kathryn & Hembrook, Deborah. (I Wish Ser.). (ENG.). 32p. (J). 2010. (gr. 4-7). pap. 7.95 *(978-1-934960-53-0(5))*; 2009. (gr. -1-3). 16.95 *(978-1-934960-52-3(7))* Continental Sales, Inc. (Raven Tree Pr.,Csi).

—I Wish I Was Strong Like Manuel/Quisiera Ser Fuerte Como Manuel. Heling, Kathryn & Hembrook, Deborah. 2008. (I Wish Ser.). (ENG.). 32p. (J). (gr. -1-3). 16.95 *(978-0-9770906-7-9(1)*, Raven Tree Pr.,Csi) Continental Sales, Inc.

—I Wish I Was Tall Like Willie. Heling, Kathryn & Hembrook, Deborah. (I Wish Ser.). (ENG.). 32p. (J). (gr. 4-7). 2010. pap. 7.95 *(978-1-934960-51-6(9))*; 2009. 16.95 *(978-1-934960-50-9(0))* Continental Sales, Inc. (Raven Tree Pr.,Csi).

—I Wish I Was Tall Like Willie/Quisiera Ser Tan Alto Como Willie. Heling, Kathryn & Hembrook, Deborah. 2008. (I Wish Ser.). (ENG & SPA.). 32p. (J). (gr. 4-7). 16.95 *(978-0-9794462-0-7(1))*; pap. 7.95 *(978-0-9794462-1-4(X))* Continental Sales, Inc. (Raven Tree Pr.,Csi).

—Postcards from Chicago/Postales Desde Chicago. Crawford, Laura. de La Vega, Eida, tr. 2008. (Traveling with Anna Ser.). (ENG.). 32p. (J). (gr. 4-7). 16.95 *(978-0-9795477-4-4(1))*; per. 7.95 *(978-0-9795477-5-1(X))* Continental Sales, Inc. (Raven Tree Pr.,Csi).

—Postcards from New York City/Postales Desde New York City. Crawford, Laura. de La Vega, Eida, tr. 2008. (Traveling with Anna Ser.). (ENG.). 32p. (J). (gr. 4-7). 16.95 *(978-0-9795477-2-0(5))*; per. 7.95 *(978-0-9795477-3-7(3))* Continental Sales, Inc. (Raven Tree Pr.,Csi).

—Postcards from Washington D. C./Postales Desde Washington D. C. Crawford, Laura. de La Vega, Eida, tr. 2008. (Traveling with Anna Ser.). (ENG.). 32p. (J). (gr. 4-7). 16.95 *(978-0-9795477-0-6(9))*; per. 7.95 *(978-0-9795477-1-3(7))* Continental Sales, Inc. (Raven Tree Pr.,Csi).

—Rutabaga Boo! Bardhan-Quallen, Sudipta. 2016. (J). *(978-1-4814-2461-5(0))* Simon & Schuster Children's Publishing.

Adamson, Ged. Meet the Mckaws. 2015. (ENG.). 32p. (J). (gr. -1-k). 16.95 *(978-1-62914-618-8(8)*, Sky Pony Pr.) Skyhorse Publishing Co., Inc.

Adamson, Ged. Elsie Clarke & the Vampire Hairdresser. Adamson, Ged. Rylance, Ulrike. 2013. (ENG.). 28p. (J). (gr. -1-1). 16.95 *(978-1-62087-983-2(2)*, 620983, Sky Pony Pr.) Skyhorse Publishing Co., Inc.

Adamson, Lynne. First Star I See. Caffrey, Jaye Andras. 2nd ed. 2010. (ENG.). 164p. (J). (gr. 2-7). pap. 12.95 *(978-1-936290-01-7(4))* Central Recovery Pr.

Adasikov, Igor. The Megalith Union. Lamar, Brad A. 2013. 344p. (YA). pap. 18.95 *(978-1-61153-070-4(9)*, Light Messages) Light Messages Publishing.

Adcock, Kerry. Bible Animal Tales: 50 Devotionals for Teen Agers. Pearson, Mary Rose. 2004. (J). pap. 13.95 *(978-0-9664803-7-5(6))* Fair Havens Pubns.

Adderley, Peter. God's Wonderful World. Godfrey, Jan. 2008. Orig. Title: Wonderful World. (J). (gr. k-3). 12.95 *(978-0-8198-8317-9(4))* Pauline Bks. & Media.

Addison, Karl. Dinosaurs Coloring Book: Artwork by Karl Addison. Addison, Karl. 2011. (ENG.). 76p. pap. 9.99 *(978-1-4663-8226-8(0))* CreateSpace Independent Publishing Platform.

Addison, Kenneth. We, 1 vol. Schertle, Alice. 2013. (ENG.). 32p. (J). (gr. 1-4). 16.95 *(978-1-58430-060-1(4))* Lee & Low Bks., Inc.

Addy, Sean. Peaceful Heroes. Winter, Jonah. 2009. (J). pap. *(978-0-439-62308-7(1)*, Levine, Arthur A. Bks.) Scholastic, Inc.

Addy, Sean & Halsey, Megan. Akira to Zoltan: Twenty-Six Men Who Changed the World. Chin-Lee, Cynthia. 2008. (ENG.). 32p. (J). (gr. 3-7). pap. 7.95 *(978-1-57091-580-2(6))* Charlesbridge Publishing, Inc.

Addy, Sean, jt. illus. see Halsey, Megan.

Adeff, Jay & Mittan, J. Barry, photos by. Joannie Rochette: Canadian Ice Princess. Dzidrums, Christine & Rendon, Leah. Allison, Elizabeth, ed. 2nd exp. rev. ed. 2010. (Skate Stars Ser.: Vol. 1). 100p. (YA). pap. 12.99 *(978-0-9826435-0-1(0))* Creative Media Publishing.

Adel, Kaveh N. The Boy & the Red Balloon. Adel, Kaveh N. Rezayazdi, Soheil & Michalopulos, Anastasios, eds. 2010. (ENG.). 32p. pap. 11.00 *(978-1-4505-7914-8(0))* CreateSpace Independent Publishing Platform.

Adele, Amy. And Then Another Sheep Turned Up. Gehl, Laura. 2015. (J). *(978-1-4677-1190-6(X))*; (ENG.). 32p. (gr. -1-3). lib. bdg. 17.95 *(978-1-4677-1188-3(8))* Lerner Publishing Group. (Kar-Ben Publishing).

Adilman, Katarzyna. Everyday Signs for the Newborn Baby. Campbell, Diana & Mosher, Nancy, eds. 2007. 20p. (J). bds. *(978-0-9791059-0-6(0))* Dakitab, Inc.

Adinolfi, JoAnn. Alfie the Apostrophe, 1 vol. Donohue, Moira Rose. 2010. (ENG.). 32p. (J). (gr. 1-4). pap. 6.99 *(978-0-8075-0256-3(1))* Whitman, Albert & Co.

—A Circle in the Sky. Wilson, Zachary. (Rookie Ready to Learn Ser.). (J). 2011. 40p. pap. 5.95 *(978-0-531-26746-2(6))*; 2011. 40p. (gr. -1-k). lib. bdg. 23.00 *(978-0-531-26446-1(7))*; 2006. (ENG.). 32p. (gr. k-2). lib. bdg. 19.50 *(978-0-531-12570-0(X))* Scholastic Library Publishing. (Children's Pr.).

—Un Circulo en el Cielo. Wilson, Zachary. 2011. (Rookie Ready to Learn Español Ser.). (SPA.). 40p. (J). pap. 5.95 *(978-0-531-26791-2(1)*, Children's Pr.) Scholastic Library Publishing.

—Here Comes Silent E! Hays, Anna Jane. 2004. (Step into Reading Ser.). (ENG.). 32p. (J). (gr. -1-1). pap. 3.99 *(978-0-375-81233-0(4)*, Random Hse. Bks. for Young Readers) Random Hse. Children's Bks.

—I Want Your Moo: A Story for Children about Self-Esteem. Weiner, Marcella Bakur & Neimark, Jill. 2nd ed. 2009. 32p. (J). (gr. -1-3). 14.95 *(978-1-4338-0542-4(1))*; pap. 9.95 *(978-1-4338-0552-3(9))* American Psychological Assn. (Magination Pr.).

—Leaping Lizards. Murphy, Stuart J. 2005. (MathStart 1 Ser.). (ENG.). 40p. (J). (gr. -1). pap. 5.99 *(978-0-06-000132-2(1))* HarperCollins Pubs.

—Leaping Lizards. Murphy, Stuart J. ed. 2005. (MathStart Level 1 Ser.). 33p. (gr. -1-3). lib. bdg. 16.00 *(978-1-4176-7758-0(9)*, Turtleback) Turtleback Bks.

—The Perfect Thanksgiving. Spinelli, Eileen. 2007. (ENG.). 32p. (J). (gr. -1-2). 7.99 *(978-0-312-37505-8(0))* Square Fish.

—This Book Is Haunted. Rocklin, Joanne. 2003. (I Can Read Book 1 Ser.). (ENG.). 48p. (J). (gr. k-3). pap. 3.99 *(978-0-06-444261-9(6))* HarperCollins Pubs.

—This Book Is Haunted. Rocklin, Joanne. 2004. (I Can Read Bks.). 48p. (gr. k-3). 14.00 *(978-0-7569-3081-3(2))* Perfection Learning Corp.

—Valentine Hearts: Holiday Poetry. Hopkins, Lee Bennett. 2004. (I Can Read Bks.). 32p. (J). (gr. k-3). 15.99 *(978-0-06-008057-0(4))* HarperCollins Pubs.

Adinolfi, JoAnn. Un Circulo en el Cielo. Adinolfi, JoAnn. Wilson, Zachary. 2011. (Rookie Ready to Learn Español Ser.). (SPA.). 40p. (J). lib. bdg. 23.00 *(978-0-531-26123-1(9)*, Children's Pr.) Scholastic Library Publishing.

Adinolfi, Joanne. Tina's Diner. Adinolfi, Joanne. 2014. (ENG.). 32p. (J). (gr. -1-3). 13.99 *(978-1-4814-4459-0(X)*, Simon & Schuster Bks. For Young Readers) Simon & Schuster Bks. For Young Readers.

Adjovi, Benoit, et al, photos by. Life & Afterlife in Benin. Enwezor, Okwui et al. rev. ed. 2005. (ENG., 136p. (gr. 8-17). 59.95 *(978-0-7148-4513-5(2))* Phaidon Pr. Ltd. GBR. Dist: Hachette Bk. Group.

Adkins, Jan. Bertha Takes a Drive. Adkins, Jan. 2015. (J). lib. bdg. *(978-1-58089-696-2(0))* Charlesbridge Publishing, Inc.

—Moving Heavy Things. Adkins, Jan. 2004. (ENG.). 48p. (J). (gr. -1-3). 13.95 *(978-0-937822-82-1(5))* WoodenBoat Pubns.

—What If You Met a Cowboy? Adkins, Jan. 2013. (ENG.). 48p. (J). (gr. 1-4). 17.99 *(978-1-59643-149-2(0))* Roaring Brook Pr.

Adkins, Loretta B. The Lottie & Annie Upside-down Book. Vogel, Cara Lynn. 2003. 8.99 *(978-1-56309-627-3(7))* Woman's Missionary Union.

Adl, Kamyar, photos by. I Is for Iran. Adl, Shirin & Quarto Generic Staff. 2012. (ENG., 32p. (J). (gr. -1-2). 17.99 *(978-1-84780-211-8(7)*, Frances Lincoln) Quarto Publishing Group UK GBR. Dist: Hachette Bk. Group.

Adl, Shirin. Let's Celebrate! Festival Poems from Around the World. Chatterjee, Debjani & D'Arcy, Brian. 2014. (ENG.). 56p. (J). (gr. 2-5). pap. 12.99 *(978-1-84780-479-2(9)*, Frances Lincoln) Quarto Publishing Group UK GBR. Dist: Hachette Bk. Group.

—Let's Celebrate! Festival Poems from Around the World. Chatterjee, Debjani & D'Arcy, Brian, eds. 2011. (ENG.). 56p. (J). (gr. 2-5). 19.99 *(978-1-84780-087-9(4)*, Frances Lincoln) Quarto Publishing Group UK GBR. Dist: Littlehampton Bk Services, Ltd.

—Let's Play! Poems about Sports & Games from Around the World. Chatterjee, Debjani & Quarto Generic Staff. D'Arcy, Brian, ed. 2014. (ENG.). 56p. (J). (gr. 1-5). 19.99 *(978-1-84780-370-2(9)*, Frances Lincoln) Quarto Publishing Group UK GBR. Dist: Hachette Bk. Group.

—Ramadan Moon. Robert, Na'ima B. 2015. (ENG.). 32p. (J). (gr. -1-2). pap. 7.95 *(978-1-84780-206-4(0)*, Frances Lincoln) Quarto Publishing Group UK GBR. Dist: Hachette Bk. Group.

—Shahnameh. Laird, Elizabeth. 2014. (ENG.). 120p. (J). (gr. 5-8). pap. 14.99 *(978-1-84780-497-6(7)*, Frances Lincoln) Quarto Publishing Group UK GBR. Dist: Hachette Bk. Group.

—Shahnameh: The Persian Book of Kings. Laird, Elizabeth. 2012. (ENG.). 120p. (J). (gr. 4-8). 24.99 *(978-1-84780-253-8(2)*, Frances Lincoln) Quarto Publishing Group UK GBR. Dist: Littlehampton Bk Services, Ltd.

Adlard, Charlie. The X-Files, Vol.1. Petrucha, Stefan et al. 2005. (X-Files Ser.: Vol. 1). (ENG.). 200p. (YA). pap. 19.95 *(978-1-933160-02-3(0))* Devil's Due Digital, Inc. - A Checker Digital Co.

Adler, Michael S. & Olofsdotter, Marie. A Picture Book of Cesar Chavez. Adler, David A. 2010. (ENG.). 32p. (J). (gr. -1-3). 17.95 *(978-0-8234-2202-9(X))* Holiday Hse., Inc.

Adlerman, Kimberly M. Rock-a-Bye Baby. Adlerman, Daniel. 2004. 32p. (J). 15.95 *(978-1-58089-082-3(2))* Charlesbridge Publishing, Inc.

Adnet, Bernard. The Ants & the Grasshopper, Vol. 4262. Williams, Rozanne Lanczak. 2005. (Reading for Fluency Ser.). 16p. (J). pap. 3.49 *(978-1-59198-162-6(X))* Creative Teaching Pr., Inc.

—Bugs in Your Backyard. Williams, Rozanne Lanczak. Hamaguchi, Carla, ed. 2003. (Sight Word Readers Ser.). 16p. (J). (gr. k-2). pap. 3.49 *(978-1-57471-968-0(8)*, 3590) Creative Teaching Pr., Inc.

—Busy Bugs: A Book about Patterns. Harvey, Jayne. 2003. (Penguin Young Readers, Level 2 Ser.: Level 1). (ENG.). 32p. (J). (gr. 1-2). pap. 3.99 *(978-0-448-43159-8(9)*, Warne, Frederick Pubs.) Penguin Bks., Ltd. GBR. Dist: Penguin Random Hse., LLC.

—Writing Dino-Mite Poems. Williams, Rozanne Lanczak. (Learn to Write Ser.). 8p. (J). 2008. (gr. -1-3). pap. 6.99 *(978-1-59198-336-1(3))*; 2006. (gr. k-2). pap. 3.49 *(978-1-59198-285-2(5)*, 6179) Creative Teaching Pr., Inc.

Adolphe, Joseph. The Night Before Christmas. Moore, Clement C. 2013. (J). 19.95 *(978-1-59530-953-2(5))* Hallmark Card, Inc.

Adrian, Marti. The Little Red Riding Book. Boudin, Jonathan. 2012. (ENG.). 94p. (J). (gr. 2-4). pap. 8.95 *(978-0-9736330-3-0(4))* JB Max Publishing CAN. Dist: Independent Pubs. Group.

Aesop. Aesop's Fables. ed. 2006. 32p. (J). (gr. -1-3). 16.95 *(978-0-7358-2068-5(6))* North-South Bks., Inc.

Aesop, jt. illus. see Zwerger, Lisbeth.

Affaya, Colette. Arkam, Numero & Numbers, 1 vol. Affaya, Colett & Affaya, Otman. 2009. 16p. pap. 24.95 *(978-1-60749-929-9(0))* America Star Bks.

AG Jatkowska. Little Seeds [Scholastic]. Ghigna, Charles. 2012. (My Little Planet Ser.). (ENG.). (J). (gr. -1 — 1). pap. 0.50 *(978-1-4795-1671-1(6)*, My Little Planet) Picture Window Bks.

Agard, Nadema. The Chichi Hoohoo Bogeyman. Sneve, Virginia Driving Hawk. 2nd ed. 2008. (ENG.). 64p. (J). (gr. -1). pap. 9.95 *(978-0-8032-1745-4(5)*, Bison Bks.) Univ. of Nebraska Pr.

Agee, Jon. Potch & Polly. Steig, William. Date not set. (J). 14.99 *(978-0-06-205144-8(X))* HarperCollins Pubs.

—Sitting in My Box, 0 vols. Lillegard, Dee. 2010. (ENG.). 32p. (J). (gr. -1-3). 15.99 *(978-0-7614-5646-9(5)*, 9780761456469, Amazon Children's Publishing) Amazon Publishing.

Agee, Jon, et al. Why Did the Chicken Cross the Road? Agee, Jon. 2006. (ENG.). 40p. (J). (gr. -1-3). 16.99 *(978-0-8037-3094-6(2)*, Dial) Penguin Publishing Group.

Agee, Jon. Nothing. Agee, Jon. 2007. (ENG.). 32p. (gr. -1-3). 16.99 *(978-0-7868-3694-9(6))* Hyperion Pr.

—The Other Side of Town. Agee, Jon. 2012. (ENG.). 32p. (J). (gr. -1-3). 17.95 *(978-0-545-16204-3(1)*, Di Capua, Michael) Scholastic, Inc.

—Palindromania! Agee, Jon. 2009. (ENG.). 112p. (J). (gr. 3-8). pap. 8.98 *(978-0-374-40025-5(3))* Square Fish.

Aggs, Patrice. Un Deux Trois: First French Rhymes. 2006. (Frances Lincoln Children's Books Dual Language Bks.). (FRE & ENG.). 24p. (J). (gr. -1-2). pap. 9.99 *(978-1-84507-623-8(0)*, Frances Lincoln Children's Bks.) Quarto Publishing Group UK GBR. Dist: Hachette Bk. Group.

—Uno Dos Tres: My First Spanish Rhymes. 2012. (SPA & ENG.). 24p. (J). (gr. k-3). 17.99 *(978-1-84780-193-7(5)*, Frances Lincoln) Quarto Publishing Group UK GBR. Dist: Hachette Bk. Group.

—My Big Brother JJ. Elliott, Odette. 2010. (ENG.). 32p. (J). (gr. -1-k). pap. 11.99 *(978-1-84853-007-2(2))* Transworld Publishers Ltd. GBR. Dist: Independent Pubs. Group.

—Yi Er San: My First Chinese Nursery Rhymes. 2014. (Frances Lincoln Children's Books Dual Language Bks.). (ENG & CHI.). 24p. (J). (gr. k-3). 19.99 *(978-1-84780-531-7(0)*, Frances Lincoln) Quarto Publishing Group UK GBR. Dist: Hachette Bk. Group.

Aggs, Patrice. Bertie Rooster. Aggs, Patrice, tr. Stewart, Maddie. 2007. (Panda Cubs Ser.: 02). (ENG.). 48p. (J). pap. 9.95 *(978-0-86278-798-1(X))* O'Brien Pr., Ltd., The IRL. Dist: Dufour Editions, Inc.

Agin, Sue. Max - a Griggstown Mystery. Shaw, Mary. Cornilliat, Francois, tr. 2004.Tr. of Max - Un Mystère de Griggstown. (ENG & FRE.). (J). (gr. k-6). pap. 18.50 *(978-0-9705404-2-3(6)*, 0-9705404-2-6) Criqueville Pr.

Agnew, Alicia. Baby Brother Goes to the Hospital. Slanina, Anne M. 2007. (Adventures of Annie Mouse Ser.: Bk. 2). 28p. (J). 18.99 *(978-0-9793379-1-8(7))*; per. 9.99 *(978-0-9793379-0-1(9))* Annie Mouse Bks.

Agnew, Lincoln. Cookiebot! A Harry & Horsie Adventure. Van Camp, Katie. 2011. (Harry & Horsie Adventures Ser.: 2). (ENG.). 32p. (J). (gr. -1-1). 16.99 *(978-0-06-197445-8(5))* HarperCollins Pubs.

—Harry & Horsie. Van Camp, Katie. 2009. (Harry & Horsie Adventures Ser.: 1). (ENG.). 32p. (J). (gr. -1-1). 16.99 *(978-0-06-175598-9(2))* HarperCollins Pubs.

—Runaway Tomato. Reeder, Kim Cooley. 2014. (ENG.). 34p. (J). (gr. -1-k). 16.99 *(978-0-8037-3694-8(0)*, Dial) Penguin Publishing Group.

Agraso, Alberto. I Am Happy. Agraso, Alberto. Dojeiji, Mony. 2013. 36p. pap. *(978-0-9878762-3-2(6))* Walking for Peace Publishing.

—Je Suis Heureuse. Agraso, Alberto. Dojeiji, Mony. 2013. 36p. pap. *(978-1-927803-01-1(2))* Walking for Peace Publishing.

—Soy Feliz. Agraso, Alberto. Dojeiji, Mony. 2013. 36p. pap. *(978-0-9878762-4-9(4))* Walking for Peace Publishing.

Agrell, Lewis. We Like to Eat Well/Nos Gusta Comer Bien. April, Elyse. 2011th alt. ed. 2011. (We Like To Ser.). (ENG.). 32p. pap. 9.95 *(978-1-935826-01-9(8))* Kalindi Pr.

Agroff, Patti. All about Us. Rosenfeld, Dina. 2008. 28p. (J). 10.95 *(978-1-929628-45-2(5))* Hachai Publishing.

Agroff, Patti. I Am a Torah: A Playful Action Rhyme. Paluch, Beily. 2014. 12p. (J). bds. 6.95 ***(978-1-929628-84-1(6))*** Hachai Publishing.

Aguila, Alicia del. Tia Tot Rules! Written By Tori Velle; Illustrated By Al. 2011. 44p. pap. 24.95 *(978-1-4241-7833-9(9))* America Star Bks.

Aguilar, Arelys. The Trouble with Cats. Ballard, George Anne & Bolton, Georgia Helen. 2012. 24p. pap. 12.00 *(978-0-9855312-1-8(5))* Bolton Publishing LLC.

Aguilar, David A. National Geographic Little Kids First Big Book of Space. Hughes, Catherine D. 2012. (National Geographic Little Kids First Big Bks.). (ENG.). 128p. (J). (gr. -1-3). 14.95 *(978-1-4263-1014-0(5))*; lib. bdg. 23.90 *(978-1-4263-1015-7(3))* National Geographic Society. (National Geographic Children's Bks.).

Aguilar, David A. Planets, Stars, & Galaxies: A Visual Encyclopedia of Our Universe. Aguilar, David A. 2007. (ENG.). 192p. (J). (gr. 5-18). lib. bdg. 38.90 *(978-1-4263-0171-1(5))*; 24.95 *(978-1-4263-0170-4(7))* National Geographic Society. (National Geographic Children's Bks.).

—Space Encyclopedia: A Tour of Our Solar System & Beyond. Aguilar, David A. 2013. (ENG.). 192p. (J). (gr. 5). 24.95 *(978-1-4263-0948-9(1))*; lib. bdg. 38.90 *(978-1-4263-1560-2(0))* National Geographic Society. (National Geographic Children's Bks.).

Aguilar, Jose. 4 Poemas de Gloria Fuertes y Una Calabaza Vestida de Luna. Fuertes, Gloria. 2007. (SPA.). 36p. (J). *(978-84-934160-9-6(6))* Atalante.

Aguilar, Laia. Bonjour Camille. Cano, Felipe. 2014. (ENG & SPA.). 32p. (J). (gr. 1-4). 12.99 *(978-1-4521-2407-0(8))* Chronicle Bks. LLC.

Aguilar, Sandra. Circus. Rider, Cynthia. 2013. (Start Reading Ser.). (ENG.). 24p. (gr. k-1). pap. 6.99 *(978-1-4765-4091-7(8))* Capstone Pr., Inc.

—The Explorers. Rider, Cynthia. 2013. (Start Reading Ser.). (ENG.). 24p. (gr. k-1). pap. 6.99 *(978-1-4765-4097-9(7))* Capstone Pr., Inc.

—Pirate Treasure, 1 vol. Rider, Cynthia. 2013. (Start Reading Ser.). (ENG.). 24p. (gr. k-1). pap. 6.99 *(978-1-4765-4129-7(9))* Capstone Pr., Inc.

—Queen Ella's Feet. Grindley, Sally. 2011. (My Phonics Readers: Level 3 Ser.). 24p. (J). (gr. -1-1). 24.25 *(978-1-84898-513-1(4))* Sea-To-Sea Pubns.

—The Spaceship. Rider, Cynthia. 2013. (Start Reading Ser.). (ENG.). 24p. (gr. k-1). pap. 6.99 *(978-1-4765-4137-2(X))* Capstone Pr., Inc.

Aguilar Sisters Staff. Count Me In: A Parade of Mexican Folk Art Numbers in English & Spanish. Weill, Cynthia. 2012. (First Concepts in Mexican Folk Art Ser.). (ENG & SPA.). 32p. (J). (gr. k-k). 14.95 *(978-1-935955-39-9(X))* Cinco Puntos Pr.

Aguiler, Manny. A Smile: B una Sonrisa. Aguiler, Manny. Smith, Michael. 2015. (SPA & ENG.). (J). ***(978-0-9913454-5-8(2))*** East West Discovery Pr.

Aguillo, Don Ellis. Boomer, the Missing Pomeranian. 2005. 34p. (J). pap. *(978-1-932864-45-8(8))* Masthof Pr.

Aguirre, Alfredo. La Almohada. Mansour, Vivian. 2nd rev. ed. 2003. (Castillo de la Lectura Verde Ser.). (SPA & ENG.). 88p. (J). pap. 7.95 *(978-970-20-0140-9(4))* Castillo, Ediciones, S. A. de C. V. MEX. Dist: Macmillan.

Aguirre, Diego, jt. illus. see Beckman, Jeff.

Aguirre, Zuriñe. Sardines of Love. Aguirre, Zuriñe. 2015. (Child's Play Library). (ENG.). 36p. (J). ***(978-1-84643-726-7(1))*** Child's Play International Ltd.

Ahern, Frank. The Good Night Book. Beckman, Amy. 2006. 28p. per. 16.95 *(978-1-59858-255-0(0))* Dog Ear Publishing, LLC.

Ahlberg, Allan, jt. illus. see Ahlberg, Janet.

Ahlberg, Janet. Adiós Pequeño! Ahlberg, Janet. Ahlberg, Allan. 2003. (Picture Books Collection).Tr. of Bye Bye Baby. (SPA.). 32p. (J). (gr. k-3). 12.95 *(978-84-372-2315-5(6))* Altea, Ediciones, S.A. - Grupo Santillana ESP. Dist: Santillana USA Publishing Co., Inc.

Ahlberg, Janet & Ahlberg, Allan. Adiós Pequeño! Ahlberg, Janet & Ahlberg, Allan. (Historias Para Dormir Ser.).Tr. of Bye Bye Baby. (SPA.). 28p. (J). (gr. k-3). 9.95 *(978-968-19-1039-6(7))* Aguilar Editorial MEX. Dist: Santillana USA Publishing Co., Inc.

Ahlberg, Jessica. Far Away Across the Sea. Tellegen, Toon. 2012. (ENG.). 160p. (J). (gr. k). 19.95 *(978-1-907152-37-5(7))* Boxer Bks., Ltd. GBR. Dist: Sterling Publishing Co., Inc.

—The Goldilocks Variations: A Pop-Up Book. Ahlberg, Allan. 2012. (ENG.). 40p. (J). (gr. k-4). 17.99 *(978-0-7636-6268-4(2))* Candlewick Pr.

—Letters to Anyone & Everyone. Tellegen, Toon. 2010. (ENG.). 156p. (J). (gr. k-6). 12.95 *(978-1-906250-95-9(2))* Boxer Bks., Ltd. GBR. Dist: Sterling Publishing Co., Inc.

—The Squirrel's Birthday & Other Parties. Tellegen, Toon. 2009. (ENG.). 156p. (J). (gr. k). 19.95 *(978-1-906250-93-5(6))* Boxer Bks., Ltd. GBR. Dist: Sterling Publishing Co., Inc.

—Yucky Worms. French, Vivian. 2012. (Read & Wonder Ser.). (ENG.). 32p. (J). (gr. -1-3). pap. 6.99 *(978-0-7636-5817-5(0))* Candlewick Pr.

Ahmad, Aadil & James, Martin. Papi, How Many Stars Are in the Sky? Vigil, Angel. 2010. (J). *(978-1-60617-151-6(8))* Teaching Strategies, Inc.

Ahmad, Maryam & Ramotar, Alexandra. One Day. Persaud, Sandhya S. 2009. 12p. pap. 12.99 *(978-1-4389-4437-1(3))* AuthorHouse.

Ahn, JiYoung. Infinity, Vol. 1. Kenyon, Sherrilyn. 2013. (Dark-Hunters Ser.: 1). (ENG.). 240p. (gr. 11-17). 13.00 *(978-0-316-19053-4(5))* Yen Pr.

Ahrends, Susan. How Willy Got His Wings: The Continuing Adventures of Wheely Willy. Turner, Deborah & Mohler, Diana. 2003. (ENG.). 32p. 15.95 *(978-0-944875-88-9(2))* i-5 Publishing LLC.

Ahrin, Jacob. Stop the Bully. Pearl, David R. & Pearl, Tamara R. 2013. 26p. pap. *(978-0-646-90104-6(4))* Be Positive Solutions.

AIC College of Design Staff. An Alphabet Trip to the Limerick Zoo. Ramirez, Jeannette. 2011. (ENG.). 62p. pap. 19.99 *(978-1-4679-3011-6(3))* CreateSpace Independent Publishing Platform.

Aihara, Miki. Hot Gimmick, 12 vols. Aihara, Miki. (Hot Gimmick Ser.). (ENG.). 2003. 184p. pap. 9.95 *(978-1-59116-227-8(0))*; Vol. 4. 2004. 192p. pap. 9.95 *(978-1-59116-389-3(7))*; Vol. 6. 2nd ed. 2004. 192p. pap. 9.99 *(978-1-56931-965-9(0))*; Vol. 7. 2004. 192p. pap. 9.99 *(978-1-59116-502-6(4))*; Vol. 9. 2005. 192p. pap. 9.99 *(978-1-59116-845-4(7))* Viz Media.

—Tokyo Boys & Girls. Aihara, Miki. (Tokyo Boys&Girls Ser.). (ENG.). Vol. 1. 2005. 200p. (YA). pap. 8.99 *(978-1-4215-0020-1(5))*; Vol. 2. 2005. 200p. pap. 8.99 *(978-1-4215-0021-8(3))*; Vol. 4. 2006. 208p. pap. 8.99 *(978-1-4215-0400-1(6))*; Vol. 5. 2006. 208p. pap. 8.99 *(978-1-4215-0589-3(4))* Viz Media.

Aikawa, Yu. Dark Edge. Aikawa, Yu. 2006. (Dark Edge Ser.). (ENG.). 200p. (YA). Vol. 5. pap. 9.95 *(978-1-59796-025-0(X))*; Vol. 6. pap. 9.95 *(978-1-59796-026-7(8))* DrMaster Pubns. Inc.

Aiken, David. Chesapeake Rainbow. Cummings, Priscilla. 2004. 32p. (J). 11.95 *(978-0-87033-556-3(1))*, Cornell Maritime Pr./Tidewater Pubs.) Schiffer Publishing, Ltd.

—Double-Talk: Word Sense & Nonsense, 1 vol. Aiken, Zora & David. 2012. (ENG.). 32p. (J). 14.99 *(978-0-7643-3962-2(1))* Schiffer Publishing, Ltd.

—Majesty from Assateague, 1 vol. Hagman, Harvey Dixon. 2003. (ENG.). 80p. (J). pap. 8.95 *(978-0-87033-552-5(9))*, Cornell Maritime Pr./Tidewater Pubs.) Schiffer Publishing, Ltd.

Aiken, David. A to Z: Pick What You'll Be. Aiken, David. Aiken, Zora. 2011. (ENG.). 32p. (J). *(978-0-7643-3701-7(7))*, Schiffer Publishing Ltd) Schiffer Publishing, Ltd.

—Camp ABC: A Place for Outdoor Fun, 1 vol. Aiken, David. Aiken, Zora. 2013. (ENG.). 32p. (J). 16.99 *(978-0-7643-4423-7(4))* Schiffer Publishing, Ltd.

Aiken, David & Aiken, David. All about Boats: A to Z, 1 vol. Aiken, Zora. 2012. (ENG.). 32p. (J). 14.99 *(978-0-7643-4184-7(7))* Schiffer Publishing, Ltd.

Aiken, David, jt. illus. see Aiken, David.

Aikins, Dave, et al. Animal Adventure. Ricci, Christine. 2007. (Little Life Lessons Ser.). (J). pap. *(978-1-4127-8922-6(2))* Publications International, Ltd.

Aikins, Dave. Baby Loves Colors. Marchesani, Laura. 2013. (Sassy Ser.). (ENG.). 12p. (J). (gr. -1 — 1). bds. 6.99 *(978-0-448-47790-9(4))*, Grosset & Dunlap) Penguin Publishing Group.

—Baby Loves Shapes. Unknown. 2014. (Sassy Ser.). (ENG.). 10p. (J). (gr. -1 — 1). bds. 6.99 *(978-0-448-48015-2(8))*, Grosset & Dunlap) Penguin Publishing Group.

—Baby's ABC. Grosset and Dunlap Staff. 2014. (Sassy Ser.). (ENG.). 36p. (J). (gr. -1 — 1). 9.99 *(978-0-448-48207-1(X))*, Grosset & Dunlap) Penguin Publishing Group.

—Baby's Busy Year: A Book of Seasons. 2014. (Sassy Ser.). (ENG.). 10p. (J). (gr. -1 — 1). bds. 6.99 *(978-0-448-48147-0(2))*, Grosset & Dunlap) Penguin Publishing Group.

—Baby's Day. Unknown. 2014. (Sassy Ser.). (ENG.). 10p. (J). (gr. -1 — 1). bds. 7.99 *(978-0-448-48013-8(1))*, Grosset & Dunlap) Penguin Publishing Group.

—Baby's First Christmas. 2014. (Sassy Ser.). (ENG.). 10p. (J). (gr. -1 — 1). bds. 7.99 *(978-0-448-48206-4(1))*, Grosset & Dunlap) Penguin Publishing Group.

—Baby's First Easter. Grosset and Dunlap Staff. 2015. (Sassy Ser.). (ENG.). 10p. (J). (— 1). bds. 7.99 *(978-0-448-48456-3(0))*, Grosset & Dunlap) Penguin Publishing Group.

—Baby's First Words. Grosset & Dunlap. 2014. (Sassy Ser.). (ENG.). 10p. (J). (gr. -1 — 1). bds. 9.99 *(978-0-448-48149-4(9))*, Grosset & Dunlap) Penguin Publishing Group.

—Baby's World: A First Book of Senses. Marchesani, Laura. 2013. (Sassy Ser.). (ENG.). 12p. (J). (gr. -1 — 1). bds. 7.99 *(978-0-448-47788-6(2))*, Grosset & Dunlap) Penguin Publishing Group.

—Bailando Al Rescate. 2005. (Dora la Exploradora Ser.). (SPA.). 24p. (J). pap. 3.99 *(978-1-4169-1504-1(4))*, Libros Para Ninos) Libros Para Ninos.

—Bedtime for Baby. Grosset & Dunlap. 2014. (Sassy Ser.). (ENG.). 10p. (J). (gr. -1 — 1). bds. 7.99 *(978-0-448-48148-7(0))*, Grosset & Dunlap) Penguin Publishing Group.

—Big! Little! A Book of Opposites. Unknown. 2014. (Sassy Ser.). (ENG.). 10p. (J). (gr. -1 — 1). bds. 6.99 *(978-0-448-48014-5(X))*, Grosset & Dunlap) Penguin Publishing Group.

—Big Sister Dora! Inches, Alison. ed. 2005. (Dora the Explorer Ser.: 13). 32p. (J). lib. bdg. 15.00 *(978-1-59054-790-8(X))* Fitzgerald Bks.

—Big Sister Dora! 2005. (Dora the Explorer Ser.). (ENG.). 24p. (J). pap. 3.99 *(978-0-689-87846-6(X))*, Simon Spotlight/Nickelodeon) Simon Spotlight/Nickelodeon.

—The Big Win. Chipponeri, Kelli. 2008. (SpongeBob SquarePants Ser.: 13). (ENG.). 32p. (J). (gr. k-2). pap. 3.99 *(978-1-4169-4938-1(0))*, Simon Spotlight/Nickelodeon) Simon Spotlight/Nickelodeon.

—The Birthday Dance Party: Daisy's Fiesta de Quinceañera. 2006. (Dora the Explorer Ser.: 19). (ENG.). 24p. (J). (gr. -1-3). pap. 3.99 *(978-1-4169-1303-0(3))*, Simon Spotlight/Nickelodeon) Simon Spotlight/Nickelodeon.

—Buddy's Teeth (Dinosaur Train) Golden Books. 2012. (Little Golden Book Ser.). (ENG.). 24p. (J). (gr. k-k). 3.99 *(978-0-375-86156-7(4))*, Golden Bks.) Random Hse. Children's Bks.

—Bunny Business. Golden Books Staff. 2011. (Color Plus Flocked Stickers Ser.). (ENG.). 64p. (J). (gr. -1-2). pap. 4.99 *(978-0-375-86818-4(6))*, Golden Bks.) Random Hse. Children's Bks.

—The Chocolate Voyage. Rabe, Tish. 2013. (Little Golden Book Ser.). (ENG.). 24p. (J). (-k). 3.99 *(978-0-307-98023-6(5))*, Golden Bks.) Random Hse. Children's Bks.

—Dance to the Rescue. Driscoll, Laura. 2005. 24p. (J). lib. bdg. 9.00 *(978-1-4242-0981-1(1))* Fitzgerald Bks.

—Demolition Derby/Class Confusion (SpongeBob SquarePants) Random House Staff. 2013. (Deluxe Pictureback Ser.). (ENG.). 32p. (J). (gr. -1-2). 4.99 *(978-0-449-81756-8(3))*, Random Hse. Bks. for Young Readers) Random Hse. Children's Bks.

—Dora salva el Reino de Cristal (Dora Saves Crystal Kingdom) Rodriguez, Daynali Flores, tr. from ENG. 2009. (Dora la Exploradora Ser.). (SPA.). 24p. (J). (gr. -1-2). pap. 3.99 *(978-1-4169-9020-8(8))*, Libros Para Ninos) Libros Para Ninos.

—Dora Saves the Snow Princess. 2008. (Dora the Explorer Ser.: 27). (ENG.). 24p. (J). (gr. -1-2). pap. 3.99 *(978-1-4169-5866-6(5))*, Simon Spotlight/Nickelodeon) Simon Spotlight/Nickelodeon.

—Dora y la Princesa de la Nieve (Dora Saves the Snow Princess) Ziegler, Argentina Palacios, tr. 2008. (Dora la Exploradora Ser.). (SPA.). 24p. (J). (gr. -1-2). pap. 3.99 *(978-1-4169-5870-3(3))*, Libros Para Ninos) Libros Para Ninos.

—Dora's Princess Party. Reisner, Molly. 2009. (Dora the Explorer Ser.). (ENG.). 12p. (J). (gr. -1-1). 6.99 *(978-1-4169-9045-1(3))*, Simon Spotlight/Nickelodeon) Simon Spotlight/Nickelodeon.

—Dress up Dora! McMahon, Kara. 2009. (Dora the Explorer Ser.). (ENG.). 12p. (J). 8.99 *(978-1-4169-6067-6(8))*, Simon Spotlight/Nickelodeon) Simon Spotlight/Nickelodeon.

—The Great Big Parade. Ricci, Christine. 2007. (J). pap. *(978-1-4127-8923-3(0))* Publications International, Ltd.

—I Love My Mami! Katschke, Judy. 2006. (Dora the Explorer Ser.: 9). (ENG.). 24p. (J). (gr. -1-k). pap. 3.99 *(978-1-4169-0650-6(9))*, Simon Spotlight/Nickelodeon) Simon Spotlight/Nickelodeon.

—Just Like Dora! Inches, Alison. 2005. (Dora the Explorer Ser.: Vol. 8). (ENG.). 24p. (J). pap. 3.99 *(978-0-689-87675-2(0))*, Simon Spotlight/Nickelodeon) Simon Spotlight/Nickelodeon.

—Let's Count! A First Book of Numbers. Unknown. 2014. (Sassy Ser.). (ENG.). 10p. (J). (gr. -1 — 1). bds. 6.99 *(978-0-448-48012-1(3))*, Grosset & Dunlap) Penguin Publishing Group.

—Meet the Animals! Ricci, Christine. 2006. (Dora the Explorer Ser.). (ENG.). 16p. (J). (gr. -1-k). 10.95 *(978-1-4169-1819-6(1))*, Simon Spotlight/Nickelodeon) Simon Spotlight/Nickelodeon.

—Nickelodeon Nursery Rhymes (Nickelodeon) Golden Books Staff. 2011. (Big Golden Book Ser.). (ENG.). 48p. (J). (gr. -1-2). 9.99 *(978-0-375-87377-5(5))*, Golden Bks.) Random Hse. Children's Bks.

—La Quinceañera. Inches, Alison. 2006. (Dora la Exploradora Ser.). (SPA.). 24p. (J). (gr. -1-3). pap. 3.99 *(978-1-4169-2462-3(0))*, Libros Para Ninos) Libros Para Ninos.

—Race to the Tower of Power. 2005. (Backyardigans Ser.: Vol. 1). (ENG.). 24p. (J). pap. 3.99 *(978-1-4169-0799-2(8))*, Simon Spotlight/Nickelodeon) Simon Spotlight/Nickelodeon.

—The Spiky Stegosaurus (Dinosaur Train) Posner-Sanchez, Andrea. 2012. (Little Golden Book Ser.). (ENG.). 24p. (J). (gr. k-k). 3.99 *(978-0-307-93022-4(X))*, Golden Bks.) Random Hse., Inc.

—A Very Crabby Christmas. Rabe, Tish. 2012. (Little Golden Book Ser.). (ENG.). 24p. (J). (gr. k-k). 4.99 *(978-0-307-97623-9(8))*, Golden Bks.) Random Hse. Children's Bks.

—A Very Krabby Christmas (SpongeBob SquarePants) Golden Books Staff. 2011. (Glitter Sticker Book Ser.). (ENG.). 64p. (J). (gr. -1-2). pap. 4.99 *(978-0-375-87392-8(9))*, Golden Bks.) Random Hse. Children's Bks.

—Watch Me Draw Dora's Favorite Adventures: Let's Draw! 2012. (J). *(978-1-936309-76-4(9))* Quarto Publishing Group USA.

—Who Says? Marchesani, Laura. 2013. (Sassy Ser.). (ENG.). 12p. (J). (gr. -1 — 1). bds. 6.99 *(978-0-448-47789-3(0))*, Grosset & Dunlap) Penguin Publishing Group.

—Who's My Baby? 2014. (Sassy Ser.). (ENG.). 10p. (J). (gr. -1 — 1). bds. 7.99 *(978-0-448-48258-3(4))*, Grosset & Dunlap) Penguin Publishing Group.

—Zoom! Things That Go. Grosset & Dunlap. 2014. (Sassy Ser.). (ENG.). 10p. (J). (gr. -1 — 1). bds. 6.99 *(978-0-448-48146-3(4))*, Grosset & Dunlap) Penguin Publishing Group.

Aikins, Dave & Miller, Victoria. Be Nice, Swiper! Ricci, Christine. 2007. (J). pap. *(978-1-4127-8925-7(7))* Publications International, Ltd.

Aikins, Dave, jt. illus. see Golden Books Staff.

Aikins, Dave, jt. illus. see Golden Books.

Aikins, Dave, jt. illus. see Random House Dictionary Staff.

Aikins, Dave, jt. illus. see Random House Editors.

Aikins, Dave, jt. illus. see Random House Staff.

Aikins, David. Dora & the Unicorn King (Dora the Explorer) Reisner, Molly. 2011. (Little Golden Book Ser.). (ENG.). 24p. (J). (gr. -1-2). 3.99 *(978-0-375-87226-6(4))*, Golden Bks.) Random Hse. Children's Bks.

—Dora's Birthday Surprise! Reisner, Molly. 2010. (Little Golden Book Ser.). (ENG.). 24p. (J). (gr. -1-2). 3.99 *(978-0-375-86163-5(7))*, Golden Bks.) Random Hse. Children's Bks.

—Dora's Puppy, Perrito! (Dora the Explorer) Random House Staff. 2013. (Step into Reading Ser.). (ENG.). 32p. (J). (gr. -1-1). 3.99 *(978-0-449-81857-2(8))*, Random Hse. Bks. for Young Readers) Random Hse. Children's Bks.

—Follow That Egg! (Team Umizoomi) Random House. 2014. (Glitter Board Book Ser.). (ENG.). 12p. (J). (-k). bds. 6.99 *(978-0-385-37518-4(2))*, Random Hse. Bks. for Young Readers) Random Hse. Children's Bks.

—The Good, the Bad, & the Krabby! Random House Editors. 2015. (Flip-It Pictureback Ser.). (ENG.). 24p. (J). (gr. -1-2). 4.99 *(978-0-385-38770-5(9))*, Random Hse. Bks. for Young Readers) Random Hse. Children's Bks.

—Halloween Hoedown! (Dora the Explorer) Reisner, Molly. 2013. (Pictureback Series.). (ENG.). 24p. (J). (gr. -1-2). 3.99 *(978-0-449-81762-9(8))*, Random Hse. Bks. for Young Readers) Random Hse. Children's Bks.

—Happy Love Day! Random House Children's Books Staff. 2013. (Pictureback Series.). (ENG.). 16p. (J). (gr. -1-2). 4.99 *(978-0-385-37519-1(0))*, Random Hse. Bks. for Young Readers) Random Hse. Children's Bks.

—I Love My Papi! (Dora the Explorer) Inches, Alison. 2014. (Step into Reading Ser.). (ENG.). 24p. (J). (gr. -1-1). 3.99 *(978-0-385-37459-0(3))*, Random Hse. Bks. for Young Readers) Random Hse. Children's Bks.

Aikins, David. Island of the Lost Horses (Dora & Friends) Depken, Kristen L. 2015. (Step into Reading Ser.). (ENG.). 24p. (J). (gr. -1-1). 4.99 ***(978-0-553-52093-4(8))***, Random Hse. Bks. for Young Readers) Random Hse. Children's Bks.

Aikins, David. Let's Save Pirate Day! (Dora & Friends) Stevens, Cara. 2014. (Pictureback Series.). (ENG.). 24p. (J). (gr. -1-2). 4.99 *(978-0-385-37440-8(2))*, Random Hse. Bks. for Young Readers) Random Hse. Children's Bks.

—Meet My Friends! (Dora & Friends) Tillworth, Mary. 2014. (Step into Reading Ser.). (ENG.). 24p. (J). (gr. -1-1). 3.99 *(978-0-385-38462-9(9))*, Random Hse. Bks. for Young Readers) Random Hse. Children's Bks.

—Mermaid Treasure Hunt (Dora & Friends) Tillworth, Mary. 2015. (Pictureback Series.). (ENG.). 24p. (J). (gr. -1-2). 3.99 *(978-0-553-51076-8(2))*, Random Hse. Bks. for Young Readers) Random Hse. Children's Bks.

—Nickelodeon Fairy Tales (Nickelodeon) Golden Books. 2012. (Big Golden Book Ser.). (ENG.). 48p. (J). (gr. k-k). 9.99 *(978-0-307-93135-1(8))*, Golden Bks.) Random Hse. Children's Bks.

Aikins, David. One Spooky Night (Dora & Friends) Golden Books. 2015. (Hologramatic Sticker Book Ser.). (ENG.). 64p. (J). (gr. -1-2). pap. 4.99 ***(978-0-553-52118-4(7))***, Golden Bks.) Random Hse. Children's Bks.

Aikins, David. Super Skates! (Dora the Explorer) Golden Books. 2013. (Hologramatic Sticker Book Ser.). (ENG.). 48p. (J). (gr. -1-2). pap. 3.99 *(978-0-385-37282-4(5))*, Golden Bks.) Random Hse. Children's Bks.

—We Love to Dance! (Dora & Friends) Depken, Kristen L. 2015. (Step into Reading Ser.). (ENG.). 24p. (J). (gr. -1-1). 4.99 *(978-0-553-50857-4(1))*, Random Hse. Bks. for Young Readers) Random Hse. Children's Bks.

Aikins, David. Welcome to Fairy World! (Dora & Friends) Tillworth, Mary. 2015. (Glitter Picturebook Ser.). (ENG.). 16p. (J). (gr. -1-2). 5.99 ***(978-0-553-52119-1(5))***, Random Hse. Bks. for Young Readers) Random Hse. Children's Bks.

Aikins, David, jt. illus. see Golden Books.

Aikins, David, jt. illus. see Random House Staff.

Aileen Co & Dayton, Melissa. In the Beginning: Catholic Bible Study for Children. Watson Manhardt, Laurie. 2008. (Come & See Kids Ser.). 108p. (J). (gr. -1-2). per. 9.95 *(978-1-931018-42-5(1))* Emmaus Road Publishing.

Aime, Luigi. The Dragon with the Girl Tattoo, 1 vol. Dahl, Michael. 2012. (Dragonborn Ser.). (ENG.). 72p. (gr. 1-3). pap. 7.10 *(978-1-4342-4257-0(9))*; lib. bdg. 22.65 *(978-1-4342-4041-5(X))* Stone Arch Bks.

—Fangs in the Mirror, 1 vol. Dahl, Michael. 2012. (Dragonborn Ser.). (ENG.). 72p. (gr. 1-3). pap. 7.10 *(978-1-4342-4255-6(2))*; lib. bdg. 22.65 *(978-1-4342-4042-2(8))* Stone Arch Bks.

—Monster Hunter, 1 vol. Dahl, Michael. 2012. (Dragonborn Ser.). (ENG.). 72p. (gr. 1-3). pap. 7.10 *(978-1-4342-4256-3(0))*; lib. bdg. 22.65 *(978-1-4342-4040-8(1))* Stone Arch Bks.

Aines, Diane. Matilda Private Eye: The Case of the Missing Socks. McClafferty, Lisa. 2012. 34p. 29.95 *(978-1-4489-5049-2(X))*; 2007. (ENG.). 31p. 24.95 *(978-1-4241-8637-2(4))* America Star Bks.

Ainslie, Tamsin. A Baby for Loving. Hathorn, Libby. 2015. (ENG.). 32p. (J). (gr. -1-k). 17.99 ***(978-1-921894-67-1(9))*** Little Hare Bks. AUS. Dist: Independent Pubs. Group.

Ainslie, Tamsin. Brigid Lucy & the Princess Tower. Norrington, Leonie. 2012. (Brigid Lucy Ser.: 2). (ENG.). 106p. (J). (gr. 2-4). pap. 8.99 *(978-1-921541-70-4(9))* Little Hare Bks. AUS. Dist: Independent Pubs. Group.

—Brigid Lucy Needs a Friend. Norrington, Leonie. 2014. (Brigid Lucy Ser.: 3). (ENG.). 112p. (J). (gr. 2-4). pap. 9.99 *(978-1-921894-24-4(5))* Little Hare Bks. AUS. Dist: Independent Pubs. Group.

—Brigid Lucy Wants a Pet. Norrington, Leonie. 2011. (Brigid Lucy Ser.: 1). (ENG.). 106p. (J). (gr. 2-4). 8.99 *(978-1-921541-69-8(5))* Little Hare Bks. AUS. Dist: Independent Pubs. Group.

—Count My Kisses, Little One. May, Ruthie. 2010. (ENG.). 24p. (J). (gr. k — 1). bds. 8.99 *(978-0-545-25281-2(4))*, Cartwheel Bks.) Scholastic, Inc.

Ainslie, Tamsin. I Can Say Please. Ainslie, Tamsin. ed. 2012. (ENG.). 26p. (J). 7.99 *(978-1-61067-037-1(X))* Kane Miller.

—I Can Say Thank You. Ainslie, Tamsin. ed. 2012. (ENG.). 26p. (J). 7.99 *(978-1-61067-038-8(8))* Kane Miller.

Aitken, Stephen. How to Cure Earth's Fever. 2011. (J). *(978-1-61641-674-4(2))* Magic Wagon.

—People in Trouble. 2011. (J). *(978-1-61641-675-1(0))* Magic Wagon.

Aizen, Marina. Mary Had a Little Lamb. (Classic Books with Holes Ser.). (ENG.). (J). 2015. 16p. ***(978-1-84643-679-6(6))***; 2012. 14p. bds. *(978-1-84643-512-6(9))*; 2012. 16p. pap. *(978-1-84643-501-0(3))* Child's Play International Ltd.

Ajhar, Brian. Book of American Heroes. Beck, Glenn. 2011. (ENG.). 276p. (J). 19.99 *(978-1-4424-2332-9(3)*, Simon & Schuster/Paula Wiseman Bks.) Simon & Schuster/Paula Wiseman Bks.

—No Pirates Allowed! Said Library Lou. Greene, Rhonda Gowler. 2013. (ENG.). 40p. (J). (gr. 1-3). 15.95 *(978-1-58536-796-2(6)*, 202364) Sleeping Bear Pr.

—Pinocchio. 2005. (Rabbit Ears Ser.). 36p. (J). (gr. k-5). 25.65 *(978-1-59679-228-9(0))* Spotlight.

Akaba, Suekichi. El Gorrion de la Lengua Cortada. Ishii, Momoko.Tr. of Tongue-Cut Sparrow. (SPA.). 40p. (J). (gr. 3-18). 14.95 *(978-980-257-073-7(7))* Ekare, Ediciones VEN. Dist: Kane Miller.

Akamatsu, Ken. A. I. Love You, 8 vols., Vol. 8. Akamatsu, Ken. Ury, David, tr. from JPN. rev. ed. 2005. 224p. (YA). pap. 14.99 *(978-1-59182-944-7(5)*, Tokyopop Adult) TOKYOPOP, Inc.

—Ai Love You, 8 vols., Vol. 7. Akamatsu, Ken. rev. ed. 2005. 216p. pap. 14.99 *(978-1-59182-943-0(7)*, Tokyopop Adult) TOKYOPOP, Inc.

—Love Hina, 14 vols., Vol. 8. Akamatsu, Ken. Rymer, Nan, tr. rev. ed. 2003. (JPN & ENG.). 184p. (gr. 9-18). pap. 14.99 *(978-1-59182-019-2(7)*, Tokyopop Adult) TOKYOPOP, Inc.

Akana, Lizzi. Playground. 50 Cent Staff. 2012. (ENG.). 320p. (YA). (gr. 7). pap. 9.99 *(978-1-59514-478-2(1)*, Razorbill) Penguin Publishing Group.

—Playground. 50 Cent Staff. ed. 2012. lib. bdg. 20.85 *(978-0-606-26633-8(X)*, Turtleback) Turtleback Bks.

Akerman, Emma. Junk Collector School. Dahlin, Adam A. Sandin, Joan, tr. from SWE. 2007. 32p. (J). (gr. -1-3). 16.00 *(978-91-29-66736-3(4))* R & S Bks. SWE. Dist: Macmillan.

Akers-Bell, Mary. Benjamin's Dog Joseph: A Three Legged Hero. Greene, Daryl C. 2003. 48p. (J). (gr. 2-4). pap. 9.95 *(978-0-9700827-4-9(6))*; lib. bdg. 17.95 *(978-0-9700827-5-6(4))* Densmore-Reid Pubns.

Akhtar, Waheed. Mouth Almighty a Play. Agbaje, Salihah. 2012. 144p. pap. *(978-0-9565861-0-0(4))* Spoken World Productions.

Aki, Katsu. Psychic Academy. Aki, Katsu. Vol. 6. rev. ed. 2005. 192p. pap. 14.99 *(978-1-59532-425-2(9))*; Vol. 8. rev. ed. 2005. 192p. pap. 14.99 *(978-1-59532-427-6(5))*; Vol. 9. 9th rev. ed. 2005. 192p. per. 14.99 *(978-1-59532-428-3(3))*; Vol. 10. 10th rev. ed. 2005. 200p. per. 14.99 *(978-1-59532-429-0(1))*; Vol. 11. 11th rev. ed. 2006. 204p. (YA). per. 14.99 *(978-1-59532-430-6(5))* TOKYOPOP, Inc. (Tokyopop Adult).

Aki, Katsu. Psychic Academy, Vol. 7. Aki, Katsu, creator. rev. ed. 2005. 192p. pap. 14.99 *(978-1-59532-426-9(7)*, Tokyopop Adult) TOKYOPOP, Inc.

Akib, Jamel. Animals Christopher Columbus Saw: An Adventure in the New World. Chronicle Books Staff & Markle, Sandra. 2008. (ENG.). 48p. (J). (gr. 2-5). 16.99 *(978-0-8118-4916-6(3))* Chronicle Bks. LLC.

—Annie Shapiro & the Clothing Workers' Strike. Brill, Marlene Targ. 2010. (History Speaks: Picture Books Plus Reader's Theater Ser.). (ENG.). 48p. (gr. 2-4). pap. 9.95 *(978-0-7613-6132-9(4))*; lib. bdg. 27.93 *(978-1-58013-672-3(9)*, Millbrook Pr.) Lerner Publishing Group.

—Around the World in 80 Days. Verne, Jules. 2007. (Classic Starts(tm) Ser.). (ENG.). 160p. (J). (gr. 2-4). 6.95 *(978-1-4027-3689-6(4))* Sterling Publishing Co., Inc.

—Divali Rose. Rahaman, Vashanti. 2008. (ENG.). 32p. (J). (gr. 2-4). 16.95 *(978-1-59078-524-9(X))* Boyds Mills Pr.

—Dracula: Retold from the Bram Stoker Original. Stoker, Bram. 2007. (Classic Starts(tm) Ser.). (ENG.). 160p. (J). (gr. 2-4). 6.95 *(978-1-4027-3690-2(8))* Sterling Publishing Co., Inc.

—Emanuel & the Hanukkah Rescue. Hyde, Heidi Smith. 2012. (Hanukkah Ser.). (SPA & ENG.). 32p. (J). (gr. k-3). 7.95 *(978-0-7613-6627-0(X)*, Kar-Ben Publishing) Lerner Publishing Group.

—Frankenstein. Shelley, Mary. 2006. (Classic Starts(tm) Ser.). (ENG.). 160p. (J). (gr. 2-4). 6.95 *(978-1-4027-2666-8(X))* Sterling Publishing Co., Inc.

—Gulliver's Travels. Swift, Jonathan. 2006. (Classic Starts(tm) Ser.). (ENG.). 160p. (J). (gr. 2-4). 6.95 *(978-1-4027-2662-0(7))* Sterling Publishing Co., Inc.

—Heidi. Spyri, Johanna. 2007. (Classic Starts(tm) Ser.). (ENG.). 160p. (J). (gr. 2-4). 6.95 *(978-1-4027-3691-9(6))* Sterling Publishing Co., Inc.

—Pollyanna. Olmstead, Kathleen & Porter, Eleanor H. 2007. (Classic Starts Ser.). 154p. (J). *(978-1-4287-4209-3(3))* Sterling Publishing Co., Inc.

—Pollyanna. Porter, Eleanor H. 2007. (Classic Starts(tm) Ser.). (ENG.). 160p. (J). (gr. 2-4). 6.95 *(978-1-4027-3692-6(4))* Sterling Publishing Co., Inc.

—The Prince & the Pauper. Twain, Mark. 2007. (Classic Starts(tm) Ser.). (ENG.). 160p. (J). (gr. 2-4). 6.95 *(978-1-4027-3687-2(8))* Sterling Publishing Co., Inc.

—Rebecca of Sunnybrook Farm. Wiggin, Kate Douglas. 2007. (Classic Starts(tm) Ser.). (ENG.). 160p. (J). (gr. 2-4). 6.95 *(978-1-4027-3693-3(2))* Sterling Publishing Co., Inc.

—The Red Badge of Courage. Crane, Stephen. 2006. (Classic Starts(tm) Ser.). (ENG.). 160p. (J). (gr. 2-4). 6.95 *(978-1-4027-2663-7(5))* Sterling Publishing Co., Inc.

—Robinson Crusoe. Defoe, Daniel. 2006. (Classic Starts(tm) Ser.). (ENG.). 160p. (J). (gr. 2-4). 6.95 *(978-1-4027-2664-4(3))* Sterling Publishing Co., Inc.

—The Strange Case of Dr. Jekyll & Mr. Hyde. Stevenson, Robert Louis. 2006. (Classic Starts(tm) Ser.). (ENG.). 160p. (J). (gr. 2-4). 6.95 *(978-1-4027-2667-5(8)*, 1252057) Sterling Publishing Co., Inc.

—The Swiss Family Robinson. Wyss, Johann David. 2007. (Classic Starts(tm) Ser.). (ENG.). 160p. (J). (gr. 2-4). 6.95 *(978-1-4027-3694-0(0))* Sterling Publishing Co., Inc.

—The Swiss Family Robinson. Tait, Chris & Wyss, Johann David. 2007. 151p. (J). *(978-1-4287-4213-0(1))* Sterling Publishing Co., Inc.

—The Swiss Family Robinson. Wyss, Johann David. abr. ed. 2010. (Classic Starts(tm) Ser.). (ENG.). 160p. (J). (gr. 2-4). pap. 9.95 incl. audio compact disk *(978-1-4027-7357-0(9))* Sterling Publishing Co., Inc.

—Tan to Tamarind: Poems about the Color Brown. Iyengar, Malathi Michelle. 2013. (ENG.). 32p. (J). (gr. k). 16.95 *(978-0-89239-227-8(4))* Lee & Low Bks., Inc.

—The Three Musketeers. Dumas, Alexandre. 2007. (Classic Starts(tm) Ser.). (ENG.). 160p. (J). (gr. 2-4). 6.95 *(978-1-4027-3695-7(9))* Sterling Publishing Co., Inc.

—Twenty-Two Cents: Muhammad Yunus & the Village Bank. Yoo, Paula. 2014. (ENG.). 40p. (J). 18.95 *(978-1-60060-658-8(X))* Lee & Low Bks., Inc.

—The War of the Worlds. Sasaki, Chris & Wells, H. G. 2007. (Classic Starts Ser.). 151p. (J). *(978-1-4287-4208-6(5))* Sterling Publishing Co., Inc.

—The War of the Worlds. Wells, H. G. 2007. (Classic Starts(tm) Ser.). (ENG.). 160p. (J). (gr. 2-4). 6.95 *(978-1-4027-3688-9(6))* Sterling Publishing Co., Inc.

—The Wind in the Willows. Woodside, Martin & Grahame, Kenneth. 2007. (Classic Starts Ser.). 152p. (J). *(978-1-4287-4210-9(7))* Sterling Publishing Co., Inc.

—The Wind in the Willows. Grahame, Kenneth. 2007. (Classic Starts(tm) Ser.). (ENG.). 160p. (J). (gr. 2-4). 6.95 *(978-1-4027-3696-4(7))* Sterling Publishing Co., Inc.

Akib, Jamel, jt. illus. see Jeyaveeran, Ruth.

Akimine, Kamijyo. Samurai Deeper Kyo, 18 vols. Akimine, Kamijyo. 192p. Vol. 3. rev. ed. 2003. (YA). pap. 14.99 *(978-1-59182-227-1(0))*; Vol. 12. 12th rev. ed. 2005. pap. 14.99 *(978-1-59532-452-8(6))* TOKYOPOP, Inc. (Tokyopop Adult).

—Samurai Deeper Kyo: Volume 15, Vol. 15. Akimine, Kamijyo. rev. ed. 2005. (Samurai Deeper Kyo Ser.). 192p. (YA). per. 14.99 *(978-1-59532-455-9(0)*, Tokyopop Adult) TOKYOPOP, Inc.

—Samurai Deeper Kyo: Volume 17, 31 vols., Vol. 17. Akimine, Kamijyo. 17th rev. ed. 2006. (Samurai Deeper Kyo Ser.). 192p. (YA). per. 14.99 *(978-1-59532-457-3(7)*, Tokyopop Adult) TOKYOPOP, Inc.

Akimoto, Nami. Miracle Girls, 9 vols., Vol. 7. Akimoto, Nami. 7th rev. ed. 2003. 192p. (gr. 2-18). pap. 9.99 *(978-1-59182-073-4(1))* TOKYOPOP, Inc.

Akin, Ian, et al. Avengers: Absolute Vision. Stern, Roger. 2014. (ENG.). 392p. (J). (gr. 4-17). pap. 39.99 *(978-0-7851-8535-2(6))* Marvel Worldwide, Inc.

Akin, Sean. Henny Penny. 2010. (J). *(978-1-60617-133-2(X))* Teaching Strategies, Inc.

Akino, Matsuri. Genju No Seiza, Vol. 1. Akino, Matsuri. 2006. (Genju No Seiza Ser.). 216p. per. 9.99 *(978-1-59816-607-1(7))* TOKYOPOP, Inc.

—Pet Shop of Horrors - Tokyo, 10 vols., Vol. 3. Akino, Matsuri. rev. ed. 2003. (Teen Ser.). 200p. (YA). (gr. 10-18). pap. 14.99 *(978-1-59182-365-0(X)*, Tokyopop Adult) TOKYOPOP, Inc.

—Pet Shop of Horrors - Tokyo, 10 vols., Vol. 4. Akino, Matsuri. Iwo, Tomoharu & Masumoto, Bryan, trs. from JPN. rev. ed. 2004. (Teen Ser.). 210p. (YA). pap. 14.99 *(978-1-59182-501-2(6)*, Tokyopop Adult) TOKYOPOP, Inc.

Akins, Tamlyn. In Grandpa's Woods. Addy, Sharon. 2004. (J). *(978-1-931599-42-9(4)*, Trails Bks.) Big Earth Publishing.

Akio, Irene. T Is for Tokyo. Akio, Irene. 2010. (ENG.). 36p. (J). (gr. k-5). 12.95 *(978-1-934159-23-1(9))* ThingsAsian Pr.

Akira, Shouko. Times Two. Akira, Shouko. 2005. (Times Two Ser.). (ENG.). 200p. (YA). pap. 9.99 *(978-1-59116-736-5(1))* Viz Media.

Akiyama, Tamayo. Mouryou Kiden, Vol. 3. Akiyama, Tamayo, creator. rev. ed. 2005. 192p. pap. 9.99 *(978-1-59532-247-0(7)*, Tokyopop Adult) TOKYOPOP, Inc.

Akridge, Bill. Intrigue at Pine Haven: Civil War in Florida. Bonner, Anne. 2006. 220p. (YA). 12.95 net. *(978-1-878398-76-5(8)*, Blue Note Bks.) Blue Note Pubns.

Al-Fakhri, Patricia. Fizza the Flamingo. Sheffield, Marilyn. 2003. 3p. pap. 7.95 *(978-1-900988-63-6(1))* Interlink Publishing Group, Inc.

—The Pearl Diver. Johnson, Julia. Stacey International Staff, ed. 2003. (ARA & ENG.). 240p. (J). (gr. 3-6). *(978-1-900988-62-9(3)*, Stacey International) Stacey Publishing.

Al-Ghani, Haitham. Baby Blue Has the Blues, 1 vol. Al-Ghani, K.I. 2011. (ENG.). 32p. (J). *(978-0-7643-3732-1(7)*, Schiffer Publishing Ltd) Schiffer Publishing, Ltd.

—Bertie Bumble Bee: Troubled by the Letter B. Al-Ghani, K.I. 2012. 44p. (J). 16.99 *(978-0-7643-3993-6(1))* Schiffer Publishing, Ltd.

—The Red Beast: Controlling Anger in Children with Asperger's Syndrome. Al-ghani, K. I. 2008. (ENG.). 48p. (J). (gr. 3-7). *(978-1-84310-943-3(3))* Kingsley, Jessica Ltd.

—Ronnie Raven Recycles, 1 vol. Al-Ghani, K.I. 2011. (ENG.). 44p. (J). 16.99 *(978-0-7643-3840-3(4)*, Schiffer Publishing Ltd) Schiffer Publishing, Ltd.

Al-Ghussinu, Wa'ad Diab. 1st Grade Learning Arabic Language Step - by - Step Approach Workbook Part 2,Third Edition: Learn Arabic Language. Tommalieh, Fakhri & Hujeer, Majeda. 2012. (ARA.). 104p. pap. 21.99 *(978-0-9853772-0-5(8))* Dar Asadeeq Publishing & Distribution, Inc.

Al-Greene, Bob. The League of Scientists: Ghost in the Water. at Science, Editors. 2014. (League of Scientists Ser.). (ENG.). 192p. (J). (gr. 5-9). pap. 12.95 *(978-0-9700106-2-9(1))* Platypus Media, L.L.C.

Al, Parker. Jane's Blanket. Miller, Arthur. 2015. (ENG.). 64p. pap. 9.99 ***(978-0-486-79682-6(5))*** Dover Pubns., Inc.

Alakija, Polly. A Stork in a Baobab Tree: An African Twelve Days of Christmas. House, Catherine & Quarto Generic Staff. 2011. (ENG.). 32p. (J). (gr. k-3). 17.95 *(978-1-84780-116-6(1)*, Frances Lincoln) Quarto Publishing Group UK GBR. Dist: Hachette Bk. Group.

Alakija, Polly. Catch That Goat! A Market Day in Nigeria. Alakija, Polly. 2007. 40p. (J). (gr. -1-3). pap. 7.99 *(978-1-84686-057-7(1))* Barefoot Bks., Inc.

Alanis, Erik Valdez Y. Rumpelstiltskin: La Novela Grafica, 1 vol. Andersen, Hans Christian & Stone Arch Books Staff. 2010. (Graphic Spin en Español Ser.). (ENG & SPA.). 40p. (gr. 1-3). pap. 5.95 *(978-1-4342-2273-2(X)*, Graphic Spin en Español) Stone Arch Bks.

—Rumpelstiltskin: The Graphic Novel, 1 vol. Stone Arch Books Staff. 2008. (Graphic Spin Ser.). (ENG.). 40p. (gr. 1-3). pap. 5.95 *(978-1-4342-0864-4(8)*, Graphic Revolve) Stone Arch Bks.

Alaniz, Adam. Germ Stories. Kolter, Roberto, photos by. Kornberg, Arthur. 2007. 70p. (J). (gr. 3-7). 34.00 *(978-1-891389-51-1(3))* Univ. Science Bks.

Alarcao, Renato. The Book of the Heart: Heaven's Mission - To Sharpen Her Senses. Asai, Carrie. 2004. (Samurai Girl Ser.: 6). (ENG.). 240p. (YA). (gr. 11). pap. 11.99 *(978-0-689-86712-5(3)*, Simon Pulse) Simon Pulse.

—The Book of the Shadow. Asai, Carrie. 2013. (Samurai Girl Ser.: 2). (ENG.). 224p. (YA). (gr. 11). pap. 13.99 *(978-1-4814-1540-8(9)*, Simon Pulse) Simon Pulse.

Alarcão, Renato. Finding the Music, 1 vol. Torres, Jennifer. 2015.Tr. of En Pos de la Música. (ENG & SPA.). 40p. (J). 18.95 *(978-0-89239-291-9(6))* Lee & Low Bks., Inc.

—Red Ridin' in the Hood: And Other Cuentos. Marcantonio, Patricia Santos et al. 2005. (ENG.). 192p. (J). (gr. 2-5). 17.99 *(978-0-374-36241-6(6)*, Farrar, Straus & Giroux (BYR)) Farrar, Straus & Giroux.

Alarcao, Renato. Roberto's Trip to the Top. Paterson Jr., John B. & Paterson Sr, John B. 2010. (ENG.). 40p. (J). (gr. -1-3). pap. 6.99 *(978-0-7636-4755-1(1))* Candlewick Pr.

—Roberto's Trip to the Top. Paterson, John B., Jr. & Paterson, John B., Sr. 2009. (ENG.). 40p. (J). (gr. -1-3). 16.99 *(978-0-7636-2708-9(9))* Candlewick Pr.

—Soccer Star. Javaherbin, Mina. 2014. (ENG.). 40p. (J). (gr. k-3). 16.99 *(978-0-7636-6056-7(6))* Candlewick Pr.

Alarcão, Renato, jt. illus. see Verhoye, Annabelle.

Alarid, Carilyn & Markel, Marilyn. Old Grandfather Teaches a Lesson: Mimbres Children Learn Respect. Alarid, Carilyn & Markel, Marilyn. 2004. 116p. (J). pap. 16.95 *(978-0-86534-418-1(3))* Sunstone Pr.

—Talks All Day Has the Courage to Speak: Mimbres Children Learn Citizenship. Alarid, Carilyn & Markel, Marilyn. 2006. 125p. (J). pap. 16.95 *(978-0-86534-470-9(1))* Sunstone Pr.

Alarid, Jason. My Kaya & Me in the Forest. Alarid, Jason. Alarid, Melissa. I.t. ed. 2011. (ENG.). 24p. pap. 9.99 *(978-1-4611-6519-4(9))* CreateSpace Independent Publishing Platform.

Alastra, Stephanie. Coo Is in Love, 1 vol. Laurent, Karine. 2012. (My Little Picture Book Ser.). (ENG.). 32p. (J). (gr. -1). pap. 6.95 *(978-2-7338-1244-0(0))* Auzou, Philippe Editions FRA. Dist: Consortium Bk. Sales & Distribution.

Alaverdy, Melissa. Introduction to Music. O'Brien, Eileen. 2004. (ENG.). 96p. (J). 7.95 *(978-0-7945-0276-8(8)*, Usborne) EDC Publishing.

Alba, Elisabeth. Fancy. Earhart, Kristin. 2010. (Stablemates Ser.). (ENG.). 48p. (J). (gr. -1-3). 4.99 *(978-0-545-12098-2(5)*, Cartwheel Bks.) Scholastic, Inc.

—Martin Luther King, Jr. Norwich, Grace. 2012. (I Am Ser.: 4). (ENG.). 128p. (J). (gr. 2-5). pap. 5.99 *(978-0-545-44780-5(1)*, Scholastic Paperbacks) Scholastic, Inc.

Albano, Jennifer. Wanda & Willie. Schultz, Brenda. 2008. 25p. pap. 24.95 *(978-1-60703-446-9(8))* America Star Bks.

Alberg, Nathan. What Happened to Marion's Book? Berg, Brook. 2003. 48p. (J). (gr. -1-2). per. 16.95 *(978-1-932146-05-9(9)*, Upstart Bks.) Highsmith Inc.

—What Marion Taught Willis. Berg, Brook. 2005. (J). 16.95 *(978-1-932146-31-8(8)*, 1242215) Highsmith Inc.

Alberini, Teresa. My Bones. Dawson, Emily C. 2015. (Inside My Body Ser.). (ENG.). 24p. (gr. 1-3). 19.95 *(978-1-60753-753-2(2))* Amicus Educational.

—My Brain. Pimentel, Annette Bay. 2015. (Inside My Body Ser.). (ENG.). 24p. (gr. 1-3). 19.95 *(978-1-60753-754-0(0))* Amicus Educational.

Alberini, Teresa. My Heart. Shaffer, Jody Jensen. 2015. (Inside My Body Ser.). (ENG.). 24p. (gr. 1-3). 19.95 ***(978-1-60753-755-7(9))*** Amicus Educational.

—My Lungs. Shaffer, Jody Jensen. 2015. (Inside My Body Ser.). (ENG.). 24p. (gr. 1-3). 19.95 ***(978-1-60753-756-4(7))*** Amicus Educational.

—My Muscles. Shaffer, Jody Jensen. 2015. (Inside My Body Ser.). (ENG.). 24p. (gr. 1-3). 19.95 ***(978-1-60753-757-1(5))*** Amicus Educational.

—My Stomach. Pimentel, Annette Bay. 2015. (Inside My Body Ser.). (ENG.). 24p. (gr. 1-3). 19.95 ***(978-1-60753-758-8(3))*** Amicus Educational.

Albert, Dar, jt. illus. see Cardillo, Linda.

Albert, Robert & Anthis, Brian. The Lost Kachina. Irbinskas, Heather. 2004. 32p. (J). 15.95 *(978-1-885772-33-6(5))* Kiva Publishing, Inc.

Alberti, Mario. Spider-Man & the Fantastic Four. Gage, Christos. 2011. (ENG.). 256p. (YA). (gr. 8-17). pap. 14.99 *(978-0-7851-4423-6(4))* Marvel Worldwide, Inc.

Albertine. At the Seaside. Zullo, Germano. 2009. (ENG.). 16p. (J). (gr. -1-3). 15.95 *(978-1-85437-862-0(7))* Tate Publishing, Ltd. GBR. Dist: Abrams.

—Jumping Jack. Zullo, Germano. 2014. (ENG.). 40p. (J). (gr. k-3). 17.99 *(978-1-4521-3152-8(X))* Chronicle Bks. LLC.

—Line 135. Zullo, Germano. 2013. (ENG.). 44p. (J). (gr. -1-1). 18.95 *(978-1-4521-1934-2(1))* Chronicle Bks. LLC.

—Little Bird. Zullo, Germano. 2012. (ENG.). 72p. (J). (gr. k). 16.95 *(978-1-59270-118-6(3))* Enchanted Lion Bks., LLC.

—Sky High. Zullo, Germano. 2012. (ENG.). 48p. 18.95 *(978-1-4521-1392-0(0))* Chronicle Bks. LLC.

Alberts, Scott. A Different Little Doggy. Whittaker, Heather. 2013. 28p. (J). 9.99 *(978-0-9820962-1-5(6))* Pen-Tech Professional.

Albon, Lucie. Little Ballerina: A Children's Book Inspired by Edgar Degas. 2011. (ENG.). 32p. 14.95 *(978-3-7913-7081-1(2))* Prestel Publishing.

Alborough, Jez. Billy the Goat's Big Breakfast. Alborough, Jez. 2014. (ENG.). 32p. (J). 12.99 *(978-1-61067-190-3(2))* Kane Miller.

—Duck in the Truck. Alborough, Jez. 2008. 32p. (J). (gr. -1-3). pap. 7.99 *(978-1-933605-76-0(6))* Kane Miller.

—The Gobble Gobble Mooooo Tractor Book. Alborough, Jez. 2010. 32p. (J). (gr. -1-1). 15.99 *(978-1-935279-66-2(1))* Kane Miller.

—Hug. Alborough, Jez. (ENG.). 32p. (J). 2009. (gr. -1-k). pap. 3.99 *(978-0-7636-4510-6(9))*; 2005. (— 1). bds. 12.99 *(978-0-7636-2893-2(X))* Candlewick Pr.

—Nat the Cat's Sunny Smile. Alborough, Jez. 2013. 32p. (J). 12.99 *(978-1-61067-177-4(5))* Kane Miller.

—Super Duck. Alborough, Jez. 2009. 32p. (J). (gr. -1-2). 10.99 *(978-1-933605-89-0(8))* Kane Miller.

—Yes. Alborough, Jez. 2006. (ENG.). 40p. (J). (gr. -1-k). 15.99 *(978-0-7636-3183-3(3))* Candlewick Pr.

Alborozo, Gabriel. Good Night, Firefly. Alborozo, Gabriel. 2015. (ENG.). 32p. (J). (gr. -1-2). 16.99 *(978-1-62779-222-6(8)*, Holt, Henry & Co. Bks. For Young Readers) Holt, Henry & Co.

Albrecht, Jeff & Jeff Albrecht Studios Staff. Presidential Pets: The Weird, Wacky, Little, Big, Scary, Strange Animals That Have Lived in the White House. Moberg, Julia. 2012. (ENG.). 96p. (J). (gr. 3-7). 14.95 *(978-1-936140-79-4(9)*, Imagine Publishing) Charlesbridge Publishing, Inc.

Albright, Ann. Samuel Sparrow & the Tree of Light. Albright, Ann. 2003. (J). *(978-0-9715472-5-4(4))* Ascension Lutheran Church.

Albright, Audrey. Rachel the Homely Rabbit: A Story about Kindness. Kaye, Christian Thomas. 2011. 30p. pap. 9.95 *(978-1-60844-763-3(4))* Dog Ear Publishing, LLC.

Albright, Tawnya, et al. Puppetry Clip Art Book & CD. rev. ed. 2003. 44p. (YA). 25.00 *(978-1-58302-229-0(5))* One Way St., Inc.

Albright, Tawnya. Travel God's Way. VonSeggen, Liz. rev. ed. 2003. 116p. (J). ring bd. 35.00 *(978-1-58302-248-1(1))* One Way St., Inc.

Albuquerque, Rafael. Road Trip, Vol. 2. Rogers, John et al. rev. ed. 2007. (Blue Beetle Ser.). (ENG.). 144p. (gr. 7-18). pap. 12.99 *(978-1-4012-1361-9(8))* DC Comics.

—The Savage Brothers. Cosby, Andrew & Stokes, Johanna. 2007. (ENG.). 128p. per. 14.99 *(978-1-934506-16-5(8))* Boom! Studios.

Albuquerque, Rafael, jt. illus. see Lyra, Rael.

Alcadia SNC Staff. A Merry Scary Holiday. Howard, Lee. 2011. (Scooby-Doo Comic Storybook Ser.: 2). (ENG.). 32p. (J). (gr. -1-3). pap. 3.99 *(978-0-545-36865-0(0))* Scholastic, Inc.

—Scooby-Doo Comic Storybook. ABDO Publishing Company Staff & Howard, Lee. 2014. (Scooby-Doo Comic Storybook Ser.: 4). (ENG.). 32p. (J). (gr. 5-9). lib. bdg. 96.84 *(978-1-61479-280-2(1)*, Graphic Planet) Magic Wagon.

Alcadia SNC Staff, jt. illus. see Scholastic, Inc. Staff.

Alcantara, Felipe Ugalde. Little Crow to the Rescue/el Cuervito al Rescate. Villasenor, Victor. Munoz, Elizabeth Cummins, tr. 2005. (SPA & ENG.). 32p. (J). (gr. -1-3). pap. 16.95 *(978-1-55885-430-7(4)*, Piñata Books) Arte Publico Pr.

Alcantara, Ignacio. Disabilities. Vision, Mutiya Sahar. 2009. 32p. 17.00 *(978-0-9659538-9-4(0))* Vision Works Publishing.

—If Only I Could! Vision, David & Vision, Mutiya Sahar. 2009. 32p. 17.00 *(978-0-9659538-8-7(2))* Vision Works Publishing.

—The Land of Expression. Vision, Mutiya & Vision, David. 2009. (ENG.). 48p. 15.00 *(978-0-9816254-0-9(1))* Vision Works Publishing.

—Missing You. Vision, David & Vision, Mutiya Sahar. 2009. 32p. 17.00 *(978-0-9659538-6-3(6))* Vision Works Publishing.

—My Choices Make Me Who I Am. Vision, Mutiya & Vision, David. 2009. 40p. (gr. 2-5). 17.00 *(978-0-9659538-2-5(3))* Vision Works Publishing.

—My Very Breast Friend. Vision, David et al. 2009. (ENG.). 40p. 17.00 *(978-0-9659538-5-6(8))* Vision Works Publishing.

—What Makes Me Beautiful? Vision, David & Vision, Mutiya Sahar. 2009. 24p. 16.00 *(978-0-9659538-4-9(X))* Vision Works Publishing.

—Who's That Crying! Vision, David. 2009. 64p. 17.00 *(978-0-9659538-1-8(5))* Vision Works Publishing.

Alcorn, John. Books! McCain, Murray. 2013. (ENG.). 42p. (J). (gr. -1). 17.95 *(978-1-62326-020-0(5))* AMMO Bks., LLC.

Alcorn, Miah. The Year of the Dog: Tales from the Chinese Zodiac. Chin, Oliver. 2006. (Tales from the Chinese Zodiac Ser.). (ENG.). 36p. (J). (gr. -1-7). 15.95 *(978-1-59702-002-2(8))* Immedium.

—The Year of the Ox: Tales from the Chinese Zodiac. Chin, Oliver. 2009. (Tales from the Chinese Zodiac Ser.). (ENG.). 36p. (J). (gr. -1-3). 15.95 *(978-1-59702-015-2(X))* Immedium.

—The Year of the Pig: Tales from the Chinese Zodiac. Chin, Oliver. 2007. (ENG.). 36p. (J). (gr. -1-3). 15.95 *(978-1-59702-007-7(9))* Immedium.

—The Year of the Rat: Tales from the Chinese Zodiac. Chin, Oliver Clyde. 2008. (Tales from the Chinese Zodiac Ser.). (ENG.). 36p. (J). (gr. -1-k). 15.95 *(978-1-59702-011-4(7))* Immedium.

Alcorn, Stephen. America at War. Hopkins, Lee Bennett, ed. 2008. (ENG.). 96p. (J). (gr. 3-7). 21.99 *(978-1-4169-1832-5(9)*, McElderry, Margaret K. Bks.) McElderry, Margaret K. Bks.

—Days to Celebrate: A Full Year of Poetry, People, Holidays, History, Fascinating Facts, & More. Hopkins, Lee Bennett. 2004. (ENG.). 112p. (J). (gr. 3-7). 18.99 *(978-0-06-000765-2(6)*, Greenwillow Bks.) HarperCollins Pubs.

—Keep On! The Story of Matthew Henson, Co-Discoverer of the North Pole, 1 vol. Hopkinson, Deborah. 2009. (ENG.). 36p. (J). (gr. 1-5). 17.95 *(978-1-56145-473-0(7))* Peachtree Pubs.

A

—Mary's Song. Hopkins, Lee Bennett. 2012. (J). 17.00 (978-0-8028-5397-4(8), Eerdmans Bks For Young Readers) Eerdmans, William B. Publishing Co.

—Yours for Justice, Ida B. Wells: The Daring Life of a Crusading Journalist, 1 vol. Dray, Philip. 2008. (ENG.). 48p. (J). (gr. 5-9). 18.95 (978-1-56145-417-4(6)) Peachtree Pubs.

Alcorn, Stephen. A Gift of Days: The Greatest Words to Live By. Alcorn, Stephen. 2009. (ENG.). 128p. (J). (gr. 3-7). 21.99 (978-1-4169-6776-7(1), Atheneum Bks. for Young Readers) Simon & Schuster Children's Publishing.

ALDEN, B. E. A. A Bad Night's Sleep. Craig, Joni. 2013. 46p. 16.95 (978-1-940224-11-4(X)) Taylor and Seale Publishing, LLC.

Alden, Carol. Paddy the Pelican Survives the Storm. Fane, Judy B. 2010. 48p. pap. 16.50 (978-1-60911-448-0(5), Eloquent Bks.) Strategic Book Publishing & Rights Agency (SBPRA).

Alder, Charlie. Katie Woo's Super Stylish Activity Book, 1 vol. Manushkin, Fran. 2013. (Katie Woo Ser.). (ENG.). 64p. (gr. k-2). pap. 4.95 (978-1-4795-2047-3(0)) Picture Window Bks.

—Toot! Hall, Kirsten. 2013. (ENG.). 24p. (J). (gr. -1-k). bds. 8.99 (978-0-448-46587-6(6), Grosset & Dunlap) Penguin Publishing Group.

—Where Is Carl the Corn Snake?, 1 vol. Dale, Jay. 2012. (Engage Literacy Green Ser.). (ENG.). 32p. (gr. k-2). pap. 5.99 (978-1-4296-8994-6(3), Engage Literacy) Capstone Pr., Inc.

Alder, Charlotte. Green Princess Saves the Day. Crowne, Alyssa. 2010. (J). (Perfectly Princess Ser.: 3). (ENG.). 80p. (gr. 2-5). 4.99 (978-0-545-20848-2(3), Scholastic Paperbacks); 71p. (978-0-545-23414-6(X)) Scholastic, Inc.

—Orange Princess Has a Ball. Crowne, Alyssa. 2010. (Perfectly Princess Ser.: 4). (ENG.). 80p. (J). (gr. 2-5). 4.99 (978-0-545-20850-5(5), Scholastic Paperbacks) Scholastic, Inc.

—Pink Princess Rules the School. Crowne, Alyssa. 2009. 80p. (J). pap. (978-0-545-16077-3(4)) Scholastic, Inc.

Alder, Kelynn. Moments of Wonder: Life with Moritz. 2008. (ENG.). 68p. (J). 22.00 (978-0-9721457-4-9(5)) Silent Moon Bks.

Alderman, Derrick & Shea, Denise. Una Bandera a Cuadros: Un Libro para Contar Sobre Carreras de Autos. Dahl, Michael. 2010. (Apréndete Tus Números/Know Your Numbers Ser.).Tr. of One Checkered Flag - A Counting Book about Racing. (SPA & MUL.). 24p. (gr. -1-2). lib. bdg. 25.99 (978-1-4048-6295-1(1)) Picture Window Bks.

—I Drive a Bulldozer, 1 vol. Bridges, Sarah. 2004. (Working Wheels Ser.). (ENG.). 24p. (gr. -1-2). 25.99 (978-1-4048-0613-9(X), Nonfiction Picture Bks.) Picture Window Bks.

—I Drive a Garbage Truck, 1 vol. Bridges, Sarah. 2004. (Working Wheels Ser.). (ENG.). 24p. (gr. -1-2). 25.99 (978-1-4048-0615-3(6), Nonfiction Picture Bks.) Picture Window Bks.

—I Drive a Snowplow, 1 vol. Bridges, Sarah. 2004. (Working Wheels Ser.). (ENG.). 24p. (gr. -1-2). 25.99 (978-1-4048-0617-7(2), Nonfiction Picture Bks.) Picture Window Bks.

—I Drive an Ambulance, 1 vol. Bridges, Sarah. 2004. (Working Wheels Ser.). (ENG.). 24p. (gr. -1-2). 25.99 (978-1-4048-0618-4(0), Nonfiction Picture Bks.) Picture Window Bks.

—On the Launch Pad: A Counting Book about Rockets, 1 vol. Dahl, Michael. 2004. (Know Your Numbers Ser.). (ENG.). 24p. (gr. -1-2). per. 7.95 (978-1-4048-1119-5(2), Nonfiction Picture Bks.) Picture Window Bks.

—Whose Food Is This? A Look at What Animals Eat - Leaves, Bugs, & Nuts. Allen, Nancy Kelly. 2004. (Whose Is It? Ser.). (ENG.). 24p. (gr. -1-2). 25.99 (978-1-4048-0607-8(5), Nonfiction Picture Bks.) Picture Window Bks.

—Whose Work Is This? A Look at Things Animals Make - Pearls, Silk, & Honey. Allen, Nancy Kelly. 2004. (Whose Is It? Ser.). (ENG.). 24p. (gr. -1-2). 25.99 (978-1-4048-0612-2(1), Nonfiction Picture Bks.) Picture Window Bks.

—Yo Manejo un Camión de la Basura. Bridges, Sarah. 2010. (Vehículos de Trabajo/Working Wheels Ser.).Tr. of I Drive a Garbage Truck. (MUL & SPA.). 24p. (gr. -1-2). lib. bdg. 25.99 (978-1-4048-6303-3(6)) Picture Window Bks.

—Yo Manejo un Camión de Volteo. Bridges, Sarah. 2010. (Vehículos de Trabajo/Working Wheels Ser.).Tr. of I Drive a Dump Truck. (MUL & SPA.). 24p. (gr. -1-2). lib. bdg. 25.99 (978-1-4048-6301-9(X)) Picture Window Bks.

—Yo Manejo Una Niveladora. Bridges, Sarah. 2010. (Vehículos de Trabajo/Working Wheels Ser.).Tr. of I Drive a Bulldozer. (MUL & SPA.). 24p. (gr. -1-2). lib. bdg. 25.99 (978-1-4048-6300-2(1)) Picture Window Bks.

Alderson, Lisa. The Night Before Christmas: Peek Inside the 3D Windows. Moore, Clement C. 2013. (ENG.). 12p. (J). (gr. -1-3). 16.99 (978-1-84322-923-0(4), Armadillo) Anness Publishing GBR. Dist: National Bk. Network.

—The Snow Family: A Winter's Tale. 2005. (ENG.). 12p. (J). 12.95 (978-1-58117-233-1(8), Intervisual/Piggy Toes) Bendon, Inc.

—The Snow Family: A Winter's Tale. Feldman, Thea & Auerbach, Annie. 2005. 12p. (J). 13.00 (978-0-7567-9460-6(9)) DIANE Publishing Co.

Alderton, John. Nerfherd. Michael, Melanie. 2011. (J). (978-0-938467-07-6(7)) Headline Bks., Inc.

Aldous, Kate. Black Beauty. Sewell, Anna. 2003. 288p. (J). 9.98 (978-1-4054-1675-7(0)) Parragon, Inc.

—A Little Princess. Burnett, Frances Hodgson. 2005. 62p. (J). (gr. 4-7). 8.95 (978-0-7945-1123-4(6), Usborne) EDC Publishing.

Aldous, Kate & McGairy, James. Little Women. 320p. (J). (978-1-4054-3772-1(3)) Parragon, Inc.

Aldredge, Terry Beckham. The Story of Jesus: Part 1. Laubach, Frank. Woodworth, Ralph, ed. 2005. per. (978-0-9749168-6-6(2)) FEA Ministries.

—The Story of Jesus: Part 2. Laubach, Frank. Woodworth, Ralph, ed. 2005. per. (978-0-9749168-8-0(9)) FEA Ministries.

Aldridge, Alan. The Butterfly Ball & the Grasshopper's Feast. Plomer, William. 2009. (ENG.). 96p. (J). (gr. k-12). 22.99 (978-0-7636-4422-2(6)) Candlewick Pr.

Aldridge, Sheila. Phoebe & Chub. Hall, Matthew Henry. 2005. (ENG.). 32p. (J). (gr. -1-3). 15.95 (978-0-87358-879-9(7)) Cooper Square Publishing Llc.

Alekos. El Leon y el Perrito: Y Otros Cuentos. Tolstoy, Leo. Montana, Francisco, tr. 2nd ed. 2003. (Cajon de Cuentos Ser.). (SPA.). 177p. (J). (gr. -1-7). (978-958-30-0333-2(6)) Panamericana Editorial.

Alekseyeva, Alla. My Sparkling Misfortune. Lond, Laura. 2011. (ENG.). 126p. pap. 9.85 (978-1-4609-2236-1(0)) CreateSpace Independent Publishing Platform.

Alemagna, Beatrice. One & Seven. Rodari, Gianni. Anglin, David, tr. from ITA. 2005. (SPA.). 26p. (J). (gr. k-3). 17.95 (978-0-9628720-6-8(7)) Iaconi, Mariuccia Bk. Imports.

—Songs from the Garden of Eden: Jewish Lullabies & Nursery Rhymes. Soussana, Nathalie et al. 2009. (ENG.). 52p. (J). (gr. -1-2). 16.95 (978-2-923163-46-8(X)) La Montagne Secrete CAN. Dist: Independent Pubs. Group.

Alemian, Kimberlee. Adventures of Dingle Dee & Lingle Dee. Masella, Rosalie Tagg. 2009. 26p. (J). 19.95 (978-0-9663730-3-5(0)) Vesper Enterprises, Inc.

Aleshina, Nonna. Cleopatra & the King's Enemies: Based on a True Story of Cleopatra in Egypt. Holub, Joan. 2011. (Young Princesses Around the World Ser.: 1). (ENG.). 48p. (J). (gr. 1-3). pap. 13.99 (978-1-4424-3088-4(5), Simon Spotlight) Simon Spotlight.

—Elizabeth & the Royal Pony: Based on a True Story of Elizabeth I of England. Holub, Joan. 2007. (Young Princesses Around the World Ser.). (ENG.). 48p. (J). (gr. 1-3). pap. 3.99 (978-0-689-87191-7(0), Simon Spotlight) Simon Spotlight.

—Isabel Saves the Prince: Based on a True Story of Isabel I of Spain. Holub, Joan. 2007. (Young Princesses Around the World Ser.). (ENG.). 48p. (J). (gr. 1-3). pap. 13.99 (978-0-689-87197-9(X), Simon Spotlight) Simon Spotlight.

—Lydia & the Island Kingdom: A Story Based on the Real Life of Princess Liliuokalani of Hawaii. Holub, Joan. 2007. (Young Princesses Around the World Ser.). (ENG.). 48p. (J). (gr. 1-3). pap. 13.99 (978-0-689-87199-3(6), Simon Spotlight) Simon Spotlight.

Alex, Ioan. My First Words. 2004. 63p. (J). 9.95 (978-1-59496-000-0(3)) Teora USA LLC.

Alex, Smith. Home. Alex, Smith. 2010. 32p. (J). (gr. -1-2). 15.95 (978-1-58925-088-8(5)) Tiger Tales.

Alexander, Claire. Back to Front & Upside Down. 2012. (J). 16.00 (978-0-8028-5414-8(1), Eerdmans Bks For Young Readers) Eerdmans, William B. Publishing Co.

Alexander, Claire. Lucy & the Bully, 1 vol. Alexander, Claire. 2008. (ENG.). 32p. (J). (gr. -1-1). 16.99 (978-0-8075-4786-1(7)) Whitman, Albert & Co.

—Small Florence, Piggy Pop Star. Alexander, Claire. 2010. (ENG.). 32p. (J). (gr. -1-3). 16.99 (978-0-8075-7455-3(4)) Whitman, Albert & Co.

Alexander, Florence, et al. Come with Me & See... A Total Eclipse in Africa. Alexander, Florence et al. 2003. (ENG & SPA.). 40p. (J). 3.99 (978-0-915960-50-7(8)) Ebon Research Systems Publishing, LLC.

Alexander, Gregory. The Jungle Book. Rowe, John, ed. 2003. (Chrysalis Childrens Classics Ser.). 159p. (YA). pap. (978-1-84365-038-6(X), Pavilion Children's Books) Pavilion Bks.

Alexander, Jason. Alice's Adventures in Wonderland. 2009. (ENG.). 12p. (J). 8.95 (978-1-58117-855-5(7), Intervisual/Piggy Toes) Bendon, Inc.

Alexander, John. The Adventures of Thunder & Avalanche: Laws of Nature. Alexander, John. 2013. 46p. 18.99 (978-0-9887625-0-3(1)) Mountain Thunder Publishing.

—The Adventures of Thunder & Avalanche: Up & Away. Alexander, John. 2013. 48p. 15.99 (978-0-9887625-1-0(X)) Mountain Thunder Publishing.

Alexander, Johnna A. An Angel's Day on Earth. Flora, B. David. 2011. 24p. pap. 24.95 (978-1-4560-9851-3(9)) PublishAmerica, Inc.

Alexander, Katie Norwood. This Little Light of Mine. Bateman, Claire Boudreaux. ed. 2005. 32p. (J). per. 18.50 (978-0-9706732-2-0(1)) Shell Beach Publishing, LLC.

Alexander, Martha. The Little Green Witch. McGrath, Barbara Barbieri. (ENG.). 32p. (J). (gr. -1-2). 2006. pap. 7.95 (978-1-58089-153-0(5)); 2005. 15.95 (978-1-58089-042-7(3)) Charlesbridge Publishing, Inc.

Alexander, Martha. A You're Adorable. Alexander, Martha. 2011. (ENG.). 20p. (J). (gr. -1 — 1). bds. 6.99 (978-0-7636-5332-3(2)) Candlewick Pr.

Alexander, Martha. Poems & Prayers for the Very Young. Alexander, Martha, selected by. 32p. (J). Random Hse. Children's Bks.

Alexander, Yvonne Rabdau. The Adventures of Super Keith! MacPherson, Lorry. 2010. 56p. pap. 19.50 (978-1-60976-268-1(1), Eloquent Bks.) Strategic Book Publishing & Rights Agency (SBPRA).

—Lynne Woke Up! MacPherson, Lorry. 2007. 20p. per. 24.95 (978-1-4137-2536-0(8)) America Star Bks.

Alexopolous, George. Go with Grace, Vol. 1. Alexopolous, George. 2006. 192p. (gr. 8-18). per. 9.99 (978-1-59816-709-2(X)) TOKYOPOP, Inc.

Alfandolo, Koffi. I Am the Blues. Gorg, Gwyn. 2012. 26p. pap. 19.95 (978-0-9840204-2-3(X)) Pacific Raven Pr.

Alfano, Wayne. Saint Bakhita of Sudan: Forever Free. Wallace, Susan Helen. 2006. (Encounter the Saints Ser.: 21). 102p. (J). pap. 7.95 (978-0-8198-7094-0(3)) Pauline Bks. & Media.

Alfano, Wayne. Saint John Bosco: Champion for the Young. Marsh, Emily Beata. 2015. 128p. (J). pap. 8.95 (978-0-8198-9045-0(6)) Pauline Bks. & Media.

Alfano, Wayne. Saint Martin de Porres: Humble Healer. Dedomenico, Elizabeth Marie. 2005. (Encounter the Saints Ser.: No. 19). 108p. (J). (gr. 3-7). per. 7.95 (978-0-8198-7091-9(9)) Pauline Bks. & Media.

Alfaro, Luis. Muu muuu dice una Vaca. Salinas, Sonia. 2007.Tr. of Moo Moo Says a Cow. (SPA.). 32p. (J). 15.99 (978-0-9794710-0-1(1)) S&S Publishing LLC.

Alfreda. Be Somebody Be Yourself Lesson Plan Reproducibles. Alfreda. 2004. 60p. (gr. 4-7). 29.95 (978-1-56820-031-6(5)) Story Time Stories That Rhyme.

Algar, James. Jack, Tommy & the Phoenix Street Firefighters. Tierney, John. 2012. 70p. pap. 11.99 (978-1-78035-416-3(9), Fastprint Publishing) Upfront Publishing Ltd. GBR. Dist: Printondemand-worldwide.com.

Alger, Liz. Naughty Norton, 1 vol. Kelly, Bernadette & Ward, Krista. (Pony Tales Ser.). (ENG.). 56p. (gr. 2-2). 2013. pap. 5.05 (978-1-4795-2067-1(5)); 2009. lib. bdg. 19.99 (978-1-4048-5504-5(1)) Picture Window Bks. (Chapter Readers).

—Norton Saves the Day, 1 vol. Kelly, Bernadette & Ward, Krista. 2009. (Pony Tales Ser.). (ENG.). 56p. (gr. 2-2). lib. bdg. 19.99 (978-1-4048-5505-2(X), Chapter Readers) Picture Window Bks.

—Norton's First Show, 1 vol. Kelly, Bernadette & Ward, Krista. (Pony Tales Ser.). (ENG.). 56p. (gr. 2-2). 2013. pap. 5.05 (978-1-4795-2068-8(3)); 2009. lib. bdg. 19.99 (978-1-4048-5506-9(8)) Picture Window Bks. (Chapter Readers).

—Pony Tales. Kelly, Bernadette & Ward, Krista. 2013. (Pony Tales Ser.). (ENG.). 56p. (gr. 2-2). pap. 9.90 (978-1-4795-3784-6(5), Chapter Readers) Picture Window Bks.

—Who Stole Norton?, 1 vol. Kelly, Bernadette & Ward, Krista. 2009. (Pony Tales Ser.). (ENG.). 56p. (gr. 2-2). lib. bdg. 19.99 (978-1-4048-5503-8(3), Chapter Readers) Picture Window Bks.

Ali, Intelaq Mohammed. The Amazing Discoveries of Ibn Sina, 1 vol. Sharafeddine, Fatima. 2015. (ENG.). 32p. (J). (gr. 1-6). 17.95 (978-1-55498-710-8(5)) Groundwood Bks. CAN. Dist: Perseus-PGW.

Alibert, Eric, jt. illus. see Hyman, Miles.

Alice, Alex. The Valykrie, Vol. 2. Alice, Alex. 2014. (Siegfried Ser.: 2). (ENG.). 144p. 24.95 (978-1-936393-79-4(4)) Boom Entertainment, Inc.

Alikhan, Salima. Lawyer's Week Before Christmas, 1 vol. Justice, Joseph. 2010. (Night Before Christmas Ser.). (ENG.). 32p. (J). (gr. 4-8). 16.99 (978-1-58980-739-6(1)) Pelican Publishing Co., Inc.

—Pieces of Another World, 1 vol. Rockliff, Mara. 2005. (ENG.). 32p. (J). (gr. k-4). 15.95 (978-0-9764943-2-4(9)) Arbordale Publishing.

—Rocky Mountain Night Before Christmas, 1 vol. Gribnau, Joe. 2007. (Night Before Christmas Ser.). (ENG.). 32p. (J). (gr. k-3). 16.99 (978-1-58980-317-6(5)) Pelican Publishing Co., Inc.

Alikhan, Salima. The Pied Piper of Austin, 1 vol. Alikhan, Salima. 2009. (ENG.). 32p. (J). (gr. k-3). 16.99 (978-1-58980-629-0(8)) Pelican Publishing Co., Inc.

Aliki. Ah, Music! Aliki. (ENG.). 48p. (J). (gr. k-5). 2005. pap. 6.99 (978-0-06-446236-5(6)); 2003. 17.99 (978-0-06-028719-1(5)) HarperCollins Pubs.

—All by Myself! Aliki. 2003. (ENG.). 32p. (J). (gr. -1-1). pap. 6.99 (978-0-06-446253-2(6)) HarperCollins Pubs.

Aliki. My Five Senses. Aliki. 2015. (Let's-Read-And-Find-Out Science 1 Ser.). (ENG.). 32p. (J). (gr. -1-3). 17.99 (978-0-06-238191-0(1)) HarperCollins Pubs.

Aliki. Play's the Thing. Aliki. 2005. (ENG.). 32p. (J). 16.99 (978-0-06-074355-0(7)) HarperCollins Pubs.

—Push Button. Aliki. 2010. (ENG.). 40p. (J). (gr. -1-k). 16.99 (978-0-06-167308-5(0), Greenwillow Bks.) HarperCollins Pubs.

—Quiet in the Garden. Aliki. 2009. 32p. (J). (gr. -1-2). (ENG.). 17.99 (978-0-06-155207-6(0)); lib. bdg. 18.89 (978-0-06-155208-3(9)) HarperCollins Pubs. (Greenwillow Bks.).

Alison, Jay & Jay, Alison. Out of the Blue. Barefoot Books Staff. 2014. 32p. (J). 16.99 (978-1-78285-042-7(2)) Barefoot Bks., Inc.

Alixe, Pascal & Klein, Nic. The Iron Nail - Captain America, Vol. 4. 2014. (ENG.). 144p. (J). (gr. 4-17). 24.99 (978-0-7851-8953-4(X)) Marvel Worldwide, Inc.

Alizadeh, Kate. All Through the Night. Hughes, John Ceiriog. Boulton, Harold, tr. from WEL. 2013. (ENG.). 24p. (J). (gr. -1-2). 12.95 (978-1-927018-09-5(9)) Simply Read Bks. CAN. Dist: Ingram Pub. Services.

Alko, Selina. The God Around Us: A Child's Garden of Prayer. Pollack-Brichto, Mira. rev. ed. 2004. (ENG & HEB.). 32p. (J). (gr. -1-1). 13.95 (978-0-8074-0701-1(1), 101072) URJ Pr.

—The God Around Us Vol. 2: The Valley of Blessings. Brichto, Mira Pollak. 2004. 32p. (gr. -1-3). 13.95 (978-0-8074-0738-7(0), 101074) URJ Pr.

—Good Morning, Boker Tov. Abraham, Michelle Shapiro. 2004. pap. 6.95 (978-0-8074-0783-7(6), 101974) URJ Pr.

—Good Night, Lilah Tov. Abraham, Michelle Shapiro. 2004. pap. 6.95 (978-0-8074-0784-4(4), 101975) URJ Pr.

—My Fathers World. 2006. 36p. (J). 14.99 (978-0-7847-1440-9(1), 04075) Standard Publishing.

—My Subway Ride. Jacobs, Paul DuBois & Swender, Jennifer. ed. 2004. (ENG.). 32p. (J). (gr. 2-3). 15.99 (978-1-58685-357-0(0)) Gibbs Smith, Publisher.

—My Taxi Ride, 1 vol. Jacobs, Paul DuBois & Swender, Jennifer. 2006. (ENG.). 32p. (J). (gr. 2-3). 17.99 (978-1-4236-0073-2(8)) Gibbs Smith, Publisher.

Alko, Selina. B Is for Brooklyn. Alko, Selina. 2012. (ENG.). 40p. (J). (gr. -1-1). 17.99 (978-0-8050-9213-4(7), Holt, Henry & Co. Bks. For Young Readers) Holt, Henry & Co.

Alko, Selina & Qualls, Sean. The Case for Loving: The Fight for Interracial Marriage. Alko, Selina. 2015. (ENG.). 40p. (J). (gr. -1-3). 18.99 (978-0-545-47853-3(7)) Scholastic, Inc.

Allan, Gill. When I Wear My Leopard Hat: Poems for Young Children. Rose, Dilys. 40p. pap. 6.95 (978-1-899827-70-1(6)) Scottish Children's Pr. GBR. Dist: Wilson & Assocs.

Allan, June. Gervelie's Journey. Robinson, Anthony & Young, Annemarie. 2009. (Refugee Diary Ser.). (ENG.). 32p. (J). (gr. 2-7). pap. 7.95 (978-1-84780-004-6(1), Frances Lincoln Children's Bks.) Quarto Publishing Group UK GBR. Dist: Littlehampton Bk Services, Ltd.

—Hamzat's Journey: A Refugee Diary. Robinson, Anthony et al. 2010. (Refugee Diary Ser.). (ENG.). 32p. (J). (gr. 3-7). 17.95 (978-1-84780-030-5(0), Frances Lincoln) Quarto Publishing Group UK GBR. Dist: Hachette Bk. Group.

Allan, Nicholas. The Bump. Kelly, Mij. 2012. (J). (978-1-58925-107-6(5)) Tiger Tales.

Allan, Nicholas. Father Christmas Needs a Wee! Allan, Nicholas. 2009. (ENG.). 32p. (J). (gr. -1-k). pap. 13.99 (978-1-86230-825-1(X), Red Fox) Random House Children's Books GBR. Dist: Independent Pubs. Group.

—More & More Rabbits. Allan, Nicholas. 2007. (ENG.). 32p. (J). (gr. k-2). 9.95 (978-0-09-947758-7(0), Red Fox) Random House Children's Books GBR. Dist: Independent Pubs. Group.

—The Royal Nappy. Allan, Nicholas. 2013. (ENG.). 32p. (J). pap. 10.99 (978-1-78295-025-7(7), Red Fox) Random House Children's Books GBR. Dist: Independent Pubs. Group.

Allanson, Patricia. Parallella's Problem. Allanson, Patricia. 2007. (J). (gr. -1-3). per. 13.99 (978-1-59879-278-2(4)) Lifevest Publishing, Inc.

Allard, Melanie. Bernadette & the Lunch Bunch, 1 vol. Glickman, Susan. 2009. (Lunch Bunch Ser.). (ENG.). 123p. (J). (gr. 1-4). pap. 6.95 (978-1-897187-51-7(3)) Second Story Pr. CAN. Dist: Orca Bk. Pubs. USA.

Allchin, Rosalind. The Frog Princess. Allchin, Rosalind. 2003. (ENG.). 32p. (J). (gr. k-3). pap. 5.95 (978-1-55337-526-5(2)) Kids Can Pr., Ltd. CAN. Dist: Univ. of Toronto Pr.

Allegri, Natasha. Adventure Time - Fionna & Cake. Allegri, Natasha, . 2013. (ENG.). 176p. (J). (gr. 4). pap. 19.99 (978-1-60886-338-9(7)) Boom! Studios.

Allegri, Natasha. Fionna & Cake Mathematical. Allegri, Natasha. 2014. (Adventure Time Ser.: 1). (ENG.). 192p. (J). (gr. 4). 39.99 (978-1-60886-391-4(3)) Boom! Studios.

Allen, A. Richard. Apes A-Go-Go! Milisic, Roman. 2015. (ENG.). 32p. (J). (gr. -1-2). 16.99 (978-0-553-53363-7(0), Knopf Bks. for Young Readers) Random Hse. Children's Bks.

Allen, Cassandra. Inside My Garden. Carriger, Candace. 2011. 46p. (J). pap. 11.95 (978-0-9816047-5-6(7)) Sadie Bks.

Allen, Chris. Booker T. Washington. Dunn, Joeming W. 2008. (Bio-Graphics Ser.). 32p. 28.50 (978-1-60270-177-9(6), Graphic Planet- Nonfiction) ABDO Publishing Co.

—George Washington Carver. Dunn, Joeming W. 2008. (Bio-Graphics Ser.). 32p. 28.50 (978-1-60270-171-7(7), Graphic Planet- Nonfiction) ABDO Publishing Co.

—Henry VIII: Graphic Novel. Shakespeare, William. 2010. (Graphic Shakespeare Set 2 Ser.). 48p. (J). (gr. 5-9). 29.93 (978-1-60270-764-1(2)) ABDO Publishing Co.

—King Lear. Farrens, Brian & Shakespeare, William. 2008. (Graphic Shakespeare Ser.). 48p. (gr. 5-10). 29.93 (978-1-60270-189-2(X), Graphic Planet- Fiction) ABDO Publishing Co.

—Martin Luther King, Jr. Dunn, Joeming W. 2008. (Bio-Graphics Ser.). 32p. 28.50 (978-1-60270-175-5(X), Graphic Planet- Nonfiction) ABDO Publishing Co.

—Othello. Goodwin, Vincent. 2008. (Graphic Shakespeare Ser.). 48p. (gr. 5-10). 29.93 (978-1-60270-192-2(X), Graphic Planet- Fiction) ABDO Publishing Co.

Allen, Dana K. Tales from Poplar Hollow. Deskins, Charlotte H. 2004. 104p. pap. (978-0-9753671-1-7(0)) Shamus B. Publishing.

Allen, Douglas, jt. illus. see Sweet, Darrell.

Allen, Elanna. Eva & Sadie & the Best Classroom Ever! Cohen, Jeff. 2015. (ENG.). 32p. (J). (gr. -1-3). 17.99 (978-0-06-224938-8(X)) HarperCollins Pubs.

—Eva & Sadie & the Worst Haircut EVER! Cohen, Jeff. 2014. (ENG.). 32p. (J). (gr. -1-3). 17.99 (978-0-06-224906-7(1)) HarperCollins Pubs.

—Violet Mackerel's Brilliant Plot. Branford, Anna. 2012. (Violet Mackerel Ser.). (ENG.). 112p. (J). (gr. 1-5). 15.99 (978-1-4424-3585-8(2)); pap. 5.99 (978-1-4424-3586-5(0)) Simon & Schuster Children's Publishing. (Atheneum Bks. for Young Readers).

—Violet Mackerel's Natural Habitat. Branford, Anna. 2013. (Violet Mackerel Ser.). (ENG.). 112p. (J). (gr. 1-5). 15.99 (978-1-4424-3594-0(1)); pap. 5.99 (978-1-4424-3595-7(X)) Simon & Schuster Children's Publishing.

—Violet Mackerel's Outside-the-Box Set: Violet Mackerel's Brilliant Plot; Violet Mackerel's Remarkable Recovery; Violet Mackerel's Natural Habita; Violet Mackerel's Personal Space. Branford, Anna. ed. 2013. (Violet Mackerel Ser.). (ENG.). 464p. (J). (gr. 1-5). pap. 19.99 (978-1-4424-8859-5(X), Atheneum Bks. for Young Readers) Simon & Schuster Children's Publishing.

—Violet Mackerel's Personal Space. Branford, Anna. 2013. (Violet Mackerel Ser.). (ENG.). 128p. (J). (gr. 1-5). 15.99 (978-1-4424-3591-9(7)); pap. 5.99 (978-1-4424-3592-6(5)) Simon & Schuster Children's Publishing. (Atheneum Bks. for Young Readers).

—Violet Mackerel's Possible Friend. Branford, Anna. 2014. (Violet Mackerel Ser.). (ENG.). 128p. (J). (gr. 1-5). 15.99 (978-1-4424-9455-8(7), Atheneum Bks. for Young Readers) Simon & Schuster Children's Publishing.

—Violet Mackerel's Remarkable Recovery. Branford, Anna. 2013. (Violet Mackerel Ser.). (ENG.). 128p. (J). (gr. 1-5). 15.99 (978-1-4424-3588-9(7)); pap. 5.99 (978-1-4424-3589-6(5)) Simon & Schuster Children's Publishing. (Atheneum Bks. for Young Readers).

Allen, Elanna. Itsy Mitsy Runs Away. Allen, Elanna. 2011. (ENG.). 40p. (J). (gr. -1-2). 16.99 (978-1-4424-0671-1(2), Atheneum Bks. for Young Readers) Simon & Schuster Children's Publishing.

Allen, Elizabeth. Be Positive! Meiners, Cheri J. 2013. (Being the Best Me Ser.). (ENG.). 40p. (J). (gr. -1-3). 14.99 (978-1-57542-452-1(5)); pap. 9.99 (978-1-57542-441-5(X)) Free Spirit Publishing, Inc.

—Bounce Back! Meiners, Cheri J. 2014. (Being the Best Me Ser.). (ENG.). 40p. (J). (gr. -1-3). 14.99 *(978-1-57542-457-6(6))* Free Spirit Publishing, Inc.
—Feel Confident! Meiners, Cheri J. 2013. (Being the Best Me Ser.). (ENG.). 40p. (J). (gr. -1-3). 14.99 *(978-1-57542-453-8(3))*; pap. 9.99 *(978-1-57542-442-2(8))* Free Spirit Publishing, Inc.
—Forgive & Let Go! A Book about Forgiveness. Meiners, Cheri J. 2015. (Being the Best Me Ser.). (ENG.). 40p. (J). (gr. -1-3). pap. 9.99 *(978-1-57542-487-3(8))* Free Spirit Publishing, Inc.
—Stand Tall! A Book about Integrity. Meiners, Cheri J. 2015. (Being the Best Me Ser.). (ENG.). 40p. (J). (gr. -1-3). pap. 9.99 *(978-1-57542-486-6(X))* Free Spirit Publishing, Inc.
Allen, Francesca. Creepy-Crawlies. 2005. 10p. (J). 4.99 *(978-0-7945-0856-2(1),* Usborne) EDC Publishing.
—First Picture Fairytales. 2008. (Usborne First Book Ser.). 14p. (J). (gr. -1). bds. 18.99 incl. audio compact disk *(978-0-7945-1832-5(X),* Usborne) EDC Publishing.
—Under the Sea. 2005. 10p. (J). 4.99 *(978-0-7945-0857-9(X),* Usborne) EDC Publishing.
—Vacation. 2006. (Usborne Look & Say Ser.). 10p. (J). (gr. -1-k). bds. 7.99 *(978-0-7945-1315-3(8),* Usborne) EDC Publishing.
Allen, Francesca, jt. illus. see Litchfield, Jo.
Allen, Jessica. Jigsaw Journey: the 50 States. Teitelbaum, Michael. 2014. (Jigsaw Journey Ser.). (ENG.). 48p. (J). (gr. 1). 15.95 *(978-1-60710-950-1(6),* Silver Dolphin Bks.) Baker & Taylor Publishing Group.
Allen, Joe. The Mission: An Angel's Most Important Assignment. Horner, Susan. 2006. pap. 10.99 *(978-1-59317-148-3(X))* Warner Pr. Pubs.
Allen, Jonathan. Hair Scare. Doyle, Malachy. 2005. (ENG.). 24p. (J). lib. bdg. 23.65 *(978-1-59646-724-8(X))* Dingles & Co.
—It's So Unfair! Thomson, Pat. 2007. (ENG.). 32p. (J). (gr. k-2). pap. 10.99 *(978-1-84270-594-0(6))* Andersen Pr. GBR. Dist: Independent Pubs. Group.
Allen, Jonathan. Banana! Allen, Jonathan. 2006. 32p. (J). pap. *(978-1-905417-02-5(0))* Boxer Bks., Ltd.
Allen, Joshua. Marissa Plans a Princess Tea Party. Hordos, Sandra. 2010. 28p. pap. 12.49 *(978-1-4520-2557-5(6))* AuthorHouse.
—Ouse the Mouse. Beverly-Barrier, Essie. 2009. 20p. pap. 12.99 *(978-1-4389-4518-7(3))* AuthorHouse.
Allen, Joy. Abigail Iris: The One & Only. Glatt, Lisa & Greenberg, Suzanne. 2010. (Abigail Iris Ser.). (ENG.). 160p. (J). (gr. 2-5). pap. 6.99 *(978-0-8027-2071-9(4))* Walker & Co.
—The Basketball Mystery, 29 vols., No. 29. Adler, David A. 2010. (Cam Jansen Ser.: 29). (ENG.). 64p. (J). (gr. 2-5). 3.99 *(978-0-14-241671-6(1),* Puffin) Penguin Publishing Group.
—Cam Jansen: The Wedding Cake Mystery, 30 vols. Adler, David A. 2011. (Cam Jansen Ser.: 30). (ENG.). 64p. (J). (gr. 2-5). 3.99 *(978-0-14-241958-8(3),* Puffin) Penguin Publishing Group.
—Cam Jansen & the Basketball Mystery. Adler, David A. 27th ed. 2008. (Cam Jansen Ser.: 27). (ENG.). 64p. (J). (gr. 2-5). 3.99 *(978-0-14-241194-0(9),* Puffin) Penguin Publishing Group.
—Cam Jansen & the Joke House Mystery. Adler, David A. 2014. (Cam Jansen Ser.: 34). (ENG.). 64p. (J). (gr. 2-5). 14.99 *(978-0-670-01262-6(9),* Viking Juvenile) Penguin Publishing Group.
—Cam Jansen & the Millionaire Mystery. Adler, David A. 2013. (Cam Jansen Ser.: 32). (ENG.). 64p. (J). (gr. 2-5). pap. 3.99 *(978-0-14-242747-7(0),* Puffin) Penguin Publishing Group.
—Cam Jansen & the Spaghetti Max Mystery. Adler, David A. (Cam Jansen Ser.: 33). (ENG.). 64p. (J). (gr. 2-5). 2014. pap. 4.99 *(978-0-14-751232-1(8),* Puffin); 2013. 14.99 *(978-0-670-01260-2(2),* Viking Juvenile) Penguin Publishing Group.
—Cam Jansen & the Sports Day Mysteries. Adler, David A. 2009. (Cam Jansen: A Super Special Ser.). 118p. 16.00 *(978-1-60686-431-9(9))* Perfection Learning Corp.
—Cam Jansen & the Sports Day Mysteries: A Super Special. Adler, David A. 2009. (Cam Jansen Ser.). (ENG.). 128p. (J). (gr. 2-5). 5.99 *(978-0-14-241225-1(2),* Puffin) Penguin Publishing Group.
—Cam Jansen & the Summer Camp Mysteries. Adler, David A. 2007. (Cam Jansen Ser.). (ENG.). 128p. (J). (gr. 2-5). 14.99 *(978-0-670-06218-8(9),* Viking Juvenile) Penguin Publishing Group.
—Carrie esta a la Altura. Aber, Linda W. 2006. (Math Matters en Espanol Ser.). 32p. (J). (gr. -1-3). pap. 5.95 *(978-1-57565-161-3(0))* Kane Pr., Inc.
—Fairy Tale Mail. Williams, Rozanne Lanczak. (Learn to Write Ser.). 16p. (J). 2007. pap. 8.99 *(978-1-59198-359-0(2))*; 2006. pap. 3.49 *(978-1-59198-301-9(0),* 6195) Creative Teaching Pr., Inc.
—The Green School Mystery, No. 28. Adler, David A. 2009. (Cam Jansen Ser.: 28). (ENG.). 64p. (J). (gr. 2-5). 3.99 *(978-0-14-241456-9(5),* Puffin) Penguin Publishing Group.
—I Am the Turkey. Spirn, Michele Sobel & Spirn, Michele S. (I Can Read Book 2 Ser.). 48p. (J). (gr. k-3). 2006. (ENG.). pap. 3.99 *(978-0-06-053232-1(7))*; 2004. 15.99 *(978-0-06-053230-7(0))* HarperCollins Pubs.
—I Am the Turkey. Spirn, Michele Sobel. 2004. (I Can Read Book 2 Ser.). 48p. (J). (gr. k-3). 16.89 *(978-0-06-053231-4(9))* HarperCollins Pubs.
—I Am the Turkey. Spirn, Michele Sobel. 2007. (I Can Read Bks.). 48p. (gr. -1-3). 14.00 *(978-0-7569-8055-9(0))* Perfection Learning Corp.
—I Can Listen. Parker, David. 2005. (J). *(978-0-439-79208-0(8))* Scholastic, Inc.
—Mud Pie Annie, 1 vol. Buchanan, Sue et al. 2008. (I Can Read!) Ser.). (ENG.). 32p. (J). (gr. -1-1). pap. 3.99 *(978-0-310-71572-6(5))* Zondervan.
—Muffin Man. Scelsa, Greg. Faulkner, Stacey, ed. 2006. (J). pap. 2.99 *(978-1-59198-321-7(5))* Creative Teaching Pr., Inc.
—The Pet Project. Glatt, Lisa & Greenberg, Suzanne. 2011. (Abigail Iris Ser.). (ENG.). 176p. (J). (gr. 2-4). pap. 6.99 *(978-0-8027-2235-5(0))* Walker & Co.
—Prayers for a Child's Day. Derico, Laura. 2003. 32p. (J). 7.99 *(978-0-7847-1273-3(5),* 04033) Standard Publishing.
—The Summer Camp Mysteries. Adler, David A. 2007. (Cam Jansen Ser.). (ENG.). 128p. (J). (gr. 2-5). 5.99 *(978-0-14-240742-4(9),* Puffin) Penguin Publishing Group.
—Tressa the Musical Princess. Simon, Charnan. 2005. 25p. (J). *(978-1-58987-112-0(X))* Kindermusik International.
—Two Stories, Two Friends. Williams, Rozanne Lanczak. 2006. (Learn to Write Ser.). 16p. (J). (gr. k-2). pap. 3.49 *(978-1-59198-295-1(2),* 6186) Creative Teaching Pr., Inc.
—Two Stories, Two Friends. Williams, Rozanne Lanczak. Maio, Barbara, ed. 2006. (J). per. 8.99 *(978-1-59198-343-9(6))* Creative Teaching Pr., Inc.
—Where Is Jake? Packard, Mary. 2003. (My First Reader Ser.). (ENG.). 32p. (J). 18.50 *(978-0-516-22957-7(5),* Children's Pr.) Scholastic Library Publishing.
Allen, Joy. Princess Party. Allen, Joy. 2009. (ENG.). 32p. (J). (gr. -1-k). 16.99 *(978-0-399-25259-4(2),* Putnam Juvenile) Penguin Publishing Group.
Allen, Judy & Humphries, Tudor. Are You a Bee? Allen, Judy. 2004. (Backyard Bks.). (ENG.). 32p. (J). (gr. k-3). pap. 6.99 *(978-0-7534-5804-4(7),* Kingfisher) Roaring Brook Pr.
Allen, Katherine E. Festival of Light: Deepavali Legends from Around India. 2005. 61p. (J). *(978-81-87111-70-2(4))* Vakils, Feffer & Simons, Ltd.
Allen, Kathy. Grandma & her Amazing Colt, Dripper! Blake, Edna L. & Boatwright, Edith. 2005. 50p. (J). 12.00 *(978-0-9668906-3-1(9))* Blake, Edna.
Allen, Kd & Giraud, Teresa. The Sleepytime Ponies Trick a Trickster. Jordan, Lana. 2004. 32p. (J). 12.95 *(978-0-9710696-1-9(1))* Jordan Publishing, Inc.
Allen Klein, Laurie. Solar System Forecast, 1 vol. Kizer Whitt, Kelly. 2014. (SPA.). 32p. (J). (gr. -1-4). pap. 9.95 ***(978-1-62855-425-0(8))*** Arbordale Publishing.
Allen, Marie. All Aboard with Noah, 1 vol. David, Juliet. 2010. (ENG.). 12p. (J). (gr. -1-k). bds. 11.99 *(978-1-85985-864-6(3),* Candle Bks.) Lion Hudson PLC GBR. Dist: Kregel Pubns.
—At the Aquarium. Suen, Anastasia. 2013. (ENG.). 24p. (gr. -1-1). 25.64 *(978-1-62169-261-4(2))*; pap. 7.95 *(978-1-62169-219-5(1))* Rourke Educational Media.
—Envelopes Everywhere! Suen, Anastasia. 2013. (ENG.). 24p. (gr. -1-1). 25.64 *(978-1-62169-262-1(0))*; pap. 7.95 *(978-1-62169-220-1(5))* Rourke Educational Media.
—The Fossil Hunt. Suen, Anastasia. 2013. (ENG.). 24p. (gr. -1-1). 25.64 *(978-1-62169-265-2(5))*; pap. 7.95 *(978-1-62169-223-2(X))* Rourke Educational Media.
—Get the Prize. Mckenzie, Precious. 2013. (ENG.). 24p. (gr. -1-1). 25.64 *(978-1-62169-256-0(6))*; pap. 7.95 *(978-1-62169-214-0(0))* Rourke Educational Media.
—Hollywood Here We Come! Suen, Anastasia. 2013. (ENG.). 24p. (gr. -1-1). 25.64 *(978-1-62169-264-5(7))*; pap. 7.95 *(978-1-62169-222-5(1))* Rourke Educational Media.
—Instrument Petting Zoo. Suen, Anastasia. 2013. (ENG.). 24p. (gr. -1-1). 25.64 *(978-1-62169-263-8(9))*; pap. 7.95 *(978-1-62169-221-8(3))* Rourke Educational Media.
—Let's Go Aquarium: A Magnetic Storybook. Pennington, Stacey & Pennington, J. C. D. 2008. 6p. (J). (gr. -1-1). bds. 10.99 *(978-2-7641-2184-9(9))* Gardner Pubns.
—Lost in the Corn Maze. Mckenzie, Precious. 2013. (ENG.). 24p. (gr. -1-1). 25.64 *(978-1-62169-257-7(4))*; pap. 7.95 *(978-1-62169-215-7(9))* Rourke Educational Media.
—My First Bedtime Stories. Baxter, Nicola. 2013. (ENG.). 16p. (J). (gr. -1-12). pap. 13.99 *(978-1-84322-685-7(5),* Armadillo) Anness Publishing GBR. Dist: National Bk. Network.
—My First Bible Stories, 1 vol. Williamson, Karen. 2014. (ENG.). 108p. (J). spiral bd. 7.99 *(978-1-85985-994-0(1),* Candle Bks.) Lion Hudson PLC GBR. Dist: Kregel Pubns.
—Off to the Yogurt Factory. Mckenzie, Precious. 2013. (ENG.). 24p. (gr. -1-1). 25.64 *(978-1-62169-258-4(2))*; pap. 7.95 *(978-1-62169-216-4(7))* Rourke Educational Media.
—To London to Visit the Queen. Robertson, J. Jean. 2013. (ENG.). 24p. (gr. -1-1). 25.64 *(978-1-62169-242-3(6))*; pap. 7.95 *(978-1-62169-200-3(0))* Rourke Educational Media.
Allen, Pamela. Brown Bread & Honey. Allen, Pamela. Carthew, Mark. 2007. (Collins Big Cat Ser.). (ENG.). 24p. (J). pap. 7.99 *(978-0-00-722877-5(5))* HarperCollins Pubs. Ltd. GBR. Dist: Independent Pubs. Group.
—Mr. Archimedes' Bath. Allen, Pamela. 2004. 81p. (J). (gr. -1-1). pap. 11.00 *(978-0-207-17285-4(4))* HarperCollins Pubs.
Allen, Peter. Ancient Egypt Jigsaw Book. 2006. (Jigsaw Bks.). 14p. (J). (gr. k-3). bds. 14.99 *(978-0-7945-1236-1(4),* Usborne) EDC Publishing.
—My First Pirate Book. Reid, Struan & Stowell, Louie. ed. 2012. (My First Book Ser.). 16p. (J). ring bd. 6.99 *(978-0-7945-3228-4(4),* Usborne) EDC Publishing.
—Pirate Jigsaw Book. Reid, Struan. 2007. (Luxury Jigsaw Bks.). 14p. (J). bds. 14.99 *(978-0-7945-1432-7(4),* Usborne) EDC Publishing.
—See Inside Space. Daynes, Katie. 2009. (See Inside Board Bks). 16p. (J). (gr. 2). bds. 12.99 *(978-0-7945-2088-5(X),* Usborne) EDC Publishing.
—Story of Astronomy & Space: Internet-Referenced. Stowell, Louie. 2009. (Science Stories Ser.). 104p. (YA). (gr. 3-18). pap. 10.99 *(978-0-7945-2139-4(8),* Usborne) EDC Publishing.
Allen, Rick. Battle Cry. Schultz, Jan Neubert. 2006. (ENG.). 240p. (YA). (gr. 6-12). 15.95 *(978-1-57505-928-0(2),* Carolrhoda Bks.) Lerner Publishing Group.
—Dark Emperor & Other Poems of the Night. Sidman, Joyce. 2010. (ENG.). 32p. (J). (gr. 1-4). 16.99 *(978-0-547-15228-8(0))* Houghton Mifflin Harcourt Publishing Co.
Allen, Russ. Now I Know the 10 Commandments. Allen, Jan. 2005. 32p. (J). (gr. k-5). *(978-0-9765514-0-9(3))* Light Bugs Publishing.
Allen, S. Joan & Graham, Jerry L. The Little Country Girl & Frisky the Squirrel. Graham, Janice C. 2008. 32p. pap. 24.95 *(978-1-60610-312-8(1))* America Star Bks.
Allen, Sandra Hutchins. Rainbows Are the Best. Pimot, Karen Hutchins. 2009. 24p. pap. 12.95 *(978-1-936051-01-4(X))* Peppertree Pr., The.
Allen, Shira. We Can Do Mitzvos from Aleph to Tav. Zoldan, Yael. 2009. 46p. (J). (gr. -1-2). 14.99 *(978-1-59826-395-4(1))* Feldheim Pubs.
Allen, Thomas B. Good-Bye for Today: The Diary of a Young Girl at Sea. Roop, Connie & Roop, Peter. 2008. (ENG.). 48p. (J). (gr. 4-6). 11.99 *(978-1-4169-7573-1(X),* Simon & Schuster/Paula Wiseman Bks.) Simon & Schuster/Paula Wiseman Bks.
—Sewing Quilts. Turner, Ann. 2012. (ENG.). 32p. (J). (gr. k-3). pap. 16.99 *(978-1-4424-6042-3(3),* Simon & Schuster Bks. For Young Readers) Simon & Schuster Bks. For Young Readers.
Allen, Timothy. The Land of Phonicia: An Enchanted Tale to Learn Phonics. McKee, Ruby. l.t. ed. 2003. 52p. (J). per. 39.95 *(978-0-9744944-0-1(2))* Jewel Publishing.
Alley. Father's Day. Heinrichs, Ann. 2013. (Holidays & Celebrations Ser.). (ENG.). 32p. (J). (gr. k-3). 27.07 *(978-1-62323-506-2(5),* 206279) Child's World, Inc., The.
—Mother's Day. Heinrichs, Ann. 2013. (Holidays & Celebrations Ser.). (ENG.). 32p. (J). (gr. k-3). 27.07 *(978-1-62323-510-9(3),* 206284) Child's World, Inc., The.
Alley, Ashleigh & Norona, Bill. My Elephant Likes to Read. Gerstler, J. C. 2013. 30p. pap. 12.00 *(978-1-4349-3548-9(5),* RoseDog Bks.) Dorrance Publishing Co., Inc.
Alley, R., jt. illus. see Alley, R. W.
Alley, R. W. Alexander Anteater's Amazing Act. deRubertis, Barbara & DeRubertis, Barbara. 2012. (Animal Antics A to Z Ser.). 32p. (J). (gr. 2 — 1). cd-rom 7.95 *(978-1-57565-394-5(X))* Kane Pr., Inc.
—Alexander Anteater's Amazing Act. deRubertis, Barbara. 2010. (Animal Antics A to Z Ser.). 32p. (J). (gr. -1-3). pap. 7.95 *(978-1-57565-300-6(1))*; (gr. k-1). lib. bdg. 22.60 *(978-1-57565-304-4(4))* Kane Pr., Inc.
—Be the Star That You Are: A Book for Kids Who Feel Different. O'Keefe, Susan Heyboer. 2005. (Elf-Help Books for Kids). (J). per. 7.95 *(978-0-87029-391-7(5))* Abbey Pr.
—Because Your Daddy Loves You. Clements, Andrew. 2009. (ENG.). 32p. (J). (gr. -1-3). pap. 6.99 *(978-0-547-23764-0(2))* Houghton Mifflin Harcourt Publishing Co.
—Because Your Grandparents Love You. Clements, Andrew. 2015. (ENG.). 32p. (J). (gr. -1-3). 16.99 *(978-0-544-14854-3(1))* Houghton Mifflin Harcourt Publishing Co.
—Because Your Mommy Loves You. Clements, Andrew. 2012. (ENG.). 32p. (J). (gr. -1-3). 16.99 *(978-0-547-25522-4(5))* Houghton Mifflin Harcourt Publishing Co.
—Being Teddy Roosevelt. Mills, Claudia. 2007. (ENG.). 96p. (J). (gr. 2-5). 16.99 *(978-0-374-30657-1(5),* Farrar, Straus & Giroux (BYR)) Farrar, Straus & Giroux.
—Being Teddy Roosevelt. Mills, Claudia. 2012. (ENG.). 112p. (J). (gr. 2-5). pap. 6.99 *(978-0-312-64018-7(8))* Square Fish.
—Bobby Baboon's Banana Be-Bop. deRubertis, Barbara & DeRubertis, Barbara. 2012. (Animal Antics A to Z Ser.). 32p. (J). (gr. 2 — 1). cd-rom 7.95 *(978-1-57565-395-2(8))* Kane Pr., Inc.
—Bobby Baboon's Banana Be-Bop. deRubertis, Barbara. 2010. (Animal Antics A to Z Ser.). 32p. (J). lib. bdg. 22.60 *(978-1-57565-305-1(2))*; (gr. -1-3). pap. 7.95 *(978-1-57565-301-3(X))* Kane Pr., Inc.
—A Book of Prayers for All Your Cares. Mundy, Michaelene. 2004. (J). per. 7.95 *(978-0-87029-382-5(6))* Abbey Pr.
—Bratty Brothers & Selfish Sisters: All about Sibling Rivalry. 2007. (Elf-Help Books for Kids Ser.). 28p. (J). (gr. -1-3). per. 7.95 *(978-0-87029-404-4(0))* Abbey Pr.
—Corky Cub's Crazy Caps. deRubertis, Barbara & DeRubertis, Barbara. 2012. (Animal Antics A to Z Ser.). 32p. (J). (gr. 2 — 1). cd-rom 7.95 *(978-1-57565-396-9(6))* Kane Pr., Inc.
—Corky Cub's Crazy Caps. deRubertis, Barbara. 2010. (Animal Antics A to Z Ser.). 32p. (J). lib. bdg. 22.60 *(978-1-57565-306-8(0))*; (gr. -1-3). pap. 7.95 *(978-1-57565-302-0(8))* Kane Pr., Inc.
—Dear Santa: The Letters of James B. Dobbins. Harley, Bill. 2005. 32p. (J). (ENG.). 15.99 *(978-0-06-623778-7(5))*; lib. bdg. 16.89 *(978-0-06-623779-4(3))* HarperCollins Pubs.
—Detective Dinosaur Undercover. Skofield, James. 2010. (I Can Read Book 2 Ser.). (ENG.). 48p. (J). (gr. -1-3). 16.99 *(978-0-06-623878-4(1))*; pap. 3.99 *(978-0-06-444319-7(1))* HarperCollins Pubs.
—Dilly Dog's Dizzy Dancing. deRubertis, Barbara & DeRubertis, Barbara. 2012. (Animal Antics A to Z Ser.). 32p. (J). (gr. 2 — 1). cd-rom 7.95 *(978-1-57565-397-6(4))* Kane Pr., Inc.
—Dilly Dog's Dizzy Dancing. deRubertis, Barbara. 2010. (Animal Antics A to Z Ser.). 32p. (J). lib. bdg. 22.60 *(978-1-57565-307-5(9))*; (gr. -1-3). pap. 7.95 *(978-1-57565-303-7(6))* Kane Pr., Inc.
—Eddie Elephant's Exciting Egg-Sitting. deRubertis, Barbara & DeRubertis, Barbara. 2012. (Animal Antics A to Z Ser.). 32p. (J). (gr. 2 — 1). cd-rom 7.95 *(978-1-57565-398-3(2))* Kane Pr., Inc.
—Eddie Elephant's Exciting Egg-Sitting. deRubertis, Barbara. 2010. (Animal Antics A to Z Ser.). 32p. (J). (gr. -1-3). pap. 7.95 *(978-1-57565-309-9(5))*; lib. bdg. 22.60 *(978-1-57565-316-7(8))* Kane Pr., Inc.
—Enzo - Races in the Rain! Stein, Garth. 2014. (ENG.). 40p. (J). (gr. -1-3). 17.99 *(978-0-06-229533-0(0))* HarperCollins Pubs.
Alley, R. W. Enzo & the Christmas Tree Hunt! Stein, Garth. 2015. (ENG.). 40p. (J). (gr. -1-3). 17.99 ***(978-0-06-229532-3(2))*** HarperCollins Pubs.
Alley, R. W. Five Days till Summer. McMullan, Kate. 2014. (Pearl & Wagner Ser.: 5). (ENG.). 48p. (J). (gr. 1-3). pap. 3.99 *(978-0-448-48137-1(5),* Warne, Frederick Pubs.) Penguin Bks., Ltd. GBR. Dist: Penguin Random Hse., LLC.
—Five Days till Summer. McMullan, Kate. 2012. (Pearl & Wagner Ser.: 5). (ENG.). 40p. (J). (gr. 1-3). 14.99 *(978-0-8037-3589-7(8),* Dial) Penguin Publishing Group.
—Forgiveness Is Smart for the Heart. Morrow, Carol. 2003. (Elf-Help Books for Kids). 32p. (J). per. 6.95 *(978-0-87029-370-2(2))* Abbey Pr.
—Four Eyes. McMullan, Kate. 2013. (Pearl & Wagner Ser.: 4). (ENG.). 48p. (J). (gr. 1-3). pap. 3.99 *(978-0-448-47781-7(5),* Warne, Frederick Pubs.) Penguin Bks., Ltd. GBR. Dist: Penguin Random Hse., LLC.
—Frances Frog's Forever Friend. deRubertis, Barbara & DeRubertis, Barbara. 2012. (Animal Antics A to Z Ser.). 32p. (J). (gr. 2 — 1). cd-rom 7.95 *(978-1-57565-399-0(0))* Kane Pr., Inc.
—Frances Frog's Forever Friend. deRubertis, Barbara. 2010. (Animal Antics A to Z Ser.). 32p. (J). (gr. -1-3). pap. 7.95 *(978-1-57565-310-5(9))*; lib. bdg. 22.60 *(978-1-57565-317-4(6))* Kane Pr., Inc.
—The Genie in the Book. Trumbore, Cindy. 2004. (ENG.). 120p. (J). (gr. -1-7). 15.95 *(978-1-59354-042-5(6),* Handprint Bks.) Chronicle Bks. LLC.
—Gertie Gorilla's Glorious Gift. deRubertis, Barbara & DeRubertis, Barbara. 2012. (Animal Antics A to Z Ser.). 32p. (J). (gr. 2 — 1). cd-rom 7.95 *(978-1-57565-400-3(8))* Kane Pr., Inc.
—Gertie Gorilla's Glorious Gift. deRubertis, Barbara. 2010. (Animal Antics A to Z Ser.). 32p. (J). (gr. -1-3). pap. 7.95 *(978-1-57565-311-2(7))*; lib. bdg. 22.60 *(978-1-57565-318-1(4))* Kane Pr., Inc.
—Halloween Surprise. Demas, Corinne. 2011. (ENG.). 32p. (J). (gr. -1-1). 12.99 *(978-0-8027-8612-8(X))* Walker & Co.
—Hanna Hippo's Horrible Hiccups. deRubertis, Barbara & DeRubertis, Barbara. 2012. (Animal Antics A to Z Ser.). 32p. (J). (gr. 2 — 1). cd-rom 7.95 *(978-1-57565-401-0(6))* Kane Pr., Inc.
—Hanna Hippo's Horrible Hiccups. deRubertis, Barbara. 2010. (Animal Antics A to Z Ser.). 32p. (J). (gr. -1-3). pap. 7.95 *(978-1-57565-312-9(5))*; lib. bdg. 22.60 *(978-1-57565-319-8(2))* Kane Pr., Inc.
—I Don't Want to Go to Church: Turning the Struggle into a Celebration. Falkenhain, John Mark. 2009. (J). pap. 7.95 *(978-0-87029-423-5(7))* Abbey Pr.
—It's Great to Be Grateful! A Kid's Guide to Being Thankful. Mundy, Michaelene. 2012. 32p. (J). pap. 7.95 *(978-0-87029-512-6(8))* Abbey Pr.
—Izzy Impala's Imaginary Illnesses. deRubertis, Barbara & DeRubertis, Barbara. 2012. (Animal Antics A to Z Ser.). 32p. (J). (gr. 2 — 1). cd-rom 7.95 *(978-1-57565-402-7(4))* Kane Pr., Inc.
—Izzy Impala's Imaginary Illnesses. deRubertis, Barbara. 2010. (Animal Antics A to Z Ser.). 32p. (J). (gr. -1-3). pap. 7.95 *(978-1-57565-313-6(3))*; lib. bdg. 22.60 *(978-1-57565-320-4(6))* Kane Pr., Inc.
—Jeremy Jackrabbit's Jumping Journey. deRubertis, Barbara & DeRubertis, Barbara. 2012. (Animal Antics A to Z Ser.). 32p. (J). (gr. 2 — 1). cd-rom 7.95 *(978-1-57565-403-4(2))* Kane Pr., Inc.
—Jeremy Jackrabbit's Jumping Journey. deRubertis, Barbara. 2010. (Animal Antics A to Z Ser.). 32p. (J). (gr. -1-3). pap. 7.95 *(978-1-57565-314-3(1))*; lib. bdg. 22.60 *(978-1-57565-321-1(4))* Kane Pr., Inc.
—Keeping Family First: A Kid's Guide. Jackson, J. S. 2004. (J). per. 7.95 *(978-0-87029-390-0(7))* Abbey Pr.
—Kylie Kangaroo's Karate Kickers. deRubertis, Barbara & DeRubertis, Barbara. 2012. (Animal Antics A to Z Ser.). 32p. (J). (gr. 2 — 1). cd-rom 7.95 *(978-1-57565-404-1(0))* Kane Pr., Inc.
—Kylie Kangaroo's Karate Kickers. deRubertis, Barbara. 2011. (Animal Antics A to Z Ser.). 32p. (J). pap. 45.32 *(978-0-7613-7657-6(7))*; (ENG.). lib. bdg. 22.60 *(978-1-57565-332-7(X))*; (gr. -1-3). pap. 7.95 *(978-1-57565-323-5(0))* Kane Pr., Inc.
—Lana Llama's Little Lamb. deRubertis, Barbara & DeRubertis, Barbara. 2012. (Animal Antics A to Z Ser.). 32p. (J). (gr. 2 — 1). cd-rom 7.95 *(978-1-57565-405-8(9))* Kane Pr., Inc.
—Lana Llama's Little Lamb. deRubertis, Barbara. 2011. (Animal Antics A to Z Ser.). 32p. (J). pap. 45.32 *(978-0-7613-7658-3(5))*; (ENG.). lib. bdg. 22.60 *(978-1-57565-333-4(8))*; (gr. -1-3). pap. 7.95 *(978-1-57565-324-2(9))* Kane Pr., Inc.
—Learning to Be a Good Friend: A Guidebook for Kids. Adams, Christine. 2004. 32p. (J). per. 7.95 *(978-0-87029-388-7(5))* Abbey Pr.
—Making Christmas Count! A Kid's Guide to Keeping the Season Sacred. 2006. (Elf-Help Books for Kids Ser.). (AFA.). 32p. (J). (gr. -1-3). per. 7.95 *(978-0-87029-401-3(6))* Abbey Pr.
—Maxwell Moose's Mountain Monster. deRubertis, Barbara & DeRubertis, Barbara. 2012. (Animal Antics A to Z Ser.). 32p. (J). (gr. 2 — 1). cd-rom 7.95 *(978-1-57565-406-5(7))* Kane Pr., Inc.
—Maxwell Moose's Mountain Monster. deRubertis, Barbara. 2011. (Animal Antics A to Z Ser.). 32p. (J). pap. 45.32 *(978-0-7613-7659-0(3))*; (ENG.). lib. bdg. 22.60 *(978-1-57565-334-1(6))*; (gr. -1-3). pap. 7.95 *(978-1-57565-325-9(7))* Kane Pr., Inc.
—Nina Nandu's Nervous Noggin. deRubertis, Barbara & DeRubertis, Barbara. 2012. (Animal Antics A to Z Ser.). 32p. (J). (gr. 2 — 1). cd-rom 7.95 *(978-1-57565-407-2(5))* Kane Pr., Inc.
—Nina Nandu's Nervous Noggin. deRubertis, Barbara. 2011. (Animal Antics A to Z Ser.). 32p. (J). pap. 45.32 *(978-0-7613-7660-6(7))*; (ENG.). lib. bdg. 22.60 *(978-1-57565-335-8(4))*; (gr. -1-3). pap. 7.95 *(978-1-57565-326-6(5))* Kane Pr., Inc.
—Oliver Otter's Own Office. deRubertis, Barbara & DeRubertis, Barbara. 2012. (Animal Antics A to Z Ser.). 32p. (J). (gr. 2 — 1). cd-rom 7.95 *(978-1-57565-408-9(3))* Kane Pr., Inc.

—Oliver Otter's Own Office. deRubertis, Barbara. 2011. (Animal Antics A to Z Ser.). 32p. (J). pap. 45.32 *(978-0-7613-7661-3(5))*; lib. bdg. 22.60 *(978-1-57565-336-5(2))*; (gr. -1-3). pap. 7.95 *(978-1-57565-327-3(3))* Kane Pr., Inc.

—One Funny Day. McMullan, Kate. 2012. (Pearl & Wagner Ser.: 1). (ENG.). 48p. (J). (gr. 1-3). pap. 3.99 *(978-0-448-45866-3(7)*, Warne, Frederick Pubs.) Penguin Bks., Ltd. GBR. Dist: Penguin Random Hse., LLC.

—One Funny Day. McMullan, Kate. 2009. (Pearl & Wagner Ser.: 1). (ENG.). 40p. (J). (gr. k-3). 14.99 *(978-0-8037-3085-4(3)*, Dial) Penguin Publishing Group.

—Paddington. Bond, Michael. (Paddington Ser.). (ENG.). 32p. (J). (gr. -1-3). 2014. 17.99 *(978-0-06-231719-3(9))*; 2007. 17.99 *(978-0-06-117074-4(7))* HarperCollins Pubs.

—Paddington & the Christmas Surprise. Bond, Michael. 2008. (Paddington Ser.). (ENG.). 32p. (J). (gr. -1-3). 16.99 *(978-0-06-168740-2(5))* HarperCollins Pubs.

—Paddington at the Beach. Bond, Michael. (Paddington Ser.). 32p. (J). (gr. -1-3). 2015. 17.99 *(978-0-06-231720-9(2))*; 2009. 17.99 *(978-0-06-168767-9(7))* HarperCollins Pubs.

—Paddington Bear All Day. Bond, Michael. 2004. 12p. (J). *(978-1-85269-442-5(4))*; *(978-1-85269-443-2(2))*; *(978-1-85269-444-9(0))*; *(978-1-85269-445-6(9))*; *(978-1-85269-456-2(4))* Mantra Lingua.

—Paddington Bear All Day Board Book. Bond, Michael. 2014. (Paddington Ser.). (ENG.). 14p. (J). (gr. -1-3). bds. 6.99 *(978-0-06-231721-6(0)*, HarperFestival) HarperCollins Pubs.

—Paddington Bear Goes to Market. Bond, Michael. 2004. 12p. (J). *(978-1-85269-451-7(3))*; *(978-1-85269-455-5(6))* Mantra Lingua.

—Paddington Bear Goes to Market Board Book. Bond, Michael. 2014. (Paddington Ser.). (ENG.). 14p. (J). (gr. -1-3). bds. 6.99 *(978-0-06-231722-3(9)*, HarperFestival) HarperCollins Pubs.

—Paddington Here & Now. Bond, Michael. 176p. (J). 2009. pap. 5.99 *(978-0-06-147366-1(9))*; 2008. (ENG.). (gr. 3-7). 15.99 *(978-0-06-147364-7(2))* HarperCollins Pubs.

—Paddington in the Garden. Bond, Michael. 2015. (Paddington Ser.). (ENG.). 32p. (J). (gr. -1-3). 17.99 *(978-0-06-231844-2(6))* HarperCollins Pubs.

—The Paddington Treasury. Bond, Michael. 2014. (Paddington Ser.). (ENG.). 160p. (J). (gr. -1-3). 21.99 *(978-0-06-231242-6(1))* HarperCollins Pubs.

—Peanut & Pearl's Picnic Adventure. Dotlich, Rebecca Kai. 2008. (My First I Can Read Ser.). (ENG.). 32p. (J). (gr. -1 — 1). pap. 3.99 *(978-0-06-054922-0(X))* HarperCollins Pubs.

—Pearl & Wagner: Two Good Friends. McMullan, Kate. 2011. (Pearl & Wagner Ser.: 2). (ENG.). 48p. (J). (gr. 1-3). pap. 3.99 *(978-0-448-45690-4(7)*, Warne, Frederick Pubs.) Penguin Bks., Ltd. GBR. Dist: Penguin Random Hse., LLC.

—Playing Fair, Having Fun: A Kid's Guide to Sports & Games. Grippo, Daniel. 2004. 32p. (J). per. 7.95 *(978-0-87029-384-9(2))* Abbey Pr.

—Police Officers on Patrol. Hamilton, Kersten. 2009. (ENG.). 32p. (J). (gr. -1-k). 15.99 *(978-0-670-06315-4(0)*, Viking Juvenile) Penguin Publishing Group.

—Polly Porcupine's Painting Prize. deRubertis, Barbara. 2011. (Animal Antics A to Z Ser.). 32p. (J). pap. 45.32 *(978-0-7613-7662-0(3))*; lib. bdg. 22.60 *(978-1-57565-337-2(0))*; (gr. -1-3). pap. 7.95 *(978-1-57565-328-0(1))* Kane Pr., Inc.

—Polly Porcupine's Painting Prizes. deRubertis, Barbara & DeRubertis, Barbara. 2012. (Animal Antics A to Z Ser.). 32p. (J). (gr. 2 — 1). cd-rom 7.95 *(978-1-57565-409-6(1))* Kane Pr., Inc.

—The Prince's Tooth Is Loose! 2005. (I'm Going to Read(r) Ser.). (ENG.). 28p. (J). (gr. -1-k). pap. 3.95 *(978-1-4027-2721-4(6))* Sterling Publishing Co., Inc.

—Quentin Quokka's Quick Questions. deRubertis, Barbara & DeRubertis, Barbara. 2012. (Animal Antics A to Z Ser.). 32p. (J). (gr. 2 — 1). cd-rom 7.95 *(978-1-57565-410-2(5))* Kane Pr., Inc.

—Quentin Quokka's Quick Questions. deRubertis, Barbara. 2011. (Animal Antics A to Z Ser.). 32p. (J). pap. 45.32 *(978-0-7613-7663-7(1))*; lib. bdg. 22.60 *(978-1-57565-338-9(9))*; (gr. -1-3). pap. 7.95 *(978-1-57565-329-7(X))* Kane Pr., Inc.

—Rosie Raccoon's Rock & Roll Raft. deRubertis, Barbara & DeRubertis, Barbara. 2012. (Animal Antics A to Z Ser.). 32p. (J). (gr. 2 — 1). cd-rom 7.95 *(978-1-57565-411-9(3))* Kane Pr., Inc.

—Rosie Raccoon's Rock & Roll Raft. deRubertis, Barbara. 2011. (Animal Antics A to Z Ser.). 32p. (J). pap. 45.32 *(978-0-7613-7664-4(X))*; lib. bdg. 22.60 *(978-1-57565-339-6(7))*; (gr. -1-3). pap. 7.95 *(978-1-57565-330-3(3))* Kane Pr., Inc.

—Sammy Skunk's Super Sniffer. Derubertis, Barbara. 2011. (Animal Antics A to Z Set III Ser.). pap. 45.32 *(978-0-7613-8428-1(6))* Kane Pr., Inc.

—Sammy Skunk's Super Sniffer. deRubertis, Barbara & DeRubertis, Barbara. 2012. (Animal Antics A to Z Ser.). 32p. (J). (gr. 2 — 1). cd-rom 7.95 *(978-1-57565-412-6(1))* Kane Pr., Inc.

—Sammy Skunk's Super Sniffer. deRubertis, Barbara. 2011. (Animal Antics A to Z Ser.). pap. 7.95 *(978-1-57565-344-0(3))*; lib. bdg. 22.60 *(978-1-57565-352-5(4))* Kane Pr., Inc.

—Saturday Is Dadurday. Pulver, Robin. 2013. (ENG.). (J). (gr. -1-3). 40p. 17.89 *(978-0-8027-8609-8(X))*; 32p. 16.99 *(978-0-8027-8691-3(X))* Walker & Co.

—Saying Good-Bye, Saying Hello... When Your Family Is Moving. Mundy, Michaelene. 2005. (Elf-Help Books for Kids). 32p. (J). (gr. -1-3). per. 7.95 *(978-0-87029-393-1(1))* Abbey Pr.

—Standing up to Peer Pressure: A Guide to Being True to You. Auer, Jim. 2003. 32p. (J). per. 7.95 *(978-0-87029-375-7(3))* Abbey Pr.

—Tessa Tiger's Temper Tantrums. Derubertis, Barbara. 2011. (Animal Antics A to Z Set III Ser.). pap. 45.32 *(978-0-7613-8429-8(4))* Kane Pr., Inc.

—Tessa Tiger's Temper Tantrums. deRubertis, Barbara & DeRubertis, Barbara. 2012. (Animal Antics A to Z Ser.). 32p. (J). (gr. 2 — 1). cd-rom 7.95 *(978-1-57565-413-3(X))* Kane Pr., Inc.

—Tessa Tiger's Temper Tantrums. deRubertis, Barbara. 2011. (Animal Antics A to Z Ser.). 32p. (J). pap. 7.95 *(978-1-57565-345-7(1))*; lib. bdg. 22.60 *(978-1-57565-353-2(2))* Kane Pr., Inc.

—Three Secrets. McMullan, Kate. 2013. (Pearl & Wagner Ser.: 3). (ENG.). 48p. (J). (gr. 1-3). pap. 3.99 *(978-0-448-46472-5(1)*, Warne, Frederick Pubs.) Penguin Bks., Ltd. GBR. Dist: Penguin Random Hse., LLC.

—The Treasure of Dead Man's Lane & Other Case Files: Saxby Smart, Private Detective: Book 2. Cheshire, Simon. 2011. (Saxby Smart, Private Detective Ser.: 2). (ENG.). 224p. (J). (gr. 3-7). pap. 8.99 *(978-0-312-67434-2(1))* Square Fish.

—Umma Ungka's Unusual Umbrella. Derubertis, Barbara. 2011. (Animal Antics A to Z Set III Ser.). pap. 45.32 *(978-0-7613-8430-4(8))* Kane Pr., Inc.

—Umma Ungka's Unusual Umbrella. deRubertis, Barbara & DeRubertis, Barbara. 2012. (Animal Antics A to Z Ser.). 32p. (J). (gr. 2 — 1). cd-rom 7.95 *(978-1-57565-414-0(8))* Kane Pr., Inc.

—Umma Ungka's Unusual Umbrella. deRubertis, Barbara. 2011. (Animal Antics A to Z Ser.). pap. 7.95 *(978-1-57565-346-4(X))*; lib. bdg. 22.60 *(978-1-57565-354-9(0))* Kane Pr., Inc.

—Valentine Surprise. Demas, Corinne. 2009. (ENG.). 34p. (J). (gr. -1-1). pap. 6.99 *(978-0-8027-2076-4(5))* Walker & Co.

—Victor Vicuna's Volcano Vacation. Derubertis, Barbara. 2011. (Animal Antics A to Z Set III Ser.). pap. 45.32 *(978-0-7613-8431-1(6))* Kane Pr., Inc.

—Victor Vicuna's Volcano Vacation. deRubertis, Barbara & DeRubertis, Barbara. 2012. (Animal Antics A to Z Ser.). 32p. (J). (gr. 2 — 1). cd-rom 7.95 *(978-1-57565-415-7(6))* Kane Pr., Inc.

—Victor Vicuna's Volcano Vacation. deRubertis, Barbara. 2011. (Animal Antics A to Z Ser.). 32p. (J). pap. 7.95 *(978-1-57565-347-1(8))*; lib. bdg. 22.60 *(978-1-57565-355-6(9))* Kane Pr., Inc.

—Walter Warthog's Wonderful Wagon. Derubertis, Barbara. 2011. (Animal Antics A to Z Set III Ser.). pap. 45.32 *(978-0-7613-8432-8(4))* Kane Pr., Inc.

—Walter Warthog's Wonderful Wagon. deRubertis, Barbara & DeRubertis, Barbara. 2012. (Animal Antics A to Z Ser.). 32p. (J). (gr. 2 — 1). cd-rom 7.95 *(978-1-57565-416-4(4))* Kane Pr., Inc.

—Walter Warthog's Wonderful Wagon. deRubertis, Barbara. 2011. (Animal Antics A to Z Ser.). 32p. (J). pap. 7.95 *(978-1-57565-348-8(6))*; lib. bdg. 22.60 *(978-1-57565-356-3(7))* Kane Pr., Inc.

—We're off to Find the Witch's House. Krieb & Krieb. 2007. (ENG.). 32p. (J). (gr. -1-2). 5.99 *(978-0-14-240854-4(9)*, Puffin) Penguin Publishing Group.

—What Does Sam Sell? Rothman, Cynthia Anne. l.t. ed. 2005. (Sadlier Phonics Reading Program). 8p. (gr. -1-1). 23.00 net. *(978-0-8215-7342-6(X))* Sadlier, William H. Inc.

—When Bad Things Happen: A Guide to Help Kids Cope. O'Neal, Ted. 2003. (Elf-Help Books for Kids). 32p. (J). per. 7.95 *(978-0-87029-371-9(0)*, 20071) Abbey Pr.

—When Dads Don't Grow Up. Parker, Marjorie Blain. 2012. (ENG.). 32p. (J). (gr. -1-k). 16.99 *(978-0-8037-3717-4(3)*, Dial) Penguin Publishing Group.

—When Mom or Dad Dies: A Book of Comfort for Kids. Grippo, Daniel. 2008. (J). pap. 7.95 *(978-0-87029-415-0(6))* Abbey Pr.

—When Someone You Love Has Cancer: A Guide to Help Kids Cope. Lewis, Alaric. 2005. (Elf-Help Books for Kids Ser.). 32p. per. 7.95 *(978-0-87029-395-5(8))* Abbey Pr.

—Worry, Worry Go Away. Adams, Christine A. 2012. 32p. (J). pap. 7.95 *(978-0-87029-471-6(7))* Abbey Pr.

—Xavier Ox's Xylophone Experiment. Derubertis, Barbara. 2011. (Animal Antics A to Z Set III Ser.). pap. 45.32 *(978-0-7613-8433-5(2))* Kane Pr., Inc.

—Xavier Ox's Xylophone Experiment. deRubertis, Barbara & DeRubertis, Barbara. 2012. (Animal Antics A to Z Ser.). 32p. (J). (gr. 2 — 1). cd-rom 7.95 *(978-1-57565-417-1(2))* Kane Pr., Inc.

—Xavier Ox's Xylophone Experiment. deRubertis, Barbara. 2011. (Animal Antics A to Z Ser.). 32p. (J). pap. 7.95 *(978-1-57565-349-5(4))*; lib. bdg. 22.60 *(978-1-57565-357-0(5))* Kane Pr., Inc.

—Yoko Yak's Yakety Yakking. deRubertis, Barbara & DeRubertis, Barbara. 2012. (Animal Antics A to Z Ser.). 32p. (J). (gr. 2 — 1). cd-rom 7.95 *(978-1-57565-418-8(0))* Kane Pr., Inc.

—Yoko Yak's Yakety Yakking. deRubertis, Barbara. 2011. (Animal Antics A to Z Ser.). pap. 7.95 *(978-1-57565-350-1(8))*; lib. bdg. 22.60 *(978-1-57565-358-7(3))* Kane Pr., Inc.

—Zachary Zebra's Zippity Zooming. Derubertis, Barbara. 2011. (Animal Antics A to Z Set III Ser.). pap. 45.32 *(978-0-7613-8435-9(9))* Kane Pr., Inc.

—Zachary Zebra's Zippity Zooming. deRubertis, Barbara & DeRubertis, Barbara. 2012. (Animal Antics A to Z Ser.). 32p. (J). (gr. 2 — 1). cd-rom 7.95 *(978-1-57565-419-5(9))* Kane Pr., Inc.

—Zachary Zebra's Zippity Zooming. deRubertis, Barbara. 2011. (Animal Antics A to Z Ser.). 32p. (J). pap. 7.95 *(978-1-57565-351-8(6))*; lib. bdg. 22.60 *(978-1-57565-359-4(1))* Kane Pr., Inc.

Alley, R. W. Because Your Daddy Loves You. Alley, R. W., tr. Clements, Andrew. 2005. (ENG.). 32p. (J). (gr. -1-3). 16.99 *(978-0-618-00361-7(4))* Houghton Mifflin Harcourt Publishing Co.

—Bye-Bye, Bully: A Kid's Guide for Dealing with Bullies. Alley, R. W., tr. Jackson, J. S. 2003. (J). per. 6.95 *(978-0-87029-369-6(9))* Abbey Pr.

Alley, R. W. & Alley, R. There's a Wolf at the Door. Alley, Zoe. 2008. (ENG.). 40p. (J). (gr. -1-3). 21.99 *(978-1-59643-275-8(6))* Roaring Brook Pr.

Alley, R. W., jt. illus. see Alley, Zoë B.

Alley, R. W., jt. illus. see Fortnum, Peggy.

Alley, R. W., jt. illus. see Ryan, Victoria.

Alley, R. W., jt. illus. see Smith, Jamie.

Alley, Zoë B. & Alley, R. W. There's a Princess in the Palace. 2010. (ENG.). 40p. (J). (gr. -1-3). 19.99 *(978-1-59643-471-4(6))* Roaring Brook Pr.

Allibone, Judith & Benson, Patrick. It's a Dog's Life. Morpurgo, Michael. 2010. 32p. (J). *(978-1-4052-1336-3(1))* Egmont Bks., Ltd.

—It's a Dog's Life. Morpurgo, Michael. 2011. (ENG.). 32p. (J). (gr. -1-2). pap. 10.99 *(978-1-4052-1337-0(X))* Egmont Bks., Ltd. GBR. Dist: Independent Pubs. Group.

Allie, Beverly. The American Schoolhouse Reader: A Colorized Children's Reading Collection from Post-Victorian America 1890-1925. Allie, Beverly, ed. 2005. (American Schoolhouse Reader Ser.). 151p. 12.95 *(978-0-9747615-3-4(2))* 45th Parallel Concepts Ltd.

—The American Schoolhouse Reader, Book II: A Colorized Children's Reading Collection from Post-Victorian America 1890-1925. Allie, Beverly, ed. 2005. (American Schoolhouse Reader Ser.). 151p. 12.95 *(978-0-9747615-2-7(4))* 45th Parallel Concepts Ltd.

Allie, Beverly & Allie, Beverly. The American Schoolhouse Reader: A Colorized Children's Reading Collection from Post-Victorian America 1890-1925. Allie, Beverly, ed. 2005. (American Schoolhouse Reader Ser.). 76p. 10.95 *(978-0-9747615-1-0(6))* 45th Parallel Concepts Ltd.

Allie, Beverly, jt. illus. see Allie, Beverly.

Alliger, Richard. Classic Literature for Teens: Every Teachers Friend Classroom Plays. Jordan, Pat. 2007. 118p. pap. 25.00 *(978-0-88734-692-7(8))* Players Pr., Inc.

—Mini-Myths for Pre-Teens & Teens Vol. 2: Every Teacher's Friend Classroom Plays. Jordan, Pat. 2008. (Every Teacher's Friend Classroom Plays Ser.: Vol. 2). 122p. pap. 25.00 *(978-0-88734-964-5(1))* Players Pr., Inc.

—Plays from Around the World: Every Teacher's Friend Classroom Plays. Jordan, Pat. 2010. (ENG.). 128p. (J). spiral bd. 25.00 *(978-0-88734-975-1(7))* Players Pr., Inc.

Allingham, Andrew. Offbeat. Ainsworth, Marlane. 2006. 128p. (Orig.). (J). pap. 13.50 *(978-1-920731-65-6(2))* Fremantle Pr. AUS. Dist: Independent Pubs. Group.

Allirol, Melusine. My Football - Buggy Buddies. ed. 2014. (ENG.). 8p. (J). (-k). bds. 7.99 *(978-1-4472-6599-3(8))* Pan Macmillan GBR. Dist: Independent Pubs. Group.

Allison, Charles T. Bobble Stories: The Bobbleup Pup. Allison, Teresa J. 2013. 42p. pap. 12.99 *(978-0-9887612-2-3(X))* Tawnsy Publishing.

—Bobble Stories: The Humbobble's Lost Hum. Allison, Teresa J. 2013. 48p. pap. 12.99 *(978-0-9887612-1-6(1))* Tawnsy Publishing.

—Bobble Stories: The Oddbobble's Visit. Allison, Teresa J. 2013. 48p. pap. 12.99 *(978-0-9887612-0-9(3))* Tawnsy Publishing.

Allison, Ralph. Where Did They Go? Allison, Ray. 2013. 36p. pap. 14.95 *(978-1-61493-191-1(7))* Peppertree Pr., The.

Allen, Katherine. Gloves down Under. Allen, Katherine. 2005. 32p. (J). 15.95 *(978-0-9747278-9-9(X))* Diakonia Publishing.

Allman, Cynthia. Olden Days of Medina: A Children's Guide to Medina History. Lucht, Susan & Wilson, Mollie. 2013. iii, 30p. (J). pap. *(978-0-578-10958-9(1))* U. S. ISBN Agency.

Allman, Howard, photos by. Children's Book of Baking. Patchett, Fiona et al. 2007. (Children's Cooking Ser.). (ENG., 96p. (J). 17.99 *(978-0-7945-1438-9(3)*, Usborne) EDC Publishing.

—First Numbers. Brooks, Felicity & Litchfield, Jo. 2006. (Usborne First Numbers Ser.). 48p. (J). (gr. -1). pap. 8.99 *(978-0-7945-0746-6(8)*, Usborne) EDC Publishing.

—The Usborne Advent Nativity Book. Doherty, Gillian, ed. 2006. 12p. (J). (gr. -1-3). bds. 14.99 *(978-0-7945-1174-6(0)*, Usborne) EDC Publishing.

—The Usborne Book of Everyday Words. Litchfield, Jo. Treays, Rebecca et al, eds. 2006. (Everyday Words Ser.). 48p. (J). (gr. -1). lib. bdg. 15.99 *(978-1-58086-964-5(5))* EDC Publishing.

—Usborne Lift-The-Flap Nitivity. Litchfield, Jo. 2004. (J). *(978-0-439-68683-9(0))* Scholastic, Inc.

Allman, Howard, jt. photos by see MMStudios.

Allman, Karl. Becoming Prince Charming. Rankin, Stephanie. 2013. (ENG.). 40p. (J). pap. 14.95 *(978-1-4497-9666-2(4)*, WestBow Pr.) Author Solutions, Inc.

Allon, Jeffrey. The Chanukah Blessing. Schram, Peninnah. 2004. (J). (gr. -1-3). 13.95 *(978-0-8074-0733-2(X)*, 101973) URJ Pr.

—The 40 Greatest Jewish Stories Ever Told, 4 vols., Set. Goldin, Barbara Diamond et al. 2005. 192p. (J). (gr. 1-4). 49.95 *(978-0-943706-89-4(0)*, Devora Publishing) Simcha Media Group.

Allred, Mike. Good Omens, Vol. 1. Milligan, Peter. 2003. (X-Statix Ser.). 128p. (YA). pap. 11.99 *(978-0-7851-1059-0(3))* Marvel Worldwide, Inc.

—X-Force: Famous, Mutant & Mortal. Milligan, Peter. 2003. (X-Statix Ser.). 352p. (YA). 29.99 *(978-0-7851-1023-1(2))* Marvel Worldwide, Inc.

Allred, Scott. How to Get Rich in the California Gold Rush: An Adventurer's Guide to the Fabulous Riches Discovered In 1848. Olson, Tod. 2008. (ENG.). 48p. (J). (gr. 5-9). lib. bdg. 25.90 *(978-1-4263-0316-6(5)*, National Geographic Children's Bks.) National Geographic Society.

Allred, Scott & Proch, Gregory. How to Get Rich on a Texas Cattle Drive: In Which I Tell the Honest Truth about Rampaging Rustlers, Stampeding Steers & Other Fateful Hazards on the Wild Chisolm Trail. Olson, Tod. 2010. (How to Get Rich Ser.). (ENG.). 48p. (J). (gr. 3-7). 18.95 *(978-1-4263-0524-5(9))*; 27.90 *(978-1-4263-0525-2(7))* National Geographic Society. (National Geographic Children's Bks.).

—How to Get Rich on the Oregon Trail. Olson, Tod. 2009. (How to Get Rich Ser.). (ENG.). 48p. (J). (gr. 5-9). 18.95 *(978-1-4263-0412-5(9))* National Geographic Society.

Allred, Scott, jt. illus. see Proch, Gregory.

Allsop, Sophie, et al. Princess: A Glittering Guide for Young Ladies. Sparklington, Madame & Gurney, Stella. 2006. (Genuine & Moste Authentic Guides: 2). (ENG.). 26p. (J). (gr. 1-4). 15.99 *(978-0-7636-3430-8(1))* Candlewick Pr.

Allsopp, Sophie. An Angel to Watch over Me: Prayers & Blessings. Piper, Sophie. 11th ed. 2011. (ENG.). 48p. (J). (gr. k-2). 9.99 *(978-0-7459-6113-2(4))* Lion Hudson PLC GBR. Dist: Independent Pubs. Group.

—The Ballerina's Handbook. Castle, Kate. 2009. (Genuine & Moste Authentic Guides). (ENG.). 22p. (J). (gr. 1-4). 14.99 *(978-0-7636-4552-6(4))* Candlewick Pr.

—The First Christmas. Rock, Lois. 2008. (ENG.). 32p. (J). (gr. k-2). 12.95 *(978-0-7459-4956-7(8))* Lion Hudson PLC GBR. Dist: Independent Pubs. Group.

—The First Rainbow. Rock, Lois. 2010. (ENG.). 28p. (J). (gr. k-2). 12.99 *(978-0-7459-6055-5(3))* Lion Hudson PLC GBR. Dist: Independent Pubs. Group.

—Flower in the Snow. Corderoy, Tracey. 2012. (ENG.). 32p. (J). (-3). 16.99 *(978-1-4022-7740-5(7)*, Sourcebooks Jabberwocky) Sourcebooks, Inc.

—Goodnight, Angels, 1 vol. Carlson, Melody. 2011. (ENG.). 32p. (J). 15.99 *(978-0-310-71687-7(X))* Zonderkidz.

Allsopp, Sophie, et al. Horse: The Essential Guide for Young Equestrians. Stoddard, Rosie & Marshall, Phillip. Hamilton, Libby, ed. 2008. (Genuine & Moste Authentic Guides: 4). (ENG.). 32p. (J). (gr. 1-4). 16.99 *(978-0-7636-3547-3(2))* Candlewick Pr.

Allsopp, Sophie. The Lion Bible to Keep for Ever. Rock, Lois. 2015. (ENG.). 320p. (J). (gr. 2-4). 19.99 *(978-0-7459-6487-4(7))* Lion Hudson PLC GBR. Dist: Independent Pubs. Group.

—The Lord's Prayer: And Other Classic Prayers for Children. Rock, Lois. 2014. (ENG.). 32p. (J). (gr. k-2). 6.99 *(978-0-7459-6322-8(6))* Lion Hudson PLC GBR. Dist: Independent Pubs. Group.

—Love Letters from God: Bible Stories, 1 vol. Nellist, Glenys. 2014. (ENG.). 40p. (J). 16.99 *(978-0-310-73384-3(7))* Zonderkidz.

—Noah's Ark. Rock, Lois. 2014. (ENG.). 32p. (J). (gr. k-2). 6.99 *(978-0-7459-6321-1(8))* Lion Hudson PLC GBR. Dist: Independent Pubs. Group.

—Our Father: And Other Classic Prayers for Children. Rock, Lois. 2010. (ENG.). 32p. (J). (gr. k-2). 12.99 *(978-0-7459-6152-1(5))* Lion Hudson PLC GBR. Dist: Independent Pubs. Group.

—Thank You, God! A Year of Blessings & Prayers for Little Ones. 2009. (ENG.). 16p. (J). (gr. -1-3). 12.99 *(978-1-4169-4754-7(X)*, Little Simon Inspirations) Little Simon Inspirations.

Allwright, Deborah. Best Pet Ever. Roberts, Victoria. 2011. 32p. pap. 7.95 *(978-1-58925-432-9(5))* Tiger Tales.

Allwright, Deborah. Dinosaur Sleepover. Edwards, Pamela Duncan. 2013. (J). ***(978-1-4351-4923-6(8))*** Barnes & Noble, Inc.

Allwright, Deborah. Dinosaur Sleepover. Edwards, Pamela Duncan. ed. 2014. (Let's Read! Ser.). (ENG.). 32p. (J). (gr. k-2). pap. 7.99 *(978-1-4472-4530-8(X))* Pan Macmillan GBR. Dist: Independent Pubs. Group.

—Dinosaur Starts School, 1 vol. Edwards, Pamela Duncan. 2010. (ENG.). 32p. (J). (gr. -1-2). pap. 6.99 *(978-0-8075-1601-0(5))* Whitman, Albert & Co.

—Don't Read This Book! Lewis, Jill. 2010. 32p. (J). (gr. -1-2). 15.95 *(978-1-58925-094-9(X))* Tiger Tales.

—The Fox in the Dark. Green, Alison. 32p. (J). (gr. -1-1). 2012. (ENG.). pap. 7.95 *(978-1-58925-437-4(6))*; 2010. 15.95 *(978-1-58925-091-8(5))* Tiger Tales.

—Hello! Is This Grandma? Whybrow, Ian. 2008. (Tiger Tales Ser.). 32p. (J). (gr. -1-2). 15.95 *(978-1-58925-072-7(9))* Tiger Tales.

—The Night Pirates. Harris, Peter. 2013. (ENG.). 14p. (J). (gr. -1-2). 22.99 *(978-1-4052-5678-0(8))* Egmont Bks., Ltd. GBR. Dist: Independent Pubs. Group.

—A Patch of Black, 8. Rooney, Rachel. ed. 2014. (ENG.). 32p. (J). (-k). pap. 9.99 *(978-0-230-71443-4(9))* Pan Macmillan GBR. Dist: Independent Pubs. Group.

—Sinclair, Wonder Bear. Blackman, Malorie. 2005. (Blue Go Bananas Ser.). (ENG.). 48p. (J). (gr. 1-2). *(978-0-7787-2653-1(3))*; lib. bdg. *(978-0-7787-2631-9(2))* Crabtree Publishing Co.

—Sinclair, Wonder Bear. Blackman, Malorie. 2003. (Blue Bananas Ser.). (ENG.). 48p. (J). (gr. k-2). pap. 5.99 *(978-1-4052-0589-4(X))* Egmont Bks., Ltd. GBR. Dist: Independent Pubs. Group.

—Where Are My Shoes? Wallace, Karen. 2005. (Reading Corner Ser.). 24p. (J). (gr. k-3). lib. bdg. 22.80 *(978-1-59771-002-2(4))* Sea-To-Sea Pubns.

Allwright, Deborah. Mrs Vickers' Knickers. Allwright, Deborah. Lebihan, Kara. 2013. (ENG.). 32p. (J). (gr. -1). pap. 10.99 *(978-1-4052-5395-6(9))* Egmont Bks., Ltd. GBR. Dist: Independent Pubs. Group.

Allyn, Virginia. Hush-a-Bye Counting: A Bedtime Book. McLeod, Kris Aro. 2008. (ENG.). 20p. (J). (gr. -1). 14.95 *(978-1-58117-785-5(2)*, Intervisual/Piggy Toes) Bendon, Inc.

Almanstotter, Susanne. Pompety-Pooh: Purplest Penguin in Zonkety Zoo. Beggs, Melissa. Laible, Steve William, ed. 2013. 52p. pap. 12.95 *(978-0-9844784-9-1(3)*, Empire Holdings) Kodel Group, LLC, The.

Almanza, Roberto. Trixie & Dixie: The Mystery of the Missing Cape. Tamez, Juliza. 2013. (ENG.). (J). 12.95 *(978-1-62086-426-5(6))* Mascot Bks., Inc.

Almara, Dono Sanchez, jt. illus. see Sanchez Almara, Dono.

Almeida, Michelangelo. Marvel Heroes Mix & Match. Teitelbaum, Michael. 2007. (Mix & Match Ser.). (ENG.). 12p. (J). (gr. -1-1). bds. 14.99 *(978-0-7944-1229-6(7))* Reader's Digest Assn., Inc., The.

Almeyda, Tonito Avalon. Billy's Mountain Adventure, 1 vol. Arnold, Ginger Fudge. 2010. 32p. pap. 24.95 *(978-1-4489-5582-4(3))* PublishAmerica, Inc.

Aloise, Frank. Experiments with MacHines & Matter. Sootin, Harry. 2012. 96p. 38.95 *(978-1-258-23744-8(X))*; pap. 23.95 *(978-1-258-24341-8(5))* Literary Licensing, LLC.

Alon Curiel, Gil-Ly. Passing By. Tepper, Yona. Guthman, Deborah, tr. from HEB. 2010. (ENG.). 40p. (J). (gr. -1-3). 9.99 *(978-1-935279-36-5(5))* Kane Miller.

Alonso, Denis. Frankly, I Never Wanted to Kiss Anybody! The Story of the Frog Prince As Told by the Frog. Loewen, Nancy. 2013. (Other Side of the Story Ser.). (ENG.). 24p. (gr. 2-3). 26.65 *(978-1-4048-8304-8(5))* Picture Window Bks.
—Frankly, I Never Wanted to Kiss Anybody! The Story of the Frog Prince, As Told by the Frog. Loewen, Nancy. 2013. (Other Side of the Story Ser.). (ENG.). 24p. (gr. 2-3). 9.95 *(978-1-4795-1948-4(0))* Picture Window Bks.
—Really, Rapunzel Needed a Haircut! The Story of Rapunzel, as Told by Dame Gothel. Gunderson, Jessica. 2013. (Other Side of the Story Ser.). (ENG.). 24p. (gr. 2-3). 26.65 *(978-1-4048-7941-6(2))* Picture Window Bks.
—Really, Rapunzel Needed a Haircut! The Story of Rapunzel As Told by Dame Gothel. Gunderson, Jessica. 2013. (Other Side of the Story Ser.). (ENG.). 24p. (gr. 2-3). 9.95 *(978-1-4795-1946-0(4))* Picture Window Bks.
Alonso, Denis & Tayal, Amit. Frankly, I Never Wanted to Kiss Anybody! The Story of the Frog Prince As Told by the Frog. Loewen, Nancy. 2013. (Other Side of the Story Ser.). (ENG.). 24p. (gr. 2-3). pap. 6.95 *(978-1-4795-1952-1(9))* Picture Window Bks.
—Really, Rapunzel Needed a Haircut! The Story of Rapunzel As Told by Dame Gothel. Gunderson, Jessica & Loewen, Nancy. 2013. (Other Side of the Story Ser.). (ENG.). 24p. (gr. 2-3). pap. 6.95 *(978-1-4795-1950-7(2))* Picture Window Bks.
Alonso Díaz-Toledo, Juan Ramón. Anastasia Tiene las Respuestas. Lowry, Lois. Bustelo, Ana, tr. 2003. (Anastasia Krupnik Ser.).Tr. of Anastasia Has the Answers. (SPA.). 160p. (J). 9.95 *(978-84-239-6334-8(9))* Espasa Calpe, S.A. ESP. Dist: Planeta Publishing Corp., Lectorum Pubns., Inc.
—Memorias de una Gallina. Narváez, Concha López et al. 11th ed.Tr. of Memoirs of a Henn. (SPA.). 96p. (J). (gr. 3-5). *(978-84-207-3531-3(0))* Grupo Anaya, S.A. ESP. Dist: Lectorum Pubns., Inc.
—Mi Hermana Gabriela. Olaizola, José Luis. (SPA.). 120p. (YA). (gr. 5-8). *(978-84-207-3065-3(3),* GS4005) Grupo Anaya, S.A. ESP. Dist: Lectorum Pubns., Inc.
Alonso, Jesus, jt. illus. see Alvarez, Jose M.
Alonso, Juan Ramon. Anastasia Vive Aqui. Lowry, Lois. 2003. (Anastasia Krupnik Ser.). (SPA.). 160p. (J). 9.95 *(978-84-670-0073-3(2))* Espasa Calpe, S.A. ESP. Dist: Planeta Publishing Corp.
—El Lugar Mas Bonito del Mundo. Cameron, Ann. 2003. (SPA.). 70p. (gr. 3-5). pap. 8.95 *(978-968-19-0402-9(8))* Santillana USA Publishing Co., Inc.
—Miguel Hernandez para Ninos. Hernández, Miguel & Hernández, Miguel. 2003. (SPA.). 178p. *(978-84-305-9548-8(1),* SU30133) Susaeta Ediciones, S.A. ESP. Dist: Lectorum Pubns., Inc.
—Por Tierras de Pan Llevar. Farias, Juan & Juan, Farias. (SPA.). 96p. (J). *(978-84-392-8726-1(7))* Gaviota Ediciones ESP. Dist: Lectorum Pubns., Inc.
Alonso, Juan Ramón. El Secreto de Gabriela. Alonso, Juan Ramón, tr. Olaizola, José Luis. 6th ed. 2003. (SPA.). 120p. *(978-84-207-3101-8(3),* GS4009) Grupo Anaya, S.A. ESP. Dist: Lectorum Pubns., Inc.
Alpern, Eliyahu. Cheesecake for Shavuot. Ofanansky, Allison. 2013. (Lag B'Omer & Shavuot Ser.). (ENG.). 32p. (J). (gr. -1-2). lib. bdg. 15.95 *(978-0-7613-8126-6(0),* Kar-Ben Publishing) Lerner Publishing Group.
Alpern, Eliyahu. Sukkot Treasure Hunt. Alpern, Eliyahu, photos by. Ofanansky, Allison. 2009. (Sukkot & Simchat Torah Ser.). (ENG.). 32p. (J). (gr. -1-5). 15.95 *(978-0-8225-8763-7(7),* Kar-Ben Publishing) Lerner Publishing Group.
Alpern, Eliyahu, photos by. Cheesecake for Shavuot. Ofanansky, Allison. 2013. (Lag B'Omer & Shavuot Ser.). (ENG., 32p. (J). (gr. -1-2). 8.95 *(978-1-4677-1411-2(9),* Kar-Ben Publishing) Lerner Publishing Group.
—Harvest of Light. Ofanansky, Allison. (Hanukkah Ser.). (ENG., 32p. (J). (gr. -1-5). 2011. pap. 8.95 *(978-0-7613-8305-5(0));* 2008. 15.95 *(978-0-8225-7389-0(X))* Lerner Publishing Group. (Kar-Ben Publishing).
—New Month, New Moon. Ofanansky, Allison. 2014. 32p. (J). (gr. -1-2). 16.95 *(978-1-4677-1945-2(5),* Kar-Ben Publishing) Lerner Publishing Group.
—What's the Buzz? Honey for a Sweet New Year. Ofanansky, Allison. 2014. 32p. (J). (gr. -1-5). 8.95 *(978-1-4677-5706-5(3),* Kar-Ben Publishing) Lerner Publishing Group.
Alphenaar, Pamela L. Crackerjack the Christmas Cat. Domer, Nancy L. 2008. 40p. pap. 16.95 *(978-0-9818488-0-8(X))* Ajoyin Publishing, Inc.
Alphona, Adrian. Runaways: Pride & Joy. Vaughn, Brian K. 2004. (X-Men Ser.). 144p. (YA). pap. 14.99 *(978-0-7851-1244-0(8))* Marvel Worldwide, Inc.
—Runaways Vol. 3: The Good Die Young. Vaughan, Brian K. 2011. (ENG.). 152p. (YA). (gr. 8-17). pap. 9.99 *(978-0-7851-5736-6(0))* Marvel Worldwide, Inc.
—Runaways - Parental Guidance, Vol. 6. 2011. (ENG.). 152p. (YA). (gr. 8-17). pap. 9.99 *(978-0-7851-5745-8(X))* Marvel Worldwide, Inc.
—Runaways - Pride & Joy, Vol. 1. 2011. (ENG.). 152p. (YA). (gr. 8-17). pap. 9.99 *(978-0-7851-5732-8(8))* Marvel Worldwide, Inc.
Alphona, Adrian & Miyazawa, Takeshi. Runaways - Teenage Wasteland, Vol. 2. 2011. (ENG.). 152p. (YA). (gr. 8-17). pap. 9.99 *(978-0-7851-5733-5(6))* Marvel Worldwide, Inc.
Alphona, Adrian & Norton, Mike. Runaways - Live Fast, Vol. 7. 2011. (ENG.). 152p. (YA). (gr. 8-17). pap. 9.99 *(978-0-7851-5748-9(4))* Marvel Worldwide, Inc.
Alsonso, Denis, jt. illus. see Tayal, Amit.
Alston, Brad. The Adventures of Abigale Green in Spain. Green, Elaine. 2012. 38p. (J). 14.95 *(978-1-937406-10-3(5))* Mascot Bks., Inc.
Alston, Sheila Y., photos by. Faith, Love & Life. Alston, Stanley E. Sharps, Angelique, ed. 48p. (YA). (gr. 4-18). pap. 12.95 *(978-0-9719897-0-2(2))* Magnatic Music.
Alter, Anna. The Ears of Corn: An Ike & Mem Story. Jennings, Patrick. 2003. (ENG.). 56p. (J). (gr. k-3). tchr. ed. 15.95 *(978-0-8234-1770-4(0))* Holiday Hse., Inc.
—The Lightning Bugs. Jennings, Patrick. 2003. (ENG.). 56p. (J). (gr. k-3). tchr. ed. 15.95 *(978-0-8234-1673-8(9))* Holiday Hse., Inc.
—Priscilla & the Hollyhocks. Broyles, Anne. 2008. (ENG.). 32p. (J). (gr. 1-4). 15.95 *(978-1-57091-675-5(6))* Charlesbridge Publishing, Inc.
Alter, Anna. Francine's Day. Alter, Anna. 2003. 32p. (J). lib. bdg. 16.89 *(978-0-06-623937-8(0))* HarperCollins Pubs.
Althea, Erin & Bertino, Mike. Recipe. Petrella, Angela et al. 2013. (ENG.). 48p. (J). (gr. -1-3). 17.95 *(978-1-936365-84-5(7))* McSweeney's Publishing.
Altman, Scott. Attack of the Shark-Headed Zombie. Doyle, Bill. 2011. (Stepping Stone Book Ser.). (ENG.). 112p. (J). (gr. 1-4). 4.99 *(978-0-375-86675-3(2),* Random Hse. Bks. for Young Readers) Random Hse. Children's Bks.
—Stampede of the Supermarket Slugs. Doyle, Bill H. 2012. (Stepping Stone Book Ser.). (ENG.). 112p. (J). (gr. 1-4). pap. 4.99 *(978-0-375-86934-1(4))* Random Hse., Inc.
Altmann, Scott. Big City Blues: Back to Wonderland. Fields, Jan. 2013. (Adventures in Extreme Reading Ser.). 112p. (J). (gr. 3-6). 27.07 *(978-1-61641-923-3(7))* Magic Wagon.
—The Calm Before the Storm: A Night in Sleepy Hollow. Fields, Jan. 2013. (Adventures in Extreme Reading Ser.). 112p. (J). (gr. 3-6). 27.07 *(978-1-61641-920-2(2))* Magic Wagon.
—Crazy Horse - Brave Warrior. Hood, Ann. 2013. (Treasure Chest Ser.: 5). (ENG.). 192p. (J). (gr. 3-7). 15.99 *(978-0-448-45738-3(5),* Grosset & Dunlap) Penguin Publishing Group.
—Fairy Fashion. 2008. (Dover Coloring Bks.). (ENG.). 32p. (J). (gr. k-5). pap. 3.99 *(978-0-486-46684-2(1))* Dover Pubns., Inc.
—Der Geheimnisvolle Mr. Spines - Wings, No. 1. Lethcoe, Jason. 2009. (Mysterious Mr. Spines Ser.: 1). (ENG.). 256p. (J). (gr. 5-18). pap. 7.99 *(978-0-448-44653-0(7),* Grosset & Dunlap) Penguin Publishing Group.
—Hack Attack: A Trip to Wonderland. Fields, Jan. 2013. (Adventures in Extreme Reading Ser.). 112p. (J). (gr. 3-6). 27.07 *(978-1-61641-919-6(9))* Magic Wagon.
—Lightning Strikes Twice: Escaping Great Expectations. Fields, Jan. 2013. (Adventures in Extreme Reading Ser.). 112p. (J). (gr. 3-6). 27.07 *(978-1-61641-922-6(9))* Magic Wagon.
—A Novel Nightmare: The Purloined Story. Fields, Jan. 2013. (Adventures in Extreme Reading Ser.). 112p. (J). (gr. 3-6). 27.07 *(978-1-61641-924-0(5))* Magic Wagon.
—Sea Monsters vs. Dragons: Showdown of the Legends, 1 vol. O'Hearn, Michael. 2011. (Monster Wars Ser.). (ENG.). 32p. (gr. 3-4). pap. 7.95 *(978-1-4296-7263-4(3));* pap. 47.70 *(978-1-4296-7264-1(1));* lib. bdg. 27.32 *(978-1-4296-6523-0(8))* Capstone Pr., Inc. (Edge Bks.).
—Song, 3 vols., No. 3. Lethcoe, Jason. 2009. (Mysterious Mr. Spines Ser.: 3). (ENG.). 208p. (J). (gr. 5-18). pap. 7.99 *(978-0-448-44655-4(3),* Grosset & Dunlap) Penguin Publishing Group.
—Trapped in Stormy Seas: Sailing to Treasure Island. Fields, Jan. 2013. (Adventures in Extreme Reading Ser.). 112p. (J). (gr. 3-6). 27.07 *(978-1-61641-921-9(0))* Magic Wagon.
Altmann, Scott & Zliber, Denis. Crazy Horse - Brave Warrior. Hood, Ann. 2013. (Treasure Chest Ser.: 5). (ENG.). 192p. (J). (gr. 3-7). pap. 6.99 *(978-0-448-45728-4(8),* Grosset & Dunlap) Penguin Publishing Group.
—Harry Houdini - Prince of Air. Hood, Ann. 2012. (Treasure Chest Ser.: 4). (ENG.). 208p. (J). (gr. 3-7). pap. 6.99 *(978-0-448-45470-2(X),* Grosset & Dunlap) Penguin Publishing Group.
—Prince of Air, No. 4. Hood, Ann. 2012. (Treasure Chest Ser.: 4). (ENG.). 208p. (J). (gr. 3-7). 15.99 *(978-0-448-45474-0(2),* Grosset & Dunlap) Penguin Publishing Group.
—Queen Liliuokalani - Royal Prisoner. Hood, Ann. 2013. (Treasure Chest Ser.: 6). (ENG.). 176p. (J). (gr. 3-7). 15.99 *(978-0-448-45739-0(3));* pap. 6.99 *(978-0-448-45729-1(6))* Penguin Publishing Group. (Grosset & Dunlap).
Alvarado, Andrea E. Selva Feliz * Happy Jungle. Alvarado, Andrea E., tr. Madelag. 2012. 88p. 22.95 *(978-9962-690-16-0(1))* Piggy Pr. Bks.
Alvarado, Carol. Harry's Last Wish: A Story about Forever. Benz, Suzanne. 2007. (ENG.). 32p. (J). 24.95 *(978-0-944963-23-4(4))* Glastonbury Pr.
Alvarado, Dalia & Pacheco, Luis Gabriel. Maraca. Romero, Alfonso Suárez. rev. ed. 2006. (Castillo de la Lectura Verde Ser.). (SPA & ENG.). 120p. (J). (gr. 2-4). pap. 7.95 *(978-970-20-0128-7(5))* Castillo, Ediciones, S. A. de C. V. MEX. Dist: Macmillan.
Alvarado, Eladia. The Adventures of Simsim: Based on a True Story. Gigi. 2010. 60p. pap. 12.99 *(978-1-4490-6524-9(4))* AuthorHouse.
Alvarado, Juan. The Adventures of Sammy the Saver In: Will Sammy Ride the World's First Space Coaster?, Vol. 2. Renick, Sam X. 2003. 32p. (J). pap. 8.95 *(978-0-9713664-1-1(1))* It's A Habit! Co., The.
Alvarado, Paulo. My Day... at the Zoo. Wagner, Jeff. 2004. 20p. (J). bds. *(978-0-9754515-0-2(2))* Wagner Entertainment.
Alvarado, Tom. Pirate Ships: Sailing the High Seas, 1 vol. O'Donnell, Liam. 2006. (Real World of Pirates Ser.). (ENG.). 32p. (gr. 3-4). 27.32 *(978-0-7368-6427-5(X),* Edge Bks.) Capstone Pr., Inc.
—Pirate Treasure: Stolen Riches, 1 vol. O'Donnell, Liam. 2006. (Real World of Pirates Ser.). (ENG.). 32p. (gr. 3-4). 27.32 *(978-0-7368-6428-2(8),* Edge Bks.) Capstone Pr., Inc.
Alvarez, David. El Mejor Es Mi Papa. Leon, Georgina Lazaro. 2003. (Yellow Ser.). (SPA.). 31p. (gr. k-3). pap. 9.95 *(978-1-57581-442-1(0))* Santillana USA Publishing Co., Inc.
Alvarez, Diego. Dentro del Cubo. Villegas, Aline Guevara. rev. ed. 2006. (Otra Escalera Ser.). (SPA & ENG.). 24p. (J). (gr. 4). pap. 9.95 *(978-968-5920-73-5(7))* Castillo, Ediciones, S. A. de C. V. MEX. Dist: Macmillan.
—El Galeon de Manila: Los Objetos Que Llegaron de Oriente. Durán, Rosa Dopazo. rev. ed. 2006. (Otra Escalera Ser.). (SPA & ENG.). 48p. (J). (gr. 4-7). pap. 10.95 *(978-968-5920-76-6(1))* Castillo, Ediciones, S. A. de C. V. MEX. Dist: Macmillan.
Alvarez, Jose M. & Alonso, Jesus. David Crockett. Santillana U. S. A. Publishing Co, Inc. Staff. 2003. (Historias de Siempre Ser.). (SPA.). 95p. (J). (gr. 5-8). pap. 12.95 *(978-84-204-5703-1(5))* Santillana USA Publishing Co., Inc.
Alvarez, Juan. Chocolate, Chipmunks, & Canoes: An American Indian Words Coloring Book. Alvarez, Juan. 2004. (ENG.). 32p. (gr. -1-3). pap. 3.95 *(978-1-878610-03-4(1))* Red Crane Bks., Inc.
—José Rabbit's Southwest Adventures: An ABC Coloring Book with Spanish Words. Alvarez, Juan. 2004. (ENG.). 32p. (Orig.). (gr. -1-3). pap. 3.95 *(978-1-878610-00-3(7))* Red Crane Bks., Inc.
Alvarez, Lamberto. Muffler Man el Hombre Mofle. Campos, Tito. 2009. 32p. *(978-1-55885-557-1(2),* Piñata Books) Arte Publico Pr.
Alvarez, Laura, jt. illus. see Luna, Tom.
Alvarez, Leticia Herrera. Dia de Reyes. Alvarez, Leticia Herrera. 2003. (SPA.). 52p. (J). (gr. 3-5). 14.95 *(978-968-19-1043-3(5))* Santillana USA Publishing Co., Inc.
Alvarez, Maria Jesus. Celebra un Powwow con Sandy Starbright. Flor Ada, Alma. 2007. (Cuentos para Celebrar / Stories to Celebrate Ser.). 30p. (gr. k-6). per. 11.95 *(978-1-59820-115-4(8),* Alfaguara) Santillana USA Publishing Co., Inc.
—Celebrate a Powwow with Sandy Starbright. Flor Ada, Alma. 2007. (Cuentos para Celebrar / Stories to Celebrate Ser.). 30p. (gr. k-6). per. 11.95 *(978-1-59820-127-7(1))* Santillana USA Publishing Co., Inc.
—La Fiesta de Las Tortillas. Argueta, Jorge. Hayes, Joe & Franco, Sharon, trs. 2013. (ENG & SPA.). 31p. (J). (gr. -1-3). pap. 15.00 *(978-0-88272-202-3(6),* Alfaguara) Santillana USA Publishing Co., Inc.
—La Fiesta de Las Tortillas: The Fiesta of the Tortillas. Argueta, Jorge. Hayes, Joe & Franco, Sharon, trs. from SPA. 2006. (Bilingual Bks). (ENG & SPA.). 32p. (gr. 3-5). 15.95 *(978-1-59820-094-2(1),* Alfaguara) Santillana USA Publishing Co., Inc.
Álvarez, Mrinali. Grano a Grano. Barceló, Josefina. 2006. (SPA.). (J). pap. 8.95 *(978-0-8477-1561-9(2))* Univ. of Puerto Rico Pr.
Alvarez, Mrinali. Mi Silla de Ruedas. Rivera, Lassen. 2006. (SPA.). 28p. 8.95 *(978-0-8477-1568-8(X))* Univ. of Puerto Rico Pr.
—Pon, Pon: ¡A Jugar con el Bebé! 2005. (SPA.). 28p. (J). 8.95 *(978-0-8477-1550-3(7))* Univ. of Puerto Rico Pr.
Álvarez, Mrinali. Pon pon, a jugar con el Bebé. Barceló, Josefina. 2006. (SPA.). (J). pap. 8.95 *(978-0-8477-1557-2(4))* Univ. of Puerto Rico Pr.
Alvarez, Mrinali. Soy Gordito. Rivera, Lassen. 2006. (SPA.). 28p. 8.95 *(978-0-8477-1565-7(5))* Univ. of Puerto Rico Pr.
Álvarez, Mrinali. Los tres reyes a Caballo. Rivera, Carmen & Maldonado, Víctor. 2006. (SPA.). (J). pap. 8.95 *(978-0-8477-1559-6(0))* Univ. of Puerto Rico Pr.
Alvarez, Mrinali. Los tres reyes a Caballo. Rivera Lassén, Carmen & Maldonado, Víctor. 2005. (SPA.). 28p. (J). 8.95 *(978-0-8477-1552-7(3))* Univ. of Puerto Rico Pr.
Álvarez, Mrinali. Vamos a Jugar. Barceló, Josefina. 2006. (SPA.). (J). 8.95 *(978-0-8477-1560-2(4))* Univ. of Puerto Rico Pr.
Alvarez O'Neill, Juan. Grano a grano... Refranes Populares. 2005. (SPA.). (J). 8.95 *(978-0-8477-1554-1(X))* Univ. of Puerto Rico Pr.
—¡Vamos a Jugar! 2005. (SPA.). 28p. (J). 8.95 *(978-0-8477-1553-4(1))* Univ. of Puerto Rico Pr.
Alves, Josh. Zeke Meeks, 1 vol. Green, D. L. (Zeke Meeks Ser.). (ENG.). 128p. (gr. 2-2). 2014. 42.64 *(978-1-4795-2045-9(4));* 2013. 170.56 *(978-1-4048-8052-8(6));* 2013. 85.28 *(978-1-4048-8053-5(4))* Picture Window Bks. (Zeke Meeks).
—Zeke Meeks vs His Big Phony Cousin, 1 vol. Green, D. L. 2014. (Zeke Meeks Ser.). (ENG.). 128p. (gr. 2-2). pap. 5.95 *(978-1-4795-3810-2(8));* 21.32 *(978-1-4795-2167-8(1))* Picture Window Bks. (Zeke Meeks).
—Zeke Meeks vs the Annoying Princess Sing-Along, 1 vol. Green, D. L. 2014. (Zeke Meeks Ser.). (ENG.). 128p. (gr. 2-2). 21.32 *(978-1-4795-4828-6(6),* Zeke Meeks) Picture Window Bks.
—Zeke Meeks vs the Big Blah-Rific Birthday, 1 vol. Green, D. L. 2013. (Zeke Meeks Ser.). (ENG.). 128p. (gr. 2-2). 8.95 *(978-1-4048-8105-1(0));* lib. bdg. 21.32 *(978-1-4048-7637-8(5))* Picture Window Bks.
—Zeke Meeks vs the Crummy Class Play, 1 vol. Green, D. L. 2014. (Zeke Meeks Ser.). (ENG.). 128p. (gr. 2-2). 21.32 *(978-1-4795-4827-9(8),* Zeke Meeks) Picture Window Bks.
—Zeke Meeks vs the Gruesome Girls, 1 vol. Green, D. L. 2012. (Zeke Meeks Ser.). (ENG.). 128p. (gr. 2-2). pap. 5.95 *(978-1-4048-7221-9(3));* lib. bdg. 21.32 *(978-1-4048-6805-2(4))* Picture Window Bks. (Zeke Meeks).
—Zeke Meeks vs the Horrendous Halloween, 1 vol. Green, D. L. 2013. (Zeke Meeks Ser.). (ENG.). 128p. (gr. 2-2). lib. bdg. 21.32 *(978-1-4048-7638-5(3))* Picture Window Bks.
—Zeke Meeks vs the Horrifying TV-Turnoff Week, 1 vol. Green, D. L. 2012. (Zeke Meeks Ser.). (ENG.). 128p. (gr. 2-2). pap. 5.95 *(978-1-4048-7220-2(5));* lib. bdg. 21.32 *(978-1-4048-6804-5(6))* Picture Window Bks. (Zeke Meeks).
—Zeke Meeks vs the Mother's Day Meltdown. Green, D. L. 2015. (Zeke Meeks Ser.). (ENG.). 128p. (gr. 2-2). 21.32 *(978-1-4795-2168-5(X))* Picture Window Bks.
—Zeke Meeks vs the No-Fun Fund-Raiser, 1 vol. Green, D. L. 2013. (Zeke Meeks Ser.). (ENG.). 128p. (gr. 2-2). lib. bdg. 21.32 *(978-1-4048-7640-8(5))* Picture Window Bks.
—Zeke Meeks vs the Pain-In-the-Neck Pets, 1 vol. Green, D. L. 2014. (Zeke Meeks Ser.). (ENG.). 128p. (gr. 2-2). 21.32 *(978-1-4795-2166-1(3),* Zeke Meeks) Picture Window Bks.
—Zeke Meeks vs the Putrid Puppet Pals, 1 vol. Green, D. L. 2012. (Zeke Meeks Ser.). (ENG.). 128p. (gr. 2-2). pap. 5.95 *(978-1-4048-7223-3(X));* lib. bdg. 21.32 *(978-1-4048-6803-8(8))* Picture Window Bks. (Zeke Meeks).
—Zeke Meeks vs the Stinkin' Science Fair, 1 vol. Green, D. L. 2012. (Zeke Meeks Ser.). (ENG.). 128p. (gr. 2-2). pap. 5.95 *(978-1-4048-7222-6(1));* lib. bdg. 21.32 *(978-1-4048-6802-1(X))* Picture Window Bks. (Zeke Meeks).
—Zeke Meeks vs the Stinky Soccer Team. Green, D. L. 2015. (Zeke Meeks Ser.). (ENG.). 128p. (gr. 2-2). 21.32 *(978-1-4795-5768-4(4))* Picture Window Bks.
—Zeke Meeks vs the Super Stressful Talent Show, 1 vol. Green, D. L. 2013. (Zeke Meeks Ser.). (ENG.). 128p. (gr. 2-2). 8.95 *(978-1-4048-8106-8(9));* lib. bdg. 21.32 *(978-1-4048-7639-2(1))* Picture Window Bks.
Alves, Wellington, et al. Marvel's Guardians of the Galaxy Prelude. Abnett, Dan & Lanning, Andy. 2014. (ENG.). 168p. (J). (gr. 4-17). pap. 14.99 *(978-0-7851-5410-5(8))* Marvel Worldwide, Inc.
Alves, Wellington. Power Man & Iron Fist: The Comedy of Death. 2011. (ENG.). 120p. (J). (gr. 4-17). pap. 16.99 *(978-0-7851-5247-7(4))* Marvel Worldwide, Inc.
—Shadowland: Blood on the Streets. 2011. (ENG.). 112p. (YA). (gr. 8-17). pap. 15.99 *(978-0-7851-5184-5(2))* Marvel Worldwide, Inc.
Alvord, Douglas. A White Heron. Jewett, Sarah Orne. 2005. (ENG.). 32p. (J). pap. 10.95 *(978-1-56792-287-5(2))* Godine, David R. Pub.
Alward, Jeff. Gold Rush. Piotrowski, Robert. 2007. 48p. (J). lib. bdg. 23.08 *(978-1-4242-1628-4(1))* Fitzgerald Bks.
—Hidden Message. Boyd, David. 2007. 48p. (J). lib. bdg. 23.08 *(978-1-4242-1637-6(0))* Fitzgerald Bks.
—In a Class of Her Own. Lundy, Kathleen Gould. 2007. 48p. (J). lib. bdg. 23.08 *(978-1-4242-1629-1(X))* Fitzgerald Bks.
Amado, Antonio. Story of a Can. Ibarrola, Begonia. 2013. (ENG.). 32p. (J). *(978-84-95923-94-3(7))* Primera Persona.
Amado, Defne. Macaroni on the Moon. Dordick, Barry. 2003. 110p. pap. 11.95 *(978-0-595-26886-3(2))* iUniverse, Inc.
Amanda, photos by. Cook School. Amanda, Grant. 2011. (ENG., 128p. *(978-1-84975-136-0(6))* Ryland Peters & Small.
Amann, Remy & Stoffel, Dominique, photos by. Face-to-Face with the Ant: Energetic Worker. Gomel, Luc. 2004. (Face to Face Ser.). 28p. (J). (gr. -1-2). 9.95 *(978-1-57091-451-5(6))* Charlesbridge Publishing, Inc.
Amano, Akira. Reborn! Amano, Akira. (Reborn! Ser.: 4). (ENG.). 2007. 184p. pap. 9.99 *(978-1-4215-0844-3(3));* Vol. 1. 2006. 200p. (gr. 11). pap. 9.99 *(978-1-4215-0671-5(8));* Vol. 2. 2007. 208p. (gr. 11). pap. 9.99 *(978-1-4215-0672-2(6));* Vol. 3. 2007. 208p. (gr. 11). pap. 9.99 *(978-1-4215-0843-6(5))* Viz Media.
Amano, Shiro. Kingdom Hearts, 4 vols., Vol. 4. Amano, Shiro. 4th rev. ed. 2006. (Disney Squaresoft Ser.). 131p. pap. 5.99 *(978-1-59816-220-2(9),* Tokyopop Kids) TOKYOPOP, Inc.
Amatisto, Brandi. Oscar: A Cat's Tale. Coleman, William L. 2012. 38p. pap. 16.97 *(978-1-61204-750-8(5),* Strategic Bk. Publishing) Strategic Book Publishing & Rights Agency (SBPRA).
Amatrula, Michele. Haven House. Olds, Barbara Anne. 2007. (ENG.). 141p. (J). pap. 8.95 *(978-0-9744446-0-4(X))* All About Kids Publishing.
Amber, Holly & Davidsson, Ashton. The Little Garden. Johnson, Rhonda & Paladin, Frank. l.t. ed. 2004. 48p. (J). per. 16.95 *(978-0-9763635-7-6(7),* TLG01) Beyond the Stars Pubns.
Amber, Holly & Lin, Melanie. Hole In My Stocking. Paladin, Frank. 2005. 24p. (J). per. 16.95 *(978-0-9763635-4-5(2))* Beyond the Stars Pubns.
Ambler, Laura & Brown, Amanda. The Rat Tank, 1 vol. Henry, Kristina. 2011. (ENG.). 40p. (J). 16.99 *(978-0-7643-3842-7(0),* Schiffer Publishing Ltd) Schiffer Publishing, Ltd.
—The Turtle Tank, 1 vol. Henry, Kristina. 2011. (ENG.). 32p. (J). 16.99 *(978-0-7643-3843-4(9),* Schiffer Publishing Ltd) Schiffer Publishing, Ltd.
Ambroz, Mark. Ben, His Helmet & Hats Off. Frances, Nelle. 2012. 16p. (Orig.). pap. *(978-0-646-43174-1(9))* Nelle Frances.
—Ben, His Helmet & the Crashing Cymbals. Frances, Nelle. 2012. 16p. (Orig.). pap. *(978-0-9751168-4-5(3))* Nelle Frances.
—Ben, His Helmet & the Too Tight Hair. Frances, Nelle. 2012. 16p. (Orig.). pap. *(978-0-9751168-1-4(9))* Nelle Frances.
Ambrus, Victor. Olaudah Equiano: From Slavery to Freedom. Thomas, Paul. 2007. (Collins Big Cat Ser.). (ENG.). 48p. (J). pap. 8.99 *(978-0-00-723096-9(6))* HarperCollins Pubs. Ltd. GBR. Dist: Independent Pubs. Group.
Ambrus, Victor G. The Iliad. 2004. (Kingfisher Epics Ser.). (ENG.). 165p. (J). (gr. 3-7). pap. 8.99 *(978-0-7534-5722-1(9),* Kingfisher) Roaring Brook Pr.
—Robin Hood: His Life & Legend. Miles, Bernard. 128p. (J). (gr. 4-18). 12.95 *(978-1-56288-412-3(3))* Checkerboard Pr., Inc.
Ambush, Peter. One Million Men & Me. Lyons, Kelly Starling. 2007. 32p. (J). (gr. -1-3). 16.95 *(978-1-933491-07-3(8))* Just Us Bks., Inc.
Amechazurra, G. Anastasia Tiene Problemas. Lowry, Lois. 2003. (Anastasia Krupnik Ser.). (SPA.). 160p. (J). (gr. 5-7). 9.95 *(978-84-239-9026-9(5))* Espasa Calpe, S.A. ESP. Dist: Planeta Publishing Corp., Lectorum Pubns., Inc.
Ameet Studio (Firm) Staff. Yoda's Secret Missions, Bk. 1. Landers, Ace. 2014. (Lego Star Wars Ser.). (ENG.). 64p. (J). (gr. 2-5). pap. 4.99 *(978-0-545-65700-6(8))* Scholastic, Inc.
Ameet Studio, Ameet. Jungle Adventure , Bk. 6. Scholastic, Inc. Staff & Hapka, Cathy. 2014. (LEGO Friends Ser.). (ENG.). 64p. (J). (gr. 2-5). pap. 4.99 *(978-0-545-79410-7(2))* Scholastic, Inc.

A

—LEGO Legends of Chima: Fire & Ice. Farshtey, Greg. 2014. (LEGO Legends of Chima Ser.). (ENG.). 64p. (J). (gr. 2-5). pap. 4.99 *(978-0-545-69526-8(0))* Scholastic, Inc.

Ameet Studio, Ameet. Vader's Secret Missions. Landers, Ace. 2015. (Lego Star Wars Ser.: 2). (ENG.). 64p. (J). (gr. 2-5). pap. 4.99 ***(978-0-545-83557-2(7))*** Scholastic, Inc.

Ameet Studio Staff. LEGO City: Space Escape Comic Reader. Kotsut, Rafat. 2013. (Lego City Ser.). (ENG.). 32p. (J). (gr. -1-3). pap. 3.99 *(978-0-545-52947-1(6))* Math Solutions.

—Lego Friends - Double Trouble. Simon, Jenne. 2014. (LEGO Friends Ser.). (ENG.). 32p. (J). (gr. 1-3). pap. 3.99 *(978-0-545-56667-4(3))* Scholastic, Inc.

—LEGO Legends of Chima: Danger in the Outlands (Chapter Book #5) Farshtey, Greg. 2014. (LEGO Legends of Chima Ser.). (ENG.). 64p. (J). (gr. 2-5). pap. 4.99 *(978-0-545-62788-7(5))* Scholastic, Inc.

—The Piece of Resistance. 2013. (ENG.). 32p. (J). (gr. 2-5). pap., act. bk. ed. 8.99 *(978-0-545-62461-9(4))* Scholastic, Inc.

—Scorpion Strike! Holmes, Anna. 2014. (LEGO Legends of Chima Ser.). (ENG.). 16p. (J). (gr. 2-5). 6.99 *(978-0-545-60587-8(3))* Scholastic, Inc.

—The Tournament of Elements. 2015. (Lego Ninjago Ser.). (ENG.). 32p. (J). (gr. 1-3). act. bk. ed. 8.99 *(978-0-545-80540-7(6))* Scholastic, Inc.

—The Warrior Within. Farshtey, Greg. 2014. (LEGO Legends of Chima Ser.). (ENG.). 64p. (J). (gr. 2-5). pap. 4.99 *(978-0-545-62787-0(7))* Scholastic, Inc.

Ameet Studio Staff. LEGO Friends: Andrea's Wish (Activity Book #3) Ameet Studio Staff. 2014. (LEGO Friends Ser.). (ENG.). 32p. (J). (gr. 2-5). pap. 8.99 *(978-0-545-64525-6(5))* Scholastic, Inc.

—LEGO Mixels: Activity Book with Figure. Ameet Studio Staff. 2014. (LEGO Mixels Ser.). (ENG.). 32p. (J). (gr. 1-3). 8.99 *(978-0-545-72573-6(9))* Scholastic, Inc.

—Ravens & Gorillas, No. 3. Ameet Studio Staff. 2014. (LEGO Legends of Chima Ser.). (ENG.). 32p. (J). (gr. 2-5). act. bk. ed. 8.99 *(978-0-545-64527-0(1))* Scholastic, Inc.

—These Aren't the Droids You're Looking For: A Search & Find Book. Ameet Studio Staff. 2014. (Lego Star Wars Ser.). (ENG.). 32p. (J). (gr. -1-3). pap. 6.99 *(978-0-545-60804-6(X))* Scholastic, Inc.

Amendola, Dominique. Krishna & the Mystery of the Stolen Calves. Greene, Joshua M. 2013. (ENG.). 24p. (gr. -1). 14.99 *(978-1-60887-173-5(8))* Mandala Publishing.

America. Waikiki Lullaby. Greenway, Bethany. 2009. pap. 7.95 *(978-1-933067-30-8(6))* Beachhouse Publishing, LLC.

Amery, Heather. Christmas Treasury. gif. ed. 2004. (Christmas Treasury Ser.). 128p. (J). act. bk. ed. 7.95 incl. audio compact disk *(978-0-7945-0224-9(5),* Usborne) EDC Publishing.

Ames, Philippe & Hop, Nguyen Thi. A Pebble for Your Pocket. Hanh, Thich Nhat. rev. ed. 2010. (ENG.). 144p. (J). (gr. k). pap. 12.95 *(978-1-935209-45-4(0),* Plum Blossom Bks.) Parallax Pr.

Amin, Heba. Extraordinary Women from the Muslim World. Maydell, Natalie & Riahi, Sep. 2008. (ENG.). (J). 17.95 *(978-0-9799901-0-6(6))* Global Content Ventures.

Amini-Holmes, Liz. Fatty Legs: A True Story. Jordan-Fenton, Christy & Pokiak-Fenton, Margaret. 2010. (ENG.). 112p. (J). (gr. 4-7). pap. 12.95 *(978-1-55451-246-1(8),* 9781554512461) Annick Pr., Ltd. CAN. Dist: Firefly Bks., Ltd.

—Fatty Legs: A True Story. Jordan-Fenton, Christy et al. 2010. (ENG.). 112p. (J). (gr. 4-7). 21.95 *(978-1-55451-247-8(6),* 9781554512478) Annick Pr., Ltd. CAN. Dist: Firefly Bks., Ltd.

—A Stranger at Home: A True Story. Jordan-Fenton, Christy & Pokiak-Fenton, Margaret. 2011. (ENG.). 128p. (J). (gr. 3-7). 21.95 *(978-1-55451-362-8(6),* 9781554513628); pap. 12.95 *(978-1-55451-361-1(8),* 9781554513611) Annick Pr., Ltd. CAN. Dist: Firefly Bks., Ltd.

Amini, Mehrdokht. Golden Domes & Silver Lanterns: A Muslim Book of Colors. Khan, Hena. 2012. (ENG.). 32p. (J). (gr. -1-2). 17.99 *(978-0-8118-7905-7(4))* Chronicle Bks. LLC.

—Golden Domes & Silver Lanterns: A Muslim Book of Colors. Khan, Hena. 2015. (ENG.). 32p. (J). (gr. -1-k). 7.99 *(978-1-4521-4121-3(5))* Chronicle Bks. LLC.

Amir, Amin Abd al-Fattah Mahmud. The Travels of Igal Shidad/Safarada Cigaal Shidaad: A Somali Folktale. Ahmed, Said Salah, tr. 2008. (J). (gr. -1-3). 28p. pap. 7.95 *(978-1-931016-15-5(1))*; 32p. 15.95 *(978-1-931016-14-8(3))* Minnesota Humanities Ctr.

—Wiil Waal: A Somali Folktale. Moriarty, Kathleen M. Adam, Jamal, tr. 2007. (SOM & ENG.). 32p. (J). (gr. -1-3). 15.95 *(978-1-931016-16-2(X))*; pap. 7.95 *(978-1-931016-17-9(8))* Minnesota Humanities Ctr.

Ammassari, Rita. Amy Carmichael - Can Brown Eyes Be Made Blue? MacKenzie, Catherine. 2006. (Little Lights Ser.). (ENG.). 24p. (J). (gr. -1-2). 7.99 *(978-1-84550-108-2(X))* Christian Focus Pubns. GBR. Dist: Send The Light Distribution LLC.

—Corrie Ten Boo - Are All of the Watches Safe? MacKenzie, Catherine. 2006. (Little Lights Ser.). (ENG.). 24p. (J). (gr. -1-2). 7.99 *(978-1-84550-109-9(8))* Christian Focus Pubns. GBR. Dist: Send The Light Distribution LLC.

—Could Somebody Pass the Salt? MacKenzie, Catherine. 2006. (Little Lights Ser.). (ENG.). 24p. (J). (gr. 4-7). 7.99 *(978-1-84550-111-2(X))* Christian Focus Pubns. GBR. Dist: Send The Light Distribution LLC.

Ammirati, Christelle & Second Story Press Staff. Princess to the Rescue, 1 vol. Souza, Cláudia. 2011. (ENG.). 24p. (J). (gr. 1-3). lib. bdg. 15.95 *(978-1-897187-93-7(9))* Second Story Pr. CAN. Dist: Orca Bk. Pubs. USA.

Amodeo, Cristina. Matisse's Garden. Friedman, Samantha & Matisse, Henri. 2014. (ENG.). 48p. (J). (gr. -1-3). 19.95 *(978-0-87070-910-4(0))* Museum of Modern Art.

Amory, Deanna & O'Hara, Cynthia. Courageous Warrior. Neuhofer, Sheri L. 2010. 28p. pap. 10.95 *(978-0-9787472-7-5(5))* Ajoyin Publishing, Inc.

Amos, Muriel & Olrun, Prudy. Animals of Nunivak Island. Amos, Muriel & Olrun, Prudy. 2006. (Animal Story Collection Ser.). 16p. (J). (gr. 2-6). pap. 9.00 *(978-1-58084-238-9(0))* Lower Kuskokwim Schl. District.

Amoss, Berthe. The Loup Garou, 1 vol. Amoss, Berthe. 2011. (ENG.). 48p. (J). (gr. 1-3). pap. 11.99 *(978-1-58980-893-5(2))* Pelican Publishing Co., Inc.

Ampel, Kenneth Robert. Alexander & the Stallion. Westra, Elizabeth. 2003. (Books for Young Learners). 16p. (J). per. 5.75 net. *(978-1-57274-534-6(7),* 2721, Bks. for Young Learners) Owen, Richard C. Pubs., Inc.

Amrein, Paul. Chasing the Pot of Gold. Soundar, Chitra. 2006. 32p. (J). E-Book 5.00 incl. cd-rom *(978-1-933090-36-8(7))* Guardian Angel Publishing, Inc.

Amstutz, Andre. Master Track's Train. Ahlberg, Allan. (ENG.). 24p. (J). pap. 6.95 *(978-0-14-037881-8(2))* Penguin Bks., Ltd. GBR. Dist: Trafalgar Square Publishing.

Amy Belle Elementary School. The Cupcake Boy. Stoll, Scott. 2012. 108p. pap. 7.95 *(978-0-9827842-4-2(4))* Argonauts, The.

Amy, Holloway. Hermione: Shipwrecked! in Ocean City, Maryland. Trimper, Marty. 2004. (J). *(978-1-886068-28-5(3))* Fruitbearer Publishing, LLC.

Amy Huntington. Adding with Sebastian Pig & Friends at the Circus. Anderson, Jill. 2013. (Math Fun with Sebastian Pig & Friends! Ser.). 32p. (J). (gr. k-3). pap. 7.95 *(978-0-7660-5973-3(1),* Enslow Elementary) Enslow Pubs., Inc.

—Counting with Sebastian Pig & Friends on the Farm. Anderson, Jill. 2013. (Math Fun with Sebastian Pig & Friends! Ser.). 32p. (J). (gr. k-3). pap. 7.95 *(978-0-7660-5980-1(4),* Enslow Elementary) Enslow Pubs., Inc.

—Finding Shapes with Sebastian Pig & Friends at the Museum. Anderson, Jill. 2013. (Math Fun with Sebastian Pig & Friends! Ser.). 32p. (J). (gr. k-3). pap. 7.95 *(978-0-7660-5981-8(2),* Enslow Elementary) Enslow Pubs., Inc.

—Measuring with Sebastian Pig & Friends on a Road Trip. Anderson, Jill. 2013. (Math Fun with Sebastian Pig & Friends! Ser.). 32p. (J). (gr. k-3). pap. 7.95 *(978-0-7660-5982-5(0),* Enslow Elementary) Enslow Pubs., Inc.

—Money Math with Sebastian Pig & Friends at the Farmer's Market. Anderson, Jill. 2013. (Math Fun with Sebastian Pig & Friends! Ser.). 32p. (J). (gr. k-3). pap. 7.95 *(978-0-7660-5983-2(9),* Enslow Elementary) Enslow Pubs., Inc.

An, Carlos. Frankenstein's Monster & Scientific Methods. Harbo, Christopher L. 2013. (Monster Science Ser.). (ENG.). 32p. (gr. 3-4). pap. 47.70 *(978-1-62065-817-8(8),* Graphic Library) Capstone Pr., Inc.

—Monster Science. Harbo, Christopher L. 2013. (Monster Science Ser.). (ENG.). 32p. (gr. 3-4). pap. 79.50 *(978-1-4765-3674-3(0),* Graphic Library) Capstone Pr., Inc.

An, Jiyoung. Barbie Loves Pets. Frazer, Rebecca. 2007. (Pictureback(R) Ser.). (ENG.). 16p. (J). (gr. -1-2). pap. 3.99 *(978-0-375-84797-4(9),* Golden Bks.) Random Hse., Inc.

—I Can Be a Pet Vet. Man-Kong, Mary. 2010. (Step into Reading Ser.). (ENG.). 32p. (J). (gr. -1-1). pap. 3.99 *(978-0-375-86581-7(0),* Random Hse. Bks. for Young Readers) Random Hse. Children's Bks.

—I Can Be a Sports Star (Barbie) Man-Kong, Mary. 2012. (3-D Pictureback Ser.). (ENG.). 16p. (J). (gr. -1-2). pap. 4.99 *(978-0-307-93130-6(7),* Random Hse. Bks. for Young Readers) Random Hse. Children's Bks.

—Secret Hearts. Frazer, Rebecca. 2008. (Pictureback Ser.). (ENG.). 16p. (J). (gr. -1-2). pap. 3.99 *(978-0-375-84633-5(6),* Golden Bks.) Random Hse. Children's Bks.

An, Jiyoung, jt. illus. see Golden Books Staff.
An, Jiyoung, jt. illus. see RH Disney Staff.

An, Sang, photos by. A Gracious Welcome: Etiquette & Ideas for Welcoming Houseguests. Nebens, Amy M. 2004. (ENG., 120p. (gr. 8-17). 19.95 *(978-0-8118-4083-5(2))* Chronicle Bks. LLC.

Anagost, Karen. The Night Before Cat-Mas. Unser, Virginia. 2007. (Petite Plush Kit Ser.). 64p. (J). (gr. -1-3). 9.95 *(978-1-59359-882-2(3))* Peter Pauper Pr. Inc.

—The Night Before Dog-Mas. Gandolfi, Claudine. 2007. (Petite Plush Kit Ser.). 64p. (J). (gr. -1-3). 9.95 *(978-1-59359-883-9(1))* Peter Pauper Pr. Inc.

Anchin, Lisa. A Penguin Named Patience: A Hurricane Katrina Rescue Story. Lewis, Suzanne. 2015. (ENG.). 24p. (J). (gr. 1-4). 15.95 *(978-1-58536-840-2(7),* 203732) Sleeping Bear Pr.

Ancona, George. Come & Eat! 2011. (ENG.). 48p. (J). (gr. k-3). 16.95 *(978-1-58089-366-4(X))* Charlesbridge Publishing, Inc.

Ancona, George. Can We Help? Kids Volunteering to Help Their Communities. Ancona, George. 2015. (ENG.). 48p. (J). (gr. k-3). 16.99 ***(978-0-7636-7367-3(6))*** Candlewick Pr.

Ancona, George. It's Our Garden: From Seeds to Harvest in a School Garden. Ancona, George. 2015. (ENG.). 48p. (J). (gr. k-3). pap. 6.99 *(978-0-7636-7691-9(8))* Candlewick Pr.

Ancona, George, photos by. Arizona. Becker, Michelle Aki. Risco, Eida del, tr. from ENG. 2004. (Rookie Readers Spanish Ser.). (SPA., 32p. (J). 19.50 *(978-0-516-25106-6(6),* Watts, Franklin) Scholastic Library Publishing.

—California. De Capua, Sarah. Risco, Eida del, tr. from ENG. 2004. (Rookie Readers Spanish Ser.). (SPA., 32p. (J). 19.50 *(978-0-516-25107-3(4),* Watts, Franklin) Scholastic Library Publishing.

—Florida. Bredeson, Carmen. Risco, Eida del, tr. from ENG. 2004. (Rookie Readers Spanish Ser.). (SPA., 32p. (J). 19.50 *(978-0-516-25108-0(2),* Watts, Franklin) Scholastic Library Publishing.

—Join Hands! The Ways We Celebrate Life. Mora, Pat. 2008. (ENG., 32p. (J). (gr. -1-3). 15.95 *(978-1-58089-202-5(7))* Charlesbridge Publishing, Inc.

Ancona, George, photos by. Come & Eat! Ancona, George. 2011. (ENG., 48p. (J). (gr. k-3). pap. 7.95 *(978-1-58089-367-1(8))* Charlesbridge Publishing, Inc.

—Olé Flamenco! Ancona, George. 2010. (ENG., 48p. (J). (gr. 2-6). 19.95 *(978-1-60060-361-7(0))* Lee & Low Bks., Inc.

—Self Portrait. Ancona, George. 2006. (Meet the Author Ser.). 32p. (J). 14.95 *(978-1-57274-860-6(5),* 733, Meet the Author) Owen, Richard C. Pubs., Inc.

Andersen, Amy Elliott. The Shroud of the Thwacker. Elliott, Chris. 2006. 368p. pap. 13.95 *(978-1-4013-6011-5(4))* Miramax Bks.

Andersen, Bethane. But God Remembered: Stories of Women from Creation to the Promised Land. Sasso, Sandy Eisenberg. 2008. (ENG.). 32p. pap. 8.99 *(978-1-58023-372-9(4),* Jewish Lights Publishing) LongHill Partners, Inc.

Andersen, Bethanne. Georgia's Bones. Bryant, Jen. 2005. 32p. (J). 16.00 *(978-0-8028-5217-5(3))* Eerdmans, William B. Publishing Co.

—Louisa. McDonough, Yona Zeldis. 2014. (ENG.). 48p. (J). (gr. 1-5). pap. 7.99 *(978-1-250-05047-2(2))* Square Fish.

—Louisa: The Life of Louisa May Alcott. McDonough, Yona Zeldis. 2009. (ENG.). 48p. (J). (gr. 1-5). 17.99 *(978-0-8050-8192-3(5),* Holt, Henry & Co. Bks. For Young Readers) Holt, Henry & Co.

—Seven Brave Women. Hearne, Betsy. 2006. (ENG.). 24p. (J). (gr. k-5). reprint ed. pap. 6.99 *(978-0-06-079921-2(8),* Greenwillow Bks.) HarperCollins Pubs.

—Seven Brave Women. Hearne, Betsy. 2006. (gr. -1-3). 17.00 *(978-0-7569-6669-0(8))* Perfection Learning Corp.

Andersen, Dana Lynne. Born with a Bang: The Universe Tells Our Cosmic Story. Morgan, Jennifer. 2004. (Sharing Nature with Children Book Ser.). 48p. (YA). (gr. 2-18). 19.95 *(978-1-58469-033-7(X))*; pap. 9.95 *(978-1-58469-032-0(1))* Dawn Pubns.

—From Lava to Life: The Universe Tells Our Earth Story. Morgan, Jennifer. (Sharing Nature with Children Book Ser.: Vol. 2). (YA). 2004. 48p. 19.95 *(978-1-58469-043-6(7))*; 2003. 47p. pap. 9.95 *(978-1-58469-042-9(9))* Dawn Pubns.

—Mammals Who Morph: The Universe Tells Our Evolution Story: Book 3. Morgan, Jennifer. 2006. (Sharing Nature with Children Book Ser.). 48p. (J). (gr. 3-7). 19.95 *(978-1-58469-084-9(4))*; pap. 9.95 *(978-1-58469-085-6(2))* Dawn Pubns.

Andersen, Flemming & Gonzalez, Jose Antonio. Donald Duck Adventures, Vol. 17. Laban, Terry. Clark, John, ed. 2006. (Walt Disney's Donald Duck Adventures Ser.). 128p. (YA). (gr. 3-7). pap. 7.95 *(978-1-888472-12-7(X))* Gemstone Publishing, Inc.

Andersen, Gregg, photos by. Adding & Subtracting in Math Club. Ayers, Amy. 2007. (Math in Our World Ser.). 24p. (gr. 1-2). lib. bdg. 22.00 *(978-0-8368-8470-8(1),* Weekly Reader Leveled Readers) Stevens, Gareth Publishing LLLP.

—Bus Drivers. Gorman, Jacqueline Laks & Laks Gorman, Jacqueline. 2010. (People in My Community Ser.). 24p. (gr. k-3). 22.60 *(978-1-4339-3335-6(7))* Stevens, Gareth Publishing LLLP.

—Bus Drivers. Gorman, Jacqueline Laks. 2010. (People in My Community Ser.). 24p. (gr. k-3). pap. 8.15 *(978-1-4339-3336-3(5))* Stevens, Gareth Publishing LLLP.

—Bus Drivers / Conductores de Autobuses. Laks Gorman, Jacqueline. 2010. (People in My Community / Mi comunidad Ser.). (SPA., 24p. (gr. k-3). pap. 8.15 *(978-1-4339-3754-5(9))* Stevens, Gareth Publishing LLLP.

—Counting at the Zoo. Rauen, Amy & Ayers, Amy. 2007. (Math in Our World Ser.). 24p. (gr. 1-2). pap. 8.15 *(978-0-8368-8478-4(7),* Weekly Reader Leveled Readers) Stevens, Gareth Publishing LLLP.

—Firefighters. Gorman, Jacqueline Laks & Laks Gorman, Jacqueline. 2010. (People in My Community Ser.). 24p. (gr. k-3). 22.60 *(978-1-4339-3338-7(1))* Stevens, Gareth Publishing LLLP.

—Firefighters. Gorman, Jacqueline Laks. 2010. (People in My Community Ser.). 24p. (gr. k-3). pap. 8.15 *(978-1-4339-3339-4(X))* Stevens, Gareth Publishing LLLP.

—Firefighters / Bomberos. Laks Gorman, Jacqueline. 2010. (People in My Community / Mi comunidad Ser.). (SPA., 24p. (gr. k-3). pap. 8.15 *(978-1-4339-3757-6(3))* Stevens, Gareth Publishing LLLP.

—Librarians. Laks Gorman, Jacqueline. 2010. (People in My Community Ser.). 24p. (gr. k-3). pap. 8.15 *(978-1-4339-3342-4(X))* Stevens, Gareth Publishing LLLP.

—Librarians. Gorman, Jacqueline Laks & Laks Gorman, Jacqueline. 2010. (People in My Community Ser.). 24p. (gr. k-3). 22.60 *(978-1-4339-3341-7(1))* Stevens, Gareth Publishing LLLP.

—Librarians / Bibliotecarios. Laks Gorman, Jacqueline. 2010. (People in My Community / Mi comunidad Ser.). (SPA., 24p. (gr. k-3). pap. 8.15 *(978-1-4339-3760-6(3))* Stevens, Gareth Publishing LLLP.

—Mail Carriers. Early Macken, JoAnn. 2010. (People in My Community Ser.). 24p. (gr. k-3). pap. 8.15 *(978-1-4339-3345-5(4))* Stevens, Gareth Publishing LLLP.

—Mail Carriers / Carteros. Early Macken, JoAnn. 2010. (People in My Community / Mi comunidad Ser.). (SPA., 24p. (gr. k-3). pap. 8.15 *(978-1-4339-3763-7(8))* Stevens, Gareth Publishing LLLP.

—Police Officers. Gorman, Jacqueline Laks & Laks Gorman, Jacqueline. 2010. (People in My Community Ser.). 24p. (gr. k-3). 22.60 *(978-1-4339-3350-9(0))* Stevens, Gareth Publishing LLLP.

—Police Officers. Gorman, Jacqueline Laks. 2010. (People in My Community Ser.). 24p. (gr. k-3). pap. 8.15 *(978-1-4339-3351-6(9))* Stevens, Gareth Publishing LLLP.

—Police Officers / Policías. Laks Gorman, Jacqueline. 2010. (People in My Community / Mi comunidad Ser.). (SPA., 24p. (gr. k-3). pap. 8.15 *(978-1-4339-3769-9(7))* Stevens, Gareth Publishing LLLP.

—Safety at Home. Knowlton, MaryLee. 2008. (Staying Safe Ser.). (ENG., 32p. (J). (gr. -1-3). lib. bdg. *(978-0-7787-4316-3(0))* Crabtree Publishing Co.

—Safety at School. Knowlton, MaryLee & Dowdy, Penny. 2008. (Staying Safe Ser.). (ENG., 32p. (J). (gr. -1-3). pap. *(978-0-7787-4322-4(5))* Crabtree Publishing Co.

—Safety at School. Knowlton, MaryLee. 2008. (Staying Safe Ser.). (ENG., 32p. (J). (gr. -1-3). lib. bdg. *(978-0-7787-4317-0(9))* Crabtree Publishing Co.

—Safety at the Playground. Knowlton, MaryLee & Dowdy, Penny. 2008. (Staying Safe Ser.). (ENG., 32p. (J). (gr. -1-3). pap. *(978-0-7787-4323-1(3))* Crabtree Publishing Co.

—Safety at the Playground. Knowlton, MaryLee. 2008. (Staying Safe Ser.). (ENG., 32p. (J). (gr. -1-3). lib. bdg. *(978-0-7787-4318-7(7))* Crabtree Publishing Co.

—Sumando y Restando en el Club de Matematicas. Rauen, Amy & Ayers, Amy. 2007. (Matemáticas en Nuestro Mundo (Math in Our World) Ser.). (SPA., 24p. (gr. 1-2). lib. bdg. 22.00 *(978-0-8368-8488-3(4),* Weekly Reader Leveled Readers) Stevens, Gareth Publishing LLLP.

—Teachers. Early Macken, JoAnn. 2010. (People in My Community Ser.). 24p. (gr. k-3). pap. 8.15 *(978-1-4339-3348-6(9))* Stevens, Gareth Publishing LLLP.

—Teachers / Maestros. Early Macken, JoAnn. 2010. (People in My Community / Mi comunidad Ser.). (SPA., 24p. (gr. k-3). pap. 8.15 *(978-1-4339-3766-8(2))* Stevens, Gareth Publishing LLLP.

—Using Math to Make Party Plans. Freese, Joan. 2008. (Math in Our World: Level 2 Ser.). 24p. (gr. 1-4). lib. bdg. 22.00 *(978-0-8368-9003-7(5),* Weekly Reader Leveled Readers) Stevens, Gareth Publishing LLLP.

—Vamos A Planear una Fiesta Con Matematicas. Freese, Joan. 2008. (Matemáticas en Nuestro Mundo - Nivel 2 (Math in Our World - Level 2) Ser.). (SPA., 24p. (gr. 1-4). lib. bdg. 22.00 *(978-0-8368-9021-1(3),* Weekly Reader Leveled Readers) Stevens, Gareth Publishing LLLP.

Andersen, Hans Christian. Thumbelina. 2004.Tr. of Tommelise. 32p. 3.99 *(978-1-894998-17-8(0))* Lake, Jack Productions, Inc. CAN. Dist: Hushion Hse. Publishing, Ltd.

Anderson, Aaron. Veterans: Heroes in Our Neighborhood. Pfundstein, Valerie. Chernesky, Felicia, ed. 2012. (ENG.). 32p. (J). 18.95 *(978-0-9837186-1-1(X))* Novanglus Publishing, LLC.

Anderson, Airlie. Cows in the Kitchen. (Classic Books with Holes Ser.). (ENG.). (gr. -1). 2013. 16p. pap. incl. audio compact disk *(978-1-84643-625-3(7))*; 2009. 16p. (J). *(978-1-84643-208-8(1))*; 2007. 16p. (J). pap. *(978-1-84643-106-7(9))*; 2007. 14p. (J). bds. *(978-1-84643-110-4(7))* Child's Play International Ltd.

—Cows in the Kitchen W/ 2009. (Classic Books with Holes US Soft Cover with CD Ser.). (ENG.). 16p. (J). *(978-1-84643-257-6(X))* Child's Play International Ltd.

—My Name Starts with J. Hayes, Larry E. 2004. (My Name Starts With Ser.). 31p. (J). spiral bd. 12.95 *(978-0-9725292-2-8(5))* Inspire Pubns.

—My Name Starts with K. Hayes, Larry. 2005. (My Name Starts With Ser.). 31p. (J). 12.95 *(978-0-9725292-6-6(8))* Inspire Pubns.

—My Name Starts with M. Hayes, Larry E., photos by. Hayes, Larry E. 2004. (My Name Starts With Ser.). 31p. (J). spiral bd. 12.95 *(978-0-9725292-3-5(3),* 1) Inspire Pubns.

—My Name Starts with S. Hayes, Larry E., photos by. Hayes, Larry E. 2003. (My Name Starts With Ser.). 31p. spiral bd. 10.95 *(978-0-9725292-1-1(7))* Inspire Pubns.

—My Name Starts with S (Library Version) Hayes, Larry E. 2004. (My Name Starts With Ser.). 32p. (J). lib. bdg. 12.95 *(978-0-9725292-8-0(4))* Inspire Pubns.

—A Very Patchy Flap Book. 2004. 10p. (J). bds. 5.95 *(978-1-58925-702-3(2))* Tiger Tales.

—A Very Spotty Flap Book. 2004. 10p. (J). bds. 5.95 *(978-1-58925-703-0(0))* Tiger Tales.

—A Very Stripy Flap Book. 2004. 10p. (J). bds. 5.95 *(978-1-58925-704-7(9))* Tiger Tales.

Anderson, Alasdair. 2011: Living in the Future. Hoyle, Geoffrey. 2010. (ENG.). 64p. 15.95 *(978-1-59583-430-0(3),* 9781595834300, Darling & Co.) Laughing Elephant.

Anderson, Amelia. Animal 123. Teckentrup, Britta. 2012. (Templar Ser.: TEMP). (ENG.). 20p. (J). (gr. -1 — 1). 12.99 *(978-1-4521-0993-0(1))* Chronicle Bks. LLC.

—Animal Spots & Stripes. Teckentrup, Britta. 2012. (Templar Ser.: TEMP). (ENG.). 20p. (J). (gr. -1 — 1). 12.99 *(978-1-4521-0994-7(X))* Chronicle Bks. LLC.

Anderson, Anya. Liv's Search for the Last Unicorn. Wreggelsworth, Irene. 2011. (ENG.). 112p. pap. 26.99 *(978-1-4538-9270-1(2))* CreateSpace Independent Publishing Platform.

Anderson, Bethan. Georgia's Bones. Bryant, Jen. 2010. 32p. (J). (gr. -1-5). pap. 7.99 *(978-0-8028-5367-7(6))* Eerdmans, William B. Publishing Co.

Anderson, Bethanne & Floca, Brian. Billy & the Rebel: Based on a True Civil War Story. Hopkinson, Deborah. 2005. (Ready-To-Reads Ser.). (ENG.). 48p. (J). (gr. 1-3). 16.99 *(978-0-689-83964-1(2),* Simon Spotlight) Simon Spotlight.

Anderson, Betheny, jt. illus. see Jackson, Helston.

Anderson, Bill. How Congress Works. Uni Photo Picture Agency Staff, photos by. Campodonica, Carol A. Miller, Bondell, ed. Date not set. (J). (gr. 4-5). pap. *(978-0-9648488-9-4(9))* Buzzard Pr. International.

—How to Build a California Mission: Santa Cruz, 20 vols. Anderson, Jay, photos by. Campodonica, Carol A. Weber, Francis J. et al, eds. Date not set. (How to Build a California Mission Ser.). (J). (gr. 4-5). pap. *(978-0-9648488-5-6(6))* Buzzard Pr. International.

—The Mesa Verde Cliff Dwellers: An Isabel Soto Archaeology Adventure, 1 vol. Collins, Terry et al. 2010. (Graphic Expeditions Ser.). (ENG.). 32p. (gr. 3-4). lib. bdg. 29.99 *(978-1-4296-3971-2(7),* Graphic Library) Capstone Pr., Inc.

Anderson, Bill & Smith, Tod G. Lessons in Science Safety with Max Axiom, Super Scientist, 1 vol. Lemke, Donald B. et al. 2007. (Graphic Science Ser.). (ENG.). 32p. (gr. 3-4). 29.99 *(978-0-7368-6834-1(8),* Graphic Library) Capstone Pr., Inc.

Anderson, Bill, jt. illus. see Hoover, Dave.

A

Anderson, Bill, jt. illus. see Martin, Cynthia.
Anderson, Bill, jt. illus. see Wyman, M. C.
Anderson, Billie Ann. My First Bus Ride. Faircloth, Harry W. Date not set. 26p. (J). (gr. -1-4). pap. 9.95 *(978-0-9668650-1-1(4))* Maximilian Pr. Pubs.
Anderson, Brent. God Loves, Man Kills. Claremont, Chris. 2011. (ENG.). 96p. (YA). (gr. 8-17). pap. 14.99 *(978-0-7851-5726-7(3))* Marvel Worldwide, Inc.
—Power Pack Classic - Volume 3. 2011. (ENG.). 280p. (J). (gr. 4-17). pap. 29.99 *(978-0-7851-5305-4(5))* Marvel Worldwide, Inc.
Anderson, Brian. Monster Chefs. Anderson, Brian. Anderson, Liam. 2014. (ENG.). 32p. (J). (gr. -1-2). 16.99 *(978-1-59643-808-8(8))* Roaring Brook Pr.
Anderson, C. W. Remus Goes to Town. Paltenghi, Madalena. 2011. 32p. 35.95 *(978-1-258-10024-7(X))* Literary Licensing, LLC.
Anderson, Constance. Smelling Sunshine, 1 vol. Anderson, Constance. 2013. (ENG.). 32p. (J). 16.99 *(978-1-59572-635-3(7))*; pap. 6.99 *(978-1-59572-636-0(5))* Star Bright Bks., Inc.
Anderson, Dale. The Tet Offensive: Turning Point of the Vietnam War, 1 vol. Anderson, Dale. 2006. (Snapshots in History Ser.). (ENG.). 96p. (gr. 7-8). lib. bdg. 33.99 *(978-0-7565-1623-9(4)*, Snapshots in History) Compass Point Bks.
Anderson, David. And the Winner Is... Amazing Animal Athletes. Kaner, Etta. 2013. (ENG.). 32p. (J). 16.95 *(978-1-55453-904-8(8))* Kids Can Pr., Ltd. CAN. Dist: Univ. of Toronto Pr.
Anderson, David. Friend or Foe: The Whole Truth about Animals People Love to Hate. Kaner, Etta. 2015. (ENG.). 48p. (J). (gr. 3-7). 16.95 ***(978-1-77147-064-3(X)**, Owlkids)* Owlkids Bks. Inc. CAN. Dist: Perseus-PGW.
Anderson, David. Pretty Ballerina. McRae, G. c. 2013. 44p. pap. *(978-0-9876845-3-0(1))* Warne, MacDonald Media.
—The Tooth. McRae, G. c. 2012. 36p. pap. *(978-0-9876845-2-3(3))* Warne, MacDonald Media.
Anderson, David. Charlie Sparrow & the Secret of Flight. Anderson, David. 2013. 98p. pap. *(978-0-9918003-2-2(X))* Underdog Bks.
Anderson, Debby. Most of All, Jesus Loves You! Piper, Noël. 2004. 24p. (J). 11.99 *(978-1-58134-630-5(1))* Crossway.
Anderson, Debby. Every Child Everywhere! Anderson, Debby. 2008. 32p. (J). pap. 11.99 *(978-1-58134-862-0(2))* Crossway.
—God Knows My Name. Anderson, Debby. 2003. 32p. (J). 12.99 *(978-1-58134-415-8(5))* Crossway.
—Jesus Is Coming Back! Anderson, Debby. 2005. 38p. (J). (gr. -1-2). 10.99 *(978-1-58134-743-2(X))* Crossway.
—Kindness Counts! Anderson, Debby. 2007. 32p. (J). (gr. -1-3). 9.99 *(978-1-58134-861-3(4))* Crossway.
—Let's Explore God's World. Anderson, Debby. 2009. 32p. (J). (gr. -1-1). 10.99 *(978-1-4335-0708-3(0))* Crossway.
Anderson, Dennis E., photos by. Hidden Treasures of San Francisco Bay. 2003. 176p. pap. 29.95 *(978-1-890771-75-1(9))* Heyday.
Anderson, Derek. Ballyhoo Bay. Sierra, Judy. 2009. (ENG.). 40p. (J). (gr. -1-3). 16.99 *(978-1-4169-5888-8(6)*, Simon & Schuster/Paula Wiseman Bks.) Simon & Schuster/Paula Wiseman Bks.
—Cuaquito (Little Quack) Thompson, Lauren. 2010. (SPA.). 34p. (J). (gr. -1-1). bds. 7.99 *(978-1-4169-9894-5(2)*, Libros Para Ninos) Libros Para Ninos.
—Happy Birthday Hamster. Lord, Cynthia. 2011. (ENG.). 40p. (J). (gr. -1-k). 16.99 *(978-0-545-25522-6(8)*, Scholastic Pr.) Scholastic, Inc.
—Hot Rod Hamster. Lord, Cynthia. 2010. (ENG.). 40p. (J). (gr. -1-k). 16.99 *(978-0-545-03530-9(9)*, Scholastic Pr.) Scholastic, Inc.
—Hot Rod Hamster & the Awesome ATV Adventure! Lord, Cynthia. 2015. (ENG.). 32p. (J). 16.99 *(978-0-545-76734-7(2))*; pap. 3.99 *(978-0-545-62680-4(3))* Scholastic, Inc. (Scholastic Pr.).
Anderson, Derek. Hot Rod Hamster & the Haunted Halloween Party! Lord, Cynthia. 2015. (ENG.). 32p. (J). (gr. -1-3). 16.99 ***(978-0-545-81529-1(0)**, Scholastic Pr.)* Scholastic, Inc.
Anderson, Derek. Hot Rod Hamster & the Wacky Whatever Race! Lord, Cynthia. 2014. (ENG.). 32p. (J). (gr. -1-3). pap. 3.99 *(978-0-545-62678-1(1)*, Scholastic Pr.) Scholastic, Inc.
—Little Quack. Thompson, Lauren. 2005. (Classic Board Bks.). (ENG.). 34p. (J). (gr. -1-k). 7.99 *(978-0-689-87645-5(9)*, Little Simon) Little Simon.
—Little Quack Counts. Thompson, Lauren. 2009. (Super Chubbies Ser.). (ENG.). 26p. (J). (gr. -1 — 1). 5.99 *(978-1-4169-6093-5(7)*, Little Simon) Little Simon.
—Little Quack Loves Colors. Thompson, Lauren. 2009. (Super Chubbies Ser.). (ENG.). 26p. (J). (gr. -1 — 1). 5.99 *(978-1-4169-6094-2(5)*, Little Simon) Little Simon.
—Little Quack's ABC's. Thompson, Lauren. 2010. (Super Chubbies Ser.). (ENG.). 26p. (J). (gr. -1 — 1). bds. 5.99 *(978-1-4169-6091-1(0)*, Little Simon) Little Simon.
—Little Quack's Bath Book. Thompson, Lauren. 2006. (ENG.). 8p. (J). (gr. -1 — 1). 8.99 *(978-1-4169-0803-6(X)*, Little Simon) Little Simon.
—Little Quack's Bedtime. Thompson, Lauren. 2005. (ENG.). 32p. (J). (gr. -1-3). 17.99 *(978-0-689-86894-8(4)*, Simon & Schuster Bks. For Young Readers) Simon & Schuster Bks. For Young Readers.
—Little Quack's New Friend. Thompson, Lauren. 2008. (Classic Board Bks.). (ENG.). 34p. (J). (gr. -1-1). 7.99 *(978-1-4169-4923-7(2)*, Little Simon) Little Simon.
—Little Quack's New Friend. Thompson, Lauren. 2006. (ENG.). 32p. (J). (gr. -1-3). 16.99 *(978-0-689-86893-1(6)*, Simon & Schuster Bks. For Young Readers) Simon & Schuster Bks. For Young Readers.
—Little Quack's Opposites. Thompson, Lauren. 2010. (Super Chubbies Ser.). (ENG.). 26p. (J). (gr. -1 — 1). bds. 5.99 *(978-1-4169-6092-8(9)*, Little Simon) Little Simon.
—Monster Truck Mania! Lord, Cynthia. 2014. (ENG.). 40p. (J). (gr. -1-k). 16.99 *(978-0-545-46261-7(4)*, Scholastic Pr.) Scholastic, Inc.
—The Potty Train. Hochman, David & Kennison, Ruth. 2008. (ENG.). 32p. (J). (gr. -1-k). 9.99 *(978-1-4169-2833-1(2)*, Simon & Schuster Bks. For Young Readers) Simon & Schuster Bks. For Young Readers.
—Waking Dragons. Yolen, Jane. 2012. (ENG.). 32p. (J). (gr. -1-3). 16.99 *(978-1-4169-9032-1(1)*, Simon & Schuster Bks. For Young Readers) Simon & Schuster Bks. For Young Readers.
Anderson, Derek. Blue Burt & Wiggles. Anderson, Derek. 2014.Tr. of Signed in American Sign Language. (ENG.). 32p. (J). (gr. -1-3). 16.99 *(978-1-4814-1933-8(1)*, Simon & Schuster Bks. For Young Readers) Simon & Schuster Bks. For Young Readers.
—Gladys Goes Out to Lunch. Anderson, Derek. 2005.Tr. of Signed in American Sign Language. (ENG.). 40p. (J). (gr. -1-3). 17.99 *(978-0-689-85688-4(1)*, Simon & Schuster Bks. For Young Readers) Simon & Schuster Bks. For Young Readers.
—How the Easter Bunny Saved Christmas. Anderson, Derek. 2006. (ENG.). 40p. (J). (gr. -1-3). 17.99 *(978-0-689-87634-9(3)*, Simon & Schuster Bks. For Young Readers) Simon & Schuster Bks. For Young Readers.
—Romeo & Lou Blast Off. Anderson, Derek. 2014. (ENG.). 32p. (J). (gr. -1-3). 16.99 *(978-1-4814-1932-1(3)*, Simon & Schuster Bks. For Young Readers) Simon & Schuster Bks. For Young Readers.
—Ten Pigs: An Epic Bath Adventure. Anderson, Derek. 2015. (ENG.). 40p. (J). (gr. -1-k). 16.99 *(978-0-545-16846-5(5))* Scholastic, Inc.
Anderson, Derek & Paprocki, Greg. Hot Rod Hamster & the Haunted Halloween Party. Lord, Cynthia. 2015. (ENG.). 32p. (J). (gr. -1-3). pap. 3.99 ***(978-0-545-81528-4(2)**, Scholastic Pr.)* Scholastic, Inc.
Anderson, Doug. 101 Best Magic Tricks. Frederick, Guy. 2012. 130p. 40.95 *(978-1-258-23095-1(X))*; pap. 25.95 *(978-1-258-23889-6(6))* Literary Licensing, LLC.
Anderson, Harold. Get 'Em Mayfield. Sherman, Harold M. 2011. 272p. 47.95 *(978-1-258-06451-8(0))* Literary Licensing, LLC.
Anderson, Ho Che, et al. Another Day, Vol. 1. Pekar, Harvey et al. rev. ed. 2007. (American Splendor Ser.). (ENG.). 136p. pap. 14.99 *(978-1-4012-1235-3(2)*, Vertigo) DC Comics.
Anderson, Irv. The Little Runaway. Hillert, Margaret. 2008. (Beginning-to-Read Bks.). 32p. (J). (gr. -1-2). lib. bdg. 19.93 *(978-1-59953-155-7(0))* Norwood Hse. Pr.
Anderson, Jan. A Wolf's Tale. Clish, Marian L. unabr. I.t. ed. (J). (gr. k-5). pap. 14.95 incl. audio compact disk *(978-1-928632-01-6(7))* Writers Marketplace:Consulting, Critiquing & Publishing.
Anderson, Jan, jt. illus. see Larkins, Mona.
Anderson, Jane A. How Do Hedgehogs Hug? Alford, Douglas J. & Alford, Pakaket. 2013. 58p. pap. 11.99 *(978-1-62495-071-1(X))* Manufacturing Application Konsulting Engineering (MAKE)in.
Anderson, Jeff. The Duke's Daughter: A Story of Faith & Love. MacKenzie, Lachlan. 2008. (Story Time Ser.). (ENG.). 24p. (J). (gr. -1-3). 7.99 *(978-1-84550-326-0(0))* Christian Focus Pubns. GBR. Dist: Send The Light Distribution LLC.
—How God Sent a Dog to Save a Family. Beeke, Joel R. & Kleyn, Diana. 2005. (Building on the Rock Ser.). (ENG.). 176p. (J). pap. 8.99 *(978-1-85792-819-8(9))* Christian Focus Pubns. GBR. Dist: Send The Light Distribution LLC.
—How God Stopped the Pirates. Beeke, Joel R. & Kleyn, Diana. 2004. (Building on the Rock Ser.). (ENG.). 176p. (J). pap. 8.99 *(978-1-85792-816-7(4))* Christian Focus Pubns. GBR. Dist: Send The Light Distribution LLC.
—How God Used a Drought & an Umbrella. Beeke, Joel R. & Kleyn, Diana. 2006. (Building on the Rock Ser.). (ENG.). 176p. (J). pap. 8.99 *(978-1-85792-818-1(0))* Christian Focus Pubns. GBR. Dist: Send The Light Distribution LLC.
—How God Used a Snowdrift. Beeke, Joel R. & Kleyn, Diana. 2005. (Building on the Rock Ser.). (ENG.). 176p. (J). pap. 8.99 *(978-1-85792-817-4(2))* Christian Focus Pubns. GBR. Dist: Send The Light Distribution LLC.
—How God Used a Thunderstorm. Beeke, Joel R. & Kleyn, Diana. 2004. (Building on the Rock Ser.). (ENG.). 176p. (J). pap. 8.99 *(978-1-85792-815-0(6))* Christian Focus Pubns. GBR. Dist: Send The Light Distribution LLC.
—Jesus: The Real Story. Mackenzie, Carine & MacKenzie, Carine. 2004. (ENG.). 148p. (J). 10.99 *(978-1-85792-930-0(6)*, Christian Focus) Christian Focus Pubns. GBR. Dist: Send The Light Distribution LLC.
—Jesus el Milagroso. Foce, Natalia, tr. from ENG. I.t. ed. 2009. Orig. Title: Jesus the Miracle Worker. (SPA & ENG.). 24p. (J). 3.49 *(978-1-932789-28-7(6))* Editorial Sendas Antiguas, LLC.
—Jesus Maestro. Foce, Natalia, tr. from ENG. I.t. ed. 2009. Orig. Title: Jesus the Teacher. (SPA & ENG.). 24p. (J). 3.49 *(978-1-932789-26-3(X))* Editorial Sendas Antiguas, LLC.
—Jesus Narrador. Foce, Natalia, tr. from ENG. I.t. ed. 2009. Orig. Title: Jesus the Storyteller. (SPA & ENG.). 24p. (J). 3.49 *(978-1-932789-25-6(1))* Editorial Sendas Antiguas, LLC.
—Jesus Niño. Foce, Natalia, tr. from ENG. I.t. ed. 2009. Orig. Title: Jesus the Child. (SPA & ENG.). 24p. (J). 3.49 *(978-1-932789-24-9(3))* Editorial Sendas Antiguas, LLC.
—Jesus Salvador. Foce, Natalia, tr. from ENG. I.t. ed. 2009. Orig. Title: Jesus the Saviour. (SPA & ENG.). 24p. (J). 3.49 *(978-1-932789-29-4(4))* Editorial Sendas Antiguas, LLC.
—Jesus Sanador. Foce, Natalia, tr. from ENG. I.t. ed. 2009. Orig. Title: Jesus the Healer. (SPA & ENG.). 24p. (J). 3.49 *(978-1-932789-27-0(8))* Editorial Sendas Antiguas, LLC.
—Queen Victoria's Request: A Story of Grace & Mercy. Spurgeon, Charles H. 2008. (Story Time Ser.). (ENG.). 24p. (J). (gr. -1-3). 7.99 *(978-1-84550-325-3(2))* Christian Focus Pubns. GBR. Dist: Send The Light Distribution LLC.
Anderson, Jesse. The Graham Cracker Kid & the Calico Girl. Overstreet, Tommy & Vest, Dale G. 2012. 46p. 12.95 *(978-1-62016-014-5(5))* AWOC.COM.
Anderson, Julie. Building Essential Vocabulary: Reproducible Photo Cards, Games, & Activities to Build Vocabulary in Any Language. Flora, Sherrill B. 2005. (ENG.). 96p. (gr. -1-3). per. 13.99 *(978-1-933052-12-0(0)*, Key Education Publishing Company, LLC) Carson-Dellosa Publishing, LLC.
Anderson, Kari A. When I Grow Up. Wilson, Jodi L. 32p. (Orig.). (J). (gr. 1-3). pap. 4.95 *(978-0-9628335-0-2(9))* Wilander Publishing Co.
Anderson, Laura Ellen. Rapunzel & the Prince of Pop. Gorman, Karyn. 2015. (ENG.). 32p. (J). ***(978-0-7787-1929-8(4))*** Crabtree Publishing Co.
Anderson, Laura Ellen & Busby, Ailie. Bad Influence. Sutcliffe, William. 2015. (ENG.). 224p. (YA). (gr. 9). pap. 15.99 *(978-1-4088-3653-8(X)*, Bloomsbury USA Childrens) Bloomsbury USA.
Anderson, Lena. Linnea in Monet's Garden. Björk, Christina. Sandin, Joan, tr. 2012. (ENG.). 48p. (J). (-3). 16.99 *(978-1-4022-7729-0(6)*, Sourcebooks Jabberwocky) Sourcebooks, Inc.
Anderson, Lesley. Gwendolyn Goes Hollywood. Rottenberg, David Ira & Rottenberg, David Ira. 2011. 40p. (J). 16.99 *(978-0-910291-11-8(X))* Cedar Crest Bks.
Anderson, Lochlin. The Adventures of Charley Mcchoochoo: Danny & the Whistling Engine. Davis, Trevor. Davis, Natalie, ed. 2012. 34p. pap. 9.99 *(978-0-9853650-5-9(6))* Mindstir Media.
Anderson, Marjorie M. A Country Christmas. Pearson, Georgene. 2005. 34p. (J). (gr. -1-3). 19.95 *(978-1-892728-08-1(7))* Tate Publishing & Enterprises, LLC.
Anderson, Mark. For Love of the Cubs: An A-to-Z Primer for Fans of All Ages. Klein, Frederick C. 2nd ed. 2004. (For the Love Of... Ser.). (ENG.). 48p. 16.95 *(978-1-57243-646-6(8))* Triumph Bks.
—For the Love of Cats: An A-to-Z Primer for Cat Lovers of All Ages. Robins, Sandy. 2011. (For the Love Of... Ser.). (ENG.). 48p. 16.95 *(978-1-60078-581-8(6))* Triumph Bks.
—For the Love of Dogs: An A-to-Z Primer for Dog Lovers of All Ages. Entrekin, Allison Weiss. 2011. (For the Love Of... Ser.). (ENG.). 48p. 16.95 *(978-1-60078-371-5(6))* Triumph Bks.
—For the Love of the Cubs: An A to Z Primer for Cubs Fans of All Ages. Klein, Frederick C. 2003. (For the Love Of... Ser.). (ENG.). 48p. 16.95 *(978-1-57243-545-2(3))* Triumph Bks.
—For the Love of the Cubs: An A-to-Z Primer for Cubs Fans of All Ages. Klein, Frederick C. 3rd ed. 2005. (For the Love Of... Ser.). (ENG.). 48p. 16.95 *(978-1-57243-795-1(2))* Triumph Bks.
—For the Love of the Red Sox: An A-to-Z Primer for Red Sox Fans of All Ages. Klein, Fredrick C. 2004. 48p. 16.95 *(978-1-57243-667-1(0))* Triumph Bks.
—For the Love of the Yankees: An A-to-Z Primer for Yankees Fans of All Ages. Klein, Fredrick C. 2003. 48p. (J). 19.95 *(978-1-57243-579-7(8))* Triumph Bks.
Anderson, Murphy, jt. illus. see Sachs, Bernard.
Anderson, Neal. Nephi, Nephi, the Scriptures Are True. Wells, Anita. 2004. 32p. (J). (gr. -1-2). 17.95 *(978-1-59038-307-0(9))* Deseret Bk. Co.
Anderson, Nicola. Planet Pop-Up: Monkey on the Moon. Litton, Jonathan. 2015. (Planet Pop-Up Ser.). (ENG.). 12p. (J). (gr. -1). 12.95 ***(978-1-62686-372-9(5)**, Silver Dolphin Bks.)* Baker & Taylor Publishing Group.
Anderson, Nicola. Planet Pop-Up: Shark Makes a Splash! Litton, Jonathan. 2015. (Planet Pop-Up Ser.). (ENG.). 12p. (J). (gr. -1). 12.95 *(978-1-62686-353-8(9)*, Silver Dolphin Bks.) Baker & Taylor Publishing Group.
—Planet Pop-Up: Sheep Rules the Roost! Litton, Jonathan. 2015. (Planet Pop-Up Ser.). (ENG.). 12p. (J). (gr. -1). 12.95 *(978-1-62686-354-5(7)*, Silver Dolphin Bks.) Baker & Taylor Publishing Group.
Anderson, Nicola. Planet Pop-Up: Tiger Takes Off. Litton, Jonathan. 2015. (Planet Pop-Up Ser.). (ENG.). 12p. (J). (gr. -1). 12.95 ***(978-1-62686-373-6(3)**, Silver Dolphin Bks.)* Baker & Taylor Publishing Group.
Anderson, Peggy Perry. To the Tub. Anderson, Peggy Perry. 2004. 52p. (gr. -1-3). 17.00 *(978-0-7569-4258-8(6))* Perfection Learning Corp.
Anderson, Peter & Brightling, Geoff. Gorilas. Redmond, Ian. 2003. (SPA.). 64p. 14.95 *(978-84-372-2323-0(7))* Altea, Ediciones, S.A. - Grupo Santillana ESP. Dist: Santillana USA Publishing Co., Inc.
Anderson, Rick. Ancient Mounds of Watson Brake: Oldest Earthworks in North America, 1 vol. Couvillon, Alice & Moore, Elizabeth. 2010. (ENG.). 32p. (J). (gr. k-3). 16.99 *(978-1-58980-656-6(5))* Pelican Publishing Co., Inc.
—M Is for Magnolia: A Mississippi Alphabet. Shoulders, Michael. 2003. (Discover America State by State Ser.). (ENG.). 40p. (J). 17.95 *(978-1-58536-129-8(1))* Sleeping Bear Pr.
—N Is for Natural State: An Arkansas Alphabet. Shoulders, Michael. 2003. (Discover America State by State Ser.). (ENG.). 40p. (J). (gr. k-6). 17.95 *(978-1-58536-067-3(8))* Sleeping Bear Pr.
—Natural Numbers: An Arkansas Number Book. Shoulders, Michael. 2008. (Count Your Way Across the U. S. A. Ser.). (ENG.). 40p. (J). 17.95 *(978-1-58536-172-4(0))* Sleeping Bear Pr.
—Racecar Driver's Night Before Christmas, 1 vol. Townsend, Una Belle. 2008. (Night Before Christmas Ser.). (ENG.). 32p. (gr. 1-3). 16.99 *(978-1-58980-565-1(8))* Pelican Publishing Co., Inc.
—1 Mississippi 2 Mississippi: A Mississippi Number Book. Shoulders, Michael. 2004. (Count Your Way Across the U. S. A. Ser.). (ENG.). 40p. (J). 16.95 *(978-1-58536-188-5(7))* Sleeping Bear Pr.
Anderson, Scott. What Is the World Series? Herman, Gail. 2015. (What Was... ? Ser.). (ENG.). 112p. (J). (gr. 3-7). 5.99 ***(978-0-448-48406-8(4)**, Grosset & Dunlap)* Penguin Publishing Group.
Anderson, Scott & Squier, Robert. Who Was Louis Braille? Frith, Margaret. 2014. (Who Was... ? Ser.). (ENG.). 112p. (J). (gr. 3-7). 5.99 *(978-0-448-47903-3(6)*, Grosset & Dunlap) Penguin Publishing Group.
Anderson, Scott, jt. illus. see Kenyon, David Grayson.
Anderson, Scoular. Bonnie Prince Charlie & All That. Burnett, Allan. 2006. (ENG.). 103p. pap. 5.00 *(978-1-84158-496-6(7))* Birlinn, Ltd. GBR. Dist: Independent Pubs. Group.
—Columba & All That. Burnett, Allan. 2007. (ENG.). 104p. pap. 5.95 *(978-1-84158-571-0(8))* Birlinn, Ltd. GBR. Dist: Independent Pubs. Group.
—The Great Exhibition Mission Vol. 3, 3. Foster, Jo. unabr. ed. 2011. (History Spies Ser.). (ENG.). 160p. (J). (gr. 4-7). pap. 7.99 *(978-0-330-44901-4(X))* Macmillan Pubs., Ltd. GBR. Dist: Independent Pubs. Group.
—Macbeth & All That. Burnett, Allan. 2007. (ENG.). 98p. (gr. 4-7). per. 4.95 *(978-1-84158-574-1(2))* Birlinn, Ltd. GBR. Dist: Independent Pubs. Group.
—Mary, Queen of Scots. Burnett, Allan. 2006. (ENG.). 128p. pap. 5.95 *(978-1-84158-499-7(1))* Birlinn, Ltd. GBR. Dist: Independent Pubs. Group.
Anderson, Scoular. The Pied Piper & the Wrong Song. North, Laura. 2015. (ENG.). 32p. (J). ***(978-0-7787-1934-2(0))*** Crabtree Publishing Co.
Anderson, Scoular. Robert the Bruce. Burnett, Allan. 2006. (ENG.). 105p. pap. 6.95 *(978-1-84158-497-3(5))* Birlinn, Ltd. GBR. Dist: Independent Pubs. Group.
—William Wallace & All That. Burnett, Allan. 2006. (ENG.). 128p. pap. 5.95 *(978-1-84158-498-0(3))* Birlinn, Ltd. GBR. Dist: Independent Pubs. Group.
Anderson, Scoular. Collins Big Cat - Where on Earth? Band 10/White. Anderson, Scoular. 2005. (Collins Big Cat Ser.). (ENG.). 32p. (J). pap. 7.99 *(978-0-00-718633-4(9))* HarperCollins Pubs. Ltd. GBR. Dist: Independent Pubs. Group.
—Fabulous Creatures - Were They Real? Anderson, Scoular. 2005. (Collins Big Cat Ser.). (ENG.). 32p. (J). pap. 7.99 *(978-0-00-718639-6(8))* HarperCollins Pubs. Ltd. GBR. Dist: Independent Pubs. Group.
—How to Be a Knight in 10 Easy Stages. Anderson, Scoular. 2007. (Collins Big Cat Ser.). (ENG.). 24p. (J). pap. 6.99 *(978-0-00-718675-4(4))* HarperCollins Pubs. Ltd. GBR. Dist: Independent Pubs. Group.
—How to Be a Tudor in 20 Easy Stages. Anderson, Scoular. 2007. (Collins Big Cat Ser.). (ENG.). 128p. (J). pap. 8.99 *(978-0-00-723090-7(7))* HarperCollins Pubs. Ltd. GBR. Dist: Independent Pubs. Group.
—How to Be a Viking in 13 Easy Stages. Anderson, Scoular. 2007. (Collins Big Cat Ser.). (ENG.). 32p. (J). pap. 7.99 *(978-0-00-723079-2(6))* HarperCollins Pubs. Ltd. GBR. Dist: Independent Pubs. Group.
—Pirate Treasure. Anderson, Scoular. 2009. (Get Set Readers Ser.). 32p. (J). (gr. -1-2). lib. bdg. 22.60 *(978-1-60754-266-7(8))* Windmill Bks.
—Space Pirates: A Map-Reading Adventure. Anderson, Scoular. 2004. (ENG.). 32p. (J). (gr. 1-4). pap., act. bk. ed. 8.95 *(978-1-55037-880-1(5)*, 9781550378801) Annick Pr., Ltd. CAN. Dist: Firefly Bks., Ltd.
Anderson, Shauna. Spoofaloof's Adventures: Rainy Day Fun. Anderson, Shel. 2008. 52p. pap. 22.50 *(978-1-4389-1689-7(2))* AuthorHouse.
Anderson-Shorter, Susan. Whitey on the Ranch. Weldon, Stayton. 2010. 52p. pap. 12.95 *(978-1-4490-5474-8(9))* AuthorHouse.
Anderson, Stephanie. Sleepy Boy. Kanevsky, Polly. 2006. (ENG.). 32p. (J). (gr. -1-k). 16.99 *(978-0-689-86735-4(2)*, Atheneum/Richard Jackson Bks.) Simon & Schuster Children's Publishing.
—Witch-Hunt: Mysteries of the Salem Witch Trials. Aronson, Marc. (ENG.). 288p. (YA). 2003. (gr. 9-18). 19.99 *(978-0-689-84864-3(1))*; 2005. (gr. 7). reprint ed. pap. 10.99 *(978-1-4169-0315-4(1))* Simon & Schuster Children's Publishing. (Atheneum Bks. for Young Readers).
—You & Me & Home Sweet Home. Lyon, George Ella. 2009. (ENG.). 48p. (J). (gr. -1-3). pap. 17.99 *(978-0-689-87589-2(4)*, Atheneum/Richard Jackson Bks.) Simon & Schuster Children's Publishing.
Anderson, Stephanie. Weaving the Rainbow. Anderson, Stephanie. Lyon, George Ella. 2004. (ENG.). 40p. (J). (gr. -1-2). 17.99 *(978-0-689-85169-8(3)*, Atheneum/Richard Jackson Bks.) Simon & Schuster Children's Publishing.
Anderson, Sue, jt. illus. see Gioulis, Sue.
Anderson, Susan. Amani's World: Amani Goes to Washington D. C. Rutledge, Eddie. 2009. 16p. pap. 8.75 *(978-1-4490-2095-8(X))* AuthorHouse.
—The Queen's 3 Jewels. Gillespie, Tonnika. 2009. 20p. pap. 13.99 *(978-1-4389-3925-4(6))* AuthorHouse.
—Star the Mermaid. Filakosky, Sandra. 2010. 20p. pap. 10.49 *(978-1-4389-8626-5(2))* AuthorHouse.
Anderson, Wayne, et al. The Dragonology Handbook: A Practical Course in Dragons. Drake, Ernest. Steer, Dugald A., ed. ed. 2005. (Ologies Ser.). (ENG.). 80p. (J). (gr. 4-7). 14.99 *(978-0-7636-2814-7(X))* Candlewick Pr.
Anderson, Wayne. Dragons: Truth, Myth & Legend. Passes, David. 2007. (ENG.). 46p. (J). (gr. 4-7). pap. 11.95 *(978-1-84458-476-5(3))* Pavilion Bks. GBR. Dist: Independent Pubs. Group.
—The Fairy-Spotter's Handbook. Kerven, Rosalind & Quarto Generic Staff. 2004. (ENG.). 48p. (J). (gr. k-4). 14.95 *(978-1-84507-152-3(2)*, Frances Lincoln) Quarto Publishing Group UK GBR. Dist: Hachette Bk. Group.
—The Secret History of Mermaids & Creatures of the Deep. Berk, Ari. 2009. (ENG.). 48p. (J). (gr. 3-7). 17.99 *(978-0-7636-4515-1(X))* Candlewick Pr.
—The Squirrel Wife. Pearce, Philippa. 2007. (ENG.). 32p. (J). (gr. k-3). 16.99 *(978-0-7636-3551-0(0))* Candlewick Pr.
—The Tin Forest. Ward, Helen. 2003. (ENG.). 32p. (J). (gr. -1-2). 7.99 *(978-0-14-250156-6(5)*, Puffin) Penguin Publishing Group.
—Twenty-five December Lane. Ward, Helen. 2007. 17p. (J). *(978-1-74178-722-1(X))* Five Mile Pr. Pty Ltd. The.
Andert, John. Good Night Cape Cod. Gamble, Adam. 2005. (J). bds. 9.95 *(978-0-9758502-5-1(3))* On Cape Pubns.

—Good Night Cape Cod. Gamble, Adam. 2007. (Good Night Our World Ser.). (ENG.). 20p. (J). (gr. k — 1). bds. 9.95 (978-1-60219-004-7(6)) Our World of Books.

Andrada, Javier. Pulgarcita. Bailer, Darice et al. 2007. (SPA & ENG.). 28p. (J). (978-0-545-02099-2(9)) Scholastic, Inc.

Andrade, Mary J., photos by. Day of the Dead A Passion for Life: Día de los Muertos Pasión por la Vida. Andrade, Mary J., . 2nd ed. 2007. (SPA., lib. bdg., stu. ed., tchr.'s training gde. ed. 29.95 (978-0-9791624-0-4(8)) La Oferta Publishing Co.

Andrade, Mary J., photos by. Day of the Dead in Mexico-Yucatan: Through the Eyes of the Soul. Andrade, Mary J. 2003. (SPA & ENG., 110p. pap. 26.95 (978-0-9665876-6-1(9)) La Oferta Publishing Co.

Andrade Valencia, Esau. A Perfect Season for Dreaming (Un Tiempo Perfecto para Soñar) Sáenz, Benjamin Alire. 2010. (ENG & SPA.). 40p. (J). (gr. 1-4). pap. 8.95 (978-1-933693-62-0(2)) Cinco Puntos Pr.

Andreasen, Dan. ABCs of Baseball. Golenbock, Peter. 2012. (ENG.). 48p. (J). (gr. 1-3). 16.99 (978-0-8037-3711-2(4), Dial) Penguin Publishing Group.

—Across the Puddingstone Dam. Wiley, Melissa. 2004. (Little House Ser.: No. 4). 224p. (J). 16.99 (978-0-06-027021-6(7)) HarperCollins Pubs.

—The Adventures of Huckleberry Finn. Twain, Mark. 2006. (Classic Starts(tm) Ser.). (ENG.). 160p. (J). (gr. 2-4). 6.95 (978-1-4027-2499-2(3)) Sterling Publishing Co., Inc.

—The Adventures of Huckleberry Finn. Twain, Mark. 2010. (Classic Starts(tm) Ser.). (ENG.). 160p. (J). (gr. 2-4). pap. 9.95 incl. audio compact disk (978-1-4027-7355-6(2)) Sterling Publishing Co., Inc.

—Alice in Wonderland & Through the Looking-Glass. Carroll, Lewis. 2009. (Classic Starts(tm) Ser.). (ENG.). 160p. (J). (gr. 2-4). 6.95 (978-1-4027-5422-7(1)) Sterling Publishing Co., Inc.

—Anne of Avonlea. Montgomery, L. M. 2009. (Classic Starts(tm) Ser.). (ENG.). 160p. (J). (gr. 2-4). 6.95 (978-1-4027-5424-1(8)) Sterling Publishing Co., Inc.

—Easter Babies: A Springtime Counting Book. Hulme, Joy N. 2012. (ENG.). 22p. (J). (gr. k — 1). bds. 6.95 (978-1-4027-9763-7(X)) Sterling Publishing Co., Inc.

—Felicity Story Collection. Tripp, Valerie. 2008. (ENG.). 404p. (J). 29.95 (978-1-59369-452-4(0)) American Girl Publishing, Inc.

—Firebears, the Rescue Team. Greene, Rhonda Gowler. 2015. (ENG.). 30p. (J). (gr. -1 — 1). bds. 7.99 (978-1-62779-240-0(6), Holt, Henry & Co. Bks. For Young Readers) Holt, Henry & Co.

—Five Little Peppers & How They Grew. Sidney, Margaret. 2009. (Classic Starts(tm) Ser.). (ENG.). 160p. (J). (gr. 2-4). 6.95 (978-1-4027-5420-3(5)) Sterling Publishing Co., Inc.

—The Forever Dog. Cochran, Bill. 2007. (ENG.). 32p. (J). (gr. -1-3). 16.99 (978-0-06-053939-9(9)) HarperCollins Pubs.

—The Hand-Me-Down Doll, 0 vols. Kroll, Steven. 2012. (ENG.). 32p. (J). (gr. k-3). 17.99 (978-0-7614-6124-1(8), 9780761461241, Amazon Children's Publishing) Amazon Publishing.

—The Happy Elf. Connick, Harry, Jr. 2011. (ENG.). 32p. (J). (gr. -1-3). 17.99 (978-0-06-128879-1(9)) HarperCollins Pubs.

—Hug a Bug. Spinelli, Eileen. 2009. 32p. (J). (gr. -1-3). lib. bdg. 17.89 (978-0-06-051833-2(2)) HarperCollins Pubs.

—Jeannette Rankin: First Lady of Congress. Marx, Trish. (ENG.). 48p. (J). 2013. (gr. 2-5). 19.99 (978-1-4424-9618-7(5)); 2006. (gr. 3-7). 18.95 (978-0-689-86290-8(3)) McElderry, Margaret K. Bks. (McElderry, Margaret K. Bks.).

—Let's Go on a Mommy Date, 1 vol. Kingsbury, Karen. 2008. (ENG.). 32p. (J). (gr. -1-3). 15.99 (978-0-310-71214-5(9)) Zonderkidz.

—Let's Have a Daddy Day, 1 vol. Kingsbury, Karen. 2010. (ENG.). 32p. (J). (gr. -1-2). 15.99 (978-0-310-71215-2(7)) Zonderkidz.

—Little Men. Alcott, Louisa May. 2009. (Classic Starts(tm) Ser.). (ENG.). 160p. (J). (gr. 2-4). 6.95 (978-1-4027-5423-4(X)) Sterling Publishing Co., Inc.

—Love Song for a Baby. Bauer, Marion Dane. 2011. (Classic Board Bks.). (ENG.). 40p. (J). (gr. -1 — 1). bds. 7.99 (978-1-4169-6395-0(2), Little Simon) Little Simon.

—Mortimer's First Garden. Wilson, Karma. 2009. (ENG.). 32p. (J). (gr. -1-3). 16.99 (978-1-4169-4203-0(3), McElderry, Margaret K. Bks.) McElderry, Margaret K. Bks.

—Needle & Thread. Martin, Ann M. 2007. 205p. (J). pap. (978-0-545-03660-3(7)) Scholastic, Inc.

—Nellie's Promise. Tripp, Valerie. England, Tamara, ed. 2004. (ENG.). 96p. (gr. 2-18). pap. 6.95 (978-1-58485-890-4(7)) American Girl Publishing, Inc.

—Oliver Twist. Dickens, Charles. 2006. (Classic Starts(tm) Ser.). (ENG.). 160p. (J). (gr. 2-4). 6.95 (978-1-4027-2665-1(1)) Sterling Publishing Co., Inc.

—Otis & Sydney & the Best Birthday Ever. Numeroff, Laura Joffe. 2010. (ENG.). 32p. (J). (gr. -1-2). 16.95 (978-0-8109-8959-7(X), Abrams Bks. for Young Readers) Abrams.

—Peter Pan. Barrie, J. M. 2009. (Classic Starts(tm) Ser.). (ENG.). 160p. (J). (gr. 2-4). 6.95 (978-1-4027-5421-0(3)) Sterling Publishing Co., Inc.

—Pilot Pups. Meadows, Michelle. 2008. (ENG.). 32p. (J). (gr. -1-3). 17.99 (978-1-4169-2484-5(1), Simon & Schuster Bks. For Young Readers) Simon & Schuster Bks. For Young Readers.

—The Punkydoos Take the Stage. Jackson, Jennifer. 2014. (Punkydoos Book Ser.). (ENG.). 32p. (J). (gr. -1-k). 17.99 (978-1-4231-4339-0(6)) Hyperion Bks. for Children.

—A Quiet Place. Wood, Douglas. 2005. (ENG.). 32p. (J). (gr. -1-3). reprint ed. 7.99 (978-0-689-87609-7(2), Simon & Schuster Bks. For Young Readers) Simon & Schuster Bks. For Young Readers.

—River Boy: The Story of Mark Twain. Anderson, William. 2003. (ENG.). 40p. (J). (gr. 2-5). 17.99 (978-0-06-028400-8(5)) HarperCollins Pubs.

—Sam & the Bag. Jeffries, Alison. 2004. (Green Light Readers Level 1 Ser.). (ENG.). 24p. (J). (gr. -1-3). pap. 3.95 (978-0-15-205151-8(1)) Houghton Mifflin Harcourt Publishing Co.

—Sam & the Bag. Jeffries, Alison. 2004. (Green Light Readers Level 1 Ser.). (gr. -1-1). 13.95 (978-0-7569-4331-8(0)) Perfection Learning Corp.

—Samantha's World: A Girl's-Eye View of the Turn of the 20th Century. Goldberg, Judy. 2009. 30p. (YA). (gr. 3-18). 24.95 (978-1-59369-554-5(3)) American Girl Publishing, Inc.

—Someone's Sleepy. Rose, Deborah Lee. 2013. (ENG.). 32p. (J). (gr. -1-1). 16.95 (978-1-4197-0539-7(3), Abrams Bks. for Young Readers) Abrams.

—The Sound of Music: A Classic Collectible Pop-Up. Rodgers and Hammerstein Organization Staff & Lindsay and Crouse Staff. 2009. (ENG.). 14p. (J). (gr. -1-3). 26.99 (978-1-4169-3655-8(6), Little Simon) Little Simon.

—Starlight. Earhart, Kristin. 2006. (Stablemates Ser.). (ENG.). 48p. (J). (gr. -1-3). 4.99 (978-0-439-72237-7(3), Cartwheel Bks.) Scholastic, Inc.

—Too Many Leprechauns: Or How That Pot O' Gold Got to the End of the Rainbow. Krensky, Stephen. 2007. (ENG.). 32p. (J). (gr. -1-1). 12.99 (978-0-689-85112-4(X), Simon & Schuster Bks. For Young Readers) Simon & Schuster Bks. For Young Readers.

—Traffic Pups. Meadows, Michelle. 2011. (ENG.). 32p. (J). (gr. -1-3). 15.99 (978-1-4169-2485-2(X), Simon & Schuster Bks. For Young Readers) Simon & Schuster Bks. For Young Readers.

—A ValueTales Treasury: Stories for Growing Good People. Johnson, Spencer. 2010. (ENG.). 96p. (J). (gr. k-5). 19.99 (978-1-4169-9838-9(1), Simon & Schuster/Paula Wiseman Bks.) Simon & Schuster/Paula Wiseman Bks.

—Very Funny, Elizabeth! Tripp, Valerie. England, Tamara, ed. 2005. (ENG.). 96p. (gr. 3). pap. 6.95 (978-1-59369-061-8(4), American Girl) American Girl Publishing, Inc.

—White Fang. London, Jack. 2006. (Classic Starts(tm) Ser.). (ENG.). 160p. (J). (gr. 2-4). 6.95 (978-1-4027-2500-5(0)) Sterling Publishing Co., Inc.

—20,000 Leagues under the Sea: Retold from the Jules Verne Original. Verne, Jules. 2006. (Classic Starts(tm) Ser.). (ENG.). 160p. (J). (gr. 2-4). 6.95 (978-1-4027-2533-3(7)) Sterling Publishing Co., Inc.

Andreasen, Dan. Saturday with Daddy. Andreasen, Dan. 2013. (ENG.). 24p. (J). (gr. -1-2). 12.99 (978-0-8050-8687-4(0), Holt, Henry & Co. Bks. For Young Readers) Holt, Henry & Co.

—The Treasure Bath. Andreasen, Dan. 2009. (ENG.). 40p. (J). (gr. -1-1). 16.99 (978-0-8050-8686-7(2), Holt, Henry & Co. Bks. For Young Readers) Holt, Henry & Co.

Andreasen, Dan & Schories, Pat. Biscuit's Pet & Play Halloween. Capucilli, Alyssa Satin. 2007. (Biscuit Ser.). (ENG.). 12p. (J). (gr. -1-1). bds. 6.99 (978-0-06-112833-2(3), HarperFestival) HarperCollins Pubs.

Andreasen, Dan, jt. illus. see LaMarche, Jim.

Andreasen, Tim. The Adventures of Hagel the Hound: And Dandy the Cat Friendship. Shelton, Carter. 2011. (ENG.). 36p. pap. 11.95 (978-1-4609-8631-8(8)) CreateSpace Independent Publishing Platform.

—The Adventures of Hagel the Hound: And Lito the Dove Homework. Shelton, Carter. 2011. (ENG.). 40p. pap. 11.95 (978-1-4635-4242-9(9)) CreateSpace Independent Publishing Platform.

—The Adventures of Hagel the Hound: And Louie the Fish Watching Too Much T. V. Shelton, Carter. 2011. (ENG.). 36p. pap. 11.95 (978-1-4610-6026-0(5)) CreateSpace Independent Publishing Platform.

—The Adventures of Hagel the Hound: And Marble the Mouse Okay to Be Small. Shelton, Carter. 2011. (ENG.). 40p. pap. 11.95 (978-1-4635-8687-4(6)) CreateSpace Independent Publishing Platform.

Andrejev, Vladislav. Saint Nicholas & the Nine Gold Coins. Forest, Jim. 2015. (J). **(978-0-88141-511-7(1))** St. Vladimir's Seminary Pr.

Andressen, Mark. Alex & the Enderson Brothers: Book One, bks. 3. Monette, Roz. 2nd ed. 2013. (ENG.). 164p. (YA). pap. 12.95 (978-0-9835077-1-0(6), Sapling Bks.) Cedar Grove Bks.

Andrew, Ian. Cleopatra: Queen of Egypt. Twist, Clint. 2012. (Historical Notebooks Ser.). (ENG.). 30p. (J). (gr. 3-7). 19.99 (978-0-7636-6095-6(7), Templar) Candlewick Pr.

Andrew, Ian, et al. Egyptology: Search for the Tomb of Osiris. Sands, Emily. 2004. (Ologies Ser.). (ENG.). 32p. (J). (gr. 3-7). 21.99 (978-0-7636-2638-9(4)) Candlewick Pr.

Andrew, Ian. The Ropemaker. Dickinson, Peter. 2004. 375p. (gr. 7). 17.95 (978-0-7569-1935-1(5)) Perfection Learning Corp.

Andrew, Ian, et al. William Shakespeare: His Life & Times. Berk, Ari & McDermott, Kristen. 2010. (Historical Notebooks Ser.). (ENG.). 30p. (J). (gr. 3-7). 21.99 (978-0-7636-4794-0(2)) Candlewick Pr.

Andrew, Ian, jt. illus. see Gilbert, Anne Yvonne.

Andrew, Ian P., et al. Egyptology: Search for the Tomb of Osiris. Sands, Emily & Anderson, Wayne. 2004. 32p. (978-1-84011-852-0(0)) Templar Publishing.

Andrew, Joe. The Three Lady Fish: A Friend in Need. Andrew, Joe. 2007. (J). (gr. -1-3). pap. 9.95 (978-0-9787995-6-4(9)) High-Pitched Hum Inc.

Andrews, Benny. Delivering Justice: W. W. Law & the Fight for Civil Rights. Haskins, James. 2008. (ENG.). 32p. (J). (gr. k-3). pap. 7.99 (978-0-7636-3880-1(3)) Candlewick Pr.

—Delivering Justice: W. W. Law & the Fight for Civil Rights. Haskins, James. 2005. (ENG.). 32p. (J). (gr. k-3). 17.99 (978-0-7636-2592-4(2)) Candlewick Pr.

—Draw What You See: The Life & Art of Benny Andrews. Benson, Kathleen. 2015. (ENG.). 32p. (J). (gr. -1-3). 16.99 (978-0-544-10487-7(0)) Houghton Mifflin Harcourt Publishing Co.

—John Lewis in the Lead: A Story of the Civil Rights Movement, 1 vol. Benson, Kathleen & Haskins, Jim. 2006. (ENG.). 40p. (gr. 2-7). 17.95 (978-1-58430-250-6(X)) Lee & Low Bks., Inc.

—Poetry for Young People: Langston Hughes. Roessel, David & Rampersad, Arnold, eds. 2013. (Poetry for Young People Ser.). (ENG.). 48p. (J). (gr. 3). 14.95 (978-1-4549-0328-4(7)) Sterling Publishing Co., Inc.

Andrews, Gary. A Christmas Carol. Dickens, Charles. 2008. (Fast Track Classics Ser.). 46p. (Orig.). (J). (gr. 4-7). pap. 10.00 (978-1-4190-5087-9(7)) Steck-Vaughn.

—The Strange Case of Dr. Jekyll & Mr. Hyde. Stevenson, Robert Louis. 2008. (Fast Track Classics Ser.). (ENG.). 48p. pap. 10.00 (978-1-4190-5082-4(6)) Steck-Vaughn.

—Tales from Shakespeare: "A Midsummer Night's Dream" Lamb, Charles & Lamb, Mary. Strang, Kay, ed. rev. ed. 2005. 40p. pap. 4.95 (978-0-9542905-3-5(4)) Capercaillie Bks., Ltd GBR. Dist: Wilson & Assocs.

—Tales from Shakespeare: "King Lear" Lamb, Charles & Lamb, Mary. Strang, Kay, ed. rev. ed. 2005. 40p. pap. 4.95 (978-0-9542905-6-6(9)) Capercaillie Bks., Ltd GBR. Dist: Wilson & Assocs.

—Tales from Shakespeare: "Othello" Lamb, Charles & Lamb, Mary. Strang, Kay, ed. rev. ed. 2005. 40p. pap. 4.95 (978-0-9542905-4-2(2)) Capercaillie Bks., Ltd GBR. Dist: Wilson & Assocs.

—Tales from Shakespeare: "Twelfth Night" Lamb, Charles & Lamb, Mary. Strang, Kay, ed. rev. ed. 2005. 40p. pap. 4.95 (978-0-9542905-7-3(7)) Capercaillie Bks., Ltd GBR. Dist: Wilson & Assocs.

Andrews, Kaare. Astonishing X-Men: Xenogenesis. 2011. (ENG.). 160p. (YA). (gr. 8-17). pap. 19.99 (978-0-7851-4033-7(6)) Marvel Worldwide, Inc.

Andrews, LaMont, Jr. Encyclopedia of Activists & Activism in America, Vol. 2 A-Z, Vol. 2. l.t. ed. 2005. 30p. (YA). pap. 10.00 (978-0-9728975-1-8(8)) JA-M Pubs., LLC.

—Encyclopedia of Activists & Activism in America, Vol. 3 A-Z, Vol. 3. Andrews-McKinney, Joyce. l.t. ed. 2006. 30p. (YA). pap. 10.00 (978-0-9728975-2-5(6)) JA-M Pubs., LLC.

Andrews, Luke. Sassafras in What Is Metamorphosis? Dontell, Susan L. 2008. 36p. pap. 24.95 (978-1-60441-776-0(5)) America Star Bks.

Andrews-McKinney, Joyce. Jentle & Jewel Fix Things. Andrews-McKinney, Joyce. l.t. ed. 2006. 17p. (J). pap. 8.00 (978-0-9728975-4-9(2)) JA-M Pubs., LLC.

Andrewson, Natalie. Nooks & Crannies. Lawson, Jessica. 2015. (ENG.). 336p. (J). (gr. 3-7). 16.99 (978-1-4814-1921-5(8), Simon & Schuster Bks. For Young Readers) Simon & Schuster Bks. For Young Readers.

Andriani, Renee. Don't Know Much about the 50 States. Davis, Kenneth C. 2004. (Don't Know Much About Ser.). (ENG.). 64p. (J). (gr. 1-4). pap. 7.99 (978-0-06-446227-3(7)) HarperCollins Pubs.

—Earth Day - Hooray!, Vol. 50. Murphy, Stuart J. 2004. (MathStart 3 Ser.). (ENG.). 40p. (J). (gr. 2-18). pap. 5.99 (978-0-06-000129-2(1)) HarperCollins Pubs.

—Earth Day — Hooray! Murphy, Stuart J. 2004. (MathStart 3 Ser.). (ENG.). 40p. (J). (gr. 2-18). 16.99 (978-0-06-000127-8(5)) HarperCollins Pubs.

—This School Year Will Be the Best! Winters, Kay. 2010. (ENG.). 32p. (J). (gr. 1-3). 16.99 (978-0-525-42275-4(7), Dutton Juvenile) Penguin Publishing Group.

—This School Year Will Be the Best! Winters, Kay. 2013. (ENG.). 32p. (J). (gr. 1-3). mass mkt. 6.99 (978-0-14-242696-8(2), Puffin) Penguin Publishing Group.

Andriani, Renee W. Annabel the Actress Starring in Camping It Up. Conford, Ellen. 2005. (Annabel the Actress Ser.). 60p. (J). (gr. 2-5). 11.65 (978-0-7569-5555-7(6)) Perfection Learning Corp.

—Annabel the Actress Starring in Camping It Up. Conford, Ellen. 2013. (ENG.). 64p. (J). (gr. 2-5). pap. 13.99 (978-1-4814-0147-0(5), Simon & Schuster Bks. For Young Readers) Simon & Schuster Bks. For Young Readers.

—Annabel the Actress Starring in Just a Little Extra. Conford, Ellen. 2013. (Annabel the Actress Ser.). (ENG.). 64p. (J). (gr. 4-6). pap. 13.99 (978-1-4814-0148-7(3), Simon & Schuster Bks. For Young Readers) Simon & Schuster Bks. For Young Readers.

—Annabel the Actress Starring in the Hound of the Barkervilles. Conford, Ellen. 2004. (Annabel the Actress Ser.). 83p. (gr. 2-5). 14.00 (978-0-7569-2180-4(5)) Perfection Learning Corp.

—Annabel the Actress Starring in the Hound of the Barkervilles. Conford, Ellen. 2003. (Annabel the Actress Ser.). (ENG.). 96p. (J). (gr. 2-5). pap. 6.99 (978-0-689-84791-2(2), Simon & Schuster/Paula Wiseman Bks.) Simon & Schuster/Paula Wiseman Bks.

—Mall Mania. Murphy, Stuart J. 2006. (MathStart Ser.). (ENG.). 40p. (J). (gr. 1-4). 15.99 (978-0-06-055776-8(1)); pap. 5.99 (978-0-06-055777-5(X)) HarperCollins Pubs.

Andriyevskaya, Yevgeniya. Stacy Takes the Train to School. Lupa, Mary R. 2009. 20p. (J). pap. 10.95 (978-1-4327-1609-7(3)) Outskirts Pr., Inc.

Andru, Ross, et al. Spider-Man: The Original Clone Saga. Conway, Gerry et al. 2011. (ENG.). 480p. (J). (gr. 4-17). pap. 39.99 (978-0-7851-5523-2(6)) Marvel Worldwide, Inc.

Andru, Ross & Kane, Gil. Marvel Masterworks: The Amazing Spider-Man Volume 16. 2014. (ENG.). 288p. (J). (gr. 4-17). 69.99 (978-0-7851-8801-8(0)) Marvel Worldwide, Inc.

Andrules, Jamie L. Why are You my Mother? A Mother's Response to Her Adopted Daughter. Hamilton, Deborah E. 2006. (J). 9.99 net. (978-0-9789202-0-3(1)) Dreams Due Media Group, Inc.

Anegon, Tamara. Waggers. Nyikos, Stacy. 2014. (ENG.). 32p. (J). (gr. -1-k). 16.95 (978-1-62914-629-4(3), Sky Pony Pr.) Skyhorse Publishing Co., Inc.

Anfuso, Dennis. The Butterfly & the Bunny's Tail. De Sena, Joseph. 2007. 60p. per. 19.95 (978-1-4327-0404-9(4)) Outskirts Pr., Inc.

Ang, Joy. Behold! a Baby. Watson, Stephanie Elaine. 2015. (ENG.). 32p. (J). (gr. -1-1). 16.99 (978-1-61963-452-7(X), Bloomsbury USA Childrens) Bloomsbury USA.

—I Will Not Read This Book. Meng, Cece. 2011. (ENG.). 32p. (J). (gr. -1-3). 16.99 (978-0-547-04971-7(4)) Houghton Mifflin Harcourt Publishing Co.

—Mustache Baby. Heos, Bridget. 2013. (ENG.). 40p. (J). (gr. -1-3). 16.99 (978-0-547-77357-5(9)) Houghton Mifflin Harcourt Publishing Co.

—Mustache Baby Meets His Match. Heos, Bridget. 2015. (ENG.). 40p. (J). (gr. -1-3). 16.99 (978-0-544-36375-5(2)) Houghton Mifflin Harcourt Publishing Co.

—Petey & Pru & the Hullabaloo. Paquette, Ammi-Joan. 2013. (ENG.). 40p. (gr. -1-3). 16.99 (978-0-544-03888-2(6)) Houghton Mifflin Harcourt Publishing Co.

—The Qalupalik, 1 vol. Kilabuk, Elisha. 2011. (ENG.). 32p. (J). (gr. 1-3). 12.95 (978-1-926569-31-4(8)) Inhabit Media Inc. CAN. Dist: Independent Pubs. Group.

Ang, Selvi. Jesus Loves Me: A Bedtime Prayer. Ranga, Katherine. 2011. 26p. pap. 11.95 (978-1-60976-989-5(9), Eloquent Bks.) Strategic Book Publishing & Rights Agency (SBPRA).

Angaramo, Roberta. The Bicklebys' Birdbath. Perry, Andrea. 2010. (ENG.). 40p. (J). (gr. -1-1). 16.99 (978-1-4169-0624-7(X), Atheneum Bks. for Young Readers) Simon & Schuster Children's Publishing.

—Dog in Boots. Gormley, Greg. 2011. (ENG.). 32p. (J). (gr. -1-1). 17.95 (978-0-8234-2347-7(6)) Holiday Hse., Inc.

—Errol & His Extraordinary Nose. Conway, David. 2010. (ENG.). 32p. (J). (gr. -1-3). 16.95 (978-0-8234-2262-3(3)) Holiday Hse., Inc.

—A Perfect Home for a Family. Harrison, David L. 2013. (ENG.). 32p. (J). 16.95 (978-0-8234-2338-5(7)) Holiday Hse., Inc.

Angel, Carl. Lakas & the Makibaka Hotel /Si Lakas at Ang Makibaka Hotel. Robles, Anthony D. de Jesus, Eloisa D., tr. from TAG. 2006. (ENG.). 32p. (J). (gr. k). 16.95 (978-0-89239-213-1(4)) Lee & Low Bks., Inc.

—Lakas & the Manilatown Fish (Si Lakas at Ang Isdang Manilatown) Robles, Anthony D. & Children's Book Press Staff. de Jesus, Eloisa D. & de Guzman, Magdalena, trs. 2003.Tr. of Si Lakas at Ang Isdang Manilatown. (ENG & TAG.). 32p. (J). 16.95 (978-0-89239-182-0(0)) Lee & Low Bks., Inc.

—Willie Wins, 1 vol. Gilles, Almira Astudillo. 2013. (ENG.). 32p. (J). (gr. -1-3). 16.95 (978-1-58430-023-6(X)) Lee & Low Bks., Inc.

—Xochitl & the Flowers. Argueta, Jorge. 2013. (ENG.). 32p. (J). (gr. k). pap. 9.95 (978-0-89239-224-7(X)) Lee & Low Bks., Inc.

—Xochitl & the Flowers (Xochitl, la Nina de Las Flores) Argueta, Jorge. 2003.Tr. of Xochitl, la Nina de Las Flores. (ENG & SPA.). 32p. (J). 16.95 (978-0-89239-181-3(2)) Lee & Low Bks., Inc.

Angela-Lago. Lucas y el Ruisenor. Ventura, Antonio. 2005. (SPA.). 24p. (J). (gr. 1-3). pap., pap. 6.99 (978-980-257-285-4(3)) Ekare, Ediciones VEN. Dist: Lectorum Pubns., Inc.

Angeletti, Roberta. Golden Goose. 2009. (Flip-Up Fairy Tales Ser.). (ENG.). 24p. (J). (gr. -1-2). pap. (978-1-84643-324-5(X)) Child's Play International Ltd.

—The Golden Goose. 2010. (Flip-Up Fairy Tales Ser.). (ENG.). 24p. (J). (gr. -1-2). (978-1-84643-330-6(4)) Child's Play International Ltd.

—The Wim Wom from the Mustard Mill. Peters, Polly. 2008. (Child's Play Library). (ENG.). 32p. (J). (gr. -1-3). pap. (978-1-84643-253-8(7)) Child's Play International Ltd.

Angelini, George. The Oak Inside the Acorn, 1 vol. Lucado, Max. 2006. (ENG.). 48p. 16.99 (978-1-4003-0601-5(9)) Nelson, Thomas Inc.

Angle, Scott. Grammar All-Stars: Parts of Speech, 6 vols. Fisher, Doris & Gibbs, D. L. 2008. (Grammar All-Stars Ser.). 32p. (gr. 2-5). pap. 10.50 (978-0-8368-8910-9(X)); pap. 10.50 (978-0-8368-8912-3(6)); pap. 10.50 (978-0-8368-8913-0(4)) Stevens, Gareth Publishing LLLP. (Gareth Stevens Learning Library).

—Half-Pipe Homonyms. Prokos, Anna & Voege, Debra. 2009. (Grammar All-Stars Ser.). 32p. (gr. 2-5). (J). lib. bdg. 26.00 (978-1-4339-0010-5(6)); pap. 10.50 (978-1-4339-0150-8(1)) Stevens, Gareth Publishing LLLP. (Gareth Stevens Learning Library).

—Hole-in-One Adverbs. Fisher, Doris & Gibbs, D. L. 2008. (Grammar All-Stars Ser.). 32p. (gr. 2-5). pap. 10.50 (978-0-8368-8909-3(6), Gareth Stevens Learning Library) Stevens, Gareth Publishing LLLP.

—Slam dunk Pronouns, 6 vols. Fisher, Doris & Gibbs, D. L. 2008. (Grammar All-Stars Ser.). 32p. (gr. 2-5). pap. 10.50 (978-0-8368-8911-6(8), Gareth Stevens Learning Library) Stevens, Gareth Publishing LLLP.

—Touchdown Nouns. Fisher, Doris & Gibbs, D. L. 2008. (Grammar All-Stars Ser.). 32p. (J). (gr. 2-5). lib. bdg. 26.00 (978-0-8368-8906-2(1), Gareth Stevens Learning Library) Stevens, Gareth Publishing LLLP.

Angle, Scott & Chandler, Jeff. Bowling Alley Adjectives. Fisher, Doris & Gibbs, D. L. 2008. (Grammar All-Stars Ser.). 32p. (J). (gr. 2-5). lib. bdg. 26.00 (978-0-8368-8901-7(0), Gareth Stevens Learning Library) Stevens, Gareth Publishing LLLP.

Angle, Scott & Roper, Robert. Home Run Verbs. Fisher, Doris & Gibbs, D. L. 2008. (Grammar All-Stars Ser.). 32p. (J). (gr. 2-5). lib. bdg. 26.00 (978-0-8368-8903-1(7), Gareth Stevens Learning Library) Stevens, Gareth Publishing LLLP.

Anglemyer, Jordan. Grandpa's Favorites: A collection of quotes, things to ponder, stories, bits of verse, & Humor. 2007. 77p. (YA). per. 10.95 (978-0-9796251-2-1(2)) Robertson Publishing.

Anglicas, Louise. Bus Troubles. Mckenzie, Precious. 2013. (ENG.). 24p. (gr. -1-1). 25.64 (978-1-62169-247-8(7)); pap. 7.95 (978-1-62169-205-8(1)) Rourke Educational Media.

—Honeybee Hills. Robertson, J. Jean. 2013. (ENG.). 24p. (gr. -1-1). 25.64 (978-1-62169-243-0(4)); pap. 7.95 (978-1-62169-201-0(9)) Rourke Educational Media.

—Lift the Flap Bible, 1 vol. Williamson, Karen. 2014. (ENG.). 16p. (J). bds. 12.99 (978-1-78128-130-7(0), Candle Bks.) Lion Hudson PLC GBR. Dist: Kregel Pubns.

—Painting Party. Greve, Meg. 2013. (ENG.). 24p. (gr. -1-1). 25.64 (978-1-62169-249-2(3)); pap. 7.95 (978-1-62169-207-2(8)) Rourke Educational Media.

—Play-Time Noah, 1 vol. Williamson, Karen. 2014. (ENG.). 8p. (J). bds. 9.99 *(978-1-78128-111-6(4)*, Candle Bks.) Lion Hudson PLC GBR. Dist: Kregel Pubns.
—River Rafting. Greve, Meg. 2013. (ENG.). 24p. (gr. -1-1). 25.64 *(978-1-62169-246-1(9))*; pap. 7.95 *(978-1-62169-204-1(3))* Rourke Educational Media.
—Volcano! Robertson, J. Jean. 2013. (ENG.). 24p. (gr. -1-1). 25.64 *(978-1-62169-244-7(2))*; pap. 7.95 *(978-1-62169-202-7(7))* Rourke Educational Media.
—Zoom to the Zoo. Mitten, Luana. 2013. (ENG.). 24p. (gr. -1-1). 25.64 *(978-1-62169-245-4(0))*; pap. 7.95 *(978-1-62169-203-4(5))* Rourke Educational Media.
Anglund, Joan Walsh. The Cowboy's Christmas. Anglund, Joan Walsh. 2004. (ENG.). 40p. (J). 8.95 *(978-0-7407-4675-8(8))* Andrews McMeel Publishing.
—Little Angels' Book of Christmas. Anglund, Joan Walsh. 2005. (ENG.). 32p. (J). (gr. -1-18). bds. 8.99 *(978-1-4169-1003-9(4))* Simon & Schuster Children's Publishing.
Angorn, Matthew. The Invasion of Planet Wampetter. Pillsbury, Samuel H. 2003. (Planet Wampetter Adventure Ser.). 133p. (J). (gr. 3-8). 15.00 *(978-0-9622036-6-4(1))*; pap. 8.95 *(978-1-930085-05-3(2))* Perspective Publishing, Inc.
Anguissola, Anna. Gatwick Bear & the Secret Plans. Cuffaro, Anna. 2009. (ENG.). 189p. (J). 18.00 *(978-1-907230-02-8(5))* Sparkling Bks. GBR. Dist: Silvermine International Bks., LLC.
Anholt, Catherine. Babies, Babies, Babies! Anholt, Laurence. 2013. (ENG.). 32p. (J). (-k). pap. 11.99 *(978-1-4083-1436-4(3))* Hodder & Stoughton GBR. Dist: Independent Pubs. Group.
—Our New Baby & Me: A First Year Record Book for New Brothers & Sisters. Anholt, Laurence. 2009. (Chimp & Zee Ser.). (ENG.). 48p. (J). (gr. -1-1). 19.95 *(978-1-84507-168-4(9)*, Frances Lincoln) Quarto Publishing Group UK GBR. Dist: Hachette Bk. Group.
Anholt, Catherine & Anholt, Laurence. Catherine & Laurence Anholt's Big Book of Little Children. Anholt, Catherine & Anholt, Laurence. 2003. (ENG.). 80p. (J). (gr. -1-k). 15.99 *(978-0-7636-2210-7(9))* Candlewick Pr.
—Chimp & Zee Play. Anholt, Catherine & Anholt, Laurence. 2007. (Chimp & Zee Ser.). (ENG.). 22p. (J). (gr. -1 — 1). bds. 3.95 *(978-1-84507-746-4(6)*, Frances Lincoln) Quarto Publishing Group UK GBR. Dist: Hachette Bk. Group.
Anholt, Catherine, jt. illus. see Anholt, Laurence.
Anholt, Laurence & Anholt, Catherine. Chimp & Zee & the Big Storm. 2008. (Chimp & Zee Ser.). (ENG.). 32p. (J). (gr. -1-1). pap. 7.95 *(978-1-84507-069-4(0)*, Frances Lincoln Children's Bks.) Quarto Publishing Group UK GBR. Dist: Hachette Bk. Group.
Anholt, Laurence, jt. illus. see Anholt, Catherine.
Ann Hollis Rife. The Little Prairie Hen. Leland, Debbie. 2003. 32p. (J). lib. bdg. 14.95 *(978-0-9667086-3-9(6))* Wildflower Run.
Annable, Graham. Stickleback. 2005. (ENG.). 48p. (gr. 8). pap. 6.95 *(978-1-891867-80-4(6))* Alternative Comics.
AnnDrewArt. The Lost Kitten & How He Was Found. Harris, Daniel C. & Harris, Donna L., photos by. Harris, Donna L. 2010. (ENG.). 32p. pap. 10.00 *(978-1-4528-4463-3(1))* CreateSpace Independent Publishing Platform.
Annelli, Nikki. Morning. Marshall, Judy. l.t. ed. 2005. 21p. (J). per. 9.99 *(978-1-59879-050-4(1))* Lifevest Publishing, Inc.
Anno, Moyoco. Flowers & Bees. Anno, Moyoco. (Flowers & Bees Ser.). (ENG.). 5. 2004. 200p. (YA). pap. 9.95 *(978-1-59116-347-3(1))*; Vol. 1. 2003. 216p. pap. 9.95 *(978-1-56931-978-9(2))*; Vol. 2. 2004. 232p. pap. 9.95 *(978-1-59116-124-0(X))*; Vol. 3. 2004. 216p. pap. 9.95 *(978-1-59116-298-8(X))*; Vol. 4. 2004. 200p. pap. 9.95 *(978-1-59116-346-6(3))*; Vol. 6. 2005. 216p. pap. 9.99 *(978-1-59116-348-0(X))*; Vol. 7. 2005. 200p. pap. 9.99 *(978-1-59116-777-8(9))* Viz Media.
—Happy Mania, 5 vols. Anno, Moyoco. 2003. Vol. 4. 4th rev. ed. 200p. pap. 9.99 *(978-1-59182-172-4(X))*; Vol. 5. 5th rev. ed. 184p. pap. 9.99 *(978-1-59182-173-1(8))* TOKYOPOP, Inc.
Anoli. The Gift of Joy & Laughter - Podarok Radosti I Smeha (in Russian Language) Po Sledam Detskogo Lepeta. Iliand, Valentina. 2011. (RUS.). 32p. pap. 9.95 *(978-1-4664-9139-7(6))* CreateSpace Independent Publishing Platform.
Ansley, Frank. Invasion of the Pig Sisters. Wheeler, Lisa. 2006. (Fitch & Chip Ser.: 4). (ENG.). 48p. (J). (gr. 1-3). 16.99 *(978-0-689-84953-4(2))*; pap. 3.99 *(978-0-689-84958-9(3))* Simon Spotlight. (Simon Spotlight).
—New Pig in Town. Wheeler, Lisa. ed. 2005. 48p. (J). lib. bdg. 15.00 *(978-1-59054-997-1(X))* Fitzgerald Bks.
—New Pig in Town. Wheeler, Lisa. 2003. (Fitch & Chip Ser.: 1). (ENG.). 48p. (J). (gr. 1-3). 16.99 *(978-0-689-84950-3(8)*, Atheneum/Richard Jackson Bks.) Simon & Schuster Children's Publishing.
—New Pig in Town. Wheeler, Lisa. 2005. (Fitch & Chip Ser.: 1). (ENG.). 48p. (J). (gr. 1-3). pap. 3.99 *(978-0-689-84955-8(9)*, Simon Spotlight) Simon Spotlight.
—Turk & Runt: A Thanksgiving Comedy. Wheeler, Lisa. 2005. (ENG.). 32p. (J). (gr. -1-2). 7.99 *(978-1-4169-0714-5(9)*, Atheneum Bks. for Young Readers) Simon & Schuster Children's Publishing.
—When Pigs Fly. Wheeler, Lisa. ed. 2005. 48p. (J). lib. bdg. 15.00 *(978-1-59054-996-4(1))* Fitzgerald Bks.
—When Pigs Fly. Wheeler, Lisa. 2005. (Fitch & Chip Ser.). 48p. (gr. 1-3). 14.00 *(978-0-7569-5472-7(X))* Perfection Learning Corp.
—When Pigs Fly. Wheeler, Lisa. 2003. (Fitch & Chip Ser.: 2). (ENG.). 48p. (J). (gr. 1-3). 16.99 *(978-0-689-84951-0(6)*, Atheneum/Richard Jackson Bks.) Simon & Schuster Children's Publishing.
—When Pigs Fly. Wheeler, Lisa. 2005. (Fitch & Chip Ser.: 2). (ENG.). 48p. (J). (gr. 1-3). pap. 3.99 *(978-0-689-84956-5(7)*, Simon Spotlight) Simon Spotlight.
—Who's Afraid of Granny Wolf? Wheeler, Lisa. 2006. (Fitch & Chip Ser.: 3). (ENG.). 48p. (J). (gr. 1-3). pap. 3.99 *(978-0-689-84957-2(5)*, Simon Spotlight) Simon Spotlight.
—Willie & Buster Take the Train. DePrisco, Dorothea. 2003. (Stories to Share Ser.). 10p. (J). 10.95 *(978-1-58117-183-9(8)*, Intervisual/Piggy Toes) Bendon, Inc.
Ansley, Frank. Who's Afraid of Granny Wolf? Ansley, Frank. Wheeler, Lisa. 2004. (Fitch & Chip Ser.: 3). (ENG.). 48p. (J). (gr. 1-3). 16.99 *(978-0-689-84952-7(4)*, Simon Spotlight) Simon Spotlight.
Anstee, Ashlyn. Are We There, Yeti? Anstee, Ashlyn. 2015. (ENG.). 40p. (J). (gr. -1-3). 17.99 *(978-1-4814-3089-0(0)*, Simon & Schuster Bks. For Young Readers) Simon & Schuster Bks. For Young Readers.
Anstey, David. Ali Baba. Clynes, Kate. 2005. 32p. (J). pap. *(978-1-84444-429-8(5))* Mantra Lingua.
—Jill & the Beanstalk. Gregory, Manju. 2004. (ENG & TUR.). (J). *(978-1-84444-495-3(3))* Mantra Lingua.
Anthis, Brian. Pauly the Adventurous Pallid Bat. Tuttle, Merlin D., photos by. Irbinskas, Heather. 2003. 32p. (J). pap. 7.95 *(978-1-58369-032-1(8))* Western National Parks Assn.
Anthis, Brian, jt. illus. see Albert, Robert.
Anthoine, Leila, et al. Trust & Obey: A Visualized Gospel Song. Cunningham, Edie. 2005. 20p. (J). pap. *(978-1-932381-20-7(1)*, 6480) Bible Visuals International, Inc.
Anthony, Alan. 190 Ready-to-Use Activities That Make Math Fun! Watson, George. 2003. (J-B Ed: Ready-To-Use Activities Ser.: 65). (ENG.). 304p. pap. 29.95 *(978-0-7879-6585-3(5)*, Jossey-Bass) Wiley, John & Sons, Inc.
Anthony, Mark. Cracking the Wall: The Struggles of the Little Rock Nine. Lucas, Eileen. 2007. pap. 37.95 incl. audio *(978-1-59519-939-3(X))*; pap. 39.95 incl. audio compact disk *(978-1-59519-943-0(8))* Live Oak Media.
Anthony, Ross. Please Don't Step on the Ants. Anthony, Ross. 2006. (ENG, CHI, SPA & JPN.). (J). per. *(978-0-9727894-4-8(8))* Arizona Blueberry Studios.
Antiporda, Enrico. The Adventures of Jimbo, the Homeless Cat. Antiporda, Enrico. 2013. 66p. pap. 14.95 *(978-0-9672793-5-0(6))* Blue Owl Editions.
Antkowski, Marygrace. What Color Is Spring? Zipf, Sean. 2008. 36p. pap. 24.95 *(978-1-60703-005-8(5))* America Star Bks.
Antle, Bhagavan. The Tiger Cubs & the Chimp: The True Story of How Anjana the Chimp Helped Raise Two Baby Tigers. Antle, Bhagavan. Bland, Barry, photos by. 2013. (ENG.). 32p. (J). (gr. -1-3). 16.99 *(978-0-8050-9319-3(2)*, Holt, Henry & Co. Bks. For Young Readers) Holt, Henry & Co.
Antle, Bhagavan & Bland, Barry. Suryia & Roscoe: The True Story of an Unlikely Friendship. Antle, Bhagavan. 2011. (ENG.). 32p. (J). (gr. -1-3). 16.99 *(978-0-8050-9316-2(8)*, Holt, Henry & Co. Bks. For Young Readers) Holt, Henry & Co.
—Suryia Swims! The True Story of How an Orangutan Learned to Swim. Antle, Bhagavan. 2012. (ENG.). 32p. (J). (gr. -1-3). 16.99 *(978-0-8050-9317-9(6)*, Holt, Henry & Co. Bks. For Young Readers) Holt, Henry & Co.
Anton, Mauricio. National Geographic Prehistoric Mammals. Turner, Alan. 2004. (ENG.). 192p. (J). (gr. 2-4). 29.95 *(978-0-7922-7134-5(3))*; 49.90 *(978-0-7922-6997-7(7)*, National Geographic Children's Bks.) National Geographic Society.
Antonelli, Gina. Who Is Ollie? Antonelli, Gina. 2006. 31p. (J). (gr. -1-3). per. 10.99 *(978-1-883573-07-2(6))* Blue Forge Pr.
Antonello, Marisa & Laidley, Victoria. Lessons from a Street Kid, 1 vol. Kielburger, Craig. 2012. (ENG.). 40p. (J). (gr. k-5). 19.95 *(978-1-55365-865-8(5)*, Greystone Bks.) Greystone Books Ltd. CAN. Dist: Perseus-PGW.
Antonenkov, Evgeny. A Little Story about a Big Turnip. Zunshine, Tatiana. 2004. (ENG.). 32p. (J). (gr. -1-3). 15.95 *(978-0-9646010-0-0(1))* Pumpkin Hse., Ltd.
—Silly Horse. Levin, Vadim. Wolfson, Tanya & Zunshine, Tatiana, trs. from RUS. 2005. (ENG.). 32p. (J). (gr. -1-4). 15.95 *(978-0-9646010-1-7(X)*, 1241074) Pumpkin Hse., Ltd.
Antonia, Miller. Baby's Very First Little Book of Bunnies. ed. 2011. (Baby's Very First Board Bks). 10p. (J). ring bd. 6.99 *(978-0-7945-2955-0(0)*, Usborne) EDC Publishing.
—Baby's Very First Little Book of Kittens. ed. 2011. (Baby's Very First Board Bks). 10p. (J). ring bd. 6.99 *(978-0-7945-2956-7(9)*, Usborne) EDC Publishing.
Antonini, Gabriele. Dudley's Muddley Day. Webb, Josh. 2011. (Red Bananas Ser.). (ENG.). 48p. (J). (gr. 1-3). pap. 5.99 *(978-1-4052-5948-4(5))* Egmont Bks., Ltd. GBR. Dist: Independent Pubs. Group.
Antonini, Gabriele. Wheels on the Bus. 2012. 22p. (J). ***(978-1-4508-3332-5(2))*** Publications International, Ltd.
Antonini, Gabriele, jt. illus. see Metzger, Steve.
Antonio & Covi. Manolo Multon y el Mago Guason. Cerda, Alfredo Gomez. 2004.Tr. of Manolo Citation & Boring the Magician. (SPA.). (J). pap. 7.99 *(978-84-236-6322-4(1))* Edebé ESP. Dist: Lectorum Pubns., Inc.
Antonishak, Tom. El Pony Express. Bailer, Darice. 2007. (Excursiones Fantásticas / Fantasy Field Trips Ser.). 48p. (gr. 3-5). pap. 8.95 *(978-1-59820-599-2(4)*, Alfaguara) Santillana USA Publishing Co., Inc.
—The Pony Express. Bailer, Darice. 3rd ed. 2003. (Soundprints' Read-and-Discover Ser.). (ENG.). 48p. (J). (gr. -1-3). pap. 3.95 *(978-1-59249-019-6(0)*, S2008) Soundprints.
Antonsson, Petur. Fork-Tongue Charmers. Durham, Paul. 2015. (Luck Uglies Ser.: 2). (ENG.). 416p. (J). (gr. 3-7). 16.99 *(978-0-06-227153-2(9))* HarperCollins Pubs.
—The Luck Uglies. Durham, Paul. 2014. (Luck Uglies Ser.: 1). (ENG.). 400p. (J). (gr. 3-7). 16.99 *(978-0-06-227150-1(4))* HarperCollins Pubs.
Antram, Dave. How to Be a Pirate. Malam, John. 2005. (How to Be Ser.). (ENG.). 32p. (J). (gr. 3-7). 14.95 *(978-0-7922-7448-3(2))*; 21.90 *(978-0-7922-7497-1(0))* National Geographic Society. (National Geographic Children's Bks.).
Antram, Dave & Bergin, Mark. How to Be an Aztec Warrior. MacDonald, Fiona. 2008. (How to Be Ser.). (ENG.). 32p. (J). (gr. 3-7). pap. 5.95 *(978-1-4263-0168-1(5)*, National Geographic Children's Bks.) National Geographic Society.
Antram, Dave, jt. illus. see Bergin, Mark.
Antram, David. Assyrian Soldier! An Ancient Army You'd Rather Not Join. Matthews, Rupert. 2007. (You Wouldn't Want to... Ser.). (ENG.). 32p. (J). (gr. 2-5). 29.00 *(978-0-531-18727-2(6))* Scholastic Library Publishing.
—Be a Mayan Soothsayer! Fortunes You'd Rather Not Tell. Matthews, Rupert. 2007. (You Wouldn't Want to...: Ancient Civilization Ser.). (ENG.). 32p. (J). (gr. 2-5). 29.00 *(978-0-531-18746-3(2)*, Watts, Franklin) Scholastic Library Publishing.
—Be a Suffragist! A Protest Movement That's Rougher Than You Expected. MacDonald, Fiona. 2008. (You Wouldn't Want to...: History of the World Ser.). (ENG.). 32p. (J). (gr. 3-12). 29.00 *(978-0-531-20701-7(3)*, Watts, Franklin) Scholastic Library Publishing.
—Be a Sumerian Slave! A Life of Hard Labor You'd Rather Avoid. Morley, Jacqueline. 2007. (You Wouldn't Want to... Ser.). (ENG.). 32p. (J). (gr. 4-7). 29.00 *(978-0-531-18728-9(4)*, Watts, Franklin); pap. 9.95 *(978-0-531-18921-4(X))* Scholastic Library Publishing.
—Be a Victorian Mill Worker! A Grueling Job You'd Rather Not Have. Malam, John. 2007. (You Wouldn't Want to...: History of the World Ser.). (ENG.). 32p. (J). (gr. 2-5). 29.00 *(978-0-531-18747-0(0))*; pap. 9.95 *(978-0-531-13928-8(X))* Scholastic Library Publishing. (Watts, Franklin).
—Be a Worker on the Statue of Liberty! A Monument You'd Rather Not Build. Malam, John. 2008. (You Wouldn't Want to...: American History Ser.). (ENG.). 32p. (J). 29.00 *(978-0-531-20700-0(5)*, Watts, Franklin) Scholastic Library Publishing.
—Be an Aristocrat in the French Revolution! A Horrible Time in Paris You'd Rather Avoid. Pipe, Jim. 2007. (You Wouldn't Want to...: History of the World Ser.). (ENG.). 32p. (J). (gr. 2-5). 29.00 *(978-0-531-18745-6(4)*, Watts, Franklin) Scholastic Library Publishing.
—Be an Inca Mummy! A One-Way Journey You'D Rather Not Make. Hynson, Colin. 2007. (You Wouldn't Want to...: Ancient Civilization Ser.). (ENG.). 32p. (J). (gr. 2-5). 29.00 *(978-0-531-18744-9(6)*, Watts, Franklin) Scholastic Library Publishing.
—Be in the First Submarine! An Undersea Expedition You'D Rather Avoid. Graham, Ian. 2008. (You Wouldn't Want to...: American History Ser.). (ENG.). 32p. (J). 29.00 *(978-0-531-20702-4(1)*, Watts, Franklin) Scholastic Library Publishing.
—Be in the Forbidden City! A Sheltered Life You'd Rather Avoid. Morley, Jacqueline. 2008. (You Wouldn't Want to Ser.). (ENG.). 32p. (J). (gr. 4-7). 29.00 *(978-0-531-18749-4(7)*, Children's Pr.) Scholastic Library Publishing.
—How to Be an Ancient Greek Athlete. Morley, Jacqueline. 2008. (How to Be Ser.). (ENG.). 32p. (J). (gr. 3-7). pap. 5.95 *(978-1-4263-0278-7(9)*, National Geographic Children's Bks.) National Geographic Society.
—Live in a Medieval Castle! A Home You'D Rather Not Inhabit. Morley, Jacqueline. 2008. (You Wouldn't Want to...: History of the World Ser.). (ENG.). 32p. (J). 29.00 *(978-0-531-20703-1(X)*, Watts, Franklin) Scholastic Library Publishing.
—Live in Pompeii! A Volcanic Eruption You'd Rather Avoid. Malam, John. 2008. (You Wouldn't Want to Ser.). (ENG.). 32p. (J). (gr. 2-5). 29.00 *(978-0-531-18748-7(9))*; pap. 9.95 *(978-0-531-16900-1(6)*, Watts, Franklin) Scholastic Library Publishing.
Antram, David, et al. Machines & Inventions. Graham, Ian. 2008. (World of Wonder Ser.). (ENG.). 32p. (J). (gr. 1-4). 29.00 *(978-0-531-24027-4(4))*; pap. 9.95 *(978-0-531-23823-3(7))* Scholastic Library Publishing. (Children's Pr.).
Antram, David. Mayan Soothsayer! Fortunes You'D Rather Not Tell. Matthews, Rupert. 2007. (You Wouldn't Want to...: Ancient Civilization Ser.). (ENG.). 32p. (J). (gr. 2-5). pap. 9.95 *(978-0-531-13925-7(5)*, Watts, Franklin) Scholastic Library Publishing.
—The Medieval Chronicles: Vikings, Knights, & Castles. Macdonald, Fiona. 2013. 92p. (J). *(978-1-4351-5067-6(8))* Barnes & Noble, Inc.
Antram, David, et al. People & Places. Chesire, Gerald. 2008. (World of Wonder Ser.). (ENG.). 32p. (J). (gr. 1-4). pap. 9.95 *(978-0-531-23824-0(5)*, Children's Pr.) Scholastic Library Publishing.
Antram, David. People & Places. Chesire, Gerald. 2008. (World of Wonder Ser.). (ENG.). 32p. (J). (gr. 1-4). 29.00 *(978-0-531-24028-1(2)*, Children's Pr.) Scholastic Library Publishing.
—Sail on a 19th-Century Whaling Ship! Grisly Tasks You'd Rather Not Do. Cook, Peter & Salariya, David. 2004. (You Wouldn't Want to Ser.). (ENG.). (J). 29.00 *(978-0-531-12356-0(1))* Scholastic Library Publishing.
—Sail on an Irish Famine Ship! A Trip Across Teh Atlantic You'd Rather Not Make. Pipe, Jim. 2008. (You Wouldn't Want to Ser.). (ENG.). 32p. (J). (gr. 4-7). 29.00 *(978-0-531-13913-4(1))* Scholastic Library Publishing.
Antram, David, et al. Scary Creatures of the Soil. Cheshire, Gerard. 2009. (Scary Creatures Ser.). (ENG.). 32p. (J). (gr. 2-4). 27.00 *(978-0-531-21821-1(X)*, Watts, Franklin); pap. 8.95 *(978-0-531-22226-3(8)*, Children's Pr.) Scholastic Library Publishing.
Antram, David, et al. The Story of the Exploration of Space. Clarke, Penny. 2013. 64p. (J). ***(978-1-4351-5030-0(9))*** Barnes & Noble, Inc.
Antram, David. Top 10 Worst Ruthless Warriors. Macdonald, Fiona. 2012. (Top 10 Worst Ser.). (ENG.). 32p. (J). (gr. 3-6). pap. 10.50 *(978-1-4339-6686-6(7))*; lib. bdg. 26.60 *(978-1-4339-6685-9(9))* Stevens, Gareth Publishing LLLP. (Gareth Stevens Learning Library).
—Top 10 Worst Things about Ancient Egypt. England, Victoria. 2012. (Top 10 Worst Ser.). (ENG.). 32p. (J). (gr. 3-6). pap. 10.50 *(978-1-4339-6689-7(1))*; lib. bdg. 26.60 *(978-1-4339-6688-0(3))* Stevens, Gareth Publishing LLLP. (Gareth Stevens Learning Library).
—Top 10 Worst Things about Ancient Greece. England, Victoria. 2012. (Top 10 Worst Ser.). (ENG.). 32p. (J). (gr. 3-6). pap. 10.50 *(978-1-4339-6692-7(1))*; lib. bdg. 26.60 *(978-1-4339-6691-0(3))* Stevens, Gareth Publishing LLLP. (Gareth Stevens Learning Library).
—Top 10 Worst Things about Ancient Rome. England, Victoria. 2012. (Top 10 Worst Ser.). (ENG.). 32p. (J). (gr. 3-6). pap. 10.50 *(978-1-4339-6695-8(6))*; lib. bdg. 26.60 *(978-1-4339-6694-1(8))* Stevens, Gareth Publishing LLLP. (Gareth Stevens Learning Library).
—Top 10 Worst Vicious Villains. Pipe, Jim. 2012. (Top 10 Worst Ser.). (ENG.). 32p. (J). (gr. 3-6). pap. 10.50 *(978-1-4339-6698-9(0))*; lib. bdg. 26.60 *(978-1-4339-6697-2(2))* Stevens, Gareth Publishing LLLP. (Gareth Stevens Learning Library).
—Top 10 Worst Wicked Rulers. Macdonald, Fiona. 2012. (Top 10 Worst Ser.). (ENG.). 32p. (J). (gr. 3-6). pap. 10.50 *(978-1-4339-6701-6(4))*; lib. bdg. 26.60 *(978-1-4339-6700-9(6))* Stevens, Gareth Publishing LLLP. (Gareth Stevens Learning Library).
—Tutankhamen! A Mummy Who Really Got Meddled With. Stewart, David. 2007. (You Wouldn't Want to... Ser.). (ENG.). 32p. (J). (gr. 2-5). 29.00 *(978-0-531-18725-8(X))* Scholastic Library Publishing.
—You Wouldn't Want to Be a 19th-Century Coal Miner in England! A Dangerous Job You'd Rather Not Have. Malam, John. 2006. (You Wouldn't Want to Ser.). (ENG.). 32p. (J). (gr. 2-5). 29.00 *(978-0-531-14971-3(4))* Scholastic Library Publishing.
—You Wouldn't Want to Be a Civil War Soldier! A War You'd Rather Not Fight. Ratliff, Thomas. 2013. (You Wouldn't Want to... Ser.). (ENG.). (J). 32p. 29.00 *(978-0-531-25947-4(1))*; 40p. pap. 9.95 *(978-0-531-24503-3(9))* Scholastic Library Publishing. (Watts, Franklin).
—You Wouldn't Want to Be a Greek Athlete! Races You'd Rather Not Run. Ford, Michael & Salariya, David. 2004. (You Wouldn't Want to Ser.). (ENG.). 32p. (J). 29.00 *(978-0-531-12352-2(9))* Scholastic Library Publishing.
—You Wouldn't Want to Be a Mammoth Hunter! Dangerous Beasts You'd Rather Not Encounter. Malam, John & Smith, Karen Barker. 2004. (You Wouldn't Want to Ser.). (ENG.). 32p. (J). (gr. 2-5). pap. 9.95 *(978-0-531-16397-9(0)*, Watts, Franklin) Scholastic Library Publishing.
—You Wouldn't Want to Be a Medieval Knight! Armor You'd Rather Not Wear. Macdonald, Fiona. 2013. (ENG.). (J). 40p. pap. 9.95 *(978-0-531-23851-6(2))*; 32p. 29.00 *(978-0-531-27100-1(5))* Scholastic Library Publishing. (Watts, Franklin).
—You Wouldn't Want to Be a Ninja Warrior! Malam, John. 2012. (You Wouldn't Want to... Ser.). (ENG.). 32p. (J). pap. 9.95 *(978-0-531-20948-6(2)*, Watts, Franklin) Scholastic Library Publishing.
—You Wouldn't Want to Be a Ninja Warrior! A Secret Job That's Your Destiny. Malam, John. 2012. (ENG.). 32p. (J). (gr. 3-12). lib. bdg. 29.00 *(978-0-531-20873-1(7))* Scholastic Library Publishing.
—You Wouldn't Want to... Be a Pirate's Prisoner! Malam, John. rev. ed. 2012. (ENG.). 32p. (J). lib. bdg. 29.00 *(978-0-531-27502-3(7))* Scholastic Library Publishing.
—You Wouldn't Want to Be a Pirate's Prisoner! Horrible Things You'd Rather Not Know. Malam, John. rev. ed. 2012. (You Wouldn't Want to...: History of the World Ser.). (ENG.). 40p. (J). pap. 9.95 *(978-0-531-28027-0(6))* Scholastic Library Publishing.
—You Wouldn't Want to Be a Pyramid Builder! A Hazardous Job You'd Rather Not Have. Morley, Jacqueline. rev. ed. 2013. (ENG.). (J). 32p. 29.00 *(978-0-531-27101-8(3))*; 40p. pap. 9.95 *(978-0-531-23852-3(0))* Scholastic Library Publishing. (Watts, Franklin).
—You Wouldn't Want to... Be a Roman Galdiator! Malam, John. rev. ed. 2012. (ENG.). 32p. (J). lib. bdg. 29.00 *(978-0-531-27503-0(5))* Scholastic Library Publishing.
—You Wouldn't Want to Be a Roman Galdiator! Malam, John. rev. ed. 2012. (You Wouldn't Want to...: Ancient Civilization Ser.). (ENG.). 40p. (J). pap. 9.95 *(978-0-531-28028-7(4))* Scholastic Library Publishing.
—You Wouldn't Want to Be a Samurai! A Deadly Career You'd Rather Not Pursue. Macdonald, Fiona. 2009. (You Wouldn't Want to Ser.). (ENG.). 32p. (J). 29.00 *(978-0-531-21325-4(0))*; (gr. 3-18). pap. 9.95 *(978-0-531-20516-7(9))* Scholastic Library Publishing.
—You Wouldn't Want to Be a Shakespearean Actor! Some Roles You Might Not Want to Play. Morley, Jacqueline & Salariya, David. 2010. (You Wouldn't Want to Ser.). (ENG.). 32p. (J). 29.00 *(978-0-531-20471-9(5))* Scholastic Library Publishing.
—You Wouldn't Want to Be a Shakespearean Actor! Some Roles You Might Not Want to Play. Morley, Jacqueline. 2010. (You Wouldn't Want to Ser.). (ENG.). 32p. (J). (gr. 3-18). pap. 9.95 *(978-0-531-22826-5(6))* Scholastic Library Publishing.
—You Wouldn't Want to Be a Slave in Ancient Greece! A Life You'd Rather Not Have. Macdonald, Fiona. rev. ed. 2013. (ENG.). (J). 32p. 29.00 *(978-0-531-27102-5(1))*; 40p. pap. 9.95 *(978-0-531-23853-0(9))* Scholastic Library Publishing. (Watts, Franklin).
—You Wouldn't Want to Be a Suffragist! A Protest Movement That's Rougher Than You Expected. MacDonald, Fiona. 2008. (You Wouldn't Want to...: History of the World Ser.). (ENG.). 32p. (J). (gr. 3-18). pap. 9.95 *(978-0-531-21911-9(9)*, Watts, Franklin) Scholastic Library Publishing.
—You Wouldn't Want to Be a Victorian Servant! A Thankless Job You'd Rather Not Have. MacDonald, Fiona & Macdonald, Fiona. 2006. (You Wouldn't Want to Ser.). (ENG.). 32p. (J). (gr. 2-5). 29.00 *(978-0-531-14972-0(2))* Scholastic Library Publishing.
—You Wouldn't Want to Be a Viking Explorer! Voyages You'd Rather Not Make. Langley, Andrew. rev. ed. 2013. (ENG.). (J). 32p. 29.00 *(978-0-531-27103-2(X))*; 40p. pap.

A

9.95 *(978-0-531-23854-7(7))* Scholastic Library Publishing. (Watts, Franklin).

—You Wouldn't Want to Be a Worker on the Statue of Liberty! A Monument You'd Rather Not Build. Malam, John. 2008. (You Wouldn't Want to...: American History Ser.). (ENG.). 32p. (J). (gr. 3-18). pap. 9.95 *(978-0-531-21910-2(0),* Watts, Franklin) Scholastic Library Publishing.

—You Wouldn't Want to Be a World War II Pilot! Air Battles You Might Not Survive. Graham, Ian. 2009. (You Wouldn't Want to Ser.). (ENG.). 32p. (J). 29.00 *(978-0-531-21326-1(9))*; (gr. 3-18). pap. 9.95 *(978-0-531-20517-4(7))* Scholastic Library Publishing.

—You Wouldn't Want to Be an 18th-Century British Convict! A Trip to Australia You'd Rather Not Take. Costain, Meredith. 2006. (You Wouldn't Want to Ser.). (ENG.). 32p. (J). (gr. 2-5). 29.00 *(978-0-531-14973-7(0))*; pap. 9.95 *(978-0-531-16998-8(7),* Watts, Franklin) Scholastic Library Publishing.

—You Wouldn't Want to Be an American Colonist! A Settlement You'd Rather Not Start. Morley, Jacqueline. 2013. (You Wouldn't Want to... Ser.). (ENG.). (J). 32p. 29.00 *(978-0-531-25946-7(3))*; 40p. pap. 9.95 *(978-0-531-24502-6(0))* Scholastic Library Publishing. (Watts, Franklin).

—You Wouldn't Want to... Be an American Pioneer! Morley, Jacqueline. rev. ed. 2012. (ENG.). (J). 40p. pap. 9.95 *(978-0-531-28025-6(X))*; 32p. lib. bdg. 29.00 *(978-0-531-27500-9(0))* Scholastic Library Publishing.

—You Wouldn't Want to Be an Aztec Sacrifice: Gruesome Things You'd Rather Not Know. Macdonald, Fiona. rev. ed. 2013. (ENG.). (J). 32p. 29.00 *(978-0-531-27104-9(8))*; 40p. pap. 9.95 *(978-0-531-23855-4(5))* Scholastic Library Publishing. (Watts, Franklin).

—You Wouldn't Want to... Be an Egyptian Mummy! Stewart, David. rev. ed. 2012. (ENG.). 32p. (J). lib. bdg. 29.00 *(978-0-531-27501-6(9))* Scholastic Library Publishing.

—You Wouldn't Want to Be an Egyptian Mummy! Disgusting Things You'd Rather Not Know. Stewart, David. rev. ed. 2012. (You Wouldn't Want to...: Ancient Civilization Ser.). (ENG.). 40p. (J). pap. 9.95 *(978-0-531-28026-3(8))* Scholastic Library Publishing.

—You Wouldn't Want to Be an Inca Mummy! A One-Way Journey You'd Rather Not Make. Hynson, Colin. 2007. (You Wouldn't Want to...: Ancient Civilization Ser.). (ENG.). 32p. (J). (gr. 2-5). pap. 9.95 *(978-0-531-13926-4(3),* Watts, Franklin) Scholastic Library Publishing.

—You Wouldn't Want to Be at the Boston Tea Party! Wharf Water You'd Rather Not Drink. Cook, Peter. 2013. (ENG.). (J). 32p. 29.00 *(978-0-531-27105-6(6))*; 40p. pap. 9.95 *(978-0-531-23856-1(3))* Scholastic Library Publishing. (Watts, Franklin).

—You Wouldn't Want to Be Cleopatra! An Egyptian Ruler You'd Rather Not Be. Pipe, Jim. 2007. (You Wouldn't Want to... Ser.). (ENG.). 32p. (J). (gr. 2-5). pap. 9.95 *(978-0-531-18923-8(6),* Watts, Franklin) Scholastic Library Publishing.

—You Wouldn't Want to Be Cleopatra! An Egyptian Ruler You'D Rather Not Be. Pipe, Jim. 2007. (You Wouldn't Want to... Ser.). (ENG.). 32p. (J). (gr. 2-5). 29.00 *(978-0-531-18726-5(8),* Watts, Franklin) Scholastic Library Publishing.

—You Wouldn't Want to Be Cursed by King Tut! Morley, Jacqueline. 2012. (You Wouldn't Want to... Ser.). (ENG.). 32p. (J). pap. 9.95 *(978-0-531-20949-3(0),* Watts, Franklin) Scholastic Library Publishing.

—You Wouldn't Want to Be Cursed by King Tut! A Mysterious Death You'd Rather Avoid. Morley, Jacqueline. 2012. (ENG.). 32p. (J). (gr. 3-12). lib. bdg. 29.00 *(978-0-531-20874-8(5))* Scholastic Library Publishing.

—You Wouldn't Want to Be in a Medieval Dungeon! Stewart, David. rev. ed. 2013. (You Wouldn't Want to... Ser.). (ENG.). 32p. (J). 29.00 *(978-0-531-25949-8(8),* Watts, Franklin) Scholastic Library Publishing.

—You Wouldn't Want to Be in a Medieval Dungeon! Prisoners You'd Rather Not Meet. MacDonald, Fiona & Macdonald, Fiona. 2003. (You Wouldn't Want to Ser.). (ENG.). 32p. (J). 29.00 *(978-0-531-12312-6(X),* Watts, Franklin) Scholastic Library Publishing.

—You Wouldn't Want to Be in a Medieval Dungeon! Prisoners You'd Rather Not Meet. Macdonald, Fiona. 2013. (You Wouldn't Want to... Ser.). (ENG.). (J). 40p. pap. 9.95 *(978-0-531-24504-0(7))*; 32p. 29.00 *(978-0-531-25948-1(X))* Scholastic Library Publishing. (Watts, Franklin).

—You Wouldn't Want to Be in Alexander the Great's Army! Miles You'd Rather Not March. Morley, Jacqueline. 2005. (You Wouldn't Want to... Ser.). (ENG.). 32p. (J). (gr. 2-5). 29.00 *(978-0-531-12410-9(X))*; (gr. 4-7). pap. 9.95 *(978-0-531-12390-4(1))* Scholastic Library Publishing. (Watts, Franklin).

—You Wouldn't Want to Be in the First Submarine! An Undersea Expedition You'd Rather Avoid. Graham, Ian. 2008. (You Wouldn't Want to...: American History Ser.). (ENG.). 32p. (J). (gr. 3-18). pap. 9.95 *(978-0-531-21912-6(7),* Watts, Franklin) Scholastic Library Publishing.

—You Wouldn't Want to Be Joan of Arc! A Mission You Might Want to Miss. Macdonald, Fiona. 2010. (You Wouldn't Want to Ser.). (ENG.). 32p. (J). 29.00 *(978-0-531-20473-3(1))*; (gr. 3-18). pap. 9.95 *(978-0-531-22828-9(2))* Scholastic Library Publishing.

—You Wouldn't Want to Be Mary Queen of Scots. MacDonald, Fiona. 2008. (You Wouldn't Want to...: History of the World Ser.). (ENG.). 32p. (J). (gr. 2-5). pap. 9.95 *(978-0-531-14853-2(X),* Watts, Franklin) Scholastic Library Publishing.

—You Wouldn't Want to Be Mary Queen of Scots: A Ruler Who Really Lost Her Head. MacDonald, Fiona. 2008. (You Wouldn't Want to Ser.). (ENG.). 32p. (J). (gr. 4-7). 29.00 *(978-0-531-13912-7(3))* Scholastic Library Publishing.

—You Wouldn't Want to Be on Apollo 13! A Mission You'd Rather Not Go On. Graham, Ian. 2003. (You Wouldn't Want to Ser.). (ENG.). 32p. (J). (gr. 2-5). pap. 9.95 *(978-0-531-16650-5(3),* Watts, Franklin) Scholastic Library Publishing.

—You Wouldn't Want to Be on the First Flying Machine! A High-Soaring Ride You'd Rather Not Take. Graham, Ian. 2013. (You Wouldn't Want to... Ser.). (ENG.). 32p. (J). 29.00 *(978-0-531-25945-0(5))*; pap. 9.95 *(978-0-531-23042-8(2))* Scholastic Library Publishing. (Watts, Franklin).

—You Wouldn't Want to Be Sir Isaac Newton! A Lonely Life You'd Rather Not Lead. Graham, Ian. 2013. (You Wouldn't Want to... Ser.). (ENG.). 32p. (J). 29.00 *(978-0-531-25943-6(9))*; pap. 9.95 *(978-0-531-23040-4(6))* Scholastic Library Publishing. (Watts, Franklin).

—You Wouldn't Want to Explore with Marco Polo! A Really Long Trip You'd Rather Not Take. Morley, Jacqueline. 2009. (You Wouldn't Want to Ser.). (ENG.). 32p. (J). (gr. 3-12). 29.00 *(978-0-531-21327-8(7))*; pap. 9.95 *(978-0-531-20518-1(5))* Scholastic Library Publishing.

—You Wouldn't Want to Explore with Sir Francis Drake! A Pirate You'd Rather Not Know. Stewart, David. 2005. (You Wouldn't Want to... Ser.). (ENG.). 32p. (J). (gr. 2-5). 29.00 *(978-0-531-12413-0(4))*; pap. 9.95 *(978-0-531-12393-5(6))* Scholastic Library Publishing. (Watts, Franklin).

—You Wouldn't Want to Live in a Wild West Town! Dust You'd Rather Not Settle. Hicks, Peter. 2013. (ENG.). (J). 32p. 29.00 *(978-0-531-27106-3(4))*; 40p. pap. 9.95 *(978-0-531-23857-8(1))* Scholastic Library Publishing. (Watts, Franklin).

—You Wouldn't Want to Live Without Antibiotics. Rooney, Anne. 2014. (You Wouldn't Want to Live Without... Ser.). (ENG.). 32p. (J). lib. bdg. 29.00 *(978-0-531-21218-9(1),* Watts, Franklin) Scholastic Library Publishing.

—You Wouldn't Want to Live Without Books! Woolf, Alex. 2014. (You Wouldn't Want to Live Without... Ser.). (ENG.). 32p. (J). lib. bdg. 29.00 *(978-0-531-21220-2(3),* Watts, Franklin) Scholastic Library Publishing.

—You Wouldn't Want to Live Without Clean Water! Canavan, Roger. 2014. (You Wouldn't Want to Live Without... Ser.). (ENG.). 32p. (J). lib. bdg. 29.00 *(978-0-531-21219-6(X),* Watts, Franklin) Scholastic Library Publishing.

Antram, David. You Wouldn't Want to Live Without Clocks & Calendars! Macdonald, Fiona. 2015. (You Wouldn't Want to Live Without... Ser.). (ENG.). 32p. (J). lib. bdg. 29.00 ***(978-0-531-21928-7(3),*** Watts, Franklin) Scholastic Library Publishing.

Antram, David. You Wouldn't Want to Live Without Dentists! Macdonald, Fiona. 2015. (You Wouldn't Want to Live Without... Ser.). (ENG.). 40p. (J). pap. 9.95 *(978-0-531-21410-7(9),* Watts, Franklin) Scholastic Library Publishing.

—You Wouldn't Want to Live Without Insects! Rooney, Anne. 2015. (You Wouldn't Want to Live Without... Ser.). (ENG.). 40p. (J). pap. 9.95 *(978-0-531-21405-3(2),* Watts, Franklin) Scholastic Library Publishing.

—You Wouldn't Want to Live Without Toilets! Macdonald, Fiona. 2014. (You Wouldn't Want to Live Without... Ser.). (ENG.). 32p. (J). lib. bdg. 29.00 *(978-0-531-21215-8(7),* Watts, Franklin) Scholastic Library Publishing.

—You Wouldn't Want to Live Without Vaccinations! Rooney, Anne. 2015. (You Wouldn't Want to Live Without... Ser.). (ENG.). 40p. (J). pap. 9.95 *(978-0-531-21409-1(5),* Watts, Franklin) Scholastic Library Publishing.

—You Wouldn't Want to Meet Typhoid Mary! A Deadly Cook You'd Rather Not Know. Morley, Jacqueline. 2013. (You Wouldn't Want to... Ser.). (ENG.). 32p. (J). 29.00 *(978-0-531-25944-3(7))*; pap. 9.95 *(978-0-531-23041-1(4))* Scholastic Library Publishing. (Watts, Franklin).

—You Wouldn't Want to Sail in the Spanish Armada! An Invasion You'd Rather Not Launch. Malam, John. 2006. (You Wouldn't Want to Ser.). (ENG.). 32p. (J). (gr. 2-5). 29.00 *(978-0-531-14974-4(9))*; pap. 9.95 *(978-0-531-16999-5(5),* Watts, Franklin) Scholastic Library Publishing.

—You Wouldn't Want to Sail on an Irish Famine Ship! A Trip Across the Atlanic You'd Rather Not Make. Pipe, Jim. 2008. (You Wouldn't Want to...: History of the World Ser.). (ENG.). 32p. (J). (gr. 4-7). pap. 9.95 *(978-0-531-14854-9(8),* Watts, Franklin) Scholastic Library Publishing.

—You Wouldn't Want to Sail on the Titanic! One Voyage You'D Rather Not Make. Stewart, David. rev. ed. 2013. (You Wouldn't Want to... Ser.). (ENG.). 40p. (J). pap. 9.95 *(978-0-531-24505-7(5),* Watts, Franklin) Scholastic Library Publishing.

—You Wouldn't Want to Work on the Great Wall of China! Defenses You'd Rather Not Build. Morley, Jacqueline. 2006. (You Wouldn't Want to Ser.). (ENG.). 32p. (J). (gr. 2-5). 29.00 *(978-0-531-12424-6(X))*; pap. 9.95 *(978-0-531-12449-9(5),* Watts, Franklin) Scholastic Library Publishing.

—You Wouldn't Want to Work on the Hoover Dam! An Explosive Job You'd Rather Not Do. Graham, Ian. 2012. (You Wouldn't Want to... Ser.). (ENG.). 32p. (J). pap. 9.95 *(978-0-531-20946-2(6),* Watts, Franklin); lib. bdg. 29.00 *(978-0-531-20871-7(0))* Scholastic Library Publishing.

Antram, David, jt. illus. see Bergin, Mark.

Anyabwile, Dawud. Monster. Sims, Guy A. & Myers, Walter Dean. 2015. (Monster Ser.). (ENG.). 160p. (YA). (gr. 8). pap. 9.99 *(978-0-06-227499-1(6))* HarperCollins Pubs.

Anzai, Nobuyuki. Flame of Recca. Anzai, Nobuyuki. Caselman, Lance. 2006. (Flame of Recca Ser.: Vol. 18). (ENG.). 208p. pap. 9.99 *(978-1-4215-0454-4(5))* Viz Media.

—Flame of Recca, Vol. 6. Anzai, Nobuyuki. 2004. (Flame of Recca Ser.). (ENG.). 200p. pap. 9.95 *(978-1-59116-316-9(1))* Viz Media.

—Flame of Recca. Anzai, Nobuyuki. Caselman, Lance. 2003. (Flame of Recca Ser.). (ENG.). Vol. 1. 184p. pap. 9.95 *(978-1-59116-066-3(9))*; Vol. 2. 200p. pap. 9.95 *(978-1-59116-067-0(7))* Viz Media.

—Flame of Recca. Anzai, Nobuyuki. (Flame of Recca Ser.). (ENG.). Vol. 3. 2003. 200p. pap. 9.95 *(978-1-59116-094-6(4))*; Vol. 4. 2004. 200p. pap. 9.95 *(978-1-59116-125-7(8))*; Vol. 5. 2004. 200p. pap. 9.95 *(978-1-59116-193-6(2))*; Vol. 7. 2004. 200p. pap. 9.95 *(978-1-59116-448-7(6))*; Vol. 8. 2004. 200p. pap. 9.95 *(978-1-59116-480-7(X))*; Vol. 9. 2004. 192p. pap. 9.95 *(978-1-59116-481-4(8))*; Vol. 10. 2005. 200p. pap. 9.95 *(978-1-59116-636-8(5))* Viz Media.

—Flame of Recca, Vol. 11. Anzai, Nobuyuki. Nobuyuki, Anzai & Caselman, Lance. 2005. (Flame of Recca Ser.). (ENG.). 200p. pap. 9.99 *(978-1-59116-741-9(8))* Viz Media.

—Flame of Recca. Anzai, Nobuyuki. Caselman, Lance. (Flame of Recca Ser.). (ENG.). Vol. 12. 2005. 192p. pap. 9.99 *(978-1-59116-796-9(5))*; Vol. 14. 2005. 184p. pap. 9.99 *(978-1-4215-0014-0(0))*; Vol. 15. 2005. 200p. pap. 9.99 *(978-1-4215-0131-4(7))*; Vol. 16. 2006. 208p. pap. 9.99 *(978-1-4215-0250-2(X))*; Vol. 17. 2006. 200p. pap. 9.99 *(978-1-4215-0381-3(6))*; Vol. 19. 2006. 208p. pap. 9.99 *(978-1-4215-0455-1(3))* Viz Media.

—MÄR, 15 vols. Anzai, Nobuyuki. 2007. (Mar Ser.: 14). (ENG.). 192p. pap. 7.99 *(978-1-4215-1322-5(6))* Viz Media.

—Märchen Awakens Romance, 15 vols. Anzai, Nobuyuki. (Mar Ser.). (ENG.). 200p. Vol. 3. 2005. pap. 7.99 *(978-1-59116-904-8(6))*; Vol. 7. 2006. pap. 7.99 *(978-1-4215-0489-6(8))* Viz Media.

Anzalone, Frank, photos by. Images & Art of Santana Row. 2nd ed. 2005. 64p. per. 19.95 *(978-0-9770788-0-6(9))* Anzalone, Frank.

Anzalone, Lori. Alligator at Saw Grass Road. Halfmann, Janet. (Smithsonian's Backyard Ser.). (ENG.). 32p. (J). 2011. (gr. -1-3). 19.95 *(978-1-60727-630-2(5))*; 2011. (gr. -1-3). 8.95 *(978-1-60727-631-9(3))*; 2006. pap. 6.95 *(978-1-59249-633-4(4))* Soundprints.

Aoki, Deb. Best Hawaiian Style Mother Goose Ever. Sullivan, Kevin. 2006. 40p. 16.95 incl. cd-rom *(978-0-9644149-6-9(1))* Hawaya, Inc.

Aoki, Takao. Beyblade. Aoki, Takao. (Beyblade Ser.). (ENG.). 2004. 200p. (YA). pap. 7.99 *(978-1-59116-621-4(7))*; Vol. 5. 2005. 192p. (YA). pap. 7.99 *(978-1-59116-793-8(0))*; Vol. 9. 2006. 208p. pap. 7.99 *(978-1-4215-0249-6(6))*; Vol. 10. 2006. 208p. pap. 7.99 *(978-1-4215-0380-6(8))* Viz Media.

—Beyblade: Beyblade Extreme Rotation Shoot, Vol. 2. Aoki, Takao. 2004. (Beyblade Ser.). (ENG.). 192p. (YA). pap. 7.99 *(978-1-59116-697-9(7))* Viz Media.

Aoki, Yuya. Fruits Basket, Volume 3. Takaya, Natsuki. 2004. (Fruits Basket Ser.). 189p. 17.65 *(978-0-7569-6009-4(6))* Perfection Learning Corp.

Aón, Carlos. Aliens & Energy, 1 vol. Biskup, Agnieszka. 2011. (Monster Science Ser.). (ENG.). 32p. (gr. 3-4). pap. 8.10 *(978-1-4296-7325-9(7))*; pap. 47.70 *(978-1-4296-7326-6(5))*; lib. bdg. 29.99 *(978-1-4296-6580-3(7))* Capstone Pr., Inc. (Graphic Library).

—Frankenstein's Monster & Scientific Methods, 1 vol. Harbo, Christopher L. 2013. (Monster Science Ser.). (ENG.). 32p. (gr. 3-4). pap. 7.95 *(978-1-62065-816-1(X),* Graphic Library); lib. bdg. 29.99 *(978-1-4296-9931-0(0))* Capstone Pr., Inc.

Aon, Carlos. Jesse & Jasmine Build a Journal. Lynette, Rachel. 2013. (ENG.). 32p. (J). lib. bdg. 25.27 *(978-1-59953-585-2(8))*; (gr. 2-4). pap. 11.94 *(978-1-60357-559-1(6))* Norwood Hse. Pr.

Aón, Carlos. Monster Science. Harbo, Christopher L. 2013. (Monster Science Ser.). (ENG.). 32p. (gr. 3-4). pap. 15.90 *(978-1-4765-3673-6(2),* Graphic Library) Capstone Pr., Inc.

Aon, Carlos & Aón, Carlos. The Legend of the Bermuda Triangle, 1 vol. Troupe, Thomas Kingsley. 2010. (Legend Has It Ser.). (ENG.). 32p. (gr. 2-4). lib. bdg. 26.65 *(978-1-4048-6034-6(7),* Nonfiction Picture Bks.) Picture Window Bks.

Aón, Carlos & Lazzati, Laura. The Lonely Existence of Asteroids & Comets. Weakland, Mark. 2012. (Adventures in Science Ser.). (ENG.). 32p. (gr. 3-4). pap. 47.70 *(978-1-4296-8465-1(8))*; lib. bdg. 29.99 *(978-1-4296-7546-8(2))* Capstone Pr., Inc. (Graphic Library).

Aón, Carlos, jt. illus. see Aon, Carlos.

Aón, Carlos, jt. illus. see Gervasio.

Aón, Carlos, jt. illus. see Lazzati, Laura.

Aoyama, Gôshô. Case Closed. Aoyama, Gôshô. (Case Closed Ser.: 49). (ENG.). 2014. 192p. pap. 9.99 *(978-1-4215-5506-5(9))*; 2008. 200p. (gr. 8-12). pap. 9.99 *(978-1-4215-1675-2(6))* Viz Media.

—Case Closed. Aoyama, Gôshô. Nakatani, Andy. 2008. (Case Closed Ser.: 21). (ENG.). 200p. pap. 9.99 *(978-1-4215-1456-7(7))* Viz Media.

—Case Closed. Aoyama, Gôshô. 2007. (Case Closed Ser.: 18). (ENG.). 192p. pap. 9.99 *(978-1-4215-0883-2(4))* Viz Media.

—Case Closed. Aoyama, Gôshô. Yamazaki, Joe, tr. from JPN. 2005. (Case Closed Ser.). (ENG.). 184p. pap. 9.95 *(978-1-59116-838-6(4))* Viz Media.

—Case Closed. Aoyama, Gôshô. 2005. (Case Closed Ser.). (ENG.). 184p. pap. 9.95 *(978-1-59116-632-0(2))* Viz Media.

—Case Closed, 20. Aoyama, Gôshô. Nakatani, Andy, ed. 2007. (Case Closed Ser.: 20). (ENG.). 192p. pap. 9.99 *(978-1-4215-0885-6(0))* Viz Media.

—Case Closed. Aoyama, Gôshô. (Case Closed Ser.). (ENG.). Vol. 1. 2004. 200p. pap. 9.99 *(978-1-59116-327-5(7))*; Vol. 2. 2004. 184p. pap. 9.95 *(978-1-59116-587-3(3))*; Vol. 3. 2005. 200p. pap. 9.95 *(978-1-59116-589-7(X))*; Vol. 5. 2005. 200p. pap. 9.95 *(978-1-59116-633-7(0))*; Vol. 7. 2005. 184p. pap. 9.95 *(978-1-59116-978-9(X))*; Vol. 8. 2005. 192p. pap. 9.95 *(978-1-4215-0111-6(2))*; Vol. 9. 2006. 184p. pap. 9.95 *(978-1-4215-0166-6(X))*; Vol. 10. 2006. 194p. pap. 9.95 *(978-1-4215-0316-5(6))*; Vol. 16. 2007. 192p. pap. 9.99 *(978-1-4215-0881-8(8))*; Vol. 19. 2007. 192p. pap. 9.99 *(978-1-4215-0884-9(2))* Viz Media.

Apa, Ivy Marie. The Adventures of Sir Ambrose Elephant: A Visit to the City. Smith, E. 2012. 19p. pap. 9.95 *(978-1-4691-8378-7(1))* Xlibris Corp.

—Harlow the Helpful Ghost. Brearley, Leeanne. 2012. 60p. pap. 31.99 *(978-1-4797-3178-7(1))* Xlibris Corp.

Aparicio, Raquel. One White Dolphin. Lewis, Gill. (ENG.). (J). (gr. 3-7). 2013. 368p. pap. 7.99 *(978-1-4424-1448-8(0))*; 2012. 352p. 15.99 *(978-1-4424-1447-1(2))* Simon & Schuster Children's Publishing. (Atheneum Bks. for Young Readers).

Apodaca, Blanca. Sight Word Poetry. Reynolds, Laureen. Migliaccio, Eric, ed. ed. 2004. (ENG.). 48p. (gr. 1-3). pap. 8.99 *(978-0-7439-3507-4(1))* Teacher Created Resources, Inc.

Apostolou, Christine Hale, jt. illus. see Hale, Christy.

Appel, Morgan. The Teacher's Classroom Companion: A Handbook for Primary Teachers. Coons, Mary H. 2003. 320p. (J). pap. 24.95 *(978-0-9634938-0-4(9))* Teachers' Handbooks.

Appelhans, Chris. Sparky! Offill, Jenny. 2014. (ENG.). 40p. (J). (gr. -1-3). 16.99 *(978-0-375-87023-1(7),* Schwartz & Wade Bks.) Random Hse. Children's Bks.

Appelt, Kenneth, photos by. Just People & Paper - Pen - Poem: A Young Writer's Way to Begin. Appelt, Kathi. 2004. (Writers & Young Writers Ser.: Vol. 1). 91p. (YA). pap. 11.95 *(978-1-888842-07-4(5),* 1020) Absey & Co.

Apperley, Dawn. The Tooth Fairy. Hall, Kirsten. (My First Reader Ser.). (ENG.). 32p. (J). (gr. k-1). 2004. pap. 3.95 *(978-0-516-24640-6(2))*; 2003. 18.50 *(978-0-516-22938-6(9))* Scholastic Library Publishing. (Children's Pr.).

Apple, Emma. Hind's Hands: A Story about Autism. Juwayriyah, Umm & Ayed, Juwayriyah. 2013. 16p. (J). pap. 6.00 *(978-1-935437-76-5(3),* As Sabr Pubns.) Imago Pr.

Apple, Margot. Birthday Pony. Haas, Jessie. 2004. 80p. (J). (gr. 2-18). 15.99 *(978-0-06-057359-1(7))*; (gr. 1-5). lib. bdg. 16.89 *(978-0-06-057360-7(0),* Greenwillow Bks.) HarperCollins Pubs.

Apple, Margot. Me First. Shaw, Nancy. 2015. 32p. pap. 7.00 ***(978-1-61003-505-7(4))*** Center for the Collaborative Classroom.

Apple, Margot. Sheep Blast Off! Shaw, Nancy E. 2011. (ENG.). 32p. (J). (gr. -1-3). pap. 5.99 *(978-0-547-52025-4(5))* Houghton Mifflin Harcourt Publishing Co.

—Sheep Go to Sleep. Shaw, Nancy. 2015. (ENG.). 32p. (J). (gr. -1-3). 16.99 *(978-0-544-30989-0(8),* HMH Books For Young Readers) Houghton Mifflin Harcourt Publishing Co.

—Sheep in a Jeep. Shaw, Nancy E. (ENG.). (J). (gr. -1-3). 2013. 32p. 26.99 *(978-0-547-99383-6(8))*; 2009. 26p. bds. 11.99 *(978-0-547-23775-6(8))*; 2006. 32p. 10.99 *(978-0-618-69522-5(2))* Houghton Mifflin Harcourt Publishing Co.

—Sheep in a Shop, 1 vol. Shaw, Nancy E. 2009. (ENG.). 32p. (J). (gr. -1-3). 10.99 *(978-0-547-23767-1(7))* Houghton Mifflin Harcourt Publishing Co.

—Sheep Out to Eat. Shaw, Nancy E. 2005. (ENG.). 28p. (J). (gr. k — 1). bds. 5.95 *(978-0-618-58339-3(4))* Houghton Mifflin Harcourt Publishing Co.

—Yours till Niagara Falls, Abby. O'Connor, Jane. 2008. (ENG.). 128p. (J). (gr. 3-7). 7.99 *(978-0-14-241151-3(5),* Puffin) Penguin Publishing Group.

Apple, Margot. Sheep Blast Off! Apple, Margot. Shaw, Nancy & Shaw, Nancy E. 2008. (ENG.). 32p. (J). (gr. k-3). 15.00 *(978-0-618-13168-6(X))* Houghton Mifflin Harcourt Publishing Co.

Applefield, Annie. The Beetle & the Berry. Applefield, Annie. 2007. 28p. (J). per. 15.95 *(978-0-9748933-9-6(0))* E & E Publishing.

Appleoff, Sandy. C Is for Cornhusker: A Nebraska Alphabet. Luebs Shepherd, Rajean. 2004. (State Ser.). (ENG.). 40p. (J). 17.95 *(978-1-58536-147-2(X))* Sleeping Bear Pr.

Apps, Fred. The Back Leg of a Goat: A Tania Abbey Adventure. Reeve, Penny. 2008. (Tania Abbey Adventure Ser.). (ENG.). 96p. pap. 6.99 *(978-1-84550-340-6(6))* Christian Focus Pubns. GBR. Dist: Send The Light Distribution LLC.

—Barnabas: The Encourager. MacKenzie, Carine. 2007. (Bible Wise Ser.). (ENG.). 32p. (J). (gr. -1-3). pap. 3.99 *(978-1-84550-290-4(6))* Christian Focus Pubns. GBR. Dist: Send The Light Distribution LLC.

—Big Book of Bible Truths, Vol. 1. Ferguson, Sinclair B. 2008. (ENG.). 64p. pap. 14.99 *(978-1-84550-371-0(6))* Christian Focus Pubns. GBR. Dist: Send The Light Distribution LLC.

—Big Book of Bible Truths 2. Ferguson, Sinclair B. 2008. (ENG.). 64p. pap. 14.99 *(978-1-84550-372-7(4))* Christian Focus Pubns. GBR. Dist: Send The Light Distribution LLC.

—Daniel: The Praying Prince. MacKenzie, Carine. 2005. (Bible Wise Ser.). (ENG.). 32p. (J). (gr. -1-3). pap. 3.99 *(978-1-85792-155-7(0))* Christian Focus Pubns. GBR. Dist: Send The Light Distribution LLC.

—Daniel, el Príncipe que Oraba, Foce, Natalia, tr. from ENG. l.t. ed. 2009. (SPA & ENG.). 32p. (J). 3.49 *(978-1-932789-19-5(7))* Editorial Sendas Antiguas, LLC.

—God's Names. Michael, Sally. 2011. (J). pap. *(978-1-59638-219-0(8))* P & R Publishing.

—La Historia de Pablo — Viajes de Aventura, 1. Foce, Natalia, tr. from ENG. l.t. ed. 2009. Orig. Title: Journeys of Adventure — the Story of Paul. (SPA & ENG.). 32p. (J). 3.49 *(978-1-932789-23-2(5))* Editorial Sendas Antiguas, LLC.

—Jesus Finds His People. MacKenzie, Catherine. 2008. (Sent to Save Ser.). (ENG.). 16p. (J). (gr. -1-3). 3.99 *(978-1-84550-324-6(4))* Christian Focus Pubns. GBR. Dist: Send The Light Distribution LLC.

—Jesus Helps His People. MacKenzie, Catherine. 2008. (Sent to Save Ser.). (ENG.). 16p. (J). (gr. -1-3). 3.99 *(978-1-84550-322-2(8))* Christian Focus Pubns. GBR. Dist: Send The Light Distribution LLC.

Apps, Fred. Jesus Is Most Special. Michael, Sally. 2014. (ENG.). 24p. (J). (gr. 4-7). 9.99 ***(978-1-62995-029-7(7))*** P & R Publishing.

Apps, Fred. Jesus Rescues His People. MacKenzie, Catherine. 2008. (Sent to Save Ser.). (ENG.). 16p. (J). (gr. 4-7). bds. 3.99 *(978-1-84550-321-5(X))* Christian Focus Pubns. GBR. Dist: Send The Light Distribution LLC.

—Jesus Saves His People. MacKenzie, Catherine. 2008. (ENG.). 16p. (J). (gr. -1-3). bds. 3.99 *(978-1-84550-323-9(6))* Christian Focus Pubns. GBR. Dist: Send The Light Distribution LLC.

—Jonah & the Big Fish. Mackenzie, Carine. 2005. (Famous Bible Stories (Board Books) Ser.). (ENG.). 12p. (J). (gr. -1-k). 3.99 *(978-1-84550-087-0(3)*, Christian Focus) Christian Focus Pubns. GBR. Dist: Send The Light Distribution LLC.

—Jonathan: The Faithful Friend. Mackenzie, Carine. 2007. (Bible Wise Ser.). (ENG.). 32p. (J). (gr. -1-2). 3.99 *(978-1-84550-289-8(2))* Christian Focus Pubns. GBR. Dist: Send The Light Distribution LLC.

—Joseph: God's Dreamer. Christian Focus Publications (CFP) Staff & MacKenzie, Carine. 2005. (Bible Wise Ser.). (ENG.). 32p. (J). (gr. k-3). pap. 3.99 *(978-1-85792-343-8(X))* Christian Focus Pubns. GBR. Dist: Send The Light Distribution LLC.

—Mary & Joseph Love Jesus. MacKenzie, Catherine. 2007. (ENG.). 16p. (gr. -1-k). 3.99 *(978-1-84550-184-6(5)*, Christian Focus) Christian Focus Pubns. GBR. Dist: Send The Light Distribution LLC.

—My Bible Story Book. Mackenzie, Carine. 2006. (Colour Bks.). (ENG.). 160p. (J). (gr. -1-3). 10.99 *(978-1-84550-129-7(2))* Christian Focus Pubns. GBR. Dist: Send The Light Distribution LLC.

—Naaman: The Soldier. MacKenzie, Carine. 2005. (Famous Bible Stories (Board Books) Ser.). (ENG.). 12p. (J). (gr. -1-k). 3.99 *(978-1-84550-085-6(7)*, Christian Focus) Christian Focus Pubns. GBR. Dist: Send The Light Distribution LLC.

—El Nacimiento de Jesús: El Niño Prometido, 1. Foce, Natalia, tr. from ENG. l.t. ed. 2009. Orig. Title: The Birth of Jesus — the Promised Child. (SPA & ENG.). 32p. (J). 3.49 *(978-1-932789-20-1(0))* Editorial Sendas Antiguas, LLC.

—The New Children's Bible. De Vries, Anne. 2005. (Colour Bks.). (ENG.). 288p. (J). 15.99 *(978-1-85792-838-9(5))* Christian Focus Pubns. GBR. Dist: Send The Light Distribution LLC.

—Noah: Rescue Plan. MacKenzie, Carine. 2007. (Bible Wise Ser.). (ENG.). 32p. (J). (gr. 1-5). pap. 3.99 *(978-1-85792-466-4(5))* Christian Focus Pubns. GBR. Dist: Send The Light Distribution LLC.

—El Plan de Rescate: La Historia de Noe, 1. Foce, Natalia, tr. from ENG. l.t. ed. 2009. Orig. Title: The Rescue Plan. (SPA & ENG.). 32p. (J). 3.49 *(978-1-932789-15-7(4))* Editorial Sendas Antiguas, LLC.

—La Resurrección: Jesús Está Vivo, 1. Foce, Natalia, tr. from ENG. l.t. ed. 2009. Orig. Title: The Resurrection — Jesus Is Alive. (SPA & ENG.). 32p. (J). 3.49 *(978-1-932789-21-8(9))* Editorial Sendas Antiguas, LLC.

—Ruth's Journey. Mackenzie, Carine. 2005. (Famous Bible Stories (Board Books) Ser.). (ENG.). 12p. (J). (gr. -1-k). 3.99 *(978-1-84550-086-3(5)*, Christian Focus) Christian Focus Pubns. GBR. Dist: Send The Light Distribution LLC.

—Samuel: The Boy Who Listened. MacKenzie, Carine. 2005. (Bible Wise Ser.). (ENG.). 32p. (J). pap. 3.99 *(978-1-85792-199-1(2))* Christian Focus Pubns. GBR. Dist: Send The Light Distribution LLC.

—Samuel, el Niño que Escuchaba. Foce, Natalia, tr. from ENG. l.t. ed. 2009. (SPA & ENG.). 32p. (J). 3.49 *(978-1-932789-17-1(0))* Editorial Sendas Antiguas, LLC.

—Samuel's Surprise. Mackenzie, Carine. 2005. (Famous Bible Stories (Board Books) Ser.). (ENG.). 12p. (J). (gr. -1-k). 3.99 *(978-1-84550-088-7(1)*, Christian Focus) Christian Focus Pubns. GBR. Dist: Send The Light Distribution LLC.

—Sara y Abraham: La maravillosa Promesa. Mackenzie, Carine. Foce, Natalia C., tr. from ENG. 2009. (Biblewise Ser.). Orig. Title: Sarah & Abraham - the Wonderful Promise. (SPA & ENG.). 32p. (J). 3.49 *(978-1-932789-14-0(6))* Editorial Sendas Antiguas, LLC.

—Sarah & Abraham: The Wonderful Promise. MacKenzie, Carine. 2007. (Bible Wise Ser.). (ENG.). 32p. (J). (gr. 4-7). pap. 3.99 *(978-1-85792-156-4(9))* Christian Focus Pubns. GBR. Dist: Send The Light Distribution LLC.

—Saul: The Miracle on the Road. Taylor, Jane & MacKenzie, Carine. 2005. (Bible Wise Ser.). (ENG.). 32p. (J). (gr. -1-k). pap. 3.99 *(978-1-85792-296-7(4))* Christian Focus Pubns. GBR. Dist: Send The Light Distribution LLC.

—Saúl — el Milagro en el Camino, 1. Foce, Natalia, tr. from ENG. l.t. ed. 2009. Orig. Title: Saul — the Miracle on the Road. (SPA & ENG.). 32p. (J). 3.49 *(978-1-932789-22-5(7))* Editorial Sendas Antiguas, LLC.

—The Shepherds Find Jesus. MacKenzie, Catherine. 2007. (ENG.). 16p. (gr. -1-k). 3.99 *(978-1-84550-185-3(3)*, Christian Focus) Christian Focus Pubns. GBR. Dist: Send The Light Distribution LLC.

—Simeon & Anna See Jesus. MacKenzie, Catherine. 2006. (Born to Be King (Board Books) Ser.). (ENG.). 16p. (gr. -1-k). 3.99 *(978-1-84550-186-0(1))* Christian Focus Pubns. GBR. Dist: Send The Light Distribution LLC.

—The Singing Soldiers: And Other Bible Stories You've Gotta Hear. Haley, Barbara. 2007. (ENG.). 112p. mass mkt. 7.99 *(978-1-84550-249-2(3))* Christian Focus Pubns. GBR. Dist: Send The Light Distribution LLC.

—Water or Goo? Reeve, Penny. 2008. (Tania Abbey Adventure Ser.). (ENG.). 96p. pap. 6.99 *(978-1-84550-341-3(4))* Christian Focus Pubns. GBR. Dist: Send The Light Distribution LLC.

—The Wise Mean Help Jesus. MacKenzie, Catherine. 2006. (Born to Be King (Board Books) Ser.). (ENG.). 16p. (gr. -1-k). 3.99 *(978-1-84550-187-7(X))* Christian Focus Pubns. GBR. Dist: Send The Light Distribution LLC.

Apsley. The Kids' Guide to Staying Awesome & in Control: Simple Stuff to Help Children Regulate Their Emotions & Senses. Brukner, Lauren. 2014. (ENG.). 112p. *(978-1-84905-997-8(7))* Kingsley, Jessica Ltd.

Aragon Art Studio. The Chocolate Man A Children's Horror Tale. Riddle, Waide Aaron. ed. 2010. (ENG.). 44p. pap. 15.00 *(978-0-615-38560-0(5))* Green Ghost Pr.

Aragon, Dolores. Grandma Lale's Tamales: A Christmas Story. García, Nasario. 2014. (SPA & ENG.). (J). *(978-1-936744-26-8(0)*, Rio Grande Bks.) LPD Pr.

Arai, Hiroyuki. Everyone Says Goodnight. 2016. (J). ***(978-1-4521-5139-7(3))*** Chronicle Bks. LLC.

Arai, Setsuo. Boy's Day in Hawaii. Ching, Tokie. 2008. 32p. (J). 12.95 *(978-1-56647-852-6(9))* Mutual Publishing LLC.

Araizumi, Rui. The Silver Beast, Vol. 5. Kanzaka, Hajime. 2005. (Slayers (Tokyopop) Ser.). 248p. pap. 7.99 *(978-1-59532-581-5(6))* TOKYOPOP, Inc.

—Slayers, Vol. 3. Kanzaka, Hajime. 2005. 232p. pap. 7.99 *(978-1-59532-579-2(4))* TOKYOPOP, Inc.

—Slayers: The Battle of Saillune, Vol. 4. Kanzaka, Hajime. 2005. 232p. pap. 7.99 *(978-1-59532-580-8(8))* TOKYOPOP, Inc.

—Slayers: The Sorcerer of Atlas, 2 vols., Vol. 2. Kanzaka, Hajime. 2004. 192p. pap. 7.99 *(978-1-59532-095-7(4))* TOKYOPOP, Inc.

—Slayers - Vezendi's Shadow, Vol. 6. Kanzaka, Hajime. 2005. (Slayers (Tokyopop) Ser.). 248p. pap. 7.99 *(978-1-59532-582-2(4))* TOKYOPOP, Inc.

Arakawa, Hiromu. The Art of Fullmetal Alchemist 2. Arakawa, Hiromu. 2007. (Fullmetal Alchemist Ser.: 1). (ENG.). 112p. (gr. 8-18). 19.99 *(978-1-4215-1408-6(7))* Viz Media.

—Fullmetal Alchemist. Arakawa, Hiromu. (ENG.). 2011. (Full Metal Alchemist 3-In-1 Ser.: 2). 576p. pap. 14.99 *(978-1-4215-4019-1(3))*; 2011. (Full Metal Alchemist 3-In-1 Ser.: 1). 576p. pap. 14.99 *(978-1-4215-4018-4(5))*; 2011. (Fullmetal Alchemist Ser.: 25). 192p. pap. 9.99 *(978-1-4215-3924-9(1))*; 2011. (Fullmetal Alchemist Ser.: 24). 192p. pap. 9.99 *(978-1-4215-3812-9(1))*; 2007. (Fullmetal Alchemist Ser.: 14). 192p. pap. 9.99 *(978-1-4215-1379-9(X))*; 2007. (Fullmetal Alchemist Ser.). 192p. pap. 9.99 *(978-1-4215-0838-2(9))*; Vol. 1. 2005. (Fullmetal Alchemist Ser.: Vol. 1). 192p. (gr. 8-18). pap. 9.99 *(978-1-59116-920-8(8))*; Vol. 2. 2005. (Fullmetal Alchemist Ser.). 192p. pap. 9.99 *(978-1-59116-923-9(2))*; Vol. 3. 2005. (Fullmetal Alchemist Ser.). 192p. pap. 9.99 *(978-1-59116-925-3(9))*; Vol. 4. 2005. (Fullmetal Alchemist Ser.). 192p. pap. 9.99 *(978-1-59116-929-1(1))*; Vol. 7. 2006. (Fullmetal Alchemist Ser.). 192p. pap. 9.99 *(978-1-4215-0458-2(8))*; Vol. 8. 2006. (Fullmetal Alchemist Ser.). 192p. pap. 9.99 *(978-1-4215-0459-9(6))*; Vol. 9. 2006. (Fullmetal Alchemist Ser.). 192p. pap. 9.99 *(978-1-4215-0460-5(X))*; Vol. 10. 2006. (Fullmetal Alchemist Ser.). 192p. pap. 9.99 *(978-1-4215-0461-2(8))*; Vol. 26. 2011. (Fullmetal Alchemist Ser.: 26). 192p. pap. 9.99 *(978-1-4215-3962-1(4))* Viz Media.

—Hana Yori Dango. Arakawa, Hiromu. 2006. (Fullmetal Alchemist Ser.: Vol. 5). (ENG.). 192p. pap. 9.99 *(978-1-4215-0175-8(9))* Viz Media.

Araki, Hirohiko. JoJo's Bizarre Adventure. Araki, Hirohiko. 2005. (JoJo's Bizarre Adventure Ser.). (ENG.). 192p. pap. 9.99 *(978-1-59116-754-9(X))* Viz Media.

—Jojo's Bizarre Adventure, Vol. 2. Araki, Hirohiko. 2006. (JoJo's Bizarre Adventure Ser.). (ENG.). 192p. pap. 9.99 *(978-1-59116-850-8(3))* Viz Media.

—JoJo's Bizarre Adventure, Vol. 3. Araki, Hirohiko. 2006. (JoJo's Bizarre Adventure Ser.). (ENG.). 208p. pap. 9.99 *(978-1-4215-0336-3(0))* Viz Media.

—Jojo's Bizarre Adventure, Vol. 4. Araki, Hirohiko. 2006. (JoJo's Bizarre Adventure Ser.). (ENG.). 208p. pap. 9.99 *(978-1-4215-0653-1(X))* Viz Media.

Araki, Mari. Tina's Mouth: An Existential Comic Diary. Kashyap, Keshni. 10th ed. 2012. (ENG.). 256p. 18.95 *(978-0-618-94519-1(9))* Houghton Mifflin Harcourt Publishing Co.

Aranda, Amira. Los Mil Anos de Pepe Corcuena. Malpica, Tono. 2010. (SPA.). 104p. (YA). (gr. 6-18). pap. *(978-607-7661-18-4(X))* Ediciones El Naranjo Sa De Cv.

Aranda, Julio C. Tierra a la Vista: La Historia de Costobal Colon. Plaza, Jose Maria & Plaza, José María. 2005. (SPA.). 202p. (J). pap. 19.95 *(978-84-670-1957-5(3))* Espasa Calpe, S.A. ESP. Dist: Planeta Publishing Corp.

Aranda, Omar. In the Playhouse, 1 vol. Giulieri, Anne. 2012. (Engage Literacy Magenta Ser.). (ENG.). 32p. (gr. k-2). pap. 5.99 *(978-1-4296-8852-9(1)*, Engage Literacy) Capstone Pr., Inc.

—Little Sea Horse & the Big Crab, 1 vol. Giulieri, Anne. 2012. (Engage Literacy Yellow Ser.). (ENG.). 32p. (gr. k-2). pap. 5.99 *(978-1-4296-8968-7(4)*, Engage Literacy) Capstone Pr., Inc.

—Little Sea Horse & the Big Storm, 1 vol. Giulieri, Anne. 2012. (Engage Literacy Blue Ser.). (ENG.). 32p. (gr. k-2). pap. 5.99 *(978-1-4296-8992-2(7)*, Engage Literacy) Capstone Pr., Inc.

—Princess Charity Sticker & Activity Book, 1 vol. Young, Jeanna & Johnson, Jacqueline Kinney. 2015. (Princess Parables Ser.). (ENG.). 16p. (J). pap. 3.99 *(978-0-310-74644-7(2))* Zonderkidz.

—Princess Charity's Courageous Heart, 1 vol. Johnson, Jacqueline & Young, Jeanna Stolle. 2012. (Princess Parables Ser.). (ENG.). 32p. (J). 14.99 *(978-0-310-72701-9(4))* Zonderkidz.

—Princess Faith Sticker & Activity Book, 1 vol. Young, Jeanna & Johnson, Jacqueline Kinney. 2015. (Princess Parables Ser.). (ENG.). 16p. (J). pap. 3.99 *(978-0-310-74658-4(2))* Zonderkidz.

—Princess Faith's Mysterious Garden, 1 vol. Johnson, Jacqueline & Young, Jeanna Stolle. 2012. (Princess Parables Ser.). (ENG.). 32p. (J). 12.99 *(978-0-310-72703-3(0))* Zonderkidz.

—Princess Grace & the Little Lost Kitten, 1 vol. Young, Jeanna Stolle & Johnson, Jacqueline Kinney. 2011. (Princess Parables Ser.). (ENG.). 32p. (J). (gr. -1-2). 14.99 *(978-0-310-71640-2(3))* Zonderkidz.

—Princess Grace Sticker & Activity Book, 1 vol. Young, Jeanna & Johnson, Jacqueline Kinney. 2015. (Princess Parables Ser.). (ENG.). 16p. (J). pap. 3.99 *(978-0-310-74741-3(4))* Zonderkidz.

—Princess Hope & the Hidden Treasure, 1 vol. Young, Jeanna Stolle & Johnson, Jacqueline. 2012. (Princess Parables Ser.). (ENG.). 32p. (J). 12.99 *(978-0-310-72699-9(9))* Zonderkidz.

—Princess Hope & the Hidden Treasure, 1 vol. Johnson, Young et al. 2012. (I Can Read! / Princess Parables Ser.). (ENG.). 32p. (J). pap. 3.99 *(978-0-310-73250-1(6))* Zondervan.

—Princess Hope Sticker & Activity Book, 1 vol. Young, Jeanna & Johnson, Jacqueline. 2015. (Princess Parables Ser.). (ENG.). 16p. (J). pap. 3.99 *(978-0-310-74665-2(5))* Zonderkidz.

—Princess Joy Sticker & Activity Book, 1 vol. Young, Jeanna & Johnson, Jacqueline. 2015. (Princess Parables Ser.). (ENG.). 16p. (J). pap. 3.99 *(978-0-310-74618-8(3))* Zonderkidz.

—Princess Joy's Birthday Blessing, 1 vol. Young, Jeanna Stolle & Johnson, Jacqueline Kinney. 2011. (Princess Parables Ser.). (ENG.). 32p. (J). (gr. -1-2). 12.99 *(978-0-310-71639-6(X))* Zonderkidz.

Aranda, Tom. The Science of Baseball with Max Axiom, Super Scientist. Dreier, David L. 2015. (Science of Sports with Max Axiom Ser.). (ENG.). 32p. (gr. 3-4). lib. bdg. 29.99 ***(978-1-4914-6083-2(0)***, Graphic Library) Capstone Pr., Inc.

Aranda, Tomás. The Science of Basketball with Max Axiom, Super Scientist. Bethea, Nikole Brooks. 2015. (Science of Sports with Max Axiom Ser.). (ENG.). 32p. (gr. 3-4). pap. 7.95 ***(978-1-4914-6088-7(1)***, Graphic Library) Capstone Pr., Inc.

Aranega, Merce. Una Medicina para No Llorar. Paloma, David. 3rd ed. (SPA.). 32p. (J). *(978-84-236-4226-7(7))* Edebé ESP. Dist: Lectorum Pubns., Inc.

Arant, Bruce. The Splinter Tree. Cleveland, Lance. 2011. (ENG.). 24p. pap. 9.99 *(978-1-4609-9701-7(8))* CreateSpace Independent Publishing Platform.

Araujo, André. Avengers A. I. , 12,000 A. D. 2014. (ENG.). 136p. (YA). (gr. 8-17). pap. 16.99 *(978-0-7851-8492-8(9))* Marvel Worldwide, Inc.

Araujo, Katie. Sage Learns to Share, 1 vol. Irwin, Gayle. 2009. 45p. pap. 24.95 *(978-1-60836-409-1(7))* America Star Bks.

Arbat, Carles. Barbazul. 2006. (Coleccion Libros para Sonar Ser.). (SPA.). 38p. (J). *(978-84-8464-194-0(5))* Kalandraka Editora, S.L.

Arbo, Cris. All Around Me, I See. Steinberg, Laya. 2005. (Sharing Nature with Children Book Ser.). 32p. (J). 16.95 *(978-1-58469-068-9(2))*; pap. 8.95 *(978-1-58469-069-6(0))* Dawn Pubns.

—All Around Me I See. Steinberg, Laya. 2008. 26p. (J). (gr. -1). bds. 7.95 *(978-1-58469-107-5(7))* Dawn Pubns.

—Champions of the Ocean. Hodgkins, Fran. 2009. (Earth Heroes Ser.). 144p. (J). (gr. 5-9). pap. 11.95 *(978-1-58469-119-8(0))* Dawn Pubns.

—The Dandelion Seed's Big Dream. Anthony, Joseph. 2014. 32p. (J). (gr. k-4). 16.95 *(978-1-58469-496-0(3))*; pap. 8.95 *(978-1-58469-497-7(1))* Dawn Pubns.

—In the Trees, Honey Bees. Mortensen, Lori. 2009. 32p. (J). (gr. -1-5). 16.95 *(978-1-58469-114-3(X))*; pap. 8.95 *(978-1-58469-115-0(8))* Dawn Pubns.

—What's in the Garden? Berkes, Marianne. 2013. (ENG.). 32p. (J). (gr. -1-4). 16.95 *(978-1-58469-189-1(1))*; pap. 8.95 *(978-1-58469-190-7(5))* Dawn Pubns.

Arbo, Hal. Tom: The Fighting Cowboy. Morgan, Leon. 2011. 426p. 56.95 *(978-1-258-10103-9(3))* Literary Licensing, LLC.

Arboleda M.Ed., Teja. What's That Pout All About? Arboleda M.Ed., Teja. 2013. 36p. pap. 11.99 *(978-0-615-80384-5(9))* Entertaining Diversity Pr.

Arbona, Marion. The Good Little Book. Maclear, Kyo. 2015. (ENG.). 40p. (J). (gr. k-4). 16.99 ***(978-1-77049-451-0(0))*** Tundra Bks. CAN. Dist: Penguin Random Hse., LLC.

Arbona, Marion. The Magic Clothesline. Poulin, Andrée. 2012. 32p. (J). 14.95 *(978-1-4338-1194-4(4))*; pap. 9.95 *(978-1-4338-1195-1(2))* American Psychological Assn. (Magination Pr.).

Arbuckle, Scott. Mr. Green's Magnificent Machine. Woolley, Bryan. 2003. 32p. 15.95 *(978-1-57168-606-0(1))* Eakin Pr.

Arcana Studio, Arcana. New Monster in School, 1 vol. O'Reilly, Sean. 2010. (Mighty Mighty Monsters Ser.). (ENG.). 48p. (gr. 2-3). lib. bdg. 22.65 *(978-1-4342-2151-3(2))* Stone Arch Bks.

Arcana Studio Staff. Demolition Day, 1 vol. Everheart, Chris. 2010. (Recon Academy Ser.). (ENG.). 64p. (gr. 3-3). 25.32 *(978-1-4342-1917-6(8)*, Recon Academy) Stone Arch Bks.

—Hide & Shriek!, 1 vol. O'Reilly, Sean. 2011. (Mighty Mighty Monsters Ser.). (ENG.). 48p. (gr. 2-3). pap. 6.10 *(978-1-4342-3417-9(7))* Stone Arch Bks.

—The King of Halloween Castle, 1 vol. O'Reilly, Sean. 2011. (Mighty Mighty Monsters Ser.). (ENG.). 48p. (gr. 2-3). pap. 5.95 *(978-1-4342-3419-3(3))* Stone Arch Bks.

—Lost in Spooky Forest, 1 vol. O'Reilly, Sean. 2011. (Mighty Mighty Monsters Ser.). (ENG.). 48p. (gr. 2-3). pap. 6.10 *(978-1-4342-3418-6(5))* Stone Arch Bks.

—The Missing Mummy, 1 vol. O'Reilly, Sean. 2012. (Mighty Mighty Monsters Ser.). (ENG.). 48p. (gr. 2-3). pap. 6.10 *(978-1-4342-4609-7(4))* Stone Arch Bks.

—Mixed Signals, 1 vol. Everheart, Chris. 2010. (Recon Academy Ser.). (ENG.). 64p. (gr. 3-3). 25.32 *(978-1-4342-1915-2(1)*, Recon Academy) Stone Arch Bks.

—Monster Beach, 1 vol. O'Reilly, Sean. 2012. (Mighty Mighty Monsters Ser.). (ENG.). 48p. (gr. 2-3). pap. 6.10 *(978-1-4342-4608-0(6))* Stone Arch Bks.

—The Monster Crooks, 1 vol. O'Reilly, Sean. 2012. (Mighty Mighty Monsters Ser.). (ENG.). 48p. (gr. 2-3). pap. 6.10 *(978-1-4342-4610-3(8))* Stone Arch Bks.

—The Scare Fair, 1 vol. O'Reilly, Sean. 2012. (Mighty Mighty Monsters Ser.). (ENG.). 48p. (gr. 2-3). pap. 6.10 *(978-1-4342-4611-0(6))* Stone Arch Bks.

—Storm Surge, 1 vol. Everheart, Chris. 2010. (Recon Academy Ser.). (ENG.). 64p. (gr. 3-3). 25.32 *(978-1-4342-1918-3(6)*, Recon Academy) Stone Arch Bks.

—Teen Agent, 1 vol. Everheart, Chris. 2010. (Recon Academy Ser.). (ENG.). 64p. (gr. 3-3). 25.32 *(978-1-4342-1916-9(X)*, Recon Academy) Stone Arch Bks.

—The Toy Snatcher, 1 vol. O'Reilly, Sean. 2012. (Mighty Mighty Monsters Ser.). (ENG.). 48p. (gr. 2-3). pap. 6.10 *(978-1-4342-4612-7(4))* Stone Arch Bks.

—The Wolfboy's Wish, 1 vol. O'Reilly, Sean. 2012. (Mighty Mighty Monsters Ser.). (ENG.). 48p. (gr. 2-3). pap. 6.10 *(978-1-4342-4613-4(2))* Stone Arch Bks.

Arcella, Steven. Carl Sandburg. Bolin, Frances Schoonmaker, ed. 2008. (Poetry for Young People Ser.). (ENG.). 48p. (J). (gr. 3-7). pap. 6.95 *(978-1-4027-5471-5(X))* Sterling Publishing Co., Inc.

Archambault, Matthew. Pat & Pea Soup. Stegall, Billy Mark. 2003. (Books for Young Learners). (ENG.). 12p. (J). 5.75 net. *(978-1-57274-278-9(X)*, 2757, Bks. for Young Learners) Owen, Richard C. Pubs., Inc.

—Saint Paul: The Thirteenth Apostle. Hill, Mary Lea. 2008. (Encounter the Saints Ser.: 22). 117p. (J). (gr. 3-7). per. 7.95 *(978-0-8198-7102-2(8))* Pauline Bks. & Media.

—Sam Collier & the Founding of Jamestown. Ransom, Candice. 2007. (On My Own History Ser.). (ENG.). 48p. (gr. 2-4). pap. 6.95 *(978-0-8225-6451-5(3)*, First Avenue Editions) Lerner Publishing Group.

Archbold, Tim. Big Liam, Little Liam. Morgan, Ruth. 2005. (ENG.). 24p. (J). lib. bdg. 23.65 *(978-1-59646-728-6(2))* Dingles & Co.

—The Dog in the Diamond Collar. Lisle, Rebecca. 2006. (ENG.). 74p. (J). (gr. 4-7). per. 8.99 *(978-1-84270-366-3(8))* Andersen Pr. GBR. Dist: Independent Pubs. Group.

—Pig in Love. French, Vivian. 2005. 32p. (J). lib. bdg. 9.00 *(978-1-4242-0889-0(0))* Fitzgerald Bks.

—Poetry. Rosen, Michael. 2007. (Collins Big Cat Ser.). (ENG.). 32p. (J). pap. 7.99 *(978-0-00-723077-8(X))* HarperCollins Pubs. Ltd. GBR. Dist: Independent Pubs. Group.

Archbold, Tim. There's a Monster in the Garden: The Best of David Harmer. Harmer, David. 2015. (ENG.). 96p. (J). (gr. 2-6). pap. 7.99 ***(978-1-84780-538-6(8)***, Frances Lincoln) Quarto Publishing Group UK GBR. Dist: Littlehampton Bk Services, Ltd.

Archembault, Matthew. Logan West, Printer's Devil. Breault, Christie Merriman. 2006. 142p. (J). pap. *(978-1-59336-762-6(7))* Mondo Publishing.

Archer, Adam. Scribblenauts Unmasked - A DC Comics Adventure. Elder, Josh. 2015. (ENG.). 192p. pap. 14.99 *(978-1-4012-4926-7(4))* DC Comics.

Archer, Angela. Popcorn. Womack, Rowena. 2013. 26p. 16.99 *(978-1-61160-595-2(4))* Whiskey Creek Restorations.

Archer, Christine. Origami Fortune Tellers. Helman, Diane & Suneby, Elizabeth. 2011. (Dover Origami Papercraft Ser.). (ENG.). 32p. (J). (gr. 2-7). pap. 6.99 *(978-0-486-47826-5(2))* Dover Pubns., Inc.

Archer, Dosh. Big Bad Wolf. Archer, Dosh. 2013. (Urgency Emergency! Ser.). (ENG.). 48p. (J). (gr. k-3). 12.99 *(978-0-8075-8352-4(9))* Whitman, Albert & Co.

Archer, Dosh. Humpty's Fall. Archer, Dosh. 2015. (Urgency Emergency! Ser.). (ENG.). 48p. (J). (gr. k-3). 12.99 ***(978-0-8075-8356-2(1))*** Whitman, Albert & Co.

Archer, Dosh. Itsy Bitsy Spider. Archer, Dosh. 2013. (Urgency Emergency! Ser.). (ENG.). 48p. (J). (gr. k-3). 12.99 *(978-0-8075-8358-6(8))* Whitman, Albert & Co.

—Little Elephant's Blocked Trunk. Archer, Dosh. 2014. (Urgency Emergency! Ser.). (ENG.). 48p. (J). (gr. k-3). 12.99 *(978-0-8075-8354-8(5))* Whitman, Albert & Co.

Archer, Mary Jane. I Am Her Ears: A Story with Pictures of a Three Year Old Rescued Dog Who Leads a New Life As a Certified Hearing Dog. Archer, Mary Jane, photos by. Peters, Jean Norman. 2004. 26p. (J). *(978-0-9749911-0-8(4)*, 1237614) Gizmo Pr.

Archer, Micha. El Fandango de Lola. Witte, Anna. 2011. (SPA.). (J). pap. 9.99 *(978-1-84686-359-2(7))*; 32p. pap. 7.99 *(978-1-78285-066-3(X))* Barefoot Bks., Inc.

—Lola's Fandango. Witte, Anna. 2011. (ENG.). 32p. (J). pap. 9.99 *(978-1-84686-681-4(2))* Barefoot Bks., Inc.

—The Wise Fool. Husain, Shahrukh. 2012. (ENG.). 64p. (J). (gr. 2-6). pap. 12.99 *(978-1-84686-938-9(2))* Barefoot Bks., Inc.

Archer, Micha, jt. illus. see Masse, Josée.

Archeval, Jose. Flying Courage. Brown, Amanda C. 2012. (ENG.). 26p. (J). pap. 9.99 *(978-1-62006-121-3(X))* Sunbury Press, Inc.

Archibald, A. L. The secret of the live Dolls. Gates, Josephine Scribner. 2007. (J). lib. bdg. 59.00 *(978-1-60304-024-2(2))* Dollworks.

Archibald, Odell. P Is for Puffin: A Newfoundland & Labrador Alphabet. Skirving, Janet. rev. ed. 2006. (Discover Canada Province by Province Ser.). (ENG.). 40p. (J). (gr. 1-3). 17.95 *(978-1-58536-287-5(5)*, 202098) Sleeping Bear Pr.

Archibold, Tim. Knock Knock! The Best Knock Knock Jokes Ever! 2004. (Sidesplitters Ser.). (ENG.). 64p. (J). (gr. 1-5). pap. 5.99 *(978-0-7534-5707-8(5)*, Kingfisher) Roaring Brook Pr.

Archipova, Anastasiya. Hansel & Gretel. Grimm, Jacob & Grimm, Wilhelm. 2008. (ENG.). 32p. (J). (gr. -1-3). *(978-0-86315-623-6(1))* Floris Bks.

Archipowa, A. Cuentos de los Hermanos Grimm. Archipowa, A. Grimm, Jacob et al. Martinez B. de Quirós, Eladio, tr. (SPA.). 102p. 19.95 *(978-84-241-5770-8(2))* Everest Editora ESP. Dist: Lectorum Pubns., Inc.

Arciero, Susan. From Sea to Shining Sea. Gingrich, Callista. 2014. (Ellis the Elephant Ser.). (ENG.). 40p. (J). (gr. -1-3). 14.99 *(978-1-62157-253-4(6)*, Regnery Kids) Regnery Publishing, Inc., An Eagle Publishing Co.

—Land of the Pilgrims Pride. Gingrich, Callista. 2012. (Ellis the Elephant Ser.). (ENG.). 28p. (J). (gr. k-3). 14.95 *(978-1-59698-829-3(0)*, Little Patriot Pr.) Regnery Publishing, Inc., An Eagle Publishing Co.

—Sweet Land of Liberty. Gingrich, Callista. 2011. (Ellis the Elephant Ser.). (ENG.). 28p. (J). (gr. -1-3). 14.95

A

(978-1-59698-292-5(6)) Regnery Publishing, Inc., An Eagle Publishing Co.
—Yankee Doodle Dandy. Gingrich, Callista. 2013. (Ellis the Elephant Ser.). (ENG.). 40p. (J). (gr. -1-3). 14.95 *(978-1-62157-087-5(8),* Regnery Kids) Regnery Publishing, Inc., An Eagle Publishing Co.
Ardizzone, Edward. The Alley. Estes, Eleanor. 2003. (ENG.). 288p. (J). (gr. 2-5). pap. 5.95 *(978-0-15-204918-8(5))* Houghton Mifflin Harcourt Publishing Co.
—The Alley. Estes, Eleanor. 2004. (Odyssey/Harcourt Young Classic Ser.). 283p. 15.95 *(978-0-7569-3475-0(3))* Perfection Learning Corp.
—Desbarolda, the Waltzing Mouse. Langley, Noel. 2008. 80p. pap. *(978-1-905946-01-3(5))* Durrant Publishing.
—Johnny the Clockmaker. Quarto Generic Staff. 2009. (ENG.). 48p. (J). (gr. -1-2). 16.95 *(978-1-84507-914-7(0),* Frances Lincoln) Quarto Publishing Group UK GBR. Dist: Hachette Bk. Group.
—The Land of Green Ginger. Langley, Noel. 2007. (ENG.). 149p. (J). (gr. 3-7). per. 11.95 *(978-1-56792-333-9(X))* Godine, David R. Pub.
—The Little Bookroom. Farjeon, Eleanor. 2003. (New York Review Children's Collection). (ENG.). 336p. (J). (gr. 4-7). 19.95 *(978-1-59017-048-9(2),* NYR Children's Collection) New York Review of Bks., Inc., The.
—Miranda the Great. Estes, Eleanor. 2005. (ENG.). 96p. (J). (gr. 2-5). pap. 5.95 *(978-0-15-205411-3(1))* Houghton Mifflin Harcourt Publishing Co.
—Nanny Mcphee: The Collected Tales of Nurse Matilda. Brand, Christianna. 2005. (ENG.). 300p. (J). (gr. 2-6). per. 7.95 *(978-1-58234-671-7(2),* Bloomsbury USA Childrens) Bloomsbury USA.
Ardizzone, Edward. Nurse Matilda Goes to Hospital. Brand, Christianna. (ENG.). 128p. ***(978-0-7475-7678-5(5))*** Bloomsbury Publishing Plc GBR. Dist: Macmillan.
Ardizzone, Edward. Sun Slower Sun Faster. Trevor, Meriol. 2nd ed. 2004. (Living History Library). 290p. (J). pap. 12.95 *(978-1-883937-41-6(8))* Bethlehem Bks.
—The Tunnel of Hugsy Goode. Estes, Eleanor. 2003. (ENG.). 256p. (J). (gr. 2-5). pap. 14.95 *(978-0-15-204916-4(9))* Houghton Mifflin Harcourt Publishing Co.
Ardizzone, Edward. Sarah & Simon & No Red Paint. Ardizzone, Edward. 2011. 48p. (J). 17.95 *(978-1-56792-410-7(7))* Godine, David R. Pub.
Arégui, Matthias & Ramstein, Anne-Margot. Before After. Arégui, Matthias & Ramstein, Anne-Margot. 2014. (ENG.). 176p. (J). (gr. -1-3). 19.99 *(978-0-7636-7621-6(7))* Candlewick Pr.
Arelys, Aguilar, jt. illus. see James, Melody A.
Arena, Felice. Sally & Dave: A Slug Story. Arena, Felice. 2008. (ENG.). 32p. (J). (gr. -1-3). 5.99 *(978-1-933605-71-5(5))* Kane Miller.
Arena, Jillayne. Playing Loteria Mexicana: El Juego de la Loteria Mexicana. Lainez, René Colato. 2005. (ENG, SPA & MUL.). 32p. (J). (gr. -1-3). 15.95 *(978-0-87358-881-2(9))* Cooper Square Publishing Llc.
Arenson, Roberta. Kids' Garden: 40 Fun Outdoor Activities & Games. Cohen, Whitney & Life Lab Science Program Staff. 2010. (ENG.). 8p. (J). (gr. 3-18). 19.99 *(978-1-84686-367-7(8))* Barefoot Bks., Inc.
—Kids' Kitchen: 40 Fun & Healthy Recipes to Make & Share. Bird, Fiona. 2009. (ENG.). 40p. (J). (gr. 3-18). 19.99 *(978-1-84686-176-5(4))* Barefoot Bks., Inc.
—The Three Billy Goats Gruff. Finch, Mary. 2007. (ENG.). 32p. (J). (gr. -1-3). 9.99 *(978-1-84686-072-0(5))* Barefoot Bks., Inc.
—Los Tres Chivitos Gruff. Finch, Mary. 2003.Tr. of Three Billy Goats Gruff. (SPA.). 32p. (J). pap. 7.99 *(978-1-84148-145-6(9))* Barefoot Bks., Inc.
Arenson, Roberta. One, Two, Skip a Few! First Number Rhymes. Arenson, Roberta. 2005. 32p. (J). pap. 6.99 *(978-1-84148-130-2(0))* Barefoot Bks., Inc.
Arenson, Roberta & Asbjørnsen, Peter Christen. The Three Billy Goats Gruff. Arenson, Roberta & Finch, Mary. 2003. (ENG.). 32p. (J). pap. 7.99 *(978-1-84148-351-1(6))* Barefoot Bks., Inc.
Arevalo, Jose Daniel. I See Many Colors Around My House: Los Colores que Veo Por Mi Casa. Layne, Carmela C. Layne, Carmela C., ed. I.t. ed. 2005. (SPA.). 24p. (J). (gr. -1-3). pap. 6.95 *(978-0-9769538-0-7(3))* Pannycake Pubn.
Argent, Kerry. Nighty Night!, 1 vol. 2014. (ENG.). 32p. (J). (gr. -1-1). 7.95 *(978-1-56145-812-7(0))* Peachtree Pubs.
—Ruby Roars. Wild, Margaret. 2009. (ENG.). 32p. (J). (gr. -1-2). pap. 12.99 *(978-1-74175-752-1(5))* Allen & Unwin AUS. Dist: Independent Pubs. Group.
Argoff, Beily. Braid the Challah: A Playful Action Rhyme. Paluch, Beily. 2004. 12p. (J). bds. 6.95 *(978-1-929628-17-9(X))* Hachai Publishing.
Argoff, Patti. Braid the Challah: A Playful Action Rhyme. Paluch, Beily. 2014. 12p. (J). bds. 6.95 ***(978-1-929628-83-4(8))*** Hachai Publishing.
Argoff, Patti. Chanukah Guess Who? A Lift the Flap Book. Stern, Ariella. 2012. (ENG.). 32p. (J). 9.95 *(978-1-929628-68-1(4))* Hachai Publishing.
—Happy Birthday to Me! - Boys' Edition. Lieberman, Channah. 2006. 32p. (J). 12.95 *(978-1-929628-27-8(7))* Hachai Publishing.
—Happy Birthday to Me! Girls' Edition. Lieberman, Channah. 2006. 32p. (J). 12.95 *(978-1-929628-31-5(5))* Hachai Publishing.
—I am a Torah: A Playful Action Rhyme. Paluch, Beily. 2004. 12p. (J). bds. 5.95 *(978-1-929628-18-6(8))* Hachai Publishing.
—Miller the Green Caterpillar. House, Darrell. I.t. ed. 2005. 32p. 16.95 *(978-0-9663276-9-4(1))* Red Engine Pr.
—What Else Do I Say? A Lift the Flap Book. Goldberg, Malky. 2007. (J). (gr. -1-k). bds. 9.95 *(978-1-929628-34-6(X))* Hachai Publishing.
—When the World Was Quiet. Nutkis, Phyllis. 2003. (J). pap. 10.95 *(978-1-929628-14-8(5))* Hachai Publishing.
Arguilé, Elisa. Kangu Va de Excursión. Nesquens, Daniel & Martos Sánchez, José Daniel. (SPA.). 18p. 11.95 *(978-84-667-1403-7(0))* Suma de Letras, S.L. ESP. Dist: Distribooks, Inc.
Aric, Nicholson. I Hope You Dance. gif. ed. 2005. 24p. (J). bds. 9.99 incl. audio compact disk *(978-1-57791-151-7(2),* Little Melody Pr.) Brighter Minds Children's Publishing.
Arif, Tasneem & Reed, Lisa. A Haunted Halloween Activity Book. Schaefer, Peggy. 2014. 16p. (J). 4.99 *(978-0-8249-5666-0(4),* Ideals Children's Bks.) Ideals Pubns.
Arihara, Shino. A Song for Cambodia, 1 vol. Lord, Michelle. 2008. (ENG.). 32p. (J). (gr. 1-6). 16.95 *(978-1-60060-139-2(1))* Lee & Low Bks., Inc.
—Zero Is the Leaves on the Tree. Franco, Betsy. 2009. (ENG.). 32p. (J). (gr. k-3). 15.99 *(978-1-58246-249-3(6),* Tricycle Pr.) Ten Speed Pr.
Arima, Keitaro. Tsukuyomi - Moon Phase, Vol. 1. Arima, Keitaro. 2005. (Tsukuyomi Ser.: Vol. 1). 192p. pap. 9.99 *(978-1-59532-948-6(X))* TOKYOPOP, Inc.
Arin, Dilara. Folktales of Anatolia: From Agri to Zelve. Ural, Serpil. 2012. (ENG.). 64p. pap. 25.99 *(978-9944-424-89-9(7))* Citlembik/Nettleberry Pubns. TUR. Dist: National Bk. Network.
—I Am Beautiful. Menase, Debra. 2012. (ENG.). 32p. (J). (gr. 3-12). pap. 17.50 *(978-9944-424-87-5(0))* Citlembik/Nettleberry Pubns. TUR. Dist: National Bk. Network.
Arinsberg, Norman. The Tush People. Favorite, Deborah. (J). 11.95 *(978-0-9722514-0-2(5))* Tush People, The.
Arisman, Marshall. The Cat Who Invented Bebop. Arisman, Marshall. 2008. (ENG.). 32p. (J). (gr. 1-3). 17.95 *(978-1-56846-152-6(6))* Creative Co., The.
Aristophane. Zabime Sisters. Aristophane. Madden, Matt, tr. from FRE. 2010. (ENG.). 96p. (YA). (gr. 7-18). pap. 16.99 *(978-1-59643-638-1(7),* First Second Bks.) Roaring Brook Pr.
Arjas, Pirkko & Butcher, Sally K. Friend Owl: A Children's Book. 1000th ed. 2005. 48p. (J). 18.00 *(978-0-9762132-0-8(6))* Old Bess Publishing Co.
Arkanov, Elvira. Princess Panny - Not Princess Nobody. Alexander, Janice Marie. 2013. 46p. pap. 21.95 *(978-0-9890410-1-0(8))* Artistic Angels Corp.
Arling, Jackie L. Grace Alone Is Enough, 1 vol. Berning, Terri J. 2010. 34p. 24.95 *(978-1-4512-9045-5(4))* PublishAmerica, Inc.
Armand, Anjale Renee. Engraved in Stone. Coleman, Alice Scovell. 2003. 152p. (J). 14.95 *(978-0-9729846-0-7(7))* Tiara Bks. LLC.
Armas, Lourdes. Diana en la Tierra Wayuu. Antillano, Laura. 2003. (SPA.). 121p. (YA). (gr. 5-8). pap. 9.95 *(978-958-24-0180-1(X))* Santillana COL. Dist: Santillana USA Publishing Co., Inc.
Armbrust, Janet. Science Fair Projects, Grades 5-8: An Inquiry-Based Guide. Galus, Pamela J. 2003. (ENG.). 80p. (gr. 5-8). per. 16.99 *(978-0-88724-949-5(3),* CD-7333) Carson-Dellosa Publishing, LLC.
—Volcanoes: A Comprehensive Hands-on Science Unit. Storey, Melinda. Mitchell, Judy & Lindeen, Mary, eds. 2007. (Nature's Fury Ser.). 32p. (J). pap. 6.95 *(978-1-57310-530-9(5))* Teaching & Learning Co.
Armbrust, Janet & Skiles, Janet. Under the Sea: A Cross-Curricular Unit for Grades 1-3. Cecchini, Marie E. Mitchell, Judy & Lindeen, Mary, eds. 2007. 32p. (J). pap. 6.95 *(978-1-57310-529-3(5))* Teaching & Learning Co.
Armer, Sidney. Waterless Mountain. Armer, Laura Adams. 2014. (ENG.). 256p. (J). (gr. 5). pap. 5.99 *(978-0-486-49288-9(5))* Dover Pubns., Inc.
Armino, Monica. At the Boardwalk. Fineman, Kelly Ramsdell. 2012. (J). *(978-1-58925-104-5(0));* pap. *(978-1-58925-431-2(7))* Tiger Tales.
Armitage, David. My Brother Sammy Is Special. Armitage, David. Edwards, Becky. 2012. (ENG.). 32p. (J). (gr. 1-3). 16.95 *(978-1-61608-480-6(4),* 608480, Sky Pony Pr.) Skyhorse Publishing Co., Inc.
Armour, Steven & Kennard, Thomas. Dr. Tootsie: A Young Girl's Dream. Knoebel, Suzanne B. 2003. 100p. (J). per. 12.97 *(978-0-9679416-1-5(X))* Alexie Bks.
Armstrong, Bev. From Caravels to the Constitution: Puzzles Trageting Historical Themes That Reinforce Logic & Problem-Solving Skills. Duby, Marjorie. 2006. (Learning Works). 112p. (J). (gr. 5-8). per. 13.99 *(978-0-88160-385-9(6),* LW405, Learning Works, The) Creative Teaching Pr., Inc.
Armstrong, Bev & Baker, Don. Centers on the Go: Fun, Creative Activity Folders to Take to Your Seat. Klawitter, Pamela Amick. VanBlaricum, Pam, ed. 2005. 192p. pap. 19.99 *(978-0-88160-378-1(3),* LW435, Learning Works, The) Creative Teaching Pr., Inc.
Armstrong, Bev & Grayson, Rick. Language Critical Thinking, Grades 2-4: Creative Puzzles to Challenge the Brain. Schwartz, Linda. 2005. 64p. (J). pap. 11.99 *(978-0-88160-384-2(8),* LW423, Learning Works, The) Creative Teaching Pr., Inc.
—Math Critical Thinking, Grades 2-4: Creative Puzzles to Challenge the Brain. Schwartz, Linda. VanBlaricum, Pam, ed. 2005. 64p. (J). pap. 11.99 *(978-0-88160-383-5(X),* LW-422) Creative Teaching Pr., Inc.
Armstrong, Beverly. Current Events: Looking at Current Issues from Different Perspectives. Sylvester, Diane. Larson, Eric, ed. 2003. 112p. (YA). (gr. 5-8). pap. 12.99 *(978-0-88160-325-5(2),* LW-1021) Creative Teaching Pr., Inc.
—Language Arts Quiz Whiz. Schwartz, Linda. Larson, Eric, ed. 2003. 128p. (YA). (gr. 5-8). pap. 13.99 *(978-0-88160-344-6(9),* LW-418) Creative Teaching Pr., Inc.
—Language Arts Quiz Whiz 3-5, Vol. 430. Schwartz, Linda. VanBlaricum, Pam, ed. 2004. 128p. (J). (gr. 3-5). pap. 14.99 *(978-0-88160-373-6(2),* LW-430) Creative Teaching Pr., Inc.
—Language Critical Thinking, Grades 5-8 Vol. 412: Creative Puzzles to Challenge the Brain. Klawitter, Pamela Amick. Schwartz, Linda, ed. 2004. 64p. (J). (gr. 5-8). pap. 11.99 *(978-0-88160-338-5(4),* LW412, Learning Works, The) Creative Teaching Pr., Inc.
—Math Critical Thinking, Grades 5-8 Vol. 413: Creative Puzzles to Challenge the Brain. Klawitter, Pamela Amick. Schwartz, Linda, ed. 2004. 64p. (J). (gr. 5-8). pap. 10.99 *(978-0-88160-339-2(2))* Creative Teaching Pr., Inc.
—Math Quiz Whiz 3-5, Vol. 431. Schwartz, Linda. VanBlaricum, Pam, ed. 2004. 128p. (J). (gr. 3-5). pap. 10.99 *(978-0-88160-374-3(0),* LW-431) Creative Teaching Pr., Inc.
—Pick a Project. Klawitter, Pamela Amick. Clark, Kimberly, ed. 2003. 96p. (J). (gr. 4-6). pap. 11.99 *(978-0-88160-337-8(6),* LW-411) Creative Teaching Pr., Inc.
—Social Studies & Science Quiz Whiz 3-5, Vol. 432. Schwartz, Linda. VanBlaricum, Pam, ed. 2004. 128p. (J). (gr. 3-5). pap. 10.99 *(978-0-88160-375-0(9),* LW-432) Creative Teaching Pr., Inc.
Armstrong, Beverly & Grayson, Rick. Conquer Spelling: Word Lists, Roles, & Activities to Help Kids Become Spelling Heros. Schwartz, Linda. Scott, Kelly, ed. 2003. 112p. (J). pap. 13.99 *(978-0-88160-362-0(7),* LW-420, Learning Works, The) Creative Teaching Pr., Inc.
—Critical Thinking Social Studies Vol. 414: Creative Puzzles to Challenge the Brain. Klawitter, Pamela Amick. Schwartz, Linda, ed. 2004. 64p. (J). (gr. 5-8). pap. 10.99 *(978-0-88160-340-8(6))* Creative Teaching Pr., Inc.
—Figuratively Speaking: Using Classic Literature to teach 40 Literary Terms, Vol. 1020. Heidrich, Delana. Clark, Kim, ed. 2004. 136p. (J). (gr. 5-8). pap. 14.99 *(978-0-88160-317-0(1),* LW-1020) Creative Teaching Pr., Inc.
Armstrong, E. J., photos by. Grill Every Day: 125 Fast-Track Recipes for Weeknights at the Grill. Morgan, Diane. 2008. (ENG., 224p. (gr. 8-17). pap. 24.95 *(978-0-8118-5208-1(3))* Chronicle Bks. LLC.
—The Wine Deck: 50 Ways to Choose, Serve, & Enjoy Great Wines. Cosmic Debris Etc., Inc. Staff & Chronicle Books Staff. 2003. (ENG., 50p. (gr. 8-17). 14.95 *(978-0-8118-3654-8(1))* Chronicle Bks. LLC.
Armstrong-Ellis, Carey. I Love You More Than Moldy Ham. 2015. (ENG.). 32p. (J). (gr. -1-3). 14.95 ***(978-1-4197-1646-1(8),*** Abrams Bks. for Young Readers) Abrams.
Armstrong-Ellis, Carey. Miss Tutu's Star. Newman, Lesléa. 2010. (ENG.). 32p. (J). (gr. -1-3). 17.95 *(978-0-8109-8396-0(6),* Abrams Bks. for Young Readers) Abrams.
—The Twelve Days of Kindergarten: A Counting Book. Rose, Deborah Lee. 2003. (ENG.). 30p. (J). (gr. -1-1). 16.95 *(978-0-8109-4512-8(6))* Abrams.
—The Twelve Days of Springtime: A School Counting Book. Rose, Deborah Lee. 2009. (ENG.). 32p. (J). (gr. -1-3). 15.95 *(978-0-8109-8330-4(3),* Abrams Bks. for Young Readers) Abrams.
Armstrong-Ellis, Carey F. The Spelling Bee Before Recess. Rose, Deborah Lee. 2013. (ENG.). 32p. (J). (gr. k-4). 16.95 *(978-1-4197-0847-3(3),* Abrams Bks. for Young Readers) Abrams.
Armstrong, Katharine. Mask Parade: Forest Animals. Trelogan, Stephanie. 2008. (ENG.). 14p. (J). (gr. -1). 12.95 *(978-1-58117-790-9(9),* Intervisual/Piggy Toes) Bendon, Inc.
Armstrong, Matthew S. The Blacksmith's Gift: A Christmas Story. Davis, Dan T. Davis, Jan, ed. 2004. 64p. (J). 14.95 *(978-0-9725977-4-6(3))* Second Star Creations.
—Flight Explorer, Vol. 1. Matte, Johane et al. Kibuishi, Kazu, ed. 2008. (ENG.). 112p. (YA). pap. 14.00 *(978-0-345-50313-8(9),* Villard Bks.) Random House Publishing Group.
—Rhino, Rhino, Sweet Potato. Prose, Francine. 2009. 32p. (J). (gr. -1-1). lib. bdg. 18.89 *(978-0-06-008079-2(5))* HarperCollins Pubs.
Armstrong, Matthew S. Jane & Mizmow. Armstrong, Matthew S. 2011. (ENG.). 32p. (J). (gr. -1-k). 16.99 *(978-0-06-117719-4(9))* HarperCollins Pubs.
Armstrong, Michelle Hartz. Little Jake Learns to Stop: A Heartwarming Tale about Determination & Succeeding with Attention Difficulties. Beyer, Pamela J. & Bilbrey, Hilary. 2006. (J). per. 9.99 *(978-0-9787074-0-8(0))* Inspired By Family.
Armstrong, Neal. Owen's Choice: The Night of the Halloween Vandals. Butler, Leah & Peters, Trudy. 2005. 64p. (J). (gr. 1-5). 18.95 *(978-0-9771666-0-2(0))* Spencer's Mill Pr.
Armstrong, Nicky. Helping Children Pursue Their Hopes & Dreams. Sunderland, Margot & Hancock, Nicky. ed. 40p. spiral bd. *(978-0-86388-455-9(5),* 002-5063) Speechmark Publishing Ltd.
—Helping Children Who Bottle up Their Feelings: A Nifflenoo Called Nevermind. Sunderland, Margot. ed. 56p. spiral bd. *(978-0-86388-457-3(1),* 002-5065) Speechmark Publishing Ltd.
—Helping Children Who Have Hardened Their Hearts or Become Bullies, 2 vols. Sunderland, Margot. 72p. spiral bd., pupil's gde. ed. *(978-0-86388-458-0(X),* 002-5061) Speechmark Publishing Ltd.
—Helping Children Who Yearn for Someone They Love: The Frog Who Longed for the Moon to Smile, 2 vols. Sunderland, Margot & Hancock, Nicky. ed. 48p. spiral bd. *(978-0-86388-456-6(3),* 002-5067) Speechmark Publishing Ltd.
Armstrong, Nicky. The Day the Sea Went Out & Never Came Back, 2 vols. Armstrong, Nicky, tr. Sunderland, Margot & Hancock, Nicky. ed. 32p. pap. *(978-0-86388-463-4(6),* 002-5147) Speechmark Publishing Ltd.
—The Frog Who Longed for the Moon to Smile, 2 vols. Armstrong, Nicky, tr. Sunderland, Margot & Hancock, Nicky. ed. 28p. pap. *(978-0-86388-495-5(4),* 002-5066) Speechmark Publishing Ltd.
—Helping Children Pursue Their Hopes & Dreams - A Pea Called Mildred, 2 vols. Armstrong, Nicky, tr. Sunderland, Margot. ed. 76p. *(978-0-86388-500-6(4),* 002-4777) Speechmark Publishing Ltd.
—Helping Children Who Are Anxious or Obsessional - Willy & the Wobbly House, 2 vols. Armstrong, Nicky, tr. Sunderland, Margot & Hancock, Nicky. ed. 100p. *(978-0-86388-499-3(7),* 002-4774) Speechmark Publishing Ltd.
—Helping Children Who Bottle up Their Feelings & a Nifflenoo Called Nevermind, 2 vols. Armstrong, Nicky, tr. Sunderland, Margot & Hancock, Nicky. ed. 88p. *(978-0-86388-501-3(2),* 002-4775) Speechmark Publishing Ltd.
—Helping Children Who Yearn for Someone They Love & the Frog Who Longed for the Moon to Smile, 2 vols. Armstrong, Nicky, tr. Sunderland, Margot & Hancock, Nicky. ed. 76p. *(978-0-86388-502-0(0),* 002-4776) Speechmark Publishing Ltd.
—How Hattie Hated Kindness. Armstrong, Nicky, tr. Sunderland, Margot & Hancock, Nicky. ed. 30p. pap. *(978-0-86388-461-0(X),* 002-5145) Speechmark Publishing Ltd.
—A Nifflenoo Called Nevermind. Armstrong, Nicky, tr. Sunderland, Margot & Hancock, Nicky. ed. 32p. pap. *(978-0-86388-496-2(2),* 002-5064) Speechmark Publishing Ltd.
—A Pea Called Mildred. Armstrong, Nicky, tr. Sunderland, Margot & Hancock, Nicky. ed. 36p. pap. *(978-0-86388-497-9(0),* 002-5062) Speechmark Publishing Ltd.
—Ruby & the Rubbish Bin. Armstrong, Nicky, tr. Sunderland, Margot & Hancock, Nicky. ed. 32p. pap. *(978-0-86388-462-7(8),* 002-5146) Speechmark Publishing Ltd.
—Teenie Weenie in a Too Big World, 2 vols. Armstrong, Nicky, tr. Sunderland, Margot & Hancock, Nicky. ed. 32p. pap. *(978-0-86388-460-3(1),* 002-5144) Speechmark Publishing Ltd.
—A Wibble Called Bipley (And a Few Honks), 2 vols. Armstrong, Nicky, tr. Sunderland, Margot & Hancock, Nicky. ed. 40p. pap. *(978-0-86388-494-8(6),* 002-5060) Speechmark Publishing Ltd.
—Willy & the Wobbly House. Armstrong, Nicky, tr. Sunderland, Margot & Hancock, Nicky. ed. 28p. pap. *(978-0-86388-498-6(9),* 002-5058) Speechmark Publishing Ltd.
Armstrong, Samuel. Gene Autry & the Lost Dogie. 2011. 30p. 35.95 *(978-1-258-02476-5(4))* Literary Licensing, LLC.
Armstrong, Shelagh. If America Were a Village: A Book about the People of the United States. Smith, David J. 2009. (CitizenKid Ser.). (ENG.). 32p. (J). (gr. 3-7). 18.95 *(978-1-55453-344-2(9))* Kids Can Pr., Ltd. CAN. Dist: Univ. of Toronto Pr.
—If the World Were a Village: A Book about the World's People. Smith, David J. 2nd ed. 2011. (CitizenKid Ser.). (ENG.). 32p. (J). 18.95 *(978-1-55453-595-8(6))* Kids Can Pr., Ltd. CAN. Dist: Univ. of Toronto Pr.
—This Child, Every Child: A Book about the World's Children. Smith, David J. 2011. (CitizenKid Ser.). (ENG.). 36p. (J). (gr. 3-7). 18.95 *(978-1-55453-466-1(6))* Kids Can Pr., Ltd. CAN. Dist: Univ. of Toronto Pr.
Arnaktauyok, Germaine. The Raven's Tale. Nicol, C. W. unabr. ed. (ENG.). 200p. (J). *(978-1-55017-083-2(X))* Harbour Publishing Co., Ltd.
—A Sled Dog for Moshi, 1 vol. Bushey, Jeanne. 2005. (ENG.). 32p. (J). pap. 8.95 *(978-1-55041-956-6(0),* 1550419560) Fitzhenry & Whiteside, Ltd. CAN. Dist: Midpoint Trade Bks., Inc.
Arnaktauyok, Germaine. Way Back Then, 1 vol. Christopher, Neil. 2015. (ENG.). 40p. (J). (gr. -1-k). 16.95 ***(978-1-77227-021-1(0))*** Inhabit Media Inc. CAN. Dist: Independent Pubs. Group.
Arnaquq-Baril, Alethea. The Blind Boy & the Loon, 1 vol. Arnaquq-Baril, Alethea. 2014. (ENG.). 48p. (J). (gr. k-2). 16.95 *(978-1-927095-57-7(3))* Inhabit Media Inc. CAN. Dist: Independent Pubs. Group.
Arnau, Marta. El cartero de los Suenos. 2004. (Cuentos con miga Ser.). 69p. pap. 12.95 *(978-84-931888-2-5(4))* Editorial Brief ESP. Dist: Independent Pubs. Group.
Arnault, Delphine. Tir na NOg: A New Adventure. Henry, William. 2009. (ENG.). 128p. (J). pap. 25.95 *(978-1-85635-597-1(7))* Mercier Pr., Ltd., The IRL. Dist: Dufour Editions, Inc.
Arndt, Charles T. A Calf Named Polly. Richardson, Lans. 2003. 38p. per. 11.95 *(978-1-59405-022-0(8))* New Age World Publishing.
Arndt, Ingo, photos by. Best Foot Forward: Exploring Feet, Flippers, & Claws. Arndt, Ingo. 2014. (ENG.). 36p. (J). (gr. k-3). 6.99 *(978-0-8234-3185-4(1))* Holiday Hse., Inc.
Arnett, Patty, photos by. Look to the Sky. Armacost, Betty. 2004. (J). 5.99 *(978-0-9760409-0-3(5))* Artist Designs.
Arno. Psalms for Young Children. Delval, Marie-Hélène. 2008. 88p. (J). (gr. -1-3). 16.50 *(978-0-8028-5322-6(6),* Eerdmans Bks For Young Readers) Eerdmans, William B. Publishing Co.
Arnold, Alli. Girl to Girl: Honest Talk about Growing up & Your Changing Body. Burningham, Sarah O'Leary. 2013. (ENG.). 136p. (J). (gr. 3-7). 12.99 *(978-1-4521-0242-9(2))* Chronicle Bks. LLC.
Arnold, Alli. Goodnight Mr. Darcy Board Book, 1 vol. Coombs, Kate. 2015. (ENG.). 22p. (J). bds. 9.99 ***(978-1-4236-4177-3(9))*** Gibbs Smith, Publisher.
Arnold, Alli. I Love You, Little Monster. Weiss, Ellen. 2012. (ENG.). 16p. (J). (gr. -1 — 1). bds. 7.99 *(978-1-4424-2850-8(3),* Little Simon) Little Simon.
—Mimi & Maty to the Rescue! Book 1: Roger the Rat Is on the Loose! Smith, Brooke. 2014. (ENG.). 88p. (J). (gr. k-4). pap. 9.95 *(978-1-62914-619-5(6),* Sky Pony Pr.) Skyhorse Publishing Co., Inc.
—Mimi & Maty to the Rescue! Book 2: Sadie the Sheep Disappears Without a Peep! Smith, Brooke. 2014. (ENG.). 96p. (J). (gr. 1-5). 14.95 *(978-1-62636-344-1(7),* Sky Pony Pr.) Skyhorse Publishing Co., Inc.
—Mimi & Maty to the Rescue! Book 3: C. C. the Parakeet Flies the Coop! Smith, Brooke. 2014. (ENG.). 96p. (J). (gr. k-4). 14.95 *(978-1-62914-620-1(X),* Sky Pony Pr.) Skyhorse Publishing Co., Inc.
—Mimi & Maty to the Rescue! Bk. 1: Roger the Rat Is on the Loose! Smith, Brooke. 2012. (ENG.). 88p. (J). (gr. 1-4).

14.95 *(978-1-62087-252-9(8)*, 620252, Sky Pony Pr.) Skyhorse Publishing Co., Inc.

Arnold, Andrew. Little Green Men at the Mercury Inn. Smith, Greg Leitich. 2014. (ENG.). 224p. (J). (gr. 4-7). 15.99 *(978-1-59643-835-4(5))* Roaring Brook Pr.

Arnold, Beth. Elijah Makes New Friends. Arnold, Beth. 2012. 30p. pap. 9.99 *(978-0-9860272-3-9(5))* Get Happy Tips, LLC.

Arnold, Caroline. Caroline Arnold's Black & White Animals. Arnold, Caroline. 2015. (Caroline Arnold's Black & White Animals Ser.). (ENG.). 20p. (gr. -1-2). bds. 31.96 ***(978-1-4795-6358-6(7))*** Picture Window Bks.

—Caroline Arnold's Habitats. Arnold, Caroline. 2015. (Caroline Arnold's Habitats Ser.). (ENG.). 24p. (gr. 2-3). lib. bdg. 109.28 ***(978-1-4795-6235-0(1))*** Picture Window Bks.

Arnold, Caroline. A Day & Night in the Desert. Arnold, Caroline. 2015. (Caroline Arnold's Habitats Ser.). (ENG.). 24p. (gr. 2-3). lib. bdg. 27.32 *(978-1-4795-6072-1(3))* Picture Window Bks.

—A Day & Night in the Forest. Arnold, Caroline. 2015. (Caroline Arnold's Habitats Ser.). (ENG.). 24p. (gr. 2-3). lib. bdg. 27.32 *(978-1-4795-6075-2(8))* Picture Window Bks.

—A Day & Night in the Rain Forest. Arnold, Caroline. 2015. (Caroline Arnold's Habitats Ser.). (ENG.). 24p. (gr. 2-3). lib. bdg. 27.32 *(978-1-4795-6074-5(X))* Picture Window Bks.

—A Day & Night on the Prairie. Arnold, Caroline. 2015. (Caroline Arnold's Habitats Ser.). (ENG.). 24p. (gr. 2-3). lib. bdg. 27.32 *(978-1-4795-6073-8(1))* Picture Window Bks.

—A Moose's World, 1 vol. Arnold, Caroline. 2010. (Caroline Arnold's Animals Ser.). (ENG.). 24p. (gr. k-2). lib. bdg. 27.32 *(978-1-4048-5742-1(7)*, Nonfiction Picture Bks.) Picture Window Bks.

Arnold, Caroline. A Panda's World. Arnold, Caroline. 2015. (Caroline Arnold's Black & White Animals Ser.). (ENG.). 20p. (gr. -1-2). bds. 7.99 ***(978-1-4795-6354-8(4))*** Picture Window Bks.

—A Penguin's World. Arnold, Caroline. (Caroline Arnold's Black & White Animals Ser.). (ENG.). 2015. 20p. (gr. -1-2). bds. 7.99 ***(978-1-4795-6356-2(0))***; 2006. 24p. (gr. k-2). 27.32 *(978-1-4048-1323-6(3)*, 1253185, Nonfiction Picture Bks.) Picture Window Bks.

Arnold, Caroline. A Polar Bear's World, 1 vol. Arnold, Caroline. (Caroline Arnold's Animals Ser.). (ENG.). 2010. 24p. (gr. k-2). lib. bdg. 27.32 *(978-1-4048-5743-8(5)*, Nonfiction Picture Bks.); 2015. 20p. (gr. -1-2). bds. 7.99 ***(978-1-4795-6357-9(9))*** Picture Window Bks.

—A Walrus' World, 1 vol. Arnold, Caroline. 2010. (Caroline Arnold's Animals Ser.). (ENG.). 24p. (gr. k-2). lib. bdg. 27.32 *(978-1-4048-5744-5(3)*, Nonfiction Picture Bks.) Picture Window Bks.

—A Wombat's World, 1 vol. Arnold, Caroline. 2008. (Caroline Arnold's Animals Ser.). (ENG.). 24p. (gr. k-2). lib. bdg. 27.32 *(978-1-4048-3986-1(0)*, Nonfiction Picture Bks.) Picture Window Bks.

Arnold, Caroline. A Zebra's World. Arnold, Caroline. 2015. (Caroline Arnold's Black & White Animals Ser.). (ENG.). 20p. (gr. -1-2). bds. 7.99 ***(978-1-4795-6355-5(2))*** Picture Window Bks.

Arnold, George "Speedy". What's an Elephant Doing in the Ausable River?!! Arnold, George "Speedy". 2012. (ENG.). 64p. (J). 20.00 *(978-0-9836925-5-3(6))* Bloated Toe Publishing.

Arnold, Jeanne. Carlos Digs to China. Stevens, Jan Romero. 2004. (Carlos Digs to China / Carlos Excava Hasta la China Ser.). (ENG, SPA & MUL.). 32p. (J). (gr. k-3). 15.95 *(978-0-87358-764-8(2))* Cooper Square Publishing Llc.

Arnold, Katya. Onions & Garlic: An Old Tale. Kimmel, Eric A. 2005. 29p. (J). (gr. k-4). reprint ed. 16.00 *(978-0-7567-9638-9(5))* DIANE Publishing Co.

Arnold, Katya, jt. photos by see Arnold, Katya R.

Arnold, Katya R. & Arnold, Katya, photos by. Elephants Can Paint Too! Arnold, Katya R. & Arnold, Katya. 2005. (ENG., 40p. (J). (gr. -1-3). 18.99 *(978-0-689-86985-3(1)*, Atheneum Bks. for Young Readers) Simon & Schuster Children's Publishing.

Arnold, Michael. Hocus Pocus Al I Mi Choo. Ross, Brad. 2012. 62p. pap. 19.95 *(978-0-9834201-0-1(6))* Illusionary Magic LLC.

Arnold, Patricia. Patchwork Trail. Kaderli, Janet. 2005. 59p. (J). 9.95 *(978-0-9754796-2-9(8))* GASLight Publishing.

Arnold, Sarah. Ugh, Eggs! Arnold, Sarah. 2010. (Child's Play Library). (ENG.). 32p. (J). (gr. -1-2). pap. *(978-1-84643-342-9(8))* Child's Play International Ltd.

Arnold, Stephen. Tobi the Little Puppy Dog. Uncle Bob. 2006. (Uncle Bob Ser.). 12p. (J). pap. 3.95 *(978-1-930596-61-0(8))* Amherst Pr.

Arnold, Tedd. Giant Children. Bagert, Brod. 2005. (ENG.). 32p. (J). (gr. -1-3). pap. 6.99 *(978-0-14-240192-7(7)*, Puffin) Penguin Publishing Group.

Arnold, Tedd, et al. Manners Mash-Up: A Goofy Guide to Good Behavior. 2011. (ENG.). 34p. (J). (gr. k-3). 16.99 *(978-0-8037-3480-7(8)*, Dial) Penguin Publishing Group.

Arnold, Tedd. Reading Placement Tests: Easy Assessments to Determine Students' Levels in Phonics, Vocabulary, & Reading Comprehension. 2003. (ENG.). 32p. pap. 8.95 *(978-0-439-40411-2(8))* Scholastic, Inc.

—Reading Placement Tests: Easy Assessments to Determine Students' Levels of Literacy Development. 2003. (ENG.). 32p. pap. 8.95 *(978-0-439-40413-6(4))* Scholastic, Inc.

Arnold, Tedd. Buzz Boy & Fly Guy. Arnold, Tedd. 2010. (Fly Guy Ser.: 9). (ENG.). 32p. (J). (gr. -1-3). 6.99 *(978-0-545-22274-7(5)*, Cartwheel Bks.) Scholastic, Inc.

—Dirty Gert. Arnold, Tedd. (ENG.). (J). 2014. 32p. (gr. 2-5). 6.99 *(978-0-8234-3054-3(5))*; 2013. 40p. 16.95 *(978-0-8234-2404-7(9))* Holiday Hse., Inc.

—Even More Parts. Arnold, Tedd. 2007. (ENG.). 40p. (J). (gr. -1-3). pap. 6.99 *(978-0-14-240714-1(3)*, Puffin) Penguin Publishing Group.

—Even More Parts: Idioms from Head to Toe. Arnold, Tedd. 2004. (ENG.). 40p. (J). (gr. -1-3). 16.99 *(978-0-8037-2938-4(3)*, Dial) Penguin Publishing Group.

—Fix This Mess! Arnold, Tedd. (I Like to Read(r) Ser.). (ENG.). (J). (gr. -1-3). 2015. 24p. 6.99 *(978-0-8234-3301-8(3))*; 2014. 32p. 14.95 *(978-0-8234-2942-4(3))* Holiday Hse., Inc.

—Fly Guy Meets Fly Girl! Arnold, Tedd. 2010. (Fly Guy Ser.: 8). (ENG.). 32p. (J). (gr. -1-3). 6.99 *(978-0-545-11029-7(7)*, Cartwheel Bks.) Scholastic, Inc.

—Fly Guy Presents: Dinosaurs. Arnold, Tedd. 2014. (Fly Guy Presents Ser.). (ENG.). 32p. (J). (gr. k-2). pap. 3.99 *(978-0-545-63159-4(9)*, Scholastic Reference) Scholastic, Inc.

—Fly Guy Presents: Firefighters. Arnold, Tedd. 2014. (Fly Guy Presents Ser.). (ENG.). 32p. (J). (gr. k-2). pap. 3.99 *(978-0-545-63160-0(2)*, Scholastic Reference) Scholastic, Inc.

—Fly Guy vs. the Flyswatter! Arnold, Tedd. 2011. (Fly Guy Ser.: 10). (ENG.). 32p. (J). (gr. -1-3). 6.99 *(978-0-545-31266-8(8)*, Cartwheel Bks.) Scholastic, Inc.

—Fly High, Fly Guy! Arnold, Tedd. 2008. (Fly Guy Ser.: 5). (ENG.). 32p. (J). (gr. -1-3). 6.99 *(978-0-545-00722-1(4))* Scholastic, Inc.

—Green Wilma, Frog in Space. Arnold, Tedd. 2009. (ENG.). 32p. (J). (gr. -1-3). 16.99 *(978-0-8037-2698-7(8)*, Dial) Penguin Publishing Group.

—Hi! Fly Guy. Arnold, Tedd. (ENG.). 32p. (J). (gr. -1-3). 2006. (Scholastic Reader Level 2 Ser.). pap. 3.99 *(978-0-439-85311-8(7))*; 2005. (Fly Guy Ser.: 1). 6.99 *(978-0-439-63903-3(4))* Scholastic, Inc. (Cartwheel Bks.).

—I Spy Fly Guy! Arnold, Tedd. 2009. (Fly Guy Ser.: 7). (ENG.). 32p. (J). (gr. -1-3). 6.99 *(978-0-545-11028-0(9))* Scholastic, Inc.

—I Spy Fly Guy! Arnold, Tedd. ed. 2009. (Fly Guy Ser.: 7). lib. bdg. 17.20 *(978-0-606-07098-0(2)*, Turtleback) Turtleback Bks.

—Insects. Arnold, Tedd. 2015. (Fly Guy Presents Ser.). (ENG.). 32p. (J). (gr. -1-3). pap. 3.99 *(978-0-545-75714-0(2)*, Scholastic Reference) Scholastic, Inc.

—A Pet for Fly Guy. Arnold, Tedd. 2014. (Fly Guy Ser.). (ENG.). 32p. (J). (gr. -1-3). 16.99 *(978-0-545-31615-6(4)*, Orchard Bks.) Scholastic, Inc.

—Sharks. Arnold, Tedd. 2013. (Fly Guy Ser.). (ENG.). 32p. (J). (gr. -1-3). pap. 3.99 *(978-0-545-50771-4(5)*, Scholastic Reference) Scholastic, Inc.

—Shoo, Fly Guy! Arnold, Tedd. 2006. (Fly Guy Ser.: 3). (ENG.). 32p. (J). (gr. -1-3). 6.99 *(978-0-439-63905-7(0)*, Cartwheel Bks.) Scholastic, Inc.

—Space. Arnold, Tedd. 2013. (ENG.). 32p. (J). (gr. -1-3). pap. 3.99 *(978-0-545-56492-2(1)*, Scholastic Reference) Scholastic, Inc.

—Super Fly Guy. Arnold, Tedd. (ENG.). 32p. (J). (gr. -1-3). 2009. (Scholastic Reader Level 2 Ser.). 3.99 *(978-0-439-90374-5(2))*; 2006. (Fly Guy Ser.: 2). 6.99 *(978-0-439-63904-0(2)*, Cartwheel Bks.) Scholastic, Inc.

—There Was an Old Lady Who Swallowed Fly Guy. Arnold, Tedd. 2007. (Fly Guy Ser.: 4). (ENG.). 32p. (J). (gr. -1-3). 6.99 *(978-0-439-63906-4(9))* Scholastic, Inc.

—The Twin Princes. Arnold, Tedd. 2007. (ENG.). 32p. (J). (gr. -1-2). 16.99 *(978-0-8037-2696-3(1)*, Dial) Penguin Publishing Group.

Arnosky, Deanna, photos by. Whole Days Outdoors: An Autobiographical Album. Arnosky, James. 2006. (Meet the Author Ser.). (ENG., 32p. (J). 14.95 *(978-1-57274-859-0(1)*, 734, Meet the Author) Owen, Richard C. Pubs., Inc.

Arnosky, Jim. Man Gave Names to All the Animals. Dylan, Bob. 2015. (ENG.). 32p. (J). (gr. -1). pap. 6.95 *(978-1-4549-1576-8(5))* Sterling Publishing Co., Inc.

—Man Gave Names to All the Animals. Dylan, Bob. 2010. (ENG.). 32p. (J). (gr. -1-2). 17.95 *(978-1-4027-6858-3(3))* Sterling Publishing Co., Inc.

Arnosky, Jim. All about Manatees. Arnosky, Jim. 2008. (All About Ser.). (ENG.). 32p. (J). (gr. -1-3). pap. 5.99 *(978-0-439-90361-5(0))* Scholastic, Inc.

—All about Turtles. Arnosky, Jim. 2008. (All About Ser.). (ENG.). 32p. (J). (gr. -1-3). pap. 5.99 *(978-0-590-69781-1(1))* Scholastic, Inc.

—Babies in the Bayou. Arnosky, Jim. (ENG.). 32p. (J). (gr. -1-k). 2010. pap. 6.99 *(978-0-14-241463-7(8)*, Puffin); 2007. 16.99 *(978-0-399-22653-3(2)*, Putnam Juvenile) Penguin Publishing Group.

—Crinkleroot's Guide to Giving Back to Nature. Arnosky, Jim. 2012. (ENG.). 32p. (J). (gr. k-3). 17.99 *(978-0-399-25520-5(6)*, Putnam Juvenile) Penguin Publishing Group.

—Crinkleroot's Guide to Knowing Animal Habitats. Arnosky, Jim. 2014. (ENG.). 32p. (J). (gr. -1-3). pap. 14.99 *(978-1-4814-2599-5(4)*, Simon & Schuster Bks. For Young Readers) Simon & Schuster Bks. For Young Readers.

—Following the Coast. Arnosky, Jim. 2004. (ENG.). 32p. (J). (gr. 3-18). 15.99 *(978-0-688-17117-9(6))* HarperCollins Pubs.

—Raccoon on His Own. Arnosky, Jim. 2003. (ENG.). 32p. (J). (gr. -1-k). 6.99 *(978-0-14-250071-2(2)*, Puffin) Penguin Publishing Group.

Aron, Bill, photos by. What You Will See Inside a Synagogue. Hoffman, Lawrence A. & Wolfson, Ron. 2008. (ENG., 32p. (J). pap. 8.99 *(978-1-59473-256-0(6)*, Skylight Paths Publishing) LongHill Partners, Inc.

Aronson, Jeff & Zephyr, Jay. Little Mike & Maddie's Black Hill's Adventure. Aronson, Jeff & Aronson, Miriam. 2007. 33p. (J). 16.00 *(978-0-9795302-1-0(0)*, CrumbGobbler Pr.) Downtown Wetmore Pr.

—Little Mike & Maddie's Christmas Book. Aronson, Jeff & Aronson, Miriam. 2007. 32p. (J). 16.00 *(978-0-9795302-2-7(9)*, CrumbGobbler Pr.) Downtown Wetmore Pr.

—Little Mike & Maddie's First Motorcycle Ride. Aronson, Jeff & Aronson, Miriam. 2007. 32p. (J). 16.00 *(978-0-9795302-0-3(2)*, CrumbGobbler Pr.) Downtown Wetmore Pr.

Arrasmith, Patrick. Attack of the Fiend. Delaney, Joseph. 2009. (Last Apprentice Ser.: 4). (ENG.). 576p. (YA). (gr. 8-18). pap. 9.99 *(978-0-06-089129-9(7)*, Greenwillow Bks.) HarperCollins Pubs.

—Clash of the Demons. Delaney, Joseph. (Last Apprentice Ser.: 6). (YA). (gr. 8). 2009. 416p. lib. bdg. 18.89 *(978-0-06-134463-3(X))*; 2009. (ENG.). 416p. 17.99 *(978-0-06-134462-6(1))*; Bk. 6. 2010. (ENG.). 432p. pap. 9.99 *(978-0-06-134464-0(8))* HarperCollins Pubs. (Greenwillow Bks.).

—A Coven of Witches. Delaney, Joseph. (Last Apprentice Short Fiction Ser.: 2). 240p. (YA). (gr. 8). 2011. (ENG.). pap. 7.99 *(978-0-06-196040-6(3))*; 2010. lib. bdg. 17.89 *(978-0-06-196039-0(X))*; 2010. (ENG.). 16.99 *(978-0-06-196038-3(1))* HarperCollins Pubs. (Greenwillow Bks.).

—Curse of the Bane. Delaney, Joseph. (Last Apprentice Ser.: 2). (YA). (gr. 8-9). 2006. (ENG.). 480p. 17.99 *(978-0-06-076621-4(2))*; Bk. 2. 2007. (ENG.). 496p. pap. 9.99 *(978-0-06-076623-8(9))*; Bk. 2. 2006. 480p. lib. bdg. 19.89 *(978-0-06-076622-1(0))* HarperCollins Pubs. (Greenwillow Bks.).

—Dark Eden. Carman, Patrick. 2012. (Dark Eden Ser.: 1). (ENG.). 336p. (YA). (gr. 8). pap. 8.99 *(978-0-06-200971-5(0)*, Tegen, Katherine Bks) HarperCollins Pubs.

—Eve of Destruction. Carman, Patrick. 2013. (Dark Eden Ser.: 2). (ENG.). 288p. (YA). (gr. 8). 17.99 *(978-0-06-210182-2(X)*, Tegen, Katherine Bks) HarperCollins Pubs.

—Fury of the Seventh Son. Delaney, Joseph. (Last Apprentice Ser.: 13). (ENG.). 480p. (YA). (gr. 8). 2014. 17.99 *(978-0-06-219231-8(0))*; Bk. 13. 2015. pap. 9.99 *(978-0-06-219232-5(9))* HarperCollins Pubs. (Greenwillow Bks.).

—Grimalkin the Witch Assassin. Delaney, Joseph. 2013. (Last Apprentice Ser.: 9). (ENG.). 416p. (YA). (gr. 8). pap. 9.99 *(978-0-06-208208-4(6)*, Greenwillow Bks.) HarperCollins Pubs.

—Grimalkin the Witch Assassin Bk. 9, Bk. 9. Delaney, Joseph. 2012. (Last Apprentice Ser.: 9). (ENG.). 400p. (YA). (gr. 8). 17.99 *(978-0-06-208207-7(8)*, Greenwillow Bks.) HarperCollins Pubs.

—The House of Dead Maids. Dunkle, Clare B. 2011. (ENG.). 176p. (YA). (gr. 7-12). pap. 14.99 *(978-0-312-55155-1(X))* Square Fish.

—I Am Alice, Bk. 12. Delaney, Joseph. 2014. (Last Apprentice Ser.: 12). (ENG.). 464p. (YA). (gr. 8). pap. 9.99 *(978-0-06-171515-0(8)*, Greenwillow Bks.) HarperCollins Pubs.

—The Last Apprentice Bk. 1: Revenge of the Witch, Bk. 1. Delaney, Joseph. 2006. (Last Apprentice Ser.: 1). (ENG.). 384p. (YA). (gr. 8). reprint ed. pap. 9.99 *(978-0-06-076620-7(4)*, Greenwillow Bks.) HarperCollins Pubs.

—The Last Apprentice Bk. 8: Rage of the Fallen. Delaney, Joseph. 2012. (Last Apprentice Ser.: 8). (ENG.). 416p. (YA). (gr. 8). pap. 9.99 *(978-0-06-202758-0(1)*, Greenwillow Bks.) HarperCollins Pubs.

—The Last Apprentice - I Am Alice, Bk. 12. Delaney, Joseph. 2013. (Last Apprentice Ser.: 12). (ENG.). 448p. (YA). (gr. 8). 17.99 *(978-0-06-171513-6(1)*, Greenwillow Bks.) HarperCollins Pubs.

—Lure of the Dead. Delaney, Joseph. (Last Apprentice Ser.: 10). (ENG.). (YA). (gr. 8). 2013. 448p. pap. 9.99 *(978-0-06-202762-7(X))*; Bk. 10. 2012. 432p. 17.99 *(978-0-06-202760-3(3))* HarperCollins Pubs. (Greenwillow Bks.).

—Night of the Soul Stealer Bk. 3. Delaney, Joseph. 2007. (Last Apprentice Ser.: 3). (ENG.). 512p. (YA). (gr. 8-9). 17.99 *(978-0-06-076624-5(7)*, Greenwillow Bks.) HarperCollins Pubs.

—Rage of the Fallen, Bk. 8. Delaney, Joseph. 2011. (Last Apprentice Ser.: 8). (ENG.). 416p. (YA). (gr. 8-18). 17.99 *(978-0-06-202756-6(5)*, Greenwillow Bks.) HarperCollins Pubs.

—Revenge of the Witch, Bk. 1. Delaney, Joseph. 2005. (Last Apprentice Ser.: 1). (ENG.). 368p. (YA). (gr. 8). 17.99 *(978-0-06-076618-4(2)*, Greenwillow Bks.) HarperCollins Pubs.

—Rise of the Huntress, Bk. 7. Delaney, Joseph. 2010. (Last Apprentice Ser.: 7). (ENG.). 448p. (YA). (gr. 8-18). 17.99 *(978-0-06-171510-5(7)*, Greenwillow Bks.) HarperCollins Pubs.

—Rise of the Huntress Bk. 7, Bk. 7. Delaney, Joseph. 2011. (Last Apprentice Ser.: 7). (ENG.). 464p. (YA). (gr. 8). pap. 7.99 *(978-0-06-171512-9(3)*, Greenwillow Bks.) HarperCollins Pubs.

Arreola Alemón, Roberto. De dos mundos = of Two Worlds: Las ranas, sapos y salamandras de la Península de Yucatán, México = the Frogs, Toads & Salamanders of the Yucatan Peninsula, Mexico. Galindo-Leal, Carlos. 2003. (SPA & ENG.). 152p. pap. 19.95 *(978-1-929165-52-0(8))* PANGAEA.

Arreola, Gil. Cesar Chavez: Changing Lives. Gotsch, Patrice. 2006. 19p. pap. 6.30 *(978-1-55501-780-4(0))* Ballard & Tighe Pubs.

—Martin Luther King, Jr: Changing Lives. Gotsch, Patrice. 2006. 19p. pap. 6.30 *(978-1-55501-779-8(7))* Ballard & Tighe Pubs.

Arreola, Manuel. Weenz the Cat: What about Me? Arreola, Perla. 2013. 30p. 14.99 *(978-0-9859298-7-9(1))* Dream&Achieve Bks.

Arrhenius, Ingela P. The World's Best Noses, Ears, & Eyes. Rundgren, Helen. 2014. (ENG.). 32p. (J). (gr. 1-5). 16.95 *(978-0-8234-3161-8(4))* Holiday Hse., Inc.

Arrigan, Mary. Milo & One Dead Angry Druid. Arrigan, Mary. 2014. (Milo Adventures Ser.: 1). (ENG.). 112p. (J). pap. 12.95 *(978-1-84717-351-5(9))* O'Brien Pr., Ltd., The IRL. Dist: Dufour Editions, Inc.

Arrington, Chiquila. Dallas: On Book One: JoJo KIDS. Arrington, Gladys. 2006. 49p. pap. 16.95 *(978-1-4241-1162-6(5))* PublishAmerica, Inc.

Arrington, Linda, photos by. Ugly Trees. Arrington, Linda. 2012. 24p. pap. 24.95 *(978-1-4626-8925-5(6))* America Star Bks.

Arriola, Ricardo Ramirez. Vivir en el Circo. Arriola, Ricardo Ramirez. rev. ed. 2006. (Otra Escalera Ser.). (SPA & ENG.). 48p. (J). (gr. 2-4). pap. 10.95 *(978-968-5920-63-6(X))* Castillo, Ediciones, S. A. de C. V. MEX. Dist: Macmillan.

Arrott, Nancy. Children's Stories from Around the World. Avalon-Pai, Phyllis. 2008. 70p. pap. 9.95 *(978-0-9788283-8-7(0))* Acacia Publishing, Inc.

Arroyo, Andrea. The Legend of the Lady Slipper. 2004. (ENG.). 32p. (J). (gr. -1-3). reprint ed. pap. 6.99 *(978-0-618-43231-8(0))* Houghton Mifflin Harcourt Publishing Co.

Arroyo, David, jt. illus. see Rio, Adam del.

Arroyo, Felipe, photos by. Healthy Taste of Corona Cookbook. Reddy, Prerana & Strauss, David, eds. Mesalles, Monica, tr. 2008.Tr. of Sabor Saludable de Corona. (ENG & SPA., 130p. (J). pap. *(978-1-929641-10-9(9))* Queens Museum of Art.

Arroyo, Fian. Bee Double Bopp: Respecting Others. Cosgrove, Stephen. 2004. (J). *(978-1-58804-350-4(9))* P C I Education.

—Big Bubba Bigg, Jr: Dealing with Bullies. Cosgrove, Stephen. 2004. (J). *(978-1-58804-352-8(5))* P C I Education.

—The Bigg Family: Getting along with Others. Cosgrove, Stephen. 2004. (J). *(978-1-58804-354-2(1))* P C I Education.

—The Bugglar Brothers: Consequences of Stealing. Cosgrove, Stephen. 2007. (J). *(978-1-58804-381-8(9))* P C I Education.

—Cricket Clickett: Finding Your Talents. Cosgrove, Stephen. 2004. (J). *(978-1-58804-382-5(7))* P C I Education.

—Flynn "Flea" Flicker: Sticking to the Truth. Cosgrove, Stephen. 2004. (J). *(978-1-58804-353-5(3))* P C I Education.

—Hickory B. Hopp: Paying Attention. Cosgrove, Stephen. 2004. (J). *(978-1-58804-379-5(7))* P C I Education.

—Katy Didd Bigg: Standing up for Yourself. Cosgrove, Stephen. 2004. (J). *(978-1-58804-378-8(9))* P C I Education.

—Melody Moth: Practice Makes Perfect. Cosgrove, Stephen. 2004. (J). *(978-1-58804-351-1(7))* P C I Education.

—Mizz Buggly: Doing Your Best. Cosgrove, Stephen. 2004. (J). *(978-1-58804-380-1(0))* P C I Education.

—Snugg N. Flitter: Facing Your Fears. Cosgrove, Stephen. 2004. (J). *(978-1-58804-377-1(0))* P C I Education.

Arscott, Dean. Spend the Day with Me. Baruch, M. P. 2009. 20p. pap. 10.95 *(978-1-936051-27-4(3))* Peppertree Pr., The.

ArsEdition. Blossom Magic: Beautiful Floral Patterns to Color. 2015. (Color Magic Ser.). (ENG.). 80p. pap. 12.99 ***(978-1-4380-0731-1(0))*** Barron's Educational Series, Inc.

—Winter Magic: Beautiful Holiday Patterns to Color. 2015. (Color Magic Ser.). (ENG.). 80p. pap. 12.99 ***(978-1-4380-0733-5(7))*** Barron's Educational Series, Inc.

Arsenault, Isabelle. Jane, the Fox & Me, 1 vol. Britt, Fanny & Ouriou, Susan. Morelli, Christelle, tr. from FRE. 2013. (ENG.). 104p. (J). (gr. 5). 19.95 *(978-1-55498-360-5(6))* Groundwood Bks. CAN. Dist: Perseus-PGW.

—Migrant, 1 vol. Trottier, Maxine. 2011. (ENG.). 40p. (J). (gr. -1-2). 18.95 *(978-0-88899-975-7(5))* Groundwood Bks. CAN. Dist: Perseus-PGW.

—My Letter to the World & Other Poems. Dickinson, Emily. 2008. (Visions in Poetry Ser.). (ENG.). 48p. (YA). (gr. 5-18). 17.95 *(978-1-55453-103-5(9))*; pap. 9.95 *(978-1-55453-339-8(2))* Kids Can Pr., Ltd. CAN. Dist: Univ. of Toronto Pr.

—That Night's Train, 1 vol. Akbarpour, Ahmad. Saghafi, Majid, tr. from PER. 2012. (ENG.). 96p. (J). (gr. 3). 14.95 *(978-1-55498-169-4(7))* Groundwood Bks. CAN. Dist: Perseus-PGW.

—Virginia Wolf. Maclear, Kyo. 2012. (ENG.). 32p. (J). 16.95 *(978-1-55453-649-8(9))* Kids Can Pr., Ltd. CAN. Dist: Univ. of Toronto Pr.

Arsenault, Isabelle. Spork. Arsenault, Isabelle. Maclear, Kyo. 2010. (ENG.). 32p. (J). (gr. -1-2). 16.95 *(978-1-55337-736-8(2))* Kids Can Pr., Ltd. CAN. Dist: Univ. of Toronto Pr.

Arseneau, Philippe & Drouin, Julie Saint-Onge. Coureurs des Bois a Clark City. Lefrancois, Viateur. 2003. (Collection des 9 Ans: Vol. 32). (FRE.). 136p. 8.95 *(978-2-922565-69-0(6))* Editions de la Paix CAN. Dist: World of Reading, Ltd.

Art Parts & Black Eye Design. Presidential Trivia: The Feats, Fates, Families, Foibles, & Firsts of Our American Presidents, 1 vol. Lederer, Richard & Gibbs Smith Publisher Staff. 2007. (ENG.). 152p. (gr. 7-18). pap. 9.99 *(978-1-4236-0210-1(2))* Gibbs Smith, Publisher.

Art&Script. Outside Fun, 1. Earley, Catherine. Earley, Catherine, ed. 2005. 12p. (J). 6.95 *(978-0-9769589-1-8(0))* Naynay Bks.

Arte y Cultura, A.C Staff. La Domadora de Miedos. Lascurain, Guadalupe Aleman. rev. ed. 2006. (Castillo de la Lectura Roja Ser.). (SPA & ENG.). 232p. (YA). (gr. 7). pap. 8.95 *(978-970-20-0182-9(X))* Castillo, Ediciones, S. A. de C. V. MEX. Dist: Macmillan.

Arte Y Diseno, Tane, jt. illus. see Sanchez, Andres.

Artell, Mike. 25 Reproducible Literature Circle Role Sheets for Fiction & Nonfiction Books, Grades 4-6 Revised & Updated. Moen, Christine Boardman. Mitchell, Judy, ed. 2004. 64p. (J). (gr. 4-6). pap., tchr. ed. 9.95 *(978-1-57310-141-7(9))* Teaching & Learning Co.

Artell, Mike & Kendrick, D. Tongue Twisters. Rosenbloom, Joseph & Artell, Mike. 2007. (Little Giant Bks.). (ENG.). 352p. (J). (gr. 2-5). pap. 6.95 *(978-1-4027-4974-2(0))* Sterling Publishing Co., Inc.

Artful Doodlers. The Devil Fish. Campbell, Tom, photos by. Williams, Geoffrey T. 2008. (Save Our Seas Adventure Bks.). (ENG.). 64p. (J). (gr. 4-7). 8.95 *(978-0-9800444-1-6(3))* Save Our Seas, Ltd.

—The Great White Red Alert. Campbell, Tom, photos by. Williams, Geoffrey T. 2008. (Save Our Seas Adventure

Bks.). (ENG.). 64p. (J). (gr. 4-7). 8.95 *(978-0-9800444-0-9(5))* Save Our Seas, Ltd.

—Picnic Day! Wax, Wendy. 2006. 24p. (J). lib. bdg. 15.00 *(978-1-4242-0952-1(8))* Fitzgerald Bks.

—Spring Is in the Air. RH Disney Staff. 2011. (Color Plus Flocked Stickers Ser.). (ENG.). 64p. (J). (gr. -1-2). pap. 4.99 *(978-0-7364-2760-9(0)*, Golden/Disney) Random Hse. Children's Bks.

—Thanksgiving Parade. Barbo, Maria S. & Bridwell, Norman. 2010. (J). *(978-0-545-25332-1(2))* Scholastic, Inc.

Artful Doodlers Limited Staff. Alvin & the Chipmunks: Alvin & the Big Art Show. Huelin, Jodi. 2013. (I Can Read Book 2 Ser.). (ENG.). 32p. (J). (gr. -1-3). pap. 3.99 *(978-0-06-225225-8(9)*, HarperFestival) HarperCollins Pubs.

—Alvin & the Chipmunks: Alvin & the Substitute Teacher. Huelin, Jodi. 2013. (I Can Read Book 2 Ser.). (ENG.). 32p. (J). (gr. -1-3). pap. 3.99 *(978-0-06-225223-4(2)*, HarperFestival) HarperCollins Pubs.

—Beastly Feast!, 1 vol. Corderoy, Tracey. 2012. (Grunt & the Grouch Ser.). (ENG.). 112p. (gr. 1-3). pap. 5.19 *(978-1-4342-4269-3(2))*; 23.99 *(978-1-4342-4603-5(5))* Stone Arch Bks.

—Big Splash!, 1 vol. Corderoy, Tracey. 2012. (Grunt & the Grouch Ser.). (ENG.). 112p. (gr. 1-3). pap. 5.19 *(978-1-4342-4268-6(4))*; 23.99 *(978-1-4342-4602-8(7))* Stone Arch Bks.

—It's Absolutely True. 2006. (Famous Fables Ser.). (J). 6.99 *(978-1-59939-029-1(9))* Cornerstone Pr.

—Puppy Love! Ackelsberg, Amy. 2014. (Strawberry Shortcake Ser.). (ENG.). 24p. (J). (gr. -1-k). 4.99 *(978-0-448-48150-0(2)*, Grosset & Dunlap) Penguin Publishing Group.

Artful Doodlers Limited Staff, et al. Royal Ride. RH Disney Staff. 2008. (Color Plus Chunky Crayons Ser.). (ENG.). 48p. (J). (gr. -1-2). pap. 3.99 *(978-0-7364-2499-8(7)*, Golden/Disney) Random Hse. Children's Bks.

Artful Doodlers Limited Staff & Carzon, Walter. Alvin & the Chipmunks: Alvin's Easter Break. Huelin, Jodi. 2014. (ENG.). 24p. (J). (gr. -1-3). pap. 3.99 *(978-0-06-225222-7(4)*, HarperFestival) HarperCollins Pubs.

Artful Doodlers Ltd. Angelina's Best Friend Dance. Grosset and Dunlap Staff. 2015. (Angelina Ballerina Ser.). (ENG.). 24p. (J). (gr. -1-k). 4.99 *(978-0-448-48455-6(2)*, Grosset & Dunlap) Penguin Publishing Group.

—A Chipping Cheddar Christmas. Grosset & Dunlap. 2014. (Angelina Ballerina Ser.). (ENG.). 24p. (J). (gr. -1-k). 4.99 *(978-0-448-48197-5(9)*, Grosset & Dunlap) Penguin Publishing Group.

Artful Doodlers Ltd Staff. The Reason for the Season. Huelin, Jodi. 2013. (Alvin & the Chipmunks Ser.). (ENG.). 24p. (J). (gr. -1-3). pap. 4.99 *(978-0-06-225221-0(6)*, HarperFestival) HarperCollins Pubs.

—Scholastic Reader Level 2: Rainbow Magic: Pet Fairies to the Rescue! Meadows, Daisy. 2013. (Scholastic Reader Level 2 Ser.). (ENG.). 32p. (J). (gr. -1-3). pap. 3.99 *(978-0-545-46295-2(9)*, Scholastic Paperbacks) Scholastic, Inc.

Arthur, Jenny. Monster Mayhem. Murphy, Rose. 2011. (Pat & Sound Stories Ser.). (ENG.). 12p. (gr. -1). 14.95 *(978-1-61524-497-3(2)*, Intervisual/Piggy Toes) Bendon, Inc.

Arthur, Jenny. Little Witch. Arthur, Jenny. 2012. (Spooky Sounds Ser.). (ENG.). 10p. (J). (gr. k — 1). 7.99 *(978-0-230-74487-5(7))* Macmillan Pubs., Ltd. GBR. Dist: Independent Pubs. Group.

Arthus-Bertrand, Yann, photos by. Kids Who Are Changing the World. Jankeliowitch, Anne. 2014. (ENG., 144p. (J). (gr. 3-6). pap. 14.99 *(978-1-4022-9532-4(4)*, Sourcebooks Jabberwocky) Sourcebooks, Inc.

Artifact Group Staff. Champions of the Sea! (SpongeBob SquarePants) Golden Books Staff. 2011. (Holographic Sticker Book Ser.). (ENG.). 48p. (J). (gr. -1-2). pap. 3.99 *(978-0-375-87322-5(8)*, Golden Bks.) Random Hse. Children's Bks.

Artigas, Alexandra. The Fuzzy Escape Artists. Isaacs, Michael. 2006. 32p. (J). (gr. -1-7). 15.95 *(978-0-9742845-8-3(0))* Mystic Ridge Bks.

—Rebecca & the Great Goat Getaway. Furfur, Christopher. 2005. 40p. (J). (gr. -1). per. 15.95 *(978-0-9742845-7-6(2))* Mystic Ridge Bks.

Artistic Book and Web Design. Adventures of My Dentist & the Tooth Fairy: Activity & Coloring Book, bk. 2. Hood, Karen Jean Matsko. Whispering Pine Press International, Inc. Staff, ed. 2013. (ENG & JPN.). 174p. (J). pap. 19.95 *(978-1-59649-535-7(9))* Whispering Pine Pr. International, Inc.

—Gaited Horse Activity & Coloring Book-English/German/Spanish Edition. Hood, Karen Jean Matsko. Whispering Pine Press International, Inc. Staff, ed. 2010. (ENG, GER & SPA.). 160p. (J). per. 19.95 *(978-1-59649-522-7(7))* Whispering Pine Pr. International, Inc.

—Girls Can Do Activity & Coloring Book. Hood, Karen Jean Matsko. Whispering Pine Press International, Inc. Staff, ed. 2010. (ENG & JPN.). 160p. (J). per. 13.95 *(978-1-59210-593-9(9))* Whispering Pine Pr. International, Inc.

—My Birth Celebration Journal: A Daily Journal, Vol. 3. Hood, Karen Jean Matsko. Whispering Pine Press International, Inc. Staff, ed. 2014. (Children's Journal Series). 164p. (J). pap. 13.95 *(978-1-59210-647-9(1))* Whispering Pine Pr. International, Inc.

Artistic Design Service. Angels, Angels Way up High, Vol. 2. Hood, Karen Jean Matsko. Whispering Pine Press International, ed. 2015. (Hood Picture Book Ser.). (J). 24.95 *(978-1-930948-81-5(6))*; pap. 15.95 *(978-1-930948-09-9(3))* Whispering Pine Pr. International, Inc.

—Lost Medal, Bk.1. Hood, Karen Jean Matsko. Whispering Pine Press International, Inc. Staff, ed. 2014. (Hood Horse Story Ser.). 160p. (J). (gr. 4-8). 25.95 *(978-1-930948-94-5(8))*; (ENG.). per. 14.95 *(978-1-930948-95-2(6))* Whispering Pine Pr. International, Inc.

—Petting Farm Fun, Bilingual English & Spanish, Bk. 3. Hood, Karen Jean Matsko. Whispering Pine Press International, ed. ed. 2015. (Hood Picture Book Ser.). (ENG & SPA.). 36p. (J). pap. 29.95 *(978-1-59808-824-3(6))* Whispering Pine Pr. International, Inc.

—Spokane Falls. Hood, Karen Jean Matsko. Whispering Pine Press International, ed. l.t. ed. 2015. (Banacek & Flannigan Mystery Ser.). 224p. pap. 22.95 *(978-1-59434-223-3(7))*; Vol. 1. 29.95 *(978-1-59434-228-8(8))*; Vol. 1. per. 19.95 *(978-1-59434-226-4(1))* Whispering Pine Pr. International, Inc.

Artistic Design Service Staff. Apple Delights Cookbook, Translated Italian: A Collection of Apple Recipes, Vol. 1. Hood, Karen Jean Matsko. Whispering Pine Press International, ed. 2014. (Cookbook Delights Translated Ser.). (ITA.). 324p. 27.95 *(978-1-59649-100-7(0))* Whispering Pine Pr. International, Inc.

—Apples: Apple Board Book, Bk.1. Hood, Karen Jean Matsko. Whispering Pine Press International, ed. 2014. (ENG.). 14p. (J). 12.99 *(978-1-59649-006-2(3))* Whispering Pine Pr. International, Inc.

—Arizona Saguaro: A Collection of Poetry, Vol. 2. Hood, Karen Jean Matsko. Whispering Pine Press International, ed. 2015. (Hood Regional Poetry Ser.). 224p. pap., tchr. ed. 19.95 *(978-1-59649-443-5(3))* Whispering Pine Pr. International, Inc.

—Arizona Saguaro: A Collection of Poetry, Vol. 2. Hood, Karen Jean Matsko. Whispering Pine Press International Staff, ed. l.t. ed. 2015. (Hood Regional Poetry Ser.). 224p. pap. 22.95 *(978-1-59649-414-5(X))* Whispering Pine Pr. International, Inc.

—Dr. James G. Hood, Author: Book, Freelance Service & Gift Catalog. Hood, James G. Whispering Pine Press International, ed. 2014. 100p. pap. 4.99 *(978-1-59210-603-5(X))* Whispering Pine Pr. International, Inc.

—Gaited Horse Activity & Coloring Book. Hood, Karen Jean Matsko. Whispering Pine Press International, ed. 2014. (Hood Activity & Coloring Book Ser.). 160p. (J). bk. 4. spiral bd. 21.95 *(978-1-59649-628-6(2))*; Vol. 4. (ENG.). per. 19.95 *(978-1-59210-591-5(2))* Whispering Pine Pr. International, Inc.

—Icelandic Horse Activity & Coloring Book, Vol. 6. Hood, Karen Jean Matsko. Whispering Pine Press International, ed. 2nd ed. 2014. (Educational Activity & Coloring Book Ser.). (ENG, ICE & GER.). 160p. (J). spiral bd. 21.95 *(978-1-59649-364-3(X))* Whispering Pine Pr. International, Inc.

—Icelandic Horse Activity & Coloring Book: Activity & Coloring Book, Vol. 6. Hood, Karen Jean Matsko. Whispering Pine Press International, ed. 2014. (Hood Activity & Coloring Book Ser.). (ENG, GER & ICE.). 160p. (J). per. 19.95 *(978-1-59210-595-3(5))* Whispering Pine Pr. International, Inc.

—Jesus Loves the Little Children: Activity & Coloring Book, Vol. 8. Hood, Karen Jean Matsko. Whispering Pine Press International, ed. ed. 2014. (Educational Activity & Coloring Book Ser.). (ENG & SPA.). (J). spiral bd. 21.95 *(978-1-59434-087-1(0))* Whispering Pine Pr. International, Inc.

—Karen Jean Matsko Hood, Inc. Parenting Book & Gift Catalog. Hood, Karen Jean Matsko. Whispering Pine Press International, ed. 2014. 50p. pap. 4.99 *(978-1-59210-715-5(X))* Whispering Pine Pr. International, Inc.

—Kids' Kindness Activity & Coloring Book, Vol. 9. Hood, Karen Jean Matsko. Whispering Pine Press International, ed. 2015. (Hood Activity & Coloring Book Ser.). 170p. (J). spiral bd. 21.95 *(978-1-59808-753-6(3))*; per. 19.95 *(978-1-59808-752-9(5))* Whispering Pine Pr. International, Inc.

—Kids' Kindness Journal: A Daily Journal, bk. 9. Hood, Karen Jean Matsko. Whispering Pine Press International, ed. 2015. (Children's Journal Series). 160p. (J). spiral bd. 15.95 *(978-1-59649-416-9(6))* Whispering Pine Pr. International, Inc.

—My Holiday Memories Scrapbook for Foster Kids: A Holiday Memories Scrapbook for Kids, Bk.1. Hood, Karen Jean Matsko. Whispering Pine Press International, ed. 2014. (Childrens Scrapbook Ser.). 124p. (J). per. 19.95 *(978-1-59649-925-6(7))* Whispering Pine Pr. International, Inc.

—My Special Care Journal for Adopted Children: A Daily Journal, Vol. 7. Hood, Karen Jean Matsko. Whispering Pine Press International, ed. 2014. (Children's Journal Series). 164p. (J). 19.95 *(978-1-59210-279-2(4))* Whispering Pine Pr. International, Inc.

—My Special Care Journal for Foster Children: A Daily Journal, bk. 8. Hood, Karen Jean Matsko. Whispering Pine Press International, ed. 2014. (Children Scrapbook Journal Ser.). 160p. (J). spiral bd. 15.95 *(978-1-59210-274-7(3))* Whispering Pine Pr. International, Inc.

—My Special Care Scrapbook for Adopted Children: A Special Care Scrapbook for Adopted Children, bk. 7. Hood, Karen Jean Matsko. Whispering Pine Press International, ed. 2014. (Childrens Scrapbook Ser.). 124p. (J). spiral bd. 21.95 *(978-1-59649-927-0(3))*; per. 19.95 *(978-1-59649-629-3(0))* Whispering Pine Pr. International, Inc.

—My Special Care Scrapbook for Adopted Children: A Special Scrapbook for Adopted Children, bk. 7. Hood, Karen Jean Matsko. Whispering Pine Press International, ed. 2014. (Childrens Scrapbook Ser.). 124p. (J). 29.95 *(978-1-59210-493-2(2))* Whispering Pine Pr. International, Inc.

—Opening Day. Hood, Karen Jean Matsko. Whispering Pine Press International, ed. l.t. ed. 2014. (Bernadette's Bakery Ser.). 224p. pap. 22.95 *(978-1-930948-27-3(1))* Whispering Pine Pr. International, Inc.

—Petting Farm Fun: Hood Picture Book Series - Book 3, bk. 3. Hood, Karen Jean Matsko. Whispering Pine Press International Staff, ed. 2015. (Hood Picture Book Ser.). (ENG.). 46p. (J). pap. 15.95 *(978-1-59434-905-8(3))* Whispering Pine Pr. International, Inc.

—Petting Farm Fun, Translated Amharic, Vol. 3. Whispering Pine Press International, ed. 2014. (Hood Picture Book Ser.). (AMH.). 42p. (J). per. 19.95 *(978-1-59649-554-8(5))* Whispering Pine Pr. International, Inc.

—Tanka Thoughts: A Collection of Poetry, bk. 11. Hood, Karen Jean Matsko. Whispering Pine Press International, ed. 2014. (Hood Poetry Ser.). 224p. pap. 19.95 *(978-1-930948-52-5(2)*, 1-930948-52-2); pap. 22.95 *(978-1-59808-648-5(0))* Whispering Pine Pr. International, Inc.

—There's a Toad in the Hole: A Big Fat Toad in the Hole, Bk.2. Hood, Karen Jean Matsko. Whispering Pine Press International, ed. 2014. (Hood Poetry Ser.). (J). 29.95 *(978-1-930948-24-2(7))*; per. 19.95 *(978-1-59649-298-1(8))* Whispering Pine Pr. International, Inc.

—Under the Lilacs: A Collection of Children's Poetry, Vol. 1. Hood, Karen Jean Matsko. Whispering Pine Press International, ed. 2014. (Hood Children's Poetry Book Ser.). 160p. (J). 29.95 *(978-1-930948-51-8(4)*, 1-930948-51-4) Whispering Pine Pr. International, Inc.

Artistic Design Services. Girls Can Do Journal: A Daily Journal, bk. 5. Hood, Karen Jean Matsko. Whispering Pine Press International, ed. 2014. (Educational Activity & Coloring Book Ser.). 164p. (J). spiral bd. 15.95 *(978-1-59649-361-2(5))* Whispering Pine Pr. International, Inc.

—Grandma Bert's Favorite Christmas Sweets Recipes: A Collection of Recipes from Grandma Bert, Vol. 8. Hood, Karen Jean Matsko. Whispering Pine Press International, ed. 2014. 324p. 34.95 *(978-1-59210-538-0(6))* Whispering Pine Pr. International, Inc.

Artistic Design Services Staff. Adventure Travel: A Daily Journal, Vol. 1. Hood, Karen Jean Matsko. Whispering Pine Press International, Inc. Staff, ed. 2014. (Hood Journal Ser.). (ENG.). 130p. (J). 19.95 *(978-1-59210-428-4(2))*; per. 13.95 *(978-1-59210-134-4(8)*, 1-59210-134-8) Whispering Pine Pr. International, Inc.

—Gaited Horse Journal: A Daily Journal, Bk.4. Hood, Karen Jean Matsko. Whispering Pine Press International, Inc. Staff, ed. 2014. (Children's Journal Series). 160p. (J). 19.95 *(978-1-59434-790-0(5))*; per. 13.95 *(978-1-59434-791-7(3))*; spiral bd. 15.95 *(978-1-59434-795-5(6))* Whispering Pine Pr. International, Inc.

—Getaway Country Kitchen Catalog: Gourmet & Country Grocery, Take-Out Food & Catering Service Products, no. 3. Hood, Karen Jean Matsko. Whispering Pine Press International, ed. 2014. 160p. pap. 4.99 *(978-1-59210-605-9(6))* Whispering Pine Pr. International, Inc.

—Icelandic Horse: A Daily Journal, bk. 6. Hood, Karen Jean Matsko. Whispering Pine Press International, ed. 2014. (Hood Activity & Coloring Book Ser.). 128p. (J). spiral bd. 15.95 *(978-1-59649-422-0(0))* Whispering Pine Pr. International, Inc.

—Kids' Kindness: Adventures in Learning, Vol. 9. Hood, Karen Jean Matsko. Whispering Pine Press International, ed. 2015. 160p. (J). 29.95 *(978-1-59808-759-8(2))*; per. 19.95 *(978-1-59808-757-4(6))* Whispering Pine Pr. International, Inc.

—Kids' Kindness Journal: A Daily Journal, bk. 9. Hood, Karen Jean Matsko. Whispering Pine Press International, ed. 2015. (Children's Journal Series). 160p. (J). 19.95 *(978-1-59649-431-2(X))* Whispering Pine Pr. International, Inc.

—Lost Medal, Christian Edition: With Bible Verses & Christian Themes. Hood, Karen Jean Matsko. Whispering Pine Press International, ed. 2014. (Hood Christian Horse Story Ser.). 160p. (J). Bk.1. pap. 19.95 *(978-1-59808-618-8(9))*; Vol. 1. 29.95 *(978-1-59808-617-1(0))* Whispering Pine Pr. International, Inc.

—My Adoption Celebration Scrapbook: A Special Celebration of My Adoption, bk. 2. Hood, Karen Jean Matsko. Whispering Pine Press International, ed. 2014. (Childrens Scrapbook Ser.). 124p. (J). 29.95 *(978-1-59210-265-5(4))*; per. 19.95 *(978-1-59649-523-4(5))* Whispering Pine Pr. International, Inc.

—My Birth Celebration Scrapbook: A Celebration of My Birth Scrapbook for Children, Vol. 3. Hood, Karen Jean Matsko. Whispering Pine Press International, Inc. Staff, ed. 2014. (Childrens Scrapbook Ser.). 128p. (J). per. 19.95 *(978-1-59649-520-3(0))* Whispering Pine Pr. International, Inc.

—My Holiday Memories Journal: A Daily Journal, bk. 5. Hood, Karen Jean Matsko. Whispering Pine Press International, ed. 2014. (Children Scrapbook Journal Ser.). 128p. (J). 19.95 *(978-1-59210-645-5(5))* Whispering Pine Pr. International, Inc.

—My Holiday Memories Scrapbook for Adopted Kids: A Holiday Memories Scrapbook for Kids, bk. 4. Hood, Karen Jean Matsko. Whispering Pine Press International, ed. 2014. (Childrens Scrapbook Ser.). 124p. (J). 29.95 *(978-1-59210-476-5(2))*; spiral bd. 21.95 *(978-1-59649-924-9(9))*; per. 19.95 *(978-1-59649-326-1(7))* Whispering Pine Pr. International, Inc.

—My Holiday Memories Scrapbook for Foster Kids: A Holiday Memories Scrapbook for Kids. Hood, Karen Jean Matsko. Whispering Pine Press International, ed. 2014. (Childrens Scrapbook Ser.). 124p. (J). Bk.1. spiral bd. 21.95 *(978-1-59649-633-0(9))*; Vol. 1. 29.95 *(978-1-59210-481-9(9))* Whispering Pine Pr. International, Inc.

—My Holiday Memories Scrapbook for Kids, bk. 5. Hood, Karen Jean Matsko. Whispering Pine Press International, ed. 2014. (Childrens Scrapbook Ser.). (ENG.). 190p. (J). 29.95 *(978-1-59210-620-2(X))* Whispering Pine Pr. International, Inc.

—My Holiday Memories Scrapbook for Kids, Bk.5. Hood, Karen Jean Matsko. Whispering Pine Press International, Inc. Staff, ed. 2014. (Childrens Scrapbook Ser.). (ENG.). 190p. (J). spiral bd. 21.95 *(978-1-59649-926-3(5))* Whispering Pine Pr. International, Inc.

—My Special Care Scrapbook for Children: A Special Scrapbook for Children, bk. 6. Hood, Karen Jean Matsko. Whispering Pine Press International, Inc. Staff, ed. 2014. (Childrens Scrapbook Ser.). 128p. (J). 29.95 *(978-1-59649-631-6(2))*; spiral bd. 21.95 *(978-1-59210-623-3(4))* Whispering Pine Pr. International, Inc.

—My Special Care Scrapbook for Foster Children: A Special Scrapbook for Foster Children, bk. 8. Hood, Kared Jean Matsko. Whispering Pine Press International, ed. 2014. (Childrens Scrapbook Ser.). (ENG.). 122p. (J). pap. 19.95 *(978-1-59649-928-7(1))* Whispering Pine Pr. International, Inc.

—Petting Farm Fun, bk. 3. Hood, Karen Jean Matsko. Whispering Pine Press International, ed. 2014. (Hood Picture Book Ser.). (ENG.). 46p. (J). 24.95 *(978-1-59434-885-3(5))* Whispering Pine Pr. International, Inc.

—Petting Farm Fun, Bilingual English & Hindi. Hood, Karen Jean Matsko. Whispering Pine Press International, ed. ed. 2015. (Hood Picture Book Ser.). (ENG & HIN.). 36p. (J). Bk. 3. pap. 29.95 *(978-1-59808-646-1(4))*; Vol. 3. 34.95 *(978-1-59808-641-6(3))*; Vol. 3. 94.99 *(978-1-59808-642-3(1))*; Vol. 3. pap. 25.95 *(978-1-59808-657-7(X))* Whispering Pine Pr. International, Inc.

—Petting Farm Fun, Bilingual English & Portuguese. Hood, Karen Jean Matsko. Whispering Pine Press International, ed. ed. 2015. (Hood Picture Book Ser.). (ENG & POR.). 36p. (J). Bk. 3. pap. 29.95 *(978-1-59808-813-7(0))*; Vol. 3. 34.95 *(978-1-59808-811-3(4))*; Vol. 3. 94.95 *(978-1-59808-812-0(2))*; Vol. 3. pap. 25.95 *(978-1-59808-814-4(9))* Whispering Pine Pr. International, Inc.

—Petting Farm Fun, Bilingual English & Spanish, Vol. 3. Hood, Karen Jean Matsko. Whispering Pine Press International, ed. ed. 2015. (Hood Picture Book Ser.). (ENG & SPA.). 36p. (J). 34.95 *(978-1-59808-822-9(X))*; 94.99 *(978-1-59808-823-6(8))*; pap. 25.95 *(978-1-59808-825-0(4))* Whispering Pine Pr. International, Inc.

—Petting Farm Fun, Translated Hindi, bk. 3. Hood, Karen Jean Matsko. Whispering Pine Press International, ed. 2014. (Hood Picture Book Ser.). (HIN.). 46p. (J). 24.95 *(978-1-59808-843-4(2))*; 84.99 *(978-1-59808-844-1(0))*; pap. 15.95 *(978-1-59808-845-8(9))*; pap. 19.95 *(978-1-59808-846-5(7))* Whispering Pine Pr. International, Inc.

—Petting Farm Fun, Translated Portuguese, bk. 3. Hood, Karen Jean Matsko. Whispering Pine Press International, ed. 2014. (Hood Picture Book Ser.). (POR.). 46p. (J). 24.95 *(978-1-59808-864-9(5))*; 84.99 *(978-1-59808-865-6(3))*; pap. 15.95 *(978-1-59808-866-3(1))*; pap. 19.95 *(978-1-59808-867-0(X))* Whispering Pine Pr. International, Inc.

Artists of the Kuru Art Project in Botswana, San. Ostrich & Lark. Nelson, Marilyn. 2012. (ENG.). 32p. (J). (gr. k-4). 16.95 *(978-1-59078-702-1(1))* Boyds Mills Pr.

Artists of Troublemaker Studios Staff. The Adventures of Shark Boy & Lava Girl in 3-D: The Illustrated Screenplay. Rodriguez, Robert. 2005. (Shark Boy & Lava Girl Adventures Ser.). 128p. (J). *(978-1-933104-01-0(5))* Troublemaker Publishing, LP.

Artists, S. I. Let's Go to the Farm (Vamos a la Granja) Froeb, Lori C. & Weiss, Ellen. 2012. (Lift-The-Flap Ser.). (ENG.). 10p. (J). (gr. -1-k). bds. 9.99 *(978-0-7944-2572-2(0))* Reader's Digest Assn., Inc., The.

—Let's Go to the Zoo! Froeb, Lori C. & Weiss, Ellen. 2012. (Lift-The-Flap Ser.). (ENG.). 10p. (J). (gr. -1-k). bds. 9.99 *(978-0-7944-2583-8(6))* Reader's Digest Assn., Inc., The.

Artists, Various. A New Take on ABCs - S Is for Smiling Sunrise: An Alphabet Book of Goodness, Beauty, & Wonder [Free Audio-Book Download Included]. Wadhwa, Vick. l.t. ed. 2014. 32p. (J). 16.95 *(978-1-940229-12-6(X))* WordsBright.

Artley, Bob. Grady's in the Silo, 1 vol. Townsend, Una Belle. 2003. (ENG.). 32p. (J). (gr. k-3). 16.99 *(978-1-58980-098-4(2))* Pelican Publishing Co., Inc.

—Step Up!, 1 vol. Hahn, Cathe. 2005. (ENG.). 32p. (J). (gr. k-3). 16.99 *(978-1-58980-214-8(4))* Pelican Publishing Co., Inc.

Artley, Bob. Christmas on the Farm, 1 vol. Artley, Bob. 2003. (ENG.). 96p. 22.95 *(978-1-58980-108-0(3))* Pelican Publishing Co., Inc.

Artist Collection Staff. The Dog from Arf! Arf! to Zzzzzz. Artist Collection Staff. 2007. (Artist Collection: the Dog Ser.). 40p. (J). (gr. -1-3). 6.99 *(978-0-06-059859-4(X))* HarperCollins Pubs.

Artman, Townsend, jt. illus. see DeJong Artman, Catherine.

Arts, Richa Kinra. Teddy Bear Princess: A Story about Sharing & Caring. Kats, Jewel. 2012. 24p. (-18). pap. 13.95 *(978-1-61599-163-1(8)*, Marvelous Spirit Pr.) Loving Healing Pr., Inc.

Aruego, Jose. Leo, el Retaño Tardío. Kraus, Robert. Mlawer, Teresa, tr.Tr. of Leo the Late Bloomer. (SPA.). (J). (gr. k-1). pap. 7.95 *(978-1-930332-02-7(5)*, LC30358) Lectorum Pubns., Inc.

—Whose Mouse Are You? Kraus, Robert. 2005. (Stories to Go! Ser.). (ENG.). 40p. (J). 4.99 *(978-1-4169-0311-6(9)*, Simon & Schuster/Paula Wiseman Bks.) Simon & Schuster/Paula Wiseman Bks.

Aruego, Jose & Dewey, Ariane. Antarctic Antics: A Book of Penguin Poems. Sierra, Judy. 2003. (ENG.). 32p. (J). (gr. -1-3). pap. 6.99 *(978-0-15-204602-6(X))* Houghton Mifflin Harcourt Publishing Co.

—The Big, Big Wall. Howard, Reginald. ed. 2003. (Green Light Readers Level 1 Ser.). (ENG.). 24p. (J). (gr. -1-3). pap.

3.95 *(978-0-15-204853-2(7))* Houghton Mifflin Harcourt Publishing Co.

—Duck, Duck, Goose! (A Coyote's on the Loose!) Beaumont, Karen. 2004. 32p. (J). (gr. -1-2). lib. bdg. 18.89 *(978-0-06-050804-3(3))* HarperCollins Pubs.

—Duck, Duck, Goose! A Coyote's on the Loose! Beaumont, Karen. 2004. (ENG.). 32p. (J). (gr. -1-2). 17.99 *(978-0-06-050802-9(7))* HarperCollins Pubs.

—How Chipmunk Got His Stripes. Bruchac, Joseph & Bruchac, James. 2003. (ENG.). 32p. (J). (gr. k-3). 6.99 *(978-0-14-250021-7(6),* Puffin) Penguin Publishing Group.

—Lizard's Guest. Shannon, George. 2003. 32p. (J). 16.89 *(978-0-06-009084-5(7))* HarperCollins Pubs.

—Turtle's Race with Beaver. Bruchac, Joseph & Bruchac, James. 2005. (ENG.). 32p. (J). (gr. k-3). pap. 5.99 *(978-0-14-240466-9(7),* Puffin) Penguin Publishing Group.

Aruego, Jose, jt. illus. see Dewey, Ariane.

Arya, Viki. The Boy Who Became King. Dutta, Arup Kumar. 2004. 122p. (J). *(978-81-291-0405-2(9))* Rupa & Co.

Aryai, Sia, photos by. 1 2 3s. (Baby Bright Board Bks.). 10p. (J). (gr. -1). 5.95 *(978-1-56565-824-0(8),* 08248W, Roxbury Park Juvenile) Lowell Hse. Juvenile.

Aryan, Kiana. The Real Beauty. Mohr, Kathryn. 2010. 106p. (J). pap. 14.95 *(978-1-61660-000-6(4))* Reflections Publishing, Inc.

Arzoumanian, Alik. So Many Houses. Bass, Hester Thompson. 2007. (Rookie Reader Repetitive Text Ser.). 32p. (gr. k-2). 14.95 *(978-0-7569-8049-8(6))* Perfection Learning Corp.

—So Many Houses. Bass, Hester Thompson & Thompson-Bass, Hester. 2006. (Rookie Reader Skill Set Ser.). (ENG.). 32p. (J). (gr. k-2). pap. 4.95 *(978-0-516-24999-5(1))* Scholastic Library Publishing.

—Tunjur! Tunjur! Tunjur! A Palestinian Folktale, 0 vols. MacDonald, Margaret Read. 2012. (ENG.). 32p. (J). (gr. -1-3). pap. 7.99 *(978-0-7614-6312-2(7),* 9780761463122, Amazon Children's Publishing) Amazon Publishing.

Asada, Hiroyuki. Tegami Bachi. Asada, Hiroyuki. 2010. (Tegami Bachi Ser.: 2). (ENG.). 200p. (gr. 8-18). pap. 9.99 *(978-1-4215-2950-9(5))* Viz Media.

—Tegami Bachi Vol. 3: Letter Bee. Asada, Hiroyuki. 2011. (Tegami Bachi Ser.: 6). (ENG.). 188p. pap. 9.99 *(978-1-4215-3339-1(1));* 192p. pap. 9.99 *(978-1-4215-3180-9(1))* Viz Media.

Asamiya, Kia. Dark Angel: The Path to Destiny, 5 bks., Bk. 1. Asamiya, Kia. rev. ed. 2003. 200p. pap. 9.99 *(978-1-58664-899-2(3),* CMX 62301MM, CPM Manga) Central Park Media Corp.

—Nadesico, 4 vols., Vol. 1. Asamiya, Kia. rev. ed. 2003. Orig. Title: Meteor Schlachtschiff Nadesico. 192p. pap. 9.99 *(978-1-56219-901-2(3),* CMX 62401MM, CPM Manga) Central Park Media Corp.

—Nadesico, 4 vols., Vol. 3. Asamiya, Kia. Cebulski, C. B. & Furuhata, Noriko, trs. from JPN. 2004. Orig. Title: Meteor Schlachtschiff Nadesico. 168p. pap. 9.99 *(978-1-58664-940-1(X),* CMX 62403MM, CPM Manga) Central Park Media Corp.

—Silent Mobius. Asamiya, Kia. 2003. (Silent Mobius Ser.: Vol. 10). (ENG.). Vol. 10. 184p. pap. 12.95 *(978-1-56931-891-1(3));* Vol. 11. 176p. pap. 12.95 *(978-1-59116-070-0(7))* Viz Media.

—Steam Detectives. Asamiya, Kia. (Steam Detectives Ser.). (ENG.). Vol. 6. 2003. 192p. pap. 12.95 *(978-1-56931-892-8(1));* Vol. 7. 2004. 184p. pap. 12.95 *(978-1-59116-208-7(4))* Viz Media.

Asare, Meshack. Sosu's Call. Asare, Meshack. 2006. (ENG.). 40p. (J). (gr. k-4). 11.99 *(978-1-929132-21-8(2))* Kane Miller.

Asbill, Annette. Mouse's Forever Christmas. Asbill, Annette. 2012. 34p. pap. *(978-0-9860247-3-3(2))* Roxby Media Ltd.

Asbjørnsen, Peter Christen, jt. illus. see Arenson, Roberta.

Asch, Devin. Mr. Maxwell's Mouse, 0 vols. Asch, Frank. 2014. (ENG.). 32p. (J). pap. 8.95 *(978-1-77138-117-8(5))* Kids Can Pr., Ltd. CAN. Dist: Univ. of Toronto Pr.

—Mrs. Marlowe's Mice. Asch, Frank. 2007. (ENG.). 32p. (J). (gr. k-4). 17.95 *(978-1-55453-022-9(9))* Kids Can Pr., Ltd. CAN. Dist: Univ. of Toronto Pr.

Asch, Devin, jt. illus. see Asch, Frank.

Asch, Frank. Gravity Buster: Journal #2 of a Cardboard Genius. Asch, Frank. 2007. (ENG.). 144p. (J). (gr. 2-5). 5.95 *(978-1-55453-069-4(5))* Kids Can Pr., Ltd. CAN. Dist: Univ. of Toronto Pr.

—Gravity Buster: Journal 2 of a Cardboard Genius. Asch, Frank. 2007. (Journals of a Cardboard Genius Ser.). (ENG.). 144p. (J). (gr. 2-5). 15.95 *(978-1-55453-068-7(7))* Kids Can Pr., Ltd. CAN. Dist: Univ. of Toronto Pr.

—Happy Birthday, Big Bad Wolf. Asch, Frank. 2011. (ENG.). 32p. (J). (gr. -1-2). 16.95 *(978-1-55337-368-1(5))* Kids Can Pr., Ltd. CAN. Dist: Univ. of Toronto Pr.

—Happy Birthday, Moon. Asch, Frank. 2014. (Moonbear Ser.). (ENG.). 32p. (J). (gr. -1-3). 7.99 *(978-1-4424-9400-8(X),* Simon & Schuster/Paula Wiseman Bks.) Simon & Schuster/Paula Wiseman Bks.

—Milk & Cookies. Asch, Frank. 2015. (Frank Asch Bear Book Ser.). (ENG.). 40p. (J). (gr. -1-3). 16.99 *(978-1-4424-6672-2(3),* Simon & Schuster/Paula Wiseman Bks.) Simon & Schuster/Paula Wiseman Bks.

—Monsieur Saguette & His Baguette. Asch, Frank. 2006. (ENG.). 32p. (J). (gr. -1-2). 6.95 *(978-1-55337-978-2(0))* Kids Can Pr., Ltd. CAN. Dist: Univ. of Toronto Pr.

—Moonbear's Bargain. Asch, Frank. 2014. (Moonbear Ser.). (ENG.). 32p. (J). (gr. -1-3). 17.99 *(978-1-4424-9436-7(0),* Simon & Schuster/Paula Wiseman Bks.) Simon & Schuster/Paula Wiseman Bks.

—Moonbear's Pet. Asch, Frank. 2014. (Moonbear Ser.). (ENG.). 32p. (J). (gr. -1-3). 17.99 *(978-1-4424-9430-5(1),* Simon & Schuster/Paula Wiseman Bks.) Simon & Schuster/Paula Wiseman Bks.

—Moonbear's Shadow. Asch, Frank. 2014. (Moonbear Ser.). (ENG.). 32p. (J). (gr. -1-3). 7.99 *(978-1-4424-9426-8(3),* Simon & Schuster/Paula Wiseman Bks.) Simon & Schuster/Paula Wiseman Bks.

—Moonbear's Skyfire. Asch, Frank. 2014. (Moonbear Ser.). (ENG.). 32p. (J). (gr. -1-3). 7.99 *(978-1-4424-9409-1(3),* Simon & Schuster/Paula Wiseman Bks.) Simon & Schuster/Paula Wiseman Bks.

—Moonbear's Sunrise. Asch, Frank. 2014. (Moonbear Ser.). (ENG.). 32p. (J). (gr. -1-3). 16.99 *(978-1-4424-6647-0(2),* Simon & Schuster/Paula Wiseman Bks.) Simon & Schuster/Paula Wiseman Bks.

—Mooncake. Asch, Frank. 2014. (Moonbear Ser.). (ENG.). 32p. (J). (gr. -1-3). 7.99 *(978-1-4424-9403-9(4),* Simon & Schuster/Paula Wiseman Bks.) Simon & Schuster/Paula Wiseman Bks.

—Moondance. Asch, Frank. 2014. (Moonbear Ser.). (ENG.). 32p. (J). (gr. -1-3). 17.99 *(978-1-4424-6659-3(6),* Simon & Schuster/Paula Wiseman Bks.) Simon & Schuster/Paula Wiseman Bks.

—Moongame. Asch, Frank. 2014. (Moonbear Ser.). (ENG.). 32p. (J). (gr. -1-3). 7.99 *(978-1-4424-9406-0(9),* Simon & Schuster/Paula Wiseman Bks.) Simon & Schuster/Paula Wiseman Bks.

—Pizza. Asch, Frank. 2015. (Frank Asch Bear Book Ser.). (ENG.). 32p. (J). (gr. -1-3). 16.99 *(978-1-4424-6675-3(8),* Simon & Schuster/Paula Wiseman Bks.) Simon & Schuster/Paula Wiseman Bks.

—Star Jumper: Journal of a Cardboard Genius. Asch, Frank. 2006. (ENG.). 128p. (J). (gr. 2-5). 14.95 *(978-1-55337-886-0(5));* pap. 7.95 *(978-1-55337-887-7(3))* Kids Can Pr., Ltd. CAN. Dist: Univ. of Toronto Pr.

—Time Twister: Journal 3 of a Cardboard Genius. Asch, Frank. 2008. (Journals of a Cardboard Genius Ser.). (ENG.). 144p. (J). (gr. 4-7). 14.95 *(978-1-55453-230-8(2));* pap. 5.95 *(978-1-55453-231-5(0))* Kids Can Pr., Ltd. CAN. Dist: Univ. of Toronto Pr.

Asch, Frank & Asch, Devin. Mr. Maxwell's Mouse. Asch, Frank & Asch, Devin. 2004. (ENG.). 32p. (J). (gr. k-4). 18.95 *(978-1-55337-486-2(X))* Kids Can Pr., Ltd. CAN. Dist: Univ. of Toronto Pr.

Asch, Frank & Asch, Frank. Happy Birthday, Moon. Asch, Frank & Asch, Frank. 2005. (Stories to Go! Ser.). (ENG.). 32p. (J). 4.99 *(978-1-4169-0307-9(0),* Simon & Schuster/Paula Wiseman Bks.) Simon & Schuster/Paula Wiseman Bks.

Asch, Frank, jt. illus. see Asch, Frank.

Asensio, Agusti. Tranquila Tragaleguas: La Tortuga Cabezota. Ende, Michael. 2003.Tr. of Tranquila Trampeltreu. (SPA.). 42p. (J). (gr. k-3). pap. 8.95 *(978-84-204-3709-5(3))* Santillana USA Publishing Co., Inc.

Ash. Imagine Travelling to the Most Mysterious & Unusual Places! Praveeta. 2011. (ENG.). 146p. (J). pap. *(978-0-9872096-0-3(4),* Travel Tales of Elves) Praveeta Kumar.

Ashby, Chris. Chocolate Milk Likes Me. Albrecht, John, Jr. 2006. 16p. (J). pap. 8.99 *(978-0-9778586-3-7(4),* CRP004); pap. 8.99 *(978-0-9778586-2-0(6),* CRP0003) Crooked River Pr. (Blue Jay Bks.).

Ashcraft Jr, D. C. Charlie Chicken Hawk, 1 vol. Hayes, Beverly. 2009. 20p. pap. 24.95 *(978-1-60836-673-6(1))* America Star Bks.

Ashcroft, Colin Michael, et al. A Field Guide to Dragons, Trolls, & Other Dangerous Monsters, 1 vol. Sautter, A. J. 2014. (Fantasy Field Guides). (ENG.). 32p. (gr. 3-4). lib. bdg. 27.32 *(978-1-4914-0691-5(7))* Capstone Pr., Inc.

—A Field Guide to Elves, Dwarves, & Other Magical Folk, 1 vol. Sautter, A. J. 2014. (Fantasy Field Guides). (ENG.). 32p. (gr. 3-4). lib. bdg. 27.32 *(978-1-4914-0692-2(5))* Capstone Pr., Inc.

—A Field Guide to Goblins, Gremlins, & Other Wicked Creatures, 1 vol. Sautter, A. J. 2014. (Fantasy Field Guides). (ENG.). 32p. (gr. 3-4). lib. bdg. 27.32 *(978-1-4914-0689-2(5))* Capstone Pr., Inc.

Ashdown, Rebecca. Bob & Flo Play Hide & Seek. 2016. (J). ***(978-0-544-59631-3(5))*** Harcourt.

Ashe, E. Happy Horse: A Children's Book of Horses. Ashe, E. 2003. 18p. (J). bds. 12.95 *(978-0-9727849-0-0(X),* 0-9727849-0-X) Happy Horse Publishing, Ltd.

Asher, James. The Adoption. Florence, Leigh Anne. 2003. (Woody: the Kentucky Wiener Ser.). 32p. (J). (gr. -1-3). per. 12.95 *(978-0-9741417-0-1(4))* HotDiggetyDog Pr.

—Kentucky's Boone: The Pioneer Spirit. Burton, K. Melissa. 2008. 30p. (J). (gr. 4-7). pap. 14.95 *(978-1-934898-03-1(1))* McClanahan Publishing Hse., Inc.

—Mr. Dogwood Goes to Washington. Florence, Leigh Anne. 2008. (Woody the Kentucky Wiener Ser.). 56p. (J). (gr. 2-8). pap. 12.95 *(978-0-9741417-5-6(5))* HotDiggetyDog Pr.

—Welcomes a Dad, Vol. 2. Florence, Leigh Anne. 2004. (Woody: the Kentucky Wiener Ser.). 32p. (J). (gr. -1-3). per. 12.95 *(978-0-9741417-1-8(2))* HotDiggetyDog Pr.

Asher, James, photos by. Now That's Interesting Kentucky's Capitol. Burton, K. Melissa. 2007. 40p. (J). per. 14.95 *(978-0-913383-96-4(1))* McClanahan Publishing Hse., Inc.

Asher, Mark J., photos by. Old Friends: Great Dogs on the Good Life. Asher, Mark J. 2003. (ENG.). 96p. (gr. 8-17). 14.95 *(978-0-8118-4002-6(6))* Chronicle Bks. LLC.

Ashford, Sylvie. A Huntsman Spider in My House... Ray, Michelle. 2014. (Morgan James Kids Ser.). (ENG.). 34p. pap. 8.95 *(978-1-61448-842-2(8),* 9781614488422) Morgan James Publishing.

Ashihara, Hinako. Sos. Ashihara, Hinako. 2005. (Sos Ser.). (ENG.). 192p. (YA). pap. 9.99 *(978-1-59116-735-8(3))* Viz Media.

Ashley, Carol. Scarum Fair. Swaim, Jessica. 2010. (ENG.). 32p. (J). (gr. 4-6). 17.95 *(978-1-59078-590-4(8),* Wordsong) Boyds Mills Pr.

Ashley Comeaux-Foret. The Day Frasier the Frog Jumped High. Guillot, Angela K. 2011. 20p. pap. 24.95 *(978-1-4626-2312-9(3))* PublishAmerica, Inc.

Ashley, Elana, photos by. Splunkunio Splunkey Detective & Peacemaker Detective y Pacificador: Case One: The Missing Friendship Bracelet Caso Primero: El Brazalete de la Amistad Desaparecido. Ashley, Elana. Nikolov, Stefan V., tr. 2005. (SPA & ENG.). 32p. (J). (gr. k-3). 17.95 *(978-0-9744812-1-0(1))* Dream Image Pr., LLC.

Ashlock, Lisel Jane. Sing a Season Song. Yolen, Jane. 2015. (ENG.). 48p. (J). (gr. 1-3). 18.99 *(978-1-56846-255-4(7),* Creative Editions) Creative Co., The.

Ashman, Iain. How to Draw Buildings. Beasant, Pam. Tatchell, Judy, ed. 2006. (Young Artist Ser.). 32p. (J). (gr. 4-7). pap. 5.99 *(978-0-7945-1371-9(9),* Usborne) EDC Publishing.

Ashton-Briggs, Shelley. Gale's Gold Ring: The Legend of Lincoln's Lost Gold. Ashton, Kenneth. 2012. (ENG.). 198p. pap. 14.95 *(978-1-4327-8224-5(X))* Outskirts Pr., Inc.

Ashworth, Nichol, jt. illus. see Cook, Katie.

Aska, Warabe. Luli, el Iceberg. Takamado, Hisako de. (SPA.). 42p. (J). (gr. k-2). *(978-84-8418-039-5(5),* ZZ5903) Zendrera Zariquiey, Editorial ESP. Dist: Lectorum Pubns., Inc.

Asker, Niklas. The City of Ember: The Graphic Novel. DuPrau, Jeanne. 2012. (Books of Ember Ser.). (ENG.). 144p. (J). (gr. 3-7). 18.99 *(978-0-375-86821-4(6));* pap. 9.99 *(978-0-375-86793-4(7))* Random Hse. Children's Bks. (Random Hse. Bks. for Young Readers).

Askin, Corrina & Clarke, Alan. Something Beginning with P: New Poems from Irish Poets. Cashman, Seamus. 2004. (ENG.). 160p. *(978-0-86278-868-1(4))* O'Brien Pr., Ltd., The.

Asner, Anne-Marie. Klutzy Boy. Asner, Anne-Marie. l.t. ed. 2007. 32p. (J). (gr. -1-2). per. 6.95 *(978-0-9753629-4-5(1))* Matzah Ball Bks.

—Kvetchy Boy. Asner, Anne-Marie. l.t. ed. 2006. 32p. (J). per. 6.95 *(978-0-9753629-3-8(3))* Matzah Ball Bks.

—Noshy Boy. Asner, Anne-Marie. l.t. ed. 2004. 32p. (J). (gr. -1-3). per. 6.95 *(978-0-9753629-1-4(7))* Matzah Ball Bks.

—Shmutzy Girl. Asner, Anne-Marie. l.t. ed. 2004. 32p. (J). (gr. -1-3). per. 6.95 *(978-0-9753629-0-7(9))* Matzah Ball Bks.

Asnong, Jocey. Nuptse & Lohtse Go to the Rockies, 1 vol. 2014. (ENG.). 40p. (J). (gr. k). pap. 12.00 ***(978-1-77160-019-4(5))*** Rocky Mountain Bks. CAN. Dist: Perseus-PGW.

Aspen, Lydia. Sparky Dog: the Pensive Pup. Holden, Susan. l.t. ed. 2011. (ENG.). 40p. pap. 9.99 *(978-1-4611-5755-7(2))* CreateSpace Independent Publishing Platform.

—Sparky Dog: the Trash Hound Beagle. Holden, Susan. l.t. ed. 2011. (ENG.). 40p. pap. 9.99 *(978-1-4611-0143-7(3))* CreateSpace Independent Publishing Platform.

Aspinall, Marc. Really, Really Big Questions about Science. Cave, Holly. ed. 2014. (Really Really Big Questions Ser.). (ENG.). 64p. (J). (gr. 4-7). 16.99 *(978-0-7534-7181-4(7),* Kingfisher) Roaring Brook Pr.

—Surprising Facts about the Human Body. Kingfisher Editors & Dods, Emma. 2014. (ENG.). 32p. (J). (gr. k-3). 15.99 *(978-0-7534-7118-0(3),* Kingfisher) Roaring Brook Pr.

—Wow, I Didn't Know That! Surprising Facts about Animals. Kingfisher Editors et al. 2013. (ENG.). 32p. (J). (gr. k-3). 15.99 *(978-0-7534-7117-3(5),* Kingfisher) Roaring Brook Pr.

—Wow, I Didn't Know That! Surprising Facts about Animals. Dodson, Emma & Woodward, John. 2013. (ENG.). 32p. (J). (gr. k-3). 8.99 *(978-0-7534-7166-1(3),* Kingfisher) Roaring Brook Pr.

—Wow! Surprising Facts about Pirates. Steele, Philip. 2014. (ENG.). 32p. (J). (gr. k-3). 15.99 *(978-0-7534-7188-3(4),* Kingfisher) Roaring Brook Pr.

—Wow! Surprising Facts about the Human Body. Dods, Emma. 2014. (ENG.). 32p. (J). (gr. k-3). 8.99 *(978-0-7534-7185-2(X),* Kingfisher) Roaring Brook Pr.

Aspinall, Neal. National Parks: A Kid's Guide to America's Parks, Monuments & Landmarks. McHugh, Erin. 2012. (ENG.). 128p. (gr. 1-8). 19.95 *(978-1-57912-884-5(X),* Black Dog & Leventhal Pubs. Inc.) Hachette Bks.

Asquith, Ros. Can It Be about Me? Moskowitz, Cheryl. 2013. (ENG.). 96p. (J). (gr. 2-5). pap. 8.99 *(978-1-84780-340-5(7),* Frances Lincoln) Quarto Publishing Group UK GBR. Dist: Hachette Bk. Group.

—The Great Big Book of Families. Hoffman, Mary. 2011. (ENG.). 40p. (J). (gr. k-3). 17.99 *(978-0-8037-3516-3(2),* Dial) Penguin Publishing Group.

—The Great Big Book of Feelings. Hoffman, Mary. 2013. (Great Big Book Ser.). (ENG.). 40p. (J). (gr. -1-2). 17.99 *(978-1-84780-281-1(8),* Frances Lincoln) Quarto Publishing Group UK GBR. Dist: Hachette Bk. Group.

—The Great Big Green Book. Hoffman, Mary Y. 2015. (Great Big Book Ser.). (ENG.). 40p. (J). (gr. -1-3). 18.99 *(978-1-84780-445-7(4),* Frances Lincoln) Quarto Publishing Group UK GBR. Dist: Hachette Bk. Group.

—It's Not Fairy. Quarto Generic Staff. 2013. (ENG.). 32p. (J). (gr. -1-3). 17.99 *(978-1-84780-236-1(2),* Frances Lincoln) Quarto Publishing Group UK GBR. Dist: Hachette Bk. Group.

—Max the Champion. Strick, Alex & Stockdale, Sean. 2014. (ENG.). 32p. (J). (gr. -1-3). 17.99 *(978-1-84780-388-7(1),* Frances Lincoln) Quarto Publishing Group UK GBR. Dist: Hachette Bk. Group.

—Max the Champion. Stockdale, Sean & Strick, Alex. 2014. 32p. (J). pap. 8.99 *(978-1-84780-519-5(1),* Frances Lincoln) Quarto Publishing Group UK GBR. Dist: Littlehampton Bk Services, Ltd.

—The Roman Beanfeast. Cross, Gillian & Quarto Generic Staff. rev. ed. 2014. (ENG.). 88p. (J). (gr. 2-5). pap. 7.99 *(978-1-84780-488-4(8),* Frances Lincoln) Quarto Publishing Group UK GBR. Dist: Hachette Bk. Group.

—Welcome to the Family. Hoffman, Mary. 2014. (ENG.). 32p. (J). (gr. k-4). 17.99 *(978-1-84780-592-8(2),* Frances Lincoln) Quarto Publishing Group UK GBR. Dist: Perseus-PGW.

Asquith, Ros. How to Draw Cartoons. Asquith, Ros. 2006. (Collins Big Cat Ser.). (ENG.). 56p. (J). pap. 6.99 *(978-0-00-718697-6(5))* HarperCollins Pubs. Ltd. GBR. Dist: Independent Pubs. Group.

Asquith, Ros. Vanishing Trick: Poems by Ros Asquith. Asquith, Ros. 2015. (ENG.). 112p. (J). (gr. 3-7). pap. 7.99 ***(978-1-84780-539-3(6),*** Frances Lincoln) Quarto Publishing Group UK GBR. Dist: Hachette Bk. Group.

Asrar, Mahmud. Shadowland: Power Man. 2011. (ENG.). 112p. (YA). (gr. 8-17). 19.99 *(978-0-7851-4397-0(1))* Marvel Worldwide, Inc.

Asrar, Mahmud & Bennett, Joe. Indestructible Hulk - Humanity Bomb, Vol. 4. 2014. (ENG.). 144p. (J). (gr. 4-17). 24.99 *(978-0-7851-5480-8(9))* Marvel Worldwide, Inc.

Assaël, Ivan. A Straggly Smile. Saint Cyr, Vanessa. Petch, Fionn, tr. 2011. (ENG.). 38p. pap. 12.00 *(978-1-4636-5605-8(X))* CreateSpace Independent Publishing Platform.

Assirelli, Francesca. Chicken Licken. (Flip-Up Fairy Tales Ser.). (ENG.). 24p. (J). (gr. -1-2). 2010. *(978-1-84643-333-7(9));* 2009. pap. *(978-1-84643-327-6(4))* Child's Play International Ltd.

—Talia & the Rude Vegetables. Marshall, Linda Elovitz. 2011. (High Holidays Ser.). (ENG.). 24p. (J). (gr. k-3). pap. 6.95 *(978-0-7613-5218-1(X),* Kar-Ben Publishing) Lerner Publishing Group.

Assirelli, Francesca. Talia & the Very YUM Kippur. Marshall, Linda Elovitz. 2015. (ENG.). 24p. (J). (gr. -1-2). 17.99 ***(978-1-4677-5236-7(3),*** Kar-Ben Publishing) Lerner Publishing Group.

—Talia & the Very Yum Kippur. Marshall, Linda Elovitz. 2015. (ENG.). 24p. (J). (gr. -1-2). pap. 7.99 ***(978-1-4677-5240-4(1),*** Kar-Ben Publishing) Lerner Publishing Group.

Astacio, Mrinali Alvarez. Pon, Pon: A Jugar con el Bebé! 2007. (SPA.). 28p. 14.95 *(978-0-8477-1575-6(2))* Univ. of Puerto Rico Pr.

Astacio, Mrinali Álvarez. Qué crees? Rivera-Lassen, Carmen Leonor. 2009. (SPA.). 30p. (J). 11.95 *(978-0-8477-1581-7(7))* Univ. of Puerto Rico Pr.

Astrella, Mark. Hello Ocean. Ryan, Pam Muñoz. 2014. 32p. pap. 8.00 *(978-1-61003-319-0(1))* Center for the Collaborative Classroom.

—Hello, Ocean (Hola Mar) Ryan, Pam Muñoz. Canetti, Yanitzia, tr. from ENG. ed. 2003. (ENG & SPA.). 32p. (J). (gr. -1-2). pap. 7.95 *(978-1-57091-372-3(2))* Charlesbridge Publishing, Inc.

Astrella, Mark, jt. illus. see Brown, Craig McFarland.

Asuao, Kelcey. Being a Boy in Samoa in the 1950s. Lesa, Ropeti F. 2003. (Polynesian Literature Ser.: Vol. 1). xiii, 197p. (J). pap. 19.95 *(978-0-9728126-3-4(6))* Isles of the Sea Pubs.

Atak. Topsy Turvy World. 2013. (ENG.). 30p. (J). (gr. -1). 18.95 *(978-1-909263-04-8(4))* Flying Eye Bks. GBR. Dist: Consortium Bk. Sales & Distribution.

Atanas. The Lost Island. Johnson, E. Pauline. 2010. (ENG.). 40p. (J). (gr. -1-3). pap. 9.95 *(978-1-897476-44-4(2))* Simply Read Bks. CAN. Dist: Ingram Pub. Services.

Atchley, Kendra. Barley & Betsy: Journey #1 A cat & dog's great adventure to the Mall. Johnson, Michael E. 2011. 36p. pap. 24.95 *(978-1-4560-4077-2(4))* America Star Bks.

Athanassiadis, Kiki. Averses et Réglisses Noires. David, Carole. 2004. (Poetry Ser.). (FRE.). 36p. (J). (gr. 7). pap. *(978-2-89021-674-7(8))* Diffusion du livre Mirabel (DLM).

Atherton, Jim. Lucky the Rubber Ducky. London, Adam. 2009. 14p. (J). pap. 14.95 *(978-0-578-00865-3(3))* AthertonCustoms.

Atkin, S. Beth. Gunstories: Life-Changing Experiences with Guns. Atkin, S. Beth. (ENG.). 256p. (gr. 8-12). 2007. (YA). per. 8.99 *(978-0-06-052661-0(0));* 2006. (J). 16.99 *(978-0-06-052659-7(9))* HarperCollins Pubs. (Tegen, Katherine Bks).

Atkins, Aimee & Franfou Studio. Billy's Boatshed - The Project. Atkins, Aimee. 2012. (ENG.). 32p. (J). (gr. -1-k). pap. 11.99 *(978-1-74275-313-3(2))* Random Hse. Australia AUS. Dist: Independent Pubs. Group.

—Billy's Boatshed: MJ Saves the Day. Atkins, Aimee. 2012. (ENG.). 32p. (J). (gr. -1-k). pap. 11.99 *(978-1-74275-314-0(0))* Random Hse. Australia AUS. Dist: Independent Pubs. Group.

Atkins, Alison. God Sent a Baby King. Henning, Heather. 2006. 31p. (J). (gr. -1-3). 14.00 *(978-0-687-49498-9(2))* Abingdon Pr.

—Humpty Dumpty & Friends. 2005. 10p. bds. *(978-1-84510-767-3(5))* Top That! Publishing PLC.

—Incy Wincy Spider & Friends. 2005. 10p. bds. *(978-1-84510-768-0(3))* Top That! Publishing PLC.

—The Magical Mermaids. Hogg, James. 2007. (Sparkling Jigsaw Book Ser.). 10p. (J). (gr. k-3). *(978-1-84666-373-4(3),* Tide Mill Pr.) Top That! Publishing PLC.

—The Midnight Fairies. Top That Publishing Staff, ed. 2007. (Sparkling Jigsaw Book Ser.). 10p. (J). (gr. -1). bds. *(978-1-84666-278-2(8),* Tide Mill Pr.) Top That! Publishing PLC.

—My First Book of Prayers, 1 vol. Freedman, Claire. 2008. 64p. (J). 7.99 *(978-0-8254-7389-0(6),* Candle Bks.) Lion Hudson PLC GBR. Dist: Kregel Pubns.

—There Were Ten Bears in a Bed: A Count-and-Feel Book. Top That Publishing Staff, ed. 2007. (Story Book Ser.). 22p. (J). (gr. -1). bds. *(978-1-84666-130-3(7),* Tide Mill Pr.) Top That! Publishing PLC.

Atkinson, Brett, jt. illus. see Atkinson, Ruth.

Atkinson, Cale. Let's Meet a Veterinarian. Bellisario, Gina. 2013. (Cloverleaf Books — Community Helpers Ser.). (ENG.). 24p. (gr. k-2). pap. 6.95 *(978-1-4677-0806-7(2));* lib. bdg. 23.93 *(978-0-7613-9030-5(8))* Lerner Publishing Group. (Millbrook Pr.).

—Muddy, Mud, Bud. Lakin, Patricia. 2014. (Penguin Young Readers, Level 1 Ser.). (ENG.). 32p. (J). (gr. k-1). pap. 3.99 *(978-0-448-47989-7(3),* Warne, Frederick Pubs.) Penguin Bks., Ltd. GBR. Dist: Penguin Random Hse., LLC.

Atkinson, Cale. To the Sea. Atkinson, Cale. 2015. (ENG.). 48p. (J). (gr. -1-k). 16.99 *(978-1-4847-0813-2(X))* Disney Publishing Worldwide.

Atkinson, Elaine. Baxter Barret Brown's Cowboy Band. McKenzie, Tim A. 2006. (ENG.). 28p. (gr. 2-4). 19.95 *(978-1-931721-77-6(7),* a4a22ca5-3fa1-4c8b-8248-2efe0591d9b2) Bright Sky Pr.

Atkinson, Ruth & Atkinson, Brett. Christmas Cutouts. Atkinson, Ruth & Atkinson, Brett. (J). (gr. k-2). pap. *(978-1-876367-20-6(2))* Wizard Bks.

—Rhyme Templates. Atkinson, Ruth & Atkinson, Brett. (J). (gr. k-2). pap. *(978-1-875739-74-5(2))* Wizard Bks.

—Stick Puppet Templates. Atkinson, Ruth & Atkinson, Brett. (J). (gr. k-2). pap. *(978-1-875739-72-1(6))* Wizard Bks.

—Story Templates. Atkinson, Ruth & Atkinson, Brett. (J). (gr. k-2). pap. *(978-1-875739-73-8(4))* Wizard Bks.

—Traditional Rhyme Templates. Atkinson, Ruth & Atkinson, Brett. (J). (gr. k-2). pap. *(978-1-875739-94-3(7))* Wizard Bks.

Aton, Barbara. Sailwind the Seabird. Knight, Betty. 2005. (J). per. 19.95 *(978-1-59858-017-4(5))* Dog Ear Publishing, LLC.

Attanasio, Fabiana. The Sweet Side of Fairy Tales. 2014. (ENG.). 54p. (gr. k). spiral bd. 19.95 *(978-88-544-0869-2(7))* White Star ITA. Dist: Sterling Publishing Co., Inc.

Attard, Enebor. Samira's Eid. Aktar, Nasreen. 2004. 24p. (J). *(978-1-85269-538-5(2)); (978-1-85269-539-2(0)); (978-1-85269-540-8(4));* (ENG & ARA.). pap. *(978-1-85269-122-6(0));* (ENG & BEN.). pap. *(978-1-85269-131-8(X));* (ENG & GUJ.). pap. *(978-1-85269-132-5(8));* (ENG & SOM.). pap. *(978-1-85269-133-2(6));* (ENG & TUR.). pap. *(978-1-85269-134-9(4));* (ENG & URD.). pap. *(978-1-85269-135-6(2));* (ENG & PAN.). pap. *(978-1-85269-183-7(2));* (ENG & FRE.). pap. *(978-1-85269-502-6(1));* (ENG & PER.). pap. *(978-1-85269-503-3(X));* (ENG & ALB.). pap. *(978-1-85269-572-9(2))* Mantra Lingua.

Atteberry, Kevan. Frankie Stein, 0 vols. Schaefer, Lola M. 2009. (ENG.). 1p. (J). (gr. k-3). pap. 6.99 *(978-0-7614-5608-7(2),* 9780761456087, Amazon Children's Publishing) Amazon Publishing.

—Frankie Stein Starts School, 0 vols. Schaefer, Lola M. 2010. (ENG.). 32p. (J). (gr. k-3). 15.99 *(978-0-7614-5656-8(2),* 9780761456568, Amazon Children's Publishing) Amazon Publishing.

—Halloween Hustle, 0 vols. Gunnufson, Charlotte. 2013. (ENG.). 32p. (J). (gr. -1-2). 16.99 *(978-1-4778-1723-0(9),* 9781477817230, Amazon Children's Publishing) Amazon Publishing.

—Lunchbox & the Aliens. Fields, Bryan W. 2009. (Froonga Ser.). (ENG.). 208p. (J). (gr. 4-7). pap. 11.99 *(978-0-312-56115-4(6))* Square Fish.

Atteberry, Kevan. Bunnies!!! Atteberry, Kevan. 2015. (ENG.). 32p. (J). (gr. -1-3). 12.99 *(978-0-06-230783-5(5))* HarperCollins Pubs.

Atteberry, Kevan J. Boogie Monster. Bissett, Josie. 2011. 36p. (J). (gr. -1-3). 16.95 *(978-1-935414-10-0(0))* Compendium, Inc., Publishing & Communications.

Attia, Caroline. David & the Worry Beast: Helping Children Cope with Anxiety. Guanci, Anne Marie. 2007. (ENG.). 48p. (J). (gr. -1-4). pap. 9.95 *(978-0-88282-275-4(6))* New Horizon Pr. Pubs., Inc.

Attinger, Billy. Baby's First Little Book of Prayers. gif. ed. 2003. (Wee Witness Ser.). 32p. (J). 7.99 *(978-0-7369-1185-6(5))* Harvest Hse. Pubs.

Attoe, Steve & Owlkids Books Inc. Staff. What's the Big Idea? Inventions That Changed Life on Earth Forever. Becker, Helaine. 2009. (ENG.). 96p. (J). (gr. 3-6). pap. 17.95 *(978-1-897349-61-8(0),* Maple Tree Pr.) Owlkids Bks. Inc. CAN. Dist: Perseus-PGW.

Atwell, Debby. Miss Moore Thought Otherwise: How Anne Carroll Moore Created Libraries for Children. Pinborough, Jan. 2013. (ENG.). 40p. (J). (gr. 1-4). 17.99 *(978-0-547-47105-1(X))* Houghton Mifflin Harcourt Publishing Co.

Auberson, Blaise. Eddy the Electron Goes Solar: A Fun & Educational Story about Photovoltaics. Auberson, Kim. 2010. (ENG.). 34p. pap. 14.95 *(978-1-4538-3544-9(X))* CreateSpace Independent Publishing Platform.

Aubert, Elena G. Mis 365 Mejores Adivinanzas. Editorial, Equipo. 2003. (SPA.). *(978-84-7630-904-9(X),* LA30439) Editorial Libsa, S.A. ESP. Dist: Lectorum Pubns., Inc.

Aubin, Antoine, jt. illus. see Shreder, Etienne.

Aubrey, Meg Kelleher, jt. illus. see Beckett, Andrew.

Auch, Herm. Beauty & the Beaks: A Turkey's Cautionary Tale. Auch, Mary Jane. 2008. (ENG.). 32p. (J). (gr. -1-3). pap. 6.95 *(978-0-8234-2164-0(3))* Holiday Hse., Inc.

—The Buk Buk Buk Festival. Auch, Mary Jane. 2015. (ENG.). 32p. (J). (gr. -1-3). 16.95 *(978-0-8234-3201-1(7))* Holiday Hse., Inc.

—Chickerella. Auch, Mary Jane. 2006. (ENG.). 32p. (J). (gr. -1-3). 6.95 *(978-0-8234-2015-5(9))* Holiday Hse., Inc.

—I Was a Third Grade Bodyguard. Auch, Mary Jane. 2003. (ENG.). 73p. (J). (gr. 4-6). tchr. ed. 16.95 *(978-0-8234-1775-9(1))* Holiday Hse., Inc.

—I Was a Third Grade Spy. Auch, Mary Jane. 2004. 86p. (gr. 2-5). 16.00 *(978-0-7569-4138-3(5))* Perfection Learning Corp.

—I Was a Third Grade Spy. Auch, Mary Jane. 2003. (ENG.). 96p. (gr. 3-7). 5.99 *(978-0-440-41871-9(2),* Yearling) Random Hse. Children's Bks.

—Souperchicken. Auch, Mary Jane. 2004. (ENG.). 32p. (J). (gr. -1-3). reprint ed. pap. 6.95 *(978-0-8234-1829-9(4))* Holiday Hse., Inc.

Auch, Herm. Chickerella. Auch, Herm, tr. Auch, Mary Jane. 2005. (ENG.). 32p. (J). 17.95 *(978-0-8234-1804-6(9))* Holiday Hse., Inc.

Auch, Herm & Auch, Mary Jane. Beauty & the Beaks: A Turkey's Cautionary Tale. Auch, Mary Jane. 2007. (ENG.). 32p. (J). (gr. -1-3). 17.95 *(978-0-8234-1990-6(8))* Holiday Hse., Inc.

Auch, Herm, jt. illus. see Auch, Mary Jane.

Auch, Herm, jt. illus. see Jane, Mary.

Auch, Mary Jane. The Plot Chickens. Auch, Mary Jane. 2010. (ENG.). 32p. (J). (gr. -1-3). pap. 7.99 *(978-0-8234-2307-1(7))* Holiday Hse., Inc.

Auch, Mary Jane & Auch, Herm. The Plot Chickens. Auch, Mary Jane. 2009. (ENG.). 32p. (J). (gr. -1-3). 16.95 *(978-0-8234-2087-2(6))* Holiday Hse., Inc.

Auch, Mary Jane, jt. illus. see Auch, Herm.

Auchter, Chris. Jenneli's Dance, 1 vol. Denny, Elizabeth. ed. 2008. (ENG.). 44p. pap. 12.95 *(978-1-894778-61-9(8))* Theytus Bks., Ltd. CAN. Dist: Univ. of Toronto Pr.

Auchter, Christopher. Chuck in the City. Wheeler, Jordan. rev. ed. 2009. (Chuck Ser.). (ENG.). 32p. (gr. -1-3). pap. 10.95 *(978-1-894778-81-7(2))* Theytus Bks., Ltd. CAN. Dist: Univ. of Toronto Pr.

Auclair, Joan. A Leer y Jugar! con Bebés y Niños Pequeños. Oppenheim, Joanne F. & Oppenheim, Stephanie. 2006.Tr. of Read It! Play It! with Babies & Toddlers. (SPA.). 102p. pap. 10.00 *(978-0-9721050-5-7(0))* Oppenheim Toy Portfolio, Inc.

—Read It! Play It! Oppenheim, Joanne F. & Oppenheim, Stephanie. 2005. 176p. pap. 10.00 *(978-0-9721050-1-9(8))* Oppenheim Toy Portfolio, Inc.

Audouin, Laurent. Diego from Madrid. Gamonal, Dulce. 2014. (AV2 Fiction Readalong Ser.: Vol. 124). (ENG.). 32p. (J). (gr. -1-3). lib. bdg. 34.28 *(978-1-4896-2280-8(2),* AV2 by Weigl) Weigl Pubs., Inc.

—Keeping It Green! 2009. (Taking Action for My Planet Ser.). 32p. (YA). (gr. 3-6). lib. bdg. 22.60 *(978-1-60754-797-6(X))* Windmill Bks.

Audrey, Colman, jt. illus. see Coleman, Audrey.

Audrey, Crosby. View from the Middle of the Road: Where the Greenest Grass Grows, 3 vols., volume I. Clark, Lucinda. Brenda, Baratto, ed. 2004. 55p. per. 9.00 *(978-0-9727703-1-6(3),* 706 855-6173) P.R.A. Publishing.

Auer, Lois. Lucy & the Red-Tailed Hawk. Cerone, Diane. 2007. 32p. (J). pap. 17.00 *(978-0-8059-7565-9(9))* Dorrance Publishing Co., Inc.

Auerbach, Adam. Edda: A Little Valkyrie's First Day of School. Auerbach, Adam. 2014. (ENG.). 40p. (J). (gr. -1-3). 16.99 *(978-0-8050-9703-0(1),* Holt, Henry & Co. Bks. For Young Readers) Holt, Henry & Co.

Auerbach, Joshua. Baby Shadows, 1. Auerbach, Joshua. 2003. 8p. (J). bds. 10.00 *(978-0-9744928-0-3(9))* Baby Shadows.

Augarde, Steve. Garage: A Pop-up Book. Augarde, Steve. 2005. 10p. (J). (gr. k-4). reprint ed. 15.00 *(978-0-7567-9299-2(1))* DIANE Publishing Co.

Auger, Dale. Mwâkwa Talks to the Loon: A Cree Story for Children, 1 vol. Auger, Dale. 2008. (ENG.). 32p. (J). pap. *(978-1-894974-32-5(8))* Heritage Hse.

Aughe, Roger. Fun Lovin' Delanie Jo. Hildreth, Ruth Erixon. 2012. 36p. pap. 24.95 *(978-1-4626-7851-8(3))* America Star Bks.

—Nicholas James & Missy. Hildreth, Joann R. 2011. 28p. pap. 24.95 *(978-1-4626-0041-0(7))* America Star Bks.

Augusseau, Stphanie. Celia. Vallat, Christelle. 2014. 36p. pap. 16.99 *(978-1-4413-1536-6(5))* Peter Pauper Pr. Inc.

Auh, Yoonil. A Guide to Practicing Repertoire: Level 1, 11 vols. Auh, Yoonil, photos by. 2003. 85p. (gr. k-12). pap. 135.00 *(978-1-882858-61-3(1))* Yoon-il Auh/Intrepid Pixels.

—A Guide to Practicing Repertoire: Level 2, 11 vols. Auh, Yoonil, photos by. 2003. 85p. (gr. k-12). pap. 135.00 *(978-1-882858-62-0(X))* Yoon-il Auh/Intrepid Pixels.

—Representation Music. Auh, Yoonil, photos by. 2003. 28p. (gr. k-12). pap., instr.'s gde. ed. 25.00 *(978-1-882858-55-2(7))* Yoon-il Auh/Intrepid Pixels.

—Representation Music: A New Approch to Creating Sound & Representing Music. Auh, Yoonil, photos by. 2003. 45p. (gr. k-12). pap. 17.00 *(978-1-882858-54-5(9))* Yoon-il Auh/Intrepid Pixels.

—Singing Hand: Study of Vibrato. Auh, Yoonil, photos by. 2003. (gr. k-12). 50p. pap. 16.00 *(978-1-882858-59-0(X));* 45p. pap. 16.00 *(978-1-882858-60-6(3))* Yoon-il Auh/Intrepid Pixels.

Aukerman, Robert J. Dream Machine: A Growing Field Adventure. Hoog, Mark E. 2007. (Growing Field Adventure Ser.). (ENG.). 35p. (J). (gr. -1-3). 16.95 *(978-0-9770391-1-1(0),* 5000) Growing Field Bks.

—Your Song: A Growing Field Adventure. Hoog, Mark. 2007. (ENG.). 43p. (J). (gr. -1-3). 16.95 *(978-0-9770391-2-8(9))* Growing Field Bks.

Auld, Francis & Joseph, Debbie. How a Young Brave Survived. Mathias, Adeline. Hamilton, Penny, ed. 2009. (ENG.). 30p. (J). pap. 5.95 *(978-1-934594-04-9(0))* Salish Kootenia College Pr.

Ault, Dane. Captain Dan Takes a Day Off. Hammond, Ashlie. l.t. ed. 2011. (ENG.). 32p. pap. 12.00 *(978-1-4637-1040-8(2))* CreateSpace Independent Publishing Platform.

Auml, Ana. Thanksgiving Day in Canada. Lewicki, Krys Val. Date not set. 48p. (J). *(978-0-929141-42-8(3),* Napoleon & Co.) Dundurn.

Aunt Judy. Chickens in the Know! Chickens of Different Occupations. Aunt Judy. 2007. 40p. (J). pap. 7.00 *(978-0-9780693-1-5(5))* McEwen, Judith A.

—Chickens on the Go! Chickens from different locations around the World. Aunt Judy. 2nd ed. 2006. 40p. (J). pap. 7.00 *(978-0-9780693-0-8(7))* McEwen, Judith A.

Aureliani, Franco. Dino-Mike & the Museum Mayhem. 2015. (J). lib. bdg. *(978-1-4062-9391-3(1))* Stone Arch Bks.

Aureliani, Franco. Dino-Mike! Aureliani, Franco. 2015. (Dino-Mike! Ser.). (ENG.). 128p. (gr. 1-3). lib. bdg. 95.96 ***(978-1-4965-0311-4(2),*** Dino-Mike!) Stone Arch Bks.

Aureliani, Franco. Dino-Mike & the Jurassic Portal. Aureliani, Franco. 2015. (Dino-Mike! Ser.). (ENG.). 128p. (gr. 1-3). lib. bdg. 23.99 *(978-1-4342-9630-6(X))* Stone Arch Bks.

Aureliani, Franco. Dino-Mike & the Museum Mayhem. Aureliani, Franco. 2015. (Dino-Mike! Ser.). (ENG.). 128p. (gr. 1-3). lib. bdg. 23.99 ***(978-1-4342-9628-3(8),*** Dino-Mike!) Stone Arch Bks.

Aureliani, Franco. Dino-Mike & the T. Rex Attack. Aureliani, Franco. 2015. (Dino-Mike! Ser.). (ENG.). 128p. (gr. 1-3). lib. bdg. 23.99 *(978-1-4342-9627-6(X))* Stone Arch Bks.

—Dino-Mike & the Underwater Dinosaurs. Aureliani, Franco. 2015. (Dino-Mike! Ser.). (ENG.). 128p. (gr. 1-3). lib. bdg. 23.99 *(978-1-4342-9629-0(6))* Stone Arch Bks.

Aureliani, Franco, jt. illus. see Baltazar, Art.

Austin, Antoinette & Wooten, Neal. The Little Lobo Who Lost His Howl. Austin, Antoinette & Austin, John. 2008.Tr. of lobito Que. (ENG & SPA.). 32p. (J). pap. 8.99 *(978-0-9817521-6-7(0))* Mirror Publishing.

Austin, Cassie Rita. Peppermint. Austin, Cassie Rita. 2011. 53p. 15.95 *(978-0-9846151-1-7(3))* Paintbrush Tales Publishing, LLC.

Austin, Heather. Many Hands: A Penobscot Indian Story. Perrow, Angeli. 2011. (ENG.). 32p. (J). (gr. -1-3). pap. 10.95 *(978-1-60893-014-2(9))* Down East Bks.

Austin, Heather. Boatyard Ducklings. Austin, Heather. ed. 2008. (ENG.). 32p. (J). (gr. -1-3). 15.95 *(978-0-89272-663-9(6))* Down East Bks.

Austin, Michael. Late for School, 1 vol. Reiss, Mike & Reiss, Mike. 2003. (ENG.). 32p. (J). (gr. k-3). 16.95 *(978-1-56145-286-6(6),* Q35957) Peachtree Pubs.

—Martina the Beautiful Cockroach, 1 vol. Deedy, Carmen Agra. 2014. (ENG.). 32p. (J). (gr. -1-3). pap. 8.95 *(978-1-56145-787-8(6))* Peachtree Pubs.

—Martina the Beautiful Cockroach: A Cuban Folktale, 1 vol. Deedy, Carmen Agra. 2007. (ENG.). 32p. (J). (gr. k-3). 16.95 *(978-1-56145-399-3(4))* Peachtree Pubs.

—Martina una Cucarachita Muy Linda: Un Cuento Cubano, 1 vol. Deedy, Carmen Agra. 2010. (SPA.). 32p. (J). pap. 8.95 *(978-1-56145-532-4(6))* Peachtree Pubs.

—Martina una Cucarachita Muy Linda: Un Cuento Cubano. Deedy, Carmen Agra. De la Torre, Cristina, tr. 2007. (SPA.). 32p. (J). (gr. -1-3). 16.95 *(978-1-56145-425-9(7))* Peachtree Pubs.

—Railroad John & the Red Rock Run, 1 vol. Crunk, Tony. 2006. (ENG.). 32p. (J). (gr. k-3). 16.95 *(978-1-56145-363-4(3))* Peachtree Pubs.

Austin, Michael Allen. Cowpoke Clyde & Dirty Dawg. Mortensen, Lori. 2013. (ENG.). 32p. (J). (gr. -1-3). 16.99 *(978-0-547-23993-4(9))* Houghton Mifflin Harcourt Publishing Co.

—Sam Patch: Daredevil Jumper. Cummins, Julie. 2009. (ENG.). 32p. (J). (gr. -1-3). 16.95 *(978-0-8234-1741-4(7))* Holiday Hse., Inc.

—Ten Rules You Absolutely Must Not Break If You Want to Survive the School Bus. Grandits, John. 2011. (ENG.). 32p. (J). (gr. 1-4). 16.99 *(978-0-618-78822-4(0))* Houghton Mifflin Harcourt Publishing Co.

Austin, Michael Allen. London Bridge Is Falling Down. Austin, Michael Allen. 2011. (Favorite Children's Songs Ser.). (ENG.). 16p. (J). (gr. -1-2). lib. bdg. 25.64 *(978-1-60954-292-4(4),* 200096) Child's World, Inc., The.

Austin, Mike. Countdown with Milo & Mouse. 2012. (ENG.). 18p. (J). (gr. k-12). 9.99 *(978-1-60905-208-9(0))* Blue Apple Bks.

—The Hidden: A Compendium of Arctic Giants, Dwarves, Gnomes, Trolls, Faeries & Other Strange Beings from Inuit Oral History, 1 vol. Christopher, Neil. 2014. (ENG.). 256p. (J). (gr. 7). 29.95 *(978-1-927095-59-1(X))* Inhabit Media Inc. CAN. Dist: Independent Pubs. Group.

—Where Is Milo's Ball? 2012. (ENG.). 16p. (J). (gr. k-12). 9.99 *(978-1-60905-209-6(9))* Blue Apple Bks.

Austin, Mike. Junkyard. Austin, Mike. 2014. (ENG.). 40p. (J). (gr. -1-3). 16.99 *(978-1-4424-5961-8(1),* Beach Lane Bks.) Beach Lane Bks.

—Monsters Love Colors. Austin, Mike. 2013. (ENG.). 40p. (J). (gr. -1-3). 15.99 *(978-0-06-212594-1(X))* HarperCollins Pubs.

—Monsters Love School. Austin, Mike. 2014. (ENG.). 40p. (J). (gr. -1-3). 15.99 *(978-0-06-228618-5(8))* HarperCollins Pubs.

Austin, Richard, photos by. Pocket Piggies Colors! The Teacup Pigs of Pennywell Farm. Austin, Richard. 2014. (ENG., 22p. (J). bds. 5.95 *(978-0-7611-7980-1(1),* 17980) Workman Publishing Co., Inc.

—Pocket Piggies Numbers! Featuring the Teacup Pigs of Pennywell Farm. Austin, Richard. 2014. (ENG., 22p. (J). bds. 5.95 *(978-0-7611-7979-5(8),* 17979) Workman Publishing Co., Inc.

Austin, Tereasa. Grandpa's Woods. McDaniel, Paula. 2008. 44p. pap. 24.95 *(978-1-60474-465-1(0))* America Star Bks.

Austin, Terry & Blevins, Bret. Balance of Power, 1 vol. McCloud, Scott. 2013. (Superman Adventures Ser.). (ENG.). 32p. (gr. 2-3). lib. bdg. 21.27 *(978-1-4342-4710-0(4))* Stone Arch Bks.

Austin, Terry & Burchett, Rick. A Big Problem!, 1 vol. McCloud, Scott. 2013. (Superman Adventures Ser.). (ENG.). 32p. (gr. 2-3). lib. bdg. 21.27 *(978-1-4342-4709-4(0))* Stone Arch Bks.

—Seonimod, 1 vol. McCloud, Scott. 2013. (Superman Adventures Ser.). (ENG.). 32p. (gr. 2-3). lib. bdg. 21.27 *(978-1-4342-4711-7(2))* Stone Arch Bks.

—Tiny Problems!, 1 vol. McCloud, Scott. 2013. (Superman Adventures Ser.). (ENG.). 32p. (gr. 2-3). lib. bdg. 21.27 *(978-1-4342-4712-4(0))* Stone Arch Bks.

Austin, Terry, jt. illus. see Burchett, Rick.

Austrew, Neva. Daddy's Girl. Jacobs, Breena. ed. 2006. 32p. (J). (gr. -1-k). 15.95 *(978-0-9749423-2-2(4))* Bookworm Pubs.

Auth, Tony. The Hoboken Chicken Emergency. Pinkwater, Daniel M. 2007. (ENG.). 112p. (J). (gr. 1-4). pap. 5.99 *(978-1-4169-2810-2(3),* Simon & Schuster/Paula Wiseman Bks.) Simon & Schuster/Paula Wiseman Bks.

—A Promise Is a Promise. Heide, Florence Parry. 2007. (ENG.). 40p. (J). (gr. k-4). 15.99 *(978-0-7636-2285-5(0))* Candlewick Pr.

—Uncle Pirate. Rees, Douglas. (ENG.). 112p. (J). (gr. 2-5). 2009. pap. 5.99 *(978-1-4169-4763-9(9));* 2008. 15.99 *(978-1-4169-4762-2(0))* McElderry, Margaret K. Bks. (McElderry, Margaret K. Bks.).

—Uncle Pirate to the Rescue. Rees, Douglas. 2010. (ENG.). 112p. (J). (gr. 2-5). pap. 6.99 *(978-1-4169-7505-2(5),* McElderry, Margaret K. Bks.) McElderry, Margaret K. Bks.

Autumn Publishing Staff. ABC Learning. 2004. (Wall Charts Ser.). (J). pap. 4.99 *(978-1-85997-302-8(7))* Byeway Bks.

—Adding Up. 2004. (Wall Charts Ser.). (J). pap. 4.99 *(978-1-85997-319-6(1))* Byeway Bks.

—Counting to 20. Byeway Wall Charts Staff. 2004. (Wall Charts Ser.). (J). pap. 4.99 *(978-1-85997-282-3(9))* Byeway Bks.

—Learn the Alphabet. 2004. (Wall Charts Ser.). (J). pap. 4.99 *(978-1-85997-290-8(X))* Byeway Bks.

—My Skeleton. 2004. (Wall Charts Ser.). (J). pap. 4.99 *(978-1-85997-268-7(3))* Byeway Bks.

—Numbers 1-100. 2004. (Wall Charts Ser.). (J). pap. 4.99 *(978-1-85997-265-4(3))* Byeway Bks.

—Solar System. 2004. (Wall Charts Ser.). (J). pap. 4.99 *(978-1-85997-257-1(8))* Byeway Bks.

—Times Table Wall Chart. 2004. (Wall Charts Ser.). (J). pap. 4.99 *(978-1-85997-114-7(8))* Byeway Bks.

—World Map. 2004. (Wall Charts Ser.). (J). pap. 4.99 *(978-1-85997-235-9(7))* Byeway Bks.

—World of Flags. 2004. (Wall Charts Ser.). (J). pap. 4.99 *(978-1-85997-277-9(2))* Byeway Bks.

Auzary-Luton, Sylvie. Going Batty! Special Glow-in-the-Dark Surprise Pictures. Auzary-Luton, Sylvie. Pottie, Marjolein. 2005. 32p. (J). 15.95 *(978-0-689-04635-3(9),* Milk & Cookies) ibooks, Inc.

Avakyan, Tatevik. Battle of the Best Friends. Dadey, Debbie. 2012. (Mermaid Tales Ser.: 2). (ENG.). 112p. (J). (gr. 1-4). 15.99 *(978-1-4424-4979-4(9));* pap. 5.99 *(978-1-4424-2982-6(8))* Simon & Schuster/Paula Wiseman Bks. (Simon & Schuster/Paula Wiseman Bks.).

—Believe Me, Goldilocks Rocks! The Story of the Three Bears As Told by Baby Bear. Loewen, Nancy. (Other Side of the Story Ser.). (ENG.). 24p. (gr. 2-3). 2013. 9.95 *(978-1-4795-1939-2(1));* 2011. pap. 6.95 *(978-1-4048-7044-4(X),* Nonfiction Picture Bks.) Picture Window Bks.

—Believe Me, Goldilocks Rocks! The Story of the Three Bears as Told by Baby Bear. Loewen, Nancy. 2011. (Other Side of the Story Ser.). (ENG.). 24p. (gr. 2-3). lib. bdg. 26.65 *(978-1-4048-6672-0(8),* Nonfiction Picture Bks.) Picture Window Bks.

—Danger in the Deep Blue Sea. Dadey, Debbie. 2013. (Mermaid Tales Ser.: 4). (ENG.). 112p. (J). (gr. 1-4). 15.99 *(978-1-4424-5319-7(2));* pap. 5.99 *(978-1-4424-2986-4(0))* Simon & Schuster/Paula Wiseman Bks. (Simon & Schuster/Paula Wiseman Bks.).

—Dream of the Blue Turtle. Dadey, Debbie. 2014. (Mermaid Tales Ser.: 7). (ENG.). 128p. (J). (gr. 1-4). 16.99 *(978-1-4424-8264-7(8));* pap. 5.99 *(978-1-4424-8263-0(X))* Simon & Schuster/Paula Wiseman Bks. (Simon & Schuster/Paula Wiseman Bks.).

—Eat a Rainbow: Healthy Foods. Kesselring, Susan. 2012. (Move & Get Healthy Ser.). 32p. (J). (gr. k-3). 28.50 *(978-1-61641-858-8(3))* Magic Wagon.

—Get Moving in the City. Heron, Jackie. 2012. (Move & Get Healthy Ser.). 32p. (J). (gr. k-3). 28.50 *(978-1-61641-859-5(1))* Magic Wagon.

—Get Moving with Friends & Family. Higgins, Nadia. 2012. (Move & Get Healthy Ser.). 32p. (J). (gr. k-3). 28.50 *(978-1-61641-860-1(5))* Magic Wagon.

—Grow a Garden: Sustainable Foods. Kesselring, Susan. 2012. (Move & Get Healthy Ser.). 32p. (J). (gr. k-3). 28.50 *(978-1-61641-861-8(3))* Magic Wagon.

—Let's Move in the Outdoors. Heron, Jackie. 2012. (Move & Get Healthy Ser.). 32p. (J). (gr. k-3). 28.50 *(978-1-61641-862-5(1))* Magic Wagon.

—The Lost Princess. Dadey, Debbie. 2013. (Mermaid Tales Ser.: 5). (ENG.). 128p. (J). (gr. 1-4). 15.99 *(978-1-4424-8258-6(3));* pap. 5.99 *(978-1-4424-8257-9(5))* Simon & Schuster/Paula Wiseman Bks. (Simon & Schuster/Paula Wiseman Bks.).

—A Mermaid Tales Sparkling Collection: Trouble at Trident Academy - Battle of the Best Friends - A Whale of a Tale - Danger in the Deep Blue Sea - The Lost Princess. Dadey, Debbie. ed. 2013. (Mermaid Tales Ser.). (ENG.). 592p. (J). (gr. 1-4). pap. 29.99 *(978-1-4814-0055-8(X),* Simon & Schuster/Paula Wiseman Bks.) Simon & Schuster/Paula Wiseman Bks.

Avakyan, Tatevik, et al. The Other Side of the Story. Loewen, Nancy et al. 2013. (Other Side of the Story Ser.). (ENG.). 24p. (gr. 2-3). 99.50 *(978-1-4795-2007-7(1))* Picture Window Bks.

Avakyan, Tatevik. The Secret Sea Horse. Dadey, Debbie. 2013. (Mermaid Tales Ser.: 6). (ENG.). 112p. (J). (gr. 1-4). 15.99 *(978-1-4424-8261-6(3));* pap. 5.99 *(978-1-4424-8260-9(5))* Simon & Schuster/Paula Wiseman Bks. (Simon & Schuster/Paula Wiseman Bks.).

—A Tail of Two Sisters. Dadey, Debbie. 2015. (Mermaid Tales Ser.: 10). (ENG.). 128p. (J). (gr. 1-4). 16.99 *(978-1-4814-0258-3(7),* Simon & Schuster/Paula Wiseman Bks.) Simon & Schuster/Paula Wiseman Bks.

—A Tale of Two Sisters. Dadey, Debbie. 2015. (Mermaid Tales Ser.: 10). (ENG.). 128p. (J). (gr. 1-4). pap. 5.99 *(978-1-4814-0257-6(9),* Simon & Schuster/Paula Wiseman Bks.) Simon & Schuster/Paula Wiseman Bks.

—Treasure in Trident City. Dadey, Debbie. 2014. (Mermaid Tales Ser.: 8). (ENG.). 128p. (J). (gr. 1-4). pap. 5.99 *(978-1-4424-8266-1(4),* Simon & Schuster/Paula Wiseman Bks.) Simon & Schuster/Paula Wiseman Bks.

—Trouble at Trident Academy. Dadey, Debbie. 2012. (Mermaid Tales Ser.: 1). (ENG.). 112p. (J). (gr. 1-4). 15.99 *(978-1-4424-4978-7(0));* pap. 5.99 *(978-1-4424-2980-2(1))* Simon & Schuster/Paula Wiseman Bks. (Simon & Schuster/Paula Wiseman Bks.).

—A Whale of a Tale. Dadey, Debbie. 2012. (Mermaid Tales Ser.: 3). (ENG.). 128p. (J). (gr. 1-4). 14.99 *(978-1-4424-5318-0(4));* pap. 5.99 *(978-1-4424-2984-0(4))* Simon & Schuster/Paula Wiseman Bks. (Simon & Schuster/Paula Wiseman Bks.).

Avant, Matthew. Diamond & the Fosters. Weis, Michael David. 2013. 64p. 21.95 *(978-1-59663-635-4(1),* Castle Keep Pr.) Rock, James A. & Co. Pubs.

Aven, Jamie H. Saints for Young Readers for Every Day, 2 vols., Vol. 1. Wallace, Susan F. S. P. & Wright, Melissa. 3rd ed. 2005. (J). pap. 15.95 *(978-0-8198-7081-0(1),* 332-377) Pauline Bks. & Media.

The check digit for ISBN-10 appears in parentheses after the full ISBN-13

—Saints for Young Readers for Every Day, 2 vols, Vol. 2. Wallace, Susan Helen & Wright, Melissa. 3rd ed. 2005. (J). pap. 15.95 *(978-0-8198-7082-7(X)*, 332-378) Pauline Bks. & Media.

Avendano, Dolores. The Joy of Giving. Testino, Mario et al, photos by. Farina von Buchwald, Martin & Prado Farina, Gabriela. 2005. 89p. (J). 18.00 *(978-0-9777266-0-8(6))* von Buchwald, Martin Farina.

Averbeck, Jim. Except If. Averbeck, Jim. 2011. (ENG.). 40p. (J). (gr. -1-1). bds. 12.99 *(978-1-4169-9544-9(7)*, Atheneum Bks. for Young Readers) Simon & Schuster Children's Publishing.

—The Market Bowl. Averbeck, Jim. 2013. (ENG.). 32p. (J). (gr. k-3). lib. bdg. 16.95 *(978-1-58089-368-8(6))* Charlesbridge Publishing, Inc.

—Oh No, Little Dragon! Averbeck, Jim. 2012. (ENG.). 40p. (J). (gr. -1-1). 14.99 *(978-1-4169-9545-6(5)*, Atheneum Bks. for Young Readers) Simon & Schuster Children's Publishing.

Averill, Esther. Captains of the City Streets. Averill, Esther. 2005. (New York Review Children's Collection Ser.). (ENG.). 164p. (J). (gr. 4-7). 18.95 *(978-1-59017-174-5(8)*, NYR Children's Collection) New York Review of Bks., Inc., The.

—The Hotel Cat. Averill, Esther. 2005. (New York Review Children's Collection Ser.). (ENG.). 180p. (J). (gr. k-4). 17.95 *(978-1-59017-159-2(4)*, NYR Children's Collection) New York Review of Bks., Inc., The.

—Jenny Goes to Sea. Averill, Esther. 2005. (New York Review Children's Collection). (ENG.). 140p. (J). (gr. k-4). reprint ed. 17.95 *(978-1-59017-155-4(1)*, NYR Children's Collection) New York Review of Bks., Inc., The.

—Jenny's Birthday Book. Averill, Esther. 2005. (New York Review Children's Collection). (ENG.). 44p. (J). (gr. -1-2). reprint ed. 15.95 *(978-1-59017-154-7(3)*, NYR Children's Collection) New York Review of Bks., Inc., The.

—Jenny's Moonlight Adventure: A Jenny's Cat Club Book. Averill, Esther. 2005. (New York Review Children's Collection). (ENG.). 32p. (J). (gr. -1-2). 12.95 *(978-1-59017-160-8(8)*, NYR Children's Collection) New York Review of Bks., Inc., The.

—The School for Cats. Averill, Esther. 2005. (New York Review Children's Collection Ser.). (ENG.). 32p. (J). (gr. -1-2). 14.00 *(978-1-59017-173-8(X)*, NYR Children's Collection) New York Review of Bks., Inc., The.

Averill, Esther H. Jenny & the Cat Club: A Collection of Favorite Stories about Jenny Linsky. Averill, Esther H. 2003. (New York Review Children's Collection Ser.). (ENG.). 176p. (J). (gr. k-4). 16.95 *(978-1-59017-047-2(4)*, NYR Children's Collection) New York Review of Bks., Inc., The.

Avery, Matt. Meriah Goes to Church. Schmaedek, Robert, photos by. Crockett, Sonja Michelle. Crockett, Sonja Michelle & Berry, Kenosha, eds. l.t. ed. 2013. (ENG.). 40p. pap. 9.99 *(978-0-615-75539-7(9))* Crockett, Sonja Michelle.

Avery, Terry. Who Will Save Mr Squeaky? 2004. 29p. (J). *(978-1-929115-11-2(3))* Azro Pr., Inc.

Avi. Doña Flautina Resuelvelotodo. Avi, tr. Canetti, Yanitzia. (SPA.). 127p. (J). (gr. 2-3). 7.60 *(978-84-236-6130-5(X)*, ED31838) Edebé ESP. Dist: Lectorum Pubns., Inc.

Avila, Jesus Villicana. A Thankful Day. Cerullo, Claudio V. 2008. 25p. pap. 24.95 *(978-1-60672-599-3(8))* America Star Bks.

Avila, Jorge, jt. illus. see Castro, Patricia.

Avilés, Martha. Abuelita Full of Life: Abuelita llena de Vida. Costales, Amy. 2007. (ENG, SPA & MUL.). 32p. (J). (gr. -1-3). 14.95 *(978-0-87358-914-7(9))* Cooper Square Publishing Llc.

Aviles, Martha. Don't Sneeze at the Wedding. Mayer, Pamela. 2013. (Life Cycle Ser.). (ENG.). 32p. (J). (gr. k-3). lib. bdg. 17.95 *(978-1-4677-0428-1(8)*, Kar-Ben Publishing) Lerner Publishing Group.

Avilés, Martha. Don't Sneeze at the Wedding. Mayer, Pamela. 2013. 32p. 17.95 *(978-1-4677-1641-3(3))*; (ENG.). (J). 7.95 *(978-1-4677-0429-8(6)*, Kar-Ben Publishing) Lerner Publishing Group.

Aviles, Martha. The Fiesta Dress: A Quinceanera Tale, 0 vols. McCormack, Caren McNelly. 2012. (ENG.). 40p. (J). (gr. k-4). pap. 7.99 *(978-0-7614-6236-1(8)*, 9780761462361, Amazon Children's Publishing) Amazon Publishing.

Avilés, Martha. Say Hello, Lily. Lakritz, Deborah. 2010. (Jewish Identity Ser.). (ENG.). 32p. (J). (gr. -1-2). pap. 7.95 *(978-0-7613-4512-1(4)*, Kar-Ben Publishing) Lerner Publishing Group.

—The Shabbat Princess. Meltzer, Amy. 2011. (Shabbat Ser.). (ENG.). 32p. (J). (gr. -1-2). pap. 7.95 *(978-0-7613-5106-1(X))*; lib. bdg. 17.95 *(978-0-7613-5142-9(6))* Lerner Publishing Group. (Kar-Ben Publishing).

Aviles, Martha. Stones for Grandpa. Londner, Renee. 2013. (ENG.). 24p. (J). (gr. k-3). pap. 7.95 *(978-0-7613-7496-1(5)*, Kar-Ben Publishing) Lerner Publishing Group.

Avrett, Judy. How the Zebra Got Its Stripes. Taylor, Janelle. 2011. (ENG.). 34p. pap. 10.95 *(978-1-4664-6574-9(3))* CreateSpace Independent Publishing Platform.

Avril, Francois. The Merchant of Noises. Rozen, Anna. Scarbrough, Carl W., tr. from FRE. 2006. (ENG.). 28p. (J). (gr. 3-7). 18.95 *(978-1-56792-321-6(6))* Godine, David R. Pub.

Avril, Francois & Duffour, Jean-Pierre. Half & Half-People of the Caves. Surget, Alain & Hirsinger, Julien. 2008. 48p. (J). 9.95 *(978-1-60115-205-3(1))*; pap. 4.99 *(978-1-60115-206-0(X))* Treasure Bay, Inc.

Avril, Lynne. Amelia Bedelia. Parish, Herman. 2013. (Amelia Bedelia Ser.: No. 2). (ENG.). 160p. (J). (gr. 1-5). pap. 4.99 *(978-0-06-209499-5(8)*, Greenwillow Bks.) HarperCollins Pubs.

Avril, Lynne. Amelia Bedelia - Sets Sail. Parish, Herman. 2015. (Amelia Bedelia Ser.). (ENG.). 160p. (J). (gr. 1-5). 15.99 ***(978-0-06-233405-3(0)***, Greenwillow Bks.) HarperCollins Pubs.

—Amelia Bedelia by the Yard. Parish, Herman. 2016. (I Can Read Book 1 Ser.). 32p. (J). (gr. -1-3). pap. 3.99 ***(978-0-06-233427-5(1)***, Greenwillow Bks.) HarperCollins Pubs.

Avril, Lynne. Amelia Bedelia Chalks It Up! Parish, Herman. 2014. (I Can Read Book 1 Ser.). (ENG.). 32p. (J). (gr. -1-3). 16.99 *(978-0-06-233422-0(0)*, Greenwillow Bks.) HarperCollins Pubs.

—Amelia Bedelia Chalks One Up. Parish, Herman. 2014. (I Can Read Book 1 Ser.). (ENG.). 32p. (J). (gr. -1-3). pap. 3.99 *(978-0-06-233421-3(2)*, Greenwillow Bks.) HarperCollins Pubs.

—Amelia Bedelia Chapter Book #5. Parish, Herman. 2014. (Amelia Bedelia Ser.). (ENG.). 160p. (J). (gr. 1-5). 9.99 *(978-0-06-233399-5(2)*, Greenwillow Bks.) HarperCollins Pubs.

—Amelia Bedelia Chapter Book #6: Amelia Bedelia Cleans Up (POB) Parish, Herman. 2015. (Amelia Bedelia Ser.). (ENG.). 160p. (J). (gr. 1-5). 9.99 *(978-0-06-233403-9(4)*, Greenwillow Bks.) HarperCollins Pubs.

—Amelia Bedelia Cleans Up. Parish, Herman. 2015. (Amelia Bedelia Ser.). (ENG.). 160p. (J). (gr. 1-5). pap. 4.99 *(978-0-06-233400-8(X)*, Greenwillow Bks.) HarperCollins Pubs.

—Amelia Bedelia Goes Wild! Parish, Herman. 2014. (Amelia Bedelia Ser.: No. 4). (ENG.). 160p. (J). (gr. 1-5). 15.99 *(978-0-06-209507-7(2))*; pap. 4.99 *(978-0-06-209506-0(4))* HarperCollins Pubs. (Greenwillow Bks.).

—Amelia Bedelia Hits the Trail. Parish, Herman. 2013. (I Can Read Book 1 Ser.). (ENG.). 32p. (J). (gr. -1-3). 16.99 *(978-0-06-209527-5(7)*, Greenwillow Bks.) HarperCollins Pubs.

—Amelia Bedelia Is for the Birds. Parish, Herman. 2015. (I Can Read Book 1 Ser.). (ENG.). 32p. (J). (gr. -1-3). pap. 3.99 *(978-0-06-233424-4(7)*, Greenwillow Bks.) HarperCollins Pubs.

—Amelia Bedelia Joins the Club. Parish, Herman. 2014. (I Can Read Book 1 Ser.). (ENG.). 32p. (J). (gr. -1-3). 16.99 *(978-0-06-222131-5(0))*; pap. 3.99 *(978-0-06-222130-8(2))* HarperCollins Pubs. (Greenwillow Bks.).

—Amelia Bedelia Makes a Friend. Parish, Herman. 2011. (I Can Read Book 1 Ser.). (ENG.). 32p. (J). (gr. k-3). 16.99 *(978-0-06-207516-1(0))*; pap. 3.99 *(978-0-06-207515-4(2))* HarperCollins Pubs. (Greenwillow Bks.).

Avril, Lynne. Amelia Bedelia Means Business. Parish, Herman. (Amelia Bedelia Ser.). (ENG.). (J). (gr. 1-5). 2015. 320p. 12.99 ***(978-0-06-240367-4(2))***; 2013. 160p. 15.99 *(978-0-06-209497-1(1))*; 2013. 149p. pap. 4.99 *(978-0-06-209496-4(3))* HarperCollins Pubs. (Greenwillow Bks.).

Avril, Lynne. Amelia Bedelia Means Business. Parish, Herman. ed. 2013. (Amelia Bedelia Chapter Book Ser.: 1). lib. bdg. 14.75 *(978-0-606-27137-0(6)*, Turtleback) Turtleback Bks.

—Amelia Bedelia Road Trip! Parish, Herman. 2013. (Amelia Bedelia Ser.: No. 3). (ENG.). 160p. (J). (gr. 1-5). 15.99 *(978-0-06-209503-9(X))*; pap. 4.99 *(978-0-06-209502-2(1))* HarperCollins Pubs. (Greenwillow Bks.).

Avril, Lynne. Amelia Bedelia Sets Sail. Parish, Herman. 2015. (Amelia Bedelia Ser.). (ENG.). 160p. (J). (gr. 1-5). pap. 4.99 ***(978-0-06-233404-6(2)***, Greenwillow Bks.) HarperCollins Pubs.

Avril, Lynne. Amelia Bedelia Shapes Up! Parish, Herman. 2014. (Amelia Bedelia Ser.). (ENG.). 160p. (J). (gr. 1-5). pap. 4.99 *(978-0-06-233396-4(8)*, Greenwillow Bks.) HarperCollins Pubs.

—Amelia Bedelia Sleeps Over. Parish, Herman. 2012. (I Can Read Book 1 Ser.). (ENG.). 32p. (J). (gr. -1-3). 16.99 *(978-0-06-209524-4(2))*; pap. 3.99 *(978-0-06-209523-7(4))* HarperCollins Pubs. (Greenwillow Bks.).

—Amelia Bedelia Storybook Treasury: Amelia Bedelia's First Day of School; Amelia Bedelia's First Field Trip; Amelia Bedelia Makes a Friend; Amelia Bedelia Sleeps over; Amelia Bedelia Hits the Trail. Parish, Herman. 2013. (ENG.). 192p. (J). (gr. -1-3). 11.99 *(978-0-06-228714-4(1)*, Greenwillow Bks.) HarperCollins Pubs.

—Amelia Bedelia Tries Her Luck. Parish, Herman. 2013. (I Can Read Book 1 Ser.). (ENG.). 32p. (J). (gr. -1-3). 16.99 *(978-0-06-222128-5(0))*; pap. 3.99 *(978-0-06-222127-8(2))* HarperCollins Pubs. (Greenwillow Bks.).

—Amelia Bedelia Unleashed. Parish, Herman. 2013. (Amelia Bedelia Ser.: No. 2). (ENG.). 160p. (J). (gr. 1-5). 15.99 *(978-0-06-209500-8(5)*, Greenwillow Bks.) HarperCollins Pubs.

—Amelia Bedelia Unleashed. Parish, Herman. ed. 2013. (Amelia Bedelia Chapter Book Ser.: 2). lib. bdg. 14.75 *(978-0-606-27138-7(4)*, Turtleback) Turtleback Bks.

—Amelia Bedelia's First Apple Pie. Parish, Herman. (Amelia Bedelia Ser.). 32p. (J). (gr. -1-3). 2012. (ENG.). pap. 6.99 *(978-0-06-196411-4(5))*; 2010. (ENG.). 16.99 *(978-0-06-196409-1(3))*; 2010. lib. bdg. 17.89 *(978-0-06-196410-7(7))* HarperCollins Pubs. (Greenwillow Bks.).

—Amelia Bedelia's First Day of School. Parish, Herman. (Amelia Bedelia Ser.). (ENG.). 32p. (J). (gr. -1-3). 2015. pap. 6.99 *(978-0-06-154457-6(4)*, Harper Trophy); 2011. 9.99 *(978-0-06-203274-4(7)*, Greenwillow Bks.); 2009. 16.99 *(978-0-06-154455-2(8)*, Greenwillow Bks.) HarperCollins Pubs.

—Amelia Bedelia's First Field Trip. Parish, Herman. (Amelia Bedelia Ser.). 32p. (J). (gr. -1-3). 2013. (ENG.). pap. 6.99 *(978-0-06-196415-2(8))*; 2011. (ENG.). 16.99 *(978-0-06-196413-8(1))*; 2011. lib. bdg. 17.89 *(978-0-06-196414-5(X))* HarperCollins Pubs. (Greenwillow Bks.).

—Amelia Bedelia's First Library Card. Parish, Herman. 2013. (Amelia Bedelia Ser.). 32p. (J). (gr. -1-3). (ENG.). 17.99 *(978-0-06-209512-1(9))*; lib. bdg. 18.89 *(978-0-06-209513-8(7))* HarperCollins Pubs. (Greenwillow Bks.).

—Amelia Bedelia's First Valentine. Parish, Herman. (Amelia Bedelia Ser.). 32p. (J). (gr. -1-3). 2014. (ENG.). pap. 6.99 *(978-0-06-154460-6(4))*; 2011. (ENG.). 9.99 *(978-0-06-203275-1(5))*; 2009. (ENG.). 16.99 *(978-0-06-154458-3(2))*; 2009. lib. bdg. 17.89 *(978-0-06-154459-0(0))* HarperCollins Pubs. (Greenwillow Bks.).

—Amelia Bedelia's First Vote. Parish, Herman. 2012. (Amelia Bedelia Ser.). 32p. (J). (gr. -1-3). (ENG.). 16.99 *(978-0-06-209405-6(X))*; lib. bdg. 17.89 *(978-0-06-209406-3(8))* HarperCollins Pubs. (Greenwillow Bks.).

—Every Cowgirl Goes to School. Janni, Rebecca. 2013. (Every Cowgirl Ser.). (ENG.). 32p. (J). (gr. -1-k). 16.99 *(978-0-8037-3937-6(0)*, Dial) Penguin Publishing Group.

—Every Cowgirl Loves a Rodeo. Janni, Rebecca. 2012. (Every Cowgirl Ser.). (ENG.). 32p. (J). (gr. -1-k). 16.99 *(978-0-8037-3734-1(3)*, Dial) Penguin Publishing Group.

—Every Cowgirl Needs a Horse. Janni, Rebecca. 2010. (Every Cowgirl Ser.). (ENG.). 32p. (J). (gr. -1-k). 16.99 *(978-0-525-42164-1(5)*, Dutton Juvenile) Penguin Publishing Group.

—Every Cowgirl Needs Dancing Boots. Janni, Rebecca. 2011. (Every Cowgirl Ser.). (ENG.). 32p. (J). (gr. -1-k). 16.99 *(978-0-525-42341-6(9)*, Dutton Juvenile) Penguin Publishing Group.

—Five Little Monkeys. 2010. (Favorite Children's Songs Ser.). (ENG.). 16p. (J). (gr. -1-2). 25.64 *(978-1-60253-530-5(2)*, 200112) Child's World, Inc., The.

—If I Ran for President. Stier, Catherine. 2012. (J). 34.28 *(978-1-61913-115-6(3))* Weigl Pubs., Inc.

—If I Ran for President. Stier, Catherine. 2007. (ENG.). 32p. (J). (gr. 1-4). 16.99 *(978-0-8075-3543-1(5))*; pap. 6.99 *(978-0-8075-3544-8(3))* Whitman, Albert & Co.

—I'm Gonna Climb a Mountain in My Patent Leather Shoes. Singer, Marilyn. 2014. (ENG.). 40p. (J). (gr. -1-3). 16.95 *(978-1-4197-0336-2(6)*, Abrams Bks. for Young Readers) Abrams.

—Nellie Sue, Happy Camper. Janni, Rebecca. 2013. (Every Cowgirl Ser.). (ENG.). 32p. (J). (gr. 1-2). 14.99 *(978-0-448-46507-4(8))*; mass mkt. 3.99 *(978-0-448-46387-2(3))* Penguin Bks., Ltd. GBR. (Warne, Frederick Pubs.). Dist: Penguin Publishing Group.

—The Pirate of Kindergarten. Lyon, George Ella. 2010. (ENG.). 40p. (J). (gr. -1-3). 17.99 *(978-1-4169-5024-0(9)*, Atheneum/Richard Jackson Bks.) Simon & Schuster Children's Publishing.

—Ruby Valentine & the Sweet Surprise. Friedman, Laurie. 2014. 32p. (J). (gr. k-3). 16.95 *(978-0-7613-8873-9(7)*, Carolrhoda Bks.) Lerner Publishing Group.

—Ruby Valentine Saves the Day. Friedman, Laurie. 2010. (Carolrhoda Picture Bks.). (ENG.). 32p. (J). (gr. k-3). lib. bdg. 16.95 *(978-0-7613-4213-7(3)*, Carolrhoda Bks.) Lerner Publishing Group.

—The Twelve Days of Christmas in Arizona. Stewart, Jennifer J. 2010. (Twelve Days of Christmas in America Ser.). (ENG.). 32p. (J). (gr. k). 12.95 *(978-1-4027-7036-4(7))* Sterling Publishing Co., Inc.

—Underpants Dance. Zapf, Marlena. 2014. (ENG.). 40p. (J). (gr. -1-k). 16.99 *(978-0-8037-3539-2(1)*, Dial) Penguin Publishing Group.

—Wagons Ho! Hallowell, George & Holub, Joan. 2014. (AV2 Fiction Readalong Ser.: Vol. 153). (ENG.). 32p. (J). (gr. -1-3). lib. bdg. 34.28 *(978-1-4896-2389-8(2)*, AV2 by Weigl) Weigl Pubs., Inc.

—Wagons Ho! Hallowell, George & Holub, Joan. 2011. (ENG.). 32p. (J). (gr. 1-4). 16.99 *(978-0-8075-8612-9(9))* Whitman, Albert & Co.

Avril, Lynne, jt. illus. see Cravath, Lynne Avril.

Awdry, Wilbert V. & Courtney, Richard. Secret of the Green Engine. Awdry, Wilbert V. 2012. (Step into Reading Ser.). (ENG.). 32p. (J). (gr. -1-2). pap. 3.99 *(978-0-307-93150-4(1)*, Random Hse. Bks. for Young Readers) Random Hse. Children's Bks.

Awes, Jennifer. It Takes a Lot of Love. Ambrosio, Michael. 2007. 32p. (J). 14.95 *(978-0-9716085-4-2(7))* LionX Publishing.

Axelsen, Stephen. The Crown Affair. Ransom, Jeanie Franz. 2015. (Nursery-Rhyme Mysteries Ser.). (ENG.). 40p. (J). (gr. 1-4). lib. bdg. 16.95 *(978-1-58089-552-1(2))* Charlesbridge Publishing, Inc.

—What Really Happened to Humpty? From the Files of a Hard-Boiled Detective. Ransom, Jeanie Franz. 2010. (Nursery-Rhyme Mysteries Ser.). (ENG.). 32p. (J). (gr. 1-4). pap. 7.95 *(978-1-58089-391-6(0))* Charlesbridge Publishing, Inc.

Axeman, Lois. I Like Things. Hillert, Margaret. 2008. (Beginning-to-Read Ser.). 32p. (J). (gr. -1-7). lib. bdg. 19.93 *(978-1-59953-150-2(X))* Norwood Hse. Pr.

Axtell, David. We're Going on a Lion Hunt. Axtell, David. 2007. (ENG.). 32p. (J). (gr. -1-1). 8.99 *(978-0-8050-8219-7(0))* Square Fish.

Axworthy, Ani. Butterflies & Caterpillars. Ganeri, Anita. 2010. (Animal Families Ser.). (ENG.). 14p. (J). bds. 10.99 *(978-1-84089-641-1(8))* Evans Brothers, Ltd. GBR. Dist: Independent Pubs. Group.

—Cats & Kittens. Ganeri, Anita. 2010. (Animal Families Ser.). (ENG.). 14p. (J). bds. 10.99 *(978-1-84089-644-2(2))* Evans Brothers, Ltd. GBR. Dist: Independent Pubs. Group.

—Ducks & Ducklings. Ganeri, Anita. 2010. (Animal Families Ser.). (ENG.). 14p. (J). bds. 10.99 *(978-1-84089-643-5(4))* Evans Brothers, Ltd. GBR. Dist: Independent Pubs. Group.

Axworthy, Ann. Butterflies & Caterpillars. Ganeri, Anita. 2012. (Animal Families Ser.). 24p. (J). (gr. -1-k). 12.79 *(978-1-60753-097-8(X))* Amicus Educational.

Axworthy, Anni. An Old Red Hat. Langford, Jane. 2004. (ENG.). 24p. (J). lib. bdg. 23.65 *(978-1-59646-676-0(6))* Dingles & Co.

—Sammy's Secret. Nash, Margaret. 2008. (Tadpoles Ser.). (ENG.). 24p. (J). (gr. -1-3). pap. *(978-0-7787-3894-7(9))*; lib. bdg. *(978-0-7787-3863-3(9))* Crabtree Publishing Co.

Axworthy, Anni. The Dragon Who Couldn't Do Sporty Things. Axworthy, Anni. 2008. (Little Dragon Ser.). (ENG.). 32p. (J). (gr. -1-k). *(978-1-84089-533-9(0))* Zero to Ten, Ltd.

—Dragon Who Couldn't Do Sporty Things. Axworthy, Anni. 2010. (Little Dragon Ser.). (ENG.). 32p. (J). (gr. -1-k). pap. *(978-1-84089-556-8(X))* Zero to Ten, Ltd.

Axworthy, Anni & Miller, Mike. Madcap Book of Brain Teasers. Brandreth, Gyles. 288p. (J). pap. 6.95 *(978-0-233-99568-7(4))* Andre Deutsch GBR. Dist: Trafalgar Square Publishing.

Ayache, Avraham. Maharal to the Rescue. Mindel, Nissan. 2010. 67p. (YA). 10.95 *(978-0-8266-0032-5(8))* Kehot Pubn. Society.

Ayagalria, Julia, et al. Animals of the River. Ayagalria, Julia et al. 2006. (Animal Story Collection Ser.). 24p. (J). (gr. 2-6). pap. 9.00 *(978-1-58084-236-5(4))* Lower Kuskokwim Schl. District.

Ayala, Joseph. Little Cloud Upset. Hertkorn, Michaela C. 2010. 28p. pap. 14.95 *(978-1-4389-9837-4(6))* AuthorHouse.

Ayalomeh, Shedrach. The Adventures of Nihu. Uwuigiaren, Omoruyi. 2007. 158p. (J). (gr. 2-8). 16.95 *(978-1-934138-15-1(0))* Bouncing Ball Bks., Inc.

Aycock, Daniel, et al. Undercover Operations. Mauro, Paul & Melton, H. Keith. 2004. (Detective Academy Ser.). 48p. (J). *(978-0-439-57183-8(9))* Scholastic, Inc.

Ayers, Linda. My Pet Mosquito. Ayers, Linda. 2004. 45p. (J). per. 6.95 *(978-0-9760505-1-3(X))* Blue Thistle Pr.

Ayers, Ryan. The Time Bridge Travelers, 3 bks., Bk. 1. Ayers, Linda. 56p. (J). 2006. 13.95 *(978-0-9760505-8-2(7))*; 2004. per. 7.95 *(978-0-9760505-0-6(1))* Blue Thistle Pr.

—The Time Bridge Travelers & the Mysterious Map, 3 bks., Bk. 2. Ayers, Linda. l.t. ed. (Time Bridge Travelers Ser.: 2). 80p. (J). 2006. 13.95 *(978-0-9760505-6-8(0))*; 2005. per. 7.95 *(978-0-9760505-3-7(6))* Blue Thistle Pr.

—The Time Bridge Travelers & the Time Travel Station, 3 bks., Bk. 3. Ayers, Linda. l.t. ed. 2007. (Time Bridge Travelers Ser.: 3). 140p. (J). lib. bdg. 16.95 *(978-0-9786302-8-7(9))*; per. 7.95 *(978-0-9786302-7-0(0))* Blue Thistle Pr.

Ayesenberg, Nina. Emma's Airport Adventure. Ehlin, Gina. l.t. ed. 2005. (Emma & Friends Ser.). 34p. (J). 15.99 *(978-1-59879-015-3(3))* Lifevest Publishing, Inc.

Ayliffe, Alex. Choo Choo Clickety-Clack! Mayo, Margaret. 2005. (ENG.). 32p. (J). (gr. k-3). 16.95 *(978-1-57505-819-1(7))* Lerner Publishing Group.

—Dig Dig Digging. Mayo, Margaret. 2006. (ENG.). 24p. (J). (gr. -1-k). bds. 7.99 *(978-0-8050-7985-2(8))*, Holt, Henry & Co. Bks. For Young Readers) Holt, Henry & Co.

—Faraway Farm. Whybrow, Ian. 2006. (ENG.). 32p. (J). (gr. -1-2). lib. bdg. 15.95 *(978-1-57505-938-9(X)*, Carolrhoda Bks.) Lerner Publishing Group.

—Looking High & Low for One Lost Sheep. Goodings, Christina. 2003. 32p. (J). pap. 9.99 *(978-0-7459-4524-8(4)*, Lion Books) Lion Hudson PLC GBR. Dist: Trafalgar Square Publishing.

—My Very First Bible & Prayers, 2 vols. Rock, Lois. 2013. (My Very First Ser.). (ENG.). 416p. (J). (gr. -1-k). 12.99 *(978-0-7459-6186-6(X))* Lion Hudson PLC GBR. Dist: Independent Pubs. Group.

—My Very First Bible Stories Bumper Sticker Book. Rock, Lois. 2014. (My Very First Sticker Bks.). (ENG.). 96p. (J). (gr. -1-k). 13.99 *(978-0-7459-6410-2(9))* Lion Hudson PLC GBR. Dist: Independent Pubs. Group.

—Zoom, Rocket, Zoom! Mayo, Margaret. 2012. (ENG.). 32p. (J). (gr. -1-1). 17.89 *(978-0-8027-2791-6(3))*; 16.99 *(978-0-8027-2790-9(5))* Walker & Co.

Aymez, Carla. Las Medidas del Tiempo. Kraselsky, Rebeca. rev. ed. 2006. (Otra Escalera Ser.). (ENG.). 48p. (J). (gr. 4). pap. 10.95 *(978-968-5920-80-3(X))* Castillo, Ediciones, S. A. de C. V. MEX. Dist: Macmillan.

Ayotte, Andie C. Molly B. Golly's Wonderful Dancing Debut. Hoppe, Bethany A. 2013. 32p. 28.00 *(978-1-937763-85-5(4))* Published by Westview, Inc.

Ayoub, Hamid. One Lost Boy. Hahn, Nancy. 2012. pap. 19.95 *(978-1-4276-5351-2(8))* Aardvark Global Publishing.

Ayres, Honor. Biblia para Niños. Wright, Sally Ann. 2007. (SPA.). 144p. 16.99 *(978-1-60255-012-4(3))* Grupo Nelson.

—A Child's Book of Prayers. Wright, Sally Ann. 2009. 96p. (J). (gr. -1). 10.99 *(978-0-7586-1662-3(7))* Concordia Publishing Hse.

—Ten Christmas Sheep. Godfrey, Jan. 2010. 28p. (J). (gr. -1-k). 12.95 *(978-0-8198-7432-0(9))* Pauline Bks. & Media.

—Where Did Grandad Go? House, Catherine. 2007. (J). 9.95 *(978-0-8198-8312-4(3))* Pauline Bks. & Media.

—Where Do Babies Come From? Wright, Sally Ann. 2007. 29p. (J). 9.95 *(978-0-8198-8311-7(5))* Pauline Bks. & Media.

—Who Made the Morning? Godfrey, Jan. ed. 2008. (ENG.). 28p. (J). (gr. -1-3). 9.99 *(978-0-9798247-0-8(2))* New Day Publishing, Inc.

Ayriss, Linda Holt. S Is for Save the Planet: A How-to-Be Green Alphabet. Herzog, Brad. 2009. (Science Ser.). (ENG.). 40p. (J). (gr. 1-5). 17.95 *(978-1-58536-428-2(2))* Sleeping Bear Pr.

Ayto, Russell. Are the Dinosaurs Dead, Dad?, 1 vol. Middleton, Julie. 2013. (ENG.). 32p. (J). (gr. -1-3). pap. 16.95 *(978-1-56145-690-1(X))* Peachtree Pubs.

—Captain Flinn & the Pirate Dinosaurs. Andreae, Giles. 2005. (Captain Flinn & the Pirate Dinosaurs Ser.). (ENG.). 32p. (J). (gr. -1-1). 17.99 *(978-1-4169-0713-8(0)*, McElderry, Margaret K. Bks.) McElderry, Margaret K. Bks.

—The Cow That Laid an Egg. Cutbill, Andy. 2008. (ENG.). 32p. (J). (gr. -1-3). 16.99 *(978-0-06-137295-7(1))* HarperCollins Pubs.

Ayto, Russell. Dustbin Dad. Bently, Peter. (ENG.). 32p. 2014. 15.99 ***(978-1-84738-873-5(6))***; 2013. (J). pap. 8.99 ***(978-1-84738-874-2(4))*** Simon & Schuster, Ltd. GBR. Dist: Simon & Schuster, Inc.

A

Ayto, Russell. First Week at Cow School. Cutbill, Andy. 2011. (ENG.). 32p. (J). (gr. -1-k). pap. 9.99 *(978-0-00-727468-0(8)*, HarperCollins Children's Bks.) HarperCollins Pubs. Ltd. GBR. Dist: HarperCollins Pubs.

—Missing Treasure! Andreae, Giles. 2008. (Captain Flinn & the Pirate Dinosaurs Ser.). (ENG.). 32p. (J). (gr. -1-3). 17.99 *(978-1-4169-6745-3(1)*, McElderry, Margaret K. Bks.) McElderry, Margaret K. Bks.

—One More Sheep. Kelly, Mij. 2006. (ENG.). 32p. (J). (gr. k-3). 16.95 *(978-1-56145-378-8(1))* Peachtree Pubs.

—The Somethingosaur. Mitton, Tony. 2014. (ENG.). 32p. (J). 17.99 *(978-0-00-758395-9(8)*, HarperCollins Children's Bks.) HarperCollins Pubs. Ltd. GBR. Dist: HarperCollins Pubs.

—Super Sue at Super School. Cowell, Cressida. 2005. (ENG.). 16p. (J). (gr. -1-2). 8.99 *(978-0-7636-2734-8(8))* Candlewick Pr.

—Tim, Ted & the Pirates. Whybrow, Ian. 2014. (ENG.). 32p. (J). 17.99 *(978-0-00-755930-5(5)*, HarperCollins Children's Bks.) HarperCollins Pubs. Ltd. GBR. Dist: HarperCollins Pubs.

—Where Teddy Bears Come From. Burgess, Mark. 2009. 32p. (J). (gr. -1-3). 16.95 *(978-1-56145-487-7(7))* Peachtree Pubs.

—Where's Tim's Ted? It's Time for Bed! Whybrow, Ian. 2014. (ENG.). 32p. (J). 17.99 *(978-0-00-755929-9(1)*, HarperCollins Children's Bks.) HarperCollins Pubs. Ltd. GBR. Dist: HarperCollins Pubs.

Ayzenberg, Nina. Emma & Friends: Emma's Airport Adventure. Ehlin, Gina. l.t. ed. 2005. 32p. (J). per. 10.99 *(978-1-59879-014-6(5))* Lifevest Publishing, Inc.

—Emma & Friends: Emma Rescues Cali. Ehlin, Gina. l.t. ed. 2006. 24p. (J). 17.99 *(978-1-59879-113-6(3))*; per. 10.99 *(978-1-59879-112-9(5))* Lifevest Publishing, Inc.

—The Story of Rap & Tap. Byrd, Bill Scott. 2006. 9.95 *(978-0-9776805-0-4(9))* Byrd, Fay T.

AZ. La Piedra de la Felicidad. Reyes, Carlos Jose. 2004. (Primer Acto: Teatro Infantil y Juvenil Ser.). (SPA.). 63p. (J). (gr. -1-7). pap. *(978-958-30-0318-9(2))* Panamericana Editorial.

Azaceta, Paul & Chee. Talent, Vol. 1. Golden, Christopher et al. 2007. (ENG.). 128p. per. 14.99 *(978-1-934506-05-9(2))* Boom! Studios.

Azaceta, Paul & Martin, Marcos. Origin of the Species. Waid, Mark & Le, Stan. 2011. (ENG.). 232p. (J). (gr. 4-17). pap. 19.99 *(978-0-7851-4622-3(9))* Marvel Worldwide, Inc.

Azaceta, Paul, jt. illus. see Ryan, Michael.

Azam, Jacques. The Book of How. Laffon, Martine & De Chabaneix, Hortense. 2007. (ENG.). 90p. (J). (gr. 4-6). 17.95 *(978-0-8109-0716-4(X)*, Abrams Bks. for Young Readers) Abrams.

Azarian, Mary. Before We Eat: From Farm to Table. Brisson, Pat. 2014. (ENG.). 32p. (J). 16.95 *(978-0-88448-352-6(5))* Tilbury Hse. Pubs.

—The Hound Dog's Haiku: And Other Poems for Dog Lovers. Rosen, Michael J. 2011. (ENG.). 56p. (J). (gr. 1-4). 17.99 *(978-0-7636-4499-4(4))* Candlewick Pr.

—Miss Bridie Chose a Shovel. Connor, Leslie. unabr. ed. 2005. (J). (gr. k-3). 27.95 incl. audio *(978-0-8045-6936-1(3)*, SAC6936); 29.95 incl. audio compact disk *(978-0-8045-4135-0(3)*, SACD4135) Spoken Arts, Inc.

—The Race of the Birkebeiners. Lunge-Larsen, Lise. 2007. (ENG.). 32p. (J). (gr. k — 1). 6.95 *(978-0-618-91599-6(0))* Houghton Mifflin Harcourt Publishing Co.

—Snowflake Bentley. Martin, Jacqueline Briggs. 2009. (ENG.). 32p. (J). (gr. -1-3). pap. 7.99 *(978-0-547-24829-5(6))* Houghton Mifflin Harcourt Publishing Co.

Azarian, Mary. Farmers Alphabet. Azarian, Mary. 2012. (ENG.). 32p. (J). (gr. -1-2). pap. 15.95 *(978-0-87923-397-6(4))* Godine, David R. Pub.

Azhderian, Cecelia. Why Is the Sea Salty? And Other Questions about the Ocean. Richmond, Benjamin. 2014. (Good Question! Ser.). (ENG.). 32p. (J). (gr. 1). pap. 5.95 *(978-1-4549-0677-3(4))* Sterling Publishing Co., Inc.

—Why Is the Sea Salty? And Other Questions about the Oceans. Richmond, Benjamin. 2014. (Good Question! Ser.). (ENG.). 32p. (J). (gr. 1). 12.95 *(978-1-4549-0676-6(6))* Sterling Publishing Co., Inc.

Aziz, Lamia. Baby Whale's Mistake, 6 pack. Holden, Pam. 2009. (Red Rocket Readers Ser.). 16p. (gr. 2-5). pap. *(978-1-877363-87-0(1))* Flying Start Bks.

—Watch Out for Whales, 6 pack. Holden, Pam. 2009. (Red Rocket Readers Ser.). 16p. (gr. 2-4). pap. *(978-1-877363-63-4(4)*, Red Rocket Readers) Flying Start Bks.

—Whale Rescue, 6 pack. Holden, Pam. 2009. (Red Rocket Readers Ser.). 16p. (gr. 2-5). pap. *(978-1-877363-79-5(0))* Flying Start Bks.

Azizi, Z., photos by. I Belong to the Muslim Faith. Dicker, K. 2009. 24p. (YA). pap. 8.25 *(978-1-4358-8624-7(0))* Rosen Publishing Group, Inc., The.

Aznar, Caridad Perez. Un Agujero en el Ala. Anastasio, Antonio. Garcia de la Viuda, Miriam, tr. 2008. (SPA.). (J). (gr. 2-5). *(978-84-7490-950-0(3))* Encuentro Ediciones, S.A.

Azzalin, Stefano. Drawing Your Pets. Colich, Abby. 2015. (Drawing Amazing Animals Ser.). (ENG.). 32p. (gr. 3-4). 27.32 *(978-1-4914-2134-5(7))* Capstone Pr., Inc.

B

B., Blair. Star Cross'd Destiny: The Fated, 5 vols., Vol. 1. B., Blair. 2005. (YA). per. 14.95 *(978-0-9767540-0-8(2)*, 121001, Star Cross'd Destiny) Bohemian Trash Studios.

B. T. B. More Beasts for Worse Children. Belloc, Hilaire. 2008. 48p. pap. *(978-1-4099-1329-0(5))* Dodo Pr.

Babajanyan, Sona. Bringing down the Wall. Reiter, David P. 2012. 32p. (J). 18.00 *(978-1-922120-19-9(7)*, IP Kidz) Interactive Pubns. Pty, Ltd. AUS. Dist: Lightning Source, Inc.

—Die Mauer Zu Fall Bringen. Reiter, David P. & Reiter, David P. Beer, Michele, tr. from ENG. 2013.Tr. of Bringing Down the Wall. (GER.). 38p. pap. *(978-1-922120-52-6(9)*, IP Kidz) Interactive Pubns. Pty, Ltd.

Babbitt, Natalie. The Devil's Storybooks: Twenty Delightfully Wicked Stories. Babbitt, Natalie. 2012. (ENG.). 224p. (J). (gr. 3-7). pap. 7.99 *(978-0-312-64158-0(3))* Square Fish.

—Elsie Times Eight. Babbitt, Natalie. 2005. 26p. (J). (gr. k-4). reprint ed. 16.00 *(978-0-7567-9640-2(7))* DIANE Publishing Co.

—Goody Hall. Babbitt, Natalie. 2007. (ENG.). 192p. (J). (gr. 3-7). per. 8.99 *(978-0-312-36983-5(2))* Square Fish.

—Kneeknock Rise. Babbitt, Natalie. 2007. (ENG.). 144p. (J). (gr. 3-7). per. 7.99 *(978-0-312-37009-1(1))* Square Fish.

—The Search for Delicious. Babbitt, Natalie. 2007. (ENG.). 192p. (J). (gr. 3-7). per. 7.99 *(978-0-312-36982-8(4))* Square Fish.

Babcock, Jeff. Bingo Bear Was Here: A Toy Bear's Climb to the Top of Africa's Highest Mountain. Newman, Gwill York. 2003. 48p. (J). pap. 8.95 *(978-0-86534-395-5(0))* Sunstone Pr.

Babeaux, Dennis, jt. photos by see Hall, Terri L.

Babel-Worth, Joyce. Let's Get Ready for Kindergarten! Spanish/English Edition. Kannenberg, Stacey. Sin Fronteras (Without Borders) et al, trs. 2008. (Let's Get Ready Ser.).Tr. of lA prepararse para Kindergarten!. (SPA & ENG.). 32p. (J). lib. bdg. 21.00 *(978-1-933476-05-6(2))* Cedar Valley Publishing.

Babineaux, Jim. Cody Cottontail Makes a Wise Choice! Babineaux, Jim. l.t. ed. 2005. 18p. (J). *(978-0-9769769-0-5(0))* ALCAPS, LLC.

Babinski, Michael. Bobby Bear Learns to Be a Cowboy. Draper, Tricia. 2004. 36p. (gr. -1-3). per. 14.95 *(978-1-58961-246-4(9))* PageFree Publishing, Inc.

Baboni, Elena. Angels among Us. Lane, Leena. 2007. 29p. (J). (gr. k-5). 17.00 *(978-0-8028-5321-9(8)*, Eerdmans Bks For Young Readers) Eerdmans, William B. Publishing Co.

—Star of Wonder. Lane, Leena. 2007. 29p. (J). (gr. -1-7). 14.00 *(978-0-687-64391-2(0))* Abingdon Pr.

Babooram, Aasha. Poco & His Missing Puppy. Babooram, Vima. 2012. 24p. pap. *(978-1-4602-0296-8(1))* FriesenPress.

Babra, Neil. Hamlet. SparkNotes Staff. 2008. (No Fear Shakespeare Illustrated Ser.). (ENG.). 216p. (gr. 5-7). per. 9.95 *(978-1-4114-9873-0(9)*, Spark Notes) Sterling Publishing Co., Inc.

Babson, Jane F. A Story of Us: The Dolls' History of People of the United States. Babson, Jane F. 2003. 56p. (J). (gr. 4-5). 10.95 *(978-0-940787-03-2(2))* Winstead Pr., Ltd.

Baca, Elena. Life! How I Love You! Murphy, Barbara & Murphy, Barbara Beasley. 2004. (ENG.). 136p. (J). 9.95 *(978-0-89013-468-9(5))* Museum of New Mexico Pr.

Baccala, Gladys. It's Holiday Time! Harrod-Eagles, Cynthia. 2012. (J). *(978-1-58925-640-8(9))* Tiger Tales.

—It's Spring Time! Harrod-Eagles, Cynthia. 2013. (ENG.). 16p. (gr. -1). bds. 8.95 *(978-1-58925-639-2(5))* Tiger Tales.

Bacchin, Giorgio. Blood Cave. Mayhew, Jon. 2014. (Collins Big Cat Progress Ser.). (ENG.). 32p. (J). pap. 7.99 *(978-0-00-751921-7(4))* HarperCollins Pubs. Ltd. GBR. Dist: Independent Pubs. Group.

Bacchin, Matteo. Giant vs. Giant: Argentinosaurus & Giganotosaurus. Signore, Marco. 2010. (Dinosaurs Ser.). (ENG.). 64p. (J). (gr. 3). 15.95 *(978-0-7892-1013-5(4)*, Abbeville Kids) Abbeville Pr., Inc.

—Growing up in the Cretaceous: Scipionyx. Signore, Marco. 2009. (Dinosaurs Ser.). (ENG.). 64p. (J). (gr. 4-9). 15.95 *(978-0-7892-1012-8(6)*, Abbeville Kids) Abbeville Pr., Inc.

—The Hunting Pack: Allosaurus. Signore, Marco. 2009. (Dinosaurs Ser.). (ENG.). 64p. (J). (gr. 4-9). 15.95 *(978-0-7892-1011-1(8)*, Abbeville Kids) Abbeville Pr., Inc.

—The Journey: Plateosaurus. Shore, Marguerite, tr. from ITA. 2008. (Dinosaurs Ser.: Vol. 1). (ENG.). 63p. (J). (gr. 4-6). 15.95 *(978-0-7892-0978-8(0)*, Abbeville Kids) Abbeville Pr., Inc.

—A Jurassic Mystery: Archaeopteryx. 2008. (Dinosaurs Ser.). (ENG.). 61p. (J). (gr. 4-6). 15.95 *(978-0-7892-0979-5(9)*, Abbeville Kids) Abbeville Pr., Inc.

—T. Rex & the Great Extinction. Signore, Marco. 2010. (Dinosaurs Ser.). (ENG.). 64p. (J). (gr. 3). 15.95 *(978-0-7892-1014-2(2)*, Abbeville Kids) Abbeville Pr., Inc.

Bach, Annie. Night-Night, Forest Friends. Bach, Annie. 2013. (ENG.). 24p. (J). (gr. -1-k). bds. 8.99 *(978-0-8431-7278-2(9)*, Grosset & Dunlap) Penguin Publishing Group.

Bachalo, Chris, et al. Generation X Classic - Volume 2. 2013. (ENG.). 248p. (J). (gr. 4-17). pap. 24.99 *(978-0-7851-6686-3(6))* Marvel Worldwide, Inc.

Bachalo, Chris. Ultimate War, 6 vols., Vol. 5. 2006. (ENG.). 112p. (YA). (gr. 8-17). pap. 10.99 *(978-0-7851-1129-0(8))* Marvel Worldwide, Inc.

Bachalo, Chris, et al. Ultimate X-Men, Bk. 3. 2009. (ENG.). 304p. (YA). (gr. 8-17). pap. 29.99 *(978-0-7851-4187-7(1))* Marvel Worldwide, Inc.

Bachalo, Chris. X-Men: With Great Power. Gischler, Victor. 2011. (ENG.). 136p. (YA). (gr. 8-17). 24.99 *(978-0-7851-4848-7(5))* Marvel Worldwide, Inc.

Bachalo, Chris, et al. X-Men: With Great Power. 2011. (ENG.). 120p. (YA). (gr. 8-17). pap. 19.99 *(978-0-7851-4849-4(3))* Marvel Worldwide, Inc.

Bachalo, Chris & Irving, Frazier. Uncanny X-Men Vol. 1: Revolution. 2013. (ENG.). 136p. (YA). (gr. 8-17). 24.99 *(978-0-7851-6846-1(X))* Marvel Worldwide, Inc.

Bachalo, Chris, jt. illus. see Bradshaw, Nick.

Bachalo, Chris, jt. illus. see Kubert, Adam.

Bachan, Krystal Ann. The Adventures of Fox Brown. Atwarie, Rossi. 2011. 62p. pap. 19.00 *(978-1-60911-845-7(6)*, Eloquent Bks.) Strategic Book Publishing & Rights Agency (SBPRA).

Bachelet, Gilles. My Cat, the Silliest Cat in the World. Bachelet, Gilles. 2006. (ENG.). 24p. (J). (gr. -1-3). 17.95 *(978-0-8109-4913-3(X))* Abrams.

Bachelier, Anne. Alice's Adventures in Wonderland, & Through the Looking Glass, 1bk. Carroll, Lewis. 2005. (J). *(978-0-9728620-8-0(0))*; *(978-0-9769071-0-7(0))*; per. *(978-0-9769071-1-4(9))*; im. lthr. *(978-0-9728620-9-7(9))* CFM.

Bachem, Paul. Anna's Blizzard, 1 vol. Hart, Alison. 2005. (ENG.). 156p. (J). (gr. 2-5). 12.95 *(978-1-56145-349-8(8))* Peachtree Pubs.

—Emma's River, 1 vol. Hart, Alison. 2010. (ENG.). 160p. (J). (gr. 2-5). 12.95 *(978-1-56145-524-9(5)*, Peachtree Junior) Peachtree Pubs.

Bachmann, B. L. Fairy Friends. Howell, Ruth. 2013. 28p. 12.95 *(978-0-9899275-2-9(0))* Ravenwood Publishing.

Bachoc, Patricia. God's Garden: A story about What Happens When We Die. Morrison, Kevin. 2009. 32p. (J). pap. 9.95 *(978-0-8091-6741-8(7)*, Ambassador Bks.) Paulist Pr.

Bachs, Ramon. The Kree-Skrull War. Disney Book Group Staff & Macri, Thomas. 2013. (World of Reading Ser.). (ENG.). 48p. (J). (gr. 1-3). pap. 3.99 *(978-1-4231-5406-8(1))* Marvel Worldwide, Inc.

Bachs, Ramon, jt. illus. see Disney Storybook Artists Staff.

Back, Francis. Champlain. Moore, Christopher. 2004. (ENG.). 56p. (J). (gr. 3-7). 18.95 *(978-0-88776-657-2(9))* Tundra Bks. CAN. Dist: Random Hse., Inc.

Back, Samee. Korean Folks Songs: Stars in the Sky & Dreams in Our Hearts. Choi, Robert. 2014. (ENG & KOR.). 32p. (J). (gr. -1-2). 15.95 *(978-0-8048-4468-0(2))* Tuttle Publishing.

Backes, Nick. Brave Emily. Tripp, Valerie. England, Tamara, ed. 2006. (ENG.). 96p. (J). (gr. 4-7). pap. 6.95 *(978-1-59369-210-0(2)*, American Girl) American Girl Publishing, Inc.

—Molly Story Collection. Tripp, Valerie. 2004. (ENG.). 388p. 29.95 *(978-1-59369-458-6(X))* American Girl Publishing, Inc.

—Molly's Cooking Studio. American Girl Editors. 2004. 54p. (gr. 3-18). 15.95 *(978-1-59369-265-0(X))* American Girl Publishing, Inc.

—Samantha's Cooking Studio. American Girl Editors. 2005. 54p. (gr. 3-18). 15.95 *(978-1-59369-268-1(4))* American Girl Publishing, Inc.

Backhouse, Carolyn. Let's Go - Boat! Rivers-Moore, Debbie. 2011. (Let's Go Bath Bks.). (ENG.). 8p. (J). (gr. -1-k). 6.99 *(978-1-4380-7116-9(7))* Barron's Educational Series, Inc.

—Let's Go - Rocket! Rivers-Moore, Debbie. 2011. (Let's Go Bath Bks.). (ENG.). 8p. (J). (gr. -1-k). 6.99 *(978-1-4380-7118-3(3))* Barron's Educational Series, Inc.

—Let's Go - Tractor! Rivers-Moore, Debbie. 2011. (Let's Go Bath Bks.). (ENG.). 8p. (J). (gr. -1-k). 6.99 *(978-1-4380-7117-6(5))* Barron's Educational Series, Inc.

Backman, Aidel. Shimmee & the Taste-Me Tree. Weinbach, Shaindel. Date not set. (J). (gr. -1-2). 2.95 *(978-0-87306-305-0(8))* Feldheim Pubs.

Backman, Aidel. The Money in the Honey. Backman, Aidel, adapted by. 2003. 32p. (J). 13.95 *(978-0-8266-0030-1(1))* Merkos L'Inyonei Chinuch.

Bacon, Irving R. You & the Ten Commandments. Cameron, William J. 2011. 210p. 44.95 *(978-1-258-08112-6(1))* Literary Licensing, LLC.

Bacon, Paul. Cats' Letters to Santa. 2004. 92p. 5.98 *(978-1-57866-005-6(X)*, Galahad Bks.) BBS Publishing Corp.

Bacon, Paul, jt. illus. see O'Sullivan, Tom.

Badalian, Lucy. George the Dragonslayer & His Friends: On Earth. Badalian, Lucy. 2003. 312p. (YA). per. 18.95 *(978-0-9725344-0-6(7)*, 9725344) Millennium Workshop Production.

Baddeley, Elizabeth. A Woman in the House (and Senate) How Women Came to the United States Congress, Broke down Barriers, & Changed the Country. Cooper, Ilene. 2014. (ENG.). 128p. (J). (gr. 3-9). 24.95 *(978-1-4197-1036-0(2)*, Abrams Bks. for Young Readers) Abrams.

Baddorf, Robert. Latin for Children. Baddorf, Robert. Perrin, Christopher. 2006. (Latin for Childred Ser.). (ENG.). 162p. (J). (gr. 4-7). pap., act. bk. ed. 16.95 *(978-1-60051-017-5(5))* Classical Academic Pr.

—Latin for Children, Primer B Activity Book! Baddorf, Robert. Perrin, Christopher. 2005. (Latin for Childred Ser.). (ENG.). 196p. (J). (gr. 4-7). pap., act. bk. ed. 16.95 *(978-1-60051-011-3(6))* Classical Academic Pr.

Bae, Hyun-Joo. New Clothes for New Year's Day. Bae, Hyun-Joo. 2007. (ENG.). 32p. (J). (gr. -1-1). 10.99 *(978-1-933605-29-6(4)*, 05296) Kane Miller.

Baek, Matthew J. In God's Hands. Kushner, Lawrence & Schmidt, Gary. 2005. (ENG.). 32p. (gr. k-3). 16.99 *(978-1-58023-224-1(8)*, Jewish Lights Publishing) LongHill Partners, Inc.

Baek, Matthew J. Panda & Polar Bear. Baek, Matthew J. 2009. (ENG.). 32p. (J). (gr. -1-k). 16.99 *(978-0-8037-3359-6(3)*, Dial) Penguin Publishing Group.

Baen, Noah. A Tree Lives. Lewis, Richard. 2006. 48p. per. 12.00 *(978-1-929299-04-1(4))* Touchstone Ctr. Pubns.

Baer, Brian. Gravelle's Land of Horror. O'Coyne, James. Whispering Pine Press International, Inc. Staff, ed. 2007. (ENG.). 120p. (J). per. 9.95 *(978-1-59649-604-0(5))* Whispering Pine Pr. International, Inc.

Baer, Julie. I Only Like What I Like. Baer, Julie, text. 2003. 32p. (J). 15.99 *(978-1-932188-00-4(2))* Bollix Bks.

Baez, Marcelo. The Amazing Work of Scientists with Max Axiom, Super Scientist, 1 vol. Biskup, Agnieszka. 2013. (Graphic Science & Engineering in Action Ser.). (ENG.). 32p. (gr. 3-4). pap. 7.95 *(978-1-62065-701-0(5))*; lib. bdg. 29.99 *(978-1-4296-9936-5(1))* Capstone Pr., Inc. (Graphic Library).

—Graphic Science & Engineering in Action. Enz, Tammy et al. 2013. (Graphic Science & Engineering in Action Ser.). (ENG.). 32p. (gr. 3-4). pap. 190.80 *(978-1-62065-708-9(2))*; pap. 31.80 *(978-1-62065-707-2(4))* Capstone Pr., Inc. (Graphic Library).

—Graphic Science & Engineering in Action. Biskup, Agnieszka et al. 2013. (Graphic Science & Engineering in Action Ser.). (ENG.). 32p. (gr. 3-4). lib. bdg. 119.96 *(978-1-4296-9938-9(8)*, Graphic Library) Capstone Pr., Inc.

—The Incredible Work of Engineers with Max Axiom, Super Scientist, 1 vol. Biskup, Agnieszka. 2013. (Graphic Science & Engineering in Action Ser.). (ENG.). 32p. (gr. 3-4). pap. 7.95 *(978-1-62065-705-8(8))*; lib. bdg. 29.99 *(978-1-4296-9937-2(X))* Capstone Pr., Inc. (Graphic Library).

Baez, Marcelo. Max Axiom Science & Engineering Activities. Biskup, Agnieszka & Enz, Tammy. 2015. (Max Axiom Science & Engineering Activities Ser.). (ENG.). 32p. (gr. 3-4). pap. 31.80 ***(978-1-4914-2536-7(9)***, Graphic Library) Capstone Pr., Inc.

—Max Axiom Science & Engineering Activities. Enz, Tammy & Biskup, Agnieszka. 2015. (Max Axiom Science & Engineering Activities Ser.). (ENG.). 32p. (gr. 3-4). lib. bdg. 119.96 ***(978-1-4914-2535-0(0)***, Graphic Library) Capstone Pr., Inc.

Baez, Marcelo. Super Cool Chemical Reaction Activities with Max Axiom. Biskup, Agnieszka. 2015. (Max Axiom Science & Engineering Activities Ser.). (ENG.). 32p. (gr. 3-4). lib. bdg. 29.99 *(978-1-4914-2077-5(4))* Capstone Pr., Inc.

—Super Cool Construction Activities with Max Axiom. Enz, Tammy. 2015. (Max Axiom Science & Engineering Activities Ser.). (ENG.). 32p. (gr. 3-4). lib. bdg. 29.99 *(978-1-4914-2078-2(2))* Capstone Pr., Inc.

Baez, Marcelo. Super Cool Forces & Motion Activities with Max Axiom. Biskup, Agnieszka. 2015. (Max Axiom Science & Engineering Activities Ser.). (ENG.). 32p. (gr. 3-4). lib. bdg. 29.99 ***(978-1-4914-2079-9(0)***, Graphic Library) Capstone Pr., Inc.

Baez, Marcelo. Super Cool Mechanical Activities with Max Axiom. Enz, Tammy. 2015. (Max Axiom Science & Engineering Activities Ser.). (ENG.). 32p. (gr. 3-4). lib. bdg. 29.99 *(978-1-4914-2080-5(4))* Capstone Pr., Inc.

Bagby, Chris, photos by. Ode to the Appalachian Trail. Bagby, Chris, ed. 2007. 55p. (YA). pap. 16.95 *(978-0-9795659-1-5(X))* Shaffer, Earl Foundation, Inc.

Bagby, Jeffrey K. What's Wrong with Grandma? A Family's Experience with Alzheimer's. Shawver, Margaret. 2003. (ENG.). 62p. (J). (gr. -1-3). pap. 16.99 *(978-1-59102-174-2(X))* Prometheus Bks., Pubs.

Baggetta, Maria. Alphathoughts. Hopkins, Lee Bennett. 2015. (ENG.). 32p. (J). (gr. k-2). 6.95 *(978-1-62091-792-3(0)*, Wordsong) Boyds Mills Pr.

—Alphathoughts: Alphabet Poems. Hopkins, Lee Bennett & Boyds Mills Press Staff. 2003. (ENG.). 32p. (J). (gr. 1-3). 16.95 *(978-1-56397-979-8(9))* Boyds Mills Pr.

Baggott, Stella. Advent Calendar to Color. ed. 2011. (Coloring Bks). (J). ring bd. 7.99 *(978-0-7945-3136-2(9)*, Usborne) EDC Publishing.

—Baby's Very First Colors Book. 2009. (Baby Board Bks). 10p. (J). bds. 6.99 *(978-0-7945-2467-8(2)*, Usborne) EDC Publishing.

—Baby's Very First Noisy Book Farm. 2013. (Baby's Very First Noisy Book Ser.). (ENG.). 10p. (gr. -1). 15.99 *(978-0-7945-2703-7(5)*, Usborne) EDC Publishing.

—Baby's Very First Noisy Christmas. ed. 2011. (Baby's Very First Noisy Book Ser.). 10p. (J). ring bd. 14.99 *(978-0-7945-3128-7(8)*, Usborne) EDC Publishing.

—Baby's Very First Outdoors Book. 2009. (Baby Board Bks). 10p. (J). bds. 6.99 *(978-0-7945-2468-5(0)*, Usborne) EDC Publishing.

Baggott, Stella. Baby's Very First Stroller Book Animals. 2015. (Baby's Very First Stroller Bks.). (ENG.). 8p. (J). 7.99 ***(978-0-7945-3535-3(6)***, Usborne) EDC Publishing.

—Baby's Very First Stroller Book Jungle. 2015. (Baby's Very First Stroller Bks.). (ENG.). 8p. (J). 7.99 ***(978-0-7945-3533-9(X)***, Usborne) EDC Publishing.

Baggott, Stella. Baby's Very First Toys Book. 2009. (Baby Board Bks). 10p. (J). bds. 6.99 *(978-0-7945-2466-1(4)*, Usborne) EDC Publishing.

—Farm Stroller Book. Watt, Fiona. 2010. 8p. (J). 7.99 *(978-0-7945-2811-9(2)*, Usborne) EDC Publishing.

—How to Knit. Allman, Howard, photos by. Watt, Fiona. 2007. (Art Ideas Ser.). 64p. (J). (gr. 4-7). pap. 14.99 *(978-0-7945-1577-5(0)*, Usborne) EDC Publishing.

Baggott, Stella. Lots of Things to Find & Color in Fairyland. 2015. (Lots of Things to Find & Color Ser.). (ENG.). 96p. (J). (gr. k-5). pap. 12.99 ***(978-0-7945-3329-8(9)***, Usborne) EDC Publishing.

Baggott, Stella. Rainy Day Stroller Book. Watt, Fiona. 2010. 8p. (J). 7.99 *(978-0-7945-2850-8(3)*, Usborne) EDC Publishing.

—Seaside Stroller Book. Watt, Fiona. 2010. 8p. (J). 7.99 *(978-0-7945-2810-2(4)*, Usborne) EDC Publishing.

—Sticker Dolly Dressing Dancers. Watt, Fiona. ed. 2011. (Sticker Dolly Dressing Ser.). 24p. (J). pap. 8.99 *(978-0-7945-2931-4(3)*, Usborne) EDC Publishing.

—Sticker Dolly Dressing Fashion Long Ago. Bowman, Lucy. 2010. (Sticker Dolly Dressing Ser.). 24p. (J). pap. 8.99 *(978-0-7945-2547-7(4)*, Usborne) EDC Publishing.

—Sticker Dolly Dressing Weddings. Watt, Fiona. ed. 2011. (Usborne Activities Ser.). 24p. (J). 8.99 *(978-0-7945-3105-8(9)*, Usborne) EDC Publishing.

—Usborne 100 Science Experiments: Internet-Linked. Allman, Howard, photos by. Andrews, Georgina & Knighton, Kate. Chisholm, Jane, ed. 2006. 96p. (J). (gr. 4-7). 15.99 *(978-0-7945-1076-3(0))* EDC Publishing.

—The Usborne Big Book of Vacation Things to Make & Do. Watt, Fiona et al. 2006. 96p. (J). (gr. 1-4). pap. 14.99 *(978-0-7945-1317-7(4)*, Usborne) EDC Publishing.

Baggott, Stella. Baby's Very First 123 Book. Baggott, Stella. 2010. (Baby's Very First Board Bks). 10p. (J). bds. 6.99 *(978-0-7945-2606-1(3)*, Usborne) EDC Publishing.

—Baby's Very First Noisy Book. Baggott, Stella. 2010. 10p. (J). bds. 14.99 *(978-0-7945-2653-5(5)*, Usborne) EDC Publishing.

—Baby's Very First Touchy-Feely Christmas Book. Baggott, Stella. 2010. (Baby's Very First Board Bks). 10p. (J). bds. 6.99 *(978-0-7945-2852-2(X)*, Usborne) EDC Publishing.

Baggott, Stella & Leyhane, Vici. Sticker Dolly Dressing Ballerinas. Pratt, Leonie. 2007. (Usborne Activities Ser.). 24p. (J). (gr. -1-3). pap. 8.99 *(978-0-7945-1392-4(1)*, Usborne) EDC Publishing.

—Sticker Dolly Dressing Fairies. Pratt, Leonie. 2007. (Usborne Activities Ser.). 24p. (J). (gr. -1-3). pap. 8.99 *(978-0-7945-1391-7(3)*, Usborne) EDC Publishing.

Baggott, Stella & Miller, Antonia. Fashion Designer Summer Collection. Watt, Fiona. 2013. (Sticker Dolly Dressing Ser.). (ENG.). 24p. (J). (gr. -1-3). 8.99 *(978-0-7945-3008-2(7)*, Usborne) EDC Publishing.

Baggott, Stella, jt. illus. see Leyhane, Vici.

Bagley, Mark. Avengers Assemble by Brian Michael Bendis. 2013. (ENG.). 184p. (YA). (gr. 8-17). pap. 29.99 *(978-0-7851-6328-2(X))*; 34.99 *(978-0-7851-6327-5(1))* Marvel Worldwide, Inc.

—Cats & Kings, Vol. 8. 2006. (ENG.). 184p. (J). (gr. 4-17). pap. 17.99 *(978-0-7851-1250-1(2))* Marvel Worldwide, Inc.

—Irresponsible, 8 vols., Vol. 7. 2006. (ENG.). 144p. (J). (gr. -1-17). pap. 12.99 *(978-0-7851-1092-7(5))* Marvel Worldwide, Inc.

—Public Scrutiny, 5, Vol. 5. 2007. (ENG.). 120p. (J). (gr. 4-17). pap. 11.99 *(978-0-7851-1087-3(9))* Marvel Worldwide, Inc.

Bagley, Mark, et al. Spider-Man - Complete Ben Reilly Epic, Bk. 1. Defalco, Tom et al. 2011. (ENG.). 120p. (J). (gr. 4-17). pap. 39.99 *(978-0-7851-5545-4(7))* Marvel Worldwide, Inc.

—Tha Amazing Spider-Man. 2011. (ENG.). 424p. (J). (gr. 4-17). pap. 39.99 *(978-0-7851-5612-3(7))* Marvel Worldwide, Inc.

—Thunderbolts Classic - Volume 1. Busiek, Kurt & David, Peter. 2011. (ENG.). 296p. (YA). (gr. 8-17). pap. 29.99 *(978-0-7851-5309-2(8))* Marvel Worldwide, Inc.

Bagley, Mark. Ultimate Six, Vol. 9. Youngquist, Jeff, ed. 2007. (ENG.). 208p. (J). (gr. 4-17). pap. 17.99 *(978-0-7851-1312-6(6))* Marvel Worldwide, Inc.

—Ultimate Spider-Man Vol. 11: Carnage. 2007. (ENG.). 144p. (J). (gr. -1-17). pap. 12.99 *(978-0-7851-1403-1(3))* Marvel Worldwide, Inc.

—Ultimate Spider-Man Vol. 12: Superstars. 2007. (ENG.). 144p. (J). (gr. -1-17). pap. 12.99 *(978-0-7851-1629-5(X))* Marvel Worldwide, Inc.

—Ultimate Spider-Man - Legacy, Vol. 4. 2006. (ENG.). 160p. (J). (gr. 4-17). pap. 14.99 *(978-0-7851-0968-6(4))* Marvel Worldwide, Inc.

—Venom, 8 vols., Vol. 6. 2006. (ENG.). 168p. (J). (gr. 4-17). pap. 15.99 *(978-0-7851-1094-1(1))* Marvel Worldwide, Inc.

Bagley, Mark & Hairsine, Trevor. Ultimate Six. Bendis, Brian Michael & Quesada, Joe. 2011. (ENG.). 208p. (J). (gr. 4-17). 24.99 *(978-0-7851-5746-5(8))* Marvel Worldwide, Inc.

Bagley, Mark & Lim, Ron. Venom: Lethal Protector. 2011. (ENG.). 144p. (J). (gr. 4-17). pap. 16.99 *(978-0-7851-5847-9(2))* Marvel Worldwide, Inc.

Bagley, Pat. Fit Kids Cookbook. Duffy, Kate & McRedmond, Sarah. 2004. 94p. (J). (gr. 4-7). spiral bd. 19.95 *(978-0-9709301-6-3(X))* Fit Kids.

—Kirby Soup for the Soul. Kirby, Robert. 2003. 127p. per. 9.95 *(978-0-9744860-2-4(7))* White Horse Bks.

Bagley, Tom. Canadian Boys Who Rocked the World, 1 vol. Kyi, Tanya Lloyd. 2010. (ENG.). 128p. (J). pap. 12.95 *(978-1-55285-799-1(9))* Whitecap Bks., Ltd. CAN. Dist: Midpoint Trade Bks., Inc.

—Canadian Girls Who Rocked the World, 1 vol. Kyi, Tanya Lloyd. 2nd rev. ed. 2010. (ENG.). 128p. (J). pap. 12.95 *(978-1-55285-986-5(X))* Whitecap Bks., Ltd. CAN. Dist: Midpoint Trade Bks., Inc.

Bagley, Val Chadwick. I Will Follow God's Plan for Me. 2004. (J). *(978-1-59156-579-6(0))* Covenant Communications.

—I Will Trust in Heavenly Father & Jesus. 2006. (J). *(978-1-59811-056-2(X))* Covenant Communications.

—I'm Reverent When- Mullins, Amy. 2005. ("Move-About" Book Ser.). (J). *(978-1-59156-951-0(6))* Covenant Communications.

Bagley, Val Chadwick. My Little Book about Prayer. Bagley, Val Chadwick, tr. Beckstrand, Tamara, tr. 2004. (J). bds. 10.95 *(978-1-59156-096-8(9))* Covenant Communications, Inc.

Bai, Durga. The Churki-Burki Book of Rhyme. 2010. (ENG.). 24p. (J). (gr. -1-3). 14.95 *(978-93-80340-06-7(0))* Tara Publishing IND. Dist: Perseus-PGW.

—The Old Animals' Forest Band. Rao, Sirish. 2008. 40p. (J). (gr. -1-3). *(978-81-86211-41-0(1))* Tara Publishing.

—The Old Animals' Forest Band. Rao, Sirish. 2008. (ENG.). 40p. (J). (gr. -1-2). 17.95 *(978-81-86211-45-8(4))* Tara Publishing IND. Dist: Perseus-PGW.

Bai, Jenny. The Adventures of Banter & Jafar: Spoiled Rotten, 1 vol. Byrd, Michael. 2009. 36p. pap. 24.95 *(978-1-60836-131-1(4))* America Star Bks.

Baicker-McKee, Carol. An Apple Pie for Dinner, 0 vols. 2009. (ENG.). 32p. (J). (gr. k-3). 17.99 *(978-0-7614-5452-6(7)*, 9780761454526, Amazon Children's Publishing) Amazon Publishing.

—Cheep! Cheep! Stiegemeyer, Julie. 2006. (ENG.). 24p. (J). (gr. k-k). 9.95 *(978-1-58234-682-3(8)*, Bloomsbury USA Childrens) Bloomsbury USA.

Baifus, Rut. Watching My Words: An Illustrated Children's Guide to the Laws of Shemiras Halashon. Grinvald, Zeev & Zryl, Laya. 2013. 63p. (J). ***(978-1-56871-539-1(0))*** Menucha Pubs. Inc.

Baikie, Constance N., jt. illus. see Fulleylove, John.

Bailey, Court. The Homeless Christmas Tree. Gordon, Leslie M. 2005. 48p. (J). 19.95 *(978-1-933285-09-2(5))* Brown Bks. Publishing Group.

—The Homeless Christmas Tree. Gordon, Leslie M. 2008. (ENG.). 42p. (J). 19.95 *(978-0-87565-384-5(7))* Texas Christian Univ. Pr.

Bailey, Frank. Hockey Canada's Learn All about Hockey: Color & Activity. Huberts, Al. 2012. (Rule 1, Sports Color & Activity Bks.). (ENG.). 176p. (gr. -1-3). pap. 9.99 *(978-1-77049-436-7(7))* Tundra Bks. CAN. Dist: Random Hse., Inc.

—Learn All about Soccer: Color & Activity. Huberts, Al. 2013. (Rule 1, Sports Color & Activity Bks.). (ENG.). 176p. (gr. -1-3). pap. 9.99 *(978-1-77049-506-7(1))* Tundra Bks. CAN. Dist: Random Hse., Inc.

Bailey, Hannah. 100 Greatest Moments in Irish History. Gallagher, Tara. 2011. (ENG.). 64p. (J). 23.95 *(978-0-7171-4970-4(6))* Gill & MacMillan, Ltd. IRL. Dist: Dufour Editions, Inc.

Bailey, K. C. The True Story of Ten Dogs - Stay. Kazmierski, Stephen, photos by. Muntean, Michaela. 2012. (ENG.). 40p. (J). (gr. -1-3). 17.99 *(978-0-545-23497-9(2)*, Scholastic Pr.) Scholastic, Inc.

Bailey, Lindsey. Peace People. Short, Robyn & Williams, Nanon McKewn. 2013. 38p. 18.95 *(978-0-9911148-2-5(5))* Goodmedia Communications, LLC.

Bailey, Loretta Dovell. I Saw a White Horse Today. Black, Janet, photos by. McMahon, V. Karen. 2011. 28p. pap. 24.95 *(978-1-4626-0282-7(7))* America Star Bks.

Bailey, Martha. New Mexico: Uno de muchos, de muchos Uno, 1. Bailey, Martha. l.t. ed. 2006. (SPA.). 96p. (J). per. *(978-0-9786448-0-2(8))* Bailey, Martha.

Bailey, Martin. Grandpa's Farm, 1 vol. Giulieri, Anne. 2012. (Engage Literacy Blue Ser.). (ENG.). 32p. (gr. k-2). pap. 5.99 *(978-1-4296-8988-5(9)*, Engage Literacy) Capstone Pr., Inc.

—The Lost Sock, 1 vol. Giulieri, Anne. 2012. (Engage Literacy Red Ser.). (ENG.). 32p. (gr. k-2). pap. 5.99 *(978-1-4296-8940-3(4)*, Engage Literacy) Capstone Pr., Inc.

—Max & the Balloons, 1 vol. Giulieri, Anne. 2012. (Engage Literacy Yellow Ser.). (ENG.). 32p. (gr. k-2). pap. 5.99 *(978-1-4296-8960-1(9)*, Engage Literacy) Capstone Pr., Inc.

—Up & Down, 1 vol. Dale, Jay. 2012. (Engage Literacy Magenta Ser.). (ENG.). 32p. (gr. k-2). pap. 5.99 *(978-1-4296-8878-9(5)*, Engage Literacy) Capstone Pr., Inc.

Bailey, Melissa. How to Be a Heroine-For Girls: Inspiration from Classic Heroines. Schuller, Kathleen. 2013. 68p. 19.95 *(978-1-4575-1649-8(7))* Dog Ear Publishing, LLC.

Bailey, Peter. The Girl with the Broken Wing. Dyer, Heather. 2005. 147p. (J). *(978-1-4156-3468-4(8))* Scholastic, Inc.

—I, Jack. Finney, Patricia. 2004. 192p. (J). 15.99 *(978-0-06-052207-0(0))*; lib. bdg. 16.89 *(978-0-06-052208-7(9))* HarperCollins Pubs.

—The Ice Child. Ward, Nick. 2004. 32p. (J). *(978-1-84458-038-5(5)*, Pavilion Children's Books) Pavilion Bks.

—Jack & Rebel, the Police Dog. 2007. 183p. (J). (gr. 3-7). 15.99 *(978-0-06-088049-1(X))* HarperCollins Pubs.

—The Magic Box: Poems for Children. Wright, Kit. unabr. ed. 2010. (ENG.). 240p. (J). (gr. 1-4). pap. 9.99 *(978-0-330-50981-7(0))* Macmillan Pubs., Ltd. GBR. Dist: Independent Pubs. Group.

—The Scarecrow & His Servant. Pullman, Philip. (ENG.). 240p. (J). (gr. 3-7). 2007. 7.99 *(978-0-440-42130-6(6)*, Yearling); 2005. 15.95 *(978-0-375-81531-7(7)*, Knopf Bks. for Young Readers) Random Hse. Children's Bks.

Bailey, Peter. The Ice Child. Bailey, Peter, tr. Ward, Nick. 2003. 32p. (YA). *(978-1-84365-004-1(5)*, Pavilion Children's Books) Pavilion Bks.

Bailey, Sally. A Is for Astoria. Leedom, Karen L. 2010. 32p. 15.00 *(978-0-9826252-0-0(0))* Rivertide Publishing.

Bailey, Sheila. Carla's Sandwich. Herman, Debbie. 2004. (ENG.). 32p. (J). (gr. k-3). 15.95 *(978-0-9729225-2-4(0))* Flashlight Pr.

—Sweetest Story Bible: Sweet Thoughts & Sweet Words for Little Girls, 1 vol. Stortz, Diane M. 2010. (ENG.). 224p. (J). 16.99 *(978-0-310-71673-0(X))* Zonderkidz.

—Sweetest Story Bible for Toddlers, 1 vol. Stortz, Diane. 2014. (ENG.). 32p. (J). bds. 9.99 *(978-0-310-74630-0(2))* Zonderkidz.

Bailey, Sian. Grandfather Mountain: Stories of Gods & Heroes from Many Cultures. Muten, Burleigh. 2004. (ENG.). 80p. (J). (gr. 3-6). 19.99 *(978-1-84148-789-2(9))* Barefoot Bks., Inc.

Bailey, Sidney. Grandma & Me Oh What Do We See When We Go to the Zoo? Ray, Sandra. 2011. 32p. 14.99 *(978-1-4520-8133-5(6))* AuthorHouse.

Bailey, Terri L. Minnow Kisses. Shank, Diane S. 2011. 34p. pap. 12.95 *(978-1-936343-60-7(6))* Peppertree Pr., The.

Bailly, Vincent. A Bag of Marbles: The Graphic Novel. Joffo, Joseph. Gauvin, Edward, tr. 2013. (ENG.). 128p. (gr. 7-12). pap. 9.95 *(978-1-4677-1516-4(6))*; lib. bdg. 29.27 *(978-1-4677-0700-8(7))* Lerner Publishing Group. (Graphic Universe).

Bainbridge, Bob, jt. illus. see Bainbridge, Shane.

Bainbridge, Shane & Bainbridge, Bob. The Hen That Couldn't Lay an Egg. Smith, Clyde. 2011. 32p. pap. 24.95 *(978-1-4626-3796-6(5))* America Star Bks.

Baines, Nigel. Alien Attack! MacDonald, Alan. 2015. (ENG.). 192p. (J). (gr. 2-4). pap. 9.99 *(978-1-4088-2524-2(4)*, Bloomsbury USA Childrens) Bloomsbury USA.

—All Things Weird & Wonderful. Henderson, Stewart. 2003. (ENG.). 96p. (J). (gr. 2-4). 19.99 *(978-0-7459-4678-8(X)*, Lion Books) Lion Hudson PLC GBR. Dist: Independent Pubs. Group.

—Dragon Hunt, 1 vol. Wallace, Karen. 2013. (Start Reading Ser.). (ENG.). 24p. (gr. k-1). pap. 6.99 *(978-1-4765-4095-5(0))* Capstone Pr., Inc.

Baines, Nigel. Supercool Snotman, No. 8. Matt and Dave. (ENG.). 112p. pap. ***(978-1-84738-288-7(6))*** Simon & Schuster, Ltd.

Baines, Nigel. Superhero School: The Revenge of the Green Meanie. MacDonald, Alan. 2015. (ENG.). 176p. (J). (gr. 2-4). pap. 9.99 *(978-1-4088-2523-5(6)*, Bloomsbury USA Childrens) Bloomsbury USA.

—Undead Ed. Ghoulstone, Rotterly. 2012. (Undead Ed Ser.: 1). (ENG.). 224p. (J). (gr. 3-7). 10.99 *(978-1-59514-531-4(1)*, Razorbill) Penguin Publishing Group.

—Yuck's Amazing Underpants. Matt & Dave. 2012. (Yuck Ser.). (ENG.). 112p. (J). (gr. 2-5). 14.99 *(978-1-4424-5121-6(1))*; pap. 4.99 *(978-1-4424-5122-3(X))* Simon & Schuster/Paula Wiseman Bks. (Simon & Schuster/Paula Wiseman Bks.).

—Yuck's Big Booger Challenge. Matt & Dave. 2013. (Yuck Ser.). (ENG.). 112p. (J). (gr. 2-5). 15.99 *(978-1-4424-8311-8(3))*; pap. 4.99 *(978-1-4424-8312-5(1))* Simon & Schuster/Paula Wiseman Bks. (Simon & Schuster/Paula Wiseman Bks.).

—Yuck's Fart Club. Morgan, Matthew et al. 2013. (Yuck Ser.). (ENG.). 112p. (J). (gr. 2-5). 15.99 *(978-1-4424-8153-4(6))*, Simon & Schuster/Paula Wiseman Bks.) Simon & Schuster/Paula Wiseman Bks.

—Yuck's Fart Club. Dave & Matt. 2013. (Yuck Ser.). (ENG.). 112p. (J). (gr. 2-5). pap. 4.99 *(978-1-4424-8152-7(8))*, Simon & Schuster/Paula Wiseman Bks.) Simon & Schuster/Paula Wiseman Bks.

Baines, Nigel. Yuck's Mega Magic Wand. Matt & Dave. 9th ed. (ENG.). 112p. pap. ***(978-1-84738-298-6(3))*** Simon & Schuster, Ltd.

Baines, Nigel. Yuck's Pet Worm. Matt & Dave. 2013. (Yuck Ser.). (ENG.). 112p. (J). (gr. 2-5). 15.99 *(978-1-4424-8150-3(1))*; pap. 4.99 *(978-1-4424-8149-7(8))* Simon & Schuster/Paula Wiseman Bks. (Simon & Schuster/Paula Wiseman Bks.).

—Yuck's Robotic Butt Blast. Matt & Dave. 2013. (Yuck Ser.). (ENG.). 112p. (J). (gr. 2-5). pap. 4.99 *(978-1-4424-8309-5(1)*, Simon & Schuster/Paula Wiseman Bks.) Simon & Schuster/Paula Wiseman Bks.

—Yuck's Robotic Butt Blast. Matthews, Morgan & Sinden, David. 2013. (Yuck Ser.). (ENG.). 112p. (J). (gr. 2-5). 15.99 *(978-1-4424-8308-8(3)*, Simon & Schuster/Paula Wiseman Bks.) Simon & Schuster/Paula Wiseman Bks.

—Yuck's Slime Monster. Matt & Dave. 2012. (Yuck Ser.). (ENG.). 112p. (J). (gr. 2-5). 14.99 *(978-1-4424-5124-7(6))*; pap. 4.99 *(978-1-4424-5126-1(2))* Simon & Schuster/Paula Wiseman Bks. (Simon & Schuster/Paula Wiseman Bks.).

Bair, Katie. NHS - Hawaii, Vol. 1. Bair, Katie. Bevard, Robby. 2006. (Ninja High School: Hawaii Ser.). 144p. (YA). pap. 12.95 *(978-0-9768043-1-4(X))* Antarctic Pr., Inc.

Bair, M. & Sadowski, Stephen. Justice Be Done, Bk. 1. Robinson, James et al. rev. ed. 2005. (Justice Society of America Ser.: Bk. 1). (ENG.). 160p. (YA). pap. 17.99 *(978-1-56389-620-0(6))* DC Comics.

Bair, Michael. Identity Crisis. Meltzer, Brad. rev. ed. 2005. (ENG.). 264p. (YA). 24.99 *(978-1-4012-0688-8(3))* DC Comics.

Baird, Roberta. The Runaway Pumpkin Pie Man, 1 vol. Town, Vicky. 2015. (ENG.). 32p. (J). (gr. k-3). 16.99 *(978-1-4556-2025-8(4))* Pelican Publishing Co., Inc.

—The Swamp Where Gator Hides. Berkes, Marianne. 2014. (ENG.). 32p. (J). (gr. k-4). 16.95 *(978-1-58469-470-0(X))*; pap. 8.95 *(978-1-58469-471-7(8))* Dawn Pubns.

Baisley, Maryann Leake. Madison's Mixed-up Flower Girl Magic & Aiden's Amazing Ring Bearer Act Aiden's Amazing Ring Bearer Act. Beach, Kathleen H. & Weeber, Stephanie B. 2009. 32p. pap. 19.95 *(978-1-4251-7059-2(5))* Trafford Publishing.

Baisley, Stephen, jt. illus. see Comfort, Mike.

Baity, Susan. Celebrations! Anderson, Gennifer. 2013. 38p. pap. 16.95 *(978-1-57258-905-6(1))* TEACH Services, Inc.

Baizer, Gayle Susan. Miss Donna's Mulberry Acres Farm. Douglas, Donna. 2011. (Mulberry Acres Farm Ser.). (ENG.). 24p. (J). (gr. -1-3). pap. 10.99 *(978-1-61036-098-2(2))* Bridge-Logos Foundation.

Bajaj, Subash. The Three Little Pigs. 2010. (J). *(978-1-60617-135-6(6))* Teaching Strategies, Inc.

Bakal, Scott. Gabriel Finley & the Raven's Riddle. Hagen, George. 2014. (ENG.). 384p. (J). (gr. 4-7). 16.99 *(978-0-385-37103-2(9)*, Schwartz & Wade Bks.) Random Hse. Children's Bks.

Baker, Alan. Animal Homes. Martin, Debbie. 2004. (Luxury Lift-the-Flap Ser.). 16p. (J). (gr. 1-18). 11.95 *(978-0-7945-0715-2(8)*, Usborne) EDC Publishing.

—North American Animals. Allette, Dawne. 2010. (ENG.). 32p. (J). (gr. k-2). pap. 9.99 *(978-1-84853-010-2(2))* Transworld Publishers Ltd. GBR. Dist: Independent Pubs. Group.

—Odyssey. 2004. (Kingfisher Epics Ser.). (ENG.). 176p. (J). (gr. 3-7). pap. 8.99 *(978-0-7534-5723-8(7)*, Kingfisher) Roaring Brook Pr.

—Two Tiny Mice: A Mouse-Eye Exploration of Nature. rev. ed. 2014. (ENG.). 40p. (J). (gr. -1-3). 16.95 *(978-1-62914-627-0(7)*, Sky Pony Pr.) Skyhorse Publishing Co., Inc.

Baker, Amanda. The Cheesehead Night Before Christmas. 2007. 40p. (J). per. 19.95 *(978-0-9797781-0-0(7))* Dreams 2 Wings LLC.

—Zack's Zany Zucchiniland. 2012. 32p. (J). 17.95 *(978-0-9832383-1-7(6))* Black Garnet Pr.

Baker, Celia M. My Tooth Fell in My Soup: And Other Poems. Korhel, Erik. 2009. 26p. (J). 14.95 *(978-1-935359-02-9(9))* Book Pubs. Network.

Baker, Darrell. Aladdin. Kreider, Karen. 2015. (Little Golden Book Ser.). (ENG.). 24p. (J). (gr. -1-2). 4.99 *(978-0-7364-2259-8(5)*, Golden/Disney) Random Hse. Children's Bks.

Baker, David. The Adventures of Sugar the Pup. T. 2011. 36p. pap. 24.95 *(978-1-4560-5724-4(3))* America Star Bks.

—The Amazing Chickens at Cliff House. Atkinson, Linda. 2011. 28p. pap. 24.95 *(978-1-4560-7744-0(9))* America Star Bks.

—Baby Dario Eats His First Carrot. Loccisano, Rina. 2012. 48p. pap. 24.95 *(978-1-4560-6100-5(3))* America Star Bks.

—Baby Dario Is Born. Loccisano, Rina. 2012. 36p. pap. 24.95 *(978-1-4560-6099-2(6))* America Star Bks.

—Blackberry Junction. Scott, Gwen. 2011. 28p. pap. 24.95 *(978-1-4560-0951-9(6))* America Star Bks.

—The Blue & Purple Egg. Smith, J. L. 2012. 28p. pap. 24.95 *(978-1-4626-6789-5(9))* America Star Bks.

—Broken Bones Are No Fun, but Broken Bones Won't Stop My Play! Scott, Molly. 2012. 32p. pap. 24.95 *(978-1-4626-7424-4(0))* America Star Bks.

—The Candy Bandit Strikes Again! Coné, Robert. 2011. 28p. pap. 24.95 *(978-1-4560-8019-8(9))* America Star Bks.

—Christmas Island. Norman, Travis D. 2011. 28p. pap. 24.95 *(978-1-4560-9800-1(4))* America Star Bks.

—Claude's Shrinking Shell. Maranhas, Jayne Ellen. 2011. 28p. pap. 24.95 *(978-1-4512-8144-6(7))* America Star Bks.

—Cooldog's Holiday Adventures. Belanger, Kathleen. 2012. 48p. 24.95 *(978-1-4626-3045-5(6))* America Star Bks.

—Dogfish on the Moon: Santa Claus & the Flying Carpet 2. Du Lac, Leo J. 2012. 26p. 24.95 *(978-1-4560-1036-2(0))* America Star Bks.

—Frankie. Phanton, Richard G. 2012. 40p. 24.95 *(978-1-4560-3509-6(9))* America Star Bks.

—Handy Sandy. Carol Hersh. 2011. 28p. pap. 24.95 *(978-1-4560-8991-7(9))* America Star Bks.

—Haylie's Haunted Hamper. Caligiuri, Susan. 2011. 28p. pap. 24.95 *(978-1-4560-0909-0(5))* America Star Bks.

—Kelli, God & New York. Dubrule, Jackie. 2013. 28p. pap. 24.95 *(978-1-4560-0969-4(9))* America Star Bks.

—The Little Mouse on the Prairie. Camp, V. Ray. 2011. 28p. pap. 24.95 *(978-1-4560-1028-7(X))* America Star Bks.

—The Loneliest Leaf. Barry, Debra R. 2011. 28p. pap. 24.95 *(978-1-4560-1002-7(6))* America Star Bks.

—Moon Fruit & the Dragons: Santa Claus & the Flying Carpet 3. Du Lac, Leo J. Washington, Victoria, ed. 2012. 26p. 24.95 *(978-1-4560-1037-9(9))* America Star Bks.

—Our New Addition. Headrick, Julianna. 2011. 28p. pap. 24.95 *(978-1-4560-0933-5(8))* America Star Bks.

—Pigeon Toed. Moore, Tijon Adamson. 2011. 28p. pap. 24.95 *(978-1-4560-0607-5(X))* America Star Bks.

—Playdance Studio. Gaulkin, Marianne Quigley. 2011. 28p. pap. 24.95 *(978-1-4560-2163-4(X))* America Star Bks.

—Rollie & Mollie: Disappearing Act. Swenson, Lynn. 2012. 26p. 24.95 *(978-1-4626-5277-8(8))* America Star Bks.

—Sam & the Tale of the Dragon Prints. Moore, Shawn. 2011. 28p. pap. 24.95 *(978-1-4560-7724-2(4))* America Star Bks.

—The Same As James. Jubilee Jr., Thomas. 2011. 28p. pap. 24.95 *(978-1-4626-0288-9(6))* America Star Bks.

—The Teddy That Went to Iraq. Sarah Taylor. 2011. 28p. pap. 24.95 *(978-1-4560-8382-3(1))* America Star Bks.

—Thunderburps. Spear, Lisa D. 2012. 26p. 24.95 *(978-1-4626-0793-8(4))* America Star Bks.

—The Travels of Chikippo. Padua, Grace. 2012. 26p. 24.95 *(978-1-4626-9782-3(8))* America Star Bks.

—While You Sleep. Dalton, Sommer. 2011. 28p. pap. 24.95 *(978-1-4560-2360-7(8))* America Star Bks.

—You're the Same As Me. Narr, Rachel K. 2012. 26p. 24.95 *(978-1-60749-472-0(8))* America Star Bks.

Baker, Don, jt. illus. see Armstrong, Bev.

Baker, Ed. The Story of Kitten Cuckoo. Baker, Ed. 2007. (ENG.). 32p. (J). (gr. -1-17). 15.95 *(978-1-933572-04-8(3))* Centro Bks., LLC.

Baker, Edmund. Another Dolphin's Tale, a Love Story. Harpan, Gaile & DiMarcello, Pete. 2012. 16p. pap. 12.95 *(978-1-61493-057-0(0))* Peppertree Pr., The.

—Panic at the Pool. Dimarcello, Pete. Harpan, Gaile, ed. 2013. 20p. pap. 12.95 *(978-1-61493-169-0(0))* Peppertree Pr., The.

Baker, Georgette, et al, photos by. We're off to the Galapagos: Nos Vamos a Las Islas Galapagos. Baker, Georgette. 2010. (ENG. 32p. pap. 12.95 *(978-1-4515-3556-3(2))* CreateSpace Independent Publishing Platform.

Baker, Janet. Living Things. Chesire, Gerald. 2008. (World of Wonder Ser.). (ENG.). 32p. (J). (gr. 1-4). pap. 9.95 *(978-0-531-23822-6(9)*, Children's Pr.) Scholastic Library Publishing.

Baker, Janet, et al. Living World. Chesire, Gerald. 2008. (World of Wonder Ser.). (ENG.). 32p. (J). (gr. 1-4). 29.00 *(978-0-531-24026-7(6)*, Children's Pr.) Scholastic Library Publishing.

—Scary Creatures of the City. Clarke, Penny. 2009. (Scary Creatures Ser.). (ENG.). 32p. (J). (gr. 2-4). 27.00 *(978-0-531-21820-4(1)*, Watts, Franklin); pap. 8.95 *(978-0-531-22225-6(X)*, Children's Pr.) Scholastic Library Publishing.

Baker, Jeannie. Belonging. Baker, Jeannie. 2004. 32p. (J). *(978-0-7445-9227-6(5))* Walker Bks., Ltd.

—Home. Baker, Jeannie. 2004. (ENG.). 32p. (J). (gr. k-5). 16.99 *(978-0-06-623935-4(4)*, Greenwillow Bks.) HarperCollins Pubs.

—Mirror. Baker, Jeannie. 2010. (ENG.). 48p. (J). (gr. k-4). 18.99 *(978-0-7636-4848-0(5))* Candlewick Pr.

Baker, Jennifer. Merlin's Island. Mann, Margaret. 2003. 147p. (gr. 4-7). pap. *(978-0-9538685-2-0(4))* Tayar Books.

Baker, Joe. The Dragon Cant. Dongweck, James. 2004. 32p. (J). per. 16.95 *(978-0-9719632-0-7(7))* Golden Monkey Publishing, LLC.

Baker, Jonathan. The Ultimate Heart. Written By Doretta Elaine Wilson; Illust. 2011. 32p. pap. 24.95 *(978-1-4626-0684-9(9))* America Star Bks.

Baker, Keith. Six Silly Foxes. Moran, Alex. 2003. (Green Light Readers Level 1 Ser.). (ENG.). 24p. (J). (gr. -1-3). pap. 3.95 *(978-0-15-204863-1(4))* Houghton Mifflin Harcourt Publishing Co.

—Six Silly Foxes. Moran, Alex. ed. 2003. (Green Light Readers — Level 1 Ser.). (gr. -1-3). lib. bdg. 13.50 *(978-0-613-64595-9(2)*, Turtleback) Turtleback Bks.

Baker, Keith. Big Fat Hen Big Book. Baker, Keith. 2010. (ENG.). 32p. (J). (gr. -1-3). 26.99 *(978-0-547-32859-1(1))* Houghton Mifflin Harcourt Publishing Co.

—Little Green Peas: A Big Book of Colors. Baker, Keith. 2014. (Peas Ser.). (ENG.). 40p. (J). (gr. -1-3). 17.99 *(978-1-4424-7660-8(5)*, Beach Lane Bks.) Beach Lane Bks.

—LMNO Peas. Baker, Keith. 2010. (Peas Ser.). (ENG.). 40p. (J). (gr. -1-3). 16.99 *(978-1-4169-9141-0(7)*, Beach Lane Bks.) Beach Lane Bks.

B

—LMNO Peas. Baker, Keith. 2014. (Peas Ser.). (ENG.). 36p. (J). (gr. -1-k). bds. 7.99 *(978-1-4424-8978-3(2)*, Little Simon) Little Simon.

—Lucky Days with Mr. & Mrs. Green. Baker, Keith. 2007. (Mr. & Mrs. Green Ser.). (ENG.). 72p. (gr. 2-4). 27.07 *(978-1-59961-300-0(X))* Spotlight.

—Meet Mr. & Mrs. Green. Baker, Keith. 2007. (Mr. & Mrs. Green Ser.). (ENG.). 71p. (gr. 2-4). 27.07 *(978-1-59961-301-7(8))* Spotlight.

—More Mr. & Mrs. Green. Baker, Keith. 2007. (Mr. & Mrs. Green Ser.). (ENG.). 68p. (gr. 2-4). 27.07 *(978-1-59961-302-4(6))* Spotlight.

—My Octopus Arms. Baker, Keith. 2013. (ENG.). 40p. (J). (gr. -1-3). 16.99 *(978-1-4424-5843-7(7)*, Beach Lane Bks.) Beach Lane Bks.

—No Two Alike. Baker, Keith. 2011. (ENG.). 40p. (J). (gr. -1-2). 16.99 *(978-1-4424-1742-7(0)*, Beach Lane Bks.) Beach Lane Bks.

—On the Go with Mr. & Mrs. Green. Baker, Keith. 2007. (Mr. & Mrs. Green Ser.). (ENG.). 72p. (gr. 2-4). 27.07 *(978-1-59961-303-1(4))* Spotlight.

—Peas in a Pod! Baker, Keith. ed. 2013. (ENG.). 80p. (J). (gr. -1-3). 33.99 *(978-1-4424-9991-1(5)*, Beach Lane Bks.) Beach Lane Bks.

—1-2-3 Peas. Baker, Keith. 2012. (Peas Ser.). (ENG.). 40p. (J). (gr. -1-3). 16.99 *(978-1-4424-4551-2(3)*, Beach Lane Bks.) Beach Lane Bks.

—1-2-3 Peas. Baker, Keith. 2014. (Peas Ser.). (ENG.). 36p. (J). (gr. -1 — 1). bds. 7.99 *(978-1-4424-9928-7(1)*, Little Simon) Little Simon.

Baker, Kyle. Truth: Red, White & Black. Morales, Robert. 2004. 168p. (YA). pap. 14.99 *(978-0-7851-1072-9(0))* Marvel Worldwide, Inc.

Baker, Leslie. A Song for Lena. Hippely, Hilary Horder. 2011. (ENG.). 40p. (J). (gr. -1-3). 19.99 *(978-1-4424-2946-8(1)*, Simon & Schuster Bks. For Young Readers) Simon & Schuster Bks. For Young Readers.

Baker, Penny. Big Purple Undies. Kelman, Louise & Kelman, Suzanne. Dowling, Jane, ed. 2004. 64p. (J). pap. *(978-0-9580869-6-7(6))* Inhoa Publishing.

Baker, Rochelle. The Boston Box. McGrath, Carmelita. 2003. (ENG.). 32p. (J). (gr. k-4). pap. *(978-1-894294-55-3(6)*, Tuckamore Bks) Creative Bk. Publishing.

Baker, Sara. The Adventures of Armadillo Baby & Annabelli. Zamenhof, Robert. 2013. 56p. pap. 9.29 *(978-0-615-80196-4(X))* RGZ Consulting.

—Do You Do a Didgeridoo. Page, Nick. 2008. 40p. (J). (gr. -1-3). bds. 15.99 *(978-1-84610-571-5(4))* Make Believe Ideas GBR. Dist: Nelson, Thomas Inc.

—Giant Sticker Activity Story Book. Page, Nick & Page, Claire. 2006. (Giant Sticker Bks.). 144p. (J). (gr. -1-k). pap. *(978-1-84610-303-2(7))* Make Believe Ideas.

—Read with Me Gingerbread Fred: Sticker Activity Book. Page, Nick & Page, Claire. 2006. (Read with Me (Make Believe Ideas) Ser.). 12p. (J). (gr. k-2). pap. *(978-1-84610-178-6(6))* Make Believe Ideas.

—Read with Me Rumpelstiltskin: Sticker Activity Book. Page, Nick & Page, Claire. 2006. (Read with Me (Make Believe Ideas) Ser.). 12p. (J). (gr. k-2). pap. *(978-1-84610-182-3(4))* Make Believe Ideas.

—Read with Me the Elves & the Shoemaker: Sticker Activity Book. Page, Nick & Page, Claire. 2006. (Read with Me (Make Believe Ideas) Ser.). 12p. (J). (gr. k-2). pap. *(978-1-84610-177-9(8))* Make Believe Ideas.

—Ready to Read Goldilocks & the Three Bears. 2007. (Ready to Read Ser.). 31p. (J). (gr. k-2). *(978-1-84610-440-4(8))* Make Believe Ideas.

—Ready to Read Sleeping Beauty. 2007. (Ready to Read Ser.). 31p. (J). (gr. k-2). *(978-1-84610-441-1(6))* Make Believe Ideas.

—The Runaway Son. Page, Nick & Page, Claire. 2006. (Read with Me Ser.). 31p. (J). (gr. k-2). *(978-1-84610-176-2(X))* Make Believe Ideas.

—Tales of Irish Enchantment. Lynch, Patricia. 2nd ed. 2011. (ENG.). 208p. (J). (gr. 3-8). 34.95 *(978-1-85635-681-7(7))* Mercier Pr., Ltd., The IRL. Dist: Dufour Editions, Inc.

Baker, Sherri. The Adventures of Drew & Ellie: The Magical Dress. Noland, Charles. 2006. (J). *(978-0-9789297-1-8(3))*; 2nd rev. ed. 84p. per. 7.95 *(978-0-9789297-0-1(5))* TMD Enterprises.

Baker-Smith, Grahame. Robin Hood. Calcutt, David. 2012. (ENG.). (J). 112p. 24.99 *(978-1-84686-357-8(0))*; 176p. (gr. 3-6). pap. 12.99 *(978-1-84686-799-6(1))* Barefoot Bks., Inc.

Baker-Smith, Grahame. FArTHER. Baker-Smith, Grahame. 2013. (ENG.). 40p. (J). (gr. k-3). 17.99 *(978-0-7636-6370-4(0)*, Templar) Candlewick Pr.

Baker, Syd & Gombinski, Rita. Gombinski's Colors in Spanish, French, & German. Wirtz, Harris et al. 2004. (J). audio compact disk 14.95 *(978-1-887371-92-6(3)*, 328C) International Linguistics Corp.

Bakker, Jenny. Get Well Soon, Grandpa. Swerts, An. 2013. (ENG.). 32p. (J). (gr. k-2). 15.95 *(978-1-60537-155-9(6))* Clavis Publishing.

Bakos, Barbara. City Street Beat. Viau, Nancy. 2014. (ENG.). 32p. (J). (gr. -1-2). 16.99 *(978-0-8075-1164-0(1))* Whitman, Albert & Co.

Bakshi, Kelly. The First Americans. Bakshi, Kelly. 2012. 16p. pap. 9.95 *(978-1-61633-278-5(6))* Guardian Angel Publishing, Inc.

Balachandran, Anitha. The Dog Who Loved Red. Balachandran, Anitha. ed. 2011. (ENG.). 28p. (J). (gr. -1-3). 8.99 *(978-1-935279-83-9(1))* Kane Miller.

Balaguer, Nuria. On One Foot. Glaser, Linda. 2015. (J). ***(978-1-4677-7842-8(7)***, Kar-Ben Publishing) Lerner Publishing Group.

Balaji, T. Mangoes & Bananas. Scott, Nathan Kumar. 2006. (ENG.). 32p. (J). 17.95 *(978-81-86211-06-9(3))* Tara Publishing IND. Dist: Perseus-PGW.

Balance, Millie. Black Dog Dream Dog, 1 vol. Superle, Michelle. 2011. (ENG.). 143p. (J). (gr. 3-6). pap. 12.95 *(978-1-896580-34-0(3))* Tradewind Bks. CAN. Dist: Orca Bk. Pubs. USA.

Balarinji. Splosh for the Billabong. Moriarty, Ros. 2015. (ENG.). 24p. (J). (— 1). 9.99 ***(978-1-76011-212-7(7))*** Allen & Unwin AUS. Dist: Independent Pubs. Group.

Balcazar, Abraham. Nina Complot. Chacek, Karen. 2009. (SPA.). 72p. (J). (gr. 3-5). pap. *(978-607-411-017-3(4))* Editorial Almadia.

Balch, Betty Neff. Tales of the Cinnamon Dragon Book I: Adventures in Farr Elvenhome. Balch, Betty Neff. Poythress, Jean Hill. 2004. 152p. (J). lib. bdg. 16.95 *(978-1-930580-46-6(0)*, Luminary Media Group) Pine Orchard, Inc.

Bald, Anna. Morgan's Boat Ride, 1 vol. MacDonald, Hugh. 2014. (ENG.). 24p. (J). (gr. -1-3). pap. 12.95 *(978-1-894838-96-2(3))* Acorn Pr., The CAN. Dist: Orca Bk. Pubs. USA.

Baldanzi, Alessandro. The Age of the Book. Rossi, Renzo. 2008. (Reading & Writing Ser.). 32p. (gr. 4-7). 28.50 *(978-0-7614-4321-6(5))* Marshall Cavendish Corp.

—A Day with Homo Erectus: Life 400,000 Years Ago. Facchini, Fiorenzo. 2003. (Early Humans Ser.). 48p. (gr. 6-18). lib. bdg. 23.90 *(978-0-7613-2766-0(5)*, Twenty-First Century Bks.) Lerner Publishing Group.

—A Day with Neanderthal Man: Life 70,000 Years Ago. Facchini, Fiorenzo. 2003. (Early Humans Ser.). 48p. (gr. 6-18). lib. bdg. 23.90 *(978-0-7613-2767-7(3)*, Twenty-First Century Bks.) Lerner Publishing Group.

—A Gift from the Gods. Rossi, Renzo. 2008. (Reading & Writing Ser.). 32p. (gr. 4-7). 28.50 *(978-0-7614-4318-6(5))* Marshall Cavendish Corp.

—How Writing Began. Rossi, Renzo. 2008. (Reading & Writing Ser.). 32p. (gr. 4-7). 28.50 *(978-0-7614-4317-9(7)*, Benchmark Bks.) Marshall Cavendish Corp.

—In Nineteenth Century London with Dickens. Rossi, Renzo. 2008. (Come See My City Ser.). 48p. (gr. 4-8). lib. bdg. 28.50 *(978-0-7614-4333-9(9)*, Benchmark Bks.) Marshall Cavendish Corp.

—In Renaissance Florence with Leonardo. Rossi, Renzo. 2008. (Come See My City Ser.). 48p. (gr. 4-8). lib. bdg. 28.50 *(978-0-7614-4329-2(0)*, Benchmark Bks.) Marshall Cavendish Corp.

—In the Sun King's Paris with Molière. Rossi, Renzo. 2008. (Come See My City Ser.). 48p. (gr. 4-8). lib. bdg. 28.50 *(978-0-7614-4332-2(0)*, Benchmark Bks.) Marshall Cavendish Corp.

—Modern Times. Silva, Patricia. 2008. (Reading & Writing Ser.). 32p. (gr. 4-7). 28.50 *(978-0-7614-4322-3(3)*, Benchmark Bks.) Marshall Cavendish Corp.

—Reading & Writing Today. Silva, Patricia. 2008. (Reading & Writing Ser.). 32p. (gr. 4-7). 28.50 *(978-0-7614-4324-7(X)*, Benchmark Bks.) Marshall Cavendish Corp.

—The Revolution of the Alphabet. Rossi, Renzo. 2008. (Reading & Writing Ser.). 32p. (gr. 4-7). 28.50 *(978-0-7614-4320-9(7)*, Benchmark Bks.) Marshall Cavendish Corp.

Baldassi, Deborah. A Cake on a Plate. Weber, K. E. 2004. 16p. (J). *(978-1-86374-325-9(1))* Era Pubns.

Baldeon, David. Nova, Vol. 3. Duggan, Gerry. 2014. (ENG.). 152p. (J). (gr. 4-17). pap. 16.99 *(978-0-7851-8957-2(2))* Marvel Worldwide, Inc.

Baldwin, Alisa. Creature Catchers. Smedman, Lisa. 2007. (ENG.). 200p. (J). (gr. 4-6). 19.95 *(978-1-55451-058-0(9)*, 9781554510580); pap. 9.95 *(978-1-55451-057-3(0)*, 9781554510573) Annick Pr., Ltd. CAN. Dist: Firefly Bks., Ltd.

—Hip Hop from A to Z: A Fresh Look at the Music, the Culture, & the Message. Dagnino, Michelle. 2007. 192p. (J). (gr. 8-12). pap. *(978-1-897073-36-0(4))* Lobster Pr.

Baldwin, Christopher. Freehand: A Young Boy's Adventures in the War Of 1812. Peterson, Mike. 2012. (ENG.). 44p. (J). pap. 6.95 *(978-1-938384-03-5(2))* Baldwin, Christopher John.

—In the Love of Animals. Geltrich, Brigitta, ed. Date not set. (Animals Ser.). 96p. (J). pap. 6.00 *(978-0-936945-64-4(8))* Creative with Words Pubns.

Balek, Dayna Courtney. Simon's Big Move. Reynolds Jr., R. A. 2008. 19p. pap. 24.95 *(978-1-60672-676-1(5))* America Star Bks.

Balian, Lecia. The Sweet Touch, 1 vol. Balian, Lorna. 2005. (ENG.). 32p. (J). (gr. -1-3). 16.95 *(978-1-59572-017-7(0))* Star Bright Bks., Inc.

Balian, Lecia & Balian, Lorna. Where in the World Is Henry?, 1 vol. Balian, Lorna. 2005. (ENG.). 32p. (J). (gr. -1-2). *(978-1-59572-035-1(9))* Star Bright Bks., Inc.

Balian, Lecia, jt. illus. see Balian, Lorna.

Balian, Lorna. Un Fiasco de Bruja, 1 vol. Balian, Lorna. 2003.Tr. of Humbug Witch. (SPA.). 32p. (J). 12.95 *(978-1-59572-010-8(3))* Star Bright Bks., Inc.

—A Garden for a Groundhog, 1 vol. Balian, Lorna. 2011. (ENG.). 32p. (J). pap. 6.95 *(978-1-59572-296-6(3))* Star Bright Bks., Inc.

—Humbug Witch, 1 vol. Balian, Lorna. 2003. (ENG.). 32p. (J). 12.95 *(978-1-932065-32-9(6)*, 1-718-784-9112) Star Bright Bks., Inc.

—Leprechauns Never Lie, 1 vol. Balian, Lorna. 2004. (ENG.). 32p. (J). 14.95 *(978-1-932065-37-4(7))* Star Bright Bks., Inc.

—A Sweetheart for Valentine, 1 vol. Balian, Lorna. 2005. (ENG.). 32p. (J). 15.95 *(978-1-932065-14-5(8))* Star Bright Bks., Inc.

Balian, Lorna & Balian, Lecia. The Aminal, 1 vol. Balian, Lorna. 2005. (ENG.). 48p. (J). 17.95 *(978-1-59572-006-1(5))* Star Bright Bks., Inc.

Balian, Lorna, jt. illus. see Balian, Lecia.

Balit, Christina. The Adventures of Odysseus. Lupton, Hugh & Morden, Daniel. 2012. (ENG.). 96p. (J). 23.99 *(978-1-84686-703-3(7))* Barefoot Bks., Inc.

—The Lion Book of Wisdom Stories from Around the World. 2009. (ENG.). 46p. (J). (gr. 2-4). 16.95 *(978-0-7459-6060-9(X))* Lion Hudson PLC GBR. Dist: Independent Pubs. Group.

—The Lion Classic Wisdom Stories. Joslin, Mary. 2013. (ENG.). 128p. (J). (gr. 2-4). 19.99 *(978-0-7459-6369-3(2))* Lion Hudson PLC GBR. Dist: Independent Pubs. Group.

—The Lion Illustrated Bible for Children. 2007. (ENG.). 224p. (J). (gr. -1-4). 17.99 *(978-0-7459-4936-9(3)*, Lion Books) Lion Hudson PLC GBR. Dist: Independent Pubs. Group.

—Once upon a Starry Night: A Book of Constellations. Mitton, Jacqueline. 2009. (ENG.). 32p. (J). (gr. 1-4). pap. 8.95 *(978-1-4263-0391-3(2)*, National Geographic Children's Bks.) National Geographic Society.

—The Planet Gods: Myths & Facts about the Solar System. Mitton, Jacqueline. 2008. (ENG.). 32p. (J). (gr. 1-4). 7.95 *(978-1-4263-0448-4(X))*; 25.90 *(978-1-4263-0449-1(8))* National Geographic Society. (National Geographic Children's Bks.).

—Saintly Tales & Legends. Rock, Lois. 2004. 100p. (J). 15.95 *(978-0-8198-7083-4(8)*, 332-379) Pauline Bks. & Media.

—Treasury of Egyptian Mythology: Classic Stories of Gods, Goddesses, Monsters & Mortals. Napoli, Donna Jo. 2013. (ENG.). 192p. (J). (gr. 3-7). 24.95 *(978-1-4263-1380-6(2))*; lib. bdg. 33.90 *(978-1-4263-1381-3(0))* National Geographic Society. (National Geographic Children's Bks.).

—Treasury of Greek Mythology: Classic Stories of Gods, Goddesses, Heroes & Monsters. Napoli, Donna Jo. 2011. (ENG.). 192p. (J). (gr. 3-7). 24.95 *(978-1-4263-0844-4(2))*; lib. bdg. 33.90 *(978-1-4263-0845-1(0))* National Geographic Society. (National Geographic Children's Bks.).

Balit, Christina. Treasury of Norse Mythology: Stories of Intrigue, Trickery, Love, & Revenge. Napoli, Donna Jo. 2015. (ENG.). 192p. (J). (gr. 3-7). 24.99 ***(978-1-4263-2098-9(1)***, National Geographic Children's Bks.) National Geographic Society.

Balit, Christina. Women of Camelot: Queens & Enchantresses at the Court of King Arthur. Hoffman, Mary. 2006. 69p. (YA). (gr. 5-9). 20.00 *(978-1-4223-5260-1(9))* DIANE Publishing Co.

—Zoo in the Sky: A Book of Animal Constellations. Mitton, Jacqueline. 2006. (ENG.). 32p. (gr. 1-4). pap. 7.95 *(978-0-7922-5935-0(1))* CENGAGE Learning.

Balkovek, James. Beanstalk: The Measure of a Giant. McCallum, Ann. 2006. (Math Adventures Ser.). (ENG.). 32p. (J). (gr. 2-5). per. 7.95 *(978-1-57091-894-0(5))* Charlesbridge Publishing, Inc.

—Makoy, the Apache Boy. Cohen, Rafael. 2013. (ENG.). (J). 14.95 *(978-1-62086-340-4(5))* Mascot Bks., Inc.

—Willa Cather. Cather, Willa. 2004. (Great American Short Stories Ser.). 80p. (gr. 4-7). lib. bdg. 24.00 *(978-0-8368-4251-7(0)*, Gareth Stevens Learning Library) Stevens, Gareth Publishing LLLP.

Balkovek, Jim. Shanaya & Friends: Litter Bugs Turn Eco H. E. R. O. S. Daughtrey, Patricia & Benson, Gary. 2011. 40p. pap. 14.95 *(978-1-60911-475-6(2)*, Eloquent Bks.) Strategic Book Publishing & Rights Agency (SBPRA).

Ball, Alexandra. Care for Our World. Robbins, Karen. 2012. (ENG.). 36p. (J). (gr. -1-3). 16.95 *(978-1-935414-61-2(5))* Compendium, Inc., Publishing & Communications.

Ball, Geoff. Trouble in Space: A First Reading Adventure Book. Baxter, Nicola. 2015. (ENG.). 24p. pap. 6.99 *(978-1-86147-491-9(1)*, Armadillo) Anness Publishing GBR. Dist: National Bk. Network.

—Trouble in Space: First Reading Books for 3-5 Year Olds. Baxter, Nicola. 2014. (ENG.). 24p. (J). (gr. -1-k). 5.99 *(978-1-84322-918-6(8)*, Armadillo) Anness Publishing GBR. Dist: National Bk. Network.

—Trouble in the Jungle: A First Reading Adventure Book. Baxter, Nicola. 2015. (ENG.). 24p. pap. 6.99 *(978-1-86147-494-0(6)*, Armadillo) Anness Publishing GBR. Dist: National Bk. Network.

—Trouble on the Ice: First Reading Books for 3-5 Year Olds. Baxter, Nicola. (ENG.). 24p. 2015. pap. 6.99 *(978-1-86147-492-6(X))*; 2014. (J). (gr. -1-k). 5.99 *(978-1-86147-323-3(0))* Anness Publishing GBR. (Armadillo). Dist: National Bk. Network.

—Trouble under the Ocean: First Reading Books for 3-5 Year Olds. Baxter, Nicola. (ENG.). 24p. 2015. bds. 6.99 *(978-1-86147-493-3(8))*; 2014. (J). (gr. -1-k). 5.99 *(978-1-84322-919-3(6))* Anness Publishing GBR. (Armadillo). Dist: National Bk. Network.

—The Trouble with Tippers. Baxter, Nicola. 2012. (ENG.). 24p. (J). (gr. -1-k). pap. 6.99 *(978-1-84322-783-0(5)*, Armadillo) Anness Publishing GBR. Dist: National Bk. Network.

—The Trouble with Tractors. Baxter, Nicola. 2012. (ENG.). 24p. pap. 6.99 *(978-1-84322-784-7(3)*, Armadillo) Anness Publishing GBR. Dist: National Bk. Network.

—The Trouble with Trains. Baxter, Nicola. 2012. (ENG.). 24p. (J). (gr. -1-k). pap. 6.99 *(978-1-84322-785-4(1)*, Armadillo) Anness Publishing GBR. Dist: National Bk. Network.

—The Trouble with Trucks. Baxter, Nicola. 2012. (ENG.). 24p. (J). (gr. -1-k). pap. 6.99 *(978-1-84322-786-1(X)*, Armadillo) Anness Publishing GBR. Dist: National Bk. Network.

Ball, Geoff, jt. illus. see Riley, Terry.

Ball, Lauren. Sam & Skully. Badeaux, Dewey. 2013. 126p. pap. 12.99 *(978-0-9884057-4-5(1))* Alligator Pr.

Ball, Liz. Bible Stories: Find-the-Picture Puzzles. 2004. (Find-the-Picture Puzzle Ser.: 1). 24p. (J). pap. 2.95 *(978-0-8198-1163-9(7)*, 332-026) Pauline Bks. & Media.

—Calling All Animals: The First Book of PunOETRY. Nathan, Jeff. 2003. 96p. per. 9.95 *(978-0-9702730-1-7(0))* Chucklebks. Publishing.

—Miracles & Parables of Jesus: Find-the-Picture Puzzles. 2004. (Find-the-Picture Puzzle Ser.: 2). 24p. (J). pap. 2.95 *(978-0-8198-4830-7(1)*, 332-221) Pauline Bks. & Media.

—A Standardbred Star: Learn about Harness Racing with Star & Friends. 2007. (YA). 3.95 *(978-0-9793891-0-8(0))* United States Trotting Association.

Ball, Liz. Frog Fun Hidden Treasures: Hidden Picture Puzzles, Vol. 8. Ball, Liz. 2008. (Hidden Treasures Ser.: Vol. 8). 56p. (YA). pap. 6.95 *(978-0-9678159-8-5(3))* Hidden Pictures.

Ball, Natalie. Can You See It?, 1 vol. Dale, Jay. 2012. (Engage Literacy Yellow Ser.). (ENG.). 32p. (gr. k-2). pap. 5.99 *(978-1-4296-8954-0(4)*, Engage Literacy) Capstone Pr., Inc.

Ball, Sara. Flip-O-Saurus. Drehsen, Britta. 2010. (ENG.). 22p. (J). (gr. -1-k). bds. 15.95 *(978-0-7892-1061-6(4)*, Abbeville Kids) Abbeville Pr., Inc.

Ball, Sara. Flip-O-Storic. Ball, Sara. 2011. (ENG.). 11p. (J). (gr. -1-k). bds. 15.95 *(978-0-7892-1099-9(1)*, Abbeville Kids) Abbeville Pr., Inc.

Ball, Victoria. Phonics Comics: Spooky Sara - Level 3, Level 3. Marks, Melanie. 2006. (ENG.). 24p. (J). (gr. 1-17). per. 3.99 *(978-1-58476-473-1(2)*, IKIDS) Innovative Kids.

Ballance, Millie. The Eco-Diary of Kiran Singer, 1 vol. Alderson, Sue Ann. 2007. (ENG.). 88p. (YA). (gr. 7-12). 15.95 *(978-1-896580-47-0(5))* Tradewind Bks. CAN. Dist: Orca Bk. Pubs. USA.

Ballard, Ben. The Be Good Fairy. Wallen-Nichols, Missy. 2013. (ENG.). 32p. (J). 16.95 *(978-0-9853523-0-1(2))* Mawco, Inc.

Ballard, George Anne & Bolton, Georgia Helen. Flowers along the Way. Ballard, George Anne. 2012. 26p. pap. 12.00 *(978-0-9855312-2-5(3))* Bolton Publishing LLC.

Ballard, Lee. Daniel's Ride/el Paseo de Daniel. P, Michael. 2nd ed. 2005. (ENG.). 36p. (J). (gr. -1-7). 18.95 *(978-0-86719-641-2(6))* Last Gasp of San Francisco.

Ballard, Merry. Pity's Porch. Crawford, Deborah & Crawford, Ryan. 2012. 24p. pap. 11.50 *(978-1-60976-796-9(9)*, Strategic Bk. Publishing) Strategic Book Publishing & Rights Agency (SBPRA).

Ballester, Arnal. Chamario. Polo, Eduardo. 2005. (SPA.). 48p. (J). 8.99 *(978-980-257-278-6(0))* Ekare, Ediciones VEN. Dist: Iaconi, Mariuccia Bk. Imports.

Ballesteros, Carles. My First Art Sticker Book. Dickens, Rosie. ed. 2013. (Art Ser.). 23p. (J). pap. 8.99 *(978-0-7945-3202-4(0)*, Usborne) EDC Publishing.

Ballhaus, Verena. David's World: A Picture Book about Living with Autism. Mueller, Dagmar H. 2012. (ENG.). 28p. (J). (gr. k-3). pap. 16.95 *(978-1-61608-962-7(8)*, 608962, Sky Pony Pr.) Skyhorse Publishing Co., Inc.

Ballinger, Bryan. God Loves You Very Much!, 1 vol. Big Idea, Inc. Staff & Kenney, Cindy. 2003. (Big Idea Books / VeggieTales Ser.). (ENG.). 18p. (J). bds. 7.99 *(978-0-310-70623-6(8))* Zondervan.

Ballinger, Carolyn. The UFB's of Bugsville, Florida USA, 1 vol. Zinner, Gennieve. 2010. 48p. pap. 24.95 *(978-1-4489-7977-6(3))* PublishAmerica, Inc.

Ballinger, Wesley. Hungry Johnny. Minnema, Cheryl. 2014. (ENG.). 32p. (J). 17.95 *(978-0-87351-926-7(4))* Minnesota Historical Society Pr.

Balmet, Jean-Paul. Edge of the Galaxy. Fry, Jason. 2014. (ENG.). 176p. (J). (gr. 3-7). pap. 6.99 *(978-1-4847-0485-1(1))* Disney Pr.

Balogh, Andras. Bubba & the Sweet Pea. Boutros, Gladys. 2013. 86p. (J). pap. *(978-0-9873334-7-6(X))* Enlife Pty, Limited.

—Bubba & the Sweet Pea: US English Edition. Boutros, Gladys. 2012. 86p. (J). pap. *(978-0-9873334-1-4(0))* Enlife Pty, Limited.

Balogh, Jared. The Adventures of Kirby. Rhodes, Jennifer. 2012. 46p. 24.95 *(978-1-4626-9473-0(X))* America Star Bks.

—Breakfast for Two. Murray, Rosalie. 2013. 32p. pap. 24.95 *(978-1-4560-7051-9(7))* America Star Bks.

—Mama Bird & Her Baby. Begum, Dilara. 2011. 28p. pap. 24.95 *(978-1-4560-6924-7(1))* America Star Bks.

—Pokey's Promise: A Charming Tale of Telling Time. Vadney, Jackie. 2011. 28p. pap. 24.95 *(978-1-4560-2850-3(2))* America Star Bks.

—What Would I Do If I Had a Zoo? McNeal, Cari. 2012. 36p. 24.95 *(978-1-4560-4006-2(5))* America Star Bks.

Balogh, Jared, jt. illus. see Jones, Tina C.

Balouch, Kristen. The Ghost Catcher: A Bengali Folktale. Hamilton, Martha & Weiss, Mitch. 2007. (ENG.). 32p. (J). (gr. -1-3). 16.95 *(978-0-87483-835-0(5))* August Hse. Pubs., Inc.

—Thank You, Trees! Karwoski, Gail & Gootman, Marilyn E. 2013. (Tu B'Shevat Ser.). (ENG.). 12p. (J). (gr. -1 — 1). bds. 5.95 *(978-1-58013-973-1(6)*, Kar-Ben Publishing) Lerner Publishing Group.

Balouch, Kristen. Feelings. Balouch, Kristen. 2011. (ENG.). 14p. (J). (gr. -1 — 1). 6.99 *(978-1-4424-1199-9(6)*, Little Simon) Little Simon.

—The Little Little Girl with the Big Big Voice. Balouch, Kristen. 2011. (ENG.). 32p. (J). (gr. -1-k). 12.99 *(978-1-4424-0808-1(1)*, Little Simon) Little Simon.

Balsano, Sean. Edison the Firefly & the Invention of the Light Bulb. Raye, Donna. 2012. 28p. pap. 9.99 *(978-0-9836771-0-9(7))* Mindstir Media.

Baltazar, Art. The Amazing Mini-Mutts, 1 vol. Lemke, Donald B. 2012. (DC Super-Pets Ser.). (ENG.). 56p. (gr. 2-2). pap. 4.95 *(978-1-4048-7218-9(3))*; lib. bdg. 22.65 *(978-1-4048-6488-7(1))* Picture Window Bks. (DC Super-Pets).

—Attack of the Invisible Cats, 1 vol. Sonneborn, Scott. 2011. (DC Super-Pets Ser.). (ENG.). 56p. (gr. 2-2). pap. 4.95 *(978-1-4048-6847-2(X))*; lib. bdg. 22.65 *(978-1-4048-6481-8(4))* Picture Window Bks. (DC Super-Pets).

—Backward Bowwow, 1 vol. Stephens, Sarah Hines. 2011. (DC Super-Pets Ser.). (ENG.). 56p. (gr. 2-2). pap. 4.95 *(978-1-4048-6845-8(3))*; lib. bdg. 22.65 *(978-1-4048-6480-1(6))* Picture Window Bks. (DC Super-Pets).

—Barnyard Brainwash, 1 vol. Sazaklis, John. 2012. (DC Super-Pets Ser.). (ENG.). 56p. (gr. 2-2). pap. 4.95 *(978-1-4048-7213-4(2))*; lib. bdg. 22.65 *(978-1-4048-6483-2(0))* Picture Window Bks. (DC Super-Pets).

—Battle Bugs of Outer Space, 1 vol. Mason, Jane B. 2011. (DC Super-Pets Ser.). (ENG.). 56p. (gr. 2-2). pap. 4.95 *(978-1-4048-6848-9(8))*; lib. bdg. 22.65 *(978-1-4048-6482-5(2))* Picture Window Bks. (DC Super-Pets).

—The Biggest Little Hero, 1 vol. Sazaklis, John. 2012. (DC Super-Pets Ser.). (ENG.). 56p. (gr. 2-2). pap. 4.95 *(978-1-4048-7664-4(2))*; lib. bdg. 22.65 *(978-1-4048-6490-0(3))* Picture Window Bks.

—Candy Store Caper, 1 vol. Sazaklis, John. 2012. (DC Super-Pets Ser.). (ENG.). 56p. (gr. 2-2). pap. 4.95 *(978-1-4048-7214-1(0))*; lib. bdg. 22.65

(978-1-4048-6484-9(9)) Picture Window Bks. (DC Super-Pets).

—The Cat Crime Club, 1 vol. Korte, Steve. 2012. (DC Super-Pets Ser.). (ENG.). 56p. (gr. 2-2). pap. 4.95 (978-1-4048-7665-1(0)); 22.65 (978-1-4048-6493-1(8)) Picture Window Bks. (DC Super-Pets).

—DC Super-Pets Character Encyclopedia, 1 vol. Korte, Steve. 2013. (DC Super-Pets Ser.). (ENG.). 128p. (gr. 1-3). pap. 7.95 (978-1-4048-8297-3(9)); 25.28 (978-1-4795-2030-5(6)) Picture Window Bks. (DC Super-Pets).

—Deep-Sea Duel, 1 vol. Sazaklis, John. 2012. (DC Super-Pets Ser.). (ENG.). 56p. (gr. 2-2). pap. 4.95 (978-1-4048-7662-0(6)); lib. bdg. 22.65 (978-1-4048-6489-4(X)) Picture Window Bks.

—The Fantastic Flexy Frog, 1 vol. Dahl, Michael. 2012. (DC Super-Pets Ser.). (ENG.). 56p. (gr. 2-2). pap. 4.95 (978-1-4048-7666-8(9)); 22.65 (978-1-4048-6494-8(6)) Picture Window Bks. (DC Super-Pets).

—The Fastest Pet on Earth, 1 vol. Bright, J. E. 2011. (DC Super-Pets Ser.). (ENG.). 56p. (gr. 2-2). pap. 4.95 (978-1-4048-6623-2(X)); lib. bdg. 22.65 (978-1-4048-6264-7(1)) Picture Window Bks. (DC Super-Pets).

—Heroes of the High Seas, 1 vol. Bright, J. E. 2011. (DC Super-Pets Ser.). (ENG.). 56p. (gr. 2-2). 22.65 (978-1-4048-6263-0(3)); pap. 4.95 (978-1-4048-6621-8(3)) Picture Window Bks. (DC Super-Pets).

—The Hopping Hero, 1 vol. Sazaklis, John. 2011. (DC Super-Pets Ser.). (ENG.). 56p. (gr. 2-2). pap. 4.95 (978-1-4048-6843-4(7)); lib. bdg. 22.65 (978-1-4048-6477-1(6)) Picture Window Bks. (DC Super-Pets).

—Midway Monkey Madness, 1 vol. Stephens, Sarah. 2011. (DC Super-Pets Ser.). (ENG.). 56p. (gr. 2-2). pap. 4.95 (978-1-4048-6619-5(1)); lib. bdg. 22.65 (978-1-4048-6305-7(2)) Picture Window Bks. (DC Super-Pets).

—Night of the Scaredy Crows, 1 vol. Stephens, Sarah Hines. 2012. (DC Super-Pets Ser.). (ENG.). 56p. (gr. 2-2). pap. 4.95 (978-1-4048-7663-7(4)); lib. bdg. 22.65 (978-1-4048-6492-4(X)) Picture Window Bks.

—Pooches of Power!, 1 vol. Stephens, Sarah. 2011. (DC Super-Pets Ser.). (ENG.). 56p. (gr. 2-2). pap. 4.95 (978-1-4048-6620-1(5)); lib. bdg. 22.65 (978-1-4048-6306-4(0)) Picture Window Bks. (DC Super-Pets).

—Royal Rodent Rescue, 1 vol. Sazaklis, John. 2011. (DC Super-Pets Ser.). (ENG.). 56p. (gr. 2-2). pap. 4.95 (978-1-4048-6622-5(1)); lib. bdg. 22.65 (978-1-4048-6307-1(9)) Picture Window Bks. (DC Super-Pets).

—Salamander Smackdown. Sazaklis, John. 2011. (DC Super-Pets Ser.). (ENG.). 56p. (gr. 2-2). pap. 4.95 (978-1-4048-6844-1(5), DC Super-Pets) Picture Window Bks.

—Salamander Smackdown!, 1 vol. Sazaklis, John. 2011. (DC Super-Pets Ser.). (ENG.). 56p. (gr. 2-2). lib. bdg. 22.65 (978-1-4048-6478-8(4), DC Super-Pets) Picture Window Bks.

—Sleepy Time Crime, 1 vol. Stephens, Sarah Hines. 2012. (DC Super-Pets Ser.). (ENG.). 56p. (gr. 2-2). pap. 4.95 (978-1-4048-7215-8(9)); lib. bdg. 22.65 (978-1-4048-6485-6(7)) Picture Window Bks. (DC Super-Pets).

—Super Hero Splash Down, 1 vol. Mason, Jane B. 2011. (DC Super-Pets Ser.). (ENG.). 56p. (gr. 2-2). pap. 4.95 (978-1-4048-6624-9(8)); lib. bdg. 22.65 (978-1-4048-6357-6(5)) Picture Window Bks. (DC Super-Pets).

—Super-Pets Showdown, 1 vol. Stephens, Sarah Hines. 2012. (DC Super-Pets Ser.). (ENG.). 56p. (gr. 2-2). pap. 4.95 (978-1-4048-7216-5(7)); lib. bdg. 22.65 (978-1-4048-6486-3(5)) Picture Window Bks. (DC Super-Pets).

—Superpowered Pony, 1 vol. Stephens, Sarah Hines. 2011. (DC Super-Pets Ser.). (ENG.). 56p. (gr. 2-2). pap. 4.95 (978-1-4048-6846-5(1)); lib. bdg. 22.65 (978-1-4048-6479-5(2)) Picture Window Bks. (DC Super-Pets).

—Swamp Thing vs the Zombie Pets, 1 vol. Sazaklis, John. 2012. (DC Super-Pets Ser.). (ENG.). 56p. (gr. 2-2). pap. 4.95 (978-1-4048-7667-5(7)); lib. bdg. 22.65 (978-1-4048-6491-7(1)) Picture Window Bks.

Baltazar, Art. Adventures Begin! Baltazar, Art. Aureliani, Franco. 2013. (Superman Family Adventures Ser.). (ENG.). 32p. (gr. 1-2). 21.27 (978-1-4342-4786-5(4)) Stone Arch Bks.

—Aw Yeah Comics! and... Action!, Vol. 1. Baltazar, Art. Aureliani, Franco. 2014. (ENG.). 152p. (gr. 5-7). pap. 12.99 (978-1-61655-558-0(0)) Dark Horse Comics.

—Menace of Metallo! Baltazar, Art. Aureliani, Franco. 2013. (Superman Family Adventures Ser.). (ENG.). 32p. (gr. 1-2). 21.27 (978-1-4342-4794-0(5)) Stone Arch Bks.

—Monkey Metropolis!, 1 vol. Baltazar, Art. Aureliani, Franco. 2013. (Superman Family Adventures Ser.). (ENG.). 32p. (gr. 1-2). 21.27 (978-1-4342-4791-9(0)) Stone Arch Bks.

—Starro & the Space Dolphins, 1 vol. Baltazar, Art. 2012. (DC Super-Pets Ser.). (ENG.). 56p. (gr. 2-2). pap. 4.95 (978-1-4048-7217-2(5)); lib. bdg. 22.65 (978-1-4048-6487-0(3)) Picture Window Bks. (DC Super-Pets).

—Super-Pets!, 1 vol. Baltazar, Art. Aureliani, Franco. 2013. (Superman Family Adventures Ser.). (ENG.). 32p. (gr. 1-2). 21.27 (978-1-4342-4792-6(9)) Stone Arch Bks.

—Who Is the Purple Superman?, 1 vol. Baltazar, Art. Aureliani, Franco. 2013. (Superman Family Adventures Ser.). (ENG.). 32p. (gr. 1-2). 21.27 (978-1-4342-4793-3(7)) Stone Arch Bks.

Baltazar, Art & Aureliani, Franco. Enter - Nightwing! Baltazar, Art & Aureliani, Franco. 2012. (Tiny Titans Ser.). (ENG.). 32p. (gr. 1-2). lib. bdg. 21.27 (978-1-4342-4540-3(3)) Stone Arch Bks.

—Meet Tiny Titans East!, 1 vol. Baltazar, Art & Aureliani, Franco. 2013. (Tiny Titans Ser.). (ENG.). 32p. (gr. 1-2). lib. bdg. 21.27 (978-1-4342-4696-7(5)) Stone Arch Bks.

—Penguins in the Batcave!, 1 vol. Baltazar, Art & Aureliani, Franco. 2012. (Tiny Titans Ser.). (ENG.). 32p. (gr. 1-2). 21.27 (978-1-4342-4539-7(X)) Stone Arch Bks.

—Report Card Pickup!, 1 vol. Baltazar, Art & Aureliani, Franco. 2013. (Tiny Titans Ser.). (ENG.). 32p. (gr. 1-2). lib. bdg. 21.27 (978-1-4342-4699-8(X)) Stone Arch Bks.

—Sidekick City Elementary, 1 vol. Baltazar, Art & Aureliani, Franco. 2012. (Tiny Titans Ser.). (ENG.). 32p. (gr. 1-2). lib. bdg. 21.27 (978-1-4342-4528-1(4)) Stone Arch Bks.

—Tiny Titans. Baltazar, Art & Aureliani, Franco. 2013. (Tiny Titans Ser.). (ENG.). 32p. (gr. 1-2). 170.16 (978-1-4342-4854-1(2)); 85.08 (978-1-4342-4853-4(4)) Stone Arch Bks.

—Tiny Titans vs. the Fearsome Five, 1 vol. Baltazar, Art & Aureliani, Franco. 2012. (Tiny Titans Ser.). (ENG.). 32p. (gr. 1-2). lib. bdg. 21.27 (978-1-4342-4538-0(1)) Stone Arch Bks.

—Titans in Space, 1 vol. Baltazar, Art & Aureliani, Franco. 2013. (Tiny Titans Ser.). (ENG.). 32p. (gr. 1-2). lib. bdg. 21.27 (978-1-4342-4698-1(1)) Stone Arch Bks.

—Welcome to the Treehouse, 1 vol. Baltazar, Art & Aureliani, Franco. 2013. (Tiny Titans Ser.). (ENG.). 32p. (gr. 1-2). lib. bdg. 21.27 (978-1-4342-4697-4(3)) Stone Arch Bks.

Baltazar, Art & Vecchio, Luciano. Batman: An Origin Story. Sazaklis, John. 2015. (DC Super Heroes Origins Ser.). (ENG.). 48p. (gr. k-2). lib. bdg. 22.65 (978-1-4342-9727-3(6)) Stone Arch Bks.

—Green Lantern: An Origin Story. Manning, Matthew K. 2015. (DC Super Heroes Origins Ser.). (ENG.). 48p. (gr. k-2). lib. bdg. 22.65 (978-1-4342-9730-3(6)) Stone Arch Bks.

—Superman: An Origin Story. Manning, Matthew K. 2015. (DC Super Heroes Origins Ser.). (ENG.). 48p. (gr. k-2). lib. bdg. 22.65 (978-1-4342-9728-0(4)) Stone Arch Bks.

—Wonder Woman: An Origin Story. Sazaklis, John. 2015. (DC Super Heroes Origins Ser.). (ENG.). 48p. (gr. k-2). lib. bdg. 22.65 (978-1-4342-9729-7(2)) Stone Arch Bks.

Baltazar, Franco. Aw Yeah Comics Vol. 2: Time for... Adventure! Baltazar, Art. 2015. (ENG.). 168p. (gr. 5-7). pap. 12.99 (978-1-61655-689-1(7)) Dark Horse Comics.

Balthazar, Flore. Freedom! Le Gall, Frank. 2012. (Miss Annie Ser.). 48p. (J). (gr. 2-4). pap. 39.62 (978-0-7613-9281-1(5), Graphic Universe) Lerner Publishing Group.

—Freedom! Le Gall, Frank & Doo, Robin. 2012. (Miss Annie Ser.: 1). (ENG.). 48p. (J). (gr. 2-4). pap. 6.95 (978-0-7613-8546-2(0), Graphic Universe) Lerner Publishing Group.

—Freedom! Le Gall, Frank. 2012. (Miss Annie Ser.: 1). (ENG.). 48p. (J). (gr. 2-4). lib. bdg. 29.27 (978-0-7613-7884-6(7), Graphic Universe) Lerner Publishing Group.

—Miss Annie. Le Gall, Frank. 2012. (Miss Annie Ser.). 48p. (J). (gr. 2-4). lib. bdg. 58.54 (978-0-7613-8902-6(4), Graphic Universe) Lerner Publishing Group.

—Miss Annie: 6Pack Set. Le Gall, Frank. 2012. (Miss Annie Ser.). 48p. (J). (gr. 2-4). pap. 79.23 (978-0-7613-9284-2(X), Graphic Universe) Lerner Publishing Group.

—Miss Annie: Single Copy Set. Le Gall, Frank. 2012. (Miss Annie Ser.). 48p. (J). (gr. 2-4). pap. 13.21 (978-0-7613-9283-5(1), Graphic Universe) Lerner Publishing Group.

—Rooftop Cat. Le Gall, Frank. 2012. (Miss Annie Ser.). (J). (gr. 2-4). 48p. pap. 39.62 (978-0-7613-9282-8(3)); (ENG.). 40p. pap. 6.95 (978-0-7613-8547-9(9)); (ENG.). 48p. lib. bdg. 29.27 (978-0-7613-7885-3(5)) Lerner Publishing Group. (Graphic Universe).

Baluschek, Hans. Peter & Anneli's Journey to the Moon. von Bassewitz, Gerdt. 2007. 110p. (J). (gr. 3-7). (978-0-88010-584-2(4), Bell Pond Bks.) SteinerBooks, Inc.

Balvanz, Gwynessa. No Cookies for Christmas: The Story of Grandma's Missing Package. delMazo, Deborah. Horsfall, Jacqueline, ed. 2010. 32p. (J). pap. 9.95 (978-0-615-32691-7(9)) Zoombird Bks.

Balzer, Jeremy. Tyler the Turtle Is Afraid of the Dark. Crawford, Deborah. 2006. 32p. (J). 14.95 (978-0-9770516-1-8(7)) Laffin Minor Pr.

Balzola, Asun. El Arbol de Mi Patio. Xirinacs, Olga. 3rd ed. (SPA.). 32p. (J). (gr. 1-3). (978-84-236-3391-3(8)) Edebé ESP. Dist: Lectorum Pubns., Inc.

—Paloma, Llegaste Por el Aire. Zubizarreta, Patxi. 2003. (SPA.). 24p. (978-84-246-5913-4(9), GL3212) La Galera, S.A. Editorial ESP. Dist: Lectorum Pubns., Inc.

Balzola, Sofia. Rosalinde Tiene Ideas en la Cabeza. Nöstlinger, Christine. 2003. (SPA.). 80p. (J). (gr. 3-5). 11.95 (978-84-204-4804-6(4)) Ediciones Alfaguara ESP. Dist: Santillana USA Publishing Co., Inc.

Bampton, Bob. Animals in the Wild. 2004. (Look & Learn about Ser.). 18p. (J). bds. 5.99 (978-1-85854-351-2(7)) Brimax Books Ltd. GBR. Dist: Byeway Bks.

—Animals on the Farm. 2004. (Look & Learn about Ser.). 18p. (J). bds. 5.99 (978-1-85854-319-2(3)) Brimax Books Ltd. GBR. Dist: Byeway Bks.

—Ocean Animals. Goldsack, Gaby. (J). (978-1-57755-508-7(2)) Flying Frog Publishing, Inc.

Banach, Virginia. Twinkle, Twinkle Little Girl. Peirce-Bale, Mary. 2005. (ENG.). 15p. (J). 6.95 (978-0-9743869-9-7(5)) Mother's Hse. Publishing.

Bancroft, Bronwyn. The Amazing A-Z Thing. Morgan, Sally. 2015. (ENG.). 32p. (J). (-k). 16.99 (978-1-921894-19-0(9)) Little Hare Bks. AUS. Dist: Independent Pubs. Group.

—An Australian ABC of Animals. 2013. (ENG.). 24p. (J). (— 1). bds. 9.99 (978-1-921894-22-0(9)) Little Hare Bks. AUS. Dist: Independent Pubs. Group.

—Malu Kangaroo. Morecroft, Judith. 2008. (ENG.). 40p. (J). (gr. k-2). pap. 11.95 (978-1-921272-51-6(1)) Little Hare Bks. AUS. Dist: Independent Pubs. Group.

—Ready to Dream. Napoli, Donna Jo & Furrow, Elena. 2009. (ENG.). 32p. (J). (gr. k-3). 16.99 (978-1-59990-049-0(1), Bloomsbury USA Childrens) Bloomsbury USA.

Bancroft, Bronwyn. An Australian 1, 2, 3 of Animals. Bancroft, Bronwyn. 2010. (ENG.). 32p. (J). (gr. -1-k). pap. 8.99 (978-1-921272-85-1(6)) Little Hare Bks. AUS. Dist: Independent Pubs. Group.

—An Australian ABC of Animals. Bancroft, Bronwyn. 2005. (ENG.). 24p. (J). (gr. -1-k). pap. 12.99 (978-1-877003-97-4(2)) Little Hare Bks. AUS. Dist: Independent Pubs. Group.

—E Is for Echidna: My Australian Word Book. Bancroft, Bronwyn. 2012. (ENG.). 24p. (J). (gr. k — 1). bds. 12.99 (978-1-921714-61-0(1)) Little Hare Bks. AUS. Dist: Independent Pubs. Group.

—Kangaroo & Crocodile: My Big Book of Australian Animals. Bancroft, Bronwyn. enl. ed. 2012. (ENG.). 48p. (J). (gr. k-k). 19.99 (978-1-921714-25-2(5)) Little Hare Bks. AUS. Dist: Independent Pubs. Group.

—Patterns of Australia. Bancroft, Bronwyn. 2005. 24p. (978-1-877003-96-7(4)); 2012. (ENG.). 32p. (J). (gr. -1). 19.95 (978-1-921894-06-0(7)) Little Hare Bks. AUS. Dist: HarperCollins Pubs. Australia, Independent Pubs. Group.

—Possum & Wattle: My Big Book of Australian Words. Bancroft, Bronwyn. 2010. (ENG.). 48p. (J). (gr. -1-1). pap. 14.99 (978-1-921541-67-4(9)) Little Hare Bks. AUS. Dist: Independent Pubs. Group.

—W Is for Wombat: My First Australian Word Book. Bancroft, Bronwyn. (ENG.). 24p. (J). (gr. k — 1). 2011. pap. 8.99 (978-1-921541-85-8(7)); 2010. bds. 8.99 (978-1-921541-17-9(2)) Little Hare Bks. AUS. Dist: Independent Pubs. Group.

—Why I Love Australia. Bancroft, Bronwyn. enl. ed. 2012. (ENG.). 32p. (J). (gr. -1-k). 22.99 (978-1-921894-05-3(9)) Little Hare Bks. AUS. Dist: Independent Pubs. Group.

Bancroft, Tom & Corley, Rob. Florence Fiasco. Sorrells, W. A. 2007. 136p. (J). (978-0-9792912-2-7(4)) KidsGive, LLC.

—Nairobi Nightmare. Sorrells, W. A. 2007. 144p. (J). (978-0-9792912-1-0(6)) KidsGive, LLC.

Bancroft, Tom, jt. illus. see Corley, Rob.

Bandelin Dacey Studios Staff, jt. illus. see Dacey, Bob.

Bandelin, Debra, et al. What's the Difference Between a Dolphin & a Porpoise?, 1 vol. Shaskan, Trisha Speed. 2010. (What's the Difference? Ser.). (ENG.). 24p. (gr. k-3). lib. bdg. 25.99 (978-1-4048-5545-8(9), Nonfiction Picture Bks.) Picture Window Bks.

—What's the Difference Between a Frog & a Toad?, 1 vol. Firestone, Mary. 2009. (What's the Difference? Ser.). (ENG.). 24p. (gr. k-3). lib. bdg. 25.99 (978-1-4048-5544-1(0), Nonfiction Picture Bks.) Picture Window Bks.

—What's the Difference Between a Leopard & a Cheetah? Bullard, Lisa. 2009. (What's the Difference? Ser.). (ENG.). 24p. (gr. k-3). lib. bdg. 25.99 (978-1-4048-5548-9(3), Nonfiction Picture Bks.) Picture Window Bks.

—What's the Difference Between a Turtle & a Tortoise?, 1 vol. Shaskan, Trisha Speed. 2010. (What's the Difference? Ser.). (ENG.). 24p. (gr. k-3). lib. bdg. 25.99 (978-1-4048-5546-5(7), Nonfiction Picture Bks.) Picture Window Bks.

Bandelin, Debra & Dacey, Bob. Abigail Adams: First Lady of the American Revolution. Lakin, Patricia. 2006. 48p. (J). lib. bdg. 15.00 (978-1-4242-1560-7(9)) Fitzgerald Bks.

—Davy Crockett: A Life on the Frontier. Krensky, Stephen. 2004. (Ready-To-read SOFA Ser.). (ENG.). 48p. (J). (gr. 1-3). pap. 3.99 (978-0-689-85944-1(9), Simon Spotlight) Simon Spotlight.

Bandelin, Debra, jt. illus. see Dacey, Bob.

Bane, Jeff. Abraham Lincoln. Haldy, Emma E. 2016. (J). **(978-1-63470-476-2(2))** Cherry Lake Publishing.

—Eleanor Roosevelt. Haldy, Emma E. 2016. (J). **(978-1-63470-483-0(5))** Cherry Lake Publishing.

—Frederick Douglass/By Emma E. Haldy; Illustrated by Jeff Bane. Haldy, Emma E. 2016. (J). **(978-1-63470-479-3(7))** Cherry Lake Publishing.

—Martin Luther King, Jr. Haldy, Emma E. 2016. (J). **(978-1-63470-477-9(0))** Cherry Lake Publishing.

—Rosa Parks. Haldy, Emma E. 2016. (J). **(978-1-63470-481-6(9))** Cherry Lake Publishing.

Bane, T. Glenn. Doodey the Combat Camel. Wardell, Joe. 2012. 20p. pap. 12.95 (978-0-615-58866-7(2)) Little Clive Pr.

Banek, Yvette. Writing Makeovers 3-4: Improving Skills - Adding Style. Hults, Alaska. Rous, Sheri, ed. 2003. 96p. (J). (gr. 3-5). pap. 11.99 (978-1-57471-956-7(4), 2261) Creative Teaching Pr., Inc.

Banerjee, Sankha. Martin Luther King. Helfand, Lewis & Teitelbaum, Michael. 2013. (Campfire Graphic Novels Ser.). (ENG.). 88p. (gr. 5). pap. 11.99 (978-93-80028-69-9(5), Campfire) Kalyani Navyug Media Pty. Ltd. IND. Dist: Random Hse., Inc.

—Stolen Hearts: The Love of Eros & Psyche. Foley, Ryan. 2011. (Campfire Graphic Novels Ser.). (ENG.). 88p. (gr. 5-9). pap. 11.99 (978-93-80028-48-4(2), Campfire) Kalyani Navyug Media Pty. Ltd. IND. Dist: Random Hse., Inc.

—The Wright Brothers. Helfand, Lewis. 2011. (Campfire Graphic Novels Ser.). (ENG.). 72p. (J). (gr. 5-9). pap. 9.99 (978-93-80028-46-0(6), Campfire) Kalyani Navyug Media Pty. Ltd. IND. Dist: Random Hse., Inc.

Banerjee, Sankha & Nagar, Sachin. Mother Teresa: Saint of the Slums. Helfand, Lewis. 2013. (Campfire Graphic Novels Ser.). (ENG.). 88p. (gr. 5). pap. 11.99 (978-93-80028-70-5(9), Campfire) Kalyani Navyug Media Pty. Ltd. IND. Dist: Random Hse., Inc.

Bang, Molly. The Day Leo Said I Hate You! Harris, Robie H. 2010. (ENG.). 32p. (J). (gr. -1-1). pap. 6.99 (978-0-316-08350-8(X)) Little, Brown Bks. for Young Readers.

Bang, Molly. Buried Sunlight: How Fossil Fuels Have Changed the Earth. Bang, Molly. Chisholm, Penny. 2014. (ENG.). 48p. (J). (gr. -1-3). 18.99 (978-0-545-57785-4(3)) Scholastic, Inc.

—Living Sunlight: How Plants Bring the Earth to Life. Bang, Molly. Chisholm, Penny. 2009. (ENG.). 40p. (J). (gr. -1-3). 18.99 (978-0-545-04422-6(7), Blue Sky Pr., The) Scholastic, Inc.

—My Light. Bang, Molly. 2004. (ENG.). 40p. (J). (gr. -1-3). 18.99 (978-0-439-48961-4(X)) Scholastic, Inc.

—Ocean Sunlight: How Tiny Plants Feed the Seas. Bang, Molly. Chisholm, Penny. 2012. (ENG.). 42p. (J). (gr. -1-3). 18.99 (978-0-545-27322-0(6), Blue Sky Pr., The) Scholastic, Inc.

—Ten, Nine, Eight. Bang, Molly. 2003. (ENG.). 24p. (J). (gr. -1-3). reprint ed. pap. 6.99 (978-0-688-10480-1(0)); 20th ed. 16.99 (978-0-688-00906-9(9)) HarperCollins Pubs. (Greenwillow Bks.).

—Wiley & the Hairy Man: Adapted from an American Folk Tale. Bang, Molly. 2009. (ENG.). 66p. (J). (gr. k-2). pap. 10.99 (978-1-4169-9843-3(8), Simon Spotlight) Simon Spotlight.

Bania, Michael. Wiggle-Waggle Woof: Counting Sled Dogs in Alaska. Stihler, Cherie B. 2009. (ENG.). 32p. (J). (gr. -1-2). pap. 10.99 (978-1-57061-559-7(4)) Sasquatch Bks.

—Wiggle-Waggle Woof 1, 2, 3. Stihler, Chérie B. 2015. (ENG.). 20p. (J). (— 1). bds. 8.99 (978-1-57061-978-6(6)) Sasquatch Bks.

Banigan, Chris. The Robber Chief: A Tale of Vengeance & Compassion. Rowe, W. W. 2003. (ENG.). 48p. (gr. 1-18). 12.95 (978-1-55939-186-3(3), Snow Lion Publications, Inc.) Shambhala Pubns., Inc.

Banis, Bud. Me & My Shadows -Shadow Puppet Fun ForKids of All Ages: Enhanced with Practical Paper Pastimes. Banis, Bud. 2012. 122p. (J). pap. 14.95 (978-1-59630-076-7(0), BeachHouse Bks.) Science & Humanities Pr.

Bankenaar, Dale. Animal Tales, Vol. 1. Von Wielligh, G. R. 2012. 96p. pap. 12.00 (978-1-86919-433-8(0)) Protea Boekhuis ZAF. Dist: Casemate Pubs. & Bk. Distributors, LLC.

—Animal Tales, Vol. 2. Von Wielligh, G. R. 2012. 96p. pap. 12.00 (978-1-86919-504-5(3)) Protea Boekhuis ZAF. Dist: Casemate Pubs. & Bk. Distributors, LLC.

Banki, Caspian & Banki, Damian. What Autism Means to Me. Banki, Caspian & Banki, Lynne. 2003. (ENG.). 40p. (J). per. 12.95 (978-0-9743801-0-0(5)) Lifelight Bks.

Banki, Damian, jt. illus. see Banki, Caspian.

Banks, Erin. The First Music. Pritchett, Dylan. 2006. (ENG.). 32p. (J). (gr. -1-3). 16.95 (978-0-87483-776-6(6)) August Hse. Pubs., Inc.

—Hush Harbor: Praying in Secret. Evans, Freddi Williams. 2008. (ENG.). 32p. (J). (gr. k-3). 16.95 (978-0-8225-7965-6(0), Carolrhoda Bks.) Lerner Publishing Group.

Banks, Pat. Appalachian Toys & Games from a to Z. Pack, Linda Hager. 2013. (ENG.). 56p. 17.95 (978-0-8131-4104-6(4)) Univ. Pr. of Kentucky.

—A Is for Appalachia: The Alphabet Book of Appalachian Heritage. Pack, Linda Hager. 2009. (ENG.). 44p. 16.95 (978-0-8131-2556-5(1)) Univ. Pr. of Kentucky.

Banks, Sandra. The Adventures of Didi & Mr Taco. Schult, Sherry. 2011. 16p. pap. 24.95 (978-1-4560-8083-9(0)) America Star Bks.

Banks, Timothy. ABCs. Wittrock, Jeni. 2013. (Wizard of Oz Ser.). (ENG.). 24p. (gr. 1-2). 27.32 (978-1-4765-3765-8(8)) Capstone Pr., Inc.

—Colors. Kalz, Jill. 2013. (Wizard of Oz Ser.). (ENG.). (gr. 1-2). 20p. bds. 7.99 (978-1-4765-3768-9(2)); 24p. 27.32 (978-1-4765-3764-1(X)) Capstone Pr., Inc.

—Counting. McCurry, Kristen. 2013. (Wizard of Oz Ser.). (ENG.). (gr. 1-2). 20p. bds. 7.99 (978-1-4765-3770-2(4)); 24p. 27.32 (978-1-4765-3766-5(6)) Capstone Pr., Inc.

—Feet First. Sonneborn, Scott. 2014. (Frankenstein Journals). (ENG.). 80p. (gr. 2-3). 21.32 (978-1-4342-8999-5(0)) Stone Arch Bks.

—The Frankenstein Journals, 1 vol. Sonneborn, Scott. 2014. (Frankenstein Journals). (ENG.). 160p. (gr. 2-3). 9.95 (978-1-4342-9130-1(8)) Stone Arch Bks.

Banks, Timothy. The Frankenstein Journals: Guts or Bust. Sonneborn, Scott. 2015. (Frankenstein Journals). (ENG.). 160p. (gr. 2-3). 9.95 **(978-1-4965-0223-0(X))** Stone Arch Bks.

Banks, Timothy. I for an Eye. Sonneborn, Scott. 2014. (Frankenstein Journals). (ENG.). 80p. (gr. 2-3). 21.32 (978-1-4342-9000-7(X)) Stone Arch Bks.

—The Land of Caring Bou. Coles, Michael Joseph et al. 2006. (J). (978-0-87483-814-5(2)) August Hse. Pubs., Inc.

Banks, Timothy. No Guts, No Gloria. Sonneborn, Scott. 2015. (Frankenstein Journals). (ENG.). 80p. (gr. 2-3). 21.32 **(978-1-4965-0221-6(3))** Stone Arch Bks.

—A Pain in the Butt. Sonneborn, Scott. 2015. (Frankenstein Journals). (ENG.). 80p. (gr. 2-3). 21.32 **(978-1-4965-0222-3(1))** Stone Arch Bks.

Banks, Timothy. Shapes. Harbo, Christopher L. 2013. (Wizard of Oz Ser.). (ENG.). (gr. 1-2). 20p. bds. 7.99 (978-1-4765-3771-9(2)); 24p. 27.32 (978-1-4765-3767-2(4)) Capstone Pr., Inc.

Banning, Greg. Go Ahead & Dream. Kingsbury, Karen & Smith, Alex. 2013. (ENG.). 32p. (J). (gr. -1-3). 17.99 (978-0-06-168625-2(5)) HarperCollins Pubs.

—Wendel & the Great One. Leonetti, Mike. 2008. 383p. (978-1-55192-812-8(4)) Raincoast Bk. Distribution.

Bannister. Book Six: The Tower of Shadows. Nykko. 2013. (ElseWhere Chronicles Ser.: 6). (ENG.). 48p. (J). (gr. 4-8). pap. 6.95 (978-1-4677-1517-1(4)); lib. bdg. 27.93 (978-1-4677-1233-0(7)) Lerner Publishing Group. (Graphic Universe).

—The Calling. Nykko. 2010. (ElseWhere Chronicles Ser.: Bk. 4). (ENG.). 48p. (J). (gr. 4-8). pap. 6.95 (978-0-7613-6069-8(7), Graphic Universe) Lerner Publishing Group.

—The Master of Shadows, 3 vols. Nykko. 2009. (ElseWhere Chronicles Ser.: Bk. 3). (ENG.). 48p. (J). (gr. 4-8). lib. bdg. 27.93 (978-0-7613-4461-2(6)) Lerner Publishing Group.

—My Amazing Dinosaur. Grimaldi. Burrell, Carol Klio, tr. from FRE. 2014. (Tib & Tumtum Ser.: 2). (ENG.). 48p. (J). (gr. 2-5). lib. bdg. 26.60 (978-1-4677-1298-9(1), Graphic Universe) Lerner Publishing Group.

—My Amazing Dinosaur. Grimaldi. Flora. Burrell, Carol Klio, tr. 2014. (Tib & Tumtum Ser.: 2). (ENG.). 48p. (J). (gr. 2-5). pap. 7.95 (978-1-4677-2181-3(6), Graphic Universe) Lerner Publishing Group.

B

—The Parting. Nykko. 2011. (ElseWhere Chronicles Ser.: 5). (ENG.). 48p. (J). (gr. 4-8). pap. 6.95 *(978-0-7613-7524-1(4)*, Graphic Universe) Lerner Publishing Group.
—The Parting, Bk. 5. Nykko. 2011. (ElseWhere Chronicles Ser.: 5). (ENG.). 48p. (J). (gr. 4-8). lib. bdg. 27.93 *(978-0-7613-6632-4(6)*, Graphic Universe) Lerner Publishing Group.
—The Shadow Door. Nykko. 2009. (ElseWhere Chronicles Ser.: Bk. 1). (ENG.). 48p. (J). (gr. 4-8). pap. 6.95 *(978-0-7613-3963-2(9))*; lib. bdg. 27.93 *(978-0-7613-4459-9(4))* Lerner Publishing Group.
—The Shadow Spies. Nykko. 2009. (ElseWhere Chronicles Ser.: Bk. 2). (ENG.). 48p. (J). (gr. 4-8). pap. 6.95 *(978-0-7613-3964-9(7))*; lib. bdg. 27.93 *(978-0-7613-4460-5(8))* Lerner Publishing Group.
—Welcome to the Tribe! Grimaldi. 2013. (Tib & Tumtum Ser.: 1). (ENG.). 48p. (J). (gr. 2-5). pap. 6.95 *(978-1-4677-1522-5(0))*; lib. bdg. 26.60 *(978-1-4677-1297-2(3))* Lerner Publishing Group. (Graphic Universe).
—Welcome to the Tribe! Grimaldi. ed. 2013. (Tib & Tumtum Ser.). (ENG.). 48p. lib. bdg. 17.15 *(978-0-606-33997-1(3)*, Turtleback) Turtleback Bks.
Bannister, A. Book One: The Shadow Door. Nykko. 2009. (ElseWhere Chronicles Ser.). (ENG.). (J). (gr. 4-8). pap. 39.62 *(978-0-7613-4904-4(9))* Lerner Publishing Group.
—Book Three: The Master of Shadows. Nykko. 2009. (ElseWhere Chronicles Ser.). (ENG.). (J). (gr. 4-8). pap. 39.62 *(978-0-7613-5087-3(X))* Lerner Publishing Group.
Bannister, Emily. Fairy Treasure Vol. 1: A Fairy Who Needs a Friend. Rees, Gwyneth. 2nd unabr. ed. 2004. (Fairy Dust Ser.: 2). (ENG.). 240p. (J). (gr. 2-4). pap. 9.99 *(978-0-330-43730-1(5))* Macmillan Pubs., Ltd. GBR. Dist: Independent Pubs. Group.
Bannon, Laura. Pecos Bill: The Greatest Cowboy of All Time. Bowman, James Cloyd. 2007. (ENG.). 296p. (J). (gr. 4-7). 18.95 *(978-1-59017-224-7(8)*, NYR Children's Collection) New York Review of Bks., Inc., The.
—Tales from a Finnish Tupa. Bowman, James Cloyd et al. Kolehmainen, Aili, tr. 2009. 288p. pap. 15.95 *(978-0-8166-6768-0(3))* Univ. of Minnesota Pr.
Bansch, Helga. Chocolate. Núñez, Marisa. 2007. (ENG.). 36p. (J). 17.95 *(978-84-96788-83-1(0))* OQO, Editora ESP. Dist: Baker & Taylor Bks.
—En Casa. Janisch, Heinz. Rodriguez Aguilar, Christina, tr. 2009. (SPA.). 32p. (J). (gr. -1-1). *(978-84-263-6857-7(3))* Vives, Luis Editorial (Edelvives).
—El Sueño del Osito Rosa. Aliaga, Roberto. (SPA.). 40p. (J). 15.95 *(978-84-96788-36-7(9))* OQO, Editora ESP. Dist: Baker & Taylor Bks.
Bansch, Helga. I Want a Dog! Bansch, Helga. 2009. (ENG.). 32p. (J). (gr. -1-3). 17.95 *(978-0-7358-2255-9(7))* North-South Bks., Inc.
—Petra. Bansch, Helga. Mejuto, Eva, tr. 2010. (SPA.). 48p. (J). 15.95 *(978-84-9871-003-8(0))* OQO, Editora ESP. Dist: Baker & Taylor Bks.
Banta, Susan. Bubble & Squeak, 1 vol. Bonnett-Rampersaud, Louise. 2006. (ENG.). 24p. (J). (gr. -1-2). 14.99 *(978-0-7614-5310-9(5))* Marshall Cavendish Corp.
—Good Morning, Little Polar Bear. Votaw, Carol J. 2005. (ENG.). 32p. (J). (gr. k-3). 15.95 *(978-1-55971-932-2(X))* Cooper Square Publishing Llc.
—Here Comes Coco. Williams, Rozanne Lanczak. 2005. (Reading for Fluency Ser.). 8p. (J). pap. 3.49 *(978-1-59198-145-9(X)*, 4245) Creative Teaching Pr., Inc.
—La Leyenda del Coqui. 2005. (SPA.). 29p. (J). (gr. k-12). 12.95 *(978-1-58173-256-6(2))* Sweetwater Pr.
—My Friends. Williams, Rozanne Lanczak. Hamaguchi, Carla, ed. 2003. (Sight Word Readers Ser.). 16p. (J). (gr. k-2). pap. 3.49 *(978-1-57471-963-5(7)*, 3585) Creative Teaching Pr., Inc.
—Peeper Has a Fever. Cowan, Charlotte. 2007. (ENG.). 32p. (J). (gr. 3-7). 17.95 *(978-0-9753516-2-8(1))* Hippocratic Pr., The.
—Waking up down Under. Votaw, Carol. 2007. (ENG.). 32p. (J). (gr. k-3). 15.95 *(978-1-55971-976-6(1))* Cooper Square Publishing Llc.
—With All My Heart. Rock, Brian. 2012. (J). *(978-1-58925-648-4(4))* Tiger Tales.
Banton, Amy Renee. Bob Tales. Morgan, Robert. 2003. 216p. (J). pap. 15.00 *(978-1-888562-06-4(4))* booksonnet.com.
Banyai, Istvan. Tap Dancing on the Roof: Sijo (Poems) Park, Linda Sue. 2007. (ENG.). 48p. (J). (gr. -1-3). 16.00 *(978-0-618-23483-7(7))* Houghton Mifflin Harcourt Publishing Co.
Baptiste, Annette Green. In the Shade of the Spade: This Tale in a Poetry Format Takes Us on a Journey. the Illustrations Are Bright & Whimsical. You Can Almost Hear Music. Lee, Deborah Baptiste & Atcheson-Melton, Patty. 2013. 48p. pap. 14.95 *(978-0-9858839-1-1(X))* Lee, Deborah I.
Barajas, Sal & Levins Morales, Ricardo. Under What Bandera? Anti-War Ofrendas from Minnesota y Califas. Ortiz, Teresa et al. Garcia Echeverria, Olga Angelina et al, eds. 2004. 44p. pap. 7.00 *(978-0-9717035-3-7(1))* Calaca Pr.
Barajas, Sal & Vélez, Gabriel J. La Calaca Review: Un Bilingual Journal of Pensamiento & Palabra. alurista et al. Vélez, Manuel J., ed. 2003. (SPA & ENG.). 152p. per. 15.00 *(978-0-9660773-9-1(3))* Calaca Pr.
Baranowski, Mark. A Day in the Life of the Shifties: Deezer's First Day of Pre-School. Baranowski, Mark. 2010. (ENG.). 34p. pap. 9.99 *(978-1-4538-1678-3(X))* CreateSpace Independent Publishing Platform.
Baranski, Marcin. Jake the Ballet Dog. LeFrak, Karen & Lefrak, Karen. 2008. (ENG.). 32p. (J). (gr. k-3). 16.99 *(978-0-8027-9658-5(3))* Walker & Co.
—Jake the Philharmonic Dog. LeFrak, Karen. 2006. (ENG.). 32p. (J). (gr. -1-2). 16.95 *(978-0-8027-9552-6(8))* Walker & Co.
Barasch, Lynne. Owney, the Mail-Pouch Pooch. Kerby, Mona. 2008. (ENG.). 40p. (J). (gr. k-3). 17.99 *(978-0-374-35685-9(8)*, Farrar, Straus & Giroux (BYR)) Farrar, Straus & Giroux.
Barasch, Lynne. First Come the Zebra. Barasch, Lynne. (ENG.). 40p. (J). 2009. (gr. 1-6). 18.95 *(978-1-60060-365-5(3))*; 2005. pap. 10.95 *(978-1-62014-029-1(2))* Lee & Low Bks., Inc.
—Hiromi's Hands, 1 vol. Barasch, Lynne. 2007. (ENG.). 40p. (J). (gr. k-6). 18.95 *(978-1-58430-275-9(5))* Lee & Low Bks., Inc.
Barasch, Lynne & McCue, Lisa. Part-Time Dog. Thayer, Jane. 2004. (ENG.). 32p. (J). (gr. -1-3). 14.99 *(978-0-06-029693-3(3))* HarperCollins Pubs.
Barb Dragony. How Do You Do? Poulter, J. R. 2014. 24p. pap. 17.99 *(978-1-62563-921-9(X))* Tate Publishing & Enterprises, LLC.
Barbaresi, Nina. The Tale of Tom Kitten: A Story about Good Behavior. 2006. (J). 6.99 *(978-1-59939-002-4(7))* Cornerstone Pr.
Barbas, Kerren. The Hero Book: Learning Lessons from the People You Admire. Sabin, Ellen. 2005. 64p. 19.95 *(978-0-9759868-1-3(3))* Watering Can.
—The Night Before Christmas dot.com. Gandolfi, Claudine. 2005. (Charming Petites Ser.). 80p. 4.95 *(978-0-88088-844-8(X))* Peter Pauper Pr. Inc.
—Princess Bella: An Art Activity Story Book for Princesses of All Ages. Peter Pauper Press Staff & Zschock, Heather. 2005. (Activity Journal Ser.). 64p. (J). (gr. -1-7). 14.99 *(978-1-59359-972-0(2))* Peter Pauper Pr. Inc.
—Super Scratch & Sketch: A Cool Art Activity Book for Budding Artists of All Ages. 2005. (Activity Journals Ser.). 60p. 12.99 *(978-0-88088-286-6(7))* Peter Pauper Pr. Inc.
—Wild Safari: An Art Activity Book for Imaginative Artists of All Ages. Zschock, Heather. 2005. (Activity Journal Ser.). 64p. (J). (gr. -1-7). 12.99 *(978-1-59359-971-3(4))* Peter Pauper Pr. Inc.
Barbas Steckler, Kerren. Knights Scratch & Sketch: For Brave Artists & Loyal Subjects of All Ages. Nemmers, Tom. 2007. (Scratch & Sketch sER.). 80p. (J). 12.99 *(978-1-59359-877-8(7))* Peter Pauper Pr. Inc.
Barbelle. Children's Cowboy Songs for Piano. Spivak, Samuel. 2011. 28p. 35.95 *(978-1-258-06408-2(1))* Literary Licensing, LLC.
Barber, Brian. My Favorite Places from A to Z. Snow, Peggy. 2007. (My Favorites Ser.). (ENG.). 32p. (J). (gr. -1). lib. bdg. 15.99 *(978-1-934277-03-4(7))* Mam Green Publishing, Inc.
Barber, Carol. Naya & Nathan. Fripp, Deborah & Fripp, Michael. Fripp, Jean, ed. 2003. (Dolphin Watch Ser.). 32p. (J). (gr. k-4). pap. 5.99 *(978-0-9701008-4-9(1))* Bicast, Inc.
Barber, David L. Custody Battle: A Workbook for Children. Martin-Finks, Nancy. 2005. 68p. per. 19.95 *(978-1-931636-42-1(7))* National Ctr. For Youth Issues.
—Tales of Temper: Grades 3-6. Sartori, Rosanne Sheritz. 2005. 128p. per. 21.95 *(978-1-931636-48-3(6))* National Ctr. For Youth Issues.
Barber, Julia. Colors Around Us. Wilcox, Michael. 2004. 32p. (J). per. 19.95 *(978-1-931780-32-2(3))* School of Color Publishing.
Barber, Shirley. The Fairies Alphabet Puzzle Tray: With Five 6-Piece Jigsaw Puzzles. 2004. 10p. (J). *(978-1-74124-437-3(4))* Five Mile Pr. Pty Ltd. The.
Barber, Shirley. The Seventh Unicorn. Barber, Shirley. ed. 32p. (J). *(978-1-74124-399-4(8))* Five Mile Pr. Pty Ltd. The.
—Spellbound & the Fairy Book: Packed with 3-D Pictures. Barber, Shirley. 2005. 64p. (J). incl. audio compact disk *(978-1-74124-486-1(2))* Five Mile Pr. Pty Ltd. The.
—Tales from Martha B. Rabbit. Barber, Shirley. 2005. 70p. (J). incl. audio compact disk *(978-1-86503-740-0(0))* Five Mile Pr. Pty Ltd. The.
Barbera, Michelle. Meerkat's Safari. Graziano, Claudia. 2007. 36p. (J). 15.99 *(978-0-9778072-0-8(7))* Meerkat's Adventures Bks.
Barbera, Tony, et al. The Chronicles of Narnia. Barbera, Tony et al, photos by. Peacock, Ann & Lewis, C. S. 2005. (Chronicles of Narnia Ser.). 64p. (J). *(978-1-4156-3678-7(8))* HarperCollins Pubs.
Barberi, Carlo. In the Dimming Light, 1 vol. Beechen, Adam & Wong, Walden. 2013. (Justice League Unlimited Ser.). (ENG.). 32p. (gr. 2-3). 21.27 *(978-1-4342-6042-0(9))* Stone Arch Bks.
—Marvel Heros: Mix & Match Storybook. Meredith, Randy. 2006. 8p. (J). 8.95 *(978-1-57791-299-6(3)*, Penny Candy Pr.) Brighter Minds Children's Publishing.
—Monitor Duty, 1 vol. Beechen, Adam & Wong, Walden. 2013. (Justice League Unlimited Ser.). (ENG.). 32p. (gr. 2-3). 21.27 *(978-1-4342-6041-3(0))* Stone Arch Bks.
—Ororo: Before the Storm. Sumerak, Marc. 2012. (Ororo: Before the Storm Ser.). 24p. (J). (gr. 2-6). lib. bdg. 24.21 *(978-1-61479-025-9(6))*; lib. bdg. 24.21 *(978-1-61479-027-3(2))*; lib. bdg. 24.21 *(978-1-61479-024-2(8))*; lib. bdg. 24.21 *(978-1-61479-026-6(4))* Spotlight.
—Who Is the Question?, 1 vol. Beechen, Adam & Wong, Walden. 2013. (Justice League Unlimited Ser.). (ENG.). 32p. (gr. 2-3). 21.27 *(978-1-4342-6044-4(5))* Stone Arch Bks.
Barberi, Carlo & Beatty, Terry. Batman Versus the Yeti!, 1 vol. Torres, J. 2013. (Batman: the Brave & the Bold Ser.). (ENG.). 32p. (gr. 2-3). 21.27 *(978-1-4342-4708-7(2))* Stone Arch Bks.
—The Case of the Fractured Fairy Tale, 1 vol. Torres, J. 2013. (Batman: the Brave & the Bold Ser.). (ENG.). 32p. (gr. 2-3). 21.27 *(978-1-4342-4705-6(8))* Stone Arch Bks.
Barberi, Carlo & Wong, Walden. Divide & Conquer, 1 vol. Beechen, Adam. 2013. (Justice League Unlimited Ser.). (ENG.). 32p. (gr. 2-3). lib. bdg. 21.27 *(978-1-4342-4713-1(9))* Stone Arch Bks.
—Local Hero, 1 vol. Beechen, Adam. 2013. (Justice League Unlimited Ser.). (ENG.). 32p. (gr. 2-3). 21.27 *(978-1-4342-4716-2(3))* Stone Arch Bks.
—Small Time, 1 vol. Beechen, Adam. 2013. (Justice League Unlimited Ser.). (ENG.). 32p. (gr. 2-3). 21.27 *(978-1-4342-4715-5(5))* Stone Arch Bks.
Barberi, Carlo, jt. illus. see Medina, Paco.
Barberis, Franco. Would You Like a Parrot? Barberis, France. 32p. (J). (gr. -1). 16.95 *(978-0-87592-060-3(8))* Scroll Pr., Inc.
Barbor, Carol. Naya & the Haunted Shipwreck. Fripp, Deborah & Fripp, Michael. Fripp, Jean, ed. 2004. 32p. (J). (gr. k-4). pap. 5.99 *(978-0-9701008-7-0(6))* Bicast, Inc.
Barborini, Robert. The Human Body: Lift the Flap & Learn. Hédelin, Pascale. 2nd ed. 2011. (Lift the Flap & Learn Ser.). (ENG.). 38p. (J). (gr. -1). spiral bd. 19.95 *(978-1-897349-86-1(6))* Owlkids Bks. Inc. CAN. Dist: Perseus-PGW.
Barbour, H. S. Pee-Wee Harris on the Briny Deep. Fitzhugh, Percy Keese. 2011. 264p. 47.95 *(978-1-258-09985-5(3))* Literary Licensing, LLC.
—Polly in Egypt: The Polly Brewster Series. Roy, Lillian Elizabeth. 2011. 226p. 44.95 *(978-1-258-09808-7(3))* Literary Licensing, LLC.
—Polly in New York. Roy, Lillian Elizabeth. 2004. reprint ed. pap. 28.95 *(978-1-4179-0068-8(7))* Kessinger Publishing, LLC.
—Polly's Southern Cruise: The Polly Brewster Series. Roy, Lillian Elizabeth. 2011. 294p. 48.95 *(978-1-258-10514-3(4))* Literary Licensing, LLC.
—The Woodcraft Girls at Camp. Roy, Lillian Elizabeth. 2011. 348p. 51.95 *(978-1-258-10242-5(0))* Literary Licensing, LLC.
Barbour, Karen. Let's Talk about Race. Lester, Julius. 2008. (ENG.). 32p. (J). (gr. 1-5). pap. 6.99 *(978-0-06-446226-6(9)*, Amistad) HarperCollins Pubs.
—Poetry for Young People: African American Poetry. Rampersad, Arnold & Blount, Marcellus, eds. 2013. (Poetry for Young People Ser.). (ENG.). 48p. (J). (gr. 3). 14.95 *(978-1-4027-1689-8(3))* Sterling Publishing Co., Inc.
—Princess Scargo & the Birthday Pumpkin. Metaxas, Eric. 2004. (Rabbit Ears-A Classic Tale Ser.). 40p. (gr. k-5). 25.65 *(978-1-59197-769-8(X))* Spotlight.
—Wonderful Words: Poems about Reading, Writing, Speaking, & Listening. 2004. (ENG.). 32p. (J). (gr. 1-6). 18.99 *(978-0-689-83588-9(4)*, Simon & Schuster Bks. For Young Readers) Simon & Schuster Bks. For Young Readers.
—You Were Loved Before You Were Born. Bunting, Eve. 2008. (J). pap. *(978-0-439-04062-4(0)*, Blue Sky Pr., The) Scholastic, Inc.
Barbour, Karen. Mr. Williams. Barbour, Karen. rev. ed. 2005. (ENG.). 32p. (J). (gr. 1-5). 18.99 *(978-0-8050-6773-6(6)*, Holt, Henry & Co. Bks. For Young Readers) Holt, Henry & Co.
Barbour Publishing Staff. Choosing Thankfulness. 2005. 94p. (J). (gr. k-5). pap. 7.99 *(978-0-9703069-5-1(4))* Train-Up A Child, LLC.
Barbra K. Mudd. The Grey Ghost of the Pharaoh. Vail, Emily Blake. 2004. 176p. (YA). per. 8.99 *(978-0-935087-27-7(3))* Wright Publishing, Inc.
Barchowsky, Damien. Teens Ask Deepak: All the Right Questions. Chopra, Deepak. 2006. (ENG.). 208p. (YA). (gr. 7). pap. 15.99 *(978-0-689-86218-2(0)*, Simon Pulse) Simon Pulse.
Barchus, Nathan, jt. illus. see Sundaravej, Sittisan.
Barcilon, Marianne. El Chupete de Gina. Naumann-Villemin, Christine & Naumann. 2004. (SPA.). 28p. (J). (gr. -1-k). 14.99 *(978-84-8470-184-2(0)*, COR33211) Corimbo, Editorial S.L. ESP. Dist: Lectorum Pubns., Inc.
Barcita, Pamela. The Little Weed Flower. Whipple, Vicky. 2010. (ENG.). 32p. (J). (gr. -1-12). lib. bdg. 16.95 *(978-1-936299-34-8(8)*, Raven Tree Pr.,Csi) Continental Sales, Inc.
—The Little Weed Flower/La Florecita de la Maleza. Whipple, Vicky. 2010. (ENG & SPA.). 32p. (J). (gr. -1-12). pap. 7.95 *(978-1-936299-33-1(X))*; lib. bdg. 16.95 *(978-1-936299-32-4(1))* Continental Sales, Inc. (Raven Tree Pr.,Csi).
—Pardon Me, It's Ham, Not Turkey. Suhay, Lisa. 2007. (J). (gr. -1-3). 17.95 *(978-1-933982-01-4(2))* Bumble Bee Publishing.
—Ruby Lee the Bumble Bee: A Bee of Possibility. Matheson, Dawn. 2006. 40p. (J). (gr. -1-3). lib. bdg. *(978-0-9754342-6-0(8))* Bumble Bee Publishing.
—Ruby Lee the Bumble Bee: A Bee's Bit of Wisdom. Matheson, Dawn. 2005. 34p. (J). (gr. -1-3). 17.95 *(978-0-9754342-1-5(7))* Bumble Bee Publishing.
—Ruby Lee the Bumble Bee: A Bee's Bit of Wisdom. Matheson, Dawn. Cindy, Huffman, ed. 2004. 40p. (J). 17.95 *(978-0-9754342-0-8(9))* Bumble Bee Publishing.
—Ruby Lee the Bumble Bee Critter Count Search & Find Game. Matheson, Dawn. Huffman, Cindy, ed. 2005. 6p. (J). 4.95 *(978-0-9754342-4-6(1))* Bumble Bee Publishing.
—Ruby Lee the Bumble Bee Promotional Coloring Book. 2005. 16p. (J). 4.95 *(978-0-9754342-3-9(3))* Bumble Bee Publishing.
—Seed Was Planted. Palazetti, Toulla. 2010. (ENG.). 32p. (J). (gr. -1-3). pap. 7.95 *(978-1-934960-10-3(1)*, Raven Tree Pr.,Csi) Continental Sales, Inc.
—A Seed Was Planted/Sembré una Semilla. Palazeti, Toulla. 2009. (ENG & SPA.). 32p. (J). (gr. -1-3). 16.95 *(978-1-932748-89-5(X))*; pap. 7.95 *(978-1-932748-88-8(1))* Continental Sales, Inc. (Raven Tree Pr.,Csi).
—A Walk with Grandpa. Solomon, Sharon K. (ENG.). 32p. (J). 2010. (gr. 4-7). pap. 7.95 *(978-1-934960-12-7(8))*; 2009. (gr. -1-3). 16.95 *(978-1-934960-11-0(X))* Continental Sales, Inc. (Raven Tree Pr.,Csi).
—A Walk With Grandpa/Un Paseo con el Abuelo. Solomon, Sharon. Del Risco, Eida, tr. 2009. (ENG & SPA.). 32p. (J). (gr. -1-3). 16.95 *(978-1-932748-91-8(1)*, Raven Tree Pr.,Csi) Continental Sales, Inc.
Barclay, Eric. Counting Dogs. Barclay, Eric. 2015. (ENG.). 16p. (J). (gr. -1-k). 10.99 ***(978-0-545-78392-7(5)***, Cartwheel Bks.) Scholastic, Inc.
Barclay, Eric. Hiding Phil. Barclay, Eric. 2013. (ENG.). 32p. (J). (gr. -1-k). 16.99 *(978-0-545-46477-2(3)*, Scholastic Pr.) Scholastic, Inc.
Barclay, Katerina. The Hand of Zeus. Barclay, Katerina. Barclay, Aegea. 2004. (J). 24.95 *(978-0-9758803-0-2(6)*, 206.612.9698); 29.95 *(978-0-9758803-1-9(4)*, 206 234 2572) Aegean Design.
Bardo, Yuyun. A, B, C Awal. Hoover, Nadine. 2013. 36p. (J). pap. 12.00 *(978-0-9828492-1-7(4))* Conscience Studio.
Bardugo, Miriam. Tales of Tzaddikim. Matov, G. Weinbach, Shaindel, tr. (J). pap. 56.99 *(978-0-89906-842-8(1))* Mesorah Pubns., Ltd.
Barella, Laura. The Brave Little Tailor. 2014. (Flip-Up Fairy Tales Ser.). (ENG.). 24p. (J). *(978-1-84643-654-3(0))* Child's Play International Ltd.
—Donkey Skin. 2011. (Flip-Up Fairy Tales Ser.). (ENG.). 24p. (J). *(978-1-84643-371-9(1))*; *(978-1-84643-410-5(6))* Child's Play International Ltd.
—The Little Mermaid. (Flip-Up Fairy Tales Ser.). (ENG.). 24p. (J). (gr. -1-2). 2010. *(978-1-84643-331-3(2))*; 2009. pap. *(978-1-84643-325-2(8))* Child's Play International Ltd.
—Sleeping Beauty. (Classic Fairy Tales Ser.). (ENG.). 24p. (J). 2012. *(978-1-84643-442-6(4))*; 2009. (gr. -1-2). pap. *(978-1-84643-252-1(9))* Child's Play International Ltd.
—The Stonecutter. 2012. (Flip-Up Fairy Tales Ser.). (ENG.). 24p. (J). *(978-1-84643-517-1(X))*; *(978-1-84643-478-5(5))* Child's Play International Ltd.
Barg, Soosoonam. All about Korea: Stories, Songs, Crafts & More. Bowler, Ann Martin. 2011. (ENG.). 64p. (J). (gr. k-4). 16.95 *(978-0-8048-4012-5(1))* Tuttle Publishing.
Barge III, John. My Hat! My Hat! Where Is My Hat? Olive, Gloria D. 2011. 28p. pap. 24.95 *(978-1-4626-0730-3(6))* America Star Bks.
Barge III, John S. I Can Choose to Be Happy. Constantine, Cara J. 2012. 32p. 24.95 *(978-1-4626-4731-6(6))* America Star Bks.
Barge III, John. The Shoes & the Laces. Dtpolk. 2011. 32p. pap. 24.95 *(978-1-4560-3141-1(4))* America Star Bks.
Barger, Jan. Community Workers. Ross, Kathy. 2005. (Crafts for Kids Who Are Learning About... Ser.). (ENG.). 48p. (gr. k-3). lib. bdg., tchr. ed. 26.60 *(978-0-7613-2743-1(6))* Lerner Publishing Group.
—Crafts for Kids Who Are Learning about Dinosaurs. Ross, Kathy. 2008. (Crafts for Kids Who Are Learning About... Ser.). (ENG.). 48p. (gr. k-3). lib. bdg. 26.60 *(978-0-8225-6809-4(8)*, Millbrook Pr.) Lerner Publishing Group.
—Crafts for Kids Who Are Learning about Farm Animals. Ross, Kathy. 2007. (Crafts for Kids Who Are Learning About... Ser.). (ENG.). 48p. (gr. k-3). lib. bdg. 26.60 *(978-0-8225-6366-2(5)*, Millbrook Pr.) Lerner Publishing Group.
—Crafts for Kids Who Are Learning about Insects. Ross, Kathy. 2008. (Crafts for Kids Who Are Learning About... Ser.). (ENG.). 48p. (gr. k-3). 26.60 *(978-0-8225-7591-7(4)*, Millbrook Pr.) Lerner Publishing Group.
—Kathy Ross Crafts Numbers. Ross, Kathy. 2003. 47p. (J). (gr. -1-3). lib. bdg. 16.40 *(978-0-613-58981-9(5)*, Turtleback) Turtleback Bks.
Barham, Timothy E. Pippi's Silent Message: Adventures of Suzy Q & You Too. Cloyd, Suzy. 2012. 24p. 24.95 *(978-1-4512-7832-3(2))* America Star Bks.
Barham, Timothy E. Blonds Blending: The Adventures of Suzy Q & You Too. Barham, Timothy E. 2011. 20p. pap. 24.95 *(978-1-4626-4458-2(9))* America Star Bks.
Barker, Charles Ferguson. Under Michigan: The Story of Michigan's Rocks & Fossils. Barker, Charles Ferguson. 2005. (Great Lakes Books Ser.). (ENG.). 56p. (J). (gr. 1-4). 18.95 *(978-0-8143-3088-3(6)*, 1092, Great Lakes Bks.) Wayne State Univ. Pr.
—Under New England: The Story of New England's Rocks & Fossils. Barker, Charles Ferguson. 2008. (ENG.). 72p. (J). (gr. 2-7). 12.95 *(978-1-58465-696-8(4))* Univ. Pr. of New England.
—Under Ohio: The Story of Ohio's Rocks & Fossils. Barker, Charles Ferguson. 2007. 56p. (J). (gr. 3-7). 17.95 *(978-0-8214-1755-3(X))* Ohio Univ. Pr.
Barker, Cicely Mary. Flower Fairies Sticker Storybook. 2011. (Flower Fairies Ser.). (ENG.). 24p. (J). (gr. -1-k). pap. 6.99 *(978-0-7232-6697-6(2)*, Warne) Penguin Publishing Group.
Barker, Clive. Abarat. Barker, Clive. (Abarat Ser.: 1). (ENG.). (YA). (gr. 8). 2011. 528p. pap. 9.99 *(978-0-06-209410-0(6))*; 2004. 496p. reprint ed. pap. 8.99 *(978-0-06-059637-8(6))* HarperCollins Pubs.
—Abarat: Days of Magic, Nights of War, 4 vols., Vol. 2. Barker, Clive. ltd. num. aut. ed. 2004. 493p. 175.00 *(978-1-890885-17-5(7))* Trice, B.E. Publishing.
—Absolute Midnight. Barker, Clive. 2013. (Abarat Ser.: 3). (ENG.). 640p. (YA). (gr. 8). pap. 9.99 *(978-0-06-440933-9(3))* HarperCollins Pubs.
—Days of Magic, Nights of War. Barker, Clive. (Abarat Ser.: 2). (ENG.). (YA). (gr. 8). 2011. 624p. pap. 9.99 *(978-0-06-209411-7(4))*; 2006. 576p. reprint ed. pap. 7.99 *(978-0-06-059638-5(4))* HarperCollins Pubs.
Barker, Gary. Garfield. Davis, Jim & Evanier, Mark. (Garfield Ser.: 3). (ENG.). 112p. (J). (gr. 2). 2014. pap. 13.99 *(978-1-60886-348-8(4))*; Vol. 1. 2012. pap. 13.99 *(978-1-60886-287-0(9))* Boom! Studios.
Barker, Gary. Garfield Vol. 2: I'll Give You All the Ten Seconds to Get off the Comic Racks! Barker, Gary. Davis, Jim & Evanier, Mark. 2013. (Garfield Ser.). (ENG.). 112p. (J). (gr. 2). pap. 13.99 *(978-1-60886-303-7(4))* Boom! Studios.
Barker, Lori, jt. illus. see Fentz, Mike.
Barker, Stephen. Chalkboard 123: Learn Your Numbers with Reusable Chalkboard Pages! Walter Foster Creative Team. 2014. (Chalk It Up! Ser.). (ENG.). 26p. (J). (gr. -1-1). 9.99 *(978-1-60058-716-0(X))* Quarto Publishing Group USA.
—Chalkboard ABC: Learn the Alphabet with Reusable Chalkboard Pages! Walter Foster Custom Creative Team. 2014. (Chalk It Up! Ser.). (ENG.). 26p. (J). (gr. -1-1). 9.99 *(978-1-60058-715-3(1))* Quarto Publishing Group USA.
—Chalkboard Shapes: Learn Your Shapes with Reusable Chalkboard Pages! Walter Foster Custom Creative Team.

The check digit for ISBN-10 appears in parentheses after the full ISBN-13

2014. (Chalk It Up! Ser.). (ENG.). 26p. (J). (gr. -1-1). 9.99 *(978-1-60058-717-7(8))* Quarto Publishing Group USA.

—My Big Bright Bible Board Book. Goodings, Christina. 2014. (ENG.). 10p. (J). (— 1). bds. 9.99 *(978-0-7459-6525-3(3))* Lion Hudson PLC GBR. Dist: Independent Pubs. Group.

Barker, Vicky, jt. illus. see Horne, Sarah.

Barkow, Henriette. That's My Mum: Voici Ma Mere. Brazell, Derek. 2004. (ENG & FRE.). 28p. (J). pap. *(978-1-85269-600-9(1))* Mantra Lingua.

Barkow, Henriette & Johnson, Richard. Don't Cry, Sly! Mos Qaj Dhelperush! 2004. (ENG & ALB.). 32p. (J). pap. *(978-1-85269-648-1(6))* Mantra Lingua.

—The Giant Turnip: Rrepa Gjigante. 2004. 24p. (J). *(978-1-85269-732-7(6))* Mantra Lingua.

Barkow, Henriette & Reed, Nathan. The Buskers of Bremen: Kengetaret Endacak Te Bremenit. 2004. (ALB & ENG.). 24p. (J). pap. *(978-1-85269-764-8(4))* Mantra Lingua.

—The Buskers of Bremen: Les Chanteurs de Rues de Bremen. 2004. (FRE & ENG.). 24p. (J). pap. *(978-1-85269-769-3(5))* Mantra Lingua.

Barks, Carl, jt. illus. see Luthi, Morgan.

Barkus, Mariona. The Flower & the Butterfly. Barkus, Mariona. 250th ed. 2003. *(978-1-932629-00-2(9))* Litkus Pr.

—Illustrated History No. 13, Vol. 13. Barkus, Mariona. 2004. 8p. 20.00 *(978-1-932629-15-6(7))* Litkus Pr.

Barley-Cohrs, Dayna. Uncle Rocky, Fireman: Fire! Brewster, James Burd. 2013. 34p. pap. 11.49 *(978-0-9911994-1-9(3))* J2B Publishing LLC.

—Uncle Rocky, Fireman: Something's Missing. Brewster, James Burd. 2013. 34p. pap. 11.49 *(978-0-9911994-2-6(1))* J2B Publishing LLC.

Barlow, Amanda. I Can Draw People. Gibson, Ray. Watt, Fiona, ed. 2004. (Usborne Playtime Ser.). (SPA.). (J). (gr. -1-18). 32p. lib. bdg., act. bk. ed. 12.95 *(978-1-58086-223-3(3))*; 1p. pap., act. bk. ed. 4.95 *(978-0-7460-3704-1(X))* EDC Publishing.

—Mini Art Ideas. Watt, Fiona. 2004. 96p. (J). 7.95 *(978-0-7945-0842-5(1)*, Usborne) EDC Publishing.

—The Usborne Book of Art Ideas. Watt, Fiona. rev. ed. 2006. (Art Ideas Ser.). 96p. (J). pap. 14.99 *(978-0-7945-0893-7(6)*, Usborne) EDC Publishing.

Barlow, Andrew. Jellytoes Misses the Bus. Barlow, Andrew. 2005. (Jellytoes Ser.). (ENG.). 32p. (J). per. 8.95 *(978-0-9764336-0-6(5))* MJS Publishing Group LLC.

Barlow, Dave. Long Long Time. Bland, Ralph. 2014. 251p. 13.50 *(978-1-933300-00-9(0))* Wandering Sage Pubns., LLC.

Barlup, Jessica. Who Could You Be at the Zoo? Zaring, Laurie. 2013. 24p. pap. 12.95 *(978-1-61244-175-7(0))* Halo Publishing International.

Barnard, Alan. Graveyards of the Dinosaurs: What It's Like to Discover Prehistoric Creatures. Tanaka, Shelley. 2010. (I Was There Ser.). (ENG.). 48p. (J). (gr. k-2). pap. 9.95 *(978-1-897330-62-3(6))* Madison Pr. Bks. CAN. Dist: Independent Pubs. Group.

—New Dinos: The Latest Finds! the Coolest Dinosaur Discoveries! Tanaka, Shelley. 2010. (ENG.). 48p. (J). (gr. k-2). pap. 9.95 *(978-1-897330-55-5(3))* Madison Pr. Bks. CAN. Dist: Independent Pubs. Group.

Barnard, Bryn. Dinosaurs. Nash, Dylan M. 2007. (ENG.). 24p. (J). (gr. 1-18). 19.95 *(978-1-58117-580-6(9)*, Intervisual/Piggy Toes) Bendon, Inc.

—Discovery in the Cave. Dubowski, Mark. 2010. (Step into Reading Ser.). (ENG.). 48p. (J). (gr. 2-4). pap. 3.99 *(978-0-375-85893-2(8)*, Random Hse. Bks. for Young Readers) Random Hse. Children's Bks.

—Sir Henry, the Polite Knight. Rovetch, L. Bob & Whitman, Emily. 2006. (J). *(978-1-58987-204-2(5))* Kindermusik International.

—Tentacles! Tales of the Giant Squid. Redmond, Shirley Raye. 2003. (Step into Reading Ser.). (ENG.). 48p. (J). (gr. k-3). pap. 3.99 *(978-0-375-81307-8(1)*, Random Hse. Bks. for Young Readers) Random Hse. Children's Bks.

—Tentacles! Tales of the Giant Squid. Redmond, Shirley Raye. 2005. (Step into Reading Ser.). (gr. k-2). 14.00 *(978-0-7569-5576-2(9))* Perfection Learning Corp.

—Tess & the Dog Star. Rotberg, Gene. 2011. (ENG.). 40p. pap. 9.99 *(978-1-4565-4745-5(3))* CreateSpace Independent Publishing Platform.

Barnard, Bryn. Outbreak: Plagues That Changed History. Barnard, Bryn. 2005. (ENG.). 48p. (J). (gr. 3-7). 17.99 *(978-0-375-82986-4(5)*, Crown Books For Young Readers) Random Hse. Children's Bks.

—Quinn's Search for the Samurai. Barnard, Bryn. Rotberg, Gene & Rotberg, Iris. 2012. 48p. (J). pap. *(978-0-615-67490-2(9))* Tower Pr.

Barnard, Frederick & Linton, J. D. The Pilgrim's Progress from This World to That Which Is to Come;Delivered under the Similitude of a Dream. Bunyan, John. 2012. 316p. *(978-1-78139-097-9(5))* Benediction Classics.

Barnard, Lucy. Do Touch! Don't Touch! Hodgman, Ann. 2012. (J). *(978-1-58925-867-9(3))* Tiger Tales.

—A Princess's Crown: A Magnetic Storybook. Lawrence, Trisha. 2008. 6p. (J). (gr. -1-1). bds. 10.99 *(978-2-7641-2186-3(5))* Gardner Pubns.

—Uh-Oh! Oh No! Hodgman, Ann. 2012. (Into-Everything Baby Stages Ser.). (ENG.). (gr. -1). bds. 7.95 *(978-1-58925-866-2(5))* Tiger Tales.

Barneda, David. Pirates vs. Cowboys. Reynolds, Aaron. 2013. (ENG.). 40p. (J). (gr. k-3). 16.99 *(978-0-375-85874-1(1))* Knopf, Alfred A. Inc.

Barner, Bob. Big Is Big & Little, Little: A Book of Contrasts. Lewis, J. Patrick. 2007. (ENG.). 32p. (J). (gr. -1-3). 16.95 *(978-0-8234-1909-8(6))* Holiday Hse., Inc.

—Sharks Have Six Senses. Waters, John F. 2015. (Let's-Read-And-Find-Out Science 2 Ser.). (ENG.). 40p. (J). (gr. -1-3). 17.99 *(978-0-06-028140-3(5))* HarperCollins Pubs.

—Where Crocodiles Have Wings. McKissack, Patricia C. 2005. (ENG.). 32p. (J). (gr. -1-3). 16.95 *(978-0-8234-1748-3(4))* Holiday Hse., Inc.

—Wiggle, Waggle, Loop-De-Loo! Todd, Traci N. 2006. (J). *(978-1-58987-009-3(3))* Kindermusik International.

Barner, Bob. Bug Safari. Barner, Bob. 2006. (ENG.). 36p. (J). (gr. -1-3). reprint ed. pap. 6.95 *(978-0-8234-2038-4(8))* Holiday Hse., Inc.

—The Day of the Dead (El Día de los Muerto) Barner, Bob. 2011. (ENG.). 32p. (J). pap. 7.99 *(978-0-8234-2381-1(6))* Holiday Hse., Inc.

—The Day of the Dead (El Día de los Muertos) Barner, Bob. 2010. (SPA & ENG.). 32p. (J). (gr. -1-3). 16.95 *(978-0-8234-2214-2(3))* Holiday Hse., Inc.

—Dinosaur Bones. Barner, Bob. unabr. ed. 2006. (J). (gr. -1-2). 29.95 *(978-0-439-90580-0(X))* Weston Woods Studios, Inc.

—I Have a Garden. Barner, Bob. (I Like to Read Ser.). (ENG.). 32p. (J). 2014. (gr. -1-3). 6.99 *(978-0-8234-3056-7(1))*; 2013. 14.95 *(978-0-8234-2527-3(4))* Holiday Hse., Inc.

Barnes, Cheryl S. House Mouse, Senate Mouse. Barnes, Peter W. 2012. (ENG.). 40p. (J). (gr. k-3). 16.95 *(978-1-59698-790-6(1)*, Little Patriot Pr.) Regnery Publishing, Inc., An Eagle Publishing Co.

—Marshall, the Courthouse Mouse: A Tail of the U. S. Supreme Court. Barnes, Peter W. 2012. (ENG.). 40p. (J). (gr. k). 16.95 *(978-1-59698-789-0(8)*, Little Patriot Pr.) Regnery Publishing, Inc., An Eagle Publishing Co.

Barnes, Cheryl S., jt. illus. see Barnes, Peter W.

Barnes, Cheryl Shaw. Little Miss Patriot. Barnes, Peter W. ed. 2007. 32p. (J). lib. bdg. 17.95 *(978-1-893622-20-3(7)*, VSP Bks.) Vacation Spot Publishing.

—Maestro Mouse: And the Mystery of the Missing Baton. Barnes, Peter W. 2005. 32p. (J). 16.95 *(978-1-893622-17-3(7)*, VSP Bks.) Vacation Spot Publishing.

—President Adams' Alligator: And Other White House Pets. Barnes, Peter W. 2003. 32p. (J). 16.95 *(978-1-893622-13-5(4)*, VSP Bks.) Vacation Spot Publishing.

—Woodrow, the White House Mouse. Barnes, Peter W. 2012. (ENG.). 40p. (J). (gr. k-3). 16.95 *(978-1-59698-788-3(X)*, Little Patriot Pr.) Regnery Publishing, Inc., An Eagle Publishing Co.

Barnes, Cheryl Shaw & Barnes, Peter W. Liberty Lee's Tail of Independence. 2012. (ENG.). 36p. (J). (gr. k-3). 16.95 *(978-1-59698-792-0(8)*, Little Patriot Pr.) Regnery Publishing, Inc., An Eagle Publishing Co.

Barnes, Garry. A Tractor Green Day. Stone, Connie. 2008. 36p. pap. 24.95 *(978-1-60474-948-9(2))* PublishAmerica, Inc.

Barnes-Murphy, Rowan. All Together. Kemp, Marion et al. Date not set. (Whizz Bang Bumper Bk.). 63p. (J). 129.15 *(978-0-582-18259-2(X))*; pap. 129.15 *(978-0-582-18258-5(1))* Addison-Wesley Longman, Ltd. GBR. Dist: Trans-Atlantic Pubns., Inc.

—Managing Money. Brennan, Linda Crotta. 2012. (Simple Economics Ser.). (ENG.). 24p. (J). (gr. 2-5). 27.07 *(978-1-61473-241-9(8)*, 204972) Child's World, Inc., The.

—Mother Goose: Treasury of Favourite Rhymes. Blyton, Enid. 2012. (ENG.). 160p. 24.95 *(978-1-84135-591-7(7))* Award Pubns. Ltd. GBR. Dist: Parkwest Pubns., Inc.

Barnes, Page. Don't Eat My Garden. Barnes, Ben. 2007. 28p. per. 24.95 *(978-1-4241-8964-9(0))* America Star Bks.

Barnes, Peter W. & Barnes, Cheryl S. Maestro Mouse: And the Mystery of the Missing Baton. 2013. (ENG.). 40p. (J). (gr. k-5). 16.95 *(978-1-62157-036-3(3)*, Little Patriot Pr.) Regnery Publishing, Inc., An Eagle Publishing Co.

—President Adams' Alligator: And Other White House Pets. 2013. (ENG.). 40p. (J). (gr. k-5). 16.95 *(978-1-62157-035-6(5)*, Little Patriot Pr.) Regnery Publishing, Inc., An Eagle Publishing Co.

Barnes, Peter W., jt. illus. see Barnes, Cheryl Shaw.

Barnes, Sarah. Nine Things Nathan Noticed at Night. Baldwin, Christy. 2005. 24p. (J). per. 13.00 *(978-0-9765072-1-5(8))* Tribute Bks.

—Remembering Wilma. Baldwin, Christy. l.t. ed. 2005. 22p. (J). per. 9.95 *(978-0-9765072-0-8(X))* Tribute Bks.

Barnes, Tom, photos by. Chicken Run: Action-Packed Storybook. David, Lawrence, ed. 2005. 48p. (gr. k-4). reprint ed. pap. 8.00 *(978-0-7567-9472-9(2))* DIANE Publishing Co.

Barnes, Trisha. Once upon A Night. Keyser, William. 2011. (J). pap. 8.99 *(978-0-9827531-1-8(X))* River Canyon Pr.

Barnes, William. A Place for All of Us. Hile, Doretta. 2007. 36p. per. 14.94 *(978-1-59858-421-9(9))* Dog Ear Publishing, LLC.

Barnet, Nancy. In the Spell of an Ibis: The Education of Minemheb the Scribe. Buchanan, Penelope. 2004. 80p. pap. *(978-0-940717-82-4(4))* Cleveland Museum of Art.

Barnett, Charles, et al. The Battle of the Alamo, 1 vol. Doeden, Matt. 2005. (Graphic History Ser.). (ENG.). 32p. (gr. 3-4). 29.99 *(978-0-7368-3832-0(5)*, Graphic Library) Capstone Pr., Inc.

Barnett, Charles, III, et al. The Brave Escape of Ellen & William Craft. Lemke, Donald B. 2005. (Graphic History Ser.). (ENG.). 32p. (gr. 3-4). 29.99 *(978-0-7368-4973-9(4)*, Graphic Library) Capstone Pr., Inc.

—Jake Burton Carpenter & the Snowboard, 1 vol. O'Hearn, Michael. 2006. (Inventions & Discovery Ser.). (ENG.). 32p. (gr. 3-4). 29.99 *(978-0-7368-6481-7(4)*, Graphic Library) Capstone Pr., Inc.

—John Sutter & the California Gold Rush, 1 vol. Doeden, Matt. 2005. (Graphic History Ser.). (ENG.). 32p. (gr. 3-4). 29.99 *(978-0-7368-4370-6(1)*, Graphic Library) Capstone Pr., Inc.

—Levi Strauss & Blue Jeans, 1 vol. Olson, Nathan. 2006. (Inventions & Discovery Ser.). (ENG.). 32p. (gr. 3-4). pap. 8.10 *(978-0-7368-9646-7(5)*, Graphic Library) Capstone Pr., Inc.

—Lords of the Sea: The Vikings Explore the North Atlantic, 1 vol. Lassieur, Allison. 2005. (Graphic History Ser.). (ENG.). 32p. (gr. 3-4). 29.99 *(978-0-7368-4974-6(2)*, Graphic Library) Capstone Pr., Inc.

Barnett, Charles, III. Political Elections, 1 vol. Miller, Davis Worth & Brevard, Katherine M. 2008. (Cartoon Nation Ser.). (ENG.). 32p. (gr. 3-4). 29.99 *(978-1-4296-1333-0(5)*, Graphic Library) Capstone Pr., Inc.

Barnett, Charles, et al. Political Parties, 1 vol. Burgan, Michael & Hoena, Blake A. 2008. (Cartoon Nation Ser.). (ENG.). 32p. (gr. 3-4). lib. bdg. 29.99 *(978-1-4296-1334-7(3)*, Graphic Library) Capstone Pr., Inc.

Barnett, Charles, III, et al. The Sinking of the Titanic, 1 vol. Doeden, Matt. 2005. (Graphic History Ser.). (ENG.). 32p. (gr. 3-4). 29.99 *(978-0-7368-3834-4(1)*, Graphic Library) Capstone Pr., Inc.

Barnett, Charles. U. S. Immigration. O'Donnell, Liam. 2008. (Cartoon Nation Ser.). (ENG.). 32p. (gr. 3-4). 29.99 *(978-1-4296-1983-7(X)*, Graphic Library) Capstone Pr., Inc.

Barnett, Charles, III & Dominguez, Richard. The Shocking World of Electricity with Max Axiom, Super Scientist, 1 vol. O'Donnell, Liam & Barnett III, Charles. 2007. (Graphic Science Ser.). (ENG.). 32p. (gr. 3-4). 29.99 *(978-0-7368-6835-8(6)*, Graphic Library) Capstone Pr., Inc.

Barnett, Charles, III & Hoover, Dave. The Boston Tea Party, 1 vol. Doeden, Matt. 2005. (Graphic History Ser.). (ENG.). 32p. (gr. 3-4). per. 8.10 *(978-0-7368-5243-2(3)*, Graphic Library) Capstone Pr., Inc.

Barnett, Charles, III & Miller, Phil. The Battle of the Alamo, 1 vol. Doeden, Matt. 2005. (Graphic History Ser.). (ENG.). 32p. (gr. 3-4). per. 8.10 *(978-0-7368-5242-5(5)*, Graphic Library) Capstone Pr., Inc.

—The Sinking of the Titanic, 1 vol. Doeden, Matt. 2005. (Graphic History Ser.). (ENG.). 32p. (gr. 3-4). per. 8.10 *(978-0-7368-5247-0(6)*, Graphic Library) Capstone Pr., Inc.

Barnett, Charles, III, jt. illus. see Dominguez, Richard.

Barnett, Charles, III, jt. illus. see Erwin, Steve.

Barnett, Charles, III, jt. illus. see Miller, Phil.

Barnett, Charles, III, jt. illus. see Whigham, Rod.

Barnett III, Charles & Hoover, Dave. The Boston Tea Party, 1 vol. Doeden, Matt. 2005. (Graphic History Ser.). (ENG.). 32p. (gr. 3-4). 29.99 *(978-0-7368-3846-7(5)*, Graphic Library) Capstone Pr., Inc.

Barnett, Isa. One World, Many People: Anthropology Made Fun for Kids. Barnett, Annette. 2006. 80p. (J). pap. 19.95 *(978-0-9787138-0-5(X))* Young Scholars Pr.

Barnett, Janet. An Adventure in Looking & Listening: Exploring Masterworks at the Albright-Knox Art Gallery. Bayles, Jennifer L. 2003. (J). *(978-1-887457-01-9(1))* Buffalo Fine Arts/Albright-Knox Art Gallery.

Barnett, Linda. Dottie the Bus Driver in Bicycle Safety. Toombs, Robert. 2013. 24p. pap. 9.99 *(978-0-9885180-6-3(6))* Mindstir Media.

Barnett, Russell. Secrets of the Oak. Taylor, Alice. 32p. 4.99 *(978-0-86322-138-5(6))* Penguin Publishing Group.

Barnett, Thora. Sally Salli & the Case of the Tic Monster: A Book for Kids Who Tic. LeBow, Michael. 2013. 75p. (J). pap. 18.95 *(978-1-59630-060-6(4))* Science & Humanities Pr.

Barney, Maginel Wright. Downright Dencey. Snedeker, Caroline. 2003. (Young Adult Library). 268p. (YA). pap. 12.95 *(978-1-883937-79-9(5))* Bethlehem Bks.

Barnhart, Nancy. The Wind in the Willows. Grahame, Kenneth. 2004. reprint ed. pap. 33.95 *(978-1-4179-1206-3(5))* Kessinger Publishing, LLC.

Barnhurst, Noel, photos by. Macaroni & Cheese. Spieler, Marlena. 2005. (ENG., 132p. (gr. 8-17). pap. 16.95 *(978-0-8118-4962-3(7))* Chronicle Bks. LLC.

—Modern Asian Flavors: A Taste of Shanghai. Wong, Richard. 2006. (ENG., 144p. (gr. 8-17). 18.95 *(978-0-8118-5110-7(9))* Chronicle Bks. LLC.

Barnoski, Karel. Melissa & the Magic Pen. Figueroa, M. A. & Figueroa, P. A. 2004. 36p. pap. 24.95 *(978-1-4137-3441-6(3))* PublishAmerica, Inc.

Barnum-Newman, Winifred. Ana & Adam Build & Acrostic. Peterson-Hilleque, Victoria. 2011. (Poetry Builders Ser.). 32p. (J). (gr. 2-4). lib. bdg. 25.27 *(978-1-59953-433-6(9))* Norwood Hse. Pr.

Barnum-Newman, Winifred, jt. illus. see Newman, Winifred Barnum.

Barnum, Tabatha. The Greatest Mousemas Ever! Quintanilla, Billie. 2012. 36p. 24.95 *(978-1-4626-9725-0(9))*; pap. 24.95 *(978-1-4626-5236-5(0))* America Star Bks.

Baron, Andrew. The Adventures of Octopus Rex. 2003. (J). per. 17.95 *(978-0-9760348-0-3(8))* BaHart Pubns. / Eight Legs Publishing.

—El Pulpo Rex. 2003. (SPA.). (J). per. 17.95 *(978-0-9760348-1-0(6))* BaHart Pubns. / Eight Legs Publishing.

Baron, Cheri Ann. Angelita's Song. Guiffre, William A. 2008. 32p. (J). (gr. -1-3). lib. bdg. 17.95 *(978-1-931650-30-4(6))* Bks. for Children Publishing.

—Angelita's Song. Guiffre, William. 2008. 32p. (J). (gr. -1-3). pap. 9.95 *(978-1-931650-36-6(5))* Bks. for Children Publishing.

—The First Gift of Christmas. Guiffre, William A. 2003. 36p. (J). (gr. -1-3). lib. bdg. 17.95 *(978-1-931650-21-2(7))* Bks. for Children Publishing.

—The First Gift of Christmas. Guiffre, William. 2008. 32p. (J). (gr. -1-3). pap. 9.95 *(978-1-931650-33-5(0))* Bks. for Children Publishing.

—The Wrong Side of the Bed. Guiffre, William A. 2003. 36p. (J). (gr. -1-3). lib. bdg. 17.95 *(978-1-931650-20-5(9))* Bks. for Children Publishing.

—The Wrong Side of the Bed. Guiffre, William. 2008. 32p. (J). (gr. -1-3). pap. 9.95 *(978-1-931650-34-2(9))* Bks. for Children Publishing.

Baron, Kathy. Possum's Three Fine Friends. Bannister, Barbara. 2006. (ENG.). 32p. (gr. 1-2). pap. 7.25 *(978-1-57874-096-3(7))* Kaeden Corp.

Barón, Lara & Torres, German. Hero City. Tsang, Evonne & Jimenez, Adan. 2012. (Twisted Journeys (r) Ser.: 22). (ENG.). 112p. (J). (gr. 4-7). lib. bdg. 27.93 *(978-0-7613-4595-4(7)*, Graphic Universe) Lerner Publishing Group.

BaróN, Lara & Torres, German. Hero City. Tsang, Evonne & Jimenez, Adan. 2012. (Twisted Journeys (r) Ser.: 22). (ENG.). 112p. (J). (gr. 4-7). pap. 7.95 *(978-1-57505-945-7(2)*, Graphic Universe) Lerner Publishing Group.

Baroncelli, Silvia. Be Safe Around Fire. Heos, Bridget. 2015. (Be Safe! Ser.). 24p. (J). 25.65 *(978-1-60753-444-0(4))* Amicus Educational.

—Be Safe Around Water. Heos, Bridget. 2015. (Be Safe! Ser.). 24p. (J). 25.65 *(978-1-60753-448-8(7))* Amicus Educational.

—Be Safe on the Internet. Heos, Bridget. 2015. (Be Safe! Ser.). 24p. (J). 25.65 *(978-1-60753-445-7(2))* Amicus Educational.

—Be Safe on the Playground. Heos, Bridget. 2015. (Be Safe! Ser.). 24p. (J). 25.65 *(978-1-60753-446-4(0))* Amicus Educational.

—Be Safe on Your Bike. Heos, Bridget. 2015. (Be Safe! Ser.). 24p. (J). 25.65 *(978-1-60753-443-3(6))* Amicus Educational.

Barone, Mark. Christ's Passion: The Way of the Cross; A Guide to Understanding Your Path. Young, Mary Beth. 2004. 100p. per. 14.00 *(978-0-9760180-1-8(2))* Young, Beth.

Barozzi, Danilo. The Amazing Voyage. Stilton, Geronimo. 2011. (Geronimo Stilton & the Kingdom of Fantasy Ser.: 3). (ENG.). 320p. (J). (gr. 2-5). 14.99 *(978-0-545-30771-0(6))* Scholastic, Inc.

—The Enchanted Charms: The Seventh Adventure in the Kingdom of Fantasy. Stilton, Geronimo & Dami, Elisabetta. 2015. (ENG.). 320p. (J). (gr. 2-5). 14.99 *(978-0-545-74615-1(9))* Scholastic, Inc.

Barr, Bailey. Diogo the Little Dinosaur. Skwara, Maike Lena. 2013. 28p. (J). *(978-0-89985-475-5(3))* R. H. Publishing.

Barr, Kristen. Creative Movement for 3-5 Year Olds: A Complete Curriculum Including 35 Lesson Plans, Dance Notations, Illustrations, Music & Poetry Suggestions Plus Detailed Prop Designs. Forbes, Ross E., photos by. Forbes, Harriet H. 2003. 241p. (J). pap., tchr. ed. 50.00 *(978-0-9659944-1-5(4))* First Steps Pr.

Barr, Kristin. Joe Boat. Riggs, Sandy. 2006. (Reader's Clubhouse Level 2 Reader Ser.). (ENG.). 24p. (J). (gr. 1-4). pap. 3.99 *(978-0-7641-3296-4(2))* Barron's Educational Series, Inc.

Barr, Loel. How & Why: A Kids' Book about the Body. Grace, Catherine O'Neill. 2011. (J). *(978-0-89043-231-0(7))* Consumers Union of U. S., Inc.

—My Dad Wears Polka-Dotted Socks! Humes, Kristin Joy. 2005. 32p. (J). (gr. -1-7). 15.95 *(978-0-9744307-2-0(2))* Merry Lane Pr.

Barr, Marilyn. A Child's Garden of Bible Stories. Gross, Arthur. 2005. 144p. (J). 10.49 *(978-0-7586-0858-1(6))* Concordia Publishing Hse.

Barr, Marilynn G. & Jeffery, Megan E. Hope Finders. Lingo, Susan L. 2006. (Power Builders Curriculum Ser.). 128p. (J). (gr. 1-5). 15.99 *(978-0-7847-1235-1(2)*, 42118) Standard Publishing.

—Joy Builders. Lingo, Susan L. 2006. (Power Builders Curriculum Ser.). 128p. (J). (gr. 1-5). 15.99 *(978-0-7847-1234-4(4)*, 42117) Standard Publishing.

—Peace Makers. Lingo, Susan L. 2006. (Power Builders Curriculum Ser.). 128p. (J). (gr. 1-5). 15.99 *(978-0-7847-1233-7(6)*, 42116) Standard Publishing.

—Power Boosters. Lingo, Susan L. 2006. (Power Builders Curriculum Ser.). 128p. (J). (gr. 1-5). 15.99 *(978-0-7847-1232-0(8)*, 42115) Standard Publishing.

Barr, Steve. The Helping, Caring, & Sharing. Schab, Lisa & Gardner, Richard. Schader, Karen, ed. 2003. (J). per., wbk. ed. 19.95 *(978-1-58815-058-5(5)*, 67238) Childswork/Childsplay.

Barradas, Leticia. Santiago & the Fox of Hatsune. Defosse, Rosana Curiel. (SPA.). 32p. (J). (gr. 3-5). pap. 7.95 *(978-970-29-0134-1(0))* Santillana USA Publishing Co., Inc.

—Santiago en el Mundo de me de la Gana. Defosse, Rosana Curiel. (SPA.). 38p. (J). (gr. 3-5). pap. 7.95 *(978-970-29-0136-5(7))* Santillana USA Publishing Co., Inc.

—Santiago en el Pantano. Defosse, Rosana Curiel. (Santiago Y Los Valores Ser.). (SPA.). 32p. (J). (gr. 3-5). pap. 7.95 *(978-970-29-0133-4(2))* Santillana USA Publishing Co., Inc.

—Santiago y el talisman de la Luz. Defosse, Rosana Curiel. (Santiago Y Los Valores Ser.). (SPA.). 32p. (J). (gr. 3-5). pap. 7.95 *(978-970-29-0131-0(6))* Santillana USA Publishing Co., Inc.

—Santiago y los Dobraks. Defosse, Rosana Curiel. (SPA.). 32p. (J). (gr. 3-5). pap. 7.95 *(978-970-29-0111-2(1))* Santillana USA Publishing Co., Inc.

Barragán, Paula. Cool Cats Counting. Shahan, Sherry. 2005. (ENG & SPA.). 24p. (J). (gr. -1-2). 16.95 *(978-0-87483-757-5(X))* August Hse. Pubs., Inc.

—Fiesta! A Celebration of Latino Festivals. Shahan, Sherry. 2008. (ENG.). 32p. (J). (gr. -1-3). 16.95 *(978-0-87483-861-9(4))* August Hse. Pubs., Inc.

—Poems to Dream Together: Poemas para soñar Juntos. Alarcón, Francisco X. 2005. (ENG & SPA.). 32p. (J). (gr. 2-5). 16.95 *(978-1-58430-233-9(X))* Lee & Low Bks., Inc.

Barrager, Brigette. Bevan vs. Evan: And Other School Rivalries. Evans, Zoe. 2012. (Cheer! Ser.: 4). (ENG.). 224p. (J). (gr. 3-7). pap. 6.99 *(978-1-4424-3364-9(7)*, Simon Spotlight) Simon Spotlight.

—Confessions of a Wannabe Cheerleader. Evans, Zoe. 2011. (Cheer! Ser.: 1). (ENG.). 240p. (J). (gr. 3-7). pap. 6.99 *(978-1-4424-2241-4(6)*, Simon Spotlight) Simon Spotlight.

—Holiday Spirit. Evans, Zoe. 2011. (Cheer! Ser.: 3). (ENG.). 224p. (J). (gr. 3-7). pap. 6.99 *(978-1-4424-3362-5(0)*, Simon Spotlight) Simon Spotlight.

—Louise Trapeze Is Totally 100% Fearless. Ostow, Micol. 2015. (Stepping Stone Book(TM) Ser.). (ENG.). 112p. (J). (gr. 1-4). 14.99 *(978-0-553-49739-7(1))* Random Hse., Inc.

—Pyramid of One. Evans, Zoe. 2011. (Cheer! Ser.: 2). (ENG.). 240p. (J). (gr. 3-7). pap. 6.99 *(978-1-4424-2239-1(4)*, Simon Spotlight) Simon Spotlight.

—Revenge of the Titan. Evans, Zoe. 2012. (Cheer! Ser.: 5). (ENG.). 224p. (J). (gr. 3-7). pap. 6.99 *(978-1-4424-4634-2(X)*, Simon Spotlight) Simon Spotlight.
—Sleeping Cinderella & Other Princess Mix-Ups. Clarkson, Stephanie. 2015. (ENG.). 40p. (J). (gr. -1-3). 17.99 *(978-0-545-56564-6(2)*, Orchard Bks.) Scholastic, Inc.
—The Twelve Dancing Princesses. Grimm, Wilhelm K. et al. 2011. (ENG.). 40p. (J). (gr. -1-3). 16.99 *(978-0-8118-7696-4(9))* Chronicle Bks. LLC.
—Uni the Unicorn. Rosenthal, Amy Krouse. 2014. (ENG.). 48p. (J). (gr. -1-3). 17.99 *(978-0-385-37555-9(7))*; lib. bdg. 20.99 *(978-0-375-97206-5(4))* Random Hse. Children's Bks. (Random Hse. Bks. for Young Readers).
—Where Does Kitty Go in the Rain? Ziefert, Harriet. 2015. (ENG.). 32p. (J). (gr. -1-3). 16.99 *(978-1-60905-519-6(5))* Blue Apple Bks.
Barrager, Brigette & Tcherevkoff, Michel. Florabelle. Quinton, Sasha. 2015. (ENG.). 40p. (J). (gr. -1-3). 15.99 *(978-0-06-229182-0(3))* HarperCollins Pubs.
Barrance, Reuben & Whatmore, Candice. Birthday. 2008. (Usborne Look & Say Ser.). 12p. (J). (gr. -1-3). bds. 7.99 *(978-0-7945-1986-9(1)*, Usborne) EDC Publishing.
Barrance, Reuben, jt. illus. see Whatmore, Candice.
Barreiro, Mike, jt. illus. see Eaton, Scot.
Barrera, F. M. Tales of the Blue Wizard: The Children of Jamornere. Barrera, F. M. 2005. 180p. (YA). (gr. 4-9). per. 10.99 *(978-0-9670848-1-7(4))* Talisman Pr.
Barreto, Eduardo. Episode IV: A New Hope, 3 vols., Vol. 3. Jones, Bruce. 2010. (Star Wars Ser.: No. 2). 24p. (J). (gr. 5-9). 24.21 *(978-1-59961-623-0(8))* Spotlight.
Barreto, Eduardo, jt. illus. see Russell, P. Craig.
Barrett, Angela. Ana Frank. Poole, Josephine. 2005. (SPA.). 32p. (J). (gr. 3-4). 17.99 *(978-1-930332-87-4(4))* Lectorum Pubns., Inc.
—Blancanieves. Poole, Josephine. 2007. (SPA.). 30p. (J). (gr. -1-5). 24.95 *(978-84-96629-17-2(1))* S.A. Kokinos ESP. Dist: Lectorum Pubns., Inc.
—The Night Before Christmas. Moore, Clement C. 2012. 30p. (J). *(978-1-4351-4416-3(3))* Barnes & Noble, Inc.
—The Night Fairy. Schlitz, Laura Amy. (ENG.). 128p. (J). (gr. 2-5). 2011. pap. 6.99 *(978-0-7636-5295-1(4))*; 2010. 16.99 *(978-0-7636-3674-6(6))* Candlewick Pr.
Barrett, Casey. Coco & Pebbles: Bath Night. Wenning, Jeremy. 2013. 20p. pap. 6.99 *(978-1-938768-16-3(7))* Gypsy Pubns.
—Coco & Pebbles: That's My Duck! Wenning, Jeremy. 2012. 16p. pap. 6.99 *(978-1-938768-04-0(3))* Gypsy Pubns.
—Tommy Fakes the Flu. Kerns, Kristen. 2013. 24p. pap. 8.99 *(978-1-938768-28-6(0))* Gypsy Pubns.
Barrett, Diana. Giuseppe's Famous Pizza Pies. Fisher, Meaghan. 2013. 24p. 17.99 *(978-1-938768-34-7(5))*; pap. 8.99 *(978-1-938768-20-0(5))* Gypsy Pubns.
Barrett, Karlish. Mary Loves Butterflies. Jonas, Gennevive. 2012. 40p. pap. 24.95 *(978-1-62709-061-2(4))* America Star Bks.
Barrett, Noah. If I Were Just a Little Taller. Anderson, Ebony. 2005. (ENG.). 48p. (J). (gr. -1-3). per. 9.99 *(978-0-9760901-8-2(X))* Morgan James Publishing.
Barrett, Peter. Day & Night in Forest. Barrett, Susan. 2009. 38p. (J). (gr. 2-5). 14.99 *(978-0-8437-0943-8(X))* Hammond World Atlas Corp.
Barrett, Peter. Dinosaur Babies. Penner, Lucille Recht. 2015. 32p. pap. 5.00 ***(978-1-61003-602-3(6))*** Center for the Collaborative Classroom.
Barrett, Peter. A Forest Tree House. Reda, Sheryl A. 2004. (Treasure Tree Ser.). 32p. (J). *(978-0-7166-1606-1(8))* World Bk., Inc.
Barrett, Peter, jt. illus. see Brown, Ruth.
Barrett, Phillip. Where's Larry? 2012. (ENG.). 32p. (J). pap. 15.95 *(978-1-84717-276-1(8))* O'Brien Pr., Ltd., The IRL. Dist: Dufour Editions, Inc.
Barrett, Rebecca. Christie Plays Softball. O'Hara, Susan. 2013. 48p. pap. 15.97 *(978-1-62516-519-0(6)*, Strategic Bk. Publishing) Strategic Book Publishing & Rights Agency (SBPRA).
—Tim's First Soccer Game. O'Hara, Susan. 2012. 38p. pap. 14.97 *(978-1-61897-199-9(9)*, Strategic Bk. Publishing) Strategic Book Publishing & Rights Agency (SBPRA).
Barrett, Robert. Michelle Obama: First Lady, 0 vols. Weatherford, Carole Boston. 2010. (ENG.). 32p. (J). (gr. k-3). 17.99 *(978-0-7614-5640-7(6)*, 9780761456407, Amazon Children's Publishing) Amazon Publishing.
—The Other Wise Man. 32p. (J). pap. 6.95 *(978-0-8249-5348-5(7)*, Ideals Children's Bks.) Ideals Pubns.
—The Other Wise Man. Van Dyke, Henry. 2008. (ENG.). 30p. (J). (gr. -1-3). 8.99 *(978-0-8249-5565-6(X)*, Ideals Children's Bks.) Ideals Pubns.
—The Real Story of the Flood. Maier, Paul. 2008. 32p. (J). (gr. 4-7). 16.99 *(978-0-7586-1267-0(2))* Concordia Publishing Hse.
—Who Were the American Pioneers? And Other Questions about Westward Expansion. Sandler, Martin W. 2014. (Good Question! Ser.). (ENG.). 32p. (J). pap. 5.95 *(978-1-4027-9047-8(3))* Sterling Publishing Co., Inc.
—Why Did the Whole World Go to War? And Other Questions about... World War II. Sandler, Martin W. 2013. (Good Question! Ser.). (ENG.). 32p. (J). (gr. 2). pap. 5.95 *(978-1-4027-9044-7(9))* Sterling Publishing Co., Inc.
—Why Did the Whole World Go to War? And Other Questions About... World War II. Sandler, Martin W. 2013. (Good Question! Ser.). (ENG.). 32p. (J). (gr. 2). 12.95 *(978-1-4027-9621-0(8))* Sterling Publishing Co., Inc.
Barrett, Robert T. The Real Story of the Creation. Maier, Paul L. 2007. 28p. (J). (gr. -1-18). 16.99 *(978-0-7586-1265-6(6))* Concordia Publishing Hse.
Barrett, Ron. Animals Series, 2 bks., Set. Barrett, Judi. (J). (gr. k-3). pap. 29.95 incl. audio *(978-0-87499-470-4(5))* Live Oak Media.
—Animals Should Definitely Not Act Like People. Barrett, Judi. pap. 35.95 incl. audio compact disk *(978-1-59112-827-4(7))*; (J). pap. 33.95 incl. audio *(978-0-87499-232-8(X))* Live Oak Media.
—Animals Should Definitely Not Wear Clothing. Barrett, Judi. 2012. (Classic Board Bks.). (ENG.). 36p. (J). (gr. -1 — 1). bds. 7.99 *(978-1-4424-3334-2(5)*, Little Simon) Little Simon.
—Cloudy with a Chance of Meatballs. Barrett, Judi. 2011. (Classic Board Bks.). (ENG.). 34p. (J). (gr. -1-k). bds. 7.99 *(978-1-4424-3023-5(0)*, Little Simon) Little Simon.
—Cloudy with a Chance of Meatballs. Barrett, Judi. ed. 2009. 9.00 *(978-1-55744-455-4(2)*, Everbind) Marco Bk. Co.
—Pickles to Pittsburgh: The Sequel to Cloudy with a Chance of Meatballs. Barrett, Judi. 2004. 26p. (gr. -1-3). 17.00 *(978-0-7569-4215-1(2))* Perfection Learning Corp.
—Superhero Joe. Weitzman, Jacqueline Preiss. 2011. (ENG.). 32p. (J). (gr. -1-3). 16.99 *(978-1-4169-9157-1(3)*, Simon & Schuster/Paula Wiseman Bks.) Simon & Schuster/Paula Wiseman Bks.
—Superhero Joe & the Creature Next Door. Weitzman, Jacqueline Preiss. 2013. (ENG.). 32p. (J). (gr. -1-3). 16.99 *(978-1-4424-1268-2(2)*, Simon & Schuster Bks. For Young Readers) Simon & Schuster Bks. For Young Readers.
Barrett, Ron. Cats Get Famous. Barrett, Ron. 2015. (ENG.). 32p. (J). (gr. -1-3). 17.99 *(978-1-4424-9453-4(0)*, Simon & Schuster Bks. For Young Readers) Simon & Schuster Bks. For Young Readers.
—The Marshmallow Incident. Barrett, Ron. Barrett, Judi. 2009. (J). pap. *(978-0-545-04654-1(8)*, Scholastic Pr.) Scholastic, Inc.
Barrett, Ronald. Cloudy with a Chance of Meatballs. Barrett, Judi. 2012. (ENG.). 32p. (J). (gr. -1-3). pap. 9.99 *(978-1-4424-4337-2(5)*, Little Simon) Little Simon.
—The Complete Cloudy with a Chance of Meatballs: Cloudy with a Chance of Meatballs; Pickles to Pittsburgh. Barrett, Judi. 2009. (ENG.). 64p. (J). (gr. -1-3). 19.99 *(978-1-4424-0199-0(0)*, Atheneum Bks. for Young Readers) Simon & Schuster Children's Publishing.
—Grandpa's Cloudy with a Chance of Meatballs Cookbook. Barrett, Judi. 2013. (ENG.). 64p. (J). (gr. -1-3). spiral bd. 17.99 *(978-1-4424-4475-1(4)*, Atheneum Bks. for Young Readers) Simon & Schuster Children's Publishing.
—Pickles to Pittsburgh: Cloudy with a Chance of Meatballs 2. Barrett, Judi. (Classic Board Bks.). (ENG.). (J). (gr. -1-k). 2013. 34p. bds. 7.99 *(978-1-4424-6493-3(3))*; 2012. 32p. pap. 9.99 *(978-1-4424-4459-1(2))* Little Simon. (Little Simon).
Barrett, Virginia. Shadows. Stott-Thornton, Janet. 2007. (Literacy 2000 Satellites: Stage 2 Ser.). 8p. (J). (gr. -1-3). pap. *(978-0-7327-1173-3(8)*, Rigby) Pearson Education Australia.
Barretta, Gene. Conrad & the Cowgirl Next Door, 1 vol. Fretz, Denette. 2014. (Next Door Ser.). (ENG.). 40p. (J). 12.99 *(978-0-310-72349-3(3))* Zonderkidz.
—Monster Trucks. Matthies, Janna. 2009. (ENG.). 14p. (J). (gr. -1-k). 9.95 *(978-1-58117-853-1(0)*, Intervisual/Piggy Toes) Bendon, Inc.
—On Christmas Morning. Pingry, Patricia A. 2007. (ENG.). 26p. (J). (gr. -1-3). bds. 6.99 *(978-0-8249-6713-0(5)*, Candy Cane Pr.) Ideals Pubns.
—On Top of Spaghetti: A Silly Song Book. 2005. 12p. (J). 12.95 *(978-1-58117-331-4(8)*, Intervisual/Piggy Toes) Bendon, Inc.
Barretta, Gene. Dear Deer: A Book of Homophones. Barretta, Gene. 2010. (ENG.). 40p. (J). (gr. -1-2). pap. 7.99 *(978-0-312-62899-4(4))* Square Fish.
—Neo Leo: The Ageless Ideas of Leonardo Da Vinci. Barretta, Gene. 2009. (ENG.). 40p. (J). (gr. -1-4). 17.99 *(978-0-8050-8703-1(6)*, Holt, Henry & Co. Bks. For Young Readers) Holt, Henry & Co.
—Now & Ben: The Modern Inventions of Benjamin Franklin. Barretta, Gene. 2006. (ENG.). 36p. (J). (gr. k-4). 18.99 *(978-0-8050-7917-3(3)*, Holt, Henry & Co. Bks. For Young Readers) Holt, Henry & Co.
—Now & Ben: The Modern Inventions of Benjamin Franklin. Barretta, Gene. 2008. (ENG.). 40p. (J). (gr. k-4). pap. 8.99 *(978-0-312-53569-8(4))* Square Fish.
—Timeless Thomas: How Thomas Edison Changed Our Lives. Barretta, Gene. 2012. (ENG.). 36p. (J). (gr. 1-5). 17.99 *(978-0-8050-9108-3(4)*, Holt, Henry & Co. Bks. For Young Readers) Holt, Henry & Co.
—Zoola Palooza: A Book of Homographs. Barretta, Gene. 2011. (ENG.). 40p. (J). (gr. k-3). 16.99 *(978-0-8050-9107-6(6)*, Holt, Henry & Co. Bks. For Young Readers) Holt, Henry & Co.
Barrette, Doris. The Christmas Song: Chestnuts Roasting on an Open Fire. Torme, Mel. 2007. 32p. (J). (gr. -1-2). lib. bdg. 17.89 *(978-0-06-072226-5(6))* HarperCollins Pubs.
—The Christmas Song: Chestnuts Roasting on an Open Fire. Tormé, Mel. 2007. (J). lib. bdg. 6.99 *(978-0-06-072227-2(4))* HarperCollins Pubs.
—Never Ask a Bear. Bonnett-Rampersaud, Louise. 2009. (ENG.). 32p. (J). (gr. -1-1). 16.99 *(978-0-06-112876-9(7))* HarperCollins Pubs.
—Thanks for Thanksgiving. Markes, Julie. (ENG.). 32p. (J). (gr. -1-3). 2008. pap. 6.99 *(978-0-06-051098-5(6))*; 2004. 12.99 *(978-0-06-051096-1(X))* HarperCollins Pubs.
—When the Wind Blew. Jackson, Alison. 2014. (ENG.). 32p. (J). (gr. -1-2). 16.99 *(978-0-8050-8688-1(9)*, Holt, Henry & Co. Bks. For Young Readers) Holt, Henry & Co.
Barrie, J. M., et al. Peter Pan. Barrie, J. M. 2009. (ENG.). 287p. *(978-1-905716-40-1(0)*, Collector's Library, The) Pan Macmillan.
Barrie, J. M. Peter Pan: Complete & Unabridged. Barrie, J. M. 2005. 176p. reprint ed. pap. 17.00 *(978-0-7567-9445-3(5))* DIANE Publishing Co.
Barringer, J. M. The Treetop Bird Family. Magden, Loretta. 2007. 28p. (J). 15.95 *(978-0-9788771-0-1(1))* Level Green Bks.
Barringer, Laura. Squirrel Dance's Plan to Relocate Buddy Raccoon: A Squirrel Dance Book. Rivers, C. 2011. (ENG.). 40p. pap. 12.99 *(978-1-4609-8151-1(0))* CreateSpace Independent Publishing Platform.
Barrio, Blanca. Paco. Carballeira, Paula. 2003. 32p. (J). 14.95 *(978-84-95730-38-1(3))* Kalandraka Catalunya, Edicions, S.L. ESP. Dist: Independent Pubs. Group.
Barrionuevo, Al. Martian Manhunter: The Others among Us. Lieberman, A. J. rev. ed. 2007. (ENG.). 208p. (YA). pap. 19.99 *(978-1-4012-1335-0(9))* DC Comics.
Barritt, Carolyn Reed. The Day the Dragon Danced. Haugaard, Kay. 2004. (Day the Dragon Danced Ser.). 32p. (J). (gr. -1-3). 16.95 *(978-1-885008-30-5(9)*, Shen's Bks.) Lee & Low Bks., Inc.
Barron, Ann. Maggie's Golden Moment. Profilet, Cynthia. 2005. (J). *(978-0-9637735-1-7(8))* Sterling Pr., Inc.
Barron, Ashley. Kyle Goes Alone. Thornhill, Jan. 2015. (ENG.). 32p. (J). (gr. -1-2). 17.95 ***(978-1-77147-075-9(5)***, Owlkids) Owlkids Bks. Inc. CAN. Dist: Perseus-PGW.
Barron, Ashley. Shaping up Summer. Flatt, Lizann. 2014. (Math in Nature Ser.: 4). (ENG.). 32p. (J). (gr. k-2). 14.95 *(978-1-926973-87-6(9)*, Owlkids) Owlkids Bks. Inc. CAN. Dist: Perseus-PGW.
—Sorting Through Spring. Flatt, Lizann. 2013. (Math in Nature Ser.: 2). (ENG.). 32p. (J). (gr. k-2). 14.95 *(978-1-926973-59-3(3))* Owlkids Bks. Inc. CAN. Dist: Perseus-PGW.
Barron, Ashley & Owlkids Books Inc. Staff. Counting on Fall. Flatt, Lizann. 2012. (Math in Nature Ser.: 1). (ENG.). 32p. (J). (gr. k-2). 15.95 *(978-1-926973-36-4(4)*, Owlkids) Owlkids Bks. Inc. CAN. Dist: Perseus-PGW.
—Sizing up Winter. Flatt, Lizann. 2013. (Math in Nature Ser.: 3). (ENG.). 32p. (J). (gr. k-2). 14.95 *(978-1-926973-82-1(8)*, Owlkids) Owlkids Bks. Inc. CAN. Dist: Perseus-PGW.
Barron, Rex. Showdown at the Food Pyramid. Barron, Rex. 2004. (ENG.). 32p. (J). (gr. -1-3). 17.99 *(978-0-399-23715-7(1)*, Putnam Juvenile) Penguin Publishing Group.
Barron, Robert, photos by. Meet Judge Patricia Barron. Barron, Patricia. 2006. 40p. per. 14.95 *(978-1-59858-301-4(8))* Dog Ear Publishing, LLC.
Barron's Educational Series Staff & Rigo, L. Off to School. 2010. (ENG.). 10p. (J). (gr. -1-1). bds. 7.99 *(978-0-7641-6363-0(9))* Barron's Educational Series, Inc.
Barroux. Bunny's Lessons. Ziefert, Harriet. 2011. (ENG.). 40p. (J). (gr. -1-3). 16.99 *(978-1-60905-028-3(2))* Blue Apple Bks.
—Draw Patterns with Barroux. 2013. (ENG.). 96p. (J). (gr. -1-3). 12.99 *(978-1-60905-300-0(1))* Blue Apple Bks.
—Draw Patterns with Barroux Drawing Book & Kit: Everything You Need to Start Drawing Shapes, Colors, & Patterns! 2014. (ENG.). 64p. (J). (gr. -1-17). 14.95 *(978-1-60058-470-1(5))* Quarto Publishing Group USA.
—Extraordinary Pets. Blue Apple Staff. 2010. (ENG.). 40p. (J). (gr. k-4). 15.99 *(978-1-60905-011-5(8))* Blue Apple Bks.
—I Could Be- Owen, Karen. 2009. (J). *(978-1-84686-289-2(2))* Barefoot Bks., Inc.
—I Could Be, You Could Be. Owen, Karen. 2010. (ENG.). 32p. (J). (gr. 1-3). 16.99 *(978-1-84686-405-6(4))* Barefoot Bks., Inc.
—It's Time to Say Good Night. Ziefert, Harriet. 2013. (ENG.). 36p. (J). (gr. -1-3). 17.99 *(978-1-60905-374-1(5))* Blue Apple Bks.
—Lucy Rescued. Ziefert, Harriet. 2012. (ENG.). 40p. (J). (gr. -1-3). 16.99 *(978-1-60905-187-7(4))* Blue Apple Bks.
—My Dog Thinks I'm a Genius. Ziefert, Harriet. 2011. (ENG.). 40p. (J). (gr. -1-3). 16.99 *(978-1-60905-059-7(2))* Blue Apple Bks.
—The Red Piano. Leblanc, André. Werner, Justine, tr. from FRE. 2010. Tr. of Piano Rouge. (ENG.). 40p. (J). (gr. 2-4). 16.99 *(978-0-9806070-1-7(9))* Wilkins Farago Pty, Ltd. AUS. Dist: Independent Pubs. Group.
—Where Is the Rocket? Ziefert, Harriet. 2014. (ENG.). 40p. (J). (gr. -1-k). 17.99 *(978-1-60905-340-6(0))* Blue Apple Bks.
Barroux. Mr Leon's Paris. Barroux. Ardizzone, Sarah, tr. from FRE. 2013. (ENG.). 32p. (J). (gr. k-2). pap. 9.99 *(978-1-907912-08-5(6))* Phoenix Yard Bks. GBR. Dist: Independent Pubs. Group.
Barroux, Gilles. Naughty & Nice. 2010. (ENG.). 32p. (J). (-k). 9.99 *(978-1-60905-013-9(4))* Blue Apple Bks.
—Plain & Fancy. 2010. (ENG.). 32p. (J). (-k). 9.99 *(978-1-60905-012-2(6))* Blue Apple Bks.
Barroux, Sophie, jt. illus. see Derenne, Juliette.
Barroux, Stephane. Mega Bunny. Vidal, Séverine. 2015. (Mega Hero Bks.). (ENG.). 28p. (J). (gr. k-2). pap. 6.95 ***(978-1-77085-654-7(4)***, 9781770856547) Firefly Bks., Ltd.
—Mega Mouse. Vidal, Séverine. 2015. (Mega Hero Bks.). (ENG.). 28p. (J). (gr. k-2). pap. 6.95 ***(978-1-77085-655-4(2)***, 9781770856554) Firefly Bks., Ltd.
—Mega Pig. Vidal, Séverine. 2015. (Mega Hero Bks.). (ENG.). 28p. (J). (gr. k-2). pap. 6.95 ***(978-1-77085-652-3(8)***, 9781770856523) Firefly Bks., Ltd.
—Mega Wolf. Vidal, Séverine. 2015. (Mega Hero Bks.). (ENG.). 28p. (J). (gr. k-2). pap. 6.95 ***(978-1-77085-653-0(6)***, 9781770856530) Firefly Bks., Ltd.
Barroux, Stephane. My Goldfish. 2009. 36p. (J). (gr. -1-2). 15.00 *(978-0-8028-5334-9(X)*, Eerdmans Bks For Young Readers) Eerdmans, William B. Publishing Co.
Barrow, Alex. London Calls. Dawnay, Gabby. 2015. (ENG.). 40p. (gr. -1-2). 13.95 *(978-1-84976-230-4(9))* Tate Publishing, Ltd. GBR. Dist: Abrams.
Barrow, Ann. Big Blue. Gill, Shelley. 2005. (ENG.). 32p. (J). (gr. k-3). 7.95 *(978-1-57091-667-0(5))* Charlesbridge Publishing, Inc.
—Doris Free. Brookins, Cara. 2006. 127p. (J). pap. *(978-1-59336-333-8(8))* Mondo Publishing.
Barrows, Laurie. The Magical, Marvelous Megan G. Beamer: A Day in the Life of A Dreamer. Burnett, Karen Gedig. 2003. (J). pap. 8.95 *(978-0-9668530-6-3(7))* G R Publishing.
—To Bee or Not to Bee: A Book for Beeings Who Feel there's More to Life than Just Making Honey. Penberthy, John. rev. l.t. ed. 2005. 112p. (J). pap. 14.95 *(978-0-9768642-0-2(7))* Panorama Pr., Inc.
Barry, Etheldred B. The Giant Scissors. Johnston, Annie Fellows. 2005. reprint ed. pap. 22.95 *(978-1-4179-0341-2(4))* Kessinger Publishing, LLC.
—The Little Colonel's Hero. Johnston, Annie Fellows. 2007. 180p. per. *(978-1-4065-3513-6(3))* Dodo Pr.
—Mary Ware, the Little Colonel's Chum, 1 vol. Johnston, Annie. 2005. (Little Colonel Ser.). (ENG.). 336p. (YA). (gr. 3-6). pap. 19.95 *(978-1-56554-813-8(2))* Pelican Publishing Co., Inc.
—Mary Ware the Little Colonel's Chum. Johnston, Annie Fellows. 2004. reprint ed. pap. 30.95 *(978-1-4179-1704-4(0))* Kessinger Publishing, LLC.
Barry, Frances. Big Yellow Sunflower. Barry, Frances. 2008. (Fold Out & Find Out Ser.). (ENG.). 22p. (J). (-k). 8.99 *(978-0-7636-3724-8(6))* Candlewick Pr.
—Let's Save the Animals. Barry, Frances. 2010. (ENG.). 40p. (J). (gr. -1-3). 12.99 *(978-0-7636-4501-4(X))* Candlewick Pr.
Barry, James. Warriors Manga - Graystripe's Adventure, 3 vols., Set. Hunter, Erin. 2009. (Warriors Ser.). 336p. (J). (gr. 3-7). pap. 16.99 *(978-0-06-178228-2(9))* HarperCollins Pubs.
Barry, James L. Beyond the Code. Hunter, Erin. 2011. (Warriors Manga Ser.: 2). (ENG.). 112p. (J). (gr. 3-7). pap. 6.99 *(978-0-06-200837-4(4))* HarperCollins Pubs.
—A Clan in Need. Hunter, Erin. 2010. (Warriors Manga Ser.: 2). (ENG.). 112p. (J). (gr. 3-7). pap. 6.99 *(978-0-06-168866-9(5))* HarperCollins Pubs.
—The Heart of a Warrior. Hunter, Erin. 2010. (Warriors Manga Ser.: 3). (ENG.). 112p. (J). (gr. 3-7). pap. 6.99 *(978-0-06-168867-6(3))* HarperCollins Pubs.
—The Rescue. Hunter, Erin. 2011. (Warriors Manga Ser.: 1). (ENG.). 112p. (J). (gr. 3-7). pap. 6.99 *(978-0-06-200836-7(6))* HarperCollins Pubs.
—Shattered Peace. Hunter, Erin. 2009. (Warriors Manga Ser.: 1). (ENG.). 112p. (J). (gr. 3-7). pap. 6.99 *(978-0-06-168865-2(7))* HarperCollins Pubs.
—Tallstar's Revenge. Hunter, Erin. (Warriors Super Edition Ser.: 6). (J). (gr. 3-7). 2014. (ENG.). 560p. pap. 7.99 *(978-0-06-221806-3(9))*; 2013. (ENG.). 544p. 18.99 *(978-0-06-221804-9(2))*; 2013. 544p. lib. bdg. 19.89 *(978-0-06-221805-6(0))* HarperCollins Pubs.
—Warrior's Refuge, 3 vols. Jolley, Dan & Hunter, Erin. 2007. (Warriors Manga Ser.: No. 2). (ENG.). 112p. (J). (gr. 3-7). pap. 6.99 *(978-0-06-125231-0(X))* HarperCollins Pubs.
—Warrior's Return, 3 vols. Hunter, Erin & Jolley, Dan. 2008. (Warriors Manga Ser.: No. 3). (ENG.). 112p. (J). (gr. 3-7). pap. 6.99 *(978-0-06-125233-4(6))* HarperCollins Pubs.
—Yellowfang's Secret. Hunter, Erin. (Warriors Super Edition Ser.: 5). (J). (gr. 3-7). 2014. (ENG.). 544p. pap. 7.99 *(978-0-06-208216-9(7))*; 2012. (ENG.). 528p. 18.99 *(978-0-06-208214-5(0))*; 2012. 528p. lib. bdg. 19.89 *(978-0-06-208215-2(9))* HarperCollins Pubs.
Barry, James L. & Hunt, John. After the Flood. Hunter, Erin. 2012. (Warriors Manga Ser.: 3). (ENG.). 112p. (J). (gr. 3-7). pap. 6.99 *(978-0-06-200838-1(2))* HarperCollins Pubs.
Barry, James L. & Richardson, Owen. Moth Flight's Vision. Hunter, Erin et al. 2015. (Warriors Super Edition Ser.: 8). (ENG.). 528p. (J). (gr. 3-7). 18.99 ***(978-0-06-229147-9(5))*** HarperCollins Pubs.
Barshaw, Ruth McNally. Best Friends Fur-Ever. Barshaw, Ruth McNally. 2013. (Ellie Mcdoodle Diaries). (ENG.). 192p. (J). (gr. 3-6). 12.99 *(978-1-61963-175-5(X)*, Bloomsbury USA Childrens) Bloomsbury USA.
—Ellie McDoodle: Best Friends Fur-Ever. Barshaw, Ruth McNally. 2011. (Ellie Mcdoodle Ser.). (ENG.). 192p. (J). (gr. 3-6). pap. 6.99 *(978-1-59990-657-7(0)*, Bloomsbury USA Childrens) Bloomsbury USA.
—Ellie McDoodle: Have Pen, Will Travel. Barshaw, Ruth McNally. 2nd ed. 2011. (Ellie Mcdoodle Ser.). (ENG.). 192p. (J). (gr. 3-6). pap. 7.99 *(978-1-59990-715-4(1)*, Bloomsbury USA Childrens) Bloomsbury USA.
—The Ellie McDoodle Diaries: Ellie for President. Barshaw, Ruth McNally. 2014. (Ellie Mcdoodle Ser.). (ENG.). 176p. (J). (gr. 3-6). 12.99 *(978-1-61963-061-1(3)*, Bloomsbury USA Childrens) Bloomsbury USA.
—The Ellie McDoodle Diaries: Most Valuable Player. Barshaw, Ruth McNally. 2013. (Ellie Mcdoodle Diaries). (ENG.). 192p. (J). (gr. 3-6). 12.99 *(978-1-61963-176-2(8)*, Bloomsbury USA Childrens) Bloomsbury USA.
—Have Pen, Will Travel. Barshaw, Ruth McNally. 2013. (Ellie Mcdoodle Diaries). (ENG.). 192p. (J). (gr. 3-6). 12.99 *(978-1-61963-173-1(3)*, Bloomsbury USA Childrens) Bloomsbury USA.
—New Kid in School. Barshaw, Ruth McNally. 2013. (Ellie Mcdoodle Diaries). (ENG.). 192p. (J). (gr. 3-6). pap. 12.99 *(978-1-61963-174-8(1)*, Bloomsbury USA Childrens) Bloomsbury USA.
—The Show Must Go On. Barshaw, Ruth McNally. 2013. (Ellie Mcdoodle Diaries). (ENG.). 176p. (J). (gr. 3-6). 12.99 *(978-1-61963-059-8(1)*, Bloomsbury USA Childrens) Bloomsbury USA.
Bart, Kathleen. Town Teddy & Country Bear Go Global. Bart, Kathleen. 2011. (J). (gr. k-3). 16.95 *(978-1-932485-60-8(0))* Reverie Publishing Co.
—Town Teddy & Country Bear Tour the USA. Bart, Kathleen. 2008. 32p. (J). (gr. -1-3). pap. 16.95 *(978-1-932485-50-9(3))* Reverie Publishing Co.
Bart, Kathleen & Hofmann, Ginnie. Doll & Teddy Bear Activity Book. Dracker, Pune. 2005. 96p. (J). pap. *(978-1-932485-24-0(4))* Reverie Publishing Co.
Bartczak, Peter. A Voice for the Redwoods. Halter, Loretta. 2010. (ENG.). 64p. (J). 18.95 *(978-0-9822942-0-8(4))* Nature's Hopes & Heroes.
Bartels, Mark. Little Robert: A True Story. Bartels, Lowell. 2011. 36p. pap. 19.95 *(978-1-4137-7171-8(8))* America Star Bks.
Barth, Alexandra. Teddy Visits the Dentist. Mahadeo Rdh, Elizabeth. 2012. 40p. pap. *(978-0-9569438-0-4(2))* Mahadeo Movement, The.
—Teddy Visits the Dentist: Teddy Gets a Filling. Mahadeo Rdh, Elizabeth. 2012. 42p. (-18). pap. *(978-0-9569438-2-8(9))* Mahadeo Movement, The.
Barthelmes, Andrew. If My Mom Were a Platypus: Mammal Babies & Their Mothers. Michels, Dia L. 2005. (ENG.). 64p. (J). (gr. 4-7). 24.95 *(978-1-930775-30-5(X))* Platypus Media, L.L.C.

—If My Mom Were a Platypus: Mammal Babies & Their Mothers. Michels, Dia L. 4th ed. 2014. (SPA, DUT, ENG & HEB.). 64p. pap. 12.95 *(978-1-938492-11-2(0))* Science, Naturally!.
—If My Mom Were A Platypus- Hebrew Language Edition. Michels, Dia L. 2006. Orig. Title: #1488;#1501; #1488;#1502;#1497; #1492;#1497;#1514;#1492; #1508;#1500;#1496;#1497;#1508;#1493;#1505;. 64p. (J). 29.95 *(978-0-9678020-9-1(1))* Science, Naturally!.
—If My Mom Were a Platypus- Hebrew Language Edition. Michels, Dia L. 2006. Orig. Title: #1488;#1501; #1488;#1502;#1497; #1492;#1497;#1514;#1492; #1508;#1500;#1496;#1497;#1508;#1493;#1505;. (HEB.). 64p. (J). 19.95 *(978-0-9678020-8-4(3))* Science, Naturally!.
—Star Wars Rebels - Ezra's Journal. Wallace, Daniel. 2014. (ENG.). 96p. (J). (gr. k-3). 9.99 *(978-0-7944-3268-3(9))* Studio Fun International.
Bartholomew. A Fun & Easy Way to Do Your Homework. Berry, Joy. 2010. (Fun & Easy Way Ser.). (ENG.). 48p. (J). (gr. 1-5). pap. 7.95 *(978-1-60577-320-9(4))* Berry, Joy Enterprises.
—A Fun & Easy Way to Get Good Grades. Berry, Joy. 2010. (Fun & Easy Way Ser.). (ENG.). 48p. (J). (gr. 1-5). pap. 7.95 *(978-1-60577-321-6(2))* Berry, Joy Enterprises.
—Good Answers to Tough Questions Disasters. Berry, Joy. 2010. (Good Answers to Tough Questions Ser.). (ENG.). 48p. (J). (gr. k-7). pap. 7.99 *(978-1-60577-510-4(X))* Berry, Joy Enterprises.
—Good Answers to Tough Questions Divorce. Berry, Joy. 2010. (Good Answers to Tough Questions Ser.). (ENG.). 48p. (J). (gr. k-7). pap. 7.99 *(978-1-60577-509-8(6))* Berry, Joy Enterprises.
—Good Answers to Tough Questions Moving. Berry, Joy. 2010. (Good Answers to Tough Questions Ser.). (ENG.). 48p. (J). (gr. k-7). pap. 7.99 *(978-1-60577-508-1(8))* Berry, Joy Enterprises.
—Good Answers to Tough Questions Trauma. Berry, Joy. 2010. (Good Answers to Tough Questions Ser.). (ENG.). 48p. (J). (gr. k-7). pap. 7.99 *(978-1-60577-507-4(X))* Berry, Joy Enterprises.
—Help Me Be Good Being a Bad Sport. Berry, Joy. 2010. (Help Me Be Good Ser.). (ENG.). 32p. (J). (gr. -1-2). pap. 4.99 *(978-1-60577-139-7(2))* Berry, Joy Enterprises.
—Help Me Be Good Being Mean. Berry, Joy. 2010. (Help Me Be Good Ser.). (ENG.). 32p. (J). (gr. -1-2). pap. 4.99 *(978-1-60577-142-7(2))* Berry, Joy Enterprises.
—Help Me Be Good Being Rude. Berry, Joy. 2010. (Help Me Be Good Ser.). (ENG.). 32p. (J). (gr. -1-2). pap. 4.99 *(978-1-60577-138-0(4))* Berry, Joy Enterprises.
—Help Me Be Good Being Selfish. Berry, Joy. 2010. (Help Me Be Good Ser.). (ENG.). 32p. (J). (gr. -1-2). pap. 4.99 *(978-1-60577-133-5(3))* Berry, Joy Enterprises.
—Help Me Be Good Bullying. Berry, Joy. 2010. (Help Me Be Good Ser.). (ENG.). 32p. (J). (gr. -1-2). pap. 4.99 *(978-1-60577-140-3(6))* Berry, Joy Enterprises.
—Help Me Be Good Disobeying. Berry, Joy. 2010. (Help Me Be Good Ser.). (ENG.). 32p. (J). (gr. -1-2). pap. 4.99 *(978-1-60577-137-3(6))* Berry, Joy Enterprises.
—Help Me Be Good Fighting. Berry, Joy. 2010. (Help Me Be Good Ser.). (ENG.). 32p. (J). (gr. -1-2). pap. 4.99 *(978-1-60577-135-9(X))* Berry, Joy Enterprises.
—Help Me Be Good Showing Off. Berry, Joy. 2010. (Help Me Be Good Ser.). (ENG.). 32p. (J). (gr. -1-2). pap. 4.99 *(978-1-60577-143-4(0))* Berry, Joy Enterprises.
—Help Me Be Good Tattling. Berry, Joy. 2010. (Help Me Be Good Ser.). (ENG.). 32p. (J). (gr. -1-2). pap. 4.99 *(978-1-60577-136-6(8))* Berry, Joy Enterprises.
—Help Me Be Good Teasing. Berry, Joy. 2010. (Help Me Be Good Ser.). (ENG.). 32p. (J). (gr. -1-2). pap. 4.99 *(978-1-60577-141-0(4))* Berry, Joy Enterprises.
—Help Me Be Good Whining. Berry, Joy. 2010. (Help Me Be Good Ser.). (ENG.). 32p. (J). (gr. -1-2). pap. 4.99 *(978-1-60577-134-2(1))* Berry, Joy Enterprises.
—I Feel Angry. Leonard, Marcia. 2003. 24p. (J). bds. 2.95 *(978-0-8249-6526-6(4))* Ideals Pubns.
—I Feel Happy. Leonard, Marcia. 2003. 24p. (J). bds. 2.95 *(978-0-8249-6523-5(X))* Ideals Pubns.
—I Feel Sad. Leonard, Marcia. 2003. 24p. (J). bds. 2.95 *(978-0-8249-6524-2(8))* Ideals Pubns.
—I Feel Scared. Leonard, Marcia. 2003. 24p. (J). bds. 2.95 *(978-0-8249-6525-9(6))* Ideals Pubns.
—The Smart Kids Allowance System: Step-by-Step Money Management Guidebook. Berry, Rob & Duey, Kathleen. Date not set. (Family Skill Builders Ser.). (J). (gr. k-6). pap. 9.95 *(978-1-883761-34-9(4))* Family Life Productions.
—Winning Skills You Can Work It! an Anthology of Six Books. Berry, Joy. 2010. (Winning Skills Ser.). (ENG.). 304p. (J). (gr. 5-7). pap. 9.95 *(978-1-60577-604-0(1))* Berry, Joy Enterprises.
Bartholomew, Al, jt. photos by see Bartholomew, Linda.
Bartholomew, Linda & Bartholomew, Al, photos by. Adventures in the Tropics. Bartholomew, Linda & Bartholomew, Al. 2005. 76p. (J). 15.00 *(978-0-9764802-1-1(2))* Solutions for Human Services, LLC.
—The Rain Forest Book for Kids. Bartholomew, Linda & Bartholomew, Al. 2005. 32p. (J). 9.00 *(978-0-9764802-0-4(4))* Solutions for Human Services, LLC.
Bartlett, Alison. Can I Play? Thomas, Janet. 2005. 32p. (J). 8.99 *(978-1-4052-0597-9(0))* Egmont Bks., Ltd. GBR. Dist: Trafalgar Square Publishing.
—Dominic Grows Sweetcorn. Ross, Mandy. 2014. (ENG.). 32p. (J). (gr. 1-5). 17.99 *(978-1-84780-327-6(X)*, Frances Lincoln) Quarto Publishing Group UK GBR. Dist: Hachette Bk. Group.
—Growing Frogs. French, Vivian. (Read, Listen, & Wonder Ser.). (ENG.). 32p. (J). (gr. -1-3). 2008. pap. 8.99 *(978-0-7636-3831-3(5))*; 2003. pap. 6.99 *(978-0-7636-2052-3(1))* Candlewick Pr.
—Growing Frogs Big Book: Read & Wonder Big Book. French, Vivian. 2003. (Read & Wonder Ser.). (ENG.). 32p. (J). (gr. k-3). pap. 24.99 *(978-0-7636-2232-9(X))* Candlewick Pr.
—T. Rex: r. French, Vivian. 2009. (Read, Listen, & Wonder Ser.). (ENG.). 32p. (J). (gr. -1-3). pap. 8.99 *(978-0-7636-3999-0(0))* Candlewick Pr.
—T. Rex: Read & Wonder. French, Vivian. 2006. (Read & Wonder Ser.). (ENG.). 32p. (J). (gr. -1-3). reprint ed. pap. 6.99 *(978-0-7636-3177-2(9))* Candlewick Pr.
—T. Rex with Audio, Peggable: Read, Listen & Wonder. French, Vivian. 2009. (Read, Listen, & Wonder Ser.). (ENG.). 32p. (J). (gr. -1-3). pap. 9.99 *(978-0-7636-4192-4(8))* Candlewick Pr.
Bartlett, Alyssa Joy. Boo Boo Kisses from the Littlest Angel, 1 vol. Penley, Janet. 2010. 34p. 24.95 *(978-1-4489-4539-9(9))* PublishAmerica, Inc.
Bartlett, Rebecca. Disappearing Diamonds: An Upton Charles Adventure. Stern, D. G. 2008. (ENG.). 126p. (J). pap. 9.99 *(978-0-9754676-9-5(7))* Yeoman Hse.
Barto, Linda ILham. Where the Ghost Camel Grins: Muslim Fables for Families of All Faiths. 2009. (ENG.). 119p. (gr. 5). 19.95 *(978-1-879402-24-9(6))* Tahrike Tarsile Quran, Inc.
Bartolini, Egle. Penguins of Madagascar Vol. 2: Operation Heist. Scott, Cavan et al. 2015. (ENG.). 64p. (gr. 1-4). pap. 6.99 ***(978-1-78276-252-2(3)**, Titan Comics)* Titan Bks. Ltd. GBR. Dist: Penguin Random Hse., LLC.
Barton, Bethany. 33 Minutes. Hasak-Lowy, Todd. (ENG.). 224p. (J). (gr. 3-7). 2014. pap. 7.99 *(978-1-4424-4501-7(7))*; 2013. 16.99 *(978-1-4424-4500-0(9))* Simon & Schuster/Paula Wiseman Bks. (Simon & Schuster/Paula Wiseman Bks.).
Barton, Bethany. I'm Trying to Love Spiders. Barton, Bethany. 2015. (ENG.). 34p. (J). (gr. -1-3). 16.99 *(978-0-670-01693-8(4))* Penguin Bks., Ltd. GBR. Dist: Penguin Random Hse., LLC.
Barton, Byron. Jump, Frog, Jump! Kalan, Robert. 2003.Tr. of Salta, Ranita, Salta!. (ENG.). 34p. (J). (gr. -1-3). bds. 7.99 *(978-0-06-008819-4(2)*, Greenwillow Bks.) HarperCollins Pubs.
—Jump, Frog, Jump! Kalan, Robert. 2004.Tr. of Salta, Ranita, Salta!. (J). (gr. -1-2). 28.95 incl. audio compact disk *(978-1-59112-728-4(9))* Live Oak Media.
Barton, Byron. Boats. Barton, Byron. 2006. 34p. (J). (gr. -1-2). 12.99 *(978-0-06-115017-3(7)*, HarperFestival) HarperCollins Pubs.
—My Bike. Barton, Byron. 2015. (ENG.). 40p. (J). (gr. -1-3). 16.99 *(978-0-06-233699-6(1)*, Collins Design) HarperCollins Pubs.
—My Bus. Barton, Byron. 2014. (ENG.). 40p. (J). (gr. -1-3). 16.99 *(978-0-06-228736-6(2)*, Greenwillow Bks.) HarperCollins Pubs.
Barton, Byron. My Bus Board Book. Barton, Byron. 2015. (ENG.). 40p. (J). (gr. -1 — 1). bds. 7.99 ***(978-0-06-228738-0(9)**, Greenwillow Bks.)* HarperCollins Pubs.
Barton, Byron. My Car. Barton, Byron. (ENG.). (J). (gr. -1-3). 2003. 36p. bds. 7.99 *(978-0-06-056045-4(2))*; 2004. 40p. reprint ed. pap. 6.99 *(978-0-06-058940-0(X))* HarperCollins Pubs. (Greenwillow Bks.).
Barton, Byron. My House. Barton, Byron. 2016. 40p. (J). (gr. -1-3). 16.99 ***(978-0-06-233703-0(3)**, Greenwillow Bks.)* HarperCollins Pubs.
Barton, Deborah. Tell Me about Our Christmas Tree. Norberg, A. 2011. (ENG.). 24p. pap. 11.95 *(978-1-4565-7745-2(X))* CreateSpace Independent Publishing Platform.
Barton, Harry. Saint Louis & the Last Crusade. Hubbard, Margaret Ann. 2013. (ENG.). 157p. pap. 9.95 *(978-1-58617-647-1(1))* Ignatius Pr.
Barton, Jill. Guess Who, Baby Duck! Hest, Amy. 2004. (ENG.). 32p. (J). (gr. k-k). 15.99 *(978-0-7636-1981-7(7))* Candlewick Pr.
—It's Quacking Time! Waddell, Martin. 2005. (ENG.). 32p. (J). (gr. -1-2). 15.99 *(978-0-7636-2738-6(0))* Candlewick Pr.
—Lady Lollipop. King-Smith, Dick. 2003. (ENG.). 128p. (J). (gr. 2-5). pap. 6.99 *(978-0-7636-2181-0(1))* Candlewick Pr.
—Puss Jekyll Cat Hyde. Dunbar, Joyce. 2013. (ENG.). 32p. (J). (gr. -1-2). 17.99 *(978-1-84780-369-6(5)*, Frances Lincoln) Quarto Publishing Group UK GBR. Dist: Hachette Bk. Group.
—Rattletrap Car. Root, Phyllis. 2004. (ENG.). 40p. (J). (gr. -1-3). reprint ed. pap. 7.99 *(978-0-7636-2007-3(6))* Candlewick Pr.
—Rattletrap Car Big Book. Root, Phyllis. 2009. (ENG.). 40p. (J). (gr. -1-3). pap. 24.99 *(978-0-7636-4139-9(1))* Candlewick Pr.
—Two Little Monkeys. Fox, Mem. 2012. (ENG.). 32p. (J). (gr. -1-3). 16.99 *(978-1-4169-8687-4(1)*, Beach Lane Bks.) Beach Lane Bks.
Barton, Patrice. I Like Old Clothes. Hoberman, Mary Ann. 2012. (ENG.). 32p. (J). (gr. k-3). 16.99 *(978-0-375-86951-8(4))* Knopf, Alfred A. Inc.
—I Pledge Allegiance. Mora, Pat & Martinez, Libby. 2014. (ENG.). 40p. (J). (gr. -1-2). 16.99 *(978-0-307-93181-8(1)*, Knopf Bks. for Young Readers) Random Hse. Children's Bks.
—The Invisible Boy. Ludwig, Trudy. 2013. (ENG.). 40p. (J). (gr. 1-4). 16.99 *(978-1-58246-450-3(2)*, Knopf Bks. for Young Readers) Random Hse. Children's Bks.
—Jessica Mcbean, Tap Dance Queen. Gerber, Carole. 2006. 144p. (J). 13.95 *(978-0-9718348-7-3(3))* Blooming Tree Pr.
—Jessica McBean, Tap Dance Queen. Gerber, Carole. 2007. (ENG.). 144p. (J). (gr. 1-5). pap. 6.95 *(978-0-9718348-9-7(X))* Blooming Tree Pr.
—Little Sleepyhead. McPike, Elizabeth. 2015. (ENG.). 26p. (J). (— 1). 16.99 *(978-0-399-16240-4(2)*, Putnam Adult) Penguin Publishing Group.
—The Looking Book. Hallinan, P. K. (J). 2015. pap. *(978-0-8249-5670-7(2))*; 2009. (ENG.). 32p. (gr. -1-2). 16.99 *(978-0-8249-5607-3(9))* Ideals Pubns. (Ideals Children's Bks.).
—Mine! Crum, Shutta. 2011. (ENG.). 32p. (J). (gr. -1-2). 16.99 *(978-0-375-86711-8(2)*, Knopf Bks. for Young Readers) Random Hse. Children's Bks.
—Mine! Crum, Shutta. 2012. (ENG.). 30p. (J). (gr. k-k). bds. 6.99 *(978-0-375-86346-2(X)*, Knopf Bks. for Young Readers) Random Hse. Children's Bks.
—Oh My! Ginny Fry! Shaw, Gina. 2010. 48p. (J). *(978-0-545-24384-1(X))* Scholastic, Inc.
—Rosie Sprout's Time to Shine. Wortche, Allison. 2011. (ENG.). 40p. (J). (gr. -1-2). 17.99 *(978-0-375-86721-7(X)*, Knopf Bks. for Young Readers) Random Hse. Children's Bks.
—Uh-Oh! Crum, Shutta. 2015. (ENG.). 32p. (J). (-k). 16.99 *(978-0-385-75268-8(7)*, Knopf Bks. for Young Readers) Random Hse. Children's Bks.
—Waiting for Snow. Shaw, Gina. 2010. 48p. (J). pap. *(978-0-545-24385-8(8))* Scholastic, Inc.
—The Year of the Baby. Cheng, Andrea. (Anna Wang Novel Ser.: 2). (ENG.). 176p. (J). (gr. 1-4). 2014. pap. 5.99 *(978-0-544-22525-1(2)*, HMH Books For Young Readers); 2013. 15.99 *(978-0-547-91067-3(3))* Houghton Mifflin Harcourt Publishing Co.
—The Year of the Fortune Cookie. Cheng, Andrea. 2014. (Anna Wang Novel Ser.: 3). (ENG.). 176p. (J). (gr. 1-4). 15.99 *(978-0-544-10519-5(2)*, HMH Books For Young Readers) Houghton Mifflin Harcourt Publishing Co.
—The Year of the Three Sisters. Cheng, Andrea. 2015. (Anna Wang Novel Ser.: 4). (ENG.). 160p. (J). (gr. 1-4). 16.99 *(978-0-544-34427-3(8)*, HMH Books For Young Readers) Houghton Mifflin Harcourt Publishing Co.
Barton, Renee. Amagestic: A Caterpillar's Journey. 2005. Orig. Title: Amagestic. (J). per. 7.99 *(978-0-9741864-2-9(2)*, 1) NT Publishing, L.L.C.
Barton, Renee L. ABC Story: Featuring: William. 2003. (J). per. 7.99 *(978-0-9741864-1-2(4)*, 1) NT Publishing, L.L.C.
Barton, Suzanne. A Guide to Sisters. Metcalf, Paula. 2015. (ENG.). 32p. (J). (gr. -1-2). 17.99 *(978-0-553-49899-8(1))* Random Hse., Inc.
Bartram, Bob & Eggers, James. Gene Autry & the Ghost Riders. Patten, Lewis B. 2011. 280p. 47.95 *(978-1-258-02621-9(X))* Literary Licensing, LLC.
Bartram, Simon. Once upon a Tomb: A Collection of Gravely Humorous Verses. Lewis, J. Patrick. 2006. (ENG.). 32p. (J). (gr. 1-4). 16.99 *(978-0-7636-1837-7(3))* Candlewick Pr.
Bartram, Simon. Man on the Moon: A Day in the Life of Bob. Bartram, Simon. 2009. (ENG.). 32p. (J). (gr. k-3). pap. 6.99 *(978-0-7636-4426-0(9)*, Templar) Candlewick Pr.
Baruffi, Andrea. Henry's Wrong Turn. 2006. (I'm Going to Read(r) Ser.). (ENG.). 32p. (J). (gr. 1-2). pap. 3.95 *(978-1-4027-2107-6(2))* Sterling Publishing Co., Inc.
—I Won't Go to Bed! Linn, Margot. 2005. (I'm Going to Read(r) Ser.: Level 3). (ENG.). 32p. (J). (gr. 1-2). pap. 3.95 *(978-1-4027-2104-5(8))* Sterling Publishing Co., Inc.
Baruzzi, Agnese. Count! Tango Books Staff. 2012. (ENG.). 12p. (J). (gr. -1-k). 15.99 *(978-1-85707-856-5(X))* Tango Bks. GBR. Dist: Independent Pubs. Group.
—Just Like My Mommy. Ikids Staff. 2009. (ENG.). 20p. (J). (gr. 1-17). 19.99 *(978-1-58476-664-3(6))* Innovative Kids.
—Tales of Mystery & Magic. Lupton, Hugh. 2010. (ENG.). 64p. (J). (gr. 3-18). 19.99 *(978-1-84686-258-8(2))* Barefoot Bks., Inc.
Baruzzi, Agnese. Aesop's Fables. Baruzzi, Agnese. Aesop Enterprise Inc. Staff. 2012. (ENG.). 16p. (J). (gr. k-2). 18.99 *(978-1-85707-895-4(0))* Tango Bks. GBR. Dist: Independent Pubs. Group.
—Opposites: A Cut-Paper Book. Baruzzi, Agnese. 2013. (ENG.). 10p. (J). (— 1). 15.99 *(978-1-85707-803-9(9))* Tango Bks. GBR. Dist: Independent Pubs. Group.
—Pinocchio: A Cut-Paper Book. Baruzzi, Agnese. Collodi, Carlo. 2013. (ENG.). 14p. (J). (— 1). 19.99 *(978-1-85707-862-6(4))* Tango Bks. GBR. Dist: Independent Pubs. Group.
Baruzzi, Agnese & Natalini, Sandro. The True Story of Little Red Riding Hood. Baruzzi, Agnese & Natalini, Sandro. 2009. (ENG.). 18p. (J). (gr. -1-3). 14.99 *(978-0-7636-4427-7(7)*, Templar) Candlewick Pr.
Baruzzi, Agnese, jt. illus. see Natalini, Sandro.
Basaluzzo, Constanza. Alef Is for Abba. Kafka, Rebecca. 2014. 24p. (J). (gr. -1-1). 17.95 *(978-1-4677-2156-1(5)*, Kar-Ben Publishing) Lerner Publishing Group.
—The Baby Bible ABCs, 1 vol. Currie, Robin. ed. 2009. (Baby Bible Ser.). (ENG.). 48p. (J). bds. 12.99 *(978-1-4347-6542-0(3))* Cook, David C.
—The Baby Bible Animals, 1 vol. Currie, Robin. ed. 2009. (Baby Bible Ser.). (ENG.). 48p. (J). bds. 9.99 *(978-1-4347-6541-3(5))* Cook, David C.
—Caleb's Hanukkah. Bullard, Lisa. 2012. (Cloverleaf Books (tm) — Fall & Winter Holidays Ser.). (ENG.). 24p. (gr. k-2). 6.95 *(978-0-7613-8587-5(8))*; lib. bdg. 23.93 *(978-0-7613-5077-4(2))* Lerner Publishing Group. (Millbrook Pr.).
—A Christmas Tree for Me: A New Holiday Tradition for Your Family. Lee, Quinlan B. 2013. (ENG.). 32p. (J). (gr. -1-2). 14.99 *(978-0-7944-3018-4(X))* Reader's Digest Assn., Inc., The.
—Emma's Easter. Bullard, Lisa. 2012. (Holidays & Special Days Ser.). 24p. (gr. k-2). (J). pap. 39.62 *(978-0-7613-9248-4(3))*; (ENG.). pap. 6.95 *(978-0-7613-8581-3(9))* Lerner Publishing Group. (Millbrook Pr.).
—Jungle Animals: Interactive Fun with Fold-Out Play Scene, Reusable Stickers, & Punch-out, Stand-up Figures! Walter Foster Custom Creative Team. 2014. (Sticker, Punch-Out, & Play! Ser.). (ENG.). 12p. (J). (gr. -1-1). pap. 6.99 *(978-1-60058-719-1(4))* Quarto Publishing Group USA.
—Kevin's Kwanzaa. Bullard, Lisa. 2012. (Cloverleaf Books (tm) — Fall & Winter Holidays Ser.). (ENG.). 24p. (gr. k-2). 6.95 *(978-0-7613-8588-2(6))*; lib. bdg. 23.93 *(978-0-7613-5075-0(6))* Lerner Publishing Group. (Millbrook Pr.).
—Sarah's Passover. Bullard, Lisa. 2012. (Holidays & Special Days Ser.). 24p. (gr. k-2). (J). pap. 39.62 *(978-0-7613-9245-3(9))*, Millbrook Pr.); (ENG.). pap. 6.95 *(978-0-7613-8582-0(7))*, Millbrook Pr.); (ENG.). lib. bdg. 23.93 *(978-0-7613-5081-1(0))* Lerner Publishing Group.
Bascle, Brian. The Adventures of Marco Polo, 1 vol. Smalley, Roger. 2005. (Graphic History Ser.). (ENG.). 32p. (gr. 3-4). per. 8.10 *(978-0-7368-5240-1(9)*, Graphic Library) Capstone Pr., Inc.
—Las Aventuras de Marco Polo. Smalley, Roger. 2006. (Historia Gráficas Ser.). (SPA.). 32p. (gr. 3-4). 29.99 *(978-0-7368-6054-3(1))* Capstone Pr., Inc.
—The Challenger Explosion, 1 vol. Adamson, Heather. 2006. (Disasters in History Ser.). (ENG.). 32p. (gr. 3-4). 29.99 *(978-0-7368-5478-8(9)*, 1252837, Graphic Library) Capstone Pr., Inc.
—Clara Barton: Angel of the Battlefield. Lassieur, Allison. 2005. (Graphic Biographies Ser.). (ENG.). 32p. (gr. 3-4). 29.99 *(978-0-7368-4632-5(8)*, Graphic Library) Capstone Pr., Inc.
—How to Draw Grotesque Monsters, 1 vol. Sautter, Aaron. 2008. (Drawing Cool Stuff Ser.). (ENG.). 32p. (gr. 3-4). 27.32 *(978-1-4296-1300-2(9)*, Edge Bks.) Capstone Pr., Inc.
—How to Draw Incredible Cars, 1 vol. Sautter, Aaron. 2007. (Drawing Cool Stuff Ser.). (ENG.). 32p. (gr. 3-4). 27.32 *(978-1-4296-0077-4(2)*, Edge Bks.) Capstone Pr., Inc.
—How to Draw Unreal Spaceships, 1 vol. Sautter, Aaron. 2008. (Drawing Cool Stuff Ser.). (ENG.). 32p. (gr. 3-4). 27.32 *(978-1-4296-1302-6(5)*, Edge Bks.) Capstone Pr., Inc.
—John F. Kennedy: American Visionary, 1 vol. Olson, Nathan & Capstone Press Staff. 2007. (Graphic Biographies Ser.). (ENG.). 32p. (gr. 3-4). 29.99 *(978-0-7368-6852-5(6)*, Graphic Library) Capstone Pr., Inc.
—John F. Kennedy: American Visionary, 1 vol. Olson, Nathan. 2007. (Graphic Biographies Ser.). (ENG.). 32p. (gr. 3-4). per. 8.10 *(978-0-7368-7904-0(8)*, 1264943, Graphic Library) Capstone Pr., Inc.
—Liberty, 1 vol. Collins, Terry. 2009. (Cartoon Nation Ser.). (ENG.). 32p. (gr. 3-4). lib. bdg. 29.99 *(978-1-4296-2340-7(3)*, Graphic Library) Capstone Pr., Inc.
—Martin Luther King, Jr: Great Civil Rights Leader, 1 vol. Fandel, Jennifer. 2006. (Graphic Biographies Ser.). (ENG.). 32p. (gr. 3-4). 29.99 *(978-0-7368-6498-5(9)*, Graphic Library) Capstone Pr., Inc.
—Muhammad Ali: American Champion, 1 vol. Burgan, Michael. 2008. (Graphic Biographies Ser.). (ENG.). 32p. (gr. 3-4). per. 8.10 *(978-1-4296-1771-0(3)*, Graphic Library) Capstone Pr., Inc.
—Muhammad Ali: American Champion. Burgan, Michael & Hoena, Blake A. 2007. (Graphic Biographies Ser.). (ENG.). 32p. (gr. 3-4). 29.99 *(978-1-4296-0153-5(1)*, Graphic Library) Capstone Pr., Inc.
—Paul Revere's Ride. Niz, Xavier & Niz, Xavier W. 2005. (Graphic History Ser.). (ENG.). 32p. (gr. 3-4). 29.99 *(978-0-7368-4965-4(3)*, Graphic Library) Capstone Pr., Inc.
—The Salem Witch Trials, 1 vol. Martin, Michael. 2005. (Graphic History Ser.). (ENG.). 32p. (gr. 3-4). per. 8.10 *(978-0-7368-5246-3(8)*, Graphic Library) Capstone Pr., Inc.
—The U. S. Congress, 1 vol. Fein, Eric. 2008. (Cartoon Nation Ser.). (ENG.). 32p. (gr. 3-4). lib. bdg. 29.99 *(978-1-4296-1335-4(1)*, Graphic Library) Capstone Pr., Inc.
—Women's Right to Vote, 1 vol. Collins, Terry. 2009. (Cartoon Nation Ser.). (ENG.). 32p. (gr. 3-4). lib. bdg. 29.99 *(978-1-4296-2341-4(1)*, Graphic Library) Capstone Pr., Inc.
Bascle, Brian, jt. illus. see Carter, Greg.
Bascle, Brian, jt. illus. see Kamerer, Justin.
Base, Graeme. The Water Hole. Base, Graeme. 2004. (ENG.). 32p. (J). (gr. k-3). reprint ed. pap. 8.99 *(978-0-14-240197-2(8)*, Puffin) Penguin Publishing Group.
Baseman, Gary. Strong Stuff: Herakles & His Labors. Harris, John. 2005. (ENG.). 32p. (gr. 3-7). 16.95 *(978-0-89236-784-9(9))* Oxford Univ. Pr., Inc.
Bash, Barbara. Shadows of Night: The Hidden World of the Little Brown Bat. Bash, Barbara. ed. 2004. (ENG.). 32p. (J). (gr. -1-3). pap. 7.95 *(978-0-87156-440-5(8))* Sierra Club Bks. for Children.
Basher, Simon. Superstars of History. Field, Jacob & Grant, R. J. 2014. (ENG.). 96p. (J). (gr. 3-7). pap. 7.99 *(978-0-545-68024-0(7)*, Scholastic Paperbacks) Scholastic, Inc.
Basher, Simon. Algebra & Geometry: Anything but Square! Basher, Simon. 2011. (Basher Science Ser.). (ENG.). 128p. (J). (gr. 5-9). pap. 8.99 *(978-0-7534-6597-4(3)*, Kingfisher) Roaring Brook Pr.
—Astronomy: Out of This World! Basher, Simon. Green, Dan. 2009. (Basher Science Ser.). (ENG.). 128p. (J). (gr. 5-9). pap. 8.99 *(978-0-7534-6290-4(7)*, Kingfisher) Roaring Brook Pr.
—Basher Basics: Creative Writing. Basher, Simon. Budzik, Mary. 2013. (Basher Basics Ser.). (ENG.). 64p. (J). (gr. 3-7). 12.99 *(978-0-7534-7054-1(3))*; pap. 7.99 *(978-0-7534-7055-8(1))* Roaring Brook Pr. (Kingfisher).
—Basher Basics: Space Exploration. Basher, Simon. 2013. (Basher Basics Ser.). (ENG.). 64p. (J). (gr. 3-7). pap. 7.99 *(978-0-7534-7165-4(5)*, Kingfisher) Roaring Brook Pr.
—Basher Science - Technology: A Byte-Sized World! Basher, Simon. Green, Dan. 2012. (Basher Science Ser.). (ENG.). 128p. (J). (gr. 5-9). 14.99 *(978-0-7534-6819-7(0)*, Kingfisher) Roaring Brook Pr.
—Basher Science: Extreme Biology. Basher, Simon. 2013. (Basher Science Ser.). (ENG.). 64p. (J). (gr. 5-9). 12.99 *(978-0-7534-7051-0(9))*; pap. 7.99 *(978-0-7534-7050-3(0))* Roaring Brook Pr. (Kingfisher).
—Basher Science: Extreme Physics. Basher, Simon. 2013. (Basher Science Ser.). (ENG.). 64p. (J). (gr. 5-9). pap. 7.99 *(978-0-7534-6956-9(1)*, Kingfisher) Roaring Brook Pr.
—Basher Science: Microbiology. Basher, Simon. Green, Dan. 2015. (Basher Science Ser.). (ENG.). 128p. (J). (gr. 5-9). pap. 8.99 *(978-0-7534-7194-4(9)*, Kingfisher) Roaring Brook Pr.

B

—Basher Science: the Complete Periodic Table: All the Elements with Style! Basher, Simon. Dingle, Adrian & Green, Dan. 2015. (Basher Science Ser.). (ENG.). 192p. (J). (gr. 5-9). pap. 11.99 (978-0-7534-7197-5(3), Kingfisher) Roaring Brook Pr.

—Basher Science: the Complete Periodic Table: All the Elements with Style. Basher, Simon. Dingle, Adrian & Green, Dan. 2015. (Basher Science Ser.). (ENG.). 192p. (J). (gr. 5-9). 16.99 (978-0-7534-7196-8(5), Kingfisher) Roaring Brook Pr.

—Biology: Life as We Know It! Basher, Simon. Green, Dan. 2008. (Basher Science Ser.). (ENG.). 128p. (J). (gr. 5-9). pap. 8.99 (978-0-7534-6253-9(2), Kingfisher) Roaring Brook Pr.

—Chemistry: Getting a Big Reaction! Basher, Simon. Green, Dan. 2010. (Basher Science Ser.). (ENG.). 128p. (J). (gr. 5-9). pap. 8.99 (978-0-7534-6413-7(6), Kingfisher) Roaring Brook Pr.

—Dinosaurs: The Bare Bones! Basher, Simon. Green, Dan. 2012. (Basher Basics Ser.). (ENG.). 64p. (J). (gr. 3-7). 12.99 (978-0-7534-6823-4(9)); pap. 7.99 (978-0-7534-6824-1(7)) Roaring Brook Pr. (Kingfisher).

—Grammar. Basher, Simon. Budzik, Mary. 2011. (Basher Basics Ser.). (ENG.). 64p. (J). (gr. 3-7). pap. 7.99 (978-0-7534-6596-7(5), Kingfisher) Roaring Brook Pr.

—Human Body: A Book with Guts! Basher, Simon. Green, Dan. 2011. (Basher Science Ser.). (ENG.). 128p. (J). (gr. 5-10). pap. 8.99 (978-0-7534-6501-1(9), Kingfisher) Roaring Brook Pr.

—Math: A Book You Can Count On! Basher, Simon. Green, Dan. 2010. (Basher Basics Ser.). (ENG.). 64p. (J). (gr. 3-7). pap. 7.99 (978-0-7534-6419-9(5), Kingfisher) Roaring Brook Pr.

—Music. Basher, Simon. Green, Dan. 2011. (Basher Basics Ser.). (ENG.). 64p. (J). (gr. 3-7). pap. 7.99 (978-0-7534-6595-0(7), Kingfisher) Roaring Brook Pr.

—Oceans: Making Waves! Basher, Simon. Green, Dan. 2012. (Basher Science Ser.). (ENG.). 128p. (J). (gr. 5-9). pap. 8.99 (978-0-7534-6822-7(0), Kingfisher) Roaring Brook Pr.

—The Periodic Table: Elements with Style! Basher, Simon. Dingle, Adrian. 2007. (Basher Science Ser.). (ENG.). 128p. (J). (gr. 5-9). pap. 8.99 (978-0-7534-6085-6(8), Kingfisher) Roaring Brook Pr.

—The Periodic Table: Elements with Style! Basher, Simon. Dingle, Adrian. 2010. (Basher Science Ser.). (ENG.). 128p. (J). (gr. 5-9). 14.99 (978-0-7534-6613-1(9), Kingfisher) Roaring Brook Pr.

—Physics: Why Matter Matters! Basher, Simon. Green, Dan. (Basher Science Ser.). (ENG.). 128p. (J). (gr. 5-9). 2010. 14.99 (978-0-7534-6612-4(0)); 2008. pap. 8.99 (978-0-7534-6214-0(1)) Roaring Brook Pr. (Kingfisher).

—Planet Earth: What Planet Are You On? Basher, Simon. Gilpin, Daniel. 2010. (Basher Science Ser.). (ENG.). 128p. (J). (gr. 5-9). pap. 8.99 (978-0-7534-6412-0(8), Kingfisher) Roaring Brook Pr.

—Planet Earth: What Planet Are You On? Basher, Simon. Gilpin, Dan. 2010. (Basher Science Ser.). (ENG.). 128p. (J). (gr. 5-9). 14.99 (978-0-7534-6616-2(3), Kingfisher) Roaring Brook Pr.

—Punctuation: The Write Stuff! Basher, Simon. Budzik, Mary. 2010. (Basher Basics Ser.). (ENG.). 64p. (J). (gr. 3-7). pap. 7.99 (978-0-7534-6420-5(9), Kingfisher) Roaring Brook Pr.

—Rocks & Minerals: A Gem of a Book! Basher, Simon. Green, Dan. 2009. (Basher Science Ser.). (ENG.). 128p. (J). (gr. 5-9). pap. 8.99 (978-0-7534-6314-7(8), Kingfisher) Roaring Brook Pr.

—Technology: A Byte-Sized World! Basher, Simon. Green, Dan. 2012. (Basher Science Ser.). (ENG.). 128p. (J). (gr. 5-9). pap. 8.99 (978-0-7534-6820-3(4), Kingfisher) Roaring Brook Pr.

—Weather: Whipping up a Storm! Basher, Simon. Green, Dan. 2012. (Basher Basics Ser.). (ENG.). 64p. (J). (gr. 3-7). 12.99 (978-0-7534-6825-8(5)); pap. 7.99 (978-0-7534-6826-5(3)) Roaring Brook Pr. (Kingfisher).

Basic, Zdenko. Las Aventuras de Pinocho. Gurney, Stella. 2012. (SPA.). 24p. (J). 24.95 (978-84-15235-19-4(4)) Roca Editorial De Libros ESP. Dist: Spanish Pubs., LLC.

Basic, Zdenko, et al. The Snow White Creativity Book: Games, Cut-Outs, Art Paper, Stickers, & Stencils. Worms, Penny. 2013. (Creativity Bks.). (ENG.). 80p. (J). (gr. 1-6). pap. 12.99 (978-1-4380-0320-7(X)) Barron's Educational Series, Inc.

Basic, Zdenko. Steampunk Charles Dickens' a Christmas Carol. 2014. (ENG.). 204p. (gr. 7). 18.95 (978-0-7624-5090-9(8), Running Pr. Kids) Running Pr. Bk. Pubs.

Basic, Zdenko & Sumberac, Manuel. Steampunk: H. G. Wells. 2013. (ENG.). 408p. (YA). 18.95 (978-0-7624-4444-1(4), Running Pr. Kids) Running Pr. Bk. Pubs.

Basil, Timothy. Despereaux. DiCamillo, Kate. 2004.Tr. of Tale of Despereaux. (SPA.). 256p. (YA). (gr. 5-8). 15.99 (978-84-279-5004-7(7)) Noguer y Caralt Editores, S. A. ESP. Dist: Lectorum Pubns., Inc.

Basile, Javier. El Cine No Fue Siempre Asi. Cerda, Marcelo. 2006. (Cosas No Fueron Siempre Asi Ser.). (SPA.). 38p. (J). pap. (978-987-1217-10-6(2)) Iamique, Ediciones.

—Preguntas que Ponen los Pelos de Punta: Sobre el Aqua y el Fuego. Baredes, Carla & Lotersztain, Ileana. 2004. (SPA.). pap. (978-987-98042-1-6(X)) Iamique, Ediciones.

—Preguntas que Ponen los Pelos de Punta: Sobre la Tierra y el Sol. Baredes, Carla & Lotersztain, Ileana. 2004. (SPA.). pap. (978-987-98042-0-9(1)) Iamique, Ediciones.

Basilico, Gabriele, photos by. Gabriele Basilico. Bonami, Francesco. rev. ed. 2005. (55s Ser.). (ENG., 128p. (gr. 8-17). 27.95 (978-0-7148-4567-8(1)) Phaidon Pr., Inc.

Baskey, Kim. Wispy Willy. Hanny, Diane. 2011. 24p. pap. 12.00 (978-1-4520-9975-0(8)) AuthorHouse.

Baskin, Jason. Ordinary Dogs, Extraordinary Friendships: Stories of Loyalty, Courage, & Compassion. Flowers, Pam. 2013. (ENG.). 144p. (YA). (gr. 5-6). pap. 12.99 (978-0-88240-916-0(6), Alaska Northwest Bks.) Graphic Arts Ctr. Publishing Co.

Baskin, Leonard. Animals That Ought to Be: Poems about Imaginary Pets. Michelson, Richard. 2011. (ENG.). 32p. (J). (gr. k-3). 16.99 (978-1-4424-3409-7(0), Simon & Schuster Bks. For Young Readers) Simon & Schuster Bks. For Young Readers.

Baskin, Lyle. The Christmas Bus. Inman, Robert. 2006. 77p. 19.95 (978-0-9760963-6-8(6)) Novello Festival Pr.

Bass, Jennifer Vogel, photos by. Edible Colors. Bass, Jennifer Vogel. 2014. (ENG., 32p. (J). (gr. -1-k). 12.99 (978-1-62672-002-2(9)) Roaring Brook Pr.

Bass, Rachel. Pamela's Plan. Noble, Kate. (Zoo Stories Ser.). 32p. (J). (gr. -1-4). 15.95 (978-0-9631798-4-5(5)) Salmon Run Pr.

Bass, Saul. Henri's Walk to Paris. 2012. (ENG.). 48p. (J). (gr. k-4). 19.95 (978-0-7893-2263-0(3)) Universe Publishing.

Bassa. El Saltamontes y Las Hormigas. Bailer, Darice et al. 2007. (SPA & ENG.). 28p. (J). (978-0-545-02965-0(1)) Scholastic, Inc.

Bassani, Srimalle. Monsters. Ahmed, Suhel. 2015. (Doodle Magic Ser.). (ENG.). 64p. (J). (gr. k). spiral bd. 14.95 (978-1-62686-478-8(0), Silver Dolphin Bks.) Baker & Taylor Publishing Group.

—Princesses. Ahmed, Suhel. Silver Dolphin Books, Silver Dolphin, ed. 2015. (Doodle Magic Ser.). (ENG.). 64p. (J). (gr. k). spiral bd. 14.95 (978-1-62686-479-5(9), Silver Dolphin Bks.) Baker & Taylor Publishing Group.

Basseches, K. B., photos by. ABeCedarios: Mexican Folk Art ABCs in English & Spanish. Weill, Cynthia. 2008. (First Concepts in Mexican Folk Art Ser.). (SPA & ENG., 32p. (J). (gr. k — 1). 14.95 (978-1-933693-13-2(4)) Cinco Puntos Pr.

Bassett, Jeni. The Biggest Christmas Tree Ever. Kroll, Steven. 2009. (ENG.). 32p. (J). (gr. -1-3). pap. 4.99 (978-0-545-12119-4(1), Cartwheel Bks.) Scholastic, Inc.

—The Biggest Easter Basket Ever. Kroll, Steven. 2008. (ENG.). 32p. (J). (gr. -1-3). pap. 4.99 (978-0-545-01702-2(5), Cartwheel Bks.) Scholastic, Inc.

—The Biggest Pumpkin Ever. Kroll, Steven. 2007. (ENG.). 32p. (J). (gr. -1-k). pap. 4.99 (978-0-439-92946-2(6)) Scholastic, Inc.

—The Biggest Pumpkin Surprise Ever. Kroll, Steven. 2012. (ENG.). 10p. (J). (gr. -1-k). bds. 6.99 (978-0-545-40285-9(9), Cartwheel Bks.) Scholastic, Inc.

—The Biggest Snowman Ever. Kroll, Steven. (ENG.). (J). (gr. -1-k). 2009. 9.95 (978-0-545-16350-7(1)); 2005. 32p. 4.99 (978-0-439-62768-9(0), Cartwheel Bks.) Scholastic, Inc.

—The Biggest Valentine Ever. Kroll, Steven. 2006. (ENG.). 32p. (J). (gr. -1-1). pap. 3.99 (978-0-439-76419-3(X)) Scholastic, Inc.

Bassett, Jeni, et al. My Christmas Treasury. Ryan, Cheryl et al. 2012. (ENG.). 96p. (J). (gr. -1-3). 8.99 (978-0-545-43647-2(8)) Scholastic, Inc.

Bassett, Madge A. At Bumblebee Farm. Bassett, Madge A. 2009. 20p. pap. 13.46 (978-1-4251-9230-3(0)) Trafford Publishing.

Basso, Bill. Beware! It's Friday the 13th. McMullan, Kate. 2005. (Dragon Slayers' Academy Ser.: 13). (ENG.). 112p. (J). (gr. 2-5). pap. 4.99 (978-0-448-43531-2(4), Grosset & Dunlap) Penguin Publishing Group.

—Beware! It's Friday the 13th. McMullan, Kate. 2006. (Dragon Slayers' Academy Ser.: No. 13). 112p. (gr. 1-7). 24.21 (978-1-59961-122-8(8)) Spotlight.

—Class Trip to the Cave of Doom, 3 vols. McMullan, Kate. 2003. (Dragon Slayers' Academy Ser.: 3). (ENG.). 112p. (J). (gr. 2-5). pap. 4.99 (978-0-448-43110-9(6), Grosset & Dunlap) Penguin Publishing Group.

—Class Trip to the Cave of Doom. McMullan, Kate. 2006. (Dragon Slayers' Academy Ser.: No. 3). 112p. (gr. 1-7). 24.21 (978-1-59961-123-5(6)) Spotlight.

—Countdown to the Year 1000. McMullan, Kate. 2003. (Dragon Slayers' Academy Ser.: 8). (ENG.). 112p. (J). (gr. 2-5). pap. 4.99 (978-0-448-43508-4(X), Grosset & Dunlap) Penguin Publishing Group.

—Countdown to the Year 1000. McMullan, Kate. 2007. (Dragon Slayers' Academy Ser.: No. 8). (ENG.). 107p. (gr. 2-5). 24.21 (978-1-59961-376-5(X)) Spotlight.

—Danger! Wizard at Work, No. 11. McMullan, Kate. 2004. (Dragon Slayers' Academy Ser.: 11). (ENG.). 112p. (J). (gr. 2-5). pap. 4.99 (978-0-448-43529-9(2), Grosset & Dunlap) Penguin Publishing Group.

—Double Dragon Trouble. McMullan, Kate. 2005. (Dragon Slayers' Academy Ser.: 15). (ENG.). 112p. (J). (gr. 2-5). pap. 4.99 (978-0-448-43821-4(6), Grosset & Dunlap) Penguin Publishing Group.

—Dragon Slayers' Academy Set 2. McMullan, Kate. 2007. (Dragon Slayers' Academy Ser.). (ENG.). 112p. 145.26 (978-1-59961-375-8(1)) Spotlight.

—The Ghost of Sir Herbert Dungeonstone, No. 12. McMullan, Kate. 2004. (Dragon Slayers' Academy Ser.: 12). (ENG.). 112p. (J). (gr. 2-5). pap. 4.99 (978-0-448-43530-5(6), Grosset & Dunlap) Penguin Publishing Group.

—The Ghost of Sir Herbert Dungeonstone. McMullan, Kate. 2006. (Dragon Slayers' Academy Ser.: No. 12). 112p. (gr. 1-7). 24.21 (978-1-59961-124-2(4)) Spotlight.

—Hail! Hail! Camp Dragononka! McMullan, Kate. 2006. (Dragon Slayers' Academy Ser.: 17). (ENG.). 224p. (J). (gr. 2-5). pap. 5.99 (978-0-448-44124-5(1), Grosset & Dunlap) Penguin Publishing Group.

—Help! It's Parent's Day at DSA. McMullan, Kate. 2004. (Dragon Slayers' Academy Ser.: 10). (ENG.). 112p. (J). (gr. 2-5). pap. 4.99 (978-0-448-43220-5(X), Grosset & Dunlap) Penguin Publishing Group.

—Help! It's Parent's Day at DSA. McMullan, Kate. 2006. (Dragon Slayers' Academy Ser.: No. 10). 112p. (gr. 1-7). 24.21 (978-1-59961-125-9(2)) Spotlight.

—Knight for a Day. McMullan, Kate. 2003. (Dragon Slayers' Academy Ser.: 5). (ENG.). 112p. (J). (gr. 2-5). mass mkt. 4.99 (978-0-448-43277-9(3), Grosset & Dunlap) Penguin Publishing Group.

—Knight for a Day. McMullan, Kate. 2007. (Dragon Slayers' Academy Ser.: No. 5). (ENG.). 109p. (gr. 2-5). 24.21 (978-1-59961-377-2(8)) Spotlight.

—Little Giant-Big Trouble, 19 vols. McMullan, Kate. 2007. (Dragon Slayers' Academy Ser.: 19). (ENG.). 112p. (J). (gr. 2-5). pap. 4.99 (978-0-448-44448-2(8), Grosset & Dunlap) Penguin Publishing Group.

—Never Trust a Troll! McMullan, Kate. 2006. (Dragon Slayers' Academy Ser.: 18). (ENG.). 112p. (J). (gr. 2-5). pap. 4.99 (978-0-448-44393-5(7), Grosset & Dunlap) Penguin Publishing Group.

—The New Kid at School. McMullan, Kate. 2006. (Dragon Slayers' Academy Ser.: No. 1). 112p. (gr. 1-7). 24.21 (978-1-59961-126-6(0)) Spotlight.

—Pig Latin - Not Just for Pigs!, No. 14. McMullan, Kate. 2005. (Dragon Slayers' Academy Ser.: 14). (ENG.). 112p. (J). (gr. 2-5). pap. 4.99 (978-0-448-43820-7(8), Grosset & Dunlap) Penguin Publishing Group.

—Pig Latin — Not Just for Pigs! McMullan, Kate. 2006. (Dragon Slayers' Academy Ser.: No. 14). 112p. (gr. 1-7). 24.21 (978-1-59961-127-3(9)) Spotlight.

—Revenge of the Dragon Lady, 2 vols. McMullan, Kate. 2003. (Dragon Slayers' Academy Ser.: 2). (ENG.). 112p. (J). (gr. 2-5). mass mkt. 4.99 (978-0-448-43109-3(2), Grosset & Dunlap) Penguin Publishing Group.

—Revenge of the Dragon Lady. McMullan, Kate. 2007. (Dragon Slayers' Academy Ser.: No. 2). (ENG.). 109p. (gr. -1-3). 24.21 (978-1-59961-378-9(6)) Spotlight.

—Sir Lancelot, Where Are You? McMullan, Kate. 2003. (Dragon Slayers' Academy Ser.: 6). (ENG.). 112p. (J). (gr. 2-5). pap. 4.99 (978-0-448-43278-6(1), Grosset & Dunlap) Penguin Publishing Group.

—Sir Lancelot, Where Are You? McMullan, Kate. 2007. (Dragon Slayers' Academy Ser.: No. 6). (ENG.). 109p. (gr. 2-5). 24.21 (978-1-59961-379-6(4)) Spotlight.

—Slime Time. Dadey, Debbie & Dadey, Nathan. 2004. 58p. (J). (978-0-439-64362-7(7)) Scholastic, Inc.

—The Slime Wars. Dadey, Debbie. 2003. (ENG.). 80p. (J). (gr. 2-5). mass mkt. 3.99 (978-0-439-42442-4(9)) Scholastic, Inc.

—A Wedding for Wiglaf?, 4 vols. McMullan, Kate. 2003. (Dragon Slayers' Academy Ser.: 4). (ENG.). 112p. (J). (gr. 2-5). pap. 4.99 (978-0-448-43111-6(4), Grosset & Dunlap) Penguin Publishing Group.

—A Wedding for Wiglaf? McMullan, Kate. 2007. (Dragon Slayers' Academy Ser.: No. 4). (ENG.). 109p. (gr. 4-7). 24.21 (978-1-59961-380-2(8)) Spotlight.

—Wheel of Misfortune. McMullan, Kate. 2003. (Dragon Slayers' Academy Ser.: 7). (ENG.). 112p. (J). (gr. 2-5). pap. 4.99 (978-0-448-43507-7(1), Grosset & Dunlap) Penguin Publishing Group.

—Wheel of Misfortune. McMullan, Kate. 2007. (Dragon Slayers' Academy Ser.: No. 7). (ENG.). 109p. (gr. 2-5). 24.21 (978-1-59961-381-9(6)) Spotlight.

—World's Oldest Living Dragon, 16 vols. McMullan, Kate. 2006. (Dragon Slayers' Academy Ser.: 16). (ENG.). 112p. (J). (gr. 2-5). pap. 4.99 (978-0-448-44112-2(8), Grosset & Dunlap) Penguin Publishing Group.

—97 Ways to Train a Dragon. McMullan, Kate. 2003. (Dragon Slayers' Academy Ser.: 9). (ENG.). 112p. (J). (gr. 2-5). pap. 4.99 (978-0-448-43177-2(7), Grosset & Dunlap) Penguin Publishing Group.

Basso, Bill & Gilpin, Stephen. The New Kid at School. McMullan, Kate. 2003. (Dragon Slayers' Academy Ser.: 1). (ENG.). 112p. (J). (gr. 2-5). mass mkt. 4.99 (978-0-448-43108-6(4), Grosset & Dunlap) Penguin Publishing Group.

—School's Out... Forever! McMullan, Kate. 2012. (Dragon Slayers' Academy Ser.: 20). (ENG.). 112p. (J). (gr. 3-7). pap. 4.99 (978-0-448-44571-7(9), Grosset & Dunlap) Penguin Publishing Group.

Basta, Mary, jt. illus. see Liddell, Daniel.

Basta, Stormie. Grandma's Traditions. Wilson, Angela. 2012. 24p. pap. 24.95 (978-1-4626-9410-5(1)) America Star Bks.

—My Aunt & Me. Wilson, Angela. 2012. 26p. 24.95 (978-1-4626-6630-0(2)) America Star Bks.

—Tara the Terrified Turtle. Wilson, Angela. 2012. 28p. pap. 24.95 (978-1-4626-7454-1(2)) America Star Bks.

Bastien, Valerie. Sing Out Loud Book II: Developing Your Voice. Hoops, Kevin, photos by. Vendera, Jaime & McGee, Anne Loader. 2012. 52p. (YA). pap. 7.99 (978-1-936307-09-8(X)) Vendera Publishing.

—Sing Out Loud Book III: Owning Your Voice. Hoops, Kevin, photos by. Vendera, Jaime & McGee, Anne Loader. 2012. 44p. (YA). pap. 7.99 (978-1-936307-10-4(3)) Vendera Publishing.

Bastien, Valerie & Bingham, Jerry. Sing Out Loud Book I: Discovering Your Voice. Hoops, Kevin, photos by. Vendera, Jaime & McGee, Anne Loader. 2012. 52p. (YA). pap. 7.99 (978-1-936307-08-1(1)) Vendera Publishing.

Basu, Suddhasattwa. Ka, the Story of Garuda: Based on the English Translation by Tim Parks of the Italian Original by Roberto Calasso. Calasso, Roberto & Parks, Tim. 2004. (J). (978-81-89020-04-0(8)) Katha.

Basulto, Rita. De carta en Carta. MacHado, Ana Maria. 2004. (SPA.). 44p. (gr. 3-5). pap. 7.95 (978-968-19-1483-7(X)) Santillana USA Publishing Co., Inc.

Bate, Helen. ABC UK. Dunn, James. 2012. (ENG.). 40p. (J). (gr. k-3). 6.99 (978-1-84780-200-2(1), Frances Lincoln) Quarto Publishing Group UK GBR. Dist: Hachette Bk. Group.

—Sita, Snake-Queen of Speed. Ewart, Franzeska G. & Quarto Generic Staff. 2012. (ENG.). 96p. (J). (gr. 3-6). pap. 8.99 (978-1-84780-330-6(X), Frances Lincoln) Quarto Publishing Group UK GBR. Dist: Hachette Bk. Group.

—There's a Hamster in My Pocket! Ewart, Francesca et al. 2012. (ENG.). 96p. (J). (gr. 3-6). pap. 7.95 (978-1-84780-118-0(8), Frances Lincoln) Quarto Publishing Group UK GBR. Dist: Hachette Bk. Group.

Bates, Amy. Adventure: Lonely Leader. Stern, Ricki & Worcester, Heidi P. 2003. (Beryl E. Bean Ser.: No. 3). 64p. (J). lib. bdg. 16.89 (978-0-06-028774-0(8)) HarperCollins Pubs.

—The Adventures of Tom Sawyer: A Song for Aunt Polly. Twain, Mark. 2008. (Easy Reader Classics Ser.). (ENG.). 32p. (gr. -1-3). lib. bdg. 24.21 (978-1-59961-334-5(4)) Spotlight.

—Bear in the Air. Meyers, Susan. 2010. (ENG.). 32p. (J). (gr. -1-3). 15.95 (978-0-8109-8398-4(2), Abrams Bks. for Young Readers) Abrams.

—The Dog Who Belonged to No One. Hest, Amy. 2008. (ENG.). 32p. (J). (gr. -1-2). 17.95 (978-0-8109-9483-6(6), Abrams Bks. for Young Readers) Abrams.

—Donavan's Double Trouble. DeGross, Monalisa. 192p. (J). (gr. 2-5). 2008. lib. bdg. 16.89 (978-0-06-077294-9(8)); 2007. (ENG.). 16.99 (978-0-06-077293-2(X)) HarperCollins Pubs. (Amistad).

—First Pooch: The Obamas Pick a Pet, 0 vols. Weatherford, Carole Boston. 2009. (ENG.). 32p. (J). (gr. -1-3). 16.99 (978-0-7614-5636-0(8), 9780761456360, Amazon Children's Publishing) Amazon Publishing.

—Hands & Hearts: With 15 Words in American Sign Language. Napoli, Donna Jo. 2014. (ENG.). 32p. (J). (gr. -1-2). 16.95 (978-1-4197-1022-3(2), Abrams Bks. for Young Readers) Abrams.

—Minette's Feast: The Delicious Story of Julia Child & Her Cat. Reich, Susanna. 2012. (ENG.). 40p. (J). (gr. -1-2). 17.95 (978-1-4197-0177-1(0), Abrams Bks. for Young Readers) Abrams.

—My Puppy's First Year. 2007. (ENG.). 24p. (gr. k-3). pap. 12.99 (978-0-8249-5571-7(4), Ideals Children's Bks.) Ideals Pubns.

—Pumpkin Cat. Turner, Ann. 2004. (ENG.). 32p. (gr. -1-2). 15.99 (978-0-7868-0494-8(7)) Hyperion Pr.

—A Song for Aunt Polly. Twain, Mark. 2004. (Adventures of Tom Sawyer Ser.: Vol. 1). 32p. (J). (978-0-7607-3963-1(3)) Barnes & Noble, Inc.

—The Spelling Bee. Twain, Mark. 2007. (Easy Reader Classics Ser.: Bk. 4). (ENG.). 32p. (J). (gr. k-2). pap. 3.95 (978-1-4027-4269-9(X)) Sterling Publishing Co., Inc.

—Susan B. Anthony: Fighter for Women's Rights. Hopkinson, Deborah. 2005. 32p. (J). lib. bdg. 15.00 (978-1-4242-1563-8(3)) Fitzgerald Bks.

Bates, Amy & Bates, Amy June. A Song for Aunt Polly. Twain, Mark. 2006. (Easy Reader Classics Ser.: Bk. 1). (ENG.). 32p. (J). (gr. k-2). pap. 3.95 (978-1-4027-3287-4(2)) Sterling Publishing Co., Inc.

Bates, Amy June. Beach House. Caswell, Deanna. 2015. (ENG.). 32p. (J). (gr. -1-k). 16.99 (978-1-4521-2408-7(6)) Chronicle Bks. LLC.

—The Birthday Boy. Twain, Mark. 2007. (Easy Reader Classics Ser.: Bk. 3). (ENG.). 32p. (J). (gr. k-2). pap. 3.95 (978-1-4027-4268-2(1)) Sterling Publishing Co., Inc.

—The Brothers Kennedy: John, Robert, Edward. Krull, Kathleen. 2010. (ENG.). 40p. (J). (gr. -1-3). 16.99 (978-1-4169-9158-8(1), Simon & Schuster Bks. For Young Readers) Simon & Schuster Bks. For Young Readers.

—Christian, the Hugging Lion. Richardson, Justin & Parnell, Peter. 2010. (ENG.). 32p. (J). (gr. -1-3). 16.99 (978-1-4169-8662-1(6), Simon & Schuster Bks. For Young Readers) Simon & Schuster Bks. For Young Readers.

—The Christmas Cat. MacDonald, Maryann. 2013. (ENG.). 32p. (J). (gr. -1-k). 16.99 (978-0-8037-3498-2(0), Dial) Penguin Publishing Group.

—Escape by Night: A Civil War Adventure. Myers, Laurie. 2011. (ENG.). 128p. (J). (gr. 3-7). 14.99 (978-0-8050-8825-0(3), Holt, Henry & Co. Bks. For Young Readers) Holt, Henry & Co.

—I Will Rejoice: Celebrating Psalm 118. Wilson, Karma. 2007. (ENG.). 32p. (J). (gr. -1-3). 14.99 (978-0-310-71117-9(7)) Zonderkidz.

—Martin's Dream. Kurtz, Jane. 2008. (Ready-To-Reads Ser.). (ENG.). 32p. (J). (gr. -1-1). pap. 3.99 (978-1-4169-2774-7(3), Simon Spotlight) Simon Spotlight.

—Red Butterfly. Sonnichsen, A. L. 2015. (ENG.). 400p. (J). (gr. 3-7). 16.99 (978-1-4814-1109-7(8)) Simon & Schuster, Inc.

—Rock-A-Bye Room. Meyers, Susan. 2013. (ENG.). 32p. (J). (gr. -1-k). 17.95 (978-1-4197-0537-3(7), Abrams Bks. for Young Readers) Abrams.

—Susan B. Anthony: Fighter for Women's Rights. Hopkinson, Deborah. 2005. (Ready-To-read SOFA Ser.). (ENG.). 32p. (J). (gr. 1-3). pap. 3.99 (978-0-689-86909-9(6), Simon Spotlight) Simon Spotlight.

—Sweet Dreams. Jewel. 2013. (ENG.). 32p. (J). (gr. -1-k). 17.99 (978-1-4424-8931-8(6), Simon & Schuster/Paula Wiseman Bks.) Simon & Schuster/Paula Wiseman Bks.

—That's What I'd Do. Jewel. 2012. (ENG.). 32p. (J). (gr. -1-k). 17.99 (978-1-4424-5813-0(5), Simon & Schuster/Paula Wiseman Bks.) Simon & Schuster/Paula Wiseman Bks.

—Waiting for the Magic. MacLachlan, Patricia. (ENG.). (J). (gr. 3-7). 2012. 176p. pap. 6.99 (978-1-4169-2746-4(8)); 2011. 160p. 16.99 (978-1-4169-2745-7(X)) Simon & Schuster Children's Publishing. (Atheneum Bks. for Young Readers).

—Wishworks, Inc. Tolan, Stephanie S. (ENG.). 160p. (J). (gr. 2-5). 2011. pap. 5.99 (978-0-545-03155-4(9)); 2009. 15.99 (978-0-545-03154-7(0)) Scholastic, Inc. (Levine, Arthur A. Bks.).

—You Can Do It! Dungy, Tony. 2008. (ENG.). 32p. (J). (gr. -1-2). 17.99 (978-1-4169-5461-3(9), Little Simon Inspirations) Little Simon Inspirations.

Bates, Amy June, jt. illus. see Bates, Amy.

Bates, Ben. Mega Man 3: Return of Dr. Wily. Flynn, Ian. 2012. (Mega Man Ser.: 3). (ENG.). 112p. (gr. 4-7). pap. 11.99 (978-1-936975-11-2(4), Archie Comics) Archie Comic Pubns., Inc.

Bates, Ben. Pinkie Pie. Anderson, Ted. 2015. (J). (978-1-61479-333-5(6)) Spotlight.

Bates, Bill. Guide Me Home, Sunny. Written By Pamela McFarland; Illustrated. 2011. 44p. pap. 24.95 (978-1-4560-8890-3(4)) America Star Bks.

Bates, Bob. Anna's Home by the River: A Children's History of Anaheim. Eastman, Gail. 2007. 199p. (J). pap. (978-0-9797419-0-6(4)) Tesoro Publishing.

Bates, Brenda J., et al. My Little Pinto, 1 vol. Tessin, Kit Elaine. 2010. 26p. pap. 24.95 (978-1-4489-9173-0(0)) PublishAmerica, Inc.

Bates, Delphine Branon & EsDesignStudio. Help Me Remember the Days of Creation. Bates, Delphine Branon. 2010. 24p. (J). 11.95 *(978-0-9799116-3-7(X))* LifeSong Pubs.

Bates, George. Chicken Bedtime Is Really Early. Perl, Erica S. 2005. (ENG.). 32p. (J). (gr. -1-1). 14.95 *(978-0-8109-4926-3(1))* Abrams.

—On a Windy Night. Day, Nancy Raines. 2010. (ENG.). 40p. (J). (gr. -1-3). 16.95 *(978-0-8109-3900-4(2),* Abrams Bks. for Young Readers) Abrams.

Bates, Harry. The Bread Bible: Beth Hensperger's 300 Favorite Recipes. Hensperger, Beth. 2004. (ENG.). 496p. (gr. 8-17). pap. 19.95 *(978-0-8118-4526-7(5))* Chronicle Bks. LLC.

Bates, Ivan. Coconut Comes to School. Doherty, Berlie. 2004. (ENG.). 32p. (J). (gr. k-2). 18.00 *(978-0-00-710433-8(2),* HarperCollins Children's Bks.) HarperCollins Pubs. Ltd. GBR. Dist: Independent Pubs. Group.

—Do Like a Duck Does! Hindley, Judy. 2007. (ENG.). 40p. (J). (gr. -1-2). 4.99 *(978-0-7636-3284-7(8))* Candlewick Pr.

—Do Like a Duck Does! Hindley, Judy. 2007. (gr. -1-k). 15.00 *(978-0-7569-8127-3(1))* Perfection Learning Corp.

—Farmer Dale's Red Pickup Truck. Wheeler, Lisa. 2014. (ENG.). 32p. (J). (— 1). bds. 7.99 *(978-0-544-24765-9(5),* HMH Books For Young Readers) Houghton Mifflin Harcourt Publishing Co.

—Grandma Elephant's in Charge. Jenkins, Martin. 2014. (ENG.). 32p. (J). (gr. k-3). 6.99 *(978-0-7636-7381-9(1))* Candlewick Pr.

—How Many Kisses Do You Want Tonight? Bajaj, Varsha. (ENG.). (J). (gr. -1 — 1). 2007. 26p. bds. 6.99 *(978-0-316-06735-5(0));* 2004. 28p. 15.99 *(978-0-316-82381-4(3))* Little, Brown Bks. for Young Readers.

—One Dark Night. Wheeler, Lisa. 2006. (ENG.). 32p. (J). (gr. -1-3). reprint ed. pap. 6.99 *(978-0-15-205888-3(5))* Houghton Mifflin Harcourt Publishing Co.

—There, There. McBratney, Sam. (ENG.). (J). 2015. 32p. (-k). bds. 7.99 *(978-0-7636-7565-3(2));* 2013. 40p. (gr. -1-2). 15.99 *(978-0-7636-6702-3(1))* Candlewick Pr. (Templar).

—Where, Oh Where, Is Santa Claus? Wheeler, Lisa. 2011. (ENG.). 32p. (J). (gr. -1-3). pap. 7.99 *(978-0-547-57675-6(7))* Houghton Mifflin Harcourt Publishing Co.

Bates, Lindsey E. & Wiggan, Desmond. Oh! I Wish. Roberts, Pauline. 2012. 24p. pap. 9.95 *(978-0-9848243-3-5(2))* Beckham Pubns. Group, Inc.

Batson, Alan. Jake & the Neverland Pirates: X Marks the Croc! La Rose, Melinda. 2014. (World of Reading Pre-1 Ser.). (ENG.). 32p. (J). (gr. 3-5). lib. bdg. 24.21 *(978-1-61479-247-5(X))* Spotlight.

Batson, Susann. Rachel Serves a Stew. Kirkle, Diane Luise. 2009. 28p. pap. 10.95 *(978-1-935137-59-7(X))* Guardian Angel Publishing, Inc.

Batson, Susann. Sparkie: A Star Afraid of the Dark. Batson, Susann. 2008. 16p. pap. 7.95 *(978-1-935137-01-6(8))* Guardian Angel Publishing, Inc.

Battaglia, Aurelius. Animal Sounds. Golden Books Staff. 2005. (Golden Sturdy Book Ser.). (ENG.). 24p. (J). (gr. k — 1). bds. 5.99 *(978-0-375-83278-9(5),* Golden Bks.) Random Hse. Children's Bks.

Batten, John D. Europa's Fairy Book. Jacobs, Joseph, ed. 2013. 330p. pap. *(978-1-909302-35-8(X))* Abela Publishing.

—Indian Fairy Tales. Jacobs, Joseph. 2011. (Dover Children's Classics Ser.). (ENG.). 288p. (J). (gr. 2-5). reprint ed. pap. 19.95 *(978-0-486-21828-1(7))* Dover Pubns., Inc.

Batti, Kimberly Rose. Charlotte Bakeman Has Her Say. Finger, Mary E. 2007. 96p. (J). 16.00 *(978-0-9746911-2-1(7))* Little Pear Pr.

—Mumsi Meets a Lion. Stegall, Kim. 2008. (gr. -1-1). pap. 7.99 *(978-1-59166-871-8(9))* BJU Pr.

Battis, Gwen. Dawn of Day. McPhail, J. A. 2012. 200p. 17.99 *(978-0-9851196-2-1(4));* pap. 10.99 *(978-0-9851196-1-4(6))* Rowe Publishing and Design.

—Hark! I Hear a Meadowlark! Bird, Roy & Harp, Kim. 2013. 34p. 16.99 *(978-1-939054-08-1(7));* 36p. pap. 10.99 *(978-1-939054-07-4(9))* Rowe Publishing and Design.

Battle, Christina. Power to the Purple! Bell, Sophie. 2013. (Ultra Violets Ser.: 2). (ENG.). 336p. (J). (gr. 3-7). 12.99 *(978-1-59514-647-2(4),* Razorbill) Penguin Publishing Group.

Battut, Éric. The Little Pea. Battut, Éric. 2011. (ENG.). 28p. (J). (gr. -1-k). 16.95 *(978-1-61608-482-0(0),* 608482, Sky Pony Pr.) Skyhorse Publishing Co., Inc.

Battuz, Christine. Hello, Goodbye, & a Very Little Lie, 1 vol. Jones, Christianne C. (Little Boost Ser.). (ENG.). 32p. (gr. k-3). 2012. 7.95 *(978-1-4048-7498-5(4));* 2010. lib. bdg. 22.65 *(978-1-4048-6167-1(X),* Little Boost) Picture Window Bks.

—My Sister Beth's Pink Birthday. Szymona, Marlene L. 2014. (J). *(978-1-4338-1654-3(7));* pap. *(978-1-4338-1655-0(5))* American Psychological Assn. (Magination Pr.).

—Shy Spaghetti & Excited Eggs: A Kid's Menu of Feelings. Nemiroff, Marc A. & Annunziata, Jane. 2011. 48p. (J). (gr. -1-3). 15.95 *(978-1-4338-0956-9(7));* pap. 10.95 *(978-1-4338-0957-6(5))* American Psychological Assn. (Magination Pr.).

Bauer, Carla. Harriet Tubman, Secret Agent: How Daring Slaves & Free Blacks Spied for the Union During the Civil War. Allen, Thomas B. 2006. (National Geographic Ser.). (ENG.). 192p. (gr. 5-8). 16.95 *(978-0-7922-7889-4(5));* lib. bdg. 25.90 *(978-0-7922-7890-0(9),* National Geographic Children's Bks.) National Geographic Society.

Bauer, Dana. An Almost True Horse Tale. Layos, Alexandra. l.t. ed. 2003. 20p. (J). (gr. 1-5). pap. 8.95 *(978-0-9655501-3-0(3))* Saddle & Bridle, Inc.

—Two Miniature Horses. Carpenter Czerw, Nancy. 2006. (Itty & Bitty Ser.). (ENG.). 32p. (J). (gr. -1-3). 15.95 *(978-0-9755618-2-9(0))* McWitty Pr., Inc.

Bauer, Dana, jt. illus. see Berlin, Rose Mary.

Bauer, Joe. Epic Fail. Bauer, Michael Gerard. 2012. 192p. *(978-1-86291-992-1(5))* Scholastic Australia.

Bauer, John. Lucifer: Good Angel Gone Bad. Wilde, Gloria. 2007. 36p. 14.95 *(978-1-57258-462-4(9),* 945-6323) TEACH Services, Inc.

—Swedish Folk Tales, 1 vol. Lundbergh, Holger, tr. from SWE. 2004. (ENG.). 240p. (J). 28.00 *(978-0-86315-457-7(3))* Floris Bks. GBR. Dist: SteinerBooks, Inc.

Bauer, Jutta. Grandpa's Angel. Bauer, Jutta. 2005. (ENG.). 48p. (J). (gr. k-12). 12.99 *(978-0-7636-2743-0(7))* Candlewick Pr.

—Selma. Bauer, Jutta. 2006. (ENG.). 56p. (J). 6.99 *(978-1-929132-50-8(6))* Kane Miller.

Bauer, Larry. Activités de Noël. Hanegar, Renee. (FRE.). 16p. pap. *(978-0-590-16904-2(1))* Scholastic Canada, Ltd.

—Activités d'Halloween. Friedman, Pamela. (FRE.). 16p. pap. *(978-0-439-00533-3(7))* Scholastic Canada, Ltd.

Bauer, Stephanie. Alligator Alphabet. Blackstone, Stella. (ENG.). (J). (gr. -1). 2007. 32p. bds. 8.99 *(978-1-84686-073-7(3));* 2005. 48p. 16.99 *(978-1-84148-494-5(6))* Barefoot Bks., Inc.

—Autumn. Hedlund, Stephanie. 2013. (Seasons Ser.). 24p. (J). (gr. k-4). lib. bdg. 27.07 *(978-1-61641-992-9(X),* Looking Glass Library- Nonfiction) Magic Wagon.

—The Best Day in Room A: Sign Language for School Activities. Prochovnic, Dawn Babb. 2009. (Story Time with Signs & Rhymes Ser.). 32p. (gr. -1-3). 28.50 *(978-1-60270-667-5(0),* Looking Glass Library) ABDO Publishing Co.

—The Big Blue Bowl: Sign Language for Food. Prochovnic, Dawn Babb. 2009. (Story Time with Signs & Rhymes Ser.). 32p. (gr. -1-3). 28.50 *(978-1-60270-668-2(9),* Looking Glass Library) ABDO Publishing Co.

—Counting Cockatoos. Blackstone, Stella. 2007. (ENG.). 24p. (J). (gr. -1-3). bds. 8.99 *(978-1-84686-061-4(X))* Barefoot Bks., Inc.

—Famous Fenton Has a Farm: Sign Language for Farm Animals. Prochovnic, Dawn Babb. 2009. (Story Time with Signs & Rhymes Ser.). 32p. (gr. -1-3). 28.50 *(978-1-60270-669-9(7),* Looking Glass Library) ABDO Publishing Co.

—Four Seasons! Five Senses! Sign Language for the Seasons & Senses. Prochovnic, Dawn Babb. 2012. 32p. 28.50 *(978-1-61641-836-6(2),* Looking Glass Library) Magic Wagon.

—Hip Hip Hooray! It's Family Day! Sign Language for Family. Prochovnic, Dawn Babb. 2012. 32p. 28.50 *(978-1-61641-837-3(0),* Looking Glass Library) Magic Wagon.

—The Nest Where I Like to Rest: Sign Language for Animals. Prochovnic, Dawn Babb. 2009. (Story Time with Signs & Rhymes Ser.). 32p. (gr. -1-3). 28.50 *(978-1-60270-670-5(0),* Looking Glass Library) ABDO Publishing Co.

—One Trick for One Treat: Sign Language for Numbers. Prochovnic, Dawn Babb. 2012. 32p. 28.50 *(978-1-61641-838-0(9),* Looking Glass Library) Magic Wagon.

—Opposites Everywhere: Sign Language for Opposites. Prochovnic, Dawn Babb. 2012. 32p. 28.50 *(978-1-61641-839-7(7),* Looking Glass Library) Magic Wagon.

—Seasons. Hedlund, Stephanie. 2013. (Seasons Ser.: 4). 24p. (J). (gr. k-4). lib. bdg. 108.28 *(978-1-61641-991-2(1),* Looking Glass Library- Nonfiction) Magic Wagon.

—See the Colors: Sign Language for Colors. Prochovnic, Dawn Babb. 2009. (Story Time with Signs & Rhymes Ser.). 32p. (gr. -1-3). 28.50 *(978-1-60270-671-2(9),* Looking Glass Library) ABDO Publishing Co.

—Shape Detective: Sign Language for Shapes. Prochovnic, Dawn Babb. 2012. 32p. 28.50 *(978-1-61641-840-3(0),* Looking Glass Library) Magic Wagon.

—Silly Sue: Sign Language for Actions. Prochovnic, Dawn Babb. 2009. (Story Time with Signs & Rhymes Ser.). 32p. (gr. -1-3). 28.50 *(978-1-60270-672-9(7),* Looking Glass Library) ABDO Publishing Co.

—So Many Feelings: Sign Language for Feelings & Emotions. Prochovnic, Dawn Babb. 2012. 32p. (J). 28.50 *(978-1-61641-841-0(9),* Looking Glass Library) Magic Wagon.

—Spring. Hedlund, Stephanie. 2013. (Seasons Ser.). 24p. (J). (gr. k-4). lib. bdg. 27.07 *(978-1-61641-993-6(8),* Looking Glass Library- Nonfiction) Magic Wagon.

—Summer. Hedlund, Stephanie. 2013. (Seasons Ser.). 24p. (J). (gr. k-4). lib. bdg. 27.07 *(978-1-61641-994-3(6),* Looking Glass Library- Nonfiction) Magic Wagon.

—There's a Story in My Head: Sign Language for Body Parts. Prochovnic, Dawn Babb. 2012. 32p. 28.50 *(978-1-61641-842-7(7),* Looking Glass Library) Magic Wagon.

—A to Z Sign with Me: Sign Language for the Alphabet. Prochovnic, Dawn Babb. 2012. 32p. 28.50 *(978-1-61641-835-9(4),* Looking Glass Library) Magic Wagon.

—Watch Me Go! Sign Language for Vehicles. Prochovnic, Dawn Babb. 2009. (Story Time with Signs & Rhymes Ser.). 32p. (gr. -1-3). 28.50 *(978-1-60270-673-6(5),* Looking Glass Library) ABDO Publishing Co.

—Wear a Silly Hat: Sign Language for Clothing. Prochovnic, Dawn Babb. 2009. (Story Time with Signs & Rhymes Ser.). 32p. (gr. -1-3). 28.50 *(978-1-60270-674-3(3),* Looking Glass Library) ABDO Publishing Co.

—Winter. Hedlund, Stephanie. 2013. (Seasons Ser.). 24p. (J). (gr. k-4). lib. bdg. 27.07 *(978-1-61641-995-0(4),* Looking Glass Library- Nonfiction) Magic Wagon.

Bauer, Stephanie. Octopus Opposites. Bauer, Stephanie. Blackstone, Stella. (ENG.). (J). 2011. 52p. bds. 8.99 *(978-1-84686-591-6(3));* 2010. 32p. (gr. -1). 16.99 *(978-1-84686-328-8(7))* Barefoot Bks., Inc.

Bauerle, Tanja. The Adventures of Salt & Soap at Grand Canyon. Rome, Lori April. 2009. (ENG.). 32p. (gr. 2-4). pap. 9.95 *(978-1-934656-04-4(6))* Grand Canyon Assn.

—The Park Our Town Built. Bertrand, Diane Gonzalez. 2011. (ENG & SPA.). 32p. (gr. -1-3). lib. bdg. 16.95 *(978-1-936299-14-0(3),* Raven Tree Pr.,Csi) Continental Sales, Inc.

—The Park Our Town Built/El Parque Que Nuestro Pueblo Construyó. Bertrand, Diane Gonzalez. 2011. (ENG & SPA.). 32p. (gr. -1-3). lib. bdg. 16.95 *(978-1-936299-12-6(7),* Raven Tree Pr.,Csi) Continental Sales, Inc.

—Wright on Time: Collection 1. Cottrell-Bentley, Lisa M. 2012. 376p. pap. 19.99 *(978-1-937848-00-2(0))* Do Life Right, Inc.

—Wright on Time: Iowa. Cottrell-Bentley, Lisa M. 2013. 164p. pap. 12.99 *(978-1-937848-06-4(X))* Do Life Right, Inc.

—Wright on Time: Minnesota. Cottrell-Bentley, Lisa M. 2012. 126p. pap. 12.99 *(978-1-937848-02-6(7))* Do Life Right, Inc.

Bauknecht, Julie. Garda Gaby: The Danger of Playing Truant. McCann, David. Brundige, Britt, ed. l.t. ed. 2003. 14p. (J). (gr. k-5). spiral bd. 5.99 *(978-1-929063-92-5(X),* 324) Moons & Stars Publishing For Children.

—My Grandma Rides a Harley: She's Cool! Davidson, Jean. 2007. (J). *(978-1-930596-79-5(0))* Amherst Pr.

Bauknight, Wilfred, jt. illus. see Blanc, Mike.

Baum, Ann. Bunny in a Basket. Baglio, Ben M. 2005. 142p. (J). *(978-0-439-68761-4(6))* Scholastic, Inc.

—Collie with a Card. Baglio, Ben M. 2004. 136p. (J). pap. *(978-0-439-68760-7(8))* Scholastic, Inc.

—Corgi in the Cupcakes. Baglio, Ben M. 2008. 142p. (J). pap. *(978-0-439-02533-1(8))* Scholastic, Inc.

—Puppy in a Puddle, No. 28. Baglio, Ben M. 2003. (Animal Ark Ser.: 28). (ENG.). 144p. (J). (gr. 3-7). mass mkt. 4.99 *(978-0-439-34389-3(5),* Scholastic Paperbacks) Scholastic, Inc.

—Tabby under the Tree. Baglio, Ben M. & Lasher, Mary Ann. 2007. 145p. (J). *(978-0-439-02532-4(X))* Scholastic, Inc.

Baum, Ann & Gregory, Jenny. Hamster in the Holly. Baglio, Ben M. 2004. (Animal Ark Ser.: 35). (ENG.). 144p. (J). (gr. 2-5). mass mkt. 4.99 *(978-0-439-44893-2(X),* Scholastic Paperbacks) Scholastic, Inc.

Baum, Ann & Lasher, Mary Ann. Colt on Christmas Eve. Baglio, Ben M. 2005. 142p. (J). pap. *(978-0-439-77522-9(1))* Scholastic, Inc.

—Dalmatian in the Daisies. Baglio, Ben M. 2007. 154p. (J). *(978-0-439-87120-4(4))* Scholastic, Inc.

Baum, Kipley, jt. photos by see Oudinot, Wanda.

Baum, L. Frank & McKowen, Scott. The Wonderful Wizard of Oz. Baum, L. Frank. 2005. (Sterling Unabridged Classics Ser.). (ENG.). 176p. (J). (gr. 5). 9.95 *(978-1-4027-2504-3(3))* Sterling Publishing Co., Inc.

Bauman, Jill. The Tale of Squirrel Nutkin. 2006. (J). 6.99 *(978-1-59939-017-8(5))* Cornerstone Pr.

Bauman, Todd. Absurd Alphabedtime Stories. Hunter, Julius K. 2nd rev. l.t. ed. 2004. 32p. (J). 16.95 *(978-0-9761422-0-1(1))* J.K.H. Enterprises.

Baumann, Marty. Phonics Comics. Katschke, Judy. 2006. (ENG.). 24p. (J). (gr. 1-17). per. 3.99 *(978-1-58476-411-3(2),* IKIDS) Innovative Kids.

Baumgardner, Julie. Crow 2. Cope, Steven R. 2012. 158p. pap. 16.00 *(978-1-936138-49-4(2))* Wind Pubns.

Baumgardner, Mary Alice. A Job for Arabella. Carolina Canines for Service & Nowak, Pat. 2007. 56p. (J). per. *(978-0-9800070-0-8(3))* Carolina Canines for Service Inc.

Baur, Laura. The Riverbank. 2012. (ENG.). 36p. (J). (gr. -1-k). 12.99 *(978-1-85103-393-5(9))* Moonlight Publishing, Ltd. GBR. Dist: Independent Pubs. Group.

Bausman, Mary. Chrissie's Shell. Keith, Brooke. 2010. 32p. (J). 14.99 *(978-1-59317-398-2(9))* Warner Pr. Pubs.

—God Loves Me Coloring Pages: For Toddlers & 2s. Standard Publishing Staff. 2006. (HeartShaper(r) Resources — Early Childhood Ser.). 192p. (J). 16.99 *(978-0-7847-1796-7(6),* 02446) Standard Publishing.

Bautista, Cisar Evangelis. Circulos y Calendarios. Mariscal, Libia E. Barajas. rev. ed. 2006. (Otra Escalera Ser.). (SPA & ENG.). 24p. (J). (gr. 2-4). pap. 9.95 *(978-968-5920-71-1(0))* Castillo, Ediciones, S. A. de C. V. MEX. Dist: Macmillan.

Bave, Terry, et al. How to Draw Cartoons & Caricatures. Tatchell, Judy. rev. ed. 2006. (How to Draw Ser.). 40p. (J). (gr. 4-7). pap. 5.99 *(978-0-7945-1374-0(3),* Usborne) EDC Publishing.

Baviera, Rocco. Earth Day: An Alphabet Book. Kowalski, Gary A. 2009. (ENG.). 1p. (J). (gr. -1-4). 12.00 *(978-1-55896-542-3(4),* 1297770, Skinner Hse. Bks.) Unitarian Universalist Assn.

Baxter, Katherine. The Kingfisher Atlas of the Ancient World. Adams, Simon. 2006. (Kingfisher Atlas Ser.). (ENG.). 48p. (J). (gr. 3-7). 15.99 *(978-0-7534-5914-0(0),* Kingfisher) Roaring Brook Pr.

Baxter, Leon. Lion First Bible. Alexander, Pat. 2015. (ENG.). 480p. (J). (gr. k-2). 14.99 *(978-0-7459-6103-3(7))* Lion Hudson PLC GBR. Dist: Independent Pubs. Group.

Baxter, Mia. Ana's Story: A Journey of Hope. Bush, Jenna. 2008. (ENG.). 304p. (YA). (gr. 9-12). pap. 9.99 *(978-0-06-137909-3(3))* HarperCollins Pubs.

—La Historia de Ana: Un Camino Lleno de Esperanza. Bush, Jenna. 2007. (ENG.). 304p. (J). 18.99 *(978-0-06-144861-4(3),* Rayo) HarperCollins Pubs.

—La Historia de Ana: Un Camino Lleno de Esperanza. Hager, Jenna Bush. de La Concha, Bertha Ruiz, tr. 2008. (SPA & ENG.). 304p. (J). (gr. 9). pap. 9.99 *(978-0-06-144862-1(1),* Rayo) HarperCollins Pubs.

Bayard, Janie Domengeaux. Ferdinand the Frog. Borland, Jerre Shadrick. 2011. 32p. pap. 24.95 *(978-1-4560-6116-6(X))* America Star Bks.

Bayley, Flo. Roast Chicken & Other Stories. Hopkinson, Simon. 2007. (ENG.). 240p. (gr. 8-17). 24.95 *(978-1-4013-0862-9(7))* Hyperion Pr.

Bayley, Nicola. The Big Snuggle-Up. Patten, Brian. ed. 2011. (ENG.). 32p. (J). 10.99 *(978-1-61067-036-4(1))* Kane Miller.

—The Tyger Voyage. Adams, Richard. 2013. 32p. 15.95 net. *(978-1-56792-491-6(3))* Godine, David R. Pub.

—Yo Subia la Escalera y Otras Rimas Infantiles. Puncel, Maria. 2003. (SPA.). 24p. 4.95 *(978-84-372-8015-8(X))* Altea, Ediciones S.A. - Grupo Santillana ESP. Dist: Santillana USA Publishing Co., Inc.

Baynes, Pauline. Bilbo's Last Song. Tolkien, J. R. R. 2012. (ENG.). 32p. (J). (gr. k-12). 12.99 *(978-0-375-82373-2(5),* Knopf Bks. for Young Readers) Random Hse. Children's Bks.

—Le Cheval et Son Ecuyer. Morgaut, Philippe, tr. 2005. (Chronicles of Narnia Ser.). (FRE.). 234p. (J). per. 21.95 *(978-2-07-054644-2(6))* Gallimard, Editions FRA. Dist: Distribooks, Inc.

—The Chronicles of Narnia. Lewis, C. S. ed. (Chronicles of Narnia Ser.). (J). 2004. (ENG.). 784p. (gr. 5). 32.99 *(978-0-06-059824-2(7));* Set. 2007. (gr. 3-18). 120.00 *(978-0-06-024488-0(7))* HarperCollins Pubs.

—The Coat of Many Colors. Koralek, Jenny. 2004. 32p. (J). 16.00 *(978-0-8028-5277-9(7))* Eerdmans, William B. Publishing Co.

—The Horse & His Boy. Lewis, C. S. (Chronicles of Narnia Ser.: 3). (ENG.). 240p. (J). (gr. 3-18). 2008. pap. 7.99 *(978-0-06-440501-0(X));* 2007. 17.99 *(978-0-06-023488-1(1))* HarperCollins Pubs.

—I Believe: The Nicene Creed. 2004. 32p. (YA). (gr. 3-18). 16.00 *(978-0-8028-5258-8(0))* Eerdmans, William B. Publishing Co.

—Las Aventuras de Tom Bombadil/the Adventures of Tom Bombadil: Y Otros Poemas de el Libro Rojo/and Other Verses from the Red Book. Tolkien, J. R. R. 2006. (SPA.). 157p. 22.95 *(978-84-450-7194-6(7))* Minotauro Ediciones ESP. Dist: Planeta Publishing Corp.

—Las Cronicas de Narnia. Lewis, C. S. 2006. (SPA & ENG.). 816p. (gr. 4-7). pap. 19.99 *(978-0-06-119900-4(1),* Rayo) HarperCollins Pubs.

—The Last Battle. Lewis, C. S. (Chronicles of Narnia Ser.: 7). (ENG.). 224p. (J). (gr. 3-18). 2008. pap. 7.99 *(978-0-06-440503-4(6));* 2007. 17.99 *(978-0-06-023493-5(8))* HarperCollins Pubs.

—The Lion, the Witch & the Wardrobe. Lewis, C. S. abr. ed. (Chronicles of Narnia Ser.: 2). 208p. (J). (gr. 3-18). 2008. (ENG.). pap. 7.99 *(978-0-06-440499-0(4));* 2007. (ENG.). 17.99 *(978-0-06-023481-2(4));* 2007. lib. bdg. 18.89 *(978-0-06-023482-9(2))* HarperCollins Pubs.

—The Lion, the Witch & the Wardrobe. Lewis, C. S. movie tie-in ed. 2005. (Chronicles of Narnia Ser.). (ENG.). 224p. (J). (gr. 3-7). pap. 6.99 *(978-0-06-076548-4(8),* HarperFestival) HarperCollins Pubs.

—The Magician's Nephew. Lewis, C. S. 2008. (Chronicles of Narnia Ser.: 1). (ENG.). 208p. (J). (gr. 3-18). pap. 7.99 *(978-0-06-440505-8(2))* HarperCollins Pubs.

—The Moses Basket. Koralek, Jenny. 2004. 32p. (J). 16.00 *(978-0-8028-5251-9(3))* Eerdmans, William B. Publishing Co.

—Prince Caspian. Lewis, C. S. 2007. (Chronicles of Narnia Ser.: 4). (ENG.). 240p. (J). (gr. 3-18). 17.99 *(978-0-06-023483-6(0))* HarperCollins Pubs.

—Prince Caspian: The Return to Narnia. Lewis, C. S. 2008. (Chronicles of Narnia Ser.: 4). (ENG.). 240p. (J). (gr. 3-18). pap. 7.99 *(978-0-06-440500-3(1))* HarperCollins Pubs.

—El Principe Caspian. Lewis, C. S. Gallart, Gemma, tr. 2008. (Narnia Ser.). (SPA & ENG.). 288p. (gr. 4-7). pap. 9.99 *(978-0-06-144078-6(7),* Rayo) HarperCollins Pubs.

—La Silla de Plata, 1 vol. Lewis, C. S. Gallart, Gemma, tr. 2005. (Chronicles of Narnia Ser.). (ESP, SPA & ENG.). 304p. (gr. 4-7). per. 9.99 *(978-0-06-088430-7(4),* Rayo) HarperCollins Pubs.

B

—The Silver Chair. Lewis, C. S. (Chronicles of Narnia Ser.: 6). (ENG.). 256p. (J). (gr. 3-18). 2008. pap. 7.99 *(978-0-06-440504-1(4));* 2007. 17.99 *(978-0-06-023495-9(4))* HarperCollins Pubs.

—The Tale of Troy. Green, Roger Lancelyn. 2012. (Puffin Classics Ser.). (ENG.). 224p. (J). pap. 4.99 *(978-0-14-134196-5(3),* Puffin) Penguin Publishing Group.

—The Voyage of the Dawn Treader. Lewis, C. S. (Chronicles of Narnia Ser.). (ENG.). 256p. (J). (gr. 3-18). 2010. 17.99 *(978-0-06-171497-9(6));* 2008. pap. 7.99 *(978-0-06-440502-7(8));* 2007. 17.99 *(978-0-06-023486-7(5))* HarperCollins Pubs.

Baynes, Pauline. Prince Caspian, Bk. 7. Baynes, Pauline. 2008. (Chronicles of Narnia Ser.). 768p. (J). (gr. 3). pap. 99.99 *(978-0-06-076552-1(6))* HarperCollins Pubs.

—Questionable Creatures: A Bestiary. Baynes, Pauline. 2006. 48p. (J). (gr. 5-18). 18.00 *(978-0-8028-5284-7(X))* Eerdmans, William B. Publishing Co.

Baynes, Pauline & Van Allsburg, Chris. The Magician's Nephew. Lewis, C. S. 2007. (Chronicles of Narnia Ser.: 1). (ENG.). 208p. (J). (gr. 3-18). 17.99 *(978-0-06-023497-3(0))* HarperCollins Pubs.

Baynton, Martin. Three's a Crowd. Baynton, Martin. 2008. (Jane & the Dragon Ser.). (ENG.). 96p. (J). (gr. 1-4). pap. 4.99 *(978-0-7636-3929-7(X))* Candlewick Pr.

Bayoc, Cbabi. Young Cornrows Callin Out the Moon. Forman, Ruth. 2007. (ENG.). 24p. (J). (gr. -1-3). lib. bdg. 16.95 *(978-0-89239-218-6(5))* Lee & Low Bks., Inc.

Bayramoglu, Hatice. Nia's Dream the Talking Tulips. Baniti, Nailah. 2nd ed. 2013. 24p. pap. 7.99 *(978-0-9853574-5-0(2))* Mountan Creek Pubns.

Bayramoglu, Hatice. Nia's Dream. Bayramoglu, Hatice. Baniti, Nailah. 2012. 26p. pap. 7.99 *(978-0-9853574-4-3(4))* Mountan Creek Pubns.

Bays, Gail, jt. illus. see Rothenberger, Boyd.

Bazzoni, Lainie M. A. Windsock Wesley & His Wild & Wonderful Weather MacHine, Living in Cloud. Fox, Alex. 2010. 48p. pap. 16.50 *(978-1-60911-873-0(1),* Eloquent Bks.) Strategic Book Publishing & Rights Agency (SBPRA).

Be-Papas. Revolutionary Girl Utena. Saito, Chiho. 2003. (Revolutionary Girl Utena Ser.: Vol. 3). (ENG.). 200p. pap. 9.95 *(978-1-56931-812-6(3))* Viz Media.

Beach, Bryan. Little Miss Daredevil. Hardman, John. 2012. (Mr. Men Little Miss Ser.: 1). (ENG.). 80p. (J). pap. 6.99 *(978-1-4215-4072-6(X))* Viz Media.

Beach, Bryan. Yogi Bear's Guide to Bugs. Weakland, Mark. 2015. (Yogi Bear's Guide to the Great Outdoors Ser.). (ENG.). 32p. (gr. 1-2). lib. bdg. 27.32 *(978-1-4914-6546-2(8))* Capstone Pr., Inc.

—Yogi Bear's Guide to Rocks. Weakland, Mark. 2015. (Yogi Bear's Guide to the Great Outdoors Ser.). (ENG.). 32p. (gr. 1-2). lib. bdg. 27.32 ***(978-1-4914-6548-6(4))*** Capstone Pr., Inc.

Beach, Bryan & Cornia, Christian. Yogi Bear's Guide to the Great Outdoors. Weakland, Mark. 2015. (Yogi Bear's Guide to the Great Outdoors Ser.). (ENG.). 32p. (gr. 1-2). 109.28 ***(978-1-4914-6967-5(6))*** Capstone Pr., Inc.

Beach, Mary FitzGerald. The Black Sheep. Harper, Stephan J. l.t. ed. 2005. 32p. (J). lib. bdg. 16.95 *(978-0-9741800-1-4(7))* Inspire Press, Inc.

Beachamp, Afiyah. The Queen of IT. Bush, Vicki-Ann. 2011. 60p. (J). pap. 9.98 *(978-0-9816949-7-9(7))* Salt of the Earth Pr.

Beacon, Dawn. Action! Writing Your Own Play, 1 vol. Loewen, Nancy. 2010. (Writer's Toolbox Ser.). (ENG.). 32p. (gr. 2-4). lib. bdg. 26.65 *(978-1-4048-6017-9(7))*; pap. 8.95 *(978-1-4048-6392-7(3))* Picture Window Bks. (Nonfiction Picture Bks.).

—Animal Fairy Tales, 1 vol. Guillain, Charlotte. (Animal Fairy Tales Ser.). (ENG.). 24p. 2014. (gr. 1-2). lib. bdg. 113.25 *(978-1-4109-6116-7(8))*; 2013. (gr. -1-2). pap. 324.70 *(978-1-4109-5527-2(3))*; 2013. (gr. -1-2). pap. 162.45 *(978-1-4109-5526-5(5))*; 2013. (gr. -1-2). pap. 32.45 *(978-1-4109-5033-8(6))*; 2013. (gr. -1-2). lib. bdg. 113.25 *(978-1-4109-5027-7(1))* Heinemann-Raintree. (NA-r).

—Animal Fairy Tales Big Book Collection. Guillain, Charlotte. 2013. (Animal Fairy Tales Ser.). (ENG.). 24p. (gr. -1-2). 130.00 *(978-1-4109-5045-1(X)*, NA-r) Heinemann-Raintree.

—Cat & the Beanstalk, 1 vol. Guillain, Charlotte. 2014. (Animal Fairy Tales Ser.). (ENG.). 24p. (gr. 1-2). lib. bdg. 22.65 *(978-1-4109-6113-6(3)*, NA-r) Heinemann-Raintree.

—The Emperor Penguin's New Clothes, 1 vol. Guillain, Charlotte. 2014. (Animal Fairy Tales Ser.). (ENG.). 24p. (gr. 1-2). pap. 6.49 *(978-1-4109-6121-1(4))*; 26.00 *(978-1-4109-6134-1(6))*; lib. bdg. 22.65 *(978-1-4109-6114-3(1))* Heinemann-Raintree. (NA-r).

—Goldiclucks & the Three Bears, 1 vol. Guillain, Charlotte. 2013. (Animal Fairy Tales Ser.). (ENG.). 24p. (gr. -1-2). pap. 6.49 *(978-1-4109-5028-4(X)*, NA-r); 26.00 *(978-1-4109-5040-6(9))*; lib. bdg. 22.65 *(978-1-4109-5022-2(0)*, NA-r) Heinemann-Raintree.

—Just the Facts: Writing Your Own Research Report, 1 vol. Loewen, Nancy. 2009. (Writer's Toolbox Ser.). (ENG.). 32p. (gr. 2-4). lib. bdg. 26.65 *(978-1-4048-5519-9(X)*, Nonfiction Picture Bks.) Picture Window Bks.

—Just the Facts [Scholastic]: Writing Your Own Research Report. Loewen, Nancy. 2010. (Writer's Toolbox Ser.). 32p. pap. 0.50 *(978-1-4048-6171-8(8)*, Nonfiction Picture Bks.) Picture Window Bks.

—The Kitten Who Cried Dog, 1 vol. Guillain, Charlotte. 2013. (Animal Fairy Tales Ser.). (ENG.). 24p. (gr. -1-2). pap. 6.49 *(978-1-4109-5029-1(8)*, NA-r) Heinemann-Raintree.

—The Kitten Who Cried Dog. Guillain, Charlotte & Aesop. 2013. (Animal Fairy Tales Ser.). (ENG.). 24p. (gr. -1-2). 26.00 *(978-1-4109-5041-3(7))* Heinemann-Raintree.

—The Kitten Who Cried Dog, 1 vol. Guillain, Charlotte. 2013. (Animal Fairy Tales Ser.). (ENG.). 24p. (gr. -1-2). lib. bdg. 22.65 *(978-1-4109-5023-9(9)*, NA-r) Heinemann-Raintree.

—Little Red Riding Duck, 1 vol. Guillain, Charlotte. 2013. (Animal Fairy Tales Ser.). (ENG.). 24p. (gr. -1-2). pap. 6.49 *(978-1-4109-5030-7(1)*, NA-r); 26.00 *(978-1-4109-5042-0(5))*; lib. bdg. 22.65 *(978-1-4109-5024-6(7)*, NA-r) Heinemann-Raintree.

—Pandarella, 1 vol. Guillain, Charlotte. 2013. (Animal Fairy Tales Ser.). (ENG.). 24p. (gr. -1-2). pap. 6.49 *(978-1-4109-5031-4(X)*, NA-r) Heinemann-Raintree.

—Pandarella. Guillain, Charlotte & Perrault, Charles. 2013. (Animal Fairy Tales Ser.). (ENG.). 24p. (gr. -1-2). 26.00 *(978-1-4109-5043-7(3))* Heinemann-Raintree.

—Pandarella, 1 vol. Guillain, Charlotte. 2013. (Animal Fairy Tales Ser.). (ENG.). 24p. (gr. -1-2). lib. bdg. 22.65 *(978-1-4109-5025-3(5)*, NA-r) Heinemann-Raintree.

—The Poodle & the Pea, 1 vol. Guillain, Charlotte. 2013. (Animal Fairy Tales Ser.). (ENG.). 24p. (gr. -1-2). pap. 6.49 *(978-1-4109-5032-1(8)*, NA-r) Heinemann-Raintree.

—The Poodle & the Pea. Guillain, Charlotte & Andersen, Hans Christian. 2013. (Animal Fairy Tales Ser.). (ENG.). 24p. (gr. -1-2). 26.00 *(978-1-4109-5044-4(1))* Heinemann-Raintree.

—The Poodle & the Pea, 1 vol. Guillain, Charlotte. 2013. (Animal Fairy Tales Ser.). (ENG.). 24p. (gr. -1-2). lib. bdg. 22.65 *(978-1-4109-5026-0(3)*, NA-r) Heinemann-Raintree.

—Ratpunzel, 1 vol. Guillain, Charlotte. 2014. (Animal Fairy Tales Ser.). (ENG.). 24p. (gr. 1-2). lib. bdg. 22.65 *(978-1-4109-6112-9(5)*, NA-r) Heinemann-Raintree.

—Rumpelsnakeskin, 1 vol. Guillain, Charlotte. 2014. (Animal Fairy Tales Ser.). (ENG.). 24p. (gr. 1-2). lib. bdg. 22.65 *(978-1-4109-6111-2(7)*, NA-r) Heinemann-Raintree.

—Sleeping Badger, 1 vol. Guillain, Charlotte. 2014. (Animal Fairy Tales Ser.). (ENG.). 24p. (gr. 1-2). lib. bdg. 22.65 *(978-1-4109-6115-0(X)*, NA-r) Heinemann-Raintree.

Beacon, Dawn. Peter Piper. Beacon, Dawn. 2011. (Favorite Mother Goose Rhymes Ser.). (ENG.). 16p. (J). (gr. -1-2). lib. bdg. 25.64 *(978-1-60954-282-5(7)*, 200234) Child's World, Inc., The.

Beacon, Dawn & Lyles, Christopher. Just the Facts: Writing Your Own Research Report, 1 vol. Loewen, Nancy. 2009. (Writer's Toolbox Ser.). (ENG.). 32p. (gr. 2-4). pap. 8.95 *(978-1-4048-5702-5(8)*, Nonfiction Picture Bks.) Picture Window Bks.

Beaky, Suzanne. The Busy Life of Ernestine Buckmeister. Lodding, Linda Ravin. 2011. (ENG.). 32p. (J). (gr. -1-1). 16.95 *(978-0-9799746-9-4(0))* Flashlight Pr.

—Hailey Twitch & the Campground Itch. Barnholdt, Lauren. 2011. (Hailey Twitch Ser.: 3). (ENG.). 144p. (J). (gr. 2-4). pap. 8.99 *(978-1-4022-2446-1(X)*, Sourcebooks Jabberwocky) Sourcebooks, Inc.

—Hailey Twitch & the Great Teacher Switch. Barnholdt, Lauren. 2010. (Hailey Twitch Ser.: 2). (ENG.). 176p. (J). (gr. 2-4). pap. 6.99 *(978-1-4022-2445-4(1)*, Sourcebooks Jabberwocky) Sourcebooks, Inc.

—Hailey Twitch & the Wedding Glitch. Barnholdt, Lauren. 2011. (Hailey Twitch Ser.: 4). (ENG.). 144p. (J). (gr. 2-4). pap. 6.99 *(978-1-4022-2447-8(8)*, Sourcebooks Jabberwocky) Sourcebooks, Inc.

—Hailey Twitch Is Not a Snitch. Barnholdt, Lauren. 2010. (Hailey Twitch Ser.: 1). (ENG.). 160p. (J). (gr. 2-4). pap. 6.99 *(978-1-4022-2444-7(3)*, Sourcebooks Jabberwocky) Sourcebooks, Inc.

—The Original Cowgirl: The Wild Adventures of Lucille Mulhall. Lang, Heather. 2015. (ENG.). 32p. (J). (gr. -1-2). 16.99 *(978-0-8075-2931-7(1))* Whitman, Albert & Co.

—Rupert the Wrong-Word Pirate. Owens, Greg. 2006. (J). *(978-1-58987-143-4(X))* Kindermusik International.

—She'll Be Comin' Round the Mountain. Schwaeber, Barbie H., ed. 2007. (American Favorites Ser.). (ENG.). 32p. (J). (gr. -1-3). 14.95 *(978-1-59249-687-7(3))* Soundprints.

—She'll Be Comin Round the Mountain. Schwaeber, Barbie H. 2007. (American Favorites Ser.). (ENG.). 32p. (J). (gr. -1-3). 9.85 *(978-1-59249-688-4(1))* Soundprints.

—She'll Be Comin' Round the Mountain. rev. ed. 2007. (ENG.). 24p. (J). (gr. -1-k). 4.99 *(978-1-59069-604-0(2))* Studio Mouse LLC.

—What's Bugging Nurse Penny? A Story about Lice. Stier, Catherine. 2013. (ENG.). 32p. (J). (gr. -1-2). 16.99 *(978-0-8075-8803-1(2))* Whitman, Albert & Co.

Béal, Marjorie. The Flea, 0 vols. Cohen, Laurie. Owlkids Books Inc. Staff & Quinn, Sarah, trs. 2014. (ENG & FRE.). 32p. (J). (gr. -1 — 1). 16.95 *(978-1-77147-056-8(9)*, Owlkids) Owlkids Bks. Inc. CAN. Dist: Perseus-PGW.

Beam, Matt. City Alphabet, 1 vol. Schwartz, Joanne. 2009. (ENG.). 60p. (gr. -1-4). 18.95 *(978-0-88899-928-3(3))* Groundwood Bks. CAN. Dist: Perseus-PGW.

Bean, Brett. Hound of Hades #2. Coats, Lucy. 2015. (Beasts of Olympus Ser.: 2). (ENG.). 144p. (J). (gr. 2-4). 5.99 *(978-0-448-46194-6(3)*, Grosset & Dunlap) Penguin Publishing Group.

—Steeds of the Gods #3. Coats, Lucy. 2015. (Beasts of Olympus Ser.: 3). (ENG.). 144p. (J). (gr. 2-4). 5.99 *(978-0-448-46195-3(1)*, Grosset & Dunlap) Penguin Publishing Group.

Bean, Izzy. St Viper's School for Super Villains. the Big Bank Burglary. Donovan, Kim. 2013. 160p. pap. *(978-0-9571300-2-9(3))* Squawk Bks.

Bean, Jonathan. The Apple Pie That Papa Baked. Thompson, Lauren. 2007. (ENG.). 32p. (J). (gr. k-3). 15.99 *(978-1-4169-1240-8(1)*, Simon & Schuster Bks. For Young Readers) Simon & Schuster Bks. For Young Readers.

—Bad Bye, Good Bye. Underwood, Deborah. 2014. (ENG.). 32p. (J). (gr. -1-3). 16.99 *(978-0-547-92852-4(1)*, HMH Books For Young Readers) Houghton Mifflin Harcourt Publishing Co.

—Emmy & the Home for Troubled Girls. Jonell, Lynne. 2010. (Emmy & the Rat Ser.: 2). (ENG.). 384p. (J). (gr. 4-7). pap. 11.99 *(978-0-312-60873-6(X))* Square Fish.

—Emmy & the Incredible Shrinking Rat. Jonell, Lynne. 2008. (Emmy & the Rat Ser.: 1). (ENG.). 368p. (J). (gr. 4-7). pap. 7.99 *(978-0-312-38460-9(2))* Square Fish.

—Emmy & the Rats in the Belfry. Jonell, Lynne. 2011. (Emmy & the Rat Ser.: 3). (ENG.). 384p. (J). (gr. 4-7). 17.99 *(978-0-8050-9183-0(1)*, Holt, Henry & Co. Bks. For Young Readers) Holt, Henry & Co.

—Mokie & Bik Go to Sea. Orr, Wendy. 2010. (ENG.). 80p. (J). (gr. 2-5). 15.99 *(978-0-8050-8174-9(7)*, Holt, Henry & Co. Bks. For Young Readers) Holt, Henry & Co.

—One Starry Night. Thompson, Lauren. (ENG.). 32p. (J). 2011. (gr. -1-3). lib. bdg. 16.99 *(978-0-689-82851-5(9))*; 2003. 6.99 *(978-0-689-84215-3(5))* McElderry, Margaret K. Bks. (McElderry, Margaret K. Bks.).

Bean, Jonathan. At Night. Bean, Jonathan. 2007. (ENG.). 32p. (J). (gr. -1-3). 17.99 *(978-0-374-30446-1(7)*, Farrar, Straus & Giroux (BYR)) Farrar, Straus & Giroux.

—Big Snow. Bean, Jonathan. 2013. (ENG.). 32p. (J). (gr. -1-1). 16.99 *(978-0-374-30696-0(6)*, Farrar, Straus & Giroux (BYR)) Farrar, Straus & Giroux.

—Building Our House. Bean, Jonathan. 2013. (ENG.). 48p. (J). (gr. -1-1). 18.99 *(978-0-374-38023-6(6)*, Farrar, Straus & Giroux (BYR)) Farrar, Straus & Giroux.

Bean, Jonathan, jt. illus. see Hoefler, Kate.

Bear, Andrea. We Are the People of This World: Book One. Santana, Sr. Stella. 2011. 40p. pap. 14.95 *(978-1-61204-643-3(6)*, Eloquent Bks.) Strategic Book Publishing & Rights Agency (SBPRA).

Beard, Lauren. The Fairytale Hairdresser: And How Rapunzel Got Her Prince! Longstaff, Abie. 2014. (Fairytale Hairdresser Ser.: 1). (ENG.). 32p. (J). (-k). pap. 9.99 *(978-0-552-56186-0(X))* Transworld Publishers Ltd. GBR. Dist: Independent Pubs. Group.

—The Fairytale Hairdresser & Cinderella. Longstaff, Abie. 2014. (Fairytale Hairdresser Ser.: 2). (ENG.). 32p. (J). (-k). pap. 13.99 *(978-0-552-56535-6(0))* Transworld Publishers Ltd. GBR. Dist: Independent Pubs. Group.

—The Fairytale Hairdresser & Father Christmas. 2014. (Fairytale Hairdresser Ser.: 5). (ENG.). 32p. (J). (-k). pap. 9.99 *(978-0-552-57052-7(4))* Transworld Publishers Ltd. GBR. Dist: Independent Pubs. Group.

—The Fairytale Hairdresser & Sleeping Beauty. Longstaff, Abie. 2014. (Fairytale Hairdresser Ser.: 3). (ENG.). 32p. (J). (-k). pap. 9.99 *(978-0-552-56755-8(8))* Transworld Publishers Ltd. GBR. Dist: Independent Pubs. Group.

—The Fairytale Hairdresser & Snow White. Longstaff, Abie. 2015. (Fairytale Hairdresser Ser.: 4). (ENG.). 32p. (J). (-k). pap. 9.99 *(978-0-552-56777-0(9))* Transworld Publishers Ltd. GBR. Dist: Independent Pubs. Group.

—Sand! Llewellyn, Claire. 2013. (Start Reading Ser.). (ENG.). 24p. (gr. k-1). pap. 41.94 *(978-1-4765-3230-1(3))*; pap. 6.99 *(978-1-4765-3187-8(0))* Capstone Pr., Inc.

—Splash! Llewellyn, Claire. 2013. (Start Reading Ser.). (ENG.). 24p. (gr. k-1). pap. 41.94 *(978-1-4765-3232-5(X))*; pap. 6.99 *(978-1-4765-3186-1(2))* Capstone Pr., Inc.

Bearden, Romare. Li'l Dan the Drummer Boy: A Civil War Story. Bearden, Romare. 2003. (ENG.). 40p. (J). (gr. -1-3). 19.99 *(978-0-689-86237-3(7)*, Simon & Schuster Bks. For Young Readers) Simon & Schuster Bks. For Young Readers.

Beardshaw, Rosalind. Funny Face, Sunny Face. Symes, Sally. 2015. (ENG.). 32p. (J). (-k). 14.99 *(978-0-7636-7606-3(3)*, Nosy Crow) Candlewick Pr.

—I Am a Spaceman! 2008. (ENG.). 12p. (J). (gr. k — 1). bds. 12.95 *(978-1-4052-2759-9(1))* Egmont Bks., Ltd. GBR. Dist: Independent Pubs. Group.

—Jack's Bed. Rickards, Lynne. 2006. (Green Bananas Ser.). (ENG.). 48p. (J). (gr. -1-k). *(978-0-7787-1044-8(0))*; lib. bdg. *(978-0-7787-1028-8(9))* Crabtree Publishing Co.

—Just Right for Christmas. Black, Birdie. 2014. (ENG.). 24p. (J). (-k). bds. 6.99 *(978-0-7636-7563-9(6)*, Nosy Crow) Candlewick Pr.

—Just Right for Two. Corderoy, Tracey. 2014. (ENG.). 32p. (J). (gr. -1-2). 15.99 *(978-0-7636-7344-4(7)*, Nosy Crow) Candlewick Pr.

Beardshaw, Rosalind. Kiss the Frog. 2013. (J). ***(978-1-4351-4925-0(4))*** Barnes & Noble, Inc.

Beardshaw, Rosalind. Lola at the Library. McQuinn, Anna. 2006. (ENG.). 32p. (J). (-k). 15.95 *(978-1-58089-113-4(6))*; 6.95 *(978-1-58089-142-4(X))* Charlesbridge Publishing, Inc.

—Lola at the Library. McQuinn, Anna. 2007. 22p. (gr. -1). 16.95 *(978-0-7569-7931-7(5))* Perfection Learning Corp.

—Lola le Lee Al Pequeño Leo. McQuinn, Anna. 2013. (SPA & ENG.). 28p. (J). (-k). pap. 7.95 *(978-1-58089-599-6(9))* Charlesbridge Publishing, Inc.

—Lola Loves Stories. McQuinn, Anna. 2010. (ENG.). 28p. (J). (gr. -1-k). pap. 6.95 *(978-1-58089-259-9(0))* Charlesbridge Publishing, Inc.

—Lola Plants a Garden. McQuinn, Anna. 2014. (ENG.). 28p. (J). (-k). 15.95 *(978-1-58089-694-8(4))* Charlesbridge Publishing, Inc.

—Lola Reads to Leo. McQuinn, Anna. 2012. (ENG.). 28p. (J). (-k). 15.95 *(978-1-58089-403-6(8))*; pap. 6.95 *(978-1-58089-404-3(6))* Charlesbridge Publishing, Inc.

—Mole's Babies. Bedford, David. 2012. (J). *(978-1-58925-108-3(3))*; pap. *(978-1-58925-435-0(X))* Tiger Tales.

—Mole's in Love. Bedford, David. 2009. 32p. (J). (gr. -1-2). 15.95 *(978-1-58925-084-0(2))*; pap. 6.95 *(978-1-58925-417-6(1))* Tiger Tales.

—Oops! Kidd, Pennie. 2011. (ENG.). 32p. (J). (gr. -1-k). pap. 8.99 *(978-0-7459-4892-8(8))* Lion Hudson PLC GBR. Dist: Independent Pubs. Group.

—Three Little Words. Pearce, Clemency. 2014. (ENG.). 32p. (J). (-k). lib. bdg. 15.99 *(978-0-375-97183-9(1)*, Doubleday Bks. for Young Readers) Random Hse. Children's Bks.

Beardshaw, Rosalind. A Lola le Encantan Los Cuentos. Beardshaw, Rosalind. McQuinn, Anna. Canetti, Yanitzia, tr. from ENG. 2012. (SPA.). 28p. (J). (-k). 16.95 *(978-1-58089-443-2(7))*; pap. 7.95 *(978-1-58089-444-9(5))* Charlesbridge Publishing, Inc.

Bearss, Patricia. The Adventures of Forealdo. Paul J McSorley; Illustrated By Patricia. 2011. 36p. pap. 24.95 *(978-1-4560-8429-5(1))* America Star Bks.

Beasley, Dion. Too Many Cheeky Dogs. Bell, Johanna. 2013. (ENG.). 32p. (J). (gr. -1-k). 22.99 *(978-1-74331-622-1(4))* Allen & Unwin AUS. Dist: Independent Pubs. Group.

Beaton, Alyson. Grow: An Environmentally Friendly Book. Beaton, Alyson. Bradley, K. J. 2009. (ENG.). 23p. (J). (gr. k-k). 16.95 *(978-0-9771992-6-6(6))* Featherproof Bks.

Beaton, Clare. Cerdota Grandota. Blackstone, Stella. 2003.Tr. of How Big Is a Pig. (SPA.). 24p. (J). (gr. k-2). pap. 6.99 *(978-1-84148-926-1(3))* Barefoot Bks., Inc.

—Clare Beaton's Action Rhymes. 2010. (ENG.). 16p. (J). bds. 6.99 *(978-1-84686-473-5(9))* Barefoot Bks., Inc.

—Clare Beaton's Animal Rhymes. Barefoot Books Staff. 16p. bds. 6.99 *(978-1-78285-080-9(5))* Barefoot Bks., Inc.

—Clare Beaton's Garden Rhymes. Barefoot Books Staff. 16p. bds. 6.99 *(978-1-78285-081-6(3))* Barefoot Bks., Inc.

—Clare Beaton's Nursery Rhymes. 2010. (ENG.). 16p. (J). bds. 6.99 *(978-1-84686-472-8(0))* Barefoot Bks., Inc.

—La Comida/Food. 2003. (Bilingual First Books/English-Spanish Ser.). (ENG & SPA.). 24p. (J). pap. 4.95 *(978-0-7641-2609-3(1))* Barron's Educational Series, Inc.

—Daisy Gets Dressed. 2005. 24p. (J). 15.99 *(978-1-84148-794-6(5))* Barefoot Bks., Inc.

—Elusive Moose. Gannij, Joan. (ENG.). (J). (gr. -1-2). 2011. 32p. pap. 7.99 *(978-1-84686-075-1(X))*; 2007. 24p. bds. 6.99 *(978-1-84686-001-0(6))* Barefoot Bks., Inc.

—English-Spanish Bilingual First Books, 6 bks. (J). lib. bdg. 86.70 *(978-1-56674-944-2(1))* Forest Hse. Publishing Co., Inc.

—First French with Superchat: Learn French the Super-Fun Way Through Games, Activities & Songs. Bruzzone, Catherine. 2007. (Teach Yourself Ser.). (ENG.). 32p. (gr. 8-12). 13.95 *(978-0-07-148101-4(X)*, 007148101X) McGraw-Hill Cos., The.

—First Spanish with Supergato: Learn Spanish the Super-Fun Way Through Games, Activities & Songs. Bruzzone, Catherine. 2007. (ENG.). 32p. (gr. -1-3). 13.95 *(978-0-07-147931-8(7)*, 0071479317) McGraw-Hill Cos., The.

—Hay una Vaca Entre las Coles. Blackstone, Stella & Bass, Jules. 2003.Tr. of There's a Cow in the Cabbage Patch. (SPA.). 32p. (J). (gr. k-2). pap. 6.99 *(978-1-84148-965-0(4))* Barefoot Bks., Inc.

—Hidden Hippo. Gannij, Joan. (ENG.). 32p. (J). 2011. (gr. -1-2). pap. 6.99 *(978-1-84686-533-6(6))*; 2009. 6.99 *(978-1-84686-329-5(5))* Barefoot Bks., Inc.

—I Dreamt I Was a Dinosaur. Blackstone, Stella. (ENG.). (J). (gr. -1-k). 2006. 24p. 6.99 *(978-1-84686-015-7(6))*; 2005. 32p. 15.99 *(978-1-84148-238-5(2))* Barefoot Bks., Inc.

—Lucy the Cat at the Farm: Lucie le Chat a la Ferme. Bruzzone, Catherine. 2005. (Lucy Cat Ser.). (ENG & FRE.). 24p. (J). (gr. -1-1). pap. 7.99 *(978-1-902915-11-1(9))* B Small Publishing GBR. Dist: Independent Pubs. Group.

—Lucy the Cat in Town: Lucie le Chat en Ville. Bruzzone, Catherine. 2005. (Lucy Cat Ser.). (ENG & FRE.). 24p. (J). (gr. -1-1). pap. 7.99 *(978-1-902915-15-9(1))* B Small Publishing GBR. Dist: Independent Pubs. Group.

—Mrs. Moon: Lullabies for Bedtime. 2003. 48p. (J). 19.99 incl. audio compact disk *(978-1-84148-176-0(9))* Barefoot Bks., Inc.

—Secret Seahorse. Blackstone, Stella. 24p. (J). 2005. pap. 6.99 *(978-1-84148-937-7(9))*; 2005. (gr. -1-2). 15.99 *(978-1-84148-704-5(X))*; 2004. (gr. -1-k). per., bds. 6.99 *(978-1-905236-15-2(8))* Barefoot Bks., Inc.

—There's a Billy Goat in the Garden. Gugler, Laurel Dee. 2003. 32p. (J). (gr. -1-2). 14.99 *(978-1-84148-089-3(4))* Barefoot Bks., Inc.

—Toys: Los Juguetes. 2003. (Bilingual First Books/English-Spanish Ser.). (ENG & SPA.). 24p. (J). pap. 4.95 *(978-0-7641-2611-6(3))* Barron's Educational Series, Inc.

—Who Are You, Baby Kangaroo? Blackstone, Stella. (J). 2005. (ENG.). 24p. (gr. -1-2). bds. 6.99 *(978-1-905236-19-0(0))*; 2004. 32p. 14.99 *(978-1-84148-217-0(X))* Barefoot Bks., Inc.

—Who Are You Baby Kangaroo? Blackstone, Stella. 2011. (ENG.). 32p. (J). (gr. -1-2). pap. 6.99 *(978-1-84686-190-1(X))* Barefoot Bks., Inc.

—Zoe & Her Zebra. Blackstone, Stella. 2011. (ENG.). 32p. (J). (gr. -1-2). pap. 6.99 *(978-1-84686-536-7(0))* Barefoot Bks., Inc.

Beaton, Clare. Un Alce, Veinte Ratones. Beaton, Clare. Blackstone, Stella. 2006.Tr. of One Moose, Twenty Mice. (ENG.). 32p. (J). (gr. -1-k). bds. 6.99 *(978-1-84686-019-5(9))* Barefoot Bks., Inc.

—Cerdota Grandota. Beaton, Clare. Blackstone, Stella. 2006.Tr. of How Big Is a Pig. (ENG.). 24p. (J). (gr. -1-k). bds. 6.99 *(978-1-84686-018-8(0))* Barefoot Bks., Inc.

—Clare Beaton's Bedtime Rhymes. Beaton, Clare. 2012. (ENG.). 14p. (J). bds. 6.99 *(978-1-84686-737-8(1))* Barefoot Bks., Inc.

—Clare Beaton's Farmyard Rhymes. Beaton, Clare. 2012. (ENG.). 14p. (J). bds. 6.99 *(978-1-84686-736-1(3))* Barefoot Bks., Inc.

—How Big Is a Pig? Beaton, Clare. Blackstone, Stella. 2003. (ENG.). 24p. (J). pap. 6.99 *(978-1-84148-702-1(3))* Barefoot Bks., Inc.

—How Loud Is a Lion? Beaton, Clare. Blackstone, Stella. 2007. (ENG.). 24p. (J). (gr. -1-k). 6.99 *(978-1-84686-000-3(8))* Barefoot Bks., Inc.

—How Loud Is a Lion? Beaton, Clare. Blackstone, Stella. 2011. (ENG.). 24p. (J). (gr. -1-2). pap. 6.99 *(978-1-84686-534-3(4))* Barefoot Bks., Inc.

—I Dreamt I Was a Dinosaur. Beaton, Clare. Blackstone, Stella. 2011. (ENG.). 32p. (J). (gr. -1-2). pap. 6.99 *(978-1-84686-025-6(3))* Barefoot Bks., Inc.

—Make & Colour Paper Planes. Beaton, Clare. 2004. (ENG.). 24p. (J). (gr. 1-4). pap. 7.99 *(978-1-874735-94-6(8))* B Small Publishing GBR. Dist: Independent Pubs. Group.

—Make Your Own Noah's Ark. Beaton, Clare. 2007. (J). (gr. k-3). 9.95 *(978-0-8198-4862-8(X))* Pauline Bks. & Media.

—Play Castles. Beaton, Clare. 2014. (Make Your Own Ser.). (ENG.). 20p. (J). (gr. k-2). pap. 7.99 *(978-1-902915-96-8(8))* B Small Publishing GBR. Dist: Independent Pubs. Group.

Beaton, Clare, jt. illus. see Harter, Debbie.

Beatrice, Chris. Casablanca. Friedman, J. S. 2013. (Maurice's Valises: Moral Tails in an Immoral World Ser.: Vol. 3). (ENG.). 45p. (J). (gr. k-4). pap. *(978-94-91613-09-8(X))* Mouse Prints Pr.

—In the Beginning. Friedman, J. S. 2013. (Maurice's Valises: Moral Tails in an Immoral World Ser.: Vol. 1). (ENG.). 45p. (J). (gr. k-4). *(978-94-91613-03-6(0))* Mouse Prints Pr.

—The Micetro of Moscow. Friedman, J. S. 2013. (Maurice's Valises: Moral Tails in an Immoral World Ser.: Vol. 2). (ENG.). 37p. (J). (gr. k-4). pap. *(978-94-91613-06-7(5))* Mouse Prints Pr.

Beatrice, Chris, jt. illus. see Whatley, Bruce.

Beattie, Steven M., II. These Are My Sensors. Beattie, Steven M., II. 2007. 32p. (gr. -1-k). 19.99 *(978-1-59879-310-9(1))*; (J). 13.99 *(978-1-59879-363-5(2))* Lifevest Publishing, Inc.

Beatty, Connie & Phillippi, Faith. Why Owls Say Who. Beatty, Connie. 2008. 20p. per. 24.95 *(978-1-4137-6715-5(X))* America Star Bks.

Beatty, Terry, et al. Batman: the Brave & the Bold. Torres, J. 2013. (Batman: the Brave & the Bold Ser.). (ENG.). 32p. (gr. 2-3). 170.16 *(978-1-4342-4858-9(5))*; 85.08 *(978-1-4342-4857-2(7))* Stone Arch Bks.

Beatty, Terry. Benedict Arnold: American Hero & Traitor, 1 vol. Burgan, Michael. 2007. (Graphic Biographies Ser.). (ENG.). 32p. (gr. 3-4). per. 8.10 *(978-0-7368-7906-4(4)*, Graphic Library) Capstone Pr., Inc.

—Jax Epoch & the Quicken Forbidden Vol. 1: Borrowed Magic. Collins, Max Allan & Rowan, Dave. 2003. 156p. (gr. 8-18). pap. 14.95 *(978-1-932051-11-7(2))* A i T/Planet Lar.

Beatty, Terry, jt. illus. see Barberi, Carlo.

Beatty, Terry, jt. illus. see Martin, Cynthia.

Beatty, Terry, jt. illus. see Purcell, Gordon.

Beaty, Lillian C. Jarod & the Mystery of the Petroglyphs: A National Park Adventure Series Book. Beaty, Janice J. 2015. (J). pap. ***(978-1-63293-071-2(4))*** Sunstone Pr.

Beaucher, Aleksandra. The Adventures of Blue Ocean Bob: Blue Ocean Bob Discovers His Purpose. Olbrys, Brooks. Hamilton, Emma Walton, ed. 2010. (Adventures of Blue Ocean Bob Ser.: Vol. 1). 32p. (J). (gr. -1-5). 16.99 *(978-0-9829613-0-8(8))* Children's Success Unlimited LLC.

Beaudesson, Emmanuel. Our Holy Father, the Pope: The Papacy from Saint Peter to the Present. Caffery, Don R. 2013. (ENG.). 44p. (J). (gr. -1-3). 14.95 *(978-1-58617-921-2(7))* Ignatius Pr.

Beaudette, Michelle. The Boss of Me. Beaudette, Cathy. 2011. 32p. pap. *(978-1-77067-350-2(4))* FriesenPress.

Beaudoin, Beau. Boetry. Beaudoin, Beau. 2007. 40p. (J). per. 15.95 *(978-0-9788401-1-2(9))* Red Ink Pr.

Beaulieu, Jimmy. L' Evasion d'Alfred le Dindon. Langlois, Annie. 2004. (Roman Jeunesse Ser.). (FRE.). 96p. (J). (gr. 4-7). pap. *(978-2-89021-687-7(X))* Diffusion du livre Mirabel (DLM).

Beaulieu, Jimmy. Mia, Matt & the Lazy Gator. Langlois, Annie. Cummins, Sarah, tr. from FRE. 2010. (Formac First Novels Ser.). (ENG.). 64p. (J). (gr. 1-4). 14.95 *(978-0-88780-938-5(3))*; pap. 5.95 *(978-0-88780-936-1(7))* Formac Publishing Co., Ltd. CAN. Dist: Casemate Pubs. & Bk. Distributors, LLC.

—Mia, Matt & the Turkey Chase, 1 vol. Langlois, Annie. Cummins, Sarah, tr. from FRE. 2008. (Formac First Novels Ser.). (ENG.). 64p. (J). (gr. 2-5). 5.95 *(978-0-88780-763-3(1))* Formac Publishing Co., Ltd. CAN. Dist: Casemate Pubs. & Bk. Distributors, LLC.

—Mia, Matt & the Turkey Chase. Langlois, Suzanne. Cummins, Sarah, tr. from FRE. 2008. (Formac First Novels Ser.). (ENG.). 64p. (J). (gr. 2-5). 14.95 *(978-0-88780-765-7(8))* Formac Publishing Co., Ltd. CAN. Dist: Casemate Pubs. & Bk. Distributors, LLC.

Beaumont, Peter. The Three Little Girls & the Giant Sea Turtle. Lowe, Lana. 2006. (J). *(978-0-9777274-0-7(8))* Lone Star Publishing Co.

Beauvais, Gailanna. How Are We Blessed? Beauvais, Gailanna. 2012. 40p. pap. 9.95 *(978-0-9884679-0-3(9))* Visual Velocity.

Beauvisage, Alice. My Blankie. Beauvisage, Alice. 2013. (ENG.). 12p. (J). (gr. -1-k). bds. 6.95 *(978-1-927018-08-8(0))* Simply Read Bks. CAN. Dist: Ingram Pub. Services.

Beauvois, Nathalie. O Little Town of Bethlehem. Traditional. 2014. 16p. (J). bds. 12.99 *(978-0-8249-1933-7(5))*, Candy Cane Pr.) Ideals Pubns.

Beaverho, Archie. The Old Man with the Otter Medicine. Blondin, John. Sundberg, Mary Rose, tr. ed. 2007. (Old Man with the Otter Medicine Ser.). (ENG, DOI & DGR.). 40p. 22.95 *(978-1-894778-49-7(9))* Theytus Bks., Ltd. CAN. Dist: Univ. of Toronto Pr.

Beavers, Ethen. Bad Weather! (DC Super Friends) Berrios, Frank. 2014. (Little Golden Book Ser.). (ENG.). 24p. (J). (-k). 3.99 *(978-0-385-38440-7(8))*, Golden Bks.) Random Hse. Children's Bks.

—Batman Shapes, 1 vol. Bird, Benjamin. 2014. (DC Board Bks.). (ENG.). 20p. (gr. -1 — 1). bds. 12.99 *(978-1-4795-5210-8(0))* Picture Window Bks.

—Batter Up! Scaletta, Kurtis. 2013. (Topps Ser.). (ENG.). 112p. (J). (gr. 2-4). pap. 5.95 *(978-1-4197-0727-8(2))*, Amulet Bks.) Abrams.

—Ben Here Before, Vol. 1. Eisinger, Justin & Simon, Alonzo, eds. 2013. (Ben 10 Classics Ser.). (ENG.). 104p. (J). (gr. 4-7). pap. 17.99 *(978-1-61377-734-3(5))* Idea & Design Works, LLC.

—The Cheerleaders of Doom, Bk. 3. Buckley, Michael. 2011. (Nerds Ser.). (ENG.). 288p. (J). (gr. 3-7). 16.95 *(978-1-4197-0024-8(3))*, Amulet Bks.) Abrams.

—Darkseid's Inferno!, 1 vol. Beechen, Adam. 2013. (Justice League Unlimited Ser.). (ENG.). 32p. (gr. 2-3). 21.27 *(978-1-4342-6043-7(7))* Stone Arch Bks.

—The Joker's Dozen. Sutton, Laurie. 2015. (You Choose Stories: Batman Ser.). (ENG.). 112p. (gr. 2-3). lib. bdg. 31.32 *(978-1-4342-9707-5(1))* Stone Arch Bks.

—M Is for Mama's Boy. Buckley, Michael. 2010. (Nerds Ser.). (ENG.). 288p. (J). (gr. 3-7). 16.95 *(978-0-8109-8986-3(7))*; pap. 6.95 *(978-0-8109-9674-8(X))* Abrams. (Amulet Bks.).

—National Espionage, Rescue, & Defense Society, Bk. 1. Buckley, Michael. 2009. (Nerds Ser.). (ENG.). 336p. (J). (gr. 3-7). 16.95 *(978-0-8109-4324-7(7))*, Amulet Bks.) Abrams.

—Poker Face, 1 vol. Beechen, Adam. 2013. (Justice League Unlimited Ser.). (ENG.). 32p. (gr. 2-3). lib. bdg. 21.27 *(978-1-4342-4714-8(7))* Stone Arch Bks.

—The Riddler's Ransom. Hoena, Blake. 2015. (You Choose Stories: Batman Ser.). (ENG.). 112p. (gr. 2-3). lib. bdg. 31.32 *(978-1-4342-9706-8(3))* Stone Arch Bks.

—Seed Bank Heist. Bright, J. E. 2015. (You Choose Stories: Batman Ser.). (ENG.). 112p. (gr. 2-3). pap. 6.95 *(978-1-4342-9709-9(8))* Stone Arch Bks.

Beavers, Ethen. Star Wars: Attack of the Clones (Star Wars) Golden Books. 2015. (Little Golden Book Ser.). (ENG.). 24p. (J). (-k). 4.99 ***(978-0-7364-3546-8(8)***, Golden Bks.) Random Hse. Children's Bks.

Beavers, Ethen. Summer Freeze! Terrell, Brandon. 2015. (You Choose Stories: Batman Ser.). (ENG.). 112p. (gr. 2-3). lib. bdg. 31.32 *(978-1-4342-9708-2(X))* Stone Arch Bks.

Beavers, Ethen. Super-Villain Smackdown! Sazaklis, John. 2015. (You Choose Stories: Batman Ser.). (ENG.). 112p. (gr. 2-3). lib. bdg. 31.32 ***(978-1-4965-0528-6(X))*** Stone Arch Bks.

Beavers, Ethen. Superman Colors, 1 vol. Bird, Benjamin. 2014. (DC Board Bks.). (ENG.). 20p. (gr. -1 — 1). bds. 5.99 *(978-1-4795-5890-2(7))* Picture Window Bks.

—Superman! (DC Super Friends) Wrecks, Billy. 2013. (Little Golden Book Ser.). (ENG.). 24p. (J). (-k). 3.99 *(978-0-307-93195-5(1))*, Golden Bks.) Random Hse. Children's Bks.

Beavers, Ethen. The Terrible Trio. Sutton, Laurie S. 2015. (You Choose Stories: Batman Ser.). (ENG.). 112p. (gr. 2-3). lib. bdg. 31.32 ***(978-1-4965-0529-3(8))*** Stone Arch Bks.

Beavers, Ethen. Wonder Woman ABCs, 1 vol. Bird, Benjamin. 2014. (DC Board Bks.). (ENG.). 20p. (gr. -1 — 1). bds. 5.99 *(978-1-4795-5889-6(3))* Picture Window Bks.

Beavers, Ethen. You Choose Stories: Batman. Bright, J. E. et al. 2015. (You Choose Stories: Batman Ser.). (ENG.). 112p. (gr. 2-3). 125.28 ***(978-1-4965-0245-2(0)***, DC Super Heroes) Stone Arch Bks.

Beavers, Ethen. You're Out! Scaletta, Kurtis. 2013. (Topps Ser.). (ENG.). 112p. (J). (gr. 2-4). pap. 5.95 *(978-1-4197-0659-2(4))*, Amulet Bks.) Abrams.

Beavers, Ethen & Schigiel, Gregg. Catwoman Counting, 1 vol. Bird, Benjamin. 2014. (DC Board Bks.). (ENG.). 20p. (gr. -1 — 1). bds. 12.99 *(978-1-4795-5209-2(7))* Picture Window Bks.

Beavers, Ethen, jt. illus. see Schoening, Dan.

Beavers, Melinda. I Want to Be a Lion. Troupe, Thomas Kingsley. 2015. (I Want to Be... Ser.). (ENG.). 24p. (gr. k-3). lib. bdg. 25.99 ***(978-1-4795-6860-4(0))*** Capstone Pr., Inc.

Beavers, Melinda. The Zoo's Annual Piggyback Race. Harrigan, Matt. 2013. 32p. (J). pap. 6.99 *(978-0-9873437-0-3(X))* Hedgebury AUS. Dist: New Shelves Distribution.

Bebirian, Helena. Good Night God, Love Olivia. Mammola-Koravos, Beth A. l.t. ed. 2006. 32p. (J). (gr. -1-1). 15.95 *(978-1-59879-110-5(9))* Lifevest Publishing, Inc.

Beccard, Helen L. Saint Catherine of Siena: The Story of the Girl Who Saw Saints in the Sky. Windeatt, Mary F. 2009. (ENG.). 65p. (J). (gr. 3-7). reprint ed. pap. 7.95 *(978-0-89555-421-5(6))* TAN Bks.

Beccia, Carlyn. Scarlatti's Cat. Lachenmeyer, Nathaniel. 2014. (ENG.). 32p. (J). (gr. -1-3). 16.95 *(978-0-7613-5472-7(7))*, Carolrhoda Bks.) Lerner Publishing Group.

Beccia, Carlyn & Marinov, Marin. Louisa May's Battle: How the Civil War Led to Little Women. Krull, Kathleen. 2013. (ENG.). 48p. (J). (gr. 2-4). 16.99 *(978-0-8027-9668-4(0)*, 161442); lib. bdg. 17.89 *(978-0-8027-9669-1(9))* Walker & Co.

Becher, Arthur. A Little Book of Christmas. Bangs, John. 2011. (ENG.). 78p. pap. 8.00 *(978-1-4611-7915-3(7))* CreateSpace Independent Publishing Platform.

Beck, Andrea. Buttercup's Lovely Day, 1 vol. Beck, Carolyn. 2009. (ENG.). 32p. (J). (gr. -1-3). pap. 9.95 *(978-1-55469-122-7(2))* Orca Bk. Pubs. USA.

Beck, Andrea. Elliot's Fire Truck, 1 vol. Beck, Andrea. 2010. (ENG.). 32p. (J). (gr. -1-3). 19.95 *(978-1-55469-143-2(5))* Orca Bk. Pubs. USA.

—Pierre in the Air!, 1 vol. Beck, Andrea. 2011. (Pierre le Poof Ser.: 3). (ENG.). 32p. (J). (gr. -1-3). 19.95 *(978-1-55469-032-9(3))* Orca Bk. Pubs. USA.

—Pierre le Poof!, 1 vol. Beck, Andrea. 2009. (Pierre le Poof Ser.: 1). (ENG.). 32p. (J). (gr. -1-3). 19.95 *(978-1-55469-028-2(5))* Orca Bk. Pubs. USA.

—Pierre's Friends, 1 vol. Beck, Andrea. 2010. (Pierre le Poof Ser.: 2). (ENG.). 32p. (J). (gr. -1-3). 19.95 *(978-1-55469-030-5(7))* Orca Bk. Pubs. USA.

Beck, Blaze. Skinni Mini & Friends in the Valley of Hope. Beck, Ernie. 2012. 74p. pap. 13.99 *(978-0-9858398-5-7(6))* Mindstir Media.

Beck, Charles. Admiral Richard E Byrd. Steinberg, Alfred. 2011. 128p. 40.95 *(978-1-258-01853-5(5))* Literary Licensing, LLC.

Beck, David Michael. Ifanti & the Orb of Prophecy. Bowyer, Clifford B. 2009. (Imperium Saga: 1). (ENG.). 416p. 19.95 *(978-0-9787782-7-9(8))* Silver Leaf Bks., LLC.

—Swords for Hire: Two of the Most Unlikely Heroes You'll Ever Meet. Allen, Will. 2003. 168p. (gr. 3-18). pap. 6.95 *(978-0-9724882-0-4(0))* Centerpunch Pr.

Beck, Ian. The Nutcracker. Doherty, Berlie. 2003. (ENG.). 32p. (J). (gr. 2-4). pap. 9.99 *(978-0-552-54834-2(0))* Transworld Publishers Ltd. GBR. Dist: Independent Pubs. Group.

—Winston the Book Wolf. McGee, Marni. 2006. (ENG.). 32p. (J). (gr. -1-3). 16.95 *(978-0-8027-9569-4(2))* Walker & Co.

Beck, Robert. Soccerland, 0 vols. Choat, Beth. 2012. (International Sports Academy Ser.: 0). (ENG.). 242p. (YA). (gr. 7-9). pap. 8.99 *(978-0-7614-6249-1(X))*, 9780761462491, Amazon Children's Publishing) Amazon Publishing.

Becker, Aaron. Journey. Becker, Aaron. 2013. (ENG.). 40p. (J). (gr. -1-3). 15.99 *(978-0-7636-6053-6(1))* Candlewick Pr.

Becker, Baruch. The Aleph Bias Ship on the Aleph Bias Trip. Altein, Chani. Rosenfeld, D. L. & Leverton, Yossi, eds. 2009. 30p. (J). 10.95 *(978-1-929628-25-4(0))* Hachai Publishing.

—Oif der Aleph Bais Shif. Altein, Chani. Brod, Chani, tr. from ENG. 2014.Tr. of Aleph Bais Trip on the Aleph Bais Ship. 32p. (J). 10.95 *(978-1-929628-77-3(3))* Hachai Publishing.

Becker, Bill. Jose & Mariano Meet Taotaomon'a, l.t. ed. 2004. 112p. (YA). per. 5.00 *(978-0-9761366-0-6(0))* Cebrano Publishing.

Becker, Boruch. Un Toque de Pesaj: A Touch of Passover. Sollish, Ari. 2005.Tr. of Touch of Passover. (SPA.). 12p. (J). bds. 8.00 *(978-0-8266-0022-6(0))* Merkos L'Inyonei Chinuch.

—Touch of Chanukah: A Touch & Feel Book. Rouss, Sylvia. 2011. (J). bds. 9.95 *(978-0-8266-0013-4(1))* Kehot Pubn. Society.

—A Touch of Passover: A Touch & Feel Book. Sollish, Ari. 2006. 12p. (J). bds. 7.95 *(978-0-8266-0021-9(2))* Merkos L'Inyonei Chinuch.

—Touch of Shabbat: A Touch & Feel Book. Krinsky, Rivkah. 2011. (J). bds. 9.95 *(978-0-8266-0019-6(0))* Kehot Pubn. Society.

Becker, Charlotte, jt. illus. see Richardson, Frederick.

Becker, Charlotte, jt. illus. see Winter, Milo.

Becker, Frank. You Can TRIUMPH over TERROR: 7 Steps to Plan, Prepare, & Persevere. Becker, Frank. 2005. per. 24.95 *(978-0-9766720-0-5(6)*, 92868) Greenbush Pr.

Becker, Ken, jt. illus. see Tilley, Scott.

Becker, Lisa E., jt. illus. see Becker, LuAnne E.

Becker, LuAnne E. Thunder on the Reservation. Winderman, Jay B. 2007. 147p. (J). (gr. 3-7). per. 13.95 *(978-0-9761623-2-2(6))* Pill Bug Pr.

Becker, LuAnne E. & Becker, Lisa E. Thunder on the Desert. Winderman, Jay B. 2005. 152p. (J). (gr. 3-7). per. 13.95 *(978-0-9761623-1-5(8))* Pill Bug Pr.

Becker, Pamela. Oil Paints, 1 vol. Bolte, Mari. 2013. (Paint It Ser.). (ENG.). 32p. (gr. 3-4). 27.32 *(978-1-4765-3110-6(2))*, Snap Bks.) Capstone Pr., Inc.

—Pastels, 1 vol. Bolte, Mari. 2013. (Paint It Ser.). (ENG.). 32p. (gr. 3-4). 27.32 *(978-1-4765-3111-3(0))*, Snap Bks.) Capstone Pr., Inc.

Becker, Paula. My Home, Your Home. Bullard, Lisa. 2015. (Cloverleaf Books (tm) — Alike & Different Ser.). (ENG.). 24p. (gr. k-2). pap. 6.99 ***(978-1-4677-6032-4(3)***, Millbrook Pr.) Lerner Publishing Group.

Becker, Rebecca J. Grobar & the Mind Control Potion. Cox, Joseph J. 2005. 168p. (J). per. 9.95 *(978-0-9764659-3-5(0))* Suckerfish Bks.

Becker, Suzy. Bud & Scooter. Becker, Suzy. Date not set. 48p. (J). (gr. k-3). 15.99 *(978-0-06-028970-6(8))*; 16.89 *(978-0-06-028971-3(6))* HarperCollins Pubs.

—Kate the Great Except When She's Not. Becker, Suzy. 2014. (Kate the Great Ser.). (ENG.). 272p. (J). (gr. 3-7). 12.99 *(978-0-385-38742-2(3))*, Crown Books For Young Readers) Random Hse. Children's Bks.

—Kate the Great, Except When She's Not. Becker, Suzy. 2014. (Kate the Great Ser.). (ENG.). 272p. (J). (gr. 3-7). lib. bdg. 15.99 *(978-0-385-38743-9(1))*, Crown Books For Young Readers) Random Hse. Children's Bks.

Becker, Toni. Sonny - the Spectacular. Keaster, Diane W. l.t. ed. 2006. (ZC Horses: Vol. 9). (ENG.). 80p. (J). per. 7.95 *(978-0-9721496-9-3(4))* ZC Horses Series of Children's Bks.

Becker, Wayne. Laugh Out Loud Jokes. Namm, Diane. 2004. (Laugh-A-Long Readers Ser.). (J). *(978-0-7607-5281-4(8))* Barnes & Noble, Inc.

—My House. Jensen, Patricia. 2003. (My First Reader Ser.). (ENG.). 32p. (J). 18.50 *(978-0-516-22934-8(6))*, Children's Pr.) Scholastic Library Publishing.

—Slithery Squirmy Jokes. Namm, Diane. 2004. (Laugh-A-Long Readers Ser.). (J). *(978-0-7607-5282-1(6))* Barnes & Noble, Inc.

—Who Says? Flaxman, Jessica & Hall, Kirsten. 2003. (My First Reader Ser.). (ENG.). 32p. (J). 18.50 *(978-0-516-22958-4(3))*, Children's Pr.) Scholastic Library Publishing.

Beckerman, Chad. Frannie in Pieces. Ephron, Delia. 2007. (YA). (gr. 7-12). 384p. 16.99 *(978-0-06-074716-9(1))*; 374p. lib. bdg. 17.89 *(978-0-06-074717-6(X))* HarperCollins Pubs. (HarperTeen).

Beckes, Shirley. Abigail's Ballet Class. James, Annabelle. 2004. 10p. (J). (gr. -1-k). 12.49 *(978-1-883043-54-4(9))* Straight Edge Pr., The.

—Abigail's Bedtime. James, Annabelle. 2004. (J). bds. 12.99 *(978-1-883043-53-7(0)*, 6022) Straight Edge Pr., The.

—The Day I Followed the Pickle. Pugliano-Martin, Carol. ed. 2004. (Reader's Theater Ser.). (J). pap. *(978-1-4108-2297-0(4)*, A22974) Benchmark Education Co.

—The Frog Prince: Imagination in a Box. Brandon, Wendy. 2004. 10p. (J). bds. 17.99 *(978-1-883043-49-0(2))* Straight Edge Pr., The.

—Halloween Math. Crawley, Brian. ed. 2004. (Reader's Theater Ser.). (J). pap. *(978-1-4108-2300-7(8)*, A23008) Benchmark Education Co.

Beckes, Shirley V. The Frog Prince: Board Book & Puppet Theater. Brandon, Wendy. 2004. (J). *(978-1-883043-46-9(8))* Straight Edge Pr., The.

Becket, Nancy. No Ordinary Cat. Sermons, Faye. 2009. 40p. pap. 16.99 *(978-1-4389-6242-9(8))* AuthorHouse.

Beckett, Andrew & Aubrey, Meg Kelleher. Searching for Sunshine. Baglio, Ben M. 2005. 158p. (J). *(978-0-439-79249-3(5))* Scholastic, Inc.

Beckett, Garner. The Cats of Grand Central. Archibald, Laura. 2004. 30p. 16.95 *(978-0-9730951-0-4(5))* Solomon's Signature CAN. Dist: Hushion Hse. Publishing, Ltd.

Beckett, Sheilah. The Nutcracker. Balducci, Rita. 2014. (Little Golden Book Ser.). (ENG.). 24p. (J). (-k). 4.99 *(978-0-385-36993-0(X))*, Golden Bks.) Random Hse. Children's Bks.

—The Twelve Days of Christmas: A Christmas Carol. Golden Books Staff. 2015. (Little Golden Book Ser.). (ENG.). 24p. (J). (gr. k-k). 4.99 *(978-0-307-00149-8(0))*, Golden Bks.) Random Hse. Children's Bks.

Beckman, Jeff & Aguirre, Diego. Amos the Elf & His Magical Pajamas. Joyce, Kelley A. 2012. 38p. pap. 9.95 *(978-0-9881822-0-2(3))* Elf Garb.

Beckstead, Lene. Color Me Baptized. 2009. 32p. pap. 6.95 *(978-0-88494-335-8(6))* Deseret Bk. Co.

Beckstrand, Jared. Baby Gets a Cake. Harris, Brooke. 2009. (Reader's Theater Nursery Rhymes & Songs Set B Ser.). 48p. (J). pap. *(978-1-60859-150-3(6))* Benchmark Education Co.

—A Fly on the Wall Street. Nelson, Sandi. 2013. (J). 19.99 *(978-1-938690-29-7(X)*, Two Harbors Press) Hillcrest Publishing Group, Inc.

Beckstrand, Karl. Crumbs on the Stairs; Migas en las Escaleras: A Mystery (in English & Spanish) Beckstrand, Karl. 2007.Tr. of Migas en las Escaleras. (ENG & SPA.). 24p. 11.00 *(978-0-9776065-0-4(3))* Premio Publishing & Gozo Bks., LLC.

Becton, Daniel Walker. Wormy Worm. Becton, Daniel Walker. Becton, Sarah Walker & Becton, Franklyn Hall. 2007. 88p. (J). 19.95 *(978-1-878398-59-8(8))*, Blue Note Bks.) Blue Note Pubns.

Bedard, Kathy. Little Lake Saga. Miller, Nelson. unabr. ed. (ENG.). 32p. (J). *(978-0-920576-58-8(3))* Caitlin Pr., Inc.

Beddows, Eric. Joyful Noise: Poems for Two Voices. Fleischman, Paul. rev. ed. 2005. (Charlotte Zolotow Bk.). (ENG.). 64p. (J). (gr. 3-7). pap. 5.99 *(978-0-06-446093-4(2))* HarperCollins Pubs.

—Night Cars, 1 vol. Jam, Teddy. 2006. (ENG.). 32p. (J). (gr k — 1). bds. 11.95 *(978-0-88899-748-7(5))* Groundwood Bks. CAN. Dist: Perseus-PGW.

—Toes. Seidler, Tor. 176p. (J). (gr. 3-18). 2004. (ENG.). 15.99 *(978-0-06-054099-9(0))*, Geringer, Laura Book); 2004. lib. bdg. 16.89 *(978-0-06-054100-2(8))*, Geringer, Laura Book); 2006. (ENG.). reprint ed. pap. 5.99 *(978-0-06-054101-9(6))* HarperCollins Pubs.

—Zoom, 1 vol. Wynne-Jones, Tim. 2009. (ENG.). 96p. (J). (gr. -1-2). 25.00 *(978-0-88899-936-8(4))* Groundwood Bks. CAN. Dist: Perseus-PGW.

—Zoom at Sea, 1 vol. Wynne-Jones, Tim. 2013. (ENG.). 32p. (J). (gr. -1-2). 14.95 *(978-1-55498-391-9(6))* Groundwood Bks. CAN. Dist: Perseus-PGW.

Bedell, Barbara. The Life Cycle of a Raccoon. Kalman, Bobbie & Crossingham, John. 2003. (Life Cycle Ser.). (ENG.). 32p. (J). (gr. 3-4). lib. bdg. *(978-0-7787-0661-8(3))* Crabtree Publishing Co.

—Refugee Child: My Memories of the 1956 Hungarian Revolution. Kalman, Bobbie. 2006. (ENG.). 224p. (J). (gr. 3-7). lib. bdg. *(978-0-7787-2760-6(2))* Crabtree Publishing Co.

Bedford, F. D. Peter Pan. Barrie, J. M. 2007. (Barnes & Noble Classics Ser.). (ENG.). 208p. 7.95 *(978-1-59308-382-3(3))* Barnes & Noble, Inc.

—Peter Pan. Barrie, J. M. 2004. (Modern Library Classics Ser.). (ENG.). 192p. (J). pap. 8.95 *(978-0-8129-7297-9(X))*, Modern Library) Random House Publishing Group.

—Peter Pan. Barrie, J. M. 2005. (Barnes & Noble Classics Ser.). (ENG.). 208p. per. 7.95 *(978-1-59308-213-0(4))* Barnes & Noble, Inc.

Bedford, F. D., jt. illus. see Rackham, Arthur.

Bedford, Francis Donkin & Rackham, Arthur. Peter Pan. Barrie, J. M. & Lindner, Brooke. 2015. (Word Cloud Classics Ser.). (ENG.). 272p. pap. 14.95 *(978-1-62686-392-7(X))*, Thunder Bay Pr.) Baker & Taylor Publishing Group.

Bedrick, Jeff. Madison Meets the Minister. Emm, David. 2010. (ENG.). 48p. (J). 12.95 *(978-1-889658-42-1(1))* New Canaan Publishing Co. LLC.

Bee, William. And the Cars Go... Bee, William. 2013. (ENG.). 32p. (J). (-k). 15.99 *(978-0-7636-6580-7(0))* Candlewick Pr.

—Migloo's Day. Bee, William. 2015. (ENG.). (J). (gr. -1-2). 14.99 *(978-0-7636-7374-1(9))* Candlewick Pr.

—Stanley the Farmer, 1 vol. Bee, William. 2015. (Stanley Ser.). (ENG.). 32p. (J). (gr. 1-2). 14.95 *(978-1-56145-803-5(1))* Peachtree Pubs.

Beebe, Robb. Judy: A Story of Divine Corners. Baldwin, Faith. 2011. 264p. 47.95 *(978-1-258-08877-4(0))* Literary Licensing, LLC.

—Tailspin Tommy: The Mystery of the Midnight Patrol. Stevens, Mark. 2011. 226p. 44.95 *(978-1-258-10164-0(5))* Literary Licensing, LLC.

Beebe, Susan. The Get Well Soon... Balloon. Parker, Vicki Sue. 2005. 16p. (J). 15.00 *(978-1-931117-35-7(7)*, BALL) Lash & Assocs. Publishing/Training, Inc.

Beebee, Dorothy. A Winter Walk. McCarroll, Tolbert. 2006. (ENG.). 160p. 14.95 *(978-0-8245-2416-6(0))* Crossroad Publishing Co., The.

Beech, Mark. Al Iltizam Bil Qawaed. Mayer, Cassie & Resl, Brigitte. Mahmoud, Ghada Mohamed, tr. 2012. (ENG & ARA.). 24p. (J). pap. 6.99 *(978-99921-94-24-9(3)*, 148136) Bloomsbury USA.

Beech, Mark. Country Money. Whitehead, William et al. 2015. (How Money Works). (ENG.). 64p. (J). (gr. 4-6). lib. bdg. 29.27 ***(978-1-59953-719-1(2))*** Norwood Hse. Pr.

Beech, Mark. Dragons at Crumbling Castle: And Other Tales. Pratchett, Terry. 2015. (ENG.). 352p. (J). (gr. 4-7). 16.99 *(978-0-544-46659-3(4))* Houghton Mifflin Harcourt Publishing Co.

Beech, Mark. Family Money. Whitehead, William. 2015. (How Money Works). (ENG.). 64p. (J). (gr. 4-6). lib. bdg. 29.27 ***(978-1-59953-717-7(6))*** Norwood Hse. Pr.

Beech, Mark. A Funeral in the Bathroom: And Other School Bathroom Poems. Dakos, Kalli. 2011. (ENG.). 48p. (J). (gr. 1-4). 14.99 *(978-0-8075-2675-0(4))* Whitman, Albert & Co.

—An Takouna Adelan. Mayer, Cassie & Resl, Brigitte. Mahmoud, Ghada Mohamed, tr. 2012.Tr. of Being Fair. (ARA & ENG.). 24p. (J). pap. 6.99 *(978-99921-94-20-1(0)*, 148146) Bloomsbury USA.

—An Takouna Masoulan. Mayer, Cassie & Resl, Brigitte. Mahmoud, Ghada Mohamed, tr. 2012.Tr. of Being Responsible. (ARA.). 24p. (J). pap. 6.99 *(978-99921-94-23-2(5)*, 148135) Bloomsbury USA.

—An Takouna Sadeqan. Mayer, Cassie & Resl, Brigitte. Mahmoud, Ghada Mohamed, tr. 2012.Tr. of Being Honest. (ARA.). 24p. (J). pap. 6.99 *(978-99921-94-22-5(7)*, 148134) Bloomsbury USA.

—Takween Sadaqat. Mayer, Cassie & Resl, Brigitte. Mahmoud, Ghada Mohamed, tr. 2012. (ENG & ARA.). 24p. (J). pap. 6.99 *(978-99921-94-25-6(1)*, 148137) Bloomsbury USA.

—An Tosaed. Mayer, Cassie & Resl, Brigitte. Mahmoud, Ghada Mohamed, tr. 2012. (ENG.). 24p. (J). pap. 6.99 *(978-99921-94-21-8(9)*, 148133) Bloomsbury USA.

—Weekend Mischief. Jackson, Robert Bradley. 2010. (ENG.). 32p. (J). (gr. 2-4). 17.95 *(978-1-59078-494-5(4))*, Wordsong) Boyds Mills Pr.

Beech, Mark. World Money. Bailey, Gerry & Law, Felicia. 2015. (How Money Works). (ENG.). 64p. (J). (gr. 4-6). lib. bdg. 29.27 ***(978-1-59953-720-7(6))*** Norwood Hse. Pr.

—Your Money. Bailey, Gerry & Law, Felicia. 2015. (How Money Works). (ENG.). 64p. (J). (gr. 4-6). lib. bdg. 29.27 ***(978-1-59953-718-4(4))*** Norwood Hse. Pr.

Beeke, Tiphanie. Changes: A Child's First Poetry Collection. Zolotow, Charlotte. 2015. (ENG.). 40p. (J). (-2). 16.99 ***(978-1-4926-0168-5(3)***, Sourcebooks Jabberwocky) Sourcebooks, Inc.

Beeke, Tiphanie. Fletcher & the Falling Leaves. Rawlinson, Julia. 2008. (ENG.). 32p. (J). (gr. -1-2). pap. 6.99 *(978-0-06-157397-2(3))*, Greenwillow Bks.) HarperCollins Pubs.

—Fletcher & the Falling Leaves. Rawlinson, Julia & Rawlinson. 2006. (ENG.). 32p. (J). (gr. -1-2). 16.99 *(978-0-06-113401-2(5))*, Greenwillow Bks.) HarperCollins Pubs.

—Fletcher & the Snowflake Christmas. Rawlinson, Julia. 2010. (ENG.). 32p. (J). (gr. -1-2). 16.99 *(978-0-06-199033-5(7))*, Greenwillow Bks.) HarperCollins Pubs.

—Fletcher & the Springtime Blossoms. Rawlinson, Julia. 2009. (ENG.). 32p. (J). (gr. -1-2). 17.99 *(978-0-06-168855-3(X))*, Greenwillow Bks.) HarperCollins Pubs.

B

—Latke, the Lucky Dog. Fischer, Ellen. 2014. 24p. (J). (gr. -1-2). 17.95 *(978-0-7613-9038-1(3)*, Kar-Ben Publishing) Lerner Publishing Group.
—Some Bunny to Talk To: A Story for Children about Going to Therapy. Conte, Paola et al. 2014. (J). *(978-1-4338-1649-9(0))*; pap. *(978-1-4338-1650-5(4))* American Psychological Assn. (Magination Pr.).
—The Stars Will Still Shine. Rylant, Cynthia. 2005. 40p. (J). lib. bdg. 17.89 *(978-0-06-054640-3(9))*; (ENG.). (gr. -1-3). 17.99 *(978-0-06-054639-7(5))* HarperCollins Pubs.
—That's How Much I Love You. Rudi, Julie A. 2013. (ENG.). 18p. (gr. -1). bds. 8.95 *(978-1-58925-644-6(1))* Tiger Tales.
Beeke, Tiphanie. The Noisy Way to Bed. Beeke, Tiphanie, tr. Whybrow, Ian. 2004. (J). *(978-0-439-55690-3(2)*, Levine, Arthur A. Bks.) Scholastic, Inc.
Beeler, Joe. The Secret of Fort Pioneer: A Bret King Mystery. Scott, Dan. 2011. 190p. 42.95 *(978-1-258-09951-0(9))* Literary Licensing, LLC.
Beene, Jason. Fish Finelli: Seagulls Don't Eat Pickles. Farber, Erica. 2013. (Fish Finelli Ser.). (ENG.). 155p. (J). (gr. 2-5). 15.99 *(978-1-4521-0820-9(X))* Chronicle Bks. LLC.
—Fish Finelli (Book 1) Seagulls Don't Eat Pickles. Farber, E. S. 2014. (Fish Finelli Ser.). (ENG.). 168p. (J). (gr. 3-7). pap. 6.99 *(978-1-4521-2853-5(7))* Chronicle Bks. LLC.
—Fish Finelli (Book 2) Operation Fireball. Farber, E. S. 2015. (Fish Finelli Ser.). (ENG.). 184p. (J). (gr. 3-7). pap. 6.99 *(978-1-4521-2875-7(8))* Chronicle Bks. LLC.
—Operation Fireball. Farber, E. S. 2014. (Fish Finelli Ser.). (ENG.). 172p. (J). (gr. 3-7). 15.99 *(978-1-4521-1083-7(2))* Chronicle Bks. LLC.
—Sophie Simon Solves Them All. Graff, Lisa. 2010. (ENG.). 112p. (J). (gr. 3-5). 14.99 *(978-0-374-37125-8(3)*, Farrar, Straus & Giroux (BYR)) Farrar, Straus & Giroux.
—Sophie Simon Solves Them All. Graff, Lisa. 2012. (ENG.). 112p. (J). (gr. 3-5). pap. 5.99 *(978-1-250-02898-3(1))* Square Fish.
—The Wednesdays. Bourbeau, Julie. (ENG.). 256p. (J). (gr. 2-5). 2013. pap. 7.99 *(978-0-375-87286-0(8))*; 2012. 16.99 *(978-0-375-86890-0(9))*; 2012. 19.99 *(978-0-375-96890-7(3))* Knopf, Alfred A. Inc.
Beer, Henry, photos by. Girl Defective. 2015. (ENG., 320p. (YA). (gr. 9). pap. 10.99 *(978-1-4424-9761-0(0))* Simon & Schuster Children's Publishing.
Beers, Robert Lee. The Batty Bat. Freeman, David. 2012. 24p. pap. 24.95 *(978-1-4241-0177-1(8))* PublishAmerica, Inc.
—Hidden Treasure. Miller, Judith J. 2013. 24p. pap. 10.95 *(978-1-61633-419-2(3))* Guardian Angel Publishing, Inc.
—The Scarecrow. Freeman, David. 2012. 24p. 24.95 *(978-1-4626-9609-3(0))*; 20p. pap. 24.95 *(978-1-4137-9543-1(9))* PublishAmerica, Inc.
—The Whispery Witch. Freeman, David. 2012. 24p. pap. 24.95 *(978-1-4137-9620-9(6))* PublishAmerica, Inc.
Beeson, Jan. Mako in My Backyard. Paul & Lady Jan. 2013. 34p. pap. 12.99 *(978-0-9890482-3-1(3))* Beeson, Jan.
—Wesley the Wobbly Bear. Paul & Lady Jan. 2013. 38p. pap. 12.99 *(978-0-9890482-4-8(1))* Beeson, Jan.
—Zeela the Zebra of a Different Color. Beeson, Paul & Beeson, Lady Jan. 2013. 38p. pap. 12.99 *(978-0-9890482-5-5(X))* Beeson, Jan.
Beeuwsaert, Matt. I Got Game. Beeuwsaert, Matt. 2003. 176p. per. 14.95 *(978-0-9724358-0-2(8))* Beex Art Bks.
BEFEC Mulguin and Associates Staff. Tres Cabezas y un Volcan. Hernandez, Alejandro. rev. ed. 2006. (Castillo de la Lectura Blanca Ser.). (SPA & ENG.). 56p. (J). (gr. k). pap. 6.95 *(978-968-5920-88-9(5))* Castillo, Ediciones, S. A. de C. V. MEX. Dist: Macmillan.
Beg, Sadiqi, jt. illus. see Sadiq bai Afshar.
Begay, Patrick. What Does 'died' Mean? Haíshą́ óolyé Daaztsą́ą? Thomas, Marjorie & Ruffenach, Jessie. 2005. (ENG & NAV.). 32p. (J). (gr. 4-7). pap. 9.00 *(978-1-893354-56-2(3))* Salina Bookshelf Inc.
Begin, Jean-Guy. Chapeau, Camomille! Richard, Martine. 2004. (Des 6 Ans Ser.). (FRE.). 64p. 7.95 *(978-2-922565-96-6(3))* Editions de la Paix CAN. Dist: World of Reading, Ltd.
—Des Legumes Pour Frank Einstein. Lavoie, Rejean. 2004. (Des 9 Ans. Ser.: Vol. 44). (FRE.). 120p. (J). 8.95 *(978-2-89599-006-2(9))* Editions de la Paix CAN. Dist: World of Reading, Ltd.
—Disparition Chez les Lutins. Mallet, C. Claire. 2003. (Collection des 6 Ans: Vol. 21). (FRE.). 64p. (J). 7.95 *(978-2-922565-64-5(5))* Editions de la Paix CAN. Dist: World of Reading, Ltd.
—La Fee Dentiste. Deslauriers, Anne. 2004. (Collection des 6 Ans). (FRE.). 64p. (J). 7.95 *(978-2-922565-99-7(8))* Editions de la Paix CAN. Dist: World of Reading, Ltd.
—OGM et Chant de Mais. Cotes, Gilles. 2004. (FRE.). 112p. (J). *(978-2-89599-002-4(6))* Editions de la Paix CAN. Dist: World of Reading, Ltd.
Begin, Mary Jane. R Is for Rhode Island Red: A Rhode Island Alphabet. Allio, Mark R. 2005. (Discover America State by State Ser.). (ENG.). 40p. (J). (gr. k-5). 17.95 *(978-1-58536-149-6(6))* Sleeping Bear Pr.
Begonia, Ruby. Don't Be a Chicken. Binks. 2013. 32p. 15.95 *(978-1-935448-22-8(6))* Lost Coast Pr.
—The Girl with Chipmunk Hands. Binks. 2013. 24p. (J). 15.95 *(978-1-935448-20-4(X))* Lost Coast Pr.
Beha, Philippe. The Best Time. Poulin, Andree. 2009. (My First Stories Ser.). 24p. (J). (gr. -1-3). 22.60 *(978-1-60754-350-3(8))*; pap. 8.15 *(978-1-60754-351-0(6))* Windmill Bks.
Béha, Philippe. Fairy Tale Breakfasts: A Cookbook for Young Readers & Eaters. Yolen, Jane. 2009. (Fairy Tale Cookbooks Ser.). 32p. (J). (gr. 2-5). 22.60 *(978-1-60754-573-6(X))*; pap. 10.55 *(978-1-60754-574-3(8))* Windmill Bks.
—Fairy Tale Desserts: A Cookbook for Young Readers & Eaters. Yolen, Jane. 2009. (Fairy Tale Cookbooks Ser.). 32p. (J). (gr. 2-5). 22.60 *(978-1-60754-583-5(7))*; pap. 10.55 *(978-1-60754-584-2(5))* Windmill Bks.
—Fairy Tale Dinners: A Cookbook for Young Readers & Eaters. Yolen, Jane. 2009. (Fairy Tale Cookbooks Ser.). 32p. (J). (gr. 2-5). 22.60 *(978-1-60754-580-4(2))*; pap. 10.55 *(978-1-60754-582-8(9))* Windmill Bks.
Beha, Philippe. Fairy Tale Feasts: A Literary Cookbook for Young Readers & Eaters. Yolen, Jane & Stemple, Heidi E. Y. (ENG.). 264p. (J). 2009. (gr. -1-3). pap. 20.00 *(978-1-56656-751-0(3)*, Crocodile Bks.); 2006. (gr. 4-7). 24.95 *(978-1-56656-643-8(6))* Interlink Publishing Group, Inc.
Béha, Philippe. Fairy Tale Lunches: A Cookbook for Young Readers & Eaters. Yolen, Jane. 2009. (Fairy Tale Cookbooks Ser.). 32p. (J). (gr. 2-5). 22.60 *(978-1-60754-576-7(4))*; pap. 10.55 *(978-1-60754-577-4(2))* Windmill Bks.
Beha, Philippe. The King Has Goat Ears, 1 vol. Jovanovic, Katarina. 2008. (ENG.). 32p. (J). (gr. k-2). 16.95 *(978-1-896580-22-7(X))* Tradewind Bks. CAN. Dist: Orca Bk. Pubs. USA.
Béha, Philippe. The Prairie Dogs, 1 vol. Goertzen, Glenda. 2004. (ENG.). 164p. pap. *(978-1-55005-113-1(X))* Fitzhenry & Whiteside, Ltd.
Beha, Philippe. The Undesirables. Brière, Paule. 2009. (ENG.). 32p. (J). (gr. -1-3). 16.95 *(978-1-894965-88-0(4))* Simply Read Bks. CAN. Dist: Ingram Pub. Services.
—The Worst Time. Poulin, Andrée. 2009. (My First Stories Ser.). 24p. (J). (gr. -1-3). 22.60 *(978-1-60754-367-1(2))*; pap. 8.15 *(978-1-60754-368-8(0))* Windmill Bks.
Beha, Philippe. City Kids: Street & Skyscraper Rhymes, 1 vol. Kennedy, X. J. 2010. (ENG.). 96p. (J). (gr. 4-7). 17.95 *(978-1-896580-44-9(0))* Tradewind Bks. CAN. Dist: Orca Bk. Pubs. USA.
Behan, Rachel A. Finding Jesus: Contemporary Children's Story. Sellers, Amy C., ed. l.t. ed. 2006. 19p. (J). 24.95 *(978-1-934194-00-3(X))* Olmstead Publishing LLC.
Behl, Anne-Kathrin. Help, I Don't Want a Babysitter! Wagner, Anke. 2015. (ENG.). 32p. (J). 17.95 *(978-0-7358-4214-4(0))* North-South Bks., Inc.
Behles, Liza. Donald Dent. Lydon, Jeff. 2003. 34p. (J). per. 10.00 *(978-0-9724922-0-1(8))* Authors & Artists Publishers of New York, Inc.
—The Smartest Kid I Ever Met. Happel, Kathleen. 2005. 57p. (J). per. 12.50 *(978-0-9763993-3-9(4))*, Ithaca Pr.) Authors & Artists Publishers of New York, Inc.
Behr, Joyce. Funny Skits & Sketches. Halligan, Terry. unabr. ed. 2003. 128p. (YA). (gr. 4-12). pap. 15.00 *(978-0-88734-688-0(X))* Players Pr., Inc.
—Humorous Monologues. Bolton, Martha. 2003. 128p. (J). (gr. 2-7). 19.00 *(978-0-8069-6750-9(1))* Sterling Publishing Co., Inc.
Beier, Ellen. Albert Einstein, Creative Genius. Mattern, Joanne & Santrey, Laurence. 2005. 45p. (J). pap. *(978-0-439-80152-2(4))* Scholastic, Inc.
—Anne of Green Gables. Helldorfer, M. C. 2003. (ENG.). 40p. (J). (gr. -1-2). pap. 7.99 *(978-0-440-41614-2(0)*, Dragonfly Bks.) Random Hse. Children's Bks.
Beier, Ellen. Brave Norman. Clements, Andrew. 2015. 32p. pap. 4.00 ***(978-1-61003-600-9(X))*** Center for the Collaborative Classroom.
Beier, Ellen. Centerfield Ballhawk. Christopher, Matt. 2009. 64p. (J). lib. bdg. 22.60 *(978-1-59953-317-9(0))* Norwood Hse. Pr.
—The Christmas Coat: Memories of My Sioux Childhood. Sneve, Virginia Driving Hawk. 2011. (ENG.). 32p. (J). 16.95 *(978-0-8234-2134-3(1))* Holiday Hse., Inc.
—Dolores & the Big Fire: A True Story. Clements, Andrew. 2003. (Pets to the Rescue Ser.). (ENG.). 32p. (J). (gr. -1-1). pap. 3.99 *(978-0-689-83440-0(3)*, Simon Spotlight) Simon Spotlight.
—Un Genio Creativo. Santrey, Laurence & Mattern, Joanne. 2007.Tr. of Albert Einstein. (SPA & ENG.). 48p. (J). (gr. k-2). pap. 4.99 *(978-0-439-87479-3(3)*, Scholastic en Espanol) Scholastic, Inc.
—Man Out at First. Christopher, Matt. 2009. 64p. (J). lib. bdg. 22.60 *(978-1-59953-319-3(7))* Norwood Hse. Pr.
—Mrs. Peachtree & the Eighth Avenue Cat. Silverman, Erica. 2011. (ENG.). 32p. (J). (gr. -1-3). pap. 16.99 *(978-1-4424-4340-2(5)*, Simon & Schuster Bks. For Young Readers) Simon & Schuster Bks. For Young Readers.
—Tara & Tiree, Fearless Friends: A True Story. Clements, Andrew. 2003. (Pets to the Rescue Ser.). (ENG.). 32p. (J). (gr. -1-2). pap. 3.99 *(978-0-689-83441-7(1)*, Simon Spotlight) Simon Spotlight.
Beier, Ellen & Cowdrey, Richard. Strike Three, Marley! Grogan, John & Hill, Susan. 2010. (I Can Read Book 2 Ser.). (ENG.). 32p. (J). (gr. k-3). 16.99 *(978-0-06-185387-6(9))* HarperCollins Pubs.
Beier, Ellen, jt. illus. see Cowdrey, Richard.
Beifus, Ruth. Round & Round the Jewish Year Vol. 1: Elul-Tishrei. Rosenberg, Tziporah. 2009. 67p. (J). (gr. 3-6). 19.99 *(978-1-59826-376-3(5))* Feldheim Pubs.
—Round & Round the Jewish Year Vol. 2: Cheshvan-Shevat. Rosenberg, Tziporah. Gross, Sherie, tr. 2008. 68p. (J). (gr. 3-6). 19.99 *(978-1-59826-281-0(5))* Feldheim Pubs.
Beighley, Marci. Strawberry Shortcake's Costume Party. 2010. (Strawberry Shortcake Ser.). (ENG.). 16p. (J). (gr. -1-k). 5.99 *(978-0-448-45380-4(0)*, Grosset & Dunlap) Penguin Publishing Group.
—We Love You, Strawberry Shortcake! Hartmann, Sierra. 2009. (Strawberry Shortcake Ser.). (ENG.). 32p. (J). (gr. 1-2). pap. 3.99 *(978-0-448-45252-4(9)*, Warne, Frederick Pubs.) Penguin Bks., Ltd. GBR. Dist: Penguin Publishing Group.
Beingessner, Laura. Our Corner Grocery Store. Schwartz, Joanne. 2009. (ENG.). 32p. (J). (gr. -1-2). 19.95 *(978-0-88776-868-2(7)*, Tundra Bks.) Tundra Bks. CAN. Dist: Penguin Random Hse., LLC.
—Rachel Carson & Her Book That Changed the World. Lawlor, Laurie. (ENG.). 32p. (J). 2014. (gr. 1-5). 7.99 *(978-0-8234-3193-9(2))*; 2012. 17.95 *(978-0-8234-2370-5(0))* Holiday Hse., Inc.
—Sail Away with Me. Collins-Philippe, Jane. 2010. (ENG.). 32p. (J). (gr. -1-2). 15.95 *(978-0-88776-842-2(3)*, Tundra Bks.) Tundra Bks. CAN. Dist: Penguin Random Hse., LLC.
Beisch, Leigh, photos by. Ice Cream Treats: Easy Ways to Transform Your Favorite Ice Cream into Spectacular Desserts. Ferreira, Charity. 2004. (ENG., 96p. (gr. 8-17). 16.95 *(978-0-8118-4102-3(2))* Chronicle Bks. LLC.
—Infused: 100+ Recipes for Infused Liqueurs & Cocktails. MacNeal, Susan Ella. 2006. (ENG., 152p. (gr. 8-17). 19.95 *(978-0-8118-4600-4(8))* Chronicle Bks. LLC.
Beith, Laura Huliska. Five Little Ladybugs with Hand Puppet. Gerth, Melanie. 2009. (ENG.). 12p. 12.95 *(978-1-58117-889-0(1)*, Intervisual/Piggy Toes) Bendon, Inc.
Beitz-Grant, Heather. The Magic Tree House, 1 vol. Shoesmith-Bateman, Amanda. 2010. 22p. 24.95 *(978-1-4489-3866-7(X))* PublishAmerica, Inc.
Belanger, Damon. Costi & the Raindrop Adventure. Khamis, Johnny. 2007. 32p. (J). (gr. -1-3). 6.95 *(978-1-60005-029-9(8))* Happy About.
Belcher, Andy & Belcher, Angie, photos by. Rally Challenge: Band 10/White. Belcher, Andy & Belcher, Angie. 2005. (Collins Big Cat Ser.). (ENG., 32p. (J). pap. 7.99 *(978-0-00-718632-7(0))* HarperCollins Pubs. Ltd. GBR. Dist: Independent Pubs. Group.
Belcher, Angie. Oceans Alive: Band 14. Belcher, Angie. Belcher, Andy. 2007. (Collins Big Cat Ser.). (ENG.). 48p. (J). pap. 8.99 *(978-0-00-723092-1(3))* HarperCollins Pubs. Ltd. GBR. Dist: Independent Pubs. Group.
Belcher, Angie, jt. photos by see Belcher, Andy.
Belisle, John. In God's Kitchen. Kavanagh, James. 2004. (ENG.). 32p. (J). 15.95 *(978-1-58355-241-4(3))* Waterford Pr., Inc.
Belkholm, Erica. The Case of the Florida Freeze. Jacobson, Ryan. l.t. ed. 2005. 80p. (J). per. 4.99 *(978-0-9774122-0-4(2))* Lake 7 Creative, LLC.
Belknap, Barbara. An Anasazi Welcome. Matthews, Kay. 2004. 40p. (gr. 4-7). pap. 6.95 *(978-1-878610-27-0(9))* Red Crane Bks., Inc.
Bell, Bill. The Night Before Christmas. Moore, Clement C. 2011. (ENG.). 32p. (J). (gr. k-2). 6.95 *(978-1-61608-470-7(7)*, 608470, Sky Pony Pr.) Skyhorse Publishing Co., Inc.
—The Selfish Giant. Wilde, Oscar & Hollingsworth, Mary. 2013. (ENG.). 40p. (J). (gr. -1-1). 14.95 *(978-1-62087-540-7(3)*, 620540, Sky Pony Pr.) Skyhorse Publishing Co., Inc.
Bell, Bill. Noah: The Incredible Voyager. Bell, Bill. 2004. 48p. (J). (gr. -1-3). per. 14.99 *(978-0-88092-801-4(8))* Royal Fireworks Publishing Co.
Bell, Cece. Bug Patrol. Mortensen, Denise Dowling. 2013. (ENG.). 32p. (J). (gr. -1-3). 16.99 *(978-0-618-79024-1(1))* Houghton Mifflin Harcourt Publishing Co.
—Crankee Doodle. Angleberger, Tom. 2013. (ENG.). 32p. (J). (gr. -1-3). 16.99 *(978-0-547-81854-2(8))* Houghton Mifflin Harcourt Publishing Co.
—The Secret of the Fortune Wookiee. Angleberger, Tom. 2012. (Origami Yoda Ser.: No. 3). (ENG.). 208p. (J). (gr. 3-7). 13.95 *(978-1-4197-0392-8(7)*, Amulet Bks.) Abrams.
Bell, Cece. Itty Bitty. Bell, Cece. 2009. (ENG.). 32p. (J). (gr. -1-2). 9.99 *(978-0-7636-3616-6(9))* Candlewick Pr.
—Rabbit & Robot: The Sleepover. Bell, Cece. 2012. (ENG.). 56p. (J). (gr. k-4). 14.99 *(978-0-7636-5475-7(2))* Candlewick Pr.
—Sock Monkey Boogie-Woogie. Bell, Cece. 2015. (ENG.). 32p. (J). (gr. -1-3). 14.00 *(978-0-7636-7758-9(2))* Candlewick Pr.
—Sock Monkey Rides Again. Bell, Cece. 2015. (ENG.). 32p. (J). (gr. -1-3). 14.00 *(978-0-7636-7760-2(4))* Candlewick Pr.
—Sock Monkey Takes a Bath. Bell, Cece. 2015. (ENG.). 32p. (J). (gr. -1-3). 14.00 *(978-0-7636-7759-6(0))* Candlewick Pr.
Bell, Corydon, jt. illus. see Diggins, Julia E.
Bell, Diana. Daisy & the Unicorn. Laguda, Kardy. 2011. (ENG.). 28p. pap. 11.99 *(978-1-4538-8935-0(3))* CreateSpace Independent Publishing Platform.
Bell, Don. Favorite Scary Stories of American Children. Young, Richard & Dockrey Young, Judy. rev. ed. 2005. (ENG.). 128p. (J). (gr. 3-6). pap. 8.95 *(978-0-87483-563-2(1))* August Hse. Pubs., Inc.
—Tales of Heroes, Vol. 4. DeSpain, Pleasant. 2005. (Books of Nine Lives: Vol. 4). (ENG.). 80p. (J). (gr. 3-6). 14.95 *(978-0-87483-666-0(2))* August Hse. Pubs., Inc.
—Tales of Holidays, Vol. 5. DeSpain, Pleasant. 2005. (Books of Nine Lives: Vol. 5). (ENG.). 80p. (J). (gr. 3-6). 14.95 *(978-0-87483-667-7(0))* August Hse. Pubs., Inc.
—Tales of Insects, Vol. 6. DeSpain, Pleasant. 2005. (Books of Nine Lives: Vol. 6). (ENG.). 80p. (J). (gr. 3-6). 14.95 *(978-0-87483-668-4(9))* August Hse. Pubs., Inc.
—Tales of Nonsense & Tomfoolery, Vol. 2. DeSpain, Pleasant. 2005. (Books of Nine Lives: Vol. 2). (ENG.). 80p. (J). (gr. 3-6). 14.95 *(978-0-87483-670-7(0))* August Hse. Pubs., Inc.
—Tales of Tricksters. DeSpain, Pleasant. 2005. (Books of Nine Lives: Vol. 1). (ENG.). 80p. (J). (gr. -1-12). 14.95 *(978-0-87483-669-1(7))* August Hse. Pubs., Inc.
—Tales of Tricksters: Books of Nine Lives, Vol. 1. DeSpain, Pleasant. 2006. (ENG.). 80p. (J). (gr. 3-6). pap. 9.95 *(978-0-87483-644-8(1))* August Hse. Pubs., Inc.
—Tales of Wisdom & Justice, Vol. 3. DeSpain, Pleasant. 2005. (Books of Nine Lives: Vol. 3). (ENG.). 80p. (J). (gr. 3-6). 14.95 *(978-0-87483-671-4(9))* August Hse. Pubs., Inc.
Bell, Don. Tales of Cats, Vol. 9. Bell, Don, tr. DeSpain, Pleasant. 2005. (ENG.). 80p. (J). (gr. 3-6). 14.95 *(978-0-87483-713-1(8))* August Hse. Pubs., Inc.
—Tales of Enchantment, Vol. 7. Bell, Don, tr. DeSpain, Pleasant. 2005. (ENG.). 80p. (J). (gr. 3-6). 14.95 *(978-0-87483-711-7(1))* August Hse. Pubs., Inc.
—Tales to Frighten & Delight, Vol. 8. Bell, Don, tr. DeSpain, Pleasant. 2005. (ENG.). 80p. (J). (gr. -1-12). 14.95 *(978-0-87483-712-4(X))* August Hse. Pubs., Inc.
Bell, Eleanor. Jack & Boo's Dinosaur Island. Bell, Philip. 2013. 32p. pap. *(978-0-9562980-3-4(6))* Beachy Bks.
Bell, Fred. Zack in the Middle. Michels, Dia L. 2005. (Newly Independent Reader Ser.). (ENG.). 48p. (J). (gr. -1-3). 9.95 *(978-1-930775-01-5(6))* Platypus Media, L.L.C.
Bell, Greg, jt. illus. see Rosen, Barry.
Bell, Jennifer. Big or Little? Stinson, Kathy. 2014. (ENG.). 24p. (J). (gr. -1 — 1). bds. 6.95 *(978-1-55451-610-0(2)*, 9781554516100) Annick Pr., Ltd. CAN. Dist: Firefly Bks., Ltd.
Bell, Jennifer. Safe in a Storm. Swinburne, Stephen R. 2016. (J). ***(978-0-545-66987-0(1))*** Scholastic, Inc.
Bell, Jennifer. Third Grade Angels. Spinelli, Jerry. 2014. (ENG.). 160p. (J). (gr. 2-5). pap. 5.99 *(978-0-545-38773-6(6)*, Levine, Arthur A. Bks.) Scholastic, Inc.
—Toe Shoe Mouse. Carr, Jan. 2014. (ENG.). 32p. (J). (gr. -1-3). 16.95 *(978-0-8234-2406-1(5))* Holiday Hse., Inc.
Bell, Jennifer A. The Emerald Berries. Green, Poppy. 2015. (Adventures of Sophie Mouse Ser.: 2). (ENG.). 128p. (J). (gr. k-4). pap. 5.99 *(978-1-4814-2835-4(7)*, Little Simon) Little Simon.
—Far Flutterby, 1 vol. Kingsbury, Karen. 2012. (ENG.). 32p. (J). 15.99 *(978-0-310-71213-8(0))* Zonderkidz.
—Forget-Me-Not Lake. Green, Poppy. 2015. (Adventures of Sophie Mouse Ser.: 3). (ENG.). 128p. (J). (gr. k-4). 16.99 *(978-1-4814-3000-5(9)*, Little Simon) Little Simon.
—The Little Bully, 1 vol. Bracken, Beth. 2012. (Little Boost Ser.). (ENG.). 32p. (gr. k-3). lib. bdg. 22.65 *(978-1-4048-6795-6(3)*, Little Boost) Picture Window Bks.
—Little Dog, Lost. Bauer, Marion Dane. (ENG.). 208p. (J). (gr. 3-7). 2013. pap. 6.99 *(978-1-4424-3424-0(4))*; 2012. 16.99 *(978-1-4424-3423-3(6))* Simon & Schuster Children's Publishing. (Atheneum Bks. for Young Readers).
Bell, Jennifer A. Looking for Winston. Green, Poppy. 2015. (Adventures of Sophie Mouse Ser.: 4). (ENG.). 128p. (J). (gr. k-4). pap. 5.99 ***(978-1-4814-3003-6(3)***, Little Simon) Little Simon.
Bell, Jennifer A. Miss You Like Crazy. Hall, Pamela. 2014. (ENG.). 32p. (J). (gr. -1-3). 15.99 *(978-1-933718-91-0(9))* Tanglewood Pr.
—My Pen Pal, Santa. Stanton, Melissa. 2013. (ENG.). 32p. (J). (gr. -1-2). 9.99 *(978-0-375-86992-1(1)*, Random Hse. Bks. for Young Readers) Random Hse. Children's Bks.
—A New Friend. Green, Poppy. 2015. (Adventures of Sophie Mouse Ser.: 1). (ENG.). 128p. (J). (gr. k-4). pap. 5.99 *(978-1-4814-2832-3(2)*, Little Simon) Little Simon.
—Rhoda's Rock Hunt. Griffin, Molly Beth. 2014. (ENG.). 32p. (J). (gr. -1-2). 16.95 *(978-0-87351-950-2(7))* Minnesota Historical Society Pr.
—Stella Batts: A Case of the Meanies. Sheinmel, Courtney. 2012. (Stella Batts Ser.: 4). (ENG.). 168p. (J). (gr. 1-3). 9.99 *(978-1-58536-198-4(4)*, 202252); pap. 5.99 *(978-1-58536-199-1(2)*, 202257) Sleeping Bear Pr.
—Stella Batts: Hair Today, Gone Tomorrow. Sheinmel, Courtney. 2012. (Stella Batts Ser.). (ENG.). 160p. (J). (gr. 1-3). lib. bdg. 9.99 *(978-1-58536-189-2(5)*, 202268) Sleeping Bear Pr.
—Stella Batts: Needs a New Name. Sheinmel, Courtney. 2012. (Stella Batts Ser.). (ENG.). 160p. (J). (gr. 1-3). lib. bdg. 9.99 *(978-1-58536-185-4(2)*, 202267) Sleeping Bear Pr.
—Stella Batts: None of Your Beeswax. Sheinmel, Courtney. 2014. (Stella Batts Ser.). (ENG.). 160p. (J). (gr. 1-3). 9.99 *(978-1-58536-853-2(9)*, 203677) Sleeping Bear Pr.
—Stella Batts: Pardon Me. Sheinmel, Courtney. 2012. (Stella Batts Ser.: 3). (ENG.). 160p. (J). (gr. 1-3). 9.99 *(978-1-58536-193-9(3)*, 202270); pap. 5.99 *(978-1-58536-194-6(1)*, 202271) Sleeping Bear Pr.
—Stella Batts - Who's in Charge? Sheinmel, Courtney. 2013. (Stella Batts Ser.). (ENG.). 152p. (J). (gr. 1-3). 9.99 *(978-1-58536-849-5(0)*, 202888) Sleeping Bear Pr.
—Stella Batts Something Blue. Sheinmel, Courtney. 2014. (Stella Batts Ser.). (ENG.). 162p. (J). (gr. 1-3). 9.99 *(978-1-58536-851-8(2)*, 203016) Sleeping Bear Pr.
—Too Shy for Show-And-Tell, 1 vol. Bracken, Beth. 2012. (Little Boost Ser.). (ENG.). 32p. (gr. k-3). 7.95 *(978-1-4048-7418-3(6))* Picture Window Bks.
—Too Shy for Show-and-Tell. Bracken, Beth. 2011. (Little Boost Ser.). (ENG.). 32p. (gr. k-3). lib. bdg. 22.65 *(978-1-4048-6654-6(X)*, Little Boost) Picture Window Bks.
—When a Dad Says "I Love You" Wood, Douglas. 2013. (ENG.). 32p. (J). (gr. -1-3). 17.99 *(978-0-689-87532-8(0)*, Simon & Schuster Bks. For Young Readers) Simon & Schuster Bks. For Young Readers.
—When a Grandpa Says I Love You. Wood, Douglas. 2014. (ENG.). 32p. (J). (gr. -1-3). 16.99 *(978-0-689-81512-6(3)*, Simon & Schuster Bks. For Young Readers) Simon & Schuster Bks. For Young Readers.
Bell, Liesl. Babytionary. Rokhsar, Lillian. 2012. (ENG.). 40p. 17.99 *(978-0-9884922-0-2(2))* Begoo Bks., LLC.
Bell, Loman. Old Glory. Bell, Loman. 2012. 40p. pap. *(978-0-9866065-8-8(8))* Wood Islands Prints.
—Old Glory Faces the Hurricane. Bell, Loman. 2013. 46p. pap. *(978-0-9918033-2-3(9))* Wood Islands Prints.
Bell-Myers, Darcy. Animal Alphabet. Mischel, Jenny Ann. 2006. (J). bds. *(978-0-9769239-0-9(4))* Perfect 4 Preschool.
—Higgledy-Piggledy: Mabel's World. D'Amico, Christine. 2005. (ENG.). 32p. (J). 16.95 *(978-0-9716631-1-4(4))* Attitude Pr. Inc.
Bell, Nick. Mary the Tooth Fairy. Bell, Nick. 32p. (J). 2008. pap. 6.95 *(978-1-60108-025-7(5))*; 2007. (gr. -1-2). 15.95 *(978-1-60108-015-8(8))* Red Cygnet Pr.
Bell, Owain. Thomas & the Hide & Seek Animals. Awdry, Wilbert V. & Awdry, W. 2007. (Thomas & Friends Ser.). (ENG.). 24p. (J). (gr. -1-k). 5.99 *(978-0-375-84173-6(3)*, Random Hse. Bks. for Young Readers) Random Hse. Children's Bks.
Bell, Rebecca. Capitano Ricco. Bell, Rebecca. 2005. 36p. (J). 9.95 *(978-1-934138-06-9(1))* Bouncing Ball Bks., Inc.
—Message from Miami: The Adventures of Sharp-Eye, Book 2. Bell, Rebecca. 2005. (Adventures of Sharp-Eye). 30p. (J). 9.95 *(978-1-934138-09-0(6))* Bouncing Ball Bks., Inc.
—Princess Sara. Bell, Rebecca. 2005. 34p. (J). 9.95 *(978-1-934138-07-6(X))* Bouncing Ball Bks., Inc.
—A Regular Bug: The Adventures of Sharp-Eye, Book 1. Bell, Rebecca. 2005. (Adventures of Sharp-Eye: Bk. 1). 25p. (J). 9.95 *(978-1-934138-08-3(8))* Bouncing Ball Bks., Inc.

Bell, Samantha. Angel Donor. Gladen, Jennifer. 2012. 24p. pap. 10.95 *(978-1-61633-274-7(3))* Guardian Angel Publishing, Inc.

—Bella Saves the Beach. Stewart, Nancy. 2013. 24p. 19.95 *(978-1-61633-370-6(7))*; pap. 11.95 *(978-1-61633-371-3(5))* Guardian Angel Publishing, Inc.

—Burgher & the Woebegone. Chatel, Kim. 2010. 102p. pap. 8.95 *(978-1-61633-061-3(9))* Guardian Angel Publishing, Inc.

—Cathy's Animal Garden: Enter at Your Own Risk. Tomio, Stacy. 2010. (J). *(978-1-934617-04-5(0))* Alma Little/ Elva Resa Publishing, LLC.

—Growing up Dreams. Berger, Susan J. 2010. 24p. pap. 10.95 *(978-1-61633-029-3(5))* Guardian Angel Publishing, Inc.

—One Pelican at a Time: A Story of the Gulf Oil Spill. Stewart, Nancy. 2011. 26p. (J). 19.95 *(978-1-61633-138-2(0))*; pap. 11.95 *(978-1-61633-139-9(9))* Guardian Angel Publishing, Inc.

—Shaping up the Year. Cox, Tracey M. 2009. 24p. pap. 10.95 *(978-1-935137-73-3(5))* Guardian Angel Publishing, Inc.

Bell, Siobhan. Hip Shapes. Blackstone, Stella. 2012. (ENG). 24p. (J). pap. 6.99 *(978-1-84686-762-0(2))* Barefoot Bks., Inc.

—Ship Shapes. Blackstone, Stella. (J). 2008. (ENG). 24p. (gr. -1-k). 6.99 *(978-1-84686-157-4(8))*; 2006. 0024p. 15.99 *(978-1-905236-34-3(4))*; 2006. *(978-1-4156-6474-2(9))* Barefoot Bks., Inc.

—We All Go Traveling By. Roberts, Sheena. (ENG). (J). 2011. 36p. pap. 9.99 *(978-1-84686-655-5(3))*; 2004. 24p. pap. 9.99 *(978-1-84148-410-5(5))*; 2003. 24p. 17.99 *(978-1-84148-168-5(8))* Barefoot Bks., Inc.

Bell, Siobhan & Fatus, Sophie. Babushka. Roberts, Sheena & Horn, Sandra Ann. 2005. 32p. (J). pap. 7.99 *(978-1-84148-411-2(3))* Barefoot Bks., Inc.

Bell, Susan. My Name Is Jake. Turner, Jennifer. 2012. 32p. (J). 14.99 *(978-1-938032-04-4(2))*; pap. 7.99 *(978-1-938032-05-9(5))* Peaks Pr. LLC.

Bellamy, Marian Meredith. Goldie & Androcles — A Fable for the 21st Century. Bellamy, Marian Meredith. 2005. 91p. (YA). per. 20.00 *(978-0-9765341-0-5(X))* Meredith Group Ltd., The.

Bellemare, Josee. The Fragrant Garden. Lee, Day's. 2005. (ENG). 32p. (J). (gr. -1-7). per. 11.95 *(978-1-894917-26-1(X))*, Napoleon & Co.) Dundurn CAN. Dist: Ingram Pub. Services.

Bellemare, Paule Trudel. Being Cool. Zephaniah, Benjamin. 2014. (Collins Big Cat Progress Ser.). (ENG). 32p. (J). pap. 7.99 *(978-0-00-751929-3(X))* HarperCollins Pubs. Ltd. GBR. Dist: Independent Pubs. Group.

Belli, Alfredo. The Good Samaritan. Morton, Sasha. 2014. (My Bible Stories Ser.). (ENG.). (J). 6.99 *(978-1-84898-831-6(1))*, TickTock Books) Octopus Publishing Group GBR. Dist: Hachette Bk. Group.

—Huckleberry Finn. Morton, Sasha. 2014. (Favorite Classics Ser.). (ENG.). (J). (gr. 2-17). 8.99 *(978-1-84898-973-3(3))*, TickTock Books) Octopus Publishing Group GBR. Dist: Hachette Bk. Group.

—Jonah & the Whale. Morton, Sasha. 2014. (My Bible Stories Ser.). (ENG.). (J). 6.99 *(978-1-84898-826-6(1))*, TickTock Books) Octopus Publishing Group GBR. Dist: Hachette Bk. Group.

—Joseph & His Coat of Many Colors. Morton, Sasha. 2014. (My Bible Stories Ser.). (ENG.). (J). 6.99 *(978-1-84898-829-3(X))*, TickTock Books) Octopus Publishing Group GBR. Dist: Hachette Bk. Group.

—Moses. Morton, Sasha. 2014. (My Bible Stories Ser.). (ENG.). (J). 6.99 *(978-1-84898-830-9(3))*, TickTock Books) Octopus Publishing Group GBR. Dist: Hachette Bk. Group.

—Oliver Twist. Dickens, Charles. 2008. (Green Apple Step Two Ser.). (ENG.). 96p. (J). (gr. 5). pap. incl. audio compact disk *(978-88-530-0580-9(7))* Cideb.

Bellinger, Marie. Pick-a-WooWoo - Wizards Words of Wisdom, 16 vols., Vol. 7. Harper, Julie-Ann. 2009. 32p. pap. *(978-0-9803669-6-9(8))* Pick-a-Woo Woo Pubs.

—Pick-a-WooWoo - Yep I See Spirit: The Gift of Sight, 16 vols., Vol. 6. Harper, Julie-Ann. 2009. 32p. pap. *(978-0-9803669-5-2(X))* Pick-a-Woo Woo Pubs.

Bellini, Ellen, photos by. Gerbils: The Complete Guide to Gerbil Care. Anastasi, Donna. 2005. (Complete Care Made Easy Ser.). 2014, 176p. per. 9.95 *(978-1-931993-56-2(4))* i-5 Publishing LLC.

Bellomy, Gail. Fun O' Licious. Clawson, Kimberly. 2007. (ENG.). 56p. per. 16.95 *(978-1-4241-5556-9(8))* America Star Bks.

Belloni, Valentina, et al. Cinderella Stories Around the World: 4 Beloved Tales, 1 vol. Meister, Cari. 2014. (Multicultural Fairy Tales Ser.). (ENG.). 32p. (gr. k-2). lib. bdg. 26.65 *(978-1-4795-5433-1(2))* Picture Window Bks.

—Rapunzel Stories Around the World: 4 Beloved Tales, 1 vol. Meister, Cari. 2014. (Multicultural Fairy Tales Ser.). (ENG.). 32p. (gr. k-2). lib. bdg. 26.65 *(978-1-4795-5436-2(7))* Picture Window Bks.

—Snow White Stories Around the World: 4 Beloved Tales, 1 vol. Gunderson, Jessica. 2014. (Multicultural Fairy Tales Ser.). (ENG.). 32p. (gr. k-2). lib. bdg. 26.65 *(978-1-4795-5434-8(0))* Picture Window Bks.

Belomlinsky, Alex. Tommy the Fishboy. Kurlander, Keith. 2012. 34p. 24.95 *(978-1-4626-4527-5(5))* America Star Bks.

Belomlinsky, M., jt. illus. see Synepolsky, I.

Below, Halina. Chestnut Dreams, 1 vol. Below, Halina. 2003. (ENG.). 40p. (J). pap. 5.95 *(978-1-55041-690-9(1))*, 1550416901) Fitzhenry & Whiteside, Ltd. CAN. Dist: Midpoint Trade Bks., Inc.

Belser, Maud Corier. Grace & Marie's Little Farm on the Hill. 2007. 32p. (J). bds. 18.00 *(978-0-9791076-0-3(1))* WebbWorks.

Belton, Robyn. Farmer John's Tractor. Sutton, Sally. 2012. 32p. (J). *(978-1-921150-94-4(7))* Walker Bks. Australia Pty, Ltd.

—Farmer John's Tractor. Sutton, Sally. 2013. (ENG). 32p. (J). (gr. -1-2). 15.99 *(978-0-7636-6430-5(8))* Candlewick Pr.

Belton, Robyn. Herbert: The True Story of a Brave Sea Dog. Belton, Robyn. 2010. (ENG). 40p. (J). (gr. -1-3). 15.99 *(978-0-7636-4741-4(1))* Candlewick Pr.

Bemelmans, Ludwig. Noodle. Leaf, Munro. 2006. 56p. (J). 15.99 *(978-0-590-04310-6(2))*, Levine, Arthur A. Bks.) Scholastic, Inc.

Bemelmans, Ludwig. Madeline's Christmas, 1 vol. Bemelmans, Ludwig. 2007. (Madeline Ser.). (ENG.). 15p. (J). (gr. -1-2). 9.99 *(978-0-14-240897-1(2))*, Puffin) Penguin Publishing Group.

Bemporad, Alex, jt. photos by see Pervan, Ivo.

Ben-Ami, Doron. Autumn Journey, 1 vol. Cummings, Priscilla. 2008. (ENG.). 120p. (YA). pap. 12.95 *(978-0-87033-606-5(1))*, Cornell Maritime Pr./Tidewater Pubs.) Schiffer Publishing, Ltd.

—Nicki, Bk. 1. Creel, Ann Howard. 2007. (ENG.). 136p. (J). (gr. 4-7). pap. 6.95 *(978-1-59369-259-9(5))*, Pleasant Co.) American Girl Publishing, Inc.

—Tornado. Byars, Betsy. 2004. (Trophy Chapter Bks.). (ENG.). 64p. (J). (gr. 1-5). pap. 4.99 *(978-0-06-442063-1(9))* HarperCollins Pubs.

—Wait until Then. Alcorn, Randy. 2007. (ENG.). 32p. (J). (gr. 1-5). 14.99 *(978-1-4143-1041-1(2))* Tyndale Hse. Pubs.

Ben-Moshe, Jana. Hebrew Through Prayer, Bk. 1. Kaye, Terry et al. Siegel, Adam, ed. 96p. (J). (gr. 4-5). pap. 6.95 *(978-0-87441-563-6(2))* Behrman Hse., Inc.

—Learn & Do Bible Book. Gurvis, Laura K. 64p. (J). (gr. k-2). pap. 4.95 *(978-0-87441-306-9(8))* Behrman Hse., Inc.

Ben-Yosef, Yoni, photos by. Edmond Lachenal & His Legacy. Eidelberg, Martin & Cass, Claire. 2009. (ENG.). 208p. 95.00 *(978-0-9788371-3-6(4))* Jason Jacques Gallery Pr. The.

Benally, Kendrick. Ch'at to Yinilo'/Frog Brings Rain. Powell, Patricia Hruby. Thomas, Peter A., tr. 2006. (NAV & ENG). 32p. (J). (gr. 4-7). 17.95 *(978-1-893354-08-1(3))* Salina Bookshelf Inc.

—Zinnia: How the Corn Was Saved. Powell, Patricia Hruby. Ruffenach, Jessie., ed. Thomas, Peter, tr. from NAV. 2004. (ENG & NAV.). 32p. (J). 17.95 *(978-1-893354-38-8(5))* Salina Bookshelf Inc.

Benatar, Raquel & Rubio, Adrian. Go, Milka, Go! The Life of Milka Duno. Benatar, Raquel & Rubio, Adrian. 2008.Tr. of Corre, Milka, Corre!. (SPA & ENG). 32p. (J). 19.95 *(978-1-56492-360-8(6))* Laredo Publishing Co., Inc.

Benatar, Raquel & Torrecilla, Pablo. Isabel Allende: Recuerdos para un Cuento. Benatar, Raquel & Torrecilla, Pablo. Petersen, Patricia, tr. 2004. (ENG & SPA.). (J). 14.95 *(978-1-56492-341-7(X)*, Piñata Books) Arte Publico Pr.

Benator, Seth. A Ballet for Bobcat. Benator, Eileen B. l.t. ed. 2005. 32p. (J). (gr. -1-2). 15.95 *(978-0-9748478-7-0(9))* Lion's Tale Pr., LLC.

—A Marching Band for Bears. Benator, Eileen. 2004. (J). lib. bdg. 15.95 *(978-0-9748478-5-6(2))* Lion's Tale Pr., LLC.

Benatova, Sibylla. The Magic Raincoat. David, Ryan. 2007. (ENG.). 40p. (J). (gr. 4-2). 17.95 *(978-1-932425-68-0(3)*, Front Street) Boyds Mills Pr.

Benchimol, Brigitte & Zlma, Siegfried. Jadyn & the Magic Bubble: Discovering India. Benchimol, Brigitte. 2007. 58p. (J). (gr. 3-4). 19.95 *(978-0-9701654-9-7(8))* East West Discovery Pr.

Benda, Wladyslaw T. A Girl of the Limberlost. Stratton-Porter, Gene. 2005. reprint ed. pap. 38.95 *(978-0-7661-9424-3(8))* Kessinger Publishing, LLC.

Bendall-Brunello, John. Big Pig. Doyle, Malachy. (ENG.). 32p. (J). (gr. -1-k). 2006. pap. 9.99 *(978-0-689-87485-7(5))*; 2005. 19.95 *(978-0-689-87484-0(7))* Simon & Schuster, Ltd. GBR. Dist: Simon & Schuster, Inc.

—The Elephant Who Was Scared. Elliot, Rachel. 2012. (When I Was Small). (ENG.). 24p. (J). (gr. -1-1). 15.99 *(978-1-60992-259-7(X))* QEB Publishing Inc.

—I Love You This Much, 1 vol. Hodges, Lynn & Buchanan, Sue. 2010. (ENG.). 36p. (J). pap. 6.99 *(978-0-310-72265-6(9))* Zonderkidz.

—I Love You This Much, 1 vol. Hodges, Lynn et al. 2005. (Songs of Gods Love Ser.). (ENG.). 16p. (J). (gr. -1). bds. 6.99 *(978-0-310-70961-9(X))* Zonderkidz.

—Lion Book of Five-Minute Animal Stories. Goodwin, John. 2009. (ENG.). 48p. (J). (gr. k-2). 16.99 *(978-0-7459-6084-5(7))* Lion Hudson PLC GBR. Dist: Independent Pubs. Group.

—Moose on the Loose. Wargin, Kathy-jo. 2009. (ENG.). 32p. (J). (gr. k-6). 15.95 *(978-1-58536-427-5(4))* Sleeping Bear Pr.

Bendall-Brunello, John. My Barnyard! A Read & Play Book! Schwartz, Betty Ann & Seresin, Lynn. 2015. (ENG.). 10p. (J). (gr. -1-k). 7.99 *(978-0-545-69077-5(3)*, Cartwheel Bks.) Scholastic, Inc.

Bendall-Brunello, John. My Dinosaurs! A Read & Play Book. Schwartz, Betty Ann & Seresin, Lynn. 2014. (ENG.). 16p. (J). (gr. -1-k). 7.99 *(978-0-545-69076-8(5)*, Cartwheel Bks.) Scholastic, Inc.

—Peep Leap, 0 vols. Verdick, Elizabeth. 2013. (ENG.). 28p. (J). (gr. -1-2). 16.99 *(978-1-4778-1640-0(2)*, 9781477816400, Amazon Children's Publishing) Amazon Publishing.

—Peter & the Wolf. Band 09/Gold. Redmond, Diane. 2007. (Collins Big Cat Ser.). (ENG.). 24p. (J). pap. 6.99 *(978-0-00-718674-7(6))* HarperCollins Pubs. Ltd. GBR. Dist: Independent Pubs. Group.

—The Tiger Who Was Angry. Elliott, Rachel. 2012. (When I Was Small). (ENG.). 24p. (J). (gr. -1-1). 15.99 *(978-1-60992-257-3(3))* QEB Publishing Inc.

—The Zebra Who Was Sad. Elliott, Rachel. 2012. (When I Was Small). (ENG.). 24p. (J). (gr. -1-1). 15.99 *(978-1-60992-258-0(1))* QEB Publishing Inc.

—100 Days of Cool. Murphy, Stuart J. 2003. (MathStart 2 Ser.). (ENG.). 40p. (J). (gr. 1-18). pap. 5.99 *(978-0-06-000123-0(2))* HarperCollins Pubs.

Bendall-Brunello, John. Archie's Amazing Adventure. Bendall-Brunello, John, tr. Grindley, Sally. 2003. 32p. (YA). *(978-1-84365-026-3(6)*, Pavilion Children's Books) Pavilion Bks.

Bendall-Brunello, John, jt. illus. see Wargin, Kathy-jo.

Bendell, Norm. Is This Normal? Girls Questions, Answered by the Editors of the Care & Keeping of You. Falligant, Erin et al, eds. 2009. (J). 112p. (YA). pap. 8.95 *(978-1-59369-483-8(0))* American Girl Publishing, Inc.

—What Would You Do? Quizzes about Real-Life Problems. Criswell, Patti Kelley. Chobanian, Elizabeth, ed. 2004. (ENG.). 64p. (J). (gr. 3-18). pap. 8.95 *(978-1-58485-874-4(5))* American Girl Publishing, Inc.

Bender, Robert. Alphabet Movers. Benzwie, Teresa. 32p. (J). (gr. -1-6). pap. *(978-1-930798-08-3(3))* National Dance Education Organization.

—By the Baobab Tree. Archambault, John. 2005. (J). *(978-1-58669-164-6(3))* Childcraft Education Corp.

—Mail Monkeys. Greene, Rhonda Gowler. 2006. (J). pap. *(978-1-58669-217-9(8))* Childcraft Education Corp.

—The Winter Witch. Evans, Clay Bonnyman. 2005. (ENG.). 32p. (J). (gr. -1-3). 16.95 *(978-0-8234-1615-8(1))* Holiday Hse., Inc.

Bendick, Jeanne. After the Sun Goes Down: The Story of Animals at Night. Blough, Glenn O. 2011. 50p. (gr. 1). 35.95 *(978-1-258-09913-8(6))* Literary Licensing, LLC.

—The Mystery of the Periodic Table. Wiker, Benjamin. 2003. (Living History Library). 170p. (YA). pap. 14.95 *(978-1-883937-71-3(X))* Bethlehem Bks.

Bendick, Jeanne. Herodotus & the Road to History. Bendick, Jeanne. 2009. (J). pap. 13.95 *(978-1-932350-20-3(9))* Bethlehem Bks.

Bendis, Keith. Calvin Can't Fly: The Story of a Bookworm Birdie. Berne, Jennifer. 2015. 40p. pap. 6.95 *(978-1-4549-1575-1(7))*; 2010. 32p. 14.95 *(978-1-4027-7323-5(4))* Sterling Publishing Co., Inc.

—Calvin, Look Out! A Bookworm Birdie Gets Glasses. Berne, Jennifer. 2014. (ENG.). 32p. (J). (gr. -1-2). 14.95 *(978-1-4549-0910-1(2))* Sterling Publishing Co., Inc.

Bendoly, Lynne. What Do You Do on a Rainy Day? Farrell, Steve. 2013. 48p. pap. 24.95 *(978-1-4626-9685-7(6))* America Star Bks.

Benenfeld, Rikki. I Go to the Ohel. Hodakov, Levi. Rosenfeld, D. L. & Leverton, Yossi, eds. 2011. (Toddler Experience Ser.). 32p. (J). 10.95 *(978-1-929628-61-2(7))* Hachai Publishing.

Benenfeld, Rikki. I Go to the Doctor. Benenfeld, Rikki. 2004. (Toddler Experience Ser.). (J). lib. bdg. 10.95 *(978-1-929628-15-5(3))* Hachai Publishing.

—Let's Go Shopping. Benenfeld, Rikki. 2005. (Toddler Experience Ser.). 24p. (J). 10.95 *(978-1-929628-20-9(X))* Hachai Publishing.

—Let's Meet Community Helpers. Benenfeld, Rikki. 2013. 32p. (J). 10.95 *(978-1-929628-75-9(7))* Hachai Publishing.

Benevenia, Rose. Dolly & Babe. Benevenia, Rose. l.t. ed. 2004. 9p. (J). (gr. k-2). pap. 9.00 *(978-0-9729044-0-7(9))* Cabbage Patch Pr.

Benfanti, Russell. Eight Spinning Planets. James, Brian. 2010. (ENG.). 16p. (J). (gr. k — 1). 10.99 *(978-0-545-23517-4(0)*, Cartwheel Bks.) Scholastic, Inc.

Benfold Haywood, Ian P. The Rule of Claw. Brindley, John. 2009. (Exceptional Reading & Language Arts Titles for Upper Grades Ser.). (ENG.). 408p. (YA). (gr. 7-12). 18.95 *(978-1-58013-608-2(7)*, Carolrhoda Bks.) Lerner Publishing Group.

Benger, Chelsi L. The Daily Adventures of Ruckus & Otis. Zabriskie, Cindy. 2008. 24p. pap. 24.95 *(978-1-60672-829-1(6))* America Star Bks.

Bengtz, Ture. White Squaw: The True Story of Jennie Wiley. Wheeler, Arville. 2011. 178p. (gr. 4-7). 42.95 *(978-1-258-05911-8(8))* Literary Licensing, LLC.

Benham, Tors. Crazy Cow. Wolfe, Jane. 2013. (ENG.). 8p. (J). (gr. -1-k). bds. 6.99 *(978-1-84322-775-5(4)*, Armadillo) Anness Publishing GBR. Dist: National Bk. Network.

—Messy Pig. Wolfe, Jane. 2013. (ENG.). 8p. (J). (gr. -1-k). bds. 6.99 *(978-1-84322-777-9(0)*, Armadillo) Anness Publishing GBR. Dist: National Bk. Network.

—Noisy Dog. Wolfe, Jane. 2013. (ENG.). 8p. (J). (gr. -1-k). bds. 6.99 *(978-1-84322-779-3(7)*, Armadillo) Anness Publishing GBR. Dist: National Bk. Network.

—Pull the Lever: Who Does What? Wolfe, Jane. 2014. (ENG.). 8p. (J). (gr. -1-2). bds. 6.99 *(978-1-86147-392-9(3)*, Armadillo) Anness Publishing GBR. Dist: National Bk. Network.

—Pull the Lever: Who's in Here? Wolfe, Jane. 2014. (ENG.). 8p. (J). (gr. -1-2). bds. 6.99 *(978-1-86147-394-3(X)*, Armadillo) Anness Publishing GBR. Dist: National Bk. Network.

—Sleepy Sheep. Wolfe, Jane. 2013. (ENG.). 8p. (J). (gr. -1-k). bds. 6.99 *(978-1-84322-778-6(9)*, Armadillo) Anness Publishing GBR. Dist: National Bk. Network.

Beniamino Brady. The Symph - in Search of Harmony. George Trad. 2012. 38p. 30.50 *(978-1-61897-519-5(6)*, Strategic Bk. Publishing) Strategic Book Publishing & Rights Agency (SBPRA)

Benicio, Angelique. Sarah's Waterfall: A Healing Story about Sexual Abuse. Akers, Ellery. 2009. (J). *(978-1-884444-79-1(2))* Safer Society Pr.

Benioff, Carol. Big Night for Salamanders. Lamstein, Sarah Marwil. 2010. (ENG.). 40p. (J). (gr. 3-7). 17.95 *(978-1-932425-96-7(5))* Boyds Mills Pr.

—Preacher's Night Before Christmas, 1 vol. Layne, Steven L. 2006. (Night Before Christmas Ser.). (ENG.). 32p. (J). (gr. k-3). 16.99 *(978-1-58980-321-3(3))* Pelican Publishing Co., Inc.

Benitez, Miguel. Freddie Ramos Makes a Splash. Jules, Jacqueline. 2013. (Zapato Power Ser.: Book 4). (ENG.). 96p. (J). (gr. 1-3). pap. 4.99 *(978-0-8075-9486-5(5))* Whitman, Albert & Co.

Benitez, Miguel. Freddie Ramos Makes a Splash Bk. 4. Jules, Jacqueline. 2012. (Zapato Power Ser.: Book 4). (ENG.). 96p. (J). (gr. 1-3). 14.99 *(978-0-8075-9485-8(7))* Whitman, Albert & Co.

Benitez, Miguel. Freddie Ramos Springs into Action. Jules, Jacqueline. 2011. (Zapato Power Ser.: Book 2). (ENG.). 92p. (J). (gr. 1-3). pap. 4.99 *(978-0-8075-9483-4(0))* Whitman, Albert & Co.

—Freddie Ramos Takes Off, Bk. 1. Jules, Jacqueline. 2011. (Zapato Power Ser.: Book 1). (ENG.). 88p. (J). (gr. 1-3). pap. 4.99 *(978-0-8075-9479-7(2))* Whitman, Albert & Co.

—Freddie Ramos Zooms to the Rescue. Jules, Jacqueline. (Zapato Power Ser.: Book 3). (ENG.). 96p. (J). (gr. 1-3). 2012. pap. 4.99 *(978-0-8075-9484-1(9))*; Bk. 3. 2011. 14.99 *(978-0-8075-9482-7(2))* Whitman, Albert & Co.

Benjamin, Christina. What Is This? Williams, Rozanne Lanczak. Hamaguchi, Carla, ed. 2003. 16p. (J). (gr. k-2). pap. 3.49 *(978-1-57471-965-9(3)*, 3587) Creative Teaching Pr., Inc.

Benjamin-Farren, Joan. Shuli & Me: From Slavery to Freedom A Storybook Omer Calendar. Benjamin-Farren, Joan. 2006. (J). 19.95 *(978-0-9788802-0-0(X))* Black Jasmine.

Bennefeld, Rikki. I Go to the Dentist. Benenfeld, Rikki. Rosenfeld, Dina & Leverton, Yossi, eds. 2011. (Toddler Experience Ser.). (ENG.). 32p. (J). 10.95 *(978-1-929628-60-5(9))* Hachai Publishing.

Bennett, Andy. Feeling Happy: A Turn-and-Learn Emotions Book. Weiss, Ellen. 2006. (PBS Kids Ser.). 10p. (J). bds. 6.95 *(978-1-57791-311-5(6))* Brighter Minds Children's Publishing.

—Fruit Salad: A Touch-and-Learn Book. Weiss, Ellen. 2006. (PBS Kids Ser.). 8p. (J). (gr. -1-k). bds. 6.95 *(978-1-57791-314-6(0))* Brighter Minds Children's Publishing.

—The Great Cake. Gerstein, Sherry. 2006. 14p. (J). (gr. -1-3). bds. 6.95 *(978-1-57791-260-6(8))* Brighter Minds Children's Publishing.

—Hide & Peek: A Lift-A-Flap Letters Book. Gerstein, Sherry. 2006. 14p. (J). (gr. -1-3). bds. 6.95 *(978-1-57791-259-0(4))* Brighter Minds Children's Publishing.

—I Don't Want to Go to School! A Fold-Out Surprise Book. Weiss, Ellen. 2006. (PBS Kids Ser.). 12p. (J). 6.95 *(978-1-57791-313-9(2))* Brighter Minds Children's Publishing.

—Imagination Vacation: A Color-Foil Shapes Book. Gerstein, Sherry. 2006. 14p. (J). (gr. -1-3). bds. 6.95 *(978-1-57791-261-3(6))* Brighter Minds Children's Publishing.

—Moo, Moo Who are You? Gerstein, Sherry. 2006. 14p. (J). (gr. -1-k). bds. 7.95 *(978-1-57791-258-3(6))* Brighter Minds Children's Publishing.

—Winter Spring Summer Fall: A Touch-and-Feel Seasons Book. Weiss, Ellen. 2006. (PBS Kids Ser.). 8p. (J). (gr. -1-k). bds. 6.95 *(978-1-57791-312-2(4))* Brighter Minds Children's Publishing.

Bennett, Brent. The Day Papa Came Home, Justus, Barbara & Starbird, Caroline. Newman, Timothy, ed. 2004. 20p. (YA). *(978-0-9755996-0-0(7))* Heifer Project International.

Bennett, Cameron. A CatFish Tale. Brodsky, Kathy. 2012. (ENG.). (J). 19.99 *(978-0-9828529-3-4(2))* Helpingwords.

—Just Sniffing Around. Brodsky, Kathy. 2009. (ENG.). 40p. 19.99 *(978-0-578-03620-5(7))* Helpingwords.

—My Bent Tree. Brodsky, Kathy. 2008. (ENG.). 44p. (J). 19.95 *(978-0-615-16066-5(2))* Helpingwords.

Bennett, Carl A., jt. illus. see Bennett, James.

Bennett, Davis, jt. illus. see Raney, Tom.

Bennett, Elizabeth. The Peanuts Guide to the Seasons: A Jumbo Activity Book. Schulz, Charles M. 2003. (Peanuts Club with Charlie Brown & Friends Ser.). 144p. (J). pap. 4.99 *(978-0-439-46826-8(4))* Scholastic, Inc.

Bennett, Erin Susanne. The Patchwork Path: A Quilt Map to Freedom. Stroud, Bettye. 2007. (ENG.). (J). (gr. k-3). pap. 7.99 *(978-0-7635-3519-0(7))* Candlewick Pr.

Bennett, Felix. The Lost World. Brenchley, Chaz & Doyle, Arthur. 2009. (Real Reads Ser.). 64p. (J). (gr. 4-8). pap. 13.55 *(978-1-60754-395-4(8))*; bdg. 29.25 *(978-1-60754-394-7(X))* Windmill Bks.

—War of the Worlds. Wells, H. G. 2013. (Classics of Science Fiction Ser.). (ENG.). 64p. pap. 6.95 *(978-1-906230-12-8(9))* Real Reads Ltd. GBR. Dist: International Publishers Marketing.

Bennett, Harry, Jr. Purple pup girls are grape jelly. Bumbalough, Jerry. 2007. 16p. (J). 8.95 *(978-0-9797960-0-5(8))* Thirsty Sponge Publishing Co.

Bennett, James. Halloween. Seinfeld, Jerry. 2008. (ENG.). 32p. (gr. -1-1). pap. 7.99 *(978-0-316-03597-2(1))* Little, Brown Bks. for Young Readers.

—Tell Me a Silly Story. Reiner, Carl. 2010. 32p. (J). (gr. -1). 16.95 *(978-1-60747-713-6(0)*, Pickwick Pr.) Phoenix Bks., Inc.

—The 2000 Year Old Man Goes to School. Brooks, Mel & Reiner, Carl. 2009. 40p. (J). (gr. 4-8). reprint ed. 18.00 *(978-1-4223-5622-7(1))* DIANE Publishing Co.

—The 2000 Year Old Man Goes to School. Brooks, Mel & Reiner, Carl. 2005. 40p. (J). (gr. -1-3). 17.99 *(978-0-06-076676-4(X))* HarperCollins Pubs.

Bennett, James & Carl A. Tell Me Another Scary Story... but Not Too Scary! Reiner, Carl. 2009. (ENG.). 32p. (J). (gr. 4-7). 16.95 *(978-1-59777-630-1(0))* Phoenix Bks., Inc.

Bennett, James, jt. illus. see Mantha, John.

Bennett, James, jt. illus. see Mortimer, Lauren.

Bennett, Jamie & Owlkids Books Inc. Staff. Weird Zone: Sports. Birmingham, Maria. 2013. (Weird Zone Ser.). (ENG.). 128p. (J). (gr. 3-7). 22.95 *(978-1-926973-60-9(7))*; pap. 12.95 *(978-1-926973-61-6(5))* Owlkids Bks. Inc. CAN. Dist: Perseus-PGW.

Bennett, Jerry. I Walk for Water. Andrews, Lindsey. 2012. (ENG.). 43p. (J). 16.95 *(978-0-615-49668-9(7))* Hilarity Waters Pr.

Bennett, Joe. Crew: Big Trouble in Little Mogadishu. Priest, Christopher. 2004. (Marvel Heroes Ser.). 160p. (YA). pap. 16.99 *(978-0-7851-1307-2(X))* Marvel Worldwide, Inc.

Bennett, Joe, et al. Spiral. Jurgens, Dan. 2011. (ENG.). 216p. (YA). (gr. 8-17). pap. 24.99 *(978-0-7851-5089-3(7))* Marvel Worldwide, Inc.

Bennett, Joe. Thor: The Death of Odin. Jurgens, Dan. 2011. (ENG.). 232p. (YA). (gr. 8-17). pap. 26.99 *(978-0-7851-4979-8(1))* Marvel Worldwide, Inc.

Bennett, Joe, jt. illus. see Asrar, Mahmud.

B

For book reviews, descriptive annotations, tables of contents, cover images, author biographies & additional information, updated daily, subscribe to **www.booksinprint2.com**

2877

Bennett, John. Old Macdonald on His Farm. Andrews, Jackie. 2012. (ENG.). 32p. pap. 6.50 *(978-1-84135-195-7(4))* Award Pubns. Ltd. GBR. Dist: Parkwest Pubns., Inc.

—Three Billy-Goat Gruff. Andrews, Jackie. 2012. (ENG.). 32p. pap. 6.50 *(978-1-84135-196-4(2))* Award Pubns. Ltd. GBR. Dist: Parkwest Pubns., Inc.

Bennett, Lorna. C Is for Chinook: An Alberta Alphabet. Welykochy, Dawn. rev. ed. 2004. (Discover Canada Province by Province Ser.). (ENG.). 40p. (J). 17.95 *(978-1-58536-223-3(9))* Sleeping Bear Pr.

Bennett, Lorna, et al. Dot-to-Dot in the Sky: Stories in the Stars, 1 vol. Bennett, Lorna & Galat, Joan Marie. 2010. (Dot to Dot in the Sky Ser.: 0). (ENG.). 64p. (J). (gr. 2-6). pap. 12.95 *(978-1-55285-182-1(6))* Whitecap Bks., Ltd. CAN. Dist: Midpoint Trade Bks., Inc.

Bennett, Lorna. L Is for Land of Living Skies: A Saskatchewan Alphabet. Aksomitis, Linda. 2010. (Discover Canada Province by Province Ser.). (ENG.). 32p. (J). (gr. 1-3). 17.95 *(978-1-58536-490-9(8)*, 202194) Sleeping Bear Pr.

—Sandwiches for Duke, 1 vol. Sadler, Judy Ann. 2007. (ENG.). 32p. (J). (gr. -1-3). 8.95 *(978-1-55005-062-2(1)*, 1550050621) Fitzhenry & Whiteside, Ltd. CAN. Dist: Midpoint Trade Bks., Inc.

—Stories of the Moon, 1 vol. Galat, Joan Marie. 2010. (Dot to Dot in the Sky Ser.: 0). (ENG.). 64p. (J). (gr. 2-6). pap. 12.95 *(978-1-55285-610-9(0))* Whitecap Bks., Ltd. CAN. Dist: Midpoint Trade Bks., Inc.

—Stories of the Zodiac, 1 vol. Galat, Joan Marie. 2010. (Dot to Dot in the Sky Ser.: 0). (ENG.). 64p. (J). (gr. 2-6). pap. 14.95 *(978-1-55285-805-9(7))* Whitecap Bks., Ltd. CAN. Dist: Midpoint Trade Bks., Inc.

—True Story. Chan, Marty. 2009. (ENG.). 32p. (J). 9.95 *(978-0-9810449-0-3(5))* Ink Jockey, Inc. CAN. Dist: Univ. of Toronto Pr.

Bennett, Lorna & Yu, Chao. Stories of the Planets, 1 vol. Galat, Joan Marie. 2003. (Dot to Dot in the Sky Ser.: 0). (ENG.). 64p. (J). (gr. 2-6). pap. 12.95 *(978-1-55285-392-4(6))* Whitecap Bks., Ltd. CAN. Dist: Midpoint Trade Bks., Inc.

Bennett, Michele & Dunlap, Joan. Backpack Cat. Bennett, Marcia. 2004. 124p. 19.95 *(978-1-932196-50-4(1))* WordWright.biz, Inc.

Bennett-Minnerly, Denise. The Color Tree. Bennett-Minnerly, Denise. 2005. (J). 14.95 *(978-1-56290-328-2(4))* Crystal Productions.

Bennett, Nneka. Vision of Beauty: The Story of Sarah Breedlove Walker. Lasky, Kathryn. 2012. (Candlewick Biographies Ser.). (ENG.). 56p. (J). (gr. 3-7). 14.99 *(978-0-7636-6428-2(6))*; pap. 4.99 *(978-0-7636-6092-5(2))* Candlewick Pr.

Bennett, Randle Paul, jt. illus. see Reed, Lisa.

Bennett, Trevor. Big Woods Bird: An Ivory-Bill Story. Luneau, Terri Robert. 2005. (ENG.). 36p. (J). (gr. -1-3). pap. 8.95 *(978-0-9768839-0-6(2))* Butler Ctr. for Arkansas Studies.

Bennington, Mark. Young Romans. Williams, Rose. 2004. (LAT & ENG.). 176p. pap., tchr. ed. 39.00 *(978-1-84331-081-5(3))* Bolchazy-Carducci Pubs.

Bennion, Anneliese. A Paper Hug. Skolmoski, Stephanie. 2006. 36p. (J). 6.95 *(978-0-9786425-0-1(3))* DesignAbility.

Benny, Mike. Just as Good: How Larry Doby Changed America's Game. Crowe, Chris. 2012. (ENG.). 32p. (J). (gr. 1-4). 16.99 *(978-0-7636-5026-1(9))* Candlewick Pr.

—The Listeners. Whelan, Gloria. 2009. (Tales of Young Americans Ser.). (ENG.). 32p. (J). (gr. k-6). 17.95 *(978-1-58536-419-0(3))* Sleeping Bear Pr.

—Oh, Brother! Grimes, Nikki. 2007. (ENG.). 32p. (J). (gr. k-5). 16.99 *(978-0-688-17294-7(6)*, Greenwillow Bks.) HarperCollins Pubs.

Benny, Mike, jt. illus. see Ellison, Chris.

Benoît, Jérôme, jt. illus. see Fayolle, Diane.

Benoit, Renné. Big City Bees, 1 vol. de Vries, Maggie. 2013. (ENG.). 48p. (J). (gr. k-3). 17.95 *(978-1-55365-906-8(6))* Greystone Books Ltd. CAN. Dist: Perseus-PGW.

—Boy in Motion: Rick Hansen's Story. Manson, Ainslie. 2009. (ENG.). 48p. (J). (gr. k-3). pap. 12.00 *(978-1-55365-427-8(7))* Greystone Books Ltd. CAN. Dist: Perseus-PGW.

Benoit, Renne. F Is for French: Un Livre d'Alphabet Sur le Quebec - A Quebec Alphabet. Arsenault, Elaine. 2013. (Discover Canada Province by Province Ser.). (FRE, ENG & MUL.). 40p. (J). (gr. 1-4). 17.95 *(978-1-58536-435-0(5)*, 202351) Sleeping Bear Pr.

Benoit, Renné. Fraser Bear: A Cub's Life. de Vries, Maggie. 2012. (ENG.). 48p. (J). (gr. k-4). pap. 10.95 *(978-1-926812-95-3(6))* Greystone Books Ltd. CAN. Dist: Perseus-PGW.

Benoit, Renne. John F. Kennedy & the Stormy Sea. Goldsmith, Howard. 2006. (Ready-To-read COFA Ser.). (ENG.). 32p. (J). (gr. 1-3). pap. 3.99 *(978-0-689-86816-0(2)*, Simon Spotlight) Simon Spotlight.

Benoit, Renné. John F. Kennedy & the Stormy Sea. Goldsmith, Howard. 2006. 32p. (J). lib. bdg. 15.00 *(978-1-4242-0958-3(7))* Fitzgerald Bks.

—Little Dance. Sleeping Bear Press. 2013. (ENG.). 20p. (J). (gr. -1-k). 8.99 *(978-1-58536-884-6(9)*, 202899) Sleeping Bear Pr.

Benoit, Renne. Mooncakes, 1 vol. Seto, Loretta. 2013. (ENG.). 32p. (J). (gr. -1-3). lib. bdg. 19.95 *(978-1-4598-0107-3(5))* Orca Bk. Pubs. USA.

Benoit, Renné. The Secret of the Village Fool, 1 vol. Upjohn, Rebecca. 2012. (ENG.). 32p. (J). (gr. 3-6). lib. bdg. 18.95 *(978-1-926920-75-7(9))* Second Story Pr. CAN. Dist: Orca Bk. Pubs. USA.

—Tale of a Great White Fish: A Sturgeon Story. de Vries, Maggie. 2010. (ENG.). 48p. (J). (gr. k-4). pap. 10.95 *(978-1-55365-303-5(3))* Greystone Books Ltd. CAN. Dist: Perseus-PGW.

Benoit, Renne. Thanksgiving: A Harvest Celebration. Stiegemeyer, Julie. 32p. (J). 2006. (gr. -1-3). per. 7.49 *(978-0-7586-0916-8(7))*; 2003. 13.49 *(978-0-7586-0530-6(7))* Concordia Publishing Hse.

—Tooling Around: Crafty Creatures & the Tools They Use. Jackson, Ellen. 2014. (ENG.). 32p. (J). (gr. -1-3). 17.95 *(978-1-58089-564-4(6))* Charlesbridge Publishing, Inc.

—When-I-Was-a-Little-Girl, 1 vol. Gilmore, Rachna. 2007. (ENG.). 24p. (J). (gr. -1-2). 14.95 *(978-1-897187-12-8(2))* Second Story Pr. CAN. Dist: Orca Bk. Pubs. USA.

Benoit, Renne & Second Story Press Staff. Lily & the Paper Man, 1 vol. Upjohn, Rebecca. 2007. (ENG.). 24p. (J). (gr. k-3). 15.95 *(978-1-897187-19-7(X))* Second Story Pr. CAN. Dist: Orca Bk. Pubs. USA.

Bensch, April. Madeline Becomes a Star. Wheeler-Cribb, Peggy. 2013. 50p. 29.95 *(978-0-9886194-1-8(5))* ProsePress.

Benson, Barbara. One. Keilbart, L. S. 2007. (ENG.). 76p. (J). (gr. k-k). per. *(978-1-85756-610-9(6))* Janus Publishing Co.

Benson, Daryl, photos by. Alberta: Images. Benson, Daryl. rev. ed. 2004. (ENG., 120p. *(978-0-9684576-2-7(2))* Cullor Bks. CAN. Dist: Lone Pine Publishing.

Benson, Patrick. Christopher Mouse: The Tale of a Small Traveler. Wise, William. 2006. (ENG.). 160p. (J). (gr. 2-5). per. 6.99 *(978-1-58234-708-0(5)*, Bloomsbury USA Childrens) Bloomsbury USA.

—Moby-Dick. Melville, Herman. 2009. (Candlewick Illustrated Classic Ser.). (ENG.). 192p. (J). (gr. 5). pap. 12.99 *(978-0-7636-4213-6(4))* Candlewick Pr.

—Moby Dick. Melville, Herman. Needle, Jan, ed. 2006. (ENG.). 192p. (J). (gr. 5-7). 21.99 *(978-0-7636-3018-8(7))* Candlewick Pr.

—Night Sky Dragons. Peet, Mal & Graham, Elspeth. 2014. (ENG.). 64p. (J). (gr. -1-3). 15.99 *(978-0-7636-6144-1(9))* Candlewick Pr.

—North: The Amazing Story of Arctic Migration. Dowson, Nick. 2013. (ENG.). 56p. (J). (gr. 2-5). 7.99 *(978-0-7636-6663-7(7))* Candlewick Pr.

—Oddly. Dunbar, Joyce. 2009. (ENG.). 40p. (J). (gr. -1-2). 16.99 *(978-0-7636-4274-7(6))* Candlewick Pr.

Benson, Patrick. Owl Babies. Waddell, Martin. 2015. (ENG.). 22p. (J). (— 1). bds. 6.99 ***(978-0-7636-7961-3(5))*** Candlewick Pr.

Benson, Patrick. Owl Babies: Book & Toy Gift Set. Waddell, Martin. 2003. (ENG.). 22p. (J). (gr. k-12). bds. 14.99 *(978-0-7636-2157-5(9))* Candlewick Pr.

—Owl Babies: Candlewick Storybook Animations. Waddell, Martin. (Candlewick Storybook Animation Ser.). (ENG.). 32p. (J). 2010. (gr. -1-2). 9.99 *(978-0-7636-5042-1(0))*; 2008. (gr. k-k). 14.99 *(978-0-7636-3538-1(3))* Candlewick Pr.

—Soon. Knapman, Timothy. 2015. (ENG.). (J). (-k). 16.99 *(978-0-7636-7476-6(8))* Candlewick Pr.

Benson, Patrick. Christopher Mouse: The Tale of a Small Traveler. Benson, Patrick, tr. Wise, William. 2004. (ENG.). 154p. (J). (gr. 3-6). 15.95 *(978-1-58234-878-0(2)*, Bloomsbury USA Childrens) Bloomsbury USA.

Benson, Patrick, jt. illus. see Allibone, Judith.

Bentley, Anita. Zoey & Bel, 1 vol. Casebolt, Christan. 2009. 14p. pap. 24.95 *(978-1-60813-220-1(X))* America Star Bks.

Bentley, Jonathan. Audrey's Tree House. Hughes, Jenny. 2015. (ENG.). 32p. (J). (gr. -1-k). 17.99 *(978-0-545-81327-3(1)*, Scholastic Pr.) Scholastic, Inc.

—The Best Kind of Kiss. Allum, Margaret. 2011. (ENG.). 24p. (J). 14.99 *(978-0-8027-2274-4(1))* Walker & Co.

—Daddy Kiss. Allum, Margaret. 2010. 24p. (J). (gr. -1). *(978-1-921541-30-8(X))* Little Hare Bks.

—Have You Seen Duck? Holmes, Janet A. 2011. (ENG.). 24p. (J). (gr. -1-3). 8.99 *(978-0-545-22488-8(8)*, Cartwheel Bks.) Scholastic, Inc.

—The Lilac Ladies. Hughes, Jenny. 2014. (ENG.). 32p. (J). (gr. -1-k). 17.99 *(978-1-921894-23-7(7))* Little Hare Bks. AUS. Dist: Independent Pubs. Group.

Bentley, Jonathan. Little Big. 2015. (J). ***(978-0-8028-5462-9(1)***, Eerdmans Bks For Young Readers) Eerdmans, William B. Publishing Co.

Bentley, Jonathan. Pink. Holmes, Janet A. 2013. (ENG.). 32p. (J). (gr. -1-k). pap. 9.99 *(978-1-921894-10-7(5))* Little Hare Bks. AUS. Dist: Independent Pubs. Group.

Bentley, Jonathan. The Ugly Duckling. 2015. (Once upon a Timeless Tale Ser.). (ENG.). 24p. (J). (gr. -1-k). 9.99 ***(978-1-921894-90-9(3))*** Little Hare Bks. AUS. Dist: Independent Pubs. Group.

Bentley, Julia Faye. What Will It Take for a Toad to Kiss a Monkey: The Adventures of Princess Gracie & Prince Wallaby. Bentley, Douglas W. 2008. 52p. per. 24.95 *(978-1-4137-8849-5(1))* America Star Bks.

Bentley, Nicolas. The Wind on the Moon. Linklater, Eric. 2004. (New York Review Children's Collection). (ENG.). 376p. (J). (gr. 4-7). 19.95 *(978-1-59017-100-4(4)*, NYR Children's Collection) New York Review of Bks., Inc., The.

Bentley, Tadgh. Little Penguin Gets the Hiccups. Bentley, Tadgh. 2015. (ENG.). 40p. (J). (gr. -1-3). 17.99 ***(978-0-06-233536-4(7))*** HarperCollins Pubs.

Bently, Peter. Blackthorn Winter. Wilson, Douglas. 2003. 141p. (J). per. 12.00 *(978-1-932168-10-5(9))* Veritas Pr., Inc.

Bently, Peter & McPhillips, Robert. Say Please, Little Bear. 2013. (J). *(978-1-4351-4727-0(8))* Barnes & Noble, Inc.

Benton, Jim. Am I the Princess or the Frog? Benton, Jim. 2005. (Dear Dumb Diary Ser.: 3). (ENG.). 160p. (J). (gr. 3-7). pap. 5.99 *(978-0-439-62907-2(1))* Scholastic, Inc.

—Attack of the 50-Ft. Cupid. Benton, Jim. (Franny K. Stein, Mad Scientist Ser.: 2). (ENG.). 112p. (J). (gr. 2-5). 2005. pap. 5.99 *(978-0-689-86296-0(2))*; 2004. 16.99 *(978-0-689-86292-2(X))* Simon & Schuster Bks. For Young Readers. (Simon & Schuster Bks. For Young Readers).

—Attack of the 50-Ft. Cupid. Benton, Jim. 2011. (Franny K. Stein, Mad Scientist Ser.). 112p. (gr. 3-6). 24.21 *(978-1-59961-818-0(4))* Spotlight.

—The Complete Franny K. Stein, Mad Scientist: Lunch Walks among Us; Attack of the 50-Ft. Cupid - The Invisible Fra - The Fran That Time Forgot - Frantastic Voyage - The Fran with Four Brains - The Frandidate. Benton, Jim. ed. 2012. (Franny K. Stein, Mad Scientist Ser.). (ENG.). 784p. (J). (gr. 2-5). pap. 34.99 *(978-1-4424-7424-6(6)*, Simon & Schuster Bks. For Young Readers) Simon & Schuster Bks. For Young Readers.

—Crate of Danger Set: Lunch Walks among Us - Attack of the 50-Ft. Cupid - The Invisible Fran - The Fran That Time Forgot. Benton, Jim. ed. 2005. (Franny K. Stein, Mad Scientist Ser.). (ENG.). 448p. (J). (gr. 2-5). pap. 19.99 *(978-1-4169-1402-0(1)*, Simon & Schuster Bks. For Young Readers) Simon & Schuster Bks. For Young Readers.

—The End (Almost) Benton, Jim. 2014. (ENG.). 40p. (J). (gr. -1-k). 16.99 *(978-0-545-17731-3(6)*, Scholastic Pr.) Scholastic, Inc.

—The Fran That Time Forgot. Benton, Jim. 4th ed. 2005. (Franny K. Stein, Mad Scientist Ser.: 4). (ENG.). 112p. (J). (gr. 2-5). mass mkt. 5.99 *(978-0-689-86298-4(9))*; 16.99 *(978-0-689-86294-6(6))* Simon & Schuster Bks. For Young Readers. (Simon & Schuster Bks. For Young Readers).

—The Fran That Time Forgot. Benton, Jim. 2011. (Franny K. Stein, Mad Scientist Ser.). 112p. (gr. 3-6). 24.21 *(978-1-59961-820-3(6))* Spotlight.

—The Fran with Four Brains. Benton, Jim. (Franny K. Stein, Mad Scientist Ser.: 6). (ENG.). 112p. (J). (gr. 2-5). 2007. pap. 5.99 *(978-1-4169-0232-4(5))*; 2006. 17.99 *(978-1-4169-0231-7(7))* Simon & Schuster Bks. For Young Readers. (Simon & Schuster Bks. For Young Readers).

—The Fran with Four Brains. Benton, Jim. 2011. (Franny K. Stein, Mad Scientist Ser.). 112p. (gr. 3-6). 24.21 *(978-1-59961-822-7(2))* Spotlight.

—The Frandidate. Benton, Jim. (Franny K. Stein, Mad Scientist Ser.: 7). (ENG.). 112p. (J). (gr. 2-5). 2009. pap. 5.99 *(978-1-4169-0234-8(1))*; No. 7. 2008. 16.99 *(978-1-4169-0233-1(3))* Simon & Schuster Bks. For Young Readers. (Simon & Schuster Bks. For Young Readers).

—The Frandidate. Benton, Jim. 2011. (Franny K. Stein, Mad Scientist Ser.). 128p. (gr. 3-6). 24.21 *(978-1-59961-823-4(0))* Spotlight.

—Frantastic Voyage. Benton, Jim. 2006. (Franny K. Stein, Mad Scientist Ser.: 5). (ENG.). 112p. (J). (gr. 2-5). pap. 5.99 *(978-1-4169-0230-0(9))*; 15.99 *(978-1-4169-0229-4(5))* Simon & Schuster Bks. For Young Readers. (Simon & Schuster Bks. For Young Readers).

—Frantastic Voyage. Benton, Jim. 2011. (Franny K. Stein, Mad Scientist Ser.). 112p. (gr. 3-6). 24.21 *(978-1-59961-821-0(4))* Spotlight.

—The Invisible Fran. Benton, Jim. (Franny K. Stein, Mad Scientist Ser.: 3). (ENG.). 112p. (J). (gr. 2-5). 2005. pap. 5.99 *(978-0-689-86297-7(0))*; 2004. 16.99 *(978-0-689-86293-9(8))* Simon & Schuster Bks. For Young Readers. (Simon & Schuster Bks. For Young Readers).

—The Invisible Fran. Benton, Jim. 2011. (Franny K. Stein, Mad Scientist Ser.). 112p. (gr. 3-6). 24.21 *(978-1-59961-819-7(2))* Spotlight.

—It's Happy Bunny. Benton, Jim. 2008. (It's Happy Bunny Ser.). (ENG.). 32p. (J). (gr. 7). pap. 7.99 *(978-0-545-06934-2(3)*, Scholastic Paperbacks) Scholastic, Inc.

—It's Not My Fault I Know Everything. Benton, Jim. 2009. (Dear Dumb Diary Ser.: 8). (ENG.). 144p. (J). (gr. 3-7). 5.99 *(978-0-439-82597-9(0)*, Scholastic Paperbacks) Scholastic, Inc.

—Let's Pretend This Never Happened. Benton, Jim. 2004. (Dear Dumb Diary Ser.: 1). (ENG.). 128p. (J). (gr. 3-7). pap. 5.99 *(978-0-439-62904-1(7)*, Scholastic Paperbacks) Scholastic, Inc.

—Let's Pretend This Never Happened. Benton, Jim. ed. 2004. (Dear Dumb Diary Ser.: 1). 95p. (gr. -1-2). 16.00 *(978-1-4176-3050-9(7)*, Turtleback) Turtleback Bks.

Benton, Jim. Live Each Day to the Dumbest. Benton, Jim. 2015. (Dear Dumb Diary Year Two Ser.: 6). (ENG.). 144p. (J). (gr. 3-7). pap. 5.99 ***(978-0-545-64258-3(2)***, Scholastic Paperbacks) Scholastic, Inc.

Benton, Jim. Lunch Walks among Us. Benton, Jim. (Franny K. Stein, Mad Scientist Ser.: 1). (ENG.). (J). (gr. 2-5). 2004. 112p. mass mkt. 5.99 *(978-0-689-86295-3(4))*; 2003. 96p. 16.99 *(978-0-689-86291-5(1))* Simon & Schuster Bks. For Young Readers. (Simon & Schuster Bks. For Young Readers).

—Lunch Walks among Us. Benton, Jim. 2011. (Franny K. Stein, Mad Scientist Ser.). 112p. (gr. 3-6). 24.21 *(978-1-59961-817-3(6))* Spotlight.

—Lunch Walks among Us. Benton, Jim. ed. 2004. (Franny K. Stein, Mad Scientist Ser.: 1). 102p. (gr. 2-5). lib. bdg. 16.00 *(978-1-4176-4054-6(5)*, Turtleback) Turtleback Bks.

—Me (Just Like You, Only Better) Benton, Jim. 2011. (Dear Dumb Diary Ser.: 12). (ENG.). 160p. (J). (gr. 3-7). pap. 5.99 *(978-0-545-11616-9(3)*, Scholastic Paperbacks) Scholastic, Inc.

—My Pants Are Haunted! Benton, Jim. 2004. (Dear Dumb Diary Ser.: 2). (ENG.). 144p. (J). (gr. 2-5). mass mkt. 5.99 *(978-0-439-62905-8(5)*, Scholastic Paperbacks) Scholastic, Inc.

—Never Do Anything, Ever. Benton, Jim. Kelly, Jamie. 2005. (Dear Dumb Diary Ser.: 4). (ENG.). 144p. (J). (gr. 3-7). pap. 5.99 *(978-0-439-62908-9(X)*, Scholastic Paperbacks) Scholastic, Inc.

—Never Underestimate Your Dumbness. Benton, Jim. Kelly, Jamie. 2008. (Dear Dumb Diary Ser.: 7). (ENG.). 160p. (J). (gr. 3-7). 5.99 *(978-0-439-82596-2(2))* Scholastic, Inc.

—Nobody's Perfect. I'm As Close As It Gets. Benton, Jim. 2013. (Dear Dumb Diary Year Two Ser.: 3). (ENG.). 144p. (J). (gr. 3-7). pap. 5.99 *(978-0-545-37764-5(1)*, Scholastic Paperbacks) Scholastic, Inc.

—Okay, So Maybe I Do Have Superpowers. Benton, Jim. 2011. (Dear Dumb Diary Ser.: 11). (ENG.). 160p. (J). (gr. 3-7). pap. 5.99 *(978-0-545-11615-2(5)*, Scholastic Paperbacks) Scholastic, Inc.

—School. Hasn't This Gone on Long Enough? Benton, Jim. 2012. (Dear Dumb Diary Year Two Ser.: 1). (ENG.). 160p. (J). (gr. 3-7). pap. 5.99 *(978-0-545-37761-4(7)*, Scholastic Paperbacks) Scholastic, Inc.

—The Super-Nice Are Super-Annoying. Benton, Jim. 2012. (Dear Dumb Diary Year Two Ser.). (ENG.). 144p. (J). (gr. 3-7). pap. 5.99 *(978-0-545-37763-8(3)*, Scholastic Paperbacks) Scholastic, Inc.

—That's What Friends Aren't For. Benton, Jim. 2010. (Dear Dumb Diary Ser.: 9). (ENG.). 144p. (J). (gr. 3-7). 5.99 *(978-0-545-11612-1(0)*, Scholastic Paperbacks) Scholastic, Inc.

—What I Don't Know Might Hurt Me. Benton, Jim. 2013. (Dear Dumb Diary Year Two Ser.: 4). (ENG.). 144p. (J). (gr. 3-7). pap. 5.99 *(978-0-545-37765-2(X)*, Scholastic Paperbacks) Scholastic, Inc.

—The Worst Things in Life Are Also Free. Benton, Jim. 2010. (Dear Dumb Diary Ser.: 10). (ENG.). 160p. (J). (gr. 3-7). pap. 5.99 *(978-0-545-11614-5(7)*, Scholastic Paperbacks) Scholastic, Inc.

—You Can Bet on That. Benton, Jim. 2014. (Dear Dumb Diary Year Two Ser.: 5). (ENG.). 160p. (J). (gr. 3-7). pap. 5.99 *(978-0-545-64257-6(4)*, Scholastic Paperbacks) Scholastic, Inc.

Benton, Marilyn. Bubba, the Busy Beaver. Folmsbee, Judi. 2013. (ENG.). 48p. (J). 20.00 *(978-1-886068-68-1(2))* Fruitbearer Publishing, LLC.

Benton, Tim. Dancing Forever. Bryant, Ann. 2006. (Ballerina Dreams Ser.). 105p. (J). lib. bdg. 4.99 *(978-0-7945-1299-6(2)*, Usborne) EDC Publishing.

—Dancing Princess. Bryant, Ann. 2006. (Ballerina Dreams Ser.). 102p. (J). per. 4.99 *(978-0-7945-1297-2(6)*, Usborne) EDC Publishing.

—Dancing with the Stars. Bryant, Ann. 2006. (Ballerina Dreams Ser.). 107p. (J). per. 4.99 *(978-0-7945-1298-9(4)*, Usborne) EDC Publishing.

—Jasmine's Lucky Star. Bryant, Ann. 2006. (Ballerina Dreams Ser.). 104p. (J). per. 4.99 *(978-0-7945-1295-8(X)*, Usborne) EDC Publishing.

—Poppy's Secret Wish. Bryant, Ann. 2006. (Ballerina Dreams Ser.). 105p. (J). per. 4.99 *(978-0-7945-1294-1(1)*, Usborne) EDC Publishing.

—Rose's Big Decision. Bryant, Ann. 2006. (Ballerina Dreams Ser.). 102p. (J). per. 4.99 *(978-0-7945-1296-5(8)*, Usborne) EDC Publishing.

Beop-Ryong, Yuy. Chronicles of the Cursed Sword, 10 vols. Hui-Jin, Park. rev. ed. 2004. 176p. Vol. 6. pap. 9.99 *(978-1-59182-423-7(0))*; Vol. 7. pap. 9.99 *(978-1-59182-424-4(9))* TOKYOPOP, Inc.

Bereal, JaeMe. In Her Hands: The Story of Sculptor Augusta Savage. Schroeder, Alan. 2009. (ENG.). 48p. (J). (gr. 1-6). 19.95 *(978-1-60060-332-7(7))* Lee & Low Bks., Inc.

Berends, Jenny. Bearen Bear & the Bunbury Tales. Due, Kirsten L. 2013. 194p. pap. *(978-0-9884916-3-2(X))* Roxby Media Ltd.

Berenstain, Jan, et al. The Berenstain Bears Lose a Friend. Berenstain, Jan et al. 2007. (Berenstain Bears Ser.). (ENG.). 32p. (J). (gr. -1-2). pap. 3.99 *(978-0-06-057389-8(9)*, HarperFestival) HarperCollins Pubs.

—The Berenstain Bears' New Kitten. Berenstain, Jan et al. 2007. (I Can Read Book 1 Ser.). (ENG.). 32p. (J). (gr. k-3). 16.99 *(978-0-06-058356-9(8))*; pap. 3.99 *(978-0-06-058357-6(6))* HarperCollins Pubs.

Berenstain, Jan. The Berenstain Bears & the Trouble with Chores. Berenstain, Jan. Berenstain, Stan. 2005. (Berenstain Bears Ser.). (ENG.). 32p. (J). (gr. -1-3). pap. 3.99 *(978-0-06-057382-9(1)*, HarperFestival) HarperCollins Pubs.

—The Berenstain Bears Go on a Ghost Walk. Berenstain, Jan. Berenstain, Stan. 2005. (Berenstain Bears Ser.). (ENG.). 32p. (J). (gr. -1-2). 10.99 *(978-0-06-057399-7(6))*; pap. 3.99 *(978-0-06-057383-6(X))* HarperCollins Pubs. (HarperFestival).

—The Berenstain Bears' New Pup. Berenstain, Jan. Berenstain, Stan. 2005. (I Can Read Book 1 Ser.). (ENG.). 32p. (J). (gr. k-3). pap. 3.99 *(978-0-06-058344-6(4))* HarperCollins Pubs.

—The Berenstain Bears' Really Big Pet Show. Berenstain, Jan. Berenstain, Mike. 2008. (Berenstain Bears Ser.). (ENG.). 32p. (J). (gr. -1-2). pap. 3.99 *(978-0-06-057390-4(2)*, HarperFestival) HarperCollins Pubs.

—The Berenstain Bears' Seashore Treasure. Berenstain, Jan. Berenstain, Stan. 2005. (I Can Read Book 1 Ser.). (ENG.). 32p. (J). (gr. k-3). pap. 3.99 *(978-0-06-058341-5(X))* HarperCollins Pubs.

Berenstain, Jan & Berenstain, Mike. All Aboard! Berenstain, Jan & Berenstain, Mike. 2010. (I Can Read Book 1 Ser.). (ENG.). 32p. (J). (gr. k-3). 16.99 *(978-0-06-168971-0(8))*; pap. 3.99 *(978-0-06-057418-5(6))* HarperCollins Pubs.

—The Berenstain Bears - We Love Trucks! Berenstain, Jan & Berenstain, Mike. 2013. (I Can Read Book 1 Ser.). (ENG.). 32p. (J). (gr. -1-3). pap. 3.99 *(978-0-06-207535-2(7))* HarperCollins Pubs.

—The Berenstain Bears & Mama for Mayor! Berenstain, Jan & Berenstain, Mike. 2012. (I Can Read Book 1 Ser.). (ENG.). 32p. (J). (gr. k-3). 16.99 *(978-0-06-207528-4(4))*; pap. 3.99 *(978-0-06-207527-7(6))* HarperCollins Pubs.

—The Berenstain Bears & the Nutcracker. Berenstain, Jan & Berenstain, Mike. 2011. (Berenstain Bears Ser.). (ENG.). 32p. (J). (gr. -1-3). pap. 3.99 *(978-0-06-057396-6(1)*, HarperFestival) HarperCollins Pubs.

—The Berenstain Bears & the Shaggy Little Pony. Berenstain, Jan & Berenstain, Mike. 2011. (I Can Read Book 1 Ser.). (ENG.). 32p. (J). (gr. k-3). 16.99 *(978-0-06-168972-7(6))*; pap. 3.99 *(978-0-06-057419-2(4))* HarperCollins Pubs.

—The Berenstain Bears & the Tooth Fairy. Berenstain, Jan & Berenstain, Mike. 2012. (Berenstain Bears Ser.). (ENG.). 24p. (J). (gr. -1-3). pap. 3.99 *(978-0-06-207549-9(7)*, HarperFestival) HarperCollins Pubs.

—The Berenstain Bears at the Aquarium. Berenstain, Jan & Berenstain, Mike. 2012. (I Can Read Book 1 Ser.). (ENG.). 32p. (J). (gr. k-3). 16.99 *(978-0-06-207525-3(X))*; pap. 3.99 *(978-0-06-207524-6(1))* HarperCollins Pubs.

—The Berenstain Bears' Baby Easter Bunny. Berenstain, Jan & Berenstain, Mike. 2008. (Berenstain Bears Ser.). (ENG.). 16p. (J). (gr. -1-1). pap. 6.99

(978-0-06-057420-8(8), HarperFestival) HarperCollins Pubs.

—The Berenstain Bears' Big Bedtime Book. Berenstain, Stan & Berenstain, Jan. Berenstain, Mike. 2008. (Berenstain Bears Ser.). 48p. (J). (gr. -1-3). 13.89 *(978-0-06-057435-2(6))* HarperCollins Pubs.

—The Berenstain Bears' Class Trip. Berenstain, Jan & Berenstain, Mike. 2009. (I Can Read Book 1 Ser.). (ENG.). 32p. (J). (gr. k-3). 16.99 *(978-0-06-168973-4(4))*;No. 4. pap., act. bk. ed. 3.99 *(978-0-06-057416-1(X))* HarperCollins Pubs.

—The Berenstain Bears Come Clean for School. Berenstain, Jan & Berenstain, Mike. 2011. (Berenstain Bears Ser.). (ENG.). 32p. (J). (gr. -1-3). pap. 3.99 *(978-0-06-057395-9(3)*, HarperFestival) HarperCollins Pubs.

—The Berenstain Bears' Computer Trouble. Berenstain, Jan & Berenstain, Mike. 2010. (Berenstain Bears Ser.). (ENG.). 32p. (J). (gr. -1-3). 10.99 *(978-0-06-057410-9(0))*; pap. 3.99 *(978-0-06-057394-2(5))* HarperCollins Pubs. (HarperFestival).

—The Berenstain Bears' Dinosaur Dig. Berenstain, Jan & Berenstain, Mike. 2012. (Berenstain Bears Ser.). (ENG.). 24p. (J). (gr. -1-3). pap. 3.99 *(978-0-06-207548-2(9)*, HarperFestival) HarperCollins Pubs.

—The Berenstain Bears' Family Reunion. Berenstain, Jan et al. 2009. (I Can Read Book 1 Ser.). (ENG.). 32p. (J). (gr. k-3). pap. 3.99 *(978-0-06-058360-6(6))* HarperCollins Pubs.

—The Berenstain Bears Get Ready for School. Berenstain, Jan & Berenstain, Mike. 2015. (Berenstain Bears Ser.). (ENG.). 16p. (J). (gr. -1-1). pap. 6.99 *(978-0-06-207552-9(7)*, HarperFestival) HarperCollins Pubs.

—The Berenstain Bears Go on Vacation. Berenstain, Jan et al. 2010. (Berenstain Bears Ser.). (ENG.). 32p. (J). (gr. -1-3). pap. 6.99 *(978-0-06-057433-8(X))* HarperCollins Pubs.

—The Berenstain Bears Go Out to Eat. Berenstain, Jan & Berenstain, Mike. 2009. (Berenstain Bears Ser.). (ENG.). 32p. (J). (gr. -1-2). pap. 3.99 *(978-0-06-057393-5(7)*, HarperFestival) HarperCollins Pubs.

—The Berenstain Bears' Old-Fashioned Christmas. Berenstain, Jan & Berenstain, Mike. 2012. (Berenstain Bears Ser.). (ENG.). 32p. (J). (gr. -1-3). 12.99 *(978-0-06-057443-7(7))* HarperCollins Pubs.

—The Berenstain Bears' Really Big Pet Show. Berenstain, Jan & Berenstain, Mike. 2008. (Berenstain Bears Ser.). 32p. (J). (gr. -1-2). 8.99 *(978-0-06-057406-2(2)*, HarperFestival) HarperCollins Pubs.

—The Berenstain Bears Say Please & Thank You. Berenstain, Jan & Berenstain, Mike. 2011. (Berenstain Bears Ser.). (ENG.). 32p. (J). (gr. -1-3). 12.99 *(978-0-06-057437-6(2))* HarperCollins Pubs.

—The Berenstain Bears' Sleepover. Berenstain, Jan & Berenstain, Mike. 2008. (I Can Read Book 1 Ser.). (ENG.). 32p. (J). (gr. k-3). 16.99 *(978-0-06-168974-1(2))* HarperCollins Pubs.

—The Berenstain Bears Trim the Tree. Berenstain, Jan & Berenstain, Mike. 2007. (Berenstain Bears Ser.). (ENG.). 16p. (J). (gr. -1-1). pap. 6.99 *(978-0-06-057417-8(8)*, HarperFestival) HarperCollins Pubs.

—The Berenstain Bears' Winter Wonderland. Berenstain, Jan & Berenstain, Mike. 2011. (Berenstain Bears Ser.). (ENG.). 16p. (J). (gr. -1-1). pap. 6.99 *(978-0-06-057427-7(5)*, HarperFestival) HarperCollins Pubs.

—Nothing Ever Happens at the South Pole. Berenstain, Stan & Berenstain, Jan. Berenstain, Mike. 2012. (ENG.). 40p. (J). (gr. -1-3). 10.99 *(978-0-06-207532-1(2))* HarperCollins Pubs.

—Safe & Sound! Berenstain, Jan & Berenstain, Mike. 2009. (Berenstain Bears Ser.). (ENG.). 32p. (J). (gr. -1-3). pap. 3.99 *(978-0-06-057391-1(0)*, HarperFestival) HarperCollins Pubs.

—Sick Days. Berenstain, Jan & Berenstain, Mike. 2009. (Berenstain Bears Ser.). (ENG.). 32p. (J). (gr. -1-3). pap. 3.99 *(978-0-06-057392-8(9)*, HarperFestival) HarperCollins Pubs.

—We Love Our Dad! Berenstain, Jan & Berenstain, Mike. 2013. (Berenstain Bears Ser.). (ENG.). 24p. (J). (gr. -1-3). pap. 3.99 *(978-0-06-207551-2(9)*, HarperFestival) HarperCollins Pubs.

—We Love Our Mom! Berenstain, Jan & Berenstain, Mike. 2012. (Berenstain Bears Ser.). (ENG.). 24p. (J). (gr. -1-3). pap. 3.99 *(978-0-06-207547-5(0)*, HarperFestival) HarperCollins Pubs.

—We Love Trucks! Berenstain, Jan & Berenstain, Mike. 2013. (I Can Read Book 1 Ser.). (ENG.). 32p. (J). (gr. -1-3). 16.99 *(978-0-06-207536-9(5))* HarperCollins Pubs.

Berenstain, Jan & Berenstain, Stan. The Big Bedtime Book. Berenstain, Jan & Berenstain, Stan. Berenstain, Mike. 2008. (Berenstain Bears Ser.). (ENG.). 48p. (J). (gr. -1-3). 12.99 *(978-0-06-057434-5(8)*, HarperFestival) HarperCollins Pubs.

Berenstain, Jan, jt. illus. see Berenstain, Mike.

Berenstain, Jan, jt. illus. see Berenstain, Stan.

Berenstain, Mike. The Berenstain Bears' Please & Thank You Book. 2015. (J). *(978-0-8249-1945-0(9))* Ideals Pubns.

—The Berenstain Bears Save Christmas. Berenstain, Stan & Berenstain, Jan. 2005. (Berenstain Bears Ser.). 48p. (J). (gr. -1-3). pap. 6.99 *(978-0-06-052672-6(6)*, HarperFestival) HarperCollins Pubs.

—The Berenstain Bears' Sleepy Time Book. 2015. (J). *(978-0-8249-1946-7(7))* Ideals Pubns.

Berenstain, Mike. The Berenstain Bears - Gone Fishin'! Berenstain, Mike. 2014. (I Can Read Book 1 Ser.). (ENG.). 32p. (J). (gr. -1-3). 16.99 *(978-0-06-207560-4(8))*; pap. 3.99 *(978-0-06-207559-8(4))* HarperCollins Pubs.

Berenstain, Mike. The Berenstain Bears Are SuperBears! Berenstain, Mike. 2015. (I Can Read Book 1 Ser.). (ENG.). 32p. (J). (gr. -1-3). pap. 3.99 ***(978-0-06-235008-4(0))*** HarperCollins Pubs.

Berenstain, Mike. The Berenstain Bears' Easter Parade. Berenstain, Mike. 2014. (Berenstain Bears Ser.). (ENG.). 24p. (J). (gr. -1-3). pap. 3.99 *(978-0-06-207554-3(3)*, HarperFestival) HarperCollins Pubs.

—The Berenstain Bears Go Back to School. Berenstain, Mike. Berenstain, Stan & Berenstain, Jan. (Berenstain Bears Ser.). (ENG.). 32p. (J). (gr. -1-3). 2009. pap. 6.99 *(978-0-06-052675-7(0))*; 2005. 15.99 *(978-0-06-052673-3(4))* HarperCollins Pubs. (HarperFestival).

—The Berenstain Bears' Graduation Day. Berenstain, Mike. 2014. (Berenstain Bears Ser.). (ENG.). 24p. (J). (gr. -1-3). pap. 3.99 *(978-0-06-207555-0(1)*, HarperFestival) HarperCollins Pubs.

—The Berenstain Bears' Lemonade Stand. Berenstain, Mike. 2014. (I Can Read Book 1 Ser.). (ENG.). 32p. (J). (gr. -1-3). 16.99 *(978-0-06-207545-1(4))*; pap. 3.99 *(978-0-06-207544-4(6))* HarperCollins Pubs.

—The Berenstain Bears' Night Before Christmas. Berenstain, Mike. 2013. (Berenstain Bears Ser.). (ENG.). 24p. (J). (gr. -1-3). pap. 3.99 *(978-0-06-207553-6(5)*, HarperFestival) HarperCollins Pubs.

—The Berenstain Bears Phonics Fun. Berenstain, Mike. 2013. (My First I Can Read Book Ser.). (ENG.). 100p. (J). (gr. -1-3). pap. 12.99 *(978-0-06-222346-3(1))* HarperCollins Pubs.

—The Berenstain Bears Save Christmas. Berenstain, Mike. Berenstain, Jan et al. 2003. (Berenstain Bears Ser.). (ENG.). 48p. (J). (gr. -1-3). 14.99 *(978-0-06-052670-2(X)*, HarperFestival) HarperCollins Pubs.

Berenstain, Mike. The Berenstain Bears: When I Grow Up. Berenstain, Mike. 2015. (Berenstain Bears Ser.). (ENG.). 24p. (J). (gr. -1-3). pap. 3.99 ***(978-0-06-235005-3(6)***, HarperFestival) HarperCollins Pubs.

Berenstain, Mike. Hospital Friends. Berenstain, Mike. 2015. (Berenstain Bears Ser.). (ENG.). 24p. (J). (gr. -1-3). pap. 3.99 *(978-0-06-207541-3(1)*, HarperFestival) HarperCollins Pubs.

—Valentine Love Bug. Berenstain, Mike. 2014. (Berenstain Bears Ser.). (ENG.). 24p. (J). (gr. -1-3). pap. 6.99 *(978-0-06-207562-8(4))* HarperCollins Pubs.

—5-Minute Berenstain Bears Stories. Berenstain, Mike. Berenstain, Jan & Berenstain, Stan. 2015. (Berenstain Bears Ser.). (ENG.). 192p. (J). (gr. -1-3). 12.99 *(978-0-06-236018-2(3)*, HarperFestival) HarperCollins Pubs.

Berenstain, Mike & Berenstain, Jan. The Berenstain Bears Lose a Friend. Berenstain, Mike & Berenstain, Jan. 2007. (Berenstain Bears Ser.). 32p. (J). (gr. -1-1). 8.99 *(978-0-06-057405-5(4)*, HarperFestival) HarperCollins Pubs.

Berenstain, Mike, jt. illus. see Berenstain, Jan.

Berenstain, Stan. The Berenstain Bears & a Job Well Done, 1 vol. Berenstain, Jan & Berenstain, Mike. 2010. (Berenstain Bears/Living Lights Ser.). (ENG.). 32p. (J). (gr. -1-2). pap. 3.99 *(978-0-310-71254-1(8))* Zonderkidz.

Berenstain, Stan, et al. The Berenstain Bears & the Bad Influence. Berenstain, Stan et al. 2008. (Berenstain Bears Ser.). 32p. (J). (gr. -1-2). 8.99 *(978-0-06-057404-8(6))*; (ENG.). pap. 3.99 *(978-0-06-057388-1(0))* HarperCollins Pubs. (HarperFestival).

—The Berenstain Bears & the Big Spelling Bee, No. 6. Berenstain, Stan et al. 2007. (Berenstain Bears Ser.). (ENG.). 32p. (J). (gr. -1-2). pap. 3.99 *(978-0-06-057386-7(4)*, HarperFestival) HarperCollins Pubs.

Berenstain, Stan. Berenstain Bears & the Gift of Courage, 1 vol. Berenstain, Jan & Berenstain, Mike. 2010. (Berenstain Bears/Living Lights Ser.). (ENG.). 32p. (J). (gr. -1-2). pap. 3.99 *(978-0-310-71256-5(4))* Zonderkidz.

Berenstain, Stan, et al. The Berenstain Bears & the Trouble with Commercials. Berenstain, Stan et al. 2007. (Berenstain Bears Ser.). (ENG.). 32p. (J). (gr. -1-2). pap. 3.99 *(978-0-06-057387-4(2)*, HarperFestival) HarperCollins Pubs.

—The Berenstain Bears Play T-Ball. Berenstain, Stan & Berenstain, Jan. (I Can Read Book 1 Ser.). (ENG.). 32p. (J). (gr. k-3). 2005. 16.99 *(978-0-06-058337-8(1))*; 2004. pap. 3.99 *(978-0-06-058338-5(X))* HarperCollins Pubs.

—The Berenstain Bears Save Christmas. Berenstain, Stan et al. 2003. (Berenstain Bears Ser.). (J). (gr. k-3). 129.90 *(978-0-06-056995-2(6))* HarperCollins Pubs.

—The Berenstain Bears' Sleepover, Vol. 3. Berenstain, Stan et al. 2008. (I Can Read Book 1 Ser.). (ENG.). 32p. (J). (gr. k-3). pap., act. bk. ed. 3.99 *(978-0-06-057415-4(1))* HarperCollins Pubs.

Berenstain, Stan. The Berenstain Bears Give Thanks, 1 vol. Berenstain, Stan. Berenstain, Mike et al. 2009. (Berenstain Bears/Living Lights Ser.). (ENG.). 32p. (J). (gr. -1-2). pap. 3.99 *(978-0-310-71251-0(3))* Zonderkidz.

—Berenstain Bears Love Their Neighbors, 1 vol. Berenstain, Stan. Berenstain, Jan et al. 2009. (Berenstain Bears/Living Lights Ser.). (ENG.). 32p. (J). (gr. -1-2). pap. 3.99 *(978-0-310-71249-7(1))* Zonderkidz.

—Faithful Friends, 1 vol. Berenstain, Stan. Berenstain, Mike et al. 2009. (Berenstain Bears/Living Lights Ser.). (ENG.). 32p. (J). (gr. -1-2). pap. 3.99 *(978-0-310-71253-4(X))* Zondervan.

Berenstain, Stan & Berenstain, Jan. The Berenstain Bears & the Baby Chipmunk. Berenstain, Stan & Berenstain, Jan. 2005. (I Can Read Book 1 Ser.). (ENG.). 32p. (J). (gr. k-3). pap. 3.99 *(978-0-06-058413-9(0))* HarperCollins Pubs.

—The Berenstain Bears & the Wishing Star. Berenstain, Stan & Berenstain, Jan. 2005. (I Can Read Book 1 Ser.). (ENG.). 32p. (J). (gr. k-3). pap. 3.99 *(978-0-06-058347-7(9))* HarperCollins Pubs.

—The Berenstain Bears & Too Much Car Trip. Berenstain, Stan & Berenstain, Jan. 2006. (Berenstain Bears Ser.). 32p. (J). (gr. -1-2). 10.99 *(978-0-06-057400-0(3))*; (ENG.). pap. 3.99 *(978-0-06-057384-3(8))* HarperCollins Pubs. (HarperFestival).

—The Berenstain Bears' Bedtime Battle. Berenstain, Stan & Berenstain, Jan. 2004. (Berenstain Bears Ser.). (ENG.). 32p. (J). (gr. -1-2). pap. 3.99 *(978-0-06-057381-2(3)*, HarperFestival) HarperCollins Pubs.

—The Berenstain Bears' Big Bedtime Book. Berenstain, Stan & Berenstain, Jan. Berenstain, Mike. 2011. (Berenstain Bears Ser.). (ENG.). 48p. (J). (gr. -1-3). pap. 6.99 *(978-0-06-057436-9(4))* HarperCollins Pubs.

—The Berenstain Bears Clean House. Berenstain, Stan & Berenstain, Jan. 2004. (I Can Read Book 1 Ser.). (ENG.). 32p. (J). (gr. k-3). pap. 3.99 *(978-0-06-058335-4(5))* HarperCollins Pubs.

—The Berenstain Bears down on the Farm. Berenstain, Stan & Berenstain, Jan. 2006. (I Can Read Book 1 Ser.). (ENG.). 32p. (J). (gr. k-3). pap. 3.99 *(978-0-06-058351-4(7))* HarperCollins Pubs.

—The Berenstain Bears God Shows the Way, 1 vol. Berenstain, Stan & Berenstain, Jan. Berenstain, Mike. 2014. (I Can Read! / Berenstain Bears / Living Lights Ser.). (ENG.). 96p. (J). 9.99 *(978-0-310-74211-1(0))* Zonderkidz.

—The Berenstain Bears Hug & Make Up. Berenstain, Stan & Berenstain, Jan. Berenstain, Mike. 2006. (Berenstain Bears Ser.). (ENG.). 32p. (J). (gr. -1-2). pap. 3.99 *(978-0-06-057385-0(6)*, HarperFestival) HarperCollins Pubs.

—The Berenstain Bears Out West. Berenstain, Stan & Berenstain, Jan. 2006. (I Can Read Book 1 Ser.). (ENG.). 32p. (J). (gr. k-3). pap. 3.99 *(978-0-06-058354-5(1))* HarperCollins Pubs.

—The Berenstain Bears Storybook Treasury. Berenstain, Stan & Berenstain, Jan. Berenstain, Mike. 2012. (Berenstain Bears Ser.). (ENG.). 192p. (J). 11.99 *(978-0-06-212014-4(X))* HarperCollins Pubs.

—The Berenstain Bears' Trouble with Pets. Berenstain, Stan & Berenstain, Jan. 2012. (Berenstain First Time Chapter Bks.). (ENG.). 32p. (J). (gr. -1-3). pap. 3.99 *(978-0-679-80848-0(5)*, Random Hse. Bks. for Young Readers) Random Hse. Children's Bks.

Berenstain, Stan, jt. illus. see Berenstain, Jan.

Berenzy, Alix. Into the Sea. Guiberson, Brenda Z. 2014. 32p. pap. 9.00 *(978-1-61003-227-8(6))* Center for the Collaborative Classroom.

Berenzy, Alix. Sammy: The Classroom Guinea Pig. Berenzy, Alix. 2008. (ENG.). 32p. (J). (gr. k-3). pap. 7.99 *(978-0-312-37964-3(1))* Square Fish.

Berg, Caroline O. Sacred Stories: Wisdom from World Religions. McFarlane, Marilyn. 2012. (ENG.). 192p. (J). (gr. 4-9). 17.99 *(978-1-58270-334-3(5))* Aladdin/Beyond Words.

Berg, Deva Jean. A Tail of Two Sisters. Berg, Deva Jean. 2013. 26p. pap. 9.95 *(978-1-939790-07-1(7))* Lorian Assn., The.

Berg, Kelly. Cassie's Creepy Candy Store. Sauvageau-Smestad, Sheila. 2006. 35p. (J). per. 17.95 *(978-0-9767732-2-1(8))* Better Be Write Pub., A.

Berg, Michelle. Dig In! Prince, April Jones. 2013. (ENG.). 14p. (J). (gr. -1 — 1). bds. 7.95 *(978-1-4197-0522-9(9))* Abrams.

—Dive In! Prince, April Jones. 2013. (ENG.). 14p. (J). (gr. -1 — 1). bds. 7.95 *(978-1-4197-0523-6(7))* Abrams.

—First Foil Poetry Love, 2 vols. Feldman, Thea. 2005. (First Foil Poetry Haikus Ser.). 10p. (J). 6.95 *(978-1-58117-189-1(7)*, Intervisual/Piggy Toes) Bendon, Inc.

—First Foil Poetry Seasons, 2 vols. Ageldis, Ida. 2005. (First Foil Poetry Haikus Ser.). 10p. (J). 6.95 *(978-1-58117-188-4(9)*, Intervisual/Piggy Toes) Bendon, Inc.

—Have You Seen Bunny? Prasadam-Halls, Smriti. 2013. (Go, Baby! Ser.). (ENG.). 12p. (J). (— 1). 7.99 *(978-1-4083-1499-9(1))* Hodder & Stoughton GBR. Dist: Independent Pubs. Group.

—Have You Seen Duck? Prasadam-Halls, Smriti. 2013. (Go, Baby! Ser.). (ENG.). 12p. (J). (— 1). bds. 7.99 *(978-1-4083-1500-2(9))* Hodder & Stoughton GBR. Dist: Independent Pubs. Group.

—Have You Seen Kitty? Prasadam-Halls, Smriti. 2013. (Go, Baby! Ser.). (ENG.). 12p. (J). (— 1). bds. 7.99 *(978-1-4083-1501-9(7))* Hodder & Stoughton GBR. Dist: Independent Pubs. Group.

—Have You Seen Puppy? Prasadam-Halls, Smriti. 2013. (Go, Baby! Ser.). (ENG.). 12p. (J). (— 1). bds. 7.99 *(978-1-4083-1506-4(8))* Hodder & Stoughton GBR. Dist: Independent Pubs. Group.

—Hey, Diddle Diddle! Ackerman, Jill. 2011. (Little Scholastic Ser.). (ENG.). 6p. (J). (gr. k — 1). 12.99 *(978-0-545-35113-3(8)*, Cartwheel Bks.) Scholastic, Inc.

—Little Monkey. Ainsworth, Kimberly. 2008. (Little Green Bks.). (ENG.). 6p. (J). (gr. -1 — 1). 9.99 *(978-1-4169-6175-8(5)*, Little Simon) Little Simon.

—Little Panda. Ainsworth, Kimberly. 2008. (Little Green Bks.). (ENG.). 6p. (J). (gr. -1 — 1). 9.99 *(978-1-4169-6173-4(9)*, Little Simon) Little Simon.

—Noah's Ark. Karr, Lily. 2007. (ENG.). 6p. (J). (gr. -1). bds. 12.99 *(978-0-439-86396-4(1))* Scholastic, Inc.

—Old MacDonald: A Hand-Puppet Board Book. Ackerman, Jill. 2007. (Little Scholastic Ser.). (ENG.). 6p. (J). (gr. k — 1). bds. 12.99 *(978-0-545-02603-1(2))* Scholastic, Inc.

—Please & Thank You! Ackerman, Jill. 2011. (Little Scholastic Ser.). (ENG.). 104p. (J). (gr. k — 1). bds. 6.99 *(978-0-545-27092-2(8)*, Cartwheel Bks.) Scholastic, Inc.

—This Little Piggy. Ackerman, Jill. 2007. (Little Scholastic Ser.). (ENG.). 6p. (J). (gr. k — 1). bds. 12.99 *(978-0-545-03038-0(2))* Scholastic, Inc.

—Uh-Oh! I'm Sorry. Ackerman, Jill. 2011. (Little Scholastic Ser.). (ENG.). 10p. (J). (gr. k — 1). bds. 6.99 *(978-0-545-30745-1(7)*, Cartwheel Bks.) Scholastic, Inc.

Berg, Ron. Flame the Desert Pony. Shire, Poppy. 2008. (Magic Pony Carousel Ser.: 5). (ENG.). 96p. (J). (gr. 2-5). pap. 3.99 *(978-0-06-083794-5(2))* HarperCollins Pubs.

—Jewel the Midnight Pony. Shire, Poppy. 2008. (Magic Pony Carousel Ser.: 4). (ENG.). 96p. (J). (gr. 2-5). pap. 3.99 *(978-0-06-083788-4(8))* HarperCollins Pubs.

—Sparkle the Circus Pony. Shire, Poppy. 2007. (Magic Pony Carousel Ser.: 1). (ENG.). 96p. (J). (gr. 2-5). pap. 3.99 *(978-0-06-083779-2(9))* HarperCollins Pubs.

—Star the Western Pony. Shire, Poppy. 2007. (Magic Pony Carousel Ser.: 3). (ENG.). 96p. (J). (gr. 2-5). pap. 3.99 *(978-0-06-083785-3(3))* HarperCollins Pubs.

Berge, Erlend. Ethiopian Voices: Tsion's Life. Bellward, Stacy. 2008. 32p. (J). (gr. 4-7). 19.99 *(978-0-9797481-1-0(9))* Amharic Kids.

Bergen, Brenda. Journey of the Phoenix. Singh, Rajinder. 2011. 24p. (J). (gr. -1-3). 10.00 *(978-0-918224-83-5(7))* Radiance Pubs.

Berger, Carin. Behold the Bold Umbrellaphant: And Other Poems. Prelutsky, Jack. 2006. (ENG.). 40p. (J). (gr. -1-4). 16.99 *(978-0-06-054317-4(5)*, Greenwillow Bks.) HarperCollins Pubs.

—The Green Mother Goose: Saving the World One Rhyme at a Time. Peck, Jan & Davis, David. 2011. (ENG.). 32p. (J). (gr. -1-3). 14.95 *(978-1-4027-6525-4(8))* Sterling Publishing Co., Inc.

—Stardines Swim High Across the Sky: And Other Poems. Prelutsky, Jack. 2013. 40p. (J). (gr. -1-3). (ENG.). 17.99 *(978-0-06-201464-1(1))*; lib. bdg. 18.89 *(978-0-06-201465-8(X))* HarperCollins Pubs. (Greenwillow Bks.).

Berger, Carin. Finding Spring. Berger, Carin. 2015. (ENG.). 40p. (J). (gr. -1-3). 17.99 *(978-0-06-225019-3(1)*, Collins Design) HarperCollins Pubs.

—Forever Friends. Berger, Carin. 2010. (ENG.). 40p. (J). (gr. -1-1). 16.99 *(978-0-06-191528-4(9)*, Greenwillow Bks.) HarperCollins Pubs.

—The Little Yellow Leaf. Berger, Carin. 2008. (ENG.). 40p. (J). (gr. -1-3). 16.99 *(978-0-06-145223-9(8)*, Greenwillow Bks.) HarperCollins Pubs.

—Ok Go. Berger, Carin. 2009. 32p. (J). (gr. -1-k). lib. bdg. 18.89 *(978-0-06-157669-0(7))*; (ENG.). 17.99 *(978-0-06-157666-9(2))* HarperCollins Pubs. (Greenwillow Bks.).

—A Perfect Day. Berger, Carin. 2012. (ENG.). 40p. (J). (gr. -1-3). 16.99 *(978-0-06-201580-8(X)*, Greenwillow Bks.) HarperCollins Pubs.

Berger, Joe. Chitty Chitty Bang Bang. Fleming, Ian. 2013. (Chitty Chitty Bang Bang Ser.). (ENG.). 160p. (J). (gr. 4-7). pap. 6.99 *(978-0-7636-6666-8(1))* Candlewick Pr.

—Chitty Chitty Bang Bang & the Race Against Time. Boyce, Frank Cottrell. (Chitty Chitty Bang Bang Ser.). (ENG.). 240p. (J). (gr. 4-7). 2014. pap. 6.99 *(978-0-7636-6931-7(8))*; 2013. 15.99 *(978-0-7636-5982-0(7))* Candlewick Pr.

—Chitty Chitty Bang Bang Flies Again. Boyce, Frank Cottrell. (Chitty Chitty Bang Bang Ser.). (ENG.). (J). (gr. 4-7). 2013. 224p. pap. 6.99 *(978-0-7636-6353-7(0))*; 2012. 192p. 15.99 *(978-0-7636-5957-8(6))* Candlewick Pr.

—Chitty Chitty Bang Bang over the Moon. Boyce, Frank Cottrell. (Chitty Chitty Bang Bang Ser.). (ENG.). (J). (gr. 4-7). 2015. 304p. pap. 6.99 *(978-0-7636-7666-7(7))*; 2014. 240p. 15.99 *(978-0-7636-5983-7(5))* Candlewick Pr.

—Dot. Zuckerberg, Randi. 2013. (ENG.). 32p. (J). (gr. -1-3). 17.99 *(978-0-06-228751-9(6))* HarperCollins Pubs.

Berger, Joe. Girl & Gorilla. Walton, Rick. 2016. 32p. (J). (gr. -1-3). 17.99 ***(978-0-06-227891-3(6))*** HarperCollins Pubs.

Berger, Joe. Hattie the Bad. Devlin, Jane V. 2010. (ENG.). 32p. (J). (gr. -1-k). 16.99 *(978-0-8037-3447-0(6)*, Dial) Penguin Publishing Group.

—Hubble Bubble, Granny Trouble. Corderoy, Tracey. 2012. (ENG.). 32p. (J). (gr. -1-2). 14.99 *(978-0-7636-5904-2(5)*, Nosy Crow) Candlewick Pr.

—Princess in Training. Sauer, Tammi. (ENG.). 40p. (J). (gr. -1-3). 2015. 6.99 *(978-0-544-45609-9(2)*, HMH Books For Young Readers); 2012. 16.99 *(978-0-15-206599-7(7))* Houghton Mifflin Harcourt Publishing Co.

—Whizz! Pop! Granny, Stop! Corderoy, Tracey. 2013. (ENG.). 32p. (J). (gr. -1-2). 14.99 *(978-0-7636-6551-7(7)*, Nosy Crow) Candlewick Pr.

Bergeron, John W. Jean-Paul Hébert Was There/Jean-Paul Hébert Etait Là, 1 vol. Hébert-Collins, Sheila. 2004. (ENG & FRE.). 32p. (J). (gr. k-3). 16.99 *(978-1-56554-928-9(7))* Pelican Publishing Co., Inc.

Berggren, Jeff. Chicken Cherries. Berggren, Jeff. Hansen, Tammy A., ed. l.t. ed. 2005. 32p. (J). per. 14.95 *(978-0-9755033-0-0(8))* Deep Dish Design.

—My Moon Lagoon. Berggren, Jeff. Hansen, Tammy A., ed. 2007. (J). per. 14.95 *(978-0-9755033-1-7(6))* Deep Dish Design.

Bergherr, Mary. Earth Day. Lowery, Linda. rev. ed. 2003. (On My Own Holidays Ser.). (ENG.). 48p. (gr. 2-4). pap. 6.95 *(978-1-57505-620-3(8))*; lib. bdg. 25.26 *(978-1-57505-700-2(X))* Lerner Publishing Group.

Bergin, Mark. How to Be a Medieval Knight. MacDonald, Fiona. 2005. (How to Be Ser.). (ENG.). 32p. (J). (gr. 3-7). 21.90 *(978-0-7922-3634-4(3)*, National Geographic Children's Bks.) National Geographic Society.

—How to Be a Pirate. Malam, John. 2008. (How to Be Ser.). (ENG.). 32p. (J). (gr. 3-7). pap. 5.95 *(978-1-4263-0283-1(5)*, National Geographic Children's Bks.) National Geographic Society.

—Inside the Beagle with Charles Darwin. MacDonald, Fiona. 2005. (ENG.). 48p. (J). (gr. 3-6). 19.95 *(978-1-59270-041-7(1))* Enchanted Lion Bks., LLC.

—It's Fun to Draw Cars, Planes, & Trains. 2015. (It's Fun to Draw Ser.). (ENG.). 32p. (J). (gr. -1-3). 5.99 *(978-1-63220-410-3(X)*, Sky Pony Pr.) Skyhorse Publishing Co., Inc.

—It's Fun to Draw Creepy-Crawlies. 2015. (It's Fun to Draw Ser.). (ENG.). 32p. (J). (gr. -1-3). 5.99 *(978-1-63220-406-6(1)*, Sky Pony Pr.) Skyhorse Publishing Co., Inc.

—It's Fun to Draw Ponies & Horses. 2015. (It's Fun to Draw Ser.). (ENG.). 32p. (J). (gr. -1-3). 5.99 *(978-1-63220-415-8(0)*, Sky Pony Pr.) Skyhorse Publishing Co., Inc.

—The Migration of a Whale. Kant, Tanya. 2008. (Amaze Ser.). (ENG.). 32p. (J). (gr. k-3). 27.00 *(978-0-531-24049-6(5))*; pap. 8.95 *(978-0-531-23803-5(2))* Scholastic Library Publishing. (Children's Pr.).

B

Bergin, Mark, et al. Scary Creatures of the Deep. Pipe, Jim. 2009. (Scary Creatures Ser.). (ENG.). 32p. (J). (gr. 2-4). 27.00 *(978-0-531-21822-8(8)*, Watts, Franklin) Scholastic Library Publishing.

Bergin, Mark. You Wouldn't Want to Be a Chicago Gangster! Some Dangerous Characters You'd Better Avoid. Matthews, Rupert & Salariya, David. 2010. (You Wouldn't Want to Ser.). (ENG.). 32p. (J). 29.00 *(978-0-531-20470-2(7))* Scholastic Library Publishing.

—You Wouldn't Want to Be a Chicago Gangster! Some Dangerous Characters You'd Better Avoid. Matthews, Rupert. 2010. (You Wouldn't Want to Ser.). (ENG.). 32p. (J). (gr. 3-18). pap. 9.95 *(978-0-531-22825-8(8))* Scholastic Library Publishing.

—You Wouldn't Want to Be a Crusader! A War You'd Rather Not Fight. MacDonald, Fiona. 2005. (You Wouldn't Want to... Ser.). (ENG.). 32p. (J). (gr. 2-5). 29.00 *(978-0-531-12412-3(6))*; pap. 9.95 *(978-0-531-12392-8(8))* Scholastic Library Publishing. (Watts, Franklin).

—You Wouldn't Want to Be a Pony Express Rider! A Dusty, Thankless Job You'd Rather Not Do. Ratliff, Thomas. 2012. (You Wouldn't Want to... Ser.). (ENG.). 32p. (J). pap. 9.95 *(978-0-531-20947-9(4)*, Watts, Franklin); lib. bdg. 29.00 *(978-0-531-20872-4(9))* Scholastic Library Publishing.

—You Wouldn't Want to Explore with Lewis & Clark! An Epic Journey You'd Rather Not Make. Morley, Jacqueline. 2013. (You Wouldn't Want to... Ser.). (ENG.). 32p. (J). 29.00 *(978-0-531-25942-9(0))*; pap. 9.95 *(978-0-531-23039-8(2))* Scholastic Library Publishing. (Watts, Franklin).

—You Wouldn't Want to Live Without Bacteria! Canavan, Roger. 2015. (You Wouldn't Want to Live Without... Ser.). (ENG.). 32p. (J). lib. bdg. 29.00 *(978-0-531-21363-6(3)*, Watts, Franklin) Scholastic Library Publishing.

Bergin, Mark. You Wouldn't Want to Live Without Soap! Woolf, Alex. 2015. (You Wouldn't Want to Live Without... Ser.). (ENG.). 32p. (J). lib. bdg. 29.00 ***(978-0-531-21927-0(5)***, Watts, Franklin) Scholastic Library Publishing.

—You Wouldn't Want to Live Without the Internet! Rooney, Anne. 2015. (You Wouldn't Want to Live Without... Ser.). (ENG.). 32p. (J). lib. bdg. 29.00 ***(978-0-531-21931-7(3)***, Watts, Franklin) Scholastic Library Publishing.

—You Wouldn't Want to Live Without the Writing! Canavan, Roger. 2015. (You Wouldn't Want to Live Without... Ser.). (ENG.). 32p. (J). lib. bdg. 29.00 ***(978-0-531-21930-0(5)***, Watts, Franklin) Scholastic Library Publishing.

Bergin, Mark. You Wouldn't Want to Work on the Brooklyn Bridge! An Enormous Project That Seemed Impossible. Ratliff, Thomas. 2009. (You Wouldn't Want to Ser.). (ENG.). 32p. (J). (gr. 3-18). pap. 9.95 *(978-0-531-20519-8(3))* Scholastic Library Publishing.

—You Wouldn't Want to Work on the Brooklyn Bridge! An Enormous Project That Seemed Impossible. Ratliff, Tom. 2009. (You Wouldn't Want to Ser.). (ENG.). 32p. (J). (gr. 3-12). 29.00 *(978-0-531-21328-5(5))* Scholastic Library Publishing.

Bergin, Mark & Antram, Dave. How to Be an Aztec Warrior. MacDonald, Fiona. 2005. (How to Be Ser.). (ENG.). 32p. (J). (gr. 3-7). lib. bdg. 21.90 *(978-0-7922-3632-0(7)*, National Geographic Children's Bks.) National Geographic Society.

Bergin, Mark & Antram, David. How to Be an Aztec Warrior. MacDonald, Fiona. 2005. (How to Be Ser.). (ENG.). 32p. (J). (gr. 3-7). 14.95 *(978-0-7922-3617-7(3)*, National Geographic Children's Bks.) National Geographic Society.

Bergin, Mark, jt. illus. see Antram, Dave.

Bergman, Shannon, jt. illus. see Ross, Sharon.

Bergmann, Sarah. Potty Palooza: A Step-by-Step Guide to Using a Potty. Gordon, Rachel & Gold, Claudia. 2013. (ENG.). 32p. (J). (gr. k — 1). bds. 8.95 *(978-0-7611-7485-1(0)*, 17485) Workman Publishing Co., Inc.

Bergna, Monica. Juguemos en el Bosque. Anónimo. 2004. (SPA.). 28p. (J). (gr. k-18). pap. 6.50 *(978-980-257-282-3(9))* Ekare, Ediciones VEN. Dist: Iaconi, Mariuccia Bk. Imports.

Bergner, Bobby. Why kitty Is afraid of Poo: A cautionary Tale. Bergner, Bobby. 2008. 20p. 12.99 *(978-0-615-21301-9(4))* Bergner, Bobby.

Bergström, Gunilla. Good Night, Alfie Atkins. Bergstrom, Gunilla. Dyssegaard, Elisabeth Kallick, tr. from SWE. 2005. 32p. (J). 15.00 *(978-91-29-66154-5(4))* R & S Bks. SWE. Dist: Macmillan.

Bergum, Constance R. Beneath the Sun, 1 vol. Stewart, Melissa. 2014. (ENG.). 32p. (J). (gr. -1-3). 16.95 *(978-1-56145-733-5(7))* Peachtree Pubs.

—Dancing with Katya, 1 vol. Chaconas, Dori. 2006. (ENG.). 32p. (J). (gr. k-3). 16.95 *(978-1-56145-376-4(5))* Peachtree Pubs.

—Daniel & His Walking Stick, 1 vol. McCormick, Wendy. 2005. (ENG.). 32p. (J). (gr. k-3). 15.95 *(978-1-56145-330-6(7))* Peachtree Pubs.

—When Rain Falls, 1 vol. Stewart, Melissa. 2008. (ENG.). 32p. (J). (gr. k-3). 16.95 *(978-1-56145-438-9(9))* Peachtree Pubs.

Bergum, Constance Rummel. Nature's Yucky! Gross Stuff That Helps Nature Work, Vol. 1. Landstrom, Lee Ann & Shragg, Karen. rev. ed. 48p. (J). (gr. k-5). pap. 10.00 *(978-0-87842-474-0(1)*, 338) Mountain Pr. Publishing Co., Inc.

—Under the Snow, 1 vol. Stewart, Melissa. 2009. (ENG.). 32p. (J). (gr. -1-3). 16.95 *(978-1-56145-493-8(1))* Peachtree Pubs.

—Who's Faster? Animals on the Move. Meyer, Eileen R. 2012. (J). *(978-0-87842-592-1(6))* Mountain Pr. Publishing Co., Inc.

Bergwerf, Barbara J. A Butterfly Called Hope, 1 vol. Monroe, Mary Alice. 2013. (ENG.). 32p. (J). (gr. -1-4). 17.95 *(978-1-60718-854-4(6))*; pap. 9.95 *(978-1-60718-856-8(2))* Arbordale Publishing.

—Carolina's Story: Sea Turtles Get Sick Too!, 1 vol. Rathmell, Donna. 2005. (ENG.). 32p. (J). (gr. -1-3). 15.95 *(978-0-9764943-0-0(2))* Arbordale Publishing.

—Turtle Summer: A Journal for My Daughter, 1 vol. Monroe, Mary Alice. 2007. (ENG.). 32p. (J). (gr. k-4). 16.95 *(978-0-9777423-5-6(0))* Arbordale Publishing.

Bergwerf, Barbara J. Carolina's Story: Sea Turtles Get Sick Too!, 1 vol. Bergwerf, Barbara J., photos by. Rathmell, Donna. 2005. (ENG.). 32p. (J). (gr. -1-3). pap. 8.95 *(978-1-934359-00-6(9))* Arbordale Publishing.

Berkeley, Jon. Uh-Oh, Cleo. Harper, Jessica. 2008. (Uh-Oh, Cleo Ser.: 1). (ENG.). 64p. (J). (gr. 1-4). 14.99 *(978-0-399-24671-5(1)*, Putnam Juvenile) Penguin Publishing Group.

Berkson, Suzanne Raphael. The Parakeet Named Dreidel. Singer, Isaac Bashevis. 2015. (J). pap. ***(978-0-374-30096-8(8))***; (ENG.). 32p. 17.99 ***(978-0-374-30094-4(1)***, Farrar, Straus & Giroux (BYR)) Farrar, Straus & Giroux.

Berlin, Rose Mary. Itty & Bitty - On the Road. Czerw, Nancy Carpenter. 2008. (Itty & Bitty Ser.: 3). (ENG.). 32p. (J). (gr. -1-3). 16.95 *(978-0-9755618-4-3(7))* McWitty Pr., Inc.

—Storytime Stickers: Baby Animals at Play. Ryals, Katherine. 2010. (Storytime Stickers Ser.). (ENG.). 16p. (J). (gr. k-2). pap. 5.95 *(978-1-4027-5933-8(9))* Sterling Publishing Co., Inc.

Berlin, Rose Mary & Bauer, Dana. Friends on the Farm. Carpenter Czerw, Nancy. 2006. (Itty & Bitty Ser.). (ENG.). 32p. (J). (gr. -1-3). 15.95 *(978-0-9755618-3-6(9))* McWitty Pr., Inc.

Berlin, Rose Mary & Schories, Pat. Biscuit Visits the Doctor. Capucilli, Alyssa Satin. 2008. (Biscuit Ser.). (ENG.). 24p. (J). (gr. -1-1). pap. 3.99 *(978-0-06-112843-1(0)*, HarperFestival) HarperCollins Pubs.

—Biscuit's First Trip. Capucilli, Alyssa Satin. 2010. (Biscuit Ser.). (ENG.). 24p. (J). (gr. -1-1). pap. 3.99 *(978-0-06-162524-4(8)*, HarperFestival) HarperCollins Pubs.

—Biscuit's Pet & Play Easter. Capucilli, Alyssa Satin. 2008. (Biscuit Ser.). (ENG.). 12p. (J). (gr. -1-3). bds. 6.99 *(978-0-06-112839-4(2)*, HarperFestival) HarperCollins Pubs.

—Where Is Love, Biscuit? A Pet & Play Book. Capucilli, Alyssa Satin. 2009. (Biscuit Ser.). (ENG.). 12p. (J). (gr. -1-1). bds. 6.99 *(978-0-06-162521-3(3)*, HarperFestival) HarperCollins Pubs.

Berlin, Rose Mary, jt. illus. see Schories, Pat.

Berlinger, Nancy A. Mother's Surprise. Templeton, Donna L. 2009. (ENG.). 32p. (J). pap. 9.99 *(978-0-9764336-6-8(4))* MJS Publishing Group LLC.

Berman, Linda. San Diego Activity & Coloring Book for All Ages. Penix, Sherry. Date not set. (J). pap. *(978-0-9670612-0-7(2))*; pap. *(978-0-9670612-1-4(0))* Sher-A-Craft.

Berman, Rachel. Bradley McGogg: The Very Fine Frog. Beiser, Tim. (ENG.). 24p. (J). (gr. k-k). 2011. pap. 7.95 *(978-1-77049-276-9(5))*; 2009. 17.95 *(978-0-88776-864-4(4))* Tundra Bks. CAN. (Tundra Bks.). Dist: Penguin Random Hse., LLC.

—Miss Mousie's Blind Date. Beiser, Tim. 2012. (ENG.). 24p. (J). (gr. -1-2). 17.95 *(978-1-77049-251-6(8)*, Tundra Bks.) Tundra Bks. CAN. Dist: Penguin Random Hse., LLC.

Bermejo, Hilbert. The Ramblings of Clyde Frog & Jasmine. Smith, Mary L. 2013. 30p. pap. 11.99 *(978-1-61286-156-2(3))* Avid Readers Publishing Group.

Bermudez, Raymund. Depth Charge, 1 vol. Sherman, M. Zachary & Lee, Raymund. 2012. (Bloodlines Ser.). (ENG.). 88p. (gr. 4-8). pap. 6.95 *(978-1-4342-3876-4(8))*; lib. bdg. 23.32 *(978-1-4342-3764-4(8))* Stone Arch Bks.

—Emergency Ops, 1 vol. Sherman, M. Zachary & Lee, Raymund. 2012. (Bloodlines Ser.). (ENG.). 88p. (gr. 4-8). pap. 6.95 *(978-1-4342-3877-1(6))*; lib. bdg. 23.32 *(978-1-4342-3766-8(4))* Stone Arch Bks.

Bernabe, Tabitha Victoria. What to Be When I Grow Up. Bernabe, Victor. 2008. 28p. pap. 24.95 *(978-1-60703-696-8(7))* America Star Bks.

Bernadin, James. Encyclopedia Brown & the Case of the Soccer Scheme. Sobol, Donald J. (Encyclopedia Brown Ser.). (ENG.). 96p. (J). (gr. 3-7). 2013. pap. 4.99 *(978-0-14-242288-5(6)*, Puffin); 2012. 16.99 *(978-0-525-42582-3(9)*, Dutton Juvenile) Penguin Publishing Group.

Bernado, Jordi, et al, photos by. Bellinzona 2001. Varini, Felice. 2003. (FRE, ENG, GER & ITA., 75p. (YA). pap. 32.00 *(978-88-87469-29-5(6))* Gabriele Capelli Editore Sagl CHE. Dist: SPD-Small Pr. Distribution.

Bernal, Mitchell. Skelanimals: Dead Animals Need Love Too, Bernal, Mitchell. l.t. ed. 2005. 22p. (J). per. 12.95 *(978-0-9766621-0-5(8)*, 818 554-8965) Kreations.

Bernal, Rafael. El Hombre de la Arena. Hoffmann, E. T. A. Toro, Jorge & Gonzalez, Carlos Mario, trs. 2004. (Cajon de Cuentos Ser.). (SPA.). 220p. (J). (gr. 4-7). *(978-958-30-0724-8(2))* Panamericana Editorial.

Bernal, Richard. Smasher. King-Smith, Dick & Fox Busters Ltd. Staff. 2006. (Stepping Stone Book(TM) Ser.). (ENG.). 80p. (J). (gr. 1-4). 3.99 *(978-0-679-88330-2(4)*, Random Hse. Bks. for Young Readers) Random Hse. Children's Bks.

Bernal, Victor Garcia. Vida y Fortuna de un Muchacho Inquieto Que Se Convirtio en Cientifico. Barajas Mariscal, Libia E. & Mariscal, Libia Barajas. rev. ed. 2006. (Otra Escalera Ser.). (SPA & ENG.). 24p. (J). (gr. 2-4). pap. 9.95 *(978-968-5920-61-2(3))* Castillo, Ediciones, S. A. de C. V. MEX. Dist: Macmillan.

Bernard, C. E. B. Tales of an Old Lumber Camp: A Story of Early Days in A Great Industry. Hamlin, John. 2011. 188p. 42.95 *(978-1-258-04052-9(2))* Literary Licensing, LLC.

Bernard, Courtney. Get Ella to the Apollo. Mullarkey, Lisa & Mullarkey, John. 2015. (J). *(978-1-62402-087-2(9))* Magic Wagon.

—Mary Molds a Monster. Mullarkey, Lisa & Mullarkey, John. 2015. (J). *(978-1-62402-088-9(7))* Magic Wagon.

—Monet Changes Mediums. Mullarkey, Lisa & Mullarkey, John. 2015. (J). *(978-1-62402-089-6(5))* Magic Wagon.

—Shakespeare Saves the Globe. Mullarkey, Lisa & Mullarkey, John. 2015. (J). *(978-1-62402-090-2(9))* Magic Wagon.

Bernard, Donna. Word Skills in Rhythm & Rhyme Level 1. Sitton, Rebecca. 2004. 122p. (gr. 1-18). spiral bd. 59.95 *(978-1-886050-62-4(7))* Egger Publishing, Inc.

—Word Skills in Rhythm & Rhyme Level 2. Sitton, Rebecca. 2004. 118p. (gr. 2-18). spiral bd. 59.95 *(978-1-886050-63-1(5))* Egger Publishing, Inc.

—Word Skills in Rhythm & Rhyme Level 3. Sitton, Rebecca. 2004. 112p. (gr. 3-18). spiral bd. 59.95 *(978-1-886050-64-8(3))* Egger Publishing, Inc.

Bernard Westcott, Nadine. Comin' down to Storytime. Reid, Rob. 2009. (J). (gr. -1-3). 17.95 *(978-1-60213-039-5(6)*, Upstart Bks.) Highsmith Inc.

—We're Going on a Book Hunt. Miller, Pat. 2008. (J). (gr. -1). 17.95 *(978-1-60213-034-0(5)*, Upstart Bks.) Highsmith Inc.

—Ziggy McFinster's Nantucket Adventure. Bagley, Conor. 2008. (ENG.). 40p. (J). (gr. -1-3). 16.95 *(978-1-56625-315-4(2))* Bonus Bks., Inc.

Bernard Westcott, Nadine & Westcott, Nadine Bernard. Miss Mary Mack. Hoberman, Mary Ann. 2003. (ENG.). 32p. (J). (gr. -1-1). pap. 7.00 *(978-0-316-07614-2(7)*, Tingley, Megan Bks.) Little, Brown Bks. for Young Readers.

Bernardin, James. Barack Obama: Out of Many, One. Corey, Shana. 2009. (Step into Reading Ser.). (ENG.). 48p. (J). (gr. k-3). pap. 3.99 *(978-0-375-86339-4(7)*, Random Hse. Bks. for Young Readers) Random Hse. Children's Bks.

—Case of the Kidnapped Cupid. Star, Nancy. 2005. (Calendar Club Mysteries Ser.). 79p. (J). *(978-0-439-67263-4(5))* Scholastic, Inc.

—The Case of the Thanksgiving Thief. Star, Nancy. 2004. 79p. (J). *(978-0-439-67261-0(9))* Scholastic, Inc.

—Encyclopedia Brown & the Case of the Secret UFOs. Sobol, Donald J. 2010. (Encyclopedia Brown Ser.). (ENG.). 128p. (J). (gr. 3-18). 16.99 *(978-0-525-42210-5(2)*, Dutton Juvenile) Penguin Publishing Group.

—Go Back to Bed! Guy, Ginger Foglesong. 2006. (ENG.). 32p. (J). (gr. k-3). 16.95 *(978-1-57505-750-7(6)*, Carolrhoda Bks.) Lerner Publishing Group.

—A Horn for Louis. Kimmel, Eric A. 2006. (Stepping Stone Book Ser.). (ENG.). 96p. (J). (gr. 2-5). per. 4.99 *(978-0-375-84005-0(2)*, Random Hse. Bks. for Young Readers) Random Hse. Children's Bks.

—I Know Who Likes You. Cooney, Doug. 2005. (ENG.). 224p. (J). (gr. 3-7). pap. 10.99 *(978-1-4169-0261-4(9)*, Simon & Schuster Bks. For Young Readers) Simon & Schuster Bks. For Young Readers.

—Lumber Camp Library. Kinsey-Warnock, Natalie. 2003. (ENG.). 96p. (J). (gr. 2-5). pap. 4.99 *(978-0-06-444292-3(6))* HarperCollins Pubs.

—Mystery of the Snow Day Bigfoot. Star, Nancy. 2005. (Calendar Club Mysteries Ser.: Vol. 3). 77p. (J). pap. 3.95 *(978-0-439-67262-7(7))* Scholastic, Inc.

—An Old-Fashioned Thanksgiving. Alcott, Louisa May. 2005. 32p. (J). (gr. -1-3). 16.99 *(978-0-06-000450-7(9))* HarperCollins Pubs.

—Say What? Haddix, Margaret Peterson. 2005. 91p. (J). 11.65 *(978-0-7569-5465-9(7))* Perfection Learning Corp.

—Say What? Haddix, Margaret Peterson. 2005. (ENG.). 96p. (J). (gr. 1-5). pap. 5.99 *(978-0-689-86256-4(3)*, Simon & Schuster Bks. For Young Readers) Simon & Schuster Bks. For Young Readers.

—The Twelve Prayers of Christmas. Chand, Candy. 2009. (HarperBlessings Ser.). (ENG.). 32p. (J). (gr. -1-2). 16.99 *(978-0-06-077636-7(6))* HarperCollins Pubs.

—Would I Trade My Parents? Numeroff, Laura Joffe. 2009. (ENG.). 32p. (J). (gr. -1-3). 16.95 *(978-0-8109-0637-2(6)*, Abrams Bks. for Young Readers) Abrams.

—Yes, Virginia: There Is a Santa Claus. Plehal, Christopher J. 2010. (ENG.). 32p. (J). (gr. -1-2). 16.99 *(978-0-06-200173-3(6))* HarperCollins Pubs.

Bernardin, James & Cowdrey, Richard. The Legend of the Candy Cane: The Inspirational Story of Our Favorite Christmas Candy, 1 vol. Walburg, Lori. ed. 2012. (ENG.). 32p. (J). 15.99 *(978-0-310-73012-5(0))* Zonderkidz.

Bernardini, Cristian. Gertrude & Reginald the Monsters Talk about Living & Nonliving, 1 vol. Braun, Eric. 2012. (In the Science Lab Ser.). (ENG.). 24p. (gr. 2-3). pap. 8.95 *(978-1-4048-7237-0(X))*; lib. bdg. 25.99 *(978-1-4048-7146-5(2))* Picture Window Bks. (Nonfiction Picture Bks.).

—No Lie, I Acted Like a Beast! The Story of Beauty & the Beast As Told by the Beast, 1 vol. Loewen, Nancy. 2013. (Other Side of the Story Ser.). (ENG.). 24p. (gr. 2-3). pap. 6.95 *(978-1-4048-8083-2(6))*; lib. bdg. 26.65 *(978-1-4048-7938-6(2))* Picture Window Bks.

—No Lie, I Acted Like a Beast: The Story of Beauty & the Beast as Told by the Beast. Loewen, Nancy. 2013. (Other Side of the Story Ser.). (ENG.). 24p. (gr. 2-3). 9.95 *(978-1-4795-1944-6(8))* Picture Window Bks.

—Trust Me, Jack's Beanstalk Stinks! The Story of Jack & the Beanstalk as Told by the Giant. Braun, Eric. 2011. (Other Side of the Story Ser.). (ENG.). 24p. (gr. 2-3). pap. 6.95 *(978-1-4048-7050-5(4))*; lib. bdg. 26.65 *(978-1-4048-6675-1(2))* Picture Window Bks. (Nonfiction Picture Bks.).

Bernardini, Cristian & Guerlais, Gérald. The Other Side of the Story. Loewen, Nancy & Gunderson, Jessica. 2013. (Other Side of the Story Ser.). (ENG.). 24p. (gr. 2-3). lib. bdg. 106.60 *(978-1-4048-8077-1(1))* Picture Window Bks.

—The Other Side of the Story. Loewen, Nancy. 2013. (Other Side of the Story Ser.). (ENG.). 24p. (gr. 2-3). pap. 13.90 *(978-1-4048-8087-0(9))*; lib. bdg. 159.90 *(978-1-4048-7939-3(0))* Picture Window Bks. (Nonfiction Picture Bks.).

Bernardini, Cristian, jt. illus. see Guerlais, Gérald.

Bernasconi, Pablo. Pumpkin Town! or, Nothing Is Better & Worse Than Pumpkins. McKy, Katie. 2008. (ENG.). 32p. (J). (gr. -1-3). pap. 6.99 *(978-0-547-18193-6(0))* Houghton Mifflin Harcourt Publishing Co.

Bernatene, Poly. Bob the Dog. Folgueira, Rodrigo. 2014. (J). ***(978-1-4351-5774-3(5))*** Barnes & Noble, Inc.

Bernatene, Poly. The Dead Family Diaz. Bracegirdle, P. J. (ENG.). 40p. (J). 2015. (gr. k-3). 8.99 *(978-0-14-751558-2(0)*, Puffin); 2012. (gr. 1-4). 16.99 *(978-0-8037-3326-8(7)*, Dial) Penguin Publishing Group.

Bernatene, Poly. Hello, Hippo! Goodbye, Bird! Crow, Kristyn. 2016. (ENG.). 32p. (J). ***(978-0-553-50990-8(X))*** Knopf, Alfred A. Inc.

Bernatene, Poly. The Princess & the Pig. Emmett, Jonathan & Dunn, David H. 2011. (ENG.). 32p. (J). (gr. k-8). 17.99 *(978-0-8027-2334-5(9)*, Bloomsbury USA Childrens) Bloomsbury USA.

—Ribbit! Folgueira, Rodrigo. 2013. (ENG.). 32p. (J). (gr. -1-k). 15.99 *(978-0-307-98146-2(0))*; lib. bdg. 18.99 *(978-0-307-98147-9(9))* Random Hse. Children's Bks. (Knopf Bks. for Young Readers).

—The Santa Trap, 1 vol. Emmett, Jonathan. 2012. (ENG.). 32p. (J). 15.95 *(978-1-56145-670-3(5))* Peachtree Pubs.

—The Second Spy. West, Jacqueline. 2013. (Books of Elsewhere Ser.: 3). (ENG.). 320p. (J). (gr. 5). pap. 6.99 *(978-0-14-242608-1(3)*, Puffin) Penguin Publishing Group.

—The Second Spy, Vol. 3. West, Jacqueline. 2012. (Books of Elsewhere Ser.: 3). (ENG.). 304p. (J). (gr. 5-18). 16.99 *(978-0-8037-3689-4(4)*, Dial) Penguin Publishing Group.

—The Shadows. West, Jacqueline. 2010. (Books of Elsewhere Ser.: 1). (ENG.). 256p. (J). (gr. 5-18). 16.99 *(978-0-8037-3440-1(9)*, Dial) Penguin Publishing Group.

—The Sorcerer's Apprentice. 2007. (Usborne Young Reading: Series One Ser.). 47p. (J). (gr. -1-3). 8.99 *(978-0-7945-1589-8(4)*, Usborne) EDC Publishing.

—Still Life. West, Jacqueline. 2014. (Books of Elsewhere Ser.: 5). (ENG.). 352p. (J). (gr. 5). 16.99 *(978-0-8037-3691-7(6)*, Dial) Penguin Publishing Group.

—Still Life: The Books of Elsewhere: Volume 5. West, Jacqueline. 2015. (Books of Elsewhere Ser.: 5). (ENG.). 352p. (J). (gr. 5). 7.99 *(978-0-14-242297-7(5)*, Puffin) Penguin Publishing Group.

—The Strangers. West, Jacqueline. (Books of Elsewhere Ser.: 4). (ENG.). (J). (gr. 5). 2014. 336p. pap. 7.99 *(978-0-14-242575-6(3)*, Puffin); 2013. 320p. 16.99 *(978-0-8037-3690-0(8)*, Dial) Penguin Publishing Group.

—The Tickle Tree. Strathie, Chae. 2008. 24p. (J). (gr. -1-1). *(978-1-84539-344-1(9))*; *(978-1-84539-345-8(7))* Meadowside Children's Bks.

—Who Did This? Hao, K. T. 2008. (ENG.). 32p. (J). (gr. -1). lib. bdg. 16.50 *(978-1-933327-33-4(2))* Purple Bear Bks., Inc.

—Who Did This? Hao, K. T. 2008. (ENG.). 32p. (J). (gr. -1). 15.95 *(978-1-933327-32-7(4))* Purple Bear Bks., Inc.

Bernatene, Poly. The Monster Diaries. Bernatene, Poly. Saracino, Luciano. 2009. 32p. (J). 15.99 *(978-1-60010-502-9(5)*, Worthwhile Bks.) Idea & Design Works, LLC.

Bernd, Penners. All Better! Lohlein, Henning. 2015. (ENG.). 16p. (J). bds. 12.99 *(978-1-61067-362-4(X))* Kane Miller.

Berner, Paulette L. The Cottontails & the Jackrabbits. Berner, R. Thomas. 2008. 22p. (J). per. 19.95 *(978-0-922993-06-2(8))* Marquette Bks., LLC.

Berner, Rotraut Susanne. The Cat: Or, How I Lost Eternity. Richter, Jutta. Brailovsky, Anna, tr. from GER. 2007. (ENG.). 80p. (J). (gr. 1-6). 14.00 *(978-1-57131-676-9(0))* Milkweed Editions.

—The Winter Book. Aldana, Patricia, ed. 2008. (ENG.). 80p. (J). (gr. 4-7). 25.00 *(978-0-88899-900-9(3))* Groundwood Bks. CAN. Dist: Perseus-PGW.

Bernhard, Durga. Green Bible Stories for Children. Lehman-Wilzig, Tami. 2011. (Bible Ser.). (ENG.). 48p. (J). (gr. 3-5). lib. bdg. 17.95 *(978-0-7613-5135-1(3)*, Kar-Ben Publishing) Lerner Publishing Group.

Bernhard, Durga. While You Are Sleeping. Bernhard, Durga. 2011. (ENG.). 24p. (J). (gr. k-3). 14.95 *(978-1-57091-473-7(7))* Charlesbridge Publishing, Inc.

Bernhard, Durga Yael. The Dreidel That Wouldn't Spin: A Toyshop Tale of Hanukkah. Simpson, Martha Seif. 2014. (ENG.). 32p. (J). (gr. -1-2). 16.95 *(978-1-937786-28-1(5)*, Wisdom Tales) World Wisdom, Inc.

—Green Bible Stories for Children. Lehman-Wilzig, Tami. 2011. (Bible Ser.). (ENG.). 48p. (J). (gr. 3-5). pap. 7.95 *(978-0-7613-5136-8(1)*, Kar-Ben Publishing) Lerner Publishing Group.

—Never Say a Mean Word Again: A Tale from Medieval Spain. Jules, Jacqueline. 2014. (ENG.). 32p. (J). (gr. -1-3). 16.95 *(978-1-937786-20-5(X)*, Wisdom Tales) World Wisdom, Inc.

Berns, J. M. Allergy Busters: A Story for Children with Autism or Related Spectrum Disorders Struggling with Allergies. Chara, Kathleen A. et al. 2004. (ENG.). 48p. (J). pap. *(978-1-84310-782-8(1))* Kingsley, Jessica Ltd.

Berns, Joel M. Sensory Smarts: A Book for Kids with ADHD or Autism Spectrum Disorders Struggling with Sensory Integration Problems. Chara, Kathleen A. & Chara, Paul J. 2004. (ENG.). 80p. (J). pap. *(978-1-84310-783-5(X))* Kingsley, Jessica Ltd.

Bernstein, Gabo León. The Legend of Black Bart, 1 vol. Guerra, Elisa Puricelli. Pernigotti, Chiara, tr. from ITA. 2014. (Minerva Mint Ser.). (ENG.). 160p. (gr. 2-4). pap. 7.99 ***(978-1-4342-6515-9(3))*** Capstone Young Readers.

Bernstein, Gabo León. The Legend of Black Bart, 1 vol. Guerra, Elisa Puricelli. Pernigotti, Chiara, tr. from ITA. 2014. (Minerva Mint Ser.). (ENG.). 160p. (gr. 2-4). 23.99 *(978-1-4342-6512-8(9))* Stone Arch Bks.

Bernstein, Gabo León. Merlin's Island, 1 vol. Guerra, Elisa Puricelli. Pernigotti, Chiara, tr. from ITA. 2014. (Minerva Mint Ser.). (ENG.). 160p. (gr. 2-4). pap. 7.99 ***(978-1-4342-6514-2(5))*** Capstone Young Readers.

Bernstein, Gabo León. Merlin's Island, 1 vol. Guerra, Elisa Puricelli. Pernigotti, Chiara, tr. from ITA. 2014. (Minerva Mint Ser.). (ENG.). 160p. (gr. 2-4). 23.99 *(978-1-4342-6511-1(0))* Stone Arch Bks.

—The Order of the Owls, 1 vol. Guerra, Elisa Puricelli. 2014. (Minerva Mint Ser.). (ENG.). 160p. (gr. 2-4). 9.95 *(978-1-62370-038-6(8))* Capstone Young Readers.

Bernstein, Gabriel León. The City of Lizards. Guerra, Elisa Puricelli. Zeni, Marco, tr. from ITA. 2015. (Minerva Mint Ser.). (ENG.). 160p. (gr. 2-4). lib. bdg. 23.99 ***(978-1-4342-9671-9(7))*** Stone Arch Bks.

—The Forest of Talking Trees. Guerra, Elisa Puricelli. Zeni, Marco, tr. 2015. (Minerva Mint Ser.). (ENG.). 160p. (gr. 2-4). lib. bdg. 23.99 ***(978-1-4342-9673-3(3))*** Stone Arch Bks.

—The Night of the Blue Turtles. Guerra, Elisa Puricelli. Zeni, Marco, tr. from ITA. 2015. (Minerva Mint Ser.). (ENG.). 160p. (gr. 2-4). lib. bdg. 23.99 ***(978-1-4342-9672-6(5))*** Stone Arch Bks.

Bernstein, Galia. Monkey & Elephant. Schaefer, Carole Lexa. (Candlewick Sparks Ser.). (ENG.). 48p. (J). (gr. k-4). 2013. pap. 3.99 *(978-0-7636-6261-5(5))*; 2012. 14.99 *(978-0-7636-4840-4(X))* Candlewick Pr.

—Monkey & Elephant & a Secret Birthday Surprise. Schaefer, Carole Lexa. 2015. (ENG.). 48p. (J). (gr. k-4). 14.99 *(978-0-7636-6131-1(7))* Candlewick Pr.

—Monkey & Elephant Get Better. Schaefer, Carole Lexa. (Candlewick Sparks Ser.). (ENG.). 48p. (J). (gr. k-4). 2014. pap. 3.99 *(978-0-7636-7180-8(0))*; 2013. 14.99 *(978-0-7636-4841-1(8))* Candlewick Pr.

Bernstein, Galia. Monkey & Elephant Go Gadding. Schaefer, Carole Lexa. 2015. (Candlewick Sparks Ser.). (ENG.). 48p. (J). (gr. k-4). pap. 3.99 ***(978-0-7636-8030-5(3))*** Candlewick Pr.

Bernstein, Galia & Ruffle, Mark. Build the Human Body. Walker, Richard. 2013. (Build It Ser.). (ENG.). 32p. (J). (gr. k). 19.95 *(978-1-60710-413-1(X)*, Silver Dolphin Bks.) Baker & Taylor Publishing Group.

—Build the T. Rex. Naish, Darren. 2013. (Build It Ser.). (ENG.). 32p. (J). (gr. k). 19.95 *(978-1-60710-415-5(6)*, Silver Dolphin Bks.) Baker & Taylor Publishing Group.

Bernstein, Galia, jt. illus. see Ruffle, Mark.

Berrett, Pat, photos by. A More Abundant Life: New Deal Artists & Public Art in New Mexico. Hoefer, Jacqueline, ed. 2003. 196p. 60.00 *(978-0-86534-305-4(5))* Sunstone Pr.

Berringer, Nick. The Super Joke Book. Brandreth, Gyles. 2009. (ENG.). 112p. (J). (gr. 2-7). pap. 4.95 *(978-1-4027-4713-7(6))* Sterling Publishing Co., Inc.

Berry, Bob. Ancient Times: Step-by-Step Instructions for 18 Ancient Characters & Civilizations. 2013. (Learn to Draw Ser.). (ENG.). 40p. (J). (gr. 1-17). pap. 4.95 *(978-1-60058-310-0(5)*, 1600583105) Quarto Publishing Group USA.

—How to Draw Steampunk: Discover the Secrets to Drawing, Painting, & Illustrating the Curious World of Science Fiction in the Victorian Age. Marsocci, Joey & DeBlasio, Allison. 2011. (Fantasy Underground Ser.). (ENG.). 128p. pap. 19.95 *(978-1-60058-240-0(0)*, 1600582400) Quarto Publishing Group USA.

—Learn to Draw Ancient Times. Phan, Sandy. 2014. (Learn to Draw (Walter Foster Library) Ser.). (ENG.). 40p. (J). (gr. 4-7). lib. bdg. 29.27 *(978-1-939581-26-6(5))* Quarto Publishing Group USA.

—Watch Me Draw - Robots: A Step-by-Step Drawing & Story Book. Torres, Jickie. 2010. (Watch Me Draw Ser.). (ENG.). 24p. (J). (gr. -1-17). pap. 4.95 *(978-1-60058-154-0(4)*, 1600581544) Quarto Publishing Group USA.

Berry, Gaynor. Where Are My Pants? A Hide-and-Seek Book W/ Flaps & Slots. Berry, Gaynor. 2005. (ENG.). 16p. (J). (gr. -1-k). 16.99 *(978-1-85707-657-8(5))* Tango Bks. GBR. Dist: Independent Pubs. Group.

Berry, Holly. Colorful Dreamer: The Story of Artist Henri Matisse. Parker, Marjorie Blain & Matisse, Henri. 2012. (ENG.). 32p. (J). (gr. -1-k). 16.99 *(978-0-8037-3758-7(0)*, Dial) Penguin Publishing Group.

—Frog Went A-Dancing. Rovetch, L. Bob. 2006. (J). *(978-1-58987-008-6(5))* Kindermusik International.

—The Gingerbread Cowboy. Squires, Janet. 2006. 32p. (J). (gr. -1-3). (ENG.). 17.99 *(978-0-06-077863-7(6))*; lib. bdg. 18.89 *(978-0-06-077864-4(4))* HarperCollins Pubs.

—I'm a Pig. Weeks, Sarah. 2005. 32p. (J). (gr. -1-2). lib. bdg. 16.89 *(978-0-06-074344-4(1)*, Geringer, Laura Book) HarperCollins Pubs.

Berry, Holly. A Passion for Elephants: The Real Life Adventure of Field Scientist Cynthia Moss. Buzzeo, Toni. 2015. (J). ***(978-0-399-18600-4(X))*** Penguin Publishing Group.

Berry, Holly. Thanksgiving on Plymouth Plantation. Stanley, Diane. 2004. (Time-Traveling Twins Ser.). (ENG.). 48p. (J). (gr. k-5). 16.99 *(978-0-06-027069-8(1))* HarperCollins Pubs.

—Woof. Weeks, Sarah. 2009. (ENG.). 32p. (J). (gr. -1-3). 16.99 *(978-0-06-025007-2(0))* HarperCollins Pubs.

Berry, Max. Meet the ANZACs. Saxby, Claire. 2014. (Meet... Ser.). (ENG.). 32p. (J). (gr. k). 19.99 *(978-0-85798-192-9(7))* Random Hse. Australia AUS. Dist: Independent Pubs. Group.

Berry, VacieAnna. Dandylion. Laible, Steve William, ed. ed. 2012. (ENG.). 38p. (J). pap. 9.95 *(978-0-9844784-6-0(9)*, Empire Holdins - Literary Division for Young Readers) Kodel Group, LLC, The.

Bersanetti, Sandra. El Pueblo de los Silencios. Brignole, Giancarla, tr. (Fabulas De Familia Ser.). (SPA.). 32p. *(978-970-20-0271-0(0))* Castillo, Ediciones, S. A. de C. V.

—Los Regalos de Tia Terciopelina. Bresanetti, Sandra & Bresanetti, S. Brignole, Giancarla, tr. rev. ed. 2006. (Fabulas De Familia Ser.). (SPA & ENG.). 32p. (J). (gr. k-4). pap. 6.95 *(978-970-20-0253-6(2))* Castillo, Ediciones, S. A. de C. V. MEX. Dist: Macmillan.

Bersani, Shennen. Animal Partners, 1 vol. Cohn, Scotti. 2015. (ENG.). 32p. (J). (gr. k-4). 17.95 *(978-1-62855-448-9(7))* Arbordale Publishing.

—Astro: The Steller Sea Lion, 1 vol. Harvey, Jeanne Walker. 2010. (ENG.). 32p. (J). (gr. -1-4). pap. 9.95 *(978-1-60718-874-2(0))* Arbordale Publishing.

—Beginnings. Watson, Lori Ann. 2009. 32p. (J). (gr. -1-1). 12.95 *(978-0-8198-1172-1(6))* Pauline Bks. & Media.

—Butterfly Colors & Counting. Pallotta, Jerry. 2013. (ENG.). 10p. (J). (— 1). bds. 5.95 *(978-1-57091-899-5(6))* Charlesbridge Publishing, Inc.

—Butterfly Counting. Pallotta, Jerry. 2015. (ENG.). 32p. (J). (gr. -1-2). 17.95 *(978-1-57091-414-0(1))* Charlesbridge Publishing, Inc.

—The Glaciers Are Melting!, 1 vol. Love, Donna. 2011. (ENG.). 32p. (J). (gr. -1-4). 16.95 *(978-1-60718-126-2(6))*; pap. 8.95 *(978-1-60718-136-1(3))* Arbordale Publishing.

—Home in the Cave, 1 vol. Halfmann, Janet. 2012. (ENG.). 32p. (J). (gr. -1-4). 17.95 *(978-1-60718-522-2(9))*; pap. 9.95 *(978-1-60718-531-4(8))* Arbordale Publishing.

—The Long & the Short of It: A Tale about Hair. Meyers, Barbara & Mays, Lydia. 2011. (ENG.). 48p. (J). (gr. 2-4). 14.95 *(978-1-60443-017-2(6))* American Cancer Society, Inc.

—My Sister, Alicia May. Tupper Ling, Nancy. 2009. (ENG.). 32p. (J). (gr. k-2). 16.95 *(978-0-9792035-9-6(7))* Pleasant St. Pr.

—Nana, What's Cancer? Fead, Beverlye Hyman et al. 2009. (ENG.). 64p. (J). (gr. -1-7). 14.95 *(978-1-60443-010-3(9)*, 1604430109) American Cancer Society, Inc.

—Ocean Counting: Odd Numbers. Pallotta, Jerry. 2005. (ENG.). 32p. (J). (gr. -1-3). pap. 7.95 *(978-0-88106-150-5(6))* Charlesbridge Publishing, Inc.

Bersani, Shennen. Salamander Season, 1 vol. Curtis, Jennifer Keats & Frederick, J. Adam. 2015. (ENG.). 32p. (J). (gr. k-3). 17.95 ***(978-1-62855-556-1(4))*** Arbordale Publishing.

Bersani, Shennen. Sea Slime: It's Eeuwy, Gooey & under the Sea, 1 vol. Prager, Ellen. 2014. (ENG.). 32p. (J). (gr. -1-3). 17.95 *(978-1-62855-210-2(7))* Arbordale Publishing.

Bersani, Shennen. Sea Slime: It's Eeuwy, Gooey & under the Sea, 1 vol. Prager, Ellen. 2014. (SPA.). 32p. (J). (gr. -1-3). pap. 9.95 ***(978-1-62855-228-7(X))*** Arbordale Publishing.

Bersani, Shennen. The Shape Family Babies, 1 vol. Haas, Kristin. 2014. (ENG.). 32p. (J). (gr. -1-3). 17.95 *(978-1-62855-211-9(5))* Arbordale Publishing.

Bersani, Shennen. Shark Baby, 1 vol. Downer, Ann. (SPA.). 32p. (J). (gr. -1-3). 2014. pap. 9.95 ***(978-1-62855-351-2(0))***; 2013. 17.95 *(978-1-60718-622-9(5))*; 2013. pap. 9.95 *(978-1-60718-634-2(9))* Arbordale Publishing.

Bersani, Shennen. Tiburoncito, 1 vol. Downer, Ann. 2013. (SPA.). 32p. (J). (gr. -1-3). 17.95 *(978-1-60718-709-7(4))* Arbordale Publishing.

Bersani, Shennen. Let My Colors Out. Bersani, Shennen. Filigenzi, Courtney. 2009. (ENG.). 16p. (J). (gr. -1-k). 11.95 *(978-1-60443-011-0(7)*, 1604430117) American Cancer Society, Inc.

—Los Bebés de la Familia Geométrica, 1 vol. Bersani, Shennen. Haas, Kristin & Toth, Rosalyna. 2014.Tr. of Shape Family Babies. (SPA.). 32p. (J). (gr. -1-3). pap. 9.95 *(978-1-62855-229-4(8))* Arbordale Publishing.

Berson, Harold. Loretta Mason Potts. Chase, Mary. 2014. (ENG.). 224p. (J). (gr. 3-7). 16.95 *(978-1-59017-757-0(6)*, NYR Children's Collection) New York Review of Bks., Inc., The.

Bersson, Robert & Trobaugh, Scott. Stripes & Stars. Bersson, Robert & Shoup, Dolores. I.t. ed. 2003. 40p. (J). (gr. 1-4). per. 16.95 *(978-0-9740585-0-4(5))* Legacy Group Productions, LLC.

Bertagnolli, Daniel. Whooo Turned Out the Lights? Bertagnolli, Daniel. 2009. 20p. pap. 9.14 *(978-1-4269-0590-2(4))* Trafford Publishing.

Bertelle, Nicoletta. Saints & Their Stories. Giraldo, Maria Loretta. Moran, Margaret Edward, tr. 2010.Tr. of I Santi: i miei primi Amici. 168p. (J). (gr. 2-5). 19.95 *(978-0-8198-7134-3(6))* Pauline Bks. & Media.

Berthoff, Bret. Leon & the Champion Chip. Kurzweil, Allen. 2005. 352p. (J). 15.99 *(978-0-06-053933-7(X))*; lib. bdg. 16.89 *(978-0-06-053934-4(8))* HarperCollins Pubs.

—Leon & the Spitting Image. Kurzweil, Allen. (ENG.). 320p. (J). (gr. 3-18). 2005. pap. 7.99 *(978-0-06-053932-0(1)*, Greenwillow Bks.); 2003. 16.99 *(978-0-06-053930-6(5))* HarperCollins Pubs.

Bertino, Mike, jt. illus. see Althea, Erin.

Bertolucci, Federico. Desert Adventure. Bordiglioni, Stephen & Bordiglioni, Stefano. 2009. (Dinodino's Dinosaur Adventures Ser.). 56p. (J). (gr. k-4). 27.95 *(978-1-60754-714-3(7))*; pap. 12.85 *(978-1-60754-721-1(X))* Windmill Bks.

—Earthquake! Bordiglioni, Stephen & Bordiglioni, Stefano. 2009. (Dinodino's Dinosaur Adventures Ser.). 56p. (J). (gr. k-4). 27.95 *(978-1-60754-713-6(9))*; pap. 12.85 *(978-1-60754-719-8(8))* Windmill Bks.

—Volcano! Bordiglioni, Stephen & Bordiglioni, Stefano. 2009. (Dinodino's Dinosaur Adventures Ser.). 56p. (J). (gr. k-4). 27.95 *(978-1-60754-712-9(0))*; pap. 12.85 *(978-1-60754-717-4(1))* Windmill Bks.

Bertoni, Oliver. The Coconut Tree. Rochelin, Ghyslaine. 2010. (HAT.). 32p. (J). pap. 14.95 *(978-1-60195-319-3(4))* International Step by Step Assn.

Bertozzi, Nick. Diabetes & Me: An Essential Guide for Kids & Parents. 2013. (ENG.). 176p. pap. 15.00 *(978-0-8090-3871-8(4)*, Hill & Wang) Farrar, Straus & Giroux.

—A Hitch at the Fairmont. Averbeck, Jim. (ENG.). 416p. (J). (gr. 3-7). 2015. pap. 7.99 *(978-1-4424-9448-0(4))*; 2014. 16.99 *(978-1-4424-9447-3(6)*, Atheneum Bks. for Young Readers) Simon & Schuster Children's Publishing.

Bertozzi, Nick. Lewis & Clark. Bertozzi, Nick. 2011. (ENG.). 144p. (YA). (gr. 7-18). pap. 17.99 *(978-1-59643-450-9(3)*, First Second Bks.) Roaring Brook Pr.

—Shackleton: Antarctic Odyssey. Bertozzi, Nick. 2014. (ENG.). 128p. (YA). (gr. 7-12). pap. 16.99 *(978-1-59643-451-6(1)*, First Second Bks.) Roaring Brook Pr.

Bertran, Nuria. Sabelotodo: 1000 Desafíos para Tu Inteligencia. Barberi, Marco et al, trs. 2003. (SPA.). 384p. 35.00 *(978-84-494-2372-7(4)*, GML07104-192209) Oceano Grupo Editoria, S.A. ESP. Dist: Cengage Gale.

Bertrand, Cécile. Stand Up! How to Stay True to Yourself. Laouénan, Christine. Moloney, Kate, ed. 2012. (ENG.). 80p. (YA). (gr. 5-9). pap. 12.95 *(978-1-4197-0198-6(3)*, Amulet Bks.) Abrams.

Bertrand, Frederique. New York in Pajamarama. Leblond, Michaël. 2013. (ENG.). 32p. (J). (gr. -1-2). 15.99 *(978-1-907912-23-8(1))* Phoenix Yard Bks. GBR. Dist: Independent Pubs. Group.

Berube, Kate. The Summer Nick Taught His Cats to Read. Manley, Curtis. 2016. (J). *(978-1-4814-3569-7(8)*, Simon & Schuster Bks. For Young Readers) Simon & Schuster Bks. For Young Readers.

Beshwathy, Steve. Adam et le Raton Dessinateur. Decary, Marie. 2004. (Premier Roman Ser.). (FRE.). 64p. (J). (gr. 1-4). pap. *(978-2-89021-643-3(8))* Diffusion du livre Mirabel (DLM).

Beshwaty, Steve. Adam's Tropical Adventure. Decary, Marie. 2005. 54p. (J). lib. bdg. 12.00 *(978-1-4242-1202-6(2))* Fitzgerald Bks.

—Adam's Tropical Adventure. Décary, Marie. Cummins, Sarah, tr. from FRE. 2005. (Formac First Novels Ser.: 56). (ENG.). 64p. (J). (gr. 2-5). 14.95 *(978-0-88780-687-2(2))*; (J). 4.95 *(978-0-88780-686-5(4))* Formac Publishing Co., Ltd. CAN. Dist: Casemate Pubs. & Bk. Distributors, LLC.

—Floop Does the Laundry. Tremblay, Carole. 2009. (Floop Ser.). 24p. (J). (gr. -1-k). 22.60 *(978-1-60754-333-6(8))*; pap. 8.15 *(978-1-60754-334-3(6))* Windmill Bks.

—Floop in the Dark. Tremblay, Carole. 2009. (Floop Ser.). 24p. (J). (gr. -1-k). 22.60 *(978-1-60754-341-1(9))*; pap. 8.15 *(978-1-60754-342-8(7))* Windmill Bks.

—Floop's Flowers. Tremblay, Carole. 2009. (Floop Ser.). 24p. (J). (gr. -1-k). 22.60 *(978-1-60754-344-2(3))*; pap. 8.15 *(978-1-60754-346-6(X))* Windmill Bks.

—Floop's New Umbrella. Tremblay, Carole. 2009. (Floop Ser.). 24p. (J). (gr. -1-k). 22.60 *(978-1-60754-347-3(8))*; pap. 8.15 *(978-1-60754-348-0(6))* Windmill Bks.

Besom, Mae. What Do You Do with an Idea? Yamada, Kobi. 2014. (ENG.). 36p. (J). (gr. -1-3). 16.95 *(978-1-938298-07-3(1))* Compendium, Inc., Publishing & Communications.

Bessey, Brandan. Peanut the Tiny Horse. Havice, L. K. 2012. 50p. *(978-1-4602-0956-1(7))*; pap. *(978-1-4602-0954-7(0))* FriesenPress.

Bessey, Vance. Fanciful Tales & Poems: For Grandchildren of Any Age. Heymann, Irene Rommel. Heyman, Frank J., ed. 2012. 102p. (-18). pap. 14.95 *(978-1-934949-63-4(9))* Just Write Bks.

Best, Cathy. Daniel's World. DeLoach, Kathleen. 2004. (J). pap. 15.95 *(978-0-9747440-5-6(0))* Three Moons Media.

—Le Monde de Daniel: Un livre sur les enfants Handicapés. DeLoach, Kathleen. 2005. (FRE.). (J). pap. 15.95 *(978-1-933514-01-7(9))* Three Moons Media.

—El Mundo de Daniel: Un libro sobre niños Minusválidos. DeLoach, Kathleen. 2005. (SPA.). 20p. (J). pap. 15.95 *(978-1-933514-00-0(0))* Three Moons Media.

Best, Roy. The Picture Story Book of Peter Pan. 2013. (Green Tiger's Illustrated Ser.). (ENG.). 96p. (J). 12.95 *(978-1-59583-661-8(6))* Laughing Elephant.

Bester, Shayle. The Cool Nguni. Bester, Maryanne. 2007. (Cool Nguni Ser.). (ENG.). 24p. (J). (gr. k-2). 12.00 *(978-1-77009-264-8(1))* Jacana Media ZAF. Dist: Independent Pubs. Group.

—I Know That! Bester, Maryanne. 2015. (ENG.). 32p. (J). (gr. -1-k). pap. 9.95 *(978-1-4314-0491-9(8))* Jacana Media ZAF. Dist: Independent Pubs. Group.

—The Long Trousers. Bester, Maryanne. 2009. (Cool Nguni Ser.). (ENG.). 32p. (J). (gr. 2-4). pap. 12.00 *(978-1-77009-499-4(7))* Jacana Media ZAF. Dist: Independent Pubs. Group.

—The Missing Ball. Bester, Maryanne. 2010. (Cool Nguni Ser.: 4). (ENG.). 32p. (J). (gr. k-2). 12.00 *(978-1-77009-704-9(X))* Jacana Media ZAF. Dist: Independent Pubs. Group.

—The Three Billy Goats Gruff. Bloch, Carole. 2011. (Best Loved Tales for Africa Ser.). (ENG.). 32p. (J). (gr. k-2). pap. 10.95 *(978-1-77009-765-0(1))* Jacana Media ZAF. Dist: Independent Pubs. Group.

—Three Friends & a Taxi. Bester, Maryanne. 2007. (Cool Nguni Ser.: 1). (ENG.). 24p. (J). (gr. k-2). 12.00 *(978-1-77009-265-5(X))* Jacana Media ZAF. Dist: Independent Pubs. Group.

—Why Dog Is Afraid of Storms. Clegg, Maryanne & Bester, Maryanne. 2012. (ENG.). 32p. (J). (gr. -1-k). pap. 12.95 *(978-1-4314-0219-9(2))* Jacana Media ZAF. Dist: Independent Pubs. Group.

Betancourt, Raymond. Everywhere Coquis. Hooper, Nancy. Quinones, Jacqueline, tr. 2003.Tr. of En Dondequiera Coquies. (ENG.). 48p. (J). 13.95 *(978-0-942929-14-0(4)*, Omni Arts Publishing) Read Street Publishing, Inc.

Betanzos, Sue. My New Backyard Garden. 2006.Tr. of Mi Nuevo Jardin del Traspatio. (SPA & ENG.). (J). *(978-0-9792253-0-7(2))* Tucson Botanical Gardens.

Beth, Shannon. One Blue Shoe. Conti, Alexis. 2013. (ENG.). (J). (gr. -1-3). 14.95 *(978-1-937406-11-0(3))* Mascot Bks., Inc.

Bethards, David. Meditation for Little People. Langford, Anne. 2003. 40p. (gr. k-4). reprint ed. 8.95 *(978-0-87516-211-9(8)*, Devorss Pubns.) DeVorss & Co.

Betiku, Olatukunbo. Gerald, Fish of the Spirit! A Caribbean Tale of Fortune & Greed. Amon, Ras Ran. ed. 2006. Orig. Title: Gerald, Fish of the Spirit! A Caribbean Tale of Fortune & Greed. (ENG.). (J). 7.99 *(978-0-9776603-0-8(3))* One Love Assn. Bks.

Betteo, Patricio. Soy el Robot. Fernández, Bernardo. 2010. (SPA.). 47p. (J). (gr. 2-4). pap. *(978-607-411-031-9(X))* Editorial Almadia.

—Un Tutu Muy Apretado. Clark, Sherryl. rev. ed. 2006. (Castillo de la Lectura Verde Ser.). (ENG.). 88p. (J). (gr. 2-4). pap. 7.95 *(978-970-20-0851-4(4))* Castillo, Ediciones, S. A. de C. V. MEX. Dist: Macmillan.

Betteridge, Deirdre. Bright Red Kisses. Toten, Teresa. 2005. (ENG.). 32p. (J). (gr. -1-k). 19.95 *(978-1-55037-909-9(7)*, 9781550379099); pap. 7.95 *(978-1-55037-908-2(9)*, 9781550379082) Annick Pr., Ltd. CAN. Dist: Firefly Bks., Ltd.

—A Pocket Can Have a Treasure in It. Stinson, Kathy. 2008. (ENG.). 32p. (J). (gr. -1-k). 18.95 *(978-1-55451-126-6(7)*, 9781554511266); pap. 6.95 *(978-1-55451-125-9(9)*, 9781554511259) Annick Pr., Ltd. CAN. Dist: Firefly Bks., Ltd.

Bettoli, Delana. This Is the Stable. Cotten, Cynthia. 2008. (ENG.). 32p. (J). (gr. -1-3). pap. 6.99 *(978-0-312-38421-0(1))* Square Fish.

Betts, Louis. Swift Fawn the Little Foundling. Wade, Mary H. 2005. reprint ed. pap. 15.95 *(978-1-4179-1811-9(X))* Kessinger Publishing, LLC.

Betz, Katy. I Forgive You: Love We Can Hear, Ask for, & Give. Lataif, Nicole. 2014. (ENG.). 40p. (J). 10.95 *(978-0-8198-3726-4(1))* Pauline Bks. & Media.

Beus, Bryan. The Hunt for Dark Infinity. Dashner, James. 2009. (13th Reality Ser.: Bk. 2). 446p. (J). 18.95 *(978-1-60641-034-9(2)*, Shadow Mountain) Shadow Mountain Publishing.

—The Hunt for Dark Infinity. Dashner, James. 2010. (13th Reality Ser.: 2). (ENG.). 432p. (J). (gr. 3-7). pap. 8.99 *(978-1-4169-9153-3(0)*, Simon & Schuster/Paula Wiseman Bks.) Simon & Schuster/Paula Wiseman Bks.

—The Journal of Curious Letters. Dashner, James. 2008. (13th Reality Ser.: Bk. 1). 434p. (J). (gr. 4-7). 17.95 *(978-1-59038-831-0(3)*, Shadow Mountain) Shadow Mountain Publishing.

—The Journal of Curious Letters. Dashner, James. 2009. (13th Reality Ser.: 1). (ENG.). 432p. (J). (gr. 3-7). pap. 7.99 *(978-1-4169-9152-6(2)*, Simon & Schuster/Paula Wiseman Bks.) Simon & Schuster/Paula Wiseman Bks.

Beus, Bryan. Westly: A Spider's Tale. Beus, Bryan. 2015. (J). 15.99 ***(978-1-62972-068-5(2)***, Shadow Mountain) Deseret Bk. Co.

Bevans Marks And Barrow. Danny Kaye's Stories from Far Away Places. Kaye, Danny. 2011. 30p. 35.95 *(978-1-258-00232-9(9))* Literary Licensing, LLC.

Beveridge, Jim, photos by. Belize Living Alphabet. Beveridge, Dorothy. 2013. 38p. pap. *(978-976-8142-51-1(0))* Producciones de la Hamaca.

—Birding in Belize with Colours. Beveridge, Dorothy. 2013. 32p. pap. *(978-976-8142-55-9(3))* Producciones de la Hamaca.

—Counting Belize Frogs & Toads. Beveridge, Dorothy. 2012. 26p. pap. *(978-976-8142-47-4(2))* Producciones de la Hamaca.

Beverley, Virginia. The Criminal Life of Effie O. An Entertainment. Savage, Sam. 2005. 216p. (YA). per. 15.00 *(978-0-9719925-6-6(8))* Papas & Nellie Pr.

Bevilacqua, Carol. Animal Defenses. Hoyt, Richard, photos by. Echols, Jean C. 2003. (Great Explorations in Math & Science Ser.). 40p. (Orig.). (J). reprint ed. pap., tchr. ed. 9.00 *(978-0-924886-88-1(9)*, GEMS) Univ. of California, Berkeley, Lawrence Hall of Science.

Bevilacqua, Carol & Klofkorn, Lisa. Fingerprinting. Hoyt, Richard, photos by. Ahouse, Jeremy John & Barber, Jacqueline. 2006. (Great Explorations in Math & Science Ser.). 72p. (J). 10.50 *(978-0-931542-06-7(6)*, GEMS) Univ. of California, Berkeley, Lawrence Hall of Science.

—Of Cabbages & Chemistry. Hoyt, Richard, photos by. Barber, Jacqueline. Bergman Publishing Co. Staff & Fairwell, Kay, eds. rev. ed. 2003. (Great Explorations in Math & Science Ser.). 80p. (J). (gr. 4-8). pap., tchr. ed. 10.50 *(978-0-924886-28-7(5)*, GEMS) Univ. of California, Berkeley, Lawrence Hall of Science.

Bevilacqua, Silvana. Rosie's Dream Cape. Freedman, Zelda. 2005. (ENG.). 116p. (J). pap. 6.95 *(978-1-55380-025-5(7))* Ronsdale Pr. CAN. Dist: Literary Pr. Group of Canada.

Bevin, Shane. Tiger Takes the Big Apple. Reiter, David P. 2014. 220p. pap. *(978-1-922120-74-8(X)*, IP Kidz) Interactive Pubns. Pty, Ltd.

Bevington, Nancy. Bruno Dreams of Ice Cream. Whitfield, Peter. 2005. (Zen Tails Ser.). (ENG.). 28p. (J). (gr. k-3). 15.95 *(978-1-894965-21-7(3))* Simply Read Bks. CAN. Dist: Ingram Pub. Services.

—No Presents Please. Whitfield, Peter. 2005. (Zen Tails Ser.). (ENG.). 28p. (J). (gr. -1-3). 15.95 *(978-1-894965-23-1(X))* Simply Read Bks. CAN. Dist: Ingram Pub. Services.

—Up & Down. Whitfield, Peter. 2005. (Zen Tails Ser.). (ENG.). 28p. (J). (gr. -1-3). 15.95 *(978-1-894965-22-4(1))* Simply Read Bks. CAN. Dist: Ingram Pub. Services.

Bevis, Mary & Powell, Consie. Old Woman Winter. Bevis, Mary. 2010. 32p. (J). (gr. 1-2). 16.95 *(978-0-9819307-7-0(8))* Raven Productions, Inc.

Bevis, Vivian. Dream Helmet. New, William. 2005. (ENG.). 32p. (J). 11.95 *(978-1-55380-021-7(4))* Ronsdale Pr. CAN. Dist: Literary Pr. Group of Canada.

—Llamas in the Laundry. New, William. 2005. (ENG.). 32p. (J). 12.95 *(978-0-921870-97-5(3))* Ronsdale Pr. CAN. Dist: Literary Pr. Group of Canada.

Bey, Charles. Rhyming on Time. Mac, Cola. 2011. 20p. pap. 24.95 *(978-1-4560-6940-7(3))* America Star Bks.

Beyer, Ramsey. Daisy to the Rescue: True Stories of Daring Dogs, Paramedic Parrots, & Other Animal Heroes. Campbell, Jeff. 2014. (ENG.). 336p. (YA). 17.99 *(978-1-936976-62-1(5))* Zest Bks.

Beyl, Charles. Annie's Plan: Taking Charge of Schoolwork & Homework. Kraus, Jeanne R. 2006. 48p. (J). (gr. 2-5). 14.95 *(978-1-59147-481-4(7))*; pap. 9.95 *(978-1-59147-482-1(5))* American Psychological Assn. (Magination Pr.).

—Learning to Slow Down & Pay Attention: A Book for Kids about ADHD. Nadeau, Kathleen G. & Dixon, Ellen B. 3rd ed. 2004. 96p. (J). 14.95 *(978-1-59147-149-3(4))*; pap. 12.95 *(978-1-59147-155-4(9))* American Psychological Assn. (Magination Pr.).

—Mind over Basketball: Coach Yourself to Handle Stress. Weierbach, Jane & Phillips-Hershey, Elizabeth. 2007. (Coach Yourself to Handle Stress Ser.). 48p. (J). (gr. 3-7). 14.95 *(978-1-4338-0135-8(3)*, 4418006); per. 9.95 *(978-1-4338-0136-5(1)*, 4418007) American Psychological Assn. (Magination Pr.).

—My Parents Are Divorced Too: A Book for Kids by Kids. 2nd ed. 2006. 71p. (J). (gr. 3-7). 14.95 *(978-1-59147-241-4(5))*; per. 9.95 *(978-1-59147-242-1(3))* American Psychological Assn. (Magination Pr.).

Bezesky, Tracy. David's Journey: The Story of David Jal, One of the Lost Boys of Sudan. Jal, David. 2012. 32p. 20.00 *(978-1-934478-30-1(X))* Sunray Publishing.

Bhabha, Shiraaz. The Closet Ghosts. Bhabha, Shiraaz. Krishnaswami, Uma. 2013. (ENG.). 32p. (J). (gr. 2). 16.95 *(978-0-89239-208-7(8))* Lee & Low Bks., Inc.

B

Bhachu, Verinder. The Usborne Science Encyclopedia: Internet-Linked. Rogers, Kirsteen et al. 2009. (Usborne Internet-Linked Encyclopedia Ser.). 448p. (J). (gr. 4-7). 19.99 *(978-0-7945-2629-0(2),* Usborne) EDC Publishing.

Bhachu, Verindr. Science Encyclopedia. Wilkes, Angela. 2009. (Library of Science Ser.). 448p. (J). 39.99 *(978-0-7945-2527-9(X),* Usborne) EDC Publishing.

Bhargava, Neirah & Dave, Vijay, photos by. What You Will See Inside a Hindu Temple. Jani, Mahendra & Jani, Vandana. 2005. (ENG., 31p. (J). (gr. 3-7). 17.99 *(978-1-59473-116-7(0),* Skylight Paths Publishing) LongHill Partners, Inc.

Bhend, Käthi. The Duck & the Owl. Johansen, Hanna & Barrett, John S. 2005. (ENG.). 72p. (J). 17.95 *(978-1-56792-285-1(6))* Godine, David R. Pub.

Bhend, Kathi. The Fairy Tale of the World. Amman, Jurg. 2010. (ENG.). 32p. (gr. 3-18). 16.95 *(978-0-7358-2316-7(2))* North-South Bks., Inc.

—In My Dreams I Can Fly. Hasler, Eveline. 2009. (ENG.). 32p. (J). (gr. -1-3). 16.95 *(978-0-7358-2259-7(X))* North-South Bks., Inc.

Bhuiyan, Julia. Mickey the Monarch. Sommers, Audrey. Mattie, Dugan, ed. 2013. 42p. pap. 14.95 *(978-0-9851996-2-3(8))* HMSI, Inc.

Bhushan, Rahul. Taj Mahal. Arnold, Caroline & Comora, Madeleine. 2007. (ENG.). 32p. (J). (gr. k-12). lib. bdg. 17.95 *(978-0-7613-2609-0(X),* Millbrook Pr.) Lerner Publishing Group.

Biagiotti, Aldo, photos by. Escape from Death Valley: A Tale of Two Burros. Biagiotti, Aldo. 2003. (Books for Young Learners). (ENG., 16p. (J). 5.75 net. *(978-1-57274-661-9(0),* 2737, Bks. for Young Learners) Owen, Richard C. Pubs., Inc.

Bianca & Annie West. Dogs Don't Wear Underwear. Carmen & Thane Johnson. 2009. 20p. pap. 12.99 *(978-1-4389-4128-8(5))* AuthorHouse.

Bianchi, Fausto. Saint Francis & the Nativity, 1 vol. Strasser, Myrna A. 2010. (ENG.). 40p. (J). (gr. -1-2). 16.99 *(978-0-310-70890-2(7))* Zonderkidz.

—The Story for Children, 1 vol. Lucado, Max et al. 2011. (Story Ser.). (ENG.). 288p. (J). (gr. -1-3). 19.99 *(978-0-310-71975-5(5))* Zonderkidz.

—The Story for Children: A Storybook Bible. Lucado, Max et al. 2011. 287p. (J). *(978-0-310-73211-2(5))* Zonderkidz.

Bianchi, John. ¡Arriba! Pitt, Marilyn & Sánchez, Lucía M. 2010. (1G Libros Papas Fritas Ser.).Tr. of Get Up. (SPA & ENG.). 12p. (J). (gr. k-1). pap. 6.50 *(978-1-61541-084-2(8))* American Reading Co.

—Bear Gets a Hat. 2012. (Bird, Bunny, & Bear Ser.). (ENG.). 12p. (J). pap. 6.50 *(978-1-61406-305-6(2))* American Reading Co.

—Bug, 1 vol. Edwards, Frank B. 2006. (ENG.). 165p. (J). (gr. 3-7). per. 6.95 *(978-1-894323-17-8(3))* Pokeweed Pr. CAN. Dist: Ingram Pub. Services.

—Come with Me. Hileman, Jane & Pitt, Marilyn. (Power 50 - Potato Chip Bks). 12p. 2011. pap. 33.92 *(978-1-61541-163-4(1));* 2010. (ENG.). (J). pap. 6.50 *(978-1-61541-162-7(3))* American Reading Co.

—Dinosaur Party. Rieger, Linda. 2007. 20p. (J). *(978-0-9779427-2-5(4))* Pathways into Science.

—Flying Animals. Rieger, Linda. ed. 2006. 20p. (J). *(978-0-9779427-1-8(6))* Pathways into Science.

—Get Up. Pitt, Marilyn & Hileman, Jane. 2010. (1G Potato Chip Bks.). (ENG.). 12p. (J). (gr. k-1). pap. 6.50 *(978-1-61541-069-9(4))* American Reading Co.

—Home Alone. Hileman, Jane & Pitt, Marilyn. (Power 50 - Potato Chip Bks). 12p. 2011. pap. 33.92 *(978-1-61541-408-6(8));* 2010. (ENG.). (J). pap. 6.50 *(978-1-61541-407-9(X))* American Reading Co.

—How Are We Alike? Rieger, Linda. ed. 2006. 20p. (J). *(978-0-9779427-0-1(8))* Pathways into Science.

—I Like My Stuff. Pitt, Marilyn & Hileman, Jane. 2009. (1G Potato Chip Bks.). (ENG.). 12p. (J). (gr. k-1). pap. 6.50 *(978-1-59301-769-9(3))* American Reading Co.

—I Love to Sleep. Hileman, Jane & Pitt, Marilyn. 2009. (1G Potato Chip Bks.). (ENG.). 12p. (J). (gr. k-1). pap. 6.50 *(978-1-59301-797-2(9))* American Reading Co.

—I Want a Dog. Hileman, Jane & Pitt, Marilyn. 2009. (1G Potato Chip Bks.). (ENG.). 12p. (J). (gr. k-1). pap. 6.50 *(978-1-59301-768-2(5))* American Reading Co.

—Let Me In. Pitt, Marilyn & Hileman, Jane. 2010. (1G Potato Chip Bks.). (ENG.). 12p. (J). (gr. k-1). pap. 6.50 *(978-1-61541-168-9(2))* American Reading Co.

—Let Me In. Hileman, Jane & Pitt, Marilyn. 2011. (Power 50 - Potato Chip Bks). 12p. pap. 33.92 *(978-1-61541-169-6(0))* American Reading Co.

—Mis Bebés. Pitt, Marilyn & Sánchez, Lucía M. 2010. (1G Libros Papas Fritas Ser.).Tr. of My Babies. (SPA & ENG.). 12p. (J). (gr. k-1). pap. 6.50 *(978-1-61541-080-4(5))* American Reading Co.

—My Babies. Pitt, Marilyn & Hileman, Jane. 2010. (1G Potato Chip Bks.). (ENG.). 12p. (J). (gr. k-1). pap. 6.50 *(978-1-61541-065-1(1))* American Reading Co.

—La Nevada: Snow Dog. Pitt, Marilyn & Sanchez, Lucia M. 2011. (poder de 50 - Libros papas fritas Ser.). (SPA.). 12p. pap. 33.92 *(978-1-61541-439-0(8))* American Reading Co.

—Perro en Apuros: Let Me In. Pitt, Marilyn & Sanchez, Lucia M. 2011. (poder de 50 - Libros papas fritas Ser.). (SPA.). 12p. pap. 33.92 *(978-1-61541-165-8(8))* American Reading Co.

—Pretty Cat. Pitt, Marilyn & Hileman, Jane. 2010. (1G Potato Chip Bks.). (ENG.). 12p. (J). (gr. k-1). pap. 6.50 *(978-1-61541-067-5(8))* American Reading Co.

—Smelling Good. Pitt, Marilyn. 2014. (1B Potato Chip Bks.). (ENG.). 16p. (J). pap. 6.50 *(978-1-61406-685-9(X))* American Reading Co.

—Snow Dog. Hileman, Jane & Pitt, Marilyn. (Power 50 - Potato Chip Bks). 12p. 2011. pap. 33.92 *(978-1-61541-298-3(0));* 2010. (ENG.). (J). pap. 6.50 *(978-1-61541-297-6(2))* American Reading Co.

—Solos en Casa. Pitt, Marilyn & Sánchez, Lucía M. 2011. (1G Libros Papas Fritas Ser.).Tr. of Home Alone. (SPA.). 12p. (J). (gr. k-1). pap. 6.50 *(978-1-61541-409-3(6))* American Reading Co.

—Start the Clean Up. Rieger, Linda. 2008. 20p. (J). *(978-0-9779427-5-6(9))* Pathways into Science.

—The Storm. Pitt, Marilyn & Hileman, Jane. 2010. (1G Potato Chip Bks.). (ENG.). 12p. (J). (gr. k-1). pap. 6.50 *(978-1-61541-232-7(8))* American Reading Co.

—The Storm. Hileman, Jane & Pitt, Marilyn. 2011. (Power 50 - Potato Chip Bks). 12p. pap. 33.92 *(978-1-61541-233-4(6))* American Reading Co.

—Time for a Bath. Hileman, Jane & Pitt, Marilyn. 2009. (1G Potato Chip Bks.). (ENG.). 12p. (J). (gr. k-1). pap. 6.50 *(978-1-59301-772-9(3))* American Reading Co.

—La Tormenta: The Storm. Pitt, Marilyn & Sanchez, Lucia M. 2011. (poder de 50 - Libros papas fritas Ser.). (SPA.). 12p. pap. 33.92 *(978-1-61541-441-3(X))* American Reading Co.

—Up Here. Pitt, Marilyn & Hileman, Jane. 2010. (1G Potato Chip Bks.). (ENG.). 12p. (J). (gr. k-1). pap. 6.50 *(978-1-61541-015-6(5))* American Reading Co.

—Water in Our House. Rieger, Linda. 2008. 20p. (J). *(978-0-9779427-6-3(7))* Pathways into Science.

—Water Party. Rieger, Linda. 2008. 20p. (J). *(978-0-9779427-3-2(2))* Pathways into Science.

—Where Is Here? 2013. (1G Bird, Bunny, & Bear Ser.). (ENG.). 12p. (J). pap. 6.50 *(978-1-61406-592-0(6))* American Reading Co.

—Where Is My Boy? Pitt, Marilyn & Hileman, Jane. 2009. (1G Potato Chip Bks.). (ENG.). 12p. (J). (gr. k-1). pap. 6.50 *(978-1-59301-766-8(9))* American Reading Co.

—Where Is That Dog? Pitt, Marilyn & Hileman, Jane. 2009. (Potato Chip Bks.). (ENG.). 12p. (J). (gr. k-1). pap. 6.50 *(978-1-59301-770-5(7))* American Reading Co.

—Will You Go? Hileman, Jane. 2014. (2G Potato Chip Bks.). (ENG.). 12p. (J). pap. 6.50 *(978-1-61406-684-2(1))* American Reading Co.

—You Can't Have It! Hileman, Jane & Pitt, Marilyn. 2009. (1G Potato Chip Bks.). (ENG.). 12p. (J). (gr. k-1). pap. 6.50 *(978-1-59301-767-5(7))* American Reading Co.

Bianchi, John. My Ride. Bianchi, John. 2014. (2G Potato Chip Bks.). (ENG.). 12p. (J). pap. 6.50 *(978-1-61406-682-8(5))* American Reading Co.

—Over & Under. Bianchi, John. 2014. (2G Bird, Bunny & Bear Ser.). (ENG.). 16p. (J). pap. 6.50 *(978-1-61406-686-6(8))* American Reading Co.

—The Sun. Bianchi, John. 2014. (2G Bird, Bunny & Bear Ser.). (ENG.). 16p. (J). pap. 6.50 *(978-1-61406-688-0(4))* American Reading Co.

—What Can You Do? Bianchi, John. 2014. (2G Bird, Bunny & Bear Ser.). (ENG.). 16p. (J). pap. 6.50 *(978-1-61406-681-1(7))* American Reading Co.

Bianchi, John & Taylor, Trace. Perro en Apuros: Let Me In. Pitt, Marilyn et al. 2010. (1G Our World Ser.). (ENG.). 24p. (J). pap. 7.50 *(978-1-61541-170-2(4))* American Reading Co.

Bianchi, Simone, jt. illus. see Williams, J. H., III.

Bianco, Francesca. St. Francis & the Christmas Miracle of Greccio. Campbell, Jeffrey. 2014. (ENG.). 28p. (J). 14.95 *(978-0-9796766-3-5(0),* Tau Publishing) Vesuvius Pr. Inc.

Bianco, Mike, jt. illus. see Larter, John.

Bibeau, Anita, photos by. My Monarch Journal. Muther, Connie. 2004. (Sharing Nature with Children Book Ser.). 32p. (gr. k-7). pap., stu. ed. 7.95 *(978-1-58469-006-1(2))* Dawn Pubns.

Bichman, David. Adventures with Rebbe Mendel. Sternfeld, Nathan. Pomerantz, Riva, tr. 230p. 21.99 *(978-1-58330-550-8(5))* Feldheim Pubs.

—All about Motti & His Adventures with Rebbe Mendel. Sternfeld, Nathan. 2004. 220p. (J). 20.99 *(978-1-58330-669-7(2))* Feldheim Pubs.

Bickel, Karla. The Animals' Debate. Bickel, Karla. l.t. ed. 2004. 16p. (J). (gr. -1-6). pap. 5.00 *(978-1-891452-16-1(9),* 10) Heart Arbor Bks.

—Easter Lights. Bickel, Karla. l.t. ed. 2004. 16p. (J). (gr. -1-6). pap. 5.00 *(978-1-891452-14-7(2),* 7) Heart Arbor Bks.

—Fishnet Valentine. Bickel, Karla. l.t. ed. 2004. 16p. (J). (gr. -1-5). pap. 5.00 *(978-1-891452-13-0(4),* 4) Heart Arbor Bks.

—Handmade Necklace. Bickel, Karla. l.t. ed. 2004. 16p. (J). (gr. -1-6). pap. 5.00 *(978-1-891452-11-6(8),* 1) Heart Arbor Bks.

—Heart Petals on the Hearth: A Collection of Children's Stories. Bickel, Karla. 2004. 64p. (J). (gr. -1-6). 20.00 *(978-1-891452-00-0(2))* Heart Arbor Bks.

—The Kite Who Was Afraid to Fly. Bickel, Karla. l.t. ed. 2004. 16p. (J). (gr. -1-6). pap. 5.00 *(978-1-891452-08-6(8),* 6) Heart Arbor Bks.

—Lilac Rose: A Flower's Lifetime. Bickel, Karla. l.t. ed. 2004. 16p. (J). (gr. -1-6). pap. 5.00 *(978-1-891452-10-9(X),* 8) Heart Arbor Bks.

—The Reading Machine. Bickel, Karla. l.t. ed. 2004. 16p. (J). (gr. -1-6). pap. 5.00 *(978-1-891452-15-4(0),* 9) Heart Arbor Bks.

—Surprise Christmas Birthday Party. Bickel, Karla. l.t. ed. 2004. 16p. (J). (gr. -1-6). pap. 5.00 *(978-1-891452-12-3(6),* 3) Heart Arbor Bks.

—Teacher's Remarkable Secret. Bickel, Karla. l.t. ed. 2004. 16p. (J). (gr. -1-6). pap. 5.00 *(978-1-891452-09-3(6),* 2) Heart Arbor Bks.

Bickford-Smith, Coralie, jt. illus. see Tenniel, John.

Bicking, Judith. Anton Finds a Treasure. Margaret I. Pascuzzo. 2008. 16p. pap. 12.00 *(978-1-4251-8683-8(1))* Trafford Publishing.

—Anton Loses a Friend. Pascuzzo, Margaret I. 2009. 20p. pap. 12.00 *(978-1-4269-0650-3(1))* Trafford Publishing.

—My Toys. Mullican, Judy. l.t. ed. 2005. (HRL Board Book Ser.). (J). (gr. -1-k). pap. 10.95 *(978-1-57332-307-9(1),* HighReach Learning, Incorporated) Carson-Dellosa Publishing, LLC.

—Tayla Takes a Trip. Zadunajsky, Donna M. 2013. (ENG.). 40p. pap. 9.99 *(978-1-938037-36-8(7))* Little T's Corner.

—Tayla's Day at the Beach. Zadunajsky, Donna M. 2013. (ENG.). 26p. pap. 6.99 *(978-1-938037-34-4(0))* Little T's Corner.

—Tayla's First Day of School. Zadunajsky, Donna M. 2013. (ENG.). 26p. pap. 9.15 *(978-1-938037-35-1(9))* Little T's Corner.

—What Daddy Did Today: A Father's Bedtime Story. Wally, Walter. 2012. (ENG.). 28p. (J). (gr. -1-3). 15.99 *(978-1-936401-08-6(8),* Two Harbors Press) Hillcrest Publishing Group, Inc.

Bicking, Judy. A Pond Full of Feelings. Bicking, Judy. Fogle, Llynda & González, Althea. 2005. (SPA.). (J). *(978-0-9760282-9-1(8))* RAPC - Sparkle & Shine Project.

Biddle, Bruce. Camping. Hooker, Karen. l.t. ed. 2003. (ENG.). 16p. (gr. k-1). pap. 5.95 *(978-1-879835-32-0(0),* Kaeden Bks.) Kaeden Corp.

—What's Inside? Hoenecke, Karen. l.t. ed. 2005. (ENG.). 16p. (gr. k-1). pap. 5.95 *(978-1-57874-009-3(6))* Kaeden Corp.

Biddlespacher, Tara. Goblinheart: A Fairy Tale. Axel, Brett. 2012. (J). 15.00 *(978-0-9769771-2-4(5))* Eastwaterfront Pr.

Biddulph, Rob. Blown Away. Biddulph, Rob. 2015. (ENG.). 40p. (J). (gr. -1-3). 17.99 *(978-0-06-236724-2(2))* HarperCollins Pubs.

Biedrzycki, David. The Beetle Alphabet Book. Pallotta, Jerry. 2004. (ENG.). 32p. (J). (gr. -1-3). 17.95 *(978-1-57091-551-2(2))* Charlesbridge Publishing, Inc.

—Dory Story. Pallotta, Jerry. 2006. (ENG.). 32p. (J). (gr. -1-3). pap. 7.95 *(978-0-88106-076-8(3))* Charlesbridge Publishing, Inc.

—How Will I Get to School This Year? Pallotta, Jerry. (J). 2013. (ENG.). 32p. (gr. -1-k). 6.99 *(978-0-545-37288-6(7),* Cartwheel Bks.); 2011. *(978-0-545-26659-8(9))* Scholastic, Inc.

—Who Will Be My Valentine This Year? Pallotta, Jerry. 2011. (ENG.). 32p. (J). (gr. -1-3). pap. 6.99 *(978-0-545-23518-1(9),* Cartwheel Bks.) Scholastic, Inc.

—Who Will See Their Shadows This Year? Pallotta, Jerry. 2013. (ENG.). 32p. (J). (gr. -1-k). pap. 6.99 *(978-0-545-47275-3(X),* Cartwheel Bks.) Scholastic, Inc.

Biedrzycki, David. Ace Lacewing: Bad Bugs Are My Business. Biedrzycki, David. 2011. (ENG.). 44p. (J). (gr. k-4). pap. 8.95 *(978-1-57091-693-9(4))* Charlesbridge Publishing, Inc.

—Ace Lacewing: Bug Detective. Biedrzycki, David. (ENG.). 40p. (J). (gr. k-4). 2008. pap. 8.95 *(978-1-57091-684-7(5));* 2005. 16.95 *(978-1-57091-569-7(5))* Charlesbridge Publishing, Inc.

—Ace Lacewing, Bug Detective: Bad Bugs Are My Business. Biedrzycki, David. 2009. (ENG.). 44p. (J). (gr. k-4). 16.95 *(978-1-57091-692-2(6))* Charlesbridge Publishing, Inc.

—Ace Lacewing, Bug Detective: The Big Swat. Biedrzycki, David. 2010. (ENG.). 44p. (J). (gr. k-4). 16.95 *(978-1-57091-747-9(7))* Charlesbridge Publishing, Inc.

—Ace Lacewing Bug Detective: The Big Swat. Biedrzycki, David. 2012. (ENG.). 44p. (J). (gr. k-4). pap. 8.95 *(978-1-57091-748-6(5))* Charlesbridge Publishing, Inc.

—Breaking News: Bear Alert. Biedrzycki, David. 2014. (Breaking News Ser.). (ENG.). 32p. (J). (gr. -1-3). 17.95 *(978-1-58089-663-4(4))* Charlesbridge Publishing, Inc.

—Me & My Dragon. Biedrzycki, David. 2011. (ENG.). 40p. (J). (gr. -1-3). 17.95 *(978-1-58089-278-0(7));* pap. 7.95 *(978-1-58089-279-7(5))* Charlesbridge Publishing, Inc.

—Me & My Dragon: Scared of Halloween. Biedrzycki, David. 2013. (ENG.). 32p. (J). (gr. -1-3). 17.95 *(978-1-58089-658-0(8));* pap. 7.95 *(978-1-58089-659-7(6))* Charlesbridge Publishing, Inc.

—Mi Dragón y Yo. Biedrzycki, David. Canetti, Yanitzia. 2014. (SPA.). 32p. (J). (gr. -1-3). pap. 7.95 *(978-1-58089-574-3(3));* lib. bdg. 17.95 *(978-1-58089-693-1(6))* Charlesbridge Publishing, Inc.

—Santa Retires. Biedrzycki, David. 2012. (ENG.). 32p. (J). (gr. -1-3). 16.95 *(978-1-58089-293-3(0));* pap. 7.95 *(978-1-58089-294-0(9))* Charlesbridge Publishing, Inc.

Biedrzycki, David. The Beetle Alphabet Book. Biedrzycki, David, tr. Pallotta, Jerry. 2004. (ENG.). 32p. (J). (gr. -1-3). pap. 7.95 *(978-1-57091-552-9(0))* Charlesbridge Publishing, Inc.

Biedrzycki, David & Bonnet, Rosalinde. Santa's New Jet. Biedrzycki, David. 2011. (ENG.). 32p. (J). (gr. -1-2). 16.95 *(978-1-58089-291-9(4));* pap. 7.95 *(978-1-58089-292-6(2))* Charlesbridge Publishing, Inc.

Bienfait, Andree. The Catholic Bible for Children. Amiot, Karine-Marie et al. 2011. (ENG.). 239p. (J). (gr. -1-3). pap. 14.99 *(978-1-58617-659-4(5))* Ignatius Pr.

Bier, Donna. I Wish I Could Fly. Bier, Andreas. 2009. 20p. pap. 9.14 *(978-1-4269-0271-0(9))* Trafford Publishing.

Biesty, Stephen. Emergency Vehicles. Green, Rod. 2015. (ENG.). 16p. (J). (gr. k-4). 15.99 ***(978-0-7636-7959-0(3),*** Templar) Candlewick Pr.

Biesty, Stephen. Giant Vehicles. Green, Rod. 2014. (ENG.). 16p. (J). (gr. k-4). 15.99 *(978-0-7636-7404-5(4),* Templar) Candlewick Pr.

—Into the Unknown: How Great Explorers Found Their Way by Land, Sea, & Air. Ross, Stewart. (ENG.). 96p. (J). (gr. 3-7). 2014. pap. 9.99 *(978-0-7636-6992-8(X));* 2011. 19.99 *(978-0-7636-4948-7(1))* Candlewick Pr.

—Stephen Biesty's Incredible Explosions: Exploded Views of Astonishing Things. Platt, Richard. 2004. 32p. (J). (gr. 2-8). reprint ed. 20.00 *(978-0-7567-7680-0(5))* DIANE Publishing Co.

—The Story of Buildings: From the Pyramids to the Sydney Opera House & Beyond. Dillon, Patrick. 2014. (ENG.). 96p. (J). (gr. 4-7). 19.99 *(978-0-7636-6990-4(3))* Candlewick Pr.

Biet, Pascal. Leo & Lester. Bloom, Becky. 2003. (J). 32p. 15.95 *(978-1-59034-582-5(7));* 33p. pap. *(978-1-59034-583-2(5))* Mondo Publishing.

Big Idea Design Staff, jt. illus. see Moore, Michael.

Big Idea, Inc. Staff. Larryboy in Tip, Top Cape Shape!, 1 vol. Poth, Karen. 2006. (Big Idea Books / LarryBoy Ser.). (ENG.). 14p. (J). (gr. -1-1). bds. 6.99 *(978-0-310-71154-4(1))* Zonderkidz.

Big Idea Productions Staff. Lost in Place: A Lesson In Overcoming Fear, 1 vol. Peterson, Doug & Kenney, Cindy. 2005. (Big Idea Books / VeggieTown Values Ser.: Bk. 4). (ENG.). 32p. (J). pap. 3.99 *(978-0-310-70629-8(7))* Zonderkidz.

Bigda, Diane. Fashion Astrology. Zenkel, Suzanne Siegel. 2005. (Charming Petites Ser.). 80p. 4.95 *(978-0-88088-842-4(3))* Peter Pauper Pr. Inc.

Bigelow, Holly. Greek Roots J-Ology. Duncan, Leonard C. Date not set. 140p. (J). (gr. 6-12). spiral bd. 25.00 *(978-0-941414-01-2(9))* L. C. D.

Biggar, Breanne. Different Kinds of Special. Koffman, Donna Carol. 2011. 36p. pap. *(978-1-55483-897-4(5))* Insomniac Pr.

Biggers, Liza. Our Daddy Is Invincible! Maxwell, Shannon. 2011. 40p. (J). 15.95 *(978-1-61751-003-8(3),* 4th Division Pr.) Kurdyla, E L Publishing LLC.

Biggin, Gary & Lipscombe, Nick. Space. Butterfield, Moira. 32p. (J). mass mkt. 8.99 *(978-0-590-24424-4(8))* Scholastic, Inc.

Biggin, Gary, jt. illus. see Lyon, Chris.

Biggs, Brian. Attack of the Tagger. Van Draanen, Wendelin. unabr. ed. 2006. (Shredderman Ser.: Bk. 2). (J). (gr. 3-6). audio 24.95 *(978-1-59519-758-0(3))* Live Oak Media.

—Attack of the Tagger. Van Draanen, Wendelin. 2006. (Shredderman Ser.: Bk. 2). (ENG.). 176p. (J). (gr. 1-4). 6.99 *(978-0-440-41913-6(1),* Yearling) Random Hse. Children's Bks.

—Brownie & Pearl Get Dolled Up. Rylant, Cynthia. 2010. (Brownie & Pearl Ser.). (ENG.). 24p. (J). (gr. -1-3). bds. 14.99 *(978-1-4169-8631-7(6),* Beach Lane Bks.) Beach Lane Bks.

—Brownie & Pearl Get Dolled Up. Rylant, Cynthia. 2014. (Brownie & Pearl Ser.). (ENG.). 24p. (J). (gr. -1-k). 16.99 *(978-1-4424-9568-5(5));* pap. 3.99 *(978-1-4424-9567-8(7))* Simon Spotlight. (Simon Spotlight).

—Brownie & Pearl Go for a Spin. Rylant, Cynthia. 2012. (Brownie & Pearl Ser.). (ENG.). 24p. (J). (gr. -1-3). bds. 14.99 *(978-1-4169-8633-1(2),* Beach Lane Bks.) Beach Lane Bks.

—Brownie & Pearl Go for a Spin. Rylant, Cynthia. 2015. (Brownie & Pearl Ser.). (ENG.). 24p. (J). (gr. -1-k). pap. 3.99 *(978-1-4814-2570-4(6),* Simon Spotlight) Simon Spotlight.

—Brownie & Pearl Grab a Bite. Rylant, Cynthia. 2011. (Brownie & Pearl Ser.). (ENG.). 24p. (J). (gr. -1-k). 13.99 *(978-1-4169-8634-8(0),* Beach Lane Bks.) Beach Lane Bks.

—Brownie & Pearl Grab a Bite. Rylant, Cynthia. 2014. (Brownie & Pearl Ser.). (ENG.). 24p. (J). (gr. -1-k). 16.99 *(978-1-4814-1717-4(7));* pap. 3.99 *(978-1-4814-1715-0(0))* Simon Spotlight. (Simon Spotlight).

—Brownie & Pearl Hit the Hay. Rylant, Cynthia. 2011. (Brownie & Pearl Ser.). (ENG.). 24p. (J). (gr. -1-k). pap. 13.99 *(978-1-4169-8635-5(9),* Beach Lane Bks.) Beach Lane Bks.

—Brownie & Pearl Hit the Hay. Rylant, Cynthia. 2013. (Brownie & Pearl Ser.). (ENG.). 24p. (J). (gr. -1-k). 16.99 *(978-1-4424-8742-0(9));* pap. 3.99 *(978-1-4424-8741-3(0))* Simon Spotlight. (Simon Spotlight).

—Brownie & Pearl Make Good. Rylant, Cynthia. 2012. (Brownie & Pearl Ser.). (ENG.). 24p. (J). (gr. -1-k). 13.99 *(978-1-4169-8636-2(7),* Beach Lane Bks.) Beach Lane Bks.

—Brownie & Pearl See the Sights. Rylant, Cynthia. 2010. (Brownie & Pearl Ser.). (ENG.). 32p. (J). (gr. -1-k). 13.99 *(978-1-4169-8637-9(5),* Beach Lane Bks.) Beach Lane Bks.

—Brownie & Pearl See the Sights. Rylant, Cynthia. 2013. (Brownie & Pearl Ser.). (ENG.). 24p. (J). (gr. -1-k). 16.99 *(978-1-4424-8744-4(5));* pap. 3.99 *(978-1-4424-8743-7(7))* Simon Spotlight. (Simon Spotlight).

—Brownie & Pearl Step Out. Rylant, Cynthia. 2009. (Brownie & Pearl Ser.). (ENG.). 24p. (J). (gr. -1-3). bds. 13.99 *(978-1-4169-8632-4(4),* Beach Lane Bks.) Beach Lane Bks.

—Brownie & Pearl Step Out. Rylant, Cynthia. 2014. (Brownie & Pearl Ser.). (ENG.). 24p. (J). (gr. -1-k). 16.99 *(978-1-4814-0314-6(1));* pap. 3.99 *(978-1-4814-0313-9(3))* Simon Spotlight. (Simon Spotlight).

—Brownie & Pearl Take a Dip. Rylant, Cynthia. 2011. (Brownie & Pearl Ser.). (ENG.). 24p. (J). (gr. -1-3). bds. 14.99 *(978-1-4169-8638-6(3),* Beach Lane Bks.) Beach Lane Bks.

—Dog Days of School. DiPucchio, Kelly. 2014. (ENG.). 40p. (J). (gr. 1-3). 16.99 *(978-0-7868-5493-6(6))* Hyperion Bks. for Children.

—Don't Swap Your Sweater for a Dog. Applegate, Katherine. 2008. (Roscoe Riley Rules Ser.: 3). (ENG.). 96p. (J). (gr. 2-5). 15.99 *(978-0-06-114886-6(5));* pap. 4.99 *(978-0-06-114885-9(7))* HarperCollins Pubs.

—Don't Tap-Dance on Your Teacher. Applegate, Katherine. 2009. (Roscoe Riley Rules Ser.: 5). (ENG.). 96p. (J). (gr. 2-5). pap. 4.99 *(978-0-06-114889-7(X))* HarperCollins Pubs.

—The Dragon Slayer! Warner, Sally. 2013. (EllRay Jakes Ser.: 4). (ENG.). 144p. (J). (gr. 1-3). 14.99 *(978-0-670-78497-4(4),* Viking Juvenile) Penguin Publishing Group.

—EllRay Jakes & the Beanstalk. Warner, Sally. 2013. (EllRay Jakes Ser.: 5). (ENG.). (J). (gr. 1-3). 128p. 14.99 *(978-0-670-78499-8(0),* Viking Juvenile); 144p. pap. 5.99 *(978-0-14-242359-2(9),* Puffin) Penguin Publishing Group.

—EllRay Jakes Is Magic. Warner, Sally. 2014. (EllRay Jakes Ser.: 6). (ENG.). (J). (gr. 1-3). 160p. 14.99 *(978-0-670-78500-1(8),* Viking Juvenile); 176p. pap. 5.99 *(978-0-14-242360-8(2),* Puffin) Penguin Publishing Group.

—Ellray Jakes Rocks the Holidays! Warner, Sally. 2014. (EllRay Jakes Ser.: 7). (ENG.). 160p. (J). (gr. 1-3). 14.99 *(978-0-451-46909-0(7))* Penguin Bks., Ltd. GBR. Dist: Penguin Publishing Group.

—Ellray Jakes the Dragon Slayer, No. 4. Warner, Sally. 2013. (EllRay Jakes Ser.: 4). (ENG.). 144p. (J). (gr. 1-3). pap. 5.99 *(978-0-14-242358-5(0),* Puffin) Penguin Publishing Group.

The check digit for ISBN-10 appears in parentheses after the full ISBN-13

—EllRay Jakes the Recess King! Warner, Sally. 2015. (EllRay Jakes Ser.: 8). (ENG.). 176p. (J). (gr. 1-3). 5.99 *(978-0-14-751252-9(2)*, Puffin); 14.99 *(978-0-451-46911-3(9)*, Viking Juvenile) Penguin Publishing Group.

—Enemy Spy. Van Draanen, Wendelin. 2006. (Shredderman Ser.: Bk. 4). (ENG.). 192p. (J). (gr. 1-4). 6.99 *(978-0-440-41915-0(8)*, Yearling) Random Hse. Children's Bks.

Biggs, Brian. Football with Dad. Berrios, Frank. 2015. (Little Golden Book Ser.). (ENG.). 24p. (J). (-k). 4.99 ***(978-0-385-37925-0(0)***, Golden Bks.) Random Hse. Children's Bks.

Biggs, Brian. Frank Einstein & the Antimatter Motor. Scieszka, Jon. 2014. (Frank Einstein Ser.: 1). (ENG.). 192p. (J). (gr. 2-6). 13.95 *(978-1-4197-1218-0(7)*, Amulet Bks.) Abrams.

Biggs, Brian. Frank Einstein & the BrainTurbo. Scieszka, Jon. 2015. (ENG.). 192p. (J). (gr. 3-7). 13.95 ***(978-1-4197-1643-0(3)***, Amulet Bks.); pap. 8.95 ***(978-1-4197-1924-0(6))*** Abrams.

Biggs, Brian. Frank Einstein & the Electro-Finger. Scieszka, Jon. 2015. (Frank Einstein Ser.: 2). (ENG.). 176p. (J). (gr. 3-7). 13.95 *(978-1-4197-1483-2(X)*, Amulet Bks.) Abrams.

—I'm a T. Rex! Shealy, Dennis. 2010. (Little Golden Book Ser.). (ENG.). 24p. (J). (gr. -1-2). 3.99 *(978-0-375-85806-2(7)*, Golden Bks.) Random Hse. Children's Bks.

—Meet the Gecko. Van Draanen, Wendelin. 2006. (Shredderman Ser.: Bk. 3). (ENG.). 176p. (J). (gr. 1-4). 5.99 *(978-0-440-41914-3(X)*, Yearling) Random Hse. Children's Bks.

—Never Glue Your Friends to Chairs. Applegate, Katherine. 2008. (Roscoe Riley Rules Ser.: 1). (ENG.). 96p. (J). (gr. 2-5). 15.99 *(978-0-06-114882-8(2))*; pap. 4.99 *(978-0-06-114881-1(4))* HarperCollins Pubs.

—Never Race a Runaway Pumpkin. Applegate, Katherine. 2009. (Roscoe Riley Rules Ser.: 7). (ENG.). 96p. (J). (gr. 2-5). 15.99 *(978-0-06-178372-2(2))*; pap. 4.99 *(978-0-06-178370-8(6))* HarperCollins Pubs.

—Never Swim in Applesauce. Applegate, Katherine. 2008. (Roscoe Riley Rules Ser.: 4). (ENG.). 96p. (J). (gr. 2-5). 15.99 *(978-0-06-114888-0(1))*; pap. 4.99 *(978-0-06-114887-3(3))* HarperCollins Pubs.

—Never Swipe a Bully's Bear. Applegate, Katherine. 2008. (Roscoe Riley Rules Ser.: 2). (ENG.). 96p. (J). (gr. 2-5). 15.99 *(978-0-06-114884-2(9))*; pap. 4.99 *(978-0-06-114883-5(0))* HarperCollins Pubs.

—Never Walk in Shoes That Talk. Applegate, Katherine. 2009. (Roscoe Riley Rules Ser.: 6). (ENG.). 96p. (J). (gr. 2-5). 14.99 *(978-0-06-114892-7(X))*; pap. 4.99 *(978-0-06-114891-0(1))* HarperCollins Pubs.

—One Beastly Beast: Two Aliens, Three Inventors, Four Fantastic Tales. Nix, Garth. 2007. 176p. (J). (gr. 2-6). lib. bdg. 16.89 *(978-0-06-084320-5(9)*, Eos) HarperCollins Pubs.

—Sammy Keyes & the Wild Things. Van Draanen, Wendelin. 2008. (Sammy Keyes Ser.: Bk. 11). (ENG.). 320p. (J). (gr. 5-7). 7.99 *(978-0-440-42112-2(8)*, Yearling) Random Hse. Children's Bks.

—Shredderman: Secret Identity. Van Draanen, Wendelin. unabr. ed. 2006. (Shredderman Ser.: Bk. 1).Tr. of Shredderman - Al Haqiqa Wara ¿Al Fatak¿. (J). (gr. 2-4). audio 24.95 *(978-1-59519-762-7(1))* Live Oak Media.

—Shredderman: Secret Identity. Van Draanen, Wendelin. 2006. (Shredderman Ser.: Bk. 1).Tr. of Shredderman - Al Haqiqa Wara ¿Al Fatak¿. (ENG.). 144p. (J). (gr. 1-4). reprint ed. 6.99 *(978-0-440-41912-9(3)*, Yearling) Random Hse. Children's Bks.

Biggs, Brian. Blue Bus, Red Balloon: A Book of Colors. Biggs, Brian. 2013. (ENG.). 24p. (J). (gr. -1 — 1). bds. 7.99 *(978-0-06-195814-4(X))* HarperCollins Pubs.

—Everything Goes: On Land. Biggs, Brian. 2011. (ENG.). 56p. (J). (gr. -1-3). 14.99 *(978-0-06-195809-0(3))* HarperCollins Pubs.

—Everything Goes: Santa Goes Everywhere! Biggs, Brian. 2013. (ENG.). 24p. (J). (gr. -1 — 1). bds. 7.99 *(978-0-06-195817-5(4))* HarperCollins Pubs.

—Everything Goes - By Sea. Biggs, Brian. 2013. (ENG.). 56p. (J). (gr. -1-3). 14.99 *(978-0-06-195811-3(5))* HarperCollins Pubs.

—Everything Goes - What Flies in the Air? Biggs, Brian. 2013. (ENG.). 24p. (J). (gr. -1 — 1). bds. 7.99 *(978-0-06-195816-8(6))* HarperCollins Pubs.

—Good Night, Trucks: A Bedtime Book. Biggs, Brian. 2013. (ENG.). 24p. (J). (gr. -1 — 1). bds. 7.99 *(978-0-06-195815-1(8))* HarperCollins Pubs.

—In the Air. Biggs, Brian. 2012. (ENG.). 56p. (J). (gr. -1-3). 14.99 *(978-0-06-195810-6(7))* HarperCollins Pubs.

—Stop! Go! Biggs, Brian. 2012. (ENG.). 24p. (J). (gr. -1 — 1). bds. 7.99 *(978-0-06-195813-7(1))* HarperCollins Pubs.

—123 Beep Beep Beep! Biggs, Brian. 2012. (ENG.). 24p. (J). (gr. -1 — 1). bds. 7.99 *(978-0-06-195812-0(3))* HarperCollins Pubs.

Biggs, Brian & Abbott, Simon. Everything Goes: Henry in a Jam. Biggs, Brian. 2012. (My First I Can Read Ser.). (ENG.). 32p. (J). (gr. -1-3). 16.99 *(978-0-06-195819-9(0))* HarperCollins Pubs.

—Henry Goes Skating. Biggs, Brian. 2012. (My First I Can Read Ser.). (ENG.). 32p. (J). (gr. -1-3). 16.99 *(978-0-06-195821-2(2))*; pap. 3.99 *(978-0-06-195820-5(4))* HarperCollins Pubs.

—Henry in a Jam. Biggs, Brian. 2012. (My First I Can Read Ser.). (ENG.). 32p. (J). (gr. -1-3). pap. 3.99 *(978-0-06-195818-2(2))* HarperCollins Pubs.

—Henry on Wheels. Biggs, Brian. 2013. (My First I Can Read Ser.). (ENG.). 32p. (J). (gr. -1-3). 16.99 *(978-0-06-195823-6(9))* HarperCollins Pubs.

Biggs, Brian & Tanguy, Elara. Camp Out! The Ultimate Kids' Guide. Brunelle, Lynn. 2007. (ENG.). 256p. (J). (gr. 4-7). pap. 13.95 *(978-0-7611-4122-8(7)*, 14122) Workman Publishing Co., Inc.

Biggs, Gene. A First Dictionary. Wittels, Harriet & Greisman, Joan. 2004. 239p. (J). (gr. 4-8). reprint ed. pap. 15.00 *(978-0-7567-8422-5(0))* DIANE Publishing Co.

Bigham, Sean. Tuniit: Mysterious Folk of the Arctic, 1 vol. Qitsualik-Tinsley, Rachel & Qitsualik-Tinsley, Sean. 2014. (ENG.). 60p. (J). (gr. 2-4). 16.95 *(978-1-927095-76-8(X))* Inhabit Media Inc. CAN. Dist: Independent Pubs. Group.

Bigly, Ashley D., jt. illus. see Bratton, Deboral B.

Bigwood, John, jt. illus. see Dreidemy, Joëlle.

Bihun, Robb. Edison's Frankenstein 1910. Yambar, Chris, ed. 2003. (YA). mass mkt. 7.95 *(978-1-929515-27-1(8))* Comic Library International.

Bilan, Edgar. Mommy Works. Bilan Hochenberg, Nerissa. 2013. 24p. pap. *(978-1-4602-2602-5(X))* FriesenPress.

Bileck, Marvin. Nobody's Birthday. Colver, Anne. 2012. 44p. 35.95 *(978-1-258-23347-1(9))*; pap. 20.95 *(978-1-258-24718-8(6))* Literary Licensing, LLC.

Bilibin, Ivan. Russian Fairy Tales. Afanasyev, Alexander. 2013. 80p. *(978-1-909115-59-0(2))*; 2012. 90p. pap. *(978-1-908478-68-9(3))* Planet, The.

—Russian Folk Tales - Russkie Narodnye Skazki. Afanasyev, Alexander. 2013. 94p. *(978-1-909115-32-3(0))* Planet, The.

—Skazki Pushkina - Fairy Tales. Pushkin, Alexander. 2013. 48p. *(978-1-909115-58-3(4))* Planet, The.

—The Tale of Tsarevich Ivan, the Firebird, & the Grey Wolf. Afanasyev, Alexander. 2013. 28p. pap. *(978-1-909115-50-7(9))* Planet, The.

Bilik-Franklin, MidiAna & Griffith, Indigo, photos by. The Carseat Tourist. 2006. (J). bds. 7.95 *(978-0-9772825-0-0(3))* Critter Camp Inc.

Bill, Graf. Nacho Money. Sparks, Candi et al. 2012. (Can I Have Some Money? Ser.). 36p. pap. 11.99 *(978-0-9789445-6-8(9))* Sparks Fly.

Billen-Frye, Paige, et al. Best-Loved Parables of Jesus. Burgdorf, Larry et al. 2014. (ENG.). 101p. (J). 9.99 *(978-0-7586-4662-0(3))* Concordia Publishing Hse.

Billen-Frye, Paige. The Wise & Foolish Builders: A Parable of Jesus, Matthew 7:24-27 & Luke 6:47-49 for Children. Burgdorf, Larry. 2007. (Arch Bks.). 16p. (J). 2.49 *(978-0-7586-1263-2(X))* Concordia Publishing Hse.

Billet, Marion. Hello! London. ed. 2014. (Hello! Ser.). (ENG.). 400p. (J). (-k). 15.99 *(978-1-4472-4682-4(9))* Pan Macmillan GBR. Dist: Independent Pubs. Group.

—London Bus. ed. 2014. (ENG.). 400p. (J). (— 1). 7.99 *(978-1-4472-5632-8(8))* Pan Macmillan GBR. Dist: Independent Pubs. Group.

—London Taxi. ed. 2014. (ENG.). 400p. (J). (— 1). 7.99 *(978-1-4472-5633-5(6))* Pan Macmillan GBR. Dist: Independent Pubs. Group.

—Noodle Loves Bedtime. Nosy Crow. 2011. (Noodle Ser.). (ENG.). 10p. (J). (gr. k — 1). bds. 8.99 *(978-0-7636-5876-2(6)*, Nosy Crow) Candlewick Pr.

—Noodle Loves the Beach. Nosy Crow. 2012. (Noodle Ser.). (ENG.). 10p. (J). (gr. k — 1). bds. 8.99 *(978-0-7636-5898-4(7)*, Nosy Crow) Candlewick Pr.

—Noodle Loves the Park. Nosy Crow. 2013. (Noodle Ser.). (ENG.). 10p. (J). (— 1). bds. 8.99 *(978-0-7636-6577-7(0)*, Nosy Crow) Candlewick Pr.

—Noodle Loves to Cuddle. Nosy Crow. 2011. (Noodle Ser.). (ENG.). 10p. (J). (gr. k — 1). bds. 8.99 *(978-0-7636-5875-5(8)*, Nosy Crow) Candlewick Pr.

—Noodle Loves to Drive. Nosy Crow. 2012. (Noodle Ser.). (ENG.). 10p. (J). (gr. k — 1). bds. 8.99 *(978-0-7636-6273-8(9)*, Nosy Crow) Candlewick Pr.

—Noodle Loves to Eat. Nosy Crow. 2012. (Noodle Ser.). (ENG.). 10p. (J). (gr. k — 1). bds. 8.99 *(978-0-7636-5897-7(9)*, Nosy Crow) Candlewick Pr.

Billet, Marion. Littleland. Billet, Marion. 2013. (ENG.). 32p. (J). (gr. k-k). 14.99 *(978-0-7636-6550-0(9)*, Nosy Crow) Candlewick Pr.

—Littleland Around the World. Billet, Marion. 2014. (ENG.). 32p. (J). (-k). 14.99 *(978-0-7636-7579-0(2)*, Nosy Crow) Candlewick Pr.

Billin-Frye, Page. Trevor el Ingenioso. Albee, Sarah. 2008. (Science Solves It! en Espanol Ser.).Tr. of Clever Trevor. (SPA.). 32p. (J). (gr. -1-3). pap. 5.95 *(978-1-57565-263-4(3))* Kane Pr., Inc.

Billin-Frye, Paige. Butterfly Express: A Book about Life Cycles. Moncure, Jane Belk. 2013. (Magic Castle Readers: Science Ser.). (ENG.). 32p. (J). (gr. -1-2). 25.64 *(978-1-62323-588-8(X)*, 206323) Child's World, Inc., The.

—Clever Trevor. Albee, Sarah. 2003. (Science Solves It! Ser.). 32p. (J). pap. 5.95 *(978-1-57565-123-1(8))* Kane Pr., Inc.

—December. Kesselring, Mari. 2009. (Months of the Year Ser.). 24p. (gr. -1-2). 27.07 *(978-1-60270-639-2(5)*, Looking Glass Library- Nonfiction) Magic Wagon.

—The Easter Victory. Rottmann, Erik. 2006. (Arch Bks.). (ENG.). 16p. (J). (gr. -1-3). 2.49 *(978-0-7586-0869-7(1))* Concordia Publishing Hse.

—February. Kesselring, Mari. 2009. (Months of the Year Ser.). 24p. (gr. -1-2). 27.07 *(978-1-60270-629-3(8)*, Looking Glass Library- Nonfiction) Magic Wagon.

—Flower Girl. Herman, Gail. 2012. (Penguin Young Readers, L3 Ser.). (ENG.). 32p. (J). (gr. 1-4). 3.99 *(978-0-448-49487-6(6)*, Grosset & Dunlap) Penguin Publishing Group.

—Forgiving a Friend. Kroll, Virginia L. 2005. (Way I ACT Ser.). (ENG.). 24p. (J). (gr. k-3). lib. bdg. 15.99 *(978-0-8075-0618-9(4))* Whitman, Albert & Co.

—The Giant Jelly Bean Jar. Aboff, Marcie. 2013. (Puffin Young Readers, L3 Ser.). (ENG.). 32p. (J). (gr. -1-3). pap. 3.99 *(978-0-448-46624-8(4)*, Puffin) Penguin Publishing Group.

—The Giant Jelly Bean Jar. Aboff, Marcie et al. 2004. (Puffin Easy-to-Read Ser.). 32p. (gr. k-3). 14.00 *(978-0-7569-2824-7(9))* Perfection Learning Corp.

—Here We Go 'Round the Year: A Book about the Months. Moncure, Jane Belk. 2013. (Magic Castle Readers: Science Ser.). (ENG.). 32p. (J). (gr. -1-2). 25.64 *(978-1-62323-582-6(0)*, 206318) Child's World, Inc., The.

—Ice Cream Cows & Mitten Sheep: A Book about Farm Animals. Moncure, Jane Belk. 2013. (Magic Castle Readers: Science Ser.). (ENG.). 32p. (J). (gr. -1-2). 25.64 *(978-1-62323-583-3(9)*, 206319) Child's World, Inc., The.

—January. Kesselring, Mari. 2009. (Months of the Year Ser.). 24p. (gr. -1-2). 27.07 *(978-1-60270-628-6(X)*, Looking Glass Library- Nonfiction) Magic Wagon.

—Patty's Pictures. Janovich, Leah. 2010. 16p. (J). *(978-0-545-24820-4(5))* Scholastic, Inc.

—A Pocketful of Pets: A Search-and-Count Adventure. Moncure, Jane Belk. 2013. (Magic Castle Readers: Science Ser.). (ENG.). 32p. (J). (gr. -1-2). 25.64 *(978-1-62323-584-0(7)*, 206317) Child's World, Inc., The.

—A Slimy Story. Knudsen, Michelle. 2004. 32p. (J). lib. bdg. 20.00 *(978-1-4242-1150-0(6))* Fitzgerald Bks.

—A Slimy Story. Knudsen, Michelle. 2004. (Science Solves It! Ser.). 32p. (J). (gr. -1-3). pap. 5.95 *(978-1-57565-144-6(0))* Kane Pr., Inc.

—Tara Pays Up! Larsen, Kirsten. 2006. (Social Studies Connects). 32p. (J). (gr. 1-3). pap. 5.95 *(978-1-57565-187-3(4))* Kane Pr., Inc.

—This Is the Dreidel. Levine, Abby. 2012. (J). 34.28 *(978-1-61913-134-7(X))* Weigl Pubs., Inc.

—This Is the Matzah. Levine, Abby. 2005. (ENG.). 32p. (J). (gr. -1-2). 16.99 *(978-0-8075-7885-8(1))* Whitman, Albert & Co.

—Todos Ganan! Bruce, Sheila. 2006. (Math Matters en Espanol Ser.). (SPA.). 32p. (J). (gr. -1-3). pap. 5.95 *(978-1-57565-162-0(9))* Kane Pr., Inc.

—Whatever Wanda. Ziglar, Christy. 2015. (J). *(978-0-8249-5668-4(0)*, Ideals Children's Bks.) Ideals Pubns.

—Where Is Baby Bear? A Book about Animal Homes. Moncure, Jane Belk. 2013. (Magic Castle Readers: Science Ser.). (ENG.). 32p. (J). (gr. -1-2). 25.64 *(978-1-62323-585-7(5)*, 206320) Child's World, Inc., The.

Billin-Frye, Paige & Frye, Paige. Pease Porridge Hot. Billin-Frye, Paige. 2011. (Favorite Children's Songs Ser.). (ENG.). 16p. (J). (gr. -1-2). lib. bdg. 25.64 *(978-1-60954-293-1(2)*, 200097) Child's World, Inc., The.

Billin-Frye, Paige & Frye, Paige Billin. Giant Jelly Bean Jar. Aboff, Marcie. 2004. (Penguin Young Readers, Level 3 Ser.). (ENG.). 32p. (J). (gr. 1-3). mass mkt. 3.99 *(978-0-14-240049-4(1)*, Puffin) Penguin Publishing Group.

Billings, David Joseph. Road Trip with Rabbit & Squash. Billings, David Joseph. 2006. 48p. (J). per. *(978-0-9789036-0-2(9))* Billings, David J.

Billingsley, Mary. The Life of Jesus: Paintings & Meditations on the Rosary. 2010. 56p. (J). 19.99 *(978-0-8028-5362-2(5)*, Eerdmans Bks For Young Readers) Eerdmans, William B. Publishing Co.

Billman, Dave, et al. Phonics. Thompson, Kim & Carder, Ken. 2009. 96p. (J). (gr. -1-3). pap. 10.99 incl. audio compact disk *(978-1-57583-820-5(6))* Twin Sisters IP, LLC.

Billout, Guy. All the World's a Stage. Hopkins, Lee Bennett. 2013. (ENG.). 40p. (J). (gr. 4-7). 19.99 *(978-1-56846-218-9(2)*, Creative Editions) Creative Co., The.

Bills, Taylor. Goldilocks & the Three Bears. 2009. 24p. 12.95 *(978-0-9776845-2-6(0))* 3D Alley, Inc.

—Jack & the Beanstalk. 2009. 24p. 12.95 *(978-0-9776845-3-3(9))* 3D Alley, Inc.

—Tear Soup: A Recipe for Healing after Loss. Schwiebert, Pat & DeKlyen, Chuck. 2nd rev. l.t. ed. 2004. (ENG.). 56p. (gr. -1-12). reprint ed. 19.95 *(978-0-9615197-6-6(2)*, 798) Grief Watch.

—Three Little Pigs. 2009. 24p. (J). 12.95 *(978-0-9776845-0-2(4))* 3D Alley, Inc.

—Twas the Night before Christmas. 2009. 24p. 12.95 *(978-0-9776845-4-0(7))* 3D Alley, Inc.

—The Ugly Duckling. 2009. 24p. 12.95 *(978-0-9776845-1-9(2))* 3D Alley, Inc.

—We Were Gonna Have a Baby, but We Had an Angel Instead. Schwiebert, Pat. 2004. 24p. pap. 7.95 *(978-0-9724241-1-0(3)*, 717) Grief Watch.

Bilyeu, Dan. Weird Rocks. Corriel, Michele. 2013. 36p. (J). 12.00 *(978-0-87842-597-6(7))* Mountain Pr. Publishing Co., Inc.

Binch, Caroline. Down by the River: Afro-Caribbean Rhymes, Games, & Songs for Children. 2011. (ENG.). 32p. (J). (gr. -1-k). pap. 7.95 *(978-1-84780-082-4(3)*, Frances Lincoln) Quarto Publishing Group UK GBR. Dist: Hachette Bk. Group.

—Gregory Cool. 2012. (ENG.). 32p. (J). (gr. k-3). pap. 8.99 *(978-1-84780-258-3(3)*, Frances Lincoln) Quarto Publishing Group UK GBR. Dist: Hachette Bk. Group.

—Hue Boy. Mitchell, Rita Phillips. 2013. (ENG.). 32p. (J). (gr. -1-2). pap. 8.99 *(978-1-84780-303-0(2)*, Frances Lincoln) Quarto Publishing Group UK GBR. Dist: Hachette Bk. Group.

—Look Back! Cooke, Trish. 2014. 32p. (J). 17.95 *(978-1-56656-980-4(X)*, Crocodile Bks.) Interlink Publishing Group, Inc.

Binch, Caroline. The Princess & the Castle. Binch, Caroline. 2005. (ENG.). 32p. (J). (gr. k-2). 8.99 *(978-0-09-943236-4(6)*, Red Fox) Random House Children's Books GBR. Dist: Independent Pubs. Group.

Binder, Lenore. Bananas & Bears, 1 vol. Binder, Anita. 2010. 24p. 24.95 *(978-1-4489-5946-4(2))* PublishAmerica, Inc.

Binder, Pat. Bluebonnet at the State Fair of Texas, 1 vol. Casad, Mary Brooke. 2010. (ENG.). 40p. (J). (gr. k-3). pap. 8.95 *(978-1-58980-830-0(4))* Pelican Publishing Co., Inc.

Bindon, John. Armored Dinosaurs. Lessem, Don. 2004. (Meet the Dinosaurs Ser.). (ENG.). 32p. (gr. 2-4). lib. bdg. 23.93 *(978-0-8225-1374-2(9))* Lerner Publishing Group.

—Carnivoros Gigantes. Lessem, Don. Translations.com Staff, tr. from ENG. 2005. (Conoce a Los Dinosaurios (Meet the Dinosaurs) Ser.).Tr. of Giant Meat-Eating Dinosaurs. (SPA.). 32p. (gr. 2-4). lib. bdg. 23.93 *(978-0-8225-2962-0(9)*, Ediciones Lerner) Lerner Publishing Group.

—The Deadliest Dinosaurs. Lessem, Don. 2005. (Meet the Dinosaurs Ser.). (ENG.). 32p. (gr. 2-4). lib. bdg. 23.93 *(978-0-8225-1421-3(4))* Lerner Publishing Group.

—Dinosaurios Acorazados. Lessem, Don. Translations.com Staff, tr. 2005. (Conoce a Los Dinosaurios (Meet the Dinosaurs) Ser.).Tr. of Armored Dinosaurs. (SPA.). 32p. (gr. 2-4). lib. bdg. 23.93 *(978-0-8225-2949-1(1)*, Ediciones Lerner) Lerner Publishing Group.

—Dinosaurios Con Plumas. Lessem, Don. Translations.com Staff, tr. from ENG. 2006. (Conoce a Los Dinosaurios (Meet the Dinosaurs) Ser.).Tr. of Feathered Dinosaurs. (SPA.). 32p. (gr. 2-4). lib. bdg. 23.93 *(978-0-8225-6242-9(1)*, Ediciones Lerner) Lerner Publishing Group.

—Los Dinosaurios Mas Rapidos. Lessem, Don. Translations.com Staff, tr. from ENG. 2006. (Conoce a Los Dinosaurios (Meet the Dinosaurs) Ser.). (SPA.). 32p. (gr. 2-4). lib. bdg. 23.93 *(978-0-8225-6241-2(3)*, Ediciones Lerner) Lerner Publishing Group.

—Dinosaurios Pico de Pato. Lessem, Don. Translations.com Staff, tr. 2005. (Conoce a Los Dinosaurios (Meet the Dinosaurs) Ser.).Tr. of Duck-Billed Dinosaurs. (SPA.). 32p. (gr. 2-4). lib. bdg. 23.93 *(978-0-8225-2959-0(9)*, Ediciones Lerner) Lerner Publishing Group.

—The Fastest Dinosaurs. Lessem, Don. 2005. (Meet the Dinosaurs Ser.). (ENG.). 32p. (gr. 2-4). lib. bdg. 23.93 *(978-0-8225-1422-0(2))* Lerner Publishing Group.

—Gigantes Marinos de la Época de los Dinosaurios. Lessem, Don. Translations.com Staff, tr. from ENG. 2006. (Conoce a Los Dinosaurios (Meet the Dinosaurs) Ser.). (SPA.). 32p. (gr. 2-4). lib. bdg. 23.93 *(978-0-8225-6244-3(8)*, Ediciones Lerner) Lerner Publishing Group.

—Gigantes Voladores de la Epoca de los Dinosaurios. Lessem, Don. Translations.com Staff, tr. from ENG. 2006. (Conoce a Los Dinosaurios (Meet the Dinosaurs) Ser.).Tr. of Flying Giants of Dinosaur Time. (SPA.). 32p. (gr. 2-4). lib. bdg. 23.93 *(978-0-8225-6243-6(X)*, Ediciones Lerner) Lerner Publishing Group.

—Herbívoros Gigantes. Lessem, Don. Translations.com Staff, tr. 2005. (Conoce a Los Dinosaurios (Meet the Dinosaurs) Ser.). (SPA.). 32p. (gr. 2-4). lib. bdg. 23.93 *(978-0-8225-2964-4(5)*, Ediciones Lerner) Lerner Publishing Group.

—Horned Dinosaurs. Lessem, Don. 2004. (Meet the Dinosaurs Ser.). (ENG.). 32p. (gr. 2-4). lib. bdg. 23.93 *(978-0-8225-1370-4(6))* Lerner Publishing Group.

—Los Dinosaurios Más Inteligentes. Lessem, Don. Translations.com Staff, tr. from ENG. 2006. (Conoce a Los Dinosaurios (Meet the Dinosaurs) Ser.). (SPA.). 32p. (gr. 2-4). lib. bdg. 23.93 *(978-0-8225-6245-0(6)*, Ediciones Lerner) Lerner Publishing Group.

—Los Dinosaurios Más Pequeños. Lessem, Don. Translations.com Staff, tr. 2005. (Conoce a Los Dinosaurios (Meet the Dinosaurs) Ser.).Tr. of Smallest Dinosaurs. (SPA.). 32p. (gr. 2-4). lib. bdg. 23.93 *(978-0-8225-2968-2(8)*, Ediciones Lerner) Lerner Publishing Group.

—Monster Fliers: From the Time of the Dinosaurs. MacLeod, Elizabeth. 2010. (ENG.). 32p. (J). (gr. k-4). 16.95 *(978-1-55453-199-8(3))* Kids Can Pr., Ltd. CAN. Dist: Univ. of Toronto Pr.

—Pterosaurs up Close: Flying Reptiles. Dodson, Peter. 2010. (Zoom in on Dinosaurs! Ser.). 24p. (J). (gr. k-3). 22.60 *(978-0-7660-3332-0(5))* Enslow Pubs., Inc.

—The Search for Antarctic Dinosaurs. Walker, Sally M. 2007. (On My Own Science Ser.). (ENG.). 48p. (gr. 2-4). lib. bdg. 25.26 *(978-0-8225-6749-3(0)*, Millbrook Pr.) Lerner Publishing Group.

—The Smartest Dinosaurs. Lessem, Don. 2005. (Meet the Dinosaurs Ser.). (ENG.). 32p. (gr. 2-4). lib. bdg. 23.93 *(978-0-8225-1373-5(0))* Lerner Publishing Group.

Bindon, John, jt. illus. see Marshall, Todd.

Bines, Gary & Boller, Gary. Freaky Facts about Natural Disasters. Fecher, Sarah & Oliver, Clare. Anderson, Jill, ed. 2006. (Freaky Facts Ser.). (ENG.). 32p. (J). (gr. 2-5). pap. 8.95 *(978-1-58728-542-4(8))* Cooper Square Publishing Llc.

Bines, Gary & Hancock, David. The Usborne Little Encyclopedia of Space. Dowswell, Paul. 2005. 64p. (J). (gr. -1-3). 6.95 *(978-0-7945-1091-6(4)*, Usborne) EDC Publishing.

Bing, Christopher. Lincoln Shot: A President's Life Remembered. Denenberg, Barry. 2008. (ENG.). 40p. (J). (gr. 5-9). 24.95 *(978-0-312-37013-8(X))* Feiwel & Friends.

—Lincoln Shot: A President's Life Remembered. Denenberg, Barry. 2011. (ENG.). 96p. (J). (gr. 5-9). pap. 12.99 *(978-0-312-60442-4(4))* Square Fish.

Bing, Christopher H. The Story of Little Red Riding Hood. Grimm, Jacob & Grimm, Wilhelm. 2010. (ENG.). 40p. (J). (gr. k-17). 18.99 *(978-0-8118-6986-7(5))* Chronicle Bks. LLC.

Bingham, Jerry. Sing Out Loud Book IV: Owning the Stage. Hoops, Kevin, photos by. Vendera, Jaime & McGee, Anne Loader. 2012. 36p. (YA). pap. 7.99 *(978-1-936307-11-1(1))* Vendera Publishing.

Bingham, Jerry, jt. illus. see Bastien, Valerie.

Bingham, Pamela E. A Thought for Thanksgiving. Stilwell, Norma Minturn. 2011. 24p. pap. 14.95 *(978-1-936343-93-5(2))* Peppertree Pr., The.

Bingham, Salina Gonzales. More Than It Seems. Bingham, Jennifer. 2011. (ENG.). 52p. pap. 14.95 *(978-1-4611-2622-5(3))* CreateSpace Independent Publishing Platform.

Binns, Chris. Razor the Vampire! Foster, Greg & Quattro, Jacquelyn. l.t. ed. 2011. (ENG.). 32p. pap. 12.99 *(978-0-615-53477-0(5))* Quattro, Jacquelyn.

Binus, Ari. Around the Shabbos Table. Berman, Seryl. 2008. 40p. (J). (gr. -1-k). pap. 10.95 *(978-1-929628-44-5(7))* Hachai Publishing.

—Hayyim's Ghost. Kimmel, Eric A. 2005. 40p. (J). 16.95 *(978-1-932687-02-6(5)*, Devora Publishing) Simcha Media Group.

—Izzy Hagbah. 2005. 37p. (J). (gr. 1-4). 16.95 *(978-1-932687-38-5(6))*; per. 9.95 *(978-1-932687-39-2(4))* Simcha Media Group. (Devora Publishing).

—Littlest Tree. Rouss, Sylvia. 2005. 32p. (J). pap. 9.95 *(978-1-932687-26-2(2)*, Devora Publishing) Simcha Media Group.

—The Littlest Tree. Rouss, Sylvia. 2005. 32p. (J). 16.95 *(978-1-932687-25-5(4)*, Devora Publishing) Simcha Media Group.

Bios Agency, photos by. The Shark: Silent Hunter. Le Bloas-Julienne, Renee. 2007. (Animal Close-Ups Ser.). 26p. (J). (gr. 1-4). pap. 6.95 (978-1-57091-631-1(4)) Charlesbridge Publishing, Inc.

Birch, Linda. Start Here. Lane, Sheila Mary & Kemp, Marion. Date not set. (Whizz Bang Bumper Bk.). 64p. (J). pap. 129.15 (978-0-582-19331-4(1)) Addison-Wesley Longman, Ltd. GBR. Dist: Trans-Atlantic Pubns., Inc.

Birch, Reginald. Little Lord Fauntleroy. Burnett, Frances Hodgson. 2004. reprint ed. pap. 27.95 (978-1-4179-4302-9(5)) Kessinger Publishing, LLC.

Birck, Jan. The Wild Soccer Bunch, Book 2, Diego the Tornado: Diego the Tornado. Masannak, Joachim. Part, Michael, ed. Schier, Helga, tr. 2011. (ENG.). 148p. (J). (gr. 4-7). 12.95 (978-0-9844257-1-6(3)) Sole Bks.

Bird, Glen. Dinosaur Jigsaw Atlas. Pearcey, Alice, ed. 2004. 20p. (J). 14.95 (978-0-7945-0913-2(4), Usborne) EDC Publishing.

Bird, Glen, jt. illus. see Cartwright, Stephen.

Bird, Jemima. Our Cat Henry Comes to the Swings. Clanchy, Kate. 2007. 32p. (J). (gr. -1-1). 16.00 (978-1-56148-563-5(2), Good Bks.) Skyhorse Publishing Co., Inc.

Bird, Matthew. Crown & Covenant, 3 bks. Bond, Doug. 2004. (Crown & Covenant Ser.). (J). per. 26.99 (978-0-87552-671-3(3)) P & R Publishing.

—First Son & President: A Story about John Quincy Adams. Gherman, Beverly. (Creative Minds Biographies Ser.). (ENG.). 64p. (gr. 4-8). 2006. pap. 8.95 (978-0-8225-3091-6(0)); 2005. lib. bdg. 22.60 (978-1-57505-756-9(5), Carolrhoda Bks.) Lerner Publishing Group.

—King's Arrow. Bond, Douglas. 2003. (Crown & Covenant Ser.). 208p. (J). per. 10.99 (978-0-87552-743-7(4)) P & R Publishing.

—Rebel's Keep. Bond, Douglas. 2004. (Crown & Covenant Ser.). 285p. (J). per. 9.99 (978-0-87552-744-4(2)) P & R Publishing.

Bird, Nikolai. Dear Principal Petunia: Word Processing. Zocchi, Judy. 2005. (Click & Squeak Ser.). 32p. (J). pap. 9.95 (978-1-59646-111-6(X)) Dingles & Co.

Bird, Richard E., photos by. Freddy in the City: Center City Sites. Bird, Janice W. Date not set. 32p. (J). (gr. 2-5). pap. 5.95 (978-0-9710071-1-6(X)) JFW, Ltd.

Birk, Sandow. Dante's Paradiso, 3 vols. Sanders, Marcus. 2005. (ENG.). 240p. (gr. 8-17). pap. 22.95 (978-0-8118-4720-9(9)) Chronicle Bks. LLC.

Birk, Sandow. Dante's Inferno, 3 vols. Birk, Sandow. Alighieri, Dante. 2003. (ENG.). 240p. (gr. 8-17). pap. 24.95 (978-0-8118-4213-6(4)) Chronicle Bks. LLC.

Birkett, Georgie. Ben's Book. Newman, Nanette. 2011. (ENG.). 32p. (J). (gr. -1-k). pap. 9.99 (978-1-84365-193-2(9), Pavilion Children's Books) Pavilion Bks. GBR. Dist: Independent Pubs. Group.

—The Bestest Baby. Simmons, Anthea. 2015. (ENG.). 24p. (J). (gr. -1). 9.95 (978-1-4549-1402-0(5)) Sterling Publishing Co., Inc.

—Clean It! 2009. (Helping Hands Ser.). (ENG.). 24p. (J). (gr. -1-k). (978-1-84643-283-5(9)) Child's Play International Ltd.

—Clean It!/a Limpiar. 2013. (Helping Hands (Bilingual) Ser.). (ENG & SPA.). 24p. (gr. -1-k). pap. (978-1-84643-569-0(2)) Child's Play International Ltd.

—Cook It! 2009. (Helping Hands Ser.). (ENG.). 24p. (J). (gr. -1-k). (978-1-84643-284-2(7)) Child's Play International Ltd.

—Cook It!/a Cocinar. 2013. (Helping Hands (Bilingual) Ser.). (ENG & SPA.). 24p. (gr. -1-k). pap. (978-1-84643-568-3(4)) Child's Play International Ltd.

—Fix It! 2009. (Helping Hands Ser.). (ENG.). 24p. (J). (gr. -1-k). (978-1-84643-286-6(3)) Child's Play International Ltd.

—Fix It!/a Reparar. 2013. (Helping Hands (Bilingual) Ser.). (ENG & SPA.). 24p. (gr. -1-k). pap. (978-1-84643-571-3(4)) Child's Play International Ltd.

—Grow It! 2009. (Helping Hands Ser.). (ENG.). 24p. (J). (gr. -1-k). (978-1-84643-285-9(5)) Child's Play International Ltd.

—Grow It!/a Sembrar. 2013. (Helping Hands (Bilingual) Ser.). (ENG & SPA.). 24p. (gr. -1-k). pap. (978-1-84643-570-6(6)) Child's Play International Ltd.

—Ha Ha, Baby! Petty, Kate. 2008. (ENG.). 32p. (J). (gr. -1-k). 14.95 (978-1-905417-12-4(8)) Boxer Bks., Ltd. GBR. Dist: Sterling Publishing Co., Inc.

—Hoppy Birthday, Jo-Jo! Goodhart, Pippa. 2005. (Green Bananas Ser.). (ENG.). 48p. (J). lib. bdg. (978-0-7787-1025-7(4)) Crabtree Publishing Co.

—How to Be Good. Toulmin & Piper, Sophie. 2009. (ENG.). 32p. (J). (gr. -1-k). 12.95 (978-0-7459-6043-2(X)) Lion Hudson PLC GBR. Dist: Independent Pubs. Group.

—A is for Apple. Tiger Tales Staff, ed. 2011. 26p. 7.95 (978-1-58925-872-3(X)) Tiger Tales.

—Is This My Nose? 2008. (ENG.). 12p. (J). (gr. -1-k). bds. 7.99 (978-0-7641-6153-7(9)) Barron's Educational Series, Inc.

—Share! Simmons, Anthea. 2014. (ENG.). 24p. (J). (gr. -1). 9.95 (978-1-4549-1403-7(3)) Sterling Publishing Co., Inc.

—Teddy Bear Hide-and-Seek. Edwards, Pamela Duncan. ed. 2008. (ENG.). 20p. (J). (gr. 2-5). 14.95 (978-0-230-01442-8(9), Macmillan) Pan Macmillan GBR. Dist: Trans-Atlantic Pubns., Inc.

—1 2 3 Count With Me. Tiger Tales Staff, ed. 2011. 26p. 7.95 (978-1-58925-873-0(8)) Tiger Tales.

Birkett, Georgie. Peekaboo! - Who Are You? Birkett, Georgie. ed. 2014. (Felty Flaps Ser.). (ENG.). 10p. (J). (gr. -1). bds. 9.99 (978-1-4472-6098-1(8)) Pan Macmillan GBR. Dist: Independent Pubs. Group.

—Red, Blue, Peekaboo! Birkett, Georgie. ed. 2015. (Felty Flaps Ser.). (ENG.). 10p. (J). (— 1). 9.99 (978-1-4472-6099-8(6)) Pan Macmillan GBR. Dist: Independent Pubs. Group.

Birkinshaw, Linda. The Amazing Pop-Up Stonehenge: All the Questions You've Always Wanted to Ask... & Some of the Answers! Richards, Julian. 2005. (ENG.). 16p. (C). (gr. 4-7). 19.95 (978-1-85074-926-4(4)) Historic England Publishing GBR. Dist: Casemate Academic.

Birky, Rachael. The Lone, Lone Cloud. Shifler, Ann. 2012. 28p. pap. 16.00 (978-1-58158-133-1(5)) McDougal Publishing Co.

Birmingham, Christian. Dear Olly. Morpurgo, Michael. 2007. (ENG.). 128p. (J). (gr. 4-7). mass mkt. 7.99 (978-0-00-675333-9(7), HarperCollins Children's Bks.) HarperCollins Pubs. Ltd. GBR. Dist: HarperCollins Pubs.

—The Night Before Christmas. Moore, Clement C. 10th anniv. ed. 2005. (ENG.). 48p. (J). (gr. -1-3). 9.95 (978-0-7624-2416-0(8)) Running Pr. Bk. Pubs.

—Thief Lord. Funke, Cornelia. 2010. (ENG.). 376p. (J). (gr. 3-7). 7.99 (978-0-545-22770-4(4), Chicken Hse., The) Scholastic, Inc.

—Wenceslas. McCaughrean, Geraldine. 2007. (ENG.). 32p. (J). (gr. k-2). 19.95 (978-0-385-60535-9(8), Doubleday Children's) Random House Children's Books GBR. Dist: Independent Pubs. Group.

Birmingham, Christian, jt. illus. see Birmingham, John.

Birmingham, John & Birmingham, Christian. Footprints on the Moon. Haddon, Mark. 2009. (ENG.). 32p. (J). (gr. -1-3). 16.99 (978-0-7636-4440-6(4)) Candlewick Pr.

Birnbach, Alece. Rise of the Undead Redhead. Dougherty, Meghan. 2014. (Dorothy's Derby Chronicles Ser.: 1). (ENG.). 256p. (J). (gr. 3-6). pap. 6.99 (978-1-4022-9535-5(9), Sourcebooks Jabberwocky) Sourcebooks, Inc.

Birnbach, Alece. Woe of Jade Doe. Dougherty, Meghan. 2015. (Dorothy's Derby Chronicles Ser.: 2). (ENG.). 288p. (J). (gr. 4-7). pap. 6.99 (978-1-4926-0147-0(0), Sourcebooks Jabberwocky) Sourcebooks, Inc.

Birnbaum, A. Little World, Hello! Savo, Jimmy. 2012. 194p. 42.95 (978-1-258-23434-8(3)); pap. 27.95 (978-1-258-24665-5(1)) Literary Licensing, LLC.

Birnbaum, A. Green Eyes. Birnbaum, A. 2011. (Family Storytime Ser.). (ENG.). 48p. (J). (gr. -1-2). pap. 7.99 (978-0-375-86201-4(3), Dragonfly Bks.) Random Hse. Children's Bks.

Biro, Val. Animal Tales for Bedtime. Jennings, Linda. 2013. (ENG.). 96p. (J). 16.50 (978-1-84135-932-8(7)) Award Pubns. Ltd. GBR. Dist: Parkwest Pubns., Inc.

Biro, Val. The Bible for Children. Fiona Fox Staff, ed. 2015. (ENG.). 280p. 33.00 (978-1-84135-827-7(4)) Award Pubns. Ltd. GBR. Dist: Parkwest Pubns., Inc.

Biro, Val. How to Draw Dinosaurs & Prehistoric Life. Claridge, Marit. Tatchell, Judy, ed. 2006. (Young Artist Ser.). 32p. (J). (gr. 4-7). pap. 5.99 (978-0-7945-1372-6(7), Usborne) EDC Publishing.

—The Lion & the Mouse with the Donkey & the Lapdog. Award, Anna & Aesop. 2014. (ENG.). 24p. (J). pap. 6.95 (978-1-84135-953-3(X)) Award Pubns. Ltd. GBR. Dist: Parkwest Pubns., Inc.

—The Secret of the Lost Necklace: 3 Great Adventure Stories. Blyton, Enid. 2013. (ENG.). 272p. (J). 16.50 (978-1-84135-587-0(9)) Award Pubns. Ltd. GBR. Dist: Parkwest Pubns., Inc.

—100 Bible Stories for Children. Andrews, Jackie. 2012. (ENG.). 208p. (J). 21.50 (978-1-84135-105-6(9)) Award Pubns. Ltd. GBR. Dist: Parkwest Pubns., Inc.

Biro, Val. Gumdrop & the Elephant. Biro, Val. 2015. (ENG.). 32p. (J). pap. 9.99 (978-1-78270-049-4(8)) Award Pubns. Ltd. GBR. Dist: Parkwest Pubns., Inc.

Birth, Ryan. What Do Monsters Look Like? Tayler, Amber. 2009. 36p. pap. 11.25 (978-1-935125-51-8(6)) Robertson Publishing.

Bisaillon, Josée. Benno & the Night of Broken Glass. Wiviott, Meg. 2010. (ENG.). 32p. (J). (gr. 2-5). pap. 7.95 (978-0-8225-9975-3(9)); lib. bdg. 17.95 (978-0-8225-9929-6(5)) Lerner Publishing Group. (Kar-Ben Publishing).

—BookSpeak! Poems about Books. Salas, Laura Purdie. 2011. (ENG.). 32p. (J). (gr. -1-3). 16.99 (978-0-547-22300-1(5)) Houghton Mifflin Harcourt Publishing Co.

—The Great Moon Hoax. Krensky, Stephen. 2011. (Carolrhoda Picture Bks). (ENG.). 32p. (J). (gr. 2-5). lib. bdg. 16.95 (978-0-7613-5110-8(8), Carolrhoda Bks.) Lerner Publishing Group.

Bisaillon, Josee. I Can't Sleep: Imagination - Bedtime. Kim, Cecil. Cowley, Joy, ed. 2015. (Step up - Creative Thinking Ser.). (ENG.). 32p. (gr. -1-2). 26.65 (978-1-925246-13-1(2)); 7.99 (978-1-925246-65-0(5)); 26.65 (978-1-925246-39-1(6)) ChoiceMaker Pty. Ltd., The AUS. (Big and SMALL). Dist: Lerner Publishing Group.

Bisaillon, Josée. Oh No, School! Chang, Hae-Kyung. 2014. 30p. (J). (978-1-4338-1333-7(5), Magination Pr.) American Psychological Assn.

—Winter's Coming: A Story of Seasonal Change. Thornhill, Jan. 2014. (ENG.). 32p. (J). (gr. k-3). 16.95 (978-1-77147-002-5(X), Owlkids) Owlkids Bks. Inc. CAN. Dist: Perseus-PGW.

Biscoe, Cee. Somebunny Loves You! Rumbaugh, Melinda. 2015. (ENG.). 16p. (J). 12.99 (978-0-8249-1950-4(5), Candy Cane Pr.) Ideals Pubns.

Biser, Dee. Forest House Firsts: Supplemental Selected Early Childhood Stories, 2 bks. Glyman, Caroline A. (J). (gr. k-3). lib. bdg. 29.90 (978-1-56674-910-7(7)) Forest Hse. Publishing Co., Inc.

Bishop, Barbara L. Children Today Around the U S A. Bishop, Barbara L. 2008. 40p. pap. 13.95 (978-1-934246-25-2(5)) Peppertree Pr., The.

Bishop, Ben. Lost Trail: Nine Days Alone in the Wilderness, 1 vol. Fendler, Donn & Plourde, Lynn. 2011. (ENG.). 72p. (J). (gr. 4-7). pap. 14.95 (978-0-89272-945-6(7)) Down East Bks.

Bishop, Christina. Enchanted Fairyland: A Sphinx & Trevi Adventure. Adam's Creations Publishing. 2007. (ENG.). 30p. (J). 19.95 (978-0-9785695-0-1(4)) Adam's Creations Publishing, LLC.

—The Puzzle Box of Nefertiti: A Sphinx & Trevi Adventure. Hayes, Celeste. 2011. 42p. (J). pap. 19.95 (978-0-9785695-3-2(9)) Adam's Creations Publishing, LLC.

Bishop, Craig. My Friend with Autism: Enhanced Edition with FREE CD of Coloring Pages! Bishop, Beverly. 2011. (ENG.). 41p. (J). pap. 14.95 (978-1-935274-18-6(X)) Future Horizons, Inc.

Bishop, Franklin, jt. illus. see Bishop, Helena Edwards.

Bishop, Gavin. Friends: Snake & Lizard. Cowley, Joy. 2011. (Gecko Press Titles Ser.). 16.95 (978-1-877579-01-1(7)) Gecko Pr. NZL. Dist: Lerner Publishing Group.

—Mister Whistler. Mahy, Margaret. 2013. 32p. (J). (gr. -1-3). 17.95 (978-1-877467-91-2(X)) Gecko Pr. NZL. Dist: Lerner Publishing Group.

—Snake & Lizard. Cowley, Joy. 2008. 104p. (J). (gr. -1-3). 9.99 (978-1-933605-83-8(9)) Kane Miller.

Bishop, Helena Edwards & Bishop, Franklin. The Wayward Haggis. 2012. 40p. pap. 18.95 (978-1-4477-6514-1(1)) Lulu Enterprises Inc.

Bishop, John E. Robber Raccoon, 1 vol. Bottiglieri, Tim. 2009. 16p. pap. 24.95 (978-1-61546-432-6(8)) America Star Bks.

Bishop, Kathleen Wong. Celebrating Holidays in Hawaii. Hayashi, Leslie Ann. 2010. (ENG.). 36p. (J). 14.95 (978-1-56647-914-1(2)) Mutual Publishing LLC.

—Fables Beneath the Rainbow. Hayashi, Leslie Ann. 2005. 32p. (J). 14.95 (978-1-56647-741-3(7), 477417) Mutual Publishing LLC.

—A Fishy Alphabet in Hawaii. Hayashi, Leslie Ann. 2007. (J). 13.95 (978-1-56647-830-4(8)) Mutual Publishing LLC.

Bishop, Megan. The Stories of Christmas: As Told by a Little Lamb. Blackburn, C. Edward. l.t. ed. 2005. 24p. (J). 9.95 (978-0-9727440-3-4(7)) Redline Bks.

Bishop, Nic. Little Monsters. Bishop, Nic. 2007. (Collins Big Cat Ser.). (ENG.). 32p. (J). pap. 7.99 (978-0-00-723080-8(X)) HarperCollins Pubs. Ltd. GBR. Dist: Independent Pubs. Group.

—Lizard, Level 2. Bishop, Nic. 2014. (Scholastic Reader Level 2 Ser.). (ENG.). 32p. (J). (gr. k-2). pap. 3.99 (978-0-545-60569-4(5), Scholastic Nonfiction) Scholastic, Inc.

—Snakes. Bishop, Nic. 2012. (Nic Bishop Ser.). (ENG.). 48p. (J). (gr. -1-3). 17.99 (978-0-545-20638-9(3), Scholastic Nonfiction) Scholastic, Inc.

Bishop, Nic. Chameleon! Bishop, Nic, photos by. 2005. (J). pap. (978-0-439-78111-4(6), Scholastic Pr.) Scholastic, Inc.

—Chameleon Chameleon. Bishop, Nic, photos by. Cowley, Joy. 2005. (ENG.). 32p. (J). (gr. -1-3). 18.99 (978-0-439-66653-4(8)) Scholastic, Inc.

—Chasing Cheetahs: The Race to Save Africa's Fastest Cats. Bishop, Nic, photos by. Montgomery, Sy. 2014. (Scientists in the Field Ser.). (ENG.). 80p. (J). (gr. 5-7). 18.99 (978-0-547-81549-7(2), HMH Books For Young Readers) Houghton Mifflin Harcourt Publishing Co.

—Kakapo Rescue: Saving the World's Strangest Parrot. Bishop, Nic, photos by. Montgomery, Sy. 2010. (Scientists in the Field Ser.). (ENG.). 80p. (J). (gr. 5-7). 18.00 (978-0-618-49417-0(0)) Houghton Mifflin Harcourt Publishing Co.

—Mysterious Universe: Supernovae, Dark Energy, & Black Holes. Bishop, Nic, photos by. Jackson, Ellen. 2008. (Scientists in the Field Ser.). (ENG.). 64p. (J). (gr. 5-7). 18.00 (978-0-618-56325-8(3)) Houghton Mifflin Harcourt Publishing Co.

—Red-Eyed Tree Frog. Bishop, Nic, photos by. Cowley, Joy. 2006. (Scholastic Bookshelf Ser.). (ENG.). 32p. (J). (gr. -1-3). mass mkt. 6.99 (978-0-439-78221-0(X), Scholastic Paperbacks) Scholastic, Inc.

—Saving the Ghost of the Mountain: An Expedition among Snow Leopards in Mongolia. Bishop, Nic, photos by. Montgomery, Sy. (Scientists in the Field Ser.). (ENG.). 80p. (J). (gr. 5-7). 2012. pap. 9.99 (978-0-547-72734-9(8)); 2009. 18.00 (978-0-618-91645-0(8)) Houghton Mifflin Harcourt Publishing Co.

Bishop, Nic, photos by. Mysterious Universe: Supernovae, Dark Energy, & Black Holes. Jackson, Ellen. 2011. (Scientists in the Field Ser.). (ENG., 64p. (J). (gr. 5-7). pap. 9.99 (978-0-547-51992-0(3)) Houghton Mifflin Harcourt Publishing Co.

—Quest for the Tree Kangaroo: An Expedition to the Cloud Forest of New Guinea. Montgomery, Sy. (Scientists in the Field Ser.). (ENG., 80p. (gr. 5-7). 2009. (YA). pap. 9.99 (978-0-547-24892-9(X)); 2006. (J). 18.99 (978-0-618-49641-9(6)) Houghton Mifflin Harcourt Publishing Co.

—The Tarantula Scientist. Montgomery, Sy. (Scientists in the Field Ser.). (ENG., 80p. (J). (gr. 5-7). 2007. pap. 9.99 (978-0-618-91577-4(X)); 2004. tchr. ed. 18.00 (978-0-618-14799-1(3)) Houghton Mifflin Harcourt Publishing Co.

Bishop, Nic, photos by. Butterflies. Bishop, Nic. 2011. (Scholastic Reader Level 2 Ser.). (ENG., 32p. (J). (gr. k-2). pap. 3.99 (978-0-545-28434-9(1), Scholastic Paperbacks) Scholastic, Inc.

—Butterflies & Moths. Bishop, Nic. 2009. (Nic Bishop Ser.). (ENG., 48p. (J). (gr. -1-3). 17.99 (978-0-439-87757-2(1)) Scholastic, Inc.

—The Cloud Forest. Bishop, Nic. 2005. (Collins Big Cat Ser.). (ENG., 32p. (J). pap. 7.99 (978-0-00-718641-9(X)) HarperCollins Pubs. Ltd. GBR. Dist: Independent Pubs. Group.

—Frogs. Bishop, Nic. 2008. (Nic Bishop Ser.). (ENG., 48p. (J). (gr. -1-3). 17.99 (978-0-439-87755-8(5)) Scholastic, Inc.

—Is There Anybody Out There? Bishop, Nic. Hughes, Jon. Moon, Cliff, ed. 2005. (Collins Big Cat Ser.). (ENG., 352p. (J). pap. 7.99 (978-0-00-718635-8(5)) HarperCollins Pubs. Ltd. GBR. Dist: Independent Pubs. Group.

—Lizards. Bishop, Nic. 2010. (Nic Bishop Ser.). (ENG., 48p. (J). (gr. -1-3). 17.99 (978-0-545-20634-1(0)) Scholastic, Inc.

—Marsupials. Bishop, Nic. 2009. (Nic Bishop Ser.). (ENG., 48p. (J). (gr. -1-3). 17.99 (978-0-439-87758-9(X)) Scholastic, Inc.

—NIC Bishop - Spiders. Bishop, Nic. 2012. (Scholastic Reader Level 2 Ser.). (ENG., 32p. (J). (gr. k-2). pap. 3.99 (978-0-545-23757-4(2), Scholastic Paperbacks) Scholastic, Inc.

—Spiders. Bishop, Nic. 2007. (Nic Bishop Ser.). (ENG., 48p. (J). (gr. -1-3). 17.99 (978-0-439-87756-5(3), Scholastic Nonfiction) Scholastic, Inc.

Bishop, Roma. Christmas Fun: Bible Activity Book. Lane, Leena. 2015. (J). pap. 9.95 (978-0-8198-1651-1(5)) Pauline Bks. & Media.

Bishop, Roma. Christmas Fun: My First Bible Activity BK. Lane, Leena. 2004. 32p. pap. 6.95 (978-1-59325-043-0(6)) Word Among Us Pr.

—Friends of God: My First Bible Activity BK. Lane, Leena. 2004. 32p. pap. 6.95 (978-1-59325-042-3(8)) Word Among Us Pr.

—Old Testament Stories. Lane, Leena. 2003. 32p. (J). 8.00 (978-0-687-06527-1(5)) Abingdon Pr.

—Stories of Jesus. Lane, Leena. 2003. 32p. (J). 8.00 (978-0-687-06537-0(2)) Abingdon Pr.

Bishop, Tracey. One Love, Two Worlds. Howard, Ian T. 2010. 36p. pap. 14.75 (978-1-60911-771-9(9), Eloquent Bks.) Strategic Book Publishing & Rights Agency (SBPRA).

Bishop, Tracy. Getting to Know Jesus for Little Ones: The Four Keys to Starting a Relationship with God. Bright, Brad et al. 2015. 32p. (J). 12.99 (978-0-7369-5401-3(5)) Harvest Hse. Pubs.

—Not the Quitting Kind. Roth, Sarra J. 2014. 32p. pap. 16.99 (978-1-4413-1415-4(6)) Peter Pauper Pr. Inc.

Bissell, Robert. Robert Bissell's Rabbits & Bears. 2013. (ENG.). (J). 7.95 (978-0-7649-6476-3(3)) Pomegranate Communications, Inc.

Bist, Vandana. The Princess with the Longest Hair. Raote, Komilla. 26p. (J). (978-81-85586-78-6(0)) Katha.

Bistricean, Claudius. The Adventures of Fergus & Lady: Home Sweet Home. Bistricean, Karen. 2006. (J). (978-0-9786975-1-8(0)) Fergus & Lady Publishing.

—The Adventures of Fergus & Lady: The Beginning. Bistricean, Karen. 2006. (J). (978-0-9786975-0-1(2)) Fergus & Lady Publishing.

Biswas, Pulak. Catch That Crocodile! Ravishankar, Anushka. 40p. (J). 2008. (ENG.). (gr. k-1). 16.95 (978-81-86211-63-2(2)); 2007. (gr. -1-2). 25.00 (978-81-86211-94-6(2)) Tara Publishing IND. Dist: Perseus-PGW, Consortium Bk. Sales & Distribution.

—The Flute, 1 vol. Gilmore, Rachna. 2012. (ENG.). 32p. (J). (gr. -1-2). 16.95 (978-1-896580-57-9(2)) Tradewind Bks. CAN. Dist: Orca Bk. Pubs. USA.

Bitetto, Marco A. V. Journal of Amateur Computing: Spring/Summer 2003 Issue. Bitetto, Marco A. V. l.t. ed. 2003. 120p. (YA). (gr. 9-12). pap. 22.00 (978-1-58578-482-0(6)) Institute of Cybernetics Research, Inc.

Bitskoff, Aleksei. Could a Penguin Ride a Bike? And Other Questions. de la Bédoyere, Camilla. 2015. (What If A Ser.). (ENG.). 24p. (J). (gr. -1-k). 15.95 (978-1-60992-734-9(6)) QEB Publishing Inc.

Bivins, Christopher. Bears Barge In. Sensel, Joni. 2003. 32p. (J). (gr. -1-18). 14.95 (978-0-9701195-0-6(X)) Dream Factory Bks.

—The Garbage Monster. Sensel, Joni. 2003. 24p. (J). (gr. -1-18). 14.95 (978-0-9701195-2-0(6)) Dream Factory Bks.

Bixby, Sean. The Goblin's Story. Dongweck, James. 2013. (J). (978-0-9719632-2-1(3)) Golden Monkey Publishing, LLC.

Bixley, Donovan. Little Bo Peep & More ... Favourite Nursery Rhymes. 2015. (ENG.). 24p. (J). (— 1). 9.99 (978-1-927262-08-5(9)) Upstart Pr. NZL. Dist: Independent Pubs. Group.

Bixley, Donovan. Maddy West & the Tongue Taker, 1 vol. Falkner, Brian. 2014. (ENG.). 256p. (gr. 4-8). 12.95 (978-1-62370-084-3(1)) Capstone Young Readers.

—Northwood, 1 vol. Falkner, Brian. 2014. (ENG.). 272p. (gr. 3-3). 26.60 (978-1-4342-8667-3(3)) Stone Arch Bks.

Bizjak, Donna. Gator & Pete - More Alike Than It Seems. McGovern, Suzanne. 2007. (J). 13.99 (978-0-9792558-0-9(5)) Hatch Ideas, Inc.

Bjarkdottir, Bjork. Your Body Is Brilliant: Body Respect for Children. Danielsdottir, Sigrun. 2014. (ENG.). 36p. (978-1-84819-221-8(5)) Kingsley, Jessica Ltd.

Bjarnason, Bjarni Thor. Raphael: The Angel Who Decided to Visit Earth. Snorradottir, Asthildur Bj. 2011. 74p. pap. 21.50 (978-1-60976-683-2(0), Strategic Bk. Publishing) Strategic Book Publishing & Rights Agency (SBPRA).

Bjorklund, L. F. Captured Words: The Story of A Great Indian. Browin, Frances Williams. 2011. 192p. 42.95 (978-1-258-09914-5(4)) Literary Licensing, LLC.

Bjorklung, Lorence. Dan Beard: Boy Scout Pioneer. Seibert, Jerry. 2012. 192p. 42.95 (978-1-258-25301-1(1)); pap. 27.95 (978-1-258-25517-6(0)) Literary Licensing, LLC.

Björkman, Steve. The Best Boat Ever Built. Larcombe, Jennifer Rees. 2004. (Best Bible Stories Ser.). 24p. (gr. -1-3). pap. 2.99 (978-1-58134-148-5(2)) Crossway.

—Coyotes All Around. Murphy, Stuart J. 2003. (MathStart 2 Ser.). (ENG.). 40p. (J). (gr. 1-18). pap. 5.99 (978-0-06-051531-7(7)) HarperCollins Pubs.

—Coyotes All Around. Murphy, Stuart J. ed. 2003. (MathStart Level 2 Ser.). 32p. (gr. -1-3). 16.00 (978-0-613-68415-6(X), Turtleback) Turtleback Bks.

—Danger on the Lonely Road. Larcombe, Jennifer Rees. 2004. (Best Bible Stories Ser.). 24p. (gr. -1-3). pap. 2.99 (978-1-58134-149-2(0)) Crossway.

—Dinosaurs Don't, Dinosaurs Do. 2011. (I Like to ReadTM Ser.). (ENG.). 24p. (J). 14.95 (978-0-8234-2355-2(7)) Holiday Hse., Inc.

—Dirt on My Shirt. Foxworthy, Jeff. 32p. (J). (gr. -1-3). 2013. (ENG.). 9.99 (978-0-06-223191-8(X)); 2009. 16.99 (978-0-06-176525-4(2)); 2008. lib. bdg. 17.89 (978-0-06-120847-8(7)); 2008. (ENG.). 17.99 (978-0-06-120846-1(9)) HarperCollins Pubs.

—Dirt on My Shirt: Selected Poems. Foxworthy, Jeff. 2009. (I Can Read Book 2 Ser.). (ENG.). 32p. (J). (gr. k-3). pap. 3.99 (978-0-06-176524-7(4)) HarperCollins Pubs.

—Easter Bunny Blues. Wallace, Carol. 2009. (ENG.). 40p. (J). (gr. k-2). 15.95 (978-0-8234-2162-6(7)) Holiday Hse., Inc.

—Emily Post's the Guide to Good Manners for Kids. Senning, Cindy Post & Post, Emily. 2004. (ENG.). 144p. (J). (gr. 3-7). 16.99 *(978-0-06-057196-2(9))* HarperCollins Pubs.
—Emily's Everyday Manners. Post, Peggy & Senning, Cindy Post. 2006. 32p. (J). (gr. -1-2). (ENG.). 16.99 *(978-0-06-076174-5(1))*; lib. bdg. 17.89 *(978-0-06-076177-6(6))* HarperCollins Pubs. (Collins).
—Emily's New Friend. Senning, Cindy Post & Post, Peggy. 2010. (ENG.). 32p. (J). (gr. -1-2). 16.99 *(978-0-06-111706-0(4)*, Collins) HarperCollins Pubs.
—The Farm Life. Spurr, Elizabeth. 2005. (ENG.). 32p. (J). (gr. k-3). tchr. ed. 16.95 *(978-0-8234-1777-3(8))* Holiday Hse., Inc.
—Farmer Brown's Field Trip. Carlson, Melody. 2004. 40p. (gr. -1-3). 9.99 *(978-1-58134-142-3(3))* Crossway.
—The Guide to Good Manners for Kids. Post, Peggy & Senning, Cindy Post. 2006. 144p. (J). (gr. 4-8). reprint ed. 16.00 *(978-1-4223-5621-0(3))* DIANE Publishing Co.
—Hide!!! Foxworthy, Jeff. 2010. (ENG.). 32p. (J). (gr. -1-2). 17.99 *(978-0-8253-0554-2(3))* Beaufort Bks., Inc.
Björkman, Steve. In the Waves. Stella, Lennon & Stella, Maisy. 2015. (ENG.). 40p. (J). (gr. -1-3). 17.99 ***(978-0-06-235939-1(8))*** HarperCollins Pubs.
Björkman, Steve. Let's Go Skating! Heller, Alyson. 2009. (After-School Sports Club Ser.). (ENG.). 32p. (J). (gr. -1-1). pap. 3.99 *(978-1-4169-9411-4(4)*, Simon Spotlight) Simon Spotlight.
—Life Strategies for Dealing with Bullies. McGraw, Jay & Björkman, Manns. 2008. (ENG.). 160p. (J). (gr. 4-8). 17.99 *(978-1-4169-7473-4(3)*, Simon & Schuster/Paula Wiseman Bks.) Simon & Schuster/Paula Wiseman Bks.
—Look Out, Mouse! 2015. (I Like to Read(r) Ser.). (ENG.). 24p. (J). (gr. -1-3). 14.95 *(978-0-8234-2953-0(9))* Holiday Hse., Inc.
—Lost in Jerusalem! Larcombe, Jennifer Rees. 2004. (Best Bible Stories Ser.). 24p. (gr. -1-3). pap. 2.99 *(978-1-58134-150-8(4))* Crossway.
—Message in a Bottle. Horn, Susan & Richardson, Philip. 2009. (ENG.). 72p. (J). pap. 19.95 *(978-1-60433-001-4(5)*, Applesauce Pr.) Cider Mill Pr. Bk. Pubs., LLC.
—My Parents Are Divorced My Elbows Have Nicknames & Other Fact. Cochran, Bill. 2009. (ENG.). 32p. (J). (gr. -1-3). 17.99 *(978-0-06-053942-9(9))* HarperCollins Pubs.
—One Nosy Pup. Wallace, Carol. 2004. (ENG.). 40p. (J). 15.95 *(978-0-8234-1917-3(7))* Holiday Hse., Inc.
—The Other Brother. Carlson, Melody. 2004. 40p. (gr. -1-3). 9.99 *(978-1-58134-122-5(9))* Crossway.
—The Pumpkin Mystery. Wallace, Carol. 2010. (ENG.). 40p. (J). (gr. k-3). 15.95 *(978-0-8234-2219-7(4))* Holiday Hse., Inc.
—Puppy Power. Cox, Judy. 2008. (ENG.). 96p. (J). (gr. 2-4). pap. 6.95 *(978-0-8234-2210-4(0))*; (gr. -1-3). 15.95 *(978-0-8234-2073-5(6))* Holiday Hse., Inc.
—Same Old Horse. Murphy, Stuart J. 2005. (MathStart Ser.). 40p. (J). 15.99 *(978-0-06-055770-6(2))*; (ENG.). (gr. 1). pap. 5.99 *(978-0-06-055771-3(0))* HarperCollins Pubs.
—The Santa Secret. Wallace, Carol. 2007. (Holiday House Readers: Level 2 Ser.). (ENG.). 40p. (J). (gr. -1-3). 15.95 *(978-0-8234-2022-3(1))*; pap. 4.95 *(978-0-8234-2126-8(0))* Holiday Hse., Inc.
—Silly Street. Foxworthy, Jeff. (I Can Read Book 2 Ser.). 32p. (J). 2010. (ENG.). (gr. k-3). pap. 3.99 *(978-0-06-176528-5(7))*; 2009. (ENG.). (gr. -1-2). 17.99 *(978-0-06-171918-9(8))*; 2009. (gr. k-2). lib. bdg. 18.89 *(978-0-06-171919-6(6))* HarperCollins Pubs.
—Soccer Day. Heller, Alyson. 2009. (After-School Sports Club Ser.). (ENG.). 32p. (J). (gr. -1-1). pap. 3.99 *(978-1-4169-9410-7(6)*, Simon Spotlight) Simon Spotlight.
—Split! Splat! Gibson, Amy. 2012. (ENG.). 32p. (J). (gr. -1-3). 16.99 *(978-0-439-58753-2(0)*, Scholastic Pr.) Scholastic, Inc.
—Sticky, Sticky, Stuck! Gutch, Michael. 2013. (ENG.). 32p. (J). (gr. -1-3). 17.99 *(978-0-06-199818-8(4))* HarperCollins Pubs.
—The Terrible Giant. Larcombe, Jennifer Rees. 2004. (Best Bible Stories Ser.). 24p. (gr. -1-3). 2.99 *(978-1-58134-054-9(0))* Crossway.
—Time for T-Ball. Heller, Alyson. 2010. (After-School Sports Club Ser.). (ENG.). 32p. (J). (gr. -1-1). pap. 3.99 *(978-1-4169-9412-1(2)*, Simon Spotlight) Simon Spotlight.
—Touchdown! Heller, Alyson. 2010. (After-School Sports Club Ser.). (ENG.). 32p. (J). (gr. -1-1). pap. 3.99 *(978-1-4169-9413-8(0)*, Simon Spotlight) Simon Spotlight.
—The Walls That Fell down Flat. Larcombe, Jennifer Rees. 2004. (Best Bible Stories Ser.). 24p. (gr. -1-3). pap. 2.99 *(978-1-58134-151-5(2))* Crossway.
—8 Class Pets + 1 Squirrel ÷ 1 Dog = Chaos. Vande Velde, Vivian. (ENG.). 80p. (J). 2012. pap. 6.99 *(978-0-8234-2594-5(0))*; 2011. 15.95 *(978-0-8234-2364-4(6))* Holiday Hse., Inc.
Björkman, Steve. Dinosaurs Don't, Dinosaurs Do. Björkman, Steve. 2012. (I Like to Read Ser.). (ENG.). 24p. (J). pap. 6.99 *(978-0-8234-2640-9(8))* Holiday Hse., Inc.
—Look Out, Mouse! Björkman, Steve. 2015. (I Like to Read(r) Ser.). (ENG.). 24p. (J). (gr. -1-3). 6.99 *(978-0-8234-3397-1(8))* Holiday Hse., Inc.
Bjornsen, Holly. A Children's Adventure Duo: Thad the Sailor & Little Miss Lavendar. White, Elga Haymon. Freudiger, Victoria, ed. 2007. 130p. (J). per. 13.95 *(978-0-9785728-2-2(3))* Entry Way Publishing.
Bjornson, Barb. A Grandma Like Yours. Rosenbaum, Andria Warmflash. 2006. (ENG.). 32p. (J). (gr. -1-1). per. 6.95 *(978-1-58013-168-1(9)*, Kar-Ben Publishing) Lerner Publishing Group.
—When It's Purim. Zolkower, Edie Stoltz. 2009. (Very First Board Bks.). (ENG.). 12p. (J). (gr. -1 — 1). bds. 5.95 *(978-0-8225-8947-1(8)*, Kar-Ben Publishing) Lerner Publishing Group.
Bjornson, Barbara. Hope-So. Hills, Jodi. 2004. (ENG.). 36p. (J). 16.95 *(978-0-9726504-2-7(3))* TRISTAN Publishing, Inc.
Blabey, Aaron. Sunday Chutney. Blabey, Aaron. 2009. (ENG.). 32p. (J). (gr. -1-k). 16.95 *(978-1-59078-597-3(5)*, Front Street) Boyds Mills Pr.
Black, Bronze. What's So Hot about Volcanoes? Duffield, Wendell A. 2011. 96p. (J). pap. 16.00 *(978-0-87842-574-7(8))* Mountain Pr. Publishing Co., Inc.
Black Eye Design, jt. illus. see Art Parts.
Black, Holly & DiTerlizzi, Tony. Arthur Spiderwick's Field Guide to the Fantastical World Around You. Black, Holly & DiTerlizzi, Tony. 2005. (Spiderwick Chronicles Ser.). (ENG.). 142p. (J). (gr. 3). 24.99 *(978-0-689-85941-0(4)*, Simon & Schuster Bks. For Young Readers) Simon & Schuster Bks. For Young Readers.
Black, Ilene. Emma Mcdougal & the Quest for Father Time. Cowden, Matt. 2008. 190p. (J). 24.95 *(978-0-9799189-0-2(1))* His Work Christian Publishing.
Black, Kieron. The Incredible Sister Brigid. Carville, Declan. 29p. pap. 7.95 *(978-0-9538222-2-5(2))* Discovery Pubns. GBR. Dist: Irish Bks. & Media, Inc.
Black, Michelle. Quincy Finds a New Home. Matthews, Camille. 2009. (Quincy the Horse Bks.). (ENG.). 40p. (J). (gr. k-2). 15.95 *(978-0-9819240-0-7(X))* Pathfinder Equine Publications.
Black, Pam. Candee Bar. 42p. (J). 2007. spiral bd. *(978-0-9800791-2-8(8))*; 2nd rev. ed. 2008. spiral bd. 18.95 *(978-0-9800791-3-5(6))* Moore Publishing.
Black, Theo. The Poison Eaters: And Other Stories. Black, Holly. 2011. (ENG.). 224p. (YA). (gr. 9). pap. 9.99 *(978-1-4424-1232-3(1)*, McElderry, Margaret K. Bks.) McElderry, Margaret K. Bks.
Black, Theodor. Ghosts & Golems: Haunting Tales of the Supernatural. Palmer, Michele. 2003. (Jps Young Adult Story Collections). (ENG.). 128p. pap. 9.95 *(978-0-8276-0763-7(6))* Jewish Pubn. Society.
Blackall, Sophie. And Two Boys Booed. Viorst, Judith. 2014. (ENG.). 32p. (J). (gr. -1-3). 16.99 *(978-0-374-30302-0(9)*, Farrar, Straus & Giroux (BYR)) Farrar, Straus & Giroux.
—Big Red Lollipop. Khan, Rukhsana. 2010. (ENG.). 40p. (J). (gr. -1-3). 16.99 *(978-0-670-06287-4(1)*, Viking Juvenile) Penguin Publishing Group.
—The Crows of Pearblossom. Huxley, Aldous. 2011. (ENG.). 40p. (J). (gr. -1-3). 17.95 *(978-0-8109-9730-1(4)*, Abrams Bks. for Young Readers) Abrams.
—Edwin Speaks Up. Stevens, April. 2011. (ENG.). 40p. (J). (gr. -1-3). 16.99 *(978-0-375-85337-1(5)*, Schwartz & Wade Bks.) Random Hse. Children's Bks.
—A Fine Dessert: Four Centuries, Four Families, One Delicious Treat. Jenkins, Emily. 2015. (ENG.). 44p. (J). (gr. -1-3). 17.99 *(978-0-375-86832-0(1))*; 20.99 *(978-0-375-96832-7(6))* Random Hse. Children's Bks. (Schwartz & Wade Bks.).
—Ivy + Bean, Bk. 1. Barrows, Annie. (Ivy & Bean Ser.: IVYB). (ENG.). 120p. (J). (gr. 1-5). 2007. pap. 5.99 *(978-0-8118-4909-8(0))*; 2006. 14.99 *(978-0-8118-4903-6(1))* Chronicle Bks. LLC.
—Ivy + Bean. Barrows, Annie. 2007. (Ivy & Bean Ser.: Bk. 1). 120p. (gr. 1-5). 16.00 *(978-0-7569-8142-6(5))* Perfection Learning Corp.
—Ivy + Bean. Barrows, Annie. ed. 2007. (Ivy & Bean Ser.: 1). lib. bdg. 16.00 *(978-1-4177-7972-7(1)*, Turtleback) Turtleback Bks.
—Ivy + Bean: No News Is Good News. Barrows, Annie. 2012. (Ivy & Bean Ser.). (ENG.). 144p. (J). (gr. 1-5). pap. 5.99 *(978-1-4521-0781-3(5))* Chronicle Bks. LLC.
—Ivy + Bean - Make the Rules. Barrows, Annie. 2012. (Ivy & Bean Ser.). (ENG.). 127p. (J). (gr. 1-5). 14.99 *(978-1-4521-0295-5(3))* Chronicle Bks. LLC.
—Ivy + Bean - What's the Big Idea? Barrows, Annie. 2011. (ENG.). 132p. (J). (gr. 1-5). pap. 5.99 *(978-1-4521-0236-8(8))* Chronicle Bks. LLC.
—Ivy + Bean & the Ghost That Had to Go. Barrows, Annie. (Ivy & Bean Ser.: IVYB). (ENG.). 136p. (J). (gr. 1-5). 2007. pap. 5.99 *(978-0-8118-4911-1(2))*; 2006. 14.99 *(978-0-8118-4910-4(4))* Chronicle Bks. LLC.
—Ivy + Bean Bound to Be Bad. Barrows, Annie. (Ivy & Bean Ser.: IVYB). (ENG.). (J). (gr. 1-5). 2009. 128p. pap. 5.99 *(978-0-8118-6857-0(5))*; 2008. 124p. 14.99 *(978-0-8118-6265-3(8))* Chronicle Bks. LLC.
—Ivy + Bean Boxed Set: Books 7-9. Barrows, Annie. 2013. (Ivy & Bean Ser.). (ENG.). 428p. (J). (gr. 1-5). 19.99 *(978-1-4521-1732-4(2))* Chronicle Bks. LLC.
—Ivy + Bean Break the Fossil Record. Barrows, Annie. 2007. (Ivy & Bean Ser.: IVYB). (ENG.). (J). (gr. 1-5). 124p. pap. 5.99 *(978-0-8118-6250-9(X))*; 132p. 14.99 *(978-0-8118-5683-6(6))* Chronicle Bks. LLC.
—Ivy + Bean Doomed to Dance. Barrows, Annie. (ENG.). 136p. (J). (gr. 1-5). 2010. pap. 5.99 *(978-0-8118-7666-7(7))*; 2009. (Ivy & Bean Ser.: IVYB). 14.99 *(978-0-8118-6266-0(6))* Chronicle Bks. LLC.
—Ivy + Bean Make the Rules, Bk. 9. Barrows, Annie. 2013. (Ivy & Bean Ser.: 9). (ENG.). 144p. (J). (gr. 1-5). pap. 5.99 *(978-1-4521-1148-3(0))* Chronicle Bks. LLC.
—Ivy + Bean No News Is Good News. Barrows, Annie. 2011. (Ivy & Bean Ser.: IVYB). (ENG.). 128p. (J). (gr. 1-5). 14.99 *(978-0-8118-6693-4(9))* Chronicle Bks. LLC.
—Ivy + Bean No News Is Good News. Barrows, Annie. ed. 2012. (Ivy & Bean Ser.: 8). lib. bdg. 16.00 *(978-0-606-26950-6(9)*, Turtleback) Turtleback Bks.
—Ivy + Bean Paper Doll Play Set. Barrows, Annie. 2011. (Ivy & Bean Ser.: IVYB). (ENG.). 11p. (J). (gr. k-5). 14.99 *(978-1-4521-0279-5(1))* Chronicle Bks. LLC.
—Ivy + Bean Take Care of the Babysitter. Barrows, Annie. (Ivy & Bean Ser.: IVYB). (ENG.). 2008. 128p. (J). (gr. 1-5). pap. 5.99 *(978-0-8118-6584-5(3))*; 2008. 144p. (J). (gr. 1-5). 14.99 *(978-0-8118-5685-0(2))*; 2007. pap., tchr. ed. *(978-0-8118-8667-3(0))* Chronicle Bks. LLC.
—Ivy + Bean Take the Case. Barrows, Annie. (ENG.). (J). (gr. 1-4). 2014. 136p. pap. 5.99 *(978-1-4521-2871-9(5))*; 2013. 128p. 14.99 *(978-1-4521-0699-1(1))* Chronicle Bks. LLC.
—Ivy + Bean What's the Big Idea? Barrows, Annie et al. 2010. (ENG.). 128p. (J). (gr. 1-5). 14.99 *(978-0-8118-6692-7(0))* Chronicle Bks. LLC.
—Ivy & Bean & the Ghost That Had to Go. Barrows, Annie. ed. 2007. (Ivy & Bean Ser.: 2). lib. bdg. 16.00 *(978-1-4177-9273-3(6)*, Turtleback) Turtleback Bks.
—Lord & Lady Bunny - Almost Royalty! Horvath, Polly. 2014. (ENG.). 304p. (J). (gr. 3-7). 16.99 *(978-0-307-98065-6(0))*; 19.99 *(978-0-307-98066-3(9))* Random Hse. Children's Bks. (Schwartz & Wade Bks.).
—Meet Wild Boars. Rosoff, Meg. 2008. (Wild Boars Ser.). (ENG.). 40p. (J). (gr. k-3). pap. 7.99 *(978-0-312-37963-6(3))* Square Fish.
—The Mighty Lalouche. Olshan, Matthew. 2013. (ENG.). 40p. (J). (gr. -1-3). 17.99 *(978-0-375-86225-0(0)*, Schwartz & Wade Bks.) Random Hse. Children's Bks.
—Mr. & Mrs. Bunny: Detectives Extraordinaire! Horvath, Polly. 2012. (ENG.). 256p. (J). (gr. 3-7). 16.99 *(978-0-375-86755-2(4)*, Schwartz & Wade Bks.) Random Hse. Children's Bks.
—Mr. & Mrs. Bunny — Detectives Extraordinaire! Horvath, Polly. 2014. (ENG.). 272p. (J). (gr. 3-7). pap. 8.99 *(978-0-375-86530-5(6)*, Ember) Random Hse. Children's Bks.
—The Nine Lives of Alexander Baddenfield. Marciano, John Bemelmans. 2013. (ENG.). 144p. (J). (gr. 5). 16.99 *(978-0-670-01406-4(0)*, Viking Juvenile) Penguin Publishing Group.
—Pecan Pie Baby. Woodson, Jacqueline. (ENG.). 32p. (J). (gr. k-3). 2013. 7.99 *(978-0-14-751128-7(3)*, Puffin); 2010. 16.99 *(978-0-399-23987-8(1)*, Putnam Juvenile) Penguin Publishing Group.
Blackall, Sophie. Ruby's Wish. Shirin Yim, Bridges. 2015. (ENG.). 36p. (J). (gr. 3-7). 7.99 ***(978-1-4521-4569-3(5))*** Chronicle Bks. LLC.
Blackall, Sophie. Spinster Goose: Twisted Rhymes for Naughty Children. Wheeler, Lisa. 2011. (ENG.). 48p. (J). (gr. k-5). 16.99 *(978-1-4169-2541-5(4)*, Atheneum Bks. for Young Readers) Simon & Schuster Children's Publishing.
—Take Two! A Celebration of Twins. Lewis, J. Patrick & Yolen, Jane. 2012. (ENG.). 72p. (J). (gr. -1-3). 17.99 *(978-0-7636-3702-6(5))* Candlewick Pr.
—Wombat Walkabout. Shields, Carol Diggory. 2009. (ENG.). 32p. (J). (gr. -1-k). 16.99 *(978-0-525-47865-2(5)*, Dutton Juvenile) Penguin Publishing Group.
—The 9 Lives of Alexander Baddenfield. Marciano, John Bemelmans. 2014. (ENG.). 144p. (J). (gr. 5). pap. 7.99 *(978-0-14-751233-8(6)*, Puffin) Penguin Publishing Group.
Blackall, Sophie. Are You Awake? Blackall, Sophie. 2011. (ENG.). 40p. (J). (gr. -1-k). 12.99 *(978-0-8050-7858-9(4)*, Holt, Henry & Co. Bks. For Young Readers) Holt, Henry & Co.
—The Baby Tree. Blackall, Sophie. 2014. (ENG.). 32p. (J). (gr. k-3). 17.99 *(978-0-399-25718-6(7)*, Nancy Paulsen Bks.) Penguin Publishing Group.
Blackbird. Mr. Hookworm. Blackbird. 2006. (J). per. 18.00 *(978-0-9789798-6-7(9)*, 978-0-9789798-6-7) Blackbird's World Publishing Co.
Blacker, Elizabeth A. Adventures on Amelia Island: A Pirate, a Princess, & Buried Treasure. Wood, Jane R. 2007. 132p. (J). (gr. 3-8). pap. 8.99 *(978-0-9792304-0-0(3))* Florida Kids Pr., Inc.
Blackford, Ami. Quest for the Dragon Stone: A Duncan Family Adventure. Blackford, Ami. 2006. 48p. (J). (gr. 3-7). 16.95 *(978-1-60108-008-0(5))* Red Cygnet Pr.
—Quest for the Elfin Elixir: A Duncan Family Adventure Book 2. Blackford, Ami. 2007. 79p. (J). (gr. 3-7). 16.95 *(978-1-60108-021-9(2))* Red Cygnet Pr.
Blackford, John. The Secret of Willow Ridge: Gabe's Dad Finds Recovery. Moore, Helen H. 2010. (ENG.). 128p. (J). (gr. 3-7). pap. 12.95 *(978-0-9818482-0-4(6))* Central Recovery Pr.
Blackington, Toni. Put Your Glasses On. Blackington, Toni. 2013. (ENG.). 70p. pap. 5.99 *(978-0-615-75922-7(X))* Blackington Publishing.
Blackley, Mary Beth. Thank You, Peter. Lundy, Charlotte. Waldrep, Evelyn L., ed. 2003. 32p. (gr. k-3). 15.95 *(978-0-9670280-8-6(5))* Bay Light Publishing.
Blackmon, Kim. Glorious Praise. Wilkinson, William L. 2012. 32p. pap. 10.00 *(978-1-62050-019-4(1))* Angels of Agape.
Blackmore, Katherine. Betsy's Day at the Game. Bancroft, Greg. 2013. (ENG.). 40p. (gr. k-5). pap. 13.95 *(978-1-938063-01-5(5)*, Mighty Media Kids) Mighty Media Pr.
—Wonderful Gifts of Winter. Mackall, Dandi. 2014. (Seasons Ser.). (ENG.). 32p. (gr. -1-3). 9.99 *(978-1-4336-8239-1(7)*, B&H Kids) B&H Publishing Group.
Blackmore, Katherine & Wiltse, Kris. A Kiss on the Keppie, 0 vols. Newman, Lesléa. 2012. (ENG.). 24p. (J). (gr. -1-2). 12.99 *(978-0-7614-6241-5(4)*, 9780761462415, Amazon Children's Publishing) Amazon Publishing.
Blackshear, Sue. Tuskaloosa Tales: Stories of Tuscaloosa & Its People. 2011. 95p. (J). *(978-0-9801113-2-3(3))* Look Again Pr., LLC.
Blacksheep, Beverly. Baby Learns about Animals. Ruffenach, Jessie, ed. Thomas, Peter, tr. from NAV. 2004. (ENG & NAV.). 16p. (J). (gr. -1-12). 7.95 *(978-1-893354-49-4(0))* Salina Bookshelf Inc.
—Baby Learns about Colors. Ruffenach, Jessie, ed. Thomas, Peter, tr. from NAV. 2004. (ENG & NAV.). 16p. (J). (gr. -1-12). 7.95 *(978-1-893354-48-7(2))* Salina Bookshelf Inc.
—Baby Learns about Seasons. Ruffenach, Jessie, ed. Thomas, Peter, tr. from ENG. 2005. (NAV & ENG.). 16p. (J). (gr. 4-7). 7.95 *(978-1-893354-61-6(X))* Salina Bookshelf Inc.
—Baby Learns about Senses. Ruffenach, Jessie, ed. Thomas, Peter, tr. from ENG. 2005. (NAV & ENG.). 16p. (J). (gr. 4-7). 7.95 *(978-1-893354-63-0(6))* Salina Bookshelf Inc.
—Baby Learns about Time. Ruffenach, Jessie, ed. Thomas, Peter, tr. from ENG. 2005. (NAV & ENG.). 16p. (J). (gr. 4-7). 7.95 *(978-1-893354-64-7(4))* Salina Bookshelf Inc.
—Baby Learns about Weather. Ruffenach, Jessie, ed. Thomas, Peter, tr. from ENG. 2005. (NAV & ENG.). 16p. (J). (gr. 4-7). 7.95 *(978-1-893354-62-3(8))* Salina Bookshelf Inc.
—Baby Learns to Count. Ruffenach, Jessie, ed. Thomas, Peter, tr. l.t. ed. 2003. (NAV & ENG.). 16p. (J). (gr. -1-12). 7.95 *(978-1-893354-47-0(4))* Salina Bookshelf Inc.
—Baby's First Laugh. Ruffenach, Jessie, ed. Thomas, Peter, tr. from ENG. 2003. (NAV & ENG.). 100p. (J). (gr. -1-12). 7.95 *(978-1-893354-39-5(3))* Salina Bookshelf Inc.
Blackstone, Stella. The Animal Boogie. Harter, Debbie. 2005. 32p. (J). (gr. -1-1). 14.99 *(978-1-84148-094-7(0))* Barefoot Bks., Inc.
Blackwell, David. Escape from the Forbidden Planet. Grasso, Julie Anne. 2012. 172p. (J). pap. *(978-0-9873725-0-5(5))* Grasso, Julie Anne AUS. Dist: INT Bks.
—Return to Cardamom. Grasso, Julie A. 2013. (Cardamom Ser.: Bk. 2). (ENG.). 136p. (J). pap. *(978-0-9873725-2-9(1))* Grasso, Julie Anne AUS. Dist: INT Bks.
Blackwood, David. Ann & Seamus, 1 vol. Major, Kevin. 2004. (ENG.). 112p. (J). 16.95 *(978-0-88899-561-2(X))* Groundwood Bks. CAN. Dist: Perseus-PGW.
Blackwood, Freya. Banjo & Ruby Red. Gleeson, Libby. 2015. (ENG.). 32p. (J). (gr. -1-k). 16.99 *(978-1-921541-08-7(3))* Little Hare Bks. AUS. Dist: Independent Pubs. Group.
—Clancy & Millie & the Very Fine House. Gleeson, Libby. (ENG.). 32p. (J). (gr. -1-k). 2011. pap. 9.99 *(978-1-921541-90-2(3))*; 2010. 14.99 *(978-1-921541-19-3(9))* Little Hare Bks. AUS. Dist: Independent Pubs. Group.
—Half a World Away. Gleeson, Libby. 2007. (J). pap. *(978-0-439-88978-0(2)*, Levine, Arthur A. Bks.) Scholastic, Inc.
—Harry & Hopper. Wild, Margaret. 2011. (ENG.). 32p. (J). (gr. -1-k). 16.99 *(978-0-312-64261-7(X))* Feiwel & Friends.
—Her Mother's Face. Doyle, Roddy. 2008. (J). pap. *(978-0-439-81502-4(9)*, Levine, Arthur A. Bks.) Scholastic, Inc.
Blackwood, Freya. My Two Blankets. Kobald, Irena. 2015. (ENG.). 32p. (J). (gr. 1-4). 16.99 ***(978-0-544-43228-4(2)***, HMH Books For Young Readers) Houghton Mifflin Harcourt Publishing Co.
Blackwood, Freya. The Runaway Hug. Bland, Nick. 2013. (ENG.). 32p. (J). (gr. -1-2). 16.99 *(978-0-449-81825-1(X))* Random Hse., Inc.
Blackwood, Freyda. Impressionists. Dickens, Rosie. 2009. (Young Reading Ser.). 64p. (J). 6.99 *(978-0-7945-2154-7(1)*, Usborne) EDC Publishing.
Blackwood, Kristin. Big Blue. Oeslchlager, Vanita. 2008. (ENG.). 32p. (J). (gr. -1-3). 17.95 *(978-0-9800162-5-3(8))* VanitaBooks.
—Carrot. Oelschlager, Vanita. 2011. (ENG.). 44p. (J). (gr. -1-3). (J). pap. 8.95 *(978-0-9826366-0-2(1))*; 15.95 *(978-0-9819714-9-0(0))* VanitaBooks.
—Elefante. Oelschlager, Vanita. 2011. 20p. (J). (gr. k-k). (SPA.). bds. 6.95 *(978-0-9826366-5-7(2))*; (ENG.). bds. 6.95 *(978-0-9826366-4-0(4))* VanitaBooks.
—Farfalla: A Story of Loss & Hope. Oelschlager, Vanita. 2012. (ENG.). 40p. (J). (gr. -1-3). 15.95 *(978-0-9832904-0-7(7))* VanitaBooks.
—Ivan's Great Fall: Poetry for Summer & Autumn from Great Poets & Writers of the Past. Oelschlager, Vanita. 2009. (ENG.). 44p. (J). (gr. -1-3). 15.95 *(978-0-9819714-1-4(5))*; pap. 8.95 *(978-0-9819714-2-1(3))* VanitaBooks.
—Ivy in Bloom: The Poetry of Spring from Great Poets & Writers from the Past. Oelschlager, Vanita. 2009. (ENG.). 40p. (J). (gr. -1-3). 17.95 *(978-0-9800162-7-7(4))* VanitaBooks.
—Let Me Bee. Oelschlager, Vanita. 2008. (ENG.). 42p. (J). (gr. -1-3). 17.95 *(978-0-9800162-1-5(5))* VanitaBooks.
—Made in China: A Story of Adoption. Oelschlager, Vanita. 2008. (ENG.). 32p. (J). (gr. -1-3). 17.95 *(978-0-9800162-3-9(1))* VanitaBooks.
—A Tale of Two Daddies. Oelschlager, Vanita. 2010. (ENG.). 42p. (J). (gr. -1-3). 15.95 *(978-0-9819714-5-2(8))*; pap. 8.95 *(978-0-9819714-6-9(6))* VanitaBooks.
—What Pet Will I Get? Oelschlager, Vanita. 2008. (ENG.). 38p. (J). (gr. -1-3). 17.95 *(978-0-9800162-2-2(3)*, 991700007) VanitaBooks.
Blackwood, Kristin & Blanc, Mike. Bonyo Bonyo. Oelschlager, Vanita. 2010. (ENG.). 42p. (J). (gr. -1-3). pap. 8.95 *(978-0-9819714-4-5(X))*; 15.95 *(978-0-9819714-3-8(1))* VanitaBooks.
Blackwood, Kristin, jt. illus. see Hegan, Robin.
Blades, Ann. A Candle for Christmas, 1 vol. Speare, Jean. (ENG.). 32p. (J). pap. 4.95 *(978-0-88899-149-2(5))* Groundwood Bks. CAN. Dist: Perseus-PGW.
—Six Darn Cows, 1 vol. Laurence, Margaret & James Lorimer and Company Ltd. Staff. 2nd rev. ed. 2011. (Kids of Canada Ser.). (ENG.). 32p. (J). (gr. k-3). 14.95 *(978-1-55277-719-0(7))* Lorimer, James & Co., Ltd., Pubs. CAN. Dist: Casemate Pubs. & Bk. Distributors, LLC.
Blades, Ann, jt. illus. see Waterton, Betty.
Bladholm, Cheri. Fear Not, Joseph. Stiegemeyer, Julie. 2008. 32p. (J). (gr. -1-3). 13.49 *(978-0-7586-1498-8(5))* Concordia Publishing Hse.
Bladimir, Trejo. Ecuador. Sojos, Catalina. 2015. 24p. (J). (gr. -1-2). pap. 12.95 ***(978-9978-07-415-2(5)***, Alfaguara Infantil) Santillana Ecuador ECU. Dist: Santillana USA Publishing Co., Inc.
Blain, Theresa A. Visualize World Geography in 7 Minutes a Day: Let Pictography Take You from Clueless to Knowing the World. Blain, Theresa A. 2003. 302p. per. 19.95 *(978-0-9741401-0-0(4))* Tender Heart Pr.
Blaine, Janice. Skookum Sal, Birling Gal. Kellerhals-Stewart, Heather. unabr. ed. (ENG.). 32p. (J). *(978-1-55017-285-0(9))* Harbour Publishing Co., Ltd.
Blair, Beth L. Five Kids & a Monkey, 3 vols., Set. Riccio, Nina M. (J). (gr. 2-6). 23.85 *(978-0-9653955-3-3(7))* Creative Attic, Inc., The.
Blair, Chris & Elliott, Mark. Room One: A Mystery or Two. Clements, Andrew. 2006. (ENG.). 224p. (J). (gr. 3-7). 17.99 *(978-0-689-86686-9(0)*, Atheneum Bks. for Young Readers) Simon & Schuster Children's Publishing.
Blair, Culverson & Simpson, Howard. Afro-Bets Book of Shapes. Brown, Margery W. 2nd ed. 2004. (Afro-Bets Ser.). 24p. (J). (gr. -1-1). pap. 3.95 *(978-0-940975-58-3(0)*, Sankofa Bks.) Just Us Bks., Inc.
—Book of Colors: Meet the Color Family. Brown, Margery W. 2nd ed. 2004. (Afro-Bets Ser.). 24p. (J). (gr. -1-1). pap. 3.95 *(978-0-940975-57-6(2)*, Sankofa Bks.) Just Us Bks., Inc.

B

Blair, Jocelyn. Little Dutch Girl in World War II. Harkes, Willy. l.t. ed. 2004. 22p. (J). pap. 13.95 (978-0-9741627-1-3(X)) Write Designs, Ltd.

Blair, Karen. Baby Animal Farm. Blair, Karen. 2014. (ENG.). 16p. (J). (— 1). bds. 6.99 (978-0-7636-7069-6(3)) Candlewick Pr.

Blair, Mary. Baby's House. Mchugh, Gelolo. 2012. (Golden Baby Ser.). (ENG.). 24p. (J). (gr. k — 1). bds. 6.99 (978-0-307-92965-5(5), Golden Bks.) Random Hse., Inc.

—I Can Fly. Krauss, Ruth. 2003. (Little Golden Book Ser.). (ENG.). 24p. (J). (gr. -1-2). 3.99 (978-0-307-00146-7(6), 312-12, Golden Bks.) Random Hse. Children's Bks.

—Walt Disney's Cinderella. Rylant, Cynthia. ed. 2015. (Walt Disney's Classic Fairytale Ser.). (ENG.). 64p. (J). (gr. -1-k). 16.99 (978-1-4847-1247-4(1)) Disney Pr.

Blair, Richard P., photos by. Point Reyes Visions Guidebook: Where to go, What to Do. Goodwin, Kathleen P. 2004. 80p. 21.95 (978-0-9671527-0-7(4)) Color & Light Editions.

Blaisdell, Elinore. Rhymes & Verses: Collected Poems for Young People. de la Mare, Walter. 2005. 351p. (J). (gr. 4-8). reprint ed. 19.00 (978-0-7567-8944-2(3)) DIANE Publishing Co.

Blake, Anne Catharine. Child's Guide to Baptism. Stanton, Sue. 2006. (Child's Guide Ser.). 32p. (J). (gr. 3-7). 9.95 (978-0-8091-6728-9(X), 6728-x) Paulist Pr.

—Child's Guide to First Holy Communion. Ficocelli, Elizabeth. 2003. 32p. 10.95 (978-0-8091-6708-1(5), 3708-5) Paulist Pr.

—Child's Guide to the Rosary. Ficocelli, Elizabeth. 2009. (J). 10.95 (978-0-8091-6736-4(0)) Paulist Pr.

—Child's Guide to the Seven Sacraments. Ficocelli, Elizabeth. 2005. 32p. (J). (978-0-8091-6723-4(9), 6723-9) Paulist Pr.

—Child's Guide to the Stations of the Cross. Stanton, Sue. 2008. 32p. (J). (gr. k-4). 10.95 (978-0-8091-6739-5(5), 6739-5) Paulist Pr.

—Josh's Smiley Faces: A Story about Anger. Ditta-Donahue, Gina. 2003. 32p. (J). pap. 9.95 (978-1-59147-001-4(3)); 14.95 (978-1-59147-000-7(5)) American Psychological Assn. (Magination Pr.).

—Katie's Premature Brother = el Hermano Prematuro de Katie. Hawkins-Walsh, Elizabeth & Pierson-Solis, Lennard. 2006. (J). (978-1-56123-197-3(5)) Centering Corp.

—Tinkle, Tinkle, Little Tot: Songs & Rhymes for Toilet Training. Lansky, Bruce & Pottle, Robert. 2005. 32p. (J). 8.95 (978-0-88166-492-8(8), 1182) Meadowbrook Pr.

Blake, Anne Catharine. Child's Guide to Reconciliation. Blake, Anne Catharine, tr. Ficocelli, Elizabeth. 2004. 32p. 9.95 (978-0-8091-6709-8(3), 6709-3) Paulist Pr.

Blake, Beccy. Clown School. Shipton, Paul. 2005. (ENG.). 24p. (J). lib. bdg. 23.65 (978-1-59646-752-1(5)) Dingles & Co.

—Detective Derek. Wallace, Karen. 2009. (Go! Readers Ser.). 48p. (J). (gr. 2-5). pap. 12.85 (978-1-60754-276-6(5)); lib. bdg. 29.25 (978-1-60754-275-9(7)) Windmill Bks.

—Ghost Mouse. Wallace, Karen. 2009. (Go! Readers Ser.). 48p. (J). (gr. 2-5). pap. 12.85 (978-1-60754-273-5(0)); lib. bdg. 29.25 (978-1-60754-272-8(2)) Windmill Bks.

—My Big, New Bed. Nash, Margaret. 2008. (Tadpoles Ser.). (ENG.). 24p. (J). (gr. -1-2). lib. bdg. (978-0-7787-3859-6(0)); pap. (978-0-7787-3890-9(6)) Crabtree Publishing Co.

—Tortoise Races Home. Atkins, Jill. 2009. (Tadpoles Ser.). (ENG.). 24p. (J). (gr. k-2). lib. bdg. (978-0-7787-3871-8(X)) Crabtree Publishing Co.

—Tortoise Races Home. Atkins, Jill. 2009. (Tadpoles Ser.). (ENG.). 24p. (J). (gr. -1-2). pap. (978-0-7787-3902-9(3)) Crabtree Publishing Co.

—What Am I? Band 00/Lilac. Kelly, Maoliosa. 2007. (Collins Big Cat Ser.). (ENG.). 16p. (J). pap. 5.99 (978-0-00-718679-2(7)) HarperCollins Pubs. Ltd. GBR. Dist: Independent Pubs. Group.

Blake, Carol. Yang the Dragon Tells His Story, Halloween Train. Wilkinson, James H. 2013. 32p. pap. 15.99 (978-0-9886360-0-2(X)) Kids At Heart Publishing & Bks.

Blake, Francis. The A to Z of Everyday Things. Weaver, Janice. 2004. (ENG.). 128p. (J). (gr. 5). pap. 8.95 (978-0-88776-671-8(4)) Tundra Bks. CAN. Dist: Random Hse., Inc.

—From Head to Toe: Bound Feet, Bathing Suits, & Other Bizarre & Beautiful Things. Weaver, Janice. 2003. (ENG.). 80p. (J). (gr. 5-9). pap. 16.95 (978-0-88776-654-1(4)) Tundra Bks. CAN. Dist: Random Hse., Inc.

—Nibbling on Einstein's Brain: The Good, the Bad & the Bogus in Science. Swanson, Diane. 2nd rev. ed. 2009. (ENG.). 112p. (gr. 1-12). 24.95 (978-1-55451-187-7(9), 9781554511877); pap. 12.95 (978-1-55451-186-0(0), 9781554511860) Annick Pr., Ltd. CAN. Dist: Firefly Bks., Ltd.

—Rude Stories. Andrews, Jan. 2010. (ENG.). 88p. (J). (gr. 1-4). 19.95 (978-0-88776-921-4(7)) Tundra Bks. CAN. Dist: Random Hse., Inc.

—What Can You Do with Only One Shoe? Reuse, Recycle, Reinvent. Shapiro, Simon & Shapiro, Sheryl. 2014. (ENG.). 32p. (J). (gr. 1-4). pap. 9.95 (978-1-55451-642-1(0), 9781554516421); lib. bdg. 22.95 (978-1-55451-643-8(9), 9781554516438) Annick Pr., Ltd. CAN. Dist: Firefly Bks., Ltd.

Blake, Jo. Behind the Scenes Christmas. Box, Su. 2006. 29p. (J). (gr. 4-7). 14.00 (978-0-687-49121-6(5)) Abingdon Pr.

—Classifying Flowering Plants, 1 vol. Galko, Francine & Heinemann Library Staff. 2nd ed. 2009. (Classifying Living Things Ser.). (ENG.). 32p. (gr. 3-5). pap. 7.99 (978-1-4329-2368-6(4), NA-h) Heinemann-Raintree.

Blake, Jocelyn. Mama Is on an Airplane. Blake, Jocelyn. ed. 2006. (J). per. 9.99 (978-0-9790572-0-5(5)) Kreativ Kaos.

Blake, Joshua Aaron. Just A Little Child. Wood, Debra. l.t. ed. 2006. 33p. (J). per. 12.95 (978-1-59879-087-0(0)) Lifevest Publishing, Inc.

—William Warrior Bear. Wood, Debra. l.t. ed. 2005. 30p. (J). per. 12.95 (978-1-59879-001-6(3)) Lifevest Publishing, Inc.

Blake, Quentin. Agu Trot. Dahl, Roald. 2003.Tr. of Esio Trot. (SPA.). 64p. (J). (gr. 3-5). pap. 9.95 (978-84-204-4436-9(7)) Santillana USA Publishing Co., Inc.

—Arabel's Raven. Aiken, Joan & Aiken, Joan. 2007. (ENG.). 160p. (J). (gr. 2-5). pap. 11.95 (978-0-15-206094-7(4)) Houghton Mifflin Harcourt Publishing Co.

—Bananas in My Ears: A Collection of Nonsense Stories, Poems, Riddles, & Rhymes. Rosen, Michael. 2012. (ENG.). 96p. (J). (gr. k-12). 15.99 (978-0-7636-6248-6(8)) Candlewick Pr.

—The Bear's Water Picnic. Yeoman, John. 2011. (ENG.). 40p. (J). (gr. k-k). pap. 10.99 (978-1-84939-004-0(5)) Andersen Pr. GBR. Dist: Independent Pubs. Group.

Blake, Quentin. The Bear's Winter House. Yeoman, John. 2012. (J). **(978-1-4351-4374-6(4))** Barnes & Noble, Inc.

Blake, Quentin. Bear's Winter House. Yeoman, John. 2010. (ENG.). 32p. (J). (gr. k-k). pap. 12.99 (978-1-84270-916-0(X)) Andersen Pr. GBR. Dist: Independent Pubs. Group.

—Beatrice & Vanessa. Yeoman, John. 2012. (ENG.). 32p. (J). (gr. -1-k). pap. 9.99 (978-1-84939-269-3(2)) Andersen Pr. GBR. Dist: Independent Pubs. Group.

—The BFG. Dahl, Roald. 30th anniv. ed. 2007. (ENG.). 208p. (J). (gr. 3-7). 7.99 (978-0-14-241038-7(1), Puffin) Penguin Publishing Group.

—Boy & Going Solo. Dahl, Roald. 2010. (ENG.). 400p. (J). (gr. 3-7). 9.99 (978-0-14-241741-6(6), Puffin) Penguin Publishing Group.

—Las Brujas. Dahl, Roald.Tr. of Witches. (SPA.). 200p. (gr. 5-8). (J). pap. 9.95 (978-84-204-4815-2(X)); 2003. (YA). pap. 12.95 (978-958-24-0100-9(1)) Santillana USA Publishing Co., Inc.

—La Casa del Arbol. Pitzorno, Bianca & Pitzorno, Bianca. 4th ed.Tr. of Casa sull'albero. (SPA.). 128p. (J). (978-84-207-7771-9(4)) Grupo Anaya, S.A. ESP. Dist: Lectorum Pubns., Inc.

—Charlie & the Chocolate Factory. Dahl, Roald. 2011. (ENG.). 24p. (J). (gr. 2-5). 29.99 (978-0-14-241930-4(3), Puffin); 2011. (ENG.). 160p. (J). (gr. 3-7). 15.99 (978-0-14-241821-5(8), Puffin); 2007. 17.00 (978-0-7569-8213-3(8)); 2007. (ENG.). 176p. (J). (gr. 3-7). 6.99 (978-0-14-241031-8(4), Puffin); 2004. (ENG.). 176p. (J). (gr. 3-7). pap. 7.99 (978-0-14-240108-8(0), Puffin) Penguin Publishing Group.

—Charlie & the Chocolate Factory. Dahl, Roald. 2014. (ENG.). (J). movie tie-in ed. 176p. (gr. 3-7). lib. bdg. 18.99 (978-0-375-91526-0(5)); 40th anniv. movie tie-in ed. 160p. (gr. k-4). 27.99 (978-0-375-83197-3(5)) Random Hse. Children's Bks. (Knopf Bks. for Young Readers).

—Charlie & the Great Glass Elevator. Dahl, Roald. 2007. (ENG.). 176p. (J). (gr. 3-7). 7.99 (978-0-14-241032-5(2), Puffin) Penguin Publishing Group.

—Charlie & the Great Glass Elevator. Dahl, Roald. 2005. (Puffin Modern Classics Ser.). (ENG.). 176p. (J). (gr. 3-7). pap. 7.99 (978-0-14-240412-6(8), Puffin) Penguin Publishing Group.

—A Christmas Carol. Dickens, Charles. unabr. ed. 2004. (Chrysalis Childrens Classics Ser.). 190p. (Orig.). (YA). pap. (978-1-84365-063-8(0), Pavilion Children's Books) Pavilion Bks.

—The Complete Adventures of Charlie & Mr. Willy Wonka. Dahl, Roald. 2010. (ENG.). 336p. (J). (gr. 3-7). 9.99 (978-0-14-241740-9(8), Puffin) Penguin Publishing Group.

—Los Cretinos. Dahl, Roald. 2005. (Infantil Ser.).Tr. of Twist. (SPA.). 106p. (gr. 3-5). per. 9.95 (978-968-19-0559-0(8)) Santillana USA Publishing Co., Inc.

—Cuentos en Verso para Niños Perversos. Dahl, Roald. 3rd ed.Tr. of Revolting Rhymes. (SPA.). 32p. (J). (gr. 5-8). pap. 10.95 (978-84-372-2183-0(8)) Santillana USA Publishing Co., Inc.

—D Is for Dahl: A Gloriumptious A-Z Guide to the World of Roald Dahl. Dahl, Roald. 2007. (ENG.). 160p. (J). (gr. 3-7). 6.99 (978-0-14-240934-3(0), Puffin) Penguin Publishing Group.

—Danny el Campeon del Mundo. Dahl, Roald. 2003.Tr. of Danny the Champion of the World. (SPA.). 200p. (YA). (gr. 5-8). 9.95 (978-84-204-4431-4(6)) Ediciones Alfaguara ESP. Dist: Santillana USA Publishing Co., Inc.

—Danny the Champion of the World. Dahl, Roald. 2007. (ENG.). 224p. (J). (gr. 3-7). 7.99 (978-0-14-241033-2(0), Puffin) Penguin Publishing Group.

—Danny the Champion of the World. Dahl, Roald. ed. 2007. 205p. (gr. 4-7). 18.40 (978-1-4177-8611-4(6), Turtleback) Turtleback Bks.

—Esio Trot. Dahl, Roald. 2009. (ENG.). 64p. (J). (gr. 3-7). 7.99 (978-0-14-241382-1(8), Puffin) Penguin Publishing Group.

Blake, Quentin. The Fabulous Foskett Family Circus. Yeoman, John. (ENG.). 32p. (J). (gr. -1-k). 2015. pap. 9.99 **(978-1-78344-035-1(X))**; 2014. 19.99 (978-1-84939-564-9(0)) Andersen Pr. GBR. Dist: Independent Pubs. Group.

Blake, Quentin. Fantastic Mr. Fox. Dahl, Roald. 2007. 17.00 (978-0-7569-8286-7(3)); (ENG.). 96p. (J). (gr. 3-7). 7.99 (978-0-14-241034-9(9), Puffin) Penguin Publishing Group.

—George's Marvelous Medicine. Dahl, Roald. 2007. (ENG.). 96p. (J). (gr. 3-7). 7.99 (978-0-14-241035-6(7), Puffin) Penguin Publishing Group.

—George's Marvelous Medicine. Dahl, Roald. 2008. 88p. (gr. 4-7). 18.00 (978-0-7569-8777-0(6)) Perfection Learning Corp.

—The Giraffe & the Pelly & Me. Dahl, Roald. 2009. (ENG.). 80p. (Orig.). (J). (gr. 3-7). 7.99 (978-0-14-241384-5(4), Puffin) Penguin Publishing Group.

—The Great Piratical Rumbustification & the Librarian & the Robbers. Mahy, Margaret. 2012. (ENG.). 64p. (J). pap. 6.95 (978-1-56792-169-4(8)) Godine, David R. Pub.

—The Heron & the Crane. Yeoman, John. 2011. (ENG.). 32p. (J). (gr. -1-k). pap. 13.99 (978-1-84939-200-6(5)) Andersen Pr. GBR. Dist: Independent Pubs. Group.

—How Tom Beat Captain Najork & His Hired Sportsmen. Hoban, Russell. 2006. (ENG.). 32p. (J). (gr. k-4). pap. 7.95 (978-1-56792-322-3(4)) Godine, David R. Pub.

—James & the Giant Peach. Dahl, Roald. 2011. (ENG.). 128p. (J). (gr. 3-7). pap. 14.99 (978-0-14-241823-9(4), Puffin) Penguin Publishing Group.

—James y el Melocoton Gigante. Dahl, Roald. 2003.Tr. of James & the Giant Peach. (SPA.). 184p. pap. 9.95 (978-968-19-0625-2(X)) Aguilar, Altea, Taurus, Alfaguara, S.A. de C.V MEX. Dist: Santillana USA Publishing Co., Inc.

—Joseph & the Amazing Technicolor Dreamcoat. Rice, Tim & Webber, Andrew Lloyd. 2012. (ENG.). 48p. (J). (gr. 2-4). 16.99 (978-1-84365-103-1(3), Pavilion Children's Books) Pavilion Bks. GBR. Dist: Independent Pubs. Group.

—The Magic Finger. Dahl, Roald. 2009. (ENG.). 64p. (J). (gr. 3-7). 7.99 (978-0-14-241385-2(2), Puffin) Penguin Publishing Group.

—The Magic Finger. Dahl, Roald. 2003. (CHI.). 133p. (J). pap. 11.70 (978-957-574-476-2(4)) Youth Cultural Publishing Co. CHN. Dist: Chinasprout, Inc.

—La Maravillosa Granja de McBroom. Fleischman, Sid. 13th ed. 2003.Tr. of McBroom's Wonderful One-Acre Farm. (SPA.). 96p. (J). (gr. 3-5). 7.95 (978-84-204-4885-5(0)) Ediciones Alfaguara ESP. Dist: Santillana USA Publishing Co., Inc.

—La Maravillosa Medicina de Jorge. Dahl, Roald. 2005. (Alfaguara Ser.).Tr. of George's Marvellous Medicine Spanish. (SPA.). 118p. (gr. 3-5). per. 11.95 (978-968-19-0547-7(4)) Santillana USA Publishing Co., Inc.

—Matilda. Dahl, Roald. (ENG.). (J). (gr. 3-7). 2007. 240p. 6.99 (978-0-14-241037-0(3)); 2004. 240p. pap. 7.99 (978-0-14-240253-5(2)); 2013. 256p. pap. 6.99 (978-0-14-242538-1(9)) Penguin Publishing Group. (Puffin).

—Michael Rosen's Sad Book. Rosen, Michael. 2005. (ENG.). 32p. (J). (gr. k-12). 16.99 (978-0-7636-2597-9(3)) Candlewick Pr.

—The Missing Golden Ticket & Other Splendiferous Secrets. Dahl, Roald. 2010. (ENG.). 128p. (J). (gr. 3-7). 7.99 (978-0-14-241742-3(4), Puffin) Penguin Publishing Group.

—More about Boy. Dahl, Roald. 2009. (ENG.). 240p. (J). (gr. 5-7). pap. 15.99 (978-0-14-241498-9(0), Puffin) Penguin Publishing Group.

—More about Boy: Roald Dahl's Tales from Childhood. Dahl, Roald. 2009. (ENG.). 240p. (J). (gr. 5-9). 24.99 (978-0-374-35055-0(8), Farrar, Straus & Giroux (BYR)) Farrar, Straus & Giroux.

—Mouse Trouble. Yeoman, John. 2011. (ENG.). 32p. (J). (gr. -1-k). pap. 9.99 (978-1-84939-201-3(3)) Andersen Pr. GBR. Dist: Independent Pubs. Group.

—Mustard, Custard, Grumble Belly & Gravy. Rosen, Michael. 2008. (ENG.). 100p. (J). (gr. -1-2). pap. 12.95 (978-0-7475-8738-5(8)) Bloomsbury Publishing Plc GBR. Dist: Independent Pubs. Group.

—A Near Thing for Captain Najork. Hoban, Russell. 2006. (ENG.). 32p. (J). (gr. -1-3). pap. 7.95 (978-1-56792-323-0(2)) Godine, David R. Pub.

—On Angel Wings. Morpurgo, Michael. 2007. (ENG.). 48p. (J). (gr. k-12). 8.99 (978-0-7636-3466-7(2)) Candlewick Pr.

—Quentin Blake's a Christmas Carol. Dickens, Charles. 2012. (ENG.). 150p. (J). (gr. 2-4). 16.99 (978-1-84365-165-9(3), Pavilion Children's Books) Pavilion Bks. GBR. Dist: Independent Pubs. Group.

—Quentin Blake's Amazing Animal Stories. Yeoman, John. (ENG.). (J). (gr. 2-4). 2014. 120p. pap. 14.99 (978-1-84365-295-3(1), Pavilion); 2012. 124p. 19.99 (978-1-84365-195-6(5), Pavilion Children's Books) Pavilion Bks. GBR. Dist: Independent Pubs. Group.

—Quentin Blake's Magical Tales. Yeoman, John. 2012. (ENG.). 112p. (J). (gr. 2-4). 19.99 (978-1-84365-155-0(6), Pavilion Children's Books) Pavilion Bks. GBR. Dist: Independent Pubs. Group.

—Quentin Blake's the Seven Voyages of Sinbad the Sailor. 2012. (ENG.). 120p. (J). (gr. 2-4). 19.99 (978-1-84365-129-1(7), Pavilion Children's Books) Pavilion Bks. GBR. Dist: Independent Pubs. Group.

—The Rights of the Reader. Pennac, Daniel. Adams, Sarah, tr. from FRE. 2008.Tr. of Comme un roman.. (ENG.). 176p. (J). (gr. 9). 16.99 (978-0-7636-3801-6(3)) Candlewick Pr.

—Roald Dahl Set: Charlie & the Chocolate Factory; Charlie & the Great Glass Elevator; Fantastic Mr. Fox; Danny the Champion of the World; James & the Giant Peach, 5 vols. Dahl, Roald. 2013. (ENG.). 224p. (J). (gr. -1-2). 79.75 (978-0-385-75367-8(5), Knopf Bks. for Young Readers) Random Hse. Children's Bks.

—Roald Dahl's Story-Sketcher: Create! Doodle! Imagine! Dahl, Roald. 2014. (ENG.). 128p. (J). (gr. 1-3). 12.99 (978-0-448-48160-9(X), Grosset & Dunlap) Penguin Publishing Group.

—Roald Dahl¿s Whipple-Scrumptious Chocolate Box, 3 vols. Dahl, Roald. 2014. (Dahl Ser.). (ENG.). 480p. (J). (gr. 3). 22.97 (978-0-14-751350-2(2), Puffin) Penguin Publishing Group.

—Rosie's Magic Horse. Hoban, Russell. 2013. (ENG.). 40p. (J). (gr. -1-3). 15.99 (978-0-7636-6400-8(6)) Candlewick Pr.

—Rumbelow's Dance. Yeoman, John. 2013. (ENG.). 32p. (J). (gr. -1-k). pap. 9.99 (978-1-84939-460-4(1)) Andersen Pr. GBR. Dist: Independent Pubs. Group.

—Santa's Last Present. Murail, Marie-aude & Murail, Elvire. 2004. (ENG.). 32p. (J). (gr. 3-7). 12.95 (978-1-56145-319-1(6)) Peachtree Pubs.

—Scrumdiddlyumptious Sticker Book. Dahl, Roald. 2012. (ENG.). 16p. (J). (gr. k-3). 6.99 (978-0-448-46172-4(2), Grosset & Dunlap) Penguin Publishing Group.

—The Seven Voyages of Sinbad the Sailor. Yeoman, John. 2003. (Chrysalis Childrens Classics Ser.). (YA). pap. (978-1-84365-040-9(1), Pavilion Children's Books) Pavilion Bks.

—Sixes & Sevens. Yeoman, John. 2012. (ENG.). 32p. (J). (gr. -1-k). pap. 11.99 (978-1-84939-308-9(7)) Andersen Pr. GBR. Dist: Independent Pubs. Group.

—Three Little Owls. Luzzati, Emanuele. Yeoman, John, tr. from ITA. 2014. (ENG.). 32p. (J). (gr. -1-17). 18.95 (978-1-84976-080-5(2)) Tate Publishing, Ltd. GBR. Dist: Hachette Bk. Group.

—The Twits. Dahl, Roald. 2007. (ENG.). 96p. (J). (gr. 3-7). 7.99 (978-0-14-241039-4(X), Puffin) Penguin Publishing Group.

—The Twits. Dahl, Roald. 2007. 76p. (gr. 4-7). 18.00 (978-0-7569-8234-8(0)) Perfection Learning Corp.

—Uncle. Martin, J. P. 2007. (New York Review Children's Collection). (ENG.). 176p. (J). (gr. 4-7). 17.95 (978-1-59017-239-1(6), NYR Children's Collection) New York Review of Bks., Inc., The.

—Uncle Cleans Up. Martin, J. P. 2008. (ENG.). 184p. (J). (gr. 4-7). 17.95 (978-1-59017-276-6(0), NYR Children's Collection) New York Review of Bks., Inc., The.

—The Wild Washerwomen. Yeoman, John. 2009. (Andersen Press Picture Bks). (ENG.). 32p. (J). (gr. k-3). 16.95 (978-0-7613-5152-8(3)) Lerner Publishing Group.

—The Witches. Dahl, Roald. 30th ed. 2013. (ENG.). 240p. (J). (gr. 3-6). 21.99 (978-0-374-38459-3(2), Farrar, Straus & Giroux (BYR)) Farrar, Straus & Giroux.

—The Witches. Dahl, Roald. 2007. (ENG.). 208p. (J). (gr. 3-7). 7.99 (978-0-14-241011-0(X), Puffin) Penguin Publishing Group.

—The Witches. Dahl, Roald. 2007. 206p. (gr. 4-7). 17.00 (978-0-7569-8229-4(4)) Perfection Learning Corp.

—Wizzil. Steig, William. 2014. 32p. pap. 8.00 (978-1-61003-221-6(7)) Center for the Collaborative Classroom.

Blake, Quentin. Loveykins. Blake, Quentin. 2003. 32p. (J). (gr. k-3). 15.95 (978-1-56145-282-8(3)) Peachtree Pubs.

—Mrs. Armitage, Queen of the Road. Blake, Quentin. 2003. (ENG.). 32p. (J). (gr. k-3). 15.95 (978-1-56145-287-3(4)) Peachtree Pubs.

—Quentin Blake's Ten Frogs: A First Book about Numbers. Blake, Quentin. 2009. (FRE & ENG.). 18p. (J). (gr. -1-k). 7.99 (978-1-84365-128-4(9)) Pavilion Bks. GBR. Dist: Independent Pubs. Group.

—Quentin Blake's Ten Frogs Diez Ranas: A Book about Counting in English & Spanish. Blake, Quentin. 2010. (SPA & ENG.). 24p. (J). (gr. -1-k). 14.99 (978-1-84365-146-8(7), Pavilion Children's Books) Pavilion Bks. GBR. Dist: Independent Pubs. Group.

—Ten Frogs: A Book about Counting in English & French. Blake, Quentin. 2008. (FRE & ENG.). 32p. (J). (gr. -1-k). 14.95 (978-1-84365-104-8(1)) Pavilion Bks. GBR. Dist: Independent Pubs. Group.

Blake, Quentin & Terrazzini, Daniela Jaglenka. Matilda. Dahl, Roald. 2013. (ENG.). 240p. (J). (gr. 3-7). 16.99 (978-0-14-242427-8(7), Puffin) Penguin Publishing Group.

Blake, Quentin, jt. illus. see Dahl, Roald.

Blake, Robert J. Victor & Hugo. 2016. (J). **(978-0-399-24324-0(0))** Penguin Publishing Group.

Blake, Robert J. Akiak: A Tale from the Iditarod. Blake, Robert J. 2004. (ENG.). 40p. (J). (gr. k-3). reprint ed. pap. 6.99 (978-0-14-240185-9(4), Puffin) Penguin Publishing Group.

—Little Devils. Blake, Robert J. 2009. (ENG.). 40p. (J). (gr. k-3). 16.99 (978-0-399-24322-6(4), Philomel) Penguin Publishing Group.

—Painter & Ugly. Blake, Robert J. 2011. (ENG.). 48p. (J). (gr. k-3). 16.99 (978-0-399-24323-3(2), Philomel) Penguin Publishing Group.

Blake, Spencer, et al. Spyology. Blake, Spencer. Steer, Dugald A., ed. 2008. (Ologies Ser.: 7). (ENG.). 32p. (J). (gr. 3-7). 22.99 (978-0-7636-4048-4(4)) Candlewick Pr.

Blake, Stephanie. No Quiero Ir a la Escuela. Blake, Stephanie. Blake. 2007. (SPA.). 40p. (gr. k-2). 17.99 (978-84-8470-268-9(5)) Corimbo, Editorial S.L. ESP. Dist: Lectorum Pubns., Inc.

—Pip Caca. Blake, Stephanie. Blake. Ros, Rafael, tr. 2006. (SPA.). 32p. (J). (978-84-8470-216-0(2)) Corimbo, Editorial S.L.

Blakemore, Sally. Lucy's Journey to the Wild West: A True Story. Piepmeier, Charlotte. 2003. 40p. (J). (gr. k-7). 19.95 (978-1-929115-07-5(5)) Azro Pr., Inc.

—Math Games That Roam the Concept Range. Bortz, Trudy & Rappaport, Josh. 2010. (Card Game Roundup Ser.: 0). (ENG.). 96p. (gr. -1-3). per. 12.95 (978-0-9659113-9-9(X)) Singing Turtle Pr.

Blakeslee, Lys. Heroes A2Z #1: (Heroes a to Z): Alien Ice Cream. Anthony, David & David, Charles. 2007. 128p. (J). pap. 4.99 (978-0-9728461-8-9(2)) Sigil Publishing.

—Heroes A2Z #13: (Heroes a to Z): Monkey Monster Truck. Anthony, David & Clasman, Charles David. 2012. 128p. (J). mass mkt. 4.99 (978-0-9846528-1-5(7)) Sigil Publishing.

—Heroes A2Z #2: (Heroes a to Z): Bowling over Halloween: Bowling over Halloween. Anthony, David & David, Charles. 2007. (Heroes A2Z Ser.). 128p. (J). pap. 4.99 (978-0-9728461-9-6(0)) Sigil Publishing.

—Natalie: School's First Day of Me, 1 vol. Mackall, Dandi Daley. 2009. (That's Nat! Ser.). (ENG.). 96p. (J). (gr. 1-4). pap. 4.99 (978-0-310-71568-9(7)) Zonderkidz.

—Natalie & the Bestest Friend Race, 1 vol. Mackall, Dandi Daley. 2009. (That's Nat! Ser.). (ENG.). 96p. (J). (gr. 1-4). pap. 4.99 (978-0-310-71570-2(9)) Zonderkidz.

—Natalie & the Downside-Up Birthday, 1 vol. Mackall, Dandi Daley. 2009. (That's Nat! Ser.). (ENG.). 96p. (J). (gr. 1-4). pap. 4.99 (978-0-310-71569-6(5)) Zonderkidz.

—Natalie & the One-of-a-Kind Wonderful Day!, 1 vol. Mackall, Dandi Daley. 2009. (That's Nat! Ser.). (ENG.). 96p. (J). (gr. 1-4). pap. 2.99 (978-0-310-71566-5(0)) Zonderkidz.

—Natalie Really Very Much Wants to Be a Star, 1 vol. Mackall, Dandi Daley. 2009. (That's Nat! Ser.). (ENG.). 96p. (J). (gr. 1-4). pap. 4.99 (978-0-310-71567-2(9)) Zonderkidz.

—Natalie Wants a Puppy, 1 vol. Mackall, Dandi Daley. 2009. (That's Nat! Ser.). (ENG.). 96p. (J). (gr. 1-4). pap. 4.99 (978-0-310-71571-9(7)) Zonderkidz.

Blakeslee, S. E. Once upon a Blue Moon: The Chronicles of the Blue Moon. Blakeslee, S. E. 2007. (ENG.). 32p. (J). 17.95 *(978-0-9798031-0-7(2))* Blaumond Pr.

Blanc, Katherine. No Dogs, Please! Blanc, Katherine. 2013. (ENG.). (J). (gr. -1-3). 14.95 *(978-1-62086-388-6(X))* Mascot Bks., Inc.

Blanc, Mike. Francesca. Oelschlager, Vanita. 2008. (ENG.). 32p. (J). (gr. -1-3). 17.95 *(978-0-9800162-4-6(X))* VanitaBooks.

—I Came from the Water: One Haitian Boy's Incredible Tale of Survival. Oelschlager, Vanita. 2012. (ENG.). 40p. (J). (gr. -1-3). 15.95 *(978-0-9832904-4-5(X))* VanitaBooks.

—Magic Words: From the Ancient Oral Tradition of the Inuit. Oelschlager, Vanita. 2013. (ENG.). 24p. (J). (gr. -1-3). 15.95 *(978-0-9832904-6-9(6))*; pap. 8.95 *(978-0-9832904-7-6(4))* VanitaBooks.

—Porcupette Finds a Family. Oelschlager, Vanita. 2010. (ENG.). 44p. (gr. -1-3). 15.95 *(978-0-9819714-7-6(4))*; pap. 8.95 *(978-0-9819714-8-3(2))* VanitaBooks.

—A Tale of Two Mommies. Oelschlager, Vanita. 2011. (ENG.). 40p. (J). (gr. -1-3). 15.95 *(978-0-9826366-6-4(0))*; pap. 8.95 *(978-0-9826366-7-1(9))* VanitaBooks.

Blanc, Mike & Bauknight, Wilfred. Postcards from a War. Oelschlager, Vanita. 2009. (ENG.). 40p. (J). (gr. 1-4). 15.95 *(978-0-9800162-9-1(0))*; pap. 8.95 *(978-0-9819714-0-7(7))* VanitaBooks.

Blanc, Mike, jt. illus. see Blackwood, Kristin.

Blanch, Ignasi. Snow White. Desclot, Miquel. 2008. (Bilingual Fairy Tales Ser.: BILI).Tr. of Blancanieves. (SPA & ENG.). 32p. (J). (gr. -1-3). 14.95 *(978-0-8118-6030-7(2))* Chronicle Bks. LLC.

Blanchart, Stephanie. Mama Bear. Quintart, Natalie. 2005. (Tiger Tales Ser.). 32p. (J). (gr. -1-2). 6.95 *(978-1-58925-394-0(9))* Tiger Tales.

Blanchin, Matthieu, jt. illus. see Moutarde.

Blanco, Martin. Attack of the Paper Bats, 1 vol. Dahl, Michael. 2007. (Library of Doom Ser.). (ENG.). 40p. (gr. 1-3). lib. bdg. 22.65 *(978-1-59889-325-0(4))*; per. 6.25 *(978-1-59889-420-2(X))* Stone Arch Bks. (Zone Bks.).

—Poison Pages. Dahl, Michael. 2007. (Library of Doom Ser.). (ENG.). 40p. (gr. 1-3). pap. 6.25 *(978-1-59889-422-6(6))*; lib. bdg. 22.65 *(978-1-59889-327-4(0))* Stone Arch Bks. (Zone Bks.).

Blanco, Migy. Cinderella's Stepsister & the Big Bad Wolf. Carey, Lorraine. 2015. (ENG.). 32p. (J). (gr. -1-2). 15.99 ***(978-0-7636-8005-3(2)***, Nosy Crow) Candlewick Pr.

Blanco, Migy. Under the Sea. Fry, Sonali. 2014. (Dream Doodle Draw! Ser.). (ENG.). 96p. (J). (gr. -1-2). pap. 7.99 *(978-1-4814-0453-2(9))*, Little Simon) Little Simon.

Bland, Barry, jt. illus. see Antle, Bhagavan.

Bland, Nick. I Lost My Kisses. Trewin, Trudie. 2008. (ENG.). 32p. (J). (gr. -1-3). 14.99 *(978-0-545-05557-4(1)*, Orchard Bks.) Scholastic, Inc.

Bland, Nick. The Very Cranky Bear. Bland, Nick. 2014. (ENG.). 32p. (J). (gr. -1-k). 16.99 *(978-0-545-61269-2(1)*, Orchard Bks.) Scholastic, Inc.

Blanden, Neale, jt. illus. see Sta.Maria, Ian.

Blander, Katy. Pride & Joy: African-American Baby Celebrations. Shepherd, Paul, photos by. Robinson, Janice. 2005. 188p. (YA). reprint ed. pap. 17.00 *(978-0-7567-9320-3(3))* DIANE Publishing Co.

Blanding, Allison. Sweet Dreams for Scotty. McKechnie, Edward. 2007. 14p. (J). spiral bd. 14.95 *(978-0-9785302-0-4(9))* Beanstalk Pubns.

Blanding, Dexter. My Life As a Third Grade Werewolf. Longmeyer, C. M. 2014. (ENG.). (J). (gr. 2-3). pap. 7.99 *(978-0-635-11144-9(6))* Gallopade International.

—My Life As a Third Grade Zombie. Longmeyer, C. M. 2013. (My Life As a Third Grade... Ser.). (ENG.). (J). (gr. -1-3). pap. 7.99 *(978-0-635-11131-9(4))* Gallopade International.

Blankenship, Robert. A Home for Ruby: Helping Children Adjust to New Families. Neer, P. J. 2015. (Let's Talk Ser.). (ENG.). 48p. (J). (gr. k-5). 9.95 *(978-0-88282-488-8(0))* New Horizon Pr. Pubs., Inc.

Blanks, Natascha Alex. Sojourner Truth: Preacher for Freedom & Equality, 1 vol. Slade, Suzanne. 2007. (Biographies Ser.). (ENG.). 24p. (gr. k-3). lib. bdg. 25.99 *(978-1-4048-3726-3(4)*, Nonfiction Picture Bks.) Picture Window Bks.

—Vietnam ABCs: A Book about the People & Places of Vietnam, 1 vol. Alberti, Theresa. 2007. (Country ABCs Ser.). (ENG.). 32p. (gr. k-5). lib. bdg. 27.32 *(978-1-4048-2251-1(8)*, Nonfiction Picture Bks.) Picture Window Bks.

Blanski, Maribeth. Would You Invite a Skunk to Your Wedding? Pate, Ginger. 2009. 32p. (J). 16.95 *(978-1-880851-73-9(3))* Greene Bark Pr., Inc.

Blaskovich, Dominique. Three Little Words. Langley, Karen. 2003. 146p. (YA). 17.95 *(978-0-9745990-0-7(X)*, 100) In Cahoots.

Blassingame, Calvin. Chinqua Where? The Spirit of Rural America, 1947-1955. McKinley, Fred B. 2003. 319p. 24.95 *(978-0-9729655-0-7(5))* Willow Creel Publishing Co.

Blasutta, Mary Lynn. School & Earth Smarts Planner. Falligant, Erin, ed. 2006. (ENG.). 112p. spiral bd. 9.95 *(978-1-59369-484-5(9))* American Girl Publishing, Inc.

Blathwayt, Benedict. Great Big Train. 2015. (J). ***(978-0-553-51289-2(7))*** Knopf, Alfred A. Inc.

Blathwayt, Benedict. Dinosaur Disaster. Blathwayt, Benedict. 2010. (ENG.). 32p. (J). (gr. -1-k). pap. 8.99 *(978-1-86230-829-9(2)*, Red Fox) Random House Children's Books GBR. Dist: Independent Pubs. Group.

—Dougal the Digger. Blathwayt, Benedict. 2009. (ENG.). 24p. (J). (gr. -1-k). pap. 12.99 *(978-1-86230-625-7(7))* Transworld Publishers Ltd. GBR. Dist: Independent Pubs. Group.

—Well Done, Dougal! Blathwayt, Benedict. 2010. (ENG.). 24p. (J). (gr. -1-k). pap. 12.99 *(978-1-84941-040-3(2)*, Red Fox) Random House Children's Books GBR. Dist: Independent Pubs. Group.

Blatz-Harvey, Elizabeth. The Windows of My World. Blatz-Harvey, Elizabeth. 2011. 32p. *(978-0-9868730-3-4(9))* Cheaper Cheeper Copy.

Blau, Aljoscha. The Fantastic Adventures of Baron Munchausen. Janisch, Heinz. Cooper, Belinda, tr. from GER. 2010. (ENG.). 32p. (J). (gr. -1-3). 17.95 *(978-1-59270-091-2(8))* Enchanted Lion Bks., LLC.

Blau, Nicole. Bedtime. Adelman, Nechama Dina. 2003. 30p. (J). 10.95 *(978-1-929628-12-4(9))* Hachai Publishing.

Blazek, Scott R. Clovis Crawfish & Bertile's Bon Voyage, 1 vol. Fontenot, Mary Alice. 2008. (Clovis Crawfish Ser.). (ENG.). 32p. (J). (gr. k-3). 16.99 *(978-1-58980-541-5(0))* Pelican Publishing Co., Inc.

—Clovis Crawfish & Michelle Mantis, 1 vol. Fontenot, Mary Alice. 2008. (Clovis Crawfish Ser.). (ENG.). 32p. (J). (gr. k-3). 16.99 *(978-1-58980-540-8(2))* Pelican Publishing Co., Inc.

Bleach, James, jt. illus. see Parlett, George.

Blecha, Aaron. All Pooped Out: And Other Gross Expressions. Larsen, C. S. 2012. (It's Just an Expression Ser.). (ENG.). 32p. (gr. 4-6). lib. bdg. 26.60 *(978-0-7613-7892-1(8)*, Lerner Pubns.) Lerner Publishing Group.

—Attack of the Tighty Whities! Krulik, Nancy. 2012. (George Brown, Class Clown Ser.: 7). (ENG.). 128p. (J). (gr. 2-4). pap. 4.99 *(978-0-448-45575-4(7)*, Grosset & Dunlap) Penguin Publishing Group.

—The Boy Who Cried Shark. Ocean, Davy. 2015. (Shark School Ser.: 4). (ENG.). 144p. (J). (gr. 1-4). 16.99 *(978-1-4814-0689-5(2)*, Simon & Schuster/Paula Wiseman Bks.) Simon & Schuster/Paula Wiseman Bks.

—Burp or Treat ... Smell My Feet! Super Special. Krulik, Nancy. 2014. (George Brown, Class Clown Ser.: No. 3). (ENG.). 208p. (J). (gr. 2-4). 5.99 *(978-0-448-46115-1(3)*, Grosset & Dunlap) Penguin Publishing Group.

—Dance Your Pants Off!, No. 9. Krulik, Nancy. 2013. (George Brown, Class Clown Ser.: 9). (ENG.). 128p. (J). (gr. 2-4). pap. 4.99 *(978-0-448-45679-9(6)*, Grosset & Dunlap) Penguin Publishing Group.

—Deep-Sea Disaster. Ocean, Davy. 2014. (Shark School Ser.: 1). (ENG.). 128p. (J). (gr. 1-4). 15.99 *(978-1-4814-0679-6(5)*, Simon & Schuster/Paula Wiseman Bks.) Simon & Schuster/Paula Wiseman Bks.

Blecha, Aaron. Deep-Sea Treasury: Deep-Sea Disaster; Lights! Camera! Hammerhead!; Squid-Napped; the Boy Who Cried Shark. Ocean, Davy. 2015. (Shark School Ser.). (ENG.). 528p. (J). (gr. 1-4). 14.99 ***(978-1-4814-5115-4(4)***, Simon & Schuster/Paula Wiseman Bks.) Simon & Schuster/Paula Wiseman Bks.

Blecha, Aaron. Eww! What's on My Shoe?, No. 11. Krulik, Nancy. 2013. (George Brown, Class Clown Ser.: 11). (ENG.). 128p. (J). (gr. 2-4). 4.99 *(978-0-448-46114-4(5)*, Grosset & Dunlap) Penguin Publishing Group.

—Hey! Who Stole the Toilet?, 8 vols. Krulik, Nancy. 2012. (George Brown, Class Clown Ser.: 8). (ENG.). 128p. (J). (gr. 2-4). pap. 4.99 *(978-0-448-45576-1(5)*, Grosset & Dunlap) Penguin Publishing Group.

—How Do You Pee in Space?, No. 13. Krulik, Nancy. 2014. (George Brown, Class Clown Ser.: 13). (ENG.). 128p. (J). (gr. 2-4). pap. 4.99 *(978-0-448-46113-7(7)*, Grosset & Dunlap) Penguin Publishing Group.

—Keep on Burpin' Krulik, Nancy. 2012. (George Brown, Class Clown Ser.: No. 2). (ENG.). 384p. (J). (gr. 2-4). pap. 8.99 *(978-0-448-46285-1(0)*, Grosset & Dunlap) Penguin Publishing Group.

—Let the Burping Begin. Krulik, Nancy. 2012. (George Brown, Class Clown Ser.). (ENG.). 384p. (J). (gr. 2-4). pap. 8.99 *(978-0-448-46284-4(2)*, Grosset & Dunlap) Penguin Publishing Group.

—Lice Check, No. 12. Krulik, Nancy. 2014. (George Brown, Class Clown Ser.: 12). (ENG.). 128p. (J). (gr. 2-4). 4.99 *(978-0-448-46112-0(9)*, Grosset & Dunlap) Penguin Publishing Group.

—Lights! Camera! Hammerhead! Ocean, Davy. 2014. (Shark School Ser.: 2). (ENG.). 128p. (J). (gr. 1-4). 15.99 *(978-1-4814-0682-6(5)*, Simon & Schuster/Paula Wiseman Bks.) Simon & Schuster/Paula Wiseman Bks.

Blecha, Aaron. A Royal Pain in the Burp #15. Krulik, Nancy. 2015. (George Brown, Class Clown Ser.: 15). (ENG.). 128p. (J). (gr. 1-3). 4.99 ***(978-0-448-48283-5(5)***, Grosset & Dunlap) Penguin Publishing Group.

Blecha, Aaron. 'Snot Funny!, No. 14. Krulik, Nancy. 2015. (George Brown, Class Clown Ser.: 14). (ENG.). 128p. (J). (gr. 2-4). 4.99 *(978-0-448-48282-8(7)*, Grosset & Dunlap) Penguin Publishing Group.

—Super Burp!, No. 1. Krulik, Nancy. 2010. (George Brown, Class Clown Ser.: 1). (ENG.). 128p. (J). (gr. 2-4). pap. 4.99 *(978-0-448-45367-5(3)*, Grosset & Dunlap) Penguin Publishing Group.

—The Tall Tale of Paul Bunyan. Stone Arch Books Staff. 2010. (Graphic Spin Ser.). (ENG.). 40p. (gr. 1-3). pap. 5.95 *(978-1-4342-2268-8(3)*, Graphic Revolve) Stone Arch Bks.

—The Tall Tale of Paul Bunyan. Capstone Press Staff. 2010. (Graphic Spin Ser.). (ENG.). 40p. (gr. 1-3). lib. bdg. 23.99 *(978-1-4342-1897-1(X)*, Graphic Revolve) Stone Arch Bks.

—The Three Little Pigs. Capstone Press Staff. (Graphic Spin Ser.). (ENG.). 40p. (gr. 1-3). 2010. pap. 5.95 *(978-1-4342-1395-2(1))*; 2009. 23.99 *(978-1-4342-1195-8(9))* Stone Arch Bks. (Graphic Revolve).

—Trouble Magnet. Krulik, Nancy. 2010. (George Brown, Class Clown Ser.: 2). (ENG.). 128p. (J). (gr. 2-4). pap. 4.99 *(978-0-448-45368-2(1)*, Grosset & Dunlap) Penguin Publishing Group.

—The Twelve Burps of Christmas. Krulik, Nancy. 2012. (George Brown, Class Clown Ser.: No. 1). (ENG.). 192p. (J). (gr. 2-4). pap. 5.99 *(978-0-448-45660-5(X)*, Grosset & Dunlap) Penguin Publishing Group.

—The Ugly Duckling: The Graphic Novel, 1 vol. Andersen, Hans Christian. 2009. (Graphic Spin Ser.). (ENG.). 40p. (gr. 1-3). pap. 5.95 *(978-1-4342-1742-4(6)*, Graphic Revolve) Stone Arch Bks.

—Until the Cows Come Home: And Other Expressions about Animals. Donovan, Sandy. 2012. (It's Just an Expression Ser.). (ENG.). 32p. (gr. 4-6). lib. bdg. 26.60 *(978-0-7613-7890-7(1)*, Lerner Pubns.) Lerner Publishing Group.

—Wet & Wild! #5, 5 vols. Krulik, Nancy. 2011. (George Brown, Class Clown Ser.: 5). (ENG.). 128p. (J). (gr. 2-4). pap. 4.99 *(978-0-448-45570-9(6)*, Grosset & Dunlap) Penguin Publishing Group.

—What's Black & White & Stinks All Over? Krulik, Nancy. 2011. (George Brown, Class Clown Ser.: 4). (ENG.). 128p. (J). (gr. 2-4). pap. 4.99 *(978-0-448-45370-5(3)*, Grosset & Dunlap) Penguin Publishing Group.

—World's Worst Wedgie. Krulik, Nancy. 2010. (George Brown, Class Clown Ser.: 3). (ENG.). 128p. (J). (gr. 2-4). pap. 4.99 *(978-0-448-45369-9(X)*, Grosset & Dunlap) Penguin Publishing Group.

—Zombiekins. Bolger, Kevin. 2011. (ENG.). 208p. (J). (gr. 3-7). 6.99 *(978-1-59514-367-9(X)*, Razorbill) Penguin Publishing Group.

—Zombiekins 2. Bolger, Kevin. 2011. (J). 10.99 *(978-1-59514-432-4(3)*, Razorbill) Penguin Publishing Group.

Blecha, Aaron. Goodnight, Grizzle Grump! Blecha, Aaron. 2015. (ENG.). 32p. (J). (gr. -1-3). 17.99 ***(978-0-06-229746-4(5))*** HarperCollins Pubs.

Blechman, Nicholas. Information Graphics: Animal Kingdom. Rogers, Simon. 2014. (ENG.). 80p. (J). (gr. 1-4). 17.99 *(978-0-7636-7122-8(3)*, Big Picture Press) Candlewick Pr.

Blechmann, R. O. The One & Only 1, 2, 3 Book. Blechmann, R. O. 2013. (ENG.). 24p. (J). (gr. -1-k). 15.99 *(978-1-56846-245-5(X)*, Creative Editions) Creative Co., The.

Bleck, Linda. A Children's Treasury of Lullabies. 2014. (ENG.). 32p. (J). (-k). pap. 6.95 *(978-1-4549-1358-0(4))* Sterling Publishing Co., Inc.

—A Children's Treasury of Mother Goose. (ENG.). (J). (-k). 2015. 32p. pap. 6.95 *(978-1-4549-1473-0(4))*; 2009. 24p. bds. 12.95 *(978-1-4027-4499-0(4))* Sterling Publishing Co., Inc.

—A Children's Treasury of Poems. 2015. (ENG.). 32p. (J). (-k). pap. 6.95 *(978-1-4549-1474-7(2))* Sterling Publishing Co., Inc.

—The Longest Day: Celebrating the Summer Solstice. Pfeffer, Wendy. 2015. (ENG.). 40p. (J). (gr. 2-4). 8.99 *(978-0-14-751556-8(4)*, Puffin) Penguin Publishing Group.

—We Gather Together: Celebrating the Harvest Season. Pfeffer, Wendy. 2014. (ENG.). 32p. (J). (gr. 1-4). 8.99 *(978-0-14-751282-6(4)*, Puffin) Penguin Publishing Group.

Bleck, Linda. Pepper Goes to School. Bleck, Linda. 2006. (Pepper Plays, Pulls, & Pops! Ser.). (ENG.). 18p. (J). (gr. -1-2). 8.99 *(978-1-4169-0944-6(3)*, Little Simon) Little Simon.

—What's in My Truck? Bleck, Linda. 2014. (ENG.). 10p. (J). (gr. -1 — 1). bds. 6.99 *(978-0-545-53525-0(5)*, Cartwheel Bks.) Scholastic, Inc.

Blecker, Lisa. The Good in Me from A to Z by Dottie. Blecker, Lisa. 2006. bds. 12.95 *(978-1-931492-21-8(2))* Discover Writing Pr.

Bledsoe, William B. Everyone Has a Story to Tell. Isbell, Rebecca & Buchanan, Marilyn. 2004. (J). 14.95 *(978-0-9755906-0-7(X))* Olde Town Publishing.

Blegvad, Erik. Ana Banana y Yo. Blegvad, Lenore. 14th ed. 2003.Tr. of Anna Banana & Me. (SPA.). 56p. (gr. k-3). pap. 10.95 *(978-84-204-0083-9(1)*, Alfaguara) Santillana USA Publishing Co., Inc.

—Mud Pies & Other Recipes: A Cookbook for Dolls. Winslow, Marjorie. 2010. (ENG.). 56p. (J). (gr. k-4). 14.95 *(978-1-59017-368-8(6)*, NYR Children's Collection) New York Review of Bks., Inc., The.

—Sea Clocks: The Story of Longitude. Borden, Louise. 2004. (ENG.). 48p. (J). (gr. 2-5). 19.99 *(978-0-689-84216-0(3)*, McElderry, Margaret K. Bks.) McElderry, Margaret K. Bks.

—The Young Hans Christian Andersen. Hesse, Karen. 2005. (ENG.). 48p. (J). (gr. 2-5). 16.99 *(978-0-439-67990-9(7))* Scholastic, Inc.

Blegvad, Erik. Ana Banana y Yo. Blegvad, Erik, tr. Blegvad, Lenore. Puncel, Maria, tr. 2003.Tr. of Anna Banana & Me. (SPA.). 56p. (J). (gr. k-3). pap. 9.95 *(978-84-204-4375-1(1))* Santillana USA Publishing Co., Inc.

Blegvad, Erik & Gilpin, Stephen. Villain's Lair. Stafford, Jean & Van Draanen, Wendelin. 2011. (Gecko & Sticky Ser.: Bk. 2). (ENG.). 208p. (J). (gr. 3-7). pap. 7.99 *(978-0-440-42242-6(6)*, Yearling) Random Hse. Children's Bks.

Blegvad, Erik & Starr, Branka. The Mushroom Center Disaster. Bodecker, N. M. 2004. (ENG.). 48p. (J). reprint ed. *(978-1-931561-98-3(2))* MacAdam/Cage Publishing, Inc.

Bleicher, David. I Can Celebrate the Jewish Holidays. Grishaver, Joel Lurie. 2010. 96p. (J). pap. 14.95 *(978-1-934527-33-7(5))* Torah Aura Productions.

Blessen, Karen. Peace One Day. Gilley, Jeremy. 2005. (ENG.). 48p. (J). (gr. -1-3). pap. 17.99 *(978-0-399-24330-1(5)*, Putnam Juvenile) Penguin Publishing Group.

Blevins, Bret. Redwall. Jacques, Brian. 2007. (Redwall Ser.). (ENG.). 148p. (J). (gr. 5-18). 12.99 *(978-0-399-24481-0(6)*, Philomel) Penguin Publishing Group.

Blevins, Bret, jt. illus. see Austin, Terry.

Bliss, Bob. The Hardest Lessons: The Lost Babies Series #3. 2007. 118p. (J). per. 5.99 *(978-0-9792499-2-1(9))* Eagle Tree Pr.

—The Ruby Hind: The Lost Babies Series #1. 2007. 116p. (J). per. 5.99 *(978-0-9792499-0-7(2))* Eagle Tree Pr.

—Too Many Parents: The Lost Babies Series #2. 2007. 109p. (J). per. 5.99 *(978-0-9792499-1-4(0))* Eagle Tree Pr.

Bliss, Harry. Anna & Solomon. Snyder, Elaine. 2014. (ENG.). 32p. (J). (gr. -1-3). 17.99 *(978-0-374-30362-4(2)*, Farrar, Straus & Giroux (BYR)) Farrar, Straus & Giroux.

—Countdown to Kindergarten. McGhee, Alison. 2006. (ENG.). 32p. (J). (gr. -1-3). reprint ed. pap. 6.99 *(978-0-15-205586-8(X))* Houghton Mifflin Harcourt Publishing Co.

—Countdown to Kindergarten. McGhee, Alison. pap. incl. audio compact disk *(978-1-59112-469-6(7))*; pap. 39.95 incl. audio *(978-1-59112-929-5(X))*; 2004. (J). 28.95 incl. audio compact disk *(978-1-59112-928-8(1))* Live Oak Media.

—Dangerous Pumpkins. Jenkins, Emily. 2012. (Invisible Inkling Ser.: 2). (ENG.). 160p. (J). (gr. 1-5). 14.99 *(978-0-06-180223-2(9))* HarperCollins Pubs.

—Diary of a Fly. Cronin, Doreen. (ENG.). 40p. (J). (gr. -1-3). 2013. 9.99 *(978-0-06-223298-4(3))*; 2007. 16.99 *(978-0-06-000156-8(9))* HarperCollins Pubs.

—Diary of a Fly. Cronin, Doreen. 2008. (J). (gr. -1-3). 25.95 incl. audio *(978-1-4301-0404-9(X))*; 28.95 incl. audio compact disk *(978-1-4301-0407-0(4))* Live Oak Media.

—Diary of a Spider. Cronin, Doreen. (ENG.). 40p. (J). (gr. -1-3). 2013. 9.99 *(978-0-06-223300-4(9))*; 2005. 16.99 *(978-0-06-000153-7(4))* HarperCollins Pubs.

—Diary of a Spider. Cronin, Doreen. unabr. ed. 2006. (Picture Book Readalong Ser.). (J). (gr. -1-2). 28.95 incl. audio compact disk *(978-1-59519-486-2(X))* Live Oak Media.

—Diary of a Spider. Cronin, Doreen. unabr. ed. 2006. (J). (gr. -1-3). 29.95 *(978-0-439-90579-4(6))* Weston Woods Studios, Inc.

—Diary of a Worm. Cronin, Doreen. 2003. 40p. (J). (gr. -1-3). (ENG.). 16.99 *(978-0-06-000150-6(X))*; lib. bdg. 18.89 *(978-0-06-000151-3(8))* HarperCollins Pubs.

—Diary of a Worm. Cronin, Doreen. pap. 16.95 incl. audio *(978-1-59112-867-0(6))*; pap. incl. audio *(978-1-59112-869-4(2))*; pap. 18.95 incl. audio compact disk *(978-1-59112-871-7(4))*; pap. incl. audio compact disk *(978-1-59112-873-1(0))* Live Oak Media.

—Diary of a Worm: Nat the Gnat. Cronin, Doreen. 2014. (I Can Read Book 1 Ser.). (ENG.). 32p. (J). (gr. -1-3). pap. 3.99 *(978-0-06-208707-2(X))* HarperCollins Pubs.

—A Fine, Fine School. Creech, Sharon. ed. 2004. (J). (gr. k-3). spiral bd. *(978-0-616-11106-2(1))* Canadian National Institute for the Blind/Institut National Canadien pour les Aveugles.

—A Fine, Fine School. Creech, Sharon. 2003. (ENG.). 32p. (J). (gr. -1-3). pap. 6.99 *(978-0-06-000728-7(1))* HarperCollins Pubs.

—A Fine, Fine School. Creech, Sharon. 2003. pap. 37.95 incl. audio *(978-1-59112-222-7(8))*; pap. 39.95 incl. audio compact disk *(978-1-59112-555-6(3))* Live Oak Media.

—A Fine, Fine School. Creech, Sharon. 2004. (J). (gr. -1-3). 14.65 *(978-0-7569-3179-7(7))* Perfection Learning Corp.

—Grandma in Blue with Red Hat. Menchin, Scott. 2015. (ENG.). 32p. (J). (gr. -1-3). 16.95 *(978-1-4197-1484-9(8)*, Abrams Bks. for Young Readers) Abrams.

—Invisible Inkling. Jenkins, Emily. (Invisible Inkling Ser.: 1). (ENG.). (J). (gr. 1-5). 2012. 176p. pap. 5.99 *(978-0-06-180222-5(0))*; 2011. 160p. 16.99 *(978-0-06-180220-1(4))* HarperCollins Pubs.

—Invisible Inkling. Jenkins, Emily. ed. 2012. (Invisible Inkling Ser.). lib. bdg. 16.00 *(978-0-606-26266-8(0)*, Turtleback) Turtleback Bks.

—Louise, the Adventures of a Chicken. DiCamillo, Kate. 2008. 56p. (J). (gr. -1-3). (ENG.). 17.99 *(978-0-06-075554-6(7))*; lib. bdg. 18.89 *(978-0-06-075555-3(5))* HarperCollins Pubs.

—Louise, the Adventures of a Chicken. DiCamillo, Kate. 2009. (J). (gr. -1-2). 29.95 incl. audio compact disk *(978-1-4301-0688-3(3))* Live Oak Media.

—Mrs. Watson Wants Your Teeth. McGhee, Alison. 2007. 32p. (J). reprint ed. 16.00 *(978-1-4223-6777-3(0))* DIANE Publishing Co.

—Mrs. Watson Wants Your Teeth. McGhee, Alison. 2008. (ENG.). 36p. (J). (gr. -1-3). pap. 6.00 *(978-0-15-206348-1(X))* Houghton Mifflin Harcourt Publishing Co.

—Mrs. Watson Wants Your Teeth. McGhee, Alison. unabr. ed. 2007. (Picture Book Readalong Ser.). (J). (gr. -1-2). 28.95 incl. audio compact disk *(978-1-59519-902-7(0))* Live Oak Media.

Bliss, Harry. My Favorite Pet by Gus W. for Ms. Smolinski's Class. Birdsall, Jeanne. 2016. (J). ***(978-0-385-75570-2(8))*** Knopf, Alfred A. Inc.

Bliss, Harry. The Sweetest Witch Around. McGhee, Alison. 2014. (ENG.). 32p. (J). (gr. -1-3). 15.99 *(978-1-4424-7833-6(0)*, Simon & Schuster/Paula Wiseman Bks.) Simon & Schuster/Paula Wiseman Bks.

—A Very Brave Witch. McGhee, Alison. 2007. (J). (gr. -1-3). 24.95 incl. audio *(978-0-545-04268-0(2))* Scholastic, Inc.

—A Very Brave Witch. McGhee, Alison. (ENG.). 32p. (J). (gr. -1-3). 2011. 7.99 *(978-0-689-86731-6(X))*; 2009. 9.99 *(978-1-4169-8670-6(7))*; 2006. 17.99 *(978-0-689-86730-9(1))* Simon & Schuster/Paula Wiseman Bks. (Simon & Schuster/Paula Wiseman Bks.).

—Which Would You Rather Be? Steig, William & Steig. 2005. (ENG.). 32p. (J). (gr. -1-3). reprint ed. pap. 8.99 *(978-0-06-443792-9(2))* HarperCollins Pubs.

—The Whoopie Pie War. Jenkins, Emily. 2013. (Invisible Inkling Ser.: 3). (ENG.). 160p. (J). (gr. 1-5). 14.99 *(978-0-06-180226-3(3))* HarperCollins Pubs.

Bliss, Harry. Bailey at the Museum. Bliss, Harry. 2012. (Bailey Ser.). (ENG.). 32p. (J). (gr. -1-k). 16.99 *(978-0-545-23345-3(3)*, Scholastic Pr.) Scholastic, Inc.

—Luke on the Loose. Bliss, Harry. (ENG.). 32p. (J). (gr. -1-3). 2014. pap. 4.99 *(978-1-935179-36-8(5))*; 2009. 12.95 *(978-1-935179-00-9(4))* TOON Books / RAW Junior, LLC.

Bliss, Harry & Nez, John. Diary of a Worm: Teacher's Pet. Cronin, Doreen. 2013. (I Can Read Book 1 Ser.). (ENG.). 32p. (J). (gr. -1-3). 16.99 *(978-0-06-208705-8(3))*; pap. 3.99 *(978-0-06-208704-1(5))* HarperCollins Pubs.

Bliss, Ryan T. Mooseclumps. Bliss, Ryan T. 2013. 58p. 15.99 *(978-0-615-75521-2(6))* Artsy Bee, LLC.

Blitt, Barry. The Adventures of Mark Twain by Huckleberry Finn. Burleigh, Robert. 2011. (ENG.). 48p. (J). (gr. 2-5). 17.99 *(978-0-689-83041-9(6)*, Atheneum Bks. for Young Readers) Simon & Schuster Children's Publishing.

—The Founding Fathers! Those Horse-Ridin', Fiddle-Playin', Book-Readin', Gun-Totin' Gentlemen Who Started America. Winter, Jonah. 2015. (ENG.). 48p. (J). (gr. k-3). 17.99 *(978-1-4424-4274-0(3))* Simon & Schuster Children's Publishing.

B

—George Washington's Birthday: A Mostly True Tale. McNamara, Margaret. 2012. (ENG.). 40p. (J). (gr. -1-3). 17.99 *(978-0-375-84499-7(6)*, Schwartz & Wade Bks.) Random Hse. Children's Bks.

—Once upon a Time, the End: Asleep in 60 Seconds. Kloske, Geoffrey. 2005. (ENG.). 40p. (J). (gr. -1-3). 17.99 *(978-0-689-86619-7(4)*, Atheneum Bks. for Young Readers) Simon & Schuster Children's Publishing.

—What's the Weather Inside? Wilson, Karma. 2009. (ENG.). 176p. (J). (gr. 1-5). 17.99 *(978-1-4169-0092-4(6)*, McElderry, Margaret K. Bks.) McElderry, Margaret K. Bks.

—While You Were Napping. Offill, Jenny. 2014. (ENG.). 40p. (J). (gr. -1-3). 16.99 *(978-0-375-86572-5(1))*; 19.99 *(978-0-375-96572-2(6)*, Schwartz & Wade Bks.) Random Hse. Children's Bks.

Bloch, Beth. My Oh My Sweet Potato Pie. Bloch, Beth. 2005. 32p. (J). 16.00 *(978-0-9771515-0-9(6))* Dream Creek Pr.

Bloch, Serge. The Big Book of Dummies, Rebels & Other Geniuses. Pouy, Jean-Bernard. Bedrick, Claudia Z., tr. from FRE. 2008. (ENG.). 128p. (J). (gr. 3-18). 19.95 *(978-1-59270-103-2(5))* Enchanted Lion Bks., LLC.

—The Enemy. Cali, Davide. 2013. Orig. Title: L' Ennemi. (ENG.). 64p. (J). (gr. 4-7). 24.99 *(978-0-9585571-8-4(7))* Wilkins Farago Pty, Ltd. AUS. Dist: Independent Pubs. Group.

—I Dare You Not to Yawn. Boudreau, Helene. 2013. (ENG.). 32p. (J). (gr. -1-3). 15.99 *(978-0-7636-5070-4(6))* Candlewick Pr.

—I Love Kissing You. Cali, Davide. 2011.Tr. of J'aime T'embrasser. (ENG.). 96p. 16.95 *(978-0-9804165-0-3(7))* Wilkins Farago Pty, Ltd. AUS. Dist: Independent Pubs. Group.

—I Scream! Ice Cream! A Book of Wordles. Rosenthal, Amy Krouse. 2013. (ENG.). 40p. (J). (gr. -1-17). 16.99 *(978-1-4521-0004-3(7))* Chronicle Bks. LLC.

—My Snake Blake. Siegel, Randy. 2012. (ENG.). 32p. (J). (gr. -1-1). 16.99 *(978-1-59643-584-1(4))* Roaring Brook Pr.

—The Underwear Salesman: And Other Jobs for Better or Verse. Lewis, J. Patrick. 2009. (ENG.). 64p. (J). (gr. 2-5). 18.99 *(978-0-689-85325-8(4)*, Atheneum Bks. for Young Readers) Simon & Schuster Children's Publishing.

Block, Ira, photos by. 1607: A New Look at Jamestown. Lange, Karen. 2007. (ENG., 48p. (J). (gr. 4-7). 17.95 *(978-1-4263-0012-7(3))*; 27.90 *(978-1-4263-0013-4(1))* National Geographic Society. (National Geographic Children's Bks.).

Block, Thomas. The Keeper & the Alabaster Chalice: Book II of the Black Ledge Series. Pendleton, Paige. 2013. (Black Ledge Ser.). (ENG.). 210p. pap. 12.50 *(978-0-615-82848-0(5))* Pig Wing Pr.

Blocksma, Mary. What's on the Beach? A Great Lakes Treasure Hunt. Blocksma, Mary. 2003. (Great Lakes Treasure Hunts Ser.: No. 1). 48p. (J). pap. 9.95 *(978-0-9708575-1-4(9))* Beaver Island Arts.

Blodau, Peter. Tina & the Tooth Fairy. Snell, Gordon. 2005. (Pandas Ser.: 31). (ENG.). 64p. (J). pap. 9.95 *(978-0-86278-601-4(0))* O'Brien Pr., Ltd., The IRL. Dist: Dufour Editions, Inc.

Blondahl, Samuel. The Outdoor Adventures of Charlie & Kaylee: Hunting Fear (book 1) Callsen, Terri. Lignor, Amy, ed. 2012. 156p. pap. 9.85 *(978-1-938634-10-9(1))* Freedom of Speech Publishing, Inc.

Blondon, Herve. The Miracle of the Myrrh. Alborghetti, Marci. 2003. (J). 16.95 *(978-0-87946-249-9(3)*, 708) ACTA Pubns.

Bloodworth, Mark. Blue Bay Mystery. 2009. (Boxcar Children Graphic Novels Ser.). (ENG.). 32p. (J). (gr. 2-5). 6.99 *(978-0-8075-2872-3(2))* Whitman, Albert & Co.

—The Castle Mystery. 2010. (Boxcar Children Graphic Novels Ser.). (ENG.). 32p. (J). (gr. 2-5). pap. 6.99 *(978-0-8075-1080-3(7))* Whitman, Albert & Co.

—The Haunted Cabin Mystery, 9 vols. Warner, Gertrude Chandler. 2010. (Boxcar Children Graphic Novels Ser.). 32p. (J). (gr. 2-5). 28.50 *(978-1-60270-717-7(0))* ABDO Publishing Co.

—Tree House Mystery, 8 vols. Long, Christopher E. & Warner, Gertrude Chandler. 2010. (Boxcar Children Graphic Novels Ser.). 32p. (J). (gr. 2-5). 28.50 *(978-1-60270-716-0(2))* ABDO Publishing Co.

Bloodworth, Mark, jt. illus. see Dubisch, Mike.

Bloom, Clive. The Scariest Thing of All. Glori, Debi. 2012. (ENG.). 32p. (J). (gr. -1-1). 17.89 *(978-0-8027-2392-5(6))* Walker & Co.

Bloom, Clive, jt. illus. see Gliori, Debi.

Bloom, Harry. Where's Father Christmas? Find Father Christmas & His Festive Helpers in 15 Fun-Filled Puzzles. Danielle, Sara & James, Danielle. 2013. (ENG.). 42p. (J). (gr. 2-5). 16.99 *(978-1-78219-476-7(2))* Blake, John Publishing, Ltd. GBR. Dist: Independent Pubs. Group.

Bloom, Lloyd. The Green Book. Walsh, Jill Paton. 2012. (ENG.). 80p. (J). (gr. 3-7). pap. 6.99 *(978-0-312-64122-1(2))* Square Fish.

Bloom, Suzanne. Girls A to Z. Bunting, Eve. 2013. (ENG.). 32p. (J). (gr. k-2). pap. 6.95 *(978-1-62091-028-3(4))* Boyds Mills Pr.

—Melissa Parkington's Beautiful, Beautiful Hair. Brisson, Pat. 2006. (ENG.). 32p. (J). (gr. 1-3). 16.95 *(978-1-59078-409-9(X))* Boyds Mills Pr.

—My Special Day at Third Street School. Bunting, Eve. 2009. (ENG.). 32p. (J). (gr. k-2). pap. 10.95 *(978-1-59078-745-8(5))* Boyds Mills Pr.

Bloom, Suzanne. Alone Together. Bloom, Suzanne. 2014. (Goose & Bear Stories Ser.). (ENG.). 32p. (J). (gr. -1-k). 16.95 *(978-1-62091-736-7(X))* Boyds Mills Pr.

—The Bus for Us. Bloom, Suzanne. 2013. (ENG.). 32p. (J). (gr. k-2). pap. 6.95 *(978-1-62091-441-0(7))* Boyds Mills Pr.

—Fox Forgets. Bloom, Suzanne. 2013. (Goose & Bear Stories Ser.). (ENG.). 32p. (J). (gr. -1-1). 16.95 *(978-1-59078-996-4(2))* Boyds Mills Pr.

—A Mighty Fine Time Machine. Bloom, Suzanne. 2014. (ENG.). 32p. (J). (gr. k-2). pap. 6.95 *(978-1-62091-605-6(3))* Boyds Mills Pr.

—No Place for a Pig. Bloom, Suzanne. 2003. (ENG.). 32p. (J). (gr. k-2). 15.95 *(978-1-59078-047-3(7))* Boyds Mills Pr.

—A Splendid Friend, Indeed. Bloom, Suzanne. (Goose & Bear Stories Ser.). (ENG.). 32p. (J). (gr. -1-k). 2009. pap. 7.95 *(978-1-59078-488-4(X))*; 2007. 24.95 *(978-1-59078-532-4(0))* Boyds Mills Pr.

Bloom, Tom. Pocketdoodles for Young Artists, 1 vol. Zimmerman, Bill. 2010. (ENG.). 272p. (J). (gr. 1). 9.99 *(978-1-4236-0466-2(0))* Gibbs Smith, Publisher.

Bloomfield, Kevin. Mr. Biggs in the City. Bloomfield, Kevin. 2011. (ENG & SPA.). 32p. (gr. -1-3). lib. bdg. 16.95 *(978-1-936299-26-3(7)*, Raven Tree Pr.,Csi) Continental Sales, Inc.

—Mr. Biggs in the City/El Sr. Grande en la Ciudad. Bloomfield, Kevin. 2011. (ENG & SPA.). 32p. (gr. -1-3). lib. bdg. 16.95 *(978-1-936299-24-9(0)*, Raven Tree Pr.,Csi) Continental Sales, Inc.

Blotnick, Elihu. Glimmins: Children of the Western Woods. Blotnick, Elihu. 2009. 72p. (J). (gr. 1-18). pap. 14.50 *(978-0-915090-18-1(X)*, California Street) Firefall Editions.

Blowars, Ryan, jt. illus. see Smale, Denise L.

Blowers, Lisa. A Cricket's Carol. Moulton, Mark Kimball. 2004. 32p. (J). 14.95 *(978-0-8249-5488-8(2))* Ideals Pubns.

Bloz. Dinosaurs: In the Beginning... Plumeri, Arnaud. 2014. (Dinosaurs Graphic Novels Ser.: 1). (ENG.). 48p. (J). (gr. 3-9). 10.99 *(978-1-59707-490-2(X))* Papercutz.

Blue, Buster. I Know a Rhino. Harrison, Kevin. 2nd rev. ed. 2006. 37p. (J). (gr. -1-3). per. 10.99 *(978-1-59092-223-1(9))* Blue Forge Pr.

—Maxwell Dreams of Trains. Anna, Jennifer. 2009. (ENG.). 88p. (J). 10.99 *(978-1-883573-05-8(X))* Blue Forge Pr.

Blue, Duck Egg, et al. 1 2 3: Touch & Trace Early Learning Fun! 2014. (ENG.). 26p. (J). pap. 13.50 *(978-1-84135-943-4(2))* Award Pubns. Ltd. GBR. Dist: Parkwest Pubns., Inc.

Bluecheese, Wally. The Little Book of Happiness. Heim, Julia & Dami, Elisabetta. 2013. 42p. (J). pap. *(978-0-545-48255-4(0))* Scholastic, Inc.

Bluedorn, Johannah. Bless the Lord: The 103rd Psalm. 2005. 32p. (J). 13.00 *(978-0-9743616-2-8(3)*, 3000) Trivium Pursuit.

Bluedorn, Johannah. Little Bitty Baby Learns Greek. Bluedorn, Johannah. 2006. (GRE & ENG.). 30p. (J). bds. *(978-1-933228-06-8(7))* Trivium Pursuit.

—Little Bitty Baby Learns Hebrew. Bluedorn, Johannah. 2005. 26p. (J). bds. 12.00 *(978-1-933228-00-6(8))* Trivium Pursuit.

—The Lord Builds the House: The 127th Psalm. 2004. 32p. (J). 10.00 *(978-0-9743616-1-1(5))* Trivium Pursuit.

—The Story of Mr. Pippin. Bluedorn, Johannah. 2004. 32p. (J). 12.00 *(978-0-9743616-8-0(2))* Trivium Pursuit.

Bluhm, Joe, jt. illus. see Joyce, William.

Blum, Julia C. What the Sea Wants. Banghart, Tracy E. 2006. 64p. (YA). kivar 16.00 *(978-0-9779753-0-3(4))* LizStar Bks.

Blume, Rebecca. Baby Whales. Blume, Rebecca. 2007. 8p. (J). 5.00 *(978-0-9785427-2-6(X))* Liberty Artists Management.

—When the World Was Green! Blume, Rebecca. 2007. 32p. (J). per. 14.00 *(978-0-9785427-1-9(1))* Liberty Artists Management.

Blundell, Kim, jt. illus. see Cartwright, Stephen.

Blundell, Tony. Chicken Licken. Strong, Jeremy. 2007. (Collins Big Cat Ser.). (ENG.). 136p. (J). pap. 6.99 *(978-0-00-718672-3(X))* HarperCollins Pubs. Ltd. GBR. Dist: Independent Pubs. Group.

—Samosa Thief. Dhami, Narinder. 2005. (ENG.). 24p. (J). lib. bdg. 23.65 *(978-1-59646-708-8(8))* Dingles & Co.

—The Sneezles. Strong, Jeremy. 2005. (Collins Big Cat Ser.). (ENG.). 32p. (J). pap. 7.99 *(978-0-00-718628-0(2))* HarperCollins Pubs. Ltd. GBR. Dist: Independent Pubs. Group.

Blunt, Fred. The Banana Bunch & the Birthday Party! Ziefert, Harriet. 2015. (I Can Read Chapters Ser.). (ENG.). 72p. (J). (gr. k-3). pap. 5.99 *(978-1-60905-460-1(1))* Blue Apple Bks.

—The Banana Bunch & the Magic Show. Ziefert, Harriet. 2015. (I Can Read Chapters Ser.). (ENG.). 72p. (J). (gr. k-3). pap. 5.99 *(978-1-60905-461-8(X))* Blue Apple Bks.

—Cow Takes a Bow. Punter, Russell. 2014. (Usborne Phonics Readers Ser.). (ENG.). (J). pap. 6.99 *(978-0-7945-3368-7(X)*, Usborne) EDC Publishing.

—Croc Gets a Shock. MacKinnon, Mairi. 2014. (Usborne Phonics Readers Ser.). (ENG.). (J). (gr. -1-3). pap. 6.99 *(978-0-7945-3395-3(7)*, Usborne) EDC Publishing.

—The Rabbit's Tale. 2013. (Usborne First Reading: Level 1 Ser.). (ENG.). 32p. (J). (gr. -1-3). 6.99 *(978-0-7945-3346-5(9)*, Usborne) EDC Publishing.

—Snail Brings the Mail. Punter, Russell & MacKinnon, Mairi. 2014. (Usborne Phonics Readers Ser.). (ENG.). (J). pap. 6.99 *(978-0-7945-3369-4(8)*, Usborne) EDC Publishing.

—Underpants for Ants. Punter, Russell. 2014. (Usborne Phonics Readers Ser.). (ENG.). (J). (gr. -1-3). pap. 6.99 *(978-0-7945-3396-0(5)*, Usborne) EDC Publishing.

Bluth, Don. Dragon's Lair, Vol. 1. Mangels, Andy et al. O'Reilly, Sean Patrick, ed. 2008. 164p. (YA). 19.95 *(978-0-9763095-5-0(6))* Arcana Studio, Inc.

Bluthenthal, Diana Cain. I'm a Kid. You're a Baby. 2020. (J). *(978-0-689-85470-5(6))* Simon & Schuster Children's Publishing.

—Just in Case. Viorst, Judith. (ENG.). 40p. (J). (gr. -1-2). 2010. 6.99 *(978-1-4424-1282-8(8))*; 2006. 15.95 *(978-0-689-87164-1(3))* Simon & Schuster Children's Publishing. (Atheneum Bks. for Young Readers).

—The Youngest Fairy Godmother Ever. Krensky, Stephen. 2003. (ENG.). 32p. (J). (gr. -1-1). 13.99 *(978-0-689-86143-7(5)*, Simon & Schuster Bks. For Young Readers) Simon & Schuster Bks. For Young Readers.

Bluthenthal, Diana Cain. I'm Not Invited? Bluthenthal, Diana Cain. 2008. (ENG.). 32p. (J). (gr. -1-2). 10.99 *(978-1-4169-7141-2(6)*, Simon & Schuster/Paula Wiseman Bks.) Simon & Schuster/Paula Wiseman Bks.

Blyth, Eileen. Healthy Air: Book C of Healthy Me, 3 books. Hawthorne, Grace. 2004. 48p. (J). pap. 73.75 *(978-0-944235-49-2(2))* American Cancer Society, Inc.

—Healthy Bodies: Book A of Healthy Me, 3 books. Hawthorne, Grace. 2004. 48p. (J). pap. 73.75 *(978-0-944235-47-8(6))* American Cancer Society, Inc.

—Healthy Food: Book B of Healthy Me, 3 bks. Hawthorne, Grace. 2004. 48p. (J). pap. 73.75 *(978-0-944235-48-5(4))* American Cancer Society, Inc.

—To Whom the Angel Spoke: A Story of the Christmas, 1 vol. Kay, Terry. 2nd ed. 2009. (ENG.). 32p. (J). (gr. k-4). 14.95 *(978-1-56145-502-7(4))* Peachtree Pubs.

Blyth, Eileen C. Healthy Me. Hawthorne, Grace. 2004. (ENG.). 144p. (J). (gr. -1-3). pap., act. bk. ed. 6.95 *(978-0-944235-46-1(8)*, 9780944235461) American Cancer Society, Inc.

Blythe, Gary. Ice Bear: In the Steps of the Polar Bear. Davies, Nicola. 2008. (Read & Wonder Ser.). (ENG.). 32p. (J). (gr. -1-3). pap. 6.99 *(978-0-7636-4149-8(9))* Candlewick Pr.

—Ice Bear with Audio, Peggable: Read, Listen, & Wonder: in the Steps of the Polar Bear. Davies, Nicola. 2009. (Read, Listen, & Wonder Ser.). (ENG.). 32p. (J). (gr. -1-3). pap. 9.99 *(978-0-7636-4441-3(2))* Candlewick Pr.

—The Moon Dragons. Sheldon, Dyan. 2015. (J). *(978-1-4677-6318-9(7))* Lerner Publishing Group.

—Moon Dragons. Sheldon, Dyan. 2015. (ENG.). 32p. (J). (gr. -1-3). 16.95 *(978-1-4677-6314-1(4))* Lerner Publishing Group.

—The Perfect Bear. Shields, Gillian. 2008. (ENG.). 32p. (J). (gr. -1-3). 16.99 *(978-1-4169-5363-0(9)*, Simon & Schuster Bks. For Young Readers) Simon & Schuster Bks. For Young Readers.

—A Treasury of Princess Stories. 2009. (ENG.). 80p. (J). (gr. 2-5). 19.99 *(978-0-7636-4478-9(1))* Candlewick Pr.

Blythe, Philip. Nature Hunt! Bewildering Puzzles of the Animal Kingdom. Blythe, Philip. 2005. 32p. pap., act. bk. ed. *(978-1-877003-82-0(4))* Little Hare Bks. AUS. Dist: HarperCollins Pubs. Australia.

Bo, Lars. The Happy Prince & Other Stories. Wilde, Oscar. 2009. (Puffin Classics Ser.). (ENG.). 224p. (J). (gr. 3-7). pap. 4.99 *(978-0-14-132779-2(0)*, Puffin) Penguin Publishing Group.

Boake, Kathy. Chitchat: Celebrating the World's Languages. Isabella, Jude. 2013. (ENG.). 44p. (J). 17.95 *(978-1-55453-787-7(8))* Kids Can Pr., Ltd. CAN. Dist: Univ. of Toronto Pr.

—You Are Weird: Your Body's Peculiar Parts & Funny Functions. Swanson, Diane. 2009. (ENG.). 40p. (J). (gr. 3-7). 16.95 *(978-1-55453-282-7(5))*; pap. 7.95 *(978-1-55453-283-4(3))* Kids Can Pr., Ltd. CAN. Dist: Univ. of Toronto Pr.

Boam, Jon. Colour Me Menagerie. 2012. (Colour Me Ser.). (ENG.). 24p. (J). (gr. -1-k). 6.00 *(978-1-907704-09-3(4))* Nobrow Ltd. GBR. Dist: Consortium Bk. Sales & Distribution.

Board, Perry. Thomas's Sheep & the Spectacular Science Project, 1 vol. Layne, Steven L. 2004. (ENG.). 32p. (J). (gr. k-3). 16.99 *(978-1-58980-210-0(1))* Pelican Publishing Co., Inc.

Boase, Susan. Lost! - A Dog Called Bear. Orr, Wendy. 2011. (Rainbow Street Shelter Ser.: 1). (ENG.). 112p. (J). (gr. 2-5). 15.99 *(978-0-8050-8931-8(4))*; pap. 5.99 *(978-0-8050-9381-0(8))* Holt, Henry & Co. (Holt, Henry & Co. Bks. For Young Readers).

—Missing! - A Cat Called Buster. Orr, Wendy. 2011. (Rainbow Street Shelter Ser.: 2). (ENG.). 128p. (J). (gr. 2-5). 15.99 *(978-0-8050-8932-5(2)*, Holt, Henry & Co. Bks. For Young Readers) Holt, Henry & Co.

Boatfield, Jonny. The New Empire of Malplaquet. Dalton, Andrew. 2009. (ENG.). 192p. (J). (gr. 4-7). 34.00 *(978-0-7188-3096-0(2))*; pap. 17.00 *(978-0-7188-3093-9(8))* Lutherworth Pr., The GBR. Dist: Casemate Academic.

—Temples of Malplaquet. Dalton, Andrew. 2005. (ENG.). 192p. (C). 34.00 *(978-0-7188-3046-5(6))*; pap. 17.00 *(978-0-7188-3047-2(4))* Lutherworth Pr., The GBR. Dist: Casemate Academic.

Bobak, Cathy. Poetry from A to Z: A Guide for Young Writers. Janeczko, Paul B. 2012. (ENG.). 144p. (J). (gr. 4-7). pap. 8.99 *(978-1-4424-6061-4(X)*, Simon & Schuster Bks. For Young Readers) Simon & Schuster Bks. For Young Readers.

Bobbish, John. Trail Fever: The Life of a Texas Cowboy. Lightfoot, D. J. exp. ed. 2003. 88p. (J). (gr. 3-18). pap. 12.95 *(978-0-9728768-0-3(4))* Seven Rivers Publishing.

Bobillo, Juan. Bird. Trillo, Carlos. 2003. 48p. (YA). (gr. 11-18). 12.95 *(978-1-931724-22-7(9))* Diamond Select Toys & Collectibles.

Bobillo, Juan & Dragotta, Nick. FF, Vol. 3. 2013. (ENG.). 128p. (J). (gr. 4-17). pap. 16.99 *(978-0-7851-6313-8(1))* Marvel Worldwide, Inc.

Bobrizky, George. Steps in Ballet: Basic Exercises at the Barre, Basic Center Exercises, Basic Allegro Steps. Mara, Thalia. 2004. (ENG.). 192p. pap. 19.95 *(978-0-87127-262-1(8)*, Elysian Editions) Princeton Bk. Co. Pubs.

Bocanfuso, Emanuele. The Gold Rush. Jeffrey, Gary. 2012. (Graphic History of the American West Ser.). (ENG.). 24p. (J). (gr. 3-8). pap. 8.15 *(978-1-4339-6741-2(3)*, Gareth Stevens Learning Library) Stevens, Gareth Publishing LLLP.

—Mermaids. Jeffrey, Gary. 2012. (Graphic Mythical Creatures Ser.). (ENG.). 24p. (J). (gr. 3-5). pap. 8.15 *(978-1-4339-6765-8(0))*; lib. bdg. 23.95 *(978-1-4339-6763-4(4))* Stevens, Gareth Publishing LLLP. (Gareth Stevens Learning Library).

Boccardo, Johanna. Sam's Sunflower. Powell, Jillian. 2008. (Tadpoles Ser.). (ENG.). 24p. (J). (gr. -1-3). pap. *(978-0-7787-3895-4(7))*; lib. bdg. *(978-0-7787-3864-0(7))* Crabtree Publishing Co.

—Sam's Sunflower. Powell, Jillian. 2008. (Tadpoles Ser.). 23p. (J). (gr. -1-3). 17.15 *(978-1-4178-0937-0(X)*, Turtleback) Turtleback Bks.

Bocchino, Serena. What Am I? the Story of an Abstract Painting. Bocchino, Serena. l.t. ed. 2005. 32p. (J). per. 19.95 *(978-0-9767674-0-4(6))* Serena Bocchino/In His Perfect Time Collection.

Bocik, Adam. Twelve upon a Time. Galluzzi, Edward. 3rd ed. 2009. 298p. (J). pap. *(978-1-926585-69-7(0))* CCB Publishing.

Bock, Janna. For the Right to Learn. Langston-George, Rebecca. 2015. (Encounter: Narrative Nonfiction Picture Bks.). (ENG.). 40p. (gr. 3-4). 15.95 ***(978-1-62370-426-1(X))*** Encounter Bks.

—For the Right to Learn: Malala Yousafzai's Story. Langston-George, Rebecca. 2015. (Encounter: Narrative Nonfiction Picture Bks.). (ENG.). 40p. (gr. 3-4). lib. bdg. 27.99 ***(978-1-4914-6071-9(7))*** Encounter Bks.

—Gustave Eiffel's Spectacular Idea: The Eiffel Tower. Cooper, Sharon Katz. 2015. (Story Behind the Name Ser.). (ENG.). 32p. (gr. 2-3). lib. bdg. 27.99 ***(978-1-4795-7136-9(9))*** Picture Window Bks.

Bock, Suzanne. In the Beginning: Angels with Attitudes, 2004. 32p. (J). 12.99 *(978-0-9758709-0-7(4)*, 11412) Journey Stone Creations, LLC.

—Meet the Angels. l.t. ed. 2004. 10p. (J). bds. 12.99 *(978-0-9758709-4-5(7)*, 13401) Journey Stone Creations, LLC.

—A Place for the King: Christmas from the Angels Point of View. Stimkorb, Patricia. 2004. 48p. (J). 15.99 *(978-0-9758709-6-9(3)*, 12420) Journey Stone Creations, LLC.

Bock, William Sauts. African Mythology. Altman, Linda Jacobs. 2003. (Mythology Ser.). 112p. (J). lib. bdg. 26.60 *(978-0-7660-2125-9(4))* Enslow Pubs., Inc.

—African Mythology Rocks! Altman, Linda Jacobs. 2011. (Mythology Rocks! Ser.). 112p. (J). (gr. 6-18). pap. 10.95 *(978-1-59845-328-7(9))*; lib. bdg. 33.27 *(978-0-7660-3896-7(3))* Enslow Pubs., Inc.

—Celtic Mythology. Bernard, Catherine. 2003. (Mythology Ser.). 104p. (J). lib. bdg. 27.94 *(978-0-7660-2204-1(8))* Enslow Pubs., Inc.

—Celtic Mythology Rocks! Bernard, Catherine. 2011. (Mythology Rocks! Ser.). 104p. (J). (gr. 6-18). pap. 10.95 *(978-1-59845-326-3(2))*; lib. bdg. 33.27 *(978-0-7660-3895-0(5))* Enslow Pubs., Inc.

—Chinese Mythology Rocks! Collier, Irene Dea. 2011. (Mythology Rocks! Ser.). 128p. (J). (gr. 6-18). pap. 10.95 *(978-1-59845-330-0(0))*; lib. bdg. 33.27 *(978-0-7660-3898-1(X))* Enslow Pubs., Inc.

—Gods & Goddesses in Greek Mythology Rock! Houle, Michelle M. 2011. (Mythology Rocks! Ser.). 128p. (J). (gr. 6-18). pap. 10.95 *(978-1-59845-329-4(7))*; lib. bdg. 33.27 *(978-0-7660-3897-4(1))* Enslow Pubs., Inc.

—Heroes in Greek Mythology Rock! Spies, Karen Bornemann. 2011. (Mythology Rocks! Ser.). 128p. (J). (gr. 6-18). pap. 10.95 *(978-1-59845-331-7(9))*; lib. bdg. 33.27 *(978-0-7660-3900-1(5))* Enslow Pubs., Inc.

—Maya & Aztec Mythology Rocks! Schuman, Michael A. 2011. (Mythology Rocks! Ser.). 128p. (J). (gr. 6-18). pap. 10.95 *(978-1-59845-327-0(0))*; lib. bdg. 33.27 *(978-0-7660-3899-8(8))* Enslow Pubs., Inc.

—The Shore Ghosts & Other Stories of New Jersey. Homer, Larona. 2005. 154p. (J). (gr. 4-8). pap. *(978-0-912608-82-2(X))* Middle Atlantic Pr.

Bocquée, Christian. Lucy & the Red Street Boyz. Collins, Paul. 2015. (Legends in Their Own Lunchbox Ser.). (ENG.). 56p. (gr. 2-3). pap. 7.99 ***(978-1-4966-0260-2(9)***, Legends in Their Own Lunchbox) Capstone Classroom.

—Lucy in a Jam. Collins, Paul. 2015. (Legends in Their Own Lunchbox Ser.). (ENG.). 48p. (gr. 1-2). pap. 7.99 ***(978-1-4966-0248-0(X)***, Legends in Their Own Lunchbox) Capstone Classroom.

—Lucy, Kung-Fu Queen. Collins, Paul. 2015. (Legends in Their Own Lunchbox Ser.). (ENG.). 48p. (gr. 1-2). pap. 7.99 ***(978-1-4966-0242-8(0)***, Legends in Their Own Lunchbox) Capstone Classroom.

—Lucy, the Boss. Collins, Paul. 2015. (Legends in Their Own Lunchbox Ser.). (ENG.). 56p. (gr. 2-3). pap. 7.99 ***(978-1-4966-0254-1(4)***, Legends in Their Own Lunchbox) Capstone Classroom.

Bodart, Denis. Green Manor: The Inconvenience of Being Dead. Vehlmann, Fabien. 2008. (ENG.). 96p. pap. 19.95 *(978-1-905460-64-9(3))* CineBook GBR. Dist: National Bk. Network.

—Green Manor Pt. 1: Assassins & Gentleman. Vehlmann, Fabien. 2008. (ENG.). 56p. pap. 13.95 *(978-1-905460-53-3(8))* CineBook GBR. Dist: National Bk. Network.

Boddy, James & Moon, Paul. Joni-Pip. King, Carrie. 2010. 476p. pap. *(978-0-9555246-9-1(5))* Bothy Bks., Corwall, A Div. of Grace & Patrick Pubs., Ltd.

Boddy, Joe. Hidden Picture Mania. Daste, Larry et al. 2006. (Dover Children's Activity Bks.). (ENG.). 96p. (J). (gr. 3-6). per. 7.95 *(978-0-486-45911-0(X))* Dover Pubns., Inc.

—Lucy Goose Goes to Texas. Bea, Holly. 2005. (ENG.). 32p. (J). (gr. -1-5). 15.95 *(978-1-932073-15-7(9))* New World Library.

Bodecker, N. M. Half Magic. Eager, Edward. 50th anniv. ed. 2004. (Tales of Magic Ser.: 1). (ENG.). 217p. (J). (gr. 2-5). 19.95 *(978-0-15-205302-4(6))* Houghton Mifflin Harcourt Publishing Co.

Bodeker, Brian. The Little Crescent Moon & the Bright Evening Star. Humann, Walter J. 2nd ed. (J). (gr. -1-5). pap. 9.95 *(978-0-9674864-1-3(6))* WJH Publishing.

Bodel, Itai, photos by. The Amazing Fishing Rod. Herzog, Pearl. 2013. 34p. (J). *(978-1-4226-1436-5(0))* Mesorah Pubns., Ltd.

Bodett, Tom. My Farm Friends. Minor, Wendell. 2012. 29.95 *(978-1-4301-1096-5(1))* Live Oak Media.

Bodger, Lorraine, jt. illus. see Montez, Michele.

Bodily, Michael. The Smart Way to Be. Knudsen, Sherilyn. 2005. 32p. (J). per. 9.95 *(978-0-9768451-0-2(5))* HPN Publishing.

Bodmer, Karl. The Piikani Blackfeet: A Culture under Siege. Catlin, George, photos by. Jackson, John C. rev. ed. 276p. (J). (gr. 4). pap. *(978-0-87842-386-6(9)*, 649) Mountain Pr. Publishing Co., Inc.

Bodoff, Janet. Eat Your Vegetables. Toscano, Leesa. 2012. 24p. pap. 24.95 *(978-1-4626-5278-5(6))* America Star Bks.

Boedoe, Geefwee. Arrowville. Boedoe, Geefwee. 2004. 40p. (J). (gr. -1-2). 16.89 *(978-0-06-055599-3(8)*, Geringer, Laura Book) HarperCollins Pubs.

Boelter, Ashaki. Diaries of the Doomed. Boelter, Ashaki. 2004. 88p. (YA). per. 6.95 *(978-0-9721067-4-0(X)*, Writing Wild & Crazy) Shakalot High Entertainment.

Boey, Stephanie. I Want to Be a Great White Shark. Troupe, Thomas Kingsley. 2015. (I Want to Be... Ser.). (ENG.). 24p. (gr. k-3). lib. bdg. 25.99 ***(978-1-4795-6859-8(7))*** Capstone Pr., Inc.

Boey, Stephanie. Little Lamb to the Rescue. Briers, Erica. 2004. (ENG.). 24p. (J). *(978-1-55168-257-0(5))* Fenn, H. B. & Co., Ltd.

—The Little Moose. Martin, Ruth. 2008. (ENG.). 35p. (J). *(978-1-55168-332-4(6))* Fenn, H. B. & Co., Ltd.

—Little Seal Finds a Friend. Harris, Sue. 2007. (ENG.). 24p. (J). *(978-1-55168-295-2(8))* Fenn, H. B. & Co., Ltd.

—Runaway Chick. Briers, Erica. 2006. (ENG.). 24p. (J). *(978-1-55168-314-0(8))* Fenn, H. B. & Co., Ltd.

Bofinger, Manfred. Charly, el Ratón Cazagatos. Bofinger, Manfred, tr. Fuchs, Gerd. 4th ed. 2007. (SPA.). 79p. (J). pap. 10.99 *(978-84-207-9006-0(0))* Lectorum Pubns., Inc.

Bogacki, Tomek. Big Box for Ben, 1 vol. Bruss, Deborah. 2011. (ENG.). 32p. (J). (gr. -1-k). bds. 6.95 *(978-1-59572-265-2(3))* Star Bright Bks., Inc.

—Cinco Criaturas. Jenkins, Emily. Cortes, Eunice, tr. 2003. (Picture Bks.).Tr. of Five Creatures. (SPA.). (J). *(978-970-690-648-9(7))* Planeta Mexicana Editorial S. A. de C. V.

—Five Creatures. Jenkins, Emily. 2005. (ENG.). 32p. (J). (gr. -1-1). reprint ed. per. 8.99 *(978-0-374-42328-5(8))* Square Fish.

—Mole Catches the Sky. Tarlow, Ellen. 2014. (ENG.). (J). 16.99 *(978-1-59572-656-8(X))* Star Bright Bks., Inc.

—El Pajaro, el Mono y la Serpiente en la Selva. Banks, Kate. (SPA.). 24p. (J). (gr. k-2). *(978-84-261-3129-4(8)*, JV2823) Juventud, Editorial ESP. Dist: Lectorum Pubns., Inc.

—Small, Medium, Large, 1 vol. Jenkins, Emily. 2011. (ENG.). 32p. (J). 19.95 *(978-1-59572-278-2(5))* Star Bright Bks., Inc.

—Small Medium Large, 1 vol. Jenkins, Emily. 2011. (ENG.). 32p. (J). pap. 12.95 *(978-1-59572-299-7(8))* Star Bright Bks., Inc.

Bogacki, Tomek. The Champion of Children: The Story of Janusz Korczak. Bogacki, Tomek. 2009. (ENG.). 40p. (J). (gr. 1-5). 17.99 *(978-0-374-34136-7(2)*, Farrar, Straus & Giroux (BYR)) Farrar, Straus & Giroux.

Bogade, Maria. Ben's Flying Flowers. Maier, Inger M. 2012. (J). 14.95 *(978-1-4338-1133-3(2))*; pap. 9.95 *(978-1-4338-1132-6(4))* American Psychological Assn. (Magination Pr.).

—Healing Days: A Guide for Kids Who Have Experienced Trauma. Straus, Susan Farber. 2013. 32p. (J). *(978-1-4338-1292-7(4))*; pap. *(978-1-4338-1293-4(2))* American Psychological Assn.

—The Lost (and Found) Balloon. Jenkins, Celeste. 2013. (ENG.). 32p. (J). (gr. -1-3). 16.99 *(978-1-4424-6697-5(9)*, Simon & Schuster/Paula Wiseman Bks.) Simon & Schuster/Paula Wiseman Bks.

Bogan, Lyuba. What God Wants for Christmas: Read along, Sing Along. Bradford, Amy L. 2006. 20p. (J). (gr. 4-7). 14.99 incl. audio compact disk *(978-1-57229-914-6(2))* FamilyLife.

Bogan, Paulette. Buffalo Wings. Reynolds, Aaron. 2007. (ENG.). 32p. (J). (gr. -1-3). 16.95 *(978-1-59990-062-9(9)*, Bloomsbury USA Childrens) Bloomsbury USA.

—Chicks & Salsa. Reynolds, Aaron. 2007. (ENG.). 32p. (J). (gr. 1-3). pap. 7.99 *(978-1-59990-099-5(8)*, Bloomsbury USA Childrens) Bloomsbury USA.

Bogdan, Enache. The Boy Who Cried Wolf. Sommer, Carl. 2014. (Sommer-Time Story Classics Ser.). (ENG.). 32p. (J). (gr. k-4). 16.95 *(978-1-57537-079-8(4))* Advance Publishing, Inc.

—The Silent Scream. Sommer, Carl & Aesop. 2009. (Quest for Success Ser.). (ENG.). 40p. (YA). pap. 4.95 *(978-1-57537-285-3(1))*; lib. bdg. 12.95 *(978-1-57537-260-0(6))* Advance Publishing, Inc.

—The Silent Scream(El Grito Silencioso) Sommer, Carl & Aesop. ed. 2009. (Quest for Success Bilingual Ser.). (SPA & ENG.). 72p. (YA). lib. bdg. 14.95 *(978-1-57537-235-8(5))* Advance Publishing, Inc.

Bogdanovic, Toma. The Snow Queen. Andersen, Hans Christian. adapted ed. 32p. (J). (gr. -1-5). 16.95 *(978-0-87592-048-1(9))* Scroll Pr., Inc.

Bogdanovic, Toma, jt. illus. see Van Nutt, Robert.

Boger-Bass, Vallerie. The Mustard Seed: A Christian Promise. Boger-Bass, Vallerie. 2003. 40p. pap. 10.00 *(978-0-8059-5640-5(9))* Dorrance Publishing Co., Inc.

Boggelen-Heutink, Ellen van. The Incredible Adventures of Captain Cameron MacDuddyfunk in Cuggermuggerland. Simons, Alan L. 2013. 98p. pap. *(978-0-9877503-8-9(0))* Baronel Bks.

Bohart, Lisa. The Blue Lobster. Taylor-Chiarello, Robin. 2011. 36p. pap. 15.95 *(978-1-936343-84-3(3))* Peppertree Pr., The.

—The Blue Lobster's Holiday! Chiarello, Robin Taylor. 2012. 40p. pap. 16.95 *(978-1-61493-053-2(8))* Peppertree Pr., The.

—The Christmas Horse. Cooper, Margaret. 2008. 32p. pap. 12.95 *(978-0-9821654-9-2(8))* Peppertree Pr., The.

—Christmas on the Internet. Bizzarro, Grace. 2013. 20p. pap. 12.95 *(978-1-61493-197-3(6))* Peppertree Pr., The.

—The Clam Diggers Ball. Chiarello, Robin Taylor. 2011. 40p. pap. 15.95 *(978-1-61493-013-6(9))* Peppertree Pr., The.

—The Croaker Sack Bunny. Harris, Dee. 2012. 24p. pap. 12.95 *(978-1-61493-043-3(0))* Peppertree Pr., The.

—Donkeys Are Special & So Are You! Krueger, T. W. 2013. (ENG.). 46p. (J). 12.99 *(978-0-9887454-0-7(2))* Donkey Publishing.

—I Am Not a Hippopotamus, I Am a Little Girl , Book. Harris, Dee. 2011. 24p. pap. 12.95 *(978-1-61493-005-1(8))* Peppertree Pr., The.

—Murky, Quirky, Beserky Math. Desjardins, Margaret M. 2013. 24p. pap. 13.95 *(978-1-61493-210-9(7))* Peppertree Pr., The.

—A Ribbon for Diego. Miranda, Edward. 2008. 28p. pap. 12.95 *(978-0-9821654-5-4(5))* Peppertree Pr., The.

—Sadie the Ladybug. Cross, Jenny. 2009. 44p. pap. 14.95 *(978-1-936051-39-7(7))* Peppertree Pr., The.

—Signs of Love. Nelson, Jan. 2009. 24p. pap. 12.95 *(978-1-936051-54-0(0))* Peppertree Pr., The.

Bohlmann, Siegfried. Dr. Rabbit. Hare, Eric B. fac. ed. 2010. 127p. per. 11.95 *(978-1-57258-278-1(2)*, 945-6131) TEACH Services, Inc.

Bohman, Jennifer White. Snowy Owls: Whoo Are They? Ford, Ansley Watson & Holt, Denver W. 2008. 68p. (J). (gr. 3-7). pap. 12.00 *(978-0-87842-543-3(8))* Mountain Pr. Publishing Co., Inc.

Bohman, Natasha. David's Big Break. Loever, Charmaine. 2008. 52p. pap. 22.99 *(978-1-4389-3173-9(5))* AuthorHouse.

Bohn, Ken & Garrison, Ron. San Diego Zoo. Bohn, Ken & Garrison, Ron, photos by. Pearce, Claudia & Worley, Karen E. 2003. (Great Zoos of the United States Ser.). 24p. (J). lib. bdg. 22.60 *(978-0-8239-6321-8(7)*, PowerKids Pr.) Rosen Publishing Group, Inc., The.

Bohn, Kendall. The Original Abstract Adventure. 2009. 54p. pap. 8.95 *(978-0-929636-99-3(6))* Syren Bk. Co.

Bohn, Klaus. Healthy Me: I Love Fruit, I Love Veggies. Bohn, Klaus. 2012. (ENG.). 44p. (J). pap. *(978-1-77143-034-0(6)*, CCB Publishing) CCB Publishing.

Bohnet, Christopher, jt. illus. see VanDeWeghe, Lindsay.

Bohrer, Joe. Red & Slim: One Hot Day. Stamp, Jeffrey. 2008. 40p. (J). 16.99 *(978-0-9794543-0-1(1))* Syllabets, LLC.

Boiger, Alexandra. Doctor All-Knowing: A Folk Tale from the Brothers Grimm. Grimm, Jacob & Grimm, Wilhelm K. 2008. (ENG.). 40p. (J). (gr. -1-1). 16.99 *(978-1-4169-1246-0(0)*, Atheneum/Richard Jackson Bks.) Simon & Schuster Children's Publishing.

—Happy Birthday, Mrs. Piggle-Wiggle. MacDonald, Betty & Canham, Anne MacDonald. 2008. (ENG.). 208p. (J). (gr. 3-7). pap. 6.99 *(978-0-06-072814-4(0))* HarperCollins Pubs.

—Happy Birthday, Mrs. Piggle-Wiggle. MacDonald, Betty. 2007. (Mrs. Piggle-Wiggle Ser.). 193p. (J). (gr. 3-7). lib. bdg. 16.89 *(978-0-06-072813-7(2))* HarperCollins Pubs.

—Happy Birthday, Mrs. Piggle-Wiggle. MacDonald, Betty & Canham, Anne MacDonald. 2007. (Mrs. Piggle-Wiggle Ser.). (ENG.). 208p. (J). (gr. 3-7). 16.99 *(978-0-06-072812-0(4))* HarperCollins Pubs.

—The Little Bit Scary People. Jenkins, Emily. 2008. (ENG.). 32p. (gr. -1-1). 16.99 *(978-1-4231-0075-1(1))* Hyperion Pr.

—The Magical Animal Adoption Agency, Book 1 Clover's Luck. George, Kallie. 2015. (Magical Animal Adoption Agency Ser.). (ENG.). 138p. (J). (gr. 2-5). 14.99 *(978-1-4231-8382-2(7))* Hyperion Bks. for Children.

—The Monster Princess. MacHale, D. J. 2010. (ENG.). 40p. (J). (gr. -1-1). 17.99 *(978-1-4169-4809-4(0)*, Simon & Schuster/Paula Wiseman Bks.) Simon & Schuster/Paula Wiseman Bks.

—Mrs. Piggle-Wiggle. MacDonald, Betty Bard. rev. ed. 2007. (Trophy Bk.). (ENG.). 144p. (J). (gr. 3-7). pap. 5.99 *(978-0-06-440148-7(0))* HarperCollins Pubs.

—Pirate vs. Pirate: The Terrific Tale of a Big, Blustery Maritime Match. Quattlebaum, Mary. 2011. (ENG.). 40p. (J). (gr. -1-3). 16.99 *(978-1-4231-2201-2(1))* Hyperion Pr.

—Poor Doreen: a Fishy Tale. Lloyd-Jones, Sally. 2014. (ENG.). 40p. (J). (gr. -1-3). 17.99 *(978-0-375-86918-1(2)*, Schwartz & Wade Bks.) Random Hse. Children's Bks.

—Roxie & the Hooligans. Naylor, Phyllis Reynolds. 2007. 115p. (gr. 2-5). 16.00 *(978-0-7569-8284-3(7))* Perfection Learning Corp.

—Roxie & the Hooligans. Naylor, Phyllis Reynolds. (ENG.). 128p. (J). 2007. (gr. 3-5). pap. 6.99 *(978-1-4169-0244-7(9)*, Simon & Schuster/Paula Wiseman Bks.); 2006. (gr. 2-5). 17.99 *(978-1-4169-0243-0(0)*, Atheneum Bks. for Young Readers) Simon & Schuster Children's Publishing.

—Take Your Mama to Work Today. Reichert, Amy. 2012. (ENG.). 40p. (J). (gr. -1-8). 16.99 *(978-1-4169-7095-8(9)*, Atheneum Bks. for Young Readers) Simon & Schuster Children's Publishing.

—Tallulah's Nutcracker. Singer, Marilyn. 2013. (ENG.). 48p. (J). (gr. -1-3). 16.99 *(978-0-547-84557-9(X))* Houghton Mifflin Harcourt Publishing Co.

—Tallulah's Solo. Singer, Marilyn. 2012. (ENG.). 40p. (J). (gr. -1-3). 16.99 *(978-0-547-33004-4(9))* Houghton Mifflin Harcourt Publishing Co.

—Tallulah's Tap Shoes. Singer, Marilyn. 2015. (ENG.). 48p. (J). (gr. -1-3). 16.99 *(978-0-544-23687-5(4))* Houghton Mifflin Harcourt Publishing Co.

—Tallulah's Toe Shoes. Singer, Marilyn. 2013. (ENG.). 48p. (J). (gr. -1-3). 16.99 *(978-0-547-48223-1(X))* Houghton Mifflin Harcourt Publishing Co.

—Tallulah's Tutu. Singer, Marilyn. 2011. (ENG.). 40p. (J). (gr. -1-3). 16.99 *(978-0-547-17353-5(9))* Houghton Mifflin Harcourt Publishing Co.

—While Mama Had a Quick Little Chat. Reichert, Amy. 2005. (ENG.). 40p. (J). (gr. -1-2). 16.99 *(978-0-689-85170-4(7)*, Atheneum/Richard Jackson Bks.) Simon & Schuster Children's Publishing.

Boiger, Alexandra, jt. illus. see Knight, Hilary.

Boisrond, H. The Sean Alexander Series: Loughngoon. Boisrond, H. 2011. (ENG.). 166p. pap. 7.99 *(978-1-4563-0563-5(8))* CreateSpace Independent Publishing Platform.

Bojesen, Niels Bo. Vitello Becomes a Businessman. Aakeson, Kim Fupz & Garde, Ruth. 2014. (ENG.). 32p. (YA). (gr. k-3). pap. 9.99 *(978-1-78269-001-6(8)*, Pushkin Children's Bks.) Pushkin Pr., Ltd. GBR. Dist: Random Hse., Inc.

—Vitello Carries a Knife. Aakeson, Kim Fupz & Garde, Ruth. 2014. (ENG.). 32p. (YA). (gr. k-3). pap. 9.99 *(978-1-78269-005-4(0)*, Pushkin Children's Bks.) Pushkin Pr., Ltd. GBR. Dist: Random Hse., Inc.

—Vitello Gets a Yucky Girlfriend. Aakeson, Kim Fupz & Garde, Ruth. 2014. (ENG.). 32p. (YA). (gr. k-3). pap. 9.99 *(978-1-78269-003-0(4)*, Pushkin Children's Bks.) Pushkin Pr., Ltd. GBR. Dist: Random Hse., Inc.

—Vitello Scratches a Car. Aakeson, Kim Fupz & Garde, Ruth. 2014. (ENG.). 32p. (YA). (gr. k-3). pap. 9.99 *(978-1-78269-002-3(6)*, Pushkin Children's Bks.) Pushkin Pr., Ltd. GBR. Dist: Random Hse., Inc.

—Vitello Wants a Dad. Aakeson, Kim Fupz & Garde, Ruth. 2014. (ENG.). 32p. (YA). (gr. k-3). pap. 9.99 *(978-1-78269-004-7(2)*, Pushkin Children's Bks.) Pushkin Pr., Ltd. GBR. Dist: Random Hse., Inc.

Bolaffio, Raffaella. The Raven & the Fox, 1 vol. Piumini, Roberto & Aesop. 2011. (Storybook Classics Ser.). (ENG.). 32p. (gr. 3-4). lib. bdg. 25.32 *(978-1-4048-6502-0(0)*, Fiction Picture Bks.) Picture Window Bks.

Bolam, Emily. Around Town. 2013. (Peekabooks Ser.). (ENG.). 8p. (J). (gr. -1 — 1). bds. 5.99 *(978-0-7641-6627-3(1))* Barron's Educational Series, Inc.

—Building Site. 2013. (Peekabooks Ser.). (ENG.). 8p. (J). (gr. -1 — 1). bds. 5.99 *(978-0-7641-6628-0(X))* Barron's Educational Series, Inc.

—Bunny Money. Krensky, Stephen. 2011. (ENG.). 16p. (J). (gr. -1-2). pap. 5.99 *(978-1-4424-0888-3(X)*, Little Simon) Little Simon.

—Can You Play?, Linn, Margot. 2005. (I'm Going to Read(r) Ser.: Level 1). (ENG.). 28p. (J). (gr. -1-k). pap. 3.95 *(978-1-4027-2094-9(7))* Sterling Publishing Co., Inc.

—Colors. 2009. 10p. (J). (gr. -1-k). 5.95 *(978-1-58925-845-7(2))* Tiger Tales.

—Counting. 2009. 10p. (J). (gr. -1-k). 5.95 *(978-1-58925-846-4(0))* Tiger Tales.

—Does a Bear Wear Boots? Ziefert, Harriet. 2014. (Think About... Ser.). (ENG.). 32p. (J). (gr. -1-2). 12.99 *(978-1-60905-424-3(5))* Blue Apple Bks.

—Does a Beaver Sleep in a Bed? Ziefert, Harriet. 2014. (Think About... Ser.). (ENG.). 32p. (J). (gr. -1-2). 12.99 *(978-1-60905-423-6(7))* Blue Apple Bks.

—Does a Camel Cook Spaghetti? Think about... How Everyone Gets Food. Ziefert, Harriet. 2014. (Think About... Ser.). (ENG.). 32p. (J). (gr. -1-2). 12.99 *(978-1-60905-422-9(9))* Blue Apple Bks.

—Does a Hippo Go to the Doctor? Ziefert, Harriet. 2014. (Think About... Ser.). (ENG.). 32p. (J). (-k). 12.99 *(978-1-60905-450-2(4))* Blue Apple Bks.

—Does a Panda Go to School? Think about... How Everyone Learns. Ziefert, Harriet. 2014. (Think About... Ser.). (ENG.). 32p. (J). (gr. -1-2). 12.99 *(978-1-60905-421-2(0))* Blue Apple Bks.

—Does a Seal Smile? Ziefert, Harriet. 2014. (Think About... Ser.). (ENG.). 32p. (J). (-k). 12.99 *(978-1-60905-449-6(0))* Blue Apple Bks.

—Does a Tiger Go to the Dentist? Ziefert, Harriet. 2014. (Think About... Ser.). (ENG.). 32p. (J). (-k). 12.99 *(978-1-60905-451-9(2))* Blue Apple Bks.

—Does a Woodpecker Use a Hammer? Ziefert, Harriet. 2014. (Think About... Ser.). (ENG.). 32p. (J). (gr. -1-2). 12.99 *(978-1-60905-428-1(8))* Blue Apple Bks.

—Does an Owl Wear Eyeglasses? Ziefert, Harriet. 2014. (Think About... Ser.). (ENG.). 32p. (J). (-k). 12.99 *(978-1-60905-470-0(9))* Blue Apple Bks.

—Down in the Daisies. Coats, Lucy. 2004. 32p. pap. 8.95 *(978-1-84255-210-0(4)*, Dolphin Paperbacks) Orion Publishing Group, Ltd. GBR. Dist: Trafalgar Square Publishing.

—Father's Day Is Coming! 2007. (I'm Going to Read(r) Ser.: No. 2). (ENG.). 32p. (J). (gr. -1-k). pap. 3.95 *(978-1-4027-4247-7(9))* Sterling Publishing Co., Inc.

—Hello, Animals! Prasadam, Smriti. 2010. (Black & White Sparklers Ser.). 10p. (J). (gr. -1). bds. 5.95 *(978-1-58925-861-7(4))* Tiger Tales.

—Hello, Bugs! Prasadam, Smriti. 2010. (Black & White Sparklers Ser.). 10p. (J). (gr. -1). bds. 5.95 *(978-1-58925-862-4(2))* Tiger Tales.

—Hey, Baby, It's Time to Come Out! Ziefert, Harriet. 2015. (ENG.). 32p. (J). (-k). 14.99 *(978-1-60905-515-8(2))* Blue Apple Bks.

—In the Beginning - Bible Stories for Little Hands. Rock, Lois. 2014. (Bible Stories for Little Hands Ser.). (ENG.). 8p. (J). (gr. -1 — 1). bds. 8.99 *(978-0-7459-6449-2(4))* Lion Hudson PLC GBR. Dist: Independent Pubs. Group.

—In the Jungle. 2013. (Peekabooks Ser.). (ENG.). 8p. (J). (gr. -1 — 1). bds. 5.99 *(978-0-7641-6629-7(8))* Barron's Educational Series, Inc.

—Jesus Is Born: A Spot-the-Difference Jigsaw Book. Rock, Lois. 2014. (Bible Stories for Little Hands Ser.). (ENG.). 8p. (J). (gr. -1 — 1). bds. 8.99 *(978-0-7459-6450-8(8))* Lion Hudson PLC GBR. Dist: Independent Pubs. Group.

—Jesus, the Good Shepherd. St. Pierre, Stephanie. 2003. 14p. (J). bds. 7.99 *(978-0-7847-1272-6(7)*, 04032) Standard Publishing.

—Jogger's Big Adventure. Simon, Francesca. 2013. (Early Reader: Buffin Street Ser.). (ENG.). 64p. (J). (gr. k-2). 7.99 *(978-1-4440-0202-7(3)*, Orion Children's Bks.) Hachette Children's Group GBR. Dist: Independent Pubs. Group.

—Look at Me. Simon, Francesca. 2013. (Early Reader: Buffin Street Ser.). (ENG.). 60p. (J). (gr. k-2). 7.99 *(978-1-4440-0468-7(9)*, Orion Children's Bks.) Hachette Children's Group GBR. Dist: Independent Pubs. Group.

—The Lost Sheep & Other Bible Stories for Little Hands. Rock, Lois. 2014. (Bible Stories for Little Hands Ser.). (ENG.). 8p. (J). (gr. -1 — 1). bds. 8.99 *(978-0-7459-6451-5(6))* Lion Hudson PLC GBR. Dist: Independent Pubs. Group.

—Miaow Miaow Bow Wow. Simon, Francesca. 2013. (Early Reader: Buffin Street Ser.). (ENG.). 64p. (J). (gr. k-2). 7.99 *(978-1-4440-0470-0(0)*, Orion Children's Bks.) Hachette Children's Group GBR. Dist: Independent Pubs. Group.

—Noah's Ark: A Spot-the-Difference Jigsaw Book. Rock, Lois. 2014. (Bible Stories for Little Hands Ser.). (ENG.). 8p. (J). (gr. -1 — 1). bds. 8.99 *(978-0-7459-6442-3(7))* Lion Hudson PLC GBR. Dist: Independent Pubs. Group.

—Rampage in Prince's Garden. Simon, Francesca. 2013. (Early Reader: Buffin Street Ser.). (ENG.). 80p. (J). (gr. k-2). 7.99 *(978-1-4440-0201-0(5)*, Orion Children's Bks.) Hachette Children's Group GBR. Dist: Independent Pubs. Group.

—Under the Sea. 2013. (Peekabooks Ser.). (ENG.). 8p. (J). (gr. -1 — 1). bds. 5.99 *(978-0-7641-6630-3(1))* Barron's Educational Series, Inc.

—Yum Yum. Simon, Francesca. 2013. (Early Reader: Buffin Street Ser.). (ENG.). 80p. (J). (gr. k-2). 7.99 *(978-1-4440-0200-3(7)*, Orion Children's Bks.) Hachette Children's Group GBR. Dist: Independent Pubs. Group.

Bolam, Emily. Bouncy Garden, 4. Bolam, Emily. 2012. (ENG.). 8p. (J). (gr. k — 1). bds. 7.99 *(978-0-230-74145-4(2))* Macmillan Pubs., Ltd. GBR. Dist: Independent Pubs. Group.

—Farmyard Friends. Bolam, Emily. 2011. (ENG.). 8p. (J). (gr. -1-k). bds. 10.99 *(978-0-230-71293-5(2))* Macmillan Pubs., Ltd. GBR. Dist: Independent Pubs. Group.

Bolam, Emily. The Copy Crocs. Bolam, Emily, tr. Bedford, David. 2004. (ENG.). 32p. (J). (gr. k-3). 15.95 *(978-1-56145-304-7(8))* Peachtree Pubs.

Bolan, Michael. Stella Eats Out. Stephens, Ann Marie. 2004. 32p. (J). per. 12.95 *(978-0-9729285-2-6(9)*, 2-9) Kinkachoo Pr., The.

Bolan, Michael P. Christmas for Bly & Ray. Stephens, Ann Marie. 2003. 45p. (J). per. 11.95 *(978-0-9729285-0-2(2)*, 0-9729285-0-2) Kinkachoo Pr., The.

—A Surprise for Ray. Stephens, Ann Marie. 2003. 47p. (J). per. 11.95 *(978-0-9729285-1-9(0)*, 0-9729285-1-0) Kinkachoo Pr., The.

Boldi, Florina. Pug in Boots. 2013. 42p. pap. 9.99 *(978-0-9829132-6-0(5))* Left Paw Pr.

Boldman, Craig. Los Marines. Entin, Cindy. 2014. (ENG & SPA.). 10p. (J). bds. 5.99 *(978-1-60433-458-6(4)*, Applesauce Pr.) Cider Mill Pr. Bk. Pubs., LLC.

—My First Counting Book: Firefighters. Entin, Cindy. 2014. (ENG.). 10p. (J). bds. 5.99 *(978-1-60433-470-8(3)*, Applesauce Pr.) Cider Mill Pr. Bk. Pubs., LLC.

—My First Counting Book: Police. Entin, Cindy. 2014. (ENG.). 10p. (J). bds. 5.99 *(978-1-60433-456-2(8)*, Applesauce Pr.) Cider Mill Pr. Bk. Pubs., LLC.

Boldt, Claudia. Star Gazers, Skyscrapers & Extraordinary Sausages. Boldt, Claudia. 2010. (Child's Play Library). (ENG.). 32p. (J). (gr. -1-3). pap. *(978-1-84643-344-3(4))* Child's Play International Ltd.

—Uugghh! Boldt, Claudia. 2011. (Child's Play Library). (ENG.). 32p. (J). *(978-1-84643-372-6(X))* Child's Play International Ltd.

Boldt, Fabienne & Wensell, Ulises. In the Meadow. Linke, Uwe. 2007. (Moving Book Ser.). (ENG.). 20p. (J). bds. 11.95 *(978-0-7358-2126-2(7))* North-South Bks., Inc.

Boldt, Mike. I Don't Want to Be a Frog. Petty, Dev. 2015. (ENG.). 32p. (J). (gr. -1-2). lib. bdg. 19.99 *(978-0-375-97334-5(6)*, Doubleday Bks. for Young Readers) Random Hse. Children's Bks.

—Tiara Saurus Rex. Sayres, Brianna Caplan. 2015. (ENG.). 32p. (J). (gr. -1-1). 16.99 *(978-1-61963-263-9(2)*, Bloomsbury USA Childrens) Bloomsbury USA.

Boldt, Mike. Colors Versus Shapes. Boldt, Mike. 2014. (ENG.). 40p. (J). (gr. -1-3). 16.99 *(978-0-06-210303-1(2))* HarperCollins Pubs.

—123 Versus ABC. Boldt, Mike. 2013. (ENG.). 32p. (J). (gr. -1-3). 17.99 *(978-0-06-210299-7(0))* HarperCollins Pubs.

Boles, Terry. I Can Do It! I Can Bowl!/I Can Ski!/I Can Do It All. Johns, Linda & Jones, Melanie Davis. 2006. (ENG.). 93p. (J). (gr. k-2). 9.95 *(978-0-531-16923-0(5)*, Children's Pr.) Scholastic Library Publishing.

—I Can Ski! Jones, Melanie Davis. 2003. (Rookie Readers Ser.). 32p. (J). 19.50 *(978-0-516-22878-5(1)*, Children's Pr.) Scholastic Library Publishing.

Bolick, Brian. So, Where do all the teeth Go? Saunders, Helen. 2006. (J). *(978-0-9763143-3-2(9))* Happy Heart Kids Publishing.

Bolland, Brian, et al. Banzai Battalion: Just Another Bug Hunt. Wagner, John. 2014. (ENG.). 160p. pap. 19.99 *(978-1-78108-218-8(9)*, 2000 AD) Rebellion GBR. Dist: Simon & Schuster, Inc.

Bolland, Brian. Doom Patrol - Magic Bus, Vol. 5. Morrison, Grant et al. rev. ed. 2007. (ENG.). 280p. pap. 19.99 *(978-1-4012-1202-5(6)*, Vertigo) DC Comics.

Bolle, Frank. My Cat Merigold. Joy, Angelica. 2008. 56p. pap. 19.95 *(978-1-59858-591-9(6))* Dog Ear Publishing, LLC.

Bollen, Roger. P. J. Funnybunny's Bag of Tricks. Sadler, Marilyn. 2005. (Step into Reading Ser.). 32p. 14.00 *(978-0-7569-5405-5(3))* Perfection Learning Corp.

—P. J. Funnybunny's Bag of Tricks. Sadler, Marilyn. 2004. (Step into Reading Ser.). (ENG.). 32p. (J). (gr. -1-1). pap. 3.99 *(978-0-375-82444-9(8)*, Random Hse. Bks. for Young Readers) Random Hse. Children's Bks.

Boller, David. Jared: Boy from the Bottom. Wallace, Patrick. 2003. 153p. (J). per. *(978-0-9740753-0-3(2))* Heritage Youth, Inc.

Boller, Gary, jt. illus. see Bines, Gary.

Bolling, Vickey. Jesus Is My Special Friend. Balika, Susan S. 2013. (Happy Day Ser.). (ENG.). 16p. (J). pap. 2.49 *(978-1-4143-9294-3(X))* Tyndale Hse. Pubs.

—Jesus Is My Special Friend. Balika, Susan. 2003. 24p. (J). 2.49 *(978-0-7847-1270-2(0))* Standard Publishing.

Bollinger, Carol. The Misadventures of Our Son Henry. Owens, Robert & Owens, Donna. 2007. 52p. per. 16.95 *(978-1-4241-8721-8(4))* America Star Bks.

Bollinger, Peter. Basilosaurus. Zabludoff, Marc. 2009. (Prehistoric Beasts Ser.). 32p. (gr. 2). 29.93 *(978-0-7614-3999-8(4))* Marshall Cavendish Corp.

—Dire Wolf. Zabludoff, Marc. 2009. (Prehistoric Beasts Ser.). 32p. (gr. 2-8). 29.93 *(978-0-7614-3998-1(6))* Marshall Cavendish Corp.

—Doedicurus. Zabludoff, Marc. 2010. (Prehistoric Beasts 2 Ser.). 32p. (gr. 2). 29.93 *(978-1-60870-033-2(X))* Marshall Cavendish Corp.

—Gastornis. Zabludoff, Marc. 2009. (Prehistoric Beasts Ser.). 32p. (gr. 2-8). 29.93 *(978-0-7614-4000-0(3))* Marshall Cavendish Corp.

—Giant Ground Sloth. Zabludoff, Marc. 2009. (Prehistoric Beasts Ser.). 32p. (gr. 2-8). 29.93 *(978-0-7614-3997-4(8))* Marshall Cavendish Corp.

—Hyracotherium. Zabludoff, Marc. 2010. (Prehistoric Beasts 2 Ser.). 32p. (gr. 2). 29.93 *(978-1-60870-034-9(8))* Marshall Cavendish GBR. Dist: Marshall Cavendish Corp.

—Kronosaurus. Zabludoff, Marc. 2010. (Prehistoric Beasts 2 Ser.). 32p. (gr. 2). 29.93 *(978-1-60870-035-6(6))* Marshall Cavendish Corp.

—Mastodon. Zabludoff, Marc. 2010. (Prehistoric Beasts 2 Ser.). 32p. (gr. 2). 29.93 *(978-1-60870-036-3(4))* Marshall Cavendish Corp.

—Saber-Toothed Cat. Zabludoff, Marc. 2010. (Prehistoric Beasts 2 Ser.). 32p. (gr. 2). 29.93 *(978-1-60870-037-0(2))* Marshall Cavendish GBR. Dist: Marshall Cavendish Corp.

—Space & the Planets. Hirschmann, Kris. 2003. (Magic School Bus Fact Finder Ser.). (ENG.). 96p. (J). pap. 4.99 *(978-0-439-38175-8(4))* Scholastic, Inc.

Bollinger, Peter. Algernon Graeves Is Scary Enough. Bollinger, Peter. 2005. 32p. (J). (gr. -1-3). lib. bdg. 15.89 *(978-0-06-052269-8(0),* Geringer, Laura Book) HarperCollins Pubs.

Bollinger/Papp. King Kong: Meet Kong & Ann. 2005. 32p. (J). lib. bdg. 13.85 *(978-1-4242-0615-5(4))* Fitzgerald Bks.

Bolognese, Don. Dinosaur Hunter. Alphin, Elaine Marie. (I Can Read Book 4 Ser.). (J). 2004. (ENG.). 48p. (gr. 3-4). pap. 3.99 *(978-0-06-444256-5(X));* 2003. 48p. 15.99 *(978-0-06-028303-2(3));* 2003. 64p. (gr. 2-3). 16.89 *(978-0-06-028304-9(1))* HarperCollins Pubs.

—Dinosaur Hunter. Alphin, Elaine Marie. 2004. (I Can Read Bks.). 48p. (gr. 2-4). 14.00 *(978-0-7569-3241-1(6))* Perfection Learning Corp.

—First Flight: The Story of Tom Tate & the Wright Brothers. Shea, George. 2003. (I Can Read Book 4 Ser.). (ENG.). 48p. (J). (gr. k-3). reprint ed. pap. 3.99 *(978-0-06-444215-2(2))* HarperCollins Pubs.

—Jimmy Takes Vanishing Lessons. Brooks, Walter R. 2007. (Freddy the Pig Ser.). (ENG.). 26p. (gr. k-3). 16.95 *(978-1-58567-895-2(3),* 856895) Overlook Pr., The.

Bolognese, Don. The Warhorse. Bolognese, Don. 2010. (ENG.). 176p. (J). (gr. 5-9). pap. 9.99 *(978-1-4424-2942-0(9),* Simon & Schuster Bks. For Young Readers) Simon & Schuster Bks. For Young Readers.

Bolster, Rob. The Addition Book. Pallotta, Jerry. 2006. 32p. (J). *(978-0-439-89637-5(1))* Scholastic, Inc.

—The Construction Alphabet Book. Pallotta, Jerry. 2006. (Jerry Pallotta's Alphabet Bks.). (ENG.). 32p. (J). (gr. -1-3). lib. bdg. 17.95 *(978-1-57091-437-9(0));* per. 7.95 *(978-1-57091-438-6(9))* Charlesbridge Publishing, Inc.

—Count by Fives. Pallotta, Jerry. 2008. 32p. (J). *(978-0-545-00245-5(1))* Scholastic, Inc.

—Count by Tens. Pallotta, Jerry. 2008. 32p. (J). *(978-0-545-07068-3(6))* Scholastic, Inc.

—Going Lobstering. Pallotta, Jerry. 2008. (ENG.). 20p. (J). (gr. -1-3). bds. 7.95 *(978-1-57091-623-6(3))* Charlesbridge Publishing, Inc.

—Hammerhead vs. Bull Shark. Pallotta, Jerry. 2011. 32p. (J). *(978-0-545-30170-1(X))* Scholastic, Inc.

—Hershey's Weights & Measures. Pallotta, Jerry. 2003. (Hershey's Ser.). (ENG.). 32p. (J). 16.99 *(978-0-439-38876-4(7),* Cartwheel Bks.) Scholastic, Inc.

Bolster, Rob. Lobster vs. Crab. Pallotta, Jerry. 2014. 32p. (J). pap. ***(978-0-545-68121-6(9))*** Scholastic, Inc.

Bolster, Rob. Multiplication. Pallotta, Jerry. 2008. 32p. (J). *(978-0-545-00686-6(4))* Scholastic, Inc.

—Pizza Fractions. Pallotta, Jerry. 2007. 32p. (J). pap. *(978-0-545-00687-3(2))* Scholastic, Inc.

—The Subtraction Book. Pallotta, Jerry. 2007. 32p. (J). *(978-0-439-89638-2(X))* Scholastic, Inc.

—U. S. Navy Alphabet Book. Garnett, Sammie & Pallotta, Jerry. 2004. (ENG.). 32p. (J). (gr. -1-3). pap. 7.95 *(978-1-57091-587-1(3))* Charlesbridge Publishing, Inc.

—Weights & Measures. Pallotta, Jerry. 2008. 32p. (J). pap. *(978-0-545-06448-4(1))* Scholastic, Inc.

—Whale vs. Giant Squid. Pallotta, Jerry. 2012. 32p. (J). pap. *(978-0-545-30173-2(4))* Scholastic, Inc.

Bolster, Rob. Wolverine vs. Tasmanian Devil. Pallotta, Jerry. 2009. 32p. (J). pap. ***(978-0-545-45189-5(2))*** Scholastic, Inc.

Bolt, Susan Collier. Gadoo the Cat: An Armenian Folktale. Gopigian, Susan Kadian. 2008. 39p. 16.95 *(978-0-9801453-0-4(9))* Wayne State Univ. Pr.

Bolton, Adam. Where's My Shoggoth? Thomas, Ian. 2012. (ENG.). 56p. (J). (gr. 2). 11.95 *(978-1-936393-56-5(5))* Boom Entertainment, Inc.

Bolton, Bill. Build Your Own Noah's Ark, 1 vol. Williamson, Karen & David, Juliet. 2011. (ENG.). 12p. (J). (gr. -1). bds. 12.99 *(978-1-85985-224-8(6),* Candle Bks.) Lion Hudson PLC GBR. Dist: Kregel Pubns.

—BusyBugz Adventures: Izzi Goes Missing. Miller, Liza. 2013. (BusyBugz Adventures Ser.). (ENG.). 16p. (J). (gr. -1). 12.95 *(978-1-60710-714-9(7),* Silver Dolphin Bks.) Baker & Taylor Publishing Group.

—Early Birdy Gets the Worm: A PictureReading Book for Young Children. Lansky, Bruce. 2014. (ENG.). 24p. (J). (gr. -1-1). 15.99 *(978-1-4424-9176-2(0))* Meadowbrook Pr.

—How Heavy? Wacky Ways to Compare Weight, 1 vol. Weakland, Mark. 2013. (Wacky Comparisons Ser.). (ENG.). 24p. (J). (gr. -1-2). 27.32 *(978-1-4048-8322-2(3));* pap. 7.95 *(978-1-4795-1912-5(X))* Picture Window Bks.

Bolton, Bill. Monkey See, Monkey Do. Lansky, Bruce. 2015. (Picture Reader Ser.). (ENG.). 32p. (J). (gr. -1-1). 7.95 ***(978-1-4767-6872-4(2))*** Meadowbrook Pr.

Bolton, Bill. My Magnetic Counting Book: Ten Dancing Dinosaurs. 2006. (Magnix Learning Fun Ser.). 12p. (J). (gr. -1-3). 9.95 *(978-1-932915-16-7(8))* Sandvik Innovations, LLC.

Bolton, Bill & Sinkovec, Igor. Wacky Comparisons. Gunderson, Jessica & Weakland, Mark. 2013. (Wacky Comparisons Ser.). (ENG.). 32p. (gr. -1-2). 14.95 *(978-1-62370-037-9(X))* Capstone Young Readers.

Bolton-Eells, Sharon. Amelia, A to Z. Hicks, Rob & Hicks, Kim. 2011. (J). *(978-0-9829908-0-3(4))* Island Media Publishing, LLC.

Bolton, Georgia Helen, jt. illus. see Ballard, George Anne.

Bolton, John, et al. 1,001 Nights of Snowfall. Willingham, Bill. rev. ed. 2006. (Fables Ser.). (ENG.). 144p. 19.99 *(978-1-4012-0367-2(1),* Vertigo) DC Comics.

Bolton, John, jt. illus. see Adams, Art.

Bolton, Kyle. Smash: Trial by Fire. Bolton, Chris A. 2013. (ENG.). 160p. (J). (gr. 4-7). 18.99 *(978-0-7636-5596-9(1))* Candlewick Pr.

Bolund, Inna. Amanda the Panda, 1 vol. Finch, Donna. 2009. (ENG.). 27p. pap. 24.95 *(978-1-61546-797-6(1))* America Star Bks.

—Amanda the Panda's ABCs: Amanda the Panda. Finch, Donna. l.t. ed. 2011. (ENG.). 58p. pap. 6.00 *(978-1-4609-0756-6(6))* CreateSpace Independent Publishing Platform.

—The Crazy, Cockeyed, Contest Between Peanut Brittle & Petit Four: Pandora Puckett. Finch, Donna. l.t. ed. 2011. (ENG.). 26p. pap. 9.25 *(978-1-4635-3760-9(3))* CreateSpace Independent Publishing Platform.

—The Perpetual, Purposeful, Pointing of Pandora Puckett's Pointer, Peanut Brittle: Pandora Puckett. Finch, Donna. l.t. ed. 2011. (ENG.). 24p. pap. 9.25 *(978-1-4637-7356-4(0))* CreateSpace Independent Publishing Platform.

—Play Day Our Way! Bulakh, Nadia. Finch, Donna, ed. 2010. (ENG.). 26p. pap. 9.25 *(978-1-4538-2830-4(3))* CreateSpace Independent Publishing Platform.

—A Very Panda Christmas: Amanda the Panda a Very Panda Christmas. Finch, Donna. 2010. (ENG.). 30p. pap. 9.25 *(978-1-4537-3010-2(9))* CreateSpace Independent Publishing Platform.

—Victoria Finch, the Poodle That's Not a Dog!! Victoria Finch, a True Story. Finch, Donna. 2010. (ENG.). 36p. pap. 9.25 *(978-1-4538-3048-2(0))* CreateSpace Independent Publishing Platform.

Boman, Erik, photos by. Blahnik by Boman: Shoes, Photographs, Conversation. Blahnik, Manolo. 2005. (ENG.). 224p. (gr. 8-17). 85.00 *(978-0-8118-5116-9(8))* Chronicle Bks. LLC.

Bonadonna, Davide & Kitzmüller, Christian. Uncover a Shark. Gordon, David George. Pringle, Betsy Henry, ed. 2004. (Uncover Bks.). (ENG.). 16p. (J). 18.95 *(978-1-59223-115-7(2),* Silver Dolphin Bks.) Baker & Taylor Publishing Group.

Bonatakis, Shannon & Disney Storybook Art Team. Sage's Story. Zappa, Ahmet & Zappa, Shane Muldoon. 2015. (Star Darlings Ser.: 1). (ENG.). 176p. (J). (gr. 3-7). pap. 6.99 *(978-1-4231-6643-6(4))* Disney Pr.

—Star Darlings Arly's Adventure. Zappa, Ahmet & Muldoon Zappa, Shana. 2015. (Star Darlings Ser.: 2). (ENG.). 176p. (J). (gr. 3-7). pap. 6.99 *(978-1-4231-7766-1(5))* Disney Pr.

Bonavita, Madison M. Theo's Special Gift. Martin, Candice J. l.t. ed. 2006. 12p. (J). per. 12.99 *(978-1-59879-190-7(7))* Lifevest Publishing, Inc.

Bond, Barbara Higgins, jt. illus. see Calitri, Susan.

Bond, Bob. President Lincoln Listened: A Story of Compassion. Moody, D. L. 2006. (Story Time Ser.). (ENG.). 24p. (J). (gr. -1-4). 7.99 *(978-1-84550-115-0(2))* Christian Focus Pubns. GBR. Dist: Send The Light Distribution LLC.

Bond, Clint & Clark, Andy. The Great Snail Race. Ostrow, Kim. ed. 2005. (SpongeBob SquarePants Ser.: No. 6). 22p. (J). lib. bdg. 15.00 *(978-1-59054-830-1(2))* Fitzgerald Bks.

—The Great Snail Race. 2005. (SpongeBob SquarePants Ser.). (ENG.). 24p. (J). pap. 3.99 *(978-0-689-87313-3(1),* Simon Spotlight/Nickelodeon) Simon Spotlight/Nickelodeon.

Bond, Denny. Mary, Did You Know? Lowry, Mark & Greene, Buddy. 2005. 24p. (J). (gr. -1-k). bds. 9.99 incl. audio compact disk *(978-1-57791-176-0(8))* Brighter Minds Children's Publishing.

Bond, Felicia. The Best Mouse Cookie. Numeroff, Laura Joffe. 2006. (If You Give... Ser.). (ENG.). 32p. (J). (gr. -1-2). 9.99 *(978-0-06-113760-0(X))* HarperCollins Pubs.

—El Gran Granero Rojo. Brown, Margaret Wise. 2003.Tr. of Big Red Barn. (SPA.). 34p. (J). (gr. -1 — 1). bds. 7.99 *(978-0-06-009107-1(X),* Rayo) HarperCollins Pubs.

—Happy Birthday, Mouse! Numeroff, Laura Joffe. 2012. (If You Give... Ser.). (ENG.). 24p. (J). (gr. -1 — 1). bds. 6.99 *(978-0-694-01425-5(7))* HarperCollins Pubs.

—Happy Easter, Mouse! Numeroff, Laura Joffe. 2010. (If You Give... Ser.). (ENG.). 24p. (J). (gr. -1 — 1). bds. 6.99 *(978-0-694-01422-4(2))* HarperCollins Pubs.

—Happy Valentine's Day, Mouse! Numeroff, Laura Joffe. 2009. (If You Give... Ser.). (ENG.). 24p. (J). (gr. -1-3). bds. 6.99 *(978-0-06-180432-8(0))* HarperCollins Pubs.

—If You Give a Bear a Brownie: Book & Doll. Numeroff, Laura Joffe. Date not set. (J). 19.99 *(978-0-694-01423-1(0))* HarperCollins Pubs.

—If You Give a Bear a Brownie Recipes. Numeroff, Laura Joffe. Date not set. 32p. (J). (gr. -1-2). 12.99 *(978-0-06-028559-3(1))* HarperCollins Pubs.

—If You Give a Cat a Cupcake. Numeroff, Laura Joffe. 2008. (If You Give... Ser.). 32p. (J). (gr. -1-3). lib. bdg. 17.89 *(978-0-06-028325-4(4))* HarperCollins Pubs.

—If You Give a Cat a Cupcake. Numeroff, Laura. 2008. (If You Give... Ser.). (ENG.). 32p. (J). (gr. -1-3). 16.99 *(978-0-06-028324-7(6))* HarperCollins Pubs.

—If You Give a Cat a Cupcake: Book & Doll. Numeroff, Laura Joffe. Date not set. (If You Give... Ser.). (J). 19.99 *(978-0-694-01431-6(1))* HarperCollins Pubs.

—If You Give a Cat a Cupcake Recipes. Numeroff, Laura Joffe. Date not set. 32p. (J). (gr. -1-2). 12.99 *(978-0-06-028560-9(5))* HarperCollins Pubs.

—If You Give a Dog a Donut. Numeroff, Laura Joffe. 2011. (If You Give... Ser.). 32p. (J). (gr. -1-3). 17.89 *(978-0-06-026684-4(8))* HarperCollins Pubs.

—If You Give a Dog a Donut. Numeroff, Laura. 2011. (If You Give... Ser.). (ENG.). 32p. (J). (gr. -1-3). 16.99 *(978-0-06-026683-7(X))* HarperCollins Pubs.

—If You Give a Moose a Muffin. Numeroff, Laura Joffe. Date not set. (J). bds. 6.99 *(978-0-694-01426-2(5))* HarperCollins Pubs.

—If You Give a Moose a Muffin: Book & Doll. Numeroff, Laura Joffe. Date not set. (J). 19.99 *(978-0-694-01421-7(4))* HarperCollins Pubs.

—If You Give a Moose a Muffin Recipe Book. Numeroff, Laura Joffe. Date not set. 32p. (J). (gr. -1-2). 12.99 *(978-0-06-028562-3(1))* HarperCollins Pubs.

—If You Give a Mouse a Cookie. Numeroff, Laura Joffe. (J). (gr. -1-2). Date not set. 32p. 4.95 *(978-0-06-443166-8(5));* 2013. (ENG.). 40p. 16.99 *(978-0-06-230594-7(8),* Balzer & Bray) HarperCollins Pubs.

—If You Give a Pig a Pancake. Numeroff, Laura Joffe. Date not set. (J). 6.99 *(978-0-694-01430-9(3))* HarperCollins Pubs.

—If You Give a Pig a Party. Numeroff, Laura Joffe. 2005. (If You Give... Ser.). (J). 32p. (J). (gr. -1-2). lib. bdg. 17.89 *(978-0-06-028327-8(0))* HarperCollins Pubs.

—If You Give a Pig a Party. Numeroff, Laura. 2005. (If You Give... Ser.). (ENG.). 32p. (J). (gr. -1-2). 16.99 *(978-0-06-028326-1(2))* HarperCollins Pubs.

—If You Give a Pig a Pumpkin: Book & Doll. Numeroff, Laura Joffe. Date not set. (J). 19.99 *(978-0-694-01432-3(X))* HarperCollins Pubs.

—If You Take a Mouse to the Movies. Numeroff, Laura Joffe. ed. 2009. (If You Give... Ser.). (ENG.). 72p. (J). (gr. -1-3). 18.99 *(978-0-06-176280-2(6))* HarperCollins Pubs.

—It's Pumpkin Day, Mouse! Numeroff, Laura Joffe. 2012. (If You Give... Ser.). (ENG.). 24p. (J). (gr. -1 — 1). bds. 6.99 *(978-0-694-01429-3(X))* HarperCollins Pubs.

—Merry Christmas, Mouse! Numeroff, Laura Joffe. 2007. (If You Give... Ser.). (ENG.). 24p. (J). (gr. -1 — 1). bds. 6.99 *(978-0-06-134499-2(0))* HarperCollins Pubs.

—Moose Stroller Songs. Numeroff, Laura Joffe. Date not set. (J). 9.99 *(978-0-694-01424-8(9))* HarperCollins Pubs.

—A Mouse Cookie First Library: If You Give a Mouse a Cookie; If You Take a Mouse to School. Numeroff, Laura Joffe. 2007. (If You Give... Ser.). (ENG.). 100p. (J). (gr. -1-2). bds. 15.99 *(978-0-06-117479-7(3),* HarperFestival) HarperCollins Pubs.

—Mouse Cookies & More: A Treasury. Numeroff, Laura. 2006. (If You Give... Ser.). (ENG.). 224p. (J). (gr. -1-3). 24.99 *(978-0-06-113763-1(4))* HarperCollins Pubs.

—Pig Pancakes. Numeroff, Laura Joffe. Date not set. 32p. (J). (gr. -1-2). 1.00 *(978-0-06-028563-0(X))* HarperCollins Pubs.

—Pig Stroller Songs. Numeroff, Laura Joffe. Date not set. (J). 10.99 *(978-0-694-01428-6(1))* HarperCollins Pubs.

—Si le das un Pastelito a un Gato. Numeroff, Laura Joffe. 2010. (If You Give... Ser.). (SPA & ENG.). 32p. (J). (gr. -1-2). 16.99 *(978-0-06-180431-1(2),* Rayo) HarperCollins Pubs.

—Si le Haces una Fiesta a una Cerdita. Numeroff, Laura Joffe. Mlawer, Teresa, tr. from ENG. 2006. (If You Give... Ser.).Tr. of If You Give a Pig a Party. (SPA.). 32p. (J). (gr. -1-2). 16.99 *(978-0-06-081532-5(9),* Rayo) HarperCollins Pubs.

—Si Llevas un Ratón a la Escuela. Numeroff, Laura Joffe. 2003. (If You Give... Ser.).Tr. of If You Take a Mouse to School. (SPA.). 32p. (J). (gr. -1-3). 16.99 *(978-0-06-052340-4(9),* Rayo) HarperCollins Pubs.

—Time for School, Mouse! Numeroff, Laura Joffe. 2008. (If You Give... Ser.). (ENG.). 24p. (J). (gr. -1 — 1). bds. 6.99 *(978-0-06-143307-8(1),* HarperFestival) HarperCollins Pubs.

Bond, Felicia. Big Hugs Little Hugs. Bond, Felicia. (ENG.). (J). (gr. -1-k). 2013. 30p. bds. 6.99 *(978-0-399-16206-0(2));* 2012. 32p. 16.99 *(978-0-399-25614-1(8))* Penguin Publishing Group. (Philomel).

—Day It Rained Hearts. Bond, Felicia. 2006. (ENG.). 36p. (J). (gr. -1-3). pap. 6.99 *(978-0-06-073123-6(0))* HarperCollins Pubs.

—The Halloween Play. Bond, Felicia. Orig. Title: The Halloween Performance. 32p. (J). (gr. -1-1). 2008. (ENG.). pap. 7.99 *(978-0-06-135796-1(0));* 2003. 6.99 *(978-0-06-054443-0(0))* HarperCollins Pubs.

—Poinsettia & the Firefighters. Bond, Felicia. 2003. (J). *(978-0-06-056871-9(2))* HarperCollins Pubs.

Bond, Felicia, jt. illus. see Cole, Henry.

Bond, Higgins. Alphabet of Space. Galvin, Laura Gates. (ENG.). 40p. 2009. 9.95 *(978-1-59249-990-8(2));* 2007. (J). (gr. -1-k). 15.95 *(978-1-59249-656-3(3))* Soundprints.

—The Christmas Pea Coat. Schneider, Richard H. 2004. 32p. (J). 14.95 *(978-0-8249-5474-1(2))* Ideals Pubns.

—Groundhog at Evergreen Road. Korman, Susan. (Smithsonian's Backyard Ser.). (ENG.). 32p. (J). (gr. -1-2). 2005. 15.95 *(978-1-59249-022-6(0),* B5024); 2003. 19.95 *(978-1-59249-025-7(5),* BC5024); 2003. 8.95 *(978-1-59249-061-5(1),* SC5024); 2003. 4.95 *(978-1-59249-023-3(9),* B5074); 2003. 6.95 *(978-1-59249-024-0(7),* S5024) Soundprints.

—Handshake in Space: The Apollo-Soyuz Test Project. Tan, Sheri. 2009. 32p. (J). (gr. 1-5). pap. 9.95 incl. audio *(978-1-60727-104-8(4));* (ENG.). 9.95 *(978-1-60727-115-4(X));* (ENG.). 17.95 *(978-1-60727-114-7(1));* pap. 9.95 incl. reel tape *(978-1-59249-203-9(7))* Soundprints.

—The Mighty Mississippi: The Life & Times of America's Greatest River. Vieira, Linda. 2005. (J). *(978-7-80802-789-7(8))* Walker & Co.

—A Place for Bats, 1 vol. Stewart, Melissa. 2012. (ENG.). 32p. (J). 16.95 *(978-1-56145-624-6(1))* Peachtree Pubs.

—A Place for Birds, 1 vol. Stewart, Melissa. 2009. (ENG.). 32p. (J). (gr. 1-5). 16.95 *(978-1-56145-474-7(5))* Peachtree Pubs.

—A Place for Birds (revised Edition), 1 vol. Stewart, Melissa. rev. ed. 2015. (Place For... Ser.). (ENG.). 32p. (gr. 1-5). 16.95 *(978-1-56145-839-4(2))* Peachtree Pubs.

—A Place for Butterflies, 1 vol. Stewart, Melissa. (ENG.). 32p. (J). 2011. pap. 7.95 *(978-1-56145-571-3(7));* 2006. (gr. 1-5). 16.95 *(978-1-56145-357-3(9))* Peachtree Pubs.

—A Place for Butterflies, Revised Edition, 1 vol. Stewart, Melissa. 2nd ed. 2014. (Place for... Ser.). (ENG.). 32p. (J). (gr. 1-5). pap. 7.95 *(978-1-56145-784-7(1))* Peachtree Pubs.

—A Place for Fish, 1 vol. Stewart, Melissa. 2011. (ENG.). 32p. (J). (gr. 1-5). 16.95 *(978-1-56145-562-1(8))* Peachtree Pubs.

—A Place for Frogs, 1 vol. Stewart, Melissa. 2010. (ENG.). 32p. (J). (gr. 1-5). 16.95 *(978-1-56145-521-8(0))* Peachtree Pubs.

—A Place for Turtles, 1 vol. Stewart, Melissa. 2013. (ENG.). 32p. (J). (gr. 1-5). pap. 16.95 *(978-1-56145-693-2(4))* Peachtree Pubs.

—Please Don't Wake the Animals: A Book about Sleep, 1 vol. Batten, Mary. 2008. (ENG.). 32p. (J). (gr. k-3). 16.95 *(978-1-56145-393-1(5))* Peachtree Pubs.

—Trails above the Tree Line: A Story of a Rocky Mountain Meadow. Fraggalosch, Audrey. 2005. (Soundprints' Wild Habitats Ser.). (ENG.). (J). (gr. 1-4). 36p. 15.95 *(978-1-56899-941-8(0),* B7021); 32p. pap. 6.95 *(978-1-56899-942-5(9),* S7021) Soundprints.

—Who Has a Belly Button?, 1 vol. Batten, Mary. 2004. (ENG.). 32p. (J). (gr. 1-5). 15.95 *(978-1-56145-235-4(1))* Peachtree Pubs.

Bond, Higgins & Sill, John. About Insects: A Guide for Children, 1 vol. Batten, Mary & Sill, Cathyrn. 2003. (About...Ser.). (ENG.). 48p. (J). (gr. k-3). pap. 7.95 *(978-1-56145-232-3(7))* Peachtree Pubs.

Bond, Nancy. Career Ideas for Kids Who Like Adventure & Travel. Reeves, Diane Lindsey. 2nd rev. ed. 2007. (Career Ideas for Kids Ser.). 208p. (gr. 4-9). 32.95 *(978-0-8160-6547-9(0),* Checkmark Bks.) Facts On File, Inc.

—Career Ideas for Kids Who Like Animals & Nature. Reeves, Diane Lindsey. 2nd rev. ed. 2007. (Career Ideas for Kids Ser.). 208p. (gr. 4-9). 32.95 *(978-0-8160-6539-4(X),* Ferguson Publishing Co.) Facts On File, Inc.

—Career Ideas for Kids Who Like Art. Reeves, Diane Lindsey. 2nd rev. ed. 2007. (Career Ideas for Kids Ser.). 208p. (gr. 4-9). 32.95 *(978-0-8160-6541-7(1),* Ferguson Publishing Co.) Facts On File, Inc.

—Career Ideas for Kids Who Like Math & Money. Reeves, Diane Lindsey. 2nd rev. ed. 2007. (Career Ideas for Kids Ser.). 208p. (gr. 4-9). 32.95 *(978-0-8160-6545-5(4),* Ferguson Publishing Co.); per. 16.95 *(978-0-8160-6546-2(2),* Checkmark Bks.) Facts On File, Inc.

—Career Ideas for Kids Who Like Science. Reeves, Diane Lindsey. 2nd rev. ed. 2007. (Career Ideas for Kids Ser.). 192p. (gr. 4-9). 32.95 *(978-0-8160-6549-3(7),* Checkmark Bks.) Facts On File, Inc.

—Career Ideas for Kids Who Like Sports. Reeves, Diane Lindsey. 2nd rev. ed. 2007. (Career Ideas for Kids Ser.). 208p. (gr. 4-9). lib. bdg. 32.95 *(978-0-8160-6551-6(9),* Checkmark Bks.) Facts On File, Inc.

—Career Ideas for Kids Who Like Talking. Reeves, Diane Lindsey. 2nd rev. ed. 2007. (Career Ideas for Kids Ser.). 192p. (gr. 4-9). 32.95 *(978-0-8160-6553-0(5),* Checkmark Bks.) Facts On File, Inc.

—Career Ideas for Kids Who Like Writing. Reeves, Diane Lindsey & Clasen, Lindsey. 2nd rev. ed. 2007. (Career Ideas for Kids Ser.). 192p. (gr. 4-9). 32.95 *(978-0-8160-6555-4(1),* Ferguson Publishing Co.) Facts On File, Inc.

Bond, Nancy. Career Ideas for Kids Who Like Computers. Bond, Nancy. Reeves, Diane Lindsey & Clasen, Lindsey. 2nd rev. ed. 2007. (Career Ideas for Kids Ser.). 208p. (gr. 4-9). 32.95 *(978-0-8160-6543-1(8),* Ferguson Publishing Co.) Facts On File, Inc.

Bond, Rebecca. The House That George Built. Slade, Suzanne. 2012. (ENG.). 32p. (J). (gr. 1-4). 16.95 *(978-1-58089-262-9(0))* Charlesbridge Publishing, Inc.

Bonder, Dianna. Black & White Blanche, 1 vol. Toews, Marj. 2006. (ENG.). 32p. (J). (gr. -1-3). 9.95 *(978-1-55005-132-2(6),* 1550051326) Fitzhenry & Whiteside, Ltd. CAN. Dist: Midpoint Trade Bks., Inc.

—Digging Canadian Dinosaurs, 1 vol. Grambo, Rebecca L. 2004. (ENG.). 64p. (J). (gr. 2-6). pap. 12.95 *(978-1-55285-395-5(0))* Whitecap Bks., Ltd. CAN. Dist: Midpoint Trade Bks., Inc.

—Leon's Song. McLellan, Stephanie Simpson. 2004. (ENG.). 32p. (J). (gr. -1-3). *(978-1-55041-813-2(0))* Fitzhenry & Whiteside, Ltd.

—Leon's Song, 1 vol. Simpson McLellan, Stephanie. 2005. (ENG.). 32p. (J). (gr. -1-3). pap. 7.95 *(978-1-55041-815-6(7),* 1550418157) Fitzhenry & Whiteside, Ltd. CAN. Dist: Midpoint Trade Bks., Inc.

—A Pacific Alphabet, 1 vol. Ruurs, Margriet. 2014. (ENG.). 32p. (J). (gr. -1-2). 9.95 *(978-1-55285-264-4(4))* Whitecap Bks., Ltd. CAN. Dist: Midpoint Trade Bks., Inc.

—Pedro, the Pirate. Hoppey, Tim. 2012. (ENG & SPA.). 32p. lib. bdg. 16.95 *(978-1-936299-18-8(6),* Raven Tree Pr.,Csi) Continental Sales, Inc.

—The Pied Piper of Hamelin: A German Folktale. StJohn, Amanda. 2011. (Folktales from Around the World Ser.). (ENG.). 24p. (J). (gr. k-3). 28.50 *(978-1-60973-142-7(5),* 201146) Child's World, Inc., The.

—The West Is Calling: Imagining British Columbia, 1 vol. Harvey, Sarah N. & Buffam, Leslie. 2008. (ENG.). 32p. (J). (gr. -1-7). 19.95 *(978-1-55143-936-5(0))* Orca Bk. Pubs. USA.

Bonder, Dianna. Accidental Alphabet, 1 vol. Bonder, Dianna. 2nd ed. 2010. (ENG.). 32p. (J). (gr. -1-2). pap. 8.95 *(978-1-55285-596-6(1))* Whitecap Bks., Ltd. CAN. Dist: Midpoint Trade Bks., Inc.

—Dogabet, 1 vol. Bonder, Dianna. (ENG.). 32p. (J). (gr. -1-2). 2010. pap. 8.95 *(978-1-55285-940-7(1));* 2008. pap. 8.95 *(978-1-55285-922-3(3),* Walrus Bks.); 2007. 16.95 *(978-1-55285-797-7(2),* Walrus Bks.) Whitecap Bks., Ltd. CAN. Dist: Midpoint Trade Bks., Inc.

Bone, J. The Collected Alison Dare Little Miss Adventures. Torres, J. 2005. (J). *(978-1-4156-1359-7(1))* Oni Pr., Inc.

—Happy Birthday, Superman!, 1 vol. Fisch, Sholly & Age, Heroic. 2014. (DC Super Friends Ser.). (ENG.). 32p. (gr. 1-2). 21.27 *(978-1-4342-9222-3(3))* Stone Arch Bks.

—The Secret of the Doomsday Design!, 1 vol. Torres, J. 2013. (Batman: the Brave & the Bold Ser.). (ENG.). 32p. (gr. 2-3). 21.27 *(978-1-4342-4707-0(4))* Stone Arch Bks.

Boné, Thomas H. The Teacher Who Would Not Retire Becomes a Movie Star. 2012. (J). *(978-0-9792918-6-9(0))* Blue Marlin Pubns.

—The Teacher Who Would Not Retire Discovers a New Planet. 2009. (J). 17.95 *(978-0-9792918-3-8(6))* Blue Marlin Pubns.

—The Teacher Who Would Not Retire Goes to Camp. 2005. (J). *(978-0-9674602-7-7(1))* Blue Marlin Pubns.

Bone, Thomas H. & LeTourneau, Anthony Alex. Mama, Can Armadillos Swim? 2004. (J). 17.00 *(978-0-9674602-6-0(3))* Blue Marlin Pubns.

Bonet, Xavier. The Doll That Waved Goodbye: And Other Scary Tales. Dahl, Michael. 2015. (J). lib. bdg. ***(978-1-4965-0595-8(6))*** Stone Arch Bks.

—Frightmares: A Creepy Collection of Scary Stories. Dahl, Michael. 2015. (J). pap. ***(978-1-4965-0598-9(0))*** Stone Arch Bks.

—Oscar & the Amazing Gravity Repellent. Peterson, Tina L. 2015. (Middle-Grade Novels Ser.). (ENG.). 224p. (gr. 3-4). lib. bdg. 25.32 ***(978-1-4965-0000-7(8))*** Stone Arch Bks.

—The Phantom on the Phone & Other Scary Tales. Dahl, Michael. 2015. (J). lib. bdg. ***(978-1-4965-0597-2(2))*** Stone Arch Bks.

—The Stranger on the Stairs: And Other Scary Tales. Dahl, Michael. 2015. (J). lib. bdg. ***(978-1-4965-0594-1(8))*** Stone Arch Bks.

—The Voice in the Boys' Room & Other Scary Tales. Dahl, Michael. 2015. (J). lib. bdg. ***(978-1-4965-0596-5(4))*** Stone Arch Bks.

Bonforte, Lisa. Ponies, Vol. 2. Pollack, Pam & Belviso, Meg. 2003. (Penguin Young Readers, Level 2 Ser.: Vol. 2). (ENG.). 32p. (J). (gr. 1-2). mass mkt. 3.99 *(978-0-448-42524-5(6)*, Warne, Frederick Pubs.) Penguin Bks., Ltd. GBR. Dist: Penguin Random Hse., LLC.

—Rainforest Animals. Smith, Kathie Billingslea. 2005. 12p. (J). (gr. k-3). 6.99 *(978-1-57755-509-4(0))* Flying Frog Publishing, Inc.

—Seal Pup Grows Up: The Story of a Harbor Seal. Zoehfeld, Kathleen Weidner. 2011. (Smithsonian Oceanic Collection Ser.). (ENG.). 32p. (J). (gr. -1-3). 19.95 *(978-1-60727-663-0(1))* Soundprints.

Bonham, Bob. Book of Mormon Numbers. Daybell, Chad. 2004. (J). bds. 8.95 *(978-1-55517-755-3(7)*, 77557) Cedar Fort, Inc./CFI Distribution.

—Sariah Mcduff: Book Three of the Sariah Mcduff Series: Valentine's Day Scrooge. Setzer, Lee Ann. 2005. (J). per. 5.95 *(978-1-55517-841-3(3))* Cedar Fort, Inc./CFI Distribution.

Bonhomme, Matthieu. William & the Lost Spirit. Bonneval, Gwen de & Smith, Owen. Smith, Anne Collins, tr. from FRE. 2013. (ENG.). 160p. (YA). (gr. 8-12). lib. bdg. 30.60 *(978-0-7613-8567-7(3)*, Graphic Universe) Lerner Publishing Group.

—William & the Lost Spirit. De Bonneval, Gwen. Smith, Anne, tr. 2013. (ENG.). 160p. (YA). (gr. 8-12). pap. 9.95 *(978-1-4677-0807-4(0)*, Graphic Universe) Lerner Publishing Group.

Boni, Simone. Sword Quest. Dixon, Andy. Brooks, Felicity, ed. rev. ed. 2005. (Usborne Fantasy Puzzle Bks.). 31p. (J). (gr. 3-7). pap., pap. 7.95 *(978-0-7945-1096-1(5)*, Usborne) EDC Publishing.

Bonita, Todd. Tae Kwon Do! Pierce, Terry. 2006. (Step into Reading Ser.). (ENG.). 32p. (J). (gr. -1-1). per. 3.99 *(978-0-375-83448-6(6)*, Random Hse. Bks. for Young Readers) Random Hse. Children's Bks.

Bonnell, B. T. The Little Looney Tales: Hatched. Jack, Lizzie. 2011. 34p. 19.95 *(978-1-4575-0665-9(3))*; pap. 14.95 *(978-1-4575-0520-1(7))* Dog Ear Publishing, LLC.

Bonner, Hannah. When Fish Got Feet, Sharks Got Teeth, & Bugs Began to Swarm: A Cartoon Prehistory of Life Long Before Dinosaurs. Bonner, Hannah. 2007. (ENG.). 48p. (J). (gr. 5-18). lib. bdg. 25.90 *(978-1-4263-0079-0(4))*; 16.95 *(978-1-4263-0078-3(6))* National Geographic Society. (National Geographic Children's Bks.).

Bonnet, Rosalinde. Alphabet Picture Book. ed. 2011. (Alphabet Picture Book Ser.). 26p. (J). ring bd. 11.99 *(978-0-7945-2954-3(2)*, Usborne) EDC Publishing.

—The Art Collector. Wahl, Jan. 2011. (ENG.). 32p. (J). (gr. k-3). 15.95 *(978-1-58089-270-4(1))* Charlesbridge Publishing, Inc.

Bonnet, Rosalinde. Ella & Penguin Stick Together. Maynor, Megan. 2016. 32p. (J). (gr. -1-3). 17.99 ***(978-0-06-233088-8(8))*** HarperCollins Pubs.

Bonnet, Rosalinde. The Little Red Elf. McGrath, Barbara Barbieri. (ENG.). 32p. (J). (gr. -1-2). 2010. pap. 7.95 *(978-1-58089-237-7(X))*; 2009. 14.95 *(978-1-58089-236-0(1))* Charlesbridge Publishing, Inc.

—My First Word Book. Brooks, Felicity. 2014. (ENG.). (J). 9.99 *(978-0-7945-3381-6(7)*, Usborne) EDC Publishing.

—Poppy's Best Paper. Eddy, Susan. 2015. (ENG.). 40p. (J). (gr. k-3). lib. bdg. 15.95 *(978-1-58089-614-6(6))* Charlesbridge Publishing, Inc.

—Sing-Along Christmas Carols. Watt, Fiona. 2010. (Baby Board Books with CD Ser.). 10p. (J). bds. 14.99 incl. audio compact disk *(978-0-7945-2660-3(8)*, Usborne) EDC Publishing.

Bonnet, Rosalinde, jt. illus. see Biedrzycki, David.

Bonnet, Rosaline. Very First Nursery Rhymes. Bonnet, Rosaline. 2010. (Very First Words Board Bks). 12p. (J). bds. 6.99 *(978-0-7945-2723-5(X)*, Usborne) EDC Publishing.

Bonnett, Rosalind. Santa Flap Book. ed. 2012. (Flap Bks). 10p. (J). bds. 7.99 *(978-0-7945-3316-8(7)*, Usborne) EDC Publishing.

Bonney, Joan, jt. illus. see Gauthier, Elizabeth.

Bonnie, Spino. Wild about Manners. Lorraine, Loria. 2013. 36p. 17.99 *(978-0-9881889-1-4(0))* Piccolo Tales.

Bono, Elena. El Sombrero de Ramito. Bono, Elena. Bono, E. Brignole, Giancarla, tr. rev. ed. 2006. (Fabulas De Familia Ser.). (SPA & ENG.). 32p. (J). (gr. k-4). pap. 6.95 *(978-970-20-0261-1(3))* Castillo, Ediciones, S. A. de C. V. MEX. Dist: Macmillan.

Bonotaux, Gilles. Dirty Rotten Bugs? Arthropods Unite to Tell Their Side of the Story. Bonotaux, Gilles. 2007. (ENG.). 48p. (J). (gr. 3-6). 14.95 *(978-1-58728-593-6(2))* Cooper Square Publishing Llc.

Booker, Carly-Jean. Jingle Bear on Ice. Hespe, Robert. 2010. (ENG.). 52p. pap. 10.00 *(978-1-4563-3576-2(6))* CreateSpace Independent Publishing Platform.

Books, Appleknobb. Charlie's Monster. Books, Appleknobb. 2013. 26p. (J). pap. 13.95 *(978-0-9890903-0-8(2))* Happy Apple Bks.

Boon, Debbie. Collins Big Cat - Tiger's Tales: Band 10/White. Morgan, Michaela. 2005. (Collins Big Cat Ser.). (ENG.). 32p. (J). pap. 7.99 *(978-0-00-718631-0(2))* HarperCollins Pubs. Ltd. GBR. Dist: Independent Pubs. Group.

—If You Go Walking in Tiger Wood. Durant, Alan. 2005. (ENG.). 100p. (J). (gr. -1-k). pap. 9.99 *(978-0-00-710390-4(5)*, HarperSport) HarperCollins Pubs. Ltd. GBR. Dist: Independent Pubs. Group.

Boone, Patti. To Be a Frog. Devol, Laura. 2010. 20p. pap. 12.95 *(978-1-60910-278-4(9))* Booklocker.com, Inc.

Boonyadhistarn, Thiranut. Origami: The Fun & Funky Art of Paper Folding, 1 vol. Boonyadhistarn, Thiranut. 2006. (Crafts Ser.). (ENG.). 32p. (gr. 3-4). 27.32 *(978-0-7368-6476-3(8)*, Snap Bks.) Capstone Pr., Inc.

Boos, Andre. Amazing Animal Puzzle Stickers: #1. 2005. (Amazing Animal Puzzle Stickers Ser.). 10p. (J). pap. 5.99 *(978-1-59496-063-5(1))* Teora USA LLC.

—Amazing Animal Puzzle Stickers: #2, Vol. 2. 2005. (Amazing Animal Puzzle Stickers Ser.). 10p. (J). pap. 5.99 *(978-1-59496-064-2(X))* Teora USA LLC.

—Amazing Animal Puzzle Stickers: #3, Vol. 3. 2005. (Amazing Animal Puzzle Stickers Ser.). 10p. (J). pap. 5.99 *(978-1-59496-065-9(8))* Teora USA LLC.

—Hi! Read, Stick & Learn about Animals. Little Bears are Brown. 2004. 20p. (J). pap. 6.99 *(978-1-59496-003-1(8))* Teora USA LLC.

—Hi! Read, Stick & Learn about Animals. Little rabbits have Fur. 2004. 20p. (J). pap. 6.99 *(978-1-59496-002-4(X))* Teora USA LLC.

Boos, Ben. Fantasy: An Artist's Realm. Boos, Ben. 2010. (ENG.). 96p. (J). (gr. 5-9). 19.99 *(978-0-7636-4056-9(5))* Candlewick Pr.

Boos, Ben & Ford, A. G. What Color Is My World? The Lost History of African-American Inventors. Abdul-Jabbar, Kareem & Obstfeld, Raymond. (ENG.). (J). (gr. 3-7). 2013. 96p. pap. 5.99 *(978-0-7636-6442-8(1))*; 2012. 44p. 17.99 *(978-0-7636-4564-9(8))* Candlewick Pr.

Booth, Anita K. Squirrels!!! An Informative & Entertaining Book about Our Favorite Mountain Mammal. Booth, Anita K., photos by. 2nd ed. 2004. 76p. 12.95 *(978-0-9748702-1-2(8))* AKB Design.

Booth, Christina. The Day I Was History. French, Jackie. 2007. (Making Tracks Ser.). (ENG.). 64p. (J). (gr. 2-4). pap. 11.95 *(978-1-876944-55-1(2))* National Museum of Australia AUS. Dist: Independent Pubs. Group.

Booth, George. Never Tease a Weasel. Soule, Jean Conder. 2011. (ENG.). 40p. (J). (gr. -1-2). pap. 6.99 *(978-0-375-87285-3(X)*, Dragonfly Bks.) Random Hse. Children's Bks.

—Nit-Pickin' Van Laan, Nancy. 2008. (ENG.). 32p. (J). (gr. -1-3). 15.99 *(978-0-689-83898-9(0)*, Atheneum Bks. for Young Readers) Simon & Schuster Children's Publishing.

—School! Adventures at the Harvey N. Trouble Elementary School. McMullan, Kate. 2012. (ENG.). 176p. (J). (gr. 1-4). pap. 6.99 *(978-0-312-55595-5(4))* Square Fish.

—Who Invited You? Fleming, Candace. 2009. (ENG.). 36p. (J). (gr. -1-3). 10.99 *(978-1-4424-0219-5(9)*, Atheneum Bks. for Young Readers) Simon & Schuster Children's Publishing.

Booth, Graham. Henry Explores the Jungle. Taylor, Mark. 2012. (ENG.). 48p. (J). (gr. -1-3). 18.95 *(978-1-930900-56-1(2))* Purple Hse. Pr.

—Henry the Castaway. Taylor, Mark. 2010. 48p. (J). (gr. -1-3). 18.95 *(978-1-930900-47-9(3))* Purple Hse. Pr.

—Henry the Explorer. Taylor, Mark. 2011. (J). 18.95 *(978-1-930900-48-6(1))* Purple Hse. Pr.

Booth, Scott. How to Draw Superheroes & Super Villains. 2003. 64p. (J). *(978-0-439-55133-5(1))* Scholastic, Inc.

Boothroyd, Sa. Before the World Was Ready: Stories of Daring Genius in Science. Eamer, Claire. 2013. (ENG.). 128p. (J). (gr. 4-7). pap. 14.95 *(978-1-55451-535-6(1)*, 9781554515356) Annick Pr., Ltd. CAN. Dist: Firefly Bks., Ltd.

—The World in Your Lunch Box: The Wacky History & Weird Science of Everyday Foods. Eamer, Claire. 2012. (ENG.). 122p. (J). (gr. 2-18). 22.95 *(978-1-55451-393-2(6)*, 9781554513932); pap. 14.95 *(978-1-55451-392-5(8)*, 9781554513925) Annick Pr., Ltd. CAN. Dist: Firefly Bks., Ltd.

Bootman, Colin. Almost to Freedom. Nelson, Vaunda Micheaux. 2003. (Carolrhoda Picture Books Ser.). (ENG.). 40p. (J). (gr. k-3). 16.95 *(978-1-57505-342-4(X))* Lerner Publishing Group.

—Climbing Lincoln's Steps: The African American Journey. Slade, Suzanne. 2010. (ENG.). 32p. (J). (gr. 2-5). 16.99 *(978-0-8075-1204-3(4))* Whitman, Albert & Co.

—Dad, Jackie, & Me, 1 vol. Uhlberg, Myron. (ENG.). 32p. (J). 2010. pap. 8.95 *(978-1-56145-531-7(8))*; 2005. 16.95 *(978-1-56145-329-0(3))* Peachtree Pubs.

—Dr. Martin Luther King, Jr: A Historical Perspective. Adler, David A. 2003. (ENG.). 48p. (J). (gr. k-3). pap. 7.99 *(978-0-8234-1803-9(0))* Holiday Hse., Inc.

—Finding Lincoln. Malaspina, Ann. 2009. (ENG.). 32p. (J). (gr. 2-4). 16.99 *(978-0-8075-2435-0(2))* Whitman, Albert & Co.

—Grandmama's Pride. Birtha, Becky. 2005. (ENG.). 32p. (J). (gr. 2-5). 16.95 *(978-0-8075-3028-3(X))* Whitman, Albert & Co.

—Hey, Charleston! The True Story of the Jenkins Orphanage Band. Rockwell, Anne F. 2013. 32p. pap. 16.95 *(978-0-7613-8843-2(5))*; (ENG.). (J). (gr. 2-5). lib. bdg. 16.95 *(978-0-7613-5565-6(0)*, Carolrhoda Bks.) Lerner Publishing Group.

—Love Twelve Miles Long, 1 vol. Armand, Glenda. 2013. (ENG.). 32p. (J). 17.95 *(978-1-60060-245-0(2))* Lee & Low Bks., Inc.

—Papa's Mark. Battle-Lavert, Gwendolyn. 2003. (ENG.). 32p. (J). (gr. k-3). tchr. ed. 17.95 *(978-0-8234-1650-9(X))* Holiday Hse., Inc.

—A Picture Book of Harriet Beecher Stowe. Adler, David A. (Picture Book Biography Ser.). (ENG.). 32p. (J). 2004. (gr. -1-3). 6.95 *(978-0-8234-1878-7(2))*; 2003. (gr. k-3). tchr. ed. 17.95 *(978-0-8234-1646-2(1))* Holiday Hse., Inc.

Bootman, Colin. A Storm Called Katrina, 1 vol. Uhlberg, Myron. (ENG.). 40p. (J). (gr. 2-4). 2015. pap. 8.95 ***(978-1-56145-887-5(2))***; 2011. 17.95 *(978-1-56145-591-1(1))* Peachtree Pubs.

Bootman, Colin. Sunday Best. Scholastic, Inc. Staff et al. 2004. (Just for You Ser.). (ENG.). 32p. pap. 3.99 *(978-0-439-56854-8(4)*, Teaching Resources) Scholastic, Inc.

Bootman, Colin. Fish for the Grand Lady. Bootman, Colin. 2006. (ENG.). 32p. (J). (gr. -1-3). 16.95 *(978-0-8234-1898-5(7))* Holiday Hse., Inc.

Borday, Irene. Mi Calle. Parramón, José María. (Coleccion Estoy En...).Tr. of My Street. (SPA.). 32p. (J). (gr. k-3). 6.36 *(978-84-342-1003-5(7))* Parramon Ediciones S.A. ESP. Dist: Lectorum Pubns., Inc.

—Mi Casa. Parramón, José María. (Coleccion Estoy En...).Tr. of My House. (SPA.). 32p. (J). (gr. k-3). 6.36 *(978-84-342-1002-8(9))* Parramon Ediciones S.A. ESP. Dist: Lectorum Pubns., Inc.

—Mi Escuela. Parramón, José María. (Coleccion Estoy En...).Tr. of My School. (SPA.). 32p. (J). (gr. k-3). 6.36 *(978-84-342-1004-2(5))* Parramon Ediciones S.A. ESP. Dist: Lectorum Pubns., Inc.

—Mi Jardin. Parramón, José María. (Coleccion Estoy En...).Tr. of My Garden. (SPA.). 32p. (J). (gr. k-3). 6.36 *(978-84-342-1005-9(3))* Parramon Ediciones S.A. ESP. Dist: Lectorum Pubns., Inc.

Bordelois, Augusto. Sunflower Promise. Hemery, Kathleen Maresh. 2005. (J). *(978-1-56123-188-1(6))* Centering Corp.

Border, Terry. Happy Birthday, Cupcake! Border, Terry. 2015. (ENG.). 32p. (J). (gr. k-3). 17.99 *(978-0-399-17160-4(6))* Penguin Publishing Group.

—Peanut Butter & Cupcake. Border, Terry. 2014. (ENG.). 32p. (J). (gr. -1-2). 17.99 *(978-0-399-16773-7(0)*, Philomel) Penguin Publishing Group.

Bordoni, Chiara. Sing-along Nursery Rhymes. Watt, Fiona. 2009. (Baby Board Books w/CD Ser.). 12p. (J). (gr. -1). bds. 15.99 *(978-0-7945-2351-0(X)*, Usborne) EDC Publishing.

Bordoy, Irene. El Patito Feo. Andersen, Hans Christian & Combel Editorial Staff. 2004. (Caballo Alado Clásico Series-Al Paso Ser.). (SPA & ENG.). 24p. (J). (gr. -1-k). 7.95 *(978-84-7864-764-4(3))* Combel Editorial, S.A. ESP. Dist: Independent Pubs. Group.

—El Patito Feo. Sarfatti, Esther, tr. 2006. (Bilingual Tales Ser.). (SPA.). 24p. (J). (gr. -1-3). pap. 3.99 *(978-0-439-77376-8(8)*, Scholastic en Espanol) Scholastic, Inc.

—La Sirenita (The Little Mermaid) Scholastic, Inc. Staff. 2007. (Bilingual Tales Ser.). (ENG & SPA.). 24p. (J). (gr. -1-3). pap. 3.99 *(978-0-439-87198-3(0))* Scholastic, Inc.

Boretzki, Anja. Animal Pants! Moses, Brian. ed. 2012. (ENG.). 24p. (J). (gr. -1-k). pap. 8.99 *(978-0-230-73614-6(9))* Macmillan Pubs., Ltd. GBR. Dist: Independent Pubs. Group.

—Doodle On! Football Doodles. Cookson, Paul. 2010. (Doodle On! Ser.). (ENG.). 80p. (J). (gr. k-4). 7.99 *(978-0-230-74851-4(1))* Macmillan Pubs., Ltd. GBR. Dist: Independent Pubs. Group.

—Doodle on! Christmas Doodles. Prasadam-Halls, Smriti. 2011. (Doodle On! Ser.). (ENG.). 160p. (J). (gr. k-4). 15.99 *(978-0-230-74421-9(4))* Macmillan Pubs., Ltd. GBR. Dist: Independent Pubs. Group.

—Scary Doodles. Prasadam-Halls, Smriti. 2011. (Doodle On! Ser.). (ENG.). 160p. (J). (gr. k-4). 15.99 *(978-0-230-73624-5(6))* Macmillan Pubs., Ltd. GBR. Dist: Independent Pubs. Group.

Borgella, Marjorie. Never Finished, Never Done! Scholastic, Inc. Staff & Brooks, Regina. 2004. (Just for You Ser.). (ENG.). 32p. pap. 3.99 *(978-0-439-56863-0(3)*, Teaching Resources) Scholastic, Inc.

Borgens, Matthew Todd, jt. illus. see Tavares, Matt.

Borgions, Mark. The Thrills & Chills of Amusement Parks. Brown, Jordan D. 2015. (Science of Fun Stuff Ser.). (ENG.). 48p. (J). (gr. 1-3). pap. 3.99 *(978-1-4814-2858-3(6)*, Simon Spotlight) Simon Spotlight.

Borgman, Jim. Chillax. Scott, Jerry. 2013. (Zits Ser.: 1). (ENG.). 256p. (YA). (gr. 8). pap. 9.99 *(978-0-06-222851-2(X)*, HarperTeen) HarperCollins Pubs.

—Shredded. Scott, Jerry. 2014. (Zits Ser.: 2). (ENG.). 224p. (YA). (gr. 8). pap. 9.99 *(978-0-06-222853-6(6)*, HarperTeen) HarperCollins Pubs.

Borgo, Deborah Colvin, jt. illus. see Goodell, Jon.

Borja, Robert. Heroes of American Explorations: Frontiers of America Series. McCall, Edith. 2011. 124p. 40.95 *(978-1-258-03255-5(4))* Literary Licensing, LLC.

—Stories of American Steamboats. McCall, Edith. 2011. 126p. 40.95 *(978-1-258-10111-4(4))* Literary Licensing, LLC.

Borkowski, Michael. X-Ray Vision! (DC Super Friends) Wrecks, Billy. 2014. (Pictureback(R) Ser.). (ENG.). 16p. (J). (gr. -1-2). 4.99 *(978-0-385-38718-7(0)*, Random Hse. Bks. for Young Readers) Random Hse. Children's Bks.

Borland, Polly, photos by. La Princesa y el Guisante. Child, Lauren. Rubio, Esther, tr. 2005. (SPA.). 48p. (J). (gr. 1-3). 22.99 *(978-84-8488-221-3(7))* Serres, Ediciones, S. L. ESP. Dist: Lectorum Pubns., Inc.

Borlasca, Hector. Big Kid Shoes. Kosara, Tori. 2011. (J). *(978-0-545-36967-1(3))* Scholastic, Inc.

—Halloween Hide & Seek: Hidden Picture Puzzles, 1 vol. Kalz, Jill. 2012. (Seek It Out Ser.). (ENG.). 32p. (gr. 1-2). 9.95 *(978-1-4048-7728-3(2))*; lib. bdg. 25.99 *(978-1-4048-7495-4(X))* Picture Window Bks.

—I Am Smart. Taylor-Butler, Christine. (My First Reader Ser.). (ENG.). 32p. (J). (gr. k-1). 2006. per. 3.95 *(978-0-516-24971-1(1))*; 2005. lib. bdg. 18.50 *(978-0-516-25176-9(7))* Scholastic Library Publishing. (Children's Pr.).

—It's Too Crowded in Here! And Other Jewish Folktales. 2010. 64p. (J). pap. 7.95 *(978-0-87441-850-7(X))* Behrman Hse., Inc.

—Jesus Loves Me, 1 vol. Zondervan Publishing Staff. 2008. (I Can Read! / Song Ser.). (ENG.). 32p. (J). (gr. -1-3). pap. 3.99 *(978-0-310-71619-8(5))* Zondervan.

—The Little Cookie Girl. Williams, Rozanne Lanczak. Hamaguchi, Carla, ed. 2003. (Sight Word Readers Ser.). 16p. (J). (gr. k-2). pap. 3.49 *(978-1-57471-967-3(X)*, 3589) Creative Teaching Pr., Inc.

—My House/Mi Casa. Rosa-Mendoza, Gladys. (English Spanish Foundations Ser.). (gr. -1-1). 2007. per. 19.95 *(978-1-931398-84-8(4))*; 2006. (ENG & SPA.). 20p. (J). bds. 6.95 *(978-1-931398-18-3(6))* Me+Mi Publishing.

—Pretend & Play Kitty: With Real Crown You Can Wear! Hapka, Cathy. 2004. (Role Play Ser.). 10p. (J). (gr. -1-18). bds. 6.99 *(978-1-57151-742-5(1))* Playhouse Publishing.

—30 Mice Are Very Nice. Fleming, Maria & Scholastic Canada Ltd. Staff. 2005. (Number Tales Ser.). (ENG.). 16p. (J). (gr. -1-1). pap. 2.99 *(978-0-439-69026-3(9))* Scholastic, Inc.

Borns, Steven, jt. illus. see Wiese, Kurt.

Borowick, Kathleen. You're the Detective! 23 Solve-Them-Yourself Mysteries. Lawrence, Treat. 2010. (ENG.). 80p. pap. 8.95 *(978-1-56792-397-1(6))* Godine, David R. Pub.

Borrajero, Judy. Snowflake's Vacation. Sprague, Howard Lee. 2011. 40p. pap. 9.95 *(978-1-881276-16-6(3))* Serey/Jones Pubs.

Borsan, Luis. Freaky Foods from Around the World: Platillos Sorprendentes de todo el Mundo. Winner, Ramana Moreno. Haake, Susana, tr. 2004. (ENG & SPA.). (J). (gr. 1-5). pap. 15.95 *(978-0-9651174-2-5(1))* BrainStorm 3000.

Borsch, Kim. Cookie's Colorful World. Kline, Joel. 2011. 32p. pap. 24.95 *(978-1-4560-7578-1(0))* America Star Bks.

Borstel, Ian von. Friends Forever: A Rachel Beth Tale, 1 vol. Marin, Dale Diane. 2009. 31p. pap. 24.95 *(978-1-61546-149-3(3))* America Star Bks.

Bosak, Virginia. Rachel & the Magic Beads. Buchanan, Johnny & Conway, Beth. 2007. 16p. (YA). pap. 7.99 *(978-0-9768772-9-5(5))* Wise Guides, LLC.

Bosch, David. Mommy Always Comes Back. Schnee-Bosch, Penny. 2013. 40p. pap. 13.95 *(978-0-9727993-6-2(2))* Athanata Arts, Ltd.

Bosch, Meritxell. BirdCatDog. Nordling, Lee. 2014. (J). lib. bdg. *(978-1-4677-4522-2(7)*, Graphic Universe) Lerner Publishing Group.

—Fishfishfish. Nordling, Lee. 2015. (Three-Story Bks.). (ENG.). 32p. (J). (gr. k-3). lib. bdg. 25.26 *(978-1-4677-4575-8(8)*, Graphic Universe) Lerner Publishing Group.

Bosch, Meritxell. FishFishFish. Nordling, Lee. 2015. (Three-Story Bks.). (ENG.). 32p. (J). (gr. k-3). pap. 6.95 ***(978-1-4677-4576-5(6)***, Graphic Universe) Lerner Publishing Group.

Bosch, Meritxell. SheHeWe. Nordling, Lee. 2015. (ENG.). 32p. (J). (gr. k-3). lib. bdg. 25.26 *(978-1-4677-4574-1(X)*, Graphic Universe) Lerner Publishing Group.

Bosch, Nicole. One-of-a-Kind Stamps & Crafts. Ross, Kathy. 2010. (Girl Crafts Ser.). (ENG.). 48p. (gr. 2-5). pap. 7.95 *(978-1-58013-885-7(3))* Lerner Publishing Group.

Bosch, Nicole in den. Beautiful Beads. Ross, Kathy. 2009. (Girl Crafts Ser.). (ENG.). 48p. (gr. 2-5). 26.60 *(978-0-8225-9214-3(2)*, Millbrook Pr.) Lerner Publishing Group.

—Bedroom Makeover Crafts. Ross, Kathy. 2008. (Girl Crafts Ser.). (ENG.). 48p. (gr. 2-5). 26.60 *(978-0-8225-7593-1(0)*, Millbrook Pr.); pap. 7.95 *(978-1-58013-823-9(3)*, First Avenue Editions) Lerner Publishing Group.

—Creative Kitchen Crafts. Ross, Kathy. 2010. (Girl Crafts Ser.). (ENG.). 48p. (gr. 2-5). lib. bdg. 26.60 *(978-0-8225-9217-4(7)*, Millbrook Pr.) Lerner Publishing Group.

—Fairy World Crafts. Ross, Kathy. 2008. (Girl Crafts Ser.). (ENG.). 48p. (gr. 2-5). lib. bdg. 26.60 *(978-0-8225-7509-2(4)*, Millbrook Pr.) Lerner Publishing Group.

—Girlfriends' Get-Together Craft Book. Ross, Kathy. 2007. (Girl Crafts Ser.). (ENG.). 48p. (gr. 2-5). pap. 7.95 *(978-0-7613-9465-5(6)*, First Avenue Editions) Lerner Publishing Group.

—Jazzy Jewelry, Pretty Purses, & More! Ross, Kathy. 2009. (Girl Crafts Ser.). (ENG.). 48p. (gr. 2-5). 26.60 *(978-0-8225-9212-9(6))*; pap. 7.95 *(978-1-58013-883-3(7)*, Millbrook Pr.) Lerner Publishing Group.

—The Mouse in the Matzah Factory. Medoff, Francine. 2003. (ENG.). 32p. (J). (gr. -1-3). pap. 6.95 *(978-1-58013-048-6(8)*, Kar-Ben Publishing) Lerner Publishing Group.

—One-of-a-Kind Stamps & Crafts. Ross, Kathy. 2010. (Girl Crafts Ser.). (ENG.). 48p. (gr. 2-5). lib. bdg. 26.60 *(978-0-8225-9216-7(9)*, Millbrook Pr.) Lerner Publishing Group.

Boscola, Carolyn. Peacock Parade. Camut, LeeAnn. 2010. (ENG.). 32p. pap. 10.99 *(978-1-4538-7915-3(3))* CreateSpace Independent Publishing Platform.

—Toe Jam. Camut, LeeAnn. 2011. (ENG.). 32p. pap. 10.99 *(978-1-4679-4977-4(9))* CreateSpace Independent Publishing Platform.

Bosgra, Johann. Diving for Colors in Hawaii: A Color Identification Book for Keiki. Hopkins, Jane. 2003. 18p. (J). bds. 7.95 *(978-0-9729905-1-6(8))* Beachhouse Publishing, LLC.

—Diving for Numbers in Hawaii. Hopkins, Jane. 2003. 20p. (J). bds. 7.95 *(978-0-9729905-0-9(X))* Beachhouse Publishing, LLC.

—Diving for Shapes in Hawaii: An Identification Book for Keiki. Gillespie, Jane. 2004. 20p. (J). bds. 7.95 *(978-1-933067-04-9(7))* Beachhouse Publishing, LLC.

Bosma, Sam. Scare Scape. Fisher, Sam. 2013. (ENG.). 352p. (J). (gr. 3-7). 16.99 *(978-0-545-52160-4(2)*, Scholastic Pr.) Scholastic, Inc.

Bosma, Sam. Stand-off. Smith, Andrew. 2015. (YA). pap. ***(978-1-4814-1830-0(0)***, Simon & Schuster Bks. For Young Readers) Simon & Schuster Bks. For Young Readers.

B

Bosma, Sam. Winger. Smith, Andrew. (ENG.). (YA). (gr. 7). 2014. 464p. pap. 11.99 *(978-1-4424-4493-5(2))*; 2013. 448p. 16.99 *(978-1-4424-4492-8(4))* Simon & Schuster Bks. For Young Readers. (Simon & Schuster Bks. For Young Readers).

Bosnia, Nella. Arturo y Clementina. Turin, Adela. (SPA.). 40p. (J). (gr. 3-5). *(978-84-264-3801-0(6))* Editorial Lumen ESP. Dist: Lectorum Pubns., Inc.

—La Herencia del Hada. Turin, Adela. (SPA.). 40p. (J). (gr. 3-5). *(978-84-264-3556-9(4))* Editorial Lumen ESP. Dist: Lectorum Pubns., Inc.

—Rosa Caramelo. Turin, Adela. (SPA.). 40p. (J). (gr. 2-4). *(978-84-264-3800-3(8))* Editorial Lumen ESP. Dist: Lectorum Pubns., Inc.

Bossi, Lisa Burnett. The Happiness Tree: Celebrating the Gifts of Trees We Treasure. Gosline, Andrea Alban. 2008. (ENG.). 40p. (J). (gr. k-3). 16.99 *(978-0-312-37017-6(2))* Feiwel & Friends.

—Ten Little Wishes: A Baby Animal Counting Book. Gosline, Andrea Alban. 2007. 40p. (J). (gr. -1-k). 16.89 *(978-0-06-053411-0(7))* HarperCollins Pubs.

Bosson, Jo-Ellen. What in the World Is a Homophone? Presson, Leslie. 192p. (J). 11.95 *(978-0-7641-2698-7(9))* Barron's Educational Series, Inc.

Bostian, Laurie. Appalachian State, A to Z. Webb, Anne Aldridge. 2010. (J). 18.95 *(978-1-933251-69-1(7))* Parkway Pubs., Inc.

Bostic, Alex. Man of Destiny: The Life of Leopold Sedar Senghor. Collin, Grace. 2006. 32p. (J). lib. bdg. 16.95 *(978-1-886366-15-2(2))* Sights Productions.

Bostock, Mike. Flip the Flaps: Whales & Dolphins. Allen, Judy. 2011. (Flip the Flaps Ser.). (ENG.). 32p. (J). (gr. -1-1). pap. 6.99 *(978-0-7534-6497-7(7))*, Kingfisher) Roaring Brook Pr.

—Gentle Giant Octopus: Read, Listen & Wonder. Wallace, Karen. 2008. (Read, Listen, & Wonder Ser.). (ENG.). 32p. (J). (gr. -1-3). pap. 8.99 *(978-0-7636-3869-6(2))* Candlewick Pr.

—Think of an Eel: Read, Listen & Wonder. Wallace, Karen. 2009. (Read, Listen & Wonder Ser.). (ENG.). 32p. (J). (gr. -1-3). pap. 8.99 *(978-0-7636-3994-5(X))* Candlewick Pr.

—Think of an Eel Big Book. Wallace, Karen. 2004. (Read & Wonder Ser.). (ENG.). 32p. (J). (gr. -1-2). pap. 24.99 *(978-0-7636-2470-5(5))* Candlewick Pr.

—Think of an Eel with Audio, Peggable: Read, Listen & Wonder. Wallace, Karen. 2009. (Read, Listen & Wonder Ser.). (ENG.). 32p. (J). (gr. -1-3). pap. 9.99 *(978-0-7636-4398-0(X))* Candlewick Pr.

Boston, David. Dancing Turtle: A Folktale from Brazil. DeSpain, Pleasant. 2005. (ENG.). 32p. (J). (gr. -1-2). 15.95 *(978-0-87483-502-1(X))* August Hse. Pubs., Inc.

—Wonder Tales from Around the World. 2006. (World Storytelling from August House Ser.). (ENG.). 158p. (J). (gr. 3-7). pap. 19.95 *(978-0-87483-422-2(8))*, AH228) August Hse. Pubs., Inc.

Boston, Peter. The Stones of Green Knowe. Boston, L. M. 2006. (Green Knowe Ser.: 6). (ENG.). 144p. (J). (gr. 2-5). pap. 5.95 *(978-0-15-205566-0(5))* Houghton Mifflin Harcourt Publishing Co.

Bostrom, Christopher. The Secret of the Twelve Days of Christmas. Bostrom, Kathleen. 2005. 68p. (gr. -1-7). per. 10.95 *(978-1-931195-74-4(9))* KiwE Publishing, Ltd.

Bostrom, Laura. I Am. Propes, Chrysti Carol. 3rd ed. 2013. 40p. 24.95 *(978-0-9790791-8-4(7))* Fig & The Vine, LLC, The.

—I Am Here. Propes, Chrysti Carol. 3rd ed. 2013. 32p. 24.95 *(978-0-9790791-9-1(5))* Fig & The Vine, LLC, The.

Bostrom, Laura L. I Am. Propes, Chrysti Carol. 2010. (ENG.). 38p. pap. 12.99 *(978-1-4505-9772-2(6))* CreateSpace Independent Publishing Platform.

Bostrom, Sally. The Magic Apple Tree. Kendall, Jack. l.t. ed. 2006. (ENG.). 48p. (J). per. 9.95 *(978-0-9787740-4-2(3))* Peppertree Pr., The.

Bosworth, David. Song of the Jackalope. Campbell, Roy. 2nd ed. 2006. 140p. (YA). pap. 12.95 *(978-1-933538-04-4(X))* Bridgeway Bks.

Bottner, Barbara. Pish & Posh. Bottner, Barbara. Kruglik, Gerald. 2004. (I Can Read Bks.). 48p. (J). (gr. k-3). pap. 15.99 *(978-0-06-051416-7(7))* HarperCollins Pubs.

—Pish & Posh Wish for Fairy Wings. Bottner, Barbara. Kruglik, Gerald. (I Can Read Book 2 Ser.). 48p. (J). 2007. (ENG.). (gr. k-3). pap. 3.99 *(978-0-06-051421-1(3))*, Tegen, Katherine Bks); 2006. (ENG.). (gr. -1-3). 15.99 *(978-0-06-051419-8(1))*, HarperCollins); 2006. (gr. -1-3). lib. bdg. 16.89 *(978-0-06-051420-4(5))* HarperCollins Pubs.

Bouchain, Nava. Los Diminutos. Suarez de la Prida, Isabel. 2003. (SPA.). 32p. (J). (gr. k-3). pap. 6.95 *(978-968-19-0631-3(4))* Santillana USA Publishing Co., Inc.

Bouchal, Renee'. The World Will Never Forget. Baurys, Tamra. 2011. 34p. pap. 12.95 *(978-0-9833354-2-9(7))* Amira Rock Publishing.

Bouchard, Jocelyne. The Kids Book of the Far North. Love, Ann & Drake, Jane. 2009. (Kids Book Of Ser.). (ENG.). 48p. (J). (gr. 3-7). 14.95 *(978-1-55453-258-2(2))* Kids Can Pr., Ltd. CAN. Dist: Univ. of Toronto Pr.

Boucher, Julie. The Little Tree That Would Be Great. Desrochers, Diane O. 2009. 36p. pap. 14.95 *(978-0-9819727-7-0(2))* Fiction Publishing, Inc.

Boucher, Michel. Enredos de Familia. Dumont, Virginie et al. 2004. (Arbol de la Vida Ser.). (SPA.). 64p. (J). 13.99 *(978-84-8488-098-1(2))* Serres, Ediciones, S. L. ESP. Dist: Lectorum Pubns., Inc.

Bouganim, Revital. The Great Adventures of Bottom the Bassett Hound. Ryshpan-Harris, Joanne. 2008. 60p. (J). pap. 5.95 *(978-1-4259-8558-5(0))* AuthorHouse.

Bouma, Paddy. Nelson Mandela: Long Walk to Freedom. 2009. (ENG.). 64p. (J). (gr. 2-6). 18.99 *(978-1-59643-566-7(6))* Roaring Brook Pr.

Bour-Chollet, Céline, et al. La Hora. Bour-Chollet, Céline et al. (Coleccion Mundo Maravilloso). (SPA.). 48p. (J). (gr. 2-4). *(978-84-348-4485-8(0))*, SM1439) SM Ediciones ESP. Dist: Lectorum Pubns., Inc.

Bourbois, J. M. The Caterpillar's Dream. Cramer, Kimberley M. 2014. (ENG.). 20p. (J). (gr. -1-3). pap. 8.99 *(978-1-63063-302-8(X))* Tate Publishing & Enterprises, LLC.

Bourbonnière, Sylvie. Dream Songs Night Songs: From China to Senegal. Lacoursiere, Patrick. 2006. (ENG.). 36p. (J). (gr. -1-2). 16.95 *(978-2-923163-24-6(9))* La Montagne Secrete CAN. Dist: Independent Pubs. Group.

—Dream Songs Night Songs: From Mali to Louisiana. Lacoursiere, Patrick. 2006. (ENG.). 36p. (J). (gr. -1-2). 16.95 *(978-2-923163-06-2(0))* La Montagne Secrete CAN. Dist: Independent Pubs. Group.

Bourbonniere, Sylvie. Tales from the Isle of Spice. Keens-Douglas, Richardo. 2004. (ENG.). 48p. (J). (gr. 2-6). 19.95 *(978-1-55037-867-2(8))*, 9781550378672) Annick Pr., Ltd. CAN. Dist: Firefly Bks., Ltd.

Bourdin, Samuel, photos by. Guy Bourdin. Gingeras, Alison M. rev. ed. 2006. (ENG., 128p. (gr. 8-17). 27.95 *(978-0-7148-4303-2(2))* Phaidon Pr., Inc.

Boureau, Silvere. A Bully Grows Up: Erik Meets the Wizard: Adult Guide Edition, 1. Hacker, Caryn Sabes. 2006. 34p. (J). tchr. ed. 15.95 *(978-0-9791046-0-2(2))* Caryn Solutions, LLC.

Bourgeau, Vincent. Help! the Wolf Is Coming! Ramadier, Cédric. Burgess, Linda, tr. from FRE. 2015.Tr. of Au Secours, Voila le Loup!. (ENG.). 22p. (J). (gr. -1 — 1). bds. 14.99 *(978-1-927271-84-1(3))* Gecko Pr. NZL. Dist: Lerner Publishing Group.

Bourgonje, Chantal. Adventures with Astro the Alien. Holcroft, Trevor. 2011. (ENG.). 92p. pap. 5.99 *(978-1-4563-6788-6(9))* CreateSpace Independent Publishing Platform.

Bourke, John-Francis. Hands Can. Willis Hudson, Cheryl. 2013. (ENG.). 32p. (J). (-k). 4.99 *(978-0-7636-6336-0(0))* Candlewick Pr.

—Las Manos. Hudson, Cheryl Willis. 2014. (ENG.). 32p. (J). (-k). pap. 4.99 *(978-0-7636-7392-5(7))* Candlewick Pr.

Bourke, John-Francis. Hands Can. Bourke, John-Francis, photos by. Hudson, Cheryl Willis. 2003. (ENG.). 32p. (J). (gr. k-k). 16.99 *(978-0-7636-1667-0(2))* Candlewick Pr.

Bourke, John-Francis, photos by. Hands Can. Hudson, Cheryl Willis. 2003. (J). (gr. k-k). 2012. 32p. pap. 24.99 *(978-0-7636-5819-9(7))*; 2007. 24p. bds. 7.99 *(978-0-7636-3292-2(9))* Candlewick Pr.

Bournakis, Maria. Everlasting Truth. Vardamaskos, Angela. 2008. 48p. pap. 24.95 *(978-1-60610-950-2(2))* America Star Bks.

Bourne, C. L. Sam the Big Blue Bear, Vol. 1. Bourne, C. L. Date not set. 24p. (J). (gr. k-4). pap. *(978-0-9651281-4-8(8))* Beach Front Bks.

Bourrouet, Jonathan. Alphabet Fun, Book 1: Coloring & Activity Book. Bumpers, Katrina B. Lopez, Eddie, ed. 2008. 64p. pap. 10.95 *(978-0-9797208-0-2(X))* K's Kids Publishing.

Bourseiller, Philippe, photos by. 50 Ways to Save the Earth. Jankéliowitch, Anne. 2008. (ENG., 144p. (J). (gr. 3-7). 19.95 *(978-0-8109-7239-1(5))*, Abrams Bks. for Young Readers) Abrams.

Bouse, Biff, jt. illus. see Mann, Derek.

Bousum, Julie. The Mouse Family Christmas, 1 vol. Johnson, Gerald J. J. 2009. 26p. pap. 24.95 *(978-1-61546-536-1(7))* America Star Bks.

Boutavant, Marc. Around the World with Mouk. 2009. (ENG.). 32p. (J). (gr. 3-17). 17.99 *(978-0-8118-6926-3(1))* Chronicle Bks. LLC.

—Edmond, the Moonlit Party. Desbordes, Astrid. 2015. (ENG.). 32p. (J). (gr. -1-3). 17.95 *(978-1-59270-174-2(4))* Enchanted Lion Bks., LLC.

—For Just One Day. Chronicle Books Staff & Leuck, Laura. 2009. (ENG.). 32p. (J). (gr. -1 — 1). 16.99 *(978-0-8118-5610-2(0))* Chronicle Bks. LLC.

—Ghosts. Goldie, Sonia. 2013. (ENG.). 40p. (J). (gr. -1-3). 16.95 *(978-1-59270-142-1(6))* Enchanted Lion Bks., LLC.

—Just a Donkey Like You & Me. Guibert, Emmanuel. 2013. (Ariol Graphic Novels Ser.: 1). (ENG.). 124p. (J). (gr. 1-5). pap. 12.99 *(978-1-59707-399-8(7))* Papercutz.

—Never Tickle a Tiger. Butchart, Pamela. 2015. (ENG.). 32p. (J). (gr. -1-1). 18.99 *(978-1-4088-3903-4(2))*, Bloomsbury USA Childrens) Bloomsbury USA.

—Thunder Horse. Guibert, Emmanuel. 2013. (Ariol Graphic Novels Ser.: 2). (ENG.). 124p. (J). (gr. 1-5). pap. 12.99 *(978-1-59707-412-4(8))* Papercutz.

—What Happens Next? Davies, Nicola. 2012. (Flip the Flap & Find Out Ser.). (ENG.). 24p. (J). (gr. -1-2). 9.99 *(978-0-7636-6264-6(X))* Candlewick Pr.

—What Will I Be? Davies, Nicola. 2012. (Flip the Flap & Find Out Ser.). (ENG.). 32p. (J). (gr. -1-2). 9.99 *(978-0-7636-5803-8(0))* Candlewick Pr.

—Who's Like Me? Davies, Nicola. 2012. (Flip the Flap & Find Out Ser.). (ENG.). 24p. (J). (gr. -1-2). 9.99 *(978-0-7636-5802-1(2))* Candlewick Pr.

Boutavant, Marc. Happy as a Pig... Boutavant, Marc. Guibert, Emmanuel. 2013. (Ariol Graphic Novels Ser.: 3). (ENG.). 124p. (J). (gr. 1-5). pap. 12.99 *(978-1-59707-487-2(X))* Papercutz.

Boutheyette, Valerie. After the Ark: Eli & Ella the Little Elephants - Children of the King! Teis, Sean P. 2013. 32p. pap. 14.99 *(978-1-937129-84-2(5))* Faithful Life Pubs.

Bouthyette, Valerie. Beauty, the Donkey-Mooing Beltie. Lindemer, C. R. 2008. 32p. (J). pap. *(978-0-9821058-2-5(7))* Shapato Publishing, LLC.

—A Change of Hats. Dowling, Iris Gray. 2012. 28p. pap. 14.99 *(978-1-937129-36-1(5))* Faithful Life Pubs.

—Gertrude & the Creature. Costello, Judi. 2008. 28p. pap. 24.95 *(978-1-60672-737-9(0))* America Star Bks.

—Isla Saves Egypt. Dewees-Gilger, Connie. 2013. (ENG.). (J). 14.95 *(978-1-62086-375-6(8))* Mascot Bks., Inc.

—The Leprechaun Trap. 2008. 40p. (J). pap. 10.95 *(978-0-9800835-0-7(8))* Clinch Media.

—Old Mean Molly, 1 vol. Arline-Hicks, Patience & Hicks, Wendi N. 2009. 38p. pap. 24.95 *(978-1-60749-678-6(X))* America Star Bks.

—A Pony for My Birthday. Dowling, Iris Gray. 2012. 36p. pap. 10.99 *(978-1-937129-50-7(0))* Faithful Life Pubs.

—Timid Timmy the Brave. Hladik, Terry L. 2008. 28p. pap. 12.95 *(978-0-9822540-5-9(9))* Peppertree Pr., The.

Boutin, Arnaud. What's New? What's Missing? What's Different? 2013. (ENG.). 96p. (J). (gr. 1-4). pap. 12.99 *(978-1-60905-352-9(4))* Blue Apple Bks.

Bové, Lorelay. No Slurping, No Burping! A Tale of Table Manners. LaReau, Kara. 2014. (ENG.). 40p. (J). (gr. -1 — 1). 16.99 *(978-1-4231-5733-5(8))* Disney Publishing Worldwide.

Bove, Neysa & Rucker, Georgia. My Favorite Shoes: A Touch-and-Feel Shoe-Stravaganza! Merberg, Julie. 2013. (ENG.). 16p. (J). (gr. -1 — 1). bds. 12.99 *(978-1-935703-64-8(1))* Downtown Bookworks.

Bowater, Charlie. Scrap City. Thornton, D. S. 2015. (Middle-Grade Novels Ser.). (ENG.). 352p. (gr. 4-8). lib. bdg. 26.65 *(978-1-4965-0475-3(5))* Stone Arch Bks.

Bowden, Cecelia. Peggy Sue & the Pepper Patch. Hopper, Missy. 2010. 32p. (J). *(978-1-57736-430-6(9))* Providence Hse Pubs.

Bowden, Rob, photos by. Sydney. Mason, Paul. 2007. (Global Cities Ser.). 64p. (gr. 5-8). lib. bdg. 30.00 *(978-0-7910-8849-4(9))*, Chelsea Hse.) Facts On File, Inc.

—Tokyo. Barber, Nicola. 2006. (Global Cities Ser.). 64p. (gr. 5-8). 30.00 *(978-0-7910-8855-5(3))*, Chelsea Hse.) Facts On File, Inc.

Bowden, Rob & Cooper, Adrian, photos by. London. Mason, Paul. 2006. (Global Cities Ser.). 64p. (gr. 5-8). 30.00 *(978-0-7910-8852-4(9))*, Chelsea Hse.) Facts On File, Inc.

Bowen, Betsy. Big Belching Bog. Root, Phyllis. 2010. (ENG.). 40p. (gr. 2-3). 15.95 *(978-0-8166-3359-3(2))* Univ. of Minnesota Pr.

—Dhegdheer: A Scary Somali Folktale. 2007. (SOM & ENG.). *(978-1-931016-18-6(6))*; *(978-1-931016-19-3(4))* Minnesota Humanities Ctr.

—Great Wolf & the Good Woodsman. Hoover, Helen. 2005. (Fesler-Lampert Minnesota Heritage Ser.). 40p. (J). (gr. -1-7). 14.95 *(978-0-8166-4445-2(4))* Univ. of Minnesota Pr.

—Plant a Pocket of Prairie. Root, Phyllis. 2014. (ENG.). 40p. 14.95 *(978-0-8166-7980-5(0))* Univ. of Minnesota Pr.

Bowen, Dean. A Song for Lorkie. Castles, Jennifer. 2012. (ENG.). 32p. (J). (gr. -1-k). 22.99 *(978-1-74237-718-6(1))* Allen & Unwin AUS. Dist: Independent Pubs. Group.

Bowen, Lance. Keiki's First Word Book. 2004. (HAW & ENG.). 32p. (J). pap. 12.95 *(978-0-9729905-5-4(0))* Beachhouse Publishing, LLC.

—Keiki's Second Word Book. 2008. 32p. 14.95 *(978-1-933067-25-4(X))* Beachhouse Publishing, LLC.

—Tons of Things to Do for Hawaii's Kids: Activities, Adventures & Excursions for Keiki Eager to Explore Oahu. Ching, Carrie. 2004. 160p. (J). pap. 14.95 *(978-0-9729905-2-3(6))* Beachhouse Publishing, LLC.

Bower, Brittany, jt. illus. see Bower, Jan.

Bower, Jan. Cody's Castle: Encouraging Others. Bower, Gary. l.t. ed. 2004. (Thinking of Others: Vol. 4). 32p. (J). 16.95 *(978-0-9704621-3-8(1))* Storybook Meadow Publishing.

—The Garden Where I Grow: And Other Poems for Cultivating a Happy Family. Bower, Gary. 2012. (Bright Future Bks.). (ENG.). 32p. (J). 11.99 *(978-0-9845236-2-7(6))* Storybook Meadow Publishing.

—I'm a Michigan Kid! Bower, Gary. 2005. 48p. (J). 17.99 *(978-0-9704621-6-9(6))* Storybook Meadow Publishing.

—Jingle in My Pocket. Bower, Gary. 2009. 32p. 11.99 *(978-0-9704621-9-0(0))* Storybook Meadow Publishing.

—Mommy Love. Bower, Gary. 2012. (Little Lovable Board Bks.). (ENG.). 16p. (J). bds. 8.50 *(978-0-9845236-0-3(X))* Storybook Meadow Publishing.

—Over Land & Sea: The Story of International Adoption, 1 vol. Layne, Steven L. 2005. (ENG.). 32p. (J). (gr. k-3). 16.99 *(978-1-58980-182-0(2))* Pelican Publishing Co., Inc.

—The Person I Marry. Bower, Gary. 2008. 32p. (J). pap. 11.99 *(978-0-9704621-7-6(4))* Storybook Meadow Publishing.

—There's a Party in Heaven! Bower, Gary. 2007. 31p. (J). 11.99 *(978-0-9704621-8-3(2))* Storybook Meadow Publishing.

Bower, Jan & Bower, Brittany. I'm a Michigan Kid Coloring & Activity Book. Bower, Gary. 2006. 48p. (J). pap. 7.95 *(978-0-9704621-5-2(8))*, Bower Bks.) Storybook Meadow Publishing.

Bower, Tamara. How the Amazon Queen Fought the Prince of Egypt. Bower, Tamara. 2014. (ENG.). 36p. (J). (gr. 2-6). 16.99 *(978-1-4814-2526-1(9))*, Atheneum Bks. for Young Readers) Simon & Schuster Children's Publishing.

—The Shipwrecked Sailor: An Egyptian Tale with Hieroglyphs. Bower, Tamara. 2014. (ENG.). 32p. (J). (gr. 2-5). 16.99 *(978-1-4814-2525-4(0))*, Atheneum Bks. for Young Readers) Simon & Schuster Children's Publishing.

Bowers, Jenny. Little Pear Tree. Williams, Rachel. 2014. (ENG.). 12p. (J). (-k). bds. 14.99 *(978-0-7636-7126-6(6))*, Big Picture Press) Candlewick Pr.

—Sticker Style: Shop. Big Picture Press, Big Picture. 2015. (ENG.). 12p. (J). (gr. k-3). pap. 12.99 *(978-0-7636-7770-1(1))*, Big Picture Press) Candlewick Pr.

Bowers, Jenny. Sticker Style: House. Bowers, Jenny. 2015. (ENG.). 12p. (J). (gr. k-3). pap. 12.99 *(978-0-7636-7983-5(6))*, Big Picture Press) Candlewick Pr.

Bowers, Tim. Acoustic Rooster & His Barnyard Band. Alexander, Kwame. 2011. (ENG.). 32p. (gr. k-5). lib. bdg. 15.95 *(978-1-58536-688-0(9))* Sleeping Bear Pr.

—Custard Surprise. Lodge, Bernard. 2007. (I Can Read Bks.). 48p. (J). (gr. -1-3). 15.99 *(978-0-06-073687-3(9))* HarperCollins Pubs.

—Dogku. Clements, Andrew. 2007. (ENG.). 40p. (J). (gr. -1-3). 17.99 *(978-0-689-85823-9(X))*, Atheneum Bks. for Young Readers) Simon & Schuster Children's Publishing.

—Dream Big, Little Pig! Yamaguchi, Kristi. 2011. (ENG.). 32p. (J). (gr. -1-3). 16.99 *(978-1-4022-5275-4(7))*, Sourcebooks Jabberwocky) Sourcebooks, Inc.

—First Dog. Lewis, J. Patrick. 2009. (ENG.). 32p. (J). (gr. k-6). 15.95 *(978-1-58536-467-1(3))* Sleeping Bear Pr.

—Fun Dog, Sun Dog, 0 vols. Heiligman, Deborah. 2011. (ENG.). 32p. (J). (gr. -1-2). pap. 7.99 *(978-0-7614-5836-4(0))*, 9780761458364, Amazon Children's Publishing) Amazon Publishing.

—Gorgonzola: A Very Stinkysaurus. Palatini, Margie. 2008. (ENG.). 32p. (J). (gr. -1-2). 17.99 *(978-0-06-073897-6(9))*, Tegen, Katherine Bks) HarperCollins Pubs.

—It's a Big World, Little Pig! Yamaguchi, Kristi. 2012. (ENG.). 32p. (J). (gr. k-3). 16.99 *(978-1-4022-6644-7(8))*, Sourcebooks Jabberwocky) Sourcebooks, Inc.

—Knuckleball Ned. Dickey, R. A. 2014. (ENG.). 32p. (J). (gr. -1-k). 17.99 *(978-0-8037-4038-9(7))*, Dial) Penguin Publishing Group.

—Little Whistle. Rylant, Cynthia. 2007. (Little Whistle Ser.). 32p. (gr. -1-3). 24.21 *(978-1-59961-253-9(4))* Spotlight.

—Little Whistle - 4 Titles. ABDO Publishing Company Staff. 2007. (Little Whistle Ser.). (ENG.). 32p. 96.84 *(978-1-59961-252-2(6))* Spotlight.

—Little Whistle's Christmas. Rylant, Cynthia. 2007. (Little Whistle Ser.). 32p. (gr. -1-3). 24.21 *(978-1-59961-254-6(2))* Spotlight.

—Little Whistle's Dinner Party. Rylant, Cynthia. 2007. (Little Whistle Ser.). 32p. (gr. -1-3). 24.21 *(978-1-59961-255-3(0))* Spotlight.

—Little Whistle's Medicine. Rylant, Cynthia. 2007. (Little Whistle Ser.). 32p. (gr. -1-2). 24.21 *(978-1-59961-256-0(9))* Spotlight.

—Memoirs of a Goldfish. Scillian, Devin. 2010. (ENG.). 32p. (J). (gr. -1-3). 15.95 *(978-1-58536-507-4(6))* Sleeping Bear Pr.

—Memoirs of a Hamster. Scillian, Devin. 2013. (ENG.). 32p. (J). (gr. -1-2). 15.99 *(978-1-58536-831-0(8))*, 202365) Sleeping Bear Pr.

—Memoirs of an Elf. Scillian, Devin. 2014. (ENG.). 32p. (J). (gr. 1-4). 16.99 *(978-1-58536-910-2(1))*, 203676) Sleeping Bear Pr.

—Pirate's Lullaby. Wessels, Marcie. 2015. (ENG.). 32p. (J). (gr. -1-2). 19.99 *(978-0-375-97352-9(4))* Random Hse., Inc.

—Puss in Boots. Findlay, Lisa. 2008. (Step into Reading Ser.). (ENG.). 48p. (J). (gr. k-3). pap. 3.99 *(978-0-375-84671-7(9))* Random Hse., Inc.

—Rappy the Raptor. Gutman, Dan. 2015. (ENG.). 40p. (J). (gr. -1-3). 17.99 *(978-0-06-229180-6(7))* HarperCollins Pubs.

—Sam & Jack: Three Stories. Moran, Alex. ed. 2003. (Green Light Readers Level 1 Ser.). (ENG.). 24p. (J). (gr. -1-3). pap. 3.95 *(978-0-15-204862-4(6))* Houghton Mifflin Harcourt Publishing Co.

—Shampoodle. Holub, Joan. 2009. (Step into Reading Ser.). (ENG.). 32p. (J). (gr. -1-1). pap. 3.99 *(978-0-375-85576-4(9))*; lib. bdg. 12.99 *(978-0-375-95576-1(3))* Random Hse., Inc.

—Snow Dog, Go Dog, 0 vols. Heiligman, Deborah. 2013. (ENG.). (J). (gr. -1-2). 15.99 *(978-1-4778-1724-7(7))*, 9781477817247, Amazon Children's Publishing) Amazon Publishing.

—Suppose You Meet a Dinosaur: A First Book of Manners. Sierra, Judy. 2012. (ENG.). 40p. (J). (gr. -1-2). 16.99 *(978-0-375-86720-0(1))*; 19.99 *(978-0-375-96720-7(6))* Knopf, Alfred A. Inc.

—10 Hungry Rabbits: Counting & Color Concepts. Lobel, Anita. 2012. (ENG.). 24p. (J). (gr. k-k). 9.99 *(978-0-375-86864-1(X))* Knopf, Alfred A. Inc.

Bowers, Tim. First Dog's White House Christmas. Bowers, Tim. Lewis, J. Patrick & Zappitello, Beth. 2010. (ENG.). 32p. (J). (gr. 1-4). 15.95 *(978-1-58536-503-6(3))*, 202197) Sleeping Bear Pr.

Bowes, Brian. Ivy, Homeless in San Francisco. Brenner, Summer. 2nd ed. 2011. (ENG.). 176p. (J). (gr. 4-7). pap. 15.00 *(978-1-60486-317-8(X))* PM Pr.

Bowker, Margie. The Adventures of Clever Kitty. Rouse, Walt. 2013. 56p. pap. *(978-1-4602-1254-7(1))* FriesenPress.

Bowler, Colin. The Big Posh Yacht. Volke, Gordon. 2004. 24p. pap. 7.00 *(978-1-84161-116-7(6))* Ravette Publishing, Ltd. GBR. Dist: Parkwest Pubns., Inc.

—The Little Lost Whale. Volke, Gordon. 2004. 24p. pap. 7.00 *(978-1-84161-118-1(2))* Ravette Publishing, Ltd. GBR. Dist: Parkwest Pubns., Inc.

—Louis the Lifeboat Activity Sticker Book. Volke, Gordon. 2004. 16p. pap. 6.00 *(978-1-84161-120-4(4))* Ravette Publishing, Ltd. GBR. Dist: Parkwest Pubns., Inc.

—The Nasty Black Stuff. Volke, Gordon. 2004. 24p. pap. 7.00 *(978-1-84161-119-8(0))* Ravette Publishing, Ltd. GBR. Dist: Parkwest Pubns., Inc.

—The Pirate's Gold. Volke, Gordon. 2004. 24p. pap. 7.00 *(978-1-84161-117-4(4))* Ravette Publishing, Ltd. GBR. Dist: Parkwest Pubns., Inc.

Bowles, Carol. Saving the Rain Forest with Cammie & Cooper. Albert, Toni Diana. l.t. ed. 2003. 32p. (J). pap. 7.95 *(978-1-929432-02-8(X))*, 800-353-2791) Trickle Creek Bks.

Bowles, Charlene. Mix-Up: Swift the Cat-Human Book 1. Bowles, Angelo. 2013. (ENG.). 78p. pap. 6.99 *(978-0-615-79424-2(6))* VAO Publishing.

—Swift the Cat-Human: Omnibus. Bowles, Angelo. 2013. (ENG.). 240p. pap. 13.99 *(978-0-615-79117-3(4))* VAO Publishing.

Bowles, Doug. The Gingerbread Man (El Hombre de Pan de Jengibre), Grades PK - 3. McCafferty, Catherine. 2007. (Keepsake Stories Ser.). (ENG & SPA.). 32p. (gr. -1-3). pap. 3.99 *(978-0-7696-5415-7(0))* Carson-Dellosa Publishing, LLC.

—Johnny Moore & the Wright Brothers' Flying Machine. Schulz, Walter A. 2011. (History Speaks: Picture Books Plus Reader's Theater Ser.). 48p. pap. 56.72 *(978-0-7613-7633-0(X))* Lerner Publishing Group.

—Johnny Moore & the Wright Brothers' Flying Machine. Schulz, Walter A. & Schultz, Walter A. 2011. (History Speaks: Picture Books Plus Reader's Theater Ser.). (ENG.). 48p. (gr. 2-4). pap. 9.95 *(978-0-7613-7117-5(6))* Lerner Publishing Group.

—Johnny Moore & the Wright Brothers' Flying Machine. Schulz, Walter A. 2011. (History Speaks: Picture Books Plus Reader's Theater Ser.). (ENG.). 48p. (gr. 2-4). lib. bdg. 27.93 *(978-0-7613-5876-3(5))*, Millbrook Pr.) Lerner Publishing Group.

—Little Baseball. Herzog, Brad. 2011. (Little Sports Ser.). (ENG.). 22p. (J). 7.95 *(978-1-58536-547-0(5))* Sleeping Bear Pr.
—Little Basketball. Herzog, Brad. 2011. (Little Sports Ser.). (ENG.). 22p. 9.95 *(978-1-58536-181-6(X))* Sleeping Bear Pr.
—Little Football. Herzog, Brad. 2011. (Little Sports Ser.). (ENG.). 22p. (J). 7.95 *(978-1-58536-546-3(7))* Sleeping Bear Pr.
—Little Soccer. Herzog, Brad. 2011. (Little Sports Ser.). (ENG.). 22p. 9.95 *(978-1-58536-197-7(6))* Sleeping Bear Pr.
—One Kansas Farmer: A Kansas Number Book. Scillian, Devin & Scillian, Corey. 2009. (Discover America State by State Ser.). (ENG.). 40p. (J). (gr. k-6). 16.95 *(978-1-58536-182-3(8))* Sleeping Bear Pr.
—P Is for Prairie Dog: A Prairie Alphabet. Fredericks, Anthony D. 2011. (Sleeping Bear Alphabets Ser.). (ENG.). 32p. (J). (gr. k-6). 16.95 *(978-1-58536-508-1(4))* Sleeping Bear Pr.
—S Is for Sunflower: A Kansas Alphabet. Scillian, Devin & Scillian, Corey. 2004. (State Ser.). (ENG.). 40p. (J). 17.95 *(978-1-58536-061-1(9)*, 1235980) Sleeping Bear Pr.
Bowles, Doug. G Is for Gold Medal: An Olympics Alphabet. Bowles, Doug. Herzog, Brad. 2011. (ENG.). 32p. (gr. k-5). 15.95 *(978-1-58536-462-6(2))* Sleeping Bear Pr.
Bowles, Janice. El primer día de escuela de Katy: Fiction-to-Fact Big Book. Jones, Tammy & Smith, Carrie. enl. ed. 2004. (SPA.). (J). pap. 26.00 *(978-1-4108-2365-6(2)*, 23652) Benchmark Education Co.
Bowles, Jennifer. Alexander & the Great Vegetable Feud. Hawkins, Linda J. 2004. 40p. (J). (gr. k-5). 19.99 *(978-0-9742806-1-5(5))* Heart to Heart Publishing, Inc.
Bowles, Michael J. N. Look What I See! Where Can I Be? In the Neighborhood. Michels, Dia L. 2005. (Look What I See! Where Can I Be? Ser.: Vol. 1). (ENG.). 32p. (J). (gr. -1-12). 9.95 *(978-1-930775-00-8(8))* Platypus Media, L.L.C.
Bowles, Michael J. N., photos by. Look What I See! Where Can I Be? At Home. Michels, Dia L. 2005. (ENG., 32p. (J). (gr. -1-12). 9.95 *(978-1-930775-06-0(7))* Platypus Media, L.L.C.
—Look What I See! Where Can I Be? At the Synagogue. Michels, Dia L. 2005. (ENG., 32p. (J). (gr. -1-3). 9.95 *(978-1-930775-16-9(4))* Platypus Media, L.L.C.
—Look What I See! Where Can I Be? Visiting China. Michels, Dia L. 2005. (Look What I See! Where Can I Be? Ser.: Vol. 5). (ENG., 32p. (J). (gr. -1-3). 9.95 *(978-1-930775-15-2(6))* Platypus Media, L.L.C.
—Look What I See! Where Can I Be? With My Animal Friends. Michels, Dia L. l.t. ed. 2005. (Look What I See! Where Can I Be? Ser.: Vol. 3). (ENG., 32p. (J). (gr. -1-12). 9.95 *(978-1-930775-07-7(5))* Platypus Media, L.L.C.
—Look What I See! Where Can I Be? 5 Book Set, 5 vols. Michels, Dia L. 2005. (Look What I See! Where Can I Be? Ser.: 1-5). (ENG., 32p. (J). (gr. -1-12). 69.95 *(978-1-930775-22-0(9))* Platypus Media, L.L.C.
Bowles, Michael J. N. & Bowles, Michael J. N., photos by. Look What I See! Where Can I Be? With My Animal Friends. Michels, Dia. 2007. (ENG., 32p. (J). 9.95 *(978-1-930775-08-4(3))* Platypus Media, L.L.C.
Bowles, Michael J. N., jt. photos by see Bowles, Michael J. N.
Bowles, Paula. What Goes Up. Bowles, Paula. 2013. (ENG.). 32p. (J). (gr. -1-1). 12.95 *(978-1-58925-119-9(9))* Tiger Tales.
Bowlsby, Tina Marie. The Adventures of LC, the Lucky Calf. Pereira, William. 2005. (J). 18.95 *(978-0-9773133-0-3(1))* Little Tule Bks.
Bowman, Anne. Count Them While You Can... Bowman, Anne. 2011. (ENG.). 24p. (J). (gr. k-2). 16.99 *(978-1-921541-60-5(1))* Little Hare Bks. AUS. Dist: Independent Pubs. Group.
Bowman, Brent. Kim the Frog. Fox, Stephen. 2003. (Little Lagoon Ser.). 22p. (J). bds. 6.95 *(978-0-9729197-0-8(8)*, Gorn Foxtail) Gorn Publishing, LLC.
Bowman, David. Beyond Bethlehem: A Book of Mormon Christmas. 2008. 32p. (J). pap. 11.95 *(978-1-59038-991-1(3))* Deseret Bk. Co.
—Who's Your Greatest Hero? A Book of Mormon Story Applied to Children. 2009. (J). *(978-1-60641-153-7(5))* Deseret Bk. Co.
Bowman, David. Who's Your Hero? Vol. 2: Book of Mormon Stories Applied to Children. Bowman, David. 2006. 80p. (J). pap. 14.95 *(978-1-59038-691-0(4))* Deseret Bk. Co.
Bowman, Ethan T. Ling Ling: The Kitten Who Changed Her Ways. Hanes, Marina C. 2010. (ENG.). 26p. pap. 10.95 *(978-1-4536-2528-6(3))* CreateSpace Independent Publishing Platform.
Bowman, Hootie. Go Hokies Go: An Interactive Book Featuring Virginia Tech University. Jones, Bryan. 2012. 1. 12p. 19.95 *(978-0-9836211-0-2(1))* Collegiate Kids Bks., LLC.
Bowman, Leslie. La Dama de Cobre. Ross, Alice & Ross, Kent. 2006. (Yo Solo: Historia (on My Own History) Ser.). (SPA.). 48p. (gr. 2-4). lib. bdg. 25.26 *(978-0-8225-6262-7(6)*, Ediciones Lerner) Lerner Publishing Group.
Bowman, Leslie W. A Name of Honor. Blasi, Kathleen McAlpin. 2006. (J). *(978-1-59336-692-6(2))* Mondo Publishing.
Bowman, Patty. The Amazing Hamweenie Escapes! Bowman, Patty. 2015. (Amazing Hamweenie Ser.: 2). (ENG.). 32p. (J). (gr. k-3). 16.99 *(978-0-399-25689-9(X)*, Philomel) Penguin Publishing Group.
Bowman, Todd A. Jay's Friend Kitty Brew. Davis, Bertha M. 2013. 28p. pap. 14.99 *(978-0-9886360-5-7(0))* Kids At Heart Publishing & Bks.
—Jay's Friend Kitty Brew Jumbo Coloring & Activity Book. Davis, Bertha. 2013. 26p. pap. 9.99 *(978-0-9899472-1-3(1))* Kids At Heart Publishing & Bks.
Bowser, Katya. Everyday Things with Morgan. Massey, K. J. 2013. 24p. 19.99 *(978-0-9910489-4-6(6))* NyreePr. Literary Group.
Bowser, Ken. Homesick Penguin: Empathy/Caring for Others. Bowser, Ken. 2014. (Funny Bone Readers: Being a Friend Ser.). 24p. (gr. -1-1). pap. 4.99 *(978-1-939656-03-2(6))* Red Chair Pr.
Bowser, Milton. Cartoon Stories from the Teachings of Buddha. l.t. ed. 2003. (Cartoon Ser.). (JPN & SPA.). 72p. (YA). 10.00 *(978-0-940178-34-2(6)*, Buddha 1) Sitare, Ltd.
Bowser, Sean T. Pear-A-Dise. Keefer, Nick T. 2013. 28p. pap. 12.95 *(978-0-9894814-6-5(8))* Warren Publishing, Inc.
Box, Marty. The Little Red Beetle Goes Shopping. Box, Marty. McKenna, Allen. 2005. (ENG.). 40p. pap. *(978-1-84401-521-4(1))* Athena Pr.
Box, Paul. Stubborn & Disobedient, 1 vol. Guinn, Dolores Hollyfield. 2009. 19p. pap. 24.95 *(978-1-4489-0902-5(3))* America Star Bks.
Boyajian, Ann. Journey to the Heart: Centering Prayer for Children. Jelenek, Frank X. 2007. (ENG.). 32p. (J). (gr. -1-5). pap. 15.99 *(978-1-55725-482-5(6))* Paraclete Pr., Inc.
—O, Say Can You See? America's Symbols, Landmarks, & Important Words. Scholastic, Inc. Staff & Keenan, Sheila. 2007. (ENG.). 64p. (J). (gr. -1-3). pap. 6.99 *(978-0-439-59360-1(3)*, Scholastic Nonfiction) Scholastic, Inc.
Boyd, Aaron. Babu's Song. Stuve-Bodeen, Stephanie. 2003. (ENG.). 32p. (J). 16.95 *(978-1-58430-058-8(2))*; (gr. -1-3). pap. 8.95 *(978-1-60060-275-7(4))* Lee & Low Bks., Inc.
—I Can't Take a Bath! Smalls, Irene. 2004. (Just for You Ser.). (ENG.). 32p. (J). (gr. 1-1). pap. 3.99 *(978-0-439-56852-4(8))* Scholastic, Inc.
—Low-Down Bad-Day Blues. Scholastic, Inc. Staff & Barnes, Derrick D. 2004. (Just for You Ser.). (ENG.). 32p. (gr. k-1). pap. 3.99 *(978-0-439-56867-8(6)*, Teaching Resources) Scholastic, Inc.
Boyd, Aaron. Luigi & the Barefoot Races, 1 vol. Paley, Daniel. 2015. (ENG.). 32p. (J). 16.95 ***(978-0-88448-397-7(5))*** Tilbury Hse. Pubs.
Boyd, Aaron. Ned Redd, World Traveler: A Search-And-Find Adventure. Kaufmann, Kelli. 2005. (J). *(978-1-58987-135-9(9))* Kindermusik International.
Boyd, Brian. Full Mouse, Empty Mouse: A Tale of Food & Feelings. Zeckhausen, Dina. 2007. 40p. (J). (gr. 2-7). 14.95 *(978-1-4338-0132-7(9)*, 4418003); pap. 9.95 *(978-1-4338-0133-4(7)*, 4418004) American Psychological Assn. (Magination Pr.).
Boyd, Lizi. I Love Daddy: Super Sturdy Picture Books. Boyd, Lizi. 2004. (Super Sturdy Picture Bks.). (ENG.). 24p. (J). (gr. -1 — 1). 8.99 *(978-0-7636-2217-6(6))* Candlewick Pr.
—I Love Grandma. Boyd, Lizi. 2009. (Super Sturdy Picture Bks.). (ENG.). 24p. (J). (gr. -1-k). 8.99 *(978-0-7636-3728-6(9))* Candlewick Pr.
—I Love Grandpa. Boyd, Lizi. 2009. (Super Sturdy Picture Bks.). (ENG.). 24p. (J). (gr. -1-k). 8.99 *(978-0-7636-3727-9(0))* Candlewick Pr.
—Inside Outside. Boyd, Lizi. 2013. (ENG.). 40p. (J). (gr. -1-1). 15.99 *(978-1-4521-0644-1(4))* Chronicle Bks. LLC.
Boyd, Patti. Magical Circus Train. Kidd, Ron. 16p. (J). (gr. -1-18). 19.95 *(978-0-9627001-5-6(0))* Futech Educational Products, Inc.
Boyd, Shelby. Run, Girl, Run! Bresheats, Alyce Park. 2013. 36p. pap. 7.95 *(978-1-60414-742-1(3))* Fideli Publishing, Inc.
Boyd, Sheree. Air: Outside, Inside, & All Around, 1 vol. Stille, Darlene R. 2004. (Amazing Science Ser.). (ENG.). 24p. (gr. k-4). 25.99 *(978-1-4048-0248-3(7)*, Nonfiction Picture Bks.) Picture Window Bks.
—El Aire: Afuera, Adentro y en Todos Lados, 1 vol. Stille, Darlene R. Robledo, Sol, tr. from ENG. 2007. (Ciencia Asombrosa Ser.). (SPA.). 24p. (gr. k-4). lib. bdg. 25.99 *(978-1-4048-3209-1(2))* Picture Window Bks.
—Easter. Haugen, Brenda. 2003. (Holidays & Celebrations Ser.). (ENG.). 24p. (gr. k-3). 25.99 *(978-1-4048-0194-3(4)*, Nonfiction Picture Bks.) Picture Window Bks.
—La Electricidad: Focos, Pilas y Chispas, 1 vol. Stille, Darlene R. & Picture Window Books Staff. Robledo, Sol, tr. 2007. (Ciencia Asombrosa Ser.). (SPA.). 24p. (gr. k-4). 25.99 *(978-1-4048-3212-1(2))* Picture Window Bks.
—Electricity: Bulbs, Batteries, & Sparks. Stille, Darlene R. 2004. (Amazing Science Ser.). (ENG.). 24p. (gr. k-4). 25.99 *(978-1-4048-0245-2(2)*, Nonfiction Picture Bks.) Picture Window Bks.
—La Energía: Calor, Luz y Combustible. Stille, Darlene R. & Picture Window Books Staff. Robledo, Sol, tr. from ENG. 2007. (Ciencia Asombrosa Ser.). (SPA.). 24p. (gr. k-4). 25.99 *(978-1-4048-3213-8(0))* Picture Window Bks.
—Energy: Heat, Light, & Fuel. Stille, Darlene R. 2004. (Amazing Science Ser.). (ENG.). 24p. (gr. k-4). 25.99 *(978-1-4048-0249-0(5)*, Nonfiction Picture Bks.) Picture Window Bks.
—Imanes: Atraen y Rechazan, 1 vol. Rosinsky, Natalie M. & Picture Window Books Staff. Robledo, Sol, tr. from ENG. 2007. (Ciencia Asombrosa Ser.).Tr. of Magnets: Pulling Together & Pushing Apart. (SPA.). 24p. (gr. k-4). 25.99 *(978-1-4048-3220-6(3))* Picture Window Bks.
—Imanes: Atraen y Rechazan, 1 vol. Rosinsky, Natalie M. Robledo, Sol, tr. from ENG. 2007. (Ciencia Asombrosa Ser.).Tr. of Magnets: Pulling Together & Pushing Apart. (SPA.). 24p. (gr. k-4). per. 8.19 *(978-1-4048-2497-3(9))* Picture Window Bks.
—La Luz: Sombras, Espejos y Arco Iris, 1 vol. Rosinsky, Natalie M. & Picture Window Books Staff. Robledo, Sol, tr. from ENG. 2007. (Ciencia Asombrosa Ser.). (SPA.). 24p. (gr. k-4). 25.99 *(978-1-4048-3219-0(X))* Picture Window Bks.
—La Materia: Mira, Toca, Prueba, Huele, 1 vol. Stille, Darlene R. & Picture Window Books Staff. Robledo, Sol, tr. from ENG. 2007. (Ciencia Asombrosa Ser.). (SPA.). 24p. (gr. k-4). 25.99 *(978-1-4048-3221-3(1))* Picture Window Bks.
—Matter: See It, Touch It, Taste It, Smell It, 1 vol. Stille, Darlene R. 2004. (Amazing Science Ser.). (ENG.). 24p. (gr. k-4). per. 7.95 *(978-1-4048-0344-2(0)*, Nonfiction Picture Bks.) Picture Window Bks.
—El Movimiento: Tira y Empuja, Rápido y Despacio. Stille, Darlene R. Robledo, Sol, tr. from ENG. 2007. (Ciencia Asombrosa Ser.). (SPA.). 24p. (gr. k-4). lib. bdg. 25.99 *(978-1-4048-3222-0(X))* Picture Window Bks.
—El Suelo: Tierra y Arena, 1 vol. Rosinsky, Natalie M. Robledo, Sol, tr. 2007. (Ciencia Asombrosa Ser.). (SPA.). 24p. (gr. k-4). lib. bdg. 25.99 *(978-1-4048-3211-4(4))* Picture Window Bks.
—La Temperatura: Caliente y Frío. Stille, Darlene R. & Picture Window Books Staff. Robledo, Sol, tr. from ENG. 2007. (Ciencia Asombrosa Ser.). (SPA.). 24p. (gr. k-4). 25.99 *(978-1-4048-3234-3(3))* Picture Window Bks.
—Temperature: Heating up & Cooling Down. Stille, Darlene R. 2004. (Amazing Science Ser.). (ENG.). 24p. (gr. k-4). 25.99 *(978-1-4048-0247-6(9)*, Nonfiction Picture Bks.) Picture Window Bks.
—Temperature: Heating up & Cooling Down, 1 vol. Stille, Darlene R. 2004. (Amazing Science Ser.). (ENG.). 24p. (gr. k-4). per. 7.95 *(978-1-4048-0345-9(9)*, Nonfiction Picture Bks.) Picture Window Bks.
Boyd, Sheree. Motion: Push & Pull, Fast & Slow. Boyd, Sheree, tr. Stille, Darlene R. 2004. (Amazing Science Ser.). (ENG.). 24p. (gr. k-4). 25.99 *(978-1-4048-0250-6(9)*, Nonfiction Picture Bks.) Picture Window Bks.
Boyden, Linda. Boy & Poi Poi Puppy. Boyden, Linda. 2013. (J). (gr. -1-2). 50p. 17.95 *(978-1-940834-00-9(7))*; 40p. pap. 11.95 *(978-0-9888568-2-0(4))* Rising Phoenix Pr.
Boyden, Robin. Joe-Joe the Wizard Brews up Solids, Liquids, & Gases, 1 vol. Braun, Eric. 2012. (In the Science Lab Ser.). (ENG.). 24p. (gr. 2-3). pap. 8.95 *(978-1-4048-7238-7(8))*; lib. bdg. 25.99 *(978-1-4048-7147-2(0))* Picture Window Bks. (Nonfiction Picture Bks.).
—Mad Margaret Experiments with the Scientific Method, 1 vol. Braun, Eric. 2012. (In the Science Lab Ser.). (ENG.). 24p. (gr. 2-3). pap. 8.95 *(978-1-4048-7710-8(X))*; lib. bdg. 25.99 *(978-1-4048-7373-5(2))* Picture Window Bks.
Boye, B. D. Easy As 1, 2, 3. Boye, B. D. l.t. ed. 2005. 22p. (J). per. 4.99 *(978-0-9768078-0-3(7))* Innerchild Publishing, Inc.
—The Look Book. Boye, B. D. l.t. ed. 2004. 20p. (J). per. 4.99 *(978-0-9768078-1-0(5)*, 100001) Innerchild Publishing, Inc.
—Our New Home. Boye, B. D. l.t. ed. 2005. 18p. (J). per. 4.99 *(978-0-9768078-2-7(3))* Innerchild Publishing, Inc.
Boyer, Cécile. Woof Meow Tweet-Tweet. 2011. (ENG.). 48p. (J). (gr. -1). 15.95 *(978-1-934734-60-5(8))* Seven Footer Pr.
Boyer, Christine M. Sweetest Joy, 1 vol. Middleton, Leeanne. 2010. 18p. pap. 24.95 *(978-1-4489-8068-0(2))* PublishAmerica, Inc.
Boyer, Lyn. Baby Bumblebee. Grudzina, Rebecca. 2010. (Rising Readers Ser.). (J). 3.49 *(978-1-60719-688-4(3))* Newmark Learning LLC.
—A Baby Bumblebee for Mommy. Grudzina, Rebecca. 2009. (Reader's Theater Nursery Rhymes & Songs Set B Ser.). 48p. (J). pap. *(978-1-60859-149-7(2))* Benchmark Education Co.
—London Bridge. Harris, Brooke. 2010. (Rising Readers Ser.). (J). 3.49 *(978-1-60719-702-7(2))* Newmark Learning LLC.
—London Bridge Has Fallen Down. Harris, Brooke. 2009. (Reader's Theater Nursery Rhymes & Songs Set B Ser.). 48p. (J). pap. *(978-1-60859-159-6(X))* Benchmark Education Co.
—Zachary's Zoo, 1 vol. Nappa, Mike et al. 2007. (I Can Read! Ser.). (ENG.). 32p. (J). (gr. -1-1). pap. 3.99 *(978-0-310-71466-8(4))* Zonderkidz.
Boyer, Lyn, jt. illus. see Hierstein, Judy.
Boyer, Robin. Alphabet Fun. Hoffman, Joan. 2006. (ENG.). 64p. (J). (gr. -1-k). 7.99 *(978-1-58947-746-9(4))* School Zone Publishing Co.
—Andrew & Allen Learn about Adverbs. Robinson, Joanna Jarc. 2015. (Language Builders Ser.). (ENG.). 32p. (J). (gr. 2-4). pap. 11.94 *(978-1-60357-704-5(1))*; lib. bdg. 25.27 *(978-1-59953-669-9(2))* Norwood Hse. Pr.
—Dot-to-Dots. School Zone Interactive Staff. 2006. (ENG.). 64p. (J). (gr. 1-2). 7.99 *(978-1-58947-302-7(7))* School Zone Publishing Co.
—First Grade Scholar. Hall, M. C. 2004. (ENG.). 32p. (J). pap. 2.99 *(978-1-58947-456-7(2))* School Zone Publishing Co.
Boyer, Robin. It's Easter, Little Bunny! Jaeger, Elizabeth. 2015. (ENG.). 16p. (J). bds. 12.99 ***(978-0-8249-1949-8(1)***, Candy Cane Pr.) Ideals Pubns.
Boyer, Robin. It's Halloween, Little Pumpkin! Jaeger, Elizabeth. 2014. 16p. (J). bds. 12.99 *(978-0-8249-1942-9(4)*, Candy Cane Pr.) Ideals Pubns.
—Kindergarten Basics. Hoffman, Joan. 2004. (ENG.). 32p. (J). pap. 2.99 *(978-1-58947-436-9(8))* School Zone Publishing Co.
—Kindergarten Scholar. Burton, Marilee R. 2004. (ENG.). 32p. (J). pap. 2.99 *(978-1-58947-455-0(4))* School Zone Publishing Co.
—Manuscript Writing. Veinje, Marie. 2005. (ENG.). 64p. (J). (gr. k-2). pap. 3.79 *(978-1-58947-397-3(3))* School Zone Publishing Co.
—Multiplication Facts. Irvin, Barbara Bando. 2005. (ENG.). 64p. (J). (gr. 3-4). pap. 3.79 *(978-1-58947-328-7(0)*, 02214) School Zone Publishing Co.
—Second Grade Scholar. Hall, M. C. 2005. (ENG.). 32p. (J). pap., wbk. ed. 2.99 *(978-1-58947-457-4(0))* School Zone Publishing Co.
—Third Grade Scholar. Giglio, Judy. 2005. (ENG.). 32p. (J). pap. 2.99 *(978-1-58947-458-1(9))* School Zone Publishing Co.
Boyer, Susy. Crazy Critters. Walker, Lois. 2007. (Collins Big Cat Ser.). (ENG.). 24p. (J). pap. 7.99 *(978-0-00-722869-0(4))* HarperCollins Pubs. Ltd. GBR. Dist: Independent Pubs. Group.
—Gone Fishing. Arena, Felice & Kettle, Phil. 2004. (J). pap. *(978-1-59336-359-8(1))* Mondo Publishing.
—Look at Me, 1 vol. Giulieri, Anne. 2012. (Engage Literacy Magenta Ser.). (ENG.). 32p. (gr. k-2). pap. 5.99 *(978-1-4296-8856-7(4)*, Engage Literacy) Capstone Pr., Inc.
—My Big Sandcastle, 1 vol. Giulieri, Anne. 2012. (Engage Literacy Magenta Ser.). (ENG.). 32p. (gr. k-2). pap. 5.99 *(978-1-4296-8870-3(X)*, Engage Literacy) Capstone Pr., Inc.
—On the Farm/By Felice Arena & Phil Kettle; Illustrated by Susy Boyer. Arena, Felice & Kettle, Phil. 2004. (J). pap. *(978-1-59336-363-5(X))* Mondo Publishing.
—Pirate Ship: By Felice Arena & Phil Kettle; Illustrated by Susy Boyer. Arena, Felice & Kettle, Phil. 2004. (J). pap. *(978-1-59336-362-8(1))* Mondo Publishing.
—The Secret Tree House, 1 vol. Giulieri, Anne. 2012. (Engage Literacy Green Ser.). (ENG.). 32p. (gr. k-2). pap. 5.99 *(978-1-4296-8999-1(4)*, Engage Literacy) Capstone Pr., Inc.
—Surprise Pancakes for Mom, 1 vol. Giulieri, Anne. 2012. (Engage Literacy Red Ser.). (ENG.). 32p. (gr. k-2). pap. 5.99 *(978-1-4296-8948-9(X)*, Engage Literacy) Capstone Pr., Inc.
—Tennis Ace. Arena, Felice & Kettle, Phil. 2004. (J). pap. *(978-1-59336-360-4(5))* Mondo Publishing.
—The Volcano Sand Hill, 1 vol. Giulieri, Anne. 2012. (Engage Literacy Blue Ser.). (ENG.). 32p. (gr. k-2). pap. 5.99 *(978-1-4296-8976-2(5)*, Engage Literacy) Capstone Pr., Inc.
Boyes, Faye. What Charlotte Ate: The Story of a Naughty Dog Who Loved to Eat. Boyes, Alison. 2012. 28p. (J). *(978-0-9808685-7-9(2))* Mono Unlimited.
Boykin, Brian, jt. illus. see Lane, Queen.
Boyle, Bob. Rosie & Rex: A Nose for Fun! Boyle, Bob. 2014. (ENG.). 40p. (J). (gr. -1-3). 15.99 *(978-0-06-221131-6(5))* HarperCollins Pubs.
Boyles, Shawn. Cavern of Babel. Packard, Albert. 2006. (J). per. 14.95 *(978-0-9790652-0-0(8))* Diamond Triple C Ranch.
Boyne, Linda. The Apple Tree. White, Cal. 2008. 48p. pap. 24.95 *(978-1-4241-8636-5(6))* America Star Bks.
Boynton, Jeannette & Holdeen, Bonnie. God Loves Variety. Boynton, Jeannette. 2007. (J). per. 10.99 *(978-1-59879-264-5(4))* Lifevest Publishing, Inc.
Boynton, Sandra. Are You a Cow? Boynton, Sandra. 2012. (ENG.). 16p. (J). (gr. -1-k). bds. 5.99 *(978-1-4424-1733-5(1)*, Little Simon) Little Simon.
—Azul el Sombrero, Verde el Sombrero. Boynton, Sandra. 2003.Tr. of Blue Hat, Green Hat. (SPA.). 14p. (J). (gr. -1 — 1). bds. 5.99 *(978-0-689-86304-2(7)*, Libros Para Ninos) Libros Para Ninos.
—Big Box of Boynton: Barnyard Dance! Pajama Time! Oh My Oh My Oh Dinosaurs! Boynton, Sandra. 2005. (ENG.). 24p. (J). (gr. k — 1). bds. 21.00 *(978-0-7611-3989-8(3)*, 13989) Workman Publishing Co., Inc.
—Boynton Set: Moo, Baa, la la La! But Not the Hippopotamus Opposite. Boynton, Sandra. 30th anniv. ed. 2012. (ENG.). 72p. (J). (gr. -1-k). bds. 31.99 *(978-1-4424-8191-6(9)*, Little Simon) Little Simon.
—Buenas Noches a Todos. Boynton, Sandra. 2004.Tr. of Going to Bed Book. (SPA.). 14p. (J). (gr. -1 — 1). bds. 5.99 *(978-0-689-86652-4(6)*, Libros Para Ninos) Libros Para Ninos.
—The Bunny Rabbit Show! Boynton, Sandra. 2014. (ENG.). 24p. (J). (gr. -1). bds. 6.95 *(978-0-7611-8060-9(5)*, 18060) Workman Publishing Co., Inc.
—But Not the Hippopotamus. Boynton, Sandra. 30th anniv. ed. 2012. (ENG.). 18p. (J). (gr. -1-k). bds. 7.99 *(978-1-4424-5408-8(3)*, Little Simon) Little Simon.
—Christmas Parade. Boynton, Sandra. 2012. (ENG.). 32p. (J). (gr. -1-1). 14.99 *(978-1-4424-6813-9(0)*, Little Simon) Little Simon.
—Consider Love. Boynton, Sandra. 2013. (ENG.). 32p. (J). (gr. -1-3). 14.99 *(978-1-4424-9465-7(4)*, Little Simon) Little Simon.
—Consider Love (Mini Edition) Its Moods & Many Ways. Boynton, Sandra. ed. 2005. (ENG.). 32p. (J). (gr. -1-3). 7.99 *(978-0-689-87814-5(1)*, Little Simon) Little Simon.
—Dinos to Go/Snoozers Vertical 2-Pack. Boynton, Sandra. 2013. (ENG.). 36p. (J). (gr. -1 — 1). bds. 17.98 *(978-1-4814-0549-2(7)*, Little Simon) Little Simon.
—Dog Train: A Wild Ride on the Rock-and-Roll Side. Boynton, Sandra. 2005. (ENG.). 64p. (J). (gr. -1-k). bds. 17.95 *(978-0-7611-3966-9(4)*, 13966) Workman Publishing Co., Inc.
—Fuzzy Fuzzy Fuzzy! A Touch, Skritch, & Tickle Book. Boynton, Sandra. 2003. (ENG.). 12p. (J). (gr. -1-k). 12.95 *(978-0-689-86363-9(2)*, Little Simon) Little Simon.
—The Going to Bed Book. Boynton, Sandra. (ENG.). (J). 2006. 14p. bds. 12.95 *(978-1-4169-2794-5(8))*; 2004. 14p. (gr. -1 — 1). bds. 9.99 *(978-0-689-87028-6(0))*; 30th anniv. ed. 2012. 18p. (gr. -1-3). bds. 7.99 *(978-1-4424-5409-5(1))* Little Simon. (Little Simon).
—Happy Hippo, Angry Duck: A Book of Moods. Boynton, Sandra. 2011. (ENG.). 16p. (J). (gr. -1-k). bds. 5.99 *(978-1-4424-1731-1(5)*, Little Simon) Little Simon.
—Hippos Go Berserk! Boynton, Sandra. 2009. (ENG.). 32p. (J). 9.99 *(978-1-4169-9619-4(2)*, Little Simon) Little Simon.
—Moo, Baa, la la La! Boynton, Sandra. (ENG.). (J). (gr. -1 — 1). 2004. 16p. bds. 9.99 *(978-0-689-87027-9(2))*; 2012. 18p. bds. 7.99 *(978-1-4424-5410-1(5))* Little Simon. (Little Simon).
—Moo Cow Book. Boynton, Sandra. 2004. (ENG.). 10p. (J). (gr. -1 — 1). 16.95 *(978-0-689-87683-7(1)*, Little Simon) Little Simon.
—Muu - Beee - ¡Así Fue! Boynton, Sandra. 2003. (SPA.). 14p. (J). (gr. -1 — 1). bds. 5.99 *(978-0-689-86302-8(0)*, Libros Para Ninos) Libros Para Ninos.
—Opposites: Special 30th Anniversary Edition! Boynton, Sandra. ed. 2012. (ENG.). 18p. (J). (gr. -1 — 1). bds. 7.99 *(978-1-4424-5411-8(3)*, Little Simon) Little Simon.
—Opuestos. Boynton, Sandra. Ziegler, Argentina Palacios, tr. 2004.Tr. of Opposites. (SPA.). 16p. (J). (gr. -1 — 1). bds. 5.99 *(978-0-689-86978-5(9)*, Libros Para Ninos) Libros Para Ninos.
—Perritos: Un Libro para Contar y Ladrar. Boynton, Sandra. 2004.Tr. of Doggies. (SPA.). 14p. (J). (gr. -1 — 1). bds. 5.99 *(978-0-689-86303-5(9)*, Libros Para Ninos) Libros Para Ninos.

B

—Rhinoceros Tap. Boynton, Sandra. 2004. (ENG.). 64p. (J). 16.95 (978-0-7611-3323-0(2), 13323) Workman Publishing Co., Inc.

—Sandra Boynton's Moo, Baa, la la La! Boynton, Sandra. ed. 2009. (ENG.). 16p. (J). bds. 16.99 (978-1-4169-5035-6(4), Little Simon) Little Simon.

Bozeman, Gary. The Broccoli Bush. Sawyer, J. Scott. 2012. 36p. pap. 24.95 (978-1-4626-2501-7(0)) America Star Bks.

Bozer, Chris. 10 Things You Should Know about Dinosaurs. Parker, Steve. Gallagher, Belinda & Borton, Paula, eds. 2004. (10 Things You Should Know Ser.). 24p. (J). 6.99 (978-1-84236-120-7(1)) Miles Kelly Publishing, Ltd. GBR. Dist: Independent Pubs. Group.

Braasch, Gary. How We Know What We Know about Our Changing Climate: Scientists & Kids Explore Global Warming. Braasch, Gary. Cherry, Lynne. 2008. 66p. (J). (gr. 5-9). 17.95 (978-1-58469-103-7(4)) Dawn Pubns.

Braasch, Gary, photos by. How We Know What We Know about Our Changing Climate: Scientists & Kids Explore Global Warming. Cherry, Lynne. 2008. (J). pap. (978-1-58469-104-4(2)) Dawn Pubns.

Brace, Eric. Please Write in This Book. Amato, Mary. (ENG.). (J). (gr. 4-7). 2008. 97p. pap. 6.95 (978-0-8234-2138-1(4)); 2006. 112p. 16.95 (978-0-8234-1932-6(0)) Holiday Hse., Inc.

Brack, Amanda. The Night Before Christmas: A Brick Story. Moore, Clement C. 2015. (ENG.). 32p. (J). (gr. -1). 12.99 **(978-1-63450-179-8(9)**, Sky Pony Pr.) Skyhorse Publishing Co., Inc.

Bracken, Carolyn. Eloise Takes a Trip. Fry, Sonali. 2007. (Eloise Ser.). (ENG.). 16p. (J). (gr. -1-1). 6.99 (978-1-4169-3343-4(3), Little Simon) Little Simon.

—Flies with the Dinosaurs. Schwabacher, Martin et al. 2008. (Magic School Bus Science Reader Ser.). (ENG.). 32p. (J). (gr. -1-3). pap. 3.99 (978-0-439-80106-5(0)) Scholastic, Inc.

—Henry & Mudge & Mrs. Hopper's House. Rylant, Cynthia. 2004. (Ready-to-Read Ser.). 40p. (gr. k-2). 14.00 (978-0-7569-2200-9(3)) Perfection Learning Corp.

—Henry & Mudge & Mrs. Hopper's House. Rylant, Cynthia. 2003. (Henry & Mudge Ser.: 22). (ENG.). 40p. (J). (gr. k-2). 15.99 (978-0-689-81153-1(5), Simon Spotlight) Simon Spotlight.

—Henry & Mudge & Mrs. Hopper's House. Rylant, Cynthia. ed. 2004. (Henry & Mudge Ready-To-Read Ser.: 22). 40p. (gr. k-2). lib. bdg. 13.55 (978-0-613-90376-9(5), Turtleback) Turtleback Bks.

—Henry & Mudge & the Funny Lunch. Rylant, Cynthia. 2005. (Henry & Mudge Ser.: 24). (ENG.). 40p. (J). (gr. k-2). pap. 3.99 (978-0-689-83444-8(6), Simon Spotlight) Simon Spotlight.

—Henry & Mudge & the Funny Lunch. Rylant, Cynthia. ed. 2005. (Henry & Mudge Ready-To-Read Ser.: 24). 40p. (gr. k-2). lib. bdg. 13.55 (978-1-4176-7107-6(6), Turtleback) Turtleback Bks.

—Henry & Mudge & the Tumbling Trip. Rylant, Cynthia. 2006. (Henry & Mudge Ser.). 40p. (gr. k-3). 14.00 (978-0-7569-6904-2(2)) Perfection Learning Corp.

—Henry & Mudge & the Tumbling Trip. Rylant, Cynthia. 2006. (Henry & Mudge Ser.: 27). (ENG.). 40p. (J). (gr. k-2). pap. 3.99 (978-0-689-83452-3(7), Simon Spotlight) Simon Spotlight.

—Henry & Mudge & the Wild Goose Chase. Rylant, Cynthia. ed. 2005. (Henry & Mudge Ser.). 40p. (J). lib. bdg. 15.00 (978-1-59054-946-9(5)) Fitzgerald Bks.

—Henry & Mudge & the Wild Goose Chase. Rylant, Cynthia. 2004. (Henry & Mudge Ser.). 40p. (gr. k-2). 14.00 (978-0-7569-3366-1(8)) Perfection Learning Corp.

—Henry & Mudge & the Wild Goose Chase. Rylant, Cynthia. ed. 2004. (Henry & Mudge Ready-To-Read Ser.: 26). 40p. (gr. k-2). lib. bdg. 13.55 (978-1-4176-4340-0(4), Turtleback) Turtleback Bks.

—The Magic School Bus & the Butterfly Bunch. Earhart, Kristin et al. 2010. 32p. (J). (978-0-545-16727-7(2)) Scholastic, Inc.

—The Magic School Bus & the Shark Adventure. Smith, Elizabeth. 2007. (Scholastic Reader Ser.). (J). (978-0-545-03464-7(7)) Scholastic, Inc.

—The Magic School Bus at the First Thanksgiving. Cole, Joanna. 2006. (J). pap. (978-0-439-89935-2(4)) Scholastic, Inc.

—The Magic School Bus Fights Germs. Egan, Kate & Cole, Joanna. 2008. pap. (978-0-545-03465-4(5), Scholastic, Inc.) Scholastic, Inc.

—The Magic School Bus Fixes a Bone. Earhart, Kristin. 2010. 32p. (J). pap. (978-0-545-23950-9(8), Cartwheel Bks.) Scholastic, Inc.

—The Magic School Bus Has a Heart. Capeci, Anne & Cole, Joanna. 2006. (Magic School Bus Science Reader Ser.). (ENG.). 32p. (J). (gr. -1-3). 3.99 (978-0-439-68402-6(1), Cartwheel Bks.) Scholastic, Inc.

Bracken, Carolyn. The Magic School Bus Inside a Volcano. Earhart, Kristin et al. 2012. 32p. (J). **(978-0-545-35685-5(7))** Scholastic, Inc.

Bracken, Carolyn. The Magic School Bus Rides the Wind, Level 2. Capeci, Anne & Cole, Joanna. 2007. (Magic School Bus Science Reader Ser.). (ENG.). 32p. (J). (gr. -1-3). pap. 4.99 (978-0-439-80108-9(7), Cartwheel Bks.) Scholastic, Inc.

—Merry Christmas, Eloise! Cheshire, Marc. 2006. (Eloise Ser.). (ENG.). 18p. (J). (gr. -1-1). pap. 6.99 (978-0-689-87155-9(4), Little Simon) Little Simon.

—Takes a Moonwalk. Cole, Joanna & Capeci, Anne. 2007. (Magic School Bus Science Reader Ser.). (ENG.). 32p. (J). (gr. -1-3). per. 4.99 (978-0-439-68400-2(5)) Scholastic, Inc.

Bracken, Carolyn. Henry & Mudge & the Funny Lunch. Bracken, Carolyn. Rylant, Cynthia. 2004. (Henry & Mudge Ser.: 24). (ENG.). 40p. (J). (gr. k-2). 16.99 (978-0-689-81178-4(0), Simon Spotlight) Simon Spotlight.

—Henry & Mudge & the Wild Goose Chase. Bracken, Carolyn. Rylant, Cynthia. 2003. (Henry & Mudge Ser.: 23). (ENG.). 40p. (J). (gr. k-2). 16.99 (978-0-689-81172-2(1), Simon Spotlight) Simon Spotlight.

Bracken, Carolyn & Glasser, Robin Preiss. Fancy Nancy's Elegant Easter. O'Connor, Jane. 2009. (Fancy Nancy Ser.). (ENG.). 16p. (J). (gr. -1-3). pap. 6.99 (978-0-06-170379-9(6), HarperFestival) HarperCollins Pubs.

Bracken, Carolyn, jt. illus. see Degen, Bruce.

Bracken, Carolyn, jt. illus. see Glasser, Robin Preiss.

Bradburn, Ryan. Conditional Following Directions Fun Deck: Fd68. 2003. (J). 11.95 (978-1-58650-290-4(5)) Super Duper Pubns.

—Using I & Me Fun Deck: Fd61. Webber, Thomas. 2003. (J). 11.95 (978-1-58650-292-8(1)) Super Duper Pubns.

Bradbury, Jack & Turner, Gil. Christmas Parade, No. 3. Connell, Del et al. Clark, John, ed. 2005. 80p. (YA). (gr. -1-3). pap. 8.95 (978-1-888472-04-2(9)) Gemstone Publishing, Inc.

Bradbury, Ray & Mugnaini, Joe. The Halloween Tree. Bradbury, Ray. Eller, Jon, ed. 2005. 494p. (J). (gr. 4-12). per. 75.00 (978-1-887368-80-3(9)) Gauntlet, Inc.

Braddock, Paige. It's Tokyo, Charlie Brown! Schulz, Charles M. & Scott, Vicki. 2012. (Peanuts Ser.). (ENG.). 96p. (J). (gr. 2). pap. 9.99 (978-1-60886-270-2(4)) Boom! Studios.

—Peanuts, Vol. 2. Schulz, Charles M. & Houghton, Shane. 2013. (Peanuts Ser.). (ENG.). 112p. (J). (gr. 1). pap. 13.99 (978-1-60886-299-3(2)) Boom! Studios.

Bradfield, Jolly Roger. Benjamin Dilley's Thirsty Camel. Bradfield, Jolly Roger. 2012. (ENG.). 64p. (J). (gr. 4-7). 18.95 (978-1-930900-60-8(0)) Purple Hse. Pr.

—Un Perfecto Caballero para Dragones. Bradfield, Jolly Roger. 2009. (SPA.). 64p. (J). (gr. 1-3). (978-84-7490-974-6(0)) Encuentro Ediciones, S.A.

Bradfield, Roger. Alvin Fernald's Incredible Buried Treasure. Hicks, Clifford B. 2009. (J). 17.95 (978-1-930900-43-1(0)) Purple Hse. Pr.

—The Pickle-Chiffon Pie Olympics. 2011. 64p. (J). (gr. -1-3). 18.95 (978-1-930900-52-3(X)) Purple Hse. Pr.

Bradford, June. Chock Full of Chocolate. MacLeod, Elizabeth. 2005. (Kids Can Do It Ser.). (ENG.). 40p. (J). (gr. 3). 6.95 (978-1-55337-763-4(X)) Kids Can Pr., Ltd. CAN. Dist: Univ. of Toronto Pr.

—Embroidery. Sadler, Judy Ann. 2006. 40p. (J). pap. (978-0-439-89943-7(5)) Scholastic, Inc.

—Hemp Jewelry. Sadler, Judy Ann & Sadler, Judy. 2005. (Kids Can Do It Ser.). (ENG.). 40p. (J). (gr. 3-18). 6.95 (978-1-55337-775-7(3)) Kids Can Pr., Ltd. CAN. Dist: Univ. of Toronto Pr.

Bradford, June, et al. The Jumbo Book of Needlecrafts. Sadler, Judy Ann et al. 2005. (Jumbo Bks.). (ENG.). 208p. (J). (gr. 3-18). 16.95 (978-1-55337-793-1(1)) Kids Can Pr., Ltd. CAN. Dist: Univ. of Toronto Pr.

Bradley, Jess. I Know Sasquatch. 2015. (Fiction Picture Bks.). (ENG.). 32p. (gr. -1-2). lib. bdg. 20.99 **(978-1-4795-6481-1(8))** Picture Window Bks.

Bradley, Jessica. Blastoff to the Secret Side of the Moon!, 1 vol. Nickel, Scott. 2013. (Comics Land Ser.). (ENG.). 32p. (gr. k-2). 7.95 (978-1-4342-4273-0(0)); lib. bdg. 23.99 (978-1-4342-4031-6(2)) Stone Arch Bks.

—Comics Land. 2013. (Comics Land Ser.). (ENG.). 32p. (gr. k-2). lib. bdg. 191.92 (978-1-4342-6063-5(1)); lib. bdg. 95.96 (978-1-4342-6062-8(3)); lib. bdg. 63.60 (978-1-4342-8516-4(2)); lib. bdg. 95.96 (978-1-4342-4104-7(1)) Stone Arch Bks.

—Dinosaurs for Breakfast, 1 vol. Lemke, Amy J. 2013. (Comics Land Ser.). (ENG.). 32p. (gr. k-2). 7.95 (978-1-4342-4270-9(6)); lib. bdg. 23.99 (978-1-4342-4029-3(0)) Stone Arch Bks.

—Frank 'n' Beans, 1 vol. Lemke, Amy J. & Lemke, Donald B. 2013. (Comics Land Ser.). (ENG.). 32p. (gr. k-2). 7.95 (978-1-4342-6284-4(7)); lib. bdg. 23.99 (978-1-4342-4988-3(3)) Stone Arch Bks.

—Goat on a Boat, 1 vol. Sazaklis, John. 2013. (Comics Land Ser.). (ENG.). 32p. (gr. k-2). 7.95 (978-1-4342-6282-0(0)); lib. bdg. 23.99 (978-1-4342-4944-9(1)) Stone Arch Bks.

—The Good, the Bad, & the Monkeys, 1 vol. Sonneborn, Scott. 2013. (Comics Land Ser.). (ENG.). 32p. (gr. k-2). 7.95 (978-1-4342-6283-7(9)); lib. bdg. 23.99 (978-1-4342-4945-6(X)) Stone Arch Bks.

—My Little Bro-Bot, 1 vol. Lemke, Amy J. & Lemke, Donald B. 2013. (Comics Land Ser.). (ENG.). 32p. (gr. k-2). 7.95 (978-1-4342-6285-1(5)); lib. bdg. 23.99 (978-1-4342-4989-0(1)) Stone Arch Bks.

—The New Kid from Planet Glorf, 1 vol. Kaplan, Arie. 2013. (Comics Land Ser.). (ENG.). 32p. (gr. k-2). 7.95 (978-1-4342-4272-3(2)); lib. bdg. 23.99 (978-1-4342-4032-3(0)) Stone Arch Bks.

—Snorkeling with Sea-Bots, 1 vol. Lemke, Amy J. 2013. (Comics Land Ser.). (ENG.). 32p. (gr. k-2). 7.95 (978-1-4342-4271-6(4)); lib. bdg. 23.99 (978-1-4342-4030-9(4)) Stone Arch Bks.

Bradley, Lois. Blind Tom: The Horse Who Helped Build the Great Railroad. Redmond, Shirley Raye. 2009. (J). pap. 10.00 (978-0-87842-558-7(6)) Mountain Pr. Publishing Co., Inc.

Bradley, Sandy. The Crows of Hidden Creek. Niemela, JoAnn Huston. 2003. 109p. (YA). 20.00 (978-0-9716786-0-6(X)) Ten Minas Publishing.

Bradley, Timothy J. Infestation. Bradley, Timothy J. 2013. (ENG.). 192p. (J). (gr. 3-7). pap. 5.99 (978-0-545-45904-4(4), Scholastic Paperbacks) Scholastic, Inc.

—Paleo Bugs: Survival of the Creepiest. Bradley, Timothy J. 2008. (Paleo Ser.: PALE). (ENG.). 48p. (J). (gr. 3-7). 15.99 (978-0-8118-6022-2(1)) Chronicle Bks. LLC.

Bradley, Vanessa. Daisy Street. Chase, Diana. 2005. 128p. (Orig.). (J). pap. 13.50 (978-1-920731-11-3(3)) Fremantle Pr. AUS. Dist: Independent Pubs. Group.

Bradshaw, Carrie. Nathan & the Really Big Bully. Renert, Gerry. 2012. (ENG.). 32p. 16.95 (978-1-62167-072-8(4), Raven Tree Pr.,Csi) Continental Sales, Inc.

Bradshaw, Carrie Anne. Nathan Saves Summer. Renert, Gerry. 2010. (ENG.). 32p. (J). (gr. -1-3). 16.95 (978-1-934960-76-9(4), Raven Tree Pr.,Csi) Continental Sales, Inc.

—Nathan Saves Summer/Nathan Rescata el Verano. Renert, Gerry. 2010. (ENG & SPA.). 32p. (J). (gr. -1-3). 16.95 (978-1-934960-74-5(8)); pap. 7.95 (978-1-934960-75-2(6)) Continental Sales, Inc. (Raven Tree Pr.,Csi).

Bradshaw, Jim. Suddenly Alligator: Adventures in Adverbs, 1 vol. Walton, Rick. 2011. (ENG.). 36p. (J). (gr. 2-3). pap. 7.99 (978-1-4236-2087-7(9)) Gibbs Smith, Publisher.

Bradshaw, Nick & Bachalo, Chris. Wolverine & the X-Men by Jason Aaron - Volume 2. 2013. (ENG.). 104p. (J). (gr. 4-17). pap. 16.99 (978-0-7851-5682-6(8), Marvel Pr.) Disney Publishing Worldwide.

Bradshaw, Nick & Roberson, Ibraim. X-Men/Steve Rogers: Escape from the Negative Zone. Asmus, James. 2011. (ENG.). 200p. (J). (gr. 4-17). 19.99 (978-0-7851-5560-7(0)) Marvel Worldwide, Inc.

Brady, Annie. Shackleton - the Boss: The Remarkable Adventures of Ernest Shackleton. Smith, Michael. 2nd rev. ed. 2010. (ENG.). 128p. (J). pap. 15.95 (978-1-905172-27-6(3)) Collins Pr., The IRL. Dist: Dufour Editions, Inc.

Brady, Irene. Illustrating Nature: Right-brain Art in a Left-Brain World. Brady, Irene. 2004. spiral bd. 25.95 (978-0-915965-09-0(7)) Nature Works Press.

Brady, Laurie. A Charm for Jo. Brady, Bill. l.t. ed. 2005. (Turtle Books). 32p. (J). (gr. 2-5). lib. bdg. 15.95 (978-0-944727-48-5(4)) Jason & Nordic Pubs.

Brady, Lisa. Here, There, & Everywhere: The Story of Sreeeeeeeet the Lorikeett. Tweti, Mira. 2008. 47p. (J). (gr. 4-7). (978-0-615-17122-7(2)) Parrot Pr.

Braffet, Holly. If You Were a Dinosaur in Hawaii. 2010. 22p. pap. 7.95 (978-1-933067-39-1(X)) Beachhouse Publishing, LLC.

—Kekoa & the Egg Mystery. 2010. (J). 14.95 (978-1-933067-35-3(7)) Beachhouse Publishing, LLC.

—Little Mouse's Hawaiian Christmas Present. Ebie, Mora. 2011. 28p. (J). (978-1-56647-956-1(8)) Mutual Publishing LLC.

—Maile & the Huli Hula Chicken. Braffet, Mary. 2010. 32p. (J). 12.95 (978-1-56647-925-7(8)) Mutual Publishing LLC.

Braga, Humberto. The Girl from Atlantis. Schenkman, Richard. 2010. 144p. (J). (gr. 2-7). 16.99 (978-0-9841809-0-5(7)) GMI Bks.

Braithwaite, Doug, jt. illus. see Ross, Alex.

Braithwaithe, Barrington. A Man Called Garvey: The Life & Times of the Great Leader Marcus Garvey. Mohamed, Paloma. l.t. ed. 2004. (Majority Press Inc., Wisdom for Children Ser.: No. 1). (ENG.). 36p. (J). 12.95 (978-0-912469-40-9(4)) Majority Pr., The.

Braithwaithe, Barry. Caribbean Mythology & Modern Life: 5 Plays for Young People. Mohamed, Paloma. 2004. (Majority Press Inc., Wisdom for Children Ser.: Vol. 2). (ENG.). 216p. (J). per. 19.95 (978-0-912469-42-3(0)) Majority Pr., The.

Braley, Shawn. Great Medieval Projects. Bordessa, Kris. 2008. (Build It Yourself Ser.). (ENG.). 128p. (J). (gr. 3-7). 21.95 (978-1-934670-26-2(X)) Nomad Pr.

—Great Medieval Projects: You Can Build Yourself. Bordessa, Kris. 2008. (Build It Yourself Ser.). (ENG.). 128p. (J). (gr. 3-7). pap. 15.95 (978-0-9792268-0-9(5)) Nomad Pr.

—Great Pioneer Projects. Dickinson, Rachel. 2007. (Build It Yourself Ser.: 1). (ENG.). 128p. (J). (gr. 3-7). pap. 15.95 (978-0-9785037-6-5(7)) Nomad Pr.

—The Human Body: 25 Fantastic Projects Illuminate How the Body Works. Reilly, Kathleen M. 2008. (Build It Yourself Ser.). (ENG.). 128p. (J). (gr. 3-7). 15.95 (978-1-934670-25-5(1)); pap. 15.95 (978-1-934670-24-8(3)) Nomad Pr.

—World Myths & Legends: 25 Projects You Can Build Yourself. Ceceri, Kathy. 2010. (Build It Yourself Ser.). (ENG.). 128p. (J). (gr. 3-7). 21.95 (978-1-934670-44-6(8)); pap. 15.95 (978-1-934670-43-9(X)) Nomad Pr.

Brallier, Christine. The Night Before Christmas. 2013. (ENG.). 32p. (J). 16.99 (978-0-9789688-2-3(4)) Brownian Bee Pr.

Bramall, Dan. The Awesome Book of Awesomeness. Frost, Adam. 2015. (ENG.). 112p. (J). (gr. 2-4). pap. 9.99 **(978-1-61963-793-1(6)**, Bloomsbury USA Childrens) Bloomsbury USA.

Bramsen, Carin. The Yellow Tutu. Bramsen, Kirsten. 2013. (ENG.). 40p. (J). (-k). pap. 7.99 (978-0-375-84393-8(0)) Random Hse., Inc.

Branam, Sandy. Kiki & the Red Shoes. Chappas, Bess. 2007. (J). 17.99 (978-1-60131-012-5(9)) Big Tent Bks.

Branch, Beverly. The Miller & the Donkey: A Tale about Thinking for Yourself. Aesop. 2006. (J). (978-1-59939-087-1(6), Reader's Digest Young Families, Inc.) Studio Fun International.

—The Nightingale. 2006. (J). 6.99 (978-1-59939-020-8(5)) Cornerstone Pr.

—Thumbelina: A Tale about Being Nice. 2006. (J). 6.99 (978-1-59939-024-6(8)) Cornerstone Pr.

Branch Jr., Robert F. Loving Danger. Williams, Eula. 2012. 20p. pap. 24.95 (978-1-4626-6954-7(9)) America Star Bks.

Brandao, Lucia. From Another World, 1 vol. MacHado, Ana Maria & Machado, Ana Maria. Baeta, Luisa, tr. from POR. 2005. (ENG.). 136p. (J). (gr. 3-7). pap. 9.95 (978-0-88899-641-1(1)) Groundwood Bks. CAN. Dist: Perseus-PGW.

Brandenburg, Claire. The Saint & His Bees. Jackson, Dessi. 2013. 28p. pap. 9.99 (978-1-62395-487-1(8)) Xist Publishing.

—Under the Grapevine: A Miracle by Saint Kendeas of Cyprus. Hart, Chrissi. 2006. 32p. (J). 15.95 (978-1-888212-84-6(5)) Conciliar Pr.

Brandi, Lillian. Encyclopedia Brown & the Case of the Midnight Visitor. Sobol, Donald J. 2015. 96p. (J). **(978-1-61479-309-0(3))** ABDO Publishing Co.

Brandi, Lillian. Encyclopedia Brown & the Case of the Midnight Visitor. Sobol, Donald J. 2008. (Encyclopedia Brown Ser.: 13). (ENG.). 96p. (J). (gr. 3-7). 4.99 (978-0-14-241106-3(X), Puffin) Penguin Publishing Group.

Brandon, Dan & Weaver, Brandon. Before You Meet Prince Charming: A Guide to Radiant Purity. Mally, Sarah. 2006. (ENG.). 272p. (YA). pap. 14.00 (978-0-9719405-4-3(1)) Tomorrow's Forefathers, Inc.

Brandon, Theresa. Year of the Dragon: The Complete Story Experience Edition. Anna, Jennifer. 2nd exp. ed. 2005. (Turtle's Back Bks.). 100p. (J). (gr. -1-6). pap. 14.99 (978-1-883573-18-8(1)) Blue Forge Pr.

Brandon, Vicky. The Wren & the Groundhog. Mcwherter, Barbara. 2011. 40p. pap. 24.95 (978-1-4560-5512-7(7)) America Star Bks.

Brandt, Linda M. Henry's Life As a Tulip Bulb: Developing an Attitude of Gratitude (Book 1) Brandt, Linda M. 2013. 24p. pap. 15.95 (978-1-61314-084-0(3)) Innovo Publishing, LLC.

Brandt, Michael. The Bunny, the Bear, the Bug & the Bee. Brandt-Taylor, Diane. 2005. (J). cd-rom 9.88 (978-0-9773236-0-9(9)) TaySysCo Publishing.

Brandt, Susan. What Am I? A Hawai'i Animal Guessing Game. Harrington, Daniel. 2006. (J). (978-1-56647-813-7(8)) Mutual Publishing LLC.

Branman, Liz. Twins. Friday, Anita. 2013. 34p. pap. 11.99 (978-0-9899544-0-2(4)) Two Chicks.

Brannen, Sarah. The Ugly Duckling. Namm, Diane. 2012. (Silver Penny Stories Ser.). (ENG.). 40p. (J). (gr. -1-1). 4.95 (978-1-4027-8437-8(6)) Sterling Publishing Co., Inc.

Brannen, Sarah S. At Home in Her Tomb: Lady Dai & the Ancient Chinese Treasures of Mawangdui. Liu-Perkins, Christine. 2014. (ENG.). 80p. (J). (gr. 4-7). lib. bdg. 19.95 (978-1-58089-370-1(8)) Charlesbridge Publishing, Inc.

—Digging for Troy: From Homer to Hisarlik. Cline, Eric H. & Rubalcaba, Jill. 2011. (ENG.). 80p. (J). (gr. 4-7). 17.95 (978-1-58089-326-8(0)); pap. 9.95 (978-1-58089-327-5(9)) Charlesbridge Publishing, Inc.

—Feathers: Not Just for Flying. Stewart, Melissa. 2014. (ENG.). 32p. (J). (gr. 1-4). pap. 7.95 (978-1-58089-431-9(3)) Charlesbridge Publishing, Inc.

—The Fox & the Grapes. Olmstead, Kathleen. 2014. (Silver Penny Stories Ser.). (ENG.). 40p. (J). (gr. -1-1). 4.95 (978-1-4027-8345-6(0)) Sterling Publishing Co., Inc.

Brannen, Sarah S. Madame Martine. 2015. (J). **(978-1-4896-3864-9(4))** Weigl Pubs., Inc.

Brannen, Sarah S. The Pied Piper of Hamelin. Olmstead, Kathleen. 2014. (Silver Penny Stories Ser.). (ENG.). 40p. (J). (gr. -1-1). 4.95 (978-1-4027-8349-4(3)) Sterling Publishing Co., Inc.

—The Pig Scramble. Kinney, Jessica. 2011. (ENG.). 36p. (J). 17.95 (978-1-934031-61-2(5), bd7fa2f2-9ea3-439a-9713-9f7979711a16) Islandport Pr., Inc.

—The Very Beary Tooth Fairy. Levine, Arthur A. 2013. (J). (978-0-439-47404-7(3)); (ENG.). 32p. (gr. -1-k). 16.99 (978-0-439-43966-4(3)) Scholastic, Inc. (Scholastic Pr.).

Brannen, Sarah S. Madame Martine. Brannen, Sarah S. 2014. (ENG.). 32p. (J). (gr. -1-2). 16.99 (978-0-8075-4905-6(3)) Whitman, Albert & Co.

Brannen, Sarah S. Madame Martine Breaks the Rules. Brannen, Sarah S. 2015. (ENG.). 32p. (J). (gr. -1-2). 16.99 **(978-0-8075-4907-0(X))** Whitman, Albert & Co.

Brannon, Tom. Abby's Pink Party. Kleinberg, Naomi. 2011. (ENG.). 12p. (J). (gr. k — 1). bds. 5.99 (978-0-307-92956-3(6), Random Hse. Bks. for Young Readers) Random Hse. Children's Bks.

—Circle of Friends (Sesame Street) Kleinberg, Naomi. 2012. (ENG.). 12p. (J). (gr. k-k). bds. 5.99 (978-0-307-93185-6(4), Random Hse. Bks. for Young Readers) Random Hse. Children's Bks.

—Elmo & Abby's Wacky Weather Day (Sesame Street) Kleinberg, Naomi. 2011. (ENG.). 12p. (J). (gr. k — 1). bds. 5.99 (978-0-375-87244-0(2), Random Hse. Bks. for Young Readers) Random Hse. Children's Bks.

—Elmo & Dorothy: Friends Forever! Tieman, Ruth Anne. 2010. (Sesame Street Ser.). (ENG.). 12p. (J). (gr. k — 1). bds. 5.99 (978-0-375-86145-1(9), Random Hse. Bks. for Young Readers) Random Hse. Children's Bks.

—Elmo & Ernie's Joke Book (Sesame Street) Random House Editors & Kleinberg, Naomi. 2012. (ENG.). 12p. (J). (gr. k-k). bds. 7.99 (978-0-307-93053-8(X), Random Hse. Bks. for Young Readers) Random Hse. Children's Bks.

—Elmo & His Friends: Brand New Readers. Sesame Workshop Staff. 2011. (Sesame Street Bks.). (ENG.). (J). (gr. -1-3). pap. 5.99 (978-0-7636-5147-3(8)) Candlewick Pr.

—Elmo & His Friends: Brand New Readers. Sesame Workshop Staff. 2011. (Sesame Street Bks.). (ENG.). 48p. (J). (gr. -1-3). 14.99 (978-0-7636-5068-1(4)) Candlewick Pr.

—Elmo's Alphabet Soup (Sesame Steet) Kleinberg, Naomi. 2011. (ENG.). 12p. (J). (gr. k — 1). bds. 6.99 (978-0-375-87179-5(9), Random Hse. Bks. for Young Readers) Random Hse. Children's Bks.

—Elmo's Christmas Hugs. Mitter, Matt. 2012. (Hugs Book Ser.). (ENG.). 12p. (J). (gr. -1-k). bds. 10.99 (978-0-7944-2703-0(0)) Reader's Digest Assn., Inc., The.

—Elmo's Christmas Snowman (Sesame Street) Kleinberg, Naomi. 2013. (ENG.). 12p. (J). (— 1). bds. 6.99 (978-0-449-81257-0(X), Random Hse. Bks. for Young Readers) Random Hse. Children's Bks.

—Elmo's Merry Christmas. 2011. (Lift-The-Flap Ser.). (ENG.). 10p. (J). (gr. -1-k). bds. 10.99 (978-0-7944-2326-1(4)) Reader's Digest Assn., Inc., The.

—Elmo's Rockin' Rhyme Time! (Sesame Street) Kleinberg, Naomi. 2012. (ENG.). 12p. (J). (gr. -1-2). bds. 6.99 (978-0-307-93184-9(6), Random Hse. Bks. for Young Readers) Random Hse. Children's Bks.

—Elmo's Walk in the Woods. Kleinberg, Naomi. 2011. (ENG.). 12p. (J). (gr. k — 1). bds. 6.99 (978-0-307-92968-6(X), Random Hse. Bks. for Young Readers) Random Hse. Children's Bks.

—Hic! Albee, Sarah. 2006. (Step-By-Step Readers Ser.). (J). pap. (978-1-59939-061-1(2), Reader's Digest Young Families, Inc.) Studio Fun International.

—Hokey Pokey Elmo. Tabby, Abigail. 2006. (Big Bird's Favorites Board Bks.). (ENG.). 24p. (J). (gr. k — 1). bds.

4.99 *(978-0-375-83507-0(5)*, Random Hse. Bks. for Young Readers) Random Hse. Children's Bks.

—Home for Christmas. Rabe, Tish. 2012. (Step into Reading Ser.). (ENG.). 48p. (J). (gr. k-3). pap. 3.99 *(978-0-307-97625-3(4))*; lib. bdg. 12.99 *(978-0-375-97119-8(X))* Random Hse. Children's Bks. (Random Hse. Bks. for Young Readers).

—Hooray for Hair! Rabe, Tish. 2013. (Step into Reading Ser.). (ENG.). 48p. (J). (gr. k-3). pap. 3.99 *(978-0-375-87048-4(2))*; lib. bdg. 12.99 *(978-0-375-97048-1(7))* Random Hse., Inc.

—I Love You Valentine Songs. 2012. (J). *(978-1-4508-3303-5(9))* Phoenix International Publications, Inc.

—Let's Help the Earth. Reader's Digest Staff. 2008. (Sesame Street Ser.). (ENG.). 12p. (J). (gr. -1-k). bds. 12.99 *(978-0-7944-1696-6(9))* Reader's Digest Assn., Inc., The.

—Me Love Cookies! Reader's Digest Staff & Mitter, Matt. 2010. (Hugs Book Ser.). (ENG.). 12p. (J). (— 1). bds. 10.99 *(978-0-7944-2176-2(8))* Reader's Digest Assn., Inc., The.

—Music Player. Reader's Digest Editors et al. 40th anniv. collector's ed. 2009. (Music Player Storybook Ser.). (ENG.). 40p. (J). (gr. -1). 19.99 *(978-0-7944-1913-4(5))* Reader's Digest Assn., Inc., The.

—Over on Sesame Street (Sesame Street) A Counting Rhyme. Kleinberg, Naomi. 2012. (ENG.). 12p. (J). (gr. k — 1). bds. 6.99 *(978-0-307-93052-1(1)*, Random Hse. Bks. for Young Readers) Random Hse. Children's Bks.

—Planet Name Game (Dr. Seuss/Cat in the Hat) Rabe, Tish. 2015. (Step into Reading Ser.). (ENG.). 32p. (J). (gr. -1-1). lib. bdg. 12.99 *(978-0-375-97373-4(7)*, Random Hse. Bks. for Young Readers) Random Hse. Children's Bks.

—Ready, Set, Brush! Mitter, Matt & Rudko, Che. 2008. (Pop-Up Book Ser.). (ENG.). 12p. (J). (gr. -1-k). bds. 12.99 *(978-0-7944-1445-0(1))* Reader's Digest Assn., Inc., The.

—Sesame Street All Aboard! 2015. (ENG.). 10p. (J). (gr. -1-k). bds. 10.99 *(978-0-7944-3329-1(4))* Studio Fun International.

—Sesame Street Grouchy Hugs! Mitter, Matt. 2012. (Hugs Book Ser.). (ENG.). 12p. (J). (gr. -1-k). bds. 10.99 *(978-0-7944-2194-6(6))* Reader's Digest Assn., Inc., The.

—Sesame Street Holiday Gift Set. Reader's Digest Editors. 2012. (Gift Set Ser.). (ENG.). 48p. (J). (gr. -1-2). 14.99 *(978-0-7944-2813-6(4))* Reader's Digest Assn., Inc., The.

—Step This Way (Dr. Seuss/Cat in the Hat) Rabe, Tish. 2013. (Step into Reading Ser.). (ENG.). 32p. (J). (gr. -1-1). 3.99 *(978-0-449-81435-2(1)*, Random Hse. Bks. for Young Readers) Random Hse. Children's Bks.

—A Tale about Tails (Dr. Seuss/Cat in the Hat) Rabe, Tish. 2014. (Step into Reading Ser.). (ENG.). 48p. (J). (gr. k-3). 3.99 *(978-0-385-37117-9(9))*; lib. bdg. 12.99 *(978-0-375-97185-3(8))* Random Hse. Children's Bks. (Random Hse. Bks. for Young Readers).

—What's the Big Idea, Charlie Brown? 2014. (ENG.). 40p. (J). (gr. -1). 16.99 *(978-1-62157-257-2(9)*, Little Patriot Pr.) Regnery Publishing, Inc., An Eagle Publishing Co.

—Where Are You Going, Charlie Brown? 2014. (ENG.). 40p. (J). (gr. -1). 16.99 *(978-1-62157-258-9(7)*, Little Patriot Pr.) Regnery Publishing, Inc., An Eagle Publishing Co.

—Who Cares, Charlie Brown? 2014. (Peanuts Great American Adventure Ser.). (ENG.). 40p. (J). (gr. -1). 16.99 *(978-1-62157-259-6(5)*, Little Patriot Pr.) Regnery Publishing, Inc., An Eagle Publishing Co.

Brannon, Tom, jt. illus. see Cooke, Tom.

Bransom, Paul. The Wind in the Willows. Grahame, Kenneth. 2013. 176p. pap. 35.00 *(978-1-927558-25-6(5))* Birch Tree Publishing.

Bransom, Paul, jt. illus. see Gleeson, J. M.

Brantley-Newton, Vanessa. Every Little Thing: Based on the Song 'Three Little Birds' by Bob Marley. Marley, Bob & Marley, Cedella. 2012. (ENG.). 32p. (J). (gr. -1-1). 16.99 *(978-1-4521-0697-7(5))* Chronicle Bks. LLC.

—Every Little Thing: Based on the Song 'Three Little Birds' by Bob Marley. Marley, Cedella & Marley, Bob. 2015. (ENG.). 24p. (J). (gr. -1-k). bds. 7.99 *(978-1-4521-4290-6(4))* Chronicle Bks. LLC.

—Hula-Hoopin' Queen. Godin, Thelma Lynne. 2014. (ENG.). 40p. (J). 18.95 *(978-1-60060-846-9(9))* Lee & Low Bks., Inc.

—Magic Trash. Shapiro, J. H. 2015. (ENG.). 32p. (J). (gr. k-3). pap. 7.95 *(978-1-58089-386-2(4))* Charlesbridge Publishing, Inc.

—My Three Best Friends & Me, Zulay. Best, Cari. 2015. (ENG.). 40p. (J). (gr. -1-3). 17.99 *(978-0-374-38819-5(9)*, Farrar, Straus & Giroux (BYR)) Farrar, Straus & Giroux.

—One Love. Marley, Cedella. 2014. (ENG.). 24p. (J). (gr. -1-k). bds. 7.99 *(978-1-4521-3855-8(9))* Chronicle Bks. LLC.

—We Shall Overcome: The Story of a Song. Levy, Debbie. 2013. (ENG.). 32p. (J). (gr. 1-3). 16.99 *(978-1-4231-1954-8(1))* Hyperion Bks. for Children.

Brantley-Newton, Vanessa. The Youngest Marcher: The Story of a Young Civil Rights Activist. Levinson, Cynthia. 2015. (J). ***(978-1-4814-0070-1(3))*** Simon & Schuster, Inc.

Branton, Molly. The Enchanted Lizard: La Lagartijita Mágica. Carter, Aubrey Smith. Nelson, Esther Whitt, ed. 2006. (ENG & SPA.). 96p. (J). 18.95 *(978-1-893271-38-8(2)*, Maverick Bks.) Trinity Univ. Pr.

Brantz, Loryn. Kindergarten Sight Word Reader. Rebboah, Julie A. 2008. (ENG.). 156p. (J). pap. 19.99 *(978-0-9817826-0-7(4))* Lightning Bug Learning Pr.

—Reproducible Kindergarten Sight Word Reader. Rebboah, Julie A. 2008. (ENG.). 156p. (J). ring bd. 39.99 *(978-0-9817826-3-8(9))* Lightning Bug Learning Pr.

Braren, Loretta Trezzo. The Little Hands Art Book: Exploring Arts & Crafts with 2-6 Year Olds. Press, Judy. 2008. (ENG.). 160p. (J). (gr. -1-1). 16.99 *(978-0-8249-6819-9(0))*; per. 12.99 *(978-0-8249-6820-5(4))* Ideals Pubns. (Williamson Bks.).

Braslavskii, Felix. Priklyuchenia L'va: Amerikanskiye i Angliiskiye Stikhi Dlya Detei. Kovner, Vladimir, tr. from ENG. 2010. (RUS.). 110p. (J). pap. *(978-1-934881-43-9(0)*, M-Graphics) M-Graphics Publishing.

Brassard, France. Lily & the Mixed-Up Letters. Hodge, Deborah. 2007. (ENG.). 32p. (J). (gr. 1-4). 18.95 *(978-0-88776-757-9(5))* Tundra Bks. CAN. Dist: Random Hse., Inc.

—Sometimes We Were Brave. Brisson, Pat. 2010. (ENG.). 32p. (J). (gr. k-2). 16.95 *(978-1-59078-586-7(X))* Boyds Mills Pr.

Brassel, Sondra. The Friendship Puzzle: Helping Kids Learn about Accepting & Including Kids with Autism. Coe, Julie L. 2009. 24p. (J). (gr. k-2). 14.95 *(978-0-9789182-4-8(X))* Larstan Publishing, Inc.

Brassey, Richard. George & the Dragon & Other Saintly Stories. 2003. 40p. *(978-1-84255-019-9(5)*, Orion Children's Bks.) Hachette Children's Group.

—Ghosts, Rogues & Highwaymen: 20 Stories from British History. McCaughrean, Geraldine. 2003. 128p. (J). pap. 9.99 *(978-1-85881-894-8(X)*, Orion) Orion Publishing Group, Ltd. GBR. Dist: Trafalgar Square Publishing.

—Rebels & Royals: 20 Stories from British History. McCaughrean, Geraldine. 2003. (Britannia Ser.). 128p. (J). pap. 9.99 *(978-1-85881-852-8(4)*, Orion) Orion Publishing Group, Ltd. GBR. Dist: Trafalgar Square Publishing.

Bratton, Ashley A., jt. illus. see Bratton, Deboral B.

Bratton, Ashley D., jt. illus. see Bratton, Deboral B.

Bratton, Deboral B. & Bigly, Ashley D. Record-a-Sport Golf Organizer. Bratton, Deborah B. & Bigly, Ashley D. Bigly, Ashley D., ed. 2003. (gr. 1-18). 18.95 *(978-1-931746-00-7(1))* Sport Your Stuff Corp.

Bratton, Deboral B. & Bratton, Ashley A. Record-a-Sport Football Sport Organizer. Bratton, Deborah B. & Bratton, Ashley A. Bratton, Ashley A., ed. 2003. (gr. 1-18). 18.95 *(978-1-931746-05-2(2))* Sport Your Stuff Corp.

Bratton, Deboral B. & Bratton, Ashley D. Record-a-Sport Baseball & Softball Organizer. Bratton, Deborah B. & Bratton, Ashley D. Bratton, Deborah B. & Bratton, Ashley D., eds. 2003. (gr. 1-18). 18.95 *(978-1-931746-03-8(6))* Sport Your Stuff Corp.

—Record-a-Sport Basketball Sport Organizer. Bratton, Deborah B. & Bratton, Ashley D. 2003. (gr. 1-18). 18.95 *(978-1-931746-02-1(8))* Sport Your Stuff Corp.

—Record-a-Sport Soccer Sport Organizer. Bratton, Deborah B. & Bratton, Ashley D. 2003. (gr. 1-18). 18.95 *(978-1-931746-04-5(4))* Sport Your Stuff Corp.

—Record-a-Sport Tennis Organizer. Bratton, Deborah B. & Bratton, Ashley D. 2003. (gr. 1-18). 18.95 *(978-1-931746-06-9(0))* Sport Your Stuff Corp.

Bratun, Katy. All Aboard Noah's Ark! Josephs, Mary. 2007. (Chunky Book Ser.). (ENG.). 22p. (J). (— 1). bds. 3.99 *(978-0-679-86054-9(1)*, Golden Inspirational) Random Hse. Children's Bks.

Bratun, Katy, et al. Alphabet of Insects. Schwaeber, Barbie Heit. 2007. (ENG.). 40p. (J). (gr. -1-3). 15.95 *(978-1-59249-725-6(X))* Soundprints.

Bratun, Katy. Josh's Halloween Pumpkin, 1 vol. Lay, Kathryn. 2008. (ENG.). 32p. (J). (gr. k-3). 16.99 *(978-1-58980-595-6(X))* Pelican Publishing Co., Inc.

—Just Mommy & Me. Morrow, Tara Jaye. 2004. 32p. (J). 13.89 *(978-0-06-000725-6(7))* HarperCollins Pubs.

—Katie Caught a Cold. Cowan, Charlotte. 2007. (ENG.). 32p. (J). (gr. 3-7). 17.95 *(978-0-9753516-3-5(X))* Hippocratic Pr., The.

—Sadie's Sore Throat. Cowan, Charlotte. 2007. (Dr. Hippo Ser.). (ENG.). 32p. (J). (gr. 3-7). 17.95 *(978-0-9753516-4-2(8))* Hippocratic Pr., The.

Bratun, Katy. Gingerbread Mouse. Bratun, Katy. 32p. (J). (gr. -1-3). 2007. (ENG.). per. 6.99 *(978-0-06-009082-1(0))*; 2003. lib. bdg. 13.89 *(978-0-06-009081-4(2))* HarperCollins Pubs.

Brauckman-Towns, Krista. Buffalo Prairie. Lee, Evelyn. (Amazing Animal Adventures Ser.). (ENG.). 32p. (J). (gr. -1-2). 19.95 *(978-1-59249-435-4(8)*, BC7110) Soundprints.

Brauckmann-Towns, Krista. Bluestem Horizon: A Story of a Tallgrass Prairie. Lee, Evelyn. 2005. (Soundprints' Wild Habitats Ser.). (ENG.). 32p. (J). (gr. 1-4). 8.95 *(978-1-59249-098-1(0))* Soundprints.

—Buffalo Prairie. Lee, Evelyn. 2005. (Amazing Animal Adventures Ser.). (ENG.). 36p. (J). (gr. -1-2). 2.95 *(978-1-59249-434-7(X)*, S7160); 15.95 *(978-1-59249-432-3(3)*, B7110); pap. 6.95 *(978-1-59249-433-0(1)*, S7110) Soundprints.

Braught, Mark. Cosmo's Moon. Scillian, Devin. 2003. (ENG.). 40p. (J). (gr. 1-4). 15.95 *(978-1-58536-123-6(2)*, 201986) Sleeping Bear Pr.

—Ellen Craft's Escape from Slavery. Moore, Cathy. 2010. (History Speaks: Picture Books Plus Reader's Theater Ser.). (ENG.). 48p. (gr. 2-4). pap. 9.95 *(978-0-7613-6672-0(5))*; lib. bdg. 27.93 *(978-0-7613-5875-6(7)*, Millbrook Pr.) Lerner Publishing Group.

—J Is for Jump Shot: A Basketball Alphabet. Ulmer, Michael. 2005. (Sports Alphabet Ser.). (ENG.). 40p. (J). (gr. -1-5). 16.95 *(978-1-58536-229-5(8))* Sleeping Bear Pr.

—J Is for Jump Shot: A Basketball Alphabet. Ulmer, Mike. rev. ed. 2006. (Sports Ser.). (ENG.). 40p. (J). (gr. k-5). pap. 7.95 *(978-1-58536-338-4(3))* Sleeping Bear Pr.

—A Peck of Peaches: A Georgia Number Book. Crane, Carol. rev. ed. 2007. (State Counting Ser.). (ENG.). 40p. (J). (gr. 1-3). 17.95 *(978-1-58536-177-9(1))* Sleeping Bear Pr.

—T Is for Touchdown: A Football Alphabet. Herzog, Brad. 2006. (Sports Ser.). (ENG.). 40p. (J). (gr. -1-3). pap. 7.95 *(978-1-58536-337-7(5))* Sleeping Bear Pr.

Braught, Mark, jt. illus. see Stacy, Alan.

Brault, Christopher. Raceboy & Super Qwok Adventures. Winkel, Andrew. 2012. (ENG.). 356p. (J). pap. 16.00 *(978-0-9837905-1-8(5))* Hierophantasm.

Braun, Chris. Galactic Treasure Hunt: Lost City of Atlantis. Childress, Jamie. 2006. 120p. (J). pap. 4.99 *(978-1-931882-62-0(2))* Adventures Unlimited Pr.

—Galactic Treasure Hunt: Lost City of the Moon. Childress, Jamie. 2005. 115p. (J). (gr. -1-7). per. 4.99 *(978-1-931882-45-3(2))* Adventures Unlimited Pr.

—Lost Universe. Childress, Jamie. 2007. (Galactic Treasure Hunt Ser.). 163p. (J). (gr. 4-7). per. 4.99 *(978-1-931882-74-3(6))* Adventures Unlimited Pr.

Braun, Chuck. How & Why Folktales: From Around the World. Egelberg, Arlene & Clark, Raymond C. 2004. 106p. (gr. 6-12). pap., stu. ed. 15.00 *(978-0-86647-180-0(4))* Pro Lingua Assocs., Inc.

Braun, Lisa. The Special Women We Call Grandmom, 1 vol. McDermott, Mary. 2010. 20p. pap. 24.95 *(978-1-4489-9749-7(6))* PublishAmerica, Inc.

Braun, Sebastein. How Many Sleeps 'til Christmas? Sperring, Mark. 2014. 32p. (J). (gr. -1-3). 16.99 *(978-1-58925-160-1(1))* Tiger Tales.

Braun, Sebastian. I Say Yes! I Say No! Ziefert, Harriet. 2015. (¡Hola, English! Ser.). (ENG & SPA.). 28p. (J). (gr. -1-3). 12.99 *(978-1-60905-513-4(6))* Blue Apple Bks.

—I'm a Clown! 2012. (Look at Me Ser.). (ENG.). 12p. (J). bds. *(978-1-84643-472-3(6))* Child's Play International Ltd.

—I'm a Monster! 2012. (Look at Me Ser.). (ENG.). 12p. (J). bds. *(978-1-84643-470-9(X))* Child's Play International Ltd.

—I'm a Robot! 2012. (Look at Me Ser.). (ENG.). 12p. (J). bds. *(978-1-84643-469-3(6))* Child's Play International Ltd.

—I'm an Alien! 2012. (Look at Me Ser.). (ENG.). 12p. (J). bds. *(978-1-84643-471-6(8))* Child's Play International Ltd.

Braun, Sebastian. Peekaboo Baby. Braun, Sebastian. 2012. (ENG.). 16p. (J). (gr. -1 — 1). bds. 6.99 *(978-0-7636-5933-2(9))* Candlewick Pr.

Braun, Sebastien. Babi Bag Siwgwr. Gates, Susan & Ceredigion, Cymdeithas Lyfrau. Williams, Dylan, tr. from ENG. 2005. (WEL.). 80p. pap. *(978-1-902416-96-0(1))* Cymdeithas Lyfrau Ceredigion.

—Be Careful What You Sniff For, No. 1. Krulik, Nancy. 2013. (Magic Bone Ser.: 1). (ENG.). 128p. (J). (gr. 1-3). pap. 4.99 *(978-0-448-46399-5(7)*, Grosset & Dunlap) Penguin Publishing Group.

—Can You Say It, Too? Arf! Arf! Nosy Crow. 2015. (ENG.). 10p. (J). (— 1). bds. 8.99 *(978-0-7636-7894-4(5)*, Nosy Crow) Candlewick Pr.

—Can You Say It, Too? Growl! Growl! Nosy Crow. 2014. (ENG.). 10p. (J). (— 1). bds. 8.99 *(978-0-7636-7396-3(X)*, Nosy Crow) Candlewick Pr.

Braun, Sebastien. Can You Say It, Too? Hoot! Hoot! Nosy Crow. 2015. (ENG.). 10p. (J). (— 1). bds. 8.99 ***(978-0-7636-7588-2(1)***, Nosy Crow) Candlewick Pr.

Braun, Sebastien. Can You Say It, Too? Moo! Moo! Crow, Nosy. 2014. (ENG.). 10p. (J). (— 1). bds. 8.99 *(978-0-7636-7066-5(9)*, Nosy Crow) Candlewick Pr.

—Can You Say It, Too? Quack! Quack! Nosy Crow. 2015. (ENG.). 10p. (J). (— 1). bds. 8.99 *(978-0-7636-7589-9(X)*, Nosy Crow) Candlewick Pr.

—Can You Say It, Too? Roar! Roar! Nosy Crow. 2014. (ENG.). 10p. (J). (— 1). bds. 8.99 *(978-0-7636-7397-0(8)*, Nosy Crow) Candlewick Pr.

—Can You Say It, Too? Woof! Woof! Crow, Nosy. 2014. (ENG.). 10p. (J). (— 1). bds. 8.99 *(978-0-7636-6605-7(X)*, Nosy Crow) Candlewick Pr.

—Catch That Wave. Krulik, Nancy. 2013. (Magic Bone Ser.: 2). (ENG.). 128p. (J). (gr. 1-3). pap. 4.99 *(978-0-448-46444-2(6)*, Grosset & Dunlap) Penguin Publishing Group.

—Dog on His Bus. Seltzer, Eric & Hall, Kirsten. 2012. (Penguin Young Readers, Level 2 Ser.). (ENG.). 32p. (J). (gr. 1-2). pap. 3.99 *(978-0-448-45904-2(3)*, Warne, Frederick Pubs.) Penguin Bks., Ltd. GBR. Dist: Penguin Random Hse., LLC.

—Dog on His Bus. Seltzer, Eric & Hall, Kirsten. ed. 2012. (Penguin Young Readers Level 2 Ser.). lib. bdg. 13.55 *(978-0-606-25815-9(9)*, Turtleback) Turtleback Bks.

—Dogs Don't Have Webbed Feet, No. 7. Krulik, Nancy. 2015. (Magic Bone Ser.: 7). (ENG.). 128p. (J). (gr. 1-3). 4.99 *(978-0-448-48096-1(4)*, Grosset & Dunlap) Penguin Publishing Group.

—Don't Mess with the Ninja Puppy!, No. 6. Krulik, Nancy. 2014. (Magic Bone Ser.: 6). (ENG.). 128p. (J). (gr. 1-3). 4.99 *(978-0-448-48095-4(6)*, Grosset & Dunlap) Penguin Publishing Group.

—First Snow. Ford, Bernette G. 2005. 32p. (J). *(978-0-9547373-3-7(4))* Boxer Bks., Ltd.

—First Snow. Ford, Bernette G. & Ford, Bernette. 2005. (ENG.). 32p. (J). (gr. -1-3). 16.95 *(978-0-8234-1937-1(1))* Holiday Hse., Inc.

—Follow That Furball. Krulik, Nancy. 2013. (Magic Bone Ser.: 3). (ENG.). 128p. (J). (gr. 1-3). 4.99 *(978-0-448-46445-9(4)*, Grosset & Dunlap) Penguin Publishing Group.

—Fox & Crow Are Not Friends. Wiley, Melissa. 2012. (Step into Reading Ser.). (ENG.). 48p. (J). (gr. k-3). pap. 3.99 *(978-0-375-86982-2(4)*, Random Hse. Bks. for Young Readers) Random Hse. Children's Bks.

—Go Fetch! Krulik, Nancy. 2014. (Magic Bone Ser.: 5). (ENG.). 128p. (J). (gr. 1-3). 4.99 *(978-0-448-48094-7(8)*, Grosset & Dunlap) Penguin Publishing Group.

—Learn to Read with Tug the Pup & Friends!, Set 1. Wood, Julie M. 2014. (My Very First I Can Read! Ser.). (ENG.). 132p. (J). (gr. -1-3). pap. 12.99 *(978-0-06-226689-7(6))* HarperCollins Pubs.

—Nice Snowing You! Krulik, Nancy. 2014. (Magic Bone Ser.: 4). (ENG.). 128p. (J). (gr. 1-3). 4.99 *(978-0-448-46446-6(2)*, Grosset & Dunlap) Penguin Publishing Group.

Braun, Sebastien. Rootin' Tootin' Cow Dog #8. Krulik, Nancy. 2015. (Magic Bone Ser.: 8). (ENG.). 128p. (J). (gr. 1-3). 4.99 ***(978-0-448-48097-8(2)***, Grosset & Dunlap) Penguin Publishing Group.

Braun, Sebastien. Santa's Noisy House. ed. 2013. (ENG.). 12p. (J). (gr. -1-k). 17.99 *(978-0-230-76411-8(8))* Pan Macmillan GBR. Dist: Independent Pubs. Group.

—Shapes & Colors. 2012. (J). *(978-1-58865-852-4(X))* Kidsbooks, LLC.

—Tigers Love to Say Goodnight. Mongredien, Sue. 2008. (ENG.). 28p. (J). (gr. -1-k). pap. 9.95 *(978-1-84362-547-6(4))* Hodder & Stoughton GBR. Dist: Independent Pubs. Group.

—Where's My Cuddly? Lobel, Gill. 2009. (ENG.). 32p. (J). (gr. k-k). 17.99 *(978-1-84616-102-5(9))* Hodder & Stoughton GBR. Dist: Independent Pubs. Group.

Braun, Sebastien. Back to Bed, Ed!, 1 vol. Braun, Sebastien. 32p. (J). (gr. -1-3). 2014. (ENG.). pap. 7.95 *(978-1-56145-775-5(2))*; 2010. 15.95 *(978-1-56145-518-8(0))* Peachtree Pubs.

—Digger & Tom! Braun, Sebastien. 2013. 32p. (J). (gr. -1-3). 16.99 *(978-0-06-207752-3(X))* HarperCollins Pubs.

—I Love My Daddy. Braun, Sebastien. 2004. (ENG.). 32p. (J). (gr. -1-2). 12.99 *(978-0-06-054311-2(6))* HarperCollins Pubs.

—I Love You More. Braun, Sebastien. 2013. (ENG.). 18p. (gr. -1). bds. 8.95 *(978-1-58925-620-0(4))* Tiger Tales.

—Toot & Pop! Braun, Sebastien. 2012. 32p. (J). (gr. -1-2). 12.99 *(978-0-06-207750-9(3))* HarperCollins Pubs.

—Who Can Jump? Braun, Sebastien. 2014. (ENG.). 14p. (J). (— 1). bds. 6.99 *(978-0-7636-6753-5(6))* Candlewick Pr.

—Who Can Swim? Braun, Sebastien. 2014. (ENG.). 14p. (J). (— 1). bds. 6.99 *(978-0-7636-6752-8(8))* Candlewick Pr.

—Whoosh & Chug! Braun, Sebastien. 2014. 32p. (J). (gr. -1-3). 16.99 *(978-0-06-207754-7(6))* HarperCollins Pubs.

Bravi, Soledad. Good Night! Marchon, Benoit. 2013. (ENG.). 40p. (J). (gr. k — 1). bds. 7.99 *(978-0-547-89314-3(0))* Houghton Mifflin Harcourt Publishing Co.

—Spoonful: A Peek-A-Boo Book. Marchon, Benoit. 2013. (ENG.). 38p. (J). (gr. k — 1). bds. 7.99 *(978-0-547-89313-6(2))* Houghton Mifflin Harcourt Publishing Co.

Bravo, Constanza. El Libro de Oro de las Fabulas. Uribe, Veronica & Esopo. 2004. (SPA.). 126p. (J). (gr. -1-3). 9.99 *(978-980-257-209-0(8))* Ekare, Ediciones VEN. Dist: Lectorum Pubns., Inc.

Bravo, Fran, jt. illus. see Bravo, Juan.

Bravo, Juan & Bravo, Fran. Un Dragon a Dieta. Cano, Carles & Carles, Cano. 2006. (Montana Encantada Ser.). (SPA.). 36p. (J). (gr. 1-2). pap. 8.50 *(978-84-241-8747-7(4))* Everest Editora ESP. Dist: Lectorum Pubns., Inc.

Bray, Pamela. Ayiana & the Hurricane Katrina Classmate. Powell, GinaMarie. 2008. 28p. pap. 24.95 *(978-1-60441-965-8(2))* America Star Bks.

Bray, Peter. One Perfect Day. French, Jackie. 2006. (Making Tracks Ser.). (ENG.). 72p. (J). (gr. 2-4). pap. 9.95 *(978-1-876944-40-7(4))* National Museum of Australia AUS. Dist: Independent Pubs. Group.

—Tibby's Leaf. Dubosarsky, Ursula. 2008. (Making Tracks Ser.). (ENG.). 64p. (J). (gr. 2-4). pap. 11.95 *(978-1-876944-68-1(4))* National Museum of Australia AUS. Dist: Independent Pubs. Group.

Bray, Phyllis. A Traveller in Time. Uttley, Alison & Singh, Mahendra. 2011. (ENG.). 336p. (J). (gr. 4-7). 17.95 *(978-1-59017-388-6(0)*, NYR Children's Collection) New York Review of Bks., Inc., The.

Brayton, Julie. You Will Be My Baby Even When. Becker, Christie. 2003. 32p. (J). (gr. -1-1). 14.95 *(978-0-9728116-0-6(5))* Becker, Christie.

Brazell, Derek. Ali Baba & the Forty Thieves. Barkow, Henriette. 2004. 28p. (J). (ENG & SWE.). pap. *(978-1-84444-539-4(9))*; (ENG, RUS, SWE & SOM.). pap. *(978-1-84444-540-0(2))*; (POL & ENG.). pap. *(978-1-84444-545-5(3))* Mantra Lingua.

—Lima's Red Hot Chilli. Mills, David. 2004. (J). 24p. *(978-1-85269-505-7(6))*; 24p. *(978-1-85269-504-0(8))*; 24p. *(978-1-85269-429-6(7))*; 24p. *(978-1-85269-534-7(X))*; 24p. *(978-1-85269-467-8(X))*; 24p. *(978-1-85269-468-5(8))*; (ENG & SPA.). 32p. pap. *(978-1-85269-942-0(6))*; (ENG & KHM.). 32p. pap. *(978-1-85269-542-2(0))*; (ENG & KOR.). 32p. pap. *(978-1-85269-543-9(9))*; (ENG & FRE.). 32p. pap. *(978-1-85269-533-0(1))*; (ENG & PER.). 32p. pap. *(978-1-85269-506-4(4))*; (ENG & TAM.). 32p. pap. *(978-1-85269-469-2(6))*; (ENG & GRE.). 32p. pap. *(978-1-85269-466-1(1))*; (ENG & ALB.). 32p. pap. *(978-1-85269-465-4(3))*; (ENG & URD.). 32p. pap. *(978-1-85269-427-2(0))*; (ENG & TUR.). 32p. pap. *(978-1-85269-426-5(2))*; (ENG & SOM.). 32p. pap. *(978-1-85269-425-8(4))*; (ENG & POR.). 32p. pap. *(978-1-85269-424-1(6))*; (ENG & GUJ.). 32p. pap. *(978-1-85269-423-4(8))*; (ENG & BEN.). 32p. pap. *(978-1-85269-421-0(1))*; (ENG & ARA.). 32p. pap. *(978-1-85269-420-3(3))* Mantra Lingua.

—Mei Ling's Hiccups. Mills, David. 2004. (J). 24p. *(978-1-85269-559-0(5))*; (CHI & ENG.). 32p. pap. *(978-1-85269-703-7(2))*; (ENG & CHI.). 32p. pap. *(978-1-85269-555-2(2))*; (ENG & ARA.). 32p. pap. *(978-1-85269-553-8(6))*; (ENG & CZE.). 32p. pap. *(978-1-85269-562-5(6))*; (ENG & POL.). 32p. pap. *(978-1-85269-626-9(5))*; (ENG & SPA.). 32p. pap. *(978-1-85269-565-1(X))*; (ENG & POR.). 32p. pap. *(978-1-85269-562-0(5))*; (ENG & JPN.). 32p. pap. *(978-1-85269-560-6(9))*; (ENG & URD.). 32p. pap. *(978-1-85269-568-2(4))*; (ENG.). 32p. pap. *(978-1-85269-563-7(3))*; (ENG & PAN.). 32p. pap. *(978-1-85269-561-3(7))*; (ENG & GUJ.). 32p. pap. *(978-1-85269-558-3(7))*; (ENG & KOR.). 32p. pap. *(978-1-85269-704-4(0))*; (ENG & VIE.). 32p. pap. *(978-1-85269-569-9(2))*; (ENG & TUR.). 32p. pap. *(978-1-85269-567-5(6))*; (ENG & TAM.). 32p. pap. *(978-1-85269-566-8(8))*; (ENG & FRE.). 32p. pap. *(978-1-85269-557-6(9))*; (ENG & PER.). 32p. pap. *(978-1-85269-556-9(0))*; (ENG & BEN.). 32p. pap. *(978-1-85269-554-5(4))*; (ENG & ALB.). 32p. pap. *(978-1-85269-552-1(8))* Mantra Lingua.

—Mei Ling's Hiccups: Higgadii Mii Linig. Mills, David. 2004. (ENG & SOM.). 32p. (J). pap. *(978-1-85269-564-4(1))* Mantra Lingua.

—That's My Mum. Barkow, Henriette. 2004. (J). 24p. *(978-1-85269-604-7(4))*; (ENG & YOR.). 28p. pap. *(978-1-84444-381-9(7))*; (ALB & ENG.). 28p. pap. *(978-1-85269-595-8(1))*; (ENG & ITA.). 28p. pap. *(978-1-85269-804-1(7))*; (GER & ENG.). 28p. pap. *(978-1-85269-803-4(9))*; (ENG & VIE.). 28p. pap. *(978-1-85269-802-7(0))*; (ENG & CZE.). 28p. pap. *(978-1-85269-628-3(1))*; (ENG & URD.). 28p. pap.

B

(978-1-85269-609-2(5)); (ENG & TUR.). 28p. pap. *(978-1-85269-608-5(7))*; (ENG & SPA.). 28p. pap. *(978-1-85269-606-1(0))*; (ENG & SOM.). 28p. pap. *(978-1-85269-605-4(2))*; (ENG & POR.). 28p. pap. *(978-1-85269-603-0(6))*; (ENG & PAN.). 28p. pap. *(978-1-85269-602-3(8))*; (ENG & GUJ.). 28p. pap. *(978-1-85269-601-6(X))*; (ENG & PER.). 28p. pap. *(978-1-85269-599-6(4))*; (ENG & CHI.). 28p. pap. *(978-1-85269-598-9(6))*; (ENG & BEN.). 28p. pap. *(978-1-85269-597-2(8))* Mantra Lingua.

—That's My Mum: Ajo Eshte Nena Ime. Barkow, Henriette. 2004. (ENG & ARA.). 28p. (J). pap. *(978-1-85269-596-5(X))* Mantra Lingua.

—Welcome to the World Baby. Robert, Na'ima Bint & Petrova-Browning, Nina. 2005. (ENG & BUL.). 32p. (J). pap. *(978-1-84444-721-3(9))* Mantra Lingua.

—Welcome to the World Baby. Robert, Na'ima Bint. 2005. 32p. (J). (WEL, ENG, KOR & KUR.). pap. *(978-1-84444-633-9(6))*; (ENG & SNA.). pap. *(978-1-84444-450-2(3))*; (YOR & ENG.). pap. *(978-1-84444-297-3(7))*; (ENG & VIE.). pap. *(978-1-84444-296-6(9))*; (ENG & URD.). pap. *(978-1-84444-295-9(0))*; (TUR & ENG.). pap. *(978-1-84444-293-5(4))*; (ENG & SWA.). pap. *(978-1-84444-290-4(X))*; (SPA & ENG.). pap. *(978-1-84444-289-8(6))*; (ENG & SOM.). pap. *(978-1-84444-288-1(8))*; (ENG & RUS.). pap. *(978-1-84444-287-4(X))*; (ENG & RUM.). pap. *(978-1-84444-286-7(1))*; (ENG & POR.). pap. *(978-1-84444-285-0(3))*; (POL & ENG.). pap. *(978-1-84444-284-3(5))*; (ENG & PAN.). pap. *(978-1-84444-283-6(7))*; (ENG & KOR.). pap. *(978-1-84444-282-9(9))*; (JPN & ENG.). pap. *(978-1-84444-281-2(0))*; (ENG & ITA.). pap. *(978-1-84444-280-5(2))*; (ENG & HIN.). pap. *(978-1-84444-279-9(9))*; (ENG & GUJ.). pap. *(978-1-84444-278-2(0))*; (ENG & GER.). pap. *(978-1-84444-276-8(4))*; (FRE & ENG.). pap. *(978-1-84444-275-1(6))*; (ENG & PER.). pap. *(978-1-84444-274-4(8))*; (ENG, HRV & SER.). pap. *(978-1-84444-273-7(X))*; (ENG & CHI.). pap. *(978-1-84444-272-0(1))*; (ENG & CHI.). pap. *(978-1-84444-271-3(3))*; (ENG & BEN.). pap. *(978-1-84444-270-6(5))*; (ENG & ARA.). pap. *(978-1-84444-269-0(1))*; (ENG & ALB.). pap. *(978-1-84444-268-3(3))* Mantra Lingua.

Bready, Jane Gilltrap. R Is for Race: A Stock Car Alphabet. Herzog, Brad. 2006. (Sports Ser.). (ENG.). 40p. (J). (gr. -1-5). 16.95 *(978-1-58536-272-1(7))* Sleeping Bear Pr.

Breakespeare, Andrew. Mole Who was Scared of the Dark. Gates, Susan. 2005. (ENG.). 24p. (J). lib. bdg. 23.65 *(978-1-59646-710-1(X))* Dingles & Co.

Breathed, Berkeley. Edward Fudwupper Fibbed Big. Breathed, Berkeley. 2003. (ENG.). 40p. (J). (gr. 1-4). pap. 8.00 *(978-0-316-14425-4(8))* Little, Brown Bks. for Young Readers.

—Flawed Dogs. Breathed, Berkeley. 2009. (ENG.). 224p. (J). (gr. 3-7). 16.99 *(978-0-399-25218-1(5)*, Philomel) Penguin Publishing Group.

—Mars Needs Moms! Breathed, Berkeley. 2007. (ENG.). 40p. (J). (gr. k-3). 16.99 *(978-0-399-24736-1(X)*, Philomel) Penguin Publishing Group.

—Pete & Pickles. Breathed, Berkeley. 2008. (ENG.). 48p. (J). (gr. -1-k). 17.99 *(978-0-399-25082-8(4)*, Philomel) Penguin Publishing Group.

Breaux, Joe Ann. Confederate Coloring & Learning Book. Walker, Gary C. 2004. 41p. (J). (gr. 1-7). pap. 4.95 *(978-0-9617898-5-5(9))* A & W Enterprises.

Breaux, Wayne, Jr., et al. Rifts Adventure Guide. Siembieda, Kevin. 2006. (Rifts RPG Ser.). (YA). pap. 22.95 *(978-1-57457-072-4(2))* Palladium Bks., Inc.

Brecke, Nicole. Airplanes & Ships You Can Draw. Brecke, Nicole. Stockland, Patricia M. 2010. (Ready, Set, Draw! Ser.). (ENG.). 32p. (gr. 2-4). lib. bdg. 25.26 *(978-0-7613-4166-6(8)*, Millbrook Pr.) Lerner Publishing Group.

—Cars, Trucks, & Motorcycles You Can Draw. Brecke, Nicole. Stockland, Patricia M. 2009. (Ready, Set, Draw! Ser.). (ENG.). 32p. (gr. 2-4). lib. bdg. 25.26 *(978-0-7613-4162-8(5)*, Millbrook Pr.) Lerner Publishing Group.

—Cats You Can Draw. Brecke, Nicole. Stockland, Patricia M. 2009. (Ready, Set, Draw! Ser.). (ENG.). 32p. (gr. 2-4). lib. bdg. 25.26 *(978-0-7613-4161-1(7)*, Millbrook Pr.) Lerner Publishing Group.

—Cool Boy Stuff You Can Draw. Brecke, Nicole. Stockland, Patricia M. 2009. (Ready, Set, Draw! Ser.). (ENG.). 32p. (gr. 2-4). lib. bdg. 25.26 *(978-0-7613-4163-5(3)*, Millbrook Pr.) Lerner Publishing Group.

—Cool Girl Stuff You Can Draw. Brecke, Nicole. Stockland, Patricia M. 2009. (Ready, Set, Draw! Ser.). (ENG.). 32p. (gr. 2-4). lib. bdg. 25.26 *(978-0-7613-4164-2(1)*, Millbrook Pr.) Lerner Publishing Group.

—Dinosaurs & Other Prehistoric Creatures You Can Draw. Brecke, Nicole. Stockland, Patricia M. 2010. (Ready, Set, Draw! Ser.). (ENG.). 32p. (gr. 2-4). lib. bdg. 25.26 *(978-0-7613-4169-7(2)*, Millbrook Pr.) Lerner Publishing Group.

—Dogs You Can Draw. Brecke, Nicole. Stockland, Patricia M. 2009. (Ready, Set, Draw! Ser.). (ENG.). 32p. (gr. 2-4). lib. bdg. 25.26 *(978-0-7613-4159-8(5)*, Millbrook Pr.) Lerner Publishing Group.

—Extinct & Endangered Animals You Can Draw. Brecke, Nicole. Stockland, Patricia M. 2010. (Ready, Set, Draw! Ser.). (ENG.). 32p. (gr. 2-4). lib. bdg. 25.26 *(978-0-7613-4165-9(X)*, Millbrook Pr.) Lerner Publishing Group.

—Horses You Can Draw. Brecke, Nicole. Stockland, Patricia M. 2009. (Ready, Set, Draw! Ser.). (ENG.). 32p. (gr. 2-4). lib. bdg. 25.26 *(978-0-7613-4160-4(9)*, Millbrook Pr.) Lerner Publishing Group.

—Insects You Can Draw. Brecke, Nicole. Stockland, Patricia M. 2010. (Ready, Set, Draw! Ser.). (ENG.). 32p. (gr. 2-4). lib. bdg. 25.26 *(978-0-7613-4170-3(6)*, Millbrook Pr.) Lerner Publishing Group.

—Sea Creatures You Can Draw. Brecke, Nicole. Stockland, Patricia M. 2010. (Ready, Set, Draw! Ser.). (ENG.). 32p. (gr. 2-4). lib. bdg. 25.26 *(978-0-7613-4168-0(4)*, Millbrook Pr.) Lerner Publishing Group.

—Spaceships, Aliens, & Robots You Can Draw. Brecke, Nicole. Stockland, Patricia M. 2010. (Ready, Set, Draw! Ser.). (ENG.). 32p. (gr. 2-4). lib. bdg. 25.26 *(978-0-7613-4167-3(6)*, Millbrook Pr.) Lerner Publishing Group.

Breckenreid, Julia. An Eye for Color: The Story of Josef Albers. Wing, Natasha. 2009. (ENG.). 40p. (J). (gr. 1-4). 18.99 *(978-0-8050-8072-8(4)*, Holt, Henry & Co. Bks. For Young Readers) Holt, Henry & Co.

Breckenridge, Scott, jt. illus. see Breckenridge, Trula.

Breckenridge, Trula & Breckenridge, Scott. Squiggly the Roach. Breckenridge, Trula & Breckenridge, Scott. 2004. (J). per. *(978-0-9749480-6-5(3)*, MSPpress) Mama Specific Productions.

Breckenridge, Trula & Lynch, Todd. Ricca the Ladybug. Breckenridge, Trula & Lynch, Todd. 2004. (J). per. *(978-0-9749480-8-9(X)*, MSPpress) Mama Specific Productions.

Breckenridge, Trula & Palmore, Iyende. FiFi the Leaf. Breckenridge, Trula & Palmore, Iyende. 2004. (J). per. *(978-0-9749480-7-2(1)*, MSPpress) Mama Specific Productions.

Brecknell, Annie. A Day to Remember. Medina, Sarah. 48p. pap. 8.99 *(978-0-7459-4770-9(0)*, Lion Books) Lion Hudson PLC GBR. Dist: Trafalgar Square Publishing.

Breckon, Brett. Dark Tales from the Woods. Morden, Daniel. 2007. (ENG.). 102p. (J). (gr. 4-6). 19.99 ***(978-1-84323-583-5(8))*** Gomer Pr. GBR. Dist: Independent Pubs. Group.

Breckon, Brett. Dragon Days. 2004. (ENG.). 82p. 17.95 *(978-1-84323-301-5(0))* Beekman Bks., Inc.

Brecon, Connah. There's This Thing. Brecon, Connah. 2014. (ENG.). 32p. (J). (gr. k-3). 16.99 *(978-0-399-16185-8(6)*, Philomel) Penguin Publishing Group.

Bredius, Rein. Little Stories. Franco, Eloise. 2003. 66p. (gr. k-5). 5.95 *(978-0-87516-384-0(X)*, Devorss Pubns.) DeVorss & Co.

Bree, Marlin. Kids' Magic Secrets: Simple Magic Tricks & Why They Work. Bree, Loris. 2003. (ENG.). 112p. (J). (gr. 2-6). pap. 10.99 *(978-1-892147-08-0(4))* Marlor Pr., Inc.

Breeden, Don. A Mako Meets a Puffer: A Reef Fish Story. Swift, Austin Christopher. 2004. (J). per. 10.95 *(978-0-9764208-0-4(5))* Austin Christopher Swift.

Breems, Beau. The Promise. Breems, Beau. 2006. (YA). 10.00 *(978-0-9768680-9-5(1))*; 20.00 *(978-0-9768680-8-8(3))* Burning Bush Creation.

Breems, Beau A. La Gran Historia: The Illustrated Gospel from Creation to Resurrection. Breems, Beau A. 2005.Tr. of His Story. (SPA.). (J). 10.99 *(978-0-9768680-5-7(9))*; 50p. 19.95 *(978-0-9768680-1-9(6)*, 1000); 50p. pre. 14.95 *(978-0-9768680-3-3(2)*, 3000) Burning Bush Creation.

—His Story: The Illustrated Gospel from Creation to Resurrection. Breems, Beau A. l.t. ed. 2005.Tr. of Gran Historia. 50p. (J). 19.95 *(978-0-9768680-0-2(8)*, 0-9768680-0-8) Burning Bush Creation.

Breems, Beau Alan. His Story: The Illustrated Gospel from Creation to Resurrection. Breems, Beau Alan. 2005. (J). per. 14.95 *(978-0-9768680-2-6(4))* Burning Bush Creation.

Breen, Steve. Big Bad Baby. Hale, Bruce. 2014. (ENG.). 32p. (J). (gr. -1-k). 16.99 *(978-0-8037-3585-9(5)*, Dial) Penguin Publishing Group.

Breen, Steve. Woodpecker Wants Waffles. 2016. 40p. (J). ***(978-0-06-234257-7(6))*** Harper & Row Ltd.

Bregoli, Jane. The Goat Lady. Bregoli, Jane. 2010. 32p. (J). (gr. 1-7). pap. 7.95 *(978-0-88448-309-0(6))* Tilbury Hse. Pubs.

Breidenthal, Kathryn. Gordon Parks: No Excuses, 1 vol. Parks, Gordon, Jr., photos by. Parr, Ann. 2006. (ENG.). 32p. (J). (gr. k-3). 16.99 *(978-1-58980-411-1(2))* Pelican Publishing Co., Inc.

Breiehagen, Per. The Tiny Wish. Evert, Lori. 2015. (ENG.). 48p. (J). (gr. -1-2). lib. bdg. 20.99 *(978-0-375-97336-9(2)*, Random Hse. Bks. for Young Readers) Random Hse. Children's Bks.

Breiehagen, Per. The Christmas Wish. Breiehagen, Per, photos by. Evert, Lori. 2013. (J). *(978-0-449-81942-5(6))*; (ENG.). 48p. (gr. -1-2). 17.99 *(978-0-449-81681-3(8))* Random Hse., Inc.

Breiehagen, Per, photos by. The Christmas Wish. Evert, Lori. 2013. (ENG.). 48p. (J). (gr. -1-2). lib. bdg. 20.99 *(978-0-375-97173-0(4))* Random Hse., Inc.

Breithaupt, Andrew. Igluvigaliurniq Qamusiurnirlu: How to Build an Iglu & a Qamutiik. Awa, Solomon. 2013. (ENG.). 40p. (J). (gr. 3-6). 9.95 *(978-1-927095-31-7(X))* Inhabit Media Inc. CAN. Dist: Independent Pubs. Group.

Brenier, Claire, jt. illus. see Fortier, Natali.

Brenn, Lisa. The Trilogy: Three Adventures of the Müsh-Mice. Grandpa Casey. 2012. 46p. 24.95 *(978-1-4626-9378-8(4))* America Star Bks.

Brennan, Anthony. Miracle Men. Downey, Glen. 2007. (Timeline Ser.). 48p. pap. 8.99 *(978-1-4190-4410-6(9))* Steck-Vaughn.

Brennan, Cait. The Virginia Giant: The True Story of Peter Francisco. Norfolk, Sherry & Norfolk, Bobby. 2014. (ENG.). 160p. (gr. 4-7). 16.99 *(978-1-62619-117-4(4)*, History Pr., The) Arcadia Publishing.

Brennan, Carla. El asma en un Minuto: Lo que usted necesita Saber. Plaut, Thomas F. Velez, Stacey, ed. Biaggi, Maria Elena, tr. 8th ed. 2008.Tr. of One Minute Asthma: What You Need to Know. (SPA & ENG.). 80p. (YA). pap. 6.00 *(978-0-914625-31-5(4))* Pedipress, Inc.

—One Minute Asthma: What You Need to Know. Plaut, Thomas F. Velez, Stacey, ed. 8th ed. 2008.Tr. of asma en un minuto: lo que usted necesita Saber. (ENG & SPA.). 80p. (YA). pap. 6.00 *(978-0-914625-30-8(6))* Pedipress, Inc.

Brennan, Craig. Mommy, Where Does Everything Come From? Samuels, Gregory Robert. 2008. 11p. pap. 24.95 *(978-1-60610-437-8(3))* America Star Bks.

Brennan, Lisa. Another Müsh-Mice Adventure. Grandpa Casey. 2012. 48p. 24.95 *(978-1-4626-9379-5(2))* America Star Bks.

—Another Müsh-Mice Adventure: Florida Vacation, 1 vol. Grandpa Casey. 2009. 45p. pap. 24.95 *(978-1-60813-329-1(X))* America Star Bks.

—Going Green: Another Mush-Mice Adventure, 1 vol. Grandpa Casey. 2010. 34p. pap. 24.95 *(978-1-4489-7375-0(9))* America Star Bks.

—I Didn't Do Nuthin' McGlotham, L. R. E. Bailin, Jill, ed. 2013. 42p. 18.99 *(978-0-9892711-5-8(3))* Mindstir Media.

—Meet the Müsh-Mice. Grandpa Casey. 2012. 28p. 24.95 *(978-1-4626-9380-1(6))* America Star Bks.

—The Trilogy: Three adventures of the Müsh-Mice. Casey, Grandpa. 2011. 48p. pap. 24.95 *(978-1-4626-2095-1(7))* America Star Bks.

Brennan, Neil. River Friendly, River Wild. Kurtz, Jane. 2007. (ENG.). 40p. (J). (gr. -1-3). 7.99 *(978-1-4169-3487-5(1)*, Simon & Schuster/Paula Wiseman Bks.) Simon & Schuster/Paula Wiseman Bks.

Brennan, Tim, jt. illus. see Turner, Dona.

Bresnahan, Patrick. The Puddinhead Story. DiBattista, Mary Ann & Finn, Sandra J. 2010. 34p. (J). 19.95 *(978-0-615-24552-2(8))* Puddinhead LLC.

Breton, Katia. The Mysterious Case of the Iws: A Story to Help Children Cope with Death. Danesh, H. B. 2012. 48p. pap. *(978-0-9782845-9-6(3))* International Education for Peace Institute (Canada).

Brett, Cathy. Boys! Orme, Helen. 2007. (Siti's Sisters Ser.). 36p. (J). per. *(978-1-84167-600-5(4))* Ransom Publishing Ltd.

—Lost! Orme, Helen. 2007. (Siti's Sisters Ser.). 36p. (J). per. *(978-1-84167-598-5(9))* Ransom Publishing Ltd.

—Mirror, Mirror, 1 vol. Wallace, Karen. 2013. (Start Reading Ser.). (ENG.). 24p. (gr. k-1). pap. 6.99 *(978-1-4765-4117-4(5))* Capstone Pr., Inc.

—Odd One Out. Orme, Helen. 2007. (Siti's Sisters Ser.). 36p. (J). per. *(978-1-84167-597-8(0))* Ransom Publishing Ltd.

—Stalker. Orme, Helen. 2007. (Siti's Sisters Ser.). 36p. (J). per. *(978-1-84167-595-4(4))* Ransom Publishing Ltd.

—Stinky Giant. Wallace, Karen. 2013. (Start Reading Ser.). (ENG.). 24p. (gr. k-1). pap. 6.99 *(978-1-4765-4139-6(6))* Capstone Pr., Inc.

—Taken for a Ride. Orme, Helen. 2007. (Siti's Sisters Ser.). 36p. (J). per. *(978-1-84167-596-1(2))* Ransom Publishing Ltd.

—Trouble with Teachers. Orme, Helen. 2007. (Siti's Sisters Ser.). 36p. (J). per. *(978-1-84167-599-2(7))* Ransom Publishing Ltd.

Brett, Harold M. The Peterkin Papers. Hale, Lucretia. 2005. reprint ed. pap. 24.95 *(978-1-4179-3265-8(1))* Kessinger Publishing, LLC.

Brett, Jan. Noelle of the Nutcracker. Jane, Pamela. 2003. (ENG.). 64p. (J). (gr. 5-7). pap. 8.95 *(978-0-618-36922-5(8))* Houghton Mifflin Harcourt Publishing Co.

—Scary, Scary Halloween, 1 vol. Bunting, Eve. 2013. (ENG.). 40p. (J). (gr. -1-3). 10.99 *(978-0-544-11114-1(1))* Houghton Mifflin Harcourt Publishing Co.

—The Secret Clocks: Time Senses of Living Things. Simon, Seymour. 2012. (Dover Children's Science Bks.). (ENG.). 80p. (J). (gr. 3-5). pap. 5.99 *(978-0-486-48866-0(7))* Dover Pubns., Inc.

Brett, Jan. The Animals' Santa. Brett, Jan. 2014. (ENG.). 32p. (J). (gr. -1-k). 17.99 *(978-0-399-25784-1(5)*, Razorbill) Penguin Publishing Group.

—Annie & the Wild Animals. Brett, Jan. 2012. (ENG.). 32p. (J). (gr. -1-k). 17.99 *(978-0-399-16104-9(X)*, Putnam Juvenile) Penguin Publishing Group.

—Armadillo Rodeo. Brett, Jan. 2004. (ENG.). 32p. (J). (gr. -1-3). pap. 6.99 *(978-0-14-240125-5(0)*, Puffin) Penguin Publishing Group.

—Beauty & the Beast. Brett, Jan. 2011. (ENG.). 32p. (J). (gr. k-3). 17.99 *(978-0-399-25731-5(4)*, Putnam Juvenile) Penguin Publishing Group.

—Cinders: A Chicken Cinderella. Brett, Jan. 2013. (ENG.). 32p. (J). (gr. k). 17.99 *(978-0-399-25783-4(7)*, Putnam Juvenile) Penguin Publishing Group.

—Daisy Comes Home. Brett, Jan. 2005. (ENG.). 32p. (J). (gr. k-3). reprint ed. pap. 6.99 *(978-0-14-240270-2(2)*, Puffin) Penguin Publishing Group.

—The Easter Egg. Brett, Jan. 2010. (ENG.). 32p. (J). (gr. -1-k). 17.99 *(978-0-399-25238-9(X)*, Putnam Juvenile) Penguin Publishing Group.

—The First Dog. Brett, Jan. 2015. (ENG.). 32p. (J). (gr. -1-k). 17.99 *(978-0-399-17270-0(X)*, Putnam Juvenile) Penguin Publishing Group.

—Gingerbread Baby. Brett, Jan. 2003. (ENG.). 32p. (J). (gr. -1 — 1). bds. 7.99 *(978-0-399-24166-6(3)*, Putnam Juvenile) Penguin Publishing Group.

—Gingerbread Friends. Brett, Jan. 2008. (ENG.). 32p. (J). (gr. -1-k). 17.99 *(978-0-399-25161-0(8)*, Putnam Juvenile) Penguin Publishing Group.

—Hedgie Blasts Off! Brett, Jan. 2006. (ENG.). 32p. (J). (gr. -1-3). 17.99 *(978-0-399-24621-0(5)*, Putnam Juvenile) Penguin Publishing Group.

—Home for Christmas. Brett, Jan. 2011. (ENG.). 32p. (J). (gr. -1-k). 17.99 *(978-0-399-25653-0(9)*, Putnam Juvenile) Penguin Publishing Group.

—Honey... Honey... Lion! Brett, Jan. 2005. (ENG.). 36p. (J). (gr. -1-3). 17.99 *(978-0-399-24463-6(8)*, Putnam Juvenile) Penguin Publishing Group.

—Honey... Honey... Lion! A Story from Africa. Brett, Jan. 2014. (ENG.). 32p. (J). (gr. -1-3). 7.99 *(978-0-14-751352-6(9)*, Puffin) Penguin Publishing Group.

—The Mitten. Brett, Jan. 20th anniv. ed. 2009. (ENG.). 32p. (J). (gr. -1-k). 17.99 *(978-0-399-25296-9(7)*, Putnam Juvenile) Penguin Publishing Group.

—The Mitten: Oversized Board Book. Brett, Jan. 2014. (ENG.). 32p. (J). (gr. -1 — 1). bds. 14.99 *(978-0-399-16981-6(4)*, Putnam Juvenile) Penguin Publishing Group.

—Mossy. Brett, Jan. 2012. (ENG.). 32p. (J). (gr. -1-k). 17.99 *(978-0-399-25782-7(9)*, Putnam Juvenile) Penguin Publishing Group.

—The Night Before Christmas. Brett, Jan. 2011. (ENG.). 32p. (J). (gr. -1-k). 20.00 *(978-0-399-25670-7(9)*, Putnam Juvenile) Penguin Publishing Group.

—On Noah's Ark. Brett, Jan. (ENG.). 32p. (J). (gr. -1 — 1). 2009. bds. 7.99 *(978-0-399-25220-4(7))*; 2003. 17.99 *(978-0-399-24028-7(4))* Penguin Publishing Group. (Putnam Juvenile).

—The Three Snow Bears. Brett, Jan. (ENG.). (J). (gr. -1-k). 2013. 32p. bds. 14.99 *(978-0-399-16326-5(3))*; 2012. 34p. bds. 7.99 *(978-0-399-26009-4(9))*; 2007. 32p. 17.99 *(978-0-399-24792-7(0))* Penguin Publishing Group. (Putnam Juvenile).

—Town Mouse Country Mouse. Brett, Jan. 2003. (ENG.). 32p. (J). (gr. -1-3). pap. 6.99 *(978-0-698-11986-4(X)*, Puffin) Penguin Publishing Group.

—The Twelve Days of Christmas. Brett, Jan. 2004. (ENG.). 32p. (J). (gr. -1 — 1). bds. 6.99 *(978-0-399-24329-5(1)*, Putnam Juvenile) Penguin Publishing Group.

—The Umbrella. Brett, Jan. (ENG.). (J). (gr. -1 — 1). 2011. 34p. bds. 7.99 *(978-0-399-25540-3(0))*; 2004. 32p. 17.99 *(978-0-399-24215-1(5))* Penguin Publishing Group. (Putnam Juvenile).

—The 3 Little Dassies. Brett, Jan. 2010. (ENG.). 32p. (J). (gr. -1-k). 17.99 *(978-0-399-25499-4(4)*, Putnam Juvenile) Penguin Publishing Group.

Brett, Jeannie. Decorated Horses. Patent, Dorothy Hinshaw. 2015. (ENG.). 48p. (J). (gr. 3-7). 17.95 *(978-1-58089-362-6(7))* Charlesbridge Publishing, Inc.

—Fishing for Numbers: A Maine Number Book. Reynolds, Cynthia Furlong. 2005. (Count Your Way Across the USA Ser.). (ENG.). 40p. (J). (gr. k-5). 16.95 *(978-1-58536-035-2(X))* Sleeping Bear Pr.

—Little New Jersey. Noble, Trinka Hakes. 2012. (My Little State Ser.). (ENG.). 20p. (J). bds. 9.95 *(978-1-58536-786-3(9))* Sleeping Bear Pr.

—Little New York. Wilbur, Helen. 2010. (My Little State Ser.). (ENG.). 22p. (J). 9.95 *(978-1-58536-491-6(6))* Sleeping Bear Pr.

—Little North Carolina. Crane, Carol. 2011. (My Little State Ser.). (ENG.). 20p. 9.95 *(978-1-58536-545-6(9))* Sleeping Bear Pr.

—Little Pennsylvania Board Book. Noble, Trinka Hakes. 2010. (My Little State Ser.). (ENG.). 22p. (J). 9.95 *(978-1-58536-506-7(8))* Sleeping Bear Pr.

—My Cat, Coon Cat, 1 vol. Fuller, Sandy Ferguson. ed. 2011. (ENG.). 36p. (J). 17.95 *(978-1-934031-32-2(1)*, 2a637e6d-ff9a-4024-93b8-7de3c891e7a9) Islandport Pr., Inc.

—One If by Land: A Massachusetts Number Book. Stemple, Heidi E. Y. 2006. (Count Your Way Across the U. S. A. Ser.). (ENG.). 40p. (J). 17.95 *(978-1-58536-186-1(0))* Sleeping Bear Pr.

Brett, Jeannie. Little Maine. Brett, Jeannie. 2010. (My Little State Ser.). (ENG.). 22p. (J). 9.95 *(978-1-58536-497-8(5))* Sleeping Bear Pr.

—Wild about Bears. Brett, Jeannie. 2014. (ENG.). 32p. (J). (gr. 1-4). pap. 7.95 *(978-1-58089-419-7(4))* Charlesbridge Publishing, Inc.

Breuer, Paul. The Coaster Cats Go to the Amusement Park. Jack Stanley. 2006. 19p. (J). pap. 5.99 *(978-0-9776284-0-7(X))* Forbes Literary Ltd. Inc.

Brevannes, Maurice. Lafayette: French-American Hero. Bishop, Claire Huchet. 2011. 82p. 37.95 *(978-1-258-03539-6(1))* Literary Licensing, LLC.

—Red Falcons of Tremoine. Peart, Hendry. 2007. (Living History Library (Bethlehem Books) Ser.). 239p. (YA). (gr. 8-12). pap. 12.95 *(978-1-932350-15-9(2))* Bethlehem Bks.

Brever, Amy. I'm So Angry. Mosby, Pamela. 2013. 28p. pap. 7.99 *(978-0-9886272-4-6(8))* Brothers N Publishing Corp.

Brewer, Dean, jt. illus. see Brewer, Sarah.

Brewer, Kathaleen. The Wonder in the Woods. Cruzan, Patricia. 2013. 250p. pap. 15.00 *(978-0-9653543-7-0(7))* Clear Creek Pubs.

Brewer, Paul. How to Trick or Treat in Outer Space. Krull, Kathleen. 2004. (ENG.). 32p. (J). (gr. k-3). tchr. ed. 16.95 *(978-0-8234-1844-2(8))* Holiday Hse., Inc.

—Robert & the Attack of the Giant Tarantula. Seuling, Barbara. 2003. (Oh No, It's Robert Ser.). (ENG.). 64p. (J). pap. 3.99 *(978-0-439-23545-7(6)*, Scholastic Paperbacks) Scholastic, Inc.

—Robert & the Great Escape. Seuling, Barbara. 2003. (Robert Bks.). (ENG.). 120p. (J). 15.95 *(978-0-8126-2700-8(8))* Cricket Bks.

—Robert & the Happy Endings. Seuling, Barbara. 2007. (Robert Bks.). (ENG.). 160p. (J). (gr. 1-4). 16.95 *(978-0-8126-2748-0(2))* Cricket Bks.

—Robert & the Lemming Problem. Seuling, Barbara. 2003. (Robert Bks.). (ENG.). 120p. (J). 15.95 *(978-0-8126-2686-5(9))* Cricket Bks.

—Robert & the Practical Jokes. Seuling, Barbara. 2006. (Robert Bks.). (ENG.). 150p. (J). (gr. k-4). 16.95 *(978-0-8126-2741-1(5))* Cricket Bks.

—Robert Finds a Way. Seuling, Barbara. 2005. (Robert Bks.). (ENG.). 150p. (J). 15.95 *(978-0-8126-2734-3(2))* Cricket Bks.

—Robert Goes to Camp. Seuling, Barbara. 2007. (Robert Bks.). (ENG.). 160p. (J). (gr. k-4). 16.95 *(978-0-8126-2753-4(9))* Cricket Bks.

—Robert Takes a Stand. Seuling, Barbara. 2004. (Robert Bks.). (ENG.). 120p. (J). 15.95 *(978-0-8126-2712-1(1))* Cricket Bks.

Brewer, Paul. You Must Be Joking, Two! Even Cooler Jokes, Plus 11 1/2 Tips for Laughing Yourself into Your Own Stand-Up Comedy Routine. Brewer, Paul. 2007. (ENG.). 128p. (J). (gr. k-5). 17.95 *(978-0-8126-2752-7(0))* Cricket Bks.

Brewer, Sarah & Brewer, Dean. Our New Garden. Brewer, Sarah. 2013. 20p. pap. 24.95 *(978-1-63004-768-9(6))* America Star Bks.

Brewer, Terry. The Monster Stick & Other Appalachian Tall Tales. Lepp, Paul & Lepp, Bil. 2006. (ENG.). 159p. (gr. 10-18). pap. 9.95 *(978-0-87483-577-9(1))* August Hse. Pubs., Inc.

Brewer, Trish, jt. illus. see Milner, Fran.

Brewster, Jane. Sarah Boone: A Lowcountry Girl, 1 vol. Adams, Michelle. 2009. (ENG.). 152p. (J). (gr. 3-6). 15.95 *(978-1-58980-657-3(0))* Pelican Publishing Co., Inc.

Brewster, Patience, jt. illus. see Murphy, Kelly.

Breyfogle, Norm. Goodbye Forever. Morgan, Melanie J. 2011. (Archie New Look Ser.). (ENG.). 112p. (J). (gr. 5). pap. 10.95 *(978-1-879794-63-4(2)*, Archie Comics) Archie Comic Pubns., Inc.

Brian, Harrold. Ingrown Tyrone. Thompson, Tolya L. 2004. (Smarties Ser.: 4). 33p. (J). 16.00 *(978-0-9708296-2-7(0))* Savor Publishing Hse., Inc.

Briant, Ed. Petal & Poppy. Clough, Lisa. 2014. (Green Light Readers Level 2 Ser.). (ENG.). 32p. (J). (gr. -1-3). pap. 3.99 *(978-0-544-11380-0(2)*, HMH Books For Young Readers) Houghton Mifflin Harcourt Publishing Co.

—Petal & Poppy & the Penguin. Clough, Lisa. 2014. (Green Light Readers Level 2 Ser.). (ENG.). 32p. (J). (gr. -1-3). 12.99 *(978-0-544-13770-7(1))*; pap. 3.99 *(978-0-544-13330-3(7))* Houghton Mifflin Harcourt Publishing Co. (HMH Books For Young Readers).

—Petal & Poppy & the Spooky Halloween! Clough, Lisa. 2014. (Green Light Readers Level 2 Ser.). (ENG.). 32p. (J). (gr. -1-3). 12.99 *(978-0-544-33602-5(X)*, HMH Books For Young Readers) Houghton Mifflin Harcourt Publishing Co.

Briant, Ed. A Day at the Beach, No. 1. Briant, Ed. 2006. 32p. (J). (gr. -1). 17.89 *(978-0-06-079982-3(X))* HarperCollins Pubs.

Bricking, Jennifer. The True Blue Scouts of Sugar Man Swamp. Appelt, Kathi. 2013. (ENG.). 336p. (J). (gr. 3-7). 16.99 *(978-1-4424-2105-9(3))* Simon & Schuster Children's Publishing.

Brickman, Robin. Leaflets Three, Let It Be! The Story of Poison Ivy. Sanchez, Anita. 2015. (ENG.). 32p. (J). (gr. -1-3). 16.95 *(978-1-62091-445-8(X))* Boyds Mills Pr.

—A Log's Life. Pfeffer, Wendy. 2007. (ENG.). 32p. (J). (gr. -1-3). 6.99 *(978-1-4169-3483-7(9)*, Simon & Schuster/Paula Wiseman Bks.) Simon & Schuster/Paula Wiseman Bks.

—One Night in the Coral Sea. Collard, Sneed B., III. 2006. (ENG.). 32p. (J). (gr. 1-4). pap. 7.95 *(978-1-57091-390-7(0))* Charlesbridge Publishing, Inc.

—One Night in the Coral Sea. Collard, Sneed B., III. 2006. 32p. (gr. 3-7). 17.95 *(978-0-7569-6969-1(7))* Perfection Learning Corp.

Brickner, Marian. I'm Lucy: A Day in the Life of a Young Bonobo. Levine, Mathea. 2008. 32p. (gr. -1-3). 19.95 *(978-0-615-18110-3(4))* Blue Bark Pr.

Bridgeman, Kristi. The Knot Fairy. Hinman, Bobbie. 2007. (ENG.). 32p. (J). (gr. -1-2). 15.95 *(978-0-9786791-0-1(5))* Best Fairy Bks.

—The Sky Tree. Page, P. K. 2009. (ENG.). 112p. (J). 19.95 *(978-0-88982-258-0(1))* Oolichan Bks. CAN. Dist: Univ. of Toronto Pr.

—The Sock Fairy. Hinman, Bobbie. 2008. (ENG.). 32p. (J). (gr. -1-2). 15.95 *(978-0-9786791-1-8(3))* Best Fairy Bks.

—Uirapurú: Based on a Brazilian Legend. Page, P. K. 2010. (ENG.). 32p. (J). 19.95 *(978-0-88982-264-1(6))* Oolichan Bks. CAN. Dist: Univ. of Toronto Pr.

Bridgen, Rachel Annie. Serious Sas & Messy Magda. Pierres, Marianne De. 2013. 32p. pap. *(978-1-909423-04-6(1))* Bks. to Treasure.

Bridges, Jeanne Rorex. Crossing Bok Chitto: A Choctaw Tale of Friendship & Freedom. Tingle, Tim. (ENG.). 40p. (J). 2008. (gr. 2-7). pap. 8.95 *(978-1-933693-20-0(7))*; 2006. (gr. 1-8). 17.95 *(978-0-938317-77-7(6))* Cinco Puntos Pr.

Bridges, John, et al. D6 Adventure. Vrtis, Nikola, ed. 2004. (ENG.). 144p. 19.99 *(978-1-932867-00-8(7)*, weg 51011, West End Games) Purgatory Publishing, Inc.

Bridges, Moire. Hermanita y el Rey: Una Parabola. Bridges, Moire. 2007. 28p. (J). (gr. -1-3). 13.99 *(978-1-59879-427-4(2))* Lifevest Publishing, Inc.

—Sissy & the King: A Parable. Bridges, Moire. 2007. (J). (gr. -1-3). 26p. 13.99 *(978-1-59879-425-0(6))*; 32p. 19.99 *(978-1-59879-403-8(5))* Lifevest Publishing, Inc.

Bridgman, L. J. The Young Puritans in King Philip's War. Smith, Mary P. Wells. 2011. 396p. 54.95 *(978-1-258-05550-9(3))* Literary Licensing, LLC.

Bridgman, L. T. Finger Plays for Nursery & Kindergarten. Poulsson, Emilie. 70th ed. 2011. (Dover Children's Activity Bks.). (ENG.). 80p. (J). (gr. 4-7). reprint ed. pap. 8.95 *(978-0-486-22588-3(7))* Dover Pubns., Inc.

Bridwell, Norman. Clifford & the Halloween Parade. Bridwell, Norman. 2004. (Scholastic Reader Level 1 Ser.). (ENG.). 32p. (J). (gr. k — 1). 3.99 *(978-0-439-09834-2(3))* Scholastic, Inc.

—Clifford at the Circus. Bridwell, Norman. 2010. (Clifford 8x8 Ser.). (ENG.). 32p. (J). (gr. -1-3). pap. 3.99 *(978-0-545-21584-8(6)*, Cartwheel Bks.) Scholastic, Inc.

—Clifford Collection. Bridwell, Norman. 2012. (ENG.). 192p. (J). (gr. -1-k). 12.99 *(978-0-545-45013-3(6))* Scholastic, Inc.

—Clifford Goes to Dog School. Bridwell, Norman. 2010. (Clifford 8x8 Ser.). (ENG.). 32p. (J). (gr. -1-3). pap. 3.99 *(978-0-545-21577-0(3)*, Cartwheel Bks.) Scholastic, Inc.

—Clifford Goes to Washington. Bridwell, Norman. 2005. (Clifford 8x8 Ser.). (ENG.). 32p. (J). (gr. -1-k). pap. 3.99 *(978-0-439-69656-2(9)*, Cartwheel Bks.) Scholastic, Inc.

—Clifford Loves His Friends. Bridwell, Norman. 2011. (Clifford Ser.). (ENG.). 16p. (J). (gr. -1-k). 6.99 *(978-0-545-35474-5(9)*, Cartwheel Bks.) Scholastic, Inc.

—Clifford Makes the Team. Bridwell, Norman. 2011. (Scholastic Reader Level 1 Ser.). (ENG.). 32p. (J). (gr. -1-2). pap. 3.99 *(978-0-545-23141-1(8))* Scholastic, Inc.

—Clifford Shares. Bridwell, Norman. 2012. (ENG.). 12p. (J). (gr. k — 1). bds. 6.99 *(978-0-545-26837-0(0)*, Cartwheel Bks.) Scholastic, Inc.

—Clifford Takes a Trip. Bridwell, Norman. (Clifford 8x8 Ser.). (ENG.). (J). (gr. -1-k). 2011. 32p. pap. 3.99 *(978-0-545-21591-6(9)*, Cartwheel Bks.); 2007. 9.95 *(978-0-545-00358-2(X))* Scholastic, Inc.

—Clifford the Big Red Dog. Bridwell, Norman. 2010. (Clifford 8x8 Ser.). (ENG.). 32p. (J). (gr. -1-3). pap. 3.99 *(978-0-545-21578-7(1)*, Cartwheel Bks.) Scholastic, Inc.

—Clifford the Big Red Dog. Bridwell, Norman. Scholastic, Inc. Staff. unabr. ed. 2006. (Clifford Ser.). (ENG.). (J). (gr. -1-3). 9.99 *(978-0-439-87587-5(0))* Scholastic, Inc.

—Clifford the Firehouse Dog. Bridwell, Norman. 2010. (Clifford 8x8 Ser.).Tr. of Clifford the Firehouse Dog. (ENG.). 32p. (J). (gr. -1-3). pap. 3.99 *(978-0-545-21580-0(3)*, Cartwheel Bks.) Scholastic, Inc.

—Clifford Va al Doctor. Bridwell, Norman. 2011. (Scholastic Reader Level 1 Ser.).Tr. of Clifford Goes to the Doctor. (SPA.). 32p. (J). (gr. -1-3). pap. 3.99 *(978-0-545-34118-9(3)*, Scholastic en Espanol) Scholastic, Inc.

—Clifford Visits the Zoo. Bridwell, Norman. 2014. (ENG.). 40p. (J). (— 1). 12.99 *(978-0-545-66896-5(4))* Scholastic, Inc.

—Clifford's Bedtime Story. Bridwell, Norman. 2013. (Clifford Ser.). (ENG.). 20p. (J). (gr. -1-k). bds. 8.99 *(978-0-545-49577-6(6))* Scholastic, Inc.

—Clifford's Bedtime Story Box. Bridwell, Norman. Scholastic, Inc. Staff. 2013. (ENG.). (J). (gr. -1-k). 10.99 *(978-0-545-61521-1(6))* Scholastic, Inc.

—Clifford's Birthday Party. Bridwell, Norman. 50th anniv. ed. 2013. (Clifford Ser.). (ENG.). 32p. (J). (gr. -1-3). pap. 4.99 *(978-0-545-47956-1(8))* Scholastic, Inc.

—Clifford's Christmas. Bridwell, Norman. 2011. (Clifford 8x8 Ser.). (ENG.). 32p. (J). (gr. -1-k). pap. 3.99 *(978-0-545-21596-1(X)*, Cartwheel Bks.) Scholastic, Inc.

—Clifford's Day with Dad. Bridwell, Norman. 2011. (Clifford 8x8 Ser.). (ENG.). 32p. (J). (gr. -1-k). pap. 3.99 *(978-0-545-21593-0(5)*, Cartwheel Bks.) Scholastic, Inc.

—Clifford's Family. Bridwell, Norman. 2010. (Clifford 8x8 Ser.). (ENG.). 32p. (J). (gr. -1-3). pap. 3.99 *(978-0-545-21585-5(4)*, Cartwheel Bks.) Scholastic, Inc.

—Clifford's First Christmas. Bridwell, Norman. 2010. (Clifford Ser.). (ENG.). 20p. (J). (gr. k — 1). bds. 6.99 *(978-0-545-21773-6(3)*, Cartwheel Bks.) Scholastic, Inc.

—Clifford's First Easter. Bridwell, Norman. 2010. (Clifford Ser.). (ENG.). 14p. (J). (gr. k — 1). bds. 6.99 *(978-0-545-20010-3(5)*, Cartwheel Bks.) Scholastic, Inc.

—Clifford's First Halloween. Bridwell, Norman. 2010. (Clifford Ser.). (ENG.). 20p. (J). (gr. k — 1). bds. 6.99 *(978-0-545-21774-3(1)*, Cartwheel Bks.) Scholastic, Inc.

—Clifford's First Valentine's Day. Bridwell, Norman. 2009. (Clifford Ser.). (ENG.). 20p. (J). (gr. k — 1). bds. 6.99 *(978-0-545-20011-0(3)*, Cartwheel Bks.) Scholastic, Inc.

—Clifford's Good Deeds. Bridwell, Norman. 2010. (Clifford 8x8 Ser.). (ENG.). 32p. (J). (gr. -1-3). pap. 3.99 *(978-0-545-21579-4(X)*, Cartwheel Bks.) Scholastic, Inc.

—Clifford's Halloween. Bridwell, Norman. 2011. (Clifford 8x8 Ser.). (ENG.). 32p. (J). (gr. -1-k). pap. 3.99 *(978-0-545-21595-4(1)*, Cartwheel Bks.) Scholastic, Inc.

—Clifford's Happy Easter. Bridwell, Norman. 2011. (Clifford 8x8 Ser.). (ENG.). 32p. (J). (gr. -1-k). pap. 3.99 *(978-0-545-21587-9(0)*, Cartwheel Bks.) Scholastic, Inc.

—Clifford's Pals. Bridwell, Norman. 2008. (Clifford Ser.). (ENG.). (J). (gr. -1-3). 9.99 *(978-0-545-05247-4(5)*, Scholastic) Scholastic, Inc.

Bridwell, Norman. Clifford's School Story Box. Bridwell, Norman. 2015. (ENG.). (J). (gr. -1-k). 10.99 *(978-0-545-83737-8(5))* Scholastic, Inc.

Bridwell, Norman. La Coleccion. Bridwell, Norman. 2012. (Clifford Ser.). (SPA.). 192p. (J). (gr. -1-k). 12.99 *(978-0-545-45692-0(4)*, Scholastic en Espanol) Scholastic, Inc.

—The Witch Next Door. Bridwell, Norman. 2013. (ENG.). 32p. (J). (gr. -1-3). pap. 3.99 *(978-0-545-54763-5(6))* Scholastic, Inc.

Bridy, Dan. Christopher Newport: Jamestown Explorer, 1 vol. Solomon, Sharon K. 2013. (ENG.). 32p. (J). (gr. k-3). 16.99 *(978-1-4556-1752-4(0))* Pelican Publishing Co., Inc.

Brieger, Ms. Kirsten. Jacob's Journey, Living with Type 1 Diabetes. Kleiman, Deanna. 2012. 28p. pap. 9.95 *(978-0-615-60112-0(X))* TwinsBooks.

Briel, Elizabeth. H Is for Hong Kong: A Primer in Pictures. Morrissey, Tricia. 2009. (Alphabetical World Ser.). (CHI & ENG.). 36p. (J). (gr. k-4). 12.95 *(978-1-934159-13-2(1))* ThingsAsian Pr.

Briere, Charity. Garden Bugs of Alberta: Gardening to Attract, Repel & Control. Macaulay, Doug et al. rev. ed. 2008. (ENG.). 224p. pap. *(978-1-55105-586-2(4))* Lone Pine Publishing.

Brigg, Cathy. Cathy's Ring: If Found, Please Call 650-266-8263. Stewart, Sean & Weisman, Jordan. 2009. (ENG.). 144p. (YA). (gr. 7-18). 17.95 *(978-0-7624-3530-2(5)*, Running Pr. Kids) Running Pr. Bk. Pubs.

Briggs, Charlotte. Sarah's Happy Harvest Time, 1 vol. Bush, Leanne. 2009. 32p. pap. 24.95 *(978-1-60813-818-0(6))* America Star Bks.

Briggs, Eleanor, photos by. The Man-Eating Tigers of Sundarbans. Montgomery, Sy. 2004. (ENG., 64p. (J). (gr. 5-7). pap. 7.99 *(978-0-618-49490-3(1))* Houghton Mifflin Harcourt Publishing Co.

—The Man-Eating Tigers of Sundarbans. Montgomery, Sy. 2004. 57p. (J). 14.60 *(978-0-7569-5180-1(1))* Perfection Learning Corp.

Briggs, Harry. Come una y Cuenta Veinte. Tang, Greg & Greg, Tang. 2003.Tr. of Grapes of Math. (SPA.). 40p. (J). (gr. 3-4). 14.99 *(978-84-241-8075-1(5))* Everest Editora ESP. Dist: Lectorum Pubns., Inc.

—The Grapes of Math. Tang, Greg. 2004. (Scholastic Bookshelf Ser.). (ENG.). 40p. (J). (gr. 2-5). pap. 6.99 *(978-0-439-59840-8(0)*, Scholastic Paperbacks) Scholastic, Inc.

—The Grapes of Math: Mind-Stretching Math Riddles. Tang, Greg. 2004. (Scholastic Bookshelf Ser.). (gr. 2-5). 17.00 *(978-0-7569-3195-7(9))* Perfection Learning Corp.

—Math Appeal. Tang, Greg. 2003. (Mind-Stretching Math Riddles Ser.). (ENG.). 40p. (J). (gr. -1-3). 18.99 *(978-0-439-21046-1(1)*, Scholastic Pr.) Scholastic, Inc.

—Math for All Seasons. Tang, Greg. 2005. (Scholastic Bookshelf Ser.). (ENG.). 40p. (J). (gr. -1-3). pap. 6.99 *(978-0-439-75537-5(9)*, Scholastic Paperbacks) Scholastic, Inc.

—Math Potatoes: Mind-Stretching Brain Food. Tang, Greg. 2005. (Math Potatoes Ser.). (ENG.). 40p. (J). (gr. 2-5). 18.99 *(978-0-439-44390-6(3)*, Scholastic Pr.) Scholastic, Inc.

—Un, Dos, Tres, el Ano Se Fue. Tang, Greg & Greg, Tang. 2003.Tr. of Math for All Seasons. (SPA.). 40p. (J). (gr. 2-3). 14.99 *(978-84-241-8074-4(7))* Everest Editora ESP. Dist: Lectorum Pubns., Inc.

Briggs, Karen. The Rain Flower. Duroux, Mary. 2005. (ENG.). 48p. pap. 13.45 *(978-0-85575-467-9(2))* Aboriginal Studies Pr. AUS. Dist: Independent Pubs. Group.

Briggs, Mayke Beckmann. Here You Are. Briggs, Mayke Beckmann. 2007. 44p. (J). 16.95 *(978-0-9776469-1-3(2))* BoathouseBooks.

Briggs, Raymond. The Puddleman. Briggs, Raymond. 2006. (ENG.). 32p. (J). (gr. k-2). pap. 16.95 *(978-0-09-945642-1(7)*, Red Fox) Random House Children's Books GBR. Dist: Independent Pubs. Group.

Briggs, Scott, photos by. Mighty Stallion 5 A Stallion's Heart. Kasten, Victoria. 2007. (J). per. 8.95 *(978-0-9788850-5-2(8))* Kasten, Victoria.

Brigham, Anthea. Henrietta, World War II Hen. Brigham, Anthea. 2008. 28p. (J). 7.00 *(978-0-9740778-2-6(8))* Whale's Jaw Publishing.

Bright, Alasdair. Bears Beware. Giff, Patricia Reilly. 2012. (Zigzag Kids Ser.). (ENG.). 80p. (J). (gr. 1-4). 12.99 *(978-0-385-73889-7(7))*; pap. 4.99 *(978-0-375-85913-7(6))* Random House Publishing Group. (Delacorte Pr).

—The Big Whopper. Giff, Patricia Reilly. 2010. (Zigzag Kids Ser.). (ENG.). 80p. (J). (gr. 3-7). pap. 4.99 *(978-0-553-49469-3(4)*, Delacorte Pr) Random House Publishing Group.

—Flying Feet. Giff, Patricia Reilly. 2011. (Zigzag Kids Ser.). (ENG.). 80p. (J). (gr. 3-7). 4.99 *(978-0-375-85911-3(X)*, Yearling) Random Hse. Children's Bks.

—The Number One Kid. Giff, Patricia Reilly. 2010. (Zigzag Kids Ser.). (ENG.). 80p. (J). (gr. 3-7). 12.99 *(978-0-385-74687-8(3))*; pap. 4.99 *(978-0-553-49468-6(6))* Random House Publishing Group. (Delacorte Pr).

—Star Time. Giff, Patricia Reilly. 2011. (Zigzag Kids Ser.). (ENG.). 80p. (J). (gr. 3-7). 4.99 *(978-0-375-85912-0(8)*, Yearling); 12.99 *(978-0-385-73888-0(9)*, Lamb, Wendy) Random Hse. Children's Bks.

—Super Surprise. Giff, Patricia Reilly. 2012. (Zigzag Kids Ser.). (ENG.). 80p. (J). (gr. 1-4). 12.99 *(978-0-385-73890-3(0))*; pap. 4.99 *(978-0-375-85914-4(4))* Random House Publishing Group. (Delacorte Pr).

—Zigzag Zoom. Giff, Patricia Reilly. 2013. (Zigzag Kids Ser.). (ENG.). 80p. (J). (gr. 1-4). 12.99 *(978-0-385-74275-7(4))*; pap. 4.99 *(978-0-307-97703-8(X))* Random House Publishing Group. (Delacorte Pr).

Bright, Bonnie. I Want to Make Friends: A Story for Kids in Preschool & Kindergarten & a Guidance Section for Parents. Rothenberg, B. Annye. 2012. 48p. (J). pap. 9.95 *(978-0-9790420-4-1(6))* Perfecting Parenting Pr.

Bright, Bonnie. The Tangle Tower. Bright, Bonnie. Elin Hirschman, Jessica. 2006. 32p. (J). (gr. k-2). 14.95 *(978-0-9701155-6-0(3))* Cookie Bear Pr., Inc.

Bright, Bonnie04. I'm Getting Ready for Kindergarten. Rothenberg, B. Annye. 2012. 48p. (J). pap. 9.95 *(978-0-9790420-5-8(4))* Perfecting Parenting Pr.

Bright, Joe. Color Yourself Smart: Masterpieces of Art. Nichols, Catherine. 2013. (Color Yourself Smart Ser.). (ENG.). 128p. 19.95 *(978-1-60710-572-5(1)*, Thunder Bay Pr.) Baker & Taylor Publishing Group.

Bright, Michael. Crash, Bang, Boom, Zing. Bright, Belle. 2009. 12p. pap. 24.95 *(978-1-60749-383-9(1))* America Star Bks.

Bright, Phyllis. Tayance, a Young Sioux Indian. Nichele, Neika. 2008. 47p. pap. 24.95 *(978-1-60703-606-7(1))* America Star Bks.

Bright, Todd, et al. Ka-Choww!/Blue Ramone. Robinson, Ty et al. 2008. (Pictureback Ser.). (ENG.). 32p. (J). (gr. -1-2). pap. 4.99 *(978-0-7364-2404-2(0)*, RH/Disney) Random Hse. Children's Bks.

Brightling, Geoff & Greenaway, Frank, photos by. Amphibian. Clarke, Barry & Dorling Kindersley Publishing Staff. 2005. (DK Eyewitness Bks.). (ENG., 72p. (J). (gr. 3-7). 16.99 *(978-0-7566-1380-8(9))* Dorling Kindersley Publishing, Inc.

Brightling, Geoff, jt. illus. see Anderson, Peter.

Brightling, Geoff, jt. photos by see Hills, Alan.

Brighton, Catherine. My Napoleon. Brighton, Catherine. 2005. 26p. (J). (gr. k-4). reprint ed. 17.00 *(978-0-7567-8931-2(1))* DIANE Publishing Co.

Brightwood, Laura. The House That Talked to Itself. 2006. (J). *(978-0-9779290-3-0(5))* 3-C Institute for Social Development.

Brightwood, Laura. Anansi & the Turtle. Brightwood, Laura, . 2006. (J). *(978-0-9779290-0-9(0))* 3-C Institute for Social Development.

—Bully Goat Grim. Brightwood, Laura, . 2006. (J). *(978-0-9779290-2-3(7))* 3-C Institute for Social Development.

—Debate in Sign Language. Brightwood, Laura, . 2006. (J). *(978-0-9779290-6-1(X))* 3-C Institute for Social Development.

—The Ghost House. Brightwood, Laura, . 2006. (J). *(978-0-9779290-1-6(9))* 3-C Institute for Social Development.

—Growing up in East L. A. Brightwood, Laura, . 2006. (J). *(978-0-9779290-8-5(6))* 3-C Institute for Social Development.

—I Am A Frog. Brightwood, Laura, . 2007. (J). DVD *(978-1-934409-02-2(2))* 3-C Institute for Social Development.

—Ka-ulu the Strong. Brightwood, Laura, . 2006. (J). *(978-0-9789871-3-8(6))* 3-C Institute for Social Development.

—King Zargon Rules. Brightwood, Laura, . 2006. (J). *(978-0-9789871-0-7(1))* 3-C Institute for Social Development.

—King's New Suit. Brightwood, Laura, . 2007. (J). DVD *(978-1-934409-05-3(7))* 3-C Institute for Social Development.

—Left Out. Brightwood, Laura, . 2006. (J). *(978-0-9779290-7-8(8))* 3-C Institute for Social Development.

—Lion & Mousie. Brightwood, Laura, . 2007. (J). DVD *(978-1-934409-00-8(6))* 3-C Institute for Social Development.

—Little Freddie & His Whistle. Brightwood, Laura, . 2007. (J). DVD *(978-1-934409-01-5(4))* 3-C Institute for Social Development.

—Look What You've Done. Brightwood, Laura, . 2007. (J). DVD *(978-1-934409-03-9(0))* 3-C Institute for Social Development.

—Mousanga Bira Mousa. Brightwood, Laura, . 2006. (J). *(978-0-9789871-1-4(X))* 3-C Institute for Social Development.

—Red Hat / Blue Hat. Brightwood, Laura, . 2006. (J). *(978-0-9779290-5-4(1))* 3-C Institute for Social Development.

—Wise People of Helm. Brightwood, Laura, . 2006. (J). *(978-0-9779290-4-7(3))* 3-C Institute for Social Development.

—Wolf under the Bed. Brightwood, Laura, . 2007. (J). DVD *(978-1-934409-04-6(9))* 3-C Institute for Social Development.

—The Woodsman & His Ax. Brightwood, Laura, . 2007. (J). DVD *(978-1-934409-07-7(3))* 3-C Institute for Social Development.

Brightwood, Laura. The Banana Fairy Fuss. Brightwood, Laura. Pifer, Kimberly, ed. 2012. (J). *(978-1-934409-34-3(0))* 3-C Institute for Social Development.

—Bee Is for Bold. Brightwood, Laura. Pifer, Kimberly, ed. 2012. (J). *(978-1-934409-40-4(5))* 3-C Institute for Social Development.

—Buzz off, Bee! Brightwood, Laura. Pifer, Kimberly, ed. 2012. (J). *(978-1-934409-45-9(6))* 3-C Institute for Social Development.

—The Cheery Garden. Brightwood, Laura. Pifer, Kimberly, ed. 2012. (J). *(978-1-934409-38-1(3))* 3-C Institute for Social Development.

—Elephant's Trunk of Confidence. Brightwood, Laura. Pifer, Kimberly, ed. 2012. (J). *(978-1-934409-33-6(2))* 3-C Institute for Social Development.

—Giraffe's Shocking Surprise. Brightwood, Laura. Pifer, Kimberly, ed. 2012. (J). *(978-1-934409-30-5(8))* 3-C Institute for Social Development.

—Knot for Singing Parrot. Brightwood, Laura. Pifer, Kimberly, ed. 2012. (J). *(978-1-934409-23-7(5))* 3-C Institute for Social Development.

—LifeStories for Kids K-2: Grades K-2. Brightwood, Laura. DeRosier, Melissa. 2007. Orig. Title: Life Skills & Character Education Through Storytelling. ring bd. incl. DVD *(978-0-9789871-8-3(7))* 3-C Institute for Social Development.

—Parrot's Winter Blues. Brightwood, Laura. Pifer, Kimberly, ed. 2012. (J). *(978-1-934409-21-3(9))* 3-C Institute for Social Development.

—Poodle's Broken E. Brightwood, Laura. Pifer, Kimberly, ed. 2012. (J). *(978-1-934409-28-2(6))* 3-C Institute for Social Development.

Briglia, Anthony. Lance Dragon Defends His Castle with Simple Machines, 1 vol. Braun, Eric. 2012. (In the Science Lab Ser.). (ENG.). 24p. (gr. 2-3). pap. 8.95 *(978-1-4048-7708-5(8))*; lib. bdg. 25.99 *(978-1-4048-7372-8(4))* Picture Window Bks.

Brigman, June. The Apprentice of Zoldex: The Imperium Saga: the Adventures of Kyria, 12 vols., Vol. 8. Bowyer, Clifford B. 2008. (Imperium Saga: 8). (ENG.). 208p. (J). 5.99 *(978-0-9787782-2-4(7)*, BK0023) Silver Leaf Bks., LLC.

—The Awakening: The Imperium Saga: the Adventures of Kyria, 12 vols., Vol. 2. Bowyer, Clifford B. 2004. (Imperium Saga: 2). (ENG.). 182p. (J). 5.99 *(978-0-9744354-1-1(4)*, BK0004) Silver Leaf Bks., LLC.

—Black Beauty. Sewell, Anna. 2005. (ENG.). 176p. (J). (gr. 3-7). 10.99 *(978-0-14-240408-9(X)*, Puffin) Penguin Publishing Group.

—The Child of Prophecy: The Imperium Saga: the Adventures of Kyria, 12 vols., Vol. 1. Bowyer, Clifford B. 2004. (Imperium Saga: 1). (ENG.). 182p. (J). 5.99 *(978-0-9744354-0-4(6)*, BK0002) Silver Leaf Bks., LLC.

—The Darkness Within: The Imperium Saga: the Adventures of Kyria, 12 vols., Vol. 9. Bowyer, Clifford B. 2009. (Imperium Saga: 9). (ENG.). (J). 5.99 *(978-0-9787782-4-8(3))* Silver Leaf Bks., LLC.

Brigman, June, et al. The Fall of the Mutants - X-Men. Simonson, Louise. ed. 2011. (ENG.). 824p. (YA). (gr. 8-17). 99.99 *(978-0-7851-5312-2(8))* Marvel Worldwide, Inc.

Brigman, June. How to Draw Cute Animals, 1 vol. Clay, Kathryn. 2009. (Drawing Fun Ser.). (ENG.). 32p. (gr. 3-4). lib. bdg. 27.32 *(978-1-4296-3405-2(7)*, Snap Bks.) Capstone Pr., Inc.

—How to Draw Flowers, 1 vol. Clay, Kathryn. 2009. (Drawing Fun Ser.). (ENG.). 32p. (gr. 3-4). lib. bdg. 27.32 *(978-1-4296-3403-8(0)*, Snap Bks.) Capstone Pr., Inc.

—How to Draw Horses, 1 vol. Clay, Kathryn. 2009. (Drawing Fun Ser.). (ENG.). 32p. (gr. 3-4). 27.32 *(978-1-4296-2306-3(3)*, Snap Bks.) Capstone Pr., Inc.

—The Mage's Council: The Imperium Saga: the Adventures of Kyria, 12 vols., Vol. 3. Bowyer, Clifford B. 2005. (Imperium Saga: 3). (ENG.). 182p. (J). 5.99 *(978-0-9744354-2-8(2)*, BK0006) Silver Leaf Bks., LLC.

—Quest for the Shard: The Imperium Saga: the Adventures of Kyria, 12 vols., Vol. 6. Bowyer, Clifford B. 2007. (Imperium Saga: 6). (ENG.). 166p. (J). 5.99 *(978-0-9744354-8-0(1)*, BK0020) Silver Leaf Bks., LLC.

—The Rescue of Nezbith: The Imperium Saga: the Adventures of Kyria, 12 vols., Vol. 10. Bowyer, Clifford B. 2009. (Imperium Saga: 10). (ENG.). 176p. (J). 7.99 *(978-0-9787782-5-5(1))* Silver Leaf Bks., LLC.

—The Shard of Time: The Imperium Saga: the Adventures of Kyria, 12 vols., Vol. 4. Bowyer, Clifford B. 2005. (Imperium Saga: 4). (ENG.). 182p. (J). 5.99 *(978-0-9744354-3-5(0)*, BK0007) Silver Leaf Bks., LLC.

B

—The Spread of Darkness: The Imperium Saga: the Adventures of Kyria, 12 vols., Vol. 7. Bowyer, Clifford B. 2007. (Imperium Saga: 7). (ENG.). 158p. (J). 5.99 (978-0-9787782-1-7(9), BK0022) Silver Leaf Bks., LLC.

—Trapped in Time: The Imperium Saga: the Adventures of Kyria, 12 vols., Vol. 5. Bowyer, Clifford B. 2006. (Imperium Saga: 5). (ENG.). 150p. (J). 5.99 (978-0-9744354-7-3(3), BK0008) Silver Leaf Bks., LLC.

Brignaud, Pierre. Baby Caillou: Good Morning! Chouette Publishing Staff. 2013. (Baby Caillou Ser.). (ENG.). 10p. (J). (gr. -1 — 1). 9.99 (978-2-89718-098-0(6)) Éditions Chouette CAN. Dist: Perseus-PGW.

—Baby Caillou: Good Night! Chouette Publishing Staff. 2013. (Baby Caillou Ser.). (ENG.). 10p. (J). (gr. -1 — 1). 9.99 (978-2-89718-099-7(4)) Éditions Chouette CAN. Dist: Perseus-PGW.

—Baby Caillou, I'm Growing! L'Heureux, Christine. 2013. (Baby Caillou Ser.). (ENG.). 10p. (J). (gr. -1 — 1). bds. 9.99 (978-2-89718-041-6(2)) Éditions Chouette CAN. Dist: Perseus-PGW.

—Baby Caillou: My Farm Friends: A Finger Fun Book. 2015. (Baby Caillou Ser.). (ENG.). 16p. (J). (— 1). bds. 6.99 (978-2-89718-177-2(X)) Éditions Chouette CAN. Dist: Perseus-PGW.

—Caillou: I Love You. L'Heureux, Christine. 2012. (Hand in Hand Ser.). (ENG.). 24p. (gr. -1-k). 5.99 (978-2-89450-860-2(3)) Éditions Chouette CAN. Dist: Perseus-PGW.

—Caillou: I'm Not Hungry! Nadeau, Nicole. 2011. (Hand in Hand Ser.). (ENG.). 24p. (J). (gr. -1-k). 5.95 (978-2-89450-829-9(8)) Éditions Chouette CAN. Dist: Perseus-PGW.

—Caillou: No More Diapers. L'Heureux, Christine. 2011. (Hand in Hand Ser.). (ENG.). 24p. (J). (gr. -1-k). 5.95 (978-2-89450-840-4(9)) Éditions Chouette CAN. Dist: Perseus-PGW.

—Caillou: Potty Time. Sanschagrin, Joceline. 4th ed. 2010. (Hand in Hand Ser.). (ENG.). 24p. (J). (gr. -1-k). 5.95 (978-2-89450-749-0(6)) Éditions Chouette CAN. Dist: Perseus-PGW.

—Caillou: Sometimes Moms Get Angry. Egar, Joann. 2014. (ENG.). 24p. (J). (gr. -1-k). 5.99 (978-2-89718-116-1(8)) Éditions Chouette CAN. Dist: Perseus-PGW.

—Caillou: The Broken Castle. Sanschagrin, Joceline. 2nd ed. 2011. (Big Dipper Ser.). (ENG.). 24p. (J). (gr. -1-k). pap. 3.99 (978-2-89450-764-3(X)) Éditions Chouette CAN. Dist: Perseus-PGW.

—Caillou - I Can Brush My Teeth. Johanson, Sarah Margaret. 2013. (Step by Step Ser.). (ENG.). 24p. (J). (gr. -1-k). bds. 5.99 (978-2-89718-032-4(3)) Éditions Chouette CAN. Dist: Perseus-PGW.

—Caillou - Let's Go to the Park. Chouette Publishing Staff. 2008. (First Word Bks.). (ENG.). 24p. (J). (gr. -1-k). bds. 7.95 (978-2-89450-660-8(0)) Éditions Chouette CAN. Dist: Perseus-PGW.

—Caillou - Merry Christmas! Mercier, Johanne. 2nd ed. 2012. (Confetti Ser.). (ENG.). 24p. (J). (gr. -1-1). pap. 4.99 (978-2-89718-020-1(X)) Éditions Chouette CAN. Dist: Perseus-PGW.

—Caillou - My Clothes. Chouette Publishing Staff. rev. ed. 2008. (First Word Bks.). (ENG.). 24p. (J). (gr. -1-k). bds. 7.95 (978-2-89450-629-5(5)) Éditions Chouette CAN. Dist: Perseus-PGW.

—Caillou - My First Dictionary. Chouette Publishing Staff. rev. ed. 2007. (My First Dictionary Ser.). (ENG.). 16p. (J). (gr. -1-k). bds. 12.95 (978-2-89450-627-1(9)) Éditions Chouette CAN. Dist: Perseus-PGW.

—Caillou - My First Dictionary / Mi Primer Diccionario: In My House / En Mi Casa. Chouette Publishing Staff. Velazquez De Leon, Mauricio, tr. 2011. (My First Dictionary Ser.). (SPA & ENG.). 16p. (J). (gr. -1-k). bds. 12.95 (978-2-89450-841-1(7)) Éditions Chouette CAN. Dist: Perseus-PGW.

—Caillou - The Shopping Trip. Nadeau, Nicole. 2010. (Big Dipper Ser.). (ENG.). 24p. (J). (gr. -1-k). pap. 3.95 (978-2-89450-718-6(6)) Éditions Chouette CAN. Dist: Perseus-PGW.

—Caillou - Toddler Essentials: 5 Books about Growing. 2015. (Caillou Ser.). (ENG.). 120p. (gr. -1-k). 12.99 (978-2-89718-171-0(0)) Éditions Chouette CAN. Dist: Perseus-PGW.

Brignaud, Pierre. Caillou & the Big Bully. L'Heureux, Christine. 2015. (Hand in Hand Ser.). (ENG.). 24p. (J). (gr. -1-k). 5.99 **(978-2-89718-199-4(0))** Éditions Chouette CAN. Dist: Perseus-PGW.

Brignaud, Pierre. Caillou Asks Nicely. 2015. (Step by Step Ser.). (ENG.). 24p. (J). (gr. k-k). bds. 5.99 (978-2-89718-175-8(3)) Éditions Chouette CAN. Dist: Perseus-PGW.

—Caillou at the Doctor. Sanschagrin, Joceline. 3rd ed. 2013. (Step by Step Ser.). (ENG.). 24p. (J). (gr. -1-k). bds. 5.99 (978-2-89718-058-4(7)) Éditions Chouette CAN. Dist: Perseus-PGW.

—Caillou, Be Careful! Sanschagrin, Joceline. 2nd ed. 2013. (Step by Step Ser.). (ENG.). 24p. (J). (gr. -1-k). bds. 5.99 (978-2-89718-039-3(0)) Éditions Chouette CAN. Dist: Perseus-PGW.

—Caillou: Happy Easter! Rudel-Tessier, Melanie. 2012. (Confetti Ser.). (ENG.). 24p. (J). (gr. -1-1). pap. 4.99 (978-2-89450-947-0(2)) Éditions Chouette CAN. Dist: Perseus-PGW.

—Caillou: It's Mine! Sanschagrin, Joceline. 3rd ed. 2013. (Step by Step Ser.). (ENG.). 24p. (J). (gr. -1-k). bds. 5.99 (978-2-89718-059-1(5)) Éditions Chouette CAN. Dist: Perseus-PGW.

—Caillou: Jobs People Do. Chouette Publishing Staff. 2011. (My First Dictionary Ser.). (ENG.). 16p. (J). (gr. -1-k). bds. 12.95 (978-2-89450-831-2(X)) Éditions Chouette CAN. Dist: Perseus-PGW.

—Caillou Meets a Princess. L'Heureux, Christine. 2014. (ENG.). 24p. (J). (gr. -1-k). 5.99 (978-2-89718-114-7(1)) Éditions Chouette CAN. Dist: Perseus-PGW.

Brignaud, Pierre. Caillou, My First ABC: The Alphabet Soup. Publishing, Chouette. 2015. (ENG.). 32p. (J). (-k). 9.99 **(978-2-89718-201-4(6))** Éditions Chouette CAN. Dist: Perseus-PGW.

Brignaud, Pierre. Caillou: My Nightlight Book. L'Heureux, Christine & Légaré, Gisèle. 2014. (ENG.). 16p. (J). (gr. -1-1). bds. 9.99 (978-2-89718-104-8(4)) Éditions Chouette CAN. Dist: Perseus-PGW.

—Caillou Takes a Bath. Sanschagrin, Joceline. 2014. (Step by Step Ser.). (ENG.). 24p. (J). (gr. -1 — 1). bds. 5.99 (978-2-89718-138-3(9)) Éditions Chouette CAN. Dist: Perseus-PGW.

—Caillou Takes a Nap. Paradis, Anne. 2014. (Step by Step Ser.). (ENG.). 24p. (J). (gr. -1 — 1). bds. 5.99 (978-2-89718-147-5(8)) Éditions Chouette CAN. Dist: Perseus-PGW.

—Caillou: Where Is Teddy? 2015. (Step by Step Ser.). (ENG.). 24p. (J). (gr. k-k). bds. 5.99 (978-2-89718-173-4(7)) Éditions Chouette CAN. Dist: Perseus-PGW.

—Le Combats des Chocolats. Decary, Marie. 2003. (Roman Jeunesse Ser.). (FRE.). 96p. (J). (gr. 4-7). pap. (978-2-89021-611-2(X)) Diffusion du livre Mirabel (DLM).

—Good Night! Légaré, Gisèle & L'Heureux, Christine. 2006. (Hand in Hand Ser.). (ENG.). 24p. (J). (gr. -1-k). 5.95 (978-2-89450-588-5(4)) Éditions Chouette CAN. Dist: Perseus-PGW.

—Happy Thanksgiving! Johanson, Sarah Margaret. 2nd ed. 2012. (Confetti Ser.). (ENG.). 24p. (J). (gr. -1-1). pap. 4.99 (978-2-89718-021-8(8)) Éditions Chouette CAN. Dist: Perseus-PGW.

—Moves Around. L'Heureux, Christine. rev. ed. 2007. (First Word Bks.). (FRE & ENG.). 24p. (J). (gr. -1-k). bds. 7.95 (978-2-89450-610-3(4)) Éditions Chouette CAN. Dist: Perseus-PGW.

—Play with Me. L'Heureux, Christine. 2009. (Big Dipper Ser.). (ENG.). 24p. (J). (gr. -1-k). pap. 3.95 (978-2-89450-679-0(1)) Éditions Chouette CAN. Dist: Perseus-PGW.

—Rose Neon Series. Decary, Marie. 2004. 96p. (J). (gr. 4-7). pap. (978-2-89021-700-3(0)) Diffusion du livre Mirabel (DLM).

—Le Visage Masqué. Sanschagrin, Joceline. 2004. (Mon Roman Ser.). (FRE.). 160p. (J). (gr. 2). pap. (978-2-89021-651-8(9)) Diffusion du livre Mirabel (DLM).

Brignaud, Pierre & Depratto, Marcel. At Grandma & Grandpa's. Sanschagrin, Joceline. 2008. (Big Dipper Ser.). (ENG.). 24p. (J). (gr. -1-k). pap. 3.99 (978-2-89450-656-1(2)) Éditions Chouette CAN. Dist: Perseus-PGW.

Brignaud, Pierre & Sévigny, Eric. Caillou - Learning for Fun: Ages 3-4. Chouette Publishing Staff. 2013. (Coloring & Activity Book Ser.). (ENG.). 64p. (J). (gr. -1-k). 6.99 (978-2-89718-049-2(8)) Éditions Chouette CAN. Dist: Perseus-PGW.

—Caillou - Learning for Fun!, Ages 4-5. Chouette Publishing Staff. 2013. (Coloring & Activity Book Ser.). (ENG.). 64p. (J). (gr. -1-k). 6.99 (978-2-89718-050-8(1)) Éditions Chouette CAN. Dist: Perseus-PGW.

Briles, Patti. My Loose Tooth. Williams, Rozanne Lanczak. Hamaguchi, Carla, ed. 2003. (Sight Word Readers Ser.). 16p. (J). (gr. k-2). pap. 3.49 (978-1-57471-972-7(6), 3594) Creative Teaching Pr., Inc.

Briles, Patty. Grandma's Lists. Williams, Rozanne Lanczak. 2006. (Learn to Write Ser.). 8p. (J). (gr. k-2). pap. 3.49 (978-1-59198-284-5(7), 6178) Creative Teaching Pr., Inc.

—Grandma's Lists. Williams, Rozanne Lanczak. Maio, Barbara & Faulkner, Stacey, eds. 2006. (J). per. 6.99 (978-1-59198-335-4(5)) Creative Teaching Pr., Inc.

—What Is the Best Pet?, Vol. 4258. Williams, Rozanne Lanczak. 2005. 16p. (J). pap. 3.49 (978-1-59198-160-2(3), 4258) Creative Teaching Pr., Inc.

—When You Go Walking. Williams, Rozanne Lanczak. 2006. (Learn to Write Ser.). 16p. (J). (gr. k-2). pap. 3.49 (978-1-59198-292-0(8), 6188) Creative Teaching Pr., Inc.

—When You Go Walking. Williams, Rozanne Lanczak. Maio, Barbara, ed. 2006. (J). per. 8.99 (978-1-59198-345-3(2)) Creative Teaching Pr., Inc.

Brim, Warren & Eglitis, Anna. Creatures of the Rainforest: Two Artists Explore Djabugay Country. Brim, Warren & Eglitis, Anna. 2005. (ENG.). 64p. (J). (gr. k). 19.95 (978-1-875641-99-4(8)) Magabala Bks. AUS. Dist: Independent Pubs. Group.

Brimberg, Sisse & Coulson, Cotton. Mayflower 1620: A New Look at a Pilgrim Village. Brimberg, Sisse & Coulson, Cotton, photos by. Arenstam, Peter et al. 2003. (ENG.). 48p. (J). (gr. 3-7). 17.95 (978-0-7922-6142-1(9)) CENGAGE Learning.

Brimberg, Sisse & Coulson, Cotton, photos by. 1621: A New Look at Thanksgiving. Grace, Catherine O'Neill & Bruchac, Margaret M. ed. 2004. 47p. (J). (gr. 3-7). 18.40 (978-1-4176-2877-3(4), Turtleback) Turtleback Bks.

Brimberg, Sisse, jt. photos by see Coulson, Cotton.

Bringle, Beverly. Rising Fawn & the Fire Mystery. Awiakta, Marilou. 2007. (ENG.). 96p. (J). (gr. 4-7). pap. 14.95 (978-1-55591-600-8(7)) Fulcrum Publishing.

Brinkman, Paula. Yoga Bear: Yoga for Youngsters. Pierce, Karen F. 2004. (ENG.). 48p. (J). (gr. -1-1). 15.95 (978-1-55971-897-4(8)) Cooper Square Publishing Llc.

Brinson, Connor J. Princess Olivia & the Leap Frog, 1 vol. Brinson, Julie L. 2009. 22p. pap. 24.95 (978-1-60813-802-9(X)) America Star Bks.

Briones, Philip. Captain America Corps. 2011. (ENG.). 128p. (YA). (gr. 8-17). pap. 16.99 (978-0-7851-5563-8(5)) Marvel Worldwide, Inc.

Brislane, Niche. Paula & the Parrot. Vaughn, J. D. 2009. 16p. pap. 8.49 (978-1-4389-8634-0(3)) AuthorHouse.

Brisley, Joyce Lankester. Adventures of the Little Wooden Horse. Williams, Ursula Moray. 2015. (Macmillan Classics Ser.). (ENG.). 256p. (J). (gr. k-2). 16.99 **(978-1-4472-7304-2(4))** Pan Macmillan GBR. Dist: Independent Pubs. Group.

Brisley, Joyce Lankester. Adventures of the Little Wooden Horse. Williams, Ursula Moray. 2013. (ENG.). 256p. (J). (gr. -1-2). 15.99 (978-0-230-75495-9(3)) Pan Macmillan GBR. Dist: Independent Pubs. Group.

Bristol, Mark. Simply Social 7 at School. Neal, Angie & Kjesbo, Rynette. 2011. 216p. (J). spiral bd. 34.95 net. (978-1-60723-005-2(4)) Super Duper Pubns.

Britt, Joanna & Edwards, Laurie J. Island Sting, Book 1. Doerr, Bonnie J. 2010. 282p. (YA). (gr. 5-11). pap. 11.99 (978-1-61603-002-5(X)) Leap Bks.

Britt, Joanna, jt. illus. see Edwards, Laurie J.

Britt, Rachel. Good Manners for Very Young Children with Rio the Rat. Lister, John C. 2005. (J). 18.00 (978-0-8059-6913-9(6)) Dorrance Publishing Co., Inc.

Britt, Stephanie. Discover Benjamin Franklin: Printer, Scientist, Statesman. Pingry, Patricia A. 2005. (Discovery Readers Ser.). (ENG.). 32p. (J). (gr. 1-2). pap. 4.35 (978-0-8249-5509-0(9)) Ideals Pubns.

—Over in the Hollow. Dickinson, Rebecca. 2009. (ENG.). 36p. (J). (gr. -1-2). 15.99 (978-0-8118-5035-3(8)) Chronicle Bks. LLC.

—Prayers at Eastertime. Kennedy, Pamela. 2009. (ENG.). 24p. (J). 8.99 (978-0-8249-5609-7(5), Ideals Children's Bks.) Ideals Pubns.

—The Story of Aloha Bear. Adair, Dick. 2008. 24p. (J). 12.95 (978-1-59700-492-3(8)) Island Heritage Publishing.

—The Story of Gettysburg. Pingry, Patricia A. 2003. (ENG.). 26p. (J). (gr. -1-k). bds. 7.69 (978-0-8249-6503-7(5)) Ideals Pubns.

—The Story of Ulysses S. Grant. Smith, Tamara. 2005. 26p. (J). bds. 7.69 (978-0-8249-6565-5(5)) Ideals Pubns.

Britt, Stephanie M. Writing Makeovers 1-2: Improving Skills - Adding Style. Hults, Alaska. Rous, Sheri, ed. 2003. 96p. (J). (gr. 1-3). pap. 11.99 (978-1-57471-955-0(6), 2260) Creative Teaching Pr., Inc.

Britt, Stephanie McFetridge. I May Be Little. Lashbrook, Marilyn. 2012. 32p. (J). pap. 8.00 (978-1-935014-41-6(2)) Hutchings, John Pubs.

—Meet Abraham Lincoln. Pingry, Patricia A. 2009. (ENG.). 32p. (J). pap. 7.99 (978-0-8249-5613-4(3), Ideals Children's Bks.) Ideals Pubns.

—Meet George Washington. Pingry, Patricia A. 2009. (ENG.). 32p. (J). pap. 7.99 (978-0-8249-5612-7(5), Ideals Children's Bks.) Ideals Pubns.

—My First Book of Prayers. 2007. (ENG.). 32p. 3.99 (978-0-8249-5570-0(6), Ideals Children's Bks.) Ideals Pubns.

—Out on a Limb. Lashbrook, Marilyn. 2012. 32p. (J). pap. 8.00 (978-1-935014-37-9(4)) Hutchings, John Pubs.

—Peter Rabbit. Potter, Beatrix. 2006. (ENG.). 32p. (J). (gr. -1-3). pap. 3.95 (978-0-8249-5533-5(1), Ideals Children's Bks.) Ideals Pubns.

—Who Needs a Boat? Lashbrook, Marilyn. 2012. 32p. (J). pap. 8.00 (978-1-935014-39-3(0)) Hutchings, John Pubs.

Brittany's Books. I Can Too! African American Girls. Brittany's Books, creator. 2006. 44p. (J). lib. bdg. 9.95 (978-0-9778796-8-7(2)) Brittany's Bks.

Brittingham, Geoffrey. Peter Cottontail & the Easter Bunny Imposter. Smith, Suzanne C. 24p. (J). pap. 3.25 (978-0-8249-5372-0(X), Ideals) Ideals Pubns.

Brittingham, Jennifer. Emily I Think I Saw Heaven. Holbrook, James. 2007. 40p. per. 14.95 (978-1-934246-56-6(5)) Peppertree Pr., The.

Britto, Romero. Color Play! An Interactive Pop Art Book. Britto, Romero. 2011. (ENG.). 12p. (J). (gr. -1-k). 10.99 (978-1-4169-9622-4(2), Little Simon) Little Simon.

—My Alphabet Playbook. Britto, Romero. 2010. (ENG.). 16p. (J). (gr. -1-k). bds. 12.99 (978-1-4169-9624-8(9), Little Simon) Little Simon.

—Where Is Friendship Bear? Britto, Romero. 2010. (ENG.). 16p. (J). (gr. -1-k). pap. 12.99 (978-1-4169-9623-1(0), Little Simon) Little Simon.

Britton, Matthew. Mr. Bump in: Lights, Camera, Bump! Hardman, John. 2012. (Mr. Men Little Miss Ser.: 1). (ENG.). 80p. (J). pap. 6.99 (978-1-4215-4074-0(6)) Viz Media.

Britton, Terre. The Otter & the Troll. Kuykendall, Anna. l.t. ed. 2011. (ENG.). 32p. pap. 10.95 (978-1-4636-9857-7(7)) CreateSpace Independent Publishing Platform.

Brizendine, Brad. Barfalloems: Much Grosser Than Poems & Ten Times More Fun. Cohen, Larry. 2011. (ENG.). 24p. pap. 9.99 (978-1-4679-7470-7(6)) CreateSpace Independent Publishing Platform.

Brizuela, Dario. April Fools, 1 vol. Fisch, Sholly. 2012. (DC Super Friends Ser.). (ENG.). 32p. (gr. 1-2). lib. bdg. 21.27 (978-1-4342-4544-1(6)) Stone Arch Bks.

—Bounty Hunter, 1 vol. Baltazar, Art & Aureliani, Franco. 2012. (Green Lantern: the Animated Ser.). (ENG.). 32p. (gr. 2-3). 21.27 (978-1-4342-4835-0(6)) Stone Arch Bks.

—Challenge of the Super Friends, 1 vol. Fisch, Sholly. 2013. (DC Super Friends Ser.). (ENG.). 32p. (gr. 1-2). lib. bdg. 21.27 (978-1-4342-4701-8(5)) Stone Arch Bks.

—Counterfeits, 1 vol. Baltazar, Art & Aureliani, Franco. 2013. (Green Lantern: the Animated Ser.). (ENG.). 32p. (gr. 2-3). 21.27 (978-1-4342-5566-2(2)) Stone Arch Bks.

—Goldface Attacks!, 1 vol. Baltazar, Art & Aureliani, Franco. 2014. (Green Lantern: the Animated Ser.). (ENG.). 32p. (gr. 2-3). 21.27 (978-1-4342-6482-4(3)) Stone Arch Bks.

—Green Lantern: the Animated Series. Baltazar, Art & Aureliani, Franco. 2013. (Green Lantern: the Animated Ser.). (ENG.). 32p. (gr. 2-3). 85.08 (978-1-4342-8828-8(5)) Stone Arch Bks.

—Hal Versus Atrocitus, 1 vol. Baltazar, Art et al. 2014. (Green Lantern: the Animated Ser.). (ENG.). 32p. (gr. 2-3). 21.27 (978-1-4342-6481-7(5)) Stone Arch Bks.

—Hungry for Power, 1 vol. Fisch, Sholly. 2012. (DC Super Friends Ser.). (ENG.). 32p. (gr. 1-2). lib. bdg. 21.27 (978-1-4342-4541-0(1)) Stone Arch Bks.

—Invisible Destroyer. Baltazar, Art & Aureliani, Franco. 2013. (Green Lantern: the Animated Ser.). (ENG.). 32p. (gr. 2-3). 21.27 (978-1-4342-4796-4(1)) Stone Arch Bks.

—Just My Luck, 1 vol. Fisch, Sholly. 2013. (DC Super Friends Ser.). (ENG.). 32p. (gr. 1-2). lib. bdg. 21.27 (978-1-4342-4702-5(3)) Stone Arch Bks.

—The Rule of Three. Manning, Matthew K. et al. 2015. (Beware the Batman Ser.). (ENG.). 32p. (gr. 2-3). lib. bdg. 21.27 (978-1-4342-9739-6(X)) Stone Arch Bks.

—Scooby-Doo! Team-Up. Fisch, Sholly. 2015. (ENG.). 128p. (J). (gr. 2-5). pap. 12.99 (978-1-4012-4946-5(9)) DC Comics.

—Season of Light, 1 vol. Fisch, Sholly & Age, Heroic. 2014. (DC Super Friends Ser.). (ENG.). 32p. (gr. 1-2). 21.27 (978-1-4342-9223-0(1)) Stone Arch Bks.

—Trouble in the Arena!, 1 vol. Baltazar, Art et al. 2014. (Green Lantern: the Animated Ser.). (ENG.). 32p. (gr. 2-3). 21.27 (978-1-4342-4787-2(2)) Stone Arch Bks.

—True Colors, 1 vol. Baltazar, Art et al. 2013. (Green Lantern: the Animated Ser.). (ENG.). 32p. (gr. 2-3). 21.27 (978-1-4342-4795-7(3)) Stone Arch Bks.

Brizuela, Dario & Staton, Joe. Dinosaur Round-Up, 1 vol. Fisch, Sholly & Ottolini, Horacio. 2012. (DC Super Friends Ser.). (ENG.). 32p. (gr. 1-2). lib. bdg. 21.27 (978-1-4342-4542-7(X)) Stone Arch Bks.

Brizuela, Dario, jt. illus. see Vecchio, Luciano.

Broad, Michael. Dodging the Donkey Doo. Wilding, Val. 2008. (Toby Tucker Ser.). (ENG.). 144p. (J). (gr. 2-4). pap. 7.95 (978-1-4052-2547-2(5)) Egmont Bks., Ltd. GBR. Dist: Independent Pubs. Group.

Broad, Michael. Ghost Diamond!, No. 1. Broad, Michael. 2011. (Agent Amelia Ser.: 1). (ENG.). 144p. (J). (gr. 2-5). pap. 5.95 (978-0-7613-8060-3(4), Darby Creek); lib. bdg. 22.60 (978-0-7613-8056-6(6)) Lerner Publishing Group.

—Hypno Hounds!, No. 3. Broad, Michael. 2011. (Agent Amelia Ser.: 3). (ENG.). 144p. (J). (gr. 2-5). pap. 5.95 (978-0-7613-8062-7(0), Darby Creek); lib. bdg. 22.60 (978-0-7613-8058-0(2)) Lerner Publishing Group.

—Spooky Ballet!, No. 4. Broad, Michael. 2011. (Agent Amelia Ser.: 4). (ENG.). 144p. (J). (gr. 2-5). pap. 5.95 (978-0-7613-8064-1(7), Darby Creek); lib. bdg. 22.60 (978-0-7613-8059-7(0)) Lerner Publishing Group.

—Zombie Cows! Broad, Michael. 2011. (Agent Amelia Ser.: 2). (ENG.). 144p. (J). (gr. 2-5). pap. 5.95 (978-0-7613-8066-5(3), Darby Creek);No. 2. lib. bdg. 22.60 (978-0-7613-8057-3(4)) Lerner Publishing Group.

Broad, Sam. The Queen & the Nobody Boy: Hodie's Journey (in Five Parts All about Bad Choices) Else, Barbara. 2013. (Tales of Fontania Ser.). (ENG.). 326p. (J). (gr. 4-7). (978-1-877579-49-3(1)) Gecko Pr.

Broadhurst, Colin. Bella's Adventures: Bella in the City. Broadhurst, Sherree. 2010. 38p. pap. 14.50 (978-1-60976-179-0(0), Eloquent Bks.) Strategic Book Publishing & Rights Agency (SBPRA).

Broadley, Leo. The Boy Who Cried Wolf, Bk. 2. Jenkins, Saffy. 2013. (Collins Big Cat Ser.). (ENG.). 16p. (J). pap. 5.99 (978-0-00-751267-6(8)) HarperCollins Pubs. Ltd. GBR. Dist: Independent Pubs. Group.

Broadnax, Charles. Time for Bed: Andrew & April's Adventures. Kearney Cooper, Nicole. 2005. (J). 7.00 (978-0-9766086-7-7(7)) nVision Publishing.

Broadway, Hannah. Doctor Monkey. Hayes, Felix. 2013. (Monkey & Robot Ser.). (ENG.). 32p. (J). (gr. -1-k). pap. 10.99 (978-1-4088-0654-8(1), 39555, Bloomsbury USA Childrens) Bloomsbury USA.

—In the Garden. Hayes, Felix. 2014. (Monkey & Robot Ser.). (ENG.). 32p. (J). (gr. -1-k). pap. 10.99 (978-1-4088-0657-9(6), 39558, Bloomsbury USA Childrens) Bloomsbury USA.

—In the Snow. Hayes, Felix. 2014. (Monkey & Robot Ser.). (ENG.). 32p. (J). (gr. -1-k). pap. 10.99 (978-1-4088-0656-2(8), 39557, Bloomsbury USA Childrens) Bloomsbury USA.

Brochard, Philippe. Le Tombeau en Peril, Vol. 56. Leblanc, Louise. 2003. (Premier Roman Ser.). (FRE.). 64p. (J). (gr. 2-5). pap. (978-2-89021-282-4(3)) Diffusion du livre Mirabel (DLM).

Brochard, Philippe, jt. illus. see Casson, Sophie.

Brock, C. E. The Railway Children. Nesbit, E. (YA). 14.95 (978-0-8118-4933-3(3)) Chronicle Bks. LLC.

—The Railway Children. Nesbit, E. 2008. (ENG.). 248p. per. (978-1-4065-9815-5(1)) Dodo Pr.

—Tales of the Norse Warrior Gods: The Heroes of Asgard. Keary, Annie & Keary, Eliza. 2005. (ENG.). 256p. (gr. 3-7). per. 9.95 (978-0-486-44053-8(2)) Dover Pubns., Inc.

Brock, Charles Edmund. Flehes an Hens Horn. Nesbit, Edith. Williams, Nicholas, tr. from ENG. 2012. (COR.). 260p. pap. (978-1-78201-003-6(3)) Evertype.

—The Railway Children. Nesbit, E. 2012. 232p. pap. (978-1-78201-004-3(1)) Evertype.

Brock, George Ann. Eagle Rock: The Memoirs of a Little Girl, 1941-1945. Monhollon, Lake Pylant. 2003. 137p. (J). 14.95 (978-0-9712142-1-7(2)) Reflection Publishing Co.

Brock, H. M. Beauty & the Beast. 2012. (ENG.). 48p. (J). 12.95 (978-1-59583-460-7(5), 9781595834607, Green Tiger Pr.) Laughing Elephant.

Brocket, Jane, photos by. Spotty, Stripy, Swirly: What Are Patterns? 2012. (Jane Brocket's Clever Concepts Ser.). (ENG., 32p. (gr. -1-2). lib. bdg. 26.60 (978-0-7613-4613-5(9)) Lerner Publishing Group.

Brocket, Jane, photos by. Circles, Stars, & Squares: Looking for Shapes. Brocket, Jane. 2012. (Jane Brocket's Clever Concepts Ser.). (ENG., 32p. (gr. -1-2). lib. bdg. 26.60 (978-0-7613-4611-1(2), Millbrook Pr.) Lerner Publishing Group.

—Cold, Crunchy, Colorful: Using Our Senses. Brocket, Jane. 2014. (Jane Brocket's Clever Concepts Ser.). (ENG., 32p. (gr. -1-2). lib. bdg. 26.60 (978-1-4677-0233-1(1), Millbrook Pr.) Lerner Publishing Group.

—Rainy, Sunny, Blowy, Snowy - What Are Seasons? Brocket, Jane. 2014. (Jane Brocket's Clever Concepts Ser.). (ENG., 32p. (gr. -1-2). lib. bdg. 26.60 (978-1-4677-0231-7(5), Millbrook Pr.) Lerner Publishing Group.

—Ruby, Violet, Lime: Looking for Color. Brocket, Jane. 2011. (Jane Brocket's Clever Concepts Ser.). (ENG., 32p. (gr. -1-2). lib. bdg. 26.60 (978-0-7613-4612-8(0)) Lerner Publishing Group.

—Spiky, Slimy, Smooth: What Is Texture? Brocket, Jane. 2011. (Jane Brocket's Clever Concepts Ser.). (ENG., 32p. (gr. -1-2). 26.60 (978-0-7613-4614-2(7)) Lerner Publishing Group.

Brocket, Jane, photos by. Stickiest, Fluffiest, Crunchiest: Super Superlatives. Brocket, Jane. 2015. (ENG., 32p. (gr. -1-2). 26.60 ***(978-1-4677-9241-7(1)***, Millbrook Pr.) Lerner Publishing Group.

Brocket, Jane, photos by. 1 Cookie, 2 Chairs, 3 Pears: Numbers Everywhere. Brocket, Jane. 2013. (Jane Brocket's Clever Concepts Ser.). (ENG., 32p. (gr. -1-2). lib. bdg. 26.60 *(978-1-4677-0232-4(3)*, Millbrook Pr.) Lerner Publishing Group.

Brockschmidt, Kev. Pocketdoodles for Christmas, 1 vol. Wood, Anita. 2015. (ENG.). 240p. pap. 9.99 ***(978-1-4236-4115-5(9))*** Gibbs Smith, Publisher.

Brockway, Harry. The Man Who Planted Trees. Giono, Jean & Giono, Aline. Bray, Barbara, tr. from FRE. 2003. (ENG.). 81p. pap. 14.95 *(978-1-86046-117-0(4)*, Harvill Pr.) Random Hse. GBR. Dist: Independent Pubs. Group.

Broda, Ron. In My Backyard. Ruurs, Margriet. 2007. (ENG.). 32p. (J). (gr. -1-3). 18.95 *(978-0-88776-775-3(3)*, Tundra Bks.) Tundra Bks. CAN. Dist: Penguin Random Hse., LLC.

Broderick, Al R. Muffy, Fluffy, & Dexter In. Broderick, Lonia R. 2013. 20p. 20.99 *(978-1-62839-255-5(X))* Salem Publishing Solutions, Inc.

Broderick, Pat. Marvel Masterworks Vol. 5: Captain Marvel. Edelman, Scott & Conway, Gerry. 2014. (ENG.). 288p. (J). (gr. 4-17). 69.99 *(978-0-7851-8892-6(4))* Marvel Worldwide, Inc.

Brodie, N. eale. In Vietnam/en Vietnam. Zocchi, Judy. 2005. (Global Adventures II Ser.).Tr. of En Vietnam. (ENG & SPA.). 32p. (J). pap. 10.95 *(978-1-59646-166-6(7))* Dingles & Co.

Brodie, Neal. Seaside Circles/Círculos a la orilla del Mar. Dingles, Molly. 2006. (Community of Shapes Ser.).Tr. of Círculos a la orilla del Mar. (ENG & SPA.). 32p. (J). per. 10.95 *(978-1-59646-259-5(0))* Dingles & Co.

Brodie, Neale. Crescent Kitchen. Dingles, Molly. 2006. (Community of Shapes Ser.). (J). *(978-1-59646-049-2(0))* Dingles & Co.

—Crescent Kitchen: Cocina de Medialuna. Dingles, Molly. 2006. (ENG & SPA.). (J). 21.65 *(978-1-59646-050-8(4))* Dingles & Co.

—In Canada. Zocchi, Judy. 2005. (Global Adventures II Ser.). 32p. (J). pap. 10.95 *(978-1-59646-168-0(3))*; lib. bdg. 21.65 *(978-1-59646-083-6(0))*; per. 10.95 *(978-1-59646-169-7(1))* Dingles & Co.

—In Canada/en Canada. Zocchi, Judy. 2005. (Global Adventures II Ser.).Tr. of En Canada. (ENG & SPA.). 32p. (J). pap. 10.95 *(978-1-59646-170-3(5))*; lib. bdg. 21.65 *(978-1-59646-084-3(9))*; per. 10.95 *(978-1-59646-171-0(3))* Dingles & Co.

—In Cuba. Zocchi, Judy. 2005. (Global Adventures II Ser.). 32p. (J). pap. 10.95 *(978-1-59646-160-4(8))*; lib. bdg. 21.65 *(978-1-59646-079-9(2))*; per. 10.95 *(978-1-59646-161-1(6))* Dingles & Co.

—In Cuba/en Cuba. Zocchi, Judy. 2005. (Global Adventures II Ser.).Tr. of En Cuba. (ENG & SPA.). 32p. (J). pap. 10.95 *(978-1-59646-162-8(4))*; lib. bdg. 21.65 *(978-1-59646-080-5(6))*; per. 10.95 *(978-1-59646-163-5(2))* Dingles & Co.

—In Germany. Zocchi, Judy. 2005. (Global Adventures II Ser.). 32p. (J). pap. 10.95 *(978-1-59646-180-2(2))*; lib. bdg. 21.65 *(978-1-59646-089-8(X))*; per. 10.95 *(978-1-59646-181-9(0))* Dingles & Co.

—In Germany/en Alemania. Zocchi, Judy. 2005. (Global Adventures II Ser.).Tr. of En Alemania. (ENG & SPA.). (J). 32p. pap. 10.95 *(978-1-59646-182-6(9))*; 28p. lib. bdg. 21.65 *(978-1-59646-090-4(3))*; 32p. per. 10.95 *(978-1-59646-183-3(7))* Dingles & Co.

—In Japan. Zocchi, Judy. 2005. (Global Adventures I Ser.). 32p. (J). pap. 10.95 *(978-1-59646-139-0(X))*; lib. bdg. 21.65 *(978-1-59646-004-1(0))*; per. 10.95 *(978-1-59646-140-6(3))* Dingles & Co.

—In Japan/en Japón. Zocchi, Judy. 2005. (Global Adventures I Ser.).Tr. of En Japón. (ENG & SPA.). 32p. (J). pap. 10.95 *(978-1-59646-141-3(1))*; lib. bdg. 21.65 *(978-1-59646-005-8(9))*; per. 10.95 *(978-1-59646-142-0(X))* Dingles & Co.

—In Mexico. Zocchi, Judy. 2005. (Global Adventures I Ser.). 32p. (J). pap. 10.95 *(978-1-59646-135-2(7))*; lib. bdg. 21.65 *(978-1-59646-002-7(4))*; per. 10.95 *(978-1-59646-136-9(5))* Dingles & Co.

—In Mexico/en México. Zocchi, Judy. 2005. (Global Adventures I Ser.).Tr. of En México. (ENG & SPA.). 32p. (J). pap. 10.95 *(978-1-59646-137-6(3))*; lib. bdg. 21.65 *(978-1-59646-003-4(2))*; per. 10.95 *(978-1-59646-138-3(1))* Dingles & Co.

—In Nigeria. Zocchi, Judy. 2005. (Global Adventures I Ser.). 32p. (J). pap. 10.95 *(978-1-59646-143-7(8))*; lib. bdg. 21.65 *(978-1-59646-010-2(5))*; per. 10.95 *(978-1-59646-144-4(6))* Dingles & Co.

—In Nigeria/en Nigeria. Zocchi, Judy. 2005. (Global Adventures I Ser.).Tr. of En Nigeria. (ENG & SPA.). 32p. (J). pap. 10.95 *(978-1-59646-145-1(4))*; lib. bdg. 21.65 *(978-1-59646-011-9(3))*; per. 10.95 *(978-1-59646-146-8(2))* Dingles & Co.

—In Scotland. Zocchi, Judy. 2005. (Global Adventures I Ser.). 32p. (J). pap. 10.95 *(978-1-59646-147-5(0))*; lib. bdg. 21.65 *(978-1-59646-012-6(1))*; per. 10.95 *(978-1-59646-149-9(7))* Dingles & Co.

—In Scotland/en Escocia. Zocchi, Judy. 2005. (Global Adventures I Ser.).Tr. of En Escocia. (ENG & SPA.). 32p. (J). pap. 10.95 *(978-1-59646-150-5(0))*; lib. bdg. *(978-1-59646-013-3(X))*; per. 10.95 *(978-1-59646-151-2(9))* Dingles & Co.

—In South Africa. Zocchi, Judith Mazzeo. 2008. (J). *(978-1-59646-642-5(1))*; pap. *(978-1-59646-643-2(X))* Dingles & Co.

—In Spain. James, Yolanda. 2008. (J). *(978-1-59646-772-9(X))* Dingles & Co.

—In Sweden. Zocchi, Judy. 2005. (Global Adventures II Ser.). 32p. (J). pap. 10.95 *(978-1-59646-176-5(4))*; lib. bdg. 21.65 *(978-1-59646-087-4(3))*; per. 10.95 *(978-1-59646-177-2(2))* Dingles & Co.

—In Sweden/en Suecia. Zocchi, Judy. 2005. (Global Adventures I Ser.).Tr. of En Japón. (ENG & SPA.). 32p. (J). pap. 10.95 *(978-1-59646-178-9(0))*; lib. bdg. 21.65 *(978-1-59646-088-1(1))*; per. 10.95 *(978-1-59646-179-6(9))* Dingles & Co.

—In Switzerland. Zocchi, Judy. 2005. (Global Adventures I Ser.). 32p. (J). pap. 10.95 *(978-1-59646-156-7(X))*; lib. bdg. 21.65 *(978-1-59646-006-5(7))*; per. 10.95 *(978-1-59646-157-4(8))* Dingles & Co.

—In Switzerland/en Suiza. Zocchi, Judy. 2005. (Global Adventures I Ser.).Tr. of En Suiza. (ENG & SPA.). 32p. (J). pap. 10.95 *(978-1-59646-158-1(6))*; lib. bdg. 21.65 *(978-1-59646-007-2(5))*; per. 10.95 *(978-1-59646-159-8(4))* Dingles & Co.

—In the United States. Zocchi, Judy. 2005. (Global Adventures II Ser.). 32p. (J). pap. 10.95 *(978-1-59646-172-7(1))*; lib. bdg. 21.65 *(978-1-59646-085-0(7))*; per. 9.95 *(978-1-59646-173-4(X))* Dingles & Co.

—In the United States/en los Estados Unidos. Zocchi, Judy. 2005. (Global Adventures II Ser.).Tr. of En los Estados Unidos. (ENG & SPA.). 32p. (J). pap. 10.95 *(978-1-59646-174-1(8))*; lib. bdg. 21.65 *(978-1-59646-086-7(5))*; per. 10.95 *(978-1-59646-175-8(6))* Dingles & Co.

—In Turkey. Zocchi, Judy. 2005. (Global Adventures I Ser.). 32p. (J). pap. 10.95 *(978-1-59646-152-9(7))*; lib. bdg. 21.65 *(978-1-59646-031-7(8))*; per. 10.95 *(978-1-59646-153-6(5))* Dingles & Co.

—In Turkey/en Turquía. Zocchi, Judy. 2005. (Global Adventures I Ser.).Tr. of En Turquía. (ENG & SPA.). 32p. (J). pap. 10.95 *(978-1-59646-154-3(3))*; lib. bdg. 21.65 *(978-1-59646-032-4(6))*; per. 10.95 *(978-1-59646-155-0(1))* Dingles & Co.

—In Vietnam. Zocchi, Judy. 2005. (Global Adventures II Ser.). 32p. (J). pap. 10.95 *(978-1-59646-164-2(0))*; lib. bdg. 21.65 *(978-1-59646-081-2(4))*; per. 10.95 *(978-1-59646-165-9(9))* Dingles & Co.

—In Vietnam/en Vietnam. Zocchi, Judy. 2005. (Global Adventures II Ser.).Tr. of En Vietnam. (ENG & SPA.). 32p. (J). lib. bdg. 21.65 *(978-1-59646-082-9(2))*; per. 10.95 *(978-1-59646-167-3(5))* Dingles & Co.

—Oval Opera. Dingles, Molly. 2006. (Community of Shapes Ser.). 29p. (J). *(978-1-59646-047-8(4))* Dingles & Co.

—Oval Opera: Ópera de óvalos. Dingles, Molly. 2006. (SPA & ENG.). (J). *(978-1-59646-048-5(2))* Dingles & Co.

—Seaside Circles. Dingles, Molly. 2006. (Community of Shapes Ser.). 32p. (J). pap. 10.95 *(978-1-59646-256-4(6))*; lib. bdg. 21.65 *(978-1-59646-033-1(4))*; per. 10.95 *(978-1-59646-257-1(4))* Dingles & Co.

—Seaside Circles/Círculos a la orilla del Mar. Dingles, Molly. 2006. (Community of Shapes Ser.).Tr. of Círculos a la orilla del Mar. (ENG & SPA.). 32p. (J). pap. 10.95 *(978-1-59646-258-8(2))*; lib. bdg. 21.65 *(978-1-59646-034-8(2))* Dingles & Co.

—Star Ship. Dingles, Molly. 2006. (Community of Shapes Ser.). 29p. (J). *(978-1-59646-039-3(3))* Dingles & Co.

—Star Ship: Barco de Estrellas. Dingles, Molly. 2006. (SPA & ENG.). (J). *(978-1-59646-040-9(7))* Dingles & Co.

—Sweet Hearts. Dingles, Molly. 2006. (Community of Shapes Ser.). (J). *(978-1-59646-037-9(7))* Dingles & Co.

—Sweet Hearts: Dulce Corazón. Dingles, Molly. 2006. (SPA & ENG.). (J). *(978-1-59646-038-6(5))* Dingles & Co.

—Town Squares. Dingles, Molly. 2006. (Community of Shapes Ser.). 32p. (J). pap. 10.95 *(978-1-59646-264-9(7))*; lib. bdg. 21.65 *(978-1-59646-041-6(5))*; per. 10.95 *(978-1-59646-265-6(5))* Dingles & Co.

—Town Squares/Cuadrados en la Plaza. Dingles, Molly. 2006. (Community of Shapes Ser.).Tr. of Cuadrados en la Plaza. (ENG & SPA.). 32p. (J). pap. 10.95 *(978-1-59646-266-3(3))*; lib. bdg. 21.65 *(978-1-59646-042-3(3))*; per. 10.95 *(978-1-59646-267-0(1))* Dingles & Co.

Brodie, Neale & McCarthy, Pat. Bertie Wiggins' Amazing Ears. James, Yolanda et al. 2008. (ENG & SPA.). 32p. (J). lib. bdg. 23.65 *(978-1-59646-774-3(6))* Dingles & Co.

Brodner, Steve. Davy Crockett. Kunstler, James Howard. 2004. (Rabbit Ears-A Classic Tale Ser.). 36p. (gr. k-5). 25.65 *(978-1-59197-762-9(2))* Spotlight.

Brody, Joyce. Cora the Caterpillar. Mann, Gerre. 2012. 20p. pap. 14.99 *(978-1-61170-088-6(4))* Robertson Publishing.

Broeck, Fabricio Vanden. Chico Rey. Bergna, Monica. rev. ed. 2006. (Otra Escalera Ser.). (ENG.). 24p. (J). (gr. -1-k). pap. 8.95 *(978-970-20-0830-9(1))* Castillo, Ediciones, S. A. de C. V. MEX. Dist: Macmillan.

—En la Ultima Frontera. Ortiz, Gilberto Rendon & Rendon, Gilberto. rev. ed. 2006. (SPA & ENG.). 268p. (YA). (gr. 8-12). pap. 8.95 *(978-970-20-0134-8(X))* Castillo, Ediciones, S. A. de C. V. MEX. Dist: Macmillan.

—My Shoes & I. Laínez, René Colato. 2010. (ENG.). 32p. (J). (gr. 2-4). 16.95 *(978-1-59078-385-6(9))* Boyds Mills Pr.

—Under the Breadfruit Tree: Island Poems. Gunning, Monica. 2004. (ENG.). 48p. (J). (gr. 2-5). pap. 9.95 *(978-1-59078-258-3(5))* Boyds Mills Pr.

Broeck, Fabricio Vanden, jt. illus. see Vigil, Luis Gerardo Sanchez.

Broekstra, Lorette. Baby Bear Goes to the Zoo. 2004. (Baby Bear Ser.). 32p. (J). pap. 4.99 *(978-1-85854-711-4(3))* Brimax Books Ltd. GBR. Dist: Byeway Bks.

—What Day Is It, Missie Mouse? Munro, Maisie. 2009. (ENG.). 16p. (J). (gr. -1-k). 9.99 *(978-1-921272-82-0(1))* Little Hare Bks. AUS. Dist: Independent Pubs. Group.

—What's That Noise? Rippin, Sally. 2009. (ENG.). 12p. (J). (gr. k — 1). bds. 7.99 *(978-1-74175-389-9(9))* Allen & Unwin AUS. Dist: Independent Pubs. Group.

Broere, Rien. I Don't Like the Dark! 2014. (Side by Side Ser.). (ENG.). 32p. (J). (gr. -1-k). pap. 10.99 *(978-1-78388-003-4(1))* Tulip Books GBR. Dist: Independent Pubs. Group.

—I Miss You, Grandad. Bode, Ann de. 2014. (Side by Side Ser.). (ENG.). 32p. (J). (gr. -1-k). pap. 10.99 *(978-1-78388-004-1(X))* Tulip Books GBR. Dist: Independent Pubs. Group.

—I Still Love You, Dad. Bode, Ann de. 2014. (Side by Side Ser.). (ENG.). 32p. (J). (gr. -1-k). pap. 10.99 *(978-1-78388-005-8(8))* Tulip Books GBR. Dist: Independent Pubs. Group.

—Leave Me Alone! Bode, Ann de. 2014. (Side by Side Ser.). (ENG.). 32p. (J). (gr. -1-k). pap. 10.99 *(978-1-78388-000-3(7))* Tulip Books GBR. Dist: Independent Pubs. Group.

Broesch, Valerie, jt. illus. see Zabel, Randy.

Brolin, Carol. Money...Cool! Fabris, Judith. l.t. ed. 2003. 155p. (YA). pap. 9.95 *(978-1-893335-12-7(7))* Archipelago Pr.

Bronfeyn, Lily. Cheese Please, Chimpanzees: Fun with Spelling. Traynor, Tracy. 2008. (Milet Wordwise Ser.). (ENG.). 28p. (J). (gr. k-2). pap. 6.95 *(978-1-84059-511-6(6))* Milet Publishing.

Bronowski, Karen Kmetz. The Golden Leaf. Rendina, Donna Rae. 2011. 24p. 20.00 *(978-1-61170-014-5(0))* Robertson Publishing.

Bronson, Jody. Fox Talk. Carmichael, L. E. 2013. 62p. *(978-0-9881638-5-0(3))*; pap. *(978-0-9881638-6-7(1))* Ashby-BP Publishing.

Bronson, Linda. Balls. Jones, Melanie Davis. 2011. (Rookie Ready to Learn - Numbers & Shapes Ser.). 32p. (J). (gr. -1-k). lib. bdg. 23.00 *(978-0-531-26445-4(9)*, Children's Pr.) Scholastic Library Publishing.

—F Is for Fireflies: God's Summertime Alphabet, 1 vol. Wargin, Kathy-jo. 2011. (ENG.). 40p. (J). (gr. -1-2). 15.99 *(978-0-310-71663-1(2))* Zonderkidz.

—Gorp's Secret: An Empowering Tale in Pumpernickel Park. Chessen, Sherri. 2008. (ENG.). 36p. (J). 16.95 *(978-0-9724249-3-6(8))* Gorp Group Pr., The.

—The Story of Halloween. Greene, Carol. 2004. 40p. (J). 15.99 *(978-0-06-027946-2(X))*; lib. bdg. 16.89 *(978-0-06-029560-8(0))* HarperCollins Pubs.

—The Three Funny Friends. Zolotow, Charlotte. 2006. 27p. (J). (gr. k-4). reprint ed. 16.00 *(978-0-7567-9860-4(4))* DIANE Publishing Co.

Bronson, Tammy Carter. Kaleidonotes & the Mixed-up Orchestra. Bronson, Tammy Carter. Bronson, Matthew Shane. 2nd rev. ed. 2003. 24p. (J). lib. bdg. 12.99 *(978-0-9678167-6-0(9))* Bookaroos Publishing, Inc.

—Polliwog. Bronson, Tammy Carter. 2006. (ENG & SPA.). (J). 7.99 *(978-0-9678167-5-3(0))* Bookaroos Publishing, Inc.

—Polliwog. Bronson, Tammy Carter. Davi, Annou, tr. 2004. (SPA & ENG.). 32p. (J). lib. bdg. 17.00 *(978-0-9678167-4-6(2))* Bookaroos Publishing, Inc.

Bronson, Wilfrid S. Cats. 2008. 84p. (J). per. 18.95 *(978-0-86534-645-1(3))* Sunstone Pr.

—The Grasshopper Book. 2009. 136p. (J). pap. 22.95 *(978-0-86534-690-1(9))* Sunstone Pr.

—Starlings. 2008. 84p. (J). pap. 18.95 *(978-0-86534-649-9(6))* Sunstone Pr.

—Stooping Hawk & Stranded Whale, Sons of Liberty. 2009. 236p. (J). pap. 22.95 *(978-0-86534-715-1(8))* Sunstone Pr.

—Turtles. 2008. 68p. (J). pap. 18.95 *(978-0-86534-651-2(8))* Sunstone Pr.

—The Wonder World of Ants. 2009. 96p. (J). pap. 19.95 *(978-0-86534-691-8(7))* Sunstone Pr.

Bronte, Jules & Oapos, Jem. The Castle Adventure. 2013. 171p. pap. *(978-1-908804-08-2(4))* Bingham Mayne & Smith, Ltd.

Brooke, Iris. A Pageant of Kings & Queens. Matthews, C. M. et al. 2011. (ENG.). 98p. pap. 22.99 *(978-0-521-23596-9(0))* Cambridge Univ. Pr.

Brooke, Janet. Mishan's Garden. Vollbracht, James. 2013. (ENG.). 32p. (J). (gr. k-9). 16.95 *(978-1-61429-112-1(8))* Wisdom Pubns.

—Prince Siddhartha: The Story of Buddha. Landaw, Jonathan. 2nd rev. ed. 2011. (ENG.). 144p. (J). (gr. 2-7). pap. 19.95 *(978-0-86171-653-1(1))* Wisdom Pubns.

Brooke, L. Leslie. Ring o' Roses, a Nursery Rhyme Picture Book. Brooke, L. Leslie. 2012. 102p. pap. 9.99 *(978-1-61720-438-8(2))* Wilder Pubns., Corp.

Brooker, Jo. Angry, 1 vol. Medina, Sarah. 2007. (Feelings Ser.). (ENG.). 24p. (gr. -1-3). 6.79 *(978-1-4034-9298-2(0)*, Heinemann Read & Learn) Heinemann-Raintree.

—Brave, 1 vol. Medina, Sarah. 2007. (Feelings Ser.). (ENG.). 24p. (gr. -1-3). pap. 6.79 *(978-1-4034-9798-7(2)*, Heinemann Read & Learn) Heinemann-Raintree.

—Jealous (Al Gheera) Medina, Sarah. Mohamed Mahmoud, Ghada, tr. 2012. (ENG & ARA.). 24p. (J). pap. 6.99 *(978-99921-94-16-4(2)*, 148144) Bloomsbury USA.

—Lonely, 1 vol. Medina, Sarah. 2007. (Feelings Ser.). (ENG.). 24p. (gr. -1-3). pap. 6.79 *(978-1-4034-9801-4(6)*, Heinemann Read & Learn) Heinemann-Raintree.

—Proud, 1 vol. Medina, Sarah. 2007. (Feelings Ser.). (ENG.). 24p. (gr. -1-k). 6.79 *(978-1-4034-9303-3(0)*, Heinemann Read & Learn) Heinemann-Raintree.

—Proud (Fakhr) Medina, Sarah. Mohamed Mahmoud, Ghada, tr. 2012. (ENG & ARA.). 24p. (J). pap. 6.99 *(978-99921-94-18-8(9)*, 161088) Bloomsbury USA.

—Sad (Al Hozn) Medina, Sarah. Mahmoud, Ghada Mohamed, tr. 2012. (ENG & ARA.). 24p. (J). pap. 6.99 *(978-99921-94-15-7(4)*, 148149) Bloomsbury USA.

—Worried, 1 vol. Medina, Sarah. 2007. (Feelings Ser.). (ENG.). 24p. (gr. -1-3). pap. 6.79 *(978-1-4034-9803-8(2)*, Heinemann Read & Learn) Heinemann-Raintree.

Brooker, Jo. Bondad, 1 vol. Brooker, Jo. Medina, Sarah. 2007. (Sentimientos Ser.). (SPA.). 24p. pap. 6.79 *(978-1-4329-0619-1(4)*, Heinemann Lee y aprende) Heinemann-Raintree.

—Celos, 1 vol. Brooker, Jo. Medina, Sarah. 2007. (Sentimientos Ser.). (SPA.). 24p. pap. 6.79 *(978-1-4329-0618-4(6)*, Heinemann Lee y aprende) Heinemann-Raintree.

—Enojo, 1 vol. Brooker, Jo. Medina, Sarah. 2007. (Sentimientos Ser.). (SPA.). 24p. pap. 6.79 *(978-1-4329-0615-3(1)*, Heinemann Lee y aprende) Heinemann-Raintree.

—Felicidad, 1 vol. Brooker, Jo. Medina, Sarah. 2007. (Sentimientos Ser.). (SPA.). 24p. pap. 6.79 *(978-1-4329-0616-0(X)*, Heinemann Lee y aprende) Heinemann-Raintree.

—Impaciencia, 1 vol. Brooker, Jo. Medina, Sarah. 2008. (Sentimientos Ser.). (SPA & ENG.). 24p. pap. 6.79 *(978-1-4329-0639-9(9)*, Heinemann Lee y aprende) Heinemann-Raintree.

—Preocupación. Brooker, Jo. Medina, Sarah. 2008. (Sentimientos Ser.). (SPA & ENG.). 24p. pap. 6.79 *(978-1-4329-0642-9(9)*, Heinemann Lee y aprende) Heinemann-Raintree.

—Soledad, 1 vol. Brooker, Jo. Medina, Sarah. 2008. (Sentimientos Ser.). (SPA & ENG.). 24p. pap. 6.79 *(978-1-4329-0640-5(2)*, Heinemann Lee y aprende) Heinemann-Raintree.

—Timidez, 1 vol. Brooker, Jo. Medina, Sarah. 2008. (Sentimientos Ser.). (SPA & ENG.). 24p. pap. 6.79 *(978-1-4329-0641-2(0)*, Heinemann Lee y aprende) Heinemann-Raintree.

—Tristeza, 1 vol. Brooker, Jo. Medina, Sarah. 2007. (Sentimientos Ser.). (SPA.). 24p. pap. 6.79 *(978-1-4329-0617-7(8)*, Heinemann Lee y aprende) Heinemann-Raintree.

—Valentía, 1 vol. Brooker, Jo. Medina, Sarah. 2008. (Sentimientos Ser.). (SPA & ENG.). 24p. pap. 6.79 *(978-1-4329-0637-5(2)*, Heinemann Lee y aprende) Heinemann-Raintree.

Brooker, Kyrsten. Chik Chak Shabbat. Rockliff, Mara. 2014. (ENG.). 32p. (J). (gr. -1-2). 15.99 *(978-0-7636-5528-0(7))* Candlewick Pr.

—Dinner with the Highbrows. Holt, Kimberly Willis. 2014. (ENG.). 36p. (J). (gr. -1-2). 17.99 *(978-0-8050-8088-9(0)*, Holt, Henry & Co. Bks. For Young Readers) Holt, Henry & Co.

—The Honeybee Man. Nargi, Lela. 2011. (ENG.). 40p. (J). (gr. -1-3). 17.99 *(978-0-375-84980-0(7)*, Schwartz & Wade Bks.) Random Hse. Children's Bks.

—Nothing Ever Happens on 90th Street. Schotter, Roni. 2014. 32p. pap. 7.00 *(978-1-61003-316-9(7))* Center for the Collaborative Classroom.

—Precious & the Boo Hag. McKissack, Patricia C. & Moss, Onawumi Jean. 2005. (ENG.). 40p. (J). (gr. -1-3). 17.99 *(978-0-689-85194-0(4)*, Atheneum Bks. for Young Readers) Simon & Schuster Children's Publishing.

—Tadeo's Search for Circles, 1 vol. Brooker, Marion. 2011. (ENG.). 32p. (J). 18.95 *(978-1-55455-173-6(0))* Fitzhenry & Whiteside, Ltd. CAN. Dist: Midpoint Trade Bks., Inc.

—They Saw the Future: Oracles, Psychics, Scientists, Great Thinkers, & Pretty Good Guessers. Krull, Kathleen. 2014. (ENG.). 112p. (J). (gr. -1-3). pap. 45.99 *(978-1-4814-3623-5(6)*, Atheneum Bks. for Young Readers) Simon & Schuster Children's Publishing.

—When We Go Walking, 0 vols. Best, Cari. 2013. (ENG.). (J). (gr. -1-3). 17.99 *(978-1-4778-1648-6(8)*, 9781477816486, Amazon Children's Publishing) Amazon Publishing.

Brookfield, Maureen. E Is for Empire: A New York State Alphabet. Burg, Ann. 2003. (Discover America State by State Ser.). (ENG.). 40p. (J). 17.95 *(978-1-58536-113-7(5))* Sleeping Bear Pr.

—N Is for Nutmeg: A Connecticut Alphabet. Elissa, Grodin. 2003. (Discover America State by State Ser.). (ENG.). 40p. (J). 17.95 *(978-1-58536-124-3(0))* Sleeping Bear Pr.

Brookfield, Maureen K. Times Square: A New York State Number Book. Burg, Ann E. 2005. (Count Your Way Across the USA Ser.). (ENG.). 40p. (J). (gr. k-6). 16.95 *(978-1-58536-195-3(X))* Sleeping Bear Pr.

—Yankee Doodle Numbers: A Connecticut Number Book. Grodin, Elissa D. rev. ed. 2007. (Count Your Way Across the U. S. A. Ser.). (ENG.). 40p. (J). (gr. 3-7). 17.95 *(978-1-58536-175-5(5))* Sleeping Bear Pr.

Brooks, Brian. Oopsy Daisy's Bad Day. Brooks, Brian. 2007. 62p. (J). reprint ed. 13.00 *(978-1-4223-9004-7(7))* DIANE Publishing Co.

Brooks, Brian, jt. illus. see Reger, Rob.

Brooks, David. A Is for Airplane. Howell, Theresa. 2003. (SPA, ENG & MUL.). 28p. (J). (gr. -1-k). 6.95 *(978-0-87358-831-7(2))* Cooper Square Publishing Llc.

—All Around Cats, , Viscardi, Dolly. 2004. (ENG.). 32p. (J). (gr. k-3). 15.95 *(978-1-55971-072-5(1))* Cooper Square Publishing Llc.

—Animals. 2005. (My First Book Ser.). 9p. (J). (gr. -1-1). bds. 3.95 *(978-1-933050-09-6(8))* Sweetwater Pr.

—Awesome Animals ABC. Biskup, Agnieszka. 2005. (J). *(978-1-58987-095-6(6))* Kindermusik International.

—Mi Primer Libro Alfabeto. Alvarez, Lourdes M. 2005. (Mi primer libro Ser.). (SPA.). 9p. (J). (gr. -1 — 1). bds. 3.95 *(978-1-933050-02-7(0))* Sweetwater Pr.

—Mi Primer Libro Animales. Alvarez, Lourdes M. 2005. (Mi primer libro Ser.). (SPA.). 9p. (J). (gr. -1 — 1). bds. 3.95 *(978-1-933050-04-1(7))* Sweetwater Pr.

—Mi Primer Libro Cosas. Alvarez, Lourdes M. 2005. (Mi primer libro Ser.). (SPA.). 9p. (J). (gr. -1 — 1). bds. 3.95 *(978-1-933050-03-4(9))* Sweetwater Pr.

—Mi Primer Libro Formas. Alvarez, Lourdes M. 2005. (Mi primer libro Ser.). (SPA.). 9p. (J). (gr. -1 — 1). bds. 3.95 *(978-1-933050-05-8(5))* Sweetwater Pr.

—Mi Primer Libro Numeros. Alvarez, Lourdes M. 2005. (Mi primer libro Ser.). (SPA.). 9p. (J). (gr. -1 — 1). bds. 3.95 *(978-1-933050-00-3(4))* Sweetwater Pr.

—Mountain Pine Beetle. Turnbaugh, Kay. 2011. (Pruett Ser.). (ENG.). 48p. (J). pap. 14.95 *(978-0-87108-958-8(0))* Pruett Publishing Co.

—My First Book Alphabet. Alvarez, Lourdes M. 2005. (My First Book Ser.). 9p. (J). (gr. -1-17). bds. 3.95 *(978-1-933050-08-9(X))* Sweetwater Pr.

—My First Book Colors. Alvarez, Lourdes M. 2005. (My First Book Ser.). 9p. (J). (gr. -1-1). bds. 3.95 *(978-1-933050-07-2(1))* Sweetwater Pr.

—My First Book Numbers. Alvarez, Lourdes M. 2005. (My First Book Ser.). 9p. (J). (gr. -1-1). bds. 3.95 *(978-1-933050-06-5(3))* Sweetwater Pr.

—My First Book Shapes. Alvarez, Lourdes M. 2005. (My First Book Ser.). 9p. (J). (gr. -1-1). bds. 3.95 *(978-1-933050-11-9(X))* Sweetwater Pr.

—My First Book Things. Alvarez, Lourdes M. 2005. (My First Book Ser.). 9p. (J). (gr. -1-1). bds. 3.95 *(978-1-933050-10-2(1))* Sweetwater Pr.

B

Brooks, David. You Can Count at the Lake. Brooks, David. 2005. (You Can Count Ser.). (ENG.). 24p. (J). (gr. -1 — 1). 6.95 *(978-1-55971-909-4(5))* Cooper Square Publishing Llc.
—You Can Count in the Desert. Brooks, David. 2005. (You Can Count Ser.). (ENG.). 24p. (J). (gr. -1 — 1). 7.95 *(978-1-55971-910-0(9))* Cooper Square Publishing Llc.
Brooks, Dominic. Is It My Turn Yet? 2008. 30p. (J). per. *(978-0-9795768-2-9(2))* Better Tomorrow Publishing, A.
Brooks, Elizabeth, et al. How to Make Historic American Costumes. Evans, Mary & Landes, William-Alan. rev. ed. 2003. 180p. (J). (gr. 8-12). pap. 22.00 *(978-0-88734-636-1(7))* Players Pr., Inc.
Brooks, Erik. Boo's Surprise. Byars, Betsy. 2009. (Boo's Dinosaur Ser.). (ENG.). 48p. (J). (gr. 1-4). 15.99 *(978-0-8050-8817-5(2))*, Holt, Henry & Co. Bks. For Young Readers) Holt, Henry & Co.
—Cat Diaries: Secret Writings of the MEOW Society. Byars, Betsy et al. 2010. (ENG.). 80p. (J). (gr. 2-5). 16.99 *(978-0-8050-8717-8(6))*, Holt, Henry & Co. Bks. For Young Readers) Holt, Henry & Co.
—Dog Diaries: Secret Writings of the WOOF Society. Byars, Betsy et al. 2007. (ENG.). 80p. (J). (gr. 3-7). 16.95 *(978-0-8050-7957-9(2))*, Holt, Henry & Co. Bks. For Young Readers) Holt, Henry & Co.
—Polar Polka: Counting Polar Bears in Alaska. Stihler, Cherie B. 2008. (ENG.). 32p. (J). (gr. -1-2). pap. 10.95 *(978-1-57061-520-7(9))* Sasquatch Bks.
Brooks, Erik. The Runaway Tortilla. Kimmel, Eric. 2015. (ENG.). 32p. (J). 16.99 ***(978-1-941821-69-5(3)***, West Winds Pr.) Graphic Arts Ctr. Publishing Co.
Brooks, Erik. Sea Star Wishes: Poems from the Coast. Ode, Eric. 2013. (ENG.). 32p. (J). (gr. -1-3). 16.99 *(978-1-57061-790-4(2))* Sasquatch Bks.
—Totem Tale: A Tall Story from Alaska. Vanasse, Deb. 2006. (Paws IV Ser.). (ENG.). 32p. (J). (gr. -1-2). pap. 10.99 *(978-1-57061-439-2(3))* Sasquatch Bks.
—What Are You Hungry For? Feed Your Tummy & Your Heart. Aronson, Emme & Aronson, Phillip. 2007. 32p. (J). (gr. -1-3). lib. bdg. 16.89 *(978-0-06-054308-2(6))* HarperCollins Pubs.
—Who Has These Feet? Hulbert, Laura. 2011. (ENG.). 44p. (J). (gr. -1-2). 16.99 *(978-0-8050-8907-3(1))*, Holt, Henry & Co. Bks. For Young Readers) Holt, Henry & Co.
—Who Has This Tail? Hulbert, Laura. 2012. (ENG.). 40p. (J). (gr. -1-2). 17.99 *(978-0-8050-9429-9(6))*, Holt, Henry & Co. Bks. For Young Readers) Holt, Henry & Co.
Brooks, Erik, jt. illus. see Palmisciano, Diane.
Brooks, Kaarina. Peikko, the Foolish Ogre. Brooks, Kaarina, tr. 2003. (Aspasia Children's Bks.). (ENG.). 61p. pap. 12.00 *(978-0-9731053-2-2(1))* Aspasia Bks. CAN. Dist: Univ. of Toronto Pr.
Brooks, Karen Stormer. Dan the Ant. Gillis, Jennifer Blizin. 2006. (Reader's Clubhouse Level 1 Reader Ser.). (ENG.). 24p. (J). (gr. 1-4). pap. 4.99 *(978-0-7641-3282-7(2))* Barron's Educational Series, Inc.
—The Magic Box: When Parents Can't Be There to Tuck You In. Sederman, Marty & Epstein, Seymour. 2003. 32p. (J). (gr. -1-3). 14.95 *(978-1-55798-807-2(2)*, Magination Pr.) American Psychological Assn.
—Sister for Sale!, 1 vol. Adams, Michelle Medlock & Adams, Michelle M. 2007. (I Can Read! Ser.). (ENG.). 32p. (J). (gr. -1-1). pap. 3.99 *(978-0-310-71469-9(9))* Zonderkidz.
Brooks, Katie. The Tale of Little Fanny Flip-Flop. Miller, R. L. 2014. (ENG.). 24p. (J). pap. 8.99 *(978-1-62994-698-6(2))* Tate Publishing & Enterprises, LLC.
Brooks, Mark. Thor: The World Eaters. 2011. (ENG.). 216p. (YA). (gr. 8-17). pap. 19.99 *(978-0-7851-4839-5(6))* Marvel Worldwide, Inc.
Brooks, Mark & Zircher, Patrick. If Looks Could Kill, Vol. 1. Youngquist, Jeff, ed. 2007. (ENG.). 136p. (YA). (gr. 8-17). pap. 14.99 *(978-0-7851-1374-4(6))* Marvel Worldwide, Inc.
Brooks, Mark, jt. illus. see Epting, Steve.
Brooks, Nan. The Ball Book. Hillert, Margaret. rev. ed. 2006. (Beginning to Read Ser.). 32p. (J). (gr. -1-3). lib. bdg. 19.93 *(978-1-59953-031-4(7))* Norwood Hse. Pr.
—The Little Reindeer. Tyrell, Melissa. enl. ed. 2005. (ENG.). 10p. (J). (gr. -1-3). 4.95 *(978-1-58117-119-8(6)*, Intervisual/Piggy Toes) Bendon, Inc.
—Make New Friends. Schwaeber, Barbie. (American Favorites Ser.). (ENG.). 32p. (J). (gr. -1-3). 2008. 14.95 *(978-1-59249-728-7(4))*; 2007. 8.95 *(978-1-59249-729-4(2))* Soundprints.
—Make New Friends. Soundprints Staff. Schwaeber, Barbie Heit & Williams, Tracee, eds. 2008. (ENG.). 24p. (J). (gr. -1). 4.99 *(978-1-59069-651-4(4))* Studio Mouse LLC.
—Making Minestrone. Blackstone, Stella. 2006. 32p. (J). (gr. k-4). reprint ed. 16.00 *(978-0-7567-9926-7(0))* DIANE Publishing Co.
—This Little Piggy. 2004. (J). 11.99 *(978-1-890647-10-0(1))* TOMY International, Inc.
—Who Goes to School? Hillert, Margaret. rev. ed. 2006. (Beginning to Read Ser.). 32p. (J). (gr. -1-3). lib. bdg. 19.93 *(978-1-59953-032-1(5))* Norwood Hse. Pr.
Brooks, Nan & Grayson, Rick. Science Tub Topics: Approaching Science Through Discovery. Morton, Debra & Stover, Elizabeth. Jennett, Pamela, ed. 2003. 128p. (J). (gr. k-3). pap. 13.99 *(978-1-57471-953-6(X)*, 2811) Creative Teaching Pr., Inc.
Brooks, Ron. The Dream of the Thylacine. Wild, Margaret. 2013. (ENG.). 32p. (J). (gr. 3-5). 23.99 *(978-1-74237-383-6(6))* Allen & Unwin AUS. Dist: Independent Pubs. Group.
—Fox. Wild, Margaret. 2006. (ENG.). 32p. (J). (gr. 1). pap. 7.99 *(978-1-933605-15-9(4))* Kane Miller.
—On the Day You Were Born. Wild, Margaret. 2014. (ENG.). 24p. (J). (— 1). 15.99 *(978-1-74114-754-4(9))* Allen & Unwin AUS. Dist: Independent Pubs. Group.
Brooks, Rosie, jt. illus. see Phillips, Mike.
Brooks, S. G. Flour Girl: A Recipe for Disaster. Slater, David Michael. 2007. (Missy Swiss & More Ser.). 32p. (gr. -1-4). 28.50 *(978-1-60270-009-3(5)*, Looking Glass Library) ABDO Publishing Co.
—Ned Breaks His Heart. Slater, David Michael. 2009. (David Michael Slater Set 2 Ser.). 32p. (gr. -1-4). 28.50 *(978-1-60270-657-6(3)*, Looking Glass Library) ABDO Publishing Co.
—Ned's Nose Is Running. Slater, David Michael. 2009. (David Michael Slater Set 2 Ser.). 32p. (gr. -1-4). 28.50 *(978-1-60270-658-3(1)*, Looking Glass Library) ABDO Publishing Co.
—Three Armadillies Tuff, 1 vol. Hopkins, Jackie Mims. 2011. (ENG.). 32p. pap. 7.95 *(978-1-56145-598-0(9)*, Peachtree Junior) Peachtree Pubs.
—Westley the Wicked & the Rascally Ring Bear. Slater, David Michael. 2012. 36p. pap. 10.95 *(978-1-61413-028-4(0))* Puddletown Publishing Group, Inc.
Brooksbank, Angela. My Busy Patterns. ed. 2008. (ENG.). 10p. (J). (gr. -1-2). bds. 11.95 *(978-0-230-52909-0(7)*, Macmillan) Pan Macmillan GBR. Dist: Trans-Atlantic Pubns., Inc.
Brookshire, Breezy. For Such a Time As This: Stories of Women from the Bible, Retold for Girls. Smith, Angie. 2014. (ENG.). 256p. (J). (gr. 1-5). 14.99 *(978-1-4336-8046-5(7)*, B&H Kids) B&H Publishing Group.
Broome, Mat. The Prophet's Oracle, 1 vol. Avery, Ben. 2008. (Z Graphic Novels / Kingdoms: a Biblical Epic Ser.). (ENG.). 160p. (YA). (gr. 8-11). pap. 6.99 *(978-0-310-71355-5(2))* Zondervan.
Broome, Shannon. I'm Thinking... My Brain Is a Pain: But Then, Maybe I Should Think Again! Miller, Sue. 2011. (ENG.). 34p. pap. 17.95 *(978-1-4564-1451-1(8))* CreateSpace Independent Publishing Platform.
Brophy, Brian, photos by. From My Eyes: Life from a Ten Year Old Boy's Perspective. Brophy, Brian. Brophy, Doris, ed. 2003. per. *(978-0-9745232-0-0(8))* Brophy, Doris Anne.
Brosgol, Vera. Anya's Ghost. Brosgol, Vera. 2011. (ENG.). 224p. (YA). (gr. 7-12). 21.99 *(978-1-59643-713-5(8))*; pap. 15.99 *(978-1-59643-552-0(6))* Roaring Brook Pr. (First Second Bks.).
—Anya's Ghost. Brosgol, Vera. 2014. (ENG.). 240p. (YA). (gr. 7). pap. 9.99 *(978-1-250-04001-5(9))* Square Fish.
Brosseau, Pat, jt. illus. see McCaig, Dave.
Brough, Hazel. The Charm of the Bearclaw Necklace. Searcy, Margaret Zehmer. 80p. (J). (gr. 3-7). pap. 7.95 *(978-1-56554-777-3(2))* Pelican Publishing Co., Inc.
Brough, Karen. Lighting the Earth. Hoffman, Diana / Lynne. 2014. 34p. (J). 23.95 ***(978-0-9891296-4-0(0)***, Aurora Books) Eco-Justice Pr., LLC.
Brougham, Jason. Inside Dinosaurs. American Museum of Natural History Staff et al. 2010. (Inside Ser.). (ENG.). 48p. (J). (gr. 4-6). 16.95 *(978-1-4027-7074-6(X))* Sterling Publishing Co., Inc.
Broughton, Ilona & Szijgyarto, Cynthia. Goats in Coats. Nagy, Jennifer. 2009. 20p. pap. 12.99 *(978-1-4389-6586-4(9))* AuthorHouse.
Brouillard, Anne. The Bathtub Prima Donna. Brouillard, Anne. 2004. 24p. (J). (gr. k-4). reprint ed. 13.00 *(978-0-7567-7755-5(0))* DIANE Publishing Co.
Broutin, Chistian. Trees. 2012. (ENG.). 38p. (J). (gr. -1-k). 12.99 *(978-1-85103-401-7(3))* Moonlight Publishing, Ltd. GBR. Dist: Independent Pubs. Group.
Broutin, Christian. In the Jungle. Broutin, Christian. 2013. (ENG.). 36p. (J). (gr. -1-k). 12.99 *(978-1-85103-417-8(X))* Moonlight Publishing, Ltd. GBR. Dist: Independent Pubs. Group.
—Let's Look at the Jungle. Broutin, Christian. Delafosse, Claude. 2012. (ENG.). 38p. (J). (gr. k-3). pap. 11.99 *(978-1-85103-332-4(7))* Moonlight Publishing, Ltd. GBR. Dist: Independent Pubs. Group.
—The Town. Broutin, Christian. 2012. (ENG.). 36p. (J). (gr. -1-k). 12.99 *(978-1-85103-395-9(5))* Moonlight Publishing, Ltd. GBR. Dist: Independent Pubs. Group.
—Tree. Broutin, Christian. 2006. (ENG & FRE.). 38p. (J). (gr. k-3). pap. 11.99 *(978-1-85103-087-3(5))* Moonlight Publishing, Ltd. GBR. Dist: Independent Pubs. Group.
Brouwer, Aafke. Ginny's Egg. Goodhart, Pippa. 142p. (J). pap. 7.50 *(978-0-7497-4557-8(6))* Egmont Bks., Ltd. GBR. Dist: Trafalgar Square Publishing.
Brower, William. Why be Normal? From Soup to Nuts, Mostly Nuts. Puscheck, Herbert Charles. 2005. 212p. (YA). per. 12.95 *(978-0-9707976-1-2(3))* Rose River Publishing Co.
Brown, Alan, et al. Bravest Warriors: the Search for Catbug. Enos, Joel, ed. 2014. (Bravest Warriors Ser.). (ENG.). 64p. (J). 14.99 *(978-1-4215-7177-5(3))* Viz Media.
Brown, Alan. Ghost Ship. Levine, Cory. 2013. (Ben 10 Ser.: 1). (ENG.). 64p. (J). pap. 7.99 *(978-1-4215-5741-0(X))* Viz Media.
—Parallel Paradox. Enos, Joel. 2014. (Ben 10 Ser.: 3). (ENG.). 64p. (J). pap. 7.99 *(978-1-4215-5743-4(6))* Viz Media.
Brown, Alison. I Love You Night & Day. Prasadam-Halls, Smriti. 2014. (ENG.). 32p. (J). (gr. -1-1). 16.99 *(978-1-61963-222-6(5)*, Bloomsbury USA Childrens) Bloomsbury USA.
Brown, Alison. Snowy Bear. Mitton, Tony. 2015. (ENG.). 32p. (J). (gr. -1-1). 16.99 ***(978-1-61963-905-8(X)***, Bloomsbury USA Childrens) Bloomsbury USA.
Brown, Amanda, jt. illus. see Ambler, Laura.
Brown, Anna. Love Is Real. Lawler, Janet. 2013. (ENG.). 32p. (J). (gr. -1-3). 15.99 *(978-0-06-224170-2(2))* HarperCollins Pubs.
Brown, Bill. Violet Makes a Splash. Mazer, Anne. 2007. (Sister Magic Ser.: 2). (ENG.). 96p. (J). (gr. 2-5). 4.99 *(978-0-439-87247-8(2))* Scholastic, Inc.
Brown, Bobby. A Midnight's Lullaby: Volume One. Hogan, Micki. 2011. 40p. pap. 24.95 *(978-1-4560-2090-3(0))* America Star Bks.
Brown, Brenda. The Pocket Guide to Mischief. King, Bart. 2008. (ENG.). 208p. (gr. 5-6). pap. 9.99 *(978-1-4236-0366-5(4))* Gibbs Smith, Publisher.
—Worst-Case Scenario Survival Handbook: College. Piven, Joshua et al. 2004. (Worst Case Scenario Ser.: WORS). (ENG.). 176p. (gr. 8-17). pap. 14.95 *(978-0-8118-4230-3(4))* Chronicle Bks. LLC.
Brown, Brett T. Haley's Comet. Brown, Brett T. Holloway, Julie M. 2013. 214p. pap. 15.00 *(978-1-62407-911-5(3))* PlatyPr.
Brown, Calef. Dragon, Robot, Gatorbunny: Pick one. Draw it. Make it Funny. 2012. (ENG.). 160p. (J). (gr. k-17). 14.99 *(978-1-4521-0364-8(X))* Chronicle Bks. LLC.
—Gertrude Is Gertrude Is Gertrude Is Gertrude. Winter, Jonah. 2009. (ENG.). 40p. (J). (gr. -1-3). 16.99 *(978-1-4169-4088-3(X)*, Atheneum Bks. for Young Readers) Simon & Schuster Children's Publishing.
—The Neddiad: How Neddie Took the Train, Went to Hollywood, & Saved Civilization. Pinkwater, Daniel M. 2009. (ENG.). 320p. (J). (gr. 5-7). pap. 7.99 *(978-0-547-13367-6(7))* Houghton Mifflin Harcourt Publishing Co.
—Pop-Up Aesop. Harris, John. 2005. (ENG.). 10p. (gr. -1-7). 19.95 *(978-0-89236-814-3(4))* Oxford Univ. Pr., Inc.
Brown, Calef. Boy Wonders. Brown, Calef. 2011. (ENG.). 40p. (J). (gr. -1-3). 16.99 *(978-1-4169-7877-0(1)*, Atheneum Bks. for Young Readers) Simon & Schuster Children's Publishing.
—Hypnotize a Tiger: Poems about Just about Everything. Brown, Calef. 2015. (ENG.). 144p. (J). (gr. 3-7). 17.99 *(978-0-8050-9928-7(X)*, Holt, Henry & Co. Bks. For Young Readers) Holt, Henry & Co.
—Pirateria: The Wonderful Plunderful Pirate Emporium. Brown, Calef. 2012. (ENG.). 40p. (J). (gr. -1-3). 16.99 *(978-1-4169-7878-7(X)*, Atheneum Bks. for Young Readers) Simon & Schuster Children's Publishing.
Brown, Chris. Chief Hawah's Book of Native American Indians. 2006. (ENG.). 32p. (J). (gr. -1-3). 14.99 *(978-0-7145-3308-7(4))* Boyars, Marion Pubs., Inc.
Brown, Chris L. My Aunt & Me. Parker, Ms. Alichia R. 2013. 24p. pap. 9.99 *(978-0-578-12712-5(1))* A PAR Educational, LLC.
Brown, Clovis. Anancy & Friends: A Grandmother's Anancy Stories for Her Grandchildren. Richmond, Beulah. 2004. (ENG.). 52p. pap. 5.99 *(978-976-8184-48-1(5))* Penguin Publishing Group.
—Naughty Eddie Larue. Wohlt, Julia. 27p. *(978-976-610-173-2(6))* Creative Links.
Brown, Craig. Mule Train Mail. Brown, Craig. 2009. (ENG.). 36p. (J). (gr. -1-3). pap. 7.95 *(978-1-58089-188-2(8))* Charlesbridge Publishing, Inc.
Brown, Craig McFarland & Astrella, Mark. How Do You Raise a Raisin? Ryan, Pam Muñoz. 2003. (ENG.). 32p. (J). (gr. k-3). pap. 7.95 *(978-1-57091-398-3(6))* Charlesbridge Publishing, Inc.
Brown, Dan. Books for Oliver. Larkin, Jim & Rambo, Lee Elliot. 2006. (J). *(978-1-59336-336-9(2))*; pap. *(978-1-59336-337-6(0))* Mondo Publishing.
—Impatient Pamela Asks: Why Are My Feet So Huge? Koski, Mary B. 2003. (Impatient Pamela Ser.). 32p. (J). (gr. -1-3). pap. 4.95 *(978-1-930650-02-2(7))* mTrellis Publishing, Inc.
—Impatient Pamela Calls 9-1-1. Koski, Mary B. (Impatient Pamela Ser.). 32p. (J). 2003. (gr. -1-3). 15.95 *(978-0-9663281-9-6(1))*; 2nd ed. 2004. (ENG.). (gr. 1-3). 14.95 *(978-1-930650-09-1(4))* mTrellis Publishing, Inc.
—I've Been Working on the Railroad. Galvin, Laura Gates. 2008. (ENG.). 32p. (J). (gr. k-2). 14.95 *(978-1-59249-771-3(3))*; 8.95 *(978-1-59249-772-0(1))* Soundprints.
—Learn to Call 911. Collins, Lori & Koski, Mary. 2007. (ENG.). 16p. (J). (gr. k-2). pap. 2.95 *(978-1-930650-05-3(1))* mTrellis Publishing, Inc.
—A Picture Book of George Washington Carver. Adler, David A. 2008. (Picture Book Biography Ser.). (J). (gr. -1-2). 28.95 incl. audio compact disk *(978-1-4301-0348-6(5))* Live Oak Media.
—A Picture Book of Sacagawea. Adler, David A. 2005. (ENG.). 32p. (J). (gr. k-3). 7.99 *(978-0-8234-1665-3(8))* Holiday Hse., Inc.
Brown, Daniel J. Billy Brown's Cat, 1 vol. Pulford, Elizabeth. 2012. (Engage Literacy Green Ser.). (ENG.). 32p. (gr. k-2). pap. 5.99 *(978-1-4296-8838-3(6)*, Engage Literacy) Capstone Pr., Inc.
Brown, Dennis L. A Gullah Alphabet. Clary, Margie Willis. 2007. (J). *(978-0-87844-184-6(0))* Sandlapper Publishing Co., Inc.
Brown, Don. A Kid's Guide to Chicago. Bartlett, Karen T. 2010. 64p. pap. 16.95 *(978-1-934907-03-0(0))* Twin Lights Pubs., Inc.
Brown, Don. All Stations! Distress! April 15, 1912 - The Day the Titanic Sank. Brown, Don. 2008. (Actual Times Ser.: 2). (ENG.). 64p. (J). (gr. 1-5). 17.99 *(978-1-59643-222-2(5))* Roaring Brook Pr.
—All Stations! Distress! April 15, 1912: the Day the Titanic Sank. Brown, Don. 2010. (Actual Times Ser.: 2). (ENG.). 64p. (J). (gr. 1-5). pap. 8.99 *(978-1-59643-644-2(1))* Square Fish.
—Dolley Madison Saves George Washington. Brown, Don. 2007. (ENG.). 32p. (J). (gr. -1-3). 16.00 *(978-0-618-41199-3(2))* Houghton Mifflin Harcourt Publishing Co.
—Gold! Gold from the American River! January 24 1848 - The Day the Gold Rush Began. Brown, Don. 2011. (Actual Times Ser.: 3). (ENG.). 64p. (J). (gr. 1-5). 17.99 *(978-1-59643-223-9(3))* Roaring Brook Pr.
—Gold! Gold from the American River! January 24, 1848: the Day the Gold Rush Began. Brown, Don. 2014. (Actual Times Ser.: 3). (ENG.). 64p. (J). (gr. 1-5). 8.99 *(978-1-250-04060-2(4))* Square Fish.
—The Great American Dust Bowl. Brown, Don. 2013. (ENG.). 80p. (J). (gr. 7). 18.99 *(978-0-547-81550-3(6))* Houghton Mifflin Harcourt Publishing Co.
—He Has Shot the President! April 14, 1865: the Day John Wilkes Booth Killed President Lincoln. Brown, Don. 2014. (Actual Times Ser.: 5). (ENG.). 64p. (J). (gr. 1-5). 17.99 *(978-1-59643-224-6(1))* Roaring Brook Pr.
—Let It Begin Here! The Day the American Revolution Began April 19, 1775. Brown, Don. 2010. (Actual Times Ser.: 1). (ENG.). 64p. (J). (gr. 1-5). pap. 9.99 *(978-1-59643-645-9(X))* Roaring Brook Pr.
—Mack Made Movies. Brown, Don. 2008. (J). (gr. 2-5). 25.95 incl. audio compact disk *(978-1-4301-0432-2(5))*; pap. 16.95 incl. audio *(978-1-4301-0431-5(7))*; pap. 39.95 incl. audio compact disk *(978-1-4301-0436-0(8))*;Set. pap. 37.95 incl. audio *(978-1-4301-0433-9(3))* Live Oak Media.
—A Wizard from the Start: The Incredible Boyhood & Amazing Inventions of Thomas Edison. Brown, Don. 2010. (ENG.). 32p. (J). (gr. -1-3). 17.99 *(978-0-547-19487-5(0))* Houghton Mifflin Harcourt Publishing Co.
Brown, Dwayne. Amy Goes Surfing. Labossiere, Julie. l.t. ed. 2010. (ENG.). 42p. pap. 10.00 *(978-1-4528-4278-3(7))* CreateSpace Independent Publishing Platform.
—Amy Plays the Violin. Labossiere, Julie. 2011. (ENG.). 26p. pap. 10.00 *(978-1-4537-9995-6(8))* CreateSpace Independent Publishing Platform.
—Amy Volunteers. Labossiere, Julie. l.t. ed. 2011. (ENG.). 34p. pap. 10.00 *(978-1-4537-9998-7(2))* CreateSpace Independent Publishing Platform.
Brown, E. Jackie. The Adventures of Fujimori-San. Kline, Spencer. 2010. 20p. 12.99 *(978-1-4520-6275-4(7))* AuthorHouse.
Brown, Elbrite. Cinnamon Brown & the Seven Dwarfs. Jackson, Ellen B. 2006. (J). *(978-0-670-06106-8(9)*, Viking Adult) Penguin Publishing Group.
—Playing to Win: The Story of Althea Gibson. Deans, Karen. 2007. (ENG.). 32p. (J). (gr. -1-3). 16.95 *(978-0-8234-1926-5(6))* Holiday Hse., Inc.
Brown, Erin. Beyond: the Coloring Book Edition: Beyond, yet Still with You (There, of Course, Is God) Jameson, Steven. 2011. (ENG.). 30p. pap. 7.99 *(978-1-4637-2801-4(8))* CreateSpace Independent Publishing Platform.
—Byen Lwen, Poutan Toujou Avèk Ou: Se Sèten, Bondye La. Jameson, Steven. Dugué, Georges, Jr., tr. l.t. ed. 2010. (HAT.). 32p. pap. 9.99 *(978-1-4563-5858-7(8))* CreateSpace Independent Publishing Platform.
Brown, Erin O'Leary. En Mi Patio. Curry, Don L. 2011. (Rookie Ready to Learn Español Ser.). (SPA.). 32p. (J). pap. 5.95 *(978-0-531-26784-4(9)*, Children's Pr.) Scholastic Library Publishing.
Brown, Fiona. How to Draw Lettering. Tatchell, Judy & Varley, Carol. 2006. (Young Artist Ser.). 32p. (J). (gr. 4-7). pap. 5.99 *(978-0-7945-1379-5(4)*, Usborne) EDC Publishing.
Brown, Gloria. What Sea Creature Is This? Allen, Nancy Kelly. 2012. (J). *(978-1-933176-41-3(5))* Red Rock Pr., Inc.
Brown, Gloria Dean. Shanleya's Quest: A Botany Adventure for Kids Ages 9 - 99, 1 vol. Elpel, Thomas J. 32p. 12.50 *(978-1-892784-16-2(5)*, 1511) HOPS Pr., LLC.
Brown, Hazel. Prince Henry St. Clair Earl of Orkney. Brown, Hazel. Bramadat, Dawn, ed. 2013. 106p. pap. 25.95 *(978-1-935786-57-3(1))* St. Clair Pubns.
Brown, Heather. Bee & Me. McGuinness, Elle J. 2008. (ENG.). 28p. (J). (gr. -1). 16.99 *(978-0-7407-7734-9(3))* Andrews McMeel Publishing.
—Hugs for You. Hannigan, Paula. 2012. (J). (-k). (ENG.). 10p. bds. 7.99 *(978-1-4494-2192-2(X))*; ***(978-1-4351-5022-5(8))*** Andrews McMeel Publishing.
—Today I'll Be a Princess. Croyle, Paula. 2015. (ENG.). 12p. (J). bds. 5.99 *(978-1-4494-6057-0(7))* Andrews McMeel Publishing.
—Under Construction. Hannigan, Paula & Accord Publishing Staff. 2012. (ENG.). 12p. (J). bds. 14.99 *(978-1-4494-0498-7(7))* Andrews McMeel Publishing.
—Under Construction. Hannigan, Paula. 2013. (ENG.). 18p. (J). bds. 5.99 *(978-1-4494-3556-1(4))* Andrews McMeel Publishing.
—Who Lives Here? A Lift-The-Flap Book. Croyle, Paula. 2013. (ENG.). 12p. (J). bds. 6.99 *(978-1-4494-3231-7(X))* Andrews McMeel Publishing.
Brown, Heather. The Robot Book. Brown, Heather. 2010. (ENG.). 12p. (J). bds. 16.99 *(978-0-7407-9725-5(5))* Andrews McMeel Publishing.
Brown, James. Farm. Brown, James. 2013. (ENG.). 16p. (J). (gr. -1 — 1). bds. 6.99 *(978-0-7636-5931-8(2))* Candlewick Pr.
Brown, Jane Clark. Marvin One Too Many. Paterson, Katherine. 2003. (I Can Read Bks.). 48p. (J). (gr. k-3). pap. 3.99 *(978-0-06-444279-4(9))* HarperCollins Pubs.
Brown, Janet & Morton, Ken. Pinocchio: My First Reading Book. Brown, Janet. 2013. (ENG.). 24p. (J). (gr. -1-k). 5.99 *(978-1-84322-831-8(9)*, Armadillo) Anness Publishing GBR. Dist: National Bk. Network.
Brown, Jason. Hanner & the Bullies. Curtiss, A. B. & Curtiss, A. B. 2012. 140p. pap. 9.99 *(978-0-932529-63-3(1))* Oldcastle Publishing.
Brown, Jeffrey. Jedi Academy. Brown, Jeffrey. 2013. (Star Wars Jedi Academy Ser.: Bk. 1). 160p. (J). (ENG.). (gr. 3-7). 12.99 *(978-0-545-50517-8(8))*; pap. *(978-0-545-60999-9(2))* Scholastic, Inc.
—Return of the Padawan. Brown, Jeffrey. 2014. (Star Wars Jedi Academy Ser.: Bk. 2). (ENG.). 176p. (J). (gr. 3-7). 12.99 *(978-0-545-62125-0(9))* Scholastic, Inc.
Brown, Jo. Hootenanny! A Festive Counting Book. Ainsworth, Kimberly. 2011. (ENG.). 32p. (J). (gr. -1-k). 12.99 *(978-1-4424-2273-5(4)*, Little Simon) Little Simon.
—Hungry Monsters: A Book of Colors. Mitter, Matt. 2008. (Halloween Ser.). (ENG.). 10p. (J). (gr. -1-k). 8.99 *(978-0-7944-1305-7(6))* Reader's Digest Assn., Inc., The.
—Penny Penguin. Mitter, Matt. 2010. (Snappy Fun Ser.). (ENG.). 10p. (J). bds. 7.99 *(978-0-7944-2014-7(1))* Reader's Digest Assn., Inc., The.
—Snappy Heads Andy Alligator. Albee, Sarah & Hood, Susan. 2009. (Snappy Fun Bks.). (ENG.). 10p. (J). (gr. -1 — 1). bds. 7.99 *(978-0-7944-1908-0(9))* Reader's Digest Assn., Inc., The.
—Snappy Heads Tommy T Rex. Albee, Sarah & Hood, Susan. 2009. (New Snappy Fun Ser.). (ENG.). 10p. (J). (gr. -1-k). bds. 7.99 *(978-0-7944-1907-3(0))* Reader's Digest Assn., Inc., The.
—This Is Our World: A Story about Taking Care of the Earth. Sollinger, Emily. 2010. (Little Green Bks.). (ENG.). 12p. (J). (gr. -1-1). bds. 7.99 *(978-1-4169-7821-3(6)*, Little Simon) Little Simon.

Brown, Jo. My Rainbow Book of Everyday Prayers. Brown, Jo. Box, Su. 2009. (ENG.). 16p. (J). (gr. k-k). bds. 9.99 *(978-0-7459-6166-8(5))* Lion Hudson PLC GBR. Dist: Independent Pubs. Group.

—Where's My Mommy? Brown, Jo. 2006. (Storytime Board Bks.). 18p. (J). (gr. -1-3). bds. 6.95 *(978-1-58925-795-5(2))* Tiger Tales.

Brown, Jonathan. Madison & the New Neighbors, 1 vol. Braver, Vanita. 2014. (ENG.). 32p. (J). 15.99 *(978-1-59572-686-5(1))* Star Bright Bks., Inc.

Brown Jr., David F. Tabby Goes to School: The First in the Tabatha Adventures Series, 1 vol. Brown Sr., David F. 2009. 20p. pap. 24.95 *(978-1-60836-181-6(0))* America Star Bks.

Brown, Judy. Creep from the Deep. Burchett, Janet & Vogler, Sara. 10th ed. (ENG.). 96p. (J). pap. *(978-0-330-37607-5(1),* Pan) Pan Macmillan.

—The Minestrone Mob. Wallace, Karen. 2006. (Read-It! Chapter Bks.). (ENG.). 52p. (gr. 2-4). lib. bdg. 21.32 *(978-1-4048-2723-3(4),* Chapter Readers) Picture Window Bks.

—No Problem! Bennett, Leonie. 2004. (ENG.). 16p. (J). lib. bdg. 23.65 *(978-1-59646-680-7(4))* Dingles & Co.

—Shiver & Deliver. Burchett, Janet & Vogler, Sara. 7th ed. 2003. (ENG.). 87p. (J). pap. *(978-0-330-37604-4(7),* Pan) Pan Macmillan.

Brown, Kalt. Tiberius Goes to School. Harvey, Keith. 2010. (Tiberius Tales Ser.). 24p. (J). (gr. -1-2). pap. 8.15 *(978-1-60754-837-9(2));* lib. bdg. 22.60 *(978-1-60754-833-1(X))* Windmill Bks.

Brown, Karen. Jessica the Furry Baroo. Moore, Judith. 2007. 44p. per. 14.95 *(978-1-59858-364-9(6))* Dog Ear Publishing, LLC.

Brown, Kate & Hickman, Paula. Tiberius Goes to School. Harvey, Keith. 2014. (ENG.). 24p. pap. 8.95 *(978-1-84135-919-9(X))* Award Pubns. Ltd. GBR. Dist: Parkwest Pubns., Inc.

Brown, Kathryn. The House That Jane Built: A Story about Jane Addams. Stone, Tanya Lee. 2015. (ENG.). 32p. (J). (gr. 1-4). 17.99 *(978-0-8050-9049-9(5),* Holt, Henry & Co. Bks. For Young Readers) Holt, Henry & Co.

—The Inside Tree. Smith, Linda. Date not set. 32p. (J). (gr. -1-3). 5.99 *(978-0-06-443542-0(3))* HarperCollins Pubs.

—Kisses on the Wind. Moser, Lisa. 2009. (ENG.). 32p. (J). (gr. -1-2). 16.99 *(978-0-7636-3110-9(8))* Candlewick Pr.

—Mama Loves. Dotlich, Rebecca Kai. 2004. 32p. (J). (gr. -1-2). lib. bdg. 15.89 *(978-0-06-029408-3(6))* HarperCollins Pubs.

—My Little Grandmother Often Forgets. Lindbergh, Reeve. 2007. (ENG.). 32p. (J). (gr. -1-1). 16.99 *(978-0-7636-1989-3(2))* Candlewick Pr.

—Nora's Chicks. MacLachlan, Patricia. 2013. (ENG.). 40p. (J). (gr. -1-2). 15.99 *(978-0-7636-4753-7(5))* Candlewick Pr.

Brown, Kathryn. The Old Woman Who Named Things. Rylant, Cynthia. 2015. 32p. pap. 7.00 ***(978-1-61003-498-2(8))*** Center for the Collaborative Classroom.

Brown, Kathryn. The Old Woman Who Named Things. Rylant, Cynthia. 2004. (gr. -1-3). 17.00 *(978-0-7569-4204-5(7))* Perfection Learning Corp.

—The Quite Contrary Man: A True American Tale. Hyatt, Patricia Rusch. 2011. (ENG.). 32p. (J). (gr. k-4). 16.95 *(978-0-8109-4065-9(5),* Abrams Bks. for Young Readers) Abrams.

Brown, Kelly. Citizenship, 1 vol. Skog, Jason. 2008. (Cartoon Nation Ser.). (ENG.). 32p. (gr. 3-4). 29.99 *(978-1-4296-1331-6(9),* Graphic Library) Capstone Pr., Inc.

—The FBI. Collins, Terry. 2008. (Cartoon Nation Ser.). (ENG.). 32p. (gr. 3-4). 29.99 *(978-1-4296-1982-0(1),* Graphic Library) Capstone Pr., Inc.

Brown, Ken. El Rey de los Bosques. Day, David. (SPA.). 27p. (J). *(978-84-236-4737-8(4))* Edebé ESP. Dist: Lectorum Pubns., Inc.

Brown, Ken. The Scarecrow's Hat, 1 vol. Brown, Ken. 2011. (ENG.). 32p. (J). (gr. -1-1). pap. 7.95 *(978-1-56145-570-6(9))* Peachtree Pubs.

Brown, Kevin. Can a Hippo Hop? Tidd, Louise Vitellaro. 2006. (ENG.). 24p. (gr. k-2). pap. 5.95 *(978-1-57874-043-7(6))* Kaeden Corp.

—Come on Down. Knowlton, Laurie Lazzaro. 2005. (J). *(978-1-933248-07-3(6))* World Quest Learning.

—God Thought of Everything Strange & Slimy. Bruno, Bonnie. 2006. 128p. (YA). (gr. 3-6). pap. 8.99 *(978-0-7847-1448-5(7),* 04084) Standard Publishing.

—God Thought of Everything Weird & Wacky. Bruno, Bonnie. 2006. 128p. (YA). (gr. 3-6). pap. 8.99 *(978-0-7847-1447-8(9),* 04083) Standard Publishing.

—Smile & Say Cheetah! Hamilton, Linda. 2005. *(978-1-933248-00-4(9))* World Quest Learning.

Brown, Kevin Christian. The Mustard Seed Prayer. Vera, J. 2012. 24p. 24.95 *(978-1-4626-5848-0(2))* America Star Bks.

Brown, Lillie Wyatt. Do I Have to Clean My Room? Rome, Jacqueline Thomas. 2011. 36p. pap. 9.95 *(978-1-936513-24-6(2))* PearlStone Publishing, Inc.

Brown, Linda L. & Brown, S. Glenn. Cats. Brown, S. Glenn. l.t. ed. 2011. (ENG.). 34p. pap. 11.99 *(978-1-4609-7158-1(2))* CreateSpace Independent Publishing Platform.

Brown, Linda L. & Brown, Steven. Cats. l.t. ed. 2011. (ENG.). 34p. pap. 11.99 *(978-0-615-45712-3(6))* Brown, Steven Glenn.

Brown, Linnea. This Is BRIEF! Or Starting Preschool & Homeschool Children Reading Naturally - at Once. Briefing Associates Staff. Khaiphus, Kosta Demetrius, ed. 2004. 136p. (gr. -1-1). pap. 24.95 *(978-0-9706105-0-8(5))* BR:IEFing Assocs. of New England.

Brown, Lisa. Baby Do My Banking. 2006. (ENG.). 12p. 6.95 *(978-1-932416-55-8(2))* McSweeney's Publishing.

—Baby Fix My Car. 2006. (ENG.). 12p. bds. 6.95 *(978-1-932416-56-5(0))* McSweeney's Publishing.

—Emily's Blue Period. Daly, Cathleen. 2014. (ENG.). 56p. (J). (gr. -1-2). 17.99 *(978-1-59643-469-1(4))* Roaring Brook Pr.

—The Latke Who Couldn't Stop Screaming: A Christmas Story. Snicket, Lemony. Scott, Daniel, ed. 2007. (ENG.). 48p. (J). (gr. 2-7). 11.00 *(978-1-932416-87-9(0))* McSweeney's Publishing.

—Mummy Cat. Ewert, Marcus. 2015. (ENG.). 48p. (J). (gr. 1-4). 16.99 *(978-0-544-34082-4(5))* Houghton Mifflin Harcourt Publishing Co.

—My First Holy Communion. Ascough, Deirdre Mary. 2013. (ENG.). 72p. (J). 17.95 *(978-1-58617-708-9(7))* Ignatius Pr.

—Sometimes You Get What You Want. Gary, Meredith. 2008. (ENG.). 32p. (J). (gr. -1 — 1). 16.99 *(978-0-06-114015-0(5))* HarperCollins Pubs.

—29 Myths on the Swinster Pharmacy. Snicket, Lemony. 2014. (ENG.). 32p. (gr. 1). 14.95 *(978-1-938073-78-6(9))* McSweeney's Publishing.

Brown, Lisa. How to Be. Brown, Lisa. 2006. (ENG.). 32p. (J). (gr. -1 — 1). 17.99 *(978-0-06-054635-9(2))* HarperCollins Pubs.

—Vampire Boy's Good Night. Brown, Lisa. 2010. (ENG.). 32p. (J). (gr. -1-2). 16.99 *(978-0-06-114011-2(2))* HarperCollins Pubs.

Brown, Lorna. The Moonlight Tooth Fairy. Frost, Lulu. 2013. (J). *(978-1-4351-4919-9(X))* Barnes & Noble, Inc.

Brown, Marc. The Banza: A Haitian Story. Wolkstein, Diane. 33p. (J). (gr. k-2). pap. 5.99 *(978-0-8072-1268-4(7),* Listening Library) Random Hse. Audio Publishing Group.

—Born to Read. Sierra, Judy. 2008. (ENG.). 40p. (J). (gr. -1-2). 16.99 *(978-0-375-84687-8(5))* Knopf, Alfred A. Inc.

—Dancing Feet! Craig, Lindsey. 2010. (ENG.). 40p. (J). (gr. -1-2). 16.99 *(978-0-375-86181-9(5),* Knopf Bks. for Young Readers) Random Hse. Children's Bks.

—Dancing Feet! Craig, Lindsey. 2012. (ENG.). 32p. (J). (gr. k-k). bds. 6.99 *(978-0-307-93081-1(5),* Knopf Bks. for Young Readers) Random Hse. Children's Bks.

—Farmyard Beat. Craig, Lindsey. (ENG.). 32p. (J). 2012. (gr. k-k). bds. 6.99 *(978-0-307-93082-8(3));* 2011. (gr. -1-2). 15.99 *(978-0-375-86455-1(5))* Random Hse. Children's Bks. (Knopf Bks. for Young Readers).

—How to Be a Friend. Brown, Laurie Krasny. 2014. 32p. pap. 7.00 *(978-1-61003-381-7(7))* Center for the Collaborative Classroom.

—If All the Animals Came Inside. Pinder, Eric. 2012. (ENG.). 40p. (J). (gr. -1-1). 16.99 *(978-0-316-09883-0(3))* Little Brown & Co.

—The Little Shop of Monsters. Stine, R. L. 2015. (ENG.). 40p. (J). (gr. -1-1). 17.00 *(978-0-316-36983-1(7))* Little Brown & Co.

—Swamp Monsters. Christian, Mary Blount. 48p. (J). (gr. 1-2). pap. 3.99 *(978-0-8072-1355-1(1),* Listening Library) Random Hse. Audio Publishing Group.

—Wild about You! Sierra, Judy. 2012. (ENG.). 40p. (J). (gr. -1-3). 17.99 *(978-0-307-93178-8(1));* lib. bdg. 20.99 *(978-0-375-97107-5(6))* Random Hse. Children's Bks. (Knopf Bks. for Young Readers).

—ZooZical. Sierra, Judy. 2011. (ENG.). 40p. (J). (gr. -1-2). 17.99 *(978-0-375-86847-4(X),* Knopf Bks. for Young Readers) Random Hse. Children's Bks.

Brown, Marc. Arthur & the 1,001 Dads, Bk. 28. Brown, Marc. 2003. (ENG.). 64p. (J). (gr. 1-4). pap. 4.25 *(978-0-316-12280-1(7))* Little, Brown Bks. for Young Readers.

—Arthur & the Baby. Brown, Marc. 2011. (Classic Arthur Adventure Ser.). (ENG.). 32p. (J). (gr. -1-1). pap. 7.00 *(978-0-316-12905-3(4))* Little Brown & Co.

—Arthur & the Big Snow. Brown, Marc. 2005. (ENG.). 24p. (J). (gr. -1-1). per. 3.99 *(978-0-316-05770-7(3))* Little, Brown Bks. for Young Readers.

—Arthur Goes to Camp. Brown, Marc. 2008. (ENG.). 32p. (J). (gr. -1-1). pap. 10.99 *(978-0-316-11870-5(2))* Little, Brown Bks. for Young Readers.

—Arthur's Mystery Babysitter. Brown, Marc. 2004. (ENG.). 24p. (J). (gr. -1-1). pap. 3.99 *(978-0-316-73394-6(6),* Tingley, Megan Bks.) Little, Brown Bks. for Young Readers.

—Arthur's Pet Business. Brown, Marc. rev. ed. 2007. (ENG.). 32p. (J). (gr. -1-1). pap. 10.99 *(978-0-316-11863-7(X))* Little, Brown Bks. for Young Readers.

—Arthur's Tooth. Brown, Marc. 2005. (ENG.). 32p. (J). (gr. -1-1). pap. 11.00 *(978-0-316-05960-2(9))* Little, Brown Bks. for Young Readers.

—D. W.'s Library Card. Brown, Marc. 2003. (ENG.). 24p. (J). (gr. -1-1). pap. 7.00 *(978-0-316-73820-0(4))* Little, Brown Bks. for Young Readers.

—D. W.'s Perfect Present. Brown, Marc. 2004. (ENG.). 24p. (J). (gr. -1-1). pap. 3.99 *(978-0-316-73386-1(5),* Tingley, Megan Bks.) Little, Brown Bks. for Young Readers.

—Good Night, D. W. Brown, Marc. 2004. (ENG.). 24p. (J). (gr. -1-1). pap. 3.99 *(978-0-316-73385-4(7))* Little, Brown Bks. for Young Readers.

Brown, Marc. Wild about Books. Brown, Marc, tr. Sierra, Judy. 2004. (ENG.). 40p. (J). (gr. -1-2). 16.95 *(978-0-375-82538-5(X));* lib. bdg. 18.99 *(978-0-375-92538-2(4))* Random Hse. Children's Bks. (Knopf Bks. for Young Readers).

Brown, Margaret. Little Raindrop. Schoeningh, Debby. 2012. 24p. pap. 9.95 *(978-0-9746360-7-8(X))* Country Side Pr., The.

Brown, Mari. Catching Boo. Rowlinson, Joanne. 2008. 24p. (J). (gr. -1-3). *(978-0-9739962-2-7(6))* Wuehr, Tina.

—Field Dance. Wuehr, Tina L. 2005. 18p. (J). (gr. -1-3). *(978-0-9739962-0-3(X))* Wuehr, Tina.

—Neela Potts Has Lots of Knots. Wuehr, Tina L. 2008. 30p. (J). (gr. -1-3). *(978-0-9739962-3-4(4))* Wuehr, Tina.

—Why Can't I Have Glue? Wuehr, Tina L. 2007. 20p. (J). (gr. -1-3). *(978-0-9739962-1-0(8))* Wuehr, Tina.

Brown, Marilyn. Girls Can! Make it Happen. Kupchella, Rick. 2004. (ENG.). 40p. (J). 16.95 *(978-0-9726504-3-4(1))* TRISTAN Publishing, Inc.

Brown, Marion, jt. illus. see McDonald, Marion.

Brown, Martin. Blood-Curdling Box, 20 vols. Deary, Terry. 2008. 2880p. pap. *(978-1-4071-0815-5(8),* Scholastic) Scholastic, Inc.

Brown, Mary Barrett. Playful Slider: The North American River Otter. Esbensen, Barbara Juster. 2011. (Fesler-Lampert Minnesota Heritage Ser.). (ENG.). 32p. pap. 11.95 *(978-0-8166-7765-8(4))* Univ. of Minnesota Pr.

Brown, Matt, photos by. Amigos en la Escuela, 1 vol. Bunnett, Rochelle. Muñoz, Yenny, tr. from ENG. 2007.Tr. of Friends at School. (SPA., 32p. (J). (gr. -1). pap. 5.95 *(978-1-59572-041-2(3))* Star Bright Bks., Inc.

Brown, Michael. The Learning Circle: A Preschool Teachers Guide to Circle Time. Claycomb, Patty. Charner, Kathleen, ed. 2004. 207p. (Orig.). (gr. -1). pap. 19.95 *(978-0-87659-115-4(2),* 10007) Gryphon Hse., Inc.

Brown, Michael D. Tanker's Adventures in Monterey. Brown, Maureen E. 2007. 24p. (J). 13.95 *(978-0-615-16200-3(2))* TankerToys.

Brown, Nick. The Watermelon Story. Miro. 2003. 103p. (J). pap. *(978-1-84426-258-8(8))* Upfront Publishing Ltd.

Brown, Palmer. Beyond the Pawpaw Trees. Brown, Palmer. 2011. (ENG.). 136p. (J). (gr. k-4). 14.95 *(978-1-59017-461-6(5),* NYR Children's Collection) New York Review of Bks., Inc., The.

—Hickory. Brown, Palmer. 2013. (ENG.). 56p. (J). (gr. -1-2). 14.95 *(978-1-59017-627-6(8),* NYRB Classics) New York Review of Bks., Inc., The.

—The Silver Nutmeg. Brown, Palmer. 2012. (ENG.). 152p. (J). (gr. k-4). 15.95 *(978-1-59017-500-2(X),* NYR Children's Collection) New York Review of Bks., Inc., The.

—Something for Christmas. Brown, Palmer. 2011. (ENG.). 40p. (J). (gr. -1-2). 12.95 *(978-1-59017-462-3(3),* NYR Children's Collection) New York Review of Bks., Inc., The.

Brown, Peter. Creepy Carrots! Reynolds, Aaron. 2012. (ENG.). 40p. (J). (gr. -1-3). 17.99 *(978-1-4424-0297-3(0),* Simon & Schuster Bks. For Young Readers) Simon & Schuster Bks. For Young Readers.

—Kaline Klattermaster's Tree House. Kimmel, Haven. 2010. (ENG.). 160p. (J). (gr. 2-7). pap. 5.99 *(978-0-689-87403-1(0),* Atheneum Bks. for Young Readers) Simon & Schuster Children's Publishing.

—The Purple Kangaroo. Black, Michael Ian. 2009. (ENG.). 32p. (J). (gr. -1-3). 16.99 *(978-1-4169-5771-3(5),* Simon & Schuster Bks. For Young Readers) Simon & Schuster Bks. For Young Readers.

Brown, Petra. The Big City. Gilmore, Grace. 2015. (Tales from Maple Ridge Ser.: 3). (ENG.). 128p. (J). (gr. k-4). pap. 5.99 *(978-1-4814-3006-7(8),* Little Simon) Little Simon.

—Conker. Morpurgo, Michael. 2011. (Red Bananas Ser.). (ENG.). 48p. (J). (gr. k-2). pap. 7.99 *(978-1-4052-5639-1(7))* Egmont Bks., Ltd. GBR. Dist: Independent Pubs. Group.

—The Ghost of Juniper Creek. Gilmore, Grace. 2015. (Tales from Maple Ridge Ser.: 4). (ENG.). 128p. (J). (gr. k-4). pap. 5.99 *(978-1-4814-3009-8(2),* Little Simon) Little Simon.

—Grandma Loves You! James, Helen Foster. 2013. (ENG.). 14.99 *(978-1-58536-836-5(9))* Sleeping Bear Pr.

—Hush, Little Baby. 2007. (Padded Hardcover Ser.). 18p. (J). 8.95 *(978-1-58925-819-8(3))* Tiger Tales.

—I Will Keep You Safe & Sound. Houran, Lori Haskins. 2013. (ENG.). 32p. (J). (gr. -1-k). 16.99 *(978-0-545-19751-9(1),* Scholastic Pr.) Scholastic, Inc.

—I Will Keep You Safe & Sound. Houran, Lori Haskins. 2013. (J). *(978-0-545-19752-6(X),* Scholastic Pr.) Scholastic, Inc.

Brown, Petra. If You Can...we Can! Shoshan, Beth. 2013. (J). ***(978-1-4351-4800-0(2))*** Barnes & Noble, Inc.

Brown, Petra. Logan Pryce Makes a Mess. Gilmore, Grace. 2015. (Tales from Maple Ridge Ser.: 1). (ENG.). 128p. (J). (gr. k-4). pap. 5.99 *(978-1-4814-2624-4(9),* Little Simon) Little Simon.

—The Lucky Wheel. Gilmore, Grace. 2015. (Tales from Maple Ridge Ser.: 2). (ENG.). 128p. (J). (gr. k-4). pap. 5.99 *(978-1-4814-2627-5(3),* Little Simon) Little Simon.

—Rags Hero Dog of WWI: A True Story. Raven, Margot Theis. 2014. (ENG.). 32p. (J). (gr. 2-5). 16.99 *(978-1-58536-258-5(1),* 203672) Sleeping Bear Pr.

Brown, Richard. A Kid's Guide to Washington, D. C. Clark, Diane C. & Harcourt, Inc Staff. rev. ed. 2008. (ENG.). 160p. (J). (gr. 1-4). pap. 14.00 *(978-0-15-206125-8(8))* Houghton Mifflin Harcourt Publishing Co.

—Surprise! Ziefert, Harriet. 2006. (I'm Going to Read(r) Ser.). (ENG.). 24p. (J). (gr. -1-3). pap. 3.95 *(978-1-4027-3410-6(7))* Sterling Publishing Co., Inc.

—Wait for Us! 2005. (I'm Going to Read(r) Ser.). (ENG.). 28p. (J). (gr. -1-k). pap. 3.95 *(978-1-4027-2506-7(X))* Sterling Publishing Co., Inc.

Brown, Richard, jt. illus. see Cordell, Matthew.

Brown, Richard E. & Prater, Linda. Afikomen Mambo. Black, Joe. 2011. (Passover Ser.). (ENG.). 24p. (J). (gr. -1 — 1). lib. bdg. 17.95 *(978-0-7613-5638-7(X),* Kar-Ben Publishing) Lerner Publishing Group.

Brown, Rick. Boker Tov! Good Morning! Black, Joe. 2009. (Kar-Ben Favorites Ser.). (ENG.). 24p. (J). (gr. -1 — 1). 16.95 *(978-0-7613-3950-2(7));* pap. 8.95 *(978-0-7613-3951-9(5))* Lerner Publishing Group. (Kar-Ben Publishing).

—Going on a Hametz Hunt. Jules, Jacqueline & Hechtkopf, Jacqueline. 2010. (Passover Ser.). (ENG.). 12p. (J). (gr. -1 — 1). bds. 5.95 *(978-0-7613-5124-5(8),* Kar-Ben Publishing) Lerner Publishing Group.

—Hooray for the 4th of July! 2007. (I'm Going to Read(r) Ser.). (ENG.). 28p. (J). (gr. k-1). pap. 3.95 *(978-1-4027-4241-5(X))* Sterling Publishing Co., Inc.

Brown, Robert. Harriet Tubman. Kudlinski, Kathleen. 2015. (History's All-Stars Ser.). (ENG.). 224p. (J). (gr. 3-7). pap. 6.99 *(978-1-4814-2510-0(2),* Simon & Schuster/Paula Wiseman Bks.) Simon & Schuster/Paula Wiseman Bks.

Brown, Roberta, jt. illus. see Call, Greg.

Brown, Rod. Freedom's a-Callin Me. Shange, Ntozake. 2012. (ENG.). 32p. (J). (gr. 3-7). 16.99 *(978-0-06-133741-3(2),* Amistad) HarperCollins Pubs.

—We Troubled the Waters. Shange, Ntozake. 2009. (ENG.). 32p. (J). (gr. 4-18). 16.99 *(978-0-06-133735-2(8),* Amistad) HarperCollins Pubs.

Brown, Ron. Holy Hum. Hauser, Sheri. aut. ed. 2005. 42p. (YA). per. 12.50 *(978-0-9766718-8-6(3))* Glorybound Publishing.

Brown, Ruth. The Christmas Mouse. Forward, Toby. 2007. (ENG.). 48p. (J). (gr. k-2). pap. 13.95 *(978-1-84270-583-4(0))* Andersen Pr. GBR. Dist: Independent Pubs. Group.

—The Christmas Mouse. 2013. (J). *(978-1-4351-5021-8(X))* Barnes & Noble, Inc.

—The Quayside Cat. Forward, Toby. 2014. (ENG.). 32p. (J). (gr. -1-3). 16.95 *(978-1-4677-3452-3(7))* Lerner Publishing Group.

—Ruggles. Fine, Anne. 2011. (ENG.). 32p. (J). (gr. k-k). pap. 8.99 *(978-1-84939-206-8(4))* Andersen Pr. GBR. Dist: Independent Pubs. Group.

Brown, Ruth. Gracie, the Lighthouse Cat. Brown, Ruth. 2011. (Andersen Press Picture Bks). (ENG.). 32p. (J). (gr. -1-3). 16.95 *(978-0-7613-7454-1(X))* Lerner Publishing Group.

—Greyfriars Bobby. Brown, Ruth. 2013. (ENG.). 32p. (J). (gr. -1-k). pap. 9.99 *(978-1-84939-632-5(9))* Andersen Pr. GBR. Dist: Independent Pubs. Group.

—Imagine. Brown, Ruth. Brown, Ruth. 2007. (ENG.). 24p. (J). (gr. -1-k). 9.99 *(978-1-84270-564-3(4))* Andersen Pr. GBR. Dist: Independent Pubs. Group.

—Monkey's Friends. Brown, Ruth. ed. 2012. (Picture Bks). (ENG.). 28p. (J). 9.99 *(978-1-61067-045-6(0),* Usborne) EDC Publishing.

—Snail Trail. Brown, Ruth. 2013. (ENG.). 20p. (J). (gr. -1-k). 10.99 *(978-1-84939-252-5(8))* Andersen Pr. GBR. Dist: Independent Pubs. Group.

—The Tale of Two Mice. Brown, Ruth. 2008. (ENG.). 32p. (J). (gr. -1-3). 17.99 *(978-0-7636-4015-6(8))* Candlewick Pr.

Brown, Ruth & Barrett, Peter. James Herriot's Treasury for Children: Warm & Joyful Tales by the Author of All Creatures Great & Small. Herriot, James. ed. 2014. (ENG.). 272p. (J). (gr. -1-3). 24.99 *(978-1-250-05813-3(9),* St. Martin's Griffin) St. Martin's Pr.

—James Herriot's Treasury of Inspirational Stories for Children: Warm & Joyful Tales by the Author of All Creatures Great & Small. Herriot, James. 2005. (ENG.). 260p. (J). (gr. -1-3). 19.99 *(978-0-312-34972-1(6),* St. Martin's Griffin) St. Martin's Pr.

Brown, S. Bugs. Brown, S. Brown, Linda. l.t. ed. 2011. (ENG.). 36p. pap. 11.99 *(978-1-4637-0775-0(4))* CreateSpace Independent Publishing Platform.

Brown, S. Glenn, jt. illus. see Brown, Linda L.

Brown, Steven, jt. illus. see Brown, Linda L.

Brown, Stevi. Glory Gone Forgotten: The Untold Story of the 12th Kentucky Cavalry. Goodall, Barry, Jr. Embry, Eugene, ed. 2nd rev. ed. 2005. 182p. *(978-0-9763932-1-4(2),* 500) Goodall, Barry.

Brown, Suzy. There's a Beetle in My Bed. Kirk, Bill. 2009. 16p. pap. 9.95 *(978-1-61633-005-7(8))* Guardian Angel Publishing, Inc.

—There's a Spider in My Sink! Kirk, Bill. 2008. 16p. pap. 9.95 *(978-1-935137-25-2(5))* Guardian Angel Publishing, Inc.

Brown, Tempe. The Little Dirt People. Brown, Tempe. 2013. 50p. pap. 14.95 *(978-1-4507-3904-7(0))* Bush Publishing Inc.

Brown, Tim. Bark & Tim: A True Story of Friendship. Vernick, Audrey Glassman & Gidaro, Ellen Glassman. 2003. 32p. (J). 14.95 *(978-1-57072-271-4(4))* Overmountain Pr.

Brown, Toni Sorenson, photos by. Heroes of the Bible. 2004. 32p. (J). 17.95 *(978-1-59156-097-5(7))* Covenant Communications, Inc.

Browne, Anita. Cycle, Children's Games & Other Songs. Rice, Ruth Mason & Villar, Rose. 2012. 56p. 36.95 *(978-1-258-23019-7(4));* pap. 21.95 *(978-1-258-24214-5(1))* Literary Licensing, LLC.

Browne, Anthony. How Do You Feel? Browne, Anthony. 2012. (ENG.). 32p. (J). (gr. -1-2). 14.99 *(978-0-7636-5862-5(6))* Candlewick Pr.

—The Little Bear Book. Browne, Anthony. 2014. (ENG.). 24p. (J). (gr. -1-2). 15.99 *(978-0-7636-7007-8(3))* Candlewick Pr.

—Little Beauty. Browne, Anthony. (ENG.). 32p. (J). (gr. -1-2). 2010. pap. 6.99 *(978-0-7636-4967-8(8));* 2008. 16.99 *(978-0-7636-3959-4(1))* Candlewick Pr.

—Me & You. Browne, Anthony. 2010. (ENG.). 32p. (J). (gr. k-3). 16.99 *(978-0-374-34908-0(8),* Farrar, Straus & Giroux (BYR)) Farrar, Straus & Giroux.

—Mi Mama. Browne, Anthony. Fuentes Silva, Andrea, tr. 2005. (Los Especiales de A la Orilla del Viento Ser.). (SPA.). 28p. (J). *(978-968-16-7375-8(1))* Fondo de Cultura Economica.

—My Mom. Browne, Anthony. 2009. (ENG.). 32p. (J). (gr. k-3). pap. 7.99 *(978-0-374-40026-2(1))* Square Fish.

—One Gorilla. Browne, Anthony. 2013. (ENG.). 32p. (J). (gr. -1-2). 16.99 *(978-0-7636-6352-0(2))* Candlewick Pr.

Browne, Anthony. One Gorilla: a Counting Book. Browne, Anthony. 2015. (ENG.). 26p. (J). (— 1). bds. 7.99 ***(978-0-7636-7915-6(1))*** Candlewick Pr.

Browne, Anthony. What If... ? Browne, Anthony. 2014. (ENG.). 32p. (J). (gr. k-3). 16.99 *(978-0-7636-7419-9(2))* Candlewick Pr.

Browne, Eileen. In a Minute. Bradman, Tony & Quarto Generic Staff. 2012. (ENG.). 32p. (J). (gr. -1-1). pap. 8.99 *(978-1-84780-180-7(3),* Frances Lincoln) Quarto Publishing Group UK GBR. Dist: Hachette Bk. Group.

—Through My Window. Bradman, Tony. 2009. (ENG.). 32p. (J). (gr. -1-1). pap. 8.99 *(978-1-84507-893-5(4),* Frances Lincoln) Quarto Publishing Group UK GBR. Dist: Hachette Bk. Group.

—Wait & See. Bradman, Tony & Quarto Generic Staff. rev. ed. 2012. (ENG.). 32p. (J). (gr. -1-1). pap. 8.99 *(978-1-84780-181-4(1),* Frances Lincoln) Quarto Publishing Group UK GBR. Dist: Hachette Bk. Group.

Browne, Eileen. Handa's Hen. Browne, Eileen. 2004. (ENG & PAN.). 32p. (J). bds. *(978-1-84444-194-5(6))* Mantra Lingua.

—Handa's Surprise. Browne, Eileen. 2011. (Reading & Math Together Ser.). (ENG.). 32p. (J). (gr. -1-2). pap. 24.99 *(978-0-7636-5385-9(3))* Candlewick Pr.

—Handa's Surprise: Read & Share. Browne, Eileen. 2004. (ENG & BEN.). 32p. (J). pap. *(978-1-85269-472-2(6));*

B

pap. *(978-1-85269-473-9(4))*; pap. *(978-1-85269-474-6(2))*; pap. *(978-1-85269-475-3(0))*; pap. *(978-1-85269-477-7(7))*; pap. *(978-1-85269-478-4(5))*; pap. *(978-1-85269-507-1(2))*; pap. *(978-1-85269-508-8(0))*; pap. *(978-1-85269-509-5(9))*; pap. *(978-1-85269-510-1(2))*; pap. *(978-1-85269-512-5(9))*; pap. *(978-1-85269-513-2(7))*; pap. *(978-1-85269-515-6(3))*; pap. *(978-1-85269-476-0(9))*; pap. *(978-1-85269-514-9(5))* Mantra Lingua.

Browne, Frank, photos by. Father Browne's Galway. O'Donnell, E. E. 2007. (ENG., 112p. 45.95 *(978-1-85607-938-9(4))* Currach Pr. IRL. Dist: Dufour Editions, Inc.

Browne, Gordon. Down the Snow Stairs: Or, from Goodnight to Goodmorning. Corkran, Alice. 2012. 278p. pap. 14.95 *(978-1-934671-12-2(6))* Salem Ridge Press LLC.

Browne, James. Return of Chancellor Paddywack: A Sequel to Magic Marmalade, A Tale of the Moonlight Fairies. Licht, Sharon. 2012. 112p. (J). pap. *(978-1-927360-69-9(2))* CCB Publishing.

Browne, Paula. El Cumpleanos de la Mona. Browne, Paula. Isabel, Isaias, tr. 2004. (Paca, la Macaca Ser.). (SPA.). 20p. pap. 4.95 *(978-85-7416-214-0(0))* Callis Editora Ltda BRA. Dist: Independent Pubs. Group.

—Paca, la macaca en la Cocina. Browne, Paula. Isabel, Isaias, tr. 2004. (Paca, la Macaca Ser.). (SPA.). 20p. pap. 4.95 *(978-85-7416-210-2(8))* Callis Editora Ltda BRA. Dist: Independent Pubs. Group.

—Paca, la Macaca va al Mercado. Browne, Paula. Isabel, Isaias, tr. 2004. (Paca, la Macaca Ser.). 20p. pap. 4.95 *(978-85-7416-215-7(9))* Callis Editora Ltda BRA. Dist: Independent Pubs. Group.

—Que Desbarajuste, Paca. Browne, Paula. Isabel, Isaias, tr. 2004. (Paca, la Macaca Ser.). 20p. pap. 6.95 *(978-85-7416-211-9(6))* Callis Editora Ltda BRA. Dist: Independent Pubs. Group.

Browning, Diane. Signed, Abiah Rose. Browning, Diane. 2010. (ENG.). 32p. (J). (gr. -1-2). 15.99 *(978-1-58246-311-7(5))*, Tricycle Pr.) Ten Speed Pr.

Browning, Dixie Burrus. North Carolina Parade: Stories of History & People. Walser, Richard & Street, Julia Montgomery. 2012. (ENG.). 216p. pap. 45.00 *(978-0-8078-3708-5(3))* Univ. of North Carolina Pr.

Browning, Lisa Marie. His Little Princess: Treasured Letters from Your King. Shepherd, Sheri Rose. 2006. (His Princess Ser.). (ENG.). 128p. (gr. 4-7). 14.99 *(978-1-59052-601-9(5))*, Multnomah Kidz) Doubleday Religious Publishing Group, The.

—His Mighty Warrior: A Treasure Map from Your King. Shepherd, Sheri Rose. 2007. (ENG.). 128p. (J). (gr. k-4). 15.99 *(978-1-60142-034-3(X))*, Multnomah) Doubleday Religious Publishing Group, The.

Browning, Suzan. Dinosaur George Pre-hysterical Adventures: What Color Were Dinosaurs? Quisenberry, Stacey. 2007. (J). 3.95 *(978-0-9797304-3-6(0))* Raining Popcorn Media.

Brownjohn, Emma. All Kinds of Fears. Safran, Sheri. 2012. (ENG.). 12p. (J). (gr. -1). 12.99 *(978-1-60887-161-2(4))* Insight Editions LP.

—All Kinds of Feelings. Safran, Sheri. 2012. (ENG.). 12p. (J). (gr. -1). 12.99 *(978-1-60887-158-2(4))* Insight Editions LP.

Brownjohn, Emma. Help Save Our Planet. Brownjohn, Emma. 2007. (Yes I Can! Ser.). (ENG.). 18p. (J). (gr. -1-k). 12.99 *(978-1-85707-701-8(6))* Tango Bks. GBR. Dist: Independent Pubs. Group.

—Yes I Can! Be Healthy. Brownjohn, Emma. 2011. (Yes I Can! Ser.). (ENG.). 18p. (J). (gr. -1-k). 12.99 *(978-1-85707-734-6(2))* Tango Bks. GBR. Dist: Independent Pubs. Group.

Brownlee, Karen. The Sakura Tree, 1 vol. McTighe, Carolyn. 2008. (ENG.). 32p. (J). (gr. 3-7). 17.95 *(978-0-88995-354-3(6))* Red Deer Pr. CAN. Dist: Ingram Pub. Services.

Brownlee, Kelly Jackson. The Boy Who Wanted to be a Dancer. Gambassi, Rod. 2007. 22p. (J). 23.95 *(978-1-889829-18-0(8))* Window Bks.

Brownlee, Sunny. Ida Claire Decorates with Flair. Rowles, Louis. 2004. 24p. (J). pap. *(978-0-9708748-1-8(2))* Rowles, Louis.

Brownlie, Ian, jt. illus. see McInturff, Linda.

Brownlie, Ian D. Until the Letter Came. St. John, Patricia. 2004. 44p. (J). pap. *(978-1-932381-14-6(7)*, 5580) Bible Visuals International, Inc.

Brownlow, Mike. Dinosaurs of Doom! 2011. (Time Pirates Ser.). (ENG.). 12p. (J). (gr. k-2). 24.99 *(978-0-230-74179-9(7))* Macmillan Pubs., Ltd. GBR. Dist: Independent Pubs. Group.

—Rocky & Daisy at the Park, 1 vol. Crow, Melinda Melton. 2013. (My Two Dogs Ser.). (ENG.). 32p. (gr. 2-3). pap. 6.25 *(978-1-4342-6118-2(2))*; lib. bdg. 21.32 *(978-1-4342-4163-4(7))* Stone Arch Bks.

—Rocky & Daisy Get Trained, 1 vol. Crow, Melinda Melton. 2013. (My Two Dogs Ser.). (ENG.). 32p. (gr. 2-3). pap. 6.25 *(978-1-4342-6116-8(6))*; lib. bdg. 21.32 *(978-1-4342-4161-0(0))* Stone Arch Bks.

—Rocky & Daisy Go Camping, 1 vol. Crow, Melinda Melton. 2013. (My Two Dogs Ser.). (ENG.). 32p. (gr. 2-3). pap. 6.25 *(978-1-4342-6117-5(4))*; lib. bdg. 21.32 *(978-1-4342-4162-7(9))* Stone Arch Bks.

—Rocky & Daisy Go Home, 1 vol. Crow, Melinda Melton. 2013. (My Two Dogs Ser.). (ENG.). 32p. (gr. 2-3). pap. 6.25 *(978-1-4342-6115-1(8))*; lib. bdg. 21.32 *(978-1-4342-4160-3(2))* Stone Arch Bks.

Broxon, Janet. The Big Blue Lake. Armstrong, Robert W. 2015. (ENG.). 32p. (J). (gr. -1). 13.95 *(978-0-9801468-3-7(6))* All About Kids Publishing.

—Every Orchard Tree. Hubbell, Patricia. 2008. (J). *(978-1-55971-986-5(9))*, NorthWord Bks. for Young Readers) T&N Children's Publishing.

Broyles, Beverly Ashley. Germs on Their Fingers! Ferrin, Wendy Wakefield. Tono, Lucia, tr. 2003.Tr. of Germenes en Tus Manos!. (SPA & ENG.). 64p. (J). (gr. 1-7). 17.95 *(978-0-9703632-1-3(4))*; pap. 12.95 *(978-0-9703632-0-6(6))* Wakefield Connection, The.

—Grandmother's Alligator: Burukenge Wa Nyanya. Ferrin, Wendy Wakefield. Mwangi, Simmon, tr. 2003. (SWA & ENG.). 56p. (J). (gr. 1-18). 17.95 *(978-0-9703632-3-7(0))* Wakefield Connection, The.

—Grandmother's Alligator/Burukenge Wa Nyanya Activity Guide. 2005. (ENG & SWA.). (J). 12.95 *(978-0-9703632-7-5(3))* Wakefield Connection, The.

Brozyna, Andrew. A Young Scientist's Guide to Defying Disasters with Skill & Daring: Includes 20 Experiments for the Sink, Bathtub & Backyard, 1 vol. Doyle, James. 2012. (ENG.). 160p. (J). (gr. 5-6). 14.99 *(978-1-4236-2440-0(8))* Gibbs Smith, Publisher.

—A Young Scientist's Guide to Faulty Freaks of Nature, 1 vol. Doyle, James. 2013. (ENG.). 160p. (J). (gr. 5-6). 14.99 *(978-1-4236-2455-4(6))* Gibbs Smith, Publisher.

Brubaker, Robert A. Cup of Glitter. Brubaker, Sherry K. 2012. (ENG.). 34p. pap. 12.95 *(978-1-4515-3523-5(6))* CreateSpace Independent Publishing Platform.

Bruce, Cindy, jt. illus. see Robertson, Elysia Hill.

Brucker, Glenn. Ice Journey. Downey, Glen. 2007. 48p. (J). lib. bdg. 23.08 *(978-1-4242-1618-5(4))* Fitzgerald Bks.

Bruckner, Wes. Lemon Path Encounter, 1 vol. Bruckner, Tai. 2009. 15p. pap. 24.95 *(978-1-60836-407-7(0))* America Star Bks.

Brudlos, Joseph. Alpha Shade Chapter One. Brudlos, Christopher. 2005. (YA). per. 24.95 net. *(978-0-9768705-0-0(9))* Alpha Shade, Inc.

Brudos, Susan E. Will You Be My Friend? — We Really Are No Different. Downey, Joni J. 2004. (J). pap. *(978-0-932991-34-8(3))* Place In The Woods, The.

Brudos, Susan E. & Rubino, Alisa A. Wayne's Trail. 2004. (J). pap. *(978-0-932991-62-1(9))* Place In The Woods, The.

Brueggeman, Bryan. Fruzzle's Mystery Talent: A Bed Time Fantasy Story for Children Ages 3-10. Brueggeman, Karen & Paddock, Briana. 2013. 48p. pap. 10.99 *(978-0-9892565-0-6(2))* Dolphins Publishing.

Brueggemann, Mindy, photos by. Who Is Lilly? Brueggemann, Mindy. 2013. 44p. pap. 9.95 *(978-0-9855676-1-3(9))* Dankworth Publishing.

Bruel, Nick. Bob & Otto. Bruel, Robert O. 2007. (ENG.). 32p. (J). (gr. -1-3). 17.99 *(978-1-59643-203-1(9))* Roaring Brook Pr.

—Dinosaur Trouble. King-Smith, Dick. 2012. (ENG.). 128p. (J). (gr. 2-5). pap. 14.99 *(978-1-59643-935-1(1))* Roaring Brook Pr.

Bruel, Nick. Bad Kitty. Bruel, Nick. unabr. ed. 2012. (Bad Kitty Ser.). (ENG.). (J). (gr. -1-3). 9.99 *(978-1-4272-1362-4(3))* Macmillan Audio.

—Bad Kitty. Bruel, Nick. (Bad Kitty Ser.). (ENG.). 40p. (J). (gr. -1-3). 2nd ed. 2007. 16.95 *(978-1-59643-299-4(3))*; 10th anniv. ed. 2015. 16.99 *(978-1-62672-245-3(5))* Roaring Brook Pr.

—A Bad Kitty Christmas. Bruel, Nick. 2011. (Bad Kitty Ser.). (ENG.). 40p. (J). (gr. -1-3). 16.99 *(978-1-59643-668-8(9))* Roaring Brook Pr.

—Bad Kitty Gets a Bath. Bruel, Nick. 2008. (Bad Kitty Ser.). (ENG.). 128p. (J). (gr. 2-5). 14.99 *(978-1-59643-341-0(8))* Roaring Brook Pr.

—Bad Kitty Gets a Bath. Bruel, Nick. 2009. (Bad Kitty Ser.). (ENG.). 144p. (J). (gr. 2-5). pap. 6.99 *(978-0-312-58138-1(6))* Square Fish.

—Bad Kitty Meets the Baby. Bruel, Nick. 2011. (Bad Kitty Ser.). (ENG.). 144p. (J). (gr. 2-5). 13.99 *(978-1-59643-597-1(6))* Roaring Brook Pr.

—Bad Kitty Meets the Baby. Bruel, Nick. 2012. (Bad Kitty Ser.). (ENG.). 160p. (J). (gr. 2-5). pap. 6.99 *(978-0-312-64121-4(4))* Square Fish.

—Bad Kitty vs. Uncle Murray. Bruel, Nick. 2010. (Bad Kitty Ser.). (ENG.). 160p. (J). (gr. 2-5). 14.99 *(978-1-59643-596-4(8))* Roaring Brook Pr.

—Bad Kitty vs. Uncle Murray. Bruel, Nick. 2011. (Bad Kitty Ser.). (ENG.). 176p. (J). (gr. 2-5). pap. 6.99 *(978-0-312-67483-0(X))* Square Fish.

—Happy Birthday, Bad Kitty. Bruel, Nick. 2009. (Bad Kitty Ser.). (ENG.). 160p. (J). (gr. 2-5). 14.99 *(978-1-59643-342-7(6))* Roaring Brook Pr.

—Happy Birthday, Bad Kitty. Bruel, Nick. 2010. (Bad Kitty Ser.). (ENG.). 176p. (J). (gr. 2-5). pap. 6.99 *(978-0-312-62902-1(8))* Square Fish.

—Little Red Bird. Bruel, Nick. 2008. (ENG.). 32p. (J). (gr. -1-1). 17.99 *(978-1-59643-339-7(6))* Roaring Brook Pr.

—Poor Puppy & Bad Kitty. Bruel, Nick. ed. 2012. (Bad Kitty Ser.). (ENG.). 40p. (J). (gr. -1-3). 17.99 *(978-1-59643-844-6(4))* Roaring Brook Pr.

—Puppy's Big Day. Bruel, Nick. 2015. (Bad Kitty Ser.). (ENG.). 160p. (J). (gr. 2-5). 13.99 *(978-1-59643-976-4(9))* Roaring Brook Pr.

—Who Is Melvin Bubble? Bruel, Nick. 2006. (ENG.). 32p. (J). (gr. -1-3). 17.99 *(978-1-59643-116-4(4))* Roaring Brook Pr.

—A Wonderful Year. Bruel, Nick. 2015. (ENG.). 40p. (J). (gr. -1-1). 17.99 *(978-1-59643-611-4(5))* Roaring Brook Pr.

Brughera, Pamela, jt. illus. see Pisapia, Blasco.

Bruha, Victor, jt. illus. see Therian, Francis Patrick.

Bruhn, Joan Z. Children's Chillers & Thrillers. Johnson, Liliane & Dufton, Jo S. 136p. (Orig.). (J). pap. 10.00 *(978-0-930069-04-9(8))* Jasmine Pr.

Brukoff, Barry, photos by. Bella Loves Bunny. McPhail, David. 2013. (David Mcphail's Love Ser.). (ENG., 22p. (J). (gr. -1 — 1). bds. 8.95 *(978-1-4197-0543-4(1)*, Abrams Appleseed) Abrams.

Brulot, Heleen. Elephants at the Airport. Wolfson, Steve. 2013. 32p. pap. 11.95 *(978-0-9798324-5-1(4))* Argami Productions, LLC.

Brumpton, Keith. Soccer Camp. Bedford, David. 3rd ed. 2004. 80p. *(978-1-877003-45-5(X))* Little Hare Bks. AUS. Dist: HarperCollins Pubs. Australia.

—The Soccer Machine. Bedford, David. 2003. 80p. *(978-1-877003-26-4(3))* Little Hare Bks. AUS. Dist: HarperCollins Pubs. Australia.

—Top of the League. Bedford, David. 2nd ed. 2003. 80p. *(978-1-877003-30-1(1))* Little Hare Bks. AUS. Dist: HarperCollins Pubs. Australia.

Brundage, Frances. Cinderella: A Fairy Story. 2004. reprint ed. pap. 15.95 *(978-1-4179-8713-9(8))* Kessinger Publishing, LLC.

—The Three Bears. 2004. (Shape Bks.). (ENG.). 16p. (J). (gr. -1-3). 9.95 *(978-1-883211-94-3(8)*, 9781883211943) Laughing Elephant.

Brundage, Frances. The Cats' Pajamas. Brundage, Frances. 2006. (Shape Bks.). (ENG.). 16p. (J). (gr. -1-3). 9.95 *(978-1-59583-054-8(5)*, 9781595830548) Laughing Elephant.

Brundage, Scott. Chase the Chupacabra. Fields, Jan. 2014. (Monster Hunters Ser.). (ENG.). 80p. (J). (gr. 8-12). 27.07 *(978-1-62402-044-5(5))* Magic Wagon.

—Hunt for Sewer Gators. Fields, Jan. 2014. (Monster Hunters Ser.). (ENG.). 80p. (J). (gr. 8-12). 27.07 *(978-1-62402-045-2(3))* Magic Wagon.

—Search for Bigfoot. Fields, Jan. 2014. (Monster Hunters Ser.). (ENG.). 80p. (J). (gr. 8-12). 27.07 *(978-1-62402-046-9(1))* Magic Wagon.

—Tame Tahoe Tessie. Fields, Jan. 2014. (Monster Hunters Ser.). (ENG.). 80p. (J). (gr. 8-12). 27.07 *(978-1-62402-047-6(X))* Magic Wagon.

Brundige, Britt & Sturgeon, Bobbi. Cats on Vacation. Johnson, Sandi. Durant, Sybrina, ed. 2014. (ENG.). 12p. (J). (gr. -1-6). pap. 12.99 *(978-1-929063-46-8(6)*, 146) Moons & Stars Publishing For Children.

Bruner, Garth. Flying High with Butterflies: A Pre-K/ K Complete Supplemental Unit. Bair, Heather. 2004. per. 9.95 *(978-1-891541-03-2(X))* Insect Lore.

—I Spy a Butterfly: A Second Grade Complete Supplemental Unit. Bair, Heather. 2005. per. 9.95 *(978-1-891541-05-6(6))* Insect Lore.

—Michael's Superheroes. Meyers, Carly J. J. 2013. 28p. (J). pap. *(978-0-8425-2845-0(8))*, BYU Creative Works) Brigham Young Univ.

—O'H Me O'H My A Butterfly: A First Grade Complete Supplemental Unit. Bair, Heather. 2005. per. 9.95 *(978-1-891541-04-9(8))* Insect Lore.

Bruner, Justine. Imagination Rocks. Edwards, Cindi. 2009. 28p. pap. 13.99 *(978-1-4490-0386-9(9))* AuthorHouse.

Bruner, Tammy. Grandad's Book. Snyder, Jennifer. (J). 2005. 8.99 *(978-1-4183-0079-1(9))*; 2004. bds. 9.99 *(978-1-4183-0015-9(2))* Christ Inspired, Inc.

Brunet, Joshua S. When Butterflies Cross the Sky: The Monarch Butterfly Migration. Cooper, Sharon Katz. 2015. (Extraordinary Migrations Ser.). (ENG.). 24p. (gr. 2-3). pap. 8.95 ***(978-1-4795-6100-1(2))***; lib. bdg. 25.99 *(978-1-4795-6076-9(6))* Picture Window Bks.

Brunetti, Ivan & Schindelman, Joseph. Charlie & the Chocolate Factory. Dahl, Roald. 2011. (Penguin Classics Deluxe Edition Ser.). (ENG.). 176p. (gr. 12). 15.00 *(978-0-14-310633-3(3)*, Penguin Classics) Penguin Publishing Group.

Bruning, Richard, et al. The Tarantula. Wagner, Matt & Seagle, Steven. Kahan, Bob, ed. rev. ed. 2004. (Sandman Mystery Theatre Ser.). (ENG.). 112p. pap. 12.99 *(978-1-56389-195-3(6))* DC Comics.

Brunkus, Denise. Aloha-Ha-Ha! Park, Barbara. (Stepping Stone Book(TM) Ser.: No. 9). (ENG.). 128p. (J). (gr. 1-4). 2007. per. 4.99 *(978-0-375-83404-2(4))*; 2006. lib. bdg. 13.95 *(978-0-375-93403-2(0))* Random Hse. Children's Bks. (Random Hse. Bks. for Young Readers).

—Boo... & I Mean It! Park, Barbara. 2005. (Junie B. Jones Ser.: Bk. 7). 86p. (gr. 1-4). 15.00 *(978-0-7569-4783-5(9))* Perfection Learning Corp.

—Boss of Lunch. Park, Barbara. 2003. (Stepping Stone Book(TM) Ser.: No. 2). (ENG.). 96p. (J). (gr. 1-4). 4.99 *(978-0-375-80294-2(0)*, Random Hse. Bks. for Young Readers) Random Hse. Children's Bks.

—Charlie Hits It Big. Blumenthal, Deborah. 2008. 32p. (J). (gr. -1). lib. bdg. 17.89 *(978-0-06-056354-7(0))* HarperCollins Pubs.

—Cheater Pants. Park, Barbara. 2003. (Stepping Stone Book(TM) Ser.: No. 4). (ENG.). 96p. (J). (gr. 1-4). lib. bdg. 13.99 *(978-0-375-92301-2(2)*, Random Hse. Bks. for Young Readers) Random Hse. Children's Bks.

—Dumb Bunny. Park, Barbara. (ENG.). 128p. (J). (gr. 1-4). 2009. (Stepping Stone Book(TM) Ser.). 4.99 *(978-0-375-83810-1(4))*; 2007. (Stepping Stone Book Ser.: No. 11). lib. bdg. 14.99 *(978-0-375-93809-2(5))*; 2007. (Stepping Stone Book Ser.: No. 27). 11.99 *(978-0-375-83809-5(0))* Random Hse. Children's Bks. (Random Hse. Bks. for Young Readers).

—The Frog Principal. Calmenson, Stephanie. 2006. (ENG.). 32p. (J). pap. 5.99 *(978-0-439-81217-7(8)*, Scholastic Paperbacks) Scholastic, Inc.

—The Green Toenails Gang. Sharmat, Marjorie Weinman & Sharmat, Mitchell. 2005. (Olivia Sharp: Agent for Secrets Ser.). (ENG.). 80p. (J). (gr. 3-7). per. 5.99 *(978-0-440-42063-7(6)*, Yearling) Random Hse. Children's Bks.

—Jingle Bells, Batman Smells! Park, Barbara. 2009. (Stepping Stone Book(TM) Ser.: No. 8). (ENG.). 128p. (J). (gr. 1-4). 4.99 *(978-0-375-82809-6(5))* Random Hse., Inc.

—Jingle Bells, Batman Smells! (P. S. So Does May.) Park, Barbara. 2005. (Stepping Stone Book(TM) Ser.: No. 8). (ENG.). 128p. (J). (gr. 1-4). 11.95 *(978-0-375-82808-9(7)*, Random Hse. Bks. for Young Readers) Random Hse. Children's Bks.

—Junie B., First Grader - Aloha-Ha-Ha! Park, Barbara. 2007. (Junie B. Jones Ser.). 119p. (gr. 1-4). 15.00 *(978-0-7569-8085-6(2))* Perfection Learning Corp.

—Junie B., First Grader - Boo...and I Mean It! Park, Barbara. (Stepping Stone Book(TM) Ser.: No. 7). (ENG.). 96p. (J). (gr. 1-4). 2005. 4.99 *(978-0-375-82807-2(9))*; 2004. lib. bdg. 13.99 *(978-0-375-92806-2(5))* Random Hse. Children's Bks. (Random Hse. Bks. for Young Readers).

—Junie B., First Grader - Boss of Lunch. Park, Barbara. 2003. (Junie B., First Grader Ser.: No. 2). 96p. (J). (gr. k-3). lib. bdg. 11.99 *(978-0-375-90294-9(5)*, Golden Bks.) Random Hse. Children's Bks.

—Junie B. Jones & the Stupid Smelly Bus. Park, Barbara. 20th anniv. ed. 2012. (Stepping Stone Book(TM) Ser.). (ENG.). 96p. (J). (gr. 1-4). 14.99 *(978-0-375-86841-2(0)*, Random Hse. Bks. for Young Readers) Random Hse. Children's Bks.

Brunkus, Denise. Junie B. Jones Books in a Bus (Books 1-28), 28 vols. Park, Barbara. 2015. (ENG.). (J). (gr. 1-4). 139.72 ***(978-1-101-93859-1(5)***, Random Hse. Bks. for Young Readers) Random Hse. Children's Bks.

Brunkus, Denise. Junie B. Jones Complete Kindergarten Collection, 17 vols. Park, Barbara. 2014. (ENG.). 96p. (J). (gr. 1-4). 84.83 *(978-0-385-37694-5(4)*, Random Hse. Bks. for Young Readers) Random Hse. Children's Bks.

—Junie B. Jones y Su Gran Bocota. Park, Barbara. 2005. (Junie B. Jones Ser.).Tr. of Junie B. Jones & Her Big Fat Mouth. (SPA.). 80p. (J). (gr. 2-5). pap. 4.99 *(978-0-439-42516-2(6)*, Scholastic en Espanol) Scholastic, Inc.

—Junie B. Jones's Fifth Boxed Set Ever!, 4 vols. Park, Barbara. 2008. (ENG.). (J). (gr. 1-4). 19.96 *(978-0-375-85570-2(X)*, Random Hse. Bks. for Young Readers) Random Hse. Children's Bks.

—Junie B. Jones's Fourth Boxed Set Ever!, 4 vols. Park, Barbara. 2004. (ENG.). (J). (gr. 1-4). 19.96 *(978-0-375-82829-4(X)*, Random Hse. Bks. for Young Readers) Random Hse. Children's Bks.

—Junie B. Jones's Third Boxed Set Ever!, 4 vols., Bks. 9-12. Park, Barbara. 2003. (Junie B. Jones Ser.). (ENG.). (J). (gr. 1-4). 19.96 *(978-0-375-82552-1(5)*, Random Hse. Bks. for Young Readers) Random Hse. Children's Bks.

—Junie B. My Valentime. Park, Barbara. 2013. (Color Plus Card Stock Ser.). (ENG.). 12p. (J). (gr. -1-2). pap. 5.99 *(978-0-385-37302-9(3)*, Random Hse. Bks. for Young Readers) Random Hse. Children's Bks.

—Junie B.'s Essential Survival Guide to School. Park, Barbara. 2013. (Stepping Stone Book(TM) Ser.). (ENG.). 144p. (J). (gr. 1-4). 12.99 *(978-0-449-81783-4(0)*, Random Hse. Bks. for Young Readers) Random Hse. Children's Bks.

—Junie B.'s These Puzzles Hurt My Brain! Park, Barbara. 2011. (Stepping Stone Book(TM) Ser.). (ENG.). 240p. (J). (gr. 1-4). 5.99 *(978-0-375-87123-8(3)*, Random Hse. Bks. for Young Readers) Random Hse. Children's Bks.

—My Teacher for President. Winters, Kay. 2008. (ENG.). 32p. (J). (gr. -1-1). pap. 6.99 *(978-0-14-241170-4(1)*, Puffin) Penguin Publishing Group.

—My Teacher for President. Winters, Kay. 2008. (gr. -1-k). 17.00 *(978-0-7569-8925-5(6))* Perfection Learning Corp.

—One-Man Band. Park, Barbara. 2003. (Stepping Stone Book(TM) Ser.: No. 5). (ENG.). 96p. (J). (gr. 1-4). lib. bdg. 13.99 *(978-0-375-92522-1(8)*, Random Hse. Bks. for Young Readers) Random Hse. Children's Bks.

—The Pizza Monster. Sharmat, Marjorie Weinman & Sharmat, Mitchell. 2nd ed. 2005. (Olivia Sharp: Agent for Secrets Ser.). (ENG.). 80p. (J). (gr. 3-7). reprint ed. 5.99 *(978-0-440-42059-0(8)*, Yearling) Random Hse. Children's Bks.

—The Princess of the Fillmore Street School. Sharmat, Marjorie Weinman & Sharmat, Mitchell. 2005. (Olivia Sharp: Agent for Secrets Ser.). (ENG.). 80p. (J). (gr. 3-7). 5.99 *(978-0-440-42060-6(1)*, Yearling) Random Hse. Children's Bks.

—Read All about It! Bush, Laura & Hager, Jenna Bush. 2010. (ENG.). 32p. (J). (gr. -1-3). pap. 6.99 *(978-0-06-156077-4(4))* HarperCollins Pubs.

—Read All about It! Bush, Laura & Hager, Jenna. 2008. (ENG.). 32p. (J). (gr. -1-3). 17.99 *(978-0-06-156075-0(8))* HarperCollins Pubs.

—Read All about It! Bush, Laura & Hager, Jenna Bush. 2008. 32p. (J). (gr. -1-3). lib. bdg. 18.89 *(978-0-06-156076-7(6))* HarperCollins Pubs.

—Shipwrecked, No. 23. Park, Barbara. 2005. (Stepping Stone Book(TM) Ser.: No. 6). (ENG.). 96p. (J). (gr. 1-4). mass mkt. 4.99 *(978-0-375-82805-8(2)*, Random Hse. Bks. for Young Readers) Random Hse. Children's Bks.

—Sloppy Joe. Keane, Dave. 2009. 32p. (J). (gr. -1-2). lib. bdg. 17.89 *(978-0-06-171021-6(0))*; (ENG.). 16.99 *(978-0-06-171020-9(2))* HarperCollins Pubs.

—The Sly Spy. Sharmat, Marjorie Weinman & Sharmat, Mitchell. 2005. (Olivia Sharp: Agent for Secrets Ser.). (ENG.). 80p. (J). (gr. 3-7). per. 4.99 *(978-0-440-42062-0(8)*, Yearling) Random Hse. Children's Bks.

—Toothless Wonder. Park, Barbara. 2003. (Junie B. Jones Ser.: Bk. 3). 80p. (gr. 1-4). 15.00 *(978-0-7569-1621-3(6))* Perfection Learning Corp.

—Toothless Wonder. Park, Barbara. 2003. (Stepping Stone Book(TM) Ser.: No. 3). (ENG.). 96p. (J). (gr. 1-4). pap. 4.99 *(978-0-375-82223-0(2)*, Random Hse. Bks. for Young Readers) Random Hse. Children's Bks.

—Turkeys We Have Loved & Eaten, No. 28. Park, Barbara. 2012. (Stepping Stone Book(TM) Ser.). (ENG.). 144p. (J). (gr. 1-4). lib. bdg. 14.99 *(978-0-375-97063-4(0)*, Random Hse. Bks. for Young Readers) Random Hse. Children's Bks.

—Turkeys We Have Loved & Eaten (And Other Thankful Stuff) Park, Barbara. 2014. (Stepping Stone Book(TM) Ser.). (ENG.). 144p. (J). (gr. 1-4). 4.99 *(978-0-375-87115-3(2)*, Random Hse. Bks. for Young Readers) Random Hse. Children's Bks.

—Turkeys We Have Loved & Eaten (and Other Thankful Stuff), No. 28. Park, Barbara. 2012. (Stepping Stone Book(TM) Ser.). (ENG.). 144p. (J). (gr. 1-4). 11.99 *(978-0-375-87063-7(6)*, Random Hse. Bks. for Young Readers) Random Hse. Children's Bks.

Brunkus, Denise. Cheater Pants. Brunkus, Denise, tr. Park, Barbara. 2004. (Stepping Stone Book(TM) Ser.: No. 4). (ENG.). 96p. (J). (gr. 1-4). 4.99 *(978-0-375-82302-2(6)*, Random Hse. Bks. for Young Readers) Random Hse. Children's Bks.

—One-Man Band. Brunkus, Denise, tr. Park, Barbara. 2004. (Stepping Stone Book Ser.: No. 5). (ENG.). 96p. (J). (gr. 1-4). 4.99 *(978-0-375-82536-1(3)*, Random Hse. Bks. for Young Readers) Random Hse. Children's Bks.

Brunner, Terry. Where Is Cecil? McCoy, M. M. Maximilian Press Publishers Staff, ed. unabr. l.t. ed. 2005. 28p. (J). lib. bdg. 12.50 *(978-1-930211-68-1(6))* Maximilian Pr. Pubs.

Bruno, Iacopo. The Ability. Vaughan, M. M. (Ability Ser.). (ENG.). (YA). (gr. 3-7). 2014. 352p. pap. 6.99 *(978-1-4424-5201-5(3))*; 2013. 336p. 15.99 *(978-1-4424-5200-8(5))* McElderry, Margaret K. Bks. (McElderry, Margaret K. Bks.).

—The Actual & Truthful Adventures of Becky Thatcher. Lawson, Jessica. 2014. (ENG.). 224p. (J). (gr. 3-7). 16.99 *(978-1-4814-0150-0(5))*, Simon & Schuster Bks. For Young Readers) Simon & Schuster Bks. For Young Readers.

—The Book of Lost Things. Voigt, Cynthia. 2013. (Mister Max Ser.: Bk. 1). (ENG.). 400p. (J). (gr. 3-7). 16.99 *(978-0-307-97681-9(5))*, Knopf Bks. for Young Readers) Random Hse. Children's Bks.

Bruno, Iacopo. The Box & the Dragonfly. Sanders, Ted. 2015. 534p. (J). ***(978-0-06-239019-6(8))*** Harper & Row Ltd.

Bruno, Iacopo. The Box & the Dragonfly. Sanders, Ted. 2015. (Keepers Ser.: 1). (ENG.). 544p. (J). (gr. 3-7). 16.99 *(978-0-06-227582-0(8))* HarperCollins Pubs.

—Brother from a Box. Kuhlman, Evan. (ENG.). 288p. (J). (gr. 4-7). 2013. pap. 6.99 *(978-1-4424-2659-7(4))*; 2012. 16.99 *(978-1-4424-2658-0(6))* Simon & Schuster Children's Publishing. (Atheneum Bks. for Young Readers).

Bruno, Iacopo. The Cathedral of Fear. Adler, Irene. McGuinness, Nanette, tr. from ITA. 2015. (Sherlock, Lupin, & Me Ser.). (ENG.). 256p. (gr. 4-8). lib. bdg. 25.32 ***(978-1-4965-0490-6(9))*** Stone Arch Bks.

Bruno, Iacopo. Compass of Dreams, 1 vol. Baccalario, Pierdomenico. Pernigotti, Chiara, tr. from ITA. 2014. (Enchanted Emporium Ser.). (ENG.). 240p. (gr. 4-8). 25.32 *(978-1-4342-6517-3(X))* Stone Arch Bks.

—The Dark Lady, 1 vol. Adler, Irene. 2014. (Sherlock, Lupin, & Me Ser.). (ENG.). 240p. (gr. 4-8). 12.95 *(978-1-62370-040-9(X))* Capstone Young Readers.

Bruno, Iacopo. Enchanted Emporium. Baccalario, Pierdomenico. Pernigotti, Chiara, tr. (Enchanted Emporium Ser.). (ENG.). 240p. (gr. 4-8). 2015. 75.96 ***(978-1-4965-0047-2(4))***; 2014. 50.64 *(978-1-4342-9603-0(2))* Stone Arch Bks.

Bruno, Iacopo. Good Night, Zombie. Preller, James. 2013. (Scary Tales Ser.: 3). (ENG.). 112p. (J). (gr. 2-5). 15.99 *(978-1-250-01890-8(0))*; pap. 5.99 *(978-1-250-01891-5(9))* Feiwel & Friends.

—Home Sweet Horror. Preller, James. 2013. (Scary Tales Ser.: 1). (ENG.). 112p. (J). (gr. 2-5). 14.99 *(978-1-250-01886-1(2))*; pap. 5.99 *(978-1-250-01887-8(0))* Feiwel & Friends.

—I Scream, You Scream! Preller, James. 2013. (Scary Tales Ser.: 2). (ENG.). 112p. (J). (gr. 2-5). 14.99 *(978-1-250-01888-5(9))*; pap. 5.99 *(978-1-250-01889-2(7))* Feiwel & Friends.

—Iron Hearted Violet. Barnhill, Kelly. 2014. (ENG.). 448p. (J). (gr. 3-7). pap. 7.00 *(978-0-316-05675-5(8))* Little, Brown Bks. for Young Readers.

—Map of the Passages. Baccalario, Pierdomenico. McGuinness, Nanette, tr. from ITA. 2015. (Enchanted Emporium Ser.). (ENG.). 240p. (gr. 4-8). 12.95 *(978-1-62370-204-5(6))* Stone Arch Bks.

—Mesmerized: How Ben Franklin Solved a Mystery That Baffled All of France. Rockliff, Mara. 2015. (ENG.). 48p. (J). (gr. 1-4). 17.99 *(978-0-7636-6351-3(4))* Candlewick Pr.

—Mindscape. Vaughan, M. M. 2015. (Ability Ser.). (ENG.). 336p. (YA). (gr. 3-7). pap. 7.99 *(978-1-4424-5205-3(6))*, McElderry, Margaret K. Bks.) McElderry, Margaret K. Bks.

—Mister Max: the Book of Lost Things: Mister Max 1. Voigt, Cynthia. 2014. (Mister Max Ser.). (ENG.). 400p. (J). (gr. 3-7). 7.99 *(978-0-307-97682-6(3))*, Yearling) Random Hse. Children's Bks.

—Mister Max: the Book of Secrets. Voigt, Cynthia. 2014. (Mister Max Ser.). (ENG.). 384p. (J). (gr. 3-7). 16.99 *(978-0-307-97684-0(X))*, Knopf Bks. for Young Readers) Random Hse. Children's Bks.

—Mister Max: the Book of Secrets: Mister Max 2. Voigt, Cynthia. 2014. (Mister Max Ser.). (ENG.). 384p. (J). (gr. 3-7). lib. bdg. 19.99 *(978-0-375-97124-2(6))*, Knopf Bks. for Young Readers) Random Hse. Children's Bks.

—The Mystery of the Scarlet Rose. Adler, Irene. McGuinness, Nanette, tr. from ITA. 2015. (Sherlock, Lupin, & Me Ser.). (ENG.). 256p. (gr. 4-8). lib. bdg. 25.32 *(978-1-4342-6524-1(2))* Stone Arch Bks.

—Nightmareland. Preller, James. 2014. (Scary Tales Ser.: 4). (ENG.). 112p. (J). (gr. 2-5). 15.99 *(978-1-250-01892-2(7))* Feiwel & Friends.

—The School for Good & Evil. Chainani, Soman. (ENG.). (J). (gr. 3-7). 2014. (School for Good & Evil Ser.: 1). 544p. pap. 6.99 *(978-0-06-210490-8(X))*; 2013. (School for Good & Evil Trilogy: No. 1). 400p. 17.99 *(978-0-06-210489-2(6))* HarperCollins Pubs.

Bruno, Iacopo. The School for Good & Evil. Chainani, Soman. 2014. (School for Good & Evil Trilogy: No. 1). 496p. lib. bdg. 17.20 ***(978-0-606-36513-0(3))*** Turtleback Bks.

Bruno, Iacopo. Sherlock, Lupin & Me, 1 vol. Adler, Irene. 2014. (Sherlock, Lupin, & Me Ser.). (ENG.). 240p. (gr. 4-8). 50.64 *(978-1-4342-9602-3(4))* Stone Arch Bks.

—The Spindlers. Oliver, Lauren. (ENG.). (J). (gr. 3-7). 2013. 272p. pap. 8.99 *(978-0-06-197809-8(4))*; 2012. 256p. 16.99 *(978-0-06-197808-1(6))* HarperCollins Pubs.

—Suitcase of Stars, 1 vol. Baccalario, P. D. Pernigotti, Chiara, tr. from ITA. 2014. (Enchanted Emporium Ser.). (ENG.). 240p. (gr. 4-8). 25.32 *(978-1-4342-6516-6(1))* Stone Arch Bks.

—Suitcase of Stars, 1 vol. Baccalario, Pierdomenico. 2014. (Enchanted Emporium Ser.). (ENG.). 240p. (gr. 4-8). 12.95 *(978-1-62370-039-3(6))* Capstone Young Readers.

—Swamp Monster. Preller, James. 2015. (Scary Tales Ser.: 6). (ENG.). 96p. (J). (gr. 2-5). 15.99 *(978-1-250-04097-8(3))* Feiwel & Friends.

—The Book of Kings. Voigt, Cynthia. 2015. (Mister Max Ser.). (ENG.). 352p. (J). (gr. 3-7). 16.99 *(978-0-307-97687-1(4))*, Knopf Bks. for Young Readers) Random Hse. Children's Bks.

Bruno, Iacopo. The Thief of Mirrors. Baccalario, Pierdomenico & McGuinness, Nanette. Pernigotti, Chiara, tr. from ITA. 2015. (Enchanted Emporium Ser.). (ENG.). 240p. (gr. 4-8). lib. bdg. 25.32 ***(978-1-4965-0516-3(6))*** Stone Arch Bks.

Bruno, Iacopo. The Tom Sawyer Collection: The Adventures of Tom Sawyer; the Adventures of Huckleberry Finn; the Actual & Truthful Adventures of Becky Thatcher. Lawson, Jessica & Twain, Mark. ed. 2014. (ENG.). 944p. (J). (gr. 3-7). 50.99 *(978-1-4814-0536-2(5))*, Simon & Schuster Bks. For Young Readers) Simon & Schuster Bks. For Young Readers.

—A World Without Princes. Chainani, Soman. 2014. (School for Good & Evil Trilogy: No. 2). (ENG.). 400p. (J). *(978-0-06-234072-6(7))* Harper & Row Ltd.

—A World Without Princes. Chainani, Soman. 2015. (School for Good & Evil Ser.: 2). (ENG.). 512p. (J). (gr. 3-7). pap. 6.99 *(978-0-06-210493-9(4))* HarperCollins Pubs.

Bruno, Iacopo, jt. illus. see Iacopo, Bruno.

Bruno, Margaret Farrell. My Little Friend Goes to the Zoo. Finnegan, Evelyn M. 2006. 32p. (J). (gr. -1-3). reprint ed. pap. 7.00 *(978-1-4223-5402-5(4))* DIANE Publishing Co.

Brunot, Katerina. Story Time with Princess Dorothy. Scretching, Dorothy/Janis. Walters, Steve, ed. 2012. 32p. (J). 20.00 *(978-0-9719767-4-0(0))*, Crowned Warrior Publishing) Walters, Steve Ministries.

Bruns, Scott. Demo: The Story of a Junkyard Dog. Bozak, Jon. 2008. (ENG.). 56p. (J). (gr. 2-4). 16.95 *(978-0-9816188-0-7(4))* Fifth Paw Pr.

Brunson, Stephanie. The Chocolate Kingdom Caper. Ballman, Swanee. 2003. 32p. (J). per. 6.95 *(978-1-59094-025-9(3))*, 1590940253) Jawbone Publishing Corp.

Brus, Mischa. Little Full Stop. Brus, Mischa. Schlitz, Matt. 2012. (ENG.). 32p. (J). *(978-0-9751837-1-7(0))* Mambooks.

Bruschetti-Weiss, Janet. A Starfish Called Rhonda. Bruschetti-Weiss, Janet. 2003. 28p. (J). *(978-0-9747716-0-1(0))* Weiss, Janet Bruschetti.

Brusco, Giulia. Kiss & Tell. Amano, Jeff. 2006. 224p. (YA). pap. 19.99 *(978-1-58240-540-7(9))* Image Comics.

Brush, Joan. Our House Is Round: A Kid's Book about Why Protecting Our Earth Matters. Kondonassis, Yolanda. 2012. (ENG.). 48p. (J). (gr. k-3). 16.95 *(978-1-61608-588-9(6))*, 608588, Sky Pony Pr.) Skyhorse Publishing Co., Inc.

Bruton, W. The Dogs' Grand Dinner Party. 2011. (American Antiquarian Society Ser.). (ENG.). 16p. (gr. 1). 24.95 *(978-1-4290-9738-3(8))* Applewood Bks.

Bryan, Ashley. All Things Bright & Beautiful. Alexander, Cecil F. 2010. (ENG.). 40p. (J). (gr. -1-3). 17.99 *(978-1-4169-8939-4(0))*, Atheneum Bks. for Young Readers) Simon & Schuster Children's Publishing.

—A Nest Full of Stars. Berry, James. 2004. 104p. (J). (gr. 2-18). 16.89 *(978-0-06-052748-8(X))* HarperCollins Pubs.

Bryan, Ashley. Sail Away. Hughes, Langston. 2015. (ENG.). 40p. (J). (gr. -1-3). 17.99 ***(978-1-4814-3085-2(8))*** Simon & Schuster Children's Publishing.

Bryan, Ashley. The Sun Is So Quiet. Giovanni, Nikki. 2014. (ENG.). 32p. (J). (gr. -1-3). 7.99 *(978-1-250-04669-7(6))* Square Fish.

Bryan, Ashley. Ashley Bryan: Words to My Life's Song. Bryan, Ashley. McGuinness, Bill, photos by. 2009. (ENG.). 64p. (J). (gr. -1-18). 19.99 *(978-1-4169-0541-7(3))*, Atheneum Bks. for Young Readers) Simon & Schuster Children's Publishing.

—Ashley Bryan's Puppets: Making Something from Everything. Bryan, Ashley. 2014. (ENG.). 80p. (J). (gr. -1). 19.99 *(978-1-4424-8728-4(3))*, Atheneum Bks. for Young Readers) Simon & Schuster Children's Publishing.

—Beautiful Blackbird. Bryan, Ashley. 2003. (ENG.). 40p. (J). (gr. -1-3). 19.99 *(978-0-689-84731-8(9))*, Atheneum Bks. for Young Readers) Simon & Schuster Children's Publishing.

—Can't Scare Me! Bryan, Ashley. 2013. (ENG.). 40p. (J). (gr. -1-3). 16.99 *(978-1-4424-7657-8(5))*, Atheneum Bks. for Young Readers) Simon & Schuster Children's Publishing.

—Let It Shine: Three Favorite Spirituals. Bryan, Ashley. 2007. (ENG.). 40p. (J). (gr. -1-3). 17.99 *(978-0-689-84732-5(7))*, Atheneum Bks. for Young Readers) Simon & Schuster Children's Publishing.

—Who Built the Stable? A Nativity Poem. Bryan, Ashley. 2012. (ENG.). 40p. (J). (gr. -1-3). 16.99 *(978-1-4424-0934-7(7))*, Atheneum Bks. for Young Readers) Simon & Schuster Children's Publishing.

Bryan, Ashley. All Night, All Day: A Child's First Book of African-American Spirituals. Bryan, Ashley, selected by. 2004. (ENG.). 48p. (J). (gr. -1-3). 7.99 *(978-0-689-86786-6(7))*, Atheneum Bks. for Young Readers) Simon & Schuster Children's Publishing.

Bryan, Diana. The Fisherman & His Wife. Grimm, Jacob & Grimm, Wilhelm K. 2005. (Rabbit Ears-A Classic Tale Set 2 Ser.). 32p. (gr. k-5). 25.65 *(978-1-59197-747-6(9))* Spotlight.

—The Monkey People. Metaxas, Eric. 2005. (Rabbit Ears Ser.). 36p. (gr. k-5). 25.65 *(978-1-59679-226-5(4))* Spotlight.

Bryan, Hendrix, jt. illus. see Hendrix, Bryan.

Bryan, Hintz. Mr. Blue a Job for You. Donahue, Laurie. 2010. 32p. (J). 15.95 *(978-0-9799116-2-0(1))* LifeSong Pubs.

Bryan-Hunt, Jan. Christmas. Trueit, Trudi Strain. 2013. (Holidays & Celebrations Ser.). (ENG.). 32p. (J). (gr. k-3). 27.07 *(978-1-62323-514-7(6))*, 206276) Child's World, Inc., The.

—J Is for Jesus: An Easter Alphabet & Activity Book. O'Neal, Debbie Trafton. 2005. 32p. (J). (gr. 3-7). per., act. bk. ed. 11.99 *(978-0-8066-5123-1(7))*, Augsburg Bks.) Augsburg Fortress, Pubs.

—Pumpkin Fever. Simon, Charnan. 2011. (Rookie Ready to Learn Ser.). 40p. (J). (ENG.). pap. 5.95 *(978-0-531-26803-2(9))*; (gr. -1-k). lib. bdg. 23.00 *(978-0-531-25643-5(X))* Scholastic Library Publishing. (Children's Pr.).

Bryan, Tayler. Walter the Dreamer in the Enchanted Wood. Kesead, Melissa. 2011. (ENG.). 34p. pap. 9.95 *(978-1-4635-6093-5(1))* CreateSpace Independent Publishing Platform.

Bryant, Carol W., jt. illus. see Klug, Leigh A.

Bryant, Julie. Right Where You Need Me. Grant, Rose. 2012. 16p. pap. 15.99 *(978-1-4685-6856-1(6))* AuthorHouse.

Bryant, Kerry. Freddie & Mee. Wales, Sid. 2013. 28p. pap. *(978-1-78222-097-8(6))* Paragon Publishing, Rothersthorpe.

Bryant, Laura. Five Little Penguins Slipping on the Ice. Metzger, Steve. 2008. (ENG.). (J). (gr. -1-3). 18.95 *(978-0-545-07408-7(8))* Scholastic, Inc.

—Five Little Sharks Swimming in the Sea. Metzger, Steve. 2004. (J). *(978-0-439-66139-3(0))*; pap. *(978-0-439-59228-4(3))* Scholastic, Inc.

Bryant, Laura & Bryant, Laura J. Kitty Cat, Kitty Cat, Are You Waking Up?, 0 vols. Sampson, Michael R. & Martin, Bill, Jr. 2008. (ENG.). 24p. (J). (gr. -1-1). 14.99 *(978-0-7614-5438-0(1))*, 9780761454380, Amazon Children's Publishing) Amazon Publishing.

Bryant, Laura J. The Bear Hug. Callahan, Sean. 2006. (ENG.). 24p. (J). (gr. -1-1). 15.95 *(978-0-8075-0596-0(X))* Whitman, Albert & Co.

—A Fairy in a Dairy, 0 vols. Nolan, Lucy. 2013. (ENG.). 29p. (J). (gr. -1-2). pap. 9.99 *(978-1-4778-1678-3(X))*, 9781477816783, Amazon Children's Publishing) Amazon Publishing.

—Five Little Penguins Slipping on the Ice. Metzger, Steve. 2008. (ENG.). (J). (gr. -1-3). 9.99 *(978-0-545-07407-0(X))* Scholastic, Inc.

—God Found Us You. Bergren, Lisa T. 2009. (J). lib. bdg. 3.99 *(978-0-06-113177-6(6))* HarperCollins Pubs.

—God Found Us You. Bergren, Lisa T. 2009. (HarperBlessings Ser.). (ENG.). 40p. (J). (gr. -1-2). 10.99 *(978-0-06-113176-9(8))* HarperCollins Pubs.

—God Gave Us Angels. Bergren, Lisa T. 2014. (ENG.). 40p. (J). (gr. -1-2). 10.99 *(978-1-60142-661-1(5))*, WaterBrook Pr.) Doubleday Religious Publishing Group, The.

—God Gave Us Love. Bergren, Lisa T. 2011. (ENG.). 22p. (J). (gr. k — 1). bds. 6.99 *(978-0-307-73027-5(1))*, WaterBrook Pr.) Doubleday Religious Publishing Group, The.

Bryant, Laura J. God Gave Us Sleep. Bergren, Lisa T. 2015. (ENG.). 40p. (J). (gr. -1-2). 10.99 ***(978-1-60142-663-5(1))***, WaterBrook Pr.) Doubleday Religious Publishing Group, The.

Bryant, Laura J. God Gave Us So Much: A Limited-Edition Three-Book Treasury. Bergren, Lisa T. 2010. (ENG.). 112p. 19.99 *(978-0-307-44629-9(8))*, WaterBrook Pr.) Doubleday Religious Publishing Group, The.

—God Gave Us the World. Bergren, Lisa T. 2011. (ENG.). 40p. (J). (gr. -1-2). 10.99 *(978-1-4000-7448-8(7))*, WaterBrook Pr.) Doubleday Religious Publishing Group, The.

—God's Light, Shining Bright. Nolan, Allia Zobel. 2006. 8p. (J). 12.99 *(978-0-8254-5527-8(8))* Kregel Pubns.

—Heaven God's Promise for Me, 1 vol. Lotz, Anne Graham & Graham Lotz, Anne. 2011. (ENG.). 40p. (J). 16.99 *(978-0-310-71601-3(2))* Zondervan.

—How Big Is God? Bergren, Lisa T. 2008. (HarperBlessings Ser.). (ENG.). 32p. (J). (gr. -1-2). 10.99 *(978-0-06-113174-5(1))* HarperCollins Pubs.

—How Many Kisses Good Night? Thomas, Jean Monrad. 2010. (ENG.). 16p. (J). (— 1). bds. 7.99 *(978-0-375-86146-8(7))*, Random Hse. Bks. for Young Readers) Random Hse. Children's Bks.

—I Need You. Murphy, Patricia J. 2003. (Rookie Readers Ser.). 31p. (J). (gr. 1-2). 12.60 *(978-0-7569-2065-4(5))* Perfection Learning Corp.

—I Need You. Murphy, Patricia J. 2003. (Rookie Reader Español Ser.). (ENG.). (J). (gr. k-2). pap. 4.95 *(978-0-516-26966-5(6))*, Children's Pr.) Scholastic Library Publishing.

—If You Were My Baby: A Wildlife Lullaby. Hodgkins, Fran. (Simply Nature Book Ser.). (J). (gr. -1 — 1). 2007. 26p. bds. 7.95 *(978-1-58469-090-0(9))*; 2005. 32p. pap. 8.95 *(978-1-58469-075-7(5))*; 2005. 32p. 16.95 *(978-1-58469-074-0(7))* Dawn Pubns.

—Jam & Honey. Morales, Melita. 2011. (ENG.). 32p. (J). (gr. -1-2). 15.99 *(978-1-58246-299-8(2))*, Tricycle Pr.) Ten Speed Pr.

—Jo MacDonald Had a Garden. Quattlebaum, Mary. 2013. (ENG.). 26p. (J). (gr. -1 — 1). bds. 7.95 *(978-1-58469-225-6(1))* Dawn Pubns.

—Jo MacDonald Hiked in the Woods. Quattlebaum, Mary. 2013. (ENG.). 32p. (J). (gr. -1-3). 16.95 *(978-1-58469-334-5(7))*; pap. 8.95 *(978-1-58469-335-2(5))* Dawn Pubns.

—Jo MacDonald Saw a Pond. Quattlebaum, Mary. (J). 2013. (ENG.). 26p. (gr. -1 — 1). bds. 7.95 *(978-1-58469-224-9(3))*; 2011. 32p. 16.95 *(978-1-58469-150-1(6))*; 2011. 32p. pap. 8.95 *(978-1-58469-151-8(4))* Dawn Pubns.

—Kitty Cat, Kitty Cat, Are You Going to School?, 0 vols. Martin, Bill, Jr. & Sampson, Michael. 2013. (ENG.). (J). (gr. -1-2). 16.99 *(978-1-4778-1722-3(0))*, 9781477817223, Amazon Children's Publishing) Amazon Publishing.

—Kitty Cat, Kitty Cat, Are You Going to Sleep?, 0 vols. Martin, Bill, Jr. & Sampson, Michael. 2011. (ENG.). 24p. (J). (gr. -1-3). 15.99 *(978-0-7614-5946-0(4))*, 9780761459460, Amazon Children's Publishing) Amazon Publishing.

—Kitty Cat, Kitty Cat, Are You Waking Up?, 0 vols. Martin, Bill, Jr. & Sampson, Michael. 2011. (ENG.). 24p. (J). (gr. -1-1). pap. 6.99 *(978-0-7614-5841-8(7))*, 9780761458418, Amazon Children's Publishing) Amazon Publishing.

—Kitty Cat, Kitty Cat, Are You Waking Up?, 0 vols. Sampson, Michael & Martin, Bill, Jr. 2011. (ENG.). 26p. (J). (gr. -1-1). bds. 7.99 *(978-0-7614-5968-2(5))*, 9780761459682, Amazon Children's Publishing) Amazon Publishing.

—Little Fox Goes to the End of the World, 0 vols. Tompert, Ann & Lister, Ralph. 2010. (ENG.). 32p. (J). (gr. -1-2). 16.99 *(978-0-7614-5703-9(8))*, 9780761457039, Amazon Children's Publishing) Amazon Publishing.

—M Is for Mountain State: A West Virginia Alphabet. Riehle, Mary Ann McCabe. 2004. (State Ser.). (ENG.). 40p. (J). 17.95 *(978-1-58536-151-9(8))* Sleeping Bear Pr.

—Patti Cake & Her New Doll. Giff, Patricia Reilly. 2014. (ENG.). 32p. (J). (gr. -1-k). 16.99 *(978-0-545-24465-7(X))*, Orchard Bks.) Scholastic, Inc.

—Seven Little Bunnies, 0 vols. Stiegemeyer, Julie. 2010. (ENG.). 24p. (J). (gr. -1-3). 15.99 *(978-0-7614-5600-1(7))*, 9780761456001, Amazon Children's Publishing) Amazon Publishing.

Bryant, Laura J. Tractor Day. Bryant, Laura J. Ransom, Candice F. 2007. (ENG.). 32p. (J). (gr. -1-k). 16.95 *(978-0-8027-8090-4(3))* Walker & Co.

Bryant, Laura J., jt. illus. see Bryant, Laura.

Bryant, Michael. Bein' with You This Way. Nikola-Lisa, W. 97th ed. 2013. (ENG.). 32p. (J). (gr. -1-3). 9.95 *(978-1-880000-26-7(1))* Lee & Low Bks., Inc.

Bryant, Ray. The Book of Space. 2013. (Questions Ser.). (ENG.). 64p. (J). (gr. k-3). 7.99 *(978-0-7534-7099-2(3))*, Kingfisher) Roaring Brook Pr.

Brycelea, Clifford & Yazzie, Johnson. The Stone Cutter & the Navajo Maiden. Browne, Vee. Manavi, Lorraine Begay, tr. from ENG. 2008. (NAV & ENG.). 32p. (J). (gr. -1-3). 17.95 *(978-1-893354-92-0(X))* Salina Bookshelf Inc.

Brychta, Alex. Camping Adventure. Hunt, Roderick. 2003. (ENG.). 24p. pap. *(978-0-19-845203-4(9))* Oxford Univ. Pr., Inc.

Bryer, Tom. Fun Poems for Kids. Bryer, Tom. 2012. 26p. *(978-1-908341-74-7(2))* Paragon Publishing, Rothersthorpe.

Bryne, Kelly. The Three Little Pigs: A Wheel-Y Silly Fairy Tale. Gallo, Tina. 2011. (Little Simon Sillies Ser.). (ENG.). 14p. (J). (gr. -1-1). 5.99 *(978-1-4424-2107-3(X))*, Little Simon) Little Simon.

Brzozowski, Christina. Sniffle, Sneeze, Cough Back Off! Grimshaw, Luke. 2008. 24p. pap. 24.95 *(978-1-60703-607-4(X))* America Star Bks.

—Sniffle, Sneeze, Cough... Back Off!, 1 vol. Grimshaw, Luke. 2010. 22p. 24.95 *(978-1-4512-1034-7(5))* America Star Bks.

Buba, Joy. Lyrico: The Only Horse of His Kind. Foster, Elizabeth Vincent. 2nd ed. 2004. 230p. (gr. 6-8). reprint ed. 8.95 *(978-0-930407-21-6(0))* Parabola Bks.

Bubar, Lorraine. Lullaby. Friedman, Debbie. 2014. (ENG.). 32p. (J). 18.99 *(978-1-58023-807-6(6))*, Jewish Lights Publishing) LongHill Partners, Inc.

Bubp, Jennifer. The Lizard Who Wanted to Be a Mouse. Russell, Allyson. 2009. 28p. pap. 12.95 *(978-1-59858-938-2(5))* Dog Ear Publishing, LLC.

Buccheri, Chiara. I'll Haunt You! - Meet a Ghost. Knudsen, Shannon. 2014. (Monster Buddies Ser.). (ENG.). 24p. (gr. k-2). lib. bdg. 23.93 *(978-0-7613-9186-9(X))*, Millbrook Pr.) Lerner Publishing Group.

—I'M a Midnight Snacker! - Meet a Vampire. Bullard, Lisa. 2014. (Monster Buddies Ser.). (ENG.). 24p. (gr. k-2). lib. bdg. 23.93 *(978-0-7613-9191-3(6))*, Millbrook Pr.) Lerner Publishing Group.

Bucci, Gino. No More Peanut Butter, Daniel! Ciccone, Tiziana & Linardi, Franca. 2012. 36p. pap. 13.95 *(978-1-61897-718-2(0))*, Strategic Bk. Publishing) Strategic Book Publishing & Rights Agency (SBPRA).

—The Pancake Princess. Ciccone, Tizania & Linardi, Franca. 2012. 36p. pap. 13.95 *(978-1-61897-720-5(2))*, Strategic Bk. Publishing) Strategic Book Publishing & Rights Agency (SBPRA).

Bucco, Joe. Everyman: Be the People. Goldman, Steven & Goldman, Dan. 2004. 96p. per. 6.00 *(978-0-9759152-0-2(7))* KINJIN Global.

Buchanan, Jessie, jt. illus. see Thoraval, Carly.

Buchanan, Yvonne. Celebremos Juneteenth! Weatherford, Carole Boston. de La Vega, Eida, tr. from ENG. 2007. (SPA.). 32p. (J). (gr. -1-3). pap. 7.95 *(978-1-60060-247-4(9))* Lee & Low Bks., Inc.

Bucher, Barbara Latini. Three Young Wild Cats. Evans, Betty J. 2008. 20p. pap. 24.95 *(978-1-60610-809-3(3))* America Star Bks.

Bucher, Cecile. Ben, the Bells & the Peacocks. Trooboff, Rhoda. 2006. (ENG.). 36p. (J). per. 15.00 *(978-0-9773536-0-6(5))* Tenley Circle Pr.

Buchheim, Su Jen. Just As You Are: The Story of Leon & Sam. Marks, Nancy Freeman. 2003. 32p. (J). 15.00 *(978-0-9722430-1-8(1))* Wave Publishing.

Buchholz, Quint. The Summer of the Pike. Richter, Jutta. Brailovsky, Anna, tr. from GER. 2006. (ENG.). 132p. (J). (gr. 2-8). 16.95 *(978-1-57131-671-4(X))*; (gr. 8-12). per. 6.95 *(978-1-57131-672-1(8))* Milkweed Editions.

Buchs, Thomas. Alphabet of Dinosaurs. Schwaeber, Barbie Heit. (ENG.). 40p. 2009. 9.95 *(978-1-59249-993-9(7))*; 2007. (J). (gr. -1-2). 15.95 *(978-1-59249-724-9(1))* Soundprints.

Buchs, Thomas, et al. Alphabet of Dinosaurs. Schwaeber, Barbie Heit. 2011. (Alphabet Bks.). (ENG.). 40p. (J). (gr. -1-3). 17.95 *(978-1-60727-671-5(2))*; 9.95 *(978-1-60727-444-5(2))* Soundprints.

Buchs, Thomas. Alphabet of Insects. Schwaeber, Barbie Heit. 2009. (ENG.). 40p. 9.95 *(978-1-59249-992-2(9))* Soundprints.

—Moon Walk. Rau, Dana Meachen. 2004. (Soundprints' Read-and-Discover Ser.). 48p. (gr. -1-3). 13.95 *(978-0-7569-3370-8(6))* Perfection Learning Corp.

—Moon Walk. Rau, Dana. 3rd ed. 2003. (Soundprints' Read-and-Discover Ser.). (ENG.). 48p. (J). (gr. -1-3). pap. 4.35 *(978-1-59249-015-8(8))*, S2006) Soundprints.

—Red Bat at Sleep Hollow Lane. Halfmann, Janet. 2004. (ENG.). 32p. (J). (gr. -1-2). 9.95 *(978-1-59249-345-6(9))*, PB5027) Soundprints.

Bucker, Jutta. Wiley & Jasper. Bucker, Jutta, tr. Moss, Miriam. 2003. (J). 25p. pap. *(978-1-59336-061-0(4))*; 32p. 15.95 *(978-1-59336-060-3(6))* Mondo Publishing.

Buckett, George. Never Talk to Strangers. Joyce, Irma. 2009. (ENG.). 32p. (J). (gr. -1-2). 9.99 *(978-0-375-84964-0(5))*, Golden Bks.) Random Hse. Children's Bks.

Buckingham, Gabriella. Head, Shoulders, Knees & Toes & Other Action Rhymes. Baxter, Nicola. 2013. (ENG.). 16p. (J). (gr. -1-6). bds. 7.99 *(978-1-84322-829-5(7))*, Armadillo) Anness Publishing GBR. Dist: National Bk. Network.

—The Wheels on the Bus & Other Action Rhymes. 2013. (ENG.). 16p. (J). (gr. -1-12). bds. 7.99

B

(978-1-84322-830-1(0), Armadillo) Anness Publishing GBR. Dist: National Bk. Network.

Buckingham, Mark, et al. Arabian Nights (And Days) Willingham, Bill. rev. ed. 2006. (Fables Ser.: Vol. 7). (ENG.). 144p. pap. 14.99 *(978-1-4012-1000-7(7),* Vertigo) DC Comics.

Buckingham, Mark. March of the Wooden Soldiers. Willingham, Bill. rev. ed. 2004. (Fables Ser.: Vol. 4). (ENG.). 240p. pap. 17.99 *(978-1-4012-0222-4(5),* Vertigo) DC Comics.

—The Mean Seasons. Willingham, Bill. rev. ed. 2005. (Fables Ser.: Vol. 5). (ENG.). 168p. pap. 17.99 *(978-1-4012-0486-0(4),* Vertigo) DC Comics.

—Storybook Love. Willingham, Bill. rev. ed. 2004. (Fables Ser.: Vol. 3). (ENG.). 192p. pap. 17.99 *(978-1-4012-0256-9(X),* Vertigo) DC Comics.

Buckingham, Matt. Bible People Factfile. Martin, Peter. 2014. (ENG.). 48p. (J). (gr. 2-4). 14.99 *(978-0-7459-6388-4(9))* Lion Hudson PLC GBR. Dist: Independent Pubs. Group.

—Nobody Laughs at a Lion!, 1 vol. Bright, Paul. 2005. (ENG.). 26p. (J). pap. 16.00 *(978-1-56148-471-3(7),* Good Bks.) Skyhorse Publishing Co., Inc.

Buckingham, Mike, jt. illus. see Wieringo, Mike.

Buckler, Rich, et al. Fantastic Four Epic Collection: Into the Timestream. Simonson, Walter et al. 2014. (ENG.). 504p. (J). (gr. 4-17). pap. 39.99 *(978-0-7851-8895-7(9))* Marvel Worldwide, Inc.

—Marvel Saga: Sub-Mariner & the Human Torch. 2014. (ENG.). 392p. (J). (gr. 4-17). pap. 39.99 *(978-0-7851-9048-6(1))* Marvel Worldwide, Inc.

Buckler, Rich & Buscema, Sal. Spider-Man: The Death of Jean Dewolff. David, Peter. 2011. (ENG.). 168p. (J). (gr. 4-17). 24.99 *(978-0-7851-5721-2(2))* Marvel Worldwide, Inc.

Buckley, Annie. The Kids' Yoga Deck: 50 Poses & Games. Buckley, Annie. 2003. (ENG.). 50p. (gr. 8-17). 14.95 *(978-0-8118-3698-2(3))* Chronicle Bks. LLC.

Buckley, Carol, photos by. Tarra & Bella: The Elephant & Dog Who Became Best Friends. Buckley, Carol. 2009. (ENG.). 32p. (J). (gr. -1-k). 16.99 *(978-0-399-25443-7(9),* Putnam Juvenile) Penguin Publishing Group.

Buckley, Harriet & Lueth, Nathan. The Doomsday Virus, 1 vol. Barlow, Steve & Skidmore, Steve. 2007. (Pathway Bks.). (ENG.). 72p. (gr. 2-3). lib. bdg. 23.99 *(978-1-59889-871-2(X),* Pathway Bks.) Stone Arch Bks.

Buckley, Joel. Adam & the Tattooed Angel. Butler, Heather. 2004. 64p. pap. *(978-1-84427-043-9(2))* Scripture Union.

—Ellie & the Clown Crisis. Butler, Heather. 2004. 64p. pap. *(978-1-84427-023-1(8))* Scripture Union.

—Peter Goes Feet First! Willoughby, R. 2004. 64p. pap. *(978-1-85999-766-6(X))* Scripture Union.

—Peter Puts His Foot in It! Willoughby, R. 2004. 64p. pap. *(978-1-85999-765-9(1))* Scripture Union.

—Peter Strides Out. Willoughby, R. 2004. 64p. pap. *(978-1-84427-022-4(X))* Scripture Union.

Buckley, Ray. Christmas Moccasins. Buckley, Ray. 2003. 32p. pap. 18.00 *(978-0-687-02738-5(1))* Abingdon Pr.

Buckner, Julie. Army Camels: Texas Ships of the Desert, 1 vol. Fisher, Doris. 2013. (ENG.). 32p. (J). (gr. k-3). 16.99 *(978-1-4556-1823-1(3))* Pelican Publishing Co., Inc.

—Jubilee!, 1 vol. Tunks, Karyn. 2012. (ENG.). 32p. (J). (gr. k-3). 16.99 *(978-1-58980-880-5(0))* Pelican Publishing Co., Inc.

Buckner, Julie Dupre. Clovis Crawfish & Echo Gecko, 1 vol. Fontenot, Mary Alice. 2003. (Clovis Crawfish Ser.). (ENG.). 32p. (J). (gr. k-3). 16.99 *(978-1-56554-708-7(X))* Pelican Publishing Co., Inc.

—Clovis Crawfish & Silvie Sulphur, 1 vol. Fontenot, Mary Alice. 2004. (Clovis Crawfish Ser.). (ENG & FRE.). 32p. (J). (gr. k-3). 16.99 *(978-1-56554-864-0(7))* Pelican Publishing Co., Inc.

Buckner, Julie Dupre, jt. illus. see Butler, Julie Dupre.

Budgen, Tim. Big Cats, Little Cats. Weaver, A. J. 2013. 32p. pap. *(978-1-909423-03-9(3))* Bks. to Treasure.

Budig, Greg. Still: A Winter's Journey. Budig, Greg. 2009. 32p. (J). (gr. 3-18). pap. 16.95 *(978-0-916144-87-6(9))* Stemmer Hse. Pubs.

Budnick, Stacy Heller. No Excuses! How What You Say Can Get in Your Way. Dyer, Wayne W. & Tracy, Kristina. 2009. (ENG.). 32p. 15.99 *(978-1-4019-2583-3(9),* 1060) Hay Hse., Inc.

—Unstoppable Me! 10 Ways to Soar Through Life. Dyer, Wayne W. & Tracy, Kristina. 2006. (ENG.). 32p. (gr. k-7). 15.99 *(978-1-4019-1186-7(2))* Hay Hse., Inc.

Budnick, Stacy Heller & Heller Budnick, Stacy. It's Not What You've Got! Lessons for Kids on Money & Abundance. Dyer, Wayne W. 2007. (ENG.). 32p. (gr. -1-3). 15.99 *(978-1-4019-1850-7(6))* Hay Hse., Inc.

Budwine, Greg. Benjamin Franklin: You Know What to Say. Uglow, Loyd. 2003. (J). lib. bdg. 23.95 incl. audio *(978-1-57537-791-9(8))* Advance Publishing, Inc.

—Can You Help Me Find My Smile? Sommer, Carl. 2003. (Another Sommer-Time Story Ser.). (ENG.). 48p. (J). (gr. k-4). lib. bdg. 23.95 incl. audio compact disk *(978-1-57537-707-0(1));* (gr. 1-4). 16.95 incl. audio compact disk *(978-1-57537-507-6(9))* Advance Publishing, Inc.

—Can You Help Me Find My Smile? Me Puedes Ayudar a Encontrar Mi Sonrisa? Sommer, Carl. ed. 2009. (Another Sommer-Time Story Bilingual Ser.). (SPA & ENG.). 48p. (J). lib. bdg. 16.95 *(978-1-57537-150-4(2))* Advance Publishing, Inc.

—Fast Forward. Sommer, Carl. 2009. (Quest for Success Ser.). (ENG.). 56p. (YA). pap. 4.95 *(978-1-57537-277-8(0));* lib. bdg. 12.95 *(978-1-57537-252-5(5))* Advance Publishing, Inc.

—Fast Forward(Avance Acelarado) Sommer, Carl. ed. 2009. (Quest for Success Bilingual Ser.). (SPA & ENG.). 104p. (YA). lib. bdg. 14.95 *(978-1-57537-227-3(4))* Advance Publishing, Inc.

Budwine, Greg. I Am a Lion! Sommer, Carl. (J). 2014. *(978-1-57537-403-1(X));* 2003. (ENG.). 48p. (gr. k-4). lib. bdg. 23.95 incl. audio compact disk *(978-1-57537-709-4(8));* 2003. (ENG.). 48p. (gr. 1-4). 16.95 incl. audio compact disk *(978-1-57537-509-0(5))* Advance Publishing, Inc.

Budwine, Greg. I Am a Lion!(Yo Soy un León!) Sommer, Carl. ed. 2009. (Another Sommer-Time Story Bilingual Ser.). (SPA & ENG.). 48p. (J). lib. bdg. 16.95 *(978-1-57537-153-5(7))* Advance Publishing, Inc.

Budwine, Greg. It's Not Fair! Sommer, Carl. (J). 2014. pap. *(978-1-57537-955-5(4));* 2003. (ENG.). 48p. 9.95 *(978-1-57537-021-7(2));* 2003. (ENG.). 48p. lib. bdg. 16.95 *(978-1-57537-070-5(0));* 2003. (ENG.). 48p. (gr. k-4). lib. bdg. 23.95 incl. audio compact disk *(978-1-57537-720-9(9));* 2003. (ENG.). 48p. (gr. 1-4). 16.95 incl. audio compact disk *(978-1-57537-520-5(6))* Advance Publishing, Inc.

Budwine, Greg. It's Not Fair!(No Es Justo) ! Sommer, Carl. ed. 2009. (Another Sommer-Time Story Bilingual Ser.). (SPA & ENG.). 48p. (J). lib. bdg. 16.95 *(978-1-57537-155-9(3))* Advance Publishing, Inc.

Budwine, Greg. King of the Pond. Sommer, Carl. (J). 2014. pap. *(978-1-57537-956-2(2));* 2003. (ENG.). 48p. (gr. k-4). lib. bdg. 23.95 incl. audio compact disk *(978-1-57537-716-2(0));* 2003. (ENG.). 48p. (gr. 1-4). 16.95 incl. audio compact disk *(978-1-57537-516-8(8))* Advance Publishing, Inc.

Budwine, Greg. King of the Pond(El Rey Del Estanque) Sommer, Carl. ed. 2009. (Another Sommer-Time Story Bilingual Ser.). (SPA & ENG.). 48p. (J). lib. bdg. 16.95 *(978-1-57537-156-6(1))* Advance Publishing, Inc.

—Lost & Found. Sommer, Carl. 2009. (Quest for Success Ser.). 56p. (YA). pap. 4.95 *(978-1-57537-280-8(0));* lib. bdg. 12.95 *(978-1-57537-255-6(X))* Advance Publishing, Inc.

—Lost & Found(Perdida y Encontrada) Sommer, Carl. ed. 2009. (Quest for Success Bilingual Ser.). (ENG & SPA.). 96p. (YA). lib. bdg. 14.95 *(978-1-57537-229-7(0))* Advance Publishing, Inc.

Budwine, Greg. No One Will Ever Know. Sommer, Carl. 2014. (J). pap. *(978-1-57537-962-3(7))* Advance Publishing, Inc.

—Proud Rooster & Little Hen. Sommer, Carl. (J). 2014. pap. *(978-1-57537-964-7(3));* 2003. (ENG.). 48p. lib. bdg. 23.95 incl. audio compact disk *(978-1-57537-710-0(1));* 2003. (ENG.). 48p. (gr. 1-4). 16.95 incl. audio compact disk *(978-1-57537-510-6(9))* Advance Publishing, Inc.

Budwine, Greg. Proud Rooster & Little Hen(Gallito Orgulloso y Gallinita) Sommer, Carl. ed. 2009. (Another Sommer-Time Story Bilingual Ser.). (SPA & ENG.). 48p. (J). 16.95 *(978-1-57537-164-1(2))* Advance Publishing, Inc.

—The Race. Sommer, Carl. 2009. (Quest for Success Ser.). (ENG.). 56p. (YA). lib. bdg. 12.95 *(978-1-57537-256-3(8))* Advance Publishing, Inc.

—The Race(La Carrera) Sommer, Carl. ed. 2009. (Quest for Success Bilingual Ser.). (SPA & ENG.). 104p. (YA). lib. bdg. 14.95 *(978-1-57537-230-3(4))* Advance Publishing, Inc.

—The Racing Fools. Sommer, Carl. 2009. (Quest for Success Ser.). (ENG.). 56p. (YA). pap. 4.95 *(978-1-57537-281-5(9))* Advance Publishing, Inc.

—The Revolt. Sommer, Carl. 2009. (Quest for Success Ser.). (ENG.). 56p. (YA). pap. 4.95 *(978-1-57537-283-9(5));* lib. bdg. 12.95 *(978-1-57537-258-7(4))* Advance Publishing, Inc.

—The Revolt(La Revuelta) Sommer, Carl. ed. 2009. (Quest for Success Bilingual Ser.). (SPA & ENG.). 104p. (YA). lib. bdg. 14.95 *(978-1-57537-232-7(0))* Advance Publishing, Inc.

—The Roar. Sommer, Carl. 2009. (Quest for Success Ser.). (ENG.). 56p. (YA). pap. 4.95 *(978-1-57537-284-6(3));* lib. bdg. 12.95 *(978-1-57537-259-4(2))* Advance Publishing, Inc.

—The Roar(El Rugido) Sommer, Carl. ed. 2009. (Quest for Success Bilingual Ser.). (SPA & ENG.). 96p. (YA). lib. bdg. 14.95 *(978-1-57537-233-4(9))* Advance Publishing, Inc.

Budwine, Greg. Three Little Pigs. Sommer, Carl. 2014. (J). pap. *(978-1-57537-968-5(6))* Advance Publishing, Inc.

Budwine, Greg. Tied up in Knots. Sommer, Carl. 2003. (Another Sommer-Time Story Ser.). (ENG.). 48p. (J). 16.95 incl. audio compact disk *(978-1-57537-503-8(6))* Advance Publishing, Inc.

—Tied up in Knots Read-along. Sommer, Carl. 2003. (Another Sommer-Time Story Ser.). (ENG.). 48p. (J). lib. bdg. 23.95 incl. audio compact disk *(978-1-57537-703-2(9))* Advance Publishing, Inc.

—Tied up in Knots(Enredados) Sommer, Carl. ed. 2009. (Another Sommer-Time Story Bilingual Ser.). (SPA & ENG.). 48p. (J). lib. bdg. 16.95 *(978-1-57537-169-6(3))* Advance Publishing, Inc.

Budwine, Greg. Time Remote! Sommer, Carl. (J). 2014. pap. *(978-1-57537-970-8(8));* 2003. (ENG.). 48p. (gr. 1-4). 16.95 incl. audio compact disk *(978-1-57537-512-0(5))* Advance Publishing, Inc.

Budwine, Greg. Time Remote! Read-along. Sommer, Carl. 2003. (Another Sommer-Time Story Ser.). (ENG.). 48p. (J). lib. bdg. 23.95 incl. audio compact disk *(978-1-57537-712-4(8))* Advance Publishing, Inc.

—Time Remote!(El Control Del Tiempo!) Sommer, Carl. ed. 2009. (Another Sommer-Time Story Bilingual Ser.). (SPA & ENG.). 48p. (J). lib. bdg. 16.95 *(978-1-57537-170-2(7))* Advance Publishing, Inc.

Budwine, Greg. The Ugly Caterpillar. Sommer, Carl. (J). 2014. pap. *(978-1-57537-971-5(6));* 2003. 48p. (gr. 1-4). 16.95 incl. audio compact disk *(978-1-57537-515-1(X))* Advance Publishing, Inc.

Budwine, Greg. The Ugly Caterpillar Read-along. Sommer, Carl. 2003. (Another Sommer-Time Story Ser.). (ENG.). 48p. (J). lib. bdg. 23.95 incl. audio compact disk *(978-1-57537-715-5(2))* Advance Publishing, Inc.

—The Ugly Caterpillar(La Oruga Fea) Sommer, Carl. ed. 2009. (Another Sommer-Time Story Bilingual Ser.). (SPA & ENG.). 48p. (J). (gr. k-3). lib. bdg. 16.95 *(978-1-57537-171-9(5))* Advance Publishing, Inc.

Budwine, Greg & Vignolo, Enrique. Three Little Pigs(Los Tres Cerditos) Sommer, Carl. ed. 2009. (Another Sommer-Time Story Bilingual Ser.). (SPA & ENG.). 48p. (J). lib. bdg. 16.95 *(978-1-57537-168-9(5))* Advance Publishing, Inc.

Buehner, Caralyn & Buehner, Mark. Fanny's Dream. Buehner, Caralyn & Buehner, Mark. 2003. (ENG.). 32p. (J). (gr. k-3). 6.99 *(978-0-14-250060-6(7),* Puffin) Penguin Publishing Group.

Buehner, Mark. Dex: The Heart of a Hero. Buehner, Caralyn. 2007. (ENG.). 32p. (J). (gr. -1-3). pap. 6.99 *(978-0-06-443845-2(7))* HarperCollins Pubs.

—Goldilocks & the Three Bears. Buehner, Caralyn. (ENG.). 32p. (J). (gr. -1-k). 2009. pap. 6.99 *(978-0-14-241275-6(9),* Puffin); 2007. 16.99 *(978-0-8037-2939-1(1),* Dial) Penguin Publishing Group.

—My Life with the Wave. Cowan, Catherine. ed. 2004. (J). (gr. k-3). spiral bd. *(978-0-616-11863-4(5))* Canadian National Institute for the Blind/Institut National Canadien pour les Aveugles.

—My Life with the Wave. Cowan, Catherine. 2004. (ENG.). 32p. (J). (gr. -1-3). reprint ed. pap. 7.99 *(978-0-06-056200-7(5))* HarperCollins Pubs.

—Snowmen All Year. Buehner, Caralyn. 2010. (ENG.). 32p. (J). (gr. -1-2). 16.99 *(978-0-8037-3383-1(6),* Dial) Penguin Publishing Group.

—Snowmen All Year Board Book. Buehner, Caralyn. 2012. (ENG.). 28p. (J). (gr. -1-k). bds. 6.99 *(978-0-8037-3905-5(2),* Dial) Penguin Publishing Group.

—Snowmen at Christmas. Buehner, Caralyn. (ENG.). (J). (gr. -1-k). 2010. 28p. bds. 6.99 *(978-0-8037-3551-4(0));* 2005. 32p. 16.99 *(978-0-8037-2995-7(2))* Penguin Publishing Group. (Dial).

—Snowmen at Night. Buehner, Caralyn. 2004. (ENG.). 26p. (J). (gr. -1-k). bds. 6.99 *(978-0-8037-3041-0(1),* Dial) Penguin Publishing Group.

—Snowmen at Play. Buehner, Caralyn. 2013. (ENG.). 16p. (J). (gr. -1-k). 6.99 *(978-0-448-47782-4(3),* Grosset & Dunlap) Penguin Publishing Group.

—Snowmen at Work. Buehner, Caralyn. 2012. (ENG.). 32p. (J). (gr. -1-2). 16.99 *(978-0-8037-3579-8(0),* Dial) Penguin Publishing Group.

—Superdog: The Heart of a Hero. Buehner, Caralyn. 2004. 32p. (J). (gr. -1-3). lib. bdg. 17.89 *(978-0-06-623621-6(5))* HarperCollins Pubs.

—This First Thanksgiving Day: A Counting Story. Melmed, Laura Krauss. 2003. (ENG.). 32p. (J). (gr. -1-3). pap. 6.99 *(978-0-06-054184-2(9))* HarperCollins Pubs.

Buehner, Mark. Mi Vida con la Ola. Buehner, Mark. Cowan, Catherine. Rubio, Esther, tr. 2004. (SPA.). 29p. (J). 19.99 *(978-84-88342-45-4(4))* S.A. Kokinos ESP. Dist: Lectorum Pubns., Inc.

Buehner, Mark, jt. illus. see Buehner, Caralyn.

Buehrle, Jackie. Sage & the Peacock. Knesek, Marian. 2011. 28p. pap. 24.95 *(978-1-4512-2211-1(4))* America Star Bks.

Buehrle, Jacquelyn. The Adventures of Hooch & Mile-A-Minute-Freebee. Signor, Priscilla M. 2011. 28p. pap. 24.95 *(978-1-4560-0936-6(2))* America Star Bks.

—A Bunny Named Apple. Tardif, Elizabeth. 2011. 28p. pap. 24.95 *(978-1-4560-0946-5(X))* America Star Bks.

—My Seeing Eye Glasses. Glass, Alberta. 2011. 28p. pap. 24.95 *(978-1-4560-2829-9(4))* PublishAmerica, Inc.

—The Rainbow in My Pocket. Hazekamp, Michelle R. 2011. 28p. pap. 24.95 *(978-1-4560-0927-4(3))* America Star Bks.

—The Story of Ocos: King of the Sky, Master of the Water. Trimoglie, Mario. 2011. 28p. pap. 24.95 *(978-1-4560-2015-6(3))* America Star Bks.

—Sylvester the One-Legged Seagull. Horstmann, Deborah McFillin. 2012. 28p. 24.95 *(978-1-4560-2308-9(X))* America Star Bks.

—Winky Sue's Peppermint Birthday. Bocanegra, Deborah. 2012. 26p. 24.95 *(978-1-4560-7282-7(X))* America Star Bks.

Buel, Hubert. The Shy Stegosaurus of Cricket Creek. Lampman, Evelyn Sibley. 2007. 218p. (J). (gr. 4-7). per. 12.00 *(978-1-930900-37-0(6))* Purple Hse. Pr.

Buell, Carl Dennis. Stickeen. Muir, John. Date not set. 94p. (J). 16.95 *(978-0-8488-2803-5(8))* Amereon LTD.

Buelt, Laura. Langur Monkey's Day. Hammerslough, Jane. 2005. (Wild Reading Adventures! Ser.). (ENG.). (J). (gr. -1-2). 36p. 2.95 *(978-1-59249-143-8(X),* S7156); 36p. 9.95 *(978-1-59249-144-5(8),* PS7156); 32p. 19.95 *(978-1-59249-221-3(5),* BC7106); 32p. 8.95 *(978-1-59249-222-0(3),* SC7106) Soundprints.

—Langur Monkey's Day. Hammerslough, Jane & Smithsonian Institution Staff. rev. ed. 2008. (ENG.). 24p. (J). (gr. -1-3). 4.99 *(978-1-59249-706-5(3),* Little Soundprints) Soundprints.

Buelt, Laura. Langur Monkey's Day. Buelt, Laura, tr. Hammerslough, Jane. 2005. (Wild Reading Adventures! Ser.). (ENG.). 36p. (J). 15.95 *(978-1-59249-141-4(3),* B7106); pap. 6.95 *(978-1-59249-142-1(1),* S7106) Soundprints.

Bueno, Lisa. Holidays with Joe. Hoffmann, Sara E. 2013. (My Reading Neighborhood: First-Grade Sight Word Stories Ser.). (ENG.). 16p. (gr. -1-1). pap. 5.95 *(978-1-4677-1169-2(1))* Lerner Publishing Group.

—A Party with Joe. Hoffmann, Sara E. 2013. (My Reading Neighborhood: First-Grade Sight Word Stories Ser.). (ENG.). 16p. (gr. -1-1). pap. 5.95 *(978-1-4677-1173-9(X))* Lerner Publishing Group.

—School for Ken. Hoffmann, Sara E. 2013. (My Reading Neighborhood: First-Grade Sight Word Stories Ser.). (ENG.). 16p. (gr. -1-1). pap. 5.95 *(978-1-4677-1171-5(3))* Lerner Publishing Group.

Buevara, Isaias. Revelation: A Visual Journey. 2005. 96p. per. 41.99 *(978-0-9763800-3-0(X),* 10) Orison Pubs.

Buffagni, Matteo. Avengers Assemble. 2014. (ENG.). 112p. (YA). (gr. 8-17). pap. 16.99 *(978-0-7851-6798-3(6))* Marvel Worldwide, Inc.

Buffagni, Matteo, et al. X-Men - X-Termination. Pak, Greg et al. 2013. (ENG.). 184p. (YA). (gr. 8-17). pap. 24.99 *(978-0-7851-8443-0(0))* Marvel Worldwide, Inc.

Buffalohead, Julie. Sacagawea. Buffalohead, Julie. Erdrich, Liselotte. 2003. (ENG.). 40p. (J). (gr. 3-6). 17.95 *(978-0-87614-646-0(9),* Carolrhoda Bks.) Lerner Publishing Group.

Buffiere, Mélanie & Lajic, Maïté. Ferrets & Ferreting Out. Mariolle, Mathieu. 2010. (Nola's Worlds Ser.: 2). (ENG.). 136p. (J). (gr. 6-9). pap. 9.95 *(978-0-7613-6542-6(7),* Graphic Universe) Lerner Publishing Group.

Buffinet, Jacqueline. I Go Exploring. Payne, Gaynell. 2012. 34p. 21.99 *(978-0-9884657-0-1(1))* DreamLand Mediaworks LLC.

Buggs, Michael A. Tabard. Buggs, Michael A. 64p. (Orig.). (J). (gr. 2-6). pap. 15.00 *(978-0-9657723-0-3(6))* Mogul Comics.

Buhagiar, Jason. Channel Blue: Riders of the Storm. Bingham, J. Z. 2014. (Salty Splashes Collection: 4). (ENG.). 40p. (gr. 1-6). 16.95 *(978-1-939454-07-2(7),* Salty Splashes Collection) Balcony 7 Media and Publishing.

Bulanadi, Danny & Cearley, Clint. El Bien y el Mal: Abraham Comic Book, Pt. 2. Pearl, Michael. 2008. (SPA & ENG.). 28p. (J). pap. 2.99 *(978-0-9786372-6-2(7))* No Greater Joy Ministries, Inc.

Bull, Carolyn. Los Tres Osos. Boase, Wendy. (Primeros Cuentos Ser.). (SPA.). 28p. (J). (gr. k-3). pap. 7.95 *(978-1-56014-475-5(0))* Santillana USA Publishing Co., Inc.

Bull, Peter. A Cool Kid's Field Guide to Space. Regan, Lisa. 2009. (Cool Kid's Field Guide Ser.). 26p. (J). (gr. 1-3). spiral bd. 6.99 *(978-0-8416-7142-3(7))* Hammond World Atlas Corp.

—Coral Reefs: In Danger. Brooke, Samantha. 2008. (Penguin Young Readers, Level 3 Ser.). (ENG.). 48p. (J). (gr. 1-3). mass mkt. 3.99 *(978-0-448-44872-5(6),* Grosset & Dunlap) Penguin Publishing Group.

—Explorers: Big Cats. Llewellyn, Claire & Johnson, Jinny. 2013. (Explorers Ser.). (ENG.). 32p. (J). (gr. 1-3). 10.99 *(978-0-7534-6744-2(5),* Kingfisher) Roaring Brook Pr.

—Explorers: Reptiles. Llewellyn, Claire. 2013. (Explorers Ser.). (ENG.). 32p. (J). (gr. 2-5). 6.99 *(978-0-7534-7064-0(0),* Kingfisher) Roaring Brook Pr.

—Explorers: Robots. Oxlade, Chris. 2013. (Explorers Ser.). (ENG.). 32p. (J). (gr. 2-5). 10.99 *(978-0-7534-6816-6(6),* Kingfisher) Roaring Brook Pr.

—Explorers: Things That Go. Gifford, Clive. 2013. (Explorers Ser.). (ENG.). 32p. (J). (gr. 2-5). 6.99 *(978-0-7534-7074-9(8),* Kingfisher) Roaring Brook Pr.

—Horses. Date not set. (Old MacDonald Stickers Ser.). 16p. (J). 2.98 *(978-0-7525-7060-0(9))* Parragon, Inc.

—How Is My Brain Like a Supercomputer? And Other Questions about ... the Human Body. Stewart, Melissa. 2014. (Good Question! Ser.). (ENG.). 32p. (J). (gr. 1). 12.95 *(978-1-4549-0680-3(4))* Sterling Publishing Co., Inc.

—How Is My Brain Like a Supercomputer? And Other Questions about The Human Body. Stewart, Melissa. 2014. (Good Question! Ser.). (ENG.). 32p. (J). (gr. 1). pap. 5.95 *(978-1-4549-0681-0(2))* Sterling Publishing Co., Inc.

—Lift & Explore: Animals. Murrell, Deborah. 2013. (Lift & Explore Ser.). (ENG.). 16p. (J). (gr. -1-1). bds. 12.99 *(978-0-7534-7115-9(9),* Kingfisher) Roaring Brook Pr.

—Lift & Explore: Dinosaurs. Kingfisher Editors & Murrell, Deborah. 2013. (Lift & Explore Ser.). (ENG.). 16p. (J). (gr. -1-1). bds. 12.99 *(978-0-7534-7080-0(2),* Kingfisher) Roaring Brook Pr.

—Lift & Explore: Oceans. Kingfisher Editors & Murrell, Deborah. 2013. (Lift & Explore Ser.). (ENG.). 16p. (J). (gr. -1-1). bds. 12.99 *(978-0-7534-7081-7(0),* Kingfisher) Roaring Brook Pr.

—Lift & Explore: Rainforests. Murrell, Deborah. 2013. (Lift & Explore Ser.). (ENG.). 16p. (J). (gr. -1-1). bds. 12.99 *(978-0-7534-7116-6(7),* Kingfisher) Roaring Brook Pr.

—Rainforests. Ganeri, Anita. 2013. (Explorers Ser.). (ENG.). 32p. (J). (gr. 2-5). 6.99 *(978-0-7534-7073-2(X),* Kingfisher) Roaring Brook Pr.

—Stars & Planets. Stott, Carole. 2013. (Explorers Ser.). (ENG.). 32p. (J). (gr. 2-5). 6.99 *(978-0-7534-7063-3(2),* Kingfisher) Roaring Brook Pr.

—Transport. (Music about Us Ser.). 64p. 9.95 *(978-1-85909-294-1(2),* Warner Bros. Pubns.) Alfred Publishing Co., Inc.

—Under the Sea. 2004. (Out & about Ser.). 12p. (J). bds. 4.99 *(978-1-85997-806-1(1))* Byeway Bks.

—Under the Sea. (J). 2.29 *(978-1-59445-061-7(7))* Dogs in Hats Children's Publishing Co.

—Under the Sea. (Puzzle Shapes Ser.). (J). 10p. bds. *(978-2-89393-938-4(4));* 8p. bds. *(978-2-7643-0146-3(4))* Phidal Publishing, Inc./Editions Phidal, Inc.

—Why Does the Earth Spin? And Other Questions about Our Planet. Carson, Mary Kay. 2014. (Good Question! Ser.). (ENG.). 32p. (J). (gr. 1). 12.95 *(978-1-4549-0674-2(X))* Sterling Publishing Co., Inc.

Bull Tellman, Gunvor. Sigurd & His Brave Companions: A Tale of Medieval Norway. Undset, Sigrid. 2013. (ENG.). 152p. pap. 16.95 *(978-0-8166-7826-6(X))* Univ. of Minnesota Pr.

Bulla, Randy. Father, Ford, $5 a Day: The Mullers from Missouri. Wells, Sherry A. 2003. 128p. lib. bdg. 14.00 *(978-0-934981-11-8(6))* Lawells Publishing.

Bullard, Joyce. Patience, 1 vol. Price, J. M. 2010. 16p. pap. 24.95 *(978-1-4489-6233-4(1))* PublishAmerica, Inc.

Bullas, Will. M Is for Masterpiece: An Art Alphabet. Domeniconi, David. rev. ed. 2006. (Art & Culture Ser.). (ENG.). 48p. (J). (gr. -1-3). 17.95 *(978-1-58536-276-9(X))* Sleeping Bear Pr.

Bullen, Marjorie. Silly Frog. Carsonie, Diane Lynn. 2008. 16p. per. 24.95 *(978-1-4241-9253-3(6))* America Star Bks.

Bullen, Marjorie J. Little Red Chicken, 1 vol. Carsonie, Diane Lynn. 2009. 17p. pap. 24.95 *(978-1-60813-495-3(4))* America Star Bks.

Buller, Jon. Simon's Dream. Schade, Susan. 2009. (Fog Mound Ser.: 3). (ENG.). 208p. (J). (gr. 3-7). pap. 12.99 *(978-0-689-87689-9(0)*, Simon & Schuster/Paula Wiseman Bks.) Simon & Schuster/Paula Wiseman Bks.

Buller, Jon, et al. Smart about the Fifty States. Buller, Jon et al. 2003. (Smart about History Ser.). (ENG.). 64p. (J). (gr. k-4). mass mkt. 6.99 *(978-0-448-43131-4(9)*, Grosset & Dunlap) Penguin Publishing Group.

—Smart about the First Ladies: Smart about History. Buller, Jon & Warner, Sally. 2004. (Smart about History Ser.). (ENG.). 78p. (J). (gr. k-4). mass mkt. 5.99 *(978-0-448-43724-8(4)*, Grosset & Dunlap) Penguin Publishing Group.

—Smart about the Presidents. Buller, Jon et al. 2004. (Smart about History Ser.). (ENG.). 64p. (J). (gr. k-4). mass mkt. 5.99 *(978-0-448-43372-1(9)*, Grosset & Dunlap) Penguin Publishing Group.

Buller, Jon. Travels of Thelonious. Schade, Susan. 2007. (Fog Mound Ser.: 1). (ENG.). 224p. (J). (gr. 3-7). pap. 10.99 *(978-0-689-87685-1(8)*, Simon & Schuster/Paula Wiseman Bks.) Simon & Schuster/Paula Wiseman Bks.

Bullock, Brad. When I Grow Up. Jasper, J. J. 2003. 16p. (J). *(978-0-9727279-8-3(1))* Pine Hill Graphics.

Bullock Jr., Michael A. Christmas & the Little Dolls. Jones, Debra. 2011. 24p. pap. 24.95 *(978-1-4560-6679-6(X))* America Star Bks.

Bullock, Kathleen. Clip-Clop, Tippity-Tap French Vocabulary on the Farm. Chatel, Kim. 2011. 24p. pap. 10.95 *(978-1-61633-136-8(4))* Guardian Angel Publishing, Inc.

—Geography Mysteries. Frank, Marjorie. 2011. (Learning Adventures Ser.). (ENG.). 112p. (gr. 5-8). pap. 14.99 *(978-0-86530-528-1(5))* Incentive Pubns., Inc.

—Graphic Organizers for Math. Frank, Marjorie & Norris, Jill. 2007. (Graphic Organizers Ser.). (ENG.). 64p. (gr. 5-8). per. 9.99 *(978-0-86530-036-1(4)*, IP 36-4) Incentive Pubns., Inc.

—Graphic Organizers for Reading. Farnette, Cherrie et al. Grayson, Cary, ed. 2006. (Graphic Organizers Ser.). (ENG.). 64p. (gr. 2-5). per. 9.99 *(978-0-86530-034-7(8)*, IP348) Incentive Pubns., Inc.

—Interactive Grammar & Usage Lessons - Sentences, Grades 6-9. Frank, Marjorie & Norris, Jill. Grayson, Cary, ed. 2011. (Interactive Digital Lessons Ser.). (ENG.). 40p. (gr. 6-9). pap. 19.99 incl. audio compact disk *(978-0-86530-661-5(3))* Incentive Pubns., Inc.

—Math Conundrums. Frank, Marjorie. MacKenzie, Joy, ed. 2011. (Learning Adventures Ser.). (ENG.). 112p. (gr. 5-8). pap. 14.99 *(978-0-86530-526-7(9))* Incentive Pubns., Inc.

—Read about It DM: Primary-Comprehension. Forte, Imogene et al. Frank, Marjorie, ed. 2011. (ENG.). 256p. (gr. 2-4). pap. 22.99 *(978-0-86530-050-7(X))* Incentive Pubns., Inc.

—U. S. History BASIC/Not Boring 6-8+ Inventive Exercises to Sharpen Skills & Raise Achievement. Forte, Imogene & Frank, Marjorie. Quinn, Anna, ed. 2nd ed. 2013. (Basic/Not Boring Ser.). (ENG.). 64p. (gr. 6-8). pap. 9.99 *(978-1-62950-024-9(0))* Incentive Pubns., Inc.

—Vocabulary Escapades. Frank, Marjorie. MacKenzie, Joy, ed. 2011. (Learning Adventures Ser.). (ENG.). 112p. (gr. 5-8). pap. 14.99 *(978-0-86530-525-0(0))* Incentive Pubns., Inc.

—Word Meaning. Frank, Marjorie & Norris, Jill. Grayson, Cary, ed. 2011. (Interactive Digital Lessons Ser.). (ENG.). 40p. (gr. 6-9). pap. 19.99 incl. audio compact disk *(978-0-86530-656-1(7))* Incentive Pubns., Inc.

—Word Structure. Frank, Marjorie & Norris, Jill. Grayson, Cary, ed. 2011. (Interactive Digital Lessons Ser.). (ENG.). 40p. (gr. 6-9). pap. 19.99 incl. audio compact disk *(978-0-86530-655-4(9))* Incentive Pubns., Inc.

Bullock, Kathleen. The Clown-Around Kids. Bullock, Kathleen. 2012. (ENG.). (J). pap. 10.95 *(978-1-61633-223-5(9))* Guardian Angel Publishing, Inc.

Bultje, Jan Willem, photos by. Estonia. Hiisjärv, Piret & Hiiepuu, Ene. 2006. (Looking at Europe Ser.). 48p. (YA). (gr. 5-8). 22.95 *(978-1-881508-32-8(3))* Oliver Pr., Inc.

—Latvia. Aizpuriete, Amanda. Hartgers, Katarina, tr. 2006. (Looking at Europe Ser.). 48p. (YA). (gr. 5-8). 22.95 *(978-1-881508-37-3(4))* Oliver Pr., Inc.

Bumstead, Debbie. Dientecito y la Placa Peligros. Nelson, James Gary. 2011. 16p. pap. 9.95 *(978-1-61633-132-0(1))* Guardian Angel Publishing, Inc.

—Smileytooth & Bushwack Plaque. Nelson, James Gary. 2009. 16p. pap. 9.95 *(978-1-61633-009-5(0))* Guardian Angel Publishing, Inc.

—Smileytooth & the Castle Hassle. Nelson, James Gary. 2008. 24p. pap. 10.95 *(978-1-933090-95-5(2))* Guardian Angel Publishing, Inc.

—Smileytooth & the Plaque Attack. Nelson, James Gary. 2008. 20p. pap. 10.95 *(978-1-935137-48-1(4))* Guardian Angel Publishing, Inc.

Bunch, Paul. Just an Ordinary Little Dog: Barnaby's Story. Mason, Alexis. 2010. (J). *(978-0-9755280-4-4(1))* Insight Technical Education.

Bunk, Tomas. Quantoons: MetaphysicalIllustrations by Tomas Bunk. Eisenkraft, Arthur & Kirkpatrick, Larry D. 2005. (ENG.). 243p. (YA). pap. 27.95 *(978-0-87355-265-3(2))* National Science Teachers Assn.

Bunker, Thomas. The Doctor Said I Have Leukemi. Bryant, Cathy. 2012. 24p. pap. 24.95 *(978-1-4560-6929-2(2))* America Star Bks.

—Eric & Wrinkles Meet the Bunnyworms. Bradford, Danette J. 2012. 28p. pap. 24.95 *(978-1-4560-4261-5(0))* America Star Bks.

—Ritzi's Bath. Goodman, Peggy. 2012. 28p. 24.95 *(978-1-4560-4138-0(X))* America Star Bks.

Bunker, Tom. Trinity Goes to Soccer Camp. Myers, Bob. 2012. 36p. 24.95 *(978-1-4560-2906-7(1))* America Star Bks.

Bunkus, Denise. Groundhog Gets a Say. Swallow, Pamela Curtis & Swallow, Pamela C. 2007. (ENG.). 40p. (J). (gr. k-3). pap. 6.99 *(978-0-14-240896-4(4)*, Puffin) Penguin Publishing Group.

Bunting, Matt, jt. illus. see Faulkner, Matt.

Burbank, Addison. Know Your Mass. Manousos, Demetrius. 2006. 96p. (YA). per. 14.95 *(978-1-892331-44-1(6))* Angelus Pr.

Burbridge, William J. Animals, Animals Everywhere. Murphy, D. Cathy. 2013. 16p. pap. 24.95 *(978-1-4626-2414-0(6))* America Star Bks.

Burch, Benjamin. Dragon Hiccups. Depken, Kristen L. 2015. (Little Golden Book Ser.). (ENG.). 24p. (J). (-k). 4.99 ***(978-0-553-52310-2(4)**, Golden Bks.)* Random Hse. Children's Bks.

Burch, Benjamin. Wally's Magical Adventures. Golden Books. 2015. (Big Golden Book Ser.). (ENG.). 48p. (J). (gr. -1-2). 9.99 *(978-0-385-38766-8(0)*, Golden Bks.) Random Hse. Children's Bks.

Burch, Deborah. God's Greatest Gift. 2007. 32p. (J). lib. bdg. 17.95 *(978-0-9796477-7-2(0))* God's Greatest Gift, LLC.

Burch, Deborah. God's Greatest Gift. Burch, Deborah. I.t. ed. 2006. (ENG.). 32p. (J). lib. bdg. *(978-0-9779445-3-8(0))* Zoe Life Publishing.

Burch, Lynda S., photos by. Meet Me at the Park! Burch, Lynda S. 2005. 64p. (J). E-Book 6.00 incl. cd-rom *(978-1-933090-15-3(4))* Guardian Angel Publishing, Inc.

—Wicky wacky Things that Go! Boats 1. Burch, Lynda S. 2004. 28p. (J). E-Book 9.95 incl. cd-rom *(978-1-933090-03-0(0))* Guardian Angel Publishing, Inc.

—Wicky Wacky Things that Go! Busses. Burch, Lynda S. 2004. 28p. (J). E-Book 9.95 incl. cd-rom *(978-1-933090-06-1(5))* Guardian Angel Publishing, Inc.

—Wicky Wacky Things that Go! Emergency Vehicles. Burch, Lynda S. 2004. 30p. (J). E-Book 9.95 incl. cd-rom *(978-1-933090-13-9(8))* Guardian Angel Publishing, Inc.

—Wicky Wacky Things that Go! Tractors. Burch, Lynda S. 2004. 28p. (J). E-Book 9.95 incl. cd-rom *(978-1-933090-09-2(X))* Guardian Angel Publishing, Inc.

—Wicky Wacky Things that Go! Trains 1. Burch, Lynda S. 2004. 16p. (J). E-Book 9.95 incl. cd-rom *(978-1-933090-02-3(2))* Guardian Angel Publishing, Inc.

—Wicky Wacky Things That Go! Trucks. Burch, Lynda S. 2004. 28p. (J). E-Book 9.95 incl. cd-rom *(978-1-933090-11-5(1))* Guardian Angel Publishing, Inc.

—Zoom Zoom Zoom Come Count with Me! Burch, Lynda S. 2005. 20p. (J). E-Book 6.00 incl. cd-rom *(978-1-933090-14-6(6))* Guardian Angel Publishing, Inc.

Burch, Lynda S. & Roberts, MarySue, photos by. I SEE Seaside Birds! 2006. 32p. (J). 16.99 *(978-1-933090-16-0(2))* Guardian Angel Publishing, Inc.

—I SEE Seaside Birds! Burch, Lynda S. 2004. 52p. (J). E-Book 9.95 incl. cd-rom *(978-1-933090-05-4(7))* Guardian Angel Publishing, Inc.

—Wicky Wacky Things that Go! Automobiles 1. Burch, Lynda S. 2004. 30p. (J). E-Book 9.95 incl. cd-rom *(978-1-933090-12-2(X))* Guardian Angel Publishing, Inc.

Burcham, David. Joseph & Snowy Joe Blue, 1 vol. Ross, Patrick. 2009. 25p. pap. 24.95 *(978-1-61582-314-7(X))* PublishAmerica, Inc.

—Oliver: The Great Escape. Ross, Patrick. 2009. 34p. pap. 24.95 *(978-1-60749-151-4(6))* America Star Bks.

—Runt River Rat's Wild Ride, 1 vol. Ross, Patrick. 2010. 24p. 24.95 *(978-1-4512-0067-6(6))* PublishAmerica, Inc.

Burchartz, Roxanne. Shamrock Sean & the Bird's Nest. Gogarty, Brian. 2007. (ENG.). 12p. (J). pap. 7.95 *(978-0-86278-969-5(9))* O'Brien Pr., Ltd., The IRL. Dist: Dufour Editions, Inc.

—Shamrock Sean & the Wishing Well. Gogarty, Brian. 2007. (ENG.). 12p. (J). pap. 7.95 *(978-0-86278-967-1(2))* O'Brien Pr., Ltd., The IRL. Dist: Dufour Editions, Inc.

Burchett, Rick. Cosmic Bounty Hunter, 1 vol. Hoena, Blake A. & Loughridge, Lee. 2010. (Superman Ser.). (ENG.). 56p. (gr. 2-3). lib. bdg. 25.32 *(978-1-4342-2133-9(4)*, DC Super Heroes) Stone Arch Bks.

—Cosmic Bounty Hunter, 1 vol. Loughridge, Lee & Hoena, Blake A. 2014. (Superman Ser.). (ENG.). 56p. (gr. 2-3). pap. 4.95 *(978-1-4342-2769-0(3)*, DC Super Heroes) Stone Arch Bks.

—Phantasm Strikes!, 1 vol. Slott, Dan et al. 2013. (Batman Adventures Ser.). (ENG.). 32p. (gr. 2-3). 21.27 *(978-1-4342-6035-2(6))* Stone Arch Bks.

—Playing with Matches, 1 vol. Slott, Dan et al. 2013. (Batman Adventures Ser.). (ENG.). 32p. (gr. 2-3). 21.27 *(978-1-4342-6034-5(8))* Stone Arch Bks.

—Prankster of Prime Time, 1 vol. Pasko, Martin & Loughridge, Lee. (Superman Ser.). (ENG.). 56p. (gr. 2-3). 2014. pap. 4.95 *(978-1-4342-2763-8(4))*; 2010. lib. bdg. 25.32 *(978-1-4342-1986-2(0))* Stone Arch Bks. (DC Super Heroes).

—The Puppet Master's Revenge, 1 vol. Lemke, Donald B. & Loughridge, Lee. 2009. (Batman Ser.). (ENG.). 56p. (gr. 2-3). 25.32 *(978-1-4342-1560-4(1)*, DC Super Heroes) Stone Arch Bks.

—Puppet Master's Revenge. Lemke, Donald & Loughridge, Lee. 2013. (Batman Ser.). (ENG.). 56p. (gr. 2-3). pap. 4.95 *(978-1-4342-1727-1(2)*, DC Super Heroes) Stone Arch Bks.

—The Shadow Masters. Kupperberg, Paul & Loughridge, Lee. (Superman Ser.). (ENG.). 56p. (gr. 2-3). 2014. pap. 4.95 *(978-1-4342-2768-3(5))*; 2010. lib. bdg. 25.32 *(978-1-4342-2079-0(6))* Stone Arch Bks. (DC Super Heroes).

Burchett, Rick. The Stolen Superpowers, 1 vol. Burchett, Rick. Powell, Martin A. & Loughridge, Lee. 2013. (Superman Ser.). (ENG.). 56p. (gr. 2-3). pap. 4.95 *(978-1-4342-1373-0(0)*, DC Super Heroes) Stone Arch Bks.

Burchett, Rick & Austin, Terry. Be Careful What You Wish For... McCloud, Scott. 2012. (Superman Adventures Ser.). (ENG.). 32p. (gr. 2-3). lib. bdg. 21.27 *(978-1-4342-4550-2(0))* Stone Arch Bks.

—Distant Thunder, 1 vol. McCloud, Scott. 2012. (Superman Adventures Ser.). (ENG.). 32p. (gr. 2-3). 21.27 *(978-1-4342-4551-9(9))* Stone Arch Bks.

—Eye to Eye, 1 vol. McCloud, Scott. 2012. (Superman Adventures Ser.). (ENG.). 32p. (gr. 2-3). lib. bdg. 21.27 *(978-1-4342-4552-6(7))* Stone Arch Bks.

—Jinx: Little Miss Steps. Torres, J. 2013. (Jinx Ser.: 2). (ENG.). (J). (gr. 5). 114p. 16.99 *(978-1-936975-42-6(4))*; 112p. pap. 9.99 *(978-1-936975-41-9(6))* Archie Comic Pubns., Inc. (Archie Comics).

—Men of Steel, 1 vol. Dini, Paul. 2012. (Superman Adventures Ser.). (ENG.). 32p. (gr. 2-3). lib. bdg. 21.27 *(978-1-4342-4549-6(7))* Stone Arch Bks.

Burchett, Rick, jt. illus. see Austin, Terry.

Burchfield, Cindy. Gimme, Gimme Moocher Marmots. Burchfield, Cindy. 2007. 48p. per. 18.95 *(978-1-59858-457-8(X))* Dog Ear Publishing, LLC.

Burchwell, Erin. Harriett's Homecoming: A High-Flying Tour of Cincinnati. Levine, Susan Sachs. 2012. (ENG.). 32p. (J). (gr. -1-3). 19.95 *(978-1-933197-97-5(8))* Orange Frazer Pr.

Burchwell, Erin McCauley. Packard Takes Flight: A Bird's-Eye View of Columbus, Ohio. Levine, Susan Sachs. 2010. (ENG.). 32p. 17.99 *(978-1-60949-051-5(7)*, History Pr., The) Arcadia Publishing.

Burckhardt, Marc. Chasing Redbird. Creech, Sharon. 2012. (ENG.). 272p. (J). (gr. 4-18). pap. 6.99 *(978-0-06-440696-3(2))* HarperCollins Pubs.

—Daddy Loves His Little Girl. Cash, John Carter. 2010. (ENG.). 32p. (J). (gr. -1-3). 16.99 *(978-1-4169-7482-6(2)*, Little Simon Inspirations) Little Simon Inspirations.

—A Drive in the Country. Rosen, Michael J. 2007. (ENG.). 32p. (J). (gr. k-4). 16.99 *(978-0-7636-2140-7(4))* Candlewick Pr.

—Momma Loves Her Little Son. Cash, John Carter. 2009. (ENG.). 32p. (J). (gr. -1-3). 16.99 *(978-1-4169-5912-0(2)*, Little Simon Inspirations) Little Simon Inspirations.

—Spring, Summer, Autumn, Winter. Siebert, Diane. 2005. (J). *(978-1-59336-299-7(4))*; pap. *(978-1-59336-300-0(1))* Mondo Publishing.

—When Bob Met Woody: The Story of the Young Bob Dylan. Golio, Gary. 2011. (ENG.). 40p. (J). (gr. 3-7). 17.99 *(978-0-316-11299-4(2))* Little, Brown Bks. for Young Readers.

Burd, Clara M. Stories of Great Adventures. Bailey, Carolyn Sherwin. 2005. reprint ed. pap. 24.95 *(978-1-4179-0215-6(9))* Kessinger Publishing, LLC.

Burden, Andrea. Birdie's Book. Bozarth, Jan. 2009. (Fairy Godmother Academy Ser.: No. 1). (ENG.). 224p. (J). (gr. 3-7). pap. 7.99 *(978-0-375-85181-0(X))* Random Hse., Inc.

—Kerka's Book. Bozarth, Jan. 2010. (Fairy Godmother Academy Ser.: No. 2). (ENG.). 224p. (J). (gr. 3-7). pap. 6.99 *(978-0-375-85183-4(6))* Random Hse., Inc.

—Zally's Book. Bozarth, Jan. 2010. (Fairy Godmother Academy Ser.: No. 3). (ENG.). 208p. (J). (gr. 3-7). pap. 6.99 *(978-0-375-85185-8(2)*, Random Hse. Bks. for Young Readers) Random Hse. Children's Bks.

Burden, P. John. Mendel Rosenbusch: Tales for Jewish Children. Weber, Ilse. Fisher, Hans, tr. from GER. 2006. Orig. Title: Mendel Rosenbusch: Geschichen Fur Jud Kinder. 128p. (J). pap. 18.00 *(978-1-933480-05-3(X))* Bunim and Bannigan Ltd.

—Mendel Rosenbusch: Tales for Jewish Children, 1 vol. Weber, Ilse. Fisher, Hans & Fisher, Ruth, trs. from GER. ed. 2006. Orig. Title: Mendel Rosenbusch: Geschichen Fur Jud Kinder. (ENG.). 58p. (J). lib. bdg. 18.95 *(978-1-933480-04-6(1))* Bunim and Bannigan Ltd.

Burfoot, Ella. Bear & Me. 2013. (J). *(978-1-4351-4753-9(7))* Barnes & Noble, Inc.

Burfoot, Ella, et al. Don't Kiss the Frog! Princess Stories with Attitude. Claybourne, Anna. 2008. (ENG.). 80p. (J). (gr. 1-5). 14.99 *(978-0-7534-5953-9(1)*, Kingfisher) Roaring Brook Pr.

Burfoot, Ella. Don't Kiss the Frog! Princess Stories with Attitude. 2013. (ENG.). 80p. (J). (gr. 1-5). pap. 8.99 *(978-0-7534-6946-0(4)*, Kingfisher) Roaring Brook Pr.

—Monsters Don't Cry! McKee, Brett. (ENG.). 32p. (J). (gr. -1-k). 2013. pap. 9.99 *(978-1-84939-313-3(3))*; 2012. 19.99 *(978-1-84939-291-4(9))* Andersen Pr. GBR. Dist: Independent Pubs. Group.

Burfoot, Ella. Louie & the Monsters. Burfoot, Ella. 2005. 32p. (J). (gr. -1-2). 6.95 *(978-1-58925-395-7(7))* Tiger Tales.

Burg, Donna. Cow Moooves Through the Books of the Bible: Genesis. Alsbrooks, Stephanie. 2004. (J). bds. 9.99 *(978-1-4183-0002-9(0))* Christ Inspired, Inc.

—Cow Moooves Through the Books of the Bible: Job. Alsbrooks, Stephanie. 2004. (J). bds. 9.99 *(978-1-4183-0006-7(3))* Christ Inspired, Inc.

—Cow Moooves Through the Books of the Bible - Exodus. Alsbrooks, Stephanie. 2004. (J). bds. 9.99 *(978-1-4183-0007-4(1))* Christ Inspired, Inc.

—Cow Moooves Through the Books of the Bible - Joshua. Alsbrooks, Stephanie. 2004. (J). bds. 9.99 *(978-1-4183-0017-3(9))* Christ Inspired, Inc.

Burgan, Michael. The Reconstruction Amendments, 1 vol. Burgan, Michael. 2006. (We the People: Civil War Era Ser.). (ENG.). 48p. (gr. 5-6). 27.99 *(978-0-7565-1636-9(6)*, We the People) Compass Point Bks.

Burgess, H. & Fitterling, Michael A. A Victorious Union. Optic, Oliver. 2005. (Blue & Gray Ser.). (ENG.). 369p. (J). (gr. -1-12). reprint ed. pap. 14.95 *(978-1-890623-13-5(X))* Lost Classic Bks.

Burgess, Kulthum. The Lost Ring: An Eid Story. Gilani-Williams, Fawzia. 2009. (ENG.). 29p. (J). (gr. 2-6). 6.95 *(978-0-86037-565-4(X))* Kube Publishing Ltd. GBR. Dist: Consortium Bk. Sales & Distribution.

Burgess, Mark. Little Toot. Gramatky, Hardie. 2015. (Little Toot Ser.). (ENG.). 32p. (J). (gr. -1-k). 7.99 *(978-0-448-48446-4(3)*, Grosset & Dunlap) Penguin Publishing Group.

—Return to the Hundred Acre Wood. Benedictus, David. 2009. (ENG.). 216p. (J). (gr. 5-18). 19.99 *(978-0-525-42160-3(2)*, Dutton Juvenile) Penguin Publishing Group.

Burgess, Mark. Mutiny at Crossbones Bay. Burgess, Mark. Cox, Phil Roxbee, ed. 2006. (Usborne Puzzle Adventures Ser.). 48p. (J). (gr. 3-7). pap. 4.99 *(978-0-7945-1407-5(3)*, Usborne) EDC Publishing.

Burgin, Norma. La Pequena Tortuga y la Cancion del Mar. Cain, Sheridan. 2003. (SPA.). 24p. (J). (gr. k-2). *(978-84-8418-037-1(9)*, ZZ30445) Zendrera Zariquiey, Editorial ESP. Dist: Lectorum Pubns., Inc.

Burgos, Carl, et al. Marvel Masterworks: Golden Age Marvel Comics - Volume 5. 2011. (ENG.). 280p. (J). (gr. -1-17). 59.99 *(978-0-7851-3367-4(4))* Marvel Worldwide, Inc.

Burick Jr., Michael, jt. illus. see Burick, Rebecca.

Burick, Rebecca & Burick Jr., Michael. Little Daisy Tutu. Burick, Rebecca. 2012. 28p. pap. 24.95 *(978-1-4560-6883-7(0))* America Star Bks.

Burke, Chris, et al. Silent Forest, 1. Beranek, Adam et al. 2004. 136p. per. 11.95 *(978-0-9752582-0-0(6))* Silent Devil Productions.

Burke, Daniel. Of Wolves & Lambs & Others. Tsallovich, Anatoly. 2005. 73p. (YA). pap. 12.99 *(978-0-9773816-0-9(9))* ATInternational Pubs.

Burke, Frank. Animal Antics. Burke, Frank. (Orig.). (J). pap. 3.59 *(978-0-927206-05-1(6))* Author's Connection Pr.

Burke, James. All Star! Honus Wagner & the Most Famous Baseball Card Ever. Yolen, Jane. 2010. (ENG.). 40p. (J). (gr. 1-3). 17.99 *(978-0-399-24661-6(4)*, Philomel) Penguin Publishing Group.

Burke, Jim. A Christmas Gift for Mama. Thompson, Lauren. 2003. (J). pap. 16.95 *(978-0-590-30726-0(6))* Scholastic, Inc.

—Johnny Appleseed: The Legend & the Truth. Yolen, Jane. (ENG.). 32p. (J). (gr. 1-4). 2011. pap. 6.99 *(978-0-06-059137-3(4))*; 2008. 16.99 *(978-0-06-059135-9(8))* HarperCollins Pubs.

—Naming Liberty. Yolen, Jane. 2008. (ENG.). 32p. (J). (gr. 1-4). 16.99 *(978-0-399-24250-2(3)*, Philomel) Penguin Publishing Group.

—Walt Whitman. Levin, Jonathan, ed. 2008. (Poetry for Young People Ser.). (ENG.). 48p. (J). (gr. 3-7). pap. 6.95 *(978-1-4027-5477-7(9))* Sterling Publishing Co., Inc.

Burke, Jim, jt. illus. see Grant, Leigh.

Burke, Kathryn Schaar. Mule Boy. Gilbert, Joan. 2004. 248p. (YA). per. 12.95 *(978-0-930973-30-8(5))* Moore, Hugh Historical Park & Museums, Inc.

Burke, Ruth Anne. Cat Tales. Brown, Pauline A. 2013. 146p. (J). pap. 9.99 *(978-0-9838653-2-2(9))* Doorlight Pubns.

—Mama's Books: An Oregon Trail Story. Nash, Nancy. 2013. (J). pap. 9.95 *(978-0-9838653-6-0(1))* Doorlight Pubns.

Burke, Shane. Tube World. Swanson, David. 2012. 158p. pap. 10.00 *(978-0-9830830-4-7(5))* Swanson, David.

—Tube World. Swanson, David C. N. 2012. 158p. pap. 25.00 *(978-0-9830830-2-3(9))* Swanson, David.

Burke, Theresa. Biggest Trivia Book Ever: And That's a Fact! Owsley, Anthony et al. 2012. (ENG.). 528p. (J). (gr. 3). pap. 16.95 *(978-1-60433-271-1(9)*, Applesauce Pr.) Cider Mill Pr. Bk. Pubs., LLC.

Burkert, Howard, photos by. Love You, Teddy - a Tail of Loss & Hope. Ulch, Virginia. 2007. 32p. per. 18.95 *(978-1-59858-354-0(9))* Dog Ear Publishing, LLC.

Burkert, Nancy E., jt. illus. see Crane, Jordan.

Burkes-Larrañaga, Dustin. Johnny Appleseed Plants Trees Across the Land, 1 vol. 2014. (American Folk Legends Ser.). (ENG.). 32p. (gr. k-2). lib. bdg. 26.65 *(978-1-4795-5428-7(6))* Picture Window Bks.

Burkes-Larrañaga, Dustin, et al. Thorns, Horns, & Crescent Moons: Reading & Writing Nature Poems, 1 vol. Fandel, Jennifer & Miller, Connie Colwell. 2014. (Poet in You Ser.). (ENG.). 32p. (gr. 2-4). lib. bdg. 26.65 *(978-1-4795-2197-5(3))* Picture Window Bks.

Burket, Sheila. Wollie the Wheelbarrow. Hunt, Debbie Colleen. 24p. 2012. 24.95 *(978-1-4626-9969-8(3))*; 2011. pap. 24.95 *(978-1-4626-2980-0(6))* America Star Bks.

Burkett, D. Brent. Dream-of-Jade: The Emperor's Cat. Alexander, Lloyd. 2005. (ENG.). 48p. (J). (gr. 3-7). 17.95 *(978-0-8126-2736-7(9))* Cricket Bks.

—Reggie. Bunting, Eve. 2006. (ENG.). 112p. (J). (gr. 1-4). 16.95 *(978-0-8126-2746-6(6))* Cricket Bks.

Burkett, Jim, photos by. My New Friends at the Zoo: Read with Me, Pops. Burkett, Pops. 2011. (ENG., 26p. pap. 9.29 *(978-1-4611-1244-0(3))* CreateSpace Independent Publishing Platform.

Burkholder, Edith. Growing with the Millers. Martin, Mildred A. 2012. 144p. (J). *(978-1-884377-23-5(8))* Green Pastures Pr.

—Missionary Stories with the Millers. Martin, Mildred A. 2009. 208p. (J). *(978-1-884377-17-4(3))*; pap. *(978-1-884377-16-7(5))* Green Pastures Pr.

—Wisdom & the Millers: Proverbs for Children. Martin, Mildred A. 2009. 159p. (J). *(978-1-884377-15-0(7))*; pap. *(978-1-884377-14-3(9))* Green Pastures Pr.

Burks, James. Itty Bitty Kitty. Holub, Joan. 2015. (ENG.). 32p. (J). (gr. -1-3). 17.99 *(978-0-06-232219-7(2))* HarperCollins Pubs.

Burks, James. Itty Bitty Kitty & the Rainy Play Day. Holub, Joan. 2016. 32p. (J). (gr. -1-3). 17.99 ***(978-0-06-232220-3(6))*** HarperCollins Pubs.

Burks, James. The Monstore. Lazar, Tara. 2013. (ENG.). 32p. (J). (gr. -1-2). 16.99 *(978-1-4424-2017-5(0))* Simon & Schuster Children's Publishing.

—Open Wide! Krensky, Stephen. 2014. (ENG.). 14p. (J). (— 1). bds. 6.99 *(978-0-545-53368-3(6)*, Cartwheel Bks.) Scholastic, Inc.

—Willy Maykit in Space. Trine, Greg. 2015. (ENG.). 208p. (J). (gr. 2-5). 13.99 *(978-0-544-31351-4(8)*, HMH Books For Young Readers) Houghton Mifflin Harcourt Publishing Co.

Burks, James. Beep & Bah. Burks, James. 2012. (Carolrhoda Picture Bks). (ENG.). 32p. (J). (gr. k-3). lib. bdg. 16.95 *(978-0-7613-6567-9(2)*, Carolrhoda Bks.) Lerner Publishing Group.

Burleson, Joe. Return of the Gypsy Witch. Leonhardt, Alice & Hart, Alison. 2003. (ENG.). 176p. (J). (gr. 3-7). pap. 9.99 *(978-0-689-85527-6(3)*, Simon & Schuster/Paula Wiseman Bks.) Simon & Schuster/Paula Wiseman Bks.

Burlinson, James & Cordner, Theo. Minecraft. Farwell, Nick. 2014. 79p. (J). ***(978-0-545-68575-7(3))*** Scholastic, Inc.

Burma, Willingham. Clang Went the Cymbals: An Onomatopoeia Alphabet Book. Jordan, Dana Hall. 2008. 32p. (J). 15.99 *(978-0-9798664-0-1(5))* Capture Bks.

Burn, Doris. Andrew Henry's Meadow. Burn, Doris. 2012. (ENG.). 48p. (J). (gr. 1-4). 15.99 *(978-0-399-25608-0(3)*, Philomel) Penguin Publishing Group.

B

Burn, Ted. Y Is for Yellowhammer: An Alabama Alphabet. Crane, Carol. 2003. (Discover America State by State Ser.). (ENG.). 40p. (J). 17.95 *(978-1-58536-118-2(6))* Sleeping Bear Pr.

Burnell Walsh, Avenda. Loophole Forest Tells Its Tale of Enchantment. Smith, Roy. Magpie, ed. 2012. 38p. *(978-1-908000-18-7(X))* Pyjama Pr.

Burnett, Anne. The Passion for Children: Bilingual (English & Spanish) Guide to the Passion of Christ, 1 bk. Turton, Karalynn Teresa. Ruiz, Jeanette, tr. 2005. (J). 3.00 *(978-0-9765180-0-6(7))* Catholic World Mission.

Burnett, Jenifer. My Jungle Quilt. Burnett, Jenifer. 2006. 32p. (J). 19.99 *(978-0-9777570-0-8(5))* Summerside Lane.

Burnett, Lindy. The Big Sled Race. Hall, Kirsten. 2003. (Hello Reader! Ser.). (J). pap. 3.99 *(978-0-439-32104-4(2))* Scholastic, Inc.

—I Live Here! 2010. (My World Ser.).Tr. of Yo Vivo Aqui!. (ENG.). 24p. (J). (gr. -1-1). pap. 8.15 *(978-1-61533-033-1(X))*; lib. bdg. 22.60 *(978-1-60754-950-5(6))* Windmill Bks.

—I Live Here!/Yo Vivo Aqui! Rosa-Mendoza, Gladys. Gonzalez, Margarita E. & Weber, Amy, eds. 2007. (# 1 Bilingual Board Book Ser.). (ENG & SPA.). 20p. (J). (gr. -1-k). bds. 6.95 *(978-1-931398-19-0(4))* Me+Mi Publishing.

—Space Trip. Williams, Rozanne Lanczak. 2005. (Reading for Fluency Ser.). 80p. (J). pap. 32.49 *(978-1-59198-142-8(5)*, 4242) Creative Teaching Pr., Inc.

—The Sunset Switch. Kudlinski, Kathleen V. 2005. (Picture Book Ser.). (ENG.). 32p. (J). (gr. k-3). 15.95 *(978-1-55971-916-2(8))* Cooper Square Publishing Llc.

Burnett, Seb. Aliens Sticker Book. Robson, Kirsteen. 2014. (Usborne Activities Ser.). (ENG.). 22p. (J). 8.99 *(978-0-7945-3101-0(6)*, Usborne) EDC Publishing.

—The Footballing Frog. Jungman, Ann. 2007. (Collins Big Cat Ser.). (ENG.). 80p. (J). pap. 8.99 *(978-0-00-723087-7(7))* HarperCollins Pubs. Ltd. GBR. Dist: Independent Pubs. Group.

Burney, Laura & Sawyer, Peter. The Outside Play & Learning Book: Activities for Young Children. Miller, Karen. Charner, Kathleen, ed. 2004. 253p. (Orig.). (gr. -1-k). pap. 24.95 *(978-0-87659-117-8(9)*, 10009) Gryphon Hse., Inc.

Burnham, Janet Hayward. Jeremy the Puny. Burnham, Janet Hayward. 2003. (J). (gr. 3-6). pap. 14.95 *(978-0-9740743-0-6(6))* My Little Jessie Pr.

Burningham, John. Cloudland. Burningham, John. 2007. (ENG.). 48p. (J). (gr. -1-2). 9.95 *(978-0-09-971161-2(3)*, Red Fox) Random House Children's Books GBR. Dist: Independent Pubs. Group.

—Granpa. Burningham, John. 2003. (ENG.). 32p. (J). (gr. -1-2). pap. 14.99 *(978-0-09-943408-5(3)*, Red Fox) Random House Children's Books GBR. Dist: Independent Pubs. Group.

—It's a Secret! Burningham, John. 2009. (ENG.). 56p. (J). (gr. -1-2). 16.99 *(978-0-7636-4275-4(4))* Candlewick Pr.

—John Burningham. Burningham, John. ltd. ed. 2009. (ENG.). 224p. (gr. k-12). 70.00 *(978-0-7636-4434-5(X))* Candlewick Pr.

—Picnic. Burningham, John. 2014. (ENG.). 32p. (J). (-k). 16.99 *(978-0-7636-6945-4(8))* Candlewick Pr.

—Tug-of-War. Burningham, John. 2013. (ENG.). 32p. (J). (gr. k-3). 16.99 *(978-0-7636-6575-3(4))* Candlewick Pr.

—The Way to the Zoo. Burningham, John. 2014. (ENG.). 40p. (J). (gr. -1-2). 15.99 *(978-0-7636-7317-8(X))* Candlewick Pr.

Burns, Charles. The Jungle. Sinclair, Upton. deluxe ed. 2006. (Penguin Classics Deluxe Edition Ser.). (ENG.). 432p. (gr. 12-18). 17.00 *(978-0-14-303958-7(X)*, Penguin Classics) Penguin Publishing Group.

Burns, Donna. Forever Buster: What a Name! What a Dog, We Exclaim! Rabbett, Martin. 2007. (J). 13.95 *(978-0-9794649-0-4(0))* Hula Moon Pr.

—Pono the Dog That Dreams. Fujii, Jocelyn. 2008. (ENG.). 40p. (YA). 14.95 *(978-0-9794649-2-8(7))* Hula Moon Pr.

Burns, John M. Wuthering Heights. Brontë, Emily. Bryant, Clive, ed. 2011. (ENG.). 160p. lib. bdg. 24.95 *(978-1-907127-80-9(1))* Classical Comics GBR. Dist: Perseus-PGW.

Burns, Mike. Your Life as a Cabin Boy on a Pirate Ship. Gunderson, Jessica. 2012. (Way It Was Ser.). (ENG.). 32p. (gr. 2-3). pap. 7.95 *(978-1-4048-7249-3(3))*; lib. bdg. 25.99 *(978-1-4048-7159-5(4))* Picture Window Bks. (Nonfiction Picture Bks.).

Burns, Raymond. The Secret of the Stone Frog. Snow, Dorothea J. 2011. 214p. 44.95 *(978-1-258-08002-0(8))* Literary Licensing, LLC.

Burns, Sandra. The Great Horned Owl. Bingamon-Haller, Mary. 2013. 28p. pap. 8.99 *(978-1-938768-12-5(4))* Gypsy Pubns.

—If You Could See Her Smile. Burkhart, Alma J. 2013. 24p. pap. 8.99 *(978-1-938768-32-3(9))* Gypsy Pubns.

—Leafy Finds a Home. Alders, Willa. 2013. 24p. pap. 8.99 *(978-1-938768-13-2(2))* Gypsy Pubns.

—Roscoe the Volunteer Emt. Wenning, Jeremy. 2013. 24p. pap. 8.99 *(978-1-938768-19-4(1))* Gypsy Pubns.

—The Stillwater River. Bingamon-Haller, Mary. 2013. 24p. pap. 8.99 *(978-1-938768-30-9(2))* Gypsy Pubns.

Burns, Taurus. Kyle Jeffries, Pilgrim. Radley, Gail. 2010. (J). pap. *(978-0-87743-712-3(2))* Baha'i Publishing Trust, U.S.

BURNS, Theresa. Sly Fly & the Gray Mare. Hoffman, Terri. 2013. 26p. 15.95 *(978-1-940224-15-2(2))* Taylor and Seale Publishing, LLC.

Burns, Theresa. The Underwater Orchestra. Gantry, Chris. 2013. 38p. 16.98 *(978-1-940224-19-0(5))* Taylor and Seale Publishing, LLC.

Burns, Theresa. Queen Emileen. Burns, Theresa. 2013. 36p. 15.50 *(978-1-949224-23-8(6))* Taylor and Seale Publishing, LLC.

Burnstine, Susan, photos by. How to Raise a Jewish Dog. Rabbi's of Boca Raton Theological Seminary Staff. rev. ed. 2007. (ENG., 176p. per. 15.00 *(978-0-316-15466-6(0))* Little Brown & Co.

Burphon, S., et al. Struggle down Under. Gilligan, Shannon. 2007. (Choose Your Own Adventure Ser.: No. 21). 123p. (J). (gr. 4-7). pap. 6.99 *(978-1-933390-21-5(2))* Chooseco LLC.

Burque, Hannah Adams. Environmental Health Narratives: A Reader for Youth. Mendenhall, Emily & Koon, Adam, eds. 2012. (ENG.). 400p. pap. 27.95 *(978-0-8263-5166-1(2))* Univ. of New Mexico Pr.

Burr, Dan. Cowboys: Voices in the Western Wind. Harrison, David L. 2012. (ENG.). 48p. (J). (gr. 2-4). 17.95 *(978-1-59078-877-6(X)*, Wordsong) Boyds Mills Pr.

—Easter Walk: A Treasure Hunt for the Real Meaning of Easter. Rowley, Deborah Pace. 2010. (J). *(978-1-60641-055-4(5))* Deseret Bk. Co.

—The Enchanted Tunnel Vol. 3: Journey to Jerusalem. Monson, Marianne. 2011. (J). (gr. 3-6). pap. 7.99 *(978-1-60908-068-6(8))* Deseret Bk. Co.

—The Enchanted Tunnel Vol. 4: Wandering in the Wilderness. Monson, Marianne. 2011. 85p. (YA). (gr. 3-6). pap. 7.99 *(978-1-60908-069-3(6))* Deseret Bk. Co.

—God Bless Your Way: A Christmas Journey. Freeman, Emily. 2007. 32p. (J). (gr. -1-3). 19.95 incl. audio compact disk *(978-1-59038-806-8(2))* Deseret Bk. Co.

—One Little Match. Monson, Thomas S. 2014. 17.99 *(978-1-60907-868-3(3))* Deseret Bk. Co.

—Pirates. Harrison, David L. (ENG.). 48p. (J). (gr. 4-6). 2012. pap. 9.95 *(978-1-59078-912-4(1))*; 2008. 17.95 *(978-1-59078-455-6(3))* Boyds Mills Pr. (Wordsong).

—Sam's Christmas Wish. Durrant, George D. 2014. (J). 17.99 *(978-1-60907-606-1(0)*, Shadow Mountain) Shadow Mountain Publishing.

—The Testimony Glove. Oaks, Kristen M. & Phillips, JoAnn. 2010. (J). (gr. -1-4). 17.99 *(978-1-60641-151-3(9))* Deseret Bk. Co.

—The White Ox. Hailstone, Ruth. 2009. (ENG.). 40p. (J). (gr. 3-7). 18.95 *(978-1-59078-555-3(X)*, Calkins Creek) Boyds Mills Pr.

Burr, Dan E. Presidential Misadventures: Poems That Poke Fun at the Man in Charge. Raczka, Bob. 2015. (ENG.). 48p. (J). (gr. 3-7). 17.99 *(978-1-59643-980-1(7))* Roaring Brook Pr.

Burrier, Sara. Nursies When the Sun Shines: A Little Book on Night Weaning. Havener, Katherine. 2nd ed. 2013. 20p. (J). pap. 9.99 *(978-0-615-75642-4(5))* Elea Pr.

Burris, Andrea. A Dog Lover's Alphabet Book. Burris, Andrea. Schad, Anna. 2007. (ENG.). 32p. (J). (gr. k-2). 14.95 *(978-0-9743294-1-3(X))* A & D Bks.

Burris, Andrea M. The Kitty Cat Alphabet Book. Burris, Andrea M. Schad, Anna M. 2004. (ENG.). 32p. (J). 14.95 *(978-0-9743294-0-6(1)*, 1230444) A & D Bks.

Burris, Priscilla. Aloha for Carol Ann. Sorenson, Margo. 2011. 32p. (J). (gr. -1-3). pap. 8.95 *(978-1-60349-027-6(2)*, Marimba Bks.) Hudson Publishing Group, The.

—Edgar's Second Word. Vernick, Audrey. 2014. (ENG.). 32p. (J). (gr. -1-3). 16.99 *(978-0-547-68462-8(2))* Houghton Mifflin Harcourt Publishing Co.

—Emily Santos, Star of the Week. Williams, Rozanne Lanczak. 2006. (Learn to Write Ser.). 16p. (J). (gr. k-2). pap. 2.99 *(978-1-59198-298-2(7)*, 6194) Creative Teaching Pr., Inc.

—Emily Santos, Star of the Week. Williams, Rozanne Lanczak. Maio, Barbara, ed. 2006. (J). per. 8.99 *(978-1-59198-358-3(4))* Creative Teaching Pr., Inc.

—Games Galore for Children's Parties & More: 80 Fun Games & Activities for Parties, Classroom, Youth Groups, Carnivals, Company Picnics, Rainy Days & Special Occasions. Pence, Shari A. Stearns, Debra & Kohout, Rosemary, eds. 2nd rev. ed. 2005. (ENG.). 121p. (J). (gr. -1-7). pap. 12.00 *(978-0-9645771-1-4(9))* Funcastle Pubns.

—Heidi Heckelbeck & the Christmas Surprise. Coven, Wanda. 2013. (Heidi Heckelbeck Ser.: 9). (ENG.). 128p. (J). (gr. k-2). 15.99 *(978-1-4424-8125-1(0))*; pap. 4.99 *(978-1-4424-8124-4(2))* Little Simon. (Little Simon).

—Heidi Heckelbeck & the Cookie Contest. Coven, Wanda. 2012. (Heidi Heckelbeck Ser.: 3). (ENG.). 128p. (J). (gr. k-2). 15.99 *(978-1-4424-4166-8(6))*; pap. 5.99 *(978-1-4424-4165-1(8))* Little Simon. (Little Simon).

—Heidi Heckelbeck & the Secret Admirer. Coven, Wanda. 2012. (Heidi Heckelbeck Ser.: 6). (ENG.). 128p. (J). (gr. k-4). 16.99 *(978-1-4424-4175-0(5))*; pap. 5.99 *(978-1-4424-4174-3(7))* Little Simon. (Little Simon).

—Heidi Heckelbeck Casts a Spell. Coven, Wanda. 2012. (Heidi Heckelbeck Ser.: 2). (ENG.). 128p. (J). (gr. k-2). 15.99 *(978-1-4424-4088-3(0))*; pap. 5.99 *(978-1-4424-3567-4(4))* Little Simon. (Little Simon).

—The Heidi Heckelbeck Collection: A Bewitching Four-Book Boxed Set: Heidi Heckelbeck Has a Secret; Heidi Hecklebeck Casts a Spell; Heidi Hecklebeck & the Cookie Contest; Heidi Hecklebeck in Disguise. Coven, Wanda. ed. 2013. (Heidi Heckelbeck Ser.). (ENG.). 512p. (J). (gr. k-4). pap. 19.99 *(978-1-4424-8976-9(6)*, Little Simon) Little Simon.

—Heidi Heckelbeck Gets Glasses. Coven, Wanda. 2012. (Heidi Heckelbeck Ser.: 5). (ENG.). 128p. (J). (gr. k-2). 15.99 *(978-1-4424-4172-9(0))*; pap. 4.99 *(978-1-4424-4171-2(2))* Little Simon. (Little Simon).

—Heidi Heckelbeck Goes to Camp! Coven, Wanda. 2013. (Heidi Heckelbeck Ser.: 8). (ENG.). 128p. (J). (gr. k-2). 15.99 *(978-1-4424-6481-0(X))*; pap. 5.99 *(978-1-4424-6480-3(1))* Little Simon. (Little Simon).

—Heidi Heckelbeck Has a Secret. Coven, Wanda. 2012. (Heidi Heckelbeck Ser.: 1). (ENG.). 128p. (J). (gr. k-2). 15.99 *(978-1-4424-4087-6(2))*; pap. 5.99 *(978-1-4424-3565-0(8))* Little Simon. (Little Simon).

—Heidi Heckelbeck Has a Secret - Heidi Heckelbeck Casts a Spell - Heidi Heckelbeck & the Cookie Contest. Coven, Wanda. 2014. (Heidi Heckelbeck Ser.). (ENG.). 384p. (J). (gr. k-4). pap. 8.99 *(978-1-4814-2771-5(7)*, Little Simon) Little Simon.

—Heidi Heckelbeck in Disguise. Coven, Wanda. 2012. (Heidi Heckelbeck Ser.: 4). (ENG.). 128p. (J). (gr. k-2). 16.99 *(978-1-4424-4169-9(0))*; pap. 5.99 *(978-1-4424-4168-2(2))* Little Simon. (Little Simon).

—Heidi Heckelbeck Is a Flower Girl. Coven, Wanda. 2014. (Heidi Heckelbeck Ser.: 11). (ENG.). 128p. (J). (gr. k-2). pap. 4.99 *(978-1-4814-0498-3(9))*, Little Simon) Little Simon.

—Heidi Heckelbeck Is Not a Thief! Coven, Wanda. 2015. (Heidi Heckelbeck Ser.: 13). (ENG.). 128p. (J). (gr. k-4). pap. 5.99 *(978-1-4814-2324-3(X)*, Little Simon) Little Simon.

—Heidi Heckelbeck Is Ready to Dance! Coven, Wanda. 2013. (Heidi Heckelbeck Ser.: 7). (ENG.). 128p. (J). (gr. k-4). 16.99 *(978-1-4424-5192-6(0)*, Little Simon) Little Simon.

—Heidi Heckelbeck Says "Cheese!" Coven, Wanda. 2015. (Heidi Heckelbeck Ser.: 14). (ENG.). 128p. (J). (gr. k-4). pap. 5.99 *(978-1-4814-2327-4(4)*, Little Simon) Little Simon.

—Humphrey's Creepy-Crawly Camping Adventure. Birney, Betty G. 2015. (Humphrey's Tiny Tales Ser.: 3). (ENG.). 96p. (J). (gr. k-3). 4.99 *(978-0-14-751459-2(2)*, Puffin); 14.99 *(978-0-399-17227-4(0)*, Putnam Adult) Penguin Publishing Group.

—Humphrey's Playful Puppy Problem. Birney, Betty G. 2014. (Humphrey's Tiny Tales Ser.: 2). (ENG.). 96p. (J). (gr. k-3). pap. 4.99 *(978-0-14-751484-4(3)*, Puffin) Penguin Publishing Group.

—Humphrey's Really Wheely Racing Day. Birney, Betty G. 2014. (Humphrey's Tiny Tales Ser.: 1). (ENG.). 96p. (J). (gr. k-3). pap. 4.99 *(978-0-14-751485-1(1)*, Puffin) Penguin Publishing Group.

—I Can Be Responsible. Burch, Regina G. & Donovan Guntly, Jenette. 2004. (Doing the Right Thing Ser.). 16p. (gr. -1-2). lib. bdg. 20.00 *(978-0-8368-4245-6(6)*, Gareth Stevens Learning Library) Stevens, Gareth Publishing LLLP.

—I Love You All Day Long. Rusackas, Francesca. 2004. (ENG.). 32p. (J). (gr. -1-k). reprint ed. pap. 6.99 *(978-0-06-050278-2(9))* HarperCollins Pubs.

—Little Book of Rules. Busath, Isabelle & Thordsen, Isabella. 2013. (ENG.). 120p. (J). (gr. 3-7). 12.99 *(978-1-4424-9980-5(X)*, Simon Spotlight) Simon Spotlight.

—Maggi & Milo. Brenning, Juli. 2014. (ENG.). 32p. (J). (gr. -1-k). 16.99 *(978-0-8037-3795-2(5)*, Dial) Penguin Publishing Group.

—Mom School. Van Slyke, Rebecca. 2015. (ENG.). 32p. (J). (gr. -1-2). 16.99 *(978-0-385-38892-4(6))* Knopf Doubleday Publishing Group.

—The Swim Lesson. Williams, Rozanne Lanczak. 2005. (Reading for Fluency Ser.). 8p. (J). pap. 3.49 *(978-1-59198-148-0(4)*, 4248) Creative Teaching Pr., Inc.

—This Is My Story. Williams, Rozanne Lanczak. 2006. (Learn to Write Ser.). 8p. (J). (gr. k-2). pap. 3.49 *(978-1-59198-280-7(4)*, 6174) Creative Teaching Pr., Inc.

—This Is My Story. Williams, Rozanne Lanczak. Maio, Barbara & Faulkner, Stacey, eds. 2006. (J). per. 6.99 *(978-1-59198-331-6(2))* Creative Teaching Pr., Inc.

—Where Have You Been? Williams, Rozanne Lanczak. Hamaguchi, Carla, ed. 2003. (Sight Word Readers Ser.). 16p. (J). (gr. k-2). pap. 3.49 *(978-1-57471-970-3(X)*, 3592) Creative Teaching Pr., Inc.

Burris, Priscilla. Daddy All Day Long. Burris, Priscilla, tr. Rusackas, Francesca. 2004. 32p. (J). (gr. -1-k). lib. bdg. 13.89 *(978-0-06-050285-0(1))* HarperCollins Pubs.

Burroughs, David. Detective Files, 1 vol. Bowkett, Steve. 2007. (Graphic Quest Ser.). (ENG.). 88p. (gr. 3-3). 23.99 *(978-1-59889-826-2(4)*, Graphic Quest) Stone Arch Bks.

Burroughs, Derrie. Baby Love. Tika. Standish, Joyce, ed. l.t. ed. 2006. 18p. (J). (gr. 1-5). pap. 15.00 *(978-0-9716244-1-2(0))* TLS Publishing.

Burroughs, Scott. Balloon Blow-Up. 2013. (Hardy Boys: the Secret Files Ser.: 13). (ENG.). 112p. (J). (gr. 1-4). pap. 5.99 *(978-1-4424-5371-5(0))*, Simon & Schuster/Paula Wiseman Bks.) Simon & Schuster/Paula Wiseman Bks.

—The Bicycle Thief. Dixon, Franklin W. 2011. (Hardy Boys: the Secret Files Ser.: 6). (ENG.). 96p. (J). (gr. 1-4). pap. 5.99 *(978-1-4169-9396-4(7)*, Simon & Schuster/Paula Wiseman Bks.) Simon & Schuster/Paula Wiseman Bks.

—The Disappearing Dog. 2011. (Hardy Boys: the Secret Files Ser.: 7). (ENG.). 96p. (J). (gr. 1-4). pap. 4.99 *(978-1-4424-2314-5(5)*, Simon & Schuster/Paula Wiseman Bks.) Simon & Schuster/Paula Wiseman Bks.

—Fossil Frenzy. 2014. (Hardy Boys: the Secret Files Ser.: 14). (ENG.). 96p. (J). (gr. 1-4). pap. 4.99 *(978-1-4424-9043-7(8)*, Simon & Schuster/Paula Wiseman Bks.) Simon & Schuster/Paula Wiseman Bks.

—God's Armor for Me. Shearer, Amelia. 2014. (Happy Day Ser.). (ENG.). 16p. (J). pap. 2.49 *(978-1-4143-9480-0(2))* Tyndale Hse. Pubs.

—God's Special Rule. Redford, Marjorie & Rice, Courtney. 2013. (Happy Day Ser.). (ENG.). 16p. (J). pap. 2.49 *(978-1-4143-9300-1(8))* Tyndale Hse. Pubs.

—The Great Coaster Caper. 2012. (Hardy Boys: the Secret Files Ser.: 9). (ENG.). 112p. (J). (gr. 1-4). pap. 4.99 *(978-1-4424-1669-7(6)*, Simon & Schuster/Paula Wiseman Bks.) Simon & Schuster/Paula Wiseman Bks.

—The Great Escape. Dixon, Franklin W. 2015. (Hardy Boys: the Secret Files Ser.: 17). (ENG.). 112p. (J). (gr. 1-4). pap. 4.99 *(978-1-4814-2267-3(7)*, Simon & Schuster/Paula Wiseman Bks.) Simon & Schuster/Paula Wiseman Bks.

—The Hardy Boys Secret Files Collection: Trouble at the Arcade - The Missing Mitt - Mystery Map - Hopping Mad - A Monster of a Mystery. ed. 2014. (Hardy Boys: the Secret Files Ser.). (ENG.). 496p. (J). (gr. 1-4). pap. 24.99 *(978-1-4814-1473-9(9)*, Simon & Schuster/Paula Wiseman Bks.) Simon & Schuster/Paula Wiseman Bks.

—The High Score & Lowdown on Video Games! Krensky, Stephen. 2015. (History of Fun Stuff Ser.). (ENG.). 48p. (J). (gr. 1-3). 16.99 *(978-1-4814-2916-0(7))*; pap. 3.99 *(978-1-4814-2915-3(9))* Simon Spotlight. (Simon Spotlight).

—Hopping Mad. 2010. (Hardy Boys: the Secret Files Ser.: 4). (ENG.). 96p. (J). (gr. 1-4). pap. 4.99 *(978-1-4169-9395-7(9)*, Simon & Schuster/Paula Wiseman Bks.) Simon & Schuster/Paula Wiseman Bks.

—Lights, Camera ... Zombies! 2013. (Hardy Boys: the Secret Files Ser.: 12). (ENG.). 96p. (J). (gr. 1-4). pap. 4.99 *(978-1-4424-5369-2(9)*, Simon & Schuster/Paula Wiseman Bks.) Simon & Schuster/Paula Wiseman Bks.

—The Missing Mitt. 2010. (Hardy Boys: the Secret Files Ser.: 2). (ENG.). 96p. (J). (gr. 1-4). pap. 4.99 *(978-1-4169-9394-0(0)*, Simon & Schuster/Paula Wiseman Bks.) Simon & Schuster/Paula Wiseman Bks.

—A Monster of a Mystery. 2011. (Hardy Boys: the Secret Files Ser.: 5). (ENG.). 96p. (J). (gr. 1-4). pap. 4.99 *(978-1-4169-9166-3(2)*, Simon & Schuster/Paula Wiseman Bks.) Simon & Schuster/Paula Wiseman Bks.

—Mystery Map. 2010. (Hardy Boys: the Secret Files Ser.: 3). (ENG.). 96p. (J). (gr. 1-4). pap. 4.99 *(978-1-4169-9165-6(4)*, Simon & Schuster/Paula Wiseman Bks.) Simon & Schuster/Paula Wiseman Bks.

—One Tiny Baby. Taylor, Mark A. 2014. (Happy Day Ser.). (ENG.). 16p. (J). pap. 2.49 *(978-1-4143-9478-7(0))* Tyndale Hse. Pubs.

—Robot Rumble. 2013. (Hardy Boys: the Secret Files Ser.: 11). (ENG.). 96p. (J). (gr. 1-4). pap. 4.99 *(978-1-4424-5367-8(2)*, Simon & Schuster/Paula Wiseman Bks.) Simon & Schuster/Paula Wiseman Bks.

—A Rockin' Mystery. 2012. (Hardy Boys: the Secret Files Ser.: 10). (ENG.). 96p. (J). (gr. 1-4). pap. 4.99 *(978-1-4424-1671-0(8)*, Simon & Schuster/Paula Wiseman Bks.) Simon & Schuster/Paula Wiseman Bks.

—A Rockin' Mystery. ed. 2012. (Hardy Boys: Secret Files Ser.: 10). lib. bdg. 14.75 *(978-0-606-26892-9(8)*, Turtleback) Turtleback Bks.

—The Scoop on Ice Cream! Williams, Bonnie. 2014. (History of Fun Stuff Ser.). (ENG.). 48p. (J). (gr. 1-3). pap. 3.99 *(978-1-4814-0981-0(6)*, Simon Spotlight) Simon Spotlight.

—Sports Sabotage. 2012. (Hardy Boys: the Secret Files Ser.: 8). (ENG.). 112p. (J). (gr. 1-4). pap. 5.99 *(978-1-4424-2316-9(1)*, Simon & Schuster/Paula Wiseman Bks.) Simon & Schuster/Paula Wiseman Bks.

Burroughs, Scott, et al. The Super Short, Amazing Story of David & Goliath. Burroughs, Chrysti & Burroughs, Scott. Burroughs, Scott A. 2005. 32p. (J). (gr. -1-3). 10.99 *(978-0-8254-2412-0(7))* Kregel Pubns.

Burroughs, Scott. Trouble at the Arcade. 2010. (Hardy Boys: the Secret Files Ser.: 1). (ENG.). 96p. (J). (gr. 1-4). pap. 4.99 *(978-1-4169-9164-9(6)*, Simon & Schuster/Paula Wiseman Bks.) Simon & Schuster/Paula Wiseman Bks.

Burrows, Jeffrey Scott. Keri Tarr - Cat Detective. Lement, Wendy. 2004. (ENG.). 80p. (J). pap. 9.95 *(978-1-891369-52-0(0))* Breakaway Bks.

Burruss, Melissa, jt. illus. see Castillo, Cesar.

Bursi, Simona. Bible Stories for Boys. Martin, Peter. 2014. (ENG.). 48p. (J). (gr. k-4). 14.99 *(978-0-7459-6370-9(6))* Lion Hudson PLC GBR. Dist: Independent Pubs. Group.

—Bible Stories for Girls. Goodings, Christina. 2014. (ENG.). 48p. (J). (gr. k-4). 14.99 *(978-0-7459-6371-6(4))* Lion Hudson PLC GBR. Dist: Independent Pubs. Group.

Bursi, Simona, et al. The Usborne Book of Greek Myths. Milbourne, Anna & Stowell, Louie. Brocklehurst, Ruth, ed. 2014. (ENG.). 301p. (J). (gr. 4-7). pap. 22.99 *(978-0-7945-2130-1(4)*, Usborne) EDC Publishing.

Burstein, Chaya M. The Kids' Catalog of Animals & the Earth. Burstein, Chaya M. 2005. (Kids' Catalog Ser.). (ENG.). 200p. (gr. 3). per. 16.95 *(978-0-8276-0785-9(7))* Jewish Pubn. Society.

Bursztyn, Dina. The Land of Lost Things: El País de las Cosas Perdidas. Bursztyn, Dina. 2011. (SPA & ENG.). 32p. (J). (gr. -1-3). 16.95 *(978-1-55885-690-5(0)*, Piñata Books) Arte Publico Pr.

Burt, Kelly. Animalimericks! Henderson, Kris. 2009. 32p. pap. 14.99 *(978-1-4389-4333-6(4))* AuthorHouse.

Burt, Mary Alice. Beginning the Walk: A Tool for Developing A Preschooler's Faith. Burt, Mary Alice. 2004. 164p. (J). cd-rom 19.95 *(978-0-9641134-2-8(2))* Products With A Purpose.

Burt-Sullivan, Neallia. Tino Turtle Travels to Beijing, China. Ahern, Carolyn L. 2011. (ENG.). 56p. (J). (gr. -1-4). 19.95 incl. audio compact disk *(978-0-9793158-4-8(0))* Tino Turtle Travels, LLC.

Burt Sullivan, Neallia. Tino Turtle Travels to Kenya - the Great Safari. Ahern, Carolyn L. 2009. (ENG & SWA.). 32p. (J). (gr. -1-4). 19.95 incl. audio compact disk *(978-0-9793158-3-1(2))* Tino Turtle Travels, LLC.

—Tino Turtle Travels to London, England. Ahern, Carolyn L. (J). 2007. 36p. 17.95 incl. audio compact disk *(978-0-9793158-0-0(8))*; 2008. (ENG.). 32p. 19.95 incl. audio compact disk *(978-0-9816297-0-4(9))* Tino Turtle Travels, LLC.

—Tino Turtle Travels to Mexico City, Mexico. Ahern, Carolyn L. 2008. (ENG & SPA.). 32p. (J). (gr. -1-4). 19.95 incl. audio compact disk *(978-0-9793158-2-4(4))* Tino Turtle Travels, LLC.

—Tino Turtle Travels to Paris, France. Ahern, Carolyn L. 2007. 36p. (J). (gr. -1-4). 17.95 incl. audio compact disk *(978-0-9793158-1-7(6))* Tino Turtle Travels, LLC.

Burton, Carl, jt. illus. see Burton, Linda.

Burton, Claudia. The Adventures of Remmington the Dog: An Unexpected Friend. Redfern, Holly. 2007. 28p. (gr. -1-3). per. 14.95 *(978-1-59858-317-5(4))* Dog Ear Publishing, LLC.

Burton, Daniel, jt. illus. see Javier, Emmanuel Xerx.

Burton, Jane & Greenaway, Frank, photos by. Cat. Rayner, Matthew & BVetMed MRCVS Staff. 2004. (I Am Your Pet Ser.). 32p. (gr. k-4). lib. bdg. 26.00 *(978-0-8368-4102-2(6)*, Gareth Stevens Learning Library) Stevens, Gareth Publishing LLLP.

—Dog. Rayner, Matthew & BVetMed MRCVS Staff. 2004. (I Am Your Pet Ser.). 32p. (gr. k-4). lib. bdg. 26.00 *(978-0-8368-4103-9(4)*, Gareth Stevens Learning Library) Stevens, Gareth Publishing LLLP.

—Rabbit. Rayner, Matthew & BVetMed MRCVS Staff. 2004. (I Am Your Pet Ser.). 32p. (gr. k-4). lib. bdg. 26.00 *(978-0-8368-4105-3(0)*, Gareth Stevens Learning Library) Stevens, Gareth Publishing LLLP.

Burton, Jane & King, Dave, photos by. Mammal: Eyewitness Books. Parker, Steve. 2004. 63p. (gr. 4-8). reprint ed. 16.00 *(978-0-7567-7286-4(9))* DIANE Publishing Co.

Burton, Jane, jt. photos by see Greenaway, Frank.

Burton, Linda & Burton, Carl. Pay Attention, Emily Brown! Burton, Linda & Burton, Carl. 2011. 32p. (J). (978-1-60613-027-8(7)) Woodbine Hse.

Burton, Nathaniel. Big Match Manager, No. 2. Sheldon, Tom. 2006. (ENG.). 224p. (YA). (gr. 7). pap. 11.99 (978-0-7475-8205-2(X)) Bloomsbury Publishing Plc GBR. Dist: Independent Pubs. Group.

Burton, Terry. Digger: A Lift-the-Flap & Stand Up. Tango Books Staff. 2011. (Mini Trucks Ser.). (ENG.). 12p. (J). (gr. -1-k). 5.99 (978-1-85707-751-3(2)) Tango Bks. GBR. Dist: Independent Pubs. Group.

—English. Award, Anna. 2012. (ENG.). 36p. (J). pap. 8.25 (978-1-84135-801-7(0)) Award Pubns. Ltd. GBR. Dist: Parkwest Pubns., Inc.

—English/French. Award, Anna. 2012. (J). (FRE & ENG.). 96p. 11.50 (978-1-84135-798-0(7)); (ENG.). 36p. pap. 8.25 (978-1-84135-802-4(9)) Award Pubns. Ltd. GBR. Dist: Parkwest Pubns., Inc.

—Fire Engine. Tango Books Staff. 2011. (Mini Trucks Ser.). (ENG.). 12p. (J). (gr. -1-k). 5.99 (978-1-85707-752-0(0)) Tango Bks. GBR. Dist: Independent Pubs. Group.

—Gingerbread Man. Andrews, Jackie. 2012. (ENG.). 32p. pap. 6.50 (978-1-84135-193-3(8)) Award Pubns. Ltd. GBR. Dist: Parkwest Pubns., Inc.

—Mini Trucks: Crane: A Lift-the-Flap & Stand Up. Tango Books. 2011. (Mini Trucks Ser.). (ENG.). 12p. (J). (gr. -1-k). 5.99 (978-1-85707-750-6(4)) Tango Bks. GBR. Dist: Independent Pubs. Group.

—Tractor: A Lift-the-Flap & Stand-Up. Tango Books. 2011. (Mini Trucks Ser.). (ENG.). 12p. (J). (gr. -1-k). 5.99 (978-1-85707-753-7(9)) Tango Bks. GBR. Dist: Independent Pubs. Group.

Burton, Terry. English. Burton, Terry. Ward, Anna. 2012. (ENG.). 96p. (J). 11.50 (978-1-84135-797-3(9)) Award Pubns. Ltd. GBR. Dist: Parkwest Pubns., Inc.

Burton, Terry & Hicks, Angela. My First Picture Dictionary. Giles, Sophie et al. 2014. (ENG.). 125p. 17.50 (978-1-84135-873-4(8)) Award Pubns. Ltd. GBR. Dist: Parkwest Pubns., Inc.

Burton, Tim. Nightmare Before Christmas. Burton, Tim. Disney Book Group Staff. 20th anniv. ed. 2013. (ENG.). 40p. (J). (gr. 1-3). 17.99 (978-1-4231-7869-9(6)) Disney Pr.

Burton, Virginia Lee. The Emperor's New Clothes. Andersen, Hans Christian & Starbright Foundation Staff. (Folk Tale Classics Ser.). (ENG.). 48p. (J). (gr. -1-3). 2014. 8.99 (978-0-544-15952-5(7), HMH Books For Young Readers); 2004. pap. 6.95 (978-0-618-34420-8(9)) Houghton Mifflin Harcourt Publishing Co.

Burton, Virginia Lee. The Little House. Burton, Virginia Lee. 2009. (ENG.). 42p. (J). (gr. -1 — 1). bds. 7.99 (978-0-547-13104-7(6)) Houghton Mifflin Harcourt Publishing Co.

—Mike Mulligan & His Steam Shovel, 1 vol. Burton, Virginia Lee. 2006. (Read along Book & CD Ser.). (ENG.). 48p. (J). (gr. -1-3). 10.99 (978-0-618-73756-7(1)) Houghton Mifflin Harcourt Publishing Co.

Busaluzzo, Constanza. The Baby Bible Sing & Pray. David C. Cook Publishing Company Staff & Currie, Robin. ed. 2008. (Baby Bible Ser.). (ENG.). 46p. (J). bds. 12.99 (978-0-7814-4893-2(X)) Cook, David C.

—The Baby Bible Storybook for Boys. Currie, Robin. ed. 2008. (Baby Bible Ser.). (ENG.). 46p. (J). bds. 12.99 (978-0-7814-3501-7(3)) Cook, David C.

—The Baby Bible Storybook for Girls. David C. Cook Publishing Company Staff & Currie, Robin. ed. 2008. (Baby Bible Ser.). (ENG.). 46p. (J). bds. 12.99 (978-1-4347-6783-7(3)) Cook, David C.

—Stories about Jesus. David C. Cook Publishing Company Staff & Currie, Robin. ed. 2008. (Baby Bible Ser.). (ENG.). 46p. (J). bds. 12.99 (978-0-7814-4889-5(1)) Cook, David C.

Busby, Allie. Elephant's Birthday Bells: Jump up & Join In. Grant, Carrie and David. 2013. 32p. (J). pap. 7.99 (978-1-61067-181-1(3)) Kane Miller.

—Henry Helps Clean His Room, 1 vol. Bracken, Beth. 2012. (Henry Helps Ser.). (ENG.). 24p. (gr. -1 — 1). pap. 4.95 (978-1-4048-7668-2(5)); lib. bdg. 21.32 (978-1-4048-7306-3(6)) Picture Window Bks.

—Henry Helps Make Cookies, 1 vol. Bracken, Beth. 2012. (Henry Helps Ser.). (ENG.). 24p. (gr. -1 — 1). pap. 4.95 (978-1-4048-7669-9(3)); lib. bdg. 21.32 (978-1-4048-7303-2(1)) Picture Window Bks.

—Henry Helps Plant a Garden, 1 vol. Bracken, Beth. 2012. (Henry Helps Ser.). (ENG.). 24p. (gr. -1 — 1). pap. 4.95 (978-1-4048-7670-5(7)); lib. bdg. 21.32 (978-1-4048-7305-6(8)) Picture Window Bks.

—Henry Helps Wash the Car, 1 vol. Bracken, Beth. 2012. (Henry Helps Ser.). (ENG.). 24p. (gr. -1 — 1). pap. 4.95 (978-1-4048-7671-2(5)); lib. bdg. 21.32 (978-1-4048-7304-9(X)) Picture Window Bks.

—Henry Helps with Dinner, 1 vol. Bracken, Beth. (Henry Helps Ser.). (ENG.). (gr. -1 — 1). 2012. 32p. pap. 4.95 (978-1-4048-7675-0(8), Henry Helps); 2012. 20p. bds. 6.95 (978-1-4048-7382-7(1)); 2011. 24p. lib. bdg. 21.32 (978-1-4048-6773-4(2), Henry Helps) Picture Window Bks.

—Henry Helps with Laundry, 1 vol. Bracken, Beth. (Henry Helps Ser.). (ENG.). (gr. -1 — 1). 2012. 24p. pap. 4.95 (978-1-4048-7674-3(X), Henry Helps); 2012. 20p. bds. 6.95 (978-1-4048-7384-1(8)); 2011. 24p. lib. bdg. 21.32 (978-1-4048-6772-7(4), Henry Helps) Picture Window Bks.

—Henry Helps with the Baby, 1 vol. Bracken, Beth. (Henry Helps Ser.). (ENG.). (gr. -1 — 1). 2012. 24p. pap. 4.95 (978-1-4048-7672-9(3), Henry Helps); 2012. 20p. bds. 6.95 (978-1-4048-7381-0(3)); 2011. 24p. lib. bdg. 21.32 (978-1-4048-6770-3(8), Henry Helps) Picture Window Bks.

—Henry Helps with the Dog, 1 vol. Bracken, Beth. (Henry Helps Ser.). (ENG.). (gr. -1 — 1). 2012. 24p. pap. 4.95 (978-1-4048-7673-6(1), Henry Helps); 2012. 20p. bds. 6.95 (978-1-4048-7383-4(X)); 2011. 24p. lib. bdg. 21.32 (978-1-4048-6771-0(6), Henry Helps) Picture Window Bks.

—Lion's Speedy Sauce: Jump up & Join In. Grant, Carrie and David. 2013. 32p. (J). pap. 7.99 (978-1-61067-180-4(5)) Kane Miller.

—Lulu Loves Colours. Reid, Camilla. 2015. (ENG.). 12p. (J). (gr. -1-k). bds. 8.99 (978-1-4088-4964-4(X), Bloomsbury USA Childrens) Bloomsbury USA.

—Lulu Loves Noises. Reid, Camilla. 2015. (ENG.). 12p. (J). (gr. -1-k). bds. 8.99 (978-1-4088-4963-7(1), Bloomsbury USA Childrens) Bloomsbury USA.

—Lulu Loves Numbers. Reid, Camilla. 2015. (ENG.). 12p. (J). (gr. -1-1). bds. 8.99 (978-1-4088-4957-6(7), Bloomsbury USA Childrens) Bloomsbury USA.

—Lulu Loves Shapes. Reid, Camilla. 2015. (ENG.). 12p. (J). (gr. -1-1). bds. 8.99 (978-1-4088-4958-3(5), Bloomsbury USA Childrens) Bloomsbury USA.

—The Quiet Woman & the Noisy Dog. Eves, Sue. 2010. (ENG.). 32p. (J). (gr. k-k). pap. 10.99 (978-1-84270-939-9(9)) Andersen Pr. GBR. Dist: Independent Pubs. Group.

Busby, Allie. Spring. Child's Play Staff. 2015. (Seasons Ser.: 4). (ENG.). 12p. (J). bds. **(978-1-84643-741-0(5))** Child's Play International Ltd.

—Summer. Child's Play Staff. 2015. (Seasons Ser.: 4). (ENG.). 12p. (J). bds. **(978-1-84643-742-7(3))** Child's Play International Ltd.

Busby, Allie. The Tooth Fairy Loses a Tooth! Metzger, Steve. 2011. (ENG.). 16p. (J). (gr. -1-1). pap. 5.99 (978-1-4424-1259-0(3), Little Simon) Little Simon.

—Who's the Boss Rhinoceros? Puttock, Simon. 32p. (J). pap. 8.99 (978-0-7497-4354-3(9)) Egmont Bks., Ltd. GBR. Dist: Trafalgar Square Publishing.

Busby, Allie. Winter. Child's Play Staff. 2015. (Seasons Ser.: 4). (ENG.). 12p. (J). bds. **(978-1-84643-745-8(8))** Child's Play International Ltd.

Busby, Allie, jt. illus. see Anderson, Laura Ellen.

Buscema, John, et al. Essential Thor, Vol. 5. Conway, Gerry & Wein, Len. 2011. (ENG.). 536p. (J). (gr. -1-17). pap. 19.99 (978-0-7851-5093-0(5)) Marvel Worldwide, Inc.

—Marvel Masterworks - The Avengers, Vol. 5. 2013. (ENG.). 288p. (J). (gr. -1-17). pap. 24.99 (978-0-7851-6758-7(7)) Marvel Worldwide, Inc.

—Nova Classic - Volume 1. Wolfman, Marv et al. 2013. (ENG.). 240p. (J). (gr. 4-17). pap. 29.99 (978-0-7851-6028-1(0)) Marvel Worldwide, Inc.

—Nova Classic Volume 3. Wolfman, Marv. 2014. (ENG.). 304p. (J). (gr. 4-17). pap. 34.99 (978-0-7851-8552-9(6)) Marvel Worldwide, Inc.

Buscema, John & Byrne, John. Avengers: The Legacy of Thanos. 2014. (ENG.). 256p. (J). (gr. 4-17). pap. 34.99 (978-0-7851-8891-9(6)) Marvel Worldwide, Inc.

Buscema, John & Hall, Bob. Avengers: Assault on Olympus. 2011. (ENG.). 192p. (J). (gr. 4-17). 29.99 (978-0-7851-5533-1(3)) Marvel Worldwide, Inc.

Buscema, John & Mooney, Jim. The Mighty Thor, Vol. 11. Conway, Gerry & Lee, Stan. 2012. (ENG.). 256p. (J). (gr. -1-17). 59.99 (978-0-7851-5885-1(5)) Marvel Worldwide, Inc.

Buscema, John, jt. illus. see Muth, Jon J.

Buscema, Sal, et al. Essential Captain America - Volume 7. 2013. (ENG.). 528p. (J). (gr. 4-17). pap. 19.99 (978-0-7851-8409-6(0)) Marvel Worldwide, Inc.

—Marvel Masterworks: The Defenders - Volume 2. 2011. (ENG.). 312p. (J). (gr. -1-17). 54.99 (978-0-7851-4216-4(9)) Marvel Worldwide, Inc.

—Marvel Masterworks Vol. 14: The Avengers. 2014. (ENG.). 264p. (J). (gr. 4-17). 69.99 (978-0-7851-8805-6(3)) Marvel Worldwide, Inc.

Buscema, Sal. Marvel Masterworks - Captain America, Vol. 7. 2014. (ENG.). 248p. (J). (gr. 4-17). 69.99 (978-0-7851-8799-8(5)) Marvel Worldwide, Inc.

—Marvel Universe Guardians of the Galaxy: Cosmic Team-Up. 2014. (ENG.). 96p. (J). (gr. -1-17). pap. 9.99 (978-0-7851-9031-8(7)) Marvel Worldwide, Inc.

—Thor by Walter Simonson Volume 2. Simonson, Walter. 2013. (ENG.). 240p. (J). (gr. 4-17). pap. 24.99 (978-0-7851-8461-4(9)) Marvel Worldwide, Inc.

—Thor by Walter Simonson Volume 3. Simonson, Walter. 2013. (ENG.). 264p. (J). (gr. 4-17). pap. 29.99 (978-0-7851-8462-1(7)) Marvel Worldwide, Inc.

Buscema, Sal & Frenz, Ron. Amazing Spider-Man Epic Collection: Ghosts of the Past. David, Peter et al. 2014. (ENG.). 472p. (J). (gr. 4-17). pap. 34.99 (978-0-7851-8916-9(5)) Marvel Worldwide, Inc.

Buscema, Sal, jt. illus. see Buckler, Rich.

Buscema, Stephanie. Name That Dog! Archer, Peggy. 2010. (ENG.). 32p. (J). (gr. -1-k). 16.99 (978-0-8037-3322-0(4), Dial) Penguin Publishing Group.

—Pugs in a Bug. Crimi, Carolyn. 2012. (ENG.). 32p. (J). (gr. -1-k). 16.99 (978-0-8037-3320-6(8), Dial) Penguin Publishing Group.

Bush, Robert Quacken. The Return of Pete Pack Rat. Bush, Robert Quacken, photos by. rev. deluxe ed. 2005. 64p. (J). (gr. 2-4). reprint ed. 12.95 (978-0-9712757-1-3(8)) Quackenbush, Robert Studios.

—The Return of Pete Pack Rat. Bush, Robert Quacken, photos by. Bush, Robert Quacken. Bush, Robert Quacken, ed. rev. deluxe ed. 2005. 64p. (J). (gr. 2-4). reprint ed. pap. 6.95 (978-0-9712757-2-0(6)) Quackenbush, Robert Studios.

Bush, Timothy. All in Just One Cookie. Goodman, Susan E. 2006. (ENG.). 32p. (J). (gr. -1-4). 17.99 (978-0-06-009092-0(8), Greenwillow Bks.) HarperCollins Pubs.

—Capital Mysteries #13: Trapped on the D. C. Train! Roy, Ron. 2011. (Stepping Stone Book(TM) Ser.). (ENG.). 96p. (J). (gr. 1-4). 4.99 (978-0-375-85926-7(8), Random Hse. Bks. for Young Readers) Random Hse. Children's Bks.

—Capital Mysteries #14: Turkey Trouble on the National Mall. Roy, Ronald. 2012. (Stepping Stone Book Ser.). (ENG.). 96p. (J). (gr. 1-4). 4.99 (978-0-307-93220-4(6), Random Hse. Bks. for Young Readers) Random Hse. Children's Bks.

—The Election-Day Disaster. Roy, Ron. 2008. (Capital Mysteries Ser.: No. 10). 87p. (gr. 1-4). 15.00 (978-0-7569-8802-9(0)) Perfection Learning Corp.

—The Election-Day Disaster. Roy, Ron. 2008. (Stepping Stone Book(TM) Ser.: No. 10). (ENG.). 96p. (J). (gr. 1-4). 4.99 (978-0-375-84805-6(3), Random Hse. Bks. for Young Readers) Random Hse. Children's Bks.

—Fireworks at the FBI. Roy, Ron. 2006. (Stepping Stone Book Ser.: No. 6). (ENG.). 96p. (J). (gr. 1-4). lib. bdg. 11.99 (978-0-375-97527-1(6)); per. 4.99 (978-0-375-87527-4(1)) Random Hse. Children's Bks. (Random Hse. Bks. for Young Readers).

—The Ghost at Camp David. Roy, Ron. 2010. (Stepping Stone Book(TM) Ser.: No. 12). (ENG.). 96p. (J). (gr. 1-4). pap. 4.99 (978-0-375-85925-0(X)) Random Hse., Inc.

—Mystery at the Washington Monument. Roy, Ron. 2007. (Capital Mysteries Ser.: No. 8). 87p. (gr. 1-4). 15.00 (978-0-7569-7845-7(9)) Perfection Learning Corp.

—Mystery at the Washington Monument. Roy, Ron. 2007. (Stepping Stone Book(TM) Ser.: No. 8). (ENG.). 96p. (J). (gr. 1-4). per. 4.99 (978-0-375-83970-2(4), Random Hse. Bks. for Young Readers) Random Hse. Children's Bks.

—The Secret at Jefferson's Mansion. Roy, Ron. 2009. (Stepping Stone Book(TM) Ser.: No. 11). (ENG.). 96p. (J). (gr. 1-4). 4.99 (978-0-375-84533-8(X)); lib. bdg. 11.99 (978-0-375-94803-9(1)) Random Hse. Children's Bks. (Random Hse. Bks. for Young Readers).

—The Skeleton in the Smithsonian. Roy, Ron. 2003. (Stepping Stone Book(TM) Ser.: No. 3). (ENG.). 96p. (J). (gr. 1-4). 4.99 (978-0-307-26517-3(X), Random Hse. Bks. for Young Readers) Random Hse. Children's Bks.

—Teddy Bear, Teddy Bear: A Traditional Rhyme. 2005. 32p. (J). 14.99 (978-0-06-057835-0(1)); (gr. -1 — 1). lib. bdg. 15.89 (978-0-06-057836-7(X)) HarperCollins Pubs.

—A Thief at the National Zoo. Roy, Ron. 2008. (Capital Mysteries Ser.: No. 9). 87p. (gr. k-3). 15.00 (978-0-7569-8329-1(0)) Perfection Learning Corp.

—A Thief at the National Zoo. Roy, Ron. 2007. (Stepping Stone Book Ser.: No. 9). (ENG.). 96p. (J). (gr. 1-4). per. 4.99 (978-0-375-84804-9(5)) Random Hse., Inc.

—Trouble at the Treasury. Roy, Ron. 2006. (Stepping Stone Book(TM) Ser.: No. 7). (ENG.). 96p. (J). (gr. 1-4). per. 4.99 (978-0-375-83969-6(0), Random Hse. Bks. for Young Readers) Random Hse. Children's Bks.

—Who Broke Lincoln's Thumb? Roy, Ron. 2005. (Stepping Stone Book Ser.: No. 5). (ENG.). 96p. (J). (gr. 1-4). per. 4.99 (978-0-375-82558-3(4), Random Hse. Bks. for Young Readers) Random Hse. Children's Bks.

Bush, Timothy. A Spy in the White House. Bush, Timothy, tr. Roy, Ron. 2004. (Stepping Stone Book(TM) Ser.: No. 4). (ENG.). 96p. (J). (gr. 1-4). 4.99 (978-0-375-82557-6(6), Random Hse. Bks. for Young Readers) Random Hse. Children's Bks.

Busquets, Carlos. Los Animales Cuentan 365 Historias. 2nd ed. 2004. (SPA.). 193p. (J). (gr. -1-7). 14.50 (978-970-22-0445-9(3)) Larousse, Ediciones, S. A. de C. V. MEX. Dist: Giron Bks.

Bustamante, Frank, et al. The Testimony of Jacob Hollow. Bustamante, Frank & Gray, Dan, eds. alt. ed. 2003. (YA). bds. 19.95 (978-0-9728526-0-9(3)) Third World Games, Inc.

Busuttil, Conor. The Magic Piano. O'Sullivan, Helen. 2013. 34p. pap. (978-1-908773-36-4(7)) Iponymous Publishing, Ltd.

Butcher, Ben. Toy Story 2, Vol. 2. Nicholas, Christopher. 2006. (Little Golden Book Ser.). (ENG.). 24p. (J). (gr. -1-2). 3.99 (978-0-7364-2394-6(X), Golden/Disney) Random Hse. Children's Bks.

Butcher, Sally K., jt. illus. see Arjas, Pirkko.

Butcher, Sam. The Gospel According to the Apostles, 1 vol. MacArthur, John. 2005. (ENG.). 288p. pap. 15.99 (978-0-7852-7180-2(5)) Nelson, Thomas Inc.

—Precious Moments: Angel Kisses & Snuggle Time Prayers with Dolly. 2003. 8.40 (978-0-7180-0575-7(9)) Nelson, Thomas Inc.

—Precious Moments: Angel Kisses & Snuggle Time Prayers with Teddy Bear. 2003. 8.40 (978-0-7180-0567-2(8)) Nelson, Thomas Inc.

—Precious Moments: Small Hands Bible with Lavender Bible Cover. 2003. 12.84 (978-0-7180-0570-2(8)) Nelson, Thomas Inc.

—Precious Moments: Small Hands Bible with Pink Bible Cover. 2003. 12.84 (978-0-7180-0576-4(7)) Nelson, Thomas Inc.

—Precious Moments: Storybook Bible & Girl Prayer Pal Set. 2003. 14.60 (978-0-7180-0569-6(4)) Nelson, Thomas Inc.

Butefish, Jennifer & Soares, Maria Fernanda, photos by. Hello Kitty Through the Seasons! Williamson, Kate T. 2006. (ENG., 96p. (J). (gr. 3-7). 14.95 (978-0-8109-5993-4(3)) Abrams.

Butler, Bryan C. E: A Tale For Everybody. Harvey, Paul, Jr. 2013. (ENG.). 44p. (J). 25.00 (978-0-9887774-0-8(1)) Aurandt, Paul H II.

Butler, Chris. My Body. 2010. (My World Ser.).Tr. of Mi Cuerpo. (ENG.). 24p. (J). (gr. -1-1). pap. 8.15 (978-1-61533-027-0(5)); lib. bdg. 22.60 (978-1-60754-947-5(6)) Windmill Bks.

—My Body/Mi Cuerpo. Rosa-Mendoza, Gladys. 2007. (English Spanish Foundations Ser.). (ENG & SPA.). 20p. (gr. -1-2). pap. 19.95 (978-1-931398-85-5(2)) Me+Mi Publishing.

Butler, Geoff. A Gift of Music: Emile Benoit & His Fiddle, 1 vol. Walsh, Alice. 2010. (ENG.). 32p. (J). (gr. k-5). 12.95 (978-1-897174-52-4(7), Tuckamore Bks) Creative Bk. Publishing CAN. Dist: Orca Bk. Pubs. USA.

Butler, Gregory J. Roscoe Goes to the Gym. Toporoff, Debi. 2007.Tr. of Rosco Va Al Gimnasio. (ENG.). 32p. (gr. -1-3). 9.99 (978-1-59979-215-6(X), Creation Hse.) Charisma Media.

Butler, Jerry. Freedom Train North: Stories of the Underground Railroad in Wisconsin. Pferdehirt, Julia. Date not set. (J). (gr. 3-8). pap. 10.00 (978-0-9664925-0-7(1)) Living History Pr.

Butler, John. Baby Animals Lift-the-Flap. Smith, Alastair. 2005. 16p. (J). (gr. 1-18). 11.95 (978-0-7945-0966-8(5), Usborne) EDC Publishing.

—Familias de Animales Libro Con Paginas Puzzle. Milbourne, Anna. 2004. (Titles in Spanish Ser.). (SPA.). 8p. (J). 8.95 (978-0-7460-6108-4(0), Usborne) EDC Publishing.

—Flip the Flaps: Pets. Wilson, Hannah. 2012. (Flip the Flaps Ser.). (ENG.). 32p. (J). (gr. -1-1). 6.99 (978-0-7534-6850-0(6), Kingfisher) Roaring Brook Pr.

—Flip the Flaps: Weather. Goldsmith, Mike. 2014. (Flip the Flaps Ser.). (ENG.). 32p. (J). (gr. -1-1). pap. 6.99 (978-0-7534-7132-6(9), Kingfisher) Roaring Brook Pr.

—Good Night, Little Bunny: A Changing-Picture Book. Hawkins, Emily. 2011. (ENG.). 14p. (J). (gr. -1-2). 12.99 (978-0-7636-5263-0(6)) Candlewick Pr.

—I Love You, Every Little Bit. Wang, Margaret. 2006. (ENG.). 10p. (gr. -1-k). bds. 9.95 (978-1-58117-482-3(9), Intervisual/Piggy Toes) Bendon, Inc.

—If Your Dreams Take off & Fly. 2013. (J). (978-1-4351-4769-0(3)) Barnes & Noble, Inc.

—Just One More? Alberts, Nancy Markham. 2007. (ENG.). 24p. (J). (gr. -1-7). 14.95 (978-1-59354-195-8(3), Handprint Bks.) Chronicle Bks. LLC.

—Little Bunny. Thompson, Lauren. 2013. (ENG.). 30p. (J). (gr. -1-k). bds. 5.99 (978-1-4424-5851-2(8), Little Simon) Little Simon.

—Little Chick. Thompson, Lauren. 2014. (ENG.). 30p. (J). (gr. -1-k). bds. 5.99 (978-1-4424-9311-7(9), Little Simon) Little Simon.

—Little Chick. Thompson, Lauren. 2014. (J). (978-1-4351-5351-6(0), Simon & Schuster Bks. For Young Readers) Simon & Schuster Bks. For Young Readers.

—Little Chick/Little Bunny Vertical 2-Pack. Thompson, Lauren. ed. 2014. (ENG.). 60p. (J). (gr. -1-k). bds. 11.98 (978-1-4814-1876-8(9), Little Simon) Little Simon.

—Little Lamb. Thompson, Lauren. 2014. (J). (978-1-4351-5352-3(9), Simon & Schuster Bks. For Young Readers) Simon & Schuster Bks. For Young Readers.

—A Mama for Owen. Bauer, Marion Dane. 2007. (ENG.). 32p. (J). (gr. -1-3). 17.99 (978-0-689-85787-4(X), Simon & Schuster Bks. For Young Readers) Simon & Schuster Bks. For Young Readers.

—Nighttime Lift-the-flap. Smith, Alastair. 2005. 16p. (J). (gr. 1-18). 11.95 (978-0-7945-0967-5(3), Usborne) EDC Publishing.

—Sharks. Parker, Steve. 2010. (I Love Animals Ser.). (ENG.). 24p. (J). (gr. 1-5). 22.60 (978-1-61533-249-6(9)); pap. 8.15 (978-1-61533-254-0(5)) Windmill Bks.

—Wee Little Bunny. Thompson, Lauren. 2010. (Wee Little Ser.). (ENG.). 32p. (J). (gr. -1-1). 14.99 (978-1-4169-7937-1(9), Simon & Schuster Bks. For Young Readers) Simon & Schuster Bks. For Young Readers.

—Wee Little Chick. Thompson, Lauren. 2008. (Wee Little Ser.). (ENG.). 32p. (J). (gr. -1-1). 15.99 (978-1-4169-3468-4(5), Simon & Schuster Bks. For Young Readers) Simon & Schuster Bks. For Young Readers.

—Wee Little Lamb. Thompson, Lauren. 2009. (Wee Little Ser.). (ENG.). 32p. (J). (gr. -1-1). 14.99 (978-1-4169-3469-1(3), Simon & Schuster Bks. For Young Readers) Simon & Schuster Bks. For Young Readers.

—When Anju Loved Being an Elephant. Henrichs, Wendy. 2011. (ENG.). 32p. (J). (gr. k-5). lib. bdg. 16.95 (978-1-58536-533-3(5)) Sleeping Bear Pr.

—Where Is Baby?, 1 vol. Galbraith, Kathryn O. 2013. (ENG.). 32p. (J). (gr. -1-1). 16.95 (978-1-56145-707-6(8)) Peachtree Pubs.

—Whose Baby Am I? 2004. (ENG.). 12p. (J). (gr. -1 — 1). bds. 4.99 (978-0-670-03696-7(X), Viking Juvenile) Penguin Publishing Group.

—10 Things You Should Know about Sharks. Parker, Steve. Gallagher, Belinda & Borton, Paula, eds. 2004. (10 Things You Should Know Ser.). (J). 6.99 (978-1-84236-118-4(X)) Miles Kelly Publishing, Ltd. GBR. Dist: Independent Pubs. Group.

Butler, John. Bedtime in the Jungle. Butler, John. 2009. 32p. (J). (gr. -1-1). 16.95 (978-1-56145-486-0(9)) Peachtree Pubs.

—Can You Cuddle Like a Koala? Butler, John. (J). (gr. k-1). 2005. (ENG.). 20p. bds. 6.95 (978-1-56145-347-4(1)); 2003. 32p. 15.95 (978-1-56145-298-9(X)) Peachtree Pubs.

—Can You Growl Like a Bear? Butler, John. (J). 2012. 20p. bds. 6.95 (978-1-56145-667-3(5)); 2007. (ENG.). 32p. 15.95 (978-1-56145-396-2(X), Peachtree Junior) Peachtree Pubs.

—Hush, Little Ones. Butler, John. 2003. 24p. (J). (gr. k-k). bds. 6.95 (978-1-56145-297-2(1)) Peachtree Pubs.

—If You See a Kitten, 1 vol. Butler, John. 24p. (J). 2015. (ENG.). (gr. 1-2). pap. 7.95 (978-1-56145-838-7(4)); 2003. (gr. k-1). 13.95 (978-1-56145-108-1(8)) Peachtree Pubs.

—Ten in the Den. Butler, John. 2005. (ENG.). 32p. (J). (gr. k-1). 15.95 (978-1-56145-344-3(7)) Peachtree Pubs.

—Ten in the Meadow. Butler, John. 2006. (ENG.). 32p. (J). (gr. k-1). 15.95 (978-1-56145-372-6(2)) Peachtree Pubs.

Butler, Julie Dupre & Buckner, Julie Dupre. Clovis Crawfish & the Twin Sister, 1 vol. Fontenot, Mary Alice & Fontenot Landry, Julie. 2007. (Clovis Crawfish Ser.). (ENG.). 32p. (J). (gr. k-3). 16.99 (978-1-58980-467-8(8)) Pelican Publishing Co., Inc.

Butler, Lindsay L. American History for Young Minds - Volume 1, Looking Towards the Sky, Book 1, the First Airplane. Cudeyro, Erica M. 2008. 20p. pap. 11.95 (978-1-934925-34-8(9), Eloquent Bks.) Strategic Book Publishing & Rights Agency (SBPRA).

Butler, Lisa. Adventures That Lead to Home. Hele, Bonita Jewel. 2012. (ENG.). 32p. (J). (gr. -1-3). 12.99 (978-0-615-50182-6(6)) Hartlyn Kids Media, LLC.

—The Bamboo Dance. Sia, Cress. 2011. (ENG.). 32p. (J). (gr. -1-3). 12.99 (978-0-615-48984-1(2)) Hartlyn Kids Media, LLC.

Butler, Nicola. Art Treasury. Dickins, Rosie. 2007. (Art Treasury Ser.). 94p. (J). 19.99 (978-0-7945-1452-5(9), Usborne) EDC Publishing.

B

Butler, Ralph M. When Mommy Had a Mastectomy. Greenfield, Nancy Reuben. 2005. 40p. (gr. -1-3). 14.95 *(978-0-910155-60-1(7))* Bartleby Pr.

Butler, Reginald. Connor & Clara Build a Concrete Poem. Atwood, Megan. 2011. (Poetry Builders Ser.). 32p. (J). (gr. 2-4). lib. bdg. 25.27 *(978-1-59953-434-3(7))* Norwood Hse. Pr.

—Inclined Planes. Marsico, Katie. 2012. (Simple Machines Ser.). (ENG.). 24p. (J). (gr. -1-2). 27.07 *(978-1-61473-273-0(6)*, 204978) Child's World, Inc., The.

—Levers. Marsico, Katie. 2012. (Simple Machines Ser.). (ENG.). 24p. (J). (gr. -1-2). 27.07 *(978-1-61473-274-7(4)*, 204979) Child's World, Inc., The.

—Pulleys. Marsico, Katie. 2012. (Simple Machines Ser.). (ENG.). 24p. (J). (gr. -1-2). 27.07 *(978-1-61473-275-4(2)*, 204980) Child's World, Inc., The.

—Screws. Sirota, Lyn. 2012. (Simple Machines Ser.). (ENG.). 24p. (J). (gr. -1-2). 27.07 *(978-1-61473-276-1(0)*, 204981) Child's World, Inc., The.

—Wedges. Marsico, Katie. 2012. (Simple Machines Ser.). (ENG.). 24p. (J). (gr. -1-2). 27.07 *(978-1-61473-277-8(9)*, 204982) Child's World, Inc., The.

—Wheels. Owings, Lisa. 2012. (Simple Machines Ser.). (ENG.). 24p. (J). (gr. -1-2). 27.07 *(978-1-61473-278-5(7)*, 204983) Child's World, Inc., The.

Butler, Rosemary. My Merry Menagerie: Lighthearted Verses & Drawings. Butler, Rosemary. 2013. 144p. 19.99 *(978-1-883378-22-6(2))* Sun on Earth Bks.

Butler, Sharon. Atop the Tree Top: A Christmas Story. Taylor, C. Brian. 2003. (J). 15.95 *(978-0-9747054-0-8(3))* Rilly Silly Bk. Co., The.

Butler, Tad. Alexander Graham Bell. McPherson, Stephanie Sammartino. 2007. (History Maker Biographies Ser.). (ENG.). 48p. (gr. 3-6). lib. bdg. 27.93 *(978-0-8225-7606-8(6)*, Lerner Pubns.) Lerner Publishing Group.

—Don't Sweat It: Ask Art & Pat. Humphrey, Art & Humphrey, Pat. pap. 11.95 *(978-0-9712305-0-7(1))* Heart Path Publishing.

—Florence Nightingale. Aller, Susan Bivin. 2007. (History Maker Biographies Ser.). (ENG.). 48p. (gr. 3-6). lib. bdg. 27.93 *(978-0-8225-7609-9(0)*, Lerner Pubns.) Lerner Publishing Group.

—Jane Goodall. Waxman, Laura Hamilton. 2007. (History Maker Biographies Ser.). (ENG.). 48p. (gr. 3-6). lib. bdg. 27.93 *(978-0-8225-7610-5(4)*, Lerner Pubns.) Lerner Publishing Group.

Butschler, Margaret, photos by. Sea Stars: Saltwater Poems. Harley, Avis. 2006. (ENG., 32p. (J). (gr. 2-7). 16.95 *(978-1-59078-429-7(4))* Boyds Mills Pr.

Butterfield, Cathy. Meerkats Don't Fly. Miller, Mark. 2007. (J). *(978-0-9794393-0-8(2))* Good Turn Publishing.

Butterfield, Ned. The Adventures of Tom Sawyer: With a Discussion of Imagination. Twain, Mark. 2003. (Values in Action Illustrated Classics Ser.). 190p. (J). *(978-1-59203-027-9(0))* Learning Challenge, Inc.

—Dad Still Smiles. Brochu, Lisa. 2003. (Books for Young Learners). (ENG.). 12p. (J). pap. 5.75 net. *(978-1-57274-601-5(7)*, 2731, Bks. for Young Learners) Owen, Richard C. Pubs., Inc.

—The Day the Circus Came to Town. Carlson, Melody. 2004. 31p. (gr. -1-3). 14.99 *(978-1-58134-158-4(X))* Crossway.

—Swiss Family Robinson: With a Discussion of Teamwork. Wyss, Johann David. 2003. (Values in Action Illustrated Classics Ser.). 191p. (J). *(978-1-59203-036-1(X))* Learning Challenge, Inc.

Butterfield, Ned. The Adventures of Sherlock Holmes: With a Discussion of Curiosity. Butterfield, Ned, tr. Doyle, Arthur. 2003. (Values in Action Illustrated Classics Ser.). (J). *(978-1-59203-045-3(9))* Learning Challenge, Inc.

—The Hunchback of Notre Dame: With a Discussion of Compassion. Butterfield, Ned, tr. Hugo, Victor. 2003. (Values in Action Illustrated Classics Ser.). (J). *(978-1-59203-049-1(1))* Learning Challenge, Inc.

Butterworth & Heath, jt. illus. see Felter.

Butterworth and Heath, jt. illus. see Felter and Gunston.

Butterworth, Nick. After the Storm. Butterworth, Nick. ed. 2003. (Percy the Park Keeper Ser.). (ENG.). 32p. (J). (gr. k-2). pap. 11.00 *(978-0-00-715515-6(8)*, HarperCollins Children's Bks.) HarperCollins Pubs. Ltd. GBR. Dist: Independent Pubs. Group.

—One Snowy Night. Butterworth, Nick. (Tales from Percy's Park Ser.). (ENG.). 32p. (J). (gr. k-2). 2008. 12.95 *(978-0-00-726024-9(5))*; 2007. 24.00 *(978-0-00-725942-7(5))*; 2011. pap. 11.00 *(978-0-00-714693-2(0)*, HarperCollins Children's Bks.) HarperCollins Pubs. Ltd. GBR. Dist: HarperCollins Pubs., Independent Pubs. Group, Independent Pubs. Group, HarperCollins Pubs.

—Percy's Bumpy Ride. Butterworth, Nick. ed. 2011. (Tales from Percy's Park Ser.). (ENG.). 32p. (J). pap. 11.00 *(978-0-00-715514-9(X)*, HarperCollins Children's Bks.) HarperCollins Pubs. Ltd. GBR. Dist: HarperCollins Pubs.

—Q Pootle 5. Butterworth, Nick. ed. 2009. (ENG.). 32p. (J). (gr. -1-k). pap. 11.95 *(978-0-00-717235-1(4)*, HarperCollins Children's Bks.) HarperCollins Pubs. Ltd. GBR. Dist: HarperCollins Pubs.

—The Rescue Party. Butterworth, Nick. ed. 2011. (Tales from Percy's Park Ser.). (ENG.). 32p. (J). (gr. k-2). pap. 11.00 *(978-0-00-715516-3(6)*, HarperSport) HarperCollins Pubs. Ltd. GBR. Dist: HarperCollins Pubs.

—The Secret Path. Butterworth, Nick. ed. 2011. (Tales from Percy's Park Ser.). (ENG.). 32p. (J). pap. 11.95 *(978-0-00-715518-7(2)*, HarperCollins Children's Bks.) HarperCollins Pubs. Ltd. GBR. Dist: HarperCollins Pubs.

—Thud! Butterworth, Nick. 2008. (ENG.). 48p. (J). (gr. -1-k). pap. 9.95 *(978-0-00-664646-4(8)*, HarperCollins Children's Bks.) HarperCollins Pubs. Ltd. GBR. Dist: HarperCollins Pubs.

—Tiger. Butterworth, Nick. 2006. (ENG.). 32p. (J). (gr. k — 1). pap. 7.95 *(978-0-00-711975-2(5)*, HarperCollins Children's Bks.) HarperCollins Pubs. Ltd. GBR. Dist: HarperCollins Pubs.

—The Treasure Hunt. Butterworth, Nick. ed. 2011. (Tales from Percy's Park Ser.). (ENG.). 32p. (J). (gr. k-2). pap. 11.00 *(978-0-00-715517-0(4)*, HarperCollins Children's Bks.) HarperCollins Pubs. Ltd. GBR. Dist: HarperCollins Pubs.

—The Whisperer. Butterworth, Nick. 2005. (ENG.). 32p. (J). (gr. k-3). pap. 15.95 *(978-0-00-712018-5(4)*, HarperCollins Children's Bks.) HarperCollins Pubs. Ltd. GBR. Dist: HarperCollins Pubs.

Buttler, Elizabeth. Me & Rolly Maloo. Wong, Janet S. 2014. (ENG.). 128p. (J). (gr. 2-5). pap. 7.95 *(978-1-58089-159-2(4))* Charlesbridge Publishing, Inc.

Buttner, Thom. Smoking Stinks!! Gosselin, Kim. 2nd ed. 2009. (Substance Free Kids Ser.). 30p. (J). (gr. -1-3). pap. 16.95 *(978-1-891383-20-5(5))* JayJo Bks., LLC.

Button, Joshua. Joshua & the Two Crabs. Button, Joshua. 2010. (ENG.). 24p. (J). (gr. k-2). pap. 12.95 *(978-1-921248-48-1(3))* Magabala Bks. AUS. Dist: Independent Pubs. Group.

Butzer, C. M. Guts & Glory: World War II. Thompson, Ben. 2016. (J). ***(978-0-316-32199-0(0))*** Little Brown & Co.

Butzer, C. M. Guts & Glory: the American Civil War. Thompson, Ben. 2014. (Guts & Glory Ser.: 1). (ENG.). 352p. (J). (gr. 3-7). 17.00 *(978-0-316-32050-4(1))* Little, Brown Bks. for Young Readers.

Butzer, C. M. The Gettysburg. Butzer, C. M. (ENG.). 80p. 2009. (YA). (gr. 4-9). pap. 9.99 *(978-0-06-156175-7(4))*; 2008. (J). (gr. 5-9). 16.99 *(978-0-06-156176-4(2))* HarperCollins Pubs.

Byars, Bob M. Ernie Tales. Woody, John. 2012. pap. 13.95 *(978-0-9848019-9-2(5))* Inkwell Productions, LLC.

Byer, Janice. The Most Unusual Pet Ever, Henry Our Great Blue Heron & His Adventures 2nd Edition. Perry, Sondra. 2014. 18.95 *(978-1-62652-432-3(7)*, Jabberwocky Bks., Inc.) Hillcrest Publishing Group, Inc.

Byer, Stacey. Fun, Fun, One Crab on the Run. Picayo, Mario. 2012. (J). *(978-1-934370-27-8(4))* Editorial Campana.

Byerly, Robbie. Ants. Byerly, Robbie. Washington, Joi. 2010. (1-3Y Bugs, Bugs, & More Bugs Ser.). (ENG.). 16p. (J). (gr. k-2). pap. 6.50 *(978-1-61541-359-1(6))* American Reading Co.

Byers, Bradley. Don't Let the Bedbugs Bite, 1 vol. Long, Samantha Gail. 2010. 24p. 24.95 *(978-1-4512-8681-6(3))* PublishAmerica, Inc.

Byers, Brian. Noah's Babies Colors & Caring. Mead, David. 2005. 22p. (J). bds. 6.95 *(978-0-9746440-7-3(2))* Virtue Bks.

—Noah's Babies Opposites & Offerings. 2005. 22p. (J). bds. 6.95 *(978-0-9746440-6-6(4))* Virtue Bks.

—Noah's Babies Shapes & Sharing. Mead, David. 2005. 22p. (J). bds. 6.95 *(978-0-9746440-5-9(6))* Virtue Bks.

Byers, Leon. Will's Bow Hunting Adventure. Busteed, Kerri J. 2012. 108p. pap. 30.00 *(978-1-61897-207-1(3)*, Strategic Bk. Publishing) Strategic Book Publishing & Rights Agency (SBPRA).

—Will's First Hunt. Busteed, Kerri J. 2010. 80p. pap. 21.50 *(978-1-60911-483-1(3)*, Eloquent Bks.) Strategic Book Publishing & Rights Agency (SBPRA).

Byers, Michael. Barbara Park, 1 vol. Kolpin, Molly. 2013. (Your Favorite Authors Ser.). (ENG.). 24p. (gr. 1-2). 24.65 *(978-1-4765-0223-6(4))*; pap. 6.95 *(978-1-4765-3438-1(1))* Capstone Pr., Inc. (First Facts).

—Dav Pilkey, 1 vol. Hicks, Kelli L. 2013. (Your Favorite Authors Ser.). (ENG.). 24p. (gr. 1-2). 24.65 *(978-1-4765-0221-2(8))*; pap. 6.95 *(978-1-4765-3436-7(5))* Capstone Pr., Inc. (First Facts).

—Encountering Bigfoot: Eyewitness Accounts, 1 vol. Krohn, Katherine. 2014. (Eyewitness to the Unexplained Ser.). (ENG.). 32p. (gr. 3-4). 29.99 *(978-1-4914-0243-6(1)*, Graphic Library) Capstone Pr., Inc.

—Grace Lin, 1 vol. Colich, Abby. 2013. (Your Favorite Authors Ser.). (ENG.). 24p. (gr. 1-2). 24.65 *(978-1-4765-3158-8(7))*; pap. 6.95 *(978-1-4765-3445-9(4))* Capstone Pr., Inc. (First Facts).

—Jeff Kinney, 1 vol. Hicks, Kelli L. 2013. (Your Favorite Authors Ser.). (ENG.). 24p. (gr. 1-2). 24.65 *(978-1-4765-0222-9(6))*; pap. 6.95 *(978-1-4765-3437-4(3))* Capstone Pr., Inc. (First Facts).

—King of Pop: The Story of Michael Jackson, 1 vol. Collins, Terry. 2012. (American Graphic Ser.). (ENG.). 32p. (gr. 3-4). pap. 8.10 *(978-1-4296-7994-7(8))*; 29.99 *(978-1-4296-6015-0(5))*; pap. 47.70 *(978-1-4296-8476-7(3))* Capstone Pr., Inc. (Graphic Library).

—Mo Willems, 1 vol. Colich, Abby. 2013. (Your Favorite Authors Ser.). (ENG.). 24p. (gr. 1-2). 24.65 *(978-1-4765-3157-1(9))*; pap. 6.95 *(978-1-4765-3444-2(6))* Capstone Pr., Inc. (First Facts).

—Shel Silverstein, 1 vol. Kolpin, Molly. 2013. (Your Favorite Authors Ser.). (ENG.). 24p. (gr. 1-2). 24.65 *(978-1-4765-0224-3(2))*; pap. 6.95 *(978-1-4765-3439-8(X))* Capstone Pr., Inc. (First Facts).

—Your Favorite Authors. Kolpin, Molly et al. 2013. (Your Favorite Authors Ser.). (ENG.). 24p. (gr. 1-2). pap. 41.70 *(978-1-4765-3648-4(1))*; lib. bdg. 147.90 *(978-1-4765-0372-1(9))* Capstone Pr., Inc. (First Facts).

Byers, Michael, jt. illus. see Kinsella, Pat.

Byj, Charlot & Richardson, Doris. Six Little Steppers Paper Dolls. Byj, Charlot. Taliadoros, Jenny, ed. 2008. 8p. pap. 12.00 *(978-0-9795053-7-9(2))* Paper Studio Pr.

Bynum, Janie. I've Got an Elephant, 1 vol. Ginkel, Anne. (ENG.). 32p. (J). 2013. (gr. -1-3). 7.95 *(978-1-56145-685-7(3))*; 2006. (gr. k-3). 16.95 *(978-1-56145-373-3(0))* Peachtree Pubs.

—One Little Flower Girl. Dussling, Jennifer. 2009. (ENG.). 32p. (J). (gr. -1-k). 12.99 *(978-0-545-09024-7(5))* Scholastic, Inc.

Bynum, Janie. The Twelve Days of Christmas in Texas. Bynum, Janie. 2009. (Twelve Days of Christmas in America Ser.). (ENG.). 32p. (J). (gr. k). 12.95 *(978-1-4027-6350-2(6))* Sterling Publishing Co., Inc.

Bynum-Nwulu, Jane. Bubbe & Gram: My Two Grandmothers. Hawxhurst, Joan C. 2003. 32p. (J). (gr. -1-2). 12.95 *(978-0-9651284-2-1(3))* Dovetail Publishing.

Bynum, Saran. Ava Lillian's Blessing. Neal, Allyson. 2012. 24p. (J). pap. 10.00 *(978-0-9714320-6-2(6))* A & L Communications, Inc.

Byous, Shawn. Sneezy Neezy. Handloser, Rick. 2006. 48p. pap. 19.97 *(978-1-59800-291-1(0))* Outskirts Pr., Inc.

Byrd, Jeff. A Tale of Two Tails, el Perro con Dos Colas: A children's story in English & Spanish. 2004.Tr. of Perro con Dos Colas. (SPA.). (J). (gr. -1-3). per. 14.95 *(978-0-9746024-0-0(X))* One Arm Publishing.

Byrd, Robert. Africa Is My Home: A Child of the Amistad. Edinger, Monica. (ENG.). 64p. (J). (gr. 5). 2015. pap. 7.99 *(978-0-7636-7647-6(0))*; 2013. 17.99 *(978-0-7636-5038-4(2))* Candlewick Pr.

—Barbarians! Kroll, Steven. 2009. (ENG.). 48p. (J). (gr. 3-7). 18.99 *(978-0-525-47958-1(9)*, Dutton Juvenile) Penguin Publishing Group.

—Good Masters! Sweet Ladies! Voices from a Medieval Village. Schlitz, Laura Amy. (ENG.). 96p. (J). (gr. 5). 2011. pap. 6.99 *(978-0-7636-5094-0(3))*; 2008. pap. 10.99 *(978-0-7636-4332-4(7))*; 2007. 19.99 *(978-0-7636-1578-9(1))* Candlewick Pr.

—The Hero Schliemann: The Dreamer Who Dug for Troy. Schlitz, Laura Amy. 2013. (ENG.). 80p. (J). (gr. 4-7). pap. 7.99 *(978-0-7636-6504-3(5))* Candlewick Pr.

—The Hero Schliemann: The Dreamer Who Dug up Troy. Schlitz, Laura Amy. 2006. (ENG.). 80p. (J). (gr. 4-7). lib. bdg. 17.99 *(978-0-7636-2283-1(4))* Candlewick Pr.

—Kubla Khan: The Emperor of Everything. Krull, Kathleen. 2010. (ENG.). 48p. (J). (gr. 3-7). 17.99 *(978-0-670-01114-8(2)*, Viking Juvenile) Penguin Publishing Group.

Byrd, Robert. Brave Chicken Little. Byrd, Robert. 2014. (ENG.). 40p. (J). (gr. -1-3). 17.99 *(978-0-670-78616-9(0)*, Viking Juvenile) Penguin Publishing Group.

—Leonardo, Hermoso Sonador. Byrd, Robert. Mendo, Miguel A., tr. 2005. (SPA.). 48p. (J). 19.99 *(978-84-8488-215-2(2))* Serres, Ediciones, S. L. ESP. Dist: Lectorum Pubns., Inc.

—Leonardo, the Beautiful Dreamer. Byrd, Robert. 2003. (ENG.). 40p. (J). (gr. 2-5). 17.99 *(978-0-525-47033-5(6)*, Dutton Juvenile) Penguin Publishing Group.

Byrd, S. Multicultural Collection. Soto, G. et al. 2003. pap. 91.95 incl. audio *(978-0-87499-673-9(2))* Live Oak Media.

Byrd, Samuel. A Picture Book of Frederick Douglass. Adler, David A. unabr. ed. 2005. (Picture Book Readalongs Ser.). (J). (gr. k-4). 25.95 incl. audio *(978-1-59519-373-5(1))*; pap. 28.95 incl. audio compact disk *(978-1-59519-377-3(4))*;Set. pap. 37.95 incl. audio *(978-1-59519-374-2(X))*;Set. pap. 39.95 incl. audio compact disk *(978-1-59519-378-0(2))* Live Oak Media.

—A Picture Book of Harriet Tubman. Adler, David A. unabr. ed. 2005. (Picture Book Readalong Ser.). (J). (gr. k-4). 25.95 incl. audio *(978-1-59519-381-0(2))*; 28.95 incl. audio compact disk *(978-1-59519-385-8(5))*;Set. pap. 37.95 incl. audio *(978-1-59519-382-7(0))*;Set. pap. 39.95 incl. audio compact disk *(978-1-59519-386-5(3))* Live Oak Media.

Byrne, Beth. Babies Are Noisy: A Book for Big Brothers & Sisters Including Those on the Autism Spectrum. Harrison, Anne-Marie. 2013. (ENG.). 40p. *(978-1-84905-459-1(2))* Kingsley, Jessica Ltd.

Byrne, Bob. The Supermarket Ghost. Snell, Gordon & Askin, Corrina. 2007. (ENG.). 80p. (J). pap. 10.95 *(978-1-84717-049-1(8))* O'Brien Pr., Ltd., The IRL. Dist: Dufour Editions, Inc.

Byrne, Emma. The Most Beautiful Letter in the World. O'Neill, Karl. 2007. (ENG.). 64p. (J). pap. 15.95 *(978-1-84717-011-8(0))* O'Brien Pr., Ltd., The IRL. Dist: Dufour Editions, Inc.

Byrne, Graham. Big Red Kangaroo. Saxby, Claire. 2015. (ENG.). 32p. (J). (gr. k-3). 16.99 *(978-0-7636-7075-7(8))* Candlewick Pr.

—Big Red Kangaroo. Saxby, Claire. 2013. 32p. *(978-1-921720-42-0(5))* Walker Bks. Australia Pty, Ltd.

—Emu. Saxby, Claire. 2015. (ENG.). 32p. (J). (gr. k-3). 16.99 *(978-0-7636-7479-3(6))* Candlewick Pr.

Byrne, John, et al. The Amazing Spider-Man. 2011. (ENG.). 392p. (J). (gr. 4-17). pap. 39.99 *(978-0-7851-5759-5(X))* Marvel Worldwide, Inc.

—Avengers: Heart of Stone. Mantlo, Bill. 2013. (ENG.). 216p. (J). (gr. 4-17). pap. 24.99 *(978-0-7851-8431-7(7))* Marvel Worldwide, Inc.

—Fantastic Four, Vol. 1. Claremont, Chris & Wolfman, Marv. 2011. (ENG.). 1080p. (J). (gr. 4-17). 125.00 *(978-0-7851-5824-0(3))* Marvel Worldwide, Inc.

Byrne, John. Spider-Man: Marvel Team-Up. 2011. (ENG.). 240p. (J). (gr. 4-17). pap. 29.99 *(978-0-7851-5866-0(9))* Marvel Worldwide, Inc.

—X-Factor, Vol. 1. Stern, Roger et al. 2005. (ENG.). 568p. (J). (gr. 4-17). pap. 19.99 *(978-0-7851-1886-2(1))* Marvel Worldwide, Inc.

Byrne, John, et al. X-Men - Phoenix Rising. Stern, Roger & Layton, Bob. 2011. (ENG.). 144p. (J). (gr. 4-17). pap. 14.99 *(978-0-7851-5786-1(7))* Marvel Worldwide, Inc.

Byrne, John & Cockrum, Dave. Essential X-Men, Vol. 2. 2005. (ENG.). 584p. (J). (gr. 4-17). pap. 19.99 *(978-0-7851-2007-0(6))* Marvel Worldwide, Inc.

Byrne, John, jt. illus. see Buscema, John.

Byrne, John, jt. illus. see Cockrum, Dave.

Byrne, John, jt. illus. see Heck, Don.

Byrne, John, jt. illus. see Smith, Paul.

Byrne, John Patrick. Donald & Benoit. Byrne, John Patrick. 2011. (ENG.). 64p. (J). (gr. 2-5). 17.95 *(978-0-7893-2084-1(3))* Universe Publishing.

Byrne, Mary Gregg. Too Many Murkles. Schmidt, Heidi. 2004. 32p. 15.95 *(978-0-9701907-7-2(8))* Illumination Arts Publishing Co., Inc.

Byrne, Mike. Animals at Home. Coult, Lucy Alice. 2014. (Magic Moving Pictures Bks.). (ENG.). 10p. (J). (gr. -1-1). 7.99 *(978-0-7641-6650-1(6))* Barron's Educational Series, Inc.

—Animals on the Farm. Graham, Oakley. 2014. (Magic Moving Pictures Bks.). (ENG.). 10p. (J). (gr. -1-1). 7.99 *(978-0-7641-6651-8(4))* Barron's Educational Series, Inc.

—At Bat. Mckenzie, Precioius. 2013. (ENG.). 24p. (gr. -1-1). 25.64 *(978-1-62169-255-3(8))*; pap. 7.95 *(978-1-62169-213-3(2))* Rourke Educational Media.

—The Best Trick: A Pet Club Story, 1 vol. Hooks, Gwendolyn. 2010. (Pet Club Ser.). (ENG.). 32p. (gr. 1-2). 21.32 *(978-1-4342-2052-3(4))*; pap. 6.25 *(978-1-4342-2794-2(4))* Stone Arch Bks.

—Brody Borrows Money. Bullard, Lisa. 2013. (Cloverleaf Books — Money Basics Ser.). (ENG.). 24p. (gr. k-2). pap. 6.95 *(978-1-4677-1508-9(5))*; lib. bdg. 23.93 *(978-1-4677-0763-3(5))* Lerner Publishing Group. (Millbrook Pr.).

—The Cat Food Mystery: A Pet Club Story, 1 vol. Hooks, Gwendolyn. 2011. (Pet Club Ser.). (ENG.). 32p. (gr. 1-2). pap. 6.25 *(978-1-4342-3051-5(1))*; lib. bdg. 21.32 *(978-1-4342-2511-5(9))* Stone Arch Bks.

—The Duck Doctor. Mckenzie, Precioius. 2013. (ENG.). 24p. (gr. -1-1). 25.64 *(978-1-62169-260-7(4))*; pap. 7.95 *(978-1-62169-218-8(3))* Rourke Educational Media.

—Find the Cat! A Pet Club Story, 1 vol. Hooks, Gwendolyn. 2010. (Pet Club Ser.). (ENG.). 32p. (gr. 1-2). 21.32 *(978-1-4342-2053-0(2))*; pap. 6.25 *(978-1-4342-2795-9(2))* Stone Arch Bks.

Byrne, Mike. Giving Thanks. Hapka, Cathy. 2014. 32p. (J). pap. ***(978-0-545-75841-3(6))*** Scholastic, Inc.

Byrne, Mike. God Helps Me, 1 vol. David, Juliet. 2014. (ENG.). 10p. (J). bds. 7.99 *(978-1-78128-112-3(2)*, Candle Bks.) Lion Hudson PLC GBR. Dist: Kregel Pubns.

—God Knows Me, 1 vol. David, Juliet. 2014. (ENG.). 10p. (J). bds. 7.99 *(978-1-78128-113-0(0)*, Candle Bks.) Lion Hudson PLC GBR. Dist: Kregel Pubns.

—God Loves Me, 1 vol. David, Juliet. 2014. (ENG.). 10p. (J). bds. 7.99 *(978-1-78128-114-7(9)*, Candle Bks.) Lion Hudson PLC GBR. Dist: Kregel Pubns.

—Hey, That's Not Trash! But Which Bin Does It Go In? Jablow, Renee. 2011. (ENG.). 16p. (J). (gr. -1). bds. 6.99 *(978-1-4169-9533-3(1)*, Little Simon) Little Simon.

—Joey & the Giant Box. Lakritz, Deborah. 2015. (J). (ENG.). 32p. (gr. -1-2). lib. bdg. 17.95 *(978-1-4677-1953-7(6))*; *(978-1-4677-6205-2(9))* Lerner Publishing Group. (Kar-Ben Publishing).

—Just Josie & the Number 7. Gale, Emily. 2010. (Picture Books Ser.). 25p. (J). (gr. -1-1). *(978-1-4075-9505-4(9))* Parragon, Inc.

—Just Josie & the Perfect Day. Gale, Emily. 2010. (Picture Books Ser.). 25p. (J). (gr. -1-1). *(978-1-4075-9506-1(7))* Parragon, Inc.

—Kyle Keeps Track of Cash. Bullard, Lisa. 2013. (Cloverleaf Books — Money Basics Ser.). (ENG.). 24p. (gr. k-2). pap. 6.95 *(978-1-4677-1510-2(7))*; lib. bdg. 23.93 *(978-1-4677-0762-6(7))* Lerner Publishing Group. (Millbrook Pr.).

—The Lucky Charm: A Pet Club Story, 1 vol. Hooks, Gwendolyn. 2011. (Pet Club Ser.). (ENG.). 32p. (gr. 1-2). pap. 6.25 *(978-1-4342-3052-2(X))*; lib. bdg. 21.32 *(978-1-4342-2512-2(7))* Stone Arch Bks.

—The Noisy Night: A Pet Club Story, 1 vol. Hooks, Gwendolyn. 2010. (Pet Club Ser.). (ENG.). 32p. (gr. 1-2). 21.32 *(978-1-4342-2049-3(4))*; pap. 6.25 *(978-1-4342-2793-5(6))* Stone Arch Bks.

—Pet Club. Hooks, Gwendolyn. 2013. (Pet Club Ser.). (ENG.). 32p. (gr. -1-1). 170.56 *(978-1-4342-8841-7(2))* Stone Arch Bks.

—Pet Costume Party: A Pet Club Story, 1 vol. Hooks, Gwendolyn. 2011. (Pet Club Ser.). (ENG.). 32p. (gr. 1-2). pap. 6.25 *(978-1-4342-3053-9(8))*; lib. bdg. 21.32 *(978-1-4342-2513-9(5))* Stone Arch Bks.

—The Pet Wash: A Pet Club Story, 1 vol. Hooks, Gwendolyn. 2011. (Pet Club Ser.). (ENG.). 32p. (gr. 1-2). pap. 6.25 *(978-1-4342-3054-6(6))*; lib. bdg. 21.32 *(978-1-4342-2514-6(3))* Stone Arch Bks.

—Pets at the Party: A Pet Club Story, 1 vol. Hooks, Gwendolyn. 2010. (Pet Club Ser.). (ENG & ABK.). 32p. (gr. 1-2). 21.32 *(978-1-4342-2054-7(0))*; pap. 6.25 *(978-1-4342-2796-6(0))* Stone Arch Bks.

—Pitch the Tent. Mckenzie, Precioius. 2013. (ENG.). 24p. (gr. -1-1). 25.64 *(978-1-62169-259-1(0))*; pap. 7.95 *(978-1-62169-217-1(5))* Rourke Educational Media.

—The Purim Superhero. Kushner, Elisabeth. 2013. (Purim Ser.). (ENG.). 32p. (J). (gr. -1-3). 7.95 *(978-0-7613-9062-6(6))*; lib. bdg. 17.95 *(978-0-7613-9061-9(8))* Lerner Publishing Group. (Kar-Ben Publishing).

—Twinkle, Twinkle, Little Star; and, Spaceship, Spaceship, Zooming. 2013. (ENG.). 24p. (J). pap. *(978-0-7787-1150-6(1))* Crabtree Publishing Co.

—Twinkle, Twinkle, Little Star; and, Spaceship, Spaceship, Zooming High. 2013. (ENG.). 24p. (J). *(978-0-7787-1132-2(3))* Crabtree Publishing Co.

Byrne, Richard. What Noise Does a Rabbit Make? Weston, Carrie. 2013. (ENG.). 32p. (J). (gr. -1-3). 16.95 *(978-1-4677-2032-8(1))* Lerner Publishing Group.

Byrne, Richard. This Book Just Ate My Dog! Byrne, Richard. 2014. (ENG.). 32p. (J). (gr. -1). 16.99 *(978-1-62779-071-0(3)*, Holt, Henry & Co. Bks. For Young Readers) Holt, Henry & Co.

Byrne, Richard. We're in the Wrong Book! Byrne, Richard. 2015. (ENG.). 32p. (J). (gr. -1-3). 16.99 ***(978-1-62779-451-0(4)***, Holt, Henry & Co. Bks. For Young Readers) Holt, Henry & Co.

Byrne-Walker, Mary Ann. The Magic Is in You. Laplante, Carole. 2012. 36p. pap. 9.95 *(978-1-62006-055-1(8))* Sunbury Press, Inc.

—Night Noises. Laplante, Carole. 2012. 40p. pap. 9.95 *(978-1-62006-046-9(9))* Sunbury Press, Inc.

Byron, Kevin, photos by. Birdology: 30 Activities & Observations for Exploring the World of Birds. Russo, Monica. 2015. (Young Naturalists Ser.). (ENG., 128p. (J). (gr. 2-4). pap. 15.95 *(978-1-61374-949-4(X))* Chicago Review Pr., Inc.

BYTE ME! ebook inc nonprofit, Georgia C. De COLORES the Song: All the Colors. Pedroza, Georgina, tr. 2007. (ENG & SPA.). 16p. (J). lib. bdg. 8.99 *(978-0-9798611-9-2(5))* Byte Me! Inc.

Byte Me! P. CLOUDWOMAN in Black & White: And in some shades of Gray. Byte Me! P. Pedroza, Georgina & Garcia, Eloisa, trs. 2007.Tr. of mujer Nube. (ENG & SPA.). 56p. (J). lib. bdg. 8.15 *(978-0-9798611-7-8(9))* Byte Me! Inc.

Byun, You. Little Baby Buttercup. Ashman, Linda. 2015. (ENG.). 32p. (J). (— 1). 16.99 *(978-0-399-16763-8(3),* Nancy Paulsen Bks.) Penguin Publishing Group.

Byun, You. Dream Friends. Byun, You. 2013. (ENG.). 32p. (J). (gr. -1-k). 16.99 *(978-0-399-25739-1(X))* Penguin Publishing Group.

Bzymek, Izabela. The Thing I Say I Saw Last Night: A Christmas Story. McKernan, Wendy. 2011. 32p. (J). *(978-0-9866204-0-9(8))*; pap. *(978-0-9866204-1-6(6))* Little Dragon Publishing.

—The 13th Floor: Colouring Outside the Lines. Stranaghan, Crystal. 2012. 34p. (-18). *(978-1-926691-25-1(3))* Gumboot Bks.

C

Caban, Carlos. Cancion de Cuna de la Virgen de Guadalupe. Caban, Carlos, tr. Stuart, Kelly. 2003. (SPA.). 28p. *(978-1-931721-18-9(1))* Bright Sky Pr.

Cabanting, Ruth. Happy Honu Takes a Bath. Gillespie, Jane. 2004. 10p. (J). 8.95 *(978-1-933067-03-2(9))* Beachhouse Publishing, LLC.

—S Went Surfing: An ABC Book for Keiki. Gillespie, Jane. 2004. 32p. (J). 12.95 *(978-1-933067-00-1(4))* Beachhouse Publishing, LLC.

Cabban, Vanessa. The Best Gift of All. Emmett, Jonathan. 2008. (ENG.). 32p. (J). (gr. -1-2). 15.99 *(978-0-7636-3860-3(9))* Candlewick Pr.

—Dear Santa Claus. Durant, Alan. ed. 2007. (ENG.). 32p. (J). (gr. -1-3). 6.99 *(978-0-7636-3465-0(4))* Candlewick Pr.

—Dear Tooth Fairy. Durant, Alan. 2004. (ENG.). 32p. (J). (gr. -1-3). 15.99 *(978-0-7636-2175-9(7))* Candlewick Pr.

—Down in the Woods at Sleepytime. Schaefer, Carole Lexa. 2004. (ENG.). 24p. (J). (— 1). bds. 8.99 *(978-0-7636-2566-5(3))* Candlewick Pr.

—Gooseberry Goose. Freedman, Claire. 2005. 32p. (J). (gr. -1-2). 6.95 *(978-1-58925-392-6(2))* Tiger Tales.

—Heaven Is Having You. Andreae, Giles. (Padded Board Bks.). (J). 2007. 18p. (gr. -1-1). bds. 7.95 *(978-1-58925-820-4(7))*; 2004. 32p. reprint ed. pap. 6.95 *(978-1-58925-388-9(4))* Tiger Tales.

—Love Is a Handful of Honey. Andreae, Giles. 2004. 32p. (J). (gr. -1-k). 5.95 *(978-1-58925-353-7(1))*; tchr. ed. 15.95 *(978-1-58925-003-1(6))* Tiger Tales.

—The Nutty Nut Chase. White, Kathryn. 2005. (ENG.). 32p. (J). (gr. -1-3). pap. 16.00 *(978-1-56148-446-1(6),* Good Bks.) Skyhorse Publishing Co., Inc.

—Where There's a Bear, There's Trouble. Catchpool, Michael. 2004. 32p. (J). pap. 6.95 *(978-1-58925-389-6(2))* Tiger Tales.

Cabell, Robert W. The Mermaid Adventures of Princess Miranda: Volume One. Cabell, Robert W. 2013. 128p. pap. 7.95 *(978-0-9890974-3-7(9),* Oceanus Bks.) Warrington Pubns.

Cable, Annette. The Day I Met You & You Met Me! Morgan, Cythia. 2008. 32p. pap. 5.95 *(978-0-9802497-0-5(8))* King'S Land Pr. Inc.

—A Forest of Trees Does Not Grow There in Rows. Wolpe, Nina. 2014. 32p. (J). 16.95 *(978-0-9860794-0-5(5))* SC & FC Publications.

—No More Rules! A Boy's Discovery of What Life is Like Without Rules. Cerny, Michele. 2013. 32p. (J). *(978-0-9860405-0-4(9))* Hat Trick Publishing.

—Postcards from George, 1763-1781: George Rogers Clark Writes Home to Virginia from the Kentucky Wilderness. Stokes, Betty Southard. 2010. (J). *(978-1-935497-12-7(X))* Butler Bk. Publishing.

Cabot, David. Trapped. Richards, Douglas E. 2005. (ENG.). 180p. (J). (gr. 4-7). pap. *(978-0-9748765-4-2(2))* DNA Pr.

Cabrera, Cozbi A. Thanks a Million. Grimes, Nikki. 2006. 32p. (J). (gr. k-3). 17.99 *(978-0-688-17292-3(X))*; 17.89 *(978-0-688-17293-0(8),* Greenwillow Bks.) HarperCollins Pubs.

Cabrera, Eva. Robinson Crusoe. Defoe, Daniel. 2015. (Graphic Revolve: Common Core Editions Ser.). (ENG.). 72p. (gr. 2-3). lib. bdg. 26.65 ***(978-1-4965-0371-8(6))*** Stone Arch Bks.

Cabrera, Eva. Romeo & Juliet, 1 vol. Gonzalez, Jorge & Shakespeare, William. 2011. (Shakespeare Graphics Ser.). (ENG.). 88p. (gr. 2-3). pap. 7.15 *(978-1-4342-3448-3(7))*; lib. bdg. 26.65 *(978-1-4342-2563-4(1))* Stone Arch Bks. (Shakespeare Graphics).

Cabrera, Giovanni. Viva el Miedo. Portorrico, Silvia. 2003. (Primer Acto: Teatro Infantil y Juvenil Ser.). (SPA.). 57p. (J). (gr. -1-7). pap. *(978-958-30-0322-6(0))* Panamericana Editorial.

Cabrera, Jane. Fetch. Cabrera, Jane. 2012. (ENG.). 32p. (J). (-k). 16.99 *(978-1-4083-1387-9(1))* Hodder & Stoughton GBR. Dist: Independent Pubs. Group.

—Here We Go Round the Mulberry Bush. Cabrera, Jane. 2010. (ENG.). 32p. (J). (gr. -1-k). 16.95 *(978-0-8234-2288-3(7))* Holiday Hse., Inc.

—If You're Happy & You Know It! Cabrera, Jane. 2010. 24p. (J). (gr. -1). bds. 7.95 *(978-0-8234-2227-2(5))* Holiday Hse., Inc.

—Mommy, Carry Me Please! Cabrera, Jane. (Jane Cabrera Board Bks.). (ENG.). (J). 2008. 24p. (gr. -1-k). bds. 6.95 *(978-0-8234-2131-2(7))*; 2006. 32p. (gr. 3-6). 16.95 *(978-0-8234-1935-7(5))* Holiday Hse., Inc.

—Row, Row, Row Your Boat. Cabrera, Jane. 2014. (ENG.). 32p. (J). (gr. -1-1). 16.95 *(978-0-8234-3050-5(2))* Holiday Hse., Inc.

—Ten in the Bed. Cabrera, Jane. (ENG.). (J). (gr. -1). 2010. 24p. bds. 7.95 *(978-0-8234-2258-6(5))*; 2006. 32p. 16.95 *(978-0-8234-2027-8(2))* Holiday Hse., Inc.

Cabrera, Marcela. Bumpy & Boo Visits the Eye Doctor: Guess Who Needs Glasses? Manson, Sheri. 2006. 32p. (J). 15.95 *(978-0-9744307-3-7(0))* Merry Lane Pr.

Cabri, Alexandra. Saving Daddy. Abdullah, Patricia Noor. 2006. 32p. (J). (gr. 2-5). 17.95 *(978-1-933193-16-8(6))* EECI, Inc.

Cabrillo, Cinthya. Money Grows with Bees. Suddard, Lisa. 2009. 24p. pap. 14.95 *(978-1-4251-8673-9(4))* Trafford Publishing.

Cabrini, Joe. Chicco's Nicedream Van - Daniel's Winning Goal. Cabrini, Joe. 2007. 32p. per. *(978-0-7552-0300-0(3))* Authors OnLine, Ltd.

—Chicco's Nicedream Van - Jessica the Superstar. Cabrini, Joe. 2007. 32p. per. *(978-0-7552-0301-7(1))* Authors OnLine, Ltd.

Cabrol, Marta. Thumbelina. 2014. (Flip-Up Fairy Tales Ser.). (ENG.). 24p. (J). *(978-1-84643-655-0(9))* Child's Play International Ltd.

Cacau, Caio. The Science of Football with Max Axiom, Super Scientist. Bethea, Nikole Brooks. 2015. (Science of Sports with Max Axiom Ser.). (ENG.). 32p. (gr. 3-4). pap. 7.95 ***(978-1-4914-6089-4(X),*** Graphic Library) Capstone Pr., Inc.

—The Science of Hockey with Max Axiom, Super Scientist. Hoena, Blake. 2015. (Science of Sports with Max Axiom Ser.). (ENG.). 32p. (gr. 3-4). pap. 7.95 ***(978-1-4914-6090-0(3),*** Graphic Library) Capstone Pr., Inc.

—The Science of Sports with Max Axiom. Bethea, Nikole Brooks et al. 2015. (Science of Sports with Max Axiom Ser.). (ENG.). 32p. (gr. 3-4). pap. 31.80 ***(978-1-4914-7342-9(8),*** Graphic Library) Capstone Pr., Inc.

—The Science of Sports with Max Axiom. Dreier, David L. & Hoena, Blake. 2015. (Science of Sports with Max Axiom Ser.). (ENG.). 32p. (gr. 3-4). 119.96 ***(978-1-4914-6914-9(5),*** Graphic Library) Capstone Pr., Inc.

Caccia, Christiane. Ma tu, che Babbo Natale Sei? Wullschleger Daldini, Elena. 2004. (ITA.). 48p. (J). 19.00 *(978-88-87469-33-2(4),* gce) Gabriele Capelli Editore Sagl CHE. Dist: SPD-Small Pr. Distribution.

Caceres, Marangelie. You May Touch Here! Puedes Tocar Aqui! Casanueva, Idilian. 2007. 16p. per. 10.95 *(978-1-59858-327-4(1))* Dog Ear Publishing, LLC.

Cadwell, Warwick Johnson. The No. 1 Car Spotter. Atinuke. ed. 2011. (ENG.). 112p. (J). pap. 4.99 *(978-1-61067-051-7(5))* Kane Miller.

Cady, Harrison. Adventures of Bob White. Burgess, Thornton W. 2011. (Dover Children's Thrift Classics Ser.). (ENG.). 96p. (J). (gr. -1-2). pap. 3.00 *(978-0-486-48109-8(3))* Dover Pubns., Inc.

—The Adventures of Mr. Mocker. Burgess, Thornton W. 2011. (Dover Children's Thrift Classics Ser.). (ENG.). 96p. (J). (gr. -1-2). pap. 3.00 *(978-0-486-48101-2(8))* Dover Pubns., Inc.

—The Adventures of Old Mr. Buzzard. Burgess, Thornton W. 2013. (Dover Children's Classics Ser.). (ENG.). 96p. (J). (gr. 1-5). pap. 3.00 *(978-0-486-49726-6(7))* Dover Pubns., Inc.

—The Adventures of Sammy Jay. Burgess, Thornton W. 2006. (Dover Children's Thrift Classics Ser.). (ENG.). 96p. (J). (gr. 3-8). per. 3.00 *(978-0-486-44946-3(7))* Dover Pubns., Inc.

—Billy Mink. Burgess, Thornton W. 2012. (Dover Children's Thrift Classics Ser.). (ENG.). 128p. (J). (gr. -1-2). pap. 3.00 *(978-0-486-48107-4(7))* Dover Pubns., Inc.

—Fifty Favorite Burgess Stories. Burgess, Thornton W. 2011. 376p. 53.95 *(978-1-258-07354-1(4))* Literary Licensing, LLC.

—Frances Hodgson Burnett Children's Stories Omnibus the Secret Garden, a Little Princess, Little Lord Fauntleroy, Racketty-Packetty House. Burnett, Frances Hodgson. 2012. 786p. *(978-1-78139-253-9(6))* Benediction Classics.

—The National Review Treasury of Classic Bedtime Stories. Burgess, Thornton W. 2004. 368p. (J). 29.95 *(978-0-9627841-8-7(4))* ISI Bks.

—Stories of the Green Forest Critters: Volume 1. Burgess, Thornton W. 2011. (ENG.). 184p. pap. 12.95 *(978-1-4565-5332-6(1))* CreateSpace Independent Publishing Platform.

—Thornton Burgess Five-Minute Bedtime Tales: From Old Mother West Wind's Library. Burgess, Thornton W. 2011. (Dover Children's Classics Ser.). (ENG.). 128p. (J). (gr. 1-5). pap. 14.99 *(978-0-486-47111-2(X))* Dover Pubns., Inc.

—Tommy & the Wishing-Stone. Burgess, Thornton W. 2012. (Dover Children's Thrift Classics Ser.). (ENG.). 240p. (J). (gr. -1-2). pap. 4.00 *(978-0-486-48105-0(0))* Dover Pubns., Inc.

—Whitefoot the Wood Mouse. Burgess, Thornton W. 2006. (Dover Children's Thrift Classics Ser.). (ENG.). 112p. (J). (gr. 3-8). per. 3.00 *(978-0-486-44944-9(0))* Dover Pubns., Inc.

Cady, Harrison & Stewart, Pat Ronson. The Adventures of Unc' Billy Possum. Burgess, Thornton W. Cady, Harrison & Stewart, Pat Ronson, trs. 2003. (Dover Children's Thrift Classics Ser.). (ENG.). 96p. (J). (gr. 3-8). pap. 3.00 *(978-0-486-43031-7(6))* Dover Pubns., Inc.

Caetano, Joao. La Flor Mas Grande del Mundo. Saramago, José. 2003. (SPA.). 26p. (J). (gr. 3-5). 14.95 *(978-84-204-4354-6(9))* Santillana USA Publishing Co., Inc.

Caez, Joshua. To Find an Ivory-billed Woodpecker. l.t. ed. 2005. 21p. (YA). 9.95 net. *(978-0-9771752-0-8(0))* Harrison, Bobby.

Caffee, Julie. Sisters, Wild Dogs & Catfish Bait. Marlow, Herb. 2005. 122p. (J). lib. bdg. 24.95 *(978-1-893595-45-3(5))*; per. 16.95 *(978-1-893595-48-4(X))* Four Seasons Bks., Inc.

Cafferata, Sue. Sound-a-Likes: Homonyms & Phonics, 4 bks., Set. Fowler, Allan. (J). (gr. k-4). lib. bdg. 73.80 *(978-1-56674-901-5(8))* Forest Hse. Publishing Co., Inc.

Cafiero, Tara. Elephants of the Tsunami. Laiz, Jana. 2005. (J). 10.00 *(978-0-9771818-3-4(9))* EarthBound Bks.

Cafu. Bringers of Storm. Parker, Jeff. 2014. (Avengers Set 4 Ser.). (ENG.). 24p. (J). (gr. 9-14). lib. bdg. 24.21 *(978-1-61479-295-6(X))* Spotlight.

Cage, Josef. Damage Control, 1 vol. Sherman, M. Zachary & Iligan, Marlon. 2012. (Bloodlines Ser.). (ENG.). 88p. (gr. 4-8). pap. 6.95 *(978-1-4342-3875-7(X))*; lib. bdg. 23.32 *(978-1-4342-3765-1(6))* Stone Arch Bks.

—Heart of the Enemy, 1 vol. Sherman, M. Zachary & Iligan, Marlon. 2012. (Bloodlines Ser.). (ENG.). 88p. (gr. 4-8). pap. 6.95 *(978-1-4342-3878-8(4))*; lib. bdg. 23.32 *(978-1-4342-3767-5(2))* Stone Arch Bks.

Cagle, Eddie. Be'Be': A Very Special Friendship. Eterno-Harris, Jacqueline. 2009. 28p. pap. 14.99 *(978-1-4389-8846-7(X))* AuthorHouse.

Cagle, Terry R. Clown Closet. Sonnenberg, Matthew Martin. 2009. 64p. pap. 12.95 *(978-1-930076-42-6(8),* Agrippina Pr.) WigWam Publishing Co.

—The Kitty Book. Gordon, Emily. 2011. 32p. (J). 14.95 *(978-1-930076-12-9(6),* New Leaf Bks.) WigWam Publishing Co.

Cagol, Andrea & Studio Iboix Staff. Ariel: The Birthday Surprise. Disney Princess Staff & Disney Book Group Staff. 2010. (Disney Princess Chapter Book: Series #1 Ser.). (ENG.). 96p. (J). (gr. 1-3). pap. 4.99 *(978-1-4231-2971-4(7))* Disney Pr.

Cagol, Andrea, jt. illus. see Laguna, Fabio.

Cagol, Andrea, jt. illus. see Lee, Grace.

Cahoon, Heather. Buzz-Buzz, Busy Bees: An Animal Sounds Book. Bentley, Dawn. 2004. (ENG.). 24p. (J). (gr. -1-1). 10.95 *(978-0-689-86848-1(0),* Little Simon) Little Simon.

—Good Night, Sweet Butterflies. Bentley, Dawn. ed. 2007. (ENG.). 14p. (J). 5.99 *(978-1-4169-1296-5(7),* Little Simon) Little Simon.

—Math Fables. Tang, Greg. 2004. (ENG.). 40p. (J). (gr. -1-3). 18.99 *(978-0-439-45399-8(2))* Scholastic, Inc.

—Speedy Little Race Cars. Bentley, Dawn. 2004. 20p. 10.99 *(978-0-9755195-1-6(4))* MELJAMES, Inc.

Caillou, Marie. Adrian & the Tree of Secrets. Hubert. 2014. (ENG.). 128p. (gr. 6). pap. 18.95 *(978-1-55152-556-3(9))* Arsenal Pulp Pr. CAN. Dist: Consortium Bk. Sales & Distribution.

Cain, David. Nature's Art Box: From T-Shirts to Twig Baskets, 65 Cool Projects for Crafty Kids to Make with Natural Materials You Can Find Anywhere. Cain, David. Martin, Laura C. 2003. (ENG.). 192p. (J). (gr. 3-9). pap. 16.95 *(978-1-58017-490-9(6),* 67490) Storey Publishing, LLC.

Cain, Doreyl Ammons. Johnny, My Favorite Mouse. Nolen, Gale. 2007. 32p. (J). per. 18.95 *(978-0-9753023-7-8(X))* Ammons Communications, Ltd.

—Sterlen: And a Mosaic of Mountain Women. Garza, Amy Ammons. Ammons, David F. & Ammons, Sherilyn, eds. 2005. 308p. (YA). per. 16.00 *(978-0-9753023-2-3(9),* Catch the Spirit of Appalachia) Ammons Communications, Ltd.

—White Feather. Pafford, Nancy McIntosh. Garza, Amy Ammons, ed. l.t. ed. 2004. 220p. (YA). per. 14.95 *(978-0-9753023-0-9(2),* Catch the Spirit of Appalachia) Ammons Communications, Ltd.

Cain, Janan. The Way I Act. Metzger, Steve. 2011. (ENG.). 32p. (J). (gr. k-5). 16.95 *(978-1-884734-99-1(5))* Parenting Pr., Inc.

Cain, Janan. Asi Me Siento Yo. Cain, Janan. Parenting Press Staff. Canetti, Yanitzia, tr. from ENG. 2009.Tr. of Way I Feel. (SPA & ENG.). 32p. (J). (gr. -1-3). 16.95 *(978-1-884734-83-0(9))* Parenting Pr., Inc.

—The Way I Feel. Cain, Janan. 2005. (ENG.). 18p. (J). (— 1). bds. 7.95 *(978-1-884734-72-4(3))* Parenting Pr., Inc.

Cain, Mary. Tale of Phoebe & Leonardo. Lobdell, Chanel Mickayla. 2012. 32p. pap. *(978-0-9859892-0-0(3))* Roxby Media Ltd.

Cairns, Julia. Grandad's Tree: Poems about Families. Bennett, Jill. 2003. 32p. (J). 16.99 *(978-1-84148-541-6(1))* Barefoot Bks., Inc.

—Las Crepes de Mama Panya: Un Relato de Kenia. Chamberlain, Mary et al. 40p. pap. 8.99 *(978-1-78285-072-4(4))* Barefoot Bks., Inc.

—Mama Panya's Pancakes. Chamberlin, Mary et al. 2005. (ENG.). 40p. (J). 16.99 *(978-1-84148-139-5(4))* Barefoot Bks., Inc.

—Mama Panya's Pancakes. Chamberlin, Richard et al. 2006. (ENG.). 40p. (J). (gr. k-2). pap. 8.99 *(978-1-905236-64-0(6))* Barefoot Bks., Inc.

—Mama Panya's Pancakes: A Market Day in Kenya. Chamberlin, Richard & Chamberlin, Mary. 2005. 40p. (J). *(978-1-84148-160-9(2))* Barefoot Bks., Inc.

—Nos Fuimos Todos de Safari: Una Aventura de Números Por Tanzania. Krebs, Laurie. 2005. (SPA & ESP.). 32p. (J). (gr. -1-2). 7.99 *(978-1-905236-08-4(5))* Barefoot Bks., Inc.

—Vamos Todos de Safari: Un Recorrido Numerico por Tanzania, Africa. Krebs, Laurie. Cortes, Eunice, tr. 2003. (SPA.). (J). *(978-970-690-873-5(0))* Planeta Mexicana Editorial S. A. de C. V.

—We All Went on Safari: A Counting Journey Through Tanzania. Krebs, Laurie. 2003. (ENG & SWA.). 32p. (J). (gr. k-3). 16.99 *(978-1-84148-478-5(4))* Barefoot Bks., Inc.

—We All Went on Safari: A Counting Journey Through Tanzania. Krebs, Laurie. 2010. (J). 18.10 *(978-0-7569-9319-1(9))* Perfection Learning Corp.

—1,2, 3, Partons en Safari! Krebs, Laurie & Barefoot Books. 2014. (FRE.). 32p. (J). pap. 7.99 *(978-1-78285-141-7(0))* Barefoot Bks., Inc.

Cairns, Julia. We All Went on Safari: A Counting Journey Through Tanzania. Cairns, Julia. Krebs, Laurie. 2004. (ENG.). 32p. (J). pap. 7.99 *(978-1-84148-119-7(X))* Barefoot Bks., Inc.

Calafiore, Jim. Rex Riders. Carlson, J. P. 2011. (ENG.). 440p. (J). (gr. 7). 16.95 *(978-0-9825796-3-3(2))* Monstrosities Inc.

Calafiore, Jim & Holdredge, Jon. Legacy, 4 vols. Winick, Judd. 2003. (Exiles Ser.: Vol. 4). 144p. (YA). pap. 12.99 *(978-0-7851-1109-2(3))* Marvel Worldwide, Inc.

Calander, Sydney. Bingo: The Black & White Dog. Danker, Mervyn. l.t. ed. 2012. (ENG.). 26p. pap. 5.95 *(978-1-4611-2371-2(2))* CreateSpace Independent Publishing Platform.

Calarnou, Yves. La Ciudad a Tu Alcance. Le Duc, Michel et al. Marti, Nuria, tr. 2006. (SPA.). 79p. (J). pap. *(978-84-9754-211-1(8))* Ediciones Oniro S.A.

Caldecott, Randolph. Jackanapes, Daddy Darwin's Dovecot & Other Stories. Ewing, Juliana Horatia. 2007. (ENG.). 112p. (J). (gr. 4-7). per. *(978-1-4065-2527-4(8))* Dodo Pr.

—Randolph Caldecott: The Man Who Could Not Stop Drawing. Marcus, Leonard S. 2013. (ENG.). 64p. (J). (gr. 5-9). 24.99 *(978-0-374-31025-7(4),* Farrar, Straus & Giroux (BYR)) Farrar, Straus & Giroux.

Calderas, Gloria. Grandma's House. Hall, Kirsten. 2004. (My First Reader Ser.). (ENG.). 32p. (J). (gr. k-1). pap. 3.95 *(978-0-516-25502-6(9),* Children's Pr.) Scholastic Library Publishing.

Calderon, Gloria. Mambru se fue a la Guerra. Iribarren, Elena, ed. 2005. (SPA.). 27p. (gr. -1-2). reprint ed. pap. 14.00 *(978-0-7567-8948-0(6))* DIANE Publishing Co.

—El Zipitio, 1 vol. Argueta, Jorge. 2003. (SPA.). 32p. (J). 16.95 *(978-0-88899-539-1(3))* Groundwood Bks. CAN. Dist: Perseus-PGW.

Calderon, Lee. There Was an Odd Princess Who Swallowed a Pea, 0 vols. Ward, Jennifer. 2011. (ENG.). 32p. (J). (gr. -1-3). 16.99 *(978-0-7614-5822-7(0),* 9780761458227, Amazon Children's Publishing) Amazon Publishing.

Calderon, Marcela. Un Dia Sin Tele. White, Amy. Kratky, Lada J., tr. 2009. (Colección Fácil de Leer Ser.). (SPA.). 16p. (gr. k-2). pap. 5.99 *(978-1-60396-409-8(6))* Ediciones Alfaguara ESP. Dist: Santillana USA Publishing Co., Inc.

—Dos Perros y una Abuela. Monkman, Olga. 2003. (SPA.). 31p. (J). (gr. k-3). pap. 9.95 *(978-950-511-642-3(X))* Santillana USA Publishing Co., Inc.

Caldwell, Ben. All-Action Classics No. 4: the Wonderful Wizard of Oz. Baum, L. Frank & Grahame, Kenneth. 2012. (All-Action Classics Ser.). (ENG.). 128p. (J). (gr. 5-9). pap. 7.95 *(978-1-4027-3153-2(1))* Sterling Publishing Co., Inc.

Caldwell, Talent. Wildcats: Nemesis. Morrison, Robbie. 2006. (ENG.). 208p. (YA). (gr. 10-18). pap. 19.99 *(978-1-4012-1105-9(4),* Wildstorm) DC Comics.

Calero, Dennis. Frankenstein, 1 vol. Shelley, Mary & Shelley, Mary. 2007. (Classic Fiction Ser.). (ENG.). 72p. (gr. 2-3). lib. bdg. 26.65 *(978-1-59889-830-9(2),* Graphic Revolve) Stone Arch Bks.

—The Invisible Man. Wells, H. G. (Classic Fiction Ser.). 72p. 2010. pap. 0.60 *(978-1-4342-3208-3(5))*; 2007. (ENG.). (gr. 2-3). lib. bdg. 26.65 *(978-1-59889-831-6(0))* Stone Arch Bks. (Graphic Revolve).

—The Invisible Man, 1 vol. Wells, H. G. 2007. (Classic Fiction Ser.). (ENG.). 72p. (gr. 2-3). per. 7.15 *(978-1-59889-887-3(6),* Graphic Revolve) Stone Arch Bks.

—The Tell-Tale Heart, 1 vol. Harper, Benjamin & Poe, Edgar Allen. 2013. (Edgar Allan Poe Graphic Novels Ser.). (ENG.). 72p. (gr. 2-3). lib. bdg. 26.65 *(978-1-4342-3023-2(6))* Stone Arch Bks.

—The Tell-Tale Heart, 1 vol. Poe, Edgar Allen & Harper, Benjamin. 2013. (Edgar Allan Poe Graphic Novels Ser.). (ENG.). 72p. (gr. 2-3). pap. 6.10 *(978-1-4342-4261-7(7))* Stone Arch Bks.

—The Tell-Tale Heart Package. Poe, Edgar Allen. 2013. (ENG.). 62p. (J). (gr. 5-8). pap. 35.70 *(978-1-4342-4285-3(4))* Stone Arch Bks.

Calero, Dennis, jt. illus. see Dimaya, Emerson.

Calero, Dennis, jt. illus. see Fabul, J. C.

Calero, Dennis, jt. illus. see Jimenz, Jim.

Caley, Isabel W. Ted Gilman. Gilman, Dorothy Foster. 2011. 200p. 44.95 *(978-1-258-06474-7(X))* Literary Licensing, LLC.

Calico World Entertainment Staff. Luigi & the Lost Wish, 1 vol. Knights, Harry B. 2003. (Nicholas Stories Ser.: 4). (ENG.). 56p. (J). (gr. k-3). 16.95 *(978-1-58980-162-2(8))* Pelican Publishing Co., Inc.

—The Maiden Voyage of Kris Kringle, 1 vol. Knights, Harry B. 2003. (Nicholas Stories Ser.: 3). (ENG.). 56p. (J). (gr. k-3). 16.95 *(978-1-58980-161-5(X))* Pelican Publishing Co., Inc.

Calindas, Marconi. Of Petals & Hope: Sunny Sunflower Triumphs over Bullying. Cafege, Adam. 2013. 36p. pap. 24.95 *(978-0-9840204-4-7(6))* Pacific Raven Pr.

Calino. ABC Snake. Calino. Abbeville Press Staff. 2008. (ENG.). 30p. (J). (gr. k-k). 8.95 *(978-0-7892-0303-8(0),* Abbeville Kids) Abbeville Pr., Inc.

—123 Caterpillar. Calino. Abbeville Press Staff. 2008. (ENG.). 30p. (J). (gr. k-k). 8.95 *(978-0-7892-0304-5(9),* Abbeville Kids) Abbeville Pr., Inc.

Calitri, Susan. Emily's Tea Party. Masurel, Claire. 2003. (Emily Ser.). (ENG.). 48p. (J). (gr. -1-k). 5.99 *(978-0-448-42643-3(9))* Penguin Publishing Group.

—Mommies & Babies on the Farm. Hawksley, Gerald. 2004. (J). bds. 11.99 *(978-1-890647-11-7(X))* TOMY International, Inc.

Calitri, Susan & Bond, Barbara Higgins. Penguins - Sticker Stories. Masurel, Claire & Bond, Barbara Higgins. 2003. (Sticker Stories Ser.). (ENG.). 16p. (J). (gr. -1-2). 4.99 *(978-0-448-42527-6(0))* Penguin Publishing Group.

Calitri, Susan Chapman. What Time Is It? Cifuentes, Carolina. 2010. (My World Ser.).Tr. of Que Hora Es?. (ENG.). 24p. (J). (gr. -1-1). lib. bdg. 22.60 *(978-1-60754-954-3(9))* Windmill Bks.

—What Time Is It? Cifuentes, Carolina, ed. 2010. (My World Ser.).Tr. of Que Hora Es?. (ENG.). 24p. (J). (gr. -1-1). pap. 8.15 *(978-1-61533-041-6(0))* Windmill Bks.

Call, Angela. Hold on to Your Horses. Tayler, Sandra. 2008. 32p. (J). per. 15.00 *(978-0-9779074-8-9(1))* Tayler Corp., The.

Call, Brian. White Shirts: A Baptism Keepsake for Boys. Rowley, Deborah Pace. 2006. 32p. (J). 16.99 *(978-1-59038-633-0(7))* Deseret Bk. Co.

Call, Brian D. Sarah's Cloud. Call, Brian D., tr. 2003. (J). 15.95 *(978-1-57008-955-8(8))* Deseret Bk. Co.

Call, Greg. The Attack of the Frozen Woodchucks. Elish, Dan. 2008. (ENG.). 256p. (J). (gr. 3-7). 16.99 *(978-0-06-113870-6(3)*, Geringer, Laura Book) HarperCollins Pubs.
—The Book of Storms. Hatfield, Ruth. 2015. (Book of Storms Trilogy Ser.). (ENG.). 368p. (J). (gr. 5-9). 16.99 *(978-0-8050-9998-0(0))*, Holt, Henry & Co. Bks. For Young Readers) Holt, Henry & Co.
—The Bridge to Never Land. Barry, Dave & Pearson, Ridley. 2012. (Peter & the Starcatchers Ser.). (ENG.). 448p. (J). (gr. 5-9). pap. 9.99 *(978-1-4231-6029-8(0))* Hyperion Pr.
—House of Secrets. Columbus, Chris & Vizzini, Ned. (J). 2014. (House of Secrets Ser.: 1). (ENG.). 512p. (gr. 3-7). pap. 7.99 *(978-0-06-219247-9(7))*; 2013. (House of Secrets Ser.: 1). (ENG.). 496p. (gr. 3-7). 17.99 *(978-0-06-219246-2(9))*; 2013. 496p. ***(978-0-06-225964-6(4))*** HarperCollins Pubs.
—House of Secrets: Battle of the Beasts. Columbus, Chris & Vizzini, Ned. 2015. (House of Secrets Ser.: 2). (ENG.). 480p. (J). (gr. 3-7). pap. 7.99 *(978-0-06-219250-9(7))* HarperCollins Pubs.
—The Last Dogs: The Vanishing. Holt, Christopher. 2012. (Last Dogs Ser.: 1). (ENG.). 384p. (J). (gr. 3-7). 16.99 *(978-0-316-20005-9(0))* Little, Brown Bks. for Young Readers.
—Peter & the Secret of Rundoon. Pearson, Ridley & Barry, Dave. rev. ed. 2009. (Peter & the Starcatchers Ser.: Bk. 3). (ENG.). 496p. (J). (gr. 5-9). pap. 8.99 *(978-1-4231-2326-2(3))* Hyperion Pr.
—Peter & the Shadow Thieves. Barry, Dave & Pearson, Ridley. 2006. (Peter & the Starcatchers Ser.). (ENG.). 576p. (J). (gr. 5-9). 18.99 *(978-0-7868-3787-8(X)*, Disney Editions) Disney Pr.
—Peter & the Shadow Thieves. Barry, Dave & Pearson, Ridley. 2007. (Starcatchers Ser.: Bk. 2). 556p. (gr. 5-9). 19.00 *(978-0-7569-8060-3(7))* Perfection Learning Corp.
—Peter & the Starcatchers. Barry, Dave & Pearson, Ridley. rev. ed. 2006. (Peter & the Starcatchers Ser.). (ENG.). 480p. (J). (gr. 5-9). reprint ed. pap. 9.99 *(978-0-7868-4907-9(X)*, Disney Editions) Disney Pr.
—Peter & the Sword of Mercy. Barry, Dave & Pearson, Ridley. 2011. (Peter & the Starcatchers Ser.: Bk. 4). (ENG.). 528p. (J). (gr. 5-9). pap. 9.99 *(978-1-4231-3070-3(7))* Hyperion Pr.
—Phantom Stallion Box Set: The Wild One; Mustang Moon; Dark Sunshine. Farley, Terri. 2004. (Phantom Stallion Ser.). 704p. (J). (gr. 5-18). pap. 14.99 *(978-0-06-059504-3(3)*, HarperCollins) HarperCollins Pubs.
—The Pirate's Coin. Malone, Marianne. (Sixty-Eight Rooms Adventures Ser.). (ENG.). (J). (gr. 3-7). 2014. 240p. 6.99 *(978-0-307-97720-5(X))*; 2013. 224p. 16.99 *(978-0-307-97717-5(X))* Random Hse., Inc.
—The Secret of the Key. Malone, Marianne. 2014. (Sixty-Eight Rooms Adventures Ser.). (ENG.). 256p. (J). (gr. 3-7). 16.99 *(978-0-307-97721-2(8))* Random Hse., Inc.
—Stealing Magic. Malone, Marianne. (Sixty-Eight Rooms Adventures Ser.). (ENG.). (J). (gr. 3-7). 2013. 272p. pap. 6.99 *(978-0-375-86790-3(2))*; 2012. 256p. 16.99 *(978-0-375-86819-1(4))* Random Hse., Inc.
—A Tale of Two Castles. Levine, Gail Carson. (J). (gr. 3-7). 2012. (ENG.). 352p. pap. 6.99 *(978-0-06-122967-1(9))*; 2011. (ENG.). 336p. 16.99 *(978-0-06-122965-7(2))*; 2011. 336p. lib. bdg. 17.89 *(978-0-06-122966-4(0))* HarperCollins Pubs.
—The Vanishing. Holt, Christopher. 2013. (Last Dogs Ser.: 1). (ENG.). 400p. (J). (gr. 3-7). pap. 8.00 *(978-0-316-20004-2(2))* Little, Brown Bks. for Young Readers.
Call, Greg & Brown, Roberta. Peter & the Shadow Thieves. Barry, Dave & Pearson, Ridley. rev. ed. 2007. (Peter & the Starcatchers Ser.). (ENG.). 592p. (J). (gr. 5-9). pap. 9.99 *(978-1-4231-0855-9(8)*, Disney Editions) Disney Pr.
Call, Greg, jt. illus. see Dorman, Brandon.
Call, Greg, jt. illus. see Triplett, Gina.
Call, Ken. Barack Obama: Presidente de Estados Unidos. Edwards, Roberta. 2009. (SPA.). 64p. (gr. 2-5). pap. 9.99 *(978-1-60396-623-8(4))* Santillana USA Publishing Co., Inc.
—Barack Obama: United States President. Edwards, Roberta. rev. exp. ed. 2009. (ENG.). 64p. (J). (gr. 1-3). mass mkt. 4.99 *(978-0-448-45234-0(0)*, Grosset & Dunlap) Penguin Publishing Group.
—Michelle Obama: Mom-in-Chief. Edwards, Roberta. 2009. (ENG.). 48p. (J). (gr. 1-3). mass mkt. 4.99 *(978-0-448-45256-2(1)*, Grosset & Dunlap) Penguin Publishing Group.
—Michelle Obama: Primera Dama y Primera Mama. Edwards, Roberta. 2010. (SPA.). 48p. (gr. 3-5). pap. 9.99 *(978-1-60396-946-8(2))* Santillana USA Publishing Co., Inc.
Callahan, Charlie. Samantha Loses Her Sweet Tooth. Callahan, Charlie. 2004. (J). *(978-0-9754019-0-3(4))* Periscope Pr.
Calle, Juan. Drawing Ocean Animals. Colich, Abby. 2015. (Drawing Amazing Animals Ser.). (ENG.). 32p. (gr. 3-4). 27.32 *(978-1-4914-2131-4(2))* Capstone Pr., Inc.
—How to Draw Incredible Dinosaurs, 1 vol. McCurry, Kristen. 2012. (Smithsonian Drawing Bks.). (ENG.). 64p. (gr. 3-4). pap. 7.19 *(978-1-4296-9450-6(5))*; pap. 41.70 *(978-1-4296-9451-3(3))*; lib. bdg. 33.32 *(978-1-4296-8750-8(9))* Capstone Pr., Inc.
Calle, Juan & Howard, Colin. Drawing Amazing Animals. Colich, Abby. 2015. (Drawing Amazing Animals Ser.). (ENG.). 32p. (gr. 3-4). lib. bdg. 109.28 ***(978-1-4914-2559-6(8)***, Snap Bks.) Capstone Pr., Inc.
Callen, Liz. Pen Pal Penguin. Scraper, Katherine. 2012. 8p. (J). *(978-0-7367-2639-9(X))* Zaner-Bloser, Inc.
—Reading, Rhyming, & 'Rithmetic. Crawley, Dave. 2010. (ENG.). 32p. (J). (gr. 2-4). 17.95 *(978-1-59078-565-2(7)*, Wordsong) Boyds Mills Pr.
Calles, Rosa M. Dodo the Bird & Other Stories. De Aragon, Ray J. 105p. (Orig.). (J). (gr. 1-12). pap. 5.95 *(978-0-932906-21-2(4))* Pan-American Publishing Co.
Callicutt, Kenny, jt. illus. see Joyce, William.
Callo, Valeria. A Quien le Toca? Peyron, Gabriela. rev. ed. 2006. (Otra Escalera Ser.). (SPA & ENG.). 24p. (J). (gr. 2-4). pap. 9.95 *(978-968-5920-57-5(5))* Castillo, Ediciones, S. A. de C. V. MEX. Dist: Macmillan.
Calo, Marcos. The Ballgame with No One at Bat. Brezenoff, Steve. 2013. (Field Trip Mysteries Ser.). (ENG.). 88p. (gr. 2-3). pap. 6.10 *(978-1-4342-6211-0(1))*; lib. bdg. 23.99 *(978-1-4342-5978-3(1))* Stone Arch Bks.
—The Bowling Lane Without Any Strikes. Brezenoff, Steve. 2013. (Field Trip Mysteries Ser.). (ENG.). 88p. (gr. 2-3). pap. 6.10 *(978-1-4342-6212-7(X))*; lib. bdg. 23.99 *(978-1-4342-5979-0(X))* Stone Arch Bks.
—The Cave That Shouldn't Collapse, 1 vol. Brezenoff, Steve. 2011. (Field Trip Mysteries Ser.). (ENG.). 88p. (gr. 2-3). pap. 6.10 *(978-1-4342-3430-8(4))*; lib. bdg. 23.99 *(978-1-4342-3227-4(1))* Stone Arch Bks.
—The Crook That Made Kids Cry, 1 vol. Brezenoff, Steve. 2013. (Field Trip Mysteries Ser.). (ENG.). 88p. (gr. 2-3). pap. 6.10 *(978-1-4342-6210-3(3))*; lib. bdg. 23.99 *(978-1-4342-5977-6(3))* Stone Arch Bks.
—The Dinosaur That Disappeared, 1 vol. Brezenoff, Steve. 2013. (Field Trip Mysteries Ser.). (ENG.). 88p. (gr. 2-3). pap. 6.10 *(978-1-4342-6213-4(8))*; lib. bdg. 23.99 *(978-1-4342-5980-6(3))* Stone Arch Bks.
—The Elves & the Shoemaker. McFadden, Deanna. 2012. (Silver Penny Stories Ser.). (ENG.). 40p. (J). (gr. -1-1). 4.95 *(978-1-4027-8334-0(5))* Sterling Publishing Co., Inc.
—The Everglades Poacher Who Pretended, 1 vol. Brezenoff, Steve. 2012. (Field Trip Mysteries Ser.). (ENG.). 88p. (gr. 2-3). pap. 6.10 *(978-1-4342-4197-9(1))*; lib. bdg. 23.99 *(978-1-4342-3790-3(7))* Stone Arch Bks.
—The Grand Canyon Burros That Broke, 1 vol. Brezenoff, Steve. 2012. (Field Trip Mysteries Ser.). (ENG.). 88p. (gr. 2-3). pap. 6.10 *(978-1-4342-4198-6(X))*; lib. bdg. 23.99 *(978-1-4342-3788-0(5))* Stone Arch Bks.
—King Arthur & His Knights. Namm, Diane. 2014. (Silver Penny Stories Ser.). (ENG.). 40p. (J). (gr. -1-1). 4.95 *(978-1-4027-8432-3(5))* Sterling Publishing Co., Inc.
—The Mount Rushmore Face That Couldn't See, 1 vol. Brezenoff, Steve. 2012. (Field Trip Mysteries Ser.). (ENG.). 88p. (gr. 2-3). pap. 6.10 *(978-1-4342-4199-3(8))*; lib. bdg. 23.99 *(978-1-4342-3787-3(7))* Stone Arch Bks.
—The Mystery Across the Secret Bridge. Paris, Harper. 2015. (Greetings from Somewhere Ser.: 7). (ENG.). 128p. (J). (gr. k-4). pap. 5.99 *(978-1-4814-2367-0(3)*, Little Simon) Little Simon.
—The Mystery at the Coral Reef. Paris, Harper. 2015. (Greetings from Somewhere Ser.: 8). (ENG.). 128p. (J). (gr. k-4). pap. 5.99 *(978-1-4814-2370-0(3)*, Little Simon) Little Simon.
—Mystery in Mayan Mexico. Wells, Marcia. 2015. (Eddie Red Undercover Ser.: 2). (ENG.). 224p. (J). (gr. 5-7). 16.99 *(978-0-544-30206-8(0)*, HMH Books For Young Readers) Houghton Mifflin Harcourt Publishing Co.
—The Mystery in the Forbidden City. Paris, Harper. 2014. (Greetings from Somewhere Ser.: 4). (ENG.). 128p. (J). (gr. k-2). pap. 5.99 *(978-1-4814-0299-6(4)*, Little Simon) Little Simon.
—The Mystery of the Gold Coin. Paris, Harper. 2014. (Greetings from Somewhere Ser.: 1). (ENG.). 128p. (J). (gr. k-4). pap. 5.99 *(978-1-4424-9718-4(1)*, Little Simon) Little Simon.
—The Mystery of the Mosaic. Paris, Harper. 2014. (Greetings from Somewhere Ser.: 2). (ENG.). 128p. (J). (gr. k-2). pap. 4.99 *(978-1-4424-9721-4(1)*, Little Simon) Little Simon.
—The Mystery of the Stolen Painting. Paris, Harper. 2014. (Greetings from Somewhere Ser.: 3). (ENG.). 128p. (J). (gr. k-2). pap. 5.99 *(978-1-4814-0296-5(X)*, Little Simon) Little Simon.
—The Mystery of the Suspicious Spices. Paris, Harper. 2014. (Greetings from Somewhere Ser.: 6). (ENG.). 128p. (J). (gr. k-4). pap. 5.99 *(978-1-4814-1467-8(4)*, Little Simon) Little Simon.
—Mystery on Museum Mile. Wells, Marcia. (Eddie Red Undercover Ser.). (ENG.). 256p. (gr. 5-7). 2015. (YA). pap. 6.99 *(978-0-544-43940-5(6))*; 2014. (J). 16.99 *(978-0-544-23833-6(8))* Houghton Mifflin Harcourt Publishing Co. (HMH Books For Young Readers).
—The Ride That Was Really Haunted, 1 vol. Brezenoff, Steve. 2011. (Field Trip Mysteries Ser.). (ENG.). 88p. (gr. 2-3). pap. 6.10 *(978-1-4342-3427-8(4))*; lib. bdg. 23.99 *(978-1-4342-3224-3(7))* Stone Arch Bks.
—Robin Hood. McFadden, Deanna. 2013. (Silver Penny Stories Ser.). (ENG.). 40p. (J). (gr. -1-1). 4.95 *(978-1-4027-8339-5(6))* Sterling Publishing Co., Inc.
—The Seals That Wouldn't Swim, 1 vol. Brezenoff, Steve. 2011. (Field Trip Mysteries Ser.). (ENG.). 88p. (gr. 2-3). pap. 6.10 *(978-1-4342-3428-5(2))*; lib. bdg. 23.99 *(978-1-4342-3225-0(5))* Stone Arch Bks.
—The Steadfast Tin Soldier. Olmstead, Kathleen & Andersen, Hans Christian. 2013. (Silver Penny Stories Ser.). (ENG.). 40p. (J). (gr. -1-1). 4.95 *(978-1-4027-8351-7(5))* Sterling Publishing Co., Inc.
—The Substitutes: An Up2U Action Adventure. Lay, Kathryn. 2015. (J). *(978-1-62402-095-7(X))* Magic Wagon.
—The Symphony That Was Silent, 1 vol. Brezenoff, Steve. 2011. (Field Trip Mysteries Ser.). (ENG.). 88p. (gr. 2-3). pap. 6.10 *(978-1-4342-3429-2(0))*; lib. bdg. 23.99 *(978-1-4342-3226-7(3))* Stone Arch Bks.
—The Yellowstone Kidnapping That Wasn't, 1 vol. Brezenoff, Steve. 2012. (Field Trip Mysteries Ser.). (ENG.). 88p. (gr. 2-3). pap. 6.10 *(978-1-4342-4200-6(5))*; lib. bdg. 23.99 *(978-1-4342-3789-7(3))* Stone Arch Bks.
Calver, Paul. Colours & Shapes. Giles, Angela & Picthall, Chez. 2015. (ENG.). 12p. (J). 9.99 ***(978-1-909763-42-5(X))*** Award Pubns. Ltd. GBR. Dist: Parkwest Pubns., Inc.
—123. Giles, Angela & Picthall, Chez. 2015. (ENG.). 12p. (J). pap. 9.99 ***(978-1-909763-29-6(2))*** Award Pubns. Ltd. GBR. Dist: Parkwest Pubns., Inc.
Calvert, Lissa. Accidental Evie. Basham, Tom. 2012. 120p. *(978-1-77097-373-2(7))*; pap. *(978-1-77097-374-9(5))* FriesenPress.
—Emily Carr's Woo. Home, Constance. 2005. (ENG.). 72p. (J). pap. 9.95 *(978-0-88982-149-1(6))* Oolichan Bks. CAN. Dist: Univ. of Toronto Pr.
—Foxes on the Ridge. Pavlick, Leon E. & PAVLICK, A. N. N. M. 2012. 48p. pap. *(978-1-77097-852-2(6))* FriesenPress.
—Sailing Home. Basham, Tom. 2012. 168p. *(978-1-77097-370-1(2))* FriesenPress.
Calvert, Trudy. ¿También Tienen Sentimientos Los Animales? Calvert, Trudy, tr. Rice, David L. & RICE, DAVID L. 2004. (SPA.). 34p. *(978-84-7720-931-7(6))* Obelisco, Ediciones S.A.
Calvert-Weyant, Linda. Abigail & the Lost Purse. Riggin, Lisa. 2012. 32p. (J). 9.95 *(978-1-59530-359-2(6))* Hallmark Card, Inc.
Calvetti, Leonello & Massini, Luca. Iguanodon. Dalla Vecchia, Fabio Marco. 2007. (Dinosaur Profiles Ser.). (ENG.). 32p. (J). (gr. 3-7). lib. bdg. 25.65 *(978-1-4103-0736-1(0)*, Blackbirch Pr., Inc.) Cengage Gale.
Camacho, Ricardo. Los Bandidos de Rio Frio. Payno, Manuel. 2003. (SPA.). 91p. (J). pap. *(978-970-643-638-2(3))* Selector, S.A. de C.V. MEX. Dist: Lectorum Pubns., Inc.
Camagni, Jacopo. Marvel Adventures Spider-Man Vol. 3: Sensational. Tobin, Paul. 2011. (ENG.). 96p. (J). (gr. -1-17). pap. 9.99 *(978-0-7851-4740-4(3))* Marvel Worldwide, Inc.
Camburn, Carol A. Ernest & Elston. Barnes, Laura T. 2005. (Ernest Ser.). 32p. (J). (gr. -1-3). 15.95 *(978-0-9674681-6-7(7))* Barnesyard Bks.
—Ernest's Special Christmas. Barnes, Laura T. 2003. (Ernest Ser.). 36p. (J). (gr. k-3). 17.95 *(978-0-9674681-3-6(2))* Barnesyard Bks.
Camcam, Princesse. Marie from Paris. Sabatier-Morel, Francoise & Pellegrini, Isabelle. 2014. (AV2 Fiction Readalong Ser.: Vol. 131). (ENG.). 32p. (J). (gr. -1-3). lib. bdg. 34.28 *(978-1-4896-2262-4(4)*, AV2 by Weigl) Weigl Pubs., Inc.
—Miyako from Tokyo. Yamada, Miho. 2014. (AV2 Fiction Readalong Ser.: Vol. 132). (ENG.). 32p. (J). (gr. -1-3). lib. bdg. 34.28 *(978-1-4896-2268-6(3)*, AV2 by Weigl) Weigl Pubs., Inc.
Camden, Jean. How to Make a Planet: A Step-by-Step Guide to Building the Earth. Kids Can Press Staff & Forbes, Scott. 2014. (ENG.). 64p. (J). 17.95 *(978-1-894786-88-1(2))* Kids Can Pr., Ltd. CAN. Dist: Univ. of Toronto Pr.
Cameron, Chad. A Day with No Crayons. Rusch, Elizabeth. 2007. (ENG.). 32p. (J). (gr. -1-3). 15.95 *(978-0-87358-910-9(6))* Cooper Square Publishing Llc.
—Fall Mixed Up. Raczka, Bob. 2011. (Carolrhoda Picture Books Ser.). (ENG.). 40p. (J). (gr. -1-3). lib. bdg. 17.95 *(978-0-7613-4606-7(6)*, Carolrhoda Bks.) Lerner Publishing Group.
Cameron, Craig. Backhoe Joe. Alexander, Lori. 2014. (ENG.). 40p. (J). (gr. -1-3). 15.99 *(978-0-06-225015-5(9))* HarperCollins Pubs.
—The Big Train. Klein, Adria F. 2013. (Train Time Ser.). (ENG.). 32p. (gr. -1-1). pap. 6.25 *(978-1-4342-4886-2(0))* Stone Arch Bks.
—The Big Train: Takes a Trip. Klein, Adria F. 2013. (Train Time Ser.). (ENG.). 32p. (gr. -1-1). lib. bdg. 21.32 *(978-1-4342-4191-7(2))* Stone Arch Bks.
—Big Train Takes a Trip, 1 vol. Klein, Adria F. 2013. (Train Time Ser.). (ENG.). 32p. (gr. -1-1). pap. 5.95 *(978-1-4342-6194-6(8))*; pap. 29.70 *(978-1-4342-6300-1(2))*; lib. bdg. 21.32 *(978-1-4342-4781-0(3))* Stone Arch Bks.
—Chico Plays Hide & Seek. Adams, Ben. 2013. (Googly Eyes Ser.). (ENG.). 12p. (J). (gr. -1-k). bds. 6.99 *(978-1-84322-280-4(9)*, Armadillo) Anness Publishing GBR. Dist: National Bk. Network.
—Circus Train, 1 vol. Klein, Adria F. 2013. (Train Time Ser.). (ENG.). 32p. (gr. -1-1). pap. 6.25 *(978-1-4342-4883-1(6))*; lib. bdg. 21.32 *(978-1-4342-4188-7(2))* Stone Arch Bks.
—Circus Train & the Clowns, 1 vol. Klein, Adria F. 2013. (Train Time Ser.). (ENG.). 32p. (gr. -1-1). pap. 5.95 *(978-1-4342-6195-3(6))*; pap. 29.70 *(978-1-4342-6303-2(7))*; lib. bdg. 21.32 *(978-1-4342-4782-7(1))* Stone Arch Bks.
—City Train, 1 vol. Klein, Adria F. 2013. (Train Time Ser.). (ENG.). 32p. (gr. -1-1). lib. bdg. 21.32 *(978-1-4342-4189-4(0))* Stone Arch Bks.
—City Train in Trouble, 1 vol. Klein, Adria F. 2013. (Train Time Ser.). (ENG.). 32p. (gr. -1-1). pap. 5.95 *(978-1-4342-6196-0(4))*; pap. 29.70 *(978-1-4342-6302-5(9))*; lib. bdg. 21.32 *(978-1-4342-4783-4(X))* Stone Arch Bks.
—Dino Detectives. Yasuda, Anita. 2013. (Dino Detectives Ser.). (ENG.). 32p. (gr. 1-3). lib. bdg. 85.28 *(978-1-4342-6058-1(5))* Stone Arch Bks.
—Freddie the Fish, Star of the Show. Baxter, Nicola & Adams, Ben. 2013. (Googly Eyes Ser.). (ENG.). 12p. (J). (gr. -1-k). bds. 6.99 *(978-1-84322-621-5(9)*, Armadillo) Anness Publishing GBR. Dist: National Bk. Network.
—Freight Train, 1 vol. Klein, Adria F. 2013. (Train Time Ser.). (ENG.). 32p. (gr. -1-1). pap. 6.25 *(978-1-4342-4885-5(2))*; lib. bdg. 21.32 *(978-1-4342-4190-0(4))* Stone Arch Bks.
—The Full Freight Train, 1 vol. Klein, Adria F. 2013. (Train Time Ser.). (ENG.). 32p. (gr. -1-1). pap. 5.95 *(978-1-4342-6197-7(2))*; pap. 29.70 *(978-1-4342-6301-8(0))*; lib. bdg. 21.32 *(978-1-4342-4784-1(8))* Stone Arch Bks.
—Happy Birthday. Hewitt, Sally. 2003. 14p. (J). pap. 10.95 *(978-1-57145-735-6(6)*, Silver Dolphin Bks.) Baker & Taylor Publishing Group.
—Happy Doctor. Hewitt, Sally. 2003. 14p. (J). pap. 10.95 *(978-1-57145-734-9(8)*, Silver Dolphin Bks.) Baker & Taylor Publishing Group.
—Happy Dresser. Hewitt, Sally. 2003. 14p. (J). pap. 10.95 *(978-1-57145-733-2(X)*, Silver Dolphin Bks.) Baker & Taylor Publishing Group.
—The Pig with the Curliest Tail. Adams, Ben. 2013. (Googly Eyes Ser.). (ENG.). 12p. (J). (gr. -1-k). bds. 6.99 *(978-1-84322-618-5(9)*, Armadillo) Anness Publishing GBR. Dist: National Bk. Network.
—Polly the Farm Puppy. Adams, Ben. 2013. (Googly Eyes Ser.). (ENG.). 12p. (J). (gr. -1-k). bds. 6.99 *(978-1-84322-319-1(8)*, Armadillo) Anness Publishing GBR. Dist: National Bk. Network.
—Train Time. Klein, Adria F. 2013. (Train Time Ser.). (ENG.). 32p. (gr. -1-1). lib. bdg. 85.28 *(978-1-4342-6055-0(0))*; lib. bdg. 170.56 *(978-1-4342-6056-7(9))* Stone Arch Bks.
Cameron, Ed. The Dog That's Not a Poodle. Schultze, Gwendolyn. 2011. 54p. (J). pap. 12.00 *(978-1-892076-97-7(7))* Dancing Moon Pr.
Cameron, Eugenia. The Basket of Seeds. St. Julian, Ska. 2013. 122p. pap. 10.99 *(978-0-9899182-0-6(3))* Chris Six Group, The.
Cameron, Marie. The Barefoot Book of Buddhist Tales. Chodzin, Sherab. 2014. (ENG.). 80p. (J). pap. 14.99 *(978-1-84686-824-5(6))* Barefoot Bks., Inc.
—Clever Katya: A Fairy Tale from Old Russia. Hoffman, Mary. 2005. 32p. (J). (gr. k-3). pap., pap. 6.99 *(978-1-905236-05-3(0))* Barefoot Bks., Inc.
Camille, Diana. The Goops Circus: A Whimsical Telling of Do-Good Tales. Ross, Barbara & Beatty, Nicholas. 2010. (Goops Ser.). 58p. (J). 19.95 incl. audio compact disk *(978-0-9712368-4-4(4))* Goops Unlimited.
—A Treasury of Goops: Timeless Manners for Every Generation. 2005. Orig. Title: Goops & How to Be Them. (ENG.). 45p. (J). 19.95 *(978-0-9712368-5-1(2)*, 8006811891) Goops Unlimited.
Camilleri, Michael. One Minute's Silence. Metzenthen, David. 2014. (ENG.). 48p. (J). (gr. k). 24.99 *(978-1-74331-624-5(0))* Allen & Unwin AUS. Dist: Independent Pubs. Group.
Camling, Candace. The Southern Twelve Days of Christmas, 1 vol. Davis, David. 2013. (ENG.). 32p. (J). (gr. k-3). 16.99 *(978-1-4556-1773-9(3))* Pelican Publishing Co., Inc.
—The Twelve Days of Christmas — In Texas, That Is, 1 vol. Davis, David. 2011. (ENG.). 32p. (J). (gr. k-3). 16.99 *(978-1-58980-924-6(6))* Pelican Publishing Co., Inc.
Camm, Martin. Day & Night in Swamp. Cheshire, Gerard. 2009. 38p. (J). (gr. 2-5). 14.99 *(978-0-8437-0974-2(X))* Hammond World Atlas Corp.
—Meyers Buch der Baeren. (GER.). 48p. *(978-3-411-07461-7(2))* Bibliographisches Institut & F. A. Brockhaus AG DEU. Dist: i. b. d., Ltd.
—Meyers Buch der Wale und Delfine. (GER.). 48p. *(978-3-411-07451-8(5))* Bibliographisches Institut & F. A. Brockhaus AG DEU. Dist: i. b. d., Ltd.
Camm, Sue. Baby Animals. 2004. 24p. (J). bds. 6.99 *(978-1-85854-728-2(8))* Brimax Books Ltd. GBR. Dist: Byeway Bks.
Cammell, Sandra. Big Red Comes to Stay. Eggleton, Jill. 2004. (Rigby Sails Early Ser.). (ENG.). 16p. (gr. 1-2). pap. 6.95 *(978-0-7578-9303-2(1))* Houghton Mifflin Harcourt Publishing Co.
—King of the Zoo, 6 pack. Holden, Pam. 2009. (Red Rocket Readers Ser.). 16p. (gr. -1-2). pap. *(978-1-877363-13-9(8)*, Red Rocket Readers) Flying Start Bks.
—Turtle's Trouble. Eggleton, Jill. 2003. (Rigby Sails Early Ser.). (ENG.). 16p. (gr. 1-2). pap. 6.95 *(978-0-7578-8672-0(8))* Houghton Mifflin Harcourt Publishing Co.
Cammuso, Frank. Otto's Orange Day. Lynch, Jay. 2013. (ENG.). 40p. (J). (gr. -1-3). pap. 4.99 *(978-1-935179-27-6(6))* TOON Books / RAW Junior, LLC.
—Otto's Orange Day. Lynch, Jay. Mouly, Francoise, ed. 2008. (ENG.). 40p. (J). (gr. -1-3). 12.95 *(978-0-9799238-2-1(4))* TOON Books / RAW Junior, LLC.
Campanelli, Mario. It's Beautiful to Be Different & Being Different Is Beautiful! Jeffrey, Dennis. I.t. ed. 2011. (ENG.). 28p. pap. 9.25 *(978-1-4663-6428-8(9))* CreateSpace Independent Publishing Platform.
Campbell, Alex & Spay, Anthony. Jackie Robinson. Raatma, Lucia & O'Hern, Kerri. (Biografias Graficas (Graphic Biographies) Ser.). 32p. (gr. 5-8). 2007. (SPA.). pap. 10.50 *(978-0-8368-7889-9(2))*; 2007. (SPA.). lib. bdg. 27.00 *(978-0-8368-7882-0(5))*; 2006. lib. bdg. 27.00 *(978-0-8368-6198-3(1))* Stevens, Gareth Publishing LLLP.
Campbell, Alex, jt. illus. see Spay, Anthony.
Campbell, Blendon. Father Abraham. Tarbell, Ida M. 2004. reprint ed. pap. 15.95 *(978-1-4179-0070-1(9))* Kessinger Publishing, LLC.
Campbell, Brent. Lobo & the Rabbit Stew. Schwartz, Marcia. 2010. (ENG.). 32p. (J). (gr. -1-12). lib. bdg. 16.95 *(978-1-936299-02-7(X)*, Raven Tree Pr.,Csi) Continental Sales, Inc.
—Lobo & the Rabbit Stew/El Lobo y el Caldo de Conejo. Schwartz, Marcia. 2010. (ENG & SPA.). 32p. (J). (gr. -1-12). pap. 7.95 *(978-1-936299-01-0(1))*; lib. bdg. 16.95 *(978-1-936299-00-3(3))* Continental Sales, Inc. (Raven Tree Pr.,Csi).
Campbell, Bruce, photos by. Buddhism in Thailand. Hawker, Frances & Sunantha Phusomsai. 2009. (ENG., 32p. (J). (gr. 3-6). *(978-0-7787-5006-2(X))*; pap. *(978-0-7787-5023-9(X))* Crabtree Publishing Co.
—Christianity in Mexico. Hawker, Frances & Paz, Noemi. 2009. (ENG., 32p. (J). (gr. 3-6). *(978-0-7787-5007-9(8))*; pap. *(978-0-7787-5024-6(8))* Crabtree Publishing Co.
—Hinduism in Bali. Hawker, Frances & Resi, Putu. 2009. (ENG., 32p. (J). (gr. 3-6). *(978-0-7787-5008-6(6))*; pap. *(978-0-7787-5025-3(6))* Crabtree Publishing Co.
—Islam in Turkey. Hawker, Frances & Alicavusoglu, Leyla. 2009. (ENG., 32p. (J). (gr. 3-6). *(978-0-7787-5009-3(4))*; pap. *(978-0-7787-5026-0(4))* Crabtree Publishing Co.
—Judaism in Israel. Hawker, Frances & Taub, Daniel. 2009. (ENG., 32p. (J). (gr. 3-6). *(978-0-7787-5010-9(8))*; pap. *(978-0-7787-5027-7(2))* Crabtree Publishing Co.
—Sikhism in India. Hawker, Frances & Bhatia, Mohini. 2009. (ENG., 32p. (J). (gr. 3-6). *(978-0-7787-5011-6(6))*; pap. *(978-0-7787-5028-4(0))* Crabtree Publishing Co.
Campbell, D. B. Lunch for Baby Elephant. Coulton, Mia. 2009. (ENG.). 12p. pap. 5.50 *(978-1-933624-49-5(3))*; pap. 5.35 *(978-1-933624-42-6(6))* Maryruth Bks., Inc.

Campbell, Donna P. Pieces of Me. Pierce, AnneMarie. (J). (gr. 1-9). *(978-0-9623937-3-0(8))* Forward.

Campbell, Eva. The Matatu. 1 vol. Walters, Eric. 2012. (ENG.). 32p. (J). (gr. -1-3). 19.95 *(978-1-55469-301-6(2))* Orca Bk. Pubs. USA.

Campbell, Jacquie. A Winter Solstice Celebration. Lemay, Didi. 2008. 56p. pap. 23.99 *(978-1-4389-0998-1(5))* AuthorHouse.

Campbell, Jenney. Zachary Z. Packrat & His Amazing Collections. Bessesen, Brooke. 2008. 40p. pap. 19.95 *(978-1-932082-83-8(2))* Arizona Highways.

Campbell, Jenny. Build-a-Skill Instant Books Math Facts To 20. Cernek, Kim & Williams, Rozanne Lanczak. Faulkner, Stacey, ed. 2007. (J). 4.99 *(978-1-59198-418-4(1))* Creative Teaching Pr., Inc.

—Build-a-Skill Instant Books Synonyms & Antonyms. Callella, Kim & Williams, Rozanne Lanczak. Faulkner, Stacey, ed. 2007. (J). 4.99 *(978-1-59198-419-1(X))* Creative Teaching Pr., Inc.

—Forever Home. Philipson, Sandra J. 2007. (ENG.). 89p. (J). (gr. 3-7). bds. 7.95 *(978-1-59624-080-3(6))* Cleveland Clinic Pr.

—Life Cycles. Cernek, Kim. Rous, Sheri, ed. 2003. (Stepping into Standards Theme Ser.). 64p. (J). (gr. 2-4). pap. 10.99 *(978-1-59198-002-5(X),* 2484) Creative Teaching Pr., Inc.

—Mapping. Cernek, Kim & Shiotsu, Vicky. Rous, Sheri, ed. 2003. (Stepping into Standards Theme Ser.). 64p. (J). (gr. 2-4). pap. 10.99 *(978-1-59198-004-9(6),* CTP2486) Creative Teaching Pr., Inc.

—Max's Rules. Philipson, Sandra. 2004. (J). 9.95 *(978-1-929821-10-5(7))* Chagrin River Publishing Co.

—Nutrition. Cernek, Kim et al. Rous, Sheri, ed. 2003. (Stepping into Standards Theme Ser.). 64p. (J). (gr. 2-4). pap. 10.99 *(978-1-59198-000-1(3),* CTP2482) Creative Teaching Pr., Inc.

—Oceans of Fun. Jordano, Kimberly & Corcoran, Tebra. Fisch, Teri L., ed. 2003. (Stepping into Standards Theme Ser.). 64p. (J). (gr. k-2). pap. 10.99 *(978-1-57471-946-8(7),* 2474) Creative Teaching Pr., Inc.

—Ollie's Monsters & Other Stories. Philipson, Sandra J. 2010. 48p. (J). pap. 10.95 *(978-1-929821-09-9(3))* Chagrin River Publishing Co.

—Plants. Lewis, Dawn & Jacks, Cyndie. Jennett, Pamela & Rous, Sheri, eds. 2003. (Stepping into Standards Theme Ser.). 64p. (J). (gr. 2-4). pap. 10.99 *(978-1-59198-006-3(2),* CTP2488) Creative Teaching Pr., Inc.

—Sight Word Puzzles & Activities. Lewis, Sue & Abrams, Suzanne. Rous, Sheri, ed. 2004. 96p. (J). pap. 11.99 *(978-1-59198-052-0(6),* CTP 2239) Creative Teaching Pr., Inc.

—Soaring into Space. Jordano, Kimberly & Corcoran, Tebra. Fisch, Teri L., ed. 2003. (Stepping into Standards Theme Ser.). 64p. (J). (gr. k-2). pap. 10.99 *(978-1-57471-952-9(1),* 2480) Creative Teaching Pr., Inc.

—A Very Special Twin Story. Alt, Susan. 2004. 32p. (J). pap. 15.95 *(978-1-891846-26-7(4),* TBSPECIAL, Twins Bks.) Sterling Investments I, LLC DBA Twins Magazine.

—Weather Wonders. Jordano, Kimberly & Corcoran, Tebra. Fisch, Teri L., ed. 2003. (Stepping into Standards Theme Ser.). 64p. (J). (gr. k-2). pap. 10.99 *(978-1-57471-950-5(5),* 2478) Creative Teaching Pr., Inc.

—Zipping Around the Zoo. Jordano, Kimberly & Corcoran, Tebra. Fisch, Teri L., ed. 2003. (Stepping into Standards Theme Ser.). 64p. (J). (gr. k-2). pap. 10.99 *(978-1-57471-948-2(3),* 2476) Creative Teaching Pr., Inc.

Campbell, Jenny & Grayson, Rick. Consonant Puzzles & Activities, Vol. 2143. Cernek, Kim. Cernek, Kim, ed. 2004. 96p. (J). pap. 12.99 *(978-1-59198-067-4(4),* 2143) Creative Teaching Pr., Inc.

—Vowel Puzzles & Activities, Vol. 2144. Lewis, Sue & Stern, Amy. Cernek, Kim, ed. 2004. 96p. (J). pap. 12.99 *(978-1-59198-068-1(2),* 2144) Creative Teaching Pr., Inc.

—Word Family Puzzles & Activities, Vol. 2145. Lewis, Sue & Stern, Amy. Cernek, Kim, ed. 2004. 96p. (J). pap. 12.99 *(978-1-59198-069-8(0),* 2145) Creative Teaching Pr., Inc.

Campbell, Jenny & Tom, Darcy. Build-a-Skill Instant Books Beginning & Ending Consonant Sounds. Shiotsu, Vicky. Faulkner, Stacey, ed. 2007. (J). 4.99 *(978-1-59198-416-0(5))* Creative Teaching Pr., Inc.

—Build-a-Skill Instant Books Color, Shape & Number Words. Cernek, Kim & Williams, Rozanne Lanczak. Shiotsu, Vicky & Faulkner, Stacey, eds. 2007. (J). 4.99 *(978-1-59198-411-5(4))* Creative Teaching Pr., Inc.

—Build-a-Skill Instant Books Consonant Blends & Digraphs. Cernak, Kim. Shiotsu, Vicky & Faulkner, Stacey, eds. 2007. (J). 4.99 *(978-1-59198-410-8(6))* Creative Teaching Pr., Inc.

—Build-a-Skill Instant Books R-Controled Vowels & Vowel Digraphs. Cernak, Kim. Shiotsu, Vicky & Faulkner, Stacey, eds. 2007. (J). 4.99 *(978-1-59198-413-9(0))* Creative Teaching Pr., Inc.

—Build-a-Skill Instant Books Short & Long Vowels. Callella, Kim. Shiotsu, Vicky & Faulkner, Stacey, eds. 2007. (J). 4.99 *(978-1-59198-412-2(2))* Creative Teaching Pr., Inc.

—Build-a-Skill Instant Books Sight Words, Part 1. Williams, Rozanne Lanczak. Faulkner, Stacey, ed. 2007. (J). 4.99 *(978-1-59198-414-6(9))* Creative Teaching Pr., Inc.

—Build-a-Skill Instant Books Sight Words, Part 2. Williams, Rozanne Lanczak. Faulkner, Stacey, ed. 2007. (J). 4.99 *(978-1-59198-415-3(7))* Creative Teaching Pr., Inc.

—Build-a-Skill Instant Books Time & Money. Cernek, Kim. Faulkner, Stacey, ed. 2007. (J). 4.99 *(978-1-59198-417-7(3))* Creative Teaching Pr., Inc.

—Build-a-Skill Instant Books Word Families-Long Vowels. Lubben, Amy & Williams, Rozanne Lanczak. Shiotsu, Vicky & Faulkner, Stacey, eds. 2007. (J). 4.99 *(978-1-59198-409-2(2))* Creative Teaching Pr., Inc.

—Build-a-Skill Instant Books Word Families-Short Vowels. Lubben, Amy & Williams, Rozanne Lanczak. Shiotsu, Vicky & Faulkner, Stacey, eds. 2007. (J). 4.99 *(978-1-59198-408-5(4))* Creative Teaching Pr., Inc.

Campbell, Jim, et al. An Inspector Calls. Priestley, J. B. Bryant, Clive, ed. 2012. (ENG.). 144p. (gr. 5). pap. 16.95 *(978-1-907127-23-6(2))* Classical Comics GBR. Dist: Perseus-PGW.

—An Inspector Calls. Priestley, J. B. Bryant, Clive, ed. 2012. (ENG.). 144p. pap. 16.95 *(978-1-907127-24-3(0))* Classical Comics GBR. Dist: Perseus-PGW.

Campbell, K. G. Flora & Ulysses: The Illuminated Adventures. DiCamillo, Kate. (ENG.). 240p. (J). (gr. 3-7). 2015. pap. 8.99 *(978-0-7636-7671-1(3));* 2013. 17.99 *(978-0-7636-6040-6(X))* Candlewick Pr.

Campbell, K. G. Who Wants a Tortoise? Keane, David. 2016. (J). ***(978-0-385-75417-0(5))*** Knopf, Alfred A. Inc.

Campbell, K. G. Lester's Dreadful Sweaters. Campbell, K. G. 2012. (ENG.). 32p. (J). 16.95 *(978-1-55453-770-9(3))* Kids Can Pr., Ltd. CAN. Dist: Univ. of Toronto Pr.

Campbell, Karen. Great Big Holy Bible: Fall Quarter, Year One. Vineyard Church of Columbus. 2007. (J). ring bd. 19.99 *(978-0-9786394-7-1(2))* Ampelon Publishing, LLC.

Campbell, Ken. Jeff & His Magic Hot Air Balloon. Cliffe, Kara. 2013. 44p. pap. 15.50 *(978-1-62212-186-1(4),* Strategic Bk. Publishing) Strategic Book Publishing & Rights Agency (SBPRA).

Campbell, Laurence. Girls in White Dresses. 2009. (ENG.). 120p. (gr. 13-17). pap. 16.99 *(978-0-7851-2520-4(5))* Marvel Worldwide, Inc.

Campbell, Lisa. The Worn-Out Backpack. Romagnoli, L. M. 2008. 15p. pap. 24.95 *(978-1-60563-934-5(6))* America Star Bks.

Campbell, Lorne, photos by. Get Cooking. Stern, Sam & Stern, Susan. 2009. (ENG.). 144p. (J). (gr. 5-18). pap. 17.99 *(978-0-7636-3926-6(5))* Candlewick Pr.

Campbell, Marie L. A Pocketful of Passage. 2007. (Great Lakes Books Ser.). (ENG.). 96p. (J). (gr. 3-7). per. 12.95 *(978-0-8143-3341-9(9),* 2078) Wayne State Univ. Pr.

Campbell-Quillen, Virginia. A Montana Love Affair: Letting Go & Being Free. McIntosh, Anne. 2005. (YA). 16.95 *(978-1-59494-008-8(8))* CPCC Pr.

Campbell, Ray. Landi of Terrebonne Bayou. Charlton, Ella Mae. 2012. 176p. 42.95 *(978-1-258-23763-9(6));* pap. 27.95 *(978-1-258-24653-2(8))* Literary Licensing, LLC.

Campbell, Richard P., photos by. Growing Patterns: Fibonacci Numbers in Nature. Campbell, Sarah C. 2010. (ENG.). 32p. (J). (gr. k-6). 17.95 *(978-1-59078-752-6(8))* Boyds Mills Pr.

Campbell, Richard P., jt. photos by see Campbell, Sarah C.

Campbell, Rod. Dear Zoo. Campbell, Rod. 2005. (Dear Zoo & Friends Ser.). (ENG.). 20p. (J). (gr. -1-k). 14.99 *(978-0-689-87751-3(X),* Little Simon) Little Simon.

—Dear Zoo. Campbell, Rod. 2004. 16p. (J). (VIE & ENG.). bds. *(978-1-84444-183-9(0));* (CHI & ENG.). bds. *(978-1-84444-171-6(7));* (RUS & ENG.). bds. *(978-1-84444-178-5(4));* (URD & ENG.). bds. *(978-1-84444-182-2(2));* (ENG & TUR.). bds. *(978-1-84444-181-5(4));* (ENG & SOM.). bds. *(978-1-84444-180-8(6));* (ENG & SPA.). bds. *(978-1-84444-179-2(2));* (ENG & POR.). bds. *(978-1-84444-177-8(6));* (ENG & PAN.). bds. *(978-1-84444-176-1(8));* (ENG & HIN.). bds. *(978-1-84444-175-4(X));* (ENG & GUJ.). bds. *(978-1-84444-174-7(1));* (ENG & FRE.). bds. *(978-1-84444-173-0(3));* (ENG & PER.). bds. *(978-1-84444-172-3(5));* (CHI & ENG.). bds. *(978-1-84444-170-9(9));* (ENG & ARA.). bds. *(978-1-84444-168-6(7));* (ENG & ALB.). bds. *(978-1-84444-167-9(9))* Mantra Lingua.

—Dear Zoo: From the Zoo. Campbell, Rod. 25th ed. 2007. (ENG.). 18p. (J). (gr. -1 — 1). bds. 6.99 *(978-1-4169-4737-0(X),* Little Simon) Little Simon.

Campbell, Ross. Leonardo. Lynch, Brian. 2015. (J). ***(978-1-61479-339-7(5))*** Spotlight.

Campbell, Ruth. Elf the Eagle. Butchart, Francis & Smith, Ron. 2007. (ENG.). 40p. 19.95 *(978-0-88982-241-2(7))* Oolichan Bks. CAN. Dist: Univ. of Toronto Pr.

—Jake, the Baker, Makes a Cake. Page, P. K. 2008. (ENG.). 40p. pap. 19.95 *(978-0-88982-245-0(X))* Oolichan Bks. CAN. Dist: Univ. of Toronto Pr.

—Mush & the Big Blue Flower. Payne, Laurie. 2007. (ENG.). 104p. (J). (gr. -1). pap. 12.95 *(978-0-88982-242-9(5))* Oolichan Bks. CAN. Dist: Univ. of Toronto Pr.

Campbell, Sarah C. & Campbell, Richard P., photos by. Mysterious Patterns: Finding Fractals in Nature. Campbell, Sarah C. 2014. (ENG.). 32p. (J). (gr. 2-5). 16.95 *(978-1-62091-627-8(4))* Boyds Mills Pr.

—Wolfsnail: A Backyard Predator. Campbell, Sarah C. 2008. (ENG.). 32p. (J). (gr. -1-2). 16.95 *(978-1-59078-554-6(1))* Boyds Mills Pr.

Campbell, Scott. East Dragon, West Dragon. Eversole, Robyn. 2012. (ENG.). 40p. (J). (gr. -1-2). 17.99 *(978-0-689-85828-4(0),* Atheneum Bks. for Young Readers) Simon & Schuster Children's Publishing.

—If Dogs Run Free. Dylan, Bob. 2013. (ENG.). 40p. (J). (gr. -1-3). 17.99 *(978-1-4516-4879-9(0))* Simon & Schuster Children's Publishing.

—Zombie in Love 2 + 1. DiPucchio, Kelly. 2014. (ENG.). 32p. (J). (gr. -1-3). 14.99 *(978-1-4424-5937-3(9),* Atheneum Bks. for Young Readers) Simon & Schuster Children's Publishing.

Campbell, Scott, jt. illus. see Joseph, Robin.

Campidelli, Maurizio, jt. illus. see Prasetya, Erwin.

Campion, Pascal. The Last Christmas Tree. Krensky, Stephen. 2014. (ENG.). 32p. (J). (gr. -1-k). 16.99 *(978-0-8037-3757-0(2),* Dial) Penguin Publishing Group.

—Me & Grandma. Catherine, Maria. 2015. (Time Together Ser.). (ENG.). 32p. (gr. -1-2). 8.95 *(978-1-4795-5795-0(1))* Picture Window Bks.

—Me & Grandpa. Catherine, Maria. 2015. (Time Together Ser.). (ENG.). 32p. (gr. -1-2). 8.95 *(978-1-4795-5796-7(X))* Picture Window Bks.

—Time Together: Me & Dad, 1 vol. Catherine, Maria. 2014. (Time Together Ser.). (ENG.). 32p. (gr. -1-2). 8.95 *(978-1-4795-2253-8(8),* Fiction Picture Bks.) Picture Window Bks.

—Time Together: Me & Mom, 1 vol. Catherine, Maria. 2014. (Time Together Ser.). (ENG.). 32p. (gr. -1-2). 8.95 *(978-1-4795-2252-1(X),* Fiction Picture Bks.) Picture Window Bks.

—We Are Twins. Driscoll, Laura. 2012. (Penguin Young Readers, Level 1 Ser.). (ENG.). 32p. (J). (gr. k-1). mass mkt. 3.99 *(978-0-448-46157-1(9),* Grosset & Dunlap) Penguin Publishing Group.

Campis, Adrian, Jr. A Journey with the Spider & Snake to Arizona. Cook, Beatrice. 2007. (J). 14.95 *(978-0-9795867-0-5(4))* Travel America Bks.

Campos F, Angel. La Conspiracion de Las Tias. Estrada, Gabriela Aguileta. rev. ed. 2007. (Castillo de la Lectura Verde Ser.). (SPA & ENG.). 136p. (J). (gr. 2-4). pap. 7.95 *(978-970-20-0174-4(9))* Castillo, Ediciones, S. A. de C. V. MEX. Dist: Macmillan.

Campos, Maria de Fatima, photos by. Cássio's Day: From Dawn to Dusk in a Brazilian Village. ed. 2010. (Child's Day Ser.). (ENG.). 32p. (J). (gr. k-3). pap. 8.95 *(978-1-84780-091-6(2),* Frances Lincoln) Quarto Publishing Group UK GBR. Dist: Hachette Bk. Group.

Camprubi, Krystal. The Magical World of Tolkien. Kloczko, Edouard. 2012. (ENG.). 28p. (J). (gr. 2). 24.95 *(978-2-7338-2151-0(2))* Auzou, Philippe Editions FRA. Dist: Consortium Bk. Sales & Distribution.

Camuncoli, Giuseppe, et al. The Amazing Spider-Man - Flying Blind. Slott, Dan & Waid, Mark. 2012. (ENG.). 120p. (J). (gr. 4-17). pap. 16.99 *(978-0-7851-6002-1(7))* Marvel Worldwide, Inc.

Camuncoli, Giuseppe, jt. illus. see Choi, Mike.

Camuncoli, Giuseppe, jt. illus. see Woods, Pete.

Canals, Mercè. La Leyenda de San Jorge. Farre, Lluis & Farré, Lluis. 2009. (SPA.). 14p. (J). (gr. -1-k). 18.95 *(978-84-9825-337-5(3))* Combel Editorial, S.A. ESP. Dist: Independent Pubs. Group.

Canals, Sonia. What Do Animals Eat for Lunch? Massey, Kay. 2009. (Little Green Footprints Ser.). 12p. (J). (gr. -1-k). bds. 11.40 *(978-1-60754-697-9(3))* Windmill Bks.

—Where Do Animals Hide? Massey, Kay. 2009. (Little Green Footprints Ser.). 12p. (J). (gr. -1-k). bds. 11.40 *(978-1-60754-696-2(5))* Windmill Bks.

Canals, Sonia & O'Toole, Jeanette. What Do You See in the Sea? Massey, Kay. 2009. (Little Green Footprints Ser.). 12p. (J). (gr. -1-k). bds. 11.40 *(978-1-60754-698-6(1))* Windmill Bks.

—What Is a Flower's Special Power? Massey, Kay. 2009. (Little Green Footprints Ser.). 12p. (J). (gr. -1-k). bds. 11.40 *(978-1-60754-695-5(7))* Windmill Bks.

Canas, Alicia. Federico Garcia Lorca para Ninos. Garcia Lorca, Federico X & Garcia Lorca, Federico. (Coleccion Grandes Autores para Ninos). (SPA.). 154p. (J). (gr. 4-6). 20.76 *(978-84-305-9302-6(0),* SU4866) Susaeta Ediciones, S.A. ESP. Dist: Lectorum Pubns., Inc.

Cañas, Alicia. El Hombre Que Perdió Su Imagen. Cañas, Alicia, tr. Sierra I. Fabra, Jordi & Sierra i Fabra, Jordi. 2nd ed. 2004.Tr. of Man Who Lost His Image. (SPA.). 128p. (J). (gr. 8-12). pap. 12.99 *(978-84-207-4478-0(6))* Grupo Anaya, S.A. ESP. Dist: Lectorum Pubns., Inc.

Canavan, Jean. Stevie Inchworm. Clinton, Ann M. 2009. 24p. (J). 31.99 *(978-1-4363-9471-0(6))* Xlibris Corp.

Cancio, Damian. Mirando y Mirando: La Gran Aventura. Gonzalez-Villariny, Natali. 2012.Tr. of Great Adventure. (SPA & ENG.). 10p. (J). 8.99 *(978-0-9765007-1-1(X))* Big-head fish.

Candace, Bonnie & Ellen. What to Do When You Worry Too Much: A Kid's Guide to Overcoming Anxiety. Huebner, Dawn. 2005. ("What to Do" Workbooks for Kids). 80p. (J). (gr. 1-7). per. 15.95 *(978-1-59147-314-5(4),* Magination Pr.) American Psychological Assn.

—Wishing Wellness: A Workbook for Children of Parents with Mental Illness. Clarke, Lisa Anne. 2006. 127p. (J). (gr. 1-7). per. 14.95 *(978-1-59147-313-8(6),* Magination Pr.) American Psychological Assn.

Candlewick Press, Candlewick & Ladybird Books Staff. Peppa Pig & the Busy Day at School. Candlewick Press, Candlewick. 2013. (Peppa Pig Ser.). (ENG.). 32p. (J). (-k). 12.99 *(978-0-7636-6525-8(8))* Candlewick Pr.

Candlewick Press Staff. Judy Moody & the Thrill Points Race. Michalak, Jamie. ed. 2011. (Judy Moody Ser.). (ENG.). 48p. (J). (gr. k-3). pap. 3.99 *(978-0-7636-5552-5(X))* Candlewick Pr.

—Out to Play. Blake, Michel. 2005. (Easy-Open Board Bks.). (ENG.). 16p. (J). (— 1). bds. 5.99 *(978-0-7636-2767-6(4))* Candlewick Pr.

Candlewick Press Staff. Peppa Pig & the Busy Day at School. Candlewick Press Staff. 2014. (Peppa Pig Ser.). (ENG.). 32p. (J). (-k). 4.99 *(978-0-7636-7227-0(0))* Candlewick Pr.

—Peppa Pig & the Lost Christmas List. Candlewick Press Staff. 2014. (Peppa Pig Ser.). (ENG.). 32p. (J). (-k). 5.99 *(978-0-7636-7456-4(7))* Candlewick Pr.

Candlewick Press Staff, jt. illus. see Reynolds, Peter H.

Candon, Jennifer. When Fuzzy Was Afraid: Of Losing His Mother. Maier, Inger M. 2004. 32p. (J). 14.95 *(978-1-59147-168-4(0));* pap. 9.95 *(978-1-59147-169-1(9))* American Psychological Assn. (Magination Pr.).

—When Fuzzy Was Afraid of Big & Loud Things. Maier, Inger M. 2005. (Fuzzy the Little Sheep Ser.). (J). (gr. -1-3). 32p. 14.95 *(978-1-59147-322-0(5));* 30p. per. 9.95 *(978-1-59147-323-7(3))* American Psychological Assn. (Magination Pr.).

—When Lizzie Was Afraid: Of Trying New Things. Maier, Inger M. 2004. 32p. (J). 14.95 *(978-1-59147-170-7(2));* pap. 9.95 *(978-1-59147-171-4(0))* American Psychological Assn. (Magination Pr.).

Canga, C. B. The Burglar Who Bit the Big Apple, 1 vol. Brezenoff, Steve. 2010. (Field Trip Mysteries Ser.). (ENG.). 88p. (gr. 2-3). 23.99 *(978-1-4342-2139-1(3));* pap. 6.10 *(978-1-4342-2771-3(5))* Stone Arch Bks.

—Celebrating Arizona: 50 States to Celebrate. Bauer, Marion Dane. 2013. (Green Light Readers Level 3 Ser.). (ENG.). 40p. (J). (gr. 1-4). 12.99 *(978-0-544-04387-9(1));* pap. 3.99 *(978-0-544-04419-7(3))* Houghton Mifflin Harcourt Publishing Co.

—Celebrating California: 50 States to Celebrate. Bauer, Marion Dane & Rucker, Justin. 2013. (Green Light Readers Level 3 Ser.). (ENG.). 40p. (J). (gr. 1-4). 12.99 *(978-0-547-98385-1(9));* pap. 3.99 *(978-0-547-89697-7(2))* Houghton Mifflin Harcourt Publishing Co.

—Celebrating Florida: 50 States to Celebrate. Bauer, Marion Dane. 2013. (Green Light Readers Level 3 Ser.). (ENG.). 40p. (J). (gr. 1-4). 12.99 *(978-0-547-89699-1(9));* pap. 3.99 *(978-0-547-89698-4(0))* Houghton Mifflin Harcourt Publishing Co.

—Celebrating Georgia: 50 States to Celebrate. Kurtz, Jane. 2015. (Green Light Readers Level 3 Ser.). (ENG.). 40p. (J). (gr. 1-4). pap. 3.99 *(978-0-544-41975-9(8),* HMH Books For Young Readers) Houghton Mifflin Harcourt Publishing Co.

—Celebrating Illinois: 50 States to Celebrate. Bauer, Marion Dane. 2014. (Green Light Readers Level 3 Ser.). (ENG.). 40p. (J). (gr. 1-4). pap. 3.99 *(978-0-544-12375-5(1),* HMH Books For Young Readers) Houghton Mifflin Harcourt Publishing Co.

—Celebrating Massachusetts: 50 States to Celebrate. Bauer, Marion Dane. 2014. (Green Light Readers Level 3 Ser.). (ENG.). 40p. (J). (gr. 1-4). 12.99 *(978-0-544-11944-4(4),* HMH Books For Young Readers) Houghton Mifflin Harcourt Publishing Co.

Canga, C. B. Celebrating New Jersey. Kurtz, Jane. 2015. (Green Light Readers Level 3 Ser.). (ENG.). 40p. (J). (gr. 1-4). 12.99 ***(978-0-544-41978-0(2),*** HMH Books For Young Readers) Houghton Mifflin Harcourt Publishing Co.

Canga, C. B. Celebrating New York: 50 States to Celebrate. Bauer, Marion Dane. 2013. (Green Light Readers Level 3 Ser.). (ENG.). 40p. (J). (gr. 1-4). 12.99 *(978-0-547-89782-0(0));* pap. 3.99 *(978-0-547-89781-3(2))* Houghton Mifflin Harcourt Publishing Co.

Canga, C. B. Celebrating Ohio. Kurtz, Jane. 2015. (Green Light Readers Level 3 Ser.). (ENG.). 40p. (J). (gr. 1-4). pap. 3.99 ***(978-0-544-41979-7(0),*** HMH Books For Young Readers) Houghton Mifflin Harcourt Publishing Co.

Canga, C. B. Celebrating Pennsylvania: 50 States to Celebrate. Kurtz, Jane. 2015. (Green Light Readers Level 3 Ser.). (ENG.). 40p. (J). (gr. 1-4). 12.99 *(978-0-544-41972-8(3),* HMH Books For Young Readers) Houghton Mifflin Harcourt Publishing Co.

—Celebrating Texas: 50 States to Celebrate. Bauer, Marion Dane. 2013. (Green Light Readers Level 3 Ser.). (ENG.). 40p. (J). (gr. 1-4). 12.99 *(978-0-547-98395-0(6));* pap. 3.99 *(978-0-547-89786-8(3))* Houghton Mifflin Harcourt Publishing Co.

—Celebrating Virginia & Washington, D. C. 50 States to Celebrate. Bauer, Marion Dane. 2013. (Green Light Readers Level 3 Ser.). (ENG.). 40p. (J). (gr. 1-4). 12.99 *(978-0-544-04407-4(X));* pap. 3.99 *(978-0-544-04417-3(7))* Houghton Mifflin Harcourt Publishing Co.

—The Crook Who Crossed the Golden Gate Bridge, 1 vol. Brezenoff, Steve. 2010. (Field Trip Mysteries Ser.). (ENG.). 88p. (gr. 2-3). 23.99 *(978-1-4342-2138-4(5));* pap. 6.10 *(978-1-4342-2770-6(7))* Stone Arch Bks.

—The Ghost Who Haunted the Capitol, 1 vol. Brezenoff, Steve. 2010. (Field Trip Mysteries Ser.). (ENG.). 88p. (gr. 2-3). 23.99 *(978-1-4342-2140-7(7));* pap. 6.10 *(978-1-4342-2772-0(3))* Stone Arch Bks.

Canga, C. B. Monica & the Bratty Stepsister, 1 vol. Gallagher, Diana G. 2010. (Monica Ser.). (ENG.). 88p. (gr. 2-3). 25.32 *(978-1-4342-1980-0(1))* Stone Arch Bks.

Canga, C. B. On the Bus, on the Case, 1 vol. Brezenoff, Steve. 2010. (Field Trip Mysteries Ser.). (ENG.). 240p. (gr. 3-6). 12.95 *(978-1-4342-2531-3(3))* Stone Arch Bks.

—The Painting That Wasn't There, 1 vol. Brezenoff, Steve. 2009. (Field Trip Mysteries Ser.). (ENG.). 88p. (gr. 2-3). lib. bdg. 23.99 *(978-1-4342-1608-3(X))* Stone Arch Bks.

Canga, C. B. Paul Bunyan vs. Hals Halson: The Giant Lumberjack Challenge! Bateman, Teresa. 2012. (J). 34.28 *(978-1-61913-126-2(9))* Weigl Pubs., Inc.

Canga, C. B. The Teacher Who Forgot Too Much, 1 vol. Brezenoff, Steve. 2009. (Field Trip Mysteries Ser.). (ENG.). 88p. (gr. 2-3). lib. bdg. 23.99 *(978-1-4342-1609-0(8))* Stone Arch Bks.

—The Village That Almost Vanished, 1 vol. Brezenoff, Steve. 2009. (Field Trip Mysteries Ser.). (ENG.). 88p. (gr. 2-3). lib. bdg. 23.99 *(978-1-4342-1611-3(X))* Stone Arch Bks.

—Your Life as a Settler in Colonial America. Troupe, Thomas Kingsley. 2012. (Way It Was Ser.). (ENG.). 32p. (gr. 2-3). pap. 7.95 *(978-1-4048-7251-6(5));* lib. bdg. 25.99 *(978-1-4048-7156-4(X))* Picture Window Bks. (Nonfiction Picture Bks.).

—The Zombie Who Visited New Orleans, 1 vol. Brezenoff, Steve. 2010. (Field Trip Mysteries Ser.). (ENG.). 88p. (gr. 2-3). 23.99 *(978-1-4342-2141-4(5));* pap. 6.10 *(978-1-4342-2773-7(1))* Stone Arch Bks.

—The Zoo with the Empty Cage, 1 vol. Brezenoff, Steve. 2009. (Field Trip Mysteries Ser.). (ENG.). 88p. (gr. 2-3). lib. bdg. 23.99 *(978-1-4342-1610-6(1))* Stone Arch Bks.

Caniac, Nina. Baby Pets Play! Caniac, Nina. 2012. (ENG.). 10p. (J). (gr. -1). 12.95 *(978-2-7338-2153-4(9))* Auzou, Philippe Editions FRA. Dist: Consortium Bk. Sales & Distribution.

Caniglia. Fuckin' Lie down Already. Piccirilli, Tom. 73p. (YA). 2005. pap. 11.95 *(978-0-9728656-6-1(7));* 2003. 45.00 *(978-0-9728656-1-6(6));* 2003. 100.00 *(978-0-9728656-0-9(8))* Endeavor Pr.

Cann, Helen. The Barefoot Book of Father & Daughter Tales. Evetts-Secker, Josephine. 2012. (ENG.). 96p. (J). 23.99 *(978-1-84686-761-3(4))* Barefoot Bks., Inc.

—Brigid's Cloak: An Ancient Irish Story. Milligan, Bryce. 32p. (J). (gr. k-17). 2005. pap., pap. 8.00 *(978-0-8028-5297-7(1),* Eerdmans Bks For Young Readers); 2004. 16.00 *(978-0-8028-5224-3(6))* Eerdmans, William B. Publishing Co.

—A Calendar of Festivals. Gilchrist, Cherry. 2006. 79p. (J). (gr. 4-8). reprint ed. pap. 10.00 *(978-1-4223-5551-0(9))* DIANE Publishing Co.

C

—Dance Stories. Stemple, Heidi E. Y. & Yolen, Jane. 2010. (ENG.). 99p. (J). (gr. 3-18). 21.99 (978-1-84686-219-9(1)) Barefoot Bks., Inc.

—A Forest of Stories. Singh, Rina. 2005. (ENG.). 80p. (J). pap. 12.99 (978-1-84148-882-0(8)) Barefoot Bks., Inc.

—A Forest of Stories: Magical Tree Tales from Around the World. Singh, Rina. 2003. 64p. (J). 19.99 (978-1-84148-963-6(8)) Barefoot Bks., Inc.

—Little Leap Forward: A Boy in Beijing. Yue, Guo & Farrow, Clare. 2008. (ENG.). 128p. (YA). (gr. 4-7). 16.99 (978-1-84686-114-7(4)) Barefoot Bks., Inc.

—Little Leap Forward: A Boy in Beijing. Yue, Gui & Farrow, Clare. 2011. (ENG.). 120p. (J). (gr. 3-6). pap. 12.99 (978-1-84686-539-8(5)) Barefoot Bks., Inc.

—Manger. Hopkins, Lee Bennett. 2014. 16.00 (978-0-8028-5419-3(2), Eerdmans Bks For Young Readers) Eerdmans, William B. Publishing Co.

—Mother & Daughter Tales. Evetts-Secker, Josephine. 2011. (ENG.). 40p. (J). 21.99 (978-1-84686-572-5(7)) Barefoot Bks., Inc.

—The Raiders Vol. 2: The Inuk Quartet. Riel, Jörn & Chodzin, Sherab. 2014. (ENG.). 112p. (J). pap. 12.99 (978-1-84686-744-6(4)) Barefoot Bks., Inc.

—Snow King. Howell, Gill. 2005. (ENG.). 24p. (J). lib. bdg. 23.65 (978-1-59646-742-2(8)) Dingles & Co.

—The Snowstorm. Riel, Jørn et al. 2012. (ENG.). 128p. (J). pap. 12.99 (978-1-84686-797-2(5)) Barefoot Bks., Inc.

—The Bible for Children. Watts, Murray. 2014. (ENG.). 352p. (J). (gr. 2-6). 17.95 (978-0-7459-4046-5(3)) Lion Hudson PLC GBR. Dist: Independent Pubs. Group.

—We're Riding on a Caravan: An Adventure on the Silk Road. Krebs, Laurie. (ENG.). 32p. (J). 2007. pap. 7.99 (978-1-84686-108-6(X)); 2005. 16.99 (978-1-84148-343-6(5)) Barefoot Bks., Inc.

Cann, Helen & Fox-Davies, Sarah. The Shipwreck: The Inuk Quartet, 4 vols. Riel, Jörn & Mason, John. 2011. (Inuk Quartet Ser.: 1). (ENG.). 36p. (J). pap. 12.99 (978-1-84686-335-6(X)) Barefoot Bks., Inc.

Cannavicci, Luigi A. Lucinda, Queen of Everything. Ciccone, Tiziana & Linardi, Franca. 2012. 36p. pap. 13.95 (978-1-61897-719-9(9), Strategic Bk. Publishing) Strategic Book Publishing & Rights Agency (SBPRA).

—Taylor, Please Stop Talking! Ciccone, Tiziana. 2013. 32p. pap. 12.95 (978-1-62516-817-7(9), Strategic Bk. Publishing) Strategic Book Publishing & Rights Agency (SBPRA).

Cannell, Jon. The Elephant from Baghdad, 0 vols. Holmes, Mary Tavener & Harris, John. 2012. (ENG.). 40p. (J). (gr. k-3). 17.99 (978-0-7614-6111-1(6), 9780761461111, Amazon Children's Publishing) Amazon Publishing.

—Get a Job at a Business. Jacobson, Ryan. 2014. (You're in Business! Ser.). (ENG.). 40p. (gr. 5-9). lib. bdg. 27.93 (978-1-4677-3838-5(7), Lerner Pubns.) Lerner Publishing Group.

—Get a Job Helping Others. Jacobson, Ryan. 2014. (You're in Business! Ser.). 40p. (J). (gr. 5-9). lib. bdg. 27.93 (978-1-4677-3836-1(0), Lerner Pubns.) Lerner Publishing Group.

—Get a Job Making Stuff to Sell. Jacobson, Ryan. 2014. (You're in Business! Ser.). 40p. (J). (gr. 5-9). lib. bdg. 27.93 (978-1-4677-3837-8(9), Lerner Pubns.) Lerner Publishing Group.

—Get a Summer Adventure Job. Jacobson, Ryan. 2014. (You're in Business! Ser.). (ENG.). 40p. (gr. 5-9). lib. bdg. 27.93 (978-1-4677-3839-2(5), Lerner Pubns.) Lerner Publishing Group.

—A Giraffe Goes to Paris, 0 vols. Holmes, Mary Tavener & Harris, John. 2010. (ENG.). 32p. (J). (gr. 1-4). 17.99 (978-0-7614-5595-0(7), 9780761455950, Amazon Children's Publishing) Amazon Publishing.

—Make It, Shake It, Mix It Up: 44 Bible Stories Brought to Life with Science. Kennedy, Nancy B. 2008. 61p. pap. 10.99 (978-0-7586-1334-9(2)) Concordia Publishing Hse.

—My Travels with Clara. Holmes, Mary Tavener. 2007. (ENG.). 32p. (gr. 3-7). 17.95 (978-0-89236-880-8(2)) Oxford Univ. Pr., Inc.

Cannella, Marco & Marron, Jose Luis. Tattoo of Death. 2007. (Choose Your Own Adventure Ser.: No. 22). 113p. (J). (gr. 4-7). pap. 6.99 (978-1-933390-22-2(0)) Chooseco LLC.

Cannella, Marco, jt. illus. see Louie, Wes.

Cannella, Marco, jt. illus. see Semionov, Vladimir.

Canning, Seán. The Cat That Loves to Eat. Canning, Seán. Canning, Erin, ed. 2005. (J). 9.95 (978-0-9773134-0-2(9)) SP Family Productions, LLC.

Cannon. Stranger Danger. Potter, Noel Gyro. 2010. (Adventures of Marshall & Art Set 2 Ser.). (ENG.). 32p. (gr. -1-4). 28.50 (978-1-60270-738-2(3), Looking Glass Library) ABDO Publishing Co.

Cannon, Annie. Horseshoe Crabs & Shorebirds: The Story of a Food Web, 1 vol. Crenson, Victoria. 2003. (ENG.). 32p. (J). (gr. 3-5). 16.95 (978-0-7614-5115-0(3)) Marshall Cavendish Corp.

—Horseshoe Crabs & Shorebirds: The Story of a Foodweb, 0 vols. Crenson, Victoria. unabr. ed. 2009. (ENG.). 32p. (J). (gr. 3-5). pap. 9.99 (978-0-7614-5552-3(3), 9780761455523, Amazon Children's Publishing) Amazon Publishing.

Cannon, Janell. Pinduli. Cannon, Janell. 2004. (ENG.). 48p. (J). (gr. -1-3). 17.99 (978-0-15-204668-2(2)) Houghton Mifflin Harcourt Publishing Co.

Cannon, Joseph. Dibble Can't Dribble. Potter, Noel Gyro. 2008. (Adventures of Marshall & Art Ser.). (ENG.). 32p. (gr. -1-4). 28.50 net. (978-1-60270-197-7(0), Looking Glass Library) ABDO Publishing Co.

—Joey Panda & His Food Allergies Save the Day. Murthy, Amishi & Chou, Vivian. 2013. (ENG.). 32p. pap. 12.95 (978-0-615-66842-0(9)) Chicago Allergist Pubns.

—Lost in the Mall. Potter, Noel Gyro. 2008. (Adventures of Marshall & Art Ser.). (ENG.). 32p. (gr. -1-4). 28.50 (978-1-60270-198-4(9), Looking Glass Library) ABDO Publishing Co.

—Plan B. Potter, Noel Gyro. 2010. (Adventures of Marshall & Art Set 2 Ser.). (ENG.). 32p. (gr. -1-4). 28.50 (978-1-60270-736-8(7), Looking Glass Library) ABDO Publishing Co.

—The Spoiled Sport. Potter, Noel Gyro. 2010. (Adventures of Marshall & Art Set 2 Ser.). (ENG.). 32p. (gr. -1-4). 28.50 (978-1-60270-737-5(5), Looking Glass Library) ABDO Publishing Co.

—A Very Sticky Situation. Potter, Noel Gyro. 2008. (Adventures of Marshall & Art Ser.). (ENG.). 32p. (gr. -1-4). 28.50 (978-1-60270-201-1(2), Looking Glass Library) ABDO Publishing Co.

—A Wheel Life Lesson. Potter, Noel Gyro. 2008. (Adventures of Marshall & Art Ser.). (ENG.). 32p. (gr. -1-4). 28.50 (978-1-60270-202-8(0), Looking Glass Library) ABDO Publishing Co.

—Writing a Wrong. Potter, Noel Gyro. 2010. (Adventures of Marshall & Art Set 2 Ser.). (ENG.). 32p. (gr. -1-4). 28.50 (978-1-60270-739-9(1), Looking Glass Library) ABDO Publishing Co.

Cannon, Kevin & Cannon, Zander. T-Minus: The Race to the Moon. Ottaviani, Jim. 2009. (ENG.). 128p. (J). (gr. 3-7). 21.99 (978-1-4169-8682-9(0), Simon & Schuster/Paula Wiseman Bks.) Simon & Schuster/Paula Wiseman Bks.

Cannon, Kevin, jt. illus. see Cannon, Zander.

Cannon, Martin. Toad Catchers' Creek. Weiner, Brian. Weintraub, Claudia & Frederick, Robin, eds. 2005. 40p. (J). lib. bdg. 17.99 (978-1-932949-58-2(5)) Illusion Factory, The.

Cannon, Nick, et al. Neon Aliens Ate My Homework: And Other Poems. Scholastic, Inc. Staff & Cannon, Nick. 2015. (ENG.). 144p. (J). (gr. 2-5). 14.99 (978-0-545-72281-0(0)) Scholastic, Inc.

Cannon, Zander & Cannon, Kevin. T-Minus: The Race to the Moon. Ottaviani, Jim. 2009. (ENG.). 128p. (J). (gr. 3-7). pap. 15.99 (978-1-4169-4960-2(7), Simon & Schuster/Paula Wiseman Bks.) Simon & Schuster/Paula Wiseman Bks.

Cannon, Zander, jt. illus. see Cannon, Kevin.

Cannone, Gregory. Rockie Rock-A-Teller on Preparing for the Loudy-Cloudy-Typhooner-Kaboomer. Mittmann, Gerald & Mittmann, Laura. 2013. 76p. 19.95 (978-1-4910-4330-1(X)) Lighthouse Publishing of the Carolinas.

Cano, Fernando. Above, 1 vol. Terrell, Brandon. 2013. (Tony Hawk: Live2Skate Ser.). (ENG.). 72p. (gr. 3-4). pap. 5.95 (978-1-4342-6186-1(7)); pap. 35.70 (978-1-4342-6266-0(9), Tony Hawk's 900 Revolution); lib. bdg. 23.99 (978-1-4342-4084-2(3)) Stone Arch Bks.

—At Large, 1 vol. Steele, Michael Anthony. 2013. (Tony Hawk: Live2Skate Ser.). (ENG.). 72p. (gr. 3-4). pap. 5.95 (978-1-4342-6189-2(1)) Stone Arch Bks.

—At Large, 1 vol. Steele, Michael A. 2013. (Tony Hawk: Live2Skate Ser.). (ENG.). 72p. (gr. 3-4). lib. bdg. 23.99 (978-1-4342-4087-3(8)) Stone Arch Bks.

—Daring, 1 vol. Hoena, Blake. 2014. (Tony Hawk: Live2Skate Ser.). (ENG.). 72p. (gr. 3-4). lib. bdg. 23.99 (978-1-4342-9139-4(1)) Stone Arch Bks.

—Fearless, 1 vol. Terrell, Brandon. 2014. (Tony Hawk: Live2Skate Ser.). (ENG.). 72p. (gr. 3-4). 23.99 (978-1-4342-9141-7(3), Tony Hawk's 900 Revolution) Stone Arch Bks.

—Fresh, 1 vol. Steele, Michael Anthony. 2014. (Tony Hawk: Live2Skate Ser.). (ENG.). 72p. (gr. 3-4). lib. bdg. 23.99 (978-1-4342-9140-0(5)) Stone Arch Bks.

—On Cue, 1 vol. Steele, Michael A. 2014. (Tony Hawk: Live2Skate Ser.). (ENG.). 72p. (gr. 3-4). pap. 5.95 (978-1-4342-6559-3(5), Tony Hawk's 900 Revolution) Stone Arch Bks.

Cano, Fernando. Peter Pan. Hoena, B. A. & Barrie, J. M. 2015. (Graphic Revolve: Common Core Editions Ser.). (ENG.). 72p. (gr. 2-3). lib. bdg. 26.65 **(978-1-4965-0372-5(4))** Stone Arch Bks.

Cano, Fernando. Raw. Hoena, Blake A. 2013. (Tony Hawk: Live2Skate Ser.). (ENG.). 72p. (gr. 3-4). pap. 35.70 (978-1-4342-6268-4(5), Tony Hawk's 900 Revolution) Stone Arch Bks.

—Raw, 1 vol. Hoena, Blake A. 2013. (Tony Hawk: Live2Skate Ser.). (ENG.). 72p. (gr. 3-4). pap. 5.95 (978-1-4342-6188-5(3)); lib. bdg. 23.99 (978-1-4342-4086-6(X)) Stone Arch Bks.

—Revive, 1 vol. Steele, Michael A. 2014. (Tony Hawk: Live2Skate Ser.). (ENG.). 72p. (gr. 3-4). pap. 5.95 (978-1-4342-6560-9(9), Tony Hawk's 900 Revolution) Stone Arch Bks.

—Rival, 1 vol. Hoena, Blake A. 2014. (Tony Hawk: Live2Skate Ser.). (ENG.). 72p. (gr. 3-4). pap. 5.95 (978-1-4342-6562-3(5), Tony Hawk's 900 Revolution) Stone Arch Bks.

—Strong, 1 vol. Manning, Matthew K. 2013. (Tony Hawk: Live2Skate Ser.). (ENG.). 72p. (gr. 3-4). pap. 5.95 (978-1-4342-6187-8(5)); lib. bdg. 23.99 (978-1-4342-4085-9(1)) Stone Arch Bks.

—Super Billy Goats Gruff. Tulien, Sean. 2015. (Far Out Fairy Tales Ser.). (ENG.). 40p. (gr. 3-4). lib. bdg. 23.99 (978-1-4342-9649-8(0)) Stone Arch Bks.

Cano, Fernando M., jt. illus. see Aburto, Jesus.

Cantalapiedra, Jose. Plumas en la Pradera. Lopez, Minia. 2006. (SPA.). (J). 10.00 (978-0-9773531-5-6(X)) Charming Pubns.

Cantell, Brenda. Digging for Buried Treasure. Thompson, Lisa. 2006. (Treasure Trackers Ser.). 80p. (J). (gr. 3-4). lib. bdg. 19.00 (978-0-7910-8872-2(3), Chelsea Hse.) Facts On File, Inc.

—In Search of the Egyptian Queen. Thompson, Lisa. 2006. (Treasure Trackers Ser.). 80p. (J). (gr. 3-4). lib. bdg. 19.00 (978-0-7910-8874-6(X)) Facts On File, Inc.

Canter, Idalia. Hansi & the Ice Man. Ebel, Julia Taylor, Jr. 2014. 32p. (YA). lib. bdg. 19.95 (978-1-933251-81-3(6)) Parkway Pubs., Inc.

—The Picture Man. Ebel, Julia Taylor. 2009. (ENG.). 32p. (J). 16.95 (978-1-933251-63-9(8)) Parkway Pubs., Inc.

Cantini, Barbara. Anyone but Ivy Pocket. Krisp, Caleb. 2015. (Ivy Pocket Ser.: 1). 400p. (J). (gr. 3-7). 17.99 (978-0-06-236434-0(0), Greenwillow Bks.) HarperCollins Pubs.

Cantone, Anna Laura. Hansel & Gretel, 1 vol. Piumini, Roberto. 2009. (Storybook Classics Ser.). (ENG.). 32p. (gr. 3-4). lib. bdg. 25.32 (978-1-4048-5500-7(9), Fiction Picture Bks.) Picture Window Bks.

Cantone, Anna-Laura. Mama Robot. Cali, Davide. Danesi, Marcel, tr. from ITA. 2008. (ENG.). 32p. (J). (gr. -1-1). 17.95 (978-0-88776-873-6(3), Tundra Bks.) Tundra Bks. CAN. Dist: Penguin Random Hse., LLC.

Cantone, AnnaLaura. Pecorino Plays Ball. Madison, Alan. 2006. (ENG.). 40p. (J). (gr. -1-3). 15.95 (978-0-689-86522-0(8), Atheneum Bks. for Young Readers) Simon & Schuster Children's Publishing.

—Pecorino's First Concert. Madison, Alan. 2010. (ENG.). 40p. (J). (gr. -1-3). 16.99 (978-1-4424-2191-2(6), Atheneum Bks. for Young Readers) Simon & Schuster Children's Publishing.

Cantor, Patricia. Christopher SAT Straight up in Bed. Long, Kathy. 2012. 32p. (J). 16.00 (978-0-8028-5359-2(5), Eerdmans Bks For Young Readers) Eerdmans, William B. Publishing Co.

—Sleeping Bootsie. Boelts, Maribeth. 2011. (Step into Reading Ser.). (ENG.). 48p. (J). (gr. k-3). pap. 3.99 (978-0-375-86678-4(7)) Random Hse. Children's Bks.

Cantrell, Katie. The Magic of Giving, 1 vol. Dunston, Marc. 2010. (ENG.). 32p. (J). (gr. k-3). 16.99 (978-1-58980-805-8(3)) Pelican Publishing Co., Inc.

Cantucci, Alessandro & Morandi, Andrea. Ancient Mesopotamian Civilization. Wildwood, Gretchen. 2009. (Ancient Civilizations & Their Myths & Legends Ser.). (YA). (gr. 5-9). lib. bdg. 29.25 (978-1-4042-8037-3(5)) Rosen Publishing Group, Inc., The.

Canty, Charlotte. Something So Big. Waddell, Martin. 2004. (ENG.). 24p. (J). lib. bdg. 23.65 (978-1-59646-706-4(1)) Dingles & Co.

Canyon, Christopher. Ancient Rhymes, a Dolphin Lullaby. Denver, John. 2004. (Sharing Nature with Children Book Ser.). 36p. (J). (gr. -1-6). 8.95 (978-1-58469-065-8(8)) Dawn Pubns.

—Ancient Rhymes, a Dolphin Lullaby: With Audio CD & Score. Denver, John. 2004. (Sharing Nature with Children Book Ser.). 36p. (J). (gr. -1-6). 19.95 incl. audio compact disk (978-1-58469-064-1(X)) Dawn Pubns.

—Earth & Me, Our Family Tree: Nature's Creatures. Lewis, J. Patrick. 2004. (Sharing Nature with Children Book Ser.). 36p. (J). (gr. -1-5). 16.95 (978-1-58469-031-3(3)); pap. 7.95 (978-1-58469-030-6(5)) Dawn Pubns.

—Earth & Us-Continuous: Earth's Past & Future. Lewis, J. Patrick. 2004. (Sharing Nature with Children Book Ser.). 36p. (J). 16.95 (978-1-58469-024-5(0)); pap. 7.95 (978-1-58469-023-8(2)) Dawn Pubns.

—Earth & You - A Closer View: Nature's Features. Lewis, J. Patrick. 2004. (Sharing Nature with Children Book Ser.). 36p. (J). (gr. -1-3). 16.95 (978-1-58469-016-0(X)); (gr. 4-7). pap. 7.95 (978-1-58469-015-3(1)) Dawn Pubns.

—Grandma's Feather Bed. Denver, John. 2007. (Sharing Nature with Children Book Ser.). 36p. (J). (gr. -1-18). pap. 8.95 (978-1-58469-096-2(8)) Dawn Pubns.

—John Denver's Grandma's Feather Bed. Denver, John. 2007. (Sharing Nature with Children Book Ser.). 36p. (J). (gr. -1-3). 19.95 incl. audio compact disk (978-1-58469-095-5(X)) Dawn Pubns.

—John Denver's Sunshine on My Shoulders. Denver, John. 2004. 32p. pap. 8.95 incl. audio compact disk (978-1-58469-050-4(X)) Dawn Pubns.

—John Denver's Take Me Home, Country Roads. 2005. (John Denver & Kids! Ser.). 32p. (J). (gr. -1-3). 8.95 (978-1-58469-073-3(9)) Dawn Pubns.

Canyon, Christopher. John Denver's Take Me Home, Country Roads. Canyon, Christopher, adapted by. 2005. (John Denver & Kids! Ser.). 32p. (J). (gr. -1-3). 19.95 incl. audio compact disk (978-1-58469-072-6(0)) Dawn Pubns.

Canyon, Christopher. Sunshine on My Shoulders. Canyon, Christopher, tr. Denver, John. 2004. 32p. 19.95 incl. audio compact disk (978-1-58469-048-1(8)) Dawn Pubns.

Canyon, Jeanette. Over in the Jungle: A Rainforest Rhyme. Berkes, Marianne. 2007. 32p. (J). (gr. -1-2). 16.95 (978-1-58469-091-7(7)) Dawn Pubns.

—Over in the Jungle: A Rainforest Rhyme. Berkes, Marianne Collins. 2007. (Sharing Nature with Children Book Ser.). 32p. (J). (gr. -1-3). 8.95 (978-1-58469-092-4(5)) Dawn Pubns.

—Over in the Ocean: In a Coral Reef. Berkes, Marianne. (Simply Nature Bks.). (J). (gr. -1). 2006. 26p. bds. 7.95 (978-1-58469-082-5(8)); 2004. 32p. 16.95 (978-1-58469-063-4(1)); 2004. 36p. pap. 8.95 (978-1-58469-062-7(3)) Dawn Pubns.

Capa, Robert, photos by. Robert Capa: The Definitive Collection. Whelan, Richard. rev. ed. 2004. (ENG., 572p. (gr. 8-17). pap. 45.00 (978-0-7148-4449-7(7)) Phaidon Pr. Ltd. GBR. Dist: Hachette Bk. Group.

Capaldi, Gina. Dancing on Grapes. Buonanno, Graziella Pacini. 2011. (ENG.). 32p. (J). (gr. k-3). 16.95 (978-1-59078-833-2(8)) Boyds Mills Pr.

—Jobs from A to Z. Mangrum, Allison. 2006. 28p. pap. 9.50 (978-1-55501-675-3(8)) Ballard & Tighe Pubs.

—Misiones Espanolas (Spanish Missions) Lilly, Melinda. 2005. (Lecturas Historicas Norteamericanas (Reading American Histor Ser.). 24p. (J). (gr. 3-7). lib. bdg. 22.79 (978-1-59515-638-9(0)) Rourke Educational Media.

—What Anna Loves. Simmons, Andra. 2006. 24p. (J). (gr. -1-3). 15.95 (978-1-59714-044-7(9)) Heyday.

Capaldi, Gina. Arts & Crafts Across the USA. Capaldi, Gina. Rife, Douglas M. Mitchell, Judith, ed. 2005. 240p. (J). pap. 19.95 (978-1-57310-445-6(0)) Teaching & Learning Co.

—A Boy Named Beckoning: The True Story of Dr. Carlos Montezuma, Native American Hero. Capaldi, Gina. 2008. (Exceptional Social Studies Titles for Intermediate Grades). (ENG.). 32p. (J). (gr. 3-6). lib. bdg. 16.95 (978-0-8225-7644-0(9)) Lerner Publishing Group.

—Red Bird Sings: The Story of Zitkala-Sa, Native American Author, Musician, & Activist. Capaldi, Gina. Pearce, Q. L. 2011. (Exceptional Social Studies Titles for Intermediate Grades Ser.). (ENG.). 32p. (J). (gr. 3-6). lib. bdg. 17.95 (978-0-7613-5257-0(0), Carolrhoda Bks.) Lerner Publishing Group.

Capaldi, Mario. Odysseus & the Wooden Horse: A Greek Legend. 2003. (Dominie Collection of Myths & Legends). (SPA.). 20p. (J). pap. (978-0-7685-2128-3(9)); lib. bdg. (978-0-7685-2425-3(3)) Dominie Pr., Inc.

Caparo, Antonio. The Secret of Rover. Wildavsky, Rachel. (ENG.). (J). 2015. 360p. (gr. 4-8). pap. 7.95 **(978-1-4197-1968-4(8))**; 2011. 368p. (gr. 5-9). 17.95 (978-0-8109-9710-3(X)) Abrams. (Amulet Bks.).

Caparo, Antonio Javier. The Circle Maker for Kids: One Prayer Can Change Everything, 1 vol. Batterson, Mark. 2013. (ENG.). 32p. (J). 15.99 (978-0-310-72492-6(9)) Zonderkidz.

—Found. Prineas, Sarah. 2011. (Magic Thief Ser.: 3). (ENG.). 384p. (J). (gr. 5). pap. 7.99 (978-0-06-137595-8(0)) HarperCollins Pubs.

Caparó, Antonio Javier. Gulliver in Lilliput. Findlay, Lisa & Swift, Jonathan. 2010. (Step into Reading Ser.). (ENG.). 48p. (J). (gr. k-3). pap. 3.99 (978-0-375-86585-5(3)) Random Hse., Inc.

—The Ice Dragon. Abbott, Tony. 2012. (Underworlds Ser.: 4). (ENG.). 128p. (J). (gr. 2-5). pap. 4.99 (978-0-545-30834-2(8), Scholastic Paperbacks) Scholastic, Inc.

Caparo, Antonio Javier. Lost. Prineas, Sarah. 2009. (Magic Thief Ser.: 2). (ENG.). 400p. (J). (gr. 5-18). 17.99 (978-0-06-137589-7(6)) HarperCollins Pubs.

—The Lost Treasure of Tuckernuck. Fairlie, Emily. (Tuckernuck Mysteries Ser.: 1). (ENG.). (J). (gr. 3-7). 2013. 320p. pap. 6.99 (978-0-06-211891-2(9)); 2012. 304p. 16.99 (978-0-06-211890-5(0)) HarperCollins Pubs. (Tegen, Katherine Bks).

—The Magic Thief. Prineas, Sarah. (Magic Thief Ser.: 1). (ENG.). (J). (gr. 5). 2009. 448p. pap. 7.99 (978-0-06-137590-3(X)); 2008. 432p. 16.99 (978-0-06-137587-3(X)) HarperCollins Pubs.

—The Magic Thief - Found. Prineas, Sarah. 2010. (Magic Thief Ser.: 3). (ENG.). 368p. (J). (gr. 5-18). 16.99 (978-0-06-137593-4(4)) HarperCollins Pubs.

Caparo, Antonio Javier. The Magic Thief - Home. Prineas, Sarah. 2015. (Magic Thief Ser.: 4). (ENG.). 416p. (J). (gr. 3-7). pap. 7.99 **(978-0-06-220956-6(6))** HarperCollins Pubs.

Caparo, Antonio Javier. The Magic Thief - Lost. Prineas, Sarah. 2010. (Magic Thief Ser.: 2). (ENG.). 416p. (J). (gr. 5). pap. 7.99 (978-0-06-137592-7(6)) HarperCollins Pubs.

—The Magic Thief: Home. Prineas, Sarah. 2014. (Magic Thief Ser.: 4). (ENG.). 416p. (J). (gr. 3-7). 17.99 (978-0-06-220954-2(X)) HarperCollins Pubs.

—The Magician's Bird. Fairlie, Emily. 2014. (Tuckernuck Mysteries Ser.: 2). (ENG.). 288p. (J). (gr. 3-7). pap. 6.99 (978-0-06-211894-3(3), Tegen, Katherine Bks) HarperCollins Pubs.

Caparó, Antonio Javier. Missing on Superstition Mountain. Broach, Elise. 2011. (Superstition Mountain Mysteries Ser.: 1). (ENG.). 272p. (J). (gr. 3-7). 15.99 (978-0-8050-9047-5(9), Holt, Henry & Co. Bks. For Young Readers) Holt, Henry & Co.

Caparo, Antonio Javier. Rudolph Shines Again. May, Robert L. 2015. (ENG.). 40p. (J). (gr. -1-1). 17.99 **(978-1-4424-7498-7(X)**, Little Simon) Little Simon.

Caparo, Antonio Javier. The Shark Rider. Prager, Ellen. 2015. (Tristan Hunt & the Sea Guardians Ser.: 2). (ENG.). 326p. (J). (gr. 3-7). pap. 9.95 (978-1-938063-51-0(1), Mighty Media Junior Readers) Mighty Media Pr.

—The Shark Whisperer. Prager, Ellen. 2014. (Tristan Hunt & the Sea Guardians Ser.). (ENG.). 288p. (J). (gr. 3-7). pap. 9.95 (978-1-938063-44-2(9), Mighty Media Junior Readers) Mighty Media Pr.

Caparó, Antonio Javier. Treasure on Superstition Mountain. Broach, Elise. 2013. (Superstition Mountain Mysteries Ser.: 2). (ENG.). 288p. (J). (gr. 3-7). 15.99 (978-0-8050-7763-6(4), Holt, Henry & Co. Bks. For Young Readers) Holt, Henry & Co.

Caparo, Antonio Javier. Treasure on Superstition Mountain. Broach, Elise. 2014. (Superstition Mountain Mysteries Ser.: 2). (ENG.). 304p. (J). (gr. 3-7). pap. 7.99 (978-1-250-03990-3(8)) Square Fish.

Capdevila, Francesc. The Little Mermaid. Andersen, Hans Christian. 2003. (Bilingual Fairy Tales Ser.: BILI).Tr. of Sirenita. (ENG & SPA.). 32p. (J). (gr. -1-7). pap. 6.99 (978-0-8118-3911-2(7)) Chronicle Bks. LLC.

—Thumbelina. Chronicle Books Staff. ed. 2004. (Bilingual Fairy Tales Ser.: BILI). (ENG & SPA.). 32p. (J). (gr. -1-7). pap. 6.99 (978-0-8118-3928-0(1)) Chronicle Bks. LLC.

—The Ugly Duckling. Bas, Mercè Escardó I & Boada, Francesc. 2004. (Bilingual Fairy Tales Ser.: BILI). (ENG.). 32p. (J). (gr. -1-7). 6.99 (978-0-8118-4455-0(2)) Chronicle Bks. LLC.

Capdevila, Roser. Aprendamos a Convivir. Ballart, Elisabet.Tr. of Let's Learn to Get Along. (SPA.). 48p. (J). (gr. 3-5). 13.56 (978-84-233-3109-3(1)) Ediciones Destino ESP. Dist: Lectorum Pubns., Inc.

—Atencion, Bebe Ataca! Joly, Fanny. 2003. (Coleccion Bebe). (SPA.). (J). (gr. 1-3). (978-84-246-3652-4(X), GL30758) La Galera, S.A. Editorial ESP. Dist: Lectorum Pubns., Inc.

—Un Bebe? Que Mala Idea! Joly, Fanny. 2003. (Coleccion Bebe). (SPA.). (J). (gr. 1-3). (978-84-246-3651-7(1), GL30757) La Galera, S.A. Editorial ESP. Dist: Lectorum Pubns., Inc.

Capelle, Joanna. Pumpkin in Hollow Countdown. Evans, Alwyn & Davis, Anne. 16p. (J). pap. 7.49 (978-1-86368-045-5(4)) Fremantle Pr. AUS. Dist: Independent Pubs. Group.

Caple, Kathy. Duck & Company. Caple, Kathy. 2007. (Holiday House Readers: Level 2 Ser.). (ENG.). 32p. (J). (gr. -1-3). pap. 4.95 (978-0-8234-2125-1(2)); (gr. k-3). 14.95 (978-0-8234-1993-7(2)) Holiday Hse., Inc.

—Duck & Company Christmas. Caple, Kathy. 2011. (ENG.). 48p. (J). 15.95 (978-0-8234-2239-5(9)) Holiday Hse., Inc.

—A Night at the Zoo. Caple, Kathy. 2014. (ENG.). 24p. (J). (gr. -1-3). 14.95 (978-0-8234-3044-4(8)) Holiday Hse., Inc.

—Termite Tales. Caple, Kathy. 2009. (Brand New Readers Ser.). (ENG.). 48p. (J). (gr. -1-3). pap. 5.99 (978-0-7636-3901-3(X)) Candlewick Pr.

—Termite Trouble: Brand New Readers. Caple, Kathy. 2005. (Brand New Readers Ser.). (ENG.). 32p. (J). (gr. -1-3). pap. 5.99 *(978-0-7636-2573-3(6))* Candlewick Pr.

Caple, Laurie. Farm Crossing: The Amazing Adventures of Addie & Zachary. Bushnell, Jack. 2005. 96p. (gr. 3-8). pap. 9.95 *(978-0-9636191-5-0(2))* Chippewa Valley Museum.

Caple, Laurie. Hungry Coyote. Blackford, Cheryl. 2015. (ENG.). 32p. (J). (gr. -1-2). 16.95 ***(978-0-87351-964-9(7))*** Minnesota Historical Society Pr.

Caple, Laurie. The Legend of Old Abe: A Civil War Eagle. Wargin, Kathy-jo. 2006. (Legend (Sleeping Bear) Ser.). (ENG.). 40p. (J). (gr. 3-7). 17.95 *(978-1-58536-232-5(8))* Sleeping Bear Pr.

—North Star Numbers: A Minnesota Number Book. Wargin, Kathy-jo. 2008. (Count Your Way Across the U. S. A. Ser.). (ENG.). 40p. (J). (gr. -1-3). 17.95 *(978-1-58536-187-8(9))* Sleeping Bear Pr.

Caple, Laurie A. Sweet Dreams, Wild Animals! A Story of Sleep. Meyer, Eileen R. 2015. (J). ***(978-0-87842-637-9(X))*** Mountain Pr. Publishing Co., Inc.

Capon, Brian. Plant Survival: Adapting to a Hostile World. Capon, Brian. 2009. (ENG.). 144p. pap. 15.95 *(978-0-88192-287-5(0),* 682287) Timber Pr., Inc.

Capon, Jenny. A Little Book of Alliterations. Arthur, Felix. 2011. (Inside Pocket Single Titles Ser.). (ENG.). 64p. (J). (gr. k-3). 7.99 *(978-0-9562315-5-0(1),* Inside Pocket Publishing) Lerner Publishing Group.

Caponigro, Laureen. Whistling Dixie. Phillips, Dixie. 2012. 16p. pap. 9.95 *(978-1-61633-272-3(7))* Guardian Angel Publishing, Inc.

Cappoen, Jennifer Tipton. Little Boys Run. Little Boys Play. Dixon, Dallas L. Williams, Nancy E., ed. 2013. 44p. (J). pap. 12.98 *(978-1-938526-40-4(6))* Laurus Bks.

—The Miracle of Susie the Puppy That Changed the Law. Lawrence, Donna. Coble, Lynn Bemer, ed. 2012. 54p. 24.95 *(978-0-9846724-2-4(7))* Paws and Claws Publishing, LLC.

—Shelby's Shoes. Dixon, Dallas L. Williams, Nancy E., ed. 2013. 24p. (J). pap. 12.98 *(978-1-938526-33-6(3))* Laurus Bks.

—The Shoe, the Necklace, & the Giant. Ghani, Samna. Williams, Nancy E., ed. 2012. 48p. (J). pap. 9.95 *(978-1-938526-18-3(X))* Roxby Media Ltd. GBR. Dist: Laurus Co., The.

—Susie's Tale Hand with Paw We Changed the Law. Lawrence, Donna. Coble, Lynn Bemer, ed. 2012. 64p. 24.95 *(978-0-9846724-1-7(9))* Paws and Claws Publishing, LLC.

—The Tooth Fairy Goes to School. Ghani, Samna. Williams, Nancy E., ed. 2013. 44p. (J). pap. 10.98 *(978-1-938526-31-2(7))* Laurus Bks.

Cappoli, Sara. Firebirds. Jeffrey, Gary. 2012. (Graphic Mythical Creatures Ser.). (ENG.). 24p. (J). (gr. 3-5). pap. 8.15 *(978-1-4339-6757-3(X))*; lib. bdg. 23.95 *(978-1-4339-6755-9(3))* Stevens, Gareth Publishing LLLP. (Gareth Stevens Learning Library).

Cappon, Manuela, et al. Everyday Life of the Aztecs, Incas & Mayans. Grant, Neil. 2003. (Uncovering History Ser.). 46p. (J). lib. bdg. 28.50 *(978-1-58340-253-5(5))* Black Rabbit Bks.

Cappon, Manuela. Everyday Life of the Celts. Grant, Neil. 2004. (Uncovering History Ser.). 46p. (J). (gr. 4-7). lib. bdg. 19.95 *(978-1-58340-252-8(7))* Black Rabbit Bks.

—In Caesar's Rome with Cicero. Leoni, Cristiana. 2008. (Come See My City Ser.). 48p. (gr. 4-8). lib. bdg. 28.50 *(978-0-7614-4328-5(2),* Benchmark Bks.) Marshall Cavendish Corp.

—In Pericles' Athens with Socrates. Leoni, Cristiana. 2008. (Come See My City Ser.). 48p. (gr. 4-8). lib. bdg. 28.50 *(978-0-7614-4326-1(6),* Benchmark Bks.) Marshall Cavendish Corp.

Cappon, Manuela. Every Day Life in Ancient Rome. Cappon, Manuela, tr. Grant, Neil. 2003. (Uncovering History Ser.). 46p. (J). lib. bdg. 28.50 *(978-1-58340-249-8(7))* Black Rabbit Bks.

Capps, Leigh. Mommy's Hat. Samuel, Lynette M. 2005. (J). per. *(978-0-9727703-3-0(X))* P.R.A. Publishing.

Caprara, Collette. Sweetpea County's Secret Quilt. Hall, Noelle Chason & Joanne Beeker Clurman. 2011. 28p. pap. 24.95 *(978-1-4626-2248-1(8))* America Star Bks.

Caprio, Pattie. The frog in the Well. Lin, Joyce, tr. 2008. (ENG & CHI.). 36p. (J). 14.95 *(978-0-9801305-1-5(4))* CE Bilingual Bks. LLC.

Caprio-Scalera, Jill & Edrington, Greg Q. Gramma's 'Jammas. Caprio-Scalera, Jill. 2013. 28p. pap. 12.50 *(978-1-60976-464-7(1),* Strategic Bk. Publishing) Strategic Book Publishing & Rights Agency (SBPRA).

Capullo, Greg & Robertson, Darick. X-Force: Assault on Graymalkin. 2011. (ENG.). 216p. (J). (gr. 4-17). 29.99 *(978-0-7851-5899-8(5))* Marvel Worldwide, Inc.

Caputo, Antonella, et al. Graphic Classics - O. Henry, Vol. 11. Henry, O. et al. Pomplun, Tom, ed. 2005. (Graphic Classics Ser.: Vol. 11). 144p. pap. 11.95 *(978-0-9746648-2-8(0))* Eureka Productions.

Caputo, James. Japan. Florence, Debbi Michiko. 2009. (Kaleidoscope Kids Ser.). (ENG.). 96p. (J). (gr. 3-8). 19.99 *(978-0-8249-6828-1(X))*; pap. 12.99 *(978-0-8249-6829-8(8))* Ideals Pubns. (Williamson Bks.).

Caputo, Jim. The Animal Zone. Chmielewski, Gary. rev. ed. 2014. (Funny Zone Ser.). (ENG.). 24p. (J). (gr. 2-4). pap. 11.94 *(978-1-60357-677-2(0))* Norwood Hse. Pr.

—Animal Zone: Jokes, Riddles, Tongue Twisters & Daffynitions. Chmielewski, Gary. rev. ed. 2007. (Funny Zone Ser.). (ENG.). 24p. (J). (gr. 2-4). lib. bdg. 22.60 *(978-1-59953-139-7(9))* Norwood Hse. Pr.

—China: Over 40 Activities to Experience China - Past & Present. Florence, Debbi Michiko. 2008. (ENG.). 96p. (J). (gr. 3-7). 16.99 *(978-0-8249-6813-7(1))*; pap. 12.99 *(978-0-8249-6814-4(X))* Ideals Pubns. (Williamson Bks.).

—The Classroom Zone. Chmielewski, Gary. rev. ed. 2014. (Funny Zone Ser.). (ENG.). 24p. (J). (gr. 2-4). pap. 11.94 *(978-1-60357-680-2(0))* Norwood Hse. Pr.

—Classroom Zone: Jokes, Riddles, Tongue Twisters & Daffynitions. Chmielewski, Gary. rev. ed. 2007. (Funny Zone Ser.). (ENG.). 24p. (J). (gr. 2-4). lib. bdg. 22.60 *(978-1-59953-145-8(3))* Norwood Hse. Pr.

—The Computer Zone. Chmielewski, Gary. rev. ed. 2014. (Funny Zone Ser.). (ENG.). 24p. (J). (gr. 2-4). pap. 11.94 *(978-1-60357-684-0(3))* Norwood Hse. Pr.

—The Computer Zone: Jokes, Riddles, Tongue Twisters & Daffynitions. Chmielewski, Gary. rev. ed. 2009. (Funny Zone Ser.). (ENG.). 24p. (J). (gr. 2-4). lib. bdg. 22.60 *(978-1-59953-300-1(6))* Norwood Hse. Pr.

—Crafts Across America. Littlefield, Cindy A. 2008. (ENG.). 128p. (J). 16.99 *(978-0-8249-6809-0(3))*; pap. 12.99 *(978-0-8249-6810-6(7))* Ideals Pubns. (Williamson Bks.).

—The Fright Zone. Chmielewski, Gary. rev. ed. 2014. (Funny Zone Ser.). (ENG.). 24p. (J). (gr. 2-4). pap. 11.94 *(978-1-60357-685-7(1))* Norwood Hse. Pr.

—The Fright Zone: Jokes, Riddles, Tongue Twisters & Daffynitions. Chmielewski, Gary. rev. ed. 2009. (Funny Zone Ser.). (ENG.). 24p. (J). (gr. 2-4). lib. bdg. 22.60 *(978-1-59953-298-1(0))* Norwood Hse. Pr.

—The Ghost Zone. Chmielewski, Gary. rev. ed. 2014. (Funny Zone Ser.). (ENG.). 24p. (J). (gr. 2-4). pap. 11.94 *(978-1-60357-686-4(X))* Norwood Hse. Pr.

—The Ghost Zone: Jokes, Riddles, Tongue Twisters & Daffynitions. Chmielewski, Gary. rev. ed. 2009. (Funny Zone Ser.). (ENG.). 24p. (J). (gr. 2-4). lib. bdg. 22.60 *(978-1-59953-297-4(2))* Norwood Hse. Pr.

—The History Zone. Chmielewski, Gary. rev. ed. 2014. (Funny Zone Ser.). (ENG.). 24p. (J). (gr. 2-4). pap. 11.94 *(978-1-60357-678-9(9))* Norwood Hse. Pr.

—History Zone: Jokes, Riddles, Tongue Twisters & Daffynitions. Chmielewski, Gary. rev. ed. 2007. (Funny Zone Ser.). (ENG.). 24p. (J). (gr. 2-4). lib. bdg. 22.60 *(978-1-59953-141-0(0))* Norwood Hse. Pr.

—Keeping Our Earth Green. Castaldo, Nancy F. 2008. (ENG.). 128p. (J). (gr. 3-8). pap. 12.99 *(978-0-8249-6825-0(5))*; (gr. 8). 16.99 *(978-0-8249-6824-3(7))* Ideals Pubns. (Williamson Bks.).

—Let's Eat in the Funny Zone. Chmielewski, Gary. rev. ed. 2014. (Funny Zone Ser.). (ENG.). 24p. (J). (gr. 2-4). pap. 11.94 *(978-1-60357-681-9(9))* Norwood Hse. Pr.

—Let's Eat in the Funny Zone: Jokes, Riddles, Tongue Twisters & Daffynitions. Chmielewski, Gary. rev. ed. 2008. (Funny Zone Ser.). (ENG.). 24p. (J). (gr. 2-4). lib. bdg. 22.60 *(978-1-59953-181-6(X))* Norwood Hse. Pr.

—Let's Go in the Funny Zone. Chmielewski, Gary. rev. ed. 2014. (Funny Zone Ser.). (ENG.). 24p. (J). (gr. 2-4). pap. 11.94 *(978-1-60357-682-6(7))* Norwood Hse. Pr.

—Let's Go in the Funny Zone: Jokes, Riddles, Tongue Twisters & Daffynitions. Chmielewski, Gary. rev. ed. 2008. (Funny Zone Ser.). (ENG.). 24p. (J). (gr. 2-4). lib. bdg. 22.60 *(978-1-59953-182-3(8))* Norwood Hse. Pr.

—The Medical Zone. Chmielewski, Gary. rev. ed. 2014. (Funny Zone Ser.). (ENG.). 24p. (J). (gr. 2-4). pap. 11.94 *(978-1-60357-687-1(8))* Norwood Hse. Pr.

—The Medical Zone: Jokes, Riddles, Tongue Twisters & Daffynitions. Chmielewski, Gary. rev. ed. 2009. (Funny Zone Ser.). (ENG.). 24p. (J). (gr. 2-4). lib. bdg. 22.60 *(978-1-59953-299-8(9))* Norwood Hse. Pr.

—The Science Zone. Chmielewski, Gary. rev. ed. 2014. (Funny Zone Ser.). (ENG.). 24p. (J). (gr. 2-4). pap. 11.94 *(978-1-60357-683-3(5))* Norwood Hse. Pr.

—The Science Zone: Jokes, Riddles, Tongue Twisters & Daffynitions. Chmielewski, Gary. rev. ed. 2008. (Funny Zone Ser.). (ENG.). 24p. (J). (gr. 2-4). lib. bdg. 22.60 *(978-1-59953-183-0(6))* Norwood Hse. Pr.

—The Sports Zone. Chmielewski, Gary. rev. ed. (Funny Zone Ser.). (ENG.). 24p. (J). (gr. 2-4). 2014. pap. 11.94 *(978-1-60357-679-6(7))*; 2007. lib. bdg. 22.60 *(978-1-59953-144-1(5))* Norwood Hse. Pr.

Caraballo, Samuel & Torrecilla, Pablo. Estrellita in the Big City/Estrellita en la Ciudad Grande. Caraballo, Samuel & Torrecilla, Pablo. 2008. (SPA & ENG.). 32p. (J). (gr. -1-4). 16.95 *(978-1-55885-498-7(3),* Piñata Books) Arte Publico Pr.

Carabelli, Francesca. The Cats on Ben Yehuda Street. Stampler, Ann Redisch. 2013. (Israel Ser.). (ENG.). 32p. (J). (gr. -1-2). 7.95 *(978-0-7613-8124-2(4))*; lib. bdg. 16.95 *(978-0-7613-8123-5(6))* Lerner Publishing Group. (Kar-Ben Publishing).

—Even Princesses Go to the Potty. Wax, Wendy A. & Wax, Naomi. 2014. (ENG.). 22p. (J). (gr. -1 — 1). bds. 7.99 *(978-1-4424-8886-1(7),* Little Simon) Little Simon.

—If You Were a Circle, 1 vol. Blaisdell, Molly. 2009. (Math Fun Ser.). (ENG.). 24p. (gr. 2-4). pap. 7.95 *(978-1-4048-5686-8(2))*; lib. bdg. 27.32 *(978-1-4048-5514-4(9))* Picture Window Bks. (Nonfiction Picture Bks.).

—If You Were a Fraction, 1 vol. Shaskan, Trisha Speed. 2008. (Math Fun Ser.). (ENG.). 24p. (gr. 2-4). 27.32 *(978-1-4048-4790-3(1))*; pap. 7.95 *(978-1-4048-4791-0(X))* Picture Window Bks. (Nonfiction Picture Bks.).

—If You Were a Minus Sign, 1 vol. Shaskan, Trisha Speed. 2008. (Math Fun Ser.). (ENG.). 24p. (gr. 2-4). 27.32 *(978-1-4048-4787-3(1))*; pap. 7.95 *(978-1-4048-4788-0(X))* Picture Window Bks. (Nonfiction Picture Bks.).

—If You Were a Minus Sign [LTD Commodities]. Shaskan, Trisha Speed. 2010. (Math Fun Ser.). 24p. pap. 3.50 *(978-1-4048-6256-2(0),* Nonfiction Picture Bks.) Picture Window Bks.

—If You Were a Minus Sign [Scholastic]. Shaskan, Trisha Speed. 2010. (Math Fun Ser.). 24p. pap. 0.52 *(978-1-4048-6173-2(4),* Nonfiction Picture Bks.) Picture Window Bks.

—If You Were a Minute, 1 vol. Shaskan, Trisha Speed. 2009. (Math Fun Ser.). (ENG.). 24p. (gr. 2-4). pap. 7.95 *(978-1-4048-5202-0(6))*; lib. bdg. 27.32 *(978-1-4048-5201-3(8))* Picture Window Bks. (Nonfiction Picture Bks.).

—If You Were a Plus Sign, 1 vol. Shaskan, Trisha Speed. 2008. (Math Fun Ser.). (ENG.). 24p. (gr. 2-4). 27.32 *(978-1-4048-4784-2(7))*; pap. 7.95 *(978-1-4048-4785-9(5))* Picture Window Bks. (Nonfiction Picture Bks.).

—If You Were a Plus Sign [LTD Commodities]. Shaskan, Trisha Speed. 2010. (Math Fun Ser.). 24p. pap. 3.50 *(978-1-4048-6257-9(9),* Nonfiction Picture Bks.) Picture Window Bks.

—If You Were a Plus Sign [Scholastic]. Shaskan, Trisha Speed. 2010. (Math Fun Ser.). 24p. pap. 0.52 *(978-1-4048-6172-5(6),* Nonfiction Picture Bks.) Picture Window Bks.

—If You Were a Pound or a Kilogram, 1 vol. Aboff, Marcie. 2009. (Math Fun Ser.). (ENG.). 24p. (gr. 2-4). pap. 7.95 *(978-1-4048-5205-1(0))*; lib. bdg. 27.32 *(978-1-4048-5204-4(2))* Picture Window Bks. (Nonfiction Picture Bks.).

—If You Were a Quadrilateral, 1 vol. Blaisdell, Molly. 2009. (Math Fun Ser.). (ENG.). 24p. (gr. 2-4). pap. 7.95 *(978-1-4048-5690-5(0),* Nonfiction Picture Bks.) Picture Window Bks.

—If You Were a Quart or a Liter, 1 vol. Aboff, Marcie. 2009. (Math Fun Ser.). (ENG.). 24p. (gr. 2-4). pap. 7.95 *(978-1-4048-5208-2(5),* Nonfiction Picture Bks.) Picture Window Bks.

Carabelli, Francesca & Dillard, Sarah. If You Were a Polygon, 1 vol. Aboff, Marcie. 2009. (Math Fun Ser.). (ENG.). 24p. (gr. 2-4). lib. bdg. 27.32 *(978-1-4048-5512-0(2),* Nonfiction Picture Bks.) Picture Window Bks.

—Math Fun, 1 vol. Aboff, Marcie & Shaskan, Trisha Speed. 2009. (Math Fun Ser.). (ENG.). 192p. (gr. 2-4). pap. 14.95 *(978-1-4048-5611-0(0),* Nonfiction Picture Bks.) Picture Window Bks.

Carabelli, Francesca, jt. illus. see Dillard, Sarah.

Caracino, Leah. Bud the Pup. Wilson, Barbara. 2012. (J). 9.00 *(978-1-56778-539-5(5))* Wilson Language Training.

—Jack & His Pal Max. Wilson, Barbara. 2012. (J). 9.00 *(978-1-56778-540-1(9))* Wilson Language Training.

—Mrs. Piglin Visits Sick Mr. Fox. Wilson, Barbara. 2012. (J). 9.00 *(978-1-56778-541-8(7))* Wilson Language Training.

—Ted & Matt. Wilson, Barbara. 2012. (J). 9.00 *(978-1-56778-544-9(1))* Wilson Language Training.

Caran, Rick. Jilli Dog - the Little Dog That Made Mr. Kranby Smile. Caran, Rick. 2011. (ENG.). 32p. pap. 10.95 *(978-0-615-47477-9(2))* Team Jilli Dog.

Caravela, Elena. The Birds of the Harbor. Italia, John. 2006. (ENG.). 32p. (J). (gr. -1-3). 15.95 *(978-0-9726614-7-8(6))* Shenanigan Bks.

—A Night of Tamales & Roses. Kraus, Joanna H. 2007. (ENG.). 32p. (J). (gr. -1-3). 15.95 *(978-0-9726614-4-7(1))* Shenanigan Bks.

Caraway, James. Ben Franklin. Friedman, Estelle. 2011. 44p. 35.95 *(978-1-258-07275-9(0))* Literary Licensing, LLC.

Carbajal, Diego. Cantemos en Español Song-Book: Spanish Learning Song-Book for Children. Dorn, Susy. 2006. (SPA.). (J). *(978-0-9764010-6-3(1))* Susy Dorn Productions, LLC.

—Sal y Pimienta Song-Book: Spanish Learning Song-Book for Children. Dorn, Susy. 2006. (SPA.). (J). *(978-0-9764010-7-0(X))* Susy Dorn Productions, LLC.

Carbajal, Richard & Stubbs, Tommy. Fun at the County Fair. Neusner, Dena. 2005. (ENG.). 10p. (J). (gr. -1-1). bds. 11.95 *(978-0-7624-2370-5(6),* Running Pr. Kids) Running Pr. Bk. Pubs.

Carbajal, Richard, jt. illus. see Hammond, Ted.

Carbajal, Richard Pimentel, jt. illus. see Hammond, Ted.

Carbaugh, Sam. Robotics: Discover the Science & Technology of the Future with 20 Projects. Ceceri, Kathy. 2012. (Build It Yourself Ser.). (ENG.). 128p. (J). (gr. 3-7). 21.95 *(978-1-936749-76-8(9))* Nomad Pr.

—Timekeeping: Explore the History & Science of Telling Time with 15 Projects. Formichelli, Linda & Martin, W. Eric. 2012. (Build It Yourself Ser.). (ENG.). 128p. (J). (gr. 3-7). 21.95 *(978-1-61930-136-8(9))* Nomad Pr.

Carbaugh, Samuel. Amazing Math: Projects You Can Build Yourself. Bardos, Laszlo C. 2010. (Build It Yourself Ser.). (ENG.). 128p. (J). (gr. 3-7). 21.95 *(978-1-934670-58-3(8))* Nomad Pr.

—Amazing Math Projects. Bardos, Laszlo C. 2010. (Build It Yourself Ser.). (ENG.). 128p. (J). (gr. 3-7). pap. 15.95 *(978-1-934670-57-6(X))* Nomad Pr.

—Food - 25 Amazing Projects: Investigate the History & Science of What We Eat. Reilly, Kathleen M. 2010. (Build It Yourself Ser.). (ENG.). 128p. (J). (gr. 3-7). 21.95 *(978-1-934670-60-6(X))* Nomad Pr.

—Forensics: Uncover the Science & Technology of Crime Scene Investigation. Mooney, Carla. 2013. (Inquire & Investigate Ser.). (ENG.). 128p. (YA). (gr. 6-10). 21.95 *(978-1-61930-188-7(1))*; pap. 16.95 *(978-1-61930-184-9(9))* Nomad Pr.

—Genetics: Breaking the Code of Your DNA. Mooney, Carla. 2014. (Inquire & Investigate Ser.). (ENG.). 128p. (J). (gr. 6-10). 21.95 *(978-1-61930-208-2(X))*; pap. 16.95 *(978-1-61930-212-9(8))* Nomad Pr.

—George Washington: 25 Great Projects You Can Build Yourself. Mooney, Carla. 2010. (Build It Yourself Ser.). (ENG.). 128p. (J). (gr. 3-7). 21.95 *(978-1-934670-64-4(2))*; pap. 15.95 *(978-1-934670-63-7(4))* Nomad Pr.

—Physics: Investigate the Forces of Nature. Gardner, Jane P. 2014. (Inquire & Investigate Ser.). (ENG.). 128p. (J). (gr. 6-10). 21.95 *(978-1-61930-227-3(6))* Nomad Pr.

—Timekeeping: Explore the History & Science of Telling Time with 15 Projects. Formichelli, Linda et al. 2012. (Build It Yourself Ser.). (ENG.). 128p. (J). (gr. 3-7). pap. 15.95 *(978-1-61930-033-0(8))* Nomad Pr.

Carbaugh, Samuel & Rizvi, Farah. Food - 25 Amazing Projects: Investigate the History & Science of What We Eat. Reilly, Kathleen M. 2010. (Build It Yourself Ser.). (ENG.). 128p. (J). (gr. 3-7). pap. 15.95 *(978-1-934670-59-0(6))* Nomad Pr.

Card, Vanessa. Christian Church. Brown, Alan & Seaman, Alison. 2004. (ENG.). 32p. pap. *(978-0-7136-5497-4(X),* A & C Black) Bloomsbury Publishing Plc.

Card, Vanessa, jt. illus. see Mukhida, Zul.

Cardemil, Carmen. Cuentos Ecologicos. Schkolnik, Saul. 2nd ed. 2003. (la Orilla del Viento Ser.).Tr. of Ecological Tales. (SPA.). 56p. (J). (gr. 3-7). per. *(978-968-16-4757-5(2),* FC6400) Fondo de Cultura Economica MEX. Dist: Lectorum Pubns., Inc.

—Gerardo y la Cama. Morábito, Fabio. 2003. (SPA.). *(978-968-494-087-1(4),* CI31141) Centro de Informacion y Desarrollo de la Comunicacion y la Literatura MEX. Dist: Lectorum Pubns., Inc.

—La Historia de Manu (Manu's Story) del Rio, Ana Maria. 2003. (Coleccion Derechos Del Nino Ser.). (SPA.). 32p. (J). (gr. 3-5). pap. 7.95 *(978-84-204-5845-8(7))* Santillana USA Publishing Co., Inc.

—Maritimi Quiere Ser Escritora. Delgado, Luis Cabrera. 2005. (SPA.). 148p. (J). 13.00 *(978-956-239-225-9(2))* Aguilar Chilena de Ediciones, Ltd. CHL. Dist: Ediciones Universal.

Cardenas, Patricia Karla, jt. illus. see Cardenas, Patricia Karla Marquez.

Cardenas, Patricia Karla Marquez & Cardenas, Patricia Karla. La Tinta de Las Moras. Hernandez, Georgina. rev. ed. 2007. (Castillo de la Lectura Roja Ser.). (SPA & ENG.). 144p. (YA). (gr. 7). pap. 8.95 *(978-968-5920-40-7(0))* Castillo, Ediciones, S. A. de C. V. MEX. Dist: Macmillan.

Cardillo, Linda & Albert, Dar. The Smallest Christmas Tree. Cardillo, Linda. 2013. 42p. pap. 9.49 *(978-0-9910861-0-8(4))* Bellastoria Pr.

Cardinal, John. I'd Rather Be Riding My Bike. Pinder, Eric. l.t. ed. 2013. 42p. (gr. k-1). pap. 10.95 *(978-1-62253-401-2(8))* Evolved Publishing.

Cardinale, Christopher. Which Side Are You On? The Story of a Song. Lyon, George Ella. 2011. (ENG.). 40p. (J). (gr. 2-4). 17.95 *(978-1-933693-96-5(7))* Cinco Puntos Pr.

Cardon, Laurent. That's What Makes a Hippopotamus Smile. Taylor, Sean. 2015. 32p. (J). pap. 8.99 ***(978-1-84780-595-9(7),*** Frances Lincoln) Quarto Publishing Group UK GBR. Dist: Littlehampton Bk Services, Ltd.

Cardon, Laurent. Wolf Wanted, 1 vol. Machado, Ana Maria. Amado, Elisa, tr. from POR. 2010. (ENG.). 40p. (J). (gr. -1-2). 18.95 *(978-0-88899-880-4(5))* Groundwood Bks. CAN. Dist: Perseus-PGW.

Cardona, Jose. Disney Sofia the First: Sweet Dreams, Sofia! Hapka, Catherine. 2015. (ENG.). 12p. (J). (gr. -1-k). 12.99 ***(978-0-7944-3383-3(9))*** Studio Fun International.

Cardona, Jose & Williams, Don. Mulan. Poindexter, Katherine & RH Disney Staff. 2013. (Pictureback Ser.). (ENG.). 24p. (J). (gr. -1-2). pap. 3.99 *(978-0-7364-2262-8(5),* RH/Disney) Random Hse. Children's Bks.

Cardoni, Paolo. Albert. Lebscky, Ibi. (Coleccion Seran Famosos).Tr. of Little Albert Einstein. (SPA.). 28p. (J). (gr. 2-4). 10.36 *(978-84-233-1400-3(6))* Ediciones Destino ESP. Dist: Lectorum Pubns., Inc.

—Amadeus. Lebscky, Ibi. (Coleccion Seran Famosos). (SPA.). 32p. (J). (gr. 2-4). 14.95 *(978-84-233-1262-7(3))* Ediciones Destino ESP. Dist: AIMS International Bks., Inc.

—Leonardo. Lebscky, Ibi. (Coleccion Seran Famosos).Tr. of Little Leonardo de Vinci. (SPA.). 28p. (J). (gr. 2-4). 10.36 *(978-84-233-1399-0(9))* Ediciones Destino ESP. Dist: Lectorum Pubns., Inc.

—Marie. Lebscky, Ibi. (Coleccion Seran Famosos).Tr. of Little Marie Curie. (SPA.). 28p. (J). (gr. 2-4). 14.95 *(978-84-233-2086-8(3))* Ediciones Destino ESP. Dist: AIMS International Bks., Inc.

—Pablito. Lebscky, Ibi. (Coleccion Seran Famosos).Tr. of Little Pablo Picasso. (SPA.). 28p. (J). (gr. 2-4). 14.95 *(978-84-233-1265-8(8))* Ediciones Destino ESP. Dist: AIMS International Bks., Inc.

—William. Lebscky, Ibi. (Coleccion Seran Famosos).Tr. of Little Wm. Shakespeare. (SPA.). 28p. (J). (gr. 2-4). 10.36 *(978-84-233-1663-2(7))* Ediciones Destino ESP. Dist: Lectorum Pubns., Inc.

Cardy, Jason. Frankenstein. Shelley, Mary & Shelley, Mary. Sutliff Sanders, Joe, tr. 2009. (ENG.). 144p. (gr. 4-18). pap. 16.95 *(978-1-906332-49-5(5),* Classical Comics, Ltd.) Classical Comics GBR. Dist: Perseus-PGW.

Cardy, Jason & Nicholson, Kat. Frankenstein. Shelley, Mary & Shelley, Mary. Sutliff Sanders, Joe, tr. 2009. (ENG.). 144p. (gr. 4-18). pap. 16.95 *(978-1-906332-50-1(9),* Classical Comics, Ltd.) Classical Comics GBR. Dist: Perseus-PGW.

Cardy, Jason, jt. illus. see Nicholson, Kat.

Carey, Bob. A Home for Dixie: The True Story of a Rescued Puppy. Jackson, Emma. 40p. (J). (gr. -1-3). 2010. (ENG.). pap. 6.99 *(978-0-06-144964-2(4),* Collins); 2008. lib. bdg. 17.89 *(978-0-06-144963-5(6))*; 2008. (ENG.). 16.99 *(978-0-06-144962-8(8),* Collins) HarperCollins Pubs.

Carey, Joseph. Jack Kat Had a Day, 1 vol. Carey, Kathleen. 2009. 21p. pap. 24.95 *(978-1-60836-314-8(7))* America Star Bks.

Carey, Katey. Firemen Don't Wear Glasses. Adams, Peyton. 2013. 26p. pap. 9.95 *(978-0-615-78508-0(5))* Steel Rooster Pr.

—Mermaids Don't Wear Glasses. Adams, Peyton. 2013. 26p. pap. 9.95 *(978-0-615-77887-7(9))* Steel Rooster Pr.

Cariello, Sergio. The Action Bible: God's Redemptive Story. Mauss, Doug, ed. ed. 2010. (Action Bible Ser.). (ENG.). 752p. (J). (gr. -1-2). 26.99 *(978-0-7814-4499-6(3))* Cook, David C.

—The Battle Begins: The Story of Creation. Seeling, Caleb. 2014. (Action Bible Graphic Novels Ser.: 1). (ENG.). 104p. (J). pap. 12.99 *(978-0-7814-1142-4(4))* Cook, David C.

—La Biblia en Acción: La Historia Redentora de Dios. Mauss, Doug, ed. 2014. Orig. Title: The Action Bible New Testament. (SPA.). 240p. (J). pap. 16.99 *(978-1-4143-8923-3(X))* Tyndale Hse. Pubs.

Cariello, Sergio, et al. Captain America: Hail Hydra. 2011. (ENG.). 120p. (YA). (gr. 8-17). pap. 14.99 *(978-0-7851-5127-2(3))* Marvel Worldwide, Inc.

Cariello, Sergio. The Heroes of God, 1 vol. Martin, Gary & Zondervan Publishing Staff. 2009. (Z Graphic Novels / Son of Samson Ser.). (ENG.). 160p. (J). pap. 6.99 *(978-0-310-71284-8(X))* Zonderkidz.

C

—The Raiders of Joppa, 1 vol. Martin, Gary & Rogers, Bud. 2008. (Z Graphic Novels / Son of Samson Ser.). (ENG.). 160p. (J). (gr. 4-7). pap. 6.99 *(978-0-310-71282-4(3))* Zondervan.

Cariello, Sergio, et al. Resurrection, Vol. 5. Dixon, Chuck. 2004. (Crux Ser.: Vol. 5). 160p. (YA). pap. 15.95 *(978-1-59314-053-3(3))* CrossGeneration Comics, Inc.

Cariello, Sergio. The Sword of Revenge, 1 vol. Martin, Gary & Zondervan Bibles Staff. Rogers, Bud, ed. 2009. (Z Graphic Novels / Son of Samson Ser.). (ENG.). 160p. (J). pap. 6.99 *(978-0-310-71285-5(8))* Zondervan.

—The Tears of Jehovah, 1 vol. Rogers, Bud & Martin, Gary. 2012. (Z Graphic Novels / Son of Samson Ser.). (ENG.). 160p. (J). pap. 6.99 *(978-0-310-71286-2(6))* Zondervan.

—Teknon & the Champion Warriors. Sapp, Brent. 2003. 7.99 *(978-1-57229-219-2(9))* FamilyLife.

—The Witch of Endor, 1 vol. Rogers, Bud & Martin, Gary. 2008. (Z Graphic Novels / Son of Samson Ser.). (ENG.). 160p. (J). pap. 6.99 *(978-0-310-71283-1(1))* Zondervan.

Cariello, Sergio & Lanphear, Dave. The Maiden of Thunder, 1 vol. Martin, Gary et al. 2008. (Z Graphic Novels / Son of Samson Ser.). (ENG.). 160p. (J). (gr. 4-7). pap. 6.99 *(978-0-310-71281-7(5))* Zondervan.

Carigiet, Alois. A Bell for Ursli: A Story from the Engadine in Switzerland. 2007. 44p. (J). *(978-0-86315-614-4(2))* Floris Bks.

Carillo, Fred. Jack London/the Call of the Wild. London, Jack. 2005. 48p. (gr. 5-8). 25.50 *(978-0-7910-9104-3(X))* Facts On File, Inc.

—The Red Badge of Courage. Crane, Stephen. 2005. 48p. (gr. 5-8). 25.50 *(978-0-7910-9103-6(1))* Facts On File, Inc.

Caringella, Rachel. Little Dead Riding Hood. Borst, Amie & Borst, Bethanie. 2014. (Scarily Ever Laughter Ser.). (ENG.). 320p. (J). (gr. 4-7). pap. 12.99 *(978-1-939967-89-3(9))* Jolly Fish Pr.

Carisse, Carissa. Buddy Boy Brooks Takes the Wheel: A Mile Wide Tale from the Mighty Mississippi. Singleton, Glynn. 2007. 32p. (J). (gr. 2-4). 12.95 *(978-1-57072-320-9(6))* Overmountain Pr.

Carle, Eric, et al. Artist to Artist: 23 Major Illustrators Talk to Children about Their Art. Eric Carle Museum of Picture Book Art Staff. Gauch, Patricia Lee et al, eds. 2007. (ENG.). 114p. (J). (gr. k-3). 30.00 *(978-0-399-24600-5(2),* Philomel) Penguin Publishing Group.

Carle, Eric. Baby Bear, Baby Bear, What Do You See? Martin, Bill, Jr. (Brown Bear & Friends Ser.). (ENG.). (J). (gr. -1-k). 2014. 28p. 12.99 *(978-0-8050-9949-2(2));* 2011. 40p. 8.99 *(978-0-8050-9291-2(9));* 2009. 26p. 7.99 *(978-0-8050-8990-5(X));* 2007. 32p. 16.95 *(978-0-8050-8336-1(7))* Holt, Henry & Co. (Holt, Henry & Co. Bks. For Young Readers).

—Baby Bear, Baby Bear, What Do You See? Big Book. Martin, Bill, Jr. 2011. (Brown Bear & Friends Ser.). (ENG.). 32p. (J). (gr. -1-k). pap. 25.99 *(978-0-8050-9345-2(1),* Holt, Henry & Co. Bks. For Young Readers) Holt, Henry & Co.

—Brown Bear & Friends. Martin, Bill, Jr. unabr. ed. 2011. (Brown Bear & Friends Ser.). (ENG.). (J). (gr. -1-k). 39.99 *(978-1-4272-1448-5(4))* Macmillan Audio.

—Brown Bear & Friends Board Book Gift Set. Martin, Bill, Jr. 2007. (Brown Bear & Friends Ser.). (ENG.). 26p. (J). (gr. -1-k). 23.95 *(978-0-8050-8273-9(5),* Holt, Henry & Co. Bks. For Young Readers) Holt, Henry & Co.

—Brown Bear Book & CD Storytime Set. Martin, Bill, Jr. unabr. ed. 2013. (ENG.). (J). (gr. -1-k). 12.99 *(978-1-4272-3510-7(4))* Macmillan Audio.

—Brown Bear, Brown Bear, What Do You See? Martin, Bill, Jr. (J). 2013. (ENG.). 128p. (gr. -1-2). 15.99 *(978-0-8050-9766-5(X));* 2012. (ENG.). 28p. (gr. -1-k). 12.99 *(978-0-8050-9577-7(2));* 2010. (ENG.). 40p. (gr. -1-2). 8.99 *(978-0-8050-9244-8(7));* 2007. 32p. pap. 7.95 *(978-0-8050-8797-0(4));* 3rd anniv. ed. 2008. (ENG.). 32p. (gr. -1-k). pap. 27.95 *(978-0-8050-8718-5(4));* 3rd anniv. ed. 2007. (ENG.). 32p. (gr. -1-k). 19.95 *(978-0-8050-8266-1(2))* Holt, Henry & Co. (Holt, Henry & Co. Bks. For Young Readers).

—Brown Bear, Brown Bear, What Do You See? Martin, Bill, Jr. (J). 2004. (SHO.). 27p. pap. *(978-1-84444-165-5(2));* 2004. (ENG & POR.). 32p. pap. *(978-1-84444-159-4(8));* 2004. (KUR & ENG.). 26p. pap. *(978-1-84444-158-7(X));* 2004. (YOR & ENG.). 25p. pap. *(978-1-84444-129-7(6));* 2004. (ENG & TUR.). 27p. pap. *(978-1-84444-127-3(X));* 2004. (TAM & ENG.). 32p. pap. *(978-1-84444-126-6(1));* 2004. (SOM & ENG.). 27p. pap. *(978-1-84444-125-9(3));* 2004. (PAN & ENG.). 32p. pap. *(978-1-84444-123-5(7));* 2004. (ENG & HIN.). 32p. pap. *(978-1-84444-122-8(9));* 2004. (GUJ & ENG.). 32p. pap. *(978-1-84444-121-1(0));* 2004. (PER & ENG.). 32p. pap. *(978-1-84444-120-4(2));* 2004. (ENG & ARA.). 32p. pap. *(978-1-84444-116-7(4));* 2004. (ALB & ENG.). 26p. pap. *(978-1-84444-115-0(6));* 2003. (URD & ENG.). 32p. pap. *(978-1-84444-128-0(8));* 2003. (CHI & ENG.). 32p. pap. *(978-1-84444-118-1(0))* Mantra Lingua.

—Brown Bear, Brown Bear, What Do You See? Martin, Bill, Jr. 2003. (VIE & ENG.). 32p. (J). pap. 12.95 *(978-1-84444-124-2(5))* Mantra Lingua GBR. Dist: Chinasprout, Inc.

—Brown Bear, Brown Bear, What Do You See? Martin, Bill, Jr. 2010. (ENG.). 24p. (J). (-1). bds. 12.99 *(978-0-312-50926-2(X),* Priddy Bks.) St. Martin's Pr.

—The Foolish Tortoise. Buckley, Richard. (ENG.). 24p. (J). (gr. -1-2). 2013. pap. 9.99 *(978-1-4424-6638-8(3));* 2009. bds. 7.99 *(978-1-4169-7916-6(6))* Little Simon. (Little Simon).

Carle, Eric. The Foolish Tortoise. Buckley, Richard. 2015. (World of Eric Carle Ser.). (ENG.). 24p. (J). (gr. k-2). pap. 3.99 ***(978-1-4814-3577-2(9),*** Simon Spotlight) Simon Spotlight.

Carle, Eric. The Foolish Tortoise: Lap Edition. Buckley, Richard. 2013. (World of Eric Carle Ser.). (ENG.). 24p. (J). (gr. -1-k). bds. 12.99 *(978-1-4424-8990-5(1),* Little Simon) Little Simon.

—The Greedy Python. Buckley, Richard. 2012. (World of Eric Carle Ser.). (ENG.). 24p. (J). (gr. -1-1). 16.99 *(978-1-4424-4577-2(7));* pap. 3.99 *(978-1-4424-4576-5(9))* Simon Spotlight. (Simon Spotlight).

—The Greedy Python. Buckley, Richard. 2009. (World of Eric Carle Ser.). (ENG.). 24p. (J). (gr. -1-k). bds. 7.99 *(978-1-4169-8290-6(6),* Little Simon) Little Simon.

—The Greedy Python: Lap Edition. Buckley, Richard. 2013. (World of Eric Carle Ser.). (ENG.). 24p. (J). (gr. -1-k). bds. 12.99 *(978-1-4424-8991-2(X),* Little Simon) Little Simon.

—The Lamb & the Butterfly. Sundgaard, Arnold. 2013. (ENG.). 32p. (J). (gr. -1-k). 17.99 *(978-0-545-44326-5(1),* Orchard Bks.) Scholastic, Inc.

—Oso Panda, Oso Panda, ¿Qué Ves Ahí? Martin, Bill, Jr. Mlawer, Teresa, tr. 2008. (Brown Bear & Friends Ser.).Tr. of Brown Bear, Brown Bear, What Do You See?. (SPA & ENG.). 32p. (J). (gr. -1-k). 17.95 *(978-0-8050-8348-4(0),* Holt, Henry & Co. Bks. For Young Readers) Holt, Henry & Co.

—Oso Panda, Oso Panda, ¿Qué Ves Ahí? Martin, Bill, Jr. Mlawer, Teresa, tr. ed. 2009. (Brown Bear & Friends Ser.).Tr. of Brown Bear, Brown Bear, What Do You See?. (SPA & ENG.). 26p. (J). (gr. -1-k). bds. 9.99 *(978-0-8050-8756-7(7),* Holt, Henry & Co. Bks. For Young Readers) Holt, Henry & Co.

—Panda Bear, Panda Bear, What Do You See? Martin, Bill, Jr. (Brown Bear & Friends Ser.). (J). 2014. (ENG.). 28p. (gr. -1-k). 12.99 *(978-0-8050-9950-8(6));* 2011. (ENG.). 40p. (gr. -1-2). 8.99 *(978-0-8050-9292-9(7));* 2007. 32p. 7.95 *(978-0-8050-8799-4(0));* 2007. (ENG.). 32p. (gr. -1-k). pap. 27.99 *(978-0-8050-8102-2(X));* 2006. (ENG.). 26p. (gr. -1-k). 7.95 *(978-0-8050-8078-0(3));* 2003. (ENG.). 32p. (gr. -1-k). 17.99 *(978-0-8050-1758-8(5))* Holt, Henry & Co. (Holt, Henry & Co. Bks. For Young Readers).

—Panda Bear, Panda Bear, What Do You See?, 1 vol. Martin, Bill, Jr. unabr. ed. 2011. (Brown Bear & Friends Ser.). (ENG.). (J). (gr. -1-k). 9.99 *(978-1-4272-1254-2(6))* Macmillan Audio.

—Panda Bear, Panda Bear, What Do You See? Martin, Bill, Jr. 2013. (Slide & Find Ser.). (ENG.). 24p. (J). (gr. -1 — 1). bds. 12.99 *(978-0-312-51581-2(2),* Priddy Bks.) St. Martin's Pr.

—Panda Bear, Panda Bear, What Do You See? 10th Anniversary Edition. Martin, Bill, Jr. 2013. (ENG.). 28p. (J). (gr. -1-k). 19.99 *(978-0-8050-9778-8(3),* Holt, Henry & Co. Bks. For Young Readers) Holt, Henry & Co.

—Polar Bear Book & CD Storytime Set. Martin, Bill, Jr. unabr. ed. 2012. (ENG.). (J). (gr. -1-k). 12.99 *(978-1-4272-3256-4(3))* Macmillan Audio.

—Polar Bear, Polar Bear, What Do You Hear? Martin, Bill, Jr. (Brown Bear & Friends Ser.). (J). 2012. (ENG.). 28p. (gr. -1-k). 12.99 *(978-0-8050-9095-6(9));* 2010. (ENG.). 40p. (gr. -1-2). 8.99 *(978-0-8050-9245-5(5));* 2007. 32p. 7.95 *(978-0-8050-8798-7(2));* 20th anniv. ed. 2011. (ENG.). 32p. (gr. -1-k). 19.99 *(978-0-8050-9066-6(5))* Holt, Henry & Co. (Holt, Henry & Co. Bks. For Young Readers).

—Polar Bear, Polar Bear, What Do You Hear? Martin, Bill, Jr. & Priddy, Roger. 2011. (ENG.). 24p. (J). (gr. -1-k). bds. 14.95 *(978-0-312-51346-7(1),* Priddy Bks.) St. Martin's Pr.

—Why Noah Chose the Dove. Singer, Isaac Bashevis. Shub, Elizabeth, tr. 2013. (ENG.). 32p. (J). (gr. 2-4). 7.99 *(978-1-250-02199-1(5))* Square Fish.

Carle, Eric. La Arana Muy Ocupada. Carle, Eric. 2004.Tr. of Very Busy Spider. (SPA & ENG.). 32p. (J). (gr. -1-k). 21.99 *(978-0-399-24241-0(4),* Philomel) Penguin Publishing Group.

—The Artist Who Painted a Blue Horse. Carle, Eric. (ENG.). (J). (gr. -1 — 1). 2013. 22p. bds. 7.99 *(978-0-399-16402-6(2));* 2011. 32p. 17.99 *(978-0-399-25713-1(6))* Penguin Publishing Group. (Philomel).

—El Canguro Tiene Mama? Carle, Eric. Mlawer, Teresa, tr. 2008.Tr. of Does a Kangaroo Have a Mother, Too?. (SPA.). 32p. (J). (gr. -1-1). pap. 6.99 *(978-0-06-001111-6(4),* Rayo) HarperCollins Pubs.

—Color My World (the World of Eric Carle) Carle, Eric. 2011. (Deluxe Paint Box Book Ser.). (ENG.). 128p. (J). (gr. -1-2). pap. 7.99 *(978-0-375-87349-2(X),* Golden Bks.) Random Hse. Children's Bks.

—Count with the Very Hungry Caterpillar. Carle, Eric. 2006. (World of Eric Carle Ser.). (ENG.). 16p. (J). (gr. -1-k). pap. 5.99 *(978-0-448-44420-8(8),* Grosset & Dunlap) Penguin Publishing Group.

—De la Cabeza a los Pies. Carle, Eric. 2007.Tr. of From Head to Toe. (SPA.). 32p. (J). (gr. -1-3). pap. 6.99 *(978-0-06-051313-9(6),* Rayo) HarperCollins Pubs.

—Does a Kangaroo Have a Mother, Too? Carle, Eric. 2005. (ENG.). 32p. (J). (gr. -1-3). reprint ed. pap. 6.99 *(978-0-06-443642-7(X))* HarperCollins Pubs.

—Eric Carle Classics: The Tiny Seed - Pancakes, Pancakes! - Walter the Baker. Carle, Eric. 2011. (World of Eric Carle Ser.). (ENG.). 112p. (J). (gr. -1-2). 19.99 *(978-1-4424-3988-7(2),* Simon & Schuster Bks. For Young Readers) Simon & Schuster Bks. For Young Readers.

—The Eric Carle Gift Set: The Tiny Seed; Pancakes, Pancakes!; a House for Hermit Crab; Rooster's off to See the World. Carle, Eric. ed. 2013. (World of Eric Carle Ser.). (ENG.). 124p. (J). (gr. -1 — 1). bds. 34.99 *(978-1-4424-8885-4(9),* Little Simon) Little Simon.

—The Eric Carle Mini Library: A Storybook Gift Set. Carle, Eric. ed. 2009. (World of Eric Carle Ser.). (ENG.). 148p. (J). 14.99 *(978-1-4169-8516-7(6),* Little Simon) Little Simon.

—The Eric Carle Ready-To-Read Collection: Have You Seen My Cat?; the Greedy Python; Pancakes, Pancakes!; Rooster Is off to See the World; a House for Hermit Crab; Walter the Baker. Carle, Eric. ed. 2014. (World of Eric Carle Ser.). (ENG.). 160p. (J). (gr. -1-2). pap. 15.99 *(978-1-4814-1632-0(4),* Simon Spotlight) Simon Spotlight.

—Eric Carle's All Around Us. Carle, Eric. 2013. (World of Eric Carle Ser.). (ENG.). 14p. (J). (gr. -1-k). bds. 7.99 *(978-0-448-47784-8(X),* Grosset & Dunlap) Penguin Publishing Group.

—Friends. Carle, Eric. (ENG.). (J). (gr. -1-k). 2015. 24p. bds. 7.99 *(978-0-399-17206-9(8));* 2013. 32p. 17.99 *(978-0-399-16533-7(9))* Penguin Publishing Group. (Philomel).

—From Head to Toe. Carle, Eric. 2007. (ENG.). 32p. (J). (gr. -1-k). pap. 24.99 *(978-0-06-111972-9(5),* HarperFestival) HarperCollins Pubs.

—Have You Seen My Cat? Carle, Eric. 2009. (World of Eric Carle Ser.). (ENG.). 16p. (J). bds. 7.99 *(978-1-4169-8514-3(X),* Little Simon) Little Simon.

—Have You Seen My Cat? Carle, Eric. 2012. (World of Eric Carle Ser.). (ENG.). 24p. (J). (gr. -1-k). 16.99 *(978-1-4424-4575-8(0));* pap. 3.99 *(978-1-4424-4574-1(2))* Simon Spotlight. (Simon Spotlight).

—A House for Hermit Crab. Carle, Eric. (World of Eric Carle Ser.). (ENG.). 32p. (J). 2013. (gr. -1-2). pap. 9.99 *(978-1-4424-7224-2(3));* 2004. (gr. k-3). bds. 8.99 *(978-0-689-87064-4(7))* Little Simon. (Little Simon).

—A House for Hermit Crab. Carle, Eric. 2014. (World of Eric Carle Ser.). (ENG.). 32p. (J). (gr. k-2). pap. 3.99 *(978-1-4814-0915-5(8),* Simon Spotlight) Simon Spotlight.

—De La Cabeza a los Pies. Carle, Eric. Simon, Seymour. 2003.Tr. of From Head to Toe. (SPA.). 32p. (J). (gr. -1-3). 17.99 *(978-0-06-051302-3(0),* Rayo) HarperCollins Pubs.

—Mister Seahorse. Carle, Eric. (ENG.). (J). (gr. -1 — 1). 2011. 28p. bds. 8.99 *(978-0-399-25490-1(0));* 2004. 32p. 17.99 *(978-0-399-24269-4(4))* Penguin Publishing Group. (Philomel).

—My Own Very Busy Spider Coloring Book. Carle, Eric. 2004. (ENG.). 32p. (J). (gr. -1-k). 5.99 *(978-0-399-24309-7(7),* Philomel) Penguin Publishing Group.

—My Own Very Hungry Caterpillar. Carle, Eric. 2003. (ENG.). 32p. (J). (gr. -1-k). 5.99 *(978-0-399-24207-6(4),* Philomel) Penguin Publishing Group.

—My Own Very Lonely Firefly Coloring Book. Carle, Eric. 2006. (ENG.). 32p. (J). (gr. -1-k). 5.99 *(978-0-399-24646-3(0),* Philomel) Penguin Publishing Group.

—My Own Very Quiet Cricket Coloring Book. Carle, Eric. 2005. (ENG.). 32p. (J). (gr. -1-k). 5.99 *(978-0-399-24475-9(1),* Philomel) Penguin Publishing Group.

—My Very First Book of Animal Homes. Carle, Eric. 2007. (ENG.). 20p. (J). (gr. -1 — 1). bds. 5.99 *(978-0-399-24647-0(9),* Philomel) Penguin Publishing Group.

—My Very First Book of Animal Sounds. Carle, Eric. 2007. (ENG.). 20p. (J). (gr. -1 — 1). bds. 5.99 *(978-0-399-24648-7(7),* Philomel) Penguin Publishing Group.

—My Very First Book of Colors. Carle, Eric. 2005. (ENG.). 20p. (J). (gr. -1 — 1). bds. 5.99 *(978-0-399-24386-8(0),* Philomel) Penguin Publishing Group.

—My Very First Book of Food. Carle, Eric. 2007. (ENG.). 18p. (J). (gr. -1 — 1). bds. 5.99 *(978-0-399-24747-7(5),* Philomel) Penguin Publishing Group.

—My Very First Book of Motion. Carle, Eric. 2007. (ENG.). 18p. (J). (gr. -1 — 1). bds. 5.99 *(978-0-399-24748-4(3),* Philomel) Penguin Publishing Group.

—My Very First Book of Numbers. Carle, Eric. 2006. (ENG.). 20p. (J). (gr. -1 — 1). bds. 5.99 *(978-0-399-24509-1(X),* Philomel) Penguin Publishing Group.

—My Very First Book of Numbers (Mi Primer Libro de Numeros) Carle, Eric. 2013. (SPA & ENG.). 20p. (J). (gr. -1 — 1). bds. 5.99 *(978-0-399-16141-4(4),* Philomel) Penguin Publishing Group.

—My Very First Book of Shapes. Carle, Eric. 2005. (ENG.). 20p. (J). (gr. -1 — 1). bds. 5.99 *(978-0-399-24387-5(9),* Philomel) Penguin Publishing Group.

—My Very First Book of Shapes / Mi Primer Libro de Figuras: Bilingual Edition. Carle, Eric. 2013. (SPA & ENG.). 20p. (J). (gr. -1 — 1). bds. 5.99 *(978-0-399-16142-1(2),* Philomel) Penguin Publishing Group.

—My Very First Book of Words. Carle, Eric. 2006. (ENG.). 20p. (J). (gr. -1 — 1). bds. 5.99 *(978-0-399-24510-7(3),* Philomel) Penguin Publishing Group.

—My Very First Library, 5 vols. Carle, Eric. 2006. (ENG.). 10p. (J). (gr. -1-k). bds. 23.99 *(978-0-399-24666-1(5),* Philomel) Penguin Publishing Group.

—Pancakes, Pancakes! Carle, Eric. 2004. (World of Eric Carle Ser.). (ENG.). 32p. (J). (gr. -1-3). bds. 8.99 *(978-0-689-87148-1(1),* Little Simon) Little Simon.

—Pancakes, Pancakes! Carle, Eric. 2013. (World of Eric Carle Ser.). (ENG.). 24p. (J). (gr. -1-1). 16.99 *(978-1-4424-7275-4(8));* pap. 3.99 *(978-1-4424-7274-7(X))* Simon Spotlight. (Simon Spotlight).

—Rooster Is off to See the World. Carle, Eric. 2013. (World of Eric Carle Ser.). (ENG.). 24p. (J). (gr. -1-1). 16.99 *(978-1-4424-7270-9(7));* pap. 3.99 *(978-1-4424-7269-3(3))* Simon Spotlight. (Simon Spotlight).

—Shapes to See, Shapes to Draw! (the World of Eric Carle) Carle, Eric. 2012. (Color Plus Stencil Ser.). (ENG.). 64p. (J). (gr. -1-2). pap. 4.99 *(978-0-375-87355-3(4),* Golden Bks.) Random Hse. Children's Bks.

—Shine with the Very Lonely Firefly. Carle, Eric. 2006. (World of Eric Carle Ser.). (ENG.). 16p. (J). (gr. -1-k). pap. 5.99 *(978-0-448-44422-2(4),* Grosset & Dunlap) Penguin Publishing Group.

—"Slowly, Slowly, Slowly," Said the Sloth. Carle, Eric. 2007. (ENG.). 32p. (J). (gr. -1-2). pap. 7.99 *(978-0-14-240847-6(6),* Puffin) Penguin Publishing Group.

—"Slowly, Slowly, Slowly," Said the Sloth. Carle, Eric. 2007. (gr. -1-3). 18.00 *(978-0-7569-8002-3(X))* Perfection Learning Corp.

—The Tiny Seed. Carle, Eric. (World of Eric Carle Ser.). (ENG.). (J). (gr. -1). 2009. 36p. 7.99 *(978-1-4169-7917-3(4));* 2005. 34p. bds. 8.99 *(978-0-689-87149-8(X))* Little Simon. (Little Simon).

Carle, Eric. The Tiny Seed. Carle, Eric. 2015. (World of Eric Carle Ser.). (ENG.). 32p. (J). (gr. k-2). pap. 3.99 ***(978-1-4814-3575-8(2),*** Simon Spotlight) Simon Spotlight.

Carle, Eric. The Very Busy Doodle Book (the World of Eric Carle) Carle, Eric. 2011. (Doodle Book Ser.). (ENG.). 128p. (J). (gr. -1-2). pap. 5.99 *(978-0-375-87350-8(3),* Golden Bks.) Random Hse. Children's Bks.

—The Very Busy Spider. Carle, Eric. 2014. (Penguin Young Readers, Level 2 Ser.). (ENG.). 32p. (J). (gr. 1-2). pap. 3.99 *(978-0-448-48052-7(2),* Warne, Frederick Pubs.) Penguin Bks., Ltd. GBR. Dist: Penguin Random Hse., LLC.

—The Very Busy Spider. Carle, Eric. 2011. (ENG.). 24p. (J). (gr. -1 — 1). bds. 15.99 *(978-0-399-25601-1(6),* Philomel) Penguin Publishing Group.

—The Very Busy Spider's Favorite Words. Carle, Eric. 2007. (World of Eric Carle Ser.). (ENG.). 20p. (J). (gr. -1-k). bds. 3.99 *(978-0-448-44703-2(7),* Grosset & Dunlap) Penguin Publishing Group.

—A Very Colorful Day (the World of Eric Carle) Carle, Eric. 2011. (Deluxe Chunky Crayon Book Ser.). (ENG.). 128p. (J). (gr. -1-2). pap. 7.99 *(978-0-375-87352-2(X),* Golden Bks.) Random Hse. Children's Bks.

—The Very Hungry Caterpilar. Carle, Eric. ed. 2011. (ENG & SPA.). 32p. (J). (gr. -1-k). 21.99 *(978-0-399-25604-2(0),* Philomel) Penguin Publishing Group.

—The Very Hungry Caterpillar. Carle, Eric. 2004. 20p. (J). (ENG & BEN.). pap. *(978-1-85269-125-7(5));* (ENG & URD.). pap. *(978-1-85269-129-5(8));* (ENG & CHI.). (gr. -1-2). pap. *(978-1-85269-126-4(3));* (ARA & ENG.). (gr. -1-5). pap. *(978-1-85269-124-0(7))* Mantra Lingua.

—The Very Hungry Caterpillar. Carle, Eric. 2007. (ENG.). 24p. (J). (gr. -1 — 1). bds., bds. 15.99 *(978-0-399-24745-3(9),* Philomel) Penguin Publishing Group.

—The Very Hungry Caterpillar (La Oruga Muy Hambrienta) Carle, Eric. 2011. (SPA & ENG.). 24p. (J). (gr. -1 — 1). bds. 10.99 *(978-0-399-25605-9(9),* Philomel) Penguin Publishing Group.

—The Very Hungry Caterpillar's Favorite Words. Carle, Eric. 2007. (World of Eric Carle Ser.). (ENG.). 20p. (J). (gr. -1-k). bds. 3.99 *(978-0-448-44704-9(5),* Grosset & Dunlap) Penguin Publishing Group.

—The Very Quiet Cricket. Carle, Eric. 2014. (Penguin Young Readers, Level 3 Ser.). (ENG.). 32p. (J). (gr. 1-3). pap. 3.99 *(978-0-448-48138-8(3),* Warne, Frederick Pubs.) Penguin Bks., Ltd. GBR. Dist: Penguin Random Hse., LLC.

—Walter the Baker. Carle, Eric. 2012. (World of Eric Carle Ser.). (ENG.). 34p. (J). (gr. -1 — 1). bds. 7.99 *(978-1-4424-4941-1(1),* Little Simon) Little Simon.

—Walter the Baker. Carle, Eric. 2014. (World of Eric Carle Ser.). (ENG.). 32p. (J). (gr. -1-2). pap. 3.99 *(978-1-4814-0917-9(4),* Simon Spotlight) Simon Spotlight.

—What's Your Favorite Animal? Carle, Eric. (ENG.). (J). (gr. -1-1). 2015. 30p. bds. 8.99 *(978-1-62779-303-2(8));* 2014. 40p. 17.99 *(978-0-8050-9641-5(8))* Holt, Henry & Co. (Holt, Henry & Co. Bks. For Young Readers).

—Where Are You Going? To See My Friend! Carle, Eric. Iwamura, Kazuo. 2003. (JPN & ENG.). 40p. (J). (gr. -1-3). 19.99 *(978-0-439-41659-7(0),* Orchard Bks.) Scholastic, Inc.

—The World of Eric Carle Big Coloring Book (the World of Eric Carle) Carle, Eric. 2011. (Big Coloring Book Ser.). (ENG.). 48p. (J). (gr. -1-2). pap. 6.99 *(978-0-375-87351-5(1),* Golden Bks.) Random Hse. Children's Bks.

—10 Little Rubber Ducks. Carle, Eric. 2005. (ENG.). 36p. (J). (gr. -1-1). 21.99 *(978-0-06-074075-7(2))* HarperCollins Pubs.

—10 Little Rubber Ducks Board Book. Carle, Eric. 2010. (ENG.). 34p. (J). (gr. -1-k). bds. 7.99 *(978-0-06-196428-2(X),* HarperFestival) HarperCollins Pubs.

Carletta-Vietes, Lisa. And I Thought about You. Kurstedt, Rosanne. 2012. (J). 14.95 *(978-1-937406-65-3(2))* Mascot Bks., Inc.

Carletti, Emanuela. In the Beginning. Goodings, Christina. 2015. (ENG.). 16p. (J). (gr. -1-k). pap. 6.99 ***(978-0-7459-6568-0(7))*** Lion Hudson PLC GBR. Dist: Independent Pubs. Group.

—Lost Sheep Story. Goodings, Christina. 2015. (ENG.). 16p. (J). (gr. -1-k). pap. 6.99 ***(978-0-7459-6571-0(7))*** Lion Hudson PLC GBR. Dist: Independent Pubs. Group.

—Noah's Ark. Goodings, Christina. 2015. (ENG.). 16p. (J). (gr. -1-k). pap. 6.99 ***(978-0-7459-6569-7(5))*** Lion Hudson PLC GBR. Dist: Independent Pubs. Group.

Carlin, Laura. The Promise. Davies, Nicola. 2014. (ENG.). 40p. (J). (gr. k-4). 16.99 *(978-0-7636-6633-0(5))* Candlewick Pr.

Carling, Amelia Lau. Alfombras de Aserrín. 2005. (SPA.). 32p. (J). 11.95 *(978-0-88899-624-4(1))* Groundwood Bks. CAN. Dist: Perseus-PGW.

—Bravo, Chico Canta! Bravo!, 1 vol. Mora, Pat & Martinez, Libby. 2014. (ENG.). 32p. (J). (gr. -1-2). 17.95 *(978-1-55498-343-8(6))* Groundwood Bks. CAN. Dist: Perseus-PGW.

—Bravo, Chico Canta! Bravo!, 1 vol. Mora, Pat & Martinez, Libby. Iribarren, Elena, tr. from ENG. 2014. (SPA.). 32p. (J). (gr. -1-2). 8.95 *(978-1-55498-344-5(4))* Groundwood Bks. CAN. Dist: Perseus-PGW.

Carlo, Sonja. The Christmasmaker: Santa's first Flight. Carlo, Sonja. 2011. (ENG.). 56p. pap. 7.89 *(978-1-4663-8631-0(2))* CreateSpace Independent Publishing Platform.

Carlow, Emma. Flora the Fairy's Magic Spells. Bradman, Tony. 2009. (Green Bananas Ser.). (ENG.). 48p. (J). (gr. k-2). pap. 5.99 *(978-1-4052-4232-5(9))* Egmont Bks., Ltd. GBR. Dist: Independent Pubs. Group.

Carlow, Emma. Flora the Fairy. Carlow, Emma. Bradman, Tony. 2005. (Green Bananas Ser.). (ENG.). 48p. (J). lib. bdg. *(978-0-7787-1022-6(X))* Crabtree Publishing Co.

—Flora the Fairy. Carlow, Emma. Bradman, Tony. 2005. (Green Bananas Ser.). (ENG.). 48p. (J). (gr. k-2). pap. 5.99 *(978-1-4052-1792-7(8))* Egmont Bks., Ltd. GBR. Dist: Independent Pubs. Group.

Carlson, jt. illus. see Carlson, Nancy.

Carlson, Al & Nicklaus, Carol. The Human Apes. Carlson, Dale. 2nd ed. 2005. (ENG.). 155p. (gr. 8-12). reprint ed. pap. 14.95 *(978-1-884158-31-5(5))* Bick Publishing Hse.

Carlson, Andy. The Amazing Action Alphabet Activities. Kehl, Esther. 2009. 40p. (J). spiral bd. 12.50 *(978-0-9788089-1-4(6))* SeeHearDo Co., LLC, The.
—American History: Presidents: Grade 4-5. Morris, Deborah & Morris, Larry. 2005. (Skill Builders (Rainbow Bridge Publishing) Ser.). 80p. per. 3.99 *(978-1-59441-267-7(7)*, RB-904000) Carson-Dellosa Publishing, LLC.
Carlson, Andy, et al. Division: Grades 4-6. Breur, Jessica. 2005. (Skill Builders (Rainbow Bridge Publishing) Ser.). 80p. per. 3.99 *(978-1-59441-268-4(5)*, RB-904001) Carson-Dellosa Publishing, LLC.
Carlson, Christine. Kaycee Kangaroo Lost in Alphabet Forest: Adventures of Kaycee Kangaroo. Tonderum, Angela. 2008. 41p. pap. 24.95 *(978-1-60672-601-3(3))* America Star Bks.
Carlson, Claudia. Avi the Ambulance Goes to School. 2015. (J). *(978-0-87441-941-2(7))*; *(978-1-68115-503-6(6))* Behrman Hse., Inc.
Carlson, Eric S. Race to Moonrise Rev. Crum, Sally. 2006. 12.95 *(978-1-932738-31-5(2))* Western Reflections Publishing Co.
Carlson, George Leonard. Peter Puzzlemaker: A John Martin Puzzle-Book. Martin, John. 2014. (ENG.). 112p. (J). (gr. 1-5). 7.99 *(978-0-486-78167-9(4))* Dover Pubns., Inc.
Carlson, Josh, jt. illus. see LeTourneau, Anthony.
Carlson, Kevin. Autism Coloring Book. Carlson, Jr. 2009. 50p. pap. 9.95 *(978-1-60264-383-3(0))* Virtualbookworm.com Publishing, Inc.
—Schizophrenia Coloring Book. Carlson, Richard. Carlson, Steven, tr. 2010. (ENG.). 50p. pap. 9.95 *(978-1-4528-6638-3(4))* CreateSpace Independent Publishing Platform.
Carlson, Kim. Elwood: A Dog with Heart. Schroeder, Frauna. 2006. 32p. (J). per. 9.95 *(978-1-892076-20-5(9))* Dancing Moon Pr.
Carlson, Kirsten. The Giraffe Who Was Afraid of Heights, 1 vol. Ufer, David A. 2006. (ENG.). 32p. (J). (gr. -1-3). 15.95 *(978-0-9768823-0-5(2))* Arbordale Publishing.
—Ocean Seasons, 1 vol. Hirschi, Ron. 2007. (ENG.). 32p. (J). (gr. k-4). 15.95 *(978-0-9777423-2-5(6))*; pap. 9.95 *(978-1-60718-863-6(5))* Arbordale Publishing.
—Sea Secrets. Cerullo, Mary M. & Simmons, Beth E. 2015. (Long Term Ecological Research Ser.). (ENG.). 32p. (J). (gr. 1-5). pap. 9.95 *(978-1-63076-075-5(7))* Taylor Trade Publishing.
Carlson, Lisa. Calamity Jane. Krensky, Stephen. 2006. (On My Own Folklore Ser.). (ENG.). 48p. (gr. 2-4). lib. bdg. 25.26 *(978-1-57505-886-3(3)*, Millbrook Pr.) Lerner Publishing Group.
—Happy Birthday, World: A Rosh Hashanah Celebration. Kropf, Latifa Berry. 2005. (Very First Board Bks.). (ENG.). 12p. (J). (gr. -1 — 1). bds. 5.95 *(978-1-929371-32-0(1)*, Kar-Ben Publishing) Lerner Publishing Group.
Carlson, Nancy. Halloween. Kessel, Joyce K. 2007. (Yo Solo: Festividades (on My Own Holidays) Ser.). (SPA.). (gr. 2-4). pap. 39.62 *(978-0-8225-9676-9(8))* Lerner Publishing Group.
—Halloween. Kessel, Joyce K. Translations.com Staff, tr. from ENG. 2007. (Yo Solo: Festividades (on My Own Holidays) Ser.). (SPA.). 48p. (gr. 2-4). lib. bdg. 25.26 *(978-0-8225-7790-4(9))*; per. 6.95 *(978-0-8225-7793-5(3))* Lerner Publishing Group. (Ediciones Lerner).
—Halloween. Kessel, Joyce K. rev. ed. 2003. (On My Own Holidays Ser.). (ENG.). 48p. (gr. 2-4). lib. bdg. 25.26 *(978-0-87614-933-1(6))* Lerner Publishing Group.
—Zip It! Lindaman, Jane. 2012. (Carolrhoda Picture Bks). (ENG.). 32p. (J). (gr. k-4). lib. bdg. 16.95 *(978-0-7613-5592-2(8)*, Carolrhoda Bks.) Lerner Publishing Group.
Carlson, Nancy. Arnie & the Skateboard Gang. Carlson, Nancy. 2012. (Nancy Carlson Picture Bks). (ENG.). 32p. (J). (gr. k-2). 9.95 *(978-0-7613-8948-4(2)*, Carolrhoda Bks.) Lerner Publishing Group.
—Arnie Goes to Camp. Carlson, Nancy. 2012. (Nancy Carlson Picture Bks). (ENG.). 32p. (J). (gr. k-2). 9.95 *(978-0-7613-8947-7(4)*, Carolrhoda Bks.) Lerner Publishing Group.
—Harriet & the Roller Coaster. Carlson, Nancy. unabr. ed. (J). (gr. k-3). 24.95 incl. audio *(978-0-941078-56-6(6))*; pap. 15.95 incl. audio *(978-0-941078-54-2(X))*; pap., tchr. ed. 31.95 incl. audio *(978-0-941078-55-9(8))* Live Oak Media.
—Harriet & Walt. Carlson, Nancy. unabr. ed. (J). (gr. k-3). 24.95 incl. audio *(978-0-941078-59-7(0))*; pap. 15.95 incl. audio *(978-0-941078-57-3(4))*; pap., tchr. ed. 31.95 incl. audio *(978-0-941078-58-0(2))* Live Oak Media.
—Harriet's Halloween Candy. Carlson, Nancy. unabr. ed. (J). pap., tchr. ed. 31.95 incl. audio *(978-0-941078-52-8(3))*; 24.95 incl. audio *(978-0-941078-53-5(1))*; pap. 15.95 incl. audio *(978-0-941078-51-1(5))* Live Oak Media.
—Henry's 100 Days of Kindergarten. Carlson, Nancy. 2007. (ENG.). 32p. (J). (gr. -1-1). pap. 5.99 *(978-0-14-240758-5(5)*, Puffin) Penguin Publishing Group.
—Henry's Show & Tell. Carlson, Nancy. 2012. (Nancy Carlson Picture Bks). (ENG.). 32p. (J). (gr. k-2). 9.95 *(978-0-7613-8953-8(9)*, Carolrhoda Bks.) Lerner Publishing Group.
—It's Going to Be Perfect! Carlson, Nancy. 2012. (Nancy Carlson Picture Bks). (ENG.). 32p. (J). (gr. k-2). 9.95 *(978-0-7613-8944-6(X)*, Carolrhoda Bks.) Lerner Publishing Group.
—Life Is Fun. Carlson, Nancy. 2012. (Nancy Carlson Picture Bks). (ENG.). 32p. (J). (gr. k-2). 9.95 *(978-0-7613-8945-3(8)*, Carolrhoda Bks.) Lerner Publishing Group.
—Look Out, Kindergarten, Here I Come! Carlson, Nancy. Mlawer, Teresa, tr. 2004.Tr. of Preparate, Kindergarten! Alla Voy!. (SPA & ENG.). 32p. (J). (gr. -1-k). 15.99 *(978-0-670-03673-8(0)*, Viking Juvenile) Penguin Publishing Group.
—Louanne Pig in Witch Lady. Carlson, Nancy. rev. ed. 2006. (ENG.). 32p. (J). (gr. k-2). per. 9.95 *(978-0-8225-6197-2(2)*, First Avenue Editions) Lerner Publishing Group.
—Loudmouth George Earns His Allowance. Carlson, Nancy. (ENG.). 32p. (J). (gr. k-2). 2013. 9.95 *(978-1-4677-0865-4(8))*; 2007. 15.95 *(978-0-8225-6560-4(9))* Lerner Publishing Group. (Carolrhoda Bks.).
—My Best Friend Moved Away. Carlson, Nancy. 2012. (Nancy Carlson Picture Bks). (ENG.). 32p. (J). (gr. k-2). 9.95 *(978-0-7613-8954-5(7)*, Carolrhoda Bks.) Lerner Publishing Group.
—My Family Is Forever. Carlson, Nancy. 2006. (ENG.). 32p. (J). (gr. -1-k). pap. 5.99 *(978-0-14-240561-1(2)*, Puffin) Penguin Publishing Group.
—No Es Mi Culpa. Carlson, Nancy. Translations.com Staff, tr. from ENG. 2006. (Spanish Picture Bks.). (SPA.). 32p. (J). (gr. k-2). lib. bdg. 15.95 *(978-0-8225-6501-7(3)*, Ediciones Lerner) Lerner Publishing Group.
—Poor Carl. Carlson, Nancy. 2012. (Nancy Carlson Picture Bks). (ENG.). 32p. (J). (gr. k-2). 9.95 *(978-0-7613-8950-7(4)*, Carolrhoda Bks.) Lerner Publishing Group.
—Sit Still! Carlson, Nancy. 2012. (Nancy Carlson Picture Bks). (ENG.). 32p. (J). (gr. k-2). 9.95 *(978-0-7613-8946-0(6)*, Carolrhoda Bks.) Lerner Publishing Group.
—Smile a Lot! Carlson, Nancy. 2012. (Nancy Carlson Picture Bks). (ENG.). 32p. (J). (gr. k-2). 9.95 *(978-0-7613-9173-9(8)*, Carolrhoda Bks.) Lerner Publishing Group.
—Snowden. Carlson, Nancy. 2012. (Nancy Carlson Picture Bks). (ENG.). 32p. (J). (gr. k-2). 9.95 *(978-0-7613-8952-1(0)*, Carolrhoda Bks.) Lerner Publishing Group.
—Sometimes You Barf. Carlson, Nancy. 2014. 32p. (J). (gr. k-2). 16.95 *(978-1-4677-1412-9(7)*, Carolrhoda Bks.) Lerner Publishing Group.
—¡Sonríe! Carlson, Nancy. Translations.com Staff, tr. from ENG. 2007. (Ediciones Lerner Single Titles Ser.).Tr. of Smile a Lot!. (SPA.). 32p. (J). (gr. k-2). 15.95 *(978-0-8225-7817-8(4)*, Ediciones Lerner) Lerner Publishing Group.
—Take Time to Relax! Carlson, Nancy. 2012. (Nancy Carlson Picture Bks). (ENG.). 32p. (J). (gr. k-2). 9.95 *(978-0-7613-8949-1(0)*, Carolrhoda Bks.) Lerner Publishing Group.
—Think Happy! Carlson, Nancy. (Nancy Carlson Picture Bks). (ENG.). 32p. (J). (gr. k-3). 2012. 9.95 *(978-0-7613-9175-3(4))*; 2009. 16.95 *(978-0-8225-8940-2(0))* Lerner Publishing Group. (Carolrhoda Bks.).
—What If It Never Stops Raining? Carlson, Nancy. 2012. (Nancy Carlson Picture Bks). (ENG.). 32p. (J). (gr. k-2). 9.95 *(978-0-7613-8951-4(2)*, Carolrhoda Bks.) Lerner Publishing Group.
Carlson, Nancy & Carlson. I Don't Like to Read! Carlson, Nancy. 2009. (ENG.). 32p. (J). (gr. -1-k). pap. 6.99 *(978-0-14-241451-4(4)*, Puffin) Penguin Publishing Group.
Carlson, Nancy Gayle. One, Two, Tie Your Shoes! Gregory, Lorraine NAR NEEDED. 2010. (J). *(978-0-545-26482-2(0))* Scholastic, Inc.
Carlson, Patrick. Albert Is Our Mascot. Wells, Jason & Wells, Jeff. 2013. (That's Not Our Mascot Ser.). (ENG.). (J). 14.95 *(978-1-62086-283-4(2))* Mascot Bks., Inc.
—Aubie Is Our Mascot. Wells, Jason & Wells, Jeff. 2013. (That's Not Our Mascot Ser.). (ENG.). (J). 14.95 *(978-1-62086-292-6(1))* Mascot Bks., Inc.
—Big Al Is Our Mascot. Wells, Jason & Wells, Jeff. 2013. (That's Not Our Mascot Ser.). (ENG.). (J). 14.95 *(978-1-62086-290-2(5))* Mascot Bks., Inc.
—Big Red Is Our Mascot. Wells, Jason & Wells, Jeff. 2013. (That's Not Our Mascot Ser.). (ENG.). (J). 14.95 *(978-1-62086-291-9(3))* Mascot Bks., Inc.
—Bully Is Our Mascot. Wells, Jason & Wells, Jeff. 2013. (That's Not Our Mascot Ser.). (ENG.). (J). 14.95 *(978-1-62086-294-0(8))* Mascot Bks., Inc.
—Cocky Is Our Mascot. Wells, Jason & Wells, Jeff. 2013. (That's Not Our Mascot Ser.). (ENG.). (J). 14.95 *(978-1-62086-287-2(5))* Mascot Bks., Inc.
—Hairy Dawg Is Our Mascot. Wells, Jason & Wells, Jeff. 2013. (That's Not Our Mascot Ser.). (ENG.). (J). 14.95 *(978-1-62086-284-1(0))* Mascot Bks., Inc.
—Mike the Tiger Is Our Mascot. Wells, Jason & Wells, Jeff. 2013. (That's Not Our Mascot Ser.). (ENG.). (J). 14.95 *(978-1-62086-293-3(X))* Mascot Bks., Inc.
—Reveille Is Our Mascot. Wells, Jason & Wells, Jeff. 2013. (That's Not Our Mascot Ser.). (ENG.). (J). 14.95 *(978-1-62086-296-4(4))* Mascot Bks., Inc.
—Scratch Is Our Mascot. Wells, Jason & Wells, Jeff. 2013. (That's Not Our Mascot Ser.). (ENG.). (J). 14.95 *(978-1-62086-285-8(9))* Mascot Bks., Inc.
—Smokey Is Our Mascot. Wells, Jason & Wells, Jeff. 2013. (That's Not Our Mascot Ser.). (ENG.). (J). 14.95 *(978-1-62086-288-9(3))* Mascot Bks., Inc.
—Truman Is Our Mascot. Wells, Jason & Wells, Jeff. 2013. (That's Not Our Mascot Ser.). (ENG.). (J). 14.95 *(978-1-62086-286-5(7))* Mascot Bks., Inc.
Carluccio, Maria. Jump into January. Blackstone, Stella. 2004. 32p. (J). 15.99 *(978-1-84148-629-1(9))* Barefoot Bks., Inc.
—Skip Through the Seasons. Blackstone, Stella. (ENG.). (J). 2010. 17p. bds. 14.99 *(978-1-84686-398-1(8))*; 2009. 32p. 16.99 *(978-1-84686-293-9(0))* Barefoot Bks., Inc.
—The Sounds Around Town. 2011. (ENG.). 24p. (J). (gr. -1-3). pap. 7.99 *(978-1-84686-430-8(5))* Barefoot Bks., Inc.
Carluccio, Maria. Un Recorrido Por Las Estaciones. Carluccio, Maria. Blackstone, Stella. 2009. (SPA.). 32p. (J). 7.99 *(978-1-84686-291-5(4))* Barefoot Bks., Inc.
—Skip Through the Seasons. Carluccio, Maria. Blackstone, Stella. 2006. (Seek-and-Find Bks.). (ENG.). 32p. (J). (gr. -1-2). pap. 7.99 *(978-1-905236-71-8(9))* Barefoot Bks., Inc.
—The Sounds Around Town. Carluccio, Maria. 2010. (ENG.). 13p. (J). 14.99 *(978-1-84686-362-2(7))* Barefoot Bks., Inc.
Carman, Debby. Cha Cha, the Dancing Dog. Carman, Debby. 2007. 28p. (J). (gr. -1-1). 14.99 *(978-0-9777340-5-4(6))* Faux Paw Media Group.
—Chewdalootie, Doing My Duty. Carman, Debby. 2007. 28p. (J). (gr. -1-1). 14.99 *(978-0-9777340-3-0(X))* Faux Paw Media Group.
—I'm Gronk & I'm Green. Carman, Debby. 2007. 28p. (J). (gr. -1-1). 14.99 *(978-0-9777340-0-9(5))* Faux Paw Media Group.
—Kittywimpuss Got Game. Carman, Debby. 2007. 28p. (J). (gr. -1-1). 14.99 *(978-0-9777340-4-7(8))* Faux Paw Media Group.
—The Nutcracker Cats of the Kremlin. Carman, Debby. 2007. 80p. (J). (gr. 1-7). 28.99 *(978-0-9777340-7-8(2))* Faux Paw Media Group.
—Purrlonia's Lullaby. Carman, Debby. 2008. 28p. (J). (gr. -1-1). 14.99 *(978-0-9777340-1-6(3))* Faux Paw Media Group.
Carmi, Giora. The Chanukkah Guest. Kimmel, Eric A. (ENG.). 32p. (J). (gr. k-3). tchr. ed. 17.95 *(978-0-8234-0788-0(8))* Holiday Hse., Inc.
—A Circle of Friends, 1 vol. 2006. (ENG.). 32p. (J). (gr. k-9). pap. 5.95 *(978-1-59572-060-3(X))* Star Bright Bks., Inc.
—A Journey to Paradise: And Other Jewish Tales. Schwartz, Howard. 2005. (Jewish Storyteller Ser.). 48p. (J). (gr. -1-3). 16.95 *(978-0-943706-21-4(1))*; pap. 9.95 *(978-0-943706-16-0(5))* Simcha Media Group. (Devora Publishing).
—Night Lights: A Sukkot Story. Goldin, Barbara Diamond. 2004. (gr. k-3). 13.95 *(978-0-8074-0803-2(4)*, 142687) URJ Pr.
—The Rooster Prince. 2005. 48p. (J). (gr. 1-4). pap. 9.95 *(978-0-943706-49-8(1))*; (gr. 2-5). 16.95 *(978-0-943706-45-0(9))* Simcha Media Group. (Devora Publishing).
Carmi, Giora. A Circle of Friends, 1 vol. Carmi, Giora. 2003. (ENG.). 32p. (J). 15.95 *(978-1-932065-00-8(8))* Star Bright Bks., Inc.
Carmichael, Peyton. The Donkey of Tarsus: His Tales about the Apostle Paul, 1 vol. Colvin, Adele. 2010. (Donkey Tales Ser.). (ENG.). 32p. (J). (gr. k-3). 16.99 *(978-1-58980-780-8(4))* Pelican Publishing Co., Inc.
—The Donkey's Easter Tale, 1 vol. Colvin, Adele Bibb. 2008. (Donkey Tales Ser.). (ENG.). 32p. (J). (gr. k-3). 16.99 *(978-1-58980-593-4(3))* Pelican Publishing Co., Inc.
Carnavas, Peter. Blue Whale Blues. Carnavas, Peter. 2016. 32p. (J). 11.99 ***(978-1-61067-458-4(8))*** Kane Miller.
Carnavas, Peter. The Boy on the Page. Carnavas, Peter. 2014. (ENG.). 32p. (J). 11.99 *(978-1-61067-245-0(3))* Kane Miller.
—The Children Who Loved Books. Carnavas, Peter. 2013. (ENG.). 32p. (J). 11.99 *(978-1-61067-145-3(7))* Kane Miller.
—Last Tree in the City (Akhr Shajara Fil Madina) Carnavas, Peter. Ibrahim, Nouran, tr. 2013. (ENG & ARA.). 32p. (J). (gr. k-3). pap. 6.99 *(978-99921-94-02-7(2)*, 149256) Bloomsbury Qatar Foundation Publishing QAT. Dist: Macmillan.
Carnehl, Jeff. Christmas Around the World. Trunkhill, Brenda. 2009. 32p. (J). (gr. k). 6.99 *(978-0-7586-1757-6(7))* Concordia Publishing Hse.
Carnesi, Mônica. Little Dog Lost: The True Story of a Brave Dog Named Baltic. Carnesi, Mônica. 2012. (ENG.). 32p. (J). (gr. -1-k). 15.99 *(978-0-399-25666-0(0)*, Nancy Paulsen Bks.) Penguin Publishing Group.
—Sleepover with Beatrice & Bear. Carnesi, Mônica. 2014. (ENG.). 32p. (J). (gr. -1-k). 15.99 *(978-0-399-25667-7(9)*, Nancy Paulsen Bks.) Penguin Publishing Group.
Carney, Deborah. Walking along with My Dog. Taeckens, Geri. 2005. (J). 16.99 *(978-0-9774546-0-0(6))* Accessibilities.
Carney, Patrick. Homes: From Start to Finish. Carney, Patrick, photos by. Kreger, Claire. 2003. 32p. (J). 24.95 *(978-1-4103-0169-7(9)*, Blackbirch Pr., Inc.) Cengage Gale.
Carol, Light. Chickensing Story Book Board. Carol, Light. 2003. 60p. (J). *(978-0-9745803-0-2(9))* Little Big Tomes.
Carol, Racklin-Siegel. Let My People Go! Goldstein, Jessica & Inker, Inna, eds. 2011. (ENG & HEB.). 32p. (J). pap. 10.95 *(978-0-939144-67-9(0))* EKS Publishing Co.
Carolan, Christine. The Ballad of Booster Bogg. Jackson, Ellen B. 2011. (J). *(978-1-934860-07-6(7))* Shenanigan Bks.
—Flowers for Pudding Street. Mannone, Christine. 2009. (ENG.). 32p. (J). 15.95 *(978-1-934860-02-1(6))* Shenanigan Bks.
—Too Much of a Good Thing. Wasserman, Mira. 2003. (ENG.). 32p. (J). (gr. -1-3). 15.95 *(978-1-58013-082-0(8)*, Kar-Ben Publishing) Lerner Publishing Group.
Carolan, Joanna. This Is My Piko. Carolan. 2009. 58p. 17.95 incl. audio compact disk *(978-0-9715333-0-1(X))* Banana Patch Pr.
Carolan, Joanna F. Where Are My Slippers? A Book of Colors. Carolan, Dr. 32p. 2007. 17.95 *(978-0-9715333-7-0(7))*; 2005. (J). pap. 16.95 *(978-0-9715333-6-3(9))* Banana Patch Pr.
Carolan, Joanna F. Old Makana Had a Taro Farm. Carolan, Joanna F. 2008. 48p. 17.95 *(978-0-9715333-9-4(3))* Banana Patch Pr.
Carole, Isaacs. Toothbugs!, Alexander, Geoff. l.t. ed. 2005. 12p. (J). bds. 12.95 *(978-0-9760944-0-1(1))* Alexander-Marcus Publishing.
Caron, Mona. The Boy Without a Name. Shah, Idries. 2007. 32p. (J). pap. 7.99 *(978-1-883536-94-7(4)*, Hoopoe Bks.) I S H K.
—The Boy Without a Name / el Nino Sin Nombre. Shah, Idries. Wirkala, Rita, tr. 2007. 32p. (J). 18.00 *(978-1-883536-92-3(8))*; pap. 7.99 *(978-1-883536-93-0(6))* I S H K. (Hoopoe Bks.).
—Many Worlds: Native Life along the Anza Trail. 2012. (ENG.). 24p. (J). pap. 7.95 *(978-1-59714-167-3(4))* Heyday.
Caron, Monique. The Smiling Scarecrow the Winter Months. Caron, Monique. l.t. ed. 2010. (ENG.). 30p. pap. 9.55 *(978-1-4563-1372-2(X))* CreateSpace Independent Publishing Platform.
Caron, Romi. Baby Turtle's Tale. McGuinness, Elle J. 2009. (ENG.). 26p. (J). (gr. -1). 19.99 *(978-0-7407-8102-5(2))* Andrews McMeel Publishing.
—Enquete Tres Speciale. Ducharme, Huguette. 2004. (Collection des 6 Ans: Vol. 32). (FRE.). 68p. (YA). 7.95 *(978-2-922565-94-2(7))* Editions de la Paix CAN. Dist: World of Reading, Ltd.
—Uumajut: Learn about Arctic Wildlife, 1 vol. Awa, Simon et al. 2010. (ENG.). 32p. (J). (gr. 1-3). pap. 9.95 *(978-1-926569-08-6(3))* Inhabit Media Inc. CAN. Dist: Independent Pubs. Group.
—Uumajut Vol. 2: Learn More about Arctic Wildlife!, Vol. 2. Awa, Simon et al. Otak, Leah, tr. 2011. (ENG.). 32p. (J). (gr. 1-3). pap. 9.95 *(978-1-926569-22-2(9))* Inhabit Media Inc. CAN. Dist: Independent Pubs. Group.
Caron, Romi & Owlkids Books Inc. Staff. Amazing Things Animals Do. Baillie, Marilyn. 2008. (ENG.). 128p. (J). (gr. k-4). 24.95 *(978-1-897066-86-7(4)*, Maple Tree Pr.) Owlkids Bks. Inc. CAN. Dist: Perseus-PGW.
Carpenter, Anthony. Big Bad Bible Giants, 1 vol. Strauss, Ed. 2005. (2:52 Ser.). (ENG.). 112p. (J). pap. 7.99 *(978-0-310-70869-8(9))* Zonderkidz.
—Creepy Creatures & Bizarre Beasts from the Bible, 1 vol. Osborne, Rick et al. 2004. (2:52 Ser.). (ENG.). 128p. (J). pap. 7.99 *(978-0-310-70654-0(8))* Zonderkidz.
Carpenter, Anthony. Weird & Gross Bible Stuff, 1 vol. Carpenter, Anthony. Osborne, Rick et al. 2003. (2:52 Ser.). (ENG.). 112p. (J). pap. 7.99 *(978-0-310-70484-3(7))* Zondervan.
Carpenter, Christopher. Lily's Heart: The Veterinary Clinic Cases Series. 2006. 32p. (J). per. 9.95 *(978-0-9766641-0-9(0))* Ichabod Ink.
Carpenter, Debra. Pete & Patricia Prairie Dog & their Pack of Prairie Pups. Lastoka, Mariann. 2003. 40p. 6.50 *(978-1-892860-05-7(8)*, 5) M R L, Inc.
Carpenter, Mark, et al. The Little Bible Storybook, 1 vol. Barfield, Maggie. 2009. 48p. (J). bds. 9.99 *(978-0-8254-7409-5(4)*, Candle Bks.) Lion Hudson PLC GBR. Dist: Kregel Pubns.
Carpenter, Mark And Anna. The Big Bible Storybook: 188 Bible Stories to Enjoy Together, 1 vol. Barfield, Maggie. 2009. 256p. (J). 18.99 *(978-0-8254-7424-8(8)*, Candle Bks.) Lion Hudson PLC GBR. Dist: Kregel Pubns.
Carpenter, Mike. Rhino Trouble. Olsen, Grant Orrin. 2015. (J). ***(978-1-4621-1665-2(5))*** Cedar Fort, Inc./CFI Distribution.
Carpenter, Nancy. Abe Lincoln: The Boy Who Loved Books. Winters, Kay. 2004. 38p. (J). (gr. -1-3). reprint ed. 17.00 *(978-0-7567-7969-6(3))* DIANE Publishing Co.
—Abe Lincoln: The Boy Who Loved Books. Winters, Kay. 2006. (ENG.). 40p. (J). (gr. k-3). reprint ed. 7.99 *(978-1-4169-1268-2(1)*, Simon & Schuster/Paula Wiseman Bks.) Simon & Schuster/Paula Wiseman Bks.
—Apples to Oregon: Being the (Slightly) True Narrative of How a Brave Pioneer Father Brought Apples, Peaches, Pears, Plums, Grapes, & Cherries (and Children) Across the Plains. Hopkinson, Deborah. 2008. (ENG.). 40p. (J). (gr. -1-3). 7.99 *(978-1-4169-6746-0(X)*, Simon & Schuster/Paula Wiseman Bks.) Simon & Schuster/Paula Wiseman Bks.
—Baby Radar. Nye, Naomi Shihab. 2003. 32p. (J). lib. bdg. 16.89 *(978-0-688-15949-8(4))* HarperCollins Pubs.
—Big Bear's Big Boat. Bunting, Eve. 2013. (ENG.). 32p. (J). (gr. -1-3). 12.99 *(978-0-618-58537-3(0))* Houghton Mifflin Harcourt Publishing Co.
—Dear Mr. Washington. Cullen, Lynn. 2015. (ENG.). 32p. (J). (gr. k-3). 16.99 *(978-0-8037-3038-0(1)*, Dial) Penguin Publishing Group.
—Emma Dilemma: Big Sister Poems. George, Kristine O'Connell. 2011. (ENG.). 48p. (J). (gr. 1-4). 16.99 *(978-0-618-42842-7(9))* Houghton Mifflin Harcourt Publishing Co.
—Fannie in the Kitchen: The Whole Story from Soup to Nuts of How Fannie Farmer Invented Recipes with Precise Measurements. Hopkinson, Deborah. 2004. (ENG.). 40p. (J). (gr. -1-4). reprint ed. 7.99 *(978-0-689-86997-6(5)*, Simon & Schuster/Paula Wiseman Bks.) Simon & Schuster/Paula Wiseman Bks.
—Heroes of the Surf. Carbone, Elisa. 2012. (ENG.). 40p. (J). (gr. -1-3). 16.99 *(978-0-670-06312-3(6)*, Viking Juvenile) Penguin Publishing Group.
—I Could Do That! Esther Morris Gets Women the Vote. White, Linda Arms. 2005. (ENG.). 40p. (J). (gr. 2-4). 17.99 *(978-0-374-33527-4(3)*, Farrar, Straus & Giroux (BYR)) Farrar, Straus & Giroux.
—Imogene's Last Stand. Fleming, Candace. (ENG.). 40p. (J). (gr. -1-3). 2014. 7.99 *(978-0-385-38654-6(0)*, Dragonfly Bks.); 2009. 16.99 *(978-0-375-83607-7(1)*, Schwartz & Wade Bks.) Random Hse. Children's Bks.
—Lucky Ducklings. Moore, Eva. 2013. (ENG.). 32p. (J). (gr. k-2). 16.99 *(978-0-439-44861-1(1)*, Orchard Bks.) Scholastic, Inc.
—M Is for Mischief: An A to Z of Naughty Children. Ashman, Linda. 2008. (ENG.). 32p. (J). (gr. 1-3). 16.99 *(978-0-525-47564-4(8)*, Dutton Juvenile) Penguin Publishing Group.
—Only a Star. Facklam, Margery. 2004. 32p. (J). (gr. -1-3). pap. 8.00 *(978-0-8028-5174-1(6))* Eerdmans, William B. Publishing Co.
—A Picnic in October. Bunting, Eve. 2004. (ENG.). 32p. (J). (gr. -1-3). reprint ed. pap. 7.99 *(978-0-15-205065-8(5))* Houghton Mifflin Harcourt Publishing Co.
—Queen Victoria's Bathing Machine. 2014. (ENG.). 40p. (J). (gr. k-3). 17.99 *(978-1-4169-2753-2(0)*, Simon & Schuster/Paula Wiseman Bks.) Simon & Schuster/Paula Wiseman Bks.
—Twister. Beard, Darleen Bailey & Beard, Darleen B. 2003. (ENG.). 32p. (J). (gr. -1-3). pap. 8.99 *(978-0-374-48014-1(1))* Square Fish.
—11 Experiments That Failed. Offill, Jenny. 2011. (ENG.). 40p. (J). (gr. -1-3). 17.99 *(978-0-375-84762-2(6)*, Schwartz & Wade Bks.) Random Hse. Children's Bks.
—17 Things I'm Not Allowed to Do Anymore. Offill, Jenny. 2011. (ENG.). 32p. (J). (gr. -1-3). pap. 6.99

C

(978-0-375-86601-2(9)), Dragonfly Bks.) Random Hse. Children's Bks.

Carpenter, Stephen. A Bad Case of the Giggles. Lansky, Bruce. 2013. (Giggle Poetry Ser.). (ENG.). 128p. (J). (gr. 1-6). per. 9.95 *(978-1-4169-5197-1(0))* Meadowbrook Pr.

—I Hope I Don't Strike Out! And Other Funny Sports Poems. Meadowbrook Press Staff. 2008. (Giggle Poetry Ser.). (ENG.). 32p. (J). (gr. k-6). 9.95 *(978-1-4169-5198-8(9))* Meadowbrook Pr.

—I Hope I Don't Strike Out! & Other Funny Sports Poems. Lansky, Bruce. 2008. 30p. *(978-0-88166-535-2(5))* Meadowbrook Pr.

—If Kids Ruled the School. Meadowbrook Press Staff. 2004. (ENG.). 80p. (J). (gr. 1-6). pap. 8.95 *(978-0-689-03273-8(0))* Meadowbrook Pr.

—If Kids Ruled the School: More Kids' Favorite Funny School Poems. 2004. 73p. (J). 8.95 *(978-0-88166-468-3(5))* Meadowbrook Pr.

—I've Been Burping in the Classroom. 2007. (Giggle Poetry Ser.). (ENG.). 32p. (J). (gr. 1-6). 9.95 *(978-1-4169-2946-8(0))* Meadowbrook Pr.

—I've Been Burping in the Classroom: And Other Silly Sing-along Songs. Lansky, Bruce, ed. 2007. 32p. (J). *(978-0-88166-521-5(5))* Meadowbrook Pr.

—Mary Had a Little Jam: And Other Silly Rhymes. Lansky, Bruce & Meadowbrook Press Staff. 2004. (ENG.). 32p. (J). (gr. -1 — 1). 9.95 *(978-0-689-03392-6(3))* Meadowbrook Pr.

—Mary Had a Little Jam, & Other Silly Rhymes. 2004. 32p. (J). *(978-0-88166-470-6(7))* Meadowbrook Pr.

—Miles of Smiles. Lansky, Bruce, ed. 2013. (Giggle Poetry Ser.). (ENG.). 126p. (J). (gr. 1-6). pap. 9.95 *(978-0-689-03461-9(X))* Meadowbrook Pr.

—Peter Peter Pizza Eater. Lansky, Bruce. 2006. (ENG.). 32p. (J). (gr. -1-1). 9.95 *(978-0-684-03166-8(3))* Meadowbrook Pr.

—Rolling in the Aisles: A Collection of Laugh-Out-Loud Poems. Lanksy, Bruce. 2004. 116p. (J). *(978-0-88166-473-7(1))* Meadowbrook Pr.

—Rolling in the Aisles (Revision) A Collection of Laugh-Out-Loud Poems. Lansky, Bruce & Wiechmann, Angela, eds. 2011. (Giggle Poetry Ser.). (ENG.). 128p. (J). (gr. 1-8). pap. 9.95 *(978-1-4424-1127-2(9))* Meadowbrook Pr.

—What I Did on My Summer Vacation: Kids' Favorite Funny Poems about Summer Vacation. Lansky, Bruce. 2009. *(978-0-88166-539-0(8))* Meadowbrook Pr.

—What I Did on My Summer Vacation: Kids' Favorite Funny Summer Vacation Poems. 2009. (Giggle Poetry Ser.). (ENG.). 80p. (J). (gr. 1-8). pap. 8.95 *(978-1-4169-7047-7(9))* Meadowbrook Pr.

Carpenter, Suzanne. Happy Christmas Sglod. Morgan, Ruth. 2003. (WEL & ENG.). 32p. pap. 12.95 *(978-1-84323-261-2(8))* Beekman Bks., Inc.

—Rapping on the Window. Stephens, Chris S. 2004. (ENG.). 48p. pap. 12.95 *(978-1-84323-360-2(6))* Beekman Bks., Inc.

—So Hungry. Morden, Daniel. 2004. (ENG.). 32p. pap. 29.95 *(978-1-84323-455-5(6))* Beekman Bks., Inc.

Carpenter, Tad. Bitty Bot. McCanna, Tim. 2016. (J). *(978-1-4814-4929-8(X)*, Simon & Schuster Bks. For Young Readers) Simon & Schuster Bks. For Young Readers.

Carpenter, Tad. Ninja, Ninja, Never Stop! Tuell, Todd. 2014. (ENG.). 32p. (J). (gr. -1-k). 14.95 *(978-1-4197-1027-8(3)*, Abrams Appleseed) Abrams.

—Pantone: Color Puzzles: 6 Color-Matching Puzzles. Pantone. 2013. (Pantone Ser.). (ENG.). 12p. (J). (gr. -1 — 1). bds. 16.95 *(978-1-4197-0939-5(9)*, Abrams Appleseed) Abrams.

—Simple Steps Toward a Healthier Earth. Natural Resources Defense Council Staff et al. 2010. (ENG.). 80p. (J). (gr. 3-17). pap., act. bk. ed. 12.99 *(978-0-8118-7141-9(X))* Chronicle Bks. LLC.

—The Summer of May. Galante, Cecilia. (ENG.). 256p. (J). (gr. 4-8). 2012. pap. 6.99 *(978-1-4169-8304-0(X))*; 2011. 16.99 *(978-1-4169-8023-0(7))* Simon & Schuster/Paula Wiseman Bks. (Simon & Schuster/Paula Wiseman Bks.).

—Trick-or-Treat: A Happy Haunter's Halloween. Leppanen, Debbie. 2013. (ENG.). 40p. (J). (gr. k-3). 16.99 *(978-1-4424-3398-4(1))* Simon & Schuster Children's Publishing.

—Zoom! Zoom! Sounds of Things That Go in the City. Burleigh, Robert. 2014. (ENG.). 32p. (J). (gr. -1-3). 17.99 *(978-1-4424-8315-6(6))*, Simon & Schuster Bks. For Young Readers) Simon & Schuster Bks. For Young Readers.

Carr, A. E. K. Alice Eats Wonderland. Imholtz, August & Tannenbaum, Alison. 2009. (ENG.). 120p. pap. 14.95 *(978-1-4290-9106-0(1))* Applewood Bks.

Carr, Greg. The Jiggleworm. Carr, Heather, ed. 2005. 18p. (J). 21.95 incl. audio compact disk *(978-0-9768450-0-3(8)*, Giggletins) Le Bk. Moderne, LLC.

Carr, Holly. What Is Pink? 2003. 24p. (J). (gr. -1-1). *(978-0-921156-92-5(8))* Rubicon Publishing, Inc.

—What Is Pink? Rossetti, Christina. 2003. 24p. pap. *(978-1-894915-13-7(5))* Rubicon Publishing, Inc.

Carr, Karen. A Busy Day for Stegosaurus. Bentley, Dawn. (ENG.). 36p. (J). (gr. -1-2). 2005. 9.95 *(978-1-59249-156-8(1)*, PS2451); 2004. 8.95 *(978-1-59249-210-7(X)*, SD2401); 2004. 14.95 *(978-1-59249-153-7(7)*, H2401); 2004. pap. 6.95 *(978-1-59249-154-4(5)*, S2401) Soundprints.

—Dino Dung: The Scoop on Fossil Feces. Chin, Karen & Holmes, Thom. 2005. (Step into Reading Ser.). 48p. (J). (gr. 2-5). 11.65 *(978-0-7569-5163-4(1))* Perfection Learning Corp.

—How Do Frogs Swallow with Their Eyes? Questions & Answers about Amphibians. Berger, Melvin & Berger, Gilda. 2003. (Scholastic Question & Answer Ser.). (ENG.). 48p. (J). (gr. 2-5). pap. 5.95 *(978-0-439-26677-2(7)*, Scholastic Reference) Scholastic, Inc.

—The Hungry T-Rex. Galvin, Laura Gates & Studiomouse Staff. 2011. (Read, Play & Go Ser.). (ENG.). 20p. (gr. -1-k). 9.99 *(978-1-60727-288-5(1))* Studio Mouse LLC.

—It's Tyrannosaurus Rex! Bentley, Dawn. (Smithsonian's Prehistoric Pals Ser.). (ENG.). 36p. (J). (gr. -1-2). 2004. 8.95 *(978-1-59249-212-1(6)*, SD2400); 2003. 9.95 *(978-1-59249-160-5(X)*, PS2450) Soundprints.

—Lead the Way, Velociraptor! Bentley, Dawn. 2004. (Read & Discover (Soundprints) Ser.). (ENG.). 32p. (J). (gr. -1-3). pap. 3.95 *(978-1-59249-304-3(1)*, S2031) Soundprints.

—Mosasaurus: Mighty Ruler of the Sea. Wagner, Karen. 2008. (ENG.). 36p. (J). (gr. k-2). 8.95 *(978-1-59249-782-9(9))*; 2.95 *(978-1-59249-783-6(7))*; 9.95 *(978-1-59249-784-3(5))*; 14.95 *(978-1-59249-780-5(2))* Soundprints.

—Pteranodon. Bailey, Gerry. 2011. (Smithsonian Prehistoric Zone Ser.). (ENG.). 32p. (J). (gr. k-3). *(978-0-7787-1800-0(X))*; pap. *(978-0-7787-1813-0(1))* Crabtree Publishing Co.

—Pteranodon Soars. Bentley, Dawn. 2005. (Smithsonian's Prehistoric Pals Ser.). (ENG.). 36p. (J). (gr. -1-2). 8.95 *(978-1-59249-371-5(8)*, SD2405); 9.95 *(978-1-59249-373-9(4)*, PS2455); 14.95 *(978-1-59249-369-2(6)*, H2405); 2.95 *(978-1-59249-372-2(6)*, S2455); pap. 6.95 *(978-1-59249-370-8(X)*, S2405) Soundprints.

—Snack Time, Tyrannosaurus Rex! Bentley, Dawn. 2004. (ENG.). 32p. (J). (gr. -1-3). pap. 3.95 *(978-1-59249-302-9(5)*, S2033) Soundprints.

—Stegosaurus. Bailey, Gerry. 2011. (Smithsonian Prehistoric Zone Ser.). (ENG.). 32p. (J). (gr. k-3). *(978-0-7787-1803-1(4))* Crabtree Publishing Co.

—Surprise, Stegosaurus! Bentley, Dawn. 2004. (ENG.). 32p. (J). (gr. -1-3). pap. 3.95 *(978-1-59249-305-0(X)*, S2032) Soundprints.

—Triceratops. Bentley, Dawn & Studio Mouse Staff. 2008. (ENG.). 24p. (J). (gr. 3-7). 4.99 *(978-1-59069-622-4(0))* Studio Mouse LLC.

—Triceratops. Bailey, Gerry. 2011. (Smithsonian Prehistoric Zone Ser.). (ENG.). 32p. (J). (gr. k-3). lib. bdg. *(978-0-7787-1804-8(2))*; pap. *(978-0-7787-1817-8(4))* Crabtree Publishing Co.

—Triceratops Gets Lost. Bentley, Dawn. (Smithsonian's Prehistoric Pals Ser.). (J). 2009. 21.95 incl. audio compact disk *(978-1-59249-544-3(3))*; 2005. (ENG.). 36p. (gr. -1-2). 8.95 *(978-1-59249-216-9(9)*, SD2403); 2004. (ENG.). 36p. (gr. -1-2). pap. 6.95 *(978-1-59249-166-7(9)*, S2403) Soundprints.

—Tylosaurus. Bailey, Gerry. 2011. (Smithsonian Prehistoric Zone Ser.). (ENG.). 32p. (J). (gr. k-3). *(978-0-7787-1805-5(0))*; pap. *(978-0-7787-1818-5(2))* Crabtree Publishing Co.

—Tyrannosaurus Rex. Bentley, Dawn & Studio Mouse Staff. 2008. (ENG.). 24p. (J). (gr. 3-7). 4.99 *(978-1-59069-621-7(2))* Studio Mouse LLC.

—Tyrannosaurus Rex. Bailey, Gerry. 2011. (Smithsonian Prehistoric Zone Ser.). (ENG.). 32p. (J). (gr. k-3). *(978-0-7787-1806-2(9))*; pap. *(978-0-7787-1819-2(0))* Crabtree Publishing Co.

—Velociraptor. Bentley, Dawn. 2005. (Smithsonian's Prehistoric Pals Ser.). (ENG.). 36p. (J). (gr. -1-2). 9.95 *(978-1-59249-168-1(5)*, PS2453) Soundprints.

—Velociraptor. Bailey, Gerry. 2011. (Smithsonian Prehistoric Zone Ser.). (ENG.). 32p. (J). (gr. k-3). *(978-0-7787-1807-9(7))*; pap. *(978-0-7787-1820-8(4))* Crabtree Publishing Co.

—Velociraptor: Small & Speedy. Bentley, Dawn. (ENG.). 36p. (J). (gr. -1-2). 2005. 9.95 *(978-1-59249-164-3(2)*, PS2452); 2004. pap. 6.95 *(978-1-59249-162-9(6)*, S2402) Soundprints.

—Velociraptor - Small & Speedy. Bentley, Dawn. 2004. (Smithsonian's Prehistoric Pals Ser.). (ENG.). 36p. (J). (gr. -1-2). 8.95 *(978-1-59249-214-5(2)*, SD2402) Soundprints.

—Watch Out, Triceratops! Bentley, Dawn. 2004. (Read & Discover (Soundprints) Ser.). (ENG.). 32p. (J). (gr. -1-3). pap. 3.95 *(978-1-59249-303-6(3)*, S2030) Soundprints.

—Woolly Mammoth. Bailey, Gerry. 2011. (Smithsonian Prehistoric Zone Ser.). (ENG.). 32p. (J). (gr. k-3). *(978-0-7787-1808-6(5))*; pap. *(978-0-7787-1821-5(2))* Crabtree Publishing Co.

—Woolly Mammoth in Trouble. Bentley, Dawn. (Smithsonian's Prehistoric Pals Ser.). (ENG.). 36p. (J). (gr. -1-2). 2005. 14.95 *(978-1-59249-364-7(5)*, H2404); 2005. 2.95 *(978-1-59249-367-8(X)*, S2454); 2005. pap. 6.95 *(978-1-59249-365-4(3)*, S2404); 2004. 8.95 *(978-1-59249-366-1(1)*, SD2404); 2004. 9.95 *(978-1-59249-368-5(8)*, PS2454) Soundprints.

Carr, Karen. Jurassic Shark. Carr, Karen. Diffily, Deborah. 2004. (ENG.). 32p. (J). (gr. -1-3). 17.99 *(978-0-06-008249-9(6))* HarperCollins Pubs.

Carr, Karen. A Busy Day for Stegosaurus. Carr, Karen, tr. Bentley, Dawn. 2005. (Smithsonian's Prehistoric Pals Ser.). (ENG.). 36p. (J). (gr. -1-2). 2.95 *(978-1-59249-155-1(3)*, S2451) Soundprints.

—It's Tyrannosaurus Rex! Carr, Karen, tr. Bentley, Dawn. 2005. (Smithsonian's Prehistoric Pals Ser.). (ENG.). 36p. (J). (gr. -1-2). 14.95 *(978-1-59249-157-5(X)*, H2400); pap. 6.95 *(978-1-59249-158-2(8)*, S2400) Soundprints.

—Triceratops Gets Lost. Carr, Karen, tr. Bentley, Dawn. 2005. (Smithsonian's Prehistoric Pals Ser.). (ENG.). 36p. (J). (gr. -1-2). 2.95 *(978-1-59249-167-4(7)*, S2453) Soundprints.

—Velociraptor: Small & Speedy. Carr, Karen, tr. Bentley, Dawn. 2005. (Smithsonian's Prehistoric Pals Ser.). (ENG.). 36p. (J). (gr. -1-2). 14.95 *(978-1-59249-161-2(8)*, H2402); 2.95 *(978-1-59249-163-6(4)*, S2452) Soundprints.

Carr, Karent. Dinosaurs & More! Bentley, Dawn & Studio Mouse Staff. rev. ed. 2006. (ENG.). 60p. (J). 12.95 *(978-1-59069-487-9(2))* Soundprints.

Carr, Stephen. The Curry Comb Caper. Carr, Debra. 2006. 48p. per. 8.95 *(978-1-933912-59-2(6))* Westview Publishing Co., Inc.

—The Feed Trough Thriller. Carr, Debra. 2007. 56p. per. 8.95 *(978-1-933912-66-0(9))* Westview Publishing Co., Inc.

—Misty Is Missing. Carr, Debra. 2008. 52p. pap. 8.95 *(978-0-9816172-7-5(1))* Westview Publishing Co., Inc.

Carr, Tabatha. A Lesson from a Tree. Mervyn, Catherine Antolino. 2008. 32p. pap. 12.95 *(978-0-9821153-2-9(6))* Living Waters Publishing Co.

Carrasco, Jose Manuel. El viaje de las semillas. 2008. 48p. *(978-84-95225-83-2(2))* Saure, Jean-Francois Editor.

Carrel, Douglas. The Dragon Diary, Vol. 2. Steer, Dugald A. 2010. (Ologies Ser.: Vol. 2). (ENG.). 272p. (J). (gr. 4-7). pap. 7.99 *(978-0-7636-4514-4(1))* Candlewick Pr.

—The Dragon Prophecy. Steer, Dugald A. 2012. (Ologies Ser.). (ENG.). 224p. (J). (gr. 4-7). pap. 7.99 *(978-0-7636-3428-5(X))* Candlewick Pr.

—Monsterology: The Complete Book of Monstrous Creatures. Drake, Ernest. Steer, Dugald A., ed. 2008. (Ologies Ser.). (ENG.). 32p. (J). (gr. 3-7). 21.99 *(978-0-7636-3940-2(0))* Candlewick Pr.

Carrell, Douglas. Alienology. Grey, Allan. Steer, Dugald A., ed. 2010. (Ologies Ser.: 10). (ENG.). 32p. (J). (gr. 3-7). 21.99 *(978-0-7636-4565-6(6))* Candlewick Pr.

Carrer, Chiara. Otto Carrotto. 2011. 26p. (J). (gr. -1-3). 16.00 *(978-0-8028-5393-6(5)*, Eerdmans Bks For Young Readers) Eerdmans, William B. Publishing Co.

Carreres, Albert. Cars: Radiator Springs. Porter, Alan J. 2010. (World of Cars Ser.). (ENG.). 112p. (J). pap. 9.99 *(978-1-60886-502-4(9))* Boom! Studios.

—Cars: The Rookie. Porter, Alan J. 2009. (World of Cars Ser.). (ENG.). 112p. (J). 24.99 *(978-1-60886-522-2(3))* Boom! Studios.

—Cars Vol. 2: Radiator Springs. Porter, Alan J. 2010. (World of Cars Ser.). (ENG.). 112p. (J). 24.99 *(978-1-60886-528-4(2))* Boom! Studios.

—Cars: the Rookie. Porter, Alan J. 2009. (World of Cars Ser.). (ENG.). 112p. (J). pap. 9.99 *(978-1-934506-84-4(2))* Boom! Studios.

Carreres, Albert, et al. Hero Overload. Smith, Brian & Moore, B. Clay. 2014. (Max Steel Ser.: 2). (ENG.). 64p. (J). pap. 7.99 *(978-1-4215-5726-7(6))* Viz Media.

Carrescia, Reid. Magic on the Wall, 1 vol. Saccheri, Josephine. 2009. 11p. pap. 24.95 *(978-1-61546-374-9(7))* America Star Bks.

Carretero, Monica. Los Latidos de Yago. Miranda, Conchita & Miranda Ros, Conchita. 2011. (Luz Ser.). (SPA & ENG.). 40p. (J). (gr. 2-4). 15.95 *(978-84-937814-4-6(4))* Cuento de Luz SL ESP. Dist: Perseus-PGW.

Carretero, Mónica. La Familia Bola. Carretero, Mónica. Carretero, M—nica. 2011. (Artistas Mini-Animalistas Ser.). (SPA & ENG.). 32p. (J). (gr. k-2). 14.95 *(978-84-938240-4-4(6))* Cuento de Luz SL ESP. Dist: Perseus-PGW.

Carretero, Monica. Flea Circus. Carretero, Monica. Carretero, M—nica & Carretero, Mónica. 2011. (Mini-Animalist Ser.). (ENG.). 32p. (J). (gr. k-2). 14.95 *(978-84-938240-0-6(3))* Cuento de Luz SL ESP. Dist: Perseus-PGW.

—Haunted Houses Handbook. Carretero, Monica. Carretero, Mónica & Carretero, M—nica. 2013. (Handbooks Ser.). (ENG.). 32p. (J). (gr. k-2). 15.95 *(978-84-15241-05-8(4))* Cuento de Luz SL ESP. Dist: Perseus-PGW.

—Roly-Polies. Carretero, Monica. Carretero, M—nica & Carretero, Mónica. 2011. (Mini-Animalist Ser.). (ENG.). 32p. (J). (gr. k-2). 14.95 *(978-84-938240-1-3(1))* Cuento de Luz SL ESP. Dist: Perseus-PGW.

Carrick, Donald. Patrick's Dinosaurs, 1 vol. Carrick, Carol. 2006. (Read along Book & CD Ser.). (ENG.). 32p. (J). (gr. -1-3). 10.99 *(978-0-618-73275-3(6))* Houghton Mifflin Harcourt Publishing Co.

Carrick, Paul. Mothers Are Like That. Carrick, Carol. 2007. (ENG.). 32p. (J). (gr. k — 1). 5.95 *(978-0-618-75241-6(2))* Houghton Mifflin Harcourt Publishing Co.

—Wired. Suen, Anastasia. 2007. (ENG.). 32p. (J). (gr. 1-4). 16.95 *(978-1-57091-599-4(7))*; pap. 7.95 *(978-1-57091-494-2(X))* Charlesbridge Publishing, Inc.

Carrick, Paul. Watch Out for Wolfgang. Carrick, Paul. 2009. (ENG.). 32p. (J). (gr. -1-3). 16.95 *(978-1-57091-689-2(6))* Charlesbridge Publishing, Inc.

Carrier, Jason. How Do Alligators Praise the Lord? Franklin, Kirk. 2005. 24p. (J). (gr. 4-7). 11.99 incl. audio compact disk *(978-1-59185-209-4(9)*, Charisma Kids) Charisma Media.

—Sprucy: The Tallest Christmas Tree. Scali, Jacob et al. 2011. 32p. (J). (gr. k-4). 14.99 *(978-1-4634-2468-8(X))* AuthorHouse.

Carrier, Tracey Dahle. Come Worship with Me: A Journey Through the Church Year. Boling, Ruth L. 2010. (J). 13.00 *(978-0-664-23717-2(7))* Westminster John Knox Pr.

Carrigg, Susan. Sally Jo Survives Sixth Grade: A Journal. Keltz, Karen. 2013. 180p. pap. 9.99 *(978-0-9857281-1-3(6))* HAPPY HOUSE PR.

Carrilho, Andre. Porch Lies: Tales of Slicksters, Tricksters, & Other Wily Characters. McKissack, Patricia C. 2006. (ENG.). 160p. (J). (gr. 3-7). 19.99 *(978-0-375-83619-0(5)*, Schwartz & Wade Bks.) Random Hse. Children's Bks.

—You Never Heard of Sandy Koufax?! Winter, Jonah. 2009. (ENG.). 40p. (J). (gr. -1-3). 17.99 *(978-0-375-83738-8(8))* Random Hse. Children's Bks.

Carrillo, Azalea & Morrissey, Kay, photos by. IV Antología Nuevo Milenio: Narració y Poesía. Kassandra, ed. l.t. ed. 2003. (SPA., 100p. (YA). pap. 12.00 *(978-1-931481-48-9(2))* LiArt-Literature & Art.

Carrillo, Charles M. Shoes for the Santo Niño. Church, Peggy Pond. 2013. 64p. 25.95 *(978-1-936744-23-7(6)*, Rio Grande Bks.) LPD Pr.

—Shoes for the Santo Niño: Zapitillos para el Santo Niño: A Bilingual Tale. Church, Peggy Pond. 2009. (SPA & ENG.). (J). pap. *(978-1-890689-64-3(5)*, Rio Grande Bks.) LPD Pr.

Carrillo, J. Raul. Use Your Noodle! The Adventures of a Hollywood Poodle Named Doodle. Messick, Maxine. Hodsdon-Carr, Sandra, ed. Urwin-Camara, Nancy, tr. 2004. (SPA.). 90p. 15.00 *(978-0-9753508-0-5(3))* Aurora Bks.

Carrington, Marsha Gray. Coriander the Contrary Hen. Chaconas, Dori. 2007. (Carolrhoda Picture Bks.). (ENG.). 32p. (J). (gr. k-3). lib. bdg. 16.95 *(978-1-57505-749-1(2)*, Carolrhoda Bks.) Lerner Publishing Group.

—Saving the Liberty Bell. McDonald, Megan. 2005. (ENG.). 32p. (J). (gr. k-3). 17.99 *(978-0-689-85167-4(7)*, Atheneum/Richard Jackson Bks.) Simon & Schuster Children's Publishing.

Carrington, Matt. The Secret Files of Professor L. Otto Funn: Or, Stop Being a Slug, Open This Book, & Make Your Brain Happy. Gors, Steven E. 2013. 159p. (J). pap. *(978-0-7166-1324-4(7))* World Bk., Inc.

Carroll, James Christopher. The Boy & the Moon. Carroll, James Christopher. 2010. (ENG.). 32p. (J). (gr. 1-4). 15.95 *(978-1-58536-521-0(1)*, 202209) Sleeping Bear Pr.

Carroll, Jr. Otis Best. Mansur, Motesem. 2011. 50p. pap. 24.95 *(978-1-4560-4910-2(0))* America Star Bks.

Carroll, Katie. Brewster's New School. Carroll, Michael Shane. 2012. 24p. pap. 5.00 *(978-1-937260-13-2(5))* Sleepytown Pr.

—Bye-Bye Brewster. Carroll, Michael Shane. 2012. 20p. pap. 5.00 *(978-1-937260-14-9(3))* Sleepytown Pr.

Carroll, Michael. Big Bang! The Tongue-Tickling Tale of a Speck That Became Spectacular. DeCristofano, Carolyn Cinami. 2005. (ENG.). 32p. (J). (gr. k-3). pap. 7.95 *(978-1-57091-619-9(5))* Charlesbridge Publishing, Inc.

—A Black Hole Is Not a Hole. DeCristofano, Carolyn Cinami. 2012. (ENG.). 80p. (J). (gr. 4-7). 18.95 *(978-1-57091-783-7(3))* Charlesbridge Publishing, Inc.

—Max Goes to Jupiter: A Science Adventure with Max the Dog. Bennett, Jeffrey et al. 2008. (Science Adventures with Max the Dog Ser.). (ENG.). 32p. (J). (gr. 2-4). 16.95 *(978-0-9721819-3-8(8))* Big Kid Science.

—Max Goes to the Space Station: A Science Adventure with Max the Dog. Bennett, Jeffrey. 2013. (Science Adventures with Max the Dog Ser.). (ENG.). 32p. (J). (gr. 2-4). 15.00 *(978-1-937548-28-5(7))* Big Kid Science.

Carroll, Pam. Golden Numbers: A California Number Book. Domeniconi, David. 2008. (Count Your Way Across the U. S. A. Ser.). (ENG.). 40p. (J). 17.95 *(978-1-58536-173-1(9))* Sleeping Bear Pr.

—M Is for Majestic: A National Parks Alphabet. Domeniconi, David. (ENG.). (J). (gr. k-6). 2007. 48p. per. 7.95 *(978-1-58536-333-9(2))*; 2003. 40p. 17.95 *(978-1-58536-138-0(0))* Sleeping Bear Pr.

—One Nation: America by the Numbers. Scillian, Devin. 2004. (ENG.). 40p. (J). (gr. k-6). pap. 7.95 *(978-1-58536-249-3(2))* Sleeping Bear Pr.

—S Is for Star: A Christmas Alphabet. Furlong, Reynolds Cynthia. 2004. (ENG.). 40p. (J). (gr. k-6). pap. 6.95 *(978-1-58536-247-9(6))* Sleeping Bear Pr.

Carroll, Raymond. Abcs of Language & Literacy. Pinestein Press. 2007. 180p. per. 19.99 *(978-0-9795364-4-1(8))* Chowder Bay Bks.

—Pre-K Prep! Pinestein Press. 2007. 180p. per. 19.99 *(978-0-9795364-3-4(X))* Chowder Bay Bks.

Carroll, Rosemary. The Golden Rules of Etiquette at the Plaza. Bloch, Lyudmila & Civitano, Tom. 2004. 48p. (J). lib. bdg. 16.95 *(978-0-9755390-0-2(0))* Fifth Ave Pr.

Carruthers, Sandy. Peril at Summerland Park. Storrie, Paul D. 2012. (Twisted Journeys Ser.: 20). (ENG.). 112p. (J). (gr. 4-7). pap. 7.95 *(978-0-7613-8551-6(7))*; pap. 45.32 *(978-0-7613-9290-3(4))*; lib. bdg. 27.93 *(978-0-7613-4935-8(9))* Lerner Publishing Group. (Graphic Universe).

—School of Evil. Croall, Marie P. 2010. (Twisted Journeys (r) Ser.: 13). (ENG.). 112p. (J). (gr. 4-7). pap. 7.95 *(978-0-8225-9271-6(1)*, Graphic Universe); lib. bdg. 27.93 *(978-0-8225-9263-1(0))* Lerner Publishing Group.

—Sunjata: Warrior King of Mali [A West African Legend]. Fontes, Justine & Fontes, Ron. 2009. (Graphic Myths & Legends Ser.). (ENG.). 48p. (gr. 4-8). pap. 8.95 *(978-1-58013-891-8(8))* Lerner Publishing Group.

—Terror in Ghost Mansion. Storrie, Paul D. 2007. (Twisted Journeys (r) Ser.: 3). (ENG.). (J). (gr. 4-7). pap. 45.32 *(978-0-8225-9467-3(6))*; 112p. lib. bdg. 27.93 *(978-0-8225-6776-9(8)*, Graphic Universe); 112p. per. 7.95 *(978-0-8225-6778-3(4)*, Twenty-First Century Bks.) Lerner Publishing Group.

—Yu the Great: Conquering the Flood. Storrie, Paul D. 2007. (Graphic Myths & Legends Ser.). (ENG.). 48p. (gr. 4-8). lib. bdg. 27.93 *(978-0-8225-3088-6(0))* Lerner Publishing Group.

—Yu the Great: Conquering the Flood - A Chinese Legend. Storrie, Paul D. 2008. (Graphic Myths & Legends Ser.). (ENG.). 48p. (gr. 4-8). per. 8.95 *(978-0-8225-6562-8(5))* Lerner Publishing Group.

Carsey, Alice. Pinocchio. 2003. (Library of Tale Ser.).Tr. of Avventure di Pinocchio. (SPA.). 12p. (J). (gr. -1-7). pap. *(978-958-30-0986-0(5))* Panamericana Editorial.

—Pinocchio. 2005.Tr. of Avventure di Pinocchio. (ENG.). 136p. (J). (gr. 2-5). 19.95 *(978-1-933327-00-6(6))* Purple Bear Bks., Inc.

—Pinocchio: the Tale of a Puppet. Collodi, C. 2007. (ENG.). 196p. per. 11.95 *(978-1-4065-1462-9(4))* Dodo Pr.

—Pinocchio, the Tale of a Puppet. 2011. 140p. pap. 12.99 *(978-1-61203-095-1(5))* Bottom of the Hill Publishing.

Carsey, Alice & Greban, Quentin. Pinocchio. Collodi, Carlo. 2010.Tr. of Avventure di Pinocchio. (ENG.). 80p. (J). (gr. k). 19.95 *(978-0-7358-2324-2(3))* North-South Bks., Inc.

Carson-Dellosa Publishing Staff. I Lost a Tooth! 2013. (ENG.). 24p. (gr. -1-5). 1.99 *(978-1-62057-266-5(4))* Carson-Dellosa Publishing, LLC.

Carson, Shawn. Keep-It-Cheap: Financially Surviving the Honey-Do List. Tompkins, Bill. 2007. (ENG.). 117p. (YA). spiral bd. *(978-0-9741647-3-1(9))* NRG Pubns.

—Miss Molly's Adventure on the Farm: Another great adventure brought to you by Miss Molly & her dog Reyburn. Tompkins, Robyn Lee. 2006. (J). per. *(978-0-9741647-7-9(1))* NRG Pubns.

Carson, Shawn K. Miss Molly's Adventure in the Park: Another Great Adventure Brought to You by Miss Molly & Her Dog Reyburn, 10 vols. Tompkins, Robyn Lee. l.t. ed. 2005. (ENG.). 60p. (J). per. *(978-0-9741647-6-2(3))* NRG Pubns.

Cart, Jen. Pea Soup Fog. Smith, Constance. 2004. (ENG.). 32p. (J). (gr. -1-17). 15.95 *(978-0-89272-643-1(1))* Down East Bks.

Carter, Abby. Andy Shane & the Barn Sale Mystery. Jacobson, Jennifer Richard. (Andy Shane Ser.: 5). (ENG.). 64p. (J). (gr. k-3). 2010. 4.99 *(978-0-7636-4827-5(2))*; 2009. 14.99 *(978-0-7636-3599-2(5))* Candlewick Pr.

—Andy Shane & the Pumpkin Trick. Jacobson, Jennifer Richard. 2007. (Andy Shane Ser.: 2). (ENG.). 64p. (J). (gr. k-3). per. 4.99 *(978-0-7636-3306-6(2))* Candlewick Pr.

—Andy Shane & the Pumpkin Trick. Jacobson, Jennifer Richard. 2008. (Andy Shane Ser.). (J). (gr. -1-3). 25.95 incl. audio *(978-1-4301-0313-4(2))*; pap. 16.95 incl. audio *(978-1-4301-0312-7(4))* Live Oak Media.

—Andy Shane & the Queen of Egypt. Jacobson, Jennifer Richard. 2009. (Andy Shane Ser.: 3). (ENG.). 64p. (J). (gr. k-3). 4.99 *(978-0-7636-4404-8(8))* Candlewick Pr.

—Andy Shane & the Very Bossy Dolores Starbuckle. Jacobson, Jennifer Richard. 2006. (Andy Shane Ser.: 1). (ENG.). 64p. (J). (gr. k-3). 4.99 *(978-0-7636-3044-7(6))* Candlewick Pr.

—Andy Shane & the Very Bossy Dolores Starbuckle. Jacobson, Jennifer Richard. 2008. (Andy Shane Ser.). (J). (gr. -1-3). 25.95 incl. audio *(978-1-4301-0321-9(3))*; pap. 16.95 incl. audio *(978-1-4301-0320-2(5))* Live Oak Media.

—Andy Shane, Hero at Last. Jacobson, Jennifer Richard. 2011. (Andy Shane Ser.: 6). (ENG.). 64p. (J). (gr. k-3). pap. 4.99 *(978-0-7636-5293-7(8))* Candlewick Pr.

—Andy Shane Is Not in Love. Jacobson, Jennifer Richard. 2009. (Andy Shane Ser.: 4). (ENG.). 64p. (J). (gr. k-3). 4.99 *(978-0-7636-4403-1(X))* Candlewick Pr.

—The Best Chef in Second Grade. Kenah, Katharine. (I Can Read Book 2 Ser.). 48p. (J). 2008. (ENG.). (gr. k-3). pap. 3.99 *(978-0-06-053563-6(6))*; 2007. (gr. -1-3). lib. bdg. 16.89 *(978-0-06-053562-9(8))* HarperCollins Pubs.

—The Best Seat in Second Grade. Kenah, Katharine. 2006. (I Can Read Book 2 Ser.). (ENG.). 48p. (J). (gr. k-3). pap. 3.99 *(978-0-06-000736-2(2))* HarperCollins Pubs.

—The Best Seat in Second Grade. Kenah, Katharine. 2006. (I Can Read Bks.). 48p. (J). (gr. -1-3). 11.65 *(978-0-7569-6979-0(4))* Perfection Learning Corp.

—The Best Teacher in Second Grade. Kenah, Katharine. (I Can Read Book 2 Ser.). 48p. (J). 2007. (ENG.). (gr. k-3). pap. 3.99 *(978-0-06-053566-7(0))*; 2006. (gr. -1-3). lib. bdg. 17.89 *(978-0-06-053565-0(2))* HarperCollins Pubs.

—The Best Teacher in Second Grade. Kenah, Katharine. 2007. (I Can Read Bks.). 48p. (J). (gr. -1-3). 14.00 *(978-0-7569-8105-1(0))* Perfection Learning Corp.

—Daddies Do It Different. Sitomer, Alan Lawrence. 2012. (ENG.). 40p. (J). (gr. -1 — 1). 16.99 *(978-1-4231-3315-5(3))* Hyperion Pr.

Carter, Abby. Daddy's Back-To-School Shopping Adventure. Sitomer, Alan Lawrence. 2015. (ENG.). 40p. (J). (gr. -1-k). 16.99 ***(978-1-4231-8421-8(1))*** Hyperion Bks. for Children.

Carter, Abby. Daddy's Zigzagging Bedtime Story. Sitomer, Alan Lawrence. 2014. (ENG.). 40p. (J). (gr. -1-k). 16.99 *(978-1-4231-8420-1(3))* Hyperion Bks. for Children.

—Emma Dilemma & the Camping Nanny, 0 vols. Hermes, Patricia. 2009. (Emma Dilemma Ser.: 0). (ENG.). 144p. (J). (gr. 3-6). 15.99 *(978-0-7614-5534-9(5))*, 9780761455349, Amazon Children's Publishing) Amazon Publishing.

—Emma Dilemma & the New Nanny, 0 vols. Hermes, Patricia. (Emma Dilemma Ser.: 0). (ENG.). 112p. (J). (gr. 3-6). 2010. pap. 6.99 *(978-0-7614-5619-3(8))*, 9780761456193); 2006. 15.95 *(978-0-7614-5286-7(9))*, 9780761452867) Amazon Publishing. (Amazon Children's Publishing).

—Emma Dilemma & the Two Nannies, 0 vols. Hermes, Patricia. 2011. (Emma Dilemma Ser.: 0). (ENG.). 117p. (J). (gr. 3-6). pap. 7.99 *(978-0-7614-5835-7(2))*, 9780761458357, Amazon Children's Publishing) Amazon Publishing.

—Emma Dilemma, the Nanny, & the Best Horse Ever, 0 vols. Hermes, Patricia. 2013. (Emma Dilemma Ser.). (ENG.). 50p. (J). (gr. 3-6). pap. 9.99 *(978-1-4778-1633-2(X))*, 9781477816332, Amazon Children's Publishing) Amazon Publishing.

—Emma Dilemma, the Nanny, & the Secret Ferret, 0 vols. Hermes, Patricia. 2010. (Emma Dilemma Ser.: 0). (ENG.). 112p. (J). (gr. 3-6). 15.99 *(978-0-7614-5650-6(3))*, 9780761456506, Amazon Children's Publishing) Amazon Publishing.

—Full House: An Invitation to Fractions. Dodds, Dayle Ann. 2012. (ENG.). 32p. (J). (gr. 1-4). pap. 24.99 *(978-0-7636-6090-1(6))* Candlewick Pr.

—Full House: An Invitation to Fractions. Dodds, Dayle Ann. 2009. (ENG.). 32p. (J). (gr. 1-4). pap. 6.99 *(978-0-7636-4130-6(8))* Candlewick Pr.

—Hero at Last. Jacobson, Jennifer Richard. 2010. (Andy Shane Ser.: 6). (ENG.). 64p. (J). (gr. k-3). 14.99 *(978-0-7636-3600-5(2))* Candlewick Pr.

—Human or Alien? Williams, Suzanne. 2004. (Marvelous Mind of Matthew Mcghee Age 8 Ser.). 57p. (J). (gr. 1-4). 11.65 *(978-0-7569-5529-8(7))* Perfection Learning Corp.

—The Lucky Penny? Williams, Suzanne. 2004. 56p. (J). lib. bdg. 15.00 *(978-1-4242-0909-5(9))* Fitzgerald Bks.

—Maggie's Monkeys. Sanders-Wells, Linda. 2009. (ENG.). 32p. (J). (gr. -1-2). 16.99 *(978-0-7636-3326-4(7))* Candlewick Pr.

—Master of Minds? Williams, Suzanne. 2004. 58p. (J). lib. bdg. 15.00 *(978-1-4242-0911-8(0))* Fitzgerald Bks.

—Master of Minds? Williams, Suzanne. 2004. (Marvelous Mind of Matthew Mcghee Age 8 Ser.). 58p. (J). 11.65 *(978-0-7569-5530-4(0))* Perfection Learning Corp.

Carter, Abby. Ollie's Class Trip: A Yes-And-No Book. Calmenson, Stephanie. 2015. (ENG.). 32p. (J). (gr. -1-1). 15.95 ***(978-0-8234-3432-9(X))*** Holiday Hse., Inc.

Carter, Abby. Ollie's School Day: A Yes-And-No Book. Calmenson, Stephanie. 2012. (ENG.). 24p. (J). *(978-0-8234-2377-4(8))* Holiday Hse., Inc.

—Scooter in the Outside. Bowen, Anne. 2012. (ENG.). 32p. (J). 16.95 *(978-0-8234-2326-2(3))* Holiday Hse., Inc.

—Slithery Jake. Provencher, Rose-Marie. 2004. (ENG.). 32p. (J). 15.99 *(978-0-06-623820-3(X))* HarperCollins Pubs.

—Too Much Noise in the Library. Chapman, Susan Margaret. 2010. 32p. (J). (gr. 1-4). 17.95 *(978-1-60213-026-5(4))*, Upstart Bks.) Highsmith Inc.

Carter, Amy. The Little Baby Snoogle- Fleejer. Carter, Jimmy. 2014. (ENG.). 24p. (J). 19.95 *(978-1-55728-671-0(X))* Univ. of Arkansas Pr.

Carter, Andi. Flutter & Float: Bringing Home Goldfish, 1 vol. Tourville, Amanda Doering. 2008. (Get a Pet Ser.). (ENG.). 24p. (gr. 1-3). lib. bdg. 25.99 *(978-1-4048-4853-5(3))*, Nonfiction Picture Bks.) Picture Window Bks.

—Purr & Pounce: Bringing Home a Cat, 1 vol. Tourville, Amanda Doering. 2008. (Get a Pet Ser.). (ENG.). 24p. (gr. 1-3). 25.99 *(978-1-4048-4856-6(8))*, Nonfiction Picture Bks.) Picture Window Bks.

—Scurry & Squeak: Bringing Home a Guinea Pig, 1 vol. Tourville, Amanda Doering. 2008. (Get a Pet Ser.). (ENG.). 24p. (gr. 1-3). lib. bdg. 25.99 *(978-1-4048-4859-7(2))*, Nonfiction Picture Bks.) Picture Window Bks.

—Skitter & Scoot: Bringing Home a Hamster, 1 vol. Tourville, Amanda Doering. 2008. (Get a Pet Ser.). (ENG.). 24p. (gr. 1-3). lib. bdg. 25.99 *(978-1-4048-4862-7(2))*, Nonfiction Picture Bks.) Picture Window Bks.

—Twitter & Tweet: Bringing Home a Bird, 1 vol. Tourville, Amanda Doering. 2008. (Get a Pet Ser.). (ENG.). 24p. (gr. 1-3). lib. bdg. 25.99 *(978-1-4048-4865-8(7))*, Nonfiction Picture Bks.) Picture Window Bks.

Carter, Anne. Unitarian Universalism Is a Really Long Name. Dant, Jennifer. 2008. (ENG.). 30p. (J). (gr. 3-7). 12.00 *(978-1-55896-508-9(4))*, Skinner Hse. Bks.) Unitarian Universalist Assn.

Carter, Barbara. Up & down with Lena Larocha. Power, Molly. 2013. 169p. pap. 15.00 *(978-1-60571-176-8(4))*, Shires Press) Northshire Pr.

Carter, Dana. The Starrigans of Little Brook Bottom, 1 vol. Davis, Harold. 2007. (ENG.). 150p. (J). (gr. 3-7). per. 8.95 *(978-1-894294-85-0(8))*, Tuckamore Bks) Creative Bk. Publishing CAN. Dist: Orca Bk. Pubs. USA.

Carter, David A. Who's under That Hat? A Lift-the-Flap Pop-up Adventure. Weeks, Sarah. 2006. 14p. (J). (gr. -1-2). 14.00 *(978-1-4223-5440-7(7))* DIANE Publishing Co.

Carter, David A. Alpha Bugs: A Pop-Up Alphabet. Carter, David A. ed. 2006. (ENG.). 28p. (J). (gr. -1-2). 12.99 *(978-1-4169-0973-6(7))*, Little Simon) Little Simon.

—B Is for Box — the Happy Little Yellow Box: A Pop-Up Book. Carter, David A. 2014. (ENG.). 18p. (J). (gr. -1). 12.99 *(978-1-4814-0295-8(1))*, Little Simon) Little Simon.

—Beach Bugs. Carter, David A. 2008. (ENG.). 16p. (J). (gr. -1-2). 12.99 *(978-1-4169-5055-4(9))*, Little Simon) Little Simon.

—The Big Bug Book. Carter, David A. 2008. (ENG.). 16p. (J). (gr. -1-2). 19.99 *(978-1-4169-4095-1(2))*, Little Simon) Little Simon.

—Birthday Bugs. Carter, David A. 2004. (ENG.). 16p. (J). (gr. -1-3). 12.99 *(978-0-689-81858-5(0))*, Little Simon) Little Simon.

—Bitsy Bee Goes to School. Carter, David A. 2014. (Ready-To-Reads Ser.). (ENG.). 24p. (J). (gr. -1-1). pap. 3.99 *(978-1-4424-9503-6(0))*, Simon Spotlight) Simon Spotlight.

—Blue 2: A Pop-Up Book for Children of All Ages. Carter, David A. ltd. ed. 2006. (ENG.). 18p. (J). 250.00 *(978-1-4169-2717-4(4))*, Little Simon) Little Simon.

—Blue 2 Vol. 2: A Pop-Up Book for Children of All Ages. Carter, David A. 2006. (ENG.). 18p. (J). (gr. 2-5). 19.95 *(978-1-4169-1781-6(0))*, Little Simon) Little Simon.

—A Box of Bugs: 4 Pop-Up Concept Books. Carter, David A. ed. 2011. (ENG.). 64p. (J). (gr. -1-3). 16.99 *(978-1-4424-2989-5(5))*, Little Simon) Little Simon.

—Bugs That Go! A Bustling Pop-Up Book. Carter, David A. 2011. (ENG.). 18p. (J). (gr. -1-1). pap. 12.99 *(978-1-4169-4097-5(9))*, Little Simon) Little Simon.

—Builder Bugs: A Busy Pop-Up Book. Carter, David A. 2012. (ENG.). 16p. (J). (gr. -1-2). pap. 12.99 *(978-1-4424-2648-1(9))*, Little Simon) Little Simon.

—Colors: A Bugs Pop-Up Concept Book. Carter, David A. 2010. (ENG.). 16p. (J). (gr. -1-1). 7.99 *(978-1-4424-0830-2(8))*, Little Simon) Little Simon.

—Counting: A Bugs Pop-Up Concept Book. Carter, David A. 2010. (ENG.). 16p. (J). (gr. -1-1). 7.99 *(978-1-4424-0828-9(6))*, Little Simon) Little Simon.

—Feely Bugs. Carter, David A. ed. 2005. (ENG.). 14p. (J). (gr. -1-2). 12.99 *(978-1-4169-0326-0(7))*, Little Simon) Little Simon.

—Halloween Bugs, Vol. 16. Carter, David A. 2003. (ENG.). 14p. (J). (gr. -1-3). 12.99 *(978-0-689-85916-8(3))*, Little Simon) Little Simon.

—The Happy Little Yellow Box: A Pop-Up Book of Opposites. Carter, David A. 2012. (ENG.). 18p. (J). (gr. -1). 12.99 *(978-1-4169-4096-8(0))*, Little Simon) Little Simon.

—How Many Bugs in a Box? Carter, David A. ed. 2006. (ENG.). 20p. (J). (gr. -1-1). 10.95 *(978-1-4169-0804-3(8))*, Little Simon) Little Simon.

—Jingle Bugs: A Merry Pop-Up Book with Lights & Music! Carter, David A. 2004. (ENG.). 22p. (J). (gr. -1-2). 11.99 *(978-0-689-87416-1(2))*, Little Simon) Little Simon.

—Love Bugs. Carter, David A. ed. 2003. (ENG.). 12p. (J). (gr. 2-5). 6.99 *(978-0-689-85815-4(9))*, Little Simon) Little Simon.

—Merry Christmas, Bugs! Carter, David A. 2014. (Ready-To-Reads Ser.). (ENG.). 24p. (J). (gr. -1-1). pap. 3.99 *(978-1-4424-9506-7(5))*, Simon Spotlight) Simon Spotlight.

—One Red Dot: A Pop-Up Book for Children of All Ages. Carter, David A. 2005. (ENG.). 18p. (J). (gr. -1-3). 22.99 *(978-0-689-87769-8(2))*, Little Simon) Little Simon.

—Opposites: A Bugs Pop-Up Concept Book. Carter, David A. 2010. (ENG.). 16p. (J). (gr. -1-1). bds. 7.99 *(978-1-4424-0829-6(4))*, Little Simon) Little Simon.

—Princess Bugs: A Touch-And-Feel Fairy Tale. Carter, David A. 2013. (ENG.). 16p. (J). (gr. -1-2). 12.99 *(978-1-4424-5055-4(X))*, Little Simon) Little Simon.

—School Bugs. Carter, David A. 2009. (ENG.). 20p. (J). (gr. -1-2). 11.99 *(978-1-4169-5056-1(7))*, Little Simon) Little Simon.

—Snow Bugs: A Wintery Pop-Up Book. Carter, David A. 2009. (ENG.). 20p. (J). (gr. -1-3). 11.99 *(978-1-4169-5054-7(0))*, Little Simon) Little Simon.

—A Snowy Day in Bugland! Carter, David A. 2012. (Ready-To-Reads Ser.). (ENG.). 24p. (J). (gr. -1-1). 15.99 *(978-1-4424-3895-8(9))*; pap. 3.99 *(978-1-4424-3894-1(0))* Simon Spotlight. (Simon Spotlight).

—Spot the Dot. Carter, David A. 2013. (ENG.). 14p. (J). (gr. -1-k). 12.99 *(978-0-545-50009-8(5))* Scholastic, Inc.

—Springtime in Bugland! Carter, David A. 2012. (Ready-To-Reads Ser.). (ENG.). 24p. (J). (gr. -1-1). 15.99 *(978-1-4424-3892-7(4))*; pap. 3.99 *(978-1-4424-3890-3(8))* Simon Spotlight. (Simon Spotlight).

—Up & Down: A Bugs Pop-Up Concept Book. Carter, David A. 2010. (ENG.). 16p. (J). (gr. -1-1). pap. 7.99 *(978-1-4424-0831-9(6))*, Little Simon) Little Simon.

—Welcome to Bugland! A Fun Foldout World from David A. Carter. Carter, David A. 2011. (ENG.). 24p. (J). (gr. -1-3). 12.99 *(978-1-4424-1962-9(8))*, Little Simon) Little Simon.

—White Noise: A Pop-Up Book for Children of All Ages. Carter, David A. 2009. (ENG.). 20p. (J). (gr. -1-3). 27.99 *(978-1-4169-4094-4(4))*, Little Simon) Little Simon.

—Yellow Square: A Pop-Up Book for Children of All Ages. Carter, David A. 2008. (ENG.). 20p. (J). (gr. -1-3). 19.99 *(978-1-4169-4093-7(6))*, Little Simon) Little Simon.

—The 12 Bugs of Christmas: A Pop-Up Christmas Counting Book. Carter, David A. 2011. (ENG.). 24p. (J). (gr. -1-1). 12.99 *(978-1-4424-2649-8(7))*, Little Simon) Little Simon.

—600 Black Spots: A Pop-Up Book for Children of All Ages. Carter, David A. 2007. (ENG.). 20p. (J). (gr. -1-2). 21.99 *(978-1-4169-4092-0(8))*, Little Simon) Little Simon.

Carter, David A. & Carter, Noelle. Little Mouse & Daddy. Carter, David A. & Carter, Noelle. 2005. (Little Mouse Ser.). 12p. (J). 7.95 *(978-1-58117-223-2(0))*, Intervisual/Piggy Toes) Bendon, Inc.

—Little Mouse & Mommy. Carter, David A. & Carter, Noelle. 2005. (Little Mouse Ser.). 12p. (J). 7.95 *(978-1-58117-224-9(9))*, Intervisual/Piggy Toes) Bendon, Inc.

—Little Mouse Plays Peek-a-Boo. Carter, David A. & Carter, Noelle. 2005. (Little Mouse Ser.). 12p. (J). 7.95 *(978-1-58117-225-6(7))*, Intervisual/Piggy Toes) Bendon, Inc.

—Little Mouse's Christmas. Carter, David A. & Carter, Noelle. 2005. 12p. (J). 7.95 *(978-1-58117-226-3(5))*, Intervisual/Piggy Toes) Bendon, Inc.

Carter, Fred, et al. The NEW Children of Color Holy Bible Hardcover Edition. Soles, Henry, ed. 2014. 880p. (gr. 2-18). 24.99 *(978-0-9638127-0-4(X))* Urban Spirit!.

Carter, Greg & Bascle, Brian. The Adventures of Marco Polo, 1 vol. Smalley, Roger. 2005. (Graphic History Ser.). (ENG.). 32p. (gr. 3-4). 29.99 *(978-0-7368-3830-6(9))*, Graphic Library) Capstone Pr., Inc.

Carter, Jill. The Great Chicken Caper. Maxwell, Andre L. & Maxwell, Amanda L. 2012. 34p. (-18). 18.00 *(978-0-9881811-1-3(8))* Maxwell, Andre.

Carter, Kelly. Roxy & Chopper Visit the Animal Shelter. Garcia, Alaycia. 2011. 44p. pap. 24.95 *(978-1-4560-7336-7(2))* America Star Bks.

—Where Dreams Are Born. Wiggins, D. L. 2012. 26p. (J). 16.95 *(978-1-60131-128-3(1))*, Castlebridge Bks.) Big Tent Bks.

Carter, Kris. Egypt. Gill, Heidi. 2012. (2 Kurious Kids Ser.: Vol. 5). (ENG.). 24p. (J). (gr. -1-5). 14.95 *(978-1-936319-93-0(4))* Mascot Bks., Inc.

—2 Kurious Kids: China. Gill, Heidi. 2012. 38p. (J). 14.95 *(978-1-936319-89-3(6))* Mascot Bks., Inc.

—2 Kurious Kids: France. Gill, Heidi. 2012. 38p. (J). 14.95 *(978-1-936319-90-9(X))* Mascot Bks., Inc.

—2 Kurious Kids: India. Gill, Heidi. 2012. 38p. (J). 14.95 *(978-1-936319-92-3(6))* Mascot Bks., Inc.

Carter, Maureen. The Tale of Jemima Puddle-Duck: A Story about Trust. 2006. (J). 6.99 *(978-1-59939-000-0(0))* Cornerstone Pr.

Carter, Noelle, jt. illus. see Carter, David A.

Carter, Paula Becker. Collect-n-Make Crafts for Kids. Lingo, Susan L. Stoker, Bruce, ed. 2006. 112p. (YA). (gr. 1-7). 15.99 *(978-0-7847-1198-9(4))*, 02432) Standard Publishing.

—Collect-n-Play Games for Kids. Lingo, Susan L. Stoker, Bruce, ed. 2006. 112p. (YA). (gr. 1-7). 15.99 *(978-0-7847-1199-6(2))*, 02433) Standard Publishing.

Carter, Robert. Windjammers: The Final Story. Carter, Robert. 2004. 258p. 59.95 *(978-1-877058-04-2(1))* Rosenberg Publishing Pty, Ltd. AUS. Dist: International Specialized Bk. Services.

Carter, Robin. Are Mountains Getting Taller? Questions & Answers about the Changing Earth. Berger, Melvin & Berger, Gilda. 2003. (Question & Answer Ser.). (ENG.). 48p. (J). pap. 5.95 *(978-0-439-26673-4(4))*, Scholastic Reference) Scholastic, Inc.

—Build the Bones Whale. Costello, Dee & Keith, Helen. ed. 2012. (Novelty Ser.). 16p. (J). 9.99 *(978-1-61067-085-2(X))* Kane Miller.

Carter, Sandy Lewis. Pookus & Buckie: A Children's Book Based on a True Story. Reed, Tom. l.t. ed. 2005. 36p. (J). per. 11.95 *(978-0-9749725-4-1(1))*, 10000, Lonestar Abilene Publishing) LoneStar Abilene Publishing, LLC.

Carter, Sharon. Let's Learn the Hawaiian Alphabet. Murray, Patricia Lei. 2005. 24p. (J). 14.95 *(978-1-59700-102-1(3))* Island Heritage Publishing.

Carter, Stephanie. If Peace Is... Baskwill, Jane. 2003. (J). 23p. pap. 7.95 *(978-1-59034-449-1(9))*; 24p. (gr. 11-18). 15.95 *(978-1-59034-448-4(0))* Mondo Publishing.

Carter, Tod, et al. Fair & Squaresville: A Lesson in Playing Fair. Nolan, Allia Zobel. 2014. (VeggieTales (Big Idea) Ser.). (ENG.). 28p. (J). (gr. -1-3). pap. 6.99 incl. audio compact disk *(978-1-61795-333-0(4))* Worthy Publishing.

Cartier, Eric, jt. illus. see Trondheim, Lewis.

Cartobaleno. Castle Caper. Depken, Kristen L. 2015. (Super Deluxe Pictureback Ser.). (ENG.). 24p. (J). (gr. -1-2). 5.99 ***(978-0-553-52313-3(9))***, Random Hse. Bks. for Young Readers) Random Hse. Children's Bks.

Cartobaleno. Dragon Quest (Winx Club) Tillworth, Mary. 2014. (Step into Reading Ser.). (ENG.). 32p. (J). (gr. k-3). 3.99 *(978-0-385-37489-7(5))*, Random Hse. Bks. for Young Readers) Random Hse. Children's Bks.

Cartobaleno Staff. P Is for Paint! Golden Books Staff. 2015. (Deluxe Paint Box Book Ser.). (ENG.). 128p. (J). (gr. -1-2). pap. 7.99 *(978-0-385-38765-1(2))*, Golden Bks.) Random Hse. Children's Bks.

Carton, Rick. Frost Bites. Ogden, Charles. 2008. (Edgar & Ellen Nodyssey Ser.: 2). (ENG.). 192p. (J). (gr. 3-7). 23.99 *(978-1-4169-5464-4(3))*, Simon & Schuster/Paula Wiseman Bks.) Simon & Schuster/Paula Wiseman Bks.

—High Wire. Ogden, Charles. 2006. (Edgar & Ellen Ser.: 5). (ENG.). 208p. (J). (gr. 3-7). 24.99 *(978-1-4169-1500-3(1))*, Simon & Schuster/Paula Wiseman Bks.) Simon & Schuster/Paula Wiseman Bks.

—Hot Air. Ogden, Charles. 2008. (Edgar & Ellen Nodyssey Ser.: 1). (ENG.). 192p. (J). (gr. 3-7). 9.99 *(978-1-4169-5465-1(1))*, Simon & Schuster/Paula Wiseman Bks.) Simon & Schuster/Paula Wiseman Bks.

—Nod's Limbs. Ogden, Charles. 2007. (Edgar & Ellen Ser.: 6). (ENG.). 224p. (J). (gr. 3-7). 24.99 *(978-1-4169-1501-0(X))*, Simon & Schuster/Paula Wiseman Bks.) Simon & Schuster/Paula Wiseman Bks.

—Pet's Revenge. Ogden, Charles. 2006. (Edgar & Ellen Ser.: 4). (ENG.). 192p. (J). (gr. 3-7). 23.99 *(978-1-4169-1408-2(0))*, Simon & Schuster/Paula Wiseman Bks.) Simon & Schuster/Paula Wiseman Bks.

—Rare Beasts. Ogden, Charles. ed. 2006. (Edgar & Ellen Ser.: 1). (ENG.). 144p. (J). (gr. 3-7). 22.99 *(978-1-4169-1409-9(9))*, Simon & Schuster/Paula Wiseman Bks.) Simon & Schuster/Paula Wiseman Bks.

—Tourist Trap. Ogden, Charles. ed. 2006. (Edgar & Ellen Ser.: 2). (ENG.). 176p. (J). (gr. 3-7). 23.99 *(978-1-4169-1411-2(0))*, Simon & Schuster/Paula Wiseman Bks.) Simon & Schuster/Paula Wiseman Bks.

—Under Town. Ogden, Charles. ed. 2006. (Edgar & Ellen Ser.: 3). (ENG.). 160p. (J). (gr. 3-7). 22.99 *(978-1-4169-1412-9(9))*, Simon & Schuster/Paula Wiseman Bks.) Simon & Schuster/Paula Wiseman Bks.

Cartoon Saloon. Blood of the Witch: Book 2. Donbavand, Tommy. 2012. 128p. (J). 24.21 *(978-1-59961-993-4(8))*, Chapter Bks.) Spotlight.

—Claw of the Werewolf: Book 6. Donbavand, Tommy. 2012. 128p. (J). 24.21 *(978-1-59961-997-2(0))*, Chapter Bks.) Spotlight.

—Fang of the Vampire: Book 1. Donbavand, Tommy. 2012. 160p. (J). 24.21 *(978-1-59961-992-7(X))*, Chapter Bks.) Spotlight.

—Flesh of the Zombie: Book 4. Donbavand, Tommy. 2012. 128p. (J). 24.21 *(978-1-59961-995-8(4))*, Chapter Bks.) Spotlight.

—Heart of the Mummy: Book 3. Donbavand, Tommy. 2012. 128p. (J). 24.21 *(978-1-59961-994-1(6))*, Chapter Bks.) Spotlight.

—Skull of the Skeleton: Book 5. Donbavand, Tommy. 2012. 128p. (J). 24.21 *(978-1-59961-996-5(2))*, Chapter Bks.) Spotlight.

Cartoon Saloon Staff. Claw of the Werewolf, Bk. 6. Donbavand, Tommy. 2010. (Scream Street Ser.: 6). (ENG.). 128p. (J). (gr. 3-7). pap. 5.99 *(978-0-7636-4638-7(5))* Candlewick Pr.

—Fang of the Vampire. Donbavand, Tommy. 2009. (Scream Street Ser.: 1). (ENG.). 160p. (J). (gr. 3-7). pap. 5.99 *(978-0-7636-4608-0(3))* Candlewick Pr.

—Flesh of the Zombie, Bk. 4. Donbavand, Tommy. 2010. (Scream Street Ser.: 4). (ENG.). 128p. (J). (gr. 3-7). pap. 5.99 *(978-0-7636-4637-0(7))* Candlewick Pr.

—Heart of the Mummy, Bk. 3. Donbavand, Tommy. 2010. (Scream Street Ser.: 3). (ENG.). 128p. (J). (gr. 3-7). pap. 5.99 *(978-0-7636-4636-3(9))* Candlewick Pr.

—Skull of the Skeleton, Bk. 5. Donbavand, Tommy. 2010. (Scream Street Ser.: 5). (ENG.). 128p. (J). (gr. 3-7). pap. 5.99 *(978-0-7636-4635-6(0))* Candlewick Pr.

Cartwright, Amy. Dreidel, Dreidel, Dreidel. 2010. (ENG.). 10p. (J). (gr. -1-k). 7.99 *(978-0-8431-9899-7(0))*, Price Stern Sloan) Penguin Publishing Group.

—Goldilocks & the Three Bears. Berger, Samantha. 2010. (ENG.). 20p. (J). (gr. -1-k). pap. 5.99 *(978-0-545-23651-5(7))*, Cartwheel Bks.) Scholastic, Inc.

—Jack & the Beanstalk. 2011. (J). pap. *(978-0-545-27434-0(6))*, Cartwheel Bks.) Scholastic, Inc.

—Pirate Potty. Berger, Samantha. 2010. (ENG.). 24p. (J). (gr. -1 — 1). pap. 5.99 *(978-0-545-17295-0(0))*, Cartwheel Bks.) Scholastic, Inc.

—Princess Potty. Berger, Samantha. 2010. (ENG.). 24p. (J). (gr. -1 — 1). pap. 5.99 *(978-0-545-17296-7(9))*, Cartwheel Bks.) Scholastic, Inc.

Cartwright, Christina. Sonja's Wish. McPherson, Heather L. A. 2012. 26p. (J). pap. 11.95 *(978-1-61863-394-1(5))* Bookstand Publishing.

Cartwright, Mary. Glug, Glug, Glug. Baggott, Stella. 2007. (Bath Bks). 5p. (J). (gr. -1-k). 14.99 *(978-0-7945-1784-7(6))*, Usborne) EDC Publishing.

Cartwright, Reg. The Three Golden Oranges. Flor Ada, Alma. 2012. (ENG.). 32p. (J). (gr. -1-3). 16.99 *(978-1-4424-7496-3(3))*, Atheneum Bks. for Young Readers) Simon & Schuster Children's Publishing.

Cartwright, Shannon. Alaska's 12 Days of Summer. Chamberlin-Calamar, Pat. 2003. (Paws IV Ser.). (ENG.). 32p. (J). (gr. -1-2). pap. 10.99 *(978-1-57061-341-8(9))* Sasquatch Bks.

—Sitka Rose. Gill, Shelley. 2005. (ENG.). 32p. (J). (gr. -1-3). per. 7.95 *(978-1-57061-364-8(1))* Charlesbridge Publishing, Inc.

—Up on Denali: Alaska's Wild Mountain. Gill, Shelley. 2006. (Paws IV Ser.). (ENG.). 32p. (J). (gr. -1-2). pap. 10.99 *(978-1-57061-365-4(6))* Sasquatch Bks.

C

Cartwright, Shannon & Love, Judy. Prickly Rose. Gill, Shelley. 2014. (ENG.). 32p. (J). (gr. -1-3). pap. 7.95 (978-1-57091-357-0(9)); lib. bdg. 17.95 (978-1-57091-356-3(0)) Charlesbridge Publishing, Inc.

Cartwright, Stephen. Big Pig on a Dig. Tyler, Jenny. 2004. (Easy Words to Read Ser.). (ENG.). 1p. (J). (gr. 1-18). pap. 6.99 (978-0-7460-3021-9(5)) EDC Publishing.

—Big Pig on a Dig. Cox, Phil Roxbee. Tyler, Jenny, ed. rev. ed. 2006. (Phonics Readers Ser.). 16p. (J). (gr. -1-3). pap. 6.99 (978-0-7945-1501-0(0), Usborne) EDC Publishing.

—Big Red Tractor. Brooks, Felicity. 2006. (Usborne Farmyard Tales Jigsaw Bks.). 10p. (J). (gr. -1-k). bds. 7.99 (978-0-7945-1130-2(9), Usborne) EDC Publishing.

—Camping Out. Amery, Heather. 2005. (Usborne Farmyard Tales Ser.). 16p. (J). (gr. -1-17). pap., pap. 5.95 (978-0-7945-0750-3(6), Usborne) EDC Publishing.

—Children's Songbook - Internet Referenced. 2004. (Songbooks Ser.). 32p. (J). pap. 6.95 (978-0-7945-0710-7(7), Usborne) EDC Publishing.

—Christmas Activities. Milbourne, Anna. 2004. (Activity Books). 32p. (J). pap. 6.95 (978-0-7945-0564-6(3), Usborne) EDC Publishing.

—Christmas Stencil Book. 2005. (Usborne Farmyard Tales Ser.). 10p. (J). (gr. -1-3). bds. 9.95 (978-0-7945-1142-5(2), Usborne) EDC Publishing.

—Cinderella. 2006. (First Stories Sticker Bks.). 16p. (J). (gr. -1-3). pap. 6.99 (978-0-7945-1311-5(5), Usborne) EDC Publishing.

—Cinderella Kid Kit with Pop Out Coach. Amery, Heather. 2006. (Usborne First Stories Ser.). 16p. (J). (gr. -1-3). pap. 8.99 (978-1-58086-877-8(0), Usborne) EDC Publishing.

—The Complete Book of First Experiences. Civardi, Anne. 2005. (Usborne First Experiences Ser.). 144p. (J). (gr. -1-3). 19.95 (978-0-7945-1012-1(4), Usborne) EDC Publishing.

—The Counting Train. Brooks, Felicity et al. 2006. (J). (978-0-439-89922-2(2)) Scholastic, Inc.

—Curly the Pig Board Book. Amery, Heather. 2004. (Young Farmyard Tales Board Books Ser.). 10p. (J). bds. 3.95 (978-0-7945-0468-7(X), Usborne) EDC Publishing.

—Curly's Friends. Cox, Phil Roxbee. rev. ed. 2005. (Usborne Farmyard Tales Touchy-Feely Ser.). 10p. (J). (gr. -1-k). bds. 7.95 (978-0-7945-1180-7(5), Usborne) EDC Publishing.

—Dolly & the Train Sticker Book. Amery, Heather. 2005. 18p. (J). pap. 6.95 (978-0-7945-1064-0(7), Usborne) EDC Publishing.

—Donkey Cards. Amery, Heather. 2004. (Farmyard Tales Card Games Ser.). 52p. (J). 8.95 (978-0-7945-0326-0(8), Usborne) EDC Publishing.

—Dragons, Stories Of. Rawson, Christopher. 2004. (Young Reading Series One Ser.). 48p. (J). (gr. 2-18). pap. 5.95 (978-0-7945-0446-5(9), Usborne) EDC Publishing.

—Duck's Bathtime. Tyler, Jenny. 2005. 4p. (J). (gr. -1-3). 7.95 (978-0-7945-0570-7(8), Usborne) EDC Publishing.

—Fairytale Jigsaw Book. 2004. (Jigsaw Books Ser.). 20p. (J). 14.95 (978-0-7945-0771-8(9), Usborne) EDC Publishing.

—Fairytale Snap. 2005. (Snap Card Games Ser.). 52p. (J). 8.95 (978-0-7945-0905-7(3), Usborne) EDC Publishing.

—The Farm. Amery, Heather. 2008. (Usborne Talkabout Bks.). 12p. (J). (gr. -1-3). bds. 8.99 (978-0-7945-1795-3(1), Usborne) EDC Publishing.

—Farm Magnet Book. Civardi, Anna. 2009. (Magnet Bks). 10p. (J). bds. 19.99 (978-0-7945-2231-5(9), Usborne) EDC Publishing.

—Farmyard Tales Treasury - Internet Referenced. Amery, Heather. 2007. 96p. (J). 19.99 (978-0-7945-1440-2(5), Usborne) EDC Publishing.

—Fat Cat on a Mat. Cox, Phil Roxbee. Tyler, Jenny, ed. rev. ed. 2006. (Phonics Readers Ser.). 16p. (J). (gr. -1-3). pap. 6.99 (978-0-7945-1502-7(9), Usborne) EDC Publishing.

—Find the Bird. Roxbee-Cox, Phil. 2004. (Treasury of Farmyard Tales Ser.). (ENG.). 1p. (J). stu. ed., bds. 3.95 (978-0-7460-3820-8(8)) EDC Publishing.

—Find the Duck. 2007. (Find-its Board Bks). 12p. (J). (gr. -1-k). bds. 6.99 (978-0-7945-1804-2(4), Usborne) EDC Publishing.

—Find the Duck. Cox, Phil Roxbee, ed. 2004. (Find It Board Bks.). (ENG.). 1p. (J). (gr. -1-18). bds. 3.95 (978-0-7460-3821-5(6)) EDC Publishing.

—Find the Kitten. 2007. (Find-its Board Bks). 12p. (J). (gr. -1-k). bds. 6.99 (978-0-7945-1803-5(6), Usborne) EDC Publishing.

—Find the Kitten. Roxbee-Cox, Phil. rev. ed. 2004. (Treasury of Farmyard Tales Ser.). (ENG.). 1p. (J). bds. 3.99 (978-0-7460-3822-2(4)) EDC Publishing.

—Find the Puppy. 2007. (Find-its Board Bks). 12p. (J). (gr. -1-k). bds. 6.99 (978-0-7945-1802-8(8), Usborne) EDC Publishing.

—Find the Puppy. Roxbee-Cox, Phil. rev. ed. 2004. (Treasury of Farmyard Tales Ser.). (ENG.). 1p. (J). bds. 3.99 (978-0-7460-3824-6(0)) EDC Publishing.

—Find the Teddy. Roxbee-Cox, Phil. 2004. (Rhyming Board Bks.). (ENG.). 1p. (J). (gr. -1-18). bds. 3.95 (978-0-7460-3825-3(9)) EDC Publishing.

—First Hundred Words. Amery, Heather. Tyler, Jenny, ed. 2006. (Usborne First Hundred Words Ser.). 32p. (J). (gr. -1). lib. bdg. 14.95 (978-1-58086-505-0(4)) EDC Publishing.

—First Thousand Words: With Internet-Linked Pronunciation Guide. Amery, Heather. MacKinnon, Mairi, ed. 2007. (Usborne Internet-Linked First Thousand Words Ser.). 63p. (J). (gr. -1). 20.99 (978-1-58086-987-4(4), Usborne) EDC Publishing.

—First Thousand Words in Arabic. Amery, Heather. 2004. (First Thousand Words Ser.). (ENG.). 64p. (J). 12.99 (978-0-7945-0030-6(7), Usborne) EDC Publishing.

—First Thousand Words in Chinese: With Internet-Linked Pronunciation Guide. Amery, Heather. MacKinnon, Mairi, ed. Asian Absolute, tr. 2007. (Usborne Internet-Linked First Thousand Words Ser.). 63p. (J). 12.99 (978-0-7945-1550-8(9), Usborne) EDC Publishing.

—First Thousand Words in English. Amery, Heather. Irving, Nicole, ed. 2003. (First Thousand Words Ser.). 63p. (J). (gr. -1). lib. bdg. 20.95 (978-1-58086-474-9(0)) EDC Publishing.

—First Thousand Words in Italian. Amery, Heather. rev. ed. 2004. (First Thousand Words Ser.). (ITA & ENG.). 64p. (J). (gr. -1-6). 12.99 (978-0-7945-0286-7(5)); lib. bdg. 20.99 (978-1-58086-560-9(7)) EDC Publishing. (Usborne).

—First Thousand Words in Japanese. Amery, Heather. rev. ed. 2004. (First Thousand Words Ser.). (JPN & ENG.). 64p. (J). (gr. -1-6). 12.95 (978-0-7945-0480-9(9)); lib. bdg. 20.95 (978-1-58086-552-4(6)) EDC Publishing. (Usborne).

—First Thousand Words in Maori. Amery, Heather. 2006. (MAO.). 64p. (J). (gr. -1-3). pap. 9.00 (978-1-86969-239-1(X)) Univ. of Hawaii Pr.

—Frog on a Log. Cox, Phil Roxbee. Tyler, Jenny, ed. rev. ed. 2006. (Phonics Readers Ser.). 16p. (J). (gr. -1). pap. 6.99 (978-0-7945-1504-1(5), Usborne) EDC Publishing.

—Gnomes & Goblins. Rawson, Christopher. 2004. (Young Reading Series One Ser.). 48p. (J). (gr. 2-18). pap. 5.95 (978-0-7945-0407-6(8), Usborne) EDC Publishing.

—Going on a Plane. Civardi, Anne. Bates, Michelle, ed. rev. ed. 2005. (Usborne First Experiences Ser.). 16p. (J). pap. 4.99 (978-0-7945-1005-3(1), Usborne) EDC Publishing.

—Going to a Party. Civardi, Anne. Watt, Fiona, ed. 2007. (Usborne First Experiences Ser.). 16p. (J). (gr. -1-3). pap. 4.99 (978-0-7945-1011-4(6), Usborne) EDC Publishing.

—Going to School. Civardi, Anne. 2005. 16p. (J). pap. 4.95 (978-0-7945-1008-4(6), Usborne) EDC Publishing.

—Going to the Dentist. Civardi, Anne. Bates, Michelle, ed. rev. ed. 2005. (First Experiences Ser.). 16p. (J). (gr. -1). per. 4.95 (978-0-7945-1007-7(8), Usborne) EDC Publishing.

—Going to the Hospital. Civardi, Anne. Bates, Michelle, ed. rev. ed. 2005. (Usborne First Experiences Ser.). 16p. (J). (gr. -1-3). per. 4.99 (978-0-7945-1006-0(X), Usborne) EDC Publishing.

—Grumpy Goat. Amery, Heather. 2004. 16p. (J). pap. 5.95 (978-0-7945-0788-6(3), Usborne) EDC Publishing.

—Hen's Pens. Cox, Phil Roxbee. Tyler, Jenny, ed. rev. ed. 2006. (Phonics Readers Ser.). 16p. (J). (gr. -1-3). pap. 6.99 (978-0-7945-1506-5(1), Usborne) EDC Publishing.

—Hercules. 2004. (Young Reading Series Two Ser.). 64p. (J). (gr. 2-18). pap. 5.95 (978-0-7945-0453-3(1), Usborne) EDC Publishing.

—Hungry Donkey. Amery, Heather. Tyler, Jenny, ed. rev. ed. 2004. (Farmyard Tales Readers Ser.). 16p. (J). pap. 5.95 (978-0-7945-0752-7(2), Usborne) EDC Publishing.

—Jason & the Golden Fleece. 2004. (Young Reading Series Two Ser.). 64p. (J). (gr. 2-18). pap. 5.95 (978-0-7945-0451-9(5), Usborne) EDC Publishing.

—Latin Words Sticker Book. Sheikh-Miller, Jonathan. 2006. (Latin Words Sticker Book Ser.). 16p. (J). (gr. 1). pap. 8.99 (978-0-7945-1145-6(7), Usborne) EDC Publishing.

—Little Red Riding Hood. Amery, Heather. Tyler, Jenny, ed. 2004. (First Stories Ser.). 16p. (J). (gr. -1). lib. bdg. 12.95 (978-1-58086-620-0(4), Usborne) EDC Publishing.

—Ludo. 2004. (Farmyard Tales Card Games Ser.). (J). 12.95 (978-0-7945-0310-9(1), Usborne) EDC Publishing.

—Market Day. Amery, Heather. 2004. 16p. (J). pap. 5.95 (978-0-7945-0783-1(2), Usborne) EDC Publishing.

—Mermaids. Watt, Fiona. 2004. 10p. (J). 15.95 (978-0-7945-0727-5(1), Usborne) EDC Publishing.

—Mouse Moves House. Cox, Phil Roxbee. Tyler, Jenny, ed. rev. ed. 2006. (Phonic Readers Ser.). 16p. (J). (gr. -1-3). pap. 6.99 (978-0-7945-1507-2(X), Usborne) EDC Publishing.

—Moving House. Civardi, Anne. Bates, Michelle, ed. rev. ed. 2005. 16p. (J). (gr. -1-17). pap. 4.95 (978-0-7945-1009-1(4), Usborne) EDC Publishing.

—Naughty Woolly. Brooks, Felicity. 2006. (Usborne Farmyard Tales Jigsaw Bks.). 10p. (J). bds. 7.99 (978-0-7945-1128-9(7), Usborne) EDC Publishing.

—The New Baby. Civardi, Anne. Bates, Michelle, ed. rev. ed. 2005. 16p. (J). (gr. -1-17). pap. 4.99 (978-0-7945-1003-9(5), Usborne) EDC Publishing.

—New Pony. Amery, Heather. rev. ed. 2004. (Farmyard Tales Readers Ser.). 16p. (J). pap. 5.95 (978-0-7945-0787-9(5), Usborne) EDC Publishing.

—The Old Steam Train. Amery, Heather. rev. ed. 2007. (Farmyard Tales Readers Ser.). 16p. (J). (gr. -1-3). pap. 5.99 (978-0-7945-0804-3(9), Usborne) EDC Publishing.

—The Old Steam Train Kid Kit. Amery, Heather. rev. ed. 2007. (Kid Kits Ser.). (J). 16p. 13.99 (978-1-60130-038-6(7)); 14p. pap. 13.99 (978-1-60130-003-4(4)) EDC Publishing. (Usborne).

—Old steam train sticker Book. Amery, Heather. 2005. 18p. (J). pap. 6.95 (978-0-7945-1066-4(3), Usborne) EDC Publishing.

—La Oveja Rizos. Amery, Heather. 2004. (Titles in Spanish Ser.). (SPA.). 10p. (J). bds. 3.99 (978-0-7460-6104-6(8), Usborne) EDC Publishing.

—Red Tractor Board Book. Amery, Heather. 2004. (Young Farmyard Tales Board Books Ser.). 10p. (J). bds. 3.95 (978-0-7945-0469-4(8), Usborne) EDC Publishing.

—Runaway Tractor. Amery, Heather. 2004. 16p. (J). pap. 5.95 (978-0-7945-0748-0(4), Usborne) EDC Publishing.

—Rusty's Friends. Brooks, Felicity. 2006. (Usborne Farmyard Tales Jigsaw Bks.). 10p. (J). bds. 7.99 (978-0-7945-1127-2(9), Usborne) EDC Publishing.

—Rusty's Train Ride. Amery, Heather. rev. ed. 2007. (Farmyard Tales Readers Ser.). 16p. (J). (gr. -1-3). pap. 5.99 (978-0-7945-0802-9(2), Usborne) EDC Publishing.

—Sam Sheep Can't Sleep. Cox, Phil Roxbee. Tyler, Jenny, ed. rev. ed. 2006. (Usborne Phonics Bks.). 16p. (J). (gr. -1-k). 6.99 (978-0-7945-1508-9(8), Usborne) EDC Publishing.

—Scarecrow's Secret. Amery, Heather. Tyler, Jenny, ed. rev. ed. 2004. (Farmyard Tales Readers Ser.). 16p. (J). pap. 5.95 (978-0-7945-0751-0(4), Usborne) EDC Publishing.

—The Seaside. Amery, Heather. 2008. (Usborne Talkabout Bks.). 12p. (J). bds. 8.99 (978-0-7945-1794-6(3), Usborne) EDC Publishing.

—Shark in the Park. Cox, Phil Roxbee. Tyler, Jenny, ed. rev. ed. 2006. (Phonics Readers Ser.). 16p. (J). (gr. -1-k). pap. 6.99 (978-0-7945-1509-6(6), Usborne) EDC Publishing.

—Sleeping Beauty. 2006. (First Stories Sticker Bks.). 16p. (J). (gr. -1-3). pap. 6.99 (978-0-7945-1313-9(1), Usborne) EDC Publishing.

—Snowy Christmas Jigsaw Book. Amery, Heather. 2004. (Jigsaw Books Ser.). 14p. (J). 8.95 (978-0-7945-0768-8(9), Usborne) EDC Publishing.

—Stories of Giants. Rawson, Christopher. 2004. (Young Reading Ser.: Vol. 1). 48p. (J). (gr. 2-18). lib. bdg. 13.95 (978-1-58086-614-9(X), Usborne) EDC Publishing.

—Stories of Witches. Rawson, Christopher. 2004. (Young Reading Ser.: Vol. 1). 48p. (J). (gr. 2-18). lib. bdg. 13.95 (978-1-58086-630-9(1), Usborne) EDC Publishing.

—The Story of Flying. Sims, Lesley. 2004. (Young Reading Series Two Ser.). 64p. (J). (gr. 2-18). pap. 5.95 (978-0-7945-0705-3(0), Usborne) EDC Publishing.

—Surprise Visitors. Amery, Heather. 2004. 16p. (J). pap. 5.95 (978-0-7945-0784-8(0), Usborne) EDC Publishing.

—Ted in a Red Bed. Cox, Phil Roxbee. Tyler, Jenny, ed. rev. ed. 2006. (Phonics Reader, A: Easy Words to Read Ser.). 16p. (J). (gr. -1-3). 6.99 (978-0-7945-1510-2(X), Usborne) EDC Publishing.

—Ted's Shed. Cox, Phil Roxbee. Tyler, Jenny, ed. rev. ed. 2006. (Phonics Readers Ser.). 16p. (J). (gr. -1-3). pap. 6.99 (978-0-7945-1511-9(8), Usborne) EDC Publishing.

—Telling the Time. Amery, Heather. Tyler, Jenny & Lacey, Minna, eds. 2007. (Usborne Farmyard Tales Ser.). 24p. (J). (gr. -1-2). bds. 12.99 (978-0-7945-1519-5(3), Usborne) EDC Publishing.

—Three Little Pigs. 2006. (First Stories Sticker Bks.). 16p. (J). (gr. -1-3). pap. 6.99 (978-0-7945-1386-3(7), Usborne) EDC Publishing.

—Toad Makes a Road. Cox, Phil Roxbee. Tyler, Jenny, ed. rev. ed. 2006. (Phonics Readers Ser.). 16p. (J). (gr. -1-k). pap. 6.99 (978-0-7945-1512-6(6), Usborne) EDC Publishing.

—Ulysses. 2004. (Young Reading Series Two Ser.). 64p. (J). (gr. 2-18). pap. 5.95 (978-0-7945-0452-6(3), Usborne) EDC Publishing.

—The Usborne 1,2,3 Jigsaw Book. Brooks, Felicity & Tyler, Jenny. 2006. (Usborne Jigsaw Bks.). 12p. (J). (gr. -1-k). bds. 15.95 (978-0-7945-1168-5(6), Usborne) EDC Publishing.

—The Usborne Farmyard Tales Songbook. Marks, Anthony. Tyler, Jenny, ed. 2005. 31p. (J). (gr. -1-7). per. 6.95 (978-0-7945-0918-7(5), Usborne) EDC Publishing.

—Usborne Stories for Bedtime. Hawthorn, Phillip. Tyler, Jenny, ed. 2007. (Stories for Bedtime Ser.). 190p. (J). (gr. -1-3). 19.99 (978-0-7945-1970-4(9), Usborne) EDC Publishing.

—What's Happening at the Seaside? Amery, Heather. rev. ed. 2006. (What's Happening Ser.). 16p. (J). (gr. -1-3). 5.99 (978-0-7945-1290-3(9), Usborne) EDC Publishing.

—What's Happening on the Farm? Amery, Heather. rev. ed. 2006. (What's Happening? Ser.). 32p. (J). (gr. -1-3). 5.99 (978-0-7945-1288-0(7), Usborne) EDC Publishing.

—Where's Curly? Amery, H. 2004. (Treasury of Farmyard Tales Ser.). 16p. (J). (gr. 1-18). pap. 7.95 (978-0-7945-0514-1(7)); lib. bdg. 15.95 (978-1-58086-563-0(1)) EDC Publishing.

—Where's Woolly? Amery, Heather. Tyler, Jenny, ed. 2006. (Treasury of Farmyard Tales Ser.). 16p. (J). (gr. -1-18). 15.95 (978-1-58086-531-9(3)) EDC Publishing.

—Who's Making That Mess? Hawthorn, Philip & Tyler, Jenny. 2008. (Luxury Flap Bks). (gr. -1-k). 9.99 (978-0-7945-1694-9(7)) EDC Publishing.

—Who's Making That Noise? Hawthorne, Philip & Tyler, Jenny. 2005. (Flap Books Ser.). 16p. (J). (gr. 1-18). pap. 7.95 (978-0-7945-0432-8(9), Usborne) EDC Publishing.

—Who's Making That Smell? Tyler, Jenny & Hawthorn, Phillip. 2007. (Luxury Flap Bks). 16p. (J). (gr. -1-3). 9.99 (978-0-7945-1696-3(3), Usborne) EDC Publishing.

—Woolly Stops the Train. Amery, Heather. 2005. 18p. (J). pap. 6.95 (978-0-7945-1063-3(9), Usborne) EDC Publishing.

—Woolly the Sheep. Amery, Heather. 2004. (Young Farmyard Tales Board Books Ser.). 10p. (J). bds. 3.95 (978-0-7945-0467-0(1), Usborne) EDC Publishing.

—Ya Se Hacer Lazos. Watt, Fiona. 2005. (SPA.). 10p. (J). 7.95 (978-0-7460-6626-3(0), Usborne) EDC Publishing.

—Zoo Talkabout Board Book. Amery, Heather. 2008. (Talkabout Board Bks). 12p. (J). bds. 8.99 (978-0-7945-1793-9(5), Usborne) EDC Publishing.

Cartwright, Stephen. Abc Floor. Cartwright, Stephen. 2006. 16p. (J). bds. 15.99 (978-0-7945-1367-2(0), Usborne) EDC Publishing.

—Noisy Animals Board Bk. Cartwright, Stephen. 2007. 12p. (J). bds. 18.99 (978-0-7945-1551-5(7), Usborne) EDC Publishing.

—Usborne Phonics Flashcards: Dog. Cartwright, Stephen. 2007. (Usborne Flashcards Ser.). 48p. (J). (gr. -1-k). 9.99 (978-0-7945-1516-4(9), Usborne) EDC Publishing.

Cartwright, Stephen & Bird, Glen. Fairies. Watt, Fiona. 2004. 10p. (J). (gr. -1 — 1). per. 15.95 (978-0-7945-0811-1(1), Usborne) EDC Publishing.

—Fairies Jigsaw Book. Watt, Fiona. 2005. (Osborne Sparkly Jigsaws Ser.). 10p. (J). bds. 14.99 (978-0-7945-1131-9(7), Usborne) EDC Publishing.

—Mermaids Jigsaw Book. Watt, Fiona. 2006. (Osborne Sparkly Jigsaws Ser.). 10p. (J). bds. 14.99 (978-0-7945-1189-0(9), Usborne) EDC Publishing.

Cartwright, Stephen & Blundell, Kim. Snakes & Ladders. 2004. (Farmyard Tales Card Games Ser.). (J). 12.95 (978-0-7945-0312-3(8), Usborne) EDC Publishing.

Cartwright, Stephen & Sage, Molly. Children's Cookbook. Watt, Fiona. 2006. (Usborne Farmyard Tales Ser.). (ENG.). 48p. (J). 6.99 (978-0-7945-1418-1(9), Usborne) EDC Publishing.

Cartwright, Steven. Farmyard Tales Sticker Coloring Book. ed. 2011. (Coloring Bks). 20p. (J). pap. 5.99 (978-0-7945-2959-8(3), Usborne) EDC Publishing.

Caruncho, Isabel. Un Topo en un Mar de Hierba. Prats, Joan de Déu. (SPA.). 31p. (978-84-236-5040-8(5)) Edebé ESP. Dist: Lectorum Pubns., Inc.

Caruso, Frank. Heart Transplant. Vachss, Andrew. 2010. (ENG.). 100p. pap. 24.99 (978-1-59582-575-9(4)) Dark Horse Comics.

Caruso, Maria Victoria. The Mystery of Leo: El misterio de Leo. Gonzalez, Aurora Adriana. Ballester Kniska, Lorena Ivonne, ed. 2008.Tr. of misterio de Leo. (ENG & SPA.). 34p. (J). per. 15.95 (978-0-9816973-0-7(5)) Spanish-Live.

Caruth, Jeannette. The Mountain Boy. Pages, Christina. 2007. (Nature Children Ser.). 39p. (J). (gr. -1-3). 12.95 (978-0-9794863-9-5(4)) Summerland Publishing.

Carvalho, Bernardo. The World in a Second. Minhós Martins, Isabel. 2015. (ENG.). 56p. (J). (gr. -1-3). 18.95 (978-1-59270-157-5(4)) Enchanted Lion Bks., LLC.

Carver, Erin. Leafy Leafs Where Is Lester?, 1 vol. Carver, David. 34p. 2010. 24.95 (978-1-4512-1069-9(8)); 2009. pap. 19.95 (978-1-4489-2203-1(8)) PublishAmerica, Inc.

—Lester Returns Home with His New Friend La'doo, 1 vol. Carver, David. 2010. 28p. 24.95 (978-1-4489-6340-9(0)) PublishAmerica, Inc.

Cary. Annie Oakley: The Shooting Star. Graves, Charles P. 2011. 80p. (gr. 4-7). 37.95 (978-1-258-01390-5(8)) Literary Licensing, LLC.

—From Barter to Gold: The Story of Money. Russell, Solveig Paulson. 2011. 66p. 36.95 (978-1-258-01865-8(9)) Literary Licensing, LLC.

—Treasure of the Revolution. Fox, Mary Virginia. 2011. 192p. 42.95 (978-1-258-09675-5(7)) Literary Licensing, LLC.

Cary, Debbi. The Lost Monster Tales. Helm, Julie G. 2010. 212p. pap. 14.49 (978-1-4490-3823-6(9)) AuthorHouse.

Cary, Debbi G., photos by. Merlin for Sherman. Helm, Julie G. 2010. 84p. pap. 26.49 (978-1-4520-5183-3(6)) AuthorHouse.

Carzon, Walter, jt. illus. see Artful Doodlers Limited Staff.

Casagrande, Donata Dal Molin. El Globo de Pablito. Brignole, Giancarla, tr. (Fabulas De Familia Ser.). (SPA.). 32p. (978-970-20-0269-7(9)) Castillo, Ediciones, S. A. de C. V.

—Joseph & Chico: The Life of Pope Benedict XVI as Told by a Cat. Perego, Jeanne. Matt, Andrew, tr. from ITA. 2008. 36p. (J). (gr. k-7). 17.95 (978-1-58617-252-7(2)) Ignatius Pr.

Casale, Paul. The Bike Race Mystery. Keene, Carolyn. 2004. (Nancy Drew Notebooks). 76p. (J). (gr. 1-4). lib. bdg. 12.10 (978-0-613-95315-3(0), Turtleback) Turtleback Bks.

—Danger! Dynamite!, 1 vol. Capeci, Anne. 2003. (Cascade Moutain Railroad Mystery Ser.: No. 1). (ENG.). 144p. (J). (gr. 2-5). 12.95 (978-1-56145-288-0(2)) Peachtree Pubs.

—Daredevils, 1 vol. Capeci, Anne. 2004. (Cascade Mountain Railroad Mysteries Ser.). (ENG.). 144p. (J). (gr. 2-5). 12.95 (978-1-56145-307-8(2)) Peachtree Pubs.

—Ghost Train, 1 vol., Vol. 3. Capeci, Anne. 2004. (Cascade Moutain Railroad Mystery Ser.: 3). (ENG.). 144p. (J). (gr. 2-5). 12.95 (978-1-56145-324-5(2)) Peachtree Pubs.

—Missing!, 1 vol. Capeci, Anne. 2005. (Cascade Mountain Railroad Mysteries Ser.). (ENG.). 144p. (J). (gr. 2-5). 12.95 (978-1-56145-334-4(X)) Peachtree Pubs.

—Sliding into Home, 1 vol. Butler, Dori Hillestad. 2003. (Peachtree Junior Publication Ser.). (ENG.). 192p. (J). (gr. 3-7). 14.95 (978-1-56145-222-4(X)) Peachtree Pubs.

—Snowman Surprise. Frost, Michael, photos by. Keene, Carolyn. 63rd ed. 2004. (Nancy Drew Notebooks Ser.: 63). (ENG.). 80p. (J). (gr. 1-4). pap. 4.99 (978-0-689-87411-6(1), Simon & Schuster/Paula Wiseman Bks.) Simon & Schuster/Paula Wiseman Bks.

—Sonshine Girls: Operation Salvation. Morris, Rene. 2009. (ENG.). 164p. (J). pap. 6.99 (978-0-9801861-5-4(3), Summertime Bks.) Summerhill Pr.

—Sonshine Girls: Summer Secret. Morris, Rene. 2008. (ENG.). 164p. (J). pap. 6.99 (978-0-9801861-2-3(9), Summertime Bks.) Summerhill Pr.

—Wild Horse Country. Diaz, Katacha. 2005. (Wild Reading Adventures! Ser.). (ENG.). (J). (gr. -1-2). 32p. 8.95 (978-1-59249-220-6(7), SC7105); 36p. 15.95 (978-1-59249-137-7(5), B7105) Soundprints.

—Wild Horse Country. Diaz, Katacha & Bosson, Jo-Ellen. 2005. (Wild Reading Adventures! Ser.). (ENG.). 36p. (J). (gr. -1-2). 9.95 (978-1-59249-140-7(5), PS7155) Soundprints.

—Wild Horse Country. Diaz, Katacha. (Wild Reading Adventures! Ser.). (ENG.). (J). 2005. 36p. (gr. -1-2). pap. 6.95 (978-1-59249-138-4(3), S7105); 2005. 32p. (gr. -1-3). 19.95 (978-1-59249-219-0(3), BC7105); 2003. 36p. (gr. 2-2). pap. 2.95 (978-1-59249-139-1(1), S7155) Soundprints.

Casale, Paul. I Have Not Yet Begun to Fight: A Story about John Paul Jones. Casale, Paul, tr. Alphin, Elaine Marie & Alphin, Arthur B. 2004. (Creative Minds Biographies Ser.). (ENG.). 64p. (gr. 4-8). pap. 8.95 (978-1-57505-635-7(6)) Lerner Publishing Group.

Casale, Roberto. Little Binky Bear. 2010. (ENM & ENG.). 18p. (J). 7.99 (978-0-9825700-0-5(7)) Show n' Tell Publishing.

Casanova, Jose Maria. Madera y Corcho. Llimos Plomer, Anna & Llimós, Anna. 2003. (Coleccion Ivamos a Crear!). (SPA.). 32p. (J). (gr. k-2). 12.00 (978-84-342-2344-8(9)) Parramon Ediciones S.A. ESP. Dist: Lectorum Pubns., Inc.

Casas, Fritz. Blood Brotherhood, 1 vol. Sherman, M. Zachary. 2011. (Bloodlines Ser.). (ENG.). 88p. (gr. 4-8). pap. 6.95 (978-1-4342-3098-0(8)); 23.32 (978-1-4342-2559-7(3)) Stone Arch Bks.

—Control under Fire, 1 vol. Sherman, M. Zachary. 2011. (Bloodlines Ser.). (ENG.). 88p. (gr. 4-8). pap. 6.95 (978-1-4342-3100-0(3)); lib. bdg. 23.32 (978-1-4342-2561-0(5)) Stone Arch Bks.

—Fighting Phantoms, 1 vol. Sherman, M. Zachary. 2011. (Bloodlines Ser.). (ENG.). 88p. (gr. 4-8). pap. 6.95 (978-1-4342-3099-7(6)); lib. bdg. 23.32 (978-1-4342-2560-3(7)) Stone Arch Bks.

—A Time for War, 1 vol. Sherman, M. Zachary. 2011. (Bloodlines Ser.). (ENG.). 88p. (gr. 4-8). pap. 6.95 (978-1-4342-3097-3(X)); 23.32 (978-1-4342-2558-0(5)) Stone Arch Bks.

Casaus, Lisa May. Grandpa's Magic Tortilla. Martinez, Demetria & Montoya-Read, Rosalee. 2010. (SPA & ENG.). 32p. (J). (gr. 1). 18.95 (978-0-8263-4862-3(9)) Univ. of New Mexico Pr.

Casciano, Christie & Moziak, Rose Mary Casciano. Haunted Hockey in Lake Placid. 2012. 72p. (J). pap. *(978-1-59531-040-8(1))* North Country Bks., Inc.

—The Puck Hog. 2011. 44p. (J). pap. 9.95 *(978-1-59531-037-8(1))* North Country Bks., Inc.

Cascino, Jennifer. The Adventures of Coco le Chat: The World's Most Fashionable Feline. Nathan, Paul, photos by. Nathan, Nadine Rubin. 2014. (ENG.). 32p. 15.00 *(978-0-9851368-5-7(5))* Pelluceo.

Cascio, Maria Cristina Lo & McNicholas, Shelagh. Little Ballerina Dancing Book. Watt, Fiona. 2007. (Little Ballerina Dancing Book Ser.). 12p. (J). bds. 15.99 incl. audio compact disk *(978-0-7945-1520-1(7),* Usborne) EDC Publishing.

Cascio, Maria Cristina Lo, jt. illus. see McNicholas, Shelagh.

Casco, Maria Cristina Lo. Saints Tell Their Stories. Mitchell, Patricia. 2009. 62p. (J). (gr. k-5). 12.95 *(978-1-59325-161-1(0))* Word Among Us Pr.

Case, Jonathan. Before Tomorrowland. Case, Jonathan. Jenson, Jeff et al. 2015. (ENG.). 336p. (YA). (gr. 7-12). 16.99 *(978-1-4847-0421-9(5))* Disney Pr.

Case, Richard, et al. Ancient History. Ennis, Garth. Kahan, Bob, ed. 4th rev. ed. 2011. (Preacher Ser.). (ENG.). 224p. (YA). pap. 17.99 *(978-1-56389-405-3(X))* DC Comics.

Caselli, Stefano. Avengers - Prelude to Infinity, Vol. 3. Spencer, Nick & Hickman, Jonathan. 2014. (ENG.). 152p. (YA). (gr. 8-17). pap. 19.99 *(978-0-7851-6654-2(8))* Marvel Worldwide, Inc.

—Avengers World Vol. 1: A. I. M. Empire. 2014. (ENG.). 120p. (J). (gr. 4-17). pap. 16.99 *(978-0-7851-8981-7(5))* Marvel Worldwide, Inc.

Casey, James, jt. illus. see Eldridge, Les.

Casey, Lukatz. Coconut Photo Journal. American Girl Editorial Staff, ed. 2005. (American Girl Today Ser.). (ENG.). 24p. (J). 9.95 *(978-1-58485-973-4(3),* American Girl) American Girl Publishing, Inc.

Casey, Quinn. My Dad Cancelled Christmas! Casey, Sean. 2008. 25p. (J). 15.95 *(978-0-9797297-0-6(X))* Cool Kids Create.

Casey, Robert, photos by. Every Kid Needs Things That Fly, 1 vol. Kinmont, Ritchie. 2005. (ENG., 136p. (J). pap. 14.95 *(978-1-58685-509-3(3),* 1241179) Gibbs Smith, Publisher.

Cash, Emory. Santa Almost Got Caught: Stories for Thanksgiving, Christmas, & the New Year. Neely, Kirk H. 2011. 152p. pap. 14.99 *(978-1-4575-0477-8(4))* Dog Ear Publishing, LLC.

Cash, Eric. Buster Tells It All: Stories from Pony Creek Ranch. Berry, Carolyn. 2011. 24p. (J). 16.99 *(978-1-61254-011-5(2))* Brown Bks. Publishing Group.

—Once upon a Time in Liverpool. Kristen, Judith. 2012. 40p. pap. 15.95 *(978-0-9849505-2-2(4))* Aquinas & Krone Publishing, LLC.

Cash, Paul. What's Wrong with Pauly? House, B. J. 2013. 36p. 11.99 *(978-0-9835843-6-0(2),* Lonely Swan Bks.) Cosmic Gargoyle Creative Solutions.

Cash-Walsh, Tina, jt. illus. see Cline, Jeff.

Cashmore-Hingley, Michael. Do Not Disturb. Gabolinscy, Jack. 2013. 24p. (gr. 3-8). pap. *(978-1-77654-019-8(0),* Red Rocket Readers) Flying Start Bks.

Casilla, Robert. Daniel & the Lord of Lions. Pinkney, Gloria Jean. 2008. 32p. 17.00 *(978-0-687-65235-8(9))* Abingdon Pr.

—Dolores Huerta: A Hero to Migrant Workers, 0 vols. Warren, Sarah E. 2012. (ENG.). 32p. (J). (gr. 2-5). 17.99 *(978-0-7614-6107-4(8),* 9780761461074, Amazon Children's Publishing) Amazon Publishing.

—The Dream on Blanca's Wall: Poems in English & Spanish. Medina, Jane & Median, Jane. 2004. (SPA & ENG.). 32p. (J). (gr. 2-4). pap. 9.95 *(978-1-59078-264-4(X))* Boyds Mills Pr.

—Jackie Robinson: He Led the Way. Prince, April Jones. 2007. (Penguin Young Readers, Level 3 Ser.). (ENG.). 48p. (J). (gr. 1-3). mass mkt. 3.99 *(978-0-448-44721-6(5),* Grosset & Dunlap) Penguin Publishing Group.

—Let's Salsa. Ruiz-Flores, Lupe & Rosales-Yeomans, Natalia. Rosales-Yeomans, Natalia, tr. 2013.Tr. of Bailemos Salsa. (SPA & ENG.). 32p. (J). 17.95 *(978-1-55885-762-9(1),* Piñata Books) Arte Publico Pr.

—The Little Painter of Sabana Grande. Markun, Patricia M. 2014. (ENG.). 32p. (J). (gr. -1-3). 13.99 *(978-1-4814-4458-3(1),* Simon & Schuster Bks. For Young Readers) Simon & Schuster Bks. For Young Readers.

—The Lunch Thief, 1 vol. Bromley, Anne C. 2009. (ENG.). 32p. (J). (gr. 1-5). 16.95 *(978-0-88448-311-3(8))* Tilbury Hse. Pubs.

—A Picture Book of Martin Luther King, Jr. Adler, David A. 2004. (Picture Book Biography Ser.). (J). (gr. -1-3). pap. 18.95 incl. audio compact disk *(978-1-59112-773-4(4))* Live Oak Media.

—A Picture Book of Rosa Parks. Adler, David A. 2004. (J). (gr. -1-2). 28.95 incl. audio compact disk *(978-1-59112-762-8(9))* Live Oak Media.

Casilla, Robert. A Picture Book of Rosa Parks. Adler, David A. 2015. 32p. pap. 8.00 ***(978-1-61003-405-0(8))*** Center for the Collaborative Classroom.

—The Remembering Day / El Día de los Muertos. Mora, Pat & Ventura, Gabriela Baeza. 2015. (SPA & ENG.). 32p. (J). (gr. k-3). 17.95 ***(978-1-55885-805-3(9),*** Piñata Books) Arte Publico Pr.

Casilla, Robert. The Train to Lulu's. Howard, Elizabeth Fitzgerald. 2007. (ENG.). 36p. (J). (gr. -1-3). 10.99 *(978-1-4169-6161-1(5),* Simon & Schuster/Paula Wiseman Bks.) Simon & Schuster/Paula Wiseman Bks.

Caso, George R. The Mission. Caso, George R. 2003. 16p. (J). (gr. -1-6). pap. 4.95 *(978-0-9719290-1-2(7))* Caso, George R.

Cass, Bill. The Survivorship Net: A Parable for the Family, Friends, & Caregivers of People with Cancer. Owens, Jim. 2010. (ENG.). 48p. (gr. 2). 14.95 *(978-1-60443-018-9(4))* American Cancer Society, Inc.

Cassaday, John. Astonishing X-Men - Gifted, Vol. 1. gif. ed. 2006. (ENG.). 152p. (YA). (gr. 8-17). pap. 14.99 *(978-0-7851-1531-1(5))* Marvel Worldwide, Inc.

—Unstoppable, Vol. 4. 2008. (ENG.). 200p. (YA). (gr. 8-17). pap. 19.99 *(978-0-7851-2254-8(0))* Marvel Worldwide, Inc.

Cassaday, John. Dangerous, Vol. 2. Cassaday, John, . 2007. (ENG.). 152p. (YA). (gr. 8-17). pap. 14.99 *(978-0-7851-1677-6(X))* Marvel Worldwide, Inc.

Cassatt, Mary. Mary Cassatt: Impressionist Painter, 1 vol. Harris, Lois V. 2007. (ENG.). 32p. (J). (gr. k-3). 16.99 *(978-1-58980-452-4(X))* Pelican Publishing Co., Inc.

Cassel, Lili. Jewish Heroes, 2 bks. Weilerstein, Sadie Rose. 208p. (J). (gr. 2-3). Bk. 1. 4.25 *(978-0-8381-0180-3(1));* Bk. 2. 4.25 *(978-0-8381-0177-3(1))* United Synagogue of America Bk. Service.

Cassels, Jean. Baby Animals. Rappoport, Bernice. 2004. (Treasure Tree Ser.). 32p. (J). *(978-0-7166-1615-3(7))* World Bk., Inc.

—The Cajun Nutcracker, 1 vol. Mock, Chara. 2011. (ENG.). 32p. (J). (gr. k-3). 16.99 *(978-1-58980-978-9(5))* Pelican Publishing Co., Inc.

—Groundhog Stays up Late. Cuyler, Margery. (ENG.). 32p. (J). 2007. (gr. k-2). pap. 6.95 *(978-0-8027-9732-2(6));* 2005. (gr. -1-2). 16.95 *(978-0-8027-8939-6(0))* Walker & Co.

Cassels, Jean. Two Bobbies. Larson, Kirby & Nethery, Mary. 2015. 36p. pap. 8.00 ***(978-1-61003-411-1(2))*** Center for the Collaborative Classroom.

Cassels, Jean. Two Bobbies: A True Story of Hurricane Katrina, Friendship, & Survival. Larson, Kirby & Nethery, Mary. 2008. (ENG.). 32p. (J). (gr. k-3). 16.99 *(978-0-8027-9754-4(7),* Bloomsbury USA Childrens) Bloomsbury USA.

—Who Is My Mom? Nicholas, Melissa. l.t. ed. 2005. (Sadlier Phonics Reading Program). 8p. (gr. -1-1). 23.00 net. *(978-0-8215-7341-9(1))* Sadlier, William H. Inc.

Cassetta, Andrea. Mr Bothers. Frost, Lesley. 2007. 52p. per. 12.95 *(978-1-934246-59-7(X))* Peppertree Pr., The.

—The Truth about Dragons & Dinosaurs. Miranda, Edward. 2007. 32p. per. 10.95 *(978-1-934246-22-1(0))* Peppertree Pr., The.

Cassidy, Al. One Misty Morning. Dean, Lani. 2004. 36p. (J). 14.95 *(978-0-9645844-9-5(2))* Manor Hse. Publishing Co., Inc.

Cassidy, Albert, Jr. The Amazing Adventures of Dr. Snappy & Sam: Dr. Snappy vs. Subluxor. Cassidy, Albert, Jr. Bennedetti, Eric. Romanchick, Jennifer, ed. 2005. 16p. (J). 9.99 *(978-0-9770527-0-7(2))* All Health Chiropractic Ctrs. Inc.

Cassidy, Amber. One Windy Day: Green Banana. Goodhart, Pippa. 2015. (Green Bananas Ser.). (ENG.). 48p. (J). pap. 7.99 ***(978-1-4052-7070-0(5))*** Egmont Bks., Ltd. GBR. Dist: Independent Pubs. Group.

Cassidy, Nancy White. The Doll of Lilac Valley. Cheney, Cora. 2003. 128p. 11.95 *(978-0-9714612-5-3(2))* Green Mansion Pr. LLC.

Cassidy, Sean. Hanna Bear's Christmas, 1 vol. Devine, Monica. 2007. (ENG.). 32p. (J). (gr. -1-1). 9.95 *(978-1-55041-585-8(9),* 1550415859) Fitzhenry & Whiteside, Ltd. CAN. Dist: Midpoint Trade Bks., Inc.

—Wake up, Henry Rooster!, 1 vol. Ruurs, Margriet. 2006. (ENG.). 32p. (J). (gr. -1-3). 9.95 *(978-1-55041-952-8(8),* 1550419528) Fitzhenry & Whiteside, Ltd. CAN. Dist: Midpoint Trade Bks., Inc.

Cassino, Mark, photos by. The Story of Snow: The Science of Winter's Wonder. Nelson, Jon. 2009. (ENG., 36p. (J). (gr. -1-2). 16.99 *(978-0-8118-6866-2(4))* Chronicle Bks. LLC.

Casson, Sophia. Toby's Very Important Question. Lemieux, Jean. 2004. 61p. (J). lib. bdg. 12.00 *(978-1-4242-1246-0(4))* Fitzgerald Bks.

Casson, Sophie. Le Fil de la Vie. Lemieux, Jean. 2004. (Premier Roman Ser.). (FRE.). 64p. (J). (gr. 1-4). pap. *(978-2-89021-644-0(6))* Diffusion du livre Mirabel (DLM).

—Toby & the Mysterious Creature. Lemieux, Jean. Cummins, Sarah, tr. from FRE. 2008. (Formac First Novels Ser.). (ENG.). 64p. (J). (gr. 2-5). 14.95 *(978-0-88780-761-9(5))* Formac Publishing Co., Ltd. CAN. Dist: Casemate Pubs. & Bk. Distributors, LLC.

—Toby Laughs Last. Lemieux, Jean. Cummins, Sarah, tr. from FRE. 2006. (Formac First Novels Ser.: 59). (ENG.). 64p. (J). (gr. 2-5). 14.95 *(978-0-88780-720-6(8))* Formac Publishing Co., Ltd. CAN. Dist: Casemate Pubs. & Bk. Distributors, LLC.

—Toby Laughs Last, 1 vol. Lemieux, Jean. Cummins, Sarah, tr. from FRE. 2006. (Formac First Novels Ser.: 59). (ENG.). 64p. (J). (gr. 2-5). 4.95 *(978-0-88780-716-9(X))* Formac Publishing Co., Ltd. CAN. Dist: Casemate Pubs. & Bk. Distributors, LLC.

—Toby Shoots for Infinity. Lemieux, Jean. 2005. 61p. (J). lib. bdg. 12.00 *(978-1-4242-1201-9(4))* Fitzgerald Bks.

—Toby Shoots for Infinity. Lemieux, Jean. Cummins, Sarah, tr. from FRE. 2005. (Formac First Novels Ser.: 55). (ENG.). 64p. (J). (gr. 2-5). 14.95 *(978-0-88780-685-8(6))* Formac Publishing Co., Ltd. CAN. Dist: Casemate Pubs. & Bk. Distributors, LLC.

—Toby Shoots for Infinity, 1 vol. Lemieux, Jean. Cummins, Sarah, tr. from FRE. 2005. (Formac First Novels Ser.: 55). (ENG.). 64p. (J). (gr. 2-5). 4.95 *(978-0-88780-684-1(8))* Formac Publishing Co., Ltd. CAN. Dist: Casemate Pubs. & Bk. Distributors, LLC.

—Toby's Best Friend. Lemieux, Jean. Cummins, Sarah, tr. from FRE. 2003. (Formac First Novels Ser.). (ENG.). 64p. (J). (gr. 2-5). 14.95 *(978-0-88780-611-7(2));* (gr. 1-5). 4.95 *(978-0-88780-610-0(4))* Formac Publishing Co., Ltd. CAN. Dist: Casemate Pubs. & Bk. Distributors, LLC.

—Toby's Very Important Question. Lemieux, Jean. Cummins, Sarah, tr. from FRE. 2004. (Formac First Novels Ser.: 51). (ENG.). 64p. (J). (gr. 1-5). 14.95 *(978-0-88780-637-7(6))* Formac Publishing Co., Ltd. CAN. Dist: Casemate Pubs. & Bk. Distributors, LLC.

Casson, Sophie. Toby & the Mysterious Creature, 1 vol. Casson, Sophie. Lemieux, Jean. Cummins, Sarah, tr. from FRE. 2008. (Formac First Novels Ser.). (ENG.). 64p. (J). (gr. 2-5). 5.95 *(978-0-88780-759-6(3))* Formac Publishing Co., Ltd. CAN. Dist: Casemate Pubs. & Bk. Distributors, LLC.

Casson, Sophie & Brochard, Philippe. Toby's Very Important Question, 1 vol. Lemieux, Jean. Cummins, Sarah, tr. from FRE. 2004. (Formac First Novels Ser.: 51). (ENG.). 64p. (J). (gr. 1-5). 4.95 *(978-0-88780-636-0(8))* Formac Publishing Co., Ltd. CAN. Dist: Casemate Pubs. & Bk. Distributors, LLC.

Castaldi, Elicia. Eighth Grade Is Making Me Sick: Ginny Davis's Year in Stuff. Holm, Jennifer L. 2015. (Ginny Davis's Year in Stuff Ser.). (ENG.). 128p. (J). (gr. 3-7). pap. 7.99 ***(978-0-375-87219-8(1),*** Yearling) Random Hse. Children's Bks.

Castaldi, Elicia. Eighth Grade Is Making Me Sick: Ginny Davis's Year in Stuff. Holm, Jennifer L. 2012. (Ginny Davis's Year in Stuff Ser.). (ENG.). 128p. (J). (gr. 3-7). 15.99 *(978-0-375-86851-1(8))* Random Hse., Inc.

—Middle School Is Worse Than Meatloaf: A Year Told Through Stuff. Holm, Jennifer L. (Babymouse Ser.). (ENG.). 128p. (J). (gr. 3-7). 2011. pap. 7.99 *(978-1-4424-3663-3(8));* 2007. 12.99 *(978-0-689-85281-7(9))* Simon & Schuster Children's Publishing. (Atheneum Bks. for Young Readers).

Castaldi, Elicia. The Food Parade: Healthy Eating with the Nutritious Food Groups. Castaldi, Elicia. 2013. (ENG.). 32p. (J). (gr. -1-2). 16.99 *(978-0-8050-9176-2(9),* Holt, Henry & Co. Bks. For Young Readers) Holt, Henry & Co.

Casteel, Kay. The Legacy of Bletchley Park. Smith, Annie Laura. Hamilton, Dianne, ed. 2004. 130p. (J). pap. 6.99 *(978-0-9700752-5-3(1),* 0-9700752-5-1) Onstage Publishing, LLC.

—The Masterpiece: An Abbie Girl Spy Mystery. Butler, Darren J. 2004. (Abbie, Girl Spy Ser.: 4). (ENG.). 278p. (J). mass mkt. 8.50 *(978-0-9753367-3-1(8))* Onstage Publishing, LLC.

—Spies: A Gander's Cove Mystery. Taylor, Mary Ann. 2006. (J). mass mkt. 5.99 *(978-0-9753367-7-9(0))* Onstage Publishing, LLC.

—Traitors: A Gander's Cove Mystery. Taylor, Mary Ann. 2006. (J). mass mkt. 5.99 *(978-0-9753367-9-3(7))* Onstage Publishing, LLC.

—Will Paris Burn? Smith, Annie Laura. 2004. (ENG.). (YA). mass mkt. 6.99 *(978-0-9753367-4-8(6))* Onstage Publishing, LLC.

Casteel, Tom. The American Revolution: Experience the Battle for Independence. Dodge Cummings, Judy. 2015. (Build It Yourself Ser.). (ENG.). 128p. (gr. 3-7). pap. 17.95 *(978-1-61930-246-4(2))* Nomad Pr.

—The Brain: Journey Through the Universe Inside Your Head. Mooney, Carla. 2015. (Inquire & Investigate Ser.). (ENG.). 128p. (gr. 6-10). 22.95 *(978-1-61930-274-7(8))* Nomad Pr.

—Cities: Discover How They Work. Reilly, Kathleen M. 2014. (Build It Yourself Ser.). (ENG.). 128p. (J). (gr. 3-7). 21.95 *(978-1-61930-213-6(6))* Nomad Pr.

—Explorers of the New World: Discover the Golden Age of Exploration with 22 Projects. Mooney, Carla. 2011. (Build It Yourself Ser.). (ENG.). 128p. (J). (gr. 3-7). 21.95 *(978-1-936313-44-0(8));* pap. 15.95 *(978-1-936313-43-3(X))* Nomad Pr.

—Maya: Amazing Inventions You Can Build Yourself. Bell-Rehwoldt, Sheri. 2nd ed. 2011. (Build It Yourself Ser.). (ENG.). 128p. (J). (gr. 3-7). 21.95 *(978-1-936749-61-4(0));* pap. 15.95 *(978-1-936749-60-7(2))* Nomad Pr.

—Maya: Inventos Increibles Que Puedes Construir Tu Mismo. Bell-Rehwoldt, Sheri. 2011. (Build It Yourself Ser.). (SPA & ENG.). 128p. (J). (gr. 3-7). pap. 15.95 *(978-1-936749-62-1(9))* Nomad Pr.

—Natural Disasters: Investigate Earth's Most Destructive Forces with 25 Projects. Reilly, Kathleen M. 2012. (Build It Yourself Ser.). (ENG.). 128p. (J). (gr. 3-7). pap. 15.95 *(978-1-61930-146-7(6));* 21.95 *(978-1-61930-147-4(4))* Nomad Pr.

Castelao, Patricia. Abandoned! - A Lion Called Kiki. Orr, Wendy. 2012. (Rainbow Street Shelter Ser.: 4). (ENG.). 128p. (J). (gr. 2-5). 15.99 *(978-0-8050-9501-2(2),* Holt, Henry & Co. Bks. For Young Readers) Holt, Henry & Co.

—Discovered! A Beagle Called Bella. Orr, Wendy. 2013. (Rainbow Street Shelter Ser.: 6). (ENG.). 128p. (J). (gr. 2-5). 15.99 *(978-0-8050-9505-0(5),* Holt, Henry & Co. Bks. For Young Readers) Holt, Henry & Co.

Castelao, Patricia. The One & Only Ivan. Applegate, Katherine. (ENG.). (J). (gr. 3-7). 2015. 352p. 24.99 ***(978-0-06-242524-9(2));*** 2015. 272p. pap. 7.99 *(978-0-06-199227-8(5));* 2012. 305p. 16.99 *(978-0-06-199225-4(9))* HarperCollins Pubs.

Castelao, Patricia. Stolen! - A Pony Called Pebbles. Orr, Wendy. 2012. (Rainbow Street Shelter Ser.: 5). (ENG.). 128p. (J). (gr. 2-5). pap. 5.99 *(978-0-8050-9504-3(7),* Holt, Henry & Co. Bks. For Young Readers) Holt, Henry & Co.

—Wanted! - A Guinea Pig Called Henry. Orr, Wendy. 2012. (Rainbow Street Shelter Ser.: 3). (ENG.). 128p. (J). (gr. 2-5). 15.99 *(978-0-8050-8933-2(0),* Holt, Henry & Co. Bks. For Young Readers) Holt, Henry & Co.

Castelao, Patricia, jt. illus. see Madrid, Erwin.

Castellan, Andrea "Casty" & Mazzon, Michelle. Mickey Mouse & the World to Come. Castellan, Andrea "Casty". 2010. (ENG.). 112p. (J). (gr. 3-6). pap. 9.99 *(978-1-60886-562-8(2))* Boom! Studios.

Castellano, Giuseppe. C Is for City: An Alphabet Book. Zuravicky, Orli. 2011. (Mister Doodle Ser.). (ENG.). 40p. (J). (gr. -1-k). bds. 7.99 *(978-1-4424-2049-6(9),* Little Simon) Little Simon.

—A Color for Sketch: A Book about Colors. Zuravicky, Orli. 2011. (Mister Doodle Ser.). (ENG.). 34p. (J). (gr. -1-k). bds. 7.99 *(978-1-4424-3154-6(7),* Little Simon) Little Simon.

Castellanos, Diana. Orfeo, Sísifo y Cía. Inkiow, Ditier. 2003. (SPA.). (J). pap. 10.99 *(978-958-04-7070-0(7))* Norma S.A. COL. Dist: Lectorum Pubns., Inc.

Castellini, Claudio. Wolverine: The End, Youngquist, Jeff, ed. 2007. (ENG.). 144p. (YA). (gr. 8-17). pap. 14.99 *(978-0-7851-1349-2(5))* Marvel Worldwide, Inc.

Castillo, Cesar & Burruss, Melissa. Crybaby: Extinction. LaRocque, Greg. 2005. (YA). per. 9.99 *(978-1-933570-86-0(5))* Aardvark Global Publishing.

Castillo, Guillermo Graco. Komok, Nokek y los Flamencos. Gomez, Mercedes. rev. ed. 2006. (Castillo de la Lectura Naranja Ser.). (SPA & ENG.). 92p. (J). (gr. 4-7). pap. 7.95 *(978-968-5920-39-1(7))* Castillo, Ediciones, S. A. de C. V. MEX. Dist: Macmillan.

—Querido Tigre Quezada. Malpica, Antonio. rev. ed. 2006. (Castillo de la Lectura Roja Ser.). (SPA & ENG.). 232p. (YA). (gr. 7). pap. 8.95 *(978-968-5920-85-8(0))* Castillo, Ediciones, S. A. de C. V. MEX. Dist: Macmillan.

Castillo, Jesus. El Encargo de Fernanda. Riveros, Gabriela. rev. ed. 2006. (Castillo de la Lectura Blanca Ser.). (SPA & ENG.). 64p. (J). (gr. k-2). pap. 6.95 *(978-970-20-0126-3(9))* Castillo, Ediciones, S. A. de C. V. MEX. Dist: Macmillan.

—Mi Hermano Paco. Riveros, Gabriela. rev. ed. 2006. (Castillo de la Lectura Blanca Ser.). (SPA & ENG.). 72p. (J). (gr. k-2). pap. 6.95 *(978-970-20-0173-7(0))* Castillo, Ediciones, S. A. de C. V. MEX. Dist: Macmillan.

Castillo, Lauren. Buffalo Music. Fern, Tracey E. 2008. (ENG.). 32p. (J). (gr. -1-3). 17.99 *(978-0-618-72341-6(2))* Houghton Mifflin Harcourt Publishing Co.

—Christmas Is Here. King James Bible Staff. 2010. (ENG.). 32p. (J). (gr. -1-2). 12.99 *(978-1-4424-0822-7(7),* Simon & Schuster Bks. For Young Readers) Simon & Schuster Bks. For Young Readers.

—City Cat. Banks, Kate. 2013. (ENG.). 48p. (J). (gr. -1-2). 17.99 *(978-0-374-31321-0(0),* Farrar, Straus & Giroux (BYR)) Farrar, Straus & Giroux.

—Happy Like Soccer. Boelts, Maribeth. 2014. (ENG.). 32p. (J). (gr. k-4). pap. 6.99 *(978-0-7636-7049-8(9))* Candlewick Pr.

—The Pig & Miss Prudence, 1 vol. Stanek, Linda. 2008. (ENG.). 32p. (J). (gr. -1-3). 15.95 *(978-1-59572-125-9(8))* Star Bright Bks., Inc.

—The Reader, 0 vols. Hest, Amy. 2012. (ENG.). 32p. (J). (gr. -1-1). 16.99 *(978-0-7614-6184-5(1),* 9780761461845, Amazon Children's Publishing) Amazon Publishing.

—Spunky Tells All. Cameron, Ann. 2011. (ENG.). 112p. (J). (gr. 3-6). 16.99 *(978-0-374-38000-7(7),* Farrar, Straus & Giroux (BYR)) Farrar, Straus & Giroux.

—That's Papa's Way. Banks, Kate. 2009. (ENG.). 32p. (J). (gr. -1-3). 16.95 *(978-0-374-37445-7(7),* Farrar, Straus & Giroux (BYR)) Farrar, Straus & Giroux.

—Yard Sale. Bunting, Eve. 2015. (ENG.). 32p. (J). (gr. -1-2). 15.99 *(978-0-7636-6542-5(8))* Candlewick Pr.

Castillo, Lauren. Melvin & the Boy. Castillo, Lauren. 2011. (ENG.). 40p. (J). (gr. -1-3). 16.99 *(978-0-8050-8929-5(2),* Holt, Henry & Co. Bks. For Young Readers) Holt, Henry & Co.

Castillo, Marcos. Hope Is Here! Kessler, Cristina. 2013. (J). ***(978-1-934370-43-8(6))*** Editorial Campana.

Castillon, Carly. I Need a Kazoo! Rovetch, L. Bob. 2006. (J). *(978-1-58987-055-0(7))* Kindermusik International.

—A Little Whale Tale. McKendry, Sam. 2005. (Stories to Share Ser.). 18p. (J). (gr. -1-k). 9.95 *(978-1-58117-146-4(3),* Intervisual/Piggy Toes) Bendon, Inc.

Castle, Frances. Pop-Up: Everything You Need to Create Your Own Pop-up Book. Wickings, Ruth. 2010. (ENG.). 16p. (J). (gr. 2-5). 19.99 *(978-0-7636-5056-8(0))* Candlewick Pr.

—Space Saver. Agnew, Kate. 2014. (Blue Bananas Ser.). (ENG.). 48p. (J). (gr. k-2). pap. 5.99 *(978-1-4052-5677-3(X))* Egmont Bks., Ltd. GBR. Dist: Independent Pubs. Group.

Castle, Lynn. A Quetzalcóatl Tale of Corn. Haberstroh, Marilyn & Panik, Sharon. 2014. (Quetzalcóatl Tales Ser.). (ENG.). 48p. (J). (gr. k-5). pap. 9.95 *(978-1-60732-345-7(1))* Univ. Pr. of Colorado.

Castles, Heather. Bit by Bit. Nejime, Shoichi. 2005. (ENG.). 32p. (J). (gr. -1-k). pap. 7.95 *(978-1-55037-906-8(2),* 9781550379068) Annick Pr., Ltd. CAN. Dist: Firefly Bks., Ltd.

—Little Land Adventures - Little Bird. James, Shilah & James, Michael. 2010. 24p. pap. *(978-1-926635-33-0(7))* Adlibbed, Ltd.

—Little Land Adventures - Little Iguan. James, Shilah & James, Michael. 2010. 24p. pap. *(978-1-926635-34-7(5))* Adlibbed, Ltd.

—Little Land Adventures - Little Pig. James, Shilah & James, Michael. 2010. 24p. pap. *(978-1-926635-35-4(3))* Adlibbed, Ltd.

—Little Land Adventures - Little Racoon. James, Shilah & James, Michael. 2010. 24p. pap. *(978-1-926635-36-1(1))* Adlibbed, Ltd.

Casto, Christina. Four Farm Boys: Turkey Times. Scholl, Jenny. 2010. 36p. (J). pap. 13.95 *(978-1-4327-5886-8(1))* Outskirts Pr., Inc.

Castrillón, Melissa. Cartwheeling in Thunderstorms. Rundell, Katherine. 2014. (ENG.). 256p. (J). (gr. 3-7). 17.99 *(978-1-4424-9061-1(6),* Simon & Schuster Bks. For Young Readers) Simon & Schuster Bks. For Young Readers.

Castro, Christopher. The Pelican Family Counting Book. Castro, Shirley. 2006. (ENG.). (J). 15.00 *(978-0-9790307-0-3(6))* Castro, Shirley.

—The Pelican Family Series — Stelly & the Sticky, Gooey Taffy. Castro, Shirley. 2011. 36p. (J). 15.00 *(978-0-9790307-3-4(0))* Castro, Shirley.

—The Pelican Family Series — Telly's Story. Castro, Shirley. 2008. 36p. (J). 15.00 *(978-0-9790307-1-0(4))* Castro, Shirley.

Castro L., Antonio. The Coyote under the Table (El Coyote Debajo de la Mesa) Hayes, Joe. 2011. (ENG & SPA.). 144p. (J). (gr. 1-7). 19.95 *(978-1-935955-21-4(7))* Cinco Puntos Pr.

—The Coyote under the Table (El Coyote Debajo de la Mesa) Hayes, Joe. 2011. (ENG & SPA.). 144p. (J). (gr. 1-7). pap. 12.95 *(978-1-935955-06-1(3))* Cinco Puntos Pr.

—The Gum-Chewing Rattler. Hayes, Joe. 2008. (ENG.). 32p. (J). (gr. k-6). pap. 7.95 (978-1-933693-19-4(3)) Cinco Puntos Pr.

—The Lovesick Skunk. Hayes, Joe. 2010. (ENG.). 32p. (J). (gr. k-7). 16.95 (978-1-933693-81-1(9)) Cinco Puntos Pr.

—My Tata's Remedies - Los Remedios de Mi Tata. Rivera-Ashford, Roni Capin. 2015. (ENG & SPA.). 40p. (J). (gr. 1-6). pap. 8.95 (978-1-935955-89-4(6)) Cinco Puntos Pr.

—Pajaro Verde. Hayes, Joe. 2005. (ENG & SPA.). 40p. (J). (gr. 4-6). pap. 8.95 (978-0-938317-90-6(3)) Cinco Puntos Pr.

—Treasure on Gold Street/El Tesoro de la Calle D'Oro: A Neighborhood Story in Spanish & English. Byrd, Lee Merrill. 2003. (ENG & SPA.). 40p. (J). (gr. 4-6). 16.95 (978-0-938317-75-3(X)) Cinco Puntos Pr.

—El Ttesoro en la Calle Oro: A Neighborhood Story in English & Spanish. Byrd, Lee Merrill. Franco, Sharon, tr. 2007.Tr. of Treasure on Gold Street. (SPA & ENG.). 40p. (J). (gr. 4-6). pap. 8.95 (978-1-933693-11-8(8)) Cinco Puntos Pr.

Castro L., Antonio, jt. illus. see Lopez, Antonio Castro.

Castro, Luis F. A House with No Mouse. Tinsley, P. S. Deans, Nora L., ed. 2003. 28p. 14.95 (978-0-9723213-1-0(4), Mousetime Bks.) Mousetime Media LLC.

Castro, Maria Elena, et al. Family Stories (Cuentos Familiares) Guerrero, Ernesto, tr. from ENG. 2006. (ENG & SPA.). 27p. 15.95 (978-0-9716580-7-3(2)) Lectura Bks.

Castro, Mima. Celebrate Chinese New Year with the Fong Family. Flor Ada, Alma. 2006. (Cuentos para Celebrar / Stories to Celebrate Ser.). 30p. (gr. k-6). per. 11.95 (978-1-59820-126-0(3)) Santillana USA Publishing Co., Inc.

—Una Fiesta Saludable. White, Amy. Kratky, Lada J., tr. 2009. (Colección Fácil de Leer Ser.). (SPA.). 16p. (gr. k-2). pap. 5.99 (978-1-60396-417-3(7)) Ediciones Alfaguara ESP. Dist: Santillana USA Publishing Co., Inc.

—La Gallinita en la Ciudad: The Little Hen in the City. Argueta, Jorge. 2006. (Bilingual Bks). 32p. (gr. 3-5). 15.95 (978-1-59820-093-5(3), Alfaguara) Santillana USA Publishing Co., Inc.

Castro, Patricia & Avila, Jorge. El Principe y el Mendigo. Twain, Mark. 2003. (Literatura Juvenil (Panamericana Editorial) Ser.).Tr. of Prince & the Pauper. (SPA.). 314p. (YA). (gr. 4-7). pap. (978-958-30-0146-8(5)) Panamericana Editorial.

Castronovo, Katy. Where Do I Live? Duehl, Kristine. 2013. (Budding Biologist Ser.). (ENG.). 32p. (J). (gr. k-2). 9.99 (978-0-9855481-1-7(8)) Budding Biologist.

Castulo Aten, Vicky Talaro & Ikaia Aten, Dayle Marc. A Mother's Prayer: A Life Changing Prayer for Children. French, Peter, photos by. Talaro, Theresa. 2007. 44p. (J). 23.99 (978-1-59879-335-2(7), Lifevest) Lifevest Publishing, Inc.

Caswell, Kelly. Hickory Dickory Dock. (Classic Books with Holes Ser.). (ENG.). (J). 2015. 16p. (978-1-84643-677-2(X)); 2012. 14p. bds. (978-1-84643-510-2(2)); 2012. 16p. pap. (978-1-84643-499-0(8)) Child's Play International Ltd.

Caszatt-Allen, Wendy. The Disappearance of Dinosaur Sue. PaleoJoe. 2006. (PaleoJoe's Dinosaur Detective Club Ser.: 1). (ENG.). 144p. (J). (gr. 2-5). pap. 7.95 (978-1-934133-03-3(5), Mackinac Island Press, Inc.) Charlesbridge Publishing, Inc.

—Mysterious Mammoths. PaleoJoe. 2008. (ENG.). 200p. (J). (gr. 2-5). pap. 7.95 (978-1-934133-43-9(4), Mackinac Island Press, Inc.) Charlesbridge Publishing, Inc.

—Secret Sabertooth. PaleoJoe. 2007. (PaleoJoe's Dinosaur Detective Club Ser.: 3). (ENG.). 168p. (J). (gr. 2-5). pap. 8.95 (978-1-934133-10-1(8), Mackinac Island Press, Inc.) Charlesbridge Publishing, Inc.

—Stolen Stegasaurus. PaleoJoe. 2006. (PaleoJoe's Dinosaur Detective Club Ser.: 2). (ENG.). 160p. (J). (gr. 2-5). pap. 7.95 (978-1-934133-04-0(3), Mackinac Island Press, Inc.) Charlesbridge Publishing, Inc.

Catagan, Tino. La Reina de las Nieves. Andersen, Hans Christian. Bravo-Villasante, Carmen, tr.Tr. of Snow Queen. (SPA.). (J). (gr. 2-4). 6.50 (978-84-355-0695-3(9)) Minon, S.A. ESP. Dist: Lectorum Pubns., Inc.

Catalano, Dominic. Bernard Wants a Baby. Goodman, Joan. 2004. (ENG.). 32p. (J). (gr. -1-k). 15.95 (978-1-59078-088-6(4)) Boyds Mills Pr.

—The Bremen Town Musicians: A Tale about Working Together. Grimm, Jacob & Grimm, Wilhelm K. 2006. (Famous Fables Ser.). (J). (978-1-59939-039-0(6), Reader's Digest Young Families, Inc.) Studio Fun International.

—Clink Clank Clunk! Aroner, Miriam. 2006. (ENG.). 32p. (J). (gr. -1-1). 15.95 (978-1-59078-270-5(4)) Boyds Mills Pr.

—My Sprig of Lilac: Remembering Abraham Lincoln. Coleman, Wim & Perrin, Pat. 2014. (Setting the Stage for Fluency Ser.). (ENG.). 40p. (gr. 3-5). lib. bdg. 27.93 (978-1-939656-54-4(0)) Red Chair Pr.

—The Shepherd's Christmas Story. Mackall, Dandi Daley. 2005. 32p. (J). (gr. 1-5). 12.99 (978-0-7586-0904-5(3)) Concordia Publishing Hse.

—Trick or Treat, Old Armadillo. Brimner, Larry Dane. 2010. (ENG.). 32p. (J). (gr. k-2). 16.95 (978-1-59078-758-8(7)) Boyds Mills Pr.

—What's So Bad about the Big Bad Wolf?, 24 vols. Williams, Rozanne Lanczak. 2005. (Reading for Fluency Ser.). 8p. (J). pap. 2.49 (978-1-59198-143-5(3), 4243) Creative Teaching Pr., Inc.

Catalano, Dominic. Mr. Basset Plays. Catalano, Dominic. (ENG.). 32p. (J). (gr. k-2). 2004. 7.95 (978-1-59078-314-6(X)); 2003. 15.95 (978-1-59078-007-7(8)) Boyds Mills Pr.

Catalanotto, Peter. Good-Bye, Sheepie, 0 vols. Burleigh, Robert. 2010. (ENG.). 32p. (J). (gr. -1-k). 16.99 (978-0-7614-5598-1(1), 9780761455981, Amazon Children's Publishing) Amazon Publishing.

—Happy Birthday, America. Osborne, Mary Pope. 2008. (ENG.). 32p. (J). (gr. -1-3). pap. 8.99 (978-0-312-38050-2(X)) Square Fish.

—My Mother's Voice. Ryder, Joanne & Ryder. 2006. (ENG.). 32p. (J). (gr. -1-3). 16.99 (978-0-06-029509-7(0)) HarperCollins Pubs.

—No Dessert Forever! Lyon, George Ella. 2006. (ENG.). 40p. (J). (gr. k-4). 17.99 (978-1-4169-0385-7(2), Atheneum/Richard Jackson Bks.) Simon & Schuster Children's Publishing.

—Sleepsong. Lyon, George Ella. 2008. (ENG.). 40p. (J). (gr. -1-k). 16.99 (978-0-689-86973-0(8), Atheneum/Richard Jackson Bks.) Simon & Schuster Children's Publishing.

Catalanotto, Peter. Daisy 1, 2, 3. Catalanotto, Peter. 2003. (ENG.). 32p. (J). (gr. -1-1). 17.99 (978-0-689-85457-6(9), Atheneum/Richard Jackson Bks.) Simon & Schuster Children's Publishing.

—Dylan's Day Out. Catalanotto, Peter. 2006. pap. 7.99 (978-0-9777720-0-1(4)) Southpaw Books LLC.

—Emily's Art. Catalanotto, Peter. 2006. (ENG.). 32p. (J). (gr. k-3). 7.99 (978-1-4169-2688-7(7), Atheneum Bks. for Young Readers) Simon & Schuster Children's Publishing.

—Ivan the Terrier. Catalanotto, Peter. 2007. (ENG.). 32p. (J). (gr. -1-3). 17.99 (978-1-4169-1247-7(9), Atheneum/Richard Jackson Bks.) Simon & Schuster Children's Publishing.

—Kitten Red, Yellow, Blue. Catalanotto, Peter. 2005. (ENG.). 32p. (J). (gr. -1-k). 17.99 (978-0-689-86562-6(7), Atheneum/Richard Jackson Bks.) Simon & Schuster Children's Publishing.

—Matthew A. B. C. Catalanotto, Peter. 2005. (ENG.). 32p. (J). (gr. -1-1). reprint ed. 7.99 (978-1-4169-0330-7(5), Atheneum Bks. for Young Readers) Simon & Schuster Children's Publishing.

—Monkey & Robot. Catalanotto, Peter. (ENG.). 64p. (J). (gr. 1-4). 2014. pap. 5.99 (978-1-4424-2979-6(8), Atheneum Bks. for Young Readers); 2013. 12.99 (978-1-4424-2978-9(X), Atheneum/Richard Jackson Bks.) Simon & Schuster Children's Publishing.

—More of Monkey & Robot. Catalanotto, Peter. 2014. (ENG.). 64p. (J). (gr. 1-4). 15.99 (978-1-4424-5251-0(X), Atheneum/Richard Jackson Bks.) Simon & Schuster Children's Publishing.

—The Newbies. Catalanotto, Peter. 2015. (ENG.). 40p. (J). (gr. -1-3). 17.99 (978-1-4814-1892-6(0)) Simon & Schuster Children's Publishing.

—Question Boy Meets Little Miss Know-It-All. Catalanotto, Peter. 2012. (ENG.). 40p. (J). (gr. -1-3). 17.99 (978-1-4424-0670-4(4), Atheneum/Richard Jackson Bks.) Simon & Schuster Children's Publishing.

—The Veterans Day Visitor. Catalanotto, Peter. Schembri, Pamela. 2008. (Second Grade Friends Ser.). (ENG.). 64p. (J). (gr. 2-5). 16.99 (978-0-8050-7840-4(1), Holt, Henry & Co. Bks. For Young Readers) Holt, Henry & Co.

Cataldo, Melanie. The Stranded Whale. Yolen, Jane. 2015. (ENG.). 32p. (J). (gr. k-4). 15.99 (978-0-7636-6953-9(9)) Candlewick Pr.

Catanese, Donna. Dirty Larry. Hamsa, Bobbie. rev. ed. 2003. (Rookie Reader Español Ser.). (ENG.). 24p. (J). (gr. k-2). pap. 4.95 (978-0-516-27493-5(7), Children's Pr.) Scholastic Library Publishing.

Catchpole, Diana. St. Patrick & the Shamrock. Mortimer, Sheila. 2004. 8p. (J). 10.95 (978-0-7171-3755-8(4)) Gill & MacMillan, Ltd. IRL. Dist: Dufour Editions, Inc.

—Trapped in the Witch's Lair: Peek Inside the Pop-Up Windows! Taylor, Dereen. 2014. (ENG.). 12p. (J). (gr. 2-7). 16.99 (978-1-86147-320-2(6), Armadillo) Anness Publishing GBR. Dist: National Bk. Network.

Cate, Annette LeBlanc. Look Up! Bird-Watching in Your Own Backyard. Cate, Annette LeBlanc. 2013. (ENG.). 64p. (J). (gr. 3-7). 15.99 (978-0-7636-4561-8(3)) Candlewick Pr.

—The Magic Rabbit. Cate, Annette LeBlanc. 2013. (ENG.). 32p. (J). (gr. -1-3). 6.99 (978-0-7636-6685-9(8)) Candlewick Pr.

Cate, Marijke Ten. Where Is My Sock? Cate, Marijke Ten. 2010. (ENG.). 24p. (J). (gr. -1-1). 16.95 (978-1-59078-808-0(7), Lemniscaat) Boyds Mills Pr.

Cater, Angela. The Adventures of Sailor Sam. Cater, Angela. 2007. (ENG.). 32p. (J). pap. (978-0-9555725-0-0(9)) Tabby Cat Pr.

—A Perfect Nest for Mrs Mallard. Cater, Angela. 2009. 32p. pap. (978-0-9555725-2-4(5)) Tabby Cat Pr.

Caterisano, Sarah. Florida Santa: Is He Real? How Do We Know It? Clark, Ruth E. 2008. (ENG.). 32p. (gr. -1-3). 16.95 (978-0-9792963-0-7(7)) Hibiscus Publishing.

Cathcart, Sharyn. The Gull That Lost the Sea. Smith, Claude Clayton. 2008. (ENG.). 34p. pap. 5.95 (978-0-9667359-7-0(8), BeanPole Bks.) Harren Communications, LLC.

Cathcart, Yvonne. Robyn Makes the News, 1 vol. Hutchins, Hazel J. & Hutchins, Hazel. 2003. (Formac First Novels Ser.: 27). (ENG.). 64p. (J). (gr. 1-5). 4.95 (978-0-88780-593-6(0)) Formac Publishing Co., Ltd. CAN. Dist: Casemate Pubs. & Bk. Distributors, LLC.

—Robyn Makes the News. Hutchins, Hazel. 2003. (Formac First Novels Ser.: 27). (ENG.). 64p. (J). (gr. 1-5). 14.95 (978-0-88780-594-3(9)) Formac Publishing Co., Ltd. CAN. Dist: Casemate Pubs. & Bk. Distributors, LLC.

—Robyn's Monster Play, 1 vol. Hutchins, Hazel. 2008. (Formac First Novels Ser.). (ENG.). 64p. (J). (gr. 2-5). 5.95 (978-0-88780-748-0(8)) Formac Publishing Co., Ltd. CAN. Dist: Casemate Pubs. & Bk. Distributors, LLC.

—Robyn's Monster Play. Hutchins, Hazel. 2008. (Formac First Novels Ser.). (ENG.). 64p. (gr. 2-5). 14.95 (978-0-88780-750-3(X)) Formac Publishing Co., Ltd. CAN. Dist: Casemate Pubs. & Bk. Distributors, LLC.

—Robyn's Party-in-the-Park. Hutchins, Hazel. 2005. 59p. (J). lib. bdg. 12.00 (978-1-4242-1203-3(0)) Fitzgerald Bks.

—Robyn's Party-in-the-Park. Hutchins, Hazel. 2005. (Formac First Novels Ser.: 31). (ENG.). 64p. (J). (gr. 2-5). 14.95 (978-0-88780-663-6(5)) Formac Publishing Co., Ltd. CAN. Dist: Casemate Pubs. & Bk. Distributors, LLC.

—Robyn's Party in the Park, 1 vol. Hutchins, Hazel. 2005. (Formac First Novels Ser.: 31). (ENG.). 64p. (J). (gr. 2-5). 4.95 (978-0-88780-662-9(7)) Formac Publishing Co., Ltd. CAN. Dist: Casemate Pubs. & Bk. Distributors, LLC.

—Skate, Robyn, Skate. Hutchins, Hazel J. & Hutchins, Hazel. 2004. (Formac First Novels Ser.: 30). (ENG.). 64p. (J). (gr. 1-5). 14.95 (978-0-88780-627-8(9)) Formac Publishing Co., Ltd. CAN. Dist: Casemate Pubs. & Bk. Distributors, LLC.

—Skate, Robyn, Skate. Hutchins, Hazel. 2004. 57p. (J). lib. bdg. 12.00 (978-1-4242-1244-6(8)) Fitzgerald Bks.

—Skate, Robyn, Skate, 1 vol. Hutchins, Hazel. 2004. (Formac First Novels Ser.: 30). (ENG.). 64p. (J). (gr. 1-5). 4.95 (978-0-88780-626-1(0)) Formac Publishing Co., Ltd. CAN. Dist: Casemate Pubs. & Bk. Distributors, LLC.

Cathcart, Yvonne. Tilt Your Head Rosie the Red, 1 vol. McCarney, Rosemary. 2015. (Rosie the Red Ser.). (ENG.). 24p. (J). (gr. 1-3). 15.95 (978-1-927583-59-3(4)) Second Story Pr. CAN. Dist: Orca Bk. Pubs. USA.

Cathy, Wilcox. I Am Jack. Gervay, Susanne. 2013. (ENG.). 144p. (J). pap. 5.99 (978-1-61067-128-6(7)) Kane Miller.

Catling, Andy. The Lost Treasure of the Sunken City. Taylor, Martin. 2012. (J). (978-1-4351-4330-2(2)) Barnes & Noble, Inc.

—The Sad Princess. Benton, Lynne. 2009. (Tadpoles Ser.). (ENG.). 24p. (J). (gr. k-2). pap. (978-0-7787-3903-6(1)); lib. bdg. (978-0-7787-3872-5(8)) Crabtree Publishing Co.

Catlow, Nikalas. Mind Your Own Business: A File of Super Secret Stuff. 2007. (ENG.). 224p. (J). 8.00 (978-1-84046-763-5(0), Wizard Books) Icon Bks., Ltd. GBR. Dist: Consortium Bk. Sales & Distribution.

Catlow, Nikalas. Oodles of Doodles: Over 200 Pictures to Complete & Create. Running Press Staff. 2009. (ENG.). 256p. (J). pap. 12.95 (978-0-7624-3324-7(8)) Running Pr. Bk. Pubs.

Catlow, Nikalas. Pirates v. Ancient Egyptians in a Haunted Museum. Catlow, Nikalas. Wesson, Tim. 2012. (Mega Mash-Up Ser.). (ENG.). 96p. (J). (gr. 2-5). pap. 6.99 (978-0-7636-5901-1(0), Nosy Crow) Candlewick Pr.

Catlow, Nikalas & Catlow, Niki. How to Be the Best at Everything. Enright, Dominique et al. Barnes, Samantha & Wingate, Philippa, eds. 2007. (Best at Everything Ser.). (ENG.). 128p. (J). (gr. 3-7). 9.99 (978-0-545-01628-5(2), Scholastic Pr.) Scholastic, Inc.

Catlow, Nikalas & Wesson, Tim. Aliens vs. Mad Scientists under the Ocean. Catlow, Nikalas & Wesson, Tim. 2011. (Mega Mash-Up Ser.). (ENG.). 96p. (J). (gr. 2-5). pap. 6.99 (978-0-7636-5874-8(X), Nosy Crow) Candlewick Pr.

—Robots vs. Gorillas in the Desert. Catlow, Nikalas & Wesson, Tim. 2011. (Mega Mash-Up Ser.). (ENG.). 96p. (J). (gr. 2-5). pap. 6.99 (978-0-7636-5873-1(1), Nosy Crow) Candlewick Pr.

—Romans vs. Dinosaurs on Mars. Catlow, Nikalas & Wesson, Tim. 2011. (Mega Mash-Up Ser.). (ENG.). 96p. (J). (gr. 2-5). pap. 6.99 (978-0-7636-5872-4(3), Nosy Crow) Candlewick Pr.

Catlow, Niki, jt. illus. see Catlow, Nikalas.

Cato, Andrea. Rosie's Pink House, 1 vol. Blair, Candice. 2010. 18p. 24.95 (978-1-4489-4619-8(0)) America Star Bks.

Cato, Nancy & Roos, Maryn. Plum Fantastic Bk. 1. Goldberg, Whoopi & Underwood, Deborah. 2008. (ENG.). 160p. (J). (gr. 1-17). pap. 4.99 (978-0-7868-5260-4(7), Jump at the Sun) Hyperion Bks. for Children.

Caton, Tim. The Book of Call & Response. Feierabend, John M. 2003. (First Steps in Music Ser.). (ENG.). 88p. (J). (gr. -1-2). pap. 13.95 (978-1-57999-215-6(3)) G I A Pubns., Inc.

—The Book of Children's Song Tales. Feierabend, John M. 2003. (First Steps in Music Ser.). (ENG.). 104p. (J). (gr. -1-2). pap. 13.95 (978-1-57999-213-2(7)) G I A Pubns., Inc.

—The Book of Echo Songs. Feierabend, John M. 2003. (First Steps in Music Ser.). (ENG.). 88p. (J). (gr. -1-2). pap. 13.95 (978-1-57999-214-9(5)) G I A Pubns., Inc.

Catrow, David. Are You Quite Polite? Silly Dilly Manners Songs. Katz, Alan. 2006. (ENG.). 32p. (J). (gr. -1-3). 17.99 (978-0-689-86970-9(3), McElderry, Margaret K. Bks.) McElderry, Margaret K. Bks.

—The Boy Who Looked Like Lincoln. Reiss, Mike & Reiss, Mike. 2006. (ENG.). 32p. (J). (gr. -1-2). reprint ed. pap. 5.99 (978-0-14-240416-4(0), Puffin) Penguin Publishing Group.

—The Boy Who Wouldn't Share. Reiss, Mike & Reiss, Mike. 2008. (ENG.). 32p. (J). (gr. 1-3). 16.99 (978-0-06-059132-8(3)) HarperCollins Pubs.

—The Boy Who Wouldn't Share. Reiss, Mike. 2008. 32p. (J). (gr. 1-3). lib. bdg. 17.89 (978-0-06-059133-5(1)) HarperCollins Pubs.

—Cinderella Skeleton. San Souci, Robert D. 2004. (ENG.). 32p. (J). (gr. -1-3). reprint ed. pap. 6.99 (978-0-15-205069-6(8)) Houghton Mifflin Harcourt Publishing Co.

—Doggone Dogs! Beaumont, Karen. 2008. (ENG.). 40p. (J). (gr. -1-k). 16.99 (978-0-8037-3157-8(4), Dial) Penguin Publishing Group.

—Don't Say That Word! Katz, Alan. 2007. (ENG.). 32p. (J). (gr. -1-3). 17.99 (978-0-689-86971-6(1), McElderry, Margaret K. Bks.) McElderry, Margaret K. Bks.

—Dozens of Cousins. Crum, Shutta. 2013. (ENG.). 32p. (J). (gr. -1-3). 16.99 (978-0-618-15874-4(X)) Houghton Mifflin Harcourt Publishing Co.

—Dream Dog. Berger, Lou. 2014. (ENG.). 40p. (J). (gr. -1-3). 17.99 (978-0-375-86655-5(8)); 20.99 (978-0-375-96655-2(2)) Random Hse. Children's Bks. (Schwartz & Wade Bks.).

—Going, Going, Gone! And Other Silly Dilly Sports Songs. Katz, Alan. 2009. (ENG.). 32p. (J). (gr. -1-3). 16.99 (978-1-4169-0696-4(7), McElderry, Margaret K. Bks.) McElderry, Margaret K. Bks.

—How Murray Saved Christmas. Reiss, Mike. 2004. (ENG.). 32p. (J). (gr. -1-2). 6.99 (978-0-14-250145-0(X), Puffin) Penguin Publishing Group.

—I Ain't Gonna Paint No More! Beaumont, Karen. (ENG.). (J). (gr. -1 — 1). 2012. 30p. bds. 11.99 (978-0-547-87035-9(3)); 2005. 32p. 17.99 (978-0-15-202488-8(3)) Houghton Mifflin Harcourt Publishing Co.

—I Like Myself! Beaumont, Karen. (ENG.). 32p. (J). (gr. -1 — 1). 2010. bds. 11.99 (978-0-547-40163-8(9)); 2004. 16.99 (978-0-15-202013-2(6)) Houghton Mifflin Harcourt Publishing Co.

—I Wanna Go Home. Orloff, Karen Kaufman. 2014. (ENG.). 32p. (J). (gr. k-3). 16.99 (978-0-399-25407-9(2), Putnam Juvenile) Penguin Publishing Group.

—I Wanna Iguana. Orloff, Karen Kaufman. 2004. (ENG.). 32p. (J). (gr. -1-3). 16.99 (978-0-399-23717-1(8), Putnam Juvenile) Penguin Publishing Group.

Catrow, David, III. I Wanna New Room. Orloff, Karen Kaufman. 2010. (ENG.). 32p. (J). (gr. k-3). 16.99 (978-0-399-25405-5(6), Putnam Juvenile) Penguin Publishing Group.

Catrow, David. I'm Still Here in the Bathtub: Brand New Silly Dilly Songs. Katz, Alan. 2003. (ENG.). 32p. (J). (gr. -1-3). 17.99 (978-0-689-84551-2(0), McElderry, Margaret K. Bks.) McElderry, Margaret K. Bks.

—Jackhammer Sam. Mandel, Peter. 2011. (ENG.). 40p. (J). (gr. -1-2). 16.99 (978-1-59643-034-1(6)) Roaring Brook Pr.

—Merry Un-Christmas. Reiss, Mike. 2006. 32p. (J). (gr. -1-2). lib. bdg. 16.89 (978-0-06-059127-4(7)) HarperCollins Pubs.

—The Middle-Child Blues. Crow, Kristyn. 2009. (ENG.). 32p. (J). (gr. k-3). 16.99 (978-0-399-24735-4(1), Putnam Juvenile) Penguin Publishing Group.

—Mosquitoes Are Ruining My Summer! And Other Silly Dilly Camp Songs. Katz, Alan. 2011. (ENG.). 32p. (J). (gr. -1-3). 16.99 (978-1-4169-5568-9(2), McElderry, Margaret K. Bks.) McElderry, Margaret K. Bks.

—My School's a Zoo! Smith, Stuart. 2004. 40p. (J). (gr. k-3). lib. bdg. 16.89 (978-0-06-028511-1(7)) HarperCollins Pubs.

—On Top of the Potty: And Other Get-up-and-Go Songs. Katz, Alan. 2008. (ENG.). 32p. (J). (gr. -1-3). 17.99 (978-0-689-86215-1(6), McElderry, Margaret K. Bks.) McElderry, Margaret K. Bks.

—Our Tree Named Steve. Zweibel, Alan. 2005. (ENG.). 32p. (J). (gr. -1-k). 15.99 (978-0-399-23722-5(4), Putnam Juvenile) Penguin Publishing Group.

—Plantzilla. Nolen, Jerdine & Keliher, Brian. 2005. (ENG.). 32p. (J). (gr. -1-3). reprint ed. pap. 7.00 (978-0-15-205392-5(1)) Houghton Mifflin Harcourt Publishing Co.

—Plantzilla Goes to Camp. Nolen, Jerdine. 2006. (ENG.). 32p. (J). (gr. k-3). 17.99 (978-0-689-86803-0(0), Simon & Schuster/Paula Wiseman Bks.) Simon & Schuster/Paula Wiseman Bks.

—Smelly Locker: Silly Dilly School Songs. Katz, Alan. (ENG.). 32p. (J). (gr. -1-3). 2010. 6.99 (978-1-4424-0251-5(2)); 2008. 16.99 (978-1-4169-0695-7(9)) McElderry, Margaret K. Bks. (McElderry, Margaret K. Bks.).

—Too Much Kissing! And Other Silly Dilly Songs about Parents. Katz, Alan. 2009. (ENG.). 32p. (J). (gr. -1-2). 16.99 (978-1-4169-4199-6(1), McElderry, Margaret K. Bks.) McElderry, Margaret K. Bks.

—Westward Ho, Carlotta! Fleming, Candace. 2009. (ENG.). 36p. (J). (gr. -1-2). 10.99 (978-1-4424-0218-8(0), Atheneum Bks. for Young Readers) Simon & Schuster Children's Publishing.

—Wet Dog! Broach, Elise. 2007. (ENG.). 32p. (J). (gr. k-3). pap. 5.99 (978-0-14-240855-1(7), Puffin) Penguin Publishing Group.

—Where Did They Hide My Presents? Silly Dilly Christmas Songs. Katz, Alan. (ENG.). 32p. (J). (gr. -1-3). 2008. 6.99 (978-1-4169-6830-6(X)); 2005. 17.99 (978-0-689-86214-4(8)) McElderry, Margaret K. Bks. (McElderry, Margaret K. Bks.).

—Where's My T-R-U-C-K? Beaumont, Karen. 2011. (ENG.). 32p. (J). (gr. -1-k). 16.99 (978-0-8037-3222-3(8), Dial) Penguin Publishing Group.

Catrow, David. The Fly Flew In. Catrow, David. 2012. (I Like to Read Ser.). (ENG.). 32p. (J). 14.95 (978-0-8234-2418-4(9)) Holiday Hse., Inc.

—Funny Lunch. Catrow, David. 2010. (Max Spaniel Ser.). (ENG.). 40p. (J). (gr. -1-3). 6.99 (978-0-545-05747-9(7), Orchard Bks.) Scholastic, Inc.

—Scholastic Reader Level 1: Max Spaniel: Best in Show. Catrow, David. 2013. (Scholastic Reader Level 1 Ser.). (ENG.). 32p. (J). (gr. -1-3). pap. 3.99 (978-0-545-05749-3(3), Orchard Bks.) Scholastic, Inc.

—We the Kids: The Preamble of the Constitution of the United States. Catrow, David. 2004. (J). (gr. k-5). 27.90 incl. audio (978-0-8045-6914-9(2)) Spoken Arts, Inc.

—We the Kids: The Preamble to the Constitution of the United States. Catrow, David. 2005. (ENG.). 32p. (J). (gr. k-3). pap. 6.99 (978-0-14-240276-4(1), Puffin) Penguin Publishing Group.

Catrow, David & David, Catrow. Our Tree Named Steve. Zweibel, Alan. 2007. (ENG.). 32p. (J). (gr. -1-k). pap. 5.99 (978-0-14-240743-1(7), Puffin) Penguin Publishing Group.

Catrow, David, jt. illus. see Lovell, Patty.

Cattish, Anna. Dude, Where's My Saxophone? Cobb, Amy. 2015. (J). (978-1-62402-073-5(9)) Magic Wagon.

—First Chair. Cobb, Amy. 2015. (J). (978-1-62402-074-2(7)) Magic Wagon.

—Notes from a Pro. Cobb, Amy. 2015. (J). (978-1-62402-075-9(5)) Magic Wagon.

—Shredding with the Geeks. Cobb, Amy. 2015. (J). (978-1-62402-076-6(3)) Magic Wagon.

—Snaring the Trumpet. Cobb, Amy. 2015. (J). (978-1-62402-077-3(1)) Magic Wagon.

—Swing Vote for Solo. Cobb, Amy. 2015. (J). (978-1-62402-078-0(X)) Magic Wagon.

Catusanu, Mircea. How to Eat an Airplane. Pearson, Peter. 2016. 40p. (J). (gr. -1-3). 17.99 (978-0-06-232062-9(9)) HarperCollins Pubs.

Catusanu, Mircea. Noah's Ark. Hazen, Barbara Shook. 2003. (Little Golden Book Ser.). (ENG.). 24p. (J). (gr. -1-2). 3.99 (978-0-307-10440-3(0), Golden Bks.) Random Hse. Children's Bks.

—Wheels on the Move: Driving with Andy. Hissom, Jennie. 2006. (J). (978-1-58987-141-0(3)) Kindermusik International.

Catusanu, Mircea & Wilkin, Eloise. Christmas Favorites. Golden Books Staff et al. 2009. (Little Golden Book Favorites Ser.). (ENG.). 80p. (J). (gr. -1-2). 6.99 *(978-0-375-85778-2(8),* Golden Bks.) Random Hse. Children's Bks.

Cauble, Christopher, photos by. What I Saw in Yellowstone: A Kid's Guide to Wonderland. Johanek, Durrae. 2012. (J). pap. 10.95 *(978-1-60639-035-1(X))* Riverbend Publishing.

Cauley, Lorinda Bryan. Double Trouble Groundhog Day. Roberts, Bethany. 2008. (ENG.). 40p. (J). (gr. -1-3). 16.95 *(978-0-8050-8280-7(8),* Holt, Henry & Co. Bks. For Young Readers) Holt, Henry & Co.

—Double Trouble Groundhog Day. Roberts, Bethany. 2011. (ENG.). 40p. (J). (gr. -1-3). pap. 6.99 *(978-0-312-55350-0(1))* Square Fish.

Caulson, Kathleen. Power Reading: Games. Caulson, Kathleen. 2005. (J). 76p. (gr. 2-4). 29.95 *(978-1-883186-98-2(6),* PPMXG2-3); 88p. (gr. 4-5). 79.95 *(978-1-883186-99-9(4),* PPMXG45) National Reading Styles Institute, Inc.

Caut, Vincent. Snowball Truce! Schmitt, Michel-Yves. 2013. (Where's Leopold? Ser.: 2). (ENG.). 32p. (J). (gr. 2-4). pap. 6.95 *(978-1-4677-1523-2(9),* Graphic Universe) Lerner Publishing Group.

—Snowball Truce! Schmitt, Michel-Yves & Burrell, Carol Klio. 2013. (Where's Leopold? Ser.: 2). (ENG.). 32p. (J). (gr. 2-4). lib. bdg. 25.26 *(978-1-4677-0770-1(8),* Graphic Universe) Lerner Publishing Group.

—Your Pajamas Are Showing! Schmitt, Michel-Yves. 2013. (Where's Leopold? Ser.: 1). (ENG.). 40p. (J). (gr. 2-4). pap. 6.95 *(978-1-4677-0871-5(2));* lib. bdg. 25.26 *(978-1-4677-0769-5(4))* Lerner Publishing Group. (Graphic Universe).

Cauthen, Tommy. The Teacher's Gift. DeBray, Sherry. 2004. 30p. *(978-1-59421-007-5(1))* Seacoast Publishing, Inc.

Cavaciuti, Susan. Someone Hurt Me. Cavaciuti, Susan. 2004. 222p. pap. 8.95 *(978-1-890995-20-1(7),* Vital Health Publishing) Square One Pubs.

Cavagnaro, Larry. Sweet Sallie's Squirrel Scarf Factory. Cavagnaro, Teresa Dunham. 2012. 36p. 24.95 *(978-1-4626-6126-8(2))* America Star Bks.

Cavallaro, Mike. Curses! Foiled Again. Yolen, Jane. 2013. (ENG.). 176p. (J). (gr. 6-9). pap. 15.99 *(978-1-59643-619-0(0),* First Second Bks.) Roaring Brook Pr.

—Foiled. Yolen, Jane. 2010. (ENG.). 160p. (J). (gr. 6-9). pap. 17.99 *(978-1-59643-279-6(9),* First Second Bks.) Roaring Brook Pr.

—The Joker Virus, 1 vol. Peterson, Scott. 2012. (Dark Knight Ser.). (ENG.). 88p. (gr. 2-3). lib. bdg. 25.32 *(978-1-4342-4096-5(7))* Stone Arch Bks.

—The Moon Bandits. Sonneborn, Scott. 2013. (Man of Steel Ser.). (ENG.). 88p. (gr. 2-3). pap. 5.95 *(978-1-4342-4223-5(4))* Stone Arch Bks.

—Parasite's Feeding Frenzy, 1 vol. Peterson, Scott. 2012. (Man of Steel Ser.). (ENG.). 88p. (gr. 2-3). lib. bdg. 25.32 *(978-1-4342-4099-6(1));* pap. 5.95 *(978-1-4342-4221-1(8))* Stone Arch Bks.

Cavallaro, Mike & DC Comics Staff. Moon Bandits. Sonneborn, Scott. 2013. (Man of Steel Ser.). (ENG.). 88p. (gr. 2-3). 25.32 *(978-1-4342-4093-4(2))* Stone Arch Bks.

Cavallaro, Mike & Levins, Tim. The Man of Gold, 1 vol. Weissburg, Paul. 2012. (Man of Steel Ser.). (ENG.). 88p. (gr. 2-3). lib. bdg. 25.32 *(978-1-4342-4095-8(9));* pap. 5.95 *(978-1-4342-4222-8(6))* Stone Arch Bks.

Cavallini, Linda. Eek! That's Creepy! Look & Find. Lobo, Julia. 2010. 24p. (J). 7.98 *(978-1-60553-898-3(1))* Publications International, Ltd.

Cavallini, Valentina. Going to Mecca. Robert, Na'ima B. & Quarto Generic Staff. 2014. (ENG.). 32p. (J). (gr. k-6). pap. 8.99 *(978-1-84780-490-7(X),* Frances Lincoln) Quarto Publishing Group UK GBR. Dist: Hachette Bk. Group.

—Going to Mecca. Robert, Na'ima B. 2012. (ENG.). 32p. (J). (gr. k-6). 17.99 *(978-1-84780-153-1(6),* Frances Lincoln Children's Bks.) Quarto Publishing Group UK GBR. Dist: Hachette Bk. Group.

Cavanaugh, Stacy. The Next Steve Erwin, 1 vol. Dalton, Matthew. 2009. 16p. pap. 24.95 *(978-1-60836-635-4(9))* America Star Bks.

Cavanaugh, Wendy & LeVesque, Sherry, photos by. Pumpkin in the Sky: Let's bake a pie together, you & I, with Auntie Wendy. Cavanaugh, Wendy. 2011. 32p. (J). spiral bd. 20.00 *(978-0-9743121-1-8(8))* Eastlight Pr.

Cave, Yvonne, photos by. The Gardener's Encyclopaedia of New Zealand Native Plants. Paddison, Valda. 2003. 320p. (J). (gr. -1-3). *(978-1-86962-043-1(7),* Godwit) Random Hse. New Zealand.

Cavender, Bernie. Hooray for Mother's Day! Lukas, Catherine. 2003. (Little Bill Ser.). (J). (gr. k-3). lib. bdg. 14.15 *(978-0-613-63298-0(2),* Turtleback) Turtleback Bks.

Caviezel, Giovanni. Little Bee. 2014. (Mini-Creatures Ser.). (ENG.). 8p. (J). (gr. -1 — 1). bds. 4.99 *(978-0-7641-6713-3(8))* Barron's Educational Series, Inc.

—Little Crab. 2014. (Mini-Creatures Ser.). (ENG.). 8p. (J). (gr. -1 — 1). bds. 4.99 *(978-0-7641-6714-0(6))* Barron's Educational Series, Inc.

—Little Snail. 2014. (Mini-Creatures Ser.). (ENG.). 8p. (J). (gr. -1 — 1). bds. 4.99 *(978-0-7641-6715-7(4))* Barron's Educational Series, Inc.

Caviezel, Giovanni & Mesturini, C. Halloween. Caviezel, Giovanni. 2009. (ENG.). 10p. (J). (gr. -1-1). bds. 6.99 *(978-0-7641-6280-0(2))* Barron's Educational Series, Inc.

Caviezel, Giovanni, jt. illus. see Rigo, L.

Cayless, Sophie. Belle's Wild Ride: The Artful Adventure of a Butterfly & a Cabbie. Corlett, Mary Lee. 2015. (ENG.). 32p. (J). (gr. 3-7). 17.95 *(978-1-907804-51-9(X))* Giles, D. Ltd. GBR. Dist: Consortium Bk. Sales & Distribution.

—Sophie's Stuff. Sasscer, Abby. 2012. 36p. pap. 9.95 *(978-0-9854729-1-7(X))* Sasscer, Abby.

Cazet, Denys. Elvis the Rooster & the Magic Words. Cazet, Denys. 2004. (I Can Read Bks.). (ENG.). 48p. (J). (gr. k-3). 15.99 *(978-0-06-000509-2(2))* HarperCollins Pubs.

—Grandpa Spanielson's Chicken Pox Stories No. 1: The Octopus. Cazet, Denys. 2005. (I Can Read Bks.). 48p. (J). (gr. -1-3). lib. bdg. 16.89 *(978-0-06-051089-3(7))* HarperCollins Pubs.

—Minnie & Moo: Hooves of Fire. Cazet, Denys. 2014. (ENG.). 208p. (J). (gr. k-6). 15.95 *(978-1-939547-08-8(3))* Creston Bks.

—Minnie & Moo: The Attack of the Easter Bunnies. Cazet, Denys. 2004. (I Can Read Bks.). 48p. (J). (gr. k-3). (ENG.). 15.99 *(978-0-06-000506-1(8));* lib. bdg. 17.89 *(978-0-06-000507-8(6))* HarperCollins Pubs.

—Minnie & Moo: The Case of the Missing Jelly Donut. Cazet, Denys. (I Can Read Bks.). (ENG.). 48p. (J). (gr. k-3). 2006. pap. 3.99 *(978-0-06-073009-3(9));* 2005. 15.99 *(978-0-06-073007-9(2))* HarperCollins Pubs.

—Minnie & Moo: The Case of the Missing Jelly Donut. Cazet, Denys. 2007. (Minnie & Moo Ser.). 45p. (J). (gr. -1-3). pap. 29.95 incl. audio *(978-1-4301-0088-1(5))* Live Oak Media.

—Minnie & Moo: The Night Before Christmas. Cazet, Denys. 2004. (Readalongs for Beginning Readers Ser.). 25.95 incl. audio *(978-1-59112-884-7(6));* (J). pap. 31.95 incl. audio compact disk *(978-1-59112-889-2(7));* (J). pap. 29.95 incl. audio *(978-1-59112-885-4(4))* Live Oak Media.

—Minnie & Moo: The Night of the Living Bed. Cazet, Denys. 2003. (I Can Read Bks.). 48p. (J). (gr. k-3). lib. bdg. 16.89 *(978-0-06-000504-7(1))* HarperCollins Pubs.

—Minnie & Moo - The Night of the Living Bed. Cazet, Denys. 2004. (I Can Read Book 3 Ser.). (ENG.). 48p. (J). (gr. k-3). pap. 3.99 *(978-0-06-000505-4(X))* HarperCollins Pubs.

—Minnie & Moo Adventure Series. Cazet, Denys. 2004. pap. 45.95 incl. audio *(978-1-59112-849-6(8));* pap. 51.95 incl. audio compact disk *(978-1-59112-850-2(1))* Live Oak Media.

—Minnie & Moo & the Haunted Sweater. Cazet, Denys. 2007. (I Can Read Bks.). 48p. (J). (gr. -1-3). lib. bdg. 17.89 *(978-0-06-073017-8(X));* (ENG.). (gr. k-3). 16.99 *(978-0-06-073016-1(1))* HarperCollins Pubs.

—Minnie & Moo & the Seven Wonders of the World. Cazet, Denys. 2003. (ENG.). 144p. (J). (gr. 2-5). 19.99 *(978-0-689-85330-2(0),* Atheneum/Richard Jackson Bks.) Simon & Schuster Children's Publishing.

—Minnie & Moo Holiday Series. Cazet, Denys. 2004. pap. 45.95 incl. audio *(978-1-59112-851-9(X));* pap. 51.95 incl. audio compact disk *(978-1-59112-852-6(8))* Live Oak Media.

—Minnie & Moo Meet Frankenswine. Cazet, Denys. 2004. (Readalongs for Beginning Readers Ser.). 28.95 incl. audio compact disk *(978-1-59112-876-2(5));* (J). 25.95 incl. audio *(978-1-59112-262-3(7));* (J). pap. 29.95 incl. audio *(978-1-59112-263-0(5))* Live Oak Media.

—The Night of the Living Bed. Cazet, Denys. unabr. ed. 2005. (Minnie & Moo Ser.). (J). (gr. k-4). 25.95 incl. audio *(978-1-59519-389-6(8));*Set. pap. 29.95 incl. audio *(978-1-59519-390-2(1));*Set. pap. 31.95 incl. audio compact disk *(978-1-59519-394-0(4))* Live Oak Media.

—The Octopus. Cazet, Denys. 2008. (Grandpa Spanielson's Chicken Pox Stories Ser.). (J). (gr. -1-3). pap. 16.95 incl. audio *(978-1-4301-0455-1(4));*Set. pap. 29.95 incl. audio *(978-1-4301-0457-5(0));*Set. pap. 31.95 incl. audio compact disk *(978-1-4301-0460-5(0))* Live Oak Media.

—The Perfect Pumpkin Pie. Cazet, Denys. 2005. (ENG.). 32p. (J). (gr. -1-1). 17.99 *(978-0-689-86467-4(1),* Atheneum/Richard Jackson Bks.) Simon & Schuster Children's Publishing.

—A Snout for Chocolate. Cazet, Denys. 2006. (I Can Read Book 2 Ser.). (ENG.). 48p. (J). (gr. k-3). pap. 4.99 *(978-0-06-051095-4(1))* HarperCollins Pubs.

—A Snout for Chocolate. Cazet, Denys. 2008. (Grandpa Spanielson's Chicken Pox Stories Ser.). (J). (gr. -1-3). pap. 16.95 incl. audio *(978-1-4301-0463-6(5));*Set. pap. 29.95 incl. audio *(978-1-4301-0465-0(1));*Set. pap. 31.95 incl. audio compact disk *(978-1-4301-0468-1(6))* Live Oak Media.

—Wanted Dead or Alive. Cazet, Denys. (I Can Read Book 3 Ser.). 48p. (J). 2007. (ENG.). (gr. k-3). pap. 3.99 *(978-0-06-073012-3(9));* 2006. (ENG.). (gr. -1-3). 15.99 *(978-0-06-073010-9(2));* 2006. (gr. -1-3). lib. bdg. 16.89 *(978-0-06-073011-6(0))* HarperCollins Pubs.

—Wanted Dead or Alive. Cazet, Denys. 2008. (Minnie & Moo Ser.). (J). (gr. -1-3). pap. 16.95 incl. audio *(978-1-4301-0471-1(6))* Live Oak Media.

—Will You Read to Me? Cazet, Denys. 2007. (ENG.). 32p. (J). (gr. -1-1). 16.99 *(978-1-4169-0935-4(4),* Atheneum/Richard Jackson Bks.) Simon & Schuster Children's Publishing.

C.B. Canga, C. B. Celebrating North Carolina: 50 States to Celebrate. Bauer, Marion Dane. 2014. (Green Light Readers Level 3 Ser.). (ENG.). 40p. (J). (gr. 1-4). 12.99 *(978-0-544-28875-1(0));* pap. 3.99 *(978-0-544-28827-0(0))* Houghton Mifflin Harcourt Publishing Co. (HMH Books For Young Readers).

—Celebrating Washington State: 50 States to Celebrate. Bauer, Marion Dane. 2014. (Green Light Readers Level 3 Ser.). (ENG.). 40p. (J). (gr. 1-4). pap. 3.99 *(978-0-544-28948-2(X),* HMH Books For Young Readers) Houghton Mifflin Harcourt Publishing Co.

Cearley, Clint, jt. illus. see Bulanadi, Danny.

Ceasar, Fady. Nolia Fasolia: Read-Along Book: Arabic & English. Akkawi, Julie. El-Ahraf, Amer, ed. 2011. (ARA & ENG.). 48p. pap. 5.99 *(978-0-9844310-1-4(2))* BigKids Bilingual Bks.

Cecchi, Lorenzo, et al. The Vikings. McRae, Anne & Agosta, Loredana. 2008. (Back to Basics Ser.). 32p. (J). (gr. 2-5). lib. bdg. *(978-88-6098-051-9(8))* McRae Bks. Srl.

Ceccoli, Nicoletta. The Barefoot Book of Fairy Tales. Doyle, Malacy. 2005. (ENG.). 160p. (J). (gr. -1-3). 19.99 *(978-1-84148-798-4(8))* Barefoot Bks., Inc.

—The Boo! Book. Lachenmeyer, Nathaniel. 2012. (ENG.). 46p. (J). (gr. -1-3). 17.99 *(978-1-4169-3513-1(4),* Atheneum Bks. for Young Readers) Simon & Schuster Children's Publishing.

—Cinderella, 0 vols. Thomson, Sarah L. 2012. (ENG.). 32p. (J). (gr. k-3). 17.99 *(978-0-7614-6170-8(1),* 9780761461708, Amazon Children's Publishing) Amazon Publishing.

—A Dignity of Dragons. Ogburn, Jacqueline K. 2010. (ENG.). 32p. (J). (gr. -1-3). 17.00 *(978-0-618-86254-2(4))* Houghton Mifflin Harcourt Publishing Co.

—The Faerie's Gift. Batt, Tanya Robyn. 32p. (J). (gr. -1-3). 2008. (ENG.). 17.99 *(978-1-84686-230-4(2));* 2003. 16.99 *(978-1-84148-998-8(0))* Barefoot Bks., Inc.

Ceccoli Nicoletta. Faeries Gift. Batt Tanya Robyn. 2006. 0032p. pap. 6.99 *(978-1-905236-73-2(5))* Barefoot Bks., Inc.

Ceccoli, Nicoletta. The Girl in the Castle Inside the Museum. Bernheimer, Kate. 2008. (ENG.). 40p. (J). (gr. -1-3). 17.99 *(978-0-375-83606-0(3),* Schwartz & Wade Bks.) Random Hse. Children's Bks.

—Horns & Wrinkles. Helgerson, Joseph. 2008. (ENG.). 240p. (J). (gr. 5-7). pap. 4.95 *(978-0-618-98178-6(0))* Houghton Mifflin Harcourt Publishing Co.

—Una Isla Bajo el Sol. Blackstone, Stella. 2003. (SPA.). 24p. (J). pap. 6.99 *(978-1-84148-144-9(0))* Barefoot Bks., Inc.

—An Island in the Sun. Blackstone, Stella & Barefoot Books Staff. 2005. (ENG.). 24p. (J). pap. 6.99 *(978-1-84148-079-4(7))* Barefoot Bks., Inc.

—Little Red Riding Hood. 2004. 32p. (J). 16.99 *(978-1-84148-621-5(3))* Barefoot Bks., Inc.

—The Princess & the White Bear King. Batt, Tanya Robyn. 2004. 40p. (J). 16.99 *(978-1-84148-339-9(7))* Barefoot Bks., Inc.

—The Princess & White Bear. Batt, Tanya Robyn. 2008. (ENG.). 40p. (J). (gr. -1-3). 17.99 *(978-1-84686-228-1(0))* Barefoot Bks., Inc.

—The Tear Thief. Duffy, Carol Ann & Stevenson, Juliet. 2011. (ENG.). (J). 9.99 *(978-1-84686-622-7(7))* Barefoot Bks., Inc.

—The Tear Thief. Duffy, Carol Ann. 2007. (ENG.). 32p. (J). (gr. -1-3). 16.99 *(978-1-84686-045-4(8))* Barefoot Bks., Inc.

Ceccolini, Danielle. What Will It Be, Penelope? Corn, Tori. 2013. (ENG.). 32p. (J). (gr. -1-1). 16.95 *(978-1-62087-542-1(X),* 620542, Sky Pony Pr.) Skyhorse Publishing Co., Inc.

Ceceri, Kathy. The Silk Road: Explore the World's Most Famous Trade Route with 20 Projects. Ceceri, Kathy. 2011. (Build It Yourself Ser.). (ENG.). 128p. (J). (gr. 3-7). 21.95 *(978-1-934670-65-1(0));* pap. 15.95 *(978-1-934670-62-0(6))* Nomad Pr.

Cecil, Jennifer, jt. illus. see Kelson, Ellen.

Cecil, Randy. Adorable You! Brown, Mae. 2011. (ENG.). 10p. (J). (gr. k — 1). bds. 6.99 *(978-0-545-34666-5(5),* Cartwheel Bks.) Scholastic, Inc.

—And Here's to You! Elliott, David. (ENG.). 32p. (J). (gr. -1-2). 2009. pap. 6.99 *(978-0-7636-4126-9(X));* 2004. 15.99 *(978-0-7636-1427-0(0))* Candlewick Pr.

—Brontorina. Howe, James. (ENG.). 32p. (J). (gr. -1-3). 2013. 6.99 *(978-0-7636-5323-1(3));* 2010. 15.99 *(978-0-7636-4437-6(4))* Candlewick Pr.

—Dusty Locks & the Three Bears. Lowell, Susan. rev. ed. 2004. (ENG.). 32p. (J). (gr. -1-3). pap. 8.99 *(978-0-8050-7534-2(8))* Square Fish.

Cecil, Randy. Evermore Dragon. Joosse, Barbara. 2015. (ENG.). 32p. (J). (gr. -1-2). 15.99 ***(978-0-7636-6882-2(6))*** Candlewick Pr.

Cecil, Randy. How Do You Wokka-Wokka? Bluemle, Elizabeth. 2012. (ENG.). 32p. (J). (gr. -1-2). pap. 6.99 *(978-0-7636-6085-7(X))* Candlewick Pr.

—Looking for a Moose. Root, Phyllis. 2008. (ENG.). 40p. (J). (gr. -1-2). pap. 6.99 *(978-0-7636-3885-6(4))* Candlewick Pr.

—Lovabye Dragon. Joosse, Barbara. 2012. (ENG.). 32p. (J). (gr. -1-2). 15.99 *(978-0-7636-5408-5(6))* Candlewick Pr.

—My Father the Dog. Bluemle, Elizabeth. (ENG.). 32p. (J). (gr. -1-3). 2008. pap. 6.99 *(978-0-7636-3077-5(2));* 2006. 15.99 *(978-0-7636-2222-0(2))* Candlewick Pr.

—One Is a Snail, Ten Is a Crab: A Counting by Feet Book. Sayre, April Pulley & Sayre, Jeff. 2006. (ENG.). 40p. (J). (gr. k-3). 6.99 *(978-0-7636-2631-0(7))* Candlewick Pr.

—One Is a Snail, Ten Is a Crab Big Book: A Counting by Feet Book. Sayre, Jeff & Sayre, April Pulley. 2010. (ENG.). 40p. (J). (gr. k-3). pap. 24.99 *(978-0-7636-4790-2(X))* Candlewick Pr.

Cecil, Randy. Duck. Cecil, Randy. 2008. (ENG.). 40p. (J). (gr. -1-2). 15.99 *(978-0-7636-3072-0(1))* Candlewick Pr.

—Gator. Cecil, Randy. 2007. (ENG.). 40p. (J). (gr. -1-2). 15.99 *(978-0-7636-2952-6(9))* Candlewick Pr.

—Horsefly & Honeybee. Cecil, Randy. 2012. (ENG.). 32p. (J). (gr. -1-3). 16.99 *(978-0-8050-9300-1(1),* Holt, Henry & Co. Bks. For Young Readers) Holt, Henry & Co.

Cedar, Emily. Miracles from Maddie. Fitzmaurice, John. 2010. 52p. pap. 21.25 *(978-1-4490-5332-1(7))* AuthorHouse.

Celeskey, Matt. Children of Time: Evolution & the Human Story. Weaver, Anne H. 2012. (ENG.). 192p. (J). 19.95 *(978-0-8263-4442-7(9))* Univ. of New Mexico Pr.

Celestino, Cleofas Ramirez. Axolotl: El Ajolote. Farfan, Flores & Antonio, Jose. 2003. (SPA.). 40p. (J). *(978-968-411-569-9(5))* Ediciones Era.

Cella, Kristen, et al. He Loves Me, He Loves Me Not. Mayhall, Robin. 2013. (My Boyfriend Is a Monster Ser.: 7). (ENG.). 128p. (YA). (gr. 7-12). pap. 9.95 *(978-0-7613-8548-6(7),* Graphic Universe) Lerner Publishing Group.

Cella, Kristen & Tiede, Dirk. He Loves Me, He Loves Me Not. Mayhall, Robin. 2013. (My Boyfriend Is a Monster Ser.: 7). (ENG.). 128p. (YA). (gr. 7-12). lib. bdg. 29.27 *(978-0-7613-6005-6(0),* Graphic Universe) Lerner Publishing Group.

Cemmick, Paul. Ben's Birthdays. Hawkins, Elizabeth. 2010. (ENG.). 40p. (J). (gr. k-2). pap. 10.99 *(978-1-84853-018-8(8))* Transworld Publishers Ltd. GBR. Dist: Independent Pubs. Group.

Cepeda, Joe. A Crazy Mixed-Up Spanglish Day. Montes, Marisa. 2004. (Get Ready for Gabi Ser.). 120p. (gr. 2-5). 14.00 *(978-0-7569-3403-3(6))* Perfection Learning Corp.

—A Crazy Mixed-Up Spanglish Day. Montes, Marisa. 2003. (Get Ready for Gabi Ser.). 128p. (J). 12.95 *(978-0-439-51710-2(9),* Scholastic Paperbacks) Scholastic, Inc.

—Cub's Big World. Thomson, Sarah L. 2013. (ENG.). 32p. (gr. -1-3). 16.99 *(978-0-544-05739-5(2))* Houghton Mifflin Harcourt Publishing Co.

—Freddy in Peril: Book Two in the Golden Hamster Saga. Reiche, Dietlof & Brownjohn, John. 2004. 202p. (J). pap. *(978-0-439-64984-1(6))* Scholastic, Inc.

—From North to South. Laínez, René Colato. 2013.Tr. of Del Norte Al Sur. (ENG & SPA.). 32p. (J). pap. 9.95 *(978-0-89239-304-6(1),* Children's Book Press) Lee & Low Bks., Inc.

—From North to South/Del Norte Al Sur. Laínez, René Colato. 2010.Tr. of Del norte al Sur. (ENG & SPA.). 32p. (J). (gr. k-3). 17.95 *(978-0-89239-231-5(2))* Lee & Low Bks., Inc.

—Get Ready for Gabi No. 5: All in the Familia. Montes, Marisa. 2004. (ENG.). 112p. (J). (gr. 2-5). pap. *(978-0-439-66156-0(0),* Scholastic Paperbacks) Scholastic, Inc.

—The Journey of Oliver K. Woodman. Pattison, Darcy. 2009. (ENG.). 52p. (J). (gr. -1-3). pap. 7.99 *(978-0-15-206118-0(5))* Houghton Mifflin Harcourt Publishing Co.

—Juan Bobo Busca Trabajo. Montes, Marisa. 2006. (SPA.). 32p. (J). (gr. -1-4). pap. 6.99 *(978-0-06-113681-8(6),* Rayo) HarperCollins Pubs.

—Koi & the Kola Nuts: A Tale from Liberia. Aardema, Verna. rev. ed. 2003. (ENG.). 32p. (J). (gr. k-3). 16.99 *(978-0-689-85677-8(6),* Simon & Schuster/Paula Wiseman Bks.) Simon & Schuster/Paula Wiseman Bks.

—Lado a Lado: La Historia de Dolores Huerta y Cesar Chavez. Brown, Monica. 2010.Tr. of Side by Side - The Story of Dolores Huerta & Cesar Chavez. (SPA & ENG.). 32p. (J). (gr. -1-3). 16.99 *(978-0-06-122781-3(1),* Rayo) HarperCollins Pubs.

—Mice & Beans. Ryan, Pam Muñoz. 2005. (gr. -1-3). lib. bdg. 17.00 *(978-0-7569-5089-7(9))* Perfection Learning Corp.

—Mice & Beans. Ryan, Pam Muñoz. 2005. (Bookshelf Ser.). (ENG.). 32p. (J). (gr. -1-3). pap. 6.99 *(978-0-439-70136-5(8),* Scholastic Paperbacks) Scholastic, Inc.

—Peeny Butter Fudge. Morrison, Toni & Morrison, Slade. 2009. (ENG.). 32p. (J). (gr. -1-3). 16.99 *(978-1-4169-8332-3(5),* Simon & Schuster/Paula Wiseman Bks.) Simon & Schuster/Paula Wiseman Bks.

—Rip's Secret Spot. Butler, Kristi T. 2003. (Green Light Readers Level 1 Ser.). (ENG.). 24p. (J). (gr. -1-3). pap. 3.95 *(978-0-15-204849-5(9))* Houghton Mifflin Harcourt Publishing Co.

—Swing Sisters: The Story of the International Sweethearts of Rhythm. Deans, Karen. 2015. (ENG.). 32p. (J). (gr. -1-3). 16.95 *(978-0-8234-1970-8(3))* Holiday Hse., Inc.

—The Tapping Tale. Giglio, Judy. 2003. (Green Light Readers Level 1 Ser.). (ENG.). 24p. (J). (gr. -1-3). pap. 3.95 *(978-0-15-204852-5(9))* Houghton Mifflin Harcourt Publishing Co.

—The Tortoise or the Hare. Morrison, Toni & Morrison, Slade. (ENG.). 32p. (J). (gr. -1-3). 2014. 7.99 *(978-1-4169-8335-4(X));* 2010. 17.99 *(978-1-4169-8334-7(1))* Simon & Schuster/Paula Wiseman Bks. (Simon & Schuster/Paula Wiseman Bks.).

—Try Your Best. McKissack, Robert L. 2004. (Green Light Readers Level 2 Ser.). (ENG.). 24p. (J). (gr. -1-3). pap. 3.95 *(978-0-15-205090-0(6))* Houghton Mifflin Harcourt Publishing Co.

—Try Your Best. McKissack, Robert L. 2005. (Green Light Readers Level 2 Ser.). (gr. k-2). 13.95 *(978-0-7569-5630-1(7))* Perfection Learning Corp.

—Two Bunny Buddies. Galbraith, Kathryn O. 2014. (ENG.). 32p. (J). (gr. -1-3). 16.99 *(978-0-544-17652-2(9),* HMH Books For Young Readers) Houghton Mifflin Harcourt Publishing Co.

Cepeda, Joseph C., photos by. Emerald's Journal: A summer with Hatchlings. Allison, Pamela S. 2007. 24p. (J). lib. bdg. 16.95 *(978-0-9793474-1-2(6))* Sand Sage Pr.

Cerato, Mattia. Amusement Park Adventure. Kalz, Jill. 2010. (A-MAZE-Ing Adventures Ser.). (ENG.). 32p. (gr. 1-2). lib. bdg. 25.99 *(978-1-4048-6023-0(1),* Nonfiction Picture Bks.) Picture Window Bks.

—Construction: Interactive Fun with Fold-Out Play Scene, Reusable Stickers, & Punch-out, Stand-up Figures! Walter Foster Custom Creative Team. 2014. (Sticker, Punch-Out, & Play! Ser.). (ENG.). 12p. (J). (gr. -1-1). pap. 6.99 *(978-1-60058-721-4(6))* Quarto Publishing Group USA.

—Dinosaurs: Interactive Fun with Reusable Stickers, Fold-Out Play Scene, & Punch-out, Stand-up Figures! Walter Foster Jr. Creative Team. 2015. (Sticker, Punch-Out, & Play! Ser.). (ENG.). 12p. (J). (gr. -1-1). pap. 6.99 *(978-1-63322-000-3(1))* Quarto Publishing Group USA.

Cerato, Mattia. Drew the Screw. 2016. (J). ***(978-0-8234-3540-1(7))*** Holiday Hse., Inc.

Cerato, Mattia. Farm Adventure. Kalz, Jill. 2010. (A-MAZE-Ing Adventures Ser.). (ENG.). 32p. (gr. 1-2). lib. bdg. 25.99 *(978-1-4048-6038-4(X),* Nonfiction Picture Bks.) Picture Window Bks.

—I'm Not Moving! Blevins, Wiley. 2014. (Family Snaps Ser.). 32p. (J). (gr. k-2). pap. 6.95 *(978-1-939656-64-3(8))* Red Chair Pr.

—Rice & Beans. Blevins, Wiley. 2014. (Family Snaps Ser.). 32p. (J). (gr. k-2). pap. 6.95 *(978-1-939656-63-6(X))* Red Chair Pr.

—School Adventure. Kalz, Jill. 2010. (A-MAZE-Ing Adventures Ser.). (ENG.). 32p. (gr. 1-2). lib. bdg. 25.99 *(978-1-4048-6039-1(8),* Nonfiction Picture Bks.) Picture Window Bks.

—Storytime Stickers: Choo Choo Trains. Plourde, Lynn. 2011. (Storytime Stickers Ser.). (ENG.). 16p. (J). (gr. k). pap. 5.95 *(978-1-4027-8186-5(5))* Sterling Publishing Co., Inc.

—Zoo Adventure. Kalz, Jill. 2010. (A-MAZE-Ing Adventures Ser.). (ENG.). 32p. (gr. 1-2). lib. bdg. 25.99 *(978-1-4048-6024-7(X),* Nonfiction Picture Bks.) Picture Window Bks.

Cerato, Mattia. Mom's New Friend. Cerato, Mattia. 2014. (Family Snaps Ser.). 32p. (J). (gr. k-2). pap. 6.95 *(978-1-939656-61-2(3))* Red Chair Pr.

C

—Sheep in the Closet. Cerato, Mattia. 2014. (Family Snaps Ser.). 32p. (J). (gr. k-2). pap. 6.95 *(978-1-939656-62-9(1))* Red Chair Pr.

—You Can Draw Construction Vehicles, 1 vol. Cerato, Mattia. 2011. (You Can Draw Ser.). (ENG.). 24p. (gr. 1-2). lib. bdg. 25.99 *(978-1-4048-6807-6(0)*, Nonfiction Picture Bks.) Picture Window Bks.

—You Can Draw Dinosaurs, 1 vol. Cerato, Mattia. Bruning, Matt. 2011. (You Can Draw Ser.). (ENG.). 24p. (gr. 1-2). lib. bdg. 25.99 *(978-1-4048-6280-7(3)*, Nonfiction Picture Bks.) Picture Window Bks.

—You Can Draw Dragons, Unicorns, & Other Magical Creatures, 1 vol. Cerato, Mattia. 2011. (You Can Draw Ser.). (ENG.). 24p. (gr. 1-2). lib. bdg. 25.99 *(978-1-4048-6809-0(7)*, Nonfiction Picture Bks.) Picture Window Bks.

—You Can Draw Flowers, 1 vol. Cerato, Mattia. Bruning, Matt. 2011. (You Can Draw Ser.). (ENG.). 24p. (gr. 1-2). lib. bdg. 25.99 *(978-1-4048-6279-1(X)*, Nonfiction Picture Bks.) Picture Window Bks.

Cerato, Mattia & Ho, Jannie. Easy to Draw Monsters, 1 vol. Capstone Press Staff & Cerato, Mattia. Ho, Jannie. 2011. (You Can Draw Ser.). (ENG.). 48p. (gr. 1-2). pap. 5.19 *(978-1-4048-6761-1(9)*, Nonfiction Picture Bks.) Picture Window Bks.

—Easy-To-Draw Monsters: A Step-By-Step Drawing Book. Cerato, Mattia & Ho, Jannie. 2014. (You Can Draw Ser.). (ENG.). 64p. (gr. 1-2). pap. 6.95 *(978-1-4795-5512-3(6))* Picture Window Bks.

Cerato, Mattia & Sexton, Brenda. Easy-to-Draw Mythical Creatures. Cerato, Mattia & Sexton, Brenda. 2011. (You Can Draw Ser.). (ENG.). 48p. (gr. 1-2). pap. 5.19 *(978-1-4048-7059-8(8)*, Nonfiction Picture Bks.) Picture Window Bks.

—Easy-to-Draw Vehicles. Cerato, Mattia & Sexton, Brenda. 2011. (You Can Draw Ser.). (ENG.). 48p. (gr. 1-2). pap. 5.19 *(978-1-4048-7058-1(X)*, Nonfiction Picture Bks.) Picture Window Bks.

—Easy-To-Draw Vehicles: A Step-By-Step Drawing Book. Cerato, Mattia & Sexton, Brenda. 2014. (You Can Draw Ser.). (ENG.). 64p. (gr. 1-2). pap. 6.95 *(978-1-4795-5513-0(4))* Picture Window Bks.

Cerda, Edward. Me & My Flea Steed, Clyde, at Home on Ralph. Merrick, Sylvia Bach. 2011. 24p. pap. 24.95 *(978-1-60813-938-5(7))* America Star Bks.

Cerisier, Emmanuel. Arab Science & Invention in the Golden Age. Blanchard, Anne. Brent, R. M., tr. from FRE. 2009. (ENG.). 80p. (J). (gr. 3). 19.95 *(978-1-59270-080-6(2))* Enchanted Lion Bks., LLC.

—Dick Whittington. Gifford, Clare. 2013. (ENG.). 64p. (J). (gr. 2-4). 21.00 *(978-1-4081-8761-6(2)*, 227541, Bloomsbury USA Childrens) Bloomsbury USA.

—Gladiators. Lacey, Minna & Davidson, Susanna. 2006. (Usborne Young Reading Ser.). 64p. (J). (gr. 3-7). 8.99 *(978-0-7945-1268-2(2)*, Usborne) EDC Publishing.

—Pompeii. Ball, Karen. 2006. (Usborne Young Reading Ser.). 64p. (J). (gr. 3-7). 8.99 *(978-0-7945-1270-5(4)*, Usborne) EDC Publishing.

Cerney, Samantha May. The Three Little Green Pigs, Llc: A Recycling Pig Tale. Oldenburg, Richard. 2013. 28p. pap. 12.50 *(978-1-62516-649-4(4)*, Strategic Bk. Publishing) Strategic Book Publishing & Rights Agency (SBPRA).

Cerniga, Kira. Vince, Boy Prince: And the Secrets of How Anyone Can Become a True Prince (or Princess), 1 vol. D'Amico, Carol. 2010. 18p. pap. 24.95 *(978-1-4489-7373-6(2))* PublishAmerica, Inc.

Cerone, Sal, jt. illus. see DeRosier, Cher.

Cerretti, Cristiana. The Enormous Turnip. 2011. (Flip-Up Fairy Tales Ser.). (ENG.). 24p. (J). *(978-1-84643-369-6(X))*; *(978-1-84643-408-2(4))* Child's Play International Ltd.

Cervantes, Valeria. The Cucuy Stole My Cascarones / el Coco Me Robó Los Cascarones. Rivas, Spelile. Baeza Ventura, Gabriela, tr. 2013. (SPA.). 32p. (J). 17.95 *(978-1-55885-771-1(0)*, Piñata Books) Arte Publico Pr.

—No Time for Monsters/No Hay Tiempo para Monstruos. Rivas, Spelile & Plascencia, Amira. 2010. (SPA & ENG.). 32p. (J). (gr. -1-3). 16.95 *(978-1-55885-445-1(2))* Arte Publico Pr.

Cesena, Denise. Respect - Companion Book. Smith, Anya. I.t. ed. 2003. 12p. (J). 2.00 *(978-0-9740418-5-8(8))* Night Light Pubns., LLC.

Cesena, Denise & Perez, Maureen T. Orderliness. Cesena, Denise. I.t. ed. 2003. 28p. (J). 10.00 *(978-0-9740418-2-7(3))* Night Light Pubns., LLC.

—Orderliness - Companion Book. Cesena, Denise. I.t. ed. 2003. 12p. (J). 2.00 *(978-0-9740418-3-4(1))* Night Light Pubns., LLC.

—Respect. Cesena, Denise. 2003. 28p. (J). *(978-0-9740418-4-1(X))* Night Light Pubns., LLC.

Cesena, Denise, jt. illus. see Perez, Maureen T.

Cestaro, Gregg, photos by. Wildly Austin: Austin's Landmark Art. Loving, Vikki. 2004. lib. bdg. 24.95 *(978-0-9753990-0-2(4))* Wildly Austin.

Ceva, Aline Cantono di. Dante's Journey. Castenetto, Christiana. 2009. (ENG.). 28p. (J). (gr. 4-7). 15.00 *(978-88-7461-113-3(7))* Mandragora ITA. Dist: National Bk. Network.

Chabot, Jacob. Sewer Squad. Golden Books. 2013. (Deluxe Stickerific Ser.). (ENG.). 64p. (J). (gr. k-3). pap. 5.99 *(978-0-307-98226-1(2)*, Golden Bks.) Random Hse. Children's Bks.

Chabot, Jean-Philippe. The Impressionists. Sorbier, Frederic. 2012. (ENG.). 32p. (J). (gr. 2-6). pap. 11.99 *(978-1-85103-296-9(7))* Moonlight Publishing, Ltd. GBR. Dist: Independent Pubs. Group.

—Paul Gauguin. 2012. (ENG.). 32p. (J). (gr. 2-6). pap. 11.99 *(978-1-85103-357-7(2))* Moonlight Publishing, Ltd. GBR. Dist: Independent Pubs. Group.

Chabrian, Deborah L. The Gift of the Christmas Cookie: Sharing the True Meaning of Jesus' Birth, 1 vol. Mackall, Dandi Daley & Kingsbury, Karen. 2008. (ENG.). 32p. (J). (gr. -1-2). 16.99 *(978-0-310-71328-9(5))* Zonderkidz.

Chacon, Pam & Chacon, Rick. Howard the Hippo & the Great Mountain Adventure. Oppenlander, Meredith. 2014. 36p. (J). pap. 11.99 *(978-1-63063-479-7(4))* Tate Publishing & Enterprises, LLC.

Chacon, Rick, jt. illus. see Chacon, Pam.

Chad, Jon. Leo Geo & His Miraculous Journey Through the Center of the Earth. Chad, Jon. 2012. (ENG.). 36p. (J). (gr. 2-5). 15.99 *(978-1-59643-661-9(1))* Roaring Brook Pr.

—Leo Geo & the Cosmic Crisis. Chad, Jon. 2013. (ENG.). 40p. (J). (gr. 2-6). 16.99 *(978-1-59643-822-4(3))* Roaring Brook Pr.

Chadwick, Cindy. Kaseybelle: The Tiniest Fairy in the Kingdom, 1 bk. Chastain, Sandra. 2004. 32p. (J). 14.95 *(978-0-9673035-6-7(7)*, 24) BelleBks., Inc.

Chadwick, Kat. Be Brave. Rochester, Karen. 2012. (ENG.). 40p. pap. 17.85 *(978-0-9808710-1-2(8))* JoJo Publishing AUS. Dist: AtlasBooks Distribution.

Chaffey, Samantha. Cinderella: A Sparkling Fairy Tale. Baxter, Nicola. 2014. (ENG.). 14p. (J). (gr. -1-1). bds. 7.99 *(978-1-84322-548-5(4)*, Armadillo) Anness Publishing GBR. Dist: National Bk. Network.

—Goldilocks & the Three Bears: A Sparkling Fairy Tale. Baxter, Nicola. 2014. (ENG.). 14p. (J). (gr. -1-1). bds. 7.99 *(978-1-84322-550-8(6)*, Armadillo) Anness Publishing GBR. Dist: National Bk. Network.

—Jewels for a Princess. Baxter, Nicola. 2012. (ENG.). 12p. (J). (gr. 1-6). 16.99 *(978-1-84322-926-1(9))* Anness Publishing GBR. Dist: National Bk. Network.

—Little Red Riding Hood: A Sparkling Fairy Tale. Baxter, Nicola. 2014. (ENG.). 14p. (J). (gr. -1-1). bds. 7.99 *(978-1-84322-547-8(6)*, Armadillo) Anness Publishing GBR. Dist: National Bk. Network.

—My Ballet Theatre: Peek Inside the 3-D Windows. Baxter, Nicola. 2014. (ENG.). 24p. (J). (gr. -1-12). 16.99 *(978-1-84322-949-0(8)*, Armadillo) Anness Publishing GBR. Dist: National Bk. Network.

—My Perfect Doll's House: Peek Inside the 3D Windows. Baxter, Nicola. 2013. (ENG.). 12p. (J). (gr. k-4). 16.99 *(978-1-84322-924-7(2)*, Armadillo) Anness Publishing GBR. Dist: National Bk. Network.

—Party at the Fairy Palace: Peek Inside the 3D Windows. Baxter, Nicola. 2013. (ENG.). 12p. 16.99 *(978-1-84322-725-0(8))* Anness Publishing GBR. Dist: National Bk. Network.

—Snow White: A Sparkling Fairy Tale. Baxter, Nicola. 2014. (ENG.). 14p. (J). (gr. -1-1). bds. 7.99 *(978-1-84322-549-2(2)*, Armadillo) Anness Publishing GBR. Dist: National Bk. Network.

Chaffin, Daniel. City Doodles - Chicago. Lewis, Anna. 2013. (ENG.). 240p. pap. 9.99 *(978-1-4236-3479-9(9))* Gibbs Smith, Publisher.

Chagall, Marc. Self-Portrait with Seven Fingers: The Life of Marc Chagall in Verse. Lewis, J. Patrick. 2011. (ENG.). 40p. (J). (gr. 4-7). 18.99 *(978-1-56846-211-0(5)*, Creative Editions) Creative Co., The.

Chaghatzbanian, Sonia. The Secret of Ferrell Savage. Gill, J. Duddy. (ENG.). 176p. (J). (gr. 3-7). 2015. pap. 7.99 *(978-1-4424-6018-8(0))*; 2014. 15.99 *(978-1-4424-6017-1(2))* Simon & Schuster Children's Publishing. (Atheneum Bks. for Young Readers).

Chaira, Francesca di. Sleepytime Stories. Taplin, Sam. ed. 2011. (Baby Board Books Ser.). 12p. (J). ring bd. 12.99 *(978-0-7945-3006-8(0)*, Usborne) EDC Publishing.

Chaisty, Chris & Lyle, Kevin. The Usborne Book of Face Painting. Moller, Ray, photos by. Caudron, Chris & Childs, Caro. Knighton, Kate, ed. 2007. (Activity Bks). 47p. (J). (gr. -1-3). 12.99 *(978-0-7945-1783-0(8)*, Usborne) EDC Publishing.

Chalek, Sarah. It's Almost Time. LaCroix, Debbie Bernstein. ed. 2011. (ENG.). 36p. (J). 9.99 *(978-1-935279-85-3(8))* Kane Miller.

Chaley, Dimitry. Marty the Martian Learns ABC. 2005. 24p. (J). bds. 6.99 *(978-0-9747387-1-0(9))* EKADOO Publishing Group.

Chalk, Gary. Big Questions: Incredible Adventures in Thinking. Morrison, Matthew. 2011. (ENG.). 204p. (J). (gr. 4-8). pap. 7.95 *(978-1-84046-670-6(7))* Icon Bks., Ltd. GBR. Dist: Consortium Bk. Sales & Distribution.

—Fire over Swallowhaven. Jones, Allan Frewin. 2012. (Six Crowns Ser.: 3). 160p. (J). (gr. 2-5). 15.99 *(978-0-06-200629-5(0)*, Greenwillow Bks.) HarperCollins Pubs.

—Firestar's Quest. Hunter, Erin. 2008. (Warriors Super Edition Ser.: 1). (ENG.). 544p. (J). (gr. 3-7). pap. 7.99 *(978-0-06-113167-7(9))* HarperCollins Pubs.

—Mariel of Redwall. Jacques, Brian. 2003. (Redwall Ser.). (ENG.). 400p. (J). (gr. 5-5). pap. 9.99 *(978-0-14-230239-2(2)*, Puffin) Penguin Publishing Group.

—Martin the Warrior. Jacques, Brian. 2004. (Redwall Ser.). (ENG.). 384p. (J). (gr. 5-18). pap. 9.99 *(978-0-14-240055-5(6)*, Puffin) Penguin Publishing Group.

—Mattimeo. Jacques, Brian. 2003. (Redwall Ser.). (ENG.). 448p. (J). (gr. 5-7). pap. 9.99 *(978-0-14-230240-8(6)*, Puffin) Penguin Publishing Group.

—The Quest Begins. Hunter, Erin. 2008. (Seekers Ser.: 1). 320p. (J). (gr. 3-7). (ENG.). 16.99 *(978-0-06-087122-2(9))*; lib. bdg. 17.89 *(978-0-06-087123-9(7))* HarperCollins Pubs.

—Redwall. Jacques, Brian. 20th anniv. ed. 2007. (Redwall Ser.). (ENG.). 352p. (J). (gr. 5-18). 23.99 *(978-0-399-24794-1(7)*, Philomel) Penguin Publishing Group.

—Salamandastron. Jacques, Brian. 2003. (Redwall Ser.). (ENG.). 400p. (J). (gr. 5-3). pap. 9.99 *(978-0-14-250152-8(2)*, Puffin) Penguin Publishing Group.

—The Six Crowns: Fair Wind to Widdershins. Jones, Allan. 2011. (Six Crowns Ser.: 2). 176p. (J). (gr. 2-5). 15.99 *(978-0-06-200626-4(6)*, Greenwillow Bks.) HarperCollins Pubs.

—The Six Crowns: Full Circle. Jones, Allan. 2013. (Six Crowns Ser.: 6). 176p. (J). (gr. 3-7). 16.99 *(978-0-06-200639-4(8)*, Greenwillow Bks.) HarperCollins Pubs.

—The Six Crowns: Sargasso Skies. Jones, Allan. 2013. (Six Crowns Ser.: 5). 176p. (J). (gr. 3-7). 16.99 *(978-0-06-200636-3(3)*, Greenwillow Bks.) HarperCollins Pubs.

—The Six Crowns: the Ice Gate of Spyre. Jones, Allan. 2012. (Six Crowns Ser.: 4). 160p. (J). (gr. 3-7). 15.99 *(978-0-06-200633-2(9)*, Greenwillow Bks.) HarperCollins Pubs.

—The Six Crowns: Trundle's Quest. Jones, Allan. 2011. (Six Crowns Ser.: 1). 176p. (J). (gr. 2-5). pap. 5.99 *(978-0-06-200625-7(8)*, Greenwillow Bks.) HarperCollins Pubs.

—Trundle's Quest. Jones, Allan Frewin. 2011. (Six Crowns Ser.: 1). 160p. (J). (gr. 2-5). 15.99 *(978-0-06-200623-3(1)*, Greenwillow Bks.) HarperCollins Pubs.

Chalk, Gary, jt. illus. see Standley, Peter.

Challoner, Audrey. Summer at the Cabin. Roberts, Johanna Lonsdorf. Shaggy Dog Press, ed. 2007. 32p. (J). per. *(978-0-9722007-2-1(X))* Shaggy Dog Pr.

Chalmers, Kirsty. Heartwood. Darling, Pollyanna. 2013. 66p. (J). pap. *(978-0-9871164-4-4(4))* Imaginaria.

Chalmers, Mary. The Crystal Tree. Lindquist, Jennie D. 2008. (J). (gr. 2-6). 25.00 *(978-0-8446-6287-9(9))* Smith, Peter Pub., Inc.

Chamberlain, Calum. The Tales of Ryan Foster: The Land of Eternal Rain. Gridley, J. 2011. (ENG.). 178p. pap. 7.99 *(978-1-4679-5272-9(9))* CreateSpace Independent Publishing Platform.

Chamberlain, Margaret. The ABCs of Thanks & Please. Ohanesian, Diane. 2011. (J). *(978-0-545-37962-5(8))* Scholastic, Inc.

Chamberlain, Margaret. Boom, Baby, Boom, Boom! Mahy, Margaret. 2015. 32p. (J). pap. 8.99 ***(978-1-84780-606-2(6)**, Frances Lincoln)* Quarto Publishing Group UK GBR. Dist: Littlehampton Bk Services, Ltd.

Chamberlain, Margaret. Boom, Baby, Boom Boom! Mahy, Margaret. 2014. (ENG.). 32p. (J). (gr. -1-k). 17.99 *(978-1-84780-410-5(1)*, Frances Lincoln Children's Bks.) Quarto Publishing Group UK GBR. Dist: Hachette Bk. Group.

—I'm Me! Sheridan, Sara. 2011. (ENG.). 32p. (J). (gr. -1-k). 17.99 *(978-0-545-28222-2(5)*, Chicken Hse., The) Scholastic, Inc.

—Lion's Lunch? Tierney, Fiona. 2010. (ENG.). 32p. (J). (gr. -1-k). 17.99 *(978-0-545-17691-0(3)*, Chicken Hse., The) Scholastic, Inc.

Chamberlain, Margaret. Made by Raffi. Pomranz, Craig. 40p. (J). 2015. pap. 9.99 ***(978-1-84780-596-6(5))***; 2014. (ENG.). 18.99 *(978-1-84780-433-4(0))* Quarto Publishing Group UK GBR. (Frances Lincoln). Dist: Littlehampton Bk Services, Ltd., Hachette Bk. Group.

Chamberlain, Margaret. Mr. Tubs Is Lost! Mooney, Bel. 2004. (Blue Bananas Ser.). (ENG.). 48p. (J). (gr. k-2). pap. 5.99 *(978-1-4052-0586-3(5))* Egmont Bks., Ltd. GBR. Dist: Independent Pubs. Group.

—My Two Grandads. Benjamin, Floella. 2011. (ENG.). 32p. (J). (gr. k-3). 16.95 *(978-1-84780-060-2(2)*, Frances Lincoln) Quarto Publishing Group UK GBR. Dist: Hachette Bk. Group.

—My Two Grannies. Benjamin, Floella. 2009. (ENG.). 32p. (J). (gr. k-3). pap. 7.95 *(978-1-84780-034-3(3)*, Frances Lincoln Children's Bks.) Quarto Publishing Group UK GBR. Dist: Hachette Bk. Group.

—Pink! Rickards, Lynne. 2009. (J). Non-ISBN Publisher.

—The Tale of Georgie Grub. Willis, Jeanne. 2012. (ENG.). 32p. (J). (gr. -1-k). pap. 12.99 *(978-1-84939-065-1(7))* Andersen Pr. GBR. Dist: Independent Pubs. Group.

—Tales from Grimm. Barber, Antonia. rev. ed. 2014. (Classics Ser.). (ENG.). 80p. (J). (gr. k-3). 19.99 *(978-1-84780-509-6(4)*, Frances Lincoln) Quarto Publishing Group UK GBR. Dist: Hachette Bk. Group.

—Tattercoats. Greaves, Margaret. 32p. (J). (gr. -1-2). pap. 9.99 *(978-0-7112-0649-6(X)*, Frances Lincoln) Quarto Publishing Group UK GBR. Dist: Perseus-PGW.

—The Very Wicked Headmistress. Mahy, Margaret. 2006. 94p. (J). (gr. 2-4). pap. 6.95 *(978-1-903015-46-9(4))* Barn Owl Bks, London GBR. Dist: Independent Pubs. Group.

Chamberlain-Pecorino, Sarah. Ugly As a Toad. Fox, Julie. 2008. 24p. pap. 12.99 *(978-1-4389-0002-5(3))* AuthorHouse.

Chamberlin, Emily Hall. The Wonderful Bed. Knevels, Gertrude. 2007. 124p. per. *(978-1-4065-2920-3(6))* Dodo Pr.

Chamberlin, Maggie. The Adventures of Penny & Tubs: The City on the Sea. May, Marcie & Zerhusen, Margaret. 2012. (ENG.). 32p. (J). 16.95 *(978-0-938467-61-8(1))* Headline Bks., Inc.

Chambers, Brent. A Bird Is a Bird. Eggleton, Jill. 2003. (Rigby Sails Early Ser.). (ENG.). 16p. (gr. 1-2). pap. 6.95 *(978-0-7578-8662-1(0))* Houghton Mifflin Harcourt Publishing Co.

Chambers-Goldberg, Micah. Daniel Boone, 1 vol. Blair, Eric. (My First Classic Story Ser.). (ENG.). 32p. (gr. k-3). 2013. pap. 7.10 *(978-1-4795-1859-3(X))*; 2011. lib. bdg. 21.32 *(978-1-4048-6578-5(0))* Picture Window Bks. (My First Classic Story).

—Even Superheroes Get Diabetes. Ganz-Schmitt, Sue. 36p. 2011. (gr. -1-3). 22.95 *(978-1-59858-303-8(4))*; 2007. (J). per. 15.95 *(978-1-59858-302-1(6))* Dog Ear Publishing, LLC.

—La Leyenda de Daniel Boone, 1 vol. Blair, Eric. Robledo, Sol, tr. 2006. (Read-It! Readers en Español: Cuentos Exagerados Ser.).Tr. of Legend of Daniel Boone. (SPA.). 32p. (gr. k-3). 19.99 *(978-1-4048-1656-5(9)*, Easy Readers) Picture Window Bks.

—Paul Bunyan, 1 vol. Blair, Eric. Robledo, Sol, tr. from ENG. 2006. (Read-It! Readers en Español: Cuentos Exagerados Ser.).Tr. of Paul Bunyan. (SPA.). 32p. (gr. k-3). 19.99 *(978-1-4048-1657-2(7)*, Easy Readers) Picture Window Bks.

—Pecos Bill, 1 vol. Blair, Eric. 2013. (My First Classic Story Ser.).Tr. of Pecos Bill. (ENG.). 32p. (gr. k-3). pap. 7.10 *(978-1-4795-1860-9(3)*, My First Classic Story) Picture Window Bks.

—Pecos Bill, 1 vol. Blair, Eric. Robledo, Sol, tr. from ENG. 2006. (Read-It! Readers en Español: Cuentos Exagerados Ser.).Tr. of Pecos Bill. (SPA.). 32p. (gr. k-3). 19.99 *(978-1-4048-1658-9(5)*, Easy Readers) Picture Window Bks.

—Stone Soup, 1 vol. Jones, Christianne C. 2005. (Read-It! Readers: Folk Tales Ser.). (ENG.). 32p. (gr. k-3). lib. bdg. 19.99 *(978-1-4048-0978-9(3)*, Easy Readers) Picture Window Bks.

Chambers-Goldberg, Micah & Monkey, Micah. Too Many Tables. Schroeder, Abraham. 2015. (ENG.). 40p. (J). (gr. -1-3). 16.99 *(978-0-9913866-1-1(2))* Ripple Grove Pr.

Chambers, Mark. Five Little Monkeys; and, Five Little Penguins. 2013. (ENG.). 24p. (J). *(978-0-7787-1133-9(1))* Crabtree Publishing Co.

—Five Little Monkeys; Five Little Penguins. 2013. (ENG.). 24p. (J). pap. *(978-0-7787-1151-3(X))* Crabtree Publishing Co.

—Kindergarten, Here I Come! Steinberg, D. J. 2012. (ENG.). 32p. (J). (gr. -1-k). pap. 3.99 *(978-0-448-45624-9(9)*, Grosset & Dunlap) Penguin Publishing Group.

—Noisy Pirates. Taplin, Sam. 2014. (ENG.). (J). 19.99 *(978-0-7945-2814-0(7)*, Usborne) EDC Publishing.

—Run! The Elephant Weighs a Ton! Frost, Adam. 2012. (ENG.). 128p. (J). (gr. -1-k). pap. 8.99 *(978-1-4088-2707-9(7)*, 136525, Bloomsbury USA Childrens) Bloomsbury USA.

—Wanda Wallaby Finds Her Bounce. Emmett, Jonathan & Dunn, David H. 2012. (ENG.). 32p. (J). (gr. -1-k). pap. 8.99 *(978-1-4088-1839-8(6)*, 39581, Bloomsbury USA Childrens) Bloomsbury USA.

Chambers, Mark, jt. illus. see Goode, Diane.

Chambers, Mark A. Chicken Pox. Powell, Jillian. 2013. (Start Reading Ser.). (ENG.). 24p. (gr. k-1). pap. 6.99 *(978-1-4765-4089-4(6))* Capstone Pr., Inc.

—Hiccup!, 1 vol. Powell, Jillian. 2013. (Start Reading Ser.). (ENG.). 24p. (gr. k-1). pap. 6.99 *(978-1-4765-4103-7(5))* Capstone Pr., Inc.

Chambers, Mark L., jt. illus. see Whitehead, Pete.

Chambers, Mary. Finding Anna Bee. Snider, Cindy Gay. 2007. 163p. (J). (gr. 3-7). per. 9.99 *(978-0-8361-9392-3(X))* Herald Pr.

Chambers, Sally. Big Cat. Shulman, Mark. 2004. 8p. (J). bds. 6.95 *(978-1-58925-737-5(5))* Tiger Tales.

—Foxy Fox. Shulman, Mark. 2004. 8p. (J). bds. 6.95 *(978-1-58925-738-2(3))* Tiger Tales.

Chambers, Tina, photos by. Pirate. Platt, Richard & Dorling Kindersley Publishing Staff. 2007. (DK Eyewitness Bks.). (ENG., 72p. (J). (gr. 3-7). 16.99 *(978-0-7566-3005-8(3))* Dorling Kindersley Publishing, Inc.

Chambers, Z. Harvey's Adventures. Santini, Philip. 2011. 44p. pap. 24.95 *(978-1-4626-2078-4(7))* America Star Bks.

Chambliss, Marilyn. The Legend of Patrick Tierney. Hecker, Cindy. 2010. (ENG.). 76p. pap. 17.67 *(978-1-4563-2739-2(9))* CreateSpace Independent Publishing Platform.

Chambliss, Matthew, et al, photos by. The Eastern Bluebird: A Guide for Young Birdwatchers. Houle, Donna Lee. 2011. 60p. (J). pap. 7.95 *(978-0-9846397-1-7(3)*, PitzlGil Pr.) PitzlGil Pubns.

Chambliss, Maxie. Baby Can. Bunting, Eve. 2007. (ENG.). 32p. (J). (gr. -1-2). 15.95 *(978-1-59078-322-1(0))* Boyds Mills Pr.

—Dog & Cat. Fehlner, Paul. 2004. (My First Reader Ser.). (ENG.). 32p. (J). (gr. k-1). pap. 3.95 *(978-0-516-24626-0(7)*, Children's Pr.) Scholastic Library Publishing.

—Hobbledy-Clop. Brisson, Pat. 2003. (ENG.). 32p. (J). (gr. -1-k). 15.95 *(978-1-56397-888-3(1))* Boyds Mills Pr.

—Monsters! Namm, Diane. 2003. (My First Reader Ser.). (ENG.). 32p. (J). 18.50 *(978-0-516-22933-1(8)*, Children's Pr.) Scholastic Library Publishing.

—My Big Boy Potty. Cole, Joanna. 2004. (ENG.). 32p. (J). (gr. -1-3). 6.99 *(978-0-688-17042-4(0))* HarperCollins Pubs.

—My Big Girl Potty. Cole, Joanna. (J). (gr. -1-k). 2006. 28p. 12.99 *(978-0-06-085410-2(3)*, HarperFestival); 2004. (ENG.). 32p. 6.99 *(978-0-688-17041-7(2))* HarperCollins Pubs.

—My Friend the Doctor. Cole, Joanna. 2005. (ENG.). 32p. (J). (gr. -1 — 1). 6.99 *(978-0-06-050500-4(1)*, HarperFestival) HarperCollins Pubs.

—One up, One Down. Snyder, Carol. 2013. (ENG.). 32p. (J). (gr. -1-3). 16.99 *(978-1-4814-2144-7(1)*, Atheneum Bks. for Young Readers) Simon & Schuster Children's Publishing.

—Six Cheers for Ladybug. Fleming, Maria. 2005. (Number Tales Ser.). (ENG.). 16p. (J). (gr. -1-1). pap. 2.99 *(978-0-439-69016-4(1))* Scholastic, Inc.

Champagne, Heather. The Adventures of Hip Hop: Hip Hop & the Blueberry Pancakes. Marshall, Denise. 2012. 36p. pap. 14.75 *(978-1-62212-331-5(X)*, Strategic Bk. Publishing) Strategic Book Publishing & Rights Agency (SBPRA).

Champagne, Heather, jt. illus. see Schley, Cheri.

Champagne, Keith. Black Vengeance. Kramer, Don & Johns, Geoff. rev. ed. 2006. (Justice Society of America Ser.). (ENG.). 208p. (YA). pap. 19.99 *(978-1-4012-0966-7(1))* DC Comics.

Champagne, Liz. The Totally Bitchin' Charlie Sheen Coloring Book. Pollack, Jeff & Steinberg, Lane. 2011. (ENG.). 58p. pap. 5.45 *(978-1-4610-7617-9(X))* CreateSpace Independent Publishing Platform.

Champagne, Melanie. My Aunt Came Back. 2008. (First Steps in Music Ser.). (ENG.). 32p. (J). (gr. -1-k). 16.95 *(978-1-57999-680-2(9))* G I A Pubns., Inc.

Champion, Daryl, jt. illus. see Champion, Dionne N.

Champion, Dionne N. & Champion, Daryl. The Spirit of the Baobab Tree. Champion, Dionne N. et al. 2008. 37p. (J). 31.99 *(978-1-4363-7842-0(7))* Xlibris Corp.

Champion, Vanessa. The Trepets Book Three Rabbit Race Day. Chance, C. 2007. 112p. per. *(978-0-9551289-2-9(7)*, Bumble Bks.) Dragonfly Bks. & Arts.

Champlin, DeeAnn. Eddie E & the Eggs. Champlin, DeeAnn. Date not set. (Little Lyrics Short Vowel Collection: Vol. 2). (J). (gr. k-2). pap. 12.00 *(978-1-893429-26-0(1))* Little Lyrics Pubns.

Chan, Harvey. Dead Man's Gold & Other Stories, 1 vol. Yee, Paul. 2004. (ENG.). 104p. (YA). pap. 7.95 *(978-0-88899-587-2(3))* Groundwood Bks. CAN. Dist: Perseus-PGW.

—Ghost Train. Yee, Paul. 2004. 29p. (J). (gr. k-4). reprint ed. 16.00 *(978-0-7567-9083-7(2))* DIANE Publishing Co.

Chan, Harvey. Petrified World, Determine Your Destiny No. 1: You Are the Hero of This Book! Storm, Jeff. 2nd ed. 2014. 160p. pap. ***(978-1-77143-159-0(8)***, CCB Publishing) CCB Publishing.

Chan, Harvey. Roses Sing on New Snow: A Delicious Tale. Yee, Paul. 32p. (J). 16.95 *(978-0-88899-144-7(4))*; 2003. (ENG.). pap. 5.95 *(978-0-88899-217-8(3))* Groundwood Bks. CAN. Dist: Perseus-PGW.

Chan, Irene. Baby Loves Aerospace Engineering! Spiro, Ruth. 2016. (J). ***(978-1-58089-541-5(7))*** Charlesbridge Publishing, Inc.

—Baby Loves Quarks! Spiro, Ruth. 2016. (J). ***(978-1-58089-540-8(9))*** Charlesbridge Publishing, Inc.

Chan, Jason. The Thief Queen's Daughter, No. 2. Haydon, Elizabeth. 2nd rev. ed. 2008. (Lost Journals of Ven Polypheme Ser.: 2). (ENG.). 320p. (J). (gr. 5-9). pap. 6.99 *(978-0-7653-4773-2(3)*, Tor Bks.) Doherty, Tom Assocs., LLC.

Chan, Jimmy. Tokyo Techno, 1 vol. Thompson, Lisa. 2006. (Read-It! Chapter Books: SWAT Ser.). (ENG.). 80p. (gr. 2-4). 21.32 *(978-1-4048-1673-2(9)*, Chapter Readers) Picture Window Bks.

Chan, San Wei. Spear & Shield. *(978-0-9744905-0-2(4))* Santoon Bks.

Chan, Suwin. Buenas Noches, Estados Unidos. Gamble, Adam. 2012. (Good Night Our World Ser.). (SPA & ENG.). 28p. (J). (gr. k — 1). bds. 9.95 *(978-1-60219-069-6(0))* Our World of Books.

—Good Night America. Gamble, Adam. 2006. (Good Night Our World Ser.). (ENG.). 28p. (J). (gr. k — 1). bds. 9.95 *(978-0-9777979-0-5(2))* Our World of Books.

—Good Night Maine. Gamble, Adam. 2007. (Good Night Our World Ser.). (ENG.). 18p. (J). (gr. k — 1). bds. 9.95 *(978-1-60219-010-8(0))* Our World of Books.

—Good Night Mermaids. Gamble, Adam & Jasper, Mark. 2015. (ENG.). 20p. (J). (— 1). bds. 9.95 *(978-1-60219-226-3(X))* Our World of Books.

Chance, Robyn. C Is for Chin. Chance, Robyn. 2012. 38p. 18.95 *(978-1-936850-31-0(1))* Rhemalda Publishing.

Chandhok, Lena. Civic Unrest: Investigate the Struggle for Social Change. Amidon Lusted, Marcia. 2015. (Inquire & Investigate Ser.). (ENG.). 128p. (gr. 6-10). 22.95 *(978-1-61930-241-9(1))* Nomad Pr.

Chandler, Alton, jt. illus. see Hayden, Seito.

Chandler, Jeff. Bowling Alley Adjectives, 6 vols. Fisher, Doris & Gibbs, D. L. 2008. (Grammar All-Stars: the Parts of Speech Ser.). 32p. (gr. 2-5). pap. 10.50 *(978-0-8368-8908-6(8)*, Gareth Stevens Learning Library) Stevens, Gareth Publishing LLLP.

—Hole-in-One Adverbs. Fisher, Doris & Gibbs, D. L. 2008. (Grammar All-Stars Ser.). 32p. (J). (gr. 2-5). lib. bdg. 26.00 *(978-0-8368-8902-4(9)*, Gareth Stevens Learning Library) Stevens, Gareth Publishing LLLP.

Chandler, Jeff, photos by. Slam Dunk Pronouns. Fisher, Doris & Gibbs, D. L. 2008. (Grammar All-Stars Ser.). 32p. (J). (gr. 2-5). lib. bdg. 26.00 *(978-0-8368-8904-8(5)*, Gareth Stevens Learning Library) Stevens, Gareth Publishing LLLP.

Chandler, Jeff, jt. illus. see Angle, Scott.

Chandler, Shannon. New York City. Hannigan, Paula. 2012. (ENG.). 12p. (J). bds. 12.99 *(978-1-4494-1876-2(7))* Andrews McMeel Publishing.

—Safari: A Build & Play Story. Riegelman, Rianna & Accord Publishing Staff. 2012. (ENG.). 10p. (J). (gr. -1-1). bds. 15.99 *(978-1-4494-2191-5(1))* Andrews McMeel Publishing.

—Washington, D. C. Hannigan, Paula & Croyle, Paula. 2013. (ENG.). 12p. (J). bds. 11.99 *(978-1-4494-2868-6(1))* Andrews McMeel Publishing.

Chandler, Terrence. Conflict Resolution in American History, Gr. 8: Lessons from the Past, Lessons for Today. Friedman-Brunt, Elyse. 2003. 48p. (YA). pap., wbk. ed. 19.95 *(978-1-878227-89-8(0))* Peace Education Foundation.

—Conflict Resolution in American History, Grade 8: Lessons from the Past, Lessons for Today. Friedman-Brunt, Elyse. 2003. 200p. pap., instr.'s training gde. ed. 29.95 *(978-1-878227-88-1(2))* Peace Education Foundation.

Chandu & Manu. Draupadi: The Fire-Born Princess. Nagpal, Saraswati. 2013. (Campfire Graphic Novels Ser.). (ENG.). 112p. (gr. 5). pap. 12.99 *(978-93-80741-09-3(X)*, Campfire) Kalyani Navyug Media Pty. Ltd. IND. Dist: Random Hse., Inc.

Chang, Bernard. Demon Knights. Cornell, Paul & Venditti, Robert. 2014. (ENG.). 144p. (YA). pap. 19.99 *(978-1-4012-4269-5(3))* DC Comics.

Chang, Chong. Jin Jin & Rain Wizard. Chang, Grace. 2009. (ENG.). 48p. (J). (gr. -1-3). 16.95 *(978-1-59270-086-8(1))* Enchanted Lion Bks., LLC.

—Jin Jin the Dragon. Chang, Grace. 2008. (ENG.). 48p. (J). (gr. -1-3). 16.95 *(978-1-59270-102-5(7))* Enchanted Lion Bks., LLC.

Chang, Michelle. Goldfish & Chrysanthemums. Cheng, Andrea. 2003. (ENG.). 32p. (J). 16.95 *(978-1-58430-057-1(4))*; pap. 8.95 *(978-1-60060-889-6(2))* Lee & Low Bks., Inc.

Chang, Roy. The Shark Man of Hana. Goldsberry, U'i. 2004. (HAW.). 32p. (J). 14.95 *(978-1-933067-01-8(2))* Beachhouse Publishing, LLC.

—Wuz Da Nite Befo: A Pidgin Christmas Story in Hawaii. Steele, Margaret. 2005. 24p. 10.95 *(978-1-56647-750-5(6))* Mutual Publishing LLC.

Chang, Tara Larsen & Gershman, Jo. Horse Happy. Miller, Sibley & Lenhard, Elizabeth. 2008. (Wind Dancers Ser.: 2). (ENG.). 80p. (J). (gr. 1-4). pap. 7.99 *(978-0-312-38281-0(2))* Feiwel & Friends.

—Horse Magic - Or Not? Miller, Sibley. 2011. (Wind Dancers Ser.: 12). (ENG.). 80p. (J). (gr. 1-4). pap. 11.99 *(978-0-312-60545-2(5))* Feiwel & Friends.

—A Horse, of Course! Miller, Sibley. 2009. (Wind Dancers Ser.: 7). (ENG.). 80p. (J). (gr. 1-4). pap. 11.99 *(978-0-312-56402-5(3))* Feiwel & Friends.

—A Horse's Best Friend. Miller, Sibley. 2011. (Wind Dancers Ser.: 9). (ENG.). 80p. (J). (gr. 1-4). pap. 6.99 *(978-0-312-60542-1(0))* Feiwel & Friends.

—Horses Her Way. Miller, Sibley. 2009. (Wind Dancers Ser.: 6). (ENG.). 80p. (J). (gr. 1-4). pap. 11.99 *(978-0-312-56279-3(9))* Feiwel & Friends.

—Horses' Night Out. Miller, Sibley & Lenhard, Elizabeth. 2008. (Wind Dancers Ser.: 4). (ENG.). 80p. (J). (gr. 1-4). pap. 11.99 *(978-0-312-38283-4(9))* Feiwel & Friends.

—Horsey Trails. Miller, Sibley. 2011. (Wind Dancers Ser.: 11). (ENG.). 80p. (J). (gr. 1-4). pap. 11.99 *(978-0-312-60544-5(7))* Feiwel & Friends.

—If Wishes Were Horses. Miller, Sibley & Lenhard, Elizabeth. 2008. (Wind Dancers Ser.: 1). (ENG.). 80p. (J). (gr. 1-4). pap. 7.99 *(978-0-312-38280-3(4))* Feiwel & Friends.

—Merry-Go-Horses. Miller, Sibley. 2011. (Wind Dancers Ser.: 10). (ENG.). 80p. (J). (gr. 1-4). pap. 6.99 *(978-0-312-60543-8(9))* Feiwel & Friends.

Chang, Warren. Encyclopedia Brown & the Case of the Slippery Salamander. Sobol, Donald J. 2003. (Encyclopedia Brown Ser.). 87p. (gr. 3-7). 16.00 *(978-0-7569-1619-0(4))* Perfection Learning Corp.

Channa, Abdul Malik. The Jinni on the Roof: A Ramadan Story. Rafi, Natasha. 2013. 40p. pap. 10.99 *(978-0-9888649-0-0(8))* Pamir LLC.

Chantler, Scott. The Captive Prince. Chantler, Scott. 2012. (Three Thieves Ser.: 3). (ENG.). 116p. (J). 17.95 *(978-1-55453-776-1(2))*; pap. 8.95 *(978-1-55453-777-8(0))* Kids Can Pr., Ltd. CAN. Dist: Univ. of Toronto Pr.

—The Sign of the Black Rock. Chantler, Scott. 2011. (Three Thieves Ser.: 2). (ENG.). 112p. (J). 17.95 *(978-1-55453-416-6(X))*; pap. 8.95 *(978-1-55453-417-3(8))* Kids Can Pr., Ltd. CAN. Dist: Univ. of Toronto Pr.

—Tower of Treasure. Chantler, Scott. 2010. (Three Thieves Ser.). (ENG.). 112p. (J). (gr. 4-7). 17.95 *(978-1-55453-414-2(3))*; pap. 8.95 *(978-1-55453-415-9(1))* Kids Can Pr., Ltd. CAN. Dist: Univ. of Toronto Pr.

Chao, Linus. Ali'i Kai. Matsuura, Richard & Matsuura, Ruth. (J). 7.95 *(978-1-887916-05-9(9))* Orchid Isle Publishing Co.

—Angels Masquerading on Earth. Matsuura, Richard & Matsuura, Ruth. (J). 7.95 *(978-1-887916-07-3(5))* Orchid Isle Publishing Co.

—Birthday Wish. Matsuura, Richard & Matsuura, Ruth. (J). 8.95 *(978-1-887916-04-2(0))* Orchid Isle Publishing Co.

—Gift from Santa. Matsuura, Richard & Matsuura, Ruth. (J). 7.95 *(978-1-887916-06-6(7))* Orchid Isle Publishing Co.

—Hawaiian Christmas Story. Matsuura, Richard & Matsuura, Ruth. (J). 8.95 *(978-1-887916-01-1(6))* Orchid Isle Publishing Co.

—Kalani & Primo. Matsuura, Richard & Matsuura, Ruth. (J). 8.95 *(978-1-887916-03-5(2))* Orchid Isle Publishing Co.

Chapin, Jimmy, jt. illus. see Craig, Branden Chapin.

Chapin, Patrick. David Goes Fishing. White, James C. 2003. 32p. (J). 6.95 *(978-0-9747752-0-3(7))* White, James C.

Chapin, Patrick O. The Seven Presidents. Giunta, Brian. Lt. ed. 2003. 24p. (J). 8.95 *(978-1-58597-172-5(3))* Leathers Publishing.

Chapman, Cat. The Frog Who Lost His Underpants. MacIver, Juliette. 2014. (ENG.). 32p. (J). (gr. -1-1). 14.99 *(978-0-7636-6782-5(X))* Candlewick Pr.

—Yak & Gnu. MacIver, Juliette. 2015. (ENG.). 32p. (J). (gr. -1-2). 14.99 *(978-0-7636-7561-5(X))* Candlewick Pr.

Chapman, Chris, et al. How to Draw Horses. Smith, Lucy. 2006. (Young Artist Ser.). 32p. (J). (gr. 4-7). pap. 5.99 *(978-0-7945-1368-9(9)*, Usborne); pap. 13.99 *(978-1-58086-969-0(6))* EDC Publishing.

Chapman, Debbie. Mommy What Is a Ceo? Harris, Angela L. 2013. 32p. pap. 10.00 *(978-0-615-62527-0(4))* ALHsiccesslines.

Chapman, Frederick T. Big John's Secret. Jewett, Eleanore M. 2nd ed. 2004. 203p. (J). pap. 12.95 *(978-1-883937-89-8(2))* Bethlehem Bks.

—Door to the North: A Saga of 14th Century America. Coatsworth, Elizabeth. 2013. 245p. (YA). pap. 15.95 *(978-1-932350-39-5(X))* Bethlehem Bks.

—Famous Horses of the Civil War. Downey, Fairfax. 2011. 128p. 40.95 *(978-1-258-00351-7(1))* Literary Licensing, LLC.

—True & Untrue & Other Norse Tales. Undset, Sigrid, ed. 2013. (ENG.). 264p. pap. 16.95 *(978-0-8166-7828-0(6))* Univ. of Minnesota Pr.

—The White Winter: A Story of Scarlet Hill. Meigs, Elizabeth Bleecker. 2011. 208p. 44.95 *(978-1-258-08230-7(6))* Literary Licensing, LLC.

Chapman, Gaye. My Sister Olive. Russell, Paula. 2012. (ENG.). 24p. (J). (gr. -1-k). 16.99 *(978-1-921272-88-2(0))* Little Hare Bks. AUS. Dist: Independent Pubs. Group.

—My Sister, Olive. Russell, Paula. gif. ed. 2013. (ENG.). 24p. (J). (gr. -1). 16.99 *(978-1-921714-51-1(4))* Little Hare Bks. AUS. Dist: Independent Pubs. Group.

Chapman, Gaye. Little Blue. Chapman, Gaye. 2009. (ENG.). 36p. (J). (gr. -1-k). 16.99 *(978-1-921049-98-9(7))* Little Hare Bks. AUS. Dist: Independent Pubs. Group.

Chapman, Gillian. Christmas. Henning, Heather. Bull, Nicola, ed. 2007. (Touch & Feel Ser.). 14p. (J). (gr. -1-3). bds. 10.49 *(978-0-7586-1383-7(0))* Concordia Publishing Hse.

—Creation. Henning, Heather. Bull, Nicola, ed. 2007. (Touch & Feel Ser.). 14p. (J). (gr. -1-3). bds. 10.49 *(978-0-7586-1384-4(9))* Concordia Publishing Hse.

—The Kids Bible. Lane, Leena. 2003. 64p. (J). 10.49 *(978-0-7586-0561-0(7))* Concordia Publishing Hse.

—My First Bible. Lane, Leena. 2005. 252p. (J). (gr. -1). 13.49 *(978-0-7586-0910-6(8))* Concordia Publishing Hse.

Chapman, Jane. Bear Counts. Wilson, Karma. 2015. (Bear Bks.). (ENG.). 32p. (J). (gr. -1-2). 16.99 *(978-1-4424-8092-6(0)*, McElderry, Margaret K. Bks.) McElderry, Margaret K. Bks.

—Bear Feels Scared. Wilson, Karma. 2011. (Bear Bks.). (ENG.). 34p. (J). (gr. -1 — 1). bds. 7.99 *(978-1-4424-2755-6(8)*, Little Simon) Little Simon.

—Bear Feels Scared. Wilson, Karma. 2008. (Bear Bks.). (ENG.). 40p. (J). (gr. -1-3). 17.99 *(978-0-689-85986-1(4)*, McElderry, Margaret K. Bks.) McElderry, Margaret K. Bks.

—Bear Feels Sick. Wilson, Karma. 2012. (Bear Bks.). (ENG.). 34p. (J). (gr. -1-2). bds. 7.99 *(978-1-4424-4093-7(7)*, Little Simon) Little Simon.

—Bear Feels Sick. Wilson, Karma. 2007. (Bear Bks.). (ENG.). 40p. (J). (gr. -1-3). 17.99 *(978-0-689-85985-4(6)*, McElderry, Margaret K. Bks.) McElderry, Margaret K. Bks.

—Bear Says Thanks. Wilson, Karma. 2012. (Bear Bks.). (ENG.). 40p. (J). (gr. -1-3). 17.99 *(978-1-4169-5856-7(8)*, McElderry, Margaret K. Bks.) McElderry, Margaret K. Bks.

—Bear Sees Colors. Wilson, Karma. 2014. (Bear Bks.). (ENG.). 32p. (J). (gr. -1-2). 16.99 *(978-1-4424-6536-7(0)*, McElderry, Margaret K. Bks.) McElderry, Margaret K. Bks.

—Bear Snores On. Wilson, Karma. 2005. (Bear Bks.). (ENG.). 34p. (J). (gr. -1-k). 7.99 *(978-1-4169-0272-0(4)*, Little Simon) Little Simon.

—Bear Stays up for Christmas. Wilson, Karma. 2011. (Bear Bks.). (ENG.). 34p. (J). (gr. -1 — 1). bds. 7.99 *(978-1-4424-2790-7(6)*, Little Simon) Little Simon.

—Bear Stays up for Christmas. Wilson, Karma. (Bear Bks.). (ENG.). 40p. (J). (gr. -1-3). 2008. 9.99 *(978-1-4169-5896-3(7))*; 2004. 17.99 *(978-0-689-85278-7(9))* McElderry, Margaret K. Bks. (McElderry, Margaret K. Bks.).

—Bear Wants More. Wilson, Karma. 2008. (Bear Bks.). (ENG.). 34p. (J). (gr. -1-2). 7.99 *(978-1-4169-4922-0(4)*, Little Simon) Little Simon.

—Bear Wants More. Wilson, Karma. 2003. (Bear Bks.). (ENG.). 40p. (J). (gr. -1-3). 17.99 *(978-0-689-84509-3(X)*, McElderry, Margaret K. Bks.) McElderry, Margaret K. Bks.

—The Bears in the Bed & the Great Big Storm, 1 vol. Bright, Paul. 2008. (ENG.). 32p. (J). (gr. -1-2). pap. 16.95 *(978-1-56148-636-6(1)*, Good Bks.) Skyhorse Publishing Co., Inc.

—Bear's Loose Tooth. Wilson, Karma. 2014. (Bear Bks.). (ENG.). 34p. (J). (gr. -1-k). bds. 7.99 *(978-1-4424-8936-3(7)*, Little Simon) Little Simon.

—Bear's Loose Tooth. Wilson, Karma. 2011. (Bear Bks.). (ENG.). 40p. (J). (gr. -1-3). 16.99 *(978-1-4169-5855-0(X)*, McElderry, Margaret K. Bks.) McElderry, Margaret K. Bks.

—Bear's New Friend. Wilson, Karma. 2009. (Bear Bks.). (ENG.). 34p. (J). (gr. -1-2). 7.99 *(978-1-4169-5438-5(4)*, Little Simon) Little Simon.

—Bear's New Friend. Wilson, Karma. 2006. (Bear Bks.). (ENG.). 40p. (J). (gr. -1-3). 17.99 *(978-0-689-85984-7(8)*, McElderry, Margaret K. Bks.) McElderry, Margaret K. Bks.

—Big Bear Little Bear. Bedford, David. 2005. (Storytime Board Bks.). 18p. (J). (gr. -1-k). bds. 6.95 *(978-1-58925-770-2(7))* Tiger Tales.

—Daddy Hug. Warnes, Tim. 2008. 32p. (J). (gr. -1-k). 17.89 *(978-0-06-058951-6(5))*; (ENG.). 17.99 *(978-0-06-058950-9(7))* HarperCollins Pubs.

—Don't Be Afraid, Little Pip. Wilson, Karma. 2009. (ENG.). 40p. (J). (gr. -1-2). 16.99 *(978-0-689-85987-8(2)*, McElderry, Margaret K. Bks.) McElderry, Margaret K. Bks.

—Dora's Chicks. Sykes, Julie. 2004. 32p. (J). pap. 6.95 *(978-1-58925-386-5(8))*; (gr. -1-2). 14.95 *(978-1-58925-015-4(X))* Tiger Tales.

—Dora's Eggs. Sykes, Julie. 2007. (Storytime Board Bks.). (J). (gr. -1-3). bds. 6.95 *(978-1-58925-801-3(0))* Tiger Tales.

—Duna y Dan. Jennings, Linda. (SPA.). 28p. (J). (gr. k-1). *(978-84-8418-027-2(1)*, ZZ4481) Zendrera Zariquiey, Editorial ESP. Dist: Lectorum Pubns., Inc.

—The Emperor's Egg. Jenkins, Martin. 2008. (Read, Listen, & Wonder Ser.). (ENG.). 32p. (J). (gr. -1-3). pap. 8.99 *(978-0-7636-3825-2(0))* Candlewick Pr.

—The Emperor's Egg Big Book: Read & Wonder Big Book. Jenkins, Martin. 2003. (Read & Wonder Ser.). (ENG.). 32p. (J). (gr. k-12). pap. 24.99 *(978-0-7636-2233-6(8))* Candlewick Pr.

Chapman, Jane. Goodnight, Ark, 1 vol. Sassi, Laura. (ENG.). (J). 2015. 24p. bds. 8.99 ***(978-0-310-74938-7(7))***; 2014. 32p. 16.99 *(978-0-310-73784-1(2))* Zonderkidz.

Chapman, Jane. A Long Way from Home. Baguley, Elizabeth. 2008. 32p. (J). (gr. 4-7). 15.95 *(978-1-58925-074-1(5))* Tiger Tales.

—Magical Snow Garden. Corderoy, Tracey. 2014. 32p. (J). (gr. -1-3). 16.99 *(978-1-58925-162-5(8))* Tiger Tales.

—Mortimer's Christmas Manger. Wilson, Karma. 2007. (ENG.). 40p. (J). (gr. -1-3). 9.99 *(978-1-4169-5049-3(4)*, McElderry, Margaret K. Bks.) McElderry, Margaret K. Bks.

—One Duck Stuck: A Mucky Ducky Counting Book. Root, Phyllis. 2003. (ENG.). 40p. (J). (gr. k-k). pap. 6.99 *(978-0-7636-1566-6(8))* Candlewick Pr.

—One Duck Stuck: A Mucky Ducky Counting Book. Root, Phyllis. 2008. (Candlewick Press Big Book Ser.). (ENG.). 40p. (J). (gr. k-k). pap. 24.99 *(978-0-7636-3817-7(X))* Candlewick Pr.

—One Tiny Turtle. Davies, Nicola. 2008. (Read, Listen, & Wonder Ser.). (ENG.). 32p. (J). (gr. -1-3). pap. 8.99 *(978-0-7636-3834-4(X))* Candlewick Pr.

—One Tiny Turtle: Read & Wonder. Davies, Nicola. 2005. (Read & Wonder Ser.). (ENG.). 32p. (J). (gr. -1-3). reprint ed. pap. 6.99 *(978-0-7636-2311-1(3))* Candlewick Pr.

—Que Noche Mas Ruidosa! Hendry, Diana. 2003. (SPA.). 28p. (J). (gr. k-2). 16.95 *(978-84-488-0865-5(7)*, BS3550) Beascoa, Ediciones S.A. ESP. Dist: Lectorum Pubns., Inc.

—Silly Dilly Duckling. Freedman, Claire. 2014. (ENG.). 18p. (gr. -1-k). bds. 8.99 *(978-1-58925-578-4(X))* Tiger Tales.

—Story of Christmas. French, Vivian. 2010. (ENG.). 22p. (J). (-k). bds. 6.99 *(978-0-7636-5045-2(5))* Candlewick Pr.

—Tigress, Pack. Dowson, Nick. 2008. (Read, Listen, & Wonder Ser.). (ENG.). 32p. (J). (gr. -1-3). pap. 9.99 *(978-0-7636-4189-4(8))* Candlewick Pr.

—Tigress: Read & Wonder. Dowson, Nick. 2007. (Read & Wonder Ser.). (ENG.). 32p. (J). (gr. -1-3). pap. 6.99 *(978-0-7636-3314-1(3))* Candlewick Pr.

—Tigress: Read, Listen & Wonder. Dowson, Nick. 2008. (Read, Listen, & Wonder Ser.). (ENG.). 32p. (J). (gr. -1-3). pap. 8.99 *(978-0-7636-3872-6(2))* Candlewick Pr.

—Time to Say Goodnight. Lloyd-Jones, Sally. 2006. (ENG.). 32p. (J). (gr. -1-2). 15.99 *(978-0-06-054328-0(0))* HarperCollins Pubs.

—The Very Snowy Christmas. Hendry, Diana. 2013. (ENG.). 16p. (gr. -1). bds. 8.95 *(978-1-58925-617-0(4))*; 2007. 32p. (J). pap. 6.95 *(978-1-58925-406-0(6))*; 2005. 32p. (J). (gr. -1-2). 15.95 *(978-1-58925-051-2(6))* Tiger Tales.

—What's in the Egg, Little Pip? Wilson, Karma. 2010. (ENG.). 40p. (J). (gr. -1-3). 16.99 *(978-1-4169-4204-7(1)*, McElderry, Margaret K. Bks.) McElderry, Margaret K. Bks.

—Where Is Home, Little Pip? Wilson, Karma. 2008. (ENG.). 40p. (J). (gr. -1-3). 17.99 *(978-0-689-85983-0(X)*, McElderry, Margaret K. Bks.) McElderry, Margaret K. Bks.

Chapman, Jane. Is It Christmas Yet? Chapman, Jane. 2013. (J). ***(978-1-58925-149-6(0))*** Tiger Tales.

—No More Cuddles! Chapman, Jane. 2015. (ENG.). 32p. (J). (gr. -1-3). 16.99 ***(978-1-58925-195-3(4))*** Tiger Tales.

Chapman, Jane. Baa! Moo! What Will We Do? Chapman, Jane, tr. Benjamin, A. H. 2003. 32p. (J). pap. 6.95 *(978-1-58925-381-0(7))* Tiger Tales.

—I Love My Mama. Chapman, Jane, tr. Kavanagh, Peter. 2003. 32p. (J). 12.95 *(978-1-85430-806-1(8)*, Simon & Schuster Bks. For Young Readers) Simon & Schuster Bks. For Young Readers.

Chapman, Jason. Who's That Singing? A Pull-the-Tab Book. Chapman, Jason. 2010. (ENG.). 12p. (J). (gr. -1-1). bds. 9.99 *(978-1-4169-8736-9(3)*, Little Simon) Little Simon.

—Who's That Snoring? A Pull-the-Tab Bedtime Book. Chapman, Jason. 2010. (ENG.). 12p. (J). (gr. -1-1). bds. 9.99 *(978-1-4169-8937-0(4)*, Little Simon) Little Simon.

Chapman, Jesse. Skating on Thick Ice. Tobin, Richard K. LeBlanc, Rebecca, ed. 2013. 122p. (J). pap. 12.00 *(978-1-929882-96-0(3))* Biographical Publishing Co.

Chapman, Jim. A Christmas Miracle, 1 vol. Chapman, Steven Curtis & Beth, Mary. 2005. (Shaoey & Dot Ser.). (ENG.). 32p. (gr. -1-7). 16.99 *(978-1-4003-0691-6(4))* Nelson, Thomas Inc.

Chapman, Katriona. Jo & Jess Go to the Dentist, 1 vol. Dale, Jay. 2012. (Wonder Words Ser.). (ENG.). 32p. (gr. k-2). pap. 5.99 *(978-1-4296-8912-0(9)*, Engage Literacy) Capstone Pr., Inc.

—The Miracle in Bethlehem: A Storyteller's Tale. Burton, Sarah. (ENG.). 64p. pap. 11.95 *(978-0-86315-663-2(0))* Floris Bks. GBR. Dist: SteinerBooks, Inc.

Chapman, Laura-Kate. The Kite Princess. Bell, Juliet Clare. 2012. (ENG.). 32p. (J). pap. 9.99 *(978-1-84686-830-6(0))* Barefoot Bks., Inc.

Chapman, Lee. Tripper's Travels: An International Scrapbook, 1 vol. Chapman, Nancy Kapp & Chapman, Nancy. 2005. (ENG.). 32p. (J). (gr. 1-5). 16.95 *(978-0-7614-5240-9(0))* Marshall Cavendish Corp.

—Who's Knocking at the Door?, 1 vol. Stevens, Carla & Stevens, Chapman. 2004. (ENG.). 32p. (J). 16.95 *(978-0-7614-5168-6(4))* Marshall Cavendish Corp.

Chapman, Lynne. Bendro Bach. Rix, Jamie. Williams, Dylan, tr. from ENG. 2005. (WEL.). 36p. *(978-1-902416-84-7(8))* Cymdeithas Lyfrau Ceredigion.

—Class Three at Sea. Jarman, Julia. 2008. (ENG.). 32p. (J). (gr. k-3). 16.95 *(978-0-8225-7617-4(1)*, Carolrhoda Bks.) Lerner Publishing Group.

—Class Two at the Zoo. Jarman, Julia. 2007. (Carolrhoda Picture Bks.). (ENG.). 32p. (J). (gr. k-2). 16.95 *(978-0-8225-7132-2(3)*, Carolrhoda Bks.) Lerner Publishing Group.

—Dos Pies Suben, Dos Pies Bajan. Love, Pamela. 2005. (Rookie Reader Español Ser.). (SPA & ESP.). 31p. (J). (gr. k-2). per. 4.95 *(978-0-516-25532-3(0)*, Children's Pr.) Scholastic Library Publishing.

—Dos pies suben, dos pies Bajan: Two Feet up, Two Feet Down. Love, Pamela. 2005. (Rookie Reader Español Ser.). 32p. (gr. k-2). 19.50 *(978-0-516-25252-0(6)*, Children's Pr.) Scholastic Library Publishing.

Chapman, Lynne. A Lark in the Ark. Bently, Peter. 2015. (ENG.). 24p. (J). (gr. -1-k). pap. 12.99 ***(978-1-4052-7508-8(1))*** Egmont Bks., Ltd. GBR. Dist: Independent Pubs. Group.

Chapman, Lynne. Mr Strongmouse & the Baby. Oram, Hiawyn. 2006. 32p. (J). pap. *(978-1-84362-588-9(1)*, Orchard Bks.) Scholastic, Inc.

—Mule School, 1 vol. Rawlinson, Julia. 2008. (ENG.). 32p. (J). (gr. -1-2). pap. 16.95 *(978-1-56148-597-0(7)*, Good Bks.) Skyhorse Publishing Co., Inc.

—The Odds Get Even. Hall, Pam. 2005. 16p. (J). 12.95 *(978-1-58117-216-4(8)*, Intervisual/Piggy Toes) Bendon, Inc.

—Two Feet up, Two Feet Down. Love, Pamela. 2005. (Rookie Reader Español Ser.). (ENG.). 32p. (J). (gr. k-2). pap. 4.95 *(978-0-516-24646-8(1)*, Children's Pr.) Scholastic Library Publishing.

Chapman, Lynne. Baby Can Bounce! Chapman, Lynne. 2013. (ENG.). 24p. (J). (— 1). pap. 7.99 *(978-1-4052-5831-9(4))* Egmont Bks., Ltd. GBR. Dist: Independent Pubs. Group.

—Baby Goes Baaaaa! Chapman, Lynne. 2013. (ENG.). 24p. (J). (— 1). 7.99 *(978-1-4052-5830-2(6))* Egmont Bks., Ltd. GBR. Dist: Independent Pubs. Group.

Chapman, Michelle. A Monster in the Attic. Crosby, June. 2011. 16p. pap. 24.95 *(978-1-4560-6959-9(4))* America Star Bks.

Chapman, Neil. The Boy with the Pudding Touch. North, Laura. 2014. (ENG.). 32p. (J). pap. *(978-0-7787-1364-7(4))* Crabtree Publishing Co.

—Pirate Pete. Benton, Lynne. 2008. (Tadpoles Ser.). (ENG.). 24p. (J). (gr. -1-2). lib. bdg. *(978-0-7787-3861-9(2))*; pap. *(978-0-7787-3892-3(2))* Crabtree Publishing Co.

C

—Pirate Pete. Benton, Lynne. 2008. (Tadpoles Ser.). 23p. (J). (gr. -1-3). 17.15 *(978-1-4178-0934-9(5)*, Turtleback) Turtleback Bks.

—Treasure Island. Stevenson, Robert Louis. 2004. 320p. (J). *(978-1-4054-3773-8(1))* Parragon, Inc.

Chapman, Neil A. Blackbeard's Treasure. Graves, Sue. 2010. (Reading Corner Phonics Ser.). (ENG.). 32p. (J). (gr. k-2). pap. 7.99 ***(978-0-7496-9182-0(4))*** Hodder & Stoughton GBR. Dist: Independent Pubs. Group.

Chapman, Robert. A Gift for Abuelita/Un Regalo para Abuelita: Celebrating the Day of the Dead/En Celebration del Día de los Muertos. Luenn, Nancy. 2004.Tr. of Un Regalo para Abuelita: En Celebration del Dia de los Muertos. (ENG, SPA & MUL.). 32p. (J). (gr. k-3). 15.95 *(978-0-87358-688-7(3))* Cooper Square Publishing Llc.

Chapman, Robert E. The Boy Who Could See. Carmona, Adela. 2008. 32p. pap. 24.95 *(978-1-60672-697-6(8))* PublishAmerica, Inc.

Chapman, Simon. In the Himalayas. Chapman, Simon. 2005. 103p. (J). lib. bdg. 20.00 *(978-1-4242-0626-1(X))* Fitzgerald Bks.

—In the Jungle. Chapman, Simon. 2005. 116p. (J). lib. bdg. 20.00 *(978-1-4242-0630-8(8))* Fitzgerald Bks.

—On Safari. Chapman, Simon. 2005. 111p. (J). lib. bdg. 20.00 *(978-1-4242-0633-9(2))* Fitzgerald Bks.

—Under the Sea. Chapman, Simon. 2005. 112p. (J). lib. bdg. 20.00 *(978-1-4242-0631-5(6))* Fitzgerald Bks.

Chapman, Susan. Monkey Business. Hood, Sue. 2005. (J). bds. *(978-1-890647-17-9(9))* TOMY International, Inc.

—Why I Praise You, God. Adams, Michelle Medlock. 2006. 20p. (J). (gr. -1). bds. 5.49 *(978-0-7586-0912-0(4))* Concordia Publishing Hse.

Chapmanworks Staff. Camping Fun. Parent, Nancy. 2004. (Barbie Glittery Window Bks.). 12p. (J). (gr. -1-1). bds. 4.99 *(978-1-57584-331-5(5)*, Reader's Digest Children's Bks.) Studio Fun International.

Chappell, Warren. The Extraordinary Education of Johnny Longfoot in His Search for the Magic Hat. Besterman, Catherine. 2011. 160p. 41.95 *(978-1-258-08544-5(5))* Literary Licensing, LLC.

—The Light in the Forest. Richter, Conrad. 2005. (Everyman's Library Children's Classics Ser.). (ENG.). 176p. (gr. -1-7). 14.95 *(978-1-4000-4426-9(X)*, Everyman's Library) Knopf Doubleday Publishing Group.

—Wolf Story. McCleery, William. 2012. (ENG.). 88p. (J). (gr. k-4). 14.95 *(978-1-59017-589-7(1)*, NYR Children's Collection) New York Review of Bks., Inc., The.

Charbonnel, Olivier & Mostyn, David. Santa's Factory. Hooper, Ruth. 2004. 6p. (J). (gr. k-4). reprint ed. 16.00 *(978-0-7567-7585-8(X))* DIANE Publishing Co.

Charette, Geraldine. Cyberbullying: And Ctrl Alt Delete It, 1 vol. MacEachern, Robyn. (Lorimer Deal with It Ser.). (ENG.). 32p. (gr. 4-6). 2010. 24.95 *(978-1-55277-496-0(1))*; 2008. (J). pap. 12.95 *(978-1-55277-037-5(0))* Lorimer, James & Co., Ltd., Pubs. CAN. Dist: Casemate Pubs. & Bk. Distributors, LLC.

Charette, Geraldine, et al. Deal with It Series Bullying & Conflict Resource Guide, 1 vol. Carmichael, Tricia & MacDonald, Allison, eds. 2011. (Lorimer Deal with It Ser.). (ENG.). 82p. (gr. 4-6). 24.95 *(978-1-55277-693-3(X))* Lorimer, James & Co., Ltd., Pubs. CAN. Dist: Casemate Pubs. & Bk. Distributors, LLC.

Charko, Kasia. Great Lakes & Rugged Ground: Imagining Ontario, 1 vol. Harvey, Sarah N. & Buffam, Leslie. 2010. (ENG.). 32p. (J). (gr. -1-7). 19.95 *(978-1-55469-105-0(2))* Orca Bk. Pubs. USA.

—Marsh Island, 1 vol. Bates, Sonya Spreen. 2009. (Orca Echoes Ser.). (ENG.). 64p. (J). (gr. 2-3). pap. 6.95 *(978-1-55469-117-3(6))* Orca Bk. Pubs. USA.

—Ospreys in Danger, 1 vol. McDowell, Pamela. 2014. (Orca Echoes Ser.). (ENG.). 64p. (J). (gr. 2-3). pap. 6.95 *(978-1-4598-0283-4(7))* Orca Bk. Pubs. USA.

—Sharing Snowy, 1 vol. Helmer, Marilyn. 2008. (Orca Echoes Ser.). (ENG.). 64p. (J). (gr. 2-3). pap. 6.95 *(978-1-55469-021-3(8))* Orca Bk. Pubs. USA.

—Smuggler's Cave, 1 vol. Bates, Sonya. 2010. (Orca Echoes Ser.). (ENG.). 64p. (J). (gr. 2-3). pap. 6.95 *(978-1-55469-308-5(X))* Orca Bk. Pubs. USA.

—The Summer of the Marco Polo, 1 vol. Manuel, Lynn. 2007. (ENG.). 32p. (J). (gr. -1-3). 17.95 *(978-1-55143-330-1(3))* Orca Bk. Pubs. USA.

—Thunder Creek Ranch, 1 vol. Bates, Sonya. 2013. (Orca Echoes Ser.). (ENG.). 64p. (J). (gr. 2-3). pap. 6.95 *(978-1-4598-0112-7(1))* Orca Bk. Pubs. USA.

—Which Way Should I Go?, 1 vol. Olsen, Sylvia & Martin, Ron. 2008. (ENG.). 40p. (J). (gr. 1-5). 19.95 *(978-1-55039-161-9(5))* Sono Nis Pr. CAN. Dist: Orca Bk. Pubs. USA.

—Wildcat Run, 1 vol. Bates, Sonya. 2011. (Orca Echoes Ser.). (ENG.). 64p. (J). (gr. 2-3). pap. 6.95 *(978-1-55469-830-1(8))* Orca Bk. Pubs. USA.

Charles, Akins. Zig the Pig Goes to School. Heiney, Sue P. l.t. ed. 2004. 32p. (J). 7.00 *(978-0-9761700-0-6(0))* Zig the Pig.

Charles, Donald. The Little Cookie. Hillert, Margaret. rev. ed. 2006. (Beginning to Read Ser.). 32p. (J). (gr. -1-2). lib. bdg. 19.93 *(978-1-59953-024-6(4))* Norwood Hse. Pr.

Charles, Joan. Lost in Lexicon: An Adventure in Words & Numbers. Noyce, Pendred. 2011. (ENG.). 368p. (J). (gr. 3). pap. 12.95 *(978-0-9830219-2-6(9))* Mighty Media Pr.

Charles Robinson. The Happy Prince & Other Tales. Oscar Wilde. 2012. 84p. pap. 3.47 *(978-1-60386-460-2(1)*, Watchmaker Publishing) Wexford College Pr.

Charles Santore. The Velveteen Rabbit (Kohl's Edition) Charles Santore. 2012. (ENG.). 48p. (J). 5.00 *(978-1-60464-032-8(4)*, Applesauce Pr.) Cider Mill Pr. Bk. Pubs., LLC.

Charles, Simpson. P'nut Butter & Rubber. Sonnebeyatta, Kemba. 2012. (ENG.). (J). *(978-0-9770904-6-4(9))* Africana Homestead Legacy Pubs., Inc.

Charlip, Remy & Rettenmund, Tamara. Little Old Big Beard & Big Young Little Beard: A Short & Tall Tale, 1 vol. Charlip, Remy. (ENG.). (J). 2006. 300p. (gr. -1-3). pap. 5.95 *(978-0-7614-5288-1(5))*; 2003. 32p. 16.95 *(978-0-7614-5142-6(0))* Marshall Cavendish Corp.

Charlotte Hansen. Those are MY Private Parts. Hansen, Diane. 2004. (J). per. *(978-0-9761988-0-2(0))* Hansen, Diane.

Charlotte, J. M. The Little Mermaid Retold. Andersen, Hans Christian. 2013. 48p. 18.00 *(978-0-9895422-0-3(3))* MHC Ministries.

Charnick, Tim. God's Zoo. Christian, Focus & Tnt Ministries Staff. 2005. (King of Clubs Ser.). (ENG.). 96p. per. 17.99 *(978-1-84550-069-6(5))* Christian Focus Pubns. GBR. Dist: Send The Light Distribution LLC.

Chartier, Normand. Elmo's Ducky Day. Albee, Sarah. 2005. (Big Bird's Favorites Board Bks.). (ENG.). 24p. (J). (gr. k — 1). bds. 4.99 *(978-0-375-83108-9(8)*, Random Hse. Bks. for Young Readers) Random Hse. Children's Bks.

—Maine Marmalade. Pochocki, Ethel. 2004. (ENG.). 32p. (J). (gr. k-17). 15.95 *(978-0-89272-558-8(3))* Down East Bks.

—'Til the Cows Come Home. Icenoggle, Jodi. 2010. (ENG.). 32p. (J). (gr. k-2). pap. 9.95 *(978-1-59078-800-4(1))* Boyds Mills Pr.

Chase, Andra. Aloha Potter! - hardcover Book. Talley, Linda. 2004. 30p. (J). *(978-1-55942-200-0(9))* Witcher Productions.

—Ludmila's Way. Talley, Linda. 2003. (J). 17.95 *(978-1-55942-190-4(8))* Witcher Productions.

Chase, Andra. Stanley's "This Is the Life!" Chase, Andra. Rebein, Alyssa Chase. 2008. (J). *(978-1-55942-570-4(9))* Witcher Productions.

Chase, Anita, et al. Tundra Adventures. Chase, Anita et al. 2006. (Adventure Story Collection Ser.). 28p. (J). (gr. 2-6). pap. 10.00 *(978-1-58084-254-9(2))* Lower Kuskokwim Schl. District.

Chase, Kit. Lulu's Party. Chase, Kit. 2015. (ENG.). 32p. (J). (gr. -1-k). 16.99 *(978-0-399-25701-8(2)*, Razorbill) Penguin Publishing Group.

—Oliver's Tree. Chase, Kit. 2014. (ENG.). 32p. (J). (gr. -1-k). 16.99 *(978-0-399-25700-1(4)*, Putnam Juvenile) Penguin Publishing Group.

Chase, Linda. Creature or Critter? Griner, Jack. 2005. 107p. (J). per. 12.95 *(978-1-59879-064-1(1))* Lifevest Publishing, Inc.

Chase, Michelle B. & Chase, Tanor R. Las Aventuras de Max, el Camión Volteador: El Mejor Día de Nieve! = the Adventures of Max the Dump Truck: The Greatest Snow Day Ever! Shea, Christine. 2007. (ENG & SPA.). (J). *(978-1-933002-01-9(8))* PublishingWorks.

Chase, Rhoda. The Christmas Reindeer. Burgess, Thornton W. 2013. (Dover Children's Classics Ser.). (ENG.). 160p. (J). (gr. -1-8). pap. 5.99 *(978-0-486-49153-0(6))* Dover Pubns., Inc.

Chase, Tanor R., jt. illus. see Chase, Michelle B.

Chast, Roz. Around the Clock. Chast, Roz. 2015. (ENG.). 32p. (J). (gr. -1-3). 17.99 *(978-1-4169-8476-4(3)*, Atheneum Bks. for Young Readers) Simon & Schuster Children's Publishing.

—Marco Goes to School. Chast, Roz. 2012. (ENG.). 32p. (J). (gr. -1-3). 16.99 *(978-1-4169-8475-7(5)*, Atheneum Bks. for Young Readers) Simon & Schuster Children's Publishing.

—Too Busy Marco. Chast, Roz. 2010. (ENG.). 32p. (J). (gr. -1-3). 16.99 *(978-1-4169-8474-0(7)*, Atheneum Bks. for Young Readers) Simon & Schuster Children's Publishing.

Chast, Roz & Feiffer, Jules. Nursery Rhyme Comics: 50 Timeless Rhymes from 50 Celebrated Cartoonists. Duffy, Chris, ed. 2011. (ENG.). 128p. (J). (gr. -1-3). 18.99 *(978-1-59643-600-8(X)*, First Second Bks.) Roaring Brook Pr.

Chastain, Madye Lee. The Cow-Tail Switch: And Other West African Stories. Courlander, Harold & Herzog, George. 2008. (ENG.). 160p. (J). (gr. 3-7). pap. 8.99 *(978-0-312-38006-9(2))* Square Fish.

Chatel, Kim, photos by. A Talent for Quiet. Chatel, Kim. 2009. 32p. pap. 10.95 *(978-1-935137-56-6(5))* Guardian Angel Publishing, Inc.

Chatelain, Éva. Green Thumbs-Up! Meyerhoff, Jenny. 2015. (Friendship Garden Ser.: 1). (ENG.). 176p. (J). (gr. 2-5). pap. 5.99 ***(978-1-4814-3904-6(9)***, Simon & Schuster/Paula Wiseman Bks.) Simon & Schuster/Paula Wiseman Bks.

Chater, Mack. Buried in Rubble: True Stories of Surviving Earthquakes. Collins, Terry. 2015. (True Stories of Survival Ser.). (ENG.). 32p. (gr. 3-4). lib. bdg. 29.99 ***(978-1-4914-6570-7(0)***, Graphic Library) Capstone Pr., Inc.

Chater, Mack, et al. True Stories of Survival. Yomtov, Nel. 2015. (True Stories of Survival Ser.). (ENG.). 32p. (gr. 3-4). 119.96 ***(978-1-4914-6915-6(3)***, Graphic Library) Capstone Pr., Inc.

Chatham, Dennis J. Professor Rock Ltd. Hatch Jr., B. J. Butch. 2003. 32p. (J). 14.95 *(978-1-56167-808-2(2))* American Literary Pr.

Chatterjee, Susnata. The Children's Garden. Talwar, Ankoor & Talwar, Abhinav. 2009. 32p. pap. 16.49 *(978-1-4389-9309-6(9))* AuthorHouse.

Chatterji, Somnath. I Am Tan! Denise, Carolyn. 2012. (ENG.). 18p. (J). (gr. -1-3). pap. 19.95 *(978-0-9835651-3-0(9))* Levi Bass Publishing.

—I Can Do It Myself! Denise, Carolyn. 2012. (ENG.). 16p. (J). (gr. -1-3). pap. 19.95 *(978-0-9835651-4-7(7))* Levi Bass Publishing.

Chatterley, Cedric N., photos by. Grace: For All the Children. 2003.Tr. of Grace: per Tutti I Bambini. (ITA., 79p. 35.00 *(978-0-9729735-2-6(4))* Luquer St. Pr.

—Sokita Celebrates the New Year: A Cambodian American Holiday. Lau, Barbara & Nesbitt, Kris. 2004. 32p. (J). per. 9.95 *(978-0-9747456-0-2(X))* Greensboro Historical Museum, Inc.

Chatterton, Chris. Kindergarten's Cool. Marshall, Linda Elovitz. 2016. (J). ***(978-0-545-65266-7(9)***, Cartwheel Bks.) Scholastic, Inc.

Chatterton, Martin. Flax the Feral Fairy. Mandrake, Tiffany. 2010. (Little Horrors Ser.: 1). (ENG.). 112p. (J). (gr. 3-7). 7.99 *(978-1-921272-70-7(8))* Little Hare Bks. AUS. Dist: Independent Pubs. Group.

—Kingfisher First Thesaurus. Beal, George. 2011. (Kingfisher First Reference Ser.). (ENG.). 144p. (J). (gr. k-3). pap. 10.99 *(978-0-7534-6586-8(8)*, Kingfisher) Roaring Brook Pr.

—Mal the Mischievous Mermaid. Mandrake, Tiffany. 2010. (Little Horrors Ser.: 2). (ENG.). 112p. (J). (gr. 3-7). 7.99 *(978-1-921272-71-4(6))* Little Hare Bks. AUS. Dist: Independent Pubs. Group.

—The Mummy Family Find Fame. Bradman, Tony. 2005. (Red Bananas Ser.). (ENG.). 48p. (J). (gr. k-2). pap. 5.99 *(978-1-4052-1877-1(0))* Egmont Bks., Ltd. GBR. Dist: Independent Pubs. Group.

—Nanda the Naughty Gnome. Mandrake, Tiffany. 2010. (Little Horrors Ser.: 3). (ENG.). 108p. (J). (gr. 2-4). 7.99 *(978-1-921541-22-3(9))* Little Hare Bks. AUS. Dist: Independent Pubs. Group.

—Prince Albert's Birthday. Clarke, Jane. 2005. 24p. (J). lib. bdg. 23.65 *(978-1-59646-748-4(7))* Dingles & Co.

—Scary Poems to Make You Shiver. Gibbs, Susie. 2007. (ENG.). 64p. (YA). (gr. 4-7). per. 10.00 *(978-0-19-272607-0(2))* Oxford Univ. Pr., Inc.

Chatterton, Martin. Technoslime Terror! Griffiths, Mark. 2013. (ENG.). 288p. (J). pap. 6.99 ***(978-0-85707-537-6(3))*** Simon & Schuster, Ltd. GBR. Dist: Simon & Schuster, Inc.

Chatterton, Martin. Tikki the Tricky Pixie. Mandrake, Tiffany. 2010. (Little Horrors Ser.: 4). (ENG.). 108p. (J). (gr. 2-4). 8.99 *(978-1-921541-32-2(6))* Little Hare Bks. AUS. Dist: Independent Pubs. Group.

—Weava the Wilful Witch. Mandrake, Tiffany. 2011. (Little Horrors Ser.: 6). (ENG.). 112p. (J). (gr. 2-4). pap. 7.99 *(978-1-921714-02-3(6))* Little Hare Bks. AUS. Dist: Independent Pubs. Group.

Chatterton, Martin. The Surprise Party. Chatterton, Martin. Bradman, Tony. 2005. (Red Bananas Ser.). (ENG.). 48p. (J). lib. bdg. *(978-0-7787-1068-4(8))* Crabtree Publishing Co.

Chatterton, Martin, jt. illus. see Trimmer, Tony.

Chatzikonstantinou, Danny. Humpty Dumpty Flip-Side Rhymes. Harbo, Christopher L. 2015. (Flip-Side Nursery Rhymes Ser.). (ENG.). 24p. (gr. -1-2). lib. bdg. 26.65 ***(978-1-4795-5986-2(5))*** Picture Window Bks.

—Little Bo Peep Flip-Side Rhymes. Harbo, Christopher L. 2015. (Flip-Side Nursery Rhymes Ser.). (ENG.). 24p. (gr. -1-2). lib. bdg. 26.65 ***(978-1-4795-5989-3(X))*** Picture Window Bks.

Chatzikonstantinou, Danny. My Grandma's a Ninja. Tarpley, Todd. 2015. (ENG.). 40p. (J). 17.95 *(978-0-7358-4199-4(3))* North-South Bks., Inc.

Chatzikonstantinou, Danny, jt. illus. see Jack, Colin.

Chau, Alina. Double Happiness. Ling, Nancy Tupper. 2015. (ENG.). 48p. (J). (gr. k-3). 16.99 ***(978-1-4521-2918-1(5))*** Chronicle Bks. LLC.

Chau, Alina. The Treehouse Heroes: The Forgotten Beast. Amara, Phil. 2012. (ENG.). 36p. (J). (gr. -1-3). 15.95 *(978-1-59702-034-3(6))* Immedium.

—The Year of the Sheep. Chin, Oliver. 2014. (Tales from the Chinese Zodiac Ser.: 10). (ENG.). 36p. (J). (gr. -1-3). 15.95 *(978-1-59702-104-3(0))* Immedium.

Chau, Ming, photos by. Walking on Solid Ground. Cheung, Shu Pui et al. Wei, Deborah & Kodish, Debora, eds. 2004. (ENG & CHI., 64p. (J). pap. 12.95 *(978-0-9644937-4-2(8)*, 09644937-4-8) Philadelphia Folklore Project.

Chaud, Benjamin. I Didn't Do My Homework Because... Cali, Davide. 2014. (ENG.). 44p. (J). (gr. 1-4). 12.99 *(978-1-4521-2551-0(1))* Chronicle Bks. LLC.

—Pomelo Begins to Grow. Badescu, Ramona & Bedrick, Claudia Z. 2011. (Pomelo the Garden Elephant Ser.). (ENG.). 48p. (J). (gr. -1-2). 16.95 *(978-1-59270-111-7(6))* Enchanted Lion Bks., LLC.

—Pomelo Explores Color. Badescu, Ramona. 2012. (Pomelo the Garden Elephant Ser.). (ENG.). 120p. (J). (gr. -1). 15.95 *(978-1-59270-126-1(4))* Enchanted Lion Bks., LLC.

—Pomelo's Big Adventure. Badescu, Ramona. 2014. (Pomelo the Garden Elephant Ser.). (ENG.). 40p. (J). (gr. -1-3). 17.95 *(978-1-59270-158-2(2))* Enchanted Lion Bks., LLC.

—Pomelo's Opposites. Badescu, Ramona. 2013. (Pomelo the Garden Elephant Ser.). (ENG.). 120p. (J). 15.95 *(978-1-59270-132-2(9))* Enchanted Lion Bks., LLC.

Chaudhary, Aman. Mo Smells Sweet Dreams: A Scentsational Journey. Hyde, Margaret E. 2012. (Mo's Nose Ser.). (ENG.). 24p. (J). (-k). 17.95 *(978-0-9816255-8-4(4))* Mo's Nose, LLC.

—Mo Smells the Ballpark. Hyde, Margaret. 2014. (ENG.). 24p. (J). (gr. -1-k). 14.95 *(978-1-62873-668-7(2)*, Sky Pony Pr.) Skyhorse Publishing Co., Inc.

Chauffrey, Celia. Little Red Riding Hood. Chauffrey, Celia. Don, Lari & Staunton, Imelda. 2012. (ENG.). 32p. (J). 16.99 *(978-1-84686-766-8(5))*; (gr. -1-4). 9.99 *(978-1-84686-768-2(1))* Barefoot Bks., Inc.

Chauncey, G. Wee Sing Around the World, 1 vol. Beall, Pamela Conn et al. 2006. (Wee Sing Ser.). (ENG.). 1p. (J). (gr. -1-2). 10.99 *(978-0-8431-2005-9(3)*, Price Stern Sloan) Penguin Publishing Group.

Chauvin, D. & Uderzo, M. The Falklands War. Rideau, J. & Asso, B. 2011. (ENG.). 48p. pap. 11.95 *(978-1-84918-056-6(3))* CineBook GBR. Dist: National Bk. Network.

Chauvin, Daniel & Uderzo, Marcel. Biggles Recounts the Falklands War: Volume 1. Asso, Bernard & Rideau, Joel. 2007. (ENG.). 48p. per. 9.99 *(978-1-905460-22-9(8))* CineBook GBR. Dist: National Bk. Network.

Chava. A Dozen Daises for Raizy: A Shavuos Story. Klempner, Rebecca. 2008. 30p. (J). (gr. -1-2). 10.95 *(978-1-929628-41-4(2))* Hachai Publishing.

Chavarri, Elisa. Christmas Traditions Around the World. Ingalls, Ann. 2013. (World Traditions Ser.). (ENG.). 32p. (J). (gr. k-3). 28.50 *(978-1-61473-425-3(9)*, 205130) Child's World, Inc., The.

—Easter Traditions Around the World. Cosson, J. 2013. (World Traditions Ser.). (ENG.). 32p. (J). (gr. k-3). 28.50 *(978-1-61473-426-0(7)*, 205131) Child's World, Inc., The.

—Fairly Fairy Tales. Codell, Esmé Raji. 2011. (ENG.). 32p. (J). (gr. -1-3). 17.99 *(978-1-4169-9086-4(0)*, Simon & Schuster/Paula Wiseman Bks.) Simon & Schuster/Paula Wiseman Bks.

—Fly Blanky Fly. Lewis, Anne Margaret. 2012. (ENG.). 40p. (J). (gr. -1-2). 16.99 *(978-0-06-199996-3(2))* HarperCollins Pubs.

—Halloween & Day of the Dead Traditions Around the World. Axelrod-Contrada, Joan. 2013. (World Traditions Ser.). (ENG.). 32p. (J). (gr. k-3). 28.50 *(978-1-61473-427-7(5)*, 205132) Child's World, Inc., The.

—National Day Traditions Around the World. Kesselring, Susan. 2013. (World Traditions Ser.). (ENG.). 32p. (J). (gr. k-3). 28.50 *(978-1-61473-428-4(3)*, 205133) Child's World, Inc., The.

—New Year Traditions Around the World. Malaspina, Ann. 2013. (World Traditions Ser.). (ENG.). 32p. (J). (gr. k-3). 28.50 *(978-1-61473-429-1(1)*, 205134) Child's World, Inc., The.

—Tooth Traditions Around the World. Malaspina, Ann. 2013. (World Traditions Ser.). (ENG.). 32p. (J). (gr. k-3). 28.50 *(978-1-61473-430-7(5)*, 205135) Child's World, Inc., The.

—Wishing Traditions Around the World. Cosson, J. 2013. (World Traditions Ser.). (ENG.). 32p. (J). (gr. k-3). 28.50 *(978-1-61473-431-4(3)*, 205136) Child's World, Inc., The.

Chaveevah, Banks Ferguson. Good Morning Lovey! Hickey, Joshalyn M. 2005. (ENG.). 28p. (J). 12.00 *(978-0-9718939-3-1(4))* BaHar Publishing, L.C.

Chaves, Guido. La Cucarachita Martina. Gonzalez, Ana Carlota. 2015. 24p. (J). (gr. -1-2). pap. 12.95 ***(978-9942-05-769-3(2)***, Alfaguara Infantil) Santillana Ecuador ECU. Dist: Santillana USA Publishing Co., Inc.

—Martina, Las Estrellas y un Cachito de Luna. Iturralde, Edna. 2015. 24p. (J). (gr. -1-2). pap. 12.95 ***(978-9942-05-068-7(X)***, Alfaguara Infantil) Santillana Ecuador ECU. Dist: Santillana USA Publishing Co., Inc.

Chawla, Neena. Bear Claws. Scheunemann, Pam. 2006. (Animal Tales Ser.). 24p. (J). (gr. k-3). (ENG.). lib. bdg. 24.21 *(978-1-59679-925-7(0)*, SandCastle); pap. 48.42 *(978-1-59679-926-4(9))* ABDO Publishing Co.

—Cat Tails. Scheunemann, Pam. 2006. (Animal Tales Ser.). 24p. (J). (gr. k-3). (ENG.). lib. bdg. 24.21 *(978-1-59679-927-1(7)*, SandCastle); pap. 48.42 *(978-1-59679-928-8(5))* ABDO Publishing Co.

—Crocodile Tears. Scheunemann, Pam. 2007. (Critter Chronicles Ser.). (ENG.). 24p. (J). (gr. k-3). lib. bdg. 24.21 *(978-1-59928-436-1(7)*, SandCastle) ABDO Publishing Co.

—Goldfish Bowl. Salzmann, Mary Elizabeth. 2006. (Animal Tales Ser.). (ENG.). 24p. (J). (gr. k-3). lib. bdg. 24.21 *(978-1-59679-939-4(0)*, SandCastle) ABDO Publishing Co.

—Goldfish Bowl (6-pack) Salzmann, Mary Elizabeth. 2006. (Fact & Fiction Ser.). 24p. (J). pap. 59.57 *(978-1-59679-940-0(4))* ABDO Publishing Co.

—Homing Pigeon. Doudna, Kelly. 2007. (Critter Chronicles Ser.). (ENG.). 24p. (J). (gr. k-3). lib. bdg. 24.21 *(978-1-59928-440-8(5)*, SandCastle) ABDO Publishing Co.

—Jellyfish Role. Doudna, Kelly. 2007. (Critter Chronicles Ser.). (ENG.). 24p. (J). (gr. k-3). lib. bdg. 24.21 *(978-1-59928-446-0(4)*, SandCastle) ABDO Publishing Co.

—Lamb Chops. Doudna, Kelly. 2006. (Animal Tales Ser.). 24p. (J). (gr. k-3). (ENG.). lib. bdg. 24.21 *(978-1-59679-947-9(1)*, SandCastle); pap. 48.42 *(978-1-59679-948-6(X))* ABDO Publishing Co.

—La Lana de la Oveja. Doudna, Kelly. 2007. (Cuentos de Animales Ser.).Tr. of Lamb Chops. (SPA & ENG.). 24p. (J). (gr. k-3). lib. bdg. 24.21 *(978-1-59928-661-7(0)*, SandCastle) ABDO Publishing Co.

—Leaping Lizards. Salzmann, Mary Elizabeth. 2007. (Critter Chronicles Ser.). (ENG.). 24p. (J). (gr. k-3). lib. bdg. 24.21 *(978-1-59928-450-7(2)*, SandCastle) ABDO Publishing Co.

—Monarch Butterfly. Kompelien, Tracy. 2007. (Critter Chronicles Ser.). (ENG.). 24p. (J). (gr. k-3). lib. bdg. 24.21 *(978-1-59928-454-5(5)*, SandCastle) ABDO Publishing Co.

—Monkey Business. Hanson, Anders. 2006. (Animal Tales Ser.). 24p. (J). (gr. k-3). (ENG.). lib. bdg. 24.21 *(978-1-59679-951-6(X)*, SandCastle); pap. 48.42 *(978-1-59679-952-3(8))* ABDO Publishing Co.

—Pack Rat. Doudna, Kelly. 2006. (Animal Tales Ser.). 24p. (J). (gr. k-3). (ENG.). lib. bdg. 24.21 *(978-1-59679-955-4(2)*, SandCastle); pap. 48.42 *(978-1-59679-956-1(0))* ABDO Publishing Co.

—Peacock Fan. Scheunemann, Pam. 2007. (Critter Chronicles Ser.). (ENG.). 24p. (J). (gr. k-3). lib. bdg. 24.21 *(978-1-59928-460-6(X)*, SandCastle) ABDO Publishing Co.

—Penguin Suit. Doudna, Kelly. 2006. (Animal Tales Ser.). 24p. (J). (gr. k-3). (ENG.). lib. bdg. 24.21 *(978-1-59679-957-8(9)*, SandCastle); pap. 48.42 *(978-1-59679-958-5(7))* ABDO Publishing Co.

—La Rata Coleccionista. Doudna, Kelly. 2007. (Cuentos de Animales Ser.).Tr. of Pack Rat. (SPA & ENG.). 24p. (J). (gr. k-3). lib. bdg. 24.21 *(978-1-59928-671-6(8)*, SandCastle) ABDO Publishing Co.

—Squirrel Hollow. Doudna, Kelly. 2006. (Animal Tales Ser.). 24p. (J). (gr. k-3). (ENG.). lib. bdg. 24.21 *(978-1-59679-967-7(6)*, SandCastle); pap. 48.42 *(978-1-59679-968-4(4))* ABDO Publishing Co.

Chayamachi, Suguro. Devil May Cry, No. 3. Chayamachi, Suguro. 2005. 168p. pap. 9.99 *(978-1-59816-031-4(1))* TOKYOPOP, Inc.

Chayka, Doug. Four Feet, Two Sandals. Williams, Karen Lynn & Mohammad, Khadra. 2007. 32p. (J). (gr. 2-5). 17.00 *(978-0-8028-5296-0(3)*, Eerdmans Bks For Young Readers) Eerdmans, William B. Publishing Co.

—The Secret Shofar of Barcelona. Greene, Jacqueline Dembar. 2009. (High Holidays Ser.). (ENG.). 32p. (J). (gr.

k-3). 17.95 *(978-0-8225-9915-9(5)*, Kar-Ben Publishing) Lerner Publishing Group.

—Waiting for Dolphins. Crowe, Carole. 2003. (ENG.). 144p. (J). (gr. 5-6). pap. 9.95 *(978-1-59078-073-2(6))* Boyds Mills Pr.

—Yasmin's Hammer. Malaspina, Ann. 2010. (ENG.). 40p. (J). (gr. k-6). 18.95 *(978-1-60060-359-4(9))* Lee & Low Bks., Inc.

Chayka, Doug & Kemly, Kathleen. Benjamin Brown & the Great Steamboat Race. Jordan, Shirley. 2011. (History Speaks: Picture Books Plus Reader's Theater Ser.). (ENG.). 48p. (gr. 2-4). lib. bdg. 27.93 *(978-1-58013-674-7(5)*, Millbrook Pr.) Lerner Publishing Group.

Chayka, Douglas. The Secret Shofar of Barcelona. Greene, Jacqueline Dembar. 2009. (High Holidays Ser.). (ENG.). 32p. (J). (gr. k-3). pap. 7.95 *(978-0-8225-9944-9(9)*, Kar-Ben Publishing) Lerner Publishing Group.

Chaykin, Howard, et al. Prisoner of War. Brubaker, Ed & Tieri, Frank. 2011. (ENG.). 192p. (YA). (gr. 8-17). 24.99 *(978-0-7851-5121-0(4))* Marvel Worldwide, Inc.

Checchetto, Marco, jt. illus. see De La Torre, Roberto.

Chee. Second Wave. Nelson, Michael Alan. 2008. (ENG.). 128p. per. 14.99 *(978-1-934506-06-6(0))* Boom! Studios.

Chee, jt. illus. see Azaceta, Paul.

Chee, Cheng-Khee. Noel. Johnston, Tony. 2005. (ENG.). 32p. (J). (gr. k-3). lib. bdg. 16.95 *(978-1-57505-752-1(2)*, Carolrhoda Bks.) Lerner Publishing Group.

Chee, Cheng-Khee, et al. Swing Around the Sun. Esbensen, Barbara Juster. 2003. (ENG.). 48p. (J). (gr. k-3). 17.95 *(978-0-87614-143-4(2)*, Carolrhoda Bks.) Lerner Publishing Group.

Cheetham, Stephen. Off to the Park! 2014. (Activity Bks.). (ENG.). 12p. (J). bds. *(978-1-84643-502-7(1))* Child's Play International Ltd.

Chelsey, Emily. Got Milk? How? Donlon, Bridget. 2012. (-18). 26p. 29.95 *(978-1-62709-613-3(2))*; 28p. pap. 24.95 *(978-1-4626-8033-7(X))* America Star Bks.

Chen, Chih-Yuan. Mimi Loves to Mimic. Chou, Yih-Fen. 2010. (ENG.). 32p. (J). (gr. -1-k). 9.95 *(978-0-9787550-8-9(1))* Heryin Publishing Corp.

Chen, Chih Yuan. Mimi Says No. Chou, Yih-Fen. 2010. (ENG.). 32p. (J). (gr. -1-k). 9.95 *(978-0-9787550-7-2(3))* Heryin Publishing Corp.

Chen, Chih-Yuan. En Camino a Comprar Huevos. Chen, Chih-Yuan. 2007. (SPA & ENG.). 32p. (J). (gr. -1-3). pap. 7.95 *(978-1-933605-55-5(3)*, Libros del Mundo) Kane Miller.

—The Featherless Chicken. Chen, Chih-Yuan. 2006. (ENG.). 40p. (J). (gr. k-2). 16.95 *(978-0-9762056-9-2(6))* Heryin Publishing Corp.

—Guji Guji. Chen, Chih-Yuan. 2004. (ENG.). 32p. (J). (gr. k-3). 11.99 *(978-1-929132-67-6(0))* Kane Miller.

Chen, Chih-Yuan, jt. illus. see Chen, Zhiyuan.

Chen, Grace. Sophie's First Dance, 1 vol. Rue, Nancy N. 2005. (Faithgirlz Ser.: No. 5). (ENG.). 128p. (J). pap. 6.99 *(978-0-310-70760-8(9))* Zonderkidz.

—Sophie's Stormy Summer, 1 vol. Rue, Nancy N. 2005. (Faithgirlz Ser.: No. 6). (ENG.). 128p. (J). pap. 6.99 *(978-0-310-70761-5(7))* Zonderkidz.

Chen, Jiang Hong. I Will Make Miracles. Morgenstern, Susie Hoch & Morgenstern, Susie. 2008. (ENG.). 32p. (J). (gr. -1-3). 18.99 *(978-1-59990-189-3(7)*, Bloomsbury USA Childrens) Bloomsbury USA.

Chen, Ju-Hong. Eliza's Cherry Trees: Japan's Gift to America, 1 vol. Zimmerman, Andrea. 2011. (ENG.). 32p. (J). (gr. k-3). 16.99 *(978-1-58980-954-3(8))* Pelican Publishing Co., Inc.

—The Jade Stone: A Chinese Folktale, 1 vol. 2005. (ENG.). 32p. (J). (gr. k-3). 16.99 *(978-1-58980-359-6(0))* Pelican Publishing Co., Inc.

Chen, Kuo Kan, et al. Forensic Science. Frith, Alex. 2007. (Forensic Science Ser.). 96p. (J). (gr. 4-7). pap. 10.99 *(978-0-7945-1689-5(0)*, Usborne) EDC Publishing.

Chen, Kuo Kang. How to Draw Robots & Aliens. Cook, Janet. Tatchell, Judy, ed. 2006. (Young Artist Ser.). 32p. (J). (gr. 4-7). pap. 5.99 *(978-0-7945-1370-2(0)*, Usborne) EDC Publishing.

—Weather. Clarke, Catriona. Ibrahim, Nouran, tr. 2013. (ENG & ARA.). 32p. (J). 6.99 *(978-99921-94-37-9(5)*, 149895) Bloomsbury USA.

—Weather: Level 7. Clarke, Catriona. 2006. (Usborne Beginners Ser.). 32p. (J). (gr. 4-7). lib. bdg. 12.99 *(978-1-58086-892-1(4)*, Usborne) EDC Publishing.

Chen, Kuo Kang, et al. The World of the Microscope. Oxlade, Chris & Stockley, Corinne. 2008. (Usborne Science & Experiments Ser.). 48p. (J). (gr. 5-11). pap. 8.99 *(978-0-7945-1524-9(X)*, Usborne) EDC Publishing.

Chen, Kuo Kang & Mayer, Uwe. Sun, Moon & Stars. Turnbull, Stephanie. 2006. (Beginners Nature: Level 2 Ser.). 32p. (J). (gr. 1-3). 4.99 *(978-0-7945-1399-3(9)*, Usborne) EDC Publishing.

Chen, Kuo Kang & Smith, Guy. Illustrated Dictionary of Biology. Stockley, Corinne. Rogers, Kirsteen, ed. 2007. (Illustrated Dictionaries Ser.). 128p. (J). (gr. 4-7). pap. 12.99 *(978-0-7945-1559-1(2)*, Usborne) EDC Publishing.

—The Usborne Illustrated Dictionary of Science. Stockley, Corinne et al. Rogers, Kirsteen, ed. rev. ed. 2007. (Illustrated Dictionaries Ser.). 382p. (J). (gr. 4-7). pap. 29.99 *(978-0-7945-1847-9(8)*, Usborne) EDC Publishing.

Chen, Kuo Kang, jt. illus. see Slane, Andrea.

Chen, Kuo Kang, jt. illus. see Spenceley, Annabel.

Chen, Sean, et al. Shadowland: Street Heroes. 2011. (ENG.). 176p. (YA). (gr. 8-17). pap. 19.99 *(978-0-7851-4888-3(4))* Marvel Worldwide, Inc.

Chen, Yong. Finding Joy. Coste, Marion. 2006. (ENG.). 32p. (J). (gr. 1-3). 16.95 *(978-1-59078-192-0(9))* Boyds Mills Pr.

Chen, Zhiyuan. Mimi Goes Potty. Chou, Yih-Fen. 2011. (J). *(978-0-9845523-9-9(1))* Heryin Publishing Corp.

—Mimi Tidies Up. Chou, Yih-Fen. 2011. (J). *(978-0-9845523-6-8(7))* Heryin Publishing Corp.

—The Potty Story. Chou, Yih-Fen. 2011. (J). *(978-0-9845523-8-2(3))* Heryin Publishing Corp.

Chen, Zhiyuan & Chen, Chih-Yuan. Artie & Julie. Chen, Chih-Yuan. 2008. (ENG.). 56p. (J). (gr. -1-k). 17.95 *(978-0-9787550-3-4(0))* Heryin Publishing Corp.

Cheng, Andrea. Etched in Clay: The Life of Dave, Enslaved Potter & Poet. Cheng, Andrea. 2013. (ENG.). 160p. (J). 17.95 *(978-1-60060-451-5(X))* Lee & Low Bks., Inc.

Cheng, Charlotte. A Moment in Time. Butenas, Jennifer. 2012. (ENG.). 40p. (J). (gr. k-2). 17.99 *(978-0-9840039-0-7(8))* Perfect Moment LLC, The.

Cheng-Liang, Zhu. A New Year's Reunion: A Chinese Story. Li-Qiong, Yu. 2013. (ENG.). 112p. (J). (gr. -1-2). 5.99 *(978-0-7636-6748-1(X))* Candlewick Pr.

Cheng, Puay Koon. I Trapped a Dolphin but It Really Wasn't My Fault. Humphreys, Neil. 2013. (Abbie Rose & the Magic Suitcase Ser.). (ENG.). 24p. (J). (gr. -1-3). pap. 15.90 *(978-981-4408-51-6(4))* Marshall Cavendish International (Asia) Private Ltd. SGP. Dist: National Bk. Network.

—Picking up a Penguin's Egg Really Got Me into Trouble. Humphreys, Neil. 2014. (Abbie Rose & the Magic Suitcase Ser.). (ENG.). 24p. (J). (gr. -1-3). pap. 15.90 *(978-981-4484-18-3(0))* Marshall Cavendish International (Asia) Private Ltd. SGP. Dist: National Bk. Network.

Chenn, Eric. Willie the Wheel. Chenn, Eric. 2006. (ENG.). 40p. (J). (gr. 2-4). 16.95 *(978-0-9762056-7-8(X))* Heryin Publishing Corp.

Cherif, Jennifer. Abbey & Friends M Is for Manners. Jesse, Mary. 2003. 48p. (J). 15.95 *(978-0-9729958-0-1(3))* Hexagon Blue.

Cherna. Patch's Country Quilt. Cherna. 2013. 54p. 25.95 *(978-1-60571-188-1(8))*; 50p. pap. 17.95 *(978-1-60571-187-4(X))* Northshire Pr.

Chernett, Dan. Malice, Bk. 1. Wooding, Chris. 2009. (Malice Ser.: 1). (ENG.). 384p. (J). (gr. 7-12). 14.99 *(978-0-545-16043-8(X))* Scholastic, Inc.

Chernichaw, Ian. Blue's Bad Dream. Albee, Sarah & Hood, Susan. 2006. (Blue's Clues Ser.: 21). (ENG.). 24p. (J). (gr. -1-2). pap. 3.99 *(978-1-4169-1553-9(2)*, Simon Spotlight/Nickelodeon) Simon Spotlight/Nickelodeon.

—Blue's Big Parade! Spelvin, Justin. 2005. (Blue's Clues Ser.). (ENG.). 24p. (J). pap. 3.99 *(978-0-689-87673-8(4)*, Simon Spotlight/Nickelodeon) Simon Spotlight/Nickelodeon.

—Blue's Checkup. Albee, Sarah. 2003. (Blue's Clues Ser.). (ENG.). 24p. (J). pap. 3.99 *(978-0-689-85449-1(8)*, Simon Spotlight/Nickelodeon) Simon Spotlight/Nickelodeon.

Chernyak, Inna. Not for All the Hamantaschen in Town. Milhander, Laura Aron. 2015. (J). ***(978-1-4677-5928-1(7)***, Kar-Ben Publishing) Lerner Publishing Group.

Cherry, Gale. The Best Book in the Library. Sue, Grandma. 2010. 20p. 12.49 *(978-1-4490-9704-2(9))* AuthorHouse.

Cherry, Lynne. Where Butterflies Grow. Ryder, Joanne. 2014. 32p. pap. 7.00 *(978-1-61003-313-8(2))* Center for the Collaborative Classroom.

Cherry, Lynne. How Groundhog's Garden Grew. Cherry, Lynne. 2003. (ENG.). 40p. (J). (gr. -1-3). 17.99 *(978-0-439-32371-0(1)*, Blue Sky Pr., The) Scholastic, Inc.

Cheryl H. Hahn. Dog Gone: Boomer's Story. Greene, Brenda. 2005. 127p. (YA). per. 8.99 *(978-0-9770279-0-3(2))* Three Willows Pr.

Chess, Victoria. Beautiful Buehla & the Zany Zoo Makeover. Hogg, Gary. 2006. 32p. (J). (gr. -1-2). 15.99 *(978-0-06-009420-1(6)*, Tegen, Katherine Bks) HarperCollins Pubs.

—The Beautiful Butterfly: A Folktale from Spain. Sierra, Judy. 2005. 32p. (J). (gr. k-4). reprint ed. 19.00 *(978-0-7567-9593-1(1))* DIANE Publishing Co.

—The Scaredy Cats. Bottner, Barbara. 2013. (ENG.). 32p. (J). (gr. -1-3). 16.99 *(978-1-4814-2166-9(2)*, Simon & Schuster Bks. For Young Readers) Simon & Schuster Bks. For Young Readers.

—Teeny Tiny Tingly Tales. Van Laan, Nancy. 2008. (ENG.). 32p. (J). (gr. -1-2). 8.99 *(978-1-4169-7572-4(1)*, Simon & Schuster/Paula Wiseman Bks.) Simon & Schuster/Paula Wiseman Bks.

—Ten Sly Piranhas: A Counting Story in Reverse (A Tale of Wickedness - And Worse!) Wise, William. 2004. (ENG.). 32p. (J). (gr. -1-k). pap. 5.99 *(978-0-14-240074-6(2)*, Puffin) Penguin Publishing Group.

Chessa, Francesca. Baby Baby Blah Blah Blah! Shipton, Jonathan. 2009. (ENG.). 32p. (J). (gr. -1-1). 16.95 *(978-0-8234-2213-5(5))* Holiday Hse., Inc.

—Library Lily. Shields, Gillian. 2011. 26p. (J). 16.00 *(978-0-8028-5401-8(X))* Eerdmans, William B. Publishing Co.

—Love-a-Duck. Brown, Alan James. 2010. (ENG.). 32p. (J). (gr. -1-1). pap. 16.95 *(978-0-8234-2263-0(1))* Holiday Hse., Inc.

—Puss in Boots, 1 vol. Piumini, Roberto. 2009. (Storybook Classics Ser.). (ENG.). 32p. (gr. 3-4). lib. bdg. 25.32 *(978-1-4048-5645-5(5)*, Fiction Picture Bks.) Picture Window Bks.

Chessa, Francesca. A Button Muddle. Chessa, Francesca. 2003. 32p. (YA). pap. *(978-1-85602-461-7(X)*, Pavilion Children's Books) Pavilion Bks.

—Holly's Red Boots. Chessa, Francesca. 2008. (ENG.). 32p. (J). (gr. -1-1). 16.95 *(978-0-8234-2158-9(9))* Holiday Hse., Inc.

Chesterman, Adrian. Ankylosaurus. Bailey, Gerry. 2011. (Smithsonian Prehistoric Zone Ser.). (ENG.). 32p. (J). (gr. k-3). *(978-0-7787-1797-3(6))*; pap. *(978-0-7787-1810-9(7))* Crabtree Publishing Co.

—Ankylosaurus Fights Back. Galvin, Laura Gates. 2007. (Smithsonian's Prehistoric Pals Ser.). (ENG.). 36p. (J). 8.95 *(978-1-59249-681-5(4))*; (J). 14.95 *(978-1-59249-679-2(2))*; (J). pap. 6.95 *(978-1-59249-680-8(6))*; (J). (gr. -1-3). 2.95 *(978-1-59249-682-2(2))*; 9.95 *(978-1-59249-683-9(0))* Soundprints.

—Polar Bear Horizon. Halfmann, Janet. (Smithsonian Oceanic Collection). (J). 2009. 24.95 incl. audio compact disk *(978-1-59249-665-5(2))*; 2006. (ENG.). 32p. 8.95 *(978-1-59249-569-6(9))*; 2006. (ENG.). 32p. 4.95 *(978-1-59249-567-2(2))*; 2006. (ENG.). 32p. (gr. -1-3). 15.95 *(978-1-59249-565-8(6))*; 2006. (ENG.). 32p. (gr. -1-3). mass mkt. 6.95 *(978-1-59249-566-5(4))* Soundprints.

—Polar Bear Horizon. Halfman, Janet. 2006. (Smithsonian Oceanic Collection). (ENG.). 32p. (J). 19.95 *(978-1-59249-568-9(0))*; (gr. -1-3). 9.95 *(978-1-59249-570-2(2))* Soundprints.

Chesterman, Al. Little Book of Dinosaurs. Winner, Cherie. 2005. (Little Bks.). (ENG.). 24p. (J). (gr. -1-2). pap. 5.95 *(978-1-58728-516-5(9))* Cooper Square Publishing Llc.

Chesterton, Peter. Macbeth. Shakespeare, William & Birch, Beverley. 2007. (Shakespeare's Tales Ser.). (ENG.). 80p. (J). (gr. 4-7). 13.95 *(978-0-7502-4965-2(X))*; per. 8.95 *(978-0-7502-5036-8(4))* Hachette Children's Group GBR. (Wayland). Dist: Independent Pubs. Group.

Chesworth, Michael. America the Musical 1776-1899: A Nation's History Through Music. Gershenson, Harold P. 2005. 21p. (J). *(978-1-58987-116-8(2))* Kindermusik International.

—America the Musical 1900-2000: A Nation's History Through Music. Gershenson, Harold P. 2006. (J). *(978-1-58987-201-1(0))* Kindermusik International.

—Como Superar los Miedos y Preocupaciones. Crist, James J. & Crist, J. J. Marti, Nuria, tr. 2004. (SPA.). 128p. *(978-84-9754-125-1(1)*, 87443) Ediciones Oniro S.A.

—Fluffy: Scourge of the Sea. Bateman, Teresa. 2006. (ENG.). 32p. (J). (gr. -1-2). pap. 7.95 *(978-1-58089-152-3(7))* Charlesbridge Publishing, Inc.

—Frieda B. & the Zillabeast. Bowers, Renata. 2013. 32p. (J). lib. bdg. 15.00 *(978-0-9843862-0-8(3))* Frieda B.

—Many Ways to Learn: A Kid's Guide to LD. Stern, Judith M. & Ben-Ami, Uzi. 2nd rev. ed. 2010. 96p. (J). (gr. 3-8). 14.95 *(978-1-4338-0739-8(4))*; pap. 9.95 *(978-1-4338-0740-4(8))* American Psychological Assn. (Magination Pr.).

—Morgy Coast to Coast. Lewis, Maggie. 2008. (ENG.). 144p. (J). (gr. 1-4). pap. 4.95 *(978-0-618-96641-7(2))* Houghton Mifflin Harcourt Publishing Co.

Chesworth, Michael D. Mom for Mayor. Edwards, Nancy. 2006. (ENG.). 96p. (J). (gr. 1-5). 16.95 *(978-0-8126-2743-5(1))* Cricket Bks.

—Truman's Loose Tooth. Wurm, Kristine. 2005. (ENG.). 32p. (J). (gr. -1-3). 16.95 *(978-0-9768513-0-1(X))* Spirited Publishing, LLC.

Chettle, Julie. Happy Misunderstanding: How Folly Gets his Name. Buller, Ginny. 2012. (ENG.). 29p. (J). pap. 16.95 *(978-1-4327-8234-4(7))* Outskirts Pr., Inc.

Cheung, Aries. The Bonsai Bear. Libster, Bernard. 2006. 31p. (J). (gr. k-4). reprint ed. 16.00 *(978-1-4223-5857-3(7))* DIANE Publishing Co.

Cheung, Charly. Macbeth. Shakespeare, William. 2013. (William Shakespeare Ser.). (ENG.). 64p. pap. 6.95 *(978-1-906230-47-0(1))* Real Reads Ltd. GBR. Dist: International Publishers Marketing.

—A Midsummer Night's Dream. Shakespeare, William. 2013. (William Shakespeare Ser.). (ENG.). 64p. pap. 6.95 *(978-1-906230-44-9(7))* Real Reads Ltd. GBR. Dist: International Publishers Marketing.

—Romeo & Juliet. Shakespeare, William. 2013. (William Shakespeare Ser.). (ENG.). 64p. pap. 6.95 *(978-1-906230-45-6(5))* Real Reads Ltd. GBR. Dist: International Publishers Marketing.

—The Tempest. Shakespeare, William. 2014. (William Shakespeare Ser.). (ENG.). 64p. pap. 6.95 *(978-1-906230-46-3(3))* Real Reads Ltd. GBR. Dist: International Publishers Marketing.

Cheung, Jim, et al. Blood for Blood, Vol. 2. Marz, Ron. 2003. (Scion Traveler Ser.: Vol. 2). 208p. (YA). (gr. 7-18). pap. 9.95 *(978-1-931484-75-6(9))* CrossGeneration Comics, Inc.

—Conflict of Conscience. Marz, Ron. 2003. (Scion Traveler Ser.: Vol. 1). 192p. (YA). (gr. 7-18). pap. 9.95 *(978-1-931484-58-9(9))* CrossGeneration Comics, Inc.

—Divided Loyalties, Vol. 3. Marz, Ron. 2003. (Scion Traveler Ser.: Vol. 3). 176p. (YA). (gr. 7-18). pap. 9.95 *(978-1-931484-94-7(5))* CrossGeneration Comics, Inc.

—The Far Kingdom, Vol. 5. Marz, Ron. 2003. (Scion Ser.: Vol. 5). 160p. (YA). (gr. 7-18). pap. 15.95 *(978-1-931484-81-7(3))* CrossGeneration Comics, Inc.

—Sanctuary, Vol. 4. Marz, Ron. (Scion Traveler Ser.: Vol. 4). 160p. (YA). 2004. pap. 9.95 *(978-1-59314-044-1(4))*; 2003. (gr. 7-18). pap. 15.95 *(978-1-931484-50-3(3))* CrossGeneration Comics, Inc.

—Scion Vol. 6: The Royal Wedding. Marz, Ron. 2004. (Scion Ser.). 160p. (YA). pap. 15.95 *(978-1-59314-034-2(7))* CrossGeneration Comics, Inc.

—Young Avengers. 2010. (ENG.). 352p. (YA). (gr. 8-17). pap. 34.99 *(978-0-7851-4907-1(4))* Marvel Worldwide, Inc.

Chewning, Randy. Ben & Bailey Build a Book Report. Lynette, Rachel. 2012. 32p. (J). lib. bdg. 25.27 *(978-1-59953-506-7(8))* Norwood Hse. Pr.

—Parade Day. Schmauss, Judy Kentor. 2006. (Reader's Clubhouse Level 2 Reader Ser.). (ENG.). 24p. (J). (gr. 1-4). pap. 3.99 *(978-0-7641-3293-3(8))* Barron's Educational Series, Inc.

—Signing at Home: Sign Language for Kids, 1 vol. Clay, Kathryn. 2013. (Time to Sign Ser.). (ENG.). 32p. (gr. 1-2). 26.65 *(978-1-62065-051-6(7)*, Aplus Bks.) Capstone Pr., Inc.

Chewning, Randy, et al. Time to Sign: Sign Language for Kids, 1 vol. Clay, Kathryn. 2013. (Time to Sign Ser.). (ENG.). 112p. (gr. 1-2). pap. 8.95 *(978-1-62065-687-7(6)*, Aplus Bks.) Capstone Pr., Inc.

Chewning, Randy. Where Does the Garbage Go? Showers, Paul. 2015. (Let's-Read-And-Find-Out Science 2 Ser.). (ENG.). 32p. (J). (gr. -1-3). pap. 6.99 ***(978-0-06-238200-9(4))*** HarperCollins Pubs.

Chiacchiera, Moreno & Todd, Michelle. Ancient Homes. Taylor, Saranne. 2014. (ENG.). 32p. (J). *(978-0-7787-1437-8(3))* Crabtree Publishing Co.

—Animal Homes. Taylor, Saranne. 2014. (ENG.). 32p. (J). *(978-0-7787-1438-5(1))* Crabtree Publishing Co.

—Futuristic Homes. Taylor, Saranne. 2014. (ENG.). 32p. (J). *(978-0-7787-1439-2(X))* Crabtree Publishing Co.

—Green Homes. Taylor, Saranne. 2014. (ENG.). 32p. (J). *(978-0-7787-1452-1(7))* Crabtree Publishing Co.

Chiacchiera, Moreno, jt. illus. see Smith, Simon.

Chiang, Andy. Harold Takes a Trip: Harold & the Purple Crayon. Marsoli, Lisa Ann. 2005. 10p. (J). 7.95 *(978-1-58117-262-1(1)*, Intervisual/Piggy Toes) Bendon, Inc.

Chiang, Shirley. Dream of the Red Chamber. Xueqin, Cao. 2013. (Chinese Classics Ser.). (ENG.). 64p. pap. 6.95 *(978-1-906230-36-4(6))* Real Reads Ltd. GBR. Dist: International Publishers Marketing.

—The Girl Who Blamed the World. MacKey, Cindy. 2013. 50p. pap. 16.50 *(978-0-9892699-0-2(6))* Cyrano Bks.

—Impressionists Sticker Book. Courtauld, Sarah & Davies, Kate, ed. 2011. (Art Ser.). 32p. (J). pap. 9.99 *(978-0-7945-2961-1(5)*, Usborne) EDC Publishing.

—Journey to the West. Cheng'en, Wu. 2013. (Chinese Classics Ser.). (ENG.). 64p. pap. 6.95 *(978-1-906230-34-0(X))* Real Reads Ltd. GBR. Dist: International Publishers Marketing.

—The Three Kingdoms. Guanzhong, Luo. 2013. (Chinese Classics Ser.). (ENG.). 64p. pap. 6.95 *(978-1-906230-35-7(8))* Real Reads Ltd. GBR. Dist: International Publishers Marketing.

—The Water Margin. Naian, Shi. 2013. (Chinese Classics Ser.). (ENG.). 64p. pap. 6.95 *(978-1-906230-37-1(4))* Real Reads Ltd. GBR. Dist: International Publishers Marketing.

Chiara, Francesca De. Little Stories for Bedtime. Taplin, Sam. 2010. (Bedtime Stories Ser.). 12p. (J). bds. 12.99 *(978-0-7945-2673-3(X)*, Usborne) EDC Publishing.

—Polar Bears. Watt, Fiona. 2010. (Luxury Touchy-Feely Board Bks). 10p. (J). bds. 15.99 *(978-0-7945-2544-6(X)*, Usborne) EDC Publishing.

Chichester Clark, Emma. Cunning Cat Tales. Cecil, Laura. 2006. 71p. (J). (gr. k-4). reprint ed. pap. 17.00 *(978-1-4223-5013-3(4))* DIANE Publishing Co.

—Enchantment: Fairy Tales, Ghost Stories & Tales of Wonder. Crossley-Holland, Kevin. 2003. 128p. (YA). reprint ed. 22.00 *(978-0-7567-6961-1(2))* DIANE Publishing Co.

—Hansel & Gretel. 2008. (ENG.). 64p. (J). (gr. 1-4). 18.99 *(978-0-7636-4012-5(3))* Candlewick Pr.

—The McElderry Book of Aesop's Fables. Morpurgo, Michael & Aesop. 2005. (ENG.). 96p. (J). (gr. 1-5). 24.99 *(978-1-4169-0290-4(2)*, McElderry, Margaret K. Bks.) McElderry, Margaret K. Bks.

—The McElderry Book of Grimms' Fairy Tales. 2006. (ENG.). 128p. (J). (gr. 1-5). 22.99 *(978-1-4169-1798-4(5)*, McElderry, Margaret K. Bks.) McElderry, Margaret K. Bks.

—Miss Wire's Christmas Surprise. Whybrow, Ian. 2007. 45p. (J). (gr. -1-3). pap. 3.95 *(978-0-7534-6136-5(6)*, Kingfisher) Roaring Brook Pr.

—The Pied Piper of Hamelin. Morpurgo, Michael. 2011. (ENG.). 64p. (J). (gr. k-4). 16.99 *(978-0-7636-4824-4(8))* Candlewick Pr.

—Thumbelina. Andersen, Hans Christian & Falloon, Jane. 2006.Tr. of Tommelise. 38p. (J). (gr. k-4). reprint ed. 16.00 *(978-1-4223-5373-8(7))* DIANE Publishing Co.

—A Treasury of Shakespeare's Verse. Shakespeare, William. Pollinger, Gina, ed. 2006. 96p. (J). (gr. 4-8). reprint ed. pap. 12.00 *(978-1-4223-5444-5(X))* DIANE Publishing Co.

—What Will You Be, Grandma? Newman, Nanette. 2012. (ENG.). 32p. (J). (gr. -1-2). 15.99 *(978-0-7636-6099-4(X)*, Templar) Candlewick Pr.

Chichester Clark, Emma. Amazing Mr. Zooty! Chichester Clark, Emma. 2008. (ENG.). 32p. (J). (gr. k — 1). pap. 10.99 *(978-1-84270-592-6(X))* Andersen Pr. GBR. Dist: Independent Pubs. Group.

—Beside the Sea. Chichester Clark, Emma. 2007. (Melrose & Croc Ser.). (ENG.). 32p. (J). (gr. -1-2). pap. 8.95 *(978-0-00-718244-2(9)*, HarperCollins Children's Bks.) HarperCollins Pubs. Ltd. GBR. Dist: HarperCollins Pubs.

—Come to School Too, Blue Kangaroo! Chichester Clark, Emma. 2013. (ENG.). 32p. (J). pap. 9.99 *(978-0-00-725868-0(2)*, HarperCollins Children's Bks.) HarperCollins Pubs. Ltd. GBR. Dist: HarperCollins Pubs.

—Friends for Life. Chichester Clark, Emma. 2006. (Melrose & Croc Ser.). (ENG.). 32p. (J). (gr. -1-2). pap. 8.95 *(978-0-00-718242-8(2)*, HarperCollins Children's Bks.) HarperCollins Pubs. Ltd. GBR. Dist: HarperCollins Pubs.

—Go to Town. Chichester Clark, Emma. 2007. (Melrose & Croc Ser.). (ENG.). 32p. (J). (gr. -1-2). pap. 8.95 *(978-0-00-718243-5(0)*, HarperCollins Children's Bks.) HarperCollins Pubs. Ltd. GBR. Dist: HarperCollins Pubs.

—Little Miss Muffet Counts to Ten. Chichester Clark, Emma. 2009. (ENG.). 32p. (J). (gr. -1-k). pap. 12.99 *(978-1-84270-955-9(0))* Andersen Pr. GBR. Dist: Independent Pubs. Group.

—Mimi's Book of Counting. Chichester Clark, Emma. 2004. 24p. (J). 9.95 *(978-1-57091-573-4(3))* Charlesbridge Publishing, Inc.

—Mimi's Book of Opposites. Chichester Clark, Emma. 2004. 24p. (J). 9.95 *(978-1-57091-574-1(1))* Charlesbridge Publishing, Inc.

—Piper. Chichester Clark, Emma. 2007. 32p. (J). (gr. k-3). 17.00 *(978-0-8028-5314-1(5)*, Eerdmans Bks For Young Readers) Eerdmans, William B. Publishing Co.

—Plum & Rabbit & Me, Bk. 3. Chichester Clark, Emma. 2010. (Humber & Plum Ser.: 3). (ENG.). 32p. (J). (gr. -1-k). pap. 9.99 *(978-0-00-727325-6(8)*, HarperCollins Children's Bks.) HarperCollins Pubs. Ltd. GBR. Dist: HarperCollins Pubs.

—We Are Not Fond of Rat! Chichester Clark, Emma. 2006. (Collins Big Cat Phonics Ser.). (ENG.). 16p. (J). pap. 5.99 *(978-0-00-723590-2(9))* HarperCollins Pubs. Ltd. GBR. Dist: Independent Pubs. Group.

Chien, Catia. A Boy & a Jaguar. Rabinowitz, Alan. 2014. (ENG.). 32p. (J). (gr. -1-3). 16.99 *(978-0-547-87507-1(X)*, HMH Books For Young Readers) Houghton Mifflin Harcourt Publishing Co.

—The Longest Night: A Passover Story. Snyder, Laurel. 2013. (ENG.). 40p. (J). (gr. -1-3). 17.99 *(978-0-375-86942-6(5)*, Schwartz & Wade Bks.) Random Hse. Children's Bks.

—My Blue Is Happy. Young, Jessica. 2013. (ENG.). 32p. (J). (gr. -1-3). 15.99 *(978-0-7636-5125-1(7))* Candlewick Pr.

C

Chikoyak, Andrew J. The Common Snipe. Joe, Anna Rose. Afcan, Paschal, ed. Afcan, Paschal, tr. 2004. (J). pap. 7.50 *(978-1-58084-224-2(0))* Lower Kuskokwim Schl. District.

—Tukutukuaralier. Joe, Anna Rose. Afcan, Paschal, ed. Afcan, Paschal, tr. 2004. (J). pap. 7.50 *(978-1-58084-225-9(9))* Lower Kuskokwim Schl. District.

Chikvaidze, Yuriy. A Brave Little Girl, Scary Chuchurella & a Christmas Tree. Troyan, Slava & Katya. 2011. (ENG.). 24p. pap. 10.30 *(978-1-4611-0803-0(9))* CreateSpace Independent Publishing Platform.

Child, Lauren. I Want a Pet. 2011. (ENG.). 24p. (J). (gr. -1-1). pap. 7.95 *(978-1-84780-289-7(3)*, Frances Lincoln Children's Bks.) Quarto Publishing Group UK GBR. Dist: Hachette Bk. Group.

—I'd Like a Little Word, Leonie! Oldfield, Jenny. 99p. (J). pap. 8.99 *(978-0-340-78501-0(2))* Macmillan Pubs., Ltd. GBR. Dist: Trafalgar Square Publishing.

—Not Now, Nathan! Oldfield, Jenny. 107p. (J). pap. 7.99 *(978-0-340-78502-7(0))* Macmillan Pubs., Ltd. GBR. Dist: Trafalgar Square Publishing.

—Pippi Longstocking. Lindgren, Astrid. Nunally, Tina, tr. (Pippi Longstocking Ser.). (ENG.). 208p. (J). (gr. 2-5). 2011. pap. 15.99 *(978-0-670-01404-0(4))*; 2007. 27.99 *(978-0-670-06276-8(6))* Penguin Publishing Group. (Viking Juvenile).

—What's the Matter, Maya? Oldfield, Jenny. 106p. (J). pap. *(978-0-340-78503-4(9))* Hodder & Stoughton.

Child, Lauren. But Excuse Me That Is My Book. Child, Lauren. 2006. (Charlie & Lola Ser.). (ENG.). 32p. (J). (gr. -1-3). 16.99 *(978-0-8037-3096-0(9)*, Dial) Penguin Publishing Group.

—Clarice Bean: The Utterly Complete Collection. Child, Lauren. 2008. (Clarice Bean Ser.). (ENG.). 656p. (J). (gr. 3-7). pap. 16.99 *(978-0-7636-4115-3(4))* Candlewick Pr.

—Clarice Bean, Don't Look Now. Child, Lauren. 2008. (Clarice Bean Ser.). (ENG.). 256p. (J). (gr. 3-7). pap. 5.99 *(978-0-7636-3935-8(4))* Candlewick Pr.

—Clarice Bean Spells Trouble. Child, Lauren. 2006. (Clarice Bean Ser.). 189p. (J). (gr. 3-6). 13.65 *(978-0-7569-7919-5(6))* Perfection Learning Corp.

—Clarice Bean, That's Me. Child, Lauren. 2010. (Clarice Bean Ser.). (ENG.). 32p. (J). (gr. 1-4). pap. 7.99 *(978-0-7636-4795-7(0))* Candlewick Pr.

—I Absolutely Must Do Coloring Now or Painting or Drawing. Child, Lauren. 2006. (Charlie & Lola Ser.). (ENG.). 24p. (J). (gr. -1-k). 3.99 *(978-0-448-44415-4(1)*, Grosset & Dunlap) Penguin Publishing Group.

—I Am Not Sleepy & I Will Not Go to Bed. Child, Lauren. (Charlie & Lola Ser.). (ENG.). (J). (gr. -1-2). 2008. 16p. 19.99 *(978-0-7636-4098-9(0))*; 2005. 32p. reprint ed. pap. 6.99 *(978-0-7636-2970-0(7))* Candlewick Pr.

—I Am Too Absolutely Small for School. Child, Lauren. (Charlie & Lola Ser.). (ENG.). 32p. (J). (gr. -1-2). 2004. 16.99 *(978-0-7636-2403-3(9))*; 2005. reprint ed. per. 6.99 *(978-0-7636-2887-1(5))* Candlewick Pr.

—I Am Too Absolutely Small for School. Child, Lauren. 2005. (ENG.). (J). (gr. -1-1). lib. bdg. 14.65 *(978-0-7569-6495-5(4))* Perfection Learning Corp.

—I Will Never Not Ever Eat a Tomato. Child, Lauren. 2003. (Charlie & Lola Ser.). (ENG.). 32p. (J). (gr. -1-3). reprint ed. 6.99 *(978-0-7636-2180-3(3))* Candlewick Pr.

—My Wobbly Tooth Must Not Ever Never Fall Out. Child, Lauren. 2006. (Charlie & Lola Ser.). (ENG.). 32p. (J). (gr. -1-2). mass mkt. 6.99 *(978-0-448-44255-6(8)*, Grosset & Dunlap) Penguin Publishing Group.

—Ruby Redfort Catch Your Death (Book #3) Child, Lauren. 2015. (Ruby Redfort Ser.: 3). (ENG.). 432p. (J). (gr. 5). 16.99 *(978-0-7636-5469-6(8))* Candlewick Pr.

—Ruby Redfort Look into My Eyes. Child, Lauren. (Ruby Redfort Ser.: 1). (ENG.). 400p. (J). (gr. 5-8). 2013. pap. 7.99 *(978-0-7636-6257-8(7))*; 2012. 16.99 *(978-0-7636-5120-6(6))* Candlewick Pr.

—Ruby Redfort Take Your Last Breath. Child, Lauren. (Ruby Redfort Ser.: 2). (ENG.). 432p. (J). (gr. 5). 2014. pap. 7.99 *(978-0-7636-6932-4(6))*; 2013. 16.99 *(978-0-7636-5468-9(X))* Candlewick Pr.

—Spells Trouble. Child, Lauren. 2006. (Clarice Bean Ser.). (ENG.). 192p. (J). (gr. 3-7). pap. 5.99 *(978-0-7636-2903-8(0))* Candlewick Pr.

—Utterly Me, Clarice Bean. Child, Lauren. 2005. (Clarice Bean Ser.). (ENG.). 208p. (J). (gr. 3-7). reprint ed. pap. 5.99 *(978-0-7636-2788-1(7))* Candlewick Pr.

—Utterly Me, Clarice Bean. Child, Lauren. 2006. (Clarice Bean Ser.). 16.00 *(978-0-7569-6567-9(5))* Perfection Learning Corp.

Childers, Basil, photos by. Tuning Up: A Visit with Eric Kimmel. Kimmel, Eric A. 2005. (Meet the Author Ser.). (ENG., 32p. (J). 14.95 *(978-1-57274-822-4(2)*, 732, Meet the Author) Owen, Richard C. Pubs., Inc.

Children of Appalachia. Teddy Bear Helps on the Farm. Children of Appalachia. 2007. 64p. (J). per. 14.95 *(978-0-929915-73-9(9))* Headline Bks., Inc.

Children-Oln. Jeremiah & the Man, 6 vols., Vol. 1. Terbay, Susan Handle. Mariants, tr. 2007. 43p. (J). (gr. 1-6). pap. *(978-0-9628309-8-3(4))* Marianist Pr.

Children's Art-Friends of Kateri, jt. illus. see McCauley, Marlene.

Childrens Books Staff & Rose, Drew. Meet OLIVIA. Ciminera, Siobhan & Testa, Maggie. 2009. (Olivia TV Tie-In Ser.). (ENG.). 32p. (J). (gr. -1-1). 4.99 *(978-1-4169-7188-7(2)*, Simon Scribbles) Simon Scribbles.

Childs, Sam. Boobela & the Belching Giant. Friedman, Joe. ed. 2010. (ENG.). 128p. 12.99 *(978-1-4440-0046-7(2))* Orion Publishing Group, Ltd. GBR. Dist: Hachette Bk. Group.

—Boobela, Worm & Potion Power. Friedman, Joe. ed. 2010. (ENG.). 128p. 12.99 *(978-1-4440-0045-0(4))* Orion Publishing Group, Ltd. GBR. Dist: Hachette Bk. Group.

—Kave-Tina Rox. Marshall, Jill. 2010. (ENG.). 32p. (J). *(978-0-340-95712-7(3)*, Hodder Children's Books) Hachette Children's Group GBR. Dist: Hachette Bk. Group.

Chilton, Noel. Pop Flop's Great Balloon Ride. Abruzzo, Nancy. 2005. (ENG.). 32p. (J). (gr. k-17). bds. 12.95 *(978-0-89013-475-7(8))* Museum of New Mexico Pr.

—The Tale of the Pronghorned Cantaloupe. Steinsiek, Sabra Brown. 2009. (SPA & ENG.). 48p. (J). (gr. -1-3). pap. 17.95 *(978-1-890689-85-8(6)*, Rio Grande Bks.) LPD Pr.

—Tia's Tamales. Baca, Ana. (ENG & SPA.). 32p. 2012. (J). pap. 16.95 *(978-0-8263-5027-5(5))*; 2011. (YA). (gr. 4-18). 16.95 *(978-0-8263-5026-8(7))* Univ. of New Mexico Pr.

Chilton, Noel Dora. The Tale of the Pronghorned Cantaloupe. Steinsiek, Sabra Brown. 2013. 48p. 24.95 *(978-1-936744-11-4(2)*, Rio Grande Bks.) LPD Pr.

Chilvers, Nigel. Demons & Dragons. Peebles, Alice. 2015. (Mythical Beasts Ser.). (ENG.). 32p. (J). (gr. 3-6). pap. 7.99 ***(978-1-4677-7651-6(3)***, Lerner Pubns.) Lerner Publishing Group.

—Giants & Trolls. Peebles, Alice. 2015. (Mythical Beasts Ser.). (ENG.). 32p. (J). (gr. 3-6). 26.65 ***(978-1-4677-6340-0(3)***, Lerner Pubns.) Lerner Publishing Group.

—Monsters of the Gods. Peebles, Alice. 2015. (Mythical Beasts Ser.). (ENG.). 32p. (J). (gr. 3-6). 26.65 ***(978-1-4677-6342-4(X)***, Lerner Pubns.) Lerner Publishing Group.

Chin, Carl & Owlkids Books Inc. Staff. Growing Up. Vermond, Kira. 2013. (ENG.). 104p. (J). (gr. 4-7). 18.95 *(978-1-926973-89-0(5))*; pap. 11.95 *(978-1-77147-004-9(6))* Owlkids Bks. Inc. CAN. Dist: Perseus-PGW.

Chin, Foo Swee. Zeet. Chin, Foo Swee. 2003. 32p. (Orig.). pap. 2.95 *(978-0-943151-75-5(9))* Slave Labor Bks.

Chin, Jason. Chinese New Year. Jango-Cohen, Judith. 2005. (On My Own Holidays Ser.). (ENG.). 48p. (gr. 2-4). pap. 6.95 *(978-1-57505-763-7(8))* Lerner Publishing Group.

—The Day the World Exploded: The Earthshaking Catastrophe at Krakatoa. Winchester, Simon. 2008. 96p. (J). (gr. 5-9). lib. bdg. 23.89 *(978-0-06-123983-0(6))* HarperCollins Pubs.

—My Big Fat Secret: How Jenna Takes Control of Her Emotions & Eating. Schechter, Lynn R. 2009. 48p. (J). (gr. 3-7). 14.95 *(978-1-4338-0540-0(5))*; pap. 9.95 *(978-1-4338-0541-7(3))* American Psychological Assn. (Magination Pr.).

—Water Is Water: A Book about the Water Cycle. Paul, Miranda. 2015. (ENG.). 40p. (J). (gr. 1-5). 17.99 *(978-1-59643-984-9(X))* Roaring Brook Pr.

—Where Do Polar Bears Live? Thomson, Sarah L. 2009. (Let's-Read-And-Find-Out Science 2 Ser.). (ENG.). 40p. (J). (gr. k-4). 16.99 *(978-0-06-157518-1(6))*; pap. 5.99 *(978-0-06-157517-4(8))* HarperCollins Pubs. (Collins).

Chin, Jason. Coral Reefs. Chin, Jason. 2011. (ENG.). 40p. (J). (gr. k-4). 16.99 *(978-1-59643-563-6(1))* Roaring Brook Pr.

—Gravity. Chin, Jason. 2014. (ENG.). 32p. (J). (gr. k-3). 16.99 *(978-1-59643-717-3(0))* Roaring Brook Pr.

—Island: A Story of the Galápagos. Chin, Jason. 2012. (ENG.). 40p. (J). (gr. k-3). 16.99 *(978-1-59643-716-6(2))* Roaring Brook Pr.

—Redwoods. Chin, Jason. 2009. (ENG.). 40p. (J). (gr. -1-3). 17.99 *(978-1-59643-430-1(9))* Roaring Brook Pr.

Chin, Lili. Don't Judge a Book by Its Cover. Fleck, Denise. 2013. 24p. pap. 14.99 *(978-1-4575-1758-7(2))* Dog Ear Publishing, LLC.

Chin, Marcos. Ella. Kasdan, Mallory. 2015. (ENG.). 56p. (J). (gr. k-3). 17.99 *(978-0-670-01675-4(6)*, Viking Juvenile) Penguin Publishing Group.

Chin, Todd. Bernice's Bad Hair Days. Cardin, Jodi. 2009. 56p. (J). pap. *(978-1-60800-004-3(4))* LifeReloaded Specialty Publishing LLC.

Chinchinian, Harry. The Princess & the Beggar II: Continuing Adventures. Chinchinian, Harry. 2005. 176p. (J). lib. bdg. 18.95 *(978-1-892476-11-1(8))* Plum Tree Pr.

Ching, Brian. Skaar: King of the Savage Land. Williams, Rob. 2011. (ENG.). 120p. (YA). (gr. 8-17). pap. 15.99 *(978-0-7851-5694-9(1))* Marvel Worldwide, Inc.

Ching, Jerry Yu. The Greatest King. Ching, Jerry Yu. Onghai, Mike. 2nd l.t. ed. 2003. 52p. *(978-0-9743215-0-9(8))* WebCartoons, LLC.

Chiodi, Maira. Monster Knows Excuse Me, 1 vol. Miller, Connie Colwell. 2014. (Monster Knows Manners Ser.). (ENG.). (J). (gr. -1-2). 20p. bds. 7.99 *(978-1-4795-2965-0(6))*; 24p. pap. 5.95 *(978-1-4795-2953-7(2))*; 24p. lib. bdg. 23.99 *(978-1-4795-2202-6(3))* Picture Window Bks.

—Monster Knows I'm Sorry. Miller, Connie Colwell. 2014. (Monster Knows Manners Ser.). (ENG.). 20p. (gr. -1-2). bds. 7.99 *(978-1-4795-2964-3(8))* Picture Window Bks.

—Monster Knows Manners, 1 vol. Miller, Connie Colwell. 2014. (Monster Knows Manners Ser.). (ENG.). 24p. (gr. -1-2). lib. bdg. 95.96 *(978-1-4795-3346-6(7))* Picture Window Bks.

—Monster Knows Please & Thank You, 1 vol. Miller, Connie Colwell. 2014. (Monster Knows Manners Ser.). (ENG.). 20p. (gr. -1-2). bds. 7.99 *(978-1-4795-2963-6(X))* Picture Window Bks.

—Monster Knows Table Manners, 1 vol. Miller, Connie Colwell. 2014. (Monster Knows Manners Ser.). (ENG.). 20p. (gr. -1-2). bds. 7.99 *(978-1-4795-2966-7(4))* Picture Window Bks.

Chiodo, Charles. Chiodo Bros.' Alien Xmas. Chiodo, Stephen & Strain, Jim. 2006. 40p. (J). (gr. -1). 17.95 *(978-0-9729388-4-6(2))* Baby Tattoo Bks.

Chiodo, Joe. The Adventures of Wonderbaby: From A to Z. Chin, Oliver Clyde. 2005. (ENG.). 32p. (J). bds. 8.95 *(978-1-59702-001-5(X))* Immedium.

Chipka, Sandy. Ok, Said Carrie Katherine, 1 vol. Flaggert, Candy. 2008. (ENG.). 25p. 24.95 *(978-1-60563-502-6(2))* America Star Bks.

Chirco, Antonella. Bible Rhymes' Christmas Story. McCardell, Kenneth/W. 2007. 32p. (J). 17.95 *(978-0-9790605-2-6(4)*, BibleRhymes) BibleRhymes Publishing, L.L.C.

—Bible Rhymes' Creation. McCardell, Kenneth/W. 2007. 32p. (J). 17.95 *(978-0-9790605-0-2(8)*, BibleRhymes) BibleRhymes Publishing, L.L.C.

—Bible Rhymes' Noah & the Ark. McCardell, Kenneth/W. 2007. 32p. (J). 17.95 *(978-0-9790605-1-9(6)*, BibleRhymes) BibleRhymes Publishing, L.L.C.

Chironna, Ronald. Galloping Gertrude: By Motorcar In 1908. Loeper, John J. 2011. 80p. (J). lib. bdg. 19.95 *(978-0-9727940-1-5(8))* Hieropub LLC.

Chitombo, Patience. From Adam to Noah in Coloring Pages: Genesis 1 To 9. Zinjiba-Nyakutya, Peshie. 2012. 64p. pap. 12.50 *(978-1-61897-769-4(5)*, Strategic Bk. Publishing) Strategic Book Publishing & Rights Agency (SBPRA).

Chitouras, Barbara. Little Women. Lindskoog, Kathryn, ed. 2003. (Classics for Young Readers Ser.). 432p. (J). per. 12.99 *(978-0-87552-734-5(5))* P & R Publishing.

Chitrakar, Manu. I See the Promised Land: A Life of Martin Luther King, Jr., 1 vol. Flowers, Arthur. rev. ed. 2013. (ENG.). 156p. (J). (gr. 6). 16.95 *(978-1-55498-328-5(2))* Groundwood Bks. CAN. Dist: Perseus-PGW.

Chitrakar, Moyna. Sita's Ramayana. Arni, Samhita & Valmiki. 2011. (ENG.). 152p. (J). (gr. 4). 24.95 *(978-1-55498-145-8(X))* Groundwood Bks. CAN. Dist: Perseus-PGW.

Chitrakar, Swarna. Monkey Photo. Rao, Sirish. 2010. (ENG.). 32p. (J). (gr. -1-1). 16.95 *(978-81-907546-2-0(9))* Tara Publishing IND. Dist: Perseus-PGW.

Chitwood, Suzanne, jt. illus. see Chitwood, Suzanne Tanner.

Chitwood, Suzanne Tanner & Chitwood, Suzanne. Boom Chicka Rock. Archambault, John. 2004. (ENG.). 32p. (J). (gr. -1-k). 16.99 *(978-0-399-23587-0(6)*, Philomel) Penguin Publishing Group.

Chiu, Bessie. Ariana Leaves San Francisco. Martha, Morales. 2011. 28p. pap. 8.50 *(978-1-61170-017-6(5))* Robertson Publishing.

Chiu, Bobby. The Familiars. Epstein, Adam Jay & Jacobson, Andrew. 2010. (Familiars Ser.: 1). (ENG.). 368p. (J). (gr. 3-7). 16.99 *(978-0-06-196108-3(6))* HarperCollins Pubs.

Chizuwa, Masayuki. My Book of Money Counting Coins: Ages 5, 6, 7. 2007. 80p. (J). (gr. -1-3). per. 7.95 *(978-1-933241-42-5(X))* Kumon Publishing North America, Inc.

—My Book of Money Counting Dollars & Cents: Ages 6, 7, 8. 2007. 80p. (J). (gr. -1-3). per. 7.95 *(978-1-933241-43-2(8))* Kumon Publishing North America, Inc.

Cho, Frank & Romita, John, Jr. Avengers vs. X-Men. Aaron, Jason. 2012. (ENG.). 568p. (YA). (gr. 8-17). 75.00 *(978-0-7851-6317-6(4))* Marvel Worldwide, Inc.

Cho, Frank, jt. illus. see Dodson, Terry.

Cho, Michael. Media Madness: An Insider's Guide to Media. Ali, Dominic. 2005. (ENG.). 64p. (J). (gr. 5-9). 9.95 *(978-1-55337-175-5(5))* Kids Can Pr., Ltd. CAN. Dist: Univ. of Toronto Pr.

Cho, Michael & Owlkids Books Inc. Staff. Gross Universe: Your Guide to All Disgusting Things under the Sun. Szpirglas, Jeff. 2006. (ENG.). 64p. (J). (gr. 3-6). pap. 9.95 *(978-1-897066-39-3(2)*, Maple Tree Pr.) Owlkids Bks. Inc. CAN. Dist: Perseus-PGW.

—Max Finder Mystery, Vol. 2. O'Donnell, Liam. 2007. (Max Finder Mystery Collected Casebook Ser.: 2). (ENG.). 96p. (J). (gr. 3-6). 9.95 *(978-2-89579-121-8(X))* Owlkids Bks. Inc. CAN. Dist: Perseus-PGW.

—Max Finder Mystery Collected Casebook, Vol. 1. O'Donnell, Liam. 2006. (Max Finder Mystery Collected Casebook Ser.: 1). (ENG.). 96p. (J). (gr. 3-6). pap. 9.95 *(978-2-89579-116-4(3))* Owlkids Bks. Inc. CAN. Dist: Perseus-PGW.

—Max Finder Mystery Collected Casebook Vol. 3, Vol. 3. O'Donnell, Liam. 2007. (Max Finder Mystery Collected Casebook Ser.: 3). (ENG.). 96p. (J). (gr. 3-6). pap. 9.95 *(978-2-89579-149-2(X))* Owlkids Bks. Inc. CAN. Dist: Perseus-PGW.

Cho, Seung-Yup. Phantom, Vol. 4. Lee, Ki-Hoon. 2008. (Phantom (Tokyopop) Ser.). 192p. (gr. 8). pap. 9.99 *(978-1-59816-773-3(1))* TOKYOPOP, Inc.

Chocheli, Niko. The Hermit, the Icon, & the Emperor: The Holy Virgin Comes to Cyprus. Hart, Chrissi. 2008. 32p. (J). 16.95 *(978-1-888212-49-5(7))* Conciliar Pr.

Chodagiri, Shanthi. The Pursuit of Pizan, 1 vol. Heap, Bridgette. 2009. 35p. pap. 24.95 *(978-1-61546-994-9(X))* America Star Bks.

Chodos-Irvine, Margaret. Apple Pie Fourth of July. Wong, Janet S. 2006. (ENG.). 40p. (J). (gr. -1-3). pap. 7.00 *(978-0-15-205708-4(0))* Houghton Mifflin Harcourt Publishing Co.

—Dinosaur Thunder. Bauer, Marion Dane. 2012. (ENG.). 32p. (J). (gr. -1-k). 16.99 *(978-0-590-45296-0(7)*, Scholastic Pr.) Scholastic, Inc.

Choi, Allan. Barbie & the Three Musketeers: A Junior Novelization. Dumas, Alexandre. 2009. 93p. (J). *(978-0-545-09413-9(5))* Scholastic, Inc.

Choi, Allan, jt. illus. see Ulkutay Design Group.

Choi, Allan Jai-Ho. Chimmy '5 in 1' Language Alphabet Book. Paigerac, Patricia. 2007. 56p. (J). 23.00 *(978-0-9801137-0-9(9))* Paigerac, Patricia M.

Choi, Il-Ho. Chrono Code, 2 vols. Shin, Eui-Cheol. 2nd rev. ed. 2005. (Chrono Code Ser.: Vol. 2). 208p. per. 9.99 *(978-1-59532-551-8(4))* TOKYOPOP, Inc.

—Chrono Code, 2 vols., Vol. I. Kim, Sarah, tr. from KOR. 2005. 192p. pap. 9.99 *(978-1-59532-550-1(6))* TOKYOPOP, Inc.

Choi, Mike. Astonishing Thor. 2011. (ENG.). 120p. (YA). (gr. 8-17). 24.99 *(978-0-7851-4876-0(0))* Marvel Worldwide, Inc.

Choi, Mike & Camuncoli, Giuseppe. Fantastic Four by Jonathan Hickman - Volume 6. Hickman, Jonathan. 2013. (ENG.). 184p. (YA). (gr. 8-17). pap. 24.99 *(978-0-7851-6155-4(4))* Marvel Worldwide, Inc.

Choi, Min-ho. Little Red Riding Hood. Brothers Grimm Staff. Cowley, Joy, ed. 2015. (World Classics Ser.). (ENG.). 32p. (gr. k-4). 26.65 ***(978-1-925246-16-2(7))***; 7.99 ***(978-1-925246-68-1(X))***; 26.65 ***(978-1-925246-42-1(6))*** ChoiceMaker Pty. Ltd., The AUS. (Big and SMALL). Dist: Lerner Publishing Group.

Choi, Stef. Ruby Lu, Star of the Show. Look, Lenore. (ENG.). 144p. (J). (gr. 1-5). 2012. pap. 6.99 *(978-1-4169-1776-2(4))*; 2011. 15.99 *(978-1-4169-1775-5(6))* Simon & Schuster Children's Publishing. (Atheneum Bks. for Young Readers).

Choi Sung Hwan, Aragon Noel. Best Friends for Life. Miller, Jennifer. 2006. (Trollz Ser.). (ENG.). 120p. (J). pap. 4.99 *(978-0-439-80311-3(X))* Scholastic, Inc.

—Ready to Glow. Ruditis, Paul. 2005. (Trollz Ser.). (ENG.). 80p. (J). pap. 5.99 *(978-0-439-80313-7(6))* Scholastic, Inc.

Choi, Yang-sook. Liang's Treasure: China. Yun, Yeo-rim. Cowley, Joy, ed. 2015. (Global Kids Storybooks Ser.). (ENG.). 32p. (gr. 1-4). 26.65 ***(978-1-925246-05-6(1))***; 26.65 ***(978-1-925246-31-5(0))***; 7.99 ***(978-1-925246-57-5(4))*** ChoiceMaker Pty. Ltd., The AUS. (Big and SMALL). Dist: Lerner Publishing Group.

Choi, Yangsook. Basket Weaver & Catches Many Mice. Gill, Janet. 2005. 30p. (J). (gr. k-4). reprint ed. 19.00 *(978-0-7567-9420-0(X))* DIANE Publishing Co.

—Gai See: What You Can See in Chinatown. Thong, Roseanne. 2007. (ENG.). 40p. (J). (gr. 1-4). 16.95 *(978-0-8109-9337-2(6)*, Abrams Bks. for Young Readers) Abrams.

—Landed. Lee, Milly. 2006. (ENG.). 40p. (J). (gr. 2-6). 17.99 *(978-0-374-34314-9(4)*, Farrar, Straus & Giroux (BYR)) Farrar, Straus & Giroux.

Choi, Yangsook. The Name Jar. Choi, Yangsook. 2003. (ENG.). 40p. (J). (gr. -1-2). pap. 7.99 *(978-0-440-41799-6(6)*, Dragonfly Bks.) Random Hse. Children's Bks.

Choksi, Nishant. Really, Really Big Questions about Space & Time. Brake, Mark. 2012. (Really Really Big Questions Ser.). (ENG.). 64p. (J). (gr. 4-7). pap. 8.99 *(978-0-7534-6747-3(X)*, Kingfisher) Roaring Brook Pr.

Chollat, Emilie. Lettuce In! And Other Knock-Knock Jokes. Gallo, Tina. 2011. (Little Simon Sillies Ser.). (ENG.). 20p. (J). (gr. -1-1). 5.99 *(978-1-4424-1404-4(9)*, Little Simon) Little Simon.

—The Please & Thank You Book. Hazen, Barbara Shook. 2009. (Little Golden Book Ser.). (ENG.). 24p. (J). (gr. -1-2). 3.99 *(978-0-375-84758-5(8)*, Golden Bks.) Random Hse. Children's Bks.

Choltus, Rebekah L. Joe's Room. Choltus, Rebekah L. 32p. (J). pap. 14.95 *(978-1-932560-40-4(8)*, Llumina Pr.) Aeon Publishing Inc.

Chomiak, Joseph, jt. illus. see Tremlin, Nathan.

Chomphootung, Rassamee. Catbird? Kundiger, Donovan & Kundiger, Marion. 2013. (ENG.). 32p. pap. 9.25 *(978-0-615-82932-6(5))* Fresh Breeze Publishing.

Chong, Luther, photos by. Counting Petals: Using Flowers of Hawaii. Whitman, Nancy C. 2009. 31p. (J). *(978-1-4363-8562-6(8))* Xlibris Corp.

Choo, Brian. The Big Picture Book. Long, John. 2005. (ENG.). 48p. (J). (gr. 4-7). 24.99 *(978-1-74114-328-7(4))* Allen & Unwin AUS. Dist: Independent Pubs. Group.

Choquette, Gabriel. Max & Voltaire Getting to Know You. Bail, Mina Mauerstein. 2015. 66p. (J). pap. 16.95 ***(978-1-59095-151-4(4))*** TotalRecall Pubns.

Chorao, Kay. All the Seasons of the Year. Rose, Deborah Lee. 2010. (ENG.). 32p. (J). (gr. -1-3). 16.95 *(978-0-8109-8395-3(8)*, Abrams Bks. for Young Readers) Abrams.

—I Could Eat You Up! Harper, Jo. 2007. (ENG.). 32p. (J). (gr. -1-3). 16.95 *(978-0-8234-1733-9(6))* Holiday Hse., Inc.

—It's Time to Sleep, It's Time to Dream. Adler, David A. 2009. (ENG.). 32p. (J). (gr. -1-k). 16.95 *(978-0-8234-1924-1(X))* Holiday Hse., Inc.

—Time for Bed, Baby Ted. Sartell, Debra. 2010. (ENG.). 32p. (J). (gr. -1). 16.95 *(978-0-8234-1968-5(1))* Holiday Hse., Inc.

Chorao, Kay. Baby's Lap Book. Chorao, Kay. ed. 2004. (ENG.). 64p. (J). (gr. -1 — 1). 18.99 *(978-0-525-47330-5(0)*, Dutton Juvenile) Penguin Publishing Group.

—D Is for Drums: A Colonial Williamsburg ABC. Chorao, Kay. 2006. 30p. (J). (gr. k-4). reprint ed. 17.00 *(978-1-4223-5240-3(4))* DIANE Publishing Co.

—Ed & Kip. Chorao, Kay. (I Like to Read(r) Ser.). (ENG.). (J). (gr. -1-3). 2015. 24p. 6.99 *(978-0-8234-3398-8(6))*; 2014. 32p. 14.95 *(978-0-8234-2903-5(2))* Holiday Hse., Inc.

—Rhymes Round the World. Chorao, Kay. 2009. (ENG.). 40p. (J). (gr. -1-k). 17.99 *(978-0-525-47875-1(2)*, Dutton Juvenile) Penguin Publishing Group.

Chou, Joey. B. Bear & Lolly: Off to School. Livingston, A. A. 2014. (ENG.). 32p. (J). (gr. -1-3). 15.99 *(978-0-06-219788-7(6))* HarperCollins Pubs.

—B. Bear & Lolly: Catch That Cookie! Livingston, A. A. 2015. (ENG.). 32p. (J). (gr. -1-3). 15.99 *(978-0-06-219791-7(6))* HarperCollins Pubs.

—Betsy B's Big Blue Bouncing Bubble. Williams, Dawn. 2007. 56p. (J). (gr. -1-3). 15.00 *(978-0-9770783-3-2(7))* SunriseHouse Pubs.

—Cyril T. Centipede Looks for New Shoes, 1. Williams, Dawn. 2006. 48p. (J). (gr. -1-3). 15.00 *(978-0-9770783-0-1(2))* SunriseHouse Pubs.

—Giraffe Rescue Company. Sagerman, Evan. 2016. (J). *(978-1-4424-1366-5(2))* Simon & Schuster Children's Publishing.

—How Hooper the Hyaena Lost His Laugh. Williams, Dawn. 2008. 56p. (J). (gr. -1-3). 15.00 *(978-0-9770783-4-9(5))* SunriseHouse Pubs.

Chou, Joey. I'm a Ballerina! Fliess, Sue. 2015. (Little Golden Book Ser.). (ENG.). 24p. (J). (-k). 4.99 ***(978-0-553-49758-8(8)***, Golden Bks.) Random Hse. Children's Bks.

Chou, Joey. It's a Small World. Disney Book Group Staff et al. 2011. (ENG.). 32p. (J). (gr. -1 — 1). 16.99 *(978-1-4231-4689-6(1))* Disney Pr.

—Say What? DiTerlizzi, Angela. 2011. (ENG.). 32p. (J). (gr. -1-k). 15.99 *(978-1-4169-8694-2(4)*, Beach Lane Bks.) Beach Lane Bks.

Chou, Joey. Thanksgiving Activity Book. Jones, Karl. 2015. (ENG.). 16p. (J). (gr. 3-7). 9.99 ***(978-0-8431-8296-5(2)***, Price Stern Sloan) Penguin Publishing Group.

Chou, Joey. Very Little Venus & the Very Friendly Fly. Williams, Dawn. 2007. 48p. (J). 15.00 *(978-0-9770783-2-5(9))* SunriseHouse Pubs.

—Winston J. Worm Hunts for a New Name. Williams, Dawn. 2010. 52p. (J). 15.00 *(978-0-9770783-5-6(3))* SunriseHouse Pubs.

Chou, Joey. Crazy by the Letters. Chou, Joey. 2006. 15.99 *(978-0-9788670-0-3(9))* Choo Choo Clan.

Chow, Candice, jt. illus. see Lee, Jenn Manley.

Chris, Healey. Jackie's Got Game! A Story about Diabetes. Steinberg, Howard. 2005. (J). 9.99 *(978-0-9777463-0-9(5))* dLife - For Your Diabetes Life.

Chris, Wright. The Legend of Skylar Swift, the Fastest Boy on Earth. Patterson, Eric. 2010. 122p. pap. 6.95 *(978-1-935105-49-7(3))* Avid Readers Publishing Group.

Chrisagis, Shawn. Who & What Am I? Good News Gang. Chrisagis, Brian. 2006. 24p. (J). 9.99 *(978-1-59958-014-2(4))* Journey Stone Creations, LLC.

Christe, Moreno. The Wild Cats of Piran. Young, Scott Alexander. 2014. (Young Europe Bks.). (ENG.). 136p. (J). (gr. 5). pap. 10.99 *(978-0-9900043-0-1(9))* New Europe Bks.

Christelow, Eileen. The Flimflam Man. Beard, Darleen Bailey. 2003. (ENG.). 96p. (J). (gr. 2-5). per. 10.99 *(978-0-374-42345-2(8)*, Sunburst) Farrar, Straus & Giroux.

Christelow, Eileen. Five Little Monkeys Bake a Birthday Cake. Christelow, Eileen. 2004. (Five Little Monkeys Story Ser.). (ENG.). 28p. (J). (gr. -1 — 1). bds. 6.99 *(978-0-618-46264-3(3))* Houghton Mifflin Harcourt Publishing Co.

—Vote! Christelow, Eileen. 2004. 48p. (J). (gr. 1-5). 47.60 *(978-0-618-51723-7(5)*, Clarion Bks.) Houghton Mifflin Harcourt Trade & Reference Pubs.

Christensen, Andrew. Canals & Dams: Investigate Feats of Engineering with 25 Projects. Latham, Donna. 2013. (Build It Yourself Ser.). (ENG.). 128p. (J). (gr. 3-7). 21.95 *(978-1-61930-169-6(5))*; pap. 16.95 *(978-1-61930-165-8(2))* Nomad Pr.

—Skyscrapers: Investigate Feats of Engineering with 25 Projects. Latham, Donna. 2013. (Build It Yourself Ser.). (ENG.). 128p. (J). (gr. 3-7). 21.95 *(978-1-61930-189-4(X))*; pap. 16.95 *(978-1-61930-193-1(8))* Nomad Pr.

Christensen, Bonnie. Breaking into Print: Before & after the Invention of the Printing Press. Krensky, Stephen. 2003. 30p. (J). (gr. 3-8). reprint ed. 18.00 *(978-0-7567-6843-0(8))* DIANE Publishing Co.

—Ida B. Wells: Let the Truth Be Told. Myers, Walter Dean. 40p. (J). (gr. -1-3). 2015. (ENG.). pap. 6.99 *(978-0-06-054468-3(6))*; 2008. (ENG.). 16.99 *(978-0-06-027705-5(X))*; 2008. lib. bdg. 17.89 *(978-0-06-027706-2(8))* HarperCollins Pubs. (Amistad).

—Moon over Tennessee: A Boy's Civil War Journal. Crist-Evans, Craig. 2003. (ENG.). 64p. (J). (gr. 5-7). pap. 8.95 *(978-0-618-31107-1(6))* Houghton Mifflin Harcourt Publishing Co.

—Pompeii: Lost & Found. Osborne, Mary Pope. 2006. (ENG.). 40p. (J). (gr. -1-2). 16.95 *(978-0-375-82889-8(3)*, Knopf Bks. for Young Readers) Random Hse. Children's Bks.

Christensen, Bonnie. Django: World's Greatest Jazz Guitarist. Christensen, Bonnie. 2011. (ENG.). 32p. (J). (gr. k-4). pap. 8.99 *(978-1-59643-696-1(4))* Roaring Brook Pr.

—Elvis: The Story of the Rock & Roll King. Christensen, Bonnie. 2015. (ENG.). 32p. (J). (gr. 1-4). 17.99 *(978-0-8050-9447-3(4)*, Holt, Henry & Co. Bks. For Young Readers) Holt, Henry & Co.

—Fabulous! A Portrait of Andy Warhol. Christensen, Bonnie. 2011. (ENG.). 40p. (J). (gr. 1-4). 16.99 *(978-0-8050-8753-6(2)*, Holt, Henry & Co. Bks. For Young Readers) Holt, Henry & Co.

—Plant a Little Seed. Christensen, Bonnie. 2012. (ENG.). 32p. (J). (gr. -1-2). 17.99 *(978-1-59643-550-6(X))* Roaring Brook Pr.

—A Single Pebble: A Story of the Silk Road. Christensen, Bonnie. 2013. (ENG.). 40p. (J). (gr. -1-2). 17.99 *(978-1-59643-715-9(4))* Roaring Brook Pr.

—Woody Guthrie: Poet of the People. Christensen, Bonnie. 2009. (ENG.). 32p. (J). (gr. -1-2). pap. 7.99 *(978-0-553-11203-0(1)*, Dragonfly Bks.) Random Hse. Children's Bks.

Christensen, D. J. Casey's Hoof Prints. McCormic, Maxine Griffith. 2006. (ENG.). 72p. (J). pap. 14.95 *(978-1-59299-217-1(X))* Inkwater Pr.

Christensen, David. All about Real Bears. Williams, Rozanne Lanczak. 2006. (Learn to Write Ser.). 8p. (J). (gr. k-2). pap. 3.49 *(978-1-59198-288-3(X)*, 6182) Creative Teaching Pr., Inc.

—All about Real Bears. Williams, Rozanne Lanczak. Maio, Barbara & Faulkner, Stacey, eds. 2006. (J). per. 6.99 *(978-1-59198-339-2(8))* Creative Teaching Pr., Inc.

Christensen, David & Leary, Catherine. Fairy Tale Rock. Williams, Rozanne Lanczak. 2005. (Reading for Fluency Ser.). 16p. (J). pap. 3.49 *(978-1-59198-153-4(0)*, 4252) Creative Teaching Pr., Inc.

Christensen, Donald. The Macaroon Moon: A Book of Poems & Rhymes for Children. Haan, Wanda. 2004. 32p. (J). 17.95 *(978-0-913337-51-6(X))* Southfarm Pr.

Christensen, Donna. Mommy, May I Hug the Fish?, 1 vol. Bowman, Crystal. (I Can Read! Ser.).Tr. of Mamá, Puedo Abrazar Al Pez?. (ENG.). 32p. (J). 2007. (gr. -1-1). pap. 3.99 *(978-0-310-71468-2(0))*; 2009. pap. 3.99 *(978-0-310-71868-0(6))* Zonderkidz.

Christenson, Emme Jo, jt. illus. see Christenson, Lisa.

Christenson, Erik. Fair Game, 1 vol. Shaskan, Trisha Speed. 2008. (Read-It! Readers: Character Education Ser.). (ENG.). 32p. (gr. k-2). 19.99 *(978-1-4048-4233-5(0)*, Easy Readers) Picture Window Bks.

Christenson, Lisa. Harley Hippo & the Crane Game. Christenson, Lisa. 2005. (J). per. *(978-0-9725311-0-8(6))* Pickled Eggs Pr.

Christenson, Lisa & Christenson, Emme Jo. Seasons on the Sofa. Christenson, Lisa & Christenson, Emme Jo. 2006. per. *(978-0-9725311-3-9(0))* Pickled Eggs Pr.

—Who Ate the Moon? Christenson, Lisa & Christenson, Emme Jo. 2006. (J). per. *(978-0-9725311-2-2(2))* Pickled Eggs Pr.

Christenson, Maren. Jingle Jangle Jungle Jeepers. Dutson, Shelly. 2009. 24p. pap. 12.50 *(978-1-4490-1061-4(X))* AuthorHouse.

Christian, Heather. Bible Awareness Series, 6 vols. Widmer, Becky. Date not set. (J). (gr. -1-18). 9.95 *(978-1-888537-00-0(0))* Publisher Plus.

Christiana, David. Fairy Haven & the Quest for the Wand. Levine, Gail Carson. 2007. 191p. (J). *(978-1-4287-6391-3(0))* Disney Pr.

—Gold & Silver, Silver & Gold: Tales of Hidden Treasure. Schwartz, Alvin. 2009. (ENG.). 144p. (J). (gr. 4-8). pap. 15.99 *(978-0-374-42582-1(5)*, Farrar, Straus & Giroux (BYR)) Farrar, Straus & Giroux.

—El Pais de Nunca Jamas y el Secreto de la Hadas. Levine, Gail Carson. Pombo, Juan Manuel, tr. 2005. (SPA.). 239p. (J). *(978-958-04-8969-6(6))* Norma S.A.

Christiane. White Gloves & Party Manners. Young, Mariabelle & Buchwald, Ann. 2012. (ENG.). 65p. (J). (gr. 4-7). pap. 14.95 *(978-0-88331-000-7(7))* Luce, Robert B. Pubs.

Christiansen, Lee. Eagle Boy: A Pacific Northwest Native Tale. Vaughan, Richard Lee. 2008. (ENG.). 32p. (J). (gr. -1-3). pap. 10.99 *(978-1-57061-592-4(6))* Sasquatch Bks.

—On This Spot: An Expedition Back Through Time. Goodman, Susan E. & Goodman, Susan. 2004. (ENG.). 32p. (J). (gr. k-5). 17.99 *(978-0-688-16913-8(9)*, Greenwillow Bks.) HarperCollins Pubs.

Christie, Gregory, jt. illus. see Christie, R.

Christie, Gregory R. The Palm of My Heart: Poetry by African American Children. Adedjouma, Davida. 2013. (ENG.). 32p. (J). (gr. -1-18). pap. 9.95 *(978-1-880000-76-2(8))* Lee & Low Bks., Inc.

—Richard Wright y el Carne de Biblioteca. Miller, William. 2003. (SPA.). (J). 32p. 16.95 *(978-1-58430-180-6(5))*; pap. 6.95 *(978-1-58430-181-3(3))* Lee & Low Bks., Inc.

Christie, R. Love to Langston, 1 vol. Medina, Tony. 2005. (ENG.). 40p. (J). (gr. 1-7). pap. 10.95 *(978-1-58430-283-4(6))* Lee & Low Bks., Inc.

Christie, R. & Christie, Gregory. A Chance to Shine. Seskin, Steve & Shamblin, Allen. 2006. (ENG.). 30p. (J). (gr. -1-2). 16.99 *(978-1-58246-167-0(8)*, Tricycle Pr.) Ten Speed Pr.

Christie, R. Gregory. Almost Zero: A Dyamonde Daniel Book. Grimes, Nikki. 2010. (Dyamonde Daniel Book Ser.: 3). (ENG.). 128p. (J). (gr. 2-4). 10.99 *(978-0-399-25177-1(4)*, Putnam Juvenile) Penguin Publishing Group.

—Bad News for Outlaws: The Remarkable Life of Bass Reeves, Deputy U. S. Marshall. Nelson, Vaunda Micheaux. 2009. (Exceptional Social Studies Titles for Intermediate Grades). (ENG.). 40p. (J). (gr. 3-6). lib. bdg. 17.95 *(978-0-8225-6764-6(4))* Lerner Publishing Group.

—The Book Itch: Freedom, Truth & Harlem's Greatest Bookstore. Nelson, Vaunda Micheaux. 2015. (ENG.). 32p. (J). (gr. 2-4). lib. bdg. 17.99 *(978-0-7613-3943-4(4)*, Carolrhoda Bks.) Lerner Publishing Group.

—Brothers in Hope: The Story of the Lost Boys of Sudan, 1 vol. Williams, Mary. 2013. (ENG.). 40p. (J). 18.95 *(978-1-58430-232-2(1))* Lee & Low Bks., Inc.

—The Champ. Bolden, Tonya. 2007. (gr. k-3). 17.00 *(978-0-7569-7940-9(4))* Perfection Learning Corp.

—The Champ: The Story of Muhammad Ali. Bolden, Tonya. 2007. (ENG.). 40p. (J). (gr. 1-4). pap. 6.99 *(978-0-440-41782-8(1)*, Dragonfly Bks.) Random Hse. Children's Bks.

—Halfway to Perfect: A Dyamonde Daniel Book, 4 vols. Grimes, Nikki. 2012. (Dyamonde Daniel Book Ser.: 4). (ENG.). 128p. (J). (gr. 2-4). 10.99 *(978-0-399-25178-8(2)*, Putnam Juvenile) Penguin Publishing Group.

—Jazz Baby. Wheeler, Lisa. 2007. (ENG.). 40p. (J). (gr. -1-3). 16.99 *(978-0-15-202522-9(7))* Houghton Mifflin Harcourt Publishing Co.

—Keep Climbing, Girls. Richards, Beah E. 2006. (ENG.). 32p. (J). (gr. -1-3). 17.99 *(978-1-4169-0264-5(3)*, Simon & Schuster Bks. For Young Readers) Simon & Schuster Bks. For Young Readers.

—Love to Langston. Medina, Tony. 2006. (J). (gr. 1-7). 17.10 *(978-0-7569-7016-1(4))* Perfection Learning Corp.

—Make Way for Dyamonde Daniel. Grimes, Nikki. (Dyamonde Daniel Book Ser.: 1). (ENG.). (J). (gr. 2-4). 2010. 112p. pap. 4.99 *(978-0-14-241555-9(3)*, Puffin); 2009. 96p. 10.99 *(978-0-399-25175-7(8)*, Putnam Juvenile) Penguin Publishing Group.

—No Crystal Stair: A Documentary Novel of the Life & Work of Lewis Michaux, Harlem Bookseller. Nelson, Vaunda Micheaux. 2012. (Carolrhoda YA Ser.). (ENG.). 192p. (YA). (gr. 7-12). 17.95 *(978-0-7613-6169-5(3)*, Carolrhoda LAB) Lerner Publishing Group.

—Rich. Grimes, Nikki. 2009. (Dyamonde Daniel Book Ser.: 2). (ENG.). 112p. (J). (gr. 2-4). 10.99 *(978-0-399-25176-4(6)*, Putnam Juvenile) Penguin Publishing Group.

—Roots & Blues: A Celebration. Adoff, Arnold. 2011. (ENG.). 96p. (J). (gr. 5-7). 17.99 *(978-0-547-23554-7(2))* Houghton Mifflin Harcourt Publishing Co.

—Sugar Hill: Harlem's Historic Neighborhood. Weatherford, Carole Boston. 2014. (ENG.). 32p. (J). (gr. k-3). 16.99 *(978-0-8075-7650-2(6))* Whitman, Albert & Co.

Christie, R. Gregory, et al. When Thunder Comes: Poems for Civil Rights Leaders. Lewis, J. Patrick. 2012. (ENG.). 44p. (J). (gr. -1-1). 16.99 *(978-1-4521-0119-4(1))* Chronicle Bks. LLC.

Christine, Grove. My Mom Has a Job. Snead, Kathi. 2004. (J). *(978-0-9747385-1-2(4))* City of Manassas Department of Social Services.

Christman, Therese. Cecil Centipede's Career. Ramsay, Betsy. 2005. 25p. (J). per. 19.99 *(978-1-4208-7870-7(0))* AuthorHouse.

Christmas, Dozay. Loon Rock. Trottier, Maxine. Sylliboy, Helen, tr. ed. (ENG.). 22p. (J). (gr. k-2). pap. *(978-0-920336-84-7(1))* Cape Breton Univ. Pr.

Christodoulou, Jean. The Night Before Christmas in Africa, 1 vol. Foster, Jesse et al. 2010. (Night Before Christmas Ser.). (ENG.). 32p. (J). (gr. k-3). 16.99 *(978-1-58980-847-8(9))* Pelican Publishing Co., Inc.

Christoph, James. Pingpong Perry Experiences How a Book Is Made, 1 vol. Donovan, Sandy. 2010. (In the Library). (ENG.). 24p. (gr. k-4). lib. bdg. 25.99 *(978-1-4048-5759-9(1)*, Nonfiction Picture Bks.) Picture Window Bks.

Christoph, Jamey. Cursive Writing: Around the World in 26 Letters. Flash Kids Editors. 2012. (ENG.). 112p. (J). (gr. 2-4). pap. 5.95 *(978-1-4114-6345-5(5)*, Spark Publishing Group) Sterling Publishing Co., Inc.

—Diggin' Dirt: Science Adventures with Kitanai the Origami Dog, 1 vol. Troupe, Thomas Kingsley. 2013. (Origami Science Adventures Ser.). (ENG.). 24p. (gr. 3-4). pap. 5.95 *(978-1-4048-8066-5(6))*; lib. bdg. 26.65 *(978-1-4048-7969-0(2))* Picture Window Bks. (Nonfiction Picture Bks.).

—Glowing with Electricity: Science Adventures with Glenda the Origami Firefly, 1 vol. Troupe, Thomas Kingsley. 2014. (Origami Science Adventures Ser.). (ENG.). 24p. (gr. 3-4). lib. bdg. 26.65 *(978-1-4795-2189-0(2))* Picture Window Bks.

—Gordon Parks: How the Photographer Captured Black & White America. Weatherford, Carole Boston. 2015. (ENG.). 32p. (J). (gr. k-3). 16.99 *(978-0-8075-3017-7(4))* Whitman, Albert & Co.

—Kitanai & Cavity Croc Brush Their Teeth. Troupe, Thomas Kingsley. 2015. (Kitanai's Healthy Habits Ser.). (ENG.). 24p. (gr. k-2). lib. bdg. 25.99 *(978-1-4795-6080-6(4))* Picture Window Bks.

—Kitanai & Filthy Flamingo Wash Up. Troupe, Thomas Kingsley. 2015. (Kitanai's Healthy Habits Ser.). (ENG.). 24p. (gr. k-2). lib. bdg. 25.99 *(978-1-4795-6081-3(2))* Picture Window Bks.

—Kitanai & Hungry Hare Eat Healthfully. Troupe, Thomas Kingsley. 2015. (Kitanai's Healthy Habits Ser.). (ENG.). 24p. (gr. k-2). pap. 8.95 *(978-1-4795-6114-8(2))* Picture Window Bks.

Christoph, Jamey. Kitanai & Lazy Lizard Get Fit. Troupe, Thomas Kingsley. 2015. (Kitanai's Healthy Habits Ser.). (ENG.). 24p. (gr. k-2). lib. bdg. 25.99 ***(978-1-4795-6083-7(9))*** Picture Window Bks.

—Kitanai's Healthy Habits. Troupe, Thomas Kingsley. 2015. (Kitanai's Healthy Habits Ser.). (ENG.). 24p. (gr. k-2). lib. bdg. 103.96 ***(978-1-4795-6255-8(6))*** Picture Window Bks.

Christoph, Jamey. Let's Rock! Science Adventures with Rudie the Origami Dinosaur, 1 vol. Braun, Eric. 2013. (Origami Science Adventures Ser.). (ENG.). 24p. (gr. 3-4). pap. 5.95 *(978-1-4048-8068-9(2))*; lib. bdg. 26.65 *(978-1-4048-7971-3(4))* Picture Window Bks. (Nonfiction Picture Bks.).

—Lookin' for Light: Science Adventures with Manny the Origami Moth, 1 vol. Braun, Eric. 2014. (Origami Science Adventures Ser.). (ENG.). 24p. (gr. 3-4). lib. bdg. 26.65 *(978-1-4795-2186-9(8))* Picture Window Bks.

—Magnet Power! Science Adventures with MAG-3000 the Origami Robot, 1 vol. Troupe, Thomas Kingsley. 2013. (Origami Science Adventures Ser.). (ENG.). 24p. (gr. 3-4). pap. 5.95 *(978-1-4048-8070-2(4))*; lib. bdg. 26.65 *(978-1-4048-7972-0(2))* Picture Window Bks. (Nonfiction Picture Bks.).

—Origami Science Adventures. Troupe, Thomas Kingsley & Braun, Eric. 2013. (Origami Science Adventures Ser.). (ENG.). 24p. (gr. 3-4). pap. 23.80 *(978-1-4048-8074-0(7))*; lib. bdg. 106.60 *(978-1-4048-7973-7(0))* Picture Window Bks. (Nonfiction Picture Bks.).

—Origami Science Adventures, 1 vol. Braun, Eric & Troupe, Thomas Kingsley. 2014. (Origami Science Adventures Ser.). (ENG.). 24p. (gr. 3-4). lib. bdg. 106.60 *(978-1-4795-3365-7(3))* Picture Window Bks.

—Plant Parts Smarts: Science Adventures with Charlie the Origami Bee, 1 vol. Braun, Eric. 2013. (Origami Science Adventures Ser.). (ENG.). 24p. (gr. 3-4). pap. 5.95 *(978-1-4048-8072-6(0))*; lib. bdg. 26.65 *(978-1-4048-7970-6(6))* Picture Window Bks. (Nonfiction Picture Bks.).

—Simply Sound: Science Adventures with Jasper the Origami Bat, 1 vol. Braun, Eric. 2014. (Origami Science Adventures Ser.). (ENG.). 24p. (gr. 3-4). lib. bdg. 26.65 *(978-1-4795-2187-6(6))* Picture Window Bks.

—Wild Weather: Science Adventures with Sonny the Origami Bird, 1 vol. Troupe, Thomas Kingsley. 2014. (Origami Science Adventures Ser.). (ENG.). 24p. (gr. 3-4). lib. bdg. 26.65 *(978-1-4795-2188-3(4))* Picture Window Bks.

Christopher, Danny. A Children's Guide to Arctic Birds, 1 vol. Pelletier, Mia. 2014. (ENG.). 32p. (J). (gr. k-2). 16.95 *(978-1-927095-67-6(0))* Inhabit Media Inc. CAN. Dist: Independent Pubs. Group.

Christopher, Jennifer, jt. illus. see Christopher, Marie.

Christopher, Lawrence. The Tickle Fingers: Where Is Pinky? Christopher, Lawrence. 2006. (ENG.). 24p. (J). (gr. -1-18). 9.95 *(978-0-9712278-3-5(7))* MF Unlimited.

Christopher, Marie & Christopher, Jennifer. What If a Fork Was a Spoon. Christopher, Jennifer R. 2006. (ENG.). 29p. (J). (gr. -1-3). per. 19.99 *(978-1-4257-0847-4(1))* Xlibris Corp.

Christopher, Wright. Something Lurking in the Bell Tower. Patterson, Eric. 2007. 99p. (J). pap. 6.95 *(978-0-9797106-1-2(6))* Avid Readers Publishing Group.

Christophersen, Christine. Kakadu Calling: Stories for Kids. Christophersen, Jane Garlil. 2007. (ENG.). 64p. (J). (gr. 2-7). pap. 9.95 *(978-1-921248-00-9(9))* Magabala Bks. AUS. Dist: Independent Pubs. Group.

Christy, Jana. And Then Comes Christmas. Brenner, Tom. 2014. (ENG.). 32p. (J). (gr. -1-3). 15.99 *(978-0-7636-5342-2(X))* Candlewick Pr.

—Around the Neighborhood: A Counting Lullaby, 0 vols. Thomson, Sarah L. 2012. (ENG.). 32p. (J). (gr. -1-3). 16.99 *(978-0-7614-6164-7(7)*, 9780761461647, Amazon Children's Publishing) Amazon Publishing.

—A Dandelion Wish. Thorpe, Kiki. 2013. (Stepping Stone Book Series: No. 3). (ENG.). 128p. (J). (gr. 1-4). 5.99 *(978-0-7364-2796-8(1)*, RH/Disney); lib. bdg. 12.99 *(978-0-7364-8139-7(7)*, Random Hse. Bks. for Young Readers) Random Hse. Children's Bks.

—A Dandelion Wish. Thorpe, Kiki. ed. 2013. (Never Girls Ser.: 3). lib. bdg. 16.00 *(978-0-606-32199-0(3)*, Turtleback) Turtleback Bks.

—From the Mist. Thorpe, Kiki. 2013. (Stepping Stone Book Series: No. 4). (ENG.). 128p. (J). (gr. 1-4). 5.99 *(978-0-7364-2797-5(X)*, RH/Disney) Random Hse. Children's Bks.

—Happy Birthday, Tree! A Tu B'Shevat Story. Rosenberg, Madelyn. 2012. (ENG.). 24p. (J). (gr. -1-2). 15.99 *(978-0-8075-3151-8(0))* Whitman, Albert & Co.

—Happy, Sad, Silly, Mad. Seven, John. 2012. (ENG.). 26p. (J). (-k). bds. 6.99 *(978-1-4494-2229-5(2))* Andrews McMeel Publishing.

—In a Blink. Thorpe, Kiki. ed. 2013. (Never Girls Ser.: No. 1). lib. bdg. 16.00 *(978-0-606-26977-3(0)*, Turtleback) Turtleback Bks.

—My Never Land Journal (Disney: the Never Girls) RH Disney Staff & Depken, Kristen L. 2014. (ENG.). 128p. (J). (gr. 1-4). 12.99 *(978-0-553-49685-7(9)*, RH/Disney) Random Hse. Children's Bks.

—Never Girls - In a Blink. RH Disney Staff. 2015. (Stepping Stone Book(TM) Ser.). (ENG.). 256p. (J). (gr. 1-4). 9.99 *(978-0-7364-3432-4(1)*, RH/Disney) Random Hse. Children's Bks.

—The Ocean Story, 1 vol. Seven, John. 2011. (Fiction Picture Bks.). (ENG.). 32p. (gr. k-2). lib. bdg. 22.65 *(978-1-4048-6785-7(6)*, Fiction Picture Bks.) Picture Window Bks.

Christy, Jana. On the Trail. Thorpe, Kiki. 2015. (Never Girls Ser.: No. 10). (ENG.). 128p. (J). (gr. 1-4). 5.99 ***(978-0-7364-3306-8(6)***, RH/Disney) Random Hse. Children's Bks.

Christy, Jana. Penelope Popper, Book Doctor. Buzzeo, Toni. 2011. 32p. (J). 17.95 *(978-1-60213-054-8(X)*, Upstart Bks.) Highsmith Inc.

—A Pinch of Magic. Thorpe, Kiki. 2014. (Never Girls Ser.: No. 7). (ENG.). 128p. (J). (gr. 1-4). 5.99 *(978-0-7364-3097-5(0))*; lib. bdg. 12.99 *(978-0-7364-8149-6(4))* Random Hse. Children's Bks. (RH/Disney).

—Pixie Puzzles, Games, & More! Posner-Sanchez, Andrea. 2014. (Stepping Stone Book Ser.). (ENG.). 256p. (J). (gr. 1-4). 6.99 *(978-0-7364-3152-1(7)*, Golden/Disney) Random Hse. Children's Bks.

—The Princess & the Pea. Golden Books. 2013. (Little Golden Book Ser.). (ENG.). 24p. (J). (-k). 3.99 *(978-0-307-97951-3(2)*, Golden Bks.) Random Hse. Children's Bks.

—The Smile That Went Around the World (Revised) New Updated Edition. Karst, Patrice. 2014. (ENG.). 22p. (J). 15.95 *(978-0-87516-875-3(2)*, Devorss Pubns.) DeVorss & Co.

—The Space Between. Thorpe, Kiki. ed. 2013. (Never Girls Ser.: No. 2). lib. bdg. 16.00 *(978-0-606-26974-2(6)*, Turtleback) Turtleback Bks.

—Wedding Wings. Thorpe, Kiki. 2014. (Stepping Stone Book Series: No. 5). (ENG.). 128p. (J). (gr. 1-4). 5.99 *(978-0-7364-3077-7(6)*, RH/Disney) Random Hse. Children's Bks.

Christy, Jana. We're Getting a Pet! Fliess, Sue. 2015. (Little Golden Book Ser.). (ENG.). 24p. (J). (-k). 4.99 ***(978-0-385-37554-2(9)***, Golden Bks.) Random Hse. Children's Bks.

Christy, Jana. When the Wind Blows. Sweeney, Linda Booth. 2015. (ENG.). 32p. (J). (gr. -1-k). 16.99 *(978-0-399-16015-8(9)*, Putnam Juvenile) Penguin Publishing Group.

—The Woods Beyond. Thorpe, Kiki. 2014. (Stepping Stone Book(TM) Ser.: No. 6). (ENG.). 128p. (J). (gr. 1-4). 5.99 *(978-0-7364-3096-8(2))*; lib. bdg. 12.99 *(978-0-7364-8148-9(6))* Random Hse. Children's Bks. (RH/Disney).

—The Woods Beyond. Thorpe, Kiki. ed. 2014. (Never Girls Ser.: 6). lib. bdg. 16.00 *(978-0-606-35545-2(6))* Turtleback Bks.

—You Are the Best Medicine. Clark, Julie Aigner. 2010. (ENG.). 32p. (J). (gr. -1-3). 16.99 *(978-0-06-195644-7(9))* HarperCollins Pubs.

—10 Items or Less. Calmenson, Stephanie. 2010. (ENG.). 16p. (J). (gr. -1 — 1). 7.99 *(978-1-4424-0720-6(4)*, Little Simon) Little Simon.

Christy, Jana & Mitchell, Jana Christy. How to Hug, 0 vols. MacDonald, Maryann. 2011. (ENG.). 32p. (J). (gr. -1-3). 16.99 *(978-0-7614-5804-3(2)*, 9780761458043, Amazon Children's Publishing) Amazon Publishing.

Christy, Jana & RH Disney Staff. From the Mist. Thorpe, Kiki & RH Disney Staff. 2013. (Stepping Stone Book(TM) Ser.: Bk. 4). (ENG.). 128p. (J). (gr. 1-4). lib. bdg. 12.99 *(978-0-7364-8140-3(0)*, RH/Disney) Random Hse. Children's Bks.

—In a Blink. Thorpe, Kiki. 2013. (Stepping Stone Book(TM) Ser.: No. 1). (ENG.). 128p. (J). (gr. 1-4). 5.99 *(978-0-7364-2794-4(5)*, RH/Disney) Random Hse. Children's Bks.

—The Never Girls Collection, 4 vols. Thorpe, Kiki. 2014. (ENG.). 640p. (J). (gr. 1-4). 24.96 *(978-0-7364-3184-2(5)*, RH/Disney) Random Hse. Children's Bks.

—The Space Between. Thorpe, Kiki. 2013. (Stepping Stone Book(TM) Ser.: No. 2). (ENG.). 128p. (J). (gr. 1-4). 5.99 *(978-0-7364-2795-1(3)*, RH/Disney) Random Hse. Children's Bks.

Christy, Jana & Zhang, Nancy. On Pins & Needles. Taylor, Chloe. 2013. (Sew Zoey Ser.: 2). (ENG.). 160p. (J). (gr. 3-7). 15.99 *(978-1-4424-7937-1(X))*; pap. 6.99 *(978-1-4424-7936-4(1))* Simon Spotlight. (Simon Spotlight).

—Ready to Wear. Taylor, Chloe. 2013. (Sew Zoey Ser.: 1). (ENG.). 176p. (J). (gr. 3-7). pap. 6.99 *(978-1-4424-7933-3(7)*, Simon Spotlight) Simon Spotlight.

Chronicle Books Staff. The Illustrated Treasury of Fairy Tales. Chronicle Books Staff. Marshall, Rita. 2003. (ENG.). 352p. (J). (gr. 1-3). 29.95 *(978-1-56846-144-1(5))* Creative Co., The.

C

Chronister, Amanda. Claim to Fame. Wallace, Nancy K. 2013. (Abby & the Book Bunch Ser.). 80p. (J). (gr. 2-5). 27.07 *(978-1-61641-912-7(1))* Magic Wagon.

—The Haunted Sleepover. Wallace, Nancy K. 2013. (Abby & the Book Bunch Ser.). 80p. (J). (gr. 2-5). 27.07 *(978-1-61641-913-4(X))* Magic Wagon.

—Movie Mishaps. Wallace, Nancy K. 2013. (Abby & the Book Bunch Ser.). 80p. (J). (gr. 2-5). 27.07 *(978-1-61641-914-1(8))* Magic Wagon.

—The Mystery of the Golden Key. Wallace, Nancy K. 2013. (Abby & the Book Bunch Ser.). 80p. (J). (gr. 2-5). 27.07 *(978-1-61641-915-8(6))* Magic Wagon.

—Out to Lunch. Wallace, Nancy K. 2013. (Abby & the Book Bunch Ser.). 80p. (J). (gr. 2-5). 27.07 *(978-1-61641-916-5(4))* Magic Wagon.

—Presumed Missing. Wallace, Nancy K. 2013. (Abby & the Book Bunch Ser.). 80p. (J). (gr. 2-5). 27.07 *(978-1-61641-917-2(2))* Magic Wagon.

Chronopoulos, Maria. La Marathonienne. Desautels, Denise. 2004. (Poetry Ser.). (FRE.). 36p. (J). (gr. 7). pap. *(978-2-89021-673-0(X))* Diffusion du livre Mirabel (DLM).

Chrustowski, Rick. Higgledy-Piggledy Chicks. Joosse, Barbara M. 2010. 40p. (J). (gr. -1-k). (ENG.). 16.99 *(978-0-06-075042-8(1))*; lib. bdg. 17.89 *(978-0-06-075043-5(X))* HarperCollins Pubs. (Greenwillow Bks.).

Chrustowski, Rick. Bee Dance. Chrustowski, Rick. 2015. (ENG.). 32p. (J). (gr. -1-3). 17.99 *(978-0-8050-9919-5(0),* Holt, Henry & Co. Bks. For Young Readers) Holt, Henry & Co.

Chrystall, Claire. ABC: A Busy Fingers Book. Harris, Sue. 2003. 10p. (J). bds. 10.95 *(978-1-57145-936-7(7),* Silver Dolphin Bks.) Baker & Taylor Publishing Group.

—Shapes. Hunt, Janie. 2003. (Busy Finger Ser.). 10p. (J). bds. 10.95 *(978-1-57145-938-1(3),* Silver Dolphin Bks.) Baker & Taylor Publishing Group.

Chu, April. Ada Byron Lovelace & the Thinking Machine. Wallmark, Laurie. 2015. (ENG.). 40p. (J). (gr. k). 17.99 ***(978-1-939547-20-0(2))*** Creston Bks.

Chu, April. In a Village by the Sea. Van, Muon. 2015. (ENG.). 32p. (J). (gr. -1-5). 16.95 *(978-1-939547-15-6(6))* Creston Bks.

—Summoning the Phoenix: Poems & Prose about Chinese Musical Instruments, 1 vol. Jiang, Emily. 2014. (ENG.). 32p. (J). 18.95 *(978-1-885008-50-3(3))* Lee & Low Bks., Inc.

Chu, Kate & Long, May. Charlotte's Garden. Partin, Charlotte Corry. Bine-Stock, Eve Heidi, ed. 2005. 29p. per. 18.95 *(978-0-9748933-3-4(1))* E & E Publishing.

Chua, Charlene. Julie Black Belt: The Kung Fu Chronicles. Chin, Oliver Clyde. 2008. (ENG.). 36p. (J). (gr. k-1). 15.95 *(978-1-59702-009-1(5))* Immedium.

—Julie Black Belt: the Belt of Fire. Chin, Oliver. 2013. (Julie Black Belt Ser.). (ENG.). 36p. (J). (gr. -1-3). 15.95 *(978-1-59702-079-4(6))* Immedium.

Chullabrahm, T. M. The Kid Who Ate Dog Food. Penner, Evelyn. 2008. 32p. (J). 15.99 *(978-0-9796500-0-0(3))* Peppernut Publishing.

Chun, C. S. Greek & Roman Mythology. Oh, Cirro. 2005. (ENG.). 192p. (J). (gr. 4-7). Vol. 1. pap. 12.95 *(978-981-05-2240-7(1))*; Vol. 2. pap. 12.95 *(978-981-05-2241-4(X))* Youngjin (Singapore) Pte Ltd. SGP. Dist: Independent Pubs. Group.

Chung, Arree. How to Pee: Potty Training for Boys. Spector, Todd. 2015. (ENG.). 40p. (J). (— 1). 12.99 *(978-0-8050-9773-3(2),* Holt, Henry & Co. Bks. For Young Readers) Holt, Henry & Co.

Chung, Arree. Ninja! Chung, Arree. 2014. (ENG.). 40p. (J). (gr. -1-2). 16.99 *(978-0-8050-9911-9(5),* Holt, Henry & Co. Bks. For Young Readers) Holt, Henry & Co.

Chung, Chi. Emily Dickinson. Bolin, Frances Schoonmaker, ed. 2008. (Poetry for Young People Ser.). (ENG.). 48p. (J). (gr. 3). pap. 6.95 *(978-1-4027-5473-9(6))* Sterling Publishing Co., Inc.

—God's Oak Tree. Nolan, Allia Zobel. 2007. 16p. (J). (gr. -1). 12.99 *(978-0-8254-5536-0(7))* Kregel Pubns.

—God's Rainbow. Nolan, Allia Zobel. 2007. 16p. (J). 12.99 *(978-0-8254-5537-7(5))* Kregel Pubns.

—Good Night Sun, Hello Moon. Viola, Karen. 2011. (ENG.). 10p. (J). (gr. -1-k). bds. 10.99 *(978-0-7944-2102-1(4))* Reader's Digest Assn., Inc., The.

—Poetry for Young People: Emily Dickinson. Bolin, Frances Schoonmaker, ed. 2014. (Poetry for Young People Ser.). (ENG.). 48p. (J). (gr. 3). 14.95 *(978-1-4549-1346-7(0))* Sterling Publishing Co., Inc.

—Rick & Rachel Build a Research Report. Lowell Gallion, Sue. 2013. (ENG.). 32p. (J). lib. bdg. 25.27 *(978-1-59953-583-8(1))*; (gr. 2-4). pap. 11.94 *(978-1-60357-557-7(X))* Norwood Hse. Pr.

—When God Tucks in the Day. Nolan, Allia Zobel. 2005. 16p. (J). 12.99 *(978-0-8254-5524-7(3))* Kregel Pubns.

Chung, Haley. Have Fun with Math. Jung, Tori. 2005. (ENG.). 192p. (J). (gr. 4-7). Vol. 1. pap. 12.95 *(978-981-05-2238-4(X))*; Vol. 2. pap. 12.95 *(978-981-05-2239-1(8))* Youngjin (Singapore) Pte Ltd. SGP. Dist: Independent Pubs. Group.

—Math Game 3, Vol. 3. Jung, Tori. 2005. (ENG.). 160p. (gr. 4-7). per. 12.95 *(978-981-05-2768-6(3))* Youngjin (Singapore) Pte Ltd. SGP. Dist: Independent Pubs. Group.

Chung, Ruth. 4,962,571. Eissler, Trevor. 2011. (ENG.). 32p. (J). 20.00 *(978-0-9835558-0-3(X))* June Bks., LLC.

Churbuck, Esther V. Tommy Sweet-Tooth & Little girl Blue. Gates, Josephine Scribner. 2007. 64p. (J). lib. bdg. 59.00 *(978-1-60304-014-3(5))* Dollworks.

Church, Anna & Taylor, Nicole. Hug-A-Bug Travels to Peru. Church, Anna. 2013. 44p. pap. 12.00 *(978-0-9831449-4-6(X))* Mighty Lion Ventures.

Church, Caroline Jayne. Dear Bunny: A Bunny Love Story. Morgan, Michaela & Hinnant, Skip. 2009. (ENG.). (J). (gr. -1-k). 9.95 *(978-0-545-13851-2(5))* Scholastic, Inc.

—La Gallina Hambrienta. Waring, Richard & Jayne, Waring -. 2003. (SPA.). 28p. (J). (gr. k-2). 17.99 *(978-84-261-3339-7(8))* Juventud, Editorial ESP. Dist: Lectorum Pubns., Inc.

—Horsey up & Down: A Book of Opposites. Bernstein, Kel. 2013. (ENG.). 12p. (J). (— 1). bds. 7.99 *(978-0-545-51204-6(2),* Cartwheel Bks.) Scholastic, Inc.

—How Do I Love You? Bauer, Marion Dane. 2009. (ENG.). 26p. (J). (gr. -1-k). bds. 8.99 *(978-0-545-07270-0(0),* Cartwheel Bks.) Scholastic, Inc.

—I Love You Through & Through. Rossetti-Shustak, Bernadette. 2005. (ENG.). 24p. (J). (gr. k — 1). bds. 8.95 *(978-0-439-67363-1(1),* Cartwheel Bks.) Scholastic, Inc.

—I Love You Through & Through: Board Book & Plush. Rossetti-Shustak, Bernadette. 2014. (ENG.). 24p. (J). (— 1). 14.99 *(978-0-545-64792-2(4),* Cartwheel Bks.) Scholastic, Inc.

—I Love You Through & Through (Te Quiero, Yo Te Quiero) Rossetti-Shustak, Bernadette. ed. 2013. (ENG & SPA.). 24p. (J). (— 1). bds. 8.95 *(978-0-545-58416-6(7))* Scholastic, Inc.

—A Kiss for You. Holub, Joan. 2011. (ENG.). 14p. (J). (gr. -1 — 1). bds. 8.99 *(978-0-545-34968-0(0),* Cartwheel Bks.) Scholastic, Inc.

—The More We Get Together. Davis, Jimmie. 2011. (ENG.). 12p. (J). (— 1). bds. 6.99 *(978-0-545-28146-1(6),* Cartwheel Bks.) Scholastic, Inc.

—Rain, Rain, Go Away. 2013. (ENG.). 12p. (J). (— 1). bds. 6.99 *(978-0-545-48542-5(8),* Cartwheel Bks.) Scholastic, Inc.

—Snuggle up, Little Penguin! Randall, Ronne. 2003. (Little Friends Ser.). 14p. (J). 12.95 *(978-1-57145-919-0(7),* Silver Dolphin Bks.) Baker & Taylor Publishing Group.

—Thank You Prayer. Page, Josephine. 2005. (ENG.). 24p. (J). (gr. -1-k). 8.99 *(978-0-439-68099-8(9),* Cartwheel Bks.) Scholastic, Inc.

—You Are My Sunshine. Davis, Jimmie. 2011. (ENG.). 12p. (J). (gr. k — 1). bds. 6.99 *(978-0-545-07552-7(1),* Cartwheel Bks.) Scholastic, Inc.

Church, Caroline Jayne. Giggle! Church, Caroline Jayne. 2013. (ENG.). 10p. (J). (— 1). bds. 7.99 *(978-0-545-35082-2(4),* Cartwheel Bks.) Scholastic, Inc.

—Goodnight, I Love You. Church, Caroline Jayne. 2012. (ENG.). 20p. (J). (gr. -1-k). bds. 8.99 *(978-0-545-39215-0(2),* Cartwheel Bks.) Scholastic, Inc.

—Here Comes Christmas! Church, Caroline Jayne. 2010. (ENG.). 14p. (J). (gr. k — 1). bds. 7.99 *(978-0-545-11817-0(4),* Cartwheel Bks.) Scholastic, Inc.

—Here Comes Easter! Church, Caroline Jayne. 2010. (ENG.). 14p. (J). (gr. k — 1). bds. 7.99 *(978-0-545-11816-3(6),* Cartwheel Bks.) Scholastic, Inc.

—Here Comes Halloween! Church, Caroline Jayne. 2009. (ENG.). 8p. (J). (gr. k — 1). bds. 7.99 *(978-0-545-11815-6(8),* Cartwheel Bks.) Scholastic, Inc.

—I Am a Big Brother! Church, Caroline Jayne. 2015. (ENG.). 24p. (J). (gr. -1 — 1). 6.99 *(978-0-545-68886-4(8),* Cartwheel Bks.) Scholastic, Inc.

—I Am a Big Sister! Church, Caroline Jayne. 2015. (ENG.). 24p. (J). (gr. -1 — 1). 6.99 *(978-0-545-68898-7(1),* Cartwheel Bks.) Scholastic, Inc.

—I Love You! Church, Caroline Jayne. 2012. (ENG.). 6p. (J). (— 1). 12.99 *(978-0-545-46140-5(5),* Cartwheel Bks.) Scholastic, Inc.

—Let's Get Dressed! Church, Caroline Jayne. 2012. (ENG.). 10p. (J). (gr. -1 — 1). bds. 7.99 *(978-0-545-43637-3(0))* Scholastic, Inc.

—Little Apple Goat. Church, Caroline Jayne. 2007. 28p. (J). (gr. k-3). 16.00 *(978-0-8028-5320-2(X),* Eerdmans Bks For Young Readers) Eerdmans, William B. Publishing Co.

—Ping Pong Pig. Church, Caroline Jayne. 2008. (ENG.). 32p. (J). (gr. -1-1). 16.95 *(978-0-8234-2176-3(7))* Holiday Hse., Inc.

—Potty Time! Church, Caroline Jayne. 2012. (ENG.). 10p. (J). (gr. -1-k). bds. 7.99 *(978-0-545-35080-8(8),* Cartwheel Bks.) Scholastic, Inc.

—Ruff! And the Wonderfully Amazing Busy Day. Church, Caroline Jayne. 2013. (ENG.). 32p. (J). (gr. k-3). 17.99 *(978-0-06-201498-6(6))* HarperCollins Pubs.

—Sweet Child of Mine: A Caroline Jayne Church Treasury. Church, Caroline Jayne. 2014. (ENG.). 26p. (J). (— 1). bds. 8.99 *(978-0-545-64771-7(1),* Cartwheel Bks.) Scholastic, Inc.

—Ten Tiny Toes. Church, Caroline Jayne. 2014. (ENG.). 22p. (J). (— 1). bds. 8.99 *(978-0-545-53601-1(4),* Cartwheel Bks.) Scholastic, Inc.

—Twinkle, Twinkle, Little Star. Church, Caroline Jayne. 2014. (ENG.). 12p. (J). (— 1). bds. 6.99 *(978-0-545-51806-2(7),* Cartwheel Bks.) Scholastic, Inc.

Church, Elizabeth Comfort. The Pancake Stories: Cuentos Del Panqueque. Church, Peggy Pond. Chilton, Noel, tr. 2013. (ENG & SPA.). 96p. (J). 19.95 *(978-0-8263-5387-0(8))* Univ. of New Mexico Pr.

Churchill, Jessica, photos by. Shalamazoo. Shaboo, Joseph R. Date not set. 56p. (J). (gr. 2-5). *(978-0-9700380-0-5(3))* Purple Pig Publishing.

Churilla, Bryan. The Engineer - Konstrukt. Churilla, Bryan. Shepherd, Jeremy. 2009. (ENG.). 128p. (YA). (gr. 7-18). 9.95 *(978-1-932386-54-7(8),* Archaia Entertainment) Boom! Studios.

Chuzzlewit, Abraham R. My Sister Is a Preemie: A Children's Guide to the NICU Experience. Vitterito, Joseph A., 2nd. 2012. 30p. (J). (-18). pap. 15.99 *(978-0-9882940-9-7(5))* Bryson Taylor Publishing.

Chwast, Seymour. Harry's Bath. Linn, Margot. 2005. (I'm Going to Read(r) Ser.: Level 2). (ENG.). 32p. (J). (gr. k-1). pap. 3.95 *(978-1-4027-2100-7(5))* Sterling Publishing Co., Inc.

—My Daddy & Me. Spinelli, Jerry. 2006. (ENG.). 40p. (J). (gr. -1-2). pap. 6.99 *(978-0-553-11303-7(8),* Dragonfly Bks.) Random Hse. Children's Bks.

—Out of the Bag: The Paper Bag Players Book of Plays. Martin, Judith. 2005. 48p. (J). (gr. k-4). reprint ed. pap. 14.00 *(978-0-7567-8530-7(8))* DIANE Publishing Co.

—Shoes, Shoes, Shoes: A Delightful Book of Imaginary Footwear for Coloring, Inspiring, & Dreaming. Chu, Carol. 2014. (ENG.). 128p. (YA). (gr. 7). pap. 12.99 *(978-0-544-30137-5(4),* HMH Books For Young Readers) Houghton Mifflin Harcourt Publishing Co.

Chwast, Seymour. Bobo's Smile. Chwast, Seymour. 2012. (ENG.). 32p. (J). (gr. 1-3). 14.99 *(978-1-56846-221-9(2),* Creative Editions) Creative Co., The.

Chwast, Seymour. Dr. Dolittle. Chwast, Seymour. Lofting, Hugh. 2015. (ENG.). 40p. (J). (gr. 4-7). 18.99 ***(978-1-56846-258-5(1),*** Creative Editions) Creative Co., The.

Chwast, Seymour. Tall City, Wide Country. Chwast, Seymour. 2013. (ENG.). 32p. (J). (gr. -1-k). 15.99 *(978-1-56846-228-8(X),* Creative Editions) Creative Co., The.

Chylak, Jolie Catherine. The Legend of the Angel Wing Shell. Steele, Kathleen Marie. 2009. 20p. pap. 24.95 *(978-1-60749-134-7(6))* America Star Bks.

Ciaffaglione, Sebastian. The Crystal Code, Bk. 4. Newsome, Richard. ed. 2013. (ENG.). 378p. (gr. 2-7). pap. 8.99 *(978-1-922079-03-9(0))* Text Publishing Co. AUS. Dist: Consortium Bk. Sales & Distribution.

—Lone Pine. Warner, Margaret & Brown, Susie. 2012. (ENG.). 32p. (J). (gr. k-2). 22.99 *(978-1-921541-34-6(2))* Little Hare Bks. AUS. Dist: Independent Pubs. Group.

—Lone Pine: First World War Centenary Edition. Warner, Margaret & Brown, Susie. 2014. 32p. (J). 22.99 *(978-1-74297-870-3(3))* Little Hare Bks. AUS. Dist: Independent Pubs. Group.

Ciaravino, Paul. Paul the Pack Rat: Helping Children Learn to Share. Belmore, Vickie J. 2009. (Let's Talk Ser.). (ENG.). 48p. (J). (gr. -1-4). pap. 8.95 *(978-0-88282-307-2(8))* New Horizon Pr. Pubs., Inc.

Ciccarelli, Gary, jt. illus. see Hillam, Corbin.

Ciccarelli, Gary, jt. illus. see Otoshi, Kathryn.

Ciccolini, Michael. The Pasta Family. Ciccolini, Marguerite. I.t. ed. 2010. (ENG.). 46p. pap. 12.00 *(978-1-4563-3686-8(X))* CreateSpace Independent Publishing Platform.

Ciccolini, Michael. The Pasta Family 2: First Day of School! Ciccolini, Michael. I.t. ed. 2010. (ENG.). 36p. pap. 12.00 *(978-1-4564-0222-8(6))* CreateSpace Independent Publishing Platform.

—The Pasta Family 5: Macaroni in Space!!! Ciccolini, Michael. I.t. ed. 2011. (ENG.). 84p. pap. 16.99 *(978-1-4610-4155-9(4))* CreateSpace Independent Publishing Platform.

Cicero, Julian. Al Reves Esta Bien. Luna, Arcadio. 2006. (Castillo de la Lectura Blanca Ser.). (ENG.). 14p. (J). (gr. -1-k). pap. 7.95 *(978-970-20-0841-5(7))* Castillo, Ediciones, S. A. de C. V. MEX. Dist: Macmillan.

—La Risa de los Cocodrilos. Baranda, Maria. 2009. (SPA.). 70p. (J). (gr. 3-6). pap. *(978-968-5389-67-9(5))* El Naranjo, Ediciones.

—Unas Vacaciones Horribles. Jinks, Catherine. rev. ed. 2007. (Castillo de la Lectura Verde Ser.). 88p. (J). (gr. 2-4). pap. 7.95 *(978-970-20-0852-1(2))* Castillo, Ediciones, S. A. de C. V. MEX. Dist: Macmillan.

—Zarabulli: Cantares de Alla y de Aqui. Masera, Mariana. rev. ed. 2006. (Otra Escalera Ser.). (SPA & ENG.). 48p. (J). (gr. k). pap. 10.95 *(978-968-5920-70-4(2))* Castillo, Ediciones, S. A. de C. V. MEX. Dist: Macmillan.

Cichos, Tomek. Bee in the Barn. Wildfong, Tonya. 2012. 22p. (J). 12.95 *(978-0-9860056-0-2(6))* TBSM Publishing.

Ciencin, Scott, et al. Trial by Fire. Salvatore, R. A. 2003. 160p. (YA). (gr. 7-18). pap. 15.95 *(978-1-931484-62-6(7))* CrossGeneration Comics, Inc.

Ciesemier, Kali. I Am Princess X. Priest, Cherie. 2015. (ENG.). 304p. (YA). (gr. 7). 18.99 ***(978-0-545-62085-7(6),*** Levine, Arthur A. Bks.) Scholastic, Inc.

Ciesinka, Izabela. The Adventures of Northern the Moose & a Dragon Named Zeus. Chapman, Karean. 2010. 38p. pap. 12.95 *(978-1-935268-44-4(9))* Halo Publishing International.

Ciesinki, Izabela. Marllow. Johnson, Cheryl. 2007. 27p. (J). 14.95 *(978-0-9785728-4-6(X))* Entry Way Publishing.

Ciesinska, Izabela. Dmitri: The Kind Storyteller Book One of Five. Karandeev, Oleg. 2006. 76p. (YA). per. 15.95 *(978-0-9785728-9-1(0))* Entry Way Publishing.

—Dmitri II: The Kind Storyteller Book Two of Five. Karandeev, Oleg. 2007. 76p. (YA). per. 15.95 *(978-0-9793944-3-0(0))* Entry Way Publishing.

—Doctor Dave's Dragon Tales. Fast, David R. 2007. 160p. (J). per. 13.95 *(978-0-9793944-8-5(1))* Entry Way Publishing.

—Kate & the Family Tree. Bernard, Margaret Mitchell. Duncan, Shirley, ed. 2009. 24p. pap. 14.99 *(978-1-4251-7408-8(6))* Trafford Publishing.

—Look at Me, a Muscian I Want to Be. Chapman, Karean. 2011. 32p. pap. 12.95 *(978-1-935268-75-8(9))* Halo Publishing International.

—Look at Me, a Veterinarian I Want to Be. Chapman, Karean. 2011. 32p. pap. 12.95 *(978-1-935268-76-5(7))* Halo Publishing International.

—Starr Light & the Christmas Story. Warren, G. A. 2009. 32p. (J). 14.95 *(978-1-935268-09-3(0))* Halo Publishing International.

Cimatoribus, Alessandra. Collins Big Cat - Mighty Mountains, Swirling Seas: Lime/Band 11. Bloom, Valerie. 2015. (Collins Big Cat Ser.). (ENG.). 32p. pap. 7.95 ***(978-0-00-759126-8(8))*** HarperCollins Pubs. Ltd. GBR. Dist: Independent Pubs. Group.

Cimatoribus, Alessandra. The Happy Prince, 1 vol. Piumini, Roberto & Wilde, Oscar. 2011. (Storybook Classics Ser.). (ENG.). 32p. (gr. 3-4). lib. bdg. 25.32 *(978-1-4048-6500-6(4),* Fiction Picture Bks.) Picture Window Bks.

—One Night in a Stable. Visconti, Guido. 2004. 32p. (J). 16.00 *(978-0-8028-5279-3(3))* Eerdmans, William B. Publishing Co.

Ciminelli, Matthew Joseph. Where's My Father? Ciminelli, Marilyn Johnson. 2006. (ENG.). 24p. per. 12.99 *(978-1-59926-657-2(1))* Xlibris Corp.

CINAR Animation Staff. Caillou, Spends the Day with Daddy. Pleau-Murissi, Marilyn. 2004. (Clubhouse Usa Ser.). 24p. (J). (gr. -1-18). 3.95 *(978-2-89450-523-6(X))* Éditions Chouette CAN. Dist: Perseus-PGW.

CINAR Corporation Staff. Caillou, What's That Noise. Johnson, Marion. 2004. (Clubhouse Usa Ser.). (ENG.). 24p. (J). pap. 3.95 *(978-2-89450-489-5(6))* Éditions Chouette CAN. Dist: Perseus-PGW.

Cinelli, Lisa. Josefina, the Christmas Cow: A Tale of Hope & Faith. Benson, P. Bryn. 2005. 35p. (J). (gr. -1-3). per. 9.95 *(978-0-929636-47-4(3))* Syren Bk. Co.

Cinelli, Lisa. Peter Fished the Springs of Galilee. Bahamon, Claire. Sampson, Anne, ed. 2015. (ENG.). 32p. (J). pap. 7.99 ***(978-0-9961139-0-8(8))*** Donkey's Quest Pr.

Cioffi, Ben. The Gospel for Children. Piantedosi, John J. 2011. (J). pap. *(978-1-56548-370-5(7))* New City Community Pr.

Cioffi, Dom. Digby & the Lake Monster. I.t. ed. 2006. 36p. (J). per. *(978-0-9745931-0-4(9))* Vermont Bookworks.

Ciraolo, Simona. Hug Me. 2014. (ENG.). 32p. (J). (gr. -1-2). 17.95 *(978-1-909263-49-9(4))* Flying Eye Bks. GBR. Dist: Consortium Bk. Sales & Distribution.

Ciresi-Abremski, M. Kathleen. Buzzy the Vegetarian Vulture. Johnson, Calvin. 2012. 28p. pap. 12.95 *(978-1-61493-109-6(7))* Peppertree Pr., The.

Cis, Valeria. Bubbe's Belated Bat Mitzvah. Pinson, Isabel. 2014. 32p. (J). (gr. -1-3). 7.95 *(978-1-4677-1950-6(1))*; (ENG.). lib. bdg. 17.95 *(978-1-4677-1949-0(8))* Lerner Publishing Group. (Kar-Ben Publishing).

Cis, Valeria. Millie's Chickens. Williams, Brenda. (J). 2015. 40ppp. (gr. -1-4). 8.99 ***(978-1-78285-083-0(X))***; 2014. 40p. 16.99 ***(978-1-78285-082-3(1))*** Barefoot Bks., Inc.

Cis, Valeria. A Tale of Two Seders. Portnoy, Mindy Avra. 2010. (ENG.). 32p. (J). (gr. k-3). pap. 7.95 *(978-0-8225-9931-9(7),* Kar-Ben Publishing) Lerner Publishing Group.

—Under the Sea: Interactive Fun with Reusable Stickers, Fold-Out Play Scene, & Punch-out, Stand-up Figures! Walter Foster Jr. Creative Team. 2015. (Sticker, Punch-Out, & Play! Ser.). (ENG.). 12p. (J). (gr. -1-1). pap. 6.99 *(978-1-63322-001-0(X))* Quarto Publishing Group USA.

Cis, Valeria. The Beeman. Cis, Valeria. Krebs, Laurie. 2008. (ENG.). 40p. (J). (gr. -1-3). 16.99 *(978-1-84686-146-8(2))* Barefoot Bks., Inc.

Cisner, Naftali. Count with Mendel. Cisner, Naftali. 2003. 10p. (J). bds. 5.95 *(978-1-880582-84-8(8),* CWMH) Judaica Pr., Inc., The.

—Get Ready for Shabbos with Mendel. Cisner, Naftali. 2003. 10p. (J). bds. 5.95 *(978-1-880582-03-9(1))* Judaica Pr., Inc., The.

Cisneros, Kevin. Shoelaces: The Secret Art of Fresco Painting. Cisneros, Kevin. Cadney, Mary, ed. collector's I.t. ed. 2004. 120p. (YA). 119.00 *(978-0-9658481-7-6(5))* Belisarian Bks.

Cissna, Kent. Clouds for Breakfast. Eisen, Laura. 2013. 60p. pap. 14.95 *(978-0-9882113-4-6(3))*; pap. 14.95 *(978-0-9882113-7-7(8))* StarryBks.

—Nubes para Desayunar. Eisen, Laura. 2013. 60p. pap. 14.95 *(978-0-9882113-2-2(7))* StarryBks.

Citro, Asia, photos by. The Curious Kid's Science Book: 100+ Creative Hands-On Activities for Ages 4-8. Citro, Asia. 2015. (ENG.). 224p. (gr. -1-3). pap. 21.95 ***(978-1-943147-00-7(0))*** Innovation Pr., The.

Cittadino, Kristen, jt. illus. see Cittadino, Kyle.

Cittadino, Kyle & Cittadino, Kristen. The Sleigh. Russo, Frank M. 2012. 24p. 24.95 *(978-1-4626-6916-5(6))*; pap. 24.95 *(978-1-4626-7662-0(6))* America Star Bks.

Civiello, Emmanuel. A Bit of Madness. Civiello, Emmanuel. Mosdi, Thomas & Civiello. 2005. (ENG.). 200p. pap. 24.95 *(978-0-9753808-9-5(3))* Devil's Due Digital, Inc. - A Checker Digital Co.

Civil War Photographers Staff, photos by. The Brothers' War: Civil War Voices in Verse. Lewis, J. Patrick. 2007. (ENG., 48p. (J). (gr. 5-9). 25.90 *(978-1-4263-0037-0(9),* National Geographic Children's Bks.) National Geographic Society.

Clack, Barbra. Good Night Cowboy. Dromgoole, Glenn. 2006. (ENG.). 24p. (J). (gr. -1-k). 15.95 *(978-1-931721-51-6(3),* 1a919f96-6211-41bc-a0b4-ea4ca94e5e4d) Bright Sky Pr.

—Good Night Little Texan. Dromgoole, Glenn. 2012. (ENG.). 24p. (gr. k-2). 15.95 *(978-1-936474-10-3(7),* 01f21916-8576-42a1-8392-f82dc1606529) Bright Sky Pr.

Clack, Barbra. Good Night Cowgirl. Clack, Barbra. Dromgoole, Glenn. 2006. (ENG.). 24p. (J). (gr. -1-k). 15.95 *(978-1-931721-80-6(7),* 2b775fed-84a0-4c63-9402-a94e6e772dbd) Bright Sky Pr.

Claerhout, Paul. Willy Nilly Volume 1. Brehm, David L. 2013. 94p. (J). pap. 19.95 *(978-0-9860669-0-0(7))* Blue Logic Publishing.

Clamp Staff. Rg Veda, Vol. 2. Furukawa, Haruko, tr. from JPN. rev. ed. 2005. 192p. pap. 14.99 *(978-1-59532-485-6(2),* Tokyopop Adult) TOKYOPOP, Inc.

—Tokyo Babylon, Vol. 6. Yoshimoto, Ray, tr. from JPN. rev. ed. 2005. 176p. pap. 9.99 *(978-1-59532-050-6(4))* TOKYOPOP, Inc.

Clamp Staff. Angelic Layer, 2 vols., Vol. 2. Clamp Staff. Horn, Carl Gustav, ed. 2013. (ENG.). 472p. pap. 19.99 *(978-1-61655-128-5(3))* Dark Horse Comics.

—Cardcaptor Sakura, 4 vols., Vol. 3. Clamp Staff. 2012. (ENG.). 600p. pap. 19.99 *(978-1-59582-808-8(7))* Dark Horse Comics.

—Cardcaptor Sakura, 6 vols., Vol. 2. Clamp Staff. Onishi, Mika, tr. rev. ed. 2004. 192p. (J). pap. 9.99 *(978-1-59182-879-2(1),* Tokyopop Kids) TOKYOPOP, Inc.

—Cardcaptor Sakura, Vol. 4. Clamp Staff. rev. ed. 2005. 200p. (J). pap. 9.99 *(978-1-59182-881-5(3),* Tokyopop Kids) TOKYOPOP, Inc.

—RG Veda, Vol. 3. Clamp Staff. 3rd rev. ed. 2005. (RG Veda Ser.). 184p. per. 14.99 *(978-1-59532-486-3(0),* Tokyopop Adult) TOKYOPOP, Inc.

Clamp Staff. Rg Veda. Clamp Staff, creator. 2005. pap. 14.99 *(978-1-59532-484-9(4),* Tokyopop Adult) TOKYOPOP, Inc.

—Tokyo Babylon, Vol. 7. Clamp Staff, creator. rev. ed. 2005. 160p. pap. 9.99 *(978-1-59532-051-3(2))* TOKYOPOP, Inc.

Clanton, Ben. Jasper John Dooley: Star of the Week. Adderson, Caroline. 2014. (ENG.). 128p. (J). pap. 7.95 *(978-1-77138-119-2(1))* Kids Can Pr., Ltd. CAN. Dist: Univ. of Toronto Pr.

—Max Finds an Egg. Blevins, Wiley. 2015. (Penguin Young Readers, Level 1 Ser.). (ENG.). 32p. (J). (gr. k-1). pap. 3.99 *(978-0-448-47993-4(1)*, Warne, Frederick Pubs.) Penguin Bks., Ltd. GBR. Dist: Penguin Random Hse., LLC.

—Max Has a Fish. Blevins, Wiley. 2012. (Penguin Young Readers, Level 1 Ser.). (ENG.). 32p. (J). (gr. k-1). pap. 3.99 *(978-0-448-46158-8(7)*, Grosset & Dunlap) Penguin Publishing Group.

Clanton, Ben. Rex Wrecks It! Clanton, Ben. 2014. (ENG.). 40p. (J). (gr. -1-2). 15.99 *(978-0-7636-6501-2(0))* Candlewick Pr.

—Something Extraordinary. Clanton, Ben. 2015. (ENG.). 40p. (J). (gr. -1-3). 17.99 *(978-1-4814-0358-0(3)*, Simon & Schuster Bks. For Young Readers) Simon & Schuster Bks. For Young Readers.

—The Table Sets Itself. Clanton, Ben. Clanton, Benjamin. 2013. (ENG.). 40p. (J). (gr. -1-3). 16.99 *(978-0-8027-3447-1(2)*, 249790) Walker & Co.

—The Table Sets Itself. Clanton, Ben. 2013. (ENG.). 40p. (J). (gr. -1-3). 17.89 *(978-0-8027-3448-8(0))* Walker & Co.

Clanton, Connie. The Boy Who Cried Wolf: The Boy Who Cried Wolf. 2012. (SGN, ARA, BOS, CHI & ENG.). 32p. (J). pap. 19.95 incl. DVD *(978-0-9818139-1-2(7))* ASL Tales.

Clar, David. Girls & Their Horses. Decaire, Carmale, ed. 2006. (ENG.). 64p. (J). (gr. 4-7). pap. 8.95 *(978-1-59369-209-4(9))* American Girl Publishing, Inc.

Clar, David Austin. The First Easter, 1 vol. DeBoer, Jesslyn. 2005. (Easter Board Bks.). (ENG.). 12p. (J). bds. 3.99 *(978-0-310-70842-1(7))* Zonderkidz.

—!Listos... Ya! Donovan, Gail. 2003. (Rainbow Fish & Friends Ser.). 24p. (J). mass mkt. 3.99 *(978-1-59014-123-6(7))* Night Sky Bks.

—My Day with Jesus, 1 vol. Davidson, Alice Joyce. 2005. (Easter Board Bks.). (ENG.). 16p. (J). bds. 3.99 *(978-0-310-70843-8(5))* Zonderkidz.

—100th Day Fun. Donovan, Gail. 2003. (Rainbow Fish & Friends Ser.). 24p. (J). lib. bdg. 9.95 *(978-1-59014-141-0(5))* Night Sky Bks.

Clar, David Austin & Hantel, Johanna. Good Food. Jensen, Patricia & Demar, Regier. 2006. (My First Reader Ser.). (ENG.). 32p. (J). (gr. k-1). per. 3.95 *(978-0-516-24969-8(X)*, Children's Pr.) Scholastic Library Publishing.

Clar, David Austin, jt. illus. see Goodell, Jon.

Clara, Miss. The Princess & the Pea. Gresham, Xanthe. 2013. (ENG.). 40p. (J). 17.99 *(978-1-84686-905-1(6))* Barefoot Bks., Inc.

—The Snow Queen. Lowes, Sarah. (ENG.). (J). 2011. 36p. pap. 9.99 *(978-1-84686-662-3(6))*; 2013. 64p. 17.99 *(978-1-84686-964-8(1))* Barefoot Bks., Inc.

—The Twelve Dancing Princesses. Hoffman, Mary. (ENG.). (J). 2013. 40p. 17.99 *(978-1-84686-966-2(8))*; 2012. 64p. pap. 9.99 *(978-1-84686-838-2(6))* Barefoot Bks., Inc.

Claremont, Heather. Thank You, Jesus. Lundy, Charlotte. Waldrep, Evelyn L., ed. 2003. 32p. (gr. k-3). 15.95 *(978-0-9670280-1-9(9))* Bay Light Publishing.

Clark, Alan M. & Koszowski, Allen. The House of the Temple. Lumley, Brian. collector's ed. 2004. 115p. (YA). 45.00 *(978-0-9728656-3-0(2))* Endeavor Pr.

Clark, Andy, jt. illus. see Bond, Clint.

Clark, Barbara Hoserman. The Tale of Rebekah Rabbit. Meade, Jean McCurdy. 2009. 28p. pap. 12.95 *(978-1-59858-970-2(9))* Dog Ear Publishing, LLC.

Clark, Bartholomew & Clark, Bill. God, I Need to Talk to You about Lying. Carr, Dan. 16p. (J). 1.19 *(978-0-7586-0512-2(9))* Concordia Publishing Hse.

—God, I Need to Talk to You about Sharing. Carr, Dan. 16p. (J). 1.19 *(978-0-7586-0511-5(0))* Concordia Publishing Hse.

—God, I Need to Talk to You about Stealing. Carr, Dan. 16p. (J). 1.19 *(978-0-7586-0509-2(9))* Concordia Publishing Hse.

—God, I Need to Talk to You about Vandalism. Carr, Dan. 16p. (J). 1.19 *(978-0-7586-0510-8(2))* Concordia Publishing Hse.

Clark, Bill. God, I Need to Talk to You about Bad Words. Leigh, Susan K. 2005. 16p. (J). pap. 1.19 *(978-0-7586-0793-5(8))* Concordia Publishing Hse.

—God, I Need to Talk to You about Bullying. Leigh, Susan K. 2005. 16p. (J). pap. 1.19 *(978-0-7586-0796-6(2))* Concordia Publishing Hse.

—God, I Need to Talk to You about Greed. Leigh, Susan K. 2005. 16p. (J). pap. 1.19 *(978-0-7586-0795-9(4))* Concordia Publishing Hse.

—God, I Need to Talk to You about Whining. Leigh, Susan K. 2005. pap. 1.19 *(978-0-7586-0794-2(6))* Concordia Publishing Hse.

—Jesus & the Woman at the Well. Busch, Melinda Kay. 2005. (Arch Bks.). (ENG.). 16p. (J). 1.99 *(978-0-7586-0675-4(3))* Concordia Publishing Hse.

—Tiny Baby Moses. Dietrich, Julie. 2003. (Arch Bks.). (ENG.). 16p. (J). (gr. k-4). 1.99 *(978-0-570-07581-3(5))* Concordia Publishing Hse.

Clark, Bill, jt. illus. see Clark, Bartholomew.

Clark, Brenda. Bravo Benjamin! Bourgeois, Paulette. ed. 2004.Tr. of Good Job Franklin!. (FRE.). (J). (gr. -1-2). spiral bd. *(978-0-616-11142-0(8))* Canadian National Institute for the Blind/Institut National Canadien pour les Aveugles.

—A Classic Franklin Story: Franklin's Thanksgiving. Jennings, Sharon & Bourgeois, Paulette. 2013. (Franklin Ser.). (ENG.). 32p. (J). pap. 5.95 *(978-1-77138-005-8(5))* Kids Can Pr., Ltd. CAN. Dist: Univ. of Toronto Pr.

—Finders Keepers for Franklin. Bourgeois, Paulette. 2013. (Franklin Ser.). (ENG.). 32p. (J). pap. 5.95 *(978-1-77138-003-4(9))* Kids Can Pr., Ltd. CAN. Dist: Univ. of Toronto Pr.

—Franklin & Harriet. Bourgeois, Paulette. 2nd ed. 2011. (Franklin Ser.). (ENG.). 32p. (J). pap. 5.95 *(978-1-55453-727-3(4))* Kids Can Pr., Ltd. CAN. Dist: Univ. of Toronto Pr.

—Franklin & the Computer. Bourgeois, Paulette. 2003. (Franklin Ser.: Bk. 16). 32p. (J). pap. 4.50 *(978-0-439-43121-7(2))* Scholastic, Inc.

—Franklin & the Thunderstorm. Bourgeois, Paulette. 2nd ed. 2011. (Franklin Ser.). (ENG.). 32p. (J). pap. 5.95 *(978-1-55453-729-7(0))* Kids Can Pr., Ltd. CAN. Dist: Univ. of Toronto Pr.

—Franklin & the Tooth Fairy. Bourgeois, Paulette. 2nd ed. 2011. (Franklin Ser.). (ENG.). 32p. (J). pap. 5.95 *(978-1-55453-734-1(7))* Kids Can Pr., Ltd. CAN. Dist: Univ. of Toronto Pr.

—Franklin Es un Mandon. Bourgeois, Paulette. Varela, Alejandra López, tr.Tr. of Franklin Is Bossy. (SPA.). 10.95 *(978-1-930332-16-4(5)*, LC6564) Lectorum Pubns., Inc.

—Franklin Fibs. Bourgeois, Paulette. 2nd ed. 2011. (Franklin Ser.). (ENG.). 32p. (J). pap. 5.95 *(978-1-55453-774-7(6))* Kids Can Pr., Ltd. CAN. Dist: Univ. of Toronto Pr.

—Franklin Goes to the Hospital. Jennings, Sharon & Bourgeois, Paulette. 2nd ed. 2011. (Franklin Ser.). (ENG.). 32p. (J). 5.95 *(978-1-55453-725-9(8))* Kids Can Pr., Ltd. CAN. Dist: Univ. of Toronto Pr.

—Franklin Has a Sleepover. Bourgeois, Paulette. 2nd ed. 2011. (Franklin Ser.). (ENG.). 32p. (J). pap. 5.95 *(978-1-55453-736-5(3))* Kids Can Pr., Ltd. CAN. Dist: Univ. of Toronto Pr.

—Franklin in the Dark. Bourgeois, Paulette. 2013. (Franklin Ser.). (ENG.). 32p. (J). pap. 5.95 *(978-1-77138-007-2(1))* Kids Can Pr., Ltd. CAN. Dist: Univ. of Toronto Pr.

—Franklin in the Dark: 25th Anniversary Edition. Bourgeois, Paulette. 2nd ed. 2011. (Franklin Ser.). (ENG.). 48p. (J). (gr. -1-3). 18.95 *(978-1-55453-616-0(2))* Kids Can Pr., Ltd. CAN. Dist: Univ. of Toronto Pr.

—Franklin Is Bossy. Bourgeois, Paulette. 2nd ed. 2011. (Franklin Ser.). (ENG.). 32p. (J). 5.95 *(978-1-55453-785-3(1))* Kids Can Pr., Ltd. CAN. Dist: Univ. of Toronto Pr.

—Franklin Is Lost. Bourgeois, Paulette. 2nd ed. 2011. (Franklin Ser.). (ENG.). 32p. (J). pap. 5.95 *(978-1-55453-735-8(5))* Kids Can Pr., Ltd. CAN. Dist: Univ. of Toronto Pr.

—Franklin Is Messy. Bourgeois, Paulette. 2013. (Franklin Ser.). (ENG.). 32p. (J). pap. 5.95 *(978-1-77138-000-3(4))* Kids Can Pr., Ltd. CAN. Dist: Univ. of Toronto Pr.

—Franklin Rides a Bike. Bourgeois, Paulette. 2nd ed. 2011. (Franklin Ser.). (ENG.). 32p. (J). pap. 5.95 *(978-1-55453-731-0(2))* Kids Can Pr., Ltd. CAN. Dist: Univ. of Toronto Pr.

—Franklin Says I Love You. Bourgeois, Paulette. 2nd ed. 2011. (Franklin Ser.). (ENG.). 32p. (J). pap. 5.95 *(978-1-55453-728-0(2))* Kids Can Pr., Ltd. CAN. Dist: Univ. of Toronto Pr.

—Franklin Wants a Badge. Bourgeois, Paulette. 2003. (Franklin TV Storybook Ser.). (ENG.). 32p. (J). 4.95 *(978-1-55337-468-8(1))*; 10.95 *(978-1-55337-467-1(3))* Kids Can Pr., Ltd. CAN. Dist: Univ. of Toronto Pr.

—Franklin Wants a Pet. Bourgeois, Paulette. 2013. (Franklin Ser.). (ENG.). 32p. (J). pap. 5.95 *(978-1-77138-004-1(7))* Kids Can Pr., Ltd. CAN. Dist: Univ. of Toronto Pr.

—Franklin y el Dia de Accion de Gracias. Bourgeois, Paulette. Varela, Alejandra López, tr.Tr. of Franklin's Thanksgiving. (SPA.). (J). (gr. k-2). 10.95 *(978-1-930332-07-2(6)*, LC30184) Lectorum Pubns., Inc.

—Franklin's Baby Sister. Bourgeois, Paulette. (Franklin Ser.). (ENG.). 32p. (J). (gr. -1-3). *(978-1-55074-858-1(0))* Kids Can Pr., Ltd.

—Franklin's Baby Sister. Bourgeois, Paulette. 2013. (Franklin Ser.). (ENG.). 32p. (J). pap. 5.95 *(978-1-77138-002-7(0))* Kids Can Pr., Ltd. CAN. Dist: Univ. of Toronto Pr.

—Franklin's Bad Day. Bourgeois, Paulette. 2nd ed. 2011. (Franklin Ser.). (ENG.). 32p. (J). pap. 5.95 *(978-1-55453-732-7(0))* Kids Can Pr., Ltd. CAN. Dist: Univ. of Toronto Pr.

—Franklin's Blanket. Bourgeois, Paulette. 2nd ed. 2011. (Franklin Ser.). (ENG.). 32p. (J). pap. 5.95 *(978-1-55453-733-4(9))* Kids Can Pr., Ltd. CAN. Dist: Univ. of Toronto Pr.

—Franklin's Christmas: A Sticker Activity Book. Bourgeois, Paulette. 2003. (ENG.). 16p. (J). 6.95 *(978-1-55337-561-6(0))*; 6.95 *(978-1-55337-506-7(8))* Kids Can Pr., Ltd. CAN. Dist: Univ. of Toronto Pr.

—Franklin's Christmas Gift. Bourgeois, Paulette. 2013. (Franklin Ser.). (ENG.). 32p. (J). pap. 5.95 *(978-1-77138-001-0(2))* Kids Can Pr., Ltd. CAN. Dist: Univ. of Toronto Pr.

—Franklin's Class Trip. Bourgeois, Paulette. 2012. (Franklin Ser.). (ENG.). 32p. (J). pap. 5.95 *(978-1-55453-936-9(6))* Kids Can Pr., Ltd. CAN. Dist: Univ. of Toronto Pr.

—Franklin's Family Treasury. Bourgeois, Paulette. 2003. (Franklin Ser.). (ENG.). 128p. (J). (gr. k-3). 15.95 *(978-1-55337-479-4(7))* Kids Can Pr., Ltd. CAN. Dist: Univ. of Toronto Pr.

—Franklin's Halloween. Bourgeois, Paulette. 2nd ed. 2011. (Franklin Ser.). (ENG.). 32p. (J). pap. 5.95 *(978-1-55453-786-0(X))* Kids Can Pr., Ltd. CAN. Dist: Univ. of Toronto Pr.

—Franklin's Neighborhood. Jennings, Sharon & Bourgeois, Paulette. 2013. (Franklin Ser.). (ENG.). 32p. (J). pap. 5.95 *(978-1-894786-98-0(X))* Kids Can Pr., Ltd. CAN. Dist: Univ. of Toronto Pr.

—Franklin's New Friend. Bourgeois, Paulette & Bourgeois, Paulette. (Franklin Ser.). (ENG.). 32p. (J). (gr. -1-3). *(978-1-55074-363-0(5))* Kids Can Pr., Ltd.

—Franklin's New Friend. Bourgeois, Paulette. 2nd ed. 2011. (Franklin Ser.). (ENG.). 32p. (J). pap. 5.95 *(978-1-55453-773-0(8))* Kids Can Pr., Ltd. CAN. Dist: Univ. of Toronto Pr.

—Franklin's School Play. Bourgeois, Paulette. 2012. (Franklin Ser.). (ENG.). 32p. (J). pap. 5.95 *(978-1-55453-935-2(8))* Kids Can Pr., Ltd. CAN. Dist: Univ. of Toronto Pr.

—Franklin's Secret Club. Bourgeois, Paulette. 2012. (Franklin Ser.). (ENG.). 32p. (J). pap. 5.95 *(978-1-55453-934-5(X))* Kids Can Pr., Ltd. CAN. Dist: Univ. of Toronto Pr.

—Franklin's Valentines. Jennings, Sharon & Bourgeois, Paulette. 2013. (Franklin Ser.). (ENG.). 32p. (J). pap. 5.95 *(978-1-77138-006-5(3))* Kids Can Pr., Ltd. CAN. Dist: Univ. of Toronto Pr.

—Fun with Franklin: A Learning to Read Book. Bourgeois, Paulette. (Franklin Ser.). (J). (gr. -1-3). *(978-1-55074-646-4(4))* Kids Can Pr., Ltd.

—Hurry up, Franklin. Bourgeois, Paulette. 2012. (Franklin Ser.). (ENG.). 32p. (J). pap. 5.95 *(978-1-55453-819-5(X))* Kids Can Pr., Ltd. CAN. Dist: Univ. of Toronto Pr.

—La Manta de Franklin. Bourgeois, Paulette. Varela, Alejandra López, tr.Tr. of Franklin's Blanket. (SPA.). (J). (gr. k-2). pap. 5.95 *(978-1-880507-98-8(6)*, LC30178); ring bd. 10.95 *(978-1-880507-99-5(4)*, LC30179) Lectorum Pubns., Inc.

Clark Brown, Jane. Marvin One Too Many. Paterson, Katherine. 2003. 25.95 incl. audio *(978-1-59112-254-8(6))*; 28.95 incl. audio compact disk *(978-1-59112-635-5(5))*; pap. 31.95 incl. audio compact disk *(978-1-59112-636-2(3))*; (J). pap. 29.95 incl. audio *(978-1-59112-255-5(4))* Live Oak Media.

Clark, Carson & Clark, Jim, photos by. The Adventures of Buddy the Beaver: Mystery of the Missing Friends. 2013. (Adventures of Buddy the Beaver Ser.). (ENG.). 48p. (J). (gr. k-2). 10.95 *(978-0-9844218-8-6(2))* Mountain Trail Pr.

Clark, Casey. Noah's Boat. Swinson, Joyce Ann. 2007. 32p. per. 24.95 *(978-1-4241-9012-6(6))* America Star Bks.

Clark, David. Bus-a-Saurus Bop. Shore, Diane Z. 2003. (ENG.). 32p. (J). (gr. k-3). 16.95 *(978-1-58234-850-6(2)*, Bloomsbury USA Childrens) Bloomsbury USA.

—Curious Creatures: Animal Poems. Polisar, Barry Louis. 2010. (Rainbow Morning Music Picture Bks.). (ENG.). 32p. (J). (gr. 2-4). 14.95 *(978-0-938663-52-2(6))* Rainbow Morning Music Alternatives.

—Fractions in Disguise: A Math Adventure. Einhorn, Edward. 2014. (ENG.). 32p. (J). (gr. 2-5). pap. 7.95 *(978-1-57091-774-5(4))*; lib. bdg. 16.95 *(978-1-57091-773-8(6))* Charlesbridge Publishing, Inc.

—Gakky Two-Feet. Dolenz, Micky. 2006. (J). *(978-1-4156-8089-6(2)*, Putnam Juvenile) Penguin Publishing Group.

—Pirate Bob. Lasky, Kathryn. alt. ed. 2008. (ENG.). 32p. (J). (gr. k-3). per. 8.95 *(978-1-57091-647-2(0))* Charlesbridge Publishing, Inc.

—Something Fishy. Polisar, Barry Louis. 2013. (Rainbow Morning Music Picture Bks.). (ENG.). 32p. (J). (gr. 2-4). 14.95 *(978-0-938663-53-9(4))* Rainbow Morning Music Alternatives.

—What's for Dinner? Quirky, Squirmy Poems from the Animal World. Hauth, Katherine B. 2011. (ENG.). 48p. (J). (gr. 2-5). pap. 8.95 *(978-1-57091-472-0(9))* Charlesbridge Publishing, Inc.

Clark, David, jt. illus. see Hohn, David.

Clark, Debbie. Alphabet of Music. Schwaeber, Barbie Heit. 2009. (ENG.). 40p. 9.95 *(978-1-59249-995-3(3))* Soundprints.

Clark, Debbie, jt. illus. see Santillan, Jorge.

Clark, Don. The Biggest Story: How the Snake Crusher Brings Us Back to the Garden. DeYoung, Kevin. 2015. 132p. (J). 17.99 *(978-1-4335-4244-2(7))* Crossway.

Clark, Donna Osborn. What about Johnson? Johnson, Harvell. Howard, Vanetta, ed. 2013. 132p. pap. 11.95 *(978-0-9885056-0-5(6))* Word on Da Street Publishing.

Clark, Elijah Brady. Who Pooped in the Park? Robson, Gary D. 2006. (J). 9.95 *(978-1-56037-388-9(1))* Farcountry Pr.

—Who Pooped in the Park? Grand Canyon National Park. Robson, Gary D. 2005. 80p. (J). pap. 11.95 *(978-1-56037-319-3(9))* Farcountry Pr.

—Who Pooped in the Park? Rocky Mountain National Park: Scats & Tracks for Kids. Robson, Gary D. 2005. 48p. (J). (gr. -1-5). per. 11.95 *(978-1-56037-320-9(2))* Farcountry Pr.

—Who Pooped in the Park? Yosemite National Park. Robson, Gary D. 2005. 80p. (J). pap. 11.95 *(978-1-56037-318-6(0))* Farcountry Pr.

Clark, Elizabeth Palmer. Lysis Goes to the Play. Snedeker, Caroline Dale. 2003. 62p. (J). per. 8.95 *(978-0-9667067-4-1(9))* American Home-School Publishing, LLC.

Clark, Emma Chicester. Tales from Hans Christian Andersen. Lewis, Naomi. rev. ed. 2014. (Classics Ser.). (ENG.). 76p. (J). (gr. -1-2). 19.99 *(978-1-84780-510-2(8)*, Frances Lincoln) Quarto Publishing Group UK GBR. Dist: Hachette Bk. Group.

Clark, Emma Chichester. Mrs. Vole the Vet. Ahlberg, Allan. (ENG.). 24p. (J). pap. 6.95 *(978-0-14-037880-1(4))* Penguin Bks., Ltd. GBR. Dist: Trafalgar Square Publishing.

Clark, Emma Chichester. Lulu & the Treasure Hunt! Clark, Emma Chichester. 2013. (Wagtail Town Ser.). (ENG.). 32p. (J). pap. 9.99 *(978-0-00-742517-4(1)*, HarperCollins Children's Bks.) HarperCollins Pubs. Ltd. GBR. Dist: HarperCollins Pubs.

—Minty & Tink. Clark, Emma Chichester. 2009. (ENG.). 32p. (J). (gr. k-k). pap. 13.99 *(978-1-84270-720-3(5))* Andersen Pr. GBR. Dist: Independent Pubs. Group.

Clark, Irene. Basic Kit - Kindergarten. Bradshaw, Georgine & Wrighton, Charlene. 2005. Orig. Title: Basic Kit II. (J). 249.95 *(978-1-886441-31-6(6))* Zoo-phonics, Inc.

—Basic Kit - Preschool. Wrighton, Charlene & Bradshaw, Georgine. 2005. Orig. Title: Basis Kit I. (J). 249.95 *(978-1-886441-30-9(8))* Zoo-phonics, Inc.

—Kindergarten Zoo-per Kit. Bradshaw, Georgine & Wrighton, Charlene. 2005. (J). 499.95 *(978-1-886441-34-7(0)*, ZOP4219) Zoo-phonics, Inc.

—Preschool Zoo-per Kit. Bradshaw, Georgine & Wrighton, Charlene. 2005. (J). 449.95 *(978-1-886441-32-3(4)*, ZOP4218) Zoo-phonics, Inc.

—Set of Color Mini-Books (29 Titles) Bradshaw, Georgine & Wrighton, Charlene. 2005. (J). 39.95 *(978-1-886441-42-2(1)*, CMB4356) Zoo-phonics, Inc.

Clark, Jeff. The Amazing Spider-Man: An Origin Story. Thomas, Rich. 2012. (Marvel Origins Ser.). 48p. (J). (gr. -1-4). lib. bdg. 24.21 *(978-1-61479-007-5(8))* Spotlight.

—The Mighty Thor: An Origin Story. Thomas, Rich. 2012. (Marvel Origins Ser.). 48p. (J). (gr. -1-4). lib. bdg. 24.21 *(978-1-61479-011-2(6))* Spotlight.

Clark, Jim, jt. photos by see Clark, Carson.

Clark, K. C. Dancing Waters. Tulley, Tara. 2004. (J). *(978-0-9759468-1-7(1))* Balanced Families.

Clark, Karen & White, Ian. Flash, Bang, Wheee! Bing, Bang, Boum! 2004. 24p. (J). *(978-1-85269-354-1(1))* Mantra Lingua.

—Flash, Bang, Wheee! Shkreptime, Gjemim Dhe Vershellime! 2004. 24p. (J). *(978-1-85269-349-7(5))* Mantra Lingua.

Clark, Leslie Ann. Peepsqueak! Clark, Leslie Ann. 2012. (ENG.). 32p. (J). (gr. -1-k). 12.99 *(978-0-06-207801-8(1))* HarperCollins Pubs.

—Peepsqueak Wants a Friend! Clark, Leslie Ann. 2013. (ENG.). 32p. (J). (gr. -1-3). 15.99 *(978-0-06-207804-9(6))* HarperCollins Pubs.

Clark, Linda. Dear Mum, I Miss You! Ross, Stewart. 54p. (J). *(978-0-237-52318-3(3))* Evans Brothers, Ltd.

Clark Mancuso, Jackie. Hudson in Provence: A Paris-Chien Adventure. Clark Mancuso, Jackie. l.t. ed. 2015. (Paris-Chien Adventure Ser.). (ENG.). 40p. (J). (gr. k-2). 17.95 *(978-0-9886058-4-8(8))* La Librairie Parisienne.

Clark, Mary. The Life & Adventures of Santa Claus. Baum, L. Frank. 2007. 156p. (gr. 4-7). 23.95 *(978-1-60206-778-3(3))*; per. 9.95 *(978-1-60206-777-6(5))* Cosimo, Inc.

Clark, Mary Cowles. The Life & Adventures of Santa Claus. Baum, L. Frank. 2011. 200p. *(978-1-84902-560-7(6))* Benediction Classics.

Clark, Matthew. Inhumans: Lunar, Vol. 1. McKeever, Sean. 2004. (Marvel Heroes Ser.). 144p. (YA). (gr. 7-18). pap. 14.99 *(978-0-7851-1303-4(7))* Marvel Worldwide, Inc.

Clark, Matthew Levi. The Substitute Teacher Named Mr King. King, Seth David. 2005. 24p. (gr. 2-6). 12.00 *(978-0-9640837-6-9(0))* Ascension Education.

Clark, Nathan. Ann Drew Jackson. Clark, Joan. 2007. 122p. per. 17.95 *(978-1-931282-45-1(5))* Autism Asperger Publishing Co.

Clark, Nicole K. Pigment the Rainbow Pig. Clark, Nicole K. Date not set. (J). (gr. -1-2). *(978-1-892176-18-9(1))* PremaNations Publishing.

Clark, Steve. All about Eels: Read Well Level K Unit 2 Storybook. Sprick, Marilyn et al. 2003. (Read Well Level K Ser.). 20p. (J). *(978-1-57035-674-2(2))* Cambium Education, Inc.

—All about Eels: Read Well Level K Unit 2 Teacher Storybook. Sprick, Marilyn et al. 2003. (Read Well Level K Ser.). 20p. (J). *(978-1-57035-697-1(1))* Cambium Education, Inc.

—Hey Diddle Diddle: Read Well Level K Unit 16 Storybook. Sprick, Marilyn & Sprick, Jessica. 2003. (Read Well Level K Ser.). 20p. (J). *(978-1-57035-687-2(4)*, 55562) Cambium Education, Inc.

Clark, Tim, photos by. Davy Asks His Dad. Clark, Harriet. 2012. 32p. pap. *(978-1-77097-977-2(8))* FriesenPress.

Clark, Warren. Lowdown on Earthworms, 1 vol. Dixon, Norma. 2005. (ENG.). 32p. (J). (gr. 2-7). pap. *(978-1-55005-119-3(9))* Fitzhenry & Whiteside, Ltd.

—Prepare to Be Amazed: The Geniuses of Modern Magic. Schendlinger, Mary. 2005. (ENG.). 80p. (J). (gr. 3-6). 24.95 *(978-1-55037-927-3(5)*, 9781550379273) Annick Pr., Ltd. CAN. Dist: Firefly Bks., Ltd.

—Turn It Loose: The Scientist in Absolutely Everybody. Swanson, Diane. 2004. (ENG.). 112p. (J). (gr. 5-18). pap. 14.95 *(978-1-55037-850-4(3)*, 9781550378504) Annick Pr., Ltd. CAN. Dist: Firefly Bks., Ltd.

Clark, Wendy. My Brother's A Pirate, 1 vol. Nannini, Randi. 2010. 14p. pap. 24.95 *(978-1-4489-8576-0(5))* America Star Bks.

Clarke & Clarke. Melusine - Hocus Pocus. Gilson. 2007. (ENG.). 48p. (J). (gr. -1-12). per. 9.99 *(978-1-905460-20-5(1))* CineBook GBR. Dist: National Bk. Network.

Clarke, jt. illus. see Clarke.

Clarke, Alan. The Big Brother. Dagg, Stephanie. 2003. (Pandas Ser.: 24). (ENG.). 64p. (J). pap. 9.95 *(978-0-86278-779-0(3))* O'Brien Pr., Ltd., The IRL. Dist: Dufour Editions, Inc.

—Eddie Lenihan's Irish Tales of Mystery. Lenihan, Eddie. 2006. (ENG.). 224p. (J). 33.95 *(978-1-85635-519-3(5))* Mercier Pr., Ltd., The IRL. Dist: Dufour Editions, Inc.

Clarke, Alan, jt. illus. see Askin, Corrina.

Clarke, Asiya. Allah Gave Me Two Ears to Hear. Arif, Amrana. 2015. (ENG.). 32p. (J). 8.95 *(978-0-86037-353-7(3))* Kube Publishing Ltd. GBR. Dist: Consortium Bk. Sales & Distribution.

—Allah Gave Me Two Hands & Feet. Bokhari, Raana. 2015. (ENG.). 32p. (J). 8.95 *(978-0-86037-348-3(7))* Kube Publishing Ltd. GBR. Dist: Consortium Bk. Sales & Distribution.

Clarke, Benjamin S. The House Who Found Its Home. Vincolisi, Marnie. 2013. 32p. pap. 10.95 *(978-0-9823732-3-1(6))* Light Internal Publishing.

Clarke, Greg. The Blood-Hungry Spleen & Other Poems about Our Parts. Wolf, Allan. 2008. (ENG.). 56p. (J). (gr. 3-7). per. 9.99 *(978-0-7636-3806-1(4))* Candlewick Pr.

Clarke, Harry & Perrault, Charles. Classic Fairy Tales of Charles Perrault. 2013. (ENG.). 224p. (J). 34.00 *(978-0-7171-5408-1(4))* Gill & MacMillan, Ltd. IRL. Dist: Dufour Editions, Inc.

Clarke, Herbert, photos by. An Introduction to Southern California Birds. Clarke, Herbert. rev. ed. 192p. (J). (gr. 4). pap. 14.00 *(978-0-87842-233-3(1)*, 413) Mountain Pr. Publishing Co., Inc.

Clarke, Judith Holmes. La Aventura de Rosetta. Papademetriou, Lisa. Pombo, Mauricio, tr. 2008.Tr. of Rosetta's Daring Day. (SPA.). 107p. (J). pap. *(978-958-45-0849-2(0))* Norma S.A.

Clarke, Lyndia A. Tidy up Tommy. Clarke, Lyndia A. 2005. (J). 1700.00 *(978-0-9762898-6-9(5))* LightHouse Pr.

Clarke, Peter. Bunyip in the Moon: A Tale from Australia. Barchers, Suzanne. 2015. (Tales of Honor Ser.). (ENG.). 32p. (gr. 1-3). lib. bdg. 26.60 *(978-1-939656-77-3(X))* Red Chair Pr.

C

Clarkson, Janet M. Petoskey Stone Soup. Mothershead, Martha Fulford. 2006. 32p. (J). 18.95 *(978-0-9785465-0-2(4))* Whaleback Pr.

Clarkson, Karen. Saltypie: A Choctaw Journey from Darkness into Light. Tingle, Tim. 2010. (ENG.). 40p. (J). (gr. 2-6). 17.95 *(978-1-933693-67-5(3))* Cinco Puntos Pr.

Class, Virginia Tyree. Auntie Silly & the Crazy Cousins Day Parade, 1 vol. Fields, Melissa. 2010. 20p. pap. 24.95 *(978-1-4489-8140-3(9))* PublishAmerica, Inc.

Claude, Jean. Henry Hyena, Why Won't You Laugh? Jantzen, Doug. 2015. (ENG.). 32p. (J). (gr. -1-2). 17.99 *(978-1-4814-2822-4(5),* Simon & Schuster/Paula Wiseman Bks.) Simon & Schuster/Paula Wiseman Bks.

Clay, Cliff. Blacks in Ohio II, Vol. 1. Moore, Mary. Caesor, Ebraska, ed. (YA). (gr. 6-18). pap. 12.95 *(978-0-913678-31-2(7))* New Day Pr.

Clay, Dorian. Freddie Loses His Game. Clay, Dorian. 2012. 64p. pap. 12.99 *(978-1-938056-03-1(5))* ARIVA Publishing.

Clay, Doris. Prince Cody Meets A Monster. Robison, Peggy. 2004. 40p. pap. 9.95 *(978-0-9708395-7-2(X))* Legacy Publishing Services, Inc.

—Prince Cody Runs Ahead of the Hurricane. Robison, Peggy. 2005. 64p. per. 9.95 *(978-0-9764982-7-8(8))* Legacy Publishing Services, Inc.

Clay, Josh. Josie's Very Unhappy Hair: Up North at Nana's. Wheadon, Bill(Beepa) & Wheadon, Bill. 2010. (ENG.). 28p. pap. 14.95 *(978-1-4528-8595-7(8))* CreateSpace Independent Publishing Platform.

Clay, Joshua. Lucy Swan's Circle. Furman, Necah Stewart & Huff, Bailey. 2005. (Friends of Fairlane Woods Ser.). (ENG.). 40p. (J). (gr. -1-3). per. 16.99 *(978-1-4134-8666-7(5))* Xlibris Corp.

Clay, Julie. Prayers for Little Girls, 1 vol. David, Juliet. 2014. 64p. (J). 12.99 *(978-1-85985-990-2(9),* Candle Bks.) Lion Hudson PLC GBR. Dist: Kregel Pubns.

Clay, Wil. Auntee Edna. Smothers, Ethel Footman. 2004. 32p. (J). pap. 8.00 *(978-0-8028-5246-5(7));* 16.00 *(978-0-8028-5154-3(1))* Eerdmans, William B. Publishing Co.

Claycomb, Norma L. Tail Talks. Hesselbein, Deborah A. 2008. 48p. per. 15.95 *(978-1-59858-560-5(6))* Dog Ear Publishing, LLC.

Clayman, Fillys, et al. Spanish Emergent Reader 1: Mira como Juego; ¡Curitas!; Los Animales del Zoológico; Construyendo una Casa; la Alberca; ¡Agua y Jabón!; Me Visto; Mi Gato, 8 bks. Libritos Mios staff et al. Elias, Annette, tr. 2003.Tr. of Emergent Reader 1. (SPA.). 8p. (J). 120.00 *(978-1-893986-24-4(1))* Keep Bks.

Clayton, Christian. Crazy Loco. Rice, David & Rice, David Talbot. 2003. (ENG.). 144p. (YA). (gr. 7-11). 5.99 *(978-0-14-250056-9(9))* Penguin Publishing Group.

Clayton, Dallas. An Awesome Book! Clayton, Dallas. 2012. (Awesome Book Ser.). (ENG.). 64p. (J). (gr. k-3). 16.99 *(978-0-06-211468-6(9))* HarperCollins Pubs.

—An Awesome Book of Love! Clayton, Dallas. 2012. (Awesome Book Ser.). (ENG.). 56p. (J). (gr. -1-3). 16.99 *(978-0-06-211666-6(5))* HarperCollins Pubs.

—Lily the Unicorn. Clayton, Dallas. 2014. (ENG.). 48p. (J). (gr. -1-3). 17.99 *(978-0-06-211668-0(1))* HarperCollins Pubs.

—Make Magic! Do Good! Clayton, Dallas. 2012. (ENG.). 112p. (J). (gr. 2-5). 17.99 *(978-0-7636-5746-8(8))* Candlewick Pr.

Clayton, Elaine. Gee Whiz. Smiley, Jane. 2013. (Horses of Oak Valley Ranch Ser.: Bk. 5). (ENG.). 272p. (J). (gr. 5). 16.99 *(978-0-375-86969-3(7));* lib. bdg. 19.99 *(978-0-375-96969-0(1))* Knopf, Alfred A. Inc.

—42 Miles. Zimmer, Tracie Vaughn. 2008. (ENG.). 80p. (J). (gr. 5-7). 16.00 *(978-0-618-61867-5(8))* Houghton Mifflin Harcourt Publishing Co.

Clayton, Henry, et al. Spider-Man: the Extremist. Tobin, Paul. 2011. (ENG.). 100p. (J). (gr. 4-17). pap., pap. 15.99 *(978-0-7851-5670-3(4))* Marvel Worldwide, Inc.

Clayton, Kim. Footprints on the Ceiling: Your Child's Footprint Completes the Story. Hetzer, Michael. 2nd ed. 2005. 32p. (J). 18.95 *(978-0-9728222-2-0(4))* Webster Henrietta Publishing.

—Footprints on the Ceiling (Collector's Edition) Your Child's Footprint Completes the Story. Hetzer, Michael. 2004. 32p. (J). 18.95 *(978-0-9728222-1-3(6))* Webster Henrietta Publishing.

—The Get Well Picture. Hetzer, Michael. 2005. (J). 2nd collector's ed. 32p. 18.95 *(978-0-9728222-5-1(9));* 3rd ed. 18.95 *(978-0-9728222-6-8(7))* Webster Henrietta Publishing.

—A Hug for Percy Porcupine. Hetzer, Michael. 2005. 32p. (J). (gr. k-2). 2nd collector's ed. 18.95 *(978-0-9728222-4-4(0));* 3rd ed. 18.95 *(978-0-9728222-3-7(2))* Webster Henrietta Publishing.

—No More Handprints: Your Child's Handprint Completes the Story. Hetzer, Michael. 2nd ed. 2005. 32p. (J). 18.95 *(978-0-9728222-0-6(8))* Webster Henrietta Publishing.

Clayton, Lew. Felina's New Home: A Florida Panther Story, 1 vol. Wlodarski, Loran. 2010. (ENG.). 32p. (J). (gr. -1-3). 16.95 *(978-1-60718-068-5(5))* Arbordale Publishing.

Clayton, Sean & Spears, Ashley. Melvin the Mailman. Clayton, Lisa. 2005. 8p. (J). 3.49 *(978-0-9773723-0-0(8))* Trent's Prints.

Clearwater, Linda. Duckling Is Patient. Simon, Mary Manz. 2006. (First Virtues for Toddlers Ser.). 20p. (J). 5.99 *(978-0-7847-1410-2(X),* 04038) Standard Publishing.

—Kitty Shows Kindness. Simon, Mary Manz. 2006. (First Virtues for Toddlers Ser.). 20p. (J). 5.99 *(978-0-7847-1408-9(8),* 04036) Standard Publishing.

Clearwater, Linda & Couri, Kathy. Bear Obeys. Simon, Mary Manz. 2006. (First Virtues for Toddlers Ser.). 20p. (J). 5.99 *(978-0-7847-1416-4(9),* 04068) Standard Publishing.

—Tiger Forgives. Simon, Mary Manz. 2006. (First Virtues for Toddlers Ser.). 20p. (J). 5.99 *(978-0-7847-1413-3(4),* 04065) Standard Publishing.

Clearwater, Linda, jt. illus. see Couri, Kathy.

Clearwater, Linda, jt. illus. see Harris, Phyllis.

Cleary, Daniel. Prickles vs. the Dust Bunnies. 2011. (ENG.). 40p. (J). (gr. 1-4). 11.99 *(978-1-60905-080-1(0))* Blue Apple Bks.

—Stop Bugging Me: That's What Friends Are For. 2010. (ENG.). 56p. (J). (gr. -1-3). 10.99 *(978-1-60905-046-7(0))* Blue Apple Bks.

Cleary, Janice. Come to Jesus: A Kids' Book for Eucharistic Adoration. Flanagan, Anne. 2006. (J). 4.50 *(978-0-8198-1577-4(2))* Pauline Bks. & Media.

Clegg, Dave. Critter Jokes & Riddles. Myers, Janet Nuzum. 2010. (ENG.). 96p. (J). pap. 4.95 *(978-1-4027-7844-5(9))* Sterling Publishing Co., Inc.

Clem, Margaret H. Elbert ein Swine, Genius Pig. Clem, Margaret H. 2003. (ENG.). 32p. (J). (gr. k-4). pap. 6.95 *(978-1-878044-12-9(5))* Mayhaven Publishing, Inc.

—Elbert ein Swine Learns Line Dancing No. 2. Clem, Margaret H. 2003. (ENG.). 32p. (J). (gr. k-4). pap. 9.95 *(978-1-878044-28-0(1))* Mayhaven Publishing, Inc.

Clemenston, John. More Little Mouse Deer Tales. Hughes, Mónica. 2005. 24p. (J). lib. bdg. 23.65 *(978-1-59646-730-9(4))* Dingles & Co.

Clement, Devyn, jt. illus. see Steele, Andrew.

Clement, Edgar. El Hombre Qve Se Convirtio en Toro: Y Otras Historias de la Inquisicion. Cortes Hernandez, Santiago & Cortes, Santiago. 2006. (Otra Escalera Ser.). (ENG.). 60p. (J). (gr. -1-k). pap. 12.95 *(978-970-20-0831-6(X))* Castillo, Ediciones, S. A. de C. V. MEX. Dist: Macmillan.

—Sonrie! McGaughrean, Geraldine et al. rev. ed. 2006. (Castillo de la Lectura Naranja Ser.). (ENG.). 120p. (J). (gr. 4-6). pap. 7.95 *(978-970-20-0853-8(0))* Castillo, Ediciones, S. A. de C. V. MEX. Dist: Macmillan.

Clement, Gary. A Coyote Solstice Tale, 1 vol. King, Thomas. 2009. (ENG.). 64p. (gr. -1). 14.95 *(978-0-88899-929-0(1))* Groundwood Bks. CAN. Dist: Perseus-PGW.

Clement, Gary, et al. Mother Goose. Lottridge, Celia. 2009. (ENG.). 64p. (J). (gr. k — 1). bds. 9.95 *(978-0-88899-933-7(X))* Groundwood Bks. CAN. Dist: Perseus-PGW.

Clement, Gary. One-Eye! Two-Eyes! Three-Eyes! A Very Grimm Fairy Tale. Shepard, Aaron. 2006. (ENG.). 32p. (J). (gr. k-2). 17.99 *(978-0-689-86740-8(9),* Atheneum Bks. for Young Readers) Simon & Schuster Children's Publishing.

—Oy, Feh, So?, 1 vol. Fagan, Cary. 2013. (ENG.). 40p. (J). (gr. -1-3). 17.95 *(978-1-55498-148-9(4))* Groundwood Bks. CAN. Dist: Perseus-PGW.

—Stories from Adam & Eve to Ezekiel, 1 vol. Lottridge, Celia Barker. 2004. (ENG.). 144p. (J). 24.95 *(978-0-88899-490-5(7))* Groundwood Bks. CAN. Dist: Perseus-PGW.

—Swimming, Swimming, 1 vol. 2015. (ENG.). 48p. (J). (gr. -1-2). 18.95 *(978-1-55498-449-7(1))* Groundwood Bks. CAN. Dist: Perseus-PGW.

—Ten Old Men & a Mouse. Fagan, Cary. 2007. (ENG.). 32p. (J). (gr. -1-1). 18.95 *(978-0-88776-716-6(8),* Tundra Bks.) Tundra Bks. CAN. Dist: Penguin Random Hse., LLC.

Clement, Marilyn. Edgar, the Near-Sighted Eagle. Bettenberg, Barbie. 2008. 27p. (J). *(978-0-9822534-0-3(0))* Cricket XPress of Minnesota.

Clement, Nathan. Big Tractor. 2015. (ENG.). 32p. (J). (gr. k-3). 16.95 *(978-1-62091-790-9(4))* Boyds Mills Pr.

Clement, Nathan. Drive. Clement, Nathan. (ENG.). 32p. (J). 2013. (gr. k-2). pap. 6.95 *(978-1-62091-030-6(6));* 2008. (gr. -1-3). 16.95 *(978-1-59078-517-1(7))* Boyds Mills Pr.

—Job Site. Clement, Nathan. 2011. (ENG.). 32p. (J). (gr. -1-1). 16.95 *(978-1-59078-769-4(2))* Boyds Mills Pr.

—Speed. Clement, Nathan. 2013. (ENG.). 32p. (J). (gr. k). 16.95 *(978-1-59078-937-7(7))* Boyds Mills Pr.

Clement, Rod. Olga the Brolga. Clement, Rod. 32p. 2005. (ENG.). pap. *(978-0-207-19758-1(X));* 2004. *(978-0-207-19701-7(6))* HarperCollins Pubs. Australia.

Clement, Stacy. God's Special Creation. Davis, Rebecca. de Papenbrock, Dervy Romero, tr. unabr. ed. 2003. (ENG & SPA.). 30p. (J). (gr. k-3). spiral bd. 8.00 *(978-0-9720881-3-8(X),* B004) His Hands, Inc.

Clements, Frida. The Wandering Goose: A Modern Fable of How Love Goes. Earnhardt, Heather L. 2013. (ENG.). 64p. 15.95 *(978-1-57061-881-9(X))* Sasquatch Bks.

Clements, Ruth Sypherd. Beasley's Christmas Party. Tarkington, Booth. 2004. reprint ed. pap. 15.95 *(978-1-4179-0186-9(1))* Kessinger Publishing, LLC.

Clemesha, David & Zimmerman, Andrea. Fire Engine Man. Clemesha, David & Zimmerman, Andrea. 2007. (ENG.). 32p. (J). (gr. -1-k). 17.99 *(978-0-8050-7905-0(X),* Holt, Henry & Co. Bks. For Young Readers) Holt, Henry & Co.

Clemesha, David, jt. illus. see Zimmerman, Andrea Griffing.

Clemesha, David, jt. illus. see Zimmerman, Andrea.

Clennell, Bobby. Watch Me Do Yoga. 2010. (ENG.). 32p. (J). (gr. -1-3). 15.95 *(978-1-930485-26-6(3))* Rodmell Pr.

Clerc, Lucille. Flip Fashion. 2013. (ENG.). 44p. spiral bd. 14.95 *(978-1-85669-923-5(4))* King, Laurence Publishing GBR. Dist: Hachette Bk. Group.

Cleveland, Fred. The Navajo Brothers & the Stolen Herd. Grammer, Maurine. 2004. 120p. (gr. 4-7). pap. 9.95 *(978-1-878610-23-2(6))* Red Crane Bks., Inc.

Cleyet-Merle, Laurence. Animal Stencil Book. 2006. (Stencil Bks.). 14p. (J). (gr. -1-3). bds. 12.99 *(978-0-7945-1140-1(6),* Usborne) EDC Publishing.

—Rhyme Bible Storybook Bible, 1 vol. Sattgast, L. J. & Sattgast, Linda. 2012. (ENG.). 344p. (J). 17.99 *(978-0-310-72602-9(6))* Zonderkidz.

—The Rhyme Bible Storybook for Toddlers, 1 vol. Sattgast, L. J. rev. ed. 2014. (ENG.). 40p. (J). bds. 9.99 *(978-0-310-73016-3(3))* Zonderkidz.

Clibbon, Lucy. Ballerina. Clibbon, Meg. 2008. (Imagine You're A ... Ser.). (ENG.). 32p. (J). pap. 9.99 *(978-1-84089-453-0(9))* Meg and Lucy Bks. GBR. Dist: Independent Pubs. Group.

—Brave Knights. Clibbon, Meg. 2010. (My World Of Ser.). (ENG.). 24p. (J). (gr. k-2). pap. 6.95 *(978-1-84089-550-6(0))* Meg and Lucy Bks. GBR. Dist: Independent Pubs. Group.

—Cowboy! Clibbon, Meg. 2008. (Imagine You're A ... Ser.). (ENG.). 32p. (J). pap. 9.99 *(978-1-84089-452-3(0))* Meg and Lucy Bks. GBR. Dist: Independent Pubs. Group.

—Fabulous Fairies. Clibbon, Meg. 2010. (My World Of Ser.). (ENG.). 32p. (J). (gr. k-2). pap. 9.99 *(978-1-84089-551-3(9))* Meg and Lucy Bks. GBR. Dist: Independent Pubs. Group.

—The Fairy Party Book: Magic Meg & Lucy Loveheart. Clibbon, Meg. 2005. (ENG.). 32p. (J). (gr. -1-4). pap. 7.95 *(978-1-55037-914-3(3),* 9781550379143) Annick Pr., Ltd. CAN. Dist: Firefly Bks., Ltd.

—The Fairyland Olympics. Clibbon, Meg et al. 2008. (ENG.). 32p. (J). (gr. k-2). *(978-1-84089-504-9(7))* Zero to Ten, Ltd.

—Imagine You're a Ballerina. Clibbon, Meg. 2006. (Imagine This! Ser.). (ENG.). 32p. (J). (gr. -1-4). 19.95 *(978-1-55451-020-7(1),* 9781554510207) Annick Pr., Ltd. CAN. Dist: Firefly Bks., Ltd.

—Imagine You're a Princess! Princess Megerella & Princess Lulubelle. Clibbon, Meg. 2005. (Imagine This! Ser.). (ENG.). 32p. (J). (gr. -1-4). pap. 7.95 *(978-1-55037-920-4(8),* 9781550379204) Annick Pr., Ltd. CAN. Dist: Firefly Bks., Ltd.

—Magical Christmas. Clibbon, Meg & Meg, Merry. 2008. (ENG.). 32p. (J). (gr. k-2). *(978-1-84089-377-9(X))* Zero to Ten, Ltd.

—Magical Creatures. Clibbon, Meg. 2006. (ENG.). 32p. (J). (gr. -1-4). 19.95 *(978-1-55451-030-6(9),* 9781554510306); pap. 8.95 *(978-1-55451-029-0(5),* 9781554510290) Annick Pr., Ltd. CAN. Dist: Firefly Bks., Ltd.

—My Beautiful Ballet Pack. Clibbon, Meg. 2008. (Imagine You're A ... Ser.). (ENG.). 32p. (J). 15.99 *(978-1-84089-485-1(7))* Meg and Lucy Bks. GBR. Dist: Independent Pubs. Group.

—My Pretty Pink Fairy Journal. Clibbon, Meg et al. 2008. (Meg & Lucy Journals). (ENG.). 112p. (J). (gr. k-2). *(978-1-84089-467-7(9))* Zero to Ten, Ltd.

—My Wicked Pirate Journal. Clibbon, Meg et al. 2008. (Meg & Lucy Journals). (ENG.). 112p. (J). (gr. k-2). *(978-1-84089-466-0(0))* Zero to Ten, Ltd.

—Shimmering Mermaids. Clibbon, Meg. 2011. (My World Of Ser.). (ENG.). 32p. (J). (gr. k-2). pap. 9.99 *(978-1-84089-594-0(2))* Meg and Lucy Bks. GBR. Dist: Independent Pubs. Group.

—Sparkly Princesses. Clibbon, Meg. 2010. (My World Of Ser.). (ENG.). 32p. (J). (gr. k-2). pap. 9.99 *(978-1-84089-542-1(X))* Meg and Lucy Bks. GBR. Dist: Independent Pubs. Group.

—Starry Ballerinas. Clibbon, Meg. 2011. (My World Of Ser.). (ENG.). 32p. (J). (gr. k-2). pap. 8.99 *(978-1-84089-593-3(4))* Meg and Lucy Bks. GBR. Dist: Independent Pubs. Group.

—Wicked Pirates. Clibbon, Meg. 2010. (My World Of Ser.). (ENG.). 32p. (J). (gr. k-2). pap. 9.99 *(978-1-84089-552-0(7))* Meg and Lucy Bks. GBR. Dist: Independent Pubs. Group.

—Wizard! Clibbon, Meg. 2003. (Imagine You're A ... Ser.). (ENG.). 32p. (J). pap. 9.99 *(978-1-84089-282-6(X))* Meg and Lucy Bks. GBR. Dist: Independent Pubs. Group.

Clibbon, Lucy & Loveheart, Lucy. Lots of Love: From Meg & Lucy. Clibbon, Meg & Meg, Mighty. 2007. (ENG.). 24p. 5.95 *(978-1-84089-376-2(1))* Meg and Lucy Bks. GBR. Dist: Independent Pubs. Group.

Clibbon, Lucy, jt. illus. see Loveheart, Lucy.

Clifford, Caroline. The Gospel on Five Fingers: The Story of Mother Theresa, 1 bk. Coming, Soon. Gosselin, Katie & Bono, Ignacio, trs. 2005. (J). 5.00 *(978-0-9765180-1-3(5))* Catholic World Mission.

—Jesus, I Trust in You! The Story of Saint Faustina, Missionary of Divine Mercy. Luetkemeyer, Jenny. Kiszkurno, Irene & Chacon, Cesar, trs. 2004. (SPA & POL.). 32p. (J). (gr. k-5). 5.00 *(978-0-9747571-2-4(8))* Catholic World Mission.

Clift, Eva. Gulliver's Travels: And A Discussion of Tolerance. Swift, Jonathan. 2003. (Values in Action Illustrated Classics Ser.). 191p. (J). *(978-1-59203-029-3(7))* Learning Challenge, Inc.

—Heidi: With a Discussion of Optimism. Spyri, Johanna. 2003. (Values in Action Illustrated Classics Ser.). 190p. (J). *(978-1-59203-030-9(0))* Learning Challenge, Inc.

—The Red Badge of Courage: With a Discussion of Self-Esteem. Crane, Stephen. 2003. (Values in Action Illustrated Classics Ser.). 190p. (J). *(978-1-59203-034-7(3))* Learning Challenge, Inc.

Clift, Eva. The Call of the Wild. Clift, Eva, tr. London, Jack. 2003. (Values in Action Illustrated Classics Ser.). (J). *(978-1-59203-047-7(5))* Learning Challenge, Inc.

—Frankenstein: With a Discussion of Tolerance. Clift, Eva, tr. Shelley, Mary. 2003. (Values in Action Illustrated Classics Ser.). (J). *(978-1-59203-048-4(3))* Learning Challenge, Inc.

—The Merry Adventures of Robin Hood: With a Discussion of Fellowship. Clift, Eva, tr. Pyle, Howard. 2003. (Values in Action Illustrated Classics Ser.). (J). *(978-1-59203-044-6(0))* Learning Challenge, Inc.

—The Strange Case of Dr. Jekyll & Mr. Hyde: With a Discussion of Moderation. Clift, Eva, tr. Stevenson, Robert Louis. 2003. (Values in Action Illustrated Classics Ser.). (J). *(978-1-59203-053-8(X))* Learning Challenge, Inc.

Clifton-Brown, Holly. Big Birthday. Hosford, Kate. 2012. (Carolrhoda Picture Bks). (ENG.). 32p. (J). (gr. k-2). lib. bdg. 16.95 *(978-0-7613-5410-9(7),* Carolrhoda Bks.) Lerner Publishing Group.

—Big Bouffant. Hosford, Kate. 2011. (ENG.). 32p. (J). (gr. k-2). 16.95 *(978-0-7613-5409-3(3),* Carolrhoda Bks.) Lerner Publishing Group.

—How to Be a Ballerina. Castor, Harriet. 2012. (ENG.). 28p. (J). (gr. 1). 19.95 *(978-1-84732-735-2(4))* Carlton Bks., Ltd. GBR. Dist: Sterling Publishing Co., Inc.

Clifton-Brown, Holly. Moo, Moo, Move Your Mood! A Guide for Kids about Mind-Body Connection. Miles, Brenda & Patterson, Colleen A. 2016. (J). ***(978-1-4338-2112-7(5),*** Magination Pr.) American Psychological Assn.

Clifton-Brown, Holly. Stella Brings the Family. Schiffer, Miriam B. 2015. (ENG.). 36p. (J). (gr. k-3). 16.99 *(978-1-4521-1190-2(1))* Chronicle Bks. LLC.

Clifton-Brown, Holly. Annie Hoot & the Knitting Extravaganza. Clifton-Brown, Holly. 2010. (Andersen Press Picture Bks). (ENG.). 32p. (J). (gr. -1-3). 16.95 *(978-0-7613-6444-3(7))* Lerner Publishing Group.

Clifton Johnson. Walking. Thoreau, Henry. 2010. 100p. pap. 3.49 *(978-1-60386-305-6(2),* Watchmaker Publishing) Wexford College Pr.

Clifton, Tom. Under One Flag: A Year at Rohwer. Parkhurst, Liz S. 2006. (ENG.). 32p. (J). (gr. 3-7). 16.95 *(978-0-87483-759-9(6),* 1241971) August Hse. Pubs., Inc.

Climo, Liz. Rory the Dinosaur Gets a Pet. 2016. (J). ***(978-0-316-27729-7(0))*** Little Brown & Co.

Climpson, Sue. Incredible Quests: Epic Journeys in Myth & Legend. Steele, Philip. 2006. (ENG.). 48p. (J). (gr. 3-7). pap. 11.99 *(978-1-84476-247-7(5))* Anness Publishing GBR. Dist: National Bk. Network.

Cline, Ian, photos by. Brownie the Monkey Visits the Zoo. Ramoutar, Tagore. 2012. 38p. pap. *(978-1-907837-48-7(5))* Longshot Ventures, Ltd.

Cline, Jeff & Cash-Walsh, Tina. The U. S. History Cookbook: Delicious Recipes & Exciting Events from the Past. D'Amico, Joan & Drummond, Karen Eich. 2003. (ENG.). 192p. (J). pap. 16.00 *(978-0-471-13602-6(6),* Jossey-Bass) Wiley, John & Sons, Inc.

Cline, Mike. Franky Fox's Fun with English Activity Book, Level A1. Cline, Mike. Yi-Cline, Nancy. Yi-Cline, Nancy, ed. 2007. 62p. pap. 7.99 *(978-0-9777419-1-5(5),* SIAB) Lingo Pr. LLC.

—Franky Fox's Fun with English Level A1. Cline, Mike. Yi-Cline, Nancy. Yi-Cline, Nancy, ed. 2007. 65p. 14.99 *(978-0-9777419-0-8(7),* SITB) Lingo Pr. LLC.

Cline, Mike, jt. illus. see Maher, Adele.

Clinedinst, B. West, jt. illus. see Varian, George.

Cliquet, Ronan, et al. Marvel Universe Thor Digest. 2013. (ENG.). 96p. (J). (gr. -1-17). pap. 9.99 *(978-0-7851-8505-5(4))* Marvel Worldwide, Inc.

Clish, Lori. Fish Don't Swim in a Tree. Clish, Marian L. (J). (gr. k-3). pap. 7.95 *(978-1-928632-12-2(2))* Writers Marketplace:Consulting, Critiquing & Publishing.

—The Owl Who Couldn't Say Whoo. Staheli, Bee, ed. l.t. ed. (J). (gr. k-5). pap. 7.95 *(978-1-928632-50-4(5))* Writers Marketplace:Consulting, Critiquing & Publishing.

Clo, Kathy. Mommy, Did I Grow in Your Tummy? Where Some Babies Come From. Gordon, Elaine R. Date not set. 28p. (Orig.). (J). (gr. -1-4). pap. 9.95 *(978-0-9634561-0-6(5))* EM Greenberg Pr., Inc.

Cloke, Rene. The Adventures of Tom Thumb. 2012. (ENG.). 24p. (J). pap. 6.50 *(978-1-84135-545-0(3))* Award Pubns. Ltd. GBR. Dist: Parkwest Pubns., Inc.

—Aladdin & His Magical Lamp. 2012. (ENG.). 24p. pap. 6.50 *(978-1-84135-534-4(8))* Award Pubns. Ltd. GBR. Dist: Parkwest Pubns., Inc.

—Bible Stories for Children. Wilkin, Wendy. 2012. (ENG.). 32p. (J). 9.95 *(978-0-86163-797-3(6))* Award Pubns. Ltd. GBR. Dist: Parkwest Pubns., Inc.

—By the River Bank, 4 vols. Bishop, Michael. 2012. (ENG.). 30p. (J). 4.95 *(978-1-84135-784-3(7))* Award Pubns. Ltd. GBR. Dist: Parkwest Pubns., Inc.

—Cinderella. 2012. (ENG.). 24p. pap. 6.50 *(978-1-84135-535-1(6))* Award Pubns. Ltd. GBR. Dist: Parkwest Pubns., Inc.

—In the Wild Wood, 4 vols. Bishop, Michael. 2012. (ENG.). 64p. (J). 4.95 *(978-1-84135-785-0(5))* Award Pubns. Ltd. GBR. Dist: Parkwest Pubns., Inc.

—Little Red Riding Hood. 2012. (ENG.). 24p. pap. 6.50 *(978-1-84135-540-5(2))* Award Pubns. Ltd. GBR. Dist: Parkwest Pubns., Inc.

—The Little Tin Soldier. 2012. (ENG.). 24p. (J). pap. 6.50 *(978-1-84135-542-9(9))* Award Pubns. Ltd. GBR. Dist: Parkwest Pubns., Inc.

—More Bible Stories for Children. Carruth, Jane. 2012. (ENG.). 32p. (J). 9.95 *(978-0-86163-770-6(4))* Award Pubns. Ltd. GBR. Dist: Parkwest Pubns., Inc.

—Mr Toad Comes Home, 4 vols. Bishop, Michael. 2012. (ENG.). 30p. (J). 4.95 *(978-1-84135-787-4(1))* Award Pubns. Ltd. GBR. Dist: Parkwest Pubns., Inc.

—Mr Toad in Trouble, 4 vols. Bishop, Michael. 2012. (ENG.). 30p. (J). 4.95 *(978-1-84135-786-7(3))* Award Pubns. Ltd. GBR. Dist: Parkwest Pubns., Inc.

—My First Picture Book of Nursery Rhymes. 2012. (ENG.). 24p. 9.95 *(978-1-84135-581-8(X))* Award Pubns. Ltd. GBR. Dist: Parkwest Pubns., Inc.

—Pinocchio. 2012. (ENG.). 24p. pap. 6.50 *(978-1-84135-538-2(0))* Award Pubns. Ltd. GBR. Dist: Parkwest Pubns., Inc.

—Puss in Boots. 2012. (ENG.). 24p. (J). pap. 6.50 *(978-1-84135-539-9(9))* Award Pubns. Ltd. GBR. Dist: Parkwest Pubns., Inc.

—Snow White & the Seven Dwarfs. 2012. (ENG.). 24p. pap. 6.50 *(978-1-84135-541-2(0))* Award Pubns. Ltd. GBR. Dist: Parkwest Pubns., Inc.

—Storytime Classics. 2012. (ENG.). 144p. (J). 12.50 *(978-1-84135-521-4(6))* Award Pubns. Ltd. GBR. Dist: Parkwest Pubns., Inc.

—The Three Little Pigs. 2012. (ENG.). 24p. pap. 6.50 *(978-1-84135-544-3(5))* Award Pubns. Ltd. GBR. Dist: Parkwest Pubns., Inc.

—The Ugly Duckling. 2012. (ENG.). 24p. (J). pap. 6.50 *(978-1-84135-543-6(7))* Award Pubns. Ltd. GBR. Dist: Parkwest Pubns., Inc.

Cloke, Rene. Favourite Bible Stories: Best-Loved Tales from the New Testament. Cloke, Rene. 2014. (ENG.). 32p. 10.50 *(978-1-84135-982-3(3))* Award Pubns. Ltd. GBR. Dist: Parkwest Pubns., Inc.

Clonts, E. M. Childrens Adoration Prayer Book. Hartley, Bob. 2012. 114p. pap. 24.95 *(978-0-615-58840-7(9))* Deeper Waters.

Close, Laura Ferraro. The Three Little Pigs. York, J. 2012. (Favorite Children's Stories Ser.). (ENG.). 24p. (J). (gr. k-3). 27.07 *(978-1-61473-216-7(7),* 204910) Child's World, Inc., The.

—5 Steps to Drawing Sea Creatures. StJohn, Amanda. 2011. (5 Steps to Drawing Ser.). (ENG.). 32p. (J). (gr. k-3). lib.

bdg. 27.07 *(978-1-60973-204-2(9)*, 201110) Child's World, Inc., The.

Clouette, Katie. Benjamin the Bear. Shakespeare, Nancy. 2013. (Benjamin the Bear Ser.). (ENG.). (J). (gr. -1-3). 14.95 *(978-1-62086-312-1(X))* Mascot Bks., Inc.

—Benjamin the Bear Gets a Sister. Shakespeare, Nancy. 2013. (Benjamin the Bear Ser.). (ENG.). (J). (gr. -1-3). 14.95 *(978-1-62086-316-9(2))* Mascot Bks., Inc.

—Benjamin the Bear Goes on a Picnic. Shakespeare, Nancy. 2013. (Benjamin the Bear Ser.). (ENG.). (J). (gr. -1-3). 14.95 *(978-1-62086-314-5(6))* Mascot Bks., Inc.

—Benjamin the Bear Goes to Kindergarten. Shakespeare, Nancy. 2013. (Benjamin the Bear Ser.). (ENG.). (J). (gr. -1-k). 14.95 *(978-1-62086-320-6(0))* Mascot Bks., Inc.

—Benjamin the Bear Rides on an Airplane. Shakespeare, Nancy. 2013. (Benjamin the Bear Ser.). (ENG.). (J). (gr. -1-3). 14.95 *(978-1-62086-318-3(9))* Mascot Bks., Inc.

Clough, Julie. The Dolphin. 2008. (Seaside Bath Bks.). (ENG.). 6p. (J). (gr. -1-k). 6.99 *(978-0-7641-9532-7(8))* Barron's Educational Series, Inc.

—The Octopus. 2008. (Seaside Bath Bks.). (ENG.). 6p. (J). (gr. -1-k). 6.99 *(978-0-7641-9530-3(1))* Barron's Educational Series, Inc.

—The Starfish. 2008. (Seaside Bath Bks.). (ENG.). 6p. (J). (gr. -1-k). 6.99 *(978-0-7641-9533-4(6))* Barron's Educational Series, Inc.

Clover, Gordon. Sammy Squirrel & Rodney Raccoon. Lawrence, Duane. 2007. (ENG.). 106p. pap. *(978-1-894694-54-4(6))* Granville Island Publishing.

Clow, Alexine. Jenny's Dreams. Clow, Alexine. 2010. 20p. pap. 10.95 *(978-1-936051-89-2(3))* Peppertree Pr., The.

Cloyne, Rachel. Snow White & Rose Red: A Pop-up Fairytale. Brothers Grimm, Becky & Brothers Grimm. 2012. (Fairytale Pop-Ups Ser.). (ENG.). 18p. (J). (gr. k-2). 19.99 *(978-1-85707-881-7(0))* Tango Bks. GBR. Dist: Independent Pubs. Group.

Clugston, Chynna. Who Is the Mystery Bat-Squad?, 1 vol. Fisch, Sholly & Age, Heroic. 2014. (DC Super Friends Ser.). (ENG.). 32p. (gr. 1-2). 21.27 *(978-1-4342-9224-7(X))* Stone Arch Bks.

Cneut, Carll. City Lullaby. Singer, Marilyn. 2007. (ENG.). 32p. (J). (gr. -1-3). 16.99 *(978-0-618-60703-7(X))* Houghton Mifflin Harcourt Publishing Co.

—Ten Moonstruck Piglets. Johnson, Lindsay Lee. 2011. (ENG.). 32p. (J). (gr. -1-3). 16.99 *(978-0-618-86866-7(6))* Houghton Mifflin Harcourt Publishing Co.

—Willy. Kockere, Geert De. 2011. 32p. (J). (gr. -1-3). 14.00 *(978-0-8028-5395-0(1)*, Eerdmans Bks For Young Readers) Eerdmans, William B. Publishing Co.

Co, Aileen & Dayton, Melissa. Friends of God: Catholic Bible Study for Children. Manhardt, Laurie Watson. 2006. (Come & See Kids Ser.). 124p. (J). (gr. -1-2). per. 9.95 *(978-1-931018-41-8(3))* Emmaus Road Publishing.

Co, Miguel. Night of the White Deer. Bushnell, Jack. 2012. (ENG.). 32p. (J). (gr. -1-3). 16.95 *(978-1-933718-80-4(3))* Tanglewood Pr.

Coalson, Glo. En Las Piernas de Mama. Scott, Ann Herbert. 2007.Tr. of On Mother's Lap. (SPA & ENG.). 14p. (J). (gr. k — 1). bds. 5.95 *(978-0-618-75247-8(1))* Houghton Mifflin Harcourt Publishing Co.

Coates, Jennifer. This Is Farmer Greg. Howard-Parham, Pam. l.t. ed. 2005. (HRL Board Book Ser.). (gr. -1-k). pap. 10.95 *(978-1-57332-305-5(5)*, HighReach Learning, Incorporated) Carson-Dellosa Publishing, LLC.

Coates, Kathy. Batty about Texas, 1 vol. Smith, J. 2008. (ENG.). 32p. (J). (gr. k-3). 16.99 *(978-1-58980-582-8(8))* Pelican Publishing Co., Inc.

—The Buzz on Honeybees, 1 vol. Kaemmerlen, Cathy. 2012. (ENG.). 32p. (J). (gr. k-3). 16.99 *(978-1-4556-1457-8(2))* Pelican Publishing Co., Inc.

Coates, Kathy, jt. illus. see Knowlton, Charlotte.

Coates, Sean. Kayla's Magic Eyes. Hinton, Cheryl. Ellis, Althia Melody, ed. 2013. 26p. 13.00 *(978-0-578-11929-8(3))* Mosaic Paradigm Group, LLC.

Cobalt Illustrations Studio Staff, jt. illus. see Low, William.

Cobb, Josh, jt. illus. see Cobb, Vicki.

Cobb, Rebecca. The Castle of Adventure. Blyton, Enid. unabr. ed. 2014. (Adventure Ser.: 2). (ENG.). 288p. (J). (gr. 4-7). pap. 9.99 *(978-1-4472-6275-6(1))* Pan Macmillan GBR. Dist: Independent Pubs. Group.

—The Circus of Adventure. Blyton, Enid. unabr. ed. 2014. (Adventure Ser.: 7). (ENG.). 288p. (J). (gr. 4-7). pap. 9.99 *(978-1-4472-6281-7(6))* Pan Macmillan GBR. Dist: Independent Pubs. Group.

—The Island of Adventure. Blyton, Enid. unabr. ed. 2014. (Adventure Ser.: 1). (ENG.). 288p. (J). (gr. 4-7). pap. 9.99 *(978-1-4472-6277-0(8))* Pan Macmillan GBR. Dist: Independent Pubs. Group.

—The Mountain of Adventure. Blyton, Enid. unabr. ed. 2014. (Adventure Ser.: 5). (ENG.). 304p. (J). (gr. 4-7). pap. 9.99 *(978-1-4472-6279-4(4))* Pan Macmillan GBR. Dist: Independent Pubs. Group.

—The River of Adventure. Blyton, Enid. unabr. ed. 2014. (Adventure Ser.: 8). (ENG.). 240p. (J). (gr. 4-7). pap. 9.99 *(978-1-4472-6282-4(4))* Pan Macmillan GBR. Dist: Independent Pubs. Group.

—The Sea of Adventure. Blyton, Enid. unabr. ed. 2014. (Adventure Ser.: 4). (ENG.). 288p. (J). (gr. 4-7). pap. 9.99 *(978-1-4472-6278-7(6))* Pan Macmillan GBR. Dist: Independent Pubs. Group.

—The Ship of Adventure. Blyton, Enid. unabr. ed. 2014. (Adventure Ser.: 6). (ENG.). 288p. (J). (gr. 4-7). pap. 9.99 *(978-1-4472-6280-0(8))* Pan Macmillan GBR. Dist: Independent Pubs. Group.

—The Valley of Adventure. Blyton, Enid. unabr. ed. 2014. (Adventure Ser.: 3). (ENG.). 288p. (J). (gr. 4-7). pap. 9.99 *(978-1-4472-6276-3(X))* Pan Macmillan GBR. Dist: Independent Pubs. Group.

Cobb, Rebecca. Missing Mommy: A Book about Bereavement. Cobb, Rebecca. 2013. (ENG.). 28p. (J). (gr. -1-3). 16.99 *(978-0-8050-9507-4(1)*, Holt, Henry & Co. Bks. For Young Readers) Holt, Henry & Co.

Cobb, Vicki & Cobb, Josh. Light Action! Amazing Experiments with Optics. 2005. (Press Monographs: PM150). 208p. (J). pap. 17.00 *(978-0-8194-5851-3(1))* SPIE.

Cobleigh, Carolynn. Edgar Allan Poe. Bagert, Brod, ed. 2008. (Poetry for Young People Ser.). (ENG.). 48p. (J). (gr. 3-7). pap. 6.95 *(978-1-4027-5472-2(8))* Sterling Publishing Co., Inc.

—Poetry for Young People: Edgar Allan Poe. Bagert, Brod, ed. 2014. (Poetry for Young People Ser.). (ENG.). 48p. (J). (gr. 3). 14.95 *(978-1-4549-1348-1(7))* Sterling Publishing Co., Inc.

Coburn, Dylan. The Boy with Wings. Cheshire, Simon. 2015. (Collins Big Cat Ser.). (ENG.). 24p. pap. 7.95 ***(978-0-00-759118-3(7))*** HarperCollins Pubs. Ltd. GBR. Dist: Independent Pubs. Group.

Cocca-Leffler, Maryann. Carl the Complainer. Knudsen, Michelle. 2005. (Social Studies Connects). 32p. (J). (gr. 1-3). pap. 5.95 *(978-1-57565-157-6(2))* Kane Pr., Inc.

—I Don't Want to Go to Camp. Bunting, Eve. 2003. (ENG.). 32p. (J). (gr. -1-1). pap. 8.95 *(978-1-59078-074-9(4))* Boyds Mills Pr.

—Spotlight on Stacey. 2007. (Social Studies Connects). 32p. (J). (gr. -1-3). pap. 5.95 *(978-1-57565-236-8(6))* Kane Pr., Inc.

Cocca-Leffler, Maryann. Thanksgiving at the Tappletons'. Spinelli, Eileen. 2015. (ENG.). 32p. (J). (gr. -1-3). pap. 6.99 ***(978-0-06-236397-8(2))*** HarperCollins Pubs.

Cocca-Leffler, Maryann. Calling All Cats. Cocca-Leffler, Maryann. 2004. (All Aboard Picture Reader Ser.). (ENG.). 32p. (J). (gr. -1-k). mass mkt. 3.99 *(978-0-448-43369-1(9)*, Grosset & Dunlap) Penguin Publishing Group.

—Dog Wash Day. Cocca-Leffler, Maryann. 2004. (All Aboard Picture Reader Ser.). (ENG.). 32p. (J). (gr. -1-k). mass mkt. 3.99 *(978-0-448-43370-7(2)*, Grosset & Dunlap) Penguin Publishing Group.

—Easter Bunny in Training. Cocca-Leffler, Maryann. 2009. (Sneak a Peek Ser.). 16p. (J). (gr. -1-3). pap. 6.99 *(978-0-06-125673-8(0))* HarperCollins Pubs.

Cocca-Leffler, Maryann. A Homemade Together Christmas. Cocca-Leffler, Maryann. 2015. (ENG.). 32p. (J). (gr. -1-2). 16.99 ***(978-0-8075-3366-6(1))*** Whitman, Albert & Co.

Cocca-Leffler, Maryann. It's Halloween Night. Cocca-Leffler, Maryann. 2009. (Sneak a Peek Ser.). (ENG.). 16p. (J). (gr. -1-3). pap. 6.99 *(978-0-06-125674-5(9)*, HarperFestival) HarperCollins Pubs.

—Jack's Talent. Cocca-Leffler, Maryann. 2007. (ENG.). 32p. (J). (gr. -1-3). 17.99 *(978-0-374-33681-3(4)*, Farrar, Straus & Giroux (BYR)) Farrar, Straus & Giroux.

—Janine. Cocca-Leffler, Maryann. 2015. (ENG.). 32p. (J). (gr. -1-2). 16.99 *(978-0-8075-3754-1(3))* Whitman, Albert & Co.

—Mr. Tanen's Ties. Cocca-Leffler, Maryann. 2004. (ENG.). 32p. (J). (gr. k-2). pap. 6.95 *(978-0-8075-5302-2(6))* Whitman, Albert & Co.

—Princess K. I. M. & the Lie That Grew. Cocca-Leffler, Maryann. 2009. (ENG.). 32p. (J). (gr. 2-4). 16.99 *(978-0-8075-4178-4(8))* Whitman, Albert & Co.

—Princess Kim & Too Much Truth. Cocca-Leffler, Maryann. 2011. (ENG.). 32p. (J). (gr. 1-4). 16.99 *(978-0-8075-6618-3(7))* Whitman, Albert & Co.

—Rain Brings Frogs: A Little Book of Hope. Cocca-Leffler, Maryann. 2011. (ENG.). 32p. (J). (gr. -1-2). 9.99 *(978-0-06-196106-9(X))* HarperCollins Pubs.

—Theo's Mood: A Book of Feelings. Cocca-Leffler, Maryann. 2013. (ENG.). 24p. (J). (gr. -1-2). 15.99 *(978-0-8075-7778-3(2))* Whitman, Albert & Co.

—A Vacation for Pooch. Cocca-Leffler, Maryann. 2013. (ENG.). 32p. (J). (gr. -1-2). 16.99 *(978-0-8050-9106-9(8)*, Holt, Henry & Co. Bks. For Young Readers) Holt, Henry & Co.

Cocciolone, Kathy Roberts. You Can't Get into More Trouble Than Gator Pervis!! Hammock, Sarah Owens. 2007. 32p. (J). 12.95 *(978-1-934246-27-6(1))* Peppertree Pr., The.

Cochard, David. The Legend of Honey Hollow. 2008. 46p. (J). 16.99 *(978-0-9799444-0-6(6))* Joey Publishing.

—Miracle in Sumatra: The Story of Gutsy Gus. McNaney, Jeanne. 2009. (ENG.). 32p. (J). (gr. -1-3). 16.95 *(978-0-9814534-6-0(5))* Ovation Bks.

Cochran, Christina. The Mini Message Man & the Great Candy Caper. Cochran, Cheryl. 2011. 40p. pap. 24.95 *(978-1-4560-7565-1(9))* America Star Bks.

Cochran, Josh. Inside & Out: New York. Cochran, Josh. 2014. (ENG.). 16p. (J). (gr. 2-5). 17.99 *(978-0-7636-7520-2(2)*, Big Picture Press) Candlewick Pr.

Cochran, Paige. Dinner for Six: A set-the-table Fable. Cochran, Gayle. 2011. (ENG.). 24p. pap. 6.00 *(978-1-4609-0987-4(9))* CreateSpace Independent Publishing Platform.

Cockburn, Gerrie L. Why Turtles Have Shells. Cockburn, Gerrie L. Cockburn, Ian, ed. (Friendship Ser.). 31p. (Orig.). (J). (gr. k-4). pap. 5.95 *(978-1-887461-00-9(0))* Cockburn Publishing.

Cockcroft, Jason. Jason & the Golden Fleece. Riordan, James. 64p. 2005. (ENG.). (J). (gr. 2-17). pap. 12.95 *(978-1-84507-061-8(5)*, Frances Lincoln Children's Bks.); 2004. (YA). 19.95 *(978-1-84507-271-1(5)*, Frances Lincoln) Quarto Publishing Group UK GBR. Dist: Hachette Bk. Group, Perseus-PGW.

—The Oxford Book of Bible Stories. Doherty, Berlie. 2014. (ENG.). 272p. 24.95 *(978-0-19-278214-4(2))*; pap. 18.95 *(978-0-19-278210-6(X))* Oxford Univ. Pr., Inc.

—Pilgrim's Progress. McCaughrean, Geraldine. 112p. (J). pap. 16.99 *(978-0-340-72754-6(3))* Hodder & Stoughton GBR. Dist: Trafalgar Square Publishing.

—Room for a Little One: A Christmas Tale. Waddell, Martin. 2008. (ENG.). 26p. (J). (gr. -1-2). bds. 7.99 *(978-1-4169-6177-2(1)*, Little Simon) Little Simon.

—Room for a Little One: A Christmas Tale. Waddell, Martin. (ENG.). 32p. (J). (gr. -1-3). 2006. 11.99 *(978-1-4169-2518-7(X))*; 2004. 17.99 *(978-0-689-86841-2(3))* McElderry, Margaret K. Bks. (McElderry, Margaret K. Bks.).

—Snow Ponies. Cotten, Cynthia. 2013. (ENG.). 32p. (J). (gr. -1-1). 6.99 *(978-1-250-03429-8(9))* Square Fish.

—A Song in Bethlehem. McGee, Marni. 2007. (ENG.). 40p. (J). (gr. -1-2). 15.99 *(978-0-375-83447-9(8)*, Knopf Bks. for Young Readers) Random Hse. Children's Bks.

Cockcroft, Jason. Jason & the Golden Fleece. Cockcroft, Jason, tr. Riordan, James. 2003. 64p. (J). 19.95 *(978-0-7112-2081-2(6)*, Frances Lincoln) Quarto Publishing Group UK GBR. Dist: Perseus-PGW.

Cockrum, Dave & Byrne, John. The Uncanny X-Men, Vol. 2. 2010. (ENG.). 192p. (J). (gr. -1-17). pap. 24.99 *(978-0-7851-3704-7(1))* Marvel Worldwide, Inc.

Cockrum, Dave, jt. illus. see Byrne, John.

Cocoretto. What's That Noise? CHOO! CHOO! Guess the Vehicle! 2015. (What's That Noise? Ser.: 4). (ENG.). 12p. (J). bds. ***(978-1-84643-746-5(6))*** Child's Play International Ltd.

—What's That Noise? SNAP! SNAP! Guess the Animal! 2015. (What's That Noise? Ser.: 4). (ENG.). 12p. (J). bds. ***(978-1-84643-748-9(2))*** Child's Play International Ltd.

—What's That Noise? TAP! TAP! Guess the Toy! 2015. (What's That Noise? Ser.: 4). (ENG.). 12p. (J). bds. ***(978-1-84643-747-2(4))*** Child's Play International Ltd.

—What's That Noise? TOOT! TOOT! Guess the Instrument! 2015. (What's That Noise? Ser.: 4). (ENG.). 12p. (J). bds. ***(978-1-84643-749-6(0))*** Child's Play International Ltd.

Cocotos, Tom Nick. Myths Busted! Just When You Thought You Knew What You Knew... Krieger, Emily. 2013. (Myths Busted Ser.). (ENG.). 208p. (J). (gr. 4-7). pap. 7.95 *(978-1-4263-1102-4(8))*; lib. bdg. 16.90 *(978-1-4263-1103-1(6))* National Geographic Society. (National Geographic Children's Bks.).

—National Geographic Kids Myths Busted! No. 2: Just When You Thought You Knew What You Knew ... Krieger, Emily. 2014. (Myths Busted Ser.). (ENG.). 208p. (J). (gr. 4-7). pap. 7.99 *(978-1-4263-1478-0(7))*, National Geographic Children's Bks.) National Geographic Society.

—National Geographic Kids Myths Busted! 2: Just When You Thought You Knew What You Knew ... Krieger, Emily. 2014. (Myths Busted Ser.). (ENG.). 208p. (J). (gr. 4-7). lib. bdg. 16.90 *(978-1-4263-1479-7(5)*, National Geographic Children's Bks.) National Geographic Society.

—Weird but True: Stupid Criminals: 100 Brainless Baddies Busted, Plus Wacky Facts. U. S. National Geographic Society Staff. 2012. (ENG.). 176p. (J). (gr. 3-7). pap. 7.95 *(978-1-4263-0861-1(2)*, National Geographic Children's Bks.) National Geographic Society.

Codell, Esmé Raji. John Pawson Works. Sudjic, Deyan. 2nd rev. ed. 2005. (ENG.). 272p. (gr. 8-17). pap. 39.95 *(978-0-7148-4382-7(2))* Phaidon Pr. Ltd. GBR. Dist: Hachette Bk. Group.

Codor, Richard. Too Many Latkes! Codor, Richard. 2011. (ENG.). 44p. (J). (gr. -1-3). pap. 9.95 *(978-0-87441-882-8(8))* Behrman Hse., Inc.

Coe, Anne. Here Is the Southwestern Desert. Dunphy, Madeleine. 2006. (Web of Life Ser.). (ENG.). 32p. (J). (gr. -1-3). 16.95 *(978-0-9773795-7-6(4))*; pap. 9.95 *(978-0-9773795-6-9(6))* Web of Life Children's Bks.

Coe, Kimberly. My Dad Is A Marine. Coe, Kimberly. 2007. 46p. (J). per. 12.00 *(978-0-9787113-1-3(9)*, Ithaca Pr.) Authors & Artists Publishers of New York, Inc.

Coevoet, Sylvie. Rouge. Averous, Helene. 2013. 38p. pap. *(978-967-1-03582-5(5))* MHC Asia Group.

Coffelt, Nancy. Aunt Ant Leaves Through the Leaves. Coffelt, Nancy. 2013. (ENG.). 32p. (J). pap. 7.99 *(978-0-8234-2761-1(7))* Holiday Hse., Inc.

—Aunt Ant Leaves Through the Leaves: A Story with Homophones & Homonyms. Coffelt, Nancy. 2012. (ENG.). 32p. (J). 16.95 *(978-0-8234-2353-8(0))* Holiday Hse., Inc.

—Big, Bigger, Biggest! Coffelt, Nancy. 2009. (ENG.). 32p. (J). (gr. -1-2). 16.95 *(978-0-8050-8089-6(9)*, Holt, Henry & Co. Bks. For Young Readers) Holt, Henry & Co.

Coffey, Anthony, jt. illus. see Labbe, Jesse.

Coffey, Durwood. Running for Home. McDiarmid, Gail S. & McGee, Marilyn S. 2013. 76p. pap. 15.95 *(978-0-9854677-0-8(3))* SunDog Enterprises.

Coffey, Kevin. Bear-Ly There with Compass. French, Mary B. 2012. 122p. pap. 6.00 *(978-0-9852821-0-3(X))* Mary B./French.

—The Candy Roses of Cape Care. Canale, Suzie Hearl. 2012. 38p. (J). 14.95 *(978-1-937406-67-7(9))* Mascot Bks., Inc.

—A Loop of String: String Stories & String Stunts: Traditional & Original String Figures & Stories. Stotter, Ruth. 2009. 110p. pap. 22.95 *(978-1-58790-170-6(6))* Regent Pr.

—New England a to Z. Baker, Alison. 2012. 38p. (J). 14.95 *(978-1-62086-065-6(1))* Mascot Bks., Inc.

—So Big yet So Small. Weiland, Peter. 2012. (J). 14.95 *(978-1-937406-16-5(4))* Mascot Bks., Inc.

Coffin, Marilyn. The Ducks' New Friends. Stephenson, Nancy Ann. l.t. ed. 2006. 34p. (J). per. 9.99 *(978-1-59879-164-8(8))* Lifevest Publishing, Inc.

Cogan, John. Belle's Star. Gotsch, Connie. 2009. 134p. (YA). pap. 8.99 *(978-1-932926-01-9(1)*, Kinkajou Pr.) Artemesia Publishing, LLC.

—Belle's Trial. Gotsch, Connie. 2010. (ENG & ABK.). 150p. (J). pap. 8.99 *(978-1-932926-12-5(7)*, Kinkajou Pr.) Artemesia Publishing, LLC.

Cogan, Kim. Cooper's Lesson. Cogan, Kim, tr. Shin, Sun Yung. Paek, Min, tr. from ENG. 2004. (ENG & KOR.). 32p. (J). 16.95 *(978-0-89239-193-6(6))* Lee & Low Bks., Inc.

Cogancherry, Helen. Floating House. Sanders, Scott Russell. 2011. 40p. (J). lib. bdg. 18.00 *(978-1-59098-425-3(0))* Wooster Bk. Co., The.

—Warm as Wool. Sanders, Scott Russell. 2007. (J). lib. bdg. 18.00 *(978-1-59098-421-5(8))* Wooster Bk. Co., The.

Cogdill, Jill K. Cracker the Crab & the Sideways Afternoon. 2003. 40p. (J). lib. bdg. 19.95 *(978-0-9725560-0-2(1))* Cracker the Crab LLC.

Cogswell, Matthew. Thor's Wedding Day: By Thialfi, the Goat Boy. Coville, Bruce. 2008. (Magic Carpet Bks.). (ENG.). 144p. (J). (gr. 2-5). pap. 6.99 *(978-0-15-205872-2(9))* Houghton Mifflin Harcourt Publishing Co.

Coh, Smiljana. Big Brave Daddy. 2012. (ENG.). 24p. (J). (gr. k-k). 10.99 *(978-1-60905-211-9(0))* Blue Apple Bks.

—I Want to Be a Ballerina. Membrino, Anna. 2014. (ENG.). 32p. (J). (gr. -1-2). lib. bdg. 17.99 *(978-0-375-97330-7(3)*, Random Hse. Bks. for Young Readers) Random Hse. Children's Bks.

Cohee, Ron. Go, Go, Go! Lagonegro, Melissa. 2011. (Step into Reading Ser.). (ENG.). 32p. (J). (gr. k-3). pap. 3.99 *(978-0-7364-2765-4(1))*; lib. bdg. 12.99 *(978-0-7364-8091-8(9))* Random Hse. Children's Bks. (RH/Disney).

—The Spooky Sound. Lagonegro, Melissa. 2010. (Step into Reading Ser.). (ENG.). 32p. (J). (gr. k-3). pap. 3.99 *(978-0-7364-2664-0(7))* Random Hse., Inc.

Cohee, Ron. Star Wars: Return of the Jedi (Star Wars) Smith, Geof. 2015. (Little Golden Book Ser.). (ENG.). 24p. (J). (-k). 4.99 ***(978-0-7364-3548-2(4)***, Golden Bks.) Random Hse. Children's Bks.

Cohee, Ron, jt. illus. see RH Disney Staff.

Cohee, Ron, jt. illus. see Webber, John.

Cohen, Brie, photos by. Awesome Snacks & Appetizers. Cornell, Kari. 2013. (You're the Chef Ser.). (ENG., 32p. (gr. 3-5). lib. bdg. 26.60 *(978-0-7613-6642-3(3)*, Millbrook Pr.) Lerner Publishing Group.

—Dandy Desserts. Cornell, Kari. 2013. (You're the Chef Ser.). (ENG., 32p. (gr. 3-5). lib. bdg. 26.60 *(978-0-7613-6644-7(X)*, Millbrook Pr.) Lerner Publishing Group.

—Delicious Vegetarian Main Dishes. Larson, Jennifer S. 2013. (You're the Chef Ser.). (ENG., 32p. (gr. 3-5). lib. bdg. 26.60 *(978-0-7613-6635-5(0)*, Millbrook Pr.) Lerner Publishing Group.

—Marvelous Muffins, Breads, & Pancakes. Cornell, Kari. 2013. (You're the Chef Ser.). (ENG., 32p. (gr. 3-5). lib. bdg. 26.60 *(978-0-7613-6636-2(9)*, Millbrook Pr.) Lerner Publishing Group.

—Meaty Main Dishes. Larson, Jennifer S. 2013. (You're the Chef Ser.). (ENG., 32p. (gr. 3-5). lib. bdg. 26.60 *(978-0-7613-6634-8(2)*, Millbrook Pr.) Lerner Publishing Group.

—Perfect Pizza Recipes. Larson, Jennifer S. 2013. (You're the Chef Ser.). (ENG., 32p. (gr. 3-5). lib. bdg. 26.60 *(978-0-7613-6637-9(7)*, Millbrook Pr.) Lerner Publishing Group.

—Slurpable Smoothies & Drinks. Cornell, Kari. 2013. (You're the Chef Ser.). (ENG., 32p. (gr. 3-5). lib. bdg. 26.60 *(978-0-7613-6639-3(3)*, Millbrook Pr.) Lerner Publishing Group.

—Super Pasta & Rice Dishes. Larson, Jennifer S. 2013. (You're the Chef Ser.). (ENG., 32p. (gr. 3-5). lib. bdg. 26.60 *(978-0-7613-6641-6(5)*, Millbrook Pr.) Lerner Publishing Group.

—Sweet Cookies & Bars. Cornell, Kari. 2013. (You're the Chef Ser.). (ENG., 32p. (gr. 3-5). lib. bdg. 26.60 *(978-0-7613-6638-6(5)*, Millbrook Pr.) Lerner Publishing Group.

—Tasty Sandwiches. Larson, Jennifer S. 2013. (You're the Chef Ser.). (ENG., 32p. (gr. 3-5). lib. bdg. 26.60 *(978-0-7613-6643-0(1)*, Millbrook Pr.) Lerner Publishing Group.

—Terrific Veggies on the Side. Cornell, Kari. 2013. (You're the Chef Ser.). (ENG., 32p. (gr. 3-5). lib. bdg. 26.60 *(978-0-7613-6640-9(7)*, Millbrook Pr.) Lerner Publishing Group.

—Yummy Soup & Salad Recipes. Larson, Jennifer S. 2013. (You're the Chef Ser.). (ENG., 32p. (gr. 3-5). lib. bdg. 26.60 *(978-0-7613-6633-1(4)*, Millbrook Pr.) Lerner Publishing Group.

Cohen, Deene. Yesterday's Child. Benjamin, Ruth. (YA). 16.95 *(978-1-56062-176-8(1)*, CFR122H); pap. 13.95 *(978-1-56062-177-5(X)*, CFR122S) C I S Communications, Inc.

Cohen, Elly. Peg Bearskin. Dinn, Philip & Jones, Andy. 2003. (ENG.). 32p. (J). pap. *(978-0-9688712-7-0(5))* Running the Goat.

Cohen, Greg A. The Littlest Maccabee: An Original Story. Rouss, Sylvia A. 2006. (J). *(978-1-932687-76-7(9)*, Pitspopany Pr.) Simcha Media Group.

Cohen, Izhar. The Wolf's Story: What Really Happened to Little Red Riding Hood. Forward, Toby. 2005. (ENG.). 32p. (J). (gr. -1-3). 17.99 *(978-0-7636-2785-0(2))* Candlewick Pr.

Cohen, Jan Barger. Four Special Questions: A Passover Story. Zucker, Jonny. 2003. (Festival Time Ser.). (ENG.). 24p. (J). (gr. -1-2). pap. 6.95 *(978-0-7641-2267-5(3))* Barron's Educational Series, Inc.

—Lanterns & Firecrackers: A Chinese New Year Story. Zucker, Jonny. 2014. (ENG.). 24p. (J). (gr. -1-k). pap. 8.99 *(978-1-84507-076-2(3)*, Frances Lincoln) Quarto Publishing Group UK GBR. Dist: Hachette Bk. Group.

—Lighting a Lamp: A Diwali Story. Zucker, Jonny. 2004. (Festival Time Ser.). (ENG.). 24p. (J). pap. 8.99 *(978-0-7641-2670-3(9))* Barron's Educational Series, Inc.

Cohen, Jesse, photos by. Elephant & Mommy. Galvin, Laura. 2003. (ENG., 16p. (J). (gr. -1-k). 5.95 *(978-1-56899-911-1(9)*, B9007) Soundprints.

Cohen, Jessie. Tamarin's Mealtime. Galvin, Laura Gates. 2005. (Let's Go to the Zoo! Ser.). (ENG.). 16p. (J). (gr. -1-k). 5.95 *(978-1-56899-858-9(9))* Soundprints.

—Tiger Cub See-and-Do. Galvin, Laura Gates. 2005. (Let's Go to the Zoo! Ser.). (ENG.). 16p. (J). (gr. -1-k). 5.95 *(978-1-56899-856-5(2)*, B9006) Soundprints.

Cohen, Jessie, photos by. Flamingo Grows Up. 2005. (Let's Go to the Zoo! Ser.). (ENG., 16p. (J). (gr. -1-k). 5.95 *(978-1-56899-974-6(7)*, B9009) Soundprints.

—New Baby Giraffe. Galvin, Laura. 2005. (ENG., 16p. (J). (gr. -1-k). 5.95 *(978-1-56899-798-8(1)*, B9003) Soundprints.

—Sea Lion Swims. Lamm, Drew. 2005. (Let's Go to the Zoo! Ser.). (ENG., 16p. (J). (gr. -1-k). 5.95 *(978-1-56899-976-0(3)*, B9010) Soundprints.

Cohen, Lynda. Beach Feet. Jackson, Marjorie. 2005. (ENG.). 8p. (J). pap. 5.75 *(978-1-57274-750-0(1)*, 2123, Bks. for Young Learners) Owen, Richard C. Pubs., Inc.

Cohen, Melissa. PuzzlePal Books: Pretty Pig. Magnayon, Megan Coy. 2013. (PuzzlePal Bks.). (ENG.). 10p. (J). (gr. -1). bds. 14.95 *(978-1-60710-698-2(1)*, Silver Dolphin Bks.) Baker & Taylor Publishing Group.

C

Cohen, Miriam. Two Little Mittens, 1 vol. Cohen, Miriam. 2006. (ENG.). 32p. (J). (gr. -1). pap. 6.95 *(978-1-59572-044-3(8))* Star Bright Bks., Inc.

Cohen, Santiago. Good Night San Francisco. Gamble, Adam. 2006. (Good Night Our World Ser.). (ENG.). 22p. (J). (gr. k — 1). bds. 9.95 *(978-0-9777979-5-0(3))* Our World of Books.

—The Yiddish Fish. 2014. (ENG.). 32p. (J). (gr. -1-k). 16.95 *(978-1-62914-633-1(1),* Sky Pony Pr.) Skyhorse Publishing Co., Inc.

Cohen, Sheldon. Kishka for Koppel, 1 vol. Davis, Aubrey. 2011. (ENG.). 32p. (J). (gr. -1-3). 19.95 *(978-1-55469-299-6(7))* Orca Bk. Pubs. USA.

Cohen, Sheldon, jt. illus. see Oberman, Sheldon.

Cohen, Tod. It's Seder Time! Cohen, Tod, photos by. Kropf, Latifa Berry. 2004. (ENG.). 24p. (J). (gr. -1-1). 12.95 *(978-1-58013-092-9(5),* Kar-Ben Publishing) Lerner Publishing Group.

Cohen, Tod, photos by. It's Hanukkah Time! Kropf, Latifa Berry. (Hanukkah Ser.). (ENG., 24p. (J). (gr. -1-1). 2011. pap. 8.95 *(978-0-7613-8306-2(9));* 2004. 12.95 *(978-1-58013-120-9(4))* Lerner Publishing Group. (Kar-Ben Publishing).

—It's Israel's Birthday! Dietrick, Ellen. 2008. (ENG., 24p. (J). (gr. -1-1). lib. bdg. 12.95 *(978-0-8225-7668-6(6),* Kar-Ben Publishing) Lerner Publishing Group.

—It's Purim Time! Kropf, Latifa Berry. 2012. (Purim Ser.). (ENG., 24p. (J). (gr. -1-1). pap. 8.95 *(978-0-7613-8493-9(6),* Kar-Ben Publishing) Lerner Publishing Group.

—It's Shofar Time! Kropf, Latifa Berry. (High Holidays Ser.). (ENG., 24p. (J). (gr. -1-1). 2011. pap. 8.95 *(978-0-7613-8307-9(7));* 2006. lib. bdg. 12.95 *(978-1-58013-158-2(1))* Lerner Publishing Group. (Kar-Ben Publishing).

—It's Sukkah Time! Kropf, Latifa Berry. 2012. (Sukkot & Simchat Torah Ser.). (ENG., 24p. (J). (gr. -1-1). 9.95 *(978-1-4677-0741-1(4),* Kar-Ben Publishing) Lerner Publishing Group.

—It's Time Set. Kropf, Latifa Berry. 24p. (J). (gr. -1-1). 58.28 *(978-1-58013-192-6(1),* Kar-Ben Publishing) Lerner Publishing Group.

—It's Tot Shabbat! Danis, Naomi. 2011. (Shabbat Ser.). (ENG., 24p. (J). (gr. -1-1). lib. bdg. 14.95 *(978-0-7613-4515-2(9),* Kar-Ben Publishing) Lerner Publishing Group.

—Ten Good Rules: A Counting Book. Topek, Susan Remick. 2007. (ENG., 24p. (J). (gr. -1-1). lib. bdg. 15.95 *(978-0-8225-7293-0(1),* Kar-Ben Publishing) Lerner Publishing Group.

—Ten Good Rules: A Ten Commandments Counting Book. Topek, Susan Remick. 2007. (ENG., 24p. (J). (gr. -1-1). per. 7.95 *(978-1-58013-209-1(X),* Kar-Ben Publishing) Lerner Publishing Group.

Cohn, Riley. Martin in the Narthex. 2011. (ENG.). 40p. (J). 14.95 *(978-0-940672-82-6(0))* Shearer Publishing.

Cohn, Scott. I Am Bane. Rosen, Lucy. 2012. (Dark Knight Rises Ser.). (ENG.). 24p. (J). (gr. -1-2). pap. 3.99 *(978-0-06-213222-2(9),* HarperFestival) HarperCollins Pubs.

Coillen, Lisa P. Time for Bed. Jarrell, Pamela R. l.t. ed. 2005. (HRL Board Book Ser.). (J). (gr. -1-k). pap. 10.95 *(978-1-57332-325-3(X),* HighReach Learning, Incorporated) Carson-Dellosa Publishing, LLC.

Cointe, François. The Book of When. Jaffé, Laura. 2008. (ENG.). 96p. (J). (gr. 3-7). 17.95 *(978-0-8109-7240-7(9),* Abrams Bks. for Young Readers) Abrams.

—Do You Wonder Why? How to Answer Life's Tough Questions. Pouilloux, David. Moloney, Kate, ed. 2012. (ENG.). 80p. (YA). (gr. 5-9). pap. 12.95 *(978-1-4197-0389-8(7),* Amulet Bks.) Abrams.

Coipel, Olivier. Siege. 2010. (ENG.). 200p. (YA). (gr. 8-17). 24.99 *(978-0-7851-4810-4(8))* Marvel Worldwide, Inc.

—Wolverine. Way, Daniel et al. 2006. (ENG.). 152p. (YA). (gr. 8-17). pap. 13.99 *(978-0-7851-1922-7(1))* Marvel Worldwide, Inc.

Coipel, Olivier. House of M. Coipel, Olivier, . 2006. (ENG.). 224p. (YA). (gr. 8-17). pap. 24.99 *(978-0-7851-1721-6(0))* Marvel Worldwide, Inc.

Coipel, Olivier & Donovan, Deric. X-Men: To Serve & Protect. 2011. (ENG.). 136p. (J). (gr. 4-17). pap. 14.99 *(978-0-7851-5228-6(8))* Marvel Worldwide, Inc.

Coipel, Olivier, jt. illus. see Marvel Comics Staff.

Coirault, Christine. Cómo se Dice... ? Wise, Sue. 2006. (How I Say That? Ser.). (ENG & SPA.). 32p. (gr. k-4). lib. bdg. 26.00 *(978-0-8368-6259-1(7),* Gareth Stevens Learning Library) Stevens, Gareth Publishing LLLP.

—How Do I Say That? (¿Cómo se Dice?) Wise, Sue. 2006. (How Do I Say That?/ Cómo se dice? Ser.). (ENG & SPA.). 32p. (gr. k-4). pap. 10.50 *(978-0-8368-6583-7(9),* Gareth Stevens Learning Library) Stevens, Gareth Publishing LLLP.

—My First Book of Learning. 2009. (J). *(978-1-74089-930-7(X))* Fog City Pr.

Coke, Sherrie. Tommy's New Shell, 2nd in series. Evangelista, Susan. 2005. 24p. (J). bds. 19.95 *(978-0-9769602-0-1(6))* Evangelista, Susan.

Coker, Carla. God's World & Me from A to Z. Langley, Judy. 2004. 32p. (gr. -1). 8.99 *(978-1-56309-367-8(7))* New Hope Pubs.

Coker, Paul, Jr. Henrietta: The Homely Duckling. Hahn, Phil. 2004. (Weewisdom Bks.). 47p. (J). 16.95 *(978-0-87159-293-4(2),* 168, Unity Hse.) Unity Schl. of Christianity.

Coker, Tom. Daredevil Noir. 2010. (ENG.). 112p. (gr. 10-17). pap. 14.99 *(978-0-7851-2154-1(4))* Marvel Worldwide, Inc.

Coker, Tomm. Avengers Assemble - Science Bros. 2013. (ENG.). 144p. (YA). (gr. 8-17). pap. 16.99 *(978-0-7851-6797-6(8))* Marvel Worldwide, Inc.

Colan, Gene, et al. Guardians of the Galaxy - Tomorrow's Avengers, Vol. 1. 2013. (ENG.). 368p. (J). (gr. 4-17). pap. 39.99 *(978-0-7851-6687-0(4))* Marvel Worldwide, Inc.

Colan, Gene & Heck, Don. The Invincible Iron Man. 2014. (ENG.). 264p. (J). (gr. -1-17). pap. 24.99 *(978-0-7851-8843-8(6))* Marvel Worldwide, Inc.

Colangione-B, Christie. That's Why They're Called Punkins. Badavino, Jimmy. 2011. (ENG.). 38p. pap. 11.95 *(978-1-4662-4138-1(1))* CreateSpace Independent Publishing Platform.

Colavecchio, Alan. Seymour & the Big Red Rhino. Powers, John. 2005. 32p. (J). (gr. -1-3). 14.95 *(978-1-929039-21-0(2))* Ambassador Bks., Inc.

Colby, Devon English, jt. illus. see Nielsen, Gwyn English.

Colby, Garry. Jack B. Nimble Jumps. Fuerst, Jeffrey B. 2009. (Reader's Theater Nursery Rhymes & Songs Set B Ser.). 48p. (J). pap. *(978-1-60859-154-1(9))* Benchmark Education Co.

—Jack Be Nimble. Fuerst, Jeffrey B. 2010. (Rising Readers Ser.). (J). 3.49 *(978-1-60719-698-3(0))* Newmark Learning LLC.

—Picture That! Bible Storybook over 65 Stories, 1 vol. Harrast, Tracy. 2011. (ENG.). 160p. (J). (gr. -1-2). pap. 9.99 *(978-0-310-72590-9(9))* Zonderkidz.

Colby, J. Z., et al. Trilogy One. Colby, J. Z. ed. 2010. (Nebador Ser.: Books One, Two, and Three). (ENG.). 641p. (YA). pupil's gde. ed. 49.95 *(978-1-936253-17-3(8))* Nebador Archives.

Colby, J. Z. & Powers, Mireille Xioulan. Flight Training, Kibi & the Search for Happiness. Colby, J. Z. & Persons, Katelynn. 2011. (Nebador Ser.: Book Four). 178p. (YA). pap. 10.95 *(978-1-936253-27-2(5))* Nebador Archives.

Cole, Al. Room for One More. Harris, Jane Ellen. 2007. 24p. (J). (gr. -1-3). pap. 11.98 *(978-0-9800733-0-0(8),* LSP) LSP Digital, LLC.

Cole, Amy, jt. illus. see Hayes, Steve.

Cole, Babette. Even My Ears Are Smiling. Rosen, Michael. 2012. (ENG.). 128p. (J). (gr. 3). 26.99 *(978-1-4088-0297-7(X),* 39635, Bloomsbury USA Childrens) Bloomsbury USA.

Cole, Babette. Instructions for Bedtime. Larsen, Mylisa. 2016. 32p. (J). (gr. -1-3). 17.99 ***(978-0-06-232064-3(5))*** HarperCollins Pubs.

Cole, Babette. The Hairy Book. Cole, Babette. 2003. (ENG.). 32p. (J). (gr. k-2). pap. 9.99 *(978-0-09-943425-2(3),* Red Fox) Random House Children's Books GBR. Dist: Independent Pubs. Group.

—Princess Smartypants. Cole, Babette. 2005. (ENG.). 32p. (J). (gr. -1-3). 16.99 *(978-0-399-24398-1(4),* Putnam Juvenile) Penguin Publishing Group.

Cole, Brock. George Washington's Teeth. Chandra, Deborah & Comora, Madeleine. 2007. (ENG.). 40p. (J). (gr. -1-3). pap. 7.99 *(978-0-312-37604-8(9))* Square Fish.

—Gully's Travels. Seidler, Tor. 2008. (ENG.). 192p. (J). (gr. -1-3). 17.95 *(978-0-545-02506-5(0),* Di Capua, Michael) Scholastic, Inc.

Cole, Brock. The Goats. Cole, Brock. 2010. (ENG.). 192p. (YA). (gr. 7-10). pap. 9.99 *(978-0-312-61191-0(9))* Square Fish.

—The Money We'll Save. Cole, Brock. 2011. (ENG.). 40p. (J). (gr. -1-3). 16.99 *(978-0-374-35011-6(6),* Farrar, Straus & Giroux (BYR)) Farrar, Straus & Giroux.

Cole, Dick. The Falling Flowers. Reed, Jennifer. 2005. (Falling Flowers Ser.). 32p. (J). (gr. -1-3). 16.95 *(978-1-885008-28-2(7),* Shen's Bks.) Lee & Low Bks., Inc.

Cole, Gina. Adapt. 2005. 40p. (J). 17.00 *(978-0-9659538-3-2(1))* Soul Vision Works Publishing.

Cole, Henry. And Tango Makes Three. Richardson, Justin & Parnell, Peter. 2005. (ENG.). 32p. (J). (gr. -1-3). 17.99 *(978-0-689-87845-9(1),* Simon & Schuster Bks. For Young Readers) Simon & Schuster Bks. For Young Readers.

Cole, Henry. And Tango Makes Three: 10th Anniversary Edition. Richardson, Justin & Parnell, Peter. 10th ed. 2015. (ENG.). 40p. (J). (gr. -1-3). 17.99 ***(978-1-4814-4884-0(6),*** Simon & Schuster Bks. For Young Readers) Simon & Schuster Bks. For Young Readers.

Cole, Henry. Bad Boys. Palatini, Margie. 40p. (J). (gr. -1-2). 2003. lib. bdg. 16.89 *(978-0-06-000103-2(8));* 2003. (ENG.). 15.99 *(978-0-06-000102-5(X),* Tegen, Katherine Bks); 2006. (ENG.). reprint ed. 6.99 *(978-0-06-000104-9(6),* Tegen, Katherine Bks) HarperCollins Pubs.

—Bad Boys Get Cookie! Palatini, Margie. 2006. 32p. (J). (gr. -1-3). 18.89 *(978-0-06-074437-3(5));* (ENG.). 17.99 *(978-0-06-074436-6(7),* Tegen, Katherine Bks) HarperCollins Pubs.

—Bad Boys Get Henpecked! Palatini, Margie. 2009. (ENG.). 32p. (J). (gr. -1-2). 17.99 *(978-0-06-074433-5(2),* Tegen, Katherine Bks) HarperCollins Pubs.

—Big Chickens. Helakoski, Leslie. 2008. (ENG.). 32p. (J). (gr. -1-k). pap. 6.99 *(978-0-14-241057-8(8),* Puffin) Penguin Publishing Group.

—Big Chickens. Helakoski, Leslie. 2008. (J). (gr. -1-3). lib. bdg. 14.65 *(978-0-7569-8913-2(2))* Perfection Learning Corp.

—Big Chickens Fly the Coop. Helakoski, Leslie. (ENG.). 32p. (J). (gr. -1-k). 2010. pap. 6.99 *(978-0-14-241464-4(6),* Puffin); 2008. 16.99 *(978-0-525-47915-4(5),* Dutton Juvenile) Penguin Publishing Group.

—Big Chickens Go to Town. Helakoski, Leslie. 2010. (ENG.). 32p. (J). (gr. -1-k). 16.99 *(978-0-525-42162-7(9),* Dutton Juvenile) Penguin Publishing Group.

—Bogart & Vinnie: A Completely Made-Up Story of True Friendship. Vernick, Audrey. 2013. (ENG.). 40p. (J). (gr. -1-3). 17.89 *(978-0-8027-2823-4(5));* 16.99 *(978-0-8027-2822-7(7))* Walker & Co.

—Chaucer's First Winter. Krensky, Stephen. (ENG.). 32p. (J). (gr. -1-1). 2010. 9.99 *(978-1-4424-1658-1(0));* 2009. 17.99 *(978-1-4169-9026-0(7))* Simon & Schuster Bks. For Young Readers. (Simon & Schuster Bks. For Young Readers).

—Chicken Butt! Perl, Erica S. 2009. (ENG.). 32p. (J). (gr. -1-1). 13.95 *(978-0-8109-8325-0(7),* Abrams Bks. for Young Readers) Abrams.

—Chicken Butt's Back! Perl, Erica S. 2011. (ENG.). 32p. (J). (gr. -1-17). 13.95 *(978-0-8109-9729-5(0),* Abrams Bks. for Young Readers) Abrams.

—City Chicken. Dorros, Arthur. 2003. 40p. (J). (gr. -1-3). 16.89 *(978-0-06-028483-1(8))* HarperCollins Pubs.

—Clara Caterpillar. Edwards, Pamela Duncan. 2004. (ENG.). 40p. (J). (gr. -1-1). reprint ed. pap. 6.99 *(978-0-06-443691-5(8))* HarperCollins Pubs.

Cole, Henry. La Gallinita de la Pradera, 1 vol. Hopkins, Jackie Mims. 2015. (SPA & ENG.). 32p. (J). (gr. 1-3). 17.95 ***(978-1-56145-841-7(4))*** Peachtree Pubs.

Cole, Henry. Honk! Duncan Edwards, Pamela. 2014. 32p. pap. 8.00 *(978-1-61003-226-1(8))* Center for the Collaborative Classroom.

—I Know a Wee Piggy. Norman, Kim. 2012. (ENG.). 32p. (J). (gr. -1-k). 16.99 *(978-0-8037-3735-8(1),* Dial) Penguin Publishing Group.

—Katy Duck. Capucilli, Alyssa Satin. 2007. (ENG.). 16p. (J). (gr. -1-k). bds. 7.99 *(978-1-4169-1901-8(5),* Little Simon) Little Simon.

—Katy Duck & the Tip-Top Tap Shoes. Capucilli, Alyssa Satin. 2013. (Ready-To-Reads Ser.). (ENG.). 24p. (J). (gr. -1-1). 16.99 *(978-1-4424-5246-6(3));* pap. 3.99 *(978-1-4424-5245-9(5))* Simon Spotlight. (Simon Spotlight).

—Katy Duck, Big Sister. Capucilli, Alyssa Satin. (ENG.). (J). (gr. -1-k). 2009. 24p. pap. 3.99 *(978-1-4169-8278-4(7));* 2007. 14p. bds. 7.99 *(978-1-4169-4209-2(2))* Little Simon. (Little Simon).

—Katy Duck Board Book 4-Pack: Katy Duck; Katy Duck, Big Sister; Katy Duck, Center Stage; Katy Duck, Dance Star. Capucilli, Alyssa Satin. 2013. (ENG.). 62p. (J). (gr. -1-k). bds. 31.99 *(978-1-4424-9023-9(3),* Little Simon) Little Simon.

—Katy Duck, Center Stage. Capucilli, Alyssa Satin. 2008. (ENG.). 14p. (J). (gr. -1-k). 7.99 *(978-1-4169-3338-0(7),* Little Simon) Little Simon.

—Katy Duck, Dance Star. Capucilli, Alyssa Satin. 2008. (ENG.). 16p. (J). (gr. -1-k). 7.99 *(978-1-4169-3337-3(9),* Little Simon) Little Simon.

—Katy Duck, Dance Star/Katy Duck, Center Stage. Capucilli, Alyssa Satin. 2009. (ENG.). 24p. (J). (gr. -1-k). pap. 3.99 *(978-1-4169-8279-1(5),* Little Simon) Little Simon.

—Katy Duck, Flower Girl. Capucilli, Alyssa Satin. 2013. (Ready-To-Reads Ser.). (ENG.). 24p. (J). (gr. -1-1). 16.99 *(978-1-4424-7279-2(0));* pap. 3.99 *(978-1-4424-7278-5(2))* Simon Spotlight. (Simon Spotlight).

—Katy Duck Goes to Work. Capucilli, Alyssa Satin. 2014. (Ready-To-Reads Ser.). (ENG.). 24p. (J). (gr. -1-1). pap. 3.99 *(978-1-4424-7281-5(2),* Simon Spotlight) Simon Spotlight.

—Katy Duck Makes a Friend. Capucilli, Alyssa Satin. 2012. (Ready-To-Reads Ser.). (ENG.). 24p. (J). (gr. -1-1). 15.99 *(978-1-4424-1977-3(6));* pap. 3.99 *(978-1-4424-1976-6(8))* Simon Spotlight. (Simon Spotlight).

—Katy Duck Meets the Babysitter. Capucilli, Alyssa Satin. 2012. (Ready-To-Reads Ser.). (ENG.). 24p. (J). (gr. -1-1). 15.99 *(978-1-4424-5242-8(0));* pap. 3.99 *(978-1-4424-5241-1(2))* Simon Spotlight. (Simon Spotlight).

—Katy Duck Meets the Babysitter. Capucilli, Alyssa Satin. ed. 2012. (Simon & Schuster Ready-To-Read Ser.). lib. bdg. 13.55 *(978-0-606-26918-6(5),* Turtleback) Turtleback Bks.

—Katy Duck Ready-To-Read Value Pack: Starring Katy Duck; Katy Duck Makes a Friend; Katy Duck Meets the Babysitter; Katy Duck & the Tip-Tip Tap Shoes; Katy Duck, Flower Girl; Katy Duck Goes to Work. Capucilli, Alyssa Satin. 2014. (Ready-To-Reads Ser.). (ENG.). 144p. (J). (gr. -1-1). pap. 15.96 *(978-1-4814-2600-8(1),* Simon Spotlight) Simon Spotlight.

—Katy Duck's Happy Halloween. Capucilli, Alyssa Satin. 2014. (Ready-To-Reads Ser.). (ENG.). 24p. (J). (gr. -1-1). pap. 3.99 *(978-1-4424-9806-8(4),* Simon Spotlight) Simon Spotlight.

—The Kiss Box. Verburg, Bonnie. 2011. (ENG.). 32p. (J). (gr. -1-k). 16.99 *(978-0-545-11284-0(2),* Orchard Bks.) Scholastic, Inc.

—The Leprechaun's Gold. Edwards, Pamela Duncan. 2006. (ENG.). 40p. (J). (gr. -1-2). reprint ed. 6.99 *(978-0-06-443878-0(3),* Tegen, Katherine Bks) HarperCollins Pubs.

—Little Bo in Italy: The Continued Adventures of Bonnie Boadicea. Andrews, Julie & Edwards, Julie Andrews. 2010. (ENG.). 112p. (J). (gr. 1-4). 19.99 *(978-0-06-008908-5(3))* HarperCollins Pubs.

—Little Bo in London, No. 2. Edwards, Julie Andrews. 2012. (ENG.). 112p. (J). (gr. 1-4). 19.99 *(978-0-06-008911-5(3))* HarperCollins Pubs.

—Mouse Was Mad. Urban, Linda. (ENG.). 40p. (J). (gr. -1-3). 2012. pap. 6.99 *(978-0-547-72750-9(X));* 2009. 16.99 *(978-0-15-205337-6(9))* Houghton Mifflin Harcourt Publishing Co.

—Mouse Was Mad Big Book. Urban, Linda. 2015. (ENG.). 40p. (J). (gr. -1-3). 26.99 *(978-0-544-45607-5(6),* HMH Books For Young Readers) Houghton Mifflin Harcourt Publishing Co.

—Naughty Little Monkeys. Aylesworth, Jim. 2006. (ENG.). 32p. (J). (gr. -1-2). reprint ed. 6.99 *(978-0-14-240562-8(0),* Puffin) Penguin Publishing Group.

—Nelly May Has Her Say. DeFelice, Cynthia C. 2013. (ENG.). 32p. (J). (gr. -1-3). 16.99 *(978-0-374-39899-6(2),* Farrar, Straus & Giroux (BYR)) Farrar, Straus & Giroux.

—Oink? Palatini, Margie. 2006. (ENG.). 40p. (J). (gr. -1-3). 17.99 *(978-0-689-86258-8(X),* Simon & Schuster Bks. For Young Readers) Simon & Schuster Bks. For Young Readers.

—One Pup's Up. Chall, Marsha Wilson. 2010. (ENG.). 32p. (J). (gr. -1 — 1). 16.99 *(978-1-4169-7960-9(3),* McElderry, Margaret K. Bks.) McElderry, Margaret K. Bks.

—Prairie Chicken Little, 1 vol. Hopkins, Jackie Mims. (ENG.). 32p. (J). 2015. (gr. 1-3). pap. 7.95 *(978-1-56145-834-9(1));* 2013. (gr. -1-3). 15.95 *(978-1-56145-694-9(2))* Peachtree Pubs.

—Princess Pigtoria & the Pea. Edwards, Pamela Duncan. 2010. (ENG.). 40p. (J). (gr. -1-3). 16.99 *(978-0-545-15625-7(4),* Orchard Bks.) Scholastic, Inc.

—Roar! A Noisy Counting Book. Edwards, Pamela Duncan. Date not set. 32p. (J). (gr. -1-2). pap. 5.99 *(978-0-06-443572-7(5))* HarperCollins Pubs.

—Santa's Stuck. Greene, Rhonda Gowler. 2006. (ENG.). 32p. (J). (gr. -1-3). pap. 5.99 *(978-0-14-240686-1(4),* Puffin) Penguin Publishing Group.

—Shiver Me Letters: A Pirate ABC. Sobel, June. (ENG.). 32p. (J). (gr. -1-3). 2009. pap. 6.99 *(978-0-15-206679-6(9));* 2006. 16.99 *(978-0-15-216732-5(3))* Houghton Mifflin Harcourt Publishing Co.

—The Sissy Duckling. Fierstein, Harvey. 2014. (ENG.). 40p. (J). (gr. -1-3). pap. 9.99 *(978-1-4424-9817-4(X),* Little Simon) Little Simon.

—The Sissy Duckling. Fierstein, Harvey. 2005. (ENG.). 40p. (J). (gr. k-3). reprint ed. 7.99 *(978-1-4169-0313-0(5),* Simon & Schuster Bks. For Young Readers) Simon & Schuster Bks. For Young Readers.

—Starring Katy Duck. Capucilli, Alyssa Satin. 2011. (Ready-To-Reads Ser.). (ENG.). 24p. (J). (gr. -1-1). pap. 3.99 *(978-1-4424-1974-2(1));* lib. bdg. 15.99 *(978-1-4424-1975-9(X))* Simon Spotlight. (Simon Spotlight).

—Surfer Chick. Dempsey, Kristy. 2012. (ENG.). 32p. (J). (gr. -1-2). 16.95 *(978-1-4197-0188-7(6),* Abrams Bks. for Young Readers) Abrams.

—Three Hens & a Peacock, 1 vol. Laminack, Lester L. 2011. (ENG.). 32p. (J). (gr. -1-3). 15.95 *(978-1-56145-564-5(4))* Peachtree Pubs.

—Three Hens & a Peacock, 1 vol. Laminack, Lester. 2014. (ENG.). 32p. (J). (gr. -1-3). pap. 7.95 *(978-1-56145-726-7(4))* Peachtree Pubs.

—Tubby the Tuba. Tripp, Paul. 2006. (ENG.). 32p. (J). (gr. -1-3). 16.99 *(978-0-525-47717-4(9),* Dutton Juvenile) Penguin Publishing Group.

—The Twelve Days of Christmas in Virginia. Corbett, Sue. 2009. (Twelve Days of Christmas in America Ser.). (ENG.). 32p. (J). (gr. k-3). 12.95 *(978-1-4027-6344-1(1))* Sterling Publishing Co., Inc.

—Who's Who? Geist, Ken. 2012. (ENG.). 28p. (J). (gr. -1 — 1). 16.99 *(978-0-312-64437-6(X))* Feiwel & Friends.

—Why Do Kittens Purr? Bauer, Marion Dane. 2007. (ENG.). 32p. (J). (gr. -1-2). 9.99 *(978-1-4169-6850-4(4),* Simon & Schuster/Paula Wiseman Bks.) Simon & Schuster/Paula Wiseman Bks.

—The Worrywarts. Edwards, Pamela Duncan. 2003. (ENG.). 32p. (J). (gr. -1-1). pap. 7.99 *(978-0-06-443516-1(4))* HarperCollins Pubs.

—Z Is for Zookeeper: A Zoo Alphabet. Smith, Roland & Smith, Marie. (ENG.). 40p. (J). (gr. k-6). 2005. 16.95 *(978-1-58536-158-8(5));* 2007. pap. 7.95 *(978-1-58536-329-2(4))* Sleeping Bear Pr.

Cole, Henry. Big Bug. Cole, Henry. 2014. (ENG.). 32p. (J). (gr. -1-2). 14.99 *(978-1-4424-9897-6(8),* Little Simon) Little Simon.

Cole, Henry. Brambleheart. Cole, Henry. 2016. 272p. (J). (gr. 3-7). 16.99 ***(978-0-06-224546-5(5))*** HarperCollins Pubs.

Cole, Henry. The Littlest Evergreen. Cole, Henry. 2011. (ENG.). 32p. (J). (gr. -1-2). 16.99 *(978-0-06-114619-0(6),* Tegen, Katherine Bks) HarperCollins Pubs.

—A Nest for Celeste: A Story about Art, Inspiration, & the Meaning of Home. Cole, Henry. (ENG.). 352p. (J). (gr. 3-7). 2012. pap. 6.99 *(978-0-06-170412-3(1));* 2010. 16.99 *(978-0-06-170410-9(5))* HarperCollins Pubs. (Tegen, Katherine Bks).

—On Meadowview Street. Cole, Henry. 2007. (ENG.). 32p. (J). (gr. -1-3). 17.99 *(978-0-06-056481-0(4),* Greenwillow Bks.) HarperCollins Pubs.

—On the Way to the Beach. Cole, Henry. 2003. (ENG.). 32p. (J). (gr. -1-3). 16.99 *(978-0-688-17515-3(5),* Greenwillow Bks.) HarperCollins Pubs.

—Trudy. Cole, Henry. 2009. 32p. (J). lib. bdg. 18.89 *(978-0-06-154268-8(7));* (ENG.). (gr. -1-3). 17.99 *(978-0-06-154267-1(9))* HarperCollins Pubs. (Greenwillow Bks.).

—Unspoken: A Story from the Underground Railroad. Cole, Henry. 2012. (Unspoken Ser.). (ENG.). 40p. (J). (gr. -1-3). 16.99 *(978-0-545-39997-5(1),* Scholastic Pr.) Scholastic, Inc.

Cole, Henry. Gigi & Lulu's Gigantic Fight. Cole, Henry, tr. Edwards, Pamela Duncan. 2004. 40p. (J). (gr. -1-2). lib. bdg. 15.89 *(978-0-06-050753-4(5))* HarperCollins Pubs.

Cole, Henry & Bond, Felicia. Jack & Jill's Treehouse. Edwards, Pamela Duncan. 2008. 24p. (J). (gr. -1-2). lib. bdg. 17.89 *(978-0-06-009078-4(2),* Tegen, Katherine Bks) HarperCollins Pubs.

Cole, Herbert. A Child's Book of Warriors. Canton, William. 2012. 290p. pap. 12.75 *(978-1-936639-21-2(1))* St. Augustine Academy Pr.

Cole, Jeff. Numbers: A Silly Slider Book. Accord Publishing Staff & Andrews McMeel Publishing, LLC Staff. 2011. (ENG.). 12p. (J). (gr. -1-k). bds. 10.99 *(978-1-4494-0174-0(0))* Andrews McMeel Publishing.

Cole, Jeff. Eyeball Animation Drawing Book: African Safari Edition. Cole, Jeff. Andrews McMeel Publishing, LLC Staff. 2009. (ENG.). 84p. (J). (gr. -1). pap. 14.99 *(978-0-7407-8101-8(4))* Andrews McMeel Publishing.

—Eyeball Animation Drawing Book: Funny Folks Edition. Cole, Jeff. Andrews McMeel Publishing, LLC Staff. 2009. (ENG.). 84p. (J). (gr. -1). pap. 14.99 *(978-0-7407-8104-9(9))* Andrews McMeel Publishing.

—Eyeball Animation Drawing Book: Underwater Safari Edition. Cole, Jeff. Andrews McMeel Publishing, LLC Staff. 2009. (ENG.). 84p. (J). (gr. -1). pap. 14.99 *(978-0-7407-8106-3(5))* Andrews McMeel Publishing.

Cole, Jess. Six Swans: A Folktale. 2006. (ENG.). 32p. (J). (gr. 1). 16.95 *(978-1-59078-056-5(6))* Boyds Mills Pr.

Cole, Joanna, jt. illus. see Cuddy, Robbin.

Cole, Lisa. Chessie of the Chesapeake Bay. Cole, Lisa. 2011. 110p. pap. 9.95 *(978-1-936343-94-2(0))* Peppertree Pr., The.

Cole, Mernie. You Let the Cat Out of the Bag! (and Other Crazy Animal Sayings) Klingel, Cynthia Fitterer & Klingel, Cynthia. 2007. (Sayings & Phrases Ser.). (ENG.). 24p. (J). (gr. 2-5). 28.50 *(978-1-59296-903-6(8),* 200791) Child's World, Inc., The.

Cole, Mernie & Gallagher-Cole, Mernie. Ack! There's a Bug in My Ear! (And Other Sayings That Just Aren't True) Klingel, Cynthia Fitterer. 2007. (Sayings & Phrases Ser.). (ENG.). 24p. (J). (gr. 2-5). 28.50 *(978-1-59296-902-9(X),* 200785) Child's World, Inc., The.

—Doctor Jokes. Rosenberg, Pam. 2010. (Hah-Larious Joke Bks.). (ENG.). 24p. (J). (gr. 1-4). 27.07 *(978-1-60253-517-6(5),* 200278) Child's World, Inc., The.

—Hold Your Horses! (And Other Peculiar Sayings) Amoroso, Cynthia. 2011. (Sayings & Phrases Ser.). (ENG.). 24p. (J). (gr. 2-5). lib. bdg. 28.50 *(978-1-60253-681-4(3),* 200780) Child's World, Inc., The.

—You're Clean as a Whistle! (And Other Silly Sayings) Klingel, Cynthia Fitterer & Klingel, Cynthia. 2007. (Sayings & Phrases Ser.). (ENG.). 24p. (J). (gr. 2-5). 28.50 *(978-1-59296-905-0(4),* 200792) Child's World, Inc., The.

Cole, Mernie Gallagher. Family Reunion. Bader, Bonnie. 2003. (Penguin Young Readers, Level 3 Ser.). (ENG.). 48p. (J). (gr. 1-3). mass mkt. 3.99 *(978-0-448-42896-3(2),* Grosset & Dunlap) Penguin Publishing Group.

Cole, Raymond A. A Slip in Time: The Book of Eventide. Cole, T. M. 2006. (YA). per. 10.75 *(978-0-9777677-0-0(1))* Silver Cloak Pubns.

Cole, Sarah. Big Fun Christmas Crafts & Activities: Over 200 Quick & Easy Activities for Holiday Fun! Press, Judy. 2006. (ENG.). 128p. (J). (gr. -1-3). 16.95 *(978-0-8249-6787-1(9));* pap. 12.95 *(978-0-8249-6786-4(0))* Ideals Pubns. (Williamson Bks.).

—Making Amazing Art! 40 Activities Using the 7 Elements of Art Design. Henry, Sandi. (ENG.). 128p. (J). (gr. 3-7). 2008. pap. 12.99 *(978-0-8249-6795-6(X));* 2007. 16.99 *(978-0-8249-6794-9(1))* Ideals Pubns. (Williamson Bks.).

Cole, Tom Clohosy. Wall. Cole, Tom Clohosy. 2014. (ENG.). 32p. (J). (gr. -1-3). 16.99 *(978-0-7636-7560-8(1),* Templar) Candlewick Pr.

Cole, Véronique. C'est Si Bon d'être un Chaton ! Cole, Véronique. 2011. (FRE.). 26p. pap. 10.99 *(978-1-4610-8389-4(3))* CreateSpace Independent Publishing Platform.

—Do You Know Your Birds?, Bk. 1. Cole, Véronique. Cole, Tim, tr. 2011. (ENG.). 40p. pap. 12.99 *(978-1-4563-5752-8(2))* CreateSpace Independent Publishing Platform.

—So Good to Be a Kitten! Cole, Véronique. Cole, Tim, tr. 2011. (ENG.). 26p. pap. 10.99 *(978-1-4610-8402-0(4))* CreateSpace Independent Publishing Platform.

Coleman, Audrey. Walter the Farting Dog: Banned from the Beach. Kotzwinkle, William et al. 2009. (ENG.). 32p. (J). (gr. k-3). pap. 6.99 *(978-0-14-241394-4(1),* Puffin) Penguin Publishing Group.

—Walter the Farting Dog Goes on a Cruise. Kotzwinkle, William et al. (ENG.). 32p. (J). (gr. k-3). 2008. pap. 6.99 *(978-0-14-241142-1(6),* Puffin); 2006. 16.99 *(978-0-525-47714-3(4),* Dutton Juvenile) Penguin Publishing Group.

Coleman, Audrey & Audrey, Colman. Walter the Farting Dog: Trouble at the Yard Sale. Kotzwinkle, William & Murray, Glenn. 2006. (ENG.). 32p. (J). (gr. k-3). reprint ed. pap. 6.99 *(978-0-14-240626-7(0),* Puffin) Penguin Publishing Group.

Coleman, Sadie. The Biggest Heart Ever. Coleman, Sadie. 2013. 24p. 14.99 *(978-0-9881969-0-2(5))* Vorpal Words, LLC.

Coleman, Winfield. The Thunder Egg. Myers, Tim J. 2015. (ENG.). 28p. (J). (gr. k-4). 15.95 ***(978-1-937786-39-7(0),*** Wisdom Tales) World Wisdom, Inc.

Coles, James. The Many Adventures of Pengey Penguin. Burns, John. 2005. 207p. (J). per. 17.95 *(978-0-9774227-0-8(4))* San Francisco Story Works.

Coles, Mary. Brontosaurus Brunch: A Smorgasbord of Dinosaur Delights. Peers, Judi. 3rd ed. 2011. *(978-0-9810964-2-1(5))* Praise Publishing.

Coleson, Julie. How Six Little Ipu Got Their Names. Coleson, Julie. Brimmer, Debi. 2005. 30p. (J). 9.95 incl. audio compact disk *(978-1-57306-186-5(7))* Bess Pr., Inc.

ColiaStudios. Gobblie Goo from the Planet Goo. Jaffe, Ilene. 2013. 30p. (J). pap. 15.95 *(978-1-62620-799-8(2))* Independent Pub.

Coll, Ivar Da. El Barbero y el Coronel. MacHado, Ana Maria.Tr. of Barber & the Colonel. (SPA.). (J). (gr. 2-3). 7.95 *(978-958-04-5035-1(8),* NR1718) Norma S.A. COL. Dist: Distribuidora Norma, Inc., Lectorum Pubns., Inc.

—Una Cama para Tres. Reyes, Yolanda. 2004. (SPA.). 36p. (J). (gr. k-3). 14.95 *(978-958-704-055-5(4))* Santillana USA Publishing Co., Inc.

Coll, Ivar Da. Carlos. Coll, Ivar Da. 2003. (SPA.). 52p. (J). (gr. k-3). pap. 9.95 *(978-958-8061-64-1(4))* Santillana USA Publishing Co., Inc.

Collar, Orpheus. The Red Pyramid, Bk. 1. Riordan, Rick. 2012. (Kane Chronicles Ser.). (ENG.). 192p. (J). (gr. 5-17). pap. 12.99 *(978-1-4231-5069-5(4))* Hyperion Pr.

Collar, Orpheus. The Red Pyramid: The Graphic Novel, Bk. 1. Collar, Orpheus. Riordan, Rick. 2012. (ENG.). 192p. (YA). (gr. 5-17). 21.99 *(978-1-4231-5068-8(6))* Hyperion Pr.

Collection/Jupiterimages Unlimited. Farm Animal Friends. Ciminera, Siobhan. 2009. (ENG.). 48p. (J). (gr. -1-2). 12.99 *(978-1-4169-6786-6(9),* Simon Scribbles) Simon Scribbles.

—Stuck on Christmas! Ciminera, Siobhan. 2008. (ENG.). 48p. (J). (gr. -1-2). 12.99 *(978-1-4169-6784-2(2),* Simon Scribbles) Simon Scribbles.

Collective Work Staff. The Arabian Nights, 7 vols. Melodie. 2012. (ENG.). 32p. (J). (gr. 1). 19.95 *(978-2-7338-2150-3(4))* Auzou, Philippe Editions FRA. Dist: Consortium Bk. Sales & Distribution.

Collenberger, Chris. The Day the Sun Called Out Sick!!! Belle, Deborah A. 2013. 30p. pap. 12.99 *(978-0-9853406-0-5(6))* Scribez, Scarebz & Vibez.

Coller, H. Seven Sisters at Queen Anne's. Smith, Evelyn. 2013. 162p. pap. *(978-1-909423-07-7(6))* Bks. to Treasure.

Collet-Derby, Pierre. The Boulder Brothers: Meet Mo & Jo. Lynn, Sarah. 2015. (Jump-Into-Chapters Ser.). (ENG.). 72p. (J). (gr. k-3). 12.99 *(978-1-60905-501-1(2))* Blue Apple Bks.

Collett, Farrell R. Jerry Lindsey: Explorer to the San Juan. Luce, Willard. 2011. 88p. 38.95 *(978-1-258-07330-5(7))* Literary Licensing, LLC.

Collett, Heather. Strike a Pose: The Planet Girl Guide to Yoga. Birkemoe, Karen. 2007. (Planet Girl Ser.). (ENG.). 96p. (J). (gr. 8-12). 12.95 *(978-1-55337-004-8(X))* Kids Can Pr., Ltd. CAN. Dist: Univ. of Toronto Pr.

Collett, Susan. The Christmas Dragon. Collett, Susan, . 2007. 64p. (J). pap. 5.95 *(978-0-9678115-1-2(1))* Dragonseed Pr.

Colley, Abdoulie, et al. The Mermaid's Dream, Internationally Illustrated Picture Book: This Is a Unique & Beautiful Fairy Tale That Resolves the Mermaid's Age-Old Dilemma of Where to Live - On the Sea or on the Land. Talic, Serkan & Sekulic, Goran, photos by. Sullivan, Marija. 2011. (ENG.). 32p. pap. 9.18 *(978-1-4610-2753-9(5))* CreateSpace Independent Publishing Platform.

Colley, Jacqui. Clubs. De Goldi, Kate. 2008. (Lolly Leopold Ser.). (ENG.). 32p. (J). (gr. 2-4). pap. 11.99 *(978-1-74114-891-6(X))* Allen & Unwin AUS. Dist: Independent Pubs. Group.

Collicott, Sharleen. The Chicken Sisters. Numeroff, Laura Joffe. abr. ed. 2003. (J). (gr. -1-2). 28.95 incl. audio compact disk *(978-1-59112-533-4(2))* Live Oak Media.

Collicott, Sharleen. Mildred & Sam. Collicott, Sharleen. (I Can Read Bks.). (J). 2008. 64p. (gr. -1-2). lib. bdg. 17.89 *(978-0-06-058115-2(8),* Geringer, Laura Book); 2004. (ENG.). 48p. (gr. k-3). pap. 3.99 *(978-0-06-000200-8(X));* 2003. 48p. (gr. -1-18). 15.99 *(978-0-06-026681-3(3))* HarperCollins Pubs.

—Mildred & Sam & Their Babies. Collicott, Sharleen. 2005. (I Can Read Bks.). 48p. (J). (gr. -1-2). 15.99 *(978-0-06-058111-4(5),* Geringer, Laura Book) HarperCollins Pubs.

Collicutt, Paul. City in Peril! Collicutt, Paul. 2009. (Robot City Ser.: 1). (ENG.). 48p. (J). (gr. 3-7). pap. 8.99 *(978-0-7636-4120-7(0))* Candlewick Pr.

—The Indestructible Metal Men. Collicutt, Paul. 2010. (Robot City Ser.: 3). (ENG.). 48p. (J). (gr. 3-7). pap. 8.99 *(978-0-7636-5014-8(5),* Templar) Candlewick Pr.

—Murder on the Robot City Express. Collicutt, Paul. 2010. (Robot City Ser.: 4). (ENG.). 48p. (J). (gr. 3-7). pap. 8.99 *(978-0-7636-5015-5(3),* Templar) Candlewick Pr.

—Rust Attack! Collicutt, Paul. 2009. (Robot City Ser.: 2). (ENG.). 48p. (J). (gr. 3-7). pap. 8.99 *(978-0-7636-4594-6(X))* Candlewick Pr.

Collier, Bryan, et al. America the Beautiful: Together We Stand. Bates, Katharine Lee. 2013. (ENG.). 32p. (J). 17.99 *(978-0-545-49207-2(6),* Orchard Bks.) Scholastic, Inc.

Collier, Bryan. Barack Obama: Son of Promise, Child of Hope. Grimes, Nikki. 2012. (ENG.). 48p. (J). (gr. k-3). pap. 9.99 *(978-1-4424-5077-6(0),* Little Simon) Little Simon.

—Barack Obama: Son of Promise, Child of Hope. Grimes, Nikki. (ENG.). 48p. (J). (gr. k-3). 2012. 7.99 *(978-1-4424-4092-0(9));* 2008. pap. 16.99 *(978-1-4169-7144-3(0))* Simon & Schuster Bks. For Young Readers. (Simon & Schuster Bks. For Young Readers).

Collier, Bryan. City Shapes. Murray, Diana. 2016. (J). ***(978-0-316-37092-9(4))*** Little Brown & Co.

Collier, Bryan. Clemente! Perdomo, Willie. 2010. (ENG.). 32p. (J). (gr. 1-5). 17.99 *(978-0-8050-8224-1(7),* Holt, Henry & Co. Bks. For Young Readers) Holt, Henry & Co.

—Dave the Potter: Artist, Poet, Slave. Hill, Laban Carrick. 2010. (ENG.). 40p. (J). (gr. -1-1). 18.00 *(978-0-316-10731-0(X))* Little, Brown Bks. for Young Readers.

—Dave the Potter: Artist, Poet, Slave. Hill, Laban Carrick. 2011. 40p. (J). (gr. -1-2). 37.75 *(978-1-4618-1710-9(2))* Recorded Bks., LLC.

—Doo-Wop Pop. Schotter, Roni. 2008. 40p. (J). (gr. -1-3). lib. bdg. 17.89 *(978-0-06-057974-6(9),* Amistad) HarperCollins Pubs.

—I, Too, Am America. Hughes, Langston. 2012. (ENG.). 40p. (J). (gr. -1-3). 16.99 *(978-1-4424-2008-3(1),* Simon & Schuster Bks. For Young Readers) Simon & Schuster Bks. For Young Readers.

—The Jump at the Sun Treasury: An African American Picture Book Collection. Price, Hope Lynne. 2004. 205p. (J). (gr. 4-8). reprint ed. 17.00 *(978-0-7567-7328-1(8))* DIANE Publishing Co.

—Lincoln & Douglass: An American Friendship. Giovanni, Nikki. 2008. (ENG.). 40p. (J). (gr. 2-6). 16.95 *(978-0-8050-8264-7(6),* Holt, Henry & Co. Bks. For Young Readers) Holt, Henry & Co.

—Lincoln & Douglass: An American Friendship. Giovanni, Nikki. 2013. (ENG.). 44p. (J). (gr. 2-6). 8.99 *(978-1-250-01869-4(2))* Square Fish.

—Lincoln & Douglass: An American Friendship. Giovanni, Nikki. 2011. (J). (gr. -1-3). 29.95 *(978-0-545-13457-6(9))* Weston Woods Studios, Inc.

—Martin's Big Words: The Life of Dr. Martin Luther King, Jr. Rappaport, Doreen. rev. ed. 2007. (Big Words Ser.). (ENG.). 40p. (J). (gr. 1-3). pap. 7.99 *(978-1-4231-0635-7(0),* Jump at the Sun) Hyperion Bks. for Children.

—My Country, 'Tis of Thee: How One Song Reveals the History of Civil Rights. Murphy, Claire Rudolf. 2014. (ENG.). 48p. (J). (gr. k-4). 17.99 *(978-0-8050-8226-5(3),* Holt, Henry & Co. Bks. For Young Readers) Holt, Henry & Co.

—Rosa. Giovanni, Nikki. rev. ed. 2005. (ENG.). 40p. (J). (gr. -1-3). 17.99 *(978-0-8050-7106-1(7),* Holt, Henry & Co. Bks. For Young Readers) Holt, Henry & Co.

—Rosa. Giovanni, Nikki. 2007. (ENG.). 40p. (J). (gr. -1-3). per. 7.99 *(978-0-312-37602-4(2))* Square Fish.

—Rosa. Giovanni, Nikki. 2011. (J). (gr. 2-5). 29.95 *(978-0-545-04261-1(5))* Weston Woods Studios, Inc.

—Rosa Storytime Set, 1 vol. Giovanni, Nikki. unabr. ed. 2014. (ENG.). 40p. (J). (gr. -1-3). 12.99 *(978-1-4272-4397-3(2))* Macmillan Audio.

—Trombone Shorty. Andrews, Troy. 2015. (ENG.). 40p. (J). (gr. -1-3). 17.95 *(978-1-4197-1465-8(1),* Abrams Bks. for Young Readers) Abrams.

—Twelve Rounds to Glory: The Story of Muhammad Ali. Smith, Charles R., Jr. (ENG.). 80p. (J). (gr. 5). 2010. pap. 10.99 *(978-0-7636-5002-5(1));* 2007. 19.99 *(978-0-7636-1692-2(3))* Candlewick Pr.

—Visiting Langston. Perdomo, Willie. 2006. (gr. -1-3). 19.00 *(978-0-7569-6802-1(X))* Perfection Learning Corp.

—Visiting Langston. Perdomo, Willie. 2005. (ENG.). 32p. (J). (gr. -1-3). reprint ed. pap. 8.99 *(978-0-8050-7881-7(9))* Square Fish.

—Welcome, Precious. Grimes, Nikki. 2006. (ENG.). 32p. (J). (gr. -1 — 1). 17.99 *(978-0-439-55702-3(X),* Orchard Bks.) Scholastic, Inc.

—Your Moon, My Moon: A Grandmother's Words to a Faraway Child. MacLachlan, Patricia. 2011. (ENG.). 32p. (J). (gr. -1-3). 16.99 *(978-1-4169-7950-0(6),* Simon & Schuster Bks. For Young Readers) Simon & Schuster Bks. For Young Readers.

Collier, Bryan. Uptown, 4 bks., Set. Collier, Bryan. 2007. (J). (gr. k-3). pap. 39.95 incl. audio compact disk *(978-1-4301-0055-3(9))* Live Oak Media.

—Uptown. Collier, Bryan. rev. ed. 2004. (ENG.). 32p. (J). (gr. -1-3). pap. 8.99 *(978-0-8050-7399-7(X))* Square Fish.

Collier, John & Morin, Paul. At Break of Day. Grimes, Nikki. 2004. 32p. (J). (gr. -1-3). 17.00 *(978-0-8028-5104-8(5))* Eerdmans, William B. Publishing Co.

Collier, Kevin. J P S Halloween Parade. Houdek, Andi. 2012. 20p. pap. 9.95 *(978-1-61633-263-1(8))* Guardian Angel Publishing, Inc.

—Magical Mea. Cole, Penelope Anne. 2013. 24p. 19.95 *(978-1-61633-394-2(4));* pap. 10.95 *(978-1-61633-395-9(2))* Guardian Angel Publishing, Inc.

—Magico Mateo. Cole, Penelope Anne. 2013. 24p. pap. 10.95 *(978-1-61633-421-5(5))* Guardian Angel Publishing, Inc.

—Michael & the Magic Dinosaur. Bloomberg, Sandi. 2012. 30p. pap. 13.95 *(978-1-61244-066-8(5))* Halo Publishing International.

—One Nutty Family. Byers, James. 2012. 16p. pap. 9.95 *(978-1-61633-200-6(X))* Guardian Angel Publishing, Inc.

—Start with Your Heart. Skordy, Anne Marie. 2011. 32p. (J). pap. 12.95 *(978-1-60131-089-7(7))* Big Tent Bks.

—Stop That Pudding! Houdek, Andi. 2010. 16p. pap. 9.95 *(978-1-61633-079-8(1))* Guardian Angel Publishing, Inc.

—What in the World Should I Be. Jones, Debra M. 2010. 16p. pap. 9.95 *(978-1-61633-037-8(6))* Guardian Angel Publishing, Inc.

Collier, Kevin Scott. The Adventures of Brutus & Baby: A Haunted Halloween. Rogers, Michelle Elizabeth. 2010. 50p. pap. 16.50 *(978-1-60860-592-7(2),* Eloquent Bks.) Strategic Book Publishing & Rights Agency (SBPRA).

—The Best Christmas Gift. Appel, Cindy. 2005. (J). E-Book 6.00 incl. cd-rom *(978-1-933090-19-1(7))* Guardian Angel Publishing, Inc.

—A Blessed Bethlehem Birth: As told by Abraham & Anna Mousenstern. McElligott, Walter Lee. 2006. 28p. (J). E-Book 5.00 incl. cd-rom *(978-1-933090-21-4(9))* Guardian Angel Publishing, Inc.

—Bobby Cottontail's Gift. James, Catherine. 2008. 28p. pap. 10.95 *(978-1-935137-07-8(7));* 2006. 32p. (J). E-Book 9.95 incl. cd-rom *(978-1-933090-24-5(3))* Guardian Angel Publishing, Inc.

—Chizzy's Topsy Tale. Shepherd, Donna J. 2008. 20p. pap. 10.95 *(978-1-935137-10-8(7))* Guardian Angel Publishing, Inc.

—Dotty's Topsy Tale. Shepherd, Donna J. 2009. 16p. pap. 9.95 *(978-1-935137-55-9(7))* Guardian Angel Publishing, Inc.

—Magical Matthew. Cole, Penelope Anne. 2012. 24p. 19.95 *(978-1-61633-325-6(1))* Guardian Angel Publishing, Inc.

—Magical Matthew. Cole, Penelope Ann. 2012. 24p. pap. 10.95 *(978-1-61633-326-3(X))* Guardian Angel Publishing, Inc.

—Mice in My Tummy. Houdek, Andrea. 2012. 16p. pap. 9.95 *(978-1-61633-219-8(0))* Guardian Angel Publishing, Inc.

—The Misadventures of Rooter & Snuffle. Lyle-Soffe, Shari. 2008. 20p. pap. 9.95 *(978-1-933090-88-7(X));* 2006. 28p. (J). E-Book 5.00 incl. cd-rom *(978-1-933090-43-6(X))* Guardian Angel Publishing, Inc.

—Nothing Stops Noah. Lyle-Soffe, Shari. 2008. 24p. pap. 10.95 *(978-1-935137-19-1(0))* Guardian Angel Publishing, Inc.

—On the Go with Rooter & Snuffle. Lyle-Soffe, Shari. 2008. 20p. pap. 9.95 *(978-1-933090-96-2(0))* Guardian Angel Publishing, Inc.

—OUCH! Sunburn. Shepherd, Donna J. 2007. 27p. (J). E-Book 9.95 incl. cd-rom *(978-1-933090-60-3(X))* Guardian Angel Publishing, Inc.

—Peaches & Cream, 1 vol. Squires, R. L. 2009. 31p. pap. 24.95 *(978-1-60749-164-8(8))* America Star Bks.

—Piccolo. Lake, Mary. 2007. (J). (gr. -1-3). 25p. 14.99 *(978-1-59879-358-1(6));* per. 10.99 *(978-1-59879-253-9(9))* Lifevest Publishing, Inc.

—The Sad Little House. James, Catherine. 2008. 24p. pap. 10.95 *(978-1-935137-06-1(9));* 2006. 28p. (J). E-Book 9.95 incl. cd-rom *(978-1-933090-18-4(9))* Guardian Angel Publishing, Inc.

—Sam Feels Better Now! An Interactive Story for Children. Osborne, Jill. 2008. 44p. (J). pap. 15.95 *(978-1-932690-60-6(3))* Loving Healing Pr., Inc.

—Sully's Topsy Tale. Shepherd, Donna J. 2010. 20p. pap. 10.95 *(978-1-61633-047-7(3))* Guardian Angel Publishing, Inc.

—Trouble Finds Rooter & Snuffle. Lyle-Soffe, Shari. 2008. 20p. pap. 9.95 *(978-1-933090-72-6(3))* Guardian Angel Publishing, Inc.

—We're Brothers & Sisters. Cahill, Bear. 2008. 20p. pap. 9.95 *(978-1-933090-70-2(7))* Guardian Angel Publishing, Inc.

Collier, Kevin Scott. Hope, the Angelfish. Collier, Kevin Scott. 2008. 24p. pap. 10.95 *(978-1-933090-17-7(0))* Guardian Angel Publishing, Inc.

—Journeys of Hope, Pearl of Wisdom. Collier, Kevin Scott. 2006. 28p. (J). E-Book 9.95 incl. cd-rom *(978-1-933090-31-3(6))* Guardian Angel Publishing, Inc.

—Professor Horace, Cryptozoologist. Collier, Kevin Scott. 2008. 20p. pap. 9.95 *(978-1-935137-14-6(X))* Guardian Angel Publishing, Inc.

Collier, Kevin Scott & LeBlanc, Giselle. The New Puppy. Hall, Raelene. 2013. 16p. pap. 9.95 *(978-1-61633-415-4(0))* Guardian Angel Publishing, Inc.

Collier, Mary. The Caterpillar. Schmauss, Judy Kentor. 2006. (Reader's Clubhouse Level 1 Reader Ser.). (ENG.). 24p. (J). (gr. 1-4). pap. 3.99 *(978-0-7641-3286-5(5))* Barron's Educational Series, Inc.

—My Clothes/Mi Ropa. Rosa-Mendoza, Gladys. Abello, Patricia & Weber, Amy, eds. 2005. (#1 Bilingual Board Book Ser.). (SPA & ENG.). 20p. (J). (gr. -1). bds. 6.95 *(978-1-931398-15-2(1))* Me+Mi Publishing.

Collier-Morales, Roberta. August. Kesselring, Mari. 2009. (Months of the Year Ser.). 24p. (gr. -1-2). 27.07 *(978-1-60270-635-4(2),* Looking Glass Library-Nonfiction) Magic Wagon.

—Inside Out. Halley, Wendy Stofan. 2003. 32p. 15.95 *(978-0-9701907-5-8(1))* Illumination Arts Publishing Co., Inc.

—July. Kesselring, Mari. 2009. (Months of the Year Ser.). 24p. (gr. -1-2). 27.07 *(978-1-60270-634-7(4),* Looking Glass Library- Nonfiction) Magic Wagon.

—June. Kesselring, Mari. 2009. (Months of the Year Ser.). 24p. (gr. -1-2). 27.07 *(978-1-60270-633-0(6),* Looking Glass Library- Nonfiction) Magic Wagon.

—The Lost Coin. Dreyer, Nicole E. 2006. 16p. (J). 1.99 *(978-0-7586-0873-4(X))* Concordia Publishing Hse.

—El Mago Que Salvo el Mundo. Bennett, Jeffrey. 2011. (SPA.). 32p. (J). (gr. 2-4). 15.00 *(978-0-9721819-5-2(4))* Big Kid Science.

—The Thankful Leper: The Story of the Ten Lepers: Luke 17:11-19 & 2 Kings 5:1-15 for Children. Hinkle, Cynthia A. 2006. (Arch Bks.). (J). 2.49 *(978-0-7586-1284-7(2))* Concordia Publishing Hse.

—The Wizard Who Saved the World. Bennett, Jeffrey. 2011. (ENG.). 32p. (J). (gr. 2-4). 15.00 *(978-0-9721819-4-5(6))* Big Kid Science.

Collier, Roberta. Frohliche Weihnachten: Learning Songs & Traditions in German. Rauenhorst, Linda. 2007. (Teach Me Ser.). (GER & ENG.). 32p. (J). (gr. -1-3). 19.95 *(978-1-59972-063-0(9))* Teach Me Tapes, Inc.

Collinet, Rob. Super Goofy Jokes. Horsfall, Jacqueline. 2010. (ENG.). 96p. (J). pap. 5.95 *(978-1-4027-7856-8(2))* Sterling Publishing Co., Inc.

Collingridge, Richard. Blackberry Blue & Other Fairy Tales. Gavin, Jamila. 2015. (ENG.). 240p. (J). (gr. 4-6). 10.99 ***(978-1-84853-107-9(9))*** Transworld Publishers Ltd. GBR. Dist: Independent Pubs. Group.

Collingridge, Richard. When It Snows. Collingridge, Richard. 2013. (ENG.). 32p. (J). (gr. -1-1). 16.99 *(978-1-250-02831-0(0))* Feiwel & Friends.

Collins, Andrew Dawe. Zombies Are Cool. Giangregorio, Anthony. 2013. 38p. pap. 9.99 *(978-1-61199-073-7(4))* Living Dead Pr.

Collins, Bernard, Jr. Beyond the Back of the Bus. Turner-Barnes, Sandra. 2011. (ENG.). 32p. (J). (gr. k-2). pap. 9.95 *(978-0-88378-295-8(2))* Third World Press.

Collins, Courtney. I Love to Exercise. Brown, Phoenix. 2008. 28p. pap. 24.95 *(978-1-60563-727-3(0))* America Star Bks.

Collins, Daryl. The Fume in the Tomb. O'neal, Katherine Pebley. 2004. 68p. (J). lib. bdg. 15.00 *(978-1-4242-0901-9(3))* Fitzgerald Bks.

Collins, Daryll. The Itsy Bity Spider. Fuerst, Jeffrey B. 2010. (Rising Readers Ser.). (J). 3.49 *(978-1-60719-689-1(1))* Newmark Learning LLC.

Collins, Daryll, et al. Laff-O-Tronic Animal Jokes!, 1 vol. Dahl, Michael. 2013. (Laff-O-Tronic Joke Books! Ser.). (ENG.). 96p. (gr. k-3). 23.99 *(978-1-4342-6020-8(8))* Stone Arch Bks.

—Laff-O-Tronic Monster Jokes!, 1 vol. Dahl, Michael. 2013. (Laff-O-Tronic Joke Books! Ser.). (ENG.). 96p. (gr. k-3). 23.99 *(978-1-4342-6021-5(6))* Stone Arch Bks.

—Laff-O-Tronic School Jokes!, 1 vol. Dahl, Michael. 2013. (Laff-O-Tronic Joke Books! Ser.). (ENG.). 96p. (gr. k-3). 23.99 *(978-1-4342-6022-2(4))* Stone Arch Bks.

—Laff-O-Tronic Sports Jokes!, 1 vol. Dahl, Michael. 2013. (Laff-O-Tronic Joke Books! Ser.). (ENG.). 96p. (gr. k-3). 23.99 *(978-1-4342-6023-9(2))* Stone Arch Bks.

Collins, Daryll. Phonics Comics: Super Sam - Level 3: Issue 1. Marks, Melanie. 2006. (ENG.). 24p. (J). (gr. 1-17). per. 3.99 *(978-1-58476-420-5(1),* IKIDS) Innovative Kids.

Collins, Daryll & Holgate, Douglas. Laff-O-Tronic Joke Books. Dahl, Michael. 2013. (Laff-O-Tronic Joke Books! Ser.). (ENG.). 96p. (gr. k-3). pap. 19.80 *(978-1-4342-6224-0(3))* Stone Arch Bks.

—Laff-O-Tronic Monster Jokes! Dahl, Michael. 2013. (Laff-O-Tronic Joke Books! Ser.). (ENG.). 96p. (gr. k-3). pap. 29.70 *(978-1-4342-6239-4(1))* Stone Arch Bks.

Collins, Daryll, jt. illus. see Holgate, Douglas.

Collins, Don. Head Case Lacrosse Goalie: Sports Fiction with a Winning Edge. Chambers, Sam T. et al. 2009. (ENG.). 95p. (gr. 4-7). pap. 9.95 *(978-1-933979-40-3(2),* b514b6ed-9361-4f2c-97bd-9aefd77b5e96) Bright Sky Pr.

—Juan Seguin. Chemerka, William R. 2012. (ENG.). 64p. (J). 16.95 *(978-1-933979-79-3(8),* 0c23ccf1-9b84-47e7-a0f6-89a6a430b039) Bright Sky Pr.

Collins, Don. David Crockett: Hero & Legend. Collins, Don. Wade, Mary Dodson. 2009. (ENG.). 63p. (J). (gr. 4-7). 16.95 *(978-1-933979-24-3(0),* 2c4983a5-462d-4837-84ce-7b1c3a301da6) Bright Sky Pr.

—Gregorio Esparza: Alamo Defender. Collins, Don. Chemerka, William R. 2009. (ENG.). 80p. (J). (gr. 4-7). 16.95 *(978-1-933979-36-6(4),* 24f605b5-70f9-4367-9cdc-1d60b5b758dc) Bright Sky Pr.

C

Collins, Erica. Aloha Activity Book. Collins, Erica. 2009. 24p. pap. 4.98 *(978-1-933735-59-7(7))* Pacifica Island Art, Inc.

Collins, Heather. The Bare Naked Book. Stinson, Kathy. 20th ed. 2006. (ENG.). 32p. (J). (gr. -1-1). 19.95 *(978-1-55451-050-4(3)*, 9781554510504); pap. 5.95 *(978-1-55451-049-8(X)*, 9781554510498) Annick Pr., Ltd. CAN. Dist: Firefly Bks., Ltd.

—Get Outside: The Kids Guide to Fun in the Great Outdoors. Drake, Jane & Love, Ann. 2012. (ENG.). 176p. (J). 16.95 *(978-1-55453-802-7(5))* Kids Can Pr., Ltd. CAN. Dist: Univ. of Toronto Pr.

—Hey Diddle Diddle. 2003. (Traditional Nursery Rhymes Ser.). (ENG.). 12p. (J). (gr. -1-k). bds. 3.95 *(978-1-55337-078-9(3))* Kids Can Pr., Ltd. CAN. Dist: Univ. of Toronto Pr.

—Jack & Jill. 2003. (Traditional Nursery Rhymes Ser.). (ENG.). 12p. (J). (gr. -1-k). bds. 3.95 *(978-1-55337-075-8(9))* Kids Can Pr., Ltd. CAN. Dist: Univ. of Toronto Pr.

—Little Miss Muffet. 2003. (Traditional Nursery Rhymes Ser.). (ENG.). 12p. (J). (gr. -1-k). bds. 3.95 *(978-1-55337-076-5(7))* Kids Can Pr., Ltd. CAN. Dist: Univ. of Toronto Pr.

—Pat-a-Cake. 2003. (Traditional Nursery Rhymes Ser.). (ENG.). 12p. (J). (gr. -1-k). bds. 3.95 *(978-1-55337-077-2(5))* Kids Can Pr., Ltd. CAN. Dist: Univ. of Toronto Pr.

—Rain Tonight: A Story of Hurricane Hazel. Pitt, Steve. 2004. (ENG.). 48p. (J). (gr. 3-7). pap. 6.95 *(978-0-88776-641-1(2))* Tundra Bks. CAN. Dist: Random Hse., Inc.

—She Dared: True Stories of Heroines, Scoundrels, & Renegades. Butts, Ed. 2005. (ENG.). 128p. (J). (gr. 5-9). pap. 8.95 *(978-0-88776-718-0(4))* Tundra Bks. CAN. Dist: Penguin Random Hse., LLC.

Collins, Heather. Out Came the Sun: A Day in Nursery Rhymes. Collins, Heather. 2007. (ENG.). 96p. (J). (gr. -1). 19.95 *(978-1-55337-881-5(4))* Kids Can Pr., Ltd. CAN. Dist: Univ. of Toronto Pr.

Collins, Heather. The Kids Book of the Night Sky. Collins, Heather, tr. Love, Ann & Drake, Jane. 2004. (Family Fun Ser.). (ENG.). 144p. (J). (gr. 4-6). pap. 16.95 *(978-1-55337-128-1(3))* Kids Can Pr., Ltd. CAN. Dist: Univ. of Toronto Pr.

Collins, Jacob. The Christmas Candle. Evans, Richard. (ENG.). 32p. (J). (gr. -1-3). 2007. 9.99 *(978-1-4169-5047-9(8))*; 2006. 7.99 *(978-1-4169-2682-5(6))* Simon & Schuster Bks. For Young Readers. (Simon & Schuster Bks. For Young Readers).

Collins, Julia B. Ohio Men, Vol. 2. Georgiady, Nicholas P. et al. 2nd rev. ed. Date not set. 44p. (J). (gr. 4-8). pap. 4.50 *(978-0-917961-04-5(8))* Argee Pubs.

Collins, Kelsey. Annie Mouse's Route 66 Adventure: A Photo Journal, vols. 6, vol. 5. Slanina, Anne Maro. 2011. (ENG.). 48p. (J). pap. 14.99 *(978-0-9793379-6-3(8))* Annie Mouse Bks.

Collins, Linda. Boppy & Me. Mazur, Gabrielle. 2013. 38p. pap. 12.95 *(978-1-4507-3906-1(7))* Bush Publishing Inc.

Collins, Matt. Basketball Belles: How Two Teams & One Scrappy Player Put Women's Hoops on the Map. Macy, Sue. 2011. (ENG.). 32p. (J). (gr. 1-5). 17.95 *(978-0-8234-2163-3(5))* Holiday Hse., Inc.

—Out in Left Field. Lemna, Don. (ENG.). (J). 2013. 217p. pap. 7.99 *(978-0-8234-2766-6(8))*; 2012. 224p. 16.95 *(978-0-8234-2313-2(1))* Holiday Hse., Inc.

—A Picture Book of Daniel Boone. Adler, David A. & Adler, Michael S. 2013. (ENG.). 32p. (J). 17.95 *(978-0-8234-2748-2(X))* Holiday Hse., Inc.

—A Picture Book of Harry Houdini. Adler, David A. & Adler, Michael S. 2009. (ENG.). 32p. (J). (gr. -1-3). 17.95 *(978-0-8234-2059-9(0))* Holiday Hse., Inc.

—A Picture Book of Sam Houston. Adler, David A. & Adler, Michael S. 2012. (ENG.). 32p. (J). 17.95 *(978-0-8234-2369-9(7))* Holiday Hse., Inc.

—Roller Derby Rivals. Macy, Sue. 2014. (ENG.). 32p. (J). (gr. 1-5). 16.95 *(978-0-8234-2923-3(7))* Holiday Hse., Inc.

—Sacajawea. Krull, Kathleen. 2015. (Women Who Broke the Rules Ser.). (ENG.). 48p. (J). (gr. 1-4). 16.99 *(978-0-8027-3799-1(4)*, Bloomsbury USA Childrens) Bloomsbury USA.

Collins, Mike, et al. A Christmas Carol the Graphic Novel - Original Text: British Edition. Dickens, Charles. 2008. 160p. (Orig.). pap. ***(978-1-906332-17-4(7))*** Classical Comics.

Collins, Mike. The Chronicles of Arthur: Sword of Fire & Ice. Matthews, John. 2009. (ENG.). (J). (gr. 3-7). 128p. 21.99 *(978-1-4169-8683-6(9))*; 123p. pap. 14.99 *(978-1-4169-5908-3(4))* Simon & Schuster/Paula Wiseman Bks. (Simon & Schuster/Paula Wiseman Bks.).

Collins, Mike & Offredi, James. A Christmas Carol. Dickens, Charles. Bryant, Clive, ed. 2012. (ENG.). 160p. (Orig.). (gr. 6). lib. bdg. 24.95 *(978-1-907127-40-3(2))* Classical Comics GBR. Dist: Perseus-PGW.

Collins, Peggy. Hungry for Math: Poems to Munch On, 1 vol. Winters, Kari-Lynn & Sherritt-Fleming, Lori. 2014. (ENG.). 32p. (J). (gr. 1-3). 18.95 *(978-1-55455-307-5(5)*, 9781554553075) Fitzhenry & Whiteside, Ltd. CAN. Dist: Midpoint Trade Bks., Inc.

—Tooter's Stinky Wish, 1 vol. Cretney, Brian. 2011. (ENG.). 32p. (J). 18.95 *(978-1-55455-165-1(X))* Fitzhenry & Whiteside, Ltd. CAN. Dist: Midpoint Trade Bks., Inc.

Collins, Peggy. In the Garden. Collins, Peggy. 2009. (ENG.). 40p. (J). 14.95 *(978-1-60433-026-7(0)*, Applesauce Pr.) Cider Mill Pr. Bk. Pubs., LLC.

Collins Powell, Judy. You Have Been Invited! Howell, Brian. 2012. (ENG.). 48p. 18.99 *(978-0-9882892-0-8(2))* Wheat State Media LLC.

Collins, Ross. Alligator Action. Sparkes, Ali. 2014. (S. W. I. T. C. H. Ser.: 14). (ENG.). 112p. (J). (gr. 2-5). lib. bdg. 27.93 *(978-1-4677-2117-2(4)*, Darby Creek) Lerner Publishing Group.

—Anaconda Adventure. Sparkes, Ali. 2014. (S. W. I. T. C. H. Ser.: 13). (ENG.). 104p. (J). (gr. 2-5). lib. bdg. 27.93 *(978-1-4677-2116-5(6)*, Darby Creek) Lerner Publishing Group.

—Ant Attack. Sparkes, Ali. 2013. (S. W. I. T. C. H. Ser.: 4). (ENG.). 104p. (J). (gr. 2-5). pap. 7.95 *(978-1-4677-0713-8(9)*, Darby Creek) Lerner Publishing Group.

—Ant Attack. Sparkes, Ali. 2013. (S. W. I. T. C. H. Ser.: 4). (ENG.). 104p. (J). (gr. 2-5). lib. bdg. 27.93 *(978-0-7613-9202-6(5))* Lerner Publishing Group.

—The Bag of Bones: The Second Tale from the Five Kingdoms. French, Vivian. 2009. (Tales from the Five Kingdoms Ser.: 2). (ENG.). 256p. (J). (gr. 3-7). 14.99 *(978-0-7636-4255-6(X))* Candlewick Pr.

—Beetle Blast. Sparkes, Ali. 2013. (S. W. I. T. C. H. Ser.: 6). (ENG.). 104p. (J). (gr. 2-5). pap. 7.95 *(978-1-4677-0715-2(5)*, Darby Creek); lib. bdg. 27.93 *(978-0-7613-9204-0(1))* Lerner Publishing Group.

—Billy Monster's Daymare. Durant, Alan. 2008. 32p. (J). (gr. -1-2). pap. 6.95 *(978-1-58925-412-1(0))* Tiger Tales.

—Chameleon Chaos. Sparkes, Ali. 2014. (S. W. I. T. C. H. Ser.: 10). (ENG.). 112p. (J). (gr. 2-5). lib. bdg. 27.93 *(978-1-4677-2113-4(1)*, Darby Creek) Lerner Publishing Group.

—Crane Fly Crash. Sparkes, Ali. 2013. (S. W. I. T. C. H. Ser.: 5). (ENG.). 104p. (J). (gr. 2-5). pap. 7.95 *(978-1-4677-0714-5(7)*, Darby Creek); lib. bdg. 27.93 *(978-0-7613-9203-3(3))* Lerner Publishing Group.

—The Flight of Dragons: The Fourth Tale from the Five Kingdoms. French, Vivian. 2011. (Tales from the Five Kingdoms Ser.: 4). (ENG.). 208p. (J). (gr. 3-7). 15.99 *(978-0-7636-5083-4(8))* Candlewick Pr.

—The Flight of Dragons: The Fourth Tale from the Five Kingdoms. French, Vivian. 2012. (Tales from the Five Kingdoms Ser.: 4). (ENG.). 256p. (J). (gr. 3-7). pap. 5.99 *(978-0-7636-5133-6(8))* Candlewick Pr.

—Fly Frenzy. Sparkes, Ali. 2013. (S. W. I. T. C. H. Ser.: 2). (ENG.). 104p. (J). (gr. 2-5). pap. 7.95 *(978-1-4677-0711-4(2)*, Darby Creek) Lerner Publishing Group.

—Fly Frenzy. Sparkes, Ali. 2013. (S. W. I. T. C. H. Ser.: 2). (ENG.). 104p. (J). (gr. 2-5). lib. bdg. 27.93 *(978-0-7613-9200-2(9))* Lerner Publishing Group.

—Frog Freakout. Sparkes, Ali. 2014. (S. W. I. T. C. H. Ser.: 7). (ENG.). 88p. (J). (gr. 2-5). lib. bdg. 27.93 *(978-1-4677-2111-0(5)*, Darby Creek) Lerner Publishing Group.

—Gecko Gladiator. Sparkes, Ali. 2014. (S. W. I. T. C. H. Ser.: 12). (ENG.). 104p. (J). (gr. 2-5). lib. bdg. 27.93 *(978-1-4677-2115-8(8)*, Darby Creek) Lerner Publishing Group.

—Grasshopper Glitch. Sparkes, Ali. 2013. (S. W. I. T. C. H. Ser.: 3). (ENG.). 104p. (J). (gr. 2-5). pap. 7.95 *(978-1-4677-0712-1(0))* Lerner Publishing Group.

—Grasshopper Glitch. Sparkes, Ali. 2013. (S. W. I. T. C. H. Ser.: 3). (ENG.). 104p. (J). (gr. 2-5). lib. bdg. 27.93 *(978-0-7613-9201-9(7))* Lerner Publishing Group.

—The Heart of Glass: The Third Tale from the Five Kingdoms. French, Vivian. (Tales from the Five Kingdoms Ser.: 3). (ENG.). 256p. (J). (gr. 3-7). 2011. pap. 5.99 *(978-0-7636-5132-9(X))*; 2010. 14.99 *(978-0-7636-4814-5(0))* Candlewick Pr.

Collins, Ross. Hugh's Blue Day. Hodgson, Karen J. 2010. (ENG.). 32p. (J). (gr. -1-k). pap. 9.99 ***(978-1-907432-00-2(0))*** Hogs Back Bks. GBR. Dist: Independent Pubs. Group.

—Littlenose Collection: The Explorer. Grant, John. 2014. (ENG.). 336p. (J). pap. 8.99 ***(978-1-4711-2135-7(6))*** Simon & Schuster, Ltd. GBR. Dist: Simon & Schuster, Inc.

—Littlenose Collection - The Magician. Grant, John. 2014. (ENG.). 352p. (J). pap. 8.99 ***(978-1-4711-2137-1(2))*** Simon & Schuster, Ltd. GBR. Dist: Simon & Schuster, Inc.

Collins, Ross. Littlenose the Magician. Grant, John. 2009. (ENG.). 128p. (J). (gr. k-12). pap. 5.99 *(978-1-84738-201-6(0))* Simon & Schuster, Ltd. GBR. Dist: Simon & Schuster, Inc.

—Lizard Loopy. Sparkes, Ali. 2014. (S. W. I. T. C. H. Ser.: 9). (ENG.). 104p. (J). (gr. 2-5). lib. bdg. 27.93 *(978-1-4677-2112-7(3)*, Darby Creek) Lerner Publishing Group.

—The Music of Zombies. French, Vivian. 2013. (Tales from the Five Kingdoms Ser.). (ENG.). 304p. (J). (gr. 3-7). 15.99 *(978-0-7636-5930-1(4))* Candlewick Pr.

—Newt Nemesis. Sparkes, Ali. 2014. (S. W. I. T. C. H. Ser.: 8). (ENG.). 88p. (J). (gr. 2-5). lib. bdg. 27.93 *(978-1-4677-3233-8(8)*, Darby Creek) Lerner Publishing Group.

—Oh, George! Graves, Sue. 2005. (Reading Corner Ser.). 24p. (J). (gr. k-3). lib. bdg. 22.80 *(978-1-59771-000-8(8))* Sea-To-Sea Pubns.

Collins, Ross. Reading Corner: Kimberley's Scary Day. Bryant, Ann. 2006. (Reading Corner Ser.). (ENG.). 32p. (J). (gr. k-2). pap. 6.99 ***(978-0-7496-6141-0(0))*** Hodder & Stoughton GBR. Dist: Independent Pubs. Group.

Collins, Ross. The Robe of Skulls: The First Tale from the Five Kingdoms. French, Vivian. 2009. (Tales from the Five Kingdoms Ser.: 1). (ENG.). 208p. (J). (gr. 3-7). pap. 5.99 *(978-0-7636-4364-5(5))* Candlewick Pr.

—Spider Stampede. Sparkes, Ali. 2013. (S. W. I. T. C. H. Ser.: 1). (ENG.). 104p. (J). (gr. 2-5). pap. 7.95 *(978-1-4677-0710-7(4))* Lerner Publishing Group.

—Spider Stampede. Sparkes, Ali. 2013. (S. W. I. T. C. H. Ser.: 1). (ENG.). 104p. (J). (gr. 2-5). lib. bdg. 27.93 *(978-0-7613-9199-9(1))* Lerner Publishing Group.

—Turtle Terror. Sparkes, Ali. 2014. (S. W. I. T. C. H. Ser.: 11). (ENG.). 104p. (J). (gr. 2-5). lib. bdg. 27.93 *(978-1-4677-2114-1(X)*, Darby Creek) Lerner Publishing Group.

—The Unlikely Adventures of Mabel Jones. Mabbitt, Will. 2015. (Mabel Jones Ser.: 1). (ENG.). 304p. (J). (gr. 3-7). 16.99 *(978-0-451-47196-3(2)*, Viking Juvenile) Penguin Publishing Group.

—When I Woke up I Was a Hippopotamus. MacRae, Tom. 2011. (Andersen Press Picture Books Ser.). (J). 16.95 *(978-0-7613-8099-3(X))* Andersen Pr. GBR. Dist: Lerner Publishing Group.

—Where Giants Hide. Kelly, Mij. 2010. (ENG.). 32p. (J). (gr. k-3). 16.99 *(978-1-4022-4270-0(0)*, Sourcebooks Jabberwocky) Sourcebooks, Inc.

Collins, Ross. Doodleday. Collins, Ross. 2011. (ENG.). 32p. (J). (gr. -1-3). 16.99 *(978-0-8075-1683-6(X))* Whitman, Albert & Co.

—The Elephantom. Collins, Ross. 2015. (ENG.). 40p. (J). (gr. -1-2). 16.99 *(978-0-7636-7591-2(1)*, Templar) Candlewick Pr.

Collins, Ross. Attila, Loolagax & the Eagle. Collins, Ross, tr. McAuliffe, Nichola. 2003. (ENG.). 128p. (J). pap. 10.99 *(978-0-7475-6499-7(X))* Bloomsbury Publishing Plc GBR. Dist: Independent Pubs. Group.

Collins, Sally J. Hamish Mchaggis & the Edinburgh Adventure. Strachan, Linda. 2005. (Hamish Mchaggis Ser.). 26p. (J). per. 9.00 *(978-0-9546701-7-7(5))* GW Publishing GBR. Dist: Wilson & Assocs.

—Hamish Mchaggis & the Ghost of Glamis. Strachan, Linda. 2005. (Hamish Mchaggis Ser.). 26p. (J). per. 9.00 *(978-0-9546701-9-1(1))* GW Publishing GBR. Dist: Wilson & Assocs.

—Hamish Mchaggis & the Search for the Loch Ness Monster. Strachan, Linda. 2005. 32p. (J). pap. 9.00 *(978-0-9546701-5-3(9))* GW Publishing GBR. Dist: Wilson & Assocs.

—Hamish Mchaggis & the Skye Surprise. Strachan, Linda. 2005. (Hamish Mchaggis Ser.). 26p. (J). pap. 9.00 *(978-0-9546701-8-4(3))* GW Publishing GBR. Dist: Wilson & Assocs.

Collins Staff. American Flag Q & A. Thomson, Sarah L. 2008. 48p. (J). (gr. k-4). 16.99 *(978-0-06-089959-2(X)*, Collins) HarperCollins Pubs.

Collins, Tami. Bats, 1 vol. Preszler, June. 2006. (World of Mammals Ser.). (ENG.). 24p. (gr. 2-3). 23.32 *(978-0-7368-5415-3(0)*, Bridgestone Bks.) Capstone Pr., Inc.

—Bearded Dragons, 1 vol. Glaser, Jason. 2006. (World of Reptiles Ser.). (ENG.). 24p. (gr. 2-3). 23.32 *(978-0-7368-5419-1(3)*, Bridgestone Bks.) Capstone Pr., Inc.

—Electricity. Richardson, Adele & Richardson, Adele D. 2006. (Questions & Answers: Physical Science Ser.). (ENG.). 32p. (gr. 3-4). 26.65 *(978-0-7368-5444-3(4)*, Fact Finders) Capstone Pr., Inc.

—Foxes, 1 vol. Richardson, Adele D. 2006. (World of Mammals Ser.). (ENG.). 24p. (gr. 2-3). 23.32 *(978-0-7368-5416-0(9)*, Bridgestone Bks.) Capstone Pr., Inc.

—Horned Lizards, 1 vol. Glaser, Jason. 2006. (World of Reptiles Ser.). (ENG.). 24p. (gr. 2-3). 23.32 *(978-0-7368-5421-4(5)*, Bridgestone Bks.) Capstone Pr., Inc.

—Komodo Dragons, 1 vol. Glaser, Jason. 2006. (World of Reptiles Ser.). (ENG.). 24p. (gr. 2-3). 23.32 *(978-0-7368-5422-1(3)*, Bridgestone Bks.) Capstone Pr., Inc.

—Sea Turtles, 1 vol. Glaser, Jason. 2006. (World of Reptiles Ser.). (ENG.). 24p. (gr. 2-3). 23.32 *(978-0-7368-5423-8(1)*, Bridgestone Bks.) Capstone Pr., Inc.

Collins, Tami & Nei, Molly. Light: A Question & Answer Book, 1 vol. Richardson, Adele D. 2006. (Questions & Answers: Physical Science Ser.). (ENG.). 32p. (gr. 3-4). 26.65 *(978-0-7368-5446-7(0)*, Fact Finders) Capstone Pr., Inc.

—Sound: A Question & Answer Book, 1 vol. Bayrock, Fiona. 2006. (Questions & Answers: Physical Science Ser.). (ENG.). 32p. (gr. 3-4). 26.65 *(978-0-7368-5449-8(5)*, Fact Finders) Capstone Pr., Inc.

Colllins, Linda. Boppy & Me. Mazur, Gabrielle. 2013. 38p. 14.97 *(978-1-4507-3897-2(4))* Bush Publishing Inc.

Colman, Audrey. Rough Weather Ahead for Walter the Farting Dog. Kotzwinkle, William et al. (ENG.). 32p. (J). (gr. k-3). 2007. pap. 6.99 *(978-0-14-240845-2(X)*, Puffin); 2005. 16.99 *(978-0-525-47218-6(5)*, Dutton Juvenile) Penguin Publishing Group.

—Walter Canis Inflatus: Walter the Farting Dog, Latin-Language Edition. Kotzwinkle, William & Murray, Glenn. Dobbin, Rob, tr. from ENG. 2004.Tr. of Walter the Farting Dog. (LAT.). 32p. (J). (gr. k-4). 15.95 *(978-1-58394-110-2(X)*, Frog Ltd.) North Atlantic Bks.

—Walter el Perro Pedorrero. Kotzwinkle, William & Murray, Glenn. Bohorquez, Eduardo, tr. from ENG. 2004.Tr. of Walter the Farting Dog. (SPA.). 32p. (J). (gr. k-4). 15.95 *(978-1-58394-103-4(7)*, Frog Ltd.) North Atlantic Bks.

—Walter le Chien Qui Pete. Kotzwinkle, William & Murray, Glenn. Choquette, Michel, tr. from ENG. 2004.Tr. of Walter the Farting Dog. (FRE.). 32p. (J). (gr. k-4). 15.95 *(978-1-58394-104-1(5)*, Frog Ltd.) North Atlantic Bks.

—Walter the Farting Dog: Banned from the Beach. Kotzwinkle, William et al. 2007. (ENG.). 32p. (J). (gr. k-3). 16.99 *(978-0-525-47812-6(4)*, Dutton Juvenile) Penguin Publishing Group.

—Walter the Farting Dog: Trouble at the Yard Sale. Kotzwinkle, William & Murray, Glenn. 2004. (ENG.). 32p. (J). (gr. k-3). 16.99 *(978-0-525-47217-9(7)*, Dutton Juvenile) Penguin Publishing Group.

—Walter the Farting Dog Goes on a Cruise. Katzwinkle, William et al. 2008. (J). 13.99 *(978-1-59319-939-5(2))* LeapFrog Enterprises, Inc.

Colnaghi, Stefania. Are We There Yet?, 1 vol. Powell, Jillian. 2013. (Start Reading Ser.). (ENG.). 24p. (gr. k-1). pap. 6.99 *(978-1-4765-4083-2(7))* Capstone Pr., Inc.

—Hurry up, Pony!, 1 vol. Powell, Jillian. 2013. (Start Reading Ser.). (ENG.). 24p. (gr. k-1). pap. 6.99 *(978-1-4765-4105-1(1))* Capstone Pr., Inc.

—Let's Say Hello. Powell, Jillian. 2013. (Start Reading Ser.). (ENG.). 24p. (gr. k-1). pap. 6.99 *(978-1-4765-4111-2(6))* Capstone Pr., Inc.

—Roller Coaster Fun!, 1 vol. Powell, Jillian. 2013. (Start Reading Ser.). (ENG.). 24p. (gr. k-1). pap. 6.99 *(978-1-4765-4135-8(3))* Capstone Pr., Inc.

Cologne, Starla. Miss Flavia & the Cookie Cottage. Schmidt, Kristina Edelkamp. 2009. 28p. pap. 7.99 *(978-1-935125-61-7(3))* Robertson Publishing.

Coloma, Lester. Tea Leaves. Coloma, Lester, tr. Lipp, Frederick J. 2003. (J). 32p. (gr. 1-6). 15.95 *(978-1-59034-998-4(9))*; 33p. pap. *(978-1-59034-999-1(7))* Mondo Publishing.

Colombo, Angelo. Alex & Penny's Italy Jigsaw Book. Francia, Giada. 2007. (ENG.). 14p. (gr. 1-3). pap. 14.95 *(978-88-544-0242-3(7)*, White Star) Rizzoli International Pubns., Inc.

—Alex & Penny's Wild West Jigsaw Book. Francia, Giada. 2007. (ENG.). 14p. (gr. 1-3). pap. 14.95 *(978-88-544-0285-0(0)*, White Star) Rizzoli International Pubns., Inc.

—Ballooning over Italy: An Extraordinary Voyage Packed with Games & Fantastic Adventures; Special Agents. Francia, Giada, ed. Ezrin, Amy, tr. 2007. (Alex & Penny Ser.). (ENG.). 80p. (J). (gr. 2-5). 14.95 *(978-88-544-0160-0(9)*, White Star) Rizzoli International Pubns., Inc.

Colombo, David. Silly Soup. Helms, Tina, photos by. Korty, Carol. Landes, William-Alan, ed. 2003. (Plays & Play Collections). 128p. (Orig.). (J). (gr. k-6). pap. 17.00 *(978-0-88734-679-8(0))* Players Pr., Inc.

Colón, Daniel, jt. illus. see Groff, David.

Colon, Ernie. Everything You Need for Simple Science Fair Projects: Grades 3-5. Friedhoffer, Bob. 2006. (Scientific American Science Fair Projects Ser.). 48p. (gr. 3-5). lib. bdg. 27.00 *(978-0-7910-9054-1(X))* Facts On File, Inc.

—Everything You Need for Winning Science Fair Projects: Grades 5-7. Friedhoffer, Bob. 2006. (Scientific American Science Fair Projects Ser.). 48p. (gr. 4-6). lib. bdg. 27.00 *(978-0-7910-9056-5(6))* Facts On File, Inc.

Colón, Ernie & Drozd, Jerzy. The Warren Commission Report: A Graphic Investigation into the Kennedy Assassination. Mishkin, Dan. 2014. (ENG.). 160p. 29.95 *(978-1-4197-1230-2(6))*; pap. 17.95 *(978-1-4197-1231-9(4))* Abrams.

Colón, Raúl. Abuelo. Dorros, Arthur. 2014. (ENG.). 32p. (J). (gr. -1-3). 17.99 *(978-0-06-168627-6(1))* HarperCollins Pubs.

—Annie & Helen. Hopkinson, Deborah. 2012. (ENG.). 48p. (J). (gr. -1-3). 17.99 *(978-0-375-85706-5(0))*; lib. bdg. 20.99 *(978-0-375-95706-2(5))* Random Hse. Children's Bks. (Schwartz & Wade Bks.).

—Any Small Goodness. Johnston, Tony. 2003. (Any Small Goodness Ser.). (ENG.). 128p. (J). (gr. 2-5). per. 5.99 *(978-0-439-23384-2(4)*, Scholastic Paperbacks) Scholastic, Inc.

—As Good As Anybody. Michelson, Richard. 2013. (ENG.). 40p. (J). (gr. 1-4). 7.99 *(978-0-385-75387-6(X)*, Dragonfly Bks.) Random Hse. Children's Bks.

—As Good as Anybody: Martin Luther King Jr. & Abraham Joshua Heschel's Amazing March Toward Freedom. Michelson, Richard. 2008. (ENG.). 40p. (J). (gr. 1-4). 16.99 *(978-0-375-83335-9(8)*, Knopf Bks. for Young Readers) Random Hse. Children's Bks.

—Baseball Is... Borden, Louise. 2014. (ENG.). 48p. (J). (gr. 2-5). 17.99 *(978-1-4169-5502-3(X)*, McElderry, Margaret K. Bks.) McElderry, Margaret K. Bks.

—Child of the Civil Rights Movement. Shelton, Paula Young. (ENG.). 48p. (J). (gr. -1-3). 2013. 7.99 *(978-0-385-37606-8(5))*; 2009. 17.99 *(978-0-375-84314-3(0))* Random Hse. Children's Bks. (Schwartz & Wade Bks.).

—Doña Flor: A Tall Tale about a Giant Woman with a Great Big Heart. Mora, Pat. (ENG & SPA.). 40p. (J). (gr. -1-2). 2010. pap. 7.99 *(978-0-375-86144-4(0)*, Dragonfly Bks.); 2005. 15.95 *(978-0-375-82337-4(9)*, Knopf Bks. for Young Readers) Random Hse. Children's Bks.

—Doña Flor: Un Cuento de una Mujer Gigante con un Gran Corazon. Mora, Pat. 2005. (SPA.). 40p. (J). (gr. -1-2). per. 7.99 *(978-0-440-41768-2(6)*, Dragonfly Bks.) Random Hse. Children's Bks.

—Good-Bye, Havana! Hola, New York! Colon, Edie. 2011. (ENG.). 32p. (J). (gr. -1-3). 16.99 *(978-1-4424-0674-2(7))*, Simon & Schuster/Paula Wiseman Bks.) Simon & Schuster/Paula Wiseman Bks.

—How to Bake an American Pie. Wilson, Karma. 2007. (ENG.). 40p. (J). (gr. -1-3). 17.99 *(978-0-689-86506-0(6)*, McElderry, Margaret K. Bks.) McElderry, Margaret K. Bks.

—José! Born to Dance: The Story of Jose Limon. Reich, Susanna. 2005. (ENG.). 32p. (J). (gr. k-3). 17.99 *(978-0-689-86576-3(7)*, Simon & Schuster/Paula Wiseman Bks.) Simon & Schuster/Paula Wiseman Bks.

—Leontyne Price: Voice of a Century. Weatherford, Carole Boston. 2014. (ENG.). 40p. (J). (gr. k-4). 17.99 *(978-0-375-85606-8(4))*; lib. bdg. 20.99 *(978-0-375-95606-5(9))* Knopf, Alfred A. Inc.

—Look Up! Henrietta Leavitt, Pioneering Woman Astronomer. Burleigh, Robert. 2013. (ENG.). 32p. (J). (gr. -1-3). 16.99 *(978-1-4169-5819-2(3)*, Simon & Schuster Bks. For Young Readers) Simon & Schuster/Paula Wiseman Bks.

—My Name Is Gabito: The Life of Gabriel Garcia Marquez. Brown, Monica. 2007. (ENG.). 32p. (J). (gr. -1-3). 15.95 *(978-0-87358-934-5(3))* Cooper Square Publishing Llc.

—My Name Is Gabito/Me Llamo Gabito: The Life of Gabriel Garcia Marquez/la Vida de Gabriel Garcia Marquez. Brown, Monica. 2007. (ENG, SPA & MUL.). 32p. (J). (gr. -1-3). 15.95 *(978-0-87358-908-6(4))* Cooper Square Publishing Llc.

—Once upon a Time: Traditional Latin American Tales. Martínez, Rueben. Unger, David, tr. from SPA. 2010. (ENG & SPA.). 96p. (J). (gr. k-5). 19.99 *(978-0-06-146895-7(9)*, Rayo) HarperCollins Pubs.

—Play Ball! Posada, Jorge. 2010. (ENG.). 32p. (J). (gr. 1-5). 6.99 *(978-1-4169-9825-9(X)*, Simon & Schuster/Paula Wiseman Bks.) Simon & Schuster/Paula Wiseman Bks.

—Portraits of Hispanic American Heroes. Herrera, Juan Felipe. 2014. (ENG.). 96p. (J). (gr. 3-7). 19.99 *(978-0-8037-3809-6(9)*, Dial) Penguin Publishing Group.

—Roberto Clemente: Pride of the Pittsburgh Pirates. Winter, Jonah. (ENG.). 40p. (J). (gr. -1-3). 2008. 7.99 *(978-1-4169-5082-0(6))*; 2005. 17.99 *(978-0-689-85643-3(1))* Simon & Schuster Children's Publishing. (Atheneum Bks. for Young Readers).

—Sí, Puedes. Posada, Jorge. 2010.Tr. of Play Ball!. (SPA.). 32p. (J). (gr. 1-5). 6.99 *(978-1-4169-9826-6(8)*, Simon &

Schuster/Paula Wiseman Bks.) Simon & Schuster/Paula Wiseman Bks.
—Tomas & the Library Lady. Mora, Pat. 2007. (gr. k-3). 18.00 *(978-0-7569-7935-5(8))* Perfection Learning Corp.
Colón, Raúl. Draw! Colón, Raúl. 2014. (ENG.). 40p. (J). (gr. -1-3). 17.99 *(978-1-4424-9492-3(1))*, Simon & Schuster/Paula Wiseman Bks.) Simon & Schuster/Paula Wiseman Bks.
Colón, Raúl & McNicholas, Shelagh. The Perfect Pony. Bradley, Kimberly Brubaker. 2007. (ENG.). 32p. (J). (gr. -1-3). 16.99 *(978-0-8037-2851-6(4))*, Dial) Penguin Publishing Group.
Colquhoun, Christine. Pick-a-WooWoo - the Little Sparkle in Me: My Sparkle Is A Gift to Feel Hear & See, 16 vols., Vol. 15. Colquhoun, Christine. 2010. 32p. pap. *(978-0-9806520-8-6(1))* Pick-a-Woo Woo Pubs.
Colson, A. W. & Renda, Joseph. Manassas, Please Slow Down. Glenn, Judith. 2010. 60p. pap. 21.99 *(978-1-4490-6682-6(8))* AuthorHouse.
Colton, Ellie. Bible Blessings. Elkins, Stephen. 2003. (Lulla-Bible Series for Little Ones). 32p. (J). 9.99 incl. audio compact disk *(978-0-8054-2761-5(9))* B&H Publishing Group.
—The Bible Prayer Collection: 30 Life Changing Prayers from the Bible for Children. Elkins, Stephen. 2003. 64p. (J). (gr. k-3). 9.99 incl. audio compact disk *(978-0-8054-2758-5(9))* B&H Publishing Group.
—Bible Prayers. Elkins, Stephen. 2003. (Lulla-Bible Series for Little Ones). 32p. (J). 9.99 incl. audio compact disk *(978-0-8054-2755-4(4))* B&H Publishing Group.
—Bible Promises. Elkins, Stephen. 2003. (Lulla-Bible Series for Little Ones). 32p. (J). 9.99 incl. audio compact disk *(978-0-8054-2756-1(2))* B&H Publishing Group.
—Bible Verses. Elkins, Stephen. 2003. (Lulla-Bible Series for Little Ones). 32p. (J). 9.99 incl. audio compact disk *(978-0-8054-2757-8(0))* B&H Publishing Group.
—First Steps in Faith: Beginning Lessons of God's Love. Elkins, Stephen. 2006. (First Steps in Faith Ser.). 25p. (J). (gr. -1-k). bds. 9.99 incl. audio compact disk *(978-0-8054-2662-5(0))* B&H Publishing Group.
—First Steps in Prayer. Elkins, Stephen. 2006. (First Steps Ser.). 32p. (J). 9.99 *(978-0-8054-2663-2(9))* B&H Publishing Group.
—First Steps to God: Beginning Lessons of God's Love. Elkins, Stephen. 2006. (First Steps Ser.). 25p. (J). (gr. -1-k). 9.99 incl. audio compact disk *(978-0-8054-2661-8(2))* B&H Publishing Group.
—The LullaBible: A Musical Treasury for Mother & Baby. Elkins, Stephen. 2004. (J). (gr. -1). 223p. 14.99 *(978-0-8054-2388-4(5))*; 224p. 19.99 incl. audio *(978-0-8054-2389-1(3))* B&H Publishing Group.
—Lullabies for Babies. Elkins, Stephen. 2005. (Jesus Loves Me Ser.). (ENG.). 32p. (J). (gr. -1-2). 6.99 *(978-1-4169-0843-2(9))*, Little Simon) Little Simon.
—My LullaBible A to Z Promise Book. Elkins, Stephen. 2007. 36p. (J). (gr. -1). bds. 14.99 incl. audio compact disk *(978-0-8054-2657-1(4))* B&H Publishing Group.
Columbin, Corey. Silly Rhymes for Fun Times. Wigden, Susan. 2011. 20p. pap. 11.95 *(978-1-60888-107-9(5))* Nimble Bks. LLC.
Colwell, Emerson/Mylon, Jr. The Fisher Cat. Colwell, Emerson/Mylon, Jr. 2009. (ENG.). 36p. (J). pap. 14.95 *(978-0-9840916-1-4(0))* TINK INK Publishing.
Combs, Bradley. Lexi's Tea Party. Tuttle, Mark. 2011. 32p. pap. 24.95 *(978-1-4560-9919-0(1))* America Star Bks.
Combs, Paul. The Floating Zoo. Scarff, Ruth. 2003. 21p. (J). pap. *(978-0-87398-289-4(4))* Sword of the Lord Pubs.
Comella, Angels. Let's Talk about God/Hablemos de Dios. Comella, Angels. Twomey, Lisa A., tr. from SPA. 2005. (SPA & ENG.). 28p. (J). (gr. -1-3). 9.95 *(978-0-8146-2361-9(1))* Liturgical Pr.
Comet, Renee, photos by. Healthy Foods from A to Z: Comida Sana de la a a la Z. Maze, Stephanie, ed. 2012. (SPA & ENG., 32p. (J). (gr. -1-k). 15.95 *(978-0-9834983-1-5(8))* Moonstone Pr., LLC.
Comfort, Louise. Fairy Unicorn Riding Stables. Bateson, Maggie. ed. 2012. (ENG.). 12p. (J). (gr. -1-k). 22.99 *(978-0-230-74331-1(5))* Macmillan Pubs., Ltd. GBR. Dist: Independent Pubs. Group.
—French-English Word Puzzle Book: 14 Fun French & English Word Games. Bruzzone, Catherine et al. 2012. (Bilingual Word Puzzle Bks.). (FRE.). 32p. (J). (gr. 3-7). pap. 5.99 *(978-1-4380-0054-1(5))* Barron's Educational Series, Inc.
—Hide & Speak French. Bruzzone, Catherine & Martinneau, Susan. 2003. (Hide & Speak Ser.). (FRE & ENG.). 32p. (J). pap. 8.99 *(978-0-7641-2588-1(5))* Barron's Educational Series, Inc.
—Hide & Speak Italian. Bruzzone, Catherine & Martinneau, Susan. 2005. (Hide & Speak Ser.). (ENG & ITA.). 32p. (J). pap. 9.99 *(978-0-7641-3151-6(6))* Barron's Educational Series, Inc.
—Hide & Speak Spanish. Bruzzone, Catherine & Martineau, Susan. 2003. (Hide & Speak Ser.). (SPA & ENG.). 32p. (J). pap. 9.99 *(978-0-7641-2589-8(3))* Barron's Educational Series, Inc.
—My Fairy Fashion Show: A Pop-up & Play Book. Bateson, Maggie. ed. 2008. (ENG.). 20p. (J). (gr. 4-8). 23.95 *(978-0-230-53035-5(4))*, Macmillan) Pan Macmillan GBR. Dist: Trans-Atlantic Pubns., Inc.
—My Fairy Princess Palace. Bateson, Maggie. 2nd ed. 2004. (ENG.). 8p. (J). (gr. k-2). 24.99 *(978-1-4050-2076-3(8))* Pan Macmillan GBR. Dist: Independent Pubs. Group.
—My Fairy Showtime. Bateson, Maggie. ed. 2011. (ENG.). 12p. (J). (gr. k-2). 24.99 *(978-0-230-01582-1(4))* Macmillan Pubs., Ltd. GBR. Dist: Independent Pubs. Group.
—My Fairytale Dream Palace. Bateson, Maggie. ed. 2013. (ENG.). 10p. (J). (gr. -1-k). bds. 26.99 *(978-0-230-74332-8(3))* Pan Macmillan GBR. Dist: Independent Pubs. Group.
—My French Sticker Dictionary: Everyday Words & Popular Themes in Colorful Sticker Scenes. Bruzzone, Catherine & Millar, Louise. 2013. (Sticker Dictionaries Ser.). (ENG.). 24p. (J). (gr. -1-1). pap. 6.99 *(978-1-4380-0253-8(X))* Barron's Educational Series, Inc.
—My Spanish Sticker Dictionary: Everyday Words & Popular Themes in Colorful Sticker Scenes. Bruzzone, Catherine & Millar, Louise. 2013. (Sticker Dictionaries Ser.). (ENG.). 24p. (J). (gr. -1-1). pap. 6.99 *(978-1-4380-0252-1(1))* Barron's Educational Series, Inc.
—El Palacio de Las Hadas. Bateson, Maggie. Sánchez Abulí, Enrique, tr. 2007. (SPA & ENG.). 14p. (J). (gr. 2-4). pap. 34.95 *(978-84-666-1678-2(0))* Ediciones B ESP. Dist: Independent Pubs. Group.
—Spanish-English Word Puzzle Book: 14 Fun Spanish & English Word Games. Bruzzone, Catherine et al. 2012. (Bilingual Word Puzzle Bks.). (SPA.). 32p. (J). (gr. 3-7). pap. 5.99 *(978-1-4380-0053-4(7))* Barron's Educational Series, Inc.
Comfort, Louise. Hide & Speak English. Comfort, Louise, tr. Bruzzone, Catherine & Martinneau, Susan. 2003. (Hide & Speak Ser.). (ENG.). 32p. (J). (gr. 1-4). pap. 9.99 *(978-1-902915-74-6(7))* B Small Publishing GBR. Dist: Independent Pubs. Group.
Comfort, Louise & Dix, Steph. French-English Picture Dictionary. Bruzzone, Catherine et al. 2011. (First Bilingual Picture Dictionaries Ser.). (FRE & ENG.). 48p. (J). (gr. -1-3). pap. 7.99 *(978-0-7641-4660-2(2))* Barron's Educational Series, Inc.
Comfort, Mike & Baisley, Stephen. Discovering Oregon. Matchette, Dennis, photos by. Matchette, Katharine E. (YA). (gr. 5-9). spiral bd. 13.00 *(978-0-9645045-4-7(5))* Deka Pr.
Comins, Andy. The Frog Scientist. Turner, Pamela S. 2011. (Scientists in the Field Ser.). (ENG.). 64p. (J). (gr. 5-7). pap. 9.99 *(978-0-547-57698-5(6))* Houghton Mifflin Harcourt Publishing Co.
—Stronger Than Steel: Spider Silk DNA & the Quest for Better Bulletproof Vests, Sutures, & Parachute Rope. Heos, Bridget. 2013. (Scientists in the Field Ser.). (ENG.). 80p. (J). (gr. 5-7). 18.99 *(978-0-547-68126-9(7))* Houghton Mifflin Harcourt Publishing Co.
Communication Design (Firm) Staff, jt. illus. see Meganck, Robert.
Compere, Janet. Louis Braille. Davidson, Margaret. (FRE.). 80p. (J). pap. 5.99 *(978-0-590-71110-4(5))* Scholastic, Inc.
Comport, Sally Wern. Ada's Violin: The Story of the Recycled Orchestra. Hood, Susan. 2016. ***(978-1-4814-3095-1(5))***, Simon & Schuster Bks. For Young Readers) Simon & Schuster Bks. For Young Readers.
Comport, Sally Wern. Bearwalker. Bruchac, Joseph. 2010. (ENG.). 240p. (J). (gr. 5). pap. 6.99 *(978-0-06-112315-3(3))* HarperCollins Pubs.
—The Dark Pond. Bruchac, Joseph. 2005. 142p. (gr. 5-9). 17.00 *(978-0-7569-5436-9(3))* Perfection Learning Corp.
—Dark Pond. Bruchac, Joseph. 2005. (ENG.). 160p. (J). (gr. 5-18). pap. 6.99 *(978-0-06-052998-7(9))* HarperCollins Pubs.
—First Kids. Davis, Gibbs. 2009. (Step into Reading Ser.). (ENG.). 48p. (J). (gr. 2-4). pap. 3.99 *(978-0-375-82218-6(6))*, Random Hse. Bks. for Young Readers) Random Hse. Children's Bks.
—For Your Paws Only. Frederick, Heather Vogel. 2006. (Spy Mice Ser.: 2). (ENG.). 272p. (J). (gr. 3-6). pap. 5.99 *(978-1-4169-4025-8(1))*, Simon & Schuster Bks. For Young Readers) Simon & Schuster Bks. For Young Readers.
—For Your Paws Only. Frederick, Heather Vogel. 2005. (Spy Mice Ser.: 2). (ENG.). 272p. (J). (gr. 4-6). 9.95 *(978-1-4169-0573-8(1))* Simon & Schuster Children's Publishing.
—Hanging off Jefferson's Nose: Growing up on Mount Rushmore. Coury, Tina Nichols. 2012. (ENG.). 40p. (J). (gr. k-3). 16.99 *(978-0-8037-3731-0(9))*, Dial) Penguin Publishing Group.
—How to Disappear Completely & Never Be Found. Nickerson, Sara. 2003. (ENG.). 288p. (J). (gr. 5-18). pap. 5.99 *(978-0-06-441027-4(7))* HarperCollins Pubs.
—Louisiana Purchase. Roop, Peter & Roop, Connie. 2004. 84p. (J). lib. bdg. 15.00 *(978-1-4242-0908-8(0))* Fitzgerald Bks.
—Louisiana Purchase. Roop, Peter & Roop, Connie. 2004. (Ready-For-Chapters Ser.). (ENG.). 80p. (J). (gr. 2-5). pap. 6.99 *(978-0-689-86443-8(4))*, Simon & Schuster/Paula Wiseman Bks.) Simon & Schuster/Paula Wiseman Bks.
—Love Will See You Through: Martin Luther King Jr.'s Six Guiding Beliefs. Watkins, Angela Farris. 2014. (ENG.). 32p. (J). (gr. 1-6). 17.99 *(978-1-4169-8693-5(6))*, Simon & Schuster Bks. For Young Readers) Simon & Schuster Bks. For Young Readers.
—Night Wings. Bruchac, Joseph. 2009. 208p. (J). (gr. 5). lib. bdg. 16.89 *(978-0-06-112319-1(6))*; (ENG.). 15.99 *(978-0-06-112318-4(8))* HarperCollins Pubs.
—On the Island. Stevenson, Robert Louis. 2007. (Easy Reader Classics Ser.). (ENG.). 32p. (J). (gr. k-2). pap. 3.95 *(978-1-4027-4119-7(7))* Sterling Publishing Co., Inc.
—Pirate Attack. Stevenson, Robert Louis. 2007. (Easy Reader Classics Ser.). (ENG.). 32p. (J). (gr. k-2). pap. 3.95 *(978-1-4027-4120-3(0))* Sterling Publishing Co., Inc.
—Pirate's Revenge. Malcolm, Jahnna N. 2003. 77p. (J). *(978-1-931020-09-1(4))* HOP, LLC.
—The Return of Skeleton Man. Bruchac, Joseph. 144p. (J). (gr. 5). 2008. (Skeleton Man Ser.: 2). (ENG.). pap. 7.99 *(978-0-06-058092-6(5))*; 2006. lib. bdg. 16.89 *(978-0-06-058091-9(7))* HarperCollins Pubs.
—Skeleton Man. Bruchac, Joseph. 2003. (Skeleton Man Ser.: 1). (ENG.). 128p. (J). (gr. 5-18). pap. 5.99 *(978-0-06-440888-2(4))* HarperCollins Pubs.
—The Story of Thanksgiving. Bartlett, Robert Merrill. rev. ed. 2004. 30p. (J). (gr. k-4). reprint ed. *(978-0-7567-7757-9(7))* DIANE Publishing Co.
—The Story of Thanksgiving. Bartlett, Robert Merrill. Date not set. 40p. (J). (gr. 2-5). 5.99 *(978-0-06-446238-9(2))* HarperCollins Pubs.
—Sware to God. Bruchac, Joseph. 2003. 114p. (J). (gr. 5). 12.65 *(978-0-7569-3399-9(4))* Perfection Learning Corp.
—Treasure Island: The Treasure Map. Stevenson, Robert Louis. 2008. (Easy Reader Classics Ser.). (ENG.). 32p. (gr. -1-3). lib. bdg. 24.21 *(978-1-59961-342-0(5))* Spotlight.
—The Treasure Map. Stevenson, Robert Louis. 2006. (Easy Reader Classics Ser.). (ENG.). 32p. (J). (gr. k-2). pap. 3.95 *(978-1-4027-3297-3(X))* Sterling Publishing Co., Inc.
—Vampire State Building. Levy, Elizabeth. 2003. (ENG.). 112p. (J). pap. 4.99 *(978-0-06-000052-3(X))* HarperCollins Pubs.
—Whisper in the Dark. Bruchac, Joseph. 2009. (ENG.). 192p. (J). (gr. 5). pap. 6.99 *(978-0-06-058089-6(5))* HarperCollins Pubs.
Compton, Annette. God's Paintbrush. Sasso, Sandy Eisenberg. 10th anniv. annot. ed. 2004. (GER & ENG.). 32p. (J). (gr. -1-2). 18.99 *(978-1-58023-195-4(0))*, Jewish Lights Publishing) LongHill Partners, Inc.
—I Am God's Paintbrush. Sasso, Sandy Eisenberg. 2009. (ENG.). 24p. (J). bds. 7.99 *(978-1-59473-265-2(5))*, Skylight Paths Publishing) LongHill Partners, Inc.
Compton, Brian L. Scoo Scoo, Bo Bo & the Dragonfly. Lindsey, Ms. Elanna T. 2013. 32p. pap. 13.50 *(978-0-615-83876-2(6))* Lindsey, Elanna.
Compton, Donna. Wood, Hay, & Pigs. Koenig, Albert. 2005. (J). 8.99 *(978-1-4183-0078-4(0))* Christ Inspired, Inc.
Comstock, Chris. The Hat Peddler. Susedik, Tina. 2014. 41p. (J). pap. 14.00 ***(978-0-9667527-7-9(5))*** Maple Lane Writing & Desktop Publishing.
Comstock, Eric. Charlie Piechart & the Case of the Missing Pizza Slice. Comstock, Eric. Sadler, Marilyn. 2015. (Charlie Piechart Ser.). (ENG.). 40p. (J). (gr. -1-3). 17.99 ***(978-0-06-237054-9(5))***, Tegen, Katherine Bks) HarperCollins Pubs.
Conahan, Carolyn Digby. All Day Long: A Book of Partner Prayers. Lund, Deb. 2004. (ENG.). 20p. pap. 10.00 *(978-0-8192-1961-9(4))*, Morehouse Publishing) Church Publishing, Inc.
—Bless This Way. Kitch, Anne E. 2003. (ENG.). 20p. 10.00 *(978-0-8192-1917-6(7))*, Morehouse Publishing) Church Publishing, Inc.
—Bubble Homes & Fish Farts. Bayrock, Fiona. 2009. (ENG.). 48p. (J). (gr. 1-4). pap. 7.95 *(978-1-57091-670-0(5))* Charlesbridge Publishing, Inc.
—The Discontented Gopher: A Prairie Tale. Baum, L. Frank. 2006. (Prairie Tales Ser.). 40p. (J). (gr. 3-7). 14.95 *(978-0-9749195-9-1(4))*, South Dakota State Historical Society Pr.) South Dakota State Historical Society Pr.
—Me & God: A Book of Partner Prayers. Lund, Deborah. 2003. (ENG.). 20p. 10.00 *(978-0-8192-1911-4(8))*, Morehouse Publishing) Church Publishing, Inc.
Conahan, Carolyn Digby. This Old Van. Norman, Kim. 2015. (ENG.). 30p. (J). (gr. -1-2). 14.95 ***(978-1-4549-1063-3(1))*** Sterling Publishing Co., Inc.
Conahan, Carolyn Digby. The Twelve Days of Christmas in Oregon. Blackaby, Susan. 2014. (Twelve Days of Christmas in America Ser.). (ENG.). 40p. (J). (gr. k). 12.95 *(978-1-4549-0891-3(2))* Sterling Publishing Co., Inc.
Conard, Vincent. Charis: A Journey to Pandora's Jar. Walters, Nicole Y. 2013. 214p. 32.95 *(978-1-62015-318-5(1))*, Booktrope Editions) Booktrope.
Conaway, Jim. The Ultimate Travel Time Bible. Elkins, Stephen. 2007. 170p. (J). (gr. -1-3). 14.99 incl. audio compact disk *(978-0-8054-2647-2(7))* B&H Publishing Group.
Concannon, Sue. The Breezes of Inspire. Ruth, Nick. 2005. (Remin Chronicles: 2). (ENG.). 264p. (J). (gr. 3-7). 16.95 *(978-0-9745603-3-5(2))* Imaginator Pr.
—The Dark Dreamweaver. Ruth, Nick. 2007. (Remin Chronicles: 1). (ENG.). 256p. (J). (gr. 4-7). per. 11.95 *(978-0-9745603-5-9(9))* Imaginator Pr.
Condé, J. M. The Hollow Tree & Deep Woods Book, Being a New Edition in One Volume of the Hollow Tree & in the Deep Woods with Several New Stories & Pictu. Paine, Albert Bigelow. 2012. 174p. *(978-1-78139-176-1(9))* Benediction Classics.
Conde, Manuel. Lost & Found. Madonna, Lenae. 2012. 38p. (J). 16.95 *(978-1-60131-115-3(X))*, Castlebridge Bks.) Big Tent Bks.
Cone, Carl. There's a Season for All. Shu, Sammy. 2006. 54p. (J). (gr. -1-3). 16.95 *(978-0-9778211-0-5(2))*, Raynestorm Bks.) Silver Rose Publishing.
Cone, Carl. There's a Season for All. Cone, Carl. 2008. (ENG.). pap. 14.95 *(978-0-9801555-6-3(8))* Argus Enterprises International, Inc.
Cone, William. The Night Before Christmas. Moore, Clement C. 2005. (Rabbit Ears: A Classic Tale Ser.). 32p. (gr. 2-7). 25.65 *(978-1-59197-751-3(7))* Spotlight.
Conforti, John W. Lucy the Elephant & Sami the Mouse: The Birthday Party. Evelyn. 2004. (J). *(978-0-9740115-1-6(7))* WeBeANS Corp.
Conforti, John W. Lucy the Elephant & Sami the Mouse: A Bedtime Story. Conforti, John W., tr. Evelyn. 2003. (J). *(978-0-9740115-0-9(9))* WeBeANS Corp.
Conger, Holli. Backyard Pirates. Feldman, Thea. 2007. (Magnix Imagination Activity Bks.). 6p. bds. 5.99 *(978-1-932915-40-2(0))* Sandvik Innovations, LLC.
—Chinese New Year. Marsico, Katie. 2009. (Cultural Holidays Ser.). 32p. (gr. -1-4). 28.50 *(978-1-60270-600-2(X))*, Looking Glass Library- Nonfiction) Magic Wagon.
—Choose Good Food! My Eating Tips. Bellisario, Gina. 2014. (Cloverleaf Books — My Healthy Habits Ser.). (ENG.). 24p. (gr. k-2). lib. bdg. 23.93 *(978-1-4677-1350-4(3))*, Millbrook Pr.) Lerner Publishing Group.
—Christmas. Owens, L. L. 2009. (Cultural Holidays Ser.). 32p. (gr. -1-4). 28.50 *(978-1-60270-601-9(8))*, Looking Glass Library- Nonfiction) Magic Wagon.
—Cinco de Mayo. Owens, L. L. 2009. (Cultural Holidays Ser.). 32p. (gr. -1-4). 28.50 *(978-1-60270-602-6(6))*, Looking Glass Library- Nonfiction) Magic Wagon.
—Daniela's Day of the Dead. Bullard, Lisa. 2012. (Cloverleaf Books (tm) — Fall & Winter Holidays Ser.). (ENG.). 24p. (gr. k-2). 6.95 *(978-0-7613-8585-1(1))*; lib. bdg. 23.93 *(978-0-7613-5084-2(5))* Lerner Publishing Group. (Millbrook Pr.).
Conger, Holli. Does the Sun Sleep? Noticing Sun, Moon, & Star Patterns. Rustad, Martha E. H. 2015. (ENG.). 24p. (J). (gr. k-2). 25.32 ***(978-1-4677-8560-0(1))***, Millbrook Pr.) Lerner Publishing Group.
Conger, Holli. Hailey's Halloween. Bullard, Lisa. 2012. (Cloverleaf Books (tm) — Fall & Winter Holidays Ser.). (ENG.). 24p. (gr. k-2). 6.95 *(978-0-7613-8586-8(X))*; lib. bdg. 23.93 *(978-0-7613-5083-5(7))* Lerner Publishing Group. (Millbrook Pr.).
—Hanukkah. Owens, L. L. 2009. (Cultural Holidays Ser.). 32p. (gr. -1-4). 28.50 *(978-1-60270-603-3(4))*, Looking Glass Library- Nonfiction) Magic Wagon.
—Is a Bald Eagle Really Bald? Rustad, Martha. 2014. (Cloverleaf Books (tm) — Our American Symbols Ser.). 24p. (gr. k-2). (J). lib. bdg. 23.93 *(978-1-4677-2138-7(7))*; pap. 6.95 *(978-1-4677-4466-9(2))* Lerner Publishing Group. (Millbrook Pr.).
—Marco's Cinco de Mayo. Bullard, Lisa. 2012. (Cloverleaf Books — Holidays & Special Days Ser.). (ENG.). 24p. (gr. k-2). lib. bdg. 23.93 *(978-0-7613-5082-8(9))* Lerner Publishing Group.
—Mitzi's Mitzvah. Koster, Gloria. 2013. (ENG.). 12p. (J). (gr. -1 — 1). bds. 5.95 *(978-1-4677-0695-7(7))*, Kar-Ben Publishing) Lerner Publishing Group.
—My Religion, Your Religion. Bullard, Lisa. 2015. (Cloverleaf Books (tm) — Alike & Different Ser.). (ENG.). 24p. (gr. k-2). (J). lib. bdg. 23.99 *(978-1-4677-4905-3(2))*; pap. 6.99 ***(978-1-4677-6033-1(1))*** Lerner Publishing Group. (Millbrook Pr.).
—Poison Alert! My Tips to Avoid Danger Zones at Home. Bellisario, Gina. 2014. (Cloverleaf Books — My Healthy Habits Ser.). (ENG.). 24p. (gr. k-2). lib. bdg. 23.93 *(978-1-4677-1353-5(8))*, Millbrook Pr.) Lerner Publishing Group.
—A Raindrop's Journey, 1 vol. Slade, Suzanne. 2011. (Follow It! Ser.). (ENG.). 24p. (gr. 1-3). lib. bdg. 25.99 *(978-1-4048-6266-1(8))*; pap. 7.49 *(978-1-4048-6712-3(0))* Picture Window Bks. (Nonfiction Picture Bks.).
—Ramadan. Anderson, Sheila. 2009. (Cultural Holidays Ser.). 32p. (gr. -1-4). 28.50 *(978-1-60270-605-7(0))*, Looking Glass Library- Nonfiction) Magic Wagon.
—Rashad's Ramadan & Eid Al-Fitr. Bullard, Lisa. 2012. (Cloverleaf Books — Holidays & Special Days Ser.). (ENG.). 24p. (gr. k-2). lib. bdg. 23.93 *(978-0-7613-5079-8(9))* Lerner Publishing Group.
—Shai's Shabbat Walk. Gellman, Ellie B. 2014. (ENG.). 12p. (gr. -1). bds. 5.95 *(978-1-4677-4949-7(4))*, Kar-Ben Publishing) Lerner Publishing Group.
—Shapes. 2013. (ENG.). 12p. (J). (gr. -1 — 1). 12.99 *(978-0-7944-2919-5(X))* Reader's Digest Assn., Inc., The.
—Take a Bath! My Tips for Keeping Clean. Bellisario, Gina. 2014. (Cloverleaf Books — My Healthy Habits Ser.). (ENG.). 24p. (gr. k-2). lib. bdg. 23.93 *(978-1-4677-1352-8(X))*, Millbrook Pr.) Lerner Publishing Group.
Conger, Holli. When Will It Rain? Noticing Weather Patterns. Rustad, Martha E. H. 2015. (ENG.). 24p. (gr. k-2). 25.32 ***(978-1-4677-8557-0(1))***, Millbrook Pr.) Lerner Publishing Group.
Conger, Holli. Why Is the Statue of Liberty Green? Rustad, Martha E. H. 2014. (Cloverleaf Books (tm) — Our American Symbols Ser.). (ENG.). 24p. (gr. k-2). lib. bdg. 23.93 *(978-1-4677-2139-4(5))*, Millbrook Pr.) Lerner Publishing Group.
—Why Is the Statue of Liberty Green? Rustad, Martha. 2014. (Cloverleaf Books (tm) — Our American Symbols Ser.). 24p. (gr. k-2). pap. 6.95 *(978-1-4677-4470-6(0))*, Millbrook Pr.) Lerner Publishing Group.
Conger, Hollli. Marco's Cinco de Mayo. Bullard, Lisa. 2012. (Holidays & Special Days Ser.). 24p. (gr. k-2). (J). pap. 39.62 *(978-0-7613-9249-1(1))*; (ENG.). pap. 6.95 *(978-0-7613-8580-6(0))* Lerner Publishing Group. (Millbrook Pr.).
—Rashad's Ramadan & Eid Al-Fitr. Bullard, Lisa. 2012. (Holidays & Special Days Ser.). 24p. (gr. k-2). (J). pap. 39.62 *(978-0-7613-9250-7(5))*; (ENG.). pap. 6.95 *(978-0-7613-8583-7(5))* Lerner Publishing Group. (Millbrook Pr.).
Conklin, Paul, photos by. Gavriel & Jemal: Two Boys of Jerusalem. Ashabranner, Brent. 2005. 94p. (J). (gr. 4-10). reprint ed. 12.00 *(978-0-7567-9758-4(6))* DIANE Publishing Co.
Conlan, Craig. Santa Claus Is on a Diet! Scott-Cameron, Nancy. 2007. (ENG.). 32p. (J). (gr. -1-k). 19.95 *(978-0-9546576-9-7(1))* Mogzilla GBR. Dist: Independent Pubs. Group.
Conley, Stephanie. My Extra Special Brother: How to Love, Understand, & Celebrate Your Sibling with Special Needs. Heyman, Carly. l.t. ed. 2003. 112p. pap. 12.95 *(978-0-9727865-0-8(3))*, 1003894) Fragile X Assn. of Georgia.
Conn, Alexandra. Turtlebird's Double Dip Shuffle. Fass, Tara. 2013. 18p. pap. 10.00 *(978-0-9838120-4-3(7))* Huqua Pr.
Connally, Perry L., Sr. Hard Heads Make Soft Bottoms. Switzer, Vern. 2007. 34p. (J). 15.95 *(978-0-9753542-2-3(1))* Rural Farm Productions.
—Lucy the Cantaloupe. Switzer, Vern. 2005. 32p. (J). 15.95 *(978-0-9753542-1-6(3))* Rural Farm Productions.
Connally, Perry L., Sr., jt. illus. see Listokin, David.
Connaught. Gator & Moose. Haynes, M. 2012. 44p. (J). pap. 19.95 *(978-1-59299-813-5(5))* Inkwater Pr.
Connell, Jacqueline. Is There Magic in the Mountains, Mamma? Cook, Maureen McNamee. 2008. 23p. pap. 24.95 *(978-1-60672-673-0(0))* America Star Bks.
Connelly, Gwen. Dayenu! A Passover Haggadah for Families & Children. Leon, Carol Boyd. 2008. 32p. (J). (gr. 1-3). 16.95 incl. audio compact disk *(978-1-60280-041-0(3))*; pap. 8.95 incl. audio compact disk *(978-1-60280-039-7(1))*; spiral bd. 16.95 incl. audio compact disk *(978-1-60280-040-3(5))*; bds. 24.95 incl. audio compact disk *(978-1-60280-042-7(1))* Ktav Publishing Hse., Inc.

C

—Little Red Riding Hood. Hillert, Margaret. rev. ed. 2006. (Beginning to Read Ser.). 32p. (J). (gr. -1-3). lib. bdg. 19.93 (978-1-59953-022-2(8)) Norwood Hse. Pr.

—No Bigger Than My Teddy Bear. Pankow, Valerie. 2nd ed. 2004. 32p. (J). 6.95 (978-0-9728460-0-4(X)) Family Bks.

—The Story of Ruth. Schur, Maxine Rose. 2005. (ENG.). 32p. (J). (gr. 1-3). per. 9.95 (978-1-58013-130-8(1), Kar-Ben Publishing) Lerner Publishing Group.

Connelly, Gwen & Holmberg, Ansgar. Days of Faith: Student Planner & Assignment Book 2004-2005. Fischer, Carl. 2004. 108p. (J). spiral bd. 3.25 (978-0-89837-199-4(6), 9805) Pflaum Publishing Group.

Connelly, Gwen, jt. illus. see Holmberg, Ansgar.

Connelly, Sheila. The Young People's Book of Saints: Sixty-Three Saints of the Western Church from the First to the Twentieth Century. Ross Williamson, Hugh. 2009. (J). 15.95 (978-1-933184-62-3(0)) Sophia Institute Pr.

Conner, Paula. Girls Who Looked under Rocks: The Lives of Six Pioneering Naturalists. Atkins, Jeannine. 2004. 64p. (YA). (gr. 4-6). pap. 8.95 (978-1-58469-011-5(9)) Dawn Pubns.

Connor, Chris. Charlotte Sometimes. Farmer, Penelope. 2007. (ENG.). 208p. (J). (gr. 4-7). 17.95 (978-1-59017-221-6(3), NYR Children's Collection) New York Review of Bks., Inc., The.

Connor, Julie. Caravan Kids. Hathorn, Libby. 2006. (Making Tracks Ser.). 64p. (J). (gr. 1-4). pap. 9.95 (978-1-876944-44-5(7)) National Museum of Australia AUS. Dist: Independent Pubs. Group.

Connor, Michael. An Buachaill Bo. Perdue, Gillian. 2006. (Sraith Sos Ser.: 13). (IRI, ENG & GLE.). 64p. (J). pap. 9.95 (978-1-84717-006-4(4)) O'Brien Pr., Ltd., The IRL. Dist: Dufour Editions, Inc.

—Conor's Canvas. Perdue, Gillian. 2007. (Pandas Ser.: 35). (ENG.). 64p. (J). pap. 9.95 (978-1-84717-043-9(9)) O'Brien Pr., Ltd., The IRL. Dist: Dufour Editions, Inc.

—Conor's Concert. Perdue, Gillian. 2003. (Pandas Ser.: 26). (ENG.). 64p. (J). pap. 9.95 (978-0-86278-847-6(1)) O'Brien Pr., Ltd., The IRL. Dist: Dufour Editions, Inc.

—Pageboy Danny. Dawson, Brianóg Brady. 2006. (Pandas Ser.: 34). (ENG.). 64p. (J). pap. 9.95 (978-0-86278-950-3(8)) O'Brien Pr., Ltd., The IRL. Dist: Dufour Editions, Inc.

Connor, Michael. Danny's Pesky Pet. Connor, Michael, tr. Dawson, Brianog Brady. 2003. (Pandas Ser.: 25). (ENG.). 64p. (J). pap. 9.95 (978-0-86278-803-2(X)) O'Brien Pr., Ltd., The IRL. Dist: Dufour Editions, Inc.

Connor, Robin. Power Reading: Classics/Jungle Book. Cole, Bob. 2004. 94p. (J). (gr. 4-18). vinyl bd. 39.95 (978-1-883186-61-6(7), PPCL2) National Reading Styles Institute, Inc.

—Power Reading: Comic Book/Jungle Book. Cole, Bob. 2005. 62p. (J). (gr. 3-18). vinyl bd. 39.95 (978-1-883186-74-6(9), PPCLC2) National Reading Styles Institute, Inc.

Connor, Sarah. Daniel & the Lions, 1 vol. Williamson, Karen. 2015. (Candle Little Lambs Ser.). (ENG.). 24p. (J). pap. 2.99 (978-1-78128-162-8(9), Candle Bks.) Lion Hudson PLC GBR. Dist: Kregel Pubns.

—David & Goliath, 1 vol. Williamson, Karen. 2015. (Candle Little Lambs Ser.). (ENG.). 24p. (J). pap. 2.99 (978-1-78128-160-4(2), Candle Bks.) Lion Hudson PLC GBR. Dist: Kregel Pubns.

Connors, Jerrold. Now, Louie! Connors, Jerrold. 2006. 40p. (J). 12.99 (978-0-9721416-1-1(8)) Alligator Boogaloo.

Connors, Mary. Mandy Miller & the Brownie Troop. Gatewood, June S. 2009. 48p. pap. 17.49 (978-1-4389-1727-6(9)) AuthorHouse.

—Patric the Pony Finds a Friend. Edmonds, Lin. 2009. 32p. pap. 12.99 (978-1-4389-5167-6(1)) AuthorHouse.

—Proto: Que faire quand un dinosaure nait dans votre Jardin? Heywood, Grand-Mere Geny. 2010. 56p. pap. 23.99 (978-1-4490-5786-2(1)) AuthorHouse.

Conover, Bret. Rope 'Em! Nyikos, Stacy. ed. 2011. (ENG.). 36p. (J). (gr. -1-3). 10.99 (978-1-935279-64-8(5)) Kane Miller.

Conrad, Didier. Asterix & the Picts. Ferri, Jean-Yves et al. 2014. (ENG.). 48p. (J). (gr. 4-6). pap. 12.99 (978-1-4440-1169-2(3), Orion) Orion Publishing Group, Ltd. GBR. Dist: Hachette Bk. Group.

—Asterix & the Picts. Ferri, Jean-Yves. 2013. (ENG.). 48p. (J). (gr. 4-7). 17.99 (978-1-4440-1167-8(7), Orion) Orion Publishing Group, Ltd. GBR. Dist: Hachette Bk. Group.

Conrad, Jeffrey. The Blue Wish (Maryoku Yummy) Random House Staff. 2012. (Step into Reading Ser.). (ENG.). 32p. (J). (gr. -1-1). pap. 3.99 (978-0-307-93005-7(X), Random Hse. Bks. for Young Readers) Random Hse. Children's Bks.

Conrad, Liz. The Baby Hustle: An Interactive Book with Wiggles & Giggles! Schoenberg, Jane. 2010. (ENG.). 12p. (J). (gr. -1 — 1). bds. 7.99 (978-1-4169-8050-6(4), Little Simon) Little Simon.

—Little Bunny. 2009. (My Sparkling Springtime Friends Ser.). (ENG.). 10p. (J). bds. 3.95 (978-1-58117-865-4(4), Intervisual/Piggy Toes) Bendon, Inc.

—Little Chick. 2009. (My Sparkling Springtime Friends Ser.). (ENG.). 10p. (J). bds. 3.95 (978-1-58117-866-1(2), Intervisual/Piggy Toes) Bendon, Inc.

—Little Duck. 2009. (My Sparkling Springtime Friends Ser.). (ENG.). 10p. (J). bds. 3.95 (978-1-58117-867-8(0), Intervisual/Piggy Toes) Bendon, Inc.

—Little Lamb. 2009. (My Sparkling Springtime Friends Ser.). (ENG.). 10p. (J). bds. 3.95 (978-1-58117-868-5(9), Intervisual/Piggy Toes) Bendon, Inc.

—Skeleton Shake. 2008. (ENG.). 12p. (J). 6.95 (978-1-58117-798-5(4), Intervisual/Piggy Toes) Bendon, Inc.

Conrad, Will, jt. illus. see Deodato, Mike.

Conroy, Robert. Emma's Memoirs: A Book of Comical Poems & Drawings with Emma as Your Hostess. Conroy, Christine. 2011. (ENG.). 84p. pap. 6.95 (978-1-4611-5982-7(2)) CreateSpace Independent Publishing Platform.

Considine, Declan. The Adventures of Feefeen & Friends. Noughton, Barbara. (978-0-9575814-1-8(6)) Universal Humourous Pubs.

Consolazio, Pamela A. Rule of Three. Archer, Nick. 2009. (Sisters Club Ser.: 2). (ENG.). 240p. (J). (gr. 3-7). 15.99 (978-0-7636-4153-5(7)) Candlewick Pr.

Constantin. Remaking the World: Pardon My Turkey. Ralph, Gordon & If. 2011. (ENG.). 48p. pap. 12.00 (978-0-615-47487-8(X)) KidsAndParentsPr..Com.

Constantin, Pascale. Al lado de una Hormiga: Next to an Ant. Rockliff, Mara. 2005. (Rookie Reader Español Ser.). (ENG & SPA.). 24p. (J). (gr. k-2). 19.50 (978-0-516-25251-3(8), Children's Pr.) Scholastic Library Publishing.

—Bible Stories for Growing Kids. Rivers, Francine & Coibion, Shannon Rivers. 2007. (ENG.). 216p. (J). (gr. 1-5). 15.99 (978-1-4143-0569-1(9)) Tyndale Hse. Pubs.

—The Facttracker. Eaton, Jason Carter. 2008. 272p. (J). (gr. 3-7). 16.99 (978-0-06-056434-6(2)) HarperCollins Pubs.

—Historias Bíblicas para Niños Bilingüe. Rivers, Francine & Coibion, Shannon Rivers. ed. 2008.Tr. of Bible Stories for Kids Bilingual. (SPA.). 216p. (J). 14.99 (978-1-4143-1981-0(9), Tyndale Espanol) Tyndale Hse. Pubs.

—Little Monster. 2007. (I'm Going to Read(r) Ser.). (ENG.). 28p. (J). (gr. -1-k). pap. 3.95 (978-1-4027-2078-9(5)) Sterling Publishing Co., Inc.

—Never Kick a Ghost & Other Silly Chillers. Sierra, Judy. 2011. (I Can Read Book 2 Ser.). (ENG.). 32p. (J). (gr. k-3). 16.99 (978-0-06-143519-5(8)); pap. 3.99 (978-0-06-143521-8(X)) HarperCollins Pubs.

—Next to an Ant. Rockliff, Mara. 2011. (Rookie Ready to Learn - Numbers & Shapes Ser.). 32p. (J). (gr. -1-k). lib. bdg. 23.00 (978-0-531-26447-8(5), Children's Pr.) Scholastic Library Publishing.

—Raising a Little Stink. Sydor, Colleen. 2006. (ENG.). 32p. (J). (gr. -1-2). 16.95 (978-1-55337-896-9(2)) Kids Can Pr., Ltd. CAN. Dist: Univ. of Toronto Pr.

Constantin, Pascale. Camilla Chameleon. Constantin, Pascale. Sydor, Colleen. 2007. (ENG.). 32p. (J). (gr. 1-4). pap. 6.95 (978-1-55453-164-6(0)) Kids Can Pr., Ltd. CAN. Dist: Univ. of Toronto Pr.

Constantine, Adam. The Usborne Illustrated Dictionary of Math. Large, Tori. 2007. 128p. (J). (gr. 4-7). pap. 12.99 (978-0-7945-1629-1(7), Usborne) EDC Publishing.

—The Usborne Illustrated Dictonary of Math. Large, Tori. Rogers, Kirsteen, ed. 2007. (Usborne Illustrated Dictionaries Ser.). 128p. (YA). (gr. 7). lib. bdg. 20.99 (978-1-60130-013-3(1), Usborne) EDC Publishing.

Consuegra, Carlos Manuel Diaz. The Czar & the Shirt. Tolstoy, Leo. Leal, Mireya Fonseca, ed. 2003. (Library of Tale Ser.). (SPA.). 12p. (J). (gr. -1-7). pap. (978-958-30-0984-6(9)) Panamericana Editorial.

Conteh-Morgan, Jane. Meet Jesus: The Life & Lessons of a Beloved Teacher. Gunney, Lynn Tuttle. 2008. (ENG.). 36p. (J). (gr. 3-7). pap. 12.00 (978-1-55896-524-9(6), Skinner Hse. Bks.) Unitarian Universalist Assn.

—Oink-Oink: And Other Animal Sounds. Cricket Magazine Editors. 2007. (ENG.). 20p. (J). (gr. k-k). bds. 7.95 (978-0-8126-7934-2(2)) Cricket Bks.

Contreras-Freeland, Gina, jt. illus. see Freeland, Devon.

Contreras, Gilbert. The Plight of the Jelly Bean. DeRosier, Cher. 2005. (J). (978-1-891685-50-7(3)) Dearborn Publishing.

Conway, Aaron. Alex the Sea Turtle. 2007. 26p. (J). (978-0-9777923-0-6(7)) Shiloh Children's Bks.

—Pamela la Impaciente y los Microbios. Overland, Sarah. Arroyo Seppa, Carmen, tr. 2006. (SPA & ENG.). 32p. (J). (gr. k-2). per. 7.95 (978-1-930650-39-8(6)) mTrellis Publishing, Inc.

Conway, Louise. Train Is on Track. Bently, Peter. 2015. (Busy Wheels Ser.). (ENG.). 24p. (J). (gr. -1-k). 14.95 (978-1-60992-790-5(7)) QEB Publishing Inc.

Conway, Tricia. Parabola O Jednom Mostu. Farah, Barbara. 2006. 44p. (gr. 4-7). per. 14.99 (978-1-59919-011-2(7)) Elim Publishing.

Conyers, Courtney. Adventures on the Farm. Jacobs, Jerry L. 2012. 38p. pap. 10.99 (978-0-9855202-6-7(4)) Kids At Heart Publishing & Bks.

Coogan, Carol. Gaia Girls: Way of Water. Welles, Lee. 2007. (Gaia Girls Ser.). (ENG.). 336p. (J). (gr. 4-7). 18.95 (978-1-933609-02-7(8)) Chelsea Green Publishing.

—Way of Water. Welles, Lee. 2007. (Gaia Girls Ser.: 2). (ENG.). 336p. (J). (gr. 4-7). pap. 19.95 (978-1-933609-03-4(6)) Chelsea Green Publishing.

Cook, Ande. Bible Heroes. Ditchfield, Christin. 2004. (Little Golden Book Ser.). (ENG.). 24p. (J). (gr. -1-2). 3.99 (978-0-375-82816-4(8), Golden Bks.) Random Hse. Children's Bks.

Cook, Danielle. Letters from Pyggles, 1. 2003. 24p. 9.00 (978-0-9729914-0-7(9)) Oden, Rachel.

Cook, Donald, jt. illus. see Walz, Richard.

Cook, Geoff. D Is for down Under: An Australia Alphabet. Scillian, Devin. 2010. (Discover the World Ser.). (ENG.). 40p. (J). (gr. 1-3). 17.95 (978-1-58536-445-9(2), 202170) Sleeping Bear Pr.

Cook, Janice. Beau, a Puppy's Tale: A Children's Book Aimed at Helping Kids Overcome Bullies & Gain Self-Esteem. Cook, Janice. 2011. (ENG.). 58p. pap. 12.95 (978-1-4635-7478-9(9)) CreateSpace Independent Publishing Platform.

Cook, Jeffrey. Sundays with Daddy. Kelly, Kelley R. 2010. 32p. pap. 13.99 (978-1-4490-6082-4(X)) AuthorHouse.

Cook, Julia & De Weerd, Kelsey. The Worst Day of My Life Ever! Cook, Julia. 2011. 32p. (J). pap. 10.95 (978-1-934490-20-4(2)); pap. 16.95 incl. audio compact disk (978-1-934490-21-1(0)) Boys Town Pr.

Cook, Katie. Star Wars: a Very Vader Valentine's Day. King, Trey. 2013. (ENG.). 16p. (J). (gr. 3-7). pap. 6.99 (978-0-545-51560-3(2)) Scholastic, Inc.

Cook, Katie & Ashworth, Nichol. Fraggle Rock: Tails & Tales. Randolph, Grace et al. Beedle, Tim, ed. 2011. (Fraggle Rock Ser.: 2). (ENG.). 136p. (J). (gr. 4). 19.95 (978-1-936393-13-8(1)) Boom Entertainment, Inc.

Cook, Laurie. Amelia Asks May I Have A Pet. Mathews, Madge. 2008. 24p. (J). 3.99 (978-0-9796536-1-2(4), EPI Kid Bks.) EPI Bks.

—Brandon's Really Bad, Really Good Day. Mathews, Madge. 2007. (J). 3.99 (978-0-9726075-1-3(X)) EPI Bks.

—Brandon's Really Big Birthday Surprise. Mathews, Madge. 2008. 24p. (J). 3.99 (978-0-9796536-0-5(6), EPI Kid Bks.) EPI Bks.

Cook, Lynette R. Faraway Worlds: Planets Beyond Our Solar System. Halpern, Paul. 2004. (ENG.). 32p. (J). (gr. 2-5). pap. 7.95 (978-1-57091-617-5(9)) Charlesbridge Publishing, Inc.

Cook, Monique. Beulah the Lunchroom Bully. Marie, K. 2011. 20p. pap. 24.95 (978-1-4560-5224-9(1)) America Star Bks.

Cook, Peter. Canada Doodles, 1 vol. Radford, Megan. ed. 2014. (ENG.). 240p. pap. 9.99 (978-1-4236-3621-2(X)) Gibbs Smith, Publisher.

Cook, Peter, photos by. Farnsworth House. Vandenberg, Maritz. rev. ed. 2005. (Architecture in Detail Ser.). (ENG., 60p. (gr. 8-17). per. 22.95 (978-0-7148-4558-6(2)) Phaidon Pr., Inc.

Cook, Terry. A Moose at the Bus Stop. Cook, Terry. 2013. 24p. pap. 10.95 (978-1-61633-378-2(2)) Guardian Angel Publishing, Inc.

Cook, Trahern. First, You Explore: The Story of Young Charles Townes. Haynie, Rachel. 2014. (Young Palmetto Bks.). (ENG.). 40p. (J). 29.95 (978-1-61117-343-7(4)) Univ. of South Carolina Pr.

Cooke, Andy. Once upon a Doodle: Fairy-Tale Pictures to Create & Complete. Cohen, Hannah, ed. 2012. (ENG.). 128p. (J). pap. 12.95 (978-0-7624-4477-9(0)) Running Pr. Bk. Pubs.

Cooke, Bev. Timmy the Tadpole, 1 vol. Wrucke, Mary. 2009. 25p. pap. 24.95 (978-1-60813-776-3(7)) America Star Bks.

Cooke, Charlotte. Lucille Gets Jealous, 1 vol. Gassman, Julie A. 2012. (Little Boost Ser.). (ENG.). 32p. (gr. k-3). lib. bdg. 22.65 (978-1-4048-6797-0(X), Little Boost) Picture Window Bks.

Cooke, Jim. Heroes & She-Roes: Poems of Amazing & Everyday Heroes. Cooke, Jim, tr. Lewis, Patrick J. Lewis, J. Patrick, tr. 2005. (ENG.). 40p. (J). (gr. -1-3). 16.99 (978-0-8037-2925-4(1), Dial) Penguin Publishing Group.

Cooke, Lucy, photos by. A Little Book of Sloth. Cooke, Lucy. 2013. (ENG., 64p. (J). (gr. k). 17.99 (978-1-4424-4557-4(2), McElderry, Margaret K. Bks.) McElderry, Margaret K. Bks.

Cooke, Tom. Elmo & Grover, Come on over! (Sesame Street) Ross, Katharine. 2013. (Step into Reading Ser.). (ENG.). 32p. (J). (gr. -1-1). 3.99 (978-0-449-81065-1(8), Random Hse. Bks. for Young Readers) Random Hse. Children's Bks.

—I Spy: A Game to Read & Play. Hayward, Linda et al. 2014. (Step into Reading Ser.). (ENG.). 32p. (J). (gr. -1-1). 12.99 (978-0-679-94979-4(8)); pap. 3.99 (978-0-679-84979-7(3)) Random Hse. Children's Bks. (Random Hse. Bks. for Young Readers).

Cooke, Tom & Brannon, Tom. Twinkle, Twinkle, Little Bug. Ross, Katharine. 2014. (Step into Reading Ser.). (ENG.). 32p. (J). (gr. -1-1). pap. 3.99 (978-0-679-87666-3(9), Random Hse. Bks. for Young Readers) Random Hse. Children's Bks.

Cool, Anna Maria, et al. Betsy Ross & the American Flag, 1 vol. Olson, Kay Melchisedech. 2005. (Graphic History Ser.). (ENG.). 32p. (gr. 3-4). 29.99 (978-0-7368-4962-3(9), Graphic Library) Capstone Pr., Inc.

Cool, Rebecca. Bog Frog Hop. Mewburn, Kyle. 2013. (ENG.). 24p. (J). (gr. -1-k). 16.99 (978-1-921714-58-0(1)) Little Hare Bks. AUS. Dist: Independent Pubs. Group.

—Isabella's Garden. Millard, Glenda. 2012. (ENG.). 32p. (J). (gr. -1-2). 16.99 (978-0-7636-6016-1(7)) Candlewick Pr.

Coombs, Jonathan. Do You Know the Cucuy? Conoces Al Cucuy? Galindo, Claudia & Pluecker, John. 2008. (SPA & ENG.). 32p. (J). (gr. -1-2). 16.95 (978-1-55885-492-5(4), Piñata Books) Arte Publico Pr.

—It's Bedtime, Cucuy!/A la Cama, Cucuy. Galindo, Claudia. Pluecker, John, tr. from ENG. 2008. (SPA & ENG.). 32p. (J). (gr. -1-2). 16.95 (978-1-55885-491-8(6), Piñata Books) Arte Publico Pr.

Coombs, Patricia. Laugh with the Moon. Coombs, Patricia. Burg, Shana. 2013. (ENG.). 256p. (J). (gr. 5-6). pap. 6.99 (978-0-440-42210-5(8), Yearling) Random Hse. Children's Bks.

Coon, Cyndi. Art That Pops! How to Make Wacky 3-D Creations That Jump, Spin, & Spring! 2006. 48p. (J). pap. (978-0-439-81337-2(9)) Scholastic, Inc.

Cooney, Barbara. El Nino Espiritu: Una Historia de la Navidad. Bierhorst, John. Aramburu, Francisco Gonzalez, tr. 2003.Tr. of Spirit Child: A Story of the Nativity. (SPA.). 26p. (J). (gr. 3-7). reprint ed. 20.00 (978-0-7567-6882-9(9)) DIANE Publishing Co.

—Roxaboxen. McLerran, Alice & Mclerran, Alice. 2004. (ENG.). 32p. (J). (gr. -1-3). pap. 6.99 (978-0-06-052633-7(5)) HarperCollins Pubs.

—Seven Little Rabbits. Becker, John E. 3rd ed. 2007. (ENG.). 32p. (J). (gr. -1-1). 7.95 (978-0-8027-9634-9(6)) Walker & Co.

—The Story of Holly & Ivy. Godden, Rumer. 2006. (ENG.). 32p. (J). (gr. k-3). 17.99 (978-0-670-06219-5(7), Viking Juvenile) Penguin Publishing Group.

Cooney, Barbara. When the Sky Is Like Lace, 1 vol. Horwitz, ElinorLander. 2015. (ENG.). 32p. 17.95 **(978-1-939017-47-5(5)**, 3ee48b7a-7a20-4033-ab13-196c42256117) Islandport Pr., Inc.

Cooney, Barbara. Miss Rumphius. Cooney, Barbara. 2004. 28p. (J). (gr. k-2). reprint ed. pap. 6.00 (978-0-7567-7107-2(2)) DIANE Publishing Co.

Coons, Dean. The Lion of Oz & the Badge of Courage. Baum, Roger S. 2nd ed. 2003. 247p. (J). 24.95 (978-1-57072-255-4(2)) Overmountain Pr.

Coope, Katy. How to Draw Manga Characters. Coope, Katy. 2008. (Collins Big Cat Ser.). (ENG.). 56p. (J). pap. 8.99 (978-0-00-723102-7(4)) HarperCollins Pubs. Ltd. GBR. Dist: Independent Pubs. Group.

—How to Draw More Manga. Coope, Katy. 2004. (ENG.). 64p. (J). (gr. 2-5). pap. 6.99 (978-0-439-58560-6(0)) Scholastic, Inc.

Cooper, Adrian, photos by. Beijing. Pellegrini, Nancy. 2007. (Global Cities Ser.). 64p. (gr. 5-8). lib. bdg. 30.00 (978-0-7910-8848-7(0), Chelsea Hse.) Facts On File, Inc.

—Los Angeles. Barber, Nicola. 2007. (Global Cities Ser.). 64p. (gr. 5-8). lib. bdg. 30.00 (978-0-7910-8847-0(2), Chelsea Hse.) Facts On File, Inc.

Cooper, Adrian, jt. photos by see Bowden, Rob.

Cooper, Blair. Hello Blue Devil! Aryal, Aimee. 2004. 22p. (J). 19.95 (978-1-932888-26-3(8)) Mascot Bks., Inc.

—Hello, Demon Deacon! Aryal, Aimee. 2004. 24p. (J). 19.95 (978-1-932888-14-0(4)) Mascot Bks., Inc.

—Hello Mr. Wuf! Aryal, Aimee. 2004. 24p. (J). 19.95 (978-1-932888-06-5(3)) Mascot Bks., Inc.

—Hello Rameses! Aryal, Aimee. 2004. 24p. (J). 19.95 (978-1-932888-17-1(9)) Mascot Bks., Inc.

—Hello Wildcat! Aryal, Aimee. 2004. 24p. (J). 19.95 (978-1-932888-33-1(0)) Mascot Bks., Inc.

Cooper, Debbie. Ancient Maya: Cultures of the Caribbean & Central America, 2 bks. l.t. ed. 2005. 32p. (J). per. 9.99 (978-0-9760406-1-3(1), A Kidz World) ABUAA, Inc.

—The Garifuna: Cultures of the Caribbean & Central America, l.t. ed. 2005. 32p. (J). 9.99 (978-0-9760406-0-6(3), 6-0-3, A Kidz World) ABUAA, Inc.

Cooper, Deborah. Searching for Grizzlies. Mangelsen, Thomas, photos by. Hirschi, Ron. 2005. (ENG.). 32p. (J). (gr. 2-7). 16.95 (978-1-59078-014-5(0)) Boyds Mills Pr.

Cooper, Deborah, jt. illus. see Mangelsen, Thomas D.

Cooper, Elisha. Beach. Cooper, Elisha. 2006. (ENG.). 40p. (J). (gr. -1-k). 17.99 (978-0-439-68785-0(3), Orchard Bks.) Scholastic, Inc.

—Bear Dreams. Cooper, Elisha. 2006. (ENG.). 40p. (J). (gr. -1-2). 16.99 (978-0-06-087428-5(7), Greenwillow Bks.) HarperCollins Pubs.

—Homer. Cooper, Elisha. 2012. (ENG.). 32p. (J). (gr. -1-3). 16.99 (978-0-06-201248-7(7), Greenwillow Bks.) HarperCollins Pubs.

Cooper, Emmanuel. A Saturday Surprise. Battle, Cleaton D. 2006. 68p. (J). pap. 11.95 (978-1-59663-504-3(5), Castle Keep Pr.) Rock, James A. & Co. Pubs.

Cooper, Floyd. Back of the Bus. Reynolds, Aaron. (ENG.). 32p. (J). (gr. 1-3). 2013. 8.99 (978-0-14-751058-7(9), Puffin); 2010. 16.99 (978-0-399-25091-0(3), Philomel) Penguin Publishing Group.

—A Beach Tail. Williams, Karen Lynn. 2010. (ENG.). 32p. (J). (gr. -1-2). 17.95 (978-1-59078-712-0(9)) Boyds Mills Pr.

—Becoming Billie Holiday. Weatherford, Carole Boston. 2008. (ENG.). 120p. (YA). (gr. 9-18). 19.95 (978-1-59078-507-2(X), Wordsong) Boyds Mills Pr.

—Ben & the Emancipation Proclamation. Sherman, Patrice. 2009. 32p. (J). (gr. 3-7). 16.99 (978-0-8028-5319-6(6), Eerdmans Bks For Young Readers) Eerdmans, William B. Publishing Co.

—The Blacker the Berry. Thomas, Joyce Carol. 2008. (ENG.). 32p. (J). (gr. -1-3). 16.99 (978-0-06-025375-2(4), Amistad) HarperCollins Pubs.

—Brick by Brick. Smith, Charles R., Jr. 2012. (ENG.). 32p. (J). (gr. -1-3). 17.99 (978-0-06-192082-0(7), Amistad) HarperCollins Pubs.

—Brick by Brick. Smith, Charles R., Jr. 2015. (ENG.). 32p. (J). (gr. -1-3). pap. 6.99 (978-0-06-192084-4(3), Amistad) HarperCollins Pubs.

—A Dance Like Starlight: One Ballerina's Dream. Dempsey, Kristy. 2014. (ENG.). 32p. (J). (gr. k-3). 16.99 (978-0-399-25284-6(3), Philomel) Penguin Publishing Group.

Cooper, Floyd. Frederick Douglass: The Lion Who Wrote History. Myers, Walter Dean. 2016. (J). **(978-0-06-027709-3(2))** Harper & Row Ltd.

Cooper, Floyd. In the Land of Milk & Honey. Thomas, Kenneth W. & Thomas, Joyce Carol. 2012. (ENG.). 32p. (J). (gr. -1-3). 16.99 (978-0-06-025383-7(5), Amistad) HarperCollins Pubs.

—Ira's Shakespeare Dream, 1 vol. Armand, Glenda. 2015. (ENG.). 40p. (J). 18.95 (978-1-62014-155-7(8), 9781620000000) Lee & Low Bks., Inc.

—The Last Stop Before Heaven. De Baun, Hillary H. 2012. 234p. (YA). 9.00 (978-0-8028-5398-1(6), Eerdmans Bks For Young Readers) Eerdmans, William B. Publishing Co.

—Miss Crandall's School for Young Ladies & Little Misses of Color. Alexander, Elizabeth & Nelson, Marilyn. 2007. (ENG.). 48p. (J). (gr. 6-9). 17.95 (978-1-59078-456-3(1), Wordsong) Boyds Mills Pr.

—Mississippi Morning. Vander Zee, Ruth. 2004. 32p. (J). 16.00 (978-0-8028-5211-3(4)) Eerdmans, William B. Publishing Co.

—The Other Double Agent: The True Story of James Armistead Lafayette, the Revolutionary Spy No One Has Ever Heard of (Because He Didn't Get Caught) Rockwell, Anne F. 2015. (J). lib. bdg. (978-1-4677-4933-6(8), Carolrhoda Bks.) Lerner Publishing Group.

—Queen of the Track: Alice Coachman, Olympic High-Jump Champion. Lang, Heather. 2012. (ENG.). 40p. (J). (gr. k). 16.95 (978-1-59078-850-9(8)) Boyds Mills Pr.

—Something to Prove: Rookie Joe Dimaggio vs. the Great Satchel Paige. Skead, Robert. 2013. (ENG.). 32p. (J). (gr. 2-5). lib. bdg. 16.95 (978-0-7613-6619-5(9), Carolrhoda Bks.) Lerner Publishing Group.

—Taneesha Never Disparaging. Perry, M. LaVora. 2008. (ENG.). 216p. (J). (gr. 2-7). pap. 8.95 (978-0-86171-550-3(0)) Wisdom Pubns.

Cooper, Floyd. These Hands. Mason, Margaret H. (ENG.). 32p. (J). (gr. -1-3). 2015. 6.99 **(978-0-544-55546-4(5)**, HMH Books For Young Readers); 2011. 16.99 (978-0-547-21566-2(5)) Houghton Mifflin Harcourt Publishing Co.

Cooper, Floyd. Tough Boy Sonatas. Crisler, Curtis L. 2007. (ENG.). 88p. (J). (gr. 8-7). 19.95 (978-1-932425-77-2(2)) Boyds Mills Pr.

Cooper, Floyd. Jump! From the Life of Michael Jordan. Cooper, Floyd. 2004. (ENG.). 40p. (J). (gr. 1-4). 17.99 *(978-0-399-24230-4(9)*, Philomel) Penguin Publishing Group.

—Juneteenth for Mazie. Cooper, Floyd. 2015. (Fiction Picture Bks.). (ENG.). 40p. (gr. 1-2). lib. bdg. 23.99 *(978-1-4795-5819-3(2))* Picture Window Bks.

—Max & the Tag-Along Moon. Cooper, Floyd. (ENG.). 32p. (J). (gr. -1-2). 2015. 8.99 *(978-0-14-751546-9(7)*, Puffin); 2013. 16.99 *(978-0-399-23342-5(3)*, Philomel) Penguin Publishing Group.

—Willie & the All-Stars. Cooper, Floyd. 2008. (ENG.). 32p. (J). (gr. 1-3). 16.99 *(978-0-399-23340-1(7)*, Philomel) Penguin Publishing Group.

Cooper, France. Oh, Do You Know? A Read-and-Sing Book. Gifford, Myrna. 2003. 12p. (J). 9.95 *(978-0-9720763-5-7(2))* Action Factor, Inc.

Cooper, Frances. Meet the Lit Kids: A Read-and-Sing Book. Gifford, Myrna. 2003. 12p. (J). 9.95 *(978-0-9720763-7-1(9))* Action Factor, Inc.

—Name Those Vowels: A Read-and-Sing Book. Gifford, Myrna. 2003. 12p. (J). 9.95 *(978-0-9720763-4-0(4))* Action Factor, Inc.

—Outlaws: A Read-and-Sing Book. Gifford, Myrna Ross. 2005. 12p. (J). 9.95 *(978-0-9754618-1-5(8))* Action Factor, Inc.

—Silent E: A Read-and-Sing Book. Gifford, Myrna Ross. 2005. 12p. (J). 9.95 *(978-0-9754618-0-8(X))* Action Factor, Inc.

—Spelling Families: A Read-and-Sing Book. Gifford, Myrna. 2003. 12p. (J). 9.95 *(978-0-9720763-6-4(0))* Action Factor, Inc.

—Talking & Walking: A Read-and-Sing Book. Gifford, Myrna. 2005. 12p. (J). 9.95 *(978-0-9720763-9-5(5))* Action Factor, Inc.

—Two Little Letters: A Read-and-Sing Book. Gifford, Myrna. 2005. 12p. (J). 9.95 *(978-0-9720763-8-8(7))* Action Factor, Inc.

—What's That Sound? A Read-and-Sing Book. Gifford, Myrna. 2003. 12p. (J). 9.95 *(978-0-9720763-3-3(6))* Action Factor, Inc.

Cooper, Gene. Who, Who... Who Is Reading My Book? Cooper, Gene. 2014. (J). 11.95 *(978-0-615-85312-3(9))* Cooper, Gene.

Cooper, Gill. Ballet Star: A Little Girl with a Big Dream. Baxter, Nicola. 2012. (ENG.). 16p. (J). (gr. -1-12). 8.99 ***(978-1-84322-687-1(1)***, Armadillo) Anness Publishing GBR. Dist: National Bk. Network.

Cooper, Helen. Delicious! Cooper, Helen. 2007. (ENG.). 32p. (J). (gr. -1-3). 16.99 *(978-0-374-31756-0(9)*, Farrar, Straus & Giroux (BYR)) Farrar, Straus & Giroux.

—Pumpkin Soup. Cooper, Helen. 2005. (ENG.). 32p. (J). (gr. -1-3). per. 6.99 *(978-0-374-46031-0(0))* Square Fish.

—Tatty-Ratty. Cooper, Helen. 2004. 28p. (J). (gr. k-3). reprint ed. 19.00 *(978-0-7567-7214-7(1))* DIANE Publishing Co.

Cooper, Jenny. The Adventures of Mali & Keela: A Virtues Book for Children. Collins, Jonathan. 2010. (ENG.). 144p. (J). (gr. k-2). pap. 15.95 *(978-1-932181-52-4(0))* Personhood Pr.

—Birds to Color. Cullis, Megan. ed. 2012. (Coloring Bks). 32p. (J). pap. 5.99 *(978-0-7945-3285-7(3)*, Usborne) EDC Publishing.

—Butterflies Coloring Book. Cullis, Megan. ed. 2012. (Coloring Bks). 32p. (J). pap. 5.99 *(978-0-7945-3113-3(X)*, Usborne) EDC Publishing.

—Flowers to Color. Meredith, Susan. ed. 2013. (Nature Coloring Bks). 32p. (J). pap. 5.99 *(978-0-7945-3058-7(3)*, Usborne) EDC Publishing.

—Forest Life to Color. ed. 2013. (Nature Coloring Bks). 32p. (J). pap. 5.99 *(978-0-7945-3305-2(1)*, Usborne) EDC Publishing.

—Fruit for You, 6 pack. Holden, Pam. 2009. (Red Rocket Readers Ser.). 16p. (gr. -1-2). pap. *(978-1-877363-01-6(4)*, Red Rocket Readers) Flying Start Bks.

—Nature to Color. Meredith, Susan & Cullis, Megan. 2013. (ENG.). 96p. (J). 9.99 *(978-0-7945-1913-1(X)*, Usborne) EDC Publishing.

—Rainforest to Color. ed. 2013. (Nature Coloring Bks). 32p. (J). pap. 5.99 *(978-0-7945-3306-9(X)*, Usborne) EDC Publishing.

—Show Me a Shape, 6 pack. Holden, Pam. 2009. (Red Rocket Readers Ser.). 16p. (gr. -1-3). pap. *(978-1-877363-27-6(8)*, Red Rocket Readers) Flying Start Bks.

—Undersea Life to Color. Meredith, Susan. 2014. (ENG.). (J). pap. 5.99 *(978-0-7945-2854-6(6)*, Usborne) EDC Publishing.

Cooper, Jenny & King, Sue. Monkeys. Bowman, Lucy. ed. 2011. (Beginner's Nature Ser.). 32p. (J). ring bd. 4.99 *(978-0-7945-2978-9(X)*, Usborne) EDC Publishing.

Cooper, Jenny & Watson, Richard. Owls. Bone, Emily. 2013. (Usborne Beginners Ser.). (ENG.). 32p. (J). 9.99 *(978-0-7945-3401-1(5)*, Usborne) EDC Publishing.

Cooper, Joseph. A Bridge to Our Tradition. Moskowitz, Nachama Skolnik. Lewy, Faye Tillis, ed. 2004. (gr. 4-6). pap., tchr. ed., tchr.'s training gde. ed. 22.95 *(978-0-8074-0761-5(5)*, 208060) URJ Pr.

—A Bridge to Our Tradition: Pirkei Avot. Moskowitz, Nachama Skolnik. Lewy, Faye Tillis, ed. 2004. (gr. 4-6). pap. 13.95 *(978-0-8074-0760-8(7)*, 160504) URJ Pr.

Cooper, Martha, photos by. The Jump Rope Book. Laredo, Elizabeth. 2004. 284p. (J). (gr. k-4). reprint ed. pap. 10.00 *(978-0-7567-7775-3(5))* DIANE Publishing Co.

—The Marble Book. Chevat, Richie. 2004. 186p. (J). (gr. k-4). reprint ed. pap. 10.00 *(978-0-7567-7776-0(3))* DIANE Publishing Co.

Cooper, Nicole. The Adventures of Ryan Lincoln. Standish, Joyce, ed. 2012. 46p. (J). pap. 10.00 *(978-0-9716244-5-0(3))* TLS Publishing.

Cooper, Paul. Seafarers: Chronicles of the Suspense & Romance of the Sea. Niedworok, Claudio O. Knight, Tori, ed. Date not set. 80p. (Orig.). (YA). pap. 11.95 *(978-1-882133-05-5(6))* Barefoot Pr.

Cooper, Sharon, jt. illus. see Kirkby, Joanne.

Cooper, Simon. Goldfish from Beyond the Grave #4. Hay, Sam. 2015. (Undead Pets Ser.: 4). (ENG.). 112p. (J). (gr. 1-3). 5.99 *(978-0-448-47798-5(X)*, Grosset & Dunlap) Penguin Publishing Group.

—Night of the Howling Hound, No. 3. Hay, Sam. 2014. (Undead Pets Ser.: 3). (ENG.). 112p. (J). (gr. 1-3). 5.99 *(978-0-448-47797-8(1)*, Grosset & Dunlap) Penguin Publishing Group.

—Return of the Hungry Hamster. Hay, Sam. 2014. (Undead Pets Ser.: 1). (ENG.). 112p. (J). (gr. 1-3). 5.99 *(978-0-448-47795-4(5)*, Grosset & Dunlap) Penguin Publishing Group.

—Revenge of the Phantom Furball, No. 2. Hay, Sam. 2014. (Undead Pets Ser.: 2). (ENG.). 112p. (J). (gr. 1-3). 5.99 *(978-0-448-47796-1(3)*, Grosset & Dunlap) Penguin Publishing Group.

Cooper, Simon. Rise of the Zombie Rabbit #5. Hay, Sam. 2015. (Undead Pets Ser.: 5). (ENG.). 112p. (J). (gr. 1-3). 5.99 ***(978-0-448-47799-2(8)***, Grosset & Dunlap) Penguin Publishing Group.

Cooper, Stephanie. Cat in the Tree. Archambault, John. 2007. (J). *(978-1-58669-230-8(5))* Childcraft Education Corp.

Cooper, Wade. Animals Around the World. Cooper, Wade. 2009. (Scholastic Reader Level 2 Ser.). (ENG.). 32p. (J). (gr. -1-3). 4.99 *(978-0-545-14092-8(7)*, Cartwheel Bks.) Scholastic, Inc.

—Farm Animals. Cooper, Wade. 2009. (Scholastic Reader Level 2 Ser.). (ENG.). 32p. (J). (gr. -1-3). pap. 3.99 *(978-0-545-09993-6(5)*, Cartwheel Bks.) Scholastic, Inc.

Coote, Mark. Pushing & Pulling. Hughes, Mónica. 2005. (Collins Big Cat Ser.). (ENG.). 16p. (J). pap. 5.99 *(978-0-00-718541-2(3))* HarperCollins Pubs. Ltd. GBR. Dist: Independent Pubs. Group.

Coover, Colleen, jt. illus. see Cruz, Roger.

Coovert, J. P. Charlie Joe Jackson's Guide to Extra Credit. Greenwald, Tommy. 2012. (Charlie Joe Jackson Ser.: 2). (ENG.). 272p. (J). (gr. 4-7). 14.99 *(978-1-59643-692-3(1))* Roaring Brook Pr.

—Charlie Joe Jackson's Guide to Extra Credit. Greenwald, Tommy. 2013. (Charlie Joe Jackson Ser.: 2). (ENG.). 288p. (J). (gr. 4-7). pap. 6.99 *(978-1-250-01670-6(3))* Square Fish.

—Charlie Joe Jackson's Guide to Making Money. Greenwald, Tommy. 2014. (Charlie Joe Jackson Ser.: 4). (ENG.). 208p. (J). (gr. 4-7). 13.99 *(978-1-59643-840-8(1))* Roaring Brook Pr.

—Charlie Joe Jackson's Guide to Not Reading. Greenwald, Tommy. 2011. (Charlie Joe Jackson Ser.: 1). (ENG.). 224p. (J). (gr. 4-7). 14.99 *(978-1-59643-691-6(3))* Roaring Brook Pr.

—Charlie Joe Jackson's Guide to Planet Girl. Greenwald, Tommy. 2015. (Charlie Joe Jackson Ser.: 5). (ENG.). 208p. (J). (gr. 4-7). 13.99 *(978-1-59643-841-5(X))* Roaring Brook Pr.

—Charlie Joe Jackson's Guide to Summer Vacation. Greenwald, Tommy. (Charlie Joe Jackson Ser.: 3). (ENG.). 240p. (J). (gr. 5-7). 2014. 13.99 *(978-1-62672-031-2(2))*; 2013. 14.99 *(978-1-59643-757-9(X))* Roaring Brook Pr.

—Katie Friedman Gives up Texting! And Lives to Tell about It. Greenwald, Tommy. 2015. (ENG.). 240p. (J). (gr. 4-7). 13.99 *(978-1-59643-837-8(1))* Roaring Brook Pr.

—The Last Invisible Boy. Kuhlman, Evan. (ENG.). 240p. (J). (gr. 5-9). 2010. pap. 6.99 *(978-1-4169-6089-8(9))*; 2008. 16.99 *(978-1-4169-5797-3(9))* Simon & Schuster Children's Publishing. (Atheneum Bks. for Young Readers).

—Why Dogs Eat Poop: Gross but True Things You Never Knew about Animals. Gould, Francesca & Haviland, David. 2013. (ENG.). 176p. (J). (gr. 3-7). pap. 8.99 *(978-0-399-16530-6(4)*, Putnam Juvenile) Penguin Publishing Group.

—Why Fish Fart: Gross but True Things You'll Wish You Didn't Know. Gould, Francesca. 2014. (ENG.). 144p. (J). (gr. 3-7). pap. 8.99 *(978-0-399-16598-6(3)*, Putnam Juvenile) Penguin Publishing Group.

Cope, Jane. Tubby Tabby. Graves, Sue. 2008. (Reading Corner Ser.). (ENG.). 24p. (J). (gr. k-2). pap. 6.99 ***(978-0-7496-7702-2(3))*** Hodder & Stoughton GBR. Dist: Independent Pubs. Group.

Cope-Robinson, Lyn. Cat Tails. Cope-Robinson, Lyn. l.t. ed. 2003. 32p. (J). lib. bdg. *(978-1-887774-14-7(9)*, Wynden) Canmore Pr.

Copeland, Cynthia L. The Wham-O Superball. Ubberball, R. 2008. (ENG.). 80p. (J). (gr. 3). pap. 12.95 *(978-1-60433-049-6(X)*, Applesauce Pr.) Cider Mill Pr. Bk. Pubs., LLC.

Copeland, Eric. The Adventures of Brer Rabbit & Friends. Dorling Kindersley Publishing Staff. 2006. (ENG.). 64p. (J). (gr. 5-12). per. 6.99 *(978-0-7566-1813-1(4))* Dorling Kindersley Publishing, Inc.

—Lewis Carroll. Mendelson, Edward, ed. 2008. (Poetry for Young People Ser.). (ENG.). 48p. (J). (gr. 3). pap. 6.95 *(978-1-4027-5474-6(4))* Sterling Publishing Co., Inc.

Copeland, Greg. The Frederick Douglass You Never Knew. 2004. (You Never Knew Ser.). (ENG.). 80p. (J). (gr. 4-6). pap. 6.95 *(978-0-516-25837-9(0)*, Children's Pr.) Scholastic Library Publishing.

—The George Washington You Never Knew. Collier, James Lincoln. 2004. (You Never Knew Ser.). (ENG.). 80p. (J). (gr. 4-6). pap. 6.95 *(978-0-516-25833-1(8)*, Children's Pr.) Scholastic Library Publishing.

—The Tecumseh You Never Knew. Collier, James Lincoln. 2004. (You Never Knew Ser.). (ENG.). (J). 25.50 *(978-0-516-24426-6(4)*, Children's Pr.) Scholastic Library Publishing.

Copeland, Gregory. Who Was Jesse Owens? Buckley, James, Jr. 2015. (Who Was... ? Ser.). (ENG.). 112p. (J). (gr. 3-7). 5.99 ***(978-0-448-48307-8(6)***, Grosset & Dunlap) Penguin Publishing Group.

Copeland, Gregory, jt. illus. see Harrison, Nancy.

Copelman, Evelyn. Once There Was a King: A Tournament of Stories. Alden, Raymond MacDonald. 2011. 194p. 42.95 *(978-1-258-08031-0(1))* Literary Licensing, LLC.

Copiel, Olivier. Red Zone, 2 vols., Vol. 2. Johns, Geoff. 2004. (Avengers Ser.). 160p. (YA). pap. 14.99 *(978-0-7851-1096-3(2))* Marvel Worldwide, Inc.

Coplestone, Jim. Two Nests. Anholt, Laurence. 2013. (ENG.). 32p. (J). (gr. -1-1). 17.99 *(978-1-84780-323-8(7)*, Frances Lincoln) Quarto Publishing Group UK GBR. Dist: Hachette Bk. Group.

—A Walk in the Wild Woods. Jones, Elisabeth & Jones, Lis. 2010. (ENG.). 32p. (J). (gr. -1-1). 16.95 *(978-1-84507-956-7(6)*, Frances Lincoln) Quarto Publishing Group UK GBR. Dist: Hachette Bk. Group.

Copplestone, Jim. Noah's Bed. Jones, Liz. 2004. 32p. (J). 14.95 *(978-1-84507-002-1(X)*, Frances Lincoln) Quarto Publishing Group UK GBR. Dist: Perseus-PGW.

Coppola, Angela, photos by. Fabulous Hair. Neuman, Maria & Dorling Kindersley Publishing Staff. 2006. (ENG.). 96p. (J). (gr. 3-9). pap. 9.99 *(978-0-7566-1589-5(5))* Dorling Kindersley Publishing, Inc.

Copter, Steve. Medikidz Explain Living with ADHD. Chilman-Blair, Kim et al. 2014. 16p. (J). pap. *(978-1-906935-84-9(X))* Medikidz Ltd.

Corace, Jen. I Hatched! Esbaum, Jill. 2014. (ENG.). 40p. (J). (gr. -1-k). 16.99 *(978-0-8037-3688-7(6)*, Dial) Penguin Publishing Group.

—Little Hoot. Rosenthal, Amy Krouse. 2007. (ENG.). 36p. (J). (gr. -1-17). 15.99 *(978-0-8118-6023-9(X))* Chronicle Bks. LLC.

—Little Oink. Rosenthal, Amy Krouse. 2009. (ENG.). (J). 36p. (gr. -1-17). 14.99 *(978-0-8118-6655-2(6))*; 14.99 *(978-0-8118-8331-3(0))* Chronicle Bks. LLC.

—Little Pea. Rosenthal, Amy Krouse. (ENG.). (J). (gr. -1-k). 2015. 32p. bds. 7.99 *(978-1-4521-4289-0(0))*; 2005. 36p. 15.99 *(978-0-8118-4658-5(X))* Chronicle Bks. LLC.

—Little Pea - Little Hoot - Little Oink, 3 vols., Set. Rosenthal, Amy Krouse. 2009. (ENG.). 80p. (J). (gr. -1 — 1). bds. 19.99 *(978-0-8118-7054-2(5))* Chronicle Bks. LLC.

—Mathilda & the Orange Balloon. de Sève, Randall. 2010. (ENG.). 32p. (J). (gr. -1-1). 16.99 *(978-0-06-172685-9(0))* HarperCollins Pubs.

—The Steadfast Tin Soldier. Rylant, Cynthia & Andersen, Hans Christian. 2013. (ENG.). 32p. (J). (gr. -1-3). 18.95 *(978-1-4197-0432-1(X)*, Abrams Bks. for Young Readers) Abrams.

—Sweet Dreams. Lewis, Rose A. 2012. (ENG.). 32p. (J). (gr. -1-2). 16.95 *(978-1-4197-0189-4(4)*, Abrams Bks. for Young Readers) Abrams.

—Telephone. Barnett, Mac. 2014. (ENG.). 40p. (J). (gr. -1-3). 16.99 *(978-1-4521-1023-3(9))* Chronicle Bks. LLC.

—This Plus That: Life's Little Equations. Rosenthal, Amy Krouse. 2011. (ENG.). 40p. (J). (gr. -1-3). 14.99 *(978-0-06-172655-2(9))* HarperCollins Pubs.

Coray, Stacy A. Cailloo Goes to the Fair. Hensley, Sarah M. l.t. ed. 2005. (HRL Board Book Ser.). (J). (gr. k-18). pap. 10.95 *(978-1-57332-328-4(4)*, HighReach Learning, Incorporated) Carson-Dellosa Publishing, LLC.

—Katie's Snacks. Hensley, Sarah M. l.t. ed. (HRL Big Book Ser.). (J). (gr. k-18). 2005. pap. 10.95 *(978-1-57332-337-6(3))*; 2004. pap. 10.95 *(978-1-57332-338-3(1))* Carson-Dellosa Publishing, LLC. (HighReach Learning, Incorporated).

Corazza, Joe. The Frog Prince: A Story about Keeping Your Word. 2006. (J). 6.99 *(978-1-59939-008-6(6))* Cornerstone Pr.

Corbera, Gabriel. Mr. Strong: Good Thing I Came Along. Kenny, Michael Daedalus. 2013. (Mr. Men Little Miss Ser.: 1). (ENG.). 80p. (J). pap. 6.99 *(978-1-4215-4073-3(8))* Viz Media.

Corbett, Barry. Gormon: The Sentinel Awakes. Corbett, Barry. 2005. per. 3.95 *(978-0-9762294-1-4(2)*, Griffin Comics) Corbett Features.

Corbett, Liza. Rabbit Tricks. Posner, Tina. 2006. 8p. (J). pap. *(978-0-439-73513-1(0))* Scholastic, Inc.

Corbin, Hillam, jt. illus. see Valko, Diane.

Corbin, Marissa. The Seasons of Life. Murray, Barbara. 2013. 36p. 19.95 *(978-0-9885370-8-8(7))* RIVERRUN BOOKSTORE INC.

Corcoran, Mark. The Three Sisters. Higgins, Kitty. ed. 2004. (Reader's Theater Ser.). (J). pap. *(978-1-4108-2312-0(1)*, A23121) Benchmark Education Co.

Cordeiro, James, et al. Iron Armory, 4 vols. Paniccia, Mark & Cosby, Nathan, eds. 2008. (ENG.). 96p. (J). (gr. -1-17). pap. 7.99 *(978-0-7851-2645-4(7))* Marvel Worldwide, Inc.

Cordell, Matthew. Bat & Rat. Jennings, Patrick. 2012. (ENG.). 40p. (J). (gr. -1-3). 16.95 *(978-1-4197-0160-3(6)*, Abrams Bks. for Young Readers) Abrams.

—First Grade Dropout. Vernick, Audrey. 2015. (ENG.). 32p. (J). (gr. -1-3). 16.99 *(978-0-544-12985-6(7))* Houghton Mifflin Harcourt Publishing Co.

—Gone Fishing: A Novel. Wissinger, Tamera Will. 2015. (ENG.). 128p. (J). (gr. 5-7). pap. 6.99 *(978-0-544-43931-3(7)*, HMH Books For Young Readers) Houghton Mifflin Harcourt Publishing Co.

—If You Were a Chocolate Mustache. Lewis, J. Patrick. 2012. (ENG.). 160p. (J). (gr. 3). 18.95 *(978-1-59078-927-8(X)*, Wordsong) Boyds Mills Pr.

—Itsy-Bitsy Baby Mouse. Meadows, Michelle. 2012. (ENG.). 40p. (J). (gr. -1-2). 15.99 *(978-1-4169-3786-9(2)*, Simon & Schuster Bks. For Young Readers) Simon & Schuster Bks. For Young Readers.

—Justin Case: School, Drool, & Other Daily Disasters. Vail, Rachel. 2010. (Justin Case Ser.: 1). (ENG.). 256p. (J). (gr. 2-4). 16.99 *(978-0-312-53290-1(3))* Feiwel & Friends.

—Justin Case: Rules, Tools, & Maybe a Bully. Vail, Rachel. 2014. (Justin Case Ser.: 3). (ENG.). 224p. (J). (gr. 2-4). 16.99 *(978-1-250-03978-1(9))* Feiwel & Friends.

—Leap Back Home to Me. Thompson, Lauren. 2011. (ENG.). 32p. (J). (gr. -1-1). 15.99 *(978-1-4169-0664-3(9)*, McElderry, Margaret K. Bks.) McElderry, Margaret K. Bks.

—Like Bug Juice on a Burger. Sternberg, Julie. 2013. (Eleanor Ser.). (ENG.). 176p. (J). (gr. 2-5). 15.95 *(978-1-4197-0190-0(8)*, Amulet Bks.) Abrams.

—Like Carrot Juice on a Cupcake. Sternberg, Julie. 2014. (Eleanor Ser.). (ENG.). 192p. (J). (gr. 2-5). 15.95 *(978-1-4197-1033-9(8)*, Amulet Bks.) Abrams.

—Like Pickle Juice on a Cookie. Sternberg, Julie. 2011. (Eleanor Ser.). (ENG.). 128p. (J). (gr. 3-5). 15.95 *(978-0-8109-8424-0(5)*, Amulet Bks.) Abrams.

—Ollie & Claire. Haber, Tiffany Strelitz. 2013. (ENG.). 40p. (J). (gr. -1-2). 16.99 *(978-0-399-25603-5(2)*, Philomel) Penguin Publishing Group.

—Rooting for You. Hood, Susan. 2014. (ENG.). 32p. (J). (gr. -1-k). 16.99 *(978-1-4231-5230-9(1))* Disney Pr.

—School, Drool, & Other Daily Disasters. Vail, Rachel. 2011. (Justin Case Ser.: 1). (ENG.). 272p. (J). (gr. 2-4). pap. 6.99 *(978-0-312-56357-8(4))* Square Fish.

—Shells, Smells, & the Horrible Flip-Flops of Doom. Vail, Rachel. 2012. (Justin Case Ser.: 2). (ENG.). 192p. (J). (gr. 2-4). 16.99 *(978-1-250-00081-1(5))* Feiwel & Friends.

—Shells, Smells, & the Horrible Flip-Flops of Doom. Vail, Rachel. 2013. (Justin Case Ser.: 2). (ENG.). 208p. (J). (gr. 2-4). pap. 6.99 *(978-1-250-02723-8(3))* Square Fish.

—Special Delivery. Stead, Philip C. 2015. (ENG.). 40p. (J). (gr. -1-2). 17.99 *(978-1-59643-931-3(9))* Roaring Brook Pr.

—Toot Toot Zoom! Root, Phyllis. 2009. (ENG.). 40p. (J). (gr. -1-2). 15.99 *(978-0-7636-3452-0(2))* Candlewick Pr.

—What Floats in a Moat? Berry, Lynne. 2013. (ENG.). 48p. (J). (gr. k-4). 17.99 *(978-1-4169-9763-4(6)*, Simon & Schuster Bks. For Young Readers) Simon & Schuster Bks. For Young Readers.

Cordell, Matthew. Another Brother. Cordell, Matthew. 2012. (ENG.). 36p. (J). (gr. -1-1). 16.99 *(978-0-312-64324-9(1))* Feiwel & Friends.

—Hello! Hello! Cordell, Matthew. 2012. (ENG.). 56p. (J). (gr. -1-4). 16.99 *(978-1-4231-5906-3(3))* Hyperion Pr.

—Trouble Gum. Cordell, Matthew. 2009. (ENG.). 48p. (J). (gr. -1-1). 16.99 *(978-0-312-38774-7(1))* Feiwel & Friends.

—Wish. Cordell, Matthew. 2015. (ENG.). 48p. (J). (gr. -1-k). 16.99 *(978-1-4847-0875-0(X))* Hyperion Bks. for Children.

Cordell, Matthew & Brown, Richard. Gone Fishing. Wissinger, Tamera Will & Long, Earlene R. ed. 2013. (ENG.). 128p. (J). (gr. 1-4). 15.99 *(978-0-547-82011-8(9))* Houghton Mifflin Harcourt Publishing Co.

Cordell, Matthew, jt. illus. see Schmid, Paul.

Cordero, Flor de Maria, photos by. M Is for Mexico. 2008. (World Alphabets Ser.). (ENG.). 32p. (J). (gr. -1-2). 16.95 *(978-1-84507-593-4(5)*, Frances Lincoln) Quarto Publishing Group UK GBR. Dist: Perseus-PGW.

Cordes, Miriam. Farewell, Grandpa Elephant: What Happens When a Loved One Dies? Abedí, Isabel. 2012. (ENG.). 28p. (J). (gr. -1-k). 16.95 *(978-1-61608-655-8(6)*, 608655, Sky Pony Pr.) Skyhorse Publishing Co., Inc.

Cordier, Severine. Gandhi: His Life, His Struggles, His Words. de Lambilly, Elisabeth. 2010. (Great Spiritual Figures of Modern Times Ser.). (ENG.). 72p. (J). (gr. 3-6). 16.95 *(978-1-59270-094-3(2))* Enchanted Lion Bks., LLC.

Cordish, Janet Luckey. Dolly Dolphin. Cordish, Janet Luckey. 2004. 32p. (J). (gr. k-3). 19.95 *(978-0-9661315-6-7(8))* FreeStar Pr.

—First Ice Cream Cone. Cordish, Janet Luckey. 2004. 32p. (J). (gr. -1-3). 19.95 *(978-0-9661315-5-0(X))* FreeStar Pr.

Cordner, Theo, jt. illus. see Burlinson, James.

Cordova, Amy. Amadito & the Hero Children: Amadito y los Ninos Heroes. Lamadrid, Enrique R. 2011. (SPA & ENG.). 60p. (J). 19.95 *(978-0-8263-4979-8(X))* Univ. of New Mexico Pr.

Córdova, Amy. Amadito & the Hero Children: Amadito y Los Niños Héroes. Lamadrid, Enrique R. 2011. (SPA & ENG.). (J). *(978-0-8263-4980-4(3))*; *(978-0-8263-4978-1(1))* Univ. of New Mexico Pr.

—Fiesta Babies. Tafolla, Carmen. 2010. (ENG & SPA.). 24p. (J). (gr. k — 1). 12.99 *(978-1-58246-319-3(0)*, Tricycle Pr.) Ten Speed Pr.

—The First Tortilla: A Bilingual Story. Anaya, Rudolfo A. & Anaya, Rudolfo. Lamadrid, Enrique R., tr. from ENG. 2007. (SPA & ENG.). 32p. (J). (gr. 4-7). 16.95 *(978-0-8263-4214-0(0))* Univ. of New Mexico Pr.

—The First Tortilla: A Bilingual Story. Anaya, Rudolfo. Lamadrid, Enrique R., tr. 2012. (ENG & SPA.). 32p. (J). pap. 16.95 *(978-0-8263-4215-7(9))* Univ. of New Mexico Pr.

—Juan the Bear & the Water of Life: La Acequia de Juan del Oso. Lamadrid, Enrique R. & Arellano, Juan Estevan. 2008. (Paso Por Aqui Ser. in the Nuevomexicano Literary Heritage Ser.). (SPA & ENG.). 48p. (J). (gr. 5-18). 17.95 *(978-0-8263-4543-1(3))* Univ. of New Mexico Pr.

—La Llorona: The Crying Woman. Anaya, Rudolfo A. Lamadrid, Enrique R., tr. 2011. (SPA & ENG.). 40p. (J). 19.95 *(978-0-8263-4460-1(7))* Univ. of New Mexico Pr.

Cordova, Amy. Namaste! Cohn, Diana. 2012. 32p. (J). pap. 9.95 *(978-1-62148-005-1(4))* SteinerBooks, Inc.

Córdova, Amy. Roses for Isabella. Cohn, Diana. 2011. 32p. (J). 17.95 *(978-0-88010-731-0(6))* SteinerBooks, Inc.

—The Santero's Miracle: A Bilingual Story. Anaya, Rudolfo A. Lamadrid, Enrique R., tr. 2004. (ENG & SPA.). 32p. (J). 17.95 *(978-0-8263-2847-2(4))* Univ. of New Mexico Pr.

—What Can You Do with a Rebozo? Tafolla, Carmen. 2008. (ENG.). 30p. (J). (gr. -1-2). 14.99 *(978-1-58246-220-2(8)*, Tricycle Pr.) Ten Speed Pr.

Córdova, Amy. Abuelita's Heart. Córdova, Amy. 2008. (ENG.). 32p. (J). (gr. -1-3). 13.99 *(978-1-4169-7576-2(4)*, Simon & Schuster/Paula Wiseman Bks.) Simon & Schuster/Paula Wiseman Bks.

Cordova, Amy. Talking Eagle & the Lady of Roses: The Story of Juan Diego & Our Lady of Guadalupe. Cordova, Amy. Gollogly, Gene. 2010. 40p. (J). (gr. k-7). 17.95 *(978-0-88010-719-8(7))* SteinerBooks, Inc.

Córdova, Amy & Cordova, Amy. What Can You Do with a Rebozo? ?Qu? Puedes Hacer con un Rebozo? Tafolla, Carmen. 2009. (SPA & ENG.). 32p. (J). (gr. -1-2). pap. 7.99 *(978-1-58246-271-4(2)*, Tricycle Pr.) Ten Speed Pr.

—What Can You Do with a Rebozo? (¿Qué Puedes Hacer Con un Rebozo?) Tafolla, Carmen. 2009. (SPA & ENG.). 30p. (J). (gr. -1-2). 14.99 *(978-1-58246-270-7(4)*, Tricycle Pr.) Ten Speed Pr.

Cordova, Amy, jt. illus. see Córdova, Amy.

Cordoves, Barbara, pseud & Cordoves, Gladys M. The Legend of Zias. Cordoves, Barbara & Cordoves, Gladys M. (Zias' Adventures Ser.). 44p. (J). pap. 7.99 *(978-0-9637252-0-2(3))* Cordoves, Barbara & Gladys M.

C

Cordoves, Gladys M., jt. illus. see Cordoves, Barbara, pseud.
Corey, Barbara. City Fun. Hillert, Margaret. 2008. (Beginning-to-Read Ser.). 32p. (J). (gr. -1-7). lib. bdg. 19.93 *(978-1-59953-147-2(X))* Norwood Hse. Pr.
Corey, Victoria. Larry the Lawnmower. Archambault, Jeanne. 2004. 32p. (J). 14.95 *(978-0-9763031-0-7(8))*; per. 10.00 *(978-0-9763031-1-4(6))* Jitterbug Bks.
Corfield, Robin Bell. Fire & Stone, Wind & Tide: Poems About the Elements. Waters, Fiona. 2006. 43p. (gr. 4-8). reprint ed. 24.00 *(978-1-4223-5595-4(0))* DIANE Publishing Co.
Corichi, Yadhira. Elisa Escuchaba el Canto de Las Ballenas. Hernandez, Ruben. rev. ed. 2003. (Castillo de la Lectura Blanca Ser.). (SPA & ENG.). 48p. (J). (gr. 1-3). pap. 6.95 *(978-970-20-0141-6(2))* Castillo, Ediciones, S. A. de C. V. MEX. Dist: Macmillan.
Corio, Paul, et al. Go Wild in New York City. Matsen, Bradford. 2005. (ENG.). 80p. (J). (gr. 3). 16.95 *(978-0-7922-7982-2(4))* CENGAGE Learning.
Corke, Estelle. Beach Socks, 1 vol. Daley, Michael J. 2013. (ENG.). 10p. (J). bds. 6.99 *(978-1-59572-637-7(3))* Star Bright Bks., Inc.
—Doodle Bug: Catch the Doodle Bug! Wright, Robin & Costello, Dee. 2010. (ENG.). 192p. (J). (gr. 2-6). 9.99 *(978-0-7641-6351-7(5))* Barron's Educational Series, Inc.
—The Gingerbread Man. 2007. (Flip-Up Fairy Tales Ser.). (ENG.). 24p. (J). *(978-1-84643-144-9(1))*; (gr. -1-2). *(978-1-84643-078-7(X))* Child's Play International Ltd.
—Goldilocks & the Three Bears. (Flip-Up Fairy Tales Ser.). (ENG.). 24p. (J). 2007. (gr. -1-2). *(978-1-84643-085-5(2))*; 2005. pap. *(978-1-904550-19-8(3))* Child's Play International Ltd.
—Long Ago in Bethlehem. Harrast, Tracy & Readers Digest Childrens Publishing Inc. Staff. 2008. 8p. 15.00 *(978-0-687-64778-1(9))* Abingdon Pr.
—The Miracles of Jesus, 1 vol. Harrast, Tracy. 2008. 10p. (J). 12.99 *(978-0-8254-5540-7(5))* Kregel Pubns.
—My New Preschool: An Interactive Playbook. Butterfield, Moira. 2010. (ENG.). 10p. (J). (gr. -1-k). 9.99 *(978-0-7641-6381-4(7))* Barron's Educational Series, Inc.
—Noah & the Animals. Froeb, Lori C. 2015. (Open Door Book Ser.: 3). (ENG.). 16p. (J). (gr. -1 — 1). bds. 9.99 *(978-0-7944-3342-0(1))* Studio Fun International.
—Noah & the Flood. Rock, Lois & Piper, Sophie. 2008. (Bible Story Time Ser.). (ENG.). 32p. (J). (gr. -1-k). 5.95 *(978-0-7459-4862-1(6))* Lion Hudson PLC GBR. Dist: Independent Pubs. Group.
—Oh Holy Night. Harrast, Tracy. 2006. 10p. (J). (gr. -1-k). bds. 10.49 *(978-0-7586-1129-1(3))* Concordia Publishing Hse.
—The Story of the Nativity, 1 vol. Harrast, Tracy. 2010. 24p. (J). (gr. -1-1). bds. 14.99 *(978-0-8254-5549-0(9))* Kregel Pubns.
—Where's My Hug? Clark, Sally. 2015. (J). *(978-0-8249-1952-8(1))* Ideals Pubns.
Corley, Rob & Bancroft, Tom. My First Message: A Devotional Bible for Kids. Peterson, Eugene H., tr. 2007. (ENG.). 384p. (J). 19.99 *(978-1-57683-448-0(4))* Tyndale Hse. Pubs.
Corley, Rob & Vollmer, Chuck. Firebird: He Lived for the Sunsine. McCorkle, Brent & Parker, Amy. 2014. (ENG.). 32p. (J). (gr. -1-3). 9.99 *(978-1-4336-8467-8(5)*, B&H Kids) B&H Publishing Group.
Corley, Rob, jt. illus. see Bancroft, Tom.
Cormack, Allan, et al. The Nature Treasury: A First Look at the Natural World. Flatt, Lizann. 2005. (ENG.). 48p. (J). (gr. -1). 16.95 *(978-1-897066-42-3(2)*, Maple Tree Pr.) Owlkids Bks. Inc. CAN. Dist: Perseus-PGW.
Cormack, Allan & Drew-Brook, Deborah. Ghost Wolf. Bradford, Karleen. 2005. 59p. (J). lib. bdg. 20.00 *(978-1-4242-1254-5(5))* Fitzgerald Bks.
—Ghost Wolf, 1 vol. Bradford, Karleen. 2005. (Orca Echoes Ser.). (ENG.). 64p. (J). (gr. 2-3). per. 6.95 *(978-1-55143-341-7(9))* Orca Bk. Pubs. USA.
Cormack, Allan, jt. illus. see Drew-Brook, Deborah.
Cornejo, Eduardo. Yo Te Quiero Aiempre. Bravo, Leonor. 2015. 24p. (J). (gr. -1-2). pap. 12.95 ***(978-9978-07-413-8(9)***, Alfaguara Infantil) Santillana Ecuador ECU. Dist: Santillana USA Publishing Co., Inc.
Cornejo, Eulalia. Mi libro, Cordova, Soledad. 2015. 24p. (J). (gr. -1-2). pap. 12.95 ***(978-9978-07-525-8(9)***, Alfaguara Infantil) Santillana Ecuador ECU. Dist: Santillana USA Publishing Co., Inc.
Cornejo, Eulalia. Verde Fue Mi Selva. Iturralde, Edna. Arroba, Doris et al, eds. 2008. (Alfaguara Infantil Ser.). 152p. (J). (gr. 5-8). pap. *(978-9978-07-097-0(4))* Ediciones Alfaguara.
Cornejo, Eulalia, et al. Verde fue mi selva. Iturralde, Edna. 154p. (J). (gr. 5-8). pap. 9.95 ***(978-607-01-1733-6(6))*** Santillana Ediciones Generales, S.A. de C.V. MEX. Dist: Santillana USA Publishing Co., Inc.
Cornejo, Eulalia. Verde Manzana. Williams, Ricardo. 2015. 24p. (J). (gr. -1-2). pap. 12.95 ***(978-9942-05-938-3(5)***, Alfaguara Infantil) Santillana Ecuador ECU. Dist: Santillana USA Publishing Co., Inc.
Cornejo, Santiago. Boucle d'or et les Trois Ours. Lomba, Ana. Wenzel, Dominique, tr. 2006.Tr. of Goldilocks & the Three Bears. (FRE & ENG.). 48p. (gr. -1-3). 17.00 *(978-0-07-146173-3(6)*, 0071461736) McGraw-Hill Cos., The.
—Le Petit Chaperon Rouge. Lomba, Ana. Wenzel, Dominique, tr. 2006.Tr. of Little Red Riding Hood/The Fun Way to Learn 50 New French Words!. (ENG & FRE.). 48p. (gr. -1-3). 17.00 incl. cd-rom *(978-0-07-146167-2(1)*, 0071461671) McGraw-Hill Cos., The.
Cornelison, Reuel. Cat Got Your Tongue? A Book of Idioms. White, Russ. l.t. ed. 2004. 44p. (J). per. *(978-0-9742885-0-5(0)*, 00) White, Russ.
Cornelison, Sue. Don't Put Yourself down in Circus Town: A Story about Self-Confidence. Sileo, Frank J. 2014. (J). pap. *(978-1-4338-1914-8(7)*, Magination Pr.) American Psychological Assn.
—Inch & Miles: The Journey to Success. Wooden, John et al. 2003. 39p. (J). pap. *(978-0-7891-6073-7(0))* Perfection Learning Corp.
—Sofia's Dream. Wilson, Land. O'Malley, Judy, ed. 2010. (ENG.). 32p. (J). (gr. -1-2). 18.95 *(978-0-9829938-1-1(1))* Little Pickle Press LLC.
Cornelison, Sue F. Inch & Miles: The Journey to Success. Wooden, John et al. 2003. (Inch & Miles Ser.). 40p. (J). (gr. k-3). 15.95 *(978-0-7569-1410-3(8)*, 3957506) Perfection Learning Corp.
—The Twelve Days of Christmas in Iowa. 2010. (Twelve Days of Christmas in America Ser.). (ENG.). 32p. (J). (gr. k). 12.95 *(978-1-4027-6710-4(2))* Sterling Publishing Co., Inc.
Cornelison, Susan F. Fiesta. Wooden, John. 2007. (Coach John Wooden for Kids Ser.). 63p. (J). (gr. k-3). lib. bdg. 11.65 *(978-0-7569-7791-7(6))*; pap., per. 4.99 *(978-0-7891-7187-0(2))* Perfection Learning Corp.
—Howard B. Wigglebottom Learns about Sportsmanship: Winning Isn't Everything. Binkow, Howard. 2012. (Howard B. Wigglebottom Ser.). 32p. (J). (gr. -1-2). 15.00 *(978-0-9826165-6-7(2)*, We Do Listen) Thunderbolt Publishing.
—Howard B. Wigglebottom Learns to Listen. Binkow, Howard. 2006. (ENG.). 32p. (J). (gr. -1-k). 15.00 *(978-0-9715390-1-3(4))* Thunderbolt Publishing.
—Howard B. Wigglebottom Listens to His Heart. Binkow, Howard. 2nd ed. 2008. (ENG.). 32p. (J). 15.00 *(978-0-9715390-2-0(2))* Thunderbolt Publishing.
Cornelius, Brad. We're Having a Tuesday. Simoneau, D. K. 2006. (ENG.). 32p. (J). 16.95 *(978-1-933302-13-3(5))* AC Pubns. Group LLC.
Cornell du Houx, Emily, jt. illus. see du Houx, Ramona.
Cornell du Houx, Emily M. D. Martin Mcmillan & the Lost Inca City. Russell, Elaine. 2005. 128p. (gr. 5-18). pap. 10.00 *(978-1-882190-86-7(6))* Polar Bear & Co.
Cornell, Kevin. The Chicken Squad: The First Misadventure. Cronin, Doreen. 2014. (Chicken Squad Ser.: 1). (ENG.). 112p. (J). (gr. 2-5). 12.99 *(978-1-4424-9676-7(2)*, Atheneum Bks. for Young Readers) Simon & Schuster Children's Publishing.
—The Legend of Diamond Lil. Cronin, Doreen. 144p. (J). (gr. 1-5). 2013. (ENG.). pap. 5.99 *(978-0-06-177997-8(0))*; 2012. (ENG.). 14.99 *(978-0-06-177996-1(2))*; 2012. lib. bdg. 15.89 *(978-0-06-198578-2(3))* HarperCollins Pubs.
—Mustache! Barnett, Mac. 2011. (ENG.). 40p. (J). (gr. -1-3). 16.99 *(978-1-4231-1671-4(2))* Hyperion Pr.
—Shark Kiss, Octopus Hug. Reed, Lynn Rowe. 2014. (ENG.). 32p. (J). (gr. -1-3). 14.99 *(978-0-06-220320-5(7))* HarperCollins Pubs.
—The Terrible Two. Barnett, Mac & John, Jory. 2015. (Terrible Two Ser.). (ENG.). 224p. (J). (gr. 3-7). 13.95 *(978-1-4197-1491-7(0)*, Amulet Bks.) Abrams.
—The Trouble with Chickens. Cronin, Doreen. (J). (gr. 1-5). 2012. (ENG.). 144p. pap. 5.99 *(978-0-06-121534-6(1))*; 2011. (ENG.). 128p. 14.99 *(978-0-06-121532-2(5))*; 2011. 128p. lib. bdg. 15.89 *(978-0-06-121533-9(3))* HarperCollins Pubs.
Cornell, Laura. A Donde Van los Globos? Curtis, Jamie Lee. 2004. (SPA.). 28p. (J). 21.99 *(978-84-8488-056-1(7))* Serres, Ediciones, S. L. ESP. Dist: Lectorum Pubns., Inc.
—Annie Bananie. Komaiko, Leah. 2003. (ENG.). 32p. (J). (gr. -1-3). pap. 6.99 *(978-0-06-051912-4(6))* HarperCollins Pubs.
—The Best Christmas Pageant Ever. Robinson, Barbara. 2011. (ENG.). 40p. (J). (gr. -1-3). 16.99 *(978-0-06-089074-2(6))* HarperCollins Pubs.
—Big Words for Little People. Curtis, Jamie Lee. 2008. (ENG.). 40p. (J). (gr. -1-3). 16.99 *(978-0-06-112759-5(0))* HarperCollins Pubs.
—Boy/Girl Book. Curtis, Jamie Lee. Date not set. 32p. (J). (gr. -1-3). 5.99 *(978-0-06-443639-7(X))* HarperCollins Pubs.
—Heather Has Two Mommies. Newman, Lesléa. 2015. (ENG.). 32p. (J). (gr. -1-2). 16.99 *(978-0-7636-6631-6(9))* Candlewick Pr.
—I'm Gonna Like Me: Letting off a Little Self-Esteem. Curtis, Jamie Lee. 2007. (ENG.). 32p. (J). (gr. -1-3). 16.99 *(978-0-06-028761-0(6))* HarperCollins Pubs.
—Is There Really a Human Race? Curtis, Jamie Lee. 2006. 40p. (gr. -1-3). (ENG.). (J). 16.99 *(978-0-06-075346-7(3))*; lib. bdg. 17.89 *(978-0-06-075348-1(X))* HarperCollins Pubs.
—It's Hard to Be Five: Learning How to Work My Control Panel. Curtis, Jamie Lee. 40p. (J). (gr. -1-3). 2007. (ENG.). 16.99 *(978-0-06-008095-2(7))*; 2004. lib. bdg. 17.89 *(978-0-06-008096-9(5)*, Cotler, Joanna Books) HarperCollins Pubs.
—Jamie Lee Curtis's Books to Grow by Treasury. Curtis, Jamie Lee. 2009. 208p. (J). (gr. -1-3). 24.99 *(978-0-06-180364-2(2))* HarperCollins Pubs.
—M. O. M. (Mom Operating Manual) Cronin, Doreen. 2011. (ENG.). 56p. (J). (gr. -1-3). 16.99 *(978-1-4169-6150-5(X)*, Atheneum Bks. for Young Readers) Simon & Schuster Children's Publishing.
—My Brave Year of Firsts: Tries, Sighs, & High Fives. Curtis, Jamie Lee. 2012. (ENG.). 40p. (J). (gr. -1-3). 16.99 *(978-0-06-144155-4(4))* HarperCollins Pubs.
—My Mommy Hung the Moon: A Love Story. Curtis, Jamie Lee. 2010. 40p. (J). (gr. -1-3). (ENG.). 16.99 *(978-0-06-029016-0(1))*; lib. bdg. 17.89 *(978-0-06-029017-7(X))* HarperCollins Pubs.
—Today I Feel Silly & Other Moods That Make My Day. Curtis, Jamie Lee. 2007. (ENG.). 40p. (J). (gr. -1-3). 16.99 *(978-0-06-024560-3(3))* HarperCollins Pubs.
Corner, Chris. Little Bear: A Folktale from Greenland. Casey, Dawn. 2014. (Collins Big Cat Progress Ser.). (ENG.). 32p. (J). pap. 7.99 *(978-0-00-751925-5(7))* HarperCollins Pubs. Ltd. GBR. Dist: Independent Pubs. Group.
Cornia, Christian, et al. Scooby-Doo! Unmasks Monsters: The Truth Behind Zombies, Werewolves, & Other Spooky Creatures. Weakland, Mark & Collins, Terry. 2015. (ENG.). 144p. (gr. 1-2). pap. 9.95 ***(978-1-62370-216-8(X))*** Capstone Pr., Inc.
Cornia, Christian. Smash! Wile E. Coyote Experiments with Simple Machines, 1 vol. Weakland, Mark. 2014. (Wile E. Coyote, Physical Science Genius Ser.). (ENG.). 32p. (gr. 3-4). 29.99 *(978-1-4765-4222-5(8))* Capstone Pr., Inc.
—Splat! Wile E. Coyote Experiments with States of Matter, 1 vol. Slade, Suzanne. 2014. (Wile E. Coyote, Physical Science Genius Ser.). (ENG.). 32p. (gr. 3-4). 29.99 *(978-1-4765-4224-9(4))* Capstone Pr., Inc.
—Thud! Wile E. Coyote Experiments with Forces & Motion, 1 vol. Weakland, Mark. 2014. (Wile E. Coyote, Physical Science Genius Ser.). (ENG.). 32p. (gr. 3-4). 29.99 *(978-1-4765-4221-8(X))* Capstone Pr., Inc.
Cornia, Christian, et al. Unmasking Monsters with Scooby-Doo! Collins, Terry & Weakland, Mark. 2015. (Unmasking Monsters with Scooby-Doo! Ser.). (ENG.). 24p. (gr. 1-2). lib. bdg. 153.90 ***(978-1-4914-1797-3(8))*** Capstone Pr., Inc.
Cornia, Christian. Yogi Bear's Guide to Animal Tracks. Weakland, Mark. 2015. (Yogi Bear's Guide to the Great Outdoors Ser.). (ENG.). 32p. (gr. 1-2). lib. bdg. 27.32 ***(978-1-4914-6545-5(X))*** Capstone Pr., Inc.
—Yogi Bear's Guide to Plants. Weakland, Mark. 2015. (Yogi Bear's Guide to the Great Outdoors Ser.). (ENG.). 32p. (gr. 1-2). lib. bdg. 27.32 ***(978-1-4914-6547-9(6))*** Capstone Pr., Inc.
Cornia, Christian & Ricci, Andrés Martínez. Wile E. Coyote, Physical Science Genius, 1 vol. Weakland, Mark & Slade, Suzanne. 2014. (Wile E. Coyote, Physical Science Genius Ser.). (ENG.). 32p. (gr. 3-4). lib. bdg. 119.96 *(978-1-4765-6199-8(0))* Capstone Pr., Inc.
Cornia, Christian, jt. illus. see Beach, Bryan.
Cornish, D. M. Foundling. Cornish, D. M. 2007. (Monster Blood Tattoo Ser.). 434p. (gr. 7-12). 20.00 *(978-0-7569-7957-7(9))* Perfection Learning Corp.
Cornish, David. Here Comes a Kiss. McCleary, Stacey. 2015. (ENG.). 24p. (J). (gr. -1-k). pap. 9.99 ***(978-1-76012-122-8(3))*** Little Hare Bks. AUS. Dist: Independent Pubs. Group.
Cornue, Don. The Firflake: A Christmas Story. Cardno, Anthony R. 2008. 56p. pap. 8.95 *(978-0-595-52468-6(0))* iUniverse, Inc.
Cornwell, Brendan W. Aesop in Goudy. 2007. 48p. (J). 20.00 *(978-0-9711321-1-5(9))* Blue Tree LLC.
Coronado, Jinky. Homecoming. Cabot, Meg. 2008. (Avalon High Coronation Ser.: Bk. 2). (ENG.). 192p. (YA). (gr. 8-18). pap. 9.99 *(978-0-06-117709-5(1))* HarperCollins Pubs.
—Hunter's Moon. Cabot, Meg. 2009. (Avalon High Coronation Ser.: Bk. 3). (ENG.). 160p. (YA). (gr. 8-18). pap. 9.99 *(978-0-06-117710-1(5))* HarperCollins Pubs.
—The Merlin Prophecy. Cabot, Meg. 2007. (Avalon High Coronation Ser.: Bk. 1). 128p. pap. 7.99 *(978-1-4278-0106-7(1))* TOKYOPOP, Inc.
Corpi, Lucha & Fields, Lisa. The Triple Banana Split Boy/El Nino Goloso. Corpi, Lucha & Fields, Lisa. 2009. (SPA & ENG.). 32p. (J). (gr. -1-4). 16.95 *(978-1-55885-504-5(1))* Arte Publico Pr.
Corpus, Mary Grace. Sergeant Bill & His Horse Bob. Dans, Peter E. 2015.Tr. of 28. (ENG.). (J). 17.95 ***(978-1-933822-97-6(X))*** Camino Bks., Inc.
Corr, Christopher. Around the World: A Colorful Atlas for Kids. Ganeri, Anita. 2015. (ENG.). 64p. (J). (gr. -1-2). 17.99 *(978-0-8075-0443-7(2))* Whitman, Albert & Co.
—Don't Spill the Milk! Davies, Stephen. 2013. 32p. 16.95 *(978-1-4677-2028-1(3))* Anderson Pr.
—Ebby Meets Felicity. Hickey, Matt. 2004. 32p. (J). 14.95 *(978-1-84458-141-2(1))* Avalon Publishing Group.
—The Goggle-Eyed Goats. Davies, Stephen. 2012. (ENG.). 32p. (J). (gr. -1-k). 22.99 *(978-1-84939-293-8(5))* Andersen Pr. GBR. Dist: Independent Pubs. Group.
—Heaven in a Poem: An Anthology of Poems. 48p. 19.99 *(978-0-7459-4259-9(8)*, Lion Books) Lion Hudson PLC GBR. Dist: Trafalgar Square Publishing.
—My Granny Went to Market: A Round-the-World Counting Rhyme. Blackstone, Stella. 2005. (ENG.). 24p. (J). 16.99 *(978-1-84148-792-2(9))* Barefoot Bks., Inc.
—My Travel Journal. Mudpuppy Press Staff. 2005. (J). 9.99 *(978-0-7353-0882-4(9))* Galison.
—Nos Vamos a Mexico! Una Aventura Bajo el Sol. Krebs, Laurie & Blackstone, Stella. Canetti, Yanitzia James, tr. from ENG. 2006. (ENG.). 32p. (J). (gr. 3-7). 7.99 *(978-1-84686-014-0(8))* Barefoot Bks., Inc.
—Off We Go to Mexico. Krebs, Laurie. 2006. (ENG.). 32p. (J). 16.99 *(978-1-905236-40-4(9))* Barefoot Bks., Inc.
—Where's Everybody Going? Samuel, Quentin. 2003. 24p. (J). *(978-1-84089-218-5(8))* Zero to Ten, Ltd.
—Whole World: PB with CD. 2010. (ENG.). 32p. (J). (gr. -1-2). pap. 9.99 *(978-1-84686-085-0(7))* Barefoot Bks., Inc.
—Why Is Everybody So Excited. Samuel, Quentin. 2003. 24p. (J). *(978-1-84089-219-2(6))* Zero to Ten, Ltd.
Corr, Christopher. Indian Tales: A Barefoot Collection. Corr, Christopher. Nanji, Shenaaz. 2007. (ENG.). 96p. (J). (gr. 2-18). 19.99 *(978-1-84686-083-6(0))* Barefoot Bks., Inc.
—Whole World. Corr, Christopher. Penner, Fred. 2007. (ENG.). 32p. (J). (gr. -1-4). 16.99 *(978-1-84686-043-0(1))* Barefoot Bks., Inc.
Correll, Gemma. Pig & Pug. Berry, Lynne. 2015. (ENG.). 40p. (J). (gr. -1-3). 16.99 *(978-1-4814-2131-7(X)*, Simon & Schuster Bks. For Young Readers) Simon & Schuster Bks. For Young Readers.
Correll, Gemma, jt. illus. see Monlongo, Jorge.
Corrette, Keith F., photos by. Sally Sue & the Hospice of Saint John. Mesplay, Gail G. 2003. 44p. (J). (gr. -1-6). pap. 15.00 *(978-0-9742849-0-3(4))* Hospice of Saint John, The.
Corrigan, Patrick. The Little Squeegy Bug, 0 vols. Martin, Bill, Jr. et al. 2005. (ENG.). 32p. (J). (gr. -1-2). reprint ed. pap. 9.99 *(978-0-7614-5243-0(5)*, 9780761452430, Amazon Children's Publishing) Amazon Publishing.
Corso, Bertina, jt. illus. see Corso, Erika.
Corso, Erika & Corso, Bertina. The Day You Came. Corso, Erika. 2006. (ENG.). 20p. (J). per. 12.95 *(978-1-59800-242-3(2))* Outskirts Pr., Inc.
Cort, Ben. Aliens in Underpants Save the World. Freedman, Claire. 2012. (Underpants Bks.). (ENG.). 32p. (J). (gr. -1-2). 15.99 *(978-1-4424-2768-6(X)*, Simon & Schuster/Paula Wiseman Bks.) Simon & Schuster/Paula Wiseman Bks.
—Aliens Love Panta Claus. Freedman, Claire. 2011. (Underpants Bks.). (ENG.). 32p. (J). (gr. -1-2). 16.99 *(978-1-4424-2830-0(9)*, Simon & Schuster/Paula Wiseman Bks.) Simon & Schuster/Paula Wiseman Bks.
—Dinosaurs Love Underpants. Freedman, Claire. 2009. (Underpants Bks.). (ENG.). 32p. (J). (gr. -1-2). 16.99 *(978-1-4169-8938-7(2)*, Simon & Schuster/Paula Wiseman Bks.) Simon & Schuster/Paula Wiseman Bks.
—Hello, Moon! Simon, Francesca. 2014. (ENG.). 32p. (J). (gr. -1-k). 16.99 *(978-0-545-64795-3(9)*, Orchard Bks.) Scholastic, Inc.
—Let's Read!/Little Ogre's Surprise Supper. Knapman, Timothy. 2014. (Let's Read! Ser.). (ENG.). 32p. (J). (gr. k-2). pap. 7.99 *(978-1-4472-4531-5(8))* Pan Macmillan GBR. Dist: Independent Pubs. Group.
—Monstersaurus! Freedman, Claire. 2011. (ENG.). 32p. *(978-1-84738-904-6(X))* Simon & Schuster, Ltd.
—Monstersaurus. Freedman, Claire. 2013. (J). *(978-1-4351-4952-6(1))* Barnes & Noble, Inc.
—Nora: The Girl Who Ate & Ate & Ate. Weale, Andrew. 2011. (ENG.). 32p. (J). (gr. -1-k). 19.99 *(978-1-84939-051-4(7))* Andersen Pr. GBR. Dist: Independent Pubs. Group.
—Nora: The Girl Who Ate & Ate & Ate ... Weale, Andrew. 2012. (ENG.). 32p. (J). (gr. -1-k). pap. 10.99 *(978-1-84939-382-9(6))* Andersen Pr. GBR. Dist: Independent Pubs. Group.
—Octopus's Garden. Starr, Ringo. 2014. (ENG.). 32p. (J). (gr. -1-3). 17.99 *(978-1-4814-0362-7(1)*, Simon & Schuster/Paula Wiseman Bks.) Simon & Schuster/Paula Wiseman Bks.
—Pirates Love Underpants. Freedman, Claire. 2013. (Underpants Bks.). (ENG.). 32p. (J). (gr. -1-2). 16.99 *(978-1-4424-8512-9(4)*, Simon & Schuster/Paula Wiseman Bks.) Simon & Schuster/Paula Wiseman Bks.
—Shark in the Dark. Bently, Peter. 2009. (ENG.). 32p. (J). (gr. -1-1). 17.99 *(978-0-8027-9841-1(1))* Walker & Co.
—The Wah-Wah Diaries: The Making of a Film. 3 CDs. Grant, Richard E. & Bently, Peter. ed. 2008. (ENG.). 32p. (J). (gr. 2-6). 23.95 *(978-0-230-01598-2(0)*, Macmillan) Pan Macmillan GBR. Dist: Trans-Atlantic Pubns., Inc.
Cortazar, Alicia Canas. Cuando Llega la Noche. Martín Anguita, Carmen & Carmen, Martín Anguita. 2008. (SPA.). 32p. (J). 10.99 *(978-84-241-5400-4(2))* Everest Editora ESP. Dist: Lectorum Pubns., Inc.
—Cuéntame un Cuento, Que Voy a Comer. Martín Anguita, Carmen & Carmen, Martín Anguita. 2008. (SPA.). 32p. (J). 10.99 *(978-84-241-5752-4(4))* Everest Editora ESP. Dist: Lectorum Pubns., Inc.
—El Cumpleaños de Laika. Martín Anguita, Carmen & Carmen, Martín Anguita. 2008. (SPA.). 32p. (J). 10.99 *(978-84-241-5803-3(2))* Everest Editora ESP. Dist: Lectorum Pubns., Inc.
—Marta y Mamá Juegan a Recordar. Martín Anguita, Carmen & Carmen, Martín Anguita. 2008. (SPA.). 32p. (J). 10.99 *(978-84-241-5390-8(1))* Everest Editora ESP. Dist: Lectorum Pubns., Inc.
—Marta y Su Dragón (Martha & Her Dragon) Martín Anguita, Carmen & Carmen, Martín Anguita. 2008. (SPA.). 32p. (J). 10.99 *(978-84-241-5444-8(4))* Everest Editora ESP. Dist: Lectorum Pubns., Inc.
—El Primer Día de Colegio de David. Martín Anguita, Carmen & Carmen, Martín Anguita. 2008. (SPA.). 32p. (J). 10.99 *(978-84-241-5790-6(7))* Everest Editora ESP. Dist: Lectorum Pubns., Inc.
—Una Tarde en el Circo. Martín Anguita, Carmen & Carmen, Martín Anguita. 2008. (SPA.). 32p. (J). 10.99 *(978-84-241-5459-2(2))* Everest Editora ESP. Dist: Lectorum Pubns., Inc.
Cortes, Mario, et al. Smash Trash! Driscoll, Laura & RH Disney Staff. 2008. (Step into Reading Ser.). (ENG.). 32p. (J). (gr. k-3). pap. 3.99 *(978-0-7364-2515-5(2)*, RH/Disney) Random Hse. Children's Bks.
Cortes, Osvaldo. Descubre la historia de los Ninos. Lara, Jose Luis Trueba. (Serie Descubre Ser.). (SPA.). 96p. (J). (gr. 3-5). pap. 18.95 *(978-970-29-1057-2(9))* Santillana USA Publishing Co., Inc.
—Descubre... La Tierra y el Cosmos. Trueba, Jose Luis. 2004. (Ser. Descubre). (SPA.). 96p. (J). (gr. 3-5). pap. 18.95 *(978-970-29-0509-7(5))* Santillana USA Publishing Co., Inc.
—Descubre... Las Raices de Mexico. Trueba, Jose Luis. 2004. (Ser. Descubre). (SPA.). 96p. (J). (gr. 3-5). pap. 18.95 *(978-970-29-0508-0(7))* Santillana USA Publishing Co., Inc.
—Descubre... Los Animales. Trueba, Jose Luis. 2004. (Ser. Descubre). 96p. (J). (gr. 3-5). pap. 18.95 *(978-970-29-0510-3(9))* Santillana USA Publishing Co., Inc.
Cortes, Paulina. Comrade, Bliss Ain't Playing: Un Cuento de la Republica Dominicana. Baez, Josefina. 2008. (Marisol Ser.: Vol. 1). (ENG.). 100p. (Orig.). (gr. k-3). pap. 12.95 *(978-1-882161-01-0(7))* I.Om.Be Pr.
Cortés, Ricardo. It's Just a Plant: A Children's Story about Marijuana. 2013. (ENG.). 48p. (J). 20.00 *(978-1-61775-186-8(3))* Akashic Bks.
Cortes, Ricardo. Relic (the Books of Eva I) Terrell, Heather. 2014. (ENG.). 288p. (J). (gr. 9). pap. 9.99 *(978-1-61695-406-2(X)*, Soho Teen) Soho Pr., Inc.
Cortés, Ricardo. Seriously, Just Go to Sleep. Mansbach, Adam. 2012. (ENG.). 36p. (gr. k-5). 15.95 *(978-1-61775-078-6(6))* Akashic Bks.
Cortez, Jess S. My Trip to the Harbor. Cortez, Jess S., photos by. ed. 2005. 16p. (J). *(978-0-9776291-0-7(4))* Jesus Estanislado.
Cortright, Robert S., photos by. Bridging the World. Cortright, Robert S. 2003. 208p. 35.00 *(978-0-9641963-3-9(6))* Bridge Ink.
Corts, Enrique. Back to the Ice Age. Nickel, Scott. 2008. (Graphic Sparks Ser.). (ENG.). 40p. (gr. 1-3). pap. 5.95 *(978-1-4342-0500-1(2)*, Graphic Sparks) Stone Arch Bks.
—T. Rex vs Robo-Dog 3000, 1 vol. Nickel, Scott. 2008. (Time Blasters Ser.). (ENG.). 40p. (gr. 1-3). 22.65 *(978-1-4342-0761-6(7))*; pap. 5.95 *(978-1-4342-0857-6(5))* Stone Arch Bks. (Graphic Sparks).

Corum, Jaime. D Is for Derby: A Kentucy Derby Alphabet. Wilbur, Helen L. 2014. (ENG.). 40p. (J). (gr. 3-6). 16.95 *(978-1-58536-813-6(X)*, 203008) Sleeping Bear Pr.

Corvaisier, Laurent. Songs in the Shade of the Flamboyant Tree: French Creole Lullabies & Nursery Rhymes, 1 vol. 2012. (ENG.). 52p. (J). (gr. -1-k). 16.95 *(978-2-923163-82-6(6))* La Montagne Secrete CAN. Dist: Independent Pubs. Group.

Corvino, Lucy. The Adventures of Robin Hood. Pyle, Howard. 2005. (Classic Starts(tm) Ser.). (ENG.). 160p. (J). (gr. 2-4). 6.95 *(978-1-4027-1257-9(X))* Sterling Publishing Co., Inc.

—The Adventures of Sherlock Holmes. Doyle, Arthur. 2005. (Classic Starts(tm) Ser.). (ENG.). 160p. (J). (gr. 2-4). 6.95 *(978-1-4027-1217-3(0))* Sterling Publishing Co., Inc.

—The Adventures of Tom Sawyer. Twain, Mark. 2005. (Classic Starts(tm) Ser.). (ENG.). 160p. (J). (gr. 2-4). 6.95 *(978-1-4027-1216-6(2))* Sterling Publishing Co., Inc.

—Anne of Green Gables. Montgomery, L. M. 2005. (Classic Starts(tm) Ser.). (ENG.). 160p. (J). (gr. 2-4). 6.95 *(978-1-4027-1130-5(1))* Sterling Publishing Co., Inc.

—Arabian Nights. 2008. (Classic Starts(tm) Ser.). (ENG.). 160p. (J). (gr. 2-4). 6.95 *(978-1-4027-4573-7(7))* Sterling Publishing Co., Inc.

—Black Beauty. Sewell, Anna. 2005. (Classic Starts(tm) Ser.). (ENG.). 160p. (J). (gr. 2-4). 6.95 *(978-1-4027-1144-2(1))* Sterling Publishing Co., Inc.

—The Call of the Wild. London, Jack. 2005. (Classic Starts(tm) Ser.). (ENG.). 160p. (J). (gr. 2-4). 6.95 *(978-1-4027-1274-6(X))* Sterling Publishing Co., Inc.

—The Hunchback of Notre-Dame. Hugo, Victor. 2008. (Classic Starts(tm) Ser.). (ENG.). 160p. (J). (gr. 2-4). 6.95 *(978-1-4027-4575-1(3))* Sterling Publishing Co., Inc.

—The Jungle Book. Kipling, Rudyard. 2008. (Classic Starts(tm) Ser.). (ENG.). 160p. (J). (gr. 2-4). 6.95 *(978-1-4027-4576-8(1))* Sterling Publishing Co., Inc.

—A Little Princess. Zamorsky, Tania & Burnett, Frances Hodgson. 2005. (Classic Starts(tm) Ser.). (ENG.). 160p. (J). (gr. 2-4). 6.95 *(978-1-4027-1275-3(8))* Sterling Publishing Co., Inc.

—Little Women. Alcott, Louisa May. 2005. (Classic Starts(tm) Ser.). (ENG.). 160p. (J). (gr. 2-4). 6.95 *(978-1-4027-1236-4(7))* Sterling Publishing Co., Inc.

—Robert Louis Stevenson. Schoonmaker, Frances, ed. 2008. (Poetry for Young People Ser.). (ENG.). 48p. (J). (gr. 3-7). pap. 6.95 *(978-1-4027-5476-0(0))* Sterling Publishing Co., Inc.

—The Secret Garden. Burnett, Frances Hodgson. 2005. (Classic Starts(tm) Ser.). (ENG.). 160p. (J). (gr. 2-4). 6.95 *(978-1-4027-1319-4(3))* Sterling Publishing Co., Inc.

—The Secret Garden. Burnett, Frances Hodgson. abr. ed. 2010. (Classic Starts(tm) Ser.). (ENG.). 160p. (J). (gr. 2-4). pap. 9.95 incl. audio compact disk *(978-1-4027-7359-4(5))* Sterling Publishing Co., Inc.

—The Adventures of Tom Sawyer. Twain, Mark. abr. ed. 2010. (Classic Starts(tm) Ser.). (ENG.). 160p. (J). (gr. 2-4). pap. 9.95 incl. audio compact disk *(978-1-4027-7356-3(0))* Sterling Publishing Co., Inc.

—Treasure Island. Stevenson, Robert Louis. 2005. (Classic Starts(tm) Ser.). (ENG.). 160p. (J). (gr. 2-4). 6.95 *(978-1-4027-1318-7(5))* Sterling Publishing Co., Inc.

—Treasure Island. Stevenson, Robert Louis. abr. ed. 2010. (Classic Starts(tm) Ser.). (ENG.). 160p. (J). (gr. 2-4). pap. 9.95 incl. audio compact disk *(978-1-4027-7358-7(7))* Sterling Publishing Co., Inc.

—The Voyages of Doctor Dolittle. Lofting, Hugh. 2008. (Classic Starts(tm) Ser.). (ENG.). 160p. (J). (gr. 2-4). 6.95 *(978-1-4027-4574-4(5))* Sterling Publishing Co., Inc.

Corvino, Lucy. The Christmas Garland. Corvino, Lucy, tr. Flinn, Lisa & Younger, Barbara. 2003. 32p. (J). 14.95 *(978-0-8249-5460-4(2)*, Ideals Children's Bks.) Ideals Pubns.

Corwin, Judith Hoffman. Native American Crafts of the Northeast & Southeast. Corwin, Judith Hoffman. 2003. (Native American Crafts Ser.). (ENG.). 48p. (J). (gr. 3-6). pap. 7.95 *(978-0-531-15593-6(5)*, Watts, Franklin) Scholastic Library Publishing.

—Native American Crafts of the Plains & Plateau. Corwin, Judith Hoffman. 2003. (Native American Crafts Ser.). (ENG.). 48p. (J). (gr. 3-6). pap. 7.95 *(978-0-531-15595-0(1)*, Watts, Franklin) Scholastic Library Publishing.

Corwin, Lena. Kids Crochet: Projects for Kids of All Ages. Gruen, John, photos by. Ronci, Kelli. 2005. (ENG.). 128p. (gr. 8-17). 21.95 *(978-1-58479-413-4(5))* Stewart, Tabori & Chang.

Corwin, Stuart. The Cryptic Cat. Corwin, Susan Simon. 2006. 99p. (YA). *(978-0-9790632-0-6(5))* Lucky Duck Designs.

Cory, Fanny Y. Sunshine Annie. Gates, Josephine Scribner. 2007. 148p. (J). lib. bdg. 59.00 *(978-1-60304-011-2(0))* Dollworks.

Cosby, Erika. Friends of a Feather: One of Life's Little Fables. Cosby, Bill. 2003. (ENG.). 64p. (gr. k-3). 16.95 *(978-0-06-009147-7(9))* HarperCollins Pubs.

Cosco, Rafaella. Little Hands Life of Jesus. Mackenzie, Carine. 2008. (ENG.). 144p. 10.99 *(978-1-84550-339-0(2))* Christian Focus Pubns. GBR. Dist: Send The Light Distribution LLC.

Cosco, Raffaella. Little Hands Story Bible. MacKenzie, Carine. 2009. (ENG.). 144p. (J). (gr. -1-3). 10.99 *(978-1-84550-435-9(6))* Christian Focus Pubns. GBR. Dist: Send The Light Distribution LLC.

Cosentino, Ralph. Batman: The Story of the Dark Knight. Cosentino, Ralph. 2008. (ENG.). 40p. (J). (gr. -1-2). 16.99 *(978-0-670-06255-3(3)*, Viking Juvenile) Penguin Publishing Group.

—Wonder Woman: The Story of the Amazon Princess. Cosentino, Ralph. 2011. (ENG.). 40p. (J). (gr. -1-2). 16.99 *(978-0-670-06256-0(1)*, Viking Juvenile) Penguin Publishing Group.

Cosford, Nina. Dublin. 2012. (Panorama Pops Ser.). (ENG.). 30p. (J). (gr. k-4). 8.99 *(978-0-7636-6153-3(8))* Candlewick Pr.

Cosgrove, Lee. Animals. Halls, Kelly Milner. 2015. (Lie Detector Ser.). (ENG.). 32p. (gr. k-3). pap. 5.95 ***(978-1-4795-8513-7(0))*** Picture Window Bks.

—Dinosaurs. Halls, Kelly Milner. 2015. (Lie Detector Ser.). (ENG.). 32p. (gr. k-3). pap. 5.95 ***(978-1-4795-8514-4(9))*** Picture Window Bks.

—Human Body. Holland, Simon. 2015. (Lie Detector Ser.). (ENG.). 32p. (gr. k-3). pap. 5.95 ***(978-1-4795-8515-1(7))*** Picture Window Bks.

—Lie Detector. Halls, Kelly Milner & Holland, Simon. 2015. (Lie Detector Ser.). (ENG.). 32p. (gr. k-3). 106.60 ***(978-1-4795-8525-0(4))*** Picture Window Bks.

—Oceans: Can You Tell the Facts from the Fibs? Holland, Simon. 2015. (Lie Detector Ser.). (ENG.). 32p. (gr. k-3). lib. bdg. 26.65 ***(978-1-4795-8512-0(2))*** Picture Window Bks.

Cosmin, Constantin. 'Remaking' the World - Hold That Hug. Ralph, Gordon & If. 2011. (ENG.). 48p. pap. 12.00 *(978-0-615-47488-5(8))* KidsAndParentsPr..Com.

Cosner, Jeff. Smoke Hole Adventure. Lough, Whitney. 2013. 36p. (J). 12.00 *(978-0-87012-833-2(7))* McClain Printing Co.

Cost, Steve. An Omelet Fit for a King. Stewart, Maria. 2013. 24p. pap. 14.99 *(978-1-936453-23-8(1))* Bezalel Bks.

Costa, Jana. Sleeping Beauty. 2007. (Usborne Young Reading: Series One Ser.). 48p. (J). 8.99 *(978-0-7945-1458-7(8)*, Usborne) EDC Publishing.

—Stories of Magic Ponies. Davidson, Susanna. 2007. (Young Reading Series 1 Gift Bks). 48p. (J). 8.99 *(978-0-7945-1790-8(0)*, Usborne) EDC Publishing.

Costa, Maria. El Patito Bello. Canetti, Yanitzia & Yanitzia, Canetti. 2009. (SPA.). 32p. (J). (gr. 1-4). 12.99 *(978-84-241-7071-4(7))* Everest Editora ESP. Dist: Lectorum Pubns., Inc.

Costa, Nicoletta. The Selfish Giant, 1 vol. Piumini, Roberto & Wilde, Oscar. 2011. (Storybook Classics Ser.). (ENG.). 32p. (gr. 3-4). lib. bdg. 25.32 *(978-1-4048-6498-6(9)*, Fiction Picture Bks.) Picture Window Bks.

—Sleeping Beauty, 1 vol. Piumini, Roberto et al. 2011. (Storybook Classics Ser.). (ENG.). 32p. (gr. 3-4). lib. bdg. 25.32 *(978-1-4048-6499-3(7)*, Fiction Picture Bks.) Picture Window Bks.

—The 3 Little Pigs, 1 vol. Piumini, Roberto. 2009. (Storybook Classics Ser.). (ENG.). 32p. (gr. 3-4). lib. bdg. 25.32 *(978-1-4048-5501-4(7)*, Fiction Picture Bks.) Picture Window Bks.

Costa, Nicoletta. Olga the Cloud. Costa, Nicoletta. 2014. (ENG.). 32p. (J). (gr. -1-k). 16.95 *(978-0-8234-3051-2(0))* Holiday Hse., Inc.

Costa, Patricia Castelao. Peter Pan: From the Story by J. M. Barrie. Barrie, J. M. 2009. (ENG.). 48p. (J). 12.95 *(978-0-7624-3543-2(7)*, Running Pr. Kids) Running Pr. Bk. Pubs.

Costanza, Stephen. The Christmas Spider's Miracle. Noble, Trinka Hakes. 2011. (ENG.). 32p. (YA). (gr. k-3). 16.95 *(978-1-58536-602-6(1))* Sleeping Bear Pr.

—Smudge & the Book of Mistakes: A Christmas Story. 2012. (ENG.). 48p. (J). (gr. 1-5). 17.95 *(978-1-58536-483-1(5))* Sleeping Bear Pr.

—Ten Big Toes & a Prince's Nose. Gow, Nancy. 2010. (ENG.). 32p. (J). (gr. -1-2). 14.95 *(978-1-4027-6396-0(4))* Sterling Publishing Co., Inc.

Costanza, Stephen. Vivaldi & the Invisible Orchestra. Costanza, Stephen. 2012. (ENG.). 40p. (J). (gr. 1-5). 16.99 *(978-0-8050-7801-5(0)*, Holt, Henry & Co. Bks. For Young Readers) Holt, Henry & Co.

Costello, David. A Crow of His Own. Lambert, Megan. 2014. (J). pap. *(978-1-58089-448-7(8))* Charlesbridge Publishing, Inc.

Costello, David & Costello, David Hyde. A Crow of His Own. Lambert, Megan Dowd. 2015. (ENG.). 32p. (J). (gr. -1-1). lib. bdg. 16.95 *(978-1-58089-447-0(X))* Charlesbridge Publishing, Inc.

Costello, David Hyde. I Can Help. Costello, David Hyde. 2010. (ENG.). 32p. (J). (gr. -1-1). 13.99 *(978-0-374-33526-7(5)*, Farrar, Straus & Giroux (BYR)) Farrar, Straus & Giroux.

—Little Pig Joins the Band. Costello, David Hyde. (ENG.). 32p. (J). (gr. -1-3). 2014. pap. 7.95 *(978-1-58089-265-0(5))*; 2011. 14.95 *(978-1-58089-264-3(7))* Charlesbridge Publishing, Inc.

—Little Pig Joins the Band. Costello, David Hyde. 2012. 29.95 incl. audio compact disk *(978-1-4301-1139-9(9))* Live Oak Media.

Costello, David Hyde, jt. illus. see Costello, David.

Costello, Jim. Nana's Quilt: Stitched in St. John'S, Newfoundland & Labrador, 1 vol. Lane, Lori & Winsor, Kathy. 2007. (ENG.). 32p. (J). (gr. -1-4). per. 8.95 *(978-1-894294-82-9(3)*, Tuckamore Bks) Creative Bk. Publishing CAN. Dist: Orca Bk. Pubs. USA.

Costello, Jim, photos by. Poppy & Allie: Hooked on St. John's, Newfoundland, 1 vol. Lane, Lori & Winsor, Kathy. 2009. (ENG., 32p. (J). (gr. 1-8). pap. 10.95 *(978-1-897174-22-7(5))* Creative Bk. Publishing CAN. Dist: Orca Bk. Pubs. USA.

Costello, Shawn. Estas Manos: Manitas de Mi Familia. Caraballo, Samuel. 2014.Tr. of These Hands: My Family's Hands. (ENG & SPA.). (J). 17.95 *(978-1-55885-795-7(6)*, Piñata Books) Arte Publico Pr.

—Luke's Mule. Schmauss, Judy Kentor. 2006. (Reader's Clubhouse Level 2 Reader Ser.). (ENG.). 24p. (J). (gr. 1-4). pap. 3.99 *(978-0-7641-3297-1(0))* Barron's Educational Series, Inc.

—Private Joel & the Sewell Mountain Seder. Fireside, Bryna J. 2008. (Passover Ser.). (ENG.). 48p. (J). (gr. 3-5). per. 6.95 *(978-0-8225-9050-7(6)*, Kar-Ben Publishing) Lerner Publishing Group.

Costner, Howard. Sixth Grade Was a Nightmare, & Seventh Is Worse: A 12-Year Old Speaks Out. Cheng, Haw. Thurman, Joann M., ed. Date not set. 128p. (J). (gr. 3-9). 11.95 *(978-0-89896-335-9(4))* Larksdale.

—The Tenth Rifle. Marvin, Isabel R. Date not set. 128p. (Orig.). (J). (gr. 3-8). pap. 9.95 *(978-0-89896-109-6(2))* Larksdale.

Cota, Cecilia. Punto y Rayo: Los Puntos Cardinales y Los Mapas. Doddoli, Consuelo. rev. ed. 2006. (Otra Escalera Ser.). (SPA & ENG.). 24p. (J). (gr. 2-4). pap. 9.95 *(978-968-5920-68-1(0))* Castillo, Ediciones, S. A. de C. V. MEX. Dist: Macmillan.

Cote, Genevieve. Ella May & the Wishing Stone. Fagan, Cary. (ENG.). 32p. (J). (gr. -1-1). 2014. pap. 8.99 *(978-1-77049-410-7(3))*; 2011. 17.95 *(978-1-77049-225-7(9))* Tundra Bks. CAN. (Tundra Bks.). Dist: Penguin Random Hse., LLC.

—Flare. George, Kallie. 2014. (ENG.). 34p. (J). (gr. -1-3). 12.95 *(978-1-927018-50-7(1))* Simply Read Bks. CAN. Dist: Ingram Pub. Services.

Côté, Geneviève. Hey Little Baby! Leigh, Heather. 2012. (ENG.). 32p. (J). (gr. -1-1). 14.99 *(978-1-4169-8979-0(X)*, Beach Lane Bks.) Beach Lane Bks.

—The Lady of Shalott. Lord Tennyson, Alfred. 2009. (Visions in Poetry Ser.). (ENG.). 48p. (YA). (gr. 5-18). 9.95 *(978-1-55453-457-9(7))* Kids Can Pr., Ltd. CAN. Dist: Univ. of Toronto Pr.

Cote, Genevieve. The Magic Beads. Nielsen-Fernlund, Susin. 2007. (ENG.). 32p. (J). (gr. -1-3). 16.95 *(978-1-894965-47-7(7))* Simply Read Bks. CAN. Dist: Ingram Pub. Services.

—Minn & Jake. Wong, Janet S. & Wong, Janet G. 2008. (ENG.). 160p. (J). (gr. 2-5). pap. 9.99 *(978-0-374-40021-7(0)*, Farrar, Straus & Giroux (BYR)) Farrar, Straus & Giroux.

Côté, Geneviève. Minn & Jake's Almost Terrible Summer. Wong, Janet S. 2008. (ENG.). 112p. (J). (gr. 2-5). 15.99 *(978-0-374-34977-6(0)*, Farrar, Straus & Giroux (BYR)) Farrar, Straus & Giroux.

—Missuk's Snow Geese. Renaud, Anne. 2008. (ENG.). 36p. (J). (gr. -1-3). 16.95 *(978-1-894965-82-8(5))* Simply Read Bks. CAN. Dist: Ingram Pub. Services.

—Noni Is Nervous. Hartt-Sussman, Heather. 2013. (ENG.). 24p. (J). (-k). 17.95 *(978-1-77049-323-0(9)*, Tundra Bks.) Tundra Bks. CAN. Dist: Penguin Random Hse., LLC.

—Noni Says No. Hartt-Sussman, Heather. 2011. (ENG.). 24p. (J). (gr. k-k). 17.95 *(978-1-77049-233-2(X)*, Tundra Bks.) Tundra Bks. CAN. Dist: Penguin Random Hse., LLC.

—Spark. George, Kallie. 2013. (ENG.). 34p. (J). (gr. -1-3). 12.95 *(978-1-927018-24-8(2))* Simply Read Bks. CAN. Dist: Ingram Pub. Services.

Cote, Genevieve. Splash. George, Kallie. 2015. (Tiny Tails Ser.: 3). (ENG.). 44p. (J). (gr. -1-3). 12.95 ***(978-1-927018-77-4(3))*** Simply Read Bks. CAN. Dist: Ingram Pub. Services.

Côté, Geneviève. W Is for Wapiti! An Alphabet Songbook. Duchesne, Christiane. 2012. (ENG.). 48p. (J). (gr. -1-k). 16.95 *(978-2-923163-83-3(4))* La Montagne Secrete CAN. Dist: Independent Pubs. Group.

Cote, Genevieve. Me & You. Cote, Genevieve. 2009. (ENG.). 32p. (J). (gr. -1). 16.95 *(978-1-55453-446-3(1))* Kids Can Pr., Ltd. CAN. Dist: Univ. of Toronto Pr.

Côté, Geneviève. Mr. King's Things. Côté, Geneviève. 2012. (Mr. King Ser.). (ENG.). 32p. (J). 16.95 *(978-1-55453-700-6(2))* Kids Can Pr., Ltd. CAN. Dist: Univ. of Toronto Pr.

Cote, Genevieve. Starring Me & You, 0 vols. Cote, Genevieve. 2014. (ENG.). 32p. (J). 16.95 *(978-1-894786-39-3(4))* Kids Can Pr., Ltd. CAN. Dist: Univ. of Toronto Pr.

Côté, Geneviève. What Elephant? Côté, Geneviève. 2008. (ENG.). 32p. (J). (gr. -1-2). pap. 7.95 *(978-1-55453-270-4(1))* Kids Can Pr., Ltd. CAN. Dist: Univ. of Toronto Pr.

Cote, Genevieve. Without You. Cote, Genevieve. 2011. (ENG.). 32p. (J). (gr. -1-k). 16.95 *(978-1-55453-620-7(0))* Kids Can Pr., Ltd. CAN. Dist: Univ. of Toronto Pr.

Côté, Geneviève & Cote, Genevieve. Mr. King's Castle. Côté, Geneviève & Cote, Genevieve. 2013. (Mr. King Ser.). (ENG.). 32p. (J). 16.95 *(978-1-55453-972-7(2))* Kids Can Pr., Ltd. CAN. Dist: Univ. of Toronto Pr.

Côté, Geneviève & Second Story Press Staff. Little Word Catcher, 1 vol. Simard, Danielle. 2008. (ENG.). 32p. (J). (gr. 1-3). 14.95 *(978-1-897187-44-9(0))* Second Story Pr. CAN. Dist: Orca Bk. Pubs. USA.

Cote, Genevieve, jt. illus. see Côté, Geneviève.

Côté, Genvièvе. Violette, la Reine Muette. Pelletier, Marthe. 2004. (Mon Roman Ser.). (FRE.). 96p. (J). (gr. 2). pap. *(978-2-89021-708-9(6))* Diffusion du livre Mirabel (DLM).

Cote, Nancy. Big Mama's Baby. Borgo, Lacy Finn. 2007. (ENG.). 32p. (J). (gr. k-2). 15.95 *(978-1-59078-187-6(2))* Boyds Mills Pr.

—Dixie Wants an Allergy. Corn, Tori. 2014. (ENG.). 32p. (J). (gr. -1-k). 16.95 *(978-1-62087-991-7(3)*, Sky Pony Pr.) Skyhorse Publishing Co., Inc.

—Good Neighbor Nicholas: A Concept Book. Kroll, Virginia. 2006. (Way I ACT Books: Vol. 5). (ENG.). 24p. (J). (gr. 1-3). lib. bdg. 15.99 *(978-0-8075-2998-0(2))* Whitman, Albert & Co.

—Gretchen Groundhog, It's Your Day! Levine, Abby. 2004. (ENG.). 32p. (J). (gr. k-3). pap. 6.95 *(978-0-8075-3059-7(X))* Whitman, Albert & Co.

—The Leprechaun Who Lost His Rainbow, 1 vol. Callahan, Sean. 2010. (ENG.). 32p. (J). (gr. 1-3). pap. 6.99 *(978-0-8075-4455-6(8))* Whitman, Albert & Co.

—Makayla Cares about Others. Kroll, Virginia. 2007. (Way I ACT Books). (ENG.). 24p. (J). (gr. k-3). lib. bdg. 15.99 *(978-0-8075-4945-2(2))* Whitman, Albert & Co.

—Mrs. Greenberg's Messy Hanukkah. Glaser, Linda. 2004. (ENG.). 32p. (J). (gr. 1-3). per. 6.95 *(978-0-8075-5298-8(4))* Whitman, Albert & Co.

—Round the Turkey: A Grateful Thanksgiving. Kimmelman, Leslie. 2012. (J). 34.28 *(978-1-61913-130-9(7))* Weigl Pubs., Inc.

—Tap-Dance Fever. Brisson, Pat. 2005. (ENG.). 32p. (J). (gr. k-2). 17.95 *(978-1-59078-290-3(9))* Boyds Mills Pr.

—When I Feel Angry. Spelman, Cornelia. 2012. (J). reprint ed. lib. bdg. 32.71 *(978-1-61913-139-2(0))* Weigl Pubs., Inc.

Cote, Nancy. It Feels Like Snow. Cote, Nancy. 2003. (ENG.). 32p. (J). (gr. k-2). 15.95 *(978-1-59078-054-1(X))* Boyds Mills Pr.

—Watch the Cookie! Cote, Nancy. 2014. (ENG.). 32p. (J). (gr. -1-k). 16.95 *(978-1-62914-630-0(7)*, Sky Pony Pr.) Skyhorse Publishing Co., Inc.

Cotes Stanley, Marsha. Gypsy the Goat. Miller, Vern. 2013. 36p. pap. 11.95 *(978-1-61153-082-7(2))* Light Messages Publishing.

Cotta-Flood, Stephanie. Harold Angel. Dahl, Steven. 2012. 40p. (J). *(978-0-9883420-0-2(6))* Thotsup LLC.

Cotter, Bill. Beard in a Box. 2016. (ENG.). 40p. (J). ***(978-0-553-50835-2(0))*** Knopf, Alfred A. Inc.

Cottin, Menena. It's Our Nature. Orozco, Rebeca. 2012. (ENG.). 24p. (J). (gr. k-3). 12.95 *(978-1-77049-283-7(6)*, Tundra Bks.) Tundra Bks. CAN. Dist: Penguin Random Hse., LLC.

Cotton, Lisa. Raindrops. Collins, Betsy. 2008. 28p. pap. 13.99 *(978-1-4343-7062-4(3))* AuthorHouse.

Cotton, Sue Lynn. The Adventures of Granville, Coming to America. MacKenzie-Krysko, Claudia & Krysko, Kenneth L. 2013. 24p. pap. 12.95 *(978-1-61493-227-7(1))* Peppertree Pr., The.

—The Adventures of the Nutters, the Tree Highway. Ringley, Patrick & Brown, Anne Corbett. 2013. 48p. pap. 19.95 *(978-1-61493-207-9(7))* Peppertree Pr., The.

—Dinky Duck's Adventure. Hattaway, Carol. 2012. 16p. pap. 12.95 *(978-1-61493-128-7(3))* Peppertree Pr., The.

—Elric's Florida Holiday. Colhoun, Sheelah. 2012. 20p. pap. 13.95 *(978-1-61493-110-2(0))* Peppertree Pr., The.

—It's Fun to Feed the Little Lambs. Colhoun, Sheelah. 2013. 32p. pap. 14.95 *(978-1-61493-185-0(2))* Peppertree Pr., The.

—Iza & Her Magic Seashell. Adrian, Mikel. 2012. 28p. 24.95 *(978-1-61493-077-8(5))* Peppertree Pr., The.

—Rounding Rescue, a Rounding Numbers Story. Lostorto, Eric. 2013. 16p. pap. 11.95 *(978-1-61493-217-8(4))* Peppertree Pr., The.

—Spaced Out Gerbil. Lang, Kathy. 2013. 20p. pap. 12.95 *(978-1-61493-190-4(9))* Peppertree Pr., The.

—The Tooth Be Told. Howell, Julie Ann. 2011. 24p. 18.95 *(978-1-61493-061-7(9))* Peppertree Pr., The.

—Waiting for Wings, Angel's Journey from Shelter Dog to Therapy Dog. Musick, Stacy. 2012. 32p. 21.95 *(978-1-61493-055-6(4))*; pap. 12.95 *(978-1-61493-054-9(6))* Peppertree Pr., The.

Cottone-Kolthoff, Carol. Chocolate, a Glacier Grizzly. Christian, Peggy. (Humane Society of the United States Animal Tales Ser.). 32p. (J). (gr. 1-5). 34.95 incl. audio *(978-1-882728-64-0(5))*; pap. 9.95 incl. audio *(978-1-882728-67-1(X))*; pap. 19.95 incl. audio *(978-1-882728-69-5(6))* Benefactory, Inc., The.

Cottrill, Peter. Mrs. McGee's Coconut. Zobel-Nolan, Allia. 2009. 32p. (J). (gr. -1-2). 15.95 *(978-1-58925-079-6(6))*; pap. 6.95 *(978-1-58925-414-5(7))* Tiger Tales.

Cotumbeanu, Alexandra. Who Stole the Hot Sauce? Carrier, Misty. l.t. ed. 2011. (ENG.). 30p. pap. 9.49 *(978-1-4679-5033-6(5))* CreateSpace Independent Publishing Platform.

Couch, Crista. Cooper's Big Bear Hug. Woo, Melissa. 2012. 32p. (J). 9.95 *(978-1-59530-352-3(9))* Hallmark Card, Inc.

Couch, Greg. Aladdin & the Magic Lamp. Kunstler, James Howard. 2005. (Rabbit Ears Ser.). 36p. (gr. k-5). 25.65 *(978-1-59679-221-0(3))* Spotlight.

—The Boy Who Invented TV: The Story of Philo Farnsworth. Krull, Kathleen. (ENG.). 40p. (J). (gr. 1-4). 2014. 7.99 *(978-0-385-75557-3(0)*, Dragonfly Bks.); 2009. 16.99 *(978-0-375-84561-1(5))* Random Hse. Children's Bks.

—Nothing but Trouble: The Story of Althea Gibson. Stauffacher, Sue. 2011. (ENG.). 40p. (J). (gr. -1-2). pap. 7.99 *(978-0-375-86544-2(6)*, Dragonfly Bks.) Random Hse. Children's Bks.

—Pretty Little Lilly & the Magical Light. Hornsby, Ashley. 2007. 32p. (J). 15.95 *(978-0-9777241-0-9(7))* Cepia LLC.

Coulson, Cotton, photos by. Mayflower 1620: A New Look at a Pilgrim Voyage. Plimoth Plantation Staff et al. 2007. (ENG., 48p. (J). (gr. 3-7). per. 6.95 *(978-0-7922-6276-3(X)*, National Geographic Children's Bks.) National Geographic Society.

Coulson, Cotton & Brimberg, Sisse, photos by. 1621: A New Look at Thanksgiving. Bruchac, Margaret M. & Grace, Catherine O'Neill. 2004. (I Am American Ser.). (ENG., 48p. (J). (gr. 3-7). pap. 7.95 *(978-0-7922-6139-1(9)*, National Geographic Children's Bks.) National Geographic Society.

Coulson, Cotton, jt. illus. see Brimberg, Sisse.

Coulson, Cotton, jt. photos by see Brimberg, Sisse.

Coulson, David. Laugh It Up! 501 Super-Silly Jokes, Riddles, & Cartoons from Highlights. Highlights for Children Editorial Staff. 2013. (Laugh Attack! Ser.). (ENG.). 256p. (J). (gr. k). pap. 5.95 *(978-1-62091-071-9(3))* Boyds Mills Pr.

Coulton, Mia, photos by. All about Danny. Coulton, Mia. 2003. (ENG., pap. 5.35 *(978-0-9720295-3-7(2))* Maryruth Bks., Inc.

—At Grandma Ruth's House. Coulton, Mia. 2008. (ENG., pap. 5.35 *(978-1-933624-32-7(9))* Maryruth Bks., Inc.

—Circus Fish. Coulton, Mia. 2008. (ENG., pap. 5.35 *(978-1-933624-29-7(9))* Maryruth Bks., Inc.

—Danny & Abby Play Tag. Coulton, Mia. 2004. (ENG., pap. 5.35 *(978-0-9746475-3-1(5))* Maryruth Bks., Inc.

—Danny & Bee's Book of Opposites. Coulton, Mia. 2006. (ENG., pap. 5.35 *(978-1-933624-02-0(7))* Maryruth Bks., Inc.

—Danny & Dad Go Shopping. Coulton, Mia. 2003. (ENG., pap. 5.35 *(978-0-9720295-4-4(0))* Maryruth Bks., Inc.

—Danny & Heather Share. Coulton, Mia. 2003. (ENG., 16p. pap. 5.35 *(978-0-9720295-8-2(3))* Maryruth Bks., Inc.

—Danny & the Little Worm. Coulton, Mia. 2004. (ENG., pap. 5.35 *(978-0-9746475-6-2(X))* Maryruth Bks., Inc.

—Danny Can Sort. Coulton, Mia. 2003. (ENG., pap. 5.35 *(978-0-9720295-6-8(7))* Maryruth Bks., Inc.

—Danny Likes Red. Coulton, Mia. 2003. (ENG., pap. 5.35 *(978-0-9720295-2-0(4))* Maryruth Bks., Inc.

—Danny Likes to Help. Coulton, Mia. 2005. (ENG., pap. 5.35 *(978-0-9746475-9-3(4))* Maryruth Bks., Inc.

—Danny Paints a Picture. Coulton, Mia. 2004. (ENG., pap. 5.35 *(978-0-9746475-5-5(1))* Maryruth Bks., Inc.

C

—Danny's Big Adventure. Coulton, Mia. 2004. (ENG., per. 9.95 *(978-0-9746475-0-0(0))* Maryruth Bks., Inc.

—Danny's Castle. Coulton, Mia. 2005. (ENG., 16p. pap. 5.35 *(978-1-933624-00-6(0))* Maryruth Bks., Inc.

—Danny's Favorite Shapes. Coulton, Mia. 2004. (ENG., pap. *(978-0-9746475-4-8(3))* Maryruth Bks., Inc.

—Danny's Party. Coulton, Mia. 2004. (ENG., (J). pap. 5.35 *(978-0-9746475-1-7(9))* Maryruth Bks., Inc.

—Danny's Rocket. Coulton, Mia. 2009. (ENG., pap. 5.35 *(978-1-933624-40-2(X))* Maryruth Bks., Inc.

—Danny's Special Tree. Coulton, Mia. 2008. (ENG., pap. 6.95 *(978-1-933624-25-9(6))* Maryruth Bks., Inc.

—Danny's Timeline. Coulton, Mia. 2004. (ENG., pap. 5.35 *(978-0-9746475-2-4(7))* Maryruth Bks., Inc.

—Danny's Window. Coulton, Mia. 2005. (ENG., pap. 5.35 *(978-0-9746475-8-6(6))* Maryruth Bks., Inc.

—Five Danny Dogs. Coulton, Mia. 2005. (ENG., pap. 5.35 *(978-1-933624-01-3(9))* Maryruth Bks., Inc.

—Get down Danny. Coulton, Mia. 2003. (ENG., pap. 5.35 *(978-0-9720295-5-1(9))* Maryruth Bks., Inc.

—I Am Danny. Coulton, Mia. 2003. (ENG., pap. 5.35 *(978-0-9720295-7-5(5))* Maryruth Bks., Inc.

—A New Home for Fish. Coulton, Mia. 2007. (ENG., pap. 5.35 *(978-1-933624-14-3(0))* Maryruth Bks., Inc.

—Pirate Fish. Coulton, Mia. 2007. (ENG., pap. 5.35 *(978-1-933624-15-0(9))* Maryruth Bks., Inc.

—Spy Danny. Coulton, Mia. 2006. (ENG., pap. 5.35 *(978-1-933624-03-7(5))* Maryruth Bks., Inc.

—Super Danny. Coulton, Mia. 2012. (ENG., 13p. bds. 6.99 *(978-1-933197-90-6(0))* Orange Frazer Pr.

Counts, Monika. Alabama Countdown to Touchdown. 2010. (Countdown to Touchdown Ser.). 20p. (J). 14.95 *(978-1-61524-080-7(2)*, Intervisual/Piggy Toes) Bendon, Inc.

—Florida Countdown to Touchdown. 2010. (Countdown to Touchdown Ser.). 20p. 14.95 *(978-1-61524-082-1(9)*, Intervisual/Piggy Toes) Bendon, Inc.

—LSU Countdown to Touchdown. 2010. (Countdown to Touchdown Ser.). 20p. 14.95 *(978-1-61524-081-4(0)*, Intervisual/Piggy Toes) Bendon, Inc.

Coupe, Peter. Zoodles! Oodles of Animal Pictures to Finish! 2010. (Doodle Factory Ser.). (ENG.). 176p. (J). (gr. 2-6). pap. 8.99 *(978-0-7641-4501-8(0))* Barron's Educational Series, Inc.

Courageous $oul. The Lonely Flower. IMyster?Ous M! & Courageous $Oul. 2011. 20p. pap. 24.95 *(978-1-4560-6950-6(0))* America Star Bks.

Courl, Kathryn A. Goodnight Bear: A Book & Night Light. Bentley, Dawn. 2005. (Stories to Share Ser.). 12p. (J). 12.95 *(978-1-58117-034-4(3)*, Intervisual/Piggy Toes) Bendon, Inc.

Courl, Kathy & Clearwater, Linda. Puppy Makes Friends. Simon, Mary Manz. 2006. (First Virtues for Toddlers Ser.). 20p. (J). 5.99 *(978-0-7847-1414-0(2)*, 04066) Standard Publishing.

—Squirrel Says Thank You. Simon, Mary Manz. 2006. (First Virtues for Toddlers Ser.). 20p. (J). 5.99 *(978-0-7847-1415-7(0)*, 04067) Standard Publishing.

Courl, Kathy, jt. illus. see Clearwater, Linda.

Court, Moira. My Superhero. Owen, Chris. 2014. (ENG.). 48p. (J). (gr. k-2). 19.95 *(978-1-921888-97-7(0))* Fremantle Pr. AUS. Dist: Independent Pubs. Group.

Courtin, Thierry. Twin to Twin. O'Hair, Margaret. 2003. (ENG.). 32p. (J). (gr. -1-3). 17.99 *(978-0-689-84494-2(8)*, McElderry, Margaret K. Bks.) McElderry, Margaret K. Bks.

Courtney-Clarke, Margaret. My Painted House, My Friendly Chicken, & Me. Angelou, Maya. 2003. (ENG.). 48p. (J). (gr. -1-2). pap. 7.99 *(978-0-375-82567-5(3)*, Crown Books For Young Readers) Random Hse. Children's Bks.

Courtney, Richard. Animals Everywhere! Awdry, W. 2011. (Step into Reading Ser.). (ENG.). 32p. (J). (gr. -1-1). pap. 3.99 *(978-0-375-86812-2(7)*, Random Hse. Bks. for Young Readers) Random Hse. Children's Bks.

—Calling All Engines! Awdry, Wilbert V. & Awdry, W. 2005. (Pictureback Ser.). (ENG.). 24p. (J). (gr. -1-2). pap. 3.99 *(978-0-375-83119-5(3)*, Random Hse. Bks. for Young Readers) Random Hse. Children's Bks.

—Christmas in Wellsworth. Awdry, W. 2010. (Thomas in Town Ser.). (ENG.). 32p. (J). (gr. -1-2). 5.99 *(978-0-375-86356-1(7)*, Random Hse. Bks. for Young Readers) Random Hse. Children's Bks.

—Down at the Docks. Awdry, Wilbert V. & Awdry, W. 2003. (Pictureback Ser.). (ENG.). 24p. (J). (gr. -1-2). pap. 3.99 *(978-0-375-82592-7(4)*, Random Hse. Bks. for Young Readers) Random Hse. Children's Bks.

—Easter Engines. Awdry, Wilbert V. 2012. (Step into Reading Ser.). (ENG.). 32p. (J). (gr. -1-1). pap. 3.99 *(978-0-307-92996-9(5)*, Random Hse. Bks. for Young Readers) Random Hse. Children's Bks.

—Five Tank Engine Tales (Thomas & Friends) Random House. 2015. (Step into Reading Ser.). (ENG.). 160p. (J). (gr. -1-1). pap. 7.99 *(978-0-385-38496-4(3)*, Random Hse. Bks. for Young Readers) Random Hse. Children's Bks.

—Flynn Saves the Day. Awdry, Wilbert V. 2011. (Step into Reading Ser.). (ENG.). 32p. (J). (gr. -1-1). pap. 3.99 *(978-0-375-86935-8(2)*, Random Hse. Bks. for Young Readers) Random Hse. Children's Bks.

—Gordon's New View. Awdry, Wilbert V. ed. 2007. (Thomas & Friends Step into Reading Ser.). 32p. (gr. -1-k). lib. bdg. 13.55 *(978-1-4177-7092-2(9)*, Turtleback) Turtleback Bks.

—Halloween in Anopha. Awdry, Wilbert V. 2008. (Thomas in Town Ser.). (ENG.). 32p. (J). (gr. -1-2). 5.99 *(978-0-375-84413-3(9)*, Random Hse. Bks. for Young Readers) Random Hse. Children's Bks.

—Henry & the Elephant. Awdry, W. 2007. (Step into Reading Ser.). (ENG.). 32p. (J). (gr. -1-1). pap. 3.99 *(978-0-375-83976-4(3)*, Random Hse. Bks. for Young Readers) Random Hse. Children's Bks.

—James Goes Buzz, Buzz. Corey, Shana. 2004. (Step into Reading Ser.). (ENG.). 32p. (J). (gr. -1-1). pap. 3.99 *(978-0-375-82860-7(5)*, Random Hse. Bks. for Young Readers) Random Hse. Children's Bks.

—Let's Find Out: Dinosaurs. Behrens, Janice. Date not set. (ENG.). 24p. (J). 8.99 *(978-0-439-87321-5(5))* Scholastic, Inc.

Courtney, Richard. The Lost Ship. Awdry, W. 2015. (Step into Reading Ser.). (ENG.). 32p. (J). (gr. -1-1). 3.99 ***(978-0-553-52171-9(3))***; lib. bdg. 12.99 ***(978-0-553-52172-6(1))*** Random Hse. Children's Bks. (Random Hse. Bks. for Young Readers).

Courtney, Richard. The Monster of Sodor (Thomas & Friends) Carbone, Courtney. 2014. (Step into Reading Ser.). (ENG.). 32p. (J). (gr. -1-1). lib. bdg. 12.99 *(978-0-375-97323-9(0)*, Random Hse. Bks. for Young Readers) Random Hse. Children's Bks.

—Not So Fast, Bash & Dash! Awdry, Wilbert V. 2013. (Step into Reading Ser.). (ENG.). 24p. (J). (gr. -1-1). 3.99 *(978-0-449-81539-7(0)*, Random Hse. Bks. for Young Readers) Random Hse. Children's Bks.

—Not So Fast, Bash & Dash! Awdry, W. 2013. (Step into Reading Ser.). (ENG.). 24p. (J). (gr. -1-1). lib. bdg. 12.99 *(978-0-375-97166-2(1)*, Random Hse. Bks. for Young Readers) Random Hse. Children's Bks.

—Railway Rhymes. Awdry, Wilbert V. & Hooke, R. Schuyler. 2005. (Lap Library). (ENG.). 36p. (J). (gr. k — 1). bds. 11.99 *(978-0-375-83175-1(4)*, Random Hse. Bks. for Young Readers) Random Hse. Children's Bks.

—Slide & Seek! Awdry, Wilbert V. 2011. (ENG.). 8p. (J). (gr. k — 1). bds. 7.99 *(978-0-375-86599-2(3)*, Random Hse. Bks. for Young Readers) Random Hse. Children's Bks.

—Stuck in the Mud. Corey, Shana & Awdry, Wilbert V. 2009. (Step into Reading Ser.). (ENG.). 32p. (J). (gr. -1-1). pap. 3.99 *(978-0-375-86177-2(7)*, Random Hse. Bks. for Young Readers) Random Hse. Children's Bks.

—Thomas' 123 Book. Awdry, Wilbert V. 2013. (Pictureback(R) Ser.). (ENG.). 24p. (J). (gr. -1-2). pap. 3.99 *(978-0-307-98203-2(3)*, Random Hse. Bks. for Young Readers) Random Hse. Children's Bks.

—Thomas & the Christmas Tree. Golden Books Staff. 2009. (Lift-The-Flap Ser.). (ENG.). 12p. (J). (gr. -1-2). 9.99 *(978-0-375-85414-9(2)*, Golden Bks.) Random Hse. Children's Bks.

—Thomas & the Shark. Awdry, Wilbert V. 2013. (Step into Reading Ser.). (ENG.). 32p. (J). (gr. -1-1). pap. 3.99 *(978-0-307-98200-1(9)*, Random Hse. Bks. for Young Readers) Random Hse. Children's Bks.

—Thomas & the Volcano (Thomas & Friends) Awdry, W. 2015. (Step into Reading Ser.). (ENG.). 24p. (J). (gr. -1-1). lib. bdg. 12.99 *(978-0-375-97378-9(8)*, Random Hse. Bks. for Young Readers) Random Hse. Children's Bks.

—Thomas Breaks a Promise. RH Disney Staff & Random House Staff. 2006. (Little Golden Book Ser.). (ENG.). 24p. (J). (gr. -1-2). lib. bdg. 3.99 *(978-0-375-83671-8(3)*, Golden Bks.) Random Hse. Children's Bks.

—Thomas Comes to Breakfast. Awdry, W. 2004. (Step into Reading Ser.). (ENG.). 32p. (J). (gr. -1-1). pap. 3.99 *(978-0-375-82892-8(3)*, Random Hse. Bks. for Young Readers) Random Hse. Children's Bks.

—Thomas Gets a Snowplow. 2004. (Pictureback(R) Ser.). (ENG.). 24p. (J). (gr. -1-2). 3.99 *(978-0-375-82783-9(8)*, Random Hse. Bks. for Young Readers) Random Hse. Children's Bks.

—Thomas Goes Fishing. Awdry, W. 2005. (Step into Reading Ser.). (ENG.). 32p. (J). (gr. -1-1). pap. 3.99 *(978-0-375-83118-8(5)*, Random Hse. Bks. for Young Readers) Random Hse. Children's Bks.

—Thomas' Night Before Christmas. Hooke, R. Schuyler. 2013. (Little Golden Book Ser.). (ENG.). 24p. (J). (gr. -1-k). 4.99 *(978-0-449-81663-9(X)*, Golden Bks.) Random Hse. Children's Bks.

—Thomas, Percy, & the Dragon. Awdry, W. 2003. (Step into Reading Ser.). (ENG.). 32p. (J). (gr. -1-1). pap. 3.99 *(978-0-375-82230-8(5)*, Random Hse. Bks. for Young Readers) Random Hse. Children's Bks.

—Treasure on the Tracks. Awdry, W. 2013. (Step into Reading Ser.). (ENG.). 32p. (J). (gr. -1-1). 3.99 *(978-0-449-81535-9(8)*, Random Hse. Bks. for Young Readers) Random Hse. Children's Bks.

Courtney, Richard & Stubbs, Tommy. Story Time Collection. Awdry, W. 2014. (ENG.). 320p. (J). (gr. -1-2). 15.99 *(978-0-553-49678-9(6)*, Random Hse. Bks. for Young Readers) Random Hse. Children's Bks.

Courtney, Richard, jt. illus. see Awdry, Wilbert V.

Courtney, Richard H. The Close Shave. Awdry, Wilbert V. 2008. (Step into Reading Ser.). (ENG.). 32p. (J). (gr. -1-1). pap. 3.99 *(978-0-375-85180-3(1)*, Random Hse. Bks. for Young Readers) Random Hse. Children's Bks.

Cousineau, Kelley & Cunningham, Kelley. Connecting Dots: Poems of My Journey. Harrison, David L. 2004. (ENG.). 64p. (J). (gr. 5-6). 15.95 *(978-1-59078-260-6(7))* Boyds Mills Pr.

Cousineau, Normand. Atalante: La Coureuse la Plus Rapide au Monde. Galloway, Priscilla. 2006. (FRE.). 75p. (J). (gr. k-4). reprint ed. pap. 15.00 *(978-1-4223-5394-3(X))* DIANE Publishing Co.

Cousins, Lucy. Bedtime Rhymes. ed. 2015. (First Nursery Rhymes Ser.). (ENG.). 16p. (J). (-k). pap. 9.99 *(978-1-4472-6106-3(2))* Pan Macmillan GBR. Dist: Independent Pubs. Group.

—Nursery Rhymes. ed. 2015. (First Nursery Rhymes Ser.). (ENG.). 16p. (J). (-k). pap. 9.99 *(978-1-4472-6105-6(4))* Pan Macmillan GBR. Dist: Independent Pubs. Group.

Cousins, Lucy. Los Alimentos de Maisy. Cousins, Lucy. 2009. (Maisy Ser.). (SPA & ENG.). 16p. (J). (gr. -1-2). bds. 5.99 *(978-0-7636-4519-9(2))* Candlewick Pr.

—Count with Maisy, Cheep, Cheep, Cheep! Cousins, Lucy. 2015. (Maisy Ser.). (ENG.). 32p. (J). (-k). 15.99 *(978-0-7636-7643-8(8))* Candlewick Pr.

—Create with Maisy: A Maisy First Arts-and-Crafts Book. Cousins, Lucy. 2012. (Maisy Ser.). (ENG.). 48p. (J). (gr. -1-3). 16.99 *(978-0-7636-6122-9(8))* Candlewick Pr.

—Fire Engine. Cousins, Lucy. 2009. (Maisy Ser.). (ENG.). 16p. (J). (gr. k-k). bds. 5.99 *(978-0-7636-4252-5(5))* Candlewick Pr.

—Hooray for Fish! Cousins, Lucy. (Candlewick Storybook Animation Ser.). (ENG.). (J). 2008. 40p. (gr. -1-k). 14.99 *(978-0-7636-3441-4(7))*; 2008. 34p. (— 1). bds. 8.99 *(978-0-7636-3918-1(4))*; 2005. 40p. (gr. k-k). 15.99 *(978-0-7636-2741-6(0))* Candlewick Pr.

—I'm the Best. Cousins, Lucy. (ENG.). 32p. (J). (-k). 2013. 6.99 *(978-0-7636-6348-3(4))*; 2010. 14.99 *(978-0-7636-4684-4(9))* Candlewick Pr.

—Jazzy in the Jungle. Cousins, Lucy. 2013. (ENG.). 32p. (J). (-k). 14.99 *(978-0-7636-6806-8(0))* Candlewick Pr.

—Los Juguetes de Maisy. Cousins, Lucy. 2009. (Maisy Ser.). (SPA & ENG.). 16p. (J). (gr. -1-2). bds. 5.99 *(978-0-7636-4520-5(6))* Candlewick Pr.

—Maisy, Charley, & the Wobbly Tooth. Cousins, Lucy. 2009. (Maisy Ser.). (ENG.). 32p. (J). (gr. k-k). pap. 6.99 *(978-0-7636-4369-0(6))* Candlewick Pr.

—Maisy Goes Camping. Cousins, Lucy. 2009. (Maisy Ser.). (ENG.). 32p. (J). (gr. k-k). pap. 6.99 *(978-0-7636-4368-3(8))* Candlewick Pr.

—Maisy Goes on a Sleepover. Cousins, Lucy. 2012. (Maisy Ser.). (ENG.). 32p. (J). (gr. -1-2). 12.99 *(978-0-7636-5883-0(9))* Candlewick Pr.

—Maisy Goes on Vacation. Cousins, Lucy. (Maisy Ser.). (ENG.). 32p. (J). (gr. -1-2). 2012. pap. 6.99 *(978-0-7636-6039-0(6))*; 2010. 12.99 *(978-0-7636-4752-0(7))* Candlewick Pr.

—Maisy Goes Swimming: A Maisy Classic Pop-up Book. Cousins, Lucy. 2011. (Maisy Ser.). (ENG.). 16p. (J). (gr. -1-2). 11.99 *(978-0-7636-5099-5(4))* Candlewick Pr.

—Maisy Goes to Bed: A Maisy Classic Pop-Up Book. Cousins, Lucy. 2010. (Maisy Ser.). (ENG.). 16p. (J). (gr. -1-2). 12.99 *(978-0-7636-5097-1(8))* Candlewick Pr.

—Maisy Goes to Preschool: A Maisy First Experiences Book. Cousins, Lucy. (Maisy Ser.). (ENG.). 32p. (J). 2010. (gr. k-k). pap. 6.99 *(978-0-7636-5086-5(2))*; 2009. (gr. -1-k). 12.99 *(978-0-7636-4254-9(1))* Candlewick Pr.

—Maisy Goes to the City. Cousins, Lucy. (Maisy Ser.). (ENG.). 32p. (J). (gr. -1-2). 2014. 6.99 *(978-0-7636-6834-1(6))*; 2011. 12.99 *(978-0-7636-5327-9(6))* Candlewick Pr.

—Maisy Goes to the Hospital. Cousins, Lucy. 2009. (Maisy Ser.). (ENG.). 32p. (J). (gr. k-k). pap. 6.99 *(978-0-7636-4372-0(6))* Candlewick Pr.

—Maisy Goes to the Library. Cousins, Lucy. 2009. (Maisy Ser.). (ENG.). 32p. (J). (gr. k-k). pap. 6.99 *(978-0-7636-4371-3(8))* Candlewick Pr.

—Maisy Goes to the Movies: A Maisy First Experiences Book. Cousins, Lucy. 2014. (Maisy Ser.). (ENG.). 32p. (J). (gr. -1-2). 6.99 *(978-0-7636-7237-9(8))* Candlewick Pr.

—Maisy Goes to the Museum. Cousins, Lucy. (Maisy Ser.). (ENG.). 32p. (J). (gr. k-k). 2009. pap. 6.99 *(978-0-7636-4370-6(X))*; 2008. 12.99 *(978-0-7636-3838-2(2))* Candlewick Pr.

—Maisy Learns to Swim. Cousins, Lucy. (Maisy Ser.). (ENG.). 32p. (J). 2015. (-k). 6.99 *(978-0-7636-7749-7(3))*; 2013. (gr. -1-k). 12.99 *(978-0-7636-6480-0(4))* Candlewick Pr.

—Maisy Plays Soccer. Cousins, Lucy. 2014. (Maisy Ser.). (ENG.). 32p. (J). (gr. -1-2). pap. 6.99 *(978-0-7636-7238-6(6))* Candlewick Pr.

—Maisy's Amazing Big Book of Words. Cousins, Lucy. 2007. (Maisy Ser.). (ENG.). 64p. (J). (gr. k-k). 14.99 *(978-0-7636-0794-4(0))* Candlewick Pr.

—Maisy's Animals (Los Animales de Maisy) Cousins, Lucy. 2009. (Maisy Ser.). (SPA & ENG.). 16p. (J). (gr. -1-2). bds. 5.99 *(978-0-7636-4517-5(6))* Candlewick Pr.

—Maisy's Band. Cousins, Lucy. 2012. (Maisy Ser.). (ENG.). 16p. (J). (gr. -1-2). 17.99 *(978-0-7636-6044-4(2))* Candlewick Pr.

—Maisy's Birthday Party Sticker Book. Cousins, Lucy. 2015. (Maisy Ser.). (ENG.). 16p. (J). (gr. -1-2). pap. 7.99 *(978-0-7636-7735-0(3))* Candlewick Pr.

—Maisy's Castle: A Maisy Pop-Up & Play Book. Cousins, Lucy. 2014. (Maisy Ser.). (ENG.). 10p. (J). (-k). 16.99 *(978-0-7636-7438-0(9))* Candlewick Pr.

—Maisy's Christmas: Sticker Book. Cousins, Lucy. 2004. (Maisy Ser.). (ENG.). 16p. (J). (-k). pap. 4.99 *(978-0-7636-2512-2(4))* Candlewick Pr.

—Maisy's Christmas Tree. Cousins, Lucy. 2014. (Maisy Ser.). (ENG.). 16p. (J). (-k). bds. 6.99 *(978-0-7636-7457-1(5))* Candlewick Pr.

—Maisy's Clothes/La Ropa de Maisy. Cousins, Lucy. 2009. (Maisy Ser.). (SPA & ENG.). 16p. (J). (gr. -1-2). bds. 5.99 *(978-0-7636-4518-2(4))* Candlewick Pr.

Cousins, Lucy. Maisy's Digger: A Go with Maisy Board Book. Cousins, Lucy. 2015. (Maisy Ser.). (ENG.). 18p. (J). (— 1). bds. 5.99 ***(978-0-7636-8010-7(9))*** Candlewick Pr.

Cousins, Lucy. Maisy's First Clock. Cousins, Lucy. 2011. (Maisy Ser.). (ENG.). 16p. (J). (gr. k-k). bds. 14.99 *(978-0-7636-5095-7(1))* Candlewick Pr.

—Maisy's First Colors: A Maisy Concept Book. Cousins, Lucy. 2013. (Maisy Ser.). (ENG.). 14p. (J). (-k). bds. 6.99 *(978-0-7636-6804-4(4))* Candlewick Pr.

Cousins, Lucy. Maisy's Pirate Ship: A Pop-Up-and-Play Book. Cousins, Lucy. 2015. (Maisy Ser.). (ENG.). 10p. (J). (-k). 16.99 ***(978-0-7636-7941-5(0))*** Candlewick Pr.

Cousins, Lucy. Maisy's Placemat Doodle Book. Cousins, Lucy. 2014. (Maisy Ser.). (ENG.). 104p. (J). (-k). pap. 11.99 *(978-0-7636-7108-2(8))* Candlewick Pr.

—Maisy's Plane. Cousins, Lucy. 2015. (Maisy Ser.). (ENG.). 18p. (J). (— 1). bds. 5.99 *(978-0-7636-7304-8(8))* Candlewick Pr.

Cousins, Lucy. Maisy's Race Car: A Go with Maisy Board Book. Cousins, Lucy. 2015. (Maisy Ser.). (ENG.). 18p. (J). (— 1). bds. 5.99 ***(978-0-7636-8011-4(7))*** Candlewick Pr.

Cousins, Lucy. Maisy's Seaside Adventure Sticker Book. Cousins, Lucy. 2015. (Maisy Ser.). (ENG.). 16p. (J). (gr. -1-2). pap. 7.99 *(978-0-7636-7734-3(5))* Candlewick Pr.

—Maisy's Seasons. Cousins, Lucy. 2011. (Maisy Ser.). (ENG.). 12p. (J). (-k). bds. 9.99 *(978-0-7636-5222-7(9))* Candlewick Pr.

—Maisy's Thanksgiving Sticker Book. Cousins, Lucy. 2006. (Maisy Ser.). (ENG.). 16p. (J). (gr. k-k). pap. 4.99 *(978-0-7636-3048-5(9))* Candlewick Pr.

—Maisy's Tractor. Cousins, Lucy. 2015. (Maisy Ser.). (ENG.). 18p. (J). (— 1). bds. 5.99 *(978-0-7636-7305-5(6))* Candlewick Pr.

—Maisy's Train. Cousins, Lucy. 2009. (Maisy Ser.). (ENG.). 16p. (J). (gr. k-k). bds. 5.99 *(978-0-7636-4251-8(7))* Candlewick Pr.

—Maisy's Valentine Sticker Book. Cousins, Lucy. 2005. (Maisy Ser.). (ENG.). 16p. (J). (gr. k-k). pap. 4.99 *(978-0-7636-2713-3(5))* Candlewick Pr.

—Maisy's Wonderful Weather Book. Cousins, Lucy. 2006. (Maisy Ser.). (ENG.). 14p. (J). (gr. -1). 11.99 *(978-0-7636-2987-8(1))* Candlewick Pr.

—Maisy's World of Animals: A Maisy First Science Book. Cousins, Lucy. 2014. (Maisy Ser.). (ENG.). 16p. (J). (gr. -1-2). 14.99 *(978-0-7636-6989-8(X))* Candlewick Pr.

—Munch Munch, Maisy: A Stroll-Along Book. Cousins, Lucy. 2008. (Maisy Ser.). (ENG.). 14p. (J). (gr. k — 1). bds. 4.99 *(978-0-7636-3914-3(1))* Candlewick Pr.

—Noah's Ark. Cousins, Lucy. 2004. (ENG.). 22p. (J). (gr. k-k). bds. 6.99 *(978-0-7636-2446-0(2))* Candlewick Pr.

—Peck, Peck, Peck. Cousins, Lucy. 2013. (ENG.). 32p. (J). (-k). 15.99 *(978-0-7636-6621-7(1))* Candlewick Pr.

—Sweet Dreams, Maisy. Cousins, Lucy. 2009. (Maisy Ser.). (ENG.). 32p. (J). (gr. -1-2). bds. 6.99 *(978-0-7636-4532-8(X))* Candlewick Pr.

—Where Are Maisy's Friends? Cousins, Lucy. 2010. (Maisy Ser.). (ENG.). 12p. (J). (-k). bds. 5.99 *(978-0-7636-4669-1(5))* Candlewick Pr.

—Where Does Maisy Live? Cousins, Lucy. 2010. (Maisy Ser.). (ENG.). 12p. (J). (-k). bds. 5.99 *(978-0-7636-4668-4(7))* Candlewick Pr.

—Where Is Maisy? Cousins, Lucy. 2010. (Maisy Ser.). (ENG.). 14p. (J). (gr. k-k). bds. 5.99 *(978-0-7636-4673-8(3))* Candlewick Pr.

—With Love from Maisy. Cousins, Lucy. ed. 2007. (Maisy Ser.). (ENG.). 16p. (J). (gr. -1-2). 4.99 *(978-0-7636-3539-8(1))* Candlewick Pr.

—Yummy: Eight Favorite Fairy Tales. Cousins, Lucy. 2009. (ENG.). 128p. (J). (gr. -1-2). 18.99 *(978-0-7636-4474-1(9))* Candlewick Pr.

Couteaud, Cheryl. A Monster for Halloween. Couteaud, Cheryl. 2009. 24p. pap. 10.96 *(978-1-4251-8563-3(0))* Trafford Publishing.

Coutts, Lisa. Hello God. Simons, Moya. 2007. 160p. (Orig.). pap. *(978-0-7322-8534-0(8))* HarperCollins Pubs. Australia.

Coverly, Dave. The Very Inappropriate Word. Tobin, Jim. 2013. (ENG.). 36p. (J). (gr. k-3). 16.99 *(978-0-8050-9474-9(1)*, Ottaviano, Christy Bks.) Holt, Henry & Co.

Covey, Rosemary Felt. Beauty & the Serpent: Thirteen Tales of Unnatural Animals. Porte, Barbara Ann. 2008. (ENG.). 128p. (YA). (gr. 7). pap. 7.99 *(978-1-4169-7579-3(9)*, Simon & Schuster/Paula Wiseman Bks.) Simon & Schuster/Paula Wiseman Bks.

Covi, jt. illus. see Antonio.

Covieo, Jeff. Saving Redwind: A Wallpaper Adventure. Yankee, Kris. 2011. (ENG.). 164p. pap. 7.95 *(978-1-4636-1667-0(8))* CreateSpace Independent Publishing Platform.

Coville, Katherine. Aliens Ate My Homework. Coville, Bruce. 2008. (Rod Allbright & the Galactic Patrol Ser.). 179p. (gr. 3-7). 17.00 *(978-0-7569-8466-3(1))* Perfection Learning Corp.

—Aliens Ate My Homework: Rod Allbright & the Galactic Patrol. Coville, Bruce. 2007. (Rod Allbright & the Galactic Patrol Ser.). (ENG.). 192p. (J). (gr. 3-7). pap. 6.99 *(978-1-4169-3883-5(4)*, Simon & Schuster/Paula Wiseman Bks.) Simon & Schuster/Paula Wiseman Bks.

—Aliens Stole My Body. Coville, Bruce. 2008. (Rod Allbright & the Galactic Patrol Ser.). (ENG.). 240p. (J). (gr. 3-7). pap. 6.99 *(978-1-4169-5359-3(0)*, Simon & Schuster/Paula Wiseman Bks.) Simon & Schuster/Paula Wiseman Bks.

—The Dragon of Doom. Coville, Bruce. 2005. (Moongobble & Me Ser.: Bk. 1). (ENG.). 80p. (J). (gr. 1-5). pap. 5.99 *(978-0-689-85757-7(8)*, Simon & Schuster/Paula Wiseman Bks.) Simon & Schuster/Paula Wiseman Bks.

—The Evil Elves. Coville, Bruce. 2006. (Moongobble & Me Ser.: Bk. 3). (ENG.). 80p. (J). (gr. 1-5). pap. 5.99 *(978-0-689-85759-1(4)*, Simon & Schuster/Paula Wiseman Bks.) Simon & Schuster/Paula Wiseman Bks.

—I Left My Sneakers in Dimension X. Coville, Bruce. 2007. (Rod Allbright & the Galactic Patrol Ser.). (ENG.). 192p. (J). (gr. 3-7). pap. 6.99 *(978-1-4169-3882-8(6)*, Simon & Schuster/Paula Wiseman Bks.) Simon & Schuster/Paula Wiseman Bks.

—The Mischief Monster. Coville, Bruce. 2008. (Moongobble & Me Ser.: Bk. 4). (ENG.). 80p. (J). (gr. 1-5). pap. 5.99 *(978-1-4169-0808-1(0)*, Simon & Schuster/Paula Wiseman Bks.) Simon & Schuster/Paula Wiseman Bks.

—The Monster's Ring. Coville, Bruce. 2008. (Magic Shop Book Ser.: 1). (ENG.). 128p. (J). (gr. 5-7). pap. 6.99 *(978-0-15-206442-6(7))* Houghton Mifflin Harcourt Publishing Co.

—More Short & Shivery: Thirty Terrifying Tales. San Souci, Robert D. 2015. (ENG.). 224p. (J). (gr. 3-7). 6.99 *(978-0-440-41857-3(7)*, Yearling) Random Hse. Children's Bks.

—The Naughty Nork. Coville, Bruce. 2009. (Moongobble & Me Ser.). (ENG.). 128p. (J). (gr. 1-5). pap. 5.99 *(978-1-4169-0810-4(2)*, Simon & Schuster/Paula Wiseman Bks.) Simon & Schuster/Paula Wiseman Bks.

—The Search for Snout. Coville, Bruce. 2007. (Rod Allbright & the Galactic Patrol Ser.). (ENG.). 224p. (J). (gr. 3-7). pap. 10.99 *(978-1-4169-4980-0(1)*, Simon & Schuster/Paula Wiseman Bks.) Simon & Schuster/Paula Wiseman Bks.

—The Weeping Werewolf. Coville, Bruce. 2006. (Moongobble & Me Ser.). 68p. (gr. 1-5). 16.00 *(978-0-7569-6582-2(9))* Perfection Learning Corp.

—The Weeping Werewolf. Coville, Bruce. 2005. (Moongobble & Me Ser.: Bk. 2). (ENG.). 80p. (J). (gr. 1-5). pap. 5.99 *(978-0-689-85758-4(6)*, Simon & Schuster/Paula Wiseman Bks.) Simon & Schuster/Paula Wiseman Bks.

Coville, Katherine, jt. illus. see Gerstein, Mordical.

Covington, Emily. Equestrian Instruction: The Integrated Approach to Teaching & Learning. Hassler-Scoop, Jill K. et al. rev. ed. (ENG.). 430p. pap. 45.00 *(978-0-9632562-6-3(2)*, 765) Goals Unlimited Pr.

Covolo, David. Ned & the General: A Lesson about Deployment. Madison, Ron. 2004. (J). 24p. 8.95 *(978-1-887206-24-2(8))*; 26p. (gr. -1-3). *(978-1-887206-25-9(6))* Ned's Head Productions.

—Ned & the World's Religions: As Seen Through the Eyes of Children. Madison, Ron. 2008. 36p. (J). 14.95 *(978-1-887206-26-6(4))* Ned's Head Productions.

—Ned Learns to Say No: A Lesson about Drugs. Madison, Ron. l.t. ed. 2003. (Health & Safety Ser.). 24p. pap. 4.95 *(978-1-887206-23-5(X))* Ned's Head Productions.

Cowcher, Helen. Desert Elephants, 1 vol. Cowcher, Helen. 2011. (ENG.). 40p. (J). (gr. k-3). 16.99 *(978-0-374-31774-4(7)*, Farrar, Straus & Giroux (BYR)) Farrar, Straus & Giroux.

Cowdrey, Richard. Animals on the Go. Brett, Jessica. 2003. (Green Light Readers Level 2 Ser.). (ENG.). 24p. (J). (gr. -1-3). pap. 3.95 *(978-0-15-204827-3(8))* Houghton Mifflin Harcourt Publishing Co.

—Animals on the Go. Brett, Jessica. ed. 2003. (Green Light Readers — Level 2 Ser.). 20p. (gr. -1-3). lib. bdg. 13.50 *(978-0-613-63248-5(6)*, Turtleback) Turtleback Bks.

—Bad Dog, Marley! Grogan, John. (ENG.). 40p. (J). (gr. -1-3). 2011. pap. 6.99 *(978-0-06-117116-1(6))*; 2007. 17.99 *(978-0-06-117114-7(X))* HarperCollins Pubs.

—Bad Dog, Marley! Beloved Book & Plush Puppy. Grogan, John. 2007. 40p. (J). (gr. -1-3). 24.99 *(978-0-06-143496-9(5))* HarperCollins Pubs.

—Bambi: A Life in the Woods. Salten, Felix. 2013. (Bambi's Classic Animal Tales Ser.). (ENG.). 272p. (J). (gr. 3-7). 16.99 *(978-1-4424-6746-0(0)*, Simon & Schuster/Paula Wiseman Bks.) Simon & Schuster/Paula Wiseman Bks.

—Bambi's Children: The Story of a Forest Family. Salten, Felix. Tilley, R. Sudgen, ed. Fles, Barthold, tr. 2014. (Bambi's Classic Animal Tales Ser.). (ENG.). 368p. (J). (gr. 3-7). pap. 7.99 *(978-1-4424-8745-1(3)*, Simon & Schuster/Paula Wiseman Bks.) Simon & Schuster/Paula Wiseman Bks.

—The Christmas Baby. Bauer, Marion Dane. 2009. (ENG.). 32p. (J). (gr. -1-k). 15.99 *(978-1-4169-7885-5(2)*, Simon & Schuster Bks. For Young Readers) Simon & Schuster Bks. For Young Readers.

—The Dog Who Cried Woof. Grogan, John. 2011. (I Can Read Book 2 Ser.). (ENG.). 32p. (J). (gr. k-3). 16.99 *(978-0-06-198944-5(4))*; pap. 3.99 *(978-0-06-198943-8(6))* HarperCollins Pubs.

—Farm Dog. Grogan, John. 2011. (I Can Read Book 2 Ser.). (ENG.). 32p. (J). (gr. k-3). 16.99 *(978-0-06-198938-4(X))*; pap. 3.99 *(978-0-06-198937-7(1))* HarperCollins Pubs.

—The Legend of St. Nicholas: A Story of Christmas Giving, 1 vol. Mackall, Dandi Daley. 2014. (ENG.). 32p. (J). 15.99 *(978-0-310-73115-3(1))* Zonderkidz.

—The Legend of the Candy Cane, 1 vol. Zondervan & Walburg, Lori. 2014. (ENG.). 30p. (J). bds. 9.99 *(978-0-310-74672-0(8))* Zonderkidz.

—Marley - Springs Ahead. Grogan, John. 2011. (Marley Ser.). (ENG.). 12p. (J). (gr. -1-1). bds. 6.99 *(978-0-06-198946-9(0)*, HarperFestival) HarperCollins Pubs.

—Marley & the Kittens. Grogan, John. 2010. (Marley Ser.). 40p. (J). (gr. -1-3). (ENG.). 17.99 *(978-0-06-171486-3(0))*; lib. bdg. 18.89 *(978-0-06-171487-0(9))* HarperCollins Pubs.

—Marley Goes to School. Grogan, John. (Marley Ser.). 40p. (J). (gr. -1-3). 2012. (ENG.). 9.99 *(978-0-06-211366-5(6))*; 2009. (ENG.). 17.99 *(978-0-06-156151-1(7))*; 2009. lib. bdg. 18.89 *(978-0-06-156152-8(5))* HarperCollins Pubs.

—Marley Learns a Lesson. Grogan, John. 2013. (I Can Read Book 2 Ser.). (ENG.). 32p. (J). (gr. -1-3). 16.99 *(978-0-06-207487-4(3))* HarperCollins Pubs.

—Marley Looks for Love. Grogan, John. 2010. (Marley Ser.). (ENG.). 16p. (J). (gr. -1-1). pap. 6.99 *(978-0-06-185590-0(1)*, HarperFestival) HarperCollins Pubs.

—Marley Storybook Treasury. Grogan, John. 2012. (I Can Read Book 2 Ser.). (ENG.). 192p. (J). (gr. k-3). 11.99 *(978-0-06-212331-2(9))* HarperCollins Pubs.

—Marley's Christmas Pageant. Grogan, John. 2013. (Marley Ser.). (ENG.). 16p. (J). (gr. -1-3). pap. 6.99 *(978-0-06-185382-1(8)*, HarperFestival) HarperCollins Pubs.

—Marley's World Reusable Sticker Book. Grogan, John. 2010. (Marley Ser.). (ENG.). 12p. (J). (gr. -1-3). pap. 6.99 *(978-0-06-185397-5(6)*, HarperFestival) HarperCollins Pubs.

—Messy Dog. Grogan, John. 2011. (I Can Read Book 2 Ser.). (ENG.). 32p. (J). (gr. k-3). 16.99 *(978-0-06-198940-7(1))*; pap. 3.99 *(978-0-06-198939-1(8))* HarperCollins Pubs.

—The Sandman. Fletcher, Ralph J. rev. ed. 2008. (ENG.). 32p. (J). (gr. -1-1). 17.99 *(978-0-8050-7726-1(X)*, Holt, Henry & Co. Bks. For Young Readers) Holt, Henry & Co.

—Snow Dog Marley. Grogan, John. 2010. (I Can Read Book 2 Ser.). (ENG.). 32p. (J). (gr. k-3). 16.99 *(978-0-06-185393-7(3))*; pap. 3.99 *(978-0-06-185392-0(5))* HarperCollins Pubs.

—Spirit Wolf. Lasky, Kathryn. 2013. (Wolves of the Beyond Ser.: 5). (ENG.). 240p. (J). (gr. 3-7). pap. 6.99 *(978-0-545-27971-0(2)*, Scholastic Pr.) Scholastic, Inc.

—Thanks, Mom & Dad! Grogan, John. 2011. (Marley Ser.). (ENG.). 24p. (J). (gr. -1-2). pap. 3.99 *(978-0-06-185381-4(X)*, HarperFestival) HarperCollins Pubs.

—This Is the Day!, 1 vol. Carlstrom, Nancy White. 2009. (ENG.). 32p. (J). (gr. -1-2). 15.99 *(978-0-310-71428-6(1))* Zonderkidz.

—Trick or Treat, Marley! Grogan, John. (Marley Ser.). (ENG.). 40p. (J). (gr. -1-3). 2013. 9.99 *(978-0-06-211368-9(2))*; 2011. 17.99 *(978-0-06-185755-3(6))* HarperCollins Pubs.

—A Very Marley Christmas. Grogan, John. (Marley Ser.). (ENG.). 40p. (J). (gr. -1-3). 2014. 9.99 *(978-0-06-211367-2(4))*; 2008. 17.99 *(978-0-06-137292-6(7))* HarperCollins Pubs.

—A Very Marley Christmas. Grogan, John. (ENG.). 32p. pap. *(978-0-00-728723-9(2)*, HarperCollins Children's Bks.) HarperCollins Pubs. Ltd.

Cowdrey, Richard & Beier, Ellen. Strike Three, Marley! Grogan, John & Hill, Susan. 2010. (I Can Read Book 2 Ser.). (ENG.). 32p. (J). (gr. k-3). pap. 3.99 *(978-0-06-185386-9(0))* HarperCollins Pubs.

Cowdrey, Richard & Halverson, Lydia. Marley: Firehouse Dog. Grogan, John. 2012. (I Can Read Book 2 Ser.). (ENG.). 32p. (J). (gr. -1-3). 16.99 *(978-0-06-207484-3(9))*; pap. 3.99 *(978-0-06-207483-6(0))* HarperCollins Pubs.

—Marley & the Runaway Pumpkin. Grogan, John & Hill, Susan. 2010. (I Can Read Book 2 Ser.). (ENG.). 32p. (J). (gr. k-3). 16.99 *(978-0-06-185391-3(7))*; pap. 3.99 *(978-0-06-185389-0(5))* HarperCollins Pubs.

—Marley's Big Adventure. Grogan, John & Hill, Susan. 2009. (I Can Read Book 2 Ser.). 32p. (J). (gr. -1-3). 16.99 *(978-0-06-185384-5(4))*; (ENG.). (gr. k-3). pap. 3.99 *(978-0-06-185383-8(6))* HarperCollins Pubs.

Cowdrey, Richard & Johnson, Steve. Bambi: A Life in the Woods. Salten, Felix. 2013. (Bambi's Classic Animal Tales Ser.). (ENG.). 272p. (J). (gr. 3-7). pap. 6.99 *(978-1-4424-6745-3(2)*, Simon & Schuster/Paula Wiseman Bks.) Simon & Schuster/Paula Wiseman Bks.

Cowdrey, Richard & Koelsch, Michael. Christmas Is Coming. Grogan, John. 2010. (Marley Ser.). (ENG.). 12p. (J). (gr. -1-1). bds. 6.99 *(978-0-06-198922-3(3)*, HarperFestival) HarperCollins Pubs.

Cowdrey, Richard & Lyon, Tammie. Marley Steals the Show. Grogan, John. 2010. (Marley Ser.). (ENG.). 24p. (J). (gr. -1-2). pap. 3.99 *(978-0-06-185377-7(1)*, HarperFestival) HarperCollins Pubs.

—Sit, Marley, Sit! Grogan, John. 2010. (Marley Ser.). (ENG.). 24p. (J). (gr. -1-2). pap. 3.99 *(978-0-06-185380-7(1)*, HarperFestival) HarperCollins Pubs.

Cowdrey, Richard & Whipple, Rick. Marley: The Dog Who Ate My Homework. Grogan, John. 2012. (I Can Read Book 2 Ser.). (ENG.). 32p. (J). (gr. k-3). pap. 3.99 *(978-0-06-207480-5(6))* HarperCollins Pubs.

—Marley - Not a Peep! Grogan, John. 2012. (I Can Read Book 2 Ser.). (ENG.). 32p. (J). (gr. k-3). pap. 3.99 *(978-0-06-207477-5(6))* HarperCollins Pubs.

—Not a Peep! Grogan, John. 2012. (I Can Read Book 2 Ser.). (ENG.). 32p. (J). (gr. k-3). 16.99 *(978-0-06-207478-2(4))* HarperCollins Pubs.

—A Thanksgiving to Remember. Grogan, John. 2011. (Marley Ser.). (ENG.). 16p. (J). (gr. -1-1). pap. 6.99 *(978-0-06-185591-7(X)*, HarperFestival) HarperCollins Pubs.

Cowdrey, Richard, jt. illus. see Beier, Ellen.

Cowdrey, Richard, jt. illus. see Bernardin, James.

Cowell, Cressida. How to Cheat a Dragon's Curse. Cowell, Cressida. 2007. (How to Train Your Dragon Ser.: 4). (ENG.). 256p. (J). (gr. 3-7). 13.99 *(978-0-316-11425-7(1))* Little, Brown Bks. for Young Readers.

Cowen-Fletcher, Jane. I Love You, Baby, from Head to Toe! Pandell, Karen. 2010. (ENG.). 16p. (J). (— 1). bds. 8.99 *(978-0-7636-5089-6(7))* Candlewick Pr.

Cowen-Fletcher, Jane. Baby Be Kind. Cowen-Fletcher, Jane. 2012. (ENG.). 18p. (J). (gr. k — 1). bds. 5.99 *(978-0-7636-5647-8(X))* Candlewick Pr.

—Hello, Puppy! Cowen-Fletcher, Jane. 2010. (ENG.). 32p. (J). (gr. -1-k). 12.99 *(978-0-7636-4303-4(3))* Candlewick Pr.

—My New Puppy. Cowen-Fletcher, Jane. 2013. (ENG.). 32p. (J). (-k). pap. 4.99 *(978-0-7636-6225-7(9))* Candlewick Pr.

—Nell's Elf. Cowen-Fletcher, Jane. 2006. (ENG.). 32p. (J). (gr. -1-3). 14.99 *(978-0-7636-2391-3(1))* Candlewick Pr.

Cowgur, Eldon. Made for Each Other, 2 vols. Storrie, Paul D. 2011. (My Boyfriend Is a Monster Ser.: 2). (ENG.). 128p. (YA). (gr. 7-12). 29.27 *(978-0-7613-5601-1(0))* Lerner Publishing Group.

—#02 Made for Each Other. Storrie, Paul D. 2011. (My Boyfriend Is a Monster Ser.). 128p. (YA). pap. 56.72 *(978-0-7613-7604-0(6)*, Graphic Universe) Lerner Publishing Group.

Cowherd, Kevin. Wild Pitch. Ripken, Cal. 2014. (Cal Ripken, Jr. 's All Stars Ser.). (ENG.). 224p. (J). (gr. 3-7). pap. 6.99 *(978-1-4231-4005-4(2))* Hyperion Bks. for Children.

Cowhey, Dennis E. Murder & Betrayal, Guzaldo, Jessica. DeFalco, Julie & Cowhey, Dennis R., eds. 2003. 72p. (YA). (gr. 7-8). pap. 9.95 *(978-0-9642823-2-2(1))* Key Answer Products, Inc.

Cowles, Rose. Achoo! Romanek, Trudee. 2003. (Mysterious You Ser.). (ENG.). 40p. (J). (gr. 4-6). pap. 8.95 *(978-1-55337-451-0(7))* Kids Can Pr., Ltd. CAN. Dist: Univ. of Toronto Pr.

—The Amazing International Space Station. Yes Magazine Editors. 2003. (ENG.). 48p. (J). (gr. 4-6). 9.95 *(978-1-55337-523-4(8))* Kids Can Pr., Ltd. CAN. Dist: Univ. of Toronto Pr.

—Puppies on Board, 1 vol. Harvey, Sarah N. 2005. (ENG.). 32p. (J). (gr. -1-3). 17.95 *(978-1-55143-390-5(7))* Orca Bk. Pubs. USA.

—The Queen, the Bear & the Bumblebee. Petty, Dini. 32p. (J). 19.95 *(978-1-55285-151-7(6))* Whitecap Bks., Ltd. CAN. Dist: Graphic Arts Ctr. Publishing Co.

—Science Detectives: How Scientists Solved Six Real-Life Mysteries. Yes Magazine Editors. 2006. (ENG.). 48p. (J). (gr. 3-7). pap. 8.95 *(978-1-55337-995-9(0))* Kids Can Pr., Ltd. CAN. Dist: Univ. of Toronto Pr.

—Squirt! The Most Interesting Book You'll Ever Read about Blood. Romanek, Trudee. 2006. (Mysterious You Ser.). (ENG.). 40p. (J). (gr. 4-9). 7.95 *(978-1-55337-777-1(X))* Kids Can Pr., Ltd. CAN. Dist: Univ. of Toronto Pr.

—Strange Times at Western High. Pohl-Weary, Emily. 2006. (Natalie Fuentes Mystery Ser.). (ENG.). 219p. (YA). (gr. 7-12). 19.95 *(978-1-55451-040-5(6)*, 9781554510405); pap. 9.95 *(978-1-55451-039-9(2)*, 9781554510399) Annick Pr., Ltd. CAN. Dist: Firefly Bks., Ltd.

—Wow! The Most Interesting Book You'll Ever Read about the Five Senses. Romanek, Trudee. 2004. (Mysterious You Ser.). (ENG.). 40p. (J). (gr. 4-9). 7.95 *(978-1-55337-630-9(7))* Kids Can Pr., Ltd. CAN. Dist: Univ. of Toronto Pr.

Cowles, Rose. Aha! The Most Interesting Book You'll Ever Read about Intelligence. Cowles, Rose, tr. Romanek, Trudee. 2004. (Mysterious You Ser.). (ENG.). 40p. (J). (gr. 4-6). 7.95 *(978-1-55337-569-2(6))* Kids Can Pr., Ltd. CAN. Dist: Univ. of Toronto Pr.

Cowley, Katz. The Wonky Donkey. Smith, Craig. 2010. (ENG.). 24p. (J). (gr. -1-k). pap. 6.99 *(978-0-545-26124-1(4)*, Scholastic Paperbacks) Scholastic, Inc.

Cowley, Ray B. First Day at Bouddi School. Bourke, Debra. 2012. 32p. pap. 18.00 *(978-1-4349-8469-2(9)*, RoseDog Bks.) Dorrance Publishing Co., Inc.

Cowman, Joseph. All in One Day. Huber, Mike. 2014. (ENG.). 32p. (gr. -1). 15.95 *(978-1-60554-207-2(5))* Redleaf Pr.

—The Amazing Erik. Huber, Mike. 2014. (ENG.). 32p. (gr. -1). 15.95 *(978-1-60554-209-6(1))* Redleaf Pr.

—Bree Finds a Friend. Huber, Mike. 2014. (ENG.). 32p. (gr. -1). 15.95 *(978-1-60554-211-9(3))* Redleaf Pr.

—Evette's Invitation. Huber, Mike. 2014. (ENG.). 32p. (gr. -1). 15.95 *(978-1-60554-212-6(1))* Redleaf Pr.

—Mama's Gloves. Huber, Mike. 2014. (ENG.). 32p. (gr. -1). 15.95 *(978-1-60554-210-2(5))* Redleaf Pr.

—Noah Chases the Wind. Worthington, Michelle. 2015. (ENG.). 32p. (J). (gr. -1-3). 16.95 *(978-1-60554-356-7(X))* Redleaf Pr.

—Rita & the Firefighters. Huber, Mike. 2014. (ENG.). 32p. (gr. -1). 15.95 *(978-1-60554-208-9(3))* Redleaf Pr.

Cowne, Joanne, jt. illus. see Levy, Ruth.

Cowper-Thomas, Wendy. Colby's New Home. Sinex, Roxana Faith. 2004. (J). pap. *(978-0-87743-705-5(X))* Baha'i Publishing Trust, U.S.

—The First Gift. Cobb, Judith A. 2008. (J). pap. *(978-0-87743-708-6(4))* Baha'i Publishing Trust, U.S.

—Something Important. 2010. (J). *(978-0-87743-711-6(4))* Baha'i Publishing Trust, U.S.

Cox, Alex. 3 Dead Princes: An Anarchist Fairy Tale. Nobacon, Danbert. 2010. (ENG.). 208p. (gr. 8-18). pap. 13.00 *(978-1-935259-06-0(7))* Exterminating Angel Pr.

Cox, Birck. The Encyclopedia of Skin & Skin Disorders. Turkington, Carol & Dover, Jeffrey S. 3rd rev. ed. 2006. (Facts on File Library of Health & Living). 480p. (C). (gr. 9). 75.00 *(978-0-8160-6403-8(2))* Facts On File, Inc.

Cox, Brain T. Lions, Lions Everywhere: The Story of Daniel as told by God's Animals. Loesch, Joe. Hutchinson, Cheryl, ed. 2004. (Bible Stories for Kids Ser.). 56p. (J). bds. 16.95 incl. audio compact disk *(978-1-932332-24-7(3))* Toy Box Productions.

Cox, Brian T. Florence Nightingale: Called to Serve with Buffalo Biff & Farley's Raiders. Wood, Jill G. 2006. (Time Traveler's Adventure Ser.). 56p. (J). 13.50 incl. audio compact disk *(978-1-932332-29-2(4))* Toy Box Productions.

—Joshua - Victory Through God: As Told by God's Animals. Loesch, Joe. 2006. 56p. (J). 13.50 incl. audio compact disk *(978-1-932332-62-9(6))* Toy Box Productions.

—Rosa Parks: Not Giving In with Buffalo Bill & Farley's Raiders. Collins, James. 2006. (Time Traveler's Adventure Ser.). 56p. (J). 13.50 incl. audio compact disk *(978-1-932332-17-9(0))* Toy Box Productions.

—Theodore Roosevelt: With Buffalo Bill & Farley's Raiders. Collins, James. 2006. (Time Traveler's Adventure Ser.). 56p. (J). 13.50 incl. audio compact disk *(978-1-932332-60-5(X))* Toy Box Productions.

Cox, Carolyn. The Lion Children's Bible: The World's Greatest Story Retold for Every Child. Rock, Lois. 2nd ed. 2012. (ENG.). 256p. (J). (gr. 2-7). 12.99 *(978-0-7459-1939-3(1))* Lion Hudson PLC GBR. Dist: Independent Pubs. Group.

—My Very Own Bible. 2010. (ENG.). 160p. (J). (gr. 2-4). 7.99 *(978-0-7459-4991-8(6))* Lion Hudson PLC GBR. Dist: Independent Pubs. Group.

—My Very Own Bible Gift. ed. 2011. (ENG.). 160p. (J). (gr. 2-4). 9.99 *(978-0-7459-6125-5(8))* Lion Hudson PLC GBR. Dist: Independent Pubs. Group.

—My Very Own Book of Prayers. Box, Su. 2011. (ENG.). 96p. (J). (gr. k-2). 7.99 *(978-0-7459-6293-1(9))* Lion Hudson PLC GBR. Dist: Independent Pubs. Group.

Cox, Chad, jt. illus. see Hillmann, Joe.

Cox, Daniel J. Borealis: A Polar Bear Cub's First Year, 1 vol. Grambo, Rebecca L. 2010. (Wild Beginnings Ser.: 0). (ENG.). 48p. (J). (gr. -1-3). pap. 9.95 *(978-1-55285-465-5(5))* Whitecap Bks., Ltd. CAN. Dist: Midpoint Trade Bks., Inc.

Cox, David. Bike Daredevils. Arena, Felice & Kettle, Phil. 2004. (J). pap. *(978-1-59336-371-0(0))* Mondo Publishing.

—Bull Riding. Arena, Felice & Kettle, Phil. 2004. (J). pap. *(978-1-59336-370-3(2))* Mondo Publishing.

—I Hate Books! Walker, Kate. 2007. (ENG.). 88p. (J). (gr. 1-4). 16.95 *(978-0-8126-2745-9(8))* Cricket Bks.

—Olympics. Arena, Felice & Kettle, Phil. 2004. (J). pap. *(978-1-59336-374-1(5))* Mondo Publishing.

—Race Car Dreamers. Arena, Felice & Kettle, Phil. 2004. (J). pap. *(978-1-59336-375-8(3))* Mondo Publishing.

—Ray's Olympics. Gleeson, Libby. 2006. (Making Tracks Ser.). (ENG.). 64p. (J). (gr. 2-4). pap. 9.95 *(978-1-876944-43-8(9))* National Museum of Australia AUS. Dist: Independent Pubs. Group.

—The Saw Doctor. Crew, Gary. 2006. (Making Tracks Ser.). (ENG.). 64p. (J). (gr. 2-4). pap. 9.95 *(978-1-876944-41-4(2))* National Museum of Australia AUS. Dist: Independent Pubs. Group.

—Turning the Page. Pulman, Felicity. 2008. (Making Tracks Ser.). (ENG.). 64p. (J). (gr. 2-4). pap. 11.95 *(978-1-876944-70-4(6))* National Museum of Australia AUS. Dist: Independent Pubs. Group.

Cox, David. The Road to Goonong. Cox, David. 2011. (ENG.). 40p. (J). (gr. -1-2). 26.95 *(978-1-74237-521-2(9))* Allen & Unwin AUS. Dist: Independent Pubs. Group.

Cox, Dorothy. Oh No! When It's OK to Be Late for School. Cox, Dorothy. 2010. (ENG.). 24p. pap. 10.00 *(978-1-4563-0455-3(0))* CreateSpace Independent Publishing Platform.

Cox, Glendyne Dewhurst. Haley Honeybee: Finds the Magic Rose. Burton M.Sc., Kathryn Mac. Diarmid. 2013. 50p. pap. *(978-0-9917941-0-2(9))* Burton, K. Publishing.

Cox, Jon. Crazy Man & the Plums. 2005. (Wind River Stories Ser.). (ENG & ARP.). 32p. (J). 14.95 *(978-0-9759806-1-3(0))* Painted Pony, Inc.

—Yuse: The Bully & the Bear. Washakie, John. 2nd ed. 2004. 47p. (J). 14.95 *(978-0-9759806-0-6(2))* Painted Pony, Inc.

Cox, Kim. Chester's Presents. McNease, Mitzy. ed. 2006. 28p. (J). 10.95 *(978-0-9779488-0-2(3))* Blancmange Publishing LLC.

Cox, Nancy. Elise the Elephant. Campbell, Jennifer. 2012. 32p. pap. 16.99 *(978-1-4567-9920-5(7))* AuthorHouse.

Cox, Palmer. The Brownies: Their Book. Cox, Palmer. 2011. (Dover Children's Classics Ser.). (ENG.). 160p. (Orig.). (J). (gr. 1-6). pap. 7.95 *(978-0-486-21265-4(3))* Dover Pubns., Inc.

Cox, Paul. The Elevator Man. Trachtenberg, Stanley. 2009. 34p. (J). (gr. -1-3). 18.00 *(978-0-8028-5315-8(3))* Eerdmans, William B. Publishing Co.

Cox, Rhonda, photos by. Best Friends. Cox, Rhonda. 2003. (ENG., 16p. (J). pap. 15.00 *(978-1-57274-699-2(8)*, BB2126, Bks. for Young Learners) Owen, Richard C. Pubs., Inc.

—Pigs Peek. Cox, Rhonda. 2003. (ENG., 12p. (J). pap. 15.00 *(978-1-57274-698-5(X)*, BB2180, Bks. for Young Learners) Owen, Richard C. Pubs., Inc.

Cox, Russ. Whatever Says Mark: Knowing & Using Punctuation, 1 vol. Collins, Terry. 2013. (Language on the Loose Ser.). (ENG.). 24p. (gr. 2-4). 27.32 *(978-1-4048-8318-5(5))*; pap. 7.95 *(978-1-4795-1917-0(0))* Picture Window Bks.

Cox, Steve. Amazing Life of Jesus. Zobel-Nolan, Allia. 2005. 10p. (J). 10.99 *(978-0-8254-5522-3(7))* Kregel Pubns.

—Ants in My Pants. Vantrease, Norma. 2004. (Rookie Readers Ser.). 31p. (J). 12.60 *(978-0-7569-4280-9(2))* Perfection Learning Corp.

—Ants in My Pants. Vantrease, Norma. 2004. (Rookie Reader Skill Set Ser.). (ENG.). 32p. (J). (gr. k-2). pap. 4.95 *(978-0-516-25839-3(7)*, Children's Pr.) Scholastic Library Publishing.

—Bible Adventures. Ellis, Gwen. 2006. 20p. (J). (gr. -1-k). bds. 9.49 *(978-0-7586-1130-7(7))* Concordia Publishing Hse.

—Boris the Boastful Frog. Hodgson, Karen J. 2015. (ENG.). 32p. (J). (gr. -1-1). pap. 9.99 *(978-1-907432-10-1(8))* Hogs Back Bks. GBR. Dist: Independent Pubs. Group.

—The Cat, the Mouse, & the Runaway Train. Bently, Peter. 2013. (J). *(978-1-4351-4968-7(8))* Barnes & Noble, Inc.

—The Diary of a Killer Cat. Fine, Anne. 2006. (Killer Cat Ser.). (ENG.). 64p. (J). (gr. 2-5). 16.99 *(978-0-374-31779-9(8)*, Farrar, Straus & Giroux (BYR)) Farrar, Straus & Giroux.

—Is That You, Alien? Check Inside the Secret Pockets If You Dare. 2014. (ENG.). 22p. (J). (gr. -1-1). 12.99 *(978-0-7641-6712-6(X))* Barron's Educational Series, Inc.

—Is That You, Monster? Check Inside the Secret Pockets If You Dare! 2013. (ENG.). 22p. (J). (gr. -1-1). 12.99 *(978-0-7641-6608-2(5))* Barron's Educational Series, Inc.

—Is That You, Wolf? BEWARE! Not a Bedtime Story. 2012. (ENG.). 22p. (J). (gr. -1-1). 12.99 *(978-0-7641-6560-3(7))* Barron's Educational Series, Inc.

—Leah & Leshawn Build a Letter. Lynette, Rachel. 2012. 32p. (J). lib. bdg. 25.27 *(978-1-59953-510-4(6))* Norwood Hse. Pr.

—The Marvelous Toy. Paxton, Tom. 2009. (ENG.). 28p. (J). (gr. k-12). 21.95 *(978-0-9822939-2-8(5)*, Imagine Publishing) Charlesbridge Publishing, Inc.

—The Marvelous Toy (Board) Paxton, Tom. 2014. (ENG.). 22p. (J). (gr. k-12). bds. 7.95 *(978-1-62354-043-2(7)*, Imagine Publishing) Charlesbridge Publishing, Inc.

—Moses' Big Adventure. Nolan, Allia Zobel. 2004. 12p. (J). bds. 10.99 *(978-0-8254-5521-6(9))* Kregel Pubns.

—Mother Goose Rhyme Time Animals. Faurot, Kimberly. 2006. 68p. (gr. -1-1). pap. 16.95 *(978-1-932146-66-0(0)*, Upstart Bks.) Highsmith Inc.

—Mother Goose Rhyme Time Night. Faurot, Kimberly. 2006. 72p. (gr. -1-1). pap. 16.95 *(978-1-932146-65-3(2)*, Upstart Bks.) Highsmith Inc.

—Mother Goose Rhyme Time People. Faurot, Kimberly. 2006. 66p. (gr. -1-1). pap. 16.95 *(978-1-932146-67-7(9)*, Upstart Bks.) Highsmith Inc.

—Peek & Find Bible Stories. Zobel-Nolan, Allia. 2003. 14p. (J). (gr. -1-k). bds. 7.49 *(978-0-7586-0413-2(0))* Concordia Publishing Hse.

—Peek & Find Christmas Story. Zobel-Nolan, Allia. 2004. 14p. (J). bds. 7.49 *(978-0-7586-0718-8(0))* Concordia Publishing Hse.

—The Puffin Book of Stories for Eight- Year- Olds. Cooling, Wendy. Cooling, Wendy, ed. (ENG.). 160p. (J). (gr. 3). pap. 8.95 *(978-0-14-038052-1(3))* Penguin Bks., Ltd. GBR. Dist: Trafalgar Square Publishing.

—The Puffin Book of Stories for Five-Year-Olds. Cooling, Wendy. (ENG.). 144p. (J). pap. 9.95 *(978-0-14-037458-2(2))* Penguin Bks., Ltd. GBR. Dist: Trafalgar Square Publishing.

—The Puffin Book of Stories for Six-Year-Olds. Cooling, Wendy. (ENG.). 144p. pap. 8.95 *(978-0-14-037459-9(0))* Penguin Bks., Ltd. GBR. Dist: Trafalgar Square Publishing.

—Stuff! Reduce, Reuse, Recycle, 0 vols. Kroll, Steven. 2012. (ENG.). 32p. (J). (gr. -1-3). pap. 7.99 *(978-0-7614-6237-8(6)*, 9780761462378, Amazon Children's Publishing) Amazon Publishing.

—The Treasure of Captain Claw. Emmett, Jonathan. 2012. (ENG.). 32p. (J). (gr. 2-4). pap. 9.99 *(978-1-84616-741-6(8))* Hodder & Stoughton GBR. Dist: Independent Pubs. Group.

Cox, Thomas. All the World's a Stage: A Novel in Five Acts. Woelfle, Gretchen. 2011. (ENG.). 176p. (YA). (gr. 5-9). 16.95 *(978-0-8234-2281-4(X))* Holiday Hse., Inc.

Cox, Tom. Things My Father Taught Me Through Sports. . . Playing the Game of Football. Maiocco, Chris & Maiocco, Kimberly. 2003. 24p. (J). 12.99 *(978-0-9720417-1-3(0))* His Kids Publishing, Inc.

—Things My Father Taught Me Through Sports... Playing the Game of Baseball: Playing the Game of Baseball.

Maiocco, Chris & Maiocco, Kimberly. 2003. 20p. (J). 12.99 *(978-0-9720417-0-6(2)*, 0-9720417-0-2) His Kids Publishing, Inc.

Cox, Val. Freaksville. Keswick, Kitty. 2010. 328p. (YA). (gr. 8-12). pap. 16.99 *(978-1-61603-001-8(1))* Leap Bks.

—Under My Skin. Graves, Judith. 2010. 328p. (YA). (gr. 8-18). pap. 16.99 *(978-1-61603-000-1(3))* Leap Bks.

Coxe, Molly. Benjamin & Bumper to the Rescue. Coxe, Molly. Toppin, Olivier, photos by. Canine, Craig, ed. 2010. (ENG.). 40p. (J). (gr. -1-k). 16.95 *(978-0-9819697-1-8(2))* BraveMouse Bks.

Coxon, Michele. Oh No, Woolly Bear!, 1 vol. McFadden, Patricia. 2008. (ENG.). 32p. (J). (gr. -1-3). 6.50 *(978-1-59572-149-5(5))* Star Bright Bks., Inc.

Coxon, Michele. Have You Fed the Cat?, 1 vol. Coxon, Michele. 2004. (ENG.). 32p. (J). 15.95 *(978-1-932065-90-9(3))* Star Bright Bks., Inc.

—Have You Fed the Cat? (Spanish/English), 1 vol. Coxon, Michele. 2004. (SPA & ENG.). 32p. (J). 15.95 *(978-1-59572-001-6(4))*; pap. 5.95 *(978-1-59572-002-3(2))* Star Bright Bks., Inc.

—Kitten's Adventure (Spanish/English), 1 vol. Coxon, Michele. 2006. (SPA.). 32p. (J). (gr. -1-k). pap. 5.95 *(978-1-59572-048-1(0))* Star Bright Bks., Inc.

—Termites on a Stick: A Chimp Learns to Use a Tool, 1 vol. Coxon, Michele. 2008. (ENG.). 32p. (J). (gr. -1-3). 17.95 *(978-1-59572-121-1(5))* Star Bright Bks., Inc.

—Termites on a Stick: A Chimpanzee Learns to Use a Tool, 1 vol. Coxon, Michele. 2008. (ENG.). 32p. (J). pap. 7.95 *(978-1-59572-183-9(5))* Star Bright Bks., Inc.

Coyle, Charissa B. D Mouse's Christmas Adventure. Ketchum, Holly. 2010. (ENG.). 106p. pap. 10.00 *(978-1-4537-1570-3(3))* CreateSpace Independent Publishing Platform.

Crabapple, Molly. The Raindrop Keeper. DePalma, Johnny. 2006. (J). per. 8.50 *(978-0-9791127-1-3(0))* Umbrelly Bks.

—The Raindrop Keeper: (Limited Edition Hardcover) DePalma, Johnny. 2006. 50p. (J). 16.50 *(978-0-9791127-8-2(8))* Umbrelly Bks.

—What Flowers Say: And Other Stories. Sand, George. Erskine Hirko, Holly, tr. from FRE. 2014. (ENG.). 208p. (J). (gr. 2-7). pap. 15.95 *(978-1-55861-857-2(0))* Feminist Pr. at The City Univ. of New York.

Crabtree, Andy. Many Moods of Maddie: Bossy Boots. Hastings, Suanne. 2006. (Baby Sitter Ser.). 24p. (J). (gr. -1-3). *(978-0-9769348-0-6(9))* Tastica, Suanne Creations Inc.

Crabtree, Marc. Gerbils. Crabtree, Marc, photos by. Sjonger, Rebecca & Kalman, Bobbie. 2003. (Pet Care Ser.). (ENG.). 32p. (J). lib. bdg. *(978-0-7787-1752-2(6))* Crabtree Publishing Co.

—Guinea Pigs. Crabtree, Marc, photos by. Kalman, Bobbie & MacAulay, Kelley. 2003. (Pet Care Ser.). (ENG.). 32p. (J). lib. bdg. *(978-0-7787-1755-3(0))* Crabtree Publishing Co.

—Hamsters. Crabtree, Marc, photos by. Sjonger, Rebecca & Kalman, Bobbie. 2003. (Pet Care Ser.). (ENG.). 32p. (J). lib. bdg. *(978-0-7787-1753-9(4))* Crabtree Publishing Co.

—Mice. Crabtree, Marc, photos by. Sjonger, Rebecca & Kalman, Bobbie. 2003. (Pet Care Ser.). (ENG.). 32p. (J). pap. *(978-0-7787-1786-7(0))*; lib. bdg. *(978-0-7787-1754-6(2))* Crabtree Publishing Co.

—Ponies. Crabtree, Marc, photos by. MacAulay, Kelley & Kalman, Bobbie. 2004. (Pet Care Ser.). (ENG.). 32p. (J). pap. *(978-0-7787-1790-4(9))* Crabtree Publishing Co.

—Rabbits. Crabtree, Marc, photos by. MacAulay, Kelley & Kalman, Bobbie. 2004. (Pet Care Ser.). (ENG.). 32p. (J). pap. *(978-0-7787-1788-1(7))* Crabtree Publishing Co.

Crabtree, Marc, photos by. Los Cachorros. Sjonger, Rebecca & Kalman, Bobbie. 2006. (Cuidado de las Mascotas Ser.). 32p. (J). (gr. 3-7). (SPA., pap. *(978-0-7787-8477-7(0))*; (ENG & SPA., lib. bdg. *(978-0-7787-8455-5(X))* Crabtree Publishing Co.

—Los Caniches o Poodles. MacAulay, Kelley & Kalman, Bobbie. rev. ed. 2007. (Cuidado de las Mascotas Ser.). (SPA & ENG., 32p. (J). (gr. -1-4). pap. *(978-0-7787-8483-8(5))* Crabtree Publishing Co.

—Los Cobayos. Kalman, Bobbie & MacAulay, Kelley. 2006. (Cuidado de las Mascotas Ser.). (SPA., 32p. (J). (gr. 3-7). pap. *(978-0-7787-8479-1(7))*; lib. bdg. *(978-0-7787-8457-9(6))* Crabtree Publishing Co.

—Los Cocker Spaniel. MacAulay, Kelley & Kalman, Bobbie. rev. ed. 2007. (Cuidado de las Mascotas Ser.). (SPA., 32p. (J). (gr. 1-5). pap. *(978-0-7787-8480-7(0))* Crabtree Publishing Co.

—Cocker Spaniels. MacAulay, Kelley & Kalman, Bobbie. 2006. (Pet Care Ser.). (ENG., 32p. (J). (gr. -1-3). pap. *(978-0-7787-1792-8(5)*, 1259503); lib. bdg. *(978-0-7787-1760-7(7)*, 1259503) Crabtree Publishing Co.

—Los Dálmatas. MacAulay, Kelley & Kalman, Bobbie. rev. ed. 2007. (Cuidado de las Mascotas Ser.). (SPA., 32p. (J). (gr. 1-5). pap. *(978-0-7787-8481-4(9))* Crabtree Publishing Co.

—Dalmatians. MacAulay, Kelley & Kalman, Bobbie. 2006. (Pet Care Ser.). (ENG., 32p. (J). (gr. -1-3). pap. *(978-0-7787-1793-5(3)*, 1259504); lib. bdg. *(978-0-7787-1761-4(5)*, 1259504) Crabtree Publishing Co.

—Los Gatitos. Walker, Niki & Kalman, Bobbie. 2006. (Cuidado de las Mascotas Ser.). (SPA., 32p. (J). (gr. 3-7). pap. *(978-0-7787-8476-0(2))*; lib. bdg. *(978-0-7787-8454-8(1))* Crabtree Publishing Co.

—Los Hamsters. Sjonger, Rebecca & Kalman, Bobbie. 2006. (Cuidado de las Mascotas Ser.). (ENG & SPA., 32p. (J). (gr. 3-7). lib. bdg. *(978-0-7787-8456-2(8))* Crabtree Publishing Co.

—Judo in Action. Crossingham, John & Kalman, Bobbie. 2005. (Sports in Action Ser.). (ENG., 32p. (J). (gr. 2-3). pap. *(978-0-7787-0362-4(2))* Crabtree Publishing Co.

—Labrador Retrievers. MacAulay, Kelley & Kalman, Bobbie. 2006. (Pet Care Ser.). (ENG., 32p. (J). (gr. -1-4). lib. bdg. *(978-0-7787-1762-1(3))* Crabtree Publishing Co.

—Los Hámsters. Sjonger, Rebecca & Kalman, Bobbie. 2006. (Cuidado de las Mascotas Ser.). (SPA & ENG., 32p. (J). (gr. 3-7). pap. *(978-0-7787-8478-4(9))* Crabtree Publishing Co.

—Los Perros Labrador. MacAulay, Kelley & Kalman, Bobbie. rev. ed. 2007. (Cuidado de las Mascotas Ser.). (SPA & ENG., 32p. (J). (gr. -1-4). pap. *(978-0-7787-8482-1(7))* Crabtree Publishing Co.

—Poodles. MacAulay, Kelley & Kalman, Bobbie. 2006. (Pet Care Ser.). (ENG., 32p. (J). (gr. -1-4). lib. bdg. *(978-0-7787-1763-8(1)*, 1259506) Crabtree Publishing Co.

—Taekwondo in Action. MacAulay, Kelley & Kalman, Bobbie. 2004. (Sports in Action Ser.). (ENG., 32p. (J). pap. *(978-0-7787-0358-7(4))* Crabtree Publishing Co.

Crabtree, Marc & Rouse, Bonna. Field Events in Action. Crabtree, Marc, photos by. Kalman, Bobbie. 2004. (Sports in Action Ser.). (ENG.). 32p. (J). lib. bdg. *(978-0-7787-0340-2(1))* Crabtree Publishing Co.

Crabtree, Marc, jt. illus. see Relach, Margaret Amy.

Crabtree Staff. Mustang. 2010. (Superstar Cars Ser.). (ENG.). 64p. (J). pap. *(978-0-7787-2152-9(3))* Crabtree Publishing Co.

Craddock, Erik. BC Mambo. Craddock, Erik. 2009. (Stone Rabbit Ser.). (ENG.). 96p. (J). (gr. 3-7). lib. bdg. 12.99 *(978-0-375-93922-8(9))*; pap. 6.99 *(978-0-375-84360-0(4))* Random Hse. Children's Bks. (Random Hse. Bks. for Young Readers).

—Deep-Space Disco. Craddock, Erik. 2009. (Stone Rabbit Ser.). (ENG.). 96p. (J). (gr. 3-7). pap. 6.99 *(978-0-375-85876-5(8))* Random Hse., Inc.

—Dragon Boogie. Craddock, Erik. 2012. (Stone Rabbit Ser.: Vol. 7). (ENG.). 96p. (J). (gr. 2-5). pap. 6.99 *(978-0-375-86912-9(3)*, Random Hse. Bks. for Young Readers) Random Hse. Children's Bks.

—Ninja Slice. Craddock, Erik. 2010. (Stone Rabbit Ser.: No. 5). (ENG.). 96p. (J). (gr. 3-7). pap. 6.99 *(978-0-375-86723-1(6))* Random Hse., Inc.

—Pirate Palooza. Craddock, Erik. 2009. (Stone Rabbit Ser.: Bk. 2). (ENG.). 96p. (J). (gr. 3-7). pap. 6.99 *(978-0-375-85660-0(9)*, Random Hse. Bks. for Young Readers) Random Hse. Children's Bks.

—Stone Rabbit #6: Night of the Living Dust Bunnies. Craddock, Erik. 2011. (Stone Rabbit Ser.). (ENG.). 96p. (J). (gr. 3-7). pap. 6.99 *(978-0-375-86724-8(4))*; lib. bdg. 12.99 *(978-0-375-96724-5(9))* Random Hse. Children's Bks. (Random Hse. Bks. for Young Readers).

—Stone Rabbit #8: Robot Frenzy. Craddock, Erik. 2013. (Stone Rabbit Ser.). (ENG.). 96p. (J). (gr. 2-5). pap. 6.99 *(978-0-375-86913-6(1))*; lib. bdg. 12.99 *(978-0-375-96913-3(6))* Random Hse. Children's Bks. (Random Hse. Bks. for Young Readers).

—Superhero Stampede. Craddock, Erik. 2010. (Stone Rabbit Ser.: No. 4). (ENG.). 96p. (J). (gr. 3-7). pap. 6.99 *(978-0-375-85877-2(6)*, Random Hse. Bks. for Young Readers) Random Hse. Children's Bks.

Craft, Danna. Sereena's Secret. Harris, Rae Ann & Weintraub, David. 2005. (ENG & YID.). 40p. (J). 16.95 *(978-1-932687-41-5(6))*; pap. 9.95 *(978-1-932687-42-2(4))* Simcha Media Group. (Devora Publishing).

Craft, Donna. Benjamin's Big Lesson. Laven, Zp. 2011. 20p. pap. 12.95 *(978-1-61493-009-9(0))* Peppertree Pr., The.

—Happy for a Honk & a Wave. McGregor, Janet C. 2010. 20p. pap. 12.95 *(978-1-936343-04-1(5))* Peppertree Pr., The.

Craft, James. Five Little Honeybees. 2009. (ENG.). 12p. 5.95 *(978-1-58117-907-1(3)*, Intervisual/Piggy Toes) Bendon, Inc.

Craft, Jerry. Looking to the Clouds for Daddy. Candelario, Margo. 2009. (J). *(978-0-9820221-7-7(4))* Hunter, Karen Media.

—The Zero Degree Zombie Zone. Bass, Patrik Henry. 2014. (ENG.). 144p. (J). (gr. 3-7). 16.99 *(978-0-545-13210-7(X)*, Scholastic Pr.) Scholastic, Inc.

Craft, Jerry. Mama's Boyz: What You Need to Succeed!: the Big Picture: the Big Picture. Craft, Jerry. 2010. 112p. (YA). (gr. 12-18). pap. 9.95 *(978-0-9796132-1-0(3))* Mama's Boyz, Inc.

Craft, K. Y. Christmas Moon. Craft, Mahlon. 2003. 32p. (J). 15.95 *(978-1-58717-056-0(6))*; lib. bdg. *(978-1-58717-057-7(4))* Chronicle Bks. LLC. (SeaStar Bks.).

Craft, Kinuko. Come Play with Me. Hillert, Margaret. 2008. (Beginning-to-Read Ser.). 30p. (J). lib. bdg. 19.93 *(978-1-59953-179-3(8))* Norwood Hse. Pr.

—The Cookie House. Hillert, Margaret. rev. exp. ed. 2006. (Beginning to Read Ser.). 32p. (J). (gr. -1-2). lib. bdg. 14.95 *(978-1-59953-051-2(1))* Norwood Hse. Pr.

Craft, Kinuko Y. The Adventures of Tom Thumb. Mayer, Marianna. 2005. 28p. (J). (gr. k-4). reprint ed. 16.00 *(978-0-7567-9642-6(3))* DIANE Publishing Co.

—King Midas & the Golden Touch. Craft, Charlotte. 2003. (ENG.). 32p. (J). (gr. -1-3). pap. 6.99 *(978-0-06-054063-0(X))* HarperCollins Pubs.

Cragg, Marcelyn Martin. Amanda & the Angel. Hutchings, Harriet Anne. 2010. 24p. pap. 9.95 *(978-1-936051-81-6(8))* Peppertree Pr., The.

Craig, Branden Chapin & Chapin, Jimmy. Thunder Is Not Scary. Rehberg, Emily. 2013. 26p. pap. 12.00 *(978-0-9800108-3-1(7))* Bilbo Bks.

Craig, Charles. Blessed John Paul II: Be Not Afraid. Wallace, Susan Helen. 2011. (Encounter the Saints Ser.). 111p. (J). (gr. 3-7). pap. 7.95 *(978-0-8198-1178-3(5))* Pauline Bks. & Media.

Craig, Charlie. Joseph from Germany: The Life of Pope Benedict XVI for Children. Mohan, Claire Jordan. 2007. (J). 8.95 *(978-0-8198-3988-6(4))* Pauline Bks. & Media.

Craig, Chris. Indigo Boy & Crystalline Girl. McCracken, Connie. 2009. 24p. pap. 10.95 *(978-1-4269-0423-3(1))* Trafford Publishing.

Craig, Dan. Mom Has Left & Gone to Vegas. Dasilva, D. 2008. 32p. pap. 19.95 *(978-1-59858-603-9(3))* Dog Ear Publishing, LLC.

Craig, David. The Alamo: Surrounded & Outnumbered, They Chose to Make a Defiant Last Stand. Tanaka, Shelley. 2010. (Day That Changed America Ser.). (ENG.). 48p. (J). (gr. 4-7). pap. 9.95 *(978-1-897330-37-1(5))* Madison Pr. Bks. CAN. Dist: Independent Pubs. Group.

—Amelia Earhart: The Legend of the Lost Aviator. Tanaka, Shelley. 2008. (ENG.). 48p. (J). (gr. 8-17). 21.95 *(978-0-8109-7095-3(3)*, Abrams Bks. for Young Readers) Abrams.

—D-Day: They Fought to Free Europe from Hitler's Tyranny. Tanaka, Shelley. 2010. (Day That Changed America Ser.). (ENG.). 48p. (J). (gr. 4-7). pap. 9.95 *(978-1-897330-38-8(3))* Madison Pr. Bks. CAN. Dist: Independent Pubs. Group.

—A Day That Changed America - The Alamo: Surrounded & Outnumbered,They Chose to Make a Defiant Last Stand. Tanaka, Shelley. 2003. (ENG.). 48p. (gr. 3-17). 16.99 *(978-0-7868-1923-2(5))* Hyperion Pr.

—Earthquake! A Day That Changed America. Tanaka, Shelley. 2006. 48p. (J). (gr. 4-8). reprint ed. 17.00 *(978-1-4223-5635-7(3))* DIANE Publishing Co.

—Earthquake! On a Peaceful Spring Morning, Disaster Strikes San Francisco. Tanaka, Shelley. 2010. (Day That Changed America Ser.). (ENG.). 48p. (J). (gr. 4-7). pap. 9.95 *(978-1-897330-39-5(1))* Madison Pr. Bks. CAN. Dist: Independent Pubs. Group.

—First to Fly: How Wilbur & Orville Wright Invented the Airplane. Busby, Peter. 2010. (ENG.). 32p. (J). (gr. 4-7). pap. 12.95 *(978-1-897330-52-4(9))* Madison Pr. Bks. CAN. Dist: Independent Pubs. Group.

—Gettysburg: The Legendary Battle & the Address That Inspired a Nation. Tanaka, Shelley. 2003. (Day That Changed America Ser.). (ENG.). 48p. 16.99 *(978-0-7868-1922-5(7))* Hyperion Pr.

—Gettysburg: The Legendary Battle & the Address that Inspired a Nation. Tanaka, Shelley. 2010. (Day That Changed America Ser.). (ENG.). 48p. (J). (gr. 4-7). pap. 9.95 *(978-1-897330-40-1(5))* Madison Pr. Bks. CAN. Dist: Independent Pubs. Group.

—Hoodwinked: Deception & Resistance. Forrester, Tina et al. 2004. (Outwitting the Enemy: Stories from World War II Ser.). (ENG.). 96p. (J). (gr. 5-18). pap. 14.95 *(978-1-55037-832-0(5)*, 9781550378320) Annick Pr., Ltd. CAN. Dist: Firefly Bks., Ltd.

—Hudson. Weaver, Janice. 2010. (ENG.). 48p. (J). (gr. 3-7). 22.95 *(978-0-88776-814-9(8))* Tundra Bks. CAN. Dist: Penguin Random Hse., LLC.

—A Is for Airplane: An Aviation Alphabet. Riehle, Mary Ann McCabe. 2009. (Science Alphabet Ser.). (ENG.). 40p. (J). (gr. 1-4). 16.95 *(978-1-58536-358-2(8)*, 202143) Sleeping Bear Pr.

—The Long White Scarf. Trottier, Maxine. 2005. (ENG.). 32p. (J). *(978-1-55005-147-6(4))* Fitzhenry & Whiteside, Ltd.

—Ultra Hush-Hush: Espionage & Special Missions. Shapiro, Stephen & Forrester, Tina. 2003. (Outwitting the Enemy: Stories from World War II Ser.). (ENG.). 96p. (J). (gr. 5-12). 29.95 *(978-1-55037-779-8(5)*, 9781550377798); pap. 14.95 *(978-1-55037-778-1(7)*, 9781550377781) Annick Pr., Ltd. CAN. Dist: Firefly Bks., Ltd.

Craig, Gary. I Can Be Anything Creative Activity Book. Craig, Gary. 2006. 41p. (J). pap. 5.99 *(978-0-9786813-2-6(0))* Elora Pr.

Craig, Helen. Amy's Three Best Things. Pearce, Philippa. 2013. (ENG.). 40p. (J). (gr. -1-3). 15.99 *(978-0-7636-6314-8(X))* Candlewick Pr.

—Angelina & Alice. Holabird, Katharine. 2006. (Angelina Ballerina Ser.). (ENG.). 32p. (J). (gr. -1-k). 12.99 *(978-0-670-06125-9(5)*, Viking Juvenile) Penguin Publishing Group.

—Angelina & Henry. Holabird, Katharine. 2006. (Angelina Ballerina Ser.). (ENG.). 32p. (J). (gr. -1-k). pap. 5.99 *(978-0-14-240590-1(6)*, Puffin) Penguin Publishing Group.

—Angelina & the Princess. Holabird, Katharine. 2006. (Angelina Ballerina Ser.). (ENG.). 32p. (J). (gr. -1-k). 15.99 *(978-0-670-06085-6(2)*, Viking Juvenile) Penguin Publishing Group.

—Angelina & the Royal Wedding. Holabird, Katharine. 2010. (Angelina Ballerina Ser.). (ENG.). 32p. (J). (gr. -1-k). 14.99 *(978-0-670-01213-8(0)*, Viking Juvenile) Penguin Publishing Group.

—Angelina at the Fair. Holabird, Katharine. 2007. (Angelina Ballerina Ser.). (ENG.). 32p. (J). (gr. -1-k). 12.99 *(978-0-670-06234-8(0)*, Viking Juvenile) Penguin Publishing Group.

—Angelina Ballerina. Holabird, Katharine. (Angelina Ballerina Ser.). (ENG.). 32p. (J). (gr. -1-k). 2006. 14.99 *(978-0-670-06026-9(7))*; 25th anniv. ed. 2008. 14.99 *(978-0-670-01117-9(7))* Penguin Publishing Group. (Viking Juvenile).

—Angelina Has the Hiccups! Holabird, Katharine. 2006. (Angelina Ballerina Ser.). (ENG.). 32p. (J). (gr. 1-2). pap. 3.99 *(978-0-448-44389-8(9)*, Grosset & Dunlap) Penguin Publishing Group.

—Angelina Ice Skates. Holabird, Katharine. (Angelina Ballerina Ser.). (ENG.). 32p. (J). (gr. -1-k). 2007. 14.99 *(978-0-670-06237-9(5)*, Viking Juvenile); 2006. 6.99 *(978-0-14-240658-8(9)*, Puffin) Penguin Publishing Group.

—Angelina Loves... Holabird, Katharine & Grosset and Dunlap Editors. 2006. (Angelina Ballerina Ser.). (ENG.). 24p. (J). (gr. -1-2). 5.99 *(978-0-448-44270-9(1)*, Grosset & Dunlap) Penguin Publishing Group.

—Angelina Takes a Bow. Holabird, Katharine. 2012. (Angelina Ballerina Ser.). (ENG.). 32p. (J). (gr. -1-k). pap. 3.99 *(978-0-448-45618-8(4)*, Warne, Frederick Pubs.) Penguin Bks., Ltd. GBR. Dist: Penguin Publishing Group.

—Angelina's Baby Sister. Holabird, Katharine. 2006. (Angelina Ballerina Ser.). (ENG.). 32p. (J). (gr. -1-k). 13.99 *(978-0-670-06146-4(8)*, Viking Juvenile) Penguin Publishing Group.

—Angelina's Big City Ballet. Holabird, Katharine. 2014. (Angelina Ballerina Ser.). (ENG.). 32p. (J). (gr. -1-2). 14.99 *(978-0-670-01560-3(1)*, Viking Adult) Penguin Publishing Group.

—Angelina's Birthday. Holabird, Katharine. 2006. (Angelina Ballerina Ser.). (ENG.). 32p. (J). (gr. -1-k). 14.99 *(978-0-670-06057-3(7)*, Viking Juvenile) Penguin Publishing Group.

—Angelina's Christmas. Holabird, Katharine. (Angelina Ballerina Ser.). (ENG.). 32p. (J). (gr. -1-k). 2008. pap. 6.99 *(978-0-14-241192-6(2)*, Puffin); 2006. 13.99 *(978-0-670-06103-7(4)*, Viking Juvenile) Penguin Publishing Group.

—Angelina's Halloween. Holabird, Katharine. 2006. (Angelina Ballerina Ser.). (ENG.). 32p. (J). (gr. -1-k). pap. 6.99 *(978-0-14-240621-2(X)*, Puffin) Penguin Publishing Group.

—Angelina's Perfect Party. Holabird, Katharine. 2011. (Angelina Ballerina Ser.). (ENG.). 24p. (J). (gr. -1-k). pap. 4.99 *(978-0-448-45617-1(6)*, Grosset & Dunlap) Penguin Publishing Group.

—Angelina's Silly Little Sister. Holabird, Katharine. 2007. (Angelina Ballerina Ser.). (ENG.). 32p. (J). (gr. 1-2). pap. 3.99 *(978-0-448-44468-0(2)*, Grosset & Dunlap) Penguin Publishing Group.

—Angelina's Surprise Show. Holabird, Katharine. 2012. (Angelina Ballerina Ser.). (ENG.). 16p. (J). (gr. -1-k). 6.99 *(978-0-448-45879-3(9)*, Grosset & Dunlap) Penguin Publishing Group.

—A Dance of Friendship. Holabird, Katharine. 2006. (Angelina Ballerina Ser.). (ENG.). 24p. (J). (gr. -1-k). 3.99 *(978-0-448-44115-3(2)*, Grosset & Dunlap) Penguin Publishing Group.

—A Day at Miss Lilly's. Holabird, Katharine. 2007. (Angelina Ballerina Ser.). (ENG.). 24p. (J). (gr. -1-1). pap. 4.99 *(978-0-448-44548-9(4)*, Grosset & Dunlap) Penguin Publishing Group.

—A Finder's Magic. Pearce, Philippa. 2009. (ENG.). 128p. (J). (gr. 2-4). 15.99 *(978-0-7636-4072-9(7))* Candlewick Pr.

—The Nutcracker. Holabird, Katharine. 2007. (Angelina Ballerina Ser.). (ENG.). 16p. (J). (gr. -1-2). 5.99 *(978-0-448-44681-3(2)*, Grosset & Dunlap) Penguin Publishing Group.

—The Rose Fairy Princess. Holabird, Katharine. 2006. (Angelina Ballerina Ser.). (ENG.). 24p. (J). (gr. -1-k). pap. 3.99 *(978-0-448-44465-9(8)*, Grosset & Dunlap) Penguin Publishing Group.

—The Shining Star Trophy. Holabird, Katharine. 2011. (Angelina Ballerina Ser.). (ENG.). 24p. (J). (gr. -1-k). pap. 4.99 *(978-0-448-45710-9(5)*, Grosset & Dunlap) Penguin Publishing Group.

—A Very Special Tea Party. Holabird, Katharine. 2007. (Angelina Ballerina Ser.). (ENG.). 16p. (J). (gr. -1-2). 5.99 *(978-0-448-44549-6(2)*, Grosset & Dunlap) Penguin Publishing Group.

—The Yellow House. Morrison, Blake. 2011. (ENG.). 32p. (J). (gr. -1-2). 15.99 *(978-0-7636-4959-3(7))* Candlewick Pr.

Craig, Karen. Be Careful, Friend! Shaw, Natalie. 2010. (Yo Gabba Gabba! Ser.). (ENG.). 26p. (J). (gr. -1 — 1). bds. 5.99 *(978-1-4169-9534-0(X)*, Simon Spotlight) Simon Spotlight.

—Blue's Beach Day. Borkin, Jeff. 2004. (Blue's Clues Ready-to-Read Ser.). (J). (gr. -1-k). lib. bdg. 8.62 *(978-1-4176-2828-5(6)*, Turtleback) Turtleback Bks.

—The Gabba Land Band. Gallo, Tina. 2010. (Yo Gabba Gabba! Ser.). (ENG.). 24p. (J). (gr. -1-k). bds. 3.99 *(978-1-4169-9716-0(4)*, Simon Spotlight) Simon Spotlight.

—One for Me, One for You: A Book about Sharing. Albee, Sarah. 2006. (Blue's Clues Ser.: 20). (ENG.). 24p. (J). (gr. -1-3). pap. 3.99 *(978-1-4169-1300-9(9)*, Simon Spotlight/Nickelodeon) Simon Spotlight/Nickelodeon.

—A Visit to the Firehouse. Tuchman, Lauryn & Silverhardt, Lauryn. 2009. (Blue's Clues Ser.). (ENG.). 24p. (J). (gr. -1-2). pap. 3.99 *(978-1-4169-7193-1(9)*, Simon Spotlight/Nickelodeon) Simon Spotlight/Nickelodeon.

Craig, Megan. Hello Big Red! Aryal, Aimee. 2004. 24p. (J). 19.95 *(978-1-932888-24-9(1))* Mascot Bks., Inc.

—Hello, Hook 'Em! Aryal, Aimee. 2004. 24p. (J). (gr. -1-3). lib. bdg. 19.95 *(978-1-932888-10-2(1))* Mascot Bks., Inc.

—Hello, Pistol Pete! Aryal, Aimee. 2007. 24p. (J). lib. bdg. 14.95 *(978-1-932888-38-6(1))* Mascot Bks., Inc.

—Howdy Reveille! Aryal, Aimee. 2004. 24p. (J). 19.95 *(978-1-932888-18-8(7))* Mascot Bks., Inc.

Craig, Michael. Counting Silly Faces: Numbers Eleven to Twenty. Carig, Michael. 2011. (ENG.). 30p. pap. 11.99 *(978-1-4538-9764-5(X))* CreateSpace Independent Publishing Platform.

Craig, Michael. Counting Silly Faces: Numbers Ninety-One to One-Hundred. Craig, Michael. 2010. (ENG.). 30p. pap. 11.99 *(978-1-4563-2598-5(1))* CreateSpace Independent Publishing Platform.

—Counting Silly Faces Numbers One to Ten: By Michael Richard Craig - Volume One. Craig, Michael. 2010. (ENG.). 30p. pap. 11.99 *(978-1-4538-6909-3(3))* CreateSpace Independent Publishing Platform.

Craigan, Charles J. Mayuk the Grizzly Bear: A Legend of the Sechelt People. braille ed. 2004. (J). (gr. k-3). spiral bd. *(978-0-616-07562-3(6))* Canadian National Institute for the Blind/Institut National Canadien pour les Aveugles.

Crain, Clayton. Carnage: Family Feud. Wells, Zeb. 2011. (ENG.). 168p. (YA). (gr. 8-17). 24.99 *(978-0-7851-5112-8(5))* Marvel Worldwide, Inc.

—Venom vs. Carnage. 2007. (ENG.). 96p. (YA). (gr. 8-17). pap. 9.99 *(978-0-7851-1524-3(2))* Marvel Worldwide, Inc.

Crain, Dale. 100 Bullets - First Shot, Last Call, 13 vols., Vol. 1. Azzarello, Brian. rev. ed. 2006. (100 Bullets Ser.). (ENG.). 128p. pap. 12.99 *(978-1-56389-645-3(1))* DC Comics.

Cramer. A Year Without Dad. Brunson, Jodi. 2003. (J). per. 10.00 *(978-0-9740683-1-2(4))* Authors & Artists Publishers of New York, Inc.

Crane, Ben. Tall Tales of the Wild West: A Humorous Collection of Cowboy Poems & Songs. Ode, Eric. 2007. 32p. *(978-0-88166-524-6(X))* Meadowbrook Pr.

Crane, Devin. Yoda: The Story of a Cat & His Kittens. Stern, Beth. 2014. (ENG.). 32p. (J). (gr. -1-3). 17.99 *(978-1-4814-4407-1(7)*, Simon & Schuster/Paula Wiseman Bks.) Simon & Schuster/Paula Wiseman Bks.

Crane, Eddie. Little Gregory. Bradex, Melissa A. 2009. 32p. pap. 14.99 *(978-1-4490-3549-5(3))* AuthorHouse.

The check digit for ISBN-10 appears in parentheses after the full ISBN-13

Crane, Jordan & Burkert, Nancy E. James & the Giant Peach. Dahl, Roald. 2011. (Penguin Classics Deluxe Edition Ser.). (ENG.). 160p. (gr. 12). 15.00 *(978-0-14-310634-0(1)*, Penguin Classics) Penguin Publishing Group.

Crane, Noelle L. The Clever Pug. Crane, Noelle L. 2013. 66p. pap. 9.99 *(978-0-9846119-8-0(3))* Pluriverse Publishing.

Crane, Walter. Beauty & the Beast. Beaumont, Jeanne Marie Le Prince De. 2013. 28p. pap. *(978-1-909115-62-0(2))* Planet, The.

—Beauty & the Beast: Beauty & the Beast a Tale for the Entertainment of Juvenile Readers. Beaumont, Jeanne-Marie Leprince De. 2010. (ENG.). 24p. pap. 9.95 *(978-1-4505-9898-9(6))* CreateSpace Independent Publishing Platform.

—The Children's Plutarch: Tales of the Romans. Gould, F. J. 2012. 260p. *(978-1-78139-160-0(2))* Benediction Classics.

—Jack & the Beanstalk. Jacobs, Joseph. 2013. 20p. pap. *(978-1-909115-63-7(0))* Planet, The.

Crane, Walter, et al. Mother Goose's Nursery Rhymes: A Collection of Alphabets, Rhymes, Tales, & Jingles. 2010. (ENG.). 324p. (gr. -1-k). pap. 19.95 *(978-1-4290-9005-6(7))* Applewood Bks.

Crane, Walter. Mr Michael Mouse Unfolds His Tale. 2011. 36p. pap. 35.95 *(978-1-258-07891-1(0))* Literary Licensing, LLC.

Crane-Yvon, Marie. Caring for Mama Bear: A Story of Love. Laflamme, Essie. 2010. 56p. (J). pap. 7.95 *(978-0-9816219-1-3(0))* Quality of Life Publishing Co.

Craner, Ben. I Can Be a Missionary, Too. Craner, Ben, tr. 2003. (J). *(978-1-57008-965-7(5))* Deseret Bk. Co.

Cranford, Darren. Aerial: A Spider's Tale. ReWalt, Nancy E. 2009. 32p. (J). 16.95 *(978-0-9821110-0-0(2))* Ronan Enterprises, Inc.

—Aerial: A Trip to Remember. ReWalt, Nancy E. 2010. 32p. (J). 16.95 *(978-0-9821110-1-7(0))* Ronan Enterprises, Inc.

—Aerial Meets Farmer Fedamore. Rewalt, Nancy E. 2012. 64p. (J). 17.95 *(978-0-9821110-3-1(7))* Ronan Enterprises, Inc.

—Jeep: The Coyote Who Flew in World War II. Moller, Sharon Chickering. 2014. (J). pap. 9.95 *(978-0-9860799-0-0(1))* Chickering-Moller Project.

—Lost & Found: Goldilocks & the Three Bears Revisited. Rewalt, Nancy E. 2012. 64p. (J). pap. 6.95 *(978-0-9821110-2-4(9))* Ronan Enterprises, Inc.

—PawPrints on Your Heart. White, Becky. 2013. 64p. (J). 18.95 *(978-0-9860169-0-5(X))* Vision Chapters Publishing Co.

Crangle, Claudine. Woolfred Does Not Eat Dandelions. 2014. (J). *(978-1-4338-1672-7(5))*; pap. *(978-1-4338-1673-4(3))* American Psychological Assn. (Magination Pr.).

Crank, Donny. Cluck, Cluck, Cluck Splash! Kruse, Donald W. 2012. 48p. pap. 12.95 *(978-1-59663-856-3(7)*, Castle Keep Pr.) Rock, James A. & Co. Pubs.

—Fleas, Please. Kruse, Donald W. 2012. 48p. pap. 12.95 *(978-1-59663-858-7(3)*, Castle Keep Pr.) Rock, James A. & Co. Pubs.

—Jasper Has Left the Building! Kruse, Donald W. 2013. 50p. pap. 12.95 *(978-1-59663-863-1(X)*, Castle Keep Pr.) Rock, James A. & Co. Pubs.

—There's a Goof on My Roof. Kruse, Donald W. 2012. 48p. pap. 12.95 *(978-1-59663-855-6(9)*, Castle Keep Pr.) Rock, James A. & Co. Pubs.

Cratty, Aaron. The Stuff in the Back of the Desk. Brink, LeeAnn. 2006. 24p. (J). per. 10.95 *(978-1-934246-05-4(0))* Peppertree Pr., The.

Cravath, Lynne Avril. Amazing You! Getting Smart about Your Private Parts. Saltz, Gail. (ENG.). 32p. (J). (gr. -1-2). 2008. pap. 6.99 *(978-0-14-241058-5(6)*, Puffin); 2005. 16.99 *(978-0-525-47389-3(0)*, Dutton Juvenile) Penguin Publishing Group.

—Big Max & the Mystery of the Missing Giraffe. Platt, Kin. (I Can Read Book 2 Ser.). 64p. (J). 2006. (ENG.). (gr. k-3). pap. 3.99 *(978-0-06-009920-6(8))*; 2005. (gr. -1). 15.99 *(978-0-06-009918-3(6))*; 2005. (gr. -1 — 1). lib. bdg. 17.89 *(978-0-06-009919-0(4))* HarperCollins Pubs.

—Changing You! A Guide to Body Changes & Sexuality. Saltz, Gail. 2009. (ENG.). 32p. (J). (gr. 1-3). pap. 6.99 *(978-0-14-241479-8(4)*, Puffin) Penguin Publishing Group.

—Love, Ruby Valentine. Friedman, Laurie. 2006. (ENG.). 32p. (J). (gr. k-3). lib. bdg. 16.95 *(978-1-57505-899-3(5)*, Carolrhoda Bks.) Lerner Publishing Group.

—The Twelve Days of Christmas in Louisiana. Cassels, Jean. 2007. (Twelve Days of Christmas in America Ser.). (ENG.). 32p. (J). (gr. k-3). 12.95 *(978-1-4027-3814-2(5))* Sterling Publishing Co., Inc.

Cravath, Lynne Avril & Avril, Lynne. The Show-and-Tell Lion. Abercrombie, Barbara. 2006. (ENG.). 32p. (J). (gr. -1-2). 17.99 *(978-0-689-86408-7(6)*, McElderry, Margaret K. Bks.) McElderry, Margaret K. Bks.

Craven, Josh. Hayrides. Craven, Josh. 2011. 16p. pap. 24.95 *(978-1-4626-1123-2(0))* America Star Bks.

Crawford, Alice. Splish, Splat!, 1 vol. Domney, Alexis. 2011. (ENG.). 24p. (J). (gr. 1-3). 15.95 *(978-1-897187-88-3(2))* Second Story Pr. CAN. Dist: Orca Bk. Pubs. USA.

Crawford, Andy, photos by. Bread & Pizza. Blake, Susannah. 2009. (Make & Eat Ser.). 24p. (J). (gr. 3-5). 25.25 *(978-1-4358-2858-2(5)*, PowerKids Pr.) Rosen Publishing Group, Inc., The.

—Cookies & Cakes. Blake, Susannah. 2009. (Make & Eat Ser.). 24p. (J). (gr. 3-5). 25.25 *(978-1-4358-2859-9(3)*, PowerKids Pr.) Rosen Publishing Group, Inc., The.

—Eyewitness Books - Crime & Detection. Lane, Brian et al. 2005. (DK Eyewitness Bks.). (ENG.). 72p. (J). (gr. 3-7). 16.99 *(978-0-7566-1386-0(8))* Dorling Kindersley Publishing, Inc.

—Sandwiches & Snacks. Blake, Susannah. 2009. (Make & Eat Ser.). 24p. (J). (gr. 5). 25.25 *(978-1-4358-2857-5(7)*, PowerKids Pr.) Rosen Publishing Group, Inc., The.

—This Is My Dump Truck. Oxlade, Chris. 2008. (Mega Machine Drivers Ser.). 30p. (J). (gr. 4-8). lib. bdg. 28.50 *(978-1-59771-105-0(5))* Sea-To-Sea Pubns.

—Vegetarian Food. Blake, Susannah. 2009. (Make & Eat Ser.). 24p. (J). (gr. 3-5). 25.25 *(978-1-4358-2860-5(7)*, PowerKids Pr.) Rosen Publishing Group, Inc., The.

Crawford, Andy, photos by. Fun with Opposites. Crawford, Andy. (J). pap. 9.99 *(978-0-590-24640-8(2))* Scholastic, Inc.

Crawford, Dale. Tales of Tails from the Blue Heron Ranch, Grandbear the Storyteller. 2nd l.t. ed. 2003. 128p. (J). per. 12.00 *(978-0-9729759-0-2(X))* Guru Graphics.

Crawford, Elizabeth. Cave: An Evocation of the Beginnings of Art. Hirose, George, photos by. Lewis, Richard. 2003. 56p. pap. 14.00 *(978-1-929299-03-4(6))* Touchstone Ctr. Pubns.

Crawford, Greg. The Flying Mouse. Otten, Charlotte. 2014. (ENG.). 32p. (J). 17.95 *(978-1-59373-152-6(3))* Bunker Hill Publishing, Inc.

Crawford, Gregory. I Can Show You I Care: Compassionate Touch for Children. Cotta, Susan. 2003. (ENG.). 32p. (J). (gr. k-4). 18.95 *(978-1-55643-433-4(2))* North Atlantic Bks.

Crawford, Gregory. Harriet's Hairballs. Crawford, Gregory, tr. Chin, Oliver Clyde. 2003. 32p. (J). 15.95 *(978-1-58394-078-5(2)*, Frog Ltd.) North Atlantic Bks.

Crawford, K. Trouble in Troublesome Creek. Allen, Nancy. 2011. (ENG.). 32p. (gr. -1-3). pap. 11.95 *(978-1-933176-36-9(9))* Red Rock Pr., Inc.

Crawford, K. Michael. The Munched-up Flower Garden. 2006. (Troublesome Creek Kids Story Ser.). (ENG.). 32p. (J). (gr. -1-3). 16.95 *(978-1-933176-04-8(0))*; pap. 10.95 *(978-1-933176-06-2(7))* Red Rock Pr., Inc.

—Trouble in Troublesome Creek: A Troublesome Creek Kids Story. Allen, Nancy Kelly. 2010. (ENG.). 32p. (J). (gr. -1-3). 16.95 *(978-1-933176-32-1(6))* Red Rock Pr., Inc.

Crawford, K. Michael. The Mystery of Journeys Crowne-an Adventure Drawing Game. Crawford, K. Michael. 2008. 52p. pap. 14.95 *(978-0-9817940-0-6(9))* Virtualbookworm.com Publishing, Inc.

Crawford, Mel. Dale Evans & the Lost Gold Mine. Hill, Monica. 2011. 32p. pap. 35.95 *(978-1-258-01715-6(6))* Literary Licensing, LLC.

—Gene Autry. Fletcher, Steffi. 2011. 32p. pap. 35.95 *(978-1-258-02076-7(9))* Literary Licensing, LLC.

—Rin Tin Tin & the Outlaw. Verral, Charles Spain. 2011. 28p. pap. 35.95 *(978-1-258-04034-5(4))* Literary Licensing, LLC.

—Roy Rogers & Cowboy Toby. Beecher, Elizabeth. 2011. 30p. 35.95 *(978-1-258-03514-3(6))* Literary Licensing, LLC.

Crawford, Mel, jt. illus. see Helweg, Hans.

Crawford, Robert. The Legend of the Old Man of the Mountain. Ortakales, Denise. 2004. (Legends Ser.). (ENG.). 40p. (J). 17.95 *(978-1-58536-236-3(0))* Sleeping Bear Pr.

—T Is for Taj Mahal: An India Alphabet. Bajaj, Varsha. 2011. (Discover the World Ser.). (ENG.). 40p. (J). (gr. k-6). 17.95 *(978-1-58536-504-3(1))* Sleeping Bear Pr.

Crawley, Annie. Plastic, Ahoy! Investigating the Great Pacific Garbage Patch. Newman, Patricia. 2014. (ENG.). 48p. (gr. 3-6). lib. bdg. 30.60 *(978-1-4677-1283-5(3)*, Millbrook Pr.) Lerner Publishing Group.

Creagh, Lachlan. Ambush at Cisco Swamp. Irwin, Robert & Wells, Jack. 2014. (Robert Irwin Dinosaur Hunter Ser.: 2). (ENG.). 92p. (J). (gr. 2-4). 7.99 *(978-1-86471-846-1(3))* Random Hse. Australia AUS. Dist: Independent Pubs. Group.

—Armoured Defence. Irwin, Robert & Wells, Jack. 2014. (Robert Irwin Dinosaur Hunter Ser.: 3). (ENG.). 90p. (J). (gr. 2-4). 7.99 *(978-1-74275-091-0(5))* Random Hse. Australia AUS. Dist: Independent Pubs. Group.

—The Dinosaur Feather. Irwin, Robert & Wells, Jack. 2014. (Robert Irwin Dinosaur Hunter Ser.: 4). (ENG.). 90p. (J). (gr. 2-4). 7.99 *(978-1-74275-092-7(3))* Random Hse. Australia AUS. Dist: Independent Pubs. Group.

—The Discovery. Irwin, Robert & Wells, Jack. 2014. (Robert Irwin Dinosaur Hunter Ser.: 1). (ENG.). 92p. (J). (gr. 2-4). 9.95 *(978-1-86471-845-4(5))* Random Hse. Australia AUS. Dist: Independent Pubs. Group.

Creamer, Joan Klatil. The Magic Sceptre - the Legend of Blue Santa Claus. Creamer, Joan Klatil. ed. 2006. (J). 16.95 *(978-0-9778476-3-1(2))* Silver Snowflake Publishing.

Creative Illustrations Studio & Good Times At Home LLC. The Night Before Christmas. Moore, Clement C. & Curto Family, The. 2012. (J). pap. 9.99 *(978-0-9840338-5-0(8))* Good Times at Home LLC.

Creek, Chris. Who Is This Jesus? A Hidden Picture Book. Creek, Lorie. 2012. (J). 18.99 *(978-1-60908-909-2(X))* Deseret Bk. Co.

Crehore, Amy. Machu Picchu: The Story of the Amazing Inkas & Their City in the Clouds. Mann, Elizabeth. 2006. (Wonders of the World Book Ser.). (ENG.). 48p. (J). (gr. 4-8). pap. 12.95 *(978-1-931414-10-4(6)*, 9781931414104) Mikaya Pr.

Crème, Aurora C. Two Tipsy Tots, 1 vol. Arnold, Ginger Fudge. 2009. 32p. pap. 24.95 *(978-1-4489-1891-1(X))* America Star Bks.

Cremeans, Robert. La Colonia de Arco Iris. Tiller, Steve. Date not set. (SPA.). (J). 15.95 *(978-1-932317-02-2(3))* Right Stuff Kids Bks.

—Connectada al Corazon. Tiller, Steve. Date not set. (SPA.). (J). 15.95 *(978-1-932317-01-5(5))* Right Stuff Kids Bks.

Crenshaw, Derek. The Dinosaurs Went Marching On. Acopiado, Ginger. 2007. 24p. (J). pap. 4.95 *(978-0-9729093-1-0(1))* Tike Time, Inc.

Cress, Michelle H. Families. Cook, Barbara L. l.t. ed. 2004. (HRL Board Book Ser.). 8p. (J). (gr. -1-1). pap. 10.95 *(978-1-57332-280-5(6)*, HighReach Learning, Incorporated) Carson-Dellosa Publishing, LLC.

—Jonah Starts School. Mullican, Judy. l.t. ed. 2003. (HRL Big Book Ser.). 8p. (J). (gr. -1-1). pap. 10.95 *(978-1-57332-268-3(7))*; pap. 10.95 *(978-1-57332-269-0(5))* Carson-Dellosa Publishing, LLC. (HighReach Learning, Incorporated).

Cressey, Roger. Owliviah. Winbolt-Lewis, Martin. 2013. 56p. (J). pap. *(978-1-78222-075-6(5))* Paragon Publishing, Rothersthorpe.

Cressey, Roger. The Talking Giraffe. Cressey, Roger. 2013. 118p. pap. *(978-1-78222-143-2(3))* Paragon Publishing, Rothersthorpe.

Cressy, Mike. The Legend of Atlantis, 1 vol. Troupe, Thomas Kingsley. 2012. (Legend Has It Ser.). (ENG.). 32p. (gr. 2-4). lib. bdg. 26.65 *(978-1-4048-6656-0(6))*, Nonfiction Picture Bks.) Picture Window Bks.

Crestan, David. Welcome to School: Helping Friends with Autism. James, Colin & Newton, Jennifer, photos by. Barrette, Melanie. James, Colin, ed. 2005. 16p. (J). (gr. k-6). pap. 12.00 *(978-1-928598-11-4(0))* Pyramid Educational Products, Inc.

Crevel, Helena. Moi, Elle & la le, Poodle Triplets Go Glam. Poulter, J. R. 2014. 38p. pap. 20.99 ***(978-1-63122-475-1(1))*** Tate Publishing & Enterprises, LLC.

Crewe, Robert. Michael & the Can of Lemon Spray. Clarke, Ashanti. 2011. (ENG.). 24p. pap. 9.50 *(978-1-4636-3021-8(2))* CreateSpace Independent Publishing Platform.

Crews, Donald. How Many Blue Birds Flew Away? A Counting Book with a Difference. Giganti, Paul. 2005. 32p. (J). lib. bdg. 16.89 *(978-0-06-000763-8(X))* HarperCollins Pubs.

Crews, Donald. Los Diez Puntos Negros. Crews, Donald. 2009. (SPA & ENG.). 32p. (J). (gr. -1-k). 16.99 *(978-0-06-177138-5(4)*, Greenwillow Bks.) HarperCollins Pubs.

—Freight Train. Crews, Donald. 2003. 24p. (J). (SPA & ENG.). lib. bdg., bds. 16.89 *(978-0-06-056203-8(X))*; (ENG.). (gr. -1-3). 16.99 *(978-0-688-80165-6(X)*, Greenwillow Bks.); (ENG.). (gr. -1-3). pap. 6.99 *(978-0-688-11701-6(5)*, Greenwillow Bks.) HarperCollins Pubs.

—Freight Train/Tren de Carga. Crews, Donald. (SPA & ENG.). 24p. (J). (gr. -1-3). 2008. pap. 7.99 *(978-0-06-056204-5(8))*; 2003. 16.99 *(978-0-06-056202-1(1))* HarperCollins Pubs. (Greenwillow Bks.).

—Ten Black Dots Board Book. Crews, Donald. 2010. (ENG.). 32p. (J). (gr. -1-3). bds. 7.99 *(978-0-06-185779-9(3)*, Greenwillow Bks.) HarperCollins Pubs.

Crews, Nina. Jack & the Beanstalk. Crews, Nina. 2011. (ENG.). 32p. (J). (gr. -1-2). 16.99 *(978-0-8050-8765-9(6)*, Holt, Henry & Co. Bks. For Young Readers) Holt, Henry & Co.

—Neighborhood Mother Goose. Crews, Nina. 2003. (ENG.). 64p. (J). (gr. -1-3). 17.99 *(978-0-06-051573-7(2)*, Greenwillow Bks.) HarperCollins Pubs.

—The Neighborhood Sing-Along. Crews, Nina. 2011. (ENG.). 64p. (J). (gr. -1-3). 17.99 *(978-0-06-185063-9(2)*, Greenwillow Bks.) HarperCollins Pubs.

Creyts, Patrick. Easter Extras: Faith-Filled Ideas for Easter Week. Schultz, Joani et al. 2007. 24p. pap. 6.99 *(978-0-7644-3694-9(5))* Group Publishing, Inc.

Crichlow, Ernest. Forever Free: The Story of the Emancipation Proclamation. Sterling, Dorothy. 2012. 216p. 44.95 *(978-1-258-25034-8(9))*; pap. 29.95 *(978-1-258-25547-3(2))* Literary Licensing, LLC.

Crilley, Mark. Autumn. Crilley, Mark. 2007. (Miki Falls Ser.: 3). (ENG.). 176p. (YA). (gr. 8-12). pap. 8.99 *(978-0-06-084618-3(6))* HarperCollins Pubs.

—Brody's Ghost Volume 6. Crilley, Mark. 2015. (ENG.). 112p. pap. 7.99 *(978-1-61655-461-3(4))* Dark Horse Comics.

—Spring. Crilley, Mark. 2007. (Miki Falls Ser.: 1). (ENG.). 176p. (YA). (gr. 8-12). pap. 8.99 *(978-0-06-084616-9(X))* HarperCollins Pubs.

—Summer. Crilley, Mark. 2007. (Miki Falls Ser.: 2). (ENG.). 176p. (YA). (gr. 8-12). pap. 8.99 *(978-0-06-084617-6(8))* HarperCollins Pubs.

—Winter. Crilley, Mark. 2008. (Miki Falls Ser.: 4). (ENG.). 176p. (YA). (gr. 8-12). pap. 8.99 *(978-0-06-084619-0(4))* HarperCollins Pubs.

Crimi-Trent, Ellen. Kitty's Color Activity Book. Priddy, Roger. 2014. (Schoolies Ser.). (ENG.). 76p. (J). (gr. -1-1). pap. 6.99 *(978-0-312-51675-8(4)*, Priddy Bks.) St. Martin's Pr.

—Schoolies: Time for Recess. Priddy, Roger. 2014. (Schoolies Ser.). (ENG.). 28p. (J). (gr. -1-1). 4.99 *(978-0-312-51661-1(4)*, Priddy Bks.) St. Martin's Pr.

—The Talent Show. Priddy, Roger. 2014. (Schoolies Ser.). (ENG.). 28p. (J). (gr. -1-1). 4.99 *(978-0-312-51664-2(9)*, Priddy Bks.) St. Martin's Pr.

Crip. Dance Class - African Folk Fever. Beka. 2012. (Dance Class Graphic Novels Ser.: 3). (ENG.). 48p. (J). 10.99 *(978-1-59707-363-9(6))* Papercutz.

—Dance Class #6: a Merry Olde Christmas. Beka. 2013. (Dance Class Graphic Novels Ser.: 6). (ENG.). 48p. (J). (gr. 1-6). 10.99 *(978-1-59707-442-1(X))* Papercutz.

—A Funny Thing Happened on the Way to Paris..., No. 4. Beka. 2013. (Dance Class Graphic Novels Ser.: 4). (ENG.). 48p. (J). (gr. 1-7). 10.99 *(978-1-59707-384-4(9))* Papercutz.

—Romeo & Juliets. Beka. 2012. (Dance Class Graphic Novels Ser.: 2). (ENG.). 48p. (J). 10.99 *(978-1-59707-317-2(2))* Papercutz.

—So, You Think You Can Hip-Hop?, No. 1. Beka. 2012. (Dance Class Graphic Novels Ser.: 1). (ENG.). 48p. (J). 10.99 *(978-1-59707-254-0(0))* Papercutz.

—To Russia, with Love. Beka. 2013. (Dance Class Graphic Novels Ser.: 5). (ENG.). 48p. (J). (gr. 1-6). 10.99 *(978-1-59707-423-0(3))* Papercutz.

Crisenbery, Casey. Ringo the Helpful Raccoon. Kelley, Khris. 2012. 38p. (J). 14.95 *(978-1-937406-70-7(9))* Mascot Bks., Inc.

Crisp, Dan. The Ants Go Marching. 2007. (Classic Books with Holes Soft Cover Ser.). (ENG.). (J). 16p. pap. *(978-1-84643-105-0(0))*; 14p. bds. *(978-1-84643-109-8(3))* Child's Play International Ltd.

—The Ants Go Marching! (Classic Books with Holes Ser.). (ENG.). 16p. (gr. -1). 2013. pap. incl. audio compact disk *(978-1-84643-622-2(2))*; 2009. (J). *(978-1-84643-207-1(3))* Child's Play International Ltd.

—Ants Go Marching W/ 2009. (Classic Books with Holes US Soft Cover with CD Ser.). (ENG.). 16p. (J). *(978-1-84643-256-9(1))* Child's Play International Ltd.

—A Bright New Star: With Color-Changing Star Light. Ranson, Erin. 2007. (Story Book Ser.). 16p. (J). (gr. -1-3). bds. *(978-1-84666-161-7(7)*, Tide Mill Pr.) Top That! Publishing PLC.

—Busy Bus. Brooks, Felicity & Durber, Matt. 2007. (Play Bks). 10p. (J). bds. 10.99 *(978-0-7945-1701-4(3)*, Usborne) EDC Publishing.

—Busy Truck. Allen, Francesca & Brooks, Felicity. 2007. (Usborne Play Bks.). 10p. (J). (gr. -1-k). bds. 10.99 *(978-0-7945-1453-2(7)*, Usborne) EDC Publishing.

—CityBLOCKS Stacking Blocks. Smartink Books Staff. 2011. (ENG.). 10p. (J). (gr. -1-17). 21.99 *(978-1-4521-0275-7(9))* Chronicle Bks. LLC.

—Farmer Jill, 1 vol. Dale, Jay. 2012. (Wonder Words Ser.). (ENG.). 32p. (gr. k-2). pap. 5.99 *(978-1-4296-8926-7(9)*, Engage Literacy) Capstone Pr., Inc.

—Five Little Men in a Flying Saucer. 2005. (Classic Books with Holes Board Book Ser.). (ENG.). (J). 14p. bds. *(978-1-904550-58-7(4))*; 16p. pap. *(978-1-904550-30-3(4))* Child's Play International Ltd.

—London: A Colourful City. 2012. (ENG.). 20p. (J). (gr. -1 — 1). bds. 9.99 *(978-1-4052-6468-6(3))* Egmont Bks., Ltd. GBR. Dist: Independent Pubs. Group.

Crisp, Dan. Santa's Missing Reindeer. Crisp, Dan. 2011. (ENG.). 12p. (J). (gr. -1-k). 12.99 *(978-0-230-71291-1(6))* Macmillan Pubs., Ltd. GBR. Dist: Independent Pubs. Group.

Crispin, Gerald W. God Speaks Through Dreams: But Who's Listening?, No. 1. Crispin, Gerald W., photos by. Crispin, Vera G., ed. unabr. ed. 2003. 160p. (gr. 10-18). reprint ed. pap. 19.95 *(978-0-9744015-1-5(X))* Benchmark Book Craft.

Crissey, Noah. The Loneliest Christmas Tree. Crissey, Brian. 2004. 32p. (J). bds. 25.00 *(978-1-893183-35-3(1)*, 598) Granite Publishing, LLC.

—The Loneliest Christmas Tree. Crissey, Brian L. 2004. (J). *(978-1-930724-12-9(8))*; *(978-1-930724-13-6(6))* Granite Publishing, LLC.

—Personal Hygiene? What's That Got to Do with Me? Crissey, Pat. 2004. (ENG.). 96p. pap. 19.95 *(978-1-84310-796-5(1))* Kingsley, Jessica Ltd. GBR. Dist: Univ. of Toronto Pr.

Crittenden, Nina Victor. Cedric & the Dragon. Raum, Elizabeth. 2010. (J). *(978-1-934617-05-2(9)*, Alma Little) Elva Resa Publishing, LLC.

Crockett-Blassingame, Linda. See the Ocean. 2006. 32p. (J). 14.95 *(978-0-9778143-0-5(0))* Inclusive Books LLC.

Crockett, Linda. Of Corn Silk & Black Braids. Johnson, Vincent L. 2005. 32p. (J). (gr. k-3). 17.95 *(978-0-9657033-2-1(0))* Marzetta Bks.

Crockett, Robert. Poetry for Young People: the Seasons. Serio, John N., ed. 2014. (Poetry for Young People Ser.). (ENG.). 48p. (J). (gr. 3). 14.95 *(978-1-4549-1347-4(9))* Sterling Publishing Co., Inc.

—The Seasons. Serio, John N., ed. 2005. (Poetry for Young People Ser.). (ENG.). 48p. (J). (gr. 3-7). 14.95 *(978-1-4027-1254-8(5))* Sterling Publishing Co., Inc.

Croft, James. Mouse Has Fun Big Book: Brand New Readers. Root, Phyllis. 2009. (Brand New Readers Ser.). (ENG.). 48p. (J). (gr. -1-3). pap. 24.99 *(978-0-7636-4209-9(6))* Candlewick Pr.

—Surprising Sharks. Davies, Nicola. 2008. (Read, Listen, & Wonder Ser.). (ENG.). 32p. (J). (gr. -1-3). pap. 8.99 *(978-0-7636-3837-5(4))* Candlewick Pr.

—Surprising Sharks: Read & Wonder. Davies, Nicola. 2005. (Read & Wonder Ser.). (ENG.). 32p. (J). (gr. -1-3). reprint ed. pap. 6.99 *(978-0-7636-2742-3(9))* Candlewick Pr.

Croft, James Lee. Meet Gator: A Picture Clues Touch & Feel Book. DePrisco, Dorothea. 2005. (Learn to Read Ser.). 10p. (J). (gr. -1-18). 10.95 *(978-1-58117-123-5(4)*, Intervisual/Piggy Toes) Bendon, Inc.

Croissant-Madden, Gayle. My Wild, Wild Hair! Croissant-Madden, Gayle. 2006. (J). 10.00 *(978-0-9786478-0-3(7))* airjam.com.

Croll, Carolyn. Cheerios Count to 100. Fontes, Justine. 2005. *(978-0-439-70341-3(7))* Scholastic, Inc.

—The Story of Christmas. ed. 2008. (ENG.). 96p. (gr. k-12). 15.95 *(978-0-7611-5250-7(4)*, 15250) Workman Publishing Co., Inc.

Croll, Carolyn. What Will the Weather Be? DeWitt, Lynda. 2015. (Let's-Read-And-Find-Out Science 2 Ser.). (ENG.). 32p. (J). (gr. -1-3). pap. 6.99 ***(978-0-06-238198-9(9))*** HarperCollins Pubs.

Cromwell, Danielle. My Ten Cents. Young, T. M. Victoria Washington and Carla Watts, ed. 2013. 24p. pap. 24.95 *(978-1-4626-5790-2(7))* America Star Bks.

—Playing Church. Young, T. M. Washington, Victoria, ed. 2012. 32p. pap. 24.95 *(978-1-4626-7883-9(1))* America Star Bks.

—What's Love Got to Do with It. Young, T. M. Vickie Washington and Carla Watts, ed. 2013. 32p. pap. 24.95 *(978-1-4626-0889-8(2))* America Star Bks.

Cronin, Janet. The Cow Party: A Story about Love (and Dancing!) Andreae, Giles & World Of Happy Staff. 2013. (World of Happy Ser.). (ENG.). 32p. (J). (gr. -1-k). pap. 5.99 *(978-1-4052-5842-5(X))* Egmont Bks., Ltd. GBR. Dist: Independent Pubs. Group.

—The Dance of Wallowy Bigness. Andreae, Giles & World Of Happy Staff. 2013. (World of Happy Ser.). (ENG.). 32p. (J). (gr. -1-k). pap. 5.99 *(978-1-4052-5839-5(X))* Egmont Bks., Ltd. GBR. Dist: Independent Pubs. Group.

—The Dog Machine. Andreae, Giles & World Of Happy Staff. 2013. (World of Happy Ser.). (ENG.). 32p. (J). (gr. -1-k). pap. 5.99 *(978-1-4052-5841-8(1))* Egmont Bks., Ltd. GBR. Dist: Independent Pubs. Group.

—The Elephant & the Spider. Andreae, Giles & World Of Happy Staff. 2013. (World of Happy Ser.). (ENG.). 32p. (J). (gr. -1-k). pap. 5.99 *(978-1-4052-5848-7(9))* Egmont Bks., Ltd. GBR. Dist: Independent Pubs. Group.

—The Knitting Gorilla. Andreae, Giles & World Of Happy Staff. 2013. (World of Happy Ser.). (ENG.). 32p. (J). (gr. -1-k). pap. 5.99 *(978-1-4052-5846-3(2))* Egmont Bks., Ltd. GBR. Dist: Independent Pubs. Group.

—The Ministry of Niceness. Andreae, Giles & World Of Happy Staff. 2013. (World of Happy Ser.). (ENG.). 32p. (J). (gr.

C

-1-k). pap. 5.99 *(978-1-4052-5843-2(8))* Egmont Bks., Ltd. GBR. Dist: Independent Pubs. Group.

—The Pink Cricket. Andreae, Giles & World Of Happy Staff. 2013. (World of Happy Ser.). (ENG.). 32p. (J). (gr. -1-k). pap. 5.99 *(978-1-4052-5840-1(3))* Egmont Bks., Ltd. GBR. Dist: Independent Pubs. Group.

—Planet of the Bears. Andreae, Giles & World Of Happy Staff. 2013. (World of Happy Ser.). (ENG.). 32p. (J). (gr. -1-k). pap. 5.99 *(978-1-4052-5845-6(4))* Egmont Bks., Ltd. GBR. Dist: Independent Pubs. Group.

—Tortoise Football. Andreae, Giles & World Of Happy Staff. 2011. (World of Happy Ser.). (ENG.). 32p. (J). (gr. -1-k). pap. 5.99 *(978-1-4052-5850-0(0))* Egmont Bks., Ltd. GBR. Dist: Independent Pubs. Group.

—Two Monkeys. Andreae, Giles & World Of Happy Staff. 2013. (World of Happy Ser.). (ENG.). 32p. (J). (gr. -1-k). pap. 5.99 *(978-1-4052-5844-9(6))* Egmont Bks., Ltd. GBR. Dist: Independent Pubs. Group.

Cronin, Laurie. Oliver's Surprise: A Boy, a Schooner, & the Great Hurricane of 1938. Cronin, Carol Newman. rev. ed. 2009. (ENG.). 150p. (J). (gr. 4-7). pap. 9.95 *(978-1-934848-62-3(X))* GemmaMedia.

Cronin, Laurie Ann. Cape Cod Surprise: Oliver Matches Wits with Hurricane Carol. Cronin, Carol Newman. 2010. (ENG.). 150p. (J). pap. 9.95 *(978-1-934848-47-0(6))* GemmaMedia.

Croom, Terry. Grandma's Here. 2013. 20p. (J). pap. 9.99 *(978-0-9888650-2-0(5))* Soar Publishing, LLC.

Crosby, Jeff. Brave Cloelia: Retold from the Account in the History of Early Rome by the Roman Historian Titus Livius. Curry, Jane Louise & Livy. 2004. (ENG.). 34p. 17.95 *(978-0-89236-763-4(6))* Oxford Univ. Pr., Inc.

—Otis Steele & the Taileebone: A Southern Tall Tale, 1 vol. McDermott, Tom. 2013. (ENG.). 32p. (J). (gr. 2-2). 16.99 *(978-1-4556-1736-4(9))* Pelican Publishing Co., Inc.

Crosby, Jeff. Wiener Wolf. Crosby, Jeff. 2011. (ENG.). 32p. (J). (gr. -1-2). 15.99 *(978-1-4231-3983-6(6))* Hyperion Pr.

Crosby, Jeff & Jackson, Shelley Ann. Little Lions, Bull Baiters & Hunting Hounds: A History of Dog Breeds. Crosby, Jeff & Jackson, Shelley Ann. 2008. (ENG.). 72p. (J). (gr. k-12). 19.95 *(978-0-88776-815-6(6))* Tundra Bks. CAN. Dist: Random Hse., Inc.

Crosby, Jeff, jt. illus. see Jackson, Shelley Ann.

Crosby, Jeff, jt. illus. see Jackson, Shelley.

Crosier, Mike. Climate Change: Discover How It Impacts Spaceship Earth. Sneideman, Joshua & Twamley, Erin. 2015. (Build It Yourself Ser.). (ENG.). 128p. (gr. 3-7). 22.95 *(978-1-61930-269-3(1))* Nomad Pr.

—Entrepreneurship: Create Your Own Business. Kahan, Alex. 2014. (Build It Yourself Ser.). (ENG.). 128p. (J). (gr. 3-7). pap. 17.95 *(978-1-61930-265-5(9))* Nomad Pr.

Cross, Chris. Nothing to Lose. David, Peter. 2003. (Captain Marvel Ser.). 144p. (YA). pap. 12.99 *(978-0-7851-1104-7(2))* Marvel Worldwide, Inc.

Cross, James. Dancing Fruit Put on a Show! Wilkes, Ruth. 2013. 48p. 18.99 *(978-1-62314-797-6(2))* Willow Publishing.

Cross, Jo Ellen. Remembering to Breathe. Chisolm, Melinda. 2009. 31p. pap. 24.95 *(978-1-60703-914-3(1))* America Star Bks.

Cross, Kevin. A Little Dachshund's Tale. Jean, April. 2012. 36p. pap. 9.95 *(978-1-61897-367-2(3)*, Strategic Bk. Publishing) Strategic Book Publishing & Rights Agency (SBPRA).

Cross, Neal. G Is for Georgia. Sullivan, E. J. 2006. 24p. (J). *(978-1-58173-524-6(3))* Sweetwater Pr.

—T Is for Tennessee. Sullivan, E. J. 2007. (State Alphabet Bks.). 24p. (J). (gr. -1-3). *(978-1-58173-527-7(8))* Sweetwater Pr.

Crossett, Warren. The Sound of the Sea. Harvey, Jacqueline. 2005. 32p. (J). *(978-0-7344-0742-9(4)*, Lothian Children's Bks.) Hachette Australia.

Crossland, Caroline. Cinderella. Umansky, Kaye. 2012. *(978-0-88734-072-7(5))* Players Pr., Inc.

—The Emperor's New Clothes. Umansky, Kaye. 2012. *(978-0-88734-074-1(1))* Players Pr., Inc.

—Sleeping Beauty. Umansky, Kaye. 2003. (Plays & Play Collections). (ENG.). 48p. (J). pap. 15.00 *(978-0-7136-5371-7(X)*, A & C Black) Bloomsbury Publishing Plc GBR. Dist: Players Pr., Inc.

—Sleeping Beauty. Umansky, Kaye. 2012. *(978-0-88734-070-3(9))* Players Pr., Inc.

Crossley, David. ABC. 2004. (Baby's First Learning Ser.). 12p. (J). bds. 4.99 *(978-1-85854-890-6(X))* Brimax Books Ltd. GBR. Dist: Byeway Bks.

—Baby's First Learning Book: 123. 2004. 10p. (J). bds. 2.99 *(978-0-681-03556-0(0))* Autumn Publishing Group, LLC.

—First Words. 2004. (Baby's First Learning Ser.). 10p. (J). bds. 4.99 *(978-1-85854-892-0(6))* Brimax Books Ltd. GBR. Dist: Byeway Bks.

—On the Farm. 2004. (Baby's First Learning Ser.). 12p. (J). bds. 4.99 *(978-1-85854-893-7(4))* Brimax Books Ltd. GBR. Dist: Byeway Bks.

—123. 2004. (Baby's First Learning Ser.). 12p. (J). bds. 4.99 *(978-1-85854-891-3(8))* Brimax Books Ltd. GBR. Dist: Byeway Bks.

Crossley, Kezzia. The Misadventures of Fink the Mink: Playground Troubles. Zielinski, David. Ballou, Miss, ed. 2013. (ENG.). 48p. pap. 12.99 *(978-0-615-69214-2(1))* Zielinski, David.

Crosson, Cierra. Rain, Rain, Come Today. Magee, Kanika. 2004. (J). *(978-0-9748834-2-7(5))* Ebenezer A.M.E. Church.

Crouch, Adele. Creations by Crouch Color Me. Crouch, Adele. 2011. (ENG.). 64p. pap. 5.95 *(978-1-4679-5588-1(4))* CreateSpace Independent Publishing Platform.

—The Dance of the Caterpillars Bilingual Japanese English. Crouch, Adele. Kohl, Carly & Ikeya, Sarah, trs. 2011. (JPN.). 52p. pap. 14.95 *(978-1-4662-0135-4(5))* CreateSpace Independent Publishing Platform.

—The Dance of the Caterpillars Bilingual Korean English. Crouch, Adele. Kim, Seong, tr. 2011. (KOR.). 54p. pap. 14.95 *(978-1-4637-9334-0(0))* CreateSpace Independent Publishing Platform.

Crouch, Frances. Alexander the Moose. Dixon, Karen S. 2004. 23p. pap. 24.95 *(978-1-4137-3626-7(2))* PublishAmerica, Inc.

Crouch, Julian. Maggot Moon. Gardner, Sally. (ENG.). 288p. (J). (gr. 7). 2014. pap. 8.99 *(978-0-7636-7169-3(X))*; 2013. 16.99 *(978-0-7636-6553-1(3))* Candlewick Pr.

Crouch, Karen Hillard. Miss Fiona's Stupendous Pumpkin Pies. Moulton, Mark Kimball. 2008. (ENG.). 28p. (J). 14.95 *(978-0-8249-5489-5(0))* Ideals Pubns.

—One Enchanted Evening. Moulton, Mark Kimball. 2003. 32p. (J). 14.95 *(978-0-8249-5480-2(7))* Ideals Pubns.

—Scarecrow Pete & His Suitcase of Dreams. Moulton, Mark Kimball. 2005. (ENG.). 36p. (J). (gr. -1-3). 14.95 *(978-0-8249-5151-1(4))* Ideals Pubns.

—A Snowman Named Just Bob. Moulton, Mark Kimball. 2008. (ENG.). 36p. (J). 14.95 *(978-0-8249-5860-2(8)*, 53876801) Ideals Pubns.

Croucher, Barry. Frogs & Toads. Whittley, Sarah & Showler, Dave. rev. ed. 2004. (Golden Guide from St. Martin's Press Ser.). (ENG.). 160p. pap. 6.95 *(978-0-312-32241-0(0)*, Golden Guides from Saint Martin's Pr.) St. Martin's Pr.

Crouth, Julia. Wibble Wobble. Mills, David. 2004. (ENG & POL.). 32p. (J). pap. *(978-1-85269-996-3(5))*; pap. *(978-1-85269-991-8(4))*; pap. *(978-1-85269-986-4(8))*; pap. *(978-1-85269-981-9(7))*; pap. *(978-1-85269-976-5(0))*; pap. *(978-1-85269-971-0(X))*; pap. *(978-1-85269-966-6(3))*; pap. *(978-1-85269-961-1(2))*; pap. *(978-1-85269-951-2(5))*; pap. *(978-1-85269-946-8(9))*; pap. *(978-1-85269-937-6(X))*; pap. *(978-1-85269-932-1(9))*; pap. *(978-1-85269-927-7(2))*; pap. *(978-1-85269-922-2(1))*; pap. *(978-1-85269-917-8(5))*; pap. *(978-1-85269-912-3(4))*; pap. *(978-1-85269-907-9(8))*; pap. *(978-1-85269-902-4(7))*; pap. *(978-1-85269-926-0(4))* Mantra Lingua.

—Wibbly Wobbly Tooth. Mills, David. 2004. (ENG & ARA.). 32p. (J). pap. *(978-1-85269-931-4(0))*; pap. *(978-1-85269-936-9(1))*; pap. *(978-1-85269-941-3(8))*; pap. *(978-1-85269-956-7(6))* Mantra Lingua.

Crovatto, Lucie, et al. Tony Baroni Loves Macaroni. Sadler, Marilyn. 2015. (ENG.). 32p. (J). (-k). 14.99 *(978-1-60905-293-5(5))* Blue Apple Bks.

Crow, Heather. Mosey's Field, 1 vol. Lockhart, Barbara. 2013. (ENG.). 32p. (J). 16.99 *(978-0-7643-4388-9(2))* Schiffer Publishing, Ltd.

Crow, Katie. The Ranch Race. Carkhuff Jr., Sam. 2012. 36p. 16.99 *(978-1-939054-03-6(6))*; pap. 11.99 *(978-1-939054-02-9(8))* Rowe Publishing and Design.

Crowe, Louise. Fergus Finds a Friend, 1 vol. Steven, Kenneth. 2010. (ENG.). 32p. (J). (gr. -1-1). 11.95 *(978-0-86315-778-3(5))* Floris Bks. GBR. Dist: SteinerBooks, Inc.

Crowell, Helen. The Little Red Present. Pierce, Brian. 2007. 32p. (J). per. 8.00 *(978-0-9793269-1-2(5))* Straub, Rick.

Crowell, Knox. Andy & Jerome. Williams, Heather L. l.t. ed. 2004. (HRL Big Book Ser.). 8p. (J). (gr. -1-1). pap. 10.95 *(978-1-57332-276-8(8))*; pap. 10.95 *(978-1-57332-277-5(6))* Carson-Dellosa Publishing, LLC. (HighReach Learning, Incorporated).

—At the Park. Hensley, Sarah M. l.t. ed. 2006. 10p. (J). (gr. -1-k). pap. 10.95 *(978-1-57332-354-3(3)*, HighReach Learning, Incorporated) Carson-Dellosa Publishing, LLC.

—Caillou Waits for Dinner. Howard-Parham, Pam. l.t. ed. 2004. (HRL Board Book Ser.). (J). (gr. -1-1). pap. 10.95 *(978-1-57332-289-8(X)*, HighReach Learning, Incorporated) Carson-Dellosa Publishing, LLC.

—A Cold Winter Day. Muench-Williams, Heather. l.t. ed. 2006. (HRL Board Book Ser.). (J). (gr. -1-k). pap. 10.95 *(978-1-57332-326-0(8)*, HighReach Learning, Incorporated) Carson-Dellosa Publishing, LLC.

—Helping Farmer Joe. Hensley, Sarah M. l.t. ed. 2004. (HRL Little Book Ser.). (J). (gr. -1). pap. 10.95 *(978-1-57332-296-6(2))*; pap. 10.95 *(978-1-57332-295-9(4))* Carson-Dellosa Publishing, LLC. (HighReach Learning, Incorporated).

—Let's Build a Snowman: Cuddle Book. Black, Jessica L. & Mullican, Judy. 6p. (J). (gr. -1-1). bds. 10.95 *(978-1-57332-222-5(9)*, HighReach Learning, Incorporated) Carson-Dellosa Publishing, LLC.

—Playing on the Playground. Howard-Parham, Pam. l.t. ed. 2005. (HRL Little Book Ser.). (J). (gr. k-18). pap. 10.95 *(978-1-57332-336-9(5))*; pap. 10.95 *(978-1-57332-335-2(7))* Carson-Dellosa Publishing, LLC. (HighReach Learning, Incorporated).

—Water Fun. Hensley, Sarah M. l.t. ed. 2005. (J). (gr. -1-k). pap. 10.95 *(978-1-57332-342-0(X))*; pap. 10.95 *(978-1-57332-343-7(8))* Carson-Dellosa Publishing, LLC. (HighReach Learning, Incorporated).

—Who Is in the Backyard? Jarrell, Pamela R. l.t. ed. 2004. (HRL Board Book Ser.). 8p. (J). (gr. -1). pap. 10.95 *(978-1-57332-281-2(4)*, HighReach Learning, Incorporated) Carson-Dellosa Publishing, LLC.

Crowell, Pers. The Whistling Stallion. Holt, Stephen. 2011. 224p. 44.95 *(978-1-258-10199-2(8))* Literary Licensing, LLC.

Crowley, Adam A., photos by. Gus Learns to Fly: Self-Defense Is Self-Discovery. Richardson, Kimberly Stanton. 2012. (ENG., 44p. (J). (gr. k). pap. 18.00 *(978-0-939165-64-3(3))* NewSage Pr., LLC.

Crowley, Ashley. Officer Panda - Fingerprint Detective. Crowley, Ashley. 2015. (Officer Panda Ser.: 1). (ENG.). 32p. (J). (gr. -1-3). 17.99 ***(978-0-06-236626-9(2))*** HarperCollins Pubs.

Crowley, Cheryl. The Adventures of Webb Ellis, a Tale from the Heart of Africa: The Return of the Protectors. Rieback, Milton. 2006. (J). lib. bdg. 19.95 *(978-0-9777440-0-8(0))* Inyati Press.

Crown Peak Publishing. Just Be You. Crown Peak Publishing. 2008. (ENG.). 40p. (J). 19.95 *(978-0-9645663-5-4(4))* Crown Peak Publishing.

Crowson, Andrew. Flip Flap Christmas. Crowson, Andrew. 2003. 12p. (J). bds. *(978-1-85602-476-1(8)*, Pavilion Children's Books) Pavilion Bks.

—Flip Flap Prehistoric. Crowson, Andrew. 2003. 12p. (J). pap. *(978-1-85602-474-7(1)*, Pavilion Children's Books) Pavilion Bks.

—Flip Flap Safari. Crowson, Andrew. 2003. 12p. (J). bds. *(978-1-85602-473-0(3)*, Pavilion Children's Books) Pavilion Bks.

—Flip Flap Spooky. Crowson, Andrew. 2003. 12p. (J). bds. *(978-1-85602-475-4(X)*, Pavilion Children's Books) Pavilion Bks.

Crowther, Jeff. Attack of the Cling-Ons, 1 vol. Ciencin, Scott. 2011. (Graphic Sparks Ser.). (ENG.). 40p. (gr. 1-3). pap. 5.95 *(978-1-4342-3067-6(8))*; lib. bdg. 22.65 *(978-1-4342-2637-2(9))* Stone Arch Bks. (Graphic Sparks).

—The Evil Echo, 1 vol. Nickel, Scott & Dahl, Michael. 2010. (Princess Candy Ser.). (ENG.). 40p. (gr. 1-3). 22.65 *(978-1-4342-1977-0(1))*; pap. 5.95 *(978-1-4342-2804-8(5))* Stone Arch Bks. (Graphic Sparks).

—The Green Queen of Mean. Dahl, Michael & Nickel, Scott. 2010. (Graphic Sparks Ser.). (ENG.). 40p. (gr. 1-3). pap. 5.95 *(978-1-4342-2803-1(7))*; lib. bdg. 22.65 *(978-1-4342-1893-3(7))* Stone Arch Bks. (Graphic Sparks).

—The Marshmallow Mermaid. Dahl, Michael. (Graphic Sparks Ser.). (ENG.). 40p. (gr. 1-3). 2010. pap. 5.95 *(978-1-4342-2802-4(9))*; 2009. lib. bdg. 22.65 *(978-1-4342-1588-8(1))* Stone Arch Bks. (Graphic Sparks).

—Sugar Hero. Dahl, Michael. (Graphic Sparks Ser.). (ENG.). 40p. (gr. 1-3). 2010. pap. 5.95 *(978-1-4342-2801-7(0))*; 2009. lib. bdg. 22.65 *(978-1-4342-1587-1(3))* Stone Arch Bks. (Graphic Sparks).

Crowther, Kitty. Scric Scrac Bibib Blub! Crowther, Kitty. Crowther. Coll-Vinent, Anna, tr. 2005. (SPA.). 36p. (J). 15.95 *(978-84-8470-197-2(2))* Corimbo, Editorial S.L. ESP. Dist: Lectorum Pubns., Inc.

Crowther, Robert. Deep down under Ground: A Pop-up Book of Amazing Facts & Feats. Crowther, Robert. 2004. 18p. (J). (gr. 3-8). reprint ed. pap. 22.00 *(978-0-7567-7179-9(X))* DIANE Publishing Co.

—The Most Amazing Hide-and-Seek Alphabet Book. Crowther, Robert. 2010. (ENG.). 12p. (J). (gr. -1-2). pap. 12.99 *(978-0-7636-5030-8(7))* Candlewick Pr.

—The Most Amazing Hide-and-Seek Numbers Book. Crowther, Robert. 2010. (ENG.). 12p. (J). (gr. -1-2). pap. 12.99 *(978-0-7636-5029-2(3))* Candlewick Pr.

—Robert Crowther's Amazing Pop-Up Big Machines. Crowther, Robert. 2010. (ENG.). 10p. (J). (gr. -1-3). 17.99 *(978-0-7636-4958-6(9))* Candlewick Pr.

—Robert Crowther's Pop-Up Dinosaur ABC. Crowther, Robert. 2015. (ENG.). 10p. (J). (gr. -1-3). 19.99 *(978-0-7636-7296-6(3))* Candlewick Pr.

—Robert Crowther's Pop-Up House of Inventions: Hundreds of Fabulous Facts about Your Home. Crowther, Robert. 2009. (ENG.). 12p. (J). (gr. 1-4). 17.99 *(978-0-7636-4253-2(3))* Candlewick Pr.

—Ships: A Pop-Up Book. Crowther, Robert. 2008. (ENG.). 10p. (J). (gr. 1-4). 17.99 *(978-0-7636-3852-8(8))* Candlewick Pr.

—Soccer: Facts & Stats & the World Cup & Superstars: A Pop-up Book. Crowther, Robert. 2004. 14p. (J). (gr. 2-8). reprint ed. 18.00 *(978-0-7567-7368-7(7))* DIANE Publishing Co.

—Trains: A Pop-Up Railroad Book. Crowther, Robert. 2006. (ENG.). 10p. (J). (gr. 1-4). 17.99 *(978-0-7636-3082-9(9))* Candlewick Pr.

Crozat, Francois. Los Gatos de Maria Tatin. Chausse, Sylvie. 2003. (SPA.). 32p. (J). (gr. k-2). *(978-84-8418-067-8(0)*, ZZ30446) Zendrera Zariquiey, Editorial ESP. Dist: Lectorum Pubns., Inc.

Cruikshank, George. Fairy Tales from the Brothers Grimm: Deluxe Hardcover Classic. Brothers Grimm, Becky et al. 2013. (Puffin Classics Ser.). (ENG.). 384p. (J). (gr. 3-7). 25.00 *(978-0-14-750949-9(1)*, Puffin) Penguin Publishing Group.

—Philosophy in Sport Made Science in Earnest: Being an Attempt to Illustrate the First Principles of Natural Philosophy by the Aid of the Popular Toys & Sports. Paris, John Ayrton. 2013. (Cambridge Library Collection - Education Ser.). (ENG.). Volume 1. 340p. pap. 35.99 *(978-1-108-05739-4(X))*; Volume 2. 328p. pap. 35.99 *(978-1-108-05740-0(3))*; Volume 3. 220p. pap. 26.99 *(978-1-108-05741-7(1))* Cambridge Univ. Pr.

—Punch & Judy. Landes, William-Alan, ed. 2003. (Classic Plays Ser.). 24p. (YA). (gr. 4-12). pap. 7.50 *(978-0-88734-290-5(6))* Players Pr., Inc.

Crum, A. M. The Lucky Farm Boy, 1 vol. Mertz, Alyssa. 2009. 28p. pap. 24.95 *(978-1-60813-892-0(5))* PublishAmerica, Inc.

Crum, Anna-Maria. The Christmas Tree Cried: The Story of the White House Christmas Tree. McAdam, Claudia Cangilla. 2004. 32p. (J). 16.95 *(978-0-9748995-5-8(0)*, 1236093) Two Sons Pr., Inc.

—Kangaroos: Read Well Level K Unit 15 Storybook. Sprick, Jessica. 2003. (Read Well Level K Ser.). 20p. (J). *(978-1-57035-686-5(6)*, 55554) Cambium Education, Inc.

—Maria's Mysterious Mission. Cangilla-McAdam, Claudia. 2007. 32p. (J). (gr. 3-7). 12.95 *(978-1-56579-588-4(1))* Fielder, John Publishing.

—Tallie's Christmas Lights Surprise!, 1 vol. Pease, Elaine. 2012. (ENG.). 32p. (J). (gr. k-3). 16.99 *(978-1-4556-1586-5(2))* Pelican Publishing Co., Inc.

Crum, Anna-Maria, jt. illus. see Shupe, Bobbi.

Crum, Shaun. The Bully & the Booger Baby: A Cautionary Tale. Ridenour, Melissa. 2013. (ENG.). 104p. pap. 7.49 *(978-0-615-82067-5(0))* Write Solution Ink.

Crump, Christopher. The Valley of Secrets. Hussey, Charmian. 2006. (ENG.). 400p. (J). (gr. 7-12). per. 17.99 *(978-1-4169-0015-3(2)*, Simon Pulse) Simon Pulse.

Crump, Fred, Jr. Three Kings & a Star. Crump, Fred, Jr. 2010. 40p. (J). (gr. -1-3). 12.95 *(978-1-932715-52-1(5))* UMI (Urban Ministries, Inc.).

Crump, Fred, Jr. The Little Mermaid. Crump, Fred, Jr., retold by. 2007. 32p. (J). 12.95 *(978-1-934056-72-1(3))*; pap. 9.95 *(978-1-60352-063-8(5))* UMI (Urban Ministries, Inc.).

Crump, Leslie. Right Guard Grant. Barbour, Ralph Henry. 2011. 304p. 48.95 *(978-1-258-10515-0(2))* Literary Licensing, LLC.

Crump, Lil. DNA Detective. Kyi, Tanya Lloyd. 2015. (ENG.). 120p. (J). (gr. 5-8). 24.95 ***(978-1-55451-774-9(5)***, 9781554517749) Annick Pr., Ltd. CAN. Dist: Firefly Bks., Ltd.

Cruse, Howard. The Swimmer with a Rope in His Teeth: A Shadow Fable. Shaffer, Jeanne E. 2004. (ENG.). 1p. pap. 15.98 *(978-1-59102-181-0(2)*, Pyr Bks.) Prometheus Bks., Pubs.

Crutchfield, Jim, jt. illus. see Laughbaum, Steve.

Cruz, Cheryl. Goodbye, Santa. Hineman, Jonathan. 2013. 26p. (J). 16.95 *(978-1-60131-172-6(9))* Big Tent Bks.

—The Million Year Meal. Lucas, Ian & Medoza, Chris. 2012. 32p. (J). 19.95 *(978-1-60131-099-6(4))* Big Tent Bks.

Cruz, D. Nina. Mis abuelos y yo / My Grandparents & I. Caraballo, Samuel. Brammer, Ethriam Cash, tr. (ENG & SPA.). 32p. 16.95 *(978-1-55885-407-9(X)*, Piñata Books) Arte Publico Pr.

—The Rowdy, Rowdy Ranch / Alla en el Rancho Grande. Brammer, Ethriam Cash. 2003. (ENG & SPA.). 32p. (J). 16.95 *(978-1-55885-409-3(6)*, Piñata Books) Arte Publico Pr.

Cruz, E. R. Mark Twain/the Adventures of Tom Sawyer. Twain, Mark. 2005. 48p. (gr. 5-8). 25.50 *(978-0-7910-9102-9(3))* Facts On File, Inc.

Cruz, Ernesto R. Two Years Before the Mast: Student Activity Book. Sohl, Marcia & Dackerman, Gerald. (Now Age Illustrated Ser.). (J). (gr. 4-12). stu. ed. 1.25 *(978-0-88301-294-9(4))* Pendulum Pr., Inc.

Cruz, María Hernández de la & López, Casimiro de la Cruz. The Journey of Tunuri & the Blue Deer: A Huichol Indian Story. Endredy, James. Cruz, María Hernández de la & López, Casimiro de la Cruz, trs. 2003. (ENG.). 32p. (J). (gr. -1-6). 15.95 *(978-1-59143-016-2(X))* Bear & Co.

Cruz, Nardo. Frankenstein. Shelley, Mary & Shelley, Mary. 2005. 48p. (gr. 5-8). 25.50 *(978-0-7910-9100-5(7))* Facts On File, Inc.

—Robert Louis Stevenson/Treasure Island. Stevenson, Robert Louis. 2005. 48p. (J). (gr. 5-8). 25.50 *(978-0-7910-9107-4(4))* Facts On File, Inc.

Cruz, Ray. Alexander & the Terrible, Horrible, No Good, Very Bad Day. Viorst, Judith. 2014. (Classic Board Bks.). (ENG.). 34p. (J). (gr. -1 — 1). bds. 7.99 *(978-1-4424-9816-7(1)*, Little Simon) Little Simon.

—Alexander & the Terrible, Horrible, No Good, Very Bad Day. Viorst, Judith. 2009. (ENG.). 32p. (J). (gr. -1-2). 17.99 *(978-1-4169-8595-2(6)*, Atheneum Bks. for Young Readers) Simon & Schuster Children's Publishing.

—Alexander & the Terrible, Horrible, No Good, Very Bad Day: Lap Edition. Viorst, Judith. 2014. (ENG.). 34p. (J). (gr. -1 — 1). bds. 12.99 *(978-1-4814-1412-8(7)*, Little Simon) Little Simon.

—Sing, Little Sack! I Canta, Saquito!: a Folktale from Puerto Rico. Jaffe, Nina. 2006. 48p. (J). (gr. 2-3). reprint ed. 19.00 *(978-1-4223-5573-2(X))* DIANE Publishing Co.

Cruz, Roger, et al. The Road to Onslaught. Davis, Alan et al. 2014. (ENG.). 440p. (J). (gr. 4-17). pap. 39.99 *(978-0-7851-8830-8(4))* Marvel Worldwide, Inc.

—X-Force: Phalanx Covenant. Lobdell, Scott et al. 2013. (ENG.). 256p. (J). (gr. 4-17). 39.99 *(978-0-7851-6271-1(2))* Marvel Worldwide, Inc.

Cruz, Roger & Coover, Colleen. X-Men First Class - Volume 2. 2011. (ENG.). 128p. (J). (gr. 4-17). pap. 14.99 *(978-0-7851-5314-6(4))* Marvel Worldwide, Inc.

Cruzan, Patricia & Solly, Gloria. Molly's Mischievous Dog. l.t. ed. 2004. 121p. (J). per. *(978-0-9653543-3-2(4))* Clear Creek Pubs.

Crysler, Ian, photos by. Seed to Sunflower: A First Look Board Book. Reid, Barbara. 2004. 12p. (J). (gr. k-2). reprint ed. 10.00 *(978-0-7567-7853-8(0))* DIANE Publishing Co.

Crystian, Carol Payne. Jas & Poetic Lucy. Crystian, Carol Payne. l.t. ed. 2006. 21p. (J). (gr. -1-3). per. 10.99 *(978-1-59879-154-9(0))* Lifevest Publishing, Inc.

Csavas, Sally. Tiny Story, Vol. 1. Price, Diane J. 2008. 28p. (J). 9.00 *(978-0-9789637-0-5(9))* Price, Diane Joan.

Csicsko, David Lee. The Skin You Live In. Tyler, Michael. 2005. (ENG.). 32p. (J). (gr. k-2). 14.95 *(978-0-9759580-0-1(3))* Chicago Children's Museum.

Csotonyi, Julius. Prehistoric Predators. Switek, Brian. 2015. (ENG.). 104p. (J). 19.95 ***(978-1-60433-552-1(1)***, Applesauce Pr.) Cider Mill Pr. Bk. Pubs., LLC.

Csotonyi, Julius. Why Does T. Rex Have Such Short Arms? And Other Questions about Dinosaurs. Stewart, Melissa. 2014. (Good Question! Ser.). (ENG.). 32p. (J). (gr. 1). 12.95 *(978-1-4549-0678-0(2))*; pap. 5.95 *(978-1-4549-0679-7(0))* Sterling Publishing Co., Inc.

Csotonyi, Julius & Marshall, Todd. Dinosaurs: And Other Prehistoric Animals. Norman, Kim & American Museum of Natural History Staff. 2012. (Storytime Stickers Ser.). (ENG.). 16p. (J). (gr. k-2). pap. 5.95 *(978-1-4027-7349-5(8))* Sterling Publishing Co., Inc.

Cubillas, Roberto. Mimosaurio! Pez, Alberto. (SPA.). (J). 8.95 *(978-958-04-6035-0(3))* Norma S.A. COL. Dist: Distribuidora Norma, Inc.

Cucca, Vincenzo, et al. The Mystery of Sheristan, Vol. 7. Kesel, Barbara. 2004. (Meridian Ser.: Vol. 7). 160p. (YA). pap. 15.95 *(978-1-59314-056-4(8))* CrossGeneration Comics, Inc.

Cucco, Giuliano. Winston & George. Miller, John. 2014. (ENG.). 56p. (J). (gr. k-3). 17.95 *(978-1-59270-145-2(0))* Enchanted Lion Bks., LLC.

Cudby, Simon, photos by. Motocross Exposure. Cudby, Simon. 2004. 24.95 *(978-0-9766918-0-8(9))* MX No Fear.

Cudd, Savannah. The True Story of the Big Red Onion. Fitzgerald, D. M. 2013. 36p. 18.99 *(978-0-9890288-7-5(9))*; pap. 10.99 *(978-0-9890288-5-1(2))* Mindstir Media.

Cuddehe, Judy Link. The Heron Chronicles. Cuddehe, Judy Link. 2013. 54p. pap. 13.00 *(978-0-9836659-6-0(6))* Found Link.

Cuddy, Robbin. Baby Meerkats. Clarke, Ginjer L. 2010. (Penguin Young Readers, Level 3 Ser.). (ENG.). 48p. (J). (gr. 1-3). mass mkt. 3.99 *(978-0-448-45106-0(9),* Grosset & Dunlap) Penguin Publishing Group.

—Clifford Helps Santa. Sander, Sonia & Bridwell, Norman. 2006. (Clifford the Big Red Dog Ser.). (J). pap. *(978-0-439-90456-8(0))* Scholastic, Inc.

Cuddy, Robbin. Learn to Draw Cats & Kittens: Step-By-Step Instructions for More Than 25 Favorite Feline Friends. Walter Foster Creative Team. 2015. (Learn to Draw: Expanded Edition Ser.). (ENG.). 64p. (J). (gr. 3-5). 33.32 ***(978-1-939581-66-2(4))*** Quarto Publishing Group USA.

—Learn to Draw Dinosaurs: Step-By-Step Instructions for More Than 25 Prehistoric Creatures. Walter Foster Creative Team. 2015. (Learn to Draw: Expanded Edition Ser.). (ENG.). 64p. (J). (gr. 3-5). 33.32 ***(978-1-939581-70-9(2))*** Quarto Publishing Group USA.

Cuddy, Robbin. Learn to Draw Dogs & Puppies: Step-By-Step Instructions for More Than 25 Different Breeds. 2015. (Learn to Draw: Expanded Edition Ser.). (ENG.). 64p. (J). (gr. k-5). 33.27 *(978-1-939581-52-5(4))* Quarto Publishing Group USA.

—Learn to Draw Farm Animals: Step-by-Step Instructions for 21 Favorite Subjects, Including a Horse, Cow & Pig! Torres, Jickie. 2011. (Learn to Draw Ser.). (ENG.). 40p. (J). (gr. 1-17). pap. 4.95 *(978-1-60058-213-4(3),* 1600582133) Quarto Publishing Group USA.

Cuddy, Robbin. Learn to Draw Forest Animals: Step-By-Step Instructions for More Than 25 Woodland Creatures. Walter Foster Creative Team. 2015. (Learn to Draw: Expanded Edition Ser.). (ENG.). 64p. (J). (gr. 3-5). 33.32 ***(978-1-939581-68-6(0))*** Quarto Publishing Group USA.

Cuddy, Robbin. Learn to Draw Forest Animals & Wildlife: Learn to Draw 20 Different Woodland Animals, Step by Easy Step, Shape by Simple Shape! Phan, Sandy. 2014. 40p. (J). *(978-1-939581-24-2(9))* Quarto Publishing Group USA.

—Learn to Draw Forest Animals & Wildlife: Step-by-Step Instructions for 25 Different Woodland Animals. 2012. (Learn to Draw Ser.). (ENG.). 40p. (J). (gr. 1-17). pap. 4.95 *(978-1-60058-308-7(3),* 1600583083) Quarto Publishing Group USA.

Cuddy, Robbin. Learn to Draw Horses & Ponies: Step-By-Step Instructions for More Than 25 Different Breeds. Walter Foster Creative Team. 2015. (Learn to Draw: Expanded Edition Ser.). (ENG.). 64p. (J). (gr. k-5). 33.32 ***(978-1-939581-65-5(6))*** Quarto Publishing Group USA.

Cuddy, Robbin. Learn to Draw Pets: Step-By-Step Instructions for More Than 25 Cute & Cuddly Animals. 2015. (Learn to Draw: Expanded Edition Ser.). (ENG.). 64p. (J). (gr. k-5). 33.27 *(978-1-939581-53-2(2))* Quarto Publishing Group USA.

—Learn to Draw Polar Animals: Draw More Than 25 Favorite Arctic & Antarctic Wildlife Critters. 2015. (Learn to Draw: Expanded Edition Ser.). (ENG.). 64p. (J). (gr. k-5). 33.27 *(978-1-939581-51-8(6))* Quarto Publishing Group USA.

—Learn to Draw Rainforest & Jungle Animals: Learn to Draw & Color 21 Different Exotic Creatures, Step by Easy Step, Shape by Simple Shape! Phan, Sandy. 2014. 40p. (J). *(978-1-939581-25-9(7))* Quarto Publishing Group USA.

—Learn to Draw Rainforest & Jungle Animals: Step-by-Step Drawing Instructions for 25 Exotic Creatures. 2013. (Learn to Draw Ser.). (ENG.). 40p. (J). (gr. 1-17). pap. 4.95 *(978-1-60058-309-4(1),* 1600583091) Quarto Publishing Group USA.

Cuddy, Robbin. Learn to Draw Safari Animals: Step-By-Step Instructions for More Than 25 Exotic Animals. Walter Foster Creative Team. 2015. (Learn to Draw: Expanded Edition Ser.). (ENG.). 64p. (J). (gr. 3-5). 33.32 ***(978-1-939581-67-9(2))*** Quarto Publishing Group USA.

Cuddy, Robbin. Learn to Draw Sea Creatures. 2015. (Learn to Draw: Expanded Edition Ser.). (ENG.). 64p. (J). (gr. k-5). 33.27 *(978-1-939581-54-9(0))* Quarto Publishing Group USA.

Cuddy, Robbin & Cole, Joanna. The Magic School Bus in the Bat Cave. Lane, Jeanette & Cole, Joanna. 2006. (J). pap. *(978-0-439-89934-5(6))* Scholastic, Inc.

Cuddy, Robin. All about Drawing: Farm & Forest Animals. Cuddy, Robbin. 2014. (All about Drawing Ser.). (ENG.). 80p. (J). (gr. 2-5). lib. bdg. 34.60 *(978-1-939581-10-5(9))* Quarto Publishing Group USA.

—Baby Otter. Clarke, Ginjer L. 2009. (Penguin Young Readers, Level 3 Ser.). (ENG.). 48p. (J). (gr. 1-3). mass mkt. 3.99 *(978-0-448-45105-3(0),* Grosset & Dunlap) Penguin Publishing Group.

—Clifford's Big Red Easter. Parent, Nancy. 2003. (Clifford Ser.). (ENG.). 7p. (J). (gr. -1-3). bds. 4.99 *(978-0-439-43428-7(9))* Scholastic, Inc.

—Simba's Moon. Weiss, Ellen. Date not set. (ENG.). 32p. (J). (gr. -1-2). 12.99 *(978-0-7868-3267-5(3))* Disney Pr.

Cuddy, Robin & Wummer, Amy. Baby Elephant. Clarke, Ginjer L. 2009. (Penguin Young Readers, Level 3 Ser.). (ENG.). 48p. (J). (gr. 1-3). mass mkt. 3.99 *(978-0-448-44825-1(4),* Warne, Frederick Pubs.) Penguin Bks., Ltd. GBR. Dist: Penguin Random Hse., LLC.

Cue, Harold. Yankee Doodle: The Story of A Pioneer Boy & His Dog. Bartlett, Arthur C. 2011. 322p. 50.95 *(978-1-258-06634-5(3))* Literary Licensing, LLC.

Cuellar, Olga. Arco Iris de Poesia: Poemmas de las Americas y Espana. Andricain, Sergio. 2008. (SPA.). 40p. (J). (gr. -1-3). 15.99 *(978-1-930332-59-1(9))* Lectorum Pubns., Inc.

—El Jardin de la Emperatriz Casia. Wang, Gabrielle. Holguin, Magdalena, tr. 2004. (SPA.). 108p. (YA). 8.95 *(978-958-04-7346-6(3))* Norma S.A. COL. Dist: Distribuidora Norma, Inc.

—Que Extranos Son Los Terricolas/Earthlings, How Weird They Are! Rodriguez, Antonio Orlando. 2006. (Bilingual Collection). (SPA.). 51p. (J). (gr. k-2). *(978-958-30-1737-7(X))* Panamericana Editorial.

—Los Siete Mejores Cuentos Chinos. Hoyos, Hector. 2004. (SPA.). (J). (gr. 3-5). *(978-958-04-7210-0(6))* Norma S.A.

—Los Siete Mejores Cuentos Indios. Hoyos, Hector. 2004. (SPA.). 55p. (J). (gr. 3-5). *(978-958-04-7213-1(0))* Norma S.A.

—El tesoro de los reyes de Irianda. Cooper, Patrick. 2012. (J). (gr. 5-8). pap. 10.99 *(978-958-04-7078-6(2))* Norma S.A. COL. Dist: Lectorum Pubns., Inc.

Cuevas, Andres Mario Ramirez. Circuito Interior: Los Deportistas Por Dentro. Santillan, Maria Luisa. rev. ed. 2006. (Otra Escalera Ser.). (SPA & ENG.). 24p. (J). (gr. 2-4). pap. 9.95 *(978-968-5920-72-8(9))* Castillo, Ediciones, S. A. de C. V. MEX. Dist: Macmillan.

Cuevas, Ernesto & Cuevas, Ernesto, Jr. Featherless: Desplumado. Herrera, Juan Felipe. 2004. (ENG & SPA.). 32p. (J). (gr. 1-4). 16.95 *(978-0-89239-195-0(2))* Lee & Low Bks., Inc.

Cuevas, Ernesto, Jr., jt. illus. see Cuevas, Ernesto.

Cuevas, Ernesto, jt. illus. see Herrera, Juan Felipe.

Culbertson, James Forrest. Louisiana: The Land & Its People, 1 vol. Eakin, Sue et al. 5th ed. 2006. (ENG.). 560p. 35.00 *(978-1-58980-303-9(5))* Pelican Publishing Co., Inc.

Culkin-Lawrence, Teresa. Daisy Sunshine. Gervay, Susanne. 2008. (Making Tracks Ser.). (ENG.). 64p. (J). (gr. 1-4). pap. 11.95 *(978-1-876944-67-4(6))* National Museum of Australia AUS. Dist: Independent Pubs. Group.

—The Red Camel. Murray, Kirsty. 2008. (Making Tracks Ser.). (ENG.). 64p. (J). (gr. 2-4). pap. 11.95 *(978-1-876944-69-8(2))* National Museum of Australia AUS. Dist: Independent Pubs. Group.

Culotta, Kent. Busy Trucks on the Go. Ode, Eric. 2014. (ENG.). 32p. (J). pap. 6.99 *(978-1-61067-287-0(9))* Kane Miller.

—Dan, the Taxi Man. Ode, Eric. ed. 2012. (Picture Book Ser.). (ENG.). 32p. (J). 14.99 *(978-1-61067-072-2(8))* Kane Miller.

Culpepper, Gina G. Felix & Culpepper, Victoria Lynn Felix. Brownie the Lonely Dragon. Culpepper, Peter Ryan & Culpepper, Gina G. Felix. Make-a-Wish Foundation Staff, ed. l.t. ed. 2003. 32p. 17.95 *(978-0-9740435-0-0(8),* 1) Culpepper, Felix International, Inc.

Culpepper, Victoria Lynn Felix, jt. illus. see Culpepper, Gina G. Felix.

Culver, Dennis. Chicken Boy: The Amazing Adventures of a Super Hero with Autism. Allen, Gregory G. 2012. 32p. pap. 9.99 *(978-0-9853441-0-8(5))* ASD Publishing.

Cumming, Hannah. The Cloud. Cumming, Hannah. 2010. (Child's Play Library). (ENG.). 32p. (J). (gr. -1-3). pap. *(978-1-84643-343-6(6))* Child's Play International Ltd.

—The Lost Stars. Cumming, Hannah. 2011. (Child's Play Library). (ENG.). 32p. (J). *(978-1-84643-416-7(5))* Child's Play International Ltd.

—The Red Boat. Cumming, Hannah. 2012. (Child's Play Library). (ENG.). 32p. (J). *(978-1-84643-493-8(9)); (978-1-84643-481-5(5))* Child's Play International Ltd.

Cummings, Maris. Seeking Serenity. Stella, Pilar. 2008. (ENG.). (J). (gr. -1-3). pap. 17.95 *(978-1-60037-451-7(4))* Morgan James Publishing.

Cummings, Pat. Beauty & the Beast. Lee, H. Chuku. 2014. (ENG.). 32p. (J). (gr. -1-3). 17.99 *(978-0-688-14819-5(0))* HarperCollins Pubs.

—Pickin' Peas. MacDonald, Margaret Read. 2014. (ENG.). 32p. pap. 8.95 *(978-1-939160-83-6(9))* August Hse. Pubs., Inc.

—The World's Wide Open. Stroud, Bettye. 2016. (J). *(978-0-689-84026-5(8))* Simon & Schuster Bks. For Young Readers.

Cummings, Pat. Harvey Moon, Museum Boy. Cummings, Pat. 2008. 32p. (J). (gr. -1-3). lib. bdg. 18.89 *(978-0-06-057861-9(0))* HarperCollins Pubs.

Cummings, Steven. Uglies-Cutters. Westerfeld, Scott & Grayson, Devin. 2012. (ENG.). 176p. (YA). (gr. 8-12). pap. 10.99 *(978-0-345-52723-3(2),* Del Rey) Random House Publishing Group.

Cummings, Terrance. We Shall Overcome: A Song That Changed the World. Stotts, Stuart. 2010. (ENG.). 80p. (J). (gr. 5-7). 18.00 *(978-0-547-18210-0(4))* Houghton Mifflin Harcourt Publishing Co.

Cummings, Troy. Captain Kidd's Crew Experiments with Sinking & Floating, 1 vol. Weakland, Mark. 2012. (In the Science Lab Ser.). (ENG.). 24p. (gr. 2-3). pap. 8.95 *(978-1-4048-7236-3(1));* lib. bdg. 25.99 *(978-1-4048-7144-1(6))* Picture Window Bks. (Nonfiction Picture Bks.).

Cummings, Troy. Mighty Truck. Barton, Chris. 2016. 32p. (J). (gr. -1-3). 17.99 ***(978-0-06-234478-6(1))*** HarperCollins Pubs.

Cummings, Troy. More Bears! Nesbitt, Kenn. 2010. (ENG.). 32p. (J). (gr. k-3). 14.99 *(978-1-4022-3835-2(5),* Sourcebooks Jabberwocky) Sourcebooks, Inc.

—The Twelve Days of Christmas in Indiana. Griffin, Donna. 2014. (Twelve Days of Christmas in America Ser.). (ENG.). 40p. (J). (gr. k). 12.95 *(978-1-4549-0888-3(2))* Sterling Publishing Co., Inc.

Cummings, Troy. Charge of the Lightning Bugs. Cummings, Troy. 2015. (Notebook of Doom Ser.: 8). (ENG.). 96p. (J). (gr. 1-3). 15.99 ***(978-0-545-79554-8(0))*** Scholastic, Inc.

Cummings, Troy. The Notebook of Doom #6: Pop of the Bumpy Mummy (a Branches Book) Cummings, Troy. 2014. (Notebook of Doom Ser.: 6). (ENG.). 96p. (J). (gr. 1-3). pap. 4.99 *(978-0-545-69898-6(7))* Scholastic, Inc.

Cummings, Troy. The Notebook of Doom #8: Charge of the Lightning Bugs (a Branches Book) Cummings, Troy. 2015. (Notebook of Doom Ser.: 8). (ENG.). 96p. (J). (gr. 1-3). pap. 4.99 ***(978-0-545-79555-5(9))*** Scholastic, Inc.

Cummins, Lucy Ruth. The Taking Tree: A Selfish Parody. Travesty, Shrill. 2010. (ENG.). 48p. (J). (gr. -1-2). 18.99 *(978-1-4424-0763-3(8),* Simon & Schuster Bks. For Young Readers) Simon & Schuster Bks. For Young Readers.

Cummins, Pat. Squashed in the Middle. Winthrop, Elizabeth. 2008. (J). (gr. k-4). 25.95 incl. audio *(978-1-4301-0440-7(6));* 28.95 incl. audio compact disk *(978-1-4301-0443-8(0))* Live Oak Media.

Cummins, Scott. The Gate of No Return. Morris, Rooster. 2004. (ENG.). (J). per. 7.95 *(978-0-9755895-1-9(2),* 0-9755895-1-2) Axle Publishing Co., Inc.

Cuniff, Joe. The Littlest Peanut: A Baby Book for the Teeny Tiny Ones. Wilson, Shannan. 2011. 32p. 16.95 *(978-1-61254-023-8(6))* Brown Bks. Publishing Group.

Cunliffe, Ian. Farm Sticker Activities. Rusling, Annette. 2014. (My First Sticker Activity Book Ser.). (ENG.). 77p. (J). (gr. -1-3). pap. 9.99 *(978-1-58925-303-2(5))* Tiger Tales.

Cunliffe, Ian. I Want to Be a Witch. Cunliffe, Ian. 2014. 32p. (J). (gr. -1-3). 16.99 *(978-1-58925-159-5(8))* Tiger Tales.

—Sunny Seaside. Cunliffe, Ian. 2011. (Match-And-Muddle Ser.). (ENG.). 10p. (J). (gr. -1-k). bds. 10.99 *(978-0-230-71297-3(5))* Macmillan Pubs., Ltd. GBR. Dist: Independent Pubs. Group.

Cunningham, Ann Elizabeth. Sadie Can Count: A Multi-sensory Book, Cunningham, Ann Elizabeth. l.t. ed. 2006. 16p. (J). bds. 29.95 *(978-0-9770054-8-2(8))* Sensational Bks.

Cunningham, Bob. Ivan the Invacar & the Cave. Boles, Jim. 2013. 52p. pap. 19.95 *(978-0-9858052-2-7(6))* People Ink Pr.

—Ivan the Invacar Helps Big Dog. Boles, Jim. 2012. 56p. pap. 19.95 *(978-0-9845983-5-9(9))* People Ink Pr.

Cunningham, Charles E. The Puzzle. Beal, Tracy Lynn. 2008. 17p. pap. 24.95 *(978-1-60610-078-3(5))* America Star Bks.

Cunningham, Imogen, et al, photos by. In Real Life: Six Women Photographers. Sills, Leslie. 2005. (ENG., 80p. (J). pap. 9.95 *(978-0-8234-1752-0(2))* Holiday Hse., Inc.

Cunningham, Kelley. The Omen & the Ghost, 1 vol. Townsend, John. 2007. (Shade Bks.). (ENG.). 80p. (gr. 2-3). 23.99 *(978-1-59889-353-3(X),* Shade Bks.) Stone Arch Bks.

—Poison Plate, 1 vol. Spirn, M. S. 2006. (Vortex Bks.). (ENG.). 112p. (gr. 2-3). 25.32 *(978-1-59889-069-3(7),* Vortex Bks.) Stone Arch Bks.

—Poison Plate, 1 vol. Sobel, M. et al. 2006. (Vortex Bks.). (ENG.). 112p. (gr. 2-3). per. 7.19 *(978-1-59889-280-2(0),* Vortex Bks.) Stone Arch Bks.

—The Ultimate How-To-Draw Real Stuff Book. 2006. 48p. (J). *(978-0-439-81336-5(0))* Scholastic, Inc.

Cunningham, Kelley, jt. illus. see Cousineau, Kelley.

Cunningham, Paul. Braving the Storm, 6 vols., Vol. 2. Dateno, Maria Grace. 2013. 70p. (J). pap. 5.95 *(978-0-8198-1204-9(8))* Pauline Bks. & Media.

—Courageous Quest. Dateno, Maria Grace. 2014. 81p. (J). pap. 5.95 *(978-0-8198-1628-3(0))* Pauline Bks. & Media.

—Danger at Sea. Dateno, Maria Grace. 2013. 80p. (J). pap. 5.95 *(978-0-8198-1891-1(7))* Pauline Bks. & Media.

—Discovery at Dawn. Dateno, Maria Grace. 2014. (ENG.). 79p. (J). pap. 5.95 *(978-0-8198-1895-9(X))* Pauline Bks. & Media.

—Mystery of the Missing Jars. Dateno, Maria Grace. 2014. 77p. (J). 5.95 *(978-0-8198-4922-9(7))* Pauline Bks. & Media.

—Shepherds to the Rescue, 6 vols., Vol. 1. Dateno, Maria Grace. 2013. 71p. (J). pap. 5.95 *(978-0-8198-7251-7(2))* Pauline Bks. & Media.

Cunningham, Rob. My Uncle Rob. Sandler, Steve. 2008. 32p. (J). pap. 12.95 *(978-0-9715721-5-7(1))* Washington Pubs.

Cupolo, Eileen. My Super Stupendous Day at the Beach. Webb, Jane K. 2012. 24p. pap. 12.95 *(978-1-61493-044-0(9))* Peppertree Pr., The.

Cupples, Pat. The Disappearing Magician. Dickson, Louise. 2007. (Kids Can Read Ser.). (ENG.). 32p. (J). (gr. 1-2). 3.95 *(978-1-55453-034-2(2))* Kids Can Pr., Ltd. CAN. Dist: Univ. of Toronto Pr.

—The Drop of Doom. Mason, Adrienne. 2007. (Kids Can Read Ser.). (ENG.). 32p. (J). (gr. 1-2). 3.95 *(978-1-55453-036-6(9));* 14.95 *(978-1-55453-035-9(0))* Kids Can Pr., Ltd. CAN. Dist: Univ. of Toronto Pr.

—Lost & Found. Mason, Adrienne. 2008. (Kids Can Read Ser.). (ENG.). 32p. (J). (gr. -1-3). pap. 3.95 *(978-1-55453-252-0(3));* (gr. 1-2). 14.95 *(978-1-55453-251-3(5))* Kids Can Pr., Ltd. CAN. Dist: Univ. of Toronto Pr.

Cupples, Pat, jt. illus. see Cupples, Patricia.

Cupples, Patricia & Cupples, Pat. Secret Spies. Mason, Adrienne. 2008. (Kids Can Read Ser.). (ENG.). 32p. (J). (gr. 1-2). 14.95 *(978-1-55453-276-6(0));* pap. 3.95 *(978-1-55453-277-3(9))* Kids Can Pr., Ltd. CAN. Dist: Univ. of Toronto Pr.

Curato, Mike. Little Elliot, Big City. Curato, Mike. 2014. (Little Elliot Ser.). (ENG.). 40p. (J). (gr. -1-3). 16.99 *(978-0-8050-9825-9(9),* Holt, Henry & Co. Bks. For Young Readers) Holt, Henry & Co.

Curlee, Lynn. Ballpark: The Story of America's Baseball Fields. Curlee, Lynn. (ENG.). 48p. (J). 2008. (gr. -1-3). 7.99 *(978-1-4169-5360-9(4));* 2005. (gr. 3-7). 19.99 *(978-0-689-86742-2(5))* Simon & Schuster Children's Publishing. (Atheneum Bks. for Young Readers).

—Capital. Curlee, Lynn. 2006. (ENG.). 48p. (J). (gr. 4-7). 22.99 *(978-1-4169-1801-1(9),* Atheneum Bks. for Young Readers) Simon & Schuster Children's Publishing.

—Liberty. Curlee, Lynn. 2003. (ENG.). 48p. (J). (gr. 2-7). 9.99 *(978-0-689-85683-9(0),* Atheneum Bks. for Young Readers) Simon & Schuster Children's Publishing.

—Mythological Creatures: A Classical Bestiary. Curlee, Lynn. 2008. (ENG.). 40p. (J). (gr. 3-7). 19.99 *(978-1-4169-1453-2(6),* Atheneum Bks. for Young Readers) Simon & Schuster Children's Publishing.

—Parthenon. Curlee, Lynn. 2011. (ENG.). 40p. (J). (gr. 3-7). 19.99 *(978-1-4424-3094-5(X),* Atheneum Bks. for Young Readers) Simon & Schuster Children's Publishing.

—Skyscraper. Curlee, Lynn. 2007. (ENG.). 48p. (J). (gr. 3-7). 19.99 *(978-0-689-84489-8(1),* Atheneum Bks. for Young Readers) Simon & Schuster Children's Publishing.

—Trains. Curlee, Lynn. 2009. (ENG.). 48p. (J). (gr. 4-6). 19.99 *(978-1-4169-4848-3(1),* Atheneum Bks. for Young Readers) Simon & Schuster Children's Publishing.

Curless, Allan. The Bellmaker. Jacques, Brian. 2004. (Redwall Ser.). (ENG.). 352p. (J). (gr. 5-18). reprint ed. pap. 8.99 *(978-0-14-240030-2(0),* Puffin) Penguin Publishing Group.

—The Long Patrol: A Tale from Redwall. Jacques, Brian. 2004. (Redwall Ser.). (ENG.). 368p. (J). (gr. 5-3). 8.99 *(978-0-14-240245-0(1),* Puffin) Penguin Publishing Group.

Curless, Allan, jt. illus. see Elliot, David.

Curley, Carol. The What If Book. Sammarco, Teresa "T". 2013. (J). lib. bdg. 16.95 *(978-1-59598-236-0(1))* HenschelHAUS Publishing.

Curmi, Serena. Smile, Principessa! Enderle, Judith Ross & Gordon, Stephanie Jacob. 2012. (ENG.). 40p. (J). (gr. -1-1). 16.99 *(978-1-4424-3096-9(6),* McElderry, Margaret K. Bks.) McElderry, Margaret K. Bks.

Currant, Gary. Code Blue Calling All Capitals! Hall, Pamela. 2009. (Grammar's Slammin' Ser.). 32p. (J). (gr. -1-3). 28.50 *(978-1-60270-614-9(X))* Magic Wagon.

—Find Your Function at Conjunction Junction. Hall, Pamela. 2009. (Grammar's Slammin' Ser.). 32p. (J). (gr. -1-3). 28.50 *(978-1-60270-615-6(8))* Magic Wagon.

—The Muscle-Bound Compounds. Hall, Pamela. 2009. (Grammar's Slammin' Ser.). 32p. (J). (gr. -1-3). 28.50 *(978-1-60270-616-3(6))* Magic Wagon.

—The Old Gray Mare. Fuerst, Jeffrey B. 2010. (Rising Readers Ser.). (J). 3.49 *(978-1-60719-692-1(1))* Newmark Learning LLC.

—The Old Gray Mare IS What She Used to Be. Fuerst, Jeffrey B. 2009. (Reader's Theater Nursery Rhymes & Songs Set B Ser.). 48p. (J). pap. *(978-1-60859-162-6(X))* Benchmark Education Co.

—Punk-Tuation Celebration. Hall, Pamela. 2009. (Grammar's Slammin' Ser.). 32p. (J). (gr. -1-3). 28.50 *(978-1-60270-617-0(4))* Magic Wagon.

—Stand-in Pronouns Save the Scene! Hall, Pamela. 2009. (Grammar's Slammin' Ser.). 32p. (J). (gr. -1-3). 28.50 *(978-1-60270-618-7(2))* Magic Wagon.

—Wheel of Subject-Verb Agreement. Hall, Pamela. 2009. (Grammar's Slammin' Ser.). 32p. (J). (gr. -1-3). 28.50 *(978-1-60270-619-4(0))* Magic Wagon.

Currant, Gary, jt. illus. see Sharp, Chris.

Currell, Augusta. My Bible: The Story of God's Love. Wright, Melissa & Currell, Augusta. 2004. 236p. (J). 24.95 *(978-0-8198-4834-5(4),* 332-223) Pauline Bks. & Media.

Currell, Augusta & Lombardo, Irina. Holy Friends: Thirty Saints & Blesseds of the Americas. Amadeo, Diana M. 2005. 134p. (J). (gr. 3-7). 19.95 *(978-0-8198-3384-6(3))* Pauline Bks. & Media.

Curren, Cindy. The Leaf That Was Left. Bryan-Brown, Kim. l.t. ed. 2006. 32p. (J). 16.95 *(978-0-9772564-0-2(5))* Them Potatoes.

Currey, Andrew K. The Littlest Ladybug. Marranzino, Sami. 2012. 32p. pap. 24.95 *(978-1-4626-7781-8(9))* America Star Bks.

Currey, Anna. Hush-a-Bye, Baby: And Other Nursery Rhymes. 2003. (ENG.). 14p. (J). bds. 8.99 *(978-0-333-78086-2(8))* Macmillan Pubs., Ltd. GBR. Dist: Trafalgar Square Publishing.

—One Ted Falls Out of Bed. Donaldson, Julia. 2014. (ENG.). 12p. (J). (gr. -1 — 1). bds. 8.99 *(978-1-4472-0995-9(8))* Pan Macmillan GBR. Dist: Independent Pubs. Group.

—Pat-a-Cake: And Other Nursery Rhymes. 2003. (ENG.). 14p. (J). bds. 6.95 *(978-0-333-78083-1(3))* Macmillan Pubs., Ltd. GBR. Dist: Trafalgar Square Publishing.

—Ring-a-Ring O' Roses: And Other Nursery Rhymes. 2003. (ENG.). 14p. (J). bds. 6.95 *(978-0-333-78084-8(1))* Macmillan Pubs., Ltd. GBR. Dist: Trafalgar Square Publishing.

—Sophie & Abigail, 1 vol. Umansky, Kaye. 2004. (Sophie Rabbit Books). (ENG.). 30p. (J). pap. 9.95 *(978-1-56148-434-8(2),* Good Bks.) Skyhorse Publishing Co., Inc.

—Sophie & the Mother's Day Card, 1 vol. Umansky, Kaye & Umansky. 2005. (ENG.). 30p. (J). pap. 3.95 *(978-1-56148-481-2(4),* Good Bks.) Skyhorse Publishing Co., Inc.

—Sophie & the Mother's Day Card. Umansky, Kaye. 2005. (ENG.). 30p. (J). pap. 9.95 *(978-1-56148-479-9(2),* Good Bks.) Skyhorse Publishing Co., Inc.

—Sophie & the Wonderful Picture. Umansky, Kaye. 2004. (Sophie Rabbit Books). (ENG.). 30p. (J). pap. 3.95 *(978-1-56148-445-4(8),* Good Bks.) Skyhorse Publishing Co., Inc.

—Sophie & the Wonderful Picture, 1 vol. Umansky, Kaye & Umansky. 2004. (Sophie Rabbit Books). (ENG.). 30p. (J). pap. 9.95 *(978-1-56148-437-9(7),* Good Bks.) Skyhorse Publishing Co., Inc.

—Sophie in Charge. Umansky, Kaye. 2005. 30p. (J). 9.95 *(978-1-56148-478-2(4));* (ENG.). pap. 3.95 *(978-1-56148-480-5(6))* Skyhorse Publishing Co., Inc. (Good Bks.).

—When the World Is Ready for Bed. Shields, Gillian. (ENG.). (J). (gr. -1 — 1). 2010. 26p. bds. 7.99 *(978-1-59990-533-4(7));* 2009. 32p. 14.99 *(978-1-59990-339-2(3))* Bloomsbury USA. (Bloomsbury USA Childrens).

—When the World Was Waiting for You. Shields, Gillian. (ENG.). (J). (gr. -1 — 1). 2012. 26p. bds. 7.99 *(978-1-59990-849-6(2));* 2011. 32p. 14.99 *(978-1-59990-531-0(0))* Bloomsbury USA. (Bloomsbury USA Childrens).

—When the World Was Waiting for You Baby Book. Shields, Gillian. 2014. (ENG.). 32p. (J). (gr. -1-1). 22.99 *(978-1-4088-4213-3(0),* 235093, Bloomsbury USA Childrens) Bloomsbury USA.

—Who Goes There? Wilson, Karma. 2013. (ENG.). 40p. (J). (gr. -1-3). 16.99 *(978-1-4169-8002-5(4),* McElderry, Margaret K. Bks.) McElderry, Margaret K. Bks.

—The Wishing Club: A Story about Fractions. Napoli, Donna Jo. rev. ed. 2007. (ENG.). 32p. (J). (gr. 1-4). 17.99

C

(978-0-8050-7665-3(4)), Holt, Henry & Co. Bks. For Young Readers) Holt, Henry & Co.

Currey, Anna. Truffle Goes to Town. Currey, Anna. 2003. 32p. (YA). *(978-1-85602-429-7(6)*, Pavilion Children's Books) Pavilion Bks.

Currey, Anna, jt. illus. see Umansky, Kaye.

Currey, Erica Leigh. Finding Nemo: Reef Rescue. Croall, Marie. 2009. (ENG.). 112p. (J). 24.99 *(978-1-60886-524-6(X))* Boom! Studios.

—Finding Nemo: Reef Rescue. Croall, Marie. 2009. (ENG.). 112p. (J). pap. 9.99 *(978-1-934506-88-2(5))* Boom! Studios.

Currie, Justin. Quackers Wants to Fly. Wolff, Susan. 2013. 32p. pap. 8.95 *(978-1-60653-074-0(7))* High Hill Pr.

Curriel, Hector. Umpire in a Skirt: The Amanda Clement Story. Kratz, Marilyn. 2011. 44p. (J). pap. 9.95 *(978-0-9845041-2-1(5)*, South Dakota State Historical Society Pr.) South Dakota State Historical Society Pr.

Curry, Garrett A. Sugarfootn' in the South with Brer' Rabbit: How Handclapping Got Started in the Church Sugarfootstrade; Tattle-Tales Series. El Wilson, Barbara. 2010. 24p. 12.99 *(978-1-4520-3145-3(2))* AuthorHouse.

Curry, Peter. This Little Bunny. Powell, R. 2004. (Mini Movers Ser.). (ENG.). 14p. (J). bds. 4.99 *(978-0-7641-5739-4(6))* Barron's Educational Series, Inc.

—This Little Doggy. Powell, R. 2004. (Mini Movers Ser.). (ENG.). 14p. (J). bds. 4.99 *(978-0-7641-5741-7(8))* Barron's Educational Series, Inc.

—This Little Lamb. Powell, R. 2004. (Mini Movers Ser.). (ENG.). 14p. (J). bds. 4.99 *(978-0-7641-5742-4(6))* Barron's Educational Series, Inc.

Curry, Tom. Buckamoo Girls. Kelley, Ellen A. 2006. (ENG.). 32p. (J). (gr. -1-3). 16.95 *(978-0-8109-5471-7(0)*, Abrams Bks. for Young Readers) Abrams.

—A Fine St. Patrick's Day. Wojciechowski, Susan. 2008. (ENG.). 40p. (J). (gr. -1-2). pap. 7.99 *(978-0-385-73640-4(1)*, Dragonfly Bks.) Random Hse. Children's Bks.

—Galileo's Universe. Lewis, J. Patrick. 2005. (Creative Editions Ser.). 18p. (YA). (gr. 4-7). 24.95 *(978-1-56846-183-0(6))* Creative Co., The.

Curtis, Bruce, photos by. Kids' Container Gardening: Year-Round Projects for Inside & Out. Krezel, Cindy. 2nd ed. 2010. (ENG.). 88p. (J). (gr. 1-6). pap. 14.95 *(978-1-883052-75-1(0))* Ball Publishing.

Curtis, E. Ends of Rainbow. Varsell, Linda. 2003. 260p. (J). per. 8.00 *(978-0-9725479-5-6(9))* Rainbow Communications.

—The Humane Touch. Varsell, Linda. 2003. 316p. per. 10.00 *(978-0-9728737-0-3(8))* Rainbow Communications.

—A Journey for Rainbows. Varsell, Linda. 2003. 166p. (YA). per. 6.00 *(978-0-9725479-1-8(6))* Rainbow Communications.

—The Rainbow Breakers. Varsell, Linda. 2003. 232p. per. 7.00 *(978-0-9725479-3-2(2))* Rainbow Communications.

—The Rainbow Circle. Varsell, Linda. 2003. 428p. (J). per. 10.00 *(978-0-9725479-9-4(1))* Rainbow Communications.

—The Rainbow Dreamers. Varsell, Linda. 2003. 262p. per. 8.00 *(978-0-9725479-4-9(0))* Rainbow Communications.

—The Rainbow Makers. Varsell, Linda. 2003. 148p. per. 6.00 *(978-0-9725479-2-5(4))* Rainbow Communications.

—The Rainbow Planet. Varsell, Linda. 2003. 162p. (J). per. 6.00 *(978-0-9725479-7-0(5))* Rainbow Communications.

—The Rainbow Remnants. Varsell, Linda. 2003. 204p. (J). per. 7.00 *(978-0-9725479-8-7(3))* Rainbow Communications.

—The Rainbow Rescue. Varsell, Linda. 2003. 200p. (J). per. 7.00 *(978-0-9725479-6-3(7))* Rainbow Communications.

—With a Human Touch. Varsell, Linda. 2003. 178p. per. 6.00 *(978-0-9725479-0-1(8))* Rainbow Communications.

Curtis King, Anna. Old Order Changes. Tshekeche. 2014. 23.99 *(978-1-63449-741-1(4))* Tate Publishing & Enterprises, LLC.

—Tsuro to the Rescue. Tshekeche. 2014. 23.99 *(978-1-63449-740-4(6))* Tate Publishing & Enterprises, LLC.

Curtis, Neil. Cat & Fish. Grant, Joan. 2005. (ENG.). 32p. (J). (gr. k-3). 16.95 *(978-1-894965-14-9(0))* Simply Read Bks. CAN. Dist: Ingram Pub. Services.

—Cat & Fish Go to See. Grant, Joan. 2006. (ENG.). 32p. (J). (gr. -1-3). 16.95 *(978-1-894965-39-2(6))* Simply Read Bks. CAN. Dist: Ingram Pub. Services.

Curtis, Stacy. Dancing Dudes. Knudson, Mike & Wilkinson, Steve. 2010. (Raymond & Graham Ser.). (ENG.). 144p. (J). (gr. 3-7). 6.99 *(978-0-14-241508-5(1)*, Puffin) Penguin Publishing Group.

—The Dragon Stone, 0 vols. Regan, Dian Curtis. 2013. (ENG.). 83p. (J). (gr. 2-4). pap. 9.99 *(978-1-4778-1632-5(1)*, 9781477816325, Amazon Children's Publishing) Amazon Publishing.

—Goob & His Grandpa. Covey, Sean. 2013. (7 Habits of Happy Kids Ser.: 7). (ENG.). 32p. (J). (gr. -1-1). 7.99 *(978-1-4424-7653-0(2)*, Simon & Schuster Bks. For Young Readers) Simon & Schuster Bks. For Young Readers.

—Just the Way I Am: Habit 1. Covey, Sean. 2009. (7 Habits of Happy Kids Ser.: 1). (ENG.). 32p. (J). (gr. -1-1). 7.99 *(978-1-4169-9423-7(8)*, Simon & Schuster Bks. For Young Readers) Simon & Schuster Bks. For Young Readers.

—Lily & the Yucky Cookies. Covey, Sean. 2013. (7 Habits of Happy Kids Ser.: 5). (ENG.). 32p. (J). (gr. -1-1). 7.99 *(978-1-4424-7649-3(4)*, Simon & Schuster Bks. For Young Readers) Simon & Schuster Bks. For Young Readers.

—Odd Ball: Hilarious, Unusual, & Bizarre Baseball Moments, 0 vols. Tocher, Timothy. 2011. (ENG.). 64p. (J). (gr. 3-6). 15.99 *(978-0-7614-5813-5(1)*, 9780761458135, Amazon Children's Publishing) Amazon Publishing.

—A Place for Everything: Habit 3. Covey, Sean. 2010. (7 Habits of Happy Kids Ser.: 3). (ENG.). 32p. (J). (gr. -1-1). bds. 7.99 *(978-1-4169-9425-1(4)*, Simon & Schuster Bks. For Young Readers) Simon & Schuster Bks. For Young Readers.

—Raymond & Graham Rule the School. Knudson, Mike & Wilkinson, Steve. 2009. (Raymond & Graham Ser.). (ENG.). 144p. (J). (gr. 3-7). 6.99 *(978-0-14-241426-2(3)*, Puffin) Penguin Publishing Group.

—Ricky Vargas: The Funniest Kid in the World. Katz, Alan. 2011. (J). pap. *(978-0-545-24583-8(4)*, Cartwheel Bks.) Scholastic, Inc.

—Sammy & the Pecan Pie. Covey, Sean. 2013. (7 Habits of Happy Kids Ser.: 4). (ENG.). 32p. (J). (gr. -1-1). 7.99 *(978-1-4424-7647-9(8)*, Simon & Schuster Bks. For Young Readers) Simon & Schuster Bks. For Young Readers.

—Snack Attack. Krensky, Stephen. 2008. (Ready-To-Reads Ser.). (ENG.). 32p. (J). (gr. -1-1). pap. 3.99 *(978-1-4169-0238-6(4)*, Simon Spotlight) Simon Spotlight.

—Sophie & the Perfect Poem. Covey, Sean. 2013. (7 Habits of Happy Kids Ser.: 6). (ENG.). 32p. (J). (gr. -1-1). 7.99 *(978-1-4424-7651-6(6)*, Simon & Schuster Bks. For Young Readers) Simon & Schuster Bks. For Young Readers.

—To Be a Cat. Haig, Matt. (ENG.). 304p. (J). (gr. 3-7). 2014. pap. 6.99 *(978-1-4424-5406-4(7))*; 2013. 16.99 *(978-1-4424-5405-7(9))* Simon & Schuster Children's Publishing.

—When I Grow Up: Habit 2. Covey, Sean. 2009. (7 Habits of Happy Kids Ser.: 2). (ENG.). 32p. (J). (gr. -1-1). 7.99 *(978-1-4169-9424-4(6)*, Simon & Schuster Bks. For Young Readers) Simon & Schuster Bks. For Young Readers.

—The 7 Habits of Happy Kids. Covey, Sean. 2008. (ENG.). 96p. (J). (gr. -1-3). 19.99 *(978-1-4169-5776-8(6)*, Simon & Schuster Bks. For Young Readers) Simon & Schuster Bks. For Young Readers.

—The 7 Habits of Happy Kids Collection: Just the Way I Am; When I Grow up; a Place for Everything; Sammy & the Pecan Pie; Lily & the Yucky Cookies; Sophie & the Perfect Poem; Goob & His Grandpa. Covey, Sean. ed. 2013. (7 Habits of Happy Kids Ser.). (ENG.). 224p. (J). (gr. -1-1). 55.99 *(978-1-4424-9617-0(7)*, Simon & Schuster Bks. For Young Readers) Simon & Schuster Bks. For Young Readers.

Curtiss, Melody. Naming: Book One of the Magic of Io Series. Robinson, Kelley. 2013. 138p. pap. 8.95 *(978-0-9745865-1-9(X)*, SarahRose Children's Bks.) SarahRose Publishing.

Curto, Rosa M. Mind Your Manners: In School. Candell, Arianna. 2005. (Mind Your Manners Ser.). (ENG.). 36p. (J). pap. 6.99 *(978-0-7641-3166-0(4))* Barron's Educational Series, Inc.

—Splash! Water. Jimenez, Nuria & Jimenez, Empar. 2010. (Taking Care of Your Planet Ser.). (ENG.). 36p. (J). (gr. k-3). pap. 6.99 *(978-0-7641-4544-5(4))* Barron's Educational Series, Inc.

Curto, Rosa M. & Curto, Rosa Maria. I Have Asthma. Moore-Malinos, Jennifer & Moore-Mallinos, Jennifer. 2007. (What Do You Know about? Bks.). (ENG.). 36p. (J). (gr. -1-2). pap. 6.99 *(978-0-7641-3785-3(9))* Barron's Educational Series, Inc.

Curto, Rosa María. La Ratita Presumida. Combel Editorial Staff & catalán, Cuento popular. 2004. (Caballo Alado Clásico Series-Al Paso Ser.). (SPA & ENG.). 24p. (J). (gr. -1-k). 7.95 *(978-84-7864-763-7(5))* Combel Editorial, S.A. ESP. Dist: Independent Pubs. Group.

Curto, Rosa Maria. La Ratita Presumida. Bailer, Darice & Domínguez, Madelca. 2007. (SPA & ENG.). 28p. (J). *(978-0-545-03031-1(5))* Scholastic, Inc.

—The Three R's: Reuse, Reduce, Recycle. Roca, Nuria. 2007. (What Do You Know about? Bks.). (ENG.). 36p. (J). (gr. -1-1). pap. 6.99 *(978-0-7641-3581-1(3))* Barron's Educational Series, Inc.

—The 5 Senses. Roca, Nuria. 2006. (Let's Learn About Ser.). (ENG.). 36p. (J). (gr. -1-3). per. 7.99 *(978-0-7641-3312-1(8))* Barron's Educational Series, Inc.

Curto, Rosa Maria, jt. illus. see Curto, Rosa M.

Curtsinger, Bill. Life under Ice. Curtsinger, Bill, photos by. Cerullo, Mary M. 2010. 40p. (J). (gr. 3-7). 16.95 *(978-0-88448-246-8(4))* Tilbury Hse. Pubs.

Curtsinger, Bill, photos by. Life under Ice, 1 vol. Cerullo, Mary M. 2010. (ENG.). 40p. (J). (gr. 4-7). 7.95 *(978-0-88448-247-5(2))* Tilbury Hse. Pubs.

—Sea Soup: Zooplankton, 1 vol. Cerullo, Mary M. 2010. (ENG., 40p. (J). (gr. 3-7). 16.95 *(978-0-88448-219-2(7))* Tilbury Hse. Pubs.

Cusack, Elizabeth. Cartwheeling. Whitaker, Joan. 2013. 24p. 22.95 *(978-1-61493-189-8(5))*; pap. 12.95 *(978-1-61493-188-1(7))* Peppertree Pr., The.

Cushman, Doug. The Amazing Trail of Seymour Snail. Hazen, Lynn E. 2009. (ENG.). 64p. (J). (gr. 1-4). 16.99 *(978-0-8050-8698-0(6)*, Holt, Henry & Co. Bks. For Young Readers) Holt, Henry & Co.

—Birthday at the Panda Palace. Calmenson, Stephanie. 2007. 32p. (J). (gr. -1-3). 15.99 *(978-0-06-052663-4(7))* HarperCollins Pubs.

—Dirk Bones & the Mystery of the Missing Books. 2009. (I Can Read Book 1 Ser.). (ENG.). 32p. (J). (gr. -1-3). 16.99 *(978-0-06-073768-9(9))* HarperCollins Pubs.

—Double Play: Monkeying Around with Addition. Franco, Betsy. 2011. (ENG.). 32p. (J). (gr. -1-2). 15.99 *(978-1-58246-384-1(0)*, Tricycle Pr.) Ten Speed Pr.

—Dracula & Frankenstein Are Friends. Tegen, Katherine. 2003. 32p. (J). (gr. -1-3). 15.99 *(978-0-06-000115-5(1))* HarperCollins Pubs.

—Ella, of Course! Weeks, Sarah. 2007. (ENG.). 32p. (J). (gr. -1-3). 16.00 *(978-0-15-204943-0(6))* Houghton Mifflin Harcourt Publishing Co.

—Feliz Cumpleanos, Gus! Williams, Jacklyn. Abello, Patricia, tr. from ENG. 2006. (Read-It! Readers en Español: Gus el Erizo Ser.). Tr. of Happy Birthday, Gus!. (SPA.). 32p. (gr. k-3). lib. bdg. 19.99 *(978-1-4048-2693-9(9)*, Easy Readers) Picture Window Bks.

—Feliz Dia de Gracias, Gus!, 1 vol. Williams, Jacklyn. Abello, Patricia, tr. from ENG. 2006. (Read-It! Readers en Español: Gus el Erizo Ser.). (SPA.). 32p. (gr. k-3). lib. bdg. 19.99 *(978-1-4048-2690-8(4)*, Easy Readers) Picture Window Bks.

—Halloween Mice! Roberts, Bethany. 2011. (ENG.). 28p. (J). (gr. k — 1). bds. 5.99 *(978-0-547-57573-5(4))* Houghton Mifflin Harcourt Publishing Co.

—Here Comes the Choo Choo! Roth, Carol. 2007. (J). *(978-0-15-205582-0(7))* Harcourt Trade Pubs.

—The Invisible Man. Yorinks, Arthur. 2011. (ENG.). 32p. (J). (gr. -1-3). 16.99 *(978-0-06-156148-1(7))* HarperCollins Pubs.

—Let's Go Fishing, Gus!, 1 vol. Williams, Jacklyn. 2006. (Read-It! Readers: Gus the Hedgehog Ser.). (ENG.). 32p. (gr. k-3). lib. bdg. 19.99 *(978-1-4048-2713-4(7)*, Easy Readers) Picture Window Bks.

—Let's Try It Out in the Air. Simon, Seymour & Fauteux, Nicole. 2003. (Let's Try It Out Ser.). 28p. (J). (gr. -1-3). lib. bdg. 14.65 *(978-0-7569-1477-6(9))* Perfection Learning Corp.

—Let's Try It Out in the Water: Hands-on Early-Learning Science Activities. Simon, Seymour & Fauteux, Nicole. 2003. (Let's Try It Out Ser.). (J). (gr. -1-3). 14.65 *(978-0-7569-1478-3(7))* Perfection Learning Corp.

—Merry Christmas, Gus!, 1 vol. Williams, Jacklyn. 2005. (Read-It! Readers: Gus the Hedgehog Ser.). (ENG.). 32p. (gr. k-3). 19.99 *(978-1-4048-0958-1(9)*, Easy Readers) Picture Window Bks.

—Nighttime: Too Dark to See. Strasser, Todd. 2008. 79p. (J). *(978-0-439-80068-6(4))* Scholastic, Inc.

—Pumpkin Time! Deàk, Erzsi. 2014. (ENG.). (J). (-3). 14.99 *(978-1-4022-9526-3(X)*, Sourcebooks Jabberwocky) Sourcebooks, Inc.

—The Snow Blew Inn. Regan, Dian Curtis. 2011. (ENG.). 32p. (J). 16.95 *(978-0-8234-2351-4(4))* Holiday Hse., Inc.

—Thanksgiving Mice! Roberts, Bethany. 2005. (ENG.). 32p. (J). (gr. -1 — 1). 5.95 *(978-0-618-60486-9(3))* Houghton Mifflin Harcourt Publishing Co.

—Too Dark to See. Strasser, Todd. 2009. (Nighttime Ser.). (ENG.). 80p. (J). (gr. 2-5). 4.99 *(978-0-545-12476-8(X)*, Scholastic Paperbacks) Scholastic, Inc.

—Tyrannosaurus Math. Markel, Michelle. 2009. (ENG.). 32p. (J). (gr. -1-2). 15.99 *(978-1-58246-282-0(8)*, Tricycle Pr.) Ten Speed Pr.

—Valentine Mice! Board Book. Roberts, Bethany. 2011. (ENG.). 28p. (J). (gr. k — 1). bds. 5.99 *(978-0-547-37144-3(6))* Houghton Mifflin Harcourt Publishing Co.

—What a Day It Was at School! Prelutsky, Jack. 40p. (J). (gr. k-5). 2009. (ENG.). pap. 6.99 *(978-0-06-082337-5(2)*, Greenwillow Bks.); 2006. 16.99 *(978-0-06-082335-1(6))* HarperCollins Pubs.

—What Grandmas Can't Do. Wood, Douglas. (ENG.). 32p. (J). (gr. -1-3). 2008. 6.99 *(978-1-4169-5483-5(X))*; 2005. 17.99 *(978-0-689-84647-2(9))* Simon & Schuster Bks. For Young Readers. (Simon & Schuster Bks. For Young Readers).

—What Santa Can't Do. Wood, Douglas. 2008. (ENG.). 32p. (J). (gr. -1-3). 16.99 *(978-1-4169-6747-7(8)*, Simon & Schuster Bks. For Young Readers) Simon & Schuster Bks. For Young Readers.

—What Time Is It, Mr. Crocodile? Sierra, Judy. 2007. (ENG.). 32p. (J). (gr. -1-3). pap. 7.00 *(978-0-15-205850-0(8))* Houghton Mifflin Harcourt Publishing Co.

Cushman, Doug. Dirk Bones & the Mystery of the Haunted House. Cushman, Doug. (I Can Read Book 1 Ser.). 32p. (J). (gr. k-3). 2009. (ENG.). pap. 3.99 *(978-0-06-073767-2(0))*; 2006. lib. bdg. 17.89 *(978-0-06-073765-8(4))* HarperCollins Pubs.

—Inspector Hopper's Mystery Year, No. 2. Cushman, Doug. 2003. (I Can Read Bks.). 64p. (J). (gr. k-3). 15.99 *(978-0-06-008962-7(8))*; 16.89 *(978-0-06-008963-4(6))* HarperCollins Pubs.

—Pigmares: Porcine Poems of the Silver Screen. Cushman, Doug. 2012. (ENG.). 44p. (J). (gr. 2-5). 12.95 *(978-1-58089-401-2(1))* Charlesbridge Publishing, Inc.

—Space Cat. Cushman, Doug. 2006. (I Can Read Book 1 Ser.). (ENG.). 32p. (J). (gr. -1-3). pap. 3.99 *(978-0-06-008967-2(9))* HarperCollins Pubs.

—Space Cat. Cushman, Doug. 2006. (I Can Read Bks.). 32p. (gr. -1-3). 14.00 *(978-0-7569-6977-6(8))* Perfection Learning Corp.

Cushman, Douglas. Never, Ever Shout in a Zoo. Wilson, Karma. 2004. (ENG.). 32p. (J). (gr. -1-1). 16.99 *(978-0-316-98564-2(3))* Little, Brown Bks. for Young Readers.

Cushner, Susie, photos by. Bride & Groom: First & Forever Cookbook. Barber, Mary Corpening et al. 2003. (ENG., 272p. (gr. 8-17). 35.00 *(978-0-8118-3493-3(X))* Chronicle Bks. LLC.

—Denyse Schmidt Quilts: 30 Colorful Quilt & Patchwork Projects. Schmidt, Denyse. 2005. (ENG., 176p. (gr. 8-17). pap. 24.95 *(978-0-8118-4442-0(0))* Chronicle Bks. LLC.

—5 Spices, 50 Dishes: Simple Indian Recipes Using Five Common Spices. Kahate, Ruta. 2007. (ENG., 132p. (gr. 8-17). pap. 19.95 *(978-0-8118-5342-2(X))* Chronicle Bks. LLC.

Custard, P. T. & Pearson, David. Kid Canine - Superhero! Custard, P. T. 2008. 32p. (J). 13.95 *(978-0-9785317-1-3(X))* Black Plum Bks.

Cutbill, Andy. Albie & the Big Race. 2004. (ENG.). 32p. (J). pap. 9.99 *(978-0-00-712212-7(8))* HarperCollins Pubs. Ltd. GBR. Dist: Trafalgar Square Publishing.

Cutchin, Marcia. Feathers: A Jewish Tale from Eastern Europe. 2005. (ENG.). 32p. (J). (gr. k-3). 16.95 *(978-0-87483-755-1(3)*, 1249133) August Hse. Pubs., Inc.

Cuthbert, R M & Vincent, Allison. Reindeer. Cuthbert, R M. 2006. 30p. (J). 12.95 *(978-1-56167-908-9(9))* American Literary Pr.

Cuthbertson, Ollie. Stranger in the Snow/L'etranger dans la Neige: French/English Edition. Barron's Educational Series & Benton, Lynne. 2010. (Let's Read! Bks.). (FRE & ENG.). 32p. (J). (gr. 3-7). pap. 4.99 *(978-0-7641-4475-2(8))* Barron's Educational Series, Inc.

Cutler, Dave. When I Wished I Was Alone. Cutler, Dave. 2003. 36p. (J). 16.95 *(978-0-9671851-0-1(6))* GreyCore Pr.

Cutler, Warren. The Seal Pup. Thach, James Otis. 2010. 128p. (J). (gr. k-7). 24.95 *(978-0-9825663-0-5(1))* Bowrider Pr.

Cutting, Ann, photos by. The Other Colors: An ABC Book. Gates, Valerie. 2013. (ENG., 56p. (J). (gr. -1-k). 14.95 *(978-1-62087-537-7(3)*, 620537, Sky Pony Pr.) Skyhorse Publishing Co., Inc.

Cutting, David. GIANTmicrobes — Cells Coloring Book. GIANTmicrobes(r). 2014. (ENG.). 32p. (J). (gr. k-5). pap. 3.99 *(978-0-486-78017-7(1))* Dover Pubns., Inc.

—GIANTmicrobes — Germs & Microbes Coloring Book. GIANTmicrobes(r). 2014. (ENG.). 32p. (J). (gr. k-5). pap. 3.99 *(978-0-486-78018-4(X))* Dover Pubns., Inc.

Cutting, David A. I Love to Sing. Matheson, Anne. 2014. (ENG.). 32p. (J). (gr. 1-5). 7.99 ***(978-1-4867-0001-1(2))*** Flowerpot Children's Pr. Inc. CAN. Dist: Cardinal Pubs. Group.

Cuxart, Bernadette. Amazing Experiments with Electricity & Magnetism. Navarro, Paula & Jimenez, Angels. 2014. (Magic Science Ser.). (ENG.). 36p. (J). (gr. 1-6). pap. 7.99 *(978-1-4380-0428-0(1))* Barron's Educational Series, Inc.

—Incredible Experiments with Chemical Reactions & Mixtures. Navarro, Paula & Jimenez, Angels. 2014. (Magic Science Ser.). (ENG.). 36p. (J). (gr. 1-6). pap. 7.99 *(978-1-4380-0427-3(3))* Barron's Educational Series, Inc.

—Magical Experiments with Light & Color. Navarro, Paula & Jimenez, Angels. 2014. (Magic Science Ser.). (ENG.). 36p. (J). (gr. 1-6). pap. 7.99 *(978-1-4380-0426-6(5))* Barron's Educational Series, Inc.

—Surprising Experiments with Sound. Navarro, Paula & Jimenez, Angels. 2014. (Magic Science Ser.). (ENG.). 36p. (J). (gr. 1-6). pap. 7.99 *(978-1-4380-0425-9(7))* Barron's Educational Series, Inc.

Cuxart, Bernardette. Cuentame un Cuento, No. 4. (SPA.). 96p. (J). (gr. k-3). *(978-84-480-1602-9(5)*, TM8095) Timun Mas, Editorial S.A. ESP. Dist: Lectorum Pubns., Inc.

Cuzik, David. Captain Cook. Levene, Rebecca. 2005. (Usborne Famous Lives Gift Bks.). 61p. (J). (gr. -1-3). 8.95 *(978-0-7945-1051-0(5)*, Usborne) EDC Publishing.

—Nelson. Lacey, Minna. 2006. (Usborne Famous Lives Gift Bks.). 64p. (J). 8.95 *(978-0-7945-1121-0(X)*, Usborne) EDC Publishing.

—The Usborne Story of Music. O'Brien, Eileen. Danes, Emma & Hooper, Caroline, eds. 2006. (Story of Music Ser.). 32p. (J). (gr. 4). lib. bdg. 15.99 *(978-1-58086-935-5(1)*, Usborne) EDC Publishing.

—The Usborne Story of Music. O'Brien, Eileen. Danes, Emma, ed. 2006. 32p. (J). (gr. 4-7). per. 7.99 *(978-0-7945-1403-7(0)*, Usborne) EDC Publishing.

Cyr, Christopher & Cyr, James. Pete-O Burrito & the Lucky Stripes. Cyr, Liz. 2012. 28p. 24.95 *(978-1-4626-5566-3(1))* America Star Bks.

Cyr, James, jt. illus. see Cyr, Christopher.

Cyrus, Kurt. Agent Q, or the Smell of Danger! Anderson, M. T. (Pals in Peril Tale Ser.). (ENG.). (J). (gr. 5-9). 2011. 320p. pap. 6.99 *(978-1-4424-2640-5(3))*; 2010. 304p. 16.99 *(978-1-4169-8640-9(5))* Beach Lane Bks. (Beach Lane Bks.).

—The Bones of Fred McFee. Bunting, Eve. 2005. (ENG.). 32p. (J). (gr. -1-3). pap. 6.99 *(978-0-15-205423-6(5))* Houghton Mifflin Harcourt Publishing Co.

—The Clue of the Linoleum Lederhosen. Anderson, M. T. 2010. (Pals in Peril Tale Ser.). (ENG.). (J). (gr. 5-9). 256p. 17.99 *(978-1-4424-0697-1(6))*; 272p. pap. 6.99 *(978-1-4424-0702-2(6))* Beach Lane Bks. (Beach Lane Bks.).

—He Laughed with His Other Mouths. Anderson, M. T. 2014. (Pals in Peril Tale Ser.). (ENG.). 304p. (J). (gr. 5-9). 17.99 *(978-1-4424-5110-0(6)*, Beach Lane Bks.) Beach Lane Bks.

—Hibernation Station. Meadows, Michelle. 2010. (ENG.). 40p. (J). (gr. -1-3). 17.99 *(978-1-4169-3788-3(9)*, Simon & Schuster Bks. For Young Readers) Simon & Schuster Bks. For Young Readers.

—Jasper Dash & the Flame-Pits of Delaware. Anderson, M. T. (Pals in Peril Tale Ser.). (ENG.). (J). (gr. 5-9). 2010. 448p. pap. 6.99 *(978-1-4424-0838-8(3))*; 2009. 432p. 16.99 *(978-1-4169-8639-3(1))* Beach Lane Bks. (Beach Lane Bks.).

—Mammoths on the Move. Wheeler, Lisa. 2006. (ENG.). 32p. (J). (gr. -1-3). 17.99 *(978-0-15-204700-9(X))* Houghton Mifflin Harcourt Publishing Co.

—Pest Fest. Durango, Julia. 2012. (ENG.). 40p. (J). (gr. -1-2). 19.99 *(978-1-4424-3095-2(8)*, Simon & Schuster Bks. For Young Readers) Simon & Schuster Bks. For Young Readers.

—Sixteen Cows. Wheeler, Lisa. 2006. (ENG.). 32p. (J). (gr. -1-3). reprint ed. pap. 6.99 *(978-0-15-205592-9(4))* Houghton Mifflin Harcourt Publishing Co.

—Twenty Big Trucks in the Middle of the Street. Lee, Mark. (ENG.). (J). 2015. 30p. (-k). bds. 7.99 *(978-0-7636-7650-6(0))*; 2013. 32p. (gr. -1-2). 15.99 *(978-0-7636-5809-0(X))* Candlewick Pr.

—Veinte Camiones Grandes en Medio de la Calle. Lee, Mark. 2015. (ENG.). 30p. (J). (-k). bds. 7.99 *(978-0-7636-7651-3(9))* Candlewick Pr.

—Whales on Stilts! Anderson, M. T. 2010. (Pals in Peril Tale Ser.). (ENG.). (J). (gr. 5-9). 2082p. 17.99 *(978-1-4424-0695-7(X))*; 224p. pap. 7.99 *(978-1-4424-0701-5(8))* Beach Lane Bks. (Beach Lane Bks.).

—Whales on Stilts! Anderson, M. T. 2006. (M. T. Anderson's Thrilling Tales Ser.). 188p. (gr. 5-9). 15.95 *(978-0-7569-7213-4(2))* Perfection Learning Corp.

—What in the World? Sets in Nature. Day, Nancy Raines. 2015. (ENG.). 32p. (J). (gr. -1-3). 17.99 *(978-1-4814-0060-2(6)*, Beach Lane Bks.) Beach Lane Bks.

—Word Builder. Paul, Ann Whitford. 2009. (ENG.). 32p. (J). (gr. k-2). 17.99 *(978-1-4169-3981-8(4)*, Simon & Schuster Bks. For Young Readers) Simon & Schuster Bks. For Young Readers.

—Zombie Mommy. Anderson, M. T. (Pals in Peril Tale Ser.). (ENG.). 224p. (J). (gr. 5-9). 2012. pap. 6.99 *(978-1-4424-5440-8(7))*; 2011. 16.99

(978-1-4169-8641-6(3)) Beach Lane Bks. (Beach Lane Bks.).

—Zombie Mommy. Anderson, M. T. 2011. (M. T. Anderson's Thrilling Tales Ser.). 240p. 16.99 *(978-1-4424-3068-6(0))* Simon & Schuster Children's Publishing.

Czekaj, Jef. The Circulatory Story. Corcoran, Mary K. 2010. (ENG.). 44p. (J). (gr. 3-7). pap. 7.95 *(978-1-58089-209-4(4))* Charlesbridge Publishing, Inc.

—Horns, Tails, Spikes, & Claws. Mills, J. Elizabeth. 2012. (ENG.). 10p. (J). (gr. -1-k). 6.99 *(978-0-545-39385-0(X),* Cartwheel Bks.) Scholastic, Inc.

—The Quest to Digest. Corcoran, Mary K. 2006. (ENG.). 32p. (J). (gr. 3-7). pap. 7.95 *(978-1-57091-665-6(9))* Charlesbridge Publishing, Inc.

Czekaj, Jef. Austin, Lost in America: A Geography Adventure. Czekaj, Jef. 2015. (ENG.). 40p. (J). (gr. -1-3). 17.99 ***(978-0-06-228017-6(1))*** HarperCollins Pubs.

Czekaj, Jef. A Call for a New Alphabet. Czekaj, Jef. 2011. (ENG.). 48p. (J). (gr. 1-4). pap. 5.95 *(978-1-58089-229-2(9))* Charlesbridge Publishing, Inc.

—Cat Secrets. Czekaj, Jef. 2011. (ENG.). 32p. (J). (gr. -1-3). 16.99 *(978-0-06-192088-2(6))* HarperCollins Pubs.

—Oink-a-Doodle-Moo. Czekaj, Jef. 2012. (ENG.). 32p. (J). (gr. -1-1). 16.99 *(978-0-06-206011-2(2))* HarperCollins Pubs.

Czernecki, Stefan. Aziz the Story Teller. Hughes, V. I. 2006. 29p. (J). (gr. k-4). reprint ed. 17.00 *(978-1-4223-5298-4(6))* DIANE Publishing Co.

—For Sure! for Sure! Andersen, Hans Christian & White, Mus. 2005. (ENG.). 32p. (J). (gr. k-3). 16.95 *(978-0-87483-742-1(1))* August Hse. Pubs., Inc.

—For Sure! for Sure! Andersen, Hans Christian. White, Mus, tr. from DAN. 2006. 29p. (J). (gr. k-4). reprint ed. 17.00 *(978-1-4223-5208-3(0))* DIANE Publishing Co.

—Holy Mole! A Folktale from Mexico. McAlister, Caroline. 2006. (ENG.). 32p. (J). (gr. k-3). 16.95 *(978-0-87483-775-9(8))* August Hse. Pubs., Inc.

—Viva Zapata!, 1 vol. Smith, Emilie & Tejada, Marguerita. 2009. (ENG.). 32p. (J). (gr. -1-3). 14.95 *(978-1-896580-55-6(6))* Tradewind Bks. CAN. Dist: Orca Bk. Pubs. USA.

—Zigzag. San Souci, Robert D. 2005. (ENG.). 32p. (J). (gr. -1-2). 16.95 *(978-0-87483-764-3(2))* August Hse. Pubs., Inc.

Czernecki, Stefan. Paper Lanterns. Czernecki, Stefan. 2004. (ENG.). 32p. (J). (gr. -1-3). pap. 7.95 *(978-1-57091-411-9(7))* Charlesbridge Publishing, Inc.

Czernichowska, Joanna. Opinions about Two Fairy Tales: Baba Yaga & Hansel & Gretel. Strom, Laura Layton et al. 2014. (Text Connections Ser.). (J). (gr. 3). *(978-1-4509-9649-5(3))* Benchmark Education Co.

Czubinski, Amber. The Many Adventures of Pig Batter: A Day at the Park, 1 vol. Czubinski, Robert. 2009. 20p. pap. 24.95 *(978-1-61546-495-1(6))* America Star Bks.

D

Da Coll, Ivar. Azucar! Da Coll, Ivar. 2005. (SPA.). (J). 14.99 *(978-1-930332-65-2(3))* Lectorum Pubns., Inc.

—Hamamelis, Miosotis y el Senor Sorpresa. Da Coll, Ivar. 2005. (SPA.). 24p. (J). *(978-958-704-218-4(2))* Ediciones Alfaguara.

—Hamamelis y el Secreto. Da Coll, Ivar. 2005. (SPA.). 24p. (J). pap. *(978-958-704-219-1(0))* Ediciones Alfaguara.

—Jose Tomillo, Maria Juana. Da Coll, Ivar. 2004. (SPA.). 53p. pap. *(978-958-04-7662-7(4))* Norma S.A.

—No, No Fui Yo! Da Coll, Ivar. 2005. (SPA.). 40p. (J). pap. *(978-958-704-220-7(4))* Ediciones Alfaguara.

Da-Young Im, Linda, jt. illus. see Ju-Young Im, Joy.

Dabbs, Douglas. The Legend's Granddaughter: Not Quite Super, Book 1. Carr, Patrick W. 2007. 281p. (J). pap. *(978-0-9793168-0-7(4))* NQSBks.

Dabcovich, Lydia. The Ghost on the Hearth. Milord, Susan. 2003. (Vermont Folklife Center Children's Book Ser.). (ENG.). 32p. (J). (gr. -1-3). 15.95 *(978-0-916718-18-3(2))* Vermont Folklife Ctr.

Dabija, Violeta. A Leaf Can Be- Salas, Laura Purdie. 2012. (Millbrook Picture Bks). (ENG.). 32p. (J). (gr. k-2). lib. bdg. 17.95 *(978-0-7613-6203-6(7),* Millbrook Pr.) Lerner Publishing Group.

—A Rock Can Be . . Salas, Laura Purdie. 2015. (ENG.). 32p. (J). (gr. k-2). lib. bdg. 17.99 *(978-1-4677-2110-3(7),* Millbrook Pr.) Lerner Publishing Group.

—The Twelve Days of Christmas. 2013. (ENG.). 24p. (J). 18.99 *(978-0-7945-3330-4(2),* Usborne) EDC Publishing.

—Water Can Be ... Salas, Laura Purdie. 2014. (ENG.). 32p. (J). (gr. k-2). 17.95 *(978-1-4677-0591-2(8),* Millbrook Pr.) Lerner Publishing Group.

Dabney, Undra & Goettling, Nickalas. My Daddy Does GOOD Things, Too! Gaffney, Linda. 2006. 55p. per. 10.99 *(978-0-9787501-0-7(1))* Gaffney, Linda.

Dacey, Bandelin, et al. What's the Difference Between a Butterfly & a Moth?, 1 vol. Koontz, Robin Michal & Koontz, Robin. 2009. (What's the Difference? Ser.). (ENG.). 24p. (gr. k-3). lib. bdg. 25.99 *(978-1-4048-5543-4(2),* Nonfiction Picture Bks.) Picture Window Bks.

Dacey, Bob. Hermit Crab's Home: Safe in a Shell. Halfmann, Janet. 2007. (ENG.). 32p. 19.95 *(978-1-59249-735-5(7));* 8.95 *(978-1-59249-736-2(5));* (J). pap. 6.95 *(978-1-59249-733-1(0))* Soundprints.

Dacey, Bob & Bandelin Dacey Studios Staff. What's the Difference Between an Alligator & a Crocodile?, 1 vol. Bullard, Lisa. 2009. (What's the Difference? Ser.). (ENG.). 24p. (gr. k-3). lib. bdg. 25.99 *(978-1-4048-5547-2(5),* Nonfiction Picture Bks.) Picture Window Bks.

Dacey, Bob & Bandelin, Debra. Abigail Adams: First Lady of the American Revolution. Lakin, Patricia. 2006. (Ready-To-read SOFA Ser.). (ENG.). 48p. (J). (gr. 1-3). pap. 3.99 *(978-0-689-87032-3(9),* Simon Spotlight) Simon Spotlight.

—Davy Crockett A Life on the Frontier. Krensky, Stephen. ed. 2005. (Ready-to-Read Ser.). 48p. (J). lib. bdg. 15.00 *(978-1-59054-959-9(7))* Fitzgerald Bks.

—Hermit Crab's Home: Safe in a Shell. Halfmann, Janet. (Smithsonian Oceanic Collection Ser.). (ENG.). 32p. (J). (gr. -1-3). 2011. 19.95 *(978-1-60727-650-0(X));* 2007. 4.95 *(978-1-59249-734-8(9));* 2007. 16.95 *(978-1-59249-732-4(2));* 2007. 9.95 *(978-1-59249-737-9(3))* Soundprints.

—Pelican's Catch. Halfmann, Janet. (Smithsonian Oceanic Collection Ser.). (ENG.). 32p. (J). 2011. (gr. -1-3). 8.95 *(978-1-60727-657-9(7));* 2011. (gr. -1-3). 19.95 *(978-1-60727-656-2(9));* 2005. (gr. -1-2). 4.95 *(978-1-59249-286-2(X),* B4076); 2005. (gr. -1-2). 19.95 *(978-1-59249-310-4(6),* BC4026); 2005. (gr. -1-2). 9.95 *(978-1-59249-311-1(4),* PB4076); 2005. (gr. -1-2). 15.95 *(978-1-59249-287-9(8),* B4026); 2004. (gr. 2-7). 8.95 *(978-1-59249-309-8(2),* SC4026); 2004. (gr. -1-3). 6.95 *(978-1-59249-285-5(1),* S4026) Soundprints.

—The Star-Spangled Banner. Winstead, Amy. 2003. (ENG.). 32p. (J). 18.65 *(978-0-8249-5462-8(9))* Ideals Pubns.

—Stars & Stripes: The Story of the American Flag. Thomson, Sarah L. 2003. 32p. (J). (gr. -1-3). 17.99 *(978-0-06-050416-8(1))* HarperCollins Pubs.

—Teddy Roosevelt: The People's President. Gayle, Sharon Shavers & Gayle, Sharon. Dacey, Bob & Bandelin, Debra, trs. 2004. (Ready-To-read SOFA Ser.). (ENG.). 32p. (J). (gr. 1-3). pap. 3.99 *(978-0-689-85825-3(6),* Simon Spotlight) Simon Spotlight.

Dacey, Bob, jt. illus. see Bandelin, Debra.

Dacus, Bobbie. Saving Emma. Willoughby, Bebe. 2005. (J). pap. 12.95 *(978-0-9763945-0-1(2))* King St Bks./Stabler-Leadbeater Apothecary Museum.

D'Adamo, Anthony. Pierre, the Young Watchmaker. Berg, Jean Horton. 2011. 190p. 42.95 *(978-1-258-08171-3(7))* Literary Licensing, LLC.

Dade, Raheem. Mommy, Why Can't I Be Rich? Ms. G. 2005. 20p. (J). 7.00 *(978-0-9724621-1-2(2))* ShaGru Entertainment, LLC.

Daff, Russ. Alien Attack. Clifford, Jack D. 2012. (Magic Game Aventures Ser.). (ENG.). 32p. (J). (gr. k-2). 5.99 ***(978-1-4451-0314-3(1))*** Hodder & Stoughton GBR. Dist: Independent Pubs. Group.

—Dragon Rock. Clifford, Jack D. 2012. (Magic Game Aventures Ser.). (ENG.). 32p. (J). (gr. k-2). 5.99 ***(978-1-4451-0315-0(X))*** Hodder & Stoughton GBR. Dist: Independent Pubs. Group.

—Egyptian Treasure Tomb. Clifford, Jack D. 2012. (Magic Game Aventures Ser.). (ENG.). 32p. (J). (gr. k-2). 5.99 ***(978-1-4451-0312-9(5))*** Hodder & Stoughton GBR. Dist: Independent Pubs. Group.

—Runaway Horses. Clifford, Jack D. 2012. (Magic Game Aventures Ser.). (ENG.). 32p. (J). (gr. k-2). 5.99 ***(978-1-4451-0313-6(3))*** Hodder & Stoughton GBR. Dist: Independent Pubs. Group.

Daff, Russ. What Has a Pointed Head & Eats Lizards? Kanner, Robert. 2008. (J). *(978-1-59646-832-0(7))* Dingles & Co.

—What Has Armor & a Tail Club? Kanner, Robert. 2008. (J). *(978-1-59646-828-3(9))* Dingles & Co.

—What Has Three Horns & a Sharp Beak? Zocchi, Judith Mazzeo. 2008. (J). *(978-1-59646-820-7(3))* Dingles & Co.

—What Weighs 70,000 Pounds & Swallows Stones? Kanner, Robert. 2008. (J). *(978-1-59646-840-5(8))* Dingles & Co.

Dages, Juliette Garesche. Learning about Virtues: A Guide to Making Good Choices. Dages, Juliette Garesche. 2009. (J). pap. 7.95 *(978-0-87029-420-4(2))* Abbey Pr.

Daggett, Irma, jt. illus. see Pighin, Marcel.

Dahl, Michael & Jensen, Brian. Caliente, Más Caliente, Muy Caliente: Animales Que Se Adaptan a Climas Calientes. Dahl, Michael & Jensen, Brian. Translations.com Staff, tr. 2012. (Los Extremos y Los Animales/Animal Extremes Ser.).Tr. of Hot, Hotter, Hottest - Animals That Adapt to Great Heat. (ENG, SPA & MUL.). 24p. (gr. k-2). lib. bdg. 25.99 *(978-1-4048-7318-6(X))* Picture Window Bks.

—Frío, Más Frío, Muy Frío: Animales Que Se Adaptan a Climas Fríos. Dahl, Michael & Jensen, Brian. Translations.com Staff, tr. 2012. (Los Extremos y Los Animales/Animal Extremes Ser.).Tr. of Cold, Colder, Coldest - Animals That Adapt to Cold Weather. (SPA, MUL & ENG.). 24p. (gr. k-2). lib. bdg. 25.99 *(978-1-4048-7316-2(3))* Picture Window Bks.

—Profundo, Más Profundo, Muy Profundo: Animales Que Van a Grandes Profundidades. Dahl, Michael & Jensen, Brian. Translations.com Staff, tr. 2012. (Los Extremos y Los Animales/Animal Extremes Ser.).Tr. of Deep, Deeper, Deepest - Animals That Go to Great Depths. (ENG, SPA & MUL.). 24p. (gr. k-2). lib. bdg. 25.99 *(978-1-4048-7319-3(8))* Picture Window Bks.

—Rápido, Más Rápido, Muy Rápido: Animales Que se Muevan a Grandes Velocidades. Dahl, Michael & Jensen, Brian. Translations.com Staff, tr. from ENG. 2012. (Los Extremos y Los Animales/Animal Extremes Ser.).Tr. of Fast, Faster, Fastest-Animals That Move at Great Speeds. (MUL & SPA.). 24p. (gr. k-2). lib. bdg. 25.99 *(978-1-4048-7317-9(1))* Picture Window Bks.

Dahl, Roald. Beastly Ballons. Top That Publishing Editors, ed. 2005. 24p. (J). pap. *(978-1-905359-55-4(1))* Top That! Publishing PLC.

—Fiendish Faces. Top That Publishing Editors, ed. 2005. 24p. (J). pap. *(978-1-905359-53-0(5))* Top That! Publishing PLC.

—Ghastly Grub. Top That Publishing Editors, ed. 2005. 24p. (J). pap. *(978-1-905359-54-7(3))* Top That! Publishing PLC.

—Magical Mischief. Top That Publishing Editors, ed. 2005. 24p. (J). pap. *(978-1-905359-51-6(9))* Top That! Publishing PLC.

—Silly Scribbles. Top That Publishing Editors, ed. 2005. 24p. (J). pap. *(978-1-905359-52-3(7))* Top That! Publishing PLC.

—Stupendous Stampers. Top That Publishing Editors, ed. 2005. 24p. (J). pap. *(978-1-905359-50-9(0))* Top That! Publishing PLC.

Dahl, Roald & Blake, Quentin. The BFG. Dahl, Roald. 2007. 17.00 *(978-0-7569-8233-1(2))* Penguin Publishing Group.

Dahl, Sarah. Hollywood Style: Fun Fashions You Can Sketch, 1 vol. Bolte, Mari. 2013. (Drawing Fun Fashions Ser.). (ENG.). 32p. (gr. 3-4). lib. bdg. 27.32 *(978-1-62065-037-0(1),* Snap Bks.) Capstone Pr., Inc.

—Rock Star Style: Fun Fashions You Can Sketch, 1 vol. Bolte, Mari. 2013. (Drawing Fun Fashions Ser.). (ENG.). 32p. (gr. 3-4). lib. bdg. 27.32 *(978-1-62065-036-3(3),* Snap Bks.) Capstone Pr., Inc.

Daigle, Brian. Texas Farm Girl. Crownover, Rebecca. 2013. (ENG.). (J). (gr. -1-3). 14.95 *(978-1-62086-265-0(4))* Mascot Bks., Inc.

Daigle, Casie. The Fish That Went Roar. Daigle, Damien. 2011. 28p. pap. 24.95 *(978-1-4560-5080-1(X))* America Star Bks.

Daigle, Stephan, jt. illus. see Galouchko, Annouchka Gravel.

Daigle, Sylvie. Tu N'es Plus Seul, Nazaire. Dube, Jasmine. 2003. (Premier Roman Ser.). (FRE.). 64p. (J). (gr. 2-5). pap. *(978-2-89021-286-2(6))* Diffusion du livre Mirabel (DLM).

Daigneault, Sylvie. The Good Garden: How One Family Went from Hunger to Having Enough. Milway, Katie Smith. 2010. (CitizenKid Ser.). (ENG.). 32p. (J). (gr. 2). 18.95 *(978-1-55453-488-3(7))* Kids Can Pr., Ltd. CAN. Dist: Univ. of Toronto Pr.

Dailey, Allison, jt. illus. see Dailey, Dan.

Dailey, Dan & Dailey, Allison. Glassigator. 2007. 33p. (J). *(978-0-935172-29-4(7))* Hudson Hills Pr. LLC.

Daily, Don. The Classic Tales of Brer Rabbit. Harris, Joel Chandler et al. 2008. (ENG.). 56p. (J). (gr. -1-3). 9.95 *(978-0-7624-3219-6(5))* Running Pr. Bk. Pubs.

—The Jungle Book. Kipling, Rudyard. 2014. (ENG.). 68p. (J). (gr. -1). 18.95 *(978-1-60433-475-3(4))* Cider Mill Pr. Bk. Pubs., LLC.

—The Velveteen Rabbit. Williams, Margery. 2007. (ENG.). 28p. (J). (gr. -1-1). pap. 5.95 *(978-0-7624-2935-6(6),* Running Pr. Kids) Running Pr. Bk. Pubs.

—The Wind in the Willows. Grahame, Kenneth. 2014. (ENG.). 64p. (J). (gr. -1). 18.95 *(978-1-60433-478-4(9),* Applesauce Pr.) Cider Mill Pr. Bk. Pubs., LLC.

Daily, Don. The Twelve Days of Christmas Cats. Daily, Don. 2014. (ENG.). 40p. (J). 18.95 *(978-1-60433-495-1(9),* Applesauce Pr.) Cider Mill Pr. Bk. Pubs., LLC.

Daily, Rick. The Ghost House. Thomas, Jesse Lee. 2011. 30p. pap. 16.00 *(978-1-4349-8472-2(9),* RoseDog Bks.) Dorrance Publishing Co., Inc.

Daines, Cameron. The Cats of Storm Mountain. Daines, McKay. 2003. 294p. (YA). 28.95 *(978-0-9749467-1-9(0));* pap. 17.99 *(978-0-9749467-0-2(2))* Shine Publishing Hse.

Daisy, April. The Lonely Dragon. Daisy, April. 2005. (J). per. 7.95 *(978-1-59466-074-0(3),* Little Ones) Port Town Publishing.

—The Monster's in My Room. Daisy, April. 2005. (J). per. 7.95 *(978-1-59466-048-1(4),* Little Ones) Port Town Publishing.

Dakins, Todd. Bobcat Bootcamp in Orange City. Pritchard, Jean. 2007. (J). *(978-0-9652491-6-4(6))* Cook, Ken Co.

—Sparky the Fire Dog. Hoffman, Don. 2011. (ENG.). 32p. (J). (gr. -1-2). 7.95 *(978-1-936140-62-6(4),* Imagine Publishing) Charlesbridge Publishing, Inc.

Dal Bello, Thiago & Tortosa, Wilson. Horizon, 1 vol. Terrell, Brandon. 2013. (Tony Hawk's 900 Revolution Ser.). (ENG.). 128p. (gr. 3-4). pap. 6.95 *(978-1-4342-6218-9(9));* lib. bdg. 25.32 *(978-1-4342-6032-1(1))* Stone Arch Bks.

Dal Chele, Egido Victor. Zoonauts: The Secret of Animalville. Mueller, Richard. Gosline, Sheldon, ed. 2003. 210p. (J). 14.95 *(978-0-9719496-6-9(2))* Shangri-La Pubns.

Dal Lago, Alberto, jt. illus. see Parks, Phil.

Dalby, Danny Brooks. Lara Ladybug. Florie, Christine. 2011. (Rookie Ready to Learn - Animals Ser.). 32p. (J). (gr. -1-k). lib. bdg. 23.00 *(978-0-531-26417-1(3),* Children's Pr.) Scholastic Library Publishing.

Dalby, Danny Brooks. La Mariquita Lara. Dalby, Danny Brooks. Florie, Christine. 2011. (Rookie Ready to Learn Español Ser.). (SPA.). 32p. (J). pap. 5.95 *(978-0-531-26783-7(0));* lib. bdg. 23.00 *(978-0-531-26115-6(8))* Scholastic Library Publishing. (Children's Pr.).

Dale, Penny. The Jamie & Angus Stories. Fine, Anne. 2007. (ENG.). 112p. (J). (gr. -1-1). per. 5.99 *(978-0-7636-3312-7(7))* Candlewick Pr.

—Jamie & Angus Together. Fine, Anne. 2007. (ENG.). 112p. (J). (gr. -1-1). 15.99 *(978-0-7636-3374-5(7))* Candlewick Pr.

Dale, Penny. Dinosaur Dig! Dale, Penny. (ENG.). (J). (gr. k-k). 2012. 14p. bds. 6.99 *(978-0-7636-6270-7(4));* 2011. 32p. 15.99 *(978-0-7636-5871-7(5))* Candlewick Pr. (Nosy Crow).

—Dinosaur Rescue! Dale, Penny. 2013. (ENG.). 32p. (J). (-k). 15.99 *(978-0-7636-6829-7(X),* Nosy Crow) Candlewick Pr.

—Dinosaur Zoom! Dale, Penny. (ENG.). (J). (-k). 2014. 24p. bds. 6.99 *(978-0-7636-7394-9(3));* 2013. 32p. 15.99 *(978-0-7636-6448-0(0))* Candlewick Pr. (Nosy Crow).

—Ten in the Bed. Dale, Penny. 2007. (ENG.). 24p. (J). (— 1). bds. 5.99 *(978-0-7636-3514-5(6))* Candlewick Pr.

Dale, Rae. Kids for Hire. Costain, Meredith. 2004. iv, 36p. (J). pap. *(978-0-7608-6748-8(8))* Sundance/Newbridge Educational Publishing.

—The Legend of Big Red. Roy, James. 2005. (UQP Children's Fiction Ser.). 96p. (J). pap. *(978-0-7022-3528-3(8))* Univ. of Queensland Pr.

Dale, Shelley. Juan Quezada. Quezada, Juan. 2003. (SPA.). 40p. (J). pap. 9.95 *(978-0-9708617-1-9(0));* (gr. -1-8). 16.95 *(978-0-9708617-0-2(2))* Norman Bks.

—Juan Quezada. Quezada, Juan. Mlawer, Teresa, tr. 2003. 40p. (J). (gr. k-6). 16.95 *(978-0-9708617-4-0(5));* pap. 9.95 *(978-0-9708617-5-7(3))* Norman Bks.

Dale, Unity-Joy. Seeds of Hope Bereavement & Loss Activity Book: Helping Children & Young People Cope with Change Through Nature. Jay, Caroline. 2014. (ENG.). 84p. pap. *(978-1-84905-546-8(7))* Kingsley, Jessica Ltd.

—What Does Dead Mean? A Book for Young Children to Help Explain Death & Dying. Jay, Caroline & Thomas, Jenni. 2012. (ENG.). 32p. *(978-1-84905-355-6(3))* Kingsley, Jessica Ltd.

Dalena, Antonello. Ernest & Rebecca Graphic Novels #1: My Best Friend Is a Germ. Bianco, Guillaume. 2011. (Ernest & Rebecca Graphic Novels Ser.: 1). (ENG.). 48p. (J). (gr. 1-7). 11.99 *(978-1-59707-286-1(9))* Papercutz.

—Grandpa Bug. Bianco, Guillaume. 2012. (Ernest & Rebecca Graphic Novels Ser.: 3). (ENG.). 48p. (J). (gr. 1-6). 10.99 *(978-1-59707-353-0(9))* Papercutz.

—The Land of Waking Stones. Bianco, Guillaume. 2013. (Ernest & Rebecca Graphic Novels Ser.: 4). (ENG.). 48p. (J). (gr. k-6). 10.99 *(978-1-59707-400-1(4))* Papercutz.

—Sam the Repulsive. Bianco, Guillaume. 2012. (Ernest & Rebecca Graphic Novels Ser.: 2). (ENG.). 48p. (J). (gr. 1-7). 11.99 *(978-1-59707-299-1(0))* Papercutz.

—Sybil the Backpack Fairy. Rodrigue, Michel & Razzi, Manuela. 2012. (Sybil the Backpack Fairy Graphic Novels Ser.: 3). (ENG.). 48p. (J). (gr. 1-6). 10.99 *(978-1-59707-369-1(5))* Papercutz.

Dalena, Antonello, et al. Tinker Bell & the Lucky Rainbow. Machetto, Augusto et al. 2012. (Disney Fairies Ser.: 10). (ENG.). 64p. (J). (gr. 1-6). 11.99 *(978-1-59707-368-4(7));* pap. 7.99 *(978-1-59707-367-7(9))* Papercutz.

Dalena, Antonello & Razzi, Manuela. Princess Nina. Rodrigue, Michel. 2013. (Sybil the Backpack Fairy Graphic Novels Ser.: 4). (ENG.). 48p. (J). (gr. 1-5). 10.99 *(978-1-59707-415-5(2))* Papercutz.

Dalena, Antonello, jt. illus. see Razzi, Manuela.

Daley-Prado, M. J. Gordon & the Magic Fishbowl, 1 vol. Nestell, Mark. 2010. 26p. pap. 24.95 *(978-1-4489-8495-4(5))* America Star Bks.

—Peanut Bunny & the Christmas Lights. Adams-Cantrell, Renee. 2009. 48p. pap. 24.95 *(978-1-60610-432-3(2))* America Star Bks.

Dalhaimer Bartkowski, Anna. Maggie Visits Grandpa: A Coloring Adventure. Dalhaimer Bartkowski, Anna. 2007. 32p. pap. 8.99 *(978-0-9790720-1-7(8))* Infinite Adventure.

Dall, Christopher M. Tell Me a Story. Grant, Susan. 2013. 56p. pap. *(978-1-4602-1356-8(4))* FriesenPress.

Dall, John. The Christmas Santa Had No Beard. H M Bricker & Bricker, Howard Michael. ed. 2011.Tr. of Navidad Que Santa Claus No Tovo Barba. (ENG & SPA.). 34p. (J). 15.45 *(978-0-615-42163-6(6))* H M Bricker.

Dalrymple, Farel. The Wrenchies. Dalrymple, Farel. 2014. (ENG.). 304p. (YA). (gr. 9). pap. 19.99 *(978-1-59643-421-9(X),* First Second Bks.) Roaring Brook Pr.

Dalton, Alex & Laguna, Fabio. Monsters vs. Aliens: the M Files. Titan Books Staff et al. 2009. (ENG.). 48p. pap. 4.95 *(978-1-84856-281-3(0),* Titan Bks.) Titan Bks. Ltd. GBR. Dist: Random Hse., Inc.

Dalton, Mar. The Night Before College. Sones, Sonya & Tramer, Ava. 2014. (Night Before Ser.). (ENG.). 48p. (J). (gr. 13). 9.99 *(978-0-448-46147-2(1),* Grosset & Dunlap) Penguin Publishing Group.

Dalton, Max. The Lonely Phone Booth. Ackerman, Peter. 2010. (ENG.). 32p. (J). (gr. k-2). 16.95 *(978-1-56792-414-5(X))* Godine, David R. Pub.

Dalton, Pamela. Brother Sun, Sister Moon. Paterson, Katherine. 2011. (ENG.). 36p. (J). (gr. -1-1). 17.99 *(978-0-8118-7734-3(5))* Chronicle Bks. LLC.

—Giving Thanks: Poems, Prayers, & Praise Songs of Thanksgiving. Paterson, Katherine. 2013. (ENG.). 56p. (J). (gr. k-17). 18.99 *(978-1-4521-1339-5(4))* Chronicle Bks. LLC.

—The Story of Christmas. 2011. (ENG.). 32p. (J). (gr. -1-17). 17.99 *(978-1-4521-0470-6(0))* Chronicle Bks. LLC.

Dalton, Pamela. The Sun with Loving Light, 1 vol. Bloomquist, Stephen, ed. 2014. Orig. Title: Der Sonne Licht. (ENG.). 110p. (J). ***(978-1-936367-63-4(7))*** Waldorf Pubns.

Dalton, Pamela. Under the Silver Moon: Lullabies, Night Songs, & Poems. 2016. (J). *(978-1-4521-1673-0(3))* Chronicle Bks. LLC.

Daly, Catherine & Leonard, Tom. Whiskers. 2015. (Step into Reading Ser.). (ENG.). 32p. (J). (gr. -1-1). pap. 3.99 *(978-0-307-26214-1(6),* Random Hse. Bks. for Young Readers) Random Hse. Children's Bks.

Daly, Dan & Gustafson, Troy. Bobby Bright's Christmas Heroics. Brooks, John R. 2010. 287p. (J). pap. 16.99 *(978-1-61663-725-5(0))* Tate Publishing & Enterprises, LLC.

Daly, Jude. Chirchir Is Singing. Cunnane, Kelly. 2011. (ENG.). 40p. (J). (gr. -1-2). 17.99 *(978-0-375-86198-7(X),* Schwartz & Wade Bks.) Random Hse. Children's Bks.

—The Dove. Stewart, Dianne & Quarto Generic Staff. 2005. (ENG.). 32p. (J). (gr. -1-3). per. 7.95 *(978-1-84507-022-9(4),* Frances Lincoln) Quarto Publishing Group UK GBR. Dist: Hachette Bk. Group.

—The Elephant's Pillow: A Chinese Bedtime Story. Roome, Diana Reynolds. 2007. (ENG.). 32p. (J). (gr. -1-2). pap. 7.95 *(978-1-84507-798-3(9),* Frances Lincoln) Quarto Publishing Group UK GBR. Dist: Hachette Bk. Group.

—Inside the Books: Readers & Libraries Around the World. Buzzeo, Toni. 2012. 32p. (J). 17.95 *(978-1-60213-058-6(2),* Upstart Bks.) Highsmith Inc.

—Lila & the Secret of Rain. Conway, David. (ENG.). 32p. (J). (gr. k-3). 2011. pap. 8.95 *(978-1-84780-035-0(1));* 2008. 16.95 *(978-1-84507-407-4(6))* Quarto Publishing Group UK GBR. (Frances Lincoln). Dist: Hachette Bk. Group, Perseus-PGW.

—Sivu's Six Wishes: A Taoist Tale. 2010. 32p. (J). (gr. 1-5). 16.99 *(978-0-8028-5369-1(2),* Eerdmans Bks For Young Readers) Eerdmans, William B. Publishing Co.

—Thank You, Jackson: How One Little Boy Makes a Big Difference. Daly, Niki. 2015. (ENG.). 32p. (J). (gr. -1-3). 17.99 *(978-1-84780-484-6(5),* Frances Lincoln) Quarto Publishing Group UK GBR. Dist: Hachette Bk. Group.

D

Daly, Jude. To Everything There Is a Season. Daly, Jude. 2006. 32p. (Orig.). (J). (gr. -1-3). 16.00 (978-0-8028-5286-1(6), Eerdmans Bks For Young Readers) Eerdmans, William B. Publishing Co.

Daly, Karen Anne. A Dinosaur under My Bed. Mitchell, Colleen. 2013. 24p. (J). pap. 7.49 (978-0-9853600-2-3(X)) Thistlewood Publishing.

—Mrs Mouse's Garden Party in Giggleswick Village. Westover, Gail. 2012. 26p. pap. 9.95 (978-0-9821507-9-5(2)) Thistlewood Publishing.

Daly, Lisa. Christmas O'Clock: A Collection. Deluca, Alison. 2013. 198p. pap. 9.99 (978-1-939296-98-6(6)) Myrddin Publishing Group.

Daly, Meghan. Little Harper Grace & the Hummingbird. Preza, Jessie. 2008. (ENG.). 36p. (J). pap. 9.95 (978-0-615-24059-6(3)) Poppy Blossom Pr.

Daly, Niki. Daddy Island. Wells, Philip. 2015. 24p. (J). (gr. -1-2). 7.99 (978-1-84148-198-2(X)) Barefoot Bks., Inc.

Daly, Niki. Fly, Eagle, Fly: An African Tale. Gregorowski, Christopher. 2008. (ENG.). 36p. (J). (gr. -1-3). 12.99 (978-1-4169-7599-1(3), Simon & Schuster/Paula Wiseman Bks.) Simon & Schuster/Paula Wiseman Bks.

—The Herd Boy. 2012. 34p. (J). 17.00 (978-0-8028-5417-9(6), Eerdmans Bks For Young Readers) Eerdmans, William B. Publishing Co.

—No More Kisses for Bernard! Quarto Generic Staff. 2012. (ENG.). 32p. (J). (gr. -1-1). 17.99 (978-1-84780-105-0(6), Frances Lincoln) Quarto Publishing Group UK GBR. Dist: Hachette Bk. Group.

—Seb & Hamish. Daly, Jude. 2014. (ENG.). 32p. (J). (gr. -1-1). 17.99 (978-1-84780-412-9(8), Frances Lincoln Children's Bks.) Quarto Publishing Group UK GBR. Dist: Hachette Bk. Group.

—A Song for Jamela. Quarto Generic Staff. 2010. (ENG.). 36p. (J). (gr. -1-2). 16.95 (978-1-84507-871-3(3), Frances Lincoln) Quarto Publishing Group UK GBR. Dist: Hachette Bk. Group.

—Where's Jamela? 2012. (ENG.). 32p. (J). (gr. -1-2). pap. 8.99 (978-1-84780-325-2(3), Frances Lincoln) Quarto Publishing Group UK GBR. Dist: Hachette Bk. Group.

Daly, Niki. The Greatest Skating Race: A World War II Story from the Netherlands. Daly, Niki. Borden, Louise. 2004. (ENG.). 48p. (J). (gr. 4-7). 19.99 (978-0-689-84502-4(2), McElderry, Margaret K. Bks.) McElderry, Margaret K. Bks.

—Next Stop — Zanzibar Road! Daly, Niki. 2012. (ENG.). 40p. (J). (gr. -1-3). 16.99 (978-0-547-68852-7(0)) Houghton Mifflin Harcourt Publishing Co.

—Pretty Salma: A Little Red Riding Hood Story from Africa. Daly, Niki. 2007. (ENG.). 32p. (J). (gr. -1-3). 16.99 (978-0-618-72345-4(5)) Houghton Mifflin Harcourt Publishing Co.

—A Song for Jamela. Daly, Niki. 2014. (ENG.). 36p. (J). (gr. -1-2). pap. 8.99 (978-1-84780-429-7(2), Frances Lincoln) Quarto Publishing Group UK GBR. Dist: Hachette Bk. Group.

Daly, Sue V. Everybody Loves Mookie. Kristen, Judith. 2008. (ENG.). 44p. (J). pap. 15.95 (978-0-9800448-4-3(7)) Aquinas & Krone Publishing, LLC.

Damant, Aurore. The Five O'Clock Ghost, No. 4. Butler, Dori Hillestad. 2015. (Haunted Library: 4). (ENG.). 144p. (J). (gr. 1-3). 4.99 (978-0-448-46248-6(6), Grosset & Dunlap) Penguin Publishing Group.

—The Ghost Backstage, No. 3. Butler, Dori Hillestad. 2014. (Haunted Library: 3). (ENG.). 128p. (J). (gr. 1-3). 4.99 (978-0-448-46246-2(X), Grosset & Dunlap) Penguin Publishing Group.

—The Ghost in the Attic, No. 2. Butler, Dori Hillestad. 2014. (Haunted Library: 2). (ENG.). 224p. (J). (gr. 1-3). 4.99 (978-0-448-46244-8(3), Grosset & Dunlap) Penguin Publishing Group.

—The Haunted Library #1. Butler, Dori Hillestad. 2014. (Haunted Library: 1). (ENG.). 128p. (J). (gr. 1-3). 4.99 (978-0-448-46242-4(7), Grosset & Dunlap) Penguin Publishing Group.

Damant, Aurore. The Secret Room #5. Butler, Dori Hillestad. 2015. (Haunted Library: 5). (ENG.). 128p. (J). (gr. 1-3). 4.99 (978-0-448-48332-0(7), Grosset & Dunlap) Penguin Publishing Group.

Dameron, Ned. The Waste Lands, 3 vols. King, Stephen. rev. ed. 2003. (Dark Tower Ser.: 3). (ENG.). (gr. 12-18). 608p. mass mkt. 8.99 (978-0-451-21086-9(7), Signet); 448p. pap. 21.00 (978-0-452-28471-5(6), Plume) Penguin Publishing Group.

Damerum, Kanako, et al. Stormbreaker. Horowitz, Anthony. 2006. (Alex Rider Ser.). (ENG.). 144p. (J). (gr. 5-18). pap. 14.99 (978-0-399-24633-3(9), Philomel) Penguin Publishing Group.

Damerum, Kanako & Parks, Paul. Abracadabra Violin, Bk. 1. Davey, Peter. Hussey, Christopher & Sebba, Jane, eds. 2nd ed. 2004. (Abracadabra Strings Ser.). (ENG.). 64p. (J). pap. 10.95 (978-0-7136-6308-2(1), A & C Black) Bloomsbury Publishing Plc GBR. Dist: Consortium Bk. Sales & Distribution.

D'Amico, Carmela & D'Amico, Steven. Ella: The Elegant Elephant. D'Amico, Carmela & D'Amico, Steven. unabr. ed. 2006. (ENG.). (J). (gr. -1-3). 9.99 (978-0-439-87589-9(7)) Scholastic, Inc.

D'Amico, Dee Densmore. Dog Heaven: Somewhere over the Rainbow Bridge. Hanson, Maria. 2012. (ENG.). 32p. (J). 15.99 (978-1-4525-4699-5(1), Balboa Pr.) Author Solutions, Inc.

D'Amico, Steven. Ella Sets the Stage. D'Amico, Carmela. 2006. 41p. (J). pap. 16.99 (978-0-439-83153-6(9), Levine, Arthur A. Bks.) Scholastic, Inc.

—The Hanukkah Hop! Silverman, Erica. 2011. (ENG.). 32p. (J). (gr. -1-3). 12.99 (978-1-4424-0604-9(6), Simon & Schuster Bks. For Young Readers) Simon & Schuster Bks. For Young Readers.

D'Amico, Steven, jt. illus. see D'Amico, Carmela.

Dammann, Anke. Chester Crumbleberry. Dammann, Anke. 2005. 32p. 15.95 (978-1-893815-11-7(0)) Pie in the Sky Publishing, LLC.

Dammer, Mike. Phonics Comics: Cave Dave - Level 1. McAdams Moore, Carol. 2007. (ENG.). 24p. (J). (gr. 1-17). per. 3.99 (978-1-58476-552-3(6)) Innovative Kids.

—Say It Again! 501 Wacky Word Puzzles from Highlights. Highlights for Children Staff. 2013. (Laugh Attack! Ser.). (ENG.). 256p. (J). (gr. k). pap. 5.95 (978-1-62091-072-6(1)) Boyds Mills Pr.

Damon Danielson. The Sleepover. Garnett, Tarreka. 2013. 32p. pap. 14.97 (978-1-62212-249-3(6), Strategic Bk. Publishing) Strategic Book Publishing & Rights Agency (SBPRA).

Damon, Emma. All Kinds of Babies. Safran, Sheri. 2007. (All Kinds Of... Ser.). (ENG.). 16p. (J). (gr. -1-k). 12.99 (978-1-85707-679-0(6)) Tango Bks. GBR. Dist: Independent Pubs. Group.

—All Kinds of Beliefs. Safran, Sheri. 2012. (ENG.). 12p. (J). (gr. -1). 12.99 (978-1-60887-159-9(2)) Insight Editions LP.

—All Kinds of People. Safran, Sheri. 2012. (ENG.). 12p. (J). (gr. -1). 12.99 (978-1-60887-160-5(6)) Insight Editions LP.

Damon, Emma. Busytime. Damon, Emma. 2010. (Pop-Up Flaps Ser.). (ENG.). 8p. (J). (gr. k-k). 10.99 (978-0-230-74454-7(0)) Macmillan Pubs., Ltd. GBR. Dist: Independent Pubs. Group.

Damone, G. L., 3rd. Interrupted Journey's: Wyoming's Haunted Historic Trails. Del Bene, Terry A. et al. 2005. (YA). per. 15.95 (978-0-9722217-5-7(1)) Horse Creek Pubns.

Dan, Houser. Creepy Kitchen. Lee, Newman. Elizabeth, Neering, ed. 2012. 40p. (J). pap. 10.00 (978-1-62314-873-7(1)) Fisticuff Publishing.

Dana, Steve. Bookworm: Discovering Idioms, Sayings & Expressions. Emigh, Karen. 2013. (ENG.). 32p. (J). pap. 9.95 (978-1-935274-88-9(0), 9781935274889) Future Horizons, Inc.

—Who Took My Shoe? Emigh, Karen. 2003. (ENG.). 19p. (J). (gr. -1-3). 9.95 (978-1-885477-95-8(3)) Future Horizons, Inc.

Danalis, John. The Girl in the Cave. Eaton, Anthony. 2004. 128p. (J). pap. (978-0-7022-3437-8(0)) Univ. of Queensland Pr.

—Licking Lizards. Risson, Toni. 2005. 128p. (Orig.). (J). pap. (978-0-7022-3524-5(5)) Univ. of Queensland Pr.

Danalis, John. Dog 37. Danalis, John. 2004. 96p. (Orig.). (J). pap. (978-0-7022-3431-6(1)) Univ. of Queensland Pr.

Danby, Aaron, jt. illus. see Martin, M. J.

Dancy, Deborah & Muirhead, Deborah. The Freedom Business: Including a Narrative of the Life & Adventures of Venture, a Native of Africa. Nelson, Marilyn. 2008. (ENG.). 72p. (YA). (gr. 6-18). 18.95 (978-1-932425-57-4(8), Wordsong) Boyds Mills Pr.

D'Anda, Carlos. Star Wars. Wood, Brian. 2014. (Star Wars: in the Shadow of Yavin Ser.: Vol. 1). (ENG.). 24p. (J). (gr. 9-14). 24.21 (978-1-61479-286-4(0)) Spotlight.

—Star Wars: In the Shadow of Yavin. ABDO Publishing Company Staff & Wood, Brian. 2014. (Star Wars: in the Shadow of Yavin Ser.: 6). (ENG.). 24p. (J). (gr. 9-14). lib. bdg. 145.26 (978-1-61479-285-7(2), Graphic Planet) Magic Wagon.

Dandan-Albano, Corazon. Filipino Celebrations: A Treasury of Feasts & Festivals. Romulo, Liana. 2012. (ENG.). 48p. (J). (gr. k-4). 16.95 (978-0-8048-3821-4(6)) Tuttle Publishing.

Dando, Marc & Hobson, Ryan. The Field Guide to Dinosaurs. Honovich, Nancy. 2014. (Field Guides). (ENG.). 32p. (J). (gr. 2). pap. 15.95 (978-1-62686-004-9(1), Silver Dolphin Bks.) Baker & Taylor Publishing Group.

D'Andrade, Hugh. The Grimm Conclusion. Gidwitz, Adam. 2013. (ENG.). 368p. (J). (gr. 5). 16.99 (978-0-525-42615-8(9), Dutton Juvenile) Penguin Publishing Group.

—In a Glass Grimmly. Gidwitz, Adam. 2012. (ENG.). 336p. (J). (gr. 5). 16.99 (978-0-525-42581-6(0), Dutton Juvenile) Penguin Publishing Group.

—A Tale Dark & Grimm. Gidwitz, Adam. 2011. (ENG.). 288p. (J). (gr. 5-18). 7.99 (978-0-14-241967-0(2), Puffin) Penguin Publishing Group.

—A Tale Dark & Grimm. Gidwitz, Adam et al. 2010. (ENG.). 272p. (J). (gr. 5-18). 16.99 (978-0-525-42334-8(6), Dutton Juvenile) Penguin Publishing Group.

Dane, Donna. Circle Time Book: For Holiday & Seasons. Wilmes, Liz et al. 2004. 128p. (J). pap. 12.95 (978-0-943452-00-5(7), 20002) Building Blocks, LLC.

—Felt Board Fun: For Everyday & Holidays. Wilmes, Liz & Wilmes, Dick. 2004. 244p. (J). pap. 16.95 (978-0-943452-02-9(3)) Building Blocks, LLC.

Danger, Chris. Stella: The Dog with the Big Heart. Feldman, Thea. 2015. (Hero Dog Ser.). (ENG.). 32p. (J). (gr. k-2). pap. 3.99 (978-1-4814-2243-7(X)) Simon & Schuster Children's Publishing.

Daniel, Alan. Bunnicula. Howe, Deborah & Howe, James. 2006. (Bunnicula & Friends Ser.). (ENG.). 128p. (J). (gr. 3-7). pap. 6.99 (978-1-4169-2817-1(0), Atheneum Bks. for Young Readers) Simon & Schuster Children's Publishing.

—Bunnicula Strikes Again! Howe, James. 2007. (Bunnicula & Friends Ser.). (ENG.). 144p. (J). (gr. 3-7). pap. 5.99 (978-1-4169-3968-9(7), Atheneum Bks. for Young Readers) Simon & Schuster Children's Publishing.

—Fireside Al's Treasury of Christmas Stories, 1 vol. 2008. (ENG.). 64p. (YA). (gr. 3-18). 19.95 (978-0-88995-382-6(1)) Red Deer Pr. CAN. Dist: Ingram Pub. Services.

—The Grand Escape. Naylor, Phyllis Reynolds. 2005. (ENG.). 160p. (J). (gr. 3-7). pap. 7.99 (978-0-689-87407-9(3), Atheneum Bks. for Young Readers) Simon & Schuster Children's Publishing.

—The Healing of Texas Jake. Naylor, Phyllis Reynolds. 2005. (ENG.). 128p. (J). (gr. 3-7). pap. 6.99 (978-0-689-87406-2(5), Atheneum Bks. for Young Readers) Simon & Schuster Children's Publishing.

—Polo's Mother. Naylor, Phyllis Reynolds. 2006. (ENG.). 176p. (J). (gr. 3-7). pap. 6.99 (978-0-689-87404-8(9), Atheneum Bks. for Young Readers) Simon & Schuster Children's Publishing.

—Return to Howliday Inn. Howe, James. 2007. (Bunnicula & Friends Ser.). (ENG.). 192p. (J). (gr. 3-7). pap. 6.99 (978-1-4169-3967-2(9), Atheneum Bks. for Young Readers) Simon & Schuster Children's Publishing.

—Return to Howliday Inn. Howe, James. ed. 2007. (Bunnicula Ser.). (gr. 4-7). lib. bdg. 17.20 (978-1-4177-9044-9(X), Turtleback) Turtleback Bks.

Daniel, Alan & Daniel, Lea. Albert Einstein: Genius of the Twentieth Century. Lakin, Patricia. 2005. (Ready-To-read SOFA Ser.). (ENG.). 48p. (J). (gr. 1-3). pap. 3.99 (978-0-689-87034-7(5), Simon Spotlight) Simon Spotlight.

—Amelia Earhart: Amelia Earhart: More Than A Flier. Lakin, Patricia. ed. 2005. 48p. (J). lib. bdg. 15.00 (978-1-59054-957-5(0)) Fitzgerald Bks.

—Amelia Earhart: More Than a Flier. Lakin, Patricia & Daniel, Alan. Daniel, Lea. 2003. (Ready-To-read SOFA Ser.). (ENG.). 48p. (J). (gr. 1-3). pap. 3.99 (978-0-689-85575-7(3), Simon Spotlight) Simon Spotlight.

—The Best Figure Skater in the Whole Wide World. Bailey, Linda. 2003. (ENG.). 32p. (J). (gr. k-3). 5.95 (978-1-55074-881-9(5)) Kids Can Pr., Ltd. CAN. Dist: Univ. of Toronto Pr.

—Roundup at the Palace, 1 vol. Waldron, Kathleen Cook. 2006. (ENG.). 32p. (J). (gr. -1). 17.95 (978-0-88995-319-2(8)) Red Deer Pr. CAN. Dist: Ingram Pub. Services.

—Under a Prairie Sky, 1 vol. Carter, Anne Laurel. 2004. (ENG.). 32p. (J). (gr. -1-3). pap. 7.95 (978-1-55143-282-3(X)) Orca Bk. Pubs. USA.

Daniel, Alan, jt. illus. see Shapiro, Deborah.

Daniel, Beverly. The Adventures of Madilyn Millicent Middleton-Mew. Daniel, Beverly. Daniel, Cindy, ed. 2013. 64p. pap. 8.95 (978-0-9789429-6-0(5)) Batelier Publishing.

Daniel, Carol. Fun to Learn Opposites: Kaleidoscope Book. Jackaman, Philippa. 16p. (J). (978-1-84322-125-8(X)) Bookmart Ltd.

Daniel, Ellen. The Twilight Ride of the Pink Fairy. Demeritt, Mary Anne. 2006. 36p. (J). pap. 17.95 (978-1-58597-410-8(2)) Leathers Publishing.

Daniel, Jennifer. Information Graphics: Space. Rogers, Simon. 2015. (ENG.). 80p. (J). (gr. 3-7). pap. 17.99 (978-0-7636-7769-5(8), Big Picture Press) Candlewick Pr.

Daniel, Lea, jt. illus. see Daniel, Alan.

Daniel, R. F. "I Can Tell You Stories, If You Gather Near"... The Big Bear of Arkansas. Sandage, Charley. 2004. 46p. (J). (gr. k-2). pap. 14.95 (978-0-9638956-7-7(2)) Archeological Assessments, Inc.

Daniel, Rick. Math Rapmatics: Mathematical Rhymes Right on Time. Van Horn, Stephanie. 2011. 24p. (J). 18.00 (978-0-9814945-9-3(5)) AK Classics, LLC.

Daniels, Gail. Pretty Princess: Words. Daniels, Gail. 2004. 12p. (J). bds. 3.99 (978-1-85997-812-2(6)); bds. 5.99 (978-1-85997-868-9(1)) Byeway Bks.

—Pretty Princess: Words. Daniels, Gail. 2003. (J). per. (978-1-884907-45-6(8)) Paradise Pr., Inc.

Daniels, Greg. I Want off This Stinkin' Plane, 1 vol. McInnes, Dawn Daniels. 2010. 18p. pap. 24.95 (978-1-4489-7809-0(2)) PublishAmerica, Inc.

Daniels, Regina. Three Days & Four Knights. Auxier, Bryan. 2004. 66p. (J). pap. 3.95 (978-0-9719144-2-1(7)) Where? Pr., Inc.

—Where Have All the Unicorns Gone? Auxier, Bryan. I.t. ed. 2003. 16p. (J). 7.95 (978-0-9719144-1-4(9)) Where? Pr., Inc.

Daniels, Sterling N., 2nd. Yas. Daniels, Sterling N., 2nd. 36p. (J). (gr. k-3). pap. 4.95 (978-0-9628081-2-8(1)) Daw Enterprises.

Danielson, Damon. Bully's Game Day Rules. Smith, Sherri Graves. 2013. (ENG.). (J). 14.95 (978-1-62086-334-3(0)) Mascot Bks., Inc.

—Cimarron's Game Day Rules. Smith, Sherri Graves. 2013. (ENG.). (J). 14.95 (978-1-62086-230-8(1)) Mascot Bks., Inc.

—Cocky's Game Day Rules. Smith, Sherri Graves. 2013. (ENG.). (J). 14.95 (978-1-62086-085-4(6)) Mascot Bks., Inc.

—Nittany Lion's Game Day Rules. Smith, Sherri Graves. 2013. (ENG.). (J). 14.95 (978-1-62086-233-9(6)) Mascot Bks., Inc.

—Reveille's Game Day Rules. Smith, Sherri Graves. 2013. (ENG.). (J). (gr. -1-3). 14.95 (978-1-62086-350-3(2)) Mascot Bks., Inc.

—Tiger's Game Day Rules. Smith, Sherri Graves. 2013. (ENG.). (J). (gr. -1-3). 14.95 (978-1-62086-086-1(4)) Mascot Bks., Inc.

Danilewicz, Jamie. Make the World Pink, I Think. Petersen, Pat. 2012. 26p. 24.95 (978-1-4626-3028-8(6)) America Star Bks.

Danioth, David. A Mother's Promise. Humphrey, Lisa. 2004. 32p. (J). per. 15.95 (978-0-9701907-9-6(4)) Illumination Arts Publishing Co., Inc.

Danker, Jennifer Anne. Max & Mila at the Beach: A Sun Safety Guide for Kids. Martin, Ms. Amalyn Persohn. 2013. 26p. pap. 14.98 (978-0-615-79018-3(6)) Children's Melanoma Education Bk., A.

Dann, Geoff. Jungle - DK Eyewitness Books. Dann, Geoff, photos by. Dorling Kindersley Publishing Staff & Greenaway, Theresa. 2009. (DK Eyewitness Bks.). (ENG.). 72p. (J). (gr. 3-7). 16.99 (978-0-7566-4544-1(1)) Dorling Kindersley Publishing, Inc.

Dann, Geoff & Gorton, Steve. Espías. Platt, Richard. 2003. (SPA.). 64p. (J). 14.95 (978-84-372-2319-3(9)) Altea, Ediciones, S.A. - Grupo Santillana ESP. Dist: Santillana USA Publishing Co., Inc.

Dann, Penny. Me Lees un Cuento, Por Favor?Tr. of Read Me a Story, Please?. (SPA.). (gr. k-3). Vol. 1. (J). (978-84-480-1622-7(X), TM7339); Vol. 3. 2003. 96p. (978-84-480-1626-5(2), TM3568) Timun Mas, Editorial S.A. ESP. Dist: Lectorum Pubns., Inc.

—Missing! Mellor, Jodie. 2010. (Mystery Pups Ser.). (ENG.). 112p. (J). (gr. k-2). pap. 6.99 (978-1-84738-226-9(6)) Simon & Schuster, Ltd. GBR. Dist: Independent Pubs. Group.

Danna Sr., Gerald. Miss Poppy & Red Jeans: Adventure to Willie Willie's Garden. Danna, Minnie. 2012. 66p. pap. 12.95 (978-0-9852608-0-4(7)) Flower Publishing.

Danner, Maggie. How Teddy Bears Find Their Homes. Waldman, David K. 2nd ed. 2015. (ENG.). 154p. (J). (gr. k-2). pap. 38.40 (978-0-945522-02-7(9)) Bk.Baby Print.

Danowski, Sonja. The Forever Flowers. Rosen, Michael J. 2014. (ENG.). 32p. (J). (gr. 1-3). 18.99 (978-1-56846-273-8(5), Creative Editions) Creative Co., The.

Danowski, Sonja. Grandma Lives in a Perfume Village. Suzhen, Fang. 2015. (ENG.). 48p. (J). 19.95 (978-0-7358-4216-8(7)) North-South Bks., Inc.

Danson, Lesley. Cairo the Camel: A Tale of Responsibility. Law, Felicia. 2010. (Animal Fair Values Ser.). (ENG.). 32p. (J). (gr. -1-3). pap. 10.55 (978-1-60754-911-6(5)); lib. bdg. 22.60 (978-1-60754-903-1(4)) Windmill Bks.

—Darwin the Dolphin: A Tale of Bravery & Courage. Law, Felicia. 2010. (Animal Fair Values Ser.). 32p. (J). (gr. -1-3). pap. 10.55 (978-1-60754-810-2(0)); lib. bdg. 22.60 (978-1-60754-806-5(2)) Windmill Bks.

—Dragon Magic. Goodhart, Pippa & Goodheart, Pippa. 2009. (Red Bananas Ser.). (ENG.). 48p. (J). (gr. k-2). pap. 5.99 (978-1-4052-4611-8(1)) Egmont Bks., Ltd. GBR. Dist: Independent Pubs. Group.

—Hide-and-Seek Bunnies. Watt, Fiona. 2007. (Touchy-Feely Flap Bks). 10p. (J). (gr. -1-k). bds. 16.99 (978-0-7945-1566-9(5), Usborne) EDC Publishing.

—Hudson the Hippo: A Tale of Self-Control. Law, Felicia. 2010. (Animal Fair Values Ser.). (ENG.). 32p. (J). (gr. -1-3). pap. 10.55 (978-1-60754-913-0(1)); lib. bdg. 22.60 (978-1-60754-904-8(2)) Windmill Bks.

—Kimberly the Koala: A Tale of Independence. Law, Felicia. 2010. (Animal Fair Values Ser.). (ENG.). 32p. (J). (gr. -1-3). pap. 10.55 (978-1-60754-909-3(3)); lib. bdg. 22.60 (978-1-60754-902-4(6)) Windmill Bks.

—Snow White. (Flip-Up Fairy Tales Ser.). (ENG.). 24p. (J). (gr. -1-2). 2007. (978-1-84643-096-1(8)); 2006. (978-1-84643-023-7(2)) Child's Play International Ltd.

Dantat, Dan & Santat, Dan. Fire! ¡Fuego! Brave Bomberos. Elya, Susan Middleton. ed. 2012. (ENG & SPA.). 40p. (J). (gr. -1-1). 16.99 (978-1-59990-461-0(6), 231375, Bloomsbury USA Childrens) Bloomsbury USA.

D'Antoni, Colleen. Cajun 'Ti Beau & the Cocodries. Gibson, Cay. 2014. (ENG.). 32p. (J). (gr. k-3). 16.99 (978-1-4556-1947-4(7)) Pelican Publishing Co., Inc.

D'Antonio, Sandra. Animals All Around, 1 vol., Set. Dahl, Michael. 2010. (Animals All Around Ser.). (ENG.). 10p. (gr. -1-2). bds. 19.98 (978-1-4048-6308-8(7)) Picture Window Bks.

—Clementine. Qualey, Marsha, ed. 2003. (Traditional Songs Ser.). (ENG.). 24p. (gr. -1-2). 25.99 (978-1-4048-0155-4(3), Nonfiction Picture Bks.) Picture Window Bks.

—Do Whales Have Wings? A Book about Animal Bodies. Dahl, Michael. 2003. (Animals All Around Ser.). (ENG.). 24p. (gr. -1-2). per. 7.95 (978-1-4048-0373-2(4), Nonfiction Picture Bks.) Picture Window Bks.

—Old MacDonald Had a Farm. Qualey, Marsha, ed. 2003. (Traditional Songs Ser.). (ENG.). 24p. (gr. -1-2). 25.99 (978-1-4048-0152-3(9), Nonfiction Picture Bks.) Picture Window Bks.

—She'll Be Coming Around the Mountain. Qualey, Marsha, ed. 2003. (Traditional Songs Ser.). (ENG.). 24p. (gr. -1-2). 25.99 (978-1-4048-0153-0(7), Nonfiction Picture Bks.) Picture Window Bks.

D'Antonio, Sandra. I've Been Working on the Railroad, 1 vol. D'Antonio, Sandra. Owen, Ann, ed. 2003. (Traditional Songs Ser.). (ENG.). 24p. (gr. -1-2). per. 7.95 (978-1-4048-0431-9(5), Nonfiction Picture Bks.) Picture Window Bks.

Daranga, Ana-Maria. Mango & His Friends Have a Party. Ionescu, Julian. 2012. (ENG.). 32p. (J). (gr. k-2). pap. 13.95 (978-0-86527-510-2(6)) Fertig, Howard Publisher.

—Tomato & Her Friends Have a Party. Ionescu, Julian. 2012. (Tomato & Her Friends Have a Party). (ENG.). (J). (gr. k-2). pap. 13.95 (978-0-86527-509-6(2)) Fertig, Howard Publisher.

Darby, Stephania Pierce, jt. illus. see Jones, C. Denise West.

Darby, Stephania Pierce, jt. illus. see Jones, Denise West.

Dardik, Helen. Lite'N Up! Laugh Yourself Skinny. Klein, Samara Q. 2009. (ENG.). 156p. pap. 14.95 (978-0-9777383-5-9(3)) Plain White Pr., LLC.

—Pantone: Colors. Pantone. 2012. (ENG.). 20p. (J). (gr. -1 — 1). bds. 9.95 (978-1-4197-0180-1(0), Abrams Appleseed) Abrams.

Dare, Bill. Topaz - Takes the Stage. Bailey, Helen. 2008. (Topaz Ser.). (ENG.). 144p. (J). (gr. 4-7). pap. 7.95 (978-0-340-91735-0(0)) Hodder & Stoughton GBR. Dist: Independent Pubs. Group.

—Topaz on Ice. Bailey, Helen. 2008. (Topaz Ser.). (ENG.). 144p. (J). (gr. 4-7). pap. 7.95 (978-0-340-91734-3(2)) Hodder & Stoughton GBR. Dist: Independent Pubs. Group.

—Topaz Takes a Chance. Bailey, Helen. 2007. (Topaz Ser.). (ENG.). 128p. (J). (gr. 4-7). pap. 7.95 (978-0-340-89347-0(8)) Hachette Children's Group GBR. Dist: Independent Pubs. Group.

Dargaud Media, jt. illus. see Ellipsanime Staff.

Dargaud Media Staff & Ellipsanime Staff. Game of Cat & Mouse. Davis, Jim et al. 2012. (Garfield Graphic Novels Ser.: 5). (ENG.). 32p. (J). (gr. 1-6). 7.99 (978-1-59707-300-4(8)) Papercutz.

—The Garfield Show #1: Unfair Weather. Davis, Jim & Michiels, Cedric. 2013. (Garfield Show Ser.: 1). (ENG.). 64p. (J). (gr. 1-5). 11.99 (978-1-59707-433-9(0)) Papercutz.

—Unfair Weather. Davis, Jim & Michiels, Cedric. 2013. (Garfield Show Ser.: 1). (ENG.). 64p. (J). (gr. 1-5). pap. 7.99 (978-1-59707-422-3(5)) Papercutz.

Dargaud Media Staff, jt. illus. see Ellipsanime Staff.

D'Argo, Laura. Suzy Season Loves Fall. Posner, Renee & Quinton, Sasha. 2003. (Be Mine Bears Ser.). (J). bds. 4.99 (978-1-58209-352-9(0)) Bks. Are Fun, Ltd.

—Suzy Season Loves Spring. Posner, Renee & Quinton, Sasha. (Be Mine Bears Ser.). (J). bds. 4.99 (978-1-58209-350-5(4)) Bks. Are Fun, Ltd.

—Suzy Season Loves Summer. Posner, Renee & Quinton, Sasha. (Be Mine Bears Ser.). (J). bds. 4.99 *(978-1-58209-351-2(2))* Bks. Are Fun, Ltd.
—Suzy Season Loves Winter. Posner, Renee & Quinton, Sasha. 2003. (Be Mine Bears Ser.). (J). bds. 4.99 *(978-1-58209-353-6(9))* Bks. Are Fun, Ltd.
—The Wright Brothers for Kid: How They Invented the Airplane, 21 Activities Exploring the Science & History of Flight. Carson, Mary Kay. 2003. (For Kids Ser.). (ENG.). 160p. (J). (gr. 4). pap. 18.95 *(978-1-55652-477-6(3))* Chicago Review Pr., Inc.
D'Ariggo, Jay, jt. illus. see Michelle, Jean.
Darling, Louis, et al. Beezus & Ramona. Cleary, Beverly. 2013. (Ramona Ser.: 1). (ENG.). 208p. (J). (gr. 3-7). 16.99 *(978-0-688-21076-2(7))* HarperCollins Pubs.
Darling, Louis. Beezus & Ramona. Cleary, Beverly. (gr. 3-5). pap. *(978-0-545-24980-5(5))* Scholastic, Inc.
Darling, Louis, et al. Henry & Beezus. Cleary, Beverly. 2014. (Henry Huggins Ser.: 2). (ENG.). 224p. (J). (gr. 3-7). 16.99 *(978-0-688-21383-1(9))*; 50th anniv. ed. pap. 6.99 *(978-0-380-70914-4(7))* HarperCollins Pubs.
—Henry & Ribsy. Cleary, Beverly. 2014. (Henry Huggins Ser.: 3). (ENG.). (J). (gr. 3-7). 192p. 16.99 *(978-0-688-21382-4(0))*; 50th anniv. ed. 208p. pap. 6.99 *(978-0-380-70917-5(1))* HarperCollins Pubs.
—Henry & the Clubhouse. Cleary, Beverly. 2014. (Henry Huggins Ser.: 5). (ENG.). 224p. (J). (gr. 3-7). 16.99 *(978-0-688-21381-7(2))*; pap. 6.99 *(978-0-380-70915-1(5))* HarperCollins Pubs.
—Henry & the Paper Route. Cleary, Beverly. 2014. (Henry Huggins Ser.: 4). (ENG.). 224p. (J). (gr. 3-7). 16.99 *(978-0-688-21380-0(4))*; reprint ed. pap. 6.99 *(978-0-380-70921-2(X))* HarperCollins Pubs.
—Henry Huggins. Cleary, Beverly. 2014. (Henry Huggins Ser.: 1). (ENG.). 208p. (J). (gr. 3-7). 16.99 *(978-0-688-21385-5(5))* HarperCollins Pubs.
Darling, Louis. Henry Huggins. Cleary, Beverly. 2004. (Henry Huggins Ser.: 1). (SPA.). 160p. (J). (gr. 3-7). pap. 7.99 *(978-0-06-073600-2(3),* Rayo) HarperCollins Pubs.
Darling, Louis, et al. Henry Huggins. Cleary, Beverly. 50th anniv. ed. 2014. (Henry Huggins Ser.: 1). (ENG.). 224p. (J). (gr. 3-7). pap. 6.99 *(978-0-380-70912-0(0))* HarperCollins Pubs.
—The Mouse & the Motorcycle. Cleary, Beverly. 2014. (Mouse & the Motorcycle Ser.). (ENG.). 208p. (J). (gr. 3-7). 16.99 *(978-0-688-21698-6(6))*; reprint ed. pap. 6.99 *(978-0-380-70924-3(4))* HarperCollins Pubs.
—Ramona la Chinche. Cleary, Beverly. 2006. (Ramona Ser.: 2).Tr. of Ramona the Pest. (SPA.). 192p. (J). (gr. 3-7). pap. 5.99 *(978-0-688-14888-1(3),* MR2295, Rayo) HarperCollins Pubs.
—Ramona the Pest. Cleary, Beverly. 2013. (Ramona Ser.: 2). (ENG.). 240p. (J). (gr. 3-7). 16.99 *(978-0-688-21721-1(4))* HarperCollins Pubs.
Darling, Louis. El Ratoncito de la Moto. Cleary, Beverly. Netto, Lydia, tr. 2006.Tr. of Mouse & the Motorcycle. (SPA.). 160p. (J). (gr. 3-7). pap. 5.99 *(978-0-06-000057-8(0),* Rayo) HarperCollins Pubs.
Darling, Louis, et al. Ribsy. Cleary, Beverly. 2014. (Henry Huggins Ser.: 6). (ENG.). 240p. (J). (gr. 3-7). 16.99 *(978-0-688-21662-7(5))*; pap. 6.99 *(978-0-380-70955-7(4))* HarperCollins Pubs.
—Runaway Ralph. Cleary, Beverly. 2014. (Mouse & the Motorcycle Ser.). (ENG.). 224p. (J). (gr. 3-7). 16.99 *(978-0-688-21701-3(X))*; pap. 6.99 *(978-0-380-70953-3(8))* HarperCollins Pubs.
Darling, Louis & Dockray, Tracy. Ellen Tebbits. Cleary, Beverly. 2008. (ENG.). 192p. (J). (gr. 3-7). 16.99 *(978-0-688-21264-3(6))*; pap. 6.99 *(978-0-380-70913-7(9))* HarperCollins Pubs.
—Otis Spofford. Cleary, Beverly. 2008. (ENG.). 208p. (J). (gr. 3-7). 16.99 *(978-0-688-21720-4(6))*; reprint ed. pap. 6.99 *(978-0-380-70919-9(8))* HarperCollins Pubs.
Darling, Louis & Rogers, Jacqueline. Beezus & Ramona. Cleary, Beverly. 2013. (Ramona Ser.: 1). (ENG.). 208p. (J). (gr. 3-7). pap. 6.99 *(978-0-380-70918-2(X))* HarperCollins Pubs.
—Ramona the Pest. Cleary, Beverly. 2013. (Ramona Ser.: 2). (SPA & ENG.). 240p. (J). (gr. 3-7). pap. 6.99 *(978-0-380-70954-0(6))* HarperCollins Pubs.
D'Armata, Frank, jt. illus. see Epting, Steve.
Darne, Txell. The Sultan & the Mice. de Boer, Joan & De Boer, Joan. 2007. (ENG.). 36p. (J). 18.95 *(978-84-96788-84-8(9))* OQO, Editora ESP. Dist: Baker & Taylor Bks.
Darnell, K. L. The American Reader. Wargin, Kathy-jo. 2006. (Readers Ser.). (ENG.). 96p. (J). (gr. 1-5). 12.95 *(978-1-58536-095-6(3))* Sleeping Bear Pr.
—The New Jersey Reader. Noble, Trinka Hakes. 2009. (Readers Ser.). (ENG.). 96p. 12.95 *(978-1-58536-438-1(X))* Sleeping Bear Pr.
—The New York Reader. Burg, Ann E. 2008. (Readers Ser.). (ENG.). 96p. (J). pap. 5.95 *(978-1-58536-349-0(9))* Sleeping Bear Pr.
—The Ohio Reader. Schonberg, Marcia. rev. ed. 2007. (State Readers Ser.). (ENG.). 96p. (J). (gr. 1-5). 12.95 *(978-1-58536-321-6(9))* Sleeping Bear Pr.
—Pennsylvania Reader. Noble, Trinka Hakes. rev. ed. 2007. (State Readers Ser.). (ENG.). 96p. (J). (gr. 1-5). 12.95 *(978-1-58536-320-9(0))* Sleeping Bear Pr.
Darnell, Kate. The Missouri Reader. Young, Judy Dockrey. 2010. (Readers Ser.). (ENG.). 96p. (J). 12.95 *(978-1-58536-437-4(1))* Sleeping Bear Pr.
Darragh, Aileen. Soda Bottle School. Slade, Suzanne & Kutner, Laura. 2014. (ENG.). 32p. (J). 16.95 *(978-0-88448-371-7(1))* Tilbury Hse. Pubs.
Darrenkamp, Julia Mary. My First Book about Mary. Orfeo, Christine Virginia. 2007. 63p. (Orig.). (J). (gr. 3-7). per. 7.95 *(978-0-8198-4861-1(1))* Pauline Bks. & Media.
—My Scriptural Rosary. Roddy, Lauren S. rev. ed. 2006. (J). 4.95 *(978-0-8198-4845-1(X))* Pauline Bks. & Media.
Darroch, Jane & Riley, Scott. The Story of Monet & Renoir. Frey, Lisa A. Frey, Lisa A. & Darroch, Jane, eds. 2004. (Color & Learn Book Ser.). 32p. (gr. k-4). pap. 12.99 *(978-0-9707110-1-4(8))* Starshell Pr., Ltd.
Darrow, Geof. Hard Boiled. Miller, Frank. Prosser, Jerry, ed. 2005. (ENG.). 128p. (gr. 11-18). pap. 16.95 *(978-1-878574-58-9(2))* Dark Horse Comics.
Dartes, Staci. Prince de'Mario's Adventure, 1 vol. Smith, Nerissia. 2009. 29p. pap. 24.95 *(978-1-61582-972-9(5))* America Star Bks.
Darwin, Beatrice, et al. Socks. Cleary, Beverly. 2008. (ENG.). 160p. (J). (gr. 3-7). 16.99 *(978-0-688-20067-1(2))* HarperCollins Pubs.
Darwin, Erwin L. Sparky Ames of the Ferry Command. Snell, Roy Judson. 2012. 246p. 46.95 *(978-1-258-25306-6(2))*; pap. 31.95 *(978-1-258-25572-5(3))* Literary Licensing, LLC.
Das, Amrita. Hope Is a Girl Selling Fruit. 2014. (ENG.). 28p. 16.95 *(978-93-83145-02-7(1))* Tara Books Agency IND. Dist: Perseus-PGW.
Das Group Staff, jt. illus. see Golden Books Staff.
Das Grup. I Can Be... a Baby Doctor (Barbie) Depken, Kristen L. 2013. (Step into Reading Ser.). (ENG.). 32p. (J). (gr. -1-1). pap. 3.99 *(978-0-307-98112-7(6),* Random Hse. Bks. for Young Readers) Random Hse. Children's Bks.
Das, Prodeepta. Kamal Goes to Trinidad. Frederick, Malcolm. 2008. (Children Return to Their Roots Ser.). (ENG.). 32p. (J). (gr. 1-4). 16.95 *(978-1-84507-702-0(4),* Frances Lincoln Children's Bks.) Quarto Publishing Group UK GBR. Dist: Hachette Bk. Group.
—R Is for Russia. Kabakov, Vladimir. 2013. (ENG.). 32p. (J). (gr. -1-2). pap. 8.99 *(978-1-84780-427-3(6),* Frances Lincoln) Quarto Publishing Group UK GBR. Dist: Hachette Bk. Group.
—S Is for South Africa. Naidoo, Beverley. 2014. (World Alphabets Ser.). (ENG.). 32p. (J). (gr. -1-2). pap. 8.99 *(978-1-84780-502-7(7),* Frances Lincoln) Quarto Publishing Group UK GBR. Dist: Hachette Bk. Group.
Das, Prodeepta. I Is for India. Das, Prodeepta. 2007. (World Alphabet Ser.). (ENG.). 32p. (J). (gr. k-3). pap. 8.99 *(978-1-84507-320-6(7),* Frances Lincoln) Quarto Publishing Group UK GBR. Dist: Littlehampton Bk Services, Ltd.
Das, Prodeepta, photos by. B Is for Bangladesh. Rahman, Urmi & Quarto Generic Staff. 2009. (World Alphabets Ser.). (ENG., 32p. (J). (gr. -1-3). 16.95 *(978-1-84507-918-5(3),* Frances Lincoln) Quarto Publishing Group UK GBR. Dist: Hachette Bk. Group.
—Geeta's Day: From Dawn to Dusk in an Indian Village. 2010. (Child's Day Ser.). (ENG., 32p. (J). (gr. k-3). pap. 8.99 *(978-1-84780-112-8(9),* Frances Lincoln) Quarto Publishing Group UK GBR. Dist: Hachette Bk. Group.
—K Is for Korea. Cheung, Hyechong. 2011. (World Alphabets Ser.). (ENG., 32p. (J). (gr. -1-2). pap. 8.95 *(978-1-84780-133-3(1),* Frances Lincoln) Quarto Publishing Group UK GBR. Dist: Hachette Bk. Group.
—P Is for Pakistan. Razzak, Shazia. 2007. (World Alphabets Ser.). (ENG., 32p. (J). (gr. -1-2). 17.95 *(978-1-84507-483-8(1),* Frances Lincoln) Quarto Publishing Group UK GBR. Dist: Hachette Bk. Group.
—P Is for Poland. Mrowczynska, Agnieszka. 2014. (World Alphabets Ser.). (ENG., 32p. (J). (gr. -1-2). pap. 8.95 *(978-1-84780-352-8(0),* Frances Lincoln) Quarto Publishing Group UK GBR. Dist: Hachette Bk. Group.
—R Is for Russia. Kabakov, Vladimir. 2011. (World Alphabets Ser.). (ENG., 32p. (J). (gr. -1-2). 17.95 *(978-1-84780-102-9(1),* Frances Lincoln) Quarto Publishing Group UK GBR. Dist: Hachette Bk. Group.
—T Is for Turkey. Tossuon, Nevin et al. 2010. (World Alphabets Ser.). (ENG., 32p. (J). (gr. k-3). 17.95 *(978-1-84507-998-7(1),* Frances Lincoln) Quarto Publishing Group UK GBR. Dist: Hachette Bk. Group.
—We Are Britain! Zephaniah, Benjamin. 2004. (ENG., 32p. (J). (gr. 1-6). pap. 8.99 *(978-1-84507-143-1(3),* Frances Lincoln) Quarto Publishing Group UK GBR. Dist: Hachette Bk. Group.
Dashiell, Margaret. Haworth Idyll: A Fantasy. Trigg, Roberta. 2012. 88p. 38.95 *(978-1-258-23556-7(0))*; pap. 23.95 *(978-1-258-24510-8(8))* Literary Licensing, LLC.
Daste, Larry. Looney Limericks. Jacobs, Frank, ed. 2011. (Dover Children's Activity Bks.). (ENG.). 64p. (gr. 3). pap. 3.00 *(978-0-486-40615-2(6))* Dover Pubns., Inc.
Dattola, Chiara. One Little Bean: Observation - Life Cycle. Kim, Cecil. Cowley, Joy, ed. 2015. (Step up - Creative Thinking Ser.). (ENG.). 32p. (gr. -1-2). 26.65 ***(978-1-925246-12-4(4))***; 7.99 ***(978-1-925246-64-3(7))***; 26.65 ***(978-1-925246-38-4(8))*** ChoiceMaker Pty. Ltd., The AUS. (Big and SMALL). Dist: Lerner Publishing Group.
Datz, Jim. Whose Tools? Buzzeo, Toni. 2015. (Whose Tools? Ser.). (ENG.). 16p. (J). (gr. -1 — 1). bds. 9.95 *(978-1-4197-1431-3(7))* Abrams.
Datz, Jim. Whose Truck? Buzzeo, Toni. 2015. (ENG.). 24p. (J). (gr. -1 — 1). bds. 9.95 ***(978-1-4197-1612-6(3))*** Abrams.
Datz, Margot. Nighttide on a Vineyard Farm. Schaal, Patty. 2010. (J). *(978-0-9827146-1-4(0))* Vineyard Stories.
Dauber, Liz. The Snow Baby. Hillert, Margaret. rev. exp. ed. 2006. (Beginning to Read-Easy Stories Ser.). 32p. (J). (gr. -1-3). lib. bdg. 14.95 *(978-1-59953-045-1(7))* Norwood Hse. Pr.
Daubney, Kate. The Airport. Goldsmith, Mike. 2015. (I Explore Ser.). (ENG.). 12p. (J). (gr. -1-k). bds. 6.95 ***(978-1-4549-1495-2(5))*** Sterling Publishing Co., Inc.
—Digging for Dinosaurs. Goldsmith, Mike. 2015. (I Explore Ser.). (ENG.). 12p. (J). (gr. -1-k). bds. 6.95 ***(978-1-4549-1501-0(3))*** Sterling Publishing Co., Inc.
Daubney, Kate. Under the Sea. Goldsmith, Mike. 2015. (I Explore Ser.). (ENG.). 12p. (J). (gr. -1-k). bds. 6.95 *(978-1-4549-1502-7(1))* Sterling Publishing Co., Inc.
—The Zoo. Dods, Emma. 2015. (I Explore Ser.). (ENG.). 12p. (J). (gr. -1-k). bds. 6.95 *(978-1-4549-1503-4(X))* Sterling Publishing Co., Inc.
Daugherty, James. Abe Lincoln Grows Up. Sandburg, Carl. 2009. (ENG.). 228p. (YA). (gr. 7-18). reprint ed. pap. 6.99 *(978-0-15-602615-4(5))* Houghton Mifflin Harcourt Publishing Co.
Dautremer, Rebecca. Nasreddine. Weulersse, Odile & Merz, Kathleen. 2013. (J). 17.00 *(978-0-8028-5416-2(8),* Eerdmans Bks For Young Readers) Eerdmans, William B. Publishing Co.
Dautremer, Rébecca. The Secret Lives of Princesses. Lechermeier, Philippe. 2010. (ENG.). 88p. (J). (gr. 2). 19.95 *(978-1-4027-6677-0(7))* Sterling Publishing Co., Inc.
—Swing Café. Norac, Carl. 2010. (ENG.). 54p. (J). (gr. k-2). 16.95 *(978-2-923163-62-8(1))* La Montagne Secrete CAN. Dist: Independent Pubs. Group.
Davalos, Felipe. Al fin en Casa. Elya, Susan Middleton. 2011.Tr. of Home at Last. (SPA.). 32p. (J). pap. 8.95 *(978-1-60060-654-0(7))* Lee & Low Bks., Inc.
Dávalos, Felipe. All the Way to Morning. Harshman, Marc. 2006. (J). per. 7.95 *(978-1-891852-49-7(3))* Quarrier Pr.
Davalos, Felipe. Eyes of the Jaguar. Flor Ada, Alma. 2004. (Puertas Al Sol / Gateways to the Sun Ser.). 48p. (gr. k-6). pap. 17.95 *(978-1-58105-970-0(1))* Santillana USA Publishing Co., Inc.
—Gone Forever: An Alphabet of Extinct Animals. Markle, Sandra & Markle, William. 2007. (ENG.). 40p. (J). (gr. 4-6). 14.99 *(978-1-4169-6138-3(0),* Simon & Schuster/Paula Wiseman Bks.) Simon & Schuster/Paula Wiseman Bks.
Dávalos, Felipe. Home at Last. Elya, Susan Middleton. 2013. (ENG.). 32p. (J). 16.95 *(978-1-58430-020-5(5))* Lee & Low Bks., Inc.
Davalos, Felipe, et al. On the Wings of the Condor. Flor Ada, Alma & Campoy, F. Isabel. (Gateways to the Sun). 48p. (J). (gr. k-6). pap. 13.95 *(978-1-58105-964-9(7))* Santillana USA Publishing Co., Inc.
Davalos, Felipe. Our Lady of Guadalupe, 1 vol. Serrano, Francisco. 2nd ed. 2011. (ENG.). 12p. (gr. -1). 22.95 *(978-1-55498-074-1(7))* Groundwood Bks. CAN. Dist: Perseus-PGW.
Dávalos, Felipe. The Secret Stars, 1 vol. Slate, Joseph & Slate. 2005. (ENG.). 32p. (J). pap. 5.95 *(978-0-7614-5152-5(8))* Marshall Cavendish Corp.
—Una Semilla de Luz. Flor Ada, Alma & Campoy, F. Isabel. 2003. (Coleccion Derechos Del Nino Ser.). (SPA.). 32p. (J). (gr. 3-5). pap. 7.95 *(978-84-204-5818-2(X))* Santillana USA Publishing Co., Inc.
Davalos, Felipe, et al. Tales Our Abuelitas Told: A Hispanic Folktale Collection. Flor Ada, Alma & Campoy, F. Isabel. 2006. (ENG.). 128p. (J). (gr. k-5). 19.95 *(978-0-689-82583-5(8),* Atheneum Bks. for Young Readers) Simon & Schuster Children's Publishing.
Dávalos, Felipe. La Virgen de Guadalupe. Serrano, Francisco.Tr. of Virgin of Guadalupe. (SPA.). (J). (gr. 2-4). 18.00 *(978-968-494-070-3(X))* Centro de Informacion y Desarrollo de la Comunicacion y la Literatura MEX. Dist: Lectorum Pubns., Inc.
Davauer, Nathaniel. Goodnight Loon. Sauer, Abe. 2014. (ENG.). 28p. (J). 9.95 *(978-0-8166-9703-8(5))* Univ. of Minnesota Pr.
Dave, Vijay, jt. photos by see Bhargava, Neirah.
Davenier, Christine. A Day with Miss Lina's Ballerinas. Maccarone, Grace. 2014. (My Readers Ser.). (ENG.). 32p. (J). (gr. k-2). 15.99 *(978-1-250-04716-8(1))* Square Fish.
—Dessert First. Durand, Hallie. (ENG.). (J). (gr. 2-5). 2010. 176p. pap. 5.99 *(978-1-4169-6386-8(3))*; 2009. 160p. 14.99 *(978-1-4169-6385-1(5))* Simon & Schuster Children's Publishing. (Atheneum Bks. for Young Readers).
—A Fairy Merry Christmas. Andrews, Julie & Hamilton, Emma Walton. 2012. (Passport to Reading Level 1 Ser.). (ENG.). 32p. (J). (gr. -1-1). pap. 4.99 *(978-0-316-21962-4(2))* Little, Brown Bks. for Young Readers.
—Iris & Walter. Guest, Elissa Haden. alt. ed. 2012. (Green Light Readers Level 3 Ser.). (ENG.). 44p. (J). (gr. 1-4). pap. 3.99 *(978-0-547-74555-8(9))* Houghton Mifflin Harcourt Publishing Co.
—Iris & Walter. Guest, Elissa Haden. 2006. (Iris & Walter Ser.). 43p. (gr. 1-4). 15.95 *(978-0-7569-7008-6(3))* Perfection Learning Corp.
—Iris & Walter: Lost & Found. Guest, Elissa Haden. 2014. (Green Light Readers Level 3 Ser.). (ENG.). 44p. (J). (gr. 1-4). pap. 3.99 *(978-0-544-22789-7(1),* HMH Books For Young Readers) Houghton Mifflin Harcourt Publishing Co.
—Iris & Walter - The School Play. Guest, Elissa Haden. 2006. (Iris & Walter Ser.). 44p. (gr. 1-4). 15.95 *(978-0-7569-6679-9(5))* Perfection Learning Corp.
—Iris & Walter & Baby Rose. Guest, Elissa Haden. 2012. (Green Light Readers Level 3 Ser.). (ENG.). 44p. (J). (gr. 1-4). pap. 3.99 *(978-0-547-85064-1(6))* Houghton Mifflin Harcourt Publishing Co.
—Iris & Walter & Baby Rose. Guest, Elissa Haden. ed. 2012. (Iris & Walter — Green Light Reader Ser.). lib. bdg. 13.55 *(978-0-606-26612-3(7),* Turtleback) Turtleback Bks.
—Iris & Walter & Cousin Howie. Guest, Elissa Haden. alt. ed. 2012. (Green Light Readers Level 3 Ser.). (ENG.). 44p. (J). (gr. 1-4). pap. 3.99 *(978-0-547-85068-9(9))* Houghton Mifflin Harcourt Publishing Co.
—Iris & Walter & the Birthday Party. Guest, Elissa Haden. 2013. (Green Light Readers Level 3 Ser.). (ENG.). 44p. (J). (gr. 1-4). pap. 3.99 *(978-0-544-10498-3(6))* Houghton Mifflin Harcourt Publishing Co.
—Iris & Walter & the Field Trip. Guest, Elissa Haden. 2013. (Green Light Readers Level 3 Ser.). (ENG.). 44p. (J). (gr. 1-4). pap. 3.99 *(978-0-544-10665-9(2))* Houghton Mifflin Harcourt Publishing Co.
—Iris & Walter & the Field Trip. Guest, Elissa Haden. 2007. (Iris & Walter Ser.). 44p. (J). (gr. 1-4). 13.60 *(978-0-7569-8041-2(0))* Perfection Learning Corp.
—Iris & Walter & the Substitute Teacher. Guest, Elissa Haden. 2006. (Iris & Walter Ser.). 44p. (gr. 1-4). 15.95 *(978-0-7569-7122-9(5))* Perfection Learning Corp.
—Iris & Walter Book & CD. Guest, Elissa Haden. 2015. (Green Light Readers Level 3 Ser.). (ENG.). 44p. (J). (gr. -1-3). 6.99 *(978-0-544-45604-4(1),* HMH Books For Young Readers) Houghton Mifflin Harcourt Publishing Co.
—Iris & Walter: Substitute Teacher. Guest, Elissa Haden. 2014. (Green Light Readers Level 3 Ser.). (ENG.). 44p. (J). (gr. 1-4). pap. 3.99 *(978-0-544-22788-0(3),* HMH Books For Young Readers) Houghton Mifflin Harcourt Publishing Co.
—Iris & Walter: the School Play. Guest, Elissa Haden. 2015. (Green Light Readers Level 3 Ser.). (ENG.). 44p. (J). (gr. 1-4). pap. 3.99 *(978-0-544-45602-0(5),* HMH Books For Young Readers) Houghton Mifflin Harcourt Publishing Co.
—Iris & Walter, the Sleepover. Guest, Elissa Haden. 2006. (Iris & Walter Ser.). 44p. (gr. 1-4). 15.95 *(978-0-7569-6681-2(7))* Perfection Learning Corp.
—Iris & Walter: the Sleepover. Guest, Elissa Haden. alt. ed. 2012. (Green Light Readers Level 3 Ser.). (ENG.). 44p. (J). (gr. 1-4). pap. 3.99 *(978-0-547-74556-5(7))* Houghton Mifflin Harcourt Publishing Co.
—Iris & Walter: True Friends. Guest, Elissa Haden. 2015. (Green Light Readers Level 3 Ser.). (ENG.). 44p. (J). (gr. 1-4). pap. 3.99 *(978-0-544-45603-7(3),* HMH Books For Young Readers) Houghton Mifflin Harcourt Publishing Co.
—Just Desserts. Durand, Hallie. (ENG.). (J). (gr. 2-5). 2011. 224p. pap. 5.99 *(978-1-4169-6388-2(X))*; 2010. 208p. 15.99 *(978-1-4169-6387-5(1))* Simon & Schuster Children's Publishing. (Atheneum Bks. for Young Readers).
—Me I Am! Prelutsky, Jack. 2007. (ENG.). 32p. (J). (gr. -1-1). 17.99 *(978-0-374-34902-8(9),* Farrar, Straus & Giroux (BYR)) Farrar, Straus & Giroux.
—Miss Lina's Ballerinas. Maccarone, Grace. 2010. (ENG.). 40p. (J). (gr. -1-1). 17.99 *(978-0-312-38243-8(X))* Feiwel & Friends.
—Miss Lina's Ballerinas & the Wicked Wish. Maccarone, Grace. 2012. (ENG.). 40p. (J). (gr. k-1). 16.99 *(978-1-250-00580-9(9))* Feiwel & Friends.
Davenier, Christine. Nadia: The Girl Who Couldn't Sit Still. Gray, Karlin. 2016. (J). ***(978-0-544-31960-8(5))*** Harcourt.
Davenier, Christine. Navy Brat. Holt, Kimberly Willis. 2011. (Piper Reed Ser.: 1). (ENG.). 176p. (J). (gr. 3-6). pap. 6.99 *(978-0-312-62548-1(0))* Square Fish.
—No Room for Dessert. Durand, Hallie. (ENG.). 192p. (J). (gr. 2-5). 2012. pap. 6.99 *(978-1-4424-0361-1(6))*; 2011. 15.99 *(978-1-4424-0360-4(8))* Simon & Schuster Children's Publishing. (Atheneum Bks. for Young Readers).
—The Other Dog. L'Engle, Madeleine. 2003. 37p. (J). (gr. 2-5). reprint ed. 16.00 *(978-0-7567-6970-3(1))* DIANE Publishing Co.
—Piper Reed - Navy Brat. Holt, Kimberly Willis. 2007. (Piper Reed Ser.: 1). (ENG.). 160p. (J). (gr. 3-6). 14.95 *(978-0-8050-8197-8(6),* Holt, Henry & Co. Bks. For Young Readers) Holt, Henry & Co.
—Piper Reed, Campfire Girl. Holt, Kimberly Willis. 2010. (Piper Reed Ser.: 4). (ENG.). 160p. (J). (gr. 3-6). 15.99 *(978-0-8050-9006-2(1),* Holt, Henry & Co. Bks. For Young Readers) Holt, Henry & Co.
—Piper Reed, Campfire Girl. Holt, Kimberly Willis. 2011. (Piper Reed Ser.: 4). (ENG.). 176p. (J). (gr. 3-6). pap. 5.99 *(978-0-312-67482-3(1))* Square Fish.
—Piper Reed, Clubhouse Queen. Holt, Kimberly Willis. 2011. (Piper Reed Ser.: 2). (ENG.). 160p. (J). (gr. 3-6). 15.99 *(978-0-8050-9431-2(8),* Holt, Henry & Co. Bks. For Young Readers) Holt, Henry & Co.
—Piper Reed, Clubhouse Queen. Holt, Kimberly Willis. 2011. (Piper Reed Ser.: 2). (ENG.). 176p. (J). (gr. 3-6). pap. 6.99 *(978-0-312-61676-2(7))* Square Fish.
—Piper Reed, Forever Friend. Holt, Kimberly Willis. 2012. (Piper Reed Ser.: 6). (ENG.). 160p. (J). (gr. 3-6). 15.99 *(978-0-8050-9008-6(8),* Holt, Henry & Co. Bks. For Young Readers) Holt, Henry & Co.
—Piper Reed, Forever Friend. Holt, Kimberly Willis. 2013. (Piper Reed Ser.: 6). (ENG.). 176p. (J). (gr. 3-6). pap. 6.99 *(978-1-250-02725-2(X))* Square Fish.
—Piper Reed Gets a Job. Holt, Kimberly Willis. 2009. (Piper Reed Ser.: 3). (ENG.). 160p. (J). (gr. 3-6). 14.99 *(978-0-8050-8199-2(2),* Holt, Henry & Co. Bks. For Young Readers) Holt, Henry & Co.
—Piper Reed, Party Planner. Holt, Kimberly Willis. 2011. (Piper Reed Ser.: 3). (ENG.). 176p. (J). (gr. 3-6). pap. 5.99 *(978-0-312-61677-9(5))* Square Fish.
—Piper Reed, Rodeo Star. Holt, Kimberly Willis. 2011. (Piper Reed Ser.: 5). (ENG.). 160p. (J). (gr. 3-6). 15.99 *(978-0-8050-9007-9(X),* Holt, Henry & Co. Bks. For Young Readers) Holt, Henry & Co.
—Piper Reed, Rodeo Star. Holt, Kimberly Willis. 2012. (Piper Reed Ser.: 5). (ENG.). 176p. (J). (gr. 3-6). pap. 5.99 *(978-1-250-00409-3(8))* Square Fish.
—Sally Jean, the Bicycle Queen. Best, Cari. 2006. (ENG.). 32p. (J). (gr. -1-3). 17.99 *(978-0-374-36386-4(2),* Melanie Kroupa Bks.) Farrar, Straus & Giroux.
—Samantha on a Roll. Ashman, Linda. 2011. (ENG.). 40p. (J). (gr. -1-4). 16.99 *(978-0-374-36399-4(4),* Farrar, Straus & Giroux (BYR)) Farrar, Straus & Giroux.
—The Very Fairy Princess. Andrews, Julie & Hamilton, Emma Walton. 2010. (Very Fairy Princess Ser.). (ENG.). 32p. (J). (gr. -1-1). 18.00 *(978-0-316-04050-1(9))* Little, Brown Bks. for Young Readers.
—The Very Fairy Princess: Here Comes the Flower Girl! Andrews, Julie & Hamilton, Emma Walton. 2012. (Very Fairy Princess Ser.). (ENG.). 32p. (J). (gr. -1-1). 16.99 *(978-0-316-18561-5(2))* Little Brown & Co.
—The Very Fairy Princess: Teacher's Pet. Andrews, Julie & Hamilton, Emma Walton. 2013. (Passport to Reading Level 1 Ser.). (ENG.). 32p. (J). (gr. -1-1). 4.99 *(978-0-316-21959-4(2))* Little Brown & Co.
—The Very Fairy Princess - Graduation Girl! Andrews, Julie et al. 2014. (Very Fairy Princess Ser.). (ENG.). 32p. (J). (gr. -1-1). 18.00 *(978-0-316-21960-0(6))* Little, Brown Bks. for Young Readers.
Davenier, Christine. The Very Fairy Princess: a Spooky, Sparkly Halloween. Andrews, Julie & Walton Hamilton, Emma. 2015. (ENG.). 32p. (J). (gr. -1-1). 18.00 ***(978-0-316-28304-5(5))*** Little, Brown Bks. for Young Readers.
Davenier, Christine. The Very Fairy Princess Doodle Book. Andrews, Julie & Walton Hamilton, Emma. 2015. (ENG.). 128p. (J). (gr. -1-17). pap. 12.99 *(978-0-316-28307-6(X))* Little, Brown Bks. for Young Readers.

D

—The Very Fairy Princess Follows Her Heart. Andrews, Julie & Hamilton, Emma Walton. 2013. (Very Fairy Princess Ser.). (ENG.). 32p. (J). (gr. -1-1). 16.99 *(978-0-316-18559-2(0))* Little Brown & Co.

—The Very Fairy Princess Sparkles in the Snow. Andrews, Julie & Hamilton, Emma Walton. 2013. (Very Fairy Princess Ser.). (ENG.). 32p. (J). (gr. -1-1). 18.00 *(978-0-316-21963-1(0))* Little Brown & Co.

Davenier, Christine & Gilbert, Rob. It's Raining, It's Pouring. Eagle, Kim. 2012. (ENG.). 32p. (J). (-k). 17.95 *(978-1-936140-77-0(2),* Imagine Publishing) Charlesbridge Publishing, Inc.

Davenport, Andy. The ABC's of Handling Money God's Way. Dayton, Howard & Dayton, Beverly. 2003. (ENG.). 96p. (J). pap., tchr. ed. 11.99 *(978-0-8024-3151-6(8))* Moody Pubs.

—The Legend of Billy Adams: A Cowboy Story with a Message for Every Child. Hawks, Robb. 2011. (ENG.). 56p. pap. 12.99 *(978-1-4663-1057-5(X))* CreateSpace Independent Publishing Platform.

—The Secret of Handling Money God's Way. Dayton, Howard & Dayton, Beverly. 2003. (ENG.). 96p. (J). pap., tchr. ed. 10.99 *(978-0-8024-3153-0(4))* Moody Pubs.

Davenport, Chris. Confronting a Bully, 1 vol. Finley, Danielle. 2009. 12p. pap. 24.95 *(978-1-61546-146-2(9))* America Star Bks.

Davey, Owen. Foxly's Feast. 2014. (ENG.). 32p. (J). (-k). 14.95 *(978-1-62914-608-9(0),* Sky Pony Pr.) Skyhorse Publishing Co., Inc.

Davey, Owen. Laika: Astronaut Dog. Davey, Owen. 2013. (ENG.). 32p. (J). (gr. k-3). 15.99 *(978-0-7636-6822-8(2),* Templar) Candlewick Pr.

—Night Knight. Davey, Owen. 2012. (ENG.). 32p. (J). (gr. k-k). 15.99 *(978-0-7636-5838-0(3),* Templar) Candlewick Pr.

Davick, Linda. Kindergarten Countdown. Hays, Anna Jane. 2013. (ENG.). 24p. (J). (gr. -1-2). 6.99 *(978-0-385-75371-5(3),* Dragonfly Bks.) Random Hse. Children's Bks.

—We Love Our School! A Read-Together Rebus Story. Sierra, Judy. 2011. (ENG.). 24p. (J). (gr. -1-2). 7.99 *(978-0-375-86728-6(7))* Knopf, Alfred A. Inc.

—10 Easter Egg Hunters: A Holiday Counting Book. Schulman, Janet. (ENG.). (J). (gr. -1 — 1). 2012. 26p. bds. 6.99 *(978-0-375-86637-1(X));* 2011. 32p. 8.99 *(978-0-375-86787-3(2))* Knopf, Alfred A. Inc.

—10 Easter Egg Hunters: A Holiday Counting Book. Schulman, Janet. 2015. (ENG.). 32p. (J). (— 1). 4.99 *(978-0-553-50784-3(2),* Dragonfly Bks.) Random Hse. Children's Bks.

—10 Trick-or-Treaters: A Halloween Counting Book. Schulman, Janet. (ENG.). (J). (gr. -1 — 1). 2009. 26p. bds. 6.99 *(978-0-375-85347-0(2),* Knopf Bks. for Young Readers); 2008. 32p. pap. 7.99 *(978-0-385-73614-5(2),* Dragonfly Bks.); 2005. 32p. 8.99 *(978-0-375-83225-3(4),* Knopf Bks. for Young Readers) Random Hse. Children's Bks.

—10 Trim-the-Tree'ers. Schulman, Janet. 2011. (ENG.). 32p. (J). (gr. -1 — 1). bds. 6.99 *(978-0-375-87302-7(3),* Knopf Bks. for Young Readers) Random Hse. Children's Bks.

—10 Trim-the-Tree'ers. Schulman, Janet. 2012. (ENG.). 32p. (J). (gr. -1 — 1). pap. 4.99 *(978-0-449-81055-2(0),* Dragonfly Bks.) Random Hse. Children's Bks.

—10 Valentine Friends. Schulman, Janet. 2011. (ENG.). 32p. (J). (gr. -1 — 1). 8.99 *(978-0-375-86967-9(0),* Knopf Bks. for Young Readers) Random Hse. Children's Bks.

—10 Valentine Friends. Schulman, Janet. 2012. (ENG.). 26p. (J). (gr. -1 — 1). bds. 6.99 *(978-0-375-87130-6(6))* Knopf, Alfred A. Inc.

Davick, Linda. I Love You, Nose! I Love You, Toes! Davick, Linda. 2013. (ENG.). 32p. (J). (gr. -1-1). 17.99 *(978-1-4424-6037-9(7),* Beach Lane Bks.) Beach Lane Bks.

—Say Hello! Davick, Linda. 2015. (ENG.). 40p. (J). (gr. -1-3). 17.99 *(978-1-4814-2867-5(5),* Beach Lane Bks.) Beach Lane Bks.

Davick, Linda. Ready, Set, Grow! A What's Happening to My Body? Book for Younger Girls. Davick, Linda, tr. Madaras, Lynda. 2003. (What's Happening to My Body? Ser.). (ENG.). 128p. (gr. 4-6). 22.00 *(978-1-55704-587-4(9),* Morrow, William & Co.) HarperCollins Pubs.

David, Amanda. Bedwin, 1 vol. Michael. 2009. (ENG.). 46p. 24.95 *(978-1-60813-258-4(7))* America Star Bks.

David, Amor. How Does God See Me? Rashad, Girmen. 2008. (Little Christian Ser.). 24p. 9.99 *(978-0-9819100-0-0(9))* Elkarez Publishing Co.

David, Catrow, jt. illus. see Catrow, David.

David, Jamie. Johann Sebastian Humpbach. David, Jamie. 2009. 167p. pap. 14.95 *(978-0-615-31840-0(1))* Chai Yo Maui Pr.

David, Jason. Red Is Beautiful: Chiih Nizhoni. John, Roberta. Ruffenach, Jessie, ed. Thomas, Peter, tr. from NAV. 2003. (ENG & NAV.). 32p. (J). (gr. 4-7). 17.95 *(978-1-893354-37-1(7))* Salina Bookshelf Inc.

David, Mark. The Case of the Graveyard Ghost & Other Mysteries. Ball, Duncan. 2005. 192p. (Orig.). *(978-0-207-20044-1(0))* HarperCollins Pubs. Australia.

David, Messing. Fill a Bucket: A Guide to Daily Happiness for the Young Children. McCloud, Carol & Martin, Katherine. 2009. (ENG.). 24p. (J). 9.95 *(978-1-933916-43-9(5),* Ferne Pr.) Nelson Publishing & Marketing.

David, Peter, et al. World War Hulk. Romita, John, Jr. 2009. (ENG.). 304p. (YA). (gr. 8-17). 34.99 *(978-0-7851-2670-6(8))* Marvel Worldwide, Inc.

David, R. Joseph & His Brothers. 2010. 12p. *(978-965-91286-0-0(6))* Sifrei Bet Shearim Ltd.

David, Racheli. Doda Golda Comes for Pesach. Paretzky, Leah. 2012. 24p. 10.95 *(978-1-60091-195-8(1))* Israel Bookshop Pubns.

—Hot! Hot! Hot! Rosenberg, Faigy & Weiss, Esti. 2013. 32p. 10.95 *(978-1-60091-268-9(0))* Israel Bookshop Pubns.

—Let's Use Them Right: Social Skills for My Hands, Feet, & Mouth. Schwartz, Sara Leah. 2013. 39p. 16.95 *(978-1-60091-276-4(1))* Israel Bookshop Pubns.

David, Racheli. Look What My Parents Give Me. Ginsburg, Sara. 2014. 29p. (J). ***(978-1-4226-1489-1(1))*** Mesorah Pubns., Ltd.

David, Racheli. Moshe Goes to Yeshiva. Levy, Rochel. 2012. 24p. 11.95 *(978-1-60091-212-2(5))* Israel Bookshop Pubns.

David, Richard. Albi the Pink Carabao. Pablo, Norma. 2011. (ENG.). 78p. pap. 15.99 *(978-1-4609-6595-5(7))* CreateSpace Independent Publishing Platform.

Daviddi, Evelyn. I Love Chocolate. Cali, Davide. 2009. (ENG.). 32p. (J). (gr. -1-k). 12.95 *(978-0-88776-912-2(8),* Tundra Bks.) Tundra Bks. CAN. Dist: Penguin Random Hse., LLC.

Davidge, Jesse. Mathemagick: The Point & the Invisible Hand. Davidge, James. 2014. (ENG.). 64p. (YA). pap. 9.95 *(978-1-897411-80-3(4))* Bayeux Arts, Inc. CAN. Dist: Chicago Distribution Ctr.

Davids, Paul, photos by. The Fountain of Youth. Davids, Paul. 56p. (Orig.). (YA). (gr. 5-9). pap. 9.95 *(978-0-939031-01-6(9))* Pictorial Legends.

Davidson, Blanche. Pancho Finds A Home. Cogan, Karen. 2007. 32p. (J). 19.95 *(978-1-929115-16-7(4))* Azro Pr., Inc.

Davidson, Chris. Family Gatherings. Owens, L. L. 2010. (Let's Be Social Ser.). 32p. 28.50 *(978-1-60270-798-6(7),* Looking Glass Library- Nonfiction) Magic Wagon.

—Go to School. Owens, L. L. 2010. (Let's Be Social Ser.). 32p. 28.50 *(978-1-60270-799-3(5),* Looking Glass Library- Nonfiction) Magic Wagon.

—Go Worship. Owens, L. L. 2010. (Let's Be Social Ser.). 32p. 28.50 *(978-1-60270-800-6(2),* Looking Glass Library- Nonfiction) Magic Wagon.

—Hide & Seek Moon: The Moon Phases, 1 vol. Koontz, Robin Michal. 2011. (First Graphics: Nature Cycles Ser.). (ENG.). 24p. (gr. 1-2). 23.32 *(978-1-4296-5365-7(5))* Capstone Pr., Inc.

—Hide & Seek Moon: The Moon Phases, 1 vol. Koontz, Robin. 2011. (First Graphics: Nature Cycles Ser.). (ENG.). 24p. (gr. 1-2). pap. 6.29 *(978-1-4296-6229-1(8));* pap. 35.70 *(978-1-4296-6398-4(7))* Capstone Pr., Inc.

—Join a Team. Owens, L. L. 2010. (Let's Be Social Ser.). 32p. 28.50 *(978-1-60270-801-3(0),* Looking Glass Library- Nonfiction) Magic Wagon.

—Make Friends. Owens, L. L. 2010. (Let's Be Social Ser.). 32p. 28.50 *(978-1-60270-802-0(9),* Looking Glass Library- Nonfiction) Magic Wagon.

—Meet Your Neighborhood. Owens, L. L. 2010. (Let's Be Social Ser.). 32p. 28.50 *(978-1-60270-803-7(7),* Looking Glass Library- Nonfiction) Magic Wagon.

—Water Goes Round: The Water Cycle, 1 vol. Koontz, Robin Michal. 2011. (First Graphics: Nature Cycles Ser.). (ENG.). 24p. (gr. 1-2). lib. bdg. 23.32 *(978-1-4296-5364-0(7))* Capstone Pr., Inc.

—Water Goes Round: The Water Cycle, 1 vol. Koontz, Robin. 2011. (First Graphics: Nature Cycles Ser.). (ENG.). 24p. (gr. 1-2). pap. 6.29 *(978-1-4296-6231-4(X));* pap. 35.70 *(978-1-4296-6400-4(2))* Capstone Pr., Inc.

Davidson, Dawn, jt. illus. see Stevenson, John.

Davidson, Jamie. On the Wings of Angels: Inspirational Verses for Everyday Living. Woodsmall, Marilyne. 2004. (YA). per. 22.00 *(978-1-892876-10-2(8))* Next Step Pr.

Davidson, Kevin. Catholic Bible Stories for Children. Ball, Ann & Will, Julianne M. 2006. 208p. (J). (gr. -1-3). 19.95 *(978-1-59276-243-9(3))* Our Sunday Visitor, Publishing Div.

—Catholic Bible Stories for Children: 1st Communion Edition. Ball, Ann & Will, Julianne M. 2006. 208p. (J). (gr. -1-3). 19.95 *(978-1-59276-221-7(2))* Our Sunday Visitor, Publishing Div.

—Making Things Right: The Sacrament of Reconciliation. Leichner, Jeannine Timko. 2005. 70p. pap. 6.95 *(978-1-59276-157-9(7))* Our Sunday Visitor, Publishing Div.

Davidson, Mary. Fiddle Me a Riddle & Bring Me the Moon. Plunkett, Windyann. 2011. 24p. pap. 24.95 *(978-1-4626-3920-5(8))* America Star Bks.

Davidson, Michael. Ready, Teddy, Go! Davidson, Michael. 2013. (ENG.). 32p. (J). (-k). 18.99 *(978-1-4083-2023-5(1))* Hodder & Stoughton GBR. Dist: Independent Pubs. Group.

Davidson, Mike, et al. Draw What? A Doodling, Drawing, & Coloring Book. 2014. (ENG.). (J). (gr. -1-3). *(978-1-74352-285-1(1))* Hinkler Bks. Pty. Ltd.

Davidson, Paul. Bugs up Close. Swanson, Diane. 2007. (ENG.). 40p. (J). (gr. 2-5). 8.95 *(978-1-55453-139-4(X));* 17.95 *(978-1-55453-138-7(1))* Kids Can Pr., Ltd. CAN. Dist: Univ. of Toronto Pr.

Davidson, Paul, et al. X-Factor: Hard Labor. 2011. (ENG.). 120p. (YA). (gr. 8-17). 19.99 *(978-0-7851-5285-9(7))* Marvel Worldwide, Inc.

—X-Men: Second Coming Revelations. Spurrier, Simon & Swierczynski, Duane. 2011. (ENG.). 208p. (YA). (gr. 8-17). pap. 19.99 *(978-0-7851-5706-9(9))* Marvel Worldwide, Inc.

Davidson, Paul. X-Men Legacy: Aftermath. 2011. (ENG.). 120p. (YA). (gr. 8-17). 19.99 *(978-0-7851-5635-2(6))* Marvel Worldwide, Inc.

Davidsson, Ashton, jt. illus. see Amber, Holly.

Davie, Helen K. Dolphin Talk: Whistles, Clicks, & Clapping Jaws. Pfeffer, Wendy. 2003. (Let's-Read-and-Find-Out Science Ser.). (ENG.). 40p. (J). (gr. k-4). 15.99 *(978-0-06-028801-3(9))* HarperCollins Pubs.

—Dolphin Talk: Whistles, Clicks, & Clapping Jaws. Pfeffer, Wendy & Pfeffer. 2003. (Let's-Read-And-Find-Out Science 2 Ser.). (ENG.). 40p. (J). (gr. k-4). pap. 5.99 *(978-0-06-445210-6(7),* Collins) HarperCollins Pubs.

—Dolphin Talk: Whistles, Clicks, & Clapping Jaws. Pfeffer, Wendy. 2003. (Let's-Read-and-Find-Out Science Ser.). 40p. (J). (gr. k-4). lib. bdg. 16.89 *(978-0-06-028802-0(7))* HarperCollins Pubs.

Davie, Helen K. What Lives in a Shell? Zoehfeld, Kathleen Weidner. 2015. (Let's-Read-And-Find-Out Science 1 Ser.). (ENG.). 32p. (J). (gr. -1-3). pap. 6.99 ***(978-0-06-238196-5(2))*** HarperCollins Pubs.

Davies, Andy Robert. Clothesline Clues to Jobs People Do. Heling, Kathryn & Hembrook, Deborah. (ENG.). 40p. (J). (gr. -1-2). 2014. pap. 7.95 *(978-1-58089-252-0(3));* 2012. 14.95 *(978-1-58089-251-3(5))* Charlesbridge Publishing, Inc.

—Clothesline Clues to Sports People Play. Heling, Kathryn & Hembrook, Deborah. 2015. (ENG.). 40p. (J). (gr. -1-2). lib. bdg. 14.95 *(978-1-58089-602-3(2))* Charlesbridge Publishing, Inc.

—Truck Stuck. Wolf, Sallie. 2009. (ENG.). 32p. (J). (-k). pap. 7.95 *(978-1-58089-257-5(4))* Charlesbridge Publishing, Inc.

Davies, Benji. Bizzy Bear: Dinosaur Safari. Nosy Crow. 2015. (Bizzy Bear Ser.). (ENG.). 8p. (J). (— 1). bds. 6.99 ***(978-0-7636-8170-8(9),*** Nosy Crow) Candlewick Pr.

Davies, Benji. Bizzy Bear: Fun on the Farm. Nosy Crow. 2011. (Bizzy Bear Ser.). (ENG.). 8p. (J). (gr. k — 1). bds. 6.99 *(978-0-7636-5879-3(0),* Nosy Crow) Candlewick Pr.

—Bizzy Bear: Knights' Castle. Nosy Crow. 2015. (Bizzy Bear Ser.). (ENG.). 8p. (J). (— 1). bds. 6.99 *(978-0-7636-7602-5(0),* Nosy Crow) Candlewick Pr.

—Bizzy Bear: Let's Get to Work! Nosy Crow. 2012. (Bizzy Bear Ser.). (ENG.). 8p. (J). (gr. k — 1). bds. 6.99 *(978-0-7636-5899-1(5),* Nosy Crow) Candlewick Pr.

—Bizzy Bear: Let's Go & Play. Nosy Crow. 2011. (Bizzy Bear Ser.). (ENG.). 8p. (J). (gr. k — 1). bds. 6.99 *(978-0-7636-5880-9(4),* Nosy Crow) Candlewick Pr.

—Bizzy Bear: off We Go! Nosy Crow. 2012. (Bizzy Bear Ser.). (ENG.). 8p. (J). (gr. k — 1). bds. 6.99 *(978-0-7636-5900-4(2),* Nosy Crow) Candlewick Pr.

—Bizzy Bear: Zookeeper. Nosy Crow. 2015. (Bizzy Bear Ser.). (ENG.). 8p. (J). (— 1). bds. 6.99 *(978-0-7636-7603-2(9),* Nosy Crow) Candlewick Pr.

—Bizzy Bear's Big Building Book. Nosy Crow. 2014. (Bizzy Bear Ser.). (ENG.). 8p. (J). (gr. -1-2). bds. 14.99 *(978-0-7636-7395-6(1),* Nosy Crow) Candlewick Pr.

—Fire Rescue! Nosy Crow. 2013. (Bizzy Bear Ser.). (ENG.). 8p. (J). (— 1). bds. 6.99 *(978-0-7636-6518-0(5),* Nosy Crow) Candlewick Pr.

—Goodnight Already! John, Jory. 2014. (ENG.). 32p. (J). (gr. -1-3). 17.99 *(978-0-06-228620-8(X))* HarperCollins Pubs.

Davies, Benji. I Love You Already! John, Jory. 2015. 32p. (J). (gr. -1-3). 17.99 ***(978-0-06-237095-2(2))*** HarperCollins Pubs.

Davies, Benji. In the Castle. Milbourne, Anna. 2006. (English Heritage Ser.). 24p. (J). (gr. -1-3). 9.99 *(978-0-7945-1243-9(7),* Usborne) EDC Publishing.

—On a Pirate Ship. Courtauld, Sarah. 2007. (Picture Bks). 24p. (J). (gr. -1-3). 9.99 *(978-0-7945-1712-0(9),* Usborne) EDC Publishing.

—Pirate Adventure. Nosy Crow. 2013. (Bizzy Bear Ser.). (ENG.). 8p. (J). (— 1). bds. 6.99 *(978-0-7636-6519-7(3),* Nosy Crow) Candlewick Pr.

Davies, Benji. The Storm Whale. Davies, Benji. 2014. (ENG.). 32p. (J). (gr. -1-3). 16.99 *(978-0-8050-9967-6(0),* Holt, Henry & Co. Bks. For Young Readers) Holt, Henry & Co.

Davies, Bronwen. Scholastic Reader Level 1: Get the Giggles: A First Joke Book. 2014. (Scholastic Reader Level 1 Ser.). (ENG.). 32p. (J). (gr. -1-2). pap. 3.99 *(978-0-545-54087-2(9))* Scholastic, Inc.

Davies, Caroline. Bunny. Child, Jeremy. 2013. (Rock & Rattle Bks.). (ENG.). 8p. (J). (gr. -1 — 1). bds. 3.99 *(978-0-7641-6589-4(5))* Barron's Educational Series, Inc.

—Duck. 2013. (Shake & Play Bath Bks.). (ENG.). 8p. (J). (gr. -1 — 1). 5.99 *(978-1-4380-7339-2(9))* Barron's Educational Series, Inc.

—Fish. 2013. (Shake & Play Bath Bks.). (ENG.). 8p. (J). (gr. -1 — 1). 5.99 *(978-1-4380-7340-8(2))* Barron's Educational Series, Inc.

—Kitty. Child, Jeremy. 2013. (Rock & Rattle Bks.). (ENG.). 8p. (J). (gr. -1 — 1). bds. 3.99 *(978-0-7641-6590-0(9))* Barron's Educational Series, Inc.

—Mouse. Child, Jeremy. 2013. (Rock & Rattle Bks.). (ENG.). 8p. (J). (gr. -1 — 1). bds. 3.99 *(978-0-7641-6591-7(7))* Barron's Educational Series, Inc.

—Puppy. Child, Jeremy. 2013. (Rock & Rattle Bks.). (ENG.). 8p. (J). (gr. -1 — 1). bds. 3.99 *(978-0-7641-6592-4(5))* Barron's Educational Series, Inc.

—Turtle. 2013. (Shake & Play Bath Bks.). (ENG.). 8p. (J). (gr. -1 — 1). 5.99 *(978-1-4380-7341-5(0))* Barron's Educational Series, Inc.

—Whale. 2013. (Shake & Play Bath Bks.). (ENG.). 8p. (J). (gr. -1 — 1). 5.99 *(978-1-4380-7342-2(9))* Barron's Educational Series, Inc.

Davies, Caroline. Hey, Diddle Diddle. Davies, Caroline, tr. 2004. (Baby's First Nursery Rhymes Ser.). 12p. (J). bds. 3.99 *(978-1-85854-622-3(2))* Brimax Books Ltd. GBR. Dist: Byeway Bks.

—Humpty Dumpty. Davies, Caroline, tr. 2004. (Baby's First Nursery Rhymes Ser.). 12p. (J). bds. 3.99 *(978-1-85854-610-0(9))* Brimax Books Ltd. GBR. Dist: Byeway Bks.

—Little Miss Muffet. Davies, Caroline, tr. 2004. (Baby's First Nursery Rhymes Ser.). 12p. (J). bds. 3.99 *(978-1-85854-623-0(0))* Brimax Books Ltd. GBR. Dist: Byeway Bks.

—Pat-A-Cake. Davies, Caroline, tr. 2004. (Baby's First Nursery Rhymes Ser.). 12p. (J). bds. 3.99 *(978-1-85854-611-7(7))* Brimax Books Ltd. GBR. Dist: Byeway Bks.

Davies, Florence S. Zeek, the Christmas Tree Mouse. Schneider, Richard H. 2004. 18.00 *(978-0-687-09465-3(8))* Abingdon Pr.

Davies, Hannah & Gunnell, Beth. Pretty Patterns: Beautiful Patterns to Color! 2013. (ENG.). 96p. (J). (gr. -1-2). 7.99 *(978-1-4424-5181-0(5),* Little Simon) Little Simon.

Davies, Hannah & Ryan, Nellie. Pretty Costumes: Beautiful Costumes to Color! 2013. (ENG.). 96p. (J). (gr. -1-2). 7.99 *(978-1-4424-5180-3(7),* Little Simon) Little Simon.

Davies, James. Polly & the Pirates. Bradman, Tony & Banana, Red. 2014. (Red Bananas Ser.). (ENG.). 48p. (J). (gr. k-2). pap. 5.99 *(978-1-4052-6412-9(8))* Egmont Bks., Ltd. GBR. Dist: Independent Pubs. Group.

Davies, James. Space Penguins. Courtenay, Lucy. 2015. (Space Penguins Ser.). (ENG.). 112p. (gr. 2-3). 85.28 ***(978-1-4965-0255-1(8),*** Space Penguins) Stone Arch Bks.

Davies, James. Space Penguins Cosmic Crash! Courtenay, L. A. 2015. (Space Penguins Ser.). (ENG.). 112p. (gr. 2-3). lib. bdg. 21.32 *(978-1-4342-9785-3(3))* Stone Arch Bks.

—Space Penguins Galaxy Race! Courtenay, L. A. 2015. (Space Penguins Ser.). (ENG.). 112p. (gr. 2-3). lib. bdg. 21.32 *(978-1-4342-9783-9(7))* Stone Arch Bks.

—Space Penguins Meteor Madness! Courtenay, L. A. 2015. (Space Penguins Ser.). (ENG.). 112p. (gr. 2-3). lib. bdg. 21.32 *(978-1-4342-9782-2(9))* Stone Arch Bks.

—Space Penguins Star Attack! Courtenay, L. A. 2015. (Space Penguins Ser.). (ENG.). 112p. (gr. 2-3). lib. bdg. 21.32 *(978-1-4342-9784-6(5))* Stone Arch Bks.

Davies, Kate. The Children's Book of Green Habits. Giles, Sophie. 2014. (ENG.). 32p. (J). pap. 10.00 *(978-1-84135-908-3(4))* Award Pubns. Ltd. GBR. Dist: Parkwest Pubns., Inc.

—The Children's Book of Healthy Habits. Giles, Sophie. 2014. (ENG.). 40p. (J). pap. 10.00 *(978-1-84135-972-4(6))* Award Pubns. Ltd. GBR. Dist: Parkwest Pubns., Inc.

Davies, Kate. Little Squeak School. 2014. (J). ***(978-1-4351-5582-4(3))*** Barnes & Noble, Inc.

Davies, Kate. Princess Tales. 2012. (ENG.). 96p. 15.00 *(978-1-84135-523-8(2))* Award Pubns. Ltd. GBR. Dist: Parkwest Pubns., Inc.

—Science in the Kitchen. Heddle, Rebecca. Edom, Helen, ed. rev. ed. 2007. (Usborne Science Activities Ser.). 24p. (J). (gr. 3-7). pap. 5.99 *(978-0-7945-1405-1(7),* Usborne) EDC Publishing.

Davies, Kate. Welcome to the Mouse House. 2014. (J). ***(978-1-4351-5583-1(1))*** Barnes & Noble, Inc.

Davies, Lauretta. God's Amazing Book. Ruckman, Kathleen. 2007. (ENG.). 28p. (J). (gr. -1-2). 10.99 *(978-1-59317-201-5(X))* Warner Pr. Pubs.

Davies, Matt. Nerdy Birdy. Reynolds, Aaron. 2015. (ENG.). 40p. (J). (gr. k-3). 16.99 ***(978-1-62672-127-2(0))*** Roaring Brook Pr.

Davies, Michelle. Debbie's Letter to God. Griffin, Marcia. 2005. (J). pap. 8.00 *(978-0-8059-6409-7(6))* Dorrance Publishing Co., Inc.

Davies, Nic, jt. illus. see Martin, Caroline.

Davies, Richard, jt. photos by see Shafran, Nigel.

Davies, Taffy. Be a Church Detective: A Young Person's Guide to Old Churches. Frewins, Clive & Open Churches Trust Staff. ed. 2005. (ENG.). 48p. (J). pap. 12.99 *(978-1-85311-628-5(9),* Canterbury Pr. Norwich) Hymns Ancient & Modern Ltd GBR. Dist: Westminster John Knox Pr.

—The Curious History of God. Stannard, Russell. 2003. 96p. 7.95 *(978-1-932031-27-0(8))* Templeton Pr.

Davies, Vanessa, photos by. Cooking with Kids. Collister, Linda. 128p. 2007. per. *(978-1-84597-488-6(3));* 2003. (ENG., (gr. 6-11). tchr. ed. *(978-1-84172-498-0(X))* Ryland Peters & Small.

—Crafting with Kids: Creative Fun for Children Aged 3-10. Woram, Catherine. 2006. (ENG., 128p. (J). (gr. 3-7). pap. *(978-1-84597-252-3(X))* Ryland Peters & Small.

Dávila, Claudia. Build It! Structures, Systems & You. Mason, Adrienne. 2006. (Primary Physical Science Ser.). (ENG.). 32p. (J). (gr. -1-2). 7.95 *(978-1-55337-836-5(9))* Kids Can Pr., Ltd. CAN. Dist: Univ. of Toronto Pr.

—Change It! Solids, Liquids, Gases & You. Mason, Adrienne. 2006. (Primary Physical Science Ser.). (ENG.). 32p. (J). (gr. -1-2). 7.95 *(978-1-55337-838-9(5));* 14.95 *(978-1-55337-837-2(7))* Kids Can Pr., Ltd. CAN. Dist: Univ. of Toronto Pr.

Dávila, Claudia. Child Soldier: When Boys & Girls Are Used in War. Humphreys, Jessica Dee & Chikwanine, Michel. 2015. (ENG.). 48p. (J). (gr. 5-9). 17.95 ***(978-1-77138-126-0(4))*** Kids Can Pr., Ltd. CAN. Dist: Univ. of Toronto Pr.

Dávila, Claudia. It's Your Room: A Decorating Guide for Real Kids. Weaver, Janice & Wishinsky, Frieda. 2006. (ENG.). 64p. (J). (gr. 4-7). per. 14.95 *(978-0-88776-711-1(7))* Tundra Bks. CAN. Dist: Random Hse., Inc.

—Magic up Your Sleeve: Amazing Illusions, Tricks, & Science Facts You'll Never Believe. Becker, Helaine. 2010. (ENG.). 64p. (J). (gr. 3-6). pap. 10.95 *(978-1-897349-76-2(9),* Maple Tree Pr.) Owlkids Bks. Inc. CAN. Dist: Perseus-PGW.

—Motion, Magnets & More. Mason, Adrienne. 2011. (ENG.). 128p. (J). 18.95 *(978-1-55453-707-5(X))* Kids Can Pr., Ltd. CAN. Dist: Univ. of Toronto Pr.

—Move It! Motion, Forces & You. Mason, Adrienne. 2005. (Primary Physical Science Ser.). (ENG.). 32p. (J). (gr. -1-3). pap. 7.95 *(978-1-55337-759-7(1))* Kids Can Pr., Ltd. CAN. Dist: Univ. of Toronto Pr.

—Sweet! The Delicious Story of Candy. Love, Ann & Drake, Jane. 2009. (ENG.). 64p. (J). (gr. 4-7). pap. 12.95 *(978-0-88776-962-7(4))* Tundra Bks. CAN. Dist: Random Hse., Inc.

—Touch It! Materials, Matter & You. Mason, Adrienne. 2005. (Primary Physical Science Ser.). (ENG.). 32p. (J). 6.95 *(978-1-55337-761-0(3))* Kids Can Pr., Ltd. CAN. Dist: Univ. of Toronto Pr.

—Viminy Crowe's Comic Book. Jocelyn, Marthe & Scrimger, Richard. 2014. (ENG.). 336p. (J). (gr. 4-7). 17.99 *(978-1-77049-479-4(0))* Tundra Bks. CAN. Dist: Random Hse., Inc.

Dávila, Claudia. Luz Sees the Light. Dávila, Claudia. 2011. (Future According to Luz Ser.: 1). (ENG.). 96p. (J). (gr. 3-7). 16.95 *(978-1-55453-581-1(6))* Kids Can Pr., Ltd. CAN. Dist: Univ. of Toronto Pr.

Dávila, Claudia & Owlkids Books Inc. Staff. The Insecto-Files: Amazing Insect Science & Bug Facts You'll Never Believe. Becker, Helaine. 2009. (ENG.). 64p. (J). (gr. 3-6). pap. 10.95 *(978-1-897349-47-2(5),* Maple Tree Pr.) Owlkids Bks. Inc. CAN. Dist: Perseus-PGW.

—Science on the Loose: Amazing Activities & Science Facts You'll Never Believe. Becker, Helaine. 2008. (ENG.). 64p.

(J). (gr. 3-6). pap. 10.95 *(978-1-897349-19-9(X)*, Maple Tree Pr.) Owlkids Bks. Inc. CAN. Dist: Perseus-PGW.

Davis, Alan. Avengers Prime. 2011. (ENG.). (YA). (gr. 8-17). 128p. pap. 16.99 *(978-0-7851-4726-8(8))*; 120p. 24.99 *(978-0-7851-4725-1(X))* Marvel Worldwide, Inc.

Davis, Alan, et al. The Mighty Thor/Journey into Mystery: Everything Burns. 2013. (ENG.). 216p. (YA). (gr. 8-17). 29.99 *(978-0-7851-6168-4(6))* Marvel Worldwide, Inc.

Davis, Alan. Righteous Ray-Ray Has a Bad Day Beginning Readers Edition. Smith, Raymond R. 2012. 26p. pap. 9.99 *(978-0-9883634-1-0(0))* Righteous Bks.

—Uncanny X-Men. 2006. (ENG.). 128p. (YA). (gr. 8-17). pap. 13.99 *(978-0-7851-1663-9(X))* Marvel Worldwide, Inc.

Davis, Alan. Killraven. Davis, Alan. 2003. (Spider-Man Ser.). 144p. (YA). pap. 16.99 *(978-0-7851-1083-5(6))* Marvel Worldwide, Inc.

Davis, Allen. Chipmunk at Hollow Tree Lane. Sherrow, Victoria. 2011. (Smithsonian's Backyard Ser.). (ENG.). 32p. (J). (gr. -1-3). 8.95 *(978-1-60727-635-7(6))*; 19.95 *(978-1-60727-634-0(8))* Soundprints.

—Cottontail at Clover Crescent. Lamm, Drew C. 2005. (Smithsonian's Backyard Ser.). (ENG.). 32p. (J). (gr. -1-2). pap. 6.95 *(978-1-59249-112-4(X)*, S5005) Soundprints.

—Why the Snake Crawls on Its Belly. Kimmel, Eric A. 2005. 32p. (J). (gr. 1-4). 14.95 *(978-1-930143-20-3(6)*, Devora Publishing) Simcha Media Group.

—Woodchuck at Blackberry Road. Lamm, C. Drew. 2011. (Smithsonian's Backyard Ser.). (ENG.). 32p. (J). (gr. -1-3). 19.95 *(978-1-60727-644-9(5))* Soundprints.

Davis, Amy. Princesses Can Be Pirates Too! Zellerhoff, Christi. 2012. 38p. 17.99 *(978-1-935961-68-0(3))*; pap. 8.99 *(978-1-935961-95-6(0))* Booktrope. (Booktrope Editions).

Davis, Anne. Bud & Gabby. Davis, Anne. 2006. 32p. (J). (gr. -1-2). lib. bdg. 16.89 *(978-0-06-075351-1(X))* HarperCollins Pubs.

—No Dogs Allowed!, No. 1. Davis, Anne. 2011. (ENG.). 32p. (J). (gr. -1-3). 16.99 *(978-0-06-075353-5(6))* HarperCollins Pubs.

Davis, Betsy, jt. illus. see Davis, Shelley.

Davis, Bill. Underneath Everything. Paul, Marcy Beller. 2015. (ENG.). 304p. (YA). (gr. 9). 17.99 ***(978-0-06-232721-5(6))*** HarperCollins Pubs.

Davis, Carol Marie. The Adventures of Moon Spirit, a Girl from Florida's Past. Davis, Carol Marie. 2008. 60p. pap. 8.95 *(978-0-9821654-2-3(0))* Peppertree Pr., The.

Davis, Carolina A. Puppy's Tail. Powell, Richard. 2003. (Animal Tails Ser.). 12p. (J). 3.95 *(978-1-58925-674-3(3))* Tiger Tales.

Davis, Caroline. Kitty's Tail. Powell, Richard. 2003. (Animal Tails Ser.). 10p. (J). 3.95 *(978-1-58925-673-6(5))* Tiger Tales.

—My Babies. Emma Treehouse Ltd. 2007. (Easy Flaps Ser.). 10p. (J). (gr. -1). bds. 6.95 *(978-1-58925-822-8(3))* Tiger Tales.

—My Friends. Emma Treehouse Ltd. 2007. (Easy Flaps Ser.). 10p. (J). (gr. -1). bds. 6.95 *(978-1-58925-823-5(1))* Tiger Tales.

—My Pets. Emma Treehouse Ltd. 2007. (Easy Flaps Ser.). 10p. (J). (gr. -1). bds. 6.95 *(978-1-58925-824-2(X))* Tiger Tales.

—My Toys. Emma Treehouse Ltd. 2007. (Easy Flaps Ser.). 10p. (J). (gr. -1). bds. 6.95 *(978-1-58925-825-9(8))* Tiger Tales.

—Old MacDonald's: Barnyard Tales. Baxter, Nicola. 256p. (J). *(978-0-7525-8771-4(4))* Parragon Bk. Service Ltd.

—Shimmery Dinkies - Ring Ring! Engel, Christiane. 2009. (Shimmery Dinkies Ser.). (ENG.). 20p. (J). (gr. k — 1). bds. 5.95 *(978-1-84616-907-6(0))* Hodder & Stoughton GBR. Dist: Independent Pubs. Group.

Davis, Caroline. Babies. Davis, Caroline. 2010. (ENG.). 20p. (J). bds. *(978-1-4083-0786-1(3)*, Orchard Bks.) Hachette Children's Group GBR. Dist: Hachette Bk. Group.

—Bugs. Davis, Caroline. 2010. (ENG.). 20p. (J). bds. *(978-1-4083-0784-7(7)*, Orchard Bks.) Hachette Children's Group GBR. Dist: Hachette Bk. Group.

—Diggers. Davis, Caroline. 2010. (ENG.). 20p. (J). bds. *(978-1-4083-0785-4(5)*, Orchard Bks.) Hachette Children's Group GBR. Dist: Hachette Bk. Group.

—Sparkly Farm. Davis, Caroline. 2008. (Tiger Tales Ser.). 8p. (J). (gr. -1). bds. 6.95 *(978-1-58925-831-0(2))* Tiger Tales.

—Sparkly Garden. Davis, Caroline. 2008. (Tiger Tales Ser.). 8p. (J). (gr. -1). bds. 6.95 *(978-1-58925-830-3(4))* Tiger Tales.

—Sparkly Ocean. Davis, Caroline. 2008. (Tiger Tales Ser.). 8p. (J). (gr. -1). bds. 6.95 *(978-1-58925-832-7(0))* Tiger Tales.

—Yum Yum! Davis, Caroline. 2010. (ENG.). 20p. (J). bds. *(978-1-4083-0787-8(1)*, Orchard Bks.) Hachette Children's Group GBR. Dist: Hachette Bk. Group.

Davis, Catherine Baptista. One Is Fun. DeRosa Bodie, Leona. 2007. 30p. (J). (gr. -1). bds. 12.95 *(978-1-4243-2961-8(2))* Independent Publisher Services.

Davis, Chad L. Little Peter & Sela. Toledo, Leila J. I.t. ed. 2004. 17p. (J). pap. 8.95 *(978-0-9753118-0-6(8))* Bimini Bks.

Davis, Christine. The Shelter Dog. Davis, Christine. 2008. 32p. (J). (gr. -1-3). 11.95 *(978-0-9659225-4-8(5))* Lighthearted Pr., Inc.

Davis, Christopher Owen, jt. illus. see Speer, Julie.

Davis, Dan. The Creepy Chef. McCann, Jesse Leon. 2005. (Scooby-Doo 8x8 Ser.). (ENG.). 24p. (J). (gr. 2-5). pap. 3.99 *(978-0-439-69643-2(7)*, Scholastic Paperbacks) Scholastic, Inc.

—Rabbit Holes, 1 vol. Weisman, Greg et al. 2013. (Young Justice Ser.). (ENG.). 32p. (gr. 2-3). 21.27 *(978-1-4342-6039-0(9))* Stone Arch Bks.

—Scooby-Doo & the Creepy Chef. McCann, Jesse Leon. 2010. (Scooby-Doo! Set 1 Ser.: No. 1). (ENG.). 24p. (gr. -1-4). lib. bdg. 24.21 *(978-1-59961-676-6(9))* Spotlight.

—Scooby-Doo & the Samurai Ghost. McCann, Jesse Leon. 2010. (Scooby-Doo! Set 1 Ser.: No. 1). (ENG.). 24p. (gr. -1-4). lib. bdg. 24.21 *(978-1-59961-679-7(3))* Spotlight.

Davis, Dan & Suriano, Andy. Charge of the Army Eternal, 1 vol. Torres, J. 2013. (Batman: the Brave & the Bold Ser.). (ENG.). 32p. (gr. 2-3). 21.27 *(978-1-4342-4706-3(6))* Stone Arch Bks.

Davis, Dan W., jt. illus. see Suriano, Andy.

Davis, Daniel M. After Halloween. McClellan, Sara, ed. 2007. 64p. (J). per. 20.00 *(978-0-9774173-4-6(4))* Steam Crow Pr.

Davis, Dennis. What God Has Always Wanted: The Bible's Big Idea from Genesis Through Revelation. Boyd, Charles F. 2006. 22p. (J). (gr. -1-3). *(978-1-57229-725-8(5))* FamilyLife.

Davis, Dick. From Here to There. Keckler, Ben. 2005. (Express Yourself Ser.). 42p. (J). (gr. 3-7). lib. bdg. 16.95 *(978-0-9769093-0-9(8))* Eagle Creek Pubns., LLC.

—Incredibly Lonely, That's Me. Keckler, Ben. 2007. (Express Yourself Ser.). 42p. (J). (gr. 3-7). 17.95 *(978-0-9769093-2-3(4))* Eagle Creek Pubns., LLC.

Davis, Eleanor. The Secret Science Alliance & the Copycat Crook. Davis, Eleanor. 2009. (ENG.). 160p. (J). (gr. 3-6). 18.99 *(978-1-59990-142-8(0))*; pap. 16.99 *(978-1-59990-396-5(2))* Bloomsbury USA. (Bloomsbury USA Childrens).

Davis, Florence S. The Blue Angel Ornament: A Story of Love & Loyalty. Schneider, Richard H. 2004. 32p. (gr. -1-18). 17.00 *(978-0-687-08181-3(5))* Abingdon Pr.

Davis, Guy & Sikoryak, Bob. Fantastic Four: Unstable Molecules. Sturm, James. 2003. (Fantastic Four Legends Ser.: Vol. 1). 128p. (YA). pap. 13.99 *(978-0-7851-1112-2(3))* Marvel Worldwide, Inc.

Davis, Jack. Crazy Campsongs. Petersen, George & Jenkins, J. J. 2003. 64p. (J). bds. 9.99 *(978-0-9726794-9-7(9))* Jenpet Publishing.

Davis, Jack & Williamson, Al. The Adventures of the Fly. Simon, Joe. 2004. (Red Circle Ser.). (ENG.). 96p. pap. 12.95 *(978-1-879794-18-4(7))* Archie Comic Pubns., Inc.

Davis, Jack E. Bunion Burt. Hayles, Marsha. 2009. (ENG.). 32p. (J). (gr. -1-3). 16.99 *(978-1-4169-4132-3(0)*, McElderry, Margaret K. Bks.) McElderry, Margaret K. Bks.

—Dirty Joe the Pirate: A True Story. Harley, Bill. 2008. (ENG.). 32p. (J). (gr. k-3). 17.99 *(978-0-06-623780-0(7))* HarperCollins Pubs.

—Don't Count on Dracula. Greenburg, Dan. 2004. (Zack Files Ser.). 58p. lib. bdg. 15.00 *(978-0-7569-2236-8(4))* Perfection Learning Corp.

—Goldie & the Three Hares. Palatini, Margie. 2011. (ENG.). 32p. (J). (gr. -1-2). 16.99 *(978-0-06-125314-0(6)*, Tegen, Katherine Bks) HarperCollins Pubs.

—Halfway Hank. Fallon, Joe & Scarborough, Ken. 2005. 40p. (J). 15.99 *(978-0-06-623636-0(3))* HarperCollins Pubs.

—Here Comes T. Rex Cottontail. Grambling, Lois G. (ENG.). 32p. (J). (gr. -1-1). 2010. pap. 6.99 *(978-0-06-053134-8(7))*; 2007. 16.99 *(978-0-06-053129-4(0))* HarperCollins Pubs. (Tegen, Katherine Bks).

—How I Went from Bad to Verse. Greenburg, Dan. 2004. (Zack Files Ser.). 59p. lib. bdg. 15.00 *(978-0-7569-2235-1(6))* Perfection Learning Corp.

—I Am the Dog. Pinkwater, Daniel M. 2010. (ENG.). 32p. (J). (gr. -1-3). 16.99 *(978-0-06-055505-4(X))* HarperCollins Pubs.

—It's Itchcraft!, 30 vols. Greenburg, Dan. 2003. (Zack Files Ser.: 30). (ENG.). 128p. (J). (gr. 2-5). pap. 4.99 *(978-0-448-42888-8(1)*, Grosset & Dunlap) Penguin Publishing Group.

—It's Itchcraft! Greenburg, Dan. 2004. (Zack Files Ser.). 118p. lib. bdg. 15.00 *(978-0-7569-2238-2(0))* Perfection Learning Corp.

—Just Add Water... & Scream! Greenburg, Dan. 2004. (Zack Files Ser.). 56p. lib. bdg. 15.00 *(978-0-7569-2239-9(9))* Perfection Learning Corp.

—Just Add Water... And Scream!, 29 vols. Greenburg, Dan. 2003. (Zack Files Ser.: 29). (ENG.). 64p. (J). (gr. 2-5). mass mkt. 4.99 *(978-0-448-42887-1(3)*, Grosset & Dunlap) Penguin Publishing Group.

—Marsupial Sue Presents the Runaway Pancake. Lithgow, John. 2008. (ENG.). 40p. (J). (gr. -1-3). 6.99 *(978-0-689-87848-0(6)*, Simon & Schuster Bks. For Young Readers) Simon & Schuster Bks. For Young Readers.

—Moose Tracks! Wilson, Karma. 2006. (ENG.). 32p. (J). (gr. -1-2). 17.99 *(978-0-689-83437-0(3)*, McElderry, Margaret K. Bks.) McElderry, Margaret K. Bks.

—Peanut Butter & Homework Sandwiches. Cook, Lisa Broadie. 2011. (ENG.). 32p. (J). (gr. -1-3). 16.99 *(978-0-399-24533-6(2)*, Putnam Juvenile) Penguin Publishing Group.

—Putting the Monkeys to Bed. Choldenko, Gennifer. 2015. (ENG.). 32p. (J). (gr. -1-k). 16.99 *(978-0-399-24623-4(1)*, Putnam Juvenile) Penguin Publishing Group.

—Stanza. Esbaum, Jill. 2009. (ENG.). 32p. (J). (gr. -1-3). 16.00 *(978-0-15-205998-9(9))* Houghton Mifflin Harcourt Publishing Co.

—T. Rex & the Mother's Day Hug. Grambling, Lois G. (ENG.). 32p. (J). (gr. -1-1). 2011. pap. 6.99 *(978-0-06-053128-7(2))*; 2008. 16.99 *(978-0-06-053126-3(6))* HarperCollins Pubs. (Tegen, Katherine Bks).

—T. Rex Trick-or-Treats. Grambling, Lois G. 32p. (J). 2008. (ENG.). (gr. -1-3). pap. 6.99 *(978-0-06-050254-6(1))*; 2005. 12.99 *(978-0-06-050252-2(5))* HarperCollins Pubs. (Tegen, Katherine Bks).

—Yo-Yo Man. Pinkwater, Daniel M. 2007. (ENG.). 32p. (J). (gr. -1-3). 16.99 *(978-0-06-055502-3(5))* HarperCollins Pubs.

Davis, Jack E. Sweet Tooth. Davis, Jack E. Palatini, Margie. 2004. (ENG.). 40p. (J). (gr. -1-3). 17.99 *(978-0-689-85159-9(6)*, Simon & Schuster Bks. For Young Readers) Simon & Schuster Bks. For Young Readers.

Davis, Jason. Hurricane Hound. Lee, Gia. 2011. 40p. pap. 24.95 *(978-1-4560-9743-1(1))* America Star Bks.

Davis, Jeff. The Hand That Scared Jenny. Rosas, Beverly. 2008. 47p. pap. 24.95 *(978-1-4241-9138-3(6))* PublishAmerica, Inc.

Davis, Jim. Garfield Out to Lunch, Bk. 12. Davis, Jim. 2006. (Garfield Ser.: 12). (ENG.). 96p. pap. 14.00 *(978-0-345-47562-6(3)*, Ballantine Bks.) Random House Publishing Group.

Davis, John Watson. The King of the Golden City: An Allegory for Children. Loyola, Mother Mary. 2nd ed. 2005. 128p. (J). per. *(978-0-9764691-0-0(3))* Little Way Pr.

Davis, Jon. The Coziest Place. Michalak, Jamie. 2013. (ENG.). 24p. (gr. -1-k). 14.99 *(978-1-58925-121-2(0))* Tiger Tales.

—Science Measurements: How Heavy? How Long? How Hot? Eboch, Chris. 2006. (Amazing Science Ser.). (ENG.). 24p. (gr. k-4). 25.99 *(978-1-4048-2197-2(X)*, Nonfiction Picture Bks.) Picture Window Bks.

—Stuck with the Blooz. Levis, Caron. 2012. (ENG.). 40p. (J). (gr. -1-3). 16.99 *(978-0-547-74560-2(5))* Houghton Mifflin Harcourt Publishing Co.

—Why Do My Teeth Fall Out? And Other Questions Kids Have about the Human Body, 1 vol. Montgomery, Heather L. 2011. (Kids' Questions Ser.). (ENG.). 24p. (gr. 1-2). pap. 7.49 *(978-1-4048-6534-1(9)*, Nonfiction Picture Bks.) Picture Window Bks.

Davis, Jon & Keiser, Paige. Two Hands to Love You. Adams, Diane. 2014. (ENG.). 40p. (J). (gr. -1 — 1). 15.99 *(978-0-8118-7797-8(3))* Chronicle Bks. LLC.

Davis, Kaley. Beau Bandit's Tale. Richardville, Carol. 2004. (J). per. 16.99 *(978-1-932503-23-4(4))* Insight Publishing Group.

Davis, Katheryn & Van Slyke, Rebecca. Storybook Art: Hands-On Art for Children in the Styles of 100 Great Picture Book Illustrators. Kohl, MaryAnn F. & Potter, Jean. 2003. (Bright Ideas for Learning (TM) Ser.: 7). (ENG.). 144p. (gr. -1-7). pap. 18.95 *(978-0-935607-03-1(X))* Bright Ring Publishing, Inc.

Davis, Kathryn Lynn, jt. illus. see Davis, Nancy.

Davis, Katie. Little Chicken's Big Day. Davis, Katie. Davis, Jerry. 2011. (ENG.). 40p. (J). (gr. -1 — 1). 14.99 *(978-1-4424-1401-3(4)*, McElderry, Margaret K. Bks.) McElderry, Margaret K. Bks.

Davis, Lambert. Seaside Dream. Bates, Janet Costa. 2013. (ENG.). 32p. (J). (gr. k-5). 17.95 *(978-1-60060-347-1(5))* Lee & Low Bks., Inc.

—Snow Bear. Stafford, Liliana. 32p. (J). pap. *(978-0-88899-441-7(9))* Groundwood Bks.

Davis, Lynne. Little Dongs for Little Souls: Sharing God's Love. Elkins, Stephen. 2005. 32p. (J). 9.99 incl. audio compact disk *(978-0-8054-2673-1(6))* B&H Publishing Group.

—Little Songs for Little Souls: God Cares for Me. Elkins, Stephen. 2005. 32p. (J). 9.99 incl. audio compact disk *(978-0-8054-2675-5(2))* B&H Publishing Group.

—Little Songs for Little Souls: I Can Be Happy in Jesus. Elkins, Stephen. 2005. 32p. (J). 9.99 incl. audio compact disk *(978-0-8054-2676-2(0))* B&H Publishing Group.

—Little Songs for Little Souls: I Can Praise the Lord. Elkins, Stephen. 2005. 32p. (J). 9.99 incl. audio compact disk *(978-0-8054-2677-9(9))* B&H Publishing Group.

Davis, Marcus. Joey & the Ancient Horn: A Mystery Revealed. Watkins, T. a. 2007. 333p. (J). (gr. -1). per. 12.95 *(978-0-9762788-0-1(4))* Great I-AM Publishing Co., The.

Davis, Nancy. Flicker Flash. Graham, Joan Bransfield. 2003. (ENG.). 32p. (J). (gr. -1-3). pap. 6.95 *(978-0-618-31102-6(5))* Houghton Mifflin Harcourt Publishing Co.

—Older Than the Stars. Fox, Karen C. 2011. (ENG.). 32p. (J). (gr. 2-5). pap. 7.95 *(978-1-57091-788-2(4))* Charlesbridge Publishing, Inc.

—Welcome Summer. Ackerman, Jill. 2010. (Little Scholastic Ser.). (ENG.). 10p. (J). (gr. k — 1). bds. 5.99 *(978-0-545-15164-1(3)*, Cartwheel Bks.) Scholastic, Inc.

Davis, Nancy. Halloween Faces. Davis, Nancy. 2010. (ENG.). 18p. (J). (gr. k — 1). bds. 6.99 *(978-0-545-16586-0(5)*, Cartwheel Bks.) Scholastic, Inc.

Davis, Nancy & Davis, Kathryn Lynn. Christmas Shapes. Gerver, Jane E. 2010. (ENG.). 14p. (J). (gr. -1 — 1). 6.99 *(978-1-4169-9759-7(8)*, Little Simon) Little Simon.

—The First Thanksgiving. Davis, Nancy & Davis, Kathryn Lynn. 2010. (ENG.). 14p. (J). (gr. -1 — 1). bds. 5.99 *(978-1-4424-0807-4(3)*, Little Simon) Little Simon.

—Wake Up! Wake Up! Davis, Nancy & Davis, Kathryn Lynn. 2011. (ENG.). 14p. (J). (gr. -1 — 1). bds. 5.99 *(978-1-4424-1217-0(8)*, Little Simon) Little Simon.

—Who's at Home? Gerver, Jane E. 2010. (ENG.). 14p. (J). (gr. -1 — 1). bds. 5.99 *(978-1-4169-9758-0(X)*, Little Simon) Little Simon.

Davis, Nelle. Eight Little Legs. Gravelle, Karen. 2004. (ENG.). 20p. (gr. k-2). pap. 5.95 *(978-1-57874-042-0(8))* Kaeden Corp.

Davis, Oslo. Henry Lawson Treasury. Lawson, Henry. 2015. 160p. (J). (gr. 6). pap. 16.99 ***(978-0-85798-513-2(2))*** Random Hse. Australia AUS. Dist: Independent Pubs. Group.

Davis, Rich. Hi-Ho, Tiny. Meister, Cari. 2015. (Tiny Ser.). (ENG.). 32p. (J). (gr. k-1). pap. 3.99 ***(978-0-448-48291-0(6)***, Warne, Frederick Pubs.) Penguin Bks., Ltd. GBR. Dist: Penguin Random Hse., LLC.

Davis, Rich. Tiny Goes Back to School. Meister, Cari. 2014. (Tiny Ser.). (ENG.). 32p. (J). (gr. k-1). pap. 3.99 *(978-0-448-48134-0(0)*, Warne, Frederick Pubs.) Penguin Bks., Ltd. GBR. Dist: Penguin Publishing Group.

—Tiny Goes Camping. Meister, Cari. 2007. (Tiny Ser.). (ENG.). 32p. (J). (gr. k-1). mass mkt. 3.99 *(978-0-14-056741-0(0)*, Puffin) Penguin Publishing Group.

—Tiny on the Farm. Meister, Cari. 2008. (Tiny Ser.). (ENG.). 32p. (J). (gr. -1-18). 16.99 *(978-0-670-06246-1(4)*, Viking Juvenile) Penguin Publishing Group.

—Tiny the Birthday Dog. Meister, Cari. 2013. (Tiny Ser.). (ENG.). 32p. (J). (gr. k-1). 14.99 *(978-0-670-01413-2(3))*; pap. 3.99 *(978-0-448-46478-7(0))* Penguin Publishing Group. (Viking Adult).

Davis, Robyn L. Good Times with Gregory: Airplanes: A Visit to A 747. Davis, Helen J. 2008. (Good Times with Gregory Ser.). 37p. (J). (gr. -1-4). 12.95 *(978-1-935122-11-1(8))* K&B Products.

—Good Times with Gregory: Birds: Rescuing a Baby Bird. Davis, Helen J. 2008. (Good Times with Gregory Ser.). 54p. (J). (gr. -1-4). 12.95 *(978-1-935122-10-4(X))* K&B Products.

Davis, Sarah. Saige. Haas, Jessie. ed. 2012. (American Girl Today Ser.: Bk. 1). lib. bdg. 17.15 *(978-0-606-31568-5(3)*, Turtleback) Turtleback Bks.

—Saige Paints the Sky. Haas, Jessie. ed. 2012. (American Girl Today Ser.: Bk. 2). lib. bdg. 17.15 *(978-0-606-31569-2(1)*, Turtleback) Turtleback Bks.

—Shawn Sheep the Soccer Star. Mirabella, Erin. 2008. (Barnsville Sports Squad Ser.). (ENG.). 32p. (J). (gr. k-3). 15.95 *(978-1-934030-16-5(3))* VeloPress.

—Sounds Spooky. Cheng, Christopher. 2012. (ENG.). 32p. (J). (gr. k-2). pap. 13.99 *(978-1-86471-880-5(3))* Random Hse. Australia AUS. Dist: Independent Pubs. Group.

—Toucan Can. MacIver, Juliette. 2014. 32p. (J). (gr. -1-2). 17.95 *(978-1-877467-53-0(7))* Gecko Pr. NZL. Dist: Lerner Publishing Group.

Davis, Shelley & Davis, Betsy. Billy's Big Tomato. White, Gene. 2013. 24p. pap. 11.00 *(978-0-9886360-9-5(3))* Kids At Heart Publishing & Bks.

Davis, Shelley L. A. The Boinking Bubble MacHine. Reece, Eva. 2013. 24p. pap. 12.99 *(978-0-9886360-2-6(6))* Kids At Heart Publishing & Bks.

Davis, Shelley La. Brownie Calf & the Barnyard Babies. Reece, Eva. 2012. 24p. pap. 12.99 *(978-0-9836641-8-5(8))* Kids At Heart Publishing & Bks.

Davis, Stephen. The Awakening: An Icelandic Classic. Chopin, Kate. 2014. (American Classics Ser.). (ENG.). 64p. pap. 6.95 *(978-1-906230-78-4(1))* Real Reads Ltd. GBR. Dist: Casemate Pubs. & Bk. Distributors, LLC.

Davis, Tim. The Case of the Purple Diamonds. 2011. 88p. pap. 9.95 *(978-1-934606-07-0(3))* TAG Publishing, LLC.

—Charlie the Chopper & the Greatest Toymaker. Yuen, Dan. 2010. 26p. (J). *(978-0-88144-480-3(4))* Yorkshire Publishing Group.

—Lunchroom Laughs Joke Book. Pellowski, Michael J. 2005. (ENG.). 128p. (gr. 2-6). per. 3.99 *(978-1-58196-032-7(8)*, Darby Creek) Lerner Publishing Group.

Davis, Will. Fairy Killer. Petty, J. T. 2011. (ENG.). 128p. (J). (gr. 3-7). pap. 7.99 *(978-1-4424-3097-6(4)*, Simon & Schuster Bks. For Young Readers) Simon & Schuster Bks. For Young Readers.

Davis, Yvonne. Tuck-Me-In Tales: Bedtime Stories from Around the World. MacDonald, Margaret Read. 2005. (ENG.). 64p. (J). (gr. -1-2). 19.95 *(978-0-87483-461-1(9))* August Hse. Pubs., Inc.

Davis, Yvonne LeBrun. The Girl Who Wore Too Much: A Folktale from Thailand. 2015. (ENG.). 32p. (J). (gr. k-3). pap. 8.95 ***(978-1-939160-93-5(6))*** August Hse. Pubs., Inc.

Davis, Yvonne LeBrun. The Round Book: Rounds Kids Love to Sing. MacDonald, Margaret Read & Jaeger, Winifred. 2006. (ENG.). 136p. (J). (gr. -1-3). per. 18.95 *(978-0-87483-786-5(3))* August Hse. Pubs., Inc.

Davisson, Vanessa. Adventures of Baroness of the Arizona Desert. Garr, Rebecca. 2010. 60p. pap. 18.95 *(978-1-60911-958-4(4)*, Eloquent Bks.) Strategic Book Publishing & Rights Agency (SBPRA).

Dawes, Will, jt. illus. see Haw, Brenda.

Dawley, Sarah. You Are Special Little Bee. Doty, Sara. 2009. 16p. pap. 10.99 *(978-1-4389-7040-0(4))* AuthorHouse.

Dawn, Baumer. The Detective Company. Baldwin, Rich & Jones, Sandie. 2004. 183p. (YA). pap. 9.95 *(978-0-9742920-0-7(1)*, 2001) Buttonwood Pr.

Dawn Phillips. Glasses for Me? Oh No! By Kaleena Ma. 2009. 40p. pap. 18.49 *(978-1-4389-5418-9(2))* AuthorHouse.

Dawson, Diane & Goodell, Jon. Mother, Mother, I Want Another. Robbins, Maria Polushkin & Polushkin Robbins, Maria. 2007. (ENG.). 32p. (J). (gr. -1-2). pap. 6.99 *(978-0-517-55947-5(1)*, Dragonfly Bks.) Random Hse. Children's Bks.

Dawson, Isabel. Stories of Mystery, Adventure & Fun from Calling All Girls. Gipson, Morrell, ed. 2011. 252p. 46.95 *(978-1-258-10497-9(0))* Literary Licensing, LLC.

Dawson, Janine. The Awful Pawful. Odgers, Darrel & Odgers, Sally. 2007. (Jack Russell: Dog Detective Ser.: 5). 96p. (J). (gr. 1-6). pap. 4.99 *(978-1-933605-53-1(7))* Kane Miller.

—The Blue Stealer. Odgers, Darrel & Odgers, Sally. 2009. (Jack Russell: Dog Detective Ser.: 9). 96p. (J). (gr. 2-6). pap. 4.99 *(978-1-935279-09-9(2))* Kane Miller.

—The Buried Biscuits. Odgers, Sally & Odgers, Darrel. 2008. (Jack Russell: Dog Detective Ser.: 7). 96p. (J). (gr. 1-6). pap. 4.99 *(978-1-933605-77-7(4))* Kane Miller.

—Cranky Paws. Odgers, Darrel & Odgers, Sally. 2009. (Pet Vet Ser.: 1). 96p. (J). (gr. 2-6). pap. 4.99 *(978-1-935279-01-3(7))* Kane Miller.

—Dog Den Mystery. Odgers, Sally & Odgers, Darrel. 2006. (Jack Russell: Dog Detective Ser.: 1). 96p. (J). (gr. 1-5). pap. 4.99 *(978-1-933605-18-0(9))* Kane Miller.

—Emma's Question. Urdahl, Catherine. 2009. (ENG.). 32p. (J). (gr. k-k). pap. 7.95 *(978-1-58089-146-2(2))* Charlesbridge Publishing, Inc.

—The Ham Heist. Odgers, Darrel & Odgers, Sally. 2010. (Jack Russell: Dog Detective Ser.: 11). 96p. (J). (gr. 2-6). pap. 4.99 *(978-1-935279-75-4(0))* Kane Miller.

—Inspector Jacques. Odgers, Darrel & Odgers, Sally. 2010. (Jack Russell: Dog Detective Ser.: 10). 96p. (J). (gr. 2-4). pap. 4.99 *(978-1-935279-17-4(3))* Kane Miller.

—The Kitnapped Creature. Odgers, Darrel & Odgers, Sally. 2008. (Jack Russell: Dog Detective Ser.: 8). 96p. (J). (gr. 2-6). pap. 4.99 *(978-1-933605-82-1(0))* Kane Miller.

—The Kitten's Tale. Odgers, Darrel & Odgers, Sally. 2010. (Pet Vet Ser.: 5). 96p. (J). (gr. 2-6). pap. 4.99 *(978-1-935279-76-1(9))* Kane Miller.

—Lily Quench 6 Hand of Manuelo, Vol. 6. Prior, Natalie Jane. 2004. (ENG.). 176p. (J). (gr. 3-7). 6.99 *(978-0-14-240222-1(2)*, Puffin) Penguin Publishing Group.

D

—Lily Quench & the Dragon of Ashby, No. 1. Prior, Natalie. 2004. (ENG.). 160p. (J). (gr. 3-7). 6.99 (978-0-14-240020-3(3), Puffin) Penguin Publishing Group.

—Lily Quench & the Hand of Manuelo. Prior, Natalie Jane. 2004. x, 166p. (Orig.). (J). pap. (978-0-7336-1654-9(2), Hodder Children's Books) Hachette Children's Group.

—The Lying Postman. Odgers, Sally & Odgers, Darrel. 2007. (Jack Russell: Dog Detective Ser.: 4). 96p. (J). pap. 4.99 (978-1-933605-31-9(6), 05319) Kane Miller.

—The Mare's Tale. Odgers, Darrel & Odgers, Sally. 2009. (Pet Vet Ser.: 2). 96p. (J). (gr. 2-6). pap. 4.99 (978-1-935279-02-0(5)) Kane Miller.

—The Mugged Pug. Odgers, Darrel & Odgers, Sally. 2007. 76p. (J). (978-0-439-88018-3(1)) Scholastic, Inc.

—The Mugged Pug. Odgers, Sally & Odgers, Darrel. 2007. (Jack Russell: Dog Detective Ser.: 3). 96p. (J). pap. 4.99 (978-1-933605-32-6(4), 05326) Kane Miller.

—The Phantom Mudder. Odgers, Sally & Odgers, Darrel. 2006. (Jack Russell: Dog Detective Ser.: 2). 96p. (J). (gr. 1-5). pap. 4.99 (978-1-933605-19-7(7)) Kane Miller.

—Pudding & Chips. Matthews, Penny. 2005. 40p. (J). (gr. k-3). (978-0-86315-496-6(4)) Floris Bks.

—The Pup's Tale: Pet Vet Book 6. Odgers, Darrel & Sally. 2015. 96p. (J). pap. 4.99 (978-1-61067-351-8(4)) Kane Miller.

—The Python Problem. Odgers, Darrel & Odgers, Sally. 2010. (Pet Vet Ser.: 4). 96p. (J). (gr. 2-4). pap. 4.99 (978-1-935279-16-7(5)) Kane Miller.

—The Sausage Situation. Odgers, Darrel & Odgers, Sally. 2007. (Jack Russell: Dog Detective Ser.: 6). 96p. (J). (gr. 1-6). pap. 4.99 (978-1-933605-54-8(5)) Kane Miller.

—The Search for King Dragon. Prior, Natalie Jane. 2005. (ENG.). 192p. (J). (gr. 3-7). 6.99 (978-0-14-240267-2(2), Puffin) Penguin Publishing Group.

Dawson, Ken. Island of Ice: And the Snowmites. James, Gilmory. 2009. 52p. pap. 20.49 (978-1-4389-1296-7(X)) AuthorHouse.

Dawson, Liz. Letts Monster Practice e Times Tables Age 5-7. Blackwood, Melissa & Monaghan, Stephen. 2014. (Letts Monster Practice Ser.). (ENG.). 32p. (J). pap. 6.99 (978-1-84419-772-9(7)) HarperCollins Pubs. Ltd. GBR. Dist: Independent Pubs. Group.

Dawson, Sandy & McGee, E. Alan, photos by. The Springer Ghost Book: A Theatre Haunting in the Deep South. Pierce, Paul. 2003. 92p. 19.99 (978-0-9741819-0-5(0)) Pierce, Paul.

Dawson, Scott. Fearless: The Story of Racing Legend Louise Smith. Rosenstock, Barb. 2010. (ENG.). 32p. (J). (gr. k-3). 16.99 (978-0-525-42173-3(4), Dutton Juvenile) Penguin Publishing Group.

—I Survived the Japanese Tsunami 2011. Tarshis, Lauren. 2013. (I Survived Ser.: No. 8). 83p. (J). (978-0-545-62981-2(0)) Scholastic, Inc.

Dawson, Sheldon. Duck's Bay. Delaronde, Deborah L. 2004. 48p. (J). pap. (978-1-894717-24-3(4), Spotlight Poets) Pemmican Pubns., Inc.

—If I Was the Mayor. Howell, Lauren. 2005. 32p. (J). per. (978-0-9735798-1-9(1)) Three Bears Publishing.

Dawson, Ted. Discovering Brachiosaurus. Korb, Rena B. 2008. (Dinosaur Digs Ser.). 32p. (gr. -1-4). 28.50 (978-1-60270-105-2(9), Looking Glass Library- Nonfiction) Magic Wagon.

—Discovering Giganotosaurus. Korb, Rena. 2008. (Dinosaur Digs Ser.). 32p. (gr. -1-5). 28.50 (978-1-60270-106-9(7), Looking Glass Library- Nonfiction) Magic Wagon.

—Discovering Ichthyosaurs. Korb, Rena. 2008. (Dinosaur Digs Ser.). 32p. (gr. -1-5). 28.50 (978-1-60270-107-6(5), Looking Glass Library- Nonfiction) Magic Wagon.

—Discovering Pteranodon. Korb, Rena B. 2008. (Dinosaur Digs Ser.). 32p. (gr. -1-4). 28.50 (978-1-60270-108-3(3), Looking Glass Library- Nonfiction) Magic Wagon.

—Discovering Tyrannosaurus Rex. Korb, Rena B. 2008. (Dinosaur Digs Ser.). 32p. (gr. -1-4). 28.50 (978-1-60270-109-0(1), Looking Glass Library- Nonfiction) Magic Wagon.

—Discovering Velociraptor. Korb, Rena B. 2008. (Dinosaur Digs Ser.). 32p. (gr. -1-4). 28.50 (978-1-60270-110-6(5), Looking Glass Library- Nonfiction) Magic Wagon.

Dawson, Willow. Avis Dolphin. 1 vol. Wishinsky, Frieda. 2015. (ENG.). 128p. (J). (gr. 3-7). 16.95 (978-1-55498-489-3(0)) Groundwood Bks. CAN. Dist: Perseus-PGW.

—The Big Green Book of the Big Blue Sea. Becker, Helaine. 2012. (ENG.). 80p. (J). 15.95 (978-1-55453-746-4(0)); pap. 9.95 (978-1-55453-747-1(9)) Kids Can Pr., Ltd. CAN. Dist: Univ. of Toronto Pr.

—No Girls Allowed: Tales of Daring Women Dressed as Men for Love, Freedom & Adventure. Hughes, Susan. 2008. (ENG.). 80p. (J). (gr. 4-7). 16.95 (978-1-55453-177-6(2)); pap. 8.95 (978-1-55453-178-3(0)) Kids Can Pr., Ltd. CAN. Dist: Univ. of Toronto Pr.

Dawson, Willow. Lila & Ecco's Do-It-Yourself Comics Club. Dawson, Willow. 2010. (ENG.). 112p. (J). (gr. 3-7). 7.95 (978-1-55453-439-5(9)); 16.95 (978-1-55453-438-8(0)) Kids Can Pr., Ltd. CAN. Dist: Univ. of Toronto Pr.

Day, Alexandra. Edens Picture Book, No. 3. Edens, Cooper. Date not set. (J). 14.99 (978-0-06-205153-0(9)) HarperCollins Pubs.

Day, Alexandra. Carl & the Puppies. Day, Alexandra. 2011. (My Readers Ser.). (ENG.). 32p. (J). (gr. -1-1). pap. 3.99 (978-0-312-62483-5(2)) Square Fish.

—Carl at the Dog Show. 1 vol. Day, Alexandra. 2012. (Carl Ser.). (ENG.). 40p. (J). (gr. -1-1). 14.99 (978-0-374-31083-7(1), Farrar, Straus & Giroux (BYR)) Farrar, Straus & Giroux.

—Carl's Halloween. Day, Alexandra. 2015. (Carl Ser.). (ENG.). 32p. (J). (gr. -1-2). 14.99 (978-0-374-31082-0(3), Farrar, Straus & Giroux (BYR)) Farrar, Straus & Giroux.

—Carl's Sleepy Afternoon. Day, Alexandra. 2005. (Carl Ser.). (ENG.). 40p. (J). (gr. -1-1). 15.99 (978-0-374-31088-2(2), Farrar, Straus & Giroux (BYR)) Farrar, Straus & Giroux.

—Carl's Snowy Afternoon. Day, Alexandra. 2009. (Carl Ser.). (ENG.). 32p. (J). (gr. -1-1). 12.99 (978-0-374-31086-8(6), Farrar, Straus & Giroux (BYR)) Farrar, Straus & Giroux.

—Carl's Summer Vacation. Day, Alexandra. 2008. (Carl Ser.). (ENG.). 32p. (J). (gr. -1-1). 13.99 (978-0-374-31085-1(8), Farrar, Straus & Giroux (BYR)) Farrar, Straus & Giroux.

—The Fairy Dogfather. Day, Alexandra. 2012. (ENG.). 32p. (J). 8.95 (978-1-59583-455-3(9), Green Tiger Pr.) Laughing Elephant.

Day, Andrew. Best in Show. LeFrak, Karen. 2011. (ENG.). 32p. (J). (gr. -1-2). 16.99 (978-0-8027-2064-1(1)) Walker & Co.

—The Leaves on the Trees. Wiley, Thom. 2011. (ENG.). 24p. (J). (gr. -1-k). pap. 6.99 (978-0-545-31290-5(6), Cartwheel Bks.) Scholastic, Inc.

Day, Betsy. Animal Habitats! Learning about North American Animals & Plants Through Art, Science & Creative Play. Press, Judy. (ENG.). 128p. (J). (gr. 3-7). 2008. per. 12.95 (978-0-8249-6756-7(9)); 2005. 14.95 (978-0-8249-6778-9(X)) Ideals Pubns. (Williamson Bks.).

—My Happy Heart Books, Set. Osteen, Victoria. 2009. (ENG.). 66p. (J). (gr. -1-k). 19.99 (978-1-4169-5549-8(6), Little Simon Inspirations) Little Simon Inspirations.

Day, Betsy. Almost-Instant Scrapbooks. Day, Betsy, tr. Check, Laura. 2004. (Quick Starts for Kids! Ser.). 64p. (J). pap. 8.95 (978-1-885593-90-0(2), Williamson Bks.) Ideals Pubns.

Day, Bruce. Rodney Robbins & the Rainy-Day Pond. Stegall, Kim. 2010. 29p. (J). (978-1-60682-058-2(3)) BJU Pr.

Day, Caroline, jt. illus. see Thompson, Josephine.

Day, J. David, photos by. Canyonlands National Park Favorite Jeep Roads & Hiking Trails. Day, J. David. 2004. (ENG., 296p. pap. 14.95 (978-0-9660858-2-2(5)) Rincon Publishing Co.

Day, Jeff. What Is Funny? Boritzer, Etan. 2004. 40p. 14.95 (978-0-9637597-8-8(7)); 32p. pap. 6.95 (978-0-9637597-9-5(5)) Lane, Veronica Bks.

Day, Larry. Bye-Bye, Baby! Morris, Richard T. 2009. (ENG.). 40p. (J). (gr. -1-1). 16.99 (978-0-8027-9772-8(5)) Walker & Co.

—Civil War Battleship: The Monitor. Thompson, Gare. 2003. (Penguin Young Readers, Level 4 Ser.). (ENG.). 48p. (J). (gr. 3-4). mass mkt. 3.99 (978-0-448-43245-8(5), Grosset & Dunlap) Penguin Publishing Group.

—Civil War Drummer Boy. Kay, Verla. 2012. (ENG.). 32p. (J). (gr. 1-3). 16.99 (978-0-399-23992-2(8), Putnam Juvenile) Penguin Publishing Group.

—Colonial Voices: Hear Them Speak. Winters, Kay. 2008. (ENG.). 32p. (J). (gr. 4-7). 17.99 (978-0-525-47872-0(8), Dutton Juvenile) Penguin Publishing Group.

—Colonial Voices - Hear Them Speak. Winters, Kay. 2015. (ENG.). 32p. (J). (gr. 4-7). 8.99 (978-0-14-751162-1(3), Puffin) Penguin Publishing Group.

—George Did It. Jurmain, Suzanne Tripp. 2007. (ENG.). 40p. (J). (gr. k-4). pap. 6.99 (978-0-14-240695-7(6), Puffin) Penguin Publishing Group.

—George Did It. Jurmain, Suzanne Tripp. 2007. (gr. -1-3). 17.00 (978-0-7569-8161-7(1)) Perfection Learning Corp.

—Let It Begin Here! Lexington & Concord - First Battles of the American Revolution. Fradin, Dennis Brindell. 2005. (ENG.). 32p. (J). (gr. 2-6). 17.99 (978-0-8027-8945-7(5)) Walker & Co.

—Lion, Lion. Busch, Miriam. 2014. (ENG.). 32p. (J). (gr. -1-3). 17.99 (978-0-06-227104-4(0)) HarperCollins Pubs.

—Nanook & Pryce: Gone Fishing. Crowley, Ned. 2009. (ENG.). 32p. (J). (gr. -1-3). 16.99 (978-0-06-133641-6(6)) HarperCollins Pubs.

—Voices from the Oregon Trail. Winters, Kay. 2014. (ENG.). 48p. (J). (gr. 2-4). 17.99 (978-0-8037-3775-4(0), Dial) Penguin Publishing Group.

—Who Was Annie Oakley? Spinner, Stephanie. 2003. (Who Was...? Ser.). 109p. (gr. 4-7). 15.00 (978-0-7569-1588-9(0)) Perfection Learning Corp.

—Worst of Friends: Thomas Jefferson, John Adams, & the True Story of an American Feud. Jurmain, Suzanne Tripp. 2011. (ENG.). 32p. (J). (gr. 1-3). 16.99 (978-0-525-47903-1(1), Dutton Juvenile) Penguin Publishing Group.

—Yankee Doodle & the Redcoats: Soldiering in the Revolutionary War. Beller, Susan Provost. 2003. (Single Titles Ser.). (ENG.). 96p. (gr. 5-8). lib. bdg. 26.60 (978-0-7613-2612-0(X), Twenty-First Century Bks.) Lerner Publishing Group.

Day, Linda S. Milestones. Darby, Joel et al. Grant, Lisa, ed. I.t. ed. 2004. 32p. (J). 12.95 (978-0-9759579-0-5(2)) Denver Broncos.

—The Pocket Fairies of Middleburg. Zern, Linda L. 2004. (J). per. 9.95 (978-0-9753098-0-3(3)) Linwood Hse. Publishing.

Day, Linda S. Frogazoom! Day, Linda S. Butterworth, MyLinda. I.t. ed. 2003. 32p. (J). (gr. k-3). pap. 16.95 (978-1-890905-03-3(8), Writers Collective, The) Day to Day Enterprises.

—There's a Frog on a Log in the Bog. Day, Linda S. Day, Robert O. 2003. (J). (gr. 3-6). 212p. pap. 8.95 (978-1-890905-50-7(X), Writers Collective, The); (Just So Wild Ser.: Vol. 1). 14.95 (978-1-890905-51-4(8), Eco Fiction Bks.) Day to Day Enterprises.

Day, Margery. The Canada Goose & You. Burrows, Jennifer S. 2009. 32p. pap. 15.95 (978-0-9791606-9-1(3)) E & E Publishing.

Day, Martin & Evans, Jamie. The Animal Parables. Methold, Graham, photos by. Day, Martin. 2011. (ENG.). 108p. pap. 10.99 (978-1-4610-6965-2(3)) CreateSpace Independent Publishing Platform.

Day, Maurice. The Animal Etiquette Book of Rhymes. LeCron, Helen Cowles. 2014. (ENG.). 64p. (J). (gr. 1-5). pap. 4.99 (978-0-486-78234-8(4)) Dover Pubns., Inc.

—Little Jack Rabbit's Favorite Bunny Tales. Cory, David. 2014. (ENG.). 320p. (J). (gr. 1-5). pap. 12.99 (978-0-486-78556-1(4)) Dover Pubns., Inc.

Day, Rob. Voices in Poetry: Walt Whitman. Whiting, Jim & Loewen, Nancy. 2015. (Voices in Poetry Ser.). (ENG.). 48p. (J). (gr. 5-8). pap. 12.00 (978-1-62832-057-2(5), Creative Paperbacks) Creative Co., The.

Day, Rob. Walt Whitman. Loewen, Nancy. 2014. 47p. 35.65 **(978-1-60818-329-6(7)**, Creative Education) Creative Co., The.

Daykin, Louise. Goldilocks & the Three Bears. 2004. 32p. (J). (978-1-84444-054-2(0)); (SER & ENG.). (978-1-84444-053-5(2)); (978-1-84444-050-4(8)); (978-1-84444-049-8(4)); (978-1-84444-047-4(8)); (978-1-84444-046-7(X)); (978-1-84444-045-0(1)); (978-1-84444-042-9(7)); (GER & ENG.). (978-1-84444-041-2(9)); (978-1-84444-039-9(7)); (978-1-84444-035-1(4)) Mantra Lingua.

—Goldilocks & the Three Bears. Clynes, Kate. 32p. (J). 2004. (ENG & PAN.). pap. (978-1-84444-043-6(5)); 2004. (ENG & POR.). pap. (978-1-84444-044-3(3)); 2004. (FRE & ENG.). pap. (978-1-84444-040-5(0)); 2004. (ENG & URD.). pap. (978-1-84444-048-1(6)); 2004. (ENG & POL.). pap. (978-1-84444-051-1(6)); 2004. (ENG & ARA.). pap. (978-1-84444-036-8(2)); 2004. (ENG & HIN.). pap. (978-1-84444-059-7(1)); 2003. (CHI & ENG.). pap. (978-1-84444-038-2(9)); 2003. (BEN & ENG.). pap. (978-1-84444-037-5(0)); 2003. (RUS & ENG.). pap. (978-1-84444-052-8(4)) Mantra Lingua.

—Not Again, Red Riding Hood! Clynes, Kate. 2004. 32p. (J). (HIN & ENG.). (978-1-85269-998-7(1)); (ENG & GUJ.). pap. (978-1-85269-993-2(0)); (GER & ENG.). pap. (978-1-85269-988-8(4)); (FRE & ENG.). pap. (978-1-85269-983-3(3)); (ENG & PER.). pap. (978-1-85269-978-9(7)); (ENG & CZE.). pap. (978-1-85269-973-4(6)); (ENG & CHI.). pap. (978-1-85269-968-0(X)); (ENG & VIE.). pap. (978-1-85269-959-8(0)); (ENG & ARA.). pap. (978-1-85269-958-1(2)); (ENG & URD.). pap. (978-1-85269-954-3(X)); (ENG & ALB.). pap. (978-1-85269-953-6(1)); (ENG & TUR.). pap. (978-1-85269-949-9(3)); (ENG & TAM.). pap. (978-1-85269-944-4(2)); (ENG & SPA.). pap. (978-1-85269-939-0(6)); (ENG & SOM.). pap. (978-1-85269-934-5(5)); (ENG & SER.). pap. (978-1-85269-929-1(9)); (ENG & RUS.). pap. (978-1-85269-924-6(8)); (POR & ENG.). pap. (978-1-85269-919-2(1)); (ENG & POL.). pap. (978-1-85269-914-7(0)); (ENG & PAN.). pap. (978-1-85269-909-3(4)); (ENG & ITA.). pap. (978-1-85269-904-8(3)) Mantra Lingua.

Daykin, Louise. Goldilocks & the Three Bears. Daykin, Louise, tr. 2004. 31p. (J). (978-1-84444-057-3(5)) Mantra Lingua.

—Goldilocks & the Three Bears. Daykin, Louise, tr. Clynes, Kate. 2003. (VIE & ENG.). 32p. (J). pap. 12.95 (978-1-84444-055-9(9)) Mantra Lingua GBR. Dist: Chinasprout, Inc.

Dayn, Penelope. Fat Rat, Fat Cat — -Because Cats & Rats Are Also People. Dyan, Penelope. 2008. 40p. pap. 11.95 (978-1-935118-11-4(0)) Bellissima Publishing, LLC.

Dayton, Melissa, jt. illus. see Aileen Co.

Dayton, Melissa, jt. illus. see Co, Aileen.

Dayton, Tyler. My Dog & My Dad. Garcia, Emerald. 2011. (ENG.). 40p. pap. 11.50 (978-1-4610-9770-9(3)) CreateSpace Independent Publishing Platform.

DC Artists Staff. DC Super Friends Heroes Unite! Reader's Digest Editors. 2012. (Shaped Fold-Out Ser.). (ENG.). 10p. (J). (gr. -1-k). bds. 6.99 (978-0-7944-2467-1(8)) Reader's Digest Assn., Inc., The.

DC Comics Staff. Emperor of the Airwaves, 1 vol. Lemke, Donald B. et al. 2013. (Batman Ser.). (ENG.). 56p. (gr. 2-3). pap. 4.95 (978-1-4342-1364-8(1), DC Super Heroes) Stone Arch Bks.

DC Comics Staff, jt. illus. see Cavallaro, Mike.

DC Comics Staff, jt. illus. see Levins, Tim.

DC Comics Staff, jt. illus. see Vecchio, Luciano.

De Angel, M. Hello, Wilbur! Olson, Lute. 2007. 24p. (J). lib. bdg. 14.95 (978-1-932888-40-9(3)) Mascot Bks., Inc.

De Angel, Miguel. Cort Spells It Out. Aryal, Aimee. 2006. (Cort the Sport Adventures Ser.). 24p. (J). (gr. -1-3). per. 5.95 (978-1-932888-62-1(4), 91-101-01) Mascot Bks., Inc.

—Go, Pack, Go! Aryal, Aimee. 2007. 24p. (J). (gr. -1-3). 14.95 (978-1-932888-94-2(2)) Mascot Bks., Inc.

—Hello, Cosmo! Edwards, Pat & Edwards, LaVell. 2006. 24p. (J). lib. bdg. 17.95 (978-1-932888-45-4(4)) Mascot Bks., Inc.

—How 'Bout Them Cowboys! Aryal, Aimee. 2007. 24p. (J). 17.95 (978-1-932888-90-4(X)) Mascot Bks., Inc.

—How 'Bout Them Dawgs! Dooley, Vince. 2006. 24p. (J). lib. bdg. 17.95 (978-1-932888-46-1(2)) Mascot Bks., Inc.

—Let's Go, Chiefs! Aryal, Aimee. 2007. 24p. (J). lib. bdg. 14.95 (978-1-932888-93-5(4)) Mascot Bks., Inc.

—Let's Go, Giants! Aryal, Aimee. 2007. 24p. (J). lib. bdg. 14.95 (978-1-932888-92-8(6)) Mascot Bks., Inc.

—Let's Go, Panthers! Aryal, Aimee. 2007. 24p. (J). (gr. -1-3). 14.95 (978-1-932888-97-3(7)) Mascot Bks., Inc.

—Let's Go, Patriots! 2007. 24p. (J). (gr. -1-3). 14.95 (978-1-932888-98-0(5)) Mascot Bks., Inc.

—Let's Go, Seahawks! Aryal, Aimee. 2007. 24p. (J). lib. bdg. 14.95 (978-1-932888-95-9(0)) Mascot Bks., Inc.

—Let's Go, Vikings! Aryal, Aimee. 2007. 24p. (J). 14.95 (978-1-932888-99-7(3)) Mascot Bks., Inc.

—Roll Tide! Stabler, Ken. 2006. 24p. (J). lib. bdg. 17.95 (978-1-932888-48-5(9)) Mascot Bks., Inc.

—War Eagle! Dye, Pat. 2006. 24p. (J). lib. bdg. 17.95 (978-1-932888-47-8(0)) Mascot Bks., Inc.

—Yea, It's Hokie Game Day! Beamer, Cheryl & Beamer, Frank. 2006. 24p. (J). lib. bdg. 17.95 (978-1-932888-44-7(6)) Mascot Bks., Inc.

De Angel, Miguel & Moore, D. Hello, Brutus! Aryal, Aimee. 2006. 24p. (J). lib. bdg. 14.95 (978-1-932888-51-5(9)) Mascot Bks., Inc.

—Let's Go, White Sox! Aryal, Aimee. 2007. 24p. (J). lib. bdg. 14.95 (978-1-932888-87-4(X)) Mascot Bks., Inc.

De Angelis, Maurizio, et al. Changing Life on Earth, 1 vol. Hartman, Eve & Meshbesher, Wendy. 2009. (Sci-Hi: Life Science Ser.). (ENG.). 48p. (gr. 4-4). lib. bdg. 32.65 (978-1-4109-3324-9(5), Sci-Hi) Heinemann-Raintree.

—Changing Life on Earth, 1 vol. Hartman, Eve et al. 2009. (Sci-Hi: Life Science Ser.). (ENG.). 48p. (gr. 4-4). pap. 8.99 (978-1-4109-3332-4(6), Sci-Hi) Heinemann-Raintree.

De Angelis, Maurizio. Earth's Biomes, 1 vol. Latham, Donna & Heinemann Library Staff. 2009. (Sci-Hi: Life Science Ser.). (ENG.). 48p. (gr. 4-4). pap. 8.99 (978-1-4109-3337-9(7), Sci-Hi) Heinemann-Raintree.

—Earth's Biomes, 1 vol. Latham, Donna. 2009. (Sci-Hi: Life Science Ser.). (ENG.). 48p. (gr. 4-4). lib. bdg. 32.65 (978-1-4109-3329-4(6), Sci-Hi) Heinemann-Raintree.

De Angelis, Maurizio, et al. Ecology, 1 vol. Latham, Donna & Heinemann Library Staff. 2009. (Sci-Hi: Life Science Ser.). (ENG.). 48p. (gr. 4-4). pap. 8.99 (978-1-4109-3336-2(9), Sci-Hi) Heinemann-Raintree.

—Ecology, 1 vol. Latham, Donna. 2009. (Sci-Hi: Life Science Ser.). (ENG.). 48p. (gr. 4-4). lib. bdg. 32.65 (978-1-4109-3328-7(8), Sci-Hi) Heinemann-Raintree.

De Angelis, Maurizio & Escott, Ian. Human Reproduction, 1 vol. Rand, Casey & Heinemann Library Staff. 2009. (Sci-Hi: Life Science Ser.). (ENG.). 48p. (gr. 4-4). pap. 8.99 (978-1-4109-3335-5(0), Sci-Hi) Heinemann-Raintree.

—Human Reproduction, 1 vol. Rand, Casey. 2009. (Sci-Hi: Life Science Ser.). (ENG.). 48p. (gr. 4-4). lib. bdg. 32.65 (978-1-4109-3327-0(X), Sci-Hi) Heinemann-Raintree.

de Beer, Hans, pseud. El Pequeno Coco. Romanelli, Serena. Lamas, Blanca Rosa, tr. from GER. 2004.Tr. of Kleiner Dodo was Spielst du?. (SPA.). 24p. (J). (gr. k-4). reprint ed. 16.00 (978-0-7567-7707-4(0)) DIANE Publishing Co.

de Beer, Hans, pseud. Little Polar Bear & the Big Balloon. de Beer, Hans. Lanning, Rosemary, tr. from GER. 2006. (Little Polar Bear Ser.). (ENG.). 32p. (J). (gr. -1-3). pap. 6.95 (978-0-7358-2077-7(5)) North-South Bks., Inc.

—Little Polar Bear Finds a Friend. de Beer, Hans. 2009. (ENG.). 12p. (J). (gr. -1-3). bds. 7.95 (978-0-7358-2239-9(5)) North-South Bks., Inc.

De Bella, Pablo. Conoce a Cristobal Colon: Get to Know Christopher Columbus. Molina, Maria I. Mendoza, Isabel C., ed. 2015. (Hispanic Biography Ser.). (ENG & SPA.). (J). pap. **(978-0-88272-330-3(8))** Ediciones Alfaguara.

De Boer, Michel. Bobby Boast a Lot. Howat, Irene. 2005. (Little Lots Ser.). (ENG.). 16p. (J). pap. 4.99 (978-1-85792-978-2(0)) Christian Focus Pubns. GBR. Dist: Send The Light Distribution LLC.

—Granny Grump a Lot. Howat, Irene. 2005. (Little Lots Ser.). (ENG.). 16p. (J). pap. 4.99 (978-1-85792-980-5(2)) Christian Focus Pubns. GBR. Dist: Send The Light Distribution LLC.

—Harry Help a Lot. Howat, Irene. 2005. (Little Lots Ser.). (ENG.). 16p. (J). pap. 4.99 (978-1-85792-976-8(4)) Christian Focus Pubns. GBR. Dist: Send The Light Distribution LLC.

—Lorna Look a Lot. Howat, Irene. 2005. (Little Lots Ser.). (ENG.). 16p. (J). pap. 4.99 (978-1-85792-979-9(9)) Christian Focus Pubns. GBR. Dist: Send The Light Distribution LLC.

—Lucy Lie a Lot. Howat, Irene. 2005. (Little Lots Ser.). (ENG.). 16p. (J). pap. 4.99 (978-1-85792-975-1(6)) Christian Focus Pubns. GBR. Dist: Send The Light Distribution LLC.

—William Work a Lot. Howat, Irene. 2005. (Little Lots Ser.). (ENG.). 16p. (J). pap. 4.99 (978-1-85792-977-5(2)) Christian Focus Pubns. GBR. Dist: Send The Light Distribution LLC.

de Brun, Brendan Joseph. The Talking Llama: la Llama Que Habla. de Brun, Kieran Christopher. 2005. (J). pap. 16.00 (978-0-8059-6910-8(1)) Dorrance Publishing Co., Inc.

de Brunhoff, Jean. Babar & Zephir. de Brunhoff, Jean. 2005. 38p. (J). (gr. k-4). reprint ed. 16.00 (978-0-7567-8935-0(4)) DIANE Publishing Co.

De Castro, Ines E. The Teddy Bear Faeries. De Castro, Ines E. 2011. 24p. (J). (gr. -1-3). 16.95 (978-1-935359-72-2(X)) Book Pubs. Network.

De Conno, Gianni. Poemas a la Luna/ Poems to the Moon. 2009. (SPA.). 28p. (YA). (gr. 5-18). (978-84-263-7338-0(0)) Vives, Luis Editorial (Edelvives).

De Dios, Susana. Ellie's Bad Hair Day. Keane, Jerome. 2012. (ENG.). 32p. (J). (gr. k-2). 15.99 (978-1-84365-140-6(8), Pavilion Children's Books) Pavilion Bks. GBR. Dist: Independent Pubs. Group.

De Gante, Guillermo. El Espejo en el Agua. Estrada, E. Gabriela Aguileta. rev. ed. 2006. (Castillo de la Lectura Naranja Ser.). (SPA & ENG.). 124p. (J). (gr. 4-7). pap. 7.95 (978-970-20-0131-7(5)) Castillo, Ediciones, S. A. de C. V. MEX. Dist: Macmillan.

de Giorgi, Sergio. Building God's Kingdom - Diggit Saves the Day, 1 vol. Holmes, Andy. 2014. (ENG.). 22p. (J). pap. 9.99 (978-0-529-11100-5(4)) Nelson, Thomas Inc.

De Giorgi, Sergio. Eight Great Planets! A Song about the Planets, 1 vol. Salas, Laura Purdie. 2010. (Science Songs Ser.). (ENG.). 24p. (gr. 1-3). lib. bdg. 25.99 (978-1-4048-5765-0(6), Nonfiction Picture Bks.) Picture Window Bks.

—I'm Exploring with My Senses: A Song about the Five Senses, 1 vol. Salas, Laura Purdie. 2010. (Science Songs Ser.). (ENG.). 24p. (gr. 1-3). lib. bdg. 25.99 (978-1-4048-5764-3(8), Nonfiction Picture Bks.) Picture Window Bks.

—Many Creatures: A Song about Animal Classifications, 1 vol. Salas, Laura Purdie. 2010. (Science Songs Ser.). (ENG.). 24p. (gr. 1-3). lib. bdg. 25.99 (978-1-4048-5763-6(X), Nonfiction Picture Bks.) Picture Window Bks.

—There Goes the Water: A Song about the Water Cycle, 1 vol. Salas, Laura Purdie. 2010. (Science Songs Ser.). (ENG.). 24p. (gr. 1-3). lib. bdg. 25.99 (978-1-4048-5766-7(4), Nonfiction Picture Bks.) Picture Window Bks.

de Giorgi, Sergio. Tipper Tells a Lie, 1 vol. Holmes, Andy. 2014. (ENG.). 22p. (J). pap. 9.99 (978-0-529-11213-2(2)) Nelson, Thomas Inc.

De Horna, Luis. El Dragon y la Mariposa. Ende, Michael. 2003.Tr. of Der Lindwurm und der Schmetterling. (SPA.). 48p. (J). (gr. k-3). pap. 8.95 (978-84-204-3710-1(7)) Santillana USA Publishing Co., Inc.

—Por Caminos Azules... varios & Varios. (SPA.). 108p. (J). (gr. 3-5). 12.99 (978-84-207-9263-7(2), EK30162) Grupo Anaya, S.A. ESP. Dist: Lectorum Pubns., Inc.

The check digit for ISBN-10 appears in parentheses after the full ISBN-13

de Hugo, Pierre. Fish Underwater. de Hugo, Pierre. 2012. (ENG.). 36p. (J). (gr. -1-k). 12.99 *(978-1-85103-409-3(9))* Moonlight Publishing, Ltd. GBR. Dist: Independent Pubs. Group.
—Polar Bears. de Hugo, Pierre. 2013. (ENG.). 36p. (J). (gr. -1-k). 12.99 *(978-1-85103-418-5(8))* Moonlight Publishing, Ltd. GBR. Dist: Independent Pubs. Group.
de Jesus Alvarez, Maria. Estoy Orgullosa de Mi Pasado. White, Amy. Kratky, Lada J., tr. 2009. (Colección Fácil de Leer Ser.). (SPA.). 16p. (gr. k-2). pap. 5.99 *(978-1-60396-421-0(5))* Ediciones Alfaguara ESP. Dist: Santillana USA Publishing Co., Inc.
De Kinder, Jan. Red. 2015. 32p. (J). 16.00 *(978-0-8028-5446-9(X),* Eerdmans Bks For Young Readers) Eerdmans, William B. Publishing Co.
de Klerk, Roger. Foxy Learns Colors. 2009. (Foxy Learns Ser.). 16p. (J). pap. 4.95 *(978-1-59496-181-6(6))* Teora USA LLC.
—Foxy Learns Shapes. 2009. (Foxy Learns Ser.). 16p. (J). pap. 4.95 *(978-1-59496-179-3(4))* Teora USA LLC.
—Foxy Learns to Add. 2009. (Foxy Learns Ser.). 16p. (J). pap. 4.95 *(978-1-59496-178-6(6))* Teora USA LLC.
—Foxy Learns to Tell Time. 2009. (Foxy Learns Ser.). 16p. (J). pap. 4.95 *(978-1-59496-180-9(8))* Teora USA LLC.
—Moses in the Bulrushes. Andrews, Jackie. 2012. (ENG.). 24p. (J). 8.50 *(978-1-84135-807-9(X))* Award Pubns. Ltd. GBR. Dist: Parkwest Pubns., Inc.
de La Cour, Gary, et al. Mother Goose Lullabies. Studio Mouse Staff. rev. ed. 2007. (ENG.). 24p. (J). 4.99 *(978-1-59069-559-3(3))* Studio Mouse LLC.
—Twinkle Twinkle: And Other Sleepy-Time Rhymes. 2005. (Mother Goose Ser.). (ENG.). 36p. (J). (gr. -1-k). 12.95 *(978-1-59249-464-4(1),* 1D016) Soundprints.
—Wheels on the Bus. rev. ed. 2007. (ENG.). 24p. (J). (gr. -1-3). 4.99 *(978-1-59069-562-3(3))* Studio Mouse LLC.
De La Cour, Gary. Counting in the Snow. De La Cour, Gary, creator. gif. ed. 2005. 10p. (J). bds. 9.99 *(978-1-57791-186-9(5))* Brighter Minds Children's Publishing.
De La Cruz, Erin Harris. Frank Is a Chihuahua. Morrison, Kevin. 2007. 32p. (J). (gr. 1-4). *(978-1-929039-43-2(3))* Ambassador Bks., Inc.
De La Fuente, Mary, jt. illus. see Horowitz, Alena Netia.
de la Fuente, Pilar. A Halloween Story: A frightfully delightful tale by a 5-year-old, for other little monsters Everywhere. Fernandez, Alberto. 2007.Tr. of Historia de Halloween. 48p. (J). *(978-0-9796465-0-8(2))* Maroma Bks.
—A Halloween Story: A frightfully-delightful tale, by a 5-year-old, for other little monsters, Everywhere. Fernandez, Alberto. 2007. (J). pap. 9.95 *(978-0-9796465-2-2(9))* Maroma Bks.
De La Torre, Roberto, et al. Prelude to Schism. Jenkins, Paul. 2011. (ENG.). 112p. (YA). (gr. 8-17). 19.99 *(978-0-7851-5689-5(5))* Marvel Worldwide, Inc.
De La Torre, Roberto & Checchetto, Marco. Shadowland - Daredevil. 2011. (ENG.). 96p. (YA). (gr. 8-17). pap. 14.99 *(978-0-7851-4522-6(2))* Marvel Worldwide, Inc.
De Leiris, Lucia. Stardust from Space. Grady, Monica et al. 2007. (ENG.). 32p. (J). (gr. 2-17). 16.95 *(978-1-84507-570-5(6),* Frances Lincoln) Quarto Publishing Group UK GBR. Dist: Hachette Bk. Group.
de los reyes Cruz, Cheryl. DemiChat & the Lost Mummy. Brisland, Toni. 2013. 142p. (J). pap. 14.95 *(978-1-60131-173-3(7))* Big Tent Bks.
De Luca, Daniela. The Animal Atlas. McRae, Anne. 2008. (ENG.). 29p. (J). (gr. -1-3). 16.95 *(978-88-88166-38-4(6))* McRae Bks. Srl ITA. Dist: Independent Pubs. Group.
—The Atlas of Ancient Civilizations. Morris, Neil. 2008. (ENG.). 28p. (J). (gr. -1-3). 17.95 *(978-88-900466-0-5(0))* McRae Bks. Srl ITA. Dist: Independent Pubs. Group.
—The Children's Pictorial Atlas of the World. Cooper, Alison & McRae, Anne. 2008. (ENG.). 45p. (J). (gr. -1-3). 17.95 *(978-88-88166-05-6(X))* McRae Bks. Srl ITA. Dist: Independent Pubs. Group.
—Meyers Bunter Weltatlas fuer Kinder. (GER.). 50p. *(978-3-411-07781-6(5))* Bibliographisches Institut & F. A. Brockhaus AG DEU. Dist: i. b. d., Ltd.
De Lucio-Brock, Anita. Grandma & Me at the Flea: Los Meros Meros Remateros. Herrera, Juan Felipe. 2013. (ENG & SPA.). 32p. (J). pap. 9.95 *(978-0-89239-279-7(7),* Children's Book Press) Lee & Low Bks., Inc.
de Marcken, Gail. Born to Pull: The Glory of Sled Dogs. Cary, Bob. 2009. (ENG.). 96p. pap. 12.95 *(978-0-8166-6773-4(X))* Univ. of Minnesota Pr.
—Princess Tales: Once upon a Time in Rhyme with Seek-and-Find Pictures. Maccarone, Grace. 2013. (ENG.). 32p. (J). (gr. -1-1). 16.99 *(978-0-312-67958-3(0))* Feiwel & Friends.
—The Quiltmaker's Journey. Brumbeau, Jeff. ed. 2005. (ENG.). 56p. (J). 18.99 *(978-0-439-51219-0(0),* Orchard Bks.) Scholastic, Inc.
De Marco, Arielle. Penny Sue the Pure Hearted. Degarmo, Serena. 2013. 30p. pap. 7.99 *(978-1-936341-55-9(7))* DeWard Publishing Co., Ltd.
de Monfreid, Dorothée. Baúl de Palabras. Girard, Franck. 2005. (Baúl de Palabras Ser.). (SPA & ENG.). 140p. (J). (gr. k-2). 19.95 *(978-84-7864-789-7(9))* Combel Editorial, S.A. ESP. Dist: Independent Pubs. Group.
De Montignie, Leon. Mudpoo & the Magic Tree Stump. Klein, Peter. 2012. (ENG.). 234p. (J). 23.49 *(978-0-9871448-5-0(5))* JoJo Publishing AUS. Dist: AtlasBooks Distribution.
De Muth, Roger. Messy Bessie: Where's My Homework? Ziefert, Harriet. 2007. (J). *(978-1-4287-4707-4(9))* Handprint Bks.
de Oaxaco, Jesus & Zarate, Jesus. My Skeleton Family. Weill, Cynthia. 2013. (ENG & SPA.). 32p. (J). (-k). 14.95 *(978-1-935955-50-4(0))* Cinco Puntos Pr.
de Polonia, Nina. The Boy Who Would Be King. Pierce, Kelly. 2011. (ENG.). 26p. pap. 11.99 *(978-1-4662-4050-6(4))* CreateSpace Independent Publishing Platform.
de Pretto, Lorenzo. The Discovery of America. Crippa, Luca et al. 2009. (Geronimo Stilton Graphic Novels Ser.: 1). (ENG.). 56p. (J). (gr. 2-6). 9.99 *(978-1-59707-158-1(7))* Papercutz.
De Saulles, Tony. Huesos, Sangre y Otros Pedazos del Cuerpo. Arnold, Nick. 2003. (Coleccion Esa Horrible Cienca). (SPA.). 156p. (YA). (gr. 5-8). *(978-84-272-2051-5(0),* ML8311) Molino, Editorial ESP. Dist: Lectorum Pubns., Inc.
De Saulles, Tony. Esa Caotica Quimica. De Saulles, Tony. Arnold, Nick. 2003. (Coleccion Esa Horrible Cienca). (SPA.). 158p. (YA). *(978-84-272-2052-2(9),* ML8312) Molino, Editorial ESP. Dist: Lectorum Pubns., Inc.
—Esa Deslumbrante Luz. De Saulles, Tony. Arnold, Nick. (SPA.). 158p. (YA). (gr. 5-8). *(978-84-272-2063-8(4))* Molino, Editorial ESP. Dist: Lectorum Pubns., Inc.
—Esa Electrizante Electricidad. De Saulles, Tony. Arnold, Nick. (SPA.). 160p. (YA). (gr. 5-8). *(978-84-272-2066-9(9))* Molino, Editorial ESP. Dist: Lectorum Pubns., Inc.
—Esas Funestas Fuerzas. De Saulles, Tony. Arnold, Nick & ARNOLD, NICK. 2003. (Coleccion Esa Horrible Cienca). (SPA.). 160p. (YA). *(978-84-272-2054-6(5),* ML8313) Molino, Editorial ESP. Dist: Lectorum Pubns., Inc.
—Esas Perversas Plantas. De Saulles, Tony. Arnold, Nick. (SPA.). 160p. (YA). (gr. 5-8). *(978-84-272-2062-1(6))* Molino, Editorial ESP. Dist: Lectorum Pubns., Inc.
—Ese Voluminoso Cerebro. De Saulles, Tony. Arnold, Nick. 2003. (Coleccion Esa Horrible Cienca). (SPA.). 158p. (YA). *(978-84-272-2065-2(0),* ML31376) Molino, Editorial ESP. Dist: Lectorum Pubns., Inc.
—Esos Microscopicos Monstruos. De Saulles, Tony. Arnold, Nick. (SPA.). 144p. (YA). (gr. 5-8). *(978-84-272-2092-8(8))* Molino, Editorial ESP. Dist: Lectorum Pubns., Inc.
de Sève, Peter. The Duchess of Whimsy. de Sève, Randall. 2009. (ENG.). 32p. (J). (gr. k-3). 17.99 *(978-0-399-25095-8(6),* Philomel) Penguin Publishing Group.
—Finn McCoul. Gleeson, Brian. 2005. (Rabbit Ears Ser.). 36p. (gr. k-5). 25.65 *(978-1-59679-223-4(X))* Spotlight.
—Pagan's Vows. Jinks, Catherine. 2004. (Pagan Chronicles Ser.: 3). (ENG.). 336p. (YA). (gr. 7-18). 16.99 *(978-0-7636-2021-9(1))* Candlewick Pr.
De, Soham. Telling Tales in Latin: A New Course & Story Book for Children. Robinson, Lorna. 2014. (ENG & LAT.). 112p. (gr. 4-7). pap. 15.95 *(978-0-285-64179-2(4))* Souvenir Pr. Ltd. GBR. Dist: Independent Pubs. Group.
De Soto, Ben. The Adventures of Dynamic Doolittle: The Problem with Paulie Python. Chachas, George & Wojtak, James. 2011. 31p. (J). pap. 9.95 *(978-0-9793144-1-4(0))* Doolittle Edutainment Corp.
—Doolittle's Very, Very Bad Day. Chachas, George & Wojtak, James. 2011. 26p. (J). pap. 9.95 *(978-0-9793144-2-1(9))* Doolittle Edutainment Corp.
—The Story of Doolittle: An Exceptional Young Gorilla. Chachas, George & Wojtak, James. 2011. 32p. (J). pap. 9.95 *(978-0-9793144-0-7(2))* Doolittle Edutainment Corp.
De Spiegeleer, Chantal, jt. illus. see Sterne, René.
De Tagyos, Paul Ratz. Barnyard Fun, 0 vols. Wright, Maureen. 2013. (ENG.). 20p. (J). (gr. -1-3). 16.99 *(978-1-4778-1643-1(7),* 9781477816431, Amazon Children's Publishing) Amazon Publishing.
De Tagyos, Paul Rátz. Ferret Fun, 0 vols. Rostoker-Gruber, Karen. 2011. (ENG.). 32p. (J). (gr. k-3). 17.99 *(978-0-7614-5817-3(4),* 9780761458173, Amazon Children's Publishing) Amazon Publishing.
—Maybelle Goes to Tea. Speck, Katie. 2008. (Maybelle Ser.). (ENG.). 64p. (J). (gr. 2-5). 16.99 *(978-0-8050-8093-3(7),* Holt, Henry & Co. Bks. For Young Readers) Holt, Henry & Co.
De Villiers Family Staff. Purple Spot Sickness. De Villiers Family Staff. 2006. (Sprout Growing with God Ser.). (ENG.). 40p. (J). (gr. -1-3). 9.99 *(978-1-4000-7196-8(8),* WaterBrook Pr.) Doubleday Religious Publishing Group, The.
De Vries, Bruce. What Do You See, Mrs Night Heron? Hasselbring, Janet. 2010. 32p. pap. 12.95 *(978-1-936343-03-4(7))* Peppertree Pr., The.
de Vries, Marloes. That 17th Hat. Eissler, Trevor. 2012. 32p. (J). 20.00 *(978-0-9835558-1-0(8))* June Bks., LLC.
De Weerd, Kelsey. I Can't Believe You Said That! Cook, Julia. 2014. 32p. (J). pap. 10.95 *(978-1-934490-67-9(9))* Boys Town Pr.
—I Just Want to Do It My Way! Cook, Julia. 2013. 32p. (J). 10.95 *(978-1-934490-43-3(1))* Boys Town Pr.
—Thanks for the Feedback, I Think. Cook, Julia. 2013. (J). pap. 10.95 *(978-1-934490-49-5(0))* Boys Town Pr.
De Weerd, Kelsey, jt. illus. see Cook, Julia.
Deach, Carol. My Grandma Died: Child's Story about Death & Loss. Britain, Lory. 2003. (ENG.). 32p. (J). (gr. -1-3). pap. 7.95 *(978-1-884734-26-7(X))* Parenting Pr., Inc.
Deacon, Alexis. Jim's Lion. Hoban, Russell. 2014. (ENG.). 64p. (J). (gr. 1-4). 15.99 *(978-0-7636-6517-3(7))* Candlewick Pr.
—Soonchild. Hoban, Russell. 2012. (ENG.). 144p. (J). (gr. 9). 15.99 *(978-0-7636-5920-2(7))* Candlewick Pr.
Deal, David, photos by. Best Behavior: A Celebration of Good Manners for Our African-American Children. Henry, Debra. 2004. (J). per. 15.00 *(978-0-9758611-0-3(7))* Black Society Pages, Inc.
Deal, L. Kate. The Boxcar Children. collector's ed. 2009. (ENG.). 168p. (J). (gr. 2-5). 18.99 *(978-0-8075-0850-3(0))* Whitman, Albert & Co.
Dean, David. Barefoot Books World Atlas. Crane, Nick. 2011. (ENG.). 56p. (J). 19.99 *(978-1-84686-333-2(3))* Barefoot Bks., Inc.
—Kentucky Thriller. St John, Lauren & St. John, Lauren. 2014. (Jóvenes Lectores. Los Misterios de Laura Ser.). (SPA.). 248p. (J). (gr. 4-7). pap. 8.95 *(978-84-8343-271-6(4),* Bambu, Editorial) Combel Editorial, S.A. ESP. Dist: Independent Pubs. Group.
—The Reluctant Rajput. Moverley, Richard. 2005. (Yellow Go Bananas Ser.). (ENG.). 48p. (J). (gr. 3-4). *(978-0-7787-2745-3(9));* lib. bdg. *(978-0-7787-2723-1(8))* Crabtree Publishing Co.
—Saying Grace: Blessings for the Family Table. McElwain, Sarah & O'Neal, John H. McElwain, Sarah, ed. 2003. (ENG.). 120p. (gr. 8-17). 14.95 *(978-0-8118-4025-5(5))* Chronicle Bks. LLC.
Dean, James. I Love My White Shoes. Litwin, Eric. 2010. (Pete the Cat Ser.). 40p. (J). (gr. -1-3). (ENG.). 17.99 *(978-0-06-190622-0(0));* lib. bdg. 17.89 *(978-0-06-190623-7(9))* HarperCollins Pubs.
—I Love My White Shoes. 2010. (Pete the Cat Ser.). (J). lib. bdg. *(978-0-06-107623-7(6))* HarperCollins Pubs.
—Mighty Dads. Holub, Joan. 2014. (ENG.). 40p. (J). (gr. -1-k). 16.99 *(978-0-545-60968-5(2),* Scholastic Pr.) Scholastic, Inc.
—Pete the Cat & His Four Groovy Buttons. Litwin, Eric. 2012. (Pete the Cat Ser.). 40p. (J). (gr. -1-2). (ENG.). 17.99 *(978-0-06-211058-9(6));* lib. bdg. 17.89 *(978-0-06-211059-6(4))* HarperCollins Pubs.
—Pete the Cat Saves Christmas. Litwin, Eric. (Pete the Cat Ser.). 40p. (J). (gr. -1-3). 2014. (ENG.). 17.99 *(978-0-06-211062-6(4));* 2012. lib. bdg. 18.89 *(978-0-06-211063-3(2))* HarperCollins Pubs.
—Rocking in My School Shoes. Litwin, Eric. 2011. (Pete the Cat Ser.). 40p. (J). (gr. -1-3). (ENG.). 17.99 *(978-0-06-191024-1(4));* lib. bdg. 17.89 *(978-0-06-191025-8(2))* HarperCollins Pubs.
—Valentine's Day Is Cool. 2013. (Pete the Cat Ser.). (ENG.). 24p. (J). (gr. -1-3). 9.99 *(978-0-06-219865-5(3),* HarperFestival) HarperCollins Pubs.
Dean, James. Cavecat Pete. Dean, James. 2015. (Pete the Cat Ser.). (ENG.). 24p. (J). (gr. -1-3). pap. 4.99 *(978-0-06-219863-1(7),* HarperFestival) HarperCollins Pubs.
—Construction Destruction. Dean, James. 2015. (Pete the Cat Ser.). (ENG.). 24p. (J). (gr. -1-3). pap. 4.99 *(978-0-06-219861-7(0),* HarperFestival) HarperCollins Pubs.
—The First Thanksgiving. Dean, James. Dean, Kimberly. 2013. (Pete the Cat Ser.). (ENG.). 16p. (J). (gr. -1-3). 6.99 *(978-0-06-219869-3(6),* HarperFestival) HarperCollins Pubs.
Dean, James. Five Little Pumpkins. Dean, James. 2015. (Pete the Cat Ser.). (ENG.). 32p. (J). (gr. -1-3). 9.99 ***(978-0-06-230418-6(6))*** HarperCollins Pubs.
Dean, James. Old MacDonald Had a Farm. Dean, James. 2014. (Pete the Cat Ser.). (ENG.). 32p. (J). (gr. -1-3). 9.99 *(978-0-06-219873-0(4))* HarperCollins Pubs.
—A Pet for Pete. Dean, James. Dean, Kimberly. 2014. (My First I Can Read Ser.). (ENG.). 32p. (J). (gr. -1-3). pap. 3.99 *(978-0-06-230379-0(1))* HarperCollins Pubs.
—Pete at the Beach. Dean, James. 2013. (My First I Can Read Ser.). (ENG.). 32p. (J). (gr. -1-3). 16.99 *(978-0-06-211073-2(X));* pap. 3.99 *(978-0-06-211072-5(1))* HarperCollins Pubs.
—Pete the Cat - Rock On, Mom & Dad! Dean, James. 2015. (Pete the Cat Ser.). (ENG.). 24p. (J). (gr. -1-3). pap. 6.99 *(978-0-06-230408-7(9),* HarperFestival) HarperCollins Pubs.
—Pete the Cat & His Magic Sunglasses. Dean, James. Dean, Kimberly. 2013. (Pete the Cat Ser.). 40p. (J). (gr. -1-3). (ENG.). 17.99 *(978-0-06-227556-1(9));* lib. bdg. 18.89 *(978-0-06-227557-8(7))* HarperCollins Pubs.
—Pete the Cat & the Bad Banana. Dean, James. 2014. (My First I Can Read Ser.). (ENG.). 32p. (J). (gr. -1-3). pap. 3.99 *(978-0-06-230382-0(1))* HarperCollins Pubs.
Dean, James. Pete the Cat & the Bedtime Blues. Dean, James. Dean, Kimberly. 2015. (Pete the Cat Ser.). (ENG.). 40p. (J). (gr. -1-3). 17.99 ***(978-0-06-230430-8(5))*** HarperCollins Pubs.
Dean, James. Pete the Cat & the New Guy. Dean, James. Dean, Kimberly. 2014. (Pete the Cat Ser.). (ENG.). 40p. (J). (gr. -1-3). 17.99 *(978-0-06-227560-8(7));* lib. bdg. 18.89 *(978-0-06-227561-5(5))* HarperCollins Pubs.
Dean, James. Pete the Cat's Big Doodle & Draw Book. Dean, James. 2015. (Pete the Cat Ser.). (ENG.). 128p. (J). (gr. -1-3). pap. 12.99 ***(978-0-06-230442-1(9),*** HarperFestival) HarperCollins Pubs.
Dean, James. Pete the Cat's Groovy Guide to Life. Dean, James. Dean, Kimberly. 2015. (Pete the Cat Ser.). (ENG.). 48p. (J). (gr. -1-3). 12.99 *(978-0-06-235135-7(4))* HarperCollins Pubs.
—Pete the Cat's Super Cool Reading Collection. Dean, James. 2014. (My First I Can Read Ser.). (ENG.). 32p. (J). (gr. -1-3). pap. 16.99 *(978-0-06-230424-7(0))* HarperCollins Pubs.
—Pete the Cat's Train Trip. Dean, James. 2015. (My First I Can Read Ser.). (ENG.). 32p. (J). (gr. -1-3). pap. 3.99 *(978-0-06-230385-1(6))* HarperCollins Pubs.
—Pete's Big Lunch. Dean, James. 2013. (My First I Can Read Ser.). (ENG.). 32p. (J). (gr. -1-3). 16.99 *(978-0-06-211070-1(5))* HarperCollins Pubs.
—Play Ball! Dean, James. 2013. (My First I Can Read Ser.). (ENG.). 32p. (J). (gr. -1-3). 16.99 *(978-0-06-211067-1(5))* HarperCollins Pubs.
Dean, James. Rock on, Mom & Dad! Dean, James. 2015. (Pete the Cat (HarperCollins) Ser.). lib. bdg. 17.20 ***(978-0-606-36490-4(0))*** Turtleback Bks.
Dean, James. Sing-Along Story Collection. Dean, James. 2014. (Pete the Cat Ser.). (ENG.). 96p. (J). (gr. -1-3). 19.99 *(978-0-06-230420-9(8))* HarperCollins Pubs.
—Twinkle, Twinkle, Little Star. Dean, James. 2014. (Pete the Cat Ser.). (ENG.). 32p. (J). (gr. -1-3). 9.99 *(978-0-06-230416-2(X))* HarperCollins Pubs.
—The Wheels on the Bus. Dean, James. 2013. (Pete the Cat Ser.). (ENG.). 32p. (J). (gr. -1-3). 9.99 *(978-0-06-219871-6(8))* HarperCollins Pubs.
Dean, James & Dean, Kimberly. Big Easter Adventure. Dean, James & Dean, Kimberly. 2014. (Pete the Cat Ser.). (ENG.). 24p. (J). (gr. -1-3). 9.99 *(978-0-06-219867-9(X))* HarperCollins Pubs.
—Too Cool for School. Dean, James & Dean, Kimberly. 2014. (My First I Can Read Ser.). (ENG.). 32p. (J). (gr. -1-3). 16.99 *(978-0-06-211076-3(4));* pap. 3.99 *(978-0-06-211075-6(6))* HarperCollins Pubs.
Dean, Karen. Kitty Kate's Tea Party. Dean, Karen. 2009. (ENG.). 48p. (J). *(978-1-934363-30-0(8))* Zoe Life Publishing.
Dean, Kimberly, jt. illus. see Dean, James.
Dean Kleven Studios & Finley, Shawn. Tonka Rescue Trucks! Joyce, Bridget & Furman, Eric. 2007. (Fold & Go Vehicles Ser.). 15.98 *(978-1-4127-2981-9(5))* Publications International, Ltd.
Dean, Venetia, jt. illus. see Scott, Kimberly.
Dean, Venitia. Forces & Motion Through Infographics. Rowell, Rebecca. 2013. (Super Science Infographics Ser.). (ENG.). 32p. (gr. 3-5). pap. 8.95 *(978-1-4677-1591-1(3));* lib. bdg. 26.60 *(978-1-4677-1291-0(4),* Lerner Pubns.) Lerner Publishing Group.
—Two Wise Children. Graves, Robert. 2014. (Classic Stories Ser.). (ENG.). 24p. (J). (gr. 3-6). 28.50 *(978-1-62323-624-3(X),* 206392) Child's World, Inc., The.
—Weather & Climate Through Infographics. Rowell, Rebecca. 2013. (Super Science Infographics Ser.). (ENG.). 32p. (gr. 3-5). pap. 8.95 *(978-1-4677-1595-9(6));* lib. bdg. 26.60 *(978-1-4677-1292-7(2),* Lerner Pubns.) Lerner Publishing Group.
DeAnguelo Hout, Sarah. Leap & Twirl. Anderson, Steven. 2012. 34p. (J). pap. 10.99 *(978-0-692-01667-1(8))* BalletMet Dance Centre.
Deas, Mike. Adventures at Camp Lots-O-Fun, 1 vol. Helmer, Marilyn. 2010. (Orca Echoes Ser.). (ENG.). 64p. (J). (gr. 2-3). pap. 6.95 *(978-1-55469-347-4(0))* Orca Bk. Pubs. USA.
—Dalen & Gole: Scandal in Port Angus, 1 vol. 2011. (ENG.). 128p. (J). (gr. 3-6). pap. 9.95 *(978-1-55469-800-4(6))* Orca Bk. Pubs. USA.
—Food Fight, 1 vol. O'Donnell, Liam. 2010. (Graphic Guides). (ENG.). 64p. (J). (gr. 3-7). pap. 9.95 *(978-1-55469-067-1(6))* Orca Bk. Pubs. USA.
—The Great Garage Sale, 1 vol. Helmer, Marilyn. 2013. (Orca Echoes Ser.). (ENG.). 64p. (J). (gr. 2-3). pap. 6.95 *(978-1-4598-0060-1(5))* Orca Bk. Pubs. USA.
—I, Witness, 1 vol. McClintock, Norah. 2012. (ENG.). 144p. (YA). (gr. 8-12). pap. 16.95 *(978-1-55469-789-2(1))* Orca Bk. Pubs. USA.
—Media Meltdown: A Graphic Guide Adventure, 1 vol. O'Donnell, Liam. 2009. (Graphic Guides). (ENG.). 64p. (J). (gr. 3-7). pap. 9.95 *(978-1-55469-065-7(X))* Orca Bk. Pubs. USA.
—Power Play, 1 vol. O'Donnell, Liam. 2011. (Graphic Guides). (ENG.). 64p. (J). (gr. 3-7). pap. 9.95 *(978-1-55469-069-5(2))* Orca Bk. Pubs. USA.
—Ramp Rats: A Graphic Guide Adventure, 1 vol. O'Donnell, Liam. 2008. (Graphic Guides). (ENG.). 64p. (J). (gr. 3-7). pap. 9.95 *(978-1-55143-880-1(1))* Orca Bk. Pubs. USA.
—Soccer Sabotage: A Graphic Guide Adventure, 1 vol. O'Donnell, Liam. 2009. (Graphic Guides). (ENG.). 64p. (J). (gr. 3-7). pap. 9.95 *(978-1-55143-884-9(4))* Orca Bk. Pubs. USA.
—Tank & Fizz: the Case of the Slime Stampede, 1 vol. O'Donnell, Liam. 2015. (Tank & Fizz Ser.: 1). (ENG.). 152p. (J). (gr. 3-6). pap. 9.95 *(978-1-4598-0810-2(X))* Orca Bk. Pubs. USA.
—Wild Ride: A Graphic Guide Adventure, 1 vol. O'Donnell, Liam. 2007. (Graphic Guides). (ENG.). 64p. (J). (gr. 3-7). pap. 9.95 *(978-1-55143-756-9(2))* Orca Bk. Pubs. USA.
Deas, Rich. 10 Fat Turkeys. Johnston, Tony. 2009. (ENG.). 28p. (J). (gr. -1-k). bds. 6.99 *(978-0-545-16469-6(9),* Cartwheel Bks.) Scholastic, Inc.
Deas, Richard F. 10 Fat Turkeys. Johnston, Tony. 2004. (ENG.). 32p. (J). (gr. -1-k). pap. 3.99 *(978-0-439-45948-8(6),* Cartwheel Bks.) Scholastic, Inc.
Deas, Robert. Macbeth. Shakespeare, William. 2008. (ENG.). 208p. (YA). (gr. 7-11). pap. 12.95 *(978-0-8109-7073-1(2),* Amulet Bks.) Abrams.
Deasey, Kevin, jt. illus. see Rice, Kaleb.
Debi Rogers. Kaylea Grows Up: Mommy & Me Days. Summer Rogers Martin. 2009. 20p. pap. 10.99 *(978-1-4389-5908-5(7))* AuthorHouse.
Debon, Nicolas. Dawn Watch, 1 vol. Pendziwol, Jean E. 2004. (ENG.). 32p. (J). 15.95 *(978-0-88899-512-4(1))* Groundwood Bks. CAN. Dist: Perseus-PGW.
—Every Single Night, 1 vol. DeMers, Dominique & Demers, Dominique. 2006. (ENG.). 40p. (J). (gr. -1-2). 17.95 *(978-0-88899-699-2(3))* Groundwood Bks. CAN. Dist: Perseus-PGW.
—Florence Nightingale. Zemlicka, Shannon. 2003. (On My Own Biography Ser.). (ENG.). 48p. (gr. 2-4). pap. 6.95 *(978-0-87614-102-1(5),* Carolrhoda Bks.) Lerner Publishing Group.
—Liberty or Death: A Story about Patrick Henry. McPherson, Stephanie Sammartino. 2003. (Creative Minds Biographies Ser.). (ENG.). 64p. (gr. 4-8). 22.60 *(978-1-57505-178-9(8));* pap. 8.95 *(978-0-87614-930-0(1))* Lerner Publishing Group. (Carolrhoda Bks.)
—The Martial Arts Book. Scandiffio, Laura. 2010. (ENG.). 64p. (J). (gr. 6-18). pap. 14.95 *(978-1-55037-776-7(0),* 9781550377767) Annick Pr., Ltd. CAN. Dist: Firefly Bks., Ltd.
—Out of the Deeps, 1 vol. Carter, Anne Laurel. 2008. (ENG.). 32p. (J). (gr. -1-3). 19.95 *(978-1-55143-559-6(4))* Orca Bk. Pubs. USA.
—The Red Sash. Pendziwol, Jean E. 2005. (ENG.). 40p. (J). (gr. k-3). 18.95 *(978-0-88899-589-6(X))* Groundwood Bks. CAN. Dist: Perseus-PGW.
—Thing-Thing. Fagan, Cary. 2008. (ENG.). 32p. (J). (gr. -1-1). 18.95 *(978-0-88776-839-2(3),* Tundra Bks.) Tundra Bks. CAN. Dist: Penguin Random Hse., LLC.
—Timmerman Was Here. Sydor, Colleen. 2009. (ENG.). 32p. (J). (gr. -1-1). 19.95 *(978-0-88776-890-3(3),* Tundra Bks.) Tundra Bks. CAN. Dist: Penguin Random Hse., LLC.
—The Warlord's Alarm, 1 vol. Pilegard, Virginia Walton. 2006. (Warlord's Ser.). (ENG.). 32p. (J). (gr. k-3). 16.99 *(978-1-58980-378-7(7))* Pelican Publishing Co., Inc.
—The Warlord's Kites, 1 vol. Pilegard, Virginia Walton. 2004. (Warlord's Ser.). (ENG.). 32p. (J). (gr. k-3). 16.99 *(978-1-58980-180-6(6))* Pelican Publishing Co., Inc.
—The Warlord's Messengers, 1 vol. Pilegard, Virginia Walton. 2005. (Warlord's Ser.). (ENG.). 32p. (J). (gr. k-3). 16.99 *(978-1-58980-271-1(3))* Pelican Publishing Co., Inc.

D

—The Warlord's Puppeteers, 1 vol. Pilegard, Virginia Walton. 2003. (Warlord's Ser.: 4). (ENG.). 32p. (J). (gr. k-3). 16.99 *(978-1-58980-077-9(X))* Pelican Publishing Co., Inc.
Deborah, Allwright. The Best Pet Ever. Victoria, Roberts. 2010. 32p. (J). (gr. -1-2). 15.95 *(978-1-58925-089-5(3))* Tiger Tales.
Deborah, Brown Armes. Grandpa Still Remembers: Life Changing Stories for Kids of All Ages from a Missionary Kid in Africa. Brown, Paul Henry. 2013. 162p. pap. 14.95 *(978-1-61153-027-8(X))* Light Messages Publishing.
DeBroech, Sarah. Beach Ball's Return. Van Tassel, Mary A. 2011. 28p. pap. 24.95 *(978-1-4512-2124-4(X))* America Star Bks.
—In Your Heart. Reyes, Cameron. 2011. 28p. pap. 24.95 *(978-1-4560-1009-6(3))* America Star Bks.
DeBroeck, Sarah. Abc People of the Bible. Collins, Chris. 2011. 44p. pap. 24.95 *(978-1-4560-2820-6(0))* America Star Bks.
—Jacub's Journey. Bailey, Leslie J. 2011. 28p. pap. 24.95 *(978-1-4560-9951-0(5))* America Star Bks.
—Moses P Rose Has Broken His Nose. Saupé, Rick. 2012. 28p. pap. 24.95 *(978-1-4626-0547-7(8))* America Star Bks.
—Small & Sassy. Atwater, Jillene. 2011. 36p. pap. 24.95 *(978-1-4489-8374-2(6))* America Star Bks.
—Thomas & the Toad King. Cardoso, Kelly. 2011. 28p. pap. 24.95 *(978-1-4560-0956-4(7))* America Star Bks.
—Working As a Team: Down to the End of the Road & Back. Lynch, Lauren Boehm. 2011. 28p. pap. 24.95 *(978-1-4560-0986-1(9))* America Star Bks.
—The Yellow Butterfly. Lynch, Lauren Boehm. 2011. 28p. pap. 24.95 *(978-1-4560-0982-3(6))* America Star Bks.
Decaire, Camela. Paper Doll Fashion Fun: Make paper doll clothes with the supplies Inside! Anton, Carrie, ed. 2007. 54p. (J). (gr. 4-7). pap. 17.95 *(978-1-59369-284-1(6))* American Girl Publishing, Inc.
DeCarlo, Mike & Tanguay, David D. Catch Catwoman! Wrecks, Billy. 2013. (Step into Reading Ser.). (ENG.). 32p. (J). (gr. -1-1). 3.99 *(978-0-449-81616-5(8)*, Random Hse. Bks. for Young Readers) Random Hse. Children's Bks.
DeCarlo, Mike, jt. illus. see Doescher, Erik.
Decedue, Julie. Frankie Goes to Fenway: The Tale of the Faithful, Red Sox-Loving Mouse. Clark, Seneca & Giardi, Sandy. 2008. 56p. (J). 18.95 *(978-0-9767276-3-7(3))* Three Bean Pr.
—Lily & the Imaginary Zoo, 1. Clark, Seneca & Giardi, Sandy. 2005. (ENG.). 30p. (J). 15.95 *(978-0-9767276-1-3(7))* Three Bean Pr.
—The Yellowest Yellow Lab. Clark, Seneca & Giardi, Sandy. 2005. 30p. (J). 11.95 *(978-0-9767276-2-0(5))* Three Bean Pr.
Decenciere, Isabelle. The Wrinkled-at-the Knees Elephant & Other Tuneful Tales. Binder, Betsy. 2008. 28p. (J). pap. 19.95 incl. audio compact disk *(978-0-615-26652-7(5))* Velvet Pony Pr.
Decis, Anne. Blanca Nieve y los Siete Gigantones. Canetti, Yanitzia & Yanitzia, Canetti. 2009. (SPA.). 32p. (J). (gr. k-2). 12.99 *(978-84-241-7061-5(X))* Everest Editora ESP. Dist: Lectorum Pubns., Inc.
—Colores que se Aman. Abril, Paco & Francisco, Abril Berán. 2004.Tr. of Colors that Love Each Other. (SPA.). 32p. (J). (gr. 2-3). 14.99 *(978-84-241-7989-2(7))* Everest Editora ESP. Dist: Lectorum Pubns., Inc.
—Cuentame un Cuento, Vol. 5. Cornelles, Salvador. 2003. (SPA.). 96p. *(978-84-480-1674-6(2)*, TM30559) Timun Mas, Editorial S.A. ESP. Dist: Lectorum Pubns., Inc.
—Me Duele la Lengua. Mainé, Margarita. 3rd ed. (SPA.). 32p. (J). (gr. 1-3). *(978-84-236-4016-4(7))* Edebé ESP. Dist: Lectorum Pubns., Inc.
Decker, C. B. Alley Oops. Levy, Janice. 2005. (ENG.). 32p. (J). (gr. k-3). 17.95 *(978-0-9729225-4-8(7))* Flashlight Pr.
—Farmer Kobi's Hanukkah Match. Rostoker-Gruber, Karen & Isaacs, Ronald H. 2015. (J). pap. *(978-0-87441-924-5(7))*; ***(978-1-68115-501-2(X))*** Behrman Hse., Inc.
Decker, Cynthia. Stories of Dinosaurs. Punter, Russell. 2006. (Usborne Young Reading: Series One Ser.). 48p. (J). (gr. 2). lib. bdg. 13.99 *(978-1-58086-940-9(8))*; per. 5.99 *(978-0-7945-1363-4(8))* EDC Publishing. (Usborne).
Decker, Jacqueline. A Kittery Kayaker. Bull, Webster. 2007. (Little Limericks Ser.). (ENG.). 24p. (J). (gr. k-3). 12.95 *(978-1-933212-36-4(5)*, Commonwealth Editions) Applewood Bks.
Decker, Tim. The Punk Ethic. Decker, Tim. 2012. (ENG.). 188p. (YA). 18.95 *(978-0-61898-120-5(7))*; pap. 9.95 *(978-1-60898-121-2(5))* namelos llc.
DeCristoforo, Jennifer. Lucky Bamboo Book of Crafts: Over 100 Projects & Ideas Celebrating Chinese Culture, vols. 2, vol. 101. DeCristoforo, Jennifer. 2013. (ENG & CHI.). 136p. 26.99 *(978-0-9884648-0-3(2))* Lucky Bamboo Crafts.
Dedering, Victoria. Snuckle-Bee & Snuckle-Bun: The Bee-Attitudes. Written By Susan J. Perry; Illustrated B. 2011. 32p. pap. 24.95 *(978-1-4560-8787-6(8))* America Star Bks.
Dee, Kati. My Secret Best Friend. Rogers-Busboom, Kimberly. 2009. 24p. lib. bdg. 16.99 *(978-0-9823145-2-4(3))* Dirks Publishing, LLC.
Deen, David. Monsters: The Hunt & the Capture. Weiss, Bobbi & Weiss, David. 2008. (ENG.). 24p. (J). (gr. 2-17). 19.99 *(978-1-58476-727-5(8))* Innovative Kids.
Dees, Leighanne. Flying Feet: A Story of Irish Dance. Burgard, Anna Marlis. 2006. 31p. (J). (gr. 4-8). 16.00 *(978-1-4223-5255-7(2))* DIANE Publishing Co.
DeFazio, Deborah. Peek-a-Boo Moon. Crick, Stephanie. 2004. 16p. (J). per. 9.95 *(978-0-9746397-3-4(7))* Pinefield Publishing.
DeFelice, Bonnie. The Adventures of Zsa-Zsa & Gabby-Lou: Dangers at the Seashore. DeFelice, Jennie & Landry, Jennifer. 2005. (J). lib. bdg. 19.95 *(978-0-9767072-0-2(9))* Two Dogz.
Defelice, Bonnie. The Adventures of Zsa Zsa & Gabby Lou in New Orleans. Defelice, Jennie & Landry, Jennifer. 2006. (J). lib. bdg. 21.95 *(978-0-9767072-1-9(7))* Two Dogz.
Defenbaugh, David. Alexander, It's Time for Bed! Lluch, Alex A. 2006. (ENG.). 30p. (J). (gr. -1-3). 14.95 *(978-1-887169-59-2(8))* WS Publishing.
—Alphabet: I Like to Learn the ABCs! Lluch, Alex A. 2014. (ENG.). 30p. (J). bds. 8.95 *(978-1-61351-077-3(2))* WS Publishing.
—Animal Alphabet: Slide & Seek the ABCs. Lluch, Alex A. 2013. (ENG.). 13p. (J). (-k). bds. 12.99 *(978-1-61351-041-4(1))* WS Publishing.
—Big Bugs, Small Bugs: If You Could Be a Bug, Which Bug Would You Be? Lluch, Alex. 2005. (ENG.). 28p. (J). (gr. -1-k). bds. 7.95 *(978-1-887169-62-2(8))* WS Publishing.
—Do I Look Good in Color? Lluch, Alex. 2006. (ENG.). (J). (gr. -1-k). 32p. 14.95 *(978-1-887169-63-9(6))*; 30p. bds. 7.95 *(978-1-887169-57-8(1))* WS Publishing.
—Numbers - I Like to Count from 1 to 10! Lluch, Alex A. 2014. (ENG.). 30p. (J). bds. 8.95 *(978-1-61351-078-0(0))* WS Publishing.
—Trace & Learn the ABCs: And Have Fun Playing Peek-A-Boo Who? Lluch, Alex A. 2014. (ENG.). 26p. (J). bds. 8.95 *(978-1-61351-082-7(9))* WS Publishing.
Deffenbaugh, Dena. Alice's ABC's: Version 2. Reid, Demetra. 2010. 66p. pap. 14.00 *(978-0-9802275-8-1(5))* Candalyse Publishing.
Degen, Bruce. At the Waterworks. Cole, Joanna. 2004. (Magic School Bus Ser.). (ENG.). 40p. (J). (gr. -1-3). pap. 6.99 *(978-0-590-40360-3(5))* Scholastic, Inc.
—Climb the Family Tree, Jesse Bear! Carlstrom, Nancy White. 2004. (ENG.). 32p. (J). (gr. -1-1). 17.99 *(978-0-689-80701-5(5)*, Simon & Schuster Bks. For Young Readers) Simon & Schuster Bks. For Young Readers.
—Guess Who's Coming, Jesse Bear. Carlstrom, Nancy White. 2012. (ENG.). 32p. (J). (gr. -1-1). 16.99 *(978-0-689-84820-9(X)*, Simon & Schuster/Paula Wiseman Bks.) Simon & Schuster/Paula Wiseman Bks.
—If You Were a Writer. Nixon, Joan Lowery. 2014. 32p. pap. 7.00 *(978-1-61003-353-4(1))* Center for the Collaborative Classroom.
—Inside the Human Body. Cole, Joanna. 2011. (Magic School Bus Ser.). (ENG.). (J). (gr. 2-5). 9.99 *(978-0-545-24083-3(2))*; pap. 18.99 incl. audio compact disk *(978-0-545-24086-4(7))* Scholastic, Inc.
—Jazzmatazz! Calmenson, Stephanie. 2008. 32p. (J). (gr. -1). lib. bdg. 17.89 *(978-0-06-077290-1(5))*; (ENG.). 16.99 *(978-0-06-077289-5(1))* HarperCollins Pubs.
—Jesse Bear, What Will You Wear? Carlstrom, Nancy White. 2nd ed. 2005. (Stories to Go! Ser.). (ENG.). 32p. (J). (gr. -1-3). 4.99 *(978-1-4169-0834-0(X)*, Simon & Schuster/Paula Wiseman Bks.) Simon & Schuster/Paula Wiseman Bks.
—The Josefina Story Quilt. Coerr, Eleanor. 2003. (I Can Read Book 3 Ser.). (ENG.). 64p. (J). (gr. k-3). pap. 3.99 *(978-0-06-444129-2(6))* HarperCollins Pubs.
—Lost in the Solar System. Cole, Joanna. 2010. (Magic School Bus Ser.). (ENG.). (J). (gr. -1-3). 18.95 *(978-0-545-22337-9(7))* Scholastic, Inc.
—The Magic School Bus & the Climate Challenge. Cole, Joanna. (Magic School Bus Ser.). (ENG.). (J). (gr. 2-5). 2014. 40p. 6.99 *(978-0-545-65599-6(4))*; 2010. 48p. 16.99 *(978-0-590-10826-3(3)*, Scholastic Pr.) Scholastic, Inc.
—Magic School Bus: Dinosaur Rescue. Simon, Jenne & Cole, Joanna. 2013. (ENG.). 16p. (J). (gr. -1-3). 6.99 *(978-0-545-49754-1(X))* Math Solutions.
—The Magic School Bus Gets Baked in a Cake: A Book about Kitchen Chemistry. Beech, Linda Ward. Duchesne, Lucie, tr. from ENG. (Magic School Bus Ser.). (FRE.). 32p. (J). (gr. 1-4). pap. 5.99 *(978-0-590-24660-6(7))* Scholastic, Inc.
Degen, Bruce. Nate Likes to Skate. 2016. (J). ***(978-0-8234-3456-5(7))*** Holiday Hse., Inc.
Degen, Bruce. On the Ocean Floor. Cole, Joanna. 2010. (Magic School Bus Ser.). (ENG.). (J). (gr. 2-5). 9.99 *(978-0-545-22751-3(8))* Scholastic, Inc.
—The Science Fair Expedition. Cole, Joanna. 2006. (Magic School Bus Ser.). (ENG.). 56p. (J). (gr. 2-5). 16.99 *(978-0-590-10824-9(7)*, Scholastic) Scholastic, Inc.
—The Time of the Dinosaurs. (Magic School Bus Ser.). (FRE.). (J). (gr. 1-4). pap. 6.99 *(978-0-590-24641-5(0))* Scholastic, Inc.
—What a Scare, Jesse Bear. Carlstrom, Nancy White. 2012. (ENG.). 32p. (J). (gr. -1-1). 16.99 *(978-0-689-85190-2(1)*, Simon & Schuster/Paula Wiseman Bks.) Simon & Schuster/Paula Wiseman Bks.
—Where Is Christmas, Jesse Bear? Carlstrom, Nancy White. 2003. (ENG.). 32p. (J). (gr. -1-1). 13.99 *(978-0-689-86233-5(4)*, Simon & Schuster/Paula Wiseman Bks.) Simon & Schuster/Paula Wiseman Bks.
Degen, Bruce. I Gotta Draw. Degen, Bruce. 2012. (ENG.). 40p. (J). (gr. k-4). 16.99 *(978-0-06-028417-6(X))* HarperCollins Pubs.
—I Said, Bed! Degen, Bruce. (I Like to Read(r) Ser.). (ENG.). (J). (gr. -1-3). 2015. 24p. 6.99 *(978-0-8234-3311-7(0))*; 2014. 32p. 14.95 *(978-0-8234-2938-7(5))* Holiday Hse., Inc.
—Jamberry. Degen, Bruce. 25th enl. anniv. ed. 2008. (I Can Read Bks.). (ENG.). 32p. (J). (gr. -1-3). pap. 7.99 *(978-0-06-443068-5(5))* HarperCollins Pubs.
—Snow Joke. Degen, Bruce. 2014. (ENG.). 24p. (J). (gr. -1-3). 14.95 *(978-0-8234-3065-9(0))* Holiday Hse., Inc.
Degen, Bruce & Bracken, Carolyn. The Human Body. Cole, Joanna et al. 2014. (Magic School Bus Presents Ser.). (ENG.). 32p. (J). (gr. 1-3). pap. 6.99 *(978-0-545-68364-7(5))* Scholastic, Inc.
—Magic School Bus Presents: Dinosaurs: A Nonfiction Companion to the Original Magic School Bus Series. Cole, Joanna & Jackson, Tom. 2014. (Magic School Bus Presents Ser.). (ENG.). 32p. (J). (gr. 1-3). pap. 6.99 *(978-0-545-68583-2(4)*, Scholastic Paperbacks) Scholastic, Inc.
—Magic School Bus Presents: Insects: A Nonfiction Companion to the Original Magic School Bus Series. Cole, Joanna & Jackson, Tom. 2014. (Magic School Bus Presents Ser.). (ENG.). 32p. (J). (gr. 1-3). pap. 6.99 *(978-0-545-68587-0(7)*, Scholastic Paperbacks) Scholastic, Inc.
—Our Solar System. Cole, Joanna & Jackson, Tom. 2014. (Magic School Bus Presents Ser.). (ENG.). 32p. (J). (gr. 1-3). pap. 6.99 *(978-0-545-68365-4(3)*, Scholastic Paperbacks) Scholastic, Inc.
—Planet Earth. Cole, Joanna & Jackson, Tom. 2014. (Magic School Bus Presents Ser.). (ENG.). 32p. (J). (gr. 1-3). pap. 6.99 *(978-0-545-68012-7(3))* Scholastic, Inc.
—Polar Animals. Cole, Joanna & O'Brien, Cynthia. 2014. (Magic School Bus Presents Ser.). (ENG.). 32p. (J). (gr. 1-3). pap. 6.99 *(978-0-545-68586-3(9)*, Scholastic Paperbacks) Scholastic, Inc.
—The Rainforest. Cole, Joanna & Jackson, Tom. 2014. (Magic School Bus Presents Ser.). (ENG.). 32p. (J). (gr. 1-3). pap. 6.99 *(978-0-545-68585-6(0)*, Scholastic Paperbacks) Scholastic, Inc.
—Sea Creatures. Cole, Joanna & Jackson, Tom. 2014. (Magic School Bus Presents Ser.). (ENG.). 32p. (J). (gr. 1-3). pap. 6.99 *(978-0-545-68366-1(1)*, Scholastic Paperbacks) Scholastic, Inc.
—Volcanoes & Earthquakes. Cole, Joanna & Jackson, Tom. 2014. (Magic School Bus Presents Ser.). (ENG.). 32p. (J). (gr. 1-3). pap. 6.99 *(978-0-545-68584-9(2)*, Scholastic Paperbacks) Scholastic, Inc.
—Wild Weather. Cole, Joanna et al. 2014. (Magic School Bus Presents Ser.). (ENG.). 32p. (J). (gr. 1-3). pap. 6.99 *(978-0-545-68367-8(X))* Scholastic, Inc.
deGennaro, Sue. The Princess & the Packet of Frozen Peas, 1 vol. Wilson, Tony. 2012. (ENG.). 32p. (J). 16.95 *(978-1-56145-635-2(7))* Peachtree Pubs.
Deghand, Tim, jt. illus. see Feyh, Alexa.
DeGraaf, Rebecca L., jt. photos by see DeGraaf, Rob L.
DeGraaf, Rob L. & DeGraaf, Rebecca L., photos by. Fat Tire Favorites: South Florida off-Road Bicycling. DeGraaf, Rob L. DeGraaf, Rebecca L., ed. 2003. Orig. Title: Guide to South Florida off-Road Bicycling. 111p. per. 12.95 *(978-0-9678385-2-6(5))* DeGraaf Publishing.
DeGrand, David. Nothing Left to Ooze. Kloepfer, John. 2014. (Zombie Chasers Ser.: 5). (ENG.). (J). (gr. 3-7). 240p. pap. 6.99 *(978-0-06-223099-7(9))*; 224p. 16.99 *(978-0-06-223098-0(0))* HarperCollins Pubs.
—The Zombie Chasers - Zombies of the Caribbean. Kloepfer, John. 2014. (Zombie Chasers Ser.: 6). (ENG.). 224p. (J). (gr. 3-7). 16.99 *(978-0-06-229024-3(X))* HarperCollins Pubs.
DeGrand, David. The Zombie Chasers #7: World Zombination. Kloepfer, John. 2015. (Zombie Chasers Ser.: 7). (ENG.). 240p. (J). (gr. 3-7). 16.99 ***(978-0-06-229027-4(4))*** HarperCollins Pubs.
DeGrand, David, jt. illus. see DeGrand, Ned.
DeGrand, Ned & DeGrand, David. Empire State of Slime. Kloepfer, John. 2013. (Zombie Chasers Ser.: 4). (ENG.). 208p. (J). (gr. 3-7). 16.99 *(978-0-06-223095-9(6))* HarperCollins Pubs.
deGroat, Diane. Bug in a Rug. Gilson, Jamie. 2003. (ENG.). 80p. (J). pap. 7.95 *(978-0-618-31670-0(1))* Houghton Mifflin Harcourt Publishing Co.
—Charlie & the Christmas Kitty. Drummond, Ree. 2012. (Charlie the Ranch Dog Ser.). (ENG.). 40p. (J). (gr. -1-3). 17.99 *(978-0-06-199657-3(2))* HarperCollins Pubs.
—Charlie & the New Baby. Drummond, Ree. 2014. (Charlie the Ranch Dog Ser.). (ENG.). 40p. (J). (gr. -1-3). 17.99 *(978-0-06-229750-1(3))* HarperCollins Pubs.
—Charlie Goes to School. Drummond, Ree. 2013. (Charlie the Ranch Dog Ser.). (ENG.). 40p. (J). (gr. -1-3). 17.99 *(978-0-06-221920-6(0))* HarperCollins Pubs.
—Charlie Plays Ball. Drummond, Ree. 2015. (Charlie the Ranch Dog Ser.). (ENG.). 40p. (J). (gr. -1-3). 17.99 *(978-0-06-229752-5(X))* HarperCollins Pubs.
—Charlie the Ranch Dog. Drummond, Ree. 2011. (Charlie the Ranch Dog Ser.). (ENG.). 40p. (J). (gr. -1-3). 16.99 *(978-0-06-199655-9(6))* HarperCollins Pubs.
—Charlie the Ranch Dog: Charlie Goes to the Doctor. Drummond, Ree. 2014. (I Can Read Book 1 Ser.). (ENG.). 32p. (J). (gr. -1-3). pap. 3.99 *(978-0-06-221917-6(0))* HarperCollins Pubs.
—Charlie the Ranch Dog: Charlie's New Friend. Drummond, Ree. 2014. (I Can Read Book 1 Ser.). (ENG.). 32p. (J). (gr. -1-3). 16.99 *(978-0-06-221915-2(4))*; pap. 3.99 *(978-0-06-221914-5(6))* HarperCollins Pubs.
—Charlie the Ranch Dog: Charlie's Snow Day. Drummond, Ree. 2013. (I Can Read Book 1 Ser.). (ENG.). 32p. (J). (gr. -1-3). pap. 3.99 *(978-0-06-221911-4(1))* HarperCollins Pubs.
—Charlie the Ranch Dog: Where's the Bacon? Drummond, Ree. 2013. (I Can Read Book 1 Ser.). (ENG.). 32p. (J). (gr. -1-3). 16.99 *(978-0-06-221909-1(X))*; pap. 3.99 *(978-0-06-221908-4(1))* HarperCollins Pubs.
—Charlie the Ranch Dog - Charlie's Snow Day. Drummond, Ree. 2013. (I Can Read Book 1 Ser.). (ENG.). 32p. (J). (gr. -1-3). 16.99 *(978-0-06-221912-1(X))* HarperCollins Pubs.
—Homer. Rotner, Shelley. 2012. (ENG.). 32p. (J). (gr. -1-3). 15.99 *(978-0-545-33272-9(9)*, Orchard Bks.) Scholastic, Inc.
—Little Rabbit's Loose Tooth. Bate, Lucy. (ENG.). 32p. (J). (gr. k-3). 2010. pap. 6.99 *(978-0-517-55122-6(5)*, Dragonfly Bks.); 2006. reprint ed. 9.95 *(978-0-375-83277-2(7)*, Crown Books For Young Readers) Random Hse. Children's Bks.
deGroat, Diane. Ants in Your Pants, Worms in Your Plants! Gilbert Goes Green. deGroat, Diane. 2011. (Gilbert Ser.). (ENG.). 32p. (J). (gr. -1-3). 16.99 *(978-0-06-176511-7(2))* HarperCollins Pubs.
—April Fool! Watch Out at School! deGroat, Diane. 2009. (Gilbert Ser.). 32p. (J). (gr. -1-3). (ENG.). 17.99 *(978-0-06-143042-8(0))*; lib. bdg. 18.89 *(978-0-06-143043-5(9))* HarperCollins Pubs.
—Brand-New Pencils, Brand-New Books. deGroat, Diane. (ENG.). 32p. (J). (gr. -1-3). 2007. pap. 6.99 *(978-0-06-072616-4(4))*; 2005. 15.99 *(978-0-06-072613-3(X))* HarperCollins Pubs.
—Brand-New Pencils, Brand-New Books. deGroat, Diane. 2007. (Gilbert & Friends Ser.). (J). (gr. -1-3). 14.65 *(978-0-7569-8087-0(9))* Perfection Learning Corp.
—Gilbert & the Lost Tooth. deGroat, Diane. 2012. (I Can Read Book 2 Ser.). (ENG.). 32p. (J). (gr. k-3). 16.99 *(978-0-06-125214-3(X))*; pap. 3.99 *(978-0-06-125216-7(6))* HarperCollins Pubs.
—Gilbert, the Surfer Dude. deGroat, Diane. (I Can Read Book 2 Ser.). (ENG.). 32p. (J). (gr. k-3). 2010. pap. 3.99 *(978-0-06-125213-6(1))*; 2009. 16.99 *(978-0-06-125211-2(5))* HarperCollins Pubs.
—Good Night, Sleep Tight, Don't Let the Bedbugs Bite! deGroat, Diane. 2008. (ENG.). 32p. (J). (gr. -1-3). pap. 6.99 *(978-0-06-134061-1(8))* HarperCollins Pubs.
—Happy Birthday to You, You Belong in a Zoo. deGroat, Diane. 2007. (Gilbert & Friends Ser.). (ENG.). 32p. (J). (gr. -1-3). pap. 6.99 *(978-0-06-001029-4(0))* HarperCollins Pubs.
—Happy Birthday to You, You Belong in a Zoo. deGroat, Diane. 2007. (Gilbert & Friends Ser.). (gr. -1-3). 17.00 *(978-0-7569-8108-2(5))* Perfection Learning Corp.
—Jingle Bells, Homework Smells. deGroat, Diane. 2003. (ENG.). 32p. (J). (gr. -1-3). pap. 6.99 *(978-0-688-17545-0(7))* HarperCollins Pubs.
—Jingle Bells, Homework Smells. deGroat, Diane. 2008. (J). (gr. -1-3). pap. 16.95 incl. audio *(978-1-4301-0419-3(8))* Live Oak Media.
—Last One in Is a Rotten Egg! deGroat, Diane. (Gilbert Ser.). 32p. (J). (gr. -1-3). 2011. (ENG.). pap. 6.99 *(978-0-06-089296-8(X))*; 2007. lib. bdg. 17.89 *(978-0-06-089295-1(1))* HarperCollins Pubs.
—Mother, You're the Best! (But Sister, You're a Pest!) deGroat, Diane. 2008. 32p. (J). (gr. -1-3). 16.99 *(978-0-06-123899-4(6))* HarperCollins Pubs.
—No More Pencils, No More Books, No More Teacher's Dirty Looks! deGroat, Diane. (Gilbert Ser.). 32p. (J). (gr. -1-3). 2009. (ENG.). pap. 6.99 *(978-0-06-079116-2(0))*; 2006. 15.99 *(978-0-06-079114-8(4))*; 2006. lib. bdg. 18.89 *(978-0-06-079115-5(2))* HarperCollins Pubs.
—Trick or Treat, Smell My Feet. deGroat, Diane. 2008. (J). (gr. -1-7). pap. 16.95 incl. audio *(978-1-4301-0425-4(2))* Live Oak Media.
deGroat, Diane & Whipple, Rick. Charlie the Ranch Dog: Stuck in the Mud. Drummond, Ree. 2015. (I Can Read Book 1 Ser.). (ENG.). 32p. (J). (gr. -1-3). pap. 3.99 *(978-0-06-234774-9(8))* HarperCollins Pubs.
—Charlie the Ranch Dog - Stuck in the Mud. Drummond, Ree. 2015. (I Can Read Book 1 Ser.). (ENG.). 32p. (J). (gr. -1-3). 16.99 *(978-0-06-234775-6(6))* HarperCollins Pubs.
Deguchi, Ryusei. Abenobashi: Magical Shopping Arcade, 2 vols. Akahori, Satoru. 2004. Vol. 1. pap. 14.99 *(978-1-59182-790-0(6))*; Vol. 2. 192p. pap. 14.99 *(978-1-59182-791-7(4))* TOKYOPOP, Inc. (Tokyopop Adult).
Dehghanpisheh, Corine. Buddy's Dream. Dehghanpisheh, Corine. 2013. 34p. pap. 12.95 *(978-0-9851930-4-1(2))* Dehghanpisheh, Corine.
—Can We Play Again? Dehghanpisheh, Corine. 2012. 32p. pap. 12.95 *(978-0-9851930-1-0(8))* Dehghanpisheh, Corine.
Deines, Brian. A Bear in War, 1 vol. Innes, Stephanie & Endrulat, Harry. 2013. (ENG.). 40p. (J). (gr. k-4). 17.95 *(978-1-927485-12-5(6))* Pajama Pr. CAN. Dist: Ingram Pub. Services.
—Bear on the Homefront, 1 vol. Innes, Stephanie & Endrulat, Harry. 2014. (ENG.). 32p. (J). (gr. k-3). 17.95 *(978-1-927485-13-2(4))* Pajama Pr. CAN. Dist: Ingram Pub. Services.
—Camping, 1 vol. Hundal, Nancy. 2006. (ENG.). 32p. (J). (gr. -1-3). 7.95 *(978-1-55041-686-2(3)*, 1550416863) Fitzhenry & Whiteside, Ltd. CAN. Dist: Midpoint Trade Bks., Inc.
—En la Granja del Tio Juan, 1 vol. Fitz-Gibbon, Sally. 2005. (SPA.). 32p. (J). 16.95 *(978-1-55041-878-1(5)*, 1550418785) Fitzhenry & Whiteside, Ltd. CAN. Dist: Midpoint Trade Bks., Inc.
—Forever: The Annual Hockey Classic, 1 vol. MacGregor, Roy. 2005. (ENG.). 64p. (J). (gr. 4-7). 22.95 *(978-0-88995-306-2(6))* Red Deer Pr. CAN. Dist: Ingram Pub. Services.
—Fox on the Ice, 1 vol. Highway, Tomson. 2011. (ENG & CRE.). 32p. (J). (gr. -1-1). pap. 12.95 *(978-1-897252-66-6(8))* Fifth Hse. Pubs. CAN. Dist: Ingram Pub. Services.
—Lullaby Berceuse: A Warm Prairie Night. Kaldor, Connie & Campagne, Carmen. 2006. (ENG & FRE.). 40p. (J). (gr. -1-2). 16.95 *(978-2-923163-22-2(2))* La Montagne Secrete CAN. Dist: Independent Pubs. Group.
—Number 21, 1 vol. Hundal, Nancy. 2004. (ENG.). 32p. (J). (gr. 1-3). pap. 9.95 *(978-1-55041-905-4(6)*, 1550419056) Fitzhenry & Whiteside, Ltd. CAN. Dist: Midpoint Trade Bks., Inc.
—On Uncle John's Farm, 1 vol. Fitz-Gibbon, Sally. 2006. (ENG.). 32p. (J). (gr. -1-k). 6.95 *(978-1-55041-886-6(6)*, 1550418866) Fitzhenry & Whiteside, Ltd. CAN. Dist: Midpoint Trade Bks., Inc.
—Prairie Summer, 1 vol. Hundal, Nancy. 2003. (ENG.). 40p. (J). (gr. k-3). pap. 9.95 *(978-1-55041-710-4(X)*, 155041710X) Fitzhenry & Whiteside, Ltd. CAN. Dist: Midpoint Trade Bks., Inc.
Deisadze, Zaur. Andy's Cherry Tree. Haxhia, Miranda. 2007. (POL & ENG.). 32p. (J). pap. 12.95 *(978-1-60195-094-9(2))* International Step by Step Assn.
—To Have a Dog. Brezinova, Ivona. 2007. (POL & ENG.). 32p. (J). pap. 12.95 *(978-1-60195-106-9(X))* International Step by Step Assn.
Deisher, Kathleen E. Beyond the Gloesmur: In the Gloesmur Scrolls. Deisher, Kathleen E. 2003. (Gloesmur Scrolls Ser.: Bk. 1). 270p. (J). pap. 13.95 *(978-1-892135-00-1(0))* Lamp Post Publishing, Inc.
DeJesus, Melissa. Fan Art. Tregay, Sarah. 2014. (ENG.). 368p. (YA). (gr. 8). 17.99 *(978-0-06-224315-7(2)*, Tegen, Katherine Bks) HarperCollins Pubs.

—Sokora Refugees. Segamu. 2006. (Sokora Refugees Ser.: Vol. 2). 192p. pap. 9.99 *(978-1-59816-551-7(8))* TOKYOPOP, Inc.

—Sokora Refugees, Vol. 1. 2005. 192p. pap. 14.99 *(978-1-59532-736-9(3),* Tokyopop Adult) TOKYOPOP, Inc.

DeJesus, Robert. Another Nastybook: The Curse of the Tweeties. Yourgrau, Barry. 2006. 171p. (J). (gr. 5-9). lib. bdg. 13.89 *(978-0-06-057982-1(X),* Cotler, Joanna Books) HarperCollins Pubs.

DeJohn, Marie. Daisy & the Girl Scouts: The Story of Juliette Gordon Low. Brown, Fern. 2005. (ENG.). 112p. (J). (gr. 3-6). pap. 8.99 *(978-0-8075-1441-2(1))* Whitman, Albert & Co.

—Gertrude Chandler Warner & the Boxcar Children. Ellsworth, Mary Ellen. 2004. (ENG.). 64p. (J). (gr. 2-7). pap. 6.95 *(978-0-8075-2838-9(2))* Whitman, Albert & Co.

DeJong Artman, Catherine & Artman, Townsend. The Further Adventures of a Lucky Dog: Owney, U. S. Rail Mail Mascot. Wales, Dirk. 2009. 32p. (J). (gr. -1-7). 17.95 *(978-0-9632459-6-0(1))* Great Plains Pr.

DeKnight, Cathy. A Family of His Own. Brown, Stacia Bradley. 2004. (J). 14.95 *(978-1-58597-283-8(5))* Leathers Publishing.

del Conte, Mia. Andy's Discovery. Benjamin, Matthew C. 2003. 78p. (J). per. 8.95 *(978-0-9744672-0-7(0))* Adventure & Discovery Pr.

—Ricky's Adventure. Benjamin, Matthew C. 2003. 94p. (J). per. 8.95 *(978-0-9744672-1-4(9))* Adventure & Discovery Pr.

Del Russo, John William, Sr. How Scooter Gets His Tail Back. Godsey, J. P. "Gus". 2014. (Morgan James Kids Ser.). (ENG.). 46p. (gr. 2-6). pap. 9.95 *(978-1-63047-003-6(1))* Morgan James Publishing.

Del Toro, Mark. Somewhere in Texas. Fitzgibbon, Diana. Gonzales, Diana, ed. 2004. 32p. (J). *(978-0-9747587-0-1(1))* Mike-Auri Bks.

del Valle, Clara J., photos by. Gisselle's Adventures in Color. Ames, Heidi L. 2010. 36p. pap. 14.95 *(978-1-60844-436-6(8))* Dog Ear Publishing, LLC.

Delaborde, Gilles, photos by. Face-to-Face with the Horse: Faster Than the Wind. Tracqui, Valérie. 2004. (Face to Face Ser.). 28p. (J). (gr. -1-2). 9.95 *(978-1-57091-450-8(8))* Charlesbridge Publishing, Inc.

Delacre, Lulu. How Far Do You Love Me? 2014. (ENG.). (J). pap. 8.95 *(978-1-62014-208-0(2))* Lee & Low Bks., Inc.

—Los Zapaticos de Rosa. Martí, José & José, Martí. 2003. (SPA.). 84p. *(978-84-241-3352-8(8),* LC4069) Everest Editora ESP. Dist: Lectorum Pubns., Inc.

Delacre, Lulu. How Far Do You Love Me?, 1 vol. Delacre, Lulu. 2013. (ENG.). 32p. (J). 11.95 *(978-1-60060-882-7(5))* Lee & Low Bks., Inc.

—Jay & Ben. Delacre, Lulu. Swanson, Katharine. 2013. (ENG.). 18p. (J). bds. 20.00 *(978-1-60060-460-7(9))* Lee & Low Bks., Inc.

—Rafi & Rosi. Delacre, Lulu. 2005. (I Can Read Bks.). 64p. (J). (gr. k-3). pap. 3.99 *(978-0-06-009897-1(X),* Rayo) HarperCollins Pubs.

—Salsa Stories. Delacre, Lulu. 2012. (ENG.). 112p. (J). (gr. 2-5). pap. 6.99 *(978-0-545-43098-2(4),* Scholastic Pr.) Scholastic, Inc.

Delacre, Lulu. Arrorro Mi Nino: Latino Lullabies & Gentle Games, 1 vol. Delacre, Lulu, compiled by. 2004. (ENG & SPA.). 32p. (J). 16.95 *(978-1-58430-159-2(7))* Lee & Low Bks., Inc.

Delafosse, Claude. Let's Look at Archimboldo's Portraits. Delafosse, Claude. 2012. (ENG.). 38p. (J). (gr. k-3). pap. 11.99 *(978-1-85103-290-7(8))* Moonlight Publishing, Ltd. GBR. Dist: Independent Pubs. Group.

DeLage, Charlene. Buds & Blossoms: A Book about Flowers, 1 vol. Blackaby, Susan. 2003. (Growing Things Ser.). (ENG.). 24p. (gr. -1-2). per. 7.95 *(978-1-4048-0388-6(2),* Nonfiction Picture Bks.) Picture Window Bks.

Delage, Charlene. Catching Sunlight: A Book about Leaves, 1 vol. Blackaby, Susan. 2003. (Growing Things Ser.). (ENG.). 24p. (gr. -1-2). per. 7.95 *(978-1-4048-0387-9(4),* Nonfiction Picture Bks.) Picture Window Bks.

DeLage, Charlene. Green & Growing: A Book about Plants. Blackaby, Susan. 2003. (Growing Things Ser.). (ENG.). 24p. (gr. -1-2). 25.99 *(978-1-4048-0107-3(3),* Nonfiction Picture Bks.) Picture Window Bks.

Delage, Charlene. El Patito Feo. Blackaby, Susan. Ruiz, Carlos, tr. from ENG. 2006. (Read-It! Readers en Español: Cuentos de Hadas Ser.). (SPA.). 32p. (gr. k-3). 19.99 *(978-1-4048-1644-2(5),* Easy Readers) Picture Window Bks.

—Plant Packages: A Book about Seeds, 1 vol. Blackaby, Susan. 2003. (Growing Things Ser.). (ENG.). 24p. (gr. -1-2). per. 7.95 *(978-1-4048-0384-8(X),* Nonfiction Picture Bks.) Picture Window Bks.

DeLage, Charlene. Plant Plumbing: A Book about Roots & Stems. Blackaby, Susan. 2003. (Growing Things Ser.). (ENG.). 24p. (gr. -1-2). 25.99 *(978-1-4048-0109-7(X));* per. 7.95 *(978-1-4048-0385-5(8))* Picture Window Bks. (Nonfiction Picture Bks.).

Delage, Charlene. La Princesa Del Guisante: Versión Del Cuento de Hans Christian Anderson. Blackaby, Susan. Abello, Patricia, tr. from ENG. 2006. (Read-It! Readers en Español: Cuentos de Hadas Ser.).Tr. of Princess & the Pea - A Retelling of the Grimm's Fairy Tale. (SPA.). 32p. (gr. k-3). 19.99 *(978-1-4048-1634-3(8),* Easy Readers) Picture Window Bks.

—Thumbelina: A Retelling of the Hans Christian Andersen Fairy Tale, 1 vol. Blackaby, Susan. 2003. (Read-It! Readers: Fairy Tales Ser.). (ENG.). 32p. (gr. k-3). 19.99 *(978-1-4048-0225-4(8),* Easy Readers) Picture Window Bks.

—El Traje Nuevo Del Emperador. Blackaby, Susan. Abello, Patricia, tr. from ENG. 2006. (Read-It! Readers en Español: Cuentos de Hadas Ser.). (SPA.). 32p. (gr. k-3). 19.99 *(978-1-4048-1629-9(1),* Easy Readers) Picture Window Bks.

Delage, Kristi, jt. illus. see Hanson, Sandy.

Delainey, James. The Savage River: Seventy-One Days with Simon Fraser, 1 vol. Campbell, Marjorie Wilkins. 2003. (ENG.). 149p. pap. 8.95 *(978-1-894856-24-9(4))* Fifth Hse. Pubs. CAN. Dist: Ingram Pub. Services.

Delandro Hardison, Brian. The Journey of Odysseus. DeHoratius, Ed. 2009. (Follow Your Fates Ser.). 116p. (J). pap. 12.00 *(978-0-86516-710-0(9))* Bolchazy-Carducci Pubs.

DeLaney, Edgar Azell. The Magical Hammock. DeLaney, Edgar Azell. 2004. (ENG.). 83p. (J). 19.95 *(978-0-9759013-0-4(3))* Special Edition Studios, Inc.

Delaney, Janine. A Friend Called Glen: A Bedtime Story for African-American Girls. Daniels, Linda. 2011. (ENG.). 26p. pap. 15.99 *(978-1-4635-9825-9(4))* CreateSpace Independent Publishing Platform.

Delaney, Molly. Mat Man Hats. Olsen, Jan Z. 2008. (ENG.). 36p. stu. ed. 13.75 *(978-1-891627-93-4(7))* Handwriting Without Tears.

—Mat Man on the Go. Olsen, Jan Z. 2010. (ENG.). stu. ed. 13.75 *(978-1-934825-39-6(5))* Handwriting Without Tears.

—Mat Man Opposites. Olsen, Jan Z. 2009. (ENG.). stu. ed. 13.75 *(978-1-891627-94-1(5))* Handwriting Without Tears.

—Mat Man Shapes. Olsen, Jan Z. 2007. (ENG.). 32p. stu. ed. 13.75 *(978-1-891627-92-7(9))* Handwriting Without Tears.

—No Peas, Please! Athey, Victoria. 2005. (ENG.). 20p. (gr. k-2). pap. 5.95 *(978-1-57874-087-1(8))* Kaeden Corp.

—Which Way Did They Go? Williams, Rozanne Lanczak. Hamaguchi, Carla, ed. 2003. (Sight Word Readers Ser.). 16p. (J). (gr. k-2). pap. 2.99 *(978-1-57471-971-0(8),* 3593) Creative Teaching Pr., Inc.

—Zero's Slider. Christopher, Matt. 2009. 64p. (J). lib. bdg. 22.60 *(978-1-59953-323-0(5))* Norwood Hse. Pr.

DeLange, Alex Pardo. The Empanadas That Abuela Made/Las Empandas Que Hacia la Abuela. Bertrand, Diane Gonzales. Ventura, Gabriela Baeza, tr. (ENG & SPA.). 32p. (J). 16.95 *(978-1-55885-388-1(X),* Piñata Books) Arte Publico Pr.

Delange, Alex Pardo. Pepita on Pepper Street/Pepita en la Calle Pepper. Lachtman, Ofelia Dumas. Monsivais, Maria Estela, tr. from ENG. 2008. (SPA & ENG.). 32p. (J). (gr. -1-3). 16.95 *(978-1-55885-443-7(6),* Piñata Books) Arte Publico Pr.

—Pepita Packs Up: Pepita Empaca. Lachtman, Ofelia Dumas. Ventura, Gabriela Baeza, tr. from ENG. 2005. 48p. (J). (gr. -1-k). lib. bdg. 16.95 *(978-1-55885-431-4(2),* Piñata Books) Arte Publico Pr.

—Sip, Slurp, Soup, Soup/Caldo, Caldo, Caldo. Bertrand, Diane Gonzales. Castilla, Julia Mercedes, tr. 2008. (SPA & ENG.). 32p. (J). (gr. -1-2). pap. 7.95 *(978-1-55885-241-9(7),* Piñata Books) Arte Publico Pr.

DeLange, Alex Pardo. Sip, Slurp, Soup Soup/Caldo Caldo Caldo: CD & Book Set. Bertrand, Diane Gonzales. 2008. 32p. (J). pap. 19.95 *(978-0-9815686-1-4(0))* Lorito Bks., Inc.

Delanssay, Cathy. Give Me Moon. Galliez, Roxane Marie. 2009. 44p. (J). (gr. -1-3). 14.99 *(978-0-8416-7138-6(9))* Hammond World Atlas Corp.

—The Secret Life of Princesses. Hanna, Virginie. 2009. 26p. (J). (gr. -1-3). 17.99 *(978-0-8437-1476-0(X))* Hammond World Atlas Corp.

Delanssay, Cathy, et al. 18 Historias de Princesas y de Hadas. Agin, Élodie et al. Oyaga, Irene, tr. from FRE. 2010. (SPA.). 118p. (J). (gr. 1-4). 24.95 *(978-84-96939-04-2(9))* Roca Editorial De Libros ESP. Dist: Spanish Pubs., LLC.

Delclos, Jordi V. Vero y el Fantasma de Canterville. Puerto, Carlos. 2005. 121p. (J). (gr. 6-10). 14.40 *(978-84-263-5180-7(8))* Vives, Luis Editorial (Edelvives) ESP. Dist: Lectorum Pubns., Inc.

Delclòs, Jordi Vila. La Bella Durmiente. Combel Editorial Staff. 2004. (Caballo Alado Clásicos-Al Trote Ser.). (SPA & ENG.). 24p. (J). (gr. -1-k). 7.95 *(978-84-7864-775-0(9))* Combel Editorial, S.A. ESP. Dist: Independent Pubs. Group.

Delcoglin, Nathan. Bella's Umbrella. Delcoglin, Gwen. 2007. 28p. (J). (gr. -1-3). per. 10.99 *(978-1-59879-315-4(2))* Lifevest Publishing, Inc.

Delderfield, Angela. The Adventures of Charlie. Moseley, Sophia. 2012. 106p. pap. *(978-1-78148-757-0(X))* Grosvenor Hse. Publishing Ltd.

Delehanty, Joan M. Manners I. Care. Bruce, David. 2006. 32p. (J). 16.95 *(978-0-9771143-2-0(5))* Child Life Bks., LLC.

—What Does the Wind Say? Silvano, Wendi. 2006. (ENG.). 32p. (J). (gr. -1-k). 15.95 *(978-1-55971-954-4(0))* Cooper Square Publishing Llc.

Delessert, Etienne. The Happy Prince. Wilde, Oscar. 2008. (Creative Short Stories Ser.). 32p. (YA). (gr. 9-18). lib. bdg. 28.50 *(978-1-58341-582-5(3),* Creative Education) Creative Co., The.

—I Hate to Read! Marshall, Rita. 2013. (ENG.). 32p. (J). (gr. k-17). 16.99 *(978-1-56846-232-5(8),* Creative Editions) Creative Co., The.

—I Hate to Read! Marshall, Rita. 2008. (J). (gr. k-3). 27.95 incl. audio *(978-0-8045-6973-6(0));* 29.95 incl. audio compact disk *(978-0-8045-4198-5(1))* Spoken Arts, Inc.

—I Still Hate to Read! Marshall, Rita. 2008. (ENG.). 32p. (J). (gr. 1-3). 19.95 *(978-1-56846-174-8(7),* Creative Editions) Creative Co., The.

—I Still Hate to Read! Marshall, Rita. 2008. (J). (gr. k-3). 27.95 incl. audio *(978-0-8045-6974-3(6));* 29.95 incl. audio compact disk *(978-0-8045-4199-2(X))* Spoken Arts, Inc.

—John Keats. Kirkpatrick, Patricia. 2005. (Voices in Poetry Ser.). 43p. (J). (gr. 5-9). 21.95 *(978-1-58341-345-6(6),* Creative Education) Creative Co., The.

—The Lonely Pine. Frisch, Aaron. 2011. (ENG.). 32p. (J). (gr. 1-3). 17.99 *(978-1-56846-214-1(X),* Creative Editions) Creative Co., The.

—Lucas. Highet, Alistair. 2011. (ENG.). 40p. (J). (gr. 4-17). pap. 8.95 *(978-0-89812-014-1(4),* Creative Paperbacks) Creative Co., The.

—The Ransom of Red Chief. Henry, O. 2008. (Creative Short Stories Ser.). 32p. (YA). (gr. 9-18). lib. bdg. 28.50 *(978-1-58341-585-6(8),* Creative Education) Creative Co., The.

—Stories 1,2,3,4. Ionesco, Eugène. 2012. (ENG.). 112p. (J). (gr. k-5). 19.95 *(978-1-936365-51-7(0))* McSweeney's Publishing.

Delessert, Etienne. A Glass. Delessert, Etienne. 2013. (ENG.). 32p. (J). (gr. 4-7). 18.99 *(978-1-56846-257-8(3),* Creative Editions) Creative Co., The.

—Night Circus. Delessert, Etienne. 2015. (ENG.). 32p. (J). (gr. 2-4). 19.99 *(978-1-56846-277-6(8),* Creative Editions) Creative Co., The.

—A Was an Apple Pie. Delessert, Etienne. 2005. (Creative Editions Ser.). 28p. (J). (gr. -1-3). 18.95 *(978-1-56846-196-0(8))* Creative Co., The.

Delezenne, Christine. Le Monde de Xéros. Plante, Raymond. 2004. (Roman Jeunesse Ser.). (FRE.). 96p. (J). (gr. 4-7). pap. *(978-2-89021-615-0(2))* Diffusion du livre Mirabel (DLM).

—Sarah & the Magic Science Project. Hutchins, Hazel. 2005. (ENG.). 152p. (J). (gr. 3-6). 18.95 *(978-1-55037-931-0(3),* 9781550379310); pap. 7.95 *(978-1-55037-930-3(5),* 9781550379303) Annick Pr., Ltd. CAN. Dist: Firefly Bks., Ltd.

—Torrie & the Pirate Queen. Johansen, K. V. 2005. (Torrie Quests Ser.). (ENG.). 160p. (J). (gr. 4-6). 18.95 *(978-1-55037-901-3(1),* 9781550379013); pap. 7.95 *(978-1-55037-900-6(3),* 9781550379006) Annick Pr., Ltd. CAN. Dist: Firefly Bks., Ltd.

—Torrie & the Snake-Prince. Johansen, K. V. 2007. (Torrie Quests Ser.). (ENG.). 192p. (J). (gr. 4-6). 18.95 *(978-1-55451-070-2(8),* 9781554510702) Annick Pr., Ltd. CAN. Dist: Firefly Bks., Ltd.

Delezenne, Christine. Torrie & the Firebird. Delezenne, Christine. 2006. (Torrie Quests Ser.). (ENG.). 195p. (J). (gr. 3-5). pap. 7.95 *(978-1-55037-960-0(7),* 9781550379600) Annick Pr., Ltd. CAN. Dist: Firefly Bks., Ltd.

Delf, Brian. Atlas Visual del Mundo. Kemp, Richard. (SPA.). 80p. (YA). (gr. 5-8). *(978-84-216-1576-8(9),* BU4606) Bruño, Editorial ESP. Dist: Lectorum Pubns., Inc.

Delgado, Francisco. ¡Sí, Se Puede! Cohn, Diana. 2009.Tr. of Yes, We Can!. (SPA & ENG.). 32p. (J). (gr. k-2). pap. 7.95 *(978-0-938317-89-0(X))* Cinco Puntos Pr.

—¡Sí, Se Puede! Cohn, Diana. Franco, Sharon, tr. from ENG. 2008.Tr. of Yes, We Can!. (SPA & ENG.). 32p. (J). (gr. 1-5). 15.95 *(978-0-938317-66-1(0))* Cinco Puntos Pr.

—Lover Boy / Juanito el Carinoso: A Bilingual Counting Book. Byrd, Lee Merrill. 2005. (ENG & SPA.). 32p. (J). (gr. -1-2). 15.95 *(978-0-938317-38-8(5))* Cinco Puntos Pr.

Delice, Shelly Meredith. A Monster Named Criney Who Makes Kids Whiney. Zuckerman, Heather. 2005. 32p. (J). (gr. -1-3). 15.95 *(978-0-9744307-0-6(6))* Merry Lane Pr.

Delinois, Alix. Eight Days: A Story of Haiti. Danticat, Edwidge. 2010. (ENG.). 32p. (J). (gr. -1-3). 17.99 *(978-0-545-27849-2(X),* Orchard Bks.) Scholastic, Inc.

—Muhammad Ali: The People's Champion. Myers, Walter Dean. 40p. (J). (gr. -1-3). 2016. pap. 6.99 *(978-0-06-443718-9(3));* 2009. (ENG.). 16.99 *(978-0-06-029131-0(1),* Collins) HarperCollins Pubs.

—Mumbet's Declaration of Independence. Woelfle, Gretchen. 2014. (ENG.). 32p. (J). (gr. 1-4). 17.95 *(978-0-7613-6589-1(3),* Carolrhoda Bks.) Lerner Publishing Group.

Delioglu, Mustafa. Kangaroo Clues. Finke, Margot. 2013. 16p. pap. 9.95 *(978-1-61633-368-3(5))* Guardian Angel Publishing, Inc.

Delios, Kim, photos by. Aussie Toddlers Can. Magabala Books Staff. l.t. ed. 2006. 10p. (J). bds. *(978-1-875641-88-8(2))* Magabala Bks.

Delisa, Patricia. Little Red Riding Hood: The Classic Grimm's Fairy Tale. Flaxman, Andrew. 2006. 32p. (J). (gr. -1-3). 14.95 *(978-0-88010-571-2(2),* Bell Pond Bks.) SteinerBooks, Inc.

Delisle, Anne-Claire & Owlkids Books Inc. Staff. Really & Truly. Rivard, Émilie & Quinn, Sarah. 2012. (ENG.). 24p. (J). (gr. -1). 15.95 *(978-1-926973-40-1(2))* Owlkids Bks. Inc. CAN. Dist: Perseus-PGW.

Delisle, Kathryn H. It's Christmas Again! Frrich, Lewandowski & Riccards, Michael. 2007. 32p. (J). 14.95 *(978-1-929039-44-9(1))* Ambassador Bks., Inc.

Delk, Chrissy. The Girl Who Owned a City: Graphic Novel. Nelson, O. T. 2012. (Single Titles Ser.). (ENG.). 128p. (YA). (gr. 5-12). lib. bdg. 29.27 *(978-0-7613-4903-7(0),* Graphic Universe) Lerner Publishing Group.

Dell, Jacob J., photos by. A Piece of Notre Dame: A pictorial guide to the University of Notre Dame, leading you on an insightful tour of the often unnoticed, yet beautifully crafted details of Campus. Dell, Jacob J. Dell, Rachel E. Wilson, Robin M., ed. 2005. 14.87 *(978-0-9744544-0-5(0))* Dell, Jacob J.

Dell, John. World War III, Bk. 6. Morrison, Grant & DeMatteis, J. M. rev. ed. 2007. (ENG.). 208p. (YA). pap. 14.99 *(978-1-56389-618-7(4))* DC Comics.

Della-Rovere, Cynthia. Bush, Blair, & Iraq: Days of Decision, 1 vol. Langley, Andrew. 2013. (Days of Decision Ser.). (ENG.). 64p. (J). (gr. 7-8). 35.00 *(978-1-4329-7633-0(8));* pap. 9.99 *(978-1-4329-7640-8(0))* Heinemann-Raintree.

Dell'edera, Werther. Thicker Than Blackwater, Vol. 2. Azzarello, Brian et al. rev. ed. 2007. (Loveless Ser.). (ENG.). 168p. pap. 14.99 *(978-1-4012-1250-6(6),* Vertigo) DC Comics.

Delmar, Natasha. The Old Woman & the Eagle. Shah, Idries. (Sounds of Afghanistan Ser.). (J). 2005. (gr. -1-3). 28.95 incl. audio compact disk *(978-1-883536-77-0(4));* 2005. 32p. (gr. -1-3). pap. 6.99 *(978-1-883536-28-2(6));* 2003. 32p. 18.00 *(978-1-883536-27-5(8),* OLWE1) I S H K. (Hoopoe Bks.).

Deloache, Shawn. Medikidz Explain Haemophilia: What's up with Louis? Chilman-Blair, Kim & Hersov, Kate. 2011. 32p. (J). pap. *(978-1-906935-29-0(7))* Medikidz Ltd.

—Medikidz Explain Inflammatory Bowel Disease: What's up with Adam? Chilman-Blair, Kim & Hersov, Kate. 2011. 32p. (J). pap. *(978-1-906935-65-8(3))* Medikidz Ltd.

deLoache, Shawn. Que le Pasa a la Abuelita de Sam? Los Medikidz Explican el Cancer de Pulmon. Chilman-Blair, Kim. 2014. (Medikidz Explain [Cancer XYZ] Ser.). (SPA.). 32p. (YA). (gr. 7). 14.95 *(978-1-60443-201-5(2))* American Cancer Society, Inc.

—Que le Pasa a Nuestro Papa? Los Medikidz Explican el Cancer Colorrectal. Chilman-Blair, Kim. 2014. (Medikidz Explain [Cancer XYZ] Ser.). (SPA.). 32p. (YA). (gr. 7). 14.95 *(978-1-60443-203-9(9))* American Cancer Society, Inc.

—¿Qué le Pasa Al Abuelito de Jerome? Los Medikidz Explican el Cancer de Prostata. Chilman-Blair, Kim. 2014. (Medikidz Explain [Cancer XYZ] Ser.). (ENG & SPA.). 32p. (YA). (gr. 7). 14.95 *(978-1-60443-199-5(7))* American Cancer Society, Inc.

—What's up with Jerome's Grandad? Medikidz Explain Prostate Cancer. Chilman-Blair, Kim. 2013. (Medikidz Explain [Cancer XYZ] Ser.). (ENG.). 32p. (J). (gr. 7). 14.95 *(978-1-60443-198-8(9))* American Cancer Society, Inc.

—What's up with Our Dad? Medikidz Explain Colorectal Cancer. Chilman-Blair, Kim. 2013. (Medikidz Explain [Cancer XYZ] Ser.). (ENG.). 32p. (J). (gr. 7). 14.95 *(978-1-60443-202-2(0))* American Cancer Society, Inc.

—What's up with Sam's Grandma? Medikidz Explain Lung Cancer. Chilman-Blair, Kim. 2013. (Medikidz Explain [Cancer XYZ] Ser.). (ENG.). 32p. (J). (gr. 7). 14.95 *(978-1-60443-200-8(4))* American Cancer Society, Inc.

Delonas, Sean. Twas the Day after Christmas. Snell, Gordon. Date not set. 32p. (J). (gr. -1-3). 5.99 *(978-0-06-443675-5(6))* HarperCollins Pubs.

Delosh, Diana Ting. Shoes! Brott, Wayne. 2013. (ENG.). (J). (gr. -1-3). 14.95 *(978-1-62086-239-1(5))* Mascot Bks., Inc.

Delsi, Dawna. Great Tastes of Michigan. Glupker, Dianne. 2006. (J). per. 9.95 *(978-0-9769846-1-0(X))* Harambee Pr.

Delsi, Dawna. Great Lights of Michigan. Delsi, Dawna. Glupker, Dianne. 2005. (J). per. 9.95 *(978-0-9769846-0-3(1),* 318924) Harambee Pr.

DeMakas, Meg, jt. illus. see Grandfield, Meg.

Demarest, Chris L. Arabic Picture Dictionary. 2011. (Kids Picture Dictionary Ser.). (ARA & ENG.). 128p. (J). pap. 14.99 *(978-981-268-579-7(0))* APA Publications Services SGP. Dist: Ingram Pub. Services.

—Breakfast at Danny's Diner: A Book about Multiplication. Stamper, Judith Bauer. 2003. (All Aboard Math Reader Ser.). 48p. (J). (gr. 2-4). 11.65 *(978-0-7569-1695-4(X))* Perfection Learning Corp.

—Ding-Dong, Trick or Treat! Ziefert, Harriet. 2004. 22p. (J). (gr. -1-3). reprint ed. pap. 12.00 *(978-0-7567-8258-0(9))* DIANE Publishing Co.

—Go, Fractions! Stamper, Judith Bauer & Stamper, Judith. 2003. (Penguin Young Readers, Level 3 Ser.). (ENG.). 48p. (J). (gr. 1-3). mass mkt. 3.99 *(978-0-448-43113-0(0),* Grosset & Dunlap) Penguin Publishing Group.

—Leaping Beauty: And Other Animal Fairy Tales. Maguire, Gregory. 2006. (ENG.). 224p. (J). (gr. 3-7). reprint ed. pap. 7.99 *(978-0-06-056419-3(9))* HarperCollins Pubs.

—Red Sled. Thomas, Patricia. (ENG.). 32p. (J). (gr. -1-1). 2013. pap. 6.95 *(978-1-62091-592-9(8));* 2008. 16.95 *(978-1-59078-559-1(2))* Boyds Mills Pr.

Demarest, Chris L. Alpha Bravo Charlie: The Military Alphabet. Demarest, Chris L. 2005. (ENG.). 40p. (J). (gr. 1-5). 17.99 *(978-0-689-86928-0(2),* McElderry, Margaret K. Bks.) McElderry, Margaret K. Bks.

—Arlington: The Story of Our Nation's Cemetery. Demarest, Chris L. 2010. (ENG.). 32p. (J). (gr. 1-5). 18.99 *(978-1-59643-517-9(8))* Roaring Brook Pr.

—Firefighters A to Z. Demarest, Chris L. 2003. (ENG.). 32p. (J). (gr. -1-3). 7.99 *(978-0-689-85999-1(6),* McElderry, Margaret K. Bks.) McElderry, Margaret K. Bks.

—Hurricane Hunters! Riders on the Storm. Demarest, Chris L. 2006. (ENG.). 40p. (J). (gr. -1-5). 19.99 *(978-0-689-86168-0(0),* McElderry, Margaret K. Bks.) McElderry, Margaret K. Bks.

—Mayday! Mayday! A Coast Guard Rescue. Demarest, Chris L. 2004. (ENG.). 40p. (J). (gr. -1-5). 17.99 *(978-0-689-85161-2(8),* McElderry, Margaret K. Bks.) McElderry, Margaret K. Bks.

Dematons, Charlotte. Holland & a Thousand Things about Holland. 2013. (ENG.). 176p. (J). (gr. 3). 29.95 *(978-1-935954-33-0(4),* 9781935954330) Lemniscaat USA.

—Raf. de Vries, Anke. 2009. (ENG.). 32p. (J). (gr. k-3). 16.95 *(978-1-59078-749-6(8),* Lemniscaat) Boyds Mills Pr.

DeMatte, Darcey. God Did Make Little Green Apples. Assunto, Cecelia. 2012. 30p. (J). pap. 12.95 *(978-1-61314-028-4(2))* Innovo Publishing, LLC.

Demers, David, photos by. My Grandpa Loves Trains: A Picture Storybook for Preschoolers. Demers, David. Demers, Lee Ann. l.t. ed. 2005. 76p. (J). 27.95 *(978-0-922993-36-9(X))* Marquette Bks., LLC.

—My Grandpa Loves Trains: A Storybook for Preschoolers. Demers, David. Demers, Lee Ann. l.t. ed. 2005. 76p. (J). per. 19.95 *(978-0-922993-23-9(8))* Marquette Bks., LLC.

Demeter, Brian. Pedro & the Coyote. 2006. (ENG.). 32p. (gr. 4-8). pap. 8.95 *(978-1-60694-925-2(X))* Rourke Educational Media.

Demetris, Alex. Grandma's Box of Memories: Helping Grandma to Remember. Demetris, Jean. 2014. (ENG.). 32p. *(978-1-84905-993-0(4))* Kingsley, Jessica Ltd.

Demi. The Conference of the Birds. 2012. (ENG.). 44p. (J). (gr. -1-3). 19.95 *(978-1-937786-02-1(1))* World Wisdom, Inc.

—Eucalyptus Wings. James, J. Alison. 2012. (ENG.). 36p. (J). (gr. k-3). 17.99 *(978-1-4424-7484-0(X),* Atheneum Bks. for Young Readers) Simon & Schuster Children's Publishing.

—Grass Sandals: The Travels of Basho. Spivak, Dawnine. 2009. (ENG.). 40p. (J). (gr. 4-6). 13.99 *(978-1-4424-0936-1(3),* Atheneum Bks. for Young Readers) Simon & Schuster Children's Publishing.

—Mahavira: The Hero of Nonviolence. Jain, Manoj. 2014. (ENG.). 28p. (J). (gr. k-4). 17.95 *(978-1-937786-21-2(8),* Wisdom Tales) World Wisdom, Inc.

D

Demi. Columbus, 0 vols. Demi. 2012. (ENG.). 64p. (J). (gr. 3-7). 19.99 *(978-0-7614-6167-8(1)*, 9780761461678, Amazon Children's Publishing) Amazon Publishing.
—The Empty Pot. Demi. 2007. (ENG.). 32p. (J). (gr. -1-3). pap. 25.99 *(978-0-8050-8227-2(1)*, Holt, Henry & Co. Bks. For Young Readers) Holt, Henry & Co.
—The Fantastic Adventures of Krishna. Demi. 2013. (ENG.). 44p. (J). (gr. -1-3). 19.95 *(978-1-937786-05-2(6)*, Wisdom Tales) World Wisdom, Inc.
—Florence Nightingale. Demi. 2014. (ENG.). 40p. (J). (gr. -1-3). 17.99 *(978-0-8050-9729-0(5)*, Holt, Henry & Co. Bks. For Young Readers) Holt, Henry & Co.
—The Girl Who Drew a Phoenix. Demi. 2008. (ENG.). 52p. (J). (gr. 2-5). 24.99 *(978-1-4169-5347-0(7)*, McElderry, Margaret K. Bks.) McElderry, Margaret K. Bks.
—The Greatest Power. Demi. 2004. (ENG.). 40p. (J). (gr. -1-3). 21.99 *(978-0-689-84503-1(0)*, McElderry, Margaret K. Bks.) McElderry, Margaret K. Bks.
—The Hungry Coat: A Tale from Turkey. Demi. 2004. (ENG.). 40p. (J). (gr. 1-5). 21.99 *(978-0-689-84680-9(0)*, McElderry, Margaret K. Bks.) McElderry, Margaret K. Bks.
—Jesus. Demi. 2005. (ENG.). 48p. (J). (gr. 2-5). 24.99 *(978-0-689-86905-1(3)*, McElderry, Margaret K. Bks.) McElderry, Margaret K. Bks.
—The Legend of Saint Nicholas. Demi. 2003. (ENG.). 40p. (J). (gr. k-5). 19.95 *(978-0-689-84681-6(9)*, McElderry, Margaret K. Bks.) McElderry, Margaret K. Bks.
—The Magic Pillow. Demi. 2008. (ENG.). 40p. (J). (gr. 2-5). 19.99 *(978-1-4169-2470-8(1)*, McElderry, Margaret K. Bks.) McElderry, Margaret K. Bks.
Demi & Demi Staff. The Boy Who Painted Dragons. Demi & Demi Staff. 2007. (ENG.). 52p. (J). (gr. 2-5). 21.99 *(978-1-4169-2469-2(8)*, McElderry, Margaret K. Bks.) McElderry, Margaret K. Bks.
Demi, Barbara. Muhammad. Demi, Barbara. 2003. (ENG.). 48p. (J). (gr. 2-5). 19.95 *(978-0-689-85264-0(9)*, McElderry, Margaret K. Bks.) McElderry, Margaret K. Bks.
Demi Staff, jt. illus. see Demi.
DeMicco, Michelle. Easy-to-Make Bible Story Puppets. Bendt, Valerie. 2005. 184p. (J). per. 24.00 *(978-1-885814-17-3(8))* Valerie Bendt.
Demirel, Selçuk. Mr. Karp's Last Glass, 1 vol. Fagan, Cary. 2009. (ENG.). 96p. (J). (gr. 2-5). pap. 6.95 *(978-0-88899-835-4(X))* Groundwood Bks. CAN. Dist: Perseus-PGW.
Demmers, Justina. Closet Creeps: A Bedtime Mystery. Mele, Leo. 2011. 20p. pap. 24.95 *(978-1-4560-9002-9(X))* America Star Bks.
Demming, Karen. Has a Donkey Ever Brought You Breakfast in Bed? Brannon, Pat. 2012. 38p. pap. 10.00 *(978-1-938634-90-1(X))* Freedom of Speech Publishing, Inc.
Demong, Todd. 100 Girls. Gallardo, Adam. 2008. (ENG.). 176p. (YA). (gr. 9-18). pap. 9.99 *(978-1-4169-6109-3(7)*, Simon Pulse) Simon Pulse.
—100 Girls Vol. 1: Vol 1: the First Girl, Vol. 1. Gallardo, Adam. 2008. (YA). 9.95 *(978-0-9763095-3-6(X))* Arcana Studio, Inc.
deMontignie, Leon. The (True) Adventures of Mudpoo. Klein, Peter. 2012. (ENG.). 48p. (J). pap. 23.49 *(978-0-9870734-9-5(4))* JoJo Publishing AUS. Dist: AtlasBooks Distribution.
Dempsey, Sheena. Bruno & Titch. Dempsey, Sheena. 2014. (ENG.). 32p. (J). (gr. -1-2). 16.99 *(978-0-7636-7316-1(1))* Candlewick Pr.
Dempster, Al, jt. illus. see Walt Disney Studios Staff.
Demski, James, Jr. Acampar, 1 vol. Jones, Christianne C. Ruiz, Carlos, tr. from ENG. 2006. (Read-It! Readers en Español: Story Collection). (SPA.). 32p. (gr. -1-3). 19.99 *(978-1-4048-1681-7(X)*, Easy Readers) Picture Window Bks.
—Elect Me!, 1 vol. Manushkin, Fran. 2008. (Read-It! Readers: Social Studies). (ENG.). 32p. (gr. k-2). 19.99 *(978-1-4048-4911-2(4)*, Easy Readers) Picture Window Bks.
—Eric No Juega, 1 vol. Jones, Christianne C. Ruiz, Carlos, tr. 2006. (Read-It! Readers en Español: Story Collection).Tr. of Eric Won't Do It. (SPA.). 24p. (gr. -1-3). 19.99 *(978-1-4048-1683-1(6)*, Easy Readers) Picture Window Bks.
Denaro, Sal. Hello, I'm Sir Frettirick! Let's Say Hello to Our New Friends! Stratten, Lou. Bennett, Judy, ed. 2006. (J). (gr. -1-2). pap. 6.95 incl. audio compact disk *(978-0-9747173-1-9(2))* Stratten, Lou.
DeNault, Shirl. Mema Has Cancer, 1 vol. McBride, Linda Ray. 2008. (ENG.). 29p. 24.95 *(978-1-60610-833-8(6))* America Star Bks.
Denchfield, Nick & Sharp, Anne. Pop-up Minibeast Adventure. 2004. 16p. (J). (gr. k-4). reprint ed. 25.00 *(978-0-7567-8204-7(X))* DIANE Publishing Co.
Denetsosie, Hoke. Little Herder in Winter: Haigo Na'nilkaadi' Ya'zhi' Clark, Ann Nolan & Harrington, John P. 2011. 116p. 39.95 *(978-1-258-03041-4(1))* Literary Licensing, LLC.
Deneux, Xavier. Hail Mary. Bus, Sabrina. 2006. 12p. (J). (gr. -1). bds. 8.00 *(978-0-8028-5312-7(9)*, Eerdmans Bks For Young Readers) Eerdmans, William B. Publishing Co.
—Our Father. Bus, Sabrina. 2nd ed. 2006. 12p. (J). (gr. -1). bds. 8.00 *(978-0-8028-5313-4(7)*, Eerdmans Bks For Young Readers) Eerdmans, William B. Publishing Co.
Deneux, Xavier. My Animals. Deneux, Xavier. 2008. (ENG.). 18p. (J). (gr. -1 — 1). bds. 9.99 *(978-0-8027-9787-2(3))* Walker & Co.
Dengo, Monica. Pick up Your Pen: The Art of Handwriting. 2012. (ENG.). 112p. (J). (gr. 1-4). pap. 14.95 *(978-1-926973-11-1(9))* Owlkids Bks. Inc. CAN. Dist: Perseus-PGW.
Denham, Caitlin. Rocketry: Investigate the Science & Technology of Rockets & Ballistics. Mooney, Carla. 2014. (Build It Yourself Ser.). (ENG.). 128p. (J). (gr. 3-7). 22.95 *(978-1-61930-232-7(2))* Nomad Pr.
Denham, Gemma. Daniel & the Lions' Den, 1 vol. David, Juliet. 2009. (Candle Playbook Ser.). 18p. (J). bds. 7.99 *(978-0-8254-7385-2(3)*, Candle Bks.) Lion Hudson PLC GBR. Dist: Kregel Pubns.
—The First Christmas, 1 vol. David, Juliet. 2008. (Candle Playbook Ser.). 18p. (J). bds. 7.99 *(978-0-8254-7377-7(2)*, Candle Bks.) Lion Hudson PLC GBR. Dist: Kregel Pubns.
—Lost Sheep, 1 vol. David, Juliet. 2009. (Candle Playbook Ser.). 18p. (J). bds. 7.99 *(978-0-8254-7430-9(2)*, Candle Bks.) Lion Hudson PLC GBR. Dist: Kregel Pubns.
—Noah & His Boat, 1 vol. David, Juliet. 2008. (Candle Playbook Ser.). 18p. (J). bds. 7.99 *(978-0-8254-7378-4(0)*, Candle Bks.) Lion Hudson PLC GBR. Dist: Kregel Pubns.
Denham, Gemma & Scott, Richard. A Stable in Bethlehem. David, Juliet. 2007. 14p. (J). (gr. -1-3). 16.99 *(978-0-8254-7341-8(1)*, Candle Bks.) Lion Hudson PLC GBR. Dist: Kregel Pubns.
Denham, Gemma & Ward, Sylvia. Lift the Flap Nativity. David, Juliet. 2007. 12p. (J). (gr. -1-3). 6.99 *(978-0-8254-7342-5(X)*, Candle Bks.) Lion Hudson PLC GBR. Dist: Kregel Pubns.
Denis, Florencia. The Best Gift. Ryan, Ann Marie. 2011. (My Phonics Readers: Level 1 Ser.). 24p. (J). (gr. -1-1). 24.25 *(978-1-84898-507-0(X))* Sea-To-Sea Pubns.
Denis, Stephane. George Most Wanted. Lee, Ingrid. 2005. 62p. (J). lib. bdg. 20.00 *(978-1-4242-1253-8(7))* Fitzgerald Bks.
—George Most Wanted, 1 vol. Lee, Ingrid. 2005. (Orca Echoes Ser.). (ENG.). 64p. (J). (gr. 2-3). per. 4.99 *(978-1-55143-472-8(5))* Orca Bk. Pubs. USA.
—George, the Best of All!, 1 vol. Lee, Ingrid. 2006. (Orca Echoes Ser.). (ENG.). 64p. (J). (gr. 2-3). per. 4.99 *(978-1-55143-623-4(X))* Orca Bk. Pubs. USA.
—The True Story of George. Lee, Ingrid. 2004. 62p. (J). lib. bdg. 20.00 *(978-1-4242-1262-0(6))* Fitzgerald Bks.
—The True Story of George, 1 vol. Lee, Ingrid. 2004. (Orca Echoes Ser.). (ENG.). 64p. (J). (gr. 2-3). pap. 6.95 *(978-1-55143-293-9(5))* Orca Bk. Pubs. USA.
Denise, Christopher. Baking Day at Grandma's. Denise, Anika. 2014. (ENG.). 32p. (J). (gr. -1-k). 16.99 *(978-0-399-24244-1(9)*, Philomel) Penguin Publishing Group.
—Bella & Stella Come Home. Denise, Anika. 2010. (ENG.). 40p. (J). (gr. -1-k). 16.99 *(978-0-399-24243-4(0)*, Philomel) Penguin Publishing Group.
—Conejo y Tortuga van a la Escuela. Floyd, Lucy. Ada, Alma Flora & Campoy, F. Isabel, trs. 2010. (Green Light Readers Level 1 Ser.).Tr. of Rabbit & Turtle Go to School. (SPA & ENG.). 28p. (J). (gr. -1-3). pap. 3.99 *(978-0-547-33898-9(8))* Houghton Mifflin Harcourt Publishing Co.
—Digger Pig & the Turnip. Cohen, Caron Lee. 2003. (Green Light Readers Level 2 Ser.). (ENG.). 24p. (J). (gr. -1-3). pap. 3.95 *(978-0-15-204829-7(4))* Houghton Mifflin Harcourt Publishing Co.
Denise, Christopher. Firefly Hollow. McGhee, Alison. 2015. (ENG.). 304p. (J). (gr. 3-7). 16.99 ***(978-1-4424-2336-7(6)***, Atheneum Bks. for Young Readers) Simon & Schuster Children's Publishing.
Denise, Christopher. Following Grandfather. Wells, Rosemary. 2012. (ENG.). 64p. (J). (gr. 1-4). 14.99 *(978-0-7636-5069-8(2))* Candlewick Pr.
—If I Could. Milord, Susan. 2009. (ENG.). 32p. (J). (gr. k-k). 15.99 *(978-0-7636-4342-3(4))* Candlewick Pr.
—Knitty Kitty. Elliott, David. 2008. (ENG.). 32p. (J). (gr. -1-3). 16.99 *(978-0-7636-3169-7(8))* Candlewick Pr.
—Me with You. Dempsey, Kristy. 2013. (Little Letters Ser.). (ENG.). (J). (gr. -1-k). 32p. 4.99 *(978-0-448-46390-2(3)*, Grosset & Dunlap); 28p. bds. 6.99 *(978-0-399-16262-6(3)*, Philomel) Penguin Publishing Group.
—Rabbit & Turtle Go to School. Floyd, Lucy. 2003. (Green Light Readers Level 1 Ser.). (ENG.). 24p. (J). (gr. -1-3). pap. 3.95 *(978-0-15-204851-8(0))* Houghton Mifflin Harcourt Publishing Co.
—The Redwall Cookbook. Jacques, Brian. 2005. (Redwall Ser.). (ENG.). 104p. (J). (gr. 5-5). pap. 24.99 *(978-0-399-23791-1(7)*, Philomel) Penguin Publishing Group.
—That's What Friends Are For. Lewis, J. Patrick. 2012. (I Am A Reader! Ser.). (ENG.). 40p. (J). (gr. k-3). pap. 3.99 *(978-1-58536-687-3(0))* Sleeping Bear Pr.
—Tugg & Teeny. Lewis, J. Patrick. 2011. (I am a Reader Ser.). (ENG.). 40p. (J). (gr. k-2). pap. 3.99 *(978-1-58536-685-9(4))*;Bk. 1. lib. bdg. 9.95 *(978-1-58536-514-2(9))* Sleeping Bear Pr.
—Tugg & Teeny: That's What Friends Are For. Lewis, J. Patrick. 2012. (I Am A Reader! Ser.). (ENG.). 40p. (gr. k-3). lib. bdg. 9.95 *(978-1-58536-516-6(5))* Sleeping Bear Pr.
—Tugg & Tweeny - Jungle Surprises, Bk. 2. Lewis, J. Patrick. 2011. (I am a Reader Ser.). (ENG.). 40p. (J). (gr. k-2). pap. 3.99 *(978-1-58536-686-6(2))*; lib. bdg. 9.95 *(978-1-58536-515-9(7))* Sleeping Bear Pr.
Denison, Susan. Jake & Josh Go Camping. Quarles, Pamela. 2007. 40p. per. 14.00 *(978-1-59858-407-3(3))* Dog Ear Publishing, LLC.
Denlinger, Sam. Marathon Mouse. Dixon, Amy. 2012. (ENG.). 32p. (J). (gr. -1-3). pap. 16.95 *(978-1-61608-966-5(0)*, 608966, Sky Pony Pr.) Skyhorse Publishing Co., Inc.
Denman, Michael, et al. Alphabet of African Animals. Galvin, Laura Gates. 2008. (ENG.). 40p. (J). (gr. -1-2). 17.95 *(978-1-59249-854-3(X))* Soundprints.
Denman, Michael. Bible Story Hidden Pictures: Coloring & Activity Book. Fogle, Robin. 2006. (J). (gr. 1-5). 1.79 *(978-1-59317-161-2(7))* Warner Pr. Pubs.
—The Miller, His Son & Their Donkey. Sommer, Carl. 2014. (Sommer-Time Story Classics Ser.). (ENG.). 32p. (J). (gr. k-4). 16.95 *(978-1-57537-085-9(9))* Advance Publishing, Inc.
—Stone Soup. Sommer, Carl. 2014. (Sommer-Time Story Classics Ser.). (ENG.). 32p. (J). (gr. k-4). 16.95 *(978-1-57537-078-1(6))* Advance Publishing, Inc.
Denman, Michael & Huiett, William. Judy the Elephant. Galvin, Laura Gates. (African Wildlife Foundation Ser.). (ENG.). 36p. (J). (gr. -1-2). 2005. 2.95 *(978-1-59249-171-1(5)*, S6552); 2005. 9.95 *(978-1-59249-172-8(3)*, PS6552); 2004. 8.95 *(978-1-59249-198-8(7)*, SD6502) Soundprints.
—Kakuda the Giraffe. Galvin, Laura Gates. (ENG.). 36p. (J). (gr. -1-2). 2006. 2.95 *(978-1-59249-187-2(1)*, S6551); 2005. 8.95 *(978-1-59249-206-0(1)*, SD6501); 2003. 9.95 *(978-1-59249-188-9(X)*, PS6551) Soundprints.
—Leperit the Zebra. Grey, Chelsea Gillian. 2005. (Internet Interactive Ser.). (ENG.). 36p. (J). (gr. -1-3). 8.95 *(978-1-59249-440-8(4)*, SD6505); (gr. 2-2). 14.95 *(978-1-59249-438-5(2)*, H6505); (gr. 2-2). pap. 6.95 *(978-1-59249-439-2(0)*, S6505) Soundprints.
Denman, Michael & Huiett, William J. Land of the Wild Llama: A Story of the Patagonian Andes. Fraggalosch, Audrey. 2005. (Wild Habitats Ser.). (ENG.). (J). (gr. 1-4). 32p. 19.95 *(978-1-931465-83-0(5)*, BC7022); 36p. 15.95 *(978-1-931465-81-6(9)*, B7022) Soundprints.
—Land of the Wild Llama: A Story of the Patagonian Andes, Including 10" Toy. Fraggalosch, Audrey. 2005. (Wild Habitats Ser.). (ENG.). 36p. (J). (gr. 1-4). 17.95 *(978-1-931465-86-1(X)*, PS7022) Soundprints.
Denman, Michael L. The Town Musicians of Bremen. Sommer, Carl. 2016. (J). ***(978-1-57537-947-0(3))*** Advance Publishing, Inc.
Denman, Michael L. & Huiett, William J. Judy the Elephant. Galvin, Laura Gates. Denman, Michael L. & Huiett, William J., trs. 2005. (African Wildlife Foundation Ser.). (ENG.). 36p. (J). (gr. -1-2). 14.95 *(978-1-59249-169-8(3)*, H6502); 6.95 *(978-1-59249-170-4(7)*, S6502) Soundprints.
—Kakuda the Giraffe. Galvin, Laura Gates. Denman, Michael L. & Huiett, William J., trs. 2005. (Meet Africa's Animals Ser.). (ENG.). 36p. (J). (gr. -1-2). 14.95 *(978-1-59249-185-8(5)*, H6501); pap. 6.95 *(978-1-59249-186-5(3)*, S6501) Soundprints.
—Leperit the Zebra: African Wildlife Foundation. Grey, Chelsea Gillian. 2005. (Meet Africa's Animals Ser.). (ENG.). 36p. (J). (gr. -1-2). 2.95 *(978-1-59249-441-5(2)*, S6555) Soundprints.
Denman, Michael L., jt. illus. see Huiett, William J.
Denmark, Thomas. Knights & Castles. Torpie, Kate. 2008. (ENG.). 24p. (J). (gr. 2-17). 19.99 *(978-1-58476-726-8(X))* Innovative Kids.
Denne, John, photos by. High Riders, Saints & Death Cars: A Life Saved by Art, 1 vol. Herrera, Nicholas. 2011. (ENG., 56p. (J). (gr. 4-18). 24.95 *(978-0-88899-854-5(6))* Groundwood Bks. CAN. Dist: Perseus-PGW.
Dennen, Sue. The Moving Book: A Kids' Survival Guide. Davis, Gabriel. 2nd ed. 2008. 160p. (J). spiral bd. 22.95 *(978-0-912301-92-1(9))* First Bks.
Dennis, Jane. Far from This Earth & Other Stories. Oliver, Chad. Olson, Priscilla, ed. 2003. (NESFA's Choice Ser.: 25). 480p. 24.00 *(978-1-886778-48-1(5)*, NESFA Pr.) New England Science Fiction Assn., Inc.
—A Star Above It & Other Stories. Oliver, Chad. Olson, Priscilla, ed. 2003. (NESFA's Choice Ser.: 24). 480p. 24.00 *(978-1-886778-45-0(0)*, NESFA Pr.) New England Science Fiction Assn., Inc.
Dennis, Nadine. Lincoln & the Lilac Lilies. Stafford, Mary. 2005. (Fantastic World of Lincoln Llama Ser.). 24p. 6.95 *(978-0-9735663-0-7(2))* Amethyst Hse Publishing, Inc. CAN. Dist: Hushion Hse. Publishing, Ltd.
—Lincoln's Day of Discovery, Vol. 2. Stafford, Mary. 2005. (Fantastic World of Lincoln Llama Ser.). 24p. 6.95 *(978-0-9735663-1-4(0))* Amethyst Hse Publishing, Inc. CAN. Dist: Hushion Hse. Publishing, Ltd.
—Lincoln's Journey of Journeys, Vol. 3. Stafford, Mary. 2005. (Fantastic World of Lincoln Llama Ser.). 24p. 6.95 *(978-0-9735663-2-1(9))* Amethyst Hse Publishing, Inc. CAN. Dist: Hushion Hse. Publishing, Ltd.
Dennis, Peter. The Adventures of King Arthur. 2003. (Young Reading Ser.). 64p. (J). (gr. k-7). pap. 5.99 *(978-0-7945-0447-2(7)*, Usborne) EDC Publishing.
—The Adventures of King Arthur. 2003. (Usborne Young Reading: Series Two Ser.). 64p. (J). (gr. k-7). 8.99 *(978-0-7945-1871-4(0)*, Usborne) EDC Publishing.
—Castle. 2006. (Leap Through Time Ser.). 31p. (J). *(978-0-7607-7523-3(0))* backpackbook.
—Conquest! Can You Build a Roman City? Bruce, Julia. 2009. (Step into History Ser.). 32p. (J). (gr. 2-5). lib. bdg. 23.94 *(978-0-7660-3478-5(X))* Enslow Pubs., Inc.
—Dinosaurs Through Time. Harris, Nicolas. 2009. (Fast Forward Ser.). 32p. (YA). (gr. 2-5). lib. bdg. 25.25 *(978-1-4358-2802-5(X))* Rosen Publishing Group, Inc., The.
—The First Humans. Harris, Nicholas. 2006. 31p. (J). *(978-0-7607-7528-8(1))* backpackbook.
—Horror of the Heights, 1 vol. Masters, Anthony. 2006. (Graphic Quest Ser.). (ENG.). 88p. (gr. 3-3). 23.99 *(978-1-59889-030-3(1)*, Graphic Quest) Stone Arch Bks.
—Hunt! Can You Survive the Stone Age? Bruce, Julia. 2009. (Step into History Ser.). 32p. (J). (gr. 2-5). lib. bdg. 23.94 *(978-0-7660-3476-1(3))* Enslow Pubs., Inc.
—Pyramid. Harris, Nicholas. 2006. 31p. (J). *(978-0-7607-7526-4(5))* backpackbook.
—Sail! Can You Command a Sea Voyage? Bruce, Julia. 2009. (Step into History Ser.). 32p. (J). (gr. 2-5). lib. bdg. 23.94 *(978-0-7660-3477-8(1))* Enslow Pubs., Inc.
—Siege! Can You Capture a Castle? Bruce, Julia. 2009. (Step into History Ser.). 32p. (J). (gr. 2-5). lib. bdg. 23.94 *(978-0-7660-3475-4(5))* Enslow Pubs., Inc.
Dennis, Peter & Draper, Richard. The Usborne Book of Explorers. Everett, Felicity & Reid, Struan. rev. ed. 2007. (Famous Lives Ser.). 47p. (J). (gr. 4-7). pap. 8.99 *(978-0-7945-1533-1(9)*, Usborne) EDC Publishing.
Dennis, Sarah. Cinderella: A Cut-Paper Book. 2015. (ENG.). 52p. (J). (gr. -1-k). 19.99 *(978-1-85707-843-5(8))* Tango Bks. GBR. Dist: Independent Pubs. Group.
Dennis, Tammy D. The Crumb Snatchers. Thompson, Debra. 2012. 24p. pap. 12.95 *(978-1-61493-037-2(6))* Peppertree Pr., The.
Dennis, Wesley. Benjamin West & His Cat Grimalkin. Henry, Marguerite. 2014. (ENG.). 160p. (J). (gr. 3-7). pap. 6.99 *(978-1-4814-0394-8(X)*, Simon & Schuster/Paula Wiseman Bks.) Simon & Schuster/Paula Wiseman Bks.
—Cinnabar, the One o'Clock Fox. Henry, Marguerite. 2014. (ENG.). 144p. (J). (gr. 3-7). pap. 5.99 *(978-1-4814-0400-6(8)*, Simon & Schuster/Paula Wiseman Bks.) Simon & Schuster/Paula Wiseman Bks.
—Justin Morgan Had a Horse. Henry, Marguerite. (ENG.). 176p. (J). (gr. 3-7). 2015. 19.99 *(978-1-4814-2562-9(5))*; 2006. pap. 6.99 *(978-1-4169-2785-3(9))* Simon & Schuster/Paula Wiseman Bks. (Simon & Schuster/Paula Wiseman Bks.).
—King of the Wind: The Story of the Godolphin Arabian. Henry, Marguerite. 2006. (ENG.). 176p. (J). (gr. 3-7). pap. 7.99 *(978-1-4169-2786-0(7)*, Simon & Schuster/Paula Wiseman Bks.) Simon & Schuster/Paula Wiseman Bks.
—Misty of Chincoteague. Henry, Marguerite. 2007. 173p. (gr. 3-7). 17.00 *(978-0-7569-8227-0(8))* Perfection Learning Corp.
—Misty of Chincoteague. Henry, Marguerite. 60th ed. 2006. (ENG.). 176p. (J). (gr. 3-7). pap. 6.99 *(978-1-4169-2783-9(2)*, Simon & Schuster/Paula Wiseman Bks.) Simon & Schuster/Paula Wiseman Bks.
—Sea Star: Orphan of Chincoteague. Henry, Marguerite. 2007. (ENG.). 176p. (J). (gr. 3-7). pap. 6.99 *(978-1-4169-2784-6(0)*, Simon & Schuster/Paula Wiseman Bks.) Simon & Schuster/Paula Wiseman Bks.
—Stormy, Misty's Foal. Henry, Marguerite. (ENG.). (J). (gr. 3-7). 2015. 256p. 19.99 *(978-1-4814-2561-2(7))*; 2007. 224p. pap. 6.99 *(978-1-4169-2788-4(3))* Simon & Schuster/Paula Wiseman Bks. (Simon & Schuster/Paula Wiseman Bks.).
—Ticktock & Jim: Famous Horse Stories. Robertson, Keith. 2011. 250p. 46.95 *(978-1-258-10102-2(5))* Literary Licensing, LLC.
—White Stallion of Lipizza. Henry, Marguerite. 2014. (ENG.). 192p. (J). (gr. 3-7). pap. 6.99 *(978-1-4814-0391-7(5)*, Simon & Schuster/Paula Wiseman Bks.) Simon & Schuster/Paula Wiseman Bks.
Denos, Julia. Clara & the Magical Charms. McNamara, Margaret. 2013. (Fairy Bell Sisters Ser.: 4). (ENG.). 128p. (J). (gr. 1-5). 15.99 *(978-0-06-222811-6(0))*; pap. 4.99 *(978-0-06-222810-9(2))* HarperCollins Pubs.
—Dotty. Perl, Erica S. 2010. (ENG.). 32p. (J). (gr. -1-3). 16.95 *(978-0-8109-8962-7(X)*, Abrams Bks. for Young Readers) Abrams.
—The Fairy Bell Sisters No. 3: Golden at the Fancy-Dress Party. McNamara, Margaret. 2013. (Fairy Bell Sisters Ser.: 3). (ENG.). 144p. (J). (gr. 1-5). pap. 4.99 *(978-0-06-222807-9(2))* HarperCollins Pubs.
—The Fairy Bell Sisters Vol. 5: Sylva & the Lost Treasure. McNamara, Margaret. 2014. (Fairy Bell Sisters Ser.: 5). (ENG.). 144p. (J). (gr. 1-5). 15.99 *(978-0-06-226721-4(3))* HarperCollins Pubs.
—The Fairy Bell Sisters #3: Golden at the Fancy-Dress Party. McNamara, Margaret. 2013. (Fairy Bell Sisters Ser.: 3). (ENG.). 144p. (J). (gr. 1-5). 15.99 *(978-0-06-222808-6(0))* HarperCollins Pubs.
—Girls Against Boys. Denton, P. J. 2013. (Sleepover Squad Ser.: 7). (ENG.). 96p. (J). (gr. 1-4). pap. 4.99 *(978-1-4169-5933-5(5)*, Simon & Schuster/Paula Wiseman Bks.) Simon & Schuster/Paula Wiseman Bks.
—Grandma's Gloves. Castellucci, Cecil. 2010. (ENG.). 32p. (J). (gr. k-3). 15.99 *(978-0-7636-3168-0(X))* Candlewick Pr.
—I Had a Favorite Dress. Ashburn, Boni. 2011. (ENG.). 32p. (J). (gr. -1-1). 16.95 *(978-1-4197-0016-3(2)*, Abrams Bks. for Young Readers) Abrams.
—Just Being Audrey. Cardillo, Margaret. 2011. (ENG.). 32p. (J). (gr. -1-3). 16.99 *(978-0-06-185283-1(X))* HarperCollins Pubs.
—Keeping Secrets. Denton, P. J. 4th ed. 2008. (Sleepover Squad Ser.: 4). (ENG.). 80p. (J). (gr. 1-4). pap. 4.99 *(978-1-4169-2801-0(4)*, Simon & Schuster/Paula Wiseman Bks.) Simon & Schuster/Paula Wiseman Bks.
—Letters to Leo. Hest, Amy. 2012. (ENG.). 160p. (J). (gr. 3-7). 14.99 *(978-0-7636-3695-1(9))* Candlewick Pr.
—Letters to Leo. Hest, Amy. 2014. (ENG.). 160p. (J). (gr. 3-7). pap. 6.99 *(978-0-7636-7165-5(7))* Candlewick Pr.
—Lexie. Couloumbis, Audrey. (ENG.). 208p. (J). (gr. 3-7). 2012. pap. 6.99 *(978-0-375-85633-4(1))*; 2011. 15.99 *(978-0-375-85632-7(3))* Random Hse., Inc.
—Pony Party! Denton, P. J. 5th ed. 2008. (Sleepover Squad Ser.: 5). (ENG.). 80p. (J). (gr. 1-4). pap. 4.99 *(978-1-4169-5931-1(9)*, Simon & Schuster/Paula Wiseman Bks.) Simon & Schuster/Paula Wiseman Bks.
—Rosy & the Secret Friend. McNamara, Margaret. 2013. (Fairy Bell Sisters Ser.: 2). (ENG.). 128p. (J). (gr. 1-5). 15.99 *(978-0-06-222805-5(6))*; pap. 4.99 *(978-0-06-222804-8(8))* HarperCollins Pubs.
—Sojourner Truth: Path to Glory. Merchant, Peter. 2007. (Ready-To-read SOFA Ser.). (ENG.). 48p. (J). (gr. 1-3). pap. 3.99 *(978-0-689-87207-5(0)*, Simon Spotlight) Simon Spotlight.
—Sylva & the Fairy Ball. McNamara, Margaret. 2013. (Fairy Bell Sisters Ser.: 1). (ENG.). 128p. (J). (gr. 1-5). 15.99 *(978-0-06-222802-4(1))*; pap. 4.99 *(978-0-06-222801-7(3))* HarperCollins Pubs.
—Sylva & the Lost Treasure. McNamara, Margaret. 2014. (Fairy Bell Sisters Ser.: 5). (ENG.). 144p. (J). (gr. 1-5). pap. 4.99 *(978-0-06-226720-7(5))* HarperCollins Pubs.
—Where Do Angels Sleep? Strong, Cynda. 2007. 24p. (J). (gr. -1-3). 14.99 *(978-0-7586-1298-4(2))* Concordia Publishing Hse.
Denslow, W. W. La Mirinda Sorchisto de Oz. Baum, L. Frank. Broadribb, Donald, tr. 2012. 276p. pap. 24.00 *(978-1-59569-245-0(2))* Mondial.
—The Wizard of Oz. Baum, L. Frank. 2012. (Stepping Stone Book Ser.). (ENG.). 112p. (J). (gr. 1-4). 4.99 *(978-0-375-86994-5(8)*, Random Hse. Bks. for Young Readers) Random Hse. Children's Bks.
—The Wonderful Wizard of Oz. Baum, L. Frank. 2015. (Dover Children's Classics Ser.). (ENG.). 308p. (J). (gr. 3-6).

reprint ed. pap. 14.99 *(978-0-486-20691-2(2))* Dover Pubns., Inc.

—The Wonderful Wizard of Oz. Baum, L. Frank. Wolstenholme, Susan, ed. 2008. (Oxford World's Classics Ser.). (ENG.). 336p. pap. 13.95 *(978-0-19-954064-8(0))* Oxford Univ. Pr., Inc.

Denslow, W. W. The Pearl & the Pumpkin: A Classic Halloween Tale. Denslow, W. W. West, Paul. 2009. (Dover Children's Classics Ser.). (ENG.). 264p. (J). (gr. 2-5). pap. 12.99 *(978-0-486-47031-3(8))* Dover Pubns., Inc.

Denslow, W. W. & Menten, Ted. The Wonderful Wizard of Oz. Baum, L. Frank. 2010. (Dover Read & Listen Ser.). (ENG.). 112p. (J). (gr. 1-5). pap. 14.99 *(978-0-486-47725-1(8))* Dover Pubns., Inc.

Denton, Ivan. Blizzard No. 5: Don't Give Up. Denton, Ivan. Sargent, Dave. 2004. 36p. (J). pap. 10.95 *(978-1-59381-009-2(1))* Ozark Publishing.

—Misty's Miracle No. 4: Overcome Fear, 6 vols. Denton, Ivan. Sargent, Dave. 2004. 36p. (J). pap. 10.95 *(978-1-59381-005-4(9))* Ozark Publishing.

—My Grandpa Is a Cowboy: Learning Is Fun #1, 6 vols. Denton, Ivan. Sargent, Dave. 2004. 36p. (J). pap. 10.95 *(978-1-59381-001-6(6))* Ozark Publishing.

Denton, Kady MacDonald. A Bedtime for Bear. Becker, Bonny. 2010. (J). (Bear & Mouse Ser.: 3). (ENG.). 48p. (gr. -1-2). 16.99 *(978-0-7636-4101-6(4))*; *(978-0-7636-5364-4(0))* Candlewick Pr.

—A Birthday for Bear. Becker, Bonny. (Candlewick Sparks Ser.). (ENG.). (J). 2013. 56p. (gr. k-4). pap. 3.99 *(978-0-7636-6861-7(3))*; 2012. 48p. (gr. -1-2). 16.99 *(978-0-7636-5823-6(5))*; 2009. 56p. (gr. -1-2). 15.99 *(978-0-7636-3746-0(7))* Candlewick Pr.

—A Child's Treasury of Nursery Rhymes. 2004. (J). (gr. k). audio compact disk 12.95 *(978-0-618-49306-7(9))* Houghton Mifflin Harcourt Trade & Reference Pubs.

—The Good-Pie Party. Scanlon, Liz Garton. 2014. (ENG.). 32p. (J). (gr. -1-3). 17.99 *(978-0-545-44870-3(0))*, Levine, Arthur A. Bks.) Scholastic, Inc.

—I Gave My Mom a Castle, 1 vol. Little, Jean. 2003. (ENG.). 80p. (J). (gr. 4-12). pap. 7.95 *(978-1-55143-253-3(6))* Orca Bk. Pubs. USA.

—A Library Book for Bear. Becker, Bonny. 2014. (Bear & Mouse Ser.). (ENG.). 32p. (J). 16.99 *(978-0-7636-4924-1(4))* Candlewick Pr.

—The Queen of France. Wadham, Tim. 2011. (ENG.). 32p. (J). (gr. -1-3). 16.99 *(978-0-7636-4102-3(2))* Candlewick Pr.

—A Sea-Wishing Day. Heidbreder, Robert. 2007. (ENG.). 32p. (J). (gr. -1-3). 15.95 *(978-1-55337-707-8(9))* Kids Can Pr., Ltd. CAN. Dist: Univ. of Toronto Pr.

—A Second Is a Hiccup: A Child's Book of Time. Hutchins, Hazel J. 2004. (ENG.). 32p. (J). *(978-0-439-97400-4(3)*, North Winds Pr) Scholastic Canada, Ltd.

—A Second Is a Hiccup: A Child's Book of Time. Hutchins, Hazel. (J). 2008. 16.99 *(978-0-439-83110-9(5))*; 2007. (ENG.). 40p. (gr. -1-3). 17.99 *(978-0-439-83106-2(7))* Scholastic, Inc. (Levine, Arthur A. Bks.).

—The Sniffles for Bear. Becker, Bonny. 2011. (Bear & Mouse Ser.). (ENG.). 32p. (J). (gr. -1-2). 16.99 *(978-0-7636-4756-8(X))* Candlewick Pr.

—Two Homes. Masurel, Claire. 2003. (ENG.). 40p. (J). (gr. -1-2). 6.99 *(978-0-7636-1984-8(1))* Candlewick Pr.

—A Visitor for Bear. Becker, Bonny. (Bear & Mouse Ser.). (ENG.). 56p. (J). 2012. (gr. k-k). pap. 6.99 *(978-0-7636-4611-0(3))*; 2008. (gr. -1-2). 16.99 *(978-0-7636-2807-9(7))* Candlewick Pr.

—A Visitor for Bear. Becker, Bonny. ed. 2012. lib. bdg. 17.20 *(978-0-606-26930-8(4)*, Turtleback) Turtleback Bks.

—You're Mean, Lily Jean! Wishinsky, Frieda. 2011. (ENG.). 32p. (J). (gr. -1-3). 16.99 *(978-0-8075-9476-6(8))* Whitman, Albert & Co.

Denton, Shannon & Denton, Shannon E. The Mystery of the Roanoke Colony, 1 vol. Niz, Xavier & Niz, Xavier W. 2006. (Graphic History Ser.). (ENG.). 32p. (gr. 3-4). 29.99 *(978-0-7368-6494-7(6)*, Graphic Library) Capstone Pr., Inc.

Denton, Shannon E. The Mystery of the Roanoke Colony, 1 vol. Englar, Xavier & Niz, Xavier W. 2006. (Graphic History Ser.). (ENG.). 32p. (gr. 3-4). per. 8.10 *(978-0-7368-9657-3(0)*, Graphic Library) Capstone Pr., Inc.

Denton, Shannon E., jt. illus. see Denton, Shannon.

Denton, Terry. Beastly Tales: Six Crazy Creature Capers. Tulloch, Richard. 2006. (ENG.). 144p. (J). (gr. k-2). pap. 13.99 *(978-1-74166-189-7(7))* Random Hse. Australia AUS. Dist: Independent Pubs. Group.

—The Big Fat Cow That Goes Kapow. Griffiths, Andy. 2010. (ENG.). 144p. (J). (gr. -1-3). pap. 7.99 *(978-0-312-65301-9(8))* Square Fish.

—The Cat on the Mat Is Flat. Griffiths, Andy. 2009. (ENG.). 192p. (J). (gr. -1-3). pap. 7.99 *(978-0-312-53584-1(8))* Square Fish.

—The Cat, the Rat, & the Baseball Bat. Griffiths, Andy. 2013. (My Readers Ser.). (ENG.). 32p. (J). (gr. -1-1). 15.99 *(978-1-250-02773-3(X))*; pap. 3.99 *(978-1-250-02774-0(8))* Square Fish.

—Ed & Ted & Ted's Dog Fred. Griffiths, Andy. 2014. (My Readers Ser.). (ENG.). 32p. (J). (gr. -1-1). 15.99 *(978-1-250-04447-1(2))* Square Fish.

—Kaleidoscope. Carthew, Mark & Rosen, Michael. 2007. (Collins Big Cat Ser.). (ENG.). 1p. (J). pap. 8.99 *(978-0-00-722870-6(8))* HarperCollins Pubs. Ltd. GBR. Dist: Independent Pubs. Group.

—Killer Koalas from Outer Space: And Lots of Other Very Bad Stuff That Will Make Your Brain Explode! Griffiths, Andy. 2011. (ENG.). 176p. (J). (gr. 3-7). 12.99 *(978-0-312-36789-3(9))* Feiwel & Friends.

—Killer Koalas from Outer Space & Lots of Other Very Bad Stuff That Will Make Your Brain Explode! Griffiths, Andy. 2012. (ENG.). 192p. (J). (gr. 3-7). pap. 6.99 *(978-1-250-01017-9(9))* Square Fish.

Denton, Terry. The Looming Lamplight. Dubosarsky, Ursula. 2015. (Cryptic Casebook of Coco Carlomagno & Alberta Ser.: 2). (ENG.). 96p. (J). (gr. 1-3). 9.99 ***(978-1-74331-259-9(8))*** Allen & Unwin AUS. Dist: Independent Pubs. Group.

—The Perplexing Pineapple. Dubosarsky, Ursula. 2015. (Cryptic Casebook of Coco Carlomagno & Alberta Ser.: 1). (ENG.). 84p. (J). (gr. 1-3). 9.99 ***(978-1-74331-257-5(1))*** Allen & Unwin AUS. Dist: Independent Pubs. Group.

Denton, Terry. What Body Part Is That? A Wacky Guide to the Funniest, Weirdest, & Most Disgustingest Parts of Your Body. Griffiths, Andy. 2012. (ENG.). 192p. (J). (gr. 3-7). 12.99 *(978-0-312-36790-9(2))* Feiwel & Friends.

—What Body Part Is That? A Wacky Guide to the Funniest, Weirdest, & Most Disgustingest Parts of Your Body. Griffiths, Andy. 2013. (ENG.). 208p. (J). (gr. 3-7). pap. 6.99 *(978-1-250-03406-9(X))* Square Fish.

—The 13-Story Treehouse. Griffiths, Andy. 2013. (Treehouse Bks.). (ENG.). 256p. (J). (gr. 1-5). 13.99 *(978-1-250-02690-3(3))* Feiwel & Friends.

—The 26-Story Treehouse. Griffiths, Andy. 2014. (Treehouse Bks.). (ENG.). 352p. (J). (gr. 1-5). 13.99 *(978-1-250-02691-0(1))* Feiwel & Friends.

—The 39-Story Treehouse. Griffiths, Andy. 2015. (Treehouse Bks.). (ENG.). 352p. (J). (gr. 1-5). 13.99 *(978-1-250-02692-7(X))* Feiwel & Friends.

Denton, Terry. The Golden Udder. Denton, Terry. 2003. (Storymaze Ser.: Vol. 4). (ENG.). 120p. (J). (gr. 3-6). pap. 11.99 *(978-1-86508-784-9(X))* Allen & Unwin AUS. Dist: Independent Pubs. Group.

—It's True! Pigs Do Fly. Denton, Terry. 2006. (It's True! Ser.). (ENG.). 96p. (J). (gr. 5-8). 19.95 *(978-1-55037-949-5(6)*, 9781550379495) Annick Pr., Ltd. CAN. Dist: Firefly Bks., Ltd.

—Summer in the City. Denton, Terry. 2008. (ENG.). 132p. (J). (gr. 2-5). pap. 11.99 *(978-1-74175-130-7(6))* Allen & Unwin AUS. Dist: Independent Pubs. Group.

—Thrillseekers. Denton, Terry. 2009. (Women's Press Classics Ser.). (ENG.). 132p. (J). (gr. 2-5). pap. 10.99 *(978-1-74175-131-4(4))* Allen & Unwin AUS. Dist: Independent Pubs. Group.

—The Ultimate Wave. Denton, Terry. 2003. (Storymaze Ser.: Vol. 1). (ENG.). 144p. (J). (gr. 3-7). pap. 11.99 *(978-1-86508-378-0(X))* Allen & Unwin AUS. Dist: Independent Pubs. Group.

—Wombat & Fox: Tales of the City. Denton, Terry. 2008. (ENG.). 130p. (Orig.). (J). (gr. -1-3). pap. 10.99 *(978-1-933605-81-4(2))* Kane Miller.

—The Wooden Cow. Denton, Terry. 2003. (Storymaze Ser.: Vol. 3). (ENG.). 120p. (J). (gr. 3-6). pap. 11.99 *(978-1-86508-783-2(1))* Allen & Unwin AUS. Dist: Independent Pubs. Group.

DeNucci, Corinne. Ava Goes to Africa. DeNucci, Sharon. 2010. 32p. pap. 16.99 *(978-1-4520-4091-2(5))* AuthorHouse.

—Grammie & the Gecko. Denucci, Sharon. 2008. 40p. pap. 16.99 *(978-1-4389-1790-0(2))* AuthorHouse.

Deodato, Mike. The Marvel Art of Mike Deodato. 2011. (ENG.). 240p. (YA). (gr. 8-17). 49.99 *(978-0-7851-4769-5(1))* Marvel Worldwide, Inc.

—Mission to Mars, Vol. 1. Brubaker, Ed. 2011. (ENG.). 168p. (YA). (gr. 8-17). pap. 19.99 *(978-0-7851-4600-1(8))* Marvel Worldwide, Inc.

Deodato, Mike & Conrad, Will. Eyes of the Dragon, Vol. 2. 2011. (ENG.). 144p. (YA). (gr. 8-17). 24.99 *(978-0-7851-4601-8(6))* Marvel Worldwide, Inc.

DePalma, Mary Newell. Bow-Wow Wiggle Waggle. 2012. 32p. (J). 14.00 *(978-0-8028-5408-7(7)*, Eerdmans Bks For Young Readers) Eerdmans, William B. Publishing Co.

—Now It Is Summer. Spinelli, Eileen. 2011. 32p. (J). (gr. -1-3). 16.00 *(978-0-8028-5340-0(4)*, Eerdmans Bks For Young Readers) Eerdmans, William B. Publishing Co.

—Now It Is Winter. Spinelli, Eileen. 2004. 32p. (J). 16.00 *(978-0-8028-5244-1(0))* Eerdmans, William B. Publishing Co.

—The Squeaky Door. MacDonald, Margaret Read. 2006. (ENG.). 40p. (J). (gr. -1-1). 16.99 *(978-0-06-028373-5(4))* HarperCollins Pubs.

—The Squeaky Door. MacDonald, Margaret Read. 2006. 40p. (J). (gr. -1-1). 17.89 *(978-0-06-028374-2(2))* HarperCollins Pubs.

—Swimming Sal. Molski, Carol. 2009. 36p. (J). (gr. -1-3). 17.00 *(978-0-8028-5327-1(7)*, Eerdmans Bks For Young Readers) Eerdmans, William B. Publishing Co.

Depalma, Victoria. This Is My Body: A Safety for Little Girls. DePalma, Vanessa. 2003. 15p. (J). (gr. -1-4). *(978-0-9728135-0-1(0))* DePalma, Vanessa.

dePaola, Tomie, et al. Brava, Strega Nona! A Heartwarming Pop-Up Book. dePaola, Tomie. 2008. (ENG.). 12p. (J). (gr. -1-k). 29.99 *(978-0-399-24453-7(0)*, Putnam Juvenile) Penguin Publishing Group.

dePaola, Tomie. Cookie's Week. Ward, Cindy. 2015. 32p. pap. 7.00 ***(978-1-61003-528-6(3))*** Center for the Collaborative Classroom.

—Erandi's Braids. Madrigal, Antonio Hernandez. 2015. 32p. pap. 7.00 ***(978-1-61003-530-9(5))*** Center for the Collaborative Classroom.

dePaola, Tomie. Frida Kahlo: The Artist Who Painted Herself. Frith, Margaret. 2003. (Smart about Art Ser.). (ENG.). 32p. (J). (gr. k-4). 5.99 *(978-0-448-42677-8(3)*, Grosset & Dunlap) Penguin Publishing Group.

—I Love You, Sun I Love You, Moon. Pandell, Karen. 2007. (ENG.). 20p. (J). (gr. k-k). bds. 6.99 *(978-0-448-44800-8(9)*, Grosset & Dunlap) Penguin Publishing Group.

DePaola, Tomie. In a Small Kingdom. 2016. (J). ***(978-0-8234-3551-7(2))*** Holiday Hse., Inc.

dePaola, Tomie. Little Poems for Tiny Ears. Oliver, Lin. 2014. (ENG.). 32p. (J). (gr. -1 — 1). 16.99 *(978-0-399-16605-1(X)*, Nancy Paulsen Bks.) Penguin Publishing Group.

DePaola, Tomie. Look & Be Grateful. 2015. (ENG.). 32p. (J). 16.95 ***(978-0-8234-3443-5(5))*** Holiday Hse., Inc.

dePaola, Tomie. Mary Had a Little Lamb. Hale, Sarah Josepha. 2004. (ENG.). 28p. (J). (gr. -1 — 1). bds. 7.99 *(978-0-399-24221-2(X)*, Putnam Juvenile) Penguin Publishing Group.

—Miracle on 34th Street. Davies, Valentine. 2004. (ENG.). 144p. (J). (gr. -1-3). 7.98 *(978-1-57866-027-8(0)*, Galahad Bks.) BBS Publishing Corp.

dePaola, Tomie. The Moon's Almost Here! MacLachlan, Patricia. 2015. (J). ***(978-1-4814-2062-4(3)***, McElderry, Margaret K. Bks.) McElderry, Margaret K. Bks.

dePaola, Tomie. The Night Before Christmas. Moore, Clement C. 2010. (ENG.). 24p. (J). (gr. -1). bds. 8.95 *(978-0-8234-2284-5(4))* Holiday Hse., Inc.

—Te Amo Sol, Te Amo Luna. Pandell, Karen. 2003.Tr. of I Love You Sun, I Love You Moon. (SPA & ENG.). 12p. (J). (gr. -1 — 1). bds. 7.99 *(978-0-399-24165-9(5)*, Putnam Juvenile) Penguin Publishing Group.

dePaola, Tomie. Adelita: A Mexican Cinderella Story. dePaola, Tomie. 2004. (SPA & ENG.). 40p. (J). (gr. -1-3). pap. 6.99 *(978-0-14-240187-3(0)*, Puffin) Penguin Publishing Group.

—The Birds of Bethlehem. dePaola, Tomie. 2012. (ENG.). 40p. (J). (gr. -1-k). 16.99 *(978-0-399-25780-3(2)*, Nancy Paulsen Bks.) Penguin Publishing Group.

—Days of the Blackbird: A Tale of Northern Italy. dePaola, Tomie. 2005. (J). 13.65 *(978-0-7569-5888-6(1))* Perfection Learning Corp.

—For the Duration: The War Years, 8 vols. dePaola, Tomie. 2009. (26 Fairmount Avenue Book Ser.: 8). (ENG.). 80p. (J). (gr. 2-5). 16.99 *(978-0-399-25209-9(6)*, Putnam Juvenile) Penguin Publishing Group.

—Four Friends at Christmas. dePaola, Tomie. 2009. (ENG.). 32p. (J). (gr. -1-1). 12.99 *(978-1-4169-9175-5(1)*, Simon & Schuster/Paula Wiseman Bks.) Simon & Schuster/Paula Wiseman Bks.

—Four Friends in Autumn. dePaola, Tomie. 2004. (ENG.). 32p. (J). (gr. -1-3). 17.99 *(978-0-689-85980-9(5)*, Simon & Schuster Bks. For Young Readers) Simon & Schuster Bks. For Young Readers.

—Four Friends in Summer. dePaola, Tomie. 2003. (ENG.). 32p. (J). (gr. -1-1). reprint ed. 16.99 *(978-0-689-85693-8(8)*, Simon & Schuster Bks. For Young Readers) Simon & Schuster Bks. For Young Readers.

—Jack. dePaola, Tomie. 2014. (ENG.). 40p. (J). (gr. -1-k). 17.99 *(978-0-399-16154-4(6)*, Nancy Paulsen Bks.) Penguin Publishing Group.

—Joy to the World: Christmas Stories & Songs. dePaola, Tomie. 2010. (ENG.). 112p. (J). (gr. -1-2). 24.99 *(978-0-399-25536-6(2)*, Putnam Juvenile) Penguin Publishing Group.

—Joy to the World: Tomie's Christmas Stories. dePaola, Tomie. 2013. (ENG.). 112p. (J). (gr. -1). 12.99 *(978-0-14-750952-9(1)*, Puffin) Penguin Publishing Group.

—Let the Whole Earth Sing Praise. dePaola, Tomie. 2011. (ENG.). 28p. (J). (gr. -1-k). 15.99 *(978-0-399-25478-9(1)*, Putnam Juvenile) Penguin Publishing Group.

—Little Grunt & the Big Egg: A Prehistoric Fairy Tale. dePaola, Tomie. 2008. (ENG.). 32p. (J). (gr. -1-3). pap. 6.99 *(978-0-14-241143-8(4)*, Puffin) Penguin Publishing Group.

—Meet the Barkers: Morgan & Moffat Go to School. dePaola, Tomie. 2003. (Barker Twins Ser.). (ENG.). 32p. (J). (gr. -1-3). 5.99 *(978-0-14-250083-5(6)*, Puffin) Penguin Publishing Group.

—More Mother Goose Favorites. dePaola, Tomie. 2007. (gr. -1-3). 14.00 *(978-0-7569-8138-9(7))* Perfection Learning Corp.

—Mother Goose Favorites. dePaola, Tomie. 2007. (ENG.). 32p. (J). (gr. -1-3). mass mkt. 3.99 *(978-0-448-44494-9(1)*, Grosset & Dunlap) Penguin Publishing Group.

—My First Chanukah. dePaola, Tomie. 2008. (ENG.). 14p. (J). (gr. -1-k). bds. 5.99 *(978-0-448-44859-6(9)*, Grosset & Dunlap) Penguin Publishing Group.

—My First Christmas. dePaola, Tomie. 2008. (ENG.). 14p. (J). (gr. -1-k). bds. 5.99 *(978-0-448-44860-2(2)*, Grosset & Dunlap) Penguin Publishing Group.

—My First Easter. dePaola, Tomie. 2008. (ENG.). 14p. (J). (gr. -1-k). bds. 5.99 *(978-0-448-44790-2(8)*, Grosset & Dunlap) Penguin Publishing Group.

—My First Passover. dePaola, Tomie. 2015. (ENG.). 14p. (J). (gr. -1-k). bds. 5.99 *(978-0-448-44791-9(6)*, Grosset & Dunlap) Penguin Publishing Group.

—My Mother Is So Smart. dePaola, Tomie. (ENG.). 32p. (J). (gr. -1-k). 2013. pap. 6.99 *(978-0-14-242536-7(2)*, Puffin); 2010. 16.99 *(978-0-399-25442-0(0)*, Putnam Juvenile) Penguin Publishing Group.

—Now One Foot, Now the Other. dePaola, Tomie. (ENG.). 48p. (J). (gr. k-3). 2006. pap. 7.99 *(978-0-14-240104-0(8)*, Puffin); 2005. reprint ed. 16.99 *(978-0-399-24259-5(7)*, Putnam Juvenile) Penguin Publishing Group.

—Pascual & the Kitchen Angels. dePaola, Tomie. 2006. (ENG.). 32p. (J). (gr. -1-3). pap. 6.99 *(978-0-14-240536-9(1)*, Puffin) Penguin Publishing Group.

—Stagestruck. dePaola, Tomie. (ENG.). 32p. (J). (gr. -1-3). 2007. pap. 6.99 *(978-0-14-240899-5(9)*, Puffin); 2005. 16.99 *(978-0-399-24338-7(0)*, Putnam Juvenile) Penguin Publishing Group.

—Stagestruck. dePaola, Tomie. 2007. (gr. -1-3). 17.00 *(978-0-7569-8159-4(X))* Perfection Learning Corp.

—Strega Nona. dePaola, Tomie. 2011. (ENG.). 40p. (J). (gr. -1-3). pap. 9.99 *(978-1-4424-3355-7(8)*, Little Simon) Little Simon.

—Strega Nona Does It Again. dePaola, Tomie. 2013. (ENG.). 40p. (J). (gr. -1-3). 17.99 *(978-0-399-25781-0(0)*, Nancy Paulsen Bks.) Penguin Publishing Group.

—Strega Nona Takes a Vacation. dePaola, Tomie. 2003. (ENG.). 32p. (J). (gr. -1-3). pap. 5.99 *(978-0-14-250076-7(3)*, Puffin) Penguin Publishing Group.

—Strega Nona Takes a Vacation. dePaola, Tomie. 2003. (J). (gr. -1-3). 13.65 *(978-0-7569-1469-1(8))* Perfection Learning Corp.

—Strega Nona's Gift. dePaola, Tomie. 2011. (ENG.). 32p. (J). (gr. -1-3). 17.99 *(978-0-399-25649-3(0)*, Nancy Paulsen Bks.) Penguin Publishing Group.

—Strega Nona's Harvest. dePaola, Tomie. (ENG.). 32p. (J). (gr. -1-3). 2012. mass mkt. 7.99 *(978-0-14-242338-7(6)*, Puffin); 2009. 16.99 *(978-0-399-25291-4(6)*, Putnam Juvenile) Penguin Publishing Group.

—Things Will Never Be the Same. dePaola, Tomie. 2004. (26 Fairmount Avenue Bks.). 69p. (J). (gr. 3-7). 13.65 *(978-0-7569-2951-0(2))* Perfection Learning Corp.

—Tomie's Baa Baa Black Sheep & Other Rhymes. dePaola, Tomie. 2004. (ENG.). 32p. (J). (gr. -1 — 1). bds. 7.99 *(978-0-399-24326-4(7)*, Putnam Juvenile) Penguin Publishing Group.

—Tomie's Three Bears & Other Tales. dePaola, Tomie. 2004. (ENG.). 32p. (J). (gr. -1 — 1). bds. 7.99 *(978-0-399-24327-1(5)*, Putnam Juvenile) Penguin Publishing Group.

—Trouble in the Barkers' Class. dePaola, Tomie. 2006. (Barker Twins Ser.). (ENG.). 32p. (J). (gr. -1-3). reprint ed. pap. 6.99 *(978-0-14-240585-7(X)*, Puffin) Penguin Publishing Group.

—What a Year. dePaola, Tomie. 2003. (26 Fairmount Avenue Bks.). 72p. (gr. 2-5). 16.00 *(978-0-7569-1546-9(5))* Perfection Learning Corp.

—26 Fairmount Avenue. dePaola, Tomie. 2005. 58p. (J). (gr. k-4). reprint ed. 14.00 *(978-0-7567-8722-6(X))* DIANE Publishing Co.

DePaolo, Daniel. Dingo & Willy's Donuts. Allen, Katy C. 2012. 74p. pap. 6.99 *(978-0-9857160-3-5(7))*; pap. 6.99 *(978-0-9857160-1-1(0))* Baysmore Bks.

DePaulo, Dorothy. Turn It Around, Sadie! McClelland, Pam. 2012. (ENG.). 208p. pap. 12.45 *(978-1-4525-5812-7(4)*, Balboa Pr.) Author Solutions, Inc.

DePauw, Sandra A. The Don't-Give-Up Kid: And Learning Differences. Gehret, Jeanne. 2003. 40p. (J). (gr. 1-5). 2nd rev. ed. 13.95 *(978-0-9625136-3-3(6))*; 3rd rev. ed. pap. 9.95 *(978-1-884281-10-5(9))* Verbal Images Pr.

DePew, Robert, jt. illus. see Vincent, Benjamin.

Depew, Robert, jt. illus. see Zapater Oliva, Carlos.

Depinet, Linda. God Just Needed Another Angel. Depinet, Linda. 2003. 32p. (J). pap. 12.95 *(978-1-59098-844-2(2))* Wooster Bk. Co., The.

DePorter, Vince. The Song That Never Ends. Banks, Steven. ed. 2005. 32p. (J). lib. bdg. 15.00 *(978-1-59054-984-1(8))* Fitzgerald Bks.

—The Song That Never Ends. Banks, Steven. 2004. (Spongebob Squarepants Ser.). 32p. (J). (gr. k-2). 11.65 *(978-0-7569-5374-4(X))* Perfection Learning Corp.

—Special Delivery! Banks, Steven. 2003. (SpongeBob SquarePants Ser.: Vol. 2). (ENG.). 32p. (J). pap. 3.99 *(978-0-689-85887-1(6)*, Simon Spotlight/Nickelodeon) Simon Spotlight/Nickelodeon.

—Special Delivery. Banks, Steven. 2005. (Ready-to-Read Ser.). 32p. (J). lib. bdg. 15.00 *(978-1-59054-986-5(4))* Fitzgerald Bks.

—Stop the Presses! Banks, Steven. 2005. 22p. (J). lib. bdg. 15.00 *(978-1-4242-0973-6(0))* Fitzgerald Bks.

Depper, Hertha. The Funny Baby. Hillert, Margaret. rev. exp. ed. 2006. (Beginning to Read Ser.). 30p. (J). (gr. -1-3). lib. bdg. 14.95 *(978-1-59953-048-2(1))* Norwood Hse. Pr.

Depratto, Marcel, jt. illus. see Brignaud, Pierre.

DePrince, Erik & Volinski, Jessica. Not Everyone Is Nice: Helping Children Learn Caution with Strangers. Tedesco, Ann & Alimonti, Frederick. 2003. (Let's Talk Ser.). (ENG.). 48p. (J). pap. 9.95 *(978-0-88282-233-4(0))* New Horizon Pr. Pubs., Inc.

Deraney, Michael J., jt. illus. see Duffy, Daniel Mark.

DeRaymond, Devaki. Who Has Seen the Sun: A Yoga Activity & Coloring Book. Dietz, Kamala. 2011. (ENG.). 50p. pap. 8.98 *(978-1-4635-8277-7(3))* CreateSpace Independent Publishing Platform.

Derby, Sarah. It's a Scamp's Life! Kezar, Wanda. 2013. 186p. pap. 14.99 *(978-1-62839-371-2(8))* Salem Publishing Solutions, Inc.

Derenne, Juliette & Barroux, Sophie. Queen Margot - The Age of Innocence. Cadic, Olivier & Gheysens, Francois. 2007. (ENG.). 48p. (J). (gr. 4-7). per. 13.95 *(978-1-905460-10-6(4))* CineBook GBR. Dist: National Bk. Network.

Dérib. Yakari & the Coyote. Job. 2012. (ENG.). 48p. (J). (gr. 1-6). pap. 11.95 *(978-1-84918-101-3(2))* CineBook GBR. Dist: National Bk. Network.

—Yakari & the Grizzly. Job. 2007. (ENG.). 46p. (J). (gr. 4-7). per. 9.99 *(978-1-905460-16-8(3))* CineBook GBR. Dist: National Bk. Network.

—Yakari Vol. 10: the River of Forgetfulness. Job. 2013. (ENG.). 48p. pap. 11.95 *(978-1-84918-140-2(3))* CineBook GBR. Dist: National Bk. Network.

Derib. Yakari Vol. 11: Yakari & Nanabozo. Job. 2014. (ENG.). 48p. pap. 11.95 *(978-1-84918-177-8(2))* CineBook GBR. Dist: National Bk. Network.

Derington, Nick. The Illuminating World of Light with Max Axiom, Super Scientist, 1 vol. Sohn, Emily. 2008. (Graphic Science Ser.). (ENG.). 32p. (gr. 3-4). pap. 8.10 *(978-1-4296-1768-0(3)*, Graphic Library) Capstone Pr., Inc.

—Understanding Viruses with Max Axiom, Super Scientist, 1 vol. Biskup, Agnieszka. 2009. (Graphic Science Ser.). (ENG.). 32p. (gr. 3-4). lib. bdg. 29.99 *(978-1-4296-2338-4(1)*, Graphic Library) Capstone Pr., Inc.

Derome, Pierre-André. La Petite Lili Est un Genie. Gauthier, Gilles. 2004. (Premier Roman Ser.). (FRE.). 64p. (J). (gr. 1-4). pap. *(978-2-89021-686-0(1))* Diffusion du livre Mirabel (DLM).

DeRosa, Dee. I'm a Princess. Hall, Kirsten. 2004. (My First Reader Ser.). (ENG.). 32p. (J). (gr. k-1). pap. 3.95 *(978-0-516-24630-7(5)*, Children's Pr.) Scholastic Library Publishing.

DeRose, Kim. Handstand Kids Mexican Cookbook. Garfield, Yvette & Azima, Cricket. 2008. 52p. (J). (gr. -1-3). 28.00 *(978-0-9792107-2-3(0))* Handstand Kids.

D

DeRosier, Cher & Cerone, Sal. The Pea & the Grape. DeRosier, Cher. 2005. (ENG.). (J). ring bd. incl. cd-rom *(978-1-891685-60-6(0))* Dearborn Publishing.

Derrick, David G., Jr. I'm the Scariest Thing in the Jungle! 2013. (ENG.). 36p. (J). (gr. -1-3). 15.95 *(978-1-59702-087-9(7))* Immedium.

d'Errico, Camilla. Camilla d'Errico's Burn. d'Errico, Camilla. Sanders, Scott. 2009. (ENG.). 176p. (YA). (gr. 7-18). pap. 9.99 *(978-1-4169-7873-2(9),* Simon Pulse) Simon Pulse.

Dershowitz, Yosef. Cartons in the Air & Other Stories. Weinbach, Shaindel. (J). 14.99 *(978-0-89906-992-0(4),* CARH) Mesorah Pubns., Ltd.

—The Friendly Persuader & Other Stories. Weinbach, Shaindel. (J). 14.99 *(978-0-89906-970-8(3),* FRIH) Mesorah Pubns., Ltd.

Derstine, Charlene. God Made Nuts. Martin, Mary. 2012. 53p. (J). *(978-0-7399-2501-0(6))* Rod & Staff Pubs., Inc.

Deru, Myriam, et al. Princess Tales, 4 bks., Set. Grimm, Jacob et al. 2007. (Abbeville Classic Fairy Tales Ser.). (ENG.). 112p. (J). (gr. 1-2). 19.95 *(978-0-7892-0950-4(0))* Abbeville Pr., Inc.

DeRungs, Tina. Isn't It Great? Oksanen, Sue & Zeisler, Riley. 2010. (ENG.). 32p. pap. 10.98 *(978-1-4528-7225-4(2))* CreateSpace Independent Publishing Platform.

DeSaix, Deborah Durland. The Grand Mosque of Paris: A Story of How Muslims Rescued Jews During the Holocaust. Ruelle, Karen Gray. 2009. (ENG.). 40p. (YA). (gr. 3-18). 18.95 *(978-0-8234-2159-6(7))* Holiday Hse., Inc.

Desaix, Deborah Durland. The Grand Mosque of Paris: A Story of How Muslims Rescued Jews During the Holocaust. Ruelle, Karen Gray. 2010. (ENG.). 40p. (YA). (gr. 3-18). pap. 8.95 *(978-0-8234-2304-0(2))* Holiday Hse., Inc.

DeSaix, Deborah Durland. Hidden on the Mountain: Stories of Children Sheltered from the Nazis in le Chambon. Ruelle, Karen Gray. 2007. (ENG.). 272p. (J). (gr. 5-18). 24.95 *(978-0-8234-1928-9(2))* Holiday Hse., Inc.

DeSaix, Deborah Durland. Peter's War. DeSaix, Deborah Durland. Ruelle, Karen Gray. Date not set. (J). *(978-0-8234-2416-0(2))* Holiday Hse., Inc.

DeSantis, Susan. Little Toot-Tall: A Book about Friendship. Moncure, Jane Belk. 2013. (Magic Castle Readers: Health & Safety Ser.). (ENG.). 32p. (J). (gr. -1-2). 25.64 *(978-1-62323-568-0(5),* 206303) Child's World, Inc., The.

—Rabbits' Habits: A Book about Good Habits. Moncure, Jane Belk. 2013. (Magic Castle Readers: Health & Safety Ser.). (ENG.). 32p. (J). (gr. -1-2). 25.64 *(978-1-62323-569-7(3),* 206304) Child's World, Inc., The.

—'Smile,' Says Little Crocodile: A Book about Good Habits. Moncure, Jane Belk. 2013. (Magic Castle Readers: Health & Safety Ser.). (ENG.). 32p. (J). (gr. -1-2). 25.64 *(978-1-62323-570-3(7),* 206305) Child's World, Inc., The.

—Yes, No, Little Hippo: A Book about Safety. Moncure, Jane Belk. 2013. (Magic Castle Readers: Health & Safety Ser.). (ENG.). 32p. (J). (gr. -1-2). 25.64 *(978-1-62323-571-0(5),* 206306) Child's World, Inc., The.

—5 Steps to Drawing Machines at Work. Kesselring, Susan. 2011. (5 Steps to Drawing Ser.). (ENG.). 32p. (J). (gr. k-3). lib. bdg. 27.07 *(978-1-60973-201-1(4),* 201106) Child's World, Inc., The.

Desautels, Stacie. Blue Bear Finds a Rainbow. Betts, McKenzie Leigh. Abbott, Candy, ed. 2011. 24p. (J). 15.00 *(978-1-886068-51-3(8))* Fruitbearer Publishing, LLC.

—Pink Bear's Journey: I Love Me, Who Do You Love? Betts, McKenzie Leigh. 2013. (ENG.). 48p. (J). 15.00 *(978-1-886068-72-8(0))* Fruitbearer Publishing, LLC.

Desharnais, Margo. An Icon for Christmas: Sophia's Gift: an Icon Christmas Story to Color. Katris Gonis, Theofania. 2005. (ENG.). 24p. (J). (gr. k-3). pap. 5.95 *(978-1-880971-94-9(1))* Light & Life Publishing Co.

DeShazo, Sharon B., jt. illus. see Jackson, April Eley.

DeSica, Melissa. Wordsworth Dances the Waltz. Kakugawa, Frances. 2007. 32p. (J). 10.95 *(978-0-9790647-3-9(2))* Watermark Publishing, LLC.

Design, Mada. Scavenger Hunt Adventure. Matheis, Mickie. 2012. (Zoobles! Ser.). (ENG.). 24p. (J). (gr. -1-k). pap. 3.99 *(978-0-448-45868-7(3),* Grosset & Dunlap) Penguin Publishing Group.

Designs, Marion, photos by. Ellen G Goes to the Haunted Planetarium. Crews, G. S. 2009. 50p. pap. 20.00 *(978-0-9795236-4-9(8))* Crews Pubns., LLC.

Desimini, Lisa. The Great Big Green. Gifford, Peggy. 2014. (ENG.). 32p. (J). (gr. -1-2). 15.95 *(978-1-62091-629-2(0))* Boyds Mills Pr.

—Iris Has a Virus. Alda, Arlene. 2008. (ENG.). 24p. (J). (gr. -1-1). 18.95 *(978-0-88776-844-6(X),* Tundra Bks.) Tundra Bks. CAN. Dist: Penguin Random Hse., LLC.

—Lulu's Piano Lesson. Alda, Arlene. 2010. (ENG.). 32p. (J). (gr. -1-1). 16.95 *(978-0-88776-930-6(6),* Tundra Bks.) Tundra Bks. CAN. Dist: Penguin Random Hse., LLC.

—She Sang Promise: The Story of Betty Mae Jumper, Seminole Tribal Leader. Annino, Jan Godown. 2010. (ENG.). 48p. (J). (gr. 1-4). 17.95 *(978-1-4263-0592-4(3))* National Geographic Society.

—She Sang Promise: The Story of Betty Mae Jumper, Seminole Tribal Leader. Annino, J G. 2010. (ENG.). 48p. (J). (gr. 1-4). 26.90 *(978-1-4263-0593-1(1),* National Geographic Children's Bks.) National Geographic Society.

—The Snowflake Sisters. Lewis, J. Patrick. 2012. (ENG.). 32p. (J). (gr. -1-3). pap. 16.99 *(978-1-4424-6719-4(3),* Atheneum Bks. for Young Readers) Simon & Schuster Children's Publishing.

DeSimone, Corkey Hay. The Planet Hue. DeSimone, Corkey Hay. 2003. (J). 14.95 *(978-0-9747921-0-1(1))* Gentle Giraffe Pr.

DeSimone, Suzanne. My Princess Boy. Kilodavis, Cheryl. 2010. (ENG.). 36p. (J). (gr. -1-3). 17.99 *(978-1-4424-2988-8(7),* Simon & Schuster/Paula Wiseman Bks.) Simon & Schuster/Paula Wiseman Bks.

Desira, Angela. A Trust of Treasures. Sinclair, Mehded Maryam. 2010. (ENG.). 29p. (J). (gr. k). 14.95 *(978-0-86037-462-6(9))* Kube Publishing Ltd. GBR. Dist: Consortium Bk. Sales & Distribution.

Desisto, Allie. Some Kids Just Can't Sit Still! Desisto, Allie. Goldstein, Sam. 2009. (ENG.). 32p. (J). (gr. 2-4). pap. 15.95 *(978-1-886941-73-1(4))* Specialty Pr., Inc.

Desjardins, Vincent. Henry Bergh: America's First Animal Advocate. Furstinger, Nancy. 2016. (ENG.). 192p. (J). *(978-0-544-65031-2(X))* Harcourt.

Desjarlait, Robert. The Creator's Game: A Story of Baaga'adowe/Lacrosse. Coulson, Art. 2013. (ENG.). 48p. (J). (gr. 3-6). pap. 6.95 *(978-0-87351-909-0(4))* Minnesota Historical Society Pr.

Deskcube. The Volcano: The Adventures of Antboy & Mr Cricket. Stevens, A. P. Finn, N. K., ed. 2008. (ENG.). 29p. pap. 9.95 *(978-0-9798886-0-1(3))* Mugsy and Sugar Pressed.

Desmet, Sara. Scared Silly. Desmet, Sara. 2006. 32p. (J). (gr. -1-3). 15.95 *(978-1-60108-009-7(3))* Red Cygnet Pr.

Desmoinaux, Christel. Passover Is Here! Pearlman, Bobby. 2005. (ENG.). 16p. (J). (gr. k-2). pap. 6.99 *(978-0-689-86587-9(2),* Little Simon) Little Simon.

Desmoineaux, Christel. Rosy Posey Is Not Dirty! Hanna, Virginie. 2012. (My Little Picture Book Ser.). (ENG.). 32p. (J). pap. 6.95 *(978-2-7338-1947-0(X))* Auzou, Philippe Editions FRA. Dist: Consortium Bk. Sales & Distribution.

Desmond, Hillary. Jake & the Big Cake Mistake. Beall, Kirsten. 2011. 36p. pap. 24.95 *(978-1-4626-4524-4(0))* America Star Bks.

Desmond, Jenni. Eric, the Boy Who Lost His Gravity. 2014. (ENG.). 40p. (J). (gr. k-3). 17.99 *(978-1-60905-348-2(6))* Blue Apple Bks.

Desplanche, Vincent. Buenas Noche. Larousse Mexico Staff, ed. 2006. (Mi Pequena Enciclopedia Ser.). (SPA.). 38p. (gr. -1-3). pap. 3.95 *(978-970-22-1190-7(5))* Larousse, Ediciones, S. A. de C. V. MEX. Dist: Houghton Mifflin Harcourt Publishing Co.

Desprès, Geneviève. Best Friend Trouble, 1 vol. Itani, Frances. 2014. (ENG.). 32p. (J). (gr. -1-3). 19.95 *(978-1-55469-891-2(X))* Orca Bk. Pubs. USA.

Despres, Genevieve. The Highest Number in the World. MacGregor, Roy. 2014. (ENG.). 32p. (J). (gr. 1-4). 17.99 *(978-1-77049-575-3(4))* Tundra Bks. CAN. Dist: Random Hse., Inc.

Desputeaux, Helene. Baby Science: How Babies Really Work! Douglas, Ann. 2004. 32p. (J). (gr. k-4). reprint ed. pap. 7.00 *(978-0-7567-8455-3(7))* DIANE Publishing Co.

Desputeaux, Helene, et al. The Munschworks Grand Treasury. Munsch, Robert & Kusugak, Michael. 2009. (ENG.). 392p. (J). (gr. -1-3). 45.00 *(978-1-55037-685-2(3),* 9781550376852) Annick Pr., Ltd. CAN. Dist: Firefly Bks., Ltd.

Desputeaux, Helene. Purple, Green & Yellow. Munsch, Robert. 2007. (Annikins Ser.). (ENG.). 32p. (J). (gr. -1-2). pap. 1.99 *(978-1-55451-113-6(5),* 9781554511136) Annick Pr., Ltd. CAN. Dist: Firefly Bks., Ltd.

Desrocher, Jack. Eat Right! How You Can Make Good Food Choices. Doeden, Matt. 2008. (Health Zone Ser.). (ENG.). 64p. (gr. 4-7). lib. bdg. 30.60 *(978-0-8225-7552-8(3))* Lerner Publishing Group.

—Keep Your Cool! What You Should Know about Stress. Leder, Jane Mersky & Donovan, Sandy. 2008. (Health Zone Ser.). (ENG.). 64p. (gr. 4-7). lib. bdg. 30.60 *(978-0-8225-7555-9(8))* Lerner Publishing Group.

—Stay Clear! What You Should Know about Skin Care. Donovan, Sandy. 2008. (Health Zone Ser.). (ENG.). 64p. (gr. 4-7). lib. bdg. 30.60 *(978-0-8225-7550-4(7))* Lerner Publishing Group.

—Stay Safe! How You Can Keep Out of Harm's Way. Nelson, Sara Kirsten. 2008. (Health Zone Ser.). (ENG.). 64p. (gr. 4-7). lib. bdg. 30.60 *(978-0-8225-7551-1(5))* Lerner Publishing Group.

Desrocher, Jack & Fairman, Jennifer. Amazing DNA. Johnson, Rebecca L. 2007. (Microquests Ser.). (ENG.). 48p. (gr. 3-5). lib. bdg. 29.27 *(978-0-8225-7139-1(0),* Millbrook Pr.) Lerner Publishing Group.

—Mighty Animal Cells. Johnson, Rebecca L. 2007. (Microquests Ser.). (ENG.). 48p. (gr. 3-5). lib. bdg. 29.27 *(978-0-8225-7137-7(4),* Millbrook Pr.) Lerner Publishing Group.

—Powerful Plant Cells. Johnson, Rebecca L. 2007. (Microquests Ser.). (ENG.). 48p. (gr. 3-5). lib. bdg. 29.27 *(978-0-8225-7141-4(2),* Millbrook Pr.) Lerner Publishing Group.

—Ultra-Organized Cell Systems. Johnson, Rebecca L. 2007. (Microquests Ser.). (ENG.). 48p. (gr. 3-5). lib. bdg. 29.27 *(978-0-8225-7138-4(2),* Millbrook Pr.) Lerner Publishing Group.

DesRosiers, Trisha. Bella's Blessings. Stokes, Brenda. 2012. (ENG.). 50p. (J). (gr. -1-3). 17.95 *(978-1-897476-61-1(2))* Simply Read Bks. CAN. Dist: Ingram Pub. Services.

DeStefano, Stephen. To Be King! Tanguay, Dave. 2015. (Billy Batson & the Magic of Shazam! Ser.). (ENG.). 32p. (gr. 2-3). lib. bdg. 21.27 ***(978-1-4342-9657-3(1))*** Stone Arch Bks.

Destiny Images Staff. Collecting Data: Pick a Pancake. Burstein, John. 2003. (Math Monsters Ser.). 24p. (gr. k-4). lib. bdg. 21.00 *(978-0-8368-3805-3(X),* Weekly Reader Leveled Readers) Stevens, Gareth Publishing LLLP.

—Keeping Track of Time: Go Fly a Kite! Burstein, John. 2003. (Math Monsters Ser.). 24p. (gr. k-4). lib. bdg. 21.00 *(978-0-8368-3810-7(6),* Weekly Reader Leveled Readers) Stevens, Gareth Publishing LLLP.

—Making Tens: Groups of Gollywomples. Burstein, John. 2003. (Math Monsters Ser.). 24p. (gr. k-4). lib. bdg. 21.00 *(978-0-8368-3812-1(2),* Weekly Reader Leveled Readers) Stevens, Gareth Publishing LLLP.

—Measuring: The Perfect Playhouse. Burstein, John. 2003. (Math Monsters Ser.). 24p. (gr. k-4). lib. bdg. 21.00 *(978-0-8368-3813-8(0),* Weekly Reader Leveled Readers) Stevens, Gareth Publishing LLLP.

—Patterns: What's on the Wall? Burstein, John. 2003. (Math Monsters Ser.). 24p. (gr. k-4). lib. bdg. 21.00 *(978-0-8368-3816-9(5),* Weekly Reader Leveled Readers) Stevens, Gareth Publishing LLLP.

—Using Computers: Machine with a Mouse. Burstein, John. 2003. (Math Monsters Ser.). 24p. (gr. k-4). lib. bdg. 21.00 *(978-0-8368-3817-6(3),* Weekly Reader Leveled Readers) Stevens, Gareth Publishing LLLP.

Deters, Kevin. Care Bears Sing & Play: Follow-the-Lights Piano Songbook. 2006. (Care Bears Ser.). 24p. (J). (gr. -1-3). bds. 13.99 *(978-1-57791-300-9(0))* Brighter Minds Children's Publishing.

Detmold, Edward J. & Detmold, Maurice. The Jungle Book. Kipling, Rudyard. 2010. (Calla Editions Ser.). (ENG.). 192p. 30.00 *(978-1-60660-009-2(5))* Dover Pubns., Inc.

Detmold, Maurice, jt. illus. see Detmold, Edward J.

Detwiler, Susan. Avanzando ... de Aquí para Allá: Migraciones Masivas, 1 vol. Cohn, Scotti. 2013. (SPA.). 32p. (gr. -1-4). 17.95 *(978-1-60718-712-7(4))* Arbordale Publishing.

—Big Cat, Little Kitty, 1 vol. Cohn, Scotti. 2011. (ENG.). 32p. (J). (gr. -1-3). 16.95 *(978-1-60718-124-8(X))*; pap. 8.95 *(978-1-60718-134-7(7))* Arbordale Publishing.

—The First Teddy Bear. Kay, Helen. 2nd enl. ed. 2005. 38p. (J). (gr. -1-3). 18.95 *(978-0-88045-154-3(8))*; per. 11.95 *(978-0-88045-153-6(X))* Stemmer Hse. Pubs.

Detwiler, Susan. On the Move: Mass Migrations, 1 vol. Cohn, Scotti. 2014. (SPA.). 32p. (J). (gr. -1-4). pap. 9.95 ***(978-1-62855-350-5(2))*** Arbordale Publishing.

Detwiler, Susan. One Wolf Howls, 1 vol. Cohn, Scotti. 2009. (ENG.). 32p. (J). (gr. -1-3). 16.95 *(978-1-934359-92-1(0))* Arbordale Publishing.

—Pandas' Earthquake Escape, 1 vol. Perry, Phyllis J. 2010. (ENG.). 32p. (J). (gr. -1-3). 16.95 *(978-1-60718-071-5(5))*; pap. 8.95 *(978-1-60718-082-1(0))* Arbordale Publishing.

Detwiler, Susan. Fine Life for a Country Mouse. Detwiler, Susan. 2014. (Penguin Core Concepts Ser.). (ENG.). 32p. (J). (gr. -1-k). 3.99 *(978-0-448-48061-9(1),* Grosset & Dunlap) Penguin Publishing Group.

Devaney, Adam. Bug Babies. Reasoner, Charles. 2009. (Baby Animal Board Bks.). 12p. (J). (gr. -1-k). bds. 7.99 *(978-1-934650-51-6(X))* Just For Kids Pr., LLC.

—Dinosaur Babies. Reasoner, Charles. 2009. (Baby Animal Board Bks.). 12p. (J). (gr. -1-k). bds. 7.99 *(978-1-934650-49-3(8))* Just For Kids Pr., LLC.

—Fan-Tab-U-Lus: Dinosaurs. Reasoner, Charles. 2011. (Fan-Tab-U-Lus Bks.). (ENG.). 12p. (J). (gr. -1). bds. 9.99 *(978-1-935498-58-2(4))* Just For Kids Pr., LLC.

—Fan-Tab-U-Lus: Jungle Animals. Reasoner, Charles. 2011. (Fan-Tab-U-Lus Bks.). (ENG.). 12p. (J). (gr. -1-3). bds. 9.99 *(978-1-935498-55-1(X))* Just For Kids Pr., LLC.

—Farm Babies. Reasoner, Charles. 2009. (Baby Animal Board Bks.). 12p. (J). (gr. -1-k). bds. 7.99 *(978-1-934650-52-3(8))* Just For Kids Pr., LLC.

—Hooray for Easter! Adams, Michelle Medlock. 2010. 16p. (J). (gr. -1-k). 12.99 *(978-0-8249-1840-8(1),* Candy Cane Pr.) Ideals Pubns.

—Jungle. Reasoner, Charles. 2009. (Learning Tab Board Bks.). 10p. (J). (gr. -1-k). bds. 9.99 *(978-1-934650-79-0(X))* Just For Kids Pr., LLC.

Devaney, Adam & Doherty, Paula. Jungle Babies. Reasoner, Charles. 2009. (Baby Animal Board Bks.). 12p. (J). (gr. -1-k). bds. 7.99 *(978-1-934650-50-9(1))* Just For Kids Pr., LLC.

Devard, Nancy. A Mom Like No Other. Scholastic, Inc. Staff & Taylor-Butler, Christine. 2004. (Just for You Ser.). (ENG.). 32p. pap. 3.99 *(978-0-439-56853-1(6),* Teaching Resources) Scholastic, Inc.

—The Mystery of the Missing Dog. Scholastic, Inc. Staff & Hooks, Gwendolyn. 2004. (Just for You Ser.). (ENG.). 32p. (gr. k-3). pap. 3.99 *(978-0-439-56864-7(1),* Teaching Resources) Scholastic, Inc.

—The Secret Olivia Told Me. Joy, N. 2007. 32p. (J). (gr. -1-3). 16.95 *(978-1-933491-08-0(6))* Just Us Bks., Inc.

Deverell, Richard. How They Lived in Bible Times. Jones, Graham. 2003. 48p. 6.49 *(978-1-85999-435-1(0))* Scripture Union GBR. Dist: Gabriel Resources.

Deverell, Richard & King, Chris. Pop-up Pets. Deverell, Christine. 2005. 12p. (J). (gr. k-4). reprint ed. 20.00 *(978-0-7567-8776-9(9))* DIANE Publishing Co.

—Sparkly Sea. 14p. (J). *(978-1-85081-374-3(4))* Frederick, Robert.

Devi, Dulari. Following My Paint Brush. 2011. (ENG.). 32p. (J). (gr. 2-18). 18.50 *(978-93-80340-11-1(7))* Tara Publishing IND. Dist: Perseus-PGW.

DeVince, James, jt. illus. see Porcheron, Tammy.

DeVito, Anthony T. The Story of Lilly & Lou: Based on a True Story. Lucia, Doriane. 2008. 56p. (J). pap. *(978-0-9809995-4-9(5),* CCB Publishing) CCB Publishing.

Devlin, Harry. Cranberry Halloween. Devlin, Wende. 2013. (Cranberryport Ser.). (ENG.). (J). (gr. -1-3). 18.95 *(978-1-930900-69-1(4))* Purple Hse. Pr.

—Cranberry Thanksgiving. Devlin, Wende. 2012. (ENG.). 32p. (J). (gr. -1-3). 18.95 *(978-1-930900-63-9(5))* Purple Hse. Pr.

—Old Black Witch! Devlin, Wende. 2012. (ENG.). 32p. (J). (gr. -1-3). 18.95 *(978-1-930900-62-2(7))* Purple Hse. Pr.

Dewan, Ted. Thomas Trew & the Hidden People. Masson, Sophie. 2008. (Thomas Trew Ser.: 1). (ENG.). 160p. (J). (gr. 4-7). pap. 7.95 *(978-0-340-89484-2(9))* Hodder & Stoughton GBR. Dist: Independent Pubs. Group.

—Thomas Trew & the Horns of Pan. Masson, Sophie. 2008. (Thomas Trew Ser.: 2). (ENG.). 208p. (J). (gr. 4-7). pap. 7.95 *(978-0-340-89485-9(7))* Hodder & Stoughton GBR. Dist: Independent Pubs. Group.

—Thomas Trew & the Island of Ghosts. Masson, Sophie. 2009. (Thomas Trew Ser.: 6). (ENG.). 244p. (J). (gr. 4-7). pap. 7.95 *(978-0-340-89489-7(X),* Hodder Faith) Hodder & Stoughton GBR. Dist: Independent Pubs. Group.

—Thomas Trew & the Klint-King's Gold. Masson, Sophie. 2008. (Thomas Trew Ser.: 3). (ENG.). 192p. (J). (gr. 4-7). pap. 7.95 *(978-0-340-89486-6(5))* Hodder & Stoughton GBR. Dist: Independent Pubs. Group.

—Thomas Trew & the Selkie's Curse. Masson, Sophie. 2009. (Thomas Trew Ser.: 4). (ENG.). 224p. (J). (gr. 4-7). pap. 7.95 *(978-0-340-89487-3(3))* Hodder & Stoughton GBR. Dist: Independent Pubs. Group.

Dewar, Bob. The Whisky Muse: Collected & Introduced by Robin Laing. Laing, Robin. 2nd ed. 2004. (ENG.). 224p. per. 14.95 *(978-1-84282-041-4(9))* Luath Pr. Ltd. GBR. Dist: Ingram Pub. Services.

Dewar, Ken. H Is for Hockey: An NHL Alumni Alphabet. Shea, Kevin. 2012. (ENG.). 32p. (J). (gr. 1-5). 16.95 *(978-1-58536-794-8(X))*; *(978-1-58536-814-3(8))* Sleeping Bear Pr.

Dewdney, Anna. All-Star Fever. Christopher, Matt. 2009. 64p. (J). lib. bdg. 22.60 *(978-1-59953-315-5(4))* Norwood Hse. Pr.

—Shadow over Second. Christopher, Matt. 2009. 64p. (J). lib. bdg. 22.60 *(978-1-59953-320-9(0))* Norwood Hse. Pr.

Dewdney, Anna. Grumpy Gloria. Dewdney, Anna. 2006. (ENG.). 32p. (J). (gr. -1-k). 16.99 *(978-0-670-06123-5(9),* Viking Juvenile) Penguin Publishing Group.

—Llama Llama - Birthday Party! Dewdney, Anna. 2013. (Llama Llama Ser.). (ENG.). 16p. (J). (gr. -1-k). 6.99 *(978-0-448-45880-9(2),* Grosset & Dunlap) Penguin Publishing Group.

—Llama Llama Easter Egg. Dewdney, Anna. 2015. (Llama Llama Ser.). (ENG.). 14p. (J). (— 1). bds. 5.99 *(978-0-451-46982-3(8),* Viking Juvenile) Penguin Publishing Group.

—Llama Llama Jingle Bells. Dewdney, Anna. 2014. (Llama Llama Ser.). (ENG.). 12p. (J). (— 1). bds. 5.99 *(978-0-451-46980-9(1),* Viking Juvenile) Penguin Publishing Group.

—Llama Llama Mad at Mama. Dewdney, Anna. 2007. (Llama Llama Ser.). (ENG.). 40p. (J). (gr. -1-k). 17.99 *(978-0-670-06240-9(5),* Viking Juvenile) Penguin Publishing Group.

—Llama Llama Red Pajama. Dewdney, Anna. (Llama Llama Ser.). (ENG.). 40p. (J). (gr. -1-k). 2014. 25.00 *(978-0-451-46990-8(9))*; 2005. 17.99 *(978-0-670-05983-6(8))* Penguin Publishing Group. (Viking Juvenile).

—Llama Llama Trick or Treat. Dewdney, Anna. 2014. (Llama Llama Ser.). (ENG.). 14p. (J). (— 1). bds. 5.99 *(978-0-451-46978-6(X),* Viking Juvenile) Penguin Publishing Group.

—Nobunny's Perfect. Dewdney, Anna. 2008. (ENG.). 32p. (J). (gr. -1-k). 15.99 *(978-0-670-06288-1(X),* Viking Juvenile) Penguin Publishing Group.

DeWeerd, Kelsey. I Just Want to Do It My Way Audio CD with Book. Cook, Julia. 2013. 32p. (J). pap. 16.95 incl. audio compact disk *(978-1-934490-44-0(X))* Boys Town Pr.

—El Peor Dia de TODA Mi Vida. Cook, Julia. 2012. (SPA.). 32p. (J). pap. 10.95 *(978-1-934490-34-1(2))* Boys Town Pr.

—Priscilla & the Perfect Storm. McCumbee, Stephie. 2014. (ENG.). 32p. (J). pap. 10.95 *(978-1-934490-60-0(1))* Boys Town Pr.

—Teamwork Isn't My Thing, & I Don't Like to Share! Cook, Julia. 2012. 32p. (J). pap. 10.95 *(978-1-934490-35-8(0))* Boys Town Pr.

Deweese, Susan. The Acorn Nuts. Beck, Bev. 2011. 32p. pap. 24.95 *(978-1-4626-2233-7(X))* America Star Bks.

DeWeese, Susan. The Birthday Present. Beck, Bev. 2011. 40p. pap. 24.95 *(978-1-4560-8398-4(8))* America Star Bks.

—The Curwood Acorns. Breece, Beverly. 2012. 40p. pap. 24.95 *(978-1-4626-8202-7(2))* America Star Bks.

Dewey, Ariane & Aruego, Jose. The Big, Big Wall. Howard, Reginald. ed. 2003. (Green Light Readers — Level 1 Ser.). (J). (gr. -1-3). 13.50 *(978-0-613-66350-2(0),* Turtleback) Turtleback Bks.

—The Big, Big Wall/No Puedo Bajar. Howard, Reginald. Ada, Alma Flora & Campoy, F. Isabel, trs. 2009. (Green Light Readers Level 1 Ser.). (SPA & ENG.). 28p. (J). (gr. -1-3). pap. 3.99 *(978-0-547-25548-4(9))* Houghton Mifflin Harcourt Publishing Co.

—Gregory, the Terrible Eater. Sharmat, Mitchell. 2009. (ENG.). 32p. (J). (gr. -1-3). pap. 6.99 *(978-0-545-12931-2(1))* Scholastic, Inc.

Dewey, Ariane, jt. illus. see Aruego, Jose.

Dewey, Jennifer Owings. Alligators & Crocodiles. Dennard, Deborah. (Our Wild World Ser.). (ENG.). 48p. (J). (gr. 2-5). 2008. pap. 8.95 *(978-1-55971-859-2(5))*; 2003. 10.95 *(978-1-55971-860-8(9))* Cooper Square Publishing Llc.

—Lizards. Dennard, Deborah. 2003. (Our Wild World Ser.). (ENG.). 48p. (J). (gr. 2-5). 10.95 *(978-1-55971-858-5(7))*; pap. 8.95 *(978-1-55971-857-8(9))* Cooper Square Publishing Llc.

—Snakes. Dennard, Deborah. 2003. (Our Wild World Ser.). (ENG.). 48p. (J). (gr. 2-5). pap. 7.95 *(978-1-55971-855-4(2))* Cooper Square Publishing Llc.

—Turtles. Dennard, Deborah. 2003. (Our Wild World Ser.). (ENG.). 48p. (J). (gr. 2-5). pap. 7.95 *(978-1-55971-861-5(7))* Cooper Square Publishing Llc.

—Winging It: A Beginner's Guide to Birds of the Southwest. Coulter, Catherine et al. 2004. (ENG.). 135p. (J). (gr. 5-18). 12.95 *(978-0-8263-3068-0(1))* Univ. of New Mexico Pr.

Dewey, Jennifer Owings. Clem: The Story of a Raven. Dewey, Jennifer Owings. 2003. (ENG.). 128p. (J). pap. 14.95 *(978-0-8263-3023-9(1))* Univ. of New Mexico Pr.

Dewey, Jennifer Owings. Reptiles: Explore the Fascinating Worlds of Alligators & Crocodiles, Lizards, Snakes, Turtles. Dewey, Jennifer Owings, tr. Dennard, Deborah. 2004. (Our Wild World Ser.). (ENG.). 192p. (J). (gr. 3-6). 16.95 *(978-1-55971-880-6(3))* Cooper Square Publishing Llc.

Dewey, Simon. I'm Trying to Be Like Jesus. Dobson, Cynthia Lund. 2010. (J). 19.99 *(978-1-60641-846-8(7))* Deseret Bk. Co.

—The Life of Our Lord: Illustrated 200th Anniversary Edition. Dickens, Charles. 2012. 17.99 *(978-1-60907-185-1(9),* Shadow Mountain) Shadow Mountain Publishing.

DeWildt, Jim. Hidden Pumpkins. Lewis, Anne Margaret. 2005. (Hidden Ser.). (ENG.). 32p. (J). (gr. -1-3). 12.95 *(978-0-9749145-5-8(X),* Mackinac Island Press, Inc.) Charlesbridge Publishing, Inc.

—What Am I? New Jersey. Lewis, Anne Margaret. 2007. 32p. (J). 9.95 *(978-1-934133-19-4(1),* Mackinac Island Press, Inc.) Charlesbridge Publishing, Inc.

Dewitt, Kenny. Sneakers Hangs Out. Gosule, Bette & Longmire, Lynda. 2012. 26p. (J). 14.95 *(978-1-60131-129-0(X),* Castlebridge Bks.) Big Tent Bks.

Dewitt, Levi. Co-Man & Poppa Meet Kanka. Wright, Mary. 2013. 24p. pap. 24.95 *(978-1-62709-328-6(1))* America Star Bks.

DeWitt, Nancy. Heroes & Heroines in Tlingit-Haida Legend. Beck, Mary Giraudo. 2003. (ENG.). 128p. (Orig.). (gr. 8-18). pap. 12.99 *(978-0-88240-334-2(6))* Graphic Arts Ctr. Publishing Co.

DeWolf, Holly. What's Going on at the Time Tonight?, 1 vol. Mercer, Gerald. ed. 2013. (ENG.). 32p. (J). (gr. -1-3). 19.95 *(978-1-77108-004-0(3))* Nimbus Publishing, Ltd. CAN. Dist: Orca Bk. Pubs. USA.

Dewyea, Glenn. The Pumpkin Se. Dohr, Robert. 2012. 32p. pap. 13.50 *(978-1-61204-337-1(2),* Strategic Bk. Publishing) Strategic Book Publishing & Rights Agency (SBPRA).

Dey, Lorraine. Maddy Patti & the Great Curiosity: Helping Children Understand Diabetes. Bilderback Abel, Mary & Borg, Stan W. 2015. (Let's Talk Ser.). (ENG.). 48p. (J). (gr. k-5). 9.95 *(978-0-88282-490-1(2))* New Horizon Pr. Pubs., Inc.

—A Sweater for Duncan. Malone, Margaret Gay. 2010. (ENG.). 32p. (J). (gr. -1-12). lib. bdg. 16.95 *(978-1-936299-06-5(2),* Raven Tree Pr.,Csi) Continental Sales, Inc.

Dey, Romi. Crazy Pizza Day. Dobkin, Bonnie. 2010. (J). *(978-1-60617-150-9(X))* Teaching Strategies, Inc.

DeYoe, Aaron, jt. illus. see DeYoe, Katie.

DeYoe, Katie & DeYoe, Aaron. The Mighty Quinn. Parnell, Robyn. 2013. (ENG.). 272p. (gr. 2-7). pap. 10.95 *(978-1-938063-10-7(4),* Mighty Media Junior Readers) Mighty Media Pr.

Dezakin, Akin. Campo Abierto (Open Field) Hagen, Oddmund. Santos, Nuria G., tr. from NOR. 2003. (Rosa y Manzana Ser.). (SPA.). 32p. 16.95 *(978-84-89804-42-5(7))* Lóguez Ediciones ESP. Dist: Baker & Taylor Bks.

Dezsö, Andrea. Lies, Knives, & Girls in Red Dresses. Koertge, Ron. 2012. (ENG.). 96p. (YA). (gr. 9). 17.99 *(978-0-7636-4406-2(4))* Candlewick Pr.

D'hamers, Heidi. Duck's Easter Egg Hunt. Richards, Dawn. 2014. (J). *(978-1-4351-5243-4(3))* Barnes & Noble, Inc.

D'Heur, Valérie. Heart in the Pocket. Bourguignon, Laurence. 2008. 26p. (J). (gr. -1-3). 16.50 *(978-0-8028-5343-1(9))* Eerdmans, William B. Publishing Co.

Di Bartolo, Jim. The Dragon's Pearl. Jordan, Devin. 2010. (ENG.). 352p. (YA). (gr. 5-9). pap. 8.99 *(978-1-4169-6411-7(8),* Simon & Schuster Bks. For Young Readers) Simon & Schuster Bks. For Young Readers.

—Lips Touch: Three Times. Taylor, Laini. (ENG.). 288p. (J). (gr. 7-7). 2011. pap. 14.99 *(978-0-545-05586-4(5));* 2009. 17.99 *(978-0-545-05585-7(7))* Scholastic, Inc. (Levine, Arthur A. Bks.).

Di Bartolo, Jim. In the Shadows. Di Bartolo, Jim. White, Kiersten. 2014. (ENG.). 384p. (J). (gr. 7). 21.99 *(978-0-545-56144-0(2),* Scholastic Pr.) Scholastic, Inc.

Di Benedetto, Angelo. How the Donkeys Came to Haiti & Other Folk Tales. 124p. (J). (gr. 4-9). 12.95 *(978-0-8159-5706-5(8))* Devin-Adair Pubs., Inc.

di Chiara, Francesca. The Sun & the Wind. 2007. (First Reading Level 1 Ser.). 32p. (J). (gr. -1-3). 8.99 *(978-0-7945-1811-0(7),* Usborne) EDC Publishing.

Di Fiori, Larry. Mouth Moths: More Classroom Tales. Evans, Douglas. 2006. (ENG.). 112p. (J). (gr. 4-6). 15.95 *(978-1-932425-23-9(3),* Lemniscaat) Boyds Mills Pr.

di Gaudesi, Andrea Ricciardi. El Girasol: Por Dentro y Por Fuera. Hipp, Andrew. Brusca, María Cristina, tr. 2004. (Explora la Naturaleza (Getting into Nature) Ser.). (SPA.). 27p. (J). (gr. 3-7). lib. bdg. 25.25 *(978-1-4042-2868-9(3))* Rosen Publishing Group, Inc., The.

—El Maíz: Por Dentro y Por Fuera. Hipp, Andrew. González, Thomas, tr. 2004. (Explora la Naturaleza (Getting into Nature) Ser.). (SPA.). 27p. lib. bdg. 25.25 *(978-1-4042-2863-4(2))* Rosen Publishing Group, Inc., The.

Di Gennaro, Andrea. Mark Twain. Carew-Miller, Anna. 2003. (Great Names Ser.). (J). 19.95 *(978-957-745-414-0(3))* Mason Crest.

Di Giacomo, Kris. Brief Thief. Escoffier, Michaël. 2013. (ENG.). 32p. (J). (gr. -1-3). 16.95 *(978-1-59270-131-5(0))* Enchanted Lion Bks., LLC.

—The Day I Lost My Superpowers. Escoffier, Michaël. 2014. (ENG.). 32p. (J). (gr. -1-3). 16.95 *(978-1-59270-144-5(2))* Enchanted Lion Bks., LLC.

—Enormous Smallness: The Story of e. e. Cummings. Burgess, Matthew. 2015. (ENG.). 64p. (J). (gr. -1-3). 17.95 *(978-1-59270-171-1(X))* Enchanted Lion Bks., LLC.

—Me First! Escoffier, Michaël. 2013. (ENG.). 24p. (J). 14.00 *(978-1-59270-136-0(1))* Enchanted Lion Bks., LLC.

—My Dad Is Big & Strong, But... A Bedtime Story. Saudo, Coralie. 2012. (ENG.). 32p. (J). (gr. -1-2). 16.95 *(978-1-59270-122-3(1))* Enchanted Lion Bks., LLC.

—Take Away the A. Escoffier, Michaël. 2014. (ENG.). 56p. (J). (gr. -1-3). 17.95 *(978-1-59270-156-8(6))* Enchanted Lion Bks., LLC.

Di Giandomenico, Carmine, et al. My Monsters, Vol. 7. Fraction, Matt. 2011. (ENG.). 200p. (J). (gr. 4-17). 19.99 *(978-0-7851-4836-4(1))* Marvel Worldwide, Inc.

Di Marco, Audrey. Little Brave Bear. Kolar, Marsha. 2005. 17p. (J). per. *(978-0-9766804-0-6(8))* CottonWood Publishing Co.

Di Salvo, Roberto. Marvel Adventures Spider-Man - Friendly Neighborhood. Tobin, Paul. 2011. (ENG.). 96p. (J). (gr. -1-17). pap. 9.99 *(978-0-7851-5257-6(1))* Marvel Worldwide, Inc.

Di Vito, Andrea. Avengers Academy: Final Exams. Gage, Christos. 2013. (ENG.). 136p. (J). (gr. 4-17). pap. 19.99 *(978-0-7851-6032-8(9))* Marvel Worldwide, Inc.

—Avengers Academy: Final Exams. Gage, Christos & Grummett, Tom. 2013. (ENG.). 136p. (J). (gr. 4-17). 24.99 *(978-0-7851-6031-1(0))* Marvel Worldwide, Inc.

Di Vito, Andrea, et al. Avengers Disassembled: Iron Man, Thor, & Captain America. Priest, Christopher. 2009. (ENG.). 456p. (YA). (gr. 8-17). 49.99 *(978-0-7851-3884-6(6))* Marvel Worldwide, Inc.

—Gladiator Triumphant, Vol. 2. Dixon, Chuck. 2004. (Brath Ser.: Vol. 2). 160p. (YA). pap. 9.95 *(978-1-59314-045-8(2))* CrossGeneration Comics, Inc.

Di Vito, Andrea. World of Reading: Black Widow This Is Black Widow. Wong, Clarissa S. 2015. (World of Reading Ser.). (ENG.). 32p. (J). (gr. 1-3). pap. 3.99 *(978-1-4847-2517-7(4),* Marvel Pr.) Disney Publishing Worldwide.

Di Vito, Andrea & Gurihiru Staff. Wolverine Comic Reader 1. 2013. (ENG.). 32p. (J). (gr. -1-17). 3.99 *(978-0-7851-5386-3(1))* Marvel Worldwide, Inc.

—Wolverine Comic Reader 2. Sumerak, Marc. 2013. (ENG.). 32p. (J). (gr. -1-17). 3.99 *(978-0-7851-5387-0(X))* Marvel Worldwide, Inc.

Diakité, Baba Wagué. The Pot of Wisdom. Badoe, Adwoa. 2008. (ENG.). 64p. (J). (gr. 1-5). pap. 12.95 *(978-0-88899-869-9(4))* Groundwood Bks. CAN. Dist: Perseus-PGW.

Diamond, Donna. Bridge to Terabithia. Paterson, Katherine. (ENG.). (J). (gr. 3-7). 2008. 208p. pap. 6.99 *(978-0-06-073401-5(9),* HarperTeen); 2006. 176p. pap. 6.99 *(978-0-06-122728-8(5),* HarperFestival); 2006. 208p. pap. 6.99 *(978-0-06-125370-6(7),* HarperFestival) HarperCollins Pubs.

—Bridge to Terabithia. Paterson, Katherine. l.t. ed. 2007. (Literacy Bridge Middle Reader Ser.). 187p. (J). (gr. 4-7). 23.95 *(978-0-7862-9620-0(8))* Thorndike Pr.

—Bridge to Terabithia. Paterson, Katherine. 2003. (Trophy Bk.). (ENG.). 176p. (J). (gr. 3-7). reprint ed. pap. 6.99 *(978-0-06-440184-5(7))* HarperCollins Pubs.

—Helen Keller: A Light for the Blind. Kudlinski, Kathleen V. 2015. (Women of Our Time Ser.). (ENG.). 80p. (J). (gr. 3-7). 7.99 *(978-0-14-751467-7(3),* Puffin) Penguin Publishing Group.

—Molly & the Sword. Shlasko, Robert. 2004. 32p. (J). 15.95 *(978-0-9745077-4-3(1))* Jane & Street Pubs. Ltd.

—Walter: The Story of a Rat. Wersba, Barbara. (ENG.). 64p. (J). (gr. 4-6). 2012. pap. 8.95 *(978-1-59078-948-3(2));* 2005. 16.95 *(978-1-932425-41-3(1),* Lemniscaat) Boyds Mills Pr.

Diamond, Donna. The Shadow. Diamond, Donna. 2010. (ENG.). 32p. (J). (gr. k-3). 15.99 *(978-0-7636-4878-7(7))* Candlewick Pr.

Diamond, Shendl. The True Story of Critter Angels by Yani. Diamond, Shendl, text. 2005. (J). 15.95 *(978-0-9764724-3-8(0))* LikeMinds Pr.

Diana. Tee Hee. Carmen, Indigo. 2008. 24p. pap. 24.95 *(978-1-4241-9959-4(X))* America Star Bks.

Diana Cox. Bebe's Big Adventure: A Bebe & Muckle Book. Laverty, Neil. 2013. 44p. pap. 17.97 *(978-1-62212-612-5(2),* Strategic Bk. Publishing) Strategic Book Publishing & Rights Agency (SBPRA).

Dias, Ron, et al. Beauty & the Beast. Slater, Teddy. 2004. (Little Golden Book Ser.). (ENG.). 24p. (J). (gr. -1-2). 3.99 *(978-0-7364-2197-3(1),* Golden/Disney) Random Hse. Children's Bks.

Dias, Ron & Lorencz, Bill. Cinderella. RH Disney Staff. 2005. (Little Golden Book Ser.). (ENG.). 24p. (J). (gr. -1-2). lib. bdg. 3.99 *(978-0-7364-2362-5(1),* Golden/Disney) Random Hse. Children's Bks.

Dias, Ron, jt. illus. see DiCicco, Sue.

Dias, Ron, jt. illus. see Langley, Bill.

Diaz, Cassandra. Pandemonium. Wooding, Chris. 2012. (ENG.). 160p. (J). (gr. 3-7). pap. 12.99 *(978-0-439-87759-6(8),* Graphix) Scholastic, Inc.

—Pandemonium. Wooding, Chris. ed. 2012. lib. bdg. 24.50 *(978-0-606-23946-2(4),* Turtleback) Turtleback Bks.

Diaz, David. Angel Face. Weeks, Sarah. 2014. (ENG.). 32p. (J). (gr. -1-2). 13.99 ***(978-1-4814-5045-4(X),*** Atheneum Bks. for Young Readers) Simon & Schuster Children's Publishing.

Diaz, David. Before You Came. Charest, Emily MacLachlan & MacLachlan, Patricia. 2011. 32p. (J). (gr. -1-3). (ENG.). 16.99 *(978-0-06-051234-7(2));* lib. bdg. 17.89 *(978-0-06-051235-4(0))* HarperCollins Pubs. (Tegen, Katherine Bks).

—The Castle Corona. Creech, Sharon. (J). 2013. (ENG.). 352p. (gr. 3-7). pap. 7.99 *(978-0-06-206395-3(2));* 2007. (ENG.). 336p. (gr. 3-7). 18.99 *(978-0-06-084621-3(6));* 2007. 336p. (gr. 4-7). lib. bdg. 19.89 *(978-0-06-084622-0(4),* Cotler, Joanna Books) HarperCollins Pubs.

—Cesar: Sí, Se Puede! Yes, We Can!, 0 vols. Bernier-Grand, Carmen T. 2011. (ENG.). 48p. (J). (gr. 3-7). pap. 7.99 *(978-0-7614-5833-3(6),* 9780761458333, Amazon Children's Publishing) Amazon Publishing.

—La Cinturita de Anansi, Level 3. Cabral, Len. Flor Ada, Alma, tr. 3rd ed. 2003. (Dejame Leer Ser.). (SPA.). 16p. (J). (gr. -1-3). 6.50 *(978-0-673-36294-0(9),* Good Year Bks.) Celebration Pr.

—Counting Ovejas. Weeks, Sarah. 2006. (ENG & SPA.). 40p. (J). (gr. -1-2). 17.99 *(978-0-689-86750-7(6),* Atheneum Bks. for Young Readers) Simon & Schuster Children's Publishing.

—Diego: Bigger Than Life, 0 vols. Bernier-Grand, Carmen. 2009. (ENG.). 64p. (J). (gr. 8-13). 18.99 *(978-0-7614-5383-3(0),* 9780761453833, Amazon Children's Publishing) Amazon Publishing.

—Feliz Navidad: Two Stories Celebrating Christmas. Feliciano, José. 2005. 23p. (J). reprint ed. 16.00 *(978-0-7567-8587-1(1))* DIANE Publishing Co.

—The Gospel Cinderella. Thomas, Joyce Carol. 2004. 40p. (J). (gr. k-5). lib. bdg. 16.89 *(978-0-06-025388-2(6),* Cotler, Joanna Books) HarperCollins Pubs.

—Let There Be Peace on Earth: And Let It Begin with Me. Jackson, Jill & Miller, Sy. 2009. (ENG.). 30p. (J). (gr. k-12). 18.99 *(978-1-58246-285-1(2),* Tricycle Pr.) Ten Speed Pr.

—The Little Scarecrow Boy. Brown, Margaret Wise. 2005. (ENG.). 40p. (J). (gr. -1-2). reprint ed. pap. 6.99 *(978-0-06-077891-0(1))* HarperCollins Pubs.

—Martin de Porres: The Rose in the Desert. Schmidt, Gary D. 2012. (ENG.). 32p. (J). (gr. 1-4). lib. bdg. 16.99 *(978-0-547-61218-8(4))* Houghton Mifflin Harcourt Publishing Co.

—Maya's Blanket, 1 vol. Brown, Monica & Domínguez, Adriana. ed. 2015. (SPA & ENG.). 32p. (J). 17.95 *(978-0-89239-292-6(4))* Lee & Low Bks., Inc.

—Me, Frida. Novesky, Amy. (ENG.). 32p. (J). (gr. -1-3). 2015. pap. 9.95 *(978-1-4197-1516-7(X));* 2010. 17.95 *(978-0-8109-8969-6(7))* Abrams. (Abrams Bks. for Young Readers).

—Neighborhood Odes. Soto, Gary. 2005. (ENG.). 80p. (J). (gr. 2-5). pap. 6.99 *(978-0-15-205364-2(6))* Houghton Mifflin Harcourt Publishing Co.

—Picasso: I the King, Yo el Rey, 0 vols. Bernier-Grand, Carmen T. 2012. (ENG.). 64p. (J). (gr. 5-10). 19.99 *(978-0-7614-6177-7(9),* 9780761461777, Amazon Children's Publishing) Amazon Publishing.

—Pocahontas: Princess of the New World. Krull, Kathleen. 2007. (ENG.). 40p. (J). (gr. 1-6). 16.95 *(978-0-8027-9554-0(4))* Walker & Co.

—The Pot That Juan Built. Andrews-Goebel, Nancy. 2013. (ENG.). 32p. (J). (gr. 1-18). 17.95 *(978-1-58430-038-0(8))* Lee & Low Bks., Inc.

—Praise Song for the Day. Alexander, Elizabeth. 2012. (ENG.). 32p. (J). (gr. 1-5). 16.99 *(978-0-06-192663-1(9),* Tegen, Katherine Bks) HarperCollins Pubs.

—Rin, Rin, Rin - Do, Re, Mi. Orozco, Jose-Luis. 2005. (Lee y Seras Ser.). (ENG.). 32p. (J). (gr. -1-k). 3.99 *(978-0-439-75531-3(X),* Orchard Bks.) Scholastic, Inc.

—Sharing the Seasons: A Book of Poems. 2010. (ENG.). 96p. (J). (gr. 3-7). 22.99 *(978-1-4169-0210-2(4),* McElderry, Margaret K. Bks.) McElderry, Margaret K. Bks.

—La Vasija Que Juan Fabrico. Andrews-Goebel, Nancy. Cortes, Eunice, tr. 2004. (SPA.). (J). 16.95 *(978-1-58430-229-2(1))* Lee & Low Bks., Inc.

—The Wanderer. Creech, Sharon. 2011. (ENG.). 304p. (J). (gr. 3-7). pap. 6.99 *(978-0-06-441032-8(3))* HarperCollins Pubs.

Diaz, David. Wilma Unlimited. Krull, Kathleen. 2015. 44p. pap. 7.00 ***(978-1-61003-502-6(X))*** Center for the Collaborative Classroom.

Diaz, David. Yes! We Are Latinos. Flor Ada, Alma & Campoy, F. Isabel. 2013. (SPA & ENG.). 96p. (J). (gr. 5). 18.95 *(978-1-58089-383-1(X))* Charlesbridge Publishing, Inc.

Diaz, David, jt. illus. see Nelson, Annika.

Diaz, Diego. I'M Casting a Spell!! Meet a Fairy-Tale Witch. Bullard, Lisa. 2014. (Monster Buddies Ser.). (ENG.). 24p. (gr. k-2). lib. bdg. 23.93 *(978-0-7613-9192-0(4),* Millbrook Pr.) Lerner Publishing Group.

Diaz, Francesca. Popigami: When Everyday Paper Pops! Diaz, James. 2007. (ENG.). 8p. (J). (gr. -1). 19.95 *(978-1-58117-641-4(4),* Intervisual/Piggy Toes) Bendon, Inc.

Diaz, Gabriel. The Hoop Kid from Elmdale Park. Bernard, Teko & Wilson, Wayne L. 2013. 126p. pap. 7.99 *(978-0-9860593-0-8(7))* Elmdale Park Books.

Diaz, Irene & Xian Nu Studio Staff. Sanctuary, Vol. 1. Marr, Melissa. 2009. (Wicked Lovely: Desert Tales Ser.: 1). (ENG.). 176p. (YA). (gr. 8-18). pap. 9.99 *(978-0-06-149354-6(6))* HarperCollins Pubs.

Diaz, James & Gerth, Melanie. Numbers: Learning Fun for Little Ones! 2007. 10p. (J). reprint ed. *(978-1-4223-6683-7(9))* DIANE Publishing Co.

Diaz, Raquel. Sapito Azul. Sánchez Beras, César. 2004. (SPA.). 32p. (J). *(978-1-58018-056-6(6))* Cambridge BrickHouse, Inc.

Diaz, Viviana. Spooky & Spookier: Four American Ghost Stories. Houran, Lori Haskins. 2015. (Step into Reading Ser.). (ENG.). 48p. (J). (gr. 2-4). 3.99 ***(978-0-553-53396-5(7),*** Random Hse. Bks. for Young Readers) Random Hse. Children's Bks.

Dibble, Traci. The Lion Pride. Zorzi, Gina & Cline, Gina. 2010. (2G Predator Animals Ser.). (ENG.). 32p. (J). (gr. k-2). pap. 8.50 *(978-1-61541-500-7(9))* American Reading Co.

Dibble, Traci. Brown Bears. Dibble, Traci. 2010. (1-3Y Wild Animals Ser.). (ENG.). 16p. (J). (gr. k-2). pap. 6.50 *(978-1-61541-375-1(8))* American Reading Co.

—Cobras. Dibble, Traci. 2010. (1-3Y Wild Animals Ser.). (ENG.). 16p. (J). (gr. k-2). pap. 6.50 *(978-1-61541-367-6(7))* American Reading Co.

—Robber Flies. Dibble, Traci. Washington, Joi. 2010. (1-3Y Bugs, Bugs, & More Bugs Ser.). (ENG.). 16p. (J). (gr. k-2). pap. 6.50 *(978-1-61541-294-5(8))* American Reading Co.

—Sea Turtles. Dibble, Traci. Johnson, Gee & Cline, Gina. 2011. (2G Marine Life Ser.). (ENG.). 32p. (J). (gr. k-2). pap. 7.50 *(978-1-61541-399-7(5))* American Reading Co.

DiBlase, Judy. More Award-Winning Science Fair Projects. Bochinski, Julianne Blair. 2004. 228p. (YA). (gr. 8-12). 24.55 *(978-0-613-81939-8(X),* Turtleback) Turtleback Bks.

—More Award-Winning Science Fair Projects. Bochinski, Julianne Blair. 2003. (ENG.). 228p. (J). pap. 22.00 *(978-0-471-27337-0(6),* Wiley) Wiley, John & Sons, Inc.

Dibley, Glin. The Case of the Missing Dinosaur Egg. Freeman, Martha. 2014. (First Kids Mystery Ser.: 5). (ENG.). 115p. (J). (gr. -1-3). pap. 6.99 *(978-0-8234-3061-1(8))* Holiday Hse., Inc.

—Joy in Mudville. Raczka, Bob. 2014. (ENG.). 32p. (J). (gr. -1-3). 17.95 *(978-0-7613-6015-5(8),* Carolrhoda Bks.) Lerner Publishing Group.

—Kid Tea, 0 vols. Ficocelli, Elizabeth. 2013. (ENG.). 36p. (J). (gr. -1-k). pap. 9.99 *(978-1-4778-4738-1(3),* 9781477847381, Amazon Children's Publishing) Amazon Publishing.

—Kid Tea. Ficocelli, Elizabeth. 2009. 32p. (J). (gr. -1). bds. 7.99 *(978-0-7614-5533-2(7))* Marshall Cavendish Corp.

—The Stupendous Dodgeball Fiasco. Rosenswelg, Jay B. & Repka, Janice. 2004. (SPA & ENG.). 160p. (J). (gr. 3-18). 16.99 *(978-0-525-47346-6(7),* Dutton Juvenile) Penguin Publishing Group.

DiCamillo, Kate & Van Dusen, Chris. Mercy Watson Fights Crime. DiCamillo, Kate. 2006. (Mercy Watson Ser.: 3). (ENG.). 80p. (J). (gr. k-3). 12.99 *(978-0-7636-2590-0(6))* Candlewick Pr.

—Mercy Watson to the Rescue. DiCamillo, Kate. 2009. (Mercy Watson Ser.: 1). (ENG.). 80p. (J). (gr. 1-4). pap. 5.99 *(978-0-7636-4504-5(4))* Candlewick Pr.

DiCianni, Ron. Tell Me about Heaven. Alcorn, Randy. 2007. 64p. 19.99 *(978-1-58134-853-8(3))* Crossway.

—Tell Me the Promises. Eareckson Tada, Joni & Jensen, Steve. 2004. 48p. (gr. 5-7). 17.99 *(978-0-89107-904-0(1))* Crossway.

—Tell Me the Story: A Story for Eternity. Lucado, Max. ed. 2015. 48p. 19.99 *(978-1-4335-4744-7(9))* Crossway.

Dicicco, Joe. Planet Baseball, Dominican Republic Edition, Volume 1: Making the Play, Vol. 1. Dicicco, Joe. Jimenez, Ruben D., tr. l.t. ed. 2009.Tr. of Beisbol de Planeta. (ENG & SPA.). 14p. (J). (gr. -1-3). 7.95 *(978-1-929528-01-1(9))* Punta Gorda Pr.

—Planet Baseball, Japanese Edition, Volume 1: Making the Play, Vol. 1. Dicicco, Joe. Jimenez, Ruben D., tr. l.t. ed. 2009. (JPN & ENG.). 14p. (J). (gr. -1-3). 7.95 *(978-1-929528-03-5(5))* Punta Gorda Pr.

—Planet Baseball, Puerto Rico: Volume 1, Making the Play, Vol. 1. Dicicco, Joe. Jimenez, Ruben D., tr. l.t. ed. 2009.Tr. of Beisbol de Planeta. (ENG & SPA.). 14p. (J). (gr. -1-3). 7.95 *(978-1-929528-02-8(7))* Punta Gorda Pr.

DiCicco, LeeAnn. Buddy & the Nature Trackers. Reader's Digest Editors & Froeb, Lori C. 2012. (Lift-The-Flap Ser.). (ENG.). 10p. (J). (gr. -1-k). bds. 9.99 *(978-0-7944-2469-5(4))* Reader's Digest Assn., Inc., The.

DiCicco, LeeAnn, jt. illus. see DiCicco, Sue.

DiCicco, Sue. Bath Time with Ariel (Disney Princess) Posner-Sanchez, Andrea. 2015. (Big Bright & Early Board Book Ser.). (ENG.). 24p. (J). (-k). bds. 6.99 *(978-0-7364-3310-5(4),* RH/Disney) Random Hse. Children's Bks.

—The Little Mermaid. Teitelbaum, Michael. 2003. (Little Golden Book Ser.). (ENG.). 24p. (J). (gr. -1-2). 3.99 *(978-0-7364-2177-5(7),* Golden/Disney) Random Hse. Children's Bks.

—Purple Monkey Rescue! (Team Umizoomi) Golden Books. 2012. (Little Golden Book Ser.). (ENG.). 24p. (J). (gr. k-k). 3.99 *(978-0-307-97589-8(4),* Golden Bks.) Random Hse. Children's Bks.

—The Shy Little Kitten. Depken, Kristen L. & Schurr, Cathleen. 2015. (Step into Reading Ser.). (ENG.). 32p. (J). (gr. -1-1). 12.99 *(978-0-375-97377-2(X))* Random Hse., Inc.

—Sleeping Beauty. RH Disney Staff & Teitelbaum, Michael. 2003. (Pictureback Ser.). (ENG.). 24p. (J). (gr. -1-2). pap. 3.99 *(978-0-7364-1318-3(9),* RH/Disney) Random Hse. Children's Bks.

DiCicco, Sue. Tawny, Scrawny Lion. Depken, Kristen L. & Jackson, Kathryn. 2016. (J). pap. ***(978-1-101-93424-1(7))*** Random Hse., Inc.

—Tidy-Up Time with Cinderella (Disney Princess) Posner-Sanchez, Andrea. 2015. (Bright & Early Board Books(TM) Ser.). (ENG.). 24p. (J). (-k). bds. 6.99 ***(978-0-7364-3408-9(9),*** RH/Disney) Random Hse. Children's Bks.

DiCicco, Sue. Totally Monster: Best Friends. 2013. (Totally Monsters Ser.). (ENG.). 14p. (J). 12.95 *(978-1-60710-643-2(4),* Silver Dolphin Bks.) Baker & Taylor Publishing Group.

—Totally Monster: Feelings. 2013. (Totally Monsters Ser.). (ENG.). 14p. (J). (gr. -1). 12.95 *(978-1-60710-644-9(2),* Silver Dolphin Bks.) Baker & Taylor Publishing Group.

—Totally Monster: Manners. 2013. (Totally Monsters Ser.). (ENG.). 14p. (J). (gr. -1). 12.95 *(978-1-60710-645-6(0),* Silver Dolphin Bks.) Baker & Taylor Publishing Group.

DiCicco, Sue. Feelings. DiCicco, Sue. 2010. 10p. 9.95 *(978-1-60747-743-3(2),* Pickwick Pr.) Phoenix Bks., Inc.

—Manners. DiCicco, Sue. 2010. 10p. 9.95 *(978-1-60747-749-5(1),* Pickwick Pr.) Phoenix Bks., Inc.

—1, 2, 3 in the Sea. DiCicco, Sue. 2012. (ENG.). 10p. (J). (— 1). bds. 6.99 *(978-0-545-43238-2(3))* Scholastic, Inc.

—1, 2 at the Zoo. DiCicco, Sue. 2012. (ENG.). 10p. (J). (— 1). bds. 6.99 *(978-0-545-43239-9(1))* Scholastic, Inc.

DiCicco, Sue & Dias, Ron. Sleeping Beauty. Teitelbaum, Michael & Golden Books Staff. 2004. (Little Golden Book Ser.). (ENG.). 24p. (J). (gr. -1-k). 3.99 *(978-0-7364-2198-0(X),* Golden/Disney) Random Hse. Children's Bks.

DiCicco, Sue & DiCicco, LeeAnn. Let's Go to Volcano Valley! Over 30 Fun Flaps to Lift. Reader's Digest Editors & Froeb, Lori C. 2011. (Lift-The-Flap Ser.). (ENG.). 10p. (J). (gr. -1-k). bds. 9.99 *(978-0-7944-2292-9(6))* Reader's Digest Assn., Inc., The.

DiCicco, Sue & Mawhinney, Art. Diego y los Dinosaurios. 2008. (Go, Diego, Go! Ser.). Orig. Title: Diego's Great Dinosaur Rescue. (SPA & ENG.). 24p. (J). (gr. -1-2). pap. 3.99 *(978-1-4169-5871-0(1),* Libros Para Ninos) Libros Para Ninos.

—Diego's Great Dinosaur Rescue. 2008. (Go, Diego, Go! Ser.). (ENG.). 24p. (J). (gr. -1-2). pap. 3.99 *(978-1-4169-5867-3(3),* Simon Spotlight/Nickelodeon) Simon Spotlight/Nickelodeon.

DiCicco, Sue, jt. illus. see RH Disney Staff.

Dick, Debra. Zoo Haiku. 2008. 84p. (YA). per. 10.00 *(978-0-9725942-3-3(X))* Paper Kite Pr.

Dick, Judy. The Seder Activity Book. Dick, Judy. 2004. 39p. (gr. k-3). pap., act. bk. ed. 9.95 *(978-0-8074-0728-8(3),* 101097) URJ Pr.

Dick, Peggy. Draw & Write Through History: Creation Through Jonah. Gressman, Carylee Anne. Wolf, Aaron D., ed. 2006. (J). per. 12.95 *(978-0-9778597-0-2(3))* CPR Pubng.

Dick, Regina Frances, jt. illus. see Richards, Virginia Helen.

Dickason, Chris. Brain Games for Clever Kids. Moore, Gareth. 2014. (ENG.). 192p. (J). (gr. 3-7). 7.99 *(978-1-78055-249-1(1))* O'Mara, Michael Bks., Ltd. GBR. Dist: Independent Pubs. Group.

Dickens, Christina. I Have a New Puppy! Now What? A Puppy Survival Guide for Kids. Hunt, James. 2007. (Fireman James & Flame Ser.). 40p. (J). (gr. 1-3). 14.99 *(978-0-9769401-0-4(8))* Hunt, J. L. Publishing.

Dickens, Earl. Real Fossils. Benanti, Carol. Frank, Michael, ed. (Real Collections). 32p. (Orig.). (J). (gr. 3-8). pap. 6.95 *(978-1-880592-06-9(1))* Pace Products, Inc.

Dickens, Frank. Albert Herbert Hawkins: The Naughtiest Boy in the World. Dickens, Frank. 32p. (J). (gr. -1-3). 12.95 *(978-0-87592-000-9(4))* Scroll Pr., Inc.

D

Dickert, Sheryl. The Night Before Christmas in New York, 1 vol. Phillips, Betty Lou & Herndon, Roblyn. 2013. (ENG.). 32p. 9.99 *(978-1-4236-3440-9(3))* Gibbs Smith, Publisher.

—The Night Before Christmas in Texas, 1 vol. Phillips, Betty Lou & Herndon, Roblyn. 2013. (ENG.). 32p. 9.99 *(978-1-4236-3509-3(4))* Gibbs Smith, Publisher.

Dickinson, Rebecca. Anybody Home?, 1 vol. Berkes, Marianne. 2013. (ENG.). 32p. (J). (gr. -1-3). 17.95 *(978-1-60718-618-2(7))*; pap. 9.95 *(978-1-60718-630-4(6))* Arbordale Publishing.

—Hay Alguien en Casa?, 1 vol. Berkes, Marianne. 2013. (SPA.). 32p. (J). (gr. -1-3). 17.95 *(978-1-60718-714-1(0))* Arbordale Publishing.

Dickison, Forrest. The Sword of Abram. 2013. (J). *(978-1-59128-046-0(X))* Canon Pr.

Dickman, Michael. The Cat & the Kids of Millbrae. Banerjee, Timir. 2011. 24p. pap. 24.95 *(978-1-4560-9721-9(0))* America Star Bks.

Dickson, Bill. Big Rig Daddy: A Ride in the Truck of All Trucks. Wildman, Dale. 2006. 24p. (J). per. 2.99 *(978-1-59958-007-4(1))* Journey Stone Creations, LLC.

—The Bremen Town Musicians: A Retelling of the Grimm's Fairy Tale, 1 vol. Blair, Eric. 2013. (My First Classic Story Ser.). (ENG.). 32p. (gr. k-3). pap. 7.10 *(978-1-4795-1848-7(4)*, My First Classic Story) Picture Window Bks.

—The Bremen Town Musicians: A Retelling of the Grimm's Fairy Tale, 1 vol. Blair, Eric et al. 2010. (My First Classic Story Ser.). (ENG.). 32p. (gr. k-3). lib. bdg. 21.32 *(978-1-4048-6076-6(2)*, My First Classic Story) Picture Window Bks.

—Daniel & the Lions. Petach, Heidi. 2013. (Happy Day Ser.). (ENG.). 16p. (J). pap. 2.49 *(978-1-4143-9298-1(2))* Tyndale Hse. Pubs.

—David & Goliath. 2013. (Happy Day Ser.). (ENG.). 16p. (J). pap. 2.49 *(978-1-4143-9324-7(5))* Tyndale Hse. Pubs.

—The Shoemaker & His Elves: A Retelling of the Grimm's Fairy Tale, 1 vol. Blair, Eric. 2013. (My First Classic Story Ser.). (ENG.). 32p. (gr. k-3). pap. 7.10 *(978-1-4795-1849-4(2)*, My First Classic Story) Picture Window Bks.

—What Kind of Cow Are You? Being Content with How God Made You. Dwire, Joyann. 2006. 24p. (J). per. 2.99 *(978-1-59958-006-7(3))* Journey Stone Creations, LLC.

Dicmas, Courtney. The Great Googly Moogly. Dicmas, Courtney. 2014. (Child's Play Library). (ENG.). 32p. (J). *(978-1-84643-640-6(0))* Child's Play International Ltd.

—Harold Finds a Voice. Dicmas, Courtney. 2013. (Child's Play Library). (ENG.). 32p. (J). *(978-1-84643-550-8(1))* Child's Play International Ltd.

Diefendorf, Cathy. Diving for el Corazon. Damitz, Charlie. 2007. (ENG.). 100p. (J). pap. 7.95 *(978-0-9744446-3-5(4))* All About Kids Publishing.

—Ginger Leads the Way. O'Donnell, Liam. (Pet Tales Ser.). (ENG.). 32p. (J). (gr. -1-2). 2005. 4.95 *(978-1-59249-358-6(0)*, 1B023); 2005. 2.95 *(978-1-59249-359-3(9)*, 1B024); 2004. 9.95 *(978-1-59249-360-9(2)*, 1B025) Soundprints.

—Pepper: A Snowy Search. O'Donnell, Liam. 2004. (Pet Tales Ser.). (ENG.). 32p. (J). (gr. -1-3). 4.95 *(978-1-59249-361-6(0)*, 1B026) Soundprints.

—Pepper, a Snowy Search. O'Donnell, Liam. (Pet Tales Ser.). (ENG.). 32p. (J). (gr. -1-2). 2005. 2.95 *(978-1-59249-362-3(9)*, 1B027); 2004. 9.95 *(978-1-59249-363-0(7)*, 1B028) Soundprints.

Diego, Rapi. La Sapita Sabia y Otros Cuentos. Ferré, Rosario. (SPA.). 48p. (J). (gr. 3-5). pap. 8.95 *(978-968-19-0353-4(6))* Santillana USA Publishing Co., Inc.

Diego, Rapi & Flores, Martha. El Jardin del Nino: Una Historia de Esperanza. Foreman, Michael. 2009. (SPA.). 30p. (J). (gr. 1-3). 14.99 *(978-1-933032-56-6(1))* Lectorum Pubns., Inc.

—El Lorito Pelon. Foreman, Michael. 2008. (SPA.). 30p. (J). (gr. 1-3). 15.99 *(978-1-930332-56-0(4))* Lectorum Pubns., Inc.

Diehl, Nichole. Old Testament Heroines of the Faith. Lo, Monica. 2007. 82p. per. 17.99 *(978-1-59879-224-9(5)*, Lifevest) Lifevest Publishing, Inc.

Diemberger, Jana. Monacello: The Little Monk. McCaughrean, Geraldine. 2013. (Monacello Trilogy Ser.: 1). (ENG.). 64p. (J). (gr. 4-7). pap. 12.99 *(978-1-907912-03-0(7))* Phoenix Yard Bks. GBR. Dist: Independent Pubs. Group.

—The Wish-Bringer. McCaughrean, Geraldine. 2014. (Monacello Trilogy Ser.). (ENG.). 56p. (J). (gr. 4-7). pap. 12.99 *(978-1-907912-06-1(1))* Phoenix Yard Bks. GBR. Dist: Independent Pubs. Group.

Dieterichs, Shelley. Ben Gives a Gift. Hoffmann, Sara E. 2013. (My Reading Neighborhood: Kindergarten Sight Word Stories Ser.). (ENG.). 16p. (gr. -1-1). pap. 5.95 *(978-1-4677-1164-7(0))* Lerner Publishing Group.

—Little Sister, Big Mess! Gerver, Jane E. 2007. (Rookie Reader Skill Set Ser.). (ENG.). 32p. (J). (gr. -1-3). 19.50 *(978-0-531-17545-3(6)*, Children's Pr.) Scholastic Library Publishing.

—Sam Is Six. Hoffmann, Sara E. 2013. (My Reading Neighborhood: Kindergarten Sight Word Stories Ser.). (ENG.). 16p. (gr. -1-1). pap. 5.95 *(978-1-4677-1163-0(2))* Lerner Publishing Group.

—Sam Sees Snow. Hoffmann, Sara E. 2013. (My Reading Neighborhood: Kindergarten Sight Word Stories Ser.). (ENG.). 16p. (gr. -1-1). pap. 5.95 *(978-1-4677-1167-8(5))* Lerner Publishing Group.

Dietrich, Andrea. Hooligan Bear Home. Toynton, Ian. 2012. 32p. (J). 15.95 *(978-1-60131-108-5(7))* Big Tent Bks.

—Hooligan Bear New Friends. Toynton, Ian. 2012. 34p. (J). 15.95 *(978-1-60131-107-8(9))* Big Tent Bks.

Dietrich, Sean. Hansel & Gretel: The Graphic Novel, 1 vol. 2008. (Graphic Spin Ser.). (ENG.). 40p. (gr. 1-3). 23.99 *(978-1-4342-0767-8(6)*, Graphic Revolve) Stone Arch Bks.

—Hansel & Gretel: The Graphic Novel, 1 vol. Stone Arch Books (Firm: Afton, Minn.) Staff. 2008. (Graphic Spin Ser.). (ENG.). 40p. (gr. 1-3). pap. 5.95 *(978-1-4342-0863-7(X)*, Graphic Revolve) Stone Arch Bks.

—Hansel y Gretel: La Novela Grafica. Andersen, Hans Christian & Stone Arch Books Staff. 2010. (Graphic Spin en Español Ser.). (SPA & ENG.). 40p. (gr. 1-3). pap. 5.95 *(978-1-4342-2271-8(3)*, Graphic Spin en Español) Stone Arch Bks.

—Hansel y Gretel: La Novela Grafica. Andersen, Hans Christian & Capstone Press Staff. 2010. (Graphic Spin en Español Ser.). (SPA.). 40p. (gr. 1-3). lib. bdg. 23.99 *(978-1-4342-1901-5(1)*, Graphic Spin en Español) Stone Arch Bks.

Dietrich, Sean, et al. Shivers, Wishes, & Wolves: Stone Arch Fairy Tales, Volume One, 1 vol. Capstone Press Staff. 2011. (Graphic Spin Ser.). (ENG.). 176p. (gr. 1-3). pap. 12.95 *(978-1-4342-3031-7(7)*, Graphic Revolve) Stone Arch Bks.

Dietrich, Sean. Sleeping Beauty. Capstone Press Staff. 2009. (Graphic Spin Ser.). (ENG.). 40p. (gr. 1-3). pap. 5.95 *(978-1-4342-1393-8(5))*; lib. bdg. 23.99 *(978-1-4342-1193-4(2))* Stone Arch Bks. (Graphic Revolve).

Dietz, Mike. Funny Boy Meets the Dumbbell Dentist from Deimos (with Dangerous Dental Decay) Gutman, Dan. 2012. (Funny Boy Ser.). (ENG.). 120p. (J). pap. 5.99 *(978-1-4532-7070-7(1))* Open Road Integrated Media, LLC.

—Funny Boy Takes on the Chit-Chatting Cheeses from Chattanooga. Gutman, Dan. 2012. (Funny Boy Ser.). (ENG.). 134p. (J). pap. 5.99 *(978-1-4532-9530-4(5))* Open Road Integrated Media, LLC.

—Funny Boy Versus the Bubble-Brained Barbers from the Big Bang. Gutman, Dan. 2012. (Funny Boy Ser.). (ENG.). 144p. (J). pap. 5.99 *(978-1-4532-9532-8(1))* Open Road Integrated Media, LLC.

Diez, Dalia Alvarado. El Secreto del Sauce. Dreser, Elena. 2003. (SPA.). 44p. (J). (gr. 3-5). pap. 6.95 *(978-968-19-0617-7(9))* Santillana USA Publishing Co., Inc.

Diez-Luckie, Cathy. Kitty Goes Splash. Hill, Merle Roddy. 2005. (ENG.). 12p. (J). 5.75 *(978-1-57274-823-1(0)*, 2171, Bks. for Young Learners) Owen, Richard C. Pubs., Inc.

—The Paper Bag. Ford, Carolyn. 2005. (ENG.). 8p. (J). 5.75 *(978-1-57274-756-2(0)*, 2494, Bks. for Young Learners) Owen, Richard C. Pubs., Inc.

DiFiori, Larry. I Can Do It! Albee, Sarah & Sesame Street Staff. 2011. (Step into Reading Ser.). (ENG.). 32p. (J). (gr. -1-1). pap. 3.99 *(978-0-679-88687-7(7)*, Random Hse. Bks. for Young Readers) Random Hse. Children's Bks.

Diggins, Julia E. & Bell, Corydon. String, Straightedge & Shadow: The Story of Geometry. Diggins, Julia E. 2003. (J). per. 16.95 *(978-1-892857-07-1(3))* Whole Spirit Pr.

Diggins, Matthew. Andrew & the Secret Gallery. Diggins, Matthew. (J). 2008. 32p. pap. 6.95 *(978-1-60108-026-4(3))*; 2007. 30p. (gr. 1-5). 15.95 *(978-1-60108-016-5(6))* Red Cygnet Pr.

Diggle, Daniel James. Barbara: A Sssslithering Adventure of Self Discovery. Diggle, David Mark. 2011. 24p. (J). pap. *(978-0-9871657-9-4(8))* Diggle de Doo Productions Pty, Ltd.

—Brian: Eats Himself Smarter. Diggle, David Mark. 2011. 24p. (J). pap. *(978-0-9871657-4-9(7))* Diggle de Doo Productions Pty, Ltd.

—Ewan: From Bullied to Superhero in One Afternoon. Diggle, David Mark. 2011. 24p. (J). pap. *(978-0-9871657-0-1(4))* Diggle de Doo Productions Pty, Ltd.

—Frederick: Thinking Makes Breathing Easy. Diggle, David Mark. 2011. 24p. (J). pap. *(978-0-9871657-8-7(X))* Diggle de Doo Productions Pty, Ltd.

—George & Toby: Won't Have A Baaa of Bed Wetting. Diggle, David Mark. 2011. 24p. (J). pap. *(978-0-9871657-5-6(5))* Diggle de Doo Productions Pty, Ltd.

—Melanie: Honestly Finds Herself Out of Her Depth. Diggle, David Mark. 2011. 24p. (J). pap. *(978-0-9871657-1-8(2))* Diggle de Doo Productions Pty, Ltd.

—Sammy: Leaves His Mark. Diggle, David Mark. 2011. 24p. (J). pap. *(978-0-9871657-3-2(9))* Diggle de Doo Productions Pty, Ltd.

Diggory, Nick. A Big Box of Bananas, 1 vol. Dale, Jay. 2012. (Engage Literacy Blue Ser.). (ENG.). 16p. (gr. k-2). pap. 5.99 *(978-1-4296-8980-9(3)*, Engage Literacy) Capstone Pr., Inc.

—Lazy Old Pirates, 1 vol. Dale, Jay. 2012. (Wonder Words Ser.). (ENG.). 32p. (gr. k-2). pap. 5.99 *(978-1-4296-8930-4(7)*, Engage Literacy) Capstone Pr., Inc.

—Two Old Pirates, 1 vol. Dale, Jay. 2012. (Wonder Words Ser.). (ENG.). 32p. (gr. k-2). pap. 5.99 *(978-1-4296-8928-1(5)*, Engage Literacy) Capstone Pr., Inc.

—What Is the Matter, Mrs. Long?, 1 vol. Dale, Jay. 2012. (Engage Literacy Green Ser.). (ENG.). 32p. (gr. k-2). pap. 5.99 *(978-1-4296-9030-0(5)*, Engage Literacy) Capstone Pr., Inc.

DiGiacomo, Kris. Rabbit & the Not-So-Big-Bad Wolf. Escoffier, Michaël. 2013. (ENG.). 32p. (J). 16.95 *(978-0-8234-2813-7(3))* Holiday Hse., Inc.

Digman, Kristina. Our Apple Tree. Digman, Kristina. Naslund, Gorel Kristina. 2006. (ENG.). 32p. (J). (gr. -1-3). pap. 8.99 *(978-1-59643-191-1(1))* Square Fish.

Dignan, James. How to Be a Villain: Evil Laughs, Secret Lairs, Master Plans, & More!!! Zawacki, Neil. 2003. (ENG.). 160p. (gr. 8-17). 12.95 *(978-0-8118-4666-0(0))* Chronicle Bks. LLC.

Dilenno, Trish. Toolbox. Ireland, Charles E. 2006. (J). *(978-1-892142-30-6(9))* Cedar Tree Bks.

Dillard, Sarah. Five Wishing Stars: Disappearing Die Cut. Runnells, Treesha. 2005. (ENG.). 12p. (J). 14.95 *(978-1-58117-265-2(6)*, Intervisual/Piggy Toes) Bendon, Inc.

—If You Were a Divided-By Sign, 1 vol. Shaskan, Trisha Speed. 2009. (Math Fun Ser.). (ENG.). 24p. (gr. 2-4). pap. 7.95 *(978-1-4048-5196-2(8))*; lib. bdg. 27.32 *(978-1-4048-5195-5(X))* Picture Window Bks. (Nonfiction Picture Bks.).

—If You Were a Polygon, 1 vol. Aboff, Marcie. 2009. (Math Fun Ser.). (ENG.). 24p. (gr. 2-4). pap. 7.95 *(978-1-4048-5692-9(7)*, Nonfiction Picture Bks.) Picture Window Bks.

—If You Were a Set, 1 vol. Aboff, Marcie. 2008. (Math Fun Ser.). (ENG.). 24p. (gr. 2-4). 27.32 *(978-1-4048-4799-6(5))*; pap. 7.95 *(978-1-4048-4800-9(2))* Picture Window Bks. (Nonfiction Picture Bks.).

—If You Were a Set [LTD Commodities]. Aboff, Marcie. 2010. (Math Fun Ser.). 24p. pap. 3.50 *(978-1-4048-6258-6(7)*, Nonfiction Picture Bks.) Picture Window Bks.

—If You Were a Times Sign, 1 vol. Shaskan, Trisha Speed. 2009. (Math Fun Ser.). (ENG.). 24p. (gr. 2-4). pap. 7.95 *(978-1-4048-5211-2(5))*; lib. bdg. 27.32 *(978-1-4048-5210-5(7))* Picture Window Bks. (Nonfiction Picture Bks.).

—If You Were a Triangle, 1 vol. Aboff, Marcie. 2009. (Math Fun Ser.). (ENG.). 24p. (gr. 2-4). pap. 7.95 *(978-1-4048-5688-2(9)*, Nonfiction Picture Bks.) Picture Window Bks.

—If You Were an Even Number, 1 vol. Aboff, Marcie. 2008. (Math Fun Ser.). (ENG.). 24p. (gr. 2-4). 27.32 *(978-1-4048-4796-5(0))*; pap. 7.95 *(978-1-4048-4797-2(9))* Picture Window Bks. (Nonfiction Picture Bks.).

—If You Were an Even Number [LTD Commodities]. Aboff, Marcie. 2010. (Math Fun Ser.). 24p. pap. 3.50 *(978-1-4048-6259-3(5)*, Nonfiction Picture Bks.) Picture Window Bks.

—If You Were an Even Number [Scholastic]. Aboff, Marcie. 2010. (Math Fun Ser.). 24p. pap. 0.47 *(978-1-4048-6547-1(0)*, Nonfiction Picture Bks.) Picture Window Bks.

—If You Were an Inch or a Centimeter, 1 vol. Aboff, Marcie. 2009. (Math Fun Ser.). (ENG.). 24p. (gr. 2-4). pap. 7.95 *(978-1-4048-5199-3(2))*; lib. bdg. 27.32 *(978-1-4048-5198-6(4))* Picture Window Bks. (Nonfiction Picture Bks.).

—If You Were an Odd Number, 1 vol. Aboff, Marcie. 2008. (Math Fun Ser.). (ENG.). 24p. (gr. 2-4). pap. 7.95 *(978-1-4048-4794-1(4)*, Nonfiction Picture Bks.) Picture Window Bks.

—If You Were an Odd Number [LTD Commodities]. Aboff, Marcie. 2010. (Math Fun Ser.). 24p. pap. 3.50 *(978-1-4048-6260-9(9)*, Nonfiction Picture Bks.) Picture Window Bks.

—If You Were an Odd Number [Scholastic]. Aboff, Marcie. 2010. (Math Fun Ser.). 24p. pap. 0.47 *(978-1-4048-6546-4(2)*, Nonfiction Picture Bks.) Picture Window Bks.

—My Magnetic Opposites: Big & Little: Best Friends. Feldman, Thea. 2007. (Magnix Learning Fun Ser.). 10p. (gr. -1-k). bds. 9.95 *(978-1-932915-39-6(7))* Sandvik Innovations, LLC.

—Ten Wishing Stars: A Countdown to Bedtime Book. Runnells, Treesha. 2006. (ENG.). 22p. (J). 9.95 *(978-1-58117-187-7(0)*, Intervisual/Piggy Toes) Bendon, Inc.

—Toca y Siente las Historias de la Biblia. Larson, Beverly. Pineda, Nancy, tr. 2003. (Touch & Feel Ser.). (SPA.). (J). (gr. -1-k). bds. 8.99 *(978-0-7899-1088-2(8))* Editorial Unilit.

—Traveling in Two's: The Journey to Noah's Ark. Auerbach, Annie. 2005. 8p. (J). 10.95 *(978-1-58117-236-2(2)*, Intervisual/Piggy Toes) Bendon, Inc.

—What Do You Say? Please & Thank You. Wax, Wendy. 2005. (J). *(978-1-58987-108-3(1))* Kindermusik International.

Dillard, Sarah. Extraordinary Warren: A Super Chicken. Dillard, Sarah. 2014. (Pix Ser.). (ENG.). 64p. (J). (gr. 1-4). 12.99 *(978-1-4424-5340-1(0)*, Simon & Schuster/Paula Wiseman Bks.) Simon & Schuster/Paula Wiseman Bks.

—First Day at Zoo School. Dillard, Sarah. 2014. (ENG.). 40p. (J). (gr. k-2). 14.99 *(978-1-58536-890-7(3)*, 203670) Sleeping Bear Pr.

Dillard, Sarah & Carabelli, Francesca. If You Were a Quadrilateral, 1 vol. Blaisdell, Molly. 2009. (Math Fun Ser.). (ENG.). 24p. (gr. 2-4). lib. bdg. 27.32 *(978-1-4048-5511-3(4)*, Nonfiction Picture Bks.) Picture Window Bks.

Dillard, Sarah, jt. illus. see Carabelli, Francesca.

Dilley, Kristi. Squiggy the Squirrel Meets Wallis the Woodpecker. Dilley, Kristi. 2013. 28p. pap. 9.99 *(978-1-937165-47-5(7))* Orange Hat Publishing.

Dillingham, Charlene. The Friendship Thief. Roach, Hesta. (J). (gr. k-5). pap. 9.99 *(978-0-9660583-3-8(X))* Sakura Pr.

Dillman, Jennifer. Tiffany at Tea Time: (A Tiffany T. Book) Gow, Kailin. 2004. (J). 14.95 *(978-1-59457-929-5(6))* Sparklesoup LLC.

—Tiffany at the Top of the World: (A Tiffany T. Book) Gow, Kailin. 2004. (J). 14.95 *(978-1-59457-928-8(8))* Sparklesoup LLC.

Dillon, Diane & Dillon, Leo. The Hundred Penny Box. Mathis, Sharon Bell. 2006. (ENG.). 48p. (J). (gr. 1-4). pap. 7.99 *(978-0-14-240702-8(X)*, Puffin) Penguin Publishing Group.

Dillon, Diane, jt. illus. see Dillon, Leo.

Dillon, Jana. Lucky O'Leprechaun in School, 1 vol. Dillon, Jana. 2003. (Lucky o'Leprechaun Ser.). (ENG.). 32p. (J). (gr. k-3). 16.99 *(978-1-58980-035-9(4))* Pelican Publishing Co., Inc.

Dillon, Julie, jt. illus. see Rayyan, Omar.

Dillon, Leo, et al. Dream: A Tale of Wonder, Wisdom & Wishes. Bosak, Susan V. 2004. 40p. (J). *(978-1-896232-04-1(3)*, TCP Pr.) Communication Project, The.

Dillon, Leo & Dillon, Diane. Ashanti to Zulu: African Traditions. Musgrove, Margaret. 2004. 28p. (YA). (gr. 4-8). reprint ed. pap. 14.00 *(978-0-7567-7106-5(4))* DIANE Publishing Co.

—The Goblin & the Empty Chair. Fox, Mem. 2009. (ENG.). 32p. (J). (gr. k-3). 17.99 *(978-1-4169-8585-3(9)*, Beach Lane Bks.) Beach Lane Bks.

—Hakon of Rogen's Saga. Haugaard, Erik Christian. 2013. (ENG.). 144p. pap. 11.95 *(978-0-8166-8127-3(9))* Univ. of Minnesota Pr.

—The Hundred Penny Box. Mathis, Sharon Bell. 2006. 47p. (gr. 1-4). 18.00 *(978-0-7569-6786-4(4))* Perfection Learning Corp.

—If Kids Ran the World. Dillon, Leo & Dillon, Diane. 2014. (ENG.). 32p. (J). 18.99 *(978-0-545-44196-4(X)*, Blue Sky Pr., The) Scholastic, Inc.

—Moses' Ark: Stories from the Bible. Bach, Alice & Exum, J. Cheryl. 2013. (ENG.). 192p. (J). (gr. 3-7). 15.99 *(978-0-385-29778-3(5)*, Delacorte Bks. for Young Readers) Random Hse. Children's Bks.

—Never Forgotten. McKissack, Patricia C. 2011. (ENG.). 48p. (J). (gr. k-12). 18.99 *(978-0-375-84384-6(1)*, Schwartz & Wade Bks.) Random Hse. Children's Bks.

—The People Could Fly: American Black Folktales. Hamilton, Virginia. 2009. (American Black Folktales Ser.). (ENG.). 192p. (J). (gr. k-12). 24.99 *(978-0-394-86925-4(7)*, Knopf Bks. for Young Readers) Random Hse. Children's Bks.

—The People Could Fly: American Black Folktales. Hamilton, Virginia. 2007. (ENG.). 32p. (J). (gr. k-12). 17.99 *(978-0-375-84553-6(4)*, Knopf Bks. for Young Readers) Random Hse. Children's Bks.

—The People Could Fly: The Picture Book. Hamilton, Virginia. (ENG.). 32p. (J). (gr. k-12). 2015. 7.99 *(978-0-553-50780-5(X)*, Dragonfly Bks.); 2004. 16.95 *(978-0-375-82405-0(7)*, Knopf Bks. for Young Readers) Random Hse. Children's Bks.

—The Porcelain Cat. Hearn, Michael Patrick. 2004. (ENG.). 32p. (J). (gr. 4-7). 16.95 *(978-1-59687-175-5(X))* IBks., Inc.

—The Porcelain Cat. Hearn, Michael Patrick. 2004. 32p. (J). (gr. -1). 16.95 *(978-0-689-03592-0(6)*, Milk & Cookies) ibooks, Inc.

—The Secret River. Rawlings, Marjorie Kinnan. 2011. (ENG.). 56p. (J). (gr. -1-3). 19.99 *(978-1-4169-1179-1(0)*, Atheneum Bks. for Young Readers) Simon & Schuster Children's Publishing.

—Switch on the Night. Bradbury, Ray. 2004. (ENG.). 40p. (J). (gr. -1-2). reprint ed. pap. 6.99 *(978-0-553-11244-3(9)*, Dragonfly Bks.) Random Hse. Children's Bks.

—The Tale of the Mandarin Ducks. Paterson, Katherine. 2004. 32p. (J). (gr. k-4). reprint ed. 15.00 *(978-0-7567-7698-5(8))* DIANE Publishing Co.

—Two Little Trains. Brown, Margaret Wise. 2003. (ENG.). 32p. (J). (gr. -1-k). pap. 6.99 *(978-0-06-443568-0(7))* HarperCollins Pubs.

—Where Have You Been? Brown, Margaret Wise. 2004. 32p. (J). (gr. -1-1). (ENG.). 16.99 *(978-0-06-028378-0(5))*; lib. bdg. 16.89 *(978-0-06-028379-7(3))* HarperCollins Pubs.

Dillon, Leo, jt. illus. see Dillon, Diane.

Dillon, Paul. Blunder or Brainstorm: Fact & Fiction of Famous Inventors & Inventions. Polette, Nancy. 2006. (YA). pap. 11.95 *(978-1-931334-91-4(9))* Pieces of Learning.

Dillon, Steve, et al. Animal Man. Morrison, Grant. Hill, Michael, ed. rev. ed. 2007. (ENG.). 240p. (YA). pap. 19.99 *(978-1-56389-005-5(4)*, Vertigo) DC Comics.

Dillon, Steve. Preacher - Gone to Texas, Vol. 1. Ennis, Garth. Kahan, Bob, ed. 2005. (Preacher Ser.). (ENG.). 200p. (YA). pap. 17.99 *(978-1-56389-261-5(8))* DC Comics.

Dimatteo, Richard. Study Strategies for Early School Success: Seven Steps to Improve Your Learning. Sirotowitz, Sandi et al. 2003. (Seven Steps Family Guides). (ENG.). 146p. pap. 18.00 *(978-1-886941-55-7(6))* Specialty Pr., Inc.

DiMatteo, Richard A. Eukee the Jumpy Jumpy Elephant. Corman, Clifford L. & Trevino, Esther. (J). 2009. (ENG.). 26p. (gr. -1-1). pap. 10.95 *(978-1-886941-75-5(0))*; 2003. 24p. (gr. 1-4). 15.00 *(978-0-9621629-8-5(1))* Specialty Pr., Inc.

—Making the Grade: An Adolescent's Struggle with ADD. Parker, Roberta N. & Parker, Harvey C. 2003. 48p. (J). (gr. 4-7). pap. 11.00 *(978-0-9621629-1-6(4))* Specialty Pr., Inc.

—Seven Steps to Homework Success: A Family Guide for Solving Common Homework Problems. Zentall, Sydney & Goldstein, Sam. 2003. (Seven Steps Family Guides Ser.). (ENG.). 138p. (J). pap. 17.00 *(978-1-886941-22-9(X))* Specialty Pr., Inc.

—Slam Dunk: A Young Boy's Struggle with Attention Defecit Disorder. Parker, Roberta N. 2003. 55p. (J). (gr. 3-7). pap. 11.00 *(978-0-9621629-4-7(9))* Specialty Pr., Inc.

—Study Strategies Made Easy: A Practical Plan for School Success. Sirotowitz, Sandi et al. 2003. (School Success Ser.). (ENG.). 160p. (J). (gr. 6-12). pap. 18.95 *(978-1-886941-03-8(3)*, 0931) Specialty Pr., Inc.

Dimaya, Emerson & Calero, Dennis. The Murders in the Rue Morgue, 1 vol. Bowen, Carl & Poe, Edgar Allen. 2013. (Edgar Allan Poe Graphic Novels Ser.). (ENG.). 72p. (gr. 2-3). 26.65 *(978-1-4342-3033-1(3))*; pap. 6.10 *(978-1-4342-4259-4(5))* Stone Arch Bks.

Dimbylow, Jube. Mr Squealy Goes to Town. Norton Kreider, Barbara. 2013. 24p. pap. *(978-1-921883-41-5(3)*, MBS Pr.) Pick-a-Woo Woo Pubs.

—Mr Squealy Makes a Friend. Norton Kreider, Barbara. 2013. 24p. pap. *(978-1-921883-52-1(9))* Pick-a-Woo Woo Pubs.

—Mr Squealy Meets Scarecrow. Norton Kreider, Barbara. 2013. 24p. pap. *(978-1-921883-53-8(7))* Pick-a-Woo Woo Pubs.

—The Surprise Party. Norton Kreider, Barbara. 2013. 30p. pap. *(978-1-921883-37-8(5)*, MBS Pr.) Pick-a-Woo Woo Pubs.

Dimitri, Simona. The Balloon Launch. Bird, Helen. 2005. 32p. (J). lib. bdg. 9.00 *(978-1-4242-0887-6(4))* Fitzgerald Bks.

—Big Yellow Balloon. Bird, Helen. 2009. (Get Set Readers Ser.). 32p. (J). (gr. -1-2). lib. bdg. 22.60 *(978-1-60754-268-1(4))* Windmill Bks.

—Peek Inside Animal Homes. Milbourne, Anna. 2014. (Peek Inside Board Bks.). (ENG.). 14p. (gr. -1). bds. 11.99 *(978-0-7945-2549-1(0)*, Usborne) EDC Publishing.

—This Is My Tractor. Brooks, Felicity. 2009. (Noisy Touchy-Feely Board Bks). 10p. (J). bds. 16.99 *(978-0-7945-2473-9(7)*, Usborne) EDC Publishing.

Dimitriadis, Nick. A Hungry Lion in My Tummy. Vollmer, Cheryl. 2009. 24p. pap. 9.99 *(978-0-9825255-9-3(1),* Epigraph Bks.) Monkfish Bk. Publishing Co.

DiMotta, Michael J. Animals at Play: Rules of the Game. Bekoff, Marc. 2008. (Animals & Ethics Ser.). (ENG.). 32p. (J). (gr. 4-6). 17.95 *(978-1-59213-551-6(X))* Temple Univ. Pr.

Dina, Madalina. The King Who Wanted More. Hodgson, Karen J. 2010. (ENG.). 32p. (J). (gr. -1-4). pap. 9.99 ***(978-1-907432-03-3(5))*** Hogs Back Bks. GBR. Dist: Independent Pubs. Group.

—The Robot Who Couldn't Cry. Hodgson, Karen J. 2010. (ENG.). 32p. (J). (gr. -1-2). pap. 9.99 ***(978-1-907432-01-9(9))*** Hogs Back Bks. GBR. Dist: Independent Pubs. Group.

Dindar, Kubra. A Day on the Farm Playing Along, 1 vol. Ochs, Tom. 2009. 25p. pap. 24.95 *(978-1-60749-405-8(1))* America Star Bks.

Dineen, Tom. Taking Hearing Impairment to School. Schneider, Elaine Ernst. Schader, Karen, ed. 2004. (Special Kids in School Ser.: Fifteenth). (J). per. 11.95 *(978-1-891383-23-6(X),* 70015) JayJo Bks., LLC.

—Taking Speech Disorders to School. Bryant, John E. Schader, Karen, ed. 2004. (Special Kids in School Ser.: Sixteenth). (J). per. 11.95 *(978-1-891383-24-3(8),* 70016) JayJo Bks., LLC.

Dion, Nathalie. Artsy Babies Wear Paint. Colman, Michelle Sinclair. 2011. (Urban Babies Wear Black Book Ser.). (ENG.). 20p. (J). (gr. k — 1). bds. 6.99 *(978-1-58246-371-1(9),* Tricycle Pr.) Ten Speed Pr.

—Beach Babies Wear Shades. Colman, Michelle Sinclair. 2007. (Urban Babies Wear Black Book Ser.). (ENG.). 18p. (J). (gr. k — 1). bds. 6.99 *(978-1-58246-204-2(6),* Tricycle Pr.) Ten Speed Pr.

—The Big Night Out. Beker, Jeanne. 2005. (ENG.). 80p. (J). (gr. 4-7). pap. 15.95 *(978-0-88776-719-7(2))* Tundra Bks. CAN. Dist: Random Hse., Inc.

—Country Babies Wear Plaid. Colman, Michelle Sinclair. 2006. (Urban Babies Wear Black Book Ser.). (ENG.). 20p. (J). (gr. k — 1). bds. 6.95 *(978-1-58246-172-4(4),* Tricycle Pr.) Ten Speed Pr.

—Foodie Babies Wear Bibs. Colman, Michelle Sinclair. 2008. (Urban Babies Wear Black Book Ser.). (ENG.). 20p. (J). (— 1). bds. 6.99 *(978-1-58246-254-7(2),* Tricycle Pr.) Ten Speed Pr.

—Passion for Fashion: Careers in Style. Beker, Jeanne. 2008. (ENG.). 80p. (J). (gr. 5-9). pap. 18.95 *(978-0-88776-800-2(8))* Tundra Bks. CAN. Dist: Random Hse., Inc.

—Rocker Babies Wear Jeans. Colman, Michelle Sinclair. 2009. (Urban Babies Wear Black Book Ser.). (ENG.). 9p. (J). (gr. -1 — 1). bds. 6.99 *(978-1-58246-291-2(7))* Ten Speed Pr.

—Sporty Babies Wear Sweats. Colman, Michelle Sinclair. 2010. (Urban Babies Wear Black Book Ser.). (ENG.). 20p. (J). (gr. -1 — 1). bds. 6.99 *(978-1-58246-313-1(1),* Tricycle Pr.) Ten Speed Pr.

—Urban Babies Wear Black. Colman, Michelle Sinclair. 2005. (Urban Babies Wear Black Book Ser.). (ENG.). 20p. (J). (gr. k — 1). bds. 6.99 *(978-1-58246-158-8(9),* Tricycle Pr.) Ten Speed Pr.

—What's in Your Purse? Samoun, Abigail. 2014. (ENG.). 12p. (J). (gr. -1-17). 17.99 *(978-1-4521-1701-0(2))* Chronicle Bks. LLC.

Dionne, Deanna. Sally Lumpkin's Party: A story of 6 true Friends. Blankenship, Julianna. 2008. 32p. pap. 15.56 *(978-1-4343-6860-7(2))* AuthorHouse.

Dionne, Nina. Samuel's Exeter Walkabout. Tomaszewski, Suzanne Lyon. 2003. 37p. (J). *(978-0-9744855-0-8(0))* Gold Charm Publishing, LLC.

DiOrio, Ariel. The Mystery of the Missing Menorahs: A Hanukkah Humdinger! 2007. 52p. (J). pap. 9.95 *(978-0-9659546-4-8(1))* Oak Leaf Systems.

Dippold, Jane. Farmers' Market Day. Trent, Shanda. 2013. (ENG.). 32p. (J). (gr. -1-1). 12.95 *(978-1-58925-115-1(6))* Tiger Tales.

—A Great Idea? An Up2U Character Education Adventure. Suen, Anastasia. 2015. (J). *(978-1-62402-093-3(3))* Magic Wagon.

—Jessica's Bear. Bennett, Donna I. 2003. (ENG.). 32p. (J). pap. 9.95 *(978-1-878044-57-0(5))* Mayhaven Publishing, Inc.

—New Girl: An Up2U Character Education Adventure. Suen, Anastasia. 2013. (Up2U Adventures Ser.). 80p. (J). (gr. 2-5). lib. bdg. 27.07 *(978-1-61641-968-4(7),* Calico Chapter Bks) Magic Wagon.

—Papa Jethro. Cohen, Deborah Bodin. 2007. (Jewish Identity Ser.). (ENG.). 32p. (J). (gr. -1-1). 9.95 *(978-1-58013-250-3(2));* per. 7.95 *(978-1-58013-252-7(9))* Lerner Publishing Group. (Kar-Ben Publishing).

—Traveling Babies. Galbraith, Kathryn Osebold. 2006. (Animal Babies Ser.). (ENG.). 32p. (J). (gr. -1-k). 16.95 *(978-1-55971-939-1(7))* Cooper Square Publishing Llc.

Dirge, Roman. It Ate Billy on Christmas. Dirge, Roman. Daily, Steven. 2007. (ENG.). 48p. (gr. 7-7). 12.95 *(978-1-59307-853-9(6))* Dark Horse Comics.

DiRocco, Carl. Dear Big, Mean, Ugly Monster. Berglin, Ruth. 2006. 40p. (J). (gr. -1-7). 14.95 *(978-1-58760-072-2(2),* Child & Family Pr.) Child Welfare League of America, Inc.

—Elliot Stone & the Mystery of the Summer Vacation Sea Monster. Chase, L. P. 2011. (ENG.). 165p. (J). pap. 8.99 *(978-0-9792918-7-6(9))* Blue Marlin Pubns.

—Madison & the Two-Wheeler, 1 vol. Braver, Vanita. 2007. (ENG.). 32p. (J). (gr. -1-3). 14.95 *(978-1-59572-109-9(6))* Star Bright Bks., Inc.

—Madison's Patriotic Project, 1 vol. Braver, Vanita. 2007. (ENG.). 32p. (J). 14.95 *(978-1-59572-110-5(X))* Star Bright Bks., Inc.

—Make Sense! Haddon, Jean. 2006. (Silly Millies Level 1 Ser.). (ENG.). 32p. (gr. k-2). lib. bdg. 21.27 *(978-0-7613-3403-3(3),* Millbrook Pr.) Lerner Publishing Group.

—Our Principal Promised to Kiss a Pig. Dakos, Kalli & DesMarteau, Alicia. 2004. (ENG.). 32p. (J). (gr. 2-5). 16.99 *(978-0-8075-6629-9(2))* Whitman, Albert & Co.

Dirr, Karen. The Back Pain Book: A Self-Help Guide for the Daily Relief of Back & Neck Pain, 1 vol. Hage, Mike. 2nd ed. 2005. (ENG.). 256p. pap. 16.95 *(978-1-56145-342-9(0))* Peachtree Pubs.

DiRubbio, Jennifer. Around One Log: Chipmunks, Spiders, & Creepy Insiders. Fredericks, Anthony D. 2011. 32p. (J). (gr. -1-5). 16.95 *(978-1-58469-137-2(9));* pap. 8.95 *(978-1-58469-138-9(7))* Dawn Pubns.

—Going Home: The Mystery of Animal Migration. Berkes, Marianne. 2010. 32p. (J). (gr. -1-5). 16.95 *(978-1-58469-126-6(3));* pap. 8.95 *(978-1-58469-127-3(1))* Dawn Pubns.

—In One Tidepool: Crabs, Snails, & Salty Tails. Fredericks, Anthony D. 2004. (Sharing Nature with Children Book Ser.). 32p. (J). (gr. -1-2). 16.95 *(978-1-58469-039-9(9));* pap. 7.95 *(978-1-58469-038-2(0))* Dawn Pubns.

—Near One Cattail: Turtles, Logs, & Leaping Frogs. Fredericks, Anthony D. 2005. (Sharing Nature with Children Book Ser.). 32p. (J). 16.95 *(978-1-58469-070-2(4));* pap. 7.95 *(978-1-58469-071-9(2))* Dawn Pubns.

—On One Flower: Butterflies, Ticks & a Few More Icks. Fredericks, Anthony D. 2006. (Sharing Nature with Children Book Ser.). 32p. (J). (gr. -1-5). 7.95 *(978-1-58469-087-0(9));* 16.95 *(978-1-58469-086-3(0))* Dawn Pubns.

—Under One Rock: Bugs, Slugs, & Other Ughs. Fredericks, Anthony D. 2004. (Sharing Nature with Children Book Ser.). 32p. (J). 16.95 *(978-1-58469-028-3(3))* Dawn Pubns.

DiRubbio, Jennifer. Around One Cactus: Owls, Bats, & Leaping Rats. DiRubbio, Jennifer, tr. Fredericks, Anthony D. 2004. (Sharing Nature with Children Book Ser.). 32p. (J). 16.95 *(978-1-58469-051-1(8));* pap. 7.95 *(978-1-58469-052-8(6))* Dawn Pubns.

DiSalvo, Len. Bully Bean. Weck, Thomas & Weck, Peter. 2013. (Lima Bear Stories Ser.). (ENG.). 32p. (J). (gr. k-2). 15.95 *(978-1-933872-05-6(5))* Lima Bear Pr LLC, The.

—The Labyrinth. Weck, Peter. 2012. (Lima Bear Stories Ser.). (ENG.). 32p. (J). (gr. k-2). 15.95 *(978-1-933872-04-9(7))* Lima Bear Pr LLC, The.

—Lima Bear's Halloween. Weck, Peter. 2012. (Lima Bear Stories Ser.). 40p. (J). 15.95 *(978-1-933872-16-2(0))* Lima Bear Pr LLC, The.

DiSalvo-Ryan, DyAnne. If I Were President. Stier, Catherine. 2004. (ENG.). 32p. (J). (gr. k-3). pap. 6.99 *(978-0-8075-3542-4(7))* Whitman, Albert & Co.

Dishaw, Karen. Cereal for Breakfast Cereal for Lunch. Cooperman, Ben. 2013. 42p. pap. *(978-0-9919356-0-4(8))* Teacherben Publishing.

Disney Animators Staff. Cinderella: A Royal Wish. Reader's Digest Editors & Miller, Sara. 2012. (Musical Toy Ser.). (ENG.). 32p. (J). (gr. -1-2). 19.99 *(978-0-7944-2701-6(4))* Reader's Digest Assn., Inc., The.

Disney Artists Staff. Cars 2 CarryAlong(r) Play Book. Stierle, Cynthia. 2011. (Carry along Play Book Ser.). (ENG.). 14p. (J). (gr. -1-k). bds. 14.99 *(978-0-7944-2323-0(X))* Reader's Digest Assn., Inc., The.

—Disney Pixar Cars 2 3-D Movie Theater. 2011. (Movie Theater Ser.). (ENG.). 32p. (J). (gr. k-2). 24.99 *(978-0-7944-2310-0(8))* Reader's Digest Assn., Inc., The.

Disney Book Club Staff & Disney Book Group Staff. Venom! Castro, Nachie. 4th ed. 2013. (ENG.). 24p. (J). (gr. -1-k). pap. 3.99 *(978-1-4231-5473-0(8))* Marvel Worldwide, Inc.

Disney Book Group Staff. The Amazing Spider-Man 2 Junior Novel. Candau, Brittany. 2014. (ENG.). 144p. (J). (gr. 3-7). pap. 5.99 *(978-1-4231-9758-4(5),* Marvel Pr.) Disney Publishing Worldwide.

—The Amazing Spider-Man vs. Green Goblin. Behling, Steve. 2012. (Marvel Super Hero vs. Book Ser.). (ENG.). 24p. (J). (gr. -1-k). pap. 3.99 *(978-1-4231-4273-7(X),* Marvel Pr.) Disney Publishing Worldwide.

—The Avengers: a Mighty Sticker Book. 2013. (Sticker-Activity Storybook Ser.). (ENG.). 88p. (J). (gr. 3-7). pap. 12.99 *(978-1-4231-8508-6(0))* Marvel Worldwide, Inc.

Disney Book Group Staff, et al. Captain America: The Tomorrow Army. Thomas, Rich, Jr. & Siglain, Michael. 2014. (Marvel Chapter Book Ser.: 2). (ENG.). 144p. (J). (gr. 1-3). pap. 5.99 *(978-1-4231-4303-1(5),* Marvel Pr.) Disney Publishing Worldwide.

Disney Book Group Staff. Captain America: The Winter Soldier - Falcon Takes Flight. Davis, Adam. 2014. (World of Reading Ser.). (ENG.). 32p. (J). (gr. 1-3). pap. 3.99 *(978-1-4231-8537-6(4),* Marvel Pr.) Disney Publishing Worldwide.

—Captain America - The Winter Soldier. Palacios, Tomas. 2014. (ENG.). 144p. (J). (gr. 3-7). pap. 5.99 *(978-1-4231-8533-8(1),* Marvel Pr.) Disney Publishing Worldwide.

—Captain America: the Winter Soldier - the Movie Storybook. Davis, Adam. 2014. (ENG.). 112p. (J). (gr. 1-3). 12.99 *(978-1-4231-8534-5(X),* Marvel Pr.) Disney Publishing Worldwide.

—Doomed! Castro, Nachie. 3rd ed. 2013. (ENG.). 24p. (J). (gr. -1-k). pap. 4.99 *(978-1-4231-5474-7(6))* Marvel Worldwide, Inc.

—Guardians of the Galaxy. Palacios, Tomas. 2014. (Beginnings Ser.). (ENG.). 48p. (J). (gr. 1-3). 12.99 *(978-1-4847-0054-9(6),* Marvel Pr.) Disney Publishing Worldwide.

Disney Book Group Staff, et al. Jingle Bell Doc. Higginson, Sheila Sweeny. 2013. (ENG.). 12p. (J). (gr. -1-k). bds. 6.99 *(978-1-4231-8386-0(X))* Disney Pr.

Disney Book Group Staff. Spider-Man: Attack of the Heroes: A Marvel Chapter Book. Thomas, Rich. 2014. (Marvel Chapter Book Ser.: 1). (ENG.). 128p. (J). (gr. 1-3). pap. 5.99 *(978-1-4231-4301-7(9),* Marvel Pr.) Disney Publishing Worldwide.

—Suits of Armor. Marvel Press Staff & Palacios, Tomas. 2013. (ENG.). 24p. (J). (gr. -1-k). pap. 3.99 *(978-1-4231-7246-8(9))* Marvel Worldwide, Inc.

—Thor: the Dark World Junior Novel. Marvel Press Staff et al. 2013. (ENG.). 128p. (J). (gr. 3-7). pap. 5.99 *(978-1-4231-7245-1(0))* Marvel Worldwide, Inc.

—Ultimate Spider-Man: the Really Big Sticker Book! Palacios, Tomas. 2014. (Really Big Sticker Book Ser.). (ENG.). 88p. (J). (gr. -1-k). pap. 12.99 *(978-1-4231-9850-5(6),* Marvel Pr.) Disney Publishing Worldwide.

—World of Reading: X-Men Days of Future Past: Level 3. Macri, Thomas. 2014. (World of Reading Ser.). (ENG.). 48p. (J). (gr. 1-3). pap. 3.99 *(978-1-4231-7213-0(2),* Marvel Pr.) Disney Publishing Worldwide.

Disney Book Group Staff. The Amazing Spider-Man 2 Movie Storybook. Disney Book Group Staff. 2014. (Movie Storybook Ser.). (ENG.). 112p. (J). (gr. 1-3). 12.99 *(978-1-4231-9757-7(7),* Marvel Pr.) Disney Publishing Worldwide.

—Flight of the Iron Spider! Based on the Hit TV Show from Marvel Animation. Disney Book Group Staff. Marvel Press Group. 2013. (ENG.). 24p. (J). (gr. -1-k). pap. 4.99 *(978-1-4231-5472-3(X))* Marvel Worldwide, Inc.

—Iron Man Fights Back, No. 3. Disney Book Group Staff. Marvel Press Group. 2013. (World of Reading Ser.). (ENG.). 32p. (J). (gr. 2-3). pap. 3.99 *(978-1-4231-7248-2(5))* Marvel Worldwide, Inc.

—Marvel Padded. Disney Book Group Staff. Marvel Book Group Staff. 2014. (Read-And-Play Storybook Ser.). (ENG.). 96p. (J). (gr. 1-3). 12.99 *(978-1-4847-0435-6(5),* Marvel Pr.) Disney Publishing Worldwide.

—Marvel Spider-Man. Disney Book Group Staff. Marvel Books Staff. 2014. (Read-And-Listen Storybook Ser.). (ENG.). 128p. (J). (gr. 1-3). 10.99 *(978-1-4847-0432-5(0),* Marvel Pr.) Disney Publishing Worldwide.

—Marvel Super Heroes. Disney Book Group Staff. Marvel Press Group. 2013. (Storybook Collection). (ENG.). 304p. (J). (gr. -1-k). 15.99 *(978-1-4231-7223-9(X))* Marvel Worldwide, Inc.

—World of Reading This Is Captain America: Level 1. Disney Book Group Staff. 2014. (World of Reading Ser.). (ENG.). 32p. (J). (gr. -1-k). pap. 3.99 *(978-1-4847-1267-2(6),* Marvel Pr.) Disney Publishing Worldwide.

—5-Minute Spider-Man Stories. Disney Book Group Staff. 2013. (5-Minute Stories Ser.). (ENG.). 192p. (J). (gr. 1-3). 12.99 *(978-1-4231-7786-9(X))* Marvel Worldwide, Inc.

Disney Book Group Staff, photos by. Stoneheart. Fletcher, Charlie. 2008. (ENG.). 480p. (J). (gr. 7-17). pap. 7.99 *(978-1-4231-0176-5(6))* Hyperion Pr.

Disney Book Group Staff & Disney Storybook Artists Staff. Doc Mcstuffins Time for Your Checkup! 2014. (ENG.). 10p. (J). (gr. -1-k). bds. 8.99 *(978-1-4231-9956-4(1))* Disney Pr.

—Super Adventure. Scollon, Bill. 2013. (ENG.). 24p. (J). (gr. -1-k). pap. 4.99 *(978-1-4231-8657-1(5))* Disney Pr.

Disney Book Group Staff & Roux, Stephane. Escape from Darth Vader, Level 1. Disney Book Group Staff & Siglain, Michael. 2014. (ENG.). 32p. (J). (gr. 1-3). pap. 3.99 *(978-1-4847-0500-1(9))* Disney Pr.

Disney Book Group Staff & Semeiks, Val. World of Reading: Thor This Is Thor: Level 1. Disney Book Group Staff & Dworkin, Brooke. 2014. (World of Reading Ser.). (ENG.). 32p. (J). (gr. -1-k). pap. 3.99 *(978-1-4847-1268-9(4),* Marvel Pr.) Disney Publishing Worldwide.

Disney Book Group Staff, jt. illus. see Disney Book Club Staff.

Disney Book Group Staff, jt. illus. see Disney Storybook Art Team.

Disney Book Group Staff, jt. illus. see Disney Storybook Artists Staff.

Disney Global Artists Staff & RH Disney Staff. Jungle Friends. Winskill, John. 2014. (Step into Reading Ser.). (ENG.). 32p. (J). (gr. -1-1). pap. 3.99 *(978-0-7364-2089-1(4),* Random Hse. Bks. for Young Readers) Random Hse. Children's Bks.

Disney Pixar Staff, jt. illus. see RH Disney Staff.

Disney Press Staff. Money Hungry. Flake, Sharon G. rev. ed. 2007. (ENG.). 192p. (J). (gr. 5-9). pap. 8.99 *(978-1-4231-0386-8(6),* Jump at the Sun) Hyperion Bks. for Children.

—The Skin I'm In. Flake, Sharon G. rev. ed. 2007. (ENG.). 176p. (J). (gr. 5-9). pap. 8.99 *(978-1-4231-0385-1(8),* Jump at the Sun) Hyperion Bks. for Children.

Disney Storybook Art Team. Ahoy, Izzy! Kelman, Marcy & Disney Book Group Staff. 2013. (ENG.). 24p. (J). (gr. -1-k). pap. 3.99 *(978-1-4231-6393-0(1))* Disney Pr.

—All Hands on Hooks. Disney Book Group Staff & Kelman, Marcy. 2014. (Flap 'n Tab Ser.). (ENG.). 10p. (J). (gr. -1-k). bds. 6.99 *(978-1-4231-8494-2(7))* Disney Pr.

—The Amulet & the Anthem. Hapka, Catherine & Disney Book Group Staff. 2013. (ENG.). 24p. (J). (gr. -1-k). pap. 4.99 *(978-1-4231-8023-4(2))* Disney Pr.

—Animal ABCs. Disney Book Group Staff & Kelman, Marcy. 2014. (ENG.). 10p. (J). (gr. -1-k). bds. 10.99 *(978-1-4231-8488-1(2))* Disney Pr.

—Aurora: The Perfect Party. Loggia, Wendy & Disney Book Group Staff. 2011. (Disney Princess Chapter Book: Series #1 Ser.). (ENG.). 96p. (J). (gr. 1-3). pap. 4.99 *(978-1-4231-2768-0(4))* Disney Pr.

—Birthday Bash! LaRose, Melinda & Disney Book Group Staff. 2014. (ENG.). 32p. (J). (gr. -1-k). pap. 4.99 *(978-1-4231-9935-9(9))* Disney Pr.

—Blue Ribbon Bunny, Level 1. Nathan, Sarah & Disney Book Group Staff. 2014. (World of Reading Ser.). (ENG.). 32p. (J). (gr. -1-k). pap. 3.99 *(978-1-4231-7158-4(6))* Disney Pr.

—Brontosaurus Breath. Higginson, Sheila Sweeny & Disney Book Group Staff. 2013. (World of Reading Ser.). (ENG.). 32p. (J). (gr. -1-k). pap. 3.99 *(978-1-4231-6894-2(1))* Disney Pr.

Disney Storybook Art Team. Captain Jake & the Never Land Pirates the Great Never Sea Conquest. Disney Book Group Staff. 2015. (ENG.). 24p. (J). (gr. -1-k). pap. 4.99 ***(978-1-4847-1150-7(5))*** Disney Pr.

Disney Storybook Art Team. Cars Storybook Collection. Disney Press Staff & Disney Book Group Staff. 2011. (Storybook Collection). (ENG.). 312p. (J). (gr. -1 — 1). 15.99 *(978-1-4231-2495-5(2))* Disney Pr.

—The Case of the Missing Sparkle-Izer, Level Pre-1. Scollon, William & Disney Book Group Staff. 2013. (World of Reading Ser.). (ENG.). 32p. (J). (gr. -1-k). pap. 3.99 *(978-1-4231-8482-9(3))* Disney Pr.

—Caught Blue-Handed. Higginson, Sheila Sweeny & Disney Book Group Staff. 2013. (World of Reading Ser.). (ENG.). 32p. (J). (gr. -1-k). pap. 3.99 *(978-1-4231-6455-5(5))* Disney Pr.

—Chilly Catches a Cold. Higginson, Sheila Sweeny & Disney Book Group Staff. 2013. (ENG.). 24p. (J). (gr. -1-k). pap. 3.99 *(978-1-4231-7509-4(3))* Disney Pr.

—Cinderella: The Great Mouse Mistake. 2010. (Disney Princess Chapter Book Ser.). (ENG.). 80p. (J). (gr. 1-3). pap. 4.99 *(978-1-4231-2978-3(4))* Disney Pr.

Disney Storybook Art Team. Descendants: Junior Novel. Disney Book Group Staff & Green, Rico. 2015. (ENG.). 176p. (J). (gr. 5-9). 10.99 ***(978-1-4847-2614-3(6))*** Disney Pr.

—Descendants: Mal's Diary. Disney Book Group. 2015. (ENG.). 192p. (J). (gr. 3-7). 9.99 ***(978-1-4847-2685-3(5))*** Disney Pr.

—Descendants: Mal's Spell Book. Disney Book Group. 2015. (ENG.). 192p. (J). (gr. 3-7). 11.99 ***(978-1-4847-2638-9(3))*** Disney Pr.

Disney Storybook Art Team. Destination - Amazon! Peterson, Scott & Disney Book Group Staff. 12th ed. 2013. (ENG.). 24p. (J). (gr. 1-3). pap. 5.99 *(978-1-4231-5151-7(8))* Disney Pr.

—Disney Baby Baby Animals. Disney Book Group Staff. 2015. (ENG.). 12p. (J). (gr. -1 — 1). bds. 7.99 *(978-1-4847-1802-5(X))* Disney Pr.

—Disney Junior 5-Minute Sofia the First & Friends Stories. Disney Book Group Staff. 2015. (5-Minute Stories Ser.). (ENG.). 192p. (J). (gr. -1-k). 12.99 *(978-1-4847-1327-3(3))* Disney Pr.

—Disney Junior Storybook Collection. Disney Book Group Staff. 2014. (Storybook Collection). (ENG.). 304p. (J). (gr. -1-k). 16.99 *(978-1-4231-7875-0(0))* Disney Pr.

—The Disney Princess Cookbook. Disney Book Group Staff. 2013. (ENG.). 144p. (J). (gr. 1-3). 15.99 *(978-1-4231-6324-4(9))* Disney Pr.

—Disney Storybook Collection. Disney Book Group Staff. 2015. (Storybook Collection). (ENG.). 304p. (J). (gr. -1-k). 16.99 *(978-1-4847-1348-8(6))* Disney Pr.

Disney Storybook Art Team. Disney Tails Figaro's Halloween Surprise. Glass, Calliope. 2015. (Disney Tails Ser.). (ENG.). 10p. (J). (gr. -1 — 1). bds. 6.99 ***(978-1-4847-1372-3(9))*** Disney Pr.

Disney Storybook Art Team. Disney*Pixar Storybook Collection. Disney Book Group Staff. 2011. (Storybook Collection). (ENG.). 312p. (J). (gr. -1 — 1). 15.99 *(978-1-4231-2423-8(5))* Disney Pr.

Disney Storybook Art Team. Doc Mcstuffins a Dragon's Best Friend. Disney Book Group. 2015. (ENG.). 40p. (J). (gr. -1-k). 8.99 ***(978-1-4847-2388-3(0))*** Disney Pr.

Disney Storybook Art Team. Doc Mcstuffins Bunny in a Basket. Disney Book Group Staff & Higginson, Sheila Sweeny. 2015. (ENG.). 12p. (J). (gr. -1-k). bds. 7.99 *(978-1-4847-0679-4(X))* Disney Pr.

—Doc Mcstuffins Dad's Favorite Toy. Disney Book Group Staff. 2015. (ENG.). 24p. (J). (gr. -1-k). pap. 4.99 *(978-1-4847-2164-3(0))* Disney Pr.

—Doc Mcstuffins Training Army Al. Disney Book Group Staff. 2014. (ENG.). 24p. (J). (gr. -1-k). pap. 3.99 *(978-1-4847-1419-5(9))* Disney Pr.

—Doctor Bag. Disney Book Group Staff & Kelman, Marcy. 2013. (ENG.). 10p. (J). (gr. -1-k). bds. 7.99 *(978-1-4231-8486-7(6))* Disney Pr.

—Dusty's Big Job. Disney Book Group Staff. 2014. (ENG.). 24p. (J). (gr. -1-k). bds. 10.99 *(978-1-4847-0654-1(4))* Disney Pr.

Disney Storybook Art Team, et al. Friends on Ice. Disney Book Group Staff & Ward, Jessica. 2013. (Minnie & Daisy Best Friends Forever Chapter Book Ser.: 4). (ENG.). 128p. (J). (gr. 1-3). pap. 6.99 *(978-1-4231-7717-3(7))* Disney Pr.

Disney Storybook Art Team. Frozen 5-Minute Frozen Stories. Disney Book Group. 2015. (5-Minute Stories Ser.). (ENG.). 192p. (J). (gr. 1-3). 12.99 ***(978-1-4847-2330-2(9))*** Disney Pr.

—Frozen Arendelle Adventures: Purchase Includes Mobile App for iPone & iPad! Disney Book Group. 2015. (Read-And-Play Storybook Ser.). (ENG.). 96p. (J). (gr. 1-3). 12.99 ***(978-1-4847-2389-0(9))*** Disney Pr.

Disney Storybook Art Team. The Great Treasure Hunt. Scollon, William & Disney Book Group Staff. 2013. (ENG.). 10p. (J). (gr. -1-k). bds. 8.99 *(978-1-4231-6396-1(6))* Disney Pr.

—The Halloween Ball. Marsoli, Lisa Ann & Disney Book Group Staff. 2013. (ENG.). 24p. (J). (gr. -1-k). pap. 5.99 *(978-1-4231-7144-7(6))* Disney Pr.

—Henry Hugglemonster Daddo in Charge. Disney Book Group Staff & Higginson, Sheila Sweeny. 2015. (ENG.). 12p. (J). (gr. -1-k). bds. 7.99 *(978-1-4847-0642-8(0))* Disney Pr.

—Holiday in Enchancia. Hapka, Catherine & Disney Book Group Staff. 2013. (ENG.). 40p. (J). (gr. -1-k). 12.99 *(978-1-4231-8396-9(7))* Disney Pr.

—Hoppy Clubhouse Easter. Kelman, Marcy & Disney Book Group Staff. 2011. (ENG.). 12p. (J). (gr. -1-k). bds. 6.99 *(978-1-4231-3910-2(0))* Disney Pr.

—Inside Out - Driven by Emotions. Disney Book Group Staff. 2015. (ENG.). 240p. (J). (gr. 3-7). 10.99 *(978-1-4847-2203-9(5))* Disney Pr.

—Jake & the Never Land Pirates - Winter Never Land. Disney Book Group Staff & LaRose, Melinda. 2014. (ENG.). 12p. (J). (gr. -1-k). bds. 7.99 *(978-1-4231-9424-8(1))* Disney Pr.

—Jake & the Never Land Pirates Battle for the Book. Disney Book Group Staff & Scollon, William. 2014. (ENG.). 24p. (J). (gr. -1-k). pap. 4.99 *(978-1-4231-8397-6(5))* Disney Pr.

—Jake & the Never Land Pirates Cubby's Mixed-Up Map. Higginson, Sheila Sweeny & Disney Book Group Staff. 2014. (ENG.). 32p. (J). (gr. -1-k). pap. 4.99 *(978-1-4231-9423-1(3))* Disney Pr.

—Jake Hatches a Plan, Pre-Level 1. LaRose, Melinda & Disney Book Group Staff. 2012. (World of Reading Ser.).

D

(ENG.). 32p. (J). (gr. -1-k). pap. 3.99 *(978-1-4231-5542-3(4))* Disney Pr.

—Junior Encyclopedia of Animated Characters. Disney Book Group Staff. 2014. (ENG.). 144p. (J). (gr. 1-3). 12.99 *(978-1-4231-8914-5(0))* Disney Pr.

—The Key to Skull Rock, Level 1. Scollon, William & Disney Book Group Staff. 2013. (World of Reading Ser.). (ENG.). 32p. (J). (gr. -1-k). pap. 3.99 *(978-1-4231-6397-8(4))* Disney Pr.

—Lady & the Tramp. Disney Book Group Staff. 2011. (Read-Along Storybook & CD Ser.). (ENG.). 32p. (J). (gr. -1-2). pap. 6.99 *(978-1-4231-6141-7(6))* Disney Pr.

—Legend of the Neverbeast. 2015. (Read-Along Storybook & CD Ser.). (ENG.). 32p. (J). (gr. 1-3). pap. 6.99 *(978-1-4847-1075-3(4))* Disney Pr.

—Let's Get Jumping! LaRose, Melinda & Disney Book Group Staff. 2012. (ENG.). 32p. (J). (gr. -1-k). pap. 3.99 *(978-1-4231-4924-8(6))* Disney Pr.

—Mater & the Easter Buggy. Larsen, Kirsten et al. 2012. (ENG.). 48p. (J). (gr. -1-k). 12.99 *(978-1-4231-3875-4(9))* Disney Pr.

—Me & Our Mom. Disney Book Group Staff & Hapka, Catherine. 2015. (ENG.). 24p. (J). (gr. -1-k). pap. 4.99 *(978-1-4847-0688-6(9))* Disney Pr.

Disney Storybook Art Team. Meeska Mooska-Tales. Disney Book Group Staff. 2015. (ENG.). 40p. (J). (gr. -1-k). 10.99 ***(978-1-4847-2189-6(6))*** Disney Pr.

Disney Storybook Art Team. Merida: Legend of the Emeralds. Bryant, Megan & Disney Book Group Staff. 2014. (ENG.). 96p. (J). (gr. 1-3). pap. 4.99 *(978-1-4231-6890-4(9))* Disney Pr.

—The Mermaid Dives In. Higginson, Sheila Sweeny & Disney Book Group Staff. 2013. (ENG.). 24p. (J). (gr. -1-k). pap. 4.99 *(978-1-4231-7132-4(2))* Disney Pr.

—Mickey & Donald Have a Farm. Scollon, William & Disney Book Group Staff. 2012. (ENG.). 32p. (J). (gr. -1-k). pap. 5.99 *(978-1-4231-4946-0(7))* Disney Pr.

—Mickey & Friends Goofy's Sledding Contest. Disney Book Group Staff & Ritchey, Kate. 2013. (World of Reading Ser.). (ENG.). 32p. (J). (gr. 1-3). pap. 3.99 *(978-1-4231-6964-2(6))* Disney Pr.

—Mickey Mouse Clubhouse a Goofy Fairy Tale. Disney Book Group Staff & Scollon, William. 2014. (ENG.). 24p. (J). (gr. -1-k). pap. 4.99 *(978-1-4231-8900-8(0))* Disney Pr.

Disney Storybook Art Team. Mickey Mouse Clubhouse Mickey's Halloween. Disney Book Group. 2015. (ENG.). 10p. (J). (gr. -1-k). bds. 8.99 ***(978-1-4847-2096-7(2))*** Disney Pr.

Disney Storybook Art Team. The Minnie & Friends Cookbook. Schmaltz, Joanne, photos by. Disney Book Group Staff & Littlefield, Cynthia. 2014. (ENG.). 64p. (J). (gr. 1-3). 10.99 *(978-1-4231-6756-3(2))* Disney Pr.

—Minnie Easter Bonnet Parade. Disney Book Group Staff. 2015. (ENG.). 24p. (J). (gr. 1-3). bds. 10.99 *(978-1-4847-0842-2(3))* Disney Pr.

—Minnie's Bow-Tastic Sticker Collection. Kelman, Marcy & Disney Book Group Staff. 2014. (ENG.). 88p. (J). (gr. -1-k). pap. 12.99 *(978-1-4231-8901-5(9))* Disney Pr.

—Minnie's Pet Salon. Scollon, William & Disney Book Group Staff. 2013. (World of Reading Ser.). (ENG.). 32p. (J). (gr. -1-k). pap. 3.99 *(978-1-4231-8481-2(5))* Disney Pr.

—Monsters, Inc. 2012. (Read-Along Storybook & CD Ser.). (ENG.). 32p. (J). (gr. -1 — 1). pap. 6.99 *(978-1-4231-4259-1(4))* Disney Pr.

—Monsters University Read-Along Storybook & CD. Glass, Calliope & Disney Book Group Staff. 2013. (Read-Along Storybook & CD Ser.). (ENG.). 32p. (J). (gr. -1 — 1). pap. 6.99 *(978-1-4231-5199-9(2))* Disney Pr.

—The Murk. Lettrick, Robert. 2015. (ENG.). 320p. (J). (gr. 5-9). 16.99 *(978-1-4231-8695-3(8))* Hyperion Bks. for Children.

—My Huggy Valentine. Disney Book Group Staff & Higginson, Sheila Sweeny. 2013. (ENG.). 24p. (J). (gr. -1-k). pap. 5.99 *(978-1-4847-0425-7(8))* Disney Pr.

—Nursery Rhymes. Scott, Denise & Disney Book Group Staff. 2012. (ENG.). 16p. (J). (gr. -1 — 1). bds. 6.99 *(978-1-4231-4844-9(4))* Disney Pr.

—Out of the Box. Kelman, Marcy & Disney Book Group Staff. 2014. (Flap 'n Tab Ser.). (ENG.). 10p. (J). (gr. -1-k). bds. 6.99 *(978-1-4231-8092-0(5))* Disney Pr.

—Palace Pets: Berry the Bunny for Snow White. Disney Book Group Staff. 2015. (ENG.). 10p. (J). (gr. -1-k). bds. 9.99 *(978-1-4847-1284-9(6))* Disney Pr.

—Peter Pan Read-Along Storybook & CD. Disney Book Group Staff. 2013. (Read-Along Storybook & CD Ser.). (ENG.). 32p. (J). (gr. -1-k). pap. 6.99 *(978-1-4231-8034-0(8))* Disney Pr.

—Planes - Fire & Rescue. Disney Book Group Staff. 2014. (Read-Along Storybook & CD Ser.). (ENG.). 32p. (J). (gr. 1-3). pap. 6.99 *(978-1-4231-7879-8(3))* Disney Pr.

—Pooh's Easter Basket. Hapka, Cathy & Disney Book Group Staff. 2012. (ENG.). 10p. (J). (gr. -1-k). bds. 5.99 *(978-1-4231-4953-8(X))* Disney Pr.

—Pooh's Secret Garden. Hapka, Catherine & Disney Book Group Staff. 2012. (ENG.). 24p. (J). (gr. -1-k). pap. 4.99 *(978-1-4231-4845-6(2))* Disney Pr.

—Pretty Princess Puzzles. Disney Book Group Staff. 2012. (Jigsaw Puzzle Book Ser.). (ENG.). 16p. (J). (gr. -1-k). bds. 14.99 *(978-1-4231-5938-4(1))* Disney Pr.

—Ready to Be a Princess. Disney Book Group Staff. 2013. (Book & Magnetic Play Set Ser.). (ENG.). 32p. (J). (gr. -1-k). 14.99 *(978-1-4231-8445-4(9))* Disney Pr.

—Road Trip. Disney Press Staff & Disney Book Group Staff. 2011. (ENG.). 10p. (J). (gr. -1-k). bds. 8.99 *(978-1-4231-4416-8(3))* Disney Pr.

—Royal Friends: A Princess Book & Magnetic Play Set. Disney Book Group Staff. 2011. (Book & Magnetic Play Set Ser.). (ENG.). 32p. (J). (gr. -1 — 1). 14.99 *(978-1-4231-4185-3(7))* Disney Pr.

—Royal Lessons. 2014. (ENG.). 10p. (J). (gr. -1-k). bds. 8.99 *(978-1-4231-8444-7(0))* Disney Pr.

—The Royal Slumber Party. Hapka, Cathy et al. 2013. (ENG.). 24p. (J). (gr. -1-k). pap. 3.99 *(978-1-4231-6410-4(5))* Disney Pr.

—The Royal Slumber Party. Disney Book Group Staff. 2014. (ENG.). 24p. (J). (gr. -1-k). bds. 10.99 *(978-1-4847-0681-7(1))* Disney Pr.

—Run-Down Racecar. Higginson, Sheila Sweeny & Disney Book Group Staff. 2013. (ENG.). 24p. (J). (gr. -1-k). pap. 3.99 *(978-1-4231-6847-8(X))* Disney Pr.

—Sheriff Callie's Wild West - The Cat Who Tamed the West. Disney Book Group Staff. 2015. (ENG.). 40p. (J). (gr. -1-k). 8.99 *(978-1-4847-1495-9(4))* Disney Pr.

—Sofia the First a Magical Match. Disney Book Group Staff. 2014. (ENG.). 24p. (J). (gr. -1-k). pap. 5.99 *(978-1-4847-2165-0(9))* Disney Pr.

Disney Storybook Art Team. Sofia the First S Is for Sofia. Disney Book Group Staff. 2015. (ENG.). 26p. (J). (gr. -1-k). bds. 12.99 ***(978-1-4847-1804-9(6))*** Disney Pr.

—Sofia the First Sofia's Princess Adventures: Board Book Boxed Set. Disney Book Group Staff. 2015. (ENG.). 40p. (J). (gr. -1-k). 10.99 ***(978-1-4847-0042-6(2))*** Disney Pr.

Disney Storybook Art Team. Sofia the First Sofia's Royal Sticker Collection. Kelman, Marcy & Disney Book Group Staff. 2014. (ENG.). 88p. (J). (gr. -1-k). pap. 12.99 *(978-1-4231-8887-2(X))* Disney Pr.

—Sofia's Cup of Tea. Disney Book Group Staff. 2015. (ENG.). 10p. (J). (gr. -1-k). bds. 7.99 *(978-1-4847-0646-6(3))* Disney Pr.

—Sweet Dreams, Roo. Hapka, Catherine & Disney Book Group Staff. 2012. (ENG.). 24p. (J). (gr. -1-k). bds. 6.99 *(978-1-4231-4843-2(6))* Disney Pr.

—Tangled. Disney Book Group Staff. 2010. (Read-Along Storybook & CD Ser.). (ENG.). 32p. (J). (gr. -1 — 1). pap. 6.99 *(978-1-4231-3742-9(6))* Disney Pr.

—Thumper & the Noisy Ducky. Disney Book Group Staff & Driscoll, Laura. 2014. (ENG.). 12p. (J). (gr. -1 — 1). bds. 6.99 *(978-1-4231-8487-4(4))* Disney Pr.

—Tiara Time. Disney Book Group Staff. 2013. (Read-Along Storybook & CD Ser.). (ENG.). 34p. (J). (gr. -1-k). bds. 10.99 *(978-1-4231-6966-6(2))* Disney Pr.

—Tinker Bell & the Pirate Fairy. Disney Book Group Staff. 2014. (Read-Along Storybook & CD Ser.). (ENG.). 32p. (J). (gr. -1-k). pap. 6.99 *(978-1-4231-7407-3(0))* Disney Pr.

—Welcome to Royal Prep, Level 1. Marsoli, Lisa Ann & Disney Book Group Staff. 2013. (World of Reading Ser.). (ENG.). 32p. (J). (gr. -1-k). pap. 3.99 *(978-1-4231-6407-4(5))* Disney Pr.

—World of Reading, Set. Disney Book Group Staff. 2014. (World of Reading Ser.: 1). (ENG.). 192p. (J). (gr. -1-k). pap. 12.99 *(978-1-4847-0433-2(9)*, Marvel Pr.) Disney Publishing Worldwide.

Disney Storybook Art Team. World of Reading: Doc Mcstuffins Peaches Pie, Take a Bath! Level Pre-1. Disney Book Group. 2015. (World of Reading Ser.). (ENG.). 32p. (J). (gr. -1-k). pap. 3.99 ***(978-1-4847-1591-8(8))*** Disney Pr.

Disney Storybook Art Team. World of Reading: Doc Mcstuffins Starry, Starry Night: Level 1. Scollon, William & Disney Book Group Staff. 2014. (World of Reading Ser.). (ENG.). 32p. (J). (gr. -1-k). pap. 3.99 *(978-1-4231-9419-4(5))* Disney Pr.

Disney Storybook Art Team. World of Reading: Sheriff Callie's Wild West Callie Asks for Help: Level Pre-1. Disney Book Group. 2015. (World of Reading Ser.). (ENG.). 32p. (J). (gr. -1-k). pap. 3.99 ***(978-1-4847-1631-1(0))*** Disney Pr.

Disney Storybook Art Team. World of Reading: Sofia the First Riches to Rags: Level 1. Disney Book Group Staff. 2015. (World of Reading Ser.). (ENG.). 32p. (J). (gr. -1-k). pap. 3.99 *(978-1-4847-0699-2(4))* Disney Pr.

—World of Reading: Sofia the First the Missing Necklace: Level Pre-1. Disney Book Group Staff & Marsoli, Lisa Ann. 2014. (World of Reading Ser.). (ENG.). 32p. (J). (gr. -1-k). pap. 3.99 *(978-1-4231-7164-5(0))* Disney Pr.

—X Marks the Croc!, Pre-Level 1. LaRose, Melinda & Disney Book Group Staff. 2013. (World of Reading Ser.). (ENG.). 32p. (J). (gr. -1-k). pap. 3.99 *(978-1-4231-6392-3(3))* Disney Pr.

Disney Storybook Art Team & Disney Book Group Staff. Cinderella: A Night at the Ball. Disney Book Group Staff & Green, Rico. 2015. (ENG.). 24p. (J). (gr. -1-k). pap. 3.99 *(978-1-4847-1111-8(4))* Disney Pr.

Disney Storybook Art Team & Houston, Lauren. Disney Baby My First Words. Disney Book Group Staff. 2014. (ENG.). 24p. (J). (gr. -1 — 1). bds. 7.99 *(978-1-4847-0915-3(2))* Disney Pr.

Disney Storybook Art Team & Mosqueda, Olga. Hide & Hug Olaf: A Fun Family Experience! Disney Book Group Staff & Lewis, Kevin. 2014. (ENG.). 48p. (J). (gr. -1-k). 26.99 *(978-1-4847-2150-6(0))* Disney Pr.

Disney Storybook Art Team & Studio Iboix Staff. The Lost Tiara. Disney Book Group Staff & Richards, Kitty. 2012. (Jewel Story Ser.). (ENG.). 96p. (J). (gr. 1-3). pap. 4.99 *(978-1-4231-5197-5(6))* Disney Pr.

Disney Storybook Art Team, jt. illus. see Bonatakis, Shannon.

Disney Storybook Art Team, jt. illus. see Disney Storybook Artists Staff.

Disney Storybook Art Team, jt. illus. see Loter Inc. Staff.

Disney Storybook Art Team Staff. Minnie Be My Sparkly Valentine. Scollon, William et al. 2014. (ENG.). 24p. (J). (gr. -1-k). pap. 5.99 *(978-1-4231-6414-2(8))* Disney Pr.

Disney Storybook Art Team Staff, jt. illus. see RH Disney Staff.

Disney Storybook Artists, jt. illus. see Lee, Grace.

Disney Storybook Artists Staff. Air Mater. Auerbach, Annie & Disney Book Group Staff. 2012. (Read-Along Storybook & CD Ser.). (ENG.). 32p. (J). (gr. -1 — 1). pap. 6.99 *(978-1-4231-6014-4(2))* Disney Pr.

Disney Storybook Artists Staff. Aladdin Read-Along Storybook & CD. Disney Book Group Staff. 2015. (Read-Along Storybook & CD Ser.). (ENG.). 32p. (J). (gr. -1-k). pap. 6.99 ***(978-1-4231-4688-9(3))*** Disney Pr.

Disney Storybook Artists Staff. Alice in Wonderland (Disney Alice in Wonderland) Bobowicz, Pamela. 2013. (Step into Reading Ser.). (ENG.). 32p. (J). (gr. -1-1). pap. 3.99 *(978-0-7364-3027-2(X))*; lib. bdg. 12.99 *(978-0-7364-8122-9(2))* Random Hse. Children's Bks. (RH/Disney).

—All Stuffed Up. Higginson, Sheila Sweeny et al. 2013. (World of Reading Ser.). (ENG.). 32p. (J). (gr. -1-k). pap. 3.99 *(978-1-4231-7135-5(7))* Disney Pr.

—Always a Princess (Disney Princess) Posner-Sanchez, Andrea. 2011. (Friendship Box Ser.). (ENG.). 48p. (J). (gr. k — 1). bds. 10.99 *(978-0-7364-2848-4(8)*, RH/Disney) Random Hse. Children's Bks.

Disney Storybook Artists Staff, et al. Around-the-World Safari. Glass, Calliope & Disney Book Group Staff. 2013. (ENG.). 24p. (J). (gr. -1 — 1). pap. 4.99 *(978-1-4231-6233-9(1))* Disney Pr.

Disney Storybook Artists Staff. Bambi. Chambers, Whittaker, tr. from GER. 2004. (Little Golden Book Ser.). (ENG.). 24p. (J). (gr. -1-2). 3.99 *(978-0-7364-2308-3(7)*, Golden/Disney) Random Hse. Children's Bks.

—Belle: The Mysterious Message. Disney Book Group Staff. 2010. (Disney Princess Chapter Book: Series #1 Ser.). (ENG.). 96p. (J). (gr. 1-3). pap. 4.99 *(978-1-4231-2977-6(6))* Disney Pr.

—Bibbidi Bobbidi Books! (Disney Princess) Posner-Sanchez, Andrea. 2012. (Friendship Box Ser.). (ENG.). 48p. (J). (gr. k-k). bds. 10.99 *(978-0-7364-3022-7(9)*, RH/Disney) Random Hse. Children's Bks.

—Blooming Bows. Scollon, William & Parent, Nancy. 2013. (ENG.). 32p. (J). (gr. -1-1). pap. 3.99 *(978-1-4231-6691-7(4))* Disney Pr.

—Bucky Makes a Splash! LaRose, Melinda & Disney Book Group Staff. 2013. (ENG.). 16p. (J). (gr. -1-k). pap. 4.99 *(978-1-4231-6389-3(3))* Disney Pr.

—Cars. Berrios, Frank & RH Disney Staff. 2006. (Read-Aloud Board Book Ser.). (ENG.). 24p. (J). (gr. k — 1). bds. 4.99 *(978-0-7364-2293-2(5)*, RH/Disney) Random Hse. Children's Bks.

—Cinderella. Disney Book Group Staff. 2012. (Read-Along Storybook & CD Ser.). (ENG.). 32p. (J). (gr. -1 — 1). pap. 6.99 *(978-1-4231-6321-3(4))* Disney Pr.

—Cinderella & the Lost Mice - Belle & the Castle Puppy. Bazaldua, Barbara. 2010. (Deluxe Pictureback Ser.). (ENG.). 32p. (J). (gr. -1-2). pap. 4.99 *(978-0-7364-2694-7(9)*, RH/Disney) Random Hse. Children's Bks.

—Cinderella (Diamond) Big Golden Book (Disney Princess) RH Disney Staff. 2012. (Big Golden Book Ser.). (ENG.). 64p. (J). (gr. -1-2). 9.99 *(978-0-7364-3002-9(4)*, Golden/Disney) Random Hse. Children's Bks.

—Color Our World. Disney Book Group Staff. 2013. (ENG.). 14p. (J). (gr. -1-k). bds. 7.99 *(978-1-4231-6009-0(6))* Disney Pr.

—Colorful Critters! (Disney Princess: Palace Pets) RH Disney Staff. 2014. (Deluxe Paint Box Book Ser.). (ENG.). 128p. (J). (gr. -1-2). pap. 7.99 *(978-0-7364-3265-8(5)*, Golden/Disney) Random Hse. Children's Bks.

—Colors All Around. Disney Book Group Staff. 2014. (Flap 'n Tab Ser.). (ENG.). 10p. (J). (gr. -1-k). bds. 6.99 *(978-1-4231-8094-4(1))* Disney Pr.

—Cozy Baby. Disney Baby Staff & Disney Book Group Staff. 2010. (ENG.). 6p. (J). (gr. -1 — 1). 7.99 *(978-1-4231-2827-4(3))* Disney Pr.

—The Croc Takes the Cake. LaRose, Melinda & Disney Book Group Staff. 2012. (World of Reading Ser.). (ENG.). 32p. (J). (gr. -1-k). pap. 3.99 *(978-1-4231-5543-0(2))* Disney Pr.

—Disney 5-Minute Fairy Tales. Disney Book Group Staff. 2013. (5-Minute Stories Ser.). (ENG.). 192p. (J). (gr. -1 — 1). 12.99 *(978-1-4231-6766-2(X))* Disney Pr.

—Disney Christmas Storybook Collection. Disney Book Group Staff et al. 2014. (Storybook Collection). (ENG.). 304p. (J). (gr. -1-k). 16.99 *(978-1-4231-8450-8(5))* Disney Pr.

—Disney Mickey & Minnie. Disney Book Group Staff. 2014. (Read-And-Listen Storybook Ser.). (ENG.). 128p. (J). (gr. 1-3). 10.99 *(978-1-4847-0436-3(3))* Disney Pr.

—Disney Mickey Mouse Clubhouse Movie Theater: Storybook & Movie Projector. 2012. (Movie Theater Ser.). (ENG.). 32p. (J). (gr. k-3). 19.99 *(978-0-7944-2587-6(9))* Reader's Digest Assn., Inc., The.

—Disney Princess Read-and-Sing - Cinderella. Disney Book Group Staff. 2015. (Read-And-Sing Ser.). (ENG.). 128p. (J). (gr. 1-3). 11.99 *(978-1-4847-0782-1(6))* Disney Pr.

Disney Storybook Artists Staff, et al. Disney's the Lion King. 2007. (Play-A-Sound Ser.). 16p. (J). (gr. -1-3). 16.98 *(978-1-4127-8776-5(9))* Publications International, Ltd.

Disney Storybook Artists Staff. Doc Mcstuffins Boo to You! Disney Book Group Staff et al. 2014. (ENG.). 12p. (J). (gr. -1-k). bds. 7.99 *(978-1-4231-8388-4(6))* Disney Pr.

—Doc Mcstuffins Doc's Big Book of Boo-Boos. Disney Book Group Staff & Higginson, Sheila Sweeny. 2014. (ENG.). 64p. (J). (gr. -1-k). 10.99 *(978-1-4231-8483-6(1))* Disney Pr.

—Doc Mcstuffins Doc's Mobile Clinic. Kelman, Marcy. 2014. (ENG.). 12p. (J). (gr. -1-k). bds. 7.99 *(978-1-4231-9420-0(9))* Disney Pr.

—Doc Mcstuffins Doctor's Helper: Purchase Includes Disney EBook! Disney Book Group Staff & Higginson, Sheila Sweeny. 2014. (ENG.). 40p. (J). (gr. -1-k). 16.99 *(978-1-4231-8390-7(8))* Disney Pr.

—Doctoring the Doc. Marsoli, Lisa Ann & Disney Book Group Staff. 2013. (Read-Along Storybook & CD Ser.). (ENG.). 32p. (J). (gr. -1-k). pap. 6.99 *(978-1-4231-7134-8(9))* Disney Pr.

—Driving Buddies. Jordan, Apple & RH Disney Staff. 2006. (Step into Reading Ser.). (ENG.). 32p. (J). (gr. k-3). pap. 3.99 *(978-0-7364-2339-7(7)*, RH/Disney) Random Hse. Children's Bks.

—Dumbo. RH Disney Staff. 2004. (Little Golden Book Ser.). (ENG.). 24p. (J). (gr. -1-2). 3.99 *(978-0-7364-2309-0(5)*, Golden/Disney) Random Hse. Children's Bks.

—Dusty's Great Race. Disney Book Group Staff & Glass, Calliope. 2013. (ENG.). 32p. (J). (gr. -1-k). 12.99 *(978-1-4231-9736-2(4))* Disney Pr.

—Easter Bonnet Parade. Scollon, William et al. 2013. (ENG.). 24p. (J). (gr. -1-k). pap. 5.99 *(978-1-4231-6416-6(4))* Disney Pr.

—Elsa's Gift. Disney Book Group Staff. 2014. (ENG.). 24p. (J). (gr. 1-3). bds. 10.99 *(978-1-4847-1699-1(X))* Disney Pr.

—Enchanted Fashions: A Magnetic Book & Playset. Bergen, Lara & Disney Book Group Staff. rev. ed. 2007. (Book & Magnetic Play Set Ser.). (ENG.). 16p. (J). (gr. -1 — 1). 14.99 *(978-1-4231-0752-1(7))* Disney Pr.

—Engine Nine, Feelin' Fine! Scollon, William et al. 2013. (ENG.). 24p. (J). (gr. -1-k). pap. 3.99 *(978-1-4231-7133-1(0))* Disney Pr.

—Fairest of All: A Tale of the Wicked Queen. Valentino, Serena & Disney Book Group Staff. 2009. (ENG.). 256p. (J). (gr. 5-9). 15.99 *(978-1-4231-0629-6(6))* Disney Pr.

—Finding Nemo. 2007. (Play-A-Sound Ser.). 15p. (J). (gr. -1-3). 15.98 *(978-1-4127-8754-3(8))* Publications International, Ltd.

—Follow That Sound! Disney Book Group Staff. 2014. (ENG.). 24p. (J). (gr. -1-k). bds. 10.99 *(978-1-4847-0658-9(7))* Disney Pr.

—Forever After. McCafferty, Catherine et al. 2012. (ENG.). 96p. (J). (gr. -1-k). 12.99 *(978-1-4231-6562-0(4))* Disney Pr.

—Frozen Read-Along Storybook & CD. Disney Book Group Staff. 2013. (Read-Along Storybook & CD Ser.). (ENG.). 32p. (J). (gr. -1-k). pap. 6.99 *(978-1-4231-7064-8(4))* Disney Pr.

—Frozen Sing-Along Storybook. Disney Book Group Staff & Marsoli, Lisa Ann. 2014. (ENG.). 128p. (J). (gr. 1-3). 17.99 *(978-1-4847-2035-6(0))* Disney Pr.

—Furry, Fluffy & Fabulous! (Disney Princess: Palace Pets) RH Disney Staff. 2014. (Big Golden Book Ser.). (ENG.). 64p. (J). (gr. -1-2). 9.99 *(978-0-7364-3263-4(9)*, Golden/Disney) Random Hse. Children's Bks.

—Furry Friends! Disney Press Staff & Disney Book Group Staff. 2011. (Touch-And-feel Book Ser.). (ENG.). 16p. (J). (gr. -1-k). bds. 7.99 *(978-1-4231-4183-9(0))* Disney Pr.

—Glamour Pets! Random House Disney Staff. 2014. (Deluxe Stickerific Ser.). (ENG.). 64p. (J). (gr. -1-2). pap. 5.99 *(978-0-7364-3196-5(9)*, Golden/Disney) Random Hse. Children's Bks.

—Guess Who! Disney Book Group Staff. 2012. (ENG.). 14p. (J). (gr. -1-k). bds. 6.99 *(978-1-4231-6008-3(8))* Disney Pr.

—Hello, World! Disney Press Staff et al. 2011. (ENG.). 14p. (J). (gr. -1-k). bds. 5.99 *(978-1-4231-4140-2(7))* Disney Pr.

—Henry Hugglemonster Welcome to Roarsville. Disney Book Group Staff & Higginson, Sheila Sweeny. 2014. (ENG.). 24p. (J). (gr. -1-k). pap. 4.99 *(978-1-4847-0264-2(6))* Disney Pr.

Disney Storybook Artists Staff. Hooray for Palace Pets! Feldman, Thea. 2015. (ENG.). 12p. (J). (gr. -1-k). bds. 10.99 ***(978-0-7944-3389-5(8))*** Studio Fun International.

Disney Storybook Artists Staff. A Horse to Love: An Enchanted Stables Story. Lagonegro, Melissa & RH Disney Staff. 2007. (Pictureback Ser.). (ENG.). 16p. (J). (gr. -1-2). pap. 3.99 *(978-0-7364-2504-9(7)*, RH/Disney) Random Hse. Children's Bks.

—I Am Ariel (Disney Princess) Posner-Sanchez, Andrea. 2011. (Shaped Board Book Ser.). (ENG.). 12p. (J). (— 1). bds. 4.99 *(978-0-7364-2819-4(4)*, Golden/Disney) Random Hse. Children's Bks.

—I Love You! Disney Book Group Staff. 2012. (ENG.). 10p. (J). (gr. -1-k). pap. 7.99 *(978-1-4231-6571-2(3))* Disney Pr.

—In Flight! Hands, Cynthia. 2013. (Color Plus Chunky Crayons Ser.). (ENG.). 48p. (J). (gr. -1-2). pap. 3.99 *(978-0-7364-2973-3(5)*, Golden/Disney) Random Hse. Children's Bks.

—Iron Man vs. Titanium Man. Disney Book Group Staff. 2013. (Marvel Super Hero vs. Book Ser.). (ENG.). 24p. (J). (gr. -1-k). pap. 3.99 *(978-1-4231-5469-3(X))* Marvel Worldwide, Inc.

—Jake & the Never Land Pirates after a While, Crocodile. LaRose, Melinda & Disney Book Group Staff. 2014. (ENG.). 32p. (J). (gr. -1-k). pap. 3.99 *(978-1-4231-8387-7(8))* Disney Pr.

—Jake & the Never Land Pirates Treasure of the Tides. LaRose, Melinda & Disney Book Group Staff. 2014. (ENG.). 32p. (J). (gr. -1-k). pap. 3.99 *(978-1-4231-9422-4(5))* Disney Pr.

—Jasmine: The Jewel Orchard. O'Ryan, Ellie & Disney Book Group Staff. 2013. (Disney Princess Chapter Book: Series #1 Ser.). (ENG.). 96p. (J). (gr. 1-3). pap. 4.99 *(978-1-4231-6978-9(6))* Disney Pr.

—Learn to Draw Disney Minnie & Daisy Best Friends Forever Fabulous Fashions. Walter Foster Creative Team. 2014. 64p. (J). (gr. 3-5). 33.27 *(978-1-939581-32-7(X))* Quarto Publishing Group USA.

—Leilani's Luau. Higginson, Sheila Sweeny. 2014. (ENG.). 32p. (J). (gr. -1-k). pap. 4.99 *(978-1-4231-9417-0(9))* Disney Pr.

—Light up the Night. RH Disney Staff & Hands, Cynthia. 2010. (Deluxe Coloring Book Ser.). (ENG.). 96p. (J). (gr. -1-2). pap. 3.99 *(978-0-7364-2720-3(1)*, Golden/Disney) Random Hse. Children's Bks.

—The Little Mermaid Read-Along Storybook & CD. Disney Book Group Staff. 2013. (Read-Along Storybook & CD Ser.). (ENG.). 32p. (J). (gr. -1-k). pap. 6.99 *(978-1-4231-6889-8(5))* Disney Pr.

—Loud Louie. Higginson, Sheila Sweeny & Disney Book Group Staff. 2013. (World of Reading Ser.). (ENG.). 32p. (J). (gr. -1-k). pap. 3.99 *(978-1-4231-6456-2(3))* Disney Pr.

—Mater Saves Christmas. Murray, Kiel & Disney Book Group Staff. 2012. (ENG.). 48p. (J). (gr. -1-2). pap. 8.99 *(978-1-4231-6570-5(5))* Disney Pr.

—Meet the Planes. Disney Book Group Staff & Disney Storybook Art Team. 2014. (Storybook Classic Ser.). (ENG.). 128p. (J). (gr. 1-3). 12.99 *(978-1-4231-7567-4(0))* Disney Pr.

—A Merry Christmas Cookbook. Disney Book Group Staff. 2014. (ENG.). 64p. (J). (gr. 1-3). 10.99 *(978-1-4231-6322-0(2))* Disney Pr.

—Mickey & Friends Goofy at Bat. Amerikaner, Susan & Disney Book Group Staff. 2013. (World of Reading Ser.). (ENG.). 32p. (J). (gr. 1-3). pap. 3.99 *(978-1-4231-6962-8(X))* Disney Pr.

—Mickey Mouse Clubhouse. Hamilton, Tisha. 2008. (Carry along Treasury Ser.). (ENG.). 14p. (J). (gr. -1-1). bds. 14.99 *(978-0-7944-1481-8(8))* Reader's Digest Assn., Inc., The.

—Mickey Mouse Clubhouse Minnie-Rella. Marsoli, Lisa Ann & Disney Book Group Staff. 2013. (World of Reading Ser.).

(ENG.). 32p. (J). (gr. -1-k). pap. 3.99 *(978-1-4231-6417-3(2))* Disney Pr.

—Mickey Saves Santa. Disney Book Group Staff. 2009. (ENG.). 24p. (J). (gr. -1-k). pap. 5.99 *(978-1-4231-1846-6(4))* Disney Pr.

—Mickey's Birthday. Driscoll, Laura & Disney Book Group Staff. 2013. (World of Reading Ser.). (ENG.). 32p. (J). (gr. 1-3). pap. 3.99 *(978-1-4231-6067-0(3))* Disney Pr.

—Mickey's Halloween Treat. Feldman, Thea & Disney Book Group Staff. 2008. (ENG.). 16p. (J). (gr. -1-k). pap. 4.99 *(978-1-4231-0983-9(X))* Disney Pr.

—Minnie a Walk in the Park, Level 1. Disney Book Group Staff & Gold, Gina. 2014. (World of Reading Ser.). (ENG.). 32p. (J). (gr. -1-k). pap. 3.99 *(978-1-4847-0678-7(1))* Disney Pr.

—Minnie & Daisy Best Friends Forever Doodle Book: Over 100 Doodle Pages! 5 Sticker Scenes! 21 Character Stencils 43 Stickers! Disney Book Group Staff. 2013. (Doodle Book Ser.). (ENG.). 112p. (J). (gr. 1-3). pap. 12.99 *(978-1-4231-7410-3(0))* Disney Pr.

—Minnie: Minnie's Costume Contest. Disney Book Group Staff & Higginson, Sheila Sweeny. 2014. (ENG.). 12p. (J). (gr. -1-k). bds. 7.99 *(978-1-4231-9427-9(6))* Disney Pr.

—Minnie: Minnie's Valentine. Disney Book Group Staff & Higginson, Sheila Sweeny. 2013. 10p. 5.99 *(978-1-4231-8811-7(X))* Disney Pr.

—Minnie Minnie's Winter Bow Show. Disney Book Group Staff et al. 2014. (ENG.). 24p. (J). (gr. -1-k). pap. 5.99 *(978-1-4231-8070-8(4))* Disney Pr.

—Minnie Wishing on a Bow. Disney Book Group Staff & Higginson, Sheila Sweeny. 2014. (ENG.). 32p. (J). (gr. -1-k). pap. 3.99 *(978-1-4231-9426-2(8))* Disney Pr.

—Minnie's Fashion & Fun. Disney Book Group Staff. 2013. (Book & Magnetic Play Set Ser.). (ENG.). 32p. (J). (gr. -1-k). 14.99 *(978-1-4231-8443-0(2))* Disney Pr.

—Minnie's Purse. Disney Book Group Staff & Kelman, Marcy. 2014. (ENG.). 20p. (J). (gr. -1-k). 9.99 *(978-1-4231-8492-8(0))* Disney Pr.

—Oodles of Princess Doodles (Disney Princess) RH Disney Staff. 2011. (Deluxe Doodle Book Ser.). (ENG.). 256p. (J). (gr. -1-2). pap. 9.99 *(978-0-7364-2825-5(9)*, Golden/Disney) Random Hse. Children's Bks.

—P Is for Princess. Auerbach, Annie & Disney Book Group Staff. 2013. (ENG.). 26p. (J). (gr. -1-k). bds. 12.99 *(978-1-4231-6471-5(7))* Disney Pr.

—Part of Their World. Disney Book Group Staff. 2013. (ENG.). 40p. (J). (gr. -1-17). 15.99 *(978-1-4231-6757-0(0))* Disney Pr.

—Perfect Princess Christmas. Disney Book Group Staff. 2014. (ENG.). 96p. (J). (gr. -1-k). 12.99 *(978-1-4231-7203-1(5))* Disney Pr.

—Planes Read-Along Storybook & CD. O'Ryan, Ellie & Disney Book Group Staff. 2013. (Read-Along Storybook & CD Ser.). (ENG.). 32p. (J). (gr. -1-k). pap. 6.99 *(978-1-4231-6888-1(7))* Disney Pr.

—Pooh's Halloween Pumpkin. Hapka, Cathy et al. 2013. (ENG.). 10p. (J). (gr. -1-k). bds. 5.99 *(978-1-4231-6767-9(8))* Disney Pr.

—Pretty in Pink. Disney Book Group Staff. 2014. (ENG.). 10p. (J). (gr. -1-k). bds. 8.99 *(978-1-4231-8522-2(6))* Disney Pr.

—Princess Adventure Stories. Disney Book Group Staff. 2013. (Storybook Collection). (ENG.). 304p. (J). (gr. -1 — 1). 15.99 *(978-1-4231-4691-9(3))* Disney Pr.

—Princess Bedtime Stories. Disney Book Group Staff. 2010. (Storybook Collection). (ENG.). 312p. (J). (gr. -1 — 1). 15.99 *(978-1-4231-2496-2(0))* Disney Pr.

—Reading Adventures Cars Level 1 Boxed Set. Disney Book Group Staff. 2013. (Reading Adventures Ser.). (ENG.). 160p. (J). (gr. 1-3). pap. 9.99 *(978-1-4231-6980-2(8))* Disney Pr.

—Run, Remy, Run! Richards, Kitty & RH Disney Staff. 2007. (Step into Reading Ser.). (ENG.). 32p. (J). (gr. k-3). pap. 3.99 *(978-0-7364-2476-9(8)*, RH/Disney) Random Hse. Children's Bks.

—Runaway Hit, No. 2. Bergen, Lara & Disney Book Group Staff. 2nd ed. 2009. (Phineas & Ferb Chapter Book Ser.: 2). (ENG.). 112p. (J). (gr. 1-3). pap. 4.99 *(978-1-4231-1797-1(2))* Disney Pr.

—Save Me, Smee! LaRose, Melinda & Disney Book Group Staff. 2013. (ENG.). 24p. (J). (gr. -1-k). pap. 3.99 *(978-1-4231-6395-4(8))* Disney Pr.

Disney Storybook Artists Staff, et al. A Sister More Like Me. Hicks, Barbara Jean & Disney Book Group Staff. 2013. (ENG.). 32p. (J). (gr. 1-3). 15.99 *(978-1-4231-7014-3(8))* Disney Pr.

Disney Storybook Artists Staff. Small Fry. Auerbach, Annie. 2012. (Read-Along Storybook & CD Ser.). (ENG.). 32p. (J). (gr. -1 — 1). pap. 6.99 *(978-1-4231-6561-3(6))* Disney Pr.

—Snow White & the Seven Dwarfs. Berrios, Frank & RH Disney Staff. 2006. (Read-Aloud Board Book Ser.). (ENG.). 24p. (J). (gr. k — 1). bds. 4.99 *(978-0-7364-2426-4(1)*, RH/Disney) Random Hse. Children's Bks.

—Sofia Makes a Friend. Hapka, Cathy & Disney Book Group Staff. 2013. (World of Reading Ser.). (ENG.). 32p. (J). (gr. -1-k). pap. 3.99 *(978-1-4231-6408-1(3))* Disney Pr.

—Sofia Takes the Lead, Level 1. Marsoli, Lisa Ann & Disney Book Group Staff. 2014. (World of Reading Ser.). (ENG.). 32p. (J). (gr. -1-k). pap. 3.99 *(978-1-4231-8345-7(2))* Disney Pr.

—Sofia the First Sofia's Purse. Disney Book Group Staff & Kelman, Marcy. 2014. (ENG.). 20p. (J). (gr. -1-k). 9.99 *(978-1-4231-8493-5(9))* Disney Pr.

—Sofia the First the Enchanted Science Fair. Disney Book Group Staff & Hapka, Catherine. 2014. (ENG.). 24p. (J). (gr. -1-k). pap. 4.99 *(978-1-4847-1309-9(5))* Disney Pr.

—Sofia the First the Royal Games. Disney Book Group Staff & Hapka, Cathy. 2014. (ENG.). 24p. (J). (gr. -1-k). pap. 3.99 *(978-1-4231-6409-8(1))* Disney Pr.

Disney Storybook Artists Staff, et al. Spring into Action! RH Disney Staff & Hands, Cynthia. 2010. (Deluxe Coloring Book Ser.). (ENG.). 96p. (J). (gr. -1-2). pap. 3.99 *(978-0-7364-2707-4(4)*, Golden/Disney) Random Hse. Children's Bks.

Disney Storybook Artists Staff. Takeoff! Hands, Cynthia. 2013. (Super Coloring Book Ser.). (ENG.). 96p. (J). (gr. -1-2). pap. 3.99 *(978-0-7364-3015-9(6)*, Golden/Disney) Random Hse. Children's Bks.

—Tangled. Disney Book Group Staff. 2014. (Read-And-Sing Ser.). (ENG.). 128p. (J). (gr. 1-3). 11.99 *(978-1-4847-0843-9(1))* Disney Pr.

—Tangled Ever After. Disney Book Group Staff & Bergen, Lara. 2012. (Read-Along Storybook & CD Ser.). (ENG.). 32p. (J). (gr. -1 — 1). pap. 6.99 *(978-1-4231-6582-8(9))* Disney Pr.

—Tiana - The Stolen Jewel: A Jewel Story. Glass, Calliope & Disney Book Group Staff. 2013. (Disney Princess Chapter Book: Series #1 Ser.). (ENG.). 96p. (J). (gr. 1-3). pap. 4.99 *(978-1-4231-6903-1(4))* Disney Pr.

—Trick or Treasure? Kelman, Marcy & Disney Book Group Staff. 2013. (ENG.). 24p. (J). (gr. -1-k). pap. 5.99 *(978-1-4231-7140-9(3))* Disney Pr.

—Trouble Times Two. Scollon, William et al. 2012. (ENG.). 32p. (J). (gr. -1-k). pap. 5.99 *(978-1-4231-6412-8(1))* Disney Pr.

—Walt Disney: Drawn from Imagination. Disney Book Group Staff & Scollon, Bill. 2014. (ENG.). 136p. (J). (gr. 3-7). pap. 14.99 *(978-1-4231-9647-1(3))* Disney Pr.

—Whose Birthday Is It? Higginson, Sheila Sweeny & Disney Book Group Staff. 2007. (ENG.). 16p. (J). (gr. -1-k). 4.99 *(978-1-4231-0652-4(0))* Disney Pr.

—Winnie the Pooh Take-Along Tunes: Book with Music Player. Reader's Digest Staff & Miller, Sara. 2011. (Take-Along Tunes Ser.). (ENG.). 32p. (J). (gr. -1 — 1). 19.99 *(978-0-7944-2179-3(2))* Reader's Digest Assn., Inc., The.

—World of Reading: Doc Mcstuffins Brave Dragon: Level Pre-1. Disney Book Group Staff et al. 2014. (World of Reading Ser.). (ENG.). 32p. (J). (gr. -1-k). pap. 3.99 *(978-1-4847-0244-4(1))* Disney Pr.

—World of Reading: Jake & the Never Land Pirates Pirate Campout: Level 1. Scollon, William et al. 2014. (World of Reading Ser.). (ENG.). 32p. (J). (gr. -1-k). pap. 3.99 *(978-1-4231-8398-3(3))* Disney Pr.

—World of Reading: Jake & the Never Land Pirates Surfin' Turf: Level 1. Disney Book Group Staff & LaRose, Melinda. 2014. (World of Reading Ser.). (ENG.). 32p. (J). (gr. -1-k). pap. 3.99 *(978-1-4231-6391-6(5))* Disney Pr.

—World of Reading: Minnie Hocus Bow-Cus! Level 1. Disney Book Group Staff & Gold, Gina. 2014. (World of Reading Ser.). (ENG.). 32p. (J). (gr. -1-k). pap. 3.99 *(978-1-4231-9428-6(4))* Disney Pr.

—World of Reading: Sofia the First Just One of the Princes: Level 1. Baer, Jill & Disney Book Group Staff. 2014. (World of Reading Ser.). (ENG.). 32p. (J). (gr. -1-k). pap. 3.99 *(978-1-4231-9432-3(2))* Disney Pr.

—5-Minute Minnie Tales. Disney Book Group Staff. 2014. (5-Minute Stories Ser.). (ENG.). 192p. (J). (gr. 1-3). 12.99 *(978-1-4847-0452-3(5))* Disney Pr.

—5-Minute Princess Stories. Disney Press Staff & Disney Book Group Staff. 2011. (5-Minute Stories Ser.). (ENG.). 192p. (J). (gr. -1 — 1). 12.99 *(978-1-4231-4657-5(3))* Disney Pr.

—5-Minute Snuggle Stories. Disney Book Group Staff. 2013. (5-Minute Stories Ser.). (ENG.). 192p. (J). (gr. -1 — 1). 12.99 *(978-1-4231-6765-5(1))* Disney Pr.

Disney Storybook Artists Staff & Bachs, Ramon. These Are the X-Men Level 1. Disney Book Group Staff & Macri, Thomas. 2013. (World of Reading Ser.). (ENG.). 32p. (J). (gr. -1-k). pap. 3.99 *(978-1-4231-7083-9(0))* Marvel Worldwide, Inc.

Disney Storybook Artists Staff & Disney Book Group Staff. Disney Bedtime Favorites. Disney Book Group Staff. 2012. (Storybook Collection). (ENG.). 312p. (J). (gr. -1 — 1). 15.99 *(978-1-4231-6034-2(7))* Disney Pr.

Disney Storybook Artists Staff & Disney Storybook Art Team. The Beast Within: A Tale of Beauty's Prince. Valentino, Serena & Disney Book Group Staff. 2014. (ENG.). 224p. (J). (gr. 5-9). 16.99 *(978-1-4231-5912-4(8))* Disney Pr.

—Bubble Trouble. Higginson, Sheila Sweeny & Disney Book Group Staff. 2013. (ENG.). 24p. (J). (gr. -1-k). pap. 4.99 *(978-1-4231-6454-8(7))* Disney Pr.

—Disney Princess Dear Princess. Disney Book Group Staff. 2014. (ENG.). 36p. (J). (gr. 1-3). 12.99 *(978-1-4847-0026-6(0))* Disney Pr.

—Doc Mcstuffins a Very Mcstuffins Christmas. Disney Book Group Staff & Higginson, Sheila Sweeny. 2014. (ENG.). 24p. (J). (gr. -1-k). pap. 5.99 *(978-1-4847-0698-5(6))* Disney Pr.

—Doc Mcstuffins Helping Hands. Disney Book Group Staff. 2014. (Sneak-A-Peek Ser.). (ENG.). 14p. (J). (gr. -1-k). bds. 8.99 *(978-1-4847-0766-1(4))* Disney Pr.

—Fly-and-Drive Read-Along Storybook. Disney Book Group Staff. 2014. (Read-Along Storybook & CD Ser.). (ENG.). 136p. (J). (gr. 1-3). 12.99 *(978-1-4847-0656-5(0))* Disney Pr.

—Gravity Falls Pining Away. Disney Book Group Staff. 2014. (Gravity Falls Chapter Book Ser.: 1). (ENG.). 112p. (J). (gr. 1-3). pap. 4.99 *(978-1-4847-1139-2(4))* Disney Pr.

—Henry Hugglemonster Pet Party. Disney Book Group Staff & Higginson, Sheila Sweeny. 2014. (ENG.). 24p. (J). (gr. -1-k). pap. 4.99 *(978-1-4847-0263-5(8))* Disney Pr.

—Jake & the Never Land Pirates Skull Rock. Disney Book Group Staff. 2014. (Sneak-A-Peek Ser.). (ENG.). 14p. (J). (gr. -1-k). bds. 8.99 *(978-1-4847-0761-6(3))* Disney Pr.

—Jake Saves Bucky. Scollon, William & Disney Book Group Staff. 2013. (Read-Along Storybook & CD Ser.). (ENG.). 32p. (J). (gr. -1-k). pap. 6.99 *(978-1-4231-7141-6(1))* Disney Pr.

—Mickey & Friends Mickey's Spooky Night: Purchase Includes Digital App! Disney Book Group Staff. 2014. (ENG.). 24p. (J). (gr. 1-3). bds. 10.99 *(978-1-4847-0841-5(5))* Disney Pr.

—Minnie Bow-Toons Trouble Times Two: Purchase Includes Digital App! - Design Bows with Minnie! Disney Book Group Staff. 2014. (ENG.). 24p. (J). (gr. -1-k). bds. 10.99 *(978-1-4847-0541-4(6))* Disney Pr.

—Minnie Busy Bow-Tique. Disney Book Group Staff. 2014. (ENG.). 14p. (J). (gr. -1-k). bds. 8.99 *(978-1-4847-0759-3(1))* Disney Pr.

—Once upon a Princess. Marsoli, Lisa Ann & Disney Book Group Staff. 2013. (Read-Along Storybook & CD Ser.). (ENG.). 32p. (J). (gr. -1-k). pap. 6.99 *(978-1-4231-6846-1(1))* Disney Pr.

—A Perfect Picnic. Ritchey, Kate & Disney Book Group Staff. 2013. (World of Reading Ser.). (ENG.). 32p. (J). (gr. 1-3). pap. 3.99 *(978-1-4231-6963-5(8))* Disney Pr.

—Royal Treasury. Disney Book Group Staff. 2014. (Read-And-Play Storybook Ser.). (ENG.). 96p. (J). (gr. 1-3). 12.99 *(978-1-4847-0434-9(7))* Disney Pr.

—Sleeping Beauty. Disney Book Group Staff. 2014. (Read-And-Sing Ser.). (ENG.). 128p. (J). (gr. 1-3). 11.99 *(978-1-4847-0431-8(2))* Disney Pr.

—Sofia the First Royal Prep Academy. Disney Book Group Staff. 2014. (ENG.). 14p. (J). (gr. -1-k). bds. 8.99 *(978-1-4847-0760-9(5))* Disney Pr.

—Thumper Finds a Friend. Disney Book Group Staff. 2010. (ENG.). 32p. (J). (gr. -1-k). pap. 3.99 *(978-1-4231-2313-2(1))* Disney Pr.

—Up, up, & Away! Higginson, Sheila Sweeny & Disney Book Group Staff. 2007. (ENG.). 24p. (J). (gr. -1-k). pap. 3.99 *(978-1-4231-0647-0(4))* Disney Pr.

—Walt Disney's Classic Storybook (Volume 3) Disney Book Group Staff. 2014. (Storybook Collection: 3). (ENG.). 304p. (J). (gr. -1-k). 16.99 *(978-1-4231-9414-9(4))* Disney Pr.

—World of Reading: Doc Mcstuffins Blame It on the Rain: Level 1. Disney Book Group Staff & Weinberg, Jennifer Liberts. 2014. (World of Reading Ser.). (ENG.). 32p. (J). (gr. -1-k). pap. 3.99 *(978-1-4847-0676-3(5))* Disney Pr.

—5-Minute Spooky Stories. Disney Book Group Staff. 2014. (5-Minute Stories Ser.). (ENG.). 192p. (J). (gr. -1-k). 12.99 *(978-1-4231-8915-2(9))* Disney Pr.

Disney Storybook Artists Staff & Kole, Nicholas. The Curse of Maleficent: The Tale of a Sleeping Beauty. Disney Book Group Staff et al. 2014. (ENG.). 240p. (J). (gr. 3-7). 9.99 *(978-1-4231-9751-5(8))* Disney Pr.

Disney Storybook Artists Staff & Lee, Britney. A Dazzling Day. RH Disney Staff & Wooster, Devin Ann. 2010. (Pictureback Ser.). (ENG.). 24p. (J). (gr. -1-2). pap. 3.99 *(978-0-7364-2721-0(X)*, RH/Disney) Random Hse. Children's Bks.

Disney Storybook Artists Staff & Lee, Grace. Sofia the First Princesses to the Rescue! Purchase Includes a Digital Song! Hapka, Catherine & Disney Book Group Staff. 2014. (ENG.). 40p. (J). (gr. -1-k). 12.99 *(978-1-4231-9431-6(4))* Disney Pr.

—Sofia the First the Enchanted Feast. Disney Book Group Staff & Hapka, Catherine. 2014. (ENG.). 40p. (J). (gr. -1-k). 12.99 *(978-1-4231-8656-4(7))* Disney Pr.

Disney Storybook Artists Staff & Legramandi, Francesco. Princess Fun & Games (Disney Princess) RH Disney Staff. 2012. (Giant Coloring Book Ser.). (ENG.). 40p. (J). (gr. -1-2). pap. 9.99 *(978-0-7364-2953-5(0)*, Golden/Disney) Random Hse. Children's Bks.

Disney Storybook Artists Staff & Mosqueda, Olga. Frozen an Amazing Snowman. Disney Book Group Staff & Hicks, Barbara Jean. 2014. (ENG.). 40p. (J). (gr. -1-k). 16.99 *(978-1-4231-8514-7(5))* Disney Pr.

Disney Storybook Artists Staff & No New Art Needed. Gravity Falls Once upon a Swine. Disney Book Group Staff. 2014. (Gravity Falls Chapter Book Ser.: 2). (ENG.). 112p. (J). (gr. 1-3). pap. 4.99 *(978-1-4847-1140-8(8))* Disney Pr.

Disney Storybook Artists Staff & Orpinas, Jean-Paul. Tangled. RH Disney Staff & Peymani, Christine. 2010. (Read-Aloud Storybook Ser.). (ENG.). 72p. (J). (gr. -1-2). 9.99 *(978-0-7364-2718-0(X)*, RH/Disney) Random Hse. Children's Bks.

Disney Storybook Artists Staff & RH Disney Staff. Lightning Fast. RH Disney Staff. 2007. (Color Plus Chunky Crayons Ser.). (ENG.). 48p. (J). (gr. -1-2). pap. 3.99 *(978-0-375-83980-1(1)*, Golden/Disney) Random Hse. Children's Bks.

Disney Storybook Artists Staff & Studio Iboix Staff. Aurora & the Helpful Dragon - Tiana & Her Furry Friend. Random House Editors & RH Disney Staff. 2011. (Deluxe Pictureback Ser.). (ENG.). 32p. (J). (gr. -1-2). pap. 4.99 *(978-0-7364-2757-9(0)*, RH/Disney) Random Hse. Children's Bks.

Disney Storybook Artists Staff & Thammavongsa, Christine. The Little Mermaid. 2007. (Play-A-Sound Bks.). 18p. (J). (gr. -1-3). bds. 16.98 *(978-1-4127-8775-8(0))* Publications International, Ltd.

Disney Storybook Artists Staff & Ying, Victoria. Tangled. RH Disney Staff & Smiley, Ben. 2010. (Little Golden Book Ser.). (ENG.). 24p. (J). (gr. -1-2). 3.99 *(978-0-7364-2684-8(1)*, Golden/Disney) Random Hse. Children's Bks.

Disney Storybook Artists Staff, jt. illus. see Disney Book Group Staff.

Disney Storybook Artists Staff, jt. illus. see Grummett, Tom.

Disney Storybook Artists Staff, jt. illus. see Lee, Grace.

Disney Storybook Artists Staff, jt. illus. see Legramandi, Francesco.

Disney Storybook Artists Staff, jt. illus. see Mawhinney, Art.

Disney Storybook Artists Staff, jt. illus. see Random House Editors.

Disney Storybook Artists Staff, jt. illus. see RH Disney Staff.

Disney Storybook Artists Staff, jt. illus. see Studio IBOIX.

Dissler, Erica. There's a World in My House. Wood, David. 2005. 37p. (J). 13.95 *(978-1-933290-90-4(0))* Tate Publishing & Enterprises, LLC.

Ditama, Bow. Mahoromatic, Vol. 5. rev. ed. 2005. 184p. pap. 14.99 *(978-1-59182-915-7(1)*, Tokyopop Adult) TOKYOPOP, Inc.

—Mahoromatic: Automatic Maiden, 4 vols., Vol. 1. Nakayama, Bunjuro. 2004. 192p. pap. 14.99 *(978-1-59182-729-0(9)*, Tokyopop Adult) TOKYOPOP, Inc.

—Mahoromatic: Automatic Maiden, 6 vols. Nakayama, Bunjuro. rev. ed. Vol. 3. 2004. 192p. pap. 14.99 *(978-1-59182-731-3(0))*; Vol. 6. 2005. 190p. pap. 14.99 *(978-1-59182-916-4(X))* TOKYOPOP, Inc. (Tokyopop Adult).

—Mahoromatic: Automatic Maiden: The Misato Residence's Maid, 6 vols., Vol. 4. Nakayama, Bunjuro. rev. ed. 2004. 192p. pap. 14.99 *(978-1-59182-732-0(9)*, Tokyopop Adult) TOKYOPOP, Inc.

DiTerlizzi, Tony. The Beloved Dearly. Cooney, Doug. 2003. (ENG.). 192p. (J). (gr. 3-7). pap. 5.99 *(978-0-689-86354-7(3)*, Simon & Schuster Bks. For Young Readers) Simon & Schuster Bks. For Young Readers.

—Dracula. Stoker, Bram. 2009. (Puffin Classics Ser.). (ENG.). 640p. (J). (gr. 3-7). 6.99 *(978-0-14-132566-8(6)*, Puffin) Penguin Publishing Group.

—Hanging Out. Johnston, Tony. 2003. (Alien & Possum Ser.). 48p. (J). 11.65 *(978-0-7569-1544-5(9))* Perfection Learning Corp.

—The Spider & the Fly: 10th Anniversary Edition. Howitt, Mary. ed. 2012. (ENG.). 40p. (J). (gr. 1-4). 17.99 *(978-1-4424-5454-5(7)*, Simon & Schuster Bks. For Young Readers) Simon & Schuster Bks. For Young Readers.

DiTerlizzi, Tony. Arthur Spiderwick's Field Guide to the Fantastical World Around You. DiTerlizzi, Tony. Black, Holly. movie tie-in ed. 2008. (Spiderwick Chronicles Ser.). (ENG.). 142p. (J). (gr. 3-7). 24.99 *(978-1-4169-6095-9(3)*, Simon & Schuster Bks. For Young Readers) Simon & Schuster Bks. For Young Readers.

—The Battle for WondLa. DiTerlizzi, Tony. 2014. (Search for WondLa Ser.: 3). (ENG.). 496p. (J). (gr. 5). 17.99 *(978-1-4169-8314-9(7)*, Simon & Schuster Bks. For Young Readers) Simon & Schuster Bks. For Young Readers.

—Big Fun! DiTerlizzi, Tony. DiTerlizzi, Angela. 2009. (Adventure of Meno Ser.: 1). (ENG.). 48p. (J). (gr. -1-k). 9.99 *(978-1-4169-7148-1(3)*, Simon & Schuster Bks. For Young Readers) Simon & Schuster Bks. For Young Readers.

—Care & Feeding of Sprites. DiTerlizzi, Tony. Black, Holly. 2006. (Spiderwick Chronicles Ser.). (ENG.). 40p. (J). (gr. 2-7). 17.99 *(978-1-4169-2757-0(3)*, Simon & Schuster Bks. For Young Readers) Simon & Schuster Bks. For Young Readers.

—The Field Guide. DiTerlizzi, Tony. Black, Holly. 2003. (Spiderwick Chronicles Ser.: 1). (ENG.). 128p. (J). (gr. 1-5). 12.99 *(978-0-689-85936-6(8)*, 53409542, Simon & Schuster Bks. For Young Readers) Simon & Schuster Bks. For Young Readers.

—The Field Guide. DiTerlizzi, Tony. Black, Holly. ed. (Spiderwick Chronicles Ser.: 1). (ENG.). (J). 2013. 128p. (gr. 1-5). 15.99 *(978-1-4424-8693-5(7))*; 2013. 144p. (gr. 1-5). pap. 7.99 *(978-1-4424-8692-8(9))*; 2008. 128p. (gr. 2-5). 10.99 *(978-1-4169-5017-2(6))* Simon & Schuster Bks. For Young Readers. (Simon & Schuster Bks. For Young Readers).

—G Is for One Gzonk! An Alpha-Number-Bet Book. DiTerlizzi, Tony. 2006. (ENG.). (J). (gr. -1-2). 64p. 16.95 *(978-0-689-85290-9(8))*; 80p. 150.00 *(978-1-4169-2471-5(X))* Simon & Schuster Bks. For Young Readers. (Simon & Schuster Bks. For Young Readers).

—A Giant Problem. DiTerlizzi, Tony. Black, Holly. 2008. (Beyond the Spiderwick Chronicles Ser.: 2). (ENG.). 160p. (J). (gr. 2-5). 12.99 *(978-0-689-87132-0(5)*, Simon & Schuster Bks. For Young Readers) Simon & Schuster Bks. For Young Readers.

—A Hero for WondLa. DiTerlizzi, Tony. (Search for WondLa Ser.: 2). (ENG.). (J). (gr. 5). 2013. 480p. pap. 8.99 *(978-1-4169-8313-2(9))*; 2012. 464p. 17.99 *(978-1-4169-8312-5(0))* Simon & Schuster Bks. For Young Readers. (Simon & Schuster Bks. For Young Readers).

—The Ironwood Tree. DiTerlizzi, Tony. Black, Holly. ed. 2013. (Spiderwick Chronicles Ser.: 4). (ENG.). (J). (gr. 1-5). 128p. 15.99 *(978-1-4424-8702-4(X))*; 144p. pap. 6.99 *(978-1-4424-8701-7(1))* Simon & Schuster Bks. For Young Readers. (Simon & Schuster Bks. For Young Readers).

—The Ironwood Tree. DiTerlizzi, Tony. Black, Holly. 4th ed. 2004. (Spiderwick Chronicles Ser.: 4). (ENG.). 128p. (J). (gr. 2-6). 10.99 *(978-0-689-85939-7(2)*, Simon & Schuster Bks. For Young Readers) Simon & Schuster Bks. For Young Readers.

—Jimmy Zangwow's Out-of-This-World Moon-Pie Adventure. DiTerlizzi, Tony. 2003. (ENG.). 40p. (J). (gr. k-3). 7.99 *(978-0-689-85563-4(X)*, Simon & Schuster Bks. For Young Readers) Simon & Schuster Bks. For Young Readers.

—Kenny & the Dragon. DiTerlizzi, Tony. 2012. (ENG.). 176p. (J). (gr. 3-7). pap. 6.99 *(978-1-4424-3651-0(4)*, Simon & Schuster Bks. For Young Readers) Simon & Schuster Bks. For Young Readers.

—Kenny & the Dragon. DiTerlizzi, Tony. 2008. 160p. (J). (gr. 3-7). 15.99 Simon & Schuster Children's Publishing.

—Lucinda's Secret. DiTerlizzi, Tony. Black, Holly. ed. 2013. (Spiderwick Chronicles Ser.: 3). (ENG.). (J). (gr. 1-5). 128p. 15.99 *(978-1-4424-8700-0(3))*; 144p. pap. 6.99 *(978-1-4424-8697-3(X))* Simon & Schuster Bks. For Young Readers. (Simon & Schuster Bks. For Young Readers).

—Lucinda's Secret, BK. 3. DiTerlizzi, Tony. Black, Holly. 3rd ed. 2003. (Spiderwick Chronicles Ser.: 3). (ENG.). 144p. (J). (gr. 2-7). 10.99 *(978-0-689-85938-0(4)*, Simon & Schuster Bks. For Young Readers) Simon & Schuster Bks. For Young Readers.

—The Nixie's Song. DiTerlizzi, Tony. Black, Holly. 2007. (Beyond the Spiderwick Chronicles Ser.: 1). (ENG.). 160p. (J). (gr. 2-6). 12.99 *(978-0-689-87131-3(7)*, Simon & Schuster Bks. For Young Readers) Simon & Schuster Bks. For Young Readers.

—The Nixies Song - A Giant Problem - The Wyrm King Set, Set. DiTerlizzi, Tony. Black, Holly. ed. 2009. (Beyond the

D

Spiderwick Chronicles Ser.: Nos. 1-3). (ENG.). 528p. (J). (gr. 2-5). 33.99 *(978-1-4169-9011-6(9),* Simon & Schuster Bks. For Young Readers) Simon & Schuster Bks. For Young Readers.

—Notebook for Fantastical Observations. DiTerlizzi, Tony. Black, Holly. 2005. (Spiderwick Chronicles Ser.). (ENG.). 240p. (J). (gr. 2-6). 14.99 *(978-1-4169-0345-1(3),* Simon & Schuster Bks. For Young Readers) Simon & Schuster Bks. For Young Readers.

—The Search for WondLa. DiTerlizzi, Tony. (Search for WondLa Ser.: 1). (ENG.). (J). (gr. 5). 2012. 512p. pap. 9.99 *(978-1-4169-8311-8(2));* 2010. 496p. 17.99 *(978-1-4169-8310-1(4))* Simon & Schuster Bks. For Young Readers. (Simon & Schuster Bks. For Young Readers).

—The Seeing Stone. DiTerlizzi, Tony. Black, Holly. (Spiderwick Chronicles Ser.: 2). (ENG.). (J). (gr. 1-5). ed. 2013. 128p. 15.99 *(978-1-4424-8695-9(3));* ed. 2013. 144p. pap. 6.99 *(978-1-4424-8694-2(5));* Bk. 2. 2nd ed. 2003. 128p. 10.99 *(978-0-689-85937-3(6),* 53409541) Simon & Schuster Bks. For Young Readers. (Simon & Schuster Bks. For Young Readers).

—The Spiderwick. DiTerlizzi, Tony. Black, Holly. 2009. (Spiderwick Chronicles Ser.). (ENG.). 608p. (J). (gr. 3-7). 29.99 *(978-1-4169-8685-0(5),* Simon & Schuster Bks. For Young Readers) Simon & Schuster Bks. For Young Readers.

—The Spiderwick Chronicles Set: The Field Guide - The Seeing Stone - Lucinda's Secret - The Ironwood Tree - The Wrath of Mulgrath. DiTerlizzi, Tony. Black, Holly. ed. 2013. (Spiderwick Chronicles Ser.). (ENG.). (J). (gr. 1-5). 752p. pap. 34.99 *(978-1-4424-8798-7(4));* 672p. 79.99 *(978-1-4424-8797-0(6))* Simon & Schuster Bks. For Young Readers. (Simon & Schuster Bks. For Young Readers).

—Ted. DiTerlizzi, Tony. 2004. (ENG.). 40p. (J). (gr. -1-3). reprint ed. 7.99 *(978-0-689-86374-5(8),* Simon & Schuster Bks. For Young Readers) Simon & Schuster Bks. For Young Readers.

—Uh-Oh Sick! DiTerlizzi, Tony. DiTerlizzi, Angela. 2010. (Adventure of Meno Ser.: 4). (ENG.). 40p. (J). (gr. -1-k). bds. 9.99 *(978-1-4169-7153-5(X),* Simon & Schuster Bks. For Young Readers) Simon & Schuster Bks. For Young Readers.

—Wet Friend! DiTerlizzi, Tony. DiTerlizzi, Angela. 2009. (Adventure of Meno Ser.: 2). (ENG.). 48p. (J). (gr. -1-k). 9.99 *(978-1-4169-7149-8(1),* Simon & Schuster Bks. For Young Readers) Simon & Schuster Bks. For Young Readers.

—The Wrath of Mulgarath. DiTerlizzi, Tony. Black, Holly. ed. 2013. (Spiderwick Chronicles Ser.: 5). (ENG.). (J). (gr. 1-5). 160p. 15.99 *(978-1-4424-8704-8(6));* 176p. pap. 6.99 *(978-1-4424-8703-1(8))* Simon & Schuster Bks. For Young Readers. (Simon & Schuster Bks. For Young Readers).

—The Wyrm King. DiTerlizzi, Tony. Black, Holly. 2009. (Beyond the Spiderwick Chronicles Ser.: 3). (ENG.). 176p. (J). (gr. 2-7). 11.99 *(978-0-689-87133-7(3),* Simon & Schuster Bks. For Young Readers) Simon & Schuster Bks. For Young Readers.

—Yummy Trip! DiTerlizzi, Tony. DiTerlizzi, Angela. 2010. (Adventure of Meno Ser.: 3). (ENG.). 48p. (J). (gr. -1-k). bds. 9.99 *(978-1-4169-7150-4(5),* Simon & Schuster Bks. For Young Readers) Simon & Schuster Bks. For Young Readers.

DiTerlizzi, Tony, jt. illus. see Black, Holly.

Ditewig, Diann. Eddie & Harry. Kretzmann, Jane. 2014. 48p. (J). *(978-0-9846739-3-3(8))* Cornerstone Pr. Chicago.

Ditko, Steve, et al. Doctor Strange, Vol. 2. Lee, Stan et al. 2013. (ENG.). 312p. (J). (gr. -1-17). pap. 24.99 *(978-0-7851-6770-9(6))* Marvel Worldwide, Inc.

—Spider-Man Through the Decades. Rude, Steve. 2011. (ENG.). 272p. (YA). (gr. 8-17). pap. 26.99 *(978-0-7851-5758-8(1))* Marvel Worldwide, Inc.

Ditko, Steve, jt. illus. see Kirby, Jack.

Ditko, Steve, jt. illus. see Romita, John.

Dittrich, Dennis. Brotherly Feelings: Me, My Emotions, & My Brother with Asperger's Syndrome. Frender, Sam & Schiffmiller, Robin. 2007. (ENG.). 64p. (J). (gr. 3-7). per. *(978-1-84310-850-4(X))* Kingsley, Jessica Ltd.

Dittus, Jade Moon. Blinky the Magical Elf. Andrew-Kollmann, Marcia. 2012. 28p. pap. 24.95 *(978-1-4626-5345-4(6))* America Star Bks.

DIVINCENZO, Yoselem G. Paisaje de Risas. Robles Echeverria, Maria De Jesus & ALONSO CURIEL, Jorge David. 2013. 72p. pap. 14.99 *(978-1-61196-924-5(7))* Divincenzo, Yoselem G.

DiVito, Andrea, et al. Brath. Dixon, Chuck. 2003. (Brath Ser.: Vol. 1). 160p. (YA). (gr. 6-18). pap. 9.95 *(978-1-931484-87-9(2))* CrossGeneration Comics, Inc.

DiVito, Anna. Eleanor Roosevelt & the Scary Basement. Merchant, Peter. 2006. (Ready-To-read COFA Ser.). (ENG.). 32p. (J). (gr. k-2). pap. 3.99 *(978-0-689-87205-1(4),* Simon & Schuster/Paula Wiseman Bks.) Simon & Schuster/Paula Wiseman Bks.

—Thomas Edison to the Rescue! Goldsmith, Howard. 2003. (Ready-To-read COFA Ser.). (ENG.). 32p. (J). (gr. k-2). pap. 3.99 *(978-0-689-85331-9(9),* Simon Spotlight) Simon Spotlight.

—Who Was Johnny Appleseed? Holub, Joan. 2005. (Who Was... ? Ser.). (ENG.). 112p. (J). (gr. 3-7). pap. 5.99 *(978-0-448-43968-6(9),* Grosset & Dunlap) Penguin Publishing Group.

—Why Do Birds Sing? Holub, Joan. 2004. (Penguin Young Readers, Level 3 Ser.). (ENG.). 48p. (J). (gr. 1-3). mass mkt. 3.99 *(978-0-14-240106-4(4),* Puffin) Penguin Publishing Group.

—Why Do Birds Sing? Holub, Joan. 2004. (Easy-to-Read Ser.). 47p. 14.00 *(978-0-7569-3114-8(2))* Perfection Learning Corp.

—Why Do Horses Neigh? Holub, Joan. 2003. (Penguin Young Readers, Level 3 Ser.). (ENG.). 48p. (J). (gr. 1-3). pap. 3.99 *(978-0-14-230119-7(1),* Puffin) Penguin Publishing Group.

—Why Do Rabbits Hop? And Other Questions about Rabbits, Guinea Pigs, Hamsters, & Gerbils. Holub, Joan. 2003. (Penguin Young Readers, Level 3 Ser.). (ENG.). 48p. (J). (gr. 1-3). pap. 3.99 *(978-0-14-230120-3(5),* Puffin) Penguin Publishing Group.

—Why Do Snakes Hiss? And Other Questions about Snakes, Lizards, & Turtles. Holub, Joan. 2004. (Penguin Young Readers, Level 3 Ser.). (ENG.). 48p. (J). (gr. 1-3). mass mkt. 3.99 *(978-0-14-240105-7(6),* Puffin) Penguin Publishing Group.

DiVito, Anna. Annie Oakley Saves the Day. DiVito, Anna. ed. 2005. 32p. (J). lib. bdg. 15.00 *(978-1-59054-939-1(2))* Fitzgerald Bks.

—Annie Oakley Saves the Day. DiVito, Anna. 2004. (Ready-To-read COFA Ser.). (ENG.). 32p. (J). (gr. 1-3). pap. 3.99 *(978-0-689-86520-6(1),* Simon Spotlight) Simon Spotlight.

Dix, Steph, jt. illus. see Comfort, Louise.

Dixey, Kay. Life in an Irish Castle: The Journal of a 17th Century Castles in Times of Peace & War. Crosbie, Duncan. 2007. (ENG.). 19p. (J). 37.95 *(978-0-7171-4273-6(6))* Gill & MacMillan, Ltd. IRL. Dist: Dufour Editions, Inc.

Dixit, Rama. Space Travelers Land at Buckingham Palace. Walker, Peter Lancaster. 2007. 275p. (J). 19.95 *(978-1-934138-12-0(6))* Bouncing Ball Bks., Inc.

Dixon, Carol. Friends with a Difference. Pope, Ellen Dittman. 2009. (J). *(978-0-929915-92-0(5))* Headline Bks., Inc.

—If I Had My Way — /By Rock S. Wilson; Illustrated by Carol Dixon. Wilson, Rock. 2010. 32p. (J). *(978-0-929915-44-9(5))* Headline Bks., Inc.

—Pros & Cons of an Outdoor John. Brooks, Karl. 2013. 36p. pap. 24.95 *(978-1-63000-813-0(3))* America Star Bks.

Dixon, Corey. Larry, Lisa & the Missing Kite, 1 vol. McLaurin, Corey F. 2009. 20p. pap. 24.95 *(978-1-61546-590-3(1))* America Star Bks.

Dixon, Darla. What Really Happened During the Middle Ages: A Collection of Historical Biographies, 4. 2007. (What Really Happened Ser.). 222p. per. 15.95 *(978-1-932786-22-4(8))* Knowledge Quest.

—What Really Happened in Ancient Times: A Collection of Historical Biographies, 4. 2007. (What Really Happened Ser.). 240p. per. 15.95 *(978-1-932786-21-7(X))* Knowledge Quest.

—What Really Happened in Colonial Times: A Collection of Historical Biographies. Johnson, Terri. 2007. (What Really Happened Ser.). 224p. (J). (gr. 4-7). per. 15.95 *(978-1-932786-23-1(6))* Knowledge Quest.

Dixon, Debra. Cooking in a Can: More Campfire Recipes for Kids, 1 vol. White, Kate. 2006. (ENG.). 64p. (J). (gr. 4-7). pap. 9.99 *(978-1-58685-814-8(9),* 1255566) Gibbs Smith, Publisher.

Dixon, Debra Spina. Splashing by the Shore: Beach Activities for Kids, 1 vol. Mullarkey, Lisa. 2007. (ENG.). 64p. (J). (gr. 1-3). pap. 9.95 *(978-1-58685-884-1(X))* Gibbs Smith, Publisher.

Dixon, Debra Spina & Spina Dixon, Debra. Painting on a Canvas: Art Adventures for Kids, 1 vol. Wheeler, Annie. 2006. (ENG.). 64p. (J). (gr. 3-7). pap. 9.95 *(978-1-58685-839-1(4))* Gibbs Smith, Publisher.

Dixon, Gary. Blackjack's Hare Raising Adventure. Papaj, Dana. 2005. (J). *(978-1-932583-20-5(3))* digital@batesjackson llc.

Dixon, Laura Emily. Talking to a Child with Bone Marrow Disease. 2004. 32p. (J). pap. *(978-0-9755572-0-4(3))* Aplastic Anemia + MDS International Foundation.

Dixon, Nehemiah F. Ryan Elias Finds: The Truth Behind Lying. Gross, Carmen. 2008. 27p. pap. 24.95 *(978-1-60474-945-8(8))* America Star Bks.

Dixon, Rachel. Bunny Hopwell's First Spring. Fritz, Jean. 2015. (G&D Vintage Ser.). (ENG.). 32p. (J). (gr. -1-k). 7.99 *(978-0-448-48463-1(3),* Grosset & Dunlap) Penguin Publishing Group.

Dixon, Tennessee. Long Johns for a Small Chicken. Blanc, Esther Silverstein & Eagle, Godeane. 2003. (J). 16.95 *(978-1-884244-23-0(8))* volcano pr.

d'Lacey, Chris. Icefire. d'Lacey, Chris. ed. 2007. (Last Dragon Chronicles Ser.: 02). lib. bdg. 18.40 *(978-1-4177-9138-5(1),* Turtleback) Turtleback Bks.

Dlugos, Pamela J. Messages from Heaven: Be a Shining Star. Dlugos, Pamela J. Date not set. 64p. (J). (gr. 4-6). pap. 10.95 *(978-0-9661564-0-9(4))* Rejoyce Pubns.

Dmitriev, Sergei. Tales of Classical Ballet. Uralskaia, Valeria et al. Talmi, Mary, ed. Loutchinina, Ekaterina, tr. from RUS. 2004. 40p. (J). *(978-0-9743082-1-0(8),* Moscow Ballet) Sports Marketing International, Inc.

Do Gam, Rin Bo. Insects & Spiders. Cowley, Joy, ed. 2015. (Science Storybooks Ser.). (ENG.). 32p. (J). (gr. k-3). 7.99 *(978-1-925246-75-9(2),* Big and SMALL) ChoiceMaker Pty. Ltd., The AUS. Dist: Lerner Publishing Group.

Doane, Pelagie. The Phantom Friend, No. 30. Sutton, Margaret. 2008. (Judy Bolton Mysteries Ser.). (ENG.). 188p. (J). (gr. 4-7). pap. 14.95 *(978-1-4290-9050-6(2))* Applewood Bks.

—The Unfinished House, No. 11. Sutton, Margaret. 2008. (Judy Bolton Mysteries Ser.). (ENG.). 264p. (gr. 4-7). pap. 14.95 *(978-1-4290-9031-5(6))* Applewood Bks.

—The Yellow Phantom: A Judy Bolton Mystery. Sutton, Margaret. 2011. 222p. 44.95 *(978-1-258-10044-5(4))* Literary Licensing, LLC.

Dob, Bob. Blimpo Vol. 3: The Third Circle of Heck. Basye, Dale E. 2011. (Heck Ser.). (ENG.). 464p. (J). (gr. 3-7). pap. 7.99 *(978-0-375-85677-8(3))* Random Hse., Inc.

—Fibble. Basye, Dale E. 2012. (Heck Ser.). (ENG.). 384p. (J). (gr. 4-7). pap. 6.99 *(978-0-375-85679-2(X))* Random Hse., Inc.

—Precocia: the Sixth Circle of Heck. Basye, Dale E. 2013. (Heck Ser.). (ENG.). 432p. (J). (gr. 3-7). 6.99 *(978-0-375-86807-8(0),* Yearling) Random Hse. Children's Bks.

—Rapacia. Basye, Dale E. 2010. (Heck Ser.). (ENG.). 384p. (J). (gr. 3-7). pap. 6.99 *(978-0-375-84078-4(8))* Random Hse., Inc.

—Snivel: the Fifth Circle of Heck. Basye, Dale E. 2013. (Heck Ser.). (ENG.). 448p. (J). (gr. 4-7). 7.99 *(978-0-375-86806-1(2),* Yearling) Random Hse. Children's Bks.

—Where the Bad Kids Go. Basye, Dale E. 2009. (Heck Ser.). (ENG.). 304p. (J). (gr. 3-7). 6.99 *(978-0-375-84076-0(1))* Random Hse., Inc.

—Wise Acres: the Seventh Circle of Heck. Basye, Dale E. (Heck Ser.). (ENG.). 448p. (J). (gr. 4-7). 2014. 8.99 *(978-0-307-98188-2(6),* Yearling); 2013. 16.99 *(978-0-307-98185-1(1),* Random Hse. Bks. for Young Readers) Random Hse. Children's Bks.

Dobbins, Erin. B Is for Baylor. Cook, Jane Hampton. 2010. (Big Bear Bks.). (ENG.). 64p. (gr. 17). 29.95 *(978-1-60258-270-5(X))* Baylor Univ. Pr.

Dobbyn, Nigel. Macbeth. Shakespeare, William. Sutliff Sanders, Joe, tr. 2008. (ENG.). 144p. (gr. 4-18). pap. 16.95 *(978-1-906332-46-4(0));* (gr. 5-18). pap. 16.95 *(978-1-906332-45-7(2));* (gr. 7-18). pap. 16.95 *(978-1-906332-44-0(4))* Classical Comics GBR. (Classical Comics, Ltd.). Dist: Perseus-PGW.

Dobi, Rob. Wish You Were Here: An Essential Guide to Your Favorite Music Scenes - From Punk to Indie & Everything in Between. Simon, Leslie & Kelley, Trevor. 2009. (ENG.). 256p. pap. 14.99 *(978-0-06-157371-2(X))* HarperCollins Pubs.

Dobler, Shirley Jean. Permilia: A Western Children's Book. Pierce, Mary E. 2013. 62p. (J). 25.00 *(978-1-936617-15-9(3))* Lemon Pr. LLC.

Dobrescu, Irina. King Thrushbeard. Bruder Grimm Staff. 2014. (ENG.). 32p. (J). 17.95 *(978-0-7358-4192-5(6))* North-South Bks., Inc.

d'Obrin, Felix. ZZ Dogs. Franks, T. S. 2003. (J). 15.99 *(978-0-9722304-0-7(8),* 5000, ZZ Dogs Pr.) That's Life Publishing, Inc.

Dobson, Clive. Jessica's X-Ray. Zonta, Pat. 2006. (ENG.). 24p. (J). (gr. 1-3). 19.95 *(978-1-55297-578-7(9),* 9781552975787); pap. 8.95 *(978-1-55297-577-0(0),* 9781552975770) Firefly Bks., Ltd.

Dobson, Clive, et al. Let's Call It Canada: Amazing Stories of Canadian Place Names. Hughes, Susan. 2009. (Wow Canada! Ser.). (ENG.). 96p. (J). (gr. 3-6). pap. 19.95 *(978-1-897349-53-3(X),* Maple Tree Pr.) Owlkids Bks. Inc. CAN. Dist: Perseus-PGW.

Dobson, Len. Diamond Downhill. Dingles, Molly. 2005. (Community of Shapes Ser.). 32p. (J). pap. 10.95 *(978-1-59646-240-3(X));* lib. bdg. 21.65 *(978-1-59646-043-0(1));* per. 10.95 *(978-1-59646-241-0(8))* Dingles & Co.

—Diamond Downhill/Cuesta abajo en forma de Rombo. Dingles, Molly. 2005. (Community of Shapes Ser.).Tr. of Cuesta abajo en forma de Rombo. (ENG & SPA.). 32p. (J). pap. 10.95 *(978-1-59646-242-7(6));* lib. bdg. 20.65 *(978-1-59646-044-7(X));* per. 10.95 *(978-1-59646-243-4(4))* Dingles & Co.

—Rectangle Ranch. Dingles, Molly. 2005. (Community of Shapes Ser.). 32p. (J). pap. 10.95 *(978-1-59646-244-1(2));* lib. bdg. 21.65 *(978-1-59646-035-5(0));* per. 10.95 *(978-1-59646-245-8(0))* Dingles & Co.

—Rectangle Ranch/Rancho Rectangular. Dingles, Molly. 2005. (Community of Shapes Ser.).Tr. of Rancho Rectangular. (ENG & SPA.). 32p. (J). pap. 10.95 *(978-1-59646-246-5(9));* lib. bdg. 20.65 *(978-1-59646-036-2(9));* per. 10.95 *(978-1-59646-247-2(7))* Dingles & Co.

Dobson, Leonard. This Little Piggy Went to Market. 2005. (ENG.). 6p. (J). (gr. -1-7). bds. 7.95 *(978-1-59354-040-1(X),* Handprint Bks.) Chronicle Bks. LLC.

Dobson, Phil, jt. illus. see Jude, Connie.

Dobson, S. Gaston. A Salute to Black Civil Rights Leaders. Green, Richard L. et al, eds. (Empak "Black History" Publication). (J). pap. 1.00 *(978-0-9616156-3-5(X))* Empak Publishing Co.

Docampo, Valeria. Always Daddy's Princess, 1 vol. Kingsbury, Karen. rev. ed. 2013. (ENG.). 32p. (J). 15.99 *(978-0-310-71647-1(0))* Zonderkidz.

—Cara & the Wizard, 2 vols. Flannigan, Liz. 2013. (ENG.). 48p. (J). pap. 7.99 *(978-1-84686-780-4(0))* Barefoot Bks., Inc.

—Celebrate Kwanzaa with Boots & Her Kittens. Flor Ada, Alma. 2007. (Cuentos para Celebrar / Stories to Celebrate Ser.). 30p. (gr. k-6). per. 11.95 *(978-1-59820-135-2(2))* Santillana USA Publishing Co., Inc.

—Dangerously Ever After. Slater, Dashka. 2012. (ENG.). 40p. (J). (gr. k-3). 16.99 *(978-0-8037-3374-9(7),* Dial) Penguin Publishing Group.

—The House at the End of Ladybug Lane. Primavera, Elise. 2012. (ENG.). 40p. (J). (gr. -1-3). 16.99 *(978-0-375-85584-9(X),* Robin Corey Bks.) Random Hse. Children's Bks.

—The Library Pages. Morton, Carlene. 2010. 32p. (J). (gr. k-4). 17.95 *(978-1-60213-045-6(0),* Upstart Bks.) Highsmith Inc.

—Medio Pollito: A Spanish Tale, 0 vols. Kimmel, Eric A. 2010. (ENG.). 32p. (J). (gr. k-3). 17.99 *(978-0-7614-5705-3(4),* 9780761457053, Amazon Children's Publishing) Amazon Publishing.

Docampo, Valeria. Oni & the Eagle. Flanagan, Liz. 2014. (J). *(978-1-84686-876-4(9))* Barefoot Bks., Ltd.

Docampo, Valeria. Penelope Crumb Never Forgets. Stout, Shawn K. 2013. (Penelope Crumb Ser.: 2). (ENG.). 208p. (J). (gr. 2-5). pap. 5.99 *(978-0-14-751009-9(0),* Puffin) Penguin Publishing Group.

—Phileas's Fortune: A Story about Self-Expression. Lestrade, Agnès de & Frank-McNeil, Julia. 2010. 40p. (J). (gr. -1-3). 14.95 *(978-1-4338-0790-9(4));* pap. 9.95 *(978-1-4338-0792-3(0))* American Psychological Assn. (Magination Pr.).

—Starlight Grey. Flannigan, Liz. 2013. (ENG.). 48p. (J). pap. 7.99 *(978-1-84686-778-1(9))* Barefoot Bks., Inc.

—The Three Little Tamales, 0 vols. Kimmel, Eric A. 2009. (ENG.). 40p. (J). (gr. -1-3). 17.99 *(978-0-7614-5519-6(1),* 9780761455196, Amazon Children's Publishing) Amazon Publishing.

—Tip-Tap Pop, 0 vols. Lynn, Sarah. 2010. (ENG.). 32p. (J). (gr. -1-4). 17.99 *(978-0-7614-5712-1(7),* 9780761457121, Amazon Children's Publishing) Amazon Publishing.

DoCampo, Valeria. Whatever You Grow up to Be, 1 vol. Kingsbury, Karen. 2015. (ENG.). 24p. (J). bds. 7.99 *(978-0-310-74512-9(8))* Zonderkidz.

Docampo, Valeria. Whatever You Grow up to Be, 1 vol. Kingsbury, Karen. rev. ed. 2014. (ENG.). 32p. (J). 15.99 *(978-0-310-71646-4(2))* Zonderkidz.

Docampo, Valeria. Celebra Kwanzaa con Botitas y Sus Gatitos. Docampo, Valeria. Flor Ada, Alma. 2007. (Cuentos para Celebrar / Stories to Celebrate Ser.). 30p. (gr. k-6). pap. 11.95 *(978-1-59820-123-9(9))* Santillana USA Publishing Co., Inc.

Docherty, Helen. The Snatchabook. Docherty, Helen. 2013. (ENG.). 32p. (J). (-2). 16.99 *(978-1-4022-9082-4(9),* Sourcebooks Jabberwocky) Sourcebooks, Inc.

Docherty, Thomas. The Lighthouse under the Clouds. Gutzschhahn, Uwe-Michael. 2008. (ENG.). 32p. (J). (gr. -1-k). 19.00 *(978-1-906367-03-9(5))* National Maritime Museum GBR. Dist: Independent Pubs. Group.

Docherty, Thomas. Big Scary Monster. Docherty, Thomas. 2010. (ENG.). 40p. (J). (gr. -1-2). 15.99 *(978-0-7636-4787-2(X),* Templar) Candlewick Pr.

—Little Boat. Docherty, Thomas. 2009. (ENG.). 40p. (J). (gr. -1-2). 15.99 *(978-0-7636-4428-4(5))* Candlewick Pr.

—To the Beach. Docherty, Thomas. 2009. (ENG.). 40p. (J). (gr. -1-2). 15.99 *(978-0-7636-4429-1(3))* Candlewick Pr.

—Wash-A-Bye Bear. Docherty, Thomas. 2013. (ENG.). 32p. (J). (gr. -1-2). 14.99 *(978-0-7636-6486-2(3),* Templar) Candlewick Pr.

Dockery, Amanda. Boogers from Beyond #3. Payne, M. D. 2014. (Monster Juice Ser.: 3). (ENG.). 192p. (J). (gr. 3-7). 5.99 *(978-0-448-46228-8(1),* Grosset & Dunlap) Penguin Publishing Group.

—Fartsunami. Payne, M. D. 2013. (Monster Juice Ser.: 2). (ENG.). 192p. (J). (gr. 3-7). pap. 5.99 *(978-0-448-46227-1(3),* Grosset & Dunlap) Penguin Publishing Group.

—Fear the Barfitron. Payne, M. D. 2013. (Monster Juice Ser.: 1). (ENG.). 192p. (J). (gr. 3-7). pap. 5.99 *(978-0-448-46226-4(5),* Grosset & Dunlap) Penguin Publishing Group.

—Sickening Secrets from Raven Hill (Books 1 And 2) Payne, M. D. 2015. (Monster Juice Ser.). (ENG.). 384p. (J). (gr. 3-7). 8.99 *(978-0-448-48911-7(2),* Grosset & Dunlap) Penguin Publishing Group.

Dockery, Amanda & Zoo, Keith. Burpstronauts, No. 4. Payne, M. D. 2014. (Monster Juice Ser.: 4). (ENG.). 192p. (J). (gr. 3-7). 5.99 *(978-0-448-46229-5(X),* Grosset & Dunlap) Penguin Publishing Group.

Dockray, Tracy. Izzy & Oscar. Estes, Allison & Stark, Dan. 2015. (ENG.). 40p. (J). (-2). 16.99 *(978-1-4926-0150-0(0),* Sourcebooks Jabberwocky) Sourcebooks, Inc.

—Jammy Dance, 1 vol. Janni, Rebecca. 2012. (ENG.). 40p. (J). (gr. -1-1). 16.99 *(978-0-374-33680-6(6),* Farrar, Straus & Giroux (BYR)) Farrar, Straus & Giroux.

—Sweet Baby Feet, 1 vol. O'Hair, Margaret. 2012. (ENG.). 28p. (J). (gr. -1 — 1). 14.99 *(978-0-374-37348-1(5),* Farrar, Straus & Giroux (BYR)) Farrar, Straus & Giroux.

—The Tushy Book. Manushkin, Fran. (ENG.). (J). (gr. -1-k). 2011. 20p. bds. 6.99 *(978-0-312-65913-4(X));* 2009. 32p. 14.99 *(978-0-312-36926-2(3))* Feiwel & Friends.

Dockray, Tracy. The Lost & Found Pony. Dockray, Tracy. 2011. (ENG.). 48p. (J). (gr. -1-3). 17.99 *(978-0-312-59259-2(0))* Feiwel & Friends.

—My Life Story. Dockray, Tracy. 2003. 40p. (J). lib. bdg. 15.95 *(978-1-58717-218-2(6),* SeaStar Bks.) Chronicle Bks. LLC.

Dockray, Tracy & Rogers, Jacqueline. Beezus & Ramona. Cleary, Beverly. movie tie-in ed. 2010. (Ramona Ser.: 1). (ENG.). 208p. (J). (gr. 3-7). pap. 5.99 *(978-0-06-191461-4(4),* HarperFestival) HarperCollins Pubs.

—The Complete Ramona Collection: Beezus & Ramona; Ramona & Her Father; Ramona & Her Mother; Ramona Quimby; Age 8; Ramona Forever; Ramona the Brave; Ramona the Pest; Ramona's World. Cleary, Beverly. 2013. (J). (gr. 3-7). pap. 44.99 *(978-0-06-196090-1(X))* HarperCollins Pubs.

—The Ramona Collection Vol. 1: Beezus & Ramona, Ramona & Her Father, Ramona the Brave, Ramona the Pest. Cleary, Beverly. 2013. (Ramona Collections). (ENG.). (J). (gr. 3-7). pap. 22.99 *(978-0-06-124647-0(6))* HarperCollins Pubs.

—The Ramona Collection Vol. 2: Ramona & Her Mother; Ramona Quimby, Age 8; Ramona Forever; Ramona's World. Cleary, Beverly. 2013. (ENG.). (J). (gr. 3-7). pap. 22.99 *(978-0-06-124648-7(4))* HarperCollins Pubs.

—Ramona's World. Cleary, Beverly. movie tie-in ed. 2010. (Ramona Ser.: 8). (ENG.). 240p. (J). (gr. 3-7). pap. 5.99 *(978-0-06-169407-7(9),* HarperFestival) HarperCollins Pubs.

Dockray, Tracy, jt. illus. see Darling, Louis.

Dockray, Tracy, jt. illus. see Tiegreen, Alan.

Dockray, Tracy Arah, jt. illus. see Howard, Linda.

Docktor, Irv. We Were There in the Klondike Gold Rush. Appel, Benjamin & Clark, Henry W. 2011. 188p. 42.95 *(978-1-258-05908-8(8))* Literary Licensing, LLC.

Dodd, Emma. All Sorts of Numbers. Reidy, Hannah. 2005. (All Sorts of Things Ser.). (ENG.). 24p. (gr. -1-1). 25.99 *(978-1-4048-1062-4(5),* Nonfiction Picture Bks.) Picture Window Bks.

—Big Brothers Don't Take Naps. Borden, Louise. 2011. (ENG.). 32p. (J). (gr. -1-3). 17.99 *(978-1-4169-5503-0(8),* McElderry, Margaret K. Bks.) McElderry, Margaret K. Bks.

—Hetty's 100 Hats, 1 vol. Slingsby, Janet. 2005. (ENG.). 40p. (J). (gr. -1-3). pap. 16.00 *(978-1-56148-456-0(3),* Good Bks.) Skyhorse Publishing Co., Inc.

—I Love My Daddy. Andreae, Giles. 2014. (ENG.). 26p. (J). (gr. -1 — 1). bds. 6.99 *(978-1-4231-9970-0(7))* Hyperion Bks. for Children.

Dodd, Emma. I Love My Grandma. Andreae, Giles. 2016. (J). *(978-1-4847-3407-0(6))* Disney Pr.

Dodd, Emma. I Love My Mommy. Andreae, Giles. 2013. (ENG.). 26p. (J). (gr. -1-k). bds. 6.99 *(978-1-4231-6825-6(9))* Hyperion Pr.

—Let's Make a Movie. Smith, Kath. 2003. (ENG.). 32p. (J). *(978-1-84089-190-4(4))* Zero to Ten, Ltd.

—My Mum's Best. Nilsen, Anna. 2011. 24p. bds. *(978-1-84089-679-4(5))* Zero to Ten, Ltd.

Dodd, Emma. Always. Dodd, Emma. 2014. (Emma Dodd's Love You Bks.). (ENG.). 24p. (J). (-k). 12.99 *(978-0-7636-7544-8(X)*, Templar) Candlewick Pr.

—Baby & Me. Dodd, Emma. Nosy Crow Staff. 2013. (ENG.). 16p. (J). (gr. -1-2). 14.99 *(978-0-7636-6544-9(4)*, Nosy Crow) Candlewick Pr.

—Cinderelephant. Dodd, Emma. 2013. (ENG.). 32p. (J). (gr. -1-3). 16.99 *(978-0-545-53285-3(X)*, Levine, Arthur A. Bks.) Scholastic, Inc.

—Dog's Colorful Day: A Messy Story about Colors & Counting. Dodd, Emma. 2003. (ENG.). 32p. (J). (gr. k-k). 5.99 *(978-0-14-250019-4(4)*, Puffin) Penguin Publishing Group.

—Everything. Dodd, Emma. 2015. (Emma Dodd's Love You Bks.). (ENG.). 24p. (J). (-k). 12.99 *(978-0-7636-7128-0(2)*, Templar) Candlewick Pr.

—Forever. Dodd, Emma. 2013. (Emma Dodd's Love You Bks.). (ENG.). 24p. (J). (-k). 12.99 *(978-0-7636-7132-7(0)*, Templar) Candlewick Pr.

—Foxy. Dodd, Emma. 2012. (ENG.). 40p. (J). (gr. -1-2). 14.99 *(978-0-06-201419-1(6))* HarperCollins Pubs.

—Foxy in Love. Dodd, Emma. 2013. (ENG.). 40p. (J). (gr. -1-3). 17.99 *(978-0-06-201422-1(6))* HarperCollins Pubs.

—Go to Bed. Dodd, Emma. 2010. (Dot & Dash Ser.). (ENG.). 12p. (J). (gr. -1 — 1). pap. 4.99 *(978-0-545-22673-8(2)*, Cartwheel Bks.) Scholastic, Inc.

—I Am Small. Dodd, Emma. 2011. (ENG.). 32p. (J). (gr. k — 1). 8.99 *(978-0-545-35370-0(X)*, Cartwheel Bks.) Scholastic, Inc.

—I Love Bugs. Dodd, Emma. (ENG.). 32p. (J). 2011. pap. 6.95 *(978-0-8234-2345-3(X))*; 2010. (gr. -1-k). 16.95 *(978-0-8234-2280-7(1))* Holiday Hse., Inc.

—Lots of Love. Dodd, Emma. 2010. (Dot & Dash Ser.). (ENG.). 14p. (J). (gr. -1 — 1). pap. 4.99 *(978-0-545-23690-4(8)*, Cartwheel Bks.) Scholastic, Inc.

—Meow Said the Cow. Dodd, Emma. 2011. (ENG.). 40p. (J). (gr. -1-3). 16.99 *(978-0-545-31861-7(0)*, Levine, Arthur A. Bks.) Scholastic, Inc.

—More & More. Dodd, Emma. 2014. (ENG.). 24p. (J). (-k). 12.99 *(978-0-7636-7543-1(1)*, Templar) Candlewick Pr.

Dodd, Emma. When I Grow Up. Dodd, Emma. 2015. (Emma Dodd's Love You Bks.). (ENG.). 24p. (J). (-k). 12.99 ***(978-0-7636-7985-9(2)***, Templar) Candlewick Pr.

Dodd, Emma. When You Were Born. Dodd, Emma. 2015. (Emma Dodd's Love You Bks.). (ENG.). 24p. (J). (-k). 12.99 *(978-0-7636-7405-2(2)*, Templar) Candlewick Pr.

Dodd, Joseph D. Kraken Ka The Komodo Dragon. Belknap, Jodi P. & Montgomery, Tamara. 2007. 32p. pap. 19.95 incl. audio compact disk *(978-0-9723420-7-0(9))* Belknap Publishing & Design.

Dodd, Lynley. Hairy Maclary's Caterwaul Caper. Dodd, Lynley. 2009. (Hairy Maclary & Friends Ser.). (ENG.). 32p. (J). (gr. -1-2). pap. 6.99 *(978-1-58246-307-0(7))* Ten Speed Pr.

—Hairy Maclary's Showbusiness. Dodd, Lynley. 2007. (Hairy Maclary & Friends Ser.). (ENG.). 32p. (J). (gr. -1-2). pap. 6.99 *(978-1-58246-208-0(9)*, Tricycle Pr.) Ten Speed Pr.

—Slinky Malinki Catflaps. Dodd, Lynley. 2006. (Slinky Malinki Ser.). (ENG.). 32p. (J). (gr. -1-2). pap. 6.99 *(978-1-58246-175-5(9)*, Tricycle Pr.) Ten Speed Pr.

—Zachary Quack Minimonster. Dodd, Lynley. 2006. (Gold Star First Readers Ser.). 32p. (gr. -1-3). lib. bdg. 23.00 *(978-0-8368-6187-7(6)*, Gareth Stevens Learning Library) Stevens, Gareth Publishing LLLP.

Dodd, Marion. Mystic by the A,B, Sea. Dodd, Marion. 2006. (J). 17.95 *(978-0-9773725-2-2(9))* Flat Hammock Pr.

Dodge, Barbara A. Counting on the Bay. Siwak, Brenda S. 2006. (J). per. 14.95 *(978-0-9790906-0-8(1))* Pleasant Plains Pr.

Dodson, Bert. An Affectionate Farewell: the Story of Old Abe & Old Bob. Krisher, Trudy. 2015. (ENG.). 32p. (J). (gr. 1-5). 17.95 ***(978-1-59373-155-7(8))*** Bunker Hill Publishing, Inc.

Dodson, Bert. Cousin John: The Story of a Boy & a Small Smart Pig. Paine, Walter. 2006. (ENG.). 96p. (J). (gr. 3-7). 17.95 *(978-1-59373-057-4(8))* Bunker Hill Publishing, Inc.

—Favor Johnson: A Christmas Story. Lange, Willem. 2009. (ENG.). 32p. (J). (gr. 1-3). 16.95 *(978-1-59373-082-6(9))* Bunker Hill Publishing, Inc.

—Finch Discoveries: An Inspiring Tale of Adaptation to a Changing Environment. Wallis, Ginger. 2013. 34p. pap. 12.95 *(978-0-9847662-2-2(7))* Dancing Journey Pr.

—Grammie's Secret Cupboard. Reynolds, Cynthia Furlong. 2007. 32p. (J). (gr. -1-3). 17.95 *(978-1-58726-310-1(6)*, Mitten Pr.) Ann Arbor Editions LLC.

—Kami & the Yaks. Stryer, Andrea Stenn. 2007. (ENG.). 48p. (J). (gr. k-2). 17.95 *(978-0-9778961-0-3(2))* Bay Otter Pr.

—Paul Revere & the Bell Ringers. Winter, Jonah. ed. 2005. 32p. (J). lib. bdg. 15.00 *(978-1-59054-952-0(X))* Fitzgerald Bks.

—Paul Revere & the Bell Ringers. Winter, Jonah. 2003. (Ready-To-read COFA Ser.). (ENG.). 32p. (J). (gr. k-2). pap. 3.99 *(978-0-689-85635-8(0)*, Simon Spotlight) Simon Spotlight.

—Stranger in Right Field. Christopher, Matt. 2009. 64p. (J). lib. bdg. 22.60 *(978-1-59953-322-3(7))* Norwood Hse. Pr.

—Super Grandpa. 2nd rev. ed. 2005. 32p. (J). (gr. -1 — 1). 18.95 *(978-1-889910-33-8(3))* Tortuga Pr.

—Superabuelo. Schwartz, David M. Guzman, Martin Luis, tr. 2005. (SPA.). (J). 32p. (gr. -1-4). pap. 18.95 incl. audio compact disk *(978-1-889910-37-6(6))*; pap. 6.95 *(978-1-889910-38-3(4))* Tortuga Pr.

—The White-Footed Mouse. Lange, Willem. 2012. (ENG.). 32p. (J). (gr. 1-3). 17.95 *(978-1-59373-109-0(4))* Bunker Hill Publishing, Inc.

Dodson, Bert. Helping Santa: My First Christmas Adventure with Grandma. Dodson, Bert. 2011. (ENG.). 32p. (J). (gr. 1-3). 17.95 *(978-1-59373-093-2(4))* Bunker Hill Publishing, Inc.

Dodson, Emma. Hattie the Dancing Hippo. Powell, Jillian. 2009. (Get Ready (Windmill Books) Ser.). 32p. (J). (gr. k-2). lib. bdg. 22.60 *(978-1-60754-264-3(1))* Windmill Bks.

—Hattie the Dancing Hippo. Powell, Jillian. 2011. 32p. pap. *(978-1-84089-709-8(0))* Zero to Ten, Ltd.

—Hooey Higgins & the Shark. Voake, Steve. 2012. (ENG.). 112p. (J). (gr. 2-5). 14.99 *(978-0-7636-5782-6(4))* Candlewick Pr.

—Hooey Higgins & the Tremendous Trousers. Voake, Steve. 2014. (ENG.). 144p. (J). (gr. 2-5). 14.99 *(978-0-7636-6923-2(7))* Candlewick Pr.

Dodson, Emma. Speckle the Spider. Dodson, Emma. 2010. (ENG.). 32p. (J). (gr. -1-2). 14.99 *(978-0-7636-4778-0(0))* Candlewick Pr.

—The Very Important Idea. Dodson, Emma. 2007. (ENG.). 32p. (J). (gr. -1-k). 19.95 *(978-0-340-87808-8(8))* Hachette Children's Group GBR. Dist: Independent Pubs. Group.

Dodson, Terry, et al. X-Men - Age of Apocalypse Omnibus Companion. Mackie, Howard et al. 2014. (ENG.). 992p. (J). (gr. 4-17). 99.99 *(978-0-7851-8514-7(3))* Marvel Worldwide, Inc.

Dodson, Terry & Cho, Frank. Spider-Man by Mark Millar Ultimate Collection. Millar, Mark & Santoro, Frank. 2011. (ENG.). 304p. (YA). (gr. 8-17). pap. 34.99 *(978-0-7851-5640-6(2))* Marvel Worldwide, Inc.

Dodson, Terry & Land, Greg. X-Men: Nation X. 2010. (ENG.). 360p. (YA). (gr. 8-17). pap. 29.99 *(978-0-7851-4103-7(0))* Marvel Worldwide, Inc.

Dodson, Terry & Pierfederici, Mirco. Defenders by Matt Fraction - Volume 2. Fraction, Matt. 2013. (ENG.). 136p. (YA). (gr. 8-17). pap. 19.99 *(978-0-7851-5853-0(7))* Marvel Worldwide, Inc.

Dodwell, Dayle. My Goat Gertrude, 1 vol. Dobson, Starr. ed. 2012. (ENG.). 32p. (J). (gr. -1-3). 18.95 *(978-1-55109-861-6(X))* Nimbus Publishing, Ltd. CAN. Dist: Orca Bk. Pubs. USA.

—My Goat Gertrude (pb), 1 vol. Dobson, Starr. ed. 2013. (ENG.). 32p. (J). (gr. -1-3). pap. 12.95 *(978-1-55109-920-0(9))* Nimbus Publishing, Ltd. CAN. Dist: Orca Bk. Pubs. USA.

Doe, Juan, jt. illus. see Haspiel, Dean.

Doehring, Aurora. The Bible According to Grandpa. Bernstein, Jordan. 2011. 34p. pap. 6.50 *(978-0-9743414-3-9(6))* Adventure in Discovery.

Doehring, Phoebe. Chip's Sharing Day. Derkez, Linda. 2012. 16p. pap. 9.95 *(978-1-61633-245-7(X))* Guardian Angel Publishing, Inc.

Doell, Glenn. Creative Coloring Books: The What If. . . series. Doell, Glenn, concept. 2003. (What If. . . ser.). 41p. (J). spiral bd. 8.95 *(978-0-9742438-0-1(9))* Curtis Elliott Designs, Ltd.

Doering, Kimber. Two Beautiful Butterflies. Moody, Gloria. l.t. ed. 2005. 25p. (YA). per. 8.99 *(978-1-59879-002-3(1))* Lifevest Publishing, Inc.

Doerrfeld, Cori. Barnyard Baby. Broach, Elise. 2013. (Baby Seasons Ser.). (ENG.). 14p. (J). (gr. -1 — 1). bds. 7.99 *(978-0-316-21203-8(2))* Little, Brown Bks. for Young Readers.

—The Cold Winter Day, 1 vol. Emerson, Carl. 2008. (Read-It! Readers: Science Ser.). (ENG.). 32p. (gr. k-2). lib. bdg. 19.99 *(978-1-4048-2627-4(0)*, Easy Readers) Picture Window Bks.

—Goalkeeper Goof, 1 vol. Meister, Cari. 2009. (My First Graphic Novel Ser.). (ENG.). 32p. (gr. k-2). pap. 6.25 *(978-1-4342-1409-6(5))*; lib. bdg. 23.32 *(978-1-4342-1292-4(0))* Stone Arch Bks. (My First Graphic Novel).

—Learning about Fiction, 1 vol. Rustad, Martha E. H. 2014. (Language Arts Ser.). (ENG.). 24p. (gr. k-1). 24.65 *(978-1-4914-0578-9(3))* Capstone Pr., Inc.

—Make Me Giggle: Writing Your Own Silly Story, 1 vol. Loewen, Nancy. 2009. (Writer's Toolbox Ser.). (ENG.). 32p. (gr. 2-4). lib. bdg. 26.65 *(978-1-4048-5518-2(1)*, Nonfiction Picture Bks.) Picture Window Bks.

—Rah-Rah Ruby!, 1 vol. Jones, Christianne C. 2009. (My First Graphic Novel Ser.). (ENG.). 32p. (gr. k-2). pap. 6.25 *(978-1-4342-1412-6(5))*; lib. bdg. 23.32 *(978-1-4342-1298-6(X))* Stone Arch Bks. (My First Graphic Novel).

—Snowflake Baby. Broach, Elise. 2011. (Baby Seasons Ser.). (ENG.). 14p. (J). (gr. -1 — 1). bds. 7.99 *(978-0-316-12926-8(7))* Little, Brown Bks. for Young Readers.

—Springtime Baby. Broach, Elise. 2014. (Baby Seasons Ser.). (ENG.). 14p. (J). (gr. -1 — 1). bds. 7.99 *(978-0-316-23526-6(1))* Little, Brown Bks. for Young Readers.

—Welcome to Your World, Baby. Shields, Brooke. 2008. 32p. (J). (gr. -1-3). lib. bdg. 17.89 *(978-0-06-125312-6(X))* HarperCollins Pubs.

Doerrfeld, Cori & Lyles, Christopher. Make Me Giggle: Writing Your Own Silly Story, 1 vol. Loewen, Nancy. 2009. (Writer's Toolbox Ser.). (ENG.). 32p. (gr. 2-4). pap. 8.95 *(978-1-4048-5704-9(4)*, Nonfiction Picture Bks.) Picture Window Bks.

Doery, Marya. The Squid Kids. Robinson, Virginia. 2008. 44p. pap. 24.95 *(978-1-4241-9901-3(8))* America Star Bks.

Doescher, Erik. Bizarro Is Born!, 1 vol. Simonson, Louise et al. 2013. (Superman Ser.). (ENG.). 56p. (gr. 2-3). pap. 4.95 *(978-1-4342-1725-7(6)*, DC Super Heroes) Stone Arch Bks.

—Bizarro Is Born!, 1 vol. Simonson, Louise et al. 2009. (Superman Ser.). (ENG.). 56p. (gr. 2-3). 25.32 *(978-1-4342-1567-3(9)*, DC Super Heroes) Stone Arch Bks.

—Captain Cold's Arctic Eruption, 1 vol. Mason, Jane B. et al. 2011. (Flash Ser.). (ENG.). 56p. (gr. 2-3). pap. 4.95 *(978-1-4342-3089-8(9))*; lib. bdg. 25.32 *(978-1-4342-2617-4(4))* Stone Arch Bks. (DC Super Heroes).

—DC Super Friends to the Rescue. Bright, J. E. 2012. (Lift-The Flap Ser.: 1). (ENG.). 10p. (J). (gr. -1-1). bds. 9.99 *(978-0-7944-2578-4(X))* Reader's Digest Assn., Inc., The.

—Gorilla Warfare, 1 vol. Sutton, Laurie S. et al. 2011. (Flash Ser.). (ENG.). 56p. (gr. 2-3). pap. 4.95 *(978-1-4342-3087-4(2))*; lib. bdg. 25.32 *(978-1-4342-2618-1(2))* Stone Arch Bks. (DC Super Heroes).

Doescher, Erik, et al. Heroes United! - Attack of the Robot! Shealy, Dennis & Random House Staff. 2008. (Pictureback Ser.). (ENG.). 32p. (J). (gr. -1-2). pap. 4.99 *(978-0-375-84409-6(0)*, Random Hse. Bks. for Young Readers) Random Hse. Children's Bks.

—Heroes vs. Villains/Space Chase! (DC Super Friends) Wrecks, Billy. 2013. (Deluxe Pictureback Ser.). (ENG.). 32p. (J). (gr. -1-2). pap. 4.99 *(978-0-307-97616-1(5)*, Random Hse. Bks. for Young Readers) Random Hse. Children's Bks.

Doescher, Erik. How to Draw Batman & His Friends & Foes. Sautter, Aaron. 2015. (Drawing DC Super Heroes Ser.). (ENG.). 32p. (gr. 3-6). lib. bdg. 27.32 *(978-1-4914-2153-6(3))* Capstone Pr., Inc.

—How to Draw Superman & His Friends & Foes. Sautter, Aaron. 2015. (Drawing DC Super Heroes Ser.). (ENG.). 32p. (gr. 3-6). lib. bdg. 27.32 *(978-1-4914-2156-7(8))* Capstone Pr., Inc.

—Reptile Rumble! Wrecks, Billy. 2014. (Step into Reading Ser.). (ENG.). 32p. (J). (gr. -1-1). 3.99 *(978-0-385-37403-3(8)*, Random Hse. Bks. for Young Readers) Random Hse. Children's Bks.

—Reptile Rumble! (DC Super Friends) Wrecks, Billy. 2014. (Step into Reading Ser.). (ENG.). 32p. (J). (gr. -1-1). lib. bdg. 12.99 *(978-0-385-37404-0(6)*, Random Hse. Bks. for Young Readers) Random Hse. Children's Bks.

—Shell Shocker, 1 vol. Sonneborn, Scott et al. 2011. (Flash Ser.). (ENG.). 56p. (gr. 2-3). pap. 4.95 *(978-1-4342-3092-8(9)*, DC Super Heroes) Stone Arch Bks.

—Shell Shocker, 1 vol. DeCarlo, Mike et al. 2011. (Flash Ser.). (ENG.). 56p. (gr. 2-3). lib. bdg. 25.32 *(978-1-4342-2615-0(8)*, DC Super Heroes) Stone Arch Bks.

—Super-Villain Showdown, 1 vol. Kupperberg, Paul et al. (Superman Ser.). (ENG.). 56p. (gr. 2-3). 2013. pap. 4.95 *(978-1-4342-1736-3(1))*; 2009. lib. bdg. 25.32 *(978-1-4342-1570-3(9))* Stone Arch Bks. (DC Super Heroes).

—Wrath of the Weather Wizard, 1 vol. Lemke, Donald B. et al. 2011. (Flash Ser.). (ENG.). 56p. (gr. 2-3). pap. 4.95 *(978-1-4342-3090-4(2))*; lib. bdg. 25.32 *(978-1-4342-2613-6(1))* Stone Arch Bks. (DC Super Heroes).

Doescher, Erik & DeCarlo, Mike. Mighty Mazes (DC Super Friends) Wrecks, Billy. 2013. (Super Color with Stickers Ser.). (ENG.). 96p. (J). (gr. -1-2). pap. 3.99 *(978-0-307-98118-9(5)*, Golden Bks.) Random Hse. Children's Bks.

Doescher, Erik & Levins, Tim. Drawing DC Super Heroes. Sautter, Aaron. 2015. (Drawing DC Super Heroes Ser.). (ENG.). 32p. (gr. 3-6). lib. bdg. 109.28 ***(978-1-4914-2553-4(9)***, DC Super Heroes) Stone Arch Bks.

Doescher, Erik & Levins, Tim. How to Draw Batman, Superman, & Other DC Super Heroes & Villains. Sautter, Aaron. 2015. (DC Super Heroes Ser.). (ENG.). 144p. (gr. 3-6). pap. 14.95 *(978-1-62370-231-1(3))* Capstone Pr., Inc.

Doescher, Erik & Marrucchi, Elisa. Battle in Space! (DC Super Friends) Wrecks, Billy. 2015. (Glow-In-the-Dark Pictureback Ser.). (ENG.). 16p. (J). (gr. -1-2). 5.99 ***(978-0-553-52467-3(4)***, Random Hse. Bks. for Young Readers) Random Hse. Children's Bks.

Doescher, Erik, jt. illus. see RH Disney Staff.

Dog Artlist Collection Staff. The Dog from Arf! Arf! to Zzzzzz. Dog Artlist Collection Staff. 2004. 40p. (J). (ENG.). 14.99 *(978-0-06-059857-0(3))*; lib. bdg. 16.89 *(978-0-06-059858-7(1))* HarperCollins Pubs.

Doggett, Al. Clara's Imagination. Edwards, Helen L. 2005. 19.95 *(978-0-9765414-0-0(8))* Bad Publishing.

Doggett, Allen B. Hans Brinker or the Silver Skates A Story of Life in Holland. Dodge, Mary Mapes. 2004. reprint ed. pap. 34.95 *(978-1-4179-4127-8(8))* Kessinger Publishing, LLC.

Doggett, W. Kirk. Physiology of the Eye. Phillips, Carey R. & Johannen, Kevin C. 2nd ed. 2005. (C). cd-rom 95.00 *(978-0-9759464-1-1(2)*, Interactive Eye, L.L.C.) Interactive Knowledge, Inc.

Dogi, Fiametta. 3D Theater: Oceans. Jewitt, Kathryn. 2011. (3D Theater Ser.). (ENG.). 20p. (J). (gr. -1-3). 19.99 *(978-0-7534-6466-3(7)*, Kingfisher) Roaring Brook Pr.

Dogi, Fiammetta. El Roble: Por Dentro y Por Fuera. Hipp, Andrew. Gonzalez, Tomas, tr. from ENG. 2004. (Explora la Naturaleza (Getting into Nature) Ser.). (SPA.). 27p. (J). (gr. 3-7). lib. bdg. 25.25 *(978-1-4042-2864-1(0))* Rosen Publishing Group, Inc., The.

—A Seed Needs Sun. Riggs, Kate. 2014. (ENG.). 14p. (J). (gr. -1-k). 7.99 *(978-1-56846-254-7(9)*, Creative Editions) Creative Co., The.

—That's Creepy! Riggs, Kate. 2013. (ENG.). 14p. (J). (gr. -1-k). bds. 7.99 *(978-1-56846-236-3(0)*, Creative Editions) Creative Co., The.

Dogi, Fiammetta & Kubinyi, Laszlo. On the Farm. Riggs, Kate. 2015. (ENG.). 14p. (J). (gr. -1 — 1). bds. 7.99 *(978-1-56846-272-1(7)*, Creative Editions) Creative Co., The.

Dogi, Flammetta. Dinosaurs. Ganeri, Anita. 2007. (Back to Basics Ser.). 32p. (J). lib. bdg. *(978-88-6098-048-9(8))* McRae Bks. Srl.

—Mammals. McRae, Anne & Agosta, Loredana. 2007. (Back to Basics Ser.). 32p. (J). lib. bdg. *(978-88-6098-047-2(X))* McRae Bks. Srl.

—The Solar System. Williams, Brian & Egan, Vicky. 2007. (Back to Basics Ser.). 32p. (J). lib. bdg. *(978-88-6098-049-6(6))* McRae Bks. Srl.

Dogliani, Daniela. Fairy Puzzles. Maidment, Stella. 2012. (Puzzle Adventures Ser.). (ENG.). 32p. (J). (gr. -1-1). 17.99 *(978-1-60992-273-3(5))* QEB Publishing Inc.

—Pirate Puzzles. Maidment, Stella. 2012. (Puzzle Adventures Ser.). (ENG.). 32p. (J). (gr. -1-k). 17.99 *(978-1-60992-270-2(0))* QEB Publishing Inc.

—Princess Puzzles. Maidment, Stella. 2012. (Puzzle Adventures Ser.). (ENG.). 32p. (J). (gr. -1-1). 17.99 *(978-1-60992-272-6(7))* QEB Publishing Inc.

Dohanish, Jason. Buddy's Bedtime. O'Shea, Pauleen. 2007. 32p. (J). 14.95 *(978-0-9778063-0-0(8))* Idlehour Entertainment.

Doherty, Ann. Prince Rama of the Solar Dynasty Pt. 1: Prince in Exile, the Journey Begins. Doherty, Vrinda & Valmiki. 2011. (ENG.). 212p. 29.95 *(978-0-9817273-1-8(X))* Torchlight Publishing.

Doherty, Catherine. Breaking Free. Mulrine, Jennifer. 2008. 112p. (YA). (gr. 7-18). pap. *(978-1-897039-32-8(8))* High Interest Publishing (HIP).

—Dancing on the Edge. Jennings, Sharon. 2007. (HIP Edge Ser.). 112p. (YA). (gr. 7-18). pap. *(978-1-897039-27-4(1))* High Interest Publishing (HIP).

—The Edge Is Burning. Kropp, Paul. 2008. 112p. (YA). (gr. 7-18). pap. *(978-1-897039-33-5(6))* High Interest Publishing (HIP).

—Foul Shot. Kropp, Paul. 96p. pap. *(978-1-897039-25-0(5))* High Interest Publishing (HIP).

—I Didn't Do It! Kropp, Paul. 72p. pap. *(978-1-897039-23-6(9))* High Interest Publishing (HIP).

—Outrage. Varrato, Tony. 2007. (HIP Edge Ser.). 112p. (YA). (gr. 7-18). pap. *(978-1-897039-28-1(X))* High Interest Publishing (HIP).

—Stealing Home. Durkin, Shawn. 96p. pap. *(978-1-897039-24-3(7))* High Interest Publishing (HIP).

Doherty, Dave. There Once Was a Place Called P.O.P. 2008. 93p. (J). 61.99 *(978-1-4363-6190-3(7))* Xlibris Corp.

Doherty, Paula. Dinosaurs. Reasoner, Charles. 2009. (Little Big Flap Bks.). 10p. (J). (gr. -1-k). 9.99 *(978-1-934650-24-0(2))* Just For Kids Pr., LLC.

—Farm Animals. Reasoner, Charles. 2009. (Little Big Flap Bks.). 10p. (J). (gr. -1-k). 9.99 *(978-1-934650-23-3(4))* Just For Kids Pr., LLC.

—Insects. Reasoner, Charles. 2009. (Little Big Flap Bks.). 10p. (J). (gr. -1-k). bds. 9.99 *(978-1-934650-21-9(8))* Just For Kids Pr., LLC.

—Jungle Animals. Reasoner, Charles. 2009. (Little Big Flap Bks.). 10p. (J). (gr. -1-k). 9.99 *(978-1-934650-22-6(6))* Just For Kids Pr., LLC.

—My Giant Fold-Out Book: Christmas. Harrast, Tracy. 2008. 10p. (J). (gr. -1). bds. 13.49 *(978-0-7586-1425-4(X))* Concordia Publishing Hse.

Doherty, Paula. My Sleepytime Bible. Godfrey, Jan. 2015. (ENG.). 96p. (J). 14.99 ***(978-1-4143-9868-6(9))*** Tyndale Hse. Pubs.

Doherty, Paula. Mi Biblia para la Hora de Dormir. Doherty, Paula. Godfrey, Jan & Urízar de Ramírez, Mayra. 2015. (SPA.). 96p. (J). 14.99 ***(978-1-4143-9874-7(3))*** Tyndale Hse. Pubs.

Doherty, Paula, jt. illus. see Devaney, Adam.

Dolan, Amy. A Boy Named Bucky, Vol. 1. Adams, Mark. 2006. 17p. (J). pap. 5.00 *(978-0-9670245-5-4(2))* Enthusi Adams, Inc.

—Bucky's Best Friend, Vol. 1. Adams, Mark. 2006. 15p. (J). pap. 5.00 *(978-0-9670245-4-7(4))* Enthusi Adams, Inc.

Dolan, Elys. Nuts in Space. Dolan, Elys. 2015. (ENG.). 32p. (J). (gr. k-3). 17.99 *(978-0-7636-7609-4(8)*, Nosy Crow) Candlewick Pr.

—Weasels. Dolan, Elys. 2014. (ENG.). 32p. (J). (gr. k-3). 17.99 *(978-0-7636-7100-6(2)*, Nosy Crow) Candlewick Pr.

Dolby, Jan. Gabby, 1 vol. Grant, Joyce. 2012. (ENG.). 32p. (J). 18.95 *(978-1-55455-250-4(8))* Fitzhenry & Whiteside, Ltd. CAN. Dist: Midpoint Trade Bks., Inc.

—Gabby Drama Queen, 1 vol. Grant, Joyce. 2013. (ENG.). 32p. (J). 18.95 *(978-1-55455-310-5(5))* Fitzhenry & Whiteside, Ltd. CAN. Dist: Midpoint Trade Bks., Inc.

Dolce, Ellen. Children's Bible Stories. Kennedy, Dana & Wilson, Etta. 2009. 160p. (J). (gr. -1). 16.99 *(978-0-7586-1634-0(1))* Concordia Publishing Hse.

Dollak, Nicholas. Frannie & Pickles. McClear, Preston. 2003. 48p. (J). (gr. k-5). 16.95 *(978-1-929084-13-5(7))* Malibu Bks. for Children.

Dollar, Diane. Johnny Kaw: The Pioneer Spirit of Kansas. Garretson, Jerri. 2011. (ENG.). 32p. (Orig.). pap. 16.95 *(978-1-4663-5038-0(5))* CreateSpace Independent Publishing Platform.

—Twister Twyla: The Kansas Cowgirl. Garretson, Jerri. 2011. (ENG.). 32p. pap. 6.95 *(978-1-4609-6481-1(0))* CreateSpace Independent Publishing Platform.

Dollar, Diane A., jt. illus. see Garretson, Jerri.

Dombek, Jeff. Caveman Art Teacher. Dombek, Jeff. 2004. 28p. (J). pap. 4.95 *(978-0-9752597-0-2(9))* Corn Tassel Pr.

Domergue, Agnes. Oh My, Oh No! Charrier, Lisa. 2014. (ENG.). 32p. (-k). 15.95 *(978-0-7624-5409-9(1)*, Running Pr. Kids) Running Pr. Bk. Pubs.

Domi. La Carrera del Sapo y el Venado. Mora, Pat. 2004. (SPA.). 32p. (J). pap. 9.95 *(978-0-88899-650-3(0))* Groundwood Bks. CAN. Dist: Perseus-PGW.

—The Honey Jar, 1 vol. Liano, Dante et al. Unger, David, tr. from SPA. 2006. (ENG.). 64p. (J). (gr. 3). 18.95 *(978-0-88899-670-1(5))* Groundwood Bks. CAN. Dist: Perseus-PGW.

—Napí, 1 vol. Ramírez, Antonio. 2004. 32p. (J). (ENG.). 15.95 *(978-0-88899-610-7(1))*; (SPA.). 15.95 *(978-0-88899-611-4(X))* Groundwood Bks. CAN. Dist: Perseus-PGW.

—Napí Funda un Pueblo. Ramírez, Antonio. Amado, Elisa, tr. ed. 2010.Tr. of Napi Makes a Village. (ENG & SPA.). 48p. (J). (gr. k-3). 18.95 *(978-0-88899-965-8(8))* Groundwood Bks. CAN. Dist: Perseus-PGW.

—Napí Va a la Montaña. Ramírez, Antonio. 2006. (SPA.). 48p. (J). (gr. k-3). 18.95 *(978-0-88899-715-9(9))* Groundwood Bks. CAN. Dist: Perseus-PGW.

—La Noche Que Se Cayó la Luna. Mora, Pat. 2009. (SPA.). 32p. (J). (gr. k-k). pap. 6.95 *(978-0-88899-963-4(1))* Groundwood Bks. CAN. Dist: Perseus-PGW.

—Senora Reganona: A Mexican Bedtime Story. Sanroman, Susana. 2006. 20p. (J). (gr. k-4). reprint ed. 15.00 *(978-1-4223-5466-7(0))* DIANE Publishing Co.

—Tamalitos. Argueta, Jorge. Amado, Elisa, tr. from SPA. 2013. (Bilingual Cooking Poems Ser.). (ENG & SPA.). 32p. (J). (gr. -1-2). 18.95 *(978-1-55498-300-1(2))* Groundwood Bks. CAN. Dist: Perseus-PGW.

Domi & Domi. Napí Goes to the Mountain. Ramirez, Antonio. Amado, Elisa, tr. from SPA. 2006. (ENG.). 48p. (J). (gr. k-3). 18.95 *(978-0-88899-713-5(2))* Groundwood Bks. CAN. Dist: Perseus-PGW.

Domi, jt. illus. see Domi.

Domi, Carlos. The Girl from Chimel, 1 vol. Menchú, Rigoberta & Liano, Dante. Unger, David, tr. from SPA. 2005. (ENG.). 56p. (J). (gr. 4-7). 18.95 *(978-0-88899-666-4(7))* Groundwood Bks. CAN. Dist: Perseus-PGW.

—The Night the Moon Fell: A Maya Myth, 1 vol. Mora, Pat. 2009. (ENG.). 32p. (J). (gr. k-k). pap. 6.95 *(978-0-88899-938-2(0))* Groundwood Bks. CAN. Dist: Perseus-PGW.

—The Secret Legacy. Menchú, Rigoberta & Liano, Dante. Unger, David, tr. from SPA. 2008. (ENG.). 64p. (J). (gr. -1). 19.95 *(978-0-88899-896-5(1))* Groundwood Bks. CAN. Dist: Perseus-PGW.

Dominguez, Angel. The Bedtime Story Book: Classic Tales from Childhood. Wainwright, Jen. 2010. (Best at Everything Ser.). (ENG.). 128p. (J). 9.99 *(978-0-545-13407-1(2))* Scholastic, Inc.

Dominguez, Angela. Carmen Learns English. Cox, Judy. 2011. (ENG.). 32p. (J). pap. 7.95 *(978-0-8234-2382-8(4))* Holiday Hse., Inc.

Dominguez, Angela. Mango, Abuela, & Me. Medina, Meg. 2015. (ENG.). 32p. (J). (gr. k-3). 15.99 ***(978-0-7636-6900-3(8))*** Candlewick Pr.

—Mango, Abuela y Yo. Medina, Meg. 2015. (ENG.). 32p. (J). (gr. k-3). 7.99 ***(978-0-7636-8099-2(0))*** Candlewick Pr.

Dominguez, Angela. La Noche Buena: A Christmas Story. Sacre, Antonio. 2010. (ENG.). 32p. (gr. -1-3). 16.95 *(978-0-8109-8967-2(0)*, Abrams Bks. for Young Readers) Abrams.

Dominguez, Angela. Quiero Ayudar! Flor Ada, Alma. 2010.Tr. of Lets Me Help!. (ENG & SPA.). 32p. (J). (gr. -1-3). 16.95 *(978-0-89239-232-2(0))* Lee & Low Bks., Inc.

Dominguez, Angela. Maria Tenía una Llamita. Dominguez, Angela. ed. 2013.Tr. of Maria Had a Little Llama. (SPA & ENG.). 28p. (J). (gr. -1-2). 16.99 *(978-0-8050-9333-9(8)*, Holt, Henry & Co. Bks. For Young Readers) Holt, Henry & Co.

Dominguez, Angela N. Carmen Learns English. Cox, Judy. 2010. (ENG.). 32p. (J). (gr. -1-3). 16.95 *(978-0-8234-2174-9(0))* Holiday Hse., Inc.

—Sonia Sotomayor: I'll Be the Judge of That! Krull, Kathleen. 2015. (Women Who Broke the Rules Ser.). (ENG.). 48p. (J). (gr. 1-4). 16.99 *(978-0-8027-3797-7(6)*, Bloomsbury USA Childrens) Bloomsbury USA.

Dominguez, Domitila. The Story of Colors (La Historia de los Colores) A Bilingual Folktale from the Jungles of Chiapas. Marcos, Subcomandante. Din, Anne Bar, tr. 2003. (ENG & SPA.). 40p. (J). (gr. 4-6). pap. 8.95 *(978-0-938317-71-5(7))* Cinco Puntos Pr.

Dominguez, Maria. Sofi & the Magic, Musical Mural. Ortiz, Raquel M. & Ventura, Gabriela Baeza. 2015. (SPA & ENG.). (J). 17.95 ***(978-1-55885-803-9(2)**, Piñata Books)* Arte Publico Pr.

Dominguez, Oliver. Electrical Wizard: How Nikola Tesla Lit up the World. Rusch, Elizabeth. (Candlewick Biographies Ser.). (ENG.). (J). 2015. 56p. (gr. 3-7). 14.99 ***(978-0-7636-7978-1(X))***; 2013. 40p. (gr. 2-5). 16.99 *(978-0-7636-5855-7(3))* Candlewick Pr.

Dominguez, Oliver. Miracle Mud: Lena Blackburne & the Secret Mud That Changed Baseball. Kelly, David A. 2013. (ENG.). 32p. (J). (gr. 2-5). lib. bdg. 16.95 *(978-0-7613-8092-4(2)*, Millbrook Pr.) Lerner Publishing Group.

Dominguez, Richard, et al. The Building of the Transcontinental Railroad, 1 vol. Olson, Nathan. 2006. (Graphic History Ser.). (ENG.). 32p. (gr. 3-4). 29.99 *(978-0-7368-6490-9(3)*, Graphic Library) Capstone Pr., Inc.

Dominguez, Richard. Cómo Comprender la Fotosíntesis con Max Axiom, Supercientífico. O'Donnell, Liam & Barnett, Charles, III. 2013. (Ciencia Gráfica Ser.). (SPA.). 32p. (gr. 3-4). pap. 8.10 *(978-1-62065-984-7(0))*; lib. bdg. 29.99 *(978-1-62065-180-3(7))* Capstone Pr., Inc.

—The Shocking World of Electricity with Max Axiom, Super Scientist, 1 vol. O'Donnell, Liam & Barnett III, Charles. 2007. (Graphic Science Ser.). (ENG.). 32p. (gr. 3-4). pap. 8.10 *(978-0-7368-7888-3(2)*, 1264936, Graphic Library) Capstone Pr., Inc.

Dominguez, Richard, et al. Understanding Photosynthesis with Max Axiom, Super Scientist, 1 vol. O'Donnell, Liam & Barnett III, Charles. 2007. (Graphic Science Ser.). (ENG.). 32p. (gr. 3-4). 29.99 *(978-0-7368-6841-9(0)*, 1264938, Graphic Library) Capstone Pr., Inc.

Dominguez, Richard & Barnett, Charles, III. Frank Zamboni & the Ice-Resurfacing Machine, 1 vol. Olson, Kay Melchisedech. 2007. (Inventions & Discovery Ser.). (ENG.). 32p. (gr. 3-4). 29.99 *(978-1-4296-0147-4(7)*, Graphic Library) Capstone Pr., Inc.

—Understanding Photosynthesis with Max Axiom, Super Scientist, 1 vol. O'Donnell, Liam. 2007. (Graphic Science Ser.). (ENG.). 32p. (gr. 3-4). per. 8.10 *(978-0-7368-7893-7(9)*, 1264938, Graphic Library) Capstone Pr., Inc.

Dominguez, Richard, jt. illus. see Barnett, Charles, III.

Dominguez, Richard, jt. illus. see Martin, Cynthia.

Dominguez, Stephanie. George Ferris' Grand Idea: The Ferris Wheel. Glatzer, Jenna. 2015. (Story Behind the Name Ser.). (ENG.). 32p. (gr. 2-3). pap. 7.95 ***(978-1-4795-7165-9(2))***; lib. bdg. 27.99 ***(978-1-4795-7135-2(0))*** Picture Window Bks.

Dominquez, Richard, et al. Madam C. J. Walker & New Cosmetics, 1 vol. Krohn, Katherine E. 2006. (Inventions & Discovery Ser.). (ENG.). 32p. (gr. 3-4). 8.10 *(978-0-7368-9647-4(3))*; 29.99 *(978-0-7368-6485-5(7))* Capstone Pr., Inc. (Graphic Library).

Dominquez, Richard, jt. illus. see Martin, Cynthia.

Domm, Jeffrey. Tangled in the Bay: The Story of a Baby Right Whale, 1 vol. Tobin, Deborah. 2003. (ENG.). 33p. (J). (gr. -1-2). pap. 8.95 *(978-1-55109-441-0(X))* Nimbus Publishing, Ltd. CAN. Dist: Orca Bk. Pubs. USA.

Domm, Jeffrey C. Atlantic Puffin: Little Brother of the North, 1 vol. Domm, Kristin Bieber. 2007. (ENG.). 32p. (J). (gr. -1-2). pap. 8.95 *(978-1-55109-518-9(1))* Nimbus Publishing, Ltd. CAN. Dist: Orca Bk. Pubs. USA.

—Eagle of the Sea, 1 vol. Domm, Kristin Bieber. ed. 2011. (ENG.). 32p. (J). (gr. -1-3). 9.95 *(978-1-55109-749-7(4))* Nimbus Publishing, Ltd. CAN. Dist: Orca Bk. Pubs. USA.

Domschke, Angelika. Stranded in Space: The Stellar Life of Jpeg the Robot Dog. Atticus, C. J. 2013. 119p. (J). pap. 6.95 *(978-0-9887780-2-3(5))* Atticus, C. J.

Donaera, Patrizia. Cats. Milbourne, Anna. 2006. (Beginners Nature: Level 1 Ser.). 32p. (J). (gr. k-2). 4.99 *(978-0-7945-1394-8(8)*, Usborne) EDC Publishing.

—The Taming. Krum, Atticus. 2014. (ENG.). 227p. (J). pap. 12.99 *(978-0-9885349-1-9(6))* Huntly Hse.

Donaera, Patrizia & Fox, Christyan. Cats. Milbourne, Anna. 2006. (Usborne Beginners Ser.). 32p. (J). (gr. 1). lib. bdg. 12.99 *(978-1-58086-942-3(4)*, Usborne) EDC Publishing.

Donaera, Patrizia & Haggerty, Tim. Seashore. Beckett-Bowman, Lucy. 2008. (Beginners Nature Ser.). 32p. (J). (gr. -1-3). 4.99 *(978-0-7945-2061-8(8)*, Usborne) EDC Publishing.

Donaera, Patrizia & Larkum, Adam. Night Animals: Level 1. Meredith, Sue. 2007. (Beginners Ser.). 32p. (J). 4.99 *(978-0-7945-1656-7(4)*, Usborne) EDC Publishing.

Donaera, Patrizia & Mayer, Uwe. Dogs. Helbrough, Emma. 2006. (Beginners Nature: Level 1 Ser.). 32p. (J). (gr. k-2). 4.99 *(978-0-7945-1395-5(6))*; (gr. 1). lib. bdg. 12.99 *(978-1-58086-943-0(2))* EDC Publishing. (Usborne).

Donaera, Patrizia & Wray, Zoe. Tadpoles & Frogs. Milbourne, Anna. 2007. (Usborne Beginners Ser.). 32p. (J). 4.99 *(978-0-7945-1345-0(X)*, Usborne) EDC Publishing.

Donahue, Jim. The Christmas Lantern. Bishop, Karen C. 2008. 32p. (J). *(978-0-615-20131-3(8))* Three River Rambler.

Donahue, Linda. A Gifted Book. Johnston, Camille. 2008. 19p. pap. 24.95 *(978-1-60563-329-9(1))* America Star Bks.

Donaldson, Jennifer. The Earth, the Alphabet, & Me. Pesout, Christine. 2011. (J). *(978-0-615-47220-1(6))* Pesout, Christine.

Donati, Giuliana. The Haunted House. Caviezel, Giovanni. 2011. (ENG.). 10p. (J). (gr. -1-k). bds. 6.99 *(978-0-7641-6474-3(0))* Barron's Educational Series, Inc.

—Little Gingerbread Man. Caviezel, Giovanni. (Mini People Shape Bks.). (ENG.). 10p. (J). (gr. -1-2). 2014. bds. 4.99 *(978-0-7641-6735-5(9))*; 2012. bds. 7.99 *(978-0-7641-6541-2(0))* Barron's Educational Series, Inc.

Donato, Janice. How Cold Was It? Barclay, Jane. ed. 2004. (J). (gr. k-3). spiral bd. *(978-0-616-11862-7(7))* Canadian National Institute for the Blind/Institut National Canadien pour les Aveugles.

—How Hot Was It? Barclay, Jane. Cole, Kathryn, ed. (ENG.). 24p. (J). 14.95 *(978-1-894222-70-9(9))* Lobster Pr. CAN. Dist: Univ. of Toronto Pr.

Donato, Michael A. Squanto & the First Thanksgiving: The Legendary American Tale. Metaxas, Eric. 2004. 36p. (J). (gr. 3-8). reprint ed. 19.00 *(978-0-7567-7123-2(4))* DIANE Publishing Co.

—Tales Alive! Milord, Susan. 2007. (ENG.). 128p. 16.99 *(978-0-8249-6804-5(2)*, Williamson Bks.) Ideals Pubns.

Donbavand, Tommy. Flame of the Dragon. Donbavand, Tommy. 2015. (Scream Street Ser.: 13). (ENG.). 192p. (J). (gr. 3-7). pap. 5.99 ***(978-0-7636-5765-9(4))*** Candlewick Pr.

—Hunger of the Yeti. Donbavand, Tommy. 2015. (Scream Street Ser.: 11). (ENG.). 128p. (J). (gr. 3-7). pap. 5.99 ***(978-0-7636-5763-5(8))*** Candlewick Pr.

—Rampage of the Goblins. Donbavand, Tommy. 2015. (Scream Street Ser.: 10). (ENG.). 128p. (J). (gr. 3-7). pap. 5.99 ***(978-0-7636-5762-8(X))*** Candlewick Pr.

—Secret of the Changeling. Donbavand, Tommy. 2015. (Scream Street Ser.: 12). (ENG.). 128p. (J). (gr. 3-7). pap. 5.99 ***(978-0-7636-5764-2(6))*** Candlewick Pr.

Donbo, Koge. Pita-Ten, Vol. 8. Donbo, Koge, creator. rev. ed. 2005. 208p. pap. 9.99 *(978-1-59532-017-9(2))* TOKYOPOP, Inc.

Donehey, Jennifer Caulfield. An Octopus Named Mom. Flaherty, Kathleen Marion. 2012. (ENG.). 32p. (J). 16.95 *(978-0-9767276-8-2(4))* Three Bean Pr.

Doner, Kim. The Buffalo in the Mall. Griffis, Molly. 32p. 8.95 *(978-1-57168-635-0(5))* Eakin Pr.

—Q Is for Quark: A Science Alphabet Book. Schwartz, David & Schwartz, David M. 2009. (ENG.). 64p. (J). (gr. 3-7). pap. 9.99 *(978-1-58246-303-2(4))* Ten Speed Pr.

—S Is for Sooner: An Oklahoma Alphabet. Scillian, Devin. 2003. (Discover America State by State Ser.). (ENG.). 40p. (J). 17.95 *(978-1-58536-062-8(7))* Sleeping Bear Pr.

Dong-Seong, Kim & Kim, Tong-Song. Waiting for Mama. Tae-Jun, Lee et al. 2007. (KOR & ENG.). 32p. (J). (gr. -1-3). 16.95 *(978-0-7358-2143-9(7))* North-South Bks., Inc.

Doniger, Nancy. Lemonade: And Other Poems Squeezed from a Single Word. Raczka, Bob. 2011. (ENG.). 48p. (J). (gr. 3-7). 16.99 *(978-1-59643-541-4(0))* Roaring Brook Pr.

Doninck, Sebastiaan Van. Cowboy Boyd & Mighty Calliope. Moser, Lisa. 2013. (ENG.). 40p. (J). (gr. -1-2). 17.99 *(978-0-375-87056-9(3))* Random Hse., Inc.

Donnelly, Jenifer. Daddy's Heroes: Gibby's Homer: the 1988 World Series. Garcia, Tom & Naga, Karun. 2007. (1988 World Ser.). 32p. (J). (gr. -1-3). pap. 9.95 *(978-0-9792111-0-2(7))* Daddy's Heroes, Inc.

Donnelly, Karen. A Christmas Carol. Dickens, Charles. 2013. (Charles Dickens Ser.). (ENG.). 64p. (Orig.). pap. 6.95 *(978-1-906230-02-9(1))* Real Reads Ltd. GBR. Dist: International Publishers Marketing.

—David Copperfield. Tavner, Gill & Dickens, Charles. 2009. (Real Reads Ser.). 64p. (J). (gr. 4-8). pap. 13.55 *(978-1-60754-383-1(4))* Windmill Bks.

—Eliza Bing Is (Not) a Big, Fat Quitter. Van Vleet, Carmella. 2014. (ENG.). 176p. (J). (gr. 2-6). 16.95 *(978-0-8234-2944-8(X))* Holiday Hse., Inc.

—Get That Ghost to Go!, 1 vol. MacPhail, C. 2006. (Pathway Bks.). (ENG.). 88p. (gr. 2-3). 23.99 *(978-1-59889-004-4(2)*, Pathway Bks.) Stone Arch Bks.

—Great Expectations. Dickens, Charles. 2013. (Charles Dickens Ser.). (ENG.). 64p. pap. 6.95 *(978-1-906230-01-2(3))* Real Reads Ltd. GBR. Dist: International Publishers Marketing.

—Hard Times. Dickens, Charles. 2014. (Charles Dickens Ser.). (ENG.). 64p. pap. 6.95 *(978-1-906230-05-0(6))* Real Reads Ltd. GBR. Dist: International Publishers Marketing.

—Hard Times. Tavner, Gill & Dickens, Charles. 2009. (Real Reads Ser.). 64p. (J). (gr. 4-8). pap. 13.55 *(978-1-60754-386-2(9))* Windmill Bks.

—Is Anybody There? Seeing Is Believing... Ure, Jean. 2004. (ENG.). 192p. (J). (gr. 4-7). pap. 9.95 *(978-0-00-716136-2(0)*, Collins) HarperCollins Pubs. Ltd. GBR. Dist: HarperCollins Pubs.

—Jesus of Nazareth. Moore, Alan & Tavner, Gill. 2014. (New Testament Ser.). (ENG.). 64p. pap. 6.95 *(978-1-906230-24-1(2))* Real Reads Ltd. GBR. Dist: International Publishers Marketing.

—Judas Iscariot. Moore, Alan & Tavner, Gill. 2014. (New Testament Ser.). (ENG.). 64p. pap. 6.95 *(978-1-906230-28-9(5))* Real Reads Ltd. GBR. Dist: International Publishers Marketing.

—Mary Magdalene. Moore, Alan & Tavner, Gill. 2014. (New Testament Ser.). (ENG.). 64p. pap. 6.95 *(978-1-906230-27-2(7))* Real Reads Ltd. GBR. Dist: International Publishers Marketing.

—Mary of Galilee. Moore, Alan & Tavner, Gill. 2014. (New Testament Ser.). (ENG.). 64p. pap. 6.95 *(978-1-906230-25-8(0))* Real Reads Ltd. GBR. Dist: International Publishers Marketing.

—Oliver Twist. Dickens, Charles. 2013. (Charles Dickens Ser.). (ENG.). 64p. pap. 6.95 *(978-1-906230-00-5(5))* Real Reads Ltd. GBR. Dist: International Publishers Marketing.

—Over the Moon. Ure, Jean. 2006. (ENG.). 192p. (J). (gr. 4-7). per. 8.99 *(978-0-00-716464-6(5)*, HarperCollins Children's Bks.) HarperCollins Pubs. Ltd. GBR. Dist: HarperCollins Pubs.

—Paul of Tarsus. Moore, Alan & Tavner, Gill. 2014. (New Testament Ser.). (ENG.). 64p. pap. 6.95 *(978-1-906230-29-6(3))* Real Reads Ltd. GBR. Dist: International Publishers Marketing.

—Simon Peter. Moore, Alan & Tavner, Gill. 2014. (New Testament Ser.). (ENG.). 64p. pap. 6.95 *(978-1-906230-26-5(9))* Real Reads Ltd. GBR. Dist: International Publishers Marketing.

Donnelly, Liza. The End of the Rainbow. Donnelly, Liza. 2015. (I Like to Read(r) Ser.). (ENG.). 24p. (J). (gr. -1-3). 6.99 *(978-0-8234-3396-4(X))*; 14.95 *(978-0-8234-3291-2(2))* Holiday Hse., Inc.

Donner, Brad, photos by. A Complete Book about Death for Kids. Grollman, Earl A. & Johnson, Joy. 2006. (ENG.). 46p. (J). pap. 7.95 *(978-1-56123-191-1(6))* Centering Corp.

Donohue, Dorothy. All in One Hour, 0 vols. Crummel, Susan Stevens. 2009. (ENG.). 40p. (J). (gr. k-3). pap. 6.99 *(978-0-7614-5537-0(X)*, 9780761455370, Amazon Children's Publishing) Amazon Publishing.

—City Dog, Country Dog, 0 vols. Crummel, Susan Stevens. 2010. (ENG.). 32p. (J). (gr. k-4). pap. 7.99 *(978-0-7614-5538-7(8)*, 9780761455387, Amazon Children's Publishing) Amazon Publishing.

—If Frogs Made the Weather. Bauer, Marion Dane. 2005. (ENG.). 32p. (J). 16.95 *(978-0-8234-1622-6(4))* Holiday Hse., Inc.

—Sherlock Bones & the Missing Cheese, 0 vols. Crummel, Susan Stevens. 2012. (ENG.). 40p. (J). (gr. k-3). 17.99 *(978-0-7614-6186-9(8)*, 9780761461869, Amazon Children's Publishing) Amazon Publishing.

—Splish, Splash, Spring. Carr, Jan. 2005. (ENG.). 32p. (J). (gr. k-3). 6.95 *(978-0-8234-1754-4(9))* Holiday Hse., Inc.

—Sweet Hearts. Carr, Jan. 2004. (ENG.). 32p. (gr. -1-1). reprint ed. 6.95 *(978-0-8234-1879-4(0))* Holiday Hse., Inc.

—Ten-Gallon Bart, 0 vols. Crummel, Susan Stevens. 2010. (ENG.). 32p. (J). (gr. k-3). pap. 7.99 *(978-0-7614-5719-0(4)*, 9780761457190, Amazon Children's Publishing) Amazon Publishing.

—Ten-Gallon Bart Beats the Heat, 0 vols. Crummel, Susan Stevens. 2010. (ENG.). 40p. (J). (gr. k-3). 17.99 *(978-0-7614-5634-6(1)*, 9780761456346, Amazon Children's Publishing) Amazon Publishing.

Donohue, Dorothy. City Dog & Country Dog. Donohue, Dorothy. Crummel, Susan Stevens. unabr. ed. 2006. (J). (gr. k-3). 27.95 incl. audio *(978-0-8045-6942-2(8)*, SAC6942) Spoken Arts, Inc.

Donoso, Marcela. Pablo. Lazaro, Georgina. 2008. (Cuando los Grandes Eran Pequenos Ser.). (SPA.). 32p. (J). (gr. 3-5). 14.99 *(978-1-933032-09-2(X))* Lectorum Pubns., Inc.

Donovan, Derec. Forget-Me-Not. Bedard, Tony. 2005. (Rogue Ser.). 144p. (YA). (gr. 8-12). pap. 14.99 *(978-0-7851-1734-6(2))* Marvel Worldwide, Inc.

Donovan, Deric, jt. illus. see Coipel, Olivier.

Donovan, Jane Monroe. Black Beauty's Early Days in the Meadow. Sewell, Anna. rev. ed. 2006. (ENG.). 32p. (J). (gr. k-6). 15.95 *(978-1-58536-296-7(4))* Sleeping Bear Pr.

—My Daddy Likes to Say. Brennan-Nelson, Denise. 2009. (ENG.). 32p. (J). (gr. k-6). 15.95 *(978-1-58536-432-9(0))* Sleeping Bear Pr.

—My Grandma Likes to Say. Brennan-Nelson, Denise. rev. ed. 2007. (ENG.). 32p. (J). (gr. k-6). 16.95 *(978-1-58536-284-4(0))* Sleeping Bear Pr.

—My Momma Likes to Say. Brennan-Nelson, Denise. 2003. (ENG.). 32p. (J). (gr. k-6). 15.95 *(978-1-58536-106-9(2))* Sleeping Bear Pr.

Donovan, Jane Monroe. Small, Medium & Large. Donovan, Jane Monroe. 2010. (ENG.). 32p. (J). (gr. 1-4). 15.95 *(978-1-58536-447-3(9)*, 202172) Sleeping Bear Pr.

Donovan, Jane Monroe, jt. illus. see Monroe Donovan, Jane.

Donovan, Patte. Tobey Boland & the Blackstone Canal. Rooney, Thomas L. 2005. 30p. (J). *(978-1-929039-30-2(1))* Ambassador Bks., Inc.

Donploypetch, Jintanan, jt. illus. see Nugent, Suzanne.

Donze, Lisa. Squanto & the First Thanksgiving. Kessel, Joyce K. rev. ed. 2003. (On My Own Holidays Ser.). (ENG.). 48p. (gr. 2-4). pap. 6.95 *(978-1-57505-585-5(6))*; lib. bdg. 25.26 *(978-0-87614-941-6(7))* Lerner Publishing Group.

—Squanto y el Primer Día de Acción de Gracias. Kessel, Joyce K. Translations.com Staff, tr. from ENG. 2007. (Yo Solo: Festividades (on My Own Holidays) Ser.). (SPA.). 48p. (gr. 2-4). lib. bdg. 25.26 *(978-0-8225-7792-8(5)*, Ediciones Lerner) Lerner Publishing Group.

Doodler, Todd H. Bear, Do You Wear Underwear? 2012. (ENG.). 12p. (J). (gr. k — 1). bds. 6.99 *(978-1-60905-259-1(5))* Blue Apple Bks.

—Bear in Long Underwear. Goldman, Todd. 2011. (ENG.). 36p. (J). (gr. -1-3). 12.99 *(978-1-60905-100-6(9))* Blue Apple Bks.

—Bear's Underwear Mystery: A Count-and-Find-It Adventure. Goldman, Todd. 2012. (ENG.). 18p. (J). (gr. k-k). bds. 9.99 *(978-1-60905-204-1(8))* Blue Apple Bks.

—Goodnight Underwear. Ziefert, Harriet. 2013. (ENG.). 36p. (J). (gr. -1-3). 12.99 *(978-1-60905-363-5(X))* Blue Apple Bks.

—Honey Bear's Blue Bathing Suit. 2012. (ENG.). 36p. (J). (gr. -1-3). 12.99 *(978-1-60905-203-4(X))* Blue Apple Bks.

Doodler, Todd H. Super Rawr! 2016. (J). ***(978-0-545-79969-0(4)**, Scholastic Pr.)* Scholastic, Inc.

Doodler, Todd H. What Color Is Bear's Underwear? Goldman, Todd. 2011. (ENG.). 18p. (J). (gr. k-k). bds. 9.99 *(978-1-60905-096-2(7))* Blue Apple Bks.

Doodler, Todd H. One Potato, Two Potato. Doodler, Todd H. 2013. (ENG.). 32p. (J). (gr. -1-k). 14.99 *(978-1-4424-8517-4(5)*, Little Simon) Little Simon.

—Rawr! Doodler, Todd H. 2013. (ENG.). 40p. (J). (gr. -1-k). 12.99 *(978-0-545-51118-6(6)*, Scholastic Pr.) Scholastic, Inc.

—Veggies with Wedgies. Doodler, Todd H. 2014. (ENG.). 32p. (J). (gr. -1-k). 14.99 *(978-1-4424-9340-7(2)*, Little Simon) Little Simon.

Dooling, Michael. The Amazing Life of Benjamin Franklin. Giblin, James Cross. 2006. 48p. (gr. -1-3). 18.00 *(978-0-7569-6551-8(9))* Perfection Learning Corp.

—The Amazing Life of Benjamin Franklin. Giblin, James Cross. 2006. (ENG.). 48p. (J). (gr. 3-7). per. 7.99 *(978-0-439-81065-4(5)*, Scholastic Paperbacks) Scholastic, Inc.

Dooling, Michael. The Great Horse-Less Carriage Race. Dooling, Michael. 2005. (ENG.). 32p. (J). (gr. k-3). tchr. ed. 16.95 *(978-0-8234-1640-0(2))* Holiday Hse., Inc.

—Young Thomas Edison. Dooling, Michael. 2005. (ENG.). 40p. (J). (gr. -1-3). 17.95 *(978-0-8234-1868-8(5))* Holiday Hse., Inc.

Dooling, Michael & Sayles, Elizabeth. Won't Papa Be Surprised! Cohlene, Terri. 2003. 32p. (J). 16.89 *(978-0-688-13094-7(1))* HarperCollins Pubs.

Doolittle, Bev. Reading the Wild. Maclay, Elise. 2005. 32p. (J). (gr. k-4). reprint ed. 17.00 *(978-0-7567-9649-5(0))* DIANE Publishing Co.

Doolittle, Michael. Monster Trucks! Goodman, Susan E. 2010. (Step into Reading Ser.). (ENG.). 48p. (J). (gr. k-3). pap. 3.99 *(978-0-375-86208-3(0)*, Random Hse. Bks. for Young Readers) Random Hse. Children's Bks.

—Motorcycles! Goodman, Susan E. 2007. (Step into Reading Ser.). (ENG.). 48p. (J). (gr. k-3). per. 3.99 *(978-0-375-84116-3(4)*, Random Hse. Bks. for Young Readers) Random Hse. Children's Bks.

—Trains! Goodman, Susan E. 2012. (Step into Reading Ser.). (ENG.). 48p. (J). (gr. 1-4). lib. bdg. 12.99 *(978-0-375-96941-6(1)*, Random Hse. Bks. for Young Readers) Random Hse. Children's Bks.

—Trains! Goodman, Susan E. 2012. (Step into Reading Ser.). (ENG.). 48p. (J). (gr. 1-4). pap. 3.99 *(978-0-375-86941-9(7))* Random Hse., Inc.

Doolittle, Michael, photos by. Choppers! Goodman, Susan E. 2004. (Step into Reading Ser.: Vol. 4). (ENG., 48p. (J). (gr. 2-4). pap. 3.99 *(978-0-375-82517-0(7)*, Random Hse. Bks. for Young Readers) Random Hse. Children's Bks.

Doolittle, Michael J. Ultimate Field Trip #5: Blasting off to Space Academy. Goodman, Susan E. 2011. (ENG.). 48p. (J). (gr. 3-7). pap. 19.99 *(978-1-4424-4345-7(6)*, Atheneum Bks. for Young Readers) Simon & Schuster Children's Publishing.

Doppert, Monika. The Streets Are Free. Kurusa. Englander, Karen, tr. 2008. (ENG.). 48p. (J). (gr. 1-4). reprint ed. pap. 11.95 *(978-1-55037-370-7(6)*, 9781550373707) Annick Pr., Ltd. CAN. Dist: Firefly Bks., Ltd.

Dorado, Steve. The Empty Pot: A Chinese Folk Tale, 1 vol. Guillain, Charlotte. 2014. (Folk Tales from Around the World Ser.). (ENG.). 24p. (gr. 1-3). pap. 6.95 *(978-1-4109-6697-1(6)*, NA-r) Heinemann-Raintree.

—Finn MacCool & the Giant's Causeway: An Irish Folk Tale, 1 vol. Guillain, Charlotte. 2014. (Folk Tales from Around the World Ser.). (ENG.). 24p. (gr. 1-3). pap. 6.95 *(978-1-4109-6699-5(2)*, NA-r) Heinemann-Raintree.

—Folk Tales from Around the World, 1 vol. Guillain, Charlotte. 2014. (Folk Tales from Around the World Ser.). (ENG.). 24p. (gr. 1-3). pap. 41.70 *(978-1-4109-6702-2(6)*, NA-r) Heinemann-Raintree.

—The Foolish, Timid Rabbit: An Indian Folk Tale, 1 vol. Guillain, Charlotte. 2014. (Folk Tales from Around the World Ser.). (ENG.). 24p. (gr. 1-3). pap. 6.95 *(978-1-4109-6700-8(X)*, NA-r) Heinemann-Raintree.

—The Tree of Life: An Amazonian Folk Tale, 1 vol. Guillain, Charlotte. 2014. (Folk Tales from Around the World Ser.). (ENG.). 24p. (gr. 1-3). pap. 6.95 (978-1-4109-6698-8(4), NA-r) Heinemann-Raintree.
—The Unhappy Stonecutter: A Japanese Folk Tale, 1 vol. Guillain, Charlotte. 2014. (Folk Tales from Around the World Ser.). (ENG.). 24p. (gr. 1-3). pap. 6.95 (978-1-4109-6696-4(8), NA-r) Heinemann-Raintree.
—Why the Spider Has Long Legs: An African Folk Tale, 1 vol. Guillain, Charlotte. 2014. (Folk Tales from Around the World Ser.). (ENG.). 24p. (gr. 1-3). pap. 6.95 (978-1-4109-6701-5(8), NA-r) Heinemann-Raintree.
Doran, Colleen. Mangaman. Lyga, Barry. 2011. (ENG.). 144p. (J). (gr. 7). 19.99 (978-0-547-42315-9(2)) Houghton Mifflin Harcourt Publishing Co.
Doran, David. Where Is God? Ferry, Therese. 2012. (ENG.). 26p. pap. 12.95 (978-1-85607-778-1(0)) Columba Pr. IRL. Dist: Dufour Editions, Inc.
Doran, Fran. The Boarding House. Melton, Marcia. 2012. 153p. (J). pap. 12.00 (978-1-937849-03-0(1)) Raven Publishing Inc. of Montana.
Dorankamp, Michelle. Why Boys & Girls Are Different. Greene, Carol. 2008. pap. 12.99 (978-0-7586-1409-4(8)) Concordia Publishing Hse.
Doré, Gustave. River Legends of the Thames & Rhine. Brabourne, Edward Hugessen Knatchbull-Hugessen. 2005. (J). pap. (978-0-486-44372-0(8)) Dover Pubns., Inc.
—The Surprising Adventures of Baron Munchausen. Raspe, Rudolf Erich. 2012. (ENG.). 208p. 20.00 (978-0-307-96147-1(8), Everyman's Library) Knopf Doubleday Publishing Group.
—A Wild Ride Through the Night. Moers, Walter. Brown, John, tr. from GER. 2008. (ENG.). 208p. (gr. 12). 23.95 (978-1-58567-873-0(2), 856873) Overlook Pr., The.
Doré, Gustavo. Cuentos Completos. Doré, Gustavo, tr. Perrault, Charles & Perrault, Charles. Eyheramonno, Jèoelle & Pascual, Emilio, trs. (SPA.). 184p. 15.95 (978-84-206-3750-1(5)) Alianza Editorial, S. A. ESP. Dist: Distribooks, Inc.
Dorémus, Gaëtan, jt. illus. see Rocco.
Doremus, Robert. Albert Einstein. 2014. (History's All-Stars Ser.). (ENG.). 208p. (J). (gr. 3-7). pap. 6.99 (978-1-4814-1496-8(8), Simon & Schuster/Paula Wiseman Bks.) Simon & Schuster/Paula Wiseman Bks.
—Jeb Stuart: Boy in the Saddle. Winders, Gertrude Hecker. 2011. 202p. 44.95 (978-1-258-08155-3(5)) Literary Licensing, LLC.
—Sacagawea. 2014. (History's All-Stars Ser.). (ENG.). 208p. (J). (gr. 3-7). pap. 6.99 (978-1-4814-1499-9(2), Simon & Schuster/Paula Wiseman Bks.) Simon & Schuster/Paula Wiseman Bks.
Dorenkamp, Michelle. The Christmas Message. Miller, Claire. 2006. (Arch Bks.). 16p. (J). 1.99 (978-0-7586-0872-7(1)) Concordia Publishing Hse.
—The Easter Day Surprise. Fryar, Jane L. 2008. 32p. (Orig.). (J). (gr. k-4). 13.49 (978-0-7586-1445-2(4)) Concordia Publishing Hse.
—From Adam to Easter. Bohnet, Eric. 2014. (Arch Bks.). (ENG.). 16p. (J). pap. 2.49 (978-0-7586-4602-6(X)) Concordia Publishing Hse.
—Get up, Lazarus! Schkade, Jonathan. 2004. (Arch Bks.). (ENG.). 16p. (J). 1.99 (978-0-7586-0480-4(7)) Concordia Publishing Hse.
—God Calls Abraham... God Calls You! Busch, Melinda Kay. 2003. (Arch Bks.). (ENG.). 16p. (J). (gr. k-4). 1.99 (978-0-7586-0502-3(1)) Concordia Publishing Hse.
—Jesus Enters Jerusalem. Fryar, Jane L. 2004. (ENG.). 16p. (J). 1.99 (978-0-7586-0641-9(9)) Concordia Publishing Hse.
—Six Dogs & a Police Officer. Sonberg, Caryn. 2006. 31p. pap. 8.40 (978-1-55501-776-7(2)) Ballard & Tighe Pubs.
Dorenkamp, Michelle. The Bear Went over the Mountain. Dorenkamp, Michelle. 2011. (Favorite Children's Songs Ser.). (ENG.). 16p. (J). (gr. -1-2). lib. bdg. 25.64 (978-1-60954-295-5(9), 200099) Child's World, Inc., The.
Dorenkamp Repa, Michelle. Lydia Believes. Hovland, Stephenie. 2014. (Arch Bks.). (ENG.). 16p. (J). (gr. k-4). pap. 2.49 (978-0-7586-4607-1(0)) Concordia Publishing Hse.
Dorfman, Elsa, photos by. No Hair Day. 2004. (Wgbh Specials Ser.). (gr. 7-18). 19.95 (978-1-57807-730-4(3), WG1205) WGBH Boston Video.
Dorian, Judith. A Tiny Little Door. Dorian, Judith. 2011. (ENG.). 62p. pap. 13.25 (978-1-4610-1146-0(9)) CreateSpace Independent Publishing Platform.
Dorland, Andrew. Harold Can't Stand to Be Alone. Cowie, Ken. 2006. 24p. per. (978-0-9781338-3-2(8)) Soul Asylum Poetry.
Dormal, Alexis. Anna Banana & the Chocolate Explosion. Roques, Dominique. 2015. (Anna Banana Ser.). (ENG.). 28p. (J). (gr. k-2). 15.99 (978-1-62672-020-6(7), First Second Bks.) Roaring Brook Pr.
—Sleep Tight, Anna Banana! Roques, Dominique. 2014. (Anna Banana Ser.). (ENG.). 28p. (J). (gr. -1-2). 15.99 (978-1-62672-019-0(3), First Second Bks.) Roaring Brook Pr.
Dorman, Brandon. Axel the Truck: Beach Race. Riley, J. D. 2013. (My First I Can Read Ser.). (ENG.). 32p. (J). (gr. -1-3). 16.99 (978-0-06-222230-5(9)); pap. 3.99 (978-0-06-222229-9(5)) HarperCollins Pubs. (Greenwillow Bks.).
—Axel the Truck - Rocky Road. Riley, J. D. 2013. (My First I Can Read Ser.). (ENG.). 32p. (J). (gr. -1-3). pap. 3.99 (978-0-06-222231-2(7), Greenwillow Bks.) HarperCollins Pubs.
—Be Glad Your Nose Is on Your Face: And Other Poems - Some of the Best of Jack Prelutsky. Prelutsky, Jack. 2008. (ENG.). 208p. (J). (gr. 1-5). 22.99 (978-0-06-157653-9(0), Greenwillow Bks.) HarperCollins Pubs.
—Between the Light. Berkeley, Jon. 2008. (Julie Andrews Collection). (J). lib. bdg. 17.89 (978-0-06-075514-0(8)) HarperCollins Pubs.
Dorman, Brandon. Beyond the Kingdoms. Colfer, Chris. 2015. (Land of Stories Ser.: Bk. 4). (ENG.). 432p. (J). (gr. 3-7). 18.00 **(978-0-316-40689-5(9))** Little, Brown Bks. for Young Readers.
Dorman, Brandon. The Blade of Shattered Hope. Dashner, James. 2011. (13th Reality Ser.: 3). (ENG.). 528p. (J). (gr. 3-7). pap. 7.99 (978-1-4424-0871-5(5), Simon & Schuster/Paula Wiseman Bks.) Simon & Schuster/Paula Wiseman Bks.
—Can You Fly High, Wright Brothers? Berger, Melvin & Berger, Gilda. 2007. (Scholastic Science Supergiants Ser.: Vol. 1). (ENG.). 48p. (J). (gr. 2-5). pap. 4.99 (978-0-439-83378-3(7)) Scholastic, Inc.
—The Christmas Sweater. Beck, Glenn et al. 2009. (ENG.). 32p. (J). (gr. -1-2). 17.99 (978-1-4169-9543-2(9), Simon & Schuster/Paula Wiseman Bks.) Simon & Schuster/Paula Wiseman Bks.
—Crashing the Party. Finn, Perdita. 2007. 109p. (J). (978-0-439-74436-2(9)) Scholastic, Inc.
—Did It Take Creativity to Find Relativity, Albert Einstein? Berger, Melvin & Berger, Gilda. 2007. (Scholastic Science Supergiants Ser.). (ENG.). 48p. (J). (gr. 2-5). pap. 4.99 (978-0-439-83384-4(1), Scholastic Nonfiction) Scholastic, Inc.
—Ends of the Earth. Hale, Bruce. 2015. (School for Spies Novel Ser.). (ENG.). 304p. (J). (gr. 3-7). 16.99 (978-1-4231-6852-2(6)) Disney Pr.
—Fablehaven. Mull, Brandon. 2007. (Fablehaven Ser.: 1). (ENG.). 384p. (J). (gr. 3-8). pap. 7.99 (978-1-4169-4720-2(5), Simon & Schuster/Paula Wiseman Bks.) Simon & Schuster/Paula Wiseman Bks.
—Fablehaven Collection Set. Mull, Brandon. ed. 2011. (Fablehaven Ser.). (ENG.). 2512p. (J). (gr. 3-8). pap. 39.95 (978-1-4424-2977-2(1), Simon & Schuster/Paula Wiseman Bks.) Simon & Schuster/Paula Wiseman Bks.
—Falcon Quinn & the Black Mirror. Boylan, Jennifer Finney. (Falcon Quinn Ser.: 1). (ENG.). (J). (gr. 5-9). 2011. 512p. pap. 7.99 (978-0-06-172834-1(9)); 2010. 496p. 16.99 (978-0-06-172832-7(2)) HarperCollins Pubs. (Tegen, Katherine Bks).
—Giant Dance Party. Bird, Betsy. 2013. (ENG.). 32p. (J). (gr. k-3). 17.99 (978-0-06-196083-3(7), Greenwillow Bks.) HarperCollins Pubs.
—Grasshopper Magic. Jonell, Lynne. (Stepping Stone Book Ser.). (ENG.). 112p. (J). (gr. 1-4). 2014. pap. 4.99 (978-0-307-93123-8(4)); 2013. 12.99 (978-0-375-87084-2(9)) Random Hse., Inc.
—Grip of the Shadow Plague. Mull, Brandon. 2008. (Fablehaven Ser.: Bk. 3). 487p. (J). (gr. 3-7). 19.95 (978-1-59038-898-3(4), Shadow Mountain) Shadow Mountain Publishing.
—Grip of the Shadow Plague. Mull, Brandon. 2009. (Fablehaven Ser.: 3). (ENG.). 512p. (J). (gr. 3-8). pap. 7.99 (978-1-4169-8603-4(0), Simon & Schuster/Paula Wiseman Bks.) Simon & Schuster/Paula Wiseman Bks.
—Halloween Night. Murray, Marjorie Dennis. (ENG.). 40p. (J). (gr. k-4). 2013. pap. 6.99 (978-0-06-185773-7(4)); 2010. 9.99 (978-0-06-201293-7(2)) HarperCollins Pubs. (Greenwillow Bks.).
—Halloween Night. Murray, Marjorie Dennis & Murray, Marjorie D. 2008. (ENG.). 40p. (J). (gr. k-4). 16.99 (978-0-06-135186-0(5), Greenwillow Bks.) HarperCollins Pubs.
—Hamster Magic. Jonell, Lynne. (Stepping Stone Book Ser.). (ENG.). 112p. (J). (gr. 1-4). 2012. pap. 4.99 (978-0-375-86616-6(7)); 2010. 12.99 (978-0-375-86660-9(4)) Random Hse., Inc.
—I Know He Is There: A Lift-A-Flap Book about Faith. Thornley, Rebecca Gundersen. 2006. (J). (978-1-59038-550-0(0)) Deseret Bk. Co.
—In the Garden. Buehner, Caralyn. 2007. (J). 18.95 (978-1-59038-403-9(2)) Deseret Bk. Co.
—Keys to the Demon Prison. Mull, Brandon. 2011. (Fablehaven Ser.: 5). (ENG.). 640p. (J). (gr. 3-8). pap. 8.99 (978-1-4169-9029-1(1), Simon & Schuster/Paula Wiseman Bks.) Simon & Schuster/Paula Wiseman Bks.
—The Lightning Key No. 3. Berkeley, Jon. 2010. (ENG.). 432p. (J). (gr. 3-7). pap. 7.99 (978-0-06-075515-7(6)) HarperCollins Pubs.
—The Not Even Once Club: My Promise to Heavenly Father. Nelson, Wendy Watson. 2013. 18.99 (978-1-60907-337-4(1)) Deseret Bk. Co.
—The Palace of Laughter. Berkeley, Jon. (Wednesday Tales Ser.: No. 1). (J). (gr. 3-7). 2007. (ENG.). 464p. pap. 8.99 (978-0-06-075509-6(1)); 2006. 427p. 16.99 (978-0-06-075507-2(5), Julie Andrews Collection) HarperCollins Pubs.
—Pingo. Mull, Brandon. 2009. (J). (gr. -1-2). 17.95 (978-1-60641-109-4(8), Shadow Mountain) Shadow Mountain Publishing.
—Pingo & the Playground Bully. Mull, Brandon. 2012. (J). 17.99 (978-1-60907-178-3(6), Shadow Mountain) Shadow Mountain Publishing.
—Rise of the Evening Star. Mull, Brandon. 2007. (Fablehaven Ser.: Bk. 2). 441p. (J). (gr. 4-7). 19.95 (978-1-59038-742-9(2), Shadow Mountain) Shadow Mountain Publishing.
—Rise of the Evening Star. Mull, Brandon. 2008. (Fablehaven Ser.: 2). (ENG.). 480p. (J). (gr. 3-8). pap. 7.99 (978-1-4169-5770-6(7), Simon & Schuster/Paula Wiseman Bks.) Simon & Schuster/Paula Wiseman Bks.
—Rocky Road. Riley, J. D. 2013. (My First I Can Read Ser.). (ENG.). 32p. (J). (gr. -1-3). 16.99 (978-0-06-222232-9(5), Greenwillow Bks.) HarperCollins Pubs.
—School for SPIES Book 2 Thicker Than Water. Hale, Bruce. 2014. (School for Spies Novel Ser.). (ENG.). 352p. (J). (gr. 3-7). 16.99 (978-1-4231-6851-5(8)) Hyperion Bks. for Children.
—School for SPIES Book One Playing with Fire. Hale, Bruce. 2014. (School for Spies Novel Ser.). (ENG.). 336p. (J). (gr. 3-7). pap. 6.99 (978-1-4231-7105-8(5)) Hyperion Bks. for Children.
Dorman, Brandon. School for SPIES Thicker Than Water. Hale, Bruce. 2015. (ENG.). 368p. (J). (gr. 3-7). pap. 6.99 **(978-1-4231-7106-5(3))** Hyperion Bks. for Children.
Dorman, Brandon. Secrets of the Dragon Sanctuary. Mull, Brandon. 2010. (Fablehaven Ser.: 4). (ENG.). 480p. (J). (gr. 3-8). pap. 8.99 (978-1-4169-9028-4(3), Simon & Schuster/Paula Wiseman Bks.) Simon & Schuster/Paula Wiseman Bks.
—The Slippery Map. 2007. 288p. (J). (gr. 3-7). lib. bdg. 17.89 (978-0-06-079109-4(8)) HarperCollins Pubs.
—The Slippery Map. Bode, N. E. 2007. (ENG.). 288p. (J). (gr. 3-7). 16.99 (978-0-06-079108-7(X)) HarperCollins Pubs.
—The Snow Angel. Beck, Glenn et al. 2011. (ENG.). 40p. (J). (gr. -1-2). 7.99 (978-1-4424-4448-5(7), Simon & Schuster/Paula Wiseman Bks.) Simon & Schuster/Paula Wiseman Bks.
—Snowman Magic. Tegen, Katherine Brown. 2012. (ENG.). 32p. (J). (gr. -1-3). 12.99 (978-0-06-201445-0(5)) HarperCollins Pubs.
—The Story of the Jack O'Lantern. Tegen, Katherine Brown. 2010. 32p. (J). (gr. -1-3). (ENG.). 12.99 (978-0-06-143088-6(9)); lib. bdg. 14.89 (978-0-06-143090-9(0)) HarperCollins Pubs.
—The Tiger's Egg. Berkeley, Jon. (Wednesday Tales Ser.: No. 2). (J). 2009. (ENG.). 432p. pap. 7.99 (978-0-06-075512-6(1), Harper Trophy); 2007. 416p. (gr. 3-7). 16.99 (978-0-06-075510-2(5), Julie Andrews Collection) HarperCollins Pubs.
—The Tree of Water. Haydon, Elizabeth. 2014. (Lost Journals of Ven Polypheme Ser.: 4). (ENG.). 400p. (J). (gr. 5-9). 17.99 (978-0-7653-2059-9(2), Starscape) Doherty, Tom Assocs., LLC.
—The Void of Mist & Thunder. Dashner, James. 2013. (13th Reality Ser.: 4). (ENG.). 496p. (J). (gr. 3-7). pap. 8.99 (978-1-4424-0873-9(1), Simon & Schuster/Paula Wiseman Bks.) Simon & Schuster/Paula Wiseman Bks.
—Wild Water Magic. Jonell, Lynne. 2014. (Stepping Stone Book(TM) Ser.). (ENG.). 112p. (J). (gr. 1-4). 12.99 (978-0-375-87085-9(7), Random Hse. Bks. for Young Readers) Random Hse. Children's Bks.
—The Wishing Spell. Colfer, Chris. 2012. (Land of Stories Ser.: Bk. 1). (ENG.). 448p. (J). (gr. 3-7). 19.00 (978-0-316-20157-5(X)) Little, Brown Bks. for Young Readers.
Dorman, Brandon. Pirates of the Sea! Dorman, Brandon. 2011. (ENG.). 32p. (J). (gr. -1-3). 16.99 (978-0-06-204068-8(5), Greenwillow Bks.) HarperCollins Pubs.
—Santa's Stowaway. Dorman, Brandon. 2009. (ENG.). 40p. (J). (gr. -1-3). 16.99 (978-0-06-135188-4(1), Greenwillow Bks.) HarperCollins Pubs.
Dorman, Brandon & Call, Greg. Up & down the Scratchy Mountains. Snyder, Laurel. 2010. (ENG.). 272p. (J). (gr. 3-7). 7.99 (978-0-375-84720-2(0), Yearling) Random Hse. Children's Bks.
Dorman, Brandon, jt. illus. see Marc, Sylvain.
Dorman, Daniel. My Angel in a Doggy Suit. Theisen, Sue. 2011. (ENG.). 36p. pap. 9.13 (978-1-4537-8201-9(X)) CreateSpace Independent Publishing Platform.
Dormer, Frank W. Aggie & Ben - Three Stories. Ries, Lori. 2007. (ENG.). 48p. (J). (gr. -1-3). 5.95 (978-1-57091-649-6(7)) Charlesbridge Publishing, Inc.
—Aggie Gets Lost. Ries, Lori. 2011. (ENG.). 48p. (J). (gr. -1-3). 12.95 (978-1-57091-633-5(0)) Charlesbridge Publishing, Inc.
—Aggie the Brave. Ries, Lori. (ENG.). 48p. (J). (gr. -1-3). 2012. pap. 5.95 (978-1-57091-636-6(5)); 2010. 12.95 (978-1-57091-635-9(7)) Charlesbridge Publishing, Inc.
—Dinos Are Forever. Trine, Greg. (Adventures of Jo Schmo Ser.: 1). (ENG.). 112p. (J). (gr. 1-4). 2014. pap. 5.99 (978-0-544-00325-5(X), HMH Books For Young Readers); 2012. 12.99 (978-0-547-76341-5(7)) Houghton Mifflin Harcourt Publishing Co.
—Good Dog, Aggie. Ries, Lori. (ENG.). 48p. (J). (gr. -1-3). 2012. pap. 5.95 (978-1-57091-646-5(2)); 2009. 12.95 (978-1-57091-645-8(4)) Charlesbridge Publishing, Inc.
—Pinkbeard's Revenge. Trine, Greg. (Adventures of Jo Schmo Ser.: 4). (ENG.). 128p. (J). (gr. 1-4). 2015. pap. 5.99 (978-0-544-45601-3(7), HMH Books For Young Readers); 2013. 12.99 (978-0-547-80797-3(X)) Houghton Mifflin Harcourt Publishing Co.
—Shifty Business. Trine, Greg. (Adventures of Jo Schmo Ser.: 3). (ENG.). 112p. (J). (gr. 1-4). 2014. pap. 5.99 (978-0-544-33911-8(8), HMH Books For Young Readers); 2013. 12.99 (978-0-547-80796-6(1)) Houghton Mifflin Harcourt Publishing Co.
—The Sword in the Stove. 2016. (J). (978-1-4814-3167-5(6)) Simon & Schuster, Inc.
—Wyatt Burp Rides Again. Trine, Greg. (Adventures of Jo Schmo Ser.: 2). (ENG.). 112p. (J). (gr. 1-4). 2014. pap. 5.99 (978-0-544-01899-0(0), HMH Books For Young Readers); 2012. 12.99 (978-0-547-80795-9(3)) Houghton Mifflin Harcourt Publishing Co.
Dormer, Frank W. Socksquatch. Dormer, Frank W. 2010. (ENG.). 32p. (J). (gr. -1-3). 14.99 (978-0-8050-8952-3(7), Holt, Henry & Co. Bks. For Young Readers) Holt, Henry & Co.
—Tita y Ben: Tres Cuentos. Dormer, Frank W. Ries, Lori & Canetti, Yanitzia. 2010. (SPA.). 48p. (J). (gr. -1-3). 13.95 (978-1-57091-934-3(8)); pap. 5.95 (978-1-57091-935-0(6)) Charlesbridge Publishing, Inc.
Dornemann, Volker. Taekwondo Kids: From White Belt to Yellow/Green Belt. Rumpf, Wolfgang. 2007. 136p. (J). pap. 14.95 (978-1-84126-214-7(5)) Meyer & Meyer Sport, Ltd. GBR. Dist: Cardinal Pubs. Group.
Dorros, Arthur. What Makes Day & Night. Branley, Franklyn M. 2015. (Let's-Read-And-Find-Out Science 2 Ser.). (ENG.). 32p. (J). (gr. -1-3). pap. 6.99 **(978-0-06-238197-2(0))** HarperCollins Pubs.
Doscher, Susan. Emmy Sue & the Blue Moo. Doscher, E. L. M. S. 2010. 20p. pap. 9.99 (978-1-935125-92-1(3)) Robertson Publishing.
Doss, Andrea. Do Your Ears Hang Low? Bell, Lucy. 2014. 20p. (J). (gr. -1-2). 8.99 **(978-1-4867-0358-6(5))** Flowerpot Children's Pr. Inc. CAN. Dist: Cardinal Pubs. Group.
D'Ottavi, Francesca. Ancient Chinese Civilization. Matthews, Rupert & Van Pelt, Todd. 2009. (Ancient Civilizations & Their Myths & Legends Ser.). 48p. (YA). (gr. 5-9). lib. bdg. 29.25 (978-1-4042-8035-9(9)) Rosen Publishing Group, Inc., The.
—Ancient Egyptian Civilization. Bell, Michael & Quie, Sarah. 2009. (Ancient Civilizations & Their Myths & Legends Ser.). 48p. (YA). (gr. 5-9). lib. bdg. 29.25 (978-1-4042-8034-2(0)) Rosen Publishing Group, Inc., The.
—Ancient Greek Civilization. Kuhtz, Cleo & Martell, Hazel. 2009. (Ancient Civilizations & Their Myths & Legends Ser.). (YA). (gr. 5-9). lib. bdg. 29.25 (978-1-4042-8033-5(2)) Rosen Publishing Group, Inc., The.
—Ancient Roman Civilization. Scurman, Ike & Malam, John. 2009. (Ancient Civilizations & Their Myths & Legends Ser.). 48p. (YA). (gr. 5-9). lib. bdg. 29.25 (978-1-4042-8038-0(3)) Rosen Publishing Group, Inc., The.
—La Biblia Juvenil Ilustrada. Griswood, John, ed. Sanz Falcon, Maria Teresa, tr. from ENG. 2006. (SPA.). 320p. (J). (gr. -1-3). 24.95 (978-1-58087-088-7(0), 0278) Stampley, C. D. Enterprises, Inc.
—Bug Life. Evans, Lynette. 2013. (Small World Ser.). (ENG.). 32p. (gr. -1). 12.99 (978-1-60887-199-5(1)) Insight Editions LP.
—The Illustrated Bible. Morris, Neil & Morris, Ting. McRae Books Staff, ed. 2008. (ENG.). 320p. (J). (gr. -1). 24.95 (978-88-88166-34-6(3)) McRae Bks. Srl ITA. Dist: Independent Pubs. Group.
—Isis & Osiris, 1 vol. 2012. (Egyptian Myths Ser.). (ENG.). 32p. (gr. 3-4). pap. 7.95 (978-1-4048-7240-0(X)); lib. bdg. 27.99 (978-1-4048-7148-9(9)) Picture Window Bks. (Nonfiction Picture Bks.).
—Sarah Palin: Political Rebel, 1 vol. Yomtov, Nelson. 2011. (American Graphic Ser.). (ENG.). 32p. (gr. 3-4). lib. bdg. 29.99 (978-1-4296-6018-1(X), Graphic Library) Capstone Pr., Inc.
—Sarah Palin: Political Rebel, 1 vol. Yomtov, Nel. 2011. (American Graphic Ser.). (ENG.). 32p. (gr. 3-4). pap. 8.10 (978-1-4296-7341-9(9)); pap. 47.70 (978-1-4296-7342-6(7)) Capstone Pr., Inc. (Graphic Library).
Dotty, Zens. The First Time I Heard the Gospel. Rolling, Greg. 2012. 24p. pap. 11.99 (978-0-9827446-9-7(2), Tamarin Pr.) Ekklesia Pr.
Doty, Eldon. Ghosts: Truth & Rumors. Shores, Lori. 2010. (Truth & Rumors Ser.). (ENG.). 32p. (gr. 3-4). lib. bdg. 27.32 (978-1-4296-3949-1(0), Edge Bks.) Capstone Pr., Inc.
—An Illustrated Timeline of Space Exploration, 1 vol. Wooster, Patricia. 2011. (Visual Timelines in History Ser.). (ENG.). 32p. (gr. 3-4). pap. 7.49 (978-1-4048-7018-5(0)); lib. bdg. 27.99 (978-1-4048-6660-7(4)) Picture Window Bks. (Nonfiction Picture Bks.).
—An Illustrated Timeline of Transportation, 1 vol. Spengler, Kremena T. 2011. (Visual Timelines in History Ser.). (ENG.). 32p. (gr. 3-4). pap. 7.49 (978-1-4048-7019-2(9)); lib. bdg. 27.99 (978-1-4048-6661-4(2)) Picture Window Bks. (Nonfiction Picture Bks.).
—Mummies: Truth & Rumors. Montgomery, Heather L. 2010. (Truth & Rumors Ser.). (ENG.). 32p. (gr. 3-4). lib. bdg. 27.32 (978-1-4296-3950-7(4), Edge Bks.) Capstone Pr., Inc.
—Pirates: Truth & Rumors, 1 vol. Price, Sean Stewart. 2010. (Truth & Rumors Ser.). (ENG.). 32p. (gr. 3-4). lib. bdg. 27.32 (978-1-4296-4746-5(9), Edge Bks.) Capstone Pr., Inc.
—Sports. Price, Sean Stewart. 2010. (Truth & Rumors Ser.). (ENG.). 32p. (gr. 3-4). lib. bdg. 27.32 (978-1-4296-4747-2(7), Edge Bks.) Capstone Pr., Inc.
—Titanic: Truth & Rumors. Burgan, Michael. 2010. (Truth & Rumors Ser.). (ENG.). 32p. (gr. 3-4). lib. bdg. 27.32 (978-1-4296-3951-4(2), Edge Bks.) Capstone Pr., Inc.
—U. S. Presidents: Truth & Rumors. Price, Sean Stewart. 2010. (Truth & Rumors Ser.). (ENG.). 32p. (gr. 3-4). lib. bdg. 27.32 (978-1-4296-3952-1(0), Edge Bks.) Capstone Pr., Inc.
Doty, Eldon C. Fast Dan. Pearson, Mary E. 2003. (Rookie Reader Skill Set Ser.). (ENG.). 32p. (J). (gr. k-2). pap. 4.95 (978-0-516-27494-2(5), Children's Pr.) Scholastic Library Publishing.
Doubleday, Dorothy. Little Bear & the Marco Polo. Minarik, Else Holmelund. 2010. (I Can Read Book 1 Ser.). (ENG.). 32p. (J). (gr. k-3). 16.99 (978-0-06-085485-0(5)); pap. 3.99 (978-0-06-085487-4(1)) HarperCollins Pubs.
Doucet, Bob. All for a Game. Abdo, Kenny. 2013. (Haven't Got a Clue! Ser.). 80p. (J). (gr. 3-6). lib. bdg. 27.07 (978-1-61641-950-9(4), Calico Chapter Bks) Magic Wagon.
—Amazing American Curls. Hengel, Katherine. 2011. (Cat Craze Set 2 Ser.). (ENG.). 24p. (J). (gr. k-3). 25.65 (978-1-61714-829-3(6)) ABDO Publishing Co.
—The Apple State Treasure Hunt: A Story about Washington. Hengel, Katherine. 2011. (Fact & Fable: State Stories Set 3 Ser.). 24p. (J). (gr. -1-2). 25.65 (978-1-61714-679-4(X)) ABDO Publishing Co.
—Awesome Abyssinians. Hanson, Anders. 2009. (Cat Craze Ser.). 24p. (J). (gr. k-3). 25.65 (978-1-60453-721-5(3)) ABDO Publishing Co.
—Bold Boxers. Hanson, Anders. 2009. (Dog Daze Ser.). 24p. 25.65 (978-1-60453-615-7(2), Super SandCastle) ABDO Publishing Co.
—Brainy Brittanys. Hengel, Katherine. 2009. (Dog Daze Ser.). 24p. 25.65 (978-1-60453-616-4(0), Super SandCastle) ABDO Publishing Co.
—Burly Bulldogs. Hengel, Katherine. 2010. (Super SandCastle Ser.). 24p. 25.65 (978-1-61613-376-4(7), Super SandCastle) ABDO Publishing Co.
—Buster's Trip to Cape Cod: A Story about Massachusetts. Gaarder-Juntti, Oona. 2010. (Fact & Fable: State Stories Set 2 Ser.). 24p. (J). (gr. -1-2). 25.65 (978-1-60453-921-9(6)) ABDO Publishing Co.

D

—Chipper Chihuahuas. Hengel, Katherine. 2010. (Super SandCastle Ser.). 24p. 25.65 *(978-1-61613-377-1(5),* Super SandCastle) ABDO Publishing Co.
—Comic Relief. Abdo, Kenny. 2013. (Haven't Got a Clue! Ser.). 80p. (J). (gr. 3-6). lib. bdg. 27.07 *(978-1-61641-951-6(2),* Calico Chapter Bks) Magic Wagon.
—Daring Dalmatians. Scheunemann, Pam. 2010. (Super SandCastle Ser.). 24p. 25.65 *(978-1-61613-378-8(3),* Super SandCastle) ABDO Publishing Co.
—Delightful Devon Rexes. Hengel, Katherine. 2011. (Cat Craze Set 2 Ser.). 24p. (J). (gr. k-3). 25.65 *(978-1-61714-830-9(X))* ABDO Publishing Co.
—Dixie's Big Heart: A Story about Alabama. Tuminelly, Nancy. 2011. (Fact & Fable: State Stories Set 3 Ser.). 24p. (J). (gr. -1-2). lib. bdg. 25.65 *(978-1-61714-680-0(3))* ABDO Publishing Co.
—Duck, Dive, Rock & Roll. Abdo, Kenny. 2013. (Haven't Got a Clue! Ser.). 80p. (J). (gr. 3-6). lib. bdg. 27.07 *(978-1-61641-952-3(0),* Calico Chapter Bks) Magic Wagon.
—Frenchy's Float: A Story about Louisiana. Scheunemann, Pam. 2010. (Fact & Fable: State Stories Set 2 Ser.). 24p. (J). (gr. -1-2). 25.65 *(978-1-60453-922-6(4))* ABDO Publishing Co.
—Give Me Liberty or Give Me Detention! Abdo, Kenny. 2013. (Haven't Got a Clue! Ser.). 80p. (J). (gr. 3-6). lib. bdg. 27.07 *(978-1-61641-953-0(9),* Calico Chapter Bks) Magic Wagon.
—The Great Lei Race: A Story about Hawaii. Salzmann, Mary Elizabeth. 2010. (Fact & Fable: State Stories Set 2 Ser.). 24p. (J). (gr. -1-2). 25.65 *(978-1-60453-923-3(2))* ABDO Publishing Co.
—Hip Himalayans. Hengel, Katherine. 2009. (Cat Craze Ser.). 24p. (J). (gr. k-3). 25.65 *(978-1-60453-722-2(1))* ABDO Publishing Co.
—Jumping Jack Russell Terriers. Scheunemann, Pam. 2009. (Dog Daze Ser.). 24p. 25.65 *(978-1-60453-617-1(9),* Super SandCastle) ABDO Publishing Co.
—Leaping Lily: A Story about Georgia. Dolphin, Colleen. 2010. (Fact & Fable: State Stories Set 2 Ser.). 24p. (J). (gr. -1-2). 25.65 *(978-1-60453-924-0(0))* ABDO Publishing Co.
—Lena & the Lady's Slippers: A Story about Minnesota. Scheunemann, Pam. 2011. (Fact & Fable: State Stories Set 3 Ser.). 24p. (J). (gr. -1-2). 25.65 *(978-1-61714-681-7(1))* ABDO Publishing Co.
—Lovely Labrador Retrievers. Scheunemann, Pam. 2009. (Dog Daze Ser.). (ENG.). 24p. 25.65 *(978-1-60453-618-8(7),* Super SandCastle) ABDO Publishing Co.
—Marvelous Maine Coons. Scheunemann, Pam. 2009. (Cat Craze Ser.). 24p. (J). (gr. k-3). 25.65 *(978-1-60453-723-9(X))* ABDO Publishing Co.
—Missy the Show-Me Mule: A Story about Missouri. Tuminelly, Nancy. 2011. (Fact & Fable: State Stories Set 3 Ser.). 24p. (J). (gr. -1-2). 25.65 *(978-1-61714-682-4(X))* ABDO Publishing Co.
—Monty's Ice Pick: A Story about Alaska. Hengel, Katherine. 2010. (Fact & Fable: State Stories Set 2 Ser.). 24p. (J). (gr. -1-2). 25.65 *(978-1-60453-925-7(9))* ABDO Publishing Co.
—Outgoing Oriental Shorthairs. Hengel, Katherine. 2011. (Cat Craze Set 2 Ser.). 24p. (J). (gr. k-3). 25.65 *(978-1-61714-831-6(8))* ABDO Publishing Co.
—Perky Poodles. Scheunemann, Pam. 2010. (Super SandCastle Ser.). 24p. 25.65 *(978-1-61613-379-5(1),* Super SandCastle) ABDO Publishing Co.
—Popular Persians. Scheunemann, Pam. 2009. (Cat Craze Ser.). 24p. (J). (gr. k-3). 25.65 *(978-1-60453-724-6(8))* ABDO Publishing Co.
—Proud Portuguese Water Dogs. Hengel, Katherine. 2010. (Super SandCastle Ser.). 24p. 25.65 *(978-1-61613-380-1(5),* Super SandCastle) ABDO Publishing Co.
—Psych-Out! Abdo, Kenny. 2013. (Haven't Got a Clue! Ser.). 80p. (J). (gr. 3-6). lib. bdg. 27.07 *(978-1-61641-954-7(7),* Calico Chapter Bks) Magic Wagon.
—Rachel's Home on Bear Mountain: A Story about Connecticut. Salzmann, Mary Elizabeth. 2011. (Fact & Fable: State Stories Set 3 Ser.). 24p. (J). (gr. -1-2). lib. bdg. 25.65 *(978-1-61714-683-1(8))* ABDO Publishing Co.
—Rocky's Outdoor Adventure: A Story about Colorado. Dolphin, Colleen. 2011. (Fact & Fable: State Stories Set 3 Ser.). 24p. (J). (gr. -1-2). lib. bdg. 25.65 *(978-1-61714-684-8(6))* ABDO Publishing Co.
—Rupert & the Liberty Bell: A Story about Pennsylvania. Hengel, Katherine. 2010. (Fact & Fable: State Stories Set 2 Ser.). 24p. (J). (gr. -1-3). 25.65 *(978-1-60453-926-4(7))* ABDO Publishing Co.
—S Is for Spirit Bear: A British Columbia Alphabet. Roberts, G. Gregory. rev. ed. 2006. (Discover Canada Province by Province Ser.). (ENG.). 40p. (J). (gr. 3-7). 18.95 *(978-1-58536-291-2(3))* Sleeping Bear Pr.
—Shaggy Shih Tzus. Hanson, Anders. 2009. (Dog Daze Ser.). (ENG.). 24p. 25.65 *(978-1-60453-619-5(5),* Super SandCastle) ABDO Publishing Co.
—Sleek Siamese. Hanson, Anders. 2009. (Cat Craze Ser.). 24p. (J). (gr. k-3). 25.65 *(978-1-60453-725-3(6))* ABDO Publishing Co.
—Smooth Sphynx. Hengel, Katherine. 2009. (Cat Craze Ser.). 24p. (J). (gr. k-3). 25.65 *(978-1-60453-726-0(4))* ABDO Publishing Co.
—Strong Siberian Huskies. Hengel, Katherine. 2009. (Dog Daze Ser.). (ENG.). 24p. 25.65 *(978-1-60453-620-1(9),* Super SandCastle) ABDO Publishing Co.
—Super Saint Bernards. Salzmann, Mary Elizabeth. 2010. (Super SandCastle Ser.). 24p. 25.65 *(978-1-61613-381-8(3),* Super SandCastle) ABDO Publishing Co.
—Sweet Scottish Folds. Hengel, Katherine. 2011. (Cat Craze Set 2 Ser.). 24p. (J). (gr. k-3). 25.65 *(978-1-61714-833-0(4))* ABDO Publishing Co.
—Terrific Tabbies. Hengel, Katherine. 2011. (Cat Craze Set 2 Ser.). (ENG.). 24p. (J). (gr. k-3). 25.65 *(978-1-61714-834-7(2))* ABDO Publishing Co.
—Triple Take. Abdo, Kenny. 2013. (Haven't Got a Clue! Ser.). 80p. (J). (gr. 3-6). lib. bdg. 27.07 *(978-1-61641-955-4(5),* Calico Chapter Bks) Magic Wagon.
Doucette, Constance. A Moose for Mackenzie. Ballard, Lisa. 2008. 32p. pap. 24.95 *(978-1-60610-123-0(4))* America Star Bks.
Dougherty, Charles L. Giant of the Western Trail: Father Peter de Smet. McHugh, Michael. 2011. 186p. 42.95 *(978-1-258-05887-6(1))* Literary Licensing, LLC.
—Priest, Patriot & Leader: The Story of Archbishop Carroll. Betz, Eva K. 2011. 188p. 42.95 *(978-1-258-03693-5(2))* Literary Licensing, LLC.
Dougherty, Dan. The Marching Band Nerds Handbook. Corchin, Dj. 2012. 136p. 22.95 *(978-0-9834876-7-8(7));* pap. 12.95 *(978-0-9819645-7-7(5))* phazelFOZ Co., LLC., The.
Dougherty, Rachel. The Twelve Days of Christmas in Pennsylvania. Peaslee Levine, Martha. 2014. (Twelve Days of Christmas in America Ser.). (ENG.). 40p. (J). (gr. k). 12.95 *(978-1-4549-0889-0(0))* Sterling Publishing Co., Inc.
—Your Life as a Cabin Attendant on the Titanic. Gunderson, Jessica. 2012. (Way It Was Ser.). (ENG.). 32p. (gr. 2-3). pap. 7.95 *(978-1-4048-7248-6(5));* lib. bdg. 25.99 *(978-1-4048-7158-8(6))* Picture Window Bks. (Nonfiction Picture Bks.).
—Your Life As a Pioneer on the Oregon Trail. Gunderson, Jessica. 2012. (Way It Was Ser.). (ENG.). 32p. (gr. 2-3). pap. 7.95 *(978-1-4048-7250-9(7));* lib. bdg. 25.99 *(978-1-4048-7157-1(8))* Picture Window Bks. (Nonfiction Picture Bks.).
Doughty, Clare, jt. illus. see Giraffe, Red.
Doughty, Rebecca. One of Those Days. Rosenthal, Amy Krouse. 2006. (ENG.). 32p. (J). (gr. -1-3). 15.99 *(978-0-399-24365-3(8),* Putnam Juvenile) Penguin Publishing Group.
—31 Usos para Mama. Ziefert, Harriet & Harriet, Ziefert. Sarfatti, Esther, tr. 2006. (Montana Encantada Ser.). (SPA.). 32p. (J). (gr. -1-k). pap. 8.50 *(978-84-241-8777-4(6))* Lectorum Pubns., Inc.
Douglas, Allen. The Last Dogs: Dark Waters. Holt, Christopher. 2013. (Last Dogs Ser.: 2). (ENG.). (J). (gr. 3-7). 352p. pap. 7.00 *(978-0-316-20009-7(3));* 336p. 17.00 *(978-0-316-20012-7(3))* Little, Brown Bks. for Young Readers.
—The Last Dogs: Journey's End. Holt, Christopher. 2014. (Last Dogs Ser.: 4). (ENG.). 320p. (J). (gr. 3-7). 17.00 *(978-0-316-20007-3(7))* Little, Brown Bks. for Young Readers.
—The Last Dogs: the Long Road. Holt, Christopher. 2014. (Last Dogs Ser.: 3). (ENG.). 352p. (J). (gr. 3-7). pap. 7.99 *(978-0-316-20016-5(6))* Little, Brown Bks. for Young Readers.
Douglas, Allen, jt. illus. see McLoughlin, Wayne.
Douglas, Allen, jt. illus. see Richardson, Owen.
Douglas, Bettye, et al. Portrait of a People: The Bettye Douglas Forum, Inc. Multicultural Resource Book. Douglas, Bettye. 222p. (YA). (gr. 5-13). 100.00 *(978-0-9703183-1-2(6))* Douglas, Bettye Forum, Inc., The.
Douglas, Garbrielle. Safari Oklahoma Presents: God Bless America Historical. Douglas, Bettye. 2003. 22p. (J). (gr. 2-7). wbk. ed. 19.95 *(978-0-9703183-6-7(7))* Douglas, Bettye Forum, Inc., The.
Douglas, Janine. The Muselings. Wicke, Ed. 2012. 212p. pap. 9.99 *(978-0-9840718-8-3(1))* Blacknblue Pr.
Douglas, Keith Cartoon Man. A Woolly Mammoth on Amelia Street: Read Aloud Poems4Kids (and Grownups Too!) St. Pierre, Todd-Michael. 2003. 164p. (J). mass mkt. 15.95 *(978-0-9742602-0-4(7))* Prytania Pr.
Douglas, Punchye. Safari Oklahoma Presents: The Magic of Christmas Around the World. Douglas, Bettye. Douglas, Bettye, ed. (Multicultural). 16p. (J). (gr. k-6). 5.00 *(978-0-9703183-4-3(0))* Douglas, Bettye Forum, Inc., The.
—Safari Oklahoma Presents Operation Safe 2000: Halloween Coloring Book. (Safari Oklahoma Presents). 16p. (J). (gr. k-6). 5.00 *(978-0-9703183-2-9(4))* Douglas, Bettye Forum, Inc., The.
Douglas, Vannick. Syler & the Sandpaper Towel. Shinno, Stephanie. 2012. 32p. 24.95 *(978-1-4626-6677-5(9))* America Star Bks.
Douglass, Ali. Girl in a Fix: Quick Beauty Solutions (and Why They Work) Flaherty, Somer & Kollmer, Jen. 2007. (ENG.). 96p. (YA). (gr. 7-18). pap. 9.95 *(978-0-9772660-2-9(8))* Zest Bks.
Dousias, Spiro. Master Stitchum & the Moon. Maher, Mickle Brandt. 2003. (J). 19.99 *(978-1-932188-01-1(0))* Bollix Bks.
Dove, Jason. First Graphics: Dinosaurs. Clay, Kathryn et al. 2012. (First Graphics: Dinosaurs Ser.). (ENG.). 24p. (gr. 1-2). pap. 25.16 *(978-1-4296-8368-5(6));* pap. 142.80 *(978-1-4296-8369-2(4));* lib. bdg. 93.28 *(978-1-4296-8143-8(8))* Capstone Pr., Inc.
—Stegosaurus: Armored Defender, 1 vol. Clay, Kathryn. 2012. (First Graphics: Dinosaurs Ser.). (ENG.). 24p. (gr. 1-2). lib. bdg. 23.32 *(978-1-4296-7604-5(3))* Capstone Pr., Inc.
—Stegosaurus: Armored Defender, 1 vol. Clay, Kathryn. 2012. (First Graphics: Dinosaurs Ser.). (ENG.). 24p. (gr. 1-2). pap. 6.29 *(978-1-4296-7929-9(8));* pap. 35.70 *(978-1-4296-8364-7(3))* Capstone Pr., Inc.
—Triceratops: Three-Horned Giant, 1 vol. Bolte, Mari. 2012. (First Graphics: Dinosaurs Ser.). (ENG.). 24p. (gr. 1-2). pap. 6.29 *(978-1-4296-7931-2(X));* pap. 35.70 *(978-1-4296-8365-4(1));* lib. bdg. 23.32 *(978-1-4296-7601-4(9))* Capstone Pr., Inc.
—Tyrannosaurus Rex: Mighty Meat-Eater, 1 vol. Hammer, Sheila. 2012. (First Graphics: Dinosaurs Ser.). (ENG.). 24p. (gr. 1-2). pap. 6.29 *(978-1-4296-7932-9(8));* pap. 35.70 *(978-1-4296-8366-1(X));* lib. bdg. 23.32 *(978-1-4296-7602-1(7))* Capstone Pr., Inc.
—Velociraptor: Clawed Hunter, 1 vol. Kolpin, Molly. 2012. (First Graphics: Dinosaurs Ser.). (ENG.). 24p. (gr. 1-2). lib. bdg. 23.32 *(978-1-4296-7603-8(5))* Capstone Pr., Inc.
—Velociraptor: Clawed Hunter, 1 vol. Kolpin, Molly. 2012. (First Graphics: Dinosaurs Ser.). (ENG.). 24p. (gr. 1-2). pap. 6.29 *(978-1-4296-7934-3(4));* pap. 35.70 *(978-1-4296-8367-8(8))* Capstone Pr., Inc.
Dow, Danica, jt. illus. see Dow, Kathy.
Dow, Kathy & Dow, Danica. Low-Down Dirty Words. 2004. 28p. (J). *(978-0-9749886-0-3(X))* KayStar Publishing.
Dow, S. B. A Day with Shapes. Heinze, Monica Bacon. 2004. (J). *(978-0-9761710-0-3(7))* Paisley Publishing.
—The Lion's Deceit. Otukile, Mpho. 2011. (ENG.). 32p. (J). pap. *(978-0-9867460-0-0(2))* Village Life Bks.
—Orville Oak & Friends. Hilgendorf, L. B. 2005. 26p. (gr. -1-1). bds. 11.95 *(978-1-58275-149-8(8))* Black Forest Pr.
Dowdle, Mary. Becoming a Ballerina: A Nutcracker Story. Dowdle, Mary, photos by. Friedman, Lise. 2012. (ENG.). 48p. (J). (gr. 2-4). 18.99 *(978-0-670-01392-0(7),* Viking Juvenile) Penguin Publishing Group.
Dowell, Larry. The Ghost of Hampton Court. Hannah, Martha. 2006. 32p. (J). 17.95 *(978-0-9779808-0-2(4))* CicadaSun.
Dowley, Coco. The Wonderful Happens. Rylant, Cynthia. 2003. (ENG.). 40p. (J). (gr. -1-3). pap. 7.99 *(978-0-689-86355-4(1),* Simon & Schuster Bks. For Young Readers) Simon & Schuster Bks. For Young Readers.
Dowling, Victor J. Joey Goes to Sea. Villiers, Alan. 2005. (Maritime Ser.). (ENG.). 70p. (J). (gr. 4-7). pap. 9.95 *(978-0-939511-10-5(X))* Mystic Seaport Museum, Inc.
Down, Alan. Beowulf: An Anglo-Saxon Epic. 2004. (J). 30p. pap. *(978-1-84444-114-3(8));* 30p. pap. *(978-1-84444-113-6(X));* 30p. pap. *(978-1-84444-112-9(1));* 30p. pap. *(978-1-84444-110-5(5));* 30p. pap. *(978-1-84444-109-9(1));* 30p. pap. *(978-1-84444-033-7(8));* 30p. pap. *(978-1-84444-032-0(X));* 32p. pap. *(978-1-84444-031-3(1));* 30p. pap. *(978-1-84444-030-6(3));* 30p. pap. *(978-1-84444-029-0(X));* 30p. pap. *(978-1-84444-028-3(1));* 30p. pap. *(978-1-84444-027-6(3));* 30p. pap. *(978-1-84444-026-9(5));* 32p. pap. *(978-1-84444-023-8(0));* 32p. pap. *(978-1-84444-022-1(2))* Mantra Lingua.
—Beowulf: An Anglo-Saxon Epic. Barkow, Henriette. 2003. (J). (URD & ENG.). 32p. pap. 12.95 *(978-1-84444-034-4(6));* (CHI & ENG.). 30p. pap. 12.95 *(978-1-84444-025-2(7));* (BEN & ENG.). 30p. pap. 12.95 *(978-1-84444-024-5(9))* Mantra Lingua GBR. Dist: Chinasprout, Inc.
Downard, Barry. Carla's Famous Traveling Feather & Fur Show. Downard, Barry. 2006. (ENG.). 32p. (J). (gr. 4-7). 16.95 *(978-1-59687-171-7(7))* IBks., Inc.
—The Race of the Century. Downard, Barry. 2008. (ENG.). 40p. (J). (gr. -1-3). 15.99 *(978-1-4169-2509-5(0),* Simon & Schuster Bks. For Young Readers) Simon & Schuster Bks. For Young Readers.
Downer, Maggie. The Lion, the Witch & the Wardrobe: Tea with Mr. Tumnus. Frantz, Jennifer. 2005. (Festival Reader Ser.). 32p. (J). 14.99 *(978-0-06-079117-9(9))* Zonderkidz.
—The Secret of Cliff Castle: 3 Great Adventure Stories. Blyton, Enid. 2013. (ENG.). 288p. (J). 16.50 *(978-1-84135-588-7(7))* Award Pubns. Ltd. GBR. Dist: Parkwest Pubns., Inc.
Downer, Romeo. Rosa's Paw-Paw Tree: An inspiring tale about a daughter's deep love for her Mother. Callender, Simone. 2011. 24p. pap. 8.99 *(978-1-4575-0596-6(7))* Dog Ear Publishing, LLC.
Downes, Belinda. Baby Days: A Quilt of Rhymes & Pictures. Downes, Belinda. 2006. (ENG.). 32p. (J). (— 1). 14.99 *(978-0-7636-2786-7(0))* Candlewick Pr.
Downey, Autumn. Idaa Trail: In the Steps of Our Ancestors, 1 vol. Stephenson, Wendy. 2005. (ENG.). 64p. (J). (gr. -1-3). 18.95 *(978-0-88899-576-6(8))* Groundwood Bks. CAN. Dist: Perseus-PGW.
Downey, Dagney, jt. illus. see Kennedy, Kelly.
Downey, Lisa. Blackberry Banquet, 1 vol. Pierce, Terry. 2008. (ENG.). 32p. (J). (gr. -1-3). pap. 8.95 *(978-1-934359-28-0(9))* Arbordale Publishing.
—Happy Birthday to Whooo? A Baby Animal Riddle Book, 1 vol. Fisher, Doris. 2006. (ENG.). 32p. (J). (gr. -1-3). 15.95 *(978-0-9768823-1-2(0));* pap. 8.95 *(978-1-934359-06-8(8))* Arbordale Publishing.
—Julie the Rockhound, 1 vol. Karwoski, Gail Langer. 2007. (ENG.). 32p. (J). (gr. k-4). 15.95 *(978-0-9764943-7-9(X))* Arbordale Publishing.
Downey, Lisa. The Pirates of Plagiarism. Downey, Lisa. Fox, Kathleen. 2010. 32p. (J). (gr. 1-4). lib. bdg. 17.95 *(978-1-60213-053-1(1),* Upstart Bks.) Highsmith Inc.
Downey, William. Deadly Ants. Simon, Seymour. 2012. (Dover Children's Science Bks.). (ENG.). 64p. (J). (gr. 3-5). pap. 5.99 *(978-0-486-48468-6(8))* Dover Pubns., Inc.
—Poisonous Snakes. Simon, Seymour. 2012. (Dover Children's Science Bks.). (ENG.). 80p. (J). (gr. 3-5). pap. 5.99 *(978-0-486-48470-9(X))* Dover Pubns., Inc.
Downie, Christopher. The Hungry Cat. Nadimi, Suzan. l.t. ed. 2005. (PER.). 32p. 5.95 net. *(978-0-9764947-0-6(1))* Nur Pubns.
Downing, Johnette. Amazon Alphabet, 1 vol. Downing, Johnette. 2011. (ENG.). 32p. (J). (gr. k-3). 16.99 *(978-1-58980-879-9(7))* Pelican Publishing Co., Inc.
—Why the Crawfish Lives in the Mud, 1 vol. Downing, Johnette. 2009. (ENG.). 32p. (J). (gr. k-3). 16.99 *(978-1-58980-678-8(6))* Pelican Publishing Co., Inc.
Downing, Julie. All the Ways I Love You. Wang, Dorothea DePrisco & Imperato, Teresa. 2005. (ENG.). 10p. (J). bds. 8.95 *(978-1-58117-190-7(0),* Intervisual/Piggy Toes) Bendon, Inc.
—All the Ways I Love You (bilingual Edition) 2005. (SPA & ENG.). 10p. (J). 8.95 *(978-1-58117-335-2(0),* Intervisual/Piggy Toes) Bendon, Inc.
—All the Way's I Love You Mini. Piggy Toes Press Staff. 2005. (ENG.). 10p. (J). 4.95 *(978-1-58117-437-3(3),* Intervisual/Piggy Toes) Bendon, Inc.
—Cabbage Rose. Helldorfer, M. C. 2013. (ENG.). 32p. (J). (gr. -1-3). 16.99 *(978-1-4814-2156-0(5),* Atheneum Bks. for Young Readers) Simon & Schuster Children's Publishing.
—The Christmas Story. Chancellor, Deborah. 12p. (J). (gr. -1-18). bds. 6.95 *(978-0-8294-1480-6(0))* Loyola Pr.
—Don't Turn the Page! Burk, Rachelle. 2014. (ENG.). 32p. (J). (gr. -1-3). 16.95 *(978-1-939547-06-4(7))* Creston Bks.
—The Firekeeper's Son. Park, Linda Sue. 2009. (ENG.). 40p. (J). (gr. -1-3). pap. 6.99 *(978-0-547-23769-5(3))* Houghton Mifflin Harcourt Publishing Co.
—First Book of Fairy Tales. Hoffman, Mary. 2006. (ENG.). 80p. (J). (gr. 3-7). pap. 9.99 *(978-0-7566-2107-0(0))* Dorling Kindersley Publishing, Inc.
—First Mothers. Gherman, Beverly. 2012. (ENG.). 64p. (J). (gr. 1-4). 17.99 *(978-0-547-22301-8(3))* Houghton Mifflin Harcourt Publishing Co.
—Ice Cream King. Metzger, Steve. 2011. 32p. (J). (gr. -1-2). 15.95 *(978-1-58925-096-3(6));* pap. 7.95 *(978-1-58925-427-5(9))* Tiger Tales.
—Lullaby & Good Night: Songs for Sweet Dreams. 2014. (ENG.). 32p. (J). (gr. -1-3). 16.99 *(978-1-4814-2528-5(5),* Simon & Schuster Bks. For Young Readers) Simon & Schuster Bks. For Young Readers.
—Spooky Friends. Feder, Jane. 2013. (ENG.). 40p. (J). (gr. k-2). 16.99 *(978-0-545-47815-1(4),* Scholastic Pr.) Scholastic, Inc.
—Spooky Friends, Level 2. Feder, Jane. 2013. (Scholastic Reader Level 2 Ser.). (ENG.). 40p. (J). (gr. 1-2). pap. 3.99 *(978-0-545-47816-8(2),* Scholastic Pr.) Scholastic, Inc.
Downing, Julie. The Night Before Christmas. Downing, Julie. 2013. (ENG.). 32p. (J). (gr. -1-3). 16.99 *(978-1-4814-2151-5(4),* Simon & Schuster Bks. For Young Readers) Simon & Schuster Bks. For Young Readers.
—Where Is My Mommy? Downing, Julie. 2003. (ENG.). 32p. (J). (gr. -1-18). 15.99 *(978-0-688-17824-6(3))* HarperCollins Pubs.
Downs, Braden. The Treasures of Christmas. Holthaus, Abbey. 2008. 126p. pap. 19.95 *(978-1-60672-152-0(6))* America Star Bks.
Doyel, Ginger. Gertrude the Albino Frog & Her Friend Rupert the Turtle. Silvermetz, Marcia A. 2003. 48p. (J). (gr. 2-3). 19.95 *(978-0-9718724-0-0(6))* Hiccup Cottage Pubns.
Doyle, Adam. Fat & Bones. Theule, Larissa. 2014. (ENG.). 112p. (J). (gr. 4-12). lib. bdg. 16.95 *(978-1-4677-0825-8(9),* Carolrhoda Bks.) Lerner Publishing Group.
Doyle, Beverly. Aliens from Earth: When Animals & Plants Invade Other Ecosystems, 1 vol. Batten, Mary. 2003. (ENG.). 32p. (J). (gr. 3-7). 15.95 *(978-1-56145-236-1(X))* Peachtree Pubs.
—Extinct! Creatures of the Past. Batten, Mary. 2004. (J). pap. *(978-0-375-82554-5(1));* lib. bdg. *(978-0-375-92554-2(6))* Random Hse. Children's Bks. (Random Hse. Bks. for Young Readers).
—What the Sea Saw, 1 vol. St. Pierre, Stephanie. 2006. (ENG.). 48p. (J). (gr. k-3). 16.95 *(978-1-56145-359-7(5))* Peachtree Pubs.
Doyle, Beverly J. Aliens from Earth: When Animals & Plants Invade Other Ecosystems, 1 vol. Batten, Mary. 2008. (ENG.). 32p. (J). (gr. 3-7). pap. 8.95 *(978-1-56145-450-1(8))* Peachtree Pubs.
Doyle, Evan Brain. Evan Brain's Christmas List & Other Shenanigans: Boy Warrior Fights Evil. Doyle, Evan Brain. Becker-Doyle, Eve. 2008. (ENG.). 64p. pap. 15.95 *(978-0-9794716-3-6(X))* BDA Publishing.
Doyle, Ming. Tantalize: Kieren's Story. Smith, Cynthia Leitich. 2011. (Tantalize Ser.). (ENG.). 192p. (YA). (gr. 9). pap. 19.99 *(978-0-7636-4114-6(6))* Candlewick Pr.
Doyle, Patrick H. T. Edgar Font's Hunt for a House to Haunt: Adventure Two: the Fakersville Power Station. Doyle, Patrick H. T. 2007. (Edgar Font's Hunt for a House to Haunt Ser.). 303p. (J). (gr. 4-7). per. 7.99 *(978-0-9786132-1-1(X))* Armadillo Bks.
Doyle, Renee. Gymnastics Competitions: On Your Way to Victory, 1 vol. Jones, Jen. 2006. (Gymnastics Ser.). (ENG.). 32p. (gr. 3-4). 27.32 *(978-0-7368-6467-1(9),* Snap Bks.) Capstone Pr., Inc.
—Gymnastics Essentials: Safety & Equipment, 1 vol. Jones, Jen. 2006. (Gymnastics Ser.). (ENG.). 32p. (gr. 3-4). 27.32 *(978-0-7368-6468-8(7),* Snap Bks.) Capstone Pr., Inc.
Doyle, Richard. Jack the Giant Killer. Doyle, Richard. 2004. 96p. (J). reprint ed. 19.00 *(978-0-7567-7478-3(0))* DIANE Publishing Co.
Doyle, Sandra. Bone Collection: Skulls. Colson, Rob Scott & de la Bédoyère, Camilla. 2014. (ENG.). 96p. (J). (gr. 3-7). pap. 14.99 *(978-0-545-72457-9(0),* Scholastic Paperbacks) Scholastic, Inc.
Dozier, Ashlyn & Dozier, Makenna Joy. The Confused Tooth Fairy. Dozier, Kim. 2005. (ENG.). 28p. (J). 10.00 *(978-0-9745839-3-8(6),* Fun to Read Bks. with Royally Good Morals) MKADesigns.
Dozier, Ashlyn McCauley. The Ear-Less Kingdom. Dozier, Kim. l.t. ed. 2003. (ENG.). 24p. (J). 7.50 *(978-0-9745839-1-4(X),* Fun to Read Bks. with Royally Good Morals) MKADesigns.
—The Forgetful Princess. Dozier, Kim. 2nd l.t. ed. 2003. (ENG.). 24p. (J). 10.00 *(978-0-9745839-0-7(1),* Fun to Read Bks. with Royally Good Morals) MKADesigns.
—Where's Dwight Dragon. Dozier, Kim. l.t. ed. 2004. (ENG.). 32p. (J). 10.00 *(978-0-9745839-2-1(8),* Fun to Read Bks. with Royally Good Morals) MKADesigns.
Dozier, Ashlyn McCauley & Dozier, Makenna Joy. The Backwards Wizard. Dozier, Kim. l.t. ed. 2005. (ENG.). 28p. (J). 10.00 *(978-0-9745839-4-5(4),* Fun to Read Bks. with Royally Good Morals) MKADesigns.
Dozier, Brendan, et al, photos by. A Book Your Baby Can Read! Titzer, Robert C. 2003. (Early Language Development Ser.: Vol. 2). 14p. (J). pap. 7.95 *(978-0-9657510-5-6(8),* 0-9657510-5-8) Infant Learning Co., The.
—A Book Your Baby Can Read! Review: Early Language Development Series. Titzer, Robert C. 2003. (Early Language Development Ser.). 14p. (J). pap. 7.95

The check digit for ISBN-10 appears in parentheses after the full ISBN-13

(978-1-931026-04-8(1), 1-931026-04-1) Infant Learning Co., The.

Dozier, Lisa, et al, photos by. A Book Your Baby Can Read! Early Language Development Series. Titzer, Robert C. 2003. (Early Language Development Ser.: Vol. 3). 14p. (J). pap. 7.95 *(978-0-9657510-9-4(0)*, 0-9657510-9-0) Infant Learning Co., The.

—A Book Your Baby Can Read! Starter: Early Language Development Series, 1, Starter Book. Titzer, Robert C. 2003. (Book Your Baby Can Read!: Starter Book). 14p. (J). pap. 7.95 *(978-1-931026-03-1(3)*, 1-931026-03-3) Infant Learning Co., The.

Dozier, Makenna Joy, jt. illus. see Dozier, Ashlyn McCauley.

Dozier, Makenna Joy, jt. illus. see Dozier, Ashlyn.

Drage, Robyn. Matson the Mouse. O'Brien, Duncan. 2011. (J). *(978-0-9686734-2-3(2))* Pier 10 Media.

Dragony, Barbara. My Tiger Cat. Frankford, Marilyn. Kaeden Corp. Staff, ed. 2006. (ENG.). 12p. (gr. k-2). pap. 5.95 *(978-1-879835-52-8(5))* Kaeden Corp.

Dragotta, Nick, et al. Captain America: Forever Allies. 2011. (ENG.). 184p. (YA). (gr. 8-17). 24.99 *(978-0-7851-5324-5(1))* Marvel Worldwide, Inc.

—Marvel Zombies Return. 2010. (ENG.). 160p. (gr. 10-17). pap. 19.99 *(978-0-7851-4238-6(X))* Marvel Worldwide, Inc.

Dragotta, Nick, jt. illus. see Bobillo, Juan.

Drainville, Beth, et al. Fancy Nancy: Pajama Day. O'Connor, Jane. 2009. (I Can Read Book 1 Ser.). (ENG.). 32p. (J). (gr. -1-3). 16.99 *(978-0-06-170371-3(0))* HarperCollins Pubs.

—Pajama Day. O'Connor, Jane. 2009. (I Can Read Book 1 Ser.). (ENG.). 32p. (J). (gr. -1-3). pap. 3.99 *(978-0-06-170370-6(2))* HarperCollins Pubs.

Drake, Lana. Woody Acorn. Drake, Lana. Clauson, Marilyn. 2012. 48p. 24.95 *(978-1-4626-9647-5(3))*; pap. 24.95 *(978-1-4626-7946-1(3))* America Star Bks.

Drake, W. H., Jr. The Jungle Book. Kipling, Rudyard. 2015. (Macmillan Classics Ser.). (ENG.). 320p. (J). (gr. 2-4). 16.99 ***(978-1-4472-7307-3(9))*** Pan Macmillan GBR. Dist: Independent Pubs. Group.

Drakeford, Philippa. Enriching Circle Time: Dream Journeys & Positive Thoughts. Weatherhead, Yvonne. 2004. (Lucky Duck Bks.). (ENG.). 86p. pap. 37.00 *(978-1-904315-26-1(7)*, B15267P) SAGE Pubns., Ltd. GBR. Dist: SAGE Pubns., Inc.

Drape, Kaitlin. Slowpoke the Turtle & Company. Finally, Lil Rose. 2005. (J). pap. 8.00 *(978-0-8059-6778-4(8))* Dorrance Publishing Co., Inc.

Draper, Richard. Bugs. Parker, Steve. 2010. (I Love Animals Ser.). (ENG.). 24p. (J). (gr. 1-5). pap. 8.15 *(978-1-61533-252-6(9))*; lib. bdg. 22.60 *(978-1-61533-246-5(4))* Windmill Bks.

—Spiders. Parker, Steve. 2010. (I Love Animals Ser.). (ENG.). 24p. (J). (gr. 1-5). pap. 8.15 *(978-1-61533-256-4(1))*; lib. bdg. 22.60 *(978-1-61533-250-2(2))* Windmill Bks.

—10 Things You Should Know about Spiders. Parker, Steve. Gallagher, Belinda & Borton, Paula, eds. 2004. (10 Things You Should Know Ser.). 24p. (J). 6.99 *(978-1-84236-122-1(8))* Miles Kelly Publishing, Ltd. GBR. Dist: Independent Pubs. Group.

Draper, Richard, jt. illus. see Dennis, Peter.

Draper, Rochelle. The Stone Wall Dragon. Draper, Rochelle. ed. 2007. (ENG.). 32p. (J). (gr. 1-17). 15.95 *(978-0-89272-690-5(3))* Down East Bks.

Drashner, Diane. Grandma & Grandpa Visit Denali. Richter, Bernd & Richter, Susan. 2008. 48p. (J). pap. 9.95 *(978-1-931353-33-5(6))* Saddle Pal Creations, Inc.

Draven, Shelly. Care for Creation. Baldwin, Christy. 2010. (ENG.). 32p. (J). lib. bdg. 16.95 *(978-0-9822565-6-5(6))* Tribute Bks.

Drawson, Blair. Arachne Speaks. Hovey, Kate. 2014. (ENG.). 40p. (J). (gr. 5). 13.99 ***(978-1-4814-5069-0(7)***, McElderry, Margaret K. Bks.) McElderry, Margaret K. Bks.

Drawson, Blair. Island of the Minotaur: The Greek Myths of Ancient Crete. Oberman, Sheldon. 2003. 96p. (J). 19.95 *(978-1-56656-531-8(6)*, Crocodile Bks.) Interlink Publishing Group, Inc.

Dray, Matt. Dougal, the Garbage Dump Bear. Dray, Matt. 2005. 32p. (J). pap. *(978-0-14-350097-1(X))* Penguin Publishing Group.

Draycott, Michelle. Daisy Wants to Go Riding, 1 vol. Dale, Jay. 2012. (Wonder Words Ser.). (ENG.). 32p. (gr. k-2). pap. 5.99 *(978-1-4296-8920-5(X)*, Engage Literacy) Capstone Pr., Inc.

—Here I Go, 1 vol. Dale, Jay. 2012. (Wonder Words Ser.). (ENG.). 32p. (gr. k-2). pap. 5.99 *(978-1-4296-8892-5(0)*, Engage Literacy) Capstone Pr., Inc.

—Pippa & the Flowers, 1 vol. Dale, Jay. 2012. (Wonder Words Ser.). (ENG.). 32p. (gr. k-2). pap. 5.99 *(978-1-4296-8908-3(0)*, Engage Literacy) Capstone Pr., Inc.

Drayton, Adrienne. Mindful Messages Mentoring Workbook: Healing Thoughts for the Hip & Hop Descendants from the Motherland. Day, Deborah A. Patterson, L. Kahlil, ed. 2nd l.t. ed. 2004. 192p. (YA). per. 14.95 *(978-0-9704048-2-4(4))* Ashay by the Bay.

Drayton, Marta. Learning to Learn: Strengthening Study Skills & Brain Power. March, Janet, photos by. Frender, Gloria. 3rd ed. 2013. (Tres Ser.). (ENG.). 288p. (J). pap. 22.99 *(978-1-62950-000-3(3))* Incentive Pubns., Inc.

Dreany, E. Joseph. Annie Oakley, Sharpshooter. Verral, Charles Spain. 2011. 28p. pap. 35.95 *(978-1-258-06762-5(5))* Literary Licensing, LLC.

—George Washington: Our First Leader. Stevenson, Augusta. 2014. (History's All-Stars Ser.). (ENG.). 208p. (J). (gr. 3-7). pap. 6.99 *(978-1-4814-0703-8(1)*, Simon & Schuster/Paula Wiseman Bks.) Simon & Schuster/Paula Wiseman Bks.

—The Lone Ranger. Fletcher, Steffi. 2013. (Little Golden Book Ser.). (ENG.). 24p. (J). (-k). 3.99 *(978-0-449-81793-3(8)*, Golden Bks.) Random Hse. Children's Bks.

Dreidemy, Joëlle, et al. Adventure Homes. Bailey, Gerry. 2013. (ENG.). 32p. (J). *(978-0-7787-0287-0(1))*; pap. *(978-0-7787-0291-7(X))* Crabtree Publishing Co.

Dreidemy, Joëlle. Cinderella: The Terrible Truth. North, Laura. 2014. (ENG.). 32p. (J). *(978-0-7787-1326-5(1))* Crabtree Publishing Co.

Dreidemy, Joëlle. Cooking Club Chaos! #4. Hiranandani, Veera. 2015. (Phoebe G. Green Ser.: 4). (ENG.). 112p. (J). (gr. 1-3). 4.99 ***(978-0-448-46701-6(1)***, Grosset & Dunlap) Penguin Publishing Group.

Dreidemy, Joëlle. Dragons Do Eat Homework. Jones, Marcia Thornton & Dadey, Debbie. 2007. 64p. (J). *(978-0-545-00234-9(6))* Scholastic, Inc.

—Ghosts Do Splash in Puddles. Jones, Marcia Thornton & Dadey, Debbie. 2006. 64p. (J). pap. *(978-0-439-87629-2(X))* Scholastic, Inc.

—Hedgehogs Do Not Like Heights. Forde, Patricia. 2011. (Blue Bananas Ser.). (ENG.). 48p. (J). (gr. k-2). pap. 5.99 *(978-1-4052-5432-8(7))* Egmont Bks., Ltd. GBR. Dist: Independent Pubs. Group.

—The Lamb Who Came for Dinner. Smallman, Steve. 2007. 32p. (J). (gr. -1-2). 15.95 *(978-1-58925-067-3(2))* Tiger Tales.

Dreidemy, Joelle. Lunch Will Never Be the Same!, No. 1. Hiranandani, Veera. 2014. (Phoebe G. Green Ser.: 1). (ENG.). 96p. (J). (gr. 1-3). 12.99 *(978-0-448-46696-5(1)*, Grosset & Dunlap) Penguin Publishing Group.

Dreidemy, Joëlle. Lunch Will Never Be the Same!, No. 1. Hiranandani, Veera. 2014. (Phoebe G. Green Ser.: 1). (ENG.). 96p. (J). (gr. 1-3). pap. 4.99 *(978-0-448-46695-8(3)*, Grosset & Dunlap) Penguin Publishing Group.

—My Explosive Diary. Gale, Emily. 2014. (Eliza Boom Ser.: 1). (ENG.). 128p. (J). (gr. 1-4). 15.99 *(978-1-4814-0650-5(7)*, Simon & Schuster/Paula Wiseman Bks.) Simon & Schuster/Paula Wiseman Bks.

—A Passport to Pastries #3. Hiranandani, Veera. 2015. (Phoebe G. Green Ser.: 3). (ENG.). 112p. (J). (gr. 1-3). 4.99 *(978-0-448-46699-6(6)*, Grosset & Dunlap) Penguin Publishing Group.

—Phoebe G. Green - Farm Fresh Fun, No. 2. Hiranandani, Veera. 2014. (Phoebe G. Green Ser.: 2). (ENG.). 96p. (J). (gr. 1-3). 12.99 *(978-0-448-46698-9(8)*, Grosset & Dunlap) Penguin Publishing Group.

Dreidemy, Joelle. Phoebe G. Green Farm Fresh Fun. Hiranandani, Veera. 2014. (Phoebe G. Green Ser.: 2). (ENG.). 96p. (J). (gr. 1-3). pap. 4.99 *(978-0-448-46697-2(X)*, Grosset & Dunlap) Penguin Publishing Group.

Dreidemy, Joëlle. Smelly Peter: The Great Pea Eater. Smallman, Steve. 2008. 32p. (J). (gr. 4-7). 15.95 *(978-1-58925-076-5(1))* Tiger Tales.

—Stinky Space Race. Collins, Tim. 2014. (Cosmic Colin Ser.: 1). (ENG.). 128p. (J). (gr. 4-6). pap. 7.99 *(978-1-78055-171-5(1))* O'Mara, Michael Bks., Ltd. GBR. Dist: Independent Pubs. Group.

—The Usborne Healthy Cookbook. Allman, Howard, photos by. Patchett, Fiona. 2008. (Children's Cooking Ser.). (ENG.). 64p. (J). (gr. 4-7). pap. 16.99 *(978-0-7945-2062-5(6)*, Usborne) EDC Publishing.

—What's in Store? Goodhart, Pippa. 2009. (ENG.). 32p. (J). (gr. -1-k). 16.99 *(978-1-4052-2760-5(5))* Egmont Bks., Ltd. GBR. Dist: Independent Pubs. Group.

—The Witch with a Twitch. Marlow, Layn. (Tiger Tales Ser.). (J). (gr. -1-2). 2006. 28p. pap. 6.95 *(978-1-58925-400-8(7))*; 2005. 32p. 15.95 *(978-1-58925-052-9(4))* Tiger Tales.

Dreidemy, Joëlle. Witches Do Not Like Bicycles. Forde, Patricia. 2015. (Blue Banana Ser.). (ENG.). 48p. (J). pap. 7.99 ***(978-1-4052-7071-7(3))*** Egmont Bks., Ltd. GBR. Dist: Independent Pubs. Group.

Dreidemy, Joëlle. Wizards Do Roast Turkeys. Jones, Marcia Thornton & Dadey, Debbie. 2007. 64p. (J). pap. *(978-0-545-00235-6(4))* Scholastic, Inc.

Dreidemy, Joëlle, et al. Working Homes. Bailey, Gerry. 2013. (ENG.). 32p. (J). *(978-0-7787-0290-0(1))* Crabtree Publishing Co.

Dreidemy, Joëlle & Bigwood, John. Sneezy Alien Attack. Collins, Tim. 2014. (Cosmic Colin Ser.: 2). (ENG.). 128p. (J). (gr. 4-6). pap. 7.99 *(978-1-78055-242-2(4))* O'Mara, Michael Bks., Ltd. GBR. Dist: Independent Pubs. Group.

Dreidemy, Joëlle & Jones, Anna. Frogs Do Not Like Dragons. Forde, Patricia & Agnew, Kate. 2010. (Blue Bananas Ser.). (ENG.). 48p. (J). (gr. k-2). pap. 5.99 *(978-1-4052-4779-5(7))* Egmont Bks., Ltd. GBR. Dist: Independent Pubs. Group.

Dreidemy, Joëlle, jt. illus. see Radford, Karen.

Dreidmy, Joelle. Press Play. Fine, Anne. ed. 2006. (Red Bananas Ser.). (ENG.). 48p. (J). (gr. k-2). pap. 5.99 *(978-1-4052-1856-6(8))* Egmont Bks., Ltd. GBR. Dist: Independent Pubs. Group.

Dreis, Stella. Happiness Is a Watermelon on Your Head. Hahn, Daniel. 2013. (ENG.). 40p. (J). (gr. k-2). pap. 9.99 *(978-1-907912-05-4(3))* Phoenix Yard Bks. GBR. Dist: Independent Pubs. Group.

Dreisbach, Kristin Wolf & Foreman, Austin Lee. Winston the Duck & His Big Orange Bill. Dreisbach, Kristin Wolf. 2013. 20p. pap. 13.97 *(978-1-62212-897-6(4)*, Strategic Bk. Publishing) Strategic Book Publishing & Rights Agency (SBPRA).

Drescher, Heather. You & Me Make Three. Stephens, Edna Cucksey et al. 2008. (Build-A-Bear Workshop Ser.). 32p. (J). (gr. -1-3). 0.00 *(978-0-9798088-0-7(4))* EDCO Publishing, Inc.

—You & Me Make Three & Accompanying Plush B. B. the Bear. Stephens, Edna Cucksey et al. 2008. 32p. (J). 35.00 *(978-0-9798088-2-1(0))* EDCO Publishing, Inc.

Drescher, Henrick. The Fool & the Flying Ship. Metaxas, Eric. 2007. (Rabbit Ears: A Classic Tale Ser.). 36p. (gr. -1-3). 25.65 *(978-1-59961-308-6(5))* Spotlight.

Drescher, Henrik. The Gruesome Guide to World Monsters. Sierra, Judy. 2005. (ENG.). 64p. (J). (gr. 2-5). 18.99 *(978-0-7636-1727-1(X))* Candlewick Pr.

—An Interview with Harry the Tarantula. Tyson, Leigh Ann. 2003. (ENG.). 32p. (J). (gr. -1-3). 15.95 *(978-0-7922-5122-4(9))* National Geographic Society.

—The Story of Brer Rabbit & the Wonderful Tar Baby. Harris, Joel Chandler. 2004. (Rabbit Ears-A Classic Tale Ser.). 52p. (gr. k-5). 25.65 *(978-1-59197-761-2(4))* Spotlight.

Drescher, Henrik. Pat the Beastie: A Pull-and-Poke Book. Drescher, Henrik. 2009. (ENG.). 11p. (J). (gr. -1-3). bds. 11.95 *(978-0-7611-5610-9(0)*, 15610) Workman Publishing Co., Inc.

Dress, Robert. The Art Contest: No Cheating Allowed! Banks, Steven. 2006. (SpongeBob SquarePants Ser.: 12). (ENG.). 24p. (J). (gr. -1-3). pap. 3.99 *(978-1-4169-0667-4(3)*, Simon Spotlight/Nickelodeon) Simon Spotlight/Nickelodeon.

—Class Confusion. Willson, Sarah. 2006. (SpongeBob SquarePants Ser.: 11). (ENG.). 24p. (J). (gr. -1-3). pap. 3.99 *(978-1-4169-1239-2(8)*, Simon Spotlight/Nickelodeon) Simon Spotlight/Nickelodeon.

—Mother Knows Best. Willson, Sarah. 2006. (SpongeBob SquarePants Chapter Bks.: Vol. 11). (ENG.). 64p. (J). (gr. 3-7). pap. 4.99 *(978-1-4169-0793-0(9)*, Simon Spotlight/Nickelodeon) Simon Spotlight/Nickelodeon.

Dress, Robert & Duddle, Johnny. Highway Robbery. Thompson, Kate. 2009. (ENG.). 128p. (J). (gr. 5-18). 15.99 *(978-0-06-173034-4(3)*, Greenwillow Bks.) HarperCollins Pubs.

Dressen-McQueen, Stacey. Behind the Museum Door: Poems to Celebrate the Wonders of Museums. Hopkins, Lee Bennett. 2007. (ENG.). 32p. (J). (gr. -1-2). 16.95 *(978-0-8109-1204-5(X)*, Abrams Bks. for Young Readers) Abrams.

—Boxes for Katje. Fleming, Candace. 2003. (ENG.). 40p. (J). (gr. -1-3). 17.99 *(978-0-374-30922-0(1)*, Farrar, Straus & Giroux (BYR)) Farrar, Straus & Giroux.

—Boxes for Katje. Fleming, Candace. 2004. (YA). 27.95 incl. audio *(978-0-8045-6930-9(4)*, SAC6930) Spoken Arts, Inc.

Drew, Benjamin. Grandma's Adventures with Benjamin. Drew, Joyce. 2013. 16p. pap. 24.95 *(978-1-63004-098-7(3))* America Star Bks.

Drew-Brook, Deborah & Cormack, Allan. Volcanoes Inside & Out. Souza, D. M. 2006. (On My Own Science Ser.). (ENG.). 48p. (gr. 2-4). per. 6.95 *(978-1-57505-853-5(7))* Lerner Publishing Group.

Drew-Brook, Deborah, jt. illus. see Cormack, Allan.

Drewes, Dan. The Case of the Missing Peanut Butter: The Adventures of Peanut Butter Bob. Seykora, Teresa. 2010. 32p. 12.99 *(978-1-4520-2678-7(5))* AuthorHouse.

—Hair Like That. Wimberly, Nikisha. 2010. 24p. 13.00 *(978-1-4520-0177-7(4))* AuthorHouse.

—Lilith Celebrates Lammas. Manderly, Lorin. 2010. 36p. pap. 15.50 *(978-1-4520-2689-3(0))* AuthorHouse.

—"You're a Meany!" Douglas, Rachel. 2011. 13p. pap. 10.19 *(978-1-4567-8643-4(1))* AuthorHouse.

Drews, Judith. Lily Loves. Lüftner, Kai. 2012. (ENG.). 32p. (J). (gr. -1-3). pap. 16.95 *(978-1-897476-94-9(9))* Simply Read Bks. CAN. Dist: Ingram Pub. Services.

Dreyer, Laura. The ABC Bible Verse Book. Scherm, Deedra. 2007. (ENG.). 26p. (J). (gr. -1-3). bds. 8.99 *(978-1-934789-04-9(6))* Lemon Vision Productions.

—Cinco Panes y un Par de Peces: Una Historia de la Fe y de Dar. Scherm, Deedra. 2008. (SPA.). 20p. (J). (gr. -1-3). bds. 7.99 *(978-1-934789-06-3(2))* Lemon Vision Productions.

—Five Loaves & a Couple of Fish: A Story of Faith & Giving. Scherm, Deedra. 2007. (ENG.). 20p. 7.99 *(978-1-934789-01-8(1))* Lemon Vision Productions.

—Only One Me: A Sweet Little Rhyme to Help Your Light Shine. Scherm, Deedra. 2008. (ENG.). 22p. (J). (gr. -1-3). 7.99 *(978-1-934789-02-5(X))* Lemon Vision Productions.

—Solo uno Como Yo: Una Rima Dulce y Pequenita para Ayudar Hacer Brillar Tu Lucecita. Scherm, Deedra. 2008. (SPA.). 22p. (J). (gr. -1-3). 7.99 *(978-1-934789-05-6(4))* Lemon Vision Productions.

—The Whale & Jonah: A Story of Obedience & Forgiveness. Scherm, Deedra. 2007. (ENG.). 20p. 7.99 *(978-1-934789-00-1(3))* Lemon Vision Productions.

Driessen, Anita. The Night after Christmas. Hebler, Michael. 2010. (ENG.). 28p. (J). 8.99 *(978-0-615-39525-8(2)*, Night After Night Pubns., Inc.) Hebler, Michael.

Driessen, Elizabeth. On the Banks of the Amazon/en las orillas del Amazonas. Allen, Nancy Kelly. de la Vega, Eida, tr. 2003.Tr. of En las orillas del Amazonas. (SPA & ENG.). 32p. (J). (gr. -1-3). 16.95 *(978-0-9720192-7-9(8)*, 626999, Raven Tree Pr.,Csi) Continental Sales, Inc.

Driscoll, Amanda. Wally Does Not Want a Haircut. 2016. (J). ***(978-0-553-53579-2(X))*** Knopf, Alfred A. Inc.

Driver, Audrey. Timmy Turtle Teaches. Takara, Kathryn Waddell. 2012. 54p. pap. 29.95 *(978-0-9840204-3-0(8))* Pacific Raven Pr.

Droney, John. The Ghost Hunter & the Ghost of the Amazon Warrior. Kline, Trish & Donev, Mary. 2003. 96p. (J). per. 7.50 *(978-0-9717234-1-2(9))* Ghost Hunter Productions.

Dronsfield, Paul. Bob-Alongs - Colors: Bath Books That Float. 2012. (Bob-Along Bks.). (ENG.). 8p. (J). (gr. -1 — 1). 5.99 *(978-1-4380-0184-5(3))* Barron's Educational Series, Inc.

—The Bulldozer. 2009. (My Shiny Little Truck Bks.). (ENG.). 10p. (J). bds. 3.95 *(978-1-58117-858-6(1)*, Intervisual/Piggy Toes) Bendon, Inc.

—The Concrete Mixer. 2009. (My Shiny Little Truck Bks.). (ENG.). 10p. (J). bds. 3.95 *(978-1-58117-859-3(X)*, Intervisual/Piggy Toes) Bendon, Inc.

—The Digger. 2009. (My Shiny Little Truck Bks.). (ENG.). 10p. (J). bds. 3.95 *(978-1-58117-860-9(3)*, Intervisual/Piggy Toes) Bendon, Inc.

—The Dump Truck. 2009. (My Shiny Little Truck Bks.). (ENG.). 10p. (J). bds. 3.95 *(978-1-58117-861-6(1)*, Intervisual/Piggy Toes) Bendon, Inc.

—Pilot Your Own Deep-Sea Submarine. Trowell, Michelle. 2007. 22p. (J). (gr. -1-3). *(978-1-84666-352-9(0)*, Tide Mill Pr.) Top That! Publishing PLC.

—Rescue Helicopter. Top That Publishing Staff, ed. 2007. (Story Book Ser.). (ENG.). 33p. (J). (gr. -1). bds. *(978-1-84666-179-2(X)*, Tide Mill Pr.) Top That! Publishing PLC.

Dronzek, Laura. Birds. Henkes, Kevin. 2009. 32p. (J). (gr. -1-k). (ENG.). 17.99 *(978-0-06-136304-7(9))*; lib. bdg. 18.89 *(978-0-06-136305-4(7))* HarperCollins Pubs. (Greenwillow Bks.).

—It Is Night. Rowand, Phyllis. 2014. (ENG.). 32p. (J). (gr. -1-3). 16.99 *(978-0-06-225024-7(8)*, Greenwillow Bks.) HarperCollins Pubs.

—Moonlight. Griffith, Helen V. 2012. (ENG.). 32p. (J). (gr. -1-k). 16.99 *(978-0-06-203285-0(2)*, Greenwillow Bks.) HarperCollins Pubs.

—Tippy-Toe Chick, Go! Shannon, George. 2003. (ENG.). 32p. (J). (gr. -1-3). 17.99 *(978-0-06-029823-4(5)*, Greenwillow Bks.) HarperCollins Pubs.

Dronzek, Laura. When Spring Comes. Henkes, Kevin. 2016. 40p. (J). (gr. -1-3). 18.89 ***(978-0-06-233140-3(X)***, Collins Design) HarperCollins Pubs.

Dronzek, Laura. White Is for Blueberry. Shannon, George. 2005. 40p. (J). (gr. -1). lib. bdg. 17.89 *(978-0-06-029276-8(8))* HarperCollins Pubs.

—White Is for Blueberry. Shannon, George & Shannon. 2005. (ENG.). 40p. (J). (gr. -1-3). 17.99 *(978-0-06-029275-1(X)*, Greenwillow Bks.) HarperCollins Pubs.

Droop, Constanza. Felix & the Flying Suitcase Adventure. Langen, Annette. 2003. 47p. (J). 14.99 *(978-1-59384-035-8(7))* Parklane Publishing.

—Felix Explores Planet Earth. Langen, Annette. 2004. (Perfect for Earth Day Promotions! Ser.). 47p. (J). 14.99 *(978-1-59384-030-3(6))* Parklane Publishing.

—Felix Travels Back in Time. Langen, Annette. 2004. 40p. (J). 14.99 *(978-1-59384-032-7(2))* Parklane Publishing.

—Felix's Christmas Around the World. Langen, Annette. 2003. 40p. (J). 14.99 *(978-1-59384-036-5(5))* Parklane Publishing.

—Jesus Is Risen. Krenzer, Rolf. Maloney, Linda M., tr. from GER. 2005. 24p. (gr. -1-3). 14.95 *(978-0-8146-2764-8(1))* Liturgical Pr.

—Letters from Felix: A Little Rabbit on a World Tour. Langen, Annette. 2003. 47p. (J). 14.99 *(978-1-59384-034-1(9))* Parklane Publishing.

Droop, Constanza. Que? Como? Por Que?: Las Estaciones del Ano. Droop, Constanza. Caballero, D., tr. 2007. (Junior (Silver Dolphin) Ser.). 16p. (J). (gr. -1). *(978-970-718-492-3(2)*, Silver Dolphin en Español) Advanced Marketing, S. de R. L. de C. V.

Drotar. Eloy the Elk & His Desert Friends. Clapp. Clapp, ed. 2009. (J). pap. 9.95 *(978-0-9825181-0-6(2))* Arizona Elk Society.

Drotleff, David J. The Littlest Elf: Marvin Mcgee & the Candle of Fate. Snedeker, Erin. 2010. 44p. pap. 15.50 *(978-1-60911-194-6(X)*, Eloquent Bks.) Strategic Book Publishing & Rights Agency (SBPRA).

Drouin, Julie Saint-Onge, jt. illus. see Arseneau, Philippe.

Drown, Eleanor J. The Wheelchair Adventures of Jeannie & the Wallpaper Children. Kraemer, Lillian Rosa. 2011. 150p. 40.95 *(978-1-258-08936-8(X))* Literary Licensing, LLC.

Drozd, Jerzy, jt. illus. see Colón, Ernie.

Drucker, Susan. Kunu's Basket: A Story of Indian Island, 1 vol. Francis, Lee DeCora. 2012. (ENG.). 32p. (J). 16.95 *(978-0-88448-330-4(4))* Tilbury Hse. Pubs.

Druckman, Joan. Memory Emory & His Hiding Places. Druckman, Michael. 2006. 24p. (gr. -1-3). per. 10.99 *(978-1-59858-060-0(4))* Dog Ear Publishing, LLC.

Drummond, Allan. The Journey That Saved Curious George: The True Wartime Escape of Margret & H. A. Rey. Borden, Louise & Borden, Louise W. 2005. (Curious George Ser.). (ENG.). 80p. (J). (gr. 2-5). 17.00 *(978-0-618-33924-2(8))* Houghton Mifflin Harcourt Publishing Co.

—The Journey That Saved Curious George: The True Wartime Escape of Margret & H. A. Rey. Borden, Louise W. 2010. (Curious George Ser.). (ENG.). 80p. (J). (gr. 2-5). pap. 8.99 *(978-0-547-41746-2(2))* Houghton Mifflin Harcourt Publishing Co.

Drummond, Allan. Energy Island: How One Community Harnessed the Wind & Changed Their World. Drummond, Allan. 2011. (ENG.). 40p. (J). (gr. 1-5). 17.99 *(978-0-374-32184-0(1)*, Farrar, Straus & Giroux (BYR)) Farrar, Straus & Giroux.

Drummond, Sarah. Raven & the Red Ball. 2013. (ENG.). 28p. (J). 9.95 *(978-0-7649-6609-5(X))* Pomegranate Communications, Inc.

Drummond, V. H. Carbonel: The King of the Cats. Sleigh, Barbara. 2004. (ENG.). 216p. (J). (gr. 4-7). reprint ed. 16.95 *(978-1-59017-126-4(8)*, NYR Children's Collection) New York Review of Bks., Inc., The.

Druschel, Bob. Finny the Friendly Shark. Janacone, Matt. 2005. 40p. (J). per. 20.99 *(978-1-58939-655-5(3))* Virtualbookworm.com Publishing, Inc.

Dry, Roland. The Pied Piper. Barkow, Henriette. 2004. 32p. (J). *(978-1-85269-990-1(6))*; (SOM & ENG.). pap. *(978-1-85269-995-6(7))*; (ENG & POR.). pap. *(978-1-85269-980-2(9))*; (ENG & POL.). pap. *(978-1-85269-975-8(2))*; (PAN & ENG.). pap. *(978-1-85269-970-3(1))*; (ENG & ITA.). pap. *(978-1-85269-965-9(5))*; (ENG & GUJ.). pap. *(978-1-85269-955-0(8))*; (ENG & GER.). pap. *(978-1-85269-950-5(7))*; (FRE & ENG.). pap. *(978-1-85269-945-1(0))*; (ENG & PER.). pap. *(978-1-85269-940-6(X))*; (ENG & CZE.). pap. *(978-1-85269-935-2(3))*; (ENG & ARA.). pap. *(978-1-85269-920-8(5))*; (URD & ENG.). pap. *(978-1-85269-916-1(7))*; (ENG & ALB.). pap. *(978-1-85269-915-4(9))*; (TUR & ENG.). pap. *(978-1-85269-911-6(6))*; (ENG & TAM.). pap. *(978-1-85269-906-2(X))*; (ENG & SPA.). pap. *(978-1-85269-901-7(9))* Mantra Lingua.

—Pied Piper. 2004. (J). E-Book incl. cd-rom *(978-1-84444-466-3(X))* Mantra Lingua.

Dryhurst, Dinah. The Railway Children. Dryhurst, Dinah, tr. Nesbit, E. 2004. 184p. 18.95 *(978-1-56792-261-5(9))* Godine, David R. Pub.

Drzewiecki, Paul. Just Like Dad. Hiris, Monica. l.t. ed. 2003. (ENG.). 8p. (gr. k-1). pap. 4.95 *(978-1-879835-76-4(2))* Kaeden Corp.

—My Native American School. Gould, Carol. l.t. ed. 2003. (ENG.). 16p. (gr. k-2). pap. 5.95 *(978-1-879835-77-1(0))* Kaeden Corp.
—Snake Hunts for Lunch. Hoenecke, Karen. l.t. ed. 2005. (ENG.). 12p. (gr. k-2). pap. 5.95 *(978-1-57874-006-2(1),* Kaeden Bks.) Kaeden Corp.
D'souza, Maris. It's Okay to Be Me! Amarsingh, Bahia. l.t. ed. 2011. (ENG.). 42p. pap. 12.99 *(978-1-4636-6023-9(5))* CreateSpace Independent Publishing Platform.
D'Souza, Mel. Emily & the Captain. Hall, Noelle. 2012. (ENG.). 32p. pap. *(978-1-894377-15-7(X))* Breakwater Bks., Ltd.
du Bois, William Pène. The Mousewife. Godden, Rumer. 2009. (ENG.). 56p. (J). (gr. -1-2). 14.95 *(978-1-59017-310-7(4),* NYR Children's Collection) New York Review of Bks., Inc., The.
du Bois, William Pène. Twenty-One Balloons. du Bois, William Pène. 2005. 180p. (J). lib. bdg. 15.00 *(978-1-4242-2270-4(2))* Fitzgerald Bks.
Du Houx, E. M. Cornell. Seasons. Kroner, David & Du Houx, Ramona. 2007. 70p. (J). per. 6.95 *(978-1-882190-54-6(8))* Polar Bear & Co.
—Two Birds in a Box. Ouilette, K. T. Valliere-Denis. 2006. 59p. (J). per. 6.95 *(978-1-882190-55-3(6))* Polar Bear & Co.
—Wisdom of Bear. Barry, Holly et al. 2006. 63p. per. 6.95 *(978-1-882190-50-8(5))* Polar Bear & Co.
du Houx, Emily. Madalynn the Monarch Butterfly & Her Quest to Michoacan. Haque, Mary Baca. Jones, Francisco Lancaster, tr. from ENG. 2003. (ENG & SPA.). 64p. pap. 14.00 *(978-1-882190-52-2(1))* Polar Bear & Co.
—A Voice for the Redwoods. Halter, Loretta. 2003. 64p. pap. 14.00 *(978-1-882190-66-9(1))* Polar Bear & Co.
du Houx, Emily C. Millicent the Magnificent. Hoffmann, Burton R. 2004. 64p. pap. 12.00 *(978-1-882190-68-3(8))* Polar Bear & Co.
du Houx, Ramona. Women Who Walk with the Sky. Levesque, Dawn Renee. 2003. 64p. pap. 14.00 *(978-1-882190-12-6(2))* Polar Bear & Co.
du Houx, Ramona & Cornell du Houx, Emily. Manitou, a Mythological Journey in Time. du Houx, Ramona et al. Cornell du Houx, Alex et al. unabr. ed. 2003. 224p. pap. 12.00 *(978-1-882190-77-5(7))* Polar Bear & Co.
Du Pont, Brittany. Chosen Last. Oehmichen, Ariel. 2012. 28p. pap. 9.99 *(978-1-937165-26-0(4))* Orange Hat Publishing.
—Invincible Me. Schmidt, Shawntay. 2013. 24p. pap. 8.99 *(978-1-937165-61-1(2))* Orange Hat Publishing.
Duarte, Pamela. Barbie - From the Heart. Silk, Courtney. 2014. (Panorama Sticker Storybook Ser.: 1). (ENG.). 16p. (J). (gr. -1-1). 5.99 *(978-0-7944-3315-4(4))* Studio Fun International.
—Barbie Loves Horses (Barbie) Man-Kong, Mary. 2013. (Color Plus Stencil Ser.). (ENG.). 64p. (J). (gr. -1-2). pap. 5.99 *(978-0-449-81612-7(5),* Golden Bks.) Random Hse. Children's Bks.
—Barbie Mix & Match. Reader's Digest Editors. 2009. (Mix & Match Ser.). (ENG.). 14p. (J). (gr. -1-k). bds. 9.99 *(978-0-7944-1776-5(0))* Reader's Digest Assn., Inc., The.
—Barbie Project Pet Park. Reader's Digest Staff & London, Olivia. 2012. (Pop & Play Ser.: 1). (ENG.). 10p. (J). (gr. -1-3). bds. 12.99 *(978-0-7944-2582-1(8))* Reader's Digest Assn., Inc., The.
—Barbie Style 'n Fun. Reader's Digest Staff & Lombardi, Kristine. 2011. (Wall Clings Ser.). (ENG.). 16p. (J). (gr. -1-1). pap. 9.99 *(978-0-7944-2331-5(0))* Reader's Digest Assn., Inc., The.
—Beyond the Clouds. Golden Books Staff. 2005. (Paint Box Book Ser.). (ENG.). 32p. (J). (gr. -1-2). pap. 3.99 *(978-0-375-83362-5(5),* Golden Bks.) Random Hse. Children's Bks.
—Dreamy Dreamhouse (Barbie: Life in the Dream House) Golden Books Staff. 2014. (Reusable Sticker Book Ser.). (ENG.). 24p. (J). (gr. -1-2). pap. 6.99 *(978-0-385-37842-0(4),* Golden Bks.) Random Hse. Children's Bks.
—An Egg-Stra Special Easter! (Barbie) Random House Staff. 2014. (Color Plus Card Stock Ser.). (ENG.). 48p. (J). (gr. -1-2). pap. 3.99 *(978-0-385-37319-7(8),* Random Hse. Bks. for Young Readers) Random Hse. Children's Bks.
—Fun with Barbie & Friends Storybook & Magnetic Playset. Reader's Digest Editors & Lombardi, Kristine. 2009. (Magnetic Playset Ser.). (ENG.). 16p. (J). (gr. k-3). bds. 15.99 *(978-0-7944-1910-3(0))* Reader's Digest Assn., Inc., The.
Duarte, Pamela & Musselman, Christian. Barbie Loves Parties (Barbie) Golden Books. 2014. (Full-Color Activity Book with Stickers Ser.). (ENG.). 32p. (J). (gr. -1-2). pap. 5.99 *(978-0-385-38495-7(5),* Golden Bks.) Random Hse. Children's Bks.
Duarte, Pamela, jt. illus. see Golden Books Staff.
Dubac, Debra. The Itchy Little Musk Ox. Brown, Tricia. 2006. (ENG.). 32p. (J). (gr. -1-3). pap. 9.99 *(978-0-88240-614-5(0),* Alaska Northwest Bks.) Graphic Arts Ctr. Publishing Co.
—Musher's Night Before Christmas, 1 vol. Brown, Tricia. 2011. (Night Before Christmas Ser.). (ENG.). 32p. (J). (gr. k-3). 16.99 *(978-1-58980-843-0(6))* Pelican Publishing Co., Inc.
Dubin, Jill. The Biggest Leaf Pile. Metzger, Steve. 2003. (J). *(978-0-439-55657-6(0))* Scholastic, Inc.
—I Can Cooperate! Parker, David. 2004. (J). *(978-0-439-62812-9(1))* Scholastic, Inc.
—I Can Share! Parker, David. 2005. (J). *(978-0-439-73587-2(4))* Scholastic, Inc.
—Over in a River: Flowing Out to the Sea. Berkes, Marianne. 2013. (ENG.). 32p. (J). (gr. -1-3). 16.95 *(978-1-58469-329-1(0));* pap. 8.95 *(978-1-58469-330-7(4))* Dawn Pubns.
—Over in Australia: Amazing Animals down Under. Berkes, Marianne. 2011. 32p. (J). (gr. -1-3). 16.95 *(978-1-58469-135-8(2));* pap. 8.95 *(978-1-58469-136-5(0))* Dawn Pubns.
—Over in the Arctic: Where the Cold Winds Blow. Berkes, Marianne. 2008. 32p. (J). (gr. -1-2). 16.95 *(978-1-58469-109-9(3));* pap. 8.95 *(978-1-58469-110-5(7))* Dawn Pubns.
—Over in the Forest: Come & Take a Peek. Berkes, Marianne. 2012. (ENG.). 32p. (J). 16.95 *(978-1-58469-162-4(X));* pap. 8.95 *(978-1-58469-163-1(8))* Dawn Pubns.
—Over on a Mountain: Somewhere in the World. Berkes, Marianne. 2015. (ENG.). 32p. (J). (gr. -1-3). 16.95 *(978-1-58469-518-9(8))* Dawn Pubns.
—Samantha Stays Safe. Mishica, Clare. 2012. 32p. (J). pap. 8.00 *(978-1-935014-40-9(4))* Hutchings, John Pubs.
Dubisch, Michael. Blue Bay Mystery, 6 vols. Warner, Gertrude Chandler. 2009. (Boxcar Children Graphic Novels Ser.). 32p. (J). (gr. 2-5). 28.50 *(978-1-60270-591-3(7))* ABDO Publishing Co.
—The Boxcar Children. Denton, Shannon Eric & Warner, Gertrude Chandler. 2009. (Boxcar Children Graphic Novels Ser.). 32p. (J). (gr. 2-5). lib. bdg. 28.50 *(978-1-60270-586-9(X))* ABDO Publishing Co.
—Mike's Mystery, 5 vols. Warner, Gertrude Chandler. 2009. (Boxcar Children Graphic Novels Ser.). 32p. (J). (gr. 2-5). 28.50 *(978-1-60270-590-6(9))* ABDO Publishing Co.
—Mystery Ranch, 4 vols. Warner, Gertrude Chandler. 2009. (Boxcar Children Graphic Novels Ser.). 32p. (J). (gr. 2-5). 28.50 *(978-1-60270-589-0(5))* ABDO Publishing Co.
—Surprise Island, 2 vols. Worley, Rob M. & Warner, Gertrude Chandler. 2009. (Boxcar Children Graphic Novels Ser.). 32p. (J). (gr. 2-5). 28.50 *(978-1-60270-587-6(9))* ABDO Publishing Co.
—The Yellow House Mystery, 3 vols. Warner, Gertrude Chandler. 2009. (Boxcar Children Graphic Novels Ser.). 32p. (J). (gr. 2-5). 28.50 *(978-1-60270-588-3(7))* ABDO Publishing Co.
Dubisch, Mike. The Amusement Park Mystery, 10 vols. Denton, Shannon Eric & Warner, Gertrude Chandler. 2010. (Boxcar Children Graphic Novels Ser.). 32p. (J). (gr. 2-5). 28.50 *(978-1-60270-718-4(9))* ABDO Publishing Co.
—The Boxcar Children: A Graphic Novel, No. 1. Denton, Shannon Eric. 2009. (Boxcar Children Graphic Novels Ser.). (ENG.). 32p. (J). (gr. 2-5). 6.99 *(978-0-8075-2867-9(6))* Whitman, Albert & Co.
—The Castle Mystery, 12 vols. Denton, Shannon Eric & Warner, Gertrude Chandler. 2010. (Boxcar Children Graphic Novels Ser.). 32p. (J). (gr. 2-5). 28.50 *(978-1-60270-720-7(0))* ABDO Publishing Co.
—The Haunted Cabin Mystery. 2009. (Boxcar Children Graphic Novels Ser.: No. 9). (ENG.). 32p. (J). (gr. 2-5). pap. 6.99 *(978-0-8075-3180-8(4))* Whitman, Albert & Co.
—Mike's Mystery, No. 5. 2009. (Boxcar Children Graphic Novels Ser.). (ENG.). 32p. (J). (gr. 2-5). 6.99 *(978-0-8075-2871-6(4))* Whitman, Albert & Co.
—Mystery Ranch. 2009. (Boxcar Children Graphic Novels Ser.). (ENG.). 32p. (J). (gr. 2-5). 6.99 *(978-0-8075-2870-9(6))* Whitman, Albert & Co.
—The Pizza Mystery. 2010. (Boxcar Children Graphic Novels Ser.). (ENG.). 32p. (J). (gr. 2-5). pap. 6.99 *(978-0-8075-6537-7(7))* Whitman, Albert & Co.
—The Pizza Mystery, 11 vols. Worley, Rob M. & Warner, Gertrude Chandler. 2010. (Boxcar Children Graphic Novels Ser.). 32p. (J). (gr. 2-5). 28.50 *(978-1-60270-719-1(7))* ABDO Publishing Co.
—Snowbound Mystery. Warner, Gertrude Chandler. 2009. (Boxcar Children Graphic Novels Ser.). (ENG.). 32p. (J). (gr. 2-5). pap. 6.99 *(978-0-8075-7515-4(1))* Whitman, Albert & Co.
—Snowbound Mystery, 7 vols. Warner, Gertrude Chandler. 2010. (Boxcar Children Graphic Novels Ser.). 32p. (J). (gr. 2-5). 28.50 *(978-1-60270-715-3(4))* ABDO Publishing Co.
—Surprise Island. 2009. (Boxcar Children Graphic Novels Ser.). (ENG.). 32p. (J). (gr. 2-5). 6.99 *(978-0-8075-2868-6(4))* Whitman, Albert & Co.
—Tree House Mystery. 2009. (Boxcar Children Graphic Novels Ser.). (ENG.). 32p. (J). (gr. 2-5). pap. 6.99 *(978-0-8075-8088-2(0))* Whitman, Albert & Co.
—The Yellow House Mystery, No. 3. Warner, Gertrude Chandler. 2009. (Boxcar Children Graphic Novels Ser.). (ENG.). 32p. (J). (gr. 2-5). 6.99 *(978-0-8075-2869-3(2))* Whitman, Albert & Co.
Dubisch, Mike & Bloodworth, Mark. The Amusement Park Mystery. 2010. (Boxcar Children Graphic Novels Ser.). (ENG.). 32p. (J). (gr. 2-5). pap. 6.99 *(978-0-8075-0321-8(5))* Whitman, Albert & Co.
DuBois, Claude. Still My Grandma. Van Den Abeele, Veronique. 2007. 32p. (J). (gr. -1-5). 16.00 *(978-0-8028-5323-3(4),* Eerdmans Bks For Young Readers) Eerdmans, William B. Publishing Co.
DuBois, Claude K. Me Quieres O No Me Quieres? Norac, Carl. 2007. (SPA.). 32p. (J). (gr. -1-k). 12.99 *(978-84-8470-155-2(7))* Corimbo, Editorial S.L. ESP. Dist: Lectorum Pubns., Inc.
Dubois, Gérard. L' Ecuyere. Gingras, Charlotte. 2004. (Picture Bks.). (FRE.). 32p. (J). (gr. -1). *(978-2-89021-666-2(7));* pap. *(978-2-89021-665-5(9))* Diffusion du livre Mirabel (DLM).
—Monsieur Marceau: Actor Without Words. Schubert, Leda. 2012. (ENG.). 40p. (J). (gr. -1-3). 17.99 *(978-1-59643-529-2(1))* Roaring Brook Pr.
Dubois, Liz Goulet. Aaron's Bar Mitzvah. Dubois, Liz Goulet, tr. Rouss, Sylvia A. 2003. (J). 14.95 *(978-0-8246-0447-9(4))* David, Jonathan Pubs., Inc.
DuBosque, Doug. ABC Nature Riddles. Joyce, Susan. 2004. (ABC Riddles Ser.). 32p. (J). (gr. -1-k). 13.95 *(978-0-939217-53-3(8))* Peel Productions, Inc.
Dubrovin, Barbara. Fantasy Fair: Bright Stories of Imagination. Dubrovin, Barbara. 2007. 128p. (J). pap. 17.50 *(978-0-9638339-6-9(0))* Storycraft Publishing.
Dubuc, Marianne. Animal Masquerade. Dubuc, Marianne. 2012. (ENG.). 120p. (J). 16.95 *(978-1-55453-782-2(7))* Kids Can Pr., Ltd. CAN. Dist: Univ. of Toronto Pr.
—In Front of My House. Dubuc, Marianne. Ghione, Yvette, tr. from FRE. 2010. (ENG.). 120p. (J). (gr. -1-2). 18.95 *(978-1-55453-641-2(3))* Kids Can Pr., Ltd. CAN. Dist: Univ. of Toronto Pr.
DuBurke, Randy. The Bravest Girls in the World. George, Olivia. 2004. 32p. (J). lib. bdg. 15.00 *(978-1-4242-0241-6(8))* Fitzgerald Bks.
—The Bravest Girls in the World. Scholastic, Inc. Staff & George, Olivia. 2004. (Just for You Ser.). (ENG.). 32p. pap. 3.99 *(978-0-439-56875-3(7),* Teaching Resources) Scholastic, Inc.
Duburke, Randy. Catching the Moon: The Story of a Young Girl's Baseball Dream, 1 vol. Hubbard, Crystal. 2005. (ENG.). 32p. (J). (gr. 1-5). 16.95 *(978-1-58430-243-8(7))* Lee & Low Bks., Inc.
DuBurke, Randy. Catching the Moon: The Story of a Young Girl's Baseball Dream. Hubbard, Crystal. 2005. (ENG.). 32p. (J). pap. 8.95 *(978-1-60060-572-7(9))* Lee & Low Bks., Inc.
—When It's Six O'Clock in San Francisco: A Trip Through Time Zones. Omololu, Cynthia Jaynes. 2009. (ENG.). 32p. (J). (gr. -1-3). 16.99 *(978-0-618-76827-1(0))* Houghton Mifflin Harcourt Publishing Co.
DuBurke, Randy & Duburke, Randy. Best Shot in the West: The Adventures of Nat Love. McKissack, Patricia C. et al. 2012. (ENG.). 136p. (YA). (gr. 8-17). 19.99 *(978-0-8118-5749-9(2))* Chronicle Bks. LLC.
Duburke, Randy, jt. illus. see DuBurke, Randy.
Duchateau. The Fascinating Madame Tussaud. Follet, René. 2008. (ENG.). 104p. pap. 19.95 *(978-1-905460-36-6(8))* CineBook GBR. Dist: National Bk. Network.
Duck Egg Blue (Firm) Staff, et al. Colours & Shapes: Touch & Trace Early Learning Fun! Hewett, Angela. 2014. (ENG.). 26p. (J). pap. 13.50 *(978-1-84135-945-8(9))* Award Pubns. Ltd. GBR. Dist: Parkwest Pubns., Inc.
Ducker Signs Plus. Fisherman Jack Meets the River Creatures, 1 vol. Wilson, Elaine Moody. 2009. 40p. pap. 24.95 *(978-1-60836-967-6(6))* PublishAmerica, Inc.
Duckworth, Jeffrey. The Wonderful World of Cupcakes. Wise-Douglas, Terri. 2011. 28p. pap. 24.95 *(978-1-4626-3570-2(9))* America Star Bks.
Duckworth, Michelle. The Moon Throws a Birthday Party. Fischer, Kelly. 2011. (ENG.). 32p. (J). 19.50 *(978-1-58385-237-8(9))* ktf-writers-studio.
—The Most Beautiful Color of All. Fischer, Kelly. 2011. (ENG.). 36p. (J). 19.50 *(978-1-58385-281-1(6))* ktf-writers-studio.
Duckworth, Ruth. Saints Adrian & Natalie. Seco, Nina S. & Pilutik, Anastasia D. Date not set. (Cloud of Witnesses Ser.). (Orig.). (J). (gr. -1-1). pap. *(978-0-913026-29-8(8))* St. Nectarios Pr.
Ducommon, Barbara. Nosy Noodles: The Curious Cow. Purkapile, Susan. 2006. 15p. (J). (gr. k-5). 13.95 *(978-1-930596-34-4(0))* Amherst Pr.
Ducommun, Barbara. Mumbles the Bumble Bee: The Bee Who Couldn't Buzz. Purkapile, Susan & Peck, Amy. 2008. (J). *(978-1-930596-87-0(1))* Amherst Pr.
Ducornet, Rikki. The Blue Rock Collection. Gander, Forrest. 2004. (ENG.). 128p. pap. 14.95 *(978-1-84471-045-4(9))* Salt Publishing GBR. Dist: SPD-Small Pr. Distribution.
Ducote, Billie Seaon. The Adventures of Artie Eco Part One: The Problem with Greed, 2 vols, Vol. 1. Ducote, Billie Seaon. 2007. (ENG.). 26p. (J). 18.95 *(978-0-9787597-5-9(3))* PureLight Pubns.
—The Adventures of Artie Eco Part Two: The Problem with Greed Artie Eco Goes to Dirtyville, 2 vols., Vol. 2. Ducote, Billie Seaon. 2007. 26p. (J). act. bk. ed. 18.95 *(978-0-9787597-1-1(0))* PureLight Pubns.
duCray, Belle Crow. Sparkle & the Light. Sullivan, Ayn Cates. 2013. (ENG.). (J). 19.99 *(978-0-9884537-0-8(3))* Infinite Light Publishing.
Ducrest, Olivier. Love Is in the Air. Sam, Amélie & Trouillot, Virgile. 2009. (Groove High Ser.). 112p. (YA). (gr. 5-8). 31.95 *(978-1-60754-212-4(9),* 1293915); pap. 15.25 *(978-1-60754-213-1(7),* 1293915) Windmill Bks.
Ducy, George. Where Is Your Name? Ms. Sue. 2009. 24p. pap. 24.95 *(978-1-60672-711-9(7))* America Star Bks.
Dudash, C. Michael. Taking Liberty: The Story of Oney Judge, George Washington's Runaway Slave. Rinaldi, Ann. 2004. (ENG.). 272p. (YA). (gr. 7). mass mkt. 6.99 *(978-0-689-85188-9(X),* Simon Pulse) Simon Pulse.
Duddle, Johnny, jt. illus. see Dress, Robert.
Duddle, Jonny. Bang Goes a Troll, Bk. 3. Sinden, David et al. 2009. (Awfully Beastly Business Ser.: 3). (ENG.). 208p. (J). (gr. 3-7). 9.99 *(978-1-4169-8651-5(0),* Simon & Schuster/Paula Wiseman Bks.) Simon & Schuster/Paula Wiseman Bks.
—The Billionaire's Curse. Newsome, Richard. 2011. (Archer Legacy Ser.). 384p. (J). (gr. 3-7). pap. 6.99 *(978-0-06-194491-8(2),* Waldon Pond Pr.) HarperCollins Pubs.
—The Emerald Casket. Newsome, Richard. (Archer Legacy Ser.). (J). (gr. 3-7). 2012. 384p. pap. 6.99 *(978-0-06-194493-2(9));* 2011. 368p. 16.99 *(978-0-06-194492-5(0))* HarperCollins Pubs. (Waldon Pond Pr.).
—The Jungle Vampire. Sinden, David et al. 2009. (Awfully Beastly Business Ser.: 4). (ENG.). 208p. (J). (gr. 3-7). 9.99 *(978-1-4169-8652-2(9),* Simon & Schuster/Paula Wiseman Bks.) Simon & Schuster/Paula Wiseman Bks.
—The Mask of Destiny. Newsome, Richard. 384p. (J). (gr. 3-7). 2013. pap. 6.99 *(978-0-06-194495-6(5));* 2012. 16.99 *(978-0-06-194494-9(7))* HarperCollins Pubs. (Waldon Pond Pr.).
—El Salteador de Caminos/Highway Robbery. Thompson, Kate. Acevedo, Adriana, tr. 2009. (SPA.). 100p. (J). (gr. 3-5). pap. *(978-84-263-7270-3(8))* Vives, Luis Editorial (Edelvives).
—Sea Monsters & Other Delicacies. Sinden, David et al. 2009. (Awfully Beastly Business Ser.: 2). (ENG.). 208p. (J). (gr. 3-7). 9.99 *(978-1-4169-8650-8(2),* Simon & Schuster/Paula Wiseman Bks.) Simon & Schuster/Paula Wiseman Bks.
—We Give a Squid a Wedgie. London, C. Alexander. 2013. (Accidental Adventure Ser.: No. 3). (ENG.). 400p. (J). (gr. 3-7). pap. 7.99 *(978-0-14-242475-9(7),* Puffin) Penguin Publishing Group.
—Werewolf Versus Dragon. Sinden, David et al. 2009. (Awfully Beastly Business Ser.: 1). (ENG.). 192p. (J). (gr. 3-7). 9.99 *(978-1-4169-8649-2(9),* Simon & Schuster/Paula Wiseman Bks.) Simon & Schuster/Paula Wiseman Bks.
Duddle, Jonny. Gigantosaurus. Duddle, Jonny. 2014. (ENG.). 32p. (J). (gr. -1-2). 16.99 *(978-0-7636-7131-0(2),* Templar) Candlewick Pr.
—King of Space. Duddle, Jonny. 2013. (ENG.). 44p. (J). (gr. -1-2). 15.99 *(978-0-7636-6435-0(9),* Templar) Candlewick Pr.
—The Pirate Cruncher. Duddle, Jonny. 2010. (ENG.). 38p. (J). (gr. -1-2). 15.99 *(978-0-7636-4876-3(0),* Templar) Candlewick Pr.
Dudley, Dick, jt. illus. see Ely, Paul.
Dudley, Peter. Bungee down Under. Ford, Sally. 2004. 40p. (J). 14.95 *(978-1-931807-26-5(4))* Randall, Peter E. Pub.
Dudley, Rebecca, photos by. Hank Has a Dream. Dudley, Rebecca. 2014. (ENG., 32p. (J). 16.99 *(978-1-4413-1572-4(1),* 9781441315724) Peter Pauper Pr. Inc.
Dudok de Wit, Michael. Oscar & Hoo. Theo. 2003. 32p. (J). (gr. -1-2). 17.99 *(978-0-00-710793-3(5),* HarperCollins Children's Bks.) HarperCollins Pubs. Ltd. GBR. Dist: Trafalgar Square Publishing.
Duendes del Sur. Scooby-Doo & the Mummy's Curse. McCann, Jesse Leon. 2010. (Scooby-Doo! Set 1 Ser.: No. 1). (ENG.). 24p. (gr. -1-4). lib. bdg. 24.21 *(978-1-59961-677-3(7))* Spotlight.
—Scooby-Doo & the Rock 'n' Roll Zombie. McCann, Jesse Leon. 2010. (Scooby-Doo! Set 1 Ser.: No. 1). (ENG.). 24p. (gr. -1-4). lib. bdg. 24.21 *(978-1-59961-678-0(5))* Spotlight.
—Scooby-Doo & the Tiki's Curse. McCann, Jesse Leon. 2010. (Scooby-Doo! Set 1 Ser.: No. 1). (ENG.). 24p. (gr. -1-4). lib. bdg. 24.21 *(978-1-59961-680-3(7))* Spotlight.
—Scooby-Doo & the Werewolf. McCann, Jesse Leon. 2010. (Scooby-Doo! Set 1 Ser.: No. 1). (ENG.). 24p. (gr. -1-4). lib. bdg. 24.21 *(978-1-59961-681-0(5))* Spotlight.
Duendes Del Sur Staff. The Anytime Bible. Simon, Mary Manz. 2009. (ENG.). 320p. (J). (gr. -1-3). 14.99 *(978-0-439-65127-1(1),* Little Shepherd) Scholastic, Inc.
—Big-Top. Howard, Kate. 2012. (Scooby-Doo Ser.). (ENG.). 80p. (J). (gr. 2-5). pap. 4.99 *(978-0-545-45717-0(3))* Scholastic, Inc.
—Big-Top Scooby-Doo! Sander, Sonia. movie tie-in ed. 2012. (Scooby-Doo Ser.). (ENG.). 32p. (J). (gr. -1-3). pap. 3.99 *(978-0-545-45718-7(1))* Scholastic, Inc.
—Chill Out, Scooby-Doo! Sander, Sonia. 2012. (Scooby-Doo! Set 2 Ser.: No. 2). (ENG.). 32p. (J). (gr. k-3). lib. bdg. 24.21 *(978-1-59961-865-4(6))* Spotlight.
—Fall Fright. Herman, Gail. 2005. (Hello Reader! Ser.). 32p. (J). pap. *(978-0-439-78358-3(5))* Scholastic, Inc.
—The Haunted Halloween Party. Herman, Gail. 2007. (Scooby-Doo Reader Ser.: 20). (ENG.). 32p. (J). (gr. 2-5). pap. 3.99 *(978-0-439-78811-3(0))* Scholastic, Inc.
—The Hotel of Horrors. Howard, Kate. 2012. (Scooby-Doo Mysteries Ser.). (ENG.). 64p. (J). (gr. 2-5). pap. 4.99 *(978-0-545-38676-0(4))* Scholastic, Inc.
—Mean Green Mystery Machine: Junior Chapter Book. Gelsey, James. 2004. (Scooby Doo Ser.). 48p. (J). mass mkt. 3.99 *(978-0-439-55711-5(9),* Scholastic Paperbacks) Scholastic, Inc.
—Mis Primeros Versículos de la Biblia. Simon, Mary Manz. 2009. (Lee y Aprende Ser.). (SPA.). 40p. (J). (gr. -1-k). 9.99 *(978-0-545-15406-2(5),* Scholastic en Espanol) Scholastic, Inc.
—My First Read & Learn Book of Prayers. Simon, Mary Manz. 2007. (Little Shepherd Book Ser.). (ENG.). 40p. (J). (gr. -1-k). bds. 9.99 *(978-0-439-90632-6(6))* Scholastic, Inc.
—Read & Learn Bible. American Bible Society Staff. 2005. (ENG.). 544p. (J). (gr. -1-3). 14.99 *(978-0-439-65126-4(3))* Scholastic, Inc.
—The Rock 'n' Roll Zombie. McCann, Jesse Leon. 2007. (Scooby-Doo 8x8 Ser.). (ENG.). 24p. (J). (gr. -1-3). pap. 3.99 *(978-0-439-78808-3(0))* Scholastic, Inc.
—Scooby-Doo & Museum Madness. McCann, Jesse Leon. 2012. (Scooby-Doo! Set 2 Ser.: No. 2). (ENG.). 24p. (J). (gr. k-3). lib. bdg. 24.21 *(978-1-59961-867-8(2))* Spotlight.
—Scooby-Doo & the Fishy Phantom. McCann, Jesse Leon. 2006. (Scooby-Doo 8x8 Ser.). (ENG.). 24p. (J). (gr. -1-3). pap. 3.99 *(978-0-439-78807-6(2),* Scholastic Paperbacks) Scholastic, Inc.
—Scooby-Doo & the Fishy Phantom. McCann, Jesse Leon. 2012. (Scooby-Doo! Set 2 Ser.: No. 2). (ENG.). 24p. (J). (gr. k-3). lib. bdg. 24.21 *(978-1-59961-866-1(4))* Spotlight.
—Scooby-Doo & the Hungry Ghost. Cunningham, Scott. 2005. (Scooby Doo Ser.). (ENG.). 12p. (J). (gr. -1-3). 8.99 *(978-0-439-74882-7(8))* Scholastic, Inc.
—Scooby-Doo & the Rotten Robot. Balaban, Mariah. 2012. (Scooby-Doo! Set 2 Ser.: No. 2). (ENG.). 24p. (J). (gr. k-3). lib. bdg. 24.21 *(978-1-59961-868-5(0))* Spotlight.
—Scooby-Doo & the Scary Snowman. Balaban, Mariah. 2012. (Scooby-Doo! Set 2 Ser.: No. 2). (ENG.). 24p. (J). (gr. k-3). lib. bdg. 24.21 *(978-1-59961-869-2(9))* Spotlight.
—Scooby-Doo & the Thanksgiving Terror. Balaban, Mariah. 2012. (Scooby-Doo! Set 2 Ser.: No. 2). (ENG.). 24p. (J). (gr. k-3). lib. bdg. 24.21 *(978-1-59961-870-8(2))* Spotlight.
—Scooby-Doo! Mystery #3: the Haunting of Pirate Cove. Howard, Kate. 2013. (Scooby-Doo! Mystery Ser.). (ENG.). 64p. (J). (gr. 2-5). pap. 4.99 *(978-0-545-38678-4(0))* Scholastic, Inc.
—Scooby-Doo Reader #31: Werewolf Watch. Sander, Sonia. 2012. (Scooby-Doo Reader Ser.: 31). (ENG.). 32p. (J). (gr. -1-3). pap. 3.99 *(978-0-545-38477-3(X))* Scholastic, Inc.
—A Scooby-Rific Reader. Herman, Gail. 2005. (Scooby Doo Ser.). 290p. (J). *(978-0-681-15349-3(0))* Scholastic, Inc.
—Stage Fright. Howard, Kate. 2013. (Scooby-Doo Ser.). (ENG.). 80p. (J). (gr. 2-5). pap. 4.99 *(978-0-545-56258-4(9))* Scholastic, Inc.
—Super Spooky Double Storybook. McCann, Jesse Leon. 2008. (Scooby-Doo Ser.). (ENG.). 48p. (J). (gr. -1-3). pap. 4.99 *(978-0-545-03153-0(2))* Scholastic, Inc.
DuFalla, Anita. Alex in Numberland. Howard, Annabelle, ed. 2004. (Reader's Theater Ser.). (J). pap. *(978-1-4108-2303-8(2),* A23032) Benchmark Education Co.
—A Bad Case of Tattle Tongue. Cook, Julia. 2008. 32p. (J). (gr. -1). pap. 9.95 *(978-1-931636-86-5(9))* National Ctr. For Youth Issues.

Dufalla, Anita. Bedtime Battles. Robertson, Jean. 2011. (ENG.). 24p. (gr. k-1). 28.50 *(978-1-61741-802-0(1))*; pap. 7.95 *(978-1-61236-006-5(8))* Rourke Educational Media.
—Best Birthday. Cleland, Jo. 2011. (ENG.). 24p. (gr. k-1). 28.50 *(978-1-61741-798-6(X))* Rourke Educational Media.
DuFalla, Anita. Blackout. Pugliano-Martin, Carol. ed. 2004. (Reader's Theater Ser.). (J). pap. *(978-1-4108-2298-7(2),* A22982) Benchmark Education Co.
—Cliques Just Don't Make Cents! Cook, Julia. 2012. 32p. (J). pap. 10.95 *(978-1-934490-39-6(3))* Boys Town Pr.
—Decibella & Her 6-Inch Voice. Cook, Julia. 2014. 32p. (J). pap. 10.95 *(978-1-934490-58-7(X))* Boys Town Pr.
DuFalla, Anita. Gas Happens! What to Do When It Happens to You. Cook, Julia. 2015. 32p. (J). pap. 10.95 ***(978-1-934490-76-1(8))*** Boys Town Pr.
Dufalla, Anita. Grandpa Comes to First Grade. Robertson, Jean. 2011. (ENG.). 24p. (gr. k-1). 28.50 *(978-1-61741-800-6(5))*; pap. 7.95 *(978-1-61236-004-1(1))* Rourke Educational Media.
—How Many Bites? Robertson, Jean. 2011. (ENG.). 24p. (gr. k-1). 28.50 *(978-1-61741-801-3(3))*; pap. 7.95 *(978-1-61236-005-8(X))* Rourke Educational Media.
DuFalla, Anita. Hygiene You Stink! Cook, Julia. 2014. (ENG.). 32p. (J). pap. 10.95 *(978-1-934490-62-4(8))* Boys Town Pr.
Dufalla, Anita. I'm the Boss. Williams, Sam. 2012. (ENG.). 24p. (gr. k-1). pap. 7.95 *(978-1-61810-297-3(4))*; lib. bdg. 28.50 *(978-1-61810-164-8(1))* Rourke Educational Media.
—It's My Turn. Williams, Sam. 2012. (ENG.). 24p. (gr. k-1). pap. 7.95 *(978-1-61810-296-6(6))*; lib. bdg. 28.50 *(978-1-61810-163-1(3))* Rourke Educational Media.
DuFalla, Anita. It's You & Me Against the Pee... & the Poop, Too! Cook, Julia & Jana, Laura. 2011. 32p. (gr. -1). pap. 9.95 *(978-1-931636-75-9(3))* National Ctr. For Youth Issues.
Dufalla, Anita. The Jungle in My Yard. Cleland, Jo. 2011. (ENG.). 24p. (gr. k-1). 28.50 *(978-1-61741-807-5(2))* Rourke Educational Media.
—Keep Your Chin Up. Hord, Colleen. 2012. (ENG.). 24p. (gr. 1-2). pap. 7.95 *(978-1-61810-315-4(6))*; lib. bdg. 28.50 *(978-1-61810-182-2(X))* Rourke Educational Media.
DuFalla, Anita. The King's New Crown. Howard, Annabelle. ed. 2004. (Reader's Theater Ser.). (J). pap. *(978-1-4108-2296-3(6),* A22966) Benchmark Education Co.
Dufalla, Anita. Kitty Come Down! Cleland, Jo. 2011. (ENG.). 24p. (gr. k-1). 28.50 *(978-1-61741-808-2(0))* Rourke Educational Media.
—Monkey Business. Robertson, Jean. 2012. (ENG.). 24p. (gr. 2-3). pap. 7.95 *(978-1-61810-322-2(9))*; lib. bdg. 28.50 *(978-1-61810-189-1(7))* Rourke Educational Media.
—My Name Is Not... Robertson, Jean. 2012. (ENG.). 24p. (gr. 1-2). pap. 7.95 *(978-1-61810-320-8(2))*; lib. bdg. 28.50 *(978-1-61810-187-7(0))* Rourke Educational Media.
—Nobody's Watching. Steinkraus, Kyla. 2012. (ENG.). 24p. (gr. 2-3). pap. 7.95 *(978-1-61810-328-4(8))*; lib. bdg. 28.50 *(978-1-61810-195-2(1))* Rourke Educational Media.
DuFalla, Anita. Owen Has Burgers & Drum: Helping to Understand & Befriend Kids with Asperger's Syndrome. Sheils, Christine M. 2013. (Let's Talk Ser.). (ENG.). 48p. (J). (gr. -1-2). 9.95 *(978-0-88282-434-5(1))* New Horizon Pr. Pubs., Inc.
Dufalla, Anita. The Pattern Hike, 6 vols. Romer, Ruth. ed. 2004. (Reader's Theater Ser.). (J). pap. *(978-1-4108-2290-1(7),* A22907) Benchmark Education Co.
—Peer Pressure Gauge. Cook, Julia. 2013. (J). pap. 10.95 *(978-1-934490-48-8(2))* Boys Town Pr.
DuFalla, Anita. The Porch Swing. Butler, Dori Hillestad. Flounders, Anne, ed. ed. 2004. (Reader's Theater Ser.). (J). pap. *(978-1-4108-2246-8(X),* A2246X) Benchmark Education Co.
—Stan the Timid Turtle: Helping Children Cope with Fears about School Violence. Fox, Laura. 2014. (ENG.). 48p. (J). (gr. -1-2). 9.95 *(978-0-88282-466-6(X))* New Horizon Pr. Pubs., Inc.
—Sumac & the Magic Lake. ed. 2004. (Reader's Theater Ser.). (J). pap. *(978-1-4108-2291-8(5),* A22915) Benchmark Education Co.
Dufalla, Anita. Swim for It! Greve, Meg. 2011. (ENG.). 24p. (gr. k-1). 28.50 *(978-1-61741-805-1(6))* Rourke Educational Media.
—Table Wars! Steinkraus, Kyla. 2012. (ENG.). 24p. (gr. 2-3). pap. 7.95 *(978-1-61810-330-7(X))*; lib. bdg. 28.50 *(978-1-61810-197-6(8))* Rourke Educational Media.
—Team Captain. Robertson, Jean. 2012. (ENG.). 24p. (gr. 1-2). pap. 7.95 *(978-1-61810-314-7(8))*; lib. bdg. 28.50 *(978-1-61810-181-5(1))* Rourke Educational Media.
DuFalla, Anita. Tease Monster: (a Book about Teasing vs. Bullying) Cook, Julia. 2013. (Building Relationships Ser.). (ENG.). 32p. (J). pap. 10.95 *(978-1-934490-47-1(4))* Boys Town Pr.
Dufalla, Anita. That's Not Fair! Reed, Jennifer. 2012. (ENG.). 24p. (gr. 1-2). pap. 7.95 *(978-1-61810-309-3(1))*; lib. bdg. 28.50 *(978-1-61810-176-1(5))* Rourke Educational Media.
—Well, I Can Top That! Cook, Julia. 2014. 32p. (J). pap. 10.95 *(978-1-934490-57-0(1))* Boys Town Pr.
—Who's Right. Picou, Lin. 2012. (ENG.). 24p. (gr. 2-3). pap. 7.95 *(978-1-61810-323-9(7))*; lib. bdg. 28.50 *(978-1-61810-190-7(0))* Rourke Educational Media.
DuFalla, Anita, jt. illus. see Heiser, Aline.
Dufey, Alexandra. What Great Music! Classical Selections to Hear & to See. Apostoli, Andrea, ed. 2011. (ENG.). 48p. (J). (-1). pap. 19.95 *(978-1-57999-841-7(0))* G I A Pubns., Inc.
Duff, Leo. Earth Story. Maddern, Eric & Quarto Generic Staff. 2004. (ENG.). 32p. (J). (gr. k-17). pap. 7.95 *(978-1-84507-185-1(9),* Frances Lincoln) Quarto Publishing Group UK GBR. Dist: Hachette Bk. Group.
Duffek, Kim Kanoa. Victor el Zopilote Renuente! Hanson, Jonathan. 2012. 36p. (J). pap. 16.95 *(978-1-886679-46-7(0))* Arizona Sonora Desert Museum Pr.
Duffour, Jean-Pierre, jt. illus. see Avril, Francois.
Duffy, Ciaran. The Lion & the Mouse. Collins Educational Staff & Robinson, Anthony. 2012. (Collins Big Cat Ser.). (ENG.). 16p. (J). pap., wbk. ed. 4.99 *(978-0-00-747292-5(7))* HarperCollins Pubs. Ltd. GBR. Dist: Independent Pubs. Group.
Duffy, Daniel Mark & Deraney, Michael J. Molly's Pilgrim. Cohen, Barbara. 97th rev. ed. 2005. (ENG.). 32p. (J). (gr. 2-5). pap. 3.99 *(978-0-688-16280-1(0))* HarperCollins Pubs.
Duforu, Sebastian. El Nino Envuelto. Bornemann, Elsa. 2003. (SPA.). 176p. (YA). (gr. 5-8). pap. 13.95 *(978-950-511-623-2(3))* Alfaguara S.A. de Ediciones ARG. Dist: Santillana USA Publishing Co., Inc.
Dugan, Alan. Grandma Can You Tell Me. Butcher, A D. 2007. 16p. per. 10.95 *(978-1-4327-1316-4(7))* Outskirts Pr., Inc.
Dugan, Karen. Camping with the President. Wadsworth, Ginger. 2009. (ENG.). 32p. (J). (gr. 4-18). 16.95 *(978-1-59078-497-6(9),* Calkins Creek) Boyds Mills Pr.
—Christmas USA. Lankford, Mary D. 2006. 48p. (J). (gr. 3-7). 16.99 *(978-0-688-15012-9(8),* Collins) HarperCollins Pubs.
—In the Spin of Things: Poetry of Motion. Dotlich, Rebecca Kai. 2010. (ENG.). 32p. (J). pap. 11.95 *(978-1-59078-828-8(1),* Wordsong) Boyds Mills Pr.
—Marie Curie, Brave Scientist. Mattern, Joanne & Brandt, Keith. 2005. 45p. (J). *(978-0-439-80153-9(2))* Scholastic, Inc.
—Mr. Tuggle's Troubles. Blankenship, LeeAnn. 2005. (ENG.). 32p. (J). (gr. k-3). 15.95 *(978-1-59078-196-8(1))* Boyds Mills Pr.
—When Riddles Come Rumbling: Poems to Ponder. Dotlich, Rebecca Kai. 2013. (ENG.). 32p. (J). (gr. 2-4). pap. 6.95 *(978-1-62091-031-3(4),* Wordsong) Boyds Mills Pr.
Dugan, Karen. Always Blue for Chicu. Dugan, Karen. 2010. (ENG.). 32p. (J). (gr. k-2). 16.95 *(978-0-940719-09-5(6))* Gryphon Pr., The.
Duggan, John M. The Action-Packed Book of Adventure Doodles: 187 Fun & Exciting Drawings You Can Finish Yourself. 2009. (ENG.). 192p. (gr. -1-3). pap. 12.95 *(978-1-56975-724-6(0))* Ulysses Pr.
Duggan, Kevin. As the Crow Flies. Keenan, Sheila. 2012. (ENG.). 40p. (J). (gr. k-1). 16.99 *(978-0-312-62156-8(6))* Feiwel & Friends.
Duggan, Micheal. Mi & Two. Soto, Manuel. 2008. 27p. pap. 24.95 *(978-1-60610-877-2(8))* America Star Bks.
Duggins, Peat. Grendel Gander the Sinister Goose. Homan, Michael. 2012. 48p. pap. 14.95 *(978-1-60808-049-6(8),* WriteLife Publishing) Boutique of Quality Books Publishing Co.
Dugina, Olga. Dragon Feathers. Dugin, Andrei. 2010. Orig. Title: Die Drachenfedern. 24p. (J). (gr. k-3). 17.95 *(978-0-86315-774-5(2))* Floris Bks. GBR. Dist: SteinerBooks, Inc.
Duhaney, Rich, jt. illus. see Habjan, Peter.
Duis, Laura. Jasper. Groce, Michelle. 2003. 174p. (J). 17.95 *(978-0-9708972-6-8(X))* Novello Festival Pr.
Duivenvoorden, Yvonne, photos by. What's for Lunch?, 1 vol. Curtis, Andrea. 2012. (ENG.). 40p. (J). pap. 12.95 *(978-0-88995-482-3(8))* Red Deer Pr. CAN. Dist: Ingram Pub. Services.
Duke, Barbara, jt. illus. see Phillips-Duke, Barbara Jean.
Duke, Kate. One Saturday Evening. Baker, Barbara. 2007. (Dutton Easy-To-Read Ser.). (J). (ENG.). 48p. (gr. 1-4). 13.99 *(978-0-525-47103-5(0))*; *(978-0-525-47850-8(7))* Penguin Publishing Group. (Dutton Juvenile).
Duke, Kate. In the Rainforest. Duke, Kate. 2014. (Let's-Read-And-Find-Out Science 2 Ser.). (ENG.). 40p. (J). (gr. -1-3). 17.99 *(978-0-06-028259-2(2))*; pap. 5.99 *(978-0-06-445197-0(6))* HarperCollins Pubs.
Duke, Marion. The Pipeline C. Y. O'Connor Built. LeFroy, Joy & Frylinck, Diana. 2003. 40p. 22.50 *(978-1-920731-60-1(1))* Fremantle Pr. AUS. Dist: Independent Pubs. Group.
—Trumpet's Kittens. Polizzotto, Carolyn & Spinks, Sarah. 2003. 32p. (YA). 22.50 *(978-1-86368-331-9(3))* Fremantle Pr. AUS. Dist: Independent Pubs. Group.
Dulac, Edmund. Dulac's Fairy Tale Illustrations in Full Color. Menges, Jeff A., ed. 2004. (Dover Fine Art, History of Art Ser.). (ENG.). 64p. pap. 12.95 *(978-0-486-43669-2(1))* Dover Pubns., Inc.
—Fairies I Have Met. Stawell, Rodolph. 2011. (ENG.). 72p. pap. 18.82 *(978-1-4681-5040-7(5))* CreateSpace Independent Publishing Platform.
—The Sleeping Beauty & Other Fairy Tales. 2011. (Calla Editions Ser.). (ENG.). 208p. 35.00 *(978-1-60660-019-1(2))* Dover Pubns., Inc.
—The Snow Queen. Andersen, Hans Christian. 2012.Tr. of ??????? ????????. (J). *(978-1-59583-459-1(1))* Laughing Elephant.
Dulemba, Elizabeth. Paco & the Giant Chile Plant/Paco y la Planta de Chile Gigante. Polette, Keith. de la Vega, Eida, tr. 2008. (SPA & ENG.). 32p. (J). (gr. k-3). lib. bdg. 16.95 *(978-0-9770906-2-4(0),* Raven Tree Pr.,Csi) Continental Sales, Inc.
Dulemba, Elizabeth O. Glitter Girl & the Crazy Cheese. Hollon, Frank Turner et al. 2006. (ENG.). 32p. (J). (gr. -1-3). *(978-1-59692-137-5(4))* MacAdam/Cage Publishing, Inc.
—The Prince's Diary. Ting, Renee. 2005. (Prince's Diary Ser.). 32p. (J). (gr. -1-3). 16.95 *(978-1-885008-27-5(9),* Shen's Bks.) Lee & Low Bks., Inc.
—The Twelve Days of Christmas in Georgia. Spain, Susan Rosson. 2010. (Twelve Days of Christmas in America Ser.). (ENG.). 32p. (J). (gr. k). 12.95 *(978-1-4027-7008-1(1))* Sterling Publishing Co., Inc.
Dulemba, Elizabeth O. Soap, Soap, Soap. Dulemba, Elizabeth O. 2010. (ENG.). 32p. (J). (gr. -1-3). pap. 7.95 *(978-1-934960-65-3(9),* Raven Tree Pr.,Csi) Continental Sales, Inc.
Dulin, Dorothy. The Fairy Babies. Smith, Laura Rountree. 2011. 126p. 40.95 *(978-1-258-09063-0(5))* Literary Licensing, LLC.
Dull, Dennis Stanley. Baby Basics & Beyond: ABC's, 123's & Shapes. Dull, Dennis Stanley. 2nd ed. 2004. (J). *(978-0-9717475-4-8(7))* Laurel Valley Graphics, Inc.
Dumas, Ryan. Art of the Ninja: Earth. Perkins, T J. 2011. (Shadow Legacy Ser.: 1). (YA). 19.95 *(978-1-60975-039-8(X))* Silver Leaf Bks., LLC.
Dumm, Brian. Henry & Hala Build a Haiku. Higgins, Nadia. 2011. (Poetry Builders Ser.). 32p. (J). (gr. 2-5). lib. bdg. 25.27 *(978-1-59953-435-0(5))* Norwood Hse. Pr.
—Piper the Elf Trains Santa. Driscoll, Colleen. 2012. (ENG.). 32p. (J). 16.95 *(978-0-938467-56-4(5))* Headline Bks., Inc.
Dumm, Brian Caleb. April. Kesselring, Mari. 2009. (Months of the Year Ser.). 24p. (gr. -1-2). 27.07 *(978-1-60270-631-6(X),* Looking Glass Library-Nonfiction) Magic Wagon.
—Firefighters at Work. Kenney, Karen L. 2009. (Meet Your Community Workers Ser.). 32p. (J). (gr. -1-2). 28.50 *(978-1-60270-648-4(4))* Magic Wagon.
—The Legend of Bigfoot, 1 vol. Troupe, Thomas Kingsley. 2010. (Legend Has It Ser.). (ENG.). 32p. (gr. 2-4). lib. bdg. 26.65 *(978-1-4048-6032-2(0),* Nonfiction Picture Bks.) Picture Window Bks.
—Librarians at Work. Kenney, Karen Latchana. 2009. (Meet Your Community Workers Ser.). 32p. (J). (gr. -1-2). 28.50 *(978-1-60270-649-1(2))* Magic Wagon.
—Life on the Mayflower, 1 vol. Gunderson, Jessica. 2011. (Thanksgiving Ser.). (ENG.). 24p. (gr. 1-2). lib. bdg. 26.65 *(978-1-4048-6284-5(6))*; pap. 7.95 *(978-1-4048-6719-2(8))* Picture Window Bks. (Nonfiction Picture Bks.).
—Mail Carriers at Work. Kenney, Karen Latchana. 2009. (Meet Your Community Workers Ser.). 32p. (J). (gr. -1-2). 28.50 *(978-1-60270-650-7(6))* Magic Wagon.
—March. Kesselring, Mari. 2009. (Months of the Year Ser.). 24p. (gr. -1-2). 27.07 *(978-1-60270-630-9(1),* Looking Glass Library- Nonfiction) Magic Wagon.
—May. Kesselring, Mari. 2009. (Months of the Year Ser.). 24p. (gr. -1-2). 27.07 *(978-1-60270-632-3(8),* Looking Glass Library- Nonfiction) Magic Wagon.
—Nurses at Work. Kenney, Karen L. 2009. (Meet Your Community Workers Ser.). 32p. (J). (gr. -1-2). 28.50 *(978-1-60270-651-4(4))* Magic Wagon.
—Police Officers at Work. Kenney, Karen L. 2009. (Meet Your Community Workers Ser.). 32p. (J). (gr. -1-2). 28.50 *(978-1-60270-652-1(2))* Magic Wagon.
—Teachers at Work. Kenney, Karen L. 2009. (Meet Your Community Workers Ser.). 32p. (J). (gr. -1-2). 28.50 *(978-1-60270-653-8(0))* Magic Wagon.
Dumont, Daniel. Les Jumeaux Bulle Series. Gauthier, Bertrand. 2004. (FRE.). 64p. (J). (gr. 1-4). pap. *(978-2-89021-684-6(5))* Diffusion du livre Mirabel (DLM).
Dumont, Jean-François. Edgar Wants to Be Alone. Mathews, Leslie. 2015. 26p. (J). 16.00 *(978-0-8028-5457-5(5),* Eerdmans Bks For Young Readers) Eerdmans, William B. Publishing Co.
Dumont, Jean-François. I Am a Bear. Mathews, Leslie. 2015. (J). ***(978-0-8028-5447-6(8),*** Eerdmans Bks For Young Readers) Eerdmans, William B. Publishing Co.
—The Sheep Go on Strike. Mathews, Leslie. 2014. (J). 16.00 ***(978-0-8028-5470-4(2),*** Eerdmans Bks For Young Readers) Eerdmans, William B. Publishing Co.
Dumont, Madeleine. Jaune. Averous, Helene. 2013. 38p. pap. *(978-981-07-5312-2(8))* MHC Asia Group.
—Yellow. Averous, Helene. 2013. 38p. pap. *(978-981-07-5311-5(X))* MHC Asia Group.
Dumortier, Marjorie. Did Dinosaurs Eat People? And Other Questions Kids Have about Dinosaurs, 1 vol. Bowman, Donna H. (Kids' Questions Ser.). (ENG.). 24p. (gr. 1-2). 2011. pap. 7.29 *(978-1-4048-6725-3(2))*; 2009. lib. bdg. 25.99 *(978-1-4048-5527-4(0))* Picture Window Bks. (Nonfiction Picture Bks.).
Dumortier, Marjorie. Whizzy Witch. Harvey, Damian. 2008. (Reading Corner Ser.). (ENG.). 24p. (J). (gr. k-2). pap. 6.99 ***(978-0-7496-7699-5(X))*** Hodder & Stoughton GBR. Dist: Independent Pubs. Group.
Dumortier, Marjorie. Zoe & Her Zany Animals. 2006. (ENG.). 32p. (J). (gr. -1-3). 14.99 *(978-0-7145-3306-3(8))* Boyars, Marion Pubs., Inc.
Dunaway, Nancy. I Scream, You Scream: A Feast of Food Rhymes. Morrison, Lillian. 2005. (ENG.). 96p. (J). (gr. -1-3). 12.95 *(978-0-87483-495-6(3))* August Hse. Pubs., Inc.
Dunbar, Eddie, photos by. Insects of Wente Scout Reservation: Mendocino County, California. 2005th ed. 2005. cd-rom 10.00 *(978-0-9764454-3-2(3),* Exploring California Insects) Insect Sciences Museum of California.
Dunbar, Geoff. High in the Clouds. Ardagh, Philip. 2007. 93p. (J). 20.00 *(978-1-4223-6720-9(7))* DIANE Publishing Co.
Dunbar, Polly. The Boy Who Climbed into the Moon. Almond, David. 2010. (ENG.). 128p. (J). (gr. 3-7). 15.99 *(978-0-7636-4217-4(7))* Candlewick Pr.
—Bubble Trouble. Mahy, Margaret. (ENG.). (J). (gr. -1-3). 2013. 40p. pap. 6.99 *(978-0-547-99483-3(4))*; 2013. 40p. 26.99 *(978-0-547-85058-0(1))*; 2011. 32p. bds. 7.99 *(978-0-547-50725-5(9))*; 2009. 40p. 16.00 *(978-0-547-07421-4(2))* Houghton Mifflin Harcourt Publishing Co.
—Here's a Little Poem: A Very First Book of Poetry. 2007. (ENG.). 112p. (J). (gr. k-12). 21.99 *(978-0-7636-3141-3(8))* Candlewick Pr.
—The Man from the Land of Fandango. Mahy, Margaret. 2012. (ENG.). 32p. (J). (gr. -1-3). 16.99 *(978-0-547-81988-4(9))* Houghton Mifflin Harcourt Publishing Co.
—My Dad's a Birdman. Almond, David. 2011. (ENG.). 128p. (J). (gr. 3-7). pap. 8.99 *(978-0-7636-5345-3(4))* Candlewick Pr.
—Pat-A-Cake Baby. Dunbar, Joyce. 2015. (ENG.). 40p. (J). (-k). 15.99 *(978-0-7636-7577-6(6))* Candlewick Pr.
Dunbar, Polly. Arthur's Dream Boat. Dunbar, Polly. 2012. (ENG.). 40p. (J). (gr. -1-k). 15.99 *(978-0-7636-5867-0(7))* Candlewick Pr.
—Doodle Bites: A Tilly & Friends Book. Dunbar, Polly. 2009. (Tilly & Friends Ser.). (ENG.). 32p. (J). (gr. -1-2). 12.99 *(978-0-7636-4327-0(0))* Candlewick Pr.
—Goodnight, Tiptoe. Dunbar, Polly. 2009. (Tilly & Friends Ser.). (ENG.). 32p. (J). (gr. -1-2). 12.99 *(978-0-7636-4328-7(9))* Candlewick Pr.
—Hello, Tilly. Dunbar, Polly. 2008. (Tilly & Friends Ser.). (ENG.). 32p. (J). (gr. -1-2). 12.99 *(978-0-7636-4109-2(X))* Candlewick Pr.
—Measuring Angels. Dunbar, Polly. Ely, Lesley. 2008. (ENG.). 32p. (J). (gr. -1-3). 16.95 *(978-1-84507-639-9(7),* Frances Lincoln) Quarto Publishing Group UK GBR. Dist: Hachette Bk. Group.
—Penguin. Dunbar, Polly. 2010. (ENG.). 40p. (J). (gr. -1-3). pap. 6.99 *(978-0-7636-4972-2(4))* Candlewick Pr.
—Pretty Pru: A Tilly & Friends Book. Dunbar, Polly. 2009. (Tilly & Friends Ser.). (ENG.). 32p. (J). (gr. -1-2). 12.99 *(978-0-7636-4272-3(X))* Candlewick Pr.
Dunbar, Polly. Looking after Louis. Dunbar, Polly, tr. Ely, Lesley. 2004. (ENG.). 32p. (J). (gr. 2-5). 16.99 *(978-0-8075-4746-5(8))* Whitman, Albert & Co.
Duncan, Beverly. Unseen Rainbows, Silent Songs: The World of Animal Senses. Goodman, Susan E. 2008. (ENG.). 40p. (J). (gr. 4-6). 12.99 *(978-1-4169-7575-5(6),* Simon & Schuster/Paula Wiseman Bks.) Simon & Schuster/Paula Wiseman Bks.
Duncan, Christa. The Story of the H Brothers. 2007. (J). 7.99 *(978-0-9792897-0-5(X))* Smartypants Publishing.
Duncan, Karen & Stringle, Sam. The Story of Armadillo. Robb, Jackie & Stringle, Berny. 2003. (Bang on the Door Ser.). 32p. (YA). pap. *(978-1-85602-337-5(0),* Pavilion Children's Books) Pavilion Bks.
—The Story of Bat. Robb, Jackie & Stringle, Berny. 2003. (Bang on the Door Ser.). 32p. (YA). pap. *(978-1-85602-316-0(8),* Pavilion Children's Books) Pavilion Bks.
—The Story of Cat. Robb, Jackie & Stringle, Berny. 2004. (Bang on the Door Ser.). 32p. (YA). pap. *(978-1-85602-314-6(1),* Pavilion Children's Books) Pavilion Bks.
—The Story of Dog. Robb, Jackie & Stringle, Berny. 2004. (Bang on the Door Ser.). 32p. (YA). pap. *(978-1-85602-315-3(X),* Pavilion Children's Books) Pavilion Bks.
—The Story of Pea Brain. Robb, Jackie & Stringle, Berny. 2004. (Bang on the Door Ser.). 32p. (YA). pap. *(978-1-85602-383-2(4),* Pavilion Children's Books) Pavilion Bks.
—The Story of Plankton. Robb, Jackie & Stringle, Berny. 2004. (Bang on the Door Ser.). 32p. (YA). pap. *(978-1-85602-336-8(2),* Pavilion Children's Books) Pavilion Bks.
—The Story of Slug. Robb, Jackie & Stringle, Berny. 2004. (Bang on the Door Ser.). 32p. (YA). pap. *(978-1-85602-317-7(6),* Pavilion Children's Books) Pavilion Bks.
—The Story of Spider. Robb, Jackie & Stringle, Berny. 2004. (Bang on the Door Ser.). 32p. (YA). pap. *(978-1-85602-318-4(4),* Pavilion Children's Books) Pavilion Bks.
Dungan, Julia. ABC Exercise with Mr. Gomes, Julie. 2005. (J). per. 7.50 *(978-0-9770207-0-6(3))* JCCJ Pr.
Dungey, Thomas. Nimble the Thimble Mouse, 1. Meek, Jeffrey/K. 2007. 21p. (J). 9.95 *(978-0-9794522-0-8(1))* Thimble Mouse Publishing, Inc.
Dunham Akiyama, Laine. Mr. Lincoln's Gift: A Civil War Story. Stewart, Whitney. 2008. 32p. (J). 19.95 *(978-0-9754917-4-4(1))* Friends of Hildene, Inc.
Dunkley, Andrew, jt. photos by see Leith, Marcus.
Dunlap, Hope. The Pied Piper of Hamelin, Illustrated by Hope Dunlap. Browning, Robert. 2008. 52p. pap. 12.95 *(978-1-59915-265-3(7))* Yesterday's Classics.
Dunlap, Joan, jt. illus. see Bennett, Michele.
Dunlavey, Rob. Counting Crows. Appelt, Kathi. 2015. (ENG.). 40p. (J). (gr. -1-3). 17.99 *(978-1-4424-2327-5(7))* Simon & Schuster Children's Publishing.
—The Dandelion's Tale. Sheehan, Kevin. 2014. (ENG.). 40p. (J). (gr. -1-2). 16.99 *(978-0-375-87032-3(6))*; 19.99 *(978-0-375-97032-0(0))* Random Hse. Children's Bks. (Schwartz & Wade Bks.).
Dunlavey, Rob. Over in the Wetlands: A Hurricane on the Bayou Story. Rose, Caroline. 2015. (ENG.). 40p. (J). (gr. -1-3). 17.99 ***(978-0-449-81016-3(X),*** Schwartz & Wade Bks.) Random Hse. Children's Bks.
Dunn, Anthony. Completely Magi-CaLL: The TRUE Secrets of Magic: A Study of the Magician's Art. Gunther, Chat, photos by. 2009. 346p. (YA). pap. 29.95 *(978-0-9729546-8-6(6))* SMC Pubns., LLC.
Dunn, Ben. The Adventure of Abbey Grange. Goodwin, Vincent. 2010. (Graphic Novel Adventures of Sherlock Holmes Ser.). 48p. (J). (gr. 4-7). 29.93 *(978-1-60270-722-1(7))* ABDO Publishing Co.
—The Adventure of the Blue Carbuncle. Goodwin, Vincent. 2012. (Graphic Novel Adventures of Sherlock Holmes Set 2 Ser.). 48p. (J). (gr. 3-8). lib. bdg. 29.93 *(978-1-61641-891-5(5),* Graphic Planet) Magic Wagon.
—The Adventure of the Cardboard Box. Goodwin, Vincent. 2013. (Graphic Novel Adventures of Sherlock Holmes Set 3 Ser.). 48p. (J). (gr. 3-8). lib. bdg. 29.93 *(978-1-61641-971-4(7),* Graphic Planet) Magic Wagon.
—The Adventure of the Copper Beeches. Goodwin, Vincent. 2012. (Graphic Novel Adventures of Sherlock Holmes Set 2 Ser.). 48p. (J). (gr. 3-8). lib. bdg. 29.93 *(978-1-61641-892-2(3),* Graphic Planet) Magic Wagon.
—The Adventure of the Dancing Men. Goodwin, Vincent. 2010. (Graphic Novel Adventures of Sherlock Holmes Ser.). 48p. (J). (gr. 4-7). 29.93 *(978-1-60270-723-8(5))* ABDO Publishing Co.
—The Adventure of the Dying Detective. Goodwin, Vincent. 2013. (Graphic Novel Adventures of Sherlock Holmes Set 3 Ser.). 48p. (J). (gr. 3-8). lib. bdg. 29.93 *(978-1-61641-972-1(5),* Graphic Planet) Magic Wagon.
—The Adventure of the Empty House. Goodwin, Vincent. 2010. (Graphic Novel Adventures of Sherlock Holmes Ser.). 48p. (J). (gr. 4-7). 29.93 *(978-1-60270-724-5(3))* ABDO Publishing Co.
—The Adventure of the Engineer's Thumb. Goodwin, Vincent. 2012. (Graphic Novel Adventures of Sherlock Holmes Set

D

2 Ser.). 48p. (J). (gr. 3-8). lib. bdg. 29.93 *(978-1-61641-893-9(1),* Graphic Planet) Magic Wagon.
—The Adventure of the Norwood Builder. Goodwin, Vincent. 2010. (Graphic Novel Adventures of Sherlock Holmes Ser.). 48p. (J). (gr. 4-7). 29.93 *(978-1-60270-725-2(1))* ABDO Publishing Co.
—The Adventure of the Priory School. Goodwin, Vincent. 2013. (Graphic Novel Adventures of Sherlock Holmes Set 3 Ser.). 48p. (J). (gr. 3-8). lib. bdg. 29.93 *(978-1-61641-973-8(3),* Graphic Planet) Magic Wagon.
—The Adventure of the Red Circle. Goodwin, Vincent. 2013. (Graphic Novel Adventures of Sherlock Holmes Set 3 Ser.). 48p. (J). (gr. 3-8). lib. bdg. 29.93 *(978-1-61641-974-5(1),* Graphic Planet) Magic Wagon.
—The Adventure of the Red-Headed League. Goodwin, Vincent. 2010. (Graphic Novel Adventures of Sherlock Holmes Ser.). 48p. (J). (gr. 4-7). 29.93 *(978-1-60270-726-9(X))* ABDO Publishing Co.
—The Adventure of the Second Stain. Goodwin, Vincent. 2013. (Graphic Novel Adventures of Sherlock Holmes Set 3 Ser.). 48p. (J). (gr. 3-8). lib. bdg. 29.93 *(978-1-61641-975-2(X),* Graphic Planet) Magic Wagon.
—The Adventure of the Six Napoleons. Goodwin, Vincent. 2013. (Graphic Novel Adventures of Sherlock Holmes Set 3 Ser.). 48p. (J). (gr. 3-8). lib. bdg. 29.93 *(978-1-61641-976-9(8),* Graphic Planet) Magic Wagon.
—The Adventure of the Solitary Cyclist. Goodwin, Vincent. 2012. (Graphic Novel Adventures of Sherlock Holmes Set 2 Ser.). 48p. (J). (gr. 3-8). lib. bdg. 29.93 *(978-1-61641-894-6(X),* Graphic Planet) Magic Wagon.
—The Adventure of the Speckled Band. Goodwin, Vincent. 2010. (Graphic Novel Adventures of Sherlock Holmes Ser.). 48p. (J). (gr. 4-7). 29.93 *(978-1-60270-727-6(8))* ABDO Publishing Co.
—The Adventure of the Three Students. Goodwin, Vincent. 2012. (Graphic Novel Adventures of Sherlock Holmes Set 2 Ser.). 48p. (J). (gr. 3-8). lib. bdg. 29.93 *(978-1-61641-895-3(8),* Graphic Planet) Magic Wagon.
—The Adventure of Wisteria Lodge. Goodwin, Vincent. 2012. (Graphic Novel Adventures of Sherlock Holmes Set 2 Ser.). 48p. (J). (gr. 3-8). lib. bdg. 29.93 *(978-1-61641-896-0(6),* Graphic Planet) Magic Wagon.
—Amelia Earhart. Dunn, Joeming W. 2008. (Bio-Graphics Ser.). 32p. (gr. 3-5). 28.50 *(978-1-60270-173-1(3),* Graphic Planet- Nonfiction) ABDO Publishing Co.
—The California Gold Rush. Dunn, Joe. 2007. (Graphic History Ser.). 32p. (gr. 3-6). 28.50 *(978-1-60270-076-5(1),* Graphic Planet- Nonfiction) ABDO Publishing Co.
Dunn, Ben. Gettysburg. Dunn, Joeming W. 2016. (J). ***(978-1-61641-981-3(4))*** Magic Wagon.
Dunn, Ben. Hamlet. Dunn, Rebecca. 2008. (Graphic Shakespeare Ser.). 48p. (gr. 5-10). 29.93 *(978-1-60270-188-5(1),* Graphic Planet- Fiction) ABDO Publishing Co.
—The Lighthouse Mystery. Dunn, Joeming. 2010. (Boxcar Children Graphic Novels Ser.). (ENG.). 32p. (J). (gr. 2-5). pap. 6.99 *(978-0-8075-4547-8(3))* Whitman, Albert & Co.
—The Lighthouse Mystery, Bk. 14. Dunn, Joeming & Warner, Gertrude Chandler. 2011. (Boxcar Children Graphic Novels Ser.). 32p. (J). (gr. 2-5). 28.50 *(978-1-61641-122-0(8))* ABDO Publishing Co.
—The Merry Adventures of Robin Hood. Pyle, Howard. 2007. (Graphic Classics). 32p. (gr. 3-6). 28.50 *(978-1-60270-053-6(2),* Graphic Planet- Fiction) ABDO Publishing Co.
—Miracle on Ice. Dunn, Joe. 2007. (Graphic History Ser.). 32p. (gr. 3-6). 28.50 *(978-1-60270-077-2(X),* Graphic Planet- Nonfiction) ABDO Publishing Co.
—Mountain Top Mystery, Bk. 15. Dunn, Joeming & Warner, Gertrude Chandler. 2011. (Boxcar Children Graphic Novels Ser.). 32p. (J). (gr. 2-5). 28.50 *(978-1-61641-123-7(6))* ABDO Publishing Co.
—Mountain Top Mystery, No. 15. Dunn, Joeming. 2010. (Boxcar Children Graphic Novels Ser.). (ENG.). 32p. (J). (gr. 2-5). pap. 6.99 *(978-0-8075-5294-0(1))* Whitman, Albert & Co.
—Mystery in the Sand, Bk. 18. Dunn, Joeming & Warner, Gertrude Chandler. 2011. (Boxcar Children Graphic Novels Ser.). 32p. (J). (gr. 2-5). 28.50 *(978-1-61641-126-8(0))* ABDO Publishing Co.
—Peter Pan. Barrie, J. M. 2007. (Graphic Classics). 32p. (gr. 3-7). 28.50 *(978-1-60270-052-9(4),* Graphic Planet- Fiction) ABDO Publishing Co.
—The Time Machine. Wells, H. G. 2007. (Graphic Classics). 32p. (gr. 4-7). 28.50 *(978-1-60270-054-3(0),* Graphic Planet- Fiction) ABDO Publishing Co.
—The Woodshed Mystery. Dunn, Joeming. 2010. (Boxcar Children Graphic Novels Ser.). (ENG.). 32p. (J). (gr. 2-5). pap. 6.99 *(978-0-8075-9208-3(0))* Whitman, Albert & Co.
—The Woodshed Mystery, Bk. 13. Dunn, Joeming & Warner, Gertrude Chandler. 2011. (Boxcar Children Graphic Novels Ser.). 32p. (J). (gr. 2-5). 28.50 *(978-1-61641-121-3(X))* ABDO Publishing Co.
—The Wright Brothers. Dunn, Joe. 2007. (Bio-Graphics Ser.). 32p. (gr. 3-6). 28.50 *(978-1-60270-071-0(0),* Graphic Planet- Nonfiction) ABDO Publishing Co.
Dunn, Ben, jt. illus. see Dunn, Joeming W.
Dunn, Ben, jt. illus. see Dunn, Joeming.
Dunn, Gary. Johnny Catbiscuit & the Stolen Secrets! Cox, Michael. 2008. (Johnny Catbiscuit Ser.). (ENG.). 160p. (J). (gr. 2-4). pap. 9.95 *(978-1-4052-3739-0(2))* Egmont Bks., Ltd. GBR. Dist: Independent Pubs. Group.
—Stop That Robot! Band 00/Lilac. Sage, Alison. 2007. (Collins Big Cat Ser.). (ENG.). 16p. (J). pap. 5.99 *(978-0-00-718678-5(9))* HarperCollins Pubs. Ltd. GBR. Dist: Independent Pubs. Group.
Dunn, Joeming & Dunn, Ben. Bicycle Mystery. 2011. (Boxcar Children Graphic Novels Ser.). (ENG.). 32p. (J). (gr. 2-5). pap. 6.99 *(978-0-8075-0710-0(5))* Whitman, Albert & Co.
—Houseboat Mystery. 2011. (Boxcar Children Graphic Novels Ser.). (ENG.). 32p. (J). (gr. 2-5). pap. 6.99 *(978-0-8075-3395-6(5))* Whitman, Albert & Co.
—Mystery in the Sand, No. 18. 2011. (Boxcar Children Graphic Novels Ser.). (ENG.). 32p. (J). (gr. 2-5). pap. 6.99 *(978-0-8075-5518-7(5))* Whitman, Albert & Co.
Dunn, Joeming W. & Dunn, Ben. Armistice Day. 2016. (J). ***(978-1-61641-978-3(4))*** Magic Wagon.
Dunn, Joeming W. & Dunn, Ben. Bicycle Mystery, Bk. 17. Warner, Gertrude Chandler. 2011. (Boxcar Children Graphic Novels Ser.). 32p. (J). (gr. 2-5). 28.50 *(978-1-61641-125-1(2))* ABDO Publishing Co.
Dunn, Joeming W. & Dunn, Ben. D-Day. Dunn, Joeming W. & Dunn, Ben. 2016. (J). ***(978-1-61641-979-0(2))*** Magic Wagon.
—Fallujah. 2016. (J). ***(978-1-61641-980-6(6))*** Magic Wagon.
Dunn, Joeming W. & Dunn, Ben. Houseboat Mystery, Bk. 16. Warner, Gertrude Chandler. 2011. (Boxcar Children Graphic Novels Ser.). 32p. (J). (gr. 2-5). 28.50 *(978-1-61641-124-4(4))* ABDO Publishing Co.
Dunn, Joeming W. & Dunn, Ben. Tet Offensive. 2016. (J). ***(978-1-61641-983-7(0))*** Magic Wagon.
Dunn Jr., Howard Alfred. The Light of the Moon. Dunn, Layne. 2012. 16p. pap. 24.95 *(978-1-4626-5501-4(7))* America Star Bks.
Dunn, Phoebe. Guess Who I Am... gif. ed. 2005. 10p. (J). (gr. -1). per., bds. 7.99 *(978-1-57791-175-3(X))* Brighter Minds Children's Publishing.
Dunn, Phoebe. Big Treasury of Little Animals. Dunn, Phoebe. 2007. (ENG.). 192p. (J). (gr. -1-2). 10.99 *(978-0-375-84177-4(6),* Random Hse. Bks. for Young Readers) Random Hse. Children's Bks.
Dunn, Phoebe. The Little Duck. Dunn, Phoebe, photos by. Dunn, Judy, photos by. 2016. (J). pap. ***(978-0-553-53352-1(5))*** Random Hse., Inc.
Dunn, Phoebe, photos by. The Little Duck. Dunn, Judy. 2014. (ENG., 14p. (J). (— 1). bds. 6.99 *(978-0-385-38521-3(8),* Golden Bks.) Random Hse. Children's Bks.
—The Little Puppy. 2015. (ENG., 14p. (J). (— 1). bds. 6.99 *(978-0-553-51139-0(4),* Random Hse. Bks. for Young Readers) Random Hse. Children's Bks.
—The Little Rabbit. Dunn, Judy. 2014. (ENG., 14p. (J). (— 1). bds. 6.99 *(978-0-385-38604-3(4),* Golden Bks.) Random Hse. Children's Bks.
Dunn, Robert. The Boardwalk Mystery. Jessell, Tim. 2013. (Boxcar Children Mysteries Ser.: 131). (ENG.). 144p. (J). (gr. 2-5). 15.99 *(978-0-8075-0802-2(0));* pap. 5.99 *(978-0-8075-0803-9(9))* Whitman, Albert & Co.
—Little Women. Alcott, Louisa May. 2013. 46p. (J). *(978-1-4351-4813-0(4))* Barnes & Noble, Inc.
—The Littlest Bunny: An Easter Adventure. Jacobs, Lily. 2015. (ENG.). 32p. (J). (-3). 9.99 *(978-1-4926-1012-0(7),* Sourcebooks Jabberwocky) Sourcebooks, Inc.
—The Littlest Bunny in Albuquerque: An Easter Adventure. Jacobs, Lily. 2015. (ENG.). 32p. (J). (-3). 9.99 *(978-1-4926-1021-2(6),* Sourcebooks Jabberwocky) Sourcebooks, Inc.
—The Littlest Bunny in Calgary: An Easter Adventure. Jacobs, Lily. 2015. (ENG.). 32p. (J). (-3). 11.99 *(978-1-4926-1039-7(9),* Sourcebooks Jabberwocky) Sourcebooks, Inc.
—The Littlest Bunny in California: An Easter Adventure. Jacobs, Lily. 2015. (ENG.). 32p. (J). (-3). 9.99 *(978-1-4926-1042-7(9),* Sourcebooks Jabberwocky) Sourcebooks, Inc.
—The Littlest Bunny in Canada: An Easter Adventure. Jacobs, Lily. 2015. (ENG.). 32p. (J). (-3). 11.99 *(978-1-4926-1045-8(3),* Sourcebooks Jabberwocky) Sourcebooks, Inc.
—The Littlest Bunny in Cincinnati: An Easter Adventure. Jacobs, Lily. 2015. (ENG.). 32p. (J). (-3). 9.99 *(978-1-4926-1054-0(2),* Sourcebooks Jabberwocky) Sourcebooks, Inc.
—The Littlest Bunny in Delaware: An Easter Adventure. Jacobs, Lily. 2015. (ENG.). 32p. (J). (-3). 9.99 *(978-1-4926-1063-2(1),* Sourcebooks Jabberwocky) Sourcebooks, Inc.
—The Littlest Bunny in Edmonton: An Easter Adventure. Jacobs, Lily. 2015. (ENG.). 32p. (J). (-3). 11.99 *(978-1-4926-1066-3(6),* Sourcebooks Jabberwocky) Sourcebooks, Inc.
—The Littlest Bunny in Florida: An Easter Adventure. Jacobs, Lily. 2015. (ENG.). 32p. (J). (-3). 9.99 *(978-1-4926-1069-4(0),* Sourcebooks Jabberwocky) Sourcebooks, Inc.
—The Littlest Bunny in Illinois: An Easter Adventure. Jacobs, Lily. 2015. (ENG.). 32p. (J). (-3). 9.99 *(978-1-4926-1081-6(X),* Sourcebooks Jabberwocky) Sourcebooks, Inc.
—The Littlest Bunny in Indiana: An Easter Adventure. Jacobs, Lily. 2015. (ENG.). 32p. (J). (-3). 9.99 *(978-1-4926-1084-7(4),* Sourcebooks Jabberwocky) Sourcebooks, Inc.
—The Littlest Bunny in Kansas City: An Easter Adventure. Jacobs, Lily. 2015. (ENG.). 32p. (J). (-3). 9.99 *(978-1-4926-1093-9(3),* Sourcebooks Jabberwocky) Sourcebooks, Inc.
—The Littlest Bunny in Kentucky: An Easter Adventure. Jacobs, Lily. 2015. (ENG.). 32p. (J). (-3). 9.99 *(978-1-4926-1096-0(8),* Sourcebooks Jabberwocky) Sourcebooks, Inc.
—The Littlest Bunny in Louisiana: An Easter Adventure. Jacobs, Lily. 2015. (ENG.). 32p. (J). (-3). 9.99 *(978-1-4926-1105-9(0),* Sourcebooks Jabberwocky) Sourcebooks, Inc.
—The Littlest Bunny in Maryland: An Easter Adventure. Jacobs, Lily. 2015. (ENG.). 32p. (J). (-3). 9.99 *(978-1-4926-1111-0(5),* Sourcebooks Jabberwocky) Sourcebooks, Inc.
—The Littlest Bunny in Michigan: An Easter Adventure. 2015. (ENG.). 32p. (J). (-3). 9.99 *(978-1-4926-1117-2(4),* Sourcebooks Jabberwocky) Sourcebooks, Inc.
—The Littlest Bunny in Minnesota: An Easter Adventure. Jacobs, Lily. 2015. (ENG.). 32p. (J). (-3). 9.99 *(978-1-4926-1120-2(4),* Sourcebooks Jabberwocky) Sourcebooks, Inc.
—The Littlest Bunny in Mississippi: An Easter Adventure. Jacobs, Lily. 2015. (ENG.). 32p. (J). (-3). 9.99 *(978-1-4926-1123-3(9),* Sourcebooks Jabberwocky) Sourcebooks, Inc.
—The Littlest Bunny in Missouri: An Easter Adventure. Jacobs, Lily. 2015. (ENG.). 32p. (J). (-3). 9.99 *(978-1-4926-1126-4(3),* Sourcebooks Jabberwocky) Sourcebooks, Inc.
—The Littlest Bunny in Montana: An Easter Adventure. Jacobs, Lily. 2015. (ENG.). 32p. (J). (-3). 9.99 *(978-1-4926-1129-5(8),* Sourcebooks Jabberwocky) Sourcebooks, Inc.
—The Littlest Bunny in Nebraska: An Easter Adventure. Jacobs, Lily. 2015. (ENG.). 32p. (J). (-3). 9.99 *(978-1-4926-1132-5(8),* Sourcebooks Jabberwocky) Sourcebooks, Inc.
—The Littlest Bunny in Nevada: An Easter Adventure. Jacobs, Lily. 2015. (ENG.). 32p. (J). (-3). 9.99 *(978-1-4926-1135-6(2),* Sourcebooks Jabberwocky) Sourcebooks, Inc.
—The Littlest Bunny in New England: An Easter Adventure. Jacobs, Lily. 2015. (ENG.). 32p. (J). (-3). 9.99 *(978-1-4926-1138-7(7),* Sourcebooks Jabberwocky) Sourcebooks, Inc.
—The Littlest Bunny in New Hampshire: An Easter Adventure. Jacobs, Lily. 2015. (ENG.). 32p. (J). (-3). 9.99 *(978-1-4926-1141-7(7),* Sourcebooks Jabberwocky) Sourcebooks, Inc.
—The Littlest Bunny in New Jersey: An Easter Adventure. Jacobs, Lily. 2015. (ENG.). 32p. (J). (-3). 9.99 *(978-1-4926-1144-8(1),* Sourcebooks Jabberwocky) Sourcebooks, Inc.
—The Littlest Bunny in New Mexico: An Easter Adventure. Jacobs, Lily. 2015. (ENG.). 32p. (J). (-3). 9.99 *(978-1-4926-1147-9(6),* Sourcebooks Jabberwocky) Sourcebooks, Inc.
—The Littlest Bunny in New York: An Easter Adventure. Jacobs, Lily. 2015. (ENG.). 32p. (J). (-3). 9.99 *(978-1-4926-1150-9(6),* Sourcebooks Jabberwocky) Sourcebooks, Inc.
—The Littlest Bunny in New York City: An Easter Adventure. Jacobs, Lily. 2015. (ENG.). 32p. (J). (-3). 9.99 *(978-1-4926-1153-0(0),* Sourcebooks Jabberwocky) Sourcebooks, Inc.
—The Littlest Bunny in North Carolina: An Easter Adventure. Jacobs, Lily. 2015. (ENG.). 32p. (J). (-3). 9.99 *(978-1-4926-1156-1(5),* Sourcebooks Jabberwocky) Sourcebooks, Inc.
—The Littlest Bunny in North Dakota: An Easter Adventure. Jacobs, Lily. 2015. (ENG.). 32p. (J). (-3). 9.99 *(978-1-4926-1159-2(X),* Sourcebooks Jabberwocky) Sourcebooks, Inc.
—The Littlest Bunny in Ohio: An Easter Adventure. Jacobs, Lily. 2015. (ENG.). 32p. (J). (-3). 9.99 *(978-1-4926-1162-2(X),* Sourcebooks Jabberwocky) Sourcebooks, Inc.
—The Littlest Bunny in Oklahoma: An Easter Adventure. Jacobs, Lily. 2015. (ENG.). 32p. (J). (-3). 9.99 *(978-1-4926-1165-3(4),* Sourcebooks Jabberwocky) Sourcebooks, Inc.
—The Littlest Bunny in Omaha: An Easter Adventure. Jacobs, Lily. 2015. (ENG.). 32p. (J). (-3). 9.99 *(978-1-4926-1168-4(9),* Sourcebooks Jabberwocky) Sourcebooks, Inc.
—The Littlest Bunny in Oregon: An Easter Adventure. Jacobs, Lily. 2015. (ENG.). 32p. (J). (-3). 9.99 *(978-1-4926-1171-4(9),* Sourcebooks Jabberwocky) Sourcebooks, Inc.
—The Littlest Bunny in Ottawa: An Easter Adventure. Jacobs, Lily. 2015. (ENG.). 32p. (J). (-3). 11.99 *(978-1-4926-1174-5(3),* Sourcebooks Jabberwocky) Sourcebooks, Inc.
—The Littlest Bunny in Pennsylvania: An Easter Adventure. Jacobs, Lily. 2015. (ENG.). 32p. (J). (-3). 9.99 *(978-1-4926-1177-6(8),* Sourcebooks Jabberwocky) Sourcebooks, Inc.
—The Littlest Bunny in Philadelphia: An Easter Adventure. Jacobs, Lily. 2015. (ENG.). 32p. (J). (-3). 9.99 *(978-1-4926-1180-6(8),* Sourcebooks Jabberwocky) Sourcebooks, Inc.
—The Littlest Bunny in Pittsburgh: An Easter Adventure. Jacobs, Lily. 2015. (ENG.). 32p. (J). (-3). 9.99 *(978-1-4926-1183-7(2),* Sourcebooks Jabberwocky) Sourcebooks, Inc.
—The Littlest Bunny in Portland: An Easter Adventure. Jacobs, Lily. 2015. (ENG.). 32p. (J). (-3). 9.99 *(978-1-4926-1186-8(7),* Sourcebooks Jabberwocky) Sourcebooks, Inc.
—The Littlest Bunny in Rhode Island: An Easter Adventure. 2015. (ENG.). 32p. (J). (-3). 9.99 *(978-1-4926-1189-9(1),* Sourcebooks Jabberwocky) Sourcebooks, Inc.
—The Littlest Bunny in San Francisco: An Easter Adventure. Jacobs, Lily. 2015. (ENG.). 32p. (J). (-3). 9.99 *(978-1-4926-1192-9(1),* Sourcebooks Jabberwocky) Sourcebooks, Inc.
—The Littlest Bunny in South Carolina: An Easter Adventure. Jacobs, Lily. 2015. (ENG.). 32p. (J). (-3). 9.99 *(978-1-4926-1195-0(6),* Sourcebooks Jabberwocky) Sourcebooks, Inc.
—The Littlest Bunny in South Dakota: An Easter Adventure. Jacobs, Lily. 2015. (ENG.). 32p. (J). (-3). 9.99 *(978-1-4926-1198-1(0),* Sourcebooks Jabberwocky) Sourcebooks, Inc.
—The Littlest Bunny in St. Louis: An Easter Adventure. Jacobs, Lily. 2015. (ENG.). 32p. (J). (-3). 9.99 *(978-1-4926-1201-8(4),* Sourcebooks Jabberwocky) Sourcebooks, Inc.
—The Littlest Bunny in Tampa Bay: An Easter Adventure. Jacobs, Lily. 2015. (ENG.). 32p. (J). (-3). 9.99 *(978-1-4926-1204-9(9),* Sourcebooks Jabberwocky) Sourcebooks, Inc.
—The Littlest Bunny in Tennessee: An Easter Adventure. Jacobs, Lily. 2015. (ENG.). 32p. (J). (-3). 9.99 *(978-1-4926-1207-0(3),* Sourcebooks Jabberwocky) Sourcebooks, Inc.
—The Littlest Bunny in Texas: An Easter Adventure. Jacobs, Lily. 2015. (ENG.). 32p. (J). (-3). 9.99 *(978-1-4926-1210-0(3),* Sourcebooks Jabberwocky) Sourcebooks, Inc.
—The Littlest Bunny in Toronto: An Easter Adventure. Jacobs, Lily. 2015. (ENG.). 32p. (J). (-3). 11.99 *(978-1-4926-1213-1(8),* Sourcebooks Jabberwocky) Sourcebooks, Inc.
—The Littlest Bunny in Tulsa: An Easter Adventure. Jacobs, Lily. 2015. (ENG.). 32p. (J). (-3). 9.99 *(978-1-4926-1216-2(2),* Sourcebooks Jabberwocky) Sourcebooks, Inc.
—The Littlest Bunny in Utah: An Easter Adventure. Jacobs, Lily. 2015. (ENG.). 32p. (J). (-3). 9.99 *(978-1-4926-1219-3(7),* Sourcebooks Jabberwocky) Sourcebooks, Inc.
—The Littlest Bunny in Vancouver: An Easter Adventure. Jacobs, Lily. 2015. (ENG.). 32p. (J). (-3). 11.99 *(978-1-4926-1222-3(7),* Sourcebooks Jabberwocky) Sourcebooks, Inc.
—The Littlest Bunny in Vermont: An Easter Adventure. Jacobs, Lily. 2015. (ENG.). 32p. (J). (-3). 9.99 *(978-1-4926-1225-4(1),* Sourcebooks Jabberwocky) Sourcebooks, Inc.
—The Littlest Bunny in Virginia: An Easter Adventure. Jacobs, Lily. 2015. (ENG.). 32p. (J). (-3). 9.99 *(978-1-4926-1228-5(6),* Sourcebooks Jabberwocky) Sourcebooks, Inc.
—Madeleine's Light: A Story of Camille Claudel. Ziarnik, Natalie. 2012. (ENG.). 32p. (J). (gr. k-2). 17.95 *(978-1-59078-855-4(9))* Boyds Mills Pr.
—Santa Is Coming to Alabama. Smallman, Steve. 2013. (ENG.). 32p. (J). (-3). 9.99 *(978-1-4022-8821-0(2),* Sourcebooks Jabberwocky) Sourcebooks, Inc.
—Santa Is Coming to Alaska. Smallman, Steve. 2013. (ENG.). 32p. (J). (-3). 9.99 *(978-1-4022-9517-1(0),* Sourcebooks Jabberwocky) Sourcebooks, Inc.
—Santa Is Coming to Albuquerque. Smallman, Steve. 2013. (ENG.). 32p. (J). (-3). 9.99 *(978-1-4022-9042-8(X),* Sourcebooks Jabberwocky) Sourcebooks, Inc.
—Santa Is Coming to Arizona. Smallman, Steve. 2012. (ENG.). 32p. (J). (-3). 9.99 *(978-1-4022-7545-6(5),* Sourcebooks Jabberwocky) Sourcebooks, Inc.
—Santa Is Coming to Arkansas. Smallman, Steve. 2013. (ENG.). 32p. (J). (-3). 9.99 *(978-1-4022-9066-4(7),* Sourcebooks Jabberwocky) Sourcebooks, Inc.
—Santa Is Coming to Asheville. Smallman, Steve. 2013. (ENG.). 32p. (J). (-3). 9.99 *(978-1-4022-9030-5(6),* Sourcebooks Jabberwocky) Sourcebooks, Inc.
—Santa Is Coming to Austin. Smallman, Steve. 2013. (ENG.). 32p. (J). (-3). 9.99 *(978-1-4022-8973-6(1),* Sourcebooks Jabberwocky) Sourcebooks, Inc.
—Santa Is Coming to Bellingham. Smallman, Steve. 2013. (ENG.). 32p. (J). (-3). 9.99 *(978-1-4022-9130-2(2),* Sourcebooks Jabberwocky) Sourcebooks, Inc.
—Santa Is Coming to Bentonville. Smallman, Steve. 2013. (ENG.). 32p. (J). (-3). 9.99 *(978-1-4022-9109-8(4),* Sourcebooks Jabberwocky) Sourcebooks, Inc.
—Santa Is Coming to Birmingham. Smallman, Steve. 2013. (ENG.). 32p. (J). (-3). 9.99 *(978-1-4022-9106-7(X),* Sourcebooks Jabberwocky) Sourcebooks, Inc.
—Santa Is Coming to Boise. Smallman, Steve. 2013. (ENG.). 32p. (J). (-3). 9.99 *(978-1-4022-9118-0(3),* Sourcebooks Jabberwocky) Sourcebooks, Inc.
—Santa Is Coming to Boston. Smallman, Steve. 2012. (ENG.). 32p. (J). (-3). 9.99 *(978-1-4022-7506-7(4),* Sourcebooks Jabberwocky) Sourcebooks, Inc.
—Santa Is Coming to Bozeman. Smallman, Steve. 2013. (ENG.). 32p. (J). (-3). 9.99 *(978-1-4022-9045-9(4),* Sourcebooks Jabberwocky) Sourcebooks, Inc.
—Santa Is Coming to Brooklyn. Smallman, Steve. 2013. (ENG.). 32p. (J). (-3). 9.99 *(978-1-4022-9003-9(9),* Sourcebooks Jabberwocky) Sourcebooks, Inc.
—Santa Is Coming to Buffalo. Smallman, Steve. 2013. (ENG.). 32p. (J). (-3). 9.99 *(978-1-4022-8858-6(1),* Sourcebooks Jabberwocky) Sourcebooks, Inc.
—Santa Is Coming to Calgary. Smallman, Steve. 2013. (ENG.). 32p. (J). (-3). 11.99 *(978-1-4022-8988-0(X),* Sourcebooks Jabberwocky) Sourcebooks, Inc.
—Santa Is Coming to California. Smallman, Steve. 2012. (ENG.). 32p. (J). (-3). 9.99 *(978-1-4022-7515-9(3),* Sourcebooks Jabberwocky) Sourcebooks, Inc.
—Santa Is Coming to Canada. Smallman, Steve. 2013. (ENG.). 32p. (J). (-3). 11.99 *(978-1-4022-8839-5(5),* Sourcebooks Jabberwocky) Sourcebooks, Inc.
—Santa Is Coming to Cape Cod. Smallman, Steve. 2013. (ENG.). 32p. (J). (-3). 9.99 *(978-1-4022-9078-7(0),* Sourcebooks Jabberwocky) Sourcebooks, Inc.
—Santa Is Coming to Charleston. Smallman, Steve. 2013. (ENG.). 32p. (J). (-3). 9.99 *(978-1-4022-8985-9(5),* Sourcebooks Jabberwocky) Sourcebooks, Inc.
—Santa Is Coming to Charlotte. Smallman, Steve. 2014. (ENG.). 32p. (J). (-3). 9.99 *(978-1-4926-0697-0(9),* Sourcebooks Jabberwocky) Sourcebooks, Inc.
—Santa Is Coming to Chicago. Smallman, Steve. 2012. (ENG.). 32p. (J). (-3). 9.99 *(978-1-4022-7509-8(9),* Sourcebooks Jabberwocky) Sourcebooks, Inc.
—Santa Is Coming to Cincinnati. Smallman, Steve. 2013. (ENG.). 32p. (J). (-3). 9.99 *(978-1-4022-8997-2(9),* Sourcebooks Jabberwocky) Sourcebooks, Inc.
—Santa Is Coming to Cleveland. Smallman, Steve. 2014. (ENG.). 32p. (J). (-3). 9.99 *(978-1-4926-0703-8(7),* Sourcebooks Jabberwocky) Sourcebooks, Inc.
—Santa Is Coming to Colorado. Smallman, Steve. 2013. (ENG.). 32p. (J). (-3). 9.99 *(978-1-4022-8815-9(8),* Sourcebooks Jabberwocky) Sourcebooks, Inc.
—Santa Is Coming to Columbus. Smallman, Steve. 2013. (ENG.). 32p. (J). (-3). 9.99 *(978-1-4022-9036-7(5),* Sourcebooks Jabberwocky) Sourcebooks, Inc.
—Santa Is Coming to Connecticut. Smallman, Steve. 2014. (ENG.). 32p. (J). (-3). 9.99 *(978-1-4926-0670-3(7),* Sourcebooks Jabberwocky) Sourcebooks, Inc.
—Santa Is Coming to Dallas. Smallman, Steve. 2014. (ENG.). 32p. (J). (-3). 9.99 *(978-1-4926-0700-7(2),* Sourcebooks Jabberwocky) Sourcebooks, Inc.
—Santa Is Coming to Delaware. Smallman, Steve. 2013. (ENG.). 32p. (J). (-3). 9.99 *(978-1-4022-9508-9(1),* Sourcebooks Jabberwocky) Sourcebooks, Inc.

—Santa Is Coming to Duluth. Smallman, Steve. 2013. (ENG.). 32p. (J). (-3). 9.99 *(978-1-4022-9027-5(6)*, Sourcebooks Jabberwocky) Sourcebooks, Inc.
—Santa Is Coming to Durango. Smallman, Steve. 2013. (ENG.). 32p. (J). (-3). 9.99 *(978-1-4022-9133-3(7)*, Sourcebooks Jabberwocky) Sourcebooks, Inc.
—Santa Is Coming to Edmonton. Smallman, Steve. 2013. (ENG.). 32p. (J). (-3). 11.99 *(978-1-4022-8991-0(X)*, Sourcebooks Jabberwocky) Sourcebooks, Inc.
—Santa Is Coming to Florida. Smallman, Steve. 2012. (ENG.). 32p. (J). (-3). 9.99 *(978-1-4022-7527-2(7)*, Sourcebooks Jabberwocky) Sourcebooks, Inc.
—Santa Is Coming to Georgia. Smallman, Steve. 2013. (ENG.). 32p. (J). (-3). 9.99 *(978-1-4022-8794-7(1)*, Sourcebooks Jabberwocky) Sourcebooks, Inc.
—Santa Is Coming to Green Bay. Smallman, Steve. 2013. (ENG.). 32p. (J). (-3). 9.99 *(978-1-4022-9112-8(4)*, Sourcebooks Jabberwocky) Sourcebooks, Inc.
—Santa Is Coming to Hawaii. Smallman, Steve. 2013. (ENG.). 32p. (J). (-3). 9.99 *(978-1-4022-9009-1(8)*, Sourcebooks Jabberwocky) Sourcebooks, Inc.
—Santa Is Coming to Idaho. Smallman, Steve. 2013. (ENG.). 32p. (J). (-3). 9.99 *(978-1-4022-9511-9(1)*, Sourcebooks Jabberwocky) Sourcebooks, Inc.
—Santa Is Coming to Illinois. Smallman, Steve. 2013. (ENG.). 32p. (J). (-3). 9.99 *(978-1-4022-9103-6(5)*, Sourcebooks Jabberwocky) Sourcebooks, Inc.
—Santa Is Coming to Indiana. Smallman, Steve. 2013. (ENG.). 32p. (J). (-3). 9.99 *(978-1-4022-8803-6(4)*, Sourcebooks Jabberwocky) Sourcebooks, Inc.
—Santa Is Coming to Iowa. Smallman, Steve. 2013. (ENG.). 32p. (J). (-3). 9.99 *(978-1-4022-8818-0(2)*, Sourcebooks Jabberwocky) Sourcebooks, Inc.
—Santa Is Coming to Jefferson City. Smallman, Steve. 2014. (ENG.). 32p. (J). (-3). 9.99 *(978-1-4926-0766-3(5)*, Sourcebooks Jabberwocky) Sourcebooks, Inc.
—Santa Is Coming to Kansas. Smallman, Steve. 2013. (ENG.). 32p. (J). (-3). 9.99 *(978-1-4022-9121-0(3)*, Sourcebooks Jabberwocky) Sourcebooks, Inc.
—Santa Is Coming to Kansas City. Smallman, Steve. 2013. (ENG.). 32p. (J). (-3). 9.99 *(978-1-4022-8855-5(7)*, Sourcebooks Jabberwocky) Sourcebooks, Inc.
—Santa Is Coming to Kentucky. Smallman, Steve. 2013. (ENG.). 32p. (J). (-3). 9.99 *(978-1-4022-8824-1(7)*, Sourcebooks Jabberwocky) Sourcebooks, Inc.
—Santa Is Coming to Las Vegas. Smallman, Steve. 2013. (ENG.). 32p. (J). (-3). 9.99 *(978-1-4022-8836-4(0)*, Sourcebooks Jabberwocky) Sourcebooks, Inc.
—Santa Is Coming to Los Angeles. Smallman, Steve. 2013. (ENG.). 32p. (J). (-3). 9.99 *(978-1-4022-8830-2(1)*, Sourcebooks Jabberwocky) Sourcebooks, Inc.
—Santa Is Coming to Louisiana. Smallman, Steve. 2012. (ENG.). 32p. (J). (-3). 9.99 *(978-1-4022-7536-4(6)*, Sourcebooks Jabberwocky) Sourcebooks, Inc.
—Santa Is Coming to Lubbock. Smallman, Steve. 2013. (ENG.). 32p. (J). (-3). 9.99 *(978-1-4022-9136-4(1)*, Sourcebooks Jabberwocky) Sourcebooks, Inc.
—Santa Is Coming to Madison. Smallman, Steve. 2014. (ENG.). 32p. (J). (-3). 9.99 *(978-1-4926-0706-9(1)*, Sourcebooks Jabberwocky) Sourcebooks, Inc.
—Santa Is Coming to Maine. Smallman, Steve. 2013. (ENG.). 32p. (J). (-3). 9.99 *(978-1-4022-9069-5(1)*, Sourcebooks Jabberwocky) Sourcebooks, Inc.
—Santa Is Coming to Manchester. Smallman, Steve. 2013. (ENG.). 32p. (J). (-3). 9.99 *(978-1-4022-9115-9(9)*, Sourcebooks Jabberwocky) Sourcebooks, Inc.
—Santa Is Coming to Maryland. Smallman, Steve. 2013. (ENG.). 32p. (J). (-3). 9.99 *(978-1-4022-8812-8(3)*, Sourcebooks Jabberwocky) Sourcebooks, Inc.
—Santa Is Coming to Massachusetts. Smallman, Steve. 2014. (ENG.). 32p. (J). (-3). 9.99 *(978-1-4926-0673-4(1)*, Sourcebooks Jabberwocky) Sourcebooks, Inc.
—Santa Is Coming to Miami. Smallman, Steve. 2013. (ENG.). 32p. (J). (-3). 9.99 *(978-1-4022-9051-0(9)*, Sourcebooks Jabberwocky) Sourcebooks, Inc.
—Santa Is Coming to Michigan. Smallman, Steve. 2012. (ENG.). 32p. (J). (-3). 9.99 *(978-1-4022-7539-5(0)*, Sourcebooks Jabberwocky) Sourcebooks, Inc.
—Santa Is Coming to Minnesota. Smallman, Steve. 2012. (ENG.). 32p. (J). (-3). 9.99 *(978-1-4022-7530-2(7)*, Sourcebooks Jabberwocky) Sourcebooks, Inc.
—Santa Is Coming to Mississippi. Smallman, Steve. 2013. (ENG.). 32p. (J). (-3). 9.99 *(978-1-4022-9015-2(2)*, Sourcebooks Jabberwocky) Sourcebooks, Inc.
—Santa Is Coming to Missouri. Smallman, Steve. 2013. (ENG.). 32p. (J). (-3). 9.99 *(978-1-4022-8809-8(3)*, Sourcebooks Jabberwocky) Sourcebooks, Inc.
—Santa Is Coming to Montana. Smallman, Steve. 2013. (ENG.). 32p. (J). (-3). 9.99 *(978-1-4022-9018-3(7)*, Sourcebooks Jabberwocky) Sourcebooks, Inc.
—Santa Is Coming to My House. Smallman, Steve. 2012. (ENG.). 32p. (J). (-3). 9.99 *(978-1-4022-7775-7(X)*, Sourcebooks Jabberwocky) Sourcebooks, Inc.
—Santa Is Coming to Naperville. Smallman, Steve. 2013. (ENG.). 32p. (J). (-3). 9.99 *(978-1-4022-9063-3(2)*, Sourcebooks Jabberwocky) Sourcebooks, Inc.
—Santa Is Coming to Naples. Smallman, Steve. 2013. (ENG.). 32p. (J). (-3). 9.99 *(978-1-4022-9048-0(9)*, Sourcebooks Jabberwocky) Sourcebooks, Inc.
—Santa Is Coming to Nashville. Smallman, Steve. 2014. (ENG.). 32p. (J). (-3). 9.99 *(978-1-4926-0718-2(5)*, Sourcebooks Jabberwocky) Sourcebooks, Inc.
—Santa Is Coming to Nebraska. Smallman, Steve. 2013. (ENG.). 32p. (J). (-3). 9.99 *(978-1-4022-9072-5(1)*, Sourcebooks Jabberwocky) Sourcebooks, Inc.
—Santa Is Coming to Nevada. Smallman, Steve. 2013. (ENG.). 32p. (J). (-3). 9.99 *(978-1-4022-9523-2(5)*, Sourcebooks Jabberwocky) Sourcebooks, Inc.
—Santa Is Coming to New Brunswick. Smallman, Steve. 2014. (ENG.). 32p. (J). (-3). 11.99 *(978-1-4926-0712-0(6)*, Sourcebooks Jabberwocky) Sourcebooks, Inc.
—Santa Is Coming to New England. Smallman, Steve. 2012. (ENG.). 32p. (J). (-3). 9.99 *(978-1-4022-7551-7(X)*, Sourcebooks Jabberwocky) Sourcebooks, Inc.
—Santa Is Coming to New Hampshire. Smallman, Steve. 2014. (ENG.). 32p. (J). (-3). 9.99 *(978-1-4926-0676-5(6)*, Sourcebooks Jabberwocky) Sourcebooks, Inc.
—Santa Is Coming to New Jersey. Smallman, Steve. 2013. (ENG.). 32p. (J). (-3). 9.99 *(978-1-4022-8797-8(6)*, Sourcebooks Jabberwocky) Sourcebooks, Inc.
—Santa Is Coming to New Mexico. Smallman, Steve. 2013. (ENG.). 32p. (J). (-3). 9.99 *(978-1-4022-9520-1(0)*, Sourcebooks Jabberwocky) Sourcebooks, Inc.
—Santa Is Coming to New Orleans. Smallman, Steve. 2014. (ENG.). 32p. (J). (-3). 9.99 *(978-1-4926-0694-9(4)*, Sourcebooks Jabberwocky) Sourcebooks, Inc.
—Santa Is Coming to New York. Smallman, Steve. 2012. (ENG.). 32p. (J). (-3). 9.99 *(978-1-4022-7503-6(X)*, Sourcebooks Jabberwocky) Sourcebooks, Inc.
—Santa Is Coming to Newfoundland. Smallman, Steve. 2014. (ENG.). 32p. (J). (-3). 11.99 *(978-1-4926-0715-1(0)*, Sourcebooks Jabberwocky) Sourcebooks, Inc.
—Santa Is Coming to North Carolina. Smallman, Steve. 2014. (ENG.). 32p. (J). (-3). 9.99 *(978-1-4926-0682-6(0)*, Sourcebooks Jabberwocky) Sourcebooks, Inc.
—Santa Is Coming to North Dakota. Smallman, Steve. 2013. (ENG.). 32p. (J). (-3). 9.99 *(978-1-4022-9514-0(6)*, Sourcebooks Jabberwocky) Sourcebooks, Inc.
—Santa Is Coming to Notre Dame. Smallman, Steve. 2013. (ENG.). 32p. (J). (-3). 9.99 *(978-1-4022-9024-4(1)*, Sourcebooks Jabberwocky) Sourcebooks, Inc.
—Santa Is Coming to Ohio. Smallman, Steve. 2012. (ENG.). 32p. (J). (-3). 9.99 *(978-1-4022-7554-8(4)*, Sourcebooks Jabberwocky) Sourcebooks, Inc.
—Santa Is Coming to Oklahoma. Smallman, Steve. 2013. (ENG.). 32p. (J). (-3). 9.99 *(978-1-4022-9012-1(8)*, Sourcebooks Jabberwocky) Sourcebooks, Inc.
—Santa Is Coming to Omaha. Smallman, Steve. 2013. (ENG.). 32p. (J). (-3). 9.99 *(978-1-4022-9006-0(3)*, Sourcebooks Jabberwocky) Sourcebooks, Inc.
—Santa Is Coming to Oregon. Smallman, Steve. 2013. (ENG.). 32p. (J). (-3). 9.99 *(978-1-4022-9075-6(6)*, Sourcebooks Jabberwocky) Sourcebooks, Inc.
—Santa Is Coming to Ottawa. Smallman, Steve. 2013. (ENG.). 32p. (J). (-3). 11.99 *(978-1-4022-8994-1(4)*, Sourcebooks Jabberwocky) Sourcebooks, Inc.
—Santa Is Coming to Pennsylvania. Smallman, Steve. 2013. (ENG.). 32p. (J). (-3). 9.99 *(978-1-4022-8791-6(7)*, Sourcebooks Jabberwocky) Sourcebooks, Inc.
—Santa Is Coming to Philadelphia. Smallman, Steve. 2012. (ENG.). 32p. (J). (-3). 9.99 *(978-1-4022-7518-0(8)*, Sourcebooks Jabberwocky) Sourcebooks, Inc.
—Santa Is Coming to Pittsburgh. Smallman, Steve. 2013. (ENG.). 32p. (J). (-3). 9.99 *(978-1-4022-8982-8(0)*, Sourcebooks Jabberwocky) Sourcebooks, Inc.
—Santa Is Coming to Portland. Smallman, Steve. 2012. (ENG.). 32p. (J). (-3). 9.99 *(978-1-4022-7772-6(5)*, Sourcebooks Jabberwocky) Sourcebooks, Inc.
—Santa Is Coming to Rhode Island. Smallman, Steve. 2014. (ENG.). 32p. (J). (-3). 9.99 *(978-1-4926-0727-4(4)*, Sourcebooks Jabberwocky) Sourcebooks, Inc.
—Santa Is Coming to San Diego. Smallman, Steve. 2014. (ENG.). 32p. (J). (-3). 9.99 *(978-1-4926-0688-8(X)*, Sourcebooks Jabberwocky) Sourcebooks, Inc.
—Santa Is Coming to San Francisco. Smallman, Steve. 2012. (ENG.). 32p. (J). (-3). 9.99 *(978-1-4022-7548-7(X)*, Sourcebooks Jabberwocky) Sourcebooks, Inc.
—Santa Is Coming to Santa Cruz. Smallman, Steve. 2013. (ENG.). 32p. (J). (-3). 9.99 *(978-1-4022-9057-2(8)*, Sourcebooks Jabberwocky) Sourcebooks, Inc.
—Santa Is Coming to Santa Fe. Smallman, Steve. 2013. (ENG.). 32p. (J). (-3). 9.99 *(978-1-4022-9124-1(8)*, Sourcebooks Jabberwocky) Sourcebooks, Inc.
—Santa Is Coming to Savannah. Smallman, Steve. 2013. (ENG.). 32p. (J). (-3). 9.99 *(978-1-4022-8979-8(0)*, Sourcebooks Jabberwocky) Sourcebooks, Inc.
—Santa Is Coming to South Carolina. Smallman, Steve. 2014. (ENG.). 32p. (J). (-3). 9.99 *(978-1-4926-0685-7(5)*, Sourcebooks Jabberwocky) Sourcebooks, Inc.
—Santa Is Coming to South Dakota. Smallman, Steve. 2013. (ENG.). 32p. (J). (-3). 9.99 *(978-1-4022-9021-3(7)*, Sourcebooks Jabberwocky) Sourcebooks, Inc.
—Santa Is Coming to St. Louis. Smallman, Steve. 2013. (ENG.). 32p. (J). (-3). 9.99 *(978-1-4022-9000-8(4)*, Sourcebooks Jabberwocky) Sourcebooks, Inc.
—Santa Is Coming to Tampa Bay & St. Petersburg. Smallman, Steve. 2013. (ENG.). 32p. (J). (-3). 9.99 *(978-1-4022-9054-1(3)*, Sourcebooks Jabberwocky) Sourcebooks, Inc.
—Santa Is Coming to Tennessee. Smallman, Steve. 2013. (ENG.). 32p. (J). (-3). 9.99 *(978-1-4022-8806-7(9)*, Sourcebooks Jabberwocky) Sourcebooks, Inc.
—Santa Is Coming to Texas. Smallman, Steve. 2012. (ENG.). 32p. (J). (-3). 9.99 *(978-1-4022-7512-8(9)*, Sourcebooks Jabberwocky) Sourcebooks, Inc.
—Santa Is Coming to the Carolinas. Smallman, Steve. 2012. (ENG.). 32p. (J). (-3). 9.99 *(978-1-4022-7586-9(2)*, Sourcebooks Jabberwocky) Sourcebooks, Inc.
—Santa Is Coming to the Great Smoky Mountains. Smallman, Steve. 2013. (ENG.). 32p. (J). (-3). 9.99 *(978-1-4022-9033-6(0)*, Sourcebooks Jabberwocky) Sourcebooks, Inc.
—Santa Is Coming to the Jersey Shore. Smallman, Steve. 2014. (ENG.). 32p. (J). (-3). 9.99 *(978-1-4926-0691-8(X)*, Sourcebooks Jabberwocky) Sourcebooks, Inc.
—Santa Is Coming to the Quad Cities. Smallman, Steve. 2013. (ENG.). 32p. (J). (-3). 9.99 *(978-1-4022-9060-2(8)*, Sourcebooks Jabberwocky) Sourcebooks, Inc.
—Santa Is Coming to the Rockies. Smallman, Steve. 2012. (ENG.). 32p. (J). (-3). 9.99 *(978-1-4022-7593-7(5)*, Sourcebooks Jabberwocky) Sourcebooks, Inc.
—Santa Is Coming to Toronto. Smallman, Steve. 2012. (ENG.). 32p. (J). (-3). 9.99 *(978-1-4022-7521-0(8)*, Sourcebooks Jabberwocky) Sourcebooks, Inc.
—Santa Is Coming to Tucson. Smallman, Steve. 2013. (ENG.). 32p. (J). (-3). 9.99 *(978-1-4022-8976-7(6)*, Sourcebooks Jabberwocky) Sourcebooks, Inc.
—Santa Is Coming to Tulsa. Smallman, Steve. 2013. (ENG.). 32p. (J). (-3). 9.99 *(978-1-4022-9039-8(X)*, Sourcebooks Jabberwocky) Sourcebooks, Inc.
—Santa Is Coming to Utah. Smallman, Steve. 2013. (ENG.). 32p. (J). (-3). 9.99 *(978-1-4022-8827-2(1)*, Sourcebooks Jabberwocky) Sourcebooks, Inc.
—Santa Is Coming to Vancouver. Smallman, Steve. 2012. (ENG.). 32p. (J). (-3). 9.99 *(978-1-4022-7542-5(0)*, Sourcebooks Jabberwocky) Sourcebooks, Inc.
—Santa Is Coming to Vermont. Smallman, Steve. 2013. (ENG.). 32p. (J). (-3). 9.99 *(978-1-4022-9127-2(2)*, Sourcebooks Jabberwocky) Sourcebooks, Inc.
—Santa Is Coming to Virginia. Smallman, Steve. 2013. (ENG.). 32p. (J). (-3). 9.99 *(978-1-4022-8800-5(X)*, Sourcebooks Jabberwocky) Sourcebooks, Inc.
—Santa Is Coming to Washington. Smallman, Steve. 2012. (ENG.). 32p. (J). (-3). 9.99 *(978-1-4022-7524-1(2)*, Sourcebooks Jabberwocky) Sourcebooks, Inc.
—Santa Is Coming to Washington DC. Smallman, Steve. 2013. (ENG.). 32p. (J). (-3). 9.99 *(978-1-4022-8833-3(6)*, Sourcebooks Jabberwocky) Sourcebooks, Inc.
—Santa Is Coming to West Virginia. Smallman, Steve. 2013. (ENG.). 32p. (J). (-3). 9.99 *(978-1-4022-9100-5(0)*, Sourcebooks Jabberwocky) Sourcebooks, Inc.
—Santa Is Coming to Wisconsin. Smallman, Steve. 2012. (ENG.). 32p. (J). (-3). 9.99 *(978-1-4022-7533-3(1)*, Sourcebooks Jabberwocky) Sourcebooks, Inc.
—Santa Is Coming to Wyoming. Smallman, Steve. 2014. (ENG.). 32p. (J). (-3). 9.99 *(978-1-4926-0679-6(0)*, Sourcebooks Jabberwocky) Sourcebooks, Inc.
—The Three Musketeers. Dumas, Alexandre. 2013. 46p. (J). *(978-1-4351-4812-3(6))* Barnes & Noble, Inc.
Dunn, Robert A. The Littlest Bunny in Washington, DC: An Easter Adventure. Jacobs, Lily. 2015. (ENG.). 32p. (J). (-3). 9.99 *(978-1-4926-1234-6(0)*, Sourcebooks Jabberwocky) Sourcebooks, Inc.
Dunn, Sandy. The Hen House: A True Story of Growing up on a Maine Farm. Dean, Carol. 2003. (ENG.). 32p. (J). (gr. -1-17). 15.95 *(978-0-89272-609-7(1))* Down East Bks.
Dunnahoe, Hugh. Prayers for Children: Sunshine Meadows. Oh! Suzannah. 2011. (ENG.). 24p. pap. 10.00 *(978-1-4610-1975-6(3))* CreateSpace Independent Publishing Platform.
Dunne, Kathleen. Hide & Seek Monsters. Williams, Rozanne Lanczak. 2005. (Reading for Fluency Ser.). 16p. (J). pap. 3.49 *(978-1-59198-154-1(9)*, 4254) Creative Teaching Pr., Inc.
Dunne, Kevin, jt. photos by see Heap, Will.
Dunne, Tom. Dude: Fun with Dude & Betty. Pliscou, Lisa. 2011. (ENG.). 40p. (J). (gr. 1-3). 14.99 *(978-0-06-175690-0(3))* HarperCollins Pubs.
Dunnick, Regan. Bad Astrid. Brennan, Eileen. 2013. (J). *(978-0-449-81427-7(0))*; (ENG.). 40p. (gr. -1-2). 15.99 *(978-0-375-85580-1(7))* Random Hse., Inc.
Dunnick, Regan. Creak! Said the Bed. Root, Phyllis. 2015. (ENG.). 32p. (J). (gr. -1-3). 6.99 ***(978-0-7636-7969-9(0))*** Candlewick Pr.
Dunnick, Regan. How Underwear Got under There: A Brief History. Shaskan, Kathy. 2015. (ENG.). 96p. (J). (gr. 2-5). 7.99 *(978-0-14-751448-6(7)*, Puffin) Penguin Publishing Group.
—The Louds Move In!, 1 vol. Crimi, Carolyn. 2006. (ENG.). 32p. (J). (gr. -1-3). 14.95 *(978-0-7614-5221-8(4))* Marshall Cavendish Corp.
Dunnier, Tina. Grandpa's a Martian. Wehrman, Tom. 2013. 28p. pap. 8.99 *(978-1-938768-27-9(2))* Gypsy Pubns.
—Mousekabitz. Fisher, Meaghan. 2013. (ENG.). 32p. (J). pap. 8.99 *(978-1-938768-31-6(0))* Gypsy Pubns.
Dunning, Joan. Seabird in the Forest: The Mystery of the Marbled Murrelet. Dunning, Joan. 2011. (ENG.). 32p. (J). (gr. k-4). 17.95 *(978-1-59078-715-1(3))* Boyds Mills Pr.
Dunningham, Jo. Michael & the Elf. Sullivan, Kathryn. 2nd ed. 2012. 24p. pap. 10.95 *(978-1-61633-356-0(1))* Guardian Angel Publishing, Inc.
Dunnington, Tom. Animal Babies. Hamsa, Bobbie. 2011. (Rookie Ready to Learn Ser.). 40p. (J). (gr. -1-k). (ENG.). pap. 5.95 *(978-0-531-26800-1(4))*; lib. bdg. 23.00 *(978-0-531-25640-4(5))* Scholastic Library Publishing. (Children's Pr.).
—The Great Bug Hunt. Dobkin, Bonnie. 2011. (Rookie Ready to Learn Ser.). 40p. (J). pap. 5.95 *(978-0-531-26696-0(6))*; (gr. -1-k). lib. bdg. 23.00 *(978-0-531-26415-7(7))* Scholastic Library Publishing. (Children's Pr.).
—Help Dress Priscilla: A Talk-along Book. Punnett, Dick. 2nd ed. 2005. (Talk-Along Bks.). 32p. (J). pap. 6.99 *(978-0-9657211-3-4(2))* Tomoka Pr.
—Help Jumbo Escape: A Talk-along Book. Punnett, Dick. 2nd ed. 2005. (Talk-Along Bks.). 32p. (J). pap. 6.99 *(978-0-9657211-2-7(4))* Tomoka Pr.
Dunrea, Olivier. The Boy Who Loved to Draw: Benjamin West. Brenner, Barbara. 2003. (ENG.). 48p. (J). (gr. -1-3). pap. 6.99 *(978-0-618-31089-0(4))* Houghton Mifflin Harcourt Publishing Co.
Dunrea, Olivier. Gossie & Friends: A First Flap Book. Dunrea, Olivier. 2006. (Gossie & Friends Ser.). (ENG.). 8p. (J). (gr. -1 — 1). 11.99 *(978-0-618-70786-7(7))* Houghton Mifflin Harcourt Publishing Co.
—Gossie & Gertie. Dunrea, Olivier. 2007. (Gossie & Friends Ser.). (ENG.). 16p. (J). (gr. -1 — 1). bds. 6.99 *(978-0-618-74793-1(1))* Houghton Mifflin Harcourt Publishing Co.
—It's Snowing! Dunrea, Olivier. 2009. (ENG.). 32p. (J). (gr. -1-1). pap. 6.99 *(978-0-312-60216-1(2))* Square Fish.
—Old Bear & His Cub. Dunrea, Olivier. 2012. (Little Cub Ser.). (ENG.). 30p. (J). (gr. -1 — 1). bds. 6.99 *(978-0-399-16035-6(3)*, Philomel) Penguin Publishing Group.
—Ollie. Dunrea, Olivier. 2003. (Gossie & Friends Ser.). (ENG.). 32p. (J). (gr. -1 — 1). tchr. ed. 9.95 *(978-0-618-33928-0(0))* Houghton Mifflin Harcourt Publishing Co.
Dunstan, David. Chester the Crab. Tovey, Peter. Hinkler Books Staff, ed. 2010. (Wiggly Eyes Ser.). 12p. (J). (gr. -1). 12.99 *(978-1-74185-405-3(9))* Ideals Pubns.
—Max the Monster. Cuthbert, Kate. Hinkler Books Staff, ed. 2010. (Wiggly Eyes Ser.). 12p. (J). (gr. -1). 12.99 *(978-1-74185-404-6(0))* Ideals Pubns.
Dunton, Trevor. Get the Fruit! Shipton, Paul. Moon, Cliff, ed. 2004. (Collins Big Cat Ser.). (ENG.). 16p. (J). pap. 5.99 *(978-0-00-718529-0(4))* HarperCollins Pubs. Ltd. GBR. Dist: Independent Pubs. Group.
—The Guinea Pigs. Shipton, Paul. 2006. (Collins Big Cat Ser.). (ENG.). 48p. (J). pap. 5.99 *(978-0-00-718648-8(7))* HarperCollins Pubs. Ltd. GBR. Dist: Independent Pubs. Group.
—In the Boat. Shipton, Paul. 2007. (Collins Big Cat Ser.). (ENG.). 16p. (J). pap. 5.99 *(978-0-00-718646-4(0))* HarperCollins Pubs. Ltd. GBR. Dist: Independent Pubs. Group.
Dunton, Trevor. Rocket Ship/the Planet. Cunningham, Anna & McClurkan, Rob. 2012. (Talk a Story Ser.). (ENG.). 16p. (J). (-k). pap. 7.99 ***(978-1-4451-0668-7(X))*** Hodder & Stoughton GBR. Dist: Independent Pubs. Group.
Duntze, Dorothee. Hansel & Gretel. Grimm, Jacob & Grimm, Wilhelm K. 2006. 24p. (J). (gr. k-4). reprint ed. 17.00 *(978-1-4223-5008-9(8))* DIANE Publishing Co.
—Rapunzel. Grimm, Jacob & Grimm, Wilhelm. Bell, Anthea, tr. from GER. 2007. (ENG.). 32p. (J). (gr. -1-3). pap. 7.95 *(978-0-7358-2113-2(5))* North-South Bks., Inc.
—The Twelve Dancing Princesses. Brothers Grimm. 2013. (ENG.). 32p. (J). (gr. -1-2). 17.95 *(978-0-7358-4121-5(7))* North-South Bks., Inc.
Dupasquier, Philippe. Billy y el Vestido Rosa. Fine, Anne. 2003.Tr. of Bill's New Frock. (SPA.). 100p. (J). (gr. 3-5). pap. 8.95 *(978-958-24-0175-7(3))* Santillana USA Publishing Co., Inc.
—Bombs & Blackberries: A World War Two Play. Donaldson, Julia. 48p. (YA). *(978-0-7502-4124-3(1)*, Wayland) Hachette Children's Group.
—The Sandal. Bradman, Tony. 32p. (J). (gr. 1-3). pap. 9.99 *(978-0-86264-843-5(2))* Andersen Pr. GBR. Dist: Trafalgar Square Publishing.
Dupasquier, Philippe. Blue. Dupasquier, Philippe. 2005. (ENG.). 32p. (J). (gr. 2-4). 16.99 *(978-1-84270-323-6(4))* Andersen Pr. GBR. Dist: Independent Pubs. Group.
Dupeyron, Sarah. The ABC's of Vermont Coloring Book. 2007. 32p. (J). 4.95 *(978-0-9793790-0-0(8))* Howard Printing, Inc.
Dupon-Martinez, Christopher. Ian's Bad Choices Turned His Life Around. Carson, Shonette. 2011. 24p. pap. 24.95 *(978-1-4560-0965-6(6))* America Star Bks.
DuPont, Brittany. Little Mouse Finds a New Home. Silvola, Liz. 2013. 24p. pap. 9.99 *(978-1-937165-42-0(6))* Orange Hat Publishing.
Dupont, Lindsay Harper. Lizzy's Ups & Downs: NOT an Ordinary School Day. Harper, Jessica. 2004. 32p. (J). (gr. -1-3). 15.99 *(978-0-06-052063-2(9))* HarperCollins Pubs.
Dupre, Kelly. The Best Part of a Sauna, 1 vol. Peterson, Sheryl. 2013. 32p. (J). (gr. 1-2). 17.95 *(978-0-9883508-0-9(7))*; (ENG.). pap. 9.95 *(978-0-9883508-1-6(5))* Raven Productions, Inc.
—How Coyote Stole the Summer: A Native American Folktale. Krensky, Stephen. 2008. (On My Own Folklore Ser.). (ENG.). 48p. (gr. 2-4). lib. bdg. 25.26 *(978-0-8225-7548-1(5)*, Millbrook Pr.) Lerner Publishing Group.
—How Coyote Stole the Summer: [A Native American Folktale]. Krensky, Stephen. 2009. (On My Own Folklore Ser.). (ENG.). 48p. (gr. 2-4). pap. 6.95 *(978-1-58013-848-2(9)*, First Avenue Editions) Lerner Publishing Group.
—The Lion's Share/Qayb Libaax: A Somali Folktale. Ahmed, Said Salah. 2006. 32p. (J). (gr. -1-3). pap. 7.95 *(978-1-931016-13-1(5))* Minnesota Humanities Ctr.
—The Littlest Christmas Kitten. Jackson, Leona Novy. 2005. 32p. (J). 16.00 *(978-0-930643-18-8(6)*, 1250560) Images Unlimited.
Dupree, Bruce. The Wild Texas Stampede!, 1 vol. McManis, Margaret. 2008. (ENG.). 32p. (J). (gr. 1-3). 16.99 *(978-1-58980-568-2(2))* Pelican Publishing Co., Inc.
Duquennoy, Jacques. Las Cataratas del Niagara. Duquennoy, Jacques. 2007. (Pandilla Fantasma Ser.). (SPA.). 27p. (J). (gr. -1). 8.95 *(978-84-263-5228-6(5))* Vives, Luis Editorial (Edelvives) ESP. Dist: Ediciones Urano S. A.
Duquet, Guy J. The Perfect Little Pumpkin. Waters, George T. l.t. ed. 2006. 30p. (J). per. 14.95 *(978-1-59879-286-7(5))* Lifevest Publishing, Inc.
Duran, Teresa. El Rey Ignacio. Tort, Pep & Josep, Tort. 2006. (Montana Encantada Ser.). (SPA.). 47p. (J). per. *(978-84-241-8558-9(7))* Everest Editora.
Duranceau, Suzanne. Follow the Moon. Weeks, Sarah. 2003. (ENG.). 32p. (J). (gr. -1-3). 17.99 *(978-0-06-055744-7(3))* HarperCollins Pubs.
—Without You. Weeks, Sarah. 40p. (J). (gr. -1-2). 2007. (ENG.). pap. 6.99 *(978-0-06-113998-7(X))*; 2003. 16.99 *(978-0-06-027816-8(1)*, Geringer, Laura Book) HarperCollins Pubs.
—Young Charles Darwin & the Voyage of the Beagle, 1 vol. Ashby, Ruth. 2009. (ENG.). 128p. (J). (gr. 2-5). 12.95 *(978-1-56145-478-5(8)*, Peachtree Junior) Peachtree Pubs.
Durand, Delphine. Al Pha's Bet. Rosenthal, Amy Krouse. 2011. (ENG.). 32p. (J). (gr. -1-k). 16.99 *(978-0-399-24601-2(0)*, Putnam Juvenile) Penguin Publishing Group.
—The Chicken of the Family. Amato, Mary. 2008. (ENG.). 32p. (J). (gr. -1-3). 16.99 *(978-0-399-24196-3(5)*, Putnam Juvenile) Penguin Publishing Group.
—The House That Jill Built: A Pop-up Book. Root, Phyllis. 2007. 18p. (J). reprint ed. 16.00 *(978-1-4223-6756-8(8))* DIANE Publishing Co.
—Welcome to Cuckooville. Chandler, Susan. 2012. (ENG.). 24p. (J). (gr. k-3). 16.95 *(978-1-61608-665-7(3)*, 608665, Sky Pony Pr.) Skyhorse Publishing Co., Inc.
Durand, Élodie. Felix from Berlin. Feuchter, Anke. 2014. (AV2 Fiction Readalong Ser.: Vol. 126). (ENG.). 32p. (J). (gr. -1-3). lib. bdg. 34.28 *(978-1-4896-2277-8(2)*, AV2 by Weigl) Weigl Pubs., Inc.

D

Durber, Matt. First ABC. 2007. (Usborne Look & Say Ser.). 22p. (J). (gr. -1-k). bds. 14.99 *(978-0-7945-1435-8(9)*, Usborne) EDC Publishing.

—First Colors. Allman, Howard & MMStudios, photos by. 2006. (Usborne Look & Say Ser.). 18p. (J). (gr. -1-k). bds. 14.99 *(978-0-7945-1348-1(4)*, Usborne) EDC Publishing.

Durber, Matt & Jones, Stephanie. First Picture Nature. MMStudios, photos by. 2007. (First Picture Board Bks). 16p. (J). (gr. -1-k). bds. 11.99 *(978-0-7945-1751-9(X)*, Usborne) EDC Publishing.

Durham, Lilly. Two Lives for Giant Jack Pumpkin: The Story of a Boy, a Jack o'Lantern & a Pie. Powell, Opal. 2nd ed. 2013. (ENG.). 24p. (J). pap. 10.95 *(978-1-59299-910-1(7))* Inkwater Pr.

Durick, Agnes York. Baby Bear, Mother Bear, Father Bear. Durick, Agnes York. 2008. (Shape Bks.). (ENG.). 48p. (J). (gr. -1-3). pap. 14.95 *(978-1-59583-289-4(0)*, 9781595832894) Laughing Elephant.

Durie, Sally. The Magic of the Dark Ravine. Wendling, Peter. 2011. 36p. pap. 13.95 *(978-1-60976-933-8(3)*, Eloquent Bks.) Strategic Book Publishing & Rights Agency (SBPRA).

Durk, Jim. Apple-Picking Day! Brooke, Samantha. 2007. (Clifford's Puppy Days Ser.). (J). *(978-0-545-02841-7(8))* Scholastic, Inc.

—Backpack Puppy. Fisch, Sarah & Bridwell, Norman. 2005. (J). pap. *(978-0-439-73379-3(0))* Scholastic, Inc.

—Brave Little Engines (Thomas & Friends) Awdry, W. 2014. (Deluxe Paint Box Book Ser.). (ENG.). 128p. (J). (gr. -1-2). pap. 7.99 *(978-0-385-38510-7(2)*, Golden Bks.) Random Hse. Children's Bks.

—Graduation Party. Kosara, Victoria. 2010. (J). pap. *(978-0-545-23400-9(X))* Scholastic, Inc.

—Hide-and-Seek Engines. Awdry, Wilbert V. 2012. (Color Plus Chunky Crayons Ser.). (ENG.). 48p. (J). (gr. -1-2). pap. 3.99 *(978-0-307-97672-7(6)*, Golden Bks.) Random Hse. Children's Bks.

—Mr. Potato Head: the Busy Day. Onish, Liane B. 2008. (Storytime Stickers Ser.). (ENG.). 16p. (J). (gr. -1-k). pap. 4.95 *(978-1-4027-5354-1(3))* Sterling Publishing Co., Inc.

Durk, Jim. Pirate Treasure. Awdry, W. 2015. (Glow-In-the-Dark Sticker Book Ser.). (ENG.). 48p. (J). (gr. -1-2). pap. 4.99 ***(978-0-553-52478-9(X)***, Golden Bks.) Random Hse. Children's Bks.

Durk, Jim. Puppy Love. Marsoli, Lisa Ann. 2003. pap. *(978-0-439-61116-9(4))* Scholastic, Inc.

—The Quest for the Golden Crown. Awdry, Wilbert V. 2013. (Paint Box Book Ser.). (ENG.). 48p. (J). (gr. -1-2). pap. 3.99 *(978-0-449-81757-5(1)*, Golden Bks.) Random Hse. Children's Bks.

—Rail Blazers! (Thomas & Friends) Awdry, W. 2011. (Paint Box Book Ser.). (ENG.). 48p. (J). (gr. -1-2). pap. 3.99 *(978-0-375-87390-4(2)*, Golden Bks.) Random Hse. Children's Bks.

—Rescue Team! Golden Books Staff. 2010. (Big Coloring Book Ser.). (ENG.). 48p. (J). (gr. -1-2). pap. 6.99 *(978-0-375-86160-4(2)*, Golden Bks.) Random Hse. Children's Bks.

—The Secret of the Mine. Awdry, Wilbert V. 2013. (Glow-In-the-Dark Sticker Book Ser.). (ENG.). 48p. (J). (gr. -1-2). pap. 3.99 *(978-0-449-81711-7(3)*, Golden Bks.) Random Hse. Children's Bks.

—Skating with Friends. Fisch, Sarah. 2007. (Little Red Reader Ser.). (J). pap. *(978-0-439-90898-6(1))* Scholastic, Inc.

—The Smallest Snowman. Fisch, Sarah. 2006. (J). *(978-0-439-81616-8(5))* Scholastic, Inc.

—Thomas' Christmas Star. Awdry, Wilbert V. 2013. (Color Plus Card Stock Ser.). (ENG.). 48p. (J). (gr. -1-2). pap. 3.99 *(978-0-449-81880-0(2)*, Golden Bks.) Random Hse. Children's Bks.

—Thomas' Giant Puzzle Book (Thomas & Friends) Awdry, Wilbert V. 2012. (Giant Coloring Book Ser.). (ENG.). 40p. (J). (gr. -1-2). pap. 9.99 *(978-0-307-97690-1(4)*, Golden Bks.) Random Hse. Children's Bks.

—Thomas' Halloween Delivery (Thomas & Friends) Awdry, W. 2011. (Glow-In-the-Dark Sticker Book Ser.). (ENG.). 48p. (J). (gr. -1-2). pap. 3.99 *(978-0-375-87229-7(9)*, Golden Bks.) Random Hse. Children's Bks.

—Thomas Saves Christmas. Awdry, W. 2011. (Glitter Sticker Book Ser.). (ENG.). 64p. (J). (gr. -1-2). pap. 4.99 *(978-0-375-87394-2(5)*, Golden Bks.) Random Hse. Children's Bks.

—Thomas Takes a Vacation (Thomas & Friends) Golden Books. 2015. (Holographic Sticker Book Ser.). (ENG.). 64p. (J). (gr. -1-2). pap. 4.99 *(978-0-553-50846-8(6)*, Golden Bks.) Random Hse. Children's Bks.

—Thomas' Valentine Party. Awdry, Wilbert V. 2011. (Full-Color Activity Book with Stickers Ser.). (ENG.). 32p. (J). (gr. -1-2). pap. 3.99 *(978-0-375-86815-3(1)*, Golden Bks.) Random Hse., Inc.

Durk, Jim & Stubbs, Tommy. Easter Eggspress! Golden Books Staff. 2011. (Color Plus Gatefold Sticker Ser.). (ENG.). 16p. (J). (gr. -1-2). pap. 3.99 *(978-0-375-86613-5(2)*, Golden Bks.) Random Hse. Children's Bks.

Durk, Jim, jt. illus. see Golden Books Staff.

Durkee, Noura. The Fall of the Giant. Durkee, Noura. 2007. (ENG.). 26p. (J). (gr. k-5). 16.00 *(978-1-879402-63-8(7))* Tahrike Tarsile Quran, Inc.

—The King, the Prince & the Naughty Sheep. Durkee, Noura. 2007. (ENG.). 24p. (J). (gr. k-5). 16.00 *(978-1-879402-58-4(0))* Tahrike Tarsile Quran, Inc.

—Yunus & the Whale. Durkee, Noura. 2007. (ENG.). 28p. (J). (gr. k-5). 16.00 *(978-1-879402-60-7(2))* Tahrike Tarsile Quran, Inc.

Durland, Maud. How the Sea Came to Marissa. Renaud, Anne. 2006. 32p. (J). *(978-1-58270-129-5(6))* Beyond Words Publishing, Inc.

Durr, Carol Atkinson. Tico's Book. Conure, Lunatico. 2008. 36p. (J). 15.00 *(978-0-9717047-8-7(3))* Bay Media, Inc.

Durrell, Julie. I Am Creative! Parker, David. 2005. (J). *(978-0-439-73586-5(6))* Scholastic, Inc.

—Jesus Rose on Easter Morn: A Listen! Look! Book. Stockstill, Gloria McQueen. 2004. 20p. (J). bds. 5.49 *(978-0-7586-0143-8(3))* Concordia Publishing Hse.

—The Night Before Kindergarten. Wing, Natasha. 2014. (Night Before Ser.). (ENG.). 32p. (J). (gr. -1-k). 12.99 *(978-0-448-48255-2(X)*, Grosset & Dunlap) Penguin Publishing Group.

—To the Town of Bethlehem. Stockstill, Gloria McQueen. 2004. 20p. (J). bds. 5.49 *(978-0-7586-0051-6(8))* Concordia Publishing Hse.

Durual, Christophe, jt. illus. see Thibault, Dominique.

Dusikova, Maja. Advent Storybook: 24 Stories to Share Before Christmas. Schneider, Antonie. Miller, Marisa, tr. from GER. 2005. (ENG.). 64p. (J). (gr. -1-3). 17.95 *(978-0-7358-1963-4(7))* North-South Bks., Inc.

—Silent Night, Holy Night Book & Advent Calendar. Mohr, Joseph. 2010. (ENG.). 32p. 9.95 *(978-0-7358-2312-9(X))* North-South Bks., Inc.

—Sleeping Beauty. Grimm, J. & W. 2012. (ENG.). 32p. (J). (gr. -1-3). 17.95 *(978-0-7358-4087-4(3))* North-South Bks., Inc.

—What the Shepherd Saw. Lagerloeff, Selma. 2014. (ENG.). 32p. (J). 17.95 *(978-0-7358-4190-1(X))* North-South Bks., Inc.

Dusikova, Maja. Heidi. Dusikova, Maja. Spyri, Johanna. 2013. (ENG.). 32p. (J). (gr. -1-3). 9.95 *(978-0-7358-4083-6(0))* North-South Bks., Inc.

Dussling, Deborah. If the Shoe Fits: Nonstandard Units of Measurement. Dussling, Jennifer. 2015. (ENG.). 32p. (J). (gr. -1-1). lib. bdg. 22.60 ***(978-1-57565-800-1(3))*** Kane Pr., Inc.

Dustin, Michael. There's a Rainbow in Me. Cooke, Pam. 2004. 30p. (J). pap. 12.95 *(978-1-892343-39-0(8))* Oak Tree Publishing.

Dutchak, Shelly. Onami: The Great Wave. Stemer, Nathan. 2007. (J). per. *(978-0-9795529-0-8(7))* 716 Productions.

Dutcher, Kieren. Chinese & English Nursery Rhymes: Share & Sing in Two Languages. Wu, Faye-Lynn. 2010. (ENG & CHI.). 32p. (J). (gr. -1-2). 16.95 *(978-0-8048-4094-1(6))* Tuttle Publishing.

Dutertre, Charles. Meet the Woolly Mammoth. Philippo, Sophie. 2005. (ENG.). 45p. (J). (gr. 4-7). 15.95 *(978-1-58728-521-9(5))* Cooper Square Publishing Llc.

Dutkiewicz, Michal. The Last Realm Dragonscarpe. McNamara, Pat & Turner, Gary. 2007. (Last Realm Ser.: Bk. 1). 320p. (YA). *(978-982-9109-01-9(1))* Angel Phoenix Publishing.

Dutrait, Vincent. The Queen's Pirate - Francis Drake. Courtauld, Sarah. 2008. (Usborne Young Reading: Series Three Ser.). 64p. (J). 8.99 *(978-0-7945-2048-9(0)*, Usborne) EDC Publishing.

—The Story of Pirates. Jones, Rob Lloyd. 2007. (Young Reading Series 3 Gift Bks). 63p. (J). (gr. 4-7). 8.99 *(978-0-7945-1618-5(1)*, Usborne) EDC Publishing.

Dutton, John. Tiger's Island. Dutton, John. unabr. ed. Date not set. (Dreamguard Ser.: Vol. 2). viii, 245p. (J). pap. 12.95 *(978-0-9577556-1-1(9))* Samara Pr.

Dutton, Mike. Donovan's Big Day. Newman, Lesléa. 2011. (ENG.). 32p. (J). (gr. -1-2). 15.99 *(978-1-58246-332-2(8)*, Tricycle Pr.) Ten Speed Pr.

Duufek, Kim Kanoa. Victor, the Reluctant Vulture. Hanson, Jonathan. 2012. 36p. (J). pap. 16.95 *(978-1-886679-45-0(2))* Arizona Sonora Desert Museum Pr.

Duverne, Evelyne. Rules of the Net, 1 vol. McKerley, Jennifer Guess. 2009. (Read-It! Readers: Character Education Ser.). (ENG.). 32p. (gr. k-2). 19.99 *(978-1-4048-5240-2(9)*, Easy Readers) Picture Window Bks.

—Saving Shadow, 1 vol. Dokas, Dara. 2009. (Read-It! Readers: Character Education Ser.). (ENG.). 32p. (gr. k-2). 19.99 *(978-1-4048-5237-2(9)*, Easy Readers) Picture Window Bks.

Duvoisin, Roger. A Doll for Marie. Fatio, Louise. 2015. (ENG.). 32p. (J). (gr. -1-2). 16.99 *(978-0-385-75596-2(1))* Knopf, Alfred A. Inc.

—The Happy Lion. Fatio, Louise. (ENG.). (J). (gr. -1-2). 2015. 32p. 6.99 *(978-0-553-50850-5(4)*, Dragonfly Bks.); 2010. 40p. pap. 7.99 *(978-0-553-11364-8(X)*, Dragonfly Bks.); 2004. 40p. 16.99 *(978-0-375-82759-4(5)*, Knopf Bks. for Young Readers) Random Hse. Children's Bks.

Duvoisin, Roger. Petunia, Beware! Duvoisin, Roger. 2011. (ENG.). 40p. (J). (gr. -1-2). reprint ed. pap. 7.99 *(978-0-679-80334-8(3)*, Dragonfly Bks.) Random Hse. Children's Bks.

Düzakin, Akin. I'm Right Here. Ørbeck-Nilssen, Constance. 2015. 28p. (J). ***(978-0-8028-5455-1(9)***, Eerdmans Bks For Young Readers) Eerdmans, William B. Publishing Co.

Dvorák, Jaroslav. Bobek, the Cat with a Pompon Tail. Dvok, Eduard & Dvorák, Eduard. 2010. 52p. pap. 17.00 *(978-1-60911-734-4(4)*, Eloquent Bks.) Strategic Book Publishing & Rights Agency (SBPRA).

Dwight, Laura, photos by. How Many? (English/Haitian Creole), 1 vol. Christian, Cheryl. 2005. (ENG., 12p. (J). 5.95 *(978-1-59572-024-5(3))* Star Bright Bks., Inc.

—How Many? (English/Russian), 1 vol. Christian, Cheryl. 2005. (Photo Flap Bks.). (RUS & ENG., 12p. (J). 5.95 *(978-1-932065-88-6(1))* Star Bright Bks., Inc.

—How Many? (Korean), 1 vol. Christian, Cheryl. Choi, Jin, tr. 2004. (KOR & ENG., 12p. (J). 5.95 *(978-1-932065-82-4(2))* Star Bright Bks., Inc.

—How Many? (Portuguese/English), 1 vol. Christian, Cheryl. 2009. (ENG & POR., 12p. (J). 5.95 *(978-1-59572-190-7(8))* Star Bright Bks., Inc.

—How Many? (Simplified Mandarin), 1 vol. Christian, Cheryl. 2004. (CHI & ENG., 12p. (J). 5.95 *(978-1-932065-70-1(9))* Star Bright Bks., Inc.

—How Many? (Traditional Cantonese) Christian, Cheryl. 2004. (CHI., 12p. (J). bds. 5.95 *(978-1-932065-64-0(4))* Star Bright Bks., Inc.

—How Many? (Vietnamese) Christian, Cheryl. 2004. (VIE., 12p. (J). bds. 5.95 *(978-1-932065-76-3(8))* Star Bright Bks., Inc.

—Toby & Tutter Therapy Dogs. DeBear, Kirsten. 2012. (ENG., 32p. (J). 17.95 *(978-0-9847812-0-1(X))* Toby & Tutter Publishing.

—What Happens Next? (Haitian Creole/English), 1 vol. Christian, Cheryl. 2005. (ENG & HAT., 12p. (J). (gr. -1). 5.95 *(978-1-59572-025-2(1))* Star Bright Bks., Inc.

—What Happens Next? (Korean), 1 vol. Christian, Cheryl. Choi, Jin, tr. 2004. (KOR & ENG., 12p. (J). 5.95 *(978-1-932065-81-7(4))* Star Bright Bks., Inc.

—What Happens Next? (Russian/English), 1 vol. Christian, Cheryl. 2005. (Photo Flap Bks.). (RUS & ENG., 12p. (J). 5.95 *(978-1-932065-87-9(3))* Star Bright Bks., Inc.

—What Happens Next? (Simplified Mandarin), 1 vol. Christian, Cheryl. 2004. (CHI & ENG., 12p. (J). 5.95 *(978-1-932065-69-5(5))* Star Bright Bks., Inc.

—What Happens Next? (Traditional Cantonese) Christian, Cheryl. 2004. (CHI., 12p. (J). bds. 5.95 *(978-1-932065-63-3(6))* Star Bright Bks., Inc.

—What Happens Next? (Vietnamese), 1 vol. Christian, Cheryl. 2004. (VIE & ENG., 12p. (J). 5.95 *(978-1-932065-75-6(X))* Star Bright Bks., Inc.

—What Happens Next (Spanish/English) Bilingual Edition, 1 vol. Christian, Cheryl. 2004. (Photoflaps Ser.). (ENG & SPA., 32p. (J). bds. 5.50 *(978-1-932065-57-2(1)*, 718-784-9112) Star Bright Bks., Inc.

—Where Does It Go? (Haitian Creole/English), 1 vol. Christian, Cheryl. 2005. (CRP & ENG., 12p. (J). 5.95 *(978-1-59572-026-9(X))* Star Bright Bks., Inc.

—Where Does It Go? (Korean), 1 vol. Christian, Cheryl. Choi, Jin, tr. from ENG. 2004. (Photo Flap Bks.). (KOR & ENG., 12p. (J). 5.95 *(978-1-932065-83-1(0))* Star Bright Bks., Inc.

—Where Does It Go? (Russian/English), 1 vol. Christian, Cheryl. 2005. (Photo Flap Bks.). (RUS & ENG., 12p. (J). 5.95 *(978-1-932065-89-3(X))* Star Bright Bks., Inc.

—Where Does It Go? (Simplified Mandarin), 1 vol. Christian, Cheryl. 2004. (CHI & ENG., 12p. (J). 5.95 *(978-1-932065-71-8(7))* Star Bright Bks., Inc.

—Where Does It Go? (Traditional Cantonese) Christian, Cheryl. 2004. (CHI., 12p. (J). bds. 5.95 *(978-1-932065-65-7(2))* Star Bright Bks., Inc.

—Where Does It Go? (Vietnamese) Christian, Cheryl. 2004. (VIE., 12p. (J). bds. 5.95 *(978-1-932065-77-0(6))* Star Bright Bks., Inc.

—Where's the Baby? (Haitian Creole/English), 1 vol. Christian, Cheryl. 2005. (Photoflaps Ser.). (HAT & ENG., 12p. (J). (gr. -1). 5.95 *(978-1-59572-027-6(8))* Star Bright Bks., Inc.

—Where's the Baby? (Korean) Christian, Cheryl. Choi, Jin, tr. 2004. (KOR., 12p. (J). bds. 5.95 *(978-1-932065-80-0(6))* Star Bright Bks., Inc.

—Where's the Baby? (Russian/English), 1 vol. Christian, Cheryl. 2005. (Photoflaps Ser.). (RUS & ENG., 24p. (J). (gr. -1). bds. 5.95 *(978-1-932065-86-2(5))* Star Bright Bks., Inc.

—Where's the Baby? (Simplified Mandarin) Christian, Cheryl. 2004. (CHI., 12p. (J). bds. 5.95 *(978-1-932065-68-8(7))* Star Bright Bks., Inc.

—Where's the Baby? (Spanish/English) Bilingual Edition, 1 vol. Christian, Cheryl. Fiol, Maria A., tr. from ENG. 2004. (SPA & ENG., 12p. (J). 5.95 *(978-1-932065-56-5(3))* Star Bright Bks., Inc.

—Where's the Baby? (Traditional Cantonese) Christian, Cheryl. 2004. (CHI., 12p. (J). bds. 5.95 *(978-1-932065-62-6(8))* Star Bright Bks., Inc.

—Where's the Baby? (Vietnamese) Christian, Cheryl. 2004. (VIE., 12p. (J). bds. 5.50 *(978-1-932065-74-9(1))* Star Bright Bks., Inc.

—Where's the Kitten? (Haitian Creole/English), 1 vol. Christian, Cheryl. 2005. (Photoflaps Ser.). (HAT & ENG., 12p. (J). (gr. -1). 5.95 *(978-1-59572-028-3(6))* Star Bright Bks., Inc.

—Where's the Kitten? (Korean), 1 vol. Christian, Cheryl. Choi, Jin, tr. 2004. (KOR & ENG., 12p. (J). 5.95 *(978-1-932065-78-7(4))* Star Bright Bks., Inc.

—Where's the Kitten? (Russian/English), 1 vol. Christian, Cheryl. 2004. (RUS & ENG., 12p. (J). 5.95 *(978-1-932065-84-8(9))* Star Bright Bks., Inc.

—Where's the Kitten? (Simplified Mandarin) Christian, Cheryl. 2004. (CHI., 12p. (J). bds. 5.95 *(978-1-932065-66-4(0))* Star Bright Bks., Inc.

—Where's the Kitten? (Spanish/English) Bilingual Edition, 1 vol. Christian, Cheryl. Fiol, Maria A., tr. 2004. (SPA & ENG., 32p. (J). bds. 5.50 *(978-1-932065-54-1(7)*, 718-784-9112) Star Bright Bks., Inc.

—Where's the Kitten? (Traditional Cantonese), 1 vol. Christian, Cheryl. 2004. (CHI & ENG., 12p. (J). 5.95 *(978-1-932065-60-2(1))* Star Bright Bks., Inc.

—Where's the Kitten? (Vietnamese) Christian, Cheryl. 2004. (VIE., 12p. (J). bds. 5.95 *(978-1-932065-72-5(5))* Star Bright Bks., Inc.

—Where's the Puppy? (Haitian Creole/English), 1 vol. Christian, Cheryl. 2005. (Photoflaps Ser.). (HAT & ENG., 12p. (J). (gr. -1). 5.95 *(978-1-59572-029-0(4))* Star Bright Bks., Inc.

—Where's the Puppy? (Korean), 1 vol. Christian, Cheryl. Choi, Jin, tr. 2004. (KOR & ENG., 12p. (J). 5.95 *(978-1-932065-79-4(2))* Star Bright Bks., Inc.

—Where's the Puppy? (Russian/English), 1 vol. Christian, Cheryl. 2005. (Photo Flap Bks.). (RUS & ENG., 12p. (J). 5.95 *(978-1-932065-85-5(7))* Star Bright Bks., Inc.

—Where's the Puppy? (Simplified Mandarin), 1 vol. Christian, Cheryl. 2004. (CHI & ENG., 12p. (J). 5.95 *(978-1-932065-67-1(9))* Star Bright Bks., Inc.

—Where's the Puppy? (Traditional Cantonese) Christian, Cheryl. 2004. (CHI., 12p. (J). bds. 5.95 *(978-1-932065-61-9(X))* Star Bright Bks., Inc.

—Where's the Puppy? (Vietnamese) Christian, Cheryl. 2004. (VIE., 12p. (J). bds. 5.50 *(978-1-932065-73-2(3))* Star Bright Bks., Inc.

—Where's the Puppy (Spanish/English) Bilingual Edition, 1 vol. Christian, Cheryl. Fiol, Maria A., tr. 2004. (Photoflaps Ser.). (ENG & SPA., 32p. (J). bds. 5.95 *(978-1-932065-55-8(5)*, 718-784-9112) Star Bright Bks., Inc.

Dwight, Laura, photos by. We Can Do It!, 1 vol. Dwight, Laura. 2005. (ENG., 32p. (J). pap. 5.95 *(978-1-59572-033-7(2))* Star Bright Bks., Inc.

Dworkin, Doug. Chain Letter. Day, Lucille. 2005. 32p. (J). (gr. 3-7). 14.95 *(978-1-59714-011-9(2))* Heyday.

Dwyer, Corinne, et al. Okay, Riders, Set 'Em Up: A Nate Walker BMX Adventure. Wielkiewicz, Richard M. 2005. 140p. (J). pap. 12.95 *(978-0-9774129-0-7(3))* Main Event Pr.

Dwyer, Kerry. Rhett's Colorful Campus Tour- Boston University A-Z. 2004. (J). 9.99 *(978-1-933069-03-6(1))* Odd Duck Ink, Inc.

Dwyer, Kieron. Captain America: The Captain. Gruenwald, Mark. 2011. (ENG.). 520p. (J). (gr. 4-17). pap., pap. 39.99 *(978-0-7851-4965-1(1))* Marvel Worldwide, Inc.

Dwyer, Michael. Barnyard Bash. Dwyer, Mary. 2006. (J). spiral bd. incl. cd-rom *(978-1-933843-00-1(4))* That's Me Publishing, LLC.

Dwyer, Mindy. Alaska's Three Little Pigs. Laverde, Arlene. 2015. (ENG.). 11p. (J). (— 1). bds. 8.99 *(978-1-57061-974-8(3))* Sasquatch Bks.

—Kayak Girl. Devine, Monica. 2012. 32p. (J). pap. 12.95 *(978-1-60223-188-7(5))* Univ. of Alaska Pr.

—Knitting with Gigi. Thalcker, Karen. 2007. (ENG.). 32p. 24.95 *(978-1-56477-816-1(9))* Martingale & Co.

Dwyer, Mindy. Alaska's Sleeping Beauty. Dwyer, Mindy. 2014. (ENG.). 32p. (J). (gr. k-3). pap. 10.99 *(978-1-57061-872-7(0))* Sasquatch Bks.

Dyan, Penelope. Bunny Ears. Dyan, Penelope. 2011. 34p. pap. 11.95 *(978-1-935630-68-5(7))* Bellissima Publishing, LLC.

Dyan, Penelope. Arianna's Shoes. Dyan, Penelope. 2008. 44p. pap. 11.95 *(978-1-935118-33-6(1))* Bellissima Publishing, LLC.

—Ba-Ba-Ba-Bad — -The Story of One Mean Moose. Dyan, Penelope. 2012. 34p. pap. 11.95 *(978-1-61477-053-4(0))* Bellissima Publishing, LLC.

—Bake a Cake, Make Two — -and Let Them Eat Cake. Dyan, Penelope. 2008. 44p. pap. 11.95 *(978-1-935118-18-3(8))* Bellissima Publishing, LLC.

—Baylee's Giraffes! Sometimes Only a Giraffe Will Do. Dyan, Penelope. 2013. 34p. pap. 11.95 *(978-1-61477-085-5(9))* Bellissima Publishing, LLC.

—Ben's Adventures — -Proof Positive That Boys Will Be Boys. Dyan, Penelope. 2008. 44p. pap. 11.95 *(978-1-935118-40-4(4))* Bellissima Publishing, LLC.

—The Big Mikey & Me Workbook. Dyan, Penelope. 2011. 48p. pap. 11.95 *(978-1-935630-72-2(5))* Bellissima Publishing, LLC.

—Blake the Cat & His Very Loose Tooth! Dyan, Penelope. 2011. 34p. pap. 10.95 *(978-1-935630-77-7(6))* Bellissima Publishing, LLC.

—Bubble Trouble — -for Boys Only (r). Dyan, Penelope. 2011. 34p. pap. 11.95 *(978-1-935630-92-0(X))* Bellissima Publishing, LLC.

—Bunny Love! a Book about Home & Bunnies. Dyan, Penelope. 2013. 34p. pap. 11.95 *(978-1-61477-084-8(0))* Bellissima Publishing, LLC.

—The Carousel. Dyan, Penelope. 2010. 34p. pap. 11.95 *(978-1-935630-26-5(1))* Bellissima Publishing, LLC.

—Changes! Dyan, Penelope. 2013. 34p. (J). pap. 11.95 *(978-1-61477-097-8(2))* Bellissima Publishing, LLC.

—The Christmas Flamingo. Dyan, Penelope. 2013. 34p. pap. 11.95 *(978-1-61477-121-0(9))* Bellissima Publishing, LLC.

—Christmas Is — -A Time to Remember, to Smile & to Share. Dyan, Penelope. 2009. 44p. pap. 11.95 *(978-1-935118-46-6(3))* Bellissima Publishing, LLC.

—Classy Nancy — A One of a Kind Girl. Dyan, Penelope. 2009. 48p. pap. 11.95 *(978-1-935118-45-9(5))* Bellissima Publishing, LLC.

—Courtney's Beach. Dyan, Penelope. 2008. 44p. pap. 11.95 *(978-1-935118-35-0(8))* Bellissima Publishing, LLC.

—The Day an Elephant Flies! Dyan, Penelope. 2013. 34p. pap. 11.95 *(978-1-61477-113-5(8))* Bellissima Publishing, LLC.

—Dear God, Thank-You! Dyan, Penelope. 2013. 34p. pap. 11.95 *(978-1-61477-072-5(7))* Bellissima Publishing, LLC.

—Don't Wake up the Bear! Dyan, Penelope. 2013. 34p. pap. 11.95 *(978-1-61477-094-7(8))* Bellissima Publishing, LLC.

—Eve. Dyan, Penelope. 2011. 34p. pap. 11.95 *(978-1-935630-95-1(4))* Bellissima Publishing, LLC.

—The Fish That Got Away — -for Boys Only(r). Dyan, Penelope. 2010. 34p. pap. 11.95 *(978-1-935630-29-6(6))* Bellissima Publishing, LLC.

—Frugal Frannie — and the Big Room Cleaning Day. Dyan, Penelope. 2009. 44p. pap. 11.95 *(978-1-935118-47-3(1))* Bellissima Publishing, LLC.

—Gabriela's Dogs — -Because Happiness Really Is a Warm Puppy! Dyan, Penelope. 2008. 44p. pap. 11.95 *(978-1-935118-37-4(4))* Bellissima Publishing, LLC.

—Gettin' Dirty! for Boys Only R. Dyan, Penelope. 2013. 34p. pap. 11.95 *(978-1-61477-083-1(2))* Bellissima Publishing, LLC.

—A Girl Named Dot. Dyan, Penelope. 2013. 34p. pap. 11.95 *(978-1-61477-102-9(2))* Bellissima Publishing, LLC.

—Go Far Star Car — Even Though Cars Are Not People. Dyan, Penelope. 2008. 44p. pap. 11.95 *(978-1-935118-12-1(9))* Bellissima Publishing, LLC.

—Go Run, Have Fun — -Because Everyone Likes Fun. Dyan, Penelope. 2008. 44p. pap. 11.95 *(978-1-935118-15-2(3))* Bellissima Publishing, LLC.

—Go to Rat House, Go to Cat House — Even Though Houses Are Not People. Dyan, Penelope. 2008. 44p. pap. 11.95 *(978-1-935118-14-5(5))* Bellissima Publishing, LLC.

—Good Luck Chuck! Dyan, Penelope. 2013. 34p. pap. 11.95 *(978-1-61477-098-5(0))* Bellissima Publishing, LLC.

—Good Night! Dyan, Penelope. 2013. 34p. pap. 11.95 *(978-1-61477-089-3(1))* Bellissima Publishing, LLC.

—Grandma's Suitcase — -Where a Kid Can Always Find a Surprise! Dyan, Penelope. 2008. 44p. pap. 11.95 *(978-1-935118-36-7(6))* Bellissima Publishing, LLC.

—Great Grandma Is Getting Old. Dyan, Penelope. 2010. 42p. pap. 11.95 *(978-1-935118-97-8(8))* Bellissima Publishing, LLC.

—Hair We Are! Dyan, Penelope. 2009. 44p. pap. 11.95 *(978-1-935118-61-9(7))* Bellissima Publishing, LLC.

—Happy Birthday! a Book about Birthdays, Dreams & Wishes. Dyan, Penelope. 2009. 42p. pap. 11.95 *(978-1-935118-73-2(0))* Bellissima Publishing, LLC.

—Happy Birthday Usa! Dyan, Penelope. 2010. 32p. pap. 11.95 *(978-1-935630-15-9(6))* Bellissima Publishing, LLC.
—The Hatchling, the Story of Stegi Stegosaurus. Dyan, Penelope. 2010. 42p. pap. 11.95 *(978-1-935630-08-1(3))* Bellissima Publishing, LLC.
—Hello Doctor! Dyan, Penelope. 2013. 34p. pap. 11.95 *(978-1-61477-096-1(4))* Bellissima Publishing, LLC.
—Hooray 4 Five! Dyan, Penelope. 2013. 34p. pap. 11.95 *(978-1-61477-103-6(0))* Bellissima Publishing, LLC.
—I Am a Monster! Dyan, Penelope. 2010. 34p. pap. 11.95 *(978-1-935630-24-1(5))* Bellissima Publishing, LLC.
—I Am Eight! Dyan, Penelope. 2010. 34p. pap. 11.95 *(978-1-935630-17-3(2))* Bellissima Publishing, LLC.
—I Am There! Dyan, Penelope. 2011. 34p. pap. 11.95 *(978-1-935630-98-2(9))* Bellissima Publishing, LLC.
—I Am Three! Dyan, Penelope. 2011. 34p. pap. 11.95 *(978-1-935630-97-5(0))* Bellissima Publishing, LLC.
—I Can't Stand the Rain! Dyan, Penelope. 2012. 34p. pap. 11.95 *(978-1-61477-040-4(9))* Bellissima Publishing, LLC.
—I Did It, & I Hid It! a Book about Taking Responsibility. Dyan, Penelope. 2009. 44p. pap. 11.95 *(978-1-935118-68-8(4))* Bellissima Publishing, LLC.
—I Like Football — for Boys Only(r). Dyan, Penelope. 2010. 34p. pap. 11.95 *(978-1-935630-27-2(X))* Bellissima Publishing, LLC.
—I Love You! Dyan, Penelope. 2012. 34p. pap. 11.95 *(978-1-61477-050-3(6))* Bellissima Publishing, LLC.
—If You Snooze! Dyan, Penelope. 2012. 34p. pap. 11.95 *(978-1-61477-059-6(X))* Bellissima Publishing, LLC.
—In Gracie's Yard! Dyan, Penelope. 2012. 34p. pap. 11.95 *(978-1-61477-067-1(0))* Bellissima Publishing, LLC.
—In My Attic. Dyan, Penelope. 2010. 34p. pap. 11.95 *(978-1-935630-23-4(7))* Bellissima Publishing, LLC.
—Introducing Fabulous Marie, a Girl with a Good Head on Her Shoulders. Dyan, Penelope. 2009. 44p. pap. 11.95 *(978-1-935118-55-8(2))* Bellissima Publishing, LLC.
—Jordan's Hair — -the Big Dilemm. Dyan, Penelope. 2008. 44p. pap. 11.95 *(978-1-935118-34-3(X))* Bellissima Publishing, LLC.
—Jump Frog, Funny Frog — -Because Frogs Are Funny. Dyan, Penelope. 2008. 44p. pap. 11.95 *(978-1-935118-19-0(6))* Bellissima Publishing, LLC.
—Just Look Out the Window! Dyan, Penelope. 2010. 34p. pap. 11.95 *(978-1-935630-25-8(3))* Bellissima Publishing, LLC.
—Ladies First, Please! a Kid's Most Important & Fun Guide to Good Manners. Dyan, Penelope. 2009. 106p. pap. 8.95 *(978-1-935118-67-1(6))* Bellissima Publishing, LLC.
—Life in the Pits. Dyan, Penelope. 2010. 34p. pap. 11.95 *(978-1-935630-18-0(0))* Bellissima Publishing, LLC.
—Life Is a Dream! Dyan, Penelope. 2013. 34p. pap. 11.95 *(978-1-61477-091-6(3))* Bellissima Publishing, LLC.
—Little Miss Chris & the Incredible Red Shoes. Dyan, Penelope. 2009. 44p. pap. 11.95 *(978-1-935118-49-7(8))* Bellissima Publishing, LLC.
—A Lot of Snot, a for Boys Only Book. Dyan, Penelope. 2008. 44p. pap. 11.95 *(978-1-935118-23-7(4))* Bellissima Publishing, LLC.
—Lovely Libby. Dyan, Penelope. 2010. 34p. pap. 11.95 *(978-1-935630-28-9(8))* Bellissima Publishing, LLC.
—Mermaids & Wishes for Tails Like Fishes. Dyan, Penelope. 2009. 44p. pap. 11.95 *(978-1-935118-50-3(1))* Bellissima Publishing, LLC.
—Mikey & Me & the Bees, the Continuing Story of a Girl & Her Dog. Dyan, Penelope. 2010. 48p. pap. 14.95 *(978-1-935118-90-9(0))* Bellissima Publishing, LLC.
—Mikey & Me & the Fly — -the Continuing Story of a Girl & Her Dog. Dyan, Penelope. 2010. 50p. pap. 14.95 *(978-1-935118-94-7(3))* Bellissima Publishing, LLC.
—Mikey & Me & the Frogs — -the Continuing Story of a Girl & Her Dog. Dyan, Penelope. 2010. 50p. pap. 14.95 *(978-1-935118-93-0(5))* Bellissima Publishing, LLC.
—Mikey & Me & the Spider — -the Continuing Story of a Girl & Her Dog. Dyan, Penelope. 2010. 50p. pap. 14.95 *(978-1-935118-95-4(1))* Bellissima Publishing, LLC.
—Mikey & Me & the Valentines — -the Continuing Story of a Girl & Her Dog. Dyan, Penelope. 2010. 50p. pap. 14.95 *(978-1-935118-96-1(X))* Bellissima Publishing, LLC.
—Molly Moose Is on the Loose. Dyan, Penelope. 2012. 34p. pap. 11.95 *(978-1-61477-025-1(5))* Bellissima Publishing, LLC.
—The Musical Family — Sometimes a Song Says It All. Dyan, Penelope. 2009. 42p. pap. 11.95 *(978-1-935118-81-7(1))* Bellissima Publishing, LLC.
—My Mother Always Says. Dyan, Penelope. 2010. 42p. pap. 11.95 *(978-1-935118-98-5(6))* Bellissima Publishing, LLC.
—A New Bag! Dyan, Penelope. 2012. 34p. pap. 11.95 *(978-1-61477-054-1(9))* Bellissima Publishing, LLC.
—New Shoes for Hand Me down Rose. Dyan, Penelope. 2012. 34p. pap. 11.95 *(978-1-61477-041-1(7))* Bellissima Publishing, LLC.
—A Nose by Any Other Name Is Still a Nose! Dyan, Penelope. 2009. 44p. pap. 11.95 *(978-1-935118-62-6(5))* Bellissima Publishing, LLC.
—Off to School. Dyan, Penelope. 2010. 34p. pap. 11.95 *(978-1-935630-21-0(0))* Bellissima Publishing, LLC.
—Olympic Gold — Because Everyone Loves a Winner! Dyan, Penelope. 2008. 44p. pap. 11.95 *(978-1-935118-20-6(X))* Bellissima Publishing, LLC.
—Out of Deepest Africa — -Another of Ben's Big Adventures — -for Boys Only (r). Dyan, Penelope. 2010. 34p. pap. 11.95 *(978-1-935630-13-5(X))* Bellissima Publishing, LLC.
—Pink Patti Pinkerton. Dyan, Penelope. 2009. 44p. pap. 11.95 *(978-1-935118-63-3(3))* Bellissima Publishing, LLC.
—Respect! Dyan, Penelope. 2012. 34p. pap. 11.95 *(978-1-61477-058-9(1))* Bellissima Publishing, LLC.
—Smile! Dyan, Penelope. 2012. 34p. pap. 11.95 *(978-1-61477-028-2(X))* Bellissima Publishing, LLC.
—Sticks — -Because Sticks Are Also People. Dyan, Penelope. 2008. 52p. pap. 11.95 *(978-1-935118-07-7(2))* Bellissima Publishing, LLC.
—Sticks — the for Boys Only Version — Because Sticks Are Also People. Dyan, Penelope. 2008. 52p. pap. 11.95 *(978-1-935118-13-8(7))* Bellissima Publishing, LLC.
—The Story of Snagatooth — -Who Is Commonly Known As the Tooth Fairy. Dyan, Penelope. 2008. 44p. pap. 11.95 *(978-1-935118-42-8(0))* Bellissima Publishing, LLC.
—The Sunny Side! Dyan, Penelope. 2012. 34p. pap. 11.95 *(978-1-61477-057-2(3))* Bellissima Publishing, LLC.
—Tammy's Left Shoe — -As Opposed to Her Right. Dyan, Penelope. 2008. 44p. pap. 11.95 *(978-1-935118-41-1(2))* Bellissima Publishing, LLC.
—Ted E Bearæs Most Unfortunate Experience to Date. Dyan, Penelope. 2009. 44p. pap. 11.95 *(978-1-935118-44-2(7))* Bellissima Publishing, LLC.
—Teeth! Dyan, Penelope. 2012. 34p. pap. 11.95 *(978-1-61477-060-2(3))* Bellissima Publishing, LLC.
—That Fat Elephant — -Because Everyone Likes Elephants. Dyan, Penelope. 2008. 44p. pap. 11.95 *(978-1-935118-16-9(1))* Bellissima Publishing, LLC.
—That Fat Rat Family — Because All Families Aren't Rats. Dyan, Penelope. 2008. 44p. pap. 11.95 *(978-1-935118-17-6(X))* Bellissima Publishing, LLC.
—There Are Bees in My Trees! Dyan, Penelope. 2009. 44p. pap. 11.95 *(978-1-935118-59-6(5))* Bellissima Publishing, LLC.
—There Are No Ants in My Pants! for Boys Only(r). Dyan, Penelope. 2010. 32p. pap. 11.95 *(978-1-935630-16-6(4))* Bellissima Publishing, LLC.
—There's a Chicken in My Kitchen! Dyan, Penelope. 2009. 44p. pap. 11.95 *(978-1-935118-60-2(9))* Bellissima Publishing, LLC.
—There's a Flea in My Te. Dyan, Penelope. 2012. 34p. pap. 11.95 *(978-1-61477-047-3(6))* Bellissima Publishing, LLC.
—There's a Racoon in My House! Dyan, Penelope. 2009. 44p. pap. 11.95 *(978-1-935118-58-9(7))* Bellissima Publishing, LLC.
—There's a Skunk in My Trunk. Dyan, Penelope. 2012. 34p. pap. 11.95 *(978-1-61477-045-9(X))* Bellissima Publishing, LLC.
—There's a Teddy Bear in My Heart! Dyan, Penelope. 2012. 34p. pap. 11.95 *(978-1-61477-048-0(4))* Bellissima Publishing, LLC.
—There's an Alligator in My Closet! Dyan, Penelope. 2009. 44p. pap. 11.95 *(978-1-935118-64-0(1))* Bellissima Publishing, LLC.
—There's No Business Like Bartholomew Bunny's Business. Dyan, Penelope. 2009. 44p. pap. 11.95 *(978-1-935118-54-1(4))* Bellissima Publishing, LLC.
—This Means War! for Boys Only. Dyan, Penelope. 2009. 44p. pap. 11.95 *(978-1-935118-65-7(X))* Bellissima Publishing, LLC.
—Thou Shalt Not Covet! Dyan, Penelope. 2012. 34p. pap. 11.95 *(978-1-61477-042-8(5))* Bellissima Publishing, LLC.
—A Thousand Stars. Dyan, Penelope. 2012. 34p. pap. 11.95 *(978-1-61477-049-7(2))* Bellissima Publishing, LLC.
—Three Strikes — -Doesn't Really Mean You Are Out. Dyan, Penelope. 2008. 44p. pap. 11.95 *(978-1-935118-39-8(0))* Bellissima Publishing, LLC.
—To See or Not to See — -the Story of Kourtney's Glasses. Dyan, Penelope. 2008. 44p. pap. 11.95 *(978-1-935118-38-1(2))* Bellissima Publishing, LLC.
—Today I Am 4! Dyan, Penelope. 2012. 34p. pap. 11.95 *(978-1-61477-043-5(3))* Bellissima Publishing, LLC.
—Today I Am Two! I Am Two Years Old Today! Dyan, Penelope. 2010. 34p. pap. 11.95 *(978-1-935630-14-2(8))* Bellissima Publishing, LLC.
—Tony Pickleloni, a Boy Full of Baloney. Dyan, Penelope. 2009. 44p. pap. 11.95 *(978-1-935118-52-7(8))* Bellissima Publishing, LLC.
—Vita Mccafee Mckay, Cat Rescuer. Dyan, Penelope. 2009. 44p. pap. 11.95 *(978-1-935118-53-4(6))* Bellissima Publishing, LLC.
—What Is a Telephant? Dyan, Penelope. 2013. 34p. pap. 11.95 *(978-1-61477-112-8(X))* Bellissima Publishing, LLC.
—What Is Truth? Dyan, Penelope. 2011. 34p. pap. 11.95 *(978-1-935630-96-8(2))* Bellissima Publishing, LLC.
—When Touching Is Bad. Dyan, Penelope. 2013. 34p. pap. 11.95 *(978-1-61477-088-6(3))* Bellissima Publishing, LLC.
—Where Is Lucy? Dyan, Penelope. 2013. 34p. pap. 11.95 *(978-1-61477-120-3(0))* Bellissima Publishing, LLC.
—The White Elephant No One Wants. Dyan, Penelope. 2012. 34p. pap. 11.95 *(978-1-61477-024-4(7))* Bellissima Publishing, LLC.
—Who Cut the Cheese? a for Boys Only Book. Dyan, Penelope. 2008. 44p. pap. 11.95 *(978-1-935118-22-0(6))* Bellissima Publishing, LLC.
—Who Deserves a Giant Chocolate Chip Cookie? Dyan, Penelope. 2009. 44p. pap. 11.95 *(978-1-935118-56-5(0))* Bellissima Publishing, LLC.
—Who's the Fairest of Them All? Dyan, Penelope. 2010. 34p. pap. 11.95 *(978-1-935630-20-3(2))* Bellissima Publishing, LLC.
—Why Angels Sing! Dyan, Penelope. 2012. 34p. pap. 11.95 *(978-1-61477-065-7(4))* Bellissima Publishing, LLC.
—Woolly Bully! Dyan, Penelope. 2013. 34p. pap. 11.95 *(978-1-61477-069-5(7))* Bellissima Publishing, LLC.
—Work It Out! Dyan, Penelope. 2012. 34p. pap. 11.95 *(978-1-61477-056-5(5))* Bellissima Publishing, LLC.
—You Are Okay! Dyan, Penelope. 2013. 34p. pap. 11.95 *(978-1-61477-070-1(0))* Bellissima Publishing, LLC.
Dyan, Penelope, photos by. Wonderful, Wonderful Copenhagen! a Kid's Guide to Copenhagen, Denmark. Weigand, John D. 2011. 34p. pap. 11.95 *(978-1-935630-62-3(8))* Bellissima Publishing, LLC.
Dyan, Penwlope. Eileen Green the Recycling Queen. Dyan, Penelope. 2009. 44p. pap. 11.95 *(978-1-935118-51-0(X))* Bellissima Publishing, LLC.
D'Yans, Masha. A Poem As Big As New York City: Little Kids Write about the Big Apple. Teachers Writers Collaborative, ed. 2012. (ENG.). 38p. (J). (gr. k-4). 19.95 *(978-0-7893-2083-4(5))* Universe Publishing.
D'yans, Masha. Razzle-Dazzle Ruby. D'yans, Masha. 2011. (ENG.). 20p. (J). (— 1). bds. 17.99 *(978-0-545-22500-7(0))* Scholastic, Inc.
Dybing, Michelle. Carlos & the Puppies, 1 vol. Dale, Jay. 2012. (Wonder Words Ser.). (ENG.). 32p. (gr. k-2). pap. 5.99 *(978-1-4296-8902-1(1),* Engage Literacy) Capstone Pr., Inc.
—Gran & Me, 1 vol. Dale, Jay. 2012. (Wonder Words Ser.). (ENG.). 32p. (gr. k-2). pap. 5.99 *(978-1-4296-8898-7(X),* Engage Literacy) Capstone Pr., Inc.
—I Am in the Park. Dale, Jay. 2012. (Wonder Words Ser.). (ENG.). 32p. (gr. k-2). pap. 5.99 *(978-1-4296-8890-1(4),* Engage Literacy) Capstone Pr., Inc.
—I Go up & Down. Dale, Jay. 2012. (Wonder Words Ser.). (ENG.). 32p. (gr. k-2). pap. 5.99 *(978-1-4296-8894-9(7),* Engage Literacy) Capstone Pr., Inc.
—To the Moon, 1 vol. Dale, Jay. 2012. (Wonder Words Ser.). (ENG.). 32p. (gr. k-2). pap. 5.99 *(978-1-4296-8904-5(8),* Engage Literacy) Capstone Pr., Inc.
Dye, Jerel. Any Two Can Be Twindollicious. Danna, Natasha. 2013. 32p. (J). 17.95 *(978-1-60131-154-2(0),* Castlebridge Bks.) Big Tent Bks.
Dyen, Don. Benjamin & the Word: Benjamín y la Palabra. Olivas, Daniel. Baeza Ventura, Gabriela, tr. 2011. 32p. (J). pap. 7.95 *(978-1-55885-687-5(0),* Piñata Books) Arte Publico Pr.
Dyer, Brooke. Mama Always Comes Home. Wilson, Karma. 32p. (J). (gr. -1-1). 2007. (ENG.). pap. 6.99 *(978-0-06-057507-6(7),* Harper Trophy); 2005. 15.99 *(978-0-06-057505-2(0))* HarperCollins Pubs.
—Sleep, Black Bear, Sleep. Yolen, Jane & Stemple, Heidi E. Y. 2007. (ENG.). 32p. (J). (gr. -1-1). 15.99 *(978-0-06-081560-8(4))* HarperCollins Pubs.
—Sleep, Black Bear, Sleep. Yolen, Jane & Stemple, Heidi Elisabet Y. 2007. 32p. (J). (gr. -1-1). lib. bdg. 16.89 *(978-0-06-081561-5(2))* HarperCollins Pubs.
Dyer, Brooke, jt. illus. see Dyer, Jane.
Dyer, Jane. Blue Moon Soup: A Family Cookbook. Goss, Gary. 2013. (ENG.). 72p. (J). (gr. 1-4). 16.95 *(978-1-62087-990-0(5),* 620990, Sky Pony Pr.) Skyhorse Publishing Co., Inc.
—Christmas Cookies: Bite-Size Holiday Lessons. Rosenthal, Amy Krouse. 2008. 40p. (J). (gr. k-5). lib. bdg. 13.89 *(978-0-06-058025-4(9));* (ENG.). 12.99 *(978-0-06-058024-7(0))* HarperCollins Pubs.
—Cookies: Bite-Size Life Lessons. Rosenthal, Amy Krouse. 2006. (ENG.). 40p. (J). (gr. -1-1). 12.99 *(978-0-06-058081-0(X))* HarperCollins Pubs.
—Cracked Corn & Snow Ice Cream: A Family Almanac. Willard, Nancy. 2005. 56p. (YA). (gr. 4-8). 18.00 *(978-0-7567-8835-3(8))* DIANE Publishing Co.
—Goodnight Goodnight Sleepyhead. Krauss, Ruth. 32p. (J). (gr. -1-3). 2007. (ENG.). bds. 7.99 *(978-0-694-01501-6(6),* HarperFestival); 2004. lib. bdg. 16.89 *(978-0-06-028895-2(7))* HarperCollins Pubs.
—Lucky & Squash. Birdsall, Jeanne. 2012. (ENG.). 32p. (J). (gr. -1-2). 16.99 *(978-0-06-083150-9(2))* HarperCollins Pubs.
—Move over, Rover! Beaumont, Karen. 2006. (ENG.). 40p. (J). (gr. -1-3). 16.99 *(978-0-15-201979-2(0))* Houghton Mifflin Harcourt Publishing Co.
—La Obra de Sofia. Spinelli, Eileen. 2004. (SPA.). 32p. (J). 16.99 *(978-84-8488-052-3(4))* Serres, Ediciones, S. L. ESP. Dist: Lectorum Pubns., Inc.
—Oh My Baby, Little One. Appelt, Kathi. (ENG.). 32p. (J). (gr. -1 — 1). 2006. pap. 3.99 *(978-0-15-206031-2(6));* 2005. reprint ed. pap. 6.99 *(978-0-15-205242-3(9))* Houghton Mifflin Harcourt Publishing Co.
—Sophie's Masterpiece: A Spider's Tale. Spinelli, Eileen. 2004. (ENG.). 32p. (J). (gr. -1-2). reprint ed. 7.99 *(978-0-689-86680-7(1),* Simon & Schuster Bks. For Young Readers) Simon & Schuster Bks. For Young Readers.
—Time for Bed. Fox, Mem. 2010. (ENG.). 28p. (J). (gr. k — 1). bds. 8.99 *(978-0-547-40856-9(0))* Houghton Mifflin Harcourt Publishing Co.
—Time for Bed: Lap-Sized Board Book. Fox, Mem. 2005. (ENG.). 28p. (J). (gr. k — 1). bds. 11.99 *(978-0-15-205349-9(2))* Houghton Mifflin Harcourt Publishing Co.
—Time for Bed (Es Hora de Dormir) Fox, Mem. 2012. (ENG & SPA.). 28p. (J). (gr. k — 1). bds. 6.99 *(978-0-547-71907-8(8))* Houghton Mifflin Harcourt Publishing Co.
—Wee Rhymes: Baby's First Poetry Book. Yolen, Jane. 2013. (ENG.). 112p. (J). (gr. -1-3). 19.99 *(978-1-4169-4898-8(8),* Simon & Schuster/Paula Wiseman Bks.) Simon & Schuster/Paula Wiseman Bks.
—A Woman for President: The Story of Victoria Woodhull. Krull, Kathleen. 2006. (J). (gr. 2-7). 14.60 *(978-0-7569-8179-2(4))* Perfection Learning Corp.
—A Woman for President: The Story of Victoria Woodhull. Krull, Kathleen. (ENG.). 32p. (J). (gr. 2-7). 2004. 16.95 *(978-0-8027-8908-2(0));* 2006. reprint ed. per. 8.99 *(978-0-8027-9615-8(X))* Walker & Co.
Dyer, Jane & Dyer, Brooke. One Smart Cookie: Bite-Size Lessons for the School Years & Beyond. Rosenthal, Amy Krouse. 2010. (ENG.). 40p. (J). (gr. k-5). 12.99 *(978-0-06-142970-5(8))* HarperCollins Pubs.
—Santa Claus & the Three Bears. Modugno, Maria. 2013. (ENG.). 40p. (J). (gr. -1-3). 17.99 *(978-0-06-170023-1(1))* HarperCollins Pubs.
—Sugar Cookies: Sweet Little Lessons on Love. Rosenthal, Amy Krouse. 2009. (ENG.). 40p. (J). (gr. k-5). 12.99 *(978-0-06-174072-5(1))* HarperCollins Pubs.
Dyer, Sarah. Bear's Best Friend. Coats, Lucy. 2014. (ENG.). 32p. (J). (gr. -1-k). 21.00 *(978-1-4088-2725-3(5),* 137577, Bloomsbury USA Childrens) Bloomsbury USA.
—Mrs. Muffly's Monster. 2008. (ENG.). 36p. (J). (gr. -1-3). 16.95 *(978-1-84507-761-7(X),* Frances Lincoln) Quarto Publishing Group UK GBR. Dist: Hachette Bk. Group.
Dyer, Sarah. Princess for a Day: A Clementine & Mungo Story. Dyer, Sarah. (ENG.). 32p. (J). (gr. -1-k). 2009. pap. 12.95 *(978-0-7475-8891-7(0));* 2007. 22.95 *(978-0-7475-8753-8(1))* Bloomsbury Publishing Plc GBR. Dist: Independent Pubs. Group.
Dykes, John S. Funny Boy Meets the Airsick Alien from Andromeda. Gutman, Dan. 2012. (Funny Boy Ser.). (ENG.). 136p. (J). pap. 5.99 *(978-1-4532-9527-4(5))* Open Road Integrated Media, LLC.
Dynamo Limited Staff. Fix That Truck! Scholastic, Inc. Staff & Steele, Michael Anthony. 2012. (Lego City Ser.). (ENG.). 24p. (J). (gr. -1-3). pap. 3.99 *(978-0-545-47061-2(7))* Scholastic, Inc.
—Rainbow Magic Special Edition: Lindsay the Luck Fairy. Meadows, Daisy. 2013. (Rainbow Magic Special Edition Ser.). (ENG.). 192p. (J). (gr. 2-5). pap. 6.99 *(978-0-545-48492-3(8),* Scholastic Paperbacks) Scholastic, Inc.
Dynamo Limited Staff, jt. illus. see Makuc, Lucy.
Dyro, Janniche. Forever Dancing. 32p. (J). (gr. 4-18). 16.00 *(978-0-9675413-8-9(7))* Libros, Encouraging Cultural Literacy.
Dyrud, Chris Wold. The Song of Christmas. Clark, Lisa. 2014. (Arch Bks.). (ENG.). 16p. (J). (gr. k-4). pap. 2.49 *(978-0-7586-4605-7(4))* Concordia Publishing Hse.
Dyrud, Chris Wold & Quackenbush, Marcia. Periodo: Guina de una Joven. Loulan, Joann & Worthen, Bonnie. 2nd ed. 2003. (Lansky, Vicki Ser.). (SPA.). 92p. pap. 9.99 *(978-0-916773-99-1(X))* Book Peddlers.
Dysinger, Stephen. William. Dysinger, Stephen. 2007. 28p. (J). (gr. -1-3). per. 12.99 *(978-1-59879-297-3(0))* Lifevest Publishing, Inc.
Dyson, Nikki. How to Be a Pirate. Fliess, Sue. 2014. (Little Golden Book Ser.). (ENG.). 24p. (J). (-k). 3.99 *(978-0-449-81309-6(6),* Golden Bks.) Random Hse. Children's Bks.
—How to Be a Superhero. Fliess, Sue. 2014. (Little Golden Book Ser.). (ENG.). 24p. (J). (-k). 3.99 *(978-0-385-38737-8(7),* Golden Bks.) Random Hse. Children's Bks.
Dyson, Nikki. 1,000 Things to Eat. 2015. (1,000 Pictures Ser.). (ENG.). 34p. (J). (gr. k-5). 14.99 *(978-0-7945-3406-6(6),* Usborne) EDC Publishing.
Dzama, Marcel, jt. illus. see Ozama, Marcel.
Dzidrums, Joseph, photos by. Cutters Don't Cry. Dzidrums, Christine. Allison, Elizabeth, ed. 2010. 132p. (YA). 24.99 *(978-0-9826435-2-5(7));* pap. 14.99 *(978-0-9826435-1-8(9))* Creative Media Publishing.
—Jennie Finch. Dzidrums, Christine & Rendon, Leah. 2013. 72p. pap. 9.99 *(978-1-938438-13-4(2))* Creative Media Publishing.
—Mike Trout: Baseball Sensation. Dzidrums, Christine. 2013. 64p. pap. 9.99 *(978-1-938438-28-8(0))* Creative Media Publishing.
Dzidrums, Joseph, et al, photos by. Yuna Kim: Ice Queen. Dzidrums, Christine. Rendon, Leah, ed. 2011. (Skate Stars Ser.: Vol. 2). 72p. (YA). pap. 10.99 *(978-0-9826435-9-4(4))* Creative Media Publishing.
Dzidrums, Joseph, jt. illus. see Lopez, Lyle.
Dziekan, Michal. Magic Delivery. Smith, Clete Barrett. 2014. (ENG.). 288p. (J). (gr. 3-7). 16.99 *(978-1-4231-6597-2(7))* Hyperion Bks. for Children.

E

Eachus, Jennifer. I'm Sorry. McBratney, Sam. 2006. (ENG.). 32p. (J). (gr. -1-2). pap. 6.99 *(978-0-06-079927-4(7))* HarperCollins Pubs.
Eaddy, Susan. First Look at Aircraft. Galvin, Laura Gates. 2008. (ENG.). 16p. (J). (gr. -1-k). bds. 6.95 *(978-1-59249-862-8(0))* Soundprints.
—First Look at Rescue Vehicles. Galvin, Laura Gates. 2009. (ENG.). 16p. (J). (gr. -1-k). 6.95 *(978-1-60727-106-2(0));* bds. 6.95 *(978-1-60727-093-5(5))* Soundprints.
—First Look at Trucks. Galvin, Laura Gates. 2008. (ENG.). 16p. (J). (gr. -1-k). 6.95 *(978-1-59249-861-1(2))* Soundprints.
—Papa Fish's Lullaby. Hubbell, Patricia. 2007. (ENG.). 32p. (J). (gr. -1-1). 16.95 *(978-1-55971-965-0(6))* Cooper Square Publishing Llc.
Eadie, Inger Sommer, jt. illus. see Grimm, Debi.
Eager, Michiko. Penny Bear's Gift of Love: A Story of Friendship Between a Grieving Young Boy & a Magical Little Bear. Wigglesworth, Penny. l.t. ed. 2004. 84p. (J). pap. 7.95 *(978-0-9675532-5-2(3))* Quality of Life Publishing Co.
Eagle, Cameron, jt. illus. see Hartelius, Margaret A.
Eagle, Cameron, jt. illus. see Tallarico, Tony.
Eagle, Joy. Chilean Mines. Ballock-Dixon, Saige J. & Medina, Sylvia M. 2013. 36p. pap. 11.49 *(978-1-939871-00-8(X))* Green Kids Club, Inc.
—Desert Mirage. Medina, Sylvia M. & Ballock-Dixon, Saige J. 2012. 32p. pap. 11.59 *(978-0-9836602-6-2(3))* Green Kids Club, Inc.
—Gorilla's Roar. Medina, Sylvia M. & B alloxk-Dixon, Saige J. 2012. 36p. pap. 11.49 *(978-0-9836602-5-5(5))* Green Kids Club, Inc.
—Green Springs Junior. Medina, Sylvia M. & Ballock-Dixon, Saige J. 2013. 36p. pap. 11.59 *(978-0-9836602-7-9(1))* Green Kids Club, Inc.
—Jade Elephant. Medina, Sylvia M. & Ballock-Dixon, Saige J. 2012. 36p. pap. 11.49 *(978-0-9836602-4-8(7))* Green Kids Club, Inc.
Eagle, Mike. Coronado's Golden Quest. Weisberg, Barbara & Haley, Alex. 2009. (Steck-Vaughn Stories of America Ser.). (ENG.). 88p. (gr. 3-8). pap. 14.20 *(978-0-8114-8072-7(0))* Houghton Mifflin Harcourt Publishing Co.
Eaglesham, Dale, et al. Perdition's Gate, Vol. 6. Dixon, Chuck. 2004. (Sigil Ser.: Vol. 6). 160p. (YA). pap. 15.95 *(978-1-59314-048-9(7))* CrossGeneration Comics, Inc.
Eaglesham, Dale. Steve Rogers - Super Soldier. Brubaker, Ed. 2011. (ENG.). 152p. (YA). (gr. 8-17). pap. 14.99 *(978-0-7851-4879-1(5))* Marvel Worldwide, Inc.
—What If? 2011. (ENG.). 184p. (YA). (gr. 8-17). pap. 24.99 *(978-0-7851-5278-1(4))* Marvel Worldwide, Inc.
Eaglesham, Dale, jt. illus. see Land, Greg.

E

Eakins, Bonny Mae & Hoffbauer, Wyng. Wonder Island. Eakins, Bonny Mae. 2nd ed. 2013. 80p. pap. 14.95 *(978-1-893660-26-7(5))* Ravenhawk Bks.

Eakle, Tayah. 3 A's & 3 B's All the Way to Z, 1 vol. Eakle, Janice. 2009. 36p. pap. 24.95 *(978-1-60813-739-8(2))* America Star Bks.

Earlenbaugh, Dennis. Puzzling over Sherlock. Senuta, Michael. 2003. (Fact-Based Bks.). 32p. (YA). (gr. 4-12). pap. 8.00 *(978-0-934468-54-1(0))* Gaslight Pubns.

—Second Thoughts about Sherlock Holmes. Senuta, Michael. 2003. (Novels, Novelas, Short Stories Ser.). 32p. (YA). (gr. 4-12). pap. 8.00 *(978-0-934468-55-8(9))* Gaslight Pubns.

Earley, Catherine M., photos by. God Makes Beautiful Things. Earley, Catherine M. 2005. 48p. (YA). per. 11.00 *(978-0-9769589-0-1(2))* Naynay Bks.

Earnhart, Jeanine. Tommy the Turtle: And His Angry Feelings. Schiller, Dawn. 2010. (ENG.). 30p. pap. 15.00 *(978-1-4505-9702-9(5))* CreateSpace Independent Publishing Platform.

Easey, Chris. Toulouse Tangled up in Lights. Thompson, Kimberly. 2011. 64p. (J). 19.95 *(978-0-9818976-1-5(4))* Little Pigeon Bks.

Easler, Kris. The Day the Mustache Took Over. Katz, Alan. 2015. (Mustache Ser.: 1). (ENG.). 208p. (J). (gr. 2-4). 13.99 *(978-1-61963-558-6(5),* Bloomsbury USA Childrens) Bloomsbury USA.

Eason, D. M. The Goodwill Vultures Club. Willard, Hugh. Holjes, Kerry, ed. 2013. 122p. pap. 9.99 *(978-1-935711-26-1(1))* Peak City Publishing, LLC.

—The Goodwill Vultures Club: No Time for Play. Willard, Hugh. Holjes, Kerry, ed. 2013. 140p. pap. 9.99 *(978-1-935711-30-8(X))* Peak City Publishing, LLC.

—The Goodwill Vultures Club: The Gift of the Vulture. Willard, Hugh. Dozier, Dolly, ed. 2013. 128p. pap. 9.99 *(978-1-935711-34-6(2))* Peak City Publishing, LLC.

—The Rusty Bucket Kids, A Behind the Scenes Look at the Rusty Bucket Kids, Lincoln, Journey To 16. Demers, Roxanna. 2010. (ENG.). 82p. (J). pap. 19.99 *(978-1-935711-04-9(0))* Peak City Publishing, LLC.

East, Jacqueline. Adeline Porcupine. Ghigna, Charles. 2015. (Tiny Tales Ser.). (ENG.). 64p. (gr. -1-2). lib. bdg. 22.65 ***(978-1-4795-6530-6(X))*** Tiny Tales.

East, Jacqueline. Baby Dinosaur Can Play, 1 vol. Dale, Jay. 2012. (Engage Literacy Red Ser.). (ENG.). 32p. (gr. k-2). pap. 5.99 *(978-1-4296-8936-6(6),* Engage Literacy) Capstone Pr., Inc.

—Baby Dinosaur Is Hiding, 1 vol. Dale, Jay. 2012. (Engage Literacy Yellow Ser.). (ENG.). 32p. (gr. k-2). pap. 5.99 *(978-1-4296-8952-6(8),* Engage Literacy) Capstone Pr., Inc.

—Baby Dinosaur Is Lost, 1 vol. Dale, Jay. 2012. (Engage Literacy Blue Ser.). (ENG.). 32p. (gr. k-2). pap. 5.99 *(978-1-4296-8972-4(2),* Engage Literacy) Capstone Pr., Inc.

—Bad Dog, Digby!, 1 vol. Llewellyn, Claire. 2013. (Start Reading Ser.). (ENG.). 24p. (gr. k-1). pap. 6.99 *(978-1-4765-4085-6(3))* Capstone Pr., Inc.

East, Jacqueline. Bobby Bear. Ghigna, Charles. 2015. (Tiny Tales Ser.). (ENG.). 64p. (gr. -1-2). lib. bdg. 22.65 ***(978-1-4795-6531-3(8))*** Tiny Tales.

East, Jacqueline. Bunnies Are for Kissing. Zobel-Nolan, Allia. 2009. 24p. (J). (gr. -1-k). 7.95 *(978-1-58925-842-6(8))* Tiger Tales.

—Cat Nap, 1 vol. Llewellyn, Claire. 2013. (Start Reading Ser.). (ENG.). 24p. (gr. k-1). pap. 6.99 *(978-1-4765-4087-0(X))* Capstone Pr., Inc.

—The Children's Book of Manners. Giles, Sophie et al. 2014. (ENG.). 32p. (J). pap. 10.00 *(978-1-84135-971-7(8))* Award Pubns. Ltd. GBR. Dist: Parkwest Pubns., Inc.

East, Jacqueline. Cuddle Bunny. Ghigna, Charles. 2015. (Tiny Tales Ser.). (ENG.). 64p. (gr. -1-2). lib. bdg. 22.65 ***(978-1-4795-6528-3(8))*** Tiny Tales.

East, Jacqueline. Easter Hop. 2008. (ENG.). 16p. (gr. -1-k). bds. 5.95 *(978-1-58117-686-5(4),* Intervisual/Piggy Toes) Bendon, Inc.

—Elephant. Elliot, Rachel. 2009. (Wiggle-Waggles Ser.). (ENG.). 8p. (J). (gr. -1). bds. 4.99 *(978-0-7641-6236-7(5))* Barron's Educational Series, Inc.

—Five Naughty Kittens. Beardsley, Martyn. 2005. (Reading Corner Ser.). 24p. (J). (gr. k-3). lib. bdg. 22.80 *(978-1-59771-006-0(7))* Sea-To-Sea Pubns.

—The Flying Monkey, 6 pack. Holden, Pam. 2009. (Red Rocket Readers Ser.). 16p. (gr. -1-3). pap. *(978-1-877363-29-0(4),* Red Rocket Readers) Flying Start Bks.

—Grumpy Old Bear, 1 vol. Dale, Jay. 2012. (Wonder Words Ser.). (ENG.). 32p. (gr. k-2). pap. 5.99 *(978-1-4296-8918-2(8),* Engage Literacy) Capstone Pr., Inc.

—Hickory Dickory Dock. Barritt, Margaret. 2006. (ENG.). 7p. (J). (gr. -1-7). bds. 7.95 *(978-1-59354-153-8(8),* Handprint Bks.) Chronicle Bks. LLC.

East, Jacqueline, et al. Hickory Dickory Dock: And Other Silly-Time Rhymes. 2005. (Mother Goose Rhymes Ser.). (ENG.). 36p. (J). (gr. -1-k). 12.95 *(978-1-59249-463-7(3),* 1D019) Soundprints.

East, Jacqueline. Learn Good Habits with Jessica: Above All, Don't Behave Like Zoe! 2008. 28p. (J). (gr. -1-3). 6.95 *(978-1-59496-163-2(8))* Teora USA LLC.

—Learn Good Manners with Charles: Above All, Don't Behave Like Trevor! 2008. 28p. (J). (gr. -1-3). 6.95 *(978-1-59496-162-5(X))* Teora USA LLC.

—Little Zebra, 1 vol. Dale, Jay. 2012. (Wonder Words Ser.). (ENG.). 32p. (gr. k-2). pap. 5.99 *(978-1-4296-8906-9(4),* Engage Literacy) Capstone Pr., Inc.

—Look at My Home, 6 vols. Holden, Pam. 2009. (Red Rocket Readers Ser.). 16p. (gr. -1-2). pap. *(978-1-877363-04-7(9),* Red Rocket Readers) Flying Start Bks.

East, Jacqueline. Lucy Goose. Ghigna, Charles. 2015. (Tiny Tales Ser.). (ENG.). 64p. (gr. -1-2). lib. bdg. 22.65 ***(978-1-4795-6529-0(6))*** Tiny Tales.

East, Jacqueline. Max Monkey, 6 pack. Holden, Pam. 2009. (Red Rocket Readers Ser.). 16p. (gr. -1-3). pap. *(978-1-877363-24-5(3),* Red Rocket Readers) Flying Start Bks.

—The Mermaid's Treasure Hunt. Taylor, Dereen. 2012. (ENG.). 12p. (J). (gr. -1-12). 16.99 *(978-1-84322-762-5(2))* Anness Publishing GBR. Dist: National Bk. Network.

—Monkey. Elliot, Rachel. 2009. (Wiggle-Waggles Ser.). (ENG.). 8p. (J). (gr. -1). bds. 4.99 *(978-0-7641-6238-1(1))* Barron's Educational Series, Inc.

—New Pet. Llewellyn, Claire. 2013. (Start Reading Ser.). (ENG.). 24p. (gr. k-1). pap. 6.99 *(978-1-4765-4123-5(X))* Capstone Pr., Inc.

—Noah's Ark. Box, Su. 2014. (Bible Dial-A-Picture Bks.). (ENG.). 8p. (J). (gr. -1-k). bds. 6.99 *(978-0-7641-6695-2(6))* Barron's Educational Series, Inc.

—Peter Cottontails Busy Day. 2009. 10p. 5.95 *(978-1-58117-862-3(X),* Intervisual/Piggy Toes) Bendon, Inc.

—Princess Palace: A Three-Demensional Playset. 2006. 8p. (J). (gr. -1-3). 22.95 *(978-1-58117-492-2(6),* Intervisual/Piggy Toes) Bendon, Inc.

—See Me Ride, 6 pack. Holden, Pam. 2009. (Red Rocket Readers Ser.). 16p. (gr. -1-2). pap. *(978-1-877363-30-6(8),* Red Rocket Readers) Flying Start Bks.

—Stickybeak the Parrot, 6 pack. Holden, Pam. 2009. (Red Rocket Readers Ser.). 16p. (gr. -1-2). pap. *(978-1-877363-28-3(6),* Red Rocket Readers) Flying Start Bks.

—Ten Little Mermaids. Williams, Becky. 2007. (Story Book Ser.). 22p. (J). (gr. -1). bds. *(978-1-84666-375-8(X),* Tide Mill Pr.) Top That! Publishing PLC.

—That's When I'm Happy. Shoshan, Beth. 2011. *(978-1-4351-3618-2(7))* Barnes & Noble, Inc.

—The Town Mouse & the Country Mouse. 2007. (Picture Book Classics Ser.). (J). (gr. -1-3). 24p. 9.99 *(978-0-7945-1877-6(X))*; 48p. 8.99 *(978-0-7945-1613-0(0))* EDC Publishing. (Usborne).

—When I Grow Up. Holden, Pam. 2009. (Red Rocket Readers Ser.). (ENG.). 16p. (gr. -1-2). pap. *(978-1-877363-06-1(5),* Red Rocket Readers) Flying Start Bks.

East, Matt. Tommy Cat & the Giant Chickens. East, Bob. 2008. 24p. per. 24.95 *(978-1-4241-9242-7(0))* America Star Bks.

East, Nick. Harry & the Monster. Mongredien, Sue. 2013. (ENG.). 32p. (gr. -1-k). 14.99 *(978-1-58925-146-5(6))* Tiger Tales.

East, Stella. The Paint Box, 1 vol. Trottier, Maxine. 2004. (ENG.). 32p. (J). pap. 8.95 *(978-1-55041-808-8(4),* 1550418084) Fitzhenry & Whiteside, Ltd. CAN. Dist: Midpoint Trade Bks., Inc.

Eastcott, John, photos by. Face to Face with Penguins. Momatiuk, Yva. 2009. (Face to Face with Animals Ser.). (ENG., 32p. (J). (gr. 2-5). 16.95 *(978-1-4263-0561-0(3))*; 25.90 *(978-1-4263-0562-7(1))* National Geographic Society. (National Geographic Children's Bks.).

—Face to Face with Wild Horses. Momatiuk, Yva. 2009. (Face to Face with Animals Ser.). (ENG., 32p. (J). (gr. 2-5). 16.95 *(978-1-4263-0466-8(8))*; lib. bdg. 25.90 *(978-1-4263-0467-5(6))* National Geographic Society. (National Geographic Children's Bks.).

Easter, Dennis. Take a Backyard Bird Walk. Kirkland, Jane. 2005. (Take a Walk Ser.). (ENG.). 32p. (J). (gr. 4-7). pap. 9.95 *(978-0-9709754-0-9(6),* Take a Walk Bk.) Stillwater Publishing.

Easter, Paige. Alphabet Rhymes for Bible Times. Augustine, Peg & Flegal, Daphna. 2004. 9.00 *(978-0-687-03021-7(8))* Abingdon Pr.

Eastley, Melanie. Scott the Starfish - an Unexpected Adventure! Fraser, Jennifer. 2012. 32p. pap. *(978-0-9868776-4-3(6))* MW Bk. Pubs.

Eastman, Dianne. One Splendid Tree. Helmer, Marilyn. 2007. (ENG.). 32p. (J). (gr. -1-3). 6.95 *(978-1-55453-166-0(7))* Kids Can Pr., Ltd. CAN. Dist: Univ. of Toronto Pr.

—Totally Human: Why We Look & Act the Way We Do. Nicolson, Cynthia Pratt. 2011. (ENG.). 40p. (J). (gr. 4-8). 16.95 *(978-1-55453-569-9(7))* Kids Can Pr., Ltd. CAN. Dist: Univ. of Toronto Pr.

Eastman, Dianne, et al. Wow Canada! Exploring This Land from Coast to Coast to Coast. Bowers, Vivien. 2nd ed. 2010. (Wow Canada! Ser.). (ENG.). 160p. (J). (gr. 3-6). 24.95 *(978-1-897349-82-3(3))*; pap. 19.95 *(978-1-897349-83-0(1))* Owlkids Bks. Inc. CAN. (Maple Tree Pr.). Dist: Perseus-PGW.

Eastman, Dianne & Owlkids Books Inc. Staff. Ha! Ha! Ha! & Much More: The Ultimate Round-Up of Jokes, Riddles, Facts, & Puzzles. Thomas, Lyn. 2008. (ENG.). 256p. (J). (gr. 3-6). per. 14.95 *(978-1-897349-23-6(8),* Maple Tree Pr.) Owlkids Bks. Inc. CAN. Dist: Perseus-PGW.

Eastman, P. D. Go, Dog. Go! Eastman, P. D. 2008. (ENG.). 64p. pap. *(978-0-00-722546-0(6))* HarperCollins Pubs. Ltd.

Eastman, P. D. & Eastman, Tony. Big Dog... Little Dog. Eastman, P. D. & Eastman, Tony. 2003. (Beginner Books(R) Ser.). (ENG.). 48p. (J). (gr. -1-2). 8.99 *(978-0-375-82297-1(6),* Random Hse. Bks. for Young Readers) Random Hse. Children's Bks.

Eastman, Peter. Fred & Ted Like to Fly. Eastman, Peter. 2007. (Beginner Books Ser.). (ENG.). 48p. (J). (gr. -1-2). 8.99 *(978-0-375-84064-7(8),* Random Hse. Bks. for Young Readers) Random Hse. Children's Bks.

Eastman, Tony, jt. illus. see Eastman, P. D.

Easton, Susan. Punkinhead's Veggie Adventure: And the Strange Contraption in the Kitchen. Rosenbaum, Elizabeth, photos by. Trooboff, Rhoda. 2013. (ENG.). 56p. (J). (gr. -1). pap. 15.00 *(978-0-9773536-7-5(2))* Tenley Circle Pr.

Easton, W. G. The Mysterious Shin Shira. Farrow, George Edward. 2007. 120p. per. *(978-1-4065-1690-6(2))* Dodo Pr.

Eastwood, John. Annie Saves the Day. Lindsay, Elizabeth. 2003. 92p. (J). *(978-0-439-44651-8(1))* Scholastic, Inc.

—The Catlady. King-Smith, Dick. 2007. (ENG.). 80p. (J). (gr. 1-4). 5.50 *(978-0-440-42031-6(8),* Yearling) Random Hse. Children's Bks.

—Funny Frank. King-Smith, Dick. 2003. (ENG.). 112p. (J). (gr. 1-4). 5.99 *(978-0-440-41880-1(1),* Yearling) Random Hse. Children's Bks.

—Titus Rules! King-Smith, Dick. 2004. (ENG.). 96p. (gr. 1-4). reprint ed. 5.50 *(978-0-440-42000-2(8),* Yearling) Random Hse. Children's Bks.

Eaton, Maxwell, III. Andy Also. 2014. (Jump-Into-Chapters Ser.). (ENG.). 96p. (J). (gr. k-3). 12.99 *(978-1-60905-457-1(1))* Blue Apple Bks.

Eaton, Maxwell, III. Okay, Andy! Eaton, Maxwell, III. 2014. (Jump-Into-Chapters Ser.). (ENG.). 96p. (J). (gr. k-3). 12.99 *(978-1-60905-350-5(8))* Blue Apple Bks.

Eaton, Scot. DoomWar. 2011. (ENG.). 160p. (YA). (gr. 8-17). pap. 15.99 *(978-0-7851-4715-2(2))* Marvel Worldwide, Inc.

Eaton, Scot, et al. Sigil, Vol. 5. Dixon, Chuck. 2003. (Sigil Ser.: Vol. 5). 160p. (YA). pap. 15.95 *(978-1-931484-83-1(X))* CrossGeneration Comics, Inc.

Eaton, Scot & Barreiro, Mike. Leonard Nimoy's Primortals Vol. 1, No. 1: Origins. Nimoy, Leonard. Chambers, James et al, eds. 36p. (Orig.). (YA). pap. 2.25 *(978-0-9645175-1-6(5))* Big Entertainment, Inc.

Eaton, Scot & Epting, Steve. Captain America by Ed Brubaker - Volume 4. 2013. (ENG.). 112p. (J). (gr. 4-17). pap. 19.99 *(978-0-7851-6078-6(7))* Marvel Worldwide, Inc.

Eaton, Scot & Robinson, Roger. Thor: Gods & Men. Jurgens, Dan. 2011. (ENG.). 144p. (YA). (gr. 8-17). pap. 29.99 *(978-0-7851-5090-9(0))* Marvel Worldwide, Inc.

Eaves, Ed. How to Catch a Dragon. Hart, Caryl. 2014. (ENG.). 32p. pap. 8.99 ***(978-0-85707-959-6(X),*** Simon & Schuster Children's) Simon & Schuster, Ltd. GBR. Dist: Simon & Schuster, Inc.

Eaves, Ed. My Pirate Adventure: A Pop-up & Play Book. Bateson, Maggie. ed. 2008. (ENG.). 20p. (J). (gr. 4-7). 23.50 *(978-0-230-53036-2(2),* Macmillan) Pan Macmillan GBR. Dist: Trans-Atlantic Pubns., Inc.

—Say Goodnight to the Sleepy Animals! Whybrow, Ian. ed. 2011. (Say Hello Ser.). (ENG.). 20p. (J). (— 1). bds. 10.99 *(978-0-230-75607-6(7))* Pan Macmillan GBR. Dist: Independent Pubs. Group.

Eaves, Ed. Say Hello to the Snowy Animals! Whybrow, Ian. ed. 2015. (Say Hello Ser.). (ENG.). 24p. (J). (gr. -1-k). pap. 10.99 ***(978-1-4472-1035-1(2))*** Pan Macmillan GBR. Dist: Independent Pubs. Group.

Eaves, Edward. Say Hello to the Snowy Animals! Whybrow, Ian. 2012. (J). *(978-0-7607-9675-7(0))* Barnes & Noble, Inc.

Ebbeler, Jeff. Battle of the Books. Slater, David Michael. 2009. (David Michael Slater Set 2 Ser.). 32p. (gr. -1-4). 28.50 *(978-1-60270-655-2(7),* Looking Glass Library) ABDO Publishing Co.

—Don't Forget! A Responsibility Story. Suen, Anastasia. 2008. (Main Street School - Kids with Character Ser.). 32p. (gr. -1-4). 28.50 *(978-1-60270-269-1(1),* Looking Glass Library) ABDO Publishing Co.

—Game Over: Dealing with Bullies. Suen, Anastasia. 2008. (Main Street School - Kids with Character Ser.). 32p. (gr. -1-4). 28.50 *(978-1-60270-270-7(5),* Looking Glass Library) ABDO Publishing Co.

—Girls Can, Too! A Tolerence Story. Suen, Anastasia. 2008. (Main Street School - Kids with Character Ser.). 32p. (gr. -1-4). 28.50 *(978-1-60270-271-4(3),* Looking Glass Library) ABDO Publishing Co.

—Lights Out Shabbat. Shulimson, Sarene. 2012. (Shabbat Ser.). (ENG.). 32p. (J). (gr. -1-2). pap. 7.95 *(978-0-7613-7565-4(1),* Kar-Ben Publishing) Lerner Publishing Group.

—Milo & the Monster. Slater, David Michael. 2009. (David Michael Slater Set 2 Ser.). 32p. (gr. -1-4). 28.50 *(978-1-60270-656-9(5),* Looking Glass Library) ABDO Publishing Co.

—Trust Me: A Loyalty Story. Suen, Anastasia. 2008. (Main Street School - Kids with Character Ser.). 32p. (gr. -1-4). 28.50 *(978-1-60270-273-8(X),* Looking Glass Library) ABDO Publishing Co.

—Vote for Isaiah! A Citizenship Story. Suen, Anastasia. 2008. (Main Street School - Kids with Character Ser.). 32p. (gr. -1-4). 28.50 *(978-1-60270-274-5(8),* Looking Glass Library) ABDO Publishing Co.

—A Warrior Prince for God. Chapman, Kelly. 2010. 32p. (J). 14.99 *(978-0-7369-2895-3(2))* Harvest Hse. Pubs.

—A Warrior Prince for God Activity Book. Chapman, Kelly. 2010. 48p. (J). 6.99 *(978-0-7369-2896-0(0))* Harvest Hse. Pubs.

—A Warrior Prince for God Curriculum Leader's Guide. Chapman, Kelly. 2009. pap. 12.99 *(978-0-7369-2899-1(5))* Harvest Hse. Pubs.

—Your Life As a Pharaoh in Ancient Egypt, 1 vol. Gunderson, Jessica Sarah. 2012. (Way It Was Ser.). (ENG.). 32p. (gr. 2-3). pap. 7.95 *(978-1-4048-7744-3(4),* Nonfiction Picture Bks.) Picture Window Bks.

—Your Life As a Pharaoh in Ancient Egypt, 1 vol. Gunderson, Jessica. 2012. (Way It Was Ser.). (ENG.). 32p. (gr. 2-3). lib. bdg. 25.99 *(978-1-4048-7371-1(6),* Nonfiction Picture Bks.) Picture Window Bks.

Ebbeler, Jeffrey. April Fools, Phyllis! Hill, Susanna Leonard. 2011. (ENG.). 32p. (J). (gr. -1-3). 16.95 *(978-0-8234-2270-8(4))* Holiday Hse., Inc.

—Cinco de Mouse-O! Cox, Judy. (SPA.). 32p. (J). 2011. pap. 6.95 *(978-0-8234-2328-6(X))*; 2010. (gr. -1-3). 16.95 *(978-0-8234-2194-7(5))* Holiday Hse., Inc.

—Cutting in Line Isn't Fair! Suen, Anastasia. 2007. (Main Street School - Kids with Character Ser.). 32p. (gr. -1-4). 28.50 *(978-1-60270-029-1(X),* Looking Glass Library) ABDO Publishing Co.

—Eli's Lie-O-Meter: A Story about Telling the Truth. Levins, Sandra. 2010. 32p. (J). (gr. -1-3). 14.95 *(978-1-4338-0735-0(1))*; pap. 9.95 *(978-1-4338-0736-7(X))* American Psychological Assn. (Magination Pr.).

—A Good Team: A Cooperation Story. Suen, Anastasia. 2008. (Main Street School - Kids with Character Ser.). 32p. (gr. -1-4). 28.50 *(978-1-60270-272-1(1),* Looking Glass Library) ABDO Publishing Co.

—Hanukkah Cookies with Sprinkles. Adler, David A. 2015. (J). *(978-0-87441-918-4(2))*; ***(978-1-68115-500-5(1))*** Behrman Hse., Inc.

—Haunted House, Haunted Mouse. Cox, Judy. (ENG.). 32p. (J). 2012. (gr. -1-2). pap. 7.99 *(978-0-8234-2544-0(4))*; 2011. 16.95 *(978-0-8234-2315-6(8))* Holiday Hse., Inc.

—Helping Sophia. Suen, Anastasia. 2007. (Main Street School - Kids with Character Ser.). 32p. (gr. -1-4). 28.50 *(978-1-60270-030-7(3),* Looking Glass Library) ABDO Publishing Co.

—Jingle Bells. 2009. (ENG.). 20p. (J). (gr. -1-k). bds. 6.99 *(978-0-8249-1827-9(4),* Candy Cane Pr.) Ideals Pubns.

—Jingle Bells - Musical. 2009. (ENG.). 20p. (J). (gr. -1-k). bds. 12.99 *(978-0-8249-1829-3(0),* Candy Cane Pr.) Ideals Pubns.

—Lights Out Shabbat. Shulimson, Sarene. 2012. (Shabbat Ser.). (ENG.). 32p. (J). (gr. -1-2). lib. bdg. 17.95 *(978-0-7613-7564-7(3),* Kar-Ben Publishing) Lerner Publishing Group.

—One Is a Feast for Mouse: A Thanksgiving Tale. Cox, Judy. (ENG.). 32p. (J). (gr. -1-3). 2009. pap. 7.99 *(978-0-8234-2231-9(3))*; 2008. 16.95 *(978-0-8234-1977-7(0))* Holiday Hse., Inc.

—The Only Alex Addleston in All These Mountains. Solheim, James. 2014. (ENG.). 32p. (J). (gr. -1-3). lib. bdg. 17.95 *(978-1-4677-0346-8(X),* Carolrhoda Bks.) Lerner Publishing Group.

—Punxsutawney Phyllis. Hill, Susanna Leonard. 2006. (ENG.). 32p. (J). (gr. -1-3). pap. 6.95 *(978-0-8234-2040-7(X))* Holiday Hse., Inc.

—Punxsutawney Phyllis. Hill, Leonard. 2005. (ENG.). 32p. (J). (gr. -1-3). 17.95 *(978-0-8234-1872-5(3))* Holiday Hse., Inc.

—Raising the Flag. Suen, Anastasia. 2007. (Main Street School - Kids with Character Ser.). 32p. (gr. -1-4). 28.50 *(978-1-60270-031-4(1),* Looking Glass Library) ABDO Publishing Co.

—Scissors, Paper & Sharing. Suen, Anastasia. 2007. (Main Street School - Kids with Character Ser.). 32p. (gr. -1-4). 28.50 *(978-1-60270-032-1(X),* Looking Glass Library) ABDO Publishing Co.

—Show Some Respect. Suen, Anastasia. 2007. (Main Street School - Kids with Character Ser.). 32p. (gr. -1-4). 28.50 *(978-1-60270-033-8(8),* Looking Glass Library) ABDO Publishing Co.

—Snow Day for Mouse. Cox, Judy. (ENG.). 32p. (J). 2013. pap. 7.99 *(978-0-8234-2913-4(X))*; 2012. 16.95 *(978-0-8234-2408-5(1))* Holiday Hse., Inc.

—The Table & the Chair. Lear, Edward. 2011. (Poetry for Children Ser.). (ENG.). 24p. (J). (gr. k-3). 27.07 *(978-1-60973-156-4(5),* 201185) Child's World, Inc., The.

—Tiger in My Soup, 1 vol. Sheth, Kashmira. 2013. (ENG.). 32p. (J). (gr. -1-3). 15.95 *(978-1-56145-696-3(9))* Peachtree Pubs.

—Times Tables Cheat. Suen, Anastasia. 2007. (Main Street School - Kids with Character Ser.). 32p. (gr. -1-4). 28.50 *(978-1-60270-034-5(6),* Looking Glass Library) ABDO Publishing Co.

—The Twelve Days of Christmas in Illinois. Bellisario, Gina. 2012. (Twelve Days of Christmas in America Ser.). (ENG.). 32p. (J). (gr. k-3). 12.95 *(978-1-4027-9733-0(8))* Sterling Publishing Co., Inc.

—The Twelve Days of Christmas in Ohio. Gerber, Carole. 2014. (Twelve Days of Christmas in America Ser.). (ENG.). 40p. (J). (gr. k). 12.95 *(978-1-4549-0890-6(4))* Sterling Publishing Co., Inc.

—We Both Read-My Sitter Is a T-Rex! (Level 1-2) Orshoski, Paul. 2011. (ENG.). 44p. (J). 9.95 *(978-1-60115-253-4(1))*; pap. 5.99 *(978-1-60115-254-1(X))* Treasure Bay, Inc.

—We Both Read-The Mouse in My House. Orshoski, Paul. 2012. 44p. (J). 9.95 *(978-1-60115-257-2(4))*; pap. 5.99 *(978-1-60115-258-9(2))* Treasure Bay, Inc.

—We Read Phonics-Ant in Her Pants. Orshoski, Paul. 2010. (ENG.). 32p. (J). pap. 4.99 *(978-1-60115-328-9(7))* Treasure Bay, Inc.

—We Read Phonics-Ants in Her Pants. Orshoski, Paul. 2010. (ENG.). 32p. (J). 9.95 *(978-1-60115-327-2(9))* Treasure Bay, Inc.

—We Read Phonics-Dad Does It All. Orshoski, Paul. 2011. 32p. (J). 9.95 *(978-1-60115-341-8(4))*; (YA). pap. 4.99 *(978-1-60115-342-5(2))* Treasure Bay, Inc.

—We Read Phonics-I Do Not Like Greens! Orshoski, Paul. 2010. (We Read Phonics Ser.). 32p. (J). (gr. 1-5). 9.95 *(978-1-60115-331-9(7))* Treasure Bay, Inc.

—We Read Phonics-Robot Man. Orshoski, Paul. 2010. (We Read Phonics Ser.). 32p. (J). (gr. 1-5). 9.95 *(978-1-60115-329-6(5))*; pap. 4.99 *(978-1-60115-330-2(9))* Treasure Bay, Inc.

—We Read Phonics-Sports Dream. Orshoski, Paul. 2011. (We Read Phonics Ser.). 32p. (J). (gr. 1-3). 9.95 *(978-1-60115-335-7(X))*; pap. 4.99 *(978-1-60115-336-4(8))* Treasure Bay, Inc.

—Your Life As an Explorer on a Viking Ship. Troupe, Thomas Kingsley. 2012. (Way It Was Ser.). (ENG.). 32p. (gr. 2-3). pap. 7.95 *(978-1-4048-7252-3(3))*; lib. bdg. 25.99 *(978-1-4048-7160-1(8))* Picture Window Bks. (Nonfiction Picture Bks.).

Ebbeler, Jeffrey, jt. illus. see Troupe, Thomas Kingsley.

Eberbach, Andrea. Ame the Elephant: Terrorized by Evil Mice. Louthain, J. A. 2nd l.t. ed. 2003. 48p. (J). 12.97 *(978-0-9679416-2-2(8),* 0-9679416-2-8) Alexie Bks.

Eberhart, Donald G. Grizzly Bear Family. Fraggalosch, Audrey M. (Soundprints' Amazing Animal Adventures! Ser.). (ENG.). (J). 2005. 36p. (gr. -1-2). 8.95 *(978-1-59249-395-1(5),* SC7103); 2005. 32p. (gr. 2-2). 19.95 *(978-1-59249-394-4(7),* BC7103); 2003. 36p. (gr. -1-3). 9.95 *(978-1-59249-059-2(X),* PS7153); 2003. 36p. (gr. -1-k). pap. 2.95 *(978-1-59249-050-9(6),* S7153) Soundprints.

Ebert, Anne. La Granja. Caballero, D., tr. 2006. (Junior (Silver Dolphin) Ser.). (SPA.). 16p. (J). (gr. -1). 9.95 *(978-970-718-345-2(4))* Baker & Taylor Publishing Group.

Ebert, Len. All about Sports with Inspector McQ. Mullins, Patty Rutland. 2004. (Treasure Tree Ser.). 32p. (J). *(978-0-7166-1645-0(9))* World Bk., Inc.

—An Amusement Park Mystery in Ohio. Wilsdon, Christina. 2006. 26p. (J). 7.99 *(978-1-59939-013-0(2))* Cornerstone Pr.

—Bible Stories to Color & Tell, Ages 6-8. Standard Publishing Staff. 2005. (HeartShaper(r) Resources — Elementary Ser.). 240p. (J). per. 16.99 *(978-0-7847-1348-8(0),* 02492) Standard Publishing.

—The Easter Cave. Wedeven, Carol. 2004. 32p. (J). (gr. -1-2). 10.49 *(978-0-570-07135-8(6))* Concordia Publishing Hse.

—The Fisherman & His Wife: A Tale about Being Happy & Satisfied. Grimm, Jacob & Grimm, Wilhelm K. 2006. (J). *(978-1-59939-097-0(3),* Reader's Digest Young Families, Inc.) Studio Fun International.

—How You Are Changing: For Boys Ages 10-12 & Parents. Graver, Jane. rev. ed. pap. 12.99 *(978-0-7586-1411-7(X))* Concordia Publishing Hse.

—It's Called Kibud Av Va'Eim: A Story about Honoring Parents. Rosenfeld, Dina. 2014. 20p. (J). 10.95 *(978-1-929628-78-0(1))* Hachai Publishing.

—Joseph's Christmas Story. Dreyer, Nicole E. 2004. (ENG.). 16p. (J). 1.99 *(978-0-570-07577-6(7))* Concordia Publishing Hse.

—Léeme Historias de la Biblia (Read to Me Bible Stories) Standard Publishing Staff. 2012. (SPA & ENG.). 64p. (J). 9.99 *(978-0-7847-3574-9(3))* Standard Publishing.

—Off to Bed. Albee, Sarah. 2006. (Step-By-Step Readers Ser.). (J). pap. *(978-1-59939-060-4(4),* Reader's Digest Young Families, Inc.) Studio Fun International.

—President George Washington, 1 vol. Allen, Kathy. 2009. (Our American Story Ser.). (ENG.). 32p. (gr. 1-3). lib. bdg. 26.65 *(978-1-4048-5539-7(4),* Nonfiction Picture Bks.) Picture Window Bks.

—The Selfish Giant: A Tale about Being Unselfish. Wilde, Oscar. 2006. (J). *(978-1-59939-085-7(X),* Reader's Digest Young Families, Inc.) Studio Fun International.

—Thomas Jefferson: A Founding Father of the United States of America, 1 vol. Mortensen, Lori. 2008. (Biographies Ser.). (ENG.). 24p. (gr. k-3). lib. bdg. 25.99 *(978-1-4048-3729-4(9),* Nonfiction Picture Bks.) Picture Window Bks.

Ebert, Roey. Mommies & Daddies Are Nurses. Wasson, E. & Strausser, A. 2011. 32p. pap. 15.99 *(978-1-4634-3451-9(0))* AuthorHouse.

Ebertsch, Ted. The Fall Free Zone. Barden, Laura. 2010. 100p. pap. 10.49 *(978-1-4520-0857-8(4))* AuthorHouse.

Eberz, Robert, jt. illus. see Scotton, Rob.

Ebin, Matthew. The Wonderfully Ridiculous Alphabet Book. 2007. 27p. (J). 10.00 *(978-0-9787628-0-3(0))* MEAR LLC.

Eccles, Jane. Hot Dogs & Dinosnores. Li, Amanda. unabr. ed. 2014. (ENG.). 400p. (J). pap. 6.99 *(978-1-4472-5373-0(6))* Pan Macmillan GBR. Dist: Independent Pubs. Group.

—What I Like! Poems for the Very Young. Phinn, Gervase. 2004. (Poetry Ser.). (ENG.). 32p. (J). (gr. -1-3). pap., pap. *(978-1-904550-12-9(6))* Child's Play International Ltd.

Echeverri, Catalina. Shmulik Paints the Town. Rose, Lisa. 2015. (J). ***(978-1-4677-5239-8(8),*** Kar-Ben Publishing) Lerner Publishing Group.

Echeverria Gyorkos, Charmaine. The EGGbees. Echeverria-Bis, Olivia. 2009. (ENG & SPA.). 32p. (J). (gr. -1-3). 16.95 *(978-1-55885-529-8(7),* Piñata Books) Arte Publico Pr.

Eck, Bernhard. Saga de la Mariposa. Martin, Ivonne. l.t. ed. 2003. (SPA.). 80p. (YA). pap. *(978-1-931481-25-0(3))* LiArt-Literature & Art.

Eckel, Jessie. Doodle Dolls: Over 300 Outfits to Design & Decorate. 2010. (ENG.). 132p. (J). pap. 12.95 *(978-0-7624-3819-8(3))* Running Pr. Bk. Pubs.

—How to Be a Princess in 7 Days or Less. 2005. (How to be A Ser.). 32p. (J). (gr. 3-5). 12.95 *(978-0-7534-5921-8(3),* Kingfisher) Roaring Brook Pr.

Eckel, Jessie & Mount, Arthur. Mama's Little Book of Tricks: Keep the Kids Entertained! Brunelle, Lynn. 2007. (ENG.). 144p. (gr. 8-17). pap. 12.95 *(978-0-8118-5571-6(6))* Chronicle Bks. LLC.

Eckerson, Margaret. The Admirable Tinker: Child of the World. Jepson, Edgar. 2007. 204p. per. *(978-1-4065-2736-0(X))* Dodo Pr.

Eckert, Charles, photos by. Eternal Spring Chi Kung. Chu, C. K. Borrelli, James, ed. 2003. 56p. 24.95 *(978-0-9616586-4-9(9))* Sunflower Pr.

Eckhardt, Jason C. Capitol Cat & Watch Dog Unite Lady Freedoms. Law, Janice. 2008. 64p. (J). *(978-1-934645-71-0(0),* Eakin Pr.) Eakin Pr.

—The Legend of the China Poblana. 2003. (J). 10.95 *(978-1-57168-731-9(9),* Eakin Pr.) Eakin Pr.

—Mystery at Jacob's Well. Bennett, Marcia Allen. 2003. 160p. (J). (gr. -1). per. 12.95 *(978-1-57168-641-1(X))* Eakin Pr.

—Paisano Pete: Snake-Killer Bird. Kornechak, Marilyn Gilbert. 2003. 100p. (J). (gr. 3-7). per. 11.95 *(978-1-57168-770-8(X),* Eakin Pr.) Eakin Pr.

Eckl-Shear, Veronica. What Is It All About? Eckl, Joseph J. & Eckl, Theresa R. 2003. (YA). (gr. 7-12). pap. 14.95 *(978-0-9746686-0-4(5),* 100103) Eckl, Joseph J.

Eckstein, Joe. Twee! Caron, Susie. 2013. 24p. (J). pap. 12.99 *(978-0-9889113-0-7(2))* Coda Grove Publishing.

—The Ultimate Friend Book: More Than Your Average Address Book for Kids. Eckstein, Kristen. 2004. 112p. (J). per. *(978-0-9761317-0-0(6))* Imagine! Studios.

—The Ultimate Friend Book: More Than Your Average Address Book for Teens. Eckstein, Kristen. 2004. 112p. (YA). per. *(978-0-9761317-1-7(4))* Imagine! Studios.

Eckstrom, Nathaniel. The Hair Ball. Lee, Spider. 2012. (ENG.). 32p. (J). 23.49 *(978-0-9873586-9-1(3))* JoJo Publishing AUS. Dist: AtlasBooks Distribution.

Ecob, Simon. Boys Only: How to Survive Anything! Oliver, Martin. 2012. (Best at Everything Ser.). (ENG.). 64p. (J). (gr. 3-7). pap. 6.99 *(978-0-545-43096-8(8),* Scholastic Paperbacks) Scholastic, Inc.

Ecob, Simon, jt. illus. see Geremia, Daniela.

Eddy, Randon T. Dillo - A Baby Armadillo's Adventure on Sanibel Island. Miller, Kyle Linda. l.t. ed. 2005. (ENG.). 64p. (J). 16.95 *(978-0-9769332-0-5(9))* Jungle Hse. Pubns.

—DILLO the Coloring Book. 2006. 53p. (J). pap. 6.95 *(978-0-9769332-1-2(7))* Jungle Hse. Pubns.

Ede, Lara. The Great Fairy Baking Competition. Snaith, Andy, photos by. Boon, Fiona, ed. 2013. (ENG.). 64p. (J). 12.99 *(978-1-78235-591-5(X))* Make Believe Ideas GBR. Dist: Nelson, Thomas Inc.

—My Easter Basket. Down, Hayley & Make Believe Ideas Staff. 2014. (ENG.). 12p. (J). (gr. -1). bds. 8.99 *(978-1-78235-074-3(8))* Make Believe Ideas GBR. Dist: Nelson, Thomas Inc.

—The Story of Jesus. Boon, Fiona. 2014. (ENG.). 22p. (J). bds. *(978-1-78235-883-1(8))* Make Believe Ideas.

Edelmann, Heinz. The Beatles Yellow Submarine. Gardner, Charlie. 2006. 37p. (J). (gr. 4-8). reprint ed. 18.00 *(978-1-4223-5184-0(X))* DIANE Publishing Co.

Edelson, Wendy. The Best Part of the Day. Ban Breathnach, Sarah. 2014. (ENG.). 40p. (J). (-k). 16.99 *(978-1-62157-252-7(8),* Regnery Kids) Regnery Publishing, Inc., An Eagle Publishing Co.

—The Christmas Story. Pingry, Patricia A. (ENG.). (J). 2008. 32p. pap. 3.95 *(978-0-8249-5512-0(9));* 2004. 26p. bds. 6.95 *(978-0-8249-6549-5(3))* Ideals Pubns.

—Easter Bunnies. Cosgrove, Stephen. 32p. (J). pap. 4.95 *(978-0-8249-5371-3(1),* Ideals) Ideals Pubns.

—Fiddler T. Bear. Cosgrove, Stephen. 2015. (Barely There Ser.). (ENG.). 32p. (J). (gr. k-4). pap. 7.95 *(978-1-941437-44-5(3))* Heritage Builders, LLC.

—Gabriel Faintheart. Cosgrove, Stephen. 2015. (Barely There Ser.). (ENG.). 32p. (J). (gr. k-4). pap. 7.95 *(978-1-941437-46-9(X))* Heritage Builders, LLC.

—GrandPa Sam. Cosgrove, Stephen. 2015. (Barely There Ser.). (ENG.). 32p. (J). (gr. k-4). pap. 7.95 *(978-1-941437-48-3(6))* Heritage Builders, LLC.

—I Believe in Genevieve. Craig, Jenny. 2013. (ENG.). 40p. (J). (gr. -1-3). 16.95 *(978-1-62157-085-1(1),* Regnery Kids) Regnery Publishing, Inc., An Eagle Publishing Co.

—One Baby Jesus/Un Nino Dios. Pingry, Patricia A. & Urbano, Aide. 2003. (ENG & SPA.). 30p. (J). pap. 3.95 *(978-0-8249-5472-7(6))* Ideals Pubns.

—Over the River & Through the Woods. Child, Lydia Maria. 2012. 16p. (J). 12.99 *(978-0-8249-1881-1(9),* Candy Cane Pr.) Ideals Pubns.

—Pretty, Pretty Prettina. Cosgrove, Stephen. 2015. (Barely There Ser.). (ENG.). 32p. (J). (gr. k-4). pap. 7.95 *(978-1-941437-50-6(8))* Heritage Builders, LLC.

—Saturn for My Birthday, 1 vol. McGranaghan, John. 2008. (ENG.). 32p. (J). (gr. -1-4). 16.95 *(978-1-934359-13-6(0));* pap. 8.95 *(978-1-934359-27-3(0))* Arbordale Publishing.

Edelstein, Racheli. Goodbye, Pacifier! Licht, S. 2013. 24p. (J). 10.95 *(978-1-60091-284-9(2))* Israel Bookshop Pubns.

—Goodbye, Thumb-Sucking! Licht, S. 2013. 24p. 10.95 *(978-1-60091-266-5(4))* Israel Bookshop Pubns.

Eden, David. The Potter's Wheel Story & Activity Book. Eden, David. 2011. (ENG.). 48p. (J). pap. 16.95 *(978-0-9841658-6-5(X),* Ignition Pr.) Publishing Services @ Thomson-Shore.

Edgar, Barrie. Up the Wooden Hill: Bedtime Stories for Little Ones. Trotter, Bob. 2011. 98p. pap. 17.99 *(978-1-60976-139-4(1),* Eloquent Bks.) Strategic Book Publishing & Rights Agency (SBPRA).

Edge, Elizabeth. A Blessing from Above. Henderson, Patti & Golden Books Staff. 2004. (Little Golden Book Ser.). (ENG.). 24p. (J). (gr. -1-2). 3.99 *(978-0-375-82866-9(4),* Golden Bks.) Random Hse. Children's Bks.

Edgerley, Ross. The Legend of Ross the Reader: A Story of How a Smart Cowboy Saved the Prairie One Book at a Time. Dailey, Reid. 2007. 32p. per. 15.95 *(978-1-59858-483-7(9))* Dog Ear Publishing, LLC.

—Ross the Reader & the Adventure of the Pirate's Treasure. Dailey, Reid. 2009. 44p. pap. 16.95 *(978-1-59858-900-9(8))* Dog Ear Publishing, LLC.

Edgson, Alison. Bear & Turtle & the Great Lake Race. Peters, Andrew Fusek. 2005. (Traditional Tales with a Twist Ser.). (ENG.). 32p. (J). per. *(978-1-904550-91-4(6))* Child's Play International Ltd.

—Bear & Turtle & the Great Lake Race. Peters, Andrew. 2010. (Traditional Tales with a Twist Ser.). (ENG.). 32p. (J). (gr. -1-2). *(978-1-84643-347-4(9))* Child's Play International Ltd.

—The Elves & the Shoemaker. 2007. (Flip-Up Fairy Tales Ser.). (ENG.). 24p. (J). *(978-1-84643-142-5(5));* (gr. -1-2). *(978-1-84643-076-3(3))* Child's Play International Ltd.

—The Emperor's New Clothes. (Flip-Up Fairy Tales Ser.). (ENG.). 24p. (J). (gr. -1-2). 2007. *(978-1-84643-093-0(3));* 2006. *(978-1-84643-020-6(8))* Child's Play International Ltd.

—I Want My Mommy! Corderoy, Tracey. 2014. 32p. (J). (gr. -1-3). mass mkt. 3.99 *(978-1-58925-453-4(8))* Tiger Tales.

—Little Puppy Lost, 1 vol. Jennings, Linda. 2008. (ENG.). 32p. (J). (gr. -1-2). pap. 16.95 *(978-1-56148-635-9(3),* Good Bks.) Skyhorse Publishing Co., Inc.

—The Magician's Apprentice. 2011. (Flip-Up Fairy Tales Ser.). (ENG.). 24p. (J). *(978-1-84643-370-2(3));* *(978-1-84643-409-9(2))* Child's Play International Ltd.

—Me & My Dad! Ritchie, Alison. 2007. (J). pap. *(978-0-545-02064-0(6))* Scholastic, Inc.

—No Time for Bed! Rusling, Annette. 2014. 18p. (J). (gr. -1-k). 12.99 *(978-1-58925-529-6(1))* Tiger Tales.

—Pirates Aren't Afraid of the Dark! Powell-Tuck, Maudie. 2014. 32p. (J). (gr. -1-3). 16.99 *(978-1-58925-165-6(2))* Tiger Tales.

—Three Billy Goats Gruff. (Flip-Up Fairy Tales Ser.). (ENG.). 24p. (J). (gr. -1-2). 2007. *(978-1-84643-089-3(5));* 2006. *(978-1-904550-72-3(X))* Child's Play International Ltd.

Edgson, Allison. I Love You All the Same, 1 vol. Keith, Donna. 2014. (ENG.). 20p. (J). bds. 9.99 *(978-0-529-10204-1(8))* Nelson, Thomas Inc.

Edgson, Allison. I Love You Even When, 1 vol. Keith, Donna. 2015. (ENG.). 20p. (J). bds. 9.99 ***(978-0-7180-3644-7(1))*** Nelson, Thomas Inc.

Eding, Bob. Mary Ann's Flying Basket. Loop, Mary Ann. 2013. 30p. pap. 12.95 *(978-0-615-68766-7(0))* Miracle Mountain Images.

Editorial El Antillano. Tai Juega Pelota. Editorial El Antillano. 2008. (J). 4.00 *(978-0-9793026-2-6(5))* Editorial El Antillano, Inc.

—Tai va de Pesca. Editorial El Antillano. 2005. (SPA.). (J). 4.00 *(978-0-9755661-9-0(9))* Editorial El Antillano, Inc.

Edleson, Wendy. One Baby Jesus. Pingry, Patricia A. 2008. (Ideals Christmas Classic Ser.). (ENG.). 30p. (J). (gr. -1-k). pap. 3.95 *(978-0-8249-5511-3(0))* Ideals Pubns.

Edmaier, Bernhard, photos by. Patterns of the Earth. Edmaier, Bernhard. Jung-Hüttl, Angelika. rev. ed. 2007. (ENG., 240p. (gr. 8-17). 19.95 *(978-0-7148-4679-8(1))* Phaidon Pr., Inc.

Edmondson, Brad. Mr. Frank's Magic School Bus: Rainbow's End Adventure. Edmondson, Frank. 2007. 20p. per. 24.95 *(978-1-4241-8617-4(X))* America Star Bks.

—Mr. Frank's Magic School Bus: Rainbow's End Adventure, 1 vol. Edmondson, Frank. 2010. 20p. 24.95 *(978-1-4512-1042-2(6))* PublishAmerica, Inc.

Edmonson, Tim. Enrique Speaks with His Hands. Fudge, Benjamin. 2008. (ENG.). 32p. (J). (gr. -1-3). 16.95 *(978-0-9800649-3-3(7))* Hilton Publishing Co.

Edmunds, Kate. Dry Bones. (Classic Books with Holes Big Book Ser.). (ENG.). (J). (gr. -1-1). 2009. 16p. *(978-1-84643-210-1(3));* 2007. 16p. pap. *(978-1-84643-108-1(5));* 2007. 14p. bds. *(978-1-84643-112-8(3))* Child's Play International Ltd.

—Dry Bones W/ 2009. (Classic Books with Holes US Soft Cover with CD Ser.). (ENG.). 16p. (J). *(978-1-84643-259-0(6))* Child's Play International Ltd.

Edmunds, Kirstie. Bruno & Lulu's Playground Adventures. Lakin, Patricia. 2014. (ENG.). 80p. (J). (gr. k-2). 16.99 *(978-0-8037-3553-8(7),* Dial) Penguin Publishing Group.

—The Monster Who Lost His Mean. Haber, Tiffany Strelitz. 2012. (ENG.). 40p. (J). (gr. -1-3). 17.99 *(978-0-8050-9375-9(3),* Holt, Henry & Co. Bks. For Young Readers) Holt, Henry & Co.

—So You Want to Be a Rock Star. Vernick, Audrey. 2012. (ENG.). 40p. (J). (gr. -1-3). 16.99 *(978-0-8027-2092-4(7),* 231361) Walker & Co.

Edrington, Greg Q., jt. illus. see Caprio-Scalera, Jill.

Edsall, Steven. The Story of Peabo, 1 vol. Prince-Stokes, Cathy. 2009. 35p. pap. 24.95 *(978-1-61582-732-9(3))* America Star Bks.

Edson, Anharad. Little One... Good Night: A Lullaby from Vermont. Vaughan, Kathryn MadeMann. 2004. (J). per. 19.95 incl. audio compact disk *(978-0-9747447-0-4(0))* Chaser Media LLC.

Eduar, Gilles. Here Comes Doctor Hippo: A Little Hippo Story. London, Jonathan. (Little Hippo Ser.). (ENG.). 32p. (J). (gr. -1-k). 2013. pap. 6.95 *(978-1-62091-595-0(2));* 2012. 15.95 *(978-1-59078-851-6(6))* Boyds Mills Pr.

—Here Comes Firefighter Hippo. London, Jonathan. 2013. (Little Hippo Ser.). (ENG.). 32p. (J). (gr. -1-1). 15.95 *(978-1-59078-968-1(7))* Boyds Mills Pr.

Edward, Aaron. Calvin Can - Be Happy. Edward, Judy. 2012. 32p. pap. *(978-1-4602-0097-1(7))* FriesenPress.

Edward J Russell Elementary School Students. Oliver Bean, Doctors Aren't Mean! Bacon, Joy. 2007. (ENG.). 32p. (J). (gr. 4-7). pap. 8.95 *(978-0-9792371-1-9(4))* Keene Publishing.

Edward, Linda. This Little Piggy. O'Brien, Eileen. Tyler, Jenny, ed. 2004. (Carry-Me Bks.). 16p. (J). 5.95 *(978-0-7945-0125-9(7),* Usborne) EDC Publishing.

Edwards, Cedric. Damaged Goods. Wheeler, Tonika Yvonne. Attaway, Anelda, ed. 2013. 100p. pap. 13.99 *(978-0-9892656-0-7(9))* Jazzy Kitty Greetings Marketing & Publishing Co.

Edwards, Frank. Is the Spaghetti Ready?, 1 vol. Bianchi, John. 2008. (New Reader Ser.). (ENG.). 32p. (J). *(978-1-894323-35-2(1))* Bungalo Bks.

Edwards, Gunvor & Felstead, Cathie. Abracadabra Piano, Bk. 1. Sebba, Jane. (ENG.). 48p. (J). pap. *(978-0-7136-3724-3(2),* 93113, A & C Black) Bloomsbury Publishing Plc.

Edwards, Jeff. The Moon, 1 vol. Oxlade, Chris. 2012. (Astronaut Travel Guides). (ENG.). 48p. (gr. 3-6). lib. bdg. 32.00 *(978-1-4109-4572-3(3),* NA-r) Heinemann-Raintree.

Edwards, Karl. Slow & Steady Wins the Race, Vol. 4260. Williams, Rozanne Lanczak. 2005. (Reading for Fluency Ser.). 16p. (J). pap. 3.49 *(978-1-59198-158-9(1),* 4260) Creative Teaching Pr., Inc.

—You Can't Catch Me. Williams, Rozanne Lanczak. 2005. (Reading for Fluency Ser.). 8p. (J). pap. 3.49 *(978-1-59198-150-3(6),* 4250) Creative Teaching Pr., Inc.

Edwards, Ken. Princess Party Paint Book. Simon-Kerr, Julia. 2005. (My Little Pony Ser.). 32p. (J). 3.99 *(978-0-06-074699-5(8),* HarperFestival) HarperCollins Pubs.

Edwards, Ken, jt. illus. see Middleton, Gayle.

Edwards, Laurie J. & Britt, Joanna. Stakeout. Doerr, Bonnie J. 2011. 310p. pap. 12.99 *(978-1-61603-007-0(0))* Leap Bks.

Edwards, Laurie J., jt. illus. see Britt, Joanna.

Edwards, Linda. Animal Picture Atlas. Maskell, Hazel. 2008. (Atlases Ser.). 48p. (J). 12.99 *(978-0-7945-2083-0(9),* Usborne) EDC Publishing.

—La Biblia para Ninos. Amery, Heather, ed. 2004.Tr. of Children's Bible. (SPA.). 144p. (J). (gr. -1-4). 19.95 *(978-0-7460-3674-7(4))* EDC Publishing.

—Greek Myths for Young Children. Amery, Heather. 2004. (Greek Myths for Young Children Ser.). 128p. (J). (gr. -1-3). lib. bdg. 26.95 *(978-1-58086-261-5(6));* 7.99 *(978-0-7945-0141-9(9),* Usborne) EDC Publishing.

—Little Book of Stories of Jesus. Amery, Heather. 2007. (ENG.). 72p. *(978-0-7460-8492-2(7))* Usborne Publishing, Ltd.

—Stories from Around the World. Amery, Heather. 2004. (Stories for Young Children Ser.). (SPA.). 128p. (J). (gr. -1-3). lib. bdg. 24.95 *(978-1-58086-330-8(2))* EDC Publishing.

—Stories of Dragons. Doherty, Gillian. Milbourne, Anna, ed. 2007. (Stories for Young Children Ser.). 96p. (J). 16.99 *(978-0-7945-1465-5(0),* Usborne) EDC Publishing.

—Stories of Wizards. Doherty, Gillian. 2008. (Stories for Young Children Ser.). 95p. (J). (gr. 1). 16.99 *(978-0-7945-1915-5(6),* Usborne) EDC Publishing.

—Usborne Children's Picture Atlas. Brocklehurst, Ruth. 2004. (Children's Picture Atlas Ser.). 48p. (J). 12.95 *(978-0-7945-0640-7(2),* Usborne) EDC Publishing.

—Usborne Greek Myths Jigsaw Book. Amery, Heather. 2006. (Usborne Jigsaw Bks.). 14p. (J). bds. 14.99 *(978-0-7945-1183-8(X),* Usborne) EDC Publishing.

Edwards, Mark. Colossal Clubs: Activities-Based Curriculum for School-Age Programs. Martinez, Kathleen & Edwards, Sue. 2006. per. 29.95 *(978-0-917505-39-3(5),* School Age Notes) Gryphon Hse., Inc.

Edwards, Mat. How to Draw Amazing Airplanes & Spacecraft, 1 vol. McCurry, Kristen. 2012. (Smithsonian Drawing Bks.). (ENG.). 64p. (gr. 3-4). pap. 7.19 *(978-1-4296-9448-3(3));* 33.32 *(978-1-4296-8749-2(5));* pap. 41.70 *(978-1-4296-9449-0(1))* Capstone Pr., Inc.

—Julius Caesar, 1 vol. Hunter, Nick. 2013. (Hero Journals). (ENG.). 48p. (gr. 4-6). pap. 8.99 *(978-1-4109-5363-6(7))* Heinemann-Raintree.

—Smithsonian Drawing Books. McCurry, Kristen. 2012. (Smithsonian Drawing Bks.). (ENG.). 64p. (gr. 3-4). pap. 83.40 *(978-1-4296-9453-7(X));* pap. 13.90 *(978-1-4296-9452-0(1))* Capstone Pr., Inc.

Edwards, Mat, et al. Smithsonian Drawing Books. McCurry, Kristen. (Smithsonian Drawing Bks.). (ENG.). 64p. (gr. 3-4). 2013. pap. 166.80 *(978-1-62065-732-4(5));* 2013. lib. bdg. 133.28 *(978-1-4296-9942-6(6));* 2012. pap. 27.80 *(978-1-62065-731-7(7))* Capstone Pr., Inc.

Edwards, Michelle. Alef-Bet. Edwards, Michelle. 2009. 32p. (J). pap. 10.95 *(978-1-58838-233-7(8))* NewSouth, Inc.

Edwards, Neil. Dark Avengers: The End Is the Beginning. Parker, Jeff et al. 2013. (ENG.). 192p. (YA). (gr. 8-17). pap. 19.99 *(978-0-7851-6172-1(4))* Marvel Worldwide, Inc.

—Spider-Man: Season One. 2012. (ENG.). 136p. (J). (gr. -1-17). 24.99 *(978-0-7851-5820-2(0))* Marvel Worldwide, Inc.

—Warriors Three: Dog Day Afternoon. 2011. (ENG.). 112p. (YA). (gr. 8-17). pap. 15.99 *(978-0-7851-5224-8(5))* Marvel Worldwide, Inc.

Edwards, Neil & Pierfederici, Mirco. Dark Avengers: Masters of Evil. 2013. (ENG.). 160p. (YA). (gr. 8-17). pap. 14.99 *(978-0-7851-6847-8(8))* Marvel Worldwide, Inc.

Edwards, Nick. Galaxy's Most Wanted. Kloepfer, John. 2014. (Galaxy's Most Wanted Ser.: 1). (ENG.). 224p. (J). (gr. 3-7). 12.99 *(978-0-06-223101-7(4))* HarperCollins Pubs.

—Into the Dorkness. Kloepfer, John. 2015. (Galaxy's Most Wanted Ser.: 2). (ENG.). 256p. (J). (gr. 3-7). 12.99 *(978-0-06-223104-8(9))* HarperCollins Pubs.

Edwards, Paul. It's My Birthday. Haworth, Margaret. 2003. 31p. (J). (gr. -1-3). pap. 10.00 *(978-0-9740313-0-9(5))* Haworth, Margaret.

—The New Kid: Rusty Book. Haworth, Margaret. l.t. ed. 2003. (Books That Help Ser.: Vol. 3). 34p. (J). (gr. k-6). pap. 9.95 *(978-0-9740313-3-0(X))* Haworth, Margaret.

—When Daddy Goes Away: Rusty Books. Haworth, Margaret. l.t. ed. 2003. (Books That Help Ser.: Vol. 2). 34p. (J). (gr. -1-5). pap. 9.95 *(978-0-9740313-1-6(3))* Haworth, Margaret.

Edwards, Rebecca. Revenge. Richardson, Duncan. 2005. 30p. (J). pap. *(978-1-876682-69-9(8))* Post Pressed.

Edwards, Tommy Lee. I Am Superman! Sudduth, Brent. 2006. (Superman Returns Ser.). 24p. (J). (gr. 4-7). pap. 3.99 *(978-0-696-22905-3(6))* Meredith Bks.

Edwards, W M. Booger Boogie. 2007. (Playdate Kids Musical Ser.). 27p. (J). (gr. -1-3). 14.95 incl. audio compact disk *(978-1-933721-13-2(8))* Playdate Kids Publishing.

—Chloe Loses Her Pet. Thiel, Annie. 2007. (Playdate Kids: Let's Be Friends! Ser.). 26p. (J). per. 6.95 *(978-1-933721-21-7(9))* Playdate Kids Publishing.

—Danny's Secret. Thiel, Annie. 2007. (Playdate Kids: Let's Be Friends! Ser.). 27p. (J). (gr. -1-3). per. 6.95 *(978-1-933721-22-4(7))* Playdate Kids Publishing.

—The I Like Me Dance! Friedlander, Tim. 2007. (Playdate Kids Musical Ser.). 27p. (J). (gr. -1-3). 14.95 incl. audio compact disk *(978-1-933721-07-1(3))* Playdate Kids Publishing.

—Island Potty Party. 2007. (Playdate Kids Musical Ser.). 27p. (J). (gr. -1-3). 14.95 incl. audio compact disk *(978-1-933721-15-6(4))* Playdate Kids Publishing.

Edwards, Wallace. You Are the Earth: Know Your World So You Can Help Make It Better. Suzuki, David & Vanderlinden, Kathy. 2nd rev. ed. 2010. (ENG.). 160p. (gr. k-7). pap. 18.95 *(978-1-55365-476-6(5))* Greystone Books Ltd. CAN. Dist: Perseus-PGW.

Edwards, Wallace. Alphabeasts. Edwards, Wallace. 2008. (ENG.). 32p. (J). (gr. -1-3). pap. 9.95 *(978-1-55453-227-8(2))* Kids Can Pr., Ltd. CAN. Dist: Univ. of Toronto Pr.

—The Cat's Pajamas. Edwards, Wallace. 2010. (ENG.). 32p. (J). (gr. -1-4). 18.95 *(978-1-55453-308-4(2))* Kids Can Pr., Ltd. CAN. Dist: Univ. of Toronto Pr.

—The Extinct Files: My Science Project. Edwards, Wallace. (ENG.). 32p. (J). (gr. k-3). 2009. 8.95 *(978-1-55453-386-2(4));* 2006. 17.95 *(978-1-55337-971-3(3))* Kids Can Pr., Ltd. CAN. Dist: Univ. of Toronto Pr.

—Mixed Beasts. Edwards, Wallace. Cox, Kenyon. 2013. (ENG.). 32p. (J). pap. 9.95 *(978-1-77138-035-5(7))* Kids Can Pr., Ltd. CAN. Dist: Univ. of Toronto Pr.

—Monkey Business. Edwards, Wallace. (ENG.). 32p. (J). 2008. pap. 8.95 *(978-1-55453-228-5(0));* 2004. (gr. -1). 18.95 *(978-1-55337-462-6(2))* Kids Can Pr., Ltd. CAN. Dist: Univ. of Toronto Pr.

—The Painted Circus: P. T. Vermin Presents a Mesmerizing Menagerie of Trickery & Illusion Guaranteed to Beguile & Bamboozle the Beholder. Edwards, Wallace. 2007.

E

(ENG.). 32p. (J). 17.95 *(978-1-55337-720-7(6))* Kids Can Pr., Ltd. CAN. Dist: Univ. of Toronto Pr.

Edwards, William M. Cosmos' Blended Family. Thiel, Annie. 2007. (Playdate Kids: Let's Be Friends! Ser.). 27p. (J). (gr. -1-3). per. 6.95 *(978-1-933721-23-1(5))* Playdate Kids Publishing.

—Dakota Gets Lost. Thiel, Annie & Fanning, Tena. 2007. (Playdate Kids: Let's Be Friends! Ser.). 27p. (J). (gr. -1-3). per. 6.95 *(978-1-933721-20-0(0))* Playdate Kids Publishing.

—Danny Is Moving. Thiel, Annie. 2006. (Playdate Kids Ser.). 32p. (J). (gr. -1-3). 14.95 *(978-1-933721-02-6(2))* Playdate Kids Publishing.

Edwards, William M. & Marjoribanks, Karen. Cosmos' Mom & Dad Are Moving Apart. Thiel, Annie. 2006. (Playdate Kids Ser.). 32p. (J). (gr. -1-3). 14.95 *(978-1-933721-04-0(9))* Playdate Kids Publishing.

—Dakota's Mom Goes to the Hospital. Thiel, Annie. 2006. (Playdate Kids Ser.). 32p. (J). (gr. -1-3). 14.95 *(978-1-933721-03-3(0))* Playdate Kids Publishing.

Edwards, William M., jt. illus. see Marjoribanks, Karen.

Edwin, Kimberly. Freddie the Fox & Peter the Cheetah. Ford, Carole S. 30p. (J). (gr. -1). pap. 4.95 *(978-1-891533-03-7(7))* Calvin Partnership, LLC.

—Timothy Turtle & Sammy Scallop. Ford, Carole S. 30p. (J). (gr. -1-k). pap. 4.95 *(978-1-891533-02-0(9))* Calvin Partnership, LLC.

Eeckhout, Emmanuelle. There's No Such Thing As Ghosts! Eeckhout, Emmanuelle. 2008. (ENG.). 32p. (J). (gr. -1-1). 10.99 *(978-1-933605-91-3(X))* Kane Miller.

Effler, Jim. A Home for Panda. Nagda, Ann Whitehead. (Amazing Animal Adventures Ser.). (ENG.). 36p. (J). 2005. (gr. -1-2). 15.95 *(978-1-59249-045-5(X)*, B7102); 2005. (gr. -1-2). pap. 6.95 *(978-1-59249-046-2(8)*, S7102); 2005. (gr. 2-2). 19.95 *(978-1-59249-392-0(0)*, BC7102); 2005. (gr. 2-2). 8.95 *(978-1-59249-393-7(9)*, SC7102); 2003. (gr. -1-3). 2.95 *(978-1-59249-047-9(6)*, S7152) Soundprints.

—A Home for Panda. Nagda, Ann Whitehead. 2003. (ENG.). 36p. (J). (gr. -1-3). 9.95 *(978-1-59249-058-5(1)*, PS7152) Soundprints.

Egan, Caroline, jt. illus. see RH Disney Staff.

Egan, Caroline LaVelle, et al. Movie Theater Vol. 2: Storybook & Movie Projector. Reader's Digest Staff. 2011. (Movie Theater Ser.). (ENG.). 32p. (J). (gr. k-2). 19.99 *(978-0-7944-2198-4(9))* Reader's Digest Assn., Inc., The.

Egan, Caroline LaVelle, jt. illus. see Ho, Winnie.

Egan, Tim. Dodsworth in London. Egan, Tim. 2010. (Dodsworth Book Ser.). (ENG.). 48p. (J). (gr. 2-5). pap. 3.99 *(978-0-547-41440-9(4))* Houghton Mifflin Harcourt Publishing Co.

—Dodsworth in Paris. Egan, Tim. 2010. (Dodsworth Book Ser.). (ENG.). 48p. (J). (gr. 1-4). pap. 3.99 *(978-0-547-33192-8(4))* Houghton Mifflin Harcourt Publishing Co.

—Dodsworth in Tokyo. Egan, Tim. (Green Light Readers Level 3 Ser.). (ENG.). 48p. (J). (gr. 1-4). 2014. pap. 3.99 *(978-0-544-33915-6(0)*, HMH Books For Young Readers); 2013. 14.99 *(978-0-547-87745-7(5))* Houghton Mifflin Harcourt Publishing Co.

Egbert, Corey. The Holy Ghost Is Like a Blanket. Hall, Annalisa. 2014. 12.99 *(978-1-4621-1419-1(9)*, Horizon Pubs.); 2013. (ENG.). 32p. (J). (gr. 3-7). 14.99 *(978-1-4621-1229-6(3))* Cedar Fort, Inc./CFI Distribution.

—I Want to Be Baptized. Hall, Annalisa. 2014. 14.99 *(978-1-4621-1461-0(X))* Cedar Fort, Inc./CFI Distribution.

—One Boy, No Water. Parker, Lehua. 2014. (Niuhi Shark Saga Ser.: 1). (ENG.). 268p. (YA). (gr. 7). pap. 12.99 *(978-1-939967-78-7(3))* Jolly Fish Pr.

Egbert, Corey. Stars, Stockings, & Shepherds. Chabot, Shersta. 2014. 14.99 ***(978-1-4621-1462-7(8)**, Horizon Pubs.) Cedar Fort, Inc./CFI Distribution.

Eger, Caroline Ruth. The Modern Story Book. Wadsworth, Wallace. 2010. (Dover Read & Listen Ser.). (ENG.). 112p. (J). (gr. 1-5). pap. 14.99 *(978-0-486-47844-9(0))* Dover Pubns., Inc.

Egger, Virginie. My Cat Isis. Austen, Catherine. 2011. (ENG.). 32p. (J). (gr. -1-2). 16.95 *(978-1-55453-413-5(5))* Kids Can Pr., Ltd. CAN. Dist: Univ. of Toronto Pr.

Eggers, James, jt. illus. see Bartram, Bob.

Eggleton, Bob. If Dinosaurs Lived in My Town. Plumridge, Marianne. 2013. (ENG.). 56p. (J). (gr. -1-3). 16.95 *(978-1-62636-176-8(2)*, 263176, Sky Pony Pr.) Skyhorse Publishing Co., Inc.

—Years in the Making: The Time Travel Stories of L. Sprague de Camp. de Camp, L. Sprague. Olson, Mark L., ed. 2005. (NESFA's Choice Ser.: 28). 384p. (YA). 25.00 *(978-1-886778-47-7(7)*, NESFA Pr.) New England Science Fiction Assn., Inc.

Egielski, Richard. The End. LaRochelle, David. 2006. (J). 16.99 *(978-0-439-64012-1(1)*, Levine, Arthur A. Bks.) Scholastic, Inc.

—The Fabulous Feud of Gilbert & Sullivan. Winter, Jonah. 2009. (J). pap. *(978-0-439-93051-2(0)*, Levine, Arthur A. Bks.) Scholastic, Inc.

—The Fierce Yellow Pumpkin. Brown, Margaret Wise & Brown. 2003. (ENG.). 32p. (J). (gr. -1-1). 16.99 *(978-0-06-024479-8(8))* HarperCollins Pubs.

—The Fierce Yellow Pumpkin. Brown, Margaret Wise. 2006. (ENG.). 32p. (J). (gr. -1-1). reprint ed. pap. 6.99 *(978-0-06-443534-5(2))* HarperCollins Pubs.

—Gumption! Broach, Elise. 2010. (ENG.). 40p. (J). (gr. k-3). 17.99 *(978-1-4169-1628-4(8)*, Atheneum Bks. for Young Readers) Simon & Schuster Children's Publishing.

—Homework. Yorinks, Arthur. 2009. (ENG.). 32p. (J). (gr. k-3). 16.99 *(978-0-8027-9585-4(4))* Walker & Co.

Egielski, Richard. Itsy Bitsy Spider. Egielski, Richard. 2012. (ENG.). 12p. (J). (gr. -1-1). 19.99 *(978-1-4169-9895-2(0)*, Atheneum Bks. for Young Readers) Simon & Schuster Children's Publishing.

—Saint Francis & the Wolf. Egielski, Richard. 2005. 40p. (J). (gr. 1-3). (ENG.). 15.99 *(978-0-06-623870-8(6))*; lib. bdg. 16.89 *(978-0-06-623871-5(4))* HarperCollins Pubs.

—The Sleepless Little Vampire. Egielski, Richard. 2011. (ENG.). 32p. (J). (gr. -1-3). 16.99 *(978-0-545-14597-8(X)*, Levine, Arthur A. Bks.) Scholastic, Inc.

—Slim & Jim. Egielski, Richard. 2005. 37p. (J). (gr. k-4). reprint ed. 16.00 *(978-0-7567-8936-7(2))* DIANE Publishing Co.

Egitim, Hasan. The All-Merciful Master: The Beautiful Names of God. Ergün, Erol. 2009. 127p. (J). pap. *(978-1-59784-223-5(0))* Tughra Bks.

Eglitis, Anna, jt. illus. see Brim, Warren.

Eguiguren, A. R., jt. illus. see Eguiguren, India J.

Eguiguren, India J. & Eguiguren, A. R. Boris: The Bengal Tiger. Jones, Thomas Rumsey. 2013. 46p. pap. 5.99 *(978-1-883378-81-3(8))* Sun on Earth Bks.

Ehlert, Lois. Chica Chica Bum Bum ABC. Martin, Bill, Jr. & Archambault, John. 2011. (SPA.). 16p. (J). (gr. -1-1). bds. 7.99 *(978-1-4424-2292-6(0)*, Libros Para Ninos) Libros Para Ninos.

—Chicka Chicka 1, 2, 3. Martin, Bill, Jr. & Sampson, Michael. 2014. (Chicka Chicka Book Ser.). (ENG.). 36p. (J). (gr. -1 — 1). bds. 7.99 *(978-1-4814-0056-5(8)*, Little Simon) Little Simon.

—Chicka Chicka 1, 2, 3. Martin, Bill, Jr. & Sampson, Michael. 2004. (Chicka Chicka Book Ser.). (ENG.). 40p. (J). (gr. -1-2). 17.99 *(978-0-689-85881-9(7)*, Simon & Schuster Bks. For Young Readers) Simon & Schuster Bks. For Young Readers.

—Chicka Chicka 1, 2, 3. Martin, Bill, Jr. & Sampson, Michael. 2005. (J). (gr. -1-3). 29.95 *(978-0-439-76677-7(X)*, WHCD669) Weston Woods Studios, Inc.

—Chicka Chicka 1, 2, 3: Lap Edition. Martin, Bill, Jr. & Sampson, Michael. 2013. (Chicka Chicka Book Ser.). (ENG.). 36p. (J). (gr. -1-1). bds. 12.99 *(978-1-4424-6613-5(8)*, Little Simon) Little Simon.

—Chicka Chicka ABC. Martin, Bill, Jr. & Archambault, John. 2009. (Chicka Chicka Book Ser.). (ENG.). 16p. (J). (gr. -1-1). 10.99 *(978-1-4169-8447-4(X)*, Little Simon) Little Simon.

—Chicka Chicka ABC. Archambault, John & Martin, Bill, Jr. 2005. (Chicka Chicka Book Ser.). (ENG.). 16p. (J). (gr. -1 — 1). bds. 9.99 *(978-0-689-87820-6(6)*, Little Simon) Little Simon.

—Chicka Chicka Boom Boom. Martin, Bill, Jr. & Archambault, John. anniv. ed. 2009. (Chicka Chicka Book Ser.). (ENG.). 40p. (J). (gr. -1-3). 17.99 *(978-1-4169-9091-8(7)*, Beach Lane Bks.) Beach Lane Bks.

—Chicka Chicka Boom Boom. Martin, Bill, Jr. et al. 2008. (J). 13.99 *(978-1-59319-935-7(X))* LeapFrog Enterprises, Inc.

—Chicka Chicka Boom Boom. Martin, Bill, Jr. & Archambault, John. (Classic Board Bks.). (ENG.). (J). (gr. -1 — 1). 2012. 36p. bds. 7.99 *(978-1-4424-5070-7(3))*; 2010. 36p. bds. 12.99 *(978-1-4169-9999-7(X))*; 2006. 40p. 10.99 *(978-1-4169-2718-1(2))* Little Simon. (Little Simon).

—Chicka Chicka Box Box! Chicka Chicka Boom Boom; Chicka Chicka 1, 2, 3. Martin, Bill, Jr. et al. ed. 2013. (Chicka Chicka Book Ser.). (ENG.). 80p. (J). (gr. -1-3). 35.99 *(978-1-4814-0223-1(4)*, Beach Lane Bks.) Beach Lane Bks.

—Mice. Fyleman, Rose. 2012. (ENG.). 40p. (J). (gr. -1-k). 16.99 *(978-1-4424-5684-6(1)*, Beach Lane Bks.) Beach Lane Bks.

—Ten Little Caterpillars. Martin, Bill, Jr. 2011. (ENG.). 40p. (J). (gr. -1-3). 17.99 *(978-1-4424-3385-4(X)*, Beach Lane Bks.) Beach Lane Bks.

Ehlert, Lois. Boo to You! Ehlert, Lois. 2009. (ENG.). 42p. (J). (gr. -1-2). 17.99 *(978-1-4169-8625-6(1)*, Beach Lane Bks.) Beach Lane Bks.

—Lots of Spots. Ehlert, Lois. 2010. (ENG.). 40p. (J). (gr. -1-3). 17.99 *(978-1-4424-0289-8(X)*, Beach Lane Bks.) Beach Lane Bks.

—Lots of Spots. Ehlert, Lois. 2014. (Classic Board Bks.). (ENG.). 40p. (J). (gr. -1 — 1). bds. 7.99 *(978-1-4424-8927-1(8)*, Little Simon) Little Simon.

—Planting a Rainbow. Ehlert, Lois. 2003. (ENG.). 32p. (J). (gr. k — 1). bds. 6.95 *(978-0-15-204633-0(X))* Houghton Mifflin Harcourt Publishing Co.

—RRRalph. Ehlert, Lois. 2011. (ENG.). 40p. (J). (gr. -1-1). 17.99 *(978-1-4424-1305-4(0)*, Beach Lane Bks.) Beach Lane Bks.

—The Scraps Book: Notes from a Colorful Life. Ehlert, Lois. 2014. (ENG.). 72p. (J). (gr. k-5). 17.99 *(978-1-4424-3571-1(2))* Simon & Schuster Children's Publishing.

Eichelberger, Jennifer. Monday I Was a Monkey: A "Tale" of Reverence. McClain, Jennie. 2011. (J). *(978-1-60861-243-7(0))* Covenant Communications.

Eichenberg, Fritz. Mistress Masham's Repose. White, T. H. 2004. (New York Review Children's Collection). (ENG.). 260p. (J). (gr. 4-7). 19.95 *(978-1-59017-103-5(9)*, NYR Children's Collection) New York Review of Bks., Inc., The.

Eid, Jean-Paul. The Smelly Story of Hazel the Weasel. Chartrand, Lili. 2009. (Rainy Day Readers Ser.). 32p. (J). (gr. -1-3). 22.60 *(978-1-60754-379-4(6))*; pap. 10.55 *(978-1-60754-380-0(X))* Windmill Bks.

Eid, Jean-Paul & Owlkids Books Inc. Staff. SOS! Titanic! Wishinsky, Frieda. 2010. (Canadian Flyer Adventures Ser.: 14). (ENG.). 96p. (J). (gr. 1-4). pap. 7.95 *(978-1-897349-78-6(5)*, Maple Tree Pr.) Owlkids Bks. Inc. CAN. Dist: Perseus-PGW.

—Stop That Stagecoach! Wishinsky, Frieda. 2009. (Canadian Flyer Adventures Ser.: 13). (ENG.). 96p. (J). (gr. 1-4). pap. 7.95 *(978-1-897349-63-2(7)*, Maple Tree Pr.) Owlkids Bks. Inc. CAN. Dist: Perseus-PGW.

Eimann, Céline. The Sky Dreamer / Le Bateau de Reves. Eimann, Céline, tr. Morgan, Anne. 2011.Tr. of Sky Dreamer. (FRE.). 36p. pap. *(978-1-921869-60-0(7)*, IP Kidz) Interactive Pubns. Pty, Ltd.

Einarson, Earl. The Moccasins. Einarson, Earl. ed. 2004. (Moccasins Ser.). (ENG.). 16p. pap. 7.95 *(978-1-894778-14-5(6))* Theytus Bks., Ltd. CAN. Dist: Univ. of Toronto Pr.

Einfeld, Aaron. Neverdark. Einfeld, C. 2012. (ENG.). 260p. pap. 9.99 *(978-1-4680-5834-5(7))* CreateSpace Independent Publishing Platform.

Einstein, Susan. Baseball Treasures. Wong, Stephen. 2007. 58p. (J). (gr. 4-7). lib. bdg. 17.89 *(978-0-06-114473-8(8))* HarperCollins Pubs.

Eisby, Lizzy. Pini the Pitcher: A Story for Hanukkah. Osterbach, Batya Kirshenbaum. 2005. 32p. (J). (gr. 1-4). 16.95 *(978-1-932687-50-7(5)*, Devora Publishing) Simcha Media Group.

Eiseman, Joan. Ricardo & the Fisherman. Eiseman, Joan. 2007. 32p. (J). per. 12.95 *(978-0-9786745-4-0(5))* Marble Hse. Editions.

Eisen, Nancy. Runaway Piggy Bank. Peck, Judith. 2003. 32p. (J). pap. 13.99 *(978-0-9746119-1-4(3))* Imagination Arts Pubns.

Eisenberg, Serge. The Ladybug & Me. Soler, Michael. 2007. 24p. (J). per. 8.99 *(978-0-9795469-0-7(7))* Soler, Michael.

Eisenfeld, Candice. The Crimson Fish. Robbins, Neal. 58p. (Orig.). (J). (gr. 1-18). pap. 4.00 *(978-1-884993-02-2(8))* Koldarana Pubns.

Eisenring, Rahel Nicole. Kiki. Schuler, Christoph. 2009. (ENG.). 32p. (J). (gr. -1-3). 14.95 *(978-0-7358-2202-3(6))* North-South Bks., Inc.

Eisner, Will. Cities of the Fantastic: Brusel. Melville, Herman. 2003. (Cities of the Fantastic Ser.). (ENG.). 120p. 19.95 *(978-1-56163-291-6(0))* NBM Publishing Co.

—Moby Dick. Melville, Herman. 2003. (ENG.). 32p. (gr. 4-7). 15.95 *(978-1-56163-293-0(7))* NBM Publishing Co.

Eisner, Will. The Princess & the Frog. Eisner, Will. Eisner, Will. 2003. (ENG.). 30p. (J). (gr. k-4). 15.95 *(978-1-56163-244-2(9))* NBM Publishing Co.

Eisner, Will. Sundiata: A Legend of Africa. Eisner, Will, retold by. 2003. (ENG.). 32p. (gr. k-3). 15.95 *(978-1-56163-332-6(1))* NBM Publishing Co.

Eitan (tchernov), Ora. Hanna's Sabbath Dress. Sschweiger-dmiel, Izhak. 2012. (ENG.). 32p. (J). (gr. -1-3). 16.99 *(978-1-4424-7439-0(4)*, Simon & Schuster Bks. For Young Readers) Simon & Schuster Bks. For Young Readers.

Eitzen, Allan. The Christmas Surprise. Moore, Ruth Nulton. 2007. 160p. (gr. 4-7). pap. 18.00 *(978-1-55635-418-2(5)*, Resource Pubns.(OR)) Wipf & Stock Pubs.

—The Clubhouse. Suen, Anastasia. 2003. (Penguin Young Readers, Level 3 Ser.). (ENG.). 32p. (J). (gr. 1-3). mass mkt. 3.99 *(978-0-14-250054-5(2)*, Puffin) Penguin Publishing Group.

—Costa Rica ABCs: A Book about the People & Places of Costa Rica, 1 vol. Cooper, Sharon Katz. 2007. (Country ABCs Ser.). (ENG.). 32p. (gr. k-5). lib. bdg. 27.32 *(978-1-4048-2249-8(6)*, Nonfiction Picture Bks.) Picture Window Bks.

Eitzen, Allan. Deadly Snakes. McCourt, Lisa. ***(978-0-439-65544-6(7)***, Scholastic) Scholastic, Inc.

Eitzen, Allan. Key to the Prison. Vernon, Louise A. 2nd ed. (Louise A. Vernon Ser.). (ENG.). (YA). (gr. 4-9). 2007. 144p. pap. 8.99 *(978-0-8361-1813-1(8))*; 2003. 146p. pap. 8.99 *(978-0-8361-1698-4(4))* Herald Pr.

—Loose Tooth. Suen, Anastasia. 2004. 28p. (gr. -1-3). 14.00 *(978-0-7569-1955-9(X))* Perfection Learning Corp.

—Tara's Flight. Eitzen, Ruth. 2008. (ENG.). 32p. (J). (gr. -1-4). 16.95 *(978-1-59078-563-8(0))* Boyds Mills Pr.

—Verdadero Cuento de Navidad. Navillus, Nell. Alvarez, Lourdes, tr. 2005. (SPA.). 28p. (J). 12.95 *(978-1-58173-250-4(3))* Sweetwater Pr.

Eklund, Håkan. My Unique Family: With JayJay & Totte. Cadeau, Michelle. Lileng, Kimberly, ed. 2011. (ENG.). 42p. pap. 9.99 *(978-1-4609-2359-7(6))* CreateSpace Independent Publishing Platform.

Ekmanis, Rena. Hawaii's Animals Do the Most Amazing Things! Coste, Marion. 2014. 47p. (J). *(978-0-8248-3962-8(5))* Univ. of Hawaii Pr.

Eko-Burgess, Carrie. The Construction Crew. Meltzer, Lynn. 2011. (ENG.). 40p. (J). (gr. -1-k). 14.99 *(978-0-8050-8884-7(9)*, Holt, Henry & Co. Bks. For Young Readers) Holt, Henry & Co.

El Fisgsn. El Profesor Ziper y la Fabulosa Guitarra Electrica. Villoro, Juan. 2005. (Infantil Ser.). (SPA.). 96p. (J). (gr. 5-8). pap. 9.95 *(978-968-19-0206-3(8))* Santillana USA Publishing Co., Inc.

El Wakil, Mohamed. The Last Night of Ramadan. Hamed, Maissa. 2007. (J). (gr. -1-3). *(978-0-88010-586-6(0)*, Bell Pond Bks.) SteinerBooks, Inc.

Elam, Brock. Naughty Nello & the Sleds. Puccinelli, Joanne. 2012. 34p. (J). pap. 12.95 *(978-1-938707-00-1(1))* Stoneydale Pr. Publishing Co.

Elden, Christian. Petunia Pepper's Picture Day. Breisacher, Cathy. 2010. 32p. (J). 14.99 *(978-1-59317-397-5(0))* Warner Pr. Pubs.

Elder, Harold. The Green Bay Area in History & Legend. Foley, Betsy, ed. 2004. xiii, 322p. 29.95 *(978-0-9641499-9-1(0))* Brown County Historical Society.

Elder, Jennifer & Thomas, Marc. Autistic Planet. Elder, Jennifer. 2007. (ENG.). 48p. (J). (gr. -1-k). *(978-1-84310-842-9(9))* Kingsley, Jessica Ltd.

—Different Like Me: My Book of Autism Heroes. Elder, Jennifer. 2005. (ENG.). 48p. *(978-1-84310-815-3(1))* Kingsley, Jessica Ltd.

Eldredge, Ernie. Bubba the Redneck Reindeer. Sullivan, E. J. 2007. 32p. (J). (gr. 4-7). 12.95 *(978-1-60261-008-8(8))* Cliff Road Bks.

—F Is for Florida. Sullivan, E. J. 2006. (State Alphabet Bks.). 24p. (J). *(978-1-58173-525-3(1))* Sweetwater Pr.

—How Santa Got His Elves. Sullivan, E. J. 2006. (J). (gr. -1-3). 9.95 *(978-1-58173-308-2(9))* Sweetwater Pr.

—A Is for Alabama. Sullivan, E. J. 2006. (State Alphabet Bks.). 24p. (J). *(978-1-58173-523-9(5))* Sweetwater Pr.

—N Is for North Carolina. Sullivan, E. J. 2007. (State Alphabet Bks.). 20p. *(978-1-58173-625-0(8))* Sweetwater Pr.

—The North Carolina Night Before Christmas. Sullivan, Ellen. 2006. (J). *(978-1-60261-163-4(7))* Sweetwater Pr.

—S Is for South Carolina. Sullivan, E. J. 2007. (State Alphabet Bks.). 20p. *(978-1-58173-626-7(6))* Sweetwater Pr.

—V Is for Virginia. Sullivan, E. J. 2006. 24p. (J). lib. bdg. *(978-1-58173-526-0(X))* Sweetwater Pr.

Eldredge, Larry. The Night Before Christmas. Moore, Clement C. 2006. (Night Before Christmas Ser.). 32p. 9.95 *(978-1-58173-306-8(2))*; 26p. bds. 9.95 *(978-1-58173-300-6(3))* Sweetwater Pr.

—La Nochebuena, 1. Moore, Clement C. Alvarez, Lourdes, tr. 2005.Tr. of Twas the Night Before Christmas. (SPA.). 28p. (J). bds. 12.95 *(978-1-58173-257-3(0))* Sweetwater Pr.

—The Tennessee Night Before Christmas. Sullivan, E. J. 2005. (Night Before Christmas Ser.). (J). (gr. -1-3). 12.95 *(978-1-58173-395-2(X))* Sweetwater Pr.

Eldridge, Crystal. When My Mommy Cries: A Story to Help Families Cope with Sadness (Book with CD) LaPoint, Crystal Godfrey. 2012. (ENG.). 32p. (J). (gr. k-6). pap. 19.99 *(978-1-4525-4241-6(4)*, Balboa Pr.) Author Solutions, Inc.

Eldridge, Jim. Atlantis & Other Lost Cities. Shone, Rob. 2006. (Graphic Mysteries Ser.). (ENG.). 48p. (YA). (gr. 5-8). lib. bdg. 31.95 *(978-1-4042-0794-3(5))* Rosen Publishing Group, Inc., The.

—Who Was Steve Irwin? Anastasio, Dina. 2015. (Who Was... ? Ser.). (ENG.). 112p. (J). (gr. 3-7). 5.99 *(978-0-448-48638-7(8)*, Grosset & Dunlap) Penguin Publishing Group.

Eldridge, Jim & Harrison, Nancy. Who Was Sitting Bull? Spinner, Stephanie. 2014. (Who Was... ? Ser.). (ENG.). 112p. (J). (gr. 3-7). 4.99 *(978-0-448-47965-1(6)*, Grosset & Dunlap) Penguin Publishing Group.

Eldridge, Les & Casey, James. Santa's Cat. Eldridge, Les. 2003. 24p. (J). *(978-1-877338-03-8(6))* Steele Roberts Aotearoa Ltd.

Eldridge, Marion. Mommy & Daddy Are Always Supposed to Say Yes — Aren't They? Rothenberg, B. Annye. 2007. 40p. (J). pap. 9.95 *(978-0-9790420-0-3(3))* Perfecting Parenting Pr.

—Shante Keys & the New Year's Peas. Piernas-Davenport, Gail. 2007. (ENG.). 32p. (J). (gr. k-4). lib. bdg. 16.99 *(978-0-8075-7330-3(2))* Whitman, Albert & Co.

—The Sparrow's Easter Song. Adams, Michelle Medlock. (ENG.). 32p. (J). 2009. pap. 7.99 *(978-0-8249-5608-0(7)*, Ideals Children's Bks.); 2003. 14.95 *(978-0-8249-5470-3(X))* Ideals Pubns.

Eldridge-Murray, Lauren. Twevven & the Horrible Big Bigger Biggest Baby Burp. Burns, Ian. 2012. 52p. pap. *(978-0-9806606-5-4(3))* Greybold Investing Pty Ltd.

Elejalde, Eliana. The Adventures of Valeria Veterinarian: Las Aventuras de Valeria Veterinaria, 1. Graziani, Maria. I.t. ed. 2004. (SPA.). 23p. (J). 7.00 *(978-0-9762361-0-8(9))* Ed. Acespanish S.A.C.- Lima, Peru.

—A Black Cat on Halloween: Un Gato Negro en Dia de Brujas. Graziani, Maria. I.t. ed. 2004. (SPA.). 23p. (J). 7.00 *(978-0-9762361-1-5(7))* Ed. Acespanish S.A.C.- Lima, Peru.

Elena, Horacio. El Superzorro. Dahl, Roald. 2003.Tr. of Fantastic Mr Fox. (SPA.). 96p. (J). (gr. 5-8). pap. 9.95 *(978-968-19-0719-8(1))* Santillana USA Publishing Co., Inc.

Elena, Horacio. Experimentos Sencillos con la Luz y el Sonido. Elena, Horacio, tr. Vecchione, Glen. 2004. (Juego de la Ciencia Ser.). (SPA.). 124p. 10.99 *(978-84-9754-043-6(3)*, 87814) Ediciones Oniro S.A. ESP. Dist: Lectorum Pubns., Inc.

Eleven. Spirit Comes to Earth: Renewing Your Heart's Mission. Eleven. 2005. 128p. (YA). per. 13.95 *(978-0-9743540-0-2(7)*, By title) Peace Love Karma Publishing.

Elfezzani, Thierry. Six Chicks. Branford, Henrietta. 2004. (ENG.). 32p. (J). (gr. k-k). pap. 8.99 *(978-0-00-664767-6(7)*, HarperCollins Children's Bks.) HarperCollins Pubs. Ltd. GBR. Dist: Independent Pubs. Group.

Elgin, Kathleen. In the Steps of the Great American Entomologist. Pallister, John C. 2014. (ENG.). 128p. (J). (gr. 2-6). pap. 11.95 *(978-1-59077-364-2(0))* Evans, M. & Co., Inc.

Eliopoulos, Chris. Bun, Onion, Burger. Mandel, Peter. 2010. (ENG.). 40p. (J). (gr. -1-1). bds. 12.99 *(978-1-4169-2466-1(3)*, Simon & Schuster Bks. For Young Readers) Simon & Schuster Bks. For Young Readers.

—Chameleon Cage Match! Lemke, Donald B. 2013. (Lucha Lizards Ser.). (ENG.). 48p. (gr. 1-3). pap. 5.95 *(978-1-4342-3874-0(1))*; lib. bdg. 22.65 *(978-1-4342-3285-4(9))* Stone Arch Bks.

—Cow Boy: A Boy & His Horse. Cosby, Nate. 2012. (Cow Boy Ser.: 1). (ENG.). 96p. (J). (gr. 2). 19.95 *(978-1-936393-67-1(0))* Boom Entertainment, Inc.

Eliopoulos, Chris. Does a Great Job, 1 vol. Eliopoulos, Chris. 2013. (Mr. Puzzle Ser.). (ENG.). 40p. (gr. 1-3). lib. bdg. 22.65 *(978-1-4342-6025-3(9))* Stone Arch Bks.

—Mr. Puzzle. Eliopoulos, Chris. 2013. (Mr. Puzzle Ser.). (ENG.). 40p. (gr. 1-3). 90.60 *(978-1-4342-6347-6(9))* Stone Arch Bks.

—Mr. Puzzle Super Collection!, 1 vol. Eliopoulos, Chris. 2013. (Mr. Puzzle Ser.). (ENG.). 128p. (gr. 3-6). pap. 7.95 *(978-1-62370-035-5(3))* Capstone Young Readers.

—No Instructions Needed, 1 vol. Eliopoulos, Chris. 2013. (Mr. Puzzle Ser.). (ENG.). 40p. (gr. 1-3). lib. bdg. 22.65 *(978-1-4342-6026-0(7))* Stone Arch Bks.

—A Perfect Fit, 1 vol. Eliopoulos, Chris. 2013. (Mr. Puzzle Ser.). (ENG.). 40p. (gr. 1-3). lib. bdg. 22.65 *(978-1-4342-6024-6(0))* Stone Arch Bks.

—Piece by Piece, 1 vol. Eliopoulos, Chris. 2013. (Mr. Puzzle Ser.). (ENG.). 40p. (gr. 1-3). lib. bdg. 22.65 *(978-1-4342-6027-7(5))* Stone Arch Bks.

Eliopoulos, Christopher. I Am Abraham Lincoln. Meltzer, Brad. 2014. (Ordinary People Change World Ser.). (ENG.). 40p. (J). (gr. k-3). 12.99 *(978-0-8037-4083-9(2)*, Dial) Penguin Publishing Group.

—I Am Albert Einstein. Meltzer, Brad. 2014. (Ordinary People Change the World Ser.). (ENG.). 40p. (J). (gr. k-3). 12.99 *(978-0-8037-4084-6(0)*, Dial) Penguin Publishing Group.

—I Am Amelia Earhart. Meltzer, Brad. 2014. (Ordinary People Change World Ser.). (ENG.). 40p. (J). (gr. k-3). 12.99 *(978-0-8037-4082-2(4)*, Dial) Penguin Publishing Group.

Eliopoulos, Christopher. I Am Helen Keller. Meltzer, Brad. 2015. (Ordinary People Change the World Ser.). (ENG.). 40p. (J). (gr. k-3). 12.99 (978-0-525-42851-0(8), Dial) Penguin Publishing Group.
Eliopoulos, Christopher. I Am Jackie Robinson. Meltzer, Brad. 2015. (Ordinary People Change the World Ser.). (ENG.). 40p. (J). (gr. k-3). 12.99 (978-0-8037-4086-0(7), Dial) Penguin Publishing Group.
—I Am Lucille Ball. Meltzer, Brad. 2015. (Ordinary People Change the World Ser.). (ENG.). 40p. (J). (gr. k-3). 12.99 (978-0-525-42855-8(0), Dial) Penguin Publishing Group.
—I Am Rosa Parks. Meltzer, Brad. 2014. (Ordinary People Change World Ser.). (ENG.). 40p. (J). (gr. -1-k). 12.99 (978-0-8037-4085-3(9), Dial) Penguin Publishing Group.
Eliseev, Sergey. My Princess Bible. Holmes, Andy. 2010. (ENG.). 66p. (J). bds. 12.99 (978-1-4143-3324-3(2)) Tyndale Hse. Pubs.
—Princess Stories: Real Bible Stories of God's Princesses. Larsen, Carolyn. 2011. (ENG.). 128p. (J). 14.99 (978-1-4143-4811-7(8), Tyndale Kids) Tyndale Hse. Pubs.
Elizabeth Mobley. My First Ride with Isaiah. Cooper, Wendy. 2006. 18p. (J). 11.95 (978-0-9772964-8-4(2)) Kingdom Publishing Group, Inc.
Elizalde, Marcelo. Harry's Hats. Tompert, Ann. 2004. (Rookie Readers Ser.). 31p. (J). 19.50 (978-0-516-23613-1(X), Children's Pr.) Scholastic Library Publishing.
—The Space Program. Metzger, Joanna. 2006. 142p. (J). (978-1-59336-695-7(7)) Mondo Publishing.
Elkerton, Andy. ABC. Watt, Fiona. 2009. (Luxury Touchy-Feely Board Bks). 10p. (J). (gr. -1). bds. 15.99 (978-0-7945-2094-6(4), Usborne) EDC Publishing.
—The Dinosaur Who Lost His Roar. Punter, Russell. 2007. (Usborne First Reading: Level 3 Ser.). 48p. (J). 8.99 (978-0-7945-1547-8(9), Usborne) EDC Publishing.
—Ella Power & the Sun Puppies: A Power Families Adventure. Moore, Suse. 2011. (ENG.). 40p. (J). 17.99 (978-0-9837863-2-0(1)) Jack Hook Publishing.
—I Can Hear!, 1 vol. John, Louise. 2013. (Start Reading Ser.). (ENG.). 24p. (gr. k-1). pap. 6.99 (978-1-4765-3199-1(4)); pap. 41.94 (978-1-4765-3219-6(2)) Capstone Pr., Inc.
—Jungle. Watt, Fiona. 2009. (Luxury Touchy-Feely Board Bks). 10p. (J). (gr. -1). bds. 15.99 (978-0-7945-2433-3(8), Usborne) EDC Publishing.
—Let's Go to the Zoo!/Vamos Al Zoologico! Rosa-Mendoza, Gladys. 2007. (English Spanish Foundations Ser.). (ENG & SPA.). 20p. (J). (gr. -1-k). bds. 6.95 (978-1-931398-20-6(8)) Me+Mi Publishing.
—My Chair. John, Louise. 2013. (Start Reading Ser.). (ENG.). 24p. (gr. k-1). pap. 41.94 (978-1-4765-3225-7(7)); pap. 6.99 (978-1-4765-3200-4(1)) Capstone Pr., Inc.
—My Mom Can't See. John, Louise. 2013. (Start Reading Ser.). (ENG.). 24p. (gr. k-1). pap. 41.94 (978-1-4765-3226-4(5)); pap. 6.99 (978-1-4765-3201-1(X)) Capstone Pr., Inc.
—Small, 1 vol. John, Louise. 2013. (Start Reading Ser.). (ENG.). 24p. (gr. k-1). pap. 6.99 (978-1-4765-3202-8(8)); pap. 41.94 (978-1-4765-3231-8(1)) Capstone Pr., Inc.
—Stinky! Bryant, Ann. 2014. (ENG.). 32p. (J). (978-0-7787-1289-3(3)) Crabtree Publishing Co.
Elkorek, Alexander. The Forgotten Daughter. Snedeker, Caroline Dale. 2005. 206p. (J). per. 14.95 (978-0-9667067-6-5(5)) American Home-School Publishing, LLC.
—The Spartan. Snedeker, Caroline Dale. 2005. (YA). per. 15.95 (978-0-9667067-8-9(1)) American Home-School Publishing, LLC.
—Twelve Bright Trumpets. 2004. 198p. (J). per. 14.95 (978-0-9667067-5-8(7)) American Home-School Publishing, LLC.
Ella, Peter Leo. Isiumanu & Manubada. Baia, Edward. 2013. 30p. pap. (978-9980-86-493-2(1)) University of Papua New Guinea Press.
Ella, Peter Leo. Class Party on the Big Yellow School Bus. Ella, Peter Leo. 2013. 28p. pap. (978-9980-86-513-7(X)) University of Papua New Guinea Press.
Ella, Peter Leo, jt. illus. see Mape, Michael.
Ellams, Victoria. Grumpy Ted: The Teds Volume One. Whitley-Kinzett, Sara. 2009. 16p. pap. 10.65 (978-1-4251-0051-3(1)) Trafford Publishing.
Ellenbogen, Keith. The Octopus Scientists. Montgomery, Sy. 2015. (Scientists in the Field Ser.). (ENG.). 80p. (J). (gr. 5-7). 18.99 (978-0-544-23270-9(4), HMH Books For Young Readers) Houghton Mifflin Harcourt Publishing Co.
Eller, Jerod R. My Grandfather's Farm. West, Stephen Earl. 2011. 20p. pap. 24.95 (978-1-4560-6628-4(5)) America Star Bks.
Eller, Sydney. Where Do Socks Go? McCord, Joseph Lennon. 2012. 32p. pap. 24.95 (978-1-4626-6624-9(8)) America Star Bks.
Ellery, Amanda, jt. illus. see Ellery, Tom.
Ellery, Tom. If I Had a Dragon. Ellery, Amanda. 2006. (ENG.). 40p. (J). (gr. -1-3). 17.99 (978-1-4169-0924-8(9), Simon & Schuster Bks. For Young Readers) Simon & Schuster Bks. For Young Readers.
—If I Were a Jungle Animal. Ellery, Amanda. 2009. (ENG.). 40p. (J). (gr. -1-3). 17.99 (978-1-4169-3778-4(1), Simon & Schuster Bks. For Young Readers) Simon & Schuster Bks. For Young Readers.
Ellery, Tom & Ellery, Amanda. If I Had a Dragon/Si Yo Tuviera un Dragon. Mlawer, Teresa. 2006. (ENG & SPA.). (J). (gr. -1-3). per. 3.99 (978-1-933032-17-7(0)); 32p. (gr. 5-6). 12.99 (978-1-933032-16-0(2)) Lectorum Pubns., Inc.
Ellie, Colton. The Lullabible Storybook. Elkins, Stephen. 2006. (Lulla-Bible Ser.). 37p. (J). (gr. -1). 14.99 incl. audio compact disk (978-0-8054-4185-7(9)) B&H Publishing Group.
Ellingsworth, Colleen. Sam's Harvest Party, 1 vol. Farrell, Connie. 2009. 29p. pap. 24.95 (978-1-60813-937-8(9)) America Star Bks.
Elliot, David. Doomwyte. Jacques, Brian. 2011. (Redwall Ser.). (ENG.). 384p. (J). (gr. 5-18). 8.99 (978-0-14-241853-6(6), Puffin) Penguin Publishing Group.
—High Rhulain. Jacques, Brian. (Redwall Ser.). (ENG.). 352p. (J). (gr. 5-18). 2008. 8.99 (978-0-14-240938-1(3), Puffin); 2005. 23.99 (978-0-399-24208-3(2), Philomel) Penguin Publishing Group.
—High Rhulain. Jacques, Brian. 2007. (Redwall Ser.). 320p. (gr. 3-7). 18.00 (978-0-7569-7763-4(0)) Perfection Learning Corp.
—Loamhedge. Jacques, Brian. 2005. (Redwall Ser.). (ENG.). 432p. (J). (gr. 5-5). 8.99 (978-0-14-240377-8(6), Puffin) Penguin Publishing Group.
—Rakkety Tam. Jacques, Brian. 2006. (Redwall Ser.). (ENG.). 384p. (J). (gr. 5-18). 8.99 (978-0-14-240683-0(X), Puffin) Penguin Publishing Group.
—The Sable Quean, 21 vols. Jacques, Brian. 2010. (Redwall Ser.: 21). (ENG.). 448p. (J). (gr. 5-18). 23.99 (978-0-399-25164-1(2), Philomel) Penguin Publishing Group.
—The Sable Quean. Jacques, Brian. ed. 2012. (Redwall Ser.: 21). lib. bdg. 19.65 (978-0-606-23646-1(5), Turtleback) Turtleback Bks.
—The Smell of Powder: A History of Duelling in New Zealand. Kerr, Donald. 2006. 160p. pap. (978-1-86941-813-7(1)) Random Hse. New Zealand.
Elliot, David. Henry's Map. Elliot, David. 2013. (ENG.). 40p. (J). (gr. -1-3). 16.99 (978-0-399-16072-1(8), Philomel) Penguin Publishing Group.
—Henry's Stars. Elliot, David. 2015. (ENG.). 40p. (J). (gr. k-3). 16.99 (978-0-399-17116-1(9)) Penguin Publishing Group.
Elliot, David & Curless, Allan. Triss. Jacques, Brian. 2004. (Redwall Ser.). (ENG.). 400p. (J). (gr. 5-7). pap. 8.99 (978-0-14-240248-1(6), Puffin) Penguin Publishing Group.
Elliot, David & Schoenherr, Ian. The Angel's Command. Jacques, Brian. 2005. (ENG.). 384p. (J). (gr. 3-7). 7.99 (978-0-14-240285-6(0), Puffin) Penguin Publishing Group.
Elliot, Gertrude. Two Little Gardeners. Hurd, Edith Thacher & Brown, Margaret Wise. 2006. (Little Golden Book Ser.). (ENG.). 24p. (J). (gr. -1-2). 3.99 (978-0-375-83529-2(6), Golden Bks.) Random Hse. Children's Bks.
Elliot, Lee, photos by. I Am Beautiful, for All the Children of the World, 1 vol. Brown, Ayanna. 2010. 20p. pap. 24.95 (978-1-4489-8112-0(3)) PublishAmerica, Inc.
Elliot, Mark. I Am Helen Keller. Norwich, Grace. 2012. (I Am Ser.). (ENG.). 128p. (J). (gr. 3-7). pap. 5.99 (978-0-545-44779-9(8), Scholastic Paperbacks) Scholastic, Inc.
—Yukon: Sled Dog, 0 vols. Presnall, Judith Janda. 2013. (ENG.). 32p. (J). (gr. 1-8). 17.99 (978-1-4778-1731-5(X), 9781477817315, Amazon Children's Publishing) Amazon Publishing.
Elliot, Rebecca. Hens Don't Crow! Benjamin, A. H. 2012. (Storytime Ser.). (ENG.). 24p. (J). (gr. -1-1). 15.99 (978-1-60992-233-7(6)) QEB Publishing Inc.
—The Last Tiger. Elliott, Rebecca. 2012. (ENG.). 32p. (J). (gr. k-2). 14.99 (978-0-7459-6384-6(6)) Lion Hudson PLC GBR. Dist: Independent Pubs. Group.
—My Daddy. Hubery, Julia. 2014. (J). (978-1-4351-5507-7(6)) Barnes & Noble, Inc.
Elliott, David. High Rhulain, 18 vols. Jacques, Brian. 2007. (Redwall Ser.: 18). (ENG.). 336p. (gr. 12-18). 7.99 (978-0-441-01436-1(4), Ace Bks.) Penguin Publishing Group.
Elliott, Jeff. The Secret Inside. Gatz, Krissandra. 2009. 34p. (J). (gr. 4-7). pap. 7.99 (978-1-60696-300-5(7)) Tate Publishing & Enterprises, LLC.
Elliott, John. Pope Pius XII: Bilingual Coloring Book. Marchione, Margherita. 2004. (SPA & ENG.). 32p. 1.00 (978-0-8091-6721-0(2), 6721-2) Paulist Pr.
Elliott, Joyce L. Heroes Were Made On 9/11, 1 vol. Rodriguez, Cindy L. 2010. 26p. 24.95 (978-1-4489-6070-5(3)) PublishAmerica, Inc.
Elliott, Julia. Where Did God Come From? Elliott, Julia. 2005. (J). 15.95 (978-0-9764129-0-8(X)) Rain Tree Bks.
Elliott, Luke. Jeffrey's Great Day. Henkel, Pat. 2012. 16p. pap. 24.95 (978-1-4626-7993-5(5)) America Star Bks.
Elliott, Mark. About Average. Clements, Andrew. (ENG.). (J). (gr. 3-7). 2014. 144p. pap. 6.99 (978-1-4169-9725-2(3)); 2012. 128p. 16.99 (978-1-4169-9724-5(5)) Simon & Schuster Children's Publishing. (Atheneum Bks. for Young Readers).
—A Day at Monticello. Chew, Elizabeth V. 2014. (ENG.). 56p. (J). (gr. 3-7). 18.95 (978-1-4197-0541-0(5), Abrams Bks. for Young Readers) Abrams.
—Dexter the Tough. Haddix, Margaret Peterson. 2008. (ENG.). 144p. (J). (gr. 2-5). pap. 6.99 (978-1-4169-1170-8(7)); 2007. 141p. pap. 7.99 (978-0-15-377020-3(1)); 2007. (ENG.). 144p. (J). (gr. 2-5). 17.99 (978-1-4169-1159-3(6)) Simon & Schuster Bks. For Young Readers. (Simon & Schuster Bks. For Young Readers).
—Extra Credit. Clements, Andrew. (ENG.). (J). (gr. 3-7). 2011. 224p. pap. 6.99 (978-1-4169-4931-2(3)); 2009. 160p. 16.99 (978-1-4169-4929-9(1)) Simon & Schuster Children's Publishing. (Atheneum Bks. for Young Readers).
—Grandpa Has a Great Big Face. Hanson, Warren. 2006. 32p. (J). (gr. -1-3). 17.89 (978-0-06-078776-9(7), Geringer, Laura Book) HarperCollins Pubs.
—Little Joe. Wallace, Sandra Neil. (ENG.). 192p. (J). (gr. 3-7). 2011. 6.99 (978-0-375-85450-7(9), Yearling); 2010. 15.99 (978-0-375-86097-3(5), Knopf Bks. for Young Readers) Random Hse. Children's Bks.
—Little Star. DeStefano, Anthony. 2013. 36p. (J). 14.99 (978-0-7369-5859-2(2)) Harvest Hse. Pubs.
—Lost & Found. Clements, Andrew. (ENG.). (J). (gr. 3-7). 2010. 192p. pap. 6.99 (978-1-4169-0986-6(9)); 2008. 160p. 16.99 (978-1-4169-0985-9(0)) Simon & Schuster Children's Publishing. (Atheneum Bks. for Young Readers).
—No Talking. Clements, Andrew. (ENG.). 160p. (J). (gr. 3-7). 2009. pap. 7.99 (978-1-4169-0984-2(2)); 2007. 17.99 (978-1-4169-0983-5(4)) Simon & Schuster Children's Publishing. (Atheneum Bks. for Young Readers).
—No Talking. Clements, Andrew. l.t. ed. 2007. (Literacy Bridge Middle Reader Ser.). 155p. (J). (gr. 3-7). 23.95 (978-1-4104-0294-3(0)) Thorndike Pr.
—The Princess Tales, No. 2. Levine, Gail Carson. 2004. (Princess Tales Ser.). (ENG.). 256p. (J). (gr. 2-7). pap. 7.99 (978-0-06-056043-0(6)) HarperCollins Pubs.
—Room One: A Mystery or Two. Clements, Andrew. 2008. (ENG.). 192p. (J). (gr. 3-7). pap. 6.99 (978-0-689-86687-6(9), Atheneum Bks. for Young Readers) Simon & Schuster Children's Publishing.
—Troublemaker. Clements, Andrew. (ENG.). (J). (gr. 3-7). 2013. 176p. pap. 6.99 (978-1-4169-4932-9(1)); 2011. 160p. lib. bdg. 16.99 (978-1-4169-4930-5(5)) Simon & Schuster Children's Publishing. (Atheneum Bks. for Young Readers).
—What Sank the World's Biggest Ship? And Other Questions About . . . The Titanic. Carson, Mary Kay. 2012. (Good Question! Ser.). (ENG.). 32p. (J). 12.95 (978-1-4027-9627-2(7)) Sterling Publishing Co., Inc.
—What Sank the World's Biggest Ship? And Other Questions About... The Titanic. Carson, Mary Kay. 2012. (Good Question! Ser.). (ENG.). 32p. (J). pap. 5.95 (978-1-4027-8733-1(2)) Sterling Publishing Co., Inc.
—When Jackie & Hank Met, 0 vols. Fishman, Cathy Goldberg. 2012. (ENG.). 40p. (J). (gr. 2-5). 17.99 (978-0-7614-6140-1(X), 9780761461401, Amazon Children's Publishing) Amazon Publishing.
Elliott, Mark & Hunt, Robert. Did It All Start with a Snowball Fight? And Other Questions about... the American Revolution. Carson, Mary Kay. 2012. (Good Question! Ser.). (ENG.). 32p. (J). 12.95 (978-1-4027-9626-5(9)) Sterling Publishing Co., Inc.
—Did It All Start with a Snowball Fight? And Other Questions about... The American Revolution. Carson, Mary Kay. 2012. (Good Question! Ser.). (ENG.). 32p. (J). pap. 5.95 (978-1-4027-8734-8(0)) Sterling Publishing Co., Inc.
Elliott, Mark, jt. illus. see Blair, Chris.
Elliott, Neil. Can You Crack Them? Bentel, Erica & Bentel Family Trust Staff. 2012. 36p. (978-0-9753548-0-3(9)) Palm Publishing LLC.
Elliott, Rebecca, et al. Atlas of Africa. Foster, Karen. 2008. (Picture Window Books World Atlases Ser.). (ENG.). 32p. (gr. 2-4). lib. bdg. 28.65 (978-1-4048-3880-2(5), Nonfiction Picture Bks.) Picture Window Bks.
—Atlas of Australia. Foster, Karen. 2008. (Picture Window Books World Atlases Ser.). (ENG.). 32p. (gr. 2-4). lib. bdg. 28.65 (978-1-4048-3881-9(3), Nonfiction Picture Bks.) Picture Window Bks.
—Atlas of Europe. Foster, Karen. 2008. (Picture Window Books World Atlases Ser.). (ENG.). 32p. (gr. 2-4). lib. bdg. 28.65 (978-1-4048-3882-6(1), Nonfiction Picture Bks.) Picture Window Bks.
—Atlas of North America. Foster, Karen. 2008. (Picture Window Books World Atlases Ser.). (ENG.). 32p. (gr. 2-4). lib. bdg. 28.65 (978-1-4048-3885-7(6), Nonfiction Picture Bks.) Picture Window Bks.
—Atlas of South America. Foster, Karen. 2008. (Picture Window Books World Atlases Ser.). (ENG.). 32p. (gr. 2-4). lib. bdg. 28.65 (978-1-4048-3887-1(2), Nonfiction Picture Bks.) Picture Window Bks.
—Atlas of Southwest & Central Asia. Law, Felicia. 2008. (Picture Window Books World Atlases Ser.). (ENG.). 32p. (gr. 2-4). lib. bdg. 28.65 (978-1-4048-3884-0(8), Nonfiction Picture Bks.) Picture Window Bks.
—Atlas of the Far East & Southeast Asia. Law, Felicia. 2008. (Picture Window Books World Atlases Ser.). (ENG.). 32p. (gr. 2-4). lib. bdg. 28.65 (978-1-4048-3883-3(X), Nonfiction Picture Bks.) Picture Window Bks.
—Atlas of the Poles & Oceans, 1 vol. Foster, Karen. 2008. (Picture Window Books World Atlases Ser.). (ENG.). 32p. (gr. 2-4). 28.65 (978-1-4048-3886-4(4), Nonfiction Picture Bks.) Picture Window Bks.
—Five Little Monkeys: And Other Counting Rhymes. 2004. (Mother Goose Ser.). (ENG.). 36p. (J). 15.95 (978-1-59249-523-6(0), 1D026) Soundprints.
—Five Little Monkeys: And Other Counting Rhymes. Studio Mouse Staff. rev. ed. 2007. (ENG.). 24p. (J). (gr. -1-k). 4.99 (978-1-59069-608-6(5)) Studio Mouse LLC.
Elliott, Rebecca. Frangoline & the Midnight Dream. Pearce, Clemency. 2011. (ENG.). 32p. (J). (gr. -1-k). 16.99 (978-0-545-31426-8(7), Chicken Hse., The) Scholastic, Inc.
—I Can Learn Times Tables: With Magnetic Numbers to Use Again & Again! Baxter, Nicola. 2013. (ENG.). 16p. (J). (gr. -1-7). bds. 17.99 (978-1-84322-986-5(2), Armadillo) Anness Publishing GBR. Dist: National Bk. Network.
—Kaleidoscope Book: My First Book of Learning. Baxter, Nicola. 2013. (ENG.). 16p. bds. 16.99 (978-1-84322-930-8(7), Armadillo) Anness Publishing GBR. Dist: National Bk. Network.
Elliott, Rebecca, et al. Kids' World Atlas: A Young Person's Guide to the Globe. Foster, Karen & Law, Felicia. 2010. (Picture Window Books World Atlases Ser.). (ENG.). 128p. (gr. 2-4). pap. 12.95 (978-1-4048-6199-2(8), Nonfiction Picture Bks.) Picture Window Bks.
Elliott, Rebecca. Kiss, Kiss Good Night. Nesbitt, Kenn. 2013. (ENG.). 12p. (J). (— 1). bds. 8.99 (978-0-545-47957-8(6), Cartwheel Bks.) Scholastic, Inc.
—Learn about Our World. Baxter, Nicola. 2013. (ENG.). 16p. (J). (gr. k-2). bds. 17.99 (978-1-84322-985-8(4), Armadillo) Anness Publishing GBR. Dist: National Bk. Network.
—Learn to Count. Baxter, Nicola. 2013. (ENG.). 16p. (J). (gr. -1-2). bds. 17.99 (978-1-84322-984-1(6), Armadillo) Anness Publishing GBR. Dist: National Bk. Network.
—Learn to Tell Time: With Magnets to Use Again & Again! Baxter, Nicola. 2013. (ENG.). 16p. (J). (gr. -1-12). bds. 17.99 (978-1-84322-638-3(3), Armadillo) Anness Publishing GBR. Dist: National Bk. Network.
—Millie the Millipede: Collects Colors as She Munches Her Way Through the Pages. Top That Publishing Staff, ed. 2007. (Story Book Ser.). 20p. (J). (gr. -1). bds. (978-1-84666-274-4(5), Tide Mill Pr.) Top That! Publishing PLC.
—Monkey Tumbles. Wang, Margaret. 2007. (ENG.). 10p. (gr. -1-k). bds. 9.95 (978-1-58117-501-1(9), Intervisual/Piggy Toes) Bendon, Inc.
—My Noah's Ark Jigsaw Book. Goodings, Christina. 2009. (ENG.). 12p. (J). (gr. -1-k). bds. 9.99 (978-0-7459-6096-8(0), Lion Children's) Lion Hudson PLC GBR. Dist: Independent Pubs. Group.
—Who Ate All the Lettuce? Munton, Gill. Top That Publishing Staff, ed. 2007. 12p. (gr. -1-k). bds. (978-1-84666-177-8(3), Tide Mill Pr.) Top That! Publishing PLC.
Elliott, Rebecca. Eva's Treetop Festival, Bk. 1. Elliott, Rebecca. 2015. (Owl Diaries: 1). (ENG.). 80p. (J). (gr. k-2). pap. 4.99 (978-0-545-68362-3(9)) Scholastic, Inc.
—The Last Tiger. Elliott, Rebecca. 2013. (ENG.). 32p. (J). (gr. k-2). pap. 8.99 (978-0-7459-6349-5(8)) Lion Hudson PLC GBR. Dist: Independent Pubs. Group.
—Missing Jack. Elliott, Rebecca. 2015. (ENG.). 32p. (J). (gr. -1-k). 16.99 (978-0-7459-6502-4(4)) Lion Hudson PLC GBR. Dist: Independent Pubs. Group.
—Sometimes. Elliott, Rebecca. (ENG.). 32p. (J). (gr. k-2). 2014. pap. 8.99 (978-0-7459-6269-6(6)); 2012. 14.99 (978-0-7459-6297-9(1)) Lion Hudson PLC GBR. Dist: Independent Pubs. Group.
—Zoo Girl. Elliott, Rebecca. (ENG.). 32p. (J). (gr. k-2). 2013. pap. 8.99 (978-0-7459-6270-2(X)); 2012. 14.99 (978-0-7459-6323-5(4)) Lion Hudson PLC GBR. Dist: Independent Pubs. Group.
Elliott, Ruth. Little Blossom, 1 disc. Elliott, Ruth. Cullquipuma, Diana y. Jose, tr. 2008. (ENG & SPA.). 26p. (J). per. 12.99 incl. DVD (978-0-9795017-2-2(5)) Edu Designs.
—The Night Princess, 1 disc. Elliott, Ruth. 2007. (SPA.). (J). per. 12.99 incl. DVD (978-0-9795017-1-5(7)) Edu Designs.
—The Richest Kid in the Poor House. Elliott, Ruth. Elliott, David. 2008. (J). pap. (978-0-9795017-4-6(1)) Edu Designs.
—See What You're Looking At. Elliott, Ruth. 2008. (J). 27.00 (978-0-9795017-0-8(9)) Edu Designs.
Elliott, Tori. The Phlunk's Worldwide Symphony. Rhodes, Lou. 2014. (ENG.). 32p. (J). pap. (978-0-9573690-2-3(6)) Strata Bks.
Ellipsanime Staff. Garfield & Co. #6: Mother Garfield. Davis, Jim et al. 2012. (Garfield Graphic Novels Ser.: 6). (ENG.). 32p. (J). (gr. 1-6). 7.99 (978-1-59707-318-9(0)) Papercutz.
Ellipsanime Staff & Dargaud Media. Catzilla. Davis, Jim & Evanier, Mark. 2011. (Garfield Graphic Novels Ser.: 3). (ENG.). 32p. (J). (gr. 1-6). 7.99 (978-1-59707-278-6(8)) Papercutz.
—Garfield & Co. #7: Home for the Holidays. Davis, Jim. 2012. (Garfield Graphic Novels Ser.: 7). (ENG.). 32p. (J). (gr. 1-6). 7.99 (978-1-59707-370-7(9)) Papercutz.
—The Garfield Show #2: Jon's Night Out. Davis, Jim & Michiels, Cedric. 2013. (Garfield Show Ser.: 2). (ENG.). 64p. (J). (gr. 1-5). 11.99 (978-1-59707-444-5(6)) Papercutz.
—Jon's Night Out. Davis, Jim & Michiels, Cedric. 2013. (Garfield Show Ser.: 2). (ENG.). 64p. (J). (gr. 1-5). pap. 7.99 (978-1-59707-443-8(8)) Papercutz.
Ellipsanime Staff & Dargaud Media Staff. The Curse of the Cat People. Magnat, Julien et al. 2011. (Garfield Graphic Novels Ser.: 2). (ENG.). 32p. (J). (gr. 1-6). 7.99 (978-1-59707-267-0(2)) Papercutz.
—Fish to Fry. Betts, Peter et al. 2011. (Garfield Graphic Novels Ser.: 1). (ENG.). 32p. (J). (gr. 1-6). 7.99 (978-1-59707-266-3(4)) Papercutz.
—Garfield & Co. #4: Caroling Capers. Davis, Jim & Evanier, Mark. 2011. (Garfield Graphic Novels Ser.: 4). (ENG.). 32p. (J). (gr. 1-6). 7.99 (978-1-59707-287-8(7)) Papercutz.
—Secret Agent X, Bk. 8. Davis, Jim et al. 2013. (Garfield Graphic Novels Ser.: 8). (ENG.). 32p. (J). (gr. 1-6). 7.99 (978-1-59707-360-8(1)) Papercutz.
Ellipsanime Staff, jt. illus. see Dargaud Media Staff.
Ellis, Amy. Job-O E: Elementary. Ferry, Francis. 3rd ed. 2003. (Job-O Ser.). (J). (978-1-887481-43-4(5)) CFKR Career Materials, Inc.
Ellis, Andy. Just for You! Leeson, Christine. (Tiger Tales Ser.). (J). 2008. 24p. (gr. -1-2). pap. 6.95 (978-1-58925-408-4(2)); 2004. 32p. tchr. ed. 15.95 (978-1-58925-042-0(7)) Tiger Tales.
—The Midnight Mouse. Baglio, Ben M. 2003. 59p. (J). (978-0-439-41916-1(6)) Scholastic, Inc.
Ellis, Andy. When Lulu Went to the Zoo. Ellis, Andy. 2010. (ENG.). 32p. (J). (gr. -1-3). 16.95 (978-0-7613-5499-4(9)) Lerner Publishing Group.
Ellis, Brendan. A Day to Remember at the Giant's Causeway. Carville, Declan. 29p. (J). (gr. 2-5). pap. 7.95 (978-0-9538222-0-1(6)) Discovery Pubns. GBR. Dist: Irish Bks. & Media, Inc.
Ellis, Carson. The Beautiful Stories of Life: Six Greek Myths, Retold. Rylant, Cynthia. 2009. (ENG.). 88p. (J). (gr. 5-7). 17.99 (978-0-15-206184-5(3)) Houghton Mifflin Harcourt Publishing Co.
—The Composer Is Dead. Snicket, Lemony & Stookey, Nathaniel. 2009. 40p. (J). (gr. k-5). (ENG.). 17.99 (978-0-06-123627-3(6)); lib. bdg. 18.89 (978-0-06-123628-0(4)) HarperCollins Pubs.
—The Mysterious Benedict Society. Stewart, Trenton Lee. (Mysterious Benedict Society Ser.: 1). (ENG.). (J). (gr. 3-7). 2008. 512p. pap. 8.99 (978-0-316-00395-7(6)); 2007. 496p. 19.00 (978-0-316-05777-6(0), Tingley, Megan Bks.); 2015. 512p. 12.99 (978-0-316-26501-0(2)) Little, Brown Bks. for Young Readers.
—The Mysterious Benedict Society. Stewart, Trenton Lee. ed. 2008. (Mysterious Benedict Society Ser.: 1). 485p. (gr. 3-7). lib. bdg. 18.45 (978-1-4178-1817-4(4), Turtleback) Turtleback Bks.
—Under Wildwood. Meloy, Colin. (Wildwood Chronicles Ser.: 2). (ENG.). (J). (gr. 3). 2013. 592p. pap. 9.99 (978-0-06-202473-2(6)); 2012. 576p. 17.99 (978-0-06-202471-8(X)) HarperCollins Pubs.
—Under Wildwood. Meloy, Colin. ed. 2013. (Wildwood Chronicles: Bk. 2). lib. bdg. 20.85 (978-0-606-32169-3(1), Turtleback) Turtleback Bks.
—Wildwood. Meloy, Colin. (Wildwood Chronicles Ser.: 1). (ENG.). (J). (gr. 3). 2012. 576p. pap. 8.99 (978-0-06-202470-1(1)); 2011. 560p. 17.99 (978-0-06-202468-8(X)) HarperCollins Pubs.

E

—Wildwood. Meloy, Colin. ed. 2012. (Wildwood Chronicles: Bk. 1). lib. bdg. 19.65 *(978-0-606-26864-6(2)*, Turtleback) Turtleback Bks.
—Wildwood Imperium. Meloy, Colin. 2014. (Wildwood Chronicles: Bk. 3). (ENG.). 592p. (J). (gr. 3). 17.99 *(978-0-06-202474-9(4))* HarperCollins Pubs.
—Wildwood Imperium: The Wildwood Chronicles, Book III. Meloy, Colin. 2015. (Wildwood Chronicles Ser.: 3). (ENG.). 592p. (J). (gr. 3). pap. 9.99 *(978-0-06-202476-3(0))* HarperCollins Pubs.
Ellis, Christina, jt. illus. see Joyce, William.
Ellis, Elina. Easter Story, 1 vol. David, Juliet & Ayliffe, Alex. 2014. (ENG.). 40p. (J). 8.99 *(978-1-78128-177-2(7)*, Candle Bks.) Lion Hudson PLC GBR. Dist: Kregel Pubns.
Ellis, Gerry. Chimpanzees. Ellis, Gerry, photos by. Kane, Karen. 2004. (Early Bird Nature Bks.). (ENG.). 48p. (gr. 2-5). 26.60 *(978-0-8225-2418-2(X)*, Lerner Pubns.) Lerner Publishing Group.
Ellis, Jan Davey. It's Back to School We Go! First Day Stories from Around the World. Jackson, Ellen B. 2003. (ENG.). 32p. (J). (gr. k-3). 17.99 *(978-0-7613-1948-1(4)*, Millbrook Pr.) Lerner Publishing Group.
—Turn of the Century: Eleven Centuries of Children & Change. Jackson, Ellen B. 2003. (ENG.). 32p. (J). (gr. k-3). pap. 8.95 *(978-0-88106-370-7(3))* Charlesbridge Publishing, Inc.
—The Winter Solstice. Jackson, Ellen B. 2003. (Traditions of the Seasons Ser.). (ENG.). 32p. (J). (gr. 3-6). pap. 7.95 *(978-0-7613-0297-1(2)*, Millbrook Pr.) Lerner Publishing Group.
Ellis, Jessica. The Gifts of the Spirit, 6 vols. Walters, David. 2005. 64p. (J). pap. 8.95 *(978-1-888081-68-8(6))* Good News Fellowship Ministries.
Ellis, Joey. A Winter's Dream. Dunn, Hunter S. 2004. 65p. (J). 19.95 *(978-0-9761732-0-5(4))* Dunn, Hunter.
Ellis, Libby. Riggeldy Jiggeldy Joggeldy Jam: Can You Guess Who I Am? Nelson, Esther & Hirsch, Davida. 2003. (J). bds. 5.95 *(978-0-7607-3278-6(7))* Barnes & Noble, Inc.
—Riggeldy Jiggeldy Joggeldy Roo: Can You Guess What I Do? Nelson, Esther & Hirsch, Davida. 2003. (J). bds. 5.95 *(978-0-7607-3279-3(5))* Barnes & Noble, Inc.
Ellis, Melissa Martin, photos by. The Redwood Review Summer 2003, 2. Van Gruisen, Janette van de Geest et al. 2003. 183p. (YA). per. 0.00 *(978-0-9708317-3-6(0))* Timshel Literature.
Ellis, Rich, jt. illus. see McHargue, Dove.
Ellison, Chris. The Christmas Tree Ship. Crane, Carol. 2011. (ENG.). 32p. (J). (gr. k-6). 15.95 *(978-1-58536-285-1(9))* Sleeping Bear Pr.
—Let Them Play. Raven, Margot Theis. 2005. (ENG.). 32p. (J). (gr. k-6). 16.95 *(978-1-58536-260-8(3))* Sleeping Bear Pr.
—The Lucky Star. Young, Judy. 2008. (Tales of Young Americans Ser.). (ENG.). 32p. (J). (gr. 3-7). 17.95 *(978-1-58536-348-3(0))* Sleeping Bear Pr.
—M Is for Mom: A Child's Alphabet. Riehle, Mary Ann McCabe. 2009. (ENG.). 32p. (J). (gr. k-6). 17.95 *(978-1-58536-458-9(4))* Sleeping Bear Pr.
—Pappy's Handkerchief. Scillian, Devin. rev. ed. 2007. (Tales of Young Americans Ser.). (ENG.). 32p. (J). (gr. 3-7). 17.95 *(978-1-58536-316-2(2))* Sleeping Bear Pr.
—Rudy Rides the Rails: A Depression Era Story. Mackall, Dandi Daley. rev. ed. 2007. (Tales of Young Americans Ser.). (ENG.). 32p. (J). (gr. -1-3). 17.95 *(978-1-58536-286-8(7))* Sleeping Bear Pr.
—Saint Nicholas: The Real Story of the Christmas Legend. Stiegemeyer, Julie. (J). 2007. 32p. (gr. -1). per. 7.49 *(978-0-7586-1341-7(5))*; 2005. 16p. (gr. -1-17). bds. 7.49 *(978-0-7586-0688-4(5))*; 2003. 32p. 13.49 *(978-0-7586-0376-0(2))* Concordia Publishing Hse.
—That's My Colt: An Easter Tale. Mackall, Dandi Daley. 2008. 24p. (J). (gr. -1). 13.49 *(978-0-7586-1423-0(3))* Concordia Publishing Hse.
Ellison, Chris, et al. Westward Journeys. Scillian, Devin & Young, Judy. 2013. (American Adventures Ser.). (ENG.). 96p. (J). (gr. 3-6). pap. 6.99 *(978-1-58536-860-0(1)*, 202367) Sleeping Bear Pr.
Ellison, Chris & Benny, Mike. America's White Table. Raven, Margot Theis. 2005. (ENG.). 48p. (J). (gr. k-6). 16.95 *(978-1-58536-216-5(6))* Sleeping Bear Pr.
Ellison, Nancy, photos by. The Book of Ballet: Learning & Appreciating the Secrets of Dance. American Ballet Theatre Staff et al. 2003. (ENG., 224p. pap. 29.95 *(978-0-7893-0865-8(7))* Universe Publishing.
Ellithorpe, Chris. Developing Reading Fluency Grade 1: Using Modeled Reading, Phrasing, & Repeated Oral Reading. Callella, Trisha. Fisch, Teri L., ed. 2003. (Developing Reading Fluency Ser.). 96p. (gr. 1-2). per. 14.99 *(978-1-57471-994-9(7)*, 2247) Creative Teaching Pr., Inc.
Ellithorpe, Chris, jt. illus. see Hilliam, Corbin.
Ells, Marcia Louise. Glips, Snodagers & Wallywogs. Ells, Marcia Louise. l.t. ed. 2006. 44p. (J). 6.99 *(978-0-9777359-0-7(7))* Marcia's Menagerie.
Ellwand, David. The Mystery of the Fool & the Vanisher. Ellwand, David, photos by. Ellwand, Ruth. 2008. (ENG.). 104p. (J). (gr. 5). 18.99 *(978-0-7636-2096-7(3))* Candlewick Pr.
Ellwand, David, photos by. Old MacDonald Had a Farm. 2010. (ENG., 14p. (J). (gr. -1). bds. 12.95 *(978-1-60710-104-8(1)*, Silver Dolphin Bks.) Baker & Taylor Publishing Group.
Ellwand, David, photos by. Cinderlily: A Floral Fairy Tale. Ellwand, David, ed. Tagg, Christine. 2006. 26p. (J). (gr. k-4). reprint ed. 17.00 *(978-1-4223-5558-9(6))* DIANE Publishing Co.
Ellwell, Tristan. A Wolf at the Door. Datlow, Ellen. Windling, Terri, ed. 2013. (ENG.). 192p. (J). (gr. 4-9). pap. 13.99 *(978-1-4814-0167-8(X)*, Simon & Schuster Bks. For Young Readers) Simon & Schuster Bks. For Young Readers.
Elmore, Larry. Penguin Comes Home. Young, Louise O. 2005. (Amazing Animal Adventures Ser.). (ENG.). 36p. (J). (gr. -1-2). 2.95 *(978-1-59249-325-8(4)*, S7158) Soundprints.
—Penguin Comes Home. Young, Louise. 2005. (Soundprints' Amazing Animal Adventures! Ser.). (ENG.). 32p. (J). (gr. -1-2). 9.95 *(978-1-59249-329-6(7)*, PS7158) Soundprints.
—Penguin Comes Home. Young, Louise O. (Amazing Animal Adventures Ser.). (ENG.). (J). (gr. -1-2). 2005. 36p. 15.95 *(978-1-59249-324-1(6)*, B7108); 2005. 32p. 19.95 *(978-1-59249-327-2(0)*, BC7108); 2004. 36p. pap. 6.95 *(978-1-59249-326-5(2)*, S7108) Soundprints.
Elphinstone, Katy. Moby Dick. Melville, Herman. 2014. (Travel & Adventure Ser.). (ENG.). 64p. pap. 6.95 *(978-1-906230-72-2(2))* Real Reads Ltd. GBR. Dist: International Publishers Marketing.
—Robinson Crusoe. Defoe, Daniel. 2014. (Travel & Adventure Ser.). (ENG.). 64p. pap. 6.95 *(978-1-906230-71-5(4))* Real Reads Ltd. GBR. Dist: International Publishers Marketing.
Elsammak, Ariane. Noodlehead Stories: World Tales Kids Can Read & Tell. Hamilton, Martha & Weiss, Mitch. 2006. (ENG.). 96p. (J). (gr. 1-6). 24.95 *(978-0-87483-584-7(4))* August Hse. Pubs., Inc.
Elsby, Lizzy. Pini the Pitcher: A Story for Hanukkah. Osterbach, Batya. 2005. 32p. (J). (gr. 1-4). per. 9.95 *(978-1-932687-51-4(3)*, Devora Publishing) Simcha Media Group.
Elsen, Janis A. As Constant As the Stars. Nees, Diane L. 2012. 36p. 24.95 *(978-1-4626-6886-1(0))*; pap. 12.99 *(978-1-4626-7919-5(6))* America Star Bks.
Elsom, Clare. Alfie's Great Escape. Irwin, Kate. 2014. (Blue Bananas Ser.). (ENG.). 48p. (J). (gr. k-2). pap. 5.99 *(978-1-4052-6212-5(5))* Egmont Bks., Ltd. GBR. Dist: Independent Pubs. Group.
—Animal Family Albums. Guillain, Charlotte & Mason, Paul. 2013. (Animal Family Albums Ser.). (ENG.). 32p. (gr. 2-4). pap. 31.96 *(978-1-4109-4944-8(3))*; lib. bdg. 119.96 *(978-1-4109-4939-4(7))* Heinemann-Raintree. (Raintree Perspectives).
Elsom, Clare. Bring on Spring! Katschke, Judy. 2015. 32p. (J). pap. ***(978-0-545-82337-1(4))*** Scholastic, Inc.
Elsom, Clare. Cats. Guillain, Charlotte. 2013. (Animal Family Albums Ser.). (ENG.). 32p. (gr. 2-4). pap. 8.29 *(978-1-4109-4940-0(0))*; 29.99 *(978-1-4109-4935-6(4))* Heinemann-Raintree. (Raintree Perspectives).
—Dogs. Mason, Paul. 2013. (Animal Family Albums Ser.). (ENG.). 32p. (gr. 2-4). pap. 8.29 *(978-1-4109-4941-7(9))*; 29.99 *(978-1-4109-4936-3(2))* Heinemann-Raintree. (Raintree Perspectives).
Elsom, Clare. First Grade Feast!/By Judy Katschke; Illustrated by Clare Elsom. Katschke, Judy. 2014. 32p. (J). pap. ***(978-0-545-75844-4(0))*** Scholastic, Inc.
Elsom, Clare. Horses & Ponies. Mason, Paul. 2013. (Animal Family Albums Ser.). (ENG.). 32p. (gr. 2-4). pap. 8.29 *(978-1-4109-4942-4(7))*; 29.99 *(978-1-4109-4937-0(0))* Heinemann-Raintree. (Raintree Perspectives).
—Rabbits. Guillain, Charlotte. 2013. (Animal Family Albums Ser.). (ENG.). 32p. (gr. 2-4). 29.99 *(978-1-4109-4938-7(9)*, Raintree Perspectives) Heinemann-Raintree.
—Rabbits - Animal Family Albums. Guillain, Charlotte. 2013. (Animal Family Albums Ser.). (ENG.). 32p. (gr. 2-4). pap. 8.29 *(978-1-4109-4943-1(5)*, Raintree Perspectives) Heinemann-Raintree.
Elsom, Clare. Ready, Set, Boo! Katschke, Judy. 2014. 32p. (J). pap. ***(978-0-545-75843-7(2))*** Scholastic, Inc.
Elsom, Clare. Zak Zoo & the Baffled Burglar. Smith, Justine. (Zak Zoo Ser.: 6). (ENG.). 32p. (J). (gr. -1-2). 2013. pap. 7.99 *(978-1-4083-1342-8(1))*; 2012. 13.99 *(978-1-4083-1334-3(0))* Hodder & Stoughton GBR. Dist: Independent Pubs. Group.
—Zak Zoo & the Birthday Bang. Smith, Justine. 2013. (Zak Zoo Ser.: 8). (ENG.). 32p. (J). (gr. -1-2). pap. 7.99 *(978-1-4083-1344-2(8))* Hodder & Stoughton GBR. Dist: Independent Pubs. Group.
—Zak Zoo & the Hectic House. Smith, Justine. 2013. (Zak Zoo Ser.: 5). (ENG.). 32p. (J). (gr. -1-2). pap. 7.99 *(978-1-4083-1341-1(3))* Hodder & Stoughton GBR. Dist: Independent Pubs. Group.
—Zak Zoo & the School Hullabaloo. Smith, Justine. 2012. (Zak Zoo Ser.: 1). (ENG.). 32p. (J). (gr. -1-2). 13.99 *(978-1-4083-1329-9(4))* Hodder & Stoughton GBR. Dist: Independent Pubs. Group.
—Zak Zoo & the Seaside SOS. Smith, Justine. 2013. (Zak Zoo Ser.: 3). (ENG.). 32p. (J). (gr. -1-2). 7.99 *(978-1-4083-1339-8(1))* Hodder & Stoughton GBR. Dist: Independent Pubs. Group.
—Zak Zoo & the Seaside Sos. Smith, Justine. 2012. (Zak Zoo Ser.: 3). (ENG.). 32p. (J). (gr. -1-2). 13.99 *(978-1-4083-1331-2(6))* Hodder & Stoughton GBR. Dist: Independent Pubs. Group.
—Zak Zoo & the TV Crew. Smith, Justine. 2013. (Zak Zoo Ser.: 7). (ENG.). 32p. (J). (gr. -1-2). pap. 7.99 *(978-1-4083-1343-5(X))* Hodder & Stoughton GBR. Dist: Independent Pubs. Group.
Elson, Richard. The Battle of Midway: The Destruction of the Japanese Fleet. Abnett, Dan. 2007. (Graphic Battles of World War II Ser.). (ENG.). 48p. (YA). (gr. 4-7). lib. bdg. 31.95 *(978-1-4042-0783-7(X))* Rosen Publishing Group, Inc., The.
Elston, James W. Battling Bigfoot. Simonson, Louise. 2007. (Extreme Monsters Ser.). 94p. (J). (gr. 2-5). per. 3.99 *(978-1-57791-275-0(6)*, Penny Candy Pr.) Brighter Minds Children's Publishing.
—Meet Mr. Hydeous, Vol. 3. Simonson, Louise. gif. ed. 2006. (Extreme Monsters Ser.). 96p. (J). per. 3.99 *(978-1-57791-255-2(1))* Brighter Minds Children's Publishing.
—What's with Wulf? Simonson, Louise. gif. ed. 2005. (Extreme Monsters Ser.). 96p. (J). (gr. 2-5). per. 3.99 *(978-1-57791-179-1(2))* Brighter Minds Children's Publishing.
Elwell, Ellen Banks & Turk, Caron. The Toddler's Songbook. 2009. (J). *(978-1-4335-0597-3(5))* Crossway.
—The Toddler's Songbook. Elwell, Ellen Banks. 2009. 48p. (J). 14.99 incl. audio compact disk *(978-1-4335-0595-9(9))* Crossway.
Elwell, Peter. My Mother Is Mine. Bauer, Marion Dane. 2009. (Classic Board Bks.). (ENG.). 36p. (J). (gr. -1-k). 7.99 *(978-1-4169-6090-4(2)*, Little Simon) Little Simon.
—My Mother Is Mine. Bauer, Marion Dane. 2004. (ENG.), 40p. (J). (gr. -1-k). reprint ed. 7.99 *(978-0-689-86695-1(X)*, Simon & Schuster Bks. For Young Readers) Simon & Schuster Bks. For Young Readers.
Elwell, Peter. A Most Remarkable Bear. Elwell, Peter. Date not set. 32p. (J). (gr. k-3). 15.95 *(978-0-7614-5008-5(4)*, Benchmark Bks.) Marshall Cavendish Corp.
Elwell, Telva. Ellasense Misses the Train. Elwell, Telva. Kelley, Barbara. 2004. 48p. (J). per. 12.95 *(978-0-9754591-0-2(4))* Cubby Hole Tales.
Elwell, Tristan. Disney after Dark. Pearson, Ridley. 2009. (Kingdom Keepers Ser.: Bk. 1). (ENG.). 336p. (J). (gr. 5-6). pap. 8.99 *(978-1-4231-2311-8(5))* Hyperion Pr.
—Disney at Dawn. Pearson, Ridley. 2008. (Kingdom Keepers Ser.: Bk. 2). (ENG.). 384p. (J). (gr. 5-9). 17.99 *(978-1-4231-0365-3(3)*, Disney Editions) Disney Pr.
—Disney at Dawn. Pearson, Ridley. 2009. (Kingdom Keepers Ser.: Bk. 2). (ENG.). 384p. (J). (gr. 5-6). pap. 8.99 *(978-1-4231-0708-8(X))* Hyperion Pr.
—Disney in Shadow. Pearson, Ridley. (Kingdom Keepers Ser.: Bk. 3). (ENG.). (J). (gr. 5-17). 2011. 576p. pap. 8.99 *(978-1-4231-3856-3(2))*; 3rd ed. 2010. 560p. 17.99 *(978-1-4231-2899-1(0))* Hyperion Pr.
—Power Play. Pearson, Ridley. 2011. (Kingdom Keepers Ser.: Bk. 4). (ENG.). 448p. (J). (gr. 5-9). 17.99 *(978-1-4231-3857-0(0))* Hyperion Pr.
Elwick, Elissa. The Princess & the Sleep Stealer. Elwick, Elissa. ed. 2012. (ENG.). 32p. (J). (gr. -1-k). pap. 9.99 *(978-0-230-75068-5(0))* Macmillan Pubs., Ltd. GBR. Dist: Independent Pubs. Group.
Elworthy, Antony. Have You Ever? Pym, Tasha. 2007. (Collins Big Cat Ser.). (ENG.). 16p. (J). pap. 5.99 *(978-0-00-718654-9(1))* HarperCollins Pubs. Ltd. GBR. Dist: Independent Pubs. Group.
—I Can Do It! Shipton, Paul. 2007. (Collins Big Cat Ser.). (ENG.). 48p. (J). pap. 5.99 *(978-0-00-718651-8(7))* HarperCollins Pubs. Ltd. GBR. Dist: Independent Pubs. Group.
—What Are You Making? Band 02b/Red B. Hawes, Alison. 2007. (Collins Big Cat Ser.). (ENG.). 16p. (J). pap. 5.99 *(978-0-00-718657-0(6))* HarperCollins Pubs. Ltd. GBR. Dist: Independent Pubs. Group.
Elworthy, Antony, photos by. Collins Big Cat - Super Sculptures: Band 05/Green. Pym, Tasha. 2006. (Collins Big Cat Ser.). (ENG., 24p. (J). pap. 6.99 *(978-0-00-718686-0(X))* HarperCollins Pubs. Ltd. GBR. Dist: Independent Pubs. Group.
Ely, Dave. Are You Smarter Than a Flying Gator? Gator Mikey over Florida! Kremer, Kevin R. 2007. 173p. per. 5.99 *(978-0-9663335-6-5(X))* Snow In Sarasota Publishing.
—Are You Smarter Than a Flying Teddy? Teddy Roosevelt Returns to North Dakota! Kremer, Kevin. 2012. (ENG.). 338p. (J). (gr. 2). pap. 8.99 *(978-0-9837685-7-9(9))* Snow In Sarasota Publishing.
—Maggie's Christmas Miracle. Pohl, Dora & Kremer, Kevin. 2010. 78p. (J). pap. 4.99 *(978-0-9824611-2-9(7))* Snow In Sarasota Publishing.
—The Most Amazing Halloween Ever. Kremer, Kevin. 2011. 90p. (J). (gr. 2-6). pap. 5.99 *(978-0-9830362-5-8(X))* Snow In Sarasota Publishing.
—Santa's Our Substitute Teacher. Kremer, Kevin. 2006. 150p. (gr. 4-7). per. 5.99 *(978-0-9663335-4-1(3)*, 703-001) Snow In Sarasota Publishing.
—The Year Our Teacher Won Super Bowl. Kremer, Kevin. 2010. (ENG.). 178p. pap. 6.50 *(978-0-9824611-1-2(9))* Snow In Sarasota Publishing.
Ely, Paul & Dudley, Dick. Eerie Feary Feeling: A Hairy Scary Pop-up Book. Hulme, Joy N. 2006. 12p. (J). (gr. k-4). reprint ed. 14.00 *(978-1-4223-5171-0(8))* DIANE Publishing Co.
Élyum Studio. The Planet of Gehom. Gaudin, Thierry. Smith, Anne & Smith, Owen, trs. from FRE. 2014. (Little Prince Ser.: 16). (ENG.). 48p. (J). (gr. 4-8). lib. bdg. 26.60 *(978-0-7613-8766-4(8)*, Graphic Universe) Lerner Publishing Group.
ÉLyum Studio. The Planet of Jade. Loisillier, Maud & Morel, Diane. Smith, Owen & Collins Smith, Anne, trs. 2012. (Little Prince Ser.: 4). (ENG.). 56p. (J). (gr. 4-8). pap. 7.95 *(978-1-4677-0263-8(3)*, Graphic Universe) Lerner Publishing Group.
Élyum Studio. The Planet of Libris. Bidaud, Agnès. 2013. (Little Prince Ser.: 11). (ENG.). 48p. (J). (gr. 4-8). pap. 7.95 *(978-1-4677-1520-1(4))*; lib. bdg. 26.60 *(978-0-7613-8761-9(7))* Lerner Publishing Group. (Graphic Universe).
—The Planet of Ludokaa. Constantine, Clélia. 2013. (Little Prince Ser.: 12). (ENG.). 48p. (J). (gr. 4-8). pap. 7.95 *(978-1-4677-1521-8(2))*; lib. bdg. 26.60 *(978-0-7613-8762-6(5))* Lerner Publishing Group. (Graphic Universe).
ÉLyum Studio. The Planet of Music. Constantine, Clélia. Smith, Owen & Collins Smith, Anne, trs. 2012. (Little Prince Ser.: 3). (ENG.). 56p. (J). (gr. 4-8). pap. 7.95 *(978-0-8225-9424-6(2)*, Graphic Universe) Lerner Publishing Group.
Élyum Studio. The Planet of Tear-Eaters. Dubos, Delphine. Smith, Anne & Smith, Owen, trs. from FRE. 2014. (Little Prince Ser.: 13). (ENG.). 48p. (J). (gr. 4-8). lib. bdg. 26.60 *(978-0-7613-8763-3(3)*, Graphic Universe) Lerner Publishing Group.
ÉLyum Studio. The Planet of the Firebird. Magnet, Julien. Klio Burrell, Carol, tr. 2012. (Little Prince Ser.: 2). (ENG.). 56p. (J). (gr. 4-8). pap. 7.95 *(978-0-8225-9423-9(4)*, Graphic Universe) Lerner Publishing Group.
Élyum Studio. The Planet of the Gargand. Costi, Vincent. Smith, Anne & Smith, Owen, trs. from FRE. 2014. (Little Prince Ser.: 15). (ENG.). 48p. (J). (gr. 4-8). lib. bdg. 26.60 *(978-0-7613-8765-7(X)*, Graphic Universe) Lerner Publishing Group.
—The Planet of the Giant. Adrien, Gilles & Broders, Alain. 2013. (Little Prince Ser.: 9). (ENG.). 56p. (J). (gr. 4-8). pap. 7.95 *(978-1-4677-1518-8(2))*; lib. bdg. 26.60 *(978-0-7613-8759-6(5))* Lerner Publishing Group. (Graphic Universe).
—The Planet of the Grand Buffoon. Cerami, Matteo et al. Smith, Anne & Smith, Owen, trs. from FRE. 2014. (Little Prince Ser.: 14). (ENG.). 48p. (J). (gr. 4-8). lib. bdg. 26.60 *(978-0-7613-8764-0(1)*, Graphic Universe) Lerner Publishing Group.
—The Planet of Trainiacs. N'Leh, Anne-Claire. 2013. (Little Prince Ser.: 10). (ENG.). 56p. (J). (gr. 4-8). pap. 7.95 *(978-1-4677-1519-5(0))*; lib. bdg. 26.60 *(978-0-7613-8760-2(9))* Lerner Publishing Group. (Graphic Universe).
—The Sin-Eater's Confession. Bick, Ilsa J. 2014. (ENG.). 296p. (YA). (gr. 9-12). pap. 9.95 *(978-1-4677-3705-0(4)*, Carolrhoda LAB) Lerner Publishing Group.
Élyum Studio Staff. The Planet of the Tortoise Driver. Benedetti, Hervé & Robin, Nicolas. 2013. (Little Prince Ser.: 8). (ENG.). 56p. (J). (gr. 4-8). pap. 7.95 *(978-1-4677-0740-4(6)*, Graphic Universe) Lerner Publishing Group.
—The Planet of the Tortoise Driver. Benedetti, Hervé et al. 2013. (Little Prince Ser.: 8). (ENG.). 56p. (J). (gr. 4-8). lib. bdg. 26.60 *(978-0-7613-8758-9(7)*, Graphic Universe) Lerner Publishing Group.
—The Planet of Wind. Dubos, Delphine. Burrell, Carol Klio, tr. 2012. (Little Prince Ser.: 1). (ENG.). 56p. (J). (gr. 4-8). pap. 7.95 *(978-0-8225-9422-2(6)*, Graphic Universe) Lerner Publishing Group.
Elzaurdia, Sharon. Let's Have a Play. Hillert, Margaret. 2008. (Beginning-to-Read Bks.). 32p. (J). (gr. -1-7). lib. bdg. 19.93 *(978-1-59953-156-4(9))* Norwood Hse. Pr.
—What Am I? Hillert, Margaret. 2008. (Beginning-to-Read Bks.). 31p. (J). (gr. 3-7). lib. bdg. 19.93 *(978-1-59953-180-9(1))* Norwood Hse. Pr.
Elzbieta & Hawcock, David. Mimi's Scary Theater: A Play in Nine Scenes for Seven Characters & an Egg. Elzbieta. 2004. 20p. (J). (gr. -1-3). reprint ed. 15.00 *(978-0-7567-8299-3(6))* DIANE Publishing Co.
Emanuel, Effie Ann. The Way to Go! Phillips, Cynthia. 2008. 17p. pap. 24.95 *(978-1-60610-455-2(1))* America Star Bks.
Ember, Dave. Alaska's Wildlife. Compton, Carrie. 2005. (Alaska Mini Book Gift Ser.). 80p. 5.95 *(978-0-9727921-6-5(3))* WW West, Inc.
Ember, Kathi. Don't Talk to Strangers. Mehlhaff, Christine. 2007. (J). *(978-0-545-00103-8(X))* Scholastic, Inc.
—A Father's Day Thank You, 1 vol. Nolan, Janet. (ENG.). 32p. (J). (gr. -1-2). 2011. 6.99 *(978-0-8075-2292-9(9))*; 2007. lib. bdg. 16.99 *(978-0-8075-2291-2(0))* Whitman, Albert & Co.
—I Can Show Respect. Burch, Regina G. & Donovan Guntly, Jenette. 2004. (Doing the Right Thing Ser.). 16p. (gr. -1-2). lib. bdg. 20.00 *(978-0-8368-4248-7(0)*, Gareth Stevens Learning Library) Stevens, Gareth Publishing LLLP.
—Mother's Day Surprise, 0 vols. Krensky, Stephen. 2010. (ENG.). 32p. (J). (gr. -1-3). 15.99 *(978-0-7614-5633-9(3)*, 9780761456339, Amazon Children's Publishing) Amazon Publishing.
—Squirrel's New Year's Resolution. Miller, Pat. 2012. (J). 34.28 *(978-1-61913-135-4(8))* Weigl Pubs., Inc.
—Squirrel's New Year's Resolution. Miller, Pat. 2010. (ENG.). 32p. (J). (gr. k-3). 16.99 *(978-0-8075-7591-8(7))* Whitman, Albert & Co.
—Substitute Groundhog. Miller, Pat. 2012. (J). *(978-1-61913-133-0(1))* Weigl Pubs., Inc.
—Substitute Groundhog, 1 vol. Miller, Pat. 2010. (ENG.). 32p. (J). (gr. k-3). pap. 6.99 *(978-0-8075-7644-1(1))* Whitman, Albert & Co.
Ember, Kathi, jt. illus. see Yamada, Jane.
Emberley, Barbara & Ed. The Moon Seems to Change. Branley, Franklyn M. 2015. (Let's-Read-And-Find-Out Science 2 Ser.). (ENG.). 32p. (J). (gr. -1-3). pap. 6.99 ***(978-0-06-238206-1(3))*** HarperCollins Pubs.
Emberley, Ed. The Ant & the Grasshopper. Emberley, Rebecca. 2012. (ENG.). 32p. (J). (gr. -1-2). 16.99 *(978-1-59643-493-6(7))* Roaring Brook Pr.
—The Crocodile & the Scorpion. Emberley, Rebecca. 2013. (ENG.). 32p. (J). (gr. -1-2). 17.99 *(978-1-59643-494-3(5))* Roaring Brook Pr.
—The Story of Paul Bunyan. Emberley, Barbara. 2015. (ENG.). 32p. 17.95 *(978-1-62326-062-0(0))* AMMO Bks., LLC.
—There Was an Old Monster! Emberley, Rebecca & Emberley, Adrian. 2009. (ENG.). 32p. (J). (gr. -1-k). 17.99 *(978-0-545-10145-5(X)*, Orchard Bks.) Scholastic, Inc.
Emberley, Ed. Bye-Bye, Big Bad Bullybug! Emberley, Ed. 2007. (ENG.). 32p. (J). (gr. -1-1). 12.99 *(978-0-316-01762-6(0))* Little, Brown Bks. for Young Readers.
—Chicken Little. Emberley, Ed. Emberley, Rebecca. 2009. (ENG.). 34p. (J). (gr. -1-2). 17.99 *(978-1-59643-464-6(3))* Roaring Brook Pr.
—Ed Emberley's Drawing Book of Trucks & Trains. Emberley, Ed. 2005. (ENG.). 32p. (J). (gr. 2-17). pap. 6.99 *(978-0-316-78967-7(4))* Little, Brown Bks. for Young Readers.
—Ed Emberley's Fingerprint Drawing Book. Emberley, Ed. 2005. (ENG.). 48p. (J). (gr. 2-17). pap., pap. 7.99 *(978-0-316-78969-1(0))* Little, Brown Bks. for Young Readers.
—Ed Emberley's Picture Pie: A Cut & Paste Drawing Book. Emberley, Ed. 2006. (ENG.). 48p. (J). (gr. 2-17). pap. 9.99 *(978-0-316-78982-0(8))* Little, Brown Bks. for Young Readers.
—If You're a Monster & You Know It... Emberley, Ed. Emberley, Rebecca. 2010. (ENG.). 32p. (J). (gr. -1-k). 16.99 *(978-0-545-21829-0(2)*, Orchard Bks.) Scholastic, Inc.
—Picture Pie Vol. 2: A Drawing Book & Stencil. Emberley, Ed. LBCL. 2005. (ENG.). 32p. (J). (gr. 2-17). pap. 10.00 *(978-0-316-78980-6(1))* Little, Brown Bks. for Young Readers.

—Red Hen. Emberley, Ed. Emberley, Rebecca. 2010. (ENG.). 32p. (J). (gr. -1-2). 18.99 *(978-1-59643-492-9(9))* Roaring Brook Pr.

Emberley, Ed, jt. illus. see Emberley, Rebecca.

Emberley, Edward R. Ed Emberley's Big Green Drawing Book. Emberley, Edward R. 2005. (ENG.). 96p. (J). (gr. 2-17). pap. 10.99 *(978-0-316-78976-9(3))* Little, Brown Bks. for Young Readers.

—Ed Emberley's Big Purple Drawing Book. Emberley, Edward R. 2005. (ENG.). 96p. (J). (gr. 2-17). pap. 10.99 *(978-0-316-78973-8(9))* Little, Brown Bks. for Young Readers.

—Ed Emberley's Drawing Book - Make a World: Learn to Draw the Ed Emberley Way! Emberley, Edward R. 2006. (ENG.). 32p. (J). (gr. 2-17). pap. 6.99 *(978-0-316-78972-1(0))* Little, Brown Bks. for Young Readers.

—Ed Emberley's Drawing Book of Animals. Emberley, Edward R. 2006. (ENG.). 32p. (J). (gr. 2-17). per. 7.00 *(978-0-316-78979-0(8))* Little, Brown Bks. for Young Readers.

—Ed Emberley's Drawing Book of Faces. Emberley, Edward R. 2006. (ENG.). 32p. (J). (gr. 2-17). pap. 7.00 *(978-0-316-78970-7(4))* Little, Brown Bks. for Young Readers.

—Ed Emberley's Great Thumbprint Drawing Book. Emberley, Edward R. 2005. (ENG.). 48p. (J). (gr. 2-17). per. 7.99 *(978-0-316-78968-4(2))* Little, Brown Bks. for Young Readers.

Emberley, Edward R., jt. illus. see Emberley, Rebecca.

Emberley, Michael. An Annoying ABC. Bottner, Barbara. 2011. (ENG.). 32p. (J). (gr. -1-2). 17.99 *(978-0-375-86708-8(2)*, Knopf Bks. for Young Readers) Random Hse. Children's Bks.

—David Dinosaur-Rrr! What It's Like to Be 3. Harris, Robie H. 2005. (Growing up Stories Ser.). (ENG.). 40p. (J). 16.95 *(978-0-689-83260-4(5)*, McElderry, Margaret K. Bks.) McElderry, Margaret K. Bks.

—Forget-Me-Nots: Poems to Learn by Heart. Hoberman, Mary Ann. 2012. (ENG.). 144p. (J). (gr. -1-17). 19.99 *(978-0-316-12947-3(X)*, Tingley, Megan Bks.) Little, Brown Bks. for Young Readers.

—It's Not the Stork! A Book about Girls, Boys, Babies, Bodies, Families & Friends. Harris, Robie H. (Family Library). (ENG.). 64p. (J). (gr. -1-3). 2008. pap. 11.99 *(978-0-7636-3331-8(3))*; 2006. 16.99 *(978-0-7636-0047-1(4))* Candlewick Pr.

—It's So Amazing! A Book about Eggs, Sperm, Birth, Babies, & Families. Harris, Robie H. 2014. (Family Library). (ENG.). 88p. (J). (gr. 2-5). 22.99 *(978-0-7636-6873-0(7))* Candlewick Pr.

—Mail Harry to the Moon! Harris, Robie H. 2008. (ENG.). 40p. (J). (gr. -1-1). 16.99 *(978-0-316-15376-8(1))* Little, Brown Bks. for Young Readers.

—Maybe a Bear Ate It! Harris, Robie H. 2008. (ENG.). 40p. (J). (gr. -1-k). 16.99 *(978-0-439-92961-5(X)*, Orchard Bks.) Scholastic, Inc.

—Miss Brooks Loves Books! (And I Don't) Bottner, Barbara. 2010. (ENG.). 32p. (J). (gr. -1-2). 17.99 *(978-0-375-84682-3(4)*, Knopf Bks. for Young Readers) Random Hse. Children's Bks.

—Miss Brooks' Story Nook (where Tales Are Told & Ogres Are Welcome) Bottner, Barbara. 2014. (ENG.). 40p. (J). (gr. k-4). 16.99 *(978-0-449-81328-7(2)*, Knopf Bks. for Young Readers) Random Hse. Children's Bks.

—Sexo: Que es? Desarrollo, Cambios Corporales, Sexo y Salud Sexual. Harris, Robie H. & Cousins, Lucy. Saslavsky, Irene, tr. 2005. (SPA.). 96p. (gr. 6-8). pap. 12.99 *(978-84-8488-181-0(4))* Serres, Ediciones, S. L. ESP. Dist: Lectorum Pubns., Inc.

—The Ultimate Guide to Grandmas & Grandpas! Lloyd-Jones, Sally. 2008. (ENG.). 32p. (J). (gr. -1-3). 14.99 *(978-0-06-075687-1(X))* HarperCollins Pubs.

—Very Short Tall Tales to Read Together. Hoberman, Mary Ann. 2014. (ENG.). 32p. (J). (gr. -1-3). 17.00 *(978-0-316-18329-1(6))* Little Brown & Co.

—You Read to Me, I'll Read to You: Very Short Fables to Read Together. Hoberman, Mary Ann. 2010. (ENG.). 32p. (J). (gr. -1-3). 16.99 *(978-0-316-04117-1(3))* Little Brown & Co.

—You Read to Me, I'll Read to You: Very Short Fairy Tales to Read Together. Hoberman, Mary Ann. 2004. (ENG.). 32p. (J). (gr. -1-3). 16.99 *(978-0-316-14611-1(0))* Little, Brown Bks. for Young Readers.

—You Read to Me, I'll Read to You: Very Short Mother Goose Tales to Read Together. Hoberman, Mary Ann. 3rd rev. ed. 2005. (ENG.). 32p. (J). (gr. -1-3). 16.99 *(978-0-316-14431-5(2))* Little, Brown Bks. for Young Readers.

—You Read to Me, I'll Read to You: Very Short Scary Tales to Read Together. Hoberman, Mary Ann. 2007. (ENG.). 32p. (J). (gr. -1-3). 16.99 *(978-0-316-01733-6(7))* Little, Brown Bks. for Young Readers.

—You Read to Me, I'll Read to You: Very Short Stories to Read Together. Hoberman, Mary Ann. 2006. 28p. (gr. -1-1). 17.00 *(978-0-7569-6581-5(0))* Perfection Learning Corp.

—You Read to Me, I'll Read to You: Very Short Stories to Read Together. Hoberman, Mary Ann. 2006. (ENG.). 32p. (J). (gr. -1-3). pap. 7.00 *(978-0-316-01316-1(1)*, Tingley, Megan Bks.) Little, Brown Bks. for Young Readers.

—You Read to Me, I'll Read to You - Very Short Mother Goose Tales to Read Together. Hoberman, Mary Ann. 3rd ed. 2012. (You Read to Me, I'll Read to You Ser.). (ENG.). 32p. (J). (gr. -1-3). pap. 7.00 *(978-0-316-20715-7(2))* Little, Brown Bks. for Young Readers.

—You Read to Me, I'll Read to You: Very Short Fables to Read Together. Hoberman, Mary Ann. 2013. (You Read to Me, I'll Read to You Ser.). (ENG.). 32p. (J). (gr. -1-3). 7.00 *(978-0-316-21847-4(2))* Little, Brown Bks. for Young Readers.

Emberley, Michael. You Read to Me, I'll Read to You No. 2: Very Short Scary Tales to Read Together. Emberley, Michael. Hoberman, Mary Ann. 2009. (ENG.). 32p. (J). (gr. -1-3). pap. 7.00 *(978-0-316-04351-9(6))* Little Brown & Co.

Emberley, Michael & Westcott, Nadine Bernard. What's in There? All about Before You Were Born. Harris, Robie H. 2013. (Let's Talk about You & Me Ser.). (ENG.). 40p. (J). (-k). 15.99 *(978-0-7636-3630-2(4))* Candlewick Pr.

Emberley, Rebecca. Flatland. Emberley, Rebecca, ed. Sayres, David. 2014. (ENG.). 32p. 18.95 *(978-0-9912935-0-6(9))* Two Little Birds Bks.

Emberley, Rebecca & Emberley, Ed. Ten Little Beasties. Emberley, Rebecca & Emberley, Ed. 2011. (ENG.). 32p. (J). (gr. -1-1). 12.99 *(978-1-59643-627-5(1))* Roaring Brook Pr.

Emberley, Rebecca & Emberley, Edward R. The Lion & the Mice. Emberley, Rebecca & Emberley, Edward R. 2012. (I Like to Read Ser.). (ENG.). 24p. (J). (gr. -1-1). pap. 6.99 *(978-0-8234-2641-6(6))* Holiday Hse., Inc.

—Mice on Ice. Emberley, Rebecca & Emberley, Edward R. 2012. (I Like to Read Ser.). (ENG.). 32p. (J). 14.95 *(978-0-8234-2576-1(2))* Holiday Hse., Inc.

Embleton-Hall, Chris. Easter, 1 vol. Williamson, Karen. 2015. (Candle Tabs Ser.). (ENG.). 12p. (J). bds. 7.99 *(978-1-78128-157-4(2)*, Candle Bks.) Lion Hudson PLC GBR. Dist: Kregel Pubns.

—Noah, 1 vol. Williamson, Karen. 2015. (Candle Tabs Ser.). (ENG.). 12p. (J). bds. 7.99 *(978-1-78128-156-7(4)*, Candle Bks.) Lion Hudson PLC GBR. Dist: Kregel Pubns.

Embleton Hall, Chris. Pull-Out David & Goliath, 1 vol. Edwards, Josh. 2014. (ENG.). 10p. (J). bds. 11.99 *(978-1-85985-997-1(6)*, Candle Bks.) Lion Hudson PLC GBR. Dist: Kregel Pubns.

Embleton-Hall, Chris. Pull-Out Jonah & the Big Fish, 1 vol. Edwards, Josh. 2014. (ENG.). 10p. (J). bds. 11.99 *(978-1-85985-998-8(4)*, Candle Bks.) Lion Hudson PLC GBR. Dist: Kregel Pubns.

Embry, Stacey. Somebody Stole My Yawn! Jones, Bryan E. 2009. 28p. pap. 24.95 *(978-1-60749-877-3(4))* America Star Bks.

Emel Alp Sari. Little Bitty Octopus. Poulter, J. R. 2014. 28p. pap. 19.99 *(978-1-62563-917-2(1))* Tate Publishing & Enterprises, LLC.

Emerling, Dorothy. The Lost Seal. McKnight, Diane. 2006. (Long Term Ecological Research Ser.). (ENG.). 40p. (J). (gr. 4-7). 19.95 *(978-0-9723422-7-8(3))* Taylor Trade Publishing.

—My Water Comes from the Rocky Mountains. Fourment, Tiffany. 2009. (Long Term Ecological Research Ser.). (ENG.). 32p. (J). (gr. 1-5). 16.95 *(978-0-9817700-0-0(2))*; pap. 9.95 *(978-0-9817700-1-7(0))* Taylor Trade Publishing.

—My Water Comes from the San Juan Mountains. Fourment, Tiffany & Gianniny, Gary. 2009. (ENG.). 32p. (J). (gr. 4-7). pap. 9.95 *(978-0-9817700-3-1(7))* Taylor Trade Publishing.

Emerson, Hunt, et al. Fight the Power! A Visual History of Protest among the English Speaking Peoples. Wilson, Sean Michael & Dickson, Benjamin. 2013. (ENG.). 192p. pap. 19.95 *(978-1-60980-492-3(9))* Seven Stories Pr.

Emerson, Zelda. Tweens Santa Surprise: How to Explain Santa to Pre-Teens. Emerson, Zelda. 2010. (ENG.). 36p. pap. 9.13 *(978-1-4528-1273-1(X))* CreateSpace Independent Publishing Platform.

Emery, Jennifer. Animal Alphabed. Ruurs, Margriet. 2005. (ENG.). 32p. (J). (gr. -1-3). 15.95 *(978-1-59078-200-2(3))* Boyds Mills Pr.

—Christmas Gifts. O'Keefe, Susan Heyboer. 2004. (ENG.). 32p. (J). (gr. -1-1). 15.95 *(978-1-59078-083-1(3))* Boyds Mills Pr.

—Moving Day. Fletcher, Ralph. 2006. (ENG.). 40p. (J). (gr. 2-7). 17.95 *(978-1-59078-339-9(5))* Boyds Mills Pr.

—Sheila Says We're Weird, 1 vol. Smalley, Ruth Ann. 2011. (ENG.). 32p. (J). 16.95 *(978-0-88448-326-7(6))* Tilbury Hse. Pubs.

—Step-By-Step Crafts for Spring. Ross, Kathy. 2007. 48p. (J). *(978-1-59078-359-7(X))*; pap. *(978-1-59078-476-1(6))* Boyds Mills Pr.

Emery, Thomas, jt. illus. see Majado, Caio.

Emery, Thomas J., jt. illus. see Majado, Caio.

Emilio, Urberuaga & Urberuaga, Emilio. Manolito Four-Eyes, 0 vols. Lindo, Elvira. 2010. (Manolito Four-Eyes Ser.: 1). (ENG.). 160p. (J). (gr. 3-7). pap. 9.99 *(978-0-7614-5729-9(1)*, 9780761457299, Amazon Children's Publishing) Amazon Publishing.

Emily, Bolam. Animals Go. Tiger Tales Staff, ed. 2010. (Touch, Look, & Learn! Ser.). 10p. (J). (gr. -1). bds. 5.95 *(978-1-58925-854-9(1))* Tiger Tales.

—Animals Talk. Tiger Tales Staff, ed. 2010. (Touch, Look, & Learn! Ser.). 10p. (J). (gr. -1). bds. 5.95 *(978-1-58925-855-6(X))* Tiger Tales.

Emison, Patricia A. & Feldman Emison, Chloë. Growing with the Grain: Dynamic Families Shaping History from Ancient Times to the Present. 2005. xix, 321p. (YA). 44.95 *(978-0-9765572-0-3(7))* Lady Illyria Pr.

Emmerson, Michael. Dump Truck Day, 1 vol. Meister, Cari. (My First Graphic Novel Ser.). (ENG.). 32p. (gr. k-2). 2010. pap. 6.25 *(978-1-4342-2288-6(8))*; 2009. 23.32 *(978-1-4342-1621-2(7))* Stone Arch Bks. (My First Graphic Novel).

Emmitt, Randy, photos by. Butterflies of the Carolinas & Virginias. Emmitt, Randy. 2005. (YA). cd-rom 19.95 *(978-0-9767239-0-5(5))* Metalmark Pr.

Empson, Jo. Never Ever. Empson, Jo. 2013. (Child's Play Library). (ENG.). 32p. (J). *(978-1-84643-552-2(8))* Child's Play International Ltd.

—Rabbityness. Empson, Jo. 2012. (Child's Play Library). (ENG.). 32p. (J). *(978-1-84643-492-1(0))*; *(978-1-84643-482-2(3))* Child's Play International Ltd.

Emroca Flores, Jose. The Room of Woe: An Up2U Horror Adventure. Wallace, Rich. 2015. (J). *(978-1-62402-094-0(1))* Magic Wagon.

Emslie, Peter & Marrucchi, Elisa. Surprise for a Princess. Weinberg, Jennifer & RH Disney Staff. 2003. (Step into Reading Ser.). (ENG.). 32p. (J). (gr. k-3). pap. 3.99 *(978-0-7364-2132-4(7)*, RH/Disney) Random Hse. Children's Bks.

Emura. W Juliet. Emura. 2006. (W Juliet Ser.). (ENG.). 208p. pap. 9.99 *(978-1-4215-0563-3(0))*; 192p. pap. 9.99 *(978-1-4215-0205-2(4))* Viz Media.

—W Juliet. Emura. Flanagan, William, tr. from JPN. 2005. (W Juliet Ser.: Vol. 5). (ENG.). 200p. pap. 9.99 *(978-1-59116-848-5(1))* Viz Media.

—W Juliet. Emura. (W Juliet Ser.). (ENG.). 2004. 184p. pap. 9.99 *(978-1-59116-598-9(9))*; Vol. 2. 2005. 184p. pap. 9.99 *(978-1-59116-602-3(0))*; Vol. 3. 2005. 200p. pap. 9.99 *(978-1-59116-600-9(4))*; Vol. 4. 2005. 200p. pap. 9.99 *(978-1-59116-781-5(7))*; Vol. 7. 2005. 208p. pap. 9.99 *(978-1-4215-0065-2(5))*; Vol. 9. 2006. 208p. pap. 9.99 *(978-1-4215-0328-8(X))* Viz Media.

Ende, Michael. Momo. Ende, Michael. 2004. (SPA.). 256p. (YA). (gr. 8-12). pap. 10.95 *(978-968-19-0255-1(6))* Santillana USA Publishing Co., Inc.

Endelman, David. The Big Squeal: A Wild, True, & Twisted Tail. Scaglione, Joanne & Small, Gail. 2005. (ENG.). 56p. pap. 31.00 *(978-1-57886-256-6(6))* Rowman & Littlefield Education.

Endersby, Frank. The First Snow. Butler, M. Christina. 2012. (J). *(978-1-4351-4320-3(5))* Barnes & Noble, Inc.

—Hugs for Little Bear: Valentine Shaker. Rivers-Moore, Debbie. 2012. (ENG.). 8p. (J). bds. 5.99 *(978-0-7641-6489-7(9))* Barron's Educational Series, Inc.

—Just Because You're Mine. Lloyd-Jones, Sally. 2011. (ENG.). 32p. (J). (gr. -1-2). 16.99 *(978-0-06-201476-4(5))* HarperCollins Pubs.

—Left Hand, Right Hand: A Hands-on Book about Left & Right. Brown, Janet Allison. 2006. (ENG.). 16p. (J). (gr. -1-1). bds. 5.99 *(978-0-7641-5924-4(0))* Barron's Educational Series, Inc.

—Maths Problem Solving: Year 1, 6 vols. Yemm, Caterhine. 2005. 106p. pap. *(978-1-903853-74-0(5))* Brilliant Pubns.

—Maths Problem Solving: Year 2, 6 vols. Yemm, Caterhine. 2005. 106p. pap. *(978-1-903853-75-7(3))* Brilliant Pubns.

—Maths Problem Solving: Year 3, 6 vols. Yemm, Caterhine. 2005. 80p. pap. *(978-1-903853-76-4(1))* Brilliant Pubns.

—Maths Problem Solving: Year 4, 6 vols. Yemm, Caterhine. 2005. 80p. pap. *(978-1-903853-77-1(X))* Brilliant Pubns.

—Maths Problem Solving: Year 5, 6 vols. Yemm, Caterhine. 2005. 80p. pap. *(978-1-903853-78-8(8))* Brilliant Pubns.

—Maths Problem Solving: Year 6, 6 vols. Yemm, Caterhine. 2006. 80p. pap. *(978-1-903853-79-5(6))* Brilliant Pubns.

—My First Book of Opposites. Brown, Janet Allison. 2004. (Early Learning Ser.). 18p. (J). bds. 5.99 *(978-1-85854-530-1(7))* Brimax Books Ltd. GBR. Dist: Byeway Bks.

—A Treasury for Little Ones: Hours of Fun for Babies & Toddlers - Stories & Rhymes, Puzzles to Solve, & Things to Make & Do. Baxter, Nicola & Birkinshaw, Marie. 2014. (ENG.). 80p. (J). (gr. -1-6). 14.99 *(978-1-86147-368-4(0)*, Armadillo) Anness Publishing GBR. Dist: National Bk. Network.

Endersly, Frank, jt. illus. see Hartung, Susan Kathleen.

Endle, Kate. Augie to Zebra: An Alphabet Book! Babypants, Caspar. 2012. (ENG.). 32p. (J). (gr. -1-2). 16.99 *(978-1-57061-750-8(3))* Sasquatch Bks.

—Bella & the Bunny. Larsen, Andrew. 2007. (ENG.). 32p. (J). (gr. -1-k). 14.95 *(978-1-55337-970-6(5))* Kids Can Pr., Ltd. CAN. Dist: Univ. of Toronto Pr.

—Big Earth, Little Me. Wiley, Thom. 2009. 16p. (J). pap. *(978-0-545-22335-5(0))* Scholastic, Inc.

—My Woodland Wish. Babypants, Caspar & Ballew, Chris. 2011. (ENG.). 32p. (J). (gr. -1-2). 16.99 *(978-1-57061-748-5(1))* Sasquatch Bks.

—Old Manhattan Has Some Farms: (E-I-E-I-Grow!) Lendroth, Susan. 2014. (ENG.). 32p. (J). (gr. -1-2). lib. bdg. 16.95 *(978-1-58089-572-9(7))* Charlesbridge Publishing, Inc.

—Trout Are Made of Trees. Sayre, April Pulley. 2008. (ENG.). 32p. (J). (gr. -1-3). 6.95 *(978-1-58089-138-7(1))* Charlesbridge Publishing, Inc.

Endoh, Minari. Dazzle, Vol. 1. Endoh, Minari. 2006. (Dazzle Ser.). 200p. (gr. 8-18). pap. 9.99 *(978-1-59816-092-5(3))* TOKYOPOP, Inc.

Endres, Patrick J., photos by. Alaska. Gill, Shelley. 2007. (ENG., 32p. (J). (gr. 1-4). pap. 7.95 *(978-0-88106-293-9(6))* Charlesbridge Publishing, Inc.

—Grizzly Bears of Alaska: Explore the Wild World of Bears. Miller, Debbie S. 2014. (ENG., 32p. (J). (gr. k-3). pap. 10.99 *(978-1-57061-932-8(8))* Sasquatch Bks.

Endres, Sharlene Duggan, jt. illus. see Schmitt, Nannette Toups.

Enersen, Adele. When My Baby Dreams. Enersen, Adele. 2012. (ENG.). 48p. (J). (gr. -1-k). 14.99 *(978-0-06-207175-0(0))* HarperCollins Pubs.

—When My Baby Dreams of Fairy Tales. Enersen, Adele. 2013. (ENG.). 48p. (J). (gr. -1-k). 15.99 *(978-0-06-207177-4(7))* HarperCollins Pubs.

Engel, Christiane. Barron's Amazing Fact-Packed, Fold-Out Atlas of the World: With Awesome Pop-Up Map! Green, Jen. 2014. (ENG.). 56p. (J). (gr. 3-6). 18.99 *(978-0-7641-6746-1(4))* Barron's Educational Series, Inc.

Engel, Christiane. Barron's Totally Wild Fact-Packed, Fold-Out Animal Atlas. Green, Jen. 2015. (ENG.). 56p. (J). (gr. 3-7). 18.99 ***(978-0-7641-6808-6(8))*** Barron's Educational Series, Inc.

Engel, Christiane. The Mitzvah Magician. Marshall, Linda Elovitz. 2012. (Kar-Ben Favorites Ser.). (ENG.). 24p. (J). (gr. -1-2). lib. bdg. 17.95 *(978-0-7613-5655-4(X)*, Kar-Ben Publishing) Lerner Publishing Group.

—The Mitzvah Magician. Elovitz Marshall, Sylvia A. & Marshall, Linda. 2012. (Kar-Ben Favorites Ser.). (ENG.). 24p. (J). (gr. -1-2). 7.95 *(978-0-7613-5656-1(8)*, Kar-Ben Publishing) Lerner Publishing Group.

Engel, Christiane. Knick Knack Paddy Whack. Engel, Christiane. Songs, Steve. 2011. (ENG.). 36p. (J). pap. 9.99 *(978-1-84686-659-3(6))* Barefoot Bks., Inc.

—My Read & Rhyme Bible Storybook. Engel, Christiane. Bowman, Crystal & Kenney, Cindy. 2009. (ENG.). 368p. (J). (gr. -1-2). 17.99 *(978-1-4143-2016-8(7)*, Tyndale Kids) Tyndale Hse. Pubs.

—We Are Moving: Louis & Bobo. Engel, Christiane. 2007. (ENG.). 28p. (J). (gr. k-2). pap. 7.99 *(978-1-84458-375-1(9))* Pavilion Bks. GBR. Dist: Independent Pubs. Group.

Engel, Tonya. Our Lady of Guadalupe, 0 vols. Bernier-Grand, Carmen T. 2012. (ENG.). 32p. (J). (gr. 3-7). 17.99 *(978-0-7614-6135-7(3)*, 9780761461357, Amazon Children's Publishing) Amazon Publishing.

Engelbreit, Mary. A Little Princess. Burnett, Frances Hodgson. 2007. (Mary Engelbreit's Classic Library). (ENG.). 304p. (J). (gr. 3-7). 9.99 *(978-0-06-008137-9(6)*, HarperFestival) HarperCollins Pubs.

—The Night Before Christmas. Moore, Clement C. (ENG.). 40p. (J). (gr. -1-3). 2011. 9.99 *(978-0-06-208944-1(7))*; 2006. 17.99 *(978-0-06-008160-7(0))*; Set. 2007. 25.00 *(978-0-06-136495-2(9)*, HarperFestival) HarperCollins Pubs.

—The Secret Garden. Burnett, Frances Hodgson. 2007. (Mary Engelbreit's Classic Library). (ENG.). 368p. (J). (gr. 3-7). 9.99 *(978-0-06-008136-2(8)*, HarperFestival) HarperCollins Pubs.

Engelbreit, Mary. Baby Booky: Honey Bunny. Engelbreit, Mary. 2004. (ENG.). 14p. (J). (gr. -1-18). 6.99 *(978-0-06-008135-5(X)*, HarperFestival) HarperCollins Pubs.

—Mary Engelbreit's A Merry Little Christmas: Celebrate from A to Z. Engelbreit, Mary. 2006. 40p. (J). (gr. -1-3). lib. bdg. 17.89 *(978-0-06-074159-4(7))* HarperCollins Pubs.

—Mary Engelbreit's a Merry Little Christmas: Celebrate from A to Z. Engelbreit, Mary. 2010. (ENG.). 40p. (J). (gr. -1-3). pap. 6.99 *(978-0-06-074160-0(0))* HarperCollins Pubs.

—Mary Engelbreit's Mother Goose. Engelbreit, Mary. 2008. (ENG.). 128p. (J). (gr. -1-3). 26.99 *(978-0-06-143153-1(2))* HarperCollins Pubs.

—Mary Engelbreit's Mother Goose: One Hundred Best-Loved Verses. Engelbreit, Mary. 2005. (ENG.). 128p. (J). (gr. -1-k). 19.99 *(978-0-06-008171-3(6))* HarperCollins Pubs.

—Mary Engelbreit's Nursery & Fairy Tales Collection. Engelbreit, Mary. 2014. (ENG.). 192p. (J). (gr. -1-3). 11.99 *(978-0-06-228707-6(9))* HarperCollins Pubs.

—Mary Engelbreit's Nutcracker. Engelbreit, Mary. (ENG.). 40p. (J). (gr. -1-3). 2014. 9.99 *(978-0-06-222417-0(4))*; 2011. 17.99 *(978-0-06-088579-3(3))* HarperCollins Pubs.

—Nursery Tales: A Treasury of Children's Classics. Engelbreit, Mary. 2008. (ENG.). 136p. (J). (gr. 4-7). 19.99 *(978-0-06-073168-7(0))* HarperCollins Pubs.

—Queen of Christmas. Engelbreit, Mary. 2003. (Ann Estelle Stories Ser.). (J). 32p. 16.99 *(978-0-06-058608-9(7))*; 159.90 *(978-0-06-056902-0(6))*; 127.92 *(978-0-06-056903-7(4))* HarperCollins Pubs.

—Queen of Easter. Engelbreit, Mary. (Ann Estelle Stories Ser.). 32p. (J). (gr. -1-3). 2009. (ENG.). pap. 6.99 *(978-0-06-008186-7(4))*; 2006. (ENG.). 15.99 *(978-0-06-008184-3(8))*; 2006. 16.89 *(978-0-06-008185-0(6))* HarperCollins Pubs.

—Queen of Halloween. Engelbreit, Mary. 2008. 32p. (J). (gr. -1-3). lib. bdg. 17.89 *(978-0-06-008191-1(0))*; (ENG.). 16.99 *(978-0-06-008190-4(2))* HarperCollins Pubs.

—Queen of Hearts. Engelbreit, Mary. 2008. (Ann Estelle Stories Ser.). (ENG.). 32p. (J). (gr. -1-3). pap. 6.99 *(978-0-06-008183-6(X))* HarperCollins Pubs.

—Queen of the Class. Engelbreit, Mary. 2007. 24p. (J). 16.00 *(978-1-4223-6705-6(3))* DIANE Publishing Co.

—Twelve Timeless Treasures. Engelbreit, Mary. 2010. (ENG.). 128p. (J). 19.99 *(978-0-06-088583-0(1))* HarperCollins Pubs.

Engelhart, Ann. Bambinelli Sunday: A Christmas Blessing. Welborn, Amy. 2013. (ENG.). 32p. (J). (gr. k-2). 15.99 *(978-1-61636-649-0(4))* Franciscan Media.

Engelhart, Ann Kissane. Adventures in Assisi: on the Path with St. Francis; On the Path with St. Francis. Welborn, Amy. 2014. (ENG.). 32p. (J). (gr. k-3). 15.99 *(978-1-61636-650-6(8))* Franciscan Media.

Engels, Christiane. Knick Knack Paddy Whack. Engel, Christiane. 2008. (ENG.). 24p. (J). (gr. -1-k). 16.99 *(978-1-84686-144-4(6))* Barefoot Bks., Inc.

England, Donald. The Sponged Stone: Or the Hunt for Christmas Yet-to-Come. Watt, Mike. 2011. (ENG.). 24p. pap. 6.49 *(978-1-4680-4988-6(7))* CreateSpace Independent Publishing Platform.

Engle, Jason. Samurai. Stowell, Louie. 2007. (Young Reading Series 3 Gift Bks). 58p. (J). (gr. 2-5). 8.99 *(978-0-7945-1719-9(6)*, Usborne) EDC Publishing.

Engle, Jenny. Big Brothers & Big Sisters Are VIP's (Very Important Persons) A Color Me Book. Palmore, Julie, III, 56p. (J). (gr. -1-1). spiral bd. 9.95 *(978-0-9722653-0-0(9))* Palmore, Julie.

Engleheart, Phil. Choreographing the Stage Musical. Sunderland, Margot & Pickering, Ken. 2003. (Musical Theatre Ser.). 152p. (YA). (gr. 4-12). pap. 20.00 *(978-0-85343-586-0(3))* Miller, J. Garnet Ltd. GBR. Dist: Empire Publishing Service.

Engler, Lori. Tiny Takes a Trip. Kennedy, Geno. 2011. 24p. pap. 24.95 *(978-1-4560-8523-0(9))* America Star Bks.

English, Sarah Jane. Secrets in Stone: All about Maya Hieroglyphs. Coulter, Laurie. 2010. (ENG.). 48p. (J). (gr. 4-7). pap. 8.95 *(978-1-897330-57-9(X))* Madison Pr. Bks. CAN. Dist: Independent Pubs. Group.

—Secrets in Stone: All about Maya Hieroglyphs. Coulter, Lavrie. 2003. 48p. (gr. 4-8). 18.00 *(978-0-7567-9000-4(X))* DIANE Publishing Co.

Englund, Jonathon. Infaeter. Brett, James. 2nd ed. 2013. 238p. pap. *(978-1-908462-03-9(5))* New Dawn Pubs.

Engman, Camilla. The Voyage, 1 vol. Salinas, Veronica. Eirheim, Jeanne, tr. from NOR. 2013. (ENG.). 40p. (J). (gr. -1-2). 16.95 *(978-1-55498-386-5(X))* Groundwood Bks. CAN. Dist: Perseus-PGW.

Enik, Ted. The Cat in the Hat Flips His Lid. Brooke, Susan Rich & Seuss, Dr. 2003. (J). *(978-0-7853-8446-5(4))* Publications International, Ltd.

—Curiosity, with a Capital S. Trimble, Tonya. 2011. 144p. (J). pap. 9.95 *(978-0-9816453-9-1(9))*; 16.95 *(978-0-9829421-5-4(X))* Tell Me Pr., LLC.

E

—Eloise in Hollywood. Stern, J. David et al. 2006. (Eloise Ser.). (ENG.). 70p. (J). (gr. -1-3). 18.99 *(978-0-689-84289-4(9))*, Simon & Schuster Bks. For Young Readers) Simon & Schuster Bks. For Young Readers.

—The Magic School Bus Gets Caught in a Web. Lane, Jeanette et al. 2007. (Scholastic Reader Ser.). (J). *(978-0-545-03587-3(2))* Scholastic, Inc.

Enik, Ted & Glasser, Robin Preiss. Fancy Nancy & the Boy from Paris. O'Connor, Jane. 2008. (I Can Read Book 1 Ser.). (ENG.). 32p. (J). (gr. -1-3). 16.99 *(978-0-06-123610-5(1))*; pap. 3.99 *(978-0-06-123609-9(8))* HarperCollins Pubs.

—Fancy Nancy at the Museum. O'Connor, Jane. 2008. (I Can Read Book 1 Ser.). (ENG.). 32p. (J). (gr. -1-3). 16.99 *(978-0-06-123608-2(X))*; pap. 3.99 *(978-0-06-123607-5(1))* HarperCollins Pubs.

—The Show Must Go On. O'Connor, Jane. 2009. (I Can Read Book 1 Ser.). (ENG.). 32p. (J). (gr. -1-3). pap. 3.99 *(978-0-06-170372-0(9))* HarperCollins Pubs.

Enik, Ted, jt. illus. see Glasser, Robin Preiss.

Enos, Daryl. Farmer Brown & His Little Red Truck. Cochran, Jean M. 2009. (ENG.). 32p. (J). (gr. -1-k). 16.95 *(978-0-9792035-0-3(3))* Pleasant St. Pr.

Enos, Randall. Inchworm & a Half. Pinczes, Elinor J. 2003. (ENG.). 32p. (J). pap. 6.99 *(978-0-618-31101-9(7))* Houghton Mifflin Harcourt Publishing Co.

—Mocha Dick: The Legend & the Fury. Heinz, Brian. 2014. (ENG.). 32p. (J). (gr. 1-3). 18.99 *(978-1-56846-242-4(5)*, Creative Editions) Creative Co., The.

Enos, Solomon. Akua Hawaii: Hawaiian Gods & Their Stories. Armitage, Kimo. 2005. 72p. (J). 16.95 *(978-1-58178-042-0(7))* Bishop Museum Pr.

Enria, Samantha. Little Brother Pumpkin Head. Panzieri, Lucia & Maccarone, Grace. 2016. (J). *(978-0-8234-3537-1(7))* Holiday Hse., Inc.

Enright, Amanda. Animals in Fall: Preparing for Winter. Rustad, Martha E. H. 2011. (Fall's Here! Ser.). pap. 39.62 *(978-0-7613-8643-8(2)*, Millbrook Pr.); (ENG.). 24p. pap. 6.95 *(978-0-7613-8506-6(1)*, Millbrook Pr.); (ENG.). 24p. lib. bdg. 23.93 *(978-0-7613-5066-8(7))* Lerner Publishing Group.

—Fall Apples: Crisp & Juicy. Rustad, Martha E. H. 2011. (Fall's Here! Ser.). pap. 39.62 *(978-0-7613-8644-5(0)*, Millbrook Pr.); (ENG.). 24p. pap. 6.95 *(978-0-7613-8507-3(X)*, Millbrook Pr.); (ENG.). 24p. lib. bdg. 23.93 *(978-0-7613-5064-4(0))* Lerner Publishing Group.

—Fall Harvests: Bringing in Food. Rustad, Martha E. H. 2011. (Fall's Here! Ser.). pap. 39.62 *(978-0-7613-8645-2(9)*, Millbrook Pr.); (ENG.). 24p. pap. 6.95 *(978-0-7613-8508-0(8)*, Millbrook Pr.); (ENG.). 24p. lib. bdg. 23.93 *(978-0-7613-5067-5(5))* Lerner Publishing Group.

—Fall Leaves: Colorful & Crunchy. Rustad, Martha E. H. 2011. (Fall's Here! Ser.). pap. 39.62 *(978-0-7613-8646-9(7)*, Millbrook Pr.); (ENG.). 24p. pap. 6.95 *(978-0-7613-8505-9(3)*, Millbrook Pr.); (ENG.). 24p. lib. bdg. 23.93 *(978-0-7613-5062-0(4))* Lerner Publishing Group.

—Fall Pumpkins: Orange & Plump. Rustad, Martha E. H. 2011. (Fall's Here! Ser.). pap. 39.62 *(978-0-7613-8647-6(5)*, Millbrook Pr.); (ENG.). 24p. pap. 6.95 *(978-0-7613-8509-7(6)*, Millbrook Pr.); (ENG.). 24p. lib. bdg. 23.93 *(978-0-7613-5065-1(9))* Lerner Publishing Group.

—Fall Weather: Cooler Temperatures. Rustad, Martha E. H. 2011. (Fall's Here! Ser.). pap. 39.62 *(978-0-7613-8648-3(3)*, Millbrook Pr.); (ENG.). 24p. pap. 6.95 *(978-0-7613-8510-3(X)*, Millbrook Pr.); (ENG.). 24p. lib. bdg. 23.93 *(978-0-7613-5063-7(2))* Lerner Publishing Group.

—The Girls' Book: How to Be the Best at Everything. Foster, Juliana. Wingate, Philippa, ed. 2007. (Best at Everything Ser.). (ENG.). 128p. (J). (gr. 3-7). 9.99 *(978-0-545-01629-2(0)*, Scholastic Pr.) Scholastic, Inc.

Enright, Amanda. I Want to Be A... Fairy. Eaton, Kait. 2014. (J). *(978-1-4351-5499-5(1))* Barnes & Noble, Inc.

Enright, Amanda. My Little Life of Jesus, 1 vol. Williamson, Karen. 2014. (ENG.). 68p. (J). 8.99 *(978-1-78128-131-4(9)*, Candle Bks.) Lion Hudson PLC GBR. Dist: Kregel Pubns.

—No More Pacifiers! With Disappearing Pacifiers! O'Brien, Melanie. 2008. (ENG.). 18p. (J). (gr. -1-k). 10.95 *(978-1-58117-684-1(8)*, Intervisual/Piggy Toes) Bendon, Inc.

Enright, Amanda & Lee, Maxine. Preschool Pirates. Wharton, Ellie. 2014. (Magnetic Play Bks.). (ENG.). 10p. (J). (gr. -1-3). *(978-1-78244-875-4(6))* Top That! Publishing PLC.

Enright, Amanda, jt. illus. see Lee, Maxine.

Enright, Elizabeth. The Four-Story Mistake. Enright, Elizabeth. 3rd ed. 2008. (Melendy Quartet Ser.: 2). (ENG.). 208p. (J). (gr. 3-7). per. 7.99 *(978-0-312-37599-7(9))* Square Fish.

—The Saturdays. Enright, Elizabeth. 3rd ed. 2008. (Melendy Quartet Ser.: 1). (ENG.). 192p. (J). (gr. 3-7). per. 7.99 *(978-0-312-37598-0(0))* Square Fish.

—Spiderweb for Two: A Melendy Maze. Enright, Elizabeth. 3rd ed. 2008. (Melendy Quartet Ser.: 4). (ENG.). 226p. (J). (gr. 3-7). per. 7.99 *(978-0-312-37601-7(4))* Square Fish.

—Then There Were Five. Enright, Elizabeth. 3rd ed. 2008. (Melendy Quartet Ser.: 3). (ENG.). 272p. (J). (gr. 3-7). per. 8.99 *(978-0-312-37600-0(6))* Square Fish.

—Thimble Summer. Enright, Elizabeth. 2008. (ENG.). 144p. (J). (gr. 3-7). pap. 6.99 *(978-0-312-38002-1(X))* Square Fish.

Enright, Maginel Wright. The Twinkle Tales. Baum, L. Frank et al. 2005. (ENG.). 270p. pap. 15.95 *(978-0-8032-6242-3(6)*, BAUTWX, Bison Bks.) Univ. of Nebraska Pr.

Enright, Vicky. Crafts to Make in the Fall. Ross, Kathy. 2003. (Crafts for All Seasons Ser.). (ENG.). 64p. (gr. k-3). pap. 9.95 *(978-0-7613-0335-0(9)*, First Avenue Editions) Lerner Publishing Group.

—Crafts to Make in the Summer. Ross, Kathy. 2003. (Crafts for All Seasons Ser.: 3). (ENG.). 64p. (gr. k-3). pap. 9.95 *(978-0-7613-0334-3(0)*, First Avenue Editions) Lerner Publishing Group.

—It's a Beautiful Day! Haddon, Jean. 2005. (Silly Millies Ser.). 32p. (J). per. 5.95 *(978-0-7613-2397-6(X)*, First Avenue Editions) Lerner Publishing Group.

—Read Anything Good Lately? Allen, Susan & Lindaman, Jane. 2006. (ENG.). 32p. (J). (gr. k-3). per. 6.95 *(978-0-8225-6470-6(X)*, First Avenue Editions) Lerner Publishing Group.

—Used Any Numbers Lately? Allen, Susan & Lindaman, Jane. 2013. (ENG.). 32p. (J). (gr. k-3). pap. 6.95 *(978-1-4677-0864-7(X)*, Millbrook Pr.) Lerner Publishing Group.

—Written Anything Good Lately? Allen, Susan & Lindaman, Jane. 2010. (ENG.). 32p. (J). (gr. k-3). pap. 6.95 *(978-0-7613-5477-2(8)*, First Avenue Editions) Lerner Publishing Group.

Enright, Vicky. It's a Beautiful Day! Enright, Vicky, tr. Haddon, Jean. 2005. (Silly Millies Level 2 Ser.). (ENG.). 32p. (gr. 1-3). lib. bdg. 21.27 *(978-0-7613-2834-6(3)*, Millbrook Pr.) Lerner Publishing Group.

Enright, Walter J. King Arthur & His Knights (Yesterday's Classics) Warren, Maude Radford. 2006. (J). per. 9.95 *(978-1-59915-194-6(4))* Yesterday's Classics.

Enrique, Sanchez. Big Enough Bastante Grande. Ofelia, Dumas Lachtman. 2008. 32p. *(978-1-55885-239-6(5))* Arte Publico Pr.

Enroc Illustrations. The Golden Egg: A Story about Adoption. Thrasher, Jenny & Thrasher, Phil. 2006. (ENG.). 24p. per. 10.95 *(978-1-59800-468-7(9))* Outskirts Pr., Inc.

Ensor, Barbara. Cinderella (As If You Didn't Already Know the Story) Ensor, Barbara. 2011. (ENG.). 128p. (J). (gr. 2-5). 5.99 *(978-0-375-87387-4(2)*, Yearling) Random Hse. Children's Bks.

Eone. Peppa Pig: Peppa Goes Swimming. 2015. (Peppa Pig Ser.). (ENG.). 24p. (J). (gr. -1-k). pap. 3.99 *(978-0-545-83491-9(0))* Scholastic, Inc.

Eone, François René. Peppa Pig: Peppa's First Sleepover. Scholastic, Inc. Staff. 2014. (Peppa Pig Ser.). (ENG.). 24p. (J). (gr. -1-k). pap. 3.99 *(978-0-545-69093-5(5))* Scholastic, Inc.

Epelbaum, Mariano. Celebrate Hanukkah with Bubbe's Tales. Flor Ada, Alma. Hayes, Joe & Franco, Sharon, trs. 2007. (Cuentos para Celebrar / Stories to Celebrate Ser.). 30p. (gr. k-6). per. 11.95 *(978-1-59820-134-5(4))* Santillana USA Publishing Co., Inc.

—Cyber Poser. Kesselring, Mari. 2014. (ENG.). 64p. (J). *(978-1-63235-036-7(X))* Pr. Room Editions LLC.

Epelbaum, Mariano. Little Red Riding Hood: An Interactive Fairy Tale Adventure. Braun, Eric. 2015. (You Choose: Fractured Fairy Tales Ser.). (ENG.). 112p. (gr. 3-4). pap. 6.95 *(978-1-4914-5929-4(8))* Capstone Pr., Inc.

Epelbaum, Mariano. Selfie Sabotage. Kesselring, Mari. 2014. (ENG.). 64p. (J). *(978-1-63235-037-4(8))* Pr. Room Editions LLC.

—Techie Cheater. Kesselring, Mari. 2014. (ENG.). 64p. (J). *(978-1-63235-038-1(6))* Pr. Room Editions LLC.

Ephraim, Shelly Ephraim. A Box of Candles. Jacobs, Laurie A. 2005. (ENG.). 40p. (J). (gr. k-3). 17.95 *(978-1-59078-169-2(4))* Boyds Mills Pr.

Epps, SArah. Alphabet for Young Eckists. Giordano, Jean. 2nd ed. 2007. (J). pap. *(978-1-57043-245-3(7))* Eckankar.

Epstein, Eugene. Arthur. Gould, Robert, photos by. Duey, Kathleen. (Time Soldiers Ser.: Vol. 4). (ENG.). (J). (gr. k-2). 2005. 96p. per. 5.95 *(978-1-929945-56-6(6))*; 2004. 48p. 15.95 *(978-1-929945-05-4(1))* Big Guy Bks., Inc.

—Bugs, Vol. 7. Gould, Robert. 2009. (Big Stuff Ser.: 7 vols.). (ENG.). 16p. (J). bds. 7.95 *(978-1-929945-66-5(3))* Big Guy Bks., Inc.

—Leonardo. Duey, Kathleen. 2009. (Time Soldiers Ser.). (ENG.). (J). (gr. k-2). 95p. 9.95 *(978-1-929945-89-4(2))*;Bk. 8. 48p. 15.95 *(978-1-929945-88-7(4))* Big Guy Bks., Inc.

—Rex. Gould, Robert, photos by. Duey, Kathleen & Gould, Robert. Windler-Cheren, Victoria, tr. 2003. (Time Soldiers Ser.: Bk. 1). (SPA & ENG.). 48p. (J). (gr. k-4). pap. 8.95 *(978-1-929945-35-1(3))* Big Guy Bks., Inc.

—Rex. Gould, Robert, photos by. Duey, Kathleen. 2003. (Time Soldiers Ser.: Bk. 1). (ENG.). 48p. (J). (gr. k-2). pap. 7.95 *(978-1-929945-20-7(5))* Big Guy Bks., Inc.

—Rex. Gould, Robert, photos by. Duey, Kathleen. 2006. (Time Soldiers Ser.: Bk. 1). (ENG.). 96p. (gr. -1-7). 24.21 *(978-1-59961-226-3(7))* Spotlight.

—Rex. Duey, Kathleen. 2006. (Time Soldiers Ser.: Bk. 1). 96p. (J). (gr. -1-7). lib. bdg. 24.21 *(978-1-59961-227-0(5))* Spotlight.

—Rex 2. Gould, Robert, photos by. Duey, Kathleen. 2003. (Time Soldiers Ser.: Bk. 2). (ENG.). 48p. (J). (gr. k-2). pap. 8.95 *(978-1-929945-27-6(2))* Big Guy Bks., Inc.

—Rex 2. Gould, Robert, photos by. Duey, Kathleen & Gould, Robert. 2003. (Soldados de Tiempo Libro: Vol. 2). (SPA & ENG.). 48p. (J). (gr. k-4). pap. 8.95 *(978-1-929945-36-8(1))* Big Guy Bks., Inc.

—Rex2. Gould, Robert, photos by. Duey, Kathleen & Gould, Robert. 2003. (Time Soldiers Ser.). 48p. (J). (gr. 4-7). 17.10 *(978-0-7569-3472-9(9))* Perfection Learning Corp.

—Rex2. Gould, Robert, photos by. Duey, Kathleen. 2007. (Time Soldiers Ser.). (ENG.). 96p. (gr. -1-7). 24.21 *(978-1-59961-228-7(3))* Spotlight.

—Samurai. Duey, Kathleen. l.t. ed. 2006. (Time Soldiers Ser.: Bk. 6). (ENG.). 48p. (J). (gr. k-2). 15.95 *(978-1-929945-62-7(0))* Big Guy Bks., Inc.

—Samurai. Gould, Robert, photos by. Duey, Kathleen. 2007. (Time Soldiers Ser.). (ENG.). 96p. (gr. k-2). 24.21 *(978-1-59961-229-4(1))* Spotlight.

—Time Soldiers, Set. Gould, Robert, photos by. Duey, Kathleen. gif. ed. 2003. (Time Soldiers Ser.). (ENG.). 144p. (J). (gr. k-2). 32.95 *(978-1-929945-23-8(X))* Big Guy Bks., Inc.

—Time Soldiers - Mummy. Gould, Robert, photos by. Duey, Kathleen. 2005. (Time Soldiers Ser.: 5). (ENG.). (J). (gr. k-2). 48p. 15.95 *(978-1-929945-50-4(7))*; 96p. per. 5.95 *(978-1-929945-57-3(4))* Big Guy Bks., Inc.

—Time Soldiers - Patch. Gould, Robert, photos by. Duey, Kathleen. (Time Soldiers Ser.: Bk. 3). (ENG.). (J). (gr. k-2). 2005. 96p. per. 5.95 *(978-1-929945-55-9(8))*; 2003. 48p. pap. 8.95 *(978-1-929945-28-3(0))*; 2003. 48p. 15.95 *(978-1-929945-02-3(7))* Big Guy Bks., Inc.

—Time Soldiers - Rex. Gould, Robert, photos by. Gould, Robert & Duey, Kathleen. 2005. (Time Soldiers Ser.: Bk. 1). (ENG.). 96p. (J). (gr. k-2). per. 5.95 *(978-1-929945-53-5(1))*; per. 5.95 *(978-1-929945-54-2(X))* Big Guy Bks., Inc.

Epstein, Eugene. Rex. Epstein, Eugene, photos by. Duey, Kathleen. 2006. (Time Soldiers Ser.: Bk. 1). (ENG.). 96p. (gr. 4-7). 24.21 *(978-1-59961-225-6(9))* Spotlight.

Epstein, Gabriela. Pierre's Stupendous Birthday Bash. Lammers, Elizabeth A. & McKinney, Dan. 2011. 48p. pap. 24.95 *(978-1-4560-4294-3(7))* America Star Bks.

—The Tale of the Black Igloo: Another Adventure of Pepe & Pierre, 1 vol. Lammers, Elizabeth A. & McKinney, Dan. 2010. 26p. pap. 24.95 *(978-1-60610-433-0(0))* PublishAmerica, Inc.

Epstein, Len. The Blue Stone Plot, 1 vol. Blackaby, Susan. 2007. (Read-It! Chapter Books: Historical Tales Ser.). (ENG.). 64p. (gr. 2-4). lib. bdg. 21.32 *(978-1-4048-4062-1(1)*, Chapter Readers) Picture Window Bks.

—Dani el Dinosaurio, 1 vol. Jones, Christianne C. Lozano, Clara, tr. from ENG. 2006. (Read-It! Readers en Español: Story Collection). (SPA.). 24p. (gr. -1-3). lib. bdg. 19.99 *(978-1-4048-2706-6(4)*, Easy Readers) Picture Window Bks.

—An Illustrated Timeline of Dinosaurs, 1 vol. Wooster, Patricia. 2012. (Visual Timelines in History Ser.). (ENG.). 32p. (gr. 3-4). pap. 7.49 *(978-1-4048-7253-0(1))*; lib. bdg. 27.99 *(978-1-4048-7162-5(4))* Picture Window Bks. (Nonfiction Picture Bks.).

—An Illustrated Timeline of U. S. Presidents, 1 vol. Englar, Mary. 2012. (Visual Timelines in History Ser.). (ENG.). 32p. (gr. 3-4). pap. 7.49 *(978-1-4048-7254-7(X))*; lib. bdg. 27.99 *(978-1-4048-7161-8(6))* Picture Window Bks. (Nonfiction Picture Bks.).

—The Secret Warning, 1 vol. Blackaby, Susan. 2008. (Read-It! Chapter Books: Historical Tales Ser.). (ENG.). 64p. (gr. 2-4). lib. bdg. 21.32 *(978-1-4048-4064-5(8)*, Chapter Readers) Picture Window Bks.

—Ted Saw an Egg. Schmauss, Judy Kentor. 2006. (Reader's Clubhouse Level 1 Reader Ser.). (ENG.). 24p. (J). (gr. 1-4). pap. 3.99 *(978-0-7641-3283-4(0))* Barron's Educational Series, Inc.

Epstein, Len & Pullan, Jack. Pretty Princess Party: Hidden Picture Puzzles, 1 vol. Kalz, Jill. 2013. (Seek It Out Ser.). (ENG.). 32p. (gr. 1-2). 9.95 *(978-1-4048-8078-8(X))*; 25.99 *(978-1-4048-7943-0(9))* Picture Window Bks.

Epstein, Len & Smith, Simon. Seek It Out. Kalz, Jill. 2013. (Seek It Out Ser.). (ENG.). 32p. (gr. 1-2). lib. bdg. 155.94 *(978-1-4048-7945-4(5))* Picture Window Bks.

Epstein, Len, jt. illus. see Smith, Simon.

Epstein, Lori, photos by. 1862 - Fredericksburg: A New Look at a Bitter Civil War Battle. Kostyal, Karen. 2011. (ENG., 48p. (J). (gr. 3-7). 17.95 *(978-1-4263-0835-2(3))*; lib. bdg. 27.90 *(978-1-4263-0836-9(1))* National Geographic Society. (National Geographic Children's Bks.).

Epting, Steve, et al. Age of Apocalypse. Hama, Larry et al. 2006. (ENG.). 376p. (YA). (gr. 8-17). pap. 29.99 *(978-0-7851-1874-9(8))* Marvel Worldwide, Inc.

—Crux, Vol. 4. Dixon, Chuck. 2003. (Crux Ser.: Vol. 4). 160p. (YA). pap. 15.95 *(978-1-931484-99-2(6))* CrossGeneration Comics, Inc.

Epting, Steve. The Death of Captain America Vol. 2: The Burden of Dreams. 2008. (ENG.). 160p. (YA). (gr. 8-17). pap. 14.99 *(978-0-7851-2424-5(1))* Marvel Worldwide, Inc.

—Fantastic Four, Vol. 1. 2011. (ENG.). 136p. (YA). (gr. 8-17). 19.99 *(978-0-7851-5144-9(3))* Marvel Worldwide, Inc.

—The Marvels Project: Birth of the Super Heroes. Brubaker, Ed. 2011. (ENG.). 224p. (YA). (gr. 8-17). pap., pap. 29.99 *(978-0-7851-4061-0(1))* Marvel Worldwide, Inc.

Epting, Steve, et al. Strangers in Atlantis, Vol. 3. Dixon, Chuck. 2003. (Crux Ser.: Vol. 3). 160p. (YA). (gr. 7-18). pap. 7.95 *(978-1-931484-63-3(5))* CrossGeneration Comics, Inc.

—X-Men: Age of Apocalypse Prelude. 2011. (ENG.). 264p. (J). (gr. 4-17). pap., pap. 29.99 *(978-0-7851-5508-9(2))* Marvel Worldwide, Inc.

Epting, Steve & Brooks, Mark. Fantastic Four, Vol. 4. Hickman, Jonathan & Dragotta, Nick. 2011. (ENG.). 184p. (J). (gr. 4-17). pap. 19.99 *(978-0-7851-5143-2(5))* Marvel Worldwide, Inc.

Epting, Steve & D'Armata, Frank. Blood Red Sea. Dixon, Chuck. 2004. (Cazador Ser.: Vol. 1). 160p. (YA). pap. 9.95 *(978-1-59314-058-8(4))* CrossGeneration Comics, Inc.

Epting, Steve, jt. illus. see Eaton, Scot.

Ercolini, David. Not Inside This House! Lewis, Kevin. 2011. (ENG.). 40p. (J). (gr. -1-3). 16.99 *(978-0-439-43981-7(7)*, Orchard Bks.) Scholastic, Inc.

Erdelji, Darka. The Sights Before Christmas, 1 vol. Malone, Beni & White, Marian Frances. 2007. (ENG.). 32p. (J). (gr. -1-2). pet. 8.95 *(978-1-894294-94-2(7)*, Tuckamore Bks) Creative Bk. Publishing CAN. Dist: Orca Bk. Pubs. USA.

Erdogan, Buket. Hello, Calico! Wilson, Karma. 2007. (ENG.). 14p. (J). (gr. -1 — 1). 7.99 *(978-1-4169-1356-6(4)*, Little Simon) Little Simon.

—Mouse Loves School. Thompson, Lauren. 2011. (Ready-To-Reads Ser.). (ENG.). 24p. (J). (gr. -1-k). lib. bdg. 16.99 *(978-1-4424-2899-7(6)*, Simon Spotlight) Simon Spotlight.

—Mouse's First Christmas. Thompson, Lauren. 2003. (ENG.). 32p. (J). (gr. -1-3). 7.99 *(978-0-689-86348-6(9))*, Simon & Schuster Bks. For Young Readers) Simon & Schuster Bks. For Young Readers.

—Mouse's First Christmas. Thompson, Lauren. ed. 2003. (gr. -1-1). lib. bdg. 18.40 *(978-0-613-91039-2(7)*, Turtleback) Turtleback Bks.

—Mouse's First Day of School. Thompson, Lauren. 2010. (Classic Board Bks.). (ENG.). 34p. (J). (gr. -1 — 1). bds. 7.99 *(978-1-4169-9476-3(9))*, Little Simon) Little Simon.

—Mouse's First Day of School. Thompson, Lauren & Jackson, Livia. 2003. (ENG.). 32p. (J). (gr. -1-3). 15.99 *(978-0-689-84727-1(0)*, Simon & Schuster Bks. For Young Readers) Simon & Schuster Bks. For Young Readers.

—Mouse's First Fall. Thompson, Lauren. 2010. (Classic Board Bks.). (ENG.). 34p. (J). (gr. -1 — 1). bds. 7.99 *(978-1-4169-9477-0(7)*, Little Simon) Little Simon.

—Mouse's First Fall. Thompson, Lauren. 2006. (ENG.). 32p. (J). (gr. -1-1). 14.99 *(978-0-689-85837-6(X)*, Simon & Schuster Bks. For Young Readers) Simon & Schuster Bks. For Young Readers.

—Mouse's First Halloween. Thompson, Lauren. 2003. (Classic Board Bks.). (ENG.). 34p. (J). (gr. -1 — 1). bds., bds. 7.99 *(978-0-689-85584-9(2)*, Little Simon) Little Simon.

—Mouse's First Snow. Thompson, Lauren. 2011. (Classic Board Bks.). (ENG.). 34p. (J). (gr. -1 — 1). bds. 7.99 *(978-1-4424-2651-1(9)*, Little Simon) Little Simon.

—Mouse's First Snow. Thompson, Lauren. 2005. (ENG.). 32p. (J). (gr. -1-3). 15.99 *(978-0-689-85836-9(1)*, Simon & Schuster Bks. For Young Readers) Simon & Schuster Bks. For Young Readers.

—Mouse's First Spring. Thompson, Lauren. 2012. (Classic Board Bks.). (ENG.). 34p. (J). (gr. -1-3). bds. 7.99 *(978-1-4424-3431-8(7)*, Little Simon) Little Simon.

—Mouse's First Spring. Thompson, Lauren. 2005. (ENG.). 32p. (J). (gr. -1-3). 15.99 *(978-0-689-85838-3(8)*, Simon & Schuster Bks. For Young Readers) Simon & Schuster Bks. For Young Readers.

—Mouse's First Summer. Thompson, Lauren. 2013. (Classic Board Bks.). (ENG.). 34p. (J). (gr. -1 — 1). bds. 7.99 *(978-1-4424-5842-0(9)*, Little Simon) Little Simon.

Erdogan, Buket. Mouse's First Summer. Thompson, Lauren. 2014. (J). *(978-1-4351-5506-0(8))* Simon & Schuster.

Erdogan, Buket. Mouse's First Summer. Thompson, Lauren. 2004. (ENG.). 32p. (J). (gr. -1-3). 16.99 *(978-0-689-85835-2(3)*, Simon & Schuster Bks. For Young Readers) Simon & Schuster Bks. For Young Readers.

—Mouse's First Valentine. Thompson, Lauren. 2004. (Classic Board Bks.). (ENG.). 34p. (J). (gr. -1 — 1). 7.99 *(978-0-689-85585-6(0)*, Little Simon) Little Simon.

—My Valentine for Jesus, 1 vol. Knowlton, Laurie Lazzaro. 2009. (ENG.). 10p. (J). bds. 4.99 *(978-0-310-71333-3(1))* Zonderkidz.

Erdogan, Buket. Trick or Treat, Calico! Wilson, Karma. 2014. (J). *(978-1-4351-5610-4(2)*, Little Simon) Little Simon.

Erdrich, Lise. Bears Make Rock Soup. Fifield, Lisa. 2013. (ENG.). 32p. (J). pap. 9.95 *(978-0-89239-300-8(9)*, Children's Book Press) Lee & Low Bks., Inc.

Erdrich, Louise. Chickadee. Erdrich, Louise. (Birchbark House Ser.: 4). (J). (gr. 3-7). 2013. (ENG.). 224p. pap. 6.99 *(978-0-06-057792-6(4))*; 2012. (ENG.). 208p. 16.99 *(978-0-06-057790-2(8))*; 2012. 208p. lib. bdg. 17.89 *(978-0-06-057791-9(6))* HarperCollins Pubs.

—The Porcupine Year. Erdrich, Louise. (Birchbark House Ser.: 3). (J). (gr. 3-7). 2010. 224p. pap. 6.99 *(978-0-06-441030-4(7))*; 2008. (ENG.). 208p. 16.99 *(978-0-06-029787-9(5))*; 2008. 208p. lib. bdg. 16.89 *(978-0-06-029788-6(3))* HarperCollins Pubs.

Eremeyev, Margarita. Mama, Don't! Merrick, Laurie K. 2008. 20p. per. 24.95 *(978-1-4241-9868-9(2))* America Star Bks.

Eric, F. Rowe. Las Minas del Rey Salomon. Haggard, H. Rider. 5th ed. (Coleccion Clasicos en Accion).Tr. of King Solomon's Mines. (SPA.). 80p. (YA). (gr. 5-8). 12.76 *(978-84-241-5779-1(6))* Everest Editora ESP. Dist: Lectorum Pubns., Inc.

—El Último Mohicano. Cooper, James Fenimore. 6th ed. (Coleccion Clasicos en Accion). (SPA.). 76p. (YA). (gr. 5-8). 15.95 *(978-84-241-5780-7(X)*, EV0655) Everest Editora ESP. Dist: Lectorum Pubns., Inc.

Eric, Kincaid. Puss in Boots. Claire, Black. 2004. 30p. pap. *(978-1-84577-074-7(9))* Berryland Bks.

Eric, Whitfield. The Gift of the Magic: And Other Enchanting Character-Building Stories for Smart Teenage Girls Who Want to Grow up to Be Strong Women. Showstack, Richard. 2004. 156p. (YA). per. 14.95 *(978-1-888725-64-3(8)*, BeachHouse Bks.) Science & Humanities Pr.

Ericksen, Barb, et al. Time at the Top & All in Good Time: Two Novels. Ormondroyd, Edward. 2011. (ENG.). 379p. (J). (gr. 4-7). pap. 12.95 *(978-1-930900-55-4(4))* Purple Hse. Pr.

Ericksen, Barbara. Time at the Top. Ormondroyd, Edward. 40th anniv. ed. 2003. 191p. (J). 17.95 *(978-1-930900-19-6(8))* Purple Hse. Pr.

Erickson, David. Brothers of the Falls. Emery, Joanna. 2004. (Adventures in America Ser.). (gr. 4). 14.95 *(978-1-893110-37-3(0))* Silver Moon Pr.

—Easter Around the World. Knudsen, Shannon. 2005. (On My Own Holidays Ser.). (ENG.). 48p. (gr. 2-4). 25.26 *(978-1-57505-655-5(0))* Lerner Publishing Group.

—Grandpa, Is There a Heaven? Bohlmann, Katharine. 2008. 32p. pap. 7.49 *(978-0-7586-1478-0(0))* Concordia Publishing Hse.

—Tell Me about God. Henley, Karyn. 2005. 24p. (J). 9.99 *(978-1-59185-616-0(7)*, Charisma Kids) Charisma Media.

Erickson, David L. Hablame de Dios. Henley, Karyn. 2005. 20p. (J). (gr. 4-7). 8.99 *(978-1-59185-825-6(9)*, Charisma Kids) Charisma Media.

Erickson, John & Klofkorn, Lisa. Color Analyzers: Investigating Light & Color. Hoyt, Richard, photos by. Erickson, John & Willard, Carolyn. rev. ed. 2005. (Great Explorations in Math & Science Ser.). 96p. (J). pap., Instr.'s gde. ed. 21.00 *(978-0-924886-89-8(7)*, GEMS) Univ. of California, Berkeley, Lawrence Hall of Science.

Erickson, John R. & Holmes, Gerald L. The Case of the Prowling Bear. 2013. 126p. (J). *(978-1-59188-261-9(3))*; pap. *(978-1-59188-161-2(7))* Maverick Bks.

The check digit for ISBN-10 appears in parentheses after the full ISBN-13

Erickson, Melissa. When the Tooth Fairy Comes... Erickson, Melissa. 2007. 15p. (J). (gr. -1-3). 10.99 *(978-1-59879-369-7(1))* Lifevest Publishing, Inc.

Erickson, Terri. April Is Born: Adventures of a New Quarter Horse Filly. Hawkins, Al. l.t. ed. 2004. 24p. (J). pap. 9.50 *(978-0-9640056-5-5(4))* Arrowhead Publishing.

Erickson, Timothy Ronald. Death's Whisper Recoil, 2. Erickson, Timothy Ronald. 2003. (YA). pap. 14.95 *(978-1-59492-001-1(X))* Erickson, Tim.

Ericson, Lisa. Dill & Bizzy: An Odd Duck & a Strange Bird. Ericson, Nora. 2016. 40p. (J). (gr. -1-3). 17.99 *(978-0-06-230452-0(6))* HarperCollins Pubs.

Ericsson, Annie Beth. What's in My Garden? A Book of Colors. Christian, Cheryl. 2009. 16p. (J). (gr. -1). bds. 6.25 *(978-1-59572-166-2(5))* Star Bright Bks., Inc.

—What's in My Toybox: A Book of Shapes, 1 vol. Christian, Cheryl. 2009. (ENG.). 32p. (J). (gr. -1). bds. 6.25 *(978-1-59572-164-8(9))* Star Bright Bks., Inc.

Eriksen, Tone. I Love You Little One. Deprisco Wang, Dorothea. 2007. (Story Book Ser.). 10p. (J). (gr. -1). bds. *(978-1-84666-173-0(0)*, Tide Mill Pr.) Top That! Publishing PLC.

Eriksson, Eva. A Day with Dad. Holmberg, Bo R. 2008. (ENG.). 32p. (J). (gr. -1-3). 15.99 *(978-0-7636-3221-2(X))* Candlewick Pr.

—Julia Wants a Pet. Lindgren, Barbro. Dyssegaard, Elisabeth Kallick, tr. 2003. 32p. (J). (gr. -1 — 1). 15.00 *(978-91-29-65940-5(X))* R & S Bks. SWE. Dist: Macmillan.

—My Happy Life. Lagercrantz, Rose. 2013. 136p. (J). (gr. k-3). 16.95 *(978-1-877579-35-6(1))* Gecko Pr. NZL. Dist: Lerner Publishing Group.

—Tim's Big Move. Wagner, Anke. 2012. (ENG.). 32p. (J). (gr. -1-3). 17.95 *(978-0-7358-4090-4(3))* North-South Bks., Inc.

Eriksson, Eva. When Dad Showed Me the Universe. Stark, Ulf. 2015.Tr. of Nar Pappa Visade Mej Varldsalltet. (ENG.). 32p. (J). (gr. 2-4). 16.99 ***(978-1-927271-81-0(9))*** Gecko Pr. NZL. Dist: Lerner Publishing Group.

—When I Am Happiest. Lagercrantz, Rose. 2015. (ENG.). 128p. (J). (gr. k-3). 16.99 ***(978-1-927271-90-2(8))*** Gecko Pr. NZL. Dist: Lerner Publishing Group.

Ering, Timothy B. The Tale of Despereaux: Being the Story of a Mouse, a Princess, Some Soup & a Spool of Thread. DiCamillo, Kate. 2013. 296p. (J). *(978-0-7636-7205-8(X))* Candlewick Pr.

Ering, Timothy Basil. The Children & the Wolves. Rapp, Adam. 2012. (ENG.). 160p. (YA). (gr. 9). 16.99 *(978-0-7636-5337-8(3))* Candlewick Pr.

—Don't Let the Peas Touch! Blumenthal, Deborah. 2004. (J). *(978-0-439-29733-2(8)*, Levine, Arthur A. Bks.) Scholastic, Inc.

—Finn Throws a Fit! Elliott, David. (ENG.). 32p. (J). 2011. (gr. k-k). pap. 6.99 *(978-0-7636-5604-1(6))*; 2009. (gr. -1-k). 16.99 *(978-0-7636-2356-2(3))* Candlewick Pr.

—Mr. & Mrs. God in the Creation Kitchen. Wood, Nancy. 2006. (ENG.). 32p. (J). (gr. k-4). 16.99 *(978-0-7636-1258-0(8))* Candlewick Pr.

—Snook Alone. Nelson, Marilyn. (ENG.). 48p. (J). (gr. -1-3). 2012. pap. 6.99 *(978-0-7636-6120-5(1))*; 2010. 16.99 *(978-0-7636-2667-9(8))* Candlewick Pr.

—The Tale of Despereaux: Being the Story of a Mouse, a Princess, Some Soup & a Spool of Thread. DiCamillo, Kate. (Tale of Despereaux Ser.). (ENG.). 272p. (J). (gr. 2-5). 2003. 17.99 *(978-0-7636-1722-6(9))*; 2008. 29.99 *(978-0-7636-2928-1(6))*; 2006. reprint ed. per. 7.99 *(978-0-7636-2529-0(9))* Candlewick Pr.

—The Tale of Despereaux: Being the Story of a Mouse, a Princess, Some Soup & a Spool of Thread. DiCamillo, Kate. l.t. ed. 2004. (Thorndike Literacy Bridge Ser.). (ENG.). 247p. (J). pap. 11.95 *(978-1-4104-1527-1(9))* Thorndike Pr.

—The Tale of Despereaux: Being the Story of a Mouse, a Princess, Some Soup & a Spool of Thread. DiCamillo, Kate. ed. 2006. 267p. (gr. 2-7). 18.40 *(978-1-4177-3322-4(5)*, Turtleback) Turtleback Bks.

—Wild Boy: The Real Life of the Savage of Aveyron. Losure, Mary. 2013. (ENG.). 176p. (J). (gr. 5). 16.99 *(978-0-7636-5669-0(0))* Candlewick Pr.

—33 Snowfish. Rapp, Adam. 2006. (ENG.). 192p. (YA). (gr. 9-12). per. 7.99 *(978-0-7636-2917-5(0))* Candlewick Pr.

Ering, Timothy Basil. The Almost Fearless Hamilton Squidlegger. Ering, Timothy Basil. 2014. (ENG.). 48p. (J). (gr. -1-2). 16.99 *(978-0-7636-2357-9(1))* Candlewick Pr.

—Necks Out for Adventure! The True Story of Edwin Wiggleskin. Ering, Timothy Basil. 2008. (ENG.). 48p. (J). (gr. -1-3). 16.99 *(978-0-7636-2355-5(5))* Candlewick Pr.

—The Story of Frog Belly Rat Bone. Ering, Timothy Basil. (ENG.). 48p. (J). (gr. -1-3). 2013. 17.99 *(978-0-7636-6661-3(0))*; 2008. pap. 6.99 *(978-0-7636-2611-2(2))* Candlewick Pr.

Erker, Robert. The Secret of the Bounce-Back Mom. Pohlmann-Eden, Bernd. Hofer, Klaus C., tr. 2013. 34p. pap. *(978-1-897462-27-0(1))* Glen Margaret Publishing.

Erkocak, Sahin. King Arthur & the Sword in the Stone, 1 vol. Meister, Cari. 2008. (Read-It! Readers: Legends Ser.). (ENG.). 32p. (gr. k-3). 19.99 *(978-1-4048-4837-5(1)*, Easy Readers) Picture Window Bks.

—No Snow for Christmas, 1 vol. Kalz, Jill. 2013. (Pfeffernut County Ser.). (ENG.). 32p. (gr. 3-4). 8.99 *(978-1-4795-2158-6(2)*, Fiction Picture Bks.) Picture Window Bks.

Erlbruch, Wolf. The Story of the Little Mole Who Knew It Was None of His Business. Holzwarth, Werner. 2012. (ENG.). 24p. (J). (gr. -1-2). bds. 17.99 *(978-1-84365-132-1(7)*, Pavilion Children's Books) Pavilion Bks. GBR. Dist: Independent Pubs. Group.

Erlich, Esther. Jonathon's Thongs. Kliman, Susie. 2013. 35p. pap. *(978-0-9875296-1-9(7))* Aly's Bks.

Ernst, Clara, jt. illus. see Madan, Fredric C.

Ernst, Clara, jt. illus. see Mingo, Norman.

Ernst, Lisa Campbell. Boots for Beth. Moran, Alex. 2003. (Green Light Readers Level 2 Ser.). (ENG.). 24p. (J). (gr. -1-3). pap. 3.95 *(978-0-15-204838-9(3))* Houghton Mifflin Harcourt Publishing Co.

—The Chick That Wouldn't Hatch. Daniel, Claire. 2003. (Green Light Readers Level 2 Ser.). (ENG.). 24p. (J). (gr. -1-3). pap. 3.95 *(978-0-15-204831-0(6))* Houghton Mifflin Harcourt Publishing Co.

—Come Here, Tiger! Moran, Alex. 2003. (Green Light Readers Level 1 Ser.). (ENG.). 24p. (J). (gr. -1-3). pap. 3.95 *(978-0-15-204860-0(X))* Houghton Mifflin Harcourt Publishing Co.

—Lucy's Quiet Book. Medearis, Angela Shelf. 2004. (Green Light Readers Level 2 Ser.). (ENG.). 24p. (J). (gr. -1-3). pap. 3.95 *(978-0-15-205143-3(0))* Houghton Mifflin Harcourt Publishing Co.

—Lucy's Quiet Book. Medearis, Angela Shelf. 2004. (Green Light Readers Level 2 Ser.). (gr. k-2). 13.95 *(978-0-7569-4310-3(8))* Perfection Learning Corp.

Ernst, Lisa Campbell. The Gingerbread Girl. Ernst, Lisa Campbell. (J). (gr. -1-k). 2009. 32p. pap. 6.99 *(978-0-14-241448-4(4)*, Puffin); 2006. (ENG.). 36p. 16.99 *(978-0-525-47667-2(9)*, Dutton Juvenile) Penguin Publishing Group.

—The Gingerbread Girl Goes Animal Crackers. Ernst, Lisa Campbell. 2011. (ENG.). 32p. (J). (gr. -1-k). 16.99 *(978-0-525-42259-4(5)*, Dutton Juvenile) Penguin Publishing Group.

—Goldilocks Returns. Ernst, Lisa Campbell. 2003. (ENG.). 40p. (J). (gr. -1-3). pap. 7.99 *(978-0-689-85705-8(5)*, Simon & Schuster Bks. For Young Readers) Simon & Schuster Bks. For Young Readers.

—El Pollito Que No Quería Salir del Huevo. Ernst, Lisa Campbell, Daniel, Claire. Flor Ada, Alma & Campoy, F. Isabel, trs. from ENG. 2009. (Green Light Readers Level 2 Ser.).Tr. of Chick That Wouldn't Hatch. (SPA & ENG.). 28p. (J). (gr. -1-3). pap. 3.99 *(978-0-15-206446-4(X))* Houghton Mifflin Harcourt Publishing Co.

—Round Like a Ball! Ernst, Lisa Campbell. 2008. (ENG.). 36p. (J). (gr. -1-3). 15.95 *(978-1-934706-01-5(9))* Blue Apple Bks.

—Sylvia Jean, Scout Supreme. Ernst, Lisa Campbell. 2010. (ENG.). 32p. (J). (gr. -1-3). 16.99 *(978-0-525-47873-7(6)*, Dutton Juvenile) Penguin Publishing Group.

—This Is the Van That Dad Cleaned. Ernst, Lisa Campbell. 2005. (ENG.). 40p. (J). (gr. -1-3). 18.99 *(978-0-689-86190-1(7)*, Simon & Schuster Bks. For Young Readers) Simon & Schuster Bks. For Young Readers.

—The Turn-Around, Upside-Down Alphabet Book. Ernst, Lisa Campbell. 2004. (ENG.). 32p. (J). (gr. -1-3). 17.99 *(978-0-689-85685-3(7)*, Simon & Schuster Bks. For Young Readers) Simon & Schuster Bks. For Young Readers.

—Wake up, It's Spring! Ernst, Lisa Campbell. 2004. (ENG.). 40p. (J). (gr. -1-3). 16.99 *(978-0-06-008985-6(7))* HarperCollins Pubs.

Ernt, Clara, jt. illus. see Mingo, Norman.

Eroglu, Aysin D. Princess Bella's Birthday Cake, 1 vol. Shaskan, Trisha Speed. 2007. (Read-It! Readers Ser.). (ENG.). 24p. (gr. -1-3). lib. bdg. 19.99 *(978-1-4048-3166-7(5)*, Easy Readers) Picture Window Bks.

Erps, Yitzy. Tell Me a Tale: 8 Great Stories. 2005. 64p. (J). *(978-1-4226-0018-4(1))* Mesorah Pubns., Ltd.

Errington, Rachael. Count Grumpula & the Wood Witch. Blackhurst, Rebecca. 2013. 18p. *(978-0-473-24899-4(9))* Cobble Creep Productions.

Erskine, Gary. The Filth. Morrison, Grant. rev. ed. 2007. (ENG.). 320p. pap. 24.99 *(978-1-4012-0013-8(3)*, Vertigo) DC Comics.

Erskine, Gary & Williams, Anthony. Island of Terror: Battle of Iwo Jima. Hama, Larry. 2006. (Graphic History Ser.: 5). (ENG.). 48p. (J). (gr. 2-4). pap. *(978-1-84603-055-0(2)*, Osprey Publishing) Bloomsbury Publishing Plc.

Erskine, Gary, jt. illus. see Spahn, Jerrold.

Ersoz, Sahin. The Mad Mysterious Mansion: Izzy & Daisy. Ersoz, Isabella. 2013. 40p. pap. 12.95 *(978-0-9912023-4-8(1))* Pep & Olie Publishing.

—Mr. Kite & the Perilous Flight: Izzy & Daisy. Lebost, Diana. 2013. 88p. pap. 18.95 *(978-0-9912023-5-5(X))* Pep & Olie Publishing.

Ervin, Keith. Charlie & Chu Chu's Day of Adventure. Ervin, Imogene. 2005. (J). 7.00 *(978-0-9771549-0-6(4))* Finer Moments.

Erwert, Scott. How to Be a Vampire: A Fangs-On Guide for the Newly Undead. Gray, Amy. 2009. (ENG.). 144p. (YA). (gr. 7-18). 14.99 *(978-0-7636-4915-9(5))* Candlewick Pr.

Erwin, J. L. Jett Smith & the Alien Grave. Orr, Andy. 2013. (ENG.). 212p. pap. 9.99 *(978-0-615-83813-7(8))* Red Planet Adventures.

Erwin, Steve, et al. The Battle of Gettysburg, 1 vol. Burgan, Michael & Hoena, Blake A. 2006. (Graphic History Ser.). (ENG.). 32p. (gr. 3-4). 29.99 *(978-0-7368-5491-7(6)*, Graphic Library) Capstone Pr., Inc.

—The Battle of Gettysburg. Burgan, Michael. 2006. (Graphic History Ser.). (ENG.). 32p. (gr. 3-4). per. 8.10 *(978-0-7368-6880-8(1)*, Graphic Library) Capstone Pr., Inc.

Erwin, Steve. Ciencia Gráfica. Biskup, Agnieszka et al. Strictly Spanish, LLC., tr. 2012. (Ciencia Gráfica Ser.). (SPA.). 32p. (gr. 3-4). lib. bdg. 179.94 *(978-1-4296-9241-0(3))* Capstone Pr., Inc.

Erwin, Steve, et al. Convergence. Friedman, Michael Jan et al. 2008. (ENG.). 176p. pap. 14.95 *(978-1-84576-320-6(3))* Titan Bks. Ltd. GBR. Dist: Random Hse., Inc.

—A Crash Course in Forces & Motion with Max Axiom, Super Scientist, 1 vol. Sohn, Emily & Barnett III, Charles. 2007. (Graphic Science Ser.). (ENG.). 32p. (gr. 3-4). 29.99 *(978-0-7368-6837-2(2)*, 1264931, Graphic Library) Capstone Pr., Inc.

Erwin, Steve. Un Curso Intensivo Sobre Fuerzas y Movimiento con Max Axiom, Supercientífico. Sohn, Emily & Barnett III, Charles. Strictly Spanish, LLC., tr. from ENG. 2012. (Ciencia Gráfica Ser.). (SPA.). 32p. (gr. 3-4). lib. bdg. 29.99 *(978-1-4296-9236-6(7))* Capstone Pr., Inc.

Erwin, Steve, et al. The Hindenburg Disaster, 1 vol. Doeden, Matt. 2006. (Disasters in History Ser.). (ENG.). 32p. (gr. 3-4). 29.99 *(978-0-7368-5481-8(9)*, Graphic Library) Capstone Pr., Inc.

—The Lewis & Clark Expedition, 1 vol. Gunderson, Jessica Sarah & Gunderson, Jessica. 2006. (Graphic History Ser.). (ENG.). 32p. (gr. 3-4). 29.99 *(978-0-7368-6493-0(8)*, Graphic Library) Capstone Pr., Inc.

—The Story of Jamestown, 1 vol. Braun, Eric. 2005. (Graphic History Ser.). (ENG.). 32p. (gr. 3-4). 29.99 *(978-0-7368-4967-8(X)*, Graphic Library) Capstone Pr., Inc.

—The Wright Brothers & the Airplane, 1 vol. Niz, Xavier et al. 2007. (Inventions & Discovery Ser.). (ENG.). 32p. (gr. 3-4). 29.99 *(978-0-7368-6845-7(3)*, Graphic Library) Capstone Pr., Inc.

Erwin, Steve. The Wright Brothers & the Airplane, 1 vol. Niz, Xavier W. et al. 2007. (Inventions & Discovery Ser.). (ENG.). 32p. (gr. 3-4). per. 8.10 *(978-0-7368-7897-5(1)*, Graphic Library) Capstone Pr., Inc.

—The Z-Boys & Skateboarding, 1 vol. Anderson, Jameson. 2007. (Inventions & Discovery Ser.). (ENG.). 32p. (gr. 3-4). 29.99 *(978-1-4296-0150-4(7)*, Graphic Library) Capstone Pr., Inc.

Erwin, Steve & Barnett, Charles, III. A Crash Course in Forces & Motion with Max Axiom, Super Scientist, 1 vol. Sohn, Emily. 2007. (Graphic Science Ser.). (ENG.). 32p. (gr. 3-4). per. 8.10 *(978-0-7368-7890-6(4)*, 1264931) Capstone Pr., Inc.

—How to Draw Ferocious Animals, 1 vol. Sautter, Aaron. 2008. (Drawing Cool Stuff Ser.). (ENG.). 32p. (gr. 3-4). 27.32 *(978-1-4296-1299-9(1)*, Edge Bks.) Capstone Pr., Inc.

—Mother Jones: Labor Leader. Miller, Connie Colwell. 2006. (Graphic Biographies Ser.). (ENG.). 32p. (gr. 3-4). 29.99 *(978-0-7368-5487-0(8)*, Graphic Library) Capstone Pr., Inc.

—Mother Jones: Labor Leader, 1 vol. Miller, Connie Colwell. 2006. (Graphic Biographies Ser.). (ENG.). 32p. (gr. 3-4). per. 8.10 *(978-0-7368-9662-7(7)*, Graphic Library) Capstone Pr., Inc.

Esberger, Trudi. The Boy Who Lost His Bumble. Esberger, Trudi. (Child's Play Library). (ENG.). 32p. (J). 2015. *(978-1-84643-662-8(1))*; 2014. ***(978-1-84643-661-1(3))*** Child's Play International Ltd.

Escher, M. C. TIDELOG 2003 Graphic Almanac for Southeastern States: Covering the Entire South Carolina Coast, North to Wilmington NC, & South to Brunswick, Ga. Born, Mark Alan. 2004. 144p. spiral bd. 14.95 *(978-1-933120-05-8(3))* Pacific Pubs.

Escobar, Antonio Rocha. El Misterio de la Casa Chueca (y el Bulto Color Mugre) The Mystery of the Crooked House. Anza, Ana Luisa. rev. ed. 2006. (Castillo de la Lectura Naranja Ser.). (SPA & ENG.). 120p. (J). (gr. 4-7). pap. 7.95 *(978-970-20-0200-0(1))* Castillo, Ediciones, S. A. de C. V. MEX. Dist: Macmillan.

—La Videocasetera YA No Esta a Dieta. Garcia, Juan Carlos Quezadas et al. rev. ed. 2007. (Castillo de la Lectura Naranja Ser.). (SPA & ENG.). 120p. (J). (gr. 4-7). pap. 7.95 *(978-970-20-0307-6(5))* Castillo, Ediciones, S. A. de C. V. MEX. Dist: Macmillan.

Escott, Esther. The Clockmaker of Mullen. Escott, Jamison. 2004. 24p. (J). pap. 8.95 *(978-1-57733-127-8(3)*, Papillon Publishing) Blue Dolphin Publishing, Inc.

Escott, Ian. Science Ethics & Controversies, 1 vol. Hartman, Eve et al. 2009. (Sci-Hi: Life Science Ser.). (ENG.). 48p. (gr. 4-4). pap. 8.99 *(978-1-4109-3338-6(5)*, Sci-Hi) Heinemann-Raintree.

Escott, Ian & Joynes, Gary. Classification of Animals, 1 vol. Rand, Casey & Heinemann Library Staff. 2009. (Sci-Hi: Life Science Ser.). (ENG.). 48p. (gr. 4-4). pap. 8.99 *(978-1-4109-3333-1(4)*, Sci-Hi) Heinemann-Raintree.

Escott, Ian, jt. illus. see De Angelis, Maurizio.

Escriva, Ana Lopez. La Familia de Mic. Pacheco, Miguel Angel. 2003. (SPA.). (J). *(978-970-690-761-5(0))* Planeta Mexicana Editorial S. A. de C. V.

—Please Do Feed the Bears. Naylor, Phyllis Reynolds. 2007. (ENG.). 40p. (J). (gr. -1-2). 11.99 *(978-1-4169-6750-7(8)*, Simon & Schuster/Paula Wiseman Bks.) Simon & Schuster/Paula Wiseman Bks.

—El Viejo Reloj. Alonso, Fernando & Fernando, Alonso. (SPA.). 48p. (J). *(978-84-392-8114-6(5))* Gaviota Ediciones ESP. Dist: Lectorum Pubns., Inc.

Escrivá, Viví. Mi Abuelita. Guy, Ginger Foglesong. 2007.Tr. of My Grandma. (ENG & SPA.). 24p. (J). (gr. -1-k). 16.99 *(978-0-06-079098-1(9)*, Rayo) HarperCollins Pubs.

—¡Muu, Moo! Rimas de Animales. Flor Ada, Alma & Campoy, F. Isabel. 2010. (SPA & ENG.). 48p. (J). (gr. -1-2). 16.99 *(978-0-06-134613-2(6)*, Rayo) HarperCollins Pubs.

—Muu, Moo! Rimas de Animales - Animal Nursery Rhymes. Flor Ada, Alma & Campoy, F. Isabel. 2010. (SPA & ENG.). 48p. (J). (gr. -1-2). lib. bdg. 17.89 *(978-0-06-134614-9(4)*, Rayo) HarperCollins Pubs.

—El Patio de Mi Casa y Otras Canciones Infantiles. Puncel, Maria. 2003. (SPA.). 32p. 4.95 *(978-84-372-8018-9(4))* Altea, Ediciones, S.A. - Grupo Santillana ESP. Dist: Santillana USA Publishing Co., Inc.

—Pio Peep! Traditional Spanish Nursery Rhymes. Ada, Alma Flor et al. 2003. (ENG & SPA.). 64p. (J). (gr. -1-1). 15.99 *(978-0-688-16019-7(0)*, Rayo) HarperCollins Pubs.

—A Rose with Wings. Flor Ada, Alma. Zubizarreta, Rosa, tr. 2005. (Cuentos para Todo el año / Stories the Year Round Ser.). 16p. (gr. k-3). pap. 9.95 *(978-1-58105-216-9(2))* Santillana USA Publishing Co., Inc.

—Tainos. Dorris, Michael. 97th ed. 2003.Tr. of Morning Girl. (SPA.). 112p. (gr. 5-8). pap. 26.30 *(978-84-204-4757-5(9)*, AF1929) Harcourt Schl. Pubs.

EsDesignStudio, jt. illus. see Bates, Delphine Branon.

Esham, Barbara. If You're So Smart, How Come You Can't Spell Mississippi? Esham, Barbara. 2008. 32p. (J). (gr. k-18). 16.95 *(978-1-60336-448-5(X)*, Adventures of Everyday Geniuses, The) Mainstream Connections Publishing.

Espadaler, Rosa. Then It Rained. Stranaghan, Crystal J. 2007. 24p. (J). *(978-0-9784047-8-9(5))* Pays et Terroirs.

Esparra, Veronica. Heaven Is All Around You. Esparra, Lydia. 2012. 28p. pap. 12.95 *(978-1-61244-071-2(1))* Halo Publishing International.

Esparza, Andres, et al. Attack of the Zorn-Bees! Sonnebom, Scott. 2013. (Tiger Moth Ser.). (ENG.). 48p. (gr. 1-3). pap. 6.19 *(978-1-4342-3871-9(7))* Stone Arch Bks.

—A Midsummer Night's Dream, 1 vol. Maese, Fares & Shakespeare, William. 2011. (Shakespeare Graphics Ser.). (ENG.). 88p. (gr. 2-3). pap. 7.15 *(978-1-4342-3449-0(5))*; lib. bdg. 26.65 *(978-1-4342-2605-1(0))* Stone Arch Bks. (Shakespeare Graphics).

—Power at the Plate, 1 vol. Ciencin, Scott & Cano, Fernando. 2011. (Sports Illustrated Kids Graphic Novels Ser.). (ENG.). 56p. (gr. 2-3). pap. 7.19 *(978-1-4342-3400-1(2))*; lib. bdg. 25.32 *(978-1-4342-2239-8(X))* Stone Arch Bks.

—Snowboard Standoff, 1 vol. Ciencin, Scott et al. 2011. (Sports Illustrated Kids Graphic Novels Ser.). (ENG.). 56p. (gr. 2-3). pap. 7.19 *(978-1-4342-3403-2(7))* Stone Arch Bks.

Esparza, Andres. Tiger Moth: Attack of the Zorn-Bees!, 1 vol. Sonnebom, Scott. 2013. (Tiger Moth Ser.). (ENG.). 48p. (gr. 1-3). lib. bdg. 22.65 *(978-1-4342-3283-0(2))* Stone Arch Bks.

Esparza, Andres & Aburto, Jesus. BMX Blitz, 1 vol. Ciencin, Scott & Maese, Fares. 2011. (Sports Illustrated Kids Graphic Novels Ser.). (ENG.). 56p. (gr. 2-3). lib. bdg. 25.32 *(978-1-4342-2222-0(5))* Stone Arch Bks.

Esparza, Andres, jt. illus. see Aburto, Jesus.

Esparza, Bob, photos by. Hadas. Haab, Rachel. Esteve, Laura, tr. 2005. (SPA., 38p. (J). spiral bd. 20.95 *(978-987-1078-27-1(7))* Klutz Latino MEX. Dist: Independent Pubs. Group.

Esperanza, Charles George. Jackie & Me: A Very Special Friendship. Grossinger, Tania. 2013. (ENG.). 32p. (J). (gr. k-4). 16.95 *(978-1-62087-683-1(3)*, 620683, Sky Pony Pr.) Skyhorse Publishing Co., Inc.

—Red, Yellow, Blue, & a Dash of White, Too! 2015. (ENG.). 40p. (J). (gr. -1-k). 16.99 *(978-1-62914-624-9(2)*, Sky Pony Pr.) Skyhorse Publishing Co., Inc.

Espina, Vito. Sometimes Boxes Make the Best Forts. Rawlings, John S. 2006. (J). pap. 15.00 *(978-0-8059-7181-1(5))* Dorrance Publishing Co., Inc.

Espinola, Nicole & Nealon, Eve. Danny & the Detention Demons. Webb, Mack H., Jr. l.t. ed. 2007. 52p. (J). per. 15.95 *(978-0-9779576-2-0(4))* Pilinut Pr., Inc.

Espinosa, Chris. The Spaniel Family Goes to the State Fair. Ellsberry, Sharon. 2004. 24p. (J). 9.00 *(978-0-9724637-2-0(0))* Sky Rocket Pr.

Espinosa, Chris. Rocket Megabyte's Texas Adventure. Espinosa, Chris. Rawlett, Robert. 2004. 68p. (J). 14.00 *(978-0-9724637-1-3(2))* Sky Rocket Pr.

Espinosa, Leo. Jackrabbit McCabe & the Electric Telegraph. Rozier, Lucy Margaret. 2015. (ENG.). 40p. (J). (gr. -1-3). 17.99 *(978-0-385-37843-7(2)*, Schwartz & Wade Bks.) Random Hse. Children's Bks.

Espinosa, Nuri. Perseo: El Joven que Venció a Medusa. Róman, Pedro. 2006. (SPA.). 32p. *(978-958-30-1958-6(5))* Panamericana Editorial.

Espinosa, Patrick, photos by. Graphing Favorite Things. Marrewa, Jennifer. 2008. (Math in Our World: Level 2 Ser.). 24p. (gr. 1-4). lib. bdg. 22.00 *(978-0-8368-9008-2(6)*, Weekly Reader Leveled Readers) Stevens, Gareth Publishing LLLP.

—Vamos a Hacer Graficas de Nuestras Cosas Favoritas. Marrewa, Jennifer. 2008. (Matemáticas en Nuestro Mundo - Nivel 2 (Math in Our World - Level 2) Ser.). (SPA., 24p. (gr. 1-4). lib. bdg. 22.00 *(978-0-8368-9026-6(4)*, Weekly Reader Leveled Readers) Stevens, Gareth Publishing LLLP.

Espinosa, Rod. Abraham Lincoln. Dunn, Joe. 2007. (Bio-Graphics Ser.). 32p. (gr. 3-6). 28.50 *(978-1-60270-064-2(8)*, Graphic Planet- Nonfiction) ABDO Publishing Co.

—Barack Obama: 44th U. S. President. Dunn, Joeming. 2011. (Presidents of the United States Bio-Graphics Ser.). 32p. (YA). (gr. 3-6). 28.50 *(978-1-61641-648-5(3))* Magic Wagon.

—Building the Transcontinental Railroad. Dunn, Joeming W. 2008. (Graphic History Ser.). 32p. 28.50 *(978-1-60270-180-9(6)*, Graphic Planet- Nonfiction) ABDO Publishing Co.

—Cesar Chavez. Dunn, Joeming W. 2008. (Bio-Graphics Ser.). 32p. (gr. 3-5). 28.50 *(978-1-60270-172-4(5)*, Graphic Planet- Nonfiction) ABDO Publishing Co.

—Clara Barton. Dunn, Joeming W. 2008. (Bio-Graphics Ser.). 32p. (gr. 3-5). 28.50 *(978-1-60270-170-0(9)*, Graphic Planet- Nonfiction) ABDO Publishing Co.

—The Comedy of Errors: Graphic Novel. Shakespeare, William. 2010. (Graphic Shakespeare Set 2 Ser.). 48p. (J). (gr. 5-9). 29.93 *(978-1-60270-762-7(6))* ABDO Publishing Co.

—The Eyes: A Graphic Novel Tour. Dunn, Joeming. 2009. (Graphic Body Ser.). 32p. (J). (gr. 3-6). 28.50 *(978-1-60270-684-2(0))* ABDO Publishing Co.

—Jackie Robinson. Dunn, Joe. 2007. (Bio-Graphics Ser.). 32p. (gr. 3-6). 28.50 *(978-1-60270-068-0(0)*, Graphic Planet- Nonfiction) ABDO Publishing Co.

—The Kidneys: A Graphic Novel Tour. Dunn, Joeming. 2009. (Graphic Body Ser.). 32p. (J). (gr. 3-6). 28.50 *(978-1-60270-686-6(7))* ABDO Publishing Co.

—The Liver: A Graphic Novel Tour. Dunn, Joeming. 2009. (Graphic Body Ser.). 32p. (J). (gr. 3-6). 28.50 *(978-1-60270-687-3(5))* ABDO Publishing Co.

—The Lungs: A Graphic Novel Tour. Dunn, Joeming. 2009. (Graphic Body Ser.). 32p. (J). (gr. 3-6). 28.50 *(978-1-60270-688-0(3))* ABDO Publishing Co.

—A MidSummer Night's Dream. Connor, Daniel. 2008. (Graphic Shakespeare Ser.). 48p. (gr. 5-10). 29.93 *(978-1-60270-191-5(1)*, Graphic Planet- Fiction) ABDO Publishing Co.

E

—Moby Dick. Melville, Herman. 2007. (Graphic Classics). 32p. (gr. 3-6). 28.50 (978-1-60270-051-2(6), Graphic Planet- Fiction) ABDO Publishing Co.

Espinosa, Rod, et al. Moon Landing. Dunn, Joe. 2007. (Graphic History Ser.). 32p. (gr. 3-6). 28.50 (978-1-60270-078-9(8), Graphic Planet- Nonfiction) ABDO Publishing Co.

Espinosa, Rod. Phantom of the Opera. Leroux, Gaston. 2009. (Graphic Horror Set 2 Ser.). 32p. (gr. 5-8). 28.50 (978-1-60270-679-8(4), Graphic Planet- Fiction) ABDO Publishing Co.

—Reaching the North Pole. Dunn, Joeming W. 2008. (Graphic History Ser.). 32p. 28.50 (978-1-60270-185-4(7), Graphic Planet- Nonfiction) ABDO Publishing Co.

—Romeo & Juliet. Dunn, Joeming. 2008. (Graphic Shakespeare Ser.). 48p. (gr. 5-10). 29.93 (978-1-60270-193-9(8), Graphic Planet- Fiction) ABDO Publishing Co.

—Sacagawea. Dunn, Joeming W. 2008. (Bio-Graphics Ser.). 32p. 28.50 (978-1-60270-176-2(8), Graphic Planet- Nonfiction) ABDO Publishing Co.

—Thomas Jefferson. Dunn, Joeming. 2008. (Bio-Graphics Ser.). 32p. 28.50 (978-1-60270-174-8(1), Graphic Planet- Nonfiction) ABDO Publishing Co.

—The Winter's Tale: Graphic Novel. Shakespeare, William. 2010. (Graphic Shakespeare Set 2 Ser.). 48p. (J). (gr. 5-9). 29.93 (978-1-60270-768-9(5)) ABDO Publishing Co.

Espinosa, Rod. The Battle of the Alamo. Espinosa, Rod. 2007. (Graphic History Ser.). 32p. (gr. 3-7). 28.50 (978-1-60270-073-4(7), Graphic Planet- Nonfiction) ABDO Publishing Co.

—Benjamin Franklin. Espinosa, Rod. 2007. (Bio-Graphics Ser.). 32p. (gr. 3-6). 28.50 (978-1-60270-066-6(4), Graphic Planet- Nonfiction) ABDO Publishing Co.

—The Boston Tea Party. Espinosa, Rod. 2007. (Graphic History Ser.). 32p. (gr. 3-6). 28.50 (978-1-60270-075-8(3), Graphic Planet- Nonfiction) ABDO Publishing Co.

—The Brain: A Graphic Novel Tour. Espinosa, Rod. Dunn, Joeming. 2009. (Graphic Body Ser.). 32p. (J). (gr. 3-6). 28.50 (978-1-60270-683-5(2)) ABDO Publishing Co.

Espinosa, Rod. Courageous Princess Vol. 1: Beyond the Hundred Kingdoms. Espinosa, Rod. 2015. (ENG.). 250p. (J). (gr. 5). 19.99 (978-1-61655-722-5(2)) Dark Horse Comics.

Espinosa, Rod. George Washington. Espinosa, Rod. 2007. (Bio-Graphics Ser.). 32p. (gr. 3-7). 28.50 (978-1-60270-067-3(2), Graphic Planet- Nonfiction) ABDO Publishing Co.

—The Heart: A Graphic Novel Tour. Espinosa, Rod. Dunn, Joeming. 2009. (Graphic Body Ser.). 32p. (J). (gr. 3-6). pap. 28.50 (978-1-60270-685-9(9)) ABDO Publishing Co.

—Lewis & Clark. Espinosa, Rod. 2007. (Bio-Graphics Ser.). 32p. (gr. 3-6). 28.50 (978-1-60270-069-7(9), Graphic Planet- Nonfiction) ABDO Publishing Co.

—Patrick Henry. Espinosa, Rod. 2007. (Bio-Graphics Ser.). 32p. (gr. 3-6). 28.50 (978-1-60270-070-3(2), Graphic Planet- Nonfiction) ABDO Publishing Co.

Espinosa, Rod. The Unremembered Lands. Espinosa, Rod. 2015. (ENG.). 166p. (J). (gr. 5). 19.99 (978-1-61655-723-2(0)) Dark Horse Comics.

Espinosa, Rod, jt. illus. see Wight, Joseph.

EspinoZa, Carlota D., jt. illus. see Espinoza, Gabbi.

Espinoza, Gabbi & EspinoZa, Carlota D. God Made a Very Big Big Bang! Espinoza, Carlota D. 2011. 32p. pap. 24.95 (978-1-4560-9582-6(X)) America Star Bks.

Espinoza, Ramon. Jungle Scout: A Vietnam War Story, 1 vol. Hoppey, Tim. 2008. (Historical Fiction Ser.). (ENG.). 56p. (gr. 2-3). pap. 6.25 (978-1-4342-0846-0(X), Graphic Flash) Stone Arch Bks.

Espluga, Maria. Fabulame un Fabula. Duran, Teresa. 2003. (SPA.). 96p. (978-84-480-1638-8(6), TM30428) Timun Mas, Editorial S.A. ESP. Dist: Lectorum Pubns., Inc.

—Ricitos de Oro. Combel Editorial Staff et al. 2005. (Caballo Alado Clásico Series-Al Paso Ser.). (SPA & ENG.). 24p. (J). (gr. -1-k). 7.95 (978-84-7864-854-2(2)) Combel Editorial, S.A. ESP. Dist: Independent Pubs. Group.

—Ricitos de Oro y Los Tres Osos. Bailer, Darice & Dominguez, Madelca. 2007. (SPA & ENG.). 28p. (J). (978-0-545-02447-1(1)) Scholastic, Inc.

Esplugas, Sonia. Magic Train Ride. Crabtree, Sally. (J). 2012. (ENG.). 32p. 9.99 (978-1-84686-657-9(X)); 2007. (ENG.). 32p. (gr. -1-k). pap. 9.99 (978-1-905236-91-6(3)); 2006. 0032p. 16.99 (978-1-905236-52-7(2)) Barefoot Bks., Inc.

Esplugas, Sonia & Espulgas, Sonia. Magic Train Ride. Crabtree, Sally. 2007. (ENG.). 32p. (J). (gr. -1-k). 6.99 (978-1-84686-132-1(2)) Barefoot Bks., Inc.

Espulgas, Sonia, jt. illus. see Esplugas, Sonia.

Esquinaldo, Virginia. My Book of Prayers. 2006. 48p. (J). 3.95 (978-0-8198-4843-7(3)) Pauline Bks. & Media.

—My First Missal. Dateno, Maria Grace. 2006. 48p. (J). pap. 3.95 (978-0-8198-4842-0(5)) Pauline Bks. & Media.

Esquinaldo, Virginia. What Did Baby Jesus Do? Esquinaldo, Virginia. 2006. 12p. (J). bds. 6.95 (978-0-8198-8310-0(7)) Pauline Bks. & Media.

Esquinaldo, Virginia. Saint Therese of Lisieux: The Way of Love. Esquinaldo, Virginia, tr. Glavich, Mary Kathleen. 2003. (Encounter the Saints Ser.). 132p. (J). pap. 5.95 (978-0-8198-7074-2(9), 332-370) Pauline Bks. & Media.

Este, James. Tres Porculi. Williams, Rose. L and L Enterprises, ed. 2006. (LAT.). spiral bd. 18.00 (978-0-9760046-5-3(8)) L & L Enterprises.

Estep, Joanna. Roadsong, Vol. 1. 2006. 200p. pap. 9.99 (978-1-59816-398-8(1)) TOKYOPOP, Inc.

Esterman, Sophia. Now for My Next Number! Songs for Multiplying Fun. Park, Margaret. 2007. 48p. (J). (gr. -1-3). 16.95 (978-0-915556-38-0(3)) Great River Bks.

Estill, Amy. Abby & the Helping Mommy. Mathisen, Michael. 2009. 28p. pap. 13.99 (978-1-4389-5327-4(5)) AuthorHouse.

Estrada, Ixchel. El Arbol del Tiempo: Para Que Sirven las Genealogias. Otero, Armando Lenero. rev. ed. 2006. (Otra Escalera Ser.). (SPA & ENG.). 24p. (J). (gr. 2-4). pap. 9.95 (978-968-5920-67-4(2)) Castillo, Ediciones, S. A. de C. V. MEX. Dist: Macmillan.

—Barriga Llena. Olivera, Martin Bonfil. rev. ed. 2006. (Otra Escalera Ser.). (SPA & ENG.). 24p. (J). (gr. 2-4). pap. 9.95 (978-968-5920-65-0(5)) Castillo, Ediciones, S. A. de C. V. MEX. Dist: Macmillan.

Estrada, Pau. Little Red Riding Hood: Caperucita Roja. Grimm, Jacob & Grimm, Wilhelm K. Surges, James, tr. 2006. 22p. (J). (gr. k-4). reprint ed. 15.00 (978-0-7567-9994-6(5)) DIANE Publishing Co.

—El Mejor Novio del Mundo. Joles, Alonso Sennell. (SPA.). 24p. 12.95 (978-84-246-1983-1(8)) Baker & Taylor Bks.

—Pedro's Burro. Capucilli, Alyssa Satin. 2007. (My First I Can Read Bks.). (ENG.). 32p. (J). (gr. -1-k). 15.99 (978-0-06-056031-7(2)) HarperCollins Pubs.

—Pippo the Fool. Fern, Tracey E. (ENG.). 48p. (J). (gr. k-3). 2011. pap. 7.95 (978-1-57091-793-6(0)); 2009. 15.95 (978-1-57091-655-7(1)) Charlesbridge Publishing, Inc.

—Princess & the Pea (La Princesa y el Guisante) Andersen, Hans Christian. 2013. (Bilingual Fairy Tales Ser.). (SPA & ENG.). 32p. (J). (gr. 1-4). lib. bdg. 28.50 (978-1-60753-357-3(X)) Amicus Educational.

—The Princess & the Pea (La Princesa y el Guisante) Boada, Francesc & Andersen, Hans Christian. ed. 2004. (Bilingual Fairy Tales Ser.: BILI). (ENG & SPA.). 32p. (J). (gr. -1-7). 14.95 (978-0-8118-4451-2(X)) Chronicle Bks. LLC.

—Princess & the Pea (la Princesa y el Guisante) A Bilingual Book! Boada, Francesc. 2004. (Bilingual Fairy Tales Ser.: BILI). (ENG.). 32p. (J). (gr. -1-7). pap. 6.99 (978-0-8118-4452-9(8)) Chronicle Bks. LLC.

—Soccer Counts! McGrath, Barbara Barbieri & Alderman, Peter. 2003. (ENG.). 32p. (J). (gr. -1-3). pap. 7.95 (978-1-57091-554-3(7)) Charlesbridge Publishing, Inc.

—Soccer Counts! (El Futbol Cuenta!) McGrath, Barbara Barbieri & Alderman, Peter. ed. 2011. (SPA & ENG.). 32p. (J). (gr. -1-3). pap. 7.95 (978-1-57091-794-3(9)) Charlesbridge Publishing, Inc.

Estrada, Pau. Pedro's Burro. Estrada, Pau. Capucilli, Alyssa Satin. 2008. (My First I Can Read Ser.). (ENG.). 32p. (J). (gr. -1 — 1). pap. 3.99 (978-0-06-056033-1(9)) HarperCollins Pubs.

—Pedro's Burro. Estrada, Pau. 2007. (My First I Can Read Bks.). 32p. (J). (gr. -1-k). lib. bdg. 16.89 (978-0-06-056032-4(0)) HarperCollins Pubs.

Estrada, Ric. It's Good to Be Clean. Pappas, Diane H. & Covey, Richard D. 2007. (J). pap. (978-0-545-01430-4(1)) Scholastic, Inc.

—Why I Need My Sleep. Pappas, Diane H. & Covey, Richard D. 2007. (J). pap. (978-0-545-01427-4(1)) Scholastic, Inc.

Estrin, James, photos by. Ballerina Dreams. Thompson, Lauren & Ferrara, Joanne. 2007. (ENG., 40p. (J). (gr. k-3). 19.99 (978-0-312-37029-9(6)) Feiwel & Friends.

Estudio Haus. The Colors of a Sunset: An Algonquin Nature Myth. Yasuda, Anita. 2012. (Short Tales Native American Myths Ser.). 32p. (J). (gr. 3-6). lib. bdg. 24.21 (978-1-61641-879-3(6)) Magic Wagon.

—Stolen Fire: A Seminole Trickster Myth. Yasuda, Anita. 2012. (Short Tales Native American Myths Ser.). 32p. (J). (gr. 3-6). lib. bdg. 24.21 (978-1-61641-883-0(4)) Magic Wagon.

Eszterhas, Suzi, photos by. Cheetah. 2012. (Eye on the Wild Ser.). (ENG., 32p. (J). (gr. -1-2). 15.99 (978-1-84780-301-6(6), Frances Lincoln Children's Bks.) Quarto Publishing Group UK GBR. Dist: Hachette Bk. Group.

—Elephant. 2014. (Eye on the Wild Ser.). (ENG., 32p. (J). (gr. -1-2). 15.99 (978-1-84780-518-8(3), Frances Lincoln) Quarto Publishing Group UK GBR. Dist: Hachette Bk. Group.

—Eye on the Wild: Lion. 2012. (Eye on the Wild Ser.). (ENG., 32p. (J). (gr. -1-2). 15.99 (978-1-84780-315-3(6), Frances Lincoln Children's Bks.) Quarto Publishing Group UK GBR. Dist: Hachette Bk. Group.

—Eye on the Wild: Sea Otter. Quarto Generic Staff. 2013. (Eye on the Wild Ser.). (ENG., 32p. (J). (gr. -1-2). 15.99 (978-1-84780-300-9(8), Frances Lincoln) Quarto Publishing Group UK GBR. Dist: Hachette Bk. Group.

—Gorilla. 2012. (Eye on the Wild Ser.). (ENG., 32p. (J). (gr. -1-2). 15.99 (978-1-84780-299-6(0), Frances Lincoln) Quarto Publishing Group UK GBR. Dist: Hachette Bk. Group.

—Tiger. 2014. (Eye on the Wild Ser.). (ENG., 32p. (J). (gr. -1-2). 15.99 (978-1-84780-517-1(5), Frances Lincoln) Quarto Publishing Group UK GBR. Dist: Hachette Bk. Group.

Etheridge, Katy, jt. illus. see Villaloz, ChiChi.

Ethier, Vicki. I Know My Nana Rosa Is an Alien. Ethier, Vicki. 2003. 20p. (J). 6.00 (978-1-928972-10-5(1)) Critter Pubns.

—Papa & the Hen. Ethier, Vicki. 2004. 36p. (J). 7.00 (978-1-928972-12-9(8)) Critter Pubns.

Ets, Marie Hall. Just Me. Ets, Marie Hall. unabr. ed. (J). (gr. k-3). pap., stu. ed. 33.95 (978-0-941078-74-0(4)); pap. 15.95 incl. audio (978-0-941078-73-3(6)) Live Oak Media.

Ettinger, Charles. Andy the Ant in Precious Cargo. Blackwell, Nancy. 2011. 40p. pap. 14.99 (978-1-937129-03-3(9)) Faithful Life Pubs.

—Jasper & Jesus at the Well. Sharpe, Charlotte. 2012. 16p. pap. 11.99 (978-1-937129-33-0(0)) Faithful Life Pubs.

Ettinger, Dorris. The Mystery of the Ancient Anchor. Price, Matt. 2010. 56p. (J). (978-0-8341-2490-5(4)) Beacon Hill Pr. of Kansas City.

Ettlinger, Doris. Abe Lincoln Loved Animals. Jackson, Ellen. 2013. (AV2 Fiction Readalong Ser.: Vol. 56). (ENG.). 32p. (J). 34.28 (978-1-62127-864-1(6), AV2 by Weigl) Weigl Pubs., Inc.

—A Book for Black-Eyed Susan. Young, Judy. 2011. (Tales of Young Americans Ser.). (ENG.). 32p. (J). (gr. k-6). lib. bdg. 16.95 (978-1-58536-463-3(0)) Sleeping Bear Pr.

—Catholic Book of Bible Stories, 1 vol. Knowlton, Laurie Lazzaro et al. 2004. (ENG.). 224p. (J). 16.99 (978-0-310-70505-5(3)) Zonderkidz.

—G Is for Garden State: A New Jersey Alphabet. Cameron, Eileen. 2004. (Discover America State by State Ser.). (ENG.). 40p. (J). 17.95 (978-1-58536-152-6(6)) Sleeping Bear Pr.

—Hazelle Boxberg. Goodman, Susan E. 2004. (Brave Kids Ser.). (ENG.). 64p. (J). (gr. 1-4). pap. 5.99 (978-0-689-84982-4(6), Simon & Schuster/Paula Wiseman Bks.) Simon & Schuster/Paula Wiseman Bks.

—Lost in the Snow. Baglio, Ben M. 2007. 153p. (J). (978-0-439-87144-0(1)) Scholastic, Inc.

—Memories of the Manger. Adams, Michelle Medlock. (J). 2009. (ENG.). 32p. (gr. -1-3). 8.99 (978-0-8249-5614-1(1), Ideals Children's Bks.); 2005. (ENG.). 32p. (gr. -1-3). 16.95 (978-0-8249-5476-5(9)); 2005. (978-0-8249-5484-0(X), Ideals Pr.) Ideals Pubns.

—Morris & Buddy: The Story of the First Seeing Eye Dog, 1 vol. Hall, Becky. 2007. (ENG.). 40p. (J). (gr. 2-5). 16.99 (978-0-8075-5284-1(4)) Whitman, Albert & Co.

—The Orange Shoes. Noble, Trinka Hakes. rev. ed. 2007. (ENG.). 40p. (J). (gr. k-6). 16.95 (978-1-58536-277-6(8)) Sleeping Bear Pr.

—Pigeon Hero! Redmond, Shirley Raye. 2005. (Ready-to-Read Ser.). 31p. (gr. k-2). 14.00 (978-0-7569-5560-1(2)) Perfection Learning Corp.

—Pigeon Hero! Redmond, Shirley Raye. 2003. (Ready-To-Reads Ser.). (ENG.). 32p. (J). lib. bdg. 11.89 (978-0-689-85487-3(0), Aladdin Library) Simon & Schuster Children's Publishing.

—Pigeon Hero! Redmond, Shirley Raye. 2003. (Ready-to-Read Ser.). 31p. (J). (gr. k-2). lib. bdg. 8.62 (978-0-613-94266-9(3), Turtleback) Turtleback Bks.

—Pilgrim Cat. Peacock, Carol Antoinette. 2004. (ENG.). 32p. (J). (gr. 2-5). 6.95 (978-0-8075-6533-9(4)) Whitman, Albert & Co.

—Robert Henry Hendershot. Goodman, Susan E. 2003. (Brave Kids Ser.). (ENG.). 64p. (J). (gr. 1-4). pap. 6.99 (978-0-689-84980-0(X), Simon & Schuster/Paula Wiseman Bks.) Simon & Schuster/Paula Wiseman Bks.

—S Is for Sea Glass: A Beach Alphabet. Michelson, Richard. 2014. (ENG.). 32p. (J). (gr. 2-5). 15.95 (978-1-58536-862-4(8), 203010) Sleeping Bear Pr.

—The Secret of the Red Shoes. Donaldson, Joan. 2006. (ENG.). 32p. (J). (gr. -1-3). 8.95 (978-0-8249-5522-9(6), Ideals Children's Bks.) Ideals Pubns.

—T Is for Teacher: A School Alphabet. Layne, Steven L. & Layne, Deborah Dover. 2007. (ENG.). 40p. (J). (gr. 1-4). per. 7.95 (978-1-58536-331-5(6), 202294) Sleeping Bear Pr.

—T Is for Teachers: A School Alphabet. Layne, Steven L. et al. 2005. (ENG.). 40p. (J). (gr. 1-4). 16.95 (978-1-58536-159-5(3), 202019) Sleeping Bear Pr.

—T Is for Teachers: A School Alphabet. Layne, Deborah & Layne, Stephen L. rev. ed. 2005. (ENG.). 40p. (J). (gr. k-6). 14.95 (978-1-58536-266-0(2)) Sleeping Bear Pr.

—Vanishing Point. Baglio, Ben M. 2007. 158p. (J). pap. (978-0-439-87145-7(X)) Scholastic, Inc.

—Welcome to America, Champ. Stier, Catherine. 2013. (Tales of the World Ser.). (ENG.). 32p. (J). (gr. 1-4). 17.95 (978-1-58536-606-4(4), 202360) Sleeping Bear Pr.

Ettlinger, Doris & Layne, Deborah. Number 1 Teacher: A School Counting Book. Layne, Steven L. 2008. (ENG.). 40p. (J). (gr. k-6). 17.95 (978-1-58536-307-0(3)) Sleeping Bear Pr.

Eubank, Patricia Reeder. Natalia's Favorite Color. Dude, Rosanna Eubank. 2008. (ENG.). 32p. (J). (gr. -1-3). 12.99 (978-0-8249-5523-6(4), Ideals Children's Bks.) Ideals Pubns.

Eubank, Patricia Reeder. ABCs of Halloween. Eubank, Patricia Reeder. 2013. 32p. (J). pap. 4.99 (978-0-8249-5658-5(3), Ideals Children's Bks.) Ideals Pubns.

—Halloween 123s. Eubank, Patricia Reeder. 2011. 22p. (J). bds. 6.99 (978-0-8249-1868-2(1)) Ideals Pubns.

—The Leprechaun's Big Pot of Gold. Eubank, Patricia Reeder. 2012. 20p. (J). bds. 6.99 (978-0-8249-1877-4(0), Candy Cane Pr.) Ideals Pubns.

—The Princess & the Snarls. Eubank, Patricia Reeder. 2006. (ENG.). 32p. (J). (gr. k-3). 16.95 (978-0-8249-5536-6(6), Ideals Children's Bks.) Ideals Pubns.

—Valentine ABCs. Eubank, Patricia Reeder. 2009. 32p. (J). (gr. -1-3). 9.99 (978-0-8249-5597-7(8), Ideals Children's Bks.) Ideals Pubns.

Eubank, Patti Reeder. Just Where You Belong. 2004. 32p. (J). 8.95 (978-0-8249-5481-9(5)) Ideals Pubns.

Eubanks, Charles. Alphabet Puke: Monsters' Medicine A-Z. Cole, Quinn. 2013. 32p. pap. 6.99 (978-1-936214-94-5(6)) Wyatt-MacKenzie Publishing.

Eudes-Pascal, Elisabeth. Monkey in the Mud. Poulin, Andrée. 2009. (Rainy Day Readers Ser.). 32p. (J). (gr. -1-3). pap. 10.55 (978-1-60754-371-8(0)) Windmill Bks.

—Monkey in the Mud. Poulin, Andrée. 2009. (Rainy Day Readers Ser.). 32p. (J). (gr. -1-3). 22.60 (978-1-60754-370-1(2)) Windmill Bks.

—Raffi's Animal Rescue. Meunier, Sylvain. Cummins, Sarah, tr. from FRE. 2007. (ENG.). 64p. (J). (gr. 2-5). (978-0-88780-742-8(9)) Formac Publishing Co., Ltd.

—Raffi's Animal Rescue, 1 vol. Meunier, Sylvain. Cummins, Sarah, tr. from FRE. 2007. (Formac First Novels Ser.). (ENG.). 64p. (J). (gr. 2-5). 4.95 (978-0-88780-740-4(2)) Formac Publishing Co., Ltd. CAN. Dist: Casemate Pubs. & Bk. Distributors, LLC.

—Raffi's Island Adventure, 1 vol. Meunier, Sylvain. Cummins, Sarah, tr. from FRE. 2008. (Formac First Novels Ser.). (ENG.). 64p. (J). (gr. 2-5). 5.95 (978-0-88780-755-8(0)); 14.95 (978-0-88780-757-2(7)) Formac Publishing Co., Ltd. CAN. Dist: Casemate Pubs. & Bk. Distributors, LLC.

Eudes-Pascal, Élisabeth. Raffi's New Friend, 1 vol. Meunier, Sylvain. Cummins, Sarah, tr. from FRE. 2010. (Formac First Novels Ser.). (ENG.). 64p. (J). (gr. 1-4). pap. 5.95 (978-0-88780-933-0(2)) Formac Publishing Co., Ltd. CAN. Dist: Casemate Pubs. & Bk. Distributors, LLC.

Eudes-Pascal, Elisabeth. The Twins & the Time Machine/Les Jumeaux et la Machine du Temps. Rabley, Stephen. Bougard, Marie-Therese, tr. 2008. (Let's Read! Bks.). (ENG & FRE.). 32p. (J). (gr. 3-7). pap. 5.99 (978-0-7641-4048-8(5)) Barron's Educational Series, Inc.

Eugenia, Maria. Cruiser & the Night Noises. Johnston, Jan. 2009. (ENG.). 20p. 12.99 (978-1-934706-51-0(5)) Blue Apple Bks.

Euvremer, Teryl. Toby, Who Are You? Steig, William. 2004. 32p. (J). (gr. -1-3). lib. bdg. 15.89 (978-0-06-000706-5(0), Cotler, Joanna Books) HarperCollins Pubs.

Evangelista, Mauro. Alice's Adventures in Wonderland. Carroll, Lewis. 2006. 63p. (J). (gr. 2). 8.99 (978-0-7945-1239-2(9), Usborne) EDC Publishing.

—The Wizard of Oz. Baum, L. Frank. (Usborne Young Reading: Series Two Ser.). 64p. (J). 2010. 6.99 (978-0-7945-2826-3(0)); 2007. (gr. 3-7). 8.99 (978-0-7945-1457-0(X), Usborne) EDC Publishing.

Evans, Andrew. The Tongue Twister Experiments Student Workbook. Densmore, Don. 2007. 60p. per. 20.00 (978-0-9787113-5-1(1), Ithaca Pr.) Authors & Artists Publishers of New York, Inc.

Evans, Antony. Don't Give up! Lap Book. Giachetti, Julia. 2014. (MySELF Ser.). (J). (gr. -1-k). 27.00 (978-1-4788-0517-5(X)) Newmark Learning LLC.

—Dylan's Questions Lap Book. Daniel, Claire. 2014. (MySELF Ser.). (J). (gr. -1-k). 27.00 (978-1-4788-0519-9(6)) Newmark Learning LLC.

—I Am a Star! Lap Book. Garcia, Ellen. 2014. (MySELF Ser.). (J). (gr. -1-k). 27.00 (978-1-4788-0516-8(1)) Newmark Learning LLC.

—I Can Make a Plan. Garcia, Ellen. 2014. (J). (gr. -1). 3.99 (978-1-4788-0478-9(5)) Newmark Learning LLC.

—I Can Make a Plan Lap Book. Garcia, Ellen. 2014. (MySELF Ser.). (J). (gr. -1-k). 27.00 (978-1-4788-0515-1(3)) Newmark Learning LLC.

—I Will Find a Way. Linde, Barbara M. 2014. (J). (gr. -1). 3.99 (978-1-4788-0483-3(1)) Newmark Learning LLC.

—I Will Find a Way Lap Book. Linde, Barbara M. 2014. (MySELF Ser.). (J). (gr. -1-k). 27.00 (978-1-4788-0520-5(X)) Newmark Learning LLC.

—Let's Get It Started. Sparks, Stacey. 2014. (J). (gr. -1). 3.99 (978-1-4788-0481-9(5)) Newmark Learning LLC.

—Let's Get It Started Lap Book. Sparks, Stacey. 2014. (MySELF Ser.). (J). (gr. -1-k). 27.00 (978-1-4788-0518-2(8)) Newmark Learning LLC.

Evans, Cambria. The One & Only Stuey Lewis: Stories from the Second Grade. Schoenberg, Jane. 2011. (Stuey Lewis Ser.: 1). (ENG.). 128p. (J). (gr. 1-4). 15.99 (978-0-374-37292-7(6), Farrar, Straus & Giroux (BYR)) Farrar, Straus & Giroux.

Evans, Cambria. Part-Time Mermaid. Underwood, Deborah. 2016. (J). (978-1-4847-2680-8(4)) Disney Pr.

Evans, Cambria. Part-Time Princess. Underwood, Deborah. 2013. (ENG.). 40p. (J). (gr. -1-k). 16.99 (978-1-4231-2485-6(5)) Hyperion Pr.

—Stuey Lewis Against All Odds: Stories from the Third Grade, 1 vol. Schoenberg, Jane. 2012. (Stuey Lewis Ser.: 2). (ENG.). 144p. (J). (gr. 1-4). 15.99 (978-0-374-39901-6(8), Farrar, Straus & Giroux (BYR)) Farrar, Straus & Giroux.

—Stuey Lewis Against All Odds: Stories from the Third Grade. Schoenberg, Jane. 2013. (Stuey Lewis Ser.: 2). (ENG.). 160p. (J). (gr. 1-4). pap. 5.99 (978-1-250-03404-5(3)) Square Fish.

Evans, Casey. Pip, Veronica & the Harmonica. Krinsky, Ed. 2013. 32p. pap. 13.00 (978-1-62516-945-7(0), Strategic Bk. Publishing) Strategic Book Publishing & Rights Agency (SBPRA).

Evans, Chadrick Michael. Johnny Lumpkin Wants a Friend. Evans, Rhonda Boone. 2007. 32p. per. 24.95 (978-1-4241-8614-3(5)) America Star Bks.

Evans, Dustin. Chasing Whales Aboard the Charles W. Morgan, Bk. 2. Specter, Baron. 2010. (Ghostly Graphic Adventures Ser.). 32p. (J). (gr. 4-6). 28.50 (978-1-60270-771-9(5), Graphic Planet- Fiction) ABDO Publishing Co.

—Costume Craziness. 2013. (Mystical Pencil Ser.). 32p. (J). (gr. 3-6). 28.50 (978-1-61641-926-4(1)) Magic Wagon.

—Dinosaur Drama. 2013. (Mystical Pencil Ser.). 32p. (J). (gr. 3-6). 28.50 (978-1-61641-927-1(X)) Magic Wagon.

—Dodging Danger on the Dartmouth, Bk. 1. Specter, Baron. 2010. (Ghostly Graphic Adventures Ser.). 32p. (J). (gr. 3-6). 28.50 (978-1-60270-770-2(7)) ABDO Publishing Co.

—Drama at Dungeon Rock: #6, 6 vols. Specter, Baron. 2010. (Ghostly Graphic Adventures Ser.). 32p. (J). (gr. 3-6). 28.50 (978-1-60270-775-7(8)) ABDO Publishing Co.

—The Lighthouse of Terror, 3 vols., Bk. 3. Specter, Baron. 2010. (Ghostly Graphic Adventures Ser.). 32p. (J). (gr. 3-6). 28.50 (978-1-60270-772-6(3)) ABDO Publishing Co.

—A Medieval Mess. 2013. (Mystical Pencil Ser.). 32p. (J). (gr. 3-6). 28.50 (978-1-61641-928-8(8)) Magic Wagon.

—Raging Robots. 2013. (Mystical Pencil Ser.). 32p. (J). (gr. 3-6). 28.50 (978-1-61641-929-5(6)) Magic Wagon.

—The Spooky Short Sands Shipwreck: #4, 4 vols. Specter, Baron. 2010. (Ghostly Graphic Adventures Ser.). 32p. (J). (gr. 3-6). 28.50 (978-1-60270-773-3(1)) ABDO Publishing Co.

—The Star Island Spirits: #5, 5 vols. Specter, Baron. 2010. (Ghostly Graphic Adventures Ser.). 32p. (J). (gr. 3-6). 28.50 (978-1-60270-774-0(X)) ABDO Publishing Co.

Evans, Fran. Gelert - A Man's Best Friend. Matthews, Cerys. 2014. (ENG.). 32p. (J). (gr. k-2). pap. 11.99 (978-1-84851-464-5(6)) Gomer Pr. GBR. Dist: Independent Pubs. Group.

Evans, Fran, et al. Green Isles of the Ocean. Francis, Marnie et al. 2005. (ENG.). 32p. pap. 12.95 (978-1-84323-421-0(1)) Beekman Bks., Inc.

Evans, Gabriel. Pick-a-WooWoo - Born to Love Frogs: All children have a Gift!, 16 vols., Vol. 8. Nicholl, Jacqueline. 2009. 32p. pap. (978-0-9803669-7-6(6)) Pick-a-Woo Woo Pubs.

—Pick-a-WooWoo - Herbie & the Tune: Deep within every moment, there is pure Joy. Kyle, Bradley. 2011. (ENG.). 32p. pap. (978-1-921883-02-6(2)) Pick-a-Woo Woo Pubs.

—Pick-a-WooWoo - Oceans Calling: An enlightening journey to the lost city of Atlantis. Nicoll, Jacqueline. 2010. 32p. pap. (978-0-9806520-1-7(4)) Pick-a-Woo Woo Pubs.

—Pick-a-WooWoo - the Star Who Lost Her Sparkle: Sprinkle here & Sparkle ther. We work with love because we Care. Lee, Patricia Mary. 2011. (ENG.). 28p. pap. (978-1-921883-03-3(0)) Pick-a-Woo Woo Pubs.

—Silly Gilly Gil - Gay L-U-V. Frantz, Donna. 2013. 30p. pap. (978-1-921883-38-5(3), MBS Pr.) Pick-a-Woo Woo Pubs.

Evans, Jamie, jt. illus. see Day, Martin.
Evans, Joyce. Just Mary Reader: Mary Grannan Selected Stories. Hume, Margaret Anne. 2006. (ENG.). 176p. (YA). pap. 24.99 *(978-1-55002-598-9(8),* Dundurn Pr.) Dundurn CAN. Dist: Ingram Pub. Services.
Evans, Kevin. The Elves of Owl's Head Mountain. Sutiff, Jamie. Blumberg, Christine A., ed. 2007. 280p. (gr. 8-12). 26.95 *(978-0-9712867-7-1(9))* Cold River Pubns.
Evans, Kevin C. The Land of Nen-Us-Yok. Sutiff, Jamie. Blumberg, Christine A., ed. 2007. 256p. pap. 10.95 *(978-0-9712867-4-0(4));* 26.95 *(978-0-9712867-6-4(0))* Cold River Pubns.
Evans, Laura. A Castle at the Straits. Panagopoulos, Janie Lynn. 2003. 48p. (J). (gr. 1-6). *(978-0-911872-83-5(3))* Mackinac State Historic Parks.
—Home to Mackinac: The Tale of Young Jack Murphy's Discovery of Loyalty, Family, & Forgiveness. Cory, Kim Delmar. 2007. (ENG.). 175p. (J). (gr. 3-7). per. 9.95 *(978-0-911872-87-3(6))* Mackinac State Historic Parks.
Evans, Leslie. At the Sea Floor Café: Odd Ocean Critter Poems, 1 vol. Bulion, Leslie. 2011. (ENG.). 48p. (J). (gr. 3-7). 14.95 *(978-1-56145-565-2(2))* Peachtree Pubs.
—Faces of the Moon. Crelin, Bob. 2009. (ENG.). 40p. (J). (gr. 1-4). 16.95 *(978-1-57091-785-1(X))* Charlesbridge Publishing, Inc.
—Grandpa & Me on Tu B'Shevat. Gold-Vukson, Marji. 2004. (ENG.). 32p. (J). (gr. -1-3). pap. 6.95 *(978-1-58013-122-3(0),* Kar-Ben Publishing) Lerner Publishing Group.
—Hey There, Stink Bug! Bulion, Leslie. (ENG.). 48p. (J). (gr. 2-5). 2008. per. 5.95 *(978-1-58089-340-4(6));* 2006. lib. bdg. 12.95 *(978-1-58089-304-6(X))* Charlesbridge Publishing, Inc.
—Leaf Jumpers. Gerber, Carole. 2006. (ENG.). 32p. (J). (gr. -1-2). per. 7.95 *(978-1-57091-498-0(2))* Charlesbridge Publishing, Inc.
—Spring Blossoms. Gerber, Carole. (ENG.). 32p. (J). (gr. -1-1). 2015. pap. 7.95 *(978-1-58089-413-5(5));* 2013. lib. bdg. 16.95 *(978-1-58089-412-8(7))* Charlesbridge Publishing, Inc.
—You Have to Be Smart If You're Going to Be Tall/Tienes Que Ser Inteligente Si Vas a Ser Alta. 2006. 46p. (J). (gr. -1-3). per. 16.99 *(978-1-59879-217-1(2))* Lifevest Publishing, Inc.
Evans, Lisa. The Flower. Light, John. (Child's Play Library). (ENG.). 32p. (J). 2011. *(978-1-84643-070-1(4));* 2007. (gr. -1-3). *(978-1-84643-072-5(0))* Child's Play International Ltd.
Evans, Lisa M. Rich Man's Song. Evans, Lisa M. 2015. 36p. (J). pap. 7.99 *(978-0-9745264-2-3(8))* Marquise Publishing.
Evans, Margaret. Tad, the Sad Tadpole, 1 vol. Shorty. 2009. 29p. pap. 19.95 *(978-1-4489-2458-5(8))* PublishAmerica, Inc.
Evans, Mark & Kun Rong, Yap. Dragon Theft Auto, 1 vol. Dahl, Michael. 2009. (Dragonblood Ser.). (ENG.). 40p. (gr. 1-3). 22.65 *(978-1-4342-1264-1(5),* Zone Bks.) Stone Arch Bks.
Evans, Mark & Vue, Tou. Claws in the Snow, 1 vol. Dahl, Michael. 2009. (Dragonblood Ser.). (ENG.). 40p. (gr. 1-3). 22.65 *(978-1-4342-1262-7(9),* Zone Bks.) Stone Arch Bks.
Evans, Melvyn. Once I Was a Cardboard Box... But Now I'm a Book about Polar Bears. Poitier, Anton. 2010. 24p. (J). (gr. k-3). 7.99 *(978-0-8416-7200-0(8))* Hammond World Atlas Corp.
—Once I Was a Comic... But Now I'm a Book about Tigers. Poitier, Anton. 2010. 24p. (J). (gr. k-3). 7.99 *(978-0-8416-7201-7(6))* Hammond World Atlas Corp.
Evans, Michael. Over in the Meadow. (Classic Books with Holes 8x8 Ser.). (ENG.). 16p. (J). 2007. (gr. -1-1). pap. *(978-1-84643-136-4(0));* 2004. pap. *(978-0-85953-692-9(0))* Child's Play International Ltd.
Evans, Michael. Poggle & the Birthday Present. Evans, Michael. 2011. (Poggle Ser.). (ENG.). 32p. (J). (gr. k — 1). pap. 8.99 *(978-1-4052-5359-8(2));* (gr. -1). 16.99 *(978-1-4052-5358-1(4))* Egmont Bks., Ltd. GBR. Dist: Independent Pubs. Group.
—Poggle & the Treasure. Evans, Michael. 2011. (Poggle Ser.). (ENG.). 32p. (J). (gr. k — 1). pap. 8.99 *(978-1-4052-4812-9(2));* (gr. -1). 16.99 *(978-1-4052-4811-2(4))* Egmont Bks., Ltd. GBR. Dist: Independent Pubs. Group.
Evans, Nicola. The Muddy Puddle. Rider, Cynthia. 2013. (Start Reading Ser.). (ENG.). 24p. (gr. k-1). pap. 41.94 *(978-1-4765-3224-0(9));* pap. 6.99 *(978-1-4765-3195-3(1))* Capstone Pr., Inc.
—Our Snowman. Rider, Cynthia. 2013. (Start Reading Ser.). (ENG.). 24p. (gr. k-1). pap. 41.94 *(978-1-4765-3229-5(X));* pap. 6.99 *(978-1-4765-3196-0(X))* Capstone Pr., Inc.
—A Sunny Day. Rider, Cynthia. 2013. (Start Reading Ser.). (ENG.). 24p. (gr. k-1). pap. 41.94 *(978-1-4765-3233-2(8));* pap. 6.99 *(978-1-4765-3197-7(8))* Capstone Pr., Inc.
—What a Windy Day!, 1 vol. Rider, Cynthia. 2013. (Start Reading Ser.). (ENG.). 24p. (gr. k-1). pap. 6.99 *(978-1-4765-3198-4(6));* pap. 41.94 *(978-1-4765-3234-9(6))* Capstone Pr., Inc.
Evans, Rowena. Brumbies. Boer, Paula. 2011. (ENG.). 148p. pap. 14.99 *(978-0-615-56093-9(8))* IFWG Publishing Inc.
Evans, Ruth Todd. The Panda Who Would Not Eat. Evans, Ruth Todd. 2007. 32p. (J). (gr. -1-3). per. 9.95 *(978-0-932653-84-0(7))* Sunbelt Pubns., Inc.
Evans, Shane. Bintou's Braids. Diouf, Sylviane. 2004. (ENG.). 40p. (J). (gr. -1-7). pap. 6.99 *(978-0-8118-4629-5(6))* Chronicle Bks. LLC.
—My Cold Plum Lemon Pie Bluesy Mood. Brown, Tameka Fryer. 2013. (ENG.). 40p. (J). (gr. -1-2). 16.99 *(978-0-670-01285-5(8),* Viking Juvenile) Penguin Publishing Group.
Evans, Shane W. Art from Her Heart: Folk Artist Clementine Hunter. Whitehead, Kathy. 2008. (ENG.). 32p. (J). (gr. 1-3). 16.99 *(978-0-399-24219-9(8),* Putnam Juvenile) Penguin Publishing Group.
—Black Jack: The Ballad of Jack Johnson. Smith, Charles R., Jr. 2010. (ENG.). 40p. (J). (gr. -1-1). 16.99 *(978-1-59643-473-8(2))* Roaring Brook Pr.
—Chocolate Me! Diggs, Taye. 2011. (ENG.). 40p. (J). (gr. -1-3). 17.99 *(978-0-312-60326-7(6))* Feiwel & Friends.
—Did I Tell You I Love You Today? Jordan, Deloris. 2004. (ENG.). 32p. (J). (gr. -1-3). 17.99 *(978-0-689-85271-8(1),* Simon & Schuster/Paula Wiseman Bks.) Simon & Schuster/Paula Wiseman Bks.
—Free at Last! Stories & Songs of Emancipation. Rappaport, Doreen. 2006. (ENG.). 64p. (J). (gr. 4-7). pap. 8.99 *(978-0-7636-3147-5(7))* Candlewick Pr.
—Hold the Flag High. Clinton, Catherine. 2005. 32p. (J). (gr. k-2). lib. bdg. 18.89 *(978-0-06-050429-8(3),* Tegen, Katherine Bks) HarperCollins Pubs.
—Li'l Rabbit's Kwanzaa. Washington, Donna L. 2010. (ENG.). 32p. (J). (gr. -1-2). 12.99 *(978-0-06-072816-8(7),* Tegen, Katherine Bks) HarperCollins Pubs.
—Lillian's Right to Vote: A Celebration of the Voting Rights Act of 1965. Winter, Jonah. 2015. (ENG.). 40p. (J). (gr. k-4). 17.99 *(978-0-385-39028-6(9),* Schwartz & Wade Bks.) Random Hse. Children's Bks.
—My Brother Charlie. Peete, Holly Robinson & Peete, Ryan Elizabeth. 2010. (ENG.). 40p. (J). (gr. 2-5). 17.99 *(978-0-545-09466-5(6),* Scholastic Pr.) Scholastic, Inc.
—No More! Stories & Songs of Slave Resistance. Rappaport, Doreen. 2005. (ENG.). 64p. (J). (gr. 4-7). reprint ed. pap. 8.99 *(978-0-7636-2876-5(X))* Candlewick Pr.
—Nobody Gonna Turn Me 'Round: Stories & Songs of the Civil Rights Movement. Rappaport, Doreen. 2006. (ENG.). 64p. (J). (gr. 4-7). 19.99 *(978-0-7636-1927-5(2))* Candlewick Pr.
—Nobody Gonna Turn Me 'Round: Stories & Songs of the Civil Rights Movement. Rappaport, Doreen. 2008. (ENG.). 64p. (J). (gr. 4-7). pap. 9.99 *(978-0-7636-3892-4(7))* Candlewick Pr.
—The Red Pencil. Pinkney, Andrea Davis. 2014. (ENG.). 336p. (J). (gr. 4-17). 17.00 *(978-0-316-24780-1(4))* Little, Brown Bks. for Young Readers.
—The Way a Door Closes. Smith, Hope Anita. 2011. (ENG.). 64p. (J). (gr. 3-7). pap. 9.99 *(978-0-312-66169-4(X))* Square Fish.
—When Harriet Met Sojourner. Clinton, Catherine. 2007. 32p. (J). (gr. k-2). (ENG.). 16.99 *(978-0-06-050425-0(0));* lib. bdg. 17.89 *(978-0-06-050426-7(9))* HarperCollins Pubs. (Tegen, Katherine Bks).
—28 Days: Moments in Black History That Changed the World. Smith, Charles R., Jr. 2015. (ENG.). 56p. (J). (gr. -1-5). 18.99 *(978-1-59643-820-0(7))* Roaring Brook Pr.
Evans, Shane W. Olu's Dream. Evans, Shane W. 2009. (ENG.). 40p. (J). (gr. -1-3). 16.99 *(978-0-06-072672-0(5),* Tegen, Katherine Bks) HarperCollins Pubs.
—Underground: Finding the Light to Freedom. Evans, Shane W. 2011. (ENG.). 32p. (J). (gr. -1-3). 16.99 *(978-1-59643-538-4(0))* Roaring Brook Pr.
—We March. Evans, Shane W. 2012. (ENG.). 32p. (J). (gr. -1-3). 16.99 *(978-1-59643-539-1(9))* Roaring Brook Pr.
Evans, Sherri. Nana & the Jabbywalker, 1 vol. Helbig-Miller, Theresa. 2008. (ENG.). 30p. 24.95 *(978-1-60703-567-1(7))* America Star Bks.
Evans, Steve, et al. Busy Ant Maths. Mumford, Jeanette et al. Clarke, Peter, ed. 2014. (ENG.). 128p. pap. 12.95 *(978-0-00-756838-3(X))* HarperCollins Pubs. Ltd. GBR. Dist: Independent Pubs. Group.
—Busy Ant Maths, Bk. 5A. Mumford, Jeanette et al. 2014. (ENG.). 128p. pap. 12.95 *(978-0-00-756833-8(9))* HarperCollins Pubs. Ltd. GBR. Dist: Independent Pubs. Group.
—Busy Ant Maths, Bk. 5C. Mumford, Jeanette et al. Clarke, Peter, ed. 2014. (ENG.). 128p. pap. 12.95 *(978-0-00-756835-2(5))* HarperCollins Pubs. Ltd. GBR. Dist: Independent Pubs. Group.
—Busy Ant Maths - Year 3, Bk. B. Mumford, Jeanette et al. Clarke, Peter, ed. 2014. (Busy Ant Maths Ser.). (ENG.). 72p. pap., stu. ed. 11.99 *(978-0-00-756238-1(1))* HarperCollins Pubs. Ltd. GBR. Dist: Independent Pubs. Group.
—Busy Ant Maths - Year 4, Bk. A. Mumford, Jeanette et al. Clarke, Peter, ed. 2014. (Busy Ant Maths Ser.). (ENG.). 72p. pap., stu. ed. 11.99 *(978-0-00-756240-4(3))* HarperCollins Pubs. Ltd. GBR. Dist: Independent Pubs. Group.
—Busy Ant Maths - Year 6 Pupil, Bk. 2. Mumford, Jeanette et al. Clarke, Peter, ed. 2014. (ENG.). 128p. pap. 12.95 *(978-0-00-756837-6(1))* HarperCollins Pubs. Ltd. GBR. Dist: Independent Pubs. Group.
—Busy Ant Maths - Year 6 Pupil, Bk. 6A. Mumford, Jeanette et al. 2014. (ENG.). 128p. pap. 12.95 *(978-0-00-756836-9(3))* HarperCollins Pubs. Ltd. GBR. Dist: Independent Pubs. Group.
—Pupil Book, Bk. 5B. Mumford, Jeanette et al. Clarke, Peter, ed. 2014. (ENG.). 128p. pap. 12.95 *(978-0-00-756834-5(7))* HarperCollins Pubs. Ltd. GBR. Dist: Independent Pubs. Group.
Evans, Wynne. Albie's First Word: A Tale Inspired by Albert Einstein's Childhood. Tourville, Jacqueline. 2014. (ENG.). 40p. (J). (gr. -1-3). 17.99 *(978-0-307-97893-6(1),* Schwartz & Wade Bks.) Random Hse. Children's Bks.
Eve Cravens Nawahine. Not Too Close. Esther Cravens Schwalger. 2009. 16p. pap. 8.49 *(978-1-4389-6987-9(2))* AuthorHouse.
Eve, Lealand. Dolly Goes on Vacation. Herman, Alison & Grossman, Lynne. 2007. 22p. (J). 24.95 *(978-0-9746153-2-5(3))* DMH Pr., Inc.
—Dolly Goes to the Beach. Herman, Alison & Grossman, Lynne. 2007. 24p. (J). 24.95 *(978-0-9746153-1-8(5))* DMH Pr., Inc.
—Dolly Goes to the Supermarket. Herman, Alison & Grossman, Lynne. 2007. 22p. (J). 24.96 *(978-0-9746153-0-1(7))* DMH Pr., Inc.
—Liberty's Journey: The Story of Our Freedom. Weigman, Matthew. 2004. 31p. (J). 16.95 *(978-0-9747981-0-3(X))* Fahnestock Pr.
Eveland, Keith & Eveland, Keith. The Yoyo & the Piggy Bank. Thoresen, Susan Werner. 2015. (ENG.). 40p. 16.95 ***(978-1-942155-05-8(0))*** Randall, Peter E. Pub.
Eveland, Keith, jt. illus. see Eveland, Keith.
Evens, Kevin C. The Elves of Owl's Head Mountain. Sutiff, Jamie. Blumberg, Christine A., ed. 2007. 276p. pap. 10.95 *(978-0-9712867-8-8(7))* Cold River Pubns.
Evenwel, Patricia L. Pierogies with the Pope: A Tribute to Pope John Paul II, & New Beginnings with Pope Benedict XVI for Young Readers, 1 vol. Barry, Todd J. 2009. 58p. pap. 16.95 *(978-1-60836-325-4(2))* America Star Bks.
—Shoofly Pie with the Pastor: A Journey Through Pennsylvania Dutch Country. Barry, Todd J. 2013. 70p. pap. 17.95 *(978-1-62709-944-8(1))* America Star Bks.
Everett-Hawkes, Bonnie. Blue Paint. Maher, Liam. 2012. 20p. pap. 9.95 *(978-1-61633-290-7(5))* Guardian Angel Publishing, Inc.
—Have You Ever Heard of a Rainbow Farm. Cousineau-Peiffer, Trisha. 2006. 32p. (J). 12.95 *(978-0-9792084-1-6(6))* Dream Ridge Pr.
—Have You Ever Heard of a Rainbow Farm: The Missing Color Kittens. Cousineau-Peiffer, Trisha. 2007. 48p. (J). per. 15.95 *(978-0-9792084-2-3(4))* Dream Ridge Pr.
Everett, J. H. & Scott-Waters, Marilyn. Haunted Histories: Creepy Castles, Dark Dungeons, & Powerful Palaces. Everett, J. H. & Scott-Waters, Marilyn. 2013. (ENG.). 160p. (J). (gr. 4-7). pap. 8.99 *(978-1-250-02726-9(8))* Square Fish.
Evergreen, Nelson. Attack of the Mud Creatures. Darke, J. A. 2015. (Spine Shivers Ser.). (ENG.). 128p. (gr. 3-4). lib. bdg. 25.32 ***(978-1-4965-0220-9(5))*** Stone Arch Bks.
Evergreen, Nelson. Death Sentence. Dahl, Michael. 2015. (Library of Doom: the Final Chapters Ser.). (ENG.). 40p. (gr. 1-3). 22.65 *(978-1-4342-9678-8(4))* Stone Arch Bks.
Evergreen, Nelson. The Grin in the Dark. Darke, J. A. 2015. (Spine Shivers Ser.). (ENG.). 128p. (gr. 3-4). lib. bdg. 25.32 ***(978-1-4965-0217-9(5))*** Stone Arch Bks.
—The House of Memories. Hulme-Cross, Benjamin. 2015. (Dark Hunter Ser.). (ENG.). 64p. (J). (gr. 4-8). pap. 4.99 ***(978-1-4677-8085-8(5))*** Lerner Publishing Group.
Evergreen, Nelson. John Henry - Hammerin' Hero. Stone Arch Books Staff. 2010. (Graphic Spin Ser.). (ENG.). 40p. (gr. 1-3). pap. 5.95 *(978-1-4342-2265-7(9),* Graphic Revolve) Stone Arch Bks.
—John Henry - Hammerin' Hero. Capstone Press Staff. 2010. (Graphic Spin Ser.). (ENG.). 40p. (gr. 1-3). lib. bdg. 23.99 *(978-1-4342-1898-8(8),* Graphic Revolve) Stone Arch Bks.
—The Lost Page. Dahl, Michael. 2015. (Library of Doom: the Final Chapters Ser.). (ENG.). 40p. (gr. 1-3). 22.65 *(978-1-4342-9679-5(2))* Stone Arch Bks.
Evergreen, Nelson. The Marsh Demon. Hulme-Cross, Benjamin. 2015. (Dark Hunter Ser.). (ENG.). 64p. (J). (gr. 4-8). 17.32 ***(978-1-4677-8658-4(6))*** Lerner Publishing Group.
—The Red Thirst. Hulme-Cross, Benjamin. 2015. (Dark Hunter Ser.). (ENG.). 64p. (J). (gr. 4-8). pap. 4.99 ***(978-1-4677-8088-9(X))*** Lerner Publishing Group.
—The Screaming Bridge. Darke, J. A. 2015. (Spine Shivers Ser.). (ENG.). 128p. (gr. 3-4). lib. bdg. 25.32 ***(978-1-4965-0219-3(1))*** Stone Arch Bks.
—Ship of Death. Hulme-Cross, Benjamin. 2015. (Dark Hunter Ser.). (ENG.). 64p. (J). (gr. 4-8). pap. 4.99 ***(978-1-4677-8090-2(1))*** Lerner Publishing Group.
Evergreen, Nelson. The Spine Tingler. Dahl, Michael. 2015. (Library of Doom: the Final Chapters Ser.). (ENG.). 40p. (gr. 1-3). 22.65 *(978-1-4342-9680-1(6))* Stone Arch Bks.
Evergreen, Nelson. The Stone Witch. Hulme-Cross, Benjamin. 2015. (Dark Hunter Ser.). (ENG.). 64p. (J). (gr. 4-8). pap. 4.99 ***(978-1-4677-8089-6(8))*** Lerner Publishing Group.
—Tech Fury. Darke, J. A. 2015. (Spine Shivers Ser.). (ENG.). 128p. (gr. 3-4). lib. bdg. 25.32 ***(978-1-4965-0218-6(3))*** Stone Arch Bks.
Evergreen, Nelson. Tome Raider. Dahl, Michael. 2015. (Library of Doom: the Final Chapters Ser.). (ENG.). 40p. (gr. 1-3). 22.65 *(978-1-4342-9677-1(6))* Stone Arch Bks.
Evergreen, Nelson. Wolf Trap. Hulme-Cross, Benjamin. 2015. (Dark Hunter Ser.). (ENG.). 64p. (J). (gr. 4-8). pap. 4.99 ***(978-1-4677-8086-5(3))*** Lerner Publishing Group.
Evergreen, Nelson & Kendall, Bradford. The Demon Card, 1 vol. Strange, Jason. 2012. (Jason Strange Ser.). (ENG.). 72p. (gr. 2-3). pap. 6.25 *(978-1-4342-3884-9(9));* lib. bdg. 23.99 *(978-1-4342-3296-0(4))* Stone Arch Bks.
—The Graveyard Plot, 1 vol. Strange, Jason. 2012. (Jason Strange Ser.). (ENG.). 72p. (gr. 2-3). pap. 6.25 *(978-1-4342-3886-3(5))* Stone Arch Bks.
—Strays, 1 vol. Strange, Jason. 2012. (Jason Strange Ser.). (ENG.). 72p. (gr. 2-3). pap. 6.25 *(978-1-4342-3883-2(0));* lib. bdg. 23.99 *(978-1-4342-3295-3(6))* Stone Arch Bks.
—23 Crow's Perch, 1 vol. Strange, Jason. 2012. (Jason Strange Ser.). (ENG.). 72p. (gr. 2-3). pap. 6.25 *(978-1-4342-3885-6(7));* lib. bdg. 23.99 *(978-1-4342-3297-7(2))* Stone Arch Bks.
Everhart, Adelaide. The Christmas Porringer (Yesterday's Classics) Stein, Evaleen. 2006. (J). per. 7.95 *(978-1-59915-193-9(6))* Yesterday's Classics.
Everidge, Channing. Catie Conrad: Faith, Friendship & Fashion Disasters. Spady, Angie. 2014. (Desperate Diva Diaries Ser.). (ENG.). 304p. (gr. 3-7). 12.99 *(978-1-4336-8460-9(8),* B&H Kids) B&H Publishing Group.
—Catie Conrad: How to Become the Most (un)Popular Girl in Jr. High. Spady, Angie. 2015. (Desperate Diva Diaries Ser.). (ENG.). 304p. (gr. 3-7). pap. 8.99 *(978-1-4336-8461-6(6),* B&H Kids) B&H Publishing Group.
Everitt, Betsy. Popcorn. Moran, Alex. 2003. (Green Light Readers Level 1 Ser.). (ENG.). 24p. (J). (gr. -1-3). pap. 3.95 *(978-0-15-204861-7(8))* Houghton Mifflin Harcourt Publishing Co.
Everitt-Stewart, Andrew. Our Baby, 1 vol. Dale, Jay. 2012. (Engage Literacy Green Ser.). (ENG.). 32p. (gr. k-2). pap. 5.99 *(978-1-4296-9023-2(2),* Engage Literacy) Capstone Pr., Inc.
—Our Special Rock Pool, 1 vol. Dale, Jay. 2012. (Engage Literacy Green Ser.). (ENG.). 32p. (gr. k-2). pap. 5.99 *(978-1-4296-9009-6(7),* Engage Literacy) Capstone Pr., Inc.
Everitt-Stewart, Andy. All Grown Up. Burlingham, Abi. 2009. (Stories to Grow with Ser.). 24p. (J). (gr. -1-2). 22.60 *(978-1-60754-469-2(5));* pap. 8.15 *(978-1-60754-470-8(9))* Windmill Bks.
—Best Friends. Burlingham, Abi. 2009. (Stories to Grow with Ser.). 24p. (J). (gr. -1-2). 22.60 *(978-1-60754-475-3(X));* pap. 8.15 *(978-1-60754-476-0(8))* Windmill Bks.
—Scaredy Bear. Nash, Sarah. 2009. (Stories to Grow with Ser.). 24p. (J). (gr. -1-2). 22.60 *(978-1-60754-472-2(5))* Windmill Bks.
—Smelly Blanket. Nash, Sarah. 2009. (Stories to Grow with Ser.). 24p. (J). (gr. -1-2). 22.60 *(978-1-60754-466-1(0));* pap. 8.15 *(978-1-60754-467-8(9))* Windmill Bks.
—3-Minute Animal Stories. Baxter, Nicola. 2013. (ENG.). 80p. (J). (gr. -1-k). pap. 9.99 *(978-1-84322-978-0(1),* Armadillo) Anness Publishing GBR. Dist: National Bk. Network.
Everson, Andy. I am Raven. Bouchard, David. 2nd ed. 2008. 28p. (J). *(978-0-9784327-0-6(3))* More Than Words Bks., Inc.
Everson, Mya. Ole Mackerel. Jacobsen, Annie. 2012. 32p. (J). 9.98 *(978-0-9778276-5-7(8))* Pickled Herring Pr.
Evrard, Gaetan. Let's Get to Work!/Vamos a Trabajar! Anderson, Jill, ed. 2005. (Word Play/Juegos con Pala Ser.). (ENG & SPA.). 20p. (J). (gr. -1-17). 6.95 *(978-1-58728-512-7(6))* Cooper Square Publishing Llc.
—Let's Go!/Vamos a Viajar! Anderson, Jill, ed. 2005. (Word Play/Juegos con Pala Ser.). (ENG & SPA.). 20p. (J). (gr. -1-17). 6.95 *(978-1-58728-513-4(4))* Cooper Square Publishing Llc.
Ewanits, Tara, photos by. Aesop's Angel. Haitz, Rochelle. 2010. (ENG., 24p. pap. 6.99 *(978-1-4538-5663-5(3))* CreateSpace Independent Publishing Platform.
Ewart, Claire. The Green Musician. Shahegh, Mahvash. 2015. (ENG.). 36p. (J). (gr. k-3). 16.95 ***(978-1-937786-42-7(0),*** Wisdom Tales) World Wisdom, Inc.
Ewart, Claire. The Olive Tree. Marston, Elsa. 2014. (ENG.). 32p. (J). (gr. -1-2). 16.95 *(978-1-937786-29-8(3),* Wisdom Tales) World Wisdom, Inc.
Ewart, Claire. The Seagoing Cowboy. Miller, Peggy Reiff. 2016. (J). ***(978-0-87178-212-0(X))*** Brethren Pr.
Ewart, Claire. Fossil. Ewart, Claire. 2014. (ENG.). 40p. (J). (gr. -1-3). 16.99 *(978-0-8027-3737-3(4))* Walker & Co.
Ewen, Caroline. Ella Moves House. Hassall, Angela. 2010. (ENG.). 32p. (J). (gr. k-2). pap. 10.99 *(978-1-84853-006-5(4))* Transworld Publishers Ltd. GBR. Dist: Independent Pubs. Group.
Ewers, Joe. The Monsters on the Bus (Sesame Street) Albee, Sarah. 2013. (Little Golden Book Ser.). (ENG.). 24p. (J). (-k). 3.99 *(978-0-307-98058-8(8),* Golden Bks.) Random Hse. Children's Bks.
—The Pied Piper: A Tale about Promises. 2006. (J). 6.99 *(978-1-59939-004-8(3))* Cornerstone Pr.
Ewers, Joe & Lopez, Paul. Everyday Heroes. Schoberle, Cecile. 2003. (Ready-to-Read Ser.). 30p. (J). (gr. k-3). lib. bdg. 9.02 *(978-0-613-66498-1(1),* Turtleback) Turtleback Bks.
Ewers, Joe, jt. illus. see Swanson, Maggie.
Ewing, John. Dezzer the Gasser. Lorraine, Florido. Shami, Susan & Crossman, Keith, eds. 2009. 32p. (J). 15.99 *(978-0-9818449-0-9(1))* Thinkus Pubs.
—Hugo the Punk. Florido, Lorraine. Shami, Susan, ed. 2013. 108p. (YA). pap. 9.98 *(978-0-9818449-6-1(0))* Thinkus Pubs.
Ewing, Richard. Spanking Shakespeare. Wizner, Jake. 2008. (ENG.). 304p. (J). (gr. 9). pap. 8.99 *(978-0-375-85594-8(7),* Random Hse. Bks. for Young Readers) Random Hse. Children's Bks.
Eyckerman, Merel. The Ant & the Grasshopper. 2013. (Usborne First Reading: Level 1 Ser.). (ENG.). 32p. (J). (gr. -1-3). 6.99 *(978-0-7945-2257-5(2),* Usborne) EDC Publishing.
Eyolfson, Norman. First Spy Case. Richler, Mordecai. 2003. (Jacob Two-Two Ser.). (ENG.). 144p. (J). (gr. 3-7). pap. 6.95 *(978-0-88776-694-7(3))* Tundra Bks. CAN. Dist: Random Hse., Inc.
—Jacob Two-Two & the Dinosaur. Richler, Mordecai. 2004. (Jacob Two-Two Ser.). (ENG.). 96p. (J). (gr. 3-7). pap. 6.95 *(978-0-88776-712-8(5))* Tundra Bks. CAN. Dist: Random Hse., Inc.
Eyre, Jane. Tyler's Halloween Horror, 1 vol. Beraducci, Deborah. 2009. 22p. pap. 24.95 *(978-1-4489-2133-1(3))* America Star Bks.
Eyre, Jane. Creatures of the New Jersey Pine Barrens Coloring Book, 1 vol. Eyre, Jane. 2004. 36p. spiral bd. 6.00 *(978-0-9762483-0-9(1))* Fun Fitness Publishing.
Eyuboglu, Melisa. Angel in a Bubble. Eyuboglu, Melisa, . 2007. 28p. (J). 10.95 *(978-1-933090-48-1(0))* Guardian Angel Publishing, Inc.

F

Faas, Linde. The Birthday Surprise. Lootens, Ann. 2013. (Wild Woods Ser.). (ENG.). 32p. (J). (gr. -1-k). 15.95 *(978-1-60537-147-4(5))* Clavis Publishing.
Faassen, Louis. A Guide to the CMMI: Interpreting the Capability Maturity Model Integration. Dymond, Kenneth. Dymond, Detta, ed. 2004. spiral bd. 20.00 *(978-0-9646008-4-3(6))* Process Transition International, Inc.
Fabbretti, Valerio. Action Movie Kid: All New Adventures Part 1. Hashimoto, Daniel & Richardville, Mandy. 2015. (ENG.). 64p. (J). (gr. -1-k). 14.99 ***(978-1-4767-9989-6(X),*** Atria Bks.) Simon & Schuster.

F

Fabbretti, Valerio. Ghost Light Burning: An Up2U Mystery Adventure. Fields, Jan. 2015. (J). (978-1-62402-092-6(5)) Magic Wagon.

Fabbretti, Valerio. Hamster Holmes: A Mystery Comes Knocking. Sadar, Albin. 2015. (Ready-To-Reads Ser.: 1). (ENG.). 32p. (J). (gr. k-2). 16.99 (978-1-4814-2037-2(2), Simon Spotlight) Simon Spotlight.

—Hamster Holmes, Combing for Clues. Sadar, Albin. 2015. (Ready-To-Reads Ser.: 2). (ENG.). 32p. (J). (gr. k-2). pap. 3.99 (978-1-4814-2039-6(9), Simon Spotlight) Simon Spotlight.

—A Mystery Comes Knocking. Sadar, Albin. 2015. (Ready-To-Reads Ser.: 1). (ENG.). 32p. (J). (gr. k-2). pap. 3.99 (978-1-4814-2036-5(4), Simon Spotlight) Simon Spotlight.

Fabbri, Daniele. Do You Really Want to Meet a Cape Buffalo? Meister, Cari. 2015. (Do You Really Want to Meet ... ? Ser.). (ENG.). 24p. (gr. 1-3). 19.95 (978-1-60753-738-0(9)) Amicus Educational.

—Do You Really Want to Meet a Crocodile? Meister, Cari. 2015. (Do You Really Want to Meet... ? Ser.). 24p. (J). 27.10 (978-1-60753-457-0(6)) Amicus Educational.

—Do You Really Want to Meet a Kangaroo? Meister, Cari. 2015. (Do You Really Want to Meet ... ? Ser.). (ENG.). 24p. (gr. 1-3). 19.95 (978-1-60753-734-2(6)) Amicus Educational.

—Do You Really Want to Meet a Lion? Meister, Cari. 2015. (Do You Really Want to Meet ... ? Ser.). (ENG.). 24p. (gr. 1-3). 19.95 (978-1-60753-735-9(4)) Amicus Educational.

—Do You Really Want to Meet a Monkey? Meister, Cari. 2015. (Do You Really Want to Meet... ? Ser.). 24p. (J). 27.10 (978-1-60753-456-3(8)) Amicus Educational.

—Do You Really Want to Meet a Moose? Meister, Cari. 2015. (Do You Really Want to Meet ... ? Ser.). (ENG.). 24p. (gr. 1-3). 19.95 (978-1-60753-736-6(2)) Amicus Educational.

—Do You Really Want to Meet a Platypus? Meister, Cari. 2014. (Do You Really Want to Meet... ? Ser.). (ENG.). 24p. (J). (gr. 1-4). 27.10 (978-1-60753-460-0(6)) Amicus Educational.

—Do You Really Want to Meet a Polar Bear? Aboff, Marcie. 2015. (Do You Really Want to Meet... ? Ser.). 24p. (J). 27.10 (978-1-60753-455-6(X)) Amicus Educational.

—Do You Really Want to Meet a Shark? Meister, Cari. 2015. (Do You Really Want to Meet ... ? Ser.). (ENG.). 24p. (gr. 1-3). 19.95 (978-1-60753-737-3(0)) Amicus Educational.

—Do You Really Want to Meet a Swan? Meister, Cari. 2014. (Do You Really Want to Meet... ? Ser.). (ENG.). 24p. (J). (gr. 1-4). 27.10 (978-1-60753-458-7(4)) Amicus Educational.

—Do You Really Want to Meet a Tiger? Meister, Cari. 2015. (Do You Really Want to Meet... ? Ser.). 24p. (J). 27.10 (978-1-60753-459-4(2)) Amicus Educational.

—Do You Really Want to Meet an Elephant? Meister, Cari. 2015. (Do You Really Want to Meet ... ? Ser.). (ENG.). 24p. (gr. 1-3). 19.95 (978-1-60753-733-5(8)) Amicus Educational.

—Do You Really Want to Visit a Coral Reef? Heos, Bridget. 2014. (Do You Really Want to Visit... ? Ser.). (ENG.). 24p. (J). (gr. 1-4). 27.10 (978-1-60753-449-5(5)) Amicus Educational.

—Do You Really Want to Visit a Prairie? Heos, Bridget. 2014. (Do You Really Want to Visit... ? Ser.). (ENG.). 24p. (J). (gr. 1-4). lib. bdg. 27.10 (978-1-60753-452-5(5)) Amicus Educational.

—Do You Really Want to Visit a Temperate Forest? Heos, Bridget. 2014. (Do You Really Want to Visit... ? Ser.). (ENG.). 24p. (J). (gr. 1-4). 27.10 (978-1-60753-451-8(7)) Amicus Educational.

—Do You Really Want to Visit a Wetland? Heos, Bridget. 2014. (Do You Really Want to Visit... ? Ser.). (ENG.). 24p. (J). (gr. 1-4). lib. bdg. 27.10 (978-1-60753-454-9(1)) Amicus Educational.

—Do You Really Want to Visit Mars? Adamson, Thomas K. 2013. (Do You Really Want to Visit... ? Ser.). (ENG.). 24p. (gr. 1-4). 27.10 (978-1-60753-198-2(4)) Amicus Educational.

—Do You Really Want to Visit Mercury? Adamson, Thomas K. 2013. (Do You Really Want to Visit... ? Ser.). (ENG.). 24p. (gr. 1-4). 27.10 (978-1-60753-195-1(X)) Amicus Educational.

—Do You Really Want to Visit Neptune? Heos, Bridget. 2013. (Do You Really Want to Visit... ? Ser.). (ENG.). 24p. (gr. 1-4). 27.10 (978-1-60753-201-9(8)) Amicus Educational.

—Do You Really Want to Visit Saturn? Heos, Bridget. 2013. (Do You Really Want to Visit... ? Ser.). (ENG.). 24p. (gr. 1-4). 27.10 (978-1-60753-200-2(X)) Amicus Educational.

—Do You Really Want to Visit the Moon? Adamson, Thomas K. 2013. (Do You Really Want to Visit... ? Ser.). (ENG.). 24p. (gr. 1-4). 27.10 (978-1-60753-197-5(6)) Amicus Educational.

—Do You Really Want to Visit Uranus? Heos, Bridget. 2013. (Do You Really Want to Visit... ? Ser.). (ENG.). 24p. (gr. 1-4). 27.10 (978-1-60753-202-6(6)) Amicus Educational.

—Do You Really Want to Visit Venus? Adamson, Thomas K. 2013. (Do You Really Want to Visit... ? Ser.). (ENG.). 24p. (gr. 1-4). 27.10 (978-1-60753-196-8(8)) Amicus Educational.

—My First Arabic Phrases, 1 vol. Kalz, Jill. TransPerfect Translations Staff, tr. 2012. (Speak Another Language! Ser.). (ARA & ENG.). 32p. (gr. 1-3). pap. 7.95 (978-1-4048-7734-4(7)); lib. bdg. 25.99 (978-1-4048-7517-3(4)) Picture Window Bks.

—My First French Phrases, 1 vol. Kalz, Jill. Translations.com Staff, tr. 2012. (Speak Another Language! Ser.). (FRE & ENG.). 32p. (gr. 1-3). pap. 7.95 (978-1-4048-7244-8(2)); lib. bdg. 25.99 (978-1-4048-7153-3(5)) Picture Window Bks. (Nonfiction Picture Bks.).

—My First German Phrases, 1 vol. Mayesky & Kalz, Jill. Translations.com Staff, tr. 2012. (Speak Another Language! Ser.). (ENG.). 32p. (gr. 1-3). pap. 7.95 (978-1-4048-7245-5(0)); lib. bdg. 25.99 (978-1-4048-7154-0(3)) Picture Window Bks. (Nonfiction Picture Bks.).

—My First Japanese Phrases, 1 vol. Kalz, Jill. TransPerfect Translations Staff, tr. 2012. (Speak Another Language! Ser.). (JPN & ENG.). 32p. (gr. 1-3). pap. 7.95 (978-1-4048-7738-2(X)); lib. bdg. 25.99 (978-1-4048-7514-2(X)) Picture Window Bks.

—My First Mandarin Chinese Phrases, 1 vol. Kalz, Jill. Advocate-Art Staff & Translations.com Staff, trs. 2012. (Speak Another Language! Ser.). (CHI & ENG.). 32p. (gr. 1-3). pap. 7.95 (978-1-4048-7246-2(9), Nonfiction Picture Bks.) Picture Window Bks.

—My First Mandarin Chinese Phrases, 1 vol. Kalz, Jill. Translations.com Staff, tr. 2012. (Speak Another Language! Ser.). (CHI & ENG.). 32p. (gr. 1-3). lib. bdg. 25.99 (978-1-4048-7155-7(1), Nonfiction Picture Bks.) Picture Window Bks.

—My First Russian Phrases, 1 vol. Kalz, Jill. TransPerfect Translations Staff, tr. 2012. (Speak Another Language! Ser.). (ENG.). 32p. (gr. 1-3). pap. 7.95 (978-1-4048-7740-5(1)); lib. bdg. 25.99 (978-1-4048-7515-9(8)) Picture Window Bks.

—My First Spanish Phrases, 1 vol. Kalz, Jill. Translations.com Staff, tr. 2012. (Speak Another Language! Ser.). (SPA & ENG.). 32p. (gr. 1-3). pap. 7.95 (978-1-4048-7247-9(7), Nonfiction Picture Bks.) Picture Window Bks.

—My First Spanish Phrases, 1 vol. Kalz, Jill. Advocate-Art Staff & Translations.com Staff, trs. 2012. (Speak Another Language! Ser.). (SPA & ENG.). 32p. (gr. 1-3). lib. bdg. 25.99 (978-1-4048-7152-6(7), Nonfiction Picture Bks.) Picture Window Bks.

Fabbri, Daniele. So You Want to Grow a Pie? Heos, Bridget. 2015. (Grow Your Food Ser.). (ENG.). 24p. (gr. 1-3). 19.95 (978-1-60753-739-7(7)) Amicus Educational.

—So You Want to Grow a Pizza? Heos, Bridget. 2015. (Grow Your Food Ser.). (ENG.). 24p. (gr. 1-3). 19.95 (978-1-60753-740-3(0)) Amicus Educational.

—So You Want to Grow a Salad? Heos, Bridget. 2015. (Grow Your Food Ser.). (ENG.). 24p. (gr. 1-3). 19.95 (978-1-60753-741-0(9)) Amicus Educational.

—So You Want to Grow a Taco? Heos, Bridget. 2015. (Grow Your Food Ser.). (ENG.). 24p. (gr. 1-3). 19.95 (978-1-60753-742-7(7)) Amicus Educational.

Fabbri, Daniele. Who Are You? Korba, Joanna & Benchmark Education Co., LLC. 2014. (Text Connections Ser.). (J). (gr. 3). (978-1-4509-9664-8(7)) Benchmark Education Co.

Fabbri, Daniele. Why Do Rainbows Have So Many Colors? Shand, Jennifer. Paiva, Johannah Gilman, ed. 2014. (ENG.). 20p. (J). (gr. k-4). 8.99 (978-1-4867-0383-8(6)) Flowerpot Children's Pr. Inc. CAN. Dist: Cardinal Pubs. Group.

—Why Do Tractors Have Such Big Tires? Shand, Jennifer. Paiva, Johannah Gilman, ed. 2014. (ENG.). 20p. (J). (gr. k-4). 8.99 (978-1-4867-0382-1(8)) Flowerpot Children's Pr. Inc. CAN. Dist: Cardinal Pubs. Group.

Faber, Rudy. Rebel with a Cause: The Daring Adventure of Dicey Langston, Girl Spy of the American Revolution. Kudlinski, Kathleen V. 2015. (Encounter: Narrative Nonfiction Picture Bks.). (ENG.). 40p. (gr. 3-4). lib. bdg. 27.99 (978-1-4914-6073-3(3)) Encounter Bks.

Fabian, Gabriella. Wishes. Morrison, Julia. 2013. 42p. pap. 10.00 (978-1-883651-65-7(4)) Winters Publishing.

Fable Vision Studios Staff, jt. illus. see Reynolds, Peter H.

FableVision Studios Staff & Reynolds, Peter H. Zebrafish. FableVision Studios Staff. 2010. (Zebrafish Ser.). (ENG.). 128p. (J). (gr. 5-9). 16.99 (978-1-4169-9525-8(0), Atheneum Bks. for Young Readers) Simon & Schuster Children's Publishing.

Fabrega, Marta. The Colors of the Rainbow. Moore-Mallinos, Jennifer. 2005. (Let's Talk about It! Bks.). (ENG.). 32p. (J). (gr. -1-2). per. 7.99 (978-0-7641-3277-3(6)) Barron's Educational Series, Inc.

—Do You Have a Secret? Moore-Mallinos, Jennifer. 2005. (Let's Talk about It! Ser.). (ENG.). 32p. (J). (gr. -1-3). pap. 7.99 (978-0-7641-3170-7(2)) Barron's Educational Series, Inc.

—I Am Deaf. Moore-Mallinos, Jennifer. 2009. (Live & Learn Ser.). (ENG.). 36p. (J). (gr. -1-2). pap. 7.99 (978-0-7641-4179-9(1)) Barron's Educational Series, Inc.

—I Can't Sit Still! Living with ADHD. Pollack, Pam & Belviso, Meg. 2009. (Live & Learn Ser.). (ENG.). 36p. (J). (gr. -1-2). pap. 6.99 (978-0-7641-4419-6(7)) Barron's Educational Series, Inc.

—It's Called Dyslexia. Moore-Mallinos, Jennifer et al. 2007. (Live & Learn Ser.). (ENG.). 32p. (J). (gr. -1-2). pap. 7.99 (978-0-7641-3794-5(8)) Barron's Educational Series, Inc.

—It's Ok to Be Me! Just Like You, I Can Do Almost Anything! Moore-Malinos, Jennifer. 2007. (Live & Learn Ser.). (ENG.). 36p. (J). (gr. -1-2). pap. 6.99 (978-0-7641-3584-2(8)) Barron's Educational Series, Inc.

—Mi Hermano Tiene Autismo. Moore-Mallinos, Jennifer & Roca, Nuria. 2008. (Hablemos de Esto Ser.).Tr. of My Brother Is Autistic. (SPA.). 32p. (J). (gr. -1-2). pap. 6.99 (978-0-7641-4045-7(0)) Barron's Educational Series, Inc.

—Mom Has Cancer! Moore-Mallinos, Jennifer & Roca, Nuria. 2008. (Let's Talk about It Ser.). (ENG.). 32p. (J). (gr. -1-2). pap. 7.99 (978-0-7641-4074-7(4)) Barron's Educational Series, Inc.

—My Brother Is Autistic. Moore-Mallinos, Jennifer & Roca, Nuria. 2008. (Let's Talk about It Bks.). (ENG.). 32p. (J). (gr. -1-2). pap. 7.99 (978-0-7641-4044-0(2)) Barron's Educational Series, Inc.

—My Friend Has down Syndrome. Moore-Mallinos, Jennifer & Roca, Nuria. 2008. (Let's Talk about It Ser.). (ENG.). 32p. (J). (gr. -1-2). pap. 7.99 (978-0-7641-4076-1(0)) Barron's Educational Series, Inc.

—¡No Puedo Estar Quieto! Mi Vida con ADHD. Pollack, Pam & Belviso, Meg. 2009. (Viva y Aprende Ser.). (SPA.). 36p. (J). (gr. -1-2). pap. 6.99 (978-0-7641-4420-2(0)) Barron's Educational Series, Inc.

Fabul, J. C. & Calero, Dennis. The Pit & the Pendulum, 1 vol. Tulien, Sean & Poe, Edgar Allen. 2013. (Edgar Allan Poe Graphic Novels Ser.). (ENG.). 72p. (gr. 2-3). pap. 6.10 (978-1-4342-4260-0(9)); lib. bdg. 26.65 (978-1-4342-4024-8(X)) Stone Arch Bks.

Faccini, Enrico. Uncle Scrooge - How Green Was My Lettuce. Faccini, Enrico. Jensen, Lars et al. Clark, John, ed. 2008. (Walt Disney's Uncle Scrooge Ser.: No. 371). 64p. pap. 7.99 (978-1-60360-001-9(9)) Gemstone Publishing, Inc.

Fach, Gernot, jt. illus. see Zengin-Karaian, Alex.

Facio, Sebastian. Swamp Sting!, 1 vol. Hoena, Blake A. 2011. (Graphic Sparks Ser.). (ENG.). 40p. (gr. 1-3). pap. 5.95 (978-1-4342-3065-2(1)); lib. bdg. 22.65 (978-1-4342-2960-1(2)) Stone Arch Bks. (Graphic Sparks).

Facklam, Paul. Snow Dance, 1 vol. Thomas, Peggy. 2008. (ENG.). 32p. (J). (gr. 1-3). 16.99 (978-1-58980-478-4(3)) Pelican Publishing Co., Inc.

Fagan, Martin. Lamhainni Glasa. Ghlinn, Aine Ni. 2004. (Sraith Sos Ser.: 11). (ENG, GLE & IRI.). 64p. (J). pap. 9.95 (978-0-86278-901-5(X)) O'Brien Pr., Ltd., The IRL. Dist: Dufour Editions, Inc.

—Mo Mhadra Beoga. Deeley, Patrick. 2005. (Sraith Sos Ser.: 12). (IRI, ENG & GLE.). 64p. (J). pap. 9.95 (978-0-86278-942-8(7)) O'Brien Pr., Ltd., The IRL. Dist: Dufour Editions, Inc.

—The Secret Life of Wally Smithers. Jenkins, Amanda & Benchmark Education Co., LLC. 2014. (Text Connections Ser.). (J). (gr. 3). (978-1-4509-9656-3(6)) Benchmark Education Co.

—A Trip to Washington, D. C. A Capital Idea. Turnage, Cyndy. 2013. (Reader's Theater Word Plays Ser.). (J). (gr. 1-2). (978-1-4509-8941-1(1)) Benchmark Education Co.

—Wolfgran Returns. O'Connor, Finbar. 2004. (ENG.). 96p. (J). pap. 10.95 (978-0-86278-884-1(6)) O'Brien Pr., Ltd., The IRL. Dist: Dufour Editions, Inc.

Fahringer, Sarah. Lessons from the Vine Second Grade Spring Quarter. Thompson, Kathy. 2012. 170p. pap. 35.00 (978-1-935014-31-7(5), Lessons From The Vine) Hutchings, John Pubs.

Fain, Cheryl. Rosa: A German Woman on the Texas Frontier. Crawford, Ann Fears. l.t. ed. 2003. 60p. (J). (gr. 3-8). 16.95 (978-1-931823-09-8(X)) Halcyon Pr.

Fair, Patricia Anne. Paddle Tail's First Winter Adventure. Legrand, H J, III. 2006. 64p. (J). per. 7.95 (978-1-59466-082-5(4), Growing Years) Port Town Publishing.

Fairbanks, Letitia. Princess April Morning-Glory: What Kind of a World Would You Create, If You Had to Do Three Dood Deeds to Make Ii Home Again? Fairbanks, Letitia. 2013. (ENG.). 66p. pap. 24.00 (978-0-9887848-0-2(7)) Sandramantos Publishing.

Fairbanks, Mark. Mikey. Pinto, Mindee & Cohen, Judy. 2013. 32p. pap. 9.99 (978-1-937165-41-3(8)) Orange Hat Publishing.

Fairchild, Vincent. Are You There? Fairchild, Dianne. 2007. 32p. (J). pap. 16.00 (978-0-8059-7535-2(7)) Dorrance Publishing Co., Inc.

Fairclough, Chris. Camping Trip. Chancellor, Deborah. 2005. (Reading Corner Ser.). 24p. (J). (gr. k-3). lib. bdg. 22.80 (978-1-59771-010-7(5)) Sea-To-Sea Pubns.

Fairclough, Chris, photos by. Dressing up Fun: Make Your Own Costumes at Home. Shirley, Rebekah Joy. 2012. (ENG., 128p. (J). pap. 9.95 (978-1-84837-915-2(3)) Arcturus Publishing GBR. Dist: AtlasBooks Distribution.

—How to Make a Card. Humphrey, Paul. 2007. (Crafty Kids Ser.). 24p. (J). (gr. -1-3). lib. bdg. 24.25 (978-1-59771-100-5(4)) Sea-To-Sea Pubns.

—How to Make a Mask. Humphrey, Paul. 2007. (Crafty Kids Ser.). 24p. (J). (gr. -1-3). lib. bdg. 24.25 (978-1-59771-101-2(2)) Sea-To-Sea Pubns.

—How to Make a Present. Humphrey, Paul. 2007. (Crafty Kids Ser.). 24p. (J). (gr. -1-3). lib. bdg. 24.25 (978-1-59771-103-6(9)) Sea-To-Sea Pubns.

—Mumbai. Green, Jen. 2007. (Global Cities Ser.). 64p. (gr. 5-8). lib. bdg. 30.00 (978-0-7910-8851-7(0), Chelsea Hse.) Facts On File, Inc.

—New York. Garrington, Sally. 2006. (Global Cities Ser.). 64p. (gr. 5-8). lib. bdg. 30.00 (978-0-7910-8853-1(7)) Facts On File, Inc.

Fairhurst, Carol. One Shining Day. Dorling, Anna et al. 2011. (Purple Elephant Tales). 66p. (J). pap. (978-1-921883-15-6(4), MBS Pr.) Pick-a-Woo Woo Pubs.

Fairhurst, Joanne. Archie & the Red Wool. Fairhurst, Joanne. 2011. 16p. pap. (978-1-908341-21-1(1)) Paragon Publishing, Rothersthorpe.

Fairman, Jennifer. El Cuerpo Humano. Beck, Paul. 2007. (SPA.). 48p. (J). (gr. k-5). 15.99 (978-970-718-436-7(1), Silver Dolphin en Español) Advanced Marketing, S. de R. L. de C. V. MEX. Dist: Perseus-PGW.

Fairman, Jennifer, jt. illus. see Desrocher, Jack.

Fairy, Meg. The Three Ants & Mother Bird. Ives, Bob. Deskov, Vladimir, ed. 2004. 40p. (J). (978-1-920832-06-3(8)) Four Heads Publishing Group Pty, Ltd.

—The Three Ants & the Cat. Ives, Bob. 2003. 40p. (J). (978-1-920832-07-0(6)) Four Heads Publishing Group Pty, Ltd.

Falcone, Fernando. The Big Book of Vampires. Despeyroux, Denise. 2012. (ENG.). 112p. (J). (gr. 4-7). 17.95 (978-1-77049-371-1(9)) Tundra Bks. CAN. Dist: Random Hse., Inc.

Falconer, Ian. Olivia Alphabet Flash Cards. 2013. (ENG.). 26p. (J). (gr. -1 — 1). 14.99 (978-1-4521-1179-7(0)) Chronicle Bks. LLC.

—Olivia Lacing Cards. 2013. (ENG.). 10p. (J). (gr. -1-1). 14.99 (978-1-4521-1177-3(4)) Chronicle Bks. LLC.

—Olivia Se Prepara para la Navidad. Mlawer, Teresa, tr. from ENG. 2008.Tr. of Olivia Helps with Christmas. (SPA.). 58p. (J). (gr. k-1). 16.99 (978-1-933032-42-9(1)) Lectorum Pubns., Inc.

Falconer, Ian. Olivia. Falconer, Ian. 2009. (ENG.). 40p. (J). (gr. -1-3). 12.99 (978-1-4169-8034-6(2), Atheneum Bks. for Young Readers) Simon & Schuster Children's Publishing.

—Olivia. Falconer, Ian. High, Amy, tr. from ENG. 2007. (LAT.). 40p. (J). (gr. 3-7). 17.99 (978-1-4169-4218-4(1), Atheneum Bks. for Young Readers) Simon & Schuster Children's Publishing.

—Olivia. Falconer, Ian. unabr. ed. 2004. (Classic Board Bks.). (ENG.). 34p. (J). (gr. -1-k). 7.99 (978-0-689-87472-7(3), Atheneum Bks. for Young Readers) Simon & Schuster Children's Publishing.

—Olivia & the Fairy Princesses. Falconer, Ian. 2012. (ENG.). 40p. (J). (gr. -1-3). 17.99 (978-1-4424-5027-1(4), Atheneum Bks. for Young Readers) Simon & Schuster Children's Publishing.

—Olivia... & the Missing Toy. Falconer, Ian. 2003. (ENG.). 42p. (J). (gr. -1-3). 18.99 (978-0-689-85291-6(6), Atheneum Bks. for Young Readers) Simon & Schuster Children's Publishing.

—The Olivia Collection: Olivia; Olivia Saves the Circus; Olivia... & the Missing Toy; Olivia Forms a Band; Olivia Helps with Christmas; Olivia Goes to Venice; Olivia & the Fairy Princesses. Falconer, Ian. Simon & Schuster Audio Firm Staff. ed. 2012. (ENG.). 322p. (J). (gr. -1-2). 128.99 (978-1-4424-8299-9(0), Atheneum Bks. for Young Readers) Simon & Schuster Children's Publishing.

—Olivia Forma una Banda. Falconer, Ian. Mlawer, Teresa, tr. from ENG. 2007. (SPA.). 39p. (J). (gr. -1-3). 17.99 (978-1-933032-23-8(5)) Lectorum Pubns., Inc.

—Olivia Forms a Band. Falconer, Ian. (ENG.). (J). (gr. -1-3). 2009. 50p. 12.99 (978-1-4169-8037-7(7)); 2006. 44p. 18.99 (978-1-4169-2454-8(X)) Simon & Schuster Children's Publishing. (Atheneum Bks. for Young Readers).

—Olivia Goes to Venice. Falconer, Ian. 2010. (ENG.). 48p. (J). (gr. -1-2). 17.99 (978-1-4169-9674-3(5), Atheneum Bks. for Young Readers) Simon & Schuster Children's Publishing.

—Olivia Helps with Christmas. Falconer, Ian. (Classic Board Bks.). (ENG.). (J). (gr. -1-2). 2013. 40p. bds. 7.99 (978-1-4424-9446-6(8)); 2007. 58p. 18.99 (978-1-4169-0786-2(6)) Simon & Schuster Children's Publishing. (Atheneum Bks. for Young Readers).

—Olivia Saves the Circus. Falconer, Ian. 2010. (Classic Board Bks.). (ENG.). 36p. (J). (gr. -1-2). bds. 7.99 (978-1-4424-1287-3(9), Atheneum Bks. for Young Readers) Simon & Schuster Children's Publishing.

—Olivia y el Juguete Desaparecido. Falconer, Ian. Mlawer, Teresa, tr. from ENG. 2004. (Olivia Ser.).Tr. of Olivia & the Missing Toy. (SPA.). 30p. (J). 16.95 (978-1-930332-71-3(8)) Lectorum Pubns., Inc.

—Teatro Olivia: Swan Lake; Romeo & Juliet; Turandot. Falconer, Ian. 2004. (Olivia Ser.). 10p. (J). 19.95 (978-0-689-87816-9(8)) Simon & Schuster, Inc.

Falk, Cathy Kennerson. Love Stories for Children. Kennerson, Vern. 2013. (ENG.). 67p. (YA). pap. 17.95 (978-1-4787-1665-5(7)) Outskirts Pr., Inc.

Falkenstern, Lisa. The Busy Tree, 0 vols. Ward, Jennifer. 2009. (ENG.). 32p. (J). (gr. k-3). 17.99 (978-0-7614-5550-9(7), 9780761455509, Amazon Children's Publishing) Amazon Publishing.

Fall, Brandon. The Bicycle Fence. Noll, Tom. 2014. (ENG.). 32p. (J). lib. bdg. 17.99 (978-1-939377-50-0(1)) Green Kids Pr., LLC.

—I Can Be an Artist (Barbie) Man-Kong, Mary. 2012. (Giant Paint Box Book Ser.). (ENG.). 40p. (J). (gr. -1-2). pap. 10.99 (978-0-307-93128-3(5), Golden Bks.) Random Hse. Children's Bks.

—The President Looks Like Me, Vol. 2. Michelle, Tanya. 2nd l.t. ed. 2010. (ENG.). 25p. (J). (978-0-615-57799-9(7)) Bee's Ink Publishing.

Faller, Regis. The Adventures of Polo. Faller, Regis. 2006. (Adventures of Polo Ser.). (ENG.). 80p. (J). (gr. -1-3). 18.99 (978-1-59643-160-7(1)) Roaring Brook Pr.

—Polo & the Dragon. Faller, Regis. 2009. (Adventures of Polo Ser.). (ENG.). 28p. (J). (gr. -1-3). 12.99 (978-1-59643-498-1(8)) Roaring Brook Pr.

Fallon, Lisa. Miss Olivia, the Little Red Poodle: Her First Big Adventure. Kaminski, Tom. 2006. (J). pap. 16.00 (978-0-8059-7253-5(6)) Dorrance Publishing Co., Inc.

Falwell, Cathryn. Butterflies for Kiri. Falwell, Cathryn. 2003. (ENG.). 32p. (J). (978-1-58430-100-4(7)) Lee & Low Bks., Inc.

—Los Dibujos de David. Falwell, Cathryn. de La Vega, Eida, tr. from ENG. 2005. (SPA.). 32p. (J). (gr. -1-5). pap. 9.95 (978-1-58430-258-2(5)) Lee & Low Bks., Inc.

—Feast for 10, 1 vol. Falwell, Cathryn. (Read along Book & CD Ser.). (ENG.). (J). (gr. -1-3). 2008. 32p. 10.99 (978-0-547-06431-4(4)); 2003. 28p. bds. 4.95 (978-0-618-38226-2(7)) Houghton Mifflin Harcourt Publishing Co.

—Gobble, Gobble. Falwell, Cathryn. 2011. 32p. (J). 16.95 (978-1-58469-148-8(4)); pap. 8.95 (978-1-58469-149-5(2)) Dawn Pubns.

—Mystery Vine. Falwell, Cathryn. 2009. 32p. (J). lib. bdg. 17.89 (978-0-06-177197-2(X), Greenwillow Bks.) HarperCollins Pubs.

—Pond Babies, 1 vol. Falwell, Cathryn. ed. 2011. (ENG.). 32p. (gr. -1-k). 15.95 (978-0-89272-920-3(1)) Down East Bks.

—Rainbow Stew, 1 vol. Falwell, Cathryn. 2013. (ENG.). 32p. (J). 17.95 (978-1-60060-847-6(7)) Lee & Low Bks., Inc.

—Scoot! Falwell, Cathryn. 2008. (ENG.). 32p. (J). (gr. -1-k). 16.99 (978-0-06-128882-1(9), Greenwillow Bks.) HarperCollins Pubs.

—Shape Capers: Shake a Shape. Falwell, Cathryn. 2007. 32p. (J). (gr. -1-k). lib. bdg. 17.89 (978-0-06-123700-3(0), Greenwillow Bks.) HarperCollins Pubs.

—Turtle Splash! Countdown at the Pond. Falwell, Cathryn. 2008. (ENG.). 32p. (J). (gr. -1-3). pap. 6.99 (978-0-06-142927-9(9), Greenwillow Bks.) HarperCollins Pubs.

—Turtle Splash! Countdown at the Pond. Falwell, Cathryn. 2008. (J). (gr. -1-3). 16.40 (978-1-4178-1399-5(7), Turtleback) Turtleback Bks.

Fan, Terry. Rooftoppers. Rundell, Katherine. 2013. (ENG.). 288p. (J). (gr. 3-7). 16.99 (978-1-4424-9058-1(6), Simon & Schuster Bks. For Young Readers) Simon & Schuster Bks. For Young Readers.

Fancher, Lou & Johnson, Steve. All God's Creatures. Hill, Karen. 2005. (ENG.). 14p. (J). (gr. -1 — 1). 9.99 (978-0-689-87819-0(2), Little Simon) Little Simon.

—Bambi: A Life in the Woods. Salten, Felix. Chambers, Whittaker, tr. 2014. (Scribner Classics Ser.). (ENG.). 192p. (J). (gr. 5). 29.99 *(978-1-4424-9345-2(3)*, Atheneum Bks. for Young Readers) Simon & Schuster Children's Publishing.

—Dolley Madison: Parties Can Be Patriotic! Krull, Kathleen. 2015. (Women Who Broke the Rules Ser.). (ENG.). 48p. (J). (gr. 1-4). 16.99 *(978-0-8027-3793-9(5)*, Bloomsbury USA Childrens) Bloomsbury USA.

—For the Love of Music: The Remarkable Story of Maria Anna Mozart. Rusch, Elizabeth. 2011. (ENG.). 32p. (J). (gr. k-3). 16.99 *(978-1-58246-326-1(3)*, Tricycle Pr.) Ten Speed Pr.

—Silver Seeds. Paolilli, Paul & Brewer, Dan. 2003. (ENG.). 32p. (J). (gr. k-4). pap. 6.99 *(978-0-14-250010-1(0)*, Puffin) Penguin Publishing Group.

—Sofia's Stoop Story: 18th Street, Brooklyn: 18th Street, Brooklyn. Bohrer, Maria. 2014. 32p. (J). 17.95 *(978-0-9885295-2-6(1))* Blue Marlin Pubns.

Fancher, Lou, jt. illus. see Johnson, Steve.

Fanelli, Sara. Pinocchio: Candlewick Illustrated Classic. Collodi, Carlo. Rose, Emma, tr. from ITA. 2010. (Candlewick Illustrated Classic Ser.). (ENG.). 192p. (J). (gr. 2-5). pap. 12.99 *(978-0-7636-4731-5(4))* Candlewick Pr.

Fang, Jade. The Twelve Days of Christmas. Accord Publishing Staff. 2011. (ENG.). 26p. (J). 17.99 *(978-1-4494-0361-4(1))* Andrews McMeel Publishing.

Fangorn. Lord Brocktree. Jacques, Brian. 2005. (Redwall Ser.). (ENG.). 384p. (J). (gr. 5-7). pap. 8.99 *(978-0-14-250110-8(7)*, Puffin) Penguin Publishing Group.

Fanlo, Africa. What's Going On? O'Callaghan, Elena. 2008. (ENG.). 32p. (J). (gr. -1-3). 10.99 *(978-1-933605-65-4(0))* Kane Miller.

Fann, Linsey. Puppy Love. Fann, Linsey. Abdulai, David, ed. Date not set. 32p. (J). (gr. 4-6). pap. 19.95 *(978-0-9647012-6-7(X)*, Dawn of a New Day Pubns., The) Konkori International.

Fannon, Chris. Eddie, the Elf Who Would Be Elvis. Guiffre, William A. 2011. (ENG.). 40p. (J). 17.95 *(978-0-9830172-0-2(4))*; pap. 9.95 *(978-0-9830172-1-9(2))* Bks. for Children Publishing.

Fanny. A Daycare for Connor. Cochard, Nadège. 2009. (My First Stories Ser.). 24p. (J). (gr. -1-3). 22.60 *(978-1-60754-353-4(2))*; pap. 8.15 *(978-1-60754-354-1(0))* Windmill Bks.

—Grandma & Grandpa Visit Connor. Cochard, Nadège. 2009. (My First Stories Ser.). 24p. (J). (gr. -1-3). 22.60 *(978-1-60754-357-2(5))* Windmill Bks.

—Grandma & Grandpa Visit Connor. Cochard, Nadège. 2009. (My First Stories Ser.). 24p. (J). (gr. -1-3). pap. 8.15 *(978-1-60754-356-5(7))* Windmill Bks.

Fanny, Nanny. The New Girl in Town: A Children's Book. Fanny, Nanny. 2013. 32p. pap. 12.99 *(978-1-62516-179-6(4)*, Strategic Bk. Publishing) Strategic Book Publishing & Rights Agency (SBPRA).

Fardell, John. The Day Louis Got Eaten. Fardell, John. 2012. (Andersen Press Picture Bks). (ENG.). 32p. (J). (gr. -1-3). 16.95 *(978-1-4677-0315-4(X))* Lerner Publishing Group.

—Jeremiah Jellyfish Flies High! Fardell, John. 2011. (ENG.). 32p. (J). (gr. -1-k). pap. 13.99 *(978-1-84939-147-4(5))* Andersen Pr. GBR. Dist: Independent Pubs. Group.

—Manfred the Baddie. Fardell, John. 2009. (ENG.). 32p. (J). (gr. -1). pap. 11.95 *(978-1-84916-044-5(9))* Quercus GBR. Dist: Independent Pubs. Group.

Fargo, Lisa J. Touched by an Angel's Tear. Santora, L. Steven. Connors, Clare & Szitas, Kathie, eds. 2008. 32p. (J). lib. bdg. 15.95 *(978-0-9818622-0-0(9))* Guilin City Publishing.

Fargo, Todd. A Charm for Jo. Brady, Bill & Brady, Laurie. l.t. ed. 2005. (Turtle Bks.). (ENG.). 32p. (J). (gr. 2-5). pap. 9.95 *(978-0-944727-47-8(6))* Jason & Nordic Pubs.

—It's Time. Mammay, Judith. l.t. ed. 2007. 32p. (J). pap. 9.95 *(978-0-944727-20-1(4))*; lib. bdg. 15.95 *(978-0-944727-21-8(2))* Jason & Nordic Pubs. (Turtle Bks.).

—Me, Hailey. Plucker, Sheri. 2005. (Turtle Books). 32p. (J). (gr. k-3). pap. 9.95 *(978-0-944727-49-2(2))*; lib. bdg. 15.95 *(978-0-944727-50-8(6)*, Turtle Bks.) Jason & Nordic Pubs.

—Peter & Friends at Camp. Scott, Rosanna. l.t. ed. 2006. (Turtle Books). 32p. (J). (gr. k-4). pap. 9.95 *(978-0-944727-51-5(4))*; lib. bdg. 15.95 *(978-0-944727-52-2(2))* Jason & Nordic Pubs. (Turtle Bks.).

—Ryan's Victory. Mammay, Judith. 2009. 32p. (J). pap. 9.95 *(978-0-944727-53-9(0))*; lib. bdg. 15.95 *(978-0-944727-54-6(9))* Jason & Nordic Pubs. (Turtle Bks.).

—Two Tracks in the Snow. Bryant, Louella. l.t. ed. 2004. (Turtle Bks.). 32p. (J). lib. bdg. 15.95 *(978-0-944727-46-1(8))*; per. 9.95 *(978-0-944727-45-4(X))* Jason & Nordic Pubs. (Turtle Bks.).

Faria, Rosana. El Libro Negro de los Colores. Cottin, Menena. Amado, Elisa, tr. 2008. (SPA.). (J). (gr. k-5). 20.99 *(978-970-825-019-1(8))* Tecolote, Ediciones, S.A. de C.V. MEX. Dist: Lectorum Pubns., Inc.

—Splash! Pantin, Yolanda. 2003. (SPA.). 16p. (J). (gr. -1-1). *(978-980-6437-19-7(5))* Playco Editores, C.A.

—Tiririca, Jararaca y Pereреca. MacHado, Ana Maria. 2003. 28p. pap. *(978-980-257-283-0(7))* Ekare, Ediciones.

Faria, Rosana & Faria, Rosana. The Black Book of Colors. Cottin, Menena. Amado, Elisa, tr. from SPA. 2008. (ENG.). 24p. (J). (gr. k-5). 17.95 *(978-0-88899-873-6(2))* Groundwood Bks. CAN. Dist: Perseus-PGW.

Faria, Rosana, jt. illus. see Faria, Rosana.

Farias, Carolina. The Truth about Fairies, 1 vol. Johnson, J. Angelique. 2010. (Fairy-Tale Superstars Ser.). (ENG.). 32p. (gr. 1-3). lib. bdg. 26.65 *(978-1-4048-5746-9(X)*, Nonfiction Picture Bks.) Picture Window Bks.

Farias, Carolina. When Christmas Feels Like Home. Griffith, Gretchen. 2013. (ENG.). 32p. (J). (gr. -1-2). 16.99 *(978-0-8075-8872-7(5))* Whitman, Albert & Co.

Farias, Susan Norberg. Think for Yourself: A Kid's Guide to Solving Life's Dilemmas & Other Sticky Problems. MacGregor, Cynthia. 2004. (ENG.). 96p. (J). (gr. 4-7). pap. 7.95 *(978-1-894222-73-0(3))* Lobster Pr. CAN. Dist: Univ. of Toronto Pr.

Faricy, Patrick. Cabin in the Snow. Hopkinson, Deborah. ed. 2005. 74p. (J). lib. bdg. 15.00 *(978-1-59054-896-7(5))* Fitzgerald Bks.

—The Clue at the Bottom of the Lake. Gregory, Kristiana. 2008. (Cabin Creek Mysteries Ser.: 2). (ENG.). 176p. (J). (gr. 2-5). 5.99 *(978-0-439-92951-6(2)*, Scholastic Paperbacks) Scholastic, Inc.

—Our Kansas Home. Hopkinson, Deborah. ed. 2005. 64p. (J). lib. bdg. 15.00 *(978-1-59054-910-0(4))* Fitzgerald Bks.

—Our Kansas Home. Hopkinson, Deborah. 2003. (Prairie Skies Ser.). 69p. (J). 11.65 *(978-0-7569-3448-4(6))* Perfection Learning Corp.

—Pioneer Summer. Hopkinson, Deborah. ed. 2005. 74p. (J). lib. bdg. 15.00 *(978-1-59054-911-7(2))* Fitzgerald Bks.

—Robert Smalls: The Boat Thief. Kennedy, Robert F., Jr. 2008. (Robert F. Kennedy, Jr.'s American Heroes Ser.). (ENG.). 48p. (gr. 5-8). 16.99 *(978-1-4231-0802-3(7))* Hyperion Pr.

—Teddy Kennedy: Lion of the Senate. Stanley, George E. 2010. (Childhood of Famous Americans Ser.). (ENG.). 224p. (J). (gr. 3-7). pap. 5.99 *(978-1-4169-9041-3(0)*, Simon & Schuster/Paula Wiseman Bks.) Simon & Schuster/Paula Wiseman Bks.

Faricy, Patrick, jt. illus. see Patrick, Jean L. S.

Farina, Kathy. Three Colors of Katie. Washington, Kathy. 2010. (J). (gr. k-2). pap. 9.95 *(978-1-932514-18-6(X))* College of DuPage Pr.

Faris, Eva. The Three Little Kittens. Stephenson, Nancy. l.t. ed. 2003. 30p. (J). per. 7.99 *(978-1-932338-13-3(6))* Lifevest Publishing, Inc.

Farish, Terry. The Alleyway. 2015. (J). ***(978-1-4677-5796-6(9)***, Carolrhoda Bks.) Lerner Publishing Group.

Fariss, Michelle. The Sad Sant. Becker, Curt. 2009. 36p. pap. 14.95 *(978-1-60844-161-7(X))* Dog Ear Publishing, LLC.

Farley, Andrew & Swan, Angela. A Circus Wish #6, 6 vols. Bentley, Sue. 2009. (Magic Kitten Ser.: 6). (ENG.). 128p. (J). (gr. 1-3). pap. 4.99 *(978-0-448-45062-9(3)*, Grosset & Dunlap) Penguin Publishing Group.

—Double Trouble, 4 vols. Bentley, Sue. 2009. (Magic Kitten Ser.: 4). (ENG.). 128p. (J). (gr. 1-3). pap. 4.99 *(978-0-448-45060-5(7)*, Grosset & Dunlap) Penguin Publishing Group.

—A Forest Charm, 6 vols. Bentley, Sue. 2010. (Magic Puppy Ser.: 6). (ENG.). 128p. (J). (gr. 1-3). pap. 4.99 *(978-0-448-45065-0(8)*, Grosset & Dunlap) Penguin Publishing Group.

—Party Dreams, 5 vols. Bentley, Sue. 2010. (Magic Puppy Ser.: 5). (ENG.). 128p. (J). (gr. 1-3). pap. 4.99 *(978-0-448-45064-3(X)*, Grosset & Dunlap) Penguin Publishing Group.

—School of Mischief, 8 vols., No. 8. Bentley, Sue. 2010. (Magic Puppy Ser.: 8). (ENG.). 128p. (J). (gr. 1-3). pap. 4.99 *(978-0-448-45067-4(4)*, Grosset & Dunlap) Penguin Publishing Group.

—Sparkling Steps #7, 7 vols. Bentley, Sue. 2009. (Magic Kitten Ser.: 7). (ENG.). 128p. (J). (gr. 1-3). pap. 4.99 *(978-0-448-45063-6(1)*, Grosset & Dunlap) Penguin Publishing Group.

—Twirling Tails, 7 vols. Bentley, Sue. 2010. (Magic Puppy Ser.: 7). (ENG.). 128p. (J). (gr. 1-3). pap. 4.99 *(978-0-448-45066-7(6)*, Grosset & Dunlap) Penguin Publishing Group.

Farley, Andrew, jt. illus. see Hull, Biz.

Farley, Andrew, jt. illus. see Swan, Angela.

Farley, Brianne. Ike's Incredible Ink. Farley, Brianne. 2013. (ENG.). 32p. (J). (gr. -1-3). 16.99 *(978-0-7636-6296-7(8))* Candlewick Pr.

Farley, Jason, jt. illus. see Seiler, Jason.

Farley, Katherine. Hope Music. Powell, Amy. 2006. 32p. (J). (gr. -1-3). per. 12.00 *(978-0-9773608-4-0(9))* Shiny Red Ball Publishing.

Farley, Rick, et al. Batman Phonics Fun! Rosen, Lucy. 2011. (My First I Can Read Ser.). (ENG.). 36p. (J). (gr. -1-3). pap. 12.99 *(978-0-06-188542-6(8))* HarperCollins Pubs.

Farley, Rick. I Am Superman. Teitelbaum, Michael. 2009. (I Can Read Book 2 Ser.). (ENG.). 32p. (J). (gr. -1-3). pap. 3.99 *(978-0-06-187857-2(X))* HarperCollins Pubs.

—I Am Wonder Woman. Stein, Erin K. 2010. (I Can Read Book 2 Ser.). (ENG.). 32p. (J). (gr. -1-3). pap. 3.99 *(978-0-06-188517-4(7))* HarperCollins Pubs.

—Paint Book. Jacobs, Lana. 2006. (Charlotte's Web Ser.). 32p. (J). 4.99 *(978-0-06-088277-8(8))* HarperCollins Pubs.

Farley, Rick & Smith, Andy. Fright Club. Sazaklis, John & Roberts, Jeremy. 2012. (ENG.). 24p. (J). (gr. -1-2). pap. 3.99 *(978-0-06-188534-1(7)*, HarperFestival) HarperCollins Pubs.

Farley, Rick & Tripp, Kanila. Batman: With Superman & Wonder Woman. Vivinetto, Gina. 2011. (ENG.). 24p. (J). (gr. -1-3). pap. 3.99 *(978-0-06-188531-0(2)*, HarperFestival) HarperCollins Pubs.

Farlow, Melissa, photos by. Wild at Heart: Mustangs & the Young People Fighting to Save Them. Farley, Terri. 2015. (ENG., 208p. (J). (gr. 5-7). 19.99 ***(978-0-544-39294-6(9)***, HMH Books For Young Readers) Houghton Mifflin Harcourt Publishing Co.

Farmer, Jonathan, photos by. Every You, Every Me. Levithan, David. ed. 2012. lib. bdg. 20.85 *(978-0-606-26816-5(2)*, Turtleback) Turtleback Bks.

Farmer, Jonathan, jt. photos by see Levithan, David.

Farmer, Libby. Polly Possum's Wandering Path. Miner, Ann. 2013. 20p. (J). pap. 12.95 *(978-1-4575-1849-2(X))* Dog Ear Publishing, LLC.

Farmer, Selina. Furbily-Furld: Takes on the World. Gotthardt, Katherine. Williams, Shane, ed. 2010. (ENG.). 50p. pap. 14.99 *(978-1-4563-5814-3(6))* CreateSpace Independent Publishing Platform.

Farmer, Suzanne. Graeme Goes Home. Pitkethly, Maggie. 2008. 32p. pap. 12.00 *(978-0-9791402-8-0(5))* Stewart, R. J. Bks.

Farmer, Zoe. The Jewel in the Attic & the Adventures of Tiger. Kimmons, Janet M. 2007. 108p. (J). (gr. 1-3). pap. *(978-1-58690-028-1(5))* Mould, Paul Publishing.

—The Magnificent Six. Bellis, Jill. 2007. 52p. pap. *(978-1-904959-47-2(4))* Mould, Paul Publishing.

—The Return of the Magnificent Six: A Christmas Adventure. Bellis, Jill. 2008. (The Magnificent Six: Vol. 2). 62p. pap. 14.00 *(978-1-58690-073-1(0))* Players Pr., Inc.

Farmer, Zoe. Practice Makes Perfect. Farmer, Zoe. 2007. 74p. (gr. -1-k). pap. *(978-1-58690-029-8(3))* Mould, Paul Publishing.

Farnsworth, Bill. The Anne Frank Case: Simon Wiesenthal's Search for the Truth. Rubin, Susan Goldman. (ENG.). 40p. (J). 2010. (gr. 1-5). pap. 8.95 *(978-0-8234-2308-8(5))*; 2009. (gr. 5-18). 18.95 *(978-0-8234-2109-1(0))* Holiday Hse., Inc.

—Bad River Boys. Sneve, Virginia Driving Hawk. 2005. (ENG.). 32p. (YA). 16.95 *(978-0-8234-1856-5(1))* Holiday Hse., Inc.

—Big-Enough Anna. Flowers, Pam. 2003. (ENG.). 32p. (J). (gr. -1-18). 15.95 *(978-0-88240-577-3(2))* Graphic Arts Ctr. Publishing Co.

—Black Beauty & the Thunderstorm. Hill, Susan & Sewell, Anna. 2011. (My Readers Ser.). (ENG.). 48p. (J). (gr. 1-3). pap. 3.99 *(978-0-312-64721-6(2))* Square Fish.

—Buffalo Song. Bruchac, Joseph. 2008. (J). Lee & Low Bks., Inc.

—By the Sword. Castroville, Selene. 2007. (ENG.). 40p. (J). (gr. 5-7). 17.95 *(978-1-59078-427-3(8))* Boyds Mills Pr.

—Eli Remembers. Vander Zee, Ruth & Sneider, Marian. 2007. 32p. (J). (gr. -1-3). 18.00 *(978-0-8028-5309-7(9)*, Eerdmans Bks For Young Readers) Eerdmans, William B. Publishing Co.

—The Flag with Fifty-Six Stars: A Gift from the Survivors of Mauthausen. Rubin, Susan Goldman. (ENG.). 40p. (J). (gr. 1-5). 2005. 17.95 *(978-0-8234-1653-0(4))*; 2006. reprint ed. 6.95 *(978-0-8234-2019-3(1))* Holiday Hse., Inc.

—El Gran Ferrocarril. Bailer, Darice. 2007. (Excursiones Fantásticas / Fantasy Field Trips Ser.). 48p. (gr. 3-5). pap. 8.95 *(978-1-59820-598-5(6)*, Alfaguara) Santillana USA Publishing Co., Inc.

—Grandpa's Music: A Story about Alzheimer's. Acheson, Alison. 2009. (ENG.). 32p. (J). (gr. 3-5). 16.99 *(978-0-8075-3052-8(2))* Whitman, Albert & Co.

—The Great Stone Face. 2005. 32p. (J). pap. 8.00 *(978-0-8028-5292-2(0))* Eerdmans, William B. Publishing Co.

—Henrietta King: La Patrona. Wade, Mary Dodson. 2012. (ENG.). 64p. 16.95 *(978-1-933979-63-2(1)*, 7e8171df-3905-4241-a084-108e6384ddaf) Bright Sky Pr.

—Henrietta King: Loving the Land. Wade, Mary Dodson. 2011. (ENG.). 24p. 16.95 *(978-1-933979-64-9(X)*, dcf39346-020e-471d-9505-349b26473e11) Bright Sky Pr.

—Heroes for Civil Rights. Adler, David A. 2007. (ENG.). 32p. (J). (gr. -1-3). 16.95 *(978-0-8234-2008-7(6))* Holiday Hse., Inc.

Farnsworth, Bill. The Hunter's Promise: An Abenaki Tale. Bruchac, Joseph. 2015. (ENG.). 32p. (J). (gr. k-3). 16.95 ***(978-1-937786-43-4(9)***, Wisdom Tales) World Wisdom, Inc.

Farnsworth, Bill. Irena Sendler & the Children of the Warsaw Ghetto. Rubin, Susan Goldman. (ENG.). 40p. (J). 2012. (gr. 4-7). pap. 8.99 *(978-0-8234-2595-2(9))*; 2011. (gr. 1-5). 18.95 *(978-0-8234-2251-7(8))* Holiday Hse., Inc.

—John Muir & the Stickeen: An Icy Adventure with a No Good Dog. Dunlap, Julie & Lorbiecki, Marybeth. 2004. (ENG.). 32p. (J). (gr. k-3). 16.95 *(978-1-55971-903-2(6))* Cooper Square Publishing Llc.

—The Long Trail. Hopkinson, Deborah. ed. 2005. 2004p. (J). lib. bdg. 15.00 *(978-1-59054-904-9(X))* Fitzgerald Bks.

—Louis Sockalexis: Native American Baseball Pioneer, 1 vol. Wise, Bill. 2007. (ENG.). 32p. (J). (gr. 1-7). 16.95 *(978-1-58430-269-8(0))* Lee & Low Bks., Inc.

—Miles of Smiles: The Story of Roxey, the Long Island Rail Road Dog. Worthington, Heather Hill. 2010. (J). *(978-0-9792918-4-5(4))*; pap. *(978-0-9792918-8-3(7))* Blue Marlin Pubns.

—Mingo, 1 vol. Strohmeier, Lenice & Strohmeier. 2003. (ENG.). 32p. (J). 16.95 *(978-0-7614-5111-2(0))* Marshall Cavendish Corp.

—Minnow & Rose: An Oregon Trail Story. Young, Judy. 2009. (Tales of Young Americans Ser.). (ENG.). 32p. (J). (gr. 1-5). 17.95 *(978-1-58536-421-3(5))* Sleeping Bear Pr.

—One Fine Day: A Radio Play. Van Steenwyk, Elizabeth. 2004. 32p. (J). (gr. 3-5). 16.00 *(978-0-8028-5234-2(3))* Eerdmans, William B. Publishing Co.

—Our Flag Was Still There: The Story of the Star-Spangled Banner. Craven, Tracy Leininger. 2004. (J). *(978-0-9724287-3-6(9))* Vision Forum, Inc., The.

—Prairie School. Avi. 2003. (I Can Read Book 4 Ser.). (ENG.). 48p. (J). (gr. 3-4). pap. 3.99 *(978-0-06-051318-4(7))* HarperCollins Pubs.

—Prairie School. Avi. 2003. (I Can Read Bks.). 47p. (gr. 3-7). 14.00 *(978-0-7569-1452-3(3))* Perfection Learning Corp.

—Railroad!, Level 3: A Story of the Transcontinental Railroad. Bailer, Darice. 3rd ed. 2004. (Soundprints' Read-and-Discover Ser.). (ENG.). 48p. (J). (gr. 1-4). pap. 3.95 *(978-1-59249-017-2(4)*, S2007) Soundprints.

—Sailing for Gold. Hopkinson, Deborah. ed. 2005. 76p. (J). lib. bdg. 15.00 *(978-1-59054-915-5(5))* Fitzgerald Bks.

—Tenth Avenue Cowboy. High, Linda Oatman. 2008. 32p. (J). (gr. 4-7). 17.00 *(978-0-8028-5330-1(7)*, Eerdmans Bks For Young Readers) Eerdmans, William B. Publishing Co.

—Valley Forge. Ammon, Richard. (ENG.). 32p. (J). 2006. (gr. 1-5). 6.95 *(978-0-8234-2016-2(7))*; 2004. (gr. 4-6). tchr. ed. 17.95 *(978-0-8234-1746-9(8))* Holiday Hse., Inc.

—The Wheat Doll, 1 vol. Randall, Alison L. 2008. (ENG.). 32p. (J). (gr. k-3). 16.95 *(978-1-56145-456-3(7))* Peachtree Pubs.

—When Abraham Talked to the Trees. Van Steenwyk, Elizabeth. 2004. 32p. (J). (gr. 2-5). 16.00 *(978-0-8028-5191-8(6))*; pap. 8.00 *(978-0-8028-5233-5(5))* Eerdmans, William B. Publishing Co.

Farnsworth, Bill. Big-Enough Anna. Farnsworth, Bill, tr. Flowers, Pam. 2003. (ENG.). 32p. (J). pap. 10.99 *(978-0-88240-580-3(2))* Graphic Arts Ctr. Publishing Co.

Farnsworth, Bill & W, Farnsworth. The Adventures of Vin Fiz. Cussler, Clive. 2007. (ENG.). 176p. (J). (gr. 3-7). 6.99 *(978-0-14-240774-5(7)*, Puffin) Penguin Publishing Group.

Farquharson, Alexander. The White House Is Burning: August 24 1814. Sutcliffe, Jane. 2014. (ENG.). 128p. (J). (gr. 4-7). 19.95 *(978-1-58089-656-6(1))* Charlesbridge Publishing, Inc.

Farr, Rich. And Then It Rained on Malcolm. Feurer, Paige. 2015. (ENG.). 40p. (J). (gr. -1-k). 16.99 ***(978-1-63450-150-7(0)***, Sky Pony Pr.) Skyhorse Publishing Co., Inc.

Farrar, Greg, photos by. Shelter Dogs: Amazing Stories of Adopted Strays. Kehret, Peg. ed. 2004. (ENG., 144p. (J). (gr. 3-8). pap. 7.99 *(978-0-8075-7336-5(1))* Whitman, Albert & Co.

Farrell, Dan. 1-2-3 Magic for Teachers: Effective Classroom Discipline Pre-K Through Grade 8. Phelan, Thomas W. & Schonour, Sarah Jane. 2004. (ENG.). 224p. (gr. -1-8). pap. 14.95 *(978-1-889140-17-9(1))* ParentMagic, Inc.

Farrell, Russell. Horses & Ponies: Step-by-Step Insructions for 25 Different Breads. 2011. (Learn to Draw Ser.). 32p. (J). (gr. 1-4). *(978-1-936309-16-0(5))* Quarto Publishing Group USA.

—Sea Creatures: Step-by-Step Insructions for 25 Ocean Animals. Walter Foster Creative Team. 2011. (Learn to Draw Ser.). 32p. (J). (gr. 1-4). 28.50 *(978-1-936309-19-1(X))* Quarto Publishing Group USA.

Farrell, Russell & Fisher, Diana. All about Drawing Sea Creatures & Animals. 2010. (All about Drawing Ser.). 80p. (J). 34.25 *(978-1-936309-08-5(4))* Quarto Publishing Group USA.

Farrelly, Linda & Hopkins, Simon. Elliot's Amazing Adventures Number 1. Farrelly, Linda. 2013. 52p. pap. *(978-0-9560331-5-4(6))* Childrens' Story Pubs.

Farrington, Teresa. Dragon Talk. Huxman, K. D. l.t. ed. 2006. 24p. (J). pap. 14.99 *(978-0-9765786-7-3(0))* Dragonfly Publishing, Inc.

Farris, Cat. Breaking the Record, Vol. 2. Reger, Rob & Huehner, Mariah. 2015. (ENG.). 1p. (gr. 5). 12.99 *(978-1-61655-598-6(X))* Dark Horse Comics.

Farris, Kim. The Happy Angel: A Fractured Fairy Tale. Cantrell, Pete. 2010. (ENG.). 32p. (J). 9.95 *(978-1-61005-010-4(X))* BookLogix.

Farris, Michael. Mr Boo Bear. Farris, Judy. 2009. 24p. pap. 15.49 *(978-1-4389-4553-8(1))* AuthorHouse.

Fasbinder, George & Jones, Bill. The Boy Who Loves Weather. Fasbinder, Susie. 2011. (ENG.). 38p. pap. 12.95 *(978-1-4610-4076-7(0))* CreateSpace Independent Publishing Platform.

Faschi, Silvia. The Adventures of Simba the Frisky Feline. McLean, Linda. 2012. (J). 14.95 *(978-1-937406-24-0(5))* Mascot Bks., Inc.

Fast, Suellen M., photos by. America's Daughters. Fast, Suellen M. 100p. (Orig.). (J). (gr. k-18). pap. 19.00 *(978-0-935281-13-2(4))* Daughter Culture Pubns.

Fatus, Sophie. The Abominable Snowman: A Story from Nepal. Parnell, Fran. 2011. (ENG.). 30p. (J). 7.99 *(978-1-84686-558-9(1))* Barefoot Bks., Inc.

—Algarabía en la Granja. MacDonald, Margaret Read. 2009. (SPA.). (J). pap. 9.99 *(978-1-84686-282-3(5))* Barefoot Bks., Inc.

—The Barefoot Book of Monsters! Parnell, Fran. 2003. (ENG.). 64p. (J). 19.99 *(978-1-84148-178-4(5))* Barefoot Bks., Inc.

—Bear in Love. Ziefert, Harriet & Davis, Samantha A. 2010. (ENG.). 40p. (J). (gr. k-12). 12.99 *(978-1-60905-044-3(4))* Blue Apple Bks.

—Can You Whoo, Too? Ziefert, Harriet. 2015. (ENG.). 32p. (J). (gr. -1-3). 16.99 *(978-1-60905-524-0(1))* Blue Apple Bks.

—The Farmyard Jamboree. MacDonald, Margaret Read. 2009. (ENG.). (J). 16.99 *(978-1-84686-290-8(6))* Barefoot Bks., Inc.

—The Feathered Ogre: A Story from Italy. Parnell, Fran. 2011. (ENG.). 30p. (J). pap. 7.99 *(978-1-84686-562-6(X))* Barefoot Bks., Inc.

—A Hen, a Chick & a String Guitar. 2005. 32p. (J). 17.99 incl. audio compact disk *(978-1-84148-796-0(1))* Barefoot Bks., Inc.

—Here We Go Round the Mulberry Bush. Penner, Fred. (ENG.). (J). 2011. 36p. pap. 9.99 *(978-1-84686-656-2(1))*; 2008. 24p. 9.99 *(978-1-84686-079-9(2))*; 2008. 24p. 6.99 *(978-1-84686-189-5(6))* Barefoot Bks., Inc.

—If a Chicken Stayed for Supper. Weston, Carrie. 2007. (ENG.). 32p. (J). (gr. -1-3). 16.95 *(978-0-8234-2067-4(1))* Holiday Hse., Inc.

—If You're Happy & You Know It. McQuinn, Anna. 2011. (ENG.). 80p. (J). pap. 6.99 *(978-1-84686-434-6(8))* Barefoot Bks., Inc.

—The Journey Home from Grandpa's. Lumley, Jemima & Penner, Fred. 2011. (ENG.). 36p. (J). pap. 9.99 *(978-1-84686-658-6(8))* Barefoot Bks., Inc.

—The Journey Home from Grandpa's. Lumley, Jemima. (ENG.). 24p. (J). 2012. (gr. -1-2). 16.99 *(978-1-84686-898-6(X))*; 2006. pap. 6.99 *(978-1-84686-029-4(6))*; 2006. (gr. -1-k). 9.99 *(978-1-84686-026-3(1))*; 2006. (gr. -1-3). 16.99 *(978-1-905236-37-4(9))* Barefoot Bks., Inc.

—The Journey Home from Grandpa's. Lumley, Jemima. 2010. (ENG.). 16p. (J). (gr. -1-3). pap. 5.99 *(978-1-84686-277-9(9))* Barefoot Bks., Inc.

—The Mother of Monsters: A Story from South Africa. Parnell, Fran. 2011. (ENG.). 30p. (J). pap. 7.99 *(978-1-84686-560-2(3))* Barefoot Bks., Inc.

—My Daddy Is a Pretzel: Yoga for Parents & Kids. Baptiste, Baron. (ENG.). 48p. (J). 2012. pap. 8.99 *(978-1-84686-899-3(8))*; 2004. (gr. -1-2). 16.99 *(978-1-84148-151-7(3))* Barefoot Bks., Inc.

—One More Friend. Flor Ada, Alma. 2007. 24p. (J). *(978-0-15-206278-1(5))* Harcourt Trade Pubs.

F

—Una Princesa Real: Un Cuento Matemagico. Williams, Brenda & Barefoot Books Staff. 40p. 8.99 *(978-1-78285-078-6(3))* Barefoot Bks., Inc.

—The Real Princess. Williams, Brenda. 2008. (ENG.). 40p. (J). (gr. -1-3). 16.99 *(978-1-905236-88-6(3))* Barefoot Bks., Inc.

—Riddle Me This! Riddles & Stories to Challenge Your Mind. Lupton, Hugh. 2003. 64p. (J). 19.99 *(978-1-84148-169-2(6))* Barefoot Bks., Inc.

—Riddle Me This! Riddles & Stories to Sharpen Your Wits. Lupton, Hugh. 2007. (ENG.). 64p. (J). pap. 12.99 *(978-1-905236-92-3(1))* Barefoot Bks., Inc.

—The Story Tree. Lupton, Hugh. 2009. (ENG.). 64p. (J). 19.99 *(978-1-84686-301-1(5))* Barefoot Bks., Inc.

—The Story Tree: Tales to Read Aloud. Lupton, Hugh. 2005. (ENG.). 64p. (J). (gr. -1-2). pap. 15.99 *(978-1-905236-13-8(1))* Barefoot Bks., Inc.

—The Story Tree Artist Card Portfolio. (J). 12.99 *(978-1-84148-543-0(8))* Barefoot Bks., Inc.

Fatus, Sophie. Grim, Grunt & Grizzle-Tail: A Story from Chile. Fatus, Sophie. Parnell, Fran. 2013. (Monsters Ser.: 6). (ENG.). 48p. (J). (gr. 3-6). pap. 7.99 *(978-1-84686-910-5(2))* Barefoot Bks., Inc.

—Here We Go Round the Mulberry Bush. Fatus, Sophie. Penner, Fred. 2007. (ENG.). 24p. (J). (gr. -1-2). 16.99 *(978-1-84686-035-5(0))* Barefoot Bks., Inc.

—If You're Happy & You Know It! Fatus, Sophie. McQuinn, Anna. 2011. (ENG.). 62p. (J). pap. 9.99 *(978-1-84686-619-7(7))* Barefoot Bks., Inc.

—My Big Barefoot Book of Wonderful Words. Fatus, Sophie. Barefoot Books. 48p. 19.99 *(978-1-78285-092-2(9))* Barefoot Bks., Inc.

—The Real Princess. Fatus, Sophie. Williams, Brenda. 2009. (ENG.). 40p. (J). 9.99 *(978-1-84686-393-6(7))* Barefoot Bks., Inc.

—Rona Long-Teeth: A Story from Tahiti. Fatus, Sophie. Parnell, Fran. 2013. (Monsters Ser.: 5). (ENG.). 48p. (J). (gr. 3-6). pap. 7.99 *(978-1-84686-908-2(0))* Barefoot Bks., Inc.

—Yoga Pretzels: 50 Fun Yoga Activities for Kids & Grownups. Fatus, Sophie. Kalish, Leah & Guber, Tara. 2005. (ENG.). (J). pap. 14.99 *(978-1-905236-04-6(2))* Barefoot Bks., Inc.

Fatus, Sophie, jt. illus. see Bell, Siobhan.

Faucher, Wayne. Rogue War. Johns, Geoff. rev. ed. 2006. (Flash (DC Comics) Ser.). (ENG.). 208p. (YA). pap. 17.99 *(978-1-4012-0924-7(6))* DC Comics.

Faulkner, Keith, et al. Time's Up! Faulkner, Keith & Tyger, Rory. 2003. (J). *(978-0-439-56155-6(8))* Scholastic, Inc.

Faulkner, Keith & Holmes, Stephen. Animal ? Math. Faulkner, Keith & Holmes, Stephen. 2003. (J). *(978-0-439-62755-9(9))* Scholastic, Inc.

Faulkner, Matt. Because I Could Not Stop My Bike: And Other Poems. Shapiro, Karen Jo. 2005. (ENG.). 32p. (J). (gr. 2-5). pap. 7.95 *(978-1-58089-105-9(5))* Charlesbridge Publishing, Inc.

—Don't Know Much about American History. Davis, Kenneth C. 2003. (Don't Know Much About Ser.). (ENG.). 224p. (J). (gr. 3-7). pap. 6.99 *(978-0-06-440836-3(1))* HarperCollins Pubs.

—Independent Dames: What You Never Knew about the Women & Girls of the American Revolution. Anderson, Laurie Halse. 2008. (ENG.). 40p. (J). (gr. 1-5). 17.99 *(978-0-689-85808-6(6))*, Simon & Schuster Bks. For Young Readers) Simon & Schuster Bks. For Young Readers.

—The Monster Who Ate My Peas, 1 vol. Schnitzlein, Danny. 2010. (ENG.). 32p. (J). pap. 7.95 *(978-1-56145-533-1(4))* Peachtree Pubs.

—The Night Henry Ford Met Santa. Hagen, Carol L. 2006. (ENG.). 32p. (J). (gr. k-6). 17.95 *(978-1-58536-132-8(1))* Sleeping Bear Pr.

—Stand Tall, Abe Lincoln. St. George, Judith. 2008. (Turning Point Bks.). (ENG.). 48p. (J). (gr. 2-5). 16.99 *(978-0-399-24174-1(4))*, Philomel) Penguin Publishing Group.

—Thank You, Sarah: The Woman Who Saved Thanksgiving. Anderson, Laurie Halse. 2005. (ENG.). 40p. (J). (gr. k-3). 7.99 *(978-0-689-85143-8(X))*, Simon & Schuster Bks. For Young Readers) Simon & Schuster Bks. For Young Readers.

—Trick or Treat on Monster Street, 1 vol. Schnitzlein, Danny. 2008. (ENG.). 32p. (J). (gr. k-3). 16.95 *(978-1-56145-465-5(6))* Peachtree Pubs.

Faulkner, Matt. A Taste of Colored Water. Faulkner, Matt. 2008. (ENG.). 48p. (J). (gr. 1-3). 17.99 *(978-1-4169-1629-1(6))*, Simon & Schuster Bks. For Young Readers) Simon & Schuster Bks. For Young Readers.

Faulkner, Matt & Bunting, Matt. S Is for Shamrock: An Ireland Alphabet. Bunting, Eve. rev. ed. 2007. (Discover the World Ser.). (ENG.). 40p. (J). (gr. -1-3). 17.95 *(978-1-58536-290-5(5))* Sleeping Bear Pr.

Faulkner, Matt, jt. illus. see Faulkner, Matthew.

Faulkner, Matthew & Faulkner, Matt. My First Book of Bedtime Prayers. Faulkner, Matt. 2008. (ENG.). 22p. (J). (gr. -1-k). bds. 6.99 *(978-0-8249-1806-4(1))*, Candy Cane Pr.) Ideals Pubns.

Faure, Florence. Geronimo, 1 vol. Spilsbury, Richard. 2013. (Hero Journals). (ENG.). 48p. (gr. 4-6). pap. 8.99 *(978-1-4109-5367-4(X))* Heinemann-Raintree.

Faust, Anke. Little Green Goose. Sansone, Adele. 2010. (ENG.). 32p. (J). (gr. -1-3). 16.95 *(978-0-7358-2292-4(1))* North-South Bks., Inc.

Faust Kalscheur, Jann, photos by. ABC's Naturally: A Child's Guide to the Alphabet Through Nature. Faust Kalscheur, Jann. Smith, Lynn. 2003. (J). 16.95 *(978-1-931599-27-6(0))*, Trails Bks.) Big Earth Publishing.

Faust, Laurie. A New Home for Honey. 2006. (Adventures of Honey Ser.). (J). pap. 9.95 *(978-0-9789227-0-2(0))* Weeping Willow Publishing.

—Pinky's Rainy Day: Pinky Padooka takes a trip to Imaginationville. Damschroder, Scott. 2004. 36p. (J). lib. bdg. 19.95 *(978-0-9754728-0-4(1))* Big Ransom Studio.

—Small Dog, Small Dog, Small, Small, Dog. Damschroder, Scott. 2004. 24p. (J). lib. bdg. 19.95 *(978-0-9754728-2-8(8))* Big Ransom Studio.

Faust, Laurie A. Cow Cake. Solomon, Michelle & Pereira, Lavinia. 2009. 24p. pap. 10.96 *(978-1-4251-8951-8(2))* Trafford Publishing.

—The Day the Trash Came Out to Play. Beadle, David M. 2004. 32p. (J). 16.95 *(978-0-9727855-0-1(7))* Ezra's Earth Publishing.

—Honey's Peanut Butter Adventure. Greer, Tom C. 2007. (Adventures of Honey Ser.). (J). per. 9.95 *(978-0-9789227-1-9(9))* Weeping Willow Publishing.

—The Magical Tree & Musical Wind. The Library Fairy. 2008. 32p. pap. 16.95 *(978-1-59858-604-6(1))* Dog Ear Publishing, LLC.

—Too Big! Solomon, Michelle & Pereira, Lavinia. 2009. 24p. pap. 10.96 *(978-1-4251-8949-5(0))* Trafford Publishing.

—Uh - Oh! Solomon, Michelle & Pereira, Lavinia. 2009. 24p. pap. 10.96 *(978-1-4251-8950-1(4))* Trafford Publishing.

—Why Is Mommy Sad? A Child's Guide to Parental Depression. Chan, Paul D. 2006. 12p. (J). pap. 6.99 *(978-1-929622-71-9(6))* Current Clinical Strategies Publishing.

Fautsch, Jackie. Catie Corn & the Corn Cops. Watson, Gayle. l.t. ed. 22p. (J). 2006. 15.99 *(978-1-59879-098-6(6))*; 2005. per. 9.99 *(978-1-59879-079-5(X))* Lifevest Publishing, Inc.

Favereau, Beatrice. Christmas with Norky the Adventure Begins... Algeier, Steve. 2007. (ENG.). 36p. (J). 17.99 *(978-0-9769209-0-8(5))* NORKY AMERICA.

Favreau, Marie-Claude. Un Dromadaire Chez Marilou Polaire. Plante, Raymond. 2003. (Premier Roman Ser.). (FRE.). 64p. (J). (gr. 1-4). pap. *(978-2-89021-608-2(X))* Diffusion du livre Mirabel (DLM).

—Le Grand Role de Marilou Polaire. Plante, Raymond. 2003. (Premier Roman Ser.). (FRE.). 64p. (J). (gr. 2-5). pap. *(978-2-89021-288-6(2))* Diffusion du livre Mirabel (DLM).

—Marilou Forecasts the Future, 1 vol. Plante, Raymond. Cummins, Sarah, tr. from FRE. 2003. (Formac First Novels Ser.: 49). (ENG.). 64p. (J). (gr. 1-5). 4.95 *(978-0-88780-614-8(7))*; (gr. 2-5). 14.95 *(978-0-88780-615-5(5))* Formac Publishing Co., Ltd. CAN. Dist: Casemate Pubs. & Bk. Distributors, LLC.

—Marilou Keeps a Camel. Plante, Raymond. 2004. 61p. (J). lib. bdg. 12.00 *(978-1-4242-1232-3(4))* Fitzgerald Bks.

—Marilou Keeps a Camel, 1 vol. Plante, Raymond. Cummins, Sarah, tr. from FRE. 2004. (Formac First Novels Ser.: 50). (ENG.). 64p. (J). (gr. 1-5). 4.95 *(978-0-88780-634-6(1))*; 14.95 *(978-0-88780-635-3(X))* Formac Publishing Co., Ltd. CAN. Dist: Casemate Pubs. & Bk. Distributors, LLC.

—Otis & Alice, 1 vol. Bertouille, Ariane. 2013. (ENG.). 32p. (J). 18.95 *(978-1-55455-294-8(X))* Fitzhenry & Whiteside, Ltd. CAN. Dist: Midpoint Trade Bks., Inc.

Fawcett, Vicki. My Arctic Circle of Friends. Belair, Brenda Brousseau, photos by. Doupe, Pauline Wood. 2009. 24p. pap. 16.98 *(978-1-4251-8097-3(3))* Trafford Publishing.

Fay, David. A. J. Puppy Learns to Swim. Rushing, John Alan. 2009. 48p. (J). pap. *(978-0-9776958-9-8(1))* CyPress Pubns.

Fayolle, Diane & Benoit, Jérôme. The Planet of the Firebird. Dorison, Guillaume et al. 2012. (Little Prince Ser.: 2). (ENG.). 56p. (J). (gr. 4-8). lib. bdg. 26.60 *(978-0-7613-8752-7(8))*, Graphic Universe) Lerner Publishing Group.

—The Planet of Wind. Dorison, Guillaume et al. 2012. (Little Prince Ser.: 1). (ENG.). 56p. (J). (gr. 4-8). lib. bdg. 26.60 *(978-0-7613-8751-0(X))*, Graphic Universe) Lerner Publishing Group.

Fazio, Michael. The Remarkable David Wordsworth. Kopley, Richard. 2013. 30p. (J). pap. *(978-1-936172-67-2(4))* Elfrig Publishing.

Fazio, Nicole. My Maine. Hersey, Suzanne Buzby. 2nd ed. 2011. (ENG.). 32p. (J). (gr. -1-1). 16.95 *(978-0-615-37246-4(5))* Little Beach Bks.

—My Massachusetts. Villa, Elisabeth. 2013. (ENG.). 32p. (J). (gr. -1-1). 16.95 *(978-0-9891340-0-2(8))* Little Beach Bks.

Fearing, Mark. The Book That Eats People. Perry, John. 2009. (ENG.). 38p. (J). (gr. -1-2). 15.99 *(978-1-58246-268-4(2))*, Tricycle Pr.) Ten Speed Pr.

Fearing, Mark. Chicken Storytime. Asher, Sandy. 2016. (J). **(978-0-8037-3944-4(3)**, Dial) Penguin Publishing Group.

Fearing, Mark. How Martha Saved Her Parents from Green Beans. LaRochelle, David. 2013. (ENG.). 32p. (J). (gr. k-3). 16.99 *(978-0-8037-3766-2(1))*, Dial) Penguin Publishing Group.

—The Three Little Aliens & the Big Bad Robot. McNamara, Margaret. 2011. (ENG.). 40p. (J). (gr. -1-3). 16.99 *(978-0-375-86689-0(2))*, Schwartz & Wade Bks.) Random Hse. Children's Bks.

—Tommy Can't Stop! Federle, Tim. 2015. (ENG.). 32p. (J). (gr. -1-k). 16.99 *(978-1-4231-6917-8(4))* Disney Pr.

—A Very Witchy Spelling Bee. Shannon, George. 2013. (ENG.). 32p. (J). (gr. -1-3). 16.99 *(978-0-15-206696-3(9))* Houghton Mifflin Harcourt Publishing Co.

Fearing, Mark. The Great Thanksgiving Escape. Fearing, Mark. 2014. (ENG.). 32p. (J). (gr. k-3). 15.99 *(978-0-7636-6306-3(9))* Candlewick Pr.

Fearn, Katrina. Christmas fairy things to make & Do. Gilpin, Rebecca. 2004. 34p. (J). pap. 6.95 *(978-0-7945-0835-7(9))*, Usborne) EDC Publishing.

—The Usborne Big Book of Christmas Things to Make & Do. Watt, Fiona & Gilpin, Rebecca. 2005. 99p. (J). *(978-0-439-81506-2(1))* Scholastic, Inc.

Fearn, Katrina. First Dot-To-Dot Dinosaurs. Fearn, Katrina, des. ed. 2013. (First Dot-To-Dot Ser.). 16p. (J). pap. 5.99 *(978-0-7945-3341-0(8))*, Usborne) EDC Publishing.

—First Dot-To-Dot Pirates. Fearn, Katrina, des. ed. 2013. (First Dot-To-Dot Ser.). 16p. (J). pap. 5.99 *(978-0-7945-3393-9(0))*, Usborne) EDC Publishing.

Fearn, Katrina & Hussain, Nelupa. Fairy Things to Stitch & Sew. Watt, Fiona. 2006. (Usborne Activities Ser.). 32p. (J). (gr. 1-4). pap. 6.99 *(978-0-7945-1235-4(6))*, Usborne) EDC Publishing.

Fearnley, Jan. Never Too Little to Love. Willis, Jeanne. 2013. (ENG.). 32p. (J). (gr. -1-2). 8.99 *(978-0-7636-6656-9(4))* Candlewick Pr.

Fearnley, Jan. Billy Tibble Moves Out! Fearnley, Jan. 2006. 29p. (J). (gr. k-4). reprint ed. 16.00 *(978-1-4223-5557-2(8))* DIANE Publishing Co.

—Mr Wolf & the Enormous Turnip. Fearnley, Jan. 2005. (ENG.). 40p. (J). (gr. k-2). pap. 10.99 *(978-1-4052-1580-0(1))* Egmont Bks., Ltd. GBR. Dist: Independent Pubs. Group.

Fearns, Georgie. Colour in Kate: Pretty Pictures of the Divine Duchess to Colour & Complete. Fearns, Georgie. Buster Books Staff. 2013. (ENG.). 32p. (J). (gr. 1-4). pap. 6.99 *(978-1-78055-158-6(4))* O'Mara, Michael Bks., Ltd. GBR. Dist: Independent Pubs. Group.

—Dress up One Direction. Fearns, Georgie. Buster Books Staff. 2013. (ENG.). 34p. (J). (gr. 1-3). pap. 7.99 *(978-1-78055-162-3(2))* O'Mara, Michael Bks., Ltd. GBR. Dist: Independent Pubs. Group.

Fearon, Merrill. Canadian Poems for Canadian Kids. Hamilton, Jen, ed. 2005. (ENG.). 64p. pap. 14.95 *(978-0-9736675-0-9(8))* Subway Bks. CAN. Dist: Univ. of Toronto Pr.

Feazell, Matt. The Amazing Cynicalman, Vol. 2. Feazell, Matt. l.t. ed. 2013. 160p. (YA). pap. 14.95 *(978-0-9744767-1-1(4)*, Not Available Books) Not Available Comics.

Fedatova, Marina. The 12 Elves: A New Christmas Tradition. 2010. (ENG.). 18p. (J). (gr. -1-k). bds. 12.99 *(978-1-4424-1684-0(X)*, Little Simon) Little Simon.

Fedhar. Como Dibujar Personajes Magicos. Fedhar. 2003. (SPA.). 160p. (J). (gr. 4-8). pap. *(978-987-550-281-9(2))* Longseller S.A. ARG. Dist: Bilingual Pubns. Co., The.

Fedigan-Linton, Katherine V. Electrum. Froimowitz, Michael P. 2003. 44p. 5.00 *(978-0-9717796-2-4(7)*, Mystic Night Bks.) Pink Stucco Pr.

Fedorov, Valentin. Moscow Ballet Great Russian Nutcracker. Herman, Mark & Apter, Ronnie, trs. from RUS. 2003. 32p. (J). *(978-0-9743082-0-3(X))* Sports Marketing International, Inc.

Fedotova, Marina. Who's My Cupcake? Guest, Elissa Haden. 2011. (ENG.). 16p. (J). (gr. -1 — 1). bds. 6.99 *(978-1-4424-2051-9(0))*, Little Simon) Little Simon.

Fee, Jim. Bad Feds. Long, Mark A. 2005. 119p. (YA). reprint ed. pap. 24.00 *(978-0-7567-9409-5(9))* DIANE Publishing Co.

Feek, Cathy. The Oglin: A Hero's Journey Across Africa... Towards the Tomorrows. Richardson, Dick. 2004. 417p. (J). 24.95 *(978-0-9759440-3-5(7))* Savanna Pr.

Feelings, Tom. Moja Means One: A Swahili Counting Book. Feelings, Muriel L. 2004. 20p. (J). (gr. k-4). reprint ed. pap. 5.00 *(978-0-7567-7108-9(0))* DIANE Publishing Co.

—To Be a Slave. Lester, Julius. 2005. (Puffin Modern Classics Ser.). (ENG.). 176p. (J). (gr. 3-7). 6.99 *(978-0-14-240386-0(5)*, Puffin) Penguin Publishing Group.

Feely, Eliza. Peka-Boo - The Smallest Bird in All the World. Feely, Eliza. 2010. (ENG.). 32p. (J). (gr. k-2). 19.99 *(978-1-74175-541-1(7))* Allen & Unwin AUS. Dist: Independent Pubs. Group.

Feeney, Betsy Franco. Amoeba Hop. Lavin, Christine. 2003. 36p. (J). (gr. 2-3). 19.95 incl. audio compact disk *(978-0-9726487-4-5(7))* Puddle Jump Pr., Ltd.

Feeney, Siri. Suffrage Sisters: The Fight for Liberty. Mead, Maggie. 2015. (Setting the Stage for Fluency Ser.). (ENG.). 40p. (gr. 3-5). lib. bdg. 27.93 **(978-1-939656-68-1(0))** Red Chair Pr.

Feeney, Siri Weber. The First American Flag, 1 vol. Allen, Kathy. 2009. (Our American Story Ser.). (ENG.). 32p. (gr. 1-3). lib. bdg. 26.65 *(978-1-4048-5541-0(6))*, Nonfiction Picture Bks.) Picture Window Bks.

—Writing the U. S. Constitution, 1 vol. Mortensen, Lori. 2009. (Our American Story Ser.). (ENG.). 32p. (gr. 1-3). lib. bdg. 26.65 *(978-1-4048-5540-3(8))*, Nonfiction Picture Bks.) Picture Window Bks.

Feeney, Tatyana. Snobby Cat. Deeley, Patrick. 2005. (Pandas Ser.: 32). (ENG.). 64p. (J). pap. 9.95 *(978-0-86278-946-6(X))* O'Brien Pr., Ltd., The IRL. Dist: Dufour Editions, Inc.

Feher, Joseph & Kane, Herb K. Hawai'i. 2010. (ENG.). 72p. pap. *(978-1-59700-839-6(7))* Island Heritage Publishing.

Fehlau, Dagmar, et al. Mother Goose & Her Animal Friends. Hopkins, Lee Bennett. 2005. (Lee Bennett Hopkins Mother Goose Ser.). (YA). (gr. -1-1). 76.50 *(978-0-8215-0470-3(3))* Sadlier, William H. Inc.

—Mother Goose & Her Children. Hopkins, Lee Bennett. 2005. (Lee Bennett Hopkins Mother Goose Ser.). (YA). (gr. -1-1). 76.50 *(978-0-8215-0460-4(6))* Sadlier, William H. Inc.

—Mother Goose Around the World. Hopkins, Lee Bennett. 2005. (Lee Bennett Hopkins Mother Goose Ser.). (YA). (gr. -1-1). 76.50 *(978-0-8215-0490-1(8))*; suppl. ed. 57.00 *(978-0-8215-0494-9(0))* Sadlier, William H. Inc.

—Mother Goose Through the Seasons. Hopkins, Lee Bennett. 2005. (Lee Bennett Hopkins Mother Goose Ser.). (YA). (gr. -1-1). 76.50 *(978-0-8215-0480-2(0))* Sadlier, William H. Inc.

Fehlau, Dagmar. My Robot. Bunting, Eve. 2006. (Green Light Readers Level 2 Ser.). (ENG.). 24p. (J). (gr. -1-3). pap. 3.95 *(978-0-15-205617-9(3))* Houghton Mifflin Harcourt Publishing Co.

—My Robot. Bunting, Eve. 2006. (Green Light Readers Level 2 Ser.). (gr. k-2). lib. bdg. 13.95 *(978-0-7569-7211-0(6))* Perfection Learning Corp.

—Snowbear's Winter Day: A Winter Wonder Book. DePrisco, Dorothea. 2005. 18p. (J). (gr. -1). 9.95 *(978-1-58117-133-4(1)*, Intervisual/Piggy Toes) Bendon, Inc.

Fehling, Leslie. What Would You Do? A Kid's Guide to Staying Safe in a World of Strangers. Ridenour, Melissa Harker. 2011. (J). *(978-0-938467-11-3(5))* Headline Bks., Inc.

Fei, Wang, jt. illus. see Louis, Catherine.

Feiffer, Jules. The Annotated Phantom Tollbooth. Juster, Norton. 2011. (ENG.). 320p. (J). (gr. 3-7). 29.99 *(978-0-375-85715-7(X))*; lib. bdg. 32.99 *(978-0-375-95715-4(4))* Random Hse. Children's Bks. (Knopf Bks. for Young Readers).

—The Birthday Ball. Lowry, Lois. (ENG.). 192p. (J). 2011. (gr. 5-7). pap. 6.99 *(978-0-547-57710-4(9))*; 2010. (gr. 2-5). 16.00 *(978-0-547-23869-2(X))* Houghton Mifflin Harcourt Publishing Co.

—Henry the Dog with No Tail. Feiffer, Kate. 2007. (ENG.). 32p. (J). (gr. -1-3). 17.99 *(978-1-4169-1614-7(8))*, Simon & Schuster/Paula Wiseman Bks.) Simon & Schuster/Paula Wiseman Bks.

—Jacob's Eye Patch. Kobliner Shaw, Beth & Shaw, Jacob. 2013. (ENG.). 32p. (J). 17.00 *(978-1-4767-3732-4(0))* Simon & Schuster.

—My Side of the Car. Feiffer, Kate. 2011. (ENG.). 32p. (J). (gr. -1-3). 16.99 *(978-0-7636-4405-5(6))* Candlewick Pr.

—No Go Sleep! Feiffer, Kate. 2012. (ENG.). 32p. (J). (gr. -1-2). 16.99 *(978-1-4424-1683-3(1))*, Simon & Schuster/Paula Wiseman Bks.) Simon & Schuster/Paula Wiseman Bks.

—The Odious Ogre. Juster, Norton. 2010. (ENG.). 32p. (J). (gr. -1-2). 17.95 *(978-0-545-16202-9(5))*, Di Capua, Michael) Scholastic, Inc.

—The Phantom Tollbooth. Juster, Norton. 2003. (J). mass mkt. 5.99 *(978-0-440-23808-9(0))*, Laurel) Random House Publishing Group.

—The Phantom Tollbooth. Juster, Norton. 256p. (J). pap. 4.99 *(978-0-8072-1400-8(0))*, Listening Library) Random Hse. Audio Publishing Group.

—Some Things Are Scary. Heide, Florence Parry. 2011. (ENG.). 40p. (J). (gr. -1-2). pap. 7.99 *(978-0-7636-5590-7(2))* Candlewick Pr.

Feiffer, Jules. The House Across the Street. Feiffer, Jules. 2003. 28p. (J). (gr. 1-4). reprint ed. 16.00 *(978-0-7567-6845-4(4))* DIANE Publishing Co.

—I'm Not Bobby! Feiffer, Jules. 2006. 28p. (J). (gr. k-4). reprint ed. 16.00 *(978-0-7567-9853-6(1))* DIANE Publishing Co.

—A Room with a Zoo. Feiffer, Jules. (ENG.). 192p. (gr. 2-7). 2007. per. 7.99 *(978-0-7868-3703-8(9))*; 2005. 16.95 *(978-0-7868-3702-1(0))* Hyperion Bks. for Children. (di Capua, Michael Bks.).

—Rupert Can Dance. Feiffer, Jules. 2014. (ENG.). 32p. (J). (gr. -1-1). 17.95 *(978-0-374-36363-5(3))*, Farrar, Straus & Giroux (BYR)) Farrar, Straus & Giroux.

Feiffer, Jules, jt. illus. see Chast, Roz.

Feiffer, Jules, jt. illus. see Feiffer, Kate.

Feiffer, Kate & Feiffer, Jules. Which Puppy? Feiffer, Kate. 2009. (ENG.). 32p. (J). (gr. -1-3). 16.99 *(978-1-4169-9147-2(6))*, Simon & Schuster/Paula Wiseman Bks.) Simon & Schuster/Paula Wiseman Bks.

Feil, Denise J. Praze B. a Growing, Loving Day: Forgiveness & Responsibility. Feil, Denise J. 2004. (J). per. 5.50 *(978-0-9741588-0-8(1))* Feil.

Feinberg, Xeth. City of Hamburgers. Reiss, Mike. 2008. 32p. 14.95 *(978-1-59299-346-8(X))* Inkwater Pr.

Feinman, Anthony, et al. Escape in a Dirigible: Or to Make the World Safe for Tea. Feinman, Myke, photos by. Feinman, Anthony & Hall, Andrew. 2004. (J). pap. *(978-0-9664974-5-8(7))* Ink & Feathers Comics.

Feister, Tom. Fact V. Fiction, Vol. 3. Vaughan, Brian K. 2006. (Ex Machina Ser.: Vol. 3). (ENG.). 144p. pap. 12.99 *(978-1-4012-0988-9(2)*, Wildstorm) DC Comics.

Fekete, Lucy. A Dragon Called Wilbur: How a Fire-Breathing Dragon Made Friends. Heeney, Bronwyn. 2012. 40p. pap. 16.97 *(978-1-61204-803-1(X)*, Strategic Bk. Publishing) Strategic Book Publishing & Rights Agency (SBPRA).

Feldman Emison, Chloë, jt. illus. see Emison, Patricia A.

Feldman, Luke. Beauty & the Beast: The Graphic Novel, 1 vol. Stone Arch Books Staff. 2008. (Graphic Spin Ser.). (ENG.). 40p. (gr. 1-3). pap. 5.95 *(978-1-4342-0861-3(3)*, Graphic Revolve) Stone Arch Bks.

—La Bella y la Bestia: La Novela Grafica, 1 vol. Andersen, Hans Christian & Stone Arch Books Staff. 2010. (Graphic Spin en Español Ser.). (SPA & ENG.). 40p. (gr. 1-3). pap. 5.95 *(978-1-4342-2269-5(1)*, Graphic Spin en Español) Stone Arch Bks.

—La Bella y la Bestia: La Novela Grafica. Andersen, Hans Christian & Capstone Press Editors. 2010. (Graphic Spin en Español Ser.). (SPA.). 40p. (gr. 1-3). lib. bdg. 23.99 *(978-1-4342-1899-5(6)*, Graphic Spin en Español) Stone Arch Bks.

—Pet's Playground: Playing Safe in a Dog-and-Cat World. Chin, Amanda. 2009. 14p. (J). pap. 11.95 *(978-1-58326-115-6(X))* American Animal Hospital Assn. Pr.

Feldman, Luke. Chaff n' Skaffs: Mai & the Lost Moskivvy. Feldman, Luke. Chin, Amanda. 2009. (ENG.). 36p. (J). (gr. -1-3). 15.95 *(978-1-59702-013-8(3))* Immedium.

Feldmeier Sims, Julie & Hartman, John. Oscar's First Flight. Zimmerman, Kathleen. 2005. 44p. (J). per. 16.95 *(978-0-9744330-0-4(4))* Kat Tales Publishing.

Felix, Monique. Bear Dance. Wahl, Jan. 2008. (ENG.). 32p. (J). (gr. k-17). 19.95 *(978-1-56846-199-1(2))*, Creative Editions) Creative Co., The.

—Good Ship Crocodile. Lewis, J. Patrick. 2013. (ENG.). 32p. (J). (gr. 1-3). 18.99 *(978-1-56846-238-7(7))*, Creative Editions) Creative Co., The.

—The Rumor. 2011. (ENG.). 24p. (J). (gr. 1-3). 19.99 *(978-1-56846-219-6(0)*, Creative Editions) Creative Co., The.

—Tuba Lessons. Bartlett, T. C. (ENG.). 32p. (J). (gr. 1-17). 2011. pap. 9.95 *(978-0-89812-522-1(7)*, Creative Paperbacks); 2009. 17.95 *(978-1-56846-209-7(3))* Creative Co., The.

—The Velveteen Rabbit. Williams, Margery. 40p. 2013. (ENG.). (J). (gr. 1-3). pap. 8.99 *(978-0-89812-831-4(5)*, Creative Paperbacks); 2005. pap. 8.95 *(978-0-89812-383-8(6))* Creative Co., The.

—The Velveteen Rabbit. Williams, Margery & Bianco, Margery Williams. 2004. (ENG.). 40p. (J). (gr. 1-3). 19.99 *(978-1-56846-217-2(4)*, Creative Editions) Creative Co., The.

Felix, Monique. Where Do I End & You Begin? Oppenheim, Shulamith. 2015. (ENG.). 32p. (J). (gr. 1-3). 17.99 ***(978-1-56846-274-5(3)***, Creative Editions) Creative Co., The.

Felix, Monique. The Alphabet. Felix, Monique. 2012. (Mouse Book Ser.). (ENG.). 32p. (J). (gr. -1-k). 12.99 *(978-1-56846-226-4(3)*, Creative Editions) Creative Co., The.

—The Colors. Felix, Monique. 2013. (ENG.). 32p. (J). (gr. -1-k). 12.99 *(978-1-56846-234-9(4)*, Creative Editions) Creative Co., The.

—Mouse Book: the Valentine. Felix, Monique. 2013. (Mouse Book Ser.). (ENG.). 32p. (J). (gr. -1-k). 12.99 *(978-1-56846-247-9(6)*, Creative Editions) Creative Co., The.

—The Numbers. Felix, Monique. 2013. (ENG.). 32p. (J). (gr. -1-k). 12.99 *(978-1-56846-235-6(2)*, Creative Editions) Creative Co., The.

Fell, H. Granville & Millar, H. R. The Book of Dragons. Nesbit, E. unabr. ed. 2004. (Dover Children's Classics Ser.). (ENG.). 176p. (gr. 3-5). pap. 7.95 *(978-0-486-43648-7(9))* Dover Pubns., Inc.

Fell, Jenny. Second Thoughts. Nuttall, Neil & Hawkins, Andy, eds. 2004. (ENG.). 64p. pap. 14.95 *(978-1-84323-046-5(1))* Beekman Bks., Inc.

Fellers, Cody. Toby & the Alien: In the Adventures of the Unusual Toys, 1 vol. Fellers, Tina. 2009. 28p. pap. 24.95 *(978-1-60672-195-7(X))* America Star Bks.

Fellows, Stan. The Cuckoo's Haiku: And Other Birding Poems. Rosen, Michael J. 2009. (ENG.). 64p. (J). (gr. 1-4). 17.99 *(978-0-7636-3049-2(7))* Candlewick Pr.

Felmang, Romano. Egyptian Myths. Jeffrey, Gary. 2006. (Graphic Mythology Ser.). (ENG.). 48p. (J). (gr. 4-7). lib. bdg. 31.95 *(978-1-4042-0800-1(3))*; (gr. 5-8). pap. 14.05 *(978-1-4042-0812-4(7))* Rosen Publishing Group, Inc., The.

Felsen, Holly. Rag Top. Felsen, Henry Gregor. 2013. 212p. pap. 15.00 *(978-1-62272-001-9(6))* Felsen Ink.

Felstead, Cathie. Earthshake: Poems from the Ground Up. Peters, Lisa Westberg & Peters. 2003. (ENG.). 32p. (J). (gr. k-5). 17.99 *(978-0-06-029265-2(2)*, Greenwillow Bks.) HarperCollins Pubs.

—Family Lullaby. Shapiro, Jody Fickes. 2007. 40p. (J). (gr. -1). lib. bdg. 17.89 *(978-0-06-051483-9(3))* HarperCollins Pubs.

—An Island Grows. Schaefer, Lola M. 2006. 40p. (J). (gr. -1-3). (ENG.). 17.99 *(978-0-06-623930-9(3))*; lib. bdg. 18.89 *(978-0-06-623931-6(1))* HarperCollins Pubs. (Greenwillow Bks.).

Felstead, Cathie, jt. illus. see Edwards, Gunvor.

Felten, Ross. Ava the Monster Slayer. Maggiore, Lisa. 2015. (ENG.). 32p. (J). (gr. -1-k). 16.99 ***(978-1-63450-151-4(9)***, Sky Pony Pr.) Skyhorse Publishing Co., Inc.

Felter & Butterworth & Heath. Glaucia the Greek Slave: A Tale of Athens in the First Century. Leslie, Emma. 2007. 308p. per. 14.95 *(978-1-934671-01-6(0))* Salem Ridge Press LLC.

Felter and Gunston & Butterworth and Heath. Out of the Mouth of the Lion: Or, the Church in the Catacombs. Leslie, Emma. 2007. 296p. 24.95 *(978-1-934671-04-7(5))*; per. 14.95 *(978-1-934671-05-4(3))* Salem Ridge Press LLC.

Feltes, Tess. Singing Crickets. Glaser, Linda. 2009. (Linda Glaser's Classic Creatures Ser.). (ENG.). 32p. (gr. k-3). 22.60 *(978-0-8225-8806-1(4)*, Millbrook Pr.) Lerner Publishing Group.

—Why Does It Rain? Jango-Cohen, Judith. 2005. (On My Own Science Ser.). (ENG.). 48p. (gr. 2-4). lib. bdg. 25.26 *(978-1-57505-762-0(X)*, Millbrook Pr.) Lerner Publishing Group.

Felton, Richard. Poor Dan. Williams, Lorraine. 2008. 36p. per. 24.95 *(978-1-60441-170-6(8))* America Star Bks.

Felts, Shirley. Sweet & Sour: Tales from China. Kendall, Carol & Li, Yao-Wen. 2007. (ENG.). 114p. (J). (gr. 5-7). per. 8.95 *(978-0-618-75245-4(5))* Houghton Mifflin Harcourt Publishing Co.

Fenderson, David. Mommy, Why Is the Sky So Blue? Fenderson, Shani. 2009. 24p. pap. 24.95 *(978-1-60749-550-5(3))* America Star Bks.

Fenech, Liza. Max Explores Chicago. Laberje, Reji. 2014. (Max Explores Ser.). (ENG.). 20p. (J). (— 1). bds. 9.95 *(978-1-62937-003-3(7))* Triumph Bks.

—Max Explores New York. Laberje, Reji. 2014. (Max Explores Ser.). (ENG.). 20p. (J). (— 1). bds. 9.95 *(978-1-62937-004-0(5))* Triumph Bks.

—Max Explores San Francisco. Laberje, Reji. 2014. (Max Explores Ser.). (ENG.). 20p. (J). (— 1). bds. 9.95 *(978-1-62937-005-7(3))* Triumph Bks.

Fenech, Liza. Max Explores Seattle. Laberje, Reji. 2015. (Max Explores Ser.). (ENG.). 20p. (J). (— 1). bds. 9.95 ***(978-1-62937-103-0(3))*** Triumph Bks.

—Max Explores the Beach. Laberje, Reji. 2015. (Max Explores Ser.). (ENG.). 20p. (J). (— 1). bds. 9.95 ***(978-1-62937-101-6(7))*** Triumph Bks.

Feng, Katherine. Panda Kindergarten. Ryder, Joanne. (ENG.). 32p. (J). (gr. -1-3). 2015. pap. 6.99 *(978-0-06-057852-7(1))*; 2009. 17.99 *(978-0-06-057850-3(5)*, Collins) HarperCollins Pubs.

Feng, Katherine, photos by. Panda Kindergarten. Ryder, Joanne. 2014. 32p. pap. 8.00 *(978-1-61003-332-9(9))* Center for the Collaborative Classroom.

Fennell, Clare. Big. Paratore, Coleen. O'Malley, Judy, ed. 2012. (ENG.). 32p. (J). (gr. -1-2). 18.95 *(978-0-9829938-5-9(4))* Little Pickle Press LLC.

Fennell, Kristen & Petruccelli, Jessica. A World of Hope: Written by Hope's Parents Laurie & Mike. I.t. ed. 2005. 18p. (J). per. 9.99 *(978-1-59879-069-6(2))* Lifevest Publishing, Inc.

Fennell, Tracy. The Qur'an & Islam. Ganeri, Anita. 2003. 30p. (J). lib. bdg. 24.25 *(978-1-58340-241-2(1))* Black Rabbit Bks.

Fennell, Tracy, jt. illus. see Morgan, Richard.

Fennewald, Joseph Grant. Wonderful White Wintery Day: The Marvelous Misadventure of Katy Bear, 1 vol. Matherly, Ashley Page. 2009. 43p. pap. 24.95 *(978-1-61546-323-7(2))* PublishAmerica, Inc.

Fenoughty, Charles. Beautiful Games. Hamley, Dennis. 2004. 104p. per. *(978-1-904529-13-2(5)*, Back to Front) Solidus.

—Haunted United. Hamley, Dennis. 2004. 148p. per. *(978-1-904529-11-8(9)*, Back to Front) Solidus.

Fenske, Jonathan. Guppy Up! Fenske, Jonathan. 2013. (Penguin Young Readers, Level 1 Ser.). (ENG.). 32p. (J). (gr. k-1). mass mkt. 3.99 *(978-0-448-49646-7(1)*, Warne, Frederick Pubs.) Penguin Bks., Ltd. GBR. Dist: Penguin Random Hse., LLC.

—Love Is in the Air. Fenske, Jonathan. 2012. (Penguin Young Readers, Level 2 Ser.). (ENG.). 32p. (J). (gr. 1-2). mass mkt. 3.99 *(978-0-448-49647-4(X)*, Grosset & Dunlap) Penguin Publishing Group.

—Love Is in the Air (HC) Fenske, Jonathan. 2012. (Penguin Young Readers, Level 2 Ser.). (ENG.). 32p. (J). (gr. 1-3). 14.99 *(978-0-448-46160-1(9)*, Grosset & Dunlap) Penguin Publishing Group.

Fenske, Jonathan. A Pig, a Fox, & a Box. Fenske, Jonathan. 2015. (Penguin Young Readers, Level 2 Ser.). (ENG.). 32p. (J). (gr. 1-2). pap. 3.99 ***(978-0-448-48510-2(9)***, Warne, Frederick Pubs.) Penguin Bks., Ltd. GBR. Dist: Penguin Random Hse., LLC.

Fenske, Jonathan. Woodward & Mctwee. Fenske, Jonathan. 2014. (Penguin Young Readers, Level 2 Ser.). (ENG.). 32p. (J). (gr. 1-2). pap. 3.99 *(978-0-448-47991-0(5)*, Warne, Frederick Pubs.) Penguin Bks., Ltd. GBR. Dist: Penguin Random Hse., LLC.

Fenton, Joe. Boo! Fenton, Joe. 2010. (ENG.). 32p. (J). (gr. -1-1). bds. 12.99 *(978-1-4169-7936-4(0)*, Simon & Schuster Bks. For Young Readers) Simon & Schuster Bks. For Young Readers.

—What's under the Bed? Fenton, Joe. 2008. (ENG.). 32p. (J). (gr. -1-2). 15.99 *(978-1-4169-4943-5(7)*, Simon & Schuster Bks. For Young Readers) Simon & Schuster Bks. For Young Readers.

Fenton, Mary Frances & Kostecke, Nancy. Worms Eat Our Garbage: Classroom Activities for a Better Environment. Appelhof, Mary et al. Harris, Barbara Loss et al. 2004. 232p. (Orig.). (gr. 4-18). pap., stu. ed. 22.95 *(978-0-942256-05-5(0))* Flowerfield Enterprises.

Fenton, Tanya. Three Silly Chickens. Fenton, Tanya. 2015. (ENG.). 32p. (J). (gr. -1-1). pap. 8.99 ***(978-1-907432-11-8(6))*** Hogs Back Bks. GBR. Dist: Independent Pubs. Group.

Fentz, Mike. Garfield & the Santa Spy. Teitelbaum, Michael. 2004. 92p. (J). *(978-0-439-70543-1(6))* Scholastic, Inc.

—Monster Trouble. Nickel, Scott. 2004. (Scholastic Reader Ser.). 22p. (J). pap. *(978-0-439-66977-1(4))* Scholastic, Inc.

Fentz, Mike & Barker, Lori. Egg Hunt. Nickel, Scott. 2005. 22p. (J). *(978-0-439-67211-5(2))* Scholastic, Inc.

Fenwick, Ray. The Great & Only Barnum: The Tremendous, Stupendous Life of Showman P. T. Barnum. Fleming, Candace. 2009. (ENG.). 160p. (J). (gr. 3-7). 18.99 *(978-0-375-84197-2(0)*, Schwartz & Wade Bks.) Random Hse. Children's Bks.

Ferchaud, Steve. Glen Robbie: A Scottish Fairy Tale. ed. 2006. (J). 22.95 *(978-1-58478-013-7(4)*, Highland Children's Pr.) Heather & Highlands Publishing.

—Gracie's Big Adventure... with Augustine the Beaver. Cobb, Debbie. 2006. (J). per. 10.95 *(978-0-9787376-0-3(1))* Laurob Pr.

—The Man Who Spoke with Cats. 2006. (ENG.). 48p. (J). 18.95 *(978-1-58478-019-9(3)*, Highland Children's Pr.) Heather & Highlands Publishing.

—Santa's Hat. Claus, Nancy. 2006. (J). *(978-0-9746747-6-6(1))* Cypress Bay Publishing.

—Santa's Prize. Claus, Nancy. 2006. (J). *(978-0-9746747-5-9(3))* Cypress Bay Publishing.

Ferenc, Bill. The Good Samaritan & Other Bible Stories. Glaser, Rebecca. 2015. (Holy Moly Bible Storybooks Ser.). (ENG.). 32p. (J). (gr. k-3). 12.99 ***(978-1-5064-0251-2(8)***, Sparkhouse Family) Augsburg Fortress, Pubs.

—The Holy Moly Christmas Story. Glaser, Rebecca. 2015. (Holy Moly Bible Storybooks Ser.). (ENG.). 32p. (J). (gr. k-3). 12.99 ***(978-1-5064-0257-4(7)***, Sparkhouse Family) Augsburg Fortress, Pubs.

—Jesus at the Temple & Other Bible Stories. Glaser, Rebecca. 2015. (Holy Moly Bible Storybooks Ser.). (ENG.). 32p. (J). (gr. k-3). 12.99 ***(978-1-5064-0250-5(X)***, Sparkhouse Family) Augsburg Fortress, Pubs.

—Jesus Feeds 5,000 & Other Bible Stories. Glaser, Rebecca. 2015. (Holy Moly Bible Storybooks Ser.). (ENG.). 32p. (J). (gr. k-3). 12.99 ***(978-1-5064-0252-9(6)***, Sparkhouse Family) Augsburg Fortress, Pubs.

—Mary & Martha & Other Bible Stories. Glaser, Rebecca. 2015. (Holy Moly Bible Storybooks Ser.). (ENG.). 32p. (J). (gr. k-3). 12.99 ***(978-1-5064-0253-6(4)***, Sparkhouse Family) Augsburg Fortress, Pubs.

Ferenic, Bill. Baby Moses & Other Bible Stories. Glaser, Rebecca. 2015. (Holy Moly Bible Storybooks Ser.). (ENG.). 32p. (J). (gr. k-3). 12.99 ***(978-1-4514-9996-4(5)***, Sparkhouse Family) Augsburg Fortress, Pubs.

—The Holy Moly Story Bible: Exploring God's Awesome Word. Glaser, Rebecca. 2015. (ENG.). 352p. (J). (gr. k-3). 22.99 ***(978-1-4514-9988-9(4)***, Sparkhouse Family) Augsburg Fortress, Pubs.

—Jonah & the Big Fish & Other Bible Stories. Glaser, Rebecca. 2015. (Holy Moly Bible Storybooks Ser.). (ENG.). 32p. (J). (gr. k-3). 12.99 ***(978-1-4514-9997-1(3)***, Sparkhouse Family) Augsburg Fortress, Pubs.

—Joseph & His Brothers & Other Bible Stories. Glaser, Rebecca. 2015. (Holy Moly Bible Storybooks Ser.). (ENG.). 32p. (J). (gr. k-3). 12.99 ***(978-1-4514-9995-7(7)***, Sparkhouse Family) Augsburg Fortress, Pubs.

—Noah's Ark & Other Bible Stories. Glaser, Rebecca. 2015. (Holy Moly Bible Storybooks Ser.). (ENG.). 32p. (J). (gr. k-3). 12.99 ***(978-1-4514-9994-0(9)***, Sparkhouse Family) Augsburg Fortress, Pubs.

Fereyra, Lucas. Penguins of Madagascar, Vol. 1. Matthews, Alex. 2015. (ENG.). 64p. (gr. 1-4). pap. 6.99 *(978-1-78276-251-5(5)*, Titan Comics) Titan Bks. Ltd. GBR. Dist: Random Hse., Inc.

Ferguson, C. Brent. Buffy the Vampire Slayer Roleplaying Game: Slayer's Handbook. Carella, C. J. et al. 2006. (Buffy RPG Ser.). 156p. 30.00 *(978-1-891153-89-1(7))* Eden Studios, Inc.

Ferguson, Chaveevah Banks. Henry the Farsighted Heron. Barbatti, Joyce. 2008. (ENG.). 24p. (J). 7.00 *(978-0-9818219-0-0(1))* BaHar Publishing, L.C.

—Travis, It's NOT Your Birthday! Hickey, Joshalyn M. 2006. (ENG.). 34p. (J). pap. 13.00 *(978-0-9718939-5-5(0))* BaHar Publishing, L.C.

Ferguson, John. Something Shiny, Something Round. Goulis, Julie. 2005. 32p. (J). (gr. 3-7). 14.99 *(978-0-9754621-1-9(3))* Bubblegum Bks.

—The Things a String Can Be. Goulis, Julie. 2005. 32p. (J). (gr. -1-3). 14.99 *(978-0-9754621-0-2(5))* Bubblegum Bks.

Ferguson, John H. The Topsy-Turvy Towel. Goulis, Julie. 2006. 32p. (J). (gr. -1-2). 14.95 *(978-0-9754621-2-6(1))* Bubblegum Bks.

Ferguson-Jones, Philip. Human Anatomy: The Fun, Visual Way to Teach Yourself about Anything & Everything. Leonard, Wendy. 2011. (ENG.). 128p. 19.95 *(978-1-60710-217-5(X)*, Thunder Bay Pr.) Baker & Taylor Publishing Group.

Ferguson, Lee. Superman - A Giant Attack. Lemke, Donald. 2015. (I Can Read Book 2 Ser.). (ENG.). 32p. (J). (gr. -1-3). pap. 3.99 *(978-0-06-234488-5(9))* HarperCollins Pubs.

Ferguson, Martha-Elizabeth. Princess Prissypants Goes to Spain. Evans, Ashley Putnam. 2009. (Princess Prissypants Ser.). (ENG & SPA.). 28p. (J). (gr. -1-k). 16.95 *(978-0-9793381-5-1(8))* Pink Angel Pr.

Ferguson, Peter. The Anybodies. Bode, N. E. 2005. (ENG.). 288p. (J). (gr. 5-8). reprint ed. pap. 6.99 *(978-0-06-055737-9(0))* HarperCollins Pubs.

—The Boy Who Cried Fabulous. Newman, Lesléa. 2007. (ENG.). 32p. (J). (gr. -1-2). pap. 7.99 *(978-1-58246-224-0(0)*, Tricycle Pr.) Ten Speed Pr.

—The Council of Mirrors. Buckley, Michael. (Sisters Grimm Ser.). (ENG.). 352p. (gr. 3-7). 2013. (YA). pap. 7.95 *(978-1-4197-0538-0(5))*; 2012. (J). 16.95 *(978-1-4197-0186-3(X))* Abrams. (Amulet Bks.).

—The Everafter War. Buckley, Michael. (Sisters Grimm Ser.: Bk. 7). (ENG.). (J). (gr. 3-7). 2010. 336p. pap. 8.95 *(978-0-8109-8429-5(6))*; 2009. 320p. 16.95 *(978-0-8109-8355-7(9))* Abrams. (Amulet Bks.).

—The Fairy-Tale Detectives. Buckley, Michael. (ENG.). (J). 2007. 312p. (gr. 2-8). pap. 7.95 *(978-0-8109-9322-8(8)*, Amulet Bks.); 2005. 288p. (gr. 3-7). 16.95 *(978-0-8109-5925-5(9)*, Abrams Bks. for Young Readers) Abrams.

—The Fairy-Tale Detectives: And the Unusual Suspects. Buckley, Michael. 2012. 580p. (J). *(978-1-4351-4487-3(2)*, Amulet Bks.) Abrams.

—The Golden Ghost. Bauer, Marion Dane. 2012. (Stepping Stone Book(TM) Ser.). (ENG.). 96p. (J). (gr. 1-4). pap. 4.99 *(978-0-375-86619-7(1))* Random Hse., Inc.

—The Green Ghost. Bauer, Marion Dane. 2009. (Stepping Stone Book(TM) Ser.). (ENG.). 96p. (J). (gr. 1-4). 4.99 *(978-0-375-84084-5(2))* Random Hse. Children's Bks.

—The Guide to the Territories of Halla. MacHale, D. J. 2005. (Pendragon Ser.). (ENG.). 48p. (J). (gr. 5-9). pap. 9.99 *(978-1-4169-0014-6(4)*, Simon & Schuster/Paula Wiseman Bks.) Simon & Schuster/Paula Wiseman Bks.

—The Inside Story. Buckley, Michael. 2010. (Sisters Grimm Ser.: Bk. 8). (ENG.). 288p. (J). (gr. 3-7). 16.95 *(978-0-8109-8430-1(X)*, Amulet Bks.) Abrams.

—Magic & Other Misdemeanors. Buckley, Michael. (Sisters Grimm Ser.). (ENG.). 304p. (gr. 3-7). 2008. (J). pap. 7.95 *(978-0-8109-7263-6(8))*; 2007. (YA). 16.95 *(978-0-8109-9358-7(9))* Abrams. (Amulet Bks.).

—My Havana: Memories of a Cuban Boyhood. Wells, Rosemary et al. 2010. (ENG.). 72p. (J). (gr. 2-5). 17.99 *(978-0-7636-4305-8(X))* Candlewick Pr.

—Once upon a Crime. Buckley, Michael. (Sisters Grimm Ser.). (ENG.). (J). 2008. 296p. (gr. 3-7). per. 7.95 *(978-0-8109-9549-9(2))*; 2007. 288p. (gr. 2-8). 16.95 *(978-0-8109-1610-4(X))* Abrams. (Amulet Bks.).

—The Problem Child. Buckley, Michael. (ENG.). 320p. (gr. 3-7). 2007. (YA). pap. 7.95 *(978-0-8109-9359-4(7))*; 2006. (J). 16.95 *(978-0-8109-4914-0(8)*, Amulet Bks.) Abrams.

—The Red Ghost. Bauer, Marion Dane. 2009. (Stepping Stone Book(TM) Ser.). (ENG.). 96p. (J). (gr. 1-4). 4.99 *(978-0-375-84082-1(6))* Random Hse., Inc.

—The Somebodies. Bode, N. E. 2006. (ENG.). 288p. (J). (gr. 5-8). 17.99 *(978-0-06-079111-7(X))* HarperCollins Pubs.

—Tales from the Hood. Buckley, Michael. 2008. (Sisters Grimm Ser.). (ENG.). 304p. (J). (gr. 3-7). 16.95 *(978-0-8109-9478-2(X)*, Amulet Bks.) Abrams.

—The Unusual Suspects. Buckley, Michael. (ENG.). (J). 2005. 290p. (gr. 3-7). 16.95 *(978-0-8109-5926-2(7)*, Abrams Bks. for Young Readers); No. 2. 2007. 320p. (gr. 2-8). pap. 7.95 *(978-0-8109-9323-5(6)*, Amulet Bks.) Abrams.

—A Very Grimm Guide. Buckley, Michael. 2012. (Sisters Grimm Ser.). (ENG.). 128p. (J). (gr. 3-7). 16.95 *(978-1-4197-0201-3(7)*, Amulet Bks.) Abrams.

—The Witches of Dredmoore Hollow, 0 vols. McKenzie, Riford. 2008. (ENG.). 272p. (J). (gr. 5-7). 16.99 *(978-0-7614-5458-8(6))*, 9780761454588, Amazon Children's Publishing) Amazon Publishing.

—Working Myself to Pieces & Bits. Kelly, Katy. 2008. (Lucy Rose Ser.). (ENG.). 208p. (J). (gr. 3-7). 6.99 *(978-0-440-42186-3(1)*, Yearling) Random Hse. Children's Bks.

Ferguson, Tamara. Did Noah Have Whales on the Ark? Hairston, Angelica. I.t. ed. 2004. 44p. (J). *(978-0-9716136-1-4(3))* Broadcast Quality Productions, Inc.

Fernandes, Eugenie. Beyond Old McDonald: Funny Poems from down on the Farm. Hoce, Charley. 2005. (ENG.). 32p. (J). (gr. -1-2). 16.95 *(978-1-59078-312-2(3))* Boyds Mills Pr.

—Hope Springs. Walters, Eric. 2014. (ENG.). 32p. (J). (gr. 1-4). 17.99 *(978-1-77049-530-2(4))* Tundra Bks. CAN. Dist: Random Hse., Inc.

—Mermaid in the Bathtub, 1 vol. Peetoom, Laura. 2006. (First Flight: Level 4 Ser.). (ENG.). 104p. (J). (gr. 4-7). pap. 4.95 *(978-1-55041-362-5(7))* Fitzhenry & Whiteside, Ltd. CAN. Dist: F&W Media, Inc.

—Mimi's Village & How Basic Health Care Transformed It. Milway, Katie Smith. 2012. (ENG.). 32p. (J). 18.95 *(978-1-55453-722-8(3))* Kids Can Pr., Ltd. CAN. Dist: Univ. of Toronto Pr.

—My Name Is Blessing. Walters, Eric. 2013. (ENG.). 32p. (J). (gr. 1-4). 17.95 *(978-1-77049-301-8(8)*, Tundra Bks.) Tundra Bks. CAN. Dist: Penguin Random Hse., LLC.

—One Hen: How One Small Loan Made a Big Difference. Milway, Katie Smith. 2008. (CitizenKid Ser.). (ENG.). 32p. (J). (gr. 2-5). 18.95 *(978-1-55453-028-1(8))* Kids Can Pr., Ltd. CAN. Dist: Univ. of Toronto Pr.

—Polar Bear, Arctic Hare: Poems of the Frozen North. Spinelli, Eileen. (ENG.). 32p. (J). (gr. -1-3). 2014. pap. 6.95 *(978-1-62979-112-8(1)*, Wordsong); 2007. 16.95 *(978-1-59078-344-3(1))* Boyds Mills Pr.

—There's a Barnyard in My Bedroom. Suzuki, David. 2010. (ENG.). 64p. (J). (gr. -1-3). pap. 10.95 *(978-1-55365-532-9(X))* Greystone Books Ltd. CAN. Dist: Perseus-PGW.

Fernandes, Eugenie. Kitten's Autumn. Fernandes, Eugenie. 2010. (ENG.). 24p. (J). (gr. -1). 14.95 *(978-1-55453-341-1(4))* Kids Can Pr., Ltd. CAN. Dist: Univ. of Toronto Pr.

—Kitten's Spring. Fernandes, Eugenie. 2010. (ENG.). 24p. (J). (gr. -1). 14.95 *(978-1-55453-340-4(6))* Kids Can Pr., Ltd. CAN. Dist: Univ. of Toronto Pr.

—Kitten's Summer. Fernandes, Eugenie. (ENG.). 24p. (J). 2013. bds. 7.95 *(978-1-55453-721-1(5))*; 2011. (gr. -1). 14.95 *(978-1-55453-342-8(2))* Kids Can Pr., Ltd. CAN. Dist: Univ. of Toronto Pr.

—Kitten's Winter. Fernandes, Eugenie. 2011. (ENG.). 24p. (J). 14.95 *(978-1-55453-343-5(0))* Kids Can Pr., Ltd. CAN. Dist: Univ. of Toronto Pr.

Fernandes, Kim. One Gray Mouse. Burton, Katherine. 2006. (ENG.). 24p. (J). (gr. -1). bds. 7.95 *(978-1-55453-026-7(1))* Kids Can Pr., Ltd. CAN. Dist: Univ. of Toronto Pr.

—Une Souris Grise. Burton, Katherine.Tr. of Souris Grise. (FRE.). 24p. (J). pap. 6.99 *(978-0-590-16023-0(0))* Scholastic, Inc.

Fernandes, Matthew. Inventions. Wyatt, Valerie. 2003. (Faq Ser.). (ENG.). 40p. (J). (gr. 4-6). 6.95 *(978-1-55337-404-6(5))* Kids Can Pr., Ltd. CAN. Dist: Univ. of Toronto Pr.

Fernandes, Roger & Point, Susan. The Spindle Whorl. McNutt, Nan. 2nd ed. 2011. (Native American Art Activity Book Ser.). (ENG.). 56p. (J). (gr. 3-5). pap. 9.95 *(978-0-88240-762-3(7)*, West Winds Pr.) Graphic Arts Ctr. Publishing Co.

Fernandez, Carina. Lily's Rainbow. Giacomo, Renee San. 2013. 28p. pap. 24.95 *(978-1-63004-174-8(2))* America Star Bks.

Fernandez, Laura & Jacobson, Rick. Little Dog Moon, 1 vol. Trottier, Maxine. 2006. (ENG.). 24p. (J). (gr. -1-5). 7.95 *(978-1-55005-160-5(1))* Stoddart Kids CAN. Dist: Ingram Pub. Services.

—Vivaldi's Ring of Mystery. Cowling, Douglas. 2004. (ENG.). 44p. (J). *(978-0-439-96904-8(2)*, North Winds Pr) Scholastic Canada, Ltd.

Fernandez, Laura, jt. illus. see Jacobson, Rick.

Fernandez, Leandro. The Punisher. 2006. (ENG.). 144p. (gr. 13-17). pap. 15.99 *(978-0-7851-1899-2(3))* Marvel Worldwide, Inc.

Fernandez, Leo. Incredible Hulk, Vol. 3. Jones, Bruce. Youngquist, Jeff, ed. 2004. (Hulk Ser.). 272p. 29.99 *(978-0-7851-1237-2(5))* Marvel Worldwide, Inc.

Fernandez, Lucia. Milagros en la Biblia. de Sturtz, Maria Ester H. 2007. (Manos a la Obra Ser.). 32p. (J). (gr. -1-4). per. 7.99 *(978-0-7586-1458-2(6))* Concordia Publishing Hse.

Fernandez, Luciana. Monstruos de Visita. Repun, Graciela. 2006. (SPA.). 24p. (J). (gr. k-2). pap. 7.50 *(978-987-1296-09-5(6))* Unaluna Ediciones ARG. Dist: Lectorum Pubns., Inc.

Fernandez, Maria Xose. A Cazar Palabras. Caccamo, Pepe. (SPA.). 142p. (J). (gr. k-2). *(978-84-95123-36-7(3)*, KA1393) Kalandraka Editora, S.L. ESP. Dist: Lectorum Pubns., Inc.

Fernández, Pablo. Chat Natacha chat (Edición Especial) Pescetti, Luis María. 2008. (Natacha Ser.). (SPA.). 124p. (gr. 3-5). pap. 12.95 *(978-970-58-0449-6(4))* Ediciones Alfaguara ESP. Dist: Santillana USA Publishing Co., Inc.

Fernandez, Pablo. Padrisimo, Natacha! Pescetti, Luis María. 2008. (Natacha! Ser.). (SPA.). 138p. (J). (gr. 2-7). pap. 12.95 *(978-970-58-0495-3(8))* Ediciones Alfaguara ESP. Dist: Santillana USA Publishing Co., Inc.

Fernandez, Raul. Breakout. Bedard, Tony. 2005. (Spider-Man Legends Ser.). 120p. (YA). pap. 13.99 *(978-0-7851-1807-7(1))* Marvel Worldwide, Inc.

Ferns, Kevin. The Spuds - the Fancy Dress Party. Haydon, David J. 2011. 20p. pap. *(978-1-908341-08-2(4))* Paragon Publishing, Rothersthorpe.

—The Spuds - the Windy Day. Haydon, David J. 2010. 20p. pap. *(978-1-907611-11-7(8))* Paragon Publishing, Rothersthorpe.

Ferran, Adriana & Ferran, Daniel. El Sabueso de Los Baskerville, 1 vol. Doyle, Arthur. 2010. (Classic Fiction Ser.). (SPA.). 72p. (gr. 2-3). 26.65 *(978-1-4342-2325-8(6)*, Graphic Revolve en Español) Stone Arch Bks.

Ferran, Adriana, et al. El Extraño Caso del Dr. Jekyll y Mr. Hyde. Stevenson, Robert L. & Facio, Sebastian. 2010. (Classic Fiction Ser.). (SPA.). 72p. (gr. 2-3). 26.65 *(978-1-4342-2323-4(X)*, Graphic Revolve en Español) Stone Arch Bks.

Ferran, Daniel. Macbeth, 1 vol. Shakespeare, William. 2011. (Shakespeare Graphics Ser.). (ENG.). 88p. (gr. 2-3). lib. bdg. 26.65 *(978-1-4342-2506-1(2)*, Shakespeare Graphics) Stone Arch Bks.

Ferran, Daniel, jt. illus. see Ferran, Adriana.

Ferran, Daniel, jt. illus. see Pérez, Daniel.

Ferrándiz, Elena. Mis Primeras 1000 Palabras/My First 1,000 Words. 2004. (ENG & SPA.). 72p. (J). (gr. -1-2). 15.95 *(978-1-58394-100-3(2),* Frog Ltd.) North Atlantic Bks.

Ferrando, Carol. Cabbages & Queens. Sullivan, Maureen. 2010. 57p. (J). pap. *(978-0-9820381-3-0(5))* MoJo InkWorks.

Ferrara, Eduardo. Sports Illustrated Kids Graphic Novels, 1 vol. Terrell, Brandon. 2014. (Sports Illustrated Kids Graphic Novels Ser.). (ENG.). 72p. (gr. 2-5). 101.28 *(978-1-4342-9528-6(1))* Stone Arch Bks.

—8-Bit Baseball, 1 vol. Terrell, Brandon. 2014. (Sports Illustrated Kids Graphic Novels Ser.). (ENG.). 72p. (gr. 2-5). 25.32 *(978-1-4342-4164-1(5))* Stone Arch Bks.

Ferrara, Eduardo, jt. illus. see Garcia, Eduardo.

Ferrara, Madeleine. The Story of Cardinal George: The Boy Who Wanted to be a Priest. the God Who Wanted Him to be a Prince. Keusal, Eugene L. 2004. 33p. (J). 5.00 *(978-0-9786605-0-5(1))* Dooley Bks., Ltd.

Ferrari, Antongionata. Apollo. Colloredo, Sabino. 2009. (Hotel Olympus Ser.). 128p. (J). (gr. 3-6). 31.95 *(978-1-60754-710-5(4))* Windmill Bks.

—Athena. Colloredo, Sabino. 2009. (Hotel Olympus Ser.). 128p. (J). (gr. 3-6). 31.95 *(978-1-60754-709-9(0))* Windmill Bks.

—Hercules. Colloredo, Sabino. 2009. (Hotel Olympus Ser.). 128p. (J). (gr. 3-6). 31.95 *(978-1-60754-708-2(2))* Windmill Bks.

—The Kindhearted Crocodile. Panzieri, Lucia. 2013. (ENG.). 32p. (J). 16.95 *(978-0-8234-2767-3(6))* Holiday Hse., Inc.

—Zeus. Colloredo, Sabino. 2009. (Hotel Olympus Ser.). 128p. (J). (gr. 3-6). 31.95 *(978-1-60754-707-5(4))* Windmill Bks.

Ferraro Close, Laura. Storytime Stickers: Farm Follies. Plourde, Lynn. 2010. (Storytime Stickers Ser.). (ENG.). 16p. (J). (gr. k-2). pap. 5.95 *(978-1-4027-7127-9(4))* Sterling Publishing Co., Inc.

Ferraro-Oster, Margaret. Freddie Q. Freckle. Messinger, Midge. Messinger, Robert, ed. unabr. ed. 2003. 40p. (gr. -1-2). 12.95 *(978-1-893237-00-1(1))* Little Mai Pr.

Ferraz, Thiago. The Golden Goose: A Grimm Graphic Novel, 1 vol. Grimm, Jacob et al. 2011. (Graphic Spin Ser.). (ENG.). 40p. (gr. 1-3). lib. bdg. 23.99 *(978-1-4342-2961-8(0),* Graphic Revolve) Stone Arch Bks.

Ferreira, Melissa. Bear's All-Night Party. Harley, Bill. 2005. (ENG.). 32p. (J). (gr. -1-2). 15.95 *(978-0-87483-572-4(0))* August Hse. Pubs., Inc.

Ferrenburg, Susie. There's Only One I in Charlie. Snyder, Sandy. 2011. 48p. pap. 24.95 *(978-1-4626-4086-7(9))* America Star Bks.

Ferrer, Isabel. Lom & the Gnatters, 1 vol. Kurusa, Monika. Amado, Elisa, tr. from SPA. 2009. (ENG.). 36p. (J). (gr. -1-k). 18.95 *(978-0-88899-944-3(5))* Groundwood Bks. CAN. Dist: Perseus-PGW.

Ferri, Francesca. Baby's Friends. Hellier, Catherine. 2010. (Baby's Bks.). (ENG.). 6p. (J). (gr. -1-k). 12.99 *(978-0-7641-4540-7(1))* Barron's Educational Series, Inc.

—Baby's World of Colors. Hellier, Catherine. 2010. (Baby's Bks.). (ENG.). 6p. (J). (gr. -1-k). 12.99 *(978-0-7641-4539-1(8))* Barron's Educational Series, Inc.

—Good Night, Teddy. 2003. (ENG.). 8p. (J). 15.99 *(978-0-7641-2595-9(8))* Barron's Educational Series, Inc.

—Peek-A-Boo. 2005. (ENG.). 10p. (J). 8.99 *(978-0-7641-5851-3(1))* Barron's Educational Series, Inc.

—Peek-A-Boo Jungle. 2006. (ENG.). 10p. (J). (gr. -1). 8.99 *(978-0-7641-5940-4(2))* Barron's Educational Series, Inc.

—Peek-a-Boo Polar Bear & Friends, 1 vol. 2008. (ENG.). 10p. (J). (gr. -1). 8.99 *(978-0-7641-6187-2(3))* Barron's Educational Series, Inc.

Ferri, Francesca. Cucu — Te veo! Mascotas. Ferri, Francesca. 2009. (SPA.). 8p. (J). (gr. -1-k). 8.99 *(978-0-7641-6972-4(6))* Barron's Educational Series, Inc.

—Peek-a-Boo Pets. Ferri, Francesca. 2009. (ENG.). 8p. (J). (gr. -1-k). 8.99 *(978-0-7641-6971-7(8))* Barron's Educational Series, Inc.

Ferri, Giuliano. Ant & Grasshopper. Gray, Luli. 2011. (ENG.). 32p. (J). (gr. -1-2). 17.99 *(978-1-4169-5140-7(7),* McElderry, Margaret K. Bks.) McElderry, Margaret K. Bks.

—Best Friends. Hao, K. T. Kung, Annie, tr. 2008. (ENG.). 32p. (J). (gr. -1). 15.95 *(978-1-933327-38-9(3));* lib. bdg. 16.50 *(978-1-933327-39-6(1))* Purple Bear Bks., Inc.

—The Easter Story. Jackson, Antonia. 2015. (ENG.). 32p. (J). (gr. k-4). 14.99 *(978-0-7459-6508-6(3))* Lion Hudson PLC GBR. Dist: Independent Pubs. Group.

—Illustrated Stories from Aesop. 2014. (ENG.). 272p. (J). 19.99 *(978-0-7945-2917-8(8),* Usborne) EDC Publishing.

—Jonah's Whale. Spinelli, Eileen. 2012. (J). 16.00 *(978-0-8028-5382-0(X),* Eerdmans Bks For Young Readers) Eerdmans, William B. Publishing Co.

—The Legend of Saint Nicholas. Grün, Anselm et al. 2014. (J). 16.00 *(978-0-8028-5434-6(6),* Eerdmans Bks For Young Readers) Eerdmans, William B. Publishing Co.

—The Magic Book. Hao, K. T. 2008. (ENG.). 32p. (J). (gr. -1). 16.50 *(978-1-933327-44-0(8));* 15.95 *(978-1-933327-43-3(X))* Purple Bear Bks., Inc.

—The Story of Daniel in the Lions' Den. McCarthy, Michael. 2003. 32p. (J). (gr. 1-3). 16.99 *(978-1-84148-209-5(9))* Barefoot Bks., Inc.

—The 100th Customer. Kim, Byung-Gyu & Hao, K. T. 2005. (ENG.). 32p. (J). (gr. -1-17). 15.95 *(978-1-933327-03-7(0))* Purple Bear Bks., Inc.

Ferri, Giuliano. A Taste of Freedom: Gandhi & the Great Salt March. Kimmel, Elizabeth Cody. 2014. (ENG.). 48p. (J). (gr. 1-3). 17.99 *(978-0-8027-9467-3(X))* Walker & Co.

Ferrier, Katherine. Wake up, Spring. Ferrier, Katherine. Ferrier, Florian & Burrell, Carol Klio. 2015. (ENG.). 40p. (J). (gr. 2-5). 26.65 *(978-1-4677-8584-6(9),* Graphic Universe) Lerner Publishing Group.

Ferrigno, Angela. Hope's Garden. Jane, Sarah. 2008. (ENG.). 32p. (J). (gr. -1-2). lib. bdg. 16.95 *(978-0-9790962-0-4(0))* Tri Valley Children's Publishing.

Ferris, Carole Anne. Donkey & the Racehorse. Johnson, Joanne Gail. 2011. (ENG.). 48p. pap. 12.00 *(978-0-230-02552-3(8),* Macmillan) Pan Macmillan GBR. Dist: Macmillan.

Ferrone, John M. Gus & the Golden Dragon. Ferrone, John M. Date not set. 36p. (gr. -1-5). pap. 16.95 *(978-1-928811-02-2(7))* Story Stuff, Inc.

—Gus & the Pirate Treasure. Ferrone, John M. Date not set. 36p. (J). (gr. -1-5). pap. 16.95 *(978-1-928811-01-5(9))* Story Stuff, Inc.

—Margo Goes on Safari. Ferrone, John M. Date not set. 36p. (J). (gr. -1-5). pap. 16.95 *(978-1-928811-04-6(3))* Story Stuff, Inc.

Ferrone, John M., photos by. Margo & the Secret Pond. Ferrone, John M. Date not set. 36p. (J). (gr. -1-5). pap. 16.95 *(978-1-928811-03-9(5))* Story Stuff, Inc.

—Margo & the Trail Ride. Ferrone, John M. Date not set. 36p. (J). (gr. -1-5). pap. 16.95 *(978-1-928811-05-3(1))* Story Stuff, Inc.

Ferry, Pasqual, et al. A+X=Awesome, Vol. 1. 2013. (ENG.). 144p. (J). (gr. 4-17). pap. 17.99 *(978-0-7851-6674-0(2))* Marvel Worldwide, Inc.

Ferry, Pasqual. Ultimate X-Men Fantastic Four. 2006. (ENG.). 152p. (J). (gr. 4-17). pap. 12.99 *(978-0-7851-2292-0(3))* Marvel Worldwide, Inc.

Ferry, Pasqual, jt. illus. see Kubert, Andy.

Fesseha, Zewditu. Lakech One: Amharic Ethiopian Script. Fesseha, Zewditu, photos by. Mammo, Rebecca et al, eds. 2005. (Lakech Two Ser.: Vol. 3). (YA). 25.00 *(978-0-9758877-0-7(X))* Orange, Michael Nicholas.

Feterl, Bill. Henry's Adventure at the Franklin Hotel. Cartwright, Nancy & Jones, Joanna. 2011. (YA). lib. bdg. *(978-0-913062-44-9(8))* Fenwyn Pr.

Fetherston, Catherine & Miller, Tom. Texas Roundup: Jake the Beagle's Crazy Adventures. Hernandez, Regina. Woods, Carol, ed. 2003. (Jake the Beagle Crazy Adventure Ser.: 2). 90p. (J). pap. 5.99 *(978-0-9727771-2-4(1))* Regal Enterprises.

Fetter, James. The Raven, the Kitty Cat, & the Mouse. Fetter, Jim. 2011. (ENG.). 28p. pap. 7.50 *(978-1-4610-1700-4(9))* CreateSpace Independent Publishing Platform.

Fetter-Vorm, Jonathan. Battle Lines: A Graphic History of the Civil War. Fetter-Vorm, Jonathan. Kelman, Ari. 2015. (ENG.). 224p. 26.00 *(978-0-8090-9474-5(6),* Hill & Wang) Farrar, Straus & Giroux.

Fetz, Ingrid. Maurice's Room. Fox, Paula. 2010. (ENG.). 64p. (J). (gr. 2-5). pap. 6.99 *(978-1-4424-1678-9(5),* Simon & Schuster/Paula Wiseman Bks.) Simon & Schuster/Paula Wiseman Bks.

Feyer, Diane Le. Words to Dream On: Bedtime Bible Stories & Prayers, 1 vol. Stortz, Diane. 2015. (ENG.). 224p. (J). 14.99 *(978-0-529-11101-2(2))* Nelson, Thomas Inc.

Feyh, Alexa & Deghand, Tim. Does God Have a Remote Control? Feyh, Janelle. l.t. ed. 2003. 66p. (J). per. 11.95 *(978-1-932344-26-4(8))* Thornton Publishing, Inc.

Fiala, Emilie. Where Do I Come From? Curtiss, Dominique. Hill, Rowland, tr. 2013. 42p. pap. *(978-2-89687-245-9(0))* chouetteditions.com.

Fiammenghi, Gioia. Chocolate Fever. Smith, Robert Kimmel. 2006. (ENG.). 96p. (J). (gr. 3-7). 4.99 *(978-0-14-240595-6(7),* Puffin) Penguin Publishing Group.

—Una Coleccion para Kate (A Collection for Kate) deRubertis, Barbara. 2007. (Math Matters Ser.). (SPA.). 29p. (J). (gr. -1-3). pap. 5.95 *(978-1-57565-240-5(4))* Kane Pr., Inc.

—I Accept You As You Are! Parker, David. 2004. (J). *(978-0-439-62811-2(3))* Scholastic, Inc.

—I Show Respect! Parker, David. 2004. (J). pap. *(978-0-439-62809-9(1))* Scholastic, Inc.

—Quien Tiene Manchas? Williams Aber, Linda. 2007. (Math Matters Ser.). (SPA.). 32p. (J). (gr. -1-3). pap. 5.95 *(978-1-57565-251-1(X))* Kane Pr., Inc.

Fickling, Phillip. Fillmore & Geary Take Off! The Adventures of a Robot Boy & a Boy Boy. Shulman, Mark. 2004. (ENG.). 40p. (J). (gr. -1-7). 14.95 *(978-1-58717-256-4(9),* SeaStar Bks.) Chronicle Bks. LLC.

Fiddy, Samantha Lane. Mr. Astley's Blueberries. Lin, Kelly Jenkins. 2012. 36p. pap. 12.95 *(978-0-615-67849-8(1))* Three Flower Farm Pr.

Fiebiger, John. The Knee Bender: Drill Sergeant Bear Volume 3, 1 vol. Hand, Reuben. 2009. 17p. pap. 24.95 *(978-1-61582-706-0(4))* America Star Bks.

—The Push Up: Drill Sergeant Bear Volume 2. Hand, Reuben. 2009. 20p. pap. 24.95 *(978-1-61546-234-6(1))* America Star Bks.

—The Turn & Bounce, 1 vol. Hand, Reuben. 2010. 18p. 24.95 *(978-1-4489-5185-7(2))* PublishAmerica, Inc.

Fiedler, Joseph Daniel. Hard Labor: The First African Americans 1619. McKissack, Fredrick L. & McKissack, Patricia C. 2004. (Milestone Ser.). (ENG.). 64p. (J). (gr. 2-5). pap. 6.99 *(978-0-689-86149-9(4),* Simon & Schuster/Paula Wiseman Bks.) Simon & Schuster/Paula Wiseman Bks.

—Juan Verdades - El Hombre Que No Sabia Mentir. Hayes, Joe. 2011.Tr. of Juan Verdades/The Man Who Couldn't Tell a Lie. (SPA & ENG.). 32p. (J). (gr. 3-6). pap. 8.95 *(978-1-933693-70-5(3))* Cinco Puntos Pr.

Fiedler, Lisa. Skin Deep. Reisfeld, Randi & Bell, Taryn. 2009. (America's Next Top Model Ser.: 3). (ENG.). 272p. (J). (gr. 7-18). 8.99 *(978-0-545-14257-1(1))* Scholastic, Inc.

—Strike a Pose. Reisfeld, Randi & Bell, Taryn. 2010. (America's Next Top Model Ser.: 4). (ENG.). 240p. (J). (gr. 7-12). 8.99 *(978-0-545-16303-3(X))* Scholastic, Inc.

Fiegenschuh, Emily, et al. A Practical Guide to Monsters. Hess, Nina. Whitman, Stacy, ed. 2007. (ENG.). 80p. (J). (gr. 1-4). 12.95 *(978-0-7869-4809-3(4),* Mirrorstone) Wizards of the Coast.

Fiegenschuh, Emily, jt. illus. see Lewis-MacDougall, Patricia Ann.

Fiegenschuh, Emily, jt. illus. see MacDougall, Larry.

Fiegenshuh, Emily. Key to the Griffon's Lair. Ransom, Candice. 2005. (Knights of the Silver Dragon Ser.: Bk. 9). 182p. (J). *(978-1-4156-3032-7(1),* Mirrorstone) Wizards of the Coast.

—The Silver Spell. Banerjee, Anjali. 2005. (Knights of the Silver Dragon Ser.: Bk. 8). 174p. (J). *(978-1-4156-1645-1(0),* Mirrorstone) Wizards of the Coast.

Field, Conrad. Alaska Ocean ABCs. Field, Conrad. 2008. 32p. (J). pap. 9.95 *(978-0-9797442-2-8(9))* Alaska Independent Pubs.

Field, Elaine. Ahora Me Toca a Mi! Bedford, David. (SPA.). 32p. (J). *(978-84-8418-051-7(4))* Corimbo, Editorial S.L. ESP. Dist: Lectorum Pubns., Inc.

Field, James. A Cool Kid's Field Guide to Dinosaurs. Crosbie, Duncan. 2009. (Cool Kid's Field Guide Ser.). 26p. (J). (gr. 1-3). spiral bd. 6.99 *(978-0-8416-7145-4(1))* Hammond World Atlas Corp.

—Defying Death in the Wilderness. Shone, Rob. 2010. (Graphic Survival Stories Ser.). 48p. (YA). 58.50 *(978-1-4488-0068-1(4));* (ENG.). pap. 14.05 *(978-1-61532-865-9(3));* (gr. 5-8). 31.95 *(978-1-4358-3531-3(X))* Rosen Publishing Group, Inc., The. (Rosen Reference).

—Dinosaurs: Discover the Awesome Lost World of the Dinosaur. Eason, Sarah. 2014. (ENG.). 64p. (J). (gr. -1-4). 14.99 *(978-1-86147-364-6(8),* Armadillo) Anness Publishing GBR. Dist: National Bk. Network.

—Diplodocus: The Whip-Tailed Dinosaur. Shone, Rob. 2008. (Graphic Dinosaurs Ser.). (ENG.). 32p. (J). 50.50 *(978-1-61532-137-7(3),* PowerKids Pr.); (gr. 2-5). lib. bdg. 26.50 *(978-1-4358-2504-8(7))* Rosen Publishing Group, Inc., The.

—Fighter Pilots. West, David. 2008. (Graphic Careers Ser.). (ENG.). 48p. (gr. 5-8). per. 14.05 *(978-1-4042-1456-9(9));* (YA). lib. bdg. 31.95 *(978-1-4042-1455-2(0))* Rosen Publishing Group, Inc., The.

—Real Ninja: Over 20 Stories of Japan's Secret Assassins. Turnbull, Stephen & Tulloch, Coral. 2008. (ENG.). 48p. (J). (gr. 3-18). 15.95 *(978-1-59270-081-3(0))* Enchanted Lion Bks., LLC.

—Real Samurai: Over 20 True Stories about the Knights of Old Japan! Turnbull, Stephen. 2007. (ENG.). 48p. (J). (gr. 3-6). 15.95 *(978-1-59270-060-8(8))* Enchanted Lion Bks., LLC.

—Stegosaurus: The Plated Dinosaur. Jeffrey, Gary. (Graphic Dinosaurs Ser.). (ENG.). 32p. 2009. (gr. 2-5). pap. 12.30 *(978-1-4042-7713-7(7),* PowerKids Pr.); 2008. (J). 50.50 *(978-1-61532-136-0(5),* PowerKids Pr.); 2008. (J). (gr. 2-5). lib. bdg. 26.50 *(978-1-4358-2503-1(9))* Rosen Publishing Group, Inc., The.

—Tyrannosaurus: The Tyrant Lizard. Shone, Rob. 2007. (Graphic Dinosaurs Ser.). (ENG.). 32p. (J). (gr. 2-5). lib. bdg. 26.50 *(978-1-4042-3897-8(2))* Rosen Publishing Group, Inc., The.

—Velociraptor: The Speedy Thief. West, David. (Graphic Dinosaurs Ser.). (ENG.). 32p. (gr. 2-5). 2008. pap. 12.30 *(978-1-4042-9628-2(X),* Rosen Classroom); 2007. (J). lib. bdg. 26.50 *(978-1-4042-3898-5(0))* Rosen Publishing Group, Inc., The.

Field, James & Weston, Steve. Deltadromeus & Other Shoreline Dinosaurs, 1 vol. Dixon, Dougal. 2004. (Dinosaur Find Ser.). (ENG.). 24p. (gr. k-3). 25.99 *(978-1-4048-0669-6(5),* Nonfiction Picture Bks.) Picture Window Bks.

—Iguanodon & Other Leaf-Eating Dinosaurs, 1 vol. 2009. (Dinosaur Find Ser.). (ENG.). 24p. (gr. k-3). 25.99 *(978-1-4048-5174-0(7),* Nonfiction Picture Bks.) Picture Window Bks.

—Triceratops & Other Forest Dinosaurs, 1 vol. Dixon, Dougal. 2004. (Dinosaur Find Ser.). (ENG.). 24p. (gr. k-3). 25.99 *(978-1-4048-0671-9(7),* Nonfiction Picture Bks.) Picture Window Bks.

Field, James, jt. illus. see Shone, Rob.

Field, James, jt. illus. see Weston, Steve.

Field, Jim. The Lion Inside. Bright, Rachel. 2016. (J). ***(978-0-545-87350-5(9),*** Scholastic Pr.) Scholastic, Inc.

Field, Jim. Pull-Back Busy Train. Watt, Fiona. ed. 2013. (Pull-Back Bks). 10p. (J). ring bd. 24.99 *(978-0-7945-3333-5(7),* Usborne) EDC Publishing.

—Rich Witch, Poor Witch. Bently, Peter. ed. 2014. (ENG.). 32p. (J). (gr. -1-k). pap. 8.99 *(978-1-4472-2018-3(8))* Pan Macmillan GBR. Dist: Independent Pubs. Group.

—There's a Lion in My Cornflakes. Robinson, Michelle. 2015. (ENG.). 32p. (J). (gr. -1-1). 16.99 *(978-0-8027-3836-3(2),* Bloomsbury USA Childrens) Bloomsbury USA.

Field, Mandy & Pearson, Maria. First Stories from the Bible. Doherty, Gillian, ed. 2007. (Bible Tales Readers Ser.). 143p. (J). (gr. -1-k). 17.99 *(978-0-7945-1668-0(8),* Usborne) EDC Publishing.

Field, Susan. The O'Brien Book of Irish Fairy Tales & Legends. Leavy, Una. 2012. (ENG.). 96p. (J). pap. 18.95 *(978-1-84717-313-3(6))* O'Brien Pr., Ltd., The IRL. Dist: Dufour Editions, Inc.

Fielder, John, photos by. Do You See What I See? 2006. (J). 14.99 *(978-1-56579-554-9(7))* Fielder, John Publishing.

Fieldhouse, Vicky. My Favorite Run. Richards, Katherine. 2013. (ENG.). 32p. (J). 16.99 *(978-0-9895095-2-7(4))* Fit Kids Publishing.

Fielding, Grace. Bilby & the Bushfire. Crawford, Joanne. 2007. 28p. (J). pap. *(978-1-921248-30-6(0))* Magabala Bks.

—Bip the Snapping Bungaroo. McRobbie, Narelle. 2nd ed. 2010. (ENG.). 36p. (J). (gr. 2-4). pap. 19.95 *(978-1-921248-07-8(6))* Magabala Bks. AUS. Dist: Independent Pubs. Group.

—A Home for Bilby. Crawford, Joanne. 2004. 28p. (J). pap. *(978-1-875641-91-8(2))* Magabala Bks.

Fields, Carole Ruth, photos by. Hurricane Dancing: Glimpses of Life with an Autistic Child. Watt, D. Alison. 2004. (ENG., 48p. (YA). 13.95 *(978-1-84310-792-7(9))* Kingsley, Jessica Ltd. GBR. Dist: Univ. of British Columbia Pr.

Fields, Laura & Walters, Bob. Velociraptor up Close: Swift Dinosaur. Dodson, Peter & Library Association Staff. 2010. (Zoom in on Dinosaurs! Ser.). 24p. (J). (gr. k-3). 22.60 *(978-0-7660-3337-5(6))* Enslow Pubs., Inc.

Fields, Laura, jt. illus. see Marshall, Todd.

Fields, Lisa. Barreling over Niagara Falls, 1 vol. Allen, Nancy Kelly. 2013. (ENG.). 40p. (J). (gr. k-3). 17.99 *(978-1-4556-1766-1(0))* Pelican Publishing Co., Inc.

—Grandma's Chocolate/El Chocolate de Abuelita. Price, Mara & Ventura, Gabriela Baeza. 2010. (SPA.). 32p. (J). (gr. -1-3). 16.95 *(978-1-55885-587-8(4),* Piñata Books) Arte Publico Pr.

—Lewis Tewanima: Born to Run, 1 vol. Solomon, Sharon. 2014. (ENG.). 32p. (J). (gr. k-3). 16.99 *(978-1-4556-1941-2(8))* Pelican Publishing Co., Inc.

—Sofia & the Purple Dress / Sofia y el Vestido Morado. Gonzales Bertrand, Diane. Baeza Ventura, Gabriela, tr. 2012. (SPA & ENG.). (J). 17.95 *(978-1-55885-701-8(X),* Piñata Books) Arte Publico Pr.

—Too Perfect. Ludwig, Trudy. 2009. (ENG.). 32p. (J). (gr. 1-4). 15.99 *(978-1-58246-258-5(5),* Tricycle Pr.) Ten Speed Pr.

Fields, Lisa, jt. illus. see Corpi, Lucha.

Fienieg, Annette. In Our Street. Meinderts, Koos. 2013. (ENG.). 32p. (J). (gr. -1). 12.95 *(978-1-935954-24-8(5),* 9781935954248) Lemniscaat USA.

—The Man in the Clouds. Meinderts, Koos. 2012. (ENG.). 38p. (J). (gr. 1). 16.95 *(978-1-935954-13-2(X),* 9781935954132) Lemniscaat USA.

Fife, Jay. Ten Dollar Words for Kids. Kennedy, Kevin. 2013. 26p. pap. 11.95 *(978-1-61244-244-0(7))* Halo Publishing International.

Fifield, Kim. Torment at Play. Dunkley, Cheryl. Drummond-Hay, Fran, ed. 2011. (ENG.). 106p. pap. 14.95 *(978-1-4563-9149-2(6))* CreateSpace Independent Publishing Platform.

Figg, Non, et al. Big Book of Things to Draw. Allman, Howard, photos by. Watt, Fiona et al. 2007. (Art Ideas Drawing School Ser.). 96p. (J). (gr. 4-7). pap. 15.99 *(978-0-7945-1328-3(X),* Usborne) EDC Publishing.

—Dibujos Paso A Paso Dinosaurios. Watt, Fiona. 2007. (Titles in Spanish Ser.). 31p. (J). 8.99 *(978-0-7460-8373-4(4),* Usborne) EDC Publishing.

Figg, Non. How to Draw Animals. Pratt, Leonie & Stowell, Louie. 2006. (Usborne Activities Ser.). 32p. (J). (gr. 1-4). pap. 8.99 *(978-0-7945-1241-5(0),* Usborne) EDC Publishing.

Figg, Non, et al. How to Draw Dinosaurs. Watt, Fiona. 2005. (Usborne Activities Ser.). 31p. (J). (gr. -1-3). pap. 8.95 *(978-0-7945-1056-5(6),* Usborne) EDC Publishing.

Figg, Non. Things to Make for Mother's Day. Gilpin, Rebecca. 2004. (ENG.). 32p. (J). pap. 8.95 *(978-0-7945-0693-3(3),* Usborne) EDC Publishing.

Figg, Non, jt. illus. see Miller, Antonia.

Figg, Non Et Al. Making Cards. Watt, Fiona. 2007. 64p. (J). pap. 14.99 *(978-0-7945-1356-6(5),* Usborne) EDC Publishing.

Fil, et al. Le Petit Frere du Chaperon Rouge. Tremblay, Marc. 2004. (était une Fois Ser.). (FRE.). 24p. (J). (gr. -1). pap. *(978-2-89021-698-3(5))* Diffusion du livre Mirabel (DLM).

Fil & Julie. La Loi du Talion. Charest, Jocelyne. 2004. (FRE.). 145p. (YA). 8.95 *(978-2-922565-85-0(8))* Editions de la Paix CAN. Dist: World of Reading, Ltd.

Fil and Julie Staff. A Duck in New York City. Kaldor, Connie. 2005. (ENG.). 36p. (J). (gr. -1-2). 16.95 *(978-2-923163-02-4(8))* La Montagne Secrete CAN. Dist: Independent Pubs. Group.

—A Poodle in Paris. Kaldor, Connie. 2006. (ENG.). 36p. (J). (gr. -1-2). 16.95 *(978-2-923163-12-3(5))* La Montagne Secrete CAN. Dist: Independent Pubs. Group.

Fil et, Julie. Graindsel et Bretel. Meunier, Sylvain & Lapierre, Steeve. 2004. (était une Fois Ser.). (FRE.). 24p. (J). (gr. -1). pap. *(978-2-89021-699-0(3))* Diffusion du livre Mirabel (DLM).

Filgate, Leonard. A Good Day for Abbey. Yost-Filgate, Susan. 2009. (ENG.). 12p. (J). (gr. -1-12). 6.99 *(978-1-934960-45-5(4),* Raven Tree Pr.,Csi) Continental Sales, Inc.

—Jesse's Book of Colors. Yost-Filgate, Susan. 2009. (ENG.). 22p. (J). (gr. -1-12). bds. 7.95 *(978-1-934960-43-1(6),* Raven Tree Pr.,Csi) Continental Sales, Inc.

—Rip Squeak & Friends: the Adventure. Yost-Filgate, Susan. 2005. (Rip Squeak Ser.). (ENG.). 32p. (J). (gr. -1-3). 16.95 *(978-0-9672422-9-3(0),* Raven Tree Pr.,Csi) Continental Sales, Inc.

—Rip Squeak & His Friends. Yost-Filgate, Susan. 2009. (ENG.). 32p. (J). (gr. -1-3). 16.95 *(978-1-934960-40-0(3),* Raven Tree Pr.,Csi) Continental Sales, Inc.

—Rip Squeak & His Friends. Yost-Filgate, Susan. 2004. 32p. (J). 16.95 *(978-1-59384-058-7(6))* Parklane Publishing.

—Rip Squeak's A to Z Book. Yost-Filgate, Susan. 2009. (ENG.). 22p. (J). (gr. -1-12). 7.95 *(978-1-934960-44-8(6),* Raven Tree Pr.,Csi) Continental Sales, Inc.

—The Treasure: A Rip Squeak Book. Yost-Filgate, Susan. 2005. (Rip Squeak Ser.). (ENG.). 32p. (J). (gr. -1-3). 16.95 *(978-0-9747825-1-5(3),* Raven Tree Pr.,Csi) Continental Sales, Inc.

Filice, Annette. My Yosemite: A Guide for Young Adventurers. Graf, Mike. 2012. (J). *(978-1-59714-170-3(4))* Heyday.

—My Yosemite: A Guide for Young Adventurers. Graf, Mike. 2012. (ENG.). 176p. (gr. 4). pap. 12.95 *(978-1-930238-30-5(4))* Yosemite Assn.

Filipak, Christine & Vargo, Joseph. Madame Endora's Fortune Cards. 2003. mass mkt. 17.99 *(978-0-9675756-3-6(X))* Monolith Graphics.

Filipina, Monika. I Say Shehechiyanu. Rocklin, Joanne. 2015. (J). (ENG.). 24p. (gr. -1-2). lib. bdg. 16.95 *(978-1-4677-3467-7(5));* *(978-1-4677-6203-8(2))* Lerner Publishing Group. (Kar-Ben Publishing).

Filippucci, Laura Francesca. The Cemetery Keepers of Gettysburg. High, Linda Oatman. 2007. (ENG.). 32p. (J). (gr. 1-6). 16.95 *(978-0-8027-8094-2(6))* Walker & Co.

—The Hidden Bestiary of Marvelous, Mysterious, & (Maybe Even) Magical Creatures. Young, Judy. 2009. (ENG.). 32p. (J). (gr. 1-4). 16.95 *(978-1-58536-433-6(9),* 202163) Sleeping Bear Pr.

Filipski, J. W., jt. photos by see Schneider, Hank.

Fillion, Susan. Pizza in Pienza. Fillion, Susan. 2013. (ENG & ITA.). 32p. (J). 17.95 *(978-1-56792-459-6(X))* Godine, David R. Pub.

Finch, David. Breakout, Vol. 1. 2006. (ENG.). 160p. (J). (gr. 4-17). pap. 14.99 *(978-0-7851-1479-6(3))* Marvel Worldwide, Inc.

—Disassembled. 2006. (ENG.). 176p. (YA). (gr. 8-17). pap. 15.99 *(978-0-7851-1482-6(3))* Marvel Worldwide, Inc.

—New Mutants. Youngquist, Jeff, ed. 2006. (ENG.). 144p. (YA). (gr. 8-17). pap. 12.99 *(978-0-7851-1161-0(1))* Marvel Worldwide, Inc.

Finch, David & Thibert, Art. Blockbuster, 7 vols., Vol. 7. Bendis, Brian Michael. 2006. (ENG.). 144p. (YA). (gr. 8-17). pap. 12.99 *(978-0-7851-1219-8(7))* Marvel Worldwide, Inc.

Finch, David, jt. illus. see Kubert, Adam.

Finch, Keith Andrew. Rudolph the Red-Nosed Reindeer Pop-Up Book. Marsoli, Lisa Ann. 2014. (ENG.). 12p. (J). (gr. -1). 19.95 *(978-1-62686-197-8(8),* Silver Dolphin Bks.) Baker & Taylor Publishing Group.

Fincher, Kathryn Andrews. Charlene's Grumpy Day: A Scoozie Tale about Patience. Carlson, Melody. Date not set. 32p. (J). 9.99 *(978-0-7369-0734-7(3))* Harvest Hse. Pubs.

—Grover Tells a Whopper: A Scoozie Tale about Honesty. Carlson, Melody. Date not set. 32p. (J). 9.99 *(978-0-7369-0733-0(5))* Harvest Hse. Pubs.

Fincher, Kathy. Baby's First Christmas. 2006. 8p. (gr. -1-k). bds. 7.95 *(978-0-88271-705-0(7))* Regina Pr., Malhame & Co.

—A Catholic's Baby's First Prayer Book. 2006. 16p. (gr. -1-k). bds. 9.95 *(978-0-88271-706-7(5))* Regina Pr., Malhame & Co.

—My Child: Boy. Waller, Steven H. 2008. 37p. (J). 11.95 *(978-0-88271-172-0(5))* Regina Pr., Malhame & Co.

—My Child: Girl. Waller, Steven H. 2009. 37p. (J). 11.95 *(978-0-88271-173-7(3))* Regina Pr., Malhame & Co.

Findley, Kelly. Puckster Goes to the Olympics. Nicholson, Lorna Schultz. 2013. (ENG.). 24p. (gr. -1-3). pap. 6.99 *(978-1-77049-594-4(0))* Tundra Bks. CAN. Dist: Random Hse., Inc.

—Puckster's First Hockey Tournament. Nicholson, Lorna Schultz. 2012. (ENG.). 24p. (gr. -1-3). pap. 6.99 *(978-1-77049-457-2(X))* Tundra Bks. CAN. Dist: Random Hse., Inc.

—Puckster's First Hockey Tryout. Nicholson, Lorna Schultz. 2013. (ENG.). 24p. (gr. -1-3). pap. 6.99 *(978-1-77049-596-8(7))* Tundra Bks. CAN. Dist: Random Hse., Inc.

Fine, Aron. Milly & Her Kittens. Wilson, Barbara. 2012. (J). 9.00 *(978-1-56778-542-5(5))* Wilson Language Training.

—Mrs. Hen & Her Six Chicks. Wilson, Barbara. 2012. (J). 9.00 *(978-1-56778-543-2(3))* Wilson Language Training.

Fine, Howard. All Aboard the Dinotrain. Lund, Deb. (ENG.). (J). (gr. -1 — 1). 2011. 30p. bds. 7.99 *(978-0-547-55415-0(X));* 2009. 40p. pap. 6.99 *(978-0-547-24825-7(3))* Houghton Mifflin Harcourt Publishing Co.

—All Aboard the Dinotrain. Lund, Deb. 2006. (ENG.). 40p. (J). (gr. -1-3). 16.99 *(978-0-15-205237-9(2))* Houghton Mifflin Harcourt Publishing Co.

—Dinosailors. Lund, Deb. (ENG.). (J). (gr. -1 — 1). 2011. 30p. bds. 7.99 *(978-0-547-55417-4(6));* 2008. 36p. pap. 6.00 *(978-0-15-206124-1(X))* Houghton Mifflin Harcourt Publishing Co.

—Dinosoaring. Lund, Deb. 2012. (ENG.). 40p. (J). (gr. -1-3). 16.99 *(978-0-15-206016-9(2))* Houghton Mifflin Harcourt Publishing Co.

—Hampire! Bardhan-Quallen, Sudipta. 2011. (ENG.). 32p. (J). (gr. -1-3). 16.99 *(978-0-06-114239-0(5))* HarperCollins Pubs.

—Piggie Pie!, 1 vol. Palatini, Margie. 2008. (Read along Book & CD Ser.). (ENG.). 32p. (J). (gr. -1-3). 10.99 *(978-0-547-18178-3(7))* Houghton Mifflin Harcourt Publishing Co.

—Snoring Beauty. Hale, Bruce. 2008. (ENG.). 44p. (J). (gr. -1-3). 16.99 *(978-0-15-216314-3(X))* Houghton Mifflin Harcourt Publishing Co.

Fine, Steve. TWIGS & the Bully. Charlton, Dennis. 2011. (ENG.). 26p. pap. 9.99 *(978-1-4635-8777-2(5))* CreateSpace Independent Publishing Platform.

Finger, Matthew. Superhero Swamp: A Slimy, Smelly Way to Find the Superhero God Placed in You!, 1 vol. Trent, John. 2007. (ENG.). 64p. (gr. -1-3). 14.99 *(978-1-59145-487-8(5))* Nelson, Thomas Inc.

Fink, Larry, photos by. Larry Fink. Dahlberg, Laurie. Hemming, Denny, ed. rev. ed. 2005. (55s Ser.). (ENG., 128p. (gr. 8-17). 27.95 *(978-0-7148-4022-2(X))* Phaidon Pr. Ltd. GBR. Dist: Hachette Bk. Group.

Fink, Sam. The Declaration of Independence: The Words That Made America. Fink, Sam. 2007. 160p. (YA). (gr. 7). 19.65 *(978-0-7569-8187-7(5))* Perfection Learning Corp.

Finkelstein, Jeff. Mazel Tov! It's a Boy: Mazel Tov! It's a Girl. Finkelstein, Jeff, photos by. Korngold, Jamie S. 2015. (J). (ENG.). 32p. (gr. -1-1). lib. bdg. 17.95 *(978-1-4677-1957-5(9)); (978-1-4677-6206-9(7))* Lerner Publishing Group. (Kar-Ben Publishing).

Finkelstein, Jeff, photos by. Seder in the Desert. Korngold, Jamie. 2014. (Passover Ser.). (ENG., 32p. (J). (gr. -1-2). 17.95 *(978-0-7613-7501-2(5));* 7.95 *(978-0-7613-7502-9(3))* Lerner Publishing Group. (Kar-Ben Publishing).

Finlay, Lizzie. Buri & the Marrow. Barkow, Henriette. 2004. (ENG & FRE.). 24p. (J). pap. *(978-1-85269-583-5(8))* Mantra Lingua.

—Buri & the Marrow. 2004. 24p. (J). pap. *(978-1-85269-587-3(0));* pap. *(978-1-85269-590-3(0));* (ENG & TUR.). pap. *(978-1-85269-591-0(9))* Mantra Lingua.

—Buri & the Marrow. Barkow, Henriette. 2004. (ENG & ARA.). 24p. (J). pap. *(978-1-85269-579-8(X));* pap. *(978-1-85269-581-1(1));* pap. *(978-1-85269-582-8(X));* pap. *(978-1-85269-584-2(6));* pap. *(978-1-85269-585-9(4));* pap. *(978-1-85269-588-0(9));* pap. *(978-1-85269-589-7(7));* pap. *(978-1-85269-592-7(7))* Mantra Lingua.

—Buri & the Marrow: Buri Dhe Kungulli. Barkow, Henriette. 2004. (ENG & ALB.). 24p. (J). pap. *(978-1-85269-578-1(1))* Mantra Lingua.

—Pony-Crazed Princess: Princess Ellie's Mystery. Kimpton, Diana. 3rd rev. ed. 2006. (ENG.). 96p. (gr. 1-4). pap. 3.99 *(978-0-7868-4872-0(3))* Hyperion Pr.

—Pony-Crazed Princess Super Special: Princess Ellie's Summer Vacation. Kimpton, Diana. 2007. (ENG.). 144p. (gr. 1-4). pap. 4.99 *(978-1-4231-0616-6(4))* Hyperion Pr.

—Princess Ellie Solves a Mystery. Kimpton, Diana. 8th rev. ed. 2007. (ENG.). 96p. (gr. 1-4). pap. 3.99 *(978-1-4231-0901-3(5))* Hyperion Pr.

—Princess Ellie to the Rescue. Kimpton, Diana. 2006. (ENG.). 96p. (gr. 1-4). pap. 3.99 *(978-0-7868-4870-6(7))* Hyperion Pr.

—Princess Ellie's Royal Jamboree No. 11. Kimpton, Diana. 11th ed. 2008. (ENG.). 96p. (gr. 1-4). pap. 3.99 *(978-1-4231-1531-1(7))* Hyperion Pr.

—Princess Ellie's Secret No. 2. Kimpton, Diana. 2nd rev. ed. 2006. (ENG.). 96p. (gr. 1-4). pap. 3.99 *(978-0-7868-4871-3(5))* Hyperion Pr.

—Princess Ellie's Snowy Ride. Kimpton, Diana. 2007. (Pony-Crazed Princess Ser.). 90p. (J). 11.65 *(978-0-7569-8352-9(5))* Perfection Learning Corp.

—Princess Ellie's Snowy Ride No. 9. Kimpton, Diana. 9th rev. ed. 2007. (ENG.). 96p. (gr. 1-4). pap. 3.99 *(978-1-4231-0902-0(3))* Hyperion Pr.

—Princess Ellie's Treasure Hunt No. 10. Kimpton, Diana. 10th ed. 2008. (ENG.). 96p. (gr. -1-3). pap. 3.99 *(978-1-4231-1414-7(0))* Hyperion Pr.

—Sam's First Day. Mills, David. 2004. 24p. (J). *(978-1-85269-630-6(3)); (978-1-85269-631-3(1));* (PER & ENG.). *(978-1-85269-634-4(6)); (978-1-85269-635-1(4)); (978-1-85269-636-8(2)); (978-1-85269-637-5(0)); (978-1-85269-639-9(7)); (978-1-85269-640-5(0)); (978-1-85269-642-9(7)); (978-1-85269-643-6(5)); (978-1-85269-645-0(1)); (978-1-85269-646-7(X)); (978-1-85269-702-0(4));* (TUR & ENG.). *(978-1-85269-644-3(3)); (978-1-84444-166-2(0))* Mantra Lingua.

—A Surprise for Princess Ellie. Kimpton, Diana. 6th rev. ed. 2006. (ENG.). 96p. (gr. 1-4). pap. 3.99 *(978-0-7868-4875-1(8))* Hyperion Pr.

Finlayson, Luke. The Clan of the Scorpion. Jones, Gareth P. 2013. (Ninja Meerkats Ser.: 1). (ENG.). 128p. (J). (gr. 2-4). pap. 5.99 *(978-1-250-01664-5(9))* Square Fish.

—The Eye of the Monkey. Jones, Gareth P. 2013. (Ninja Meerkats Ser.: 2). (ENG.). 128p. (J). (gr. 2-4). pap. 5.99 *(978-1-250-01665-2(7))* Square Fish.

—Ninja Meerkats (#3): Escape from Ice Mountain. Jones, Gareth P. 2013. (Ninja Meerkats Ser.: 3). (ENG.). 128p. (J). (gr. 2-4). pap. 5.99 *(978-1-250-02931-7(7))* Square Fish.

—Ninja Meerkats (#4): Hollywood Showdown. Jones, Gareth P. 2013. (Ninja Meerkats Ser.: 4). (ENG.). 128p. (J). (gr. 2-4). pap. 5.99 *(978-1-250-02932-4(5))* Square Fish.

—Ninja Meerkats (#5): the Tomb of Doom. Jones, Gareth P. 2013. (Ninja Meerkats Ser.: 5). (ENG.). 128p. (J). (gr. 2-4). pap. 5.99 *(978-1-250-03402-1(7))* Square Fish.

—Ninja Meerkats (#6): Big City Bust-Up. Jones, Gareth P. 2013. (Ninja Meerkats Ser.: 6). (ENG.). 128p. (J). (gr. 2-4). pap. 5.99 *(978-1-250-03403-8(5))* Square Fish.

—Ninja Meerkats (#7) the Ultimate Dragon Warrior. Jones, Gareth P. 2014. (Ninja Meerkats Ser.: 7). (ENG.). 128p. (J). (gr. 2-4). pap. 5.99 *(978-1-250-04665-9(3))* Square Fish.

—Ninja Meerkats (#8) Outback Attack. Jones, Gareth P. 2014. (Ninja Meerkats Ser.: 8). (ENG.). 128p. (J). (gr. 2-4). pap. 5.99 *(978-1-250-04667-3(X))* Square Fish.

Finlayson, Luke & Mazzara, Mauro. Dirty Rotten Pirates. Breed, Simon & Butterfield, Moira. 2014. (ENG.). 64p. (J). pap. 8.99 *(978-1-78325-048-6(8),* TickTock Books) Octopus Publishing Group GBR. Dist: Hachette Bk. Group.

Finley, Shawn, jt. illus. see Dean Kleven Studios.

Finley, Thomas Murray. Danger Dolphin. Kernan, Martin James. 2012. 28p. pap. 14.95 *(978-1-4675-2428-5(X))* Independent Pub.

—Entertaining Elephant. Kernan, Martin James. 2012. (ENG.). 28p. (J). pap. 9.95 *(978-1-4675-4149-7(4))* Independent Pub.

Finn, Ann-Marie. Start of the Ocean. Worthington, Michelle. 2013. 32p. pap. *(978-0-9874160-1-8(4))* Wybble Publishing.

Finn, Ann-Marie. Captain Kieron. Finn, Ann-Marie. 2013. 32p. pap. *(978-0-9874160-3-2(0))* Wybble Publishing.

Finn, Christine. Little Mozarts Go to Hollywood, Pop Book 1 And 2: 10 Favorites from TV, Movies & Radio. Barden, Christine H. et al. 2008. (Music for Little Mozarts Ser.: Bk 1-2). (ENG.). 24p. (J). pap. 8.99 *(978-0-7390-5013-2(3))* Alfred Publishing Co., Inc.

Finn, Jenny. Tales from Hallowed Hollow: Karma. Watt, Marg. 2012. 34p. (YA). pap. *(978-0-9872715-8-7(X))* Moonrra Pubns.

Finn, Rebecca. Airport. Sterling Children's, Sterling. 2015. (Busy Bks.). (ENG.). 10p. (J). (— 1). bds. 8.95 ***(978-1-4549-1732-8(6))*** Sterling Publishing Co., Inc.

Finn, Rebecca. Bedtime Lullabies: Fall Asleep to Your Free Cd. Baxter, Nicola. 2014. (ENG.). 12p. (J). (gr. -1-12). bds. 14.99 *(978-1-86147-360-8(5),* Armadillo) Anness Publishing GBR. Dist: National Bk. Network.

Finn, Rebecca. Builders. Sterling Children's, Sterling. 2015. (Busy Bks.). (ENG.). 10p. (J). (— 1). bds. 8.95 ***(978-1-4549-1733-5(4))*** Sterling Publishing Co., Inc.

Finn, Rebecca. Christmas Lullabies for Children. Baxter, Nicola, ed. 2014. (ENG.). 12p. (J). (gr. k-5). 14.99 *(978-1-84322-931-5(5),* Armadillo) Anness Publishing GBR. Dist: National Bk. Network.

—First Sticker Book Princesses. Greenwall, Jessica. ed. 2013. (First Sticker Bks). 16p. (J). pap. 6.99 *(978-0-7945-3357-1(4),* Usborne) EDC Publishing.

Finn, Rebecca. Garage. Sterling Publishing Co., Inc. Staff. 2015. (Busy Bks.). (ENG.). 10p. (J). (— 1). bds. 8.95 ***(978-1-4549-1734-2(2))*** Sterling Publishing Co., Inc.

Finn, Rebecca. Jolly Snowman. 2005. (Cuddly Cuffstm Ser.). 6p. (J). (gr. -1-13). 6.95 *(978-1-58925-754-2(5))* Tiger Tales.

—Little Bunny. (Cuddly Cuffstm Ser.). 6p. (J). 6.95 *(978-1-58925-767-2(7))* Tiger Tales.

—Little Ducky. (Cuddly Cuffstm Ser.). 6p. (J). 6.95 *(978-1-58925-766-5(9))* Tiger Tales.

—Little Kitty. (Cuddly Cuffstm Ser.). 6p. (J). 6.95 *(978-1-58925-764-1(2))* Tiger Tales.

—Little Puppy. (Cuddly Cuffstm Ser.). 6p. (J). 6.95 *(978-1-58925-765-8(0))* Tiger Tales.

—My Fairy Glade. Prasadam, Smriti. 2008. (Peep Through Play Bks.). (ENG.). 12p. (J). (gr. k-k). bds. 7.95 *(978-0-7475-8809-2(0))* Bloomsbury Publishing Plc GBR. Dist: Independent Pubs. Group.

—Ponies (First Sticker Book) Patchett, Fiona. ed. 2011. (First Sticker Book Ser.). 24p. (J). pap. 6.99 *(978-0-7945-2921-5(6),* Usborne) EDC Publishing.

Finn, Rebecca. Railway. Sterling Children's, Sterling. 2015. (Busy Bks.). (ENG.). 10p. (J). (— 1). bds. 8.95 ***(978-1-4549-1735-9(0))*** Sterling Publishing Co., Inc.

Finn, Rebecca. Santa's Day. 2005. (Cuddly Cuffstm Ser.). 6p. (J). (gr. -1-13). 6.95 *(978-1-58925-755-9(3))* Tiger Tales.

—Sing-Along Songs for Children: Join in with Your Free CD. Baxter, Nicola. 2014. (ENG.). 12p. (J). (gr. -1-k). bds. 14.99 *(978-1-84322-892-9(0),* Armadillo) Anness Publishing GBR. Dist: National Bk. Network.

—Toys (Cuddly Cuffs W/Hang Tag) Field, Elaine. (Cuddly Cuffs Ser.). 12p. (J). tchr. ed. 5.95 *(978-1-58925-709-2(X))* Tiger Tales.

Finn, Rebecca, jt. illus. see Richards, Lucy.

Finnell-Acosta, B. C. The Search for the Missing Ball: Norman G. Bear. Pwob. 2010. 64p. pap. 25.49 *(978-1-4520-3952-7(6))* AuthorHouse.

Finnell, Cyndy, jt. illus. see Stephens, Sherry.

Finney, Kathryn. Little Louie. 2014. (ENG.). 32p. (J). (gr. -1-k). 16.95 *(978-1-62914-615-7(3),* Sky Pony Pr.) Skyhorse Publishing Co., Inc.

Finney, Kathryn Kunz. Rising above the Storm Clouds: What It's Like to Forgive. Enright, Robert D. 2004. 32p. (J). 14.95 *(978-1-59147-075-5(7));* pap. 9.95 *(978-1-59147-076-2(5))* American Psychological Assn. (Magination Pr.).

Finney, Pat. Sam Houston: I Am Houston. Finney, Pat. Wade, Mary Dodson. 2009. (ENG.). 64p. (J). (gr. 4-7). 16.95 *(978-1-933979-37-3(2),* 69142d3c-afed-48b8-9ae8-3c9533f77117) Bright Sky Pr.

—Stephen F. Austin: The Son Becomes Father of Texas. Finney, Pat. Wade, Mary Dodson. 2009. (ENG.). 64p. (J). (gr. 4-7). 16.95 *(978-1-933979-45-8(3),* b2874897-f07d-47b8-83fa-a611da26c6bb) Bright Sky Pr.

Finney, Simone. My Daddy Is A Deputy Sheriff. Beckler, Bruce. l.t. ed. 2004. 14p. (J). per. 5.59 *(978-0-9745210-4-6(3))* Myers Publishing Co.

—My Daddy Is a Police Officer: My Daddy Wears a Star. Beckler, Bruce. l.t. ed. 2004. 14p. (J). per. 5.59 *(978-0-9745210-3-9(5))* Myers Publishing Co.

—My Daddy Is A Police Officer: Wears A Badge, 8 bks. Beckler, Bruce. l.t. ed. 2004. 14p. (J). per. 5.59 *(978-0-9745210-2-2(7))* Myers Publishing Co.

—My Mommy Is A Deputy Sheriff. Beckler, Bruce. l.t. ed. 2004. 14p. (J). 5.59 *(978-0-9745210-7-7(8))* Myers Publishing Co.

—My Mommy Is A Police Officer: My Mommy Wears A Badge. Beckler, Bruce. l.t. ed. 2004. 14p. (J). per. 5.59 *(978-0-9745210-5-3(1))* Myers Publishing Co.

—My Mommy Is A Police Officer: My Mommy Wears A Star. Beckler, Bruce. l.t. ed. 2004. 14p. (J). 5.59 *(978-0-9745210-6-0(X))* Myers Publishing Co.

Fino, Roberto. Awake in the Dark! McMillan, Dawn. 2009. (Rigby PM Stars Bridge Bks.). (ENG.). 24p. (gr. 2-3). pap. 8.70 *(978-1-4190-5527-0(5))* Rigby Education.

Fiore, Peter M. Henry David's House. Schnur, Steven. 2007. (ENG.). 32p. (J). (gr. k-3). pap. 7.95 *(978-0-88106-117-8(4))* Charlesbridge Publishing, Inc.

—When Washington Crossed the Delaware: A Wintertime Story for Young Patriots. Cheney, Lynne. 2012. (ENG.). 40p. (J). (gr. k-4). 7.99 *(978-1-4424-4423-2(1),* Simon & Schuster/Paula Wiseman Bks.) Simon & Schuster/Paula Wiseman Bks.

Fiore, Peter M. Touching the Sky: The Flying Adventures of Wilbur & Orville Wright. Fiore, Peter M. Borden, Louise & Marx, Trish. 2003. (ENG.). 64p. (J). (gr. k-3). 19.99 *(978-0-689-84876-6(5),* McElderry, Margaret K. Bks.) McElderry, Margaret K. Bks.

Fiore, Rob. First Fairytales. Zakarin, Debra Mostow. 2010. 10p. 9.95 *(978-1-60747-746-4(7),* Pickwick Pr.) Phoenix Bks., Inc.

Fiorentino, Al. Betsy Ross: Creator of Our Flag. Weil, Ann. 2014. (History's All-Stars Ser.). (ENG.). 208p. (J). (gr. 3-7). pap. 6.99 *(978-1-4814-0706-9(6),* Simon & Schuster/Paula Wiseman Bks.) Simon & Schuster/Paula Wiseman Bks.

Fiorentino, Fabrizio, et al. Master Class, Vol. 5. Bedard, Tony. 2003. (Mystic Ser.: Vol. 5). 160p. (YA). (gr. 7-18). pap. 9.95 *(978-1-931484-79-4(1))* CrossGeneration Comics, Inc.

—Out All Night, Vol. 4. Bedard, Tony. 2003. (Mystic Ser.: Vol. 4). 160p. (YA). (gr. 7-18). pap. 7.95 *(978-1-931484-46-6(5))* CrossGeneration Comics, Inc.

Fiorin, Fabiano. Big Book of Dinosaurs Internet Referenced. Frith, Alex. 2010. (Big Bks.). 16p. (J). bds. 13.99 *(978-0-7945-2770-9(1),* Usborne) EDC Publishing.

—Hide-and-Seek Dragons. Watt, Fiona. 2007. (Touchy-Feely Flap Bks). 10p. (J). (gr. -1-k). bds. 16.99 *(978-0-7945-1590-4(8),* Usborne) EDC Publishing.

—No Wobbly Teeth, 1 vol. Rooney, Anne. 2013. (Start Reading Ser.). (ENG.). 24p. (gr. k-1). pap. 6.99 *(978-1-4765-4125-9(6))* Capstone Pr., Inc.

—Noisy Books. Harrison, Paul. 2009. (Get Ready (Windmill Books) Ser.). 32p. (J). (gr. k-2). lib. bdg. 22.60 *(978-1-60754-258-2(7))* Windmill Bks.

—Stories of Cowboys. Punter, Russell. 2008. (Usborne Young Reading: Series One Ser.). 48p. (J). 8.99 *(978-0-7945-1822-6(2),* Usborne) EDC Publishing.

—The Usborne Big Book of Big Monsters. Stowell, Louie. 2013. (Usborne Big Book Of... Ser.). (ENG.). 16p. (J). (gr. -1-3). 14.99 *(978-0-7945-3025-9(7),* Usborne) EDC Publishing.

—Wanted: Prince Charming. Benjamin, A. H. 2014. (ENG.). 32p. (J). *(978-0-7787-1313-5(X))* Crabtree Publishing Co.

Fiorini, Nancy. La Nube Traicionera. Walsh, Maria Elena. 2003. (SPA.). 88p. (YA). (gr. 5-8). 14.95 *(978-950-511-616-4(0))* Alfaguara S.A. de Ediciones ARG. Dist: Santillana USA Publishing Co., Inc.

Firebrace, Francis. More Stories from the Billabong. Marshall, James Vance. 2013. 80p. (J). *(978-1-921720-48-2(4))* Walker Bks. Australia Pty, Ltd.

—Stories from the Billabong. Marshall, James Vance. 2010. (ENG.). 64p. (J). (gr. k-3). pap. 9.99 *(978-1-84780-124-1(2),* Frances Lincoln) Quarto Publishing Group UK GBR. Dist: Hachette Bk. Group.

Firehammer, Karla. The Flea's Sneeze. Downey, Lynn. 2005. (ENG.). 32p. (J). (gr. -1-1). reprint ed. pap. 8.99 *(978-0-8050-7756-8(1))* Square Fish.

Firenze, Inklink. A Day in the Life of a Knight. Hopkins, Andrea. 2007. (Day in the Life Ser.: Vol. 4). 32p. (J). (gr. 4-7). lib. bdg. 25.25 *(978-1-4042-3851-0(4))* Rosen Publishing Group, Inc., The.

—A Day in the Life of a Native American. Helbrough, Emma. 2007. (Day in the Life Ser.: Vol. 4). 32p. (J). (gr. 3-7). lib. bdg. 25.25 *(978-1-4042-3854-1(9))* Rosen Publishing Group, Inc., The.

—A Day in the Life of a Pirate. Helbrough, Emma. 2007. (Day in the Life Ser.: Vol. 4). 32p. (J). (gr. 3-7). lib. bdg. 25.25 *(978-1-4042-3853-4(0))* Rosen Publishing Group, Inc., The.

—Medieval world - internet Linked. Bingham, Jane. rev. ed. 2004. 96p. (J). pap. 14.95 *(978-0-7945-0815-9(4),* Usborne) EDC Publishing.

—The Usborne Internet-Linked Prehistoric World. Chandler, Fiona et al. 2005. 96p. (J). pap. *(978-0-439-78504-4(9))* Scholastic, Inc.

Firenze, Inklink, jt. illus. see Galante, Studio.

Firmin, Hannah. Prayers for Your Confirmation. Rock, Lois. 2007. (ENG.). 48p. (J). (gr. 4). 9.95 *(978-0-7459-6045-6(6))* Lion Hudson PLC GBR. Dist: Independent Pubs. Group.

Firmin, Peter. Then & Now. Amery, Heather. 2008. (Then & Now Ser.). 24p. (J). (gr. -1-3). pap. 4.99 *(978-0-7945-2211-7(4),* Usborne) EDC Publishing.

Firos, Daphne. Square Bear Meets Round Hound: A Fairytale of Shapes. Penn, M. W. 2012. (ENG.). 38p. (J). pap. 11.95 *(978-0-9840425-8-6(X))* MathWord Pr., LLC.

—A Tangram ABC: Shaping the Alphabet from an Ancient Chinese Puzzle. McKay, Chelsea. 2013. 60p. (J). pap. 13.95 *(978-1-939431-04-2(2))* MathWord Pr., LLC.

—2 Lines. Penn, M. W. 2011. (ENG.). 32p. (J). pap. 11.95 *(978-0-9840425-0-0(4))* MathWord Pr., LLC.

Firpo, Ethan. Custer Brown in Marshmallow Madness. Costley, Kirk. 2012. 34p. pap. 15.95 *(978-1-893075-85-6(0))* Spirit Pr., LLC.

Firsova, Yuliya. Why Mommy Is a Democrat. Zilber, Jeremy. 2005. 28p. (J). 8.00 *(978-0-9786688-0-8(4))* Zilber, Jeremy.

First Choice Productions Staff, photos by. Almost There: A Series of Monologues. Darnell, Yolanda. 2003. 51p. (YA). (gr. 8-18). pap. 12.99 *(978-1-884429-13-2(0))* Papillon Pr.

Firth, Barbara. Bears in the Forest: Read & Wonder. Wallace, Karen. 2009. (Read & Wonder Ser.). (ENG.). 32p. (J). (gr. -1-3). pap. 6.99 *(978-0-7636-4522-9(2))* Candlewick Pr.

—Can't You Sleep, Little Bear? Waddell, Martin. 2011. (Candlewick Storybook Audio Ser.). (ENG.). 32p. (J). (gr. k-k). 8.99 *(978-0-7636-5114-5(1))* Candlewick Pr.

—Can't You Sleep, Little Bear?: Candlewick Storybook Animations. Waddell, Martin. 2008. (Candlewick Storybook Animation Ser.). (ENG.). 32p. (J). (gr. k-k). 14.99 *(978-0-7636-3537-4(5))* Candlewick Pr.

Firth, Barbara, jt. illus. see Parkins, David.

Firtl, Mary Meehan. The Broken Doll. Zuber, Diane C. 2006. (ENG.). 32p. (J). (gr. -1-3). incl. audio compact disk *(978-0-9785551-1-5(2))* Zuber Publishing.

Fischer, Chuck. Great American Houses & Gardens: A Pop-up Book. Fischer, Chuck. 2005. 12p. (J). (gr. 4-8). reprint ed. 40.00 *(978-0-7567-9193-3(6))* DIANE Publishing Co.

Fischer, Jeff. Johnny Appleseed. 2006. (Famous Fables Ser.). (J). 6.99 *(978-1-59939-028-4(0))* Cornerstone Pr.

Fischer, Sandi. Where the Leprechauns Hide. Hoyt, Charlene. 2007. (ENG.). 40p. per. 12.99 *(978-0-9792258-9-5(2))* Bezalel Bks.

Fischer, Scott M. Animals Anonymous. Michelson, Richard. 2008. (ENG.). 96p. (YA). (gr. 9-18). 14.99 *(978-1-4169-1424-2(2),* Simon & Schuster Bks. For Young Readers) Simon & Schuster Bks. For Young Readers.

—Lottie Paris & the Best Place. Johnson, Angela. 2013. (ENG.). 32p. (J). (gr. k-4). 16.99 *(978-0-689-87378-2(6),* Simon & Schuster Bks. For Young Readers) Simon & Schuster Bks. For Young Readers.

—Lottie Paris Lives Here. Johnson, Angela. 2011. (ENG.). 32p. (J). (gr. k-4). 16.99 *(978-0-689-87377-5(8),* Simon & Schuster Bks. For Young Readers) Simon & Schuster Bks. For Young Readers.

Fischer, Scott M., et al. Mars Trilogy: A Princess of Mars - The Gods of Mars - The Warlord of Mars. Burroughs, Edgar Rice. 2012. (ENG.). 704p. (YA). (gr. 7). pap. 12.99 *(978-1-4424-2387-9(0),* Simon & Schuster Bks. For Young Readers) Simon & Schuster Bks. For Young Readers.

Fischer, Scott M. Monsters on the March. Derek the Ghost Staff. (Scary School Ser.: 2). (ENG.). (J). (gr. 3-7). 2013. 272p. pap. 6.99 *(978-0-06-196097-0(7));* 2012. 256p. 15.99 *(978-0-06-196095-6(0))* HarperCollins Pubs.

—The Northern Frights. Derek the Ghost Staff. 2013. (Scary School Ser.: 3). (ENG.). 272p. (J). (gr. 3-7). 16.99 *(978-0-06-196098-7(5))* HarperCollins Pubs.

—Peter Pan in Scarlet. McCaughrean, Geraldine. (ENG.). 320p. (J). (gr. 4-9). 2008. pap. 6.99 *(978-1-4169-1809-7(4));* 2006. 19.99 *(978-1-4169-1808-0(6))* McElderry, Margaret K. Bks. (McElderry, Margaret K. Bks.).

—Scary School. Derek the Ghost Staff. (Scary School Ser.: 1). (ENG.). (J). (gr. 3-7). 2012. 272p. pap. 6.99 *(978-0-06-196094-9(2))*; 2011. 256p. 16.99 *(978-0-06-196092-5(6))* HarperCollins Pubs.

—Secrets of Dripping Fang: Attack of the Giant Octopus. Greenburg, Dan. 2009. (Secrets of Dripping Fang Ser.). (ENG.). 160p. 25.65 *(978-1-59961-537-0(1))* Spotlight.

—Secrets of Dripping Fang: Fall of the House of Mandible. Greenburg, Dan. 2009. (Secrets of Dripping Fang Ser.). (ENG.). 160p. 25.65 *(978-1-59961-535-6(5))* Spotlight.

—Secrets of Dripping Fang: Please Don't Eat the Children: Book 7: Book 7. Greenburg, Dan. 2009. (Secrets of Dripping Fang Ser.). (ENG.). 160p. 25.65 *(978-1-59961-538-7(X))* Spotlight.

—Secrets of Dripping Fang: The Onts. Greenburg, Dan. 2009. (Secrets of Dripping Fang Ser.). (ENG.). 144p. 25.65 *(978-1-59961-532-5(0))* Spotlight.

—Secrets of Dripping Fang: The Shluffmuffin Boy Is History. Greenburg, Dan. 2009. (Secrets of Dripping Fang Ser.). (ENG.). 176p. 25.65 *(978-1-59961-536-3(3))* Spotlight.

—Secrets of Dripping Fang: The Vampire's Curse: Book 3: Book 3. Greenburg, Dan. 2009. (Secrets of Dripping Fang Ser.). (ENG.). 144p. 25.65 *(978-1-59961-534-9(7))* Spotlight.

—Secrets of Dripping Fang: Treachery & Betrayal at Jolly Days. Greenburg, Dan. 2009. (Secrets of Dripping Fang Ser.). (ENG.). 144p. 25.65 *(978-1-59961-533-2(9))* Spotlight.

—Secrets of Dripping Fang: When Bad Snakes Attack Good Children. Greenburg, Dan. 2009. (Secrets of Dripping Fang Ser.). (ENG.). 144p. 25.65 *(978-1-59961-539-4(8))* Spotlight.

—Secrets of Dripping Fang, Book Eight: When Bad Snakes Attack Good Children. Greenburg, Dan. 2007. (Secrets of Dripping Fang Ser.: Bk. 8). (ENG.). 144p. (J). (gr. 2-5). 11.99 *(978-0-15-206056-5(1))* Houghton Mifflin Harcourt Publishing Co.

—Secrets of Dripping Fang, Book Four: Fall of the House of Mandible. Greenburg, Dan. 2006. (Secrets of Dripping Fang Ser.: Bk. 4). (ENG.). 160p. (J). (gr. 2-5). 11.95 *(978-0-15-205475-5(8))* Houghton Mifflin Harcourt Publishing Co.

—Secrets of Dripping Fang, Book One: The Onts. Greenburg, Dan. 2005. (Secrets of Dripping Fang Ser.: Bk. 1). (ENG.). 144p. (J). (gr. 2-5). 12.99 *(978-0-15-205457-1(X))* Houghton Mifflin Harcourt Publishing Co.

—Secrets of Dripping Fang, Book Seven: Please Don't Eat the Children. Greenburg, Dan. 2007. (Secrets of Dripping Fang Ser.: Bk. 7). (ENG.). 160p. (J). (gr. 2-5). 11.95 *(978-0-15-206047-3(2))* Houghton Mifflin Harcourt Publishing Co.

—Secrets of Dripping Fang, Book Six: Attack of the Giant Octopus. Greenburg, Dan. 2007. (Secrets of Dripping Fang Ser.: Bk. 6). (ENG.). 160p. (J). (gr. 2-5). 12.99 *(978-0-15-206041-1(3))* Houghton Mifflin Harcourt Publishing Co.

—Secrets of Dripping Fang, Book Two: Treachery & Betrayal at Jolly Days. Greenburg, Dan. 2006. (Secrets of Dripping Fang Ser.: Bk. 2). (ENG.). 144p. (J). (gr. 2-5). 12.99 *(978-0-15-205463-2(4))* Houghton Mifflin Harcourt Publishing Co.

—The Shluffmuffin Boy Is History, Bk. 5. Greenburg, Dan. 2006. (Secrets of Dripping Fang Ser.: Bk. 5). (ENG.). 176p. (J). (gr. 2-5). 12.99 *(978-0-15-206035-0(9))* Houghton Mifflin Harcourt Publishing Co.

—The Vampire's Curse, Bk. 3. Greenburg, Dan & DiTerlizzi, Angela. 2006. (Secrets of Dripping Fang Ser.: Bk. 3). (ENG.). 144p. (J). (gr. 2-5). 12.99 *(978-0-15-205469-4(3))* Houghton Mifflin Harcourt Publishing Co.

Fischer, Scott M. Jump! Fischer, Scott M. 2010. (ENG.). 32p. (J). (gr. -1-1). 14.99 *(978-1-4169-7884-8(4)*, Simon & Schuster Bks. For Young Readers) Simon & Schuster Bks. For Young Readers.

Fischer, Shan. The Back Alley Pupsters: Zac & Roxie for the Win. Layne, Casey & Jordan, Cedar. 2013. (ENG.). (J). (gr. -1-3). 14.95 *(978-1-62086-300-8(6))* Mascot Bks., Inc.

Fish, Lori Flying. One Shining Starfish. Fish, Lori Flying. 2010. 16p. pap. 9.95 *(978-1-936343-12-6(6))* Peppertree Pr., The.

Fish, Mister. Snerfy Cat Meets Prancy Finch. Fish, Mister, . 2007. 80p. (J). 14.99 *(978-0-9794753-0-6(9))* Children's Classic Book Pubs.

Fisher, Bonnie & Wolski, Bobbi. Charles Gordon Willingham. Whitlow, Crystal K. 2006. per. *(978-0-9777361-0-2(5))* Day3 Productions, Inc.

Fisher, Carolyn. Good Night, World. Perlman, Willa. 2011. (ENG.). 40p. (J). (gr. -1-k). 16.99 *(978-1-4424-0197-6(4)*, Beach Lane Bks.) Beach Lane Bks.

—Two Old Potatoes & Me. Coy, John. 2013. (ENG.). (J). (gr. k-3). pap. 7.99 *(978-1-935666-46-2(0))* Nodin Pr.

—Weeds Find a Way. Jenson-Elliott, Cindy. 2014. (ENG.). 40p. (J). (gr. -1-3). 16.99 *(978-1-4424-1260-6(7))* Simon & Schuster Children's Publishing.

Fisher, Chris. Ballet Magic, Vol. 1. Castor, Harriet. 64p. (J). pap. 7.95 *(978-0-14-038479-6(0))* Penguin Publishing Group.

—Mountain Mona: Band 09/Gold. French, Vivian. 2006. (Collins Big Cat Ser.). (ENG.). 24p. (J). pap. 6.99 *(978-0-00-718700-3(9))* HarperCollins Pubs. Ltd. GBR. Dist: Independent Pubs. Group.

—Pets, Pets, Pets! Henderson, Kathy. 2004. (ENG.). 32p. (J). (gr. -1-17). 14.95 *(978-1-84507-021-2(6)*, Frances Lincoln) Quarto Publishing Group UK GBR. Dist: Hachette Bk. Group.

—Royston Knapper: Return of the Rogue. Phinn, Gervase. 2005. (Child's Play Library - First Chapter Bks.). (ENG.). 126p. (J). *(978-0-85953-024-8(8))* Child's Play International Ltd.

—The Snow Dragon. French, Vivian. 2003. (ENG.). 32p. (J). pap. 11.99 *(978-0-552-54595-2(3))* Transworld Publishers Ltd. GBR. Dist: Trafalgar Square Publishing.

Fisher, Cynthia. The Biggest Pest on Eighth Avenue. Lawlor, Laurie. (Holiday House Reader Ser.). (ENG.). 47p. (J). (gr. k-3). tchr. ed. 14.95 *(978-0-8234-1321-8(7))* Holiday Hse., Inc.

—Friends, Like You. Griswold, Melissa. 2007. (J). 24.95 *(978-0-9797287-2-3(X))*; 32p. 15.00 *(978-0-9797287-3-0(8))* Mainstream Ctr., Schl. for the Deaf, The.

—Friends, Like You: Children's Activity Book. Griswold, Melissa. 2007. 16p. (J). *(978-0-9797287-4-7(6))* Mainstream Ctr., Schl. for the Deaf, The.

—How to Survive a Totally Boring Summer. DeLaCroix, Alice. 2007. (ENG.). 96p. (J). (gr. 1-4). 16.95 *(978-0-8234-2024-7(8))* Holiday Hse., Inc.

Fisher, Cynthia, jt. illus. see Holub, Joan.

Fisher, Diana. Animals: Step-by-Step Instructions for 26 Captivating Creatures. Walter Foster Creative Team. 2011. (Learn to Draw Ser.). 32p. (J). (gr. 1-4). 28.50 *(978-1-936309-20-7(3))* Quarto Publishing Group USA.

—Cats & Kittens. Foster, Walter, ed. 2004. (Learn to Draw Ser.). (ENG.). 40p. (J). (gr. 1-17). pap. 4.95 *(978-1-56010-844-3(4)*, 1560108444) Quarto Publishing Group USA.

—Dinosaurs. Winterberg, Jenna. 2006. (Watch Me Draw Ser.). (ENG.). 24p. (J). (gr. 1-17). pap. 4.95 *(978-1-56010-951-8(3)*, 1560109513) Quarto Publishing Group USA.

—Dogs & Puppies: Step-by-Step Insructions for 25 Different Breads. Walter Foster Creative Team. 2011. (Learn to Draw Ser.). 32p. (J). (gr. 1-4). 28.50 *(978-1-936309-18-4(1))* Quarto Publishing Group USA.

—Dolphins, Whales, Fish & More. Winterberg, Jenna. 2006. (Watch Me Draw Ser.). (ENG.). 24p. (J). (gr. 1-17). pap. 4.95 *(978-1-56010-949-5(1)*, 1560109491) Quarto Publishing Group USA.

—Dolphins, Whales, Fish & More. Winterberg, Jenna. 2015. (J). *(978-1-939581-34-1(6))* Quarto Publishing Group USA.

—Favorite Pets: A Step-By-step Drawing & Story Book for Preschoolers. Winterberg, Jenna. 2006. (Watch Me Draw Ser.). (ENG.). 24p. (J). (gr. 1-17). pap. 4.95 *(978-1-56010-948-8(3)*, 1560109483) Quarto Publishing Group USA.

—I Love Cats! Activity Book: Meow-velous stickers, trivia, step-by-step drawing projects, & more for the cat lover in You! Creative Team at Walter Foster Publishing Staff. 2011. (I Love Activity Bks.). (ENG.). 112p. (J). (gr. 1-17). pap. 9.95 *(978-1-60058-224-0(9)*, 1600582249) Quarto Publishing Group USA.

—I Love Dogs! Pup-Tacular Stickers, Trivia, Step-by-Step Drawing Projects, & More for the Dog Lover in You! Creative Team at Walter Foster Publishing Staff. 2011. (I Love Activity Bks.). (ENG.). 112p. (J). (gr. 1-17). pap., act. bk. ed. 9.95 *(978-1-60058-225-7(7)*, 1600582257) Quarto Publishing Group USA.

—I Love Horses! Giddy-Up Great Stickers, Trivia, Step-by-Step Drawing Projects, & More for the Horse Lover in You! Farrell, Russell & Creative Team at Walter Foster Publishing Staff. 2011. (I Love Activity Bks.). (ENG.). 112p. (J). (gr. 1-17). pap. 9.95 *(978-1-60058-226-4(5)*, 1600582265) Quarto Publishing Group USA.

—Learn to Draw Cats & Kittens. 2012. (J). *(978-1-936309-51-1(3))* Quarto Publishing Group USA.

—Learn to Draw Insects. 2012. (J). *(978-1-936309-52-8(1))* Quarto Publishing Group USA.

—Learn to Draw Reptiles & Amphibians. 2012. (J). *(978-1-936309-50-4(5))* Quarto Publishing Group USA.

—A Magical Fairy World: A Step-by-Step Drawing & Story Book. Fitzgerald, Stephanie. 2010. (Watch Me Draw Ser.). (ENG.). 24p. (J). (gr. -1-17). pap. 4.95 *(978-1-60058-191-5(9)*, 1600581919) Quarto Publishing Group USA.

—The Monsters under My Bed. Razo, Rebecca J. 2014. 24p. (J). (gr. k-2). 23.93 *(978-1-939581-37-2(0))* Quarto Publishing Group USA.

—Outer Space: A Step-by-Step Drawing & Story Book. Winterberg, Jenna. 2006. (Watch Me Draw Ser.). (ENG.). 24p. (J). (gr. 1-17). pap. 4.95 *(978-1-56010-797-2(9)*, 1560107979) Quarto Publishing Group USA.

—Things Girls Love. Winterberg, Jenna. 2006. (Watch Me Draw Ser.). (ENG.). 24p. (J). (gr. -1-17). pap. 4.95 *(978-1-56010-950-1(5)*, 1560109505, Walter Foster Jr) Quarto Publishing Group USA.

—Watch Me Draw a Boy's Adventure. 2012. (J). *(978-1-936309-79-5(3))* Quarto Publishing Group USA.

—Watch Me Draw a Magical Fairy World. 2013. (Watch Me Draw Ser.). 24p. (J). (gr. -1-2). 25.65 *(978-1-936309-91-7(2))* Quarto Publishing Group USA.

—Watch Me Draw Dinosaurs. 2013. (Watch Me Draw Ser.). 24p. (J). (gr. -1-2). 25.65 *(978-1-936309-89-4(0))* Quarto Publishing Group USA.

—Watch Me Draw Disney's Little Einsteins Amazing Missions. 2012. (J). *(978-1-936309-43-6(2))* Quarto Publishing Group USA.

—Watch Me Draw Favorite Pets. 2012. (J). *(978-1-936309-77-1(7))* Quarto Publishing Group USA.

—Watch Me Draw the Monsters under My Bed: A Step-by-Step Drawing & Story Book. Razo, Rebecca J. 2009. (Watch Me Draw Ser.). (ENG.). 24p. (J). (gr. -1-1). pap. 4.95 *(978-1-60058-608-8(2)*, 1600586082) Quarto Publishing Group USA.

—Watch Me Draw the Zoo. 2013. (Watch Me Draw Ser.). 24p. (J). (gr. -1-2). 25.65 *(978-1-936309-90-0(4))* Quarto Publishing Group USA.

—Watch Me Draw Things Girls Love. 2012. (J). *(978-1-936309-78-8(5))* Quarto Publishing Group USA.

—The Zoo: A Step-by-Step Drawing & Story Book. Winterberg, Jenna. 2006. (Watch Me Draw Ser.). (ENG.). 24p. (J). (gr. 1-17). pap. 4.95 *(978-1-56010-798-9(7)*, 1560107987) Quarto Publishing Group USA.

Fisher, Diana & Shelly, Jeff. All about Dinosaurs & Reptiles. 2010. (All about Drawing Ser.). 80p. (J). 34.25 *(978-1-936309-07-8(6))* Quarto Publishing Group USA.

Fisher, Diana, jt. illus. see Farrell, Russell.

Fisher, Douglas W., jt. illus. see Fisher, Phyllis Mae Richardson.

Fisher, G. W., jt. illus. see Malbrough, Michael.

Fisher Hein, Joy. Bloomin' Tales: Seven Favorite Wildflower Legends. Foster Colburn, Cherie. 2012. (ENG.). 64p. pap. 9.95 *(978-1-936474-36-3(0)*, 1987c76b-83d5-44af-9831-cd68dda6cbfd) Bright Sky Pr.

—Sam Houston: Standing Firm. Wade, Mary Dodson. 2009. (ENG.). 24p. (J). (gr. k-2). 16.95 *(978-1-933979-13-7(5)*, b21386f0-913f-4469-aac4-6dc1e0ccf68c) Bright Sky Pr.

Fisher, Henry. The Night Before Christmas. Moore, Clement C. 2013. 26p. (J). ***(978-1-4351-4927-4(0))*** Barnes & Noble, Inc.

Fisher, Henry. ABC Dreams. Fisher, Henry. 2014. (Turn & Learn Ser.). (ENG.). 12p. (J). (gr. -1-3). *(978-1-78244-535-7(8))* Top That! Publishing PLC.

Fisher, Jeff. A Picture Book of Amelia Earhart. Adler, David A. 2015. 32p. pap. 8.00 ***(978-1-61003-403-6(1))*** Center for the Collaborative Classroom.

Fisher, Jeffrey. Birds Notecards. 2005. (ENG.). (gr. 8-17). 14.95 *(978-0-8118-4988-3(0))* Chronicle Bks. LLC.

Fisher, Jessie, jt. illus. see Santy, Elizabeth.

Fisher-Johnson, Paul. Can You Survive an Alien Invasion? An Interactive Doomsday Adventure. Hoena, B. A. 2015. (You Choose: Doomsday Ser.). (ENG.). 112p. (gr. 3-4). lib. bdg. 31.32 ***(978-1-4914-5853-2(4))*** Capstone Pr., Inc.

Fisher, Julie, photos by. Baby Massage: The Calming Power of Touch. Heath, Alan & Bainbridge, Nicki. 2nd rev. ed. 2004. (ENG., 96p. pap. 15.00 *(978-0-7566-0246-8(7))* Dorling Kindersley Publishing, Inc.

Fisher, Leonard Everett. A Horse Named Justin Morgan. Felton, Harold W. 2011. 162p. 41.95 *(978-1-258-07855-3(4))* Literary Licensing, LLC.

—The Military History of Civil War Land Battles. Dupuy, Trevor Nevitt. 2011. 98p. 38.95 *(978-1-258-07607-8(1))*; 38.95 *(978-1-258-01405-6(X))* Literary Licensing, LLC.

—The Queen's Most Honorable Pirate. Wood, James Playsted. 2011. 192p. 42.95 *(978-1-258-09722-6(2))* Literary Licensing, LLC.

—The Three Princes. Kimmel, Eric A. 2005. (Ala Notable Book Ser.). (ENG.). 32p. (J). (gr. k-3). pap. 6.95 *(978-0-8234-1553-3(8))* Holiday Hse., Inc.

Fisher, Leonard Everett. William Tell. Fisher, Leonard Everett. 2006. 28p. (J). reprint ed. 16.00 *(978-0-7567-9880-2(9))* DIANE Publishing Co.

Fisher, Leonard Everett & Waltrip, Mildred. The First Book of the Indian Wars. Morris, Richard B. 2011. 94p. 38.95 *(978-1-258-01128-4(X))* Literary Licensing, LLC.

Fisher, Marianne. The Last Pacifier. Oliveri, Lisa L. 2013. 36p. pap. 24.95 *(978-1-62709-860-1(7))* America Star Bks.

Fisher, Nell. One Suprising Night/una Noche Sorprendente! Augustine, Peg. Vargas, Emmanuel, tr. 2007. 16p. (J). (gr. -1-3). pap. 5.00 *(978-0-687-49250-3(5))* Abingdon Pr.

Fisher, Pat. Walk a Mile in Our Shoes. Fisher, Pat, photos by. Fisher, D. H., photos by. Fisher, D. H., ed. l.t. ed. 2005. 288p. reprint ed. pap. 19.99 *(978-0-9677231-4-3(0))* ITSMEEE Industries.

Fisher, Patrica A. I Want to Live. Fisher, Patrica A. Fisher, Patrica A., ed. 2004. 200p. (YA). 20.00 *(978-0-9677231-5-0(9))* ITSMEEE Industries.

Fisher, Phyllis Mae Richardson. Chrissy (#1 in the 1989 Family Friends Paper Doll Set) l.t. ed. 2004. 24p. (J). 10.00 *(978-0-9745615-5-4(X))* PJs Corner.

—Janae, #3 in the 1989 Family Friends Paper Doll Set, Vol. 3. l.t. ed. 2003. 24p. (J). 10.00 *(978-0-9745615-7-8(6))* PJs Corner.

—Melly, #2 in the 1989 Family Friends Paper Doll Set, Vols. 3, Vol. 2. l.t. ed. 2004. 24p. (J). 10.00 *(978-0-9745615-6-1(8))* PJs Corner.

—Natasha, an International Friends Paper Doll from Russia. 2004. 15p. (J). 10.00 *(978-0-9745615-8-5(4))* PJs Corner.

—Tess, an International Friends Paper Doll from Africa. 2004. (J). 10.00 *(978-0-9745615-9-2(2))* PJs Corner.

Fisher, Phyllis Mae Richardson. Rueben & Rachel's Paper Doll Coloring Book. Fisher, Phyllis Mae Richardson, . 2003. (J). 8.00 *(978-0-9745615-0-9(9))* PJs Corner.

Fisher, Phyllis Mae Richardson & Fisher, Douglas W. Twiglet the Little Christmas Tree. Fisher, Phyllis Mae Richardson. 2003. (J). 30.00 *(978-0-9745615-1-6(7)*, Twiglet The Little Christmas Tree); 186p. 12.00 *(978-0-9745615-4-7(1))* PJs Corner.

Fisher, Sandy. The Adventures of CJ & Angel; the Scary Helicopter Ride. 2008. 24p. (J). *(978-0-9779072-1-2(X))* Creative Life Publishing.

Fisher, Sean, jt. illus. see Menking, Amanda.

Fisher, Todd. The Snake with a Bellyache. Schwartz, Jean. 2007. 20p. per. 10.95 *(978-1-934246-41-2(7))* Peppertree Pr., The.

Fisher, Valorie. Moxy Maxwell Does Not Love Writing Thank-You Notes. Gifford, Peggy. 2009. (Moxy Maxwell Ser.). (ENG.). 192p. (J). (gr. 2-5). 6.99 *(978-0-375-84343-3(4)*, Yearling) Random Hse. Children's Bks.

Fisher, Valorie. Ellsworth's Extraordinary Electric Ears: And Other Amazing Alphabet Anecdotes. Fisher, Valorie. 2009. (ENG.). 36p. (J). (gr. -1-3). 10.99 *(978-1-4424-0658-2(5)*, Atheneum Bks. for Young Readers) Simon & Schuster Children's Publishing.

—Everything I Need to Know Before I'm Five. Fisher, Valorie. 2011. (ENG.). 40p. (J). (gr. k-k). 17.99 *(978-0-375-86865-8(8)*, Schwartz & Wade Bks.) Random Hse. Children's Bks.

—I Can Do It Myself. Fisher, Valorie. 2014. (ENG.). 40p. (J). (gr. -1-2). 17.99 *(978-0-449-81593-9(5)*, Schwartz & Wade Bks.) Random Hse. Children's Bks.

Fisher, Valorie, photos by. Moxy Maxwell Does Not Love Stuart Little. Gifford, Peggy. 2008. (Moxy Maxwell Ser.). (ENG., 112p. (J). (gr. 2-5). 5.99 *(978-0-440-42230-3(2)*, Yearling) Random Hse. Children's Bks.

Fisher, Valorie, photos by. My Big Sister. Fisher, Valorie. 2003. (ENG., 40p. (J). (gr. -1-3). 17.99 *(978-0-689-85479-8(X)*, Atheneum Bks. for Young Readers) Simon & Schuster Children's Publishing.

Fisk, David. Hooga Booga Presents the Little Pumpkin. Fisk, Cindy. 2013. 28p. pap. 11.95 *(978-1-938743-02-3(4))* Reimann Bks.

—Melvin Pickles. Fisk, Cindy. 2013. 26p. pap. 11.95 *(978-1-938743-03-0(2))* Reimann Bks.

Fitch, Rik. Hershel the Dog. Tysseland, Elsie. 2008. (ENG.). 32p. pap. 12.99 *(978-1-4389-2130-3(6))* AuthorHouse.

Fithian, Catherine. The Magical Merry-Go-Round. 2008. (ENG.). (J). lib. bdg. *(978-0-9754867-2-6(1))* Snodgrass, Ruth M.

Fitterling, Michael. The Elson Readers. Newcomer, Mary Jane et al. 2005. (ENG.). (J). (gr. -1-12). Bk. 4. 193p. tchr. ed., per. 17.95 *(978-1-890623-28-9(8))*; Bk. 5. 267p. tchr. ed., per. 18.95 *(978-1-890623-29-6(6))* Lost Classic Bks.

Fitterling, Michael A., jt. illus. see Burgess, H.

Fitterling, Michael A., jt. illus. see Shute, A. B.

Fitts, Seth. Birds I've Met Through the Alphabet. Tietjen, Amy. 2013. 32p. pap. 17.95 *(978-1-938230-33-2(7))* Vabella Publishing.

Fitzgerald, Anita. Dancing in the Moonlight. Fitzgerald, Kevin. 2005. (J). *(978-0-9765987-4-9(4))* Foundation, Pr. The.

—The EGG-Cellent Adventure. Fitzgerald, Kevin. 2005. (J). *(978-0-9765987-3-2(6))* Foundation, Pr. The.

Fitzgerald, Anne. Being Mad: A Book about Anger... Just for Me! Wigand, Molly. 2012. 32p. (J). pap. 7.95 *(978-0-87029-502-7(0))* Abbey Pr.

—Being Sad When Someone Dies: A Book about Grief... Just for Me! Mundy, Linus. 2012. 32p. (J). pap. 7.95 *(978-0-87029-501-0(2))* Abbey Pr.

—How to Be a Friend: A Book about Friendship... Just for Me! Wigand, Molly. 2012. 32p. (J). pap. 7.95 *(978-0-87029-503-4(9))* Abbey Pr.

—Making Good Choices: Just for Me Book. Engelhardt, Lisa O. 2012. 32p. (J). pap. 7.95 *(978-0-87029-514-0(4))* Abbey Pr.

—My Family Is Changing: A Book about Divorce. Menéndez-Aponte, Emily. 2013. 32p. (J). pap. 7.95 *(978-0-87029-555-3(1))* Abbey Pr.

—Sometimes I'm Afraid: A Book about Fear... Just for Me! Mundy, Michaelene. 2012. 32p. (J). pap. 7.95 *(978-0-87029-500-3(4))* Abbey Pr.

—We Are Different & Alike: A Book about Diversity. Geisen, Cynthia. 2013. 32p. (J). 7.95 *(978-0-87029-557-7(8))* Abbey Pr.

—What Is God Like? Just for Me Book. Geisen, Cynthia. 2012. 32p. (J). pap. 7.95 *(978-0-87029-516-4(0))* Abbey Pr.

Fitzgerald, Brian. The Boy & the Fish. Mannion, Mary. 2010. 52p. pap. *(978-1-907276-62-0(9))* Lapwing Pubns.

—Roaring Rory. Mannion, Mary. 2010. 68p. pap. *(978-1-907276-63-7(7))* Lapwing Pubns.

—Ruckus on the Ranch. Ziefert, Harriet & Texas Tenors Staff. 2015. (ENG.). 36p. (J). (gr. -1-2). 17.99 *(978-1-60905-534-9(9))* Blue Apple Bks.

Fitzgerald, Brian. The Korean War: America's Forgotten War, 1 vol. Fitzgerald, Brian. 2006. (Snapshots in History Ser.). (ENG.). 96p. (gr. 7-8). lib. bdg. 33.99 *(978-0-7565-1625-3(0)*, Snapshots in History) Compass Point Bks.

Fitzgerald, Gerald. Flying over Brooklyn, 1 vol. Uhlberg, Myron. 2003. (ENG.). 32p. (J). (gr. k-3). pap. 7.95 *(978-1-56145-294-1(7))* Peachtree Pubs.

Fitzgerald, Jennifer. Marley's Treasure. Yerrid, Gable. 2007. 28p. (J). (gr. -1-3). 15.95 *(978-0-9767442-6-9(0))* Yorkville Pr.

Fitzgerald, Joanne. Emily's House, 1 vol. Scharer, Niko. 2010. (ENG.). 24p. (J). (gr. k — 1). bds. 7.95 *(978-0-88899-831-6(7))* Groundwood Bks. CAN. Dist: Perseus-PGW.

Fitzgerald, Joanne. Este Soy Yo y lo Que Me Rodea, 1 vol. Fitzgerald, Joanne. 2008. (SPA.). 32p. (J). pap. 7.95 *(978-1-55455-108-8(0)*, 1554551080) Fitzhenry & Whiteside, Ltd. CAN. Dist: Midpoint Trade Bks., Inc.

Fitzgerald, Royce. The Genie King. Abbott, Tony & Jessell, Tim. ed. 2010. (Secrets of Droon Ser.: 7). (ENG.). 176p. (J). (gr. 2-5). 6.99 *(978-0-545-09884-7(X)*, Scholastic Paperbacks) Scholastic, Inc.

—Lucy's Holiday Surprise. Cooper, Ilene. 2015. (Stepping Stone Book(TM) Ser.). (ENG.). 112p. (J). (gr. 1-4). 12.99 *(978-0-385-39131-3(5))* Random Hse., Inc.

—Slumpbuster. Markey, Kevin. 2010. (Super Sluggers Ser.). (ENG.). 208p. (J). (gr. 3-7). pap. 5.99 *(978-0-06-115220-7(X))* HarperCollins Pubs.

Fitzgerald, Stephanie. Pearl Harbor: Day of Infamy, 1 vol. Fitzgerald, Stephanie. 2006. (Snapshots in History Ser.). (ENG.). 96p. (gr. 7-8). 33.99 *(978-0-7565-1622-2(6)*, Snapshots in History) Compass Point Bks.

Fitzl, Richelle Kristi. Grandma's Garden. 2004. (J). *(978-0-9741657-1-4(9))* Galaxia Publishing Group, LLC.

Fitzpatrick, Audrey. Jamaal's Lucky Day. Little, Robert. 2003. 32p. (J). (gr. 2-6). 15.95 *(978-0-9701863-4-8(7))* Relde Publishing.

Fitzpatrick, Brad. Cansada de Esperar, 1 vol. Meachen Rau, Dana. Ruíz, Carlos, tr. 2006. (Read-It! Readers en Español: Story Collection).Tr. of Tired of Waiting. (SPA.). 32p. (gr. -1-3). 19.99 *(978-1-4048-1695-4(X)*, Easy Readers) Picture Window Bks.

—In the Money: A Book about Banking, 1 vol. Loewen, Nancy. 2010. (Money Matters Ser.). (ENG.). 32p. lib. bdg. 9.95 *(978-1-4048-6036-0(3)*, Nonfiction Picture Bks.) Picture Window Bks.

—Taxes, Taxes! Where the Money Goes. Loewen, Nancy. 2005. (Money Matters Ser.). (ENG.). 24p. (gr. 1-3). lib. bdg. 25.99 *(978-1-4048-1158-4(3)*, Nonfiction Picture Bks.) Picture Window Bks.

—Ups & Downs: A Book about the Stock Market. Loewen, Nancy. 2005. (Money Matters Ser.). (ENG.). 24p. (gr. 1-3). 25.99 *(978-1-4048-0954-3(6)*, Nonfiction Picture Bks.) Picture Window Bks.

Fitzpatrick, Brad & Jensen, Brian. Lemons & Lemonade: A Book about Supply & Demand. Loewen, Nancy. 2005. (Money Matters Ser.). (ENG.). 24p. (gr. 1-3). 25.99 *(978-1-4048-0956-7(2)*, Nonfiction Picture Bks.) Picture Window Bks.

—Save, Spend, or Donate? A Book about Managing Money. Loewen, Nancy. 2005. (Money Matters Ser.). (ENG.). 24p. (gr. 1-3). 25.99 *(978-1-4048-0952-9(X)*, Nonfiction Picture Bks.) Picture Window Bks.

Fitzpatrick, Marie-Louise. Jasmine's Lion. McAllister, Angela. 2005. (ENG.). 32p. (J). (gr. k-4). 20.00 *(978-0-385-60505-2(6))*, Doubleday Children's) Random House Children's Books GBR. Dist: Independent Pubs. Group.

—Silly Baby. 2010. (ENG.). 32p. (J). (gr. -1-k). 16.95 *(978-1-84507-951-2(5))*, Frances Lincoln Children's Bks.) Quarto Publishing Group UK GBR. Dist: Hachette Bk. Group.

Fitzpatrick, Marie-Louise. There. Fitzpatrick, Marie-Louise. 2009. (ENG.). 32p. (J). (gr. -1-2). 17.99 *(978-1-59643-087-7(7))* Roaring Brook Pr.

Fitzpatrick, Meg & Ravenhill, John A. The World of Bridgett & Emily. Friederich, Uve. 2004. 41p. (J). mass mkt. 8.95 *(978-0-9747532-4-9(6))* Taylor-Dth Publishing.

Fiumara, Sebastian. Thor: The Trials of Loki. 2011. (ENG.). 120p. (YA). (gr. 8-17). 19.99 *(978-0-7851-5165-4(6))* Marvel Worldwide, Inc.

Five Mile Press Staff. Renaissance Artists. deluxe ed. 2007. ***(978-1-74178-336-0(4))*** Five Mile Pr. Pty Ltd. The.

Five Mile Press Staff. The Seven Continents of the World. Mappin, Jennifer. 2008. 12p. (J). (gr. -1-3). *(978-1-74124-473-1(0))* Five Mile Pr. Pty Ltd. The.

Flack, Marjorie. The Country Bunny & the Little Gold Shoes 75th Anniversary Edition. Heyward, DuBose. 2014. (ENG.). 56p. (J). (gr. -1-3). 14.99 *(978-0-544-25197-7(0))*, HMH Books For Young Readers) Houghton Mifflin Harcourt Publishing Co.

—The Country Bunny & the Little Gold Shoes Gift Edition with Charm. Heyward, DuBose. 2010. (ENG.). 56p. (J). (gr. -1-3). 9.99 *(978-0-547-14418-4(0))* Houghton Mifflin Harcourt Publishing Co.

Flaherty, Tom, photos by. Continuing the Passion. Bowyer, Clifford B. 2009. 360p. (J). 18.95 *(978-0-9787782-6-2(X))* Silver Leaf Bks., LLC.

Flamini, Lorella. The Bible for Little Ones. Prestofillipo, Mary Nazarene, tr. 2004. 38p. (J). 9.95 *(978-0-8198-1166-0(1)*, 332-029) Pauline Bks. & Media.

—Growing in Love: Virtues for Little Ones. 2006. 40p. (J). (gr. -1-k). bds. 11.95 *(978-0-8198-3105-7(0))* Pauline Bks. & Media.

—The Story of Creation. Prestofillipo, Mary Nazarene, tr. 2005. Orig. Title: Piccola storia della Creazione. (ITA.). 36p. (J). pap. 12.95 *(978-0-8198-7093-3(5))* Pauline Bks. & Media.

—The Story of Noah's Ark. Prestofillopo, Mary Nazarene, tr. 2003. 38p. (J). 9.95 *(978-0-8198-7084-1(6)*, 332-380) Pauline Bks. & Media.

—Thank You Dear God! Prayers for Little Ones. 2006. 40p. (J). (gr. -1-k). bds. 11.95 *(978-0-8198-7417-7(5))* Pauline Bks. & Media.

Flanagan, Jeff. Pass It On. Fantasia, Kathryn. 2009. 28p. pap. 18.65 *(978-1-4415-5446-8(7))* Xlibris Corp.

Flass, E. C. The Turkey Doll. Gates, Josephine Scribner. 2007. 62p. (J). lib. bdg. 59.00 *(978-1-60304-016-7(1))* Dollworks.

Flather, Lisa. Caribou Journey. French, Vivian. 2003. (Fantastic Journeys Ser.). 32p. (J). *(978-1-84089-216-1(1))* Zero to Ten, Ltd.

Flavin, Teresa. All Families Are Special. Simon, Norma. 2013. (AV2 Fiction Readalong Ser.: Vol. 59). (ENG.). 32p. (J). (gr. k-3). 34.28 *(978-1-62127-867-2(0)*, AV2 by Weigl) Weigl Pubs., Inc.

—All Families Are Special. Simon, Norma. 2003. (ENG.). 32p. (J). (gr. k-3). 16.99 *(978-0-8075-2175-5(2))* Whitman, Albert & Co.

—Fly High! The Story of Bessie Coleman. Borden, Louise & Kroeger, Mary Kay. 2004. (ENG.). 40p. (J). (gr. 3-7). 7.99 *(978-0-689-86462-9(0))*, Simon & Schuster/Paula Wiseman Bks.) Simon & Schuster/Paula Wiseman Bks.

—The Old Cotton Blues. England, Linda. 2011. (ENG.). 32p. (J). (gr. -1-2). 14.99 *(978-1-4424-2945-1(3))*, McElderry, Margaret K. Bks.) McElderry, Margaret K. Bks.

Flavin, Teresa. Pushing up the Sky. Bruchac, Joseph. 2015. 96p. pap. 10.00 ***(978-1-61003-552-1(6))*** Center for the Collaborative Classroom.

Fleecs, Tony. Fluttershy. Kesel, Barbara. 2015. (J). ***(978-1-61479-332-8(8))*** Spotlight.

—Rainbow Dash. Lindsay, Ryan K. 2015. (J). ***(978-1-61479-334-2(4))*** Spotlight.

Fleishman, Seymour. Babe Ruth. Van Riper, Guernsey, Jr. 2015. (History's All-Stars Ser.). (ENG.). 208p. (J). (gr. 3-7). pap. 6.99 *(978-1-4814-2507-0(2))*, Simon & Schuster/Paula Wiseman Bks.) Simon & Schuster/Paula Wiseman Bks.

Fleming, Christopher. Wires, 1 vol. Long, Tyler. 2009. 28p. pap. 24.95 *(978-1-60836-217-2(5))* America Star Bks.

Fleming, Denise. 5 Little Ducks. 2015. (J). ***(978-1-4814-2422-6(X)***, Beach Lane Bks.) Beach Lane Bks.

Fleming, Denise. Alphabet under Construction. Fleming, Denise. 2006. (ENG.). 32p. (J). (gr. -1-k). reprint ed. pap. 7.99 *(978-0-8050-8112-1(7))* Square Fish.

—Barnyard Banter. Fleming, Denise. 2008. (ENG.). 32p. (J). (gr. -1-k). pap. 25.95 *(978-0-8050-8778-9(8))*, Holt, Henry & Co. Bks. For Young Readers) Holt, Henry & Co.

—Buster Goes to Cowboy Camp. Fleming, Denise. 2008. (ENG.). 40p. (J). (gr. -1-2). 16.95 *(978-0-8050-7892-3(4))*, Holt, Henry & Co. Bks. For Young Readers) Holt, Henry & Co.

—The Cow Who Clucked. Fleming, Denise. rev. ed. 2006. (ENG.). 40p. (J). (gr. -1-2). 18.99 *(978-0-8050-7265-5(9))*, Holt, Henry & Co. Bks. For Young Readers) Holt, Henry & Co.

—The Everything Book. Fleming, Denise. (ENG.). (J). (— 1). 2009. 32p. pap. 25.99 *(978-0-8050-8869-4(5))*; 2004. 26p. bds. 7.95 *(978-0-8050-7709-4(X))* Holt, Henry & Co. (Holt, Henry & Co. Bks. For Young Readers).

—The First Day of Winter. Fleming, Denise. rev. ed. 2005. (ENG.). 32p. (J). (gr. -1-1). 17.99 *(978-0-8050-7384-3(1))*, Holt, Henry & Co. Bks. For Young Readers) Holt, Henry & Co.

—The First Day of Winter. Fleming, Denise. 2012. (ENG.). 32p. (J). (gr. -1-1). 7.99 *(978-0-312-37138-8(1))* Square Fish.

—Go, Shapes, Go! Fleming, Denise. 2014. (ENG.). 40p. (J). (gr. -1-3). 17.99 *(978-1-4424-8240-1(0))*, Beach Lane Bks.) Beach Lane Bks.

—In the Small, Small Pond. Fleming, Denise. 2007. (ENG.). 32p. (J). (gr. -1-k). pap. 27.99 *(978-0-8050-8117-6(8))*, Holt, Henry & Co. Bks. For Young Readers) Holt, Henry & Co.

—Pumpkin Eye. Fleming, Denise. rev. ed. 2005. (ENG.). 32p. (J). (gr. -1-k). reprint ed. pap. 7.99 *(978-0-8050-7635-6(2))* Square Fish.

—Shout! Shout It Out! Fleming, Denise. 2011. (ENG.). 40p. (J). (gr. -1-1). 16.99 *(978-0-8050-9237-0(4))*, Holt, Henry & Co. Bks. For Young Readers) Holt, Henry & Co.

—Sleepy, Oh So Sleepy. Fleming, Denise. 2010. (ENG.). 32p. (J). (gr. -1-k). 16.99 *(978-0-8050-8126-8(7))*, Holt, Henry & Co. Bks. For Young Readers) Holt, Henry & Co.

—UnderGROUND. Fleming, Denise. 2012. (ENG.). 40p. (J). (gr. -1-3). 17.99 *(978-1-4424-5882-6(8))*, Beach Lane Bks.) Beach Lane Bks.

Fleming, Diana Trucks. Nine Goldfish in David's Pond. Calvert, Ellen Hasenecz. 2013. 36p. pap. 14.99 *(978-1-936745-18-0(6))* Nuevo Bks.

Fleming, Garry. Look at the Animals, 1 vol. Dale, Jay. 2012. (Engage Literacy Magenta Ser.). (ENG.). 32p. (J). (gr. k-2). pap. 5.99 *(978-1-4296-8880-2(7))*, Engage Literacy) Capstone Pr., Inc.

—The School Garden, 1 vol. Giulieri, Anne. 2012. (Engage Literacy Yellow Ser.). (ENG.). 32p. (J). (gr. k-2). pap. 5.99 *(978-1-4296-8958-8(7))*, Engage Literacy) Capstone Pr., Inc.

Fleming, Jeanie Puleston. Zozobra! The Story of Old Man Gloom. Fleming, Jeanie Puleston, photos by. Dewey, Jennifer Owings. 2004. (ENG.). 32p. (J). (gr. 3-18). pap. 14.95 *(978-0-8263-3279-0(X))* Univ. of New Mexico Pr.

Fleming, Jesse, jt. illus. see Matsunaga, Judd.

Fleming, Kye. The Friendship Seed. Hull, Bunny. 2007. (Young Masters Ser.). 28p. (J). (gr. -1-2). per. 13.95 incl. audio compact disk *(978-0-9721478-6-6(1))*, Dream A World) BrassHeart Music.

—The Hidden Treasure. Bunny, Hull. 2007. (Young Masters Ser.). (J). (gr. -1). 13.95 incl. audio compact disk *(978-0-9721478-8-0(8))* BrassHeart Music.

—Young Masters: The Magic Eye. Hull, Bunny. 2007. (Young Masters Ser.). (J). (gr. -1). 13.95 incl. audio compact disk *(978-0-9721478-7-3(X))* BrassHeart Music.

Fleming, Lucy. Ghosts & Gummy Worms: A Readers' Theater Script & Guide. Wallace, Nancy K. 2016. (J). ***(978-1-62402-113-8(1))*** Magic Wagon.

—Groundhogs & Guinea Pigs: A Readers' Theater Script & Guide. Wallace, Nancy K. 2016. (J). ***(978-1-62402-114-5(X))*** Magic Wagon.

—Pickles & Parks: A Readers' Theater Script & Guide. Wallace, Nancy K. 2016. (J). ***(978-1-62402-116-9(6))*** Magic Wagon.

—Turkey & Take-Out: A Readers' Theater Script & Guide. Wallace, Nancy K. 2016. (J). ***(978-1-62402-117-6(4))*** Magic Wagon.

Fleming, Michael. Ten Eggs in a Nest. Sadler, Marilyn. 2014. (Bright & Early Books Series). (ENG.). 48p. (J). (gr. -1-2). 9.99 *(978-0-449-81082-8(8))*; lib. bdg. 13.99 *(978-0-375-97151-8(3))* Random Hse. Children's Bks. (Random Hse. Bks. for Young Readers).

—Twinky the Dinky Dog. Klimo, Kate. 2013. (Step into Reading Ser.). (ENG.). 48p. (J). (gr. k-3). pap. 3.99 *(978-0-307-97667-3(X))* Random Hse., Inc.

Fleming, Michael. 10 Busy Brooms. Gerber, Carole. 2016. (J). ***(978-0-553-53341-5(X))*** Knopf Doubleday Publishing Group.

Fleming, Yvonne B. Going Home with Jesus, 1 vol. Fleming, Theresa. 2009. 22p. pap. 24.95 *(978-1-60813-703-9(1))* America Star Bks.

Flener, Sheila S. Sidney's Bedtime Stories. Flener, Bettie D. 2011. 44p. pap. 24.95 *(978-1-4560-3226-5(7))* America Star Bks.

Flensted, Christian, et al. Counting Chickens. 2010. (ENG.). 36p. (J). (gr. -1-3). 16.99 *(978-1-60905-033-7(9))* Blue Apple Bks.

Flesher, Vivienne. East of the Sun, West of the Moon. MacHale, D. J. 2007. (Rabbit Ears: A Classic Tale Ser.). 36p. (gr. -1-3). 25.65 *(978-1-59961-306-2(3))* Spotlight.

Flesher, Vivienne. Alfred's Nose. Flesher, Vivienne. 2008. 32p. (J). (gr. -1-2). lib. bdg. 17.89 *(978-0-06-084314-4(4))* HarperCollins Pubs.

Fletcher, Ashlee. My Dog, My Cat. Fletcher, Ashlee. 2011. (ENG.). 32p. (J). (gr. -1-3). 13.95 *(978-1-933718-22-4(6))* Tanglewood Pr.

Fletcher, Bob. I Grew up on a Farm. Lewis, Alan K. 2005. (ENG.). 32p. (J). (gr. -1-3). 19.95 *(978-0-9766805-2-9(1))* Keene Publishing.

Fletcher, Corina, jt. illus. see Roberts, David.

Fletcher, Lyn. Merry Christmas, Rarity! Shepherd, Jodie. 2006. (My Little Pony Ser.). 32p. (J). (gr. -1-1). pap., act. bk. ed. 3.99 *(978-0-06-079472-9(0))*, HarperFestival) HarperCollins Pubs.

Fletcher, Robert A. Jeeps at War. Fletcher, Robert A. Naples, Thomas R. et al, eds. 2008. 36p. (J). 19.95 *(978-0-9722961-1-3(5))* Iron Mountain Pr.

Fletcher, Rusty. God Bless America. Beveridge, Amy. 2006. 16p. (J). pap. 1.99 *(978-0-7847-1509-3(2)*, 22136) Standard Publishing.

—God Made Dinosaurs. Head, Heno. 2013. (Happy Day Ser.). (ENG.). 16p. (J). pap. 2.49 *(978-1-4143-9296-7(6))* Tyndale Hse. Pubs.

—Ice Skating. Weil, Ann. 2004. (Elements of Reading: Phonics Ser.). 16p. pap. 40.00 *(978-0-7398-9010-3(7))* Houghton Mifflin Harcourt Supplemental Pubs.

—My Pink Piggy Bank. Williams, Rozanne Lanczak. 2005. (Reading for Fluency Ser.). 8p. (J). pap. 2.49 *(978-1-59198-144-2(1)*, 4244) Creative Teaching Pr., Inc.

—Thank You, God, for This Day. Bowman, Crystal. 2014. (Happy Day Ser.). (ENG.). 16p. (J). pap. 2.49 *(978-1-4143-9486-2(1))* Tyndale Hse. Pubs.

—The Weather. George, Olivia. 2005. (My First Reader Ser.). (ENG.). 32p. (J). (gr. k-1). lib. bdg. 18.50 *(978-0-516-24880-6(4))*, Children's Pr.) Scholastic Library Publishing.

Flett, Julie. Dolphin Sos, 1 vol. Miki, Roy & Miki, Slavia. 2014. (ENG.). 32p. (J). (gr. 1-4). 16.95 *(978-1-896580-76-0(9))* Tradewind Bks. CAN. Dist: Orca Bk. Pubs. USA.

—Little You, 1 vol. Van Camp, Richard. 2013. (ENG.). 24p. (J). (gr. -1-k). bds. 9.95 *(978-1-4598-0248-3(9))* Orca Bk. Pubs. USA.

—Zoe & the Fawn. Jameson, Catherine. ed. 2006. (ENG.). 32p. pap. 11.95 *(978-1-894778-43-5(X))* Theytus Bks., Ltd. CAN. Dist: Univ. of Toronto Pr.

Flett, Julie. Wild Berries. Flett, Julie. Cook, Earl N., tr. 2013. (ENG.). 32p. (J). (gr. -1-3). pap. 16.95 *(978-1-897476-89-5(2))* Simply Read Bks. CAN. Dist: Ingram Pub. Services.

Fletter, Sharon Sofia. My Guardian Angel. Fletter, Sharon Sofia. I.t. ed. 2007.Tr. of Mi Angel Guardian, il Mio Angelo, Meu Anjo Da Guarda, Mein Schutzengel, Mon Ange Guardian. (SPA, ITA, POR, GER & FRE.). 44p. (J). per. 17.95 *(978-0-9793113-0-7(6))* SoulSong Publishing.

Flinn, Hannah. Dashing Duke & His Dodgy Adventures. Albuquerque, Blossom. 2011. 36p. pap. 13.95 *(978-1-60911-743-6(3))*, Strategic Bk. Publishing) Strategic Book Publishing & Rights Agency (SBPRA).

Flint, Russ. Christian Reader's Theater. Ewald, Thomas. 2005. 64p. (J). per. 8.99 *(978-1-59441-077-2(1)*, CD-204004) Carson-Dellosa Publishing, LLC.

—Taking Godly Care of My Money: Stewardship Lessons in Money Matters, Grades 2-5. Sharp, Anna Layton. 2005. (Resource Bks.). 80p. (J). (gr. 2-5). per. 9.99 *(978-1-59441-082-6(8)*, CD-204009) Carson-Dellosa Publishing, LLC.

Flint, Stacie. Ten Pigs Fiddling. Atlas, Ron. 2006. (ENG.). 32p. (J). (gr. -1-k). 16.00 *(978-0-9630243-8-1(8)*, 1249130) Amberwood Pr.

—Ten Pigs Fiddling. Atlas, Ron. 2nd rev. ed. 2006. (ENG.). 32p. (J). (gr. -1-k). 17.95 *(978-0-9630243-3-6(7))* Amberwood Pr.

Flintham, Thomas. Mameshiba Love Winter. VIZ Media Staff. 2011. (Mameshiba Ser.). (ENG.). 16p. (J). 12.99 *(978-1-4215-4110-5(6))* Viz Media.

—Mesmerizing Math. Litton, Jonathan. 2013. (ENG.). 16p. (J). (gr. 2-5). 18.99 *(978-0-7636-6881-5(8))*, Templar) Candlewick Pr.

Flintham, Thomas. Thomas Flintham's Book of Mazes & Puzzles. Flintham, Thomas. 2015. (ENG.). 192p. (J). (gr. 1-3). pap. 12.99 ***(978-0-545-81981-7(4)***, Cartwheel Bks.) Scholastic, Inc.

Flintman, Thomas. Super Science: Matter Matters! Adams, Tom. 2012. (ENG.). 18p. (J). (gr. 2-5). 18.99 *(978-0-7636-6096-3(5))*, Templar) Candlewick Pr.

Flintoft, Anthony. My First Day at Nursery School. Edwards, Becky. 2004. (ENG.). 32p. (J). (gr. -1-1). pap. 7.99 *(978-1-58234-909-1(6))*, Bloomsbury USA Childrens) Bloomsbury USA.

Floca, Brian. Ballet for Martha: Making Appalachian Spring. Greenberg, Jan & Jordan, Sandra. 2010. (ENG.). 48p. (J). (gr. 1-5). 18.99 *(978-1-59643-338-0(8))* Roaring Brook Pr.

—Billy & the Rebel: Based on a True Civil War Story. Hopkinson, Deborah. 2005. 44p. (J). lib. bdg. 15.00 *(978-1-4242-1148-7(4))* Fitzgerald Bks.

—Billy & the Rebel: Based on a True Civil War Story. Hopkinson, Deborah. 2006. (Ready-to-Read Ser.). 44p. (gr. 1-3). 14.00 *(978-0-7569-6390-3(7))* Perfection Learning Corp.

—Billy & the Rebel: Based on a True Civil War Story. Hopkinson, Deborah. 2006. (Ready-To-Reads Ser.). (ENG.). 48p. (J). (gr. 1-3). pap. 3.99 *(978-0-689-83396-0(2))*, Simon Spotlight) Simon Spotlight.

—City of Light, City of Dark. Avi. 2013. (ENG.). 192p. (J). (gr. 3-7). 19.99 *(978-0-545-54256-2(1))*; pap. 10.99 *(978-0-545-39880-0(0))* Scholastic, Inc. (Graphix).

—Elizabeth, Queen of the Seas. Cox, Lynne. 2014. (ENG.). 48p. (J). (gr. -1-3). 17.99 *(978-0-375-85888-8(1))*; 20.99 *(978-0-375-95888-5(6))* Random Hse. Children's Bks. (Schwartz & Wade Bks.).

—Ereth's Birthday. Avi. 2006. (Poppy Stories Ser.). (ENG.). 224p. (J). (gr. 3-7). pap. 6.99 *(978-0-380-80490-0(5))* HarperCollins Pubs.

—Ethan Out & about Big Book: Brand New Readers. Hurwitz, Johanna. 2010. (Brand New Readers Ser.). (ENG.). 48p. (J). (gr. -1-3). pap. 24.99 *(978-0-7636-4811-4(6))* Candlewick Pr.

—From Slave to Soldier: Based on a True Civil War Story. Hopkinson, Deborah. (Ready-To-Reads Ser.). (ENG.). 48p. (J). (gr. 1-3). 2007. pap. 3.99 *(978-0-689-83966-5(9))*; 2005. 16.99 *(978-0-689-83965-8(0))* Simon Spotlight. (Simon Spotlight).

—The Hinky-Pink: An Old Tale. 2008. (ENG.). 48p. (J). (gr. -1-3). 16.99 *(978-0-689-87588-5(6))*, Atheneum/Richard Jackson Bks.) Simon & Schuster Children's Publishing.

—Marty McGuire. Messner, Kate. 2011. (ENG.). 144p. (J). (gr. 2-5). pap. 5.99 *(978-0-545-14246-5(6))*, Scholastic Pr.) Scholastic, Inc.

—Marty McGuire Digs Worms! Messner, Kate. 2012. (ENG.). 176p. (J). (gr. -1-3). 17.99 *(978-0-545-14245-8(8))*; pap. 5.99 *(978-0-545-14247-2(4))* Scholastic, Inc. (Scholastic Pr.).

—Marty McGuire Has Too Many Pets! Messner, Kate. (Marty Mcguire Ser.). (ENG.). 176p. (J). (gr. -1-3). 2015. pap. 5.99 *(978-0-545-53560-1(3))*; 2014. 15.99 *(978-0-545-53559-5(X))* Scholastic, Inc. (Scholastic Pr.).

—Max & Mo Go Apple Picking. Lakin, Patricia. 2007. (Ready-To-Reads Ser.). (ENG.). 32p. (J). (gr. -1-1). pap. 3.99 *(978-1-4169-2535-4(X))*, Simon Spotlight) Simon Spotlight.

—Max & Mo Make a Snowman. Lakin, Patricia. 2007. (Ready-To-Reads Ser.). (ENG.). 32p. (J). (gr. -1-1). pap. 3.99 *(978-1-4169-2537-8(6))*, Simon Spotlight) Simon Spotlight.

—Max & Mo's First Day at School. Lakin, Patricia. 2007. (Ready-To-Reads Ser.). (ENG.). 32p. (J). (gr. -1-1). pap. 3.99 *(978-1-4169-2533-0(3))*, Simon Spotlight) Simon Spotlight.

—Max & Mo's Halloween Surprise. Lakin, Patricia. 2008. (Ready-To-Reads Ser.). (ENG.). 32p. (J). (gr. -1-1). pap. 3.99 *(978-1-4169-2539-2(2))*, Simon Spotlight) Simon Spotlight.

—The Mayor of Central Park. Avi. 2003. tchr. ed. *(978-0-06-057254-9(X))*; 2003. (ENG.). 208p. (J). (gr. 3-6). 15.99 *(978-0-06-000682-2(X))*; 2005. (ENG.). 208p. (J). (gr. 3-7). reprint ed. pap. 6.99 *(978-0-06-051557-7(0))* HarperCollins Pubs.

—The Mayor of Central Park. Avi. 2005. 193p. (J). (gr. 3-7). 13.65 *(978-0-7569-5125-2(9))* Perfection Learning Corp.

—Old Wolf. Avi. 2015. (ENG.). 160p. (J). (gr. 3-7). 16.99 *(978-1-4424-9921-8(4))* Simon & Schuster Children's Publishing.

—Poppy. Avi. 2006. (Poppy Stories Ser.). (ENG.). 192p. (J). (gr. 3-7). pap. 6.99 *(978-0-380-72769-8(2))* HarperCollins Pubs.

—Poppy & Ereth. Avi. (Poppy Stories Ser.). 224p. (J). (gr. 3-7). 2011. (ENG.). pap. 6.99 *(978-0-06-111971-2(7))*; 2009. (ENG.). 15.99 *(978-0-06-111969-9(5))*; 2009. lib. bdg. 16.89 *(978-0-06-111970-5(9))* HarperCollins Pubs.

—Poppy & Rye. Avi. 2006. (Poppy Stories Ser.). (ENG.). 240p. (J). (gr. 3-7). pap. 6.99 *(978-0-380-79717-2(8))* HarperCollins Pubs.

—Poppy's Return. Avi. (Poppy Stories Ser.). (J). 2006. (ENG.). 256p. (gr. 3-7). pap. 6.99 *(978-0-06-000014-1(7))*; 2005. 240p. lib. bdg. 16.89 *(978-0-06-000013-4(9))* HarperCollins Pubs.

—Ragweed. Avi. Howard, E., ed. 2006. (Poppy Stories Ser.). (ENG.). 224p. (J). (gr. 3-7). pap. 6.99 *(978-0-380-80167-1(1))* HarperCollins Pubs.

—The True Gift. MacLachlan, Patricia. 2013. (ENG.). 112p. (J). (gr. 2-6). pap. 5.99 *(978-1-4424-8858-8(1))*, Atheneum Bks. for Young Readers) Simon & Schuster Children's Publishing.

—The True Gift: A Christmas Story. MacLachlan, Patricia. 2009. (ENG.). 96p. (J). (gr. 2-6). 14.99 *(978-1-4169-9081-9(X))*, Atheneum Bks. for Young Readers) Simon & Schuster Children's Publishing.

—Uncles & Antlers. Wheeler, Lisa. 2014. (ENG.). 40p. (J). (gr. -1-3). 17.99 *(978-1-4814-3018-0(1))*, Atheneum Bks. for Young Readers) Simon & Schuster Children's Publishing.

Floca, Brian. Five Trucks. Floca, Brian. 2014. (ENG.). 32p. (J). (gr. -1-3). 17.99 *(978-1-4814-0593-5(4))*, Atheneum Bks. for Young Readers) Simon & Schuster Children's Publishing.

—The Frightful Story of Harry Walfish. Floca, Brian. 2004. 26p. (J). (gr. k-4). reprint ed. pap. *(978-0-7567-7852-1(2))* DIANE Publishing Co.

—Lightship. Floca, Brian. 2007. (ENG.). 48p. (J). (gr. -1-3). 17.99 *(978-1-4169-2436-4(1))*, Atheneum/Richard Jackson Bks.) Simon & Schuster Children's Publishing.

—Locomotive. Floca, Brian. 2013. (ENG.). 64p. (J). (gr. -1-5). 17.99 *(978-1-4169-9415-2(7))*, Atheneum/Richard Jackson Bks.) Simon & Schuster Children's Publishing.

—Moonshot: The Flight of Apollo 11. Floca, Brian. 2009. (ENG.). 48p. (J). (gr. -1-5). 18.99 *(978-1-4169-5046-2(X))*, Atheneum/Richard Jackson Bks.) Simon & Schuster Children's Publishing.

—The Racecar Alphabet. Floca, Brian. 2003. (ENG.). 40p. (J). (gr. -1-2). 18.99 *(978-0-689-85091-2(3))*, Atheneum/Richard Jackson Bks.) Simon & Schuster Children's Publishing.

Floca, Brian, jt. illus. see Anderson, Bethanne.

Floerchinger, Jeremy. Ocean of Dreams. Floerchinger, Lori Liddic. 2008. 36p. pap. 24.95 *(978-1-60703-003-4(9))* America Star Bks.

Floeter, Nell. A Year in the Life of the Kingwood Bunnies. Wood, David. 2010. 54p. pap. 15.95 *(978-1-936343-07-2(X))* Peppertree Pr., The.

Flook, Helen. The Boy Who Cried Horse, 1 vol. Deary, Terry. 2008. (Read-It! Chapter Books: Historical Tales Ser.). (ENG.). 64p. (gr. 2-4). lib. bdg. 21.32 *(978-1-4048-4049-2(4))*, Chapter Readers) Picture Window Bks.

—Bruno for Real, 1 vol. Adderson, Caroline. 2009. (Orca Echoes Ser.). (ENG.). 64p. (J). (gr. 2-3). pap. 6.95 *(978-1-55469-023-7(4))* Orca Bk. Pubs. USA.

—I, Bruno, 1 vol. Adderson, Caroline. 2007. (Orca Echoes Ser.). (ENG.). 64p. (J). (gr. 2-3). per. 6.95 *(978-1-55143-501-5(2))* Orca Bk. Pubs. USA.

—The Middle School Survival Guide. Erlbach, Arlene. 2003. (ENG.). 160p. (J). (gr. 5-9). per. 8.95 *(978-0-8027-7657-0(4))* Walker & Co.

—Pocket Rocks, 1 vol. Fitch, Sheree. 2004. (ENG.). 32p. (J). (gr. -1-3). 16.95 *(978-1-55143-289-2(7)*, 1234125) Orca Bk. Pubs. USA.

—Queen Carrion's Big Bear Hug, 1 vol. Wallace, Karen & Mackey, James. 2007. (Read-It! Chapter Books: the Crunchbone Castle Chronicles Ser.). (ENG.). 64p. (gr. 2-4). lib. bdg. 21.32 *(978-1-4048-3709-6(4))*, Chapter Readers) Picture Window Bks.

—Quirky Times at Quagmire Castle, 1 vol. Wallace, Karen. 2006. (Pathway Bks.). (ENG.). 112p. (gr. 2-3). lib. bdg. 23.99 *(978-1-59889-112-6(X))*, Pathway Bks.) Stone Arch Bks.

—Silas' Seven Grandparents, 1 vol. Horrocks, Anita. 2010. (ENG.). 32p. (J). (gr. -1-3). 19.95 *(978-1-55143-561-9(6))* Orca Bk. Pubs. USA.

—Vinny Drake Is One. Hopkins, Audrey. 2007. (Tiger Ser.). (ENG.). 64p. (J). (gr. 2-4). pap. 9.95 *(978-1-84270-437-0(0))* Andersen Pr. GBR. Dist: Independent Pubs. Group.

Flook, Helen. Welsh Cakes & Custard. White, Wendy. 2013. (ENG.). 63p. (J). (gr. 2-4). pap. 9.99 ***(978-1-84851-712-7(2))*** Gomer Pr. GBR. Dist: Independent Pubs. Group.

Floor, Guus. The Bombing of Pearl Harbor. Uschan, Michael V. & Goff, Elizabeth Hudson. 2006. (Graphic Histories Ser.). 32p. (gr. 5-8). lib. bdg. 27.00 *(978-0-8368-6206-5(6))* Stevens, Gareth Publishing LLLP.

—The California Gold Rush. Goff, Elizabeth Hudson et al. 2006. (Graphic Histories Ser.). 32p. (gr. 5-8). lib. bdg.

F

27.00 *(978-0-8368-6202-7(3))* Stevens, Gareth Publishing LLLP.

Floor, Guus & Spay, Anthony. The First Moon Landing. Anderson, Dale & Goff, Elizabeth Hudson. 2006. (Graphic Histories Ser.). 32p. (gr. 5-8). lib. bdg. 27.00 *(978-0-8368-6203-4(1))* Stevens, Gareth Publishing LLLP.

Floor, Guus & Timmons, Jonathan. Anne Frank. Brown, Jonatha A. & Goff, Elizabeth Hudson. 2006. (Graphic Biographies (World Almanac Library (Firm))). 32p. (gr. 5-8). lib. bdg. 27.00 *(978-0-8368-6196-9(5))* Stevens, Gareth Publishing LLLP.

Florence, Tyler & Frazier, Craig. Tyler Makes Pancakes! Florence, Tyler & Frazier, Craig. 2012. (ENG.). 40p. (J). (gr. -1-2). 16.99 *(978-0-06-204752-6(3))* HarperCollins Pubs.

Florendo, R. M. The Lonesome Dreidel: A Chanukah Adventure. Feinglass, Arthur. 2010. (ENG.). 24p. pap. 12.00 *(978-1-4528-8042-6(5))* CreateSpace Independent Publishing Platform.

Flores, Carolyn Dee. Dale, Dale, Dale / Hit It, Hit It, Hit It: Una Fiesta de Numeros / a Fiesta of Numbers. Saldana, Rene. 2014. (ENG & SPA.). (J). 17.95 *(978-1-55885-782-7(6))*, Piñata Books) Arte Publico Pr.

—Daughters of Two Nations. Caravantes, Peggy. 2013. 144p. (J). pap. 14.00 *(978-0-87842-610-2(8))* Mountain Pr. Publishing Co., Inc.

Flores, Carolyn Dee. Canta, Rana, Canta. Flores, Carolyn Dee. Rosales-Yeomans, Natalia, tr. from SPA. 2013.Tr. of Sing, Froggie, Sing. (ENG & SPA.). 32p. (J). 16.95 *(978-1-55885-764-3(8))*, Piñata Books) Arte Publico Pr.

Flores, Catty. Les Misérables. Hugo, Victor. adapted ed. 2014. (ENG.). 64p. pap. 6.95 *(978-1-906230-79-1(X))* Real Reads Ltd. GBR. Dist: International Publishers Marketing.

Flores, Cory. Bugs on Parade: A Counting Book. 2006. 8p. (J). *(978-1-58970-400-8(2))* Lakeshore Learning Materials.

Flores, Enrique. The Harvest Birds: Los Pajaros de la Cosecha. de Mariscal, Blanca Lopez. 2013. (ENG & SPA.). 32p. (J). (gr. 1-18). pap. 8.95 *(978-0-89239-169-1(3))*, Children's Book Press) Lee & Low Bks., Inc.

Flores, Heyliana. Entre Amigos. Chimal, Monica Genis. rev. ed. 2006. (Otra Escalera Ser.). (SPA & ENG.). 24p. (J). (gr. 2-4). pap. 9.95 *(978-968-5920-65-0(6))* Castillo, Ediciones, S. A. de C. V. MEX. Dist: Macmillan.

Flores, Joe, et al. Math Bridge Enriching Classroom Skills: 4th Grade. Moore, Jennifer et al. Willie, Kirsten et al, eds. 2004. (Math & Reading Bridge Ser.). 96p. (gr. 4-18). wbk. ed. 9.95 *(978-1-887923-16-3(0))* Rainbow Bridge Publishing.

—Math Bridge Enriching Classroom Skills: 5th Grade. Moore, Jennifer et al. Willie, Kirsten et al, eds. 2004. (Math & Reading Bridge Ser.). 96p. (gr. 5-18). wbk. ed. 9.95 *(978-1-887923-17-0(9))* Rainbow Bridge Publishing.

—Math Bridge Enriching Classroom Skills: 6th Grade. Dankberg, Tracy & Graham, Leland. Willie, Kirsten et al, eds. 2004. (Math & Reading Bridge Ser.). 96p. (gr. 6-18). wbk. ed. 9.95 *(978-1-887923-18-7(7))* Rainbow Bridge Publishing.

—Math Bridge Enriching Classroom Skills: 8th Grade. Dankberg, Tracy & Graham, Leland. Willie, Kirsten et al, eds. 2004. (Math & Reading Bridge Ser.). 96p. (gr. 8-18). wbk. ed. 9.95 *(978-1-887923-20-0(9))* Rainbow Bridge Publishing.

—Reading Bridge Enriching Classroom Skills: 5th Grade. Moore, Jennifer. Willie, Kirsten et al, eds. 2004. (Math & Reading Bridge Ser.). 96p. (gr. 5-18). wbk. ed. 9.95 *(978-1-887923-12-5(8))* Rainbow Bridge Publishing.

—Reading Bridge Enriching Classroom Skills: 6th Grade. Ledbetter, Darril & Graham, Leland. Willie, Kirsten et al, eds. 2004. (Math & Reading Bridge Ser.). 96p. (gr. 6-18). wbk. ed. 9.95 *(978-1-887923-13-2(6))* Rainbow Bridge Publishing.

—Reading Bridge Enriching Classroom Skills: 7th Grade. Ledbetter, Darril & Graham, Leland. Willie, Kirsten et al, eds. 2004. (Math & Reading Bridge Ser.). 96p. (gr. 7-18). wbk. ed. 9.95 *(978-1-887923-14-9(4))* Rainbow Bridge Publishing.

—Reading Bridge Enriching Classroom Skills: 8th Grade. Ledbetter, Darril & Graham, Leland. Willie, Kirsten et al, eds. 2004. (Math & Reading Bridge Ser.). 96p. (gr. 8-18). wbk. ed. 9.95 *(978-1-887923-15-6(2))* Rainbow Bridge Publishing.

Flores, Justin. Henry & Dale. Schwinn, Ruth E. 2010. 24p. (J). 14.95 *(978-0-578-04719-5(5))* PRF Pubs.

Flores, Lupita. La Vida Util de Pillo Polilla. Manzur, Vivian Mansour & Mansour, Vivian. rev. ed. 2005. (Castillo de la Lectura Naranja Ser.). (SPA & ENG.). 112p. (J). (gr. -1-7). pap. 7.95 *(978-970-20-0129-4(3))* Castillo, Ediciones, S. A. de C. V. MEX. Dist: Macmillan.

Flores, Martha, jt. illus. see Diego, Rapi.

Florian, Douglas. Autumnblings. Florian, Douglas. 2003. (ENG.). 48p. (J). (gr. k-5). 16.99 *(978-0-06-009278-5(5))*, Greenwillow Bks.) HarperCollins Pubs.

—Dinothesaurus: Prehistoric Poems & Paintings. Florian, Douglas. 2009. (ENG.). 56p. (J). (gr. 1-5). 17.99 *(978-1-4169-7978-4(6))*, Beach Lane Bks.) Beach Lane Bks.

—How to Draw a Dragon. Florian, Douglas. 2015. (ENG.). 42p. (J). (gr. -1-3). 17.99 *(978-1-4424-7399-7(1))*, Beach Lane Bks.) Beach Lane Bks.

—Laugh-Eteria. Florian, Douglas. 2008. (ENG.). 160p. (J). (gr. 1-4). pap. 8.00 *(978-0-15-206148-7(7))* Houghton Mifflin Harcourt Publishing Co.

Florian, Douglas. Pig Is Big on Books. Florian, Douglas. (I Like to Read(r) Ser.). (ENG.). 24p. (J). (gr. -1-3). 6.99 ***(978-0-8234-3424-4(9))*** Holiday Hse., Inc.

Florian, Douglas. Poetrees. Florian, Douglas. 2010. (ENG.). 48p. (J). (gr. 1-5). 16.99 *(978-1-4169-8672-0(3))*, Beach Lane Bks.) Beach Lane Bks.

—UnBEElievables: Honeybee Poems & Paintings. Florian, Douglas. 2012. (ENG.). 32p. (J). (gr. k-3). 17.99 *(978-1-4424-2652-8(7))*, Beach Lane Bks.) Beach Lane Bks.

Florian, Douglas & Taplinger, Lee, photos by. See for Your Self. Florian, Douglas. 2005. (Meet the Author Ser.). (ENG., 32p. (J). 14.95 *(978-1-57274-821-7(4))*, 731, Meet the Author) Owen, Richard C. Pubs., Inc.

Florian, Melanie. Emma, the Extra Ordinary Princess. Rennert, Laura Joy. 2009. (J). *(978-0-525-42152-8(1))*, Dutton Juvenile) Penguin Publishing Group.

Florian, Mélanie. Princess Addison Gets Angry, 1 vol. Martin, Molly. 2013. (Princess Heart Ser.). (ENG.). 24p. (gr. -1-1). 6.95 *(978-1-4048-8107-5(7))*; lib. bdg. 21.32 *(978-1-4048-7851-8(3))* Picture Window Bks.

—Princess Harper Gets Happy, 1 vol. Martin, Molly. 2013. (Princess Heart Ser.). (ENG.). 24p. (gr. -1-1). 6.95 *(978-1-4048-8108-2(5))*; lib. bdg. 21.32 *(978-1-4048-7852-5(1))* Picture Window Bks.

—Princess Heart. Martin, Molly. 2013. (Princess Heart Ser.). (ENG.). 24p. (gr. -1-1). 85.28 *(978-1-4048-8056-6(9))* Picture Window Bks.

—Princess Sophia Gets Scared, 1 vol. Martin, Molly. 2013. (Princess Heart Ser.). (ENG.). 24p. (gr. -1-1). 6.95 *(978-1-4048-8110-5(7))*; lib. bdg. 21.32 *(978-1-4048-7854-9(8))* Picture Window Bks.

—Princess Stella Gets Sad, 1 vol. Martin, Molly. 2013. (Princess Heart Ser.). (ENG.). 24p. (gr. -1-1). 6.95 *(978-1-4048-8109-9(3))*; lib. bdg. 21.32 *(978-1-4048-7853-2(X))* Picture Window Bks.

—Sleepy Little Caterpillar, 1 vol. Giulieri, Anne. 2012. (Engage Literacy Red Ser.). (ENG.). 32p. (gr. k-2). pap. 5.99 *(978-1-4296-8932-6(3))*, Engage Literacy) Capstone Pr., Inc.

—To the Shops, 1 vol. Giulieri, Anne. 2012. (Engage Literacy Magenta Ser.). (ENG.). 32p. (gr. k-2). pap. 5.99 *(978-1-4296-8882-6(3))*, Engage Literacy) Capstone Pr., Inc.

Florian, Melanie. A Day with Mommy. Florian, Melanie. 2010. (Sticker Stories Ser.). (ENG.). 16p. (J). (gr. -1-2). pap. 5.99 *(978-0-448-45342-2(8))*, Grosset & Dunlap) Penguin Publishing Group.

Florian, Mlanie. God's Amazing World! Spinelli, Eileen. 2014. 32p. (J). 15.99 *(978-0-8249-5661-5(3))*, Ideals Children's Bks.) Ideals Pubns.

Flory, Jane. The Too Little Fire Engine. Flory, Jane. 2015. (G&d Vintage Ser.). (ENG.). 24p. (J). (gr. -1-k). 7.99 *(978-0-448-48217-0(7))*, Grosset & Dunlap) Penguin Publishing Group.

Flotte, Eddie. Angkat: The Cambodian Cinderella. Coburn, Jewell Reinhart. 2014. (ENG.). 32p. (J). pap. 9.95 *(978-1-885008-42-8(2))*, Shen's Bks.) Lee & Low Bks., Inc.

Flournoy, L. Diana. Learning Through Symbolism & Celebrations. Love, Mary A. 2nd rev. ed. 2011. (ENG.). 168p. pap. 24.00 *(978-1-929548-00-2(1))* Love's Creative Resources.

Flowers, Tony. The Battle for the Golden Egg. Falk, Nick. 2015. (Samurai vs Ninja Ser.: 1). (ENG.). 96p. (J). (gr. 1-3). pap. 7.99 ***(978-0-85798-605-4(8))*** Random Hse. Australia AUS. Dist: Independent Pubs. Group.

Flowers, Tony. Eaten Alive! Falk, Nick. 2014. (Billy Is a Dragon Ser.: 4). (ENG.). 153p. (J). (gr. 1-3). pap. 10.99 *(978-0-85798-317-6(2))* Random Hse. Australia AUS. Dist: Independent Pubs. Group.

—First Bite. Falk, Nick. 2014. 1. 135p. (J). (gr. 1-3). 10.99 *(978-0-85798-305-3(9))* Random Hse. Australia AUS. Dist: Independent Pubs. Group.

Flowers, Tony. The Race for the Shogun's Treasure. Falk, Nick. 2015. (Samurai vs Ninja Ser.: 2). (ENG.). 96p. (J). (gr. 1-3). pap. 7.99 ***(978-0-85798-636-8(8))*** Random Hse. Australia AUS. Dist: Independent Pubs. Group.

Flowers, Tony. Shadow Shifter. Falk, Nick. 2014. 3. 137p. (J). (gr. 1-3). 10.99 *(978-0-85798-315-2(6))* Random Hse. Australia AUS. Dist: Independent Pubs. Group.

—Werewolves Beware! Falk, Nick. 2014. 2. 137p. (J). (gr. 1-3). 10.99 *(978-0-85798-307-7(5))* Random Hse. Australia AUS. Dist: Independent Pubs. Group.

Floyd, Claire. Stupid Alabama: A Laugh-So-Hard-You-Will-Snot about Growing up to Discover Not All Things Are Stupid but a Lot of Them Are. Wines, Michael P. Gierhart, Steve, ed. 2013. (ENG.). 244p. (YA). pap. 17.95 *(978-1-938667-13-8(1))* Ardent Writer Pr., LLC, The.

Floyd, John, Jr. A Bedtime Lullaby. Heath, Beverly C. 2006. 9p. (J). (gr. -1). bds. 5.95 *(978-0-9752860-1-2(3))* OurRainbow Pr., LLC.

—Counting with Colors. Heath, Beverly C. 2005. 8p. (J). (gr. -1). bds. 5.95 *(978-0-9752860-0-5(5))* OurRainbow Pr., LLC.

—I Like Dressing Up. Collins, Elaine Banks. 2005. (J). bds. 5.95 *(978-0-9752860-5-0(6))* OurRainbow Pr., LLC.

—Let's Potty! Lewis, Bisa. 2006. (J). bds. 6.99 *(978-1-934214-12-1(4))* OurRainbow Pr., LLC.

—My Parts Equal Me! Heath, Beverly C. 2005. 15p. (J). (gr. -1). bds. 5.95 *(978-0-9752860-2-9(1))* OurRainbow Pr., LLC.

—Neeko's Angel: A Story about Kindness. Mims, Melanie. 2006. (Fruit of the Spirit Ser.). 24p. (J). (gr. -1-1). 6.95 *(978-0-9752860-7-4(2))* OurRainbow Pr., LLC.

—Not All Angels Have Wings. Mims, Melanie. 2006. (Fruit of the Spirit Ser.). 24p. (J). (gr. -1-1). 6.95 *(978-0-9752860-6-7(4))* OurRainbow Pr., LLC.

—Opposites. Heath, Beverly C. 2006. 8p. (J). (gr. -1). bds. 5.95 *(978-0-9752860-3-6(X))* OurRainbow Pr., LLC.

—See What I Can Do. Collins, Elaine Banks. 2006. 10p. (J). (gr. -1). bds. 5.95 *(978-0-9752860-4-3(8))* OurRainbow Pr., LLC.

Fluharty, Kristi & Fluharty, T. Lively. Fool Moon Rising. Fluharty, Kristi & Fluharty, T. Lively. 2009. 40p. (J). 16.99 *(978-1-4335-0682-6(3))* Crossway.

Fluharty, T. Lively. The Barber Who Wanted to Pray. Sproul, R. C. 2011. 40p. (J). 17.99 *(978-1-4335-2703-6(0))* Crossway.

Fluharty, T. Lively, jt. illus. see Fluharty, Kristi.

Flynn, Noel. Summer Dance of the Fireflies. Connolly, Ed. 2003. 44p. (J). per. 10.95 *(978-1-888996-64-7(1))* Red Hen Pr.

Flynn, Samantha. Friends in a Storm. Seymour, Mary Sue. 2013. 20p. pap. 9.95 *(978-1-61633-376-8(6))* Guardian Angel Publishing, Inc.

Fochesato, Giorgio. Untold. Brennan, Sarah Rees. 2014. (Lynburn Legacy Ser.: Bk. 2). (ENG.). 400p. (J). (gr. 7). pap. 9.99 *(978-0-375-87104-7(7))*, Ember) Random Hse. Children's Bks.

—Untold. Brennan, Sarah Rees. 2013. (Lynburn Legacy Ser.: Bk. 2). (ENG.). 384p. (J). (gr. 7). 18.99 *(978-0-375-87042-2(3))* Random Hse., Inc.

Fochtman, Omra Jo. What's on the Other Side of the Rainbow? The Secret of the Golden Mirror. Masterson, Carla Jo. 2006. 40p. (J). 24.95 *(978-1-59975-228-0(X))* Father & Son Publishing.

Fodi, Lee Edward. Gwynne, Fair & Shining. Tara, Stephanie L. 2006. (J). (gr. -1-3). 16.95 *(978-1-933285-62-7(1))* Brown Bks. Publishing Group.

—I'll Follow the Moon. Tara, Stephanie. 2005. 40p. (J). 20.95 *(978-1-933285-13-9(3))* Brown Bks. Publishing Group.

—I'll Follow the Moon. Tara, Stephanie Lisa. 2011. 48p. (J). 12.99 *(978-1-61254-016-0(3))* Brown Bks. Publishing Group.

Födi, Lee Edward. Kendra Kandlestar & the Box of Whispers. 2013. (Kendra Kandlestar Ser.: 1). (ENG.). 228p. (J). (gr. 3-6). pap. 8.95 *(978-1-927018-25-5(0))* Simply Read Bks. CAN. Dist: Ingram Pub. Services.

—Kendra Kandlestar & the Door to Unger. 2013. (Kendra Kandlestar Ser.: 2). (ENG.). 260p. (J). (gr. 2-5). pap. 8.95 *(978-1-927018-26-2(9))* Simply Read Bks. CAN. Dist: Ingram Pub. Services.

Fodi, Lee Edward. Martha Ann's Quilt for Queen Victoria. Hicks, Kyra E. 2006. 28p. (J). (gr. -1-3). 16.95 *(978-1-933285-59-7(1))* Brown Bks. Publishing Group.

Födi, Lee Edward. Martha Ann's Quilt for Queen Victoria. Hicks, Kyra E. 2012. 32p. (J). pap. 12.95 *(978-0-9824796-8-1(9))* Black Threads Pr.

Fodi, Lee Edward. Kendra Kandlestar & the Box of Whispers. Fodi, Lee Edward. 2005. 227p. (J). (gr. 2). 16.95 *(978-1-933285-10-8(9))*; per. 8.95 *(978-1-933285-11-5(7))* Brown Bks. Publishing Group.

—Kendra Kandlestar & the Crack in Kazah. Fodi, Lee Edward. 2011. (ENG.). 282p. (J). (gr. 4-7). 16.95 *(978-1-61254-018-4(X))* Brown Bks. Publishing Group.

—Kendra Kandlestar & the Shard from Greeve. Fodi, Lee Edward. 2009. 304p. (J). (gr. 3-18). 16.95 *(978-1-934812-37-2(4))* Brown Bks. Publishing Group.

Fogarty, Alexandria, jt. illus. see Little Airplane Productions.

Fogden, Katherine, photos by. Meet Christopher: An Osage Indian Boy from Oklahoma. Simermeyer, Genevieve. 2008. (My World — Young Native Americans Today Ser.). (ENG., 48p. (J). 15.95 *(978-1-57178-217-5(6))* Council Oak Bks.

Fogel, Seymour. Among the River Pirates. Lloyd, Hugh. 2011. 204p. 44.95 *(978-1-258-06703-8(X))* Literary Licensing, LLC.

—Held for Ransom: A Skippy Dare Mystery Story. Lloyd, Hugh. 2011. 228p. 46.95 *(978-1-258-07879-9(1))* Literary Licensing, LLC.

Fogelin, Adrian. Sorta Sisters, 1 vol. Fogelin, Adrian. 2011. (ENG.). 288p. pap. 7.95 *(978-1-56145-592-8(X))*, Peachtree Junior) Peachtree Pubs.

Fogg, Paul. He Leads Me. 2008. 24p. pap. 9.95 *(978-0-9814878-1-6(5))* Little Hands Bk. Co., LLC.

—Jesus Said. 2008. 36p. pap. 10.95 *(978-0-9814878-2-3(3))* Little Hands Bk. Co., LLC.

Folch, Sergio. Good-bye Diaper! Geis, Patricia. 2009. (Good Habits with Coco & Tula Ser.). 16p. (J). (gr. -1-k). bds. 11.40 *(978-1-60754-404-3(0))* Windmill Bks.

—Good-bye Pacifier! Geis, Patricia. 2009. (Good Habits with Coco & Tula Ser.). 16p. (J). (gr. -1-k). bds. 11.40 *(978-1-60754-405-0(9))* Windmill Bks.

—Let's Eat! Geis, Patricia. 2009. (Good Habits with Coco & Tula Ser.). 16p. (J). (gr. -1-k). bds. 11.40 *(978-1-60754-411-1(3))* Windmill Bks.

—Let's Get Dressed! Geis, Patricia. 2009. (Good Habits with Coco & Tula Ser.). 16p. (J). (gr. -1-k). bds. 11.40 *(978-1-60754-409-8(1))* Windmill Bks.

—Let's Get Well! Geis, Patricia. 2009. (Good Habits with Coco & Tula Ser.). 16p. (J). (gr. -1-k). bds. 11.40 *(978-1-60754-407-4(5))* Windmill Bks.

—Let's Go to Sleep! Geis, Patricia. 2009. (Good Habits with Coco & Tula Ser.). 16p. (J). (gr. -1-k). bds. 11.40 *(978-1-60754-408-1(3))* Windmill Bks.

—Let's Help! Geis, Patricia. 2009. (Good Habits with Coco & Tula Ser.). 16p. (J). (gr. -1-k). bds. 11.40 *(978-1-60754-406-7(7))* Windmill Bks.

—Let's Wash Up! Geis, Patricia. 2009. (Good Habits with Coco & Tula Ser.). 16p. (J). (gr. -1-k). bds. 11.40 *(978-1-60754-410-4(5))* Windmill Bks.

Foley, Greg. Don't Worry Bear. Foley, Greg. 2008. (ENG.). 32p. (J). (gr. -1-k). 15.99 *(978-0-670-06245-4(6))*, Viking Juvenile) Penguin Publishing Group.

—Purple Little Bird. Foley, Greg. 2011. (ENG.). 32p. (J). (gr. -1-2). 14.99 *(978-0-06-200828-2(5))* HarperCollins Pubs.

—Thank You Bear. Foley, Greg. 2007. (ENG.). 32p. (J). (gr. -1-k). 15.99 *(978-0-670-06165-5(4))*, Viking Juvenile) Penguin Publishing Group.

—Thank You Bear Board Book. Foley, Greg. 2012. (ENG.). 30p. (J). (gr. -1-k). bds. 6.99 *(978-0-670-78507-0(5))*, Viking Juvenile) Penguin Publishing Group.

—Willoughby & the Lion. Foley, Greg. 2009. 40p. (J). (gr. -1-2). (ENG.). 17.99 *(978-0-06-154750-8(6))*; lib. bdg. 18.89 *(978-0-06-154751-5(4))* HarperCollins Pubs.

—Willoughby & the Moon. Foley, Greg. 2010. (ENG.). 40p. (J). (gr. -1-2). 18.99 *(978-0-06-154753-9(0))* HarperCollins Pubs.

Foley, Niki. Blaze of Glory (Blaze & the Monster Machines) Random House Staff. 2015. (Pictureback(R) Ser.). (ENG.). 16p. (J). (gr. -1-2). 4.99 ***(978-0-553-52457-4(7))***, Random Hse. Bks. for Young Readers) Random Hse. Children's Bks.

Foley, Tim. The Bambino: The Story of Babe Ruth's Legendary 1927 Season, 1 vol. Yomtov, Nelson. 2011. (American Graphic Ser.). (ENG.). 32p. (gr. 3-4). lib. bdg. 29.99 *(978-1-4296-5473-9(2))*, Graphic Library) Capstone Pr., Inc.

—The Bambino: The Story of Babe Ruth's Legendary 1927 Season, 1 vol. Yomtov, Nel. 2011. (American Graphic Ser.). (ENG.). 32p. (gr. 3-4). pap. 8.10 *(978-1-4296-6265-9(4))*; pap. 47.70 *(978-1-4296-6433-2(9))* Capstone Pr., Inc. (Graphic Library).

—What Was the Lewis & Clark Expedition? St. George, Judith. 2014. (What Was... ? Ser.). (ENG.). 112p. (J). (gr. 3-7). pap. 5.99 *(978-0-448-47901-9(X))*, Grosset & Dunlap) Penguin Publishing Group.

—Who Was Julius Caesar? Medina, Nico. 2014. (Who Was... ? Ser.). (ENG.). 112p. (J). (gr. 3-7). pap. 5.99 *(978-0-448-48083-1(2))*, Grosset & Dunlap) Penguin Publishing Group.

Foley, Tim & Harper, Fred. What Is the Panama Canal? Pascal, Janet B. 2014. (What Was... ? Ser.). (ENG.). 112p. (J). (gr. 3-7). 5.99 *(978-0-448-47899-9(4))*, Grosset & Dunlap) Penguin Publishing Group.

Foley, Tim & Harrison, Nancy. Who Was Isaac Newton? Pascal, Janet. 2014. (Who Was... ? Ser.). (ENG.). 112p. (J). (gr. 3-7). pap. 5.99 *(978-0-448-47913-2(3))*, Grosset & Dunlap) Penguin Publishing Group.

—Who Was Robert Ripley? Anderson, Kirsten. 2015. (Who Was... ? Ser.). (ENG.). 112p. (J). (gr. 3-7). 5.99 *(978-0-448-48298-9(3))*, Grosset & Dunlap) Penguin Publishing Group.

—Who Were the Wright Brothers? Buckley, James, Jr. 2014. (Who Was... ? Ser.). (ENG.). 112p. (J). (gr. 3-7). 5.99 *(978-0-448-47951-4(6))*, Grosset & Dunlap) Penguin Publishing Group.

Foli, Gianluca. The Bear with the Sword. Cali, Davide. 2010. (ENG.). 32p. (J). (gr. -1-3). 15.99 *(978-0-9806070-4-8(3))* Wilkins Farago Pty, Ltd. AUS. Dist: Independent Pubs. Group.

Folkard, Charles. Pinocchio, As First Translated into English by M a Murray & Illustrated by Charles Folkard. Murray, M. A., tr. 2009. 280p. pap. 11.95 *(978-1-59915-177-9(4))* Yesterday's Classics.

Folkerts, Jason. The Mystery of the Round Rocks. Meierhenry, Mark V. & Volk, David. 2007. 44p. (J). (gr. 2-5). pap. 13.95 *(978-0-9777955-3-6(5))*, South Dakota State Historical Society Pr.) South Dakota State Historical Society Pr.

—The Mystery of the Tree Rings. Meierhenry, Mark V. & Volk, David. 2008. 44p. (J). 13.95 *(978-0-9798940-0-8(X))*, South Dakota State Historical Society Pr.) South Dakota State Historical Society Pr.

Folmsbee, Patricia. Happy Anderson & Connie Clam. Custureri, Mary. 2006. 36p. (J). spiral bd. 24.95 *(978-1-933190-00-6(0))* HighPoint Publishing, Inc.

Foltz, Susan Convery. Jan Napjus & the Ghost. Foltz, Sharon Terpstra. 2009. 24p. (J). 15.99 *(978-1-4415-5097-2(6))* Xlibris Corp.

Fonseca-Hughes, Sarah. The Grape Escape: Call 9-1-1, the Grapes Are on the Run! Debowksi, Sharon. 2007. 32p. (J). 14.95 *(978-1-60227-472-3(X))* Above the Clouds Publishing.

Fontana, Ugo. The Rabbit Catcher & Other Fairy Tales. Bechstein, Ludwig. Jarrell, Randall, tr. 2011. 42p. 35.95 *(978-1-258-08375-5(2))* Literary Licensing, LLC.

Fontanez, Edwin. En esta hermosa Isla. Fontanez, Edwin. 2nd rev. ed. 2005. (SPA.). 32p. (J). 16.95 *(978-0-9640868-7-6(5))* Exit Studio.

—Hadas, Sirenas y Sapos: Un ramito de poemas Encantados. Fontanez, Edwin. 2008. (SPA.). 32p. (J). lib. bdg. 19.99 *(978-0-9640868-8-3(3))* Exit Studio.

—On This Beautiful Island. Fontanez, Edwin. l.t. ed. 2004. 32p. (J). 16.95 *(978-0-9640868-6-9(7))*, 1241077) Exit Studio.

Foote, Dan. Jack Hayford Presenta Hechos una Historia de la Biblia. Hayford, Jack W. 2005. 60p. (J). (gr. -1-5). 9.99 *(978-1-59185-487-6(3))*, Charisma Kids) Charisma Media.

—The Land of Havala. Moores, Katie. 2006. (ENG.). 64p. pap. 6.99 *(978-1-59185-910-9(7))*, Creation Hse.) Charisma Media.

Foote, David. Modern Fairies, Dwarves, Goblins, & Other Nasties: A Practical Guide by Miss Edythe McFate. Blume, Lesley M. M. 2012. (ENG.). 256p. (J). (gr. 3-7). pap. 7.99 *(978-0-375-85493-4(2))* Knopf, Alfred A. Inc.

—Modern Fairies, Dwarves, Goblins, & Other Nasties: A Practical Guide by Miss Edythe McFate. Blume, Lesley M. M. 2010. (ENG.). 256p. (J). (gr. 3-7). 16.99 *(978-0-375-86203-8(X))*, Knopf Bks. for Young Readers) Random Hse. Children's Bks.

—The Wondrous Journals of Dr. Wendell Wellington Wiggins. Blume, Lesley M. 2012. (ENG.). 256p. (J). (gr. 3-7). 16.99 *(978-0-375-86850-4(X))*, Knopf Bks. for Young Readers) Random Hse. Children's Bks.

—The Wondrous Journals of Dr. Wendell Wiggins. Blume, Lesley M. M. 2013. (ENG.). 256p. (J). (gr. 3-7). pap. 7.99 *(978-0-375-87218-1(3))* Knopf, Alfred A. Inc.

Foott, Jeff, photos by. A Pod of Killer Whales: The Mysterious Life of the Intelligent Orca. León, Vicki. 2nd ed. 2006. (Jean-Michel Cousteau Presents Ser.). (ENG.). 48p. (J). (gr. 4-9). pap. 9.95 *(978-0-9766134-7-3(6))* London Town Pr.

Forberg, Ati. Samurai of Gold Hill. Uchida, Yoshiko. 2005. 119p. (J). (gr. 2). per. 8.95 *(978-1-59714-015-7(5))* Heyday.

Forbes, Ashley. Pet Preacher. Forbes, Ashley. 2003. 20p. pap. 5.95 *(978-0-9711564-6-3(8))* Pendleton Publishing, Inc.

Forbes, Justin. Under the Faithful Watch of the River Hawk. Forbes, J. L. 2013. 20p. pap. 24.95 *(978-1-62709-899-1(2))* America Star Bks.

Forbush, Lisa. Alaska's Wild Animals Coloring Book. Forbush, Kyle. 2003. (J). 3.95 *(978-1-57833-232-8(X))* Todd Communications.

—Balto: The Dog Hero. Forbush, Kyle. 2004. (J). pap. 14.95 *(978-1-57833-267-0(2))* Todd Communications.

—A Is for Alaska - an ABC Book. Forbush, Kyle & Forbush, Kyle. 2004. (J). bds. 6.95 *(978-1-57833-287-8(7))* Todd Communications.
—The Sourdoughs' Five Children. Forbush, Kyle. 2004. (J). bds. 6.95 *(978-1-57833-258-8(3))* Todd Communications.
—Who Is Alaska's Favorite Bear? Forbush, Kyle. 2003. (J). bds. 6.95 *(978-1-57833-211-3(7))* Todd Communications.
Forcada, Adiela & Giron, Elizabeth. Lambyro. Olesen, Demetria Vassiliou. 2011. (ENG.). 32p. (J). 19.00 *(978-0-615-47664-3(3))* Elissian Publishing Co.
Ford, A. G. Barack. Winter, Jonah. 32p. (J). (gr. -1-2). 2010. (ENG.). pap. 6.99 *(978-0-06-170396-6(6)*, Tegen, Katherine Bks); 2008. lib. bdg. 18.89 *(978-0-06-170393-5(1))*; 2008. (ENG.). 17.99 *(978-0-06-170392-8(3)*, Tegen, Katherine Bks) HarperCollins Pubs.
—Desmond & the Very Mean Word. Tutu, Desmond. 2012. (ENG.). 32p. (J). (gr. 1-4). 15.99 *(978-0-7636-5229-6(6))* Candlewick Pr.
—First Family. Hopkinson, Deborah. 2009. (ENG.). 32p. (J). (gr. -1-2). 17.99 *(978-0-06-189680-4(2)*, Tegen, Katherine Bks) HarperCollins Pubs.
—Goal! Javaherbin, Mina. 2012. (ENG.). 40p. (J). (gr. 1-4). pap. 6.99 *(978-0-7636-5822-9(7))* Candlewick Pr.
—Hello, I'm Johnny Cash. Neri, G. 2014. (ENG.). 40p. (J). (gr. 4-7). 16.99 *(978-0-7636-6245-5(3))* Candlewick Pr.
—JFK. Winter, Jonah. 2013. (ENG.). 32p. (J). (gr. -1-3). 17.99 *(978-0-06-176807-1(3))* HarperCollins Pubs.
—Malcolm Little: The Boy Who Grew up to Become Malcolm X. Shabazz, Ilyasah. 2014. (ENG.). 48p. (J). (gr. 1-5). 17.99 *(978-1-4424-1216-3(X))* Simon & Schuster Children's Publishing.
—Michelle. Hopkinson, Deborah. 2009. 32p. (J). (gr. -1-2). 17.99 *(978-0-06-182739-6(8))*; lib. bdg. 18.89 *(978-0-06-182743-3(6)*, Tegen, Katherine Bks) HarperCollins Pubs.
—My Daddy, Dr. Martin Luther King, Jr. King, Martin Luther, III. 2013. 32p. (J). (gr. -1-3). (ENG.). 17.99 *(978-0-06-028075-8(1))*; 18.89 *(978-0-06-028076-5(X))* HarperCollins Pubs. (Amistad).
Ford, A. G., et al. Our Children Can Soar: A Celebration of Rosa, Barack, & the Pioneers of Change. Cook, Michelle. 2009. (ENG.). 32p. (J). (gr. -1-3). 16.99 *(978-1-59990-418-4(7)*, Bloomsbury USA Childrens) Bloomsbury USA.
Ford, A. G. Roc & Roe's Twelve Days of Christmas. Cannon, Nick & Carey, Mariah. 2014. (ENG.). 32p. (J). (gr. -1-k). 17.99 *(978-0-545-51950-2(0)*, Orchard Bks.) Scholastic, Inc.
—Summer Jackson: Grown Up. Harris, Teresa E. 2011. (ENG.). 32p. (J). (gr. -1-2). 16.99 *(978-0-06-185757-7(2)*, Tegen, Katherine Bks) HarperCollins Pubs.
—Under the Same Sun. Robinson, Sharon. 2014. (ENG.). 40p. (J). (gr. -1-3). 17.99 *(978-0-545-16672-0(1)*, Scholastic Pr.) Scholastic, Inc.
Ford, A. G., jt. illus. see Boos, Ben.
Ford, Christina. A Button for a Crown. Lawrence, Ava. l.t. ed. 2003. 84p. (J). 14.95 *(978-0-9651048-4-5(2))* Papillon Publishing.
Ford, Christopher. An Epic Doodle, Bk. 1. Ford, Christopher. 2011. (Stickman Odyssey Ser.: 1). (ENG.). 208p. (J). (gr. 3-7). 12.99 *(978-0-399-25426-0(9)*, Philomel) Penguin Publishing Group.
—The Wrath of Zozimos, 2 vols., Bk. 2. Ford, Christopher. 2012. (Stickman Odyssey Ser.: 2). (ENG.). 224p. (J). (gr. 3-7). 12.99 *(978-0-399-25427-7(7)*, Philomel) Penguin Publishing Group.
Ford, David. Power Reading: Chapter/Sci-Fi/Dr. Little 2. Cole, Bob. 2005. 25p. (J). (gr. 3-4). vinyl bd. 39.95 *(978-1-883186-76-0(5)*, PPSF4) National Reading Styles Institute, Inc.
—Power Reading: Chapter/Sci-Fi/Superhero. Cole, Bob. 2004. 25p. (J). (gr. 3-4). vinyl bd. 39.95 *(978-1-883186-62-3(5)*, PPSF2) National Reading Styles Institute, Inc.
—Power Reading: Chapter/Sci-Fi/Time Warp. Cole, Bob. 2004. 25p. (J). (gr. 4-18). vinyl bd. 39.95 *(978-1-883186-60-9(9)*, PPSF3) National Reading Styles Institute, Inc.
—Power Reading: Chapter/Sci-Fi/Time Warp 2. Cole, Bob. 2005. 52p. (J). (gr. 4-18). vinyl bd. 39.95 *(978-1-883186-75-3(7)*, PPSF5) National Reading Styles Institute, Inc.
—Power Reading: Comic Book/Superhero. Cole, Bob. 2005. 34p. (J). (gr. 2-4). vinyl bd. 29.95 *(978-1-883186-79-1(X)*, PPSFC2) National Reading Styles Institute, Inc.
—Power Reading: Comic Book/Time Warp. Cole, Bob. 2005. 36p. (J). (gr. 3-4). vinyl bd. 29.95 *(978-1-883186-69-2(2)*, PPSFC3) National Reading Styles Institute, Inc.
—Power Reading: Comic Book/Time Warp 2. Cole, Bob. 2005. 36p. (J). (gr. 3-4). vinyl bd. 29.95 *(978-1-933533-01-8(3)*, PPSFC3A) National Reading Styles Institute, Inc.
Ford, Emily. Jesus Loves Trucks. Haluska, David. 2014. 32p. (J). 7.99 *(978-0-8280-2719-9(6))* Review & Herald Publishing Assn.
Ford, George. Paul Robeson. Greenfield, Eloise. 2009. (ENG.). 40p. (J). (gr. 1-6). pap. 10.95 *(978-1-60060-262-7(2))* Lee & Low Bks., Inc.
—The Story of Ruby Bridges. Coles, Robert. 50th anniv. ed. 2010. (ENG.). 32p. (J). (gr. -1-3). pap. 6.99 *(978-0-439-47226-5(1)*, Scholastic Paperbacks) Scholastic, Inc.
Ford, Gilbert. Moonpenny Island. Springstubb, Tricia. 2015. (ENG.). 304p. (J). (gr. 3-7). 16.99 *(978-0-06-211293-4(7))* HarperCollins Pubs.
—Mr. Ferris & His Wheel. Davis, Kathryn Gibbs. 2014. (ENG.). 40p. (J). (gr. -1-3). 17.99 *(978-0-547-95922-1(2)*, HMH Books For Young Readers) Houghton Mifflin Harcourt Publishing Co.
—The Name of This Book Is Secret. Bosch, Pseudonymous. rev. ed. 2007. (Secret Ser.: 1). (ENG.). 384p. (J). (gr. 3-7). 16.99 *(978-0-316-11366-3(2))* Little, Brown Bks. for Young Readers.
—12 Days of New York. Bolden, Tonya. 2013. (ENG.). 32p. (J). (gr. -1-k). 17.95 *(978-1-4197-0542-7(3)*, Abrams Bks. for Young Readers) Abrams.
Ford, H. J. The Book of Romance. Lang, Andrew, ed. 2004. reprint ed. pap. 34.95 *(978-1-4179-1718-1(0))* Kessinger Publishing, LLC.
—The Book of Saints & Heroes. Lang, Leonora Blanche. Lang, Andrew, ed. 2012. 344p. pap. 13.50 *(978-1-936639-18-2(1))* St. Augustine Academy Pr.
—Tales of Troy & Greece. Lang, Andrew. 2006. (Dover Children's Classics Ser.). (ENG.). 336p. (gr. 9-12). per. 9.95 *(978-0-486-44917-3(3))* Dover Pubns., Inc.
Ford, H. J. The Tale of the Cid: And Other Stories of Knights & Chivalry. Ford, H. J. Lang, Andrew. 2007. (Dover Children's Classics Ser.). (ENG.). 208p. (J). (gr. 4-7). per. 9.95 *(978-0-486-45470-2(3))* Dover Pubns., Inc.
Ford, Henry J. The Red Book of Animal Stories 1899. Lang, Andrew, ed. 2004. reprint ed. pap. 34.95 *(978-1-4179-8249-3(7))* Kessinger Publishing, LLC.
Ford, Kate. How to Be a Wizard at Grammer. Yates, Irene. 48p. (J). (gr. 3-6). pap. *(978-1-876367-29-9(6))* Wizard Bks.
—How to Be a Wizard at Nursery Rhymes. Laurence, Jo. 48p. (J). (gr. 1-3). pap. *(978-1-876367-28-2(8))* Wizard Bks.
—How to Be Brilliant at Science Investigations. Hughes, Colin & Wade, Winnie. 2004. 48p. pap. 30.00 *(978-1-897675-11-3(9))* Brilliant Pubns. GBR. Dist: Parkwest Pubns., Inc.
—How to Be Brilliant at Writing Poetry. Yates, Irene Dorothy. 2004. 48p. pap. 30.00 *(978-1-897675-01-4(1))* Brilliant Pubns. GBR. Dist: Parkwest Pubns., Inc.
—How to Sparkle at Assessing Science. Burton, Neil. 2004. 48p. pap. 30.00 *(978-1-897675-20-5(8))* Brilliant Pubns. GBR. Dist: Parkwest Pubns., Inc.
Ford, Sandy Lee. Gullah, the Nawleans Cat Meets Katrina. 2007. 32p. (J). *(978-0-9793637-0-2(5))* Hart Street Pubs.
Ford, Stephanie. Confederate Night Before Christmas, 1 vol. Vogl, Mark. 2015. (ENG.). 32p. (J). (gr. k-3). 16.99 ***(978-1-4556-2075-3(0))*** Pelican Publishing Co., Inc.
Ford, Stephanie. Nadine, My Funny & Trusty Guide Dog, 1 vol. Fleischman, Carol. 2015. 32p. (J). 16.99 *(978-1-4556-1927-6(2))* Pelican Publishing Co., Inc.
—Willy the Texas Longhorn, 1 vol. Elliott, Alan. 2013. (ENG.). 32p. (J). (gr. k-3). 16.99 *(978-1-4556-1870-5(5))* Pelican Publishing Co., Inc.
Ford, Stephanie A. Confederate Alphabet, 1 vol. Pittman, Rickey E. 2011. (ENG.). 32p. (J). (gr. k-3). 16.99 *(978-1-58980-760-0(X))* Pelican Publishing Co., Inc.
Ford, Yvonne. Farm Days A-Z Coloring Book. Marsh, Carole. 2009. 28p. (J). 5.99 *(978-0-635-07421-8(4))* Gallopade International.
Fore, Elizabeth. Maude, the Flop-Eared Mule. Wilson, Douglas. 2012. 38p. 24.95 *(978-1-4626-7455-8(0))* America Star Bks.
Foreman, A. Skeeter Sneeter Doodlebop. Smith, C. Michelle. 2009. 24p. pap. 15.63 *(978-1-934840-54-2(8))* Nimble Bks. LLC.
—Skeeter Uses Manners. Smith, C. Michelle. 2010. 28p. pap. 17.36 *(978-1-60888-017-1(6))* Nimble Bks. LLC.
Foreman, Austin Lee, jt. illus. see Dreisbach, Kristin Wolf.
Foreman, Gabe. Halifax Hal. Thran, Nick. 2013. (ENG.). 46p. (YA). (gr. 5). pap. 9.95 *(978-1-897411-77-3(4))* Bayeux Arts, Inc. CAN. Dist: Chicago Distribution Ctr.
Foreman, Michael. Animal Tales. Jones, Terry. 2013. (Fantastic World of Terry Jones Ser.). (ENG.). 120p. (J). (gr. 4-7). 16.99 *(978-1-84365-163-5(7)*, Pavilion) Pavilion Bks. GBR. Dist: Independent Pubs. Group.
—Beowulf. Morpurgo, Michael. 2015. (ENG.). 160p. (J). (gr. 3-7). pap. 6.99 *(978-0-7636-7297-3(1))* Candlewick Pr.
—The Best Christmas Present in the World. Morpurgo, Michael. 2004. (ENG.). 48p. (J). (gr. k-4). 9.99 *(978-1-4052-1518-3(6))* Egmont Bks., Ltd. GBR. Dist: Independent Pubs. Group.
—Billy the Kid. Morpurgo, Michael. 2013. (ENG.). 80p. (J). (gr. 2-4). pap. 11.99 *(978-1-84365-260-1(9)*, Pavilion) Pavilion Bks. GBR. Dist: Independent Pubs. Group.
—El Caballo de Arena. Turnbull, Ann. (Barril Sin Fondo Ser.).Tr. of Sand Horse. (SPA.). (J). (gr. 3-5). pap. *(978-968-6465-00-6(6))* Casa de Estudios de Literatura y Talleres Artisticos Amaquemecan A.C. MEX. Dist: Lectorum Pubns., Inc.
—El Delfín de Luis. Morpurgo, Michael & Foreman. 2004.Tr. of Dolphin Boy. (SPA.). 32p. (J). (gr. 1-2). 19.99 *(978-84-261-3401-1(7)*, JV32953) Juventud, Editorial ESP. Dist: Lectorum Pubns., Inc.
—Dolphin Boy. Morpurgo, Michael. 2005. (ENG.). 32p. (J). (gr. k-2). pap. 13.99 *(978-1-84270-448-6(6))*; 14.99 *(978-1-84270-320-5(X))* Andersen Pr. GBR. Dist: Independent Pubs. Group, Trafalgar Square Publishing.
—Fairy Tales. Jones, Terry. 2013. (Fantastic World of Terry Jones Ser.). (ENG.). 120p. (J). (gr. 4-7). 16.99 *(978-1-84365-161-1(0)*, Pavilion) Pavilion Bks. GBR. Dist: Independent Pubs. Group.
—Fantastic Stories. Jones, Terry. 2013. (Fantastic World of Terry Jones Ser.). (ENG.). 120p. (J). (gr. 4-7). 16.99 *(978-1-84365-162-8(9)*, Pavilion) Pavilion Bks. GBR. Dist: Independent Pubs. Group.
—Farm Boy. Morpurgo, Michael. 2007. (ENG.). 76p. (J). (gr. 4-7). pap. 15.99 *(978-1-84365-090-4(8))* Pavilion Bks. GBR. Dist: Independent Pubs. Group.
—The General. Charters, Janet. 2010. (ENG.). 48p. (J). (gr. k-12). 16.99 *(978-0-7636-4875-6(2))* Candlewick Pr.
—Gentle Giant. Morpurgo, Michael. 2006. 28p. (J). reprint ed. (gr. k-4). pap. 12.00 *(978-1-4223-5667-8(1))*; (gr. 4-8). 19.00 *(978-1-4223-5398-1(2))* DIANE Publishing Co.
—Gentle Giant. Morpurgo, Michael. 2003. (ENG.). 32p. (J). 16.95 *(978-0-00-711064-3(2)*, HarperCollins Children's Bks.) HarperCollins Pubs. Ltd. GBR. Dist: Trafalgar Square Publishing.
—Kaspar the Titanic Cat. Morpurgo, Michael. 2012. 208p. (J). (gr. 3-7). 16.99 *(978-0-06-200618-9(5))* HarperCollins Pubs.
—Little Albatross. Morpurgo, Michael. 2006. (ENG.). 32p. (J). pap. 8.99 *(978-0-552-54698-0(4))* Transworld Publishers Ltd. GBR. Dist: Independent Pubs. Group.
—The Little Ships: The Heroic Rescue at Dunkirk in World War II. Borden, Louise. 2003. (ENG.). 32p. (J). (gr. 4-7). 7.99 *(978-0-689-85396-8(3)*, McElderry, Margaret K. Bks.) McElderry, Margaret K. Bks.
—Long Neck & Thunder Foot. Piers, Helen. 2013. (ENG.). 32p. (J). (gr. -1-k). pap. 8.99 *(978-1-84939-482-6(2))* Andersen Pr. GBR. Dist: Independent Pubs. Group.
—Michael Foreman's Alice's Adventures in Wonderland. Carroll, Lewis. 2010. (ENG.). 176p. (J). (gr. 2-7). 19.99 *(978-1-84365-142-0(4)*, Pavilion Children's Books) Pavilion Bks. GBR. Dist: Independent Pubs. Group.
—Michael Foreman's the Wonderful Wizard of Oz. Baum, L. Frank. 2010. (ENG.). 160p. (J). (gr. 2-7). 19.99 *(978-1-84365-157-4(2)*, Pavilion Children's Books) Pavilion Bks. GBR. Dist: Independent Pubs. Group.
—Michael Foreman's Treasure Island. Stevenson, Robert Louis. 2010. (ENG.). 232p. (J). (gr. 2-7). 19.99 *(978-1-84365-117-8(3)*, Pavilion Children's Books) Pavilion Bks. GBR. Dist: Independent Pubs. Group.
—The Mozart Question. Morpurgo, Michael. 2008. (ENG.). 80p. (J). (gr. 3-7). 15.99 *(978-0-7636-3552-7(9))* Candlewick Pr.
—Peter Pan & Wendy. Barrie, J. M. 2003. (Chrysalis Childrens Classics Ser.). 176p. (YA). pap. *(978-1-84365-039-3(8)*, Pavilion Children's Books) Pavilion Bks.
—Peter Pan & Wendy. Barrie, J. M. 2010. (ENG.). 160p. (J). (gr. 2-7). 19.99 *(978-1-84365-136-9(X)*, Pavilion Children's Books) Pavilion Bks. GBR. Dist: Independent Pubs. Group.
—El Reino de Kensuke. Morpurgo, Michael. Aguilar, Carmen, tr. 2006.Tr. of Kensuke's Kingdom. (SPA.). 155p. (J). (gr. 5-8). 16.99 *(978-84-7901-420-9(2))* RBA Libros, S.A. ESP. Dist: Santillana USA Publishing Co., Inc.
—The Saga of Erik the Viking. Jones, Terry. 30th ed. 2013. (ENG.). 250p. (J). (gr. 4-7). 16.99 *(978-1-84365-224-3(2)*, Pavilion) Pavilion Bks. GBR. Dist: Independent Pubs. Group.
—Say Hello. Foreman, Jack. (ENG.). (J). (gr. -1-2). 2012. 40p. pap. 6.99 *(978-0-7636-6087-1(6))*; 2008. 32p. 15.99 *(978-0-7636-3657-9(6))* Candlewick Pr.
—Team Trouble. Smiley, Sophie. 2007. (ENG.). 64p. (J). (gr. 2-4). pap. 9.95 *(978-1-84270-684-8(5))* Andersen Pr. GBR. Dist: Independent Pubs. Group.
—Toro! Toro! Morpurgo, Michael. 2007. (ENG.). 128p. (J). (gr. 4-7). pap. 8.99 *(978-0-00-710718-6(8)*, HarperSport) HarperCollins Pubs. Ltd. GBR. Dist: HarperCollins Pubs.
Foreman, Michael. The White Horse of Zennor & Other Stories. Morpurgo, Michael. 2015. (ENG.). 176p. (J). (gr. 2-4). pap. 10.99 ***(978-1-4052-7301-5(1))*** Egmont Bks., Ltd. GBR. Dist: Independent Pubs. Group.
Foreman, Michael. White Owl, Barn Owl: Read & Wonder. Davies, Nicola. 2009. (Read & Wonder Ser.). (ENG.). 32p. (J). (gr. -1-3). pap. 6.99 *(978-0-7636-4143-6(X))* Candlewick Pr.
—White Owl, Barn Owl with Audio, Peggable. Davies, Nicola. 2009. (Read, Listen, & Wonder Ser.). (ENG.). 32p. (J). (gr. -1-3). pap. 9.99 *(978-0-7636-4194-8(4))* Candlewick Pr.
Foreman, Michael. Cat & Dog. Foreman, Michael. 2014. (ENG.). 32p. (J). (gr. -1-3). 16.95 *(978-1-4677-5124-7(3))* Lerner Publishing Group.
—Fortunately, Unfortunately. Foreman, Michael. 2011. (Andersen Press Picture Bks). (ENG.). 32p. (J). (gr. -1-3). 16.95 *(978-0-7613-7460-2(4))* Lerner Publishing Group.
—Friends. Foreman, Michael. 2012. (Andersen Press Picture Bks). (ENG.). 32p. (J). (gr. -1-3). 16.95 *(978-1-4677-0317-8(6))* Lerner Publishing Group.
—I Love You, Too! Foreman, Michael. 2014. (ENG.). 32p. (J). (gr. -1-3). 16.95 *(978-1-4677-3451-6(9))* Lerner Publishing Group.
—Newspaper Boy & Origami Girl! Foreman, Michael. 2013. (Origami Girl Ser.). (ENG.). 32p. (J). (gr. -1-k). 16.99 *(978-1-84939-451-2(2))* Andersen Pr. GBR. Dist: Independent Pubs. Group.
—Norman's Ark. Foreman, Michael. 2006. (Tiger Tales Ser.). 24p. (J). (gr. -1-3). pap. 6.95 *(978-1-58925-401-5(5))* Tiger Tales.
—Oh! If Only... Foreman, Michael. 2013. 32p. (gr. -1-3). 16.95 *(978-1-4677-1213-2(2))* Andersen Pr. GBR. Dist: Lerner Publishing Group.
—Seal Surfer. Foreman, Michael. 2007. (ENG.). 36p. (J). (gr. k-4). pap. 10.99 *(978-1-84270-578-0(4))* Andersen Pr. GBR. Dist: Independent Pubs. Group.
Foreman, Michael. The Seeds of Friendship. Foreman, Michael. 2015. (ENG.). 32p. (J). (gr. -1-3). 16.99 ***(978-0-7636-7834-0(1))*** Candlewick Pr.
Foreman, Michael. Superfrog! Foreman, Michael. 2012. (ENG.). 32p. (J). (gr. -1-k). pap. 10.99 *(978-1-84939-219-8(6))* Andersen Pr. GBR. Dist: Independent Pubs. Group.
—Superfrog & the Big Stink! Foreman, Michael. 2014. (ENG.). 32p. (J). (gr. -1-k). pap. 9.99 *(978-1-78344-030-6(9))* Andersen Pr. GBR. Dist: Independent Pubs. Group.
—Wonder Goal! Foreman, Michael. 2010. (ENG.). 32p. (J). (gr. k-2). pap. 12.99 *(978-1-84270-934-4(8))* Andersen Pr. GBR. Dist: Independent Pubs. Group.
Foreman, Michael. Classic Christmas Tales. Foreman, Michael, compiled by. 2014. (ENG.). 120p. (J). (gr. 3). 16.99 *(978-1-84365-266-3(8)*, Pavilion) Pavilion Bks. GBR. Dist: Independent Pubs. Group.
Foreman, Michael. Classic Fairy Tales. Foreman, Michael, retold by. 2005. (ENG.). 176p. (J). (gr. 2-5). 12.95 *(978-1-4027-2865-5(4))* Sterling Publishing Co., Inc.
Foreman, Michael, jt. illus. see Jones, Terry.
Forest, Crista. Let's Explore, Moose! Fraggalosch, Audrey. (ENG.). 32p. (J). (gr. -1-1). 2005. pap. 3.95 *(978-1-59249-151-3(0)*, S2017); 2003. 12.95 *(978-1-59249-152-0(9)*, PS2017) Soundprints.
—Moon in Bear's Eyes. Swinburne, Stephen R. 2005. (ENG.). 32p. (J). (gr. k-7). pap. 9.95 *(978-1-59078-330-6(1))* Boyds Mills Pr.
Forgas-Davis, Melissa. After Dark. Forgas, Christine. 2004. 17p. (J). (gr. 1-6). pap. *(978-1-930200-27-2(7))* Martell Publishing Co.
Forlati, Anna. Yoga for Kids: Simple Animal Poses for Any Age. Pajalunga, Lorena V. 2015. (ENG.). 32p. (J). (gr. -1-2). 16.99 ***(978-0-8075-9172-7(6))*** Whitman, Albert & Co.
Formello, Lorri. If You Sleep with a Cat on Your Head. Starling, Landa. 2008. 27p. pap. 24.95 *(978-1-60703-318-9(6))* America Star Bks.
Formosa, Natasha. Potato Boy. Rate, Kristina. 2005. 32p. (J). (gr. -1). per. *(978-0-9549372-0-1(1))* Fastback TV Ltd.
Fornari, Giuliano. Panoramas Human Body. 2006. (J). *(978-0-7607-8155-5(9))* backpackbook.
Forney, Ellen. The Absolutely True Diary of a Part-Time Indian. Alexie, Sherman. (ENG.). (YA). (gr. 7-17). 2009. 288p. pap. 15.00 *(978-0-316-01369-7(2))*; 2007. 240p. 20.00 *(978-0-316-01368-0(4))* Little, Brown Bks. for Young Readers.
—The Absolutely True Diary of a Part-Time Indian. Alexie, Sherman. 2008. 230p. 25.00 *(978-1-60686-072-4(0))* Perfection Learning Corp.
—The Absolutely True Diary of a Part-Time Indian. Alexie, Sherman. l.t. ed. 2008. (Thorndike Literacy Bridge Ser.). (ENG.). 302p. (YA). (gr. 7-12). 23.95 *(978-1-4104-0499-2(4))* Thorndike Pr.
Forney, Ellen. Monkey Food: The Complete I was Seven in '75 Collection. Forney, Ellen. 2005. 142p. (YA). reprint ed. pap. 13.00 *(978-0-7567-8610-6(X))* DIANE Publishing Co.
Forrest, A. S. Our Island Story (Yesterday's Classics) Marshall, H. E. l.t. ed. 2006. 676p. (J). per. 19.95 *(978-1-59915-009-3(3))* Yesterday's Classics.
Forrest, Amber. Butterflies & Dragon Tears: A Pacific Northwest Quileute Legand Come to Life for Children. Ludvik, Elizabeth. 2011. (ENG.). 38p. pap. 9.40 *(978-1-4662-8597-2(4))* CreateSpace Independent Publishing Platform.
—The Toymakers New Job: The Story of Why Santa Claus Dedicated His Life to Serving the Children Around the World. Ludvik, Elizabeth. 2010. (ENG.). 28p. pap. 10.13 *(978-1-4564-4496-9(4))* CreateSpace Independent Publishing Platform.
Forrest, Chris. One-Eyed Jack. Miller, Paula. (J). 2007. (ENG.). 133p. (gr. 2-7). pap. 8.95 *(978-0-9769417-0-5(8))*; 2006. 144p. 13.95 *(978-0-9718348-8-0(1))* Blooming Tree Pr.
Forrest, Genevieve. Pick-a-WooWoo -the Happy Little Spirit: Each of us has a Spirit but what Is it & where did it come From?, 16 vols., Vol. 2. Harper, Julie-Ann. 2008. 32p. (J). pap. *(978-0-9803669-1-4(7))* Pick-a-Woo Woo Pubs.
Forrest, Grace Metzger. Shelby's Collection Day. Dixon, Dallas L. Williams, Nancy E., ed. 2013. 24p. (J). pap. 12.98 *(978-1-938526-54-1(6))* Laurus Bks.
—Silas Watts: The Highly Electric Lightning Bug. Barnes, Brenda J. Williams, Nancy E., ed. 2013. 28p. (J). pap. 17.98 *(978-1-938526-36-7(8))* Roxby Media Ltd. GBR. Dist: Laurus Co., The.
Forrest, James. Eric & the Angrrry Frog, Vol. 2. Sprecher, John. l.t. ed. Date not set. (Special Kids "Special Message" Book Ser.). 32p. (J). (gr. k-4). pap. 10.00 *(978-1-892186-01-0(2))* Anythings Possible, Inc.
—Tori & Cassandra & the Pelican in Peril. Sprecher, John. l.t. ed. Date not set. (Special Kids "Special Message" Book Ser.: Vol. 3). 32p. (J). (gr. k-4). pap. 10.00 *(978-1-892186-02-7(0))* Anythings Possible, Inc.
—Zoe & the Very Unmerry Bear. Sprecher, John. l.t. ed. Date not set. (Special Kids "Special Message" Book Ser.). 32p. (J). (gr. k-4). pap. 10.00 *(978-1-892186-03-4(9)*, SKPB4) Anythings Possible, Inc.
Forrest, Nancy. What Is Beautiful? Boritzer, Etan. 2004. (gr. -1-5). 40p. 14.95 *(978-0-9637597-6-4(0))*; 32p. pap. *(978-0-9637597-7-1(9))* Lane, Veronica Bks.
—What Is Death? Boritzer, Etan. 2004. (What Is? Ser.). 40p. (J). (gr. k-5). pap. 6.95 *(978-0-9637597-5-7(2))* Lane, Veronica Bks.
Forrester, Anne Marie. Wild Girls: The Path of the Young Goddess. Monaghan, Patricia & Managhan, Patricia. 2nd exp. ed. 2005. (ENG.). 258p. pap. 15.95 *(978-0-9760604-1-3(8))* Creatrix! LLC.
Forrester Baldy, Sherri. Daria Rose & the Day She Chose. Capitelli, Yvonne. 2008. (ENG.). 32p. (J). 16.95 *(978-0-9818366-0-7(7))* ASunnyDay Publishing.
Forrester, Kate. Adventures with Waffles. Parr, Maria. 2015. (ENG.). 240p. (J). (gr. 2-4). 15.99 *(978-0-7636-7281-2(5))* Candlewick Pr.
Forsey, Chris. Martin Luther King Jr: The Life of a Civil Rights Leader. Jeffrey, Gary. 2007. (Graphic Nonfiction Biographies Ser.). (ENG.). 48p. (YA). (gr. 4-7). lib. bdg. 31.95 *(978-1-4042-0858-2(5))* Rosen Publishing Group, Inc., The.
—War Correspondents. Shone, Rob. 2008. (Graphic Careers Ser.). (ENG.). 48p. (gr. 5-8). per. 14.05 *(978-1-4042-1450-7(X))*; (YA). lib. bdg. 31.95 *(978-1-4042-1449-1(6))* Rosen Publishing Group, Inc., The.
Forsey, Chris, jt. illus. see Ganeri, Anita.
Forsey, Christopher. Martin Luther King Jr: The Life of a Civil Rights Leader. Jeffrey, Gary. 2007. (Graphic Biographies Ser.). (ENG.). 48p. (gr. 5-8). pap. 14.05 *(978-1-4042-0921-3(2))* Rosen Publishing Group, Inc., The.
Forshall, Rose. Pirate Gran. Durrant, Geraldine. 2009. 32p. (J). 19.95 *(978-0-948065-96-5(6))* National Maritime Museum GBR. Dist: Independent Pubs. Group.
Forshaw, Andy. The What on Earth? Wallbook of Natural History. Lloyd, Christopher. ed. 2013. (ENG.). 16p. (J). (gr. 2-7). 12.99 *(978-0-565-09309-9(6))* Natural History Museum Pubns. GBR. Dist: Independent Pubs. Group.
—The What on Earth? Wallbook of the Natural World: From the Dawn of Life to the Present Day. Lloyd, Christopher. 2013. (ENG.). 16p. (J). (gr. 2-7). 29.95 *(978-0-565-09297-9(9))* Natural History Museum Pubns. GBR. Dist: Independent Pubs. Group.
Forshaw, John. The Beast of Didley Dale. Popper, Garry. 2004. (Bret the Vet Ser.). 40p. 7.00 *(978-1-84161-024-5(0))* Ravette Publishing, Ltd. GBR. Dist: Parkwest Pubns., Inc.

F

—High Noon in Didley Pidley. Popper, Garry. 2004. (Bret the Vet Ser.). 40p. 7.00 *(978-1-84161-013-9(5))* Ravette Publishing, Ltd. GBR. Dist: Parkwest Pubns., Inc.

—Scary Monkeys: Going Ape. Popper, Garry. 2004. 48p. 9.00 *(978-1-84161-014-6(3))* Ravette Publishing, Ltd. GBR. Dist: Parkwest Pubns., Inc.

—Worm's Eye View: A Witch's Tale. Popper, Garry. 2004. 48p. 7.00 *(978-1-84161-025-2(9))* Ravette Publishing, Ltd. GBR. Dist: Parkwest Pubns., Inc.

Forshaw, Louise. Dinosaur Safari. Bateson, Maggie. 2014. (ENG.). 10p. (J). 14.99 ***(978-1-4711-2121-0(6))*** Simon & Schuster, Ltd. GBR. Dist: Simon & Schuster, Inc.

Forshay, Christina. Goodnight Baseball. Dahl, Michael. 2013. (Sports Illustrated Kids Bedtime Bks.). (ENG.). 32p. (gr. -1-2). pap. 7.19 *(978-1-4795-4975-7(4))*; lib. bdg. 20.99 *(978-1-4048-7979-9(X))* Picture Window Bks.

Forshay, Christina. Goodnight Hockey. Dahl, Michael. 2015. (Sports Illustrated Kids Bedtime Bks.). (ENG.). 32p. (gr. -1-2). lib. bdg. 20.99 ***(978-1-4795-6526-9(1))*** Capstone Young Readers.

Forshay, Christina. The Really Groovy Story of the Tortoise & the Hare. Crow, Kristyn & Aesop. 2012. (J). *(978-1-61913-128-6(5))* Weigl Pubs., Inc.

—The Really Groovy Story of the Tortoise & the Hare. Crow, Kristyn. 2011. (ENG.). 32p. (J). (gr. -1-3). 16.99 *(978-0-8075-6911-5(9))* Whitman, Albert & Co.

Forshay, Christina E. Goodnight Baseball, 1 vol. Dahl, Michael. 2013. (Sports Illustrated Kids Bedtime Bks.). (ENG.). 32p. (gr. -1-2). 14.95 *(978-1-62370-000-3(0))* Capstone Young Readers.

Forshay, Christina E. Sports Illustrated Kids Bedtime Books. Dahl, Michael. 2015. (Sports Illustrated Kids Bedtime Bks.). (ENG.). 32p. (gr. -1-2). 62.97 ***(978-1-4795-8261-7(1))*** Capstone Pr., Inc.

Forss, Ian. Un Año del Arco Iris. Perez, Marlene. enl. ed. 2004. (SPA.). (J). pap. 26.00 *(978-1-4108-2367-0(9), 23679)* Benchmark Education Co.

—Apúrate, Teddy: Fiction-to-Fact Big Book. Holl, Robert. enl. ed. 2004. (SPA.). (J). pap. 26.00 *(978-1-4108-2362-5(8), 23628)* Benchmark Education Co.

Forsyth, Robert. A Song of Life 1922. Morley, Margaret Warner. 2004. reprint ed. pap. 21.95 *(978-1-4179-7842-7(2))* Kessinger Publishing, LLC.

Forsythe, Matthew. My Name Is Elizabeth! Dunklee, Annika. 2011. (ENG.). 24p. (J). 14.95 *(978-1-55453-560-6(3))* Kids Can Pr., Ltd. CAN. Dist: Univ. of Toronto Pr.

—Warning - Do Not Open This Book! Lehrhaupt, Adam. 2013. (ENG.). 40p. (J). (gr. -1-3). 17.99 *(978-1-4424-3582-7(8)*, Simon & Schuster Bks. For Young Readers) Simon & Schuster Bks. For Young Readers.

Forte, Helen. Minimus Secundus Pupil's Book: Moving on in Latin. Bell, Barbara. 2004. (Minimus Ser.). (LAT & ENG.). 96p. pap., stu. ed. 29.00 *(978-0-521-75545-0(X))* Cambridge Univ. Pr.

—Minimus Secundus Teacher's Resource Book: Moving on in Latin. Bell, Barbara. 2004. (Minimus Ser.). (LAT & ENG.). 96p. tchr. ed., spiral bd. 82.75 *(978-0-521-75546-7(8))* Cambridge Univ. Pr.

Fortenberry, Julie. Pippa at the Parade. Roosa, Karen. 2009. (ENG.). 32p. (J). (gr. -1 — 1). 16.95 *(978-1-59078-567-6(3))* Boyds Mills Pr.

—Pirate Boy. Bunting, Eve. (ENG.). 32p. (J). (gr. -1-2). 2012. pap. 7.99 *(978-0-8234-2546-4(0))*; 2011. 16.95 *(978-0-8234-2321-7(2))* Holiday Hse., Inc.

—Sadie & the Big Mountain. Korngold, Jamie. 2012. (Lag B'Omer & Shavuot Ser.). (ENG.). 32p. (J). (gr. -1-1). pap. 7.95 *(978-0-7613-6494-8(3))*; lib. bdg. 17.95 *(978-0-7613-6492-4(7))* Lerner Publishing Group. (Kar-Ben Publishing).

—Sadie, Ori, & Nuggles Go to Camp. Korngold, Jamie. 2014. 24p. (J). (gr. -1-1). 17.95 *(978-1-4677-0424-3(5)*, Kar-Ben Publishing) Lerner Publishing Group.

—Sadie's Almost Marvelous Menorah. Korngold, Jamie. 2013. 24p. 17.95 *(978-1-4677-0051-1(7))*; (ENG.). (J). (gr. -1-1). 7.95 *(978-0-7613-6495-5(1)*, Kar-Ben Publishing) Lerner Publishing Group.

—Sadie's Lag Ba'Omer Mystery. Korngold, Jamie. 2014. (Lag Ba'Omer & Shavuot Ser.). (ENG.). 32p. (J). (gr. -1-3). 17.95 *(978-0-7613-9047-3(2))*; 7.95 *(978-0-7613-9048-0(0))* Lerner Publishing Group. (Kar-Ben Publishing).

—Sadie's Sukkah Breakfast. Korngold, Jamie S. 2011. (Sukkot & Simchat Torah Ser.). (ENG.). 24p. (J). (gr. -1-1). pap. 7.95 *(978-0-7613-5648-6(7))*; lib. bdg. 16.95 *(978-0-7613-5647-9(9))* Lerner Publishing Group. (Kar-Ben Publishing).

Fortier, Natali & Brenier, Claire. Half & Half-A Doctor for the Animals. Moncomble, Gerard & Van den Dries, Sidonie. 32p. (J). 2009. 9.95 *(978-1-60115-203-9(5))*; 2008. pap. 4.99 *(978-1-60115-204-6(3))* Treasure Bay, Inc.

Fortnum, Peggy. More about Paddington. Bond, Michael. 2015. (Paddington Ser.). 176p. (J). (gr. 3-7). 9.99 *(978-0-06-231220-4(0))* HarperCollins Pubs.

—Paddington Helps Out. Bond, Michael. 2015. (Paddington Ser.). 160p. (J). (gr. 3-7). 9.99 *(978-0-06-231230-3(8))* HarperCollins Pubs.

Fortnum, Peggy & Alley, R. W. Love from Paddington. Bond, Michael. 2014. (Paddington Ser.). (ENG.). 144p. (J). (gr. 3-7). 9.99 *(978-0-06-236816-4(8))* HarperCollins Pubs.

Fortune, Eric. Bunnicula Meets Edgar Allan Crow. Howe, James. (Bunnicula & Friends Ser.). (ENG.). 160p. (J). (gr. 3-7). 2008. pap. 6.99 *(978-1-4169-1473-0(0))*; 2006. 15.95 *(978-1-4169-1458-7(7))* Simon & Schuster Children's Publishing. (Atheneum Bks. for Young Readers).

—Magickeepers: The Eternal Hourglass. Kirov, Erica. 2010. (ENG.). 256p. (J). (gr. 4-7). pap. 10.99 *(978-1-4022-3855-0(X)*, Sourcebooks Jabberwocky) Sourcebooks, Inc.

—The Shadow Thieves. Ursu, Anne. (Cronus Chronicles Ser.: 1). (ENG.). (J). (gr. 3-7). 2007. 432p. pap. 7.99 *(978-1-4169-0588-2(X))*; 2006. 416p. 17.99 *(978-1-4169-0587-5(1))* Simon & Schuster Children's Publishing. (Atheneum Bks. for Young Readers).

—The Siren Song. Ursu, Anne. (Cronus Chronicles Ser.: 2). (ENG.). 448p. (J). (gr. 3-7). 2008. pap. 7.99 *(978-1-4169-0590-5(1))*; 2007. 19.99 *(978-1-4169-0589-9(8))* Simon & Schuster Children's Publishing. (Atheneum Bks. for Young Readers).

Fortune, Eric & Swaab, Neil. The Immortal Fire. Ursu, Anne. 2009. (Cronus Chronicles Ser.: 3). (ENG.). 448p. (J). (gr. 3-7). 17.99 *(978-1-4169-0591-2(X)*, Atheneum Bks. for Young Readers) Simon & Schuster Children's Publishing.

Fortune, Leslie. Petey the Pigasaurus. Nordquist, Donna M. 2011. 32p. pap. 24.95 *(978-1-4560-6051-0(1))* America Star Bks.

Forward, Max. The Legend of Baeoh: How Baeoh Got His Stripes. Lee, Lucas Taekwon. 2007. (ENG.). 36p. (J). 17.95 *(978-1-931741-88-0(3))* Reed, Robert D. Pubs.

Foss, Timothy. Rocks & the People Who Love Them, 1 vol. Yomtov, Nelson. 2012. (Adventures in Science Ser.). (ENG.). 32p. (gr. 3-4). lib. bdg. 29.99 *(978-1-4296-7687-8(6)*, Graphic Library) Capstone Pr., Inc.

—Rocks & the People Who Love Them, 1 vol. Yomtov, Nel. 2012. (Adventures in Science Ser.). (ENG.). 32p. (gr. 3-4). pap. 8.10 *(978-1-4296-7988-6(3))*; pap. 47.70 *(978-1-4296-8466-8(6))* Capstone Pr., Inc. (Graphic Library).

Fossey, Wietse. The Clever Little Witch. Baeten, Lieve. 2012. (ENG.). 32p. (J). (gr. -1-1). 16.95 *(978-0-7358-4079-9(2))* North-South Bks., Inc.

Foster, Angela. Grandma's Story: the Singing Mouse. Foster, Angela. 2011. (ENG.). 24p. pap. 6.95 *(978-1-4611-3651-4(2))* CreateSpace Independent Publishing Platform.

Foster, Brad W. & Simmons, Mark. Flight to Freedom! Nickolas Flux & the Underground Railroad, 1 vol. Bolte, Mari. 2014. (Nickolas Flux History Chronicles Ser.). (ENG.). 32p. (gr. 3-4). lib. bdg. 29.99 *(978-1-4914-0254-2(7))* Capstone Pr., Inc.

Foster, Dara, photos by. Now You See It! Pupstyle Red Carpet Pups. Foster, Dara. 2013. (ENG., 64p. (J). (gr. 2-5). pap. 5.99 *(978-0-545-53245-7(0))* Math Solutions.

Foster, Frank. Run Farrah Run: Detecting, Ditching & Dealing with Dating Dopes. Taylor, Paula. von Seeburg, Kate, ed. 2004. 128p. (YA). pap. 12.95 *(978-0-9749173-0-6(3))* Tea Party Pr.

Foster, Jack. Cobbledom's Curse. Kennedy, J. Aday. 2012. 20p. pap. 9.95 *(978-1-61633-265-5(4))* Guardian Angel Publishing, Inc.

—Come Inside the Ark. Harrah, Judith. 2012. (J). pap. 17.99 *(978-1-937331-12-2(1))* ShadeTree Publishing, LLC.

—Doodle Girl. Reed, Jennifer Bond. 2012. 20p. pap. 9.95 *(978-1-61633-341-6(3))* Guardian Angel Publishing, Inc.

—Itcha Itcha Goo Goo Blues. Kennedy, J. Aday. 2012. 20p. pap. 10.95 *(978-1-61633-294-5(8))* Guardian Angel Publishing, Inc.

—Little Isaac's Big Adventure. Helixon, Tracy Schuldt. 2012. 16p. pap. 9.95 *(978-1-61633-321-8(9))* Guardian Angel Publishing, Inc.

—One in a Buzzillion. Schreiber, Hannah & Hartsock, Conner. 2011. 16p. pap. 9.95 *(978-1-61633-154-2(2))* Guardian Angel Publishing, Inc.

—Ridiculously Ridiculous. Tucker, Susan K. 2012. 16p. pap. 9.95 *(978-1-61633-346-1(4))* Guardian Angel Publishing, Inc.

—Sh Sh Sh Let the Baby Sleep. Sternke, Kathy. 2011. 20p. pap. 10.95 *(978-1-61633-156-6(9))* Guardian Angel Publishing, Inc.

—Shoo Cat. Lyle-Soffe, Shari. 2010. 16p. pap. 9.95 *(978-1-61633-033-0(3))* Guardian Angel Publishing, Inc.

—Stella, the Fire Farting Dragon. Kennedy, J. Aday. 2011. 20p. pap. 10.95 *(978-1-61633-149-8(6))* Guardian Angel Publishing, Inc.

—Zippy y Las Rayas de Valor. Sullivan, Candida. 2013. 40p. pap. 13.99 *(978-1-937331-51-1(2))* ShadeTree Publishing, LLC.

Foster, Janet. Elmer the Elf & the Magical Jingle Bells, 1 vol. Robinson, George. 2008. (ENG.). 33p. 24.95 *(978-1-60610-606-8(6))* America Star Bks.

Foster, John. The Foundry's Edg. Baity, Cameron & Zelkowicz, Benny. 2014. (Books of Ore Ser.). (ENG.). 448p. (J). (gr. 3-7). 16.99 *(978-1-4231-6227-8(7))* Hyperion Bks. for Children.

Foster, Jon. The Islands of the Blessed. Farmer, Nancy. 2009. (ENG.). 496p. (YA). (gr. 7-9). 18.99 *(978-1-4169-0737-4(8)*, Atheneum/Richard Jackson Bks.) Simon & Schuster Children's Publishing.

Foster, Jonathan. Sleep, 1 vol. Spiritworks. 2010. 18p. 24.95 *(978-1-4489-4930-4(0))* PublishAmerica, Inc.

Foster, Michael K. The Donkey in the Living Room: A Tradition That Celebrates the Real Meaning of Christmas. Cunningham, Sarah. 2014. (ENG.). 32p. (J). (gr. -1-3). 14.99 *(978-1-4336-8317-6(2)*, B&H Kids) B&H Publishing Group.

—The Donkey in the Living Room Nativity Set: A Tradition That Celebrates the True Meaning of Christmas. Cunningham, Sarah. 2014. (ENG.). 32p. (J). (gr. -1-3). 29.99 *(978-1-4336-8448-7(9)*, B&H Kids) B&H Publishing Group.

Foster, Peggy. Wild Logging: Sustainable Forestry among Western Woodlot Owners. Foster, Bryan. rev. ed. 161p. (J). (gr. 4). pap. *(978-0-87842-448-1(2)*, 335) Mountain Pr. Publishing Co., Inc.

Foster, Ron. I Like Rain. 2007. 28p. (J). (gr. 1-4). *(978-1-929039-39-5(5))* Ambassador Bks., Inc.

—I Like Snow! 2006. 28p. (J). (gr. -1-3). *(978-1-929039-37-1(9))* Ambassador Bks., Inc.

—I Like Sunshine! O'Day, Joseph E. 2007. (J). *(978-1-929039-41-8(7))* Ambassador Bks., Inc.

—I Like Wind! Joseph, O'Day E. 2007. 28p. (J). (gr. -1-3). *(978-1-929039-42-5(5))* Ambassador Bks., Inc.

Foster, Teresa. Let's Learn French. Watson, Carol & Moyle, Philippa. 2003. (Let's Learn Ser.). (ENG.). 32p. pap. 9.95 *(978-0-7818-1014-2(0))* Hippocrene Bks., Inc.

Foster, Travis. I Can Doodle - Dots. 2013. (ENG.). 96p. (J). (gr. -1-1). pap. 9.99 *(978-1-60905-349-9(4))* Blue Apple Bks.

—The Princess and... The Peas & Carrots. Ziefert, Harriet. 2012. (ENG.). 40p. (J). (gr. -1-3). 16.99 *(978-1-60905-250-8(1))* Blue Apple Bks.

—What's New at the Zoo? Comden, Betty & Green, Adolph. 2011. (ENG.). 36p. (J). (gr. -1-3). 16.99 *(978-1-60905-088-7(6))* Blue Apple Bks.

Foster, Trista, photos by. Animals of the Ark: (for a boy named Clay) Reynolds, Loralyn & Caldwell, Christiana Marie Melvin. 2011. 36p. pap. 15.14 *(978-1-4634-3328-4(X))* AuthorHouse.

Foster, William. Nonsense Drolleries: The Owl & the Pussy-Cat, the Duck & the Kangaroo. Lear, Edward. 2007. 32p. pap. 10.95 *(978-1-60355-050-5(X))* Juniper Grove.

Foston, Desirae. The Hawaiian Hiatus of Herkimer Street. Foston, Desirae. 2013. 24p. 24.00 *(978-1-940021-00-3(6))* Bliss Group.

Fotheringham, Ed. Tony Baloney: Buddy Trouble. Ryan, Pam Muñoz. 2013. 38p. (J). pap. ***(978-0-545-48170-0(8))*** Scholastic, Inc.

Fotheringham, Ed. Tony Baloney: Pen Pal. Ryan, Pam Muñoz. 2014. 39p. (J). pap. *(978-0-545-69227-4(X)*, Scholastic Pr.) Scholastic, Inc.

Fotheringham, Edwin. The Extraordinary Mark Twain (According to Susy) Kerley, Barbara. 2010. (ENG.). 48p. (J). (gr. 2-5). 17.99 *(978-0-545-12508-6(1)*, Scholastic Pr.) Scholastic, Inc.

—The "Extrodinary" Mark Twain (According to Susy) Kerley, Barbara. 2010. (J). *(978-0-545-12509-3(X)*, Scholastic Pr.) Scholastic, Inc.

—A Home for Mr. Emerson. Kerley, Barbara. 2014. (ENG.). 48p. (J). (gr. 3-7). 18.99 *(978-0-545-35088-4(3)*, Scholastic Pr.) Scholastic, Inc.

—Mermaid Queen: The Spectacular True Story of Annette Kellerman, Who Swam Her Way to Fame, Fortune, & Swimsuit History. Corey, Shana. 2009. (Mermaid Queen Ser.). (ENG.). 48p. (J). (gr. 1-3). 17.99 *(978-0-439-69835-1(9)*, Scholastic Pr.) Scholastic, Inc.

—Monkey & Duck Quack Up! Hamburg, Jennifer. 2015. (ENG.). 32p. (J). (gr. -1-3). 17.99 *(978-0-545-64514-0(X)*, Scholastic Pr.) Scholastic, Inc.

—Those Rebels, John & Tom. Kerley, Barbara. 2012. (ENG.). 48p. (J). (gr. 2-5). 17.99 *(978-0-545-22268-6(0)*, Scholastic Pr.) Scholastic, Inc.

—Tony Baloney. Ryan, Pam Muñoz. 2011. (ENG.). 40p. (J). (gr. -1-k). 16.99 *(978-0-545-23135-0(3)*, Scholastic Pr.) Scholastic, Inc.

—Tony Baloney: Buddy Trouble. Ryan, Pam Muñoz. 2014. (ENG.). 40p. (J). (gr. k-2). 6.99 *(978-0-545-48169-4(4)*, Scholastic Pr.) Scholastic, Inc.

—Tony Baloney: School Rules. Ryan, Pam Muñoz. (J). (gr. k-2). 2013. (ENG.). 40p. 6.99 *(978-0-545-48166-3(X))*; 2012. pap. *(978-0-545-48167-0(8))* Scholastic, Inc.

Fotheringham, Edwin. Tony Baloney: Pen Pal. Ryan, Pam Muñoz. 2015. (Tony Baloney Ser.). (ENG.). 40p. (J). (gr. k-2). 6.99 ***(978-0-545-65037-3(2)***, Scholastic Pr.) Scholastic, Inc.

Fotheringham, Edwin. What to Do about Alice? How Alice Roosevelt Broke the Rules, Charmed the World, & Drove Her Father Teddy Crazy! Kerley, Barbara. 2008. (ENG.). 48p. (J). (gr. 2-5). 16.99 *(978-0-439-92231-9(3)*, Scholastic Pr.) Scholastic, Inc.

Foti, Anthony J. Emma's New Beginning. Gunderson, Jessica. 2015. (U. S. Immigration in The 1900s Ser.). (ENG.). 96p. (gr. 3-4). pap. 7.95 ***(978-1-4965-0501-9(8))*** Stone Arch Bks.

—Mars for Humanity. Terrell, Brandon. 2015. (Exploring Space & Beyond Ser.). (ENG.). 96p. (gr. 3-4). lib. bdg. 25.32 ***(978-1-4965-0502-6(6))*** Stone Arch Bks.

Fotolia, photos by. Animal Babies. Apsley, Brenda. 2012. (Animal Snapshots Ser.). (ENG., 10p. (J). (gr. -1 — 1). bds. 7.99 *(978-0-7641-6554-2(2))* Barron's Educational Series, Inc.

—Animal Families. Apsley, Brenda. 2012. (Animal Snapshots Ser.). (ENG., 10p. (J). (gr. -1-k). bds. 7.99 *(978-0-7641-6537-5(2))* Barron's Educational Series, Inc.

—Animal Friends. Apsley, Brenda. 2012. (Animal Snapshots Ser.). (ENG., 10p. (J). (gr. -1 — 1). bds. 7.99 *(978-0-7641-6555-9(0))* Barron's Educational Series, Inc.

—Animal Fun. Apsley, Brenda. 2012. (Animal Snapshots Ser.). (ENG., 10p. (J). (gr. -1 — 1). bds. 7.99 *(978-0-7641-6538-2(0))* Barron's Educational Series, Inc.

Fotos, Jay, jt. illus. see Moreno, Chris.

Foulke, Nancy. How Many Spots Have I Got? McCabe, Lauren A. 2005. (J). 16.00 *(978-1-893516-02-1(4))* Our Child Pr.

Foulkes, Fiona, et al. Period Costume for Stage & Screen Vol. 5: Dominos, Dolmans, Coats, Pelisses, Spencers, Callashes, Hoods & Bonnets. Hunnisett, Jean. 2003. 176p. (gr. 8-12). 59.00 *(978-0-88734-670-5(7))* Players Pr., Inc.

Fountain, John. Birthday Wishes. Phillips, Leigh Hope. 2005. (J). pap. *(978-1-933156-10-1(4))*; per. *(978-1-933156-03-3(1))* GSVQ Publishing. (VisionQuest Kids).

Fournier, Laure. The Merchant & the Thief: A Folktale from India, 1 vol. Zacharias, Ravi. 2012. (ENG.). 32p. (J). 15.99 *(978-0-310-71636-5(5))* Zonderkidz.

—My First Prayers. Mcclure, Gillian. 2009. (ENG.). 24p. (J). (gr. k-k). 16.95 *(978-1-84507-535-4(8)*, Frances Lincoln) Quarto Publishing Group UK GBR. Dist: Perseus-PGW.

Fowkes, Charlie. Harry the Clever Spider at School. Jarman, Julia. 2007. (Collins Big Cat Ser.). (ENG.). 128p. (J). pap. 6.99 *(978-0-00-718670-9(3))* HarperCollins Pubs. Ltd. GBR. Dist: Independent Pubs. Group.

Fowler, Charlie, photos by. Mountain Star: A Story about a Mountaineer That Will Teach You How to Draw a Star! Fowler Hicks, Ginny. 2008. 24p. (J). 18.95 *(978-0-9763309-3-6(8))* Mountain World Media LLC.

Fowler, Claire. My Sister Saarah. Talhah, Abu & Books, Greenbird. 2013. 30p. pap. *(978-0-9576379-6-2(9))* Greenbird Bks.

Fowler, Elizabeth. Luke & Nana, 1 vol. Whitby, Rozene. 2010. 16p. 24.95 *(978-1-4489-3826-1(0))* PublishAmerica, Inc.

Fowler, Faith. Sissy Goes to Washington. Goguen, Martha. 2013. 36p. pap. *(978-1-897435-59-5(2))* Agio Publishing Hse.

Fowler, Jim. Arctic Aesop's Fables: Twelve Retold Tales. Fowler, Susi Gregg. 2013. (Paws IV Ser.). (ENG.). 32p. (J). (gr. 1-4). pap. 10.99 *(978-1-57061-861-1(5))* Sasquatch Bks.

—Patsy Ann of Alaska: The True Story of a Dog. Brown, Tricia. 2011. (ENG.). 32p. (J). (gr. -1-2). pap. 10.99 *(978-1-57061-697-6(3))* Paws Four Publishing.

Fowler, Richard. The Toy Cupboard. Wood, David. 2005. 14p. (J). (gr. -1-3). 14.95 *(978-1-58117-103-7(X)*, Intervisual/Piggy Toes) Bendon, Inc.

Fowler, Romana, jt. illus. see Martins, Ann-Kathrin.

Fowler, Rosamund. Home for a Tiger, Home for a Bear. Williams, Brenda. 2009. (ENG.). 32p. (J). pap. 7.99 *(978-1-84686-353-0(8))* Barefoot Bks., Inc.

Fowles, Shelley. The Most Magnificent Mosque. Jungman, Ann & Quarto Generic Staff. 2007. (ENG.). 32p. (J). (gr. 1-4). pap. 8.99 *(978-1-84507-085-4(2)*, Frances Lincoln) Quarto Publishing Group UK GBR. Dist: Hachette Bk. Group.

—The Ogress & the Snake: And Other Stories from Somalia. Laird, Elizabeth & Quarto Generic Staff. 2009. (Folktales from Around the World Ser.). (ENG.). 96p. (J). (gr. 3-6). pap. 7.95 *(978-1-84507-870-6(5)*, Frances Lincoln) Quarto Publishing Group UK GBR. Dist: Hachette Bk. Group.

Fox, Charles Philip, photos by. Sweet Sue's Adventures. Campbell, Sam. 2010. 119p. reprint ed. pap. 10.95 *(978-1-57258-210-1(3))* TEACH Services, Inc.

Fox, Christyan. The Cat, the Dog, Little Red, the Exploding Eggs, the Wolf, & Grandma. Fox, Diane. 2014. (ENG.). 32p. (J). (gr. -1-3). 16.99 *(978-0-545-69481-0(7)*, Scholastic Pr.) Scholastic, Inc.

—Cats & Kittens. Burton, Jane, photos by. Starke, Katherine & Watt, Fiona. 2006. 30p. (J). pap. *(978-0-439-78492-4(1))* Scholastic, Inc.

—Creaky Castle. Clarke, Jane. 2013. *(978-1-4351-4951-9(3))* Barnes & Noble, Inc.

—Dogs & Puppies. Starke, Katherine & Watt, Fiona. 2004. 31p. (J). *(978-0-439-78715-4(7))* Scholastic, Inc.

—Farm Animals. Daynes, Katie. 2006. (Beginners Nature: Level 1 Ser.). 32p. (J). (gr. k-2). 4.99 *(978-0-7945-1396-2(4)*, Usborne) EDC Publishing.

—Firefighters. Daynes Katie et al. 2006. (Usborne Beginners Ser.). 32p. (J). *(978-0-439-88992-6(8))* Scholastic, Inc.

—Firefighters. Daynes, Katie. 2007. (Beginners Social Studies). 32p. (J). (gr. -1-3). 4.99 *(978-0-7945-1658-1(0)*, Usborne) EDC Publishing.

—Gerbils. Burton, Jane, photos by. Howell, Laura. 2005. (Usborne First Pets Ser.). 32p. (J). (gr. k-4). pap. 5.95 *(978-0-7945-1116-6(3)*, Usborne) EDC Publishing.

—Guinea Pigs. Burton, James, photos by. Howell, Laura. 2005. (Usborne First Pets Ser.). 32p. (J). (gr. k-4). pap. 5.95 *(978-0-7945-1115-9(5)*, Usborne) EDC Publishing.

—Hamsters. Meredith, Susan et al. 2004. 30p. (J). *(978-0-439-78698-0(3))* Scholastic, Inc.

—Pirate Adventures. Punter, Russell. 2007. (Usborne Young Reading: Series One Ser.). 48p. (J). (gr. 2). 13.99 *(978-1-58086-985-0(8))*; (gr. 4-7). pap. 5.99 *(978-0-7945-1447-1(2))* EDC Publishing. (Usborne).

—Rain or Shine. Fox, Diane. 2014. (Snip & Snap Ser.). (ENG.). 20p. (J). (-k). pap. 9.99 *(978-1-4083-1613-9(7))* Hodder & Stoughton GBR. Dist: Independent Pubs. Group.

—Red or Blue. Fox, Diane. 2013. (Snip & Snap Ser.). (ENG.). 20p. (J). (-k). 16.99 *(978-1-4083-1614-6(5))* Hodder & Stoughton GBR. Dist: Independent Pubs. Group.

—Trash & Recycling. Turnbull, Stephanie. 2006. (Beginners Science: Level 2 Ser.). 32p. (J). (gr. 1-3). 4.99 *(978-0-7945-1400-6(6)*, Usborne) EDC Publishing.

—Understanding Your Brain - Internet Linked. Treays, Rebecca. rev. ed. 2004. (Science for Beginners Ser.). 32p. (J). pap. 7.95 *(978-0-7945-0853-1(7)*, Usborne) EDC Publishing.

—Understanding Your Muscles & Bones: Internet-Linked. Treays, Rebecca. rev. ed. 2006. (Usborne Science for Beginners Ser.). 32p. (J). (gr. 3-7). per. 7.99 *(978-0-7945-0813-5(8)*, Usborne) EDC Publishing.

—Understanding Your Senses - Internet Linked. Treays, Rebecca. rev. ed. 2004. (Science for Beginners Ser.). 32p. (J). pap. 7.95 *(978-0-7945-0852-4(9)*, Usborne) EDC Publishing.

—Wind-Up Pirate Ship. Stowell, Louie. 2010. (Wind-up Bks). 13p. (J). bds. 29.99 *(978-0-7945-2835-5(X)*, Usborne) EDC Publishing.

Fox, Christyan & Fox, Diane. Enzo the Racing Car. Fox, Christyan & Fox, Diane. 2008. (Wheelyworld Ser.). (ENG.). 32p. (J). (gr. -1-k). pap. 8.95 *(978-1-4052-2742-1(7))* Egmont Bks., Ltd. GBR. Dist: Independent Pubs. Group.

—Monty the Rally Car. Fox, Christyan & Fox, Diane. 2008. (Wheelyworld Ser.). (ENG.). 32p. (J). (gr. -1-k). pap. 8.95 *(978-1-4052-2743-8(5))* Egmont Bks., Ltd. GBR. Dist: Independent Pubs. Group.

Fox, Christyan & Pang, Alex. Life in Space. Daynes, Katie & Wray, Zoe. 2008. (Usborne Beginners Ser.). 32p. (J). *(978-0-545-06963-2(7))* Scholastic, Inc.

—Living in Space. Daynes, Katie. 2003. (Usborne Beginners Ser.). 32p. (J). (gr. 1). lib. bdg. 12.99 *(978-1-58086-930-0(0)*, Usborne) EDC Publishing.

Fox, Christyan, jt. illus. see Donaera, Patrizia.

Fox, Christyan, jt. illus. see Wray, Zoe.

Fox, Culpeo S. The Fox & the Crow. 2014. (ENG.). 28p. (J). (gr. -1). 17.95 *(978-81-8190-303-7(X))* Karadi Tales Co. Pvt. Ltd. IND. Dist: Consortium Bk. Sales & Distribution.

Fox, Dave. Satan's Prep: A Graphic Novel. Guarente, Gabe. 2014. (ENG.). 112p. (J). (gr. 6). 17.95 *(978-1-62873-592-5(9)*, Sky Pony Pr.) Skyhorse Publishing Co., Inc.

Fox-Davies, Sarah. Bat Loves the Night. Davies, Nicola. 2008. (Read, Listen, & Wonder Ser.). (ENG.). 32p. (J). (gr. -1-3). pap. 8.99 *(978-0-7636-3863-4(3))* Candlewick Pr.

—Bat Loves the Night. Davies, Nicola. 2006. (Read & Wonder Ser.). 17.00 *(978-0-7569-6561-7(6))* Perfection Learning Corp.

—Bat Loves the Night: Read & Wonder. Davies, Nicola. 2004. (Read & Wonder Ser.). (ENG.). 32p. (J). (gr. -1-3). pap. 6.99 *(978-0-7636-2438-5(1))* Candlewick Pr.

—Do Rabbits Have Christmas?, YOU. Fisher, Aileen. 2007. (ENG.). 32p. (J). (gr. -1-2). 16.95 *(978-0-8050-7491-8(0),* Holt, Henry & Co. Bks. For Young Readers) Holt, Henry & Co.

—Walk with a Wolf: Read, Listen & Wonder. Howker, Janni. 2008. (Read, Listen, & Wonder Ser.). (ENG.). 32p. (J). (gr. -1-3). pap. 8.99 *(978-0-7636-3875-7(7))* Candlewick Pr.

Fox-Davies, Sarah, jt. illus. see Cann, Helen.

Fox, Diane. Tyson the Terrible. Fox, Diane. Fox, Christyan. 2006. (ENG.). 24p. (J). (gr. -1-1). 12.95 *(978-1-58234-734-9(4),* Bloomsbury USA Childrens) Bloomsbury USA.

Fox, Diane, jt. illus. see Fox, Christyan.

Fox, Lisa. Josie the Giraffe & the Starry Night. Baxter, Nicola. 2012. (ENG.). 16p. (J). (gr. -1 — 1). 9.99 ***(978-1-84322-776-2(2),*** Armadillo) Anness Publishing GBR. Dist: National Bk. Network.

Fox, Lisa. Lamb Loves Springtime. Rivers-Moore, Debbie. 2012. (Springtime Shakers Ser.). (ENG.). 8p. (J). bds. 5.99 *(978-0-7641-6487-3(2))* Barron's Educational Series, Inc.

—Little Bunny's Butterflies. Rivers-Moore, Debbie. 2012. (Springtime Shakers Ser.). (ENG.). 8p. (J). bds. 5.99 *(978-0-7641-6488-0(0))* Barron's Educational Series, Inc.

—Noah's Ark. McCombs, Margi. 2014. (ENG.). 10p. (J). (gr. -1-k). bds. 7.99 *(978-0-545-60557-1(1),* Little Shepherd) Scholastic, Inc.

—You Go Away. Corey, Dorothy. 2010. (ENG.). 16p. (J). (gr. -1-k). bds. 7.99 *(978-0-8075-9440-7(7))* Whitman, Albert & Co.

Fox, Nathan. Dogs of War. Keenan, Sheila. 2013. (ENG.). 176p. (J). (gr. 3-7). 22.99 *(978-0-545-12887-2(0));* pap. 12.99 *(978-0-545-12888-9(9))* Scholastic, Inc. (Graphix).

Fox, Peter, photos by. Insectos Insolitos. Hutnick, Theresa & Phillips, Karen. 2005. (SPA., 38p. (J). spiral bd. 17.95 *(978-987-1078-43-1(9))* Klutz Latino MEX. Dist: Independent Pubs. Group.

Fox, Rebecca. Circle. Smallwood, Sally & Jones, Bryony. 2011. (Shapes Are Fun Ser.). (ENG.). 24p. (J). (gr. k — 1). bds. *(978-1-84089-610-7(8))* Zero to Ten, Ltd.

—Rectangle. Smallwood, Sally & Jones, Bryony. 2011. (Shapes Are Fun Ser.). (ENG.). 14p. (J). (gr. k — 1). bds. *(978-1-84089-613-8(2))* Zero to Ten, Ltd.

—Square. Smallwood, Sally & Jones, Bryony. 2011. (Shapes Are Fun Ser.). (ENG.). 14p. (J). (gr. k — 1). bds. *(978-1-84089-612-1(4))* Zero to Ten, Ltd.

—Triangle. Smallwood, Sally & Jones, Bryony. 2011. (Shapes Are Fun Ser.). (ENG.). 14p. (J). (gr. k — 1). bds. *(978-1-84089-611-4(6))* Zero to Ten, Ltd.

Fox, Tom Paul. Bullying Is Wrong. Anderson, Georgia Lee. 2012. (ENG.). 26p. pap. 14.95 *(978-1-57258-882-0(9),* Aspect Bk.) TEACH Services, Inc.

Fox, Will. Bertie Bolt. Fox, Will. 2013. (ENG.). 20p. (J). pap. *(978-1-908865-20-5(2))* Beecroft Publishing.

—Billy Brush. Fox, Will. 2013. (ENG.). 20p. (J). pap. *(978-1-908865-25-0(3))* Beecroft Publishing.

—Hector Hacksaw. Fox, Will. 2013. (ENG.). 20p. (J). pap. *(978-1-908865-28-1(8))* Beecroft Publishing.

—Molly Mallet. Fox, Will. 2013. (ENG.). 20p. (J). pap. *(978-1-908865-27-4(X))* Beecroft Publishing.

—Peggy Peg. Fox, Will. 2013. (ENG.). 20p. (J). pap. *(978-1-908865-22-9(9))* Beecroft Publishing.

—Rusty Nail. Fox, Will. 2013. (ENG.). 20p. (J). pap. *(978-1-908865-21-2(0))* Beecroft Publishing.

—Sally Screw. Fox, Will. 2013. (ENG.). 20p. (J). pap. *(978-1-908865-23-6(7))* Beecroft Publishing.

—Spiky Saw. Fox, Will. 2013. (ENG.). 16p. (J). pap. *(978-1-908865-26-7(1))* Beecroft Publishing.

—Suzy Scissors. Fox, Will. 2013. (ENG.). 20p. (J). pap. *(978-1-908865-29-8(6))* Beecroft Publishing.

—Twisty Drill. Fox, Will. 2013. (ENG.). 16p. (J). pap. *(978-1-908865-24-3(5))* Beecroft Publishing.

Fox, Woody. Alice Again. Curtin, Judi. 2006. (ENG.). 240p. (J). pap. 12.95 *(978-0-86278-956-5(7))* O'Brien Pr., Ltd., The IRL. Dist: Dufour Editions, Inc.

Fox, Woody. Alice in the Middle. Curtin, Judi. 2nd rev. ed. 2015. (ENG.). 256p. (J). 13.00 ***(978-1-84717-673-8(9))*** O'Brien Pr., Ltd., The IRL. Dist: Dufour Editions, Inc.

Fox, Woody. Alice Next Door. Curtin, Judi. 2005. (ENG.). 208p. (J). pap. 12.95 *(978-0-86278-898-8(6))* O'Brien Pr., Ltd., The IRL. Dist: Dufour Editions, Inc.

—Don't Ask Alice. Curtin, Judi. (ENG.). 256p. (J). 2007. pap. 12.95 *(978-1-84717-023-1(4));* 2nd rev. ed. 2015. 13.00 ***(978-1-84717-672-1(0))*** O'Brien Pr., Ltd., The IRL. Dist: Dufour Editions, Inc.

—Emma Says Boo. Donovan, Anna. 2003. (Panda Cubs Ser.: 03). (ENG.). 48p. (J). pap. 9.95 *(978-0-86278-795-0(5))* O'Brien Pr., Ltd., The IRL. Dist: Dufour Editions, Inc.

—Emma Says Oops! Donovan, Anna. 2004. (Panda Cubs Ser.: 04). (ENG.). 48p. (J). pap. 9.95 *(978-0-86278-902-2(8))* O'Brien Pr., Ltd., The IRL. Dist: Dufour Editions, Inc.

—Eva & the Hidden Diary. Curtin, Judi. 2013. (ENG.). 240p. (J). pap. 13.95 *(978-1-84717-588-5(0))* O'Brien Pr., Ltd., The IRL. Dist: Dufour Editions, Inc.

—What Do Rabbits Think? And Other Fun Poems for Kids. Reddin, Brian. 2006. (ENG.). 64p. (J). pap. 17.95 *(978-1-85635-517-9(9))* Mercier Pr., Ltd., The IRL. Dist: Dufour Editions, Inc.

Foy, Denis. Dear God, Are There Any Flies in Heaven? Gallina, Danielle. 2013. (ENG.). (J). 15.98 *(978-1-62086-380-0(4))* Mascot Bks., Inc.

Foye, Lloyd. Basketball Showdown. Arena, Jacqueline. 2005. (Girlz Rock! Ser.). (J). pap. *(978-1-59336-704-6(X))* Mondo Publishing.

—Bowling Buddies. Dinbergs, Holly Smith. 2005. (Girlz Rock! Ser.). (J). pap. *(978-1-59336-699-5(X))* Mondo Publishing.

—The Sleepover. Mullins, Julie. 2005. (Girlz Rock! Ser.). (J). pap. *(978-1-59336-707-7(4))* Mondo Publishing.

Fra, Irene. Diario del Autobus a de la Linea 3. Montes, Juan Mari & Montes Gonzalo, Juan Mari. 2006. (SPA.). 96p. (J). *(978-84-667-5192-6(0))* Grupo Anaya, S.A.

—Los Inventores de Cuentos. Garcia-Castellano, Ana. 2009. (SPA.). 76p. (J). (gr. 3-6). pap. *(978-607-11-0102-0(6))* Aguilar, Altea, Taurus, Alfaguara, S.A. de C.V.

Fractured Pixels Staff. Minions: Seek & Find. Universal Books (Panama) Staff & King, Trey. 2015. (ENG.). 24p. (J). (gr. 1-4). 8.99 ***(978-0-316-29997-8(9))*** Little, Brown Bks. for Young Readers.

Fraggalosch, Crista. Northern Refuge: A Story of a Canadian Boreal Forest. Fraggalosch, Audrey. 2005. (Soundprints' Wild Habitats Ser.). (ENG.). 36p. (J). (gr. 1-4). 8.95 *(978-1-59249-100-1(6),* SC7012) Soundprints.

Frahm, Paul. Caleb Takes a Ride on the Staten Island Ferry. St. Jean, Catherine. 2011. (ENG.). 26p. pap. 10.00 *(978-1-4663-9158-1(8))* CreateSpace Independent Publishing Platform.

—A Staten Island Ferry Tale. St Jean, Catherine Avery. 2006. 32p. (J). per. 26.99 *(978-1-4134-0262-9(3))* Xlibris Corp.

Frake, Barbara. Tales from Falmac Farm. Falcone, Karen. 2005. (ENG.). 47p. (J). per. *(978-1-933002-08-8(5))* PublishingWorks.

Framestore. The Creature Department. Weston, Robert Paul. 2014. (Creature Department Ser.: 1). (ENG.). 346p. (J). (gr. 3-7). pap. 8.99 *(978-1-59514-684-7(9),* Razorbill) Penguin Publishing Group.

—Gobbled by Ghorks. Weston, Robert Paul. 2014. (Creature Department Ser.: 2). (ENG.). 234p. (J). (gr. 3-7). 16.99 *(978-1-59514-750-9(0),* Razorbill) Penguin Publishing Group.

Frampton, David. At Jerusalem's Gate: Poems of Easter. Grimes, Nikki. 2005. 48p. (J). 20.00 *(978-0-8028-5183-3(5))* Eerdmans, William B. Publishing Co.

—The Song of Francis & the Animals. Mora, Pat. 2005. 32p. (J). (gr. -1-2). 16.00 *(978-0-8028-5253-3(X))* Eerdmans, William B. Publishing Co.

Frampton, David. Beastie ABC. Frampton, David. Date not set. 32p. (J). (gr. -1-1). pap. 5.99 *(978-0-06-443653-3(5))* HarperCollins Pubs.

—Mr. Ferlinghetti's Poem. Frampton, David. 2006. 32p. (J). (gr. k-4). 18.00 *(978-0-8028-5290-8(4),* Eerdmans Bks For Young Readers) Eerdmans, William B. Publishing Co.

—The Whole Night Through. Frampton, David. Date not set. 32p. (J). (gr. -1-1). pap. 5.99 *(978-0-06-443652-6(7))* HarperCollins Pubs.

—The Whole Night Through: A Lullaby. Frampton, David. 2004. 30p. (J). (gr. k-4). reprint ed. *(978-0-7567-7723-4(2))* DIANE Publishing Co.

Frampton, Otis, et al. Far Out Fairy Tales. Comeau, Joey et al. 2015. (Far Out Fairy Tales Ser.). (ENG.). 40p. (gr. 3-4). 95.96 ***(978-1-4965-0283-4(3),*** Far Out Fairy Tales) Stone Arch Bks.

Frampton, Otis. Soul Mates. Downer, Denise. 2013. (Tombstone Twins Ser.). (ENG.). 48p. (gr. 1-3). lib. bdg. 22.65 *(978-1-4342-2248-0(9))* Stone Arch Bks.

—Tombstone Twins: Soul Mates, 1 vol. Downer, Denise. 2013. (Tombstone Twins Ser.). (ENG.). 48p. (gr. 1-3). pap. 5.95 *(978-1-4342-3873-3(3))* Stone Arch Bks.

—Tombstone Twins Package: Soul Mates. Downer, Denise. 2013. (ENG.). 41p. (J). (gr. 2-4). pap. 35.70 *(978-1-4342-3955-6(1))* Stone Arch Bks.

Frampton, Otis. Red Riding Hood, Superhero. Frampton, Otis. 2015. (Far Out Fairy Tales Ser.). (ENG.). 40p. (gr. 3-4). lib. bdg. 23.99 *(978-1-4342-9650-4(4))* Stone Arch Bks.

Francais, Isabelle, photos by. Puppies: A Guide to Caring for Your Puppy. Fernandez, Amy. 2006. (Complete Care Made Easy Ser.). (ENG., 200p. (gr. 3-7). per. 9.95 *(978-1-931993-76-0(9))* I-5 Publishing LLC.

Francavilla, Francesco. Cry of the Banshee! Ciencin, Scott. 2008. 48p. (J). pap. *(978-0-545-03981-9(9))* Scholastic, Inc.

—Escape from Blackbeard's Curse! Ciencin, Scott. 2007. 48p. (J). pap. *(978-0-545-03767-9(0))* Scholastic, Inc.

—The Man Without Fear Vol. 1: Urban Jungle. 2011. (ENG.). 144p. (YA). (gr. 8-17). pap. 16.99 *(978-0-7851-4523-3(0))* Marvel Worldwide, Inc.

France, Mark. The Horsosaurus. Stanley, Dean. 2008. 32p. pap. 14.62 *(978-1-4251-8158-1(9))* Trafford Publishing.

Francine Ngardab, Riches. What Makes a Tree Smile? Pitt, Tamina & Tem, Janke. 2003. (Uupababa Ser.). 24p. (J). pap. *(978-1-875641-80-2(7))* Magabala Bks.

Francis, Amber Rose. Jeanettie Is Called Retard, 1 vol. Blackmore, Charlotte Lozano. 2010. 34p. 24.95 *(978-1-4489-4096-7(6))* PublishAmerica, Inc.

Francis, David. The Secret of the Ginger Mice. Watts, Frances. 2012. (ENG.). 304p. (J). 12.95 *(978-0-7624-4410-6(X))* Running Pr. Bk. Pubs.

Francis, Guy. Afraid of the Dark. Hale, Bruce. 2015. (Clark the Shark Ser.). (ENG.). 32p. (J). (gr. -1-3). 17.99 ***(978-0-06-237450-9(8))*** HarperCollins Pubs.

Francis, Guy. The Alien, the Giant, & Rocketman. Perry, Phyllis Jean. 2006. (J). pap. *(978-1-59336-723-7(6))* Mondo Publishing.

—Angus MacMouse Brings down the House. Teitel, Linda & Teitel, Linda Phillips. 2010. (ENG.). 208p. (J). (gr. 2-4). 15.99 *(978-1-59990-493-1(4),* Bloomsbury USA Childrens) Bloomsbury USA.

—Angus MacMouse Brings down the House. Teitel, Linda Phillips. 2010. (ENG.). 208p. (J). (gr. 2-4). pap. 5.99 *(978-1-59990-490-0(X),* Bloomsbury USA Childrens) Bloomsbury USA.

—Basketball Disasters. Mills, Claudia. (Mason Dixon Ser.). (ENG.). 176p. (J). (gr. 2-5). 2013. pap. 6.99 *(978-0-375-87276-1(0));* 2012. 12.99 *(978-0-375-86875-7(5))* Random Hse. Children's Bks. (Knopf Bks. for Young Readers).

—Ben Franklin's Fame. Deutsch, Stacia & Cohon, Rhody. 2006. (Blast to the Past Ser.: 6). (ENG.). 128p. (J). (gr. 2-5). pap. 7.99 *(978-1-4169-1804-2(3),* Simon & Schuster/Paula Wiseman Bks.) Simon & Schuster/Paula Wiseman Bks.

—Clark the Shark. Hale, Bruce. 2013. (Clark the Shark Ser.). (ENG.). 32p. (J). (gr. -1-3). 17.99 *(978-0-06-219226-4(4))* HarperCollins Pubs.

—Clark the Shark - Tooth Trouble. Hale, Bruce. 2014. (I Can Read Book 1 Ser.). (ENG.). 32p. (J). (gr. -1-3). 16.99 *(978-0-06-227908-8(4));* pap. 3.99 *(978-0-06-227906-4(8))* HarperCollins Pubs.

—Clark the Shark Dares to Share. Hale, Bruce. 2013. (Clark the Shark Ser.). (ENG.). 32p. (J). (gr. -1-3). 17.99 *(978-0-06-227905-7(X))* HarperCollins Pubs.

—Clark the Shark Takes Heart. Hale, Bruce. 2014. (Clark the Shark Ser.). (ENG.). 32p. (J). (gr. -1-3). 17.99 *(978-0-06-219227-1(2))* HarperCollins Pubs.

—Dance by the Light of the Moon. Ryder, Joanne. 2006. (ENG.). 40p. (gr. -1-1). 15.99 *(978-0-7868-1820-4(4))* Hyperion Pr.

—Guys & Ghouls. Jones, Marcia Thornton & Dadey, Debbie. 2006. (Ghostville Elementary Ser.: Bk. 13). 81p. *(978-0-439-79402-2(1))* Scholastic, Inc.

—Mason Dixon: Fourth-Grade Disasters. Mills, Claudia. 2012. (Mason Dixon Ser.). (ENG.). 176p. (J). (gr. 4-7). 6.99 *(978-0-375-87275-4(2),* Yearling) Random Hse. Children's Bks.

—Monkey See, Monkey Zoo. Soderberg, Erin. 2010. (ENG.). 160p. (J). (gr. 2-4). pap. 5.99 *(978-1-59990-558-7(2),* Bloomsbury USA Childrens) Bloomsbury USA.

—Never Ever Talk to Strangers. Pace, Anne Marie. 2010. (J). *(978-0-545-24229-5(0))* Scholastic, Inc.

—Pet Disasters. Mills, Claudia. 2012. (Mason Dixon Ser.). (ENG.). 176p. (J). (gr. 4-7). 6.99 *(978-0-375-87274-7(4),* Yearling) Random Hse. Children's Bks.

—Pets. Ikids Staff. 2009. (ENG.). 10p. (J). (gr. -1-1). 15.99 *(978-1-58476-940-8(8))* Innovative Kids.

—The Pup Who Cried Wolf. Kurtz, Chris. 2010. (ENG.). 144p. (J). (gr. 2-4). 15.99 *(978-1-59990-497-9(7));* pap. 5.99 *(978-1-59990-492-4(6))* Bloomsbury USA. (Bloomsbury USA Childrens).

—Red, White, & Boo! Jones, Marcia Thornton & Dadey, Debbie. 2007. (Ghostville Elementary Ser.: Bk. 16). 64p. (J). *(978-0-439-88364-1(4))* Scholastic, Inc.

—The Top Secret Toys. Kehoe, Tim. 2013. (Vincent Shadow Ser.: 2). (ENG.). 272p. (J). (gr. 3-7). pap. 6.99 *(978-0-316-05668-7(5))* Little, Brown Bks. for Young Readers.

—The View at the Zoo. Bostrom, Kathleen Long. 2011. 32p. (J). (gr. -1-3). 14.99 *(978-0-8249-5629-5(X),* Ideals Children's Bks.) Ideals Pubns.

—A View at the Zoo. Bostrom, Kathleen Long. 2015. (J). pap. *(978-0-8249-5669-1(9),* Ideals Children's Bks.) Ideals Pubns.

Francis, Guy & Wohnoutka, Mike. The Unusual Mind of Vincent Shadow. Kehoe, Tim. 2009. (Vincent Shadow Ser.: 1). (ENG.). 192p. (J). (gr. 3-7). 9.99 *(978-0-316-05665-6(0))* Little, Brown Bks. for Young Readers.

—Vincent Shadow: Toy Inventor. Kehoe, Tim. 2011. (Vincent Shadow Ser.: 1). (ENG.). 224p. (J). (gr. 3-7). pap. 6.99 *(978-0-316-05666-3(9))* Little, Brown Bks. for Young Readers.

Francis, Jamie, et al. Big Keep Books- Spanish Caption Books: Dinosaurios; Camiones; ¿Qué Es lo Que Veo?; el Tráfico; Globos; la Granja, 8 bks., Set. deLeon Diaz, Rosa et al. deLeon Diaz, Rosa et al, trs. enl. ed. 2005.Tr. of Caption Books. (SPA.). 8p. (J). 20.00 *(978-1-893986-41-1(1))* Keep Bks.

Francis, John. My Big Dinosaur World. Mugford, Simon. 2008. 60p. (J). *(978-1-84332-594-9(2),* Priddy Bks.) St. Martin's Pr.

—Prehistoric Animals. Franklin, Carolyn. 2013. (World of Wonder Ser.). (ENG.). 32p. (J). (gr. 4-7). lib. bdg. *(978-1-904642-65-7(9))* Book Hse.

Francis, John, et al. Scary Creatures of the River. Cheshire, Gerard. 2009. (Scary Creatures Ser.). (ENG.). 32p. (J). (gr. 2-4). 27.00 *(978-0-531-21823-5(6),* Watts, Franklin); pap. 8.95 *(978-0-531-22228-7(4),* Children's Pr.) Scholastic Library Publishing.

Francis, John. The Truth about Animal Communication. Stonehouse, Bernard. & Bertram, Esther. 2003. (Animals Exposed! Ser.). 48p. (J). 11.99 *(978-0-439-54329-3(0))* Scholastic, Inc.

Francis, John & Scott, Kimberley. Wolves. MacLaine, James. 2013. (Usborne Beginners Ser.). (ENG.). 32p. (J). 4.99 *(978-0-7945-3402-8(3),* Usborne) EDC Publishing.

Francis, John & Testar, Sue. Dogs Sticker Book. Glover, Harry. 2007. (Spotter's Guides Sticker Books - New Format Ser.). 24p. (J). (gr. -1-3). pap. 8.99 *(978-0-7945-1690-1(4),* Usborne) EDC Publishing.

Francis, Lauren. Hannah's Sunday Hats. Yoxen, Jackie. l.t. ed. 2006. 32p. (J). 19.95 *(978-1-59879-184-6(2))* Lifevest Publishing, Inc.

Francis, Michael Harlowe, photos by. Watching Yellowstone & Grand Teton Wildlife. Wilkinson, Todd. 2004. 96p. per. 12.95 *(978-1-931832-27-4(7))* Riverbend Publishing.

Francis, Peter. Butterfly Blues. Keene, Carolyn. 2015. (Nancy Drew & the Clue Crew Ser.: 40). (ENG.). 96p. (J). (gr. 1-4). pap. 4.99 *(978-1-4814-1470-8(4),* Simon & Schuster/Paula Wiseman Bks.) Simon & Schuster/Paula Wiseman Bks.

—Pool Party Puzzler. Keene, Carolyn. 2015. (Nancy Drew Clue Book Ser.: 1). (ENG.). 96p. (J). (gr. 1-4). 16.99 *(978-1-4814-3896-4(4),* Simon & Schuster/Paula Wiseman Bks.) Simon & Schuster/Paula Wiseman Bks.

Francisco, Manny. Learn Filipino: Book One, Book One. Romero, Victor Eclar. 2004. 384p. per. 29.95 *(978-1-932956-41-2(7))* Magsimba Pr.

Francisco, Wendy. Animal Alphabet: On the Land, in the Sky or Sea, Meet God's Creatures from a to Z. Hopkins, Mary Rice. 2003. 32p. (gr. -1-1). 12.99 *(978-0-89107-968-2(8))* Crossway.

—David & His Giant Battle, 5 vols. Hansen, Janis. 2003. (Bible Adventure Club Ser.). 36p. wbk. ed. 19.99 incl. audio, cd-rom *(978-1-58134-321-2(3))* Crossway.

—Jesus: The Birthday of the King, 5 vols. Hansen, Janis. 2003. (Bible Adventure Club Ser.). 36p. wbk. ed. 19.99 incl. audio, cd-rom *(978-1-58134-331-1(0))* Crossway.

—Jonah & His Amazing Voyage, 5 vols. Hansen, Janis. 2003. (Bible Adventure Club Ser.). 36p. wbk. ed. 19.99 incl. audio, cd-rom *(978-1-58134-326-7(4))* Crossway.

—Noah & the Incredible Flood, 5 vols. Carlson, Melody. 2003. (Bible Adventure Club Ser.). 36p. wbk. ed. 19.99 incl. audio, cd-rom *(978-1-58134-336-6(1))* Crossway.

Franco. Return to the Treehouse. Baltazar, Art. 2015. (ENG.). 128p. (gr. 2-5). pap. 12.99 *(978-1-4012-5492-6(6))* DC Comics.

Franco, Betsy, jt. illus. see Franco, Tom.

Franco-Feeney, Betsy. Hole in the Bottom of the Sea. Franco-Feeney, Betsy. Lavin, Christine. McHugh, Patricia & Feeney, Kathryn, eds. 2012. (ENG.). 32p. (J). 18.95 incl. audio compact disk *(978-0-9726487-8-3(X))* Puddle Jump Pr., Ltd.

Franco, Franco. Dino-Mike! Franco, Franco. 2015. (Dino-Mike! Ser.). (ENG.). 128p. (gr. 1-3). pap. 23.80 ***(978-1-4965-2233-7(8),*** Dino-Mike!) Stone Arch Bks.

Franco, Liliana. Cogito Pt. 1: Antoine & Liliana, the Separation. Franco, Liliana. Bacha, Antoine. 2007. 293p. pap. 24.95 *(978-0-9794618-1-1(2))* AJL Publishers.

Franco, Mauricio. Cuentos para Ninos de la Candelaria. Mzjica, Elisa. 2004. (Literatura Juvenil (Panamericana Editorial) Ser.). (SPA.). 125p. (YA). (gr. 4-7). pap. *(978-958-30-0303-5(4))* Panamericana Editorial.

Franco, Paula. Ashley Goes Viral. Jones, Jen. 2015. (Sleepover Girls Ser.). (ENG.). 128p. (gr. 3-5). pap. 6.95 ***(978-1-62370-306-6(9))*** Stone Arch Bks.

Franco, Paula. Awesome Recipes You Can Make & Share, 1 vol. Bolte, Mari. 2014. (Sleepover Girls Crafts Ser.). (ENG.). 32p. (gr. 3-4). 27.32 *(978-1-4914-1733-1(1))* Capstone Pr., Inc.

Franco, Paula. Carly. Mullarkey, Lisa. 2016. (J). ***(978-1-62402-127-5(1))*** Magic Wagon.

Franco, Paula. Colorful Creations You Can Make & Share, 1 vol. Bolte, Mari. 2014. (Sleepover Girls Crafts Ser.). (ENG.). 32p. (gr. 3-4). 27.32 *(978-1-4914-1734-8(X))* Capstone Pr., Inc.

Franco, Paula. Daniela. Mullarkey, Lisa. 2016. (J). ***(978-1-62402-128-2(X))*** Magic Wagon.

—Delaney vs. the Bully. Jones, Jen. 2015. (Sleepover Girls Ser.). (ENG.). 128p. (gr. 3-5). lib. bdg. 21.32 ***(978-1-4965-0541-5(7))*** Stone Arch Bks.

Franco, Paula. Dog Days for Delaney. Jones, Jen. 2014. (Sleepover Girls Ser.). (ENG.). 128p. (gr. 3-5). 21.32 *(978-1-4342-9756-3(X))* Stone Arch Bks.

—Fab Fashions You Can Make & Share, 1 vol. Bolte, Mari. 2014. (Sleepover Girls Crafts Ser.). (ENG.). 32p. (gr. 3-4). lib. bdg. 27.32 *(978-1-4914-1735-5(8))* Capstone Pr., Inc.

Franco, Paula. Gabriela. Mullarkey, Lisa. 2016. (J). ***(978-1-62402-129-9(8))*** Magic Wagon.

—Kianna. Mullarkey, Lisa. 2016. (J). ***(978-1-62402-130-5(1))*** Magic Wagon.

Franco, Paula. Maren Loves Luke Lewis. Jones, Jen. 2014. (Sleepover Girls Ser.). (ENG.). 128p. (gr. 3-5). lib. bdg. 21.32 *(978-1-4342-9755-6(1))* Stone Arch Bks.

Franco, Paula. Maren's New Family. Jones, Jen. 2015. (Sleepover Girls Ser.). (ENG.). 128p. (gr. 3-5). lib. bdg. 21.32 ***(978-1-4965-0540-8(9))*** Stone Arch Bks.

Franco, Paula. The New Ashley. Jones, Jen. 2014. (Sleepover Girls Ser.). (ENG.). 128p. (gr. 3-5). lib. bdg. 21.32 *(978-1-4342-9758-7(6))* Stone Arch Bks.

—Saving the Team. Morgan, Alex. 2013. (Kicks Ser.). (ENG.). 176p. (J). (gr. 3-7). 16.99 *(978-1-4424-8570-9(1),* Simon & Schuster Bks. For Young Readers) Simon & Schuster Bks. For Young Readers.

—Sleepover Girls. Bolte, Mari. 2014. (Sleepover Girls Crafts Ser.). (ENG.). 64p. (gr. 3-4). pap. 51.80 *(978-1-62370-201-4(1))* Capstone Young Readers.

—Sleepover Girls. Jones, Jen. 2014. (Sleepover Girls Ser.). (ENG.). 128p. (gr. 3-5). 85.28 *(978-1-4965-0316-9(3))* Stone Arch Bks.

—Sleepover Girls Crafts, 1 vol. Bolte, Mari. 2014. (Sleepover Girls Crafts Ser.). (ENG.). 32p. (gr. 3-4). 109.28 *(978-1-4914-1737-9(4),* Snap Bks.) Capstone Pr., Inc.

—Sleepover Girls Crafts: Amazing Recipes You Can Make & Share, 1 vol. Bolte, Mari. 2014. (Sleepover Girls Crafts Ser.). (ENG.). 64p. (gr. 3-4). pap. 9.95 *(978-1-62370-197-0(X))* Capstone Pr., Inc.

—Sleepover Girls Crafts: Colorful Creations You Can Make & Share, 1 vol. Bolte, Mari. 2014. (Sleepover Girls Crafts Ser.). (ENG.). 64p. (gr. 3-4). pap. 9.95 *(978-1-62370-198-7(8))* Capstone Pr., Inc.

—Sleepover Girls Crafts: Fab Fashions You Can Make & Share, 1 vol. Bolte, Mari. 2014. (Sleepover Girls Crafts Ser.). (ENG.). 64p. (gr. 3-4). pap. 9.95 *(978-1-62370-199-4(6))* Capstone Pr., Inc.

—Sleepover Girls Crafts: Spa Projects You Can Make & Share, 1 vol. Bolte, Mari. 2014. (Sleepover Girls Crafts Ser.). (ENG.). 64p. (gr. 3-4). pap. 9.95 *(978-1-62370-200-7(3))* Capstone Pr., Inc.

—Spa Projects You Can Make & Share, 1 vol. Bolte, Mari. 2014. (Sleepover Girls Crafts Ser.). (ENG.). 32p. (gr. 3-4). lib. bdg. 27.32 *(978-1-4914-1736-2(6))* Capstone Pr., Inc.

Franco, Paula. Willow's: Spring Break Adventure. Jones, Jen. 2015. (Sleepover Girls Ser.). (ENG.). 128p. (gr. 3-5). pap. 6.95 ***(978-1-62370-305-9(0))*** Stone Arch Bks.

Franco, Paula. Willow's Boy-Crazy Birthday. Jones, Jen. 2014. (Sleepover Girls Ser.). (ENG.). 128p. (gr. 3-5). lib. bdg. 21.32 *(978-1-4342-9757-0(8))* Stone Arch Bks.

Franco, Tom & Franco, Betsy. Metamorphosis: Junior Year. Franco, Betsy. 2009. (ENG.). 128p. (YA). (gr. 9-18). 16.99 *(978-0-7636-3765-1(3))* Candlewick Pr.

François, André. Little Boy Brown. Harris, Isobel. 2013. (ENG.). 48p. (J). (gr. -1-3). 15.95 *(978-1-59270-135-3(3))* Enchanted Lion Bks., LLC.

Francour, Kathleen. Charmed. Book Company Staff. 2003. (Stationery Ser.). (J). bds. 19.95 *(978-1-74047-380-4(9))* Book Co. Publishing Pty, Ltd., The AUS. Dist: Penton Overseas, Inc.

—Flitterbyes Photo Frames. Book Company Staff. 2003. (Stationery Ser.). (J). 9.95 *(978-1-74047-354-5(X))* Book Co. Publishing Pty, Ltd., The AUS. Dist: Penton Overseas, Inc.

F

—Friends Forever. 2003. (Puzzles Ser.). (J). bds. 10.95 (978-1-74047-342-2(6)) Book Co. Publishing Pty, Ltd., The AUS. Dist: Penton Overseas, Inc.

—Little Treasures. Book Company Staff. 2003. (Stationery Ser.). (J). 14.95 (978-1-74047-311-8(6)) Book Co. Publishing Pty, Ltd., The AUS. Dist: Penton Overseas, Inc.

Francour, Kathleen, photos by. The Friends in My Garden. Appel, Dee. Date not set. (Tiny Times Board Book Ser.). 10p. (J). bds. 5.99 (978-0-7369-0564-0(2)) Harvest Hse. Pubs.

—Let's Play Dress Up. Appel, Dee. Date not set. (Tiny Times Board Book Ser.). 10p. (J). bds. 5.99 (978-0-7369-0563-3(4)) Harvest Hse. Pubs.

Francq, Philippe. The Heir. Van Hamme, Jean. 2008. (ENG.). 96p. pap. 19.95 (978-1-905460-48-9(1)) CineBook GBR. Dist: National Bk. Network.

Franfou. Melvin et le Grand Match de Hockey. Burke, Christina. Minguet, Anne, tr. 2013. 52p. (978-0-9918561-3-8(9)); pap. (978-0-9918561-2-1(0)) Stars Aligned Publishing.

Franfou Studio. The Color of People. Labuda, Scott A. 2011. (ENG.). 34p. (J). (gr. -1-3). 15.95 (978-1-935268-94-9(5)) Halo Publishing International.

Franfou Studio, jt. illus. see Atkins, Aimee.

Frangouli, Rena. My Greek Reader. Papaloizos, Theodore C. 2004. (GRE & ENG.). 124p. (Orig.). (YA). (gr. 2). pap. (978-0-932416-46-9(2)) Papaloizos Pubns., Inc.

Frank, Dave. I Went to the Party in Kalamazoo. Shankman, Ed. 2013. (ENG.). 40p. pap. 12.95 (978-1-938700-22-4(8), Commonwealth Editions) Applewood Bks.

Frank, Remkiewicz, jt. illus. see Remkiewicz, Frank.

Frankel, Alona. Once upon a Potty - - Girl. Frankel, Alona. 2007. (Once upon a Potty Ser.). (ENG.). 40p. (J). (gr. -1 — 1). 7.95 (978-1-55407-284-2(0), 9781554072842) Firefly Bks., Ltd.

—Once upon a Potty - Boy. Frankel, Alona. 2007. (Once upon a Potty Ser.). (ENG.). 40p. (J). (gr. -1 — 1). 7.95 (978-1-55407-283-5(2), 9781554072835) Firefly Bks., Ltd.

Frankenberg, Robert. Fire Canoe. Falk, Elsa. 2012. 188p. 42.95 (978-1-258-23680-9(X)); pap. 27.95 (978-1-258-24375-3(X)) Literary Licensing, LLC.

—Owls in the Family. Mowat, Farley. ed. 2004. 91p. (gr. 5-9). lib. bdg. 16.00 (978-0-88103-863-7(6), Turtleback) Turtleback Bks.

Frankenhuyzen, Gijsbert van. Challenger: America's Favorite Eagle. Raven, Margot Theis. 2005. (ENG.). 40p. (J). (gr. k-6). 17.95 (978-1-58536-261-5(1)) Sleeping Bear Pr.

—I Love You Just Enough. Frankenhuyzen, Robbyn Smith van. 2014. (Hazel Ridge Farm Stories Ser.). (ENG.). 36p. (J). (gr. 1-4). 16.95 (978-1-58536-839-6(3), 203009) Sleeping Bear Pr.

—Jasper's Story: Saving Moon Bears. Robinson, Jill & Bekoff, Marc. 2013. (ENG.). 40p. (J). (gr. 1-4). 16.99 (978-1-58536-798-6(2), 202359) Sleeping Bear Pr.

—S Is for Sleeping Bear Dunes: A National Lakeshore Alphabet. Wargin, Kathy-jo. 2015. (ENG.). 32p. (J). (gr. 2-4). 16.99 (978-1-58536-917-1(9), 203818) Sleeping Bear Pr.

—S Is for Smithsonian: America's Museum Alphabet. Smith, Roland & Smith, Marie. 2010. (Sleeping Bear Alphabets Ser.). (ENG.). 32p. (J). (gr. 1-5). 17.95 (978-1-58536-314-8(6)) Sleeping Bear Pr.

Frankenhuyzen, Gijsbert van, et al. Voices for Freedom. Swain, Gwenyth. 2013. (American Adventures Ser.). (ENG.). 72p. (J). (gr. 3-6). 6.99 (978-1-58536-886-0(5), 202900) Sleeping Bear Pr.

Frankenhuyzen, Gijsbert van. W Is for Woof: A Dog Alphabet. Strother, Ruth. 2009. (ENG.). 40p. (J). (gr. k-6). pap. 7.95 (978-1-58536-477-0(0)) Sleeping Bear Pr.

Frankeny, Frankie, jt. photos by see Stojanovic, Laura.

Frankfeldt, Gwen & Morrow, Glenn. Dateline: Troy. Fleischman, Paul. ed. 2006. (ENG.). 80p. (YA). (gr. 7-10). 18.99 (978-0-7636-3083-6(7)) Candlewick Pr.

—Dateline - Troy. Frankfeldt, Gwen & Fleischman, Paul. ed. 2006. (ENG.). 80p. (YA). (gr. 7-10). pap. 8.99 (978-0-7636-3084-3(5)) Candlewick Pr.

Franklin, Carolyn. How a Caterpillar Grows into a Butterfly. Kant, Tanya. 2008. (Amaze Ser.). (ENG.). 32p. (J). 27.00 (978-0-531-24046-5(0)); (gr. -1-3). pap. 8.95 (978-0-531-23800-4(8)) Scholastic Library Publishing. (Children's Pr.).

—How a Seed Grows into a Sunflower. Stewart, David. 2008. (Amaze Ser.). (ENG.). 32p. (J). (gr. k-3). 27.00 (978-0-531-20442-9(1), Children's Pr.) Scholastic Library Publishing.

—How a Tadpole Grows into a Frog. Stewart, David. 2008. (Amaze Ser.). (ENG.). 32p. (J). (gr. k-3). 27.00 (978-0-531-20443-6(X)); pap. 8.95 (978-0-531-20454-2(5)) Scholastic Library Publishing. (Children's Pr.).

—How an Egg Grows into a Chicken. Kant, Tanya. 2008. (Amaze Ser.). (ENG.). 32p. (J). (gr. -1-3). pap. 8.95 (978-0-531-23801-1(6)); (gr. k-3). 27.00 (978-0-531-24047-2(9)) Scholastic Library Publishing. (Children's Pr.).

—How Your Body Works: A Good Look Inside You Insides. Stewart, David. 2008. (Amaze Ser.). (ENG.). 32p. (J). (gr. k-3). pap. 8.95 (978-0-531-20455-9(3), Children's Pr.) Scholastic Library Publishing.

—How Your Body Works: A Good Look Inside Your Insides. Stewart, David. 2008. (Amaze Ser.). (ENG.). 32p. (J). (gr. k-3). 27.00 (978-0-531-20444-3(8), Children's Pr.) Scholastic Library Publishing.

—The Migration of a Butterfly. Kant, Tanya. 2008. (Amaze Ser.). (ENG.). 32p. (J). 27.00 (978-0-531-24048-9(7)); (gr. -1-3). pap. 8.95 (978-0-531-23802-8(4)) Scholastic Library Publishing. (Children's Pr.).

Franklin, Carolyn. Ocean Life. Franklin, Carolyn. Stewart, David. 2008. (World of Wonder Ser.). (ENG.). 32p. (J). (gr. 1-4). 29.00 (978-0-531-20451-1(0), Children's Pr.) Scholastic Library Publishing.

—Rain Forest Animals. Franklin, Carolyn. Stewart, David. 2008. (World of Wonder Ser.). (ENG.). 32p. (J). (gr. 1-4). 29.00 (978-0-531-20452-8(9), Children's Pr.) Scholastic Library Publishing.

Franklin, Mark. Color Yourself Smart: Geography. Cowling, Dan. 2012. (Color Yourself Smart Ser.). (ENG.). 128p. 19.95 (978-1-60710-216-8(1), Thunder Bay Pr.) Baker & Taylor Publishing Group.

Franks, C. J. The Virginia Night Before Christmas. Sullivan, Ellen & Moore, Clement C. 2005. (J). (978-1-58173-392-1(5)) Sweetwater Pr.

Fransisco, Tina. Race Against Time (Mr. Peabody & Sherman) Golden Books. 2014. (Super Color with Stickers Ser.). (ENG.). 96p. (J). (gr. -1-2). pap. 3.99 (978-0-385-37151-3(9), Golden Bks.) Random Hse. Children's Bks.

Fransisco, Wendy. Creation: God's Wonderful Gift, 5 vols. Hansen, Janis. 2003. (Bible Adventure Club Ser.). 36p. wbk. ed. 19.99 incl. audio, cd-rom (978-1-58134-292-5(6)) Crossway.

Franson, Leanne. Best Wishes for Eddie. Nayer, Judy. 2012. (First Chapters: Set 2 Ser.: Vol. 8). (ENG.). 64p. (J). (gr. 2-3). pap. 9.50 (978-0-7652-0884-2(9)) Modern Curriculum Pr.

—Flood Warning, 1 vol. Pearce, Jacqueline. 2012. (Orca Echoes Ser.). (ENG.). 64p. (J). (gr. 2-3). pap. 6.95 (978-1-4598-0068-7(0)) Orca Bk. Pubs. USA.

—The Girl Who Hated Books, 1 vol. Pawagi, Manjusha. 24p. (J). (gr. k-3). 2010. (ENG.). pap. 7.95 (978-1-896764-09-2(6)); 2005. 12.95 (978-1-896764-11-5(8)) Second Story Pr. CAN. Dist: Orca Bk. Pubs. USA.

—It's a Baby, Andy Russell. Adler, David A. 2006. (Andy Russell Ser.: Bk. 6). (ENG.). 128p. (J). (gr. 1-4). pap. 9.95 (978-0-15-205610-0(6)) Houghton Mifflin Harcourt Publishing Co.

—Not Wanted by the Police. Adler, David A. 2005. (Andy Russell Ser.: Bk. 5). (ENG.). 128p. (J). (gr. 1-4). pap. 5.99 (978-0-15-216719-6(6)) Houghton Mifflin Harcourt Publishing Co.

Franson, Leanne, et al. On the Case. Wishinsky, Frieda. 2009. (Canadian Flyer Adventures Ser.: 12). (ENG.). 96p. (J). (gr. 1-4). pap. 7.95 (978-1-897349-55-7(6), Maple Tree Pr.) Owlkids Bks. Inc. CAN. Dist: Perseus-PGW.

Franson, Leanne. Ripley's Believe It or Not! Awesome Collection. Packard, Mary. ed. 361p. (J). pap. (978-0-681-15435-3(7)) Scholastic, Inc.

—Ripley's Believe It or Not! Bizarre Collection. Packard, Mary. 2004. 361p. (J). pap. 3.99 (978-0-681-02479-3(8)) Scholastic, Inc.

—Thumb & the Bad Guys, 1 vol. Roberts, Ken. 2011. (ENG.). 120p. (J). (gr. 1-5). pap. 7.95 (978-0-88899-917-7(8)) Groundwood Bks. CAN. Dist: Perseus-PGW.

—Thumb on a Diamond, 1 vol. Roberts, Ken. 2007. (ENG.). 128p. (J). (gr. 2-5). pap. 7.95 (978-0-88899-705-0(1)) Groundwood Bks. CAN. Dist: Perseus-PGW.

—Totally Gross. Packard, Mary. 2004. 85p. (J). (978-0-439-71739-7(6)) Scholastic, Inc.

Franson, Leanne & Owlkids Books Inc. Staff. Far from Home. Wishinsky, Frieda & Griffiths, Dean. 2008. (Canadian Flyer Adventures Ser.: 11). (ENG.). 96p. (J). (gr. 1-4). pap. 7.95 (978-1-897349-43-4(2), Maple Tree Pr.) Owlkids Bks. Inc. CAN. Dist: Perseus-PGW.

—Lost in the Snow. Wishinsky, Frieda & Griffiths, Dean. 2008. (Canadian Flyer Adventures Ser.: 10). (ENG.). 96p. (J). (gr. 1-4). pap. 7.95 (978-1-897349-41-0(6), Maple Tree Pr.) Owlkids Bks. Inc. CAN. Dist: Perseus-PGW.

Fransoy, Monse. Cinderella (Cenicienta) Perrault, Charles. 2013. (Bilingual Fairy Tales Ser.). (ENG & SPA.). 32p. (gr. 1-4). lib. bdg. 28.50 (978-1-60753-356-6(1)) Amicus Educational.

Franzen, Sean, photos by. Busy Kitties. Schindel, John. 2004. (Busy Book Ser.). (ENG., 20p. (J). (— 1). bds. 6.99 (978-1-58246-130-4(9), Tricycle Pr.) Ten Speed Pr.

Franzese, Nora Tapp. I Want to Learn to Dance. Wigden, Susan. 2012. 36p. pap. 11.99 (978-1-60820-725-1(0)) MLR Pr., LLC.

Fraser-Allen, Johnny. The Squickerwonkers. Lilly, Evangeline. 2014. (ENG.). 42p. (gr. k-3). 16.99 (978-1-78329-545-6(7), Titan Bks.) Titan Bks. Ltd. GBR. Dist: Random Hse., Inc.

Fraser, Betty. A House Is a House for Me. Hoberman, Mary Ann. 2007. (ENG.). 48p. (J). (gr. -1-1). pap. 7.99 (978-0-14-240773-8(9), Puffin) Penguin Publishing Group.

—The Llama Who Had No Pajama: 100 Favorite Poems. Hoberman, Mary Ann. 2006. (ENG.). 68p. (J). (gr. 1-4). pap. 8.00 (978-0-15-205571-4(1)) Houghton Mifflin Harcourt Publishing Co.

—Sounds Are High, Sounds Are Low: I Wonder Why, Lowery, Lawrence F. 2014. (ENG.). 36p. (J). pap. 11.95 (978-1-941316-04-7(2)) National Science Teachers Assn.

Fraser, Frank. Bearista: A Grand Adventure. Fraser, Frank. 2003. (J). pap. 14.95 (978-0-9726394-0-8(3)) Starbucks Coffee Co.

Fraser, Jess. Gleedus the Happy Grasshopper. Wright, Bill, Sr. 2006. (J). cd-rom 9.99 (978-0-9795190-6-2(3)) Color & Learn.

—Henry's New Home. Fraser, Lynne. 2007. (J). cd-rom 9.99 (978-0-9795190-9-3(8)) Color & Learn.

—Jungle Jingles. 2007. (J). cd-rom 9.99 (978-0-9795190-8-6(X)) Color & Learn.

—The Legend of the Cosmic Cowboy. 2007. (J). cd-rom 12.99 (978-0-9795190-7-9(1)) Color & Learn.

Fraser, Kara-Anne. Brave Dave & the Dragons. Reed, Janet. 2009. 12p. (J). (978-0-545-16142-8(8)) Scholastic, Inc.

Fraser, Kay. Finn Reeder, Flu Fighter: How I Survived a Worldwide Pandemic, the School Bully, & the Craziest Game of Dodge Ball Ever. Stevens, Eric. 2009. (Finn Reeder Ser.). (ENG.). 80p. (gr. 2-3). lib. bdg. 25.32 (978-1-4342-2450-7(3)) Capstone Digital.

—Flu Fighter: How I Survived a Worldwide Pandemic, the School Bully, & the Craziest Game of Dodge Ball Ever. Stevens, Eric. 2010. (Finn Reeder Ser.). (ENG.). 80p. (gr. 3-4). 9.99 (978-1-4342-2562-7(3)) Capstone Digital.

Fraser, Kevin. Ants? in My Pants? An Animated Tale. Bahz, Kahanni. 2005. 72p. (J). (gr. k-4). reprint ed. 22.00 (978-0-7567-8705-9(X)) DIANE Publishing Co.

Fraser, Mary Ann. Hey Diddle Diddle. Bunting, Eve. 2011. (ENG.). 32p. (J). (gr. -1-k). 16.95 (978-1-59078-768-7(4)) Boyds Mills Pr.

—Life with Mammoth, 0 vols. Fraser, Ian. (Ogg & Bob Ser.). (ENG.). 64p. (J). (gr. k-3). 2013. pap. 9.99 (978-1-4778-1615-8(1), 9781477816158); 2010. 14.99 (978-0-7614-5722-0(4), 9780761457220) Amazon Publishing. (Amazon Children's Publishing).

—Meet Mammoth, 0 vols. Fraser, Ian. (Ogg & Bob Ser.). (ENG.). (J). (gr. 1-3). 2013. 65p. pap. 9.99 (978-1-4778-1617-2(8), 9781477816172); 2010. 64p. 14.99 (978-0-7614-5721-3(6), 9780761457213) Amazon Publishing. (Amazon Children's Publishing).

Fraser, Mary Ann. No Yeti Yet. 2015. (ENG.). 32p. (J). 16.99 (978-1-4413-0855-9(5), 9781441308559) Peter Pauper Pr. Inc.

Fraser, Mary Ann. I. Q., It's Time. Fraser, Mary Ann. 2005. (ENG.). 32p. (J). (gr. -1-3). 15.95 (978-0-8027-8978-5(1)) Walker & Co.

—I. Q. Goes to the Library. Fraser, Mary Ann. 2003. (I. Q Book Ser.). (ENG.). 32p. (J). (gr. -1-3). 15.95 (978-0-8027-8877-1(7)) Walker & Co.

—Pet Shop Lullaby. Fraser, Mary Ann. 2009. (ENG.). 32p. (J). (gr. -1-1). 16.95 (978-1-59078-618-5(1)) Boyds Mills Pr.

Fraser, Richard M. The Boy Who Saved a Cape Cod Town: And Other Cape Cod Stories. Clark, Admont G. 2006. 56p. (J). (gr. 6-12). per. 12.95 (978-0-9785766-0-8(8)) On Cape Pubns.

Fraser, Sigmund. Smile Bright. Wallace, Jazey. 2012. 24p. pap. 11.50 (978-1-61897-755-7(5), Strategic Bk. Publishing) Strategic Book Publishing & Rights Agency (SBPRA).

Frasier, Debra. A Fabulous Fair Alphabet. Frasier, Debra. 2010. (ENG.). 40p. (J). (gr. k-6). 16.99 (978-1-4169-9817-4(9), Beach Lane Bks.) Beach Lane Bks.

—Miss Alaineus: A Vocabulary Disaster. Frasier, Debra. 2007. (ENG.). 40p. (J). (gr. -1-3). pap. 7.00 (978-0-15-206053-4(7)) Houghton Mifflin Harcourt Publishing Co.

—Spike: Ugliest Dog in the Universe. Frasier, Debra. 2013. (ENG.). 40p. (J). (gr. -1-3). 16.99 (978-1-4424-1452-5(9), Beach Lane Bks.) Beach Lane Bks.

Fravel, Harold. Fellsmere the Pirate, Chipley's Adventure. Fravel, Gale. 2011. 28p. pap. 12.95 (978-1-936343-79-9(7)) Peppertree Pr., The.

Frawley, Keith. Super Schnoz & the Invasion of the Snore Snatchers. Urey, Gary. 2014. (Super Schnoz Ser.: 2). (ENG.). 160p. (J). (gr. 3-6). 14.99 (978-0-8075-7557-4(7)) Whitman, Albert & Co.

Frawley, Keith, jt. illus. see Marlet, Nico.

Frazao, Catia. The Story of Señor Pico. Guatemala, Anne. 2007.Tr. of Historia del Señor Pico. (ENG & SPA.). 32p. (J). pap. 17.00 (978-0-8059-7818-6(6)) Dorrance Publishing Co., Inc.

Frazee, Marla. All the World. Scanlon, Liz Garton. 2009. (ENG.). 40p. (J). (gr. -1-3). 17.99 (978-1-4169-8580-8(8), Beach Lane Bks.) Beach Lane Bks.

Frazee, Marla. All the World. Scanlon, Liz Garton. 2015. (Classic Board Bks.). (ENG.). 44p. (J). (gr. -1-k). bds. 7.99 (978-1-4814-3121-7(8), Little Simon) Little Simon.

Frazee, Marla. All the World. Scanlon, Liz Garton. 2011. (J). (gr. -1-2). 29.95 (978-0-545-32716-9(4)) Weston Woods Studios, Inc.

—Clementine. Pennypacker, Sara. (ENG.). (J). 2008. 160p. (gr. 2-5). pap. 5.99 (978-0-7868-3883-7(3)); 2006. 144p. (gr. 1-3). 14.99 (978-0-7868-3882-0(5)) Hyperion Pr.

—Clementine & the Family Meeting. Pennypacker, Sara. (ENG.). 176p. (J). (gr. 2-5). 2012. pap. 5.99 (978-1-4231-2436-8(7)); 2011. 14.99 (978-1-4231-2356-9(5)) Hyperion Pr.

—Clementine & the Spring Trip. Pennypacker, Sara. 2013. (ENG.). 160p. (J). (gr. 2-5). 14.99 (978-1-4231-2357-6(3)) Hyperion Pr.

—Clementine, Friend of the Week. Pennypacker, Sara. (Clementine Book Ser.). (ENG.). 176p. (J). 2011. (gr. 1-3). pap. 5.99 (978-1-4231-1560-1(0)); 2010. (gr. 2-5). 14.99 (978-1-4231-1355-3(1)) Hyperion Pr.

—Clementine's Letter. Pennypacker, Sara. (Clementine Book Ser.). (ENG.). 160p. (J). (gr. 1-3). 2009. pap. 5.99 (978-0-7868-3885-1(X)); 2008. 16.99 (978-0-7868-3884-4(1)) Hyperion Pr.

—Completely Clementine. Pennypacker, Sara. 2015. (Clementine Book Ser.). (ENG.). 192p. (J). (gr. 1-3). 14.99 (978-1-4231-2358-3(1)) Disney Pr.

—Everywhere Babies. Meyers, Susan. 2011. (ENG.). 30p. (J). (gr. -1 — 1). bds. 11.99 (978-0-547-51074-3(8)) Houghton Mifflin Harcourt Publishing Co.

—Everywhere Babies. Meyers, Susan. 2004. (ENG.). 30p. (J). (gr. k — 1). bds. 6.95 (978-0-15-205315-4(8)) Houghton Mifflin Harcourt Publishing Co.

—God Got a Dog. Rylant, Cynthia. 2013. (ENG.). 48p. (J). (gr. 5-5). 17.99 (978-1-4424-6518-3(2), Beach Lane Bks.) Beach Lane Bks.

—Harriet, You'll Drive Me Wild! Fox, Mem. 2003. (ENG.). 32p. (J). (gr. -1-3). pap. 7.00 (978-0-15-204598-2(8)) Houghton Mifflin Harcourt Publishing Co.

—Mrs. Biddlebox: Her Bad Day & What She Did about It. Smith, Linda. Date not set. 32p. (J). (gr. -1-3). pap. 5.99 (978-0-06-443620-5(9)) HarperCollins Pubs.

—On the Mom of Mayfest. Silverman, Erica. 2011. (ENG.). 32p. (J). (gr. -1-2). pap. 13.99 (978-1-4424-4341-9(3), Simon & Schuster Bks. For Young Readers) Simon & Schuster Bks. For Young Readers.

—The Seven Silly Eaters. Hoberman, Mary Ann. ed. 2004. (J). (gr. k-3). spiral bd. (978-0-616-14576-0(4)) Canadian National Institute for the Blind/Institut National Canadien pour les Aveugles.

Frazee, Marla, et al. Sweet Stories for Baby Gift Set. Meyers, Susan & Fox, Mem. 2015. (ENG.). 128p. (J). (— 1). 16.99 (978-0-544-53121-5(3), HMH Books For Young Readers) Houghton Mifflin Harcourt Publishing Co.

Frazee, Marla. The Talented Clementine. Pennypacker, Sara. (Clementine Book Ser.). (ENG.). (J). 2008. 160p. (gr. 1-3). pap. 5.99 (978-0-7868-3871-4(X)); 2007. 144p. (gr. 2-5). 14.99 (978-0-7868-3870-7(1)) Hyperion Pr.

Frazee, Marla. Boot & Shoe. Frazee, Marla. 2012. (ENG.). 40p. (J). (gr. -1-3). 16.99 (978-1-4424-2247-6(5), Beach Lane Bks.) Beach Lane Bks.

—The Boss Baby. Frazee, Marla. 2010. (ENG.). 40p. (J). (gr. -1-3). 17.99 (978-1-4424-0167-9(2), Beach Lane Bks.) Beach Lane Bks.

—The Boss Baby. Frazee, Marla. 2013. (Classic Board Bks.). (ENG.). 36p. (J). (gr. -1 — 1). bds. 7.99 (978-1-4424-8779-6(8), Little Simon) Little Simon.

—Roller Coaster. Frazee, Marla. 2003. (ENG.). 32p. (J). (gr. -1-3). 16.99 (978-0-15-204554-8(6)) Houghton Mifflin Harcourt Publishing Co.

—Walk On! A Guide for Babies of All Ages. Frazee, Marla. 2006. (ENG.). 40p. (J). (gr. -1-k). 16.00 (978-0-15-205573-8(8)) Houghton Mifflin Harcourt Publishing Co.

Frazee, Marla & Pedersen, Janet. Bully Buster. Clements, Andrew. 2008. (Jake Drake Ser.: Bk. 1). 67p. (gr. 2-5). 15.00 (978-0-7569-9001-5(7)) Perfection Learning Corp.

—Jake Drake, Know-It-All. Clements, Andrew. 2007. (Jake Drake Ser.: Bk. 2). 88p. (gr. 2-5). 15.00 (978-0-7569-8212-6(X)) Perfection Learning Corp.

Frazee, Marla, jt. illus. see Pedersen, Janet.

Frazier, Craig. The Tiny Brown Seed. Frazier, Daniele. 2003. 24p. (J). (gr. -1-1). 14.95 (978-1-932026-11-5(8)) Graphis, U.S., Inc.

—Trucks Roll! Lyon, George Ella. 2007. (ENG.). 40p. (J). (gr. -1-2). 17.99 (978-1-4169-2435-7(3), Atheneum/Richard Jackson Bks.) Simon & Schuster Children's Publishing.

Frazier, Craig. Tyler Makes a Birthday Cake! Florence, Tyler. 2014. (J). lib. bdg. (978-0-06-204761-8(2)) Harper & Row Ltd.

Frazier, Craig. Tyler Makes a Birthday Cake! Florence, Tyler. 2014. (ENG.). 40p. (J). (gr. -1-3). 17.99 (978-0-06-204760-1(4)) HarperCollins Pubs.

—Tyler Makes Spaghetti! Florence, Tyler. 2013. (ENG.). 40p. (J). (gr. -1-3). 17.99 (978-0-06-204756-4(6)) HarperCollins Pubs.

Frazier, Craig, jt. illus. see Florence, Tyler.

Frazier, James J. Pennsylvania Fireside Tales Volume V Vol. V: Origins & Foundations of Pennsylvania Mountains Folktales, Legends, & Folklore. Frazier, Jeffrey R. 2003. (ENG.). 250p. 15.00 (978-0-9652351-6-7(5)) Egg Hill Pubns.

Fred. The Suspended Castle: a Philemon Adventure: A TOON Graphic. Kutner, Richard, tr. from FRE. 2015. (Philemon Adventures Ser.). (ENG.). 56p. (J). (gr. 2). 16.95 (978-1-935179-86-3(1)) TOON Books / RAW Junior, LLC.

Fred. The Wild Piano. Kutner, Richard, tr. from FRE. 2015. (Philemon Adventures Ser.). (ENG.). 48p. (J). (gr. 2-7). pap. 16.95 (978-1-935179-83-2(7)) TOON Books / RAW Junior, LLC.

Fred. Cast Away on the Letter A. Fred. 2013. (Philemon Adventures Ser.). (ENG.). 48p. (J). (gr. 2-7). 16.95 (978-1-935179-63-4(2)) TOON Books / RAW Junior, LLC.

Frederick-Frost, Alexis. Explore Spring! 25 Great Ways to Learn about Spring. Anderson, Maxine & Berkenkamp, Lauri. 2007. (Explore Your World Ser.). (ENG.). 96p. (J). (gr. k-4). per. 12.95 (978-0-9785037-4-1(0)) Nomad Pr.

—Explore Winter! 25 Great Ways to Learn about Winter. Anderson, Maxine. 2007. (Explore Your World Ser.). (ENG.). 96p. (J). (gr. k-4). pap. 12.95 (978-0-9785037-5-8(9)) Nomad Pr.

Frederick, Sarah. School is Not for Me, Jeremy James Conor McGee. Mahony, Mary. 2009. (J). pap. 7.95 (978-0-9658879-4-6(4)) Redding Pr.

Fredericks, Karen & Rix, Fred. How to Build Your Own Country. Wyatt, Valerie. 2009. (CitizenKid Ser.). (ENG.). 40p. (J). (gr. 3-7). 17.95 (978-1-55453-310-7(4)) Kids Can Pr., Ltd. CAN. Dist: Univ. of Toronto Pr.

Fredericks, Rob. The Adventures of Tyler the Dinosaur, 1 vol. Fredericks, Eleanor. 2009. 31p. pap. 24.95 (978-1-61546-233-9(3)) America Star Bks.

Fredrich, Volker. Rechtschreibtraining fuer die 1. Klasse. (Duden-Lernminuten Ser.). (GER.). 32p. (J). wbk. ed. (978-3-411-70831-4(X)) Bibliographisches Institut & F. A. Brockhaus AG DEU. Dist: International Bk. Import Service, Inc.

—Rechtschreibtraining fuer die 1. und 2. Klasse. (Duden-Lernminuten Ser.). (GER.). 32p. (J). wbk. ed. (978-3-411-70841-3(7)) Bibliographisches Institut & F. A. Brockhaus AG DEU. Dist: International Bk. Import Service, Inc.

Freeberg, Eric. Animal Stories. 2010. (Classic Starts(tm) Ser.). (ENG.). 160p. (J). (gr. 2-4). 6.95 (978-1-4027-6646-6(7)) Sterling Publishing Co., Inc.

—Ballet Stories. 2010. (Classic Starts(tm) Ser.). (ENG.). 160p. (J). (gr. 2-4). 6.95 (978-1-4027-6663-3(7)) Sterling Publishing Co., Inc.

—Classic Starts - The Iliad. Homer. 2014. (Classic Starts(tm) Ser.). (ENG.). 160p. (J). (gr. 2-4). 6.95 (978-1-4549-0612-4(X)) Sterling Publishing Co., Inc.

—Great Expectations. Dickens, Charles. 2010. (Classic Starts(tm) Ser.). (ENG.). 160p. (J). (gr. 2-4). 6.95 (978-1-4027-6645-9(9)) Sterling Publishing Co., Inc.

—Greek Myths. 2011. (Classic Starts(tm) Ser.). (ENG.). 160p. (J). (gr. 2-4). 6.95 (978-1-4027-7312-9(9)) Sterling Publishing Co., Inc.

—Grimm's Fairy Tales. Grimm, Jakob & Grimm, Wilhelm K. 2011. (Classic Starts(tm) Ser.). (ENG.). 160p. (J). (gr. 2-4). 6.95 (978-1-4027-7311-2(0)) Sterling Publishing Co., Inc.

—Journey to the Center of the Earth. Verne, Jules. 2011. (Classic Starts(tm) Ser.). (ENG.). 160p. (J). (gr. 2-4). 6.95 (978-1-4027-7313-6(7)) Sterling Publishing Co., Inc.

—Moby-Dick. Melville, Herman. 2010. (Classic Starts(tm) Ser.). (ENG.). 160p. (J). (gr. 2-4). 6.95 (978-1-4027-6644-2(0)) Sterling Publishing Co., Inc.

—The Odyssey. Homer. 2011. (Classic Starts(tm) Ser.). (ENG.). 160p. (J). (gr. 2-4). 6.95 (978-1-4027-7334-1(X)) Sterling Publishing Co., Inc.

—Roman Myths. Namm, Diane. 2014. (Classic Starts(tm) Ser.). (ENG.). 160p. (J). (gr. 2-4). 6.95 *(978-1-4549-0611-7(1))* Sterling Publishing Co., Inc.

Freeborn, Andrew J. Colorways: For Days. abr. ed. 2005. 32p. pap. *(978-0-9769575-0-8(7))* N8TIVE.

Freed, Margaret. The View from under the Pew. Winters-Johnson, Diane. 2008. 30p. (gr. -1-3). pap. 14.99 *(978-0-687-64478-0(X))* Abingdon Pr.

Freedman, Deborah. By Mouse & Frog. Freedman, Deborah. 2015. (ENG.). 32p. (J). (gr. -1-k). 16.99 *(978-0-670-78490-5(7),* Viking Juvenile) Penguin Publishing Group.

Freel, Mirle. Zigzag the Rocking Roadrunner. O'Toole-Freel, Judy. 2012. 40p. 24.95 *(978-1-4626-9970-4(7))* America Star Bks.

Freeland, Devon & Contreras-Freeland, Gina. A Boy & His Wizard. Smith, M. a. & Smith, M. A. 2009. 32p. pap. 8.95 *(978-1-60076-152-2(6))* StoneGarden.net Publishing.

Freeman, Angela. Just Inn Time. Angelo, Tony. 2011. 24p. pap. 24.95 *(978-1-4560-6828-8(8))* America Star Bks.

Freeman, Don. The Day Is Waiting, 1 vol. Zuckerman, Linda. 2015. (ENG.). 32p. (J). 9.99 *(978-0-310-74054-4(1))* Zonderkidz.

Freeman, Don. Corduroy. Freeman, Don. 40th anniv. ed. 2008. (Corduroy Ser.). (ENG.). 40p. (J). (gr. -1-k). 19.99 *(978-0-670-06336-9(3),* Viking Juvenile) Penguin Publishing Group.

—Earl the Squirrel. Freeman, Don. 2008. (J). (gr. -1-2). pap. 16.95 incl. audio *(978-1-4301-0411-7(2))* Live Oak Media.

—Earl the Squirrel. Freeman, Don. 2007. (ENG.). 48p. (J). (gr. -1-2). pap. 6.99 *(978-0-14-240893-3(X),* Puffin) Penguin Publishing Group.

—Fly High, Fly Low. Freeman, Don. (ENG.). 64p. (J). (gr. -1-k). 2004. reprint ed. 16.99 *(978-0-670-03685-1(4),* Viking Juvenile); 50th anniv. ed. 2007. 7.99 *(978-0-14-240817-9(4),* Puffin) Penguin Publishing Group.

—Fly High, Fly Low. Freeman, Don. 2007. 56p. (gr. -1-3). 18.00 *(978-0-7569-8001-6(1))* Perfection Learning Corp.

—Gregory's Shadow. Freeman, Don. 2003. pap. 39.95 incl. audio compact disk *(978-1-59112-536-5(7))*; (J). 25.95 incl. audio *(978-1-59112-238-8(4))*; (J). pap. 37.95 incl. audio *(978-1-59112-239-5(2))* Live Oak Media.

Freeman, Don & McCue, Lisa. Corduroy Series Boxed Set: Corduroy; A Pocket for Corduroy; Corduroy's Busy Street; Corduroy Goes to the Doctor; Corduroy's Day; Corduroy's Party, Set. Freeman, Don & McCue, Lisa. (Corduroy Ser.). (J). (gr. k-1). pap. 30.95 incl. audio *(978-0-87499-471-1(3))* Live Oak Media.

Freeman, Julie. In the Garden with the LittleWeeds: A Counting Book for Little Ones. Weisenfluh, C. C. 2004. 26p. (J). 11.95 *(978-0-9746782-0-7(1))* B'Squeak Productions.

Freeman, Kathryn S. Loon Chase, 1 vol. Diehl, Jean Heilprin. 2006. (ENG.). 32p. (J). (gr. 1-5). 15.95 *(978-0-9764943-8-6(8))* Arbordale Publishing.

Freeman, Laura. Be Love, Baby Love. Hooks, Bell. 2007. (ENG.). (J). (gr. -1-17). 15.99 *(978-0-7868-0943-1(4),* Jump at the Sun) Hyperion Bks. for Children.

—Birthday Blues. English, Karen. 2010. (ENG.). 96p. (J). (gr. 1-4). pap. 5.99 *(978-0-547-24893-6(8))* Houghton Mifflin Harcourt Publishing Co.

—The Boy at the Dike: A Dutch Folktale. York, J. 2012. (Folktales from Around the World Ser.). (ENG.). 24p. (J). (gr. k-3). 28.50 *(978-1-61473-219-8(1),* 204914) Child's World, Inc., The.

—Dog Days. English, Karen. 2014. (Carver Chronicles Ser.). (ENG.). 128p. (J). (gr. 1-4). pap. 5.99 *(978-0-544-33912-5(6),* HMH Books For Young Readers) Houghton Mifflin Harcourt Publishing Co.

—The Little Red Hen. York, J. 2012. (Favorite Children's Stories Ser.). (ENG.). 24p. (J). (gr. k-3). 27.07 *(978-1-61473-214-3(0),* 204908) Child's World, Inc., The.

—The Newsy News Newsletter. English, Karen. 2011. (ENG.). 96p. (J). (gr. 1-4). pap. 5.99 *(978-0-547-40626-8(6))* Houghton Mifflin Harcourt Publishing Co.

—Nikki & Deja. English, Karen. 2009. (ENG.). 80p. (J). (gr. -1-3). pap. 5.99 *(978-0-547-13362-1(6))* Houghton Mifflin Harcourt Publishing Co.

—Nikki & Deja: Substitute Trouble. English, Karen. 2014. (ENG.). 112p. (J). (gr. 1-4). pap. 4.99 *(978-0-544-22388-2(8),* HMH Books For Young Readers) Houghton Mifflin Harcourt Publishing Co.

—Skateboard Party: The Carver Chronicles, Book Two. English, Karen. 2014. (Carver Chronicles Ser.). (ENG.). 128p. (J). (gr. 1-4). 14.99 *(978-0-544-28306-0(6))* Houghton Mifflin Harcourt Publishing Co.

—Wedding Drama. English, Karen. 2013. (ENG.). 112p. (J). (gr. 1-4). pap. 5.99 *(978-0-544-00324-8(1))* Houghton Mifflin Harcourt Publishing Co.

Freeman, Laura. Here We Go Looby Loo. Freeman, Laura. 2011. (Favorite Children's Songs Ser.). (ENG.). 16p. (J). (gr. -1-2). lib. bdg. 25.64 *(978-1-60954-291-7(6),* 200095) Child's World, Inc., The.

Freeman, Melita. The Knight of Lord Greengate's Castle. Freeman, Melita. 2012. 28p. pap. 10.00 *(978-1-936750-90-0(2))* Yorkshire Publishing Group.

Freeman, Mike, photos by. Rocks & Minerals Spotter's Guide: With Internet Links. Woolley, Alan. rev. ed. 2007. (Spotter's Guides). 64p. (J). pap. 5.99 *(978-0-7945-1304-7(2),* Usborne) EDC Publishing.

Freeman, Mike & Julings, Emma, photos by. Usborne Rocks & Minerals Sticker Book. Miles, Lisa. Khan, Sarah & Armstrong, Carrie, eds. rev. ed. 2006. (Spotter's Guides Sticker Books - New Format Ser.). 16p. (J). (gr. 2-5). pap. 8.99 *(978-0-7945-1413-6(8),* Usborne) EDC Publishing.

Freeman, Mylo. Every Girl Is a Princess. Freeman, Mylo. 2011. (ENG.). 30p. (J). (gr. -1-k). 14.95 *(978-1-60537-087-3(8))* Clavis Publishing.

Freeman, Patricia. Where Is God? Stevens, Sherri. 2005. 24p. (YA). 15.95 *(978-0-9769541-0-1(9),* 2005-1) Enlightened Bks.

Freeman, T. R. The Lark in the Morn. Vipont, Elfrida. 2007. 196p. (YA). pap. 12.95 *(978-1-932350-22-7(5))* Bethlehem Bks.

—The Lark on the Wing. Vipont, Elfrida. 2008. 233p. (J). pap. 12.95 *(978-1-932350-11-1(X))* Bethlehem Bks.

Freeman, Tina. Ten Little Monkeys. 2004. (Classic Books with Holes Giant Board Book Ser.). (ENG.). 16p. (J). bds. *(978-0-85953-450-5(2))* Child's Play International Ltd.

—Ten Little Monkeys: Jumping on the Bed. Twinn, A. 2007. (Classic Books with Holes 8x8 with CD Ser.). (ENG.). 16p. (J). (gr. -1-1). *(978-1-904550-67-9(3))* Child's Play International Ltd.

Freeman, Tina. Ten Little Monkeys Jumping on the Bed. Freeman, Tina, tr. 2003. (Classic Books with Holes 8x8 Ser.). (ENG.). 16p. (J). pap. *(978-0-85953-137-5(6))* Child's Play International Ltd.

Freeman, Tor. Olive & the Bad Mood. Freeman, Tor. 2013. (ENG.). 32p. (J). (gr. -1-3). 15.99 *(978-0-7636-6657-6(2),* Templar) Candlewick Pr.

—Olive & the Big Secret. Freeman, Tor. 2012. (ENG.). 32p. (J). (gr. -1-3). 15.99 *(978-0-7636-6149-6(X))* Candlewick Pr.

—Olive & the Embarrassing Gift. Freeman, Tor. 2014. (ENG.). 32p. (J). (gr. -1-3). 15.99 *(978-0-7636-7406-9(0),* Templar) Candlewick Pr.

Freeman, Troy. All Dried Out. Brodland, Rita, ed. l.t. ed. 2006. (WeWrite Kids! Ser.: 50). 68p. (J). pap. 11.95 *(978-1-57635-063-8(0))* WeWrite LLC.

Freeswick, Jill. Making Mouth Sounds All Day Long. Clayton, Darcy M. 2013. 36p. pap. 9.95 *(978-1-889131-90-0(3),* Castlebridge Bks.) Big Tent Bks.

Freisager, Katrin, photos by. The Seventh Generation: Images of the Lakota Today. Seals, David. 2005. 144p. (gr. 1-18). 45.00 *(978-1-57687-031-0(6),* powerHouse Bks.) powerHouse Cultural Entertainment, Inc.

Freitag, Charles. The Christmas Tractor. Aumann, Jane & Ladage, Cindy. 2003. 30p. (J). (gr. k-4). pap. 8.95 *(978-0-9703319-2-2(4))* Roots & Wings.

French, David. Dear God, Will You Give Me A Dog?, 1 vol. Pierro, Rita. 2009. 35p. pap. 19.95 *(978-1-61582-589-9(4))* PublishAmerica, Inc.

—The Duck Who Couldn't Swim, 1 vol. Pierro, Rita. 2010. 26p. 24.95 *(978-1-4489-6405-5(9))* PublishAmerica, Inc.

—A Horse in the House, 1 vol. Pierro, Rita. 2009. 29p. pap. 24.95 *(978-1-60836-410-7(0))* America Star Bks.

French, Fiona. Pepi & the Secret Names: Help Pepi Crack the Hieroglyphic Code. Walsh, Jill Paton. 2009. (ENG.). 32p. (J). (gr. k-3). pap. 9.99 *(978-1-84507-873-7(X),* Frances Lincoln) Quarto Publishing Group UK GBR. Dist: Hachette Bk. Group.

French, Martin. Sophisticated Ladies: The Great Women of Jazz. Gourse, Leslie. 2007. (ENG.). 64p. (J). (gr. 4-7). 19.99 *(978-0-525-47198-1(7),* Dutton Juvenile) Penguin Publishing Group.

—Stompin' at the Savoy: The Story of Norma Miller. 2006. (ENG.). 64p. (J). (gr. 4-7). 15.99 *(978-0-7636-2244-2(3))* Candlewick Pr.

French, Phyllis. The Chocolate Chip Ghost. Peifer, Meighan. 2004. (J). 14.95 *(978-1-58597-245-6(2))* Leathers Publishing.

French, Renee, et al. The Adventure Time Encyclopaedia: Inhabitants, Lore, Spells, & Ancient Crypt Warnings of the Land of Ooo Circa 19. 56 B. G. E. - 501 A. G. E. Olson, Martin. 2013. (ENG.). 160p. 19.95 *(978-1-4197-0564-9(4),* Abrams Image) Abrams.

French, Renee. The Soap Lady. French, Renee. 2005. 111p. (J). (gr. 4-8). reprint ed. 20.00 *(978-0-7567-9419-4(6))* DIANE Publishing Co.

Frenette, Cynthia. Get Hooked Again: Simple Steps to Crochet More Cool Stuff. Fama, Angela & Bethel, Pamela, photos by. Werker, Kim Piper & Werker, Kim. 2007. (ENG.). 96p. (YA). (gr. 7-11). pap. 11.95 *(978-0-8230-5110-6(2))* Watson-Guptill Pubns., Inc.

Frenkel, Yetti. Andre the Famous Harbor Seal. Hodgkins, Fran. 2003. (ENG.). 32p. (J). (gr. k-17). 16.95 *(978-0-89272-594-6(X))* Down East Bks.

Frenkel, Yetti. The Big, Blue Lump. Frenkel, Yetti. 2004. 32p. (J). 16.95 *(978-0-9749006-0-5(5))* Snow Tree Bks.

—Libby & the Cat. Frenkel, Yetti. 2005. 32p. (J). 16.95 *(978-0-9749006-2-9(1))* Snow Tree Bks.

—Trudy & the Captain's Cat. Frenkel, Yetti. 2005. 32p. (J). 16.95 *(978-0-9749006-1-2(3))* Snow Tree Bks.

Frenz, Ron, et al. The Donner Party, 1 vol. Welvaert, Scott R. & Welvaert, Scott R. 2006. (Disasters in History Ser.). (ENG.). 32p. (gr. 3-4). 29.99 *(978-0-7368-5479-5(7),* Graphic Library) Capstone Pr., Inc.

—Fantastic Four: The World's Greatest Comics Magazine. 2011. (ENG.). 280p. (J). (gr. 4-17). 34.99 *(978-0-7851-5607-9(0))* Marvel Worldwide, Inc.

Frenz, Ron. Spider-Man - Lizard: No Turning Back. Slott, Dan & Busiek, Kurt. 2013. (ENG.). 112p. (J). (gr. 4-17). pap. 16.99 *(978-0-7851-6008-3(6),* Marvel Pr.) Disney Publishing Worldwide.

—Thor: Black Galaxy Saga. Defalco, Tom. 2011. (ENG.). 168p. (J). (gr. 4-17). pap. 19.99 *(978-0-7851-5095-4(1))* Marvel Worldwide, Inc.

Frenz, Ron, et al. Thor Epic Collection: War of the Pantheons. Defalco, Tom et al. 2013. (ENG.). 472p. (J). (gr. 4-17). pap. 34.99 *(978-0-7851-8788-2(X))* Marvel Worldwide, Inc.

Frenz, Ron & Nauck, Todd. Thunderstrike: Youth in Revolt. 2011. (ENG.). 136p. (J). (gr. 4-17). pap., pap. 14.99 *(978-0-7851-5271-2(7))* Marvel Worldwide, Inc.

Frenz, Ron, jt. illus. see Buscema, Sal.

Freschet, Gina. Beto & the Bone Dance. Freschet, Gina. 2005. 30p. (J). (gr. 4-8). reprint ed. 16.00 *(978-0-7567-8933-6(8))* DIANE Publishing Co.

Freshman, Floris R., jt. illus. see James, Larry W.

Fretczak-Rodak, Monika. Farm. Miedzybrodzka, Wiktoria. 2014. (Mommy & Me Bath Bks.). (ENG.). 6p. (J). (gr. -1 — 1). 4.99 *(978-1-4380-7484-9(0))* Barron's Educational Series, Inc.

—Jungle. Miedzybrodzka, Wiktoria. 2014. (Mommy & Me Bath Bks.). (ENG.). 6p. (J). (gr. -1 — 1). 4.99 *(978-1-4380-7485-6(9))* Barron's Educational Series, Inc.

Frey, Ben. My Friend Jamal. McQuinn, Anna, photos by. McQuinn, Anna. 2008. (My Friend Ser.). (ENG.). 32p. (J). (gr. -1-2). 17.95 *(978-1-55451-123-5(2),* 9781554511235); pap. 8.95 *(978-1-55451-122-8(4),* 9781554511228) Annick Pr., Ltd. CAN. Dist: Firefly Bks., Ltd.

—My Friend Mei Jing. Cheung, Irvin, photos by. McQuinn, Anna. 2009. (My Friend Ser.: 2). (ENG.). 32p. (J). (gr. -1-1). 17.95 *(978-1-55451-153-2(4),* 9781554511532); pap. 8.95 *(978-1-55451-152-5(6),* 9781554511525) Annick Pr., Ltd. CAN. Dist: Firefly Bks., Ltd.

—Runaway Alphabet. Winters, Kari-Lynn. 2010. (ENG.). 32p. (J). (gr. -1-3). 17.95 *(978-1-897476-24-6(8))* Simply Read Bks. CAN. Dist: Ingram Pub. Services.

Frey, Daniel. Jacy Meets Betsy: Jacy's Search for Jesus Book 2. Edwards, Carol. 2006. 32p. (J). 15.95 *(978-0-9755314-1-9(7))* Majestic Publishing, LLC.

Frey, Daniel J. Jacy Faces Evil: Jacy's Search for Jesus Book III. Edwards, Carol. 2008. 32p. (J). 15.95 *(978-0-9755314-3-3(3))* Majestic Publishing, LLC.

—Jacy's Coloring & Activity Book. 2006. 32p. (J). 3.00 *(978-0-9755314-2-6(5))* Majestic Publishing, LLC.

—Jacy's Search for Jesus. Edwards, Carol. 2005. 31p. (J). (gr. -1-3). 15.95 *(978-0-9755314-0-2(9))* Majestic Publishing, LLC.

Freysinger, Karen. Adventures of Countess Pigula Her Royal Imagination. Freysinger, Karen. 2006. (J). 15.95 *(978-0-9786729-0-4(9))* Aha! Elora Danan Productions.

freysinger, karen. Adventures of Countess Pigula up, up & Away. freysinger, karen. 2009. 32p. (J). 16.99 *(978-0-9786729-1-1(7))* Aha! Elora Danan Productions.

Freytag, Lorna. My Humongous Hamster. Freytag, Lorna. 2014. (My Humongous Hamster Ser.). (ENG.). 32p. (J). (gr. -1-3). 15.99 *(978-0-8050-9918-8(2),* Holt, Henry & Co. Bks. For Young Readers) Holt, Henry & Co.

—My Humongous Hamster Goes to School. Freytag, Lorna. 2015. (My Humongous Hamster Ser.). (ENG.). 32p. (J). (gr. -1-3). 16.99 *(978-1-62779-140-3(X),* Holt, Henry & Co. Bks. For Young Readers) Holt, Henry & Co.

Friar, Joanne. Freedom Quilt. Helmso, Candy Grant. 2003. (Books for Young Learners). (ENG.). 16p. (J). 5.75 net. *(978-1-57274-529-2(0),* 2744, Bks. for Young Learners) Owen, Richard C. Pubs., Inc.

—My Favorite Place. Heller, Maryellen. 2005. (ENG.). 16p. (J). 5.75 *(978-1-57274-535-3(5),* 2771, Bks. for Young Learners) Owen, Richard C. Pubs., Inc.

—My Mom's Apron. O'Brien, Claudia Moore. 2005. (ENG.). 12p. (J). 5.75 *(978-1-57274-753-1(6),* 2772, Bks. for Young Learners) Owen, Richard C. Pubs., Inc.

—Nathan of Yesteryear & Michael of Today. Heinz, Brian J. 2006. (Exceptional Social Studies Titles for Intermediate Grades). (ENG.). 32p. (J). (gr. 3-6). lib. bdg. 22.60 *(978-0-7613-2893-3(9),* Millbrook Pr.) Lerner Publishing Group.

—O Christmas Tree: Its History & Holiday Traditions. Farmer, Jacqueline. 2010. (ENG.). 32p. (J). (gr. k-3). pap. 7.95 *(978-1-58089-239-1(6))* Charlesbridge Publishing, Inc.

Friar, Joanne H. A Place for Elijah. Easton, Kelly. 2015. (J). **(978-1-4677-7841-1(9),** Kar-Ben Publishing) Lerner Publishing Group.

Fricker, Steve. Como Funcionan los Animales. Ganeri, Anita. (Coleccion Como Funcionan). (SPA.). 30p. (J). (gr. 1-3). 18.95 *(978-84-272-4092-6(9),* ML30534) Molino, Editorial ESP. Dist: Lectorum Pubns., Inc.

Fricker, Steve & Holder, John. Como Funcionan los Huesos y Otras Partes del Cuerpo. Ganeri, Anita. (Coleccion Como Funcionan). (SPA.). 30p. (J). (gr. 1-3). *(978-84-272-4091-9(0),* ML30533) Molino, Editorial ESP. Dist: Lectorum Pubns., Inc.

Friday, Arthur. Peter Pan: An Illustrated Classic for Kids & Young Readers (Excellent for Bedtime & Young Readers) Barrie, J. M. eMusic, Tom, ed. 2013. 38p. pap. 6.99 *(978-1-62321-067-0(4))* Tommye-music Corp. DBA Tom eMusic.

Fridell, Pat. Thar She Blows! Whaling in The 1860s. Kassirer, Sue. 2007. 32p. (J). 15.00 *(978-1-4223-6721-6(5))* DIANE Publishing Co.

Fried, Janice. Where Is Grandpa Dennis? Abraham, Michelle Shapiro. 2009. (J). *(978-0-8074-1083-7(7))* URJ Pr.

Friedericy Dolls. Into the Woods: Favorite Fairy Tales from the World of Friedericy Dolls. Greer, Rob, photos by. 2009. 74p. (J). *(978-0-9824812-0-2(9))* POCEE Publishing.

Friedl, Peter. Social Behaviour. Holland, Stephanie. ed. 44p. *(978-0-86388-422-1(9),* 001-5126) Speechmark Publishing Ltd.

Friedlander, Randolyn. The Mystery at Area 51. Marsh, Carole. 2011. (Carole Marsh Mysteries Ser.). 32p. pap. 7.99 *(978-0-635-07961-9(5),* Marsh, Carole Mysteries) Gallopade International.

—The Mystery at Cape Cod. Marsh, Carole. 2010. (Real Kids, Real Places Teacher Guides). 32p. (J). pap. 7.99 *(978-0-635-07600-7(4))* Gallopade International.

—The Mystery at Fort Sumter. Marsh, Carole. 2010. (Real Kids, Real Places Ser.). 32p. (J). pap. 7.99 *(978-0-635-07432-4(X),* Marsh, Carole Mysteries) Gallopade International.

—The Mystery at Motown. Marsh, Carole. 2011. (Carole Marsh Mysteries Ser.). 32p. pap. 7.99 *(978-0-635-07962-6(3),* Marsh, Carole Mysteries) Gallopade International.

—The Mystery at Mount Vernon. Marsh, Carole. 2010. (Real Kids, Real Places Ser.). 32p. pap. 7.99 *(978-0-635-07444-7(3),* Marsh, Carole Mysteries) Gallopade International.

—The Mystery in Hawaii. Marsh, Carole. 2010. (Real Kids, Real Places Ser.). 32p. pap. 7.99 *(978-0-635-07447-8(8),* Marsh, Carole Mysteries) Gallopade International.

—The Mystery on the Oregon Trail. Marsh, Carole. 2010. (Real Kids, Real Places Ser.). 32p. pap. 7.99 *(978-0-635-07441-6(9),* Marsh, Carole Mysteries) Gallopade International.

Friedman, Carol. Nicky the Jazz Cat. Friedman, Carol. 2005. (ENG.). 32p. (J). (-k). 16.95 *(978-1-57687-248-2(3),* PowerHouse Kids) powerHouse Cultural Entertainment, Inc.

Friedman, Jeffrey. Will Allen & the Great Monster Detective: Chronicles of the Monster Detective Agency Volume 1. Edwards, Jason. l.t. ed. 2007. (ENG.). 82p. (J). per. 5.95 *(978-0-9789512-0-7(4))* Rogue Bear Pr.

Friedman, Judith. Aidan of Oren: The Journey Begins. St. Jean, Alan. 2004. (ENG.). 208p. (J). (gr. 4-7). 19.95 *(978-0-9724853-5-7(X))* Keene Publishing.

—One Incredible Dog! Boone. Williams, Christopher. 2005. (One Incredible Dog! Ser.). (ENG.). 32p. (J). (gr. -1-3). lib. bdg. 15.95 *(978-0-9724853-9-5(2))* Keene Publishing.

—One Incredible Dog! Kizzy. Williams, Christopher. 2006. (One Incredible Dog! Ser.). (ENG.). 32p. (J). (gr. -1-3). lib. bdg. 15.95 *(978-0-9766805-5-0(6))* Keene Publishing.

—One Incredible Dog! Lady. Williams, Christopher. 2004. (ENG.). 32p. (J). (gr. -1-3). 15.95 *(978-0-9724853-3-3(3),* 845-987-7750) Keene Publishing.

Friedman, Laura. Henry the Steinway a Star Is Born. Coveleskie, Sally & Peter, Goodrich. 2003. (Henry the Steinway Ser.: Vol. 2). 32p. (J). (gr. k-3). *(978-0-9729427-1-3(8))* Yorkville Pr.

—Henry the Steinway & the Piano Recital. Coveleskie, Sally et al. 2003. (Henry the Steinway Ser.: Vol. 1). 32p. (J). (gr. k-3). *(978-1-931721-05-9(X))* Bright Sky Pr.

—Henry the Steinway Tours the World. Coveleskie, Sally & Goodrich, Peter. 2005. (Henry the Steinway Ser.: 3). 32p. (J). (gr. -1-3). 15.95 *(978-0-9729427-8-2(5))* Yorkville Pr.

Friedman, Michael (Myk). Echoes of the Lost Boys of Sudan, 4 vols., Vol. 1. Clark, Susan, ed. 2nd l.t. ed. 2004. 36p. (YA). 4.95 *(978-0-9759995-0-9(8))* Echoes Joint Venture.

Friend, Alison. Bramble & Maggie: Give & Take. Haas, Jessie. 2013. (ENG.). 56p. (J). (gr. k-3). 14.99 *(978-0-7636-5021-6(8))* Candlewick Pr.

—Bramble & Maggie: Horse Meets Girl. Haas, Jessie. 2013. (Candlewick Sparks Ser.). (ENG.). 56p. (J). (gr. k-3). pap. 3.99 *(978-0-7636-6251-6(8))* Candlewick Pr.

—Bramble & Maggie Give & Take. Haas, Jessie. 2015. (Candlewick Sparks Ser.). (ENG.). 56p. (J). (gr. k-4). pap. 3.99 *(978-0-7636-7787-9(6))* Candlewick Pr.

—Horse Meets Girl. Haas, Jessie. 2012. (ENG.). 56p. (J). (gr. k-3). 14.99 *(978-0-7636-4955-5(4))* Candlewick Pr.

—Scrawny Cat. Root, Phyllis. 2011. (ENG.). 40p. (J). (gr. -1-3). 16.99 *(978-0-7636-4164-1(2))* Candlewick Pr.

—Spooky Season. Haas, Jessie. 2014. (ENG.). 56p. (J). (gr. k-3). 14.99 *(978-0-7636-6450-3(2))* Candlewick Pr.

—What Color Is Caesar? Kumin, Maxine. 2010. (ENG.). 56p. (J). (gr. -1-k). 16.99 *(978-0-7636-3432-2(8))* Candlewick Pr.

Friend, Alison. Freddy & Frito & the Clubhouse Rules. Friend, Alison. 2015. (ENG.). 40p. (J). (gr. -1-3). 17.99 *(978-0-06-228580-5(7))* HarperCollins Pubs.

Friend, Bonnie. The Little Carrot, 1 vol. Waxman, Melanie Brown. 2009. 39p. pap. 24.95 *(978-1-61546-046-5(2))* America Star Bks.

Friend, David Michael. The Scrivener Bees. Petty, J. T. 2014. (ENG.). 176p. (J). (gr. 3-7). 9.99 *(978-1-4814-4491-0(3),* Simon & Schuster Bks. For Young Readers) Simon & Schuster Bks. For Young Readers.

Friend, David Michael. Blueberry Mouse. Friend, David Michael, tr. Low, Alice. 2004. (J). 15.95 *(978-1-59336-111-2(4))*; pap. *(978-1-59336-112-9(2))* Mondo Publishing.

Friese, Diane Lynn. Martoose, the Pampered Mouse: A Story of Love & Friendship. Friese, Diane Lynn. Rivers, Mary Anne & Dressig, Don. 2010. (ENG.). 26p. pap. 11.95 *(978-1-4528-6704-5(6))* CreateSpace Independent Publishing Platform.

Friesen, Anni. A Big Change, 1 vol. Unrau, Adela. 2010. 16p. pap. 24.95 *(978-1-4489-7672-0(3))* PublishAmerica, Inc.

—That Was a Nice Surprise, 1 vol. Unrau, Adela. 2010. 16p. 24.95 *(978-1-4489-5744-6(3))* PublishAmerica, Inc.

Friesen, Ray. Giant Mike & the Four Fairies. Osborn, Linda. 2013. 24p. (J). mass mkt. 12.95 *(978-0-9887329-5-7(5))* Don't Eat Any Bugs Prodns.

Friesen, Wayne. Dino Treasure Hunt, 1 vol. Henry, LaTosha. 2010. 16p. 24.95 *(978-1-4489-3966-4(6))* PublishAmerica, Inc.

Friestad, Kathleen M. & Kline, Michael. The Kids' Book of Weather Forecasting. Friestad, Kathleen M. et al. Breen, Mark et al. 2008. (ENG.). 160p. (J). pap. 12.99 *(978-0-8249-6823-6(9),* Williamson Bks.) Ideals Pubns.

Friis, Karen. Ethan's Butterflies: A Spiritual Book for Parents & Young Children after a Baby's Passing. Jonas-Simpson, Christine. 2006. 16p. (J). pap. 9.95 *(978-1-4120-8850-3(X))* Trafford Publishing.

Frink, Phil, photos by. What's the Difference? Costa, David. 2004. 24p. (J). per. 26.99 *(978-1-4134-4855-9(0))* Xlibris Corp.

Frisk, Maria, jt. illus. see Perkins, Nicole.

Fritz, Kathleen Cheney. Tears of Mother Bear. Lewis, Anne Margaret. 2012. (ENG.). 32p. (J). (gr. -1-3). pap. 8.95 *(978-1-934133-62-0(0),* Mackinac Island Press, Inc.) Charlesbridge Publishing, Inc.

Fritz, Ronald. Sam y Sus Cuadrados de Zapatos. Gabriel, Nat & Ramirez, Alma. 2009. (Math Matters en Espanol Ser.). (SPA.). 32p. (J). (gr. 1-3). pap. 5.95 *(978-1-57565-276-4(5))* Kane Pr., Inc.

Fritz, Siegfried. Katie's Day. Iverson, Gregory. 2006. 48p. (J). *(978-0-9755184-1-0(0))* Sandbox Bks.

—Tyler's Big Blue Truck. Iverson, Gregory. 2006. 40p. (J). *(978-0-9755184-0-3(2))* Sandbox Bks.

Fröhlich, Lorenz & Pedersen, Vilhelm. Hans Andersen's Fairy Tales: A Selection. Andersen, Hans Christian. Kingsland, L. W., tr. from DAN. 2009. (Oxford World's Classics Ser.). (ENG.). 384p. pap. 10.95 *(978-0-19-955585-7(0))* Oxford Univ. Pr., Inc.

Frongia, Daniela. Allah's Gifts. Nazeer, Tasnim & Publishing, Greenbirdbooks Childrens. 2012. 26p. pap. *(978-0-9562141-7-1(7))* Greenbird Bks.

—A Beautiful Husky Needs a Home. Orcutt, Cherie. 2012. 32p. pap. 21.00 *(978-1-4685-7156-1(7))* AuthorHouse.

—Mister D. Stevens, Elizabeth. 2012. 24p. (J). 16.95 *(978-1-60131-114-6(1))* Big Tent Bks.

F

Front, Charles. Carbonel & Calidor: Being the Further Adventures of a Royal Cat. Sleigh, Barbara. 2009. (ENG.). 224p. (J). (gr. 4-7). 17.95 *(978-1-59017-333-6(3),* NYR Children's Collection) New York Review of Bks., Inc., The.

Fronty, Aurélia. Animals of the Bible. Delval, Marie-Hélène. 2010. 88p. (J). (gr. -1-3). 16.50 *(978-0-8028-5376-9(5),* Eerdmans Bks For Young Readers) Eerdmans, William B. Publishing Co.

—Hilo de Hada. Lechermeier, Philippe. Rozarena, P., tr. from FRE. 2009. (SPA.). 89p. (J). (gr. 4-7). *(978-84-263-7257-4(0))* Vives, Luis Editorial (Edelvives).

—I Have the Right to Be a Child, 1 vol. Serres, Alain. Mixter, Helen, tr. from FRE. 2012. (ENG.). 48p. (J). (gr. -1-2). 18.95 *(978-1-55498-149-6(2))* Groundwood Bks. CAN. Dist: Perseus-PGW.

—One City, Two Brothers. Smith, Chris. 2007. (ENG.). 32p. (J). (gr. -1-3). 16.99 *(978-1-84686-042-3(3))* Barefoot Bks., Inc.

—Songs from a Journey with a Parrot: Lullabies & Nursery Rhymes from Portugal & Brazil. Lerasle, Magdeleine. 2013. (POR & ENG.). 52p. (J). (gr. -1-k). 16.95 *(978-2-923163-99-4(0))* La Montagne Secrete CAN. Dist: Independent Pubs. Group.

—Sube y Baja Por Los Andes: Un Cuento de un Festival Peruano. Krebs, Laurie. 2011. (SPA.). 32p. (J). (gr. 1-6). pap. 7.99 *(978-1-84686-548-0(4))* Barefoot Bks., Inc.

—Up & down the Andes. Krebs, Laurie. 2011. (ENG.). 32p. (J). (gr. 1-6). pap. 7.99 *(978-1-84686-468-1(2))* Barefoot Bks., Inc.

—Up & down the Andes: A Peruvian Festival Tale. Krebs, Laurie. 2008. (ENG.). 32p. (J). (gr. -1-5). 16.99 *(978-1-84686-203-8(5))* Barefoot Bks., Inc.

Frossard, Claire. Basil Becomes a Big Brother. Renoult, Armelle. 2012. (My Little Picture Book Ser.). (ENG.). 32p. (J). (gr. -1). 6.95 *(978-2-7338-2143-5(1))* Auzou, Philippe Editions FRA. Dist: Consortium Bk. Sales & Distribution.

—Emma's Journey. Frossard, Etienne, photos by. 2010. (ENG.). 56p. (J). (gr. -1-3). 17.95 *(978-1-59270-099-8(3))* Enchanted Lion Bks., LLC.

Frost, Adam. Paw Prints in the Snow. Grindley, Sally. 2012. (ENG.). 105p. (J). (gr. 3-5). pap. 11.99 *(978-1-4088-1945-6(7),* 43049, Bloomsbury USA Childrens) Bloomsbury USA.

Frost, Justine. Squeaks Narrow Squeaks. Davey, Keith Peter. 2009. 32p. pap. 14.62 *(978-1-4120-4402-8(2))* Trafford Publishing.

Frost, Michael. The Scarlet Macaw Scandal. Keene, Carolyn. 8th ed. 2004. (Nancy Drew (All New) Girl Detective Ser.: 8). (ENG.). 160p. (J). (gr. 3-7). pap. 5.99 *(978-0-689-86844-3(8),* Simon & Schuster/Paula Wiseman Bks.) Simon & Schuster/Paula Wiseman Bks.

Frost, Michael, photos by. Boo Who? A Foldout Halloween Adventure. Schaefer, Lola M. 2009. (ENG., 12p. (J). (gr. -1-k). bds. 7.99 *(978-1-4169-5911-3(4),* Little Simon) Little Simon.

—Private Killer, Bk. 2. 2010. (Hardy Boys (All New) Undercover Brothers Ser.: 32). (ENG.). 160p. (J). (gr. 3-7). pap. 5.99 *(978-1-4169-8697-3(9),* Simon & Schuster/Paula Wiseman Bks.) Simon & Schuster/Paula Wiseman Bks.

—The Vincent Brothers. Glines, Abbi. 2012. (ENG., 304p. (YA). (gr. 11). 17.99 *(978-1-4424-8529-7(9));* pap. 9.99 *(978-1-4424-8528-0(0))* Simon Pulse. (Simon Pulse).

—When I Was the Greatest. Reynolds, Jason. 2014. (ENG., 240p. (YA). (gr. 7). 17.99 *(978-1-4424-5947-2(6),* Atheneum Bks. for Young Readers) Simon & Schuster Children's Publishing.

Froud, Brian. Chelsea Morning. 2004. (ENG.). 32p. (J). (gr. -1-3). 17.95 *(978-1-59687-178-6(4))* IBks., Inc.

—Chelsea Morning. 2004. 32p. (J). *(978-0-689-03593-7(4),* Milk & Cookies) ibooks, Inc.

Froud, Wendy. Midsummer Night's Faery Tale. Jones, John Lawrence, photos by. Windling, Terri. 2005. 52p. (J). (gr. k-4). reprint ed. 18.00 *(978-0-7567-8759-2(9))* DIANE Publishing Co.

Fruchter, Jason. Big Brother Daniel. Santomero, Angela C. 2015. (Daniel Tiger's Neighborhood Ser.). (ENG.). 14p. (J). (gr. -1-k). bds. 5.99 *(978-1-4814-3172-9(2),* Simon Spotlight) Simon Spotlight.

—The Big Pony Race. David, Erica. 2006. 27p. (J). *(978-0-7172-9869-3(8))* Scholastic, Inc.

—Buddy's Big Bite. Reader's Digest Staff & Froeb, Lori C. 2013. (Snappy Fun Bks.: 1). (ENG.). 10p. (J). (gr. -1-k). bds. 8.99 *(978-0-7944-2790-0(1))* Reader's Digest Assn., Inc., The.

—Christmas Countdown (Team Umizoomi) Golden Books. 2013. (Paint Box Book Ser.). (ENG.). 48p. (J). (gr. -1-2). pap. 3.99 *(978-0-449-81853-4(5),* Golden Bks.) Random Hse. Children's Bks.

—Christmas Fiesta. Golden Books Staff. 2009. (Giant Coloring Book Ser.). (ENG.). 40p. (J). (gr. -1-2). pap. 9.99 *(978-0-375-85466-8(5),* Golden Bks.) Random Hse. Children's Bks.

—Daniel Goes Out for Dinner. 2015. (Daniel Tiger's Neighborhood Ser.). (ENG.). 32p. (J). (gr. -1-k). 16.99 *(978-1-4814-2872-9(1),* Simon Spotlight) Simon Spotlight.

—Daniel's First Sleepover. 2015. (Daniel Tiger's Neighborhood Ser.). (ENG.). 24p. (J). (gr. -1-2). pap. 3.99 *(978-1-4814-2893-4(4),* Simon Spotlight) Simon Spotlight.

—Un Dia en la Playa. Silverhardt, Lauryn. Ziegler, Argentina Palacios, tr. 2004. (Dora la Exploradora Ser.).Tr. of Day at the Beach. (SPA.). 22p. (J). bds. 4.99 *(978-0-689-86976-1(2),* Libros Para Ninos) Libros Para Ninos.

—Dora Goes for a Ride. Beinstein, Phoebe. 2004. (Dora the Explorer Ser.). (ENG.). 22p. (J). bds. 4.99 *(978-0-689-86372-1(1),* Simon Spotlight/Nickelodeon) Simon Spotlight/Nickelodeon.

—Dora the Explorer Mix & Match Dress-Up. Reader's Digest Staff & Roe, David. 2012. (Mix & Match Ser.). (ENG.). 12p. (J). (gr. -1-2). bds. 14.99 *(978-0-7944-2475-6(9))* Reader's Digest Assn., Inc., The.

—Dora's Nursery Rhyme Adventure. Ricci, Christine. 2005. (Dora the Explorer Ser.). (J). *(978-0-7172-9819-8(1))* Scholastic, Inc.

—Fairy Magic (Dora the Explorer) Golden Books Staff. 2012. (Color Plus Chunky Crayons Ser.). (ENG.). 48p. (J). (gr. -1-2). pap. 3.99 *(978-0-307-93030-9(0),* Golden Bks.) Random Hse., Inc.

—Farm Alarm! (Team Umizoomi) Random House. 2014. (Step into Reading Ser.). (ENG.). 24p. (J). (gr. -1-1). pap. 3.99 *(978-0-385-38508-4(0),* Random Hse. Bks. for Young Readers) Random Hse. Children's Bks.

—Friends Help Each Other. 2014. (Daniel Tiger's Neighborhood Ser.). (ENG.). 32p. (J). (gr. -1-k). pap. 3.99 *(978-1-4814-0366-5(4),* Simon Spotlight) Simon Spotlight.

—Hey, Buddy! Miller, Mona. 2010. (Super Coloring Book Ser.). (ENG.). 96p. (J). (gr. -1-2). pap. 3.99 *(978-0-375-86155-0(6),* Golden Bks.) Random Hse. Children's Bks.

—Kite Riders! (Team Umizoomi) Golden Books Staff. 2012. (Color Plus Chunky Crayons Ser.). (ENG.). 48p. (J). (gr. -1-2). pap. 3.99 *(978-0-375-86119-2(X),* Golden Bks.) Random Hse., Inc.

—Lalaloopsy: Halloween Surprise. Cecil, Lauren. 2012. (Lalaloopsy Ser.). (ENG.). 24p. (J). (gr. -1-3). pap. 3.99 *(978-0-545-43388-4(6))* Scholastic, Inc.

—Legend of the Blue Mermaid (Team Umizoomi) Random House Staff. 2013. (Pictureback Series.). (ENG.). 24p. (J). (gr. -1-2). 3.99 *(978-0-449-81758-2(X),* Random Hse. Bks. for Young Readers) Random Hse. Children's Bks.

—Let's Dance! Golden Books Staff. 2005. (Paint Box Book Ser.). (ENG.). 32p. (J). (gr. -1-2). pap. 3.99 *(978-0-375-83478-3(8),* Golden Bks.) Random Hse. Children's Bks.

—Lovestruck! Lewman, David. 2004. (Fairly Oddparents Ser.). (J). (gr. -1-3). 11.15 *(978-0-7569-1992-4(4))* Perfection Learning Corp.

—Mighty Adventures (Team Umizoomi) Golden Books. 2012. (Super Color with Stickers Ser.). (ENG.). 96p. (J). (gr. -1-2). pap. 3.99 *(978-0-307-93085-9(8),* Golden Bks.) Random Hse. Children's Bks.

—My Heart Is Happy! Golden Books Staff. 2009. (Holographic Sticker Book Ser.). (ENG.). 48p. (J). (gr. -1-2). pap. 3.99 *(978-0-375-85723-2(0),* Golden Bks.) Random Hse. Children's Bks.

—My Name Is Tiny! Reader's Digest Staff. 2013. (Snappy Fun Bks.: 1). (ENG.). 10p. (J). (gr. -1-k). bds. 8.99 *(978-0-7944-2791-7(X))* Reader's Digest Assn., Inc., The.

—Outer-Space Chase (Team Umizoomi) Random House Staff. 2013. (Step into Reading Ser.). (ENG.). 32p. (J). (gr. -1-1). 3.99 *(978-0-449-81890-9(X));* lib. bdg. 12.99 *(978-0-449-81891-6(8))* Random Hse. Children's Bks. (Random Hse. Bks. for Young Readers).

—Painting Power! (Team Umizoomi) Golden Books Staff. 2012. (Deluxe Paint Box Book Ser.). (ENG.). 128p. (J). (gr. -1-2). pap. 7.99 *(978-0-375-86161-1(0),* Golden Bks.) Random Hse., Inc.

—Pets Are the Best! (Dora the Explorer) Golden Books Staff. 2011. (Color Plus Flocked Stickers Ser.). (ENG.). 64p. (J). (gr. -1-2). pap. 4.99 *(978-0-375-87194-8(2),* Golden Bks.) Random Hse. Children's Bks.

—Ride the Holiday Train! Reader's Digest Editors. 2012. (Lift-The-Flap Ser.). (ENG.). 10p. (J). (gr. -1-k). bds. 9.99 *(978-0-7944-2712-2(X))* Reader's Digest Assn., Inc., The.

—The Science Project. McCann, Jesse Leon. 2003. 61p. (J). *(978-0-439-56271-3(6))* Scholastic, Inc.

—Silly Costume Contest (Team Umizoomi) Golden Books. 2014. (Glow-In-the-Dark Sticker Book Ser.). (ENG.). 48p. (J). (gr. -1-2). pap. 3.99 *(978-0-385-38413-1(0),* Golden Bks.) Random Hse. Children's Bks.

Fruchter, Jason. T Is for Troll! Golden Books. 2015. (Color & Paint Plus Stickers Ser.). (ENG.). 128p. (J). (gr. -1-2). pap. 9.99 **(978-0-553-52312-6(0),** Golden Bks.) Random Hse. Children's Bks.

—Time to Fly! (Disney Junior: Sheriff Callie's Wild West) Posner-Sanchez, Andrea. 2015. (Little Golden Book Ser.). (ENG.). 24p. (J). (-k). 4.99 **(978-0-7364-3362-4(7),** Golden/Disney) Random Hse. Children's Bks.

Fruchter, Jason. Top Cops (Team Umizoomi) Random House. 2014. (Step into Reading Ser.). (ENG.). 24p. (J). (gr. -1-1). pap. 3.99 *(978-0-385-37494-1(1),* Random Hse. Bks. for Young Readers) Random Hse. Children's Bks.

—¡Vámonos! / Let's Go! Beinstein, Phoebe. Ziegler, Argentina Palacios, tr. 2007. (Dora la Exploradora Ser.). (SPA & ENG.). 14p. (J). bds. 4.99 *(978-1-4169-3367-0(0),* Libros Para Ninos) Libros Para Ninos.

—We Love Halloween! Golden Books Staff. 2010. (Glow-In-the-Dark Sticker Book Ser.). (ENG.). 48p. (J). (gr. -1-2). pap. 3.99 *(978-0-375-86513-8(6),* Golden Bks.) Random Hse. Children's Bks.

—Who's Hatching? (Dinosaur Train) Golden Books. 2013. (Holographic Sticker Book Ser.). (ENG.). 48p. (J). (gr. -1-2). pap. 3.99 *(978-0-307-98102-8(9),* Golden Bks.) Random Hse. Children's Bks.

—Zoom to the Rescue! (Team Umizoomi) Golden Books. 2013. (Paint Box Book Ser.). (ENG.). 48p. (J). (gr. -1-2). pap. 3.99 *(978-0-307-98198-1(3),* Golden Bks.) Random Hse. Children's Bks.

Fruchter, Jason & Golden Books Staff. Ready, Set, Race! Golden Books Staff. 2008. (Color Plus Ser.). (ENG.). 48p. (J). (gr. -1-2). pap. 4.99 *(978-0-375-84577-2(1),* Golden Bks.) Random Hse. Children's Bks.

Fruchter, Jason, jt. illus. see Golden Books Staff.

Fruchter, Jason, jt. illus. see RH Disney Staff.

Fruchter, Jason, jt. illus. see Style Guide Staff.

Fruchter, Jason, jt. illus. see Style Guide, Style.

Fruisen, Catherine Myler. Alice & Her Fabulous Teeth! Maconie, Robin. 2004. 32p. (J). per. *(978-1-893974-21-0(9),* Design Pr. Bks.) Savannah College of Art & Design Exhibitions.

—Rick & Rocky. Wallace, Paula S. 2004. 32p. (J). pap. *(978-1-893974-22-7(7),* Design Pr. Bks.) Savannah College of Art & Design Exhibitions.

Fry, Debbie. Donkeywise & Otherwise: The Story of Daisy Doo & Dudley Duz. 2004. 44p. (J). *(978-0-9759647-0-5(4),* 1238040) Fry, Debbie.

Fry, Michael. The Naughty List. Fry, Michael. Jackson, Bradley. 2015. (ENG.). 240p. (J). (gr. 3-7). 12.99 **(978-0-06-235475-4(2))** HarperCollins Pubs.

Fry, Michael. The Odd Squad Bully Bait. Fry, Michael. 2013. (Odd Squad Book Ser.). (ENG.). 224p. (J). (gr. 3-7). 12.99 *(978-1-4231-6924-6(7))* Hyperion Pr.

—The Odd Squad King Karl. Fry, Michael. 2014. (Odd Squad Book Ser.). (ENG.). 208p. (J). (gr. 3-7). 12.99 *(978-1-4231-9958-8(8))* Hyperion Bks. for Children.

—Zero Tolerance. Fry, Michael. 2013. (Odd Squad Book Ser.). (ENG.). 240p. (J). (gr. 3-7). 12.99 *(978-1-4231-7099-0(7))* Hyperion Pr.

Frye, Paige, jt. illus. see Billin-Frye, Paige.

Frye, Paige Billin, jt. illus. see Billin-Frye, Paige.

Fu, Sherwin, jt. illus. see Abboreno, Joseph F.

Fuchs, Bernie. The Wolves. Heinz, Brian. 2005. 32p. (J). lib. bdg. 15.99 *(978-0-936335-11-7(4))* Ballyhoo BookWorks, Inc.

Fuchs, Kaitlyn. Puppies & Poems. Sack, Nancy. 2012. (ENG.). 32p. (J). 19.95 *(978-1-4327-8470-6(6))* Outskirts Pr., Inc.

Fucíková, Renata. Madame Butterfly. Puccini, Giacomo. 2005. (ENG.). 40p. (Orig.). (J). 15.95 *(978-1-933327-04-4(9))* Purple Bear Bks., Inc.

Fucile, Tony. Best Friends Forever. DiCamillo, Kate & McGhee, Alison. 2013. (Bink & Gollie Ser.). (ENG.). 96p. (J). (gr. 1-4). 15.99 *(978-0-7636-3497-1(2))* Candlewick Pr.

—Bink & Gollie. DiCamillo, Kate & McGhee, Alison. (Bink & Gollie Ser.). (ENG.). (J). (gr. 1-4). 2012. 88p. pap. 6.99 *(978-0-7636-5954-7(1));* 2010. 96p. 15.99 *(978-0-7636-3266-3(X))* Candlewick Pr.

—Bink & Gollie - The Completely Marvelous Collection. DiCamillo, Kate & McGhee, Alison. 2014. (Bink & Gollie Ser.). (ENG.). (J). (gr. 1-4). pap. 19.99 *(978-0-7636-7536-3(9))* Candlewick Pr.

—Bink & Gollie - Two for One. DiCamillo, Kate & McGhee, Alison. 2012. (Bink & Gollie Ser.). (ENG.). 96p. (J). (gr. 1-4). 15.99 *(978-0-7636-3361-5(5))* Candlewick Pr.

—Bink & Gollie: Best Friends Forever. DiCamillo, Kate & McGhee, Alison. 2014. (Bink & Gollie Ser.). (ENG.). 88p. (J). (gr. 1-4). pap. 6.99 *(978-0-7636-7092-4(8))* Candlewick Pr.

—Mitchell Goes Bowling. Durand, Hallie. 2013. (ENG.). 40p. (J). (gr. -1-2). 15.99 *(978-0-7636-6049-9(3))* Candlewick Pr.

—Mitchell Goes Driving. Durand, Hallie. 2013. (ENG.). 40p. (J). (gr. -1-2). pap. 6.99 *(978-0-7636-6737-5(4))* Candlewick Pr.

—Mitchell's License. Durand, Hallie. 2011. (ENG.). 40p. (J). (gr. -1-2). 15.99 *(978-0-7636-4496-3(X))* Candlewick Pr.

—Two for One. DiCamillo, Kate & McGhee, Alison. 2013. (Bink & Gollie Ser.). (ENG.). 96p. (J). (gr. 1-4). pap. 6.99 *(978-0-7636-6445-9(6))* Candlewick Pr.

Fucile, Tony. Let's Do Nothing! Fucile, Tony. (ENG.). 40p. (J). (gr. -1-3). 2012. pap. 6.99 *(978-0-7636-5269-2(5));* 2009. 16.99 *(978-0-7636-3440-7(9))* Candlewick Pr.

Fuenmayor, Morella. Rosaura en Bicicleta. Barbot, Daniel. 2005. (SPA.). 23p. (J). (gr. -1-2). reprint ed. pap. 14.00 *(978-0-7567-8947-3(8))* DIANE Publishing Co.

Fuentes, Benny, jt. illus. see Tortosa, Wilson.

Fuentes, Mikel. How You Were Born. Calaf, Monica. 2014. (ENG.). 48p. (J). (gr. -1-3). 9.99 *(978-1-78066-125-4(8))* Pinter & Martin Ltd. GBR. Dist: National Bk. Network.

—You, Me & the Breast. Calaf, Monica. 2012. (ENG.). 40p. (J). (gr. -1-12). pap. 9.99 *(978-1-905177-52-3(6))* Pinter & Martin Ltd. GBR. Dist: National Bk. Network.

Fuert, L. A. & Woodbury et al, Charles H. Fresh Fields. Burroughs, John. 2008. 196p. pap. *(978-1-4099-2065-6(8))* Dodo Pr.

Fuertes, Louis Agassiz. The Burgess Animal Book for Children. Burgess, Thornton W. 2008. 284p. (gr. 4-7). pap. *(978-1-4099-2052-6(6))* Dodo Pr.

—The Burgess Animal Book for Children. Burgess, Thornton W. 2011. 478p. 52.95 *(978-1-169-84273-1(9));* 2010. 478p. 42.36 *(978-1-163-21392-6(6));* 2010. 478p. pap. 30.36 *(978-1-162-64734-0(5));* 2004. 476p. (gr. 4-7). 52.95 *(978-1-4326-2165-0(3));* 2004. reprint ed. pap. 37.95 *(978-1-4179-2978-8(2))* Kessinger Publishing, LLC.

—The Burgess Animal Book for Children (Yesterday's Classics) Burgess, Thornton W. 2006. (J). per. 13.95 *(978-1-59915-171-7(5))* Yesterday's Classics.

—The Burgess Bird Book for Children. Burgess, Thornton W. 2008. 168p. (gr. -1-7). pap. 7.99 *(978-1-4209-3052-8(4))* Digireads.com.

—The Burgess Bird Book for Children. Burgess, Thornton W. 2003. (Dover Children's Classics Ser.). (ENG.). 272p. (J). (gr. 3-8). pap. 9.95 *(978-0-486-42840-6(0))* Dover Pubns., Inc.

—The Burgess Bird Book for Children (Yesterday's Classics) Burgess, Thornton W. 2006. (J). per. 13.95 *(978-1-59915-170-0(7))* Yesterday's Classics.

—Citizen Bird: Scenes from Bird-Life in Plain English for Beginners. Wright, Mabel Osgood & Coues, Elliott. 2009. 386p. pap. *(978-1-4099-8625-6(X))* Dodo Pr.

—Citizen Bird: Scenes from Bird Life in Plain English for Beginners (1897) Wright, Mabel Osgood & Coues, Elliott. 2010. 446p. 41.56 *(978-1-164-42138-2(7));* 2010. 446p. pap. 29.56 *(978-1-164-13374-2(8));* 2008. 444p. 51.95 *(978-1-4366-1564-8(X));* 2008. (ENG.). 448p. per. 36.95 *(978-0-548-81704-9(9))* Kessinger Publishing, LLC.

Fuge, Charles. Adventures of Little Wombat. Churchill, Vicki & McAllister, Angela. 2008. (ENG.). 96p. (J). (gr. k-k). 17.95 *(978-1-4027-6322-9(0))* Sterling Publishing Co., Inc.

—Bedtime Hullabaloo. Conway, David. 2010. (ENG.). 32p. (J). (gr. -1-3). 16.99 *(978-0-8027-2170-9(2))* Walker & Co.

—I Love It When You Smile. McBratney, Sam. 2012. 32p. (J). (gr. -1-3). 9.99 *(978-0-06-222133-9(7))* HarperCollins Pubs.

—A Lullaby for Little One. Casey, Dawn. 2015. (ENG.). 32p. (J). (-k). 12.99 *(978-0-7636-7608-7(X),* Nosy Crow) Candlewick Pr.

—Who Will You Meet on Scary Street? Nine Pop-up Nightmares! Tagg, Christine. 2004. 20p. (J). reprint ed. 15.00 *(978-0-7567-8003-6(9))* DIANE Publishing Co.

Fuglestad, R. A. Over the Rainbow with Joey. Acopiado, Ginger. l.t. ed. 2004. 22p. (J). bds. 8.99 *(978-0-9729093-0-3(3))* Tike Time, Inc.

Fuhr, Ute & Sautai, Raoul. Los Indios. Fuhr, Ute & Sautai, Raoul. Jeunesse, Gallimard. (Coleccion Mundo Maravilloso). (SPA.). 86p. (J). (gr. 2-4). *(978-84-348-4654-8(3),* SM6992) SM Ediciones ESP. Dist: Lectorum Pubns., Inc.

Fuhriman, Raphael Scott. Jake the Puppy & Emma the Cat. Oakes, Krista Ralston. 2012. 36p. (J). 19.99 *(978-0-9838321-2-6(9))* Higher Ground Pr.

Fuijkschot, Edo. Agent Boo, Vol. 1. de Campi, Alex. 2006. 96p. pap. 4.99 *(978-1-59816-802-0(9))* TOKYOPOP, Inc.

Fujikawa, Gyo. A Child's Book of Poems. 2007. (ENG.). 128p. (J). (gr. -1-2). 9.95 *(978-1-4027-5061-8(7))* Sterling Publishing Co., Inc.

—A Child's Garden of Verses: A Collection of Scriptures, Prayers & Poems. Stevenson, Robert Louis. 2007. (ENG.). 104p. (J). (gr. -1-2). 9.95 *(978-1-4027-5062-5(5))* Sterling Publishing Co., Inc.

—Fairy Tales & Fables. 2008. (ENG.). 128p. (J). (gr. -1-2). 9.95 *(978-1-4027-5698-6(4))* Sterling Publishing Co., Inc.

—Let's Play. 2010. (ENG.). 20p. (J). (gr. k-k). bds. 5.95 *(978-1-4027-6821-7(4))* Sterling Publishing Co., Inc.

—Mother Goose. 2007. (ENG.). 130p. (J). (gr. -1-2). 9.95 *(978-1-4027-5064-9(1))* Sterling Publishing Co., Inc.

—The Night Before Christmas. Moore, Clement C. 2007. (ENG.). 32p. (J). (gr. -1-2). 9.95 *(978-1-4027-5065-6(X))* Sterling Publishing Co., Inc.

—Sleepy Time. 2011. (ENG.). 20p. (J). (gr. k-k). bds. 5.95 *(978-1-4027-6820-0(6))* Sterling Publishing Co., Inc.

Fujikawa, Gyo. Baby Animals. Fujikawa, Gyo. 2008. (ENG.). 24p. (J). (gr. -1-2). bds. 5.95 *(978-1-4027-5701-3(8))* Sterling Publishing Co., Inc.

—Sunny Books - Four-Favorite Tales, 4 bks., Set. Fujikawa, Gyo. (J). (gr. -1). reprint ed. *(978-1-55987-042-9(7),* Sunny Bks.) J B Communications, Inc.

—Ten Little Babies. Fujikawa, Gyo. 2008. (ENG.). 24p. (J). (gr. -1-2). bds. 5.95 *(978-1-4027-5700-6(X))* Sterling Publishing Co., Inc.

Fujisaki, Ryu. Hoshin Engi, Vol. 1. Fujisaki, Ryu. 2007. (Hoshin Engi Ser.). (ENG.). 192p. (gr. 8-12). pap. 7.99 *(978-1-4215-1362-1(5))* Viz Media.

—The Sennin World War. Fujisaki, Ryu. 2009. (Hoshin Engi Ser.: 13). (ENG.). 200p. pap. 7.99 *(978-1-4215-2402-3(3))* Viz Media.

—Waqwaq, Vol. 4. Fujisaki, Ryu. 2010. (WaqWaq Ser.: 4). (ENG.). 208p. (gr. 8-18). pap. 9.99 *(978-1-4215-2741-3(3))* Viz Media.

Fujisawa, Tohru. GTO: Great Teacher Onizuka, 25 vols., Vol. 21. Fujisawa, Tohru, compiled by. rev. ed. 2004. 192p. pap. 9.99 *(978-1-59182-455-8(9),* Tokyopop Adult) TOKYOPOP, Inc.

Fujita, Artur, jt. illus. see Hart, Sam.

Fujita, Goro. The Junkyard Bot, Bk. 7. Richards, C. J. 2014. (Robots Rule Ser.: 1). (ENG.). 208p. (J). (gr. 5-7). 13.99 *(978-0-544-33936-1(3),* HMH Books For Young Readers) Houghton Mifflin Harcourt Publishing Co.

—Lots of Bots. Richards, C. J. 2015. (Robots Rule Ser.: 2). (ENG.). 224p. (J). (gr. 2-5). 13.99 *(978-0-544-33934-7(7),* HMH Books For Young Readers) Houghton Mifflin Harcourt Publishing Co.

Fujita, Goro. Your Alien. Sauer, Tammi. 2015. (ENG.). 32p. (J). (gr. -1). 14.95 **(978-1-4549-1129-6(8))** Sterling Publishing Co., Inc.

Fujita, Mikiko. Strange Light Afar: Tales of the Supernatural from Old Japan, 1 vol. Umezawa, Rui. 2015. (ENG.). 144p. (J). (gr. 6). 18.95 **(978-1-55498-723-8(7))** Groundwood Bks. CAN. Dist: Perseus-PGW.

Fujiwara, Hiroko. Different Croaks for Different Folks: All about Children with Special Learning Needs. Ochiai, Midori & Oyama, Shigeki. Sanders, Esther, tr. from JPN. 2006. (ENG.). 96p. (J). (gr. -1-3). *(978-1-84310-392-9(3))* Kingsley, Jessica Ltd.

Fujiwara, Kim. My Name is Leona. Harris, Carol Gahara. 2013. 24p. (J). 19.95 *(978-0-9860324-0-0(9))* Snowy Night Pub.

Fuka, Vladimír. New York: A Mod Portrait of the City. Mahler, Zdenek. 2014. (ENG.). 128p. 24.95 *(978-0-7893-2727-7(9))* Universe Publishing.

Fukuda, Toyofumi, photos by. Life-Size Zoo: From Tiny Rodents to Gigantic Elephants, an Actual Size Animal Encyclopedia. Earhart, Kristin, ed. 2009. (ENG., 48p. (gr. -1). 17.95 *(978-1-934734-20-9(9))* Seven Footer Pr.

Fukuoka, Aki. The Bad Butterfly. Rippin, Sally. 2012. 44p. (J). *(978-1-61067-132-3(5))* Kane Miller.

—The Bad Butterfly: Billie B. Brown. Rippin, Sally. 2013. (ENG.). 48p. (J). pap. 4.99 *(978-1-61067-095-1(7))* Kane Miller.

—The Beautiful Haircut. Rippin, Sally. 2014. (ENG.). 48p. (J). pap. 4.99 *(978-1-61067-100-2(7))* Kane Miller.

—The Best Project. Rippin, Sally. (J). 2015. (ENG.). 48p. pap. 4.99 *(978-1-61067-258-0(5));* 2014. 43p. *(978-1-61067-292-4(5))* Kane Miller.

—The Big Sister: Billie B. Brown. Rippin, Sally. 2014. (ENG.). 48p. (J). pap. 4.99 *(978-1-61067-184-2(8))* Kane Miller.

—The Birthday Mix-Up. Rippin, Sally. 2013. 43p. (J). *(978-1-61067-232-0(1))* Kane Miller.

—The Birthday Mix-Up: Billie B. Brown. Rippin, Sally. 2014. (ENG.). 48p. (J). pap. 4.99 *(978-1-61067-182-8(1))* Kane Miller.

—Code Breakers. Rippin, Sally. 2015. (ENG.). 96p. (J). pap. 4.99 *(978-1-61067-312-9(3))* Kane Miller.

—The Extra-Special Helper. Rippin, Sally. 2014. (ENG.). 48p. (J). pap. 4.99 *(978-1-61067-099-9(X))* Kane Miller.

—The Little Lie. Rippin, Sally. 2014. 43p. (J). *(978-1-61067-291-7(7))* Kane Miller.

—The Midnight Feast. Rippin, Sally. (J). 2013. (ENG.). 48p. pap. 4.99 *(978-1-61067-097-5(3));* 2012. 44p. *(978-1-61067-134-7(1))* Kane Miller.

—The Second-Best Friend: Billie B. Brown. Rippin, Sally. 2014. (ENG.). 48p. (J). pap. 4.99 *(978-1-61067-098-2(1))* Kane Miller.

—The Soccer Star. Rippin, Sally. (J). 2013. (ENG.). 48p. pap. 4.99 *(978-1-61067-096-8(5))*; 2012. 44p. *(978-1-61067-133-0(3))* Kane Miller.

—Spooky House. Rippin, Sally. 2015. (ENG.). 96p. (J). pap. 4.99 *(978-1-61067-311-2(5))* Kane Miller.

—The Spotty Vacation. Rippin, Sally. 2013. 43p. (J). *(978-1-61067-233-7(X))* Kane Miller.

—The Spotty Vacation: Billie B. Brown. Rippin, Sally. 2014. (ENG.). 48p. (J). pap. 4.99 *(978-1-61067-183-5(X))* Kane Miller.

Fulcher, Roz. First Look at Farm Animals. Galvin, Laura Gates. 2009. (ENG.). 16p. bds. 6.95 *(978-1-59249-999-1(6))* Soundprints.

—First Look at Zoo Animals. Galvin, Laura Gates. 2009. (ENG.). 16p. (J). bds. 6.95 *(978-1-59249-998-4(8))* Studio Mouse LLC.

—Months of the Year. Scelsa, Greg. Faulkner, Stacey, ed. 2006. (J). pap. 2.99 *(978-1-59198-320-0(7))* Creative Teaching Pr., Inc.

Fulco, Haley. Elephant Hips Are Expensive! A Tale of the Sooner State. Hudson, Marilyn A. 2007. 50p. (J). per. *(978-0-9778850-2-2(X),* WhorlBooks Thumbprints) Whorl Bks.

Fuller Baldwin, Fran. What Animal Needs a Wig?, 1 vol. Wollman, Neil & Fuller, Abigail. 2014. (ENG.). 32p. (J). pap. 6.99 *(978-1-59572-677-3(2))* Star Bright Bks., Inc.

Fuller, Bob. The Costume Trunk. 2011. (J). *(978-1-936169-01-6(0))* Paddywhack Lane LLC.

Fuller, Bob. Lauren & the Leaky Pail. Fuller, Bob. 2010. 32p. (J). (gr. -1-3). 15.99 *(978-1-936169-00-9(2))* Paddywhack Lane LLC.

Fuller, Cari. Bobby Dog & the Flying Frog. Pepin, Rebecca. 2004. (J). (gr. 4-18). 16.99 *(978-0-9760684-0-2(0))*; pap. 11.99 *(978-0-9760684-1-9(9))* FullofPep Pubns.

Fuller, E. My Best Friend Fred. Webster, S. 2011. (ENG.). 26p. pap. 14.95 *(978-1-4515-4185-4(6))* CreateSpace Independent Publishing Platform.

Fuller, Elizabeth. Mrs. Wishy-Washy's Farm. Cowley, Joy. (ENG.). 32p. (J). (gr. -1-k). 2006. 5.99 *(978-0-14-240299-3(0),* Puffin); 2003. 16.99 *(978-0-399-23872-7(7),* Philomel) Penguin Publishing Group.

Fuller, Harvey. Tommy & the Island. Fuller, Harvey. 2007. (J). pap. 18.95 *(978-0-9773725-7-7(X))* Flat Hammock Pr.

Fuller, Jeremy. Puff Flies. Grindley, Sally. 2011. (My Phonics Readers: Level 3 Ser.). 24p. (J). (gr. -1-1). 24.25 *(978-1-84898-514-8(2))* Sea-To-Sea Pubns.

Fuller, Laurie. Who Goes with That Nose? The Wild Adventures of Juicy Coppertoes. Kobert, Michael Gilead & Donato, Dona. 2005. 40p. (J). per. 9.95 *(978-0-9770700-0-8(X))* Giggling Gorilla Productions, LLC.

Fuller, Rachel. All Kinds of Festivals. Safran, Sheri. 2012. (ENG.). 12p. (J). (gr. -1). 12.99 *(978-1-60887-162-9(2))* Insight Editions LP.

—Let's Dress! Safran, Sheri. 2011. (ENG.). 20p. (J). (gr. -1-2). 18.99 *(978-1-85707-725-4(3))* Tango Bks. GBR. Dist: Independent Pubs. Group.

—Look at Me! 2009. (New Baby Ser.). (ENG.). 12p. (J). (gr. -1). bds. *(978-1-84643-278-1(2))* Child's Play International Ltd.

—My New Baby. 2009. (New Baby Ser.). (ENG.). 12p. (J). (gr. -1). bds. *(978-1-84643-276-7(6))* Child's Play International Ltd.

—Waiting for Baby. 2009. (New Baby Ser.). (ENG.). 12p. (J). (gr. -1). bds. *(978-1-84643-275-0(8))* Child's Play International Ltd.

—You & Me. 2009. (New Baby Ser.). (ENG.). 12p. (J). (gr. -1). bds. *(978-1-84643-277-4(4))* Child's Play International Ltd.

Fuller, Sandy Ferguson. Hannah & the Perfect Picture Pony: A Story of the Great Depression. Zimet, Sara Goodman. 2005. 24p. (J). lib. bdg. 16.95 *(978-0-9645159-2-5(X))* Discovery Pr. Pubns., Inc.

Fuller, Steve. Johnny Tractor's Fun Farm Day. Neusner, Dena & Running Press Staff. 2006. (ENG.). 10p. (J). (gr. -1). pap. 6.95 *(978-0-7624-2630-0(6),* Running Pr. Kids) Running Pr. Bk. Pubs.

Fulleylove, John & Baikie, Constance N. Peeps at Many Lands: Ancient Greece (Yesterday's Classics) Baikie, James. 2008. 128p. pap. 8.95 *(978-1-59915-289-9(4))* Yesterday's Classics.

Fulmer, Patrick. My Angel Next Door. Holt, Madeline. Kovalevich, Denise, ed. 2003. 20p. 10.00 *(978-0-9740016-0-9(0))* Holt Enterprise, LLC.

Fulton, Parker. Small One's Adventure. Mueller, Doris. Guevara, Linda L., ed. 2004. 32p. (J). (gr. k-5). 16.95 *(978-0-9710278-1-7(1))* All About Kids Publishing.

Fulvimari, Jeffrey. Being Binah, No. 6. Madonna. 2008. (English Roses Ser.: 6). (ENG.). 128p. (J). (gr. 3-7). 9.99 *(978-0-14-241095-0(0),* Puffin) Penguin Publishing Group.

—Big-Sister Blues, No. 5. Madonna. 2008. (English Roses Ser.: 5). (ENG.). 128p. (J). (gr. 3-7). 10.99 *(978-0-14-241093-6(4),* Puffin) Penguin Publishing Group.

—Friends for Life! Madonna. 2007. (English Roses Ser.: 1). (ENG.). 96p. (J). (gr. 3-7). 10.99 *(978-0-14-241114-8(0),* Puffin) Penguin Publishing Group.

—Good-Bye, Grace?, No. 2. Madonna. 2007. (English Roses Ser.: 2). (ENG.). 144p. (J). (gr. 3-7). 10.99 *(978-0-14-240883-4(2),* Puffin) Penguin Publishing Group.

—The New Girl, Vol. 3. Madonna. 2007. (English Roses Ser.: 3). (ENG.). 144p. (J). (gr. 3-7). 9.99 *(978-0-14-240884-1(0),* Puffin) Penguin Publishing Group.

—A Perfect Pair, No. 8. Ciccone, Madonna L. & Madonna. 2008. (English Roses Ser.: 8). (ENG.). 128p. (J). (gr. 3-7). 9.99 *(978-0-14-241125-4(6),* Puffin) Penguin Publishing Group.

—A Rose by Any Other Name. Madonna. 2007. (English Roses Ser.: 4). (ENG.). 144p. (J). (gr. 3-7). 10.99 *(978-0-14-240885-8(9),* Puffin) Penguin Publishing Group.

Fumizuki, Kou. Ai Yori Aoshi, 9 vols. Fumizuki, Kou, creator. rev. ed. Vol. 6. 2004. 196p. pap. 9.99 *(978-1-59182-650-7(0))*; Vol. 9. 2005. 192p. pap. 9.99 *(978-1-59532-372-9(4))* TOKYOPOP, Inc.

Fundora, Yolanda V. My Brain Won't Float Away / Mi cerebro no va a salir Flotando. Perez, Annette. Herranz Brooks, Jacqueline, tr. 2007. (ENG & SPA.). 32p. (J). 19.95 *(978-0-9725611-2-9(9),* Campanita Bks.) Editorial Campana.

Fundora, Yolanda V. Sand, Sea & Poetry. Moolenaar Bernier, Ashley-Ruth. 2014. (J). pap. *(978-1-934370-35-3(5))* Editorial Campana.

Fundora, Yolanda V. A Very Smart Cat: Una Gata Muy Inteligente. Picayo, Mario. 2008. (SPA & ENG.). 32p. (J). *(978-1-934370-00-1(2))* Editorial Campana.

Funk, Clotilde Embree. Flowers & Their Travels. Fox, Frances Margaret. 2011. 230p. 46.95 *(978-1-258-07400-5(1))* Literary Licensing, LLC.

—The Three Tripps. Moore, Margaret & Moore, John Travers. 2011. 158p. 41.95 *(978-1-258-08478-3(3))* Literary Licensing, LLC.

Funk, Debbie. My Dog, Eddie. Holzer, Angela. 2009. 36p. (J). lib. bdg. 8.99 *(978-0-9821563-5-3(9))* Good Sound Publishing.

Funke, Cornelia. Corazón De Tinta. Funke, Cornelia. Blanco, Rosa Pilar, tr. from GER. 2006.Tr. of Tintenherz. (SPA.). 598p. (J). *(978-84-7844-235-5(9))* Siruela, Ediciones S.A.

—Igraine the Brave. Funke, Cornelia. Bell, Anthea, tr. l.t. ed. 2008. (Thorndike Literacy Bridge Middle Reader Ser.). 259p. (J). (gr. 4-7). 23.95 *(978-1-4104-0341-4(6))* Thorndike Pr.

Funke, Peggy. Ellie Saves the Day, 1 vol. Johnson, Gerald J. J. 2009. 12p. pap. 24.95 *(978-1-60836-709-2(6))* America Star Bks.

Funnell, Sonja. Timmy the Goat: Spelunking Adventure. Anderson, Henry Morgan. Falk, Wendy & Makepeace, Jonathan, eds. 2011. (Adventures of Henry Ser.). 48p. 14.99 *(978-1-936813-00-1(9))* Adventures of Henry, LLC.

Fur, Emil. Ronny. Vujadinovic, Nenad. 2007. (POL & ENG.). 32p. (J). pap. 12.95 *(978-1-60195-105-2(1))* International Step by Step Assn.

Furchgott, Eve. Naughty Elepaio. Kruger, Malia. 2008. 32p. 14.95 *(978-0-87336-158-3(X))* Kamehameha Publishing.

Furie, Matt. The Night Riders. 2013. (ENG.). 48p. (J). (gr. -1-3). 8.95 *(978-1-938073-72-4(X))* McSweeney's Publishing.

Furlong, Frank. Not Yet: Poems for Kids Five & Up. 2011. 24p. pap. 14.95 *(978-1-4575-0467-9(7))* Dog Ear Publishing, LLC.

—Pop Pop's Magic Chair. 2010. 24p. pap. 12.95 *(978-1-60844-658-2(1))* Dog Ear Publishing, LLC.

Furniss, Harry. Sylvie & Bruno Concluded. Carroll, Lewis. 462p. 2010. 42.36 *(978-1-167-13605-4(5))*; 2010. pap. 30.36 *(978-1-167-01946-3(6))*; 2009. 52.95 *(978-1-120-84142-1(9))*; 2009. pap. 37.95 *(978-1-120-71925-6(9))* Kessinger Publishing, LLC.

Furnival, Keith. Introduction to Weather & Climate Change. Howell, Laura. 2004. (Geography Ser.). 96p. (J). (gr. 5). lib. bdg. 22.95 *(978-1-58086-613-2(1),* Usborne) EDC Publishing.

—The Usborne Internet-Linked Mysteries & Marvels of Science. Clarke, Phillip et al. 2005. 96p. (J). *(978-0-439-81568-0(1))* Scholastic, Inc.

Furnival, Keith, jt. illus. see Scott, Peter David.

Furukawa, Masumi, et al. Baby & Toddler Treasury. Davidson, Susanna. 2007. (Baby & Toddler Treasury Ser.). 95p. (J). (gr. -1-k). 19.99 *(978-0-7945-1150-0(3),* Usborne) EDC Publishing.

Furukawa, Masumi. Bears. Courtauld, Sarah. 2010. (First Reading Level 2 Ser.). 32p. (J). 6.99 *(978-0-7945-2735-8(3),* Usborne) EDC Publishing.

—Growing Green: A Young Person's Guide to Taking Care of the Planet. Goodings, Christina. 2008. (ENG.). 32p. (J). (gr. k-2). 12.95 *(978-0-7459-6171-2(1))* Lion Hudson PLC GBR. Dist: Independent Pubs. Group.

—Growing Strong: A Book about Taking Care of Yourself. Goodings, Christina. 2010. (ENG.). 32p. (J). (gr. k-2). 12.99 *(978-0-7459-6158-3(4))* Lion Hudson PLC GBR. Dist: Independent Pubs. Group.

—Johnny Appleseed. Shepherd, Jodie. 2010. (ENG.). 32p. (J). (gr. -1-3). pap. 3.99 *(978-0-545-22306-5(7),* Cartwheel Bks.) Scholastic, Inc.

—Let's Be Friends. Choi, SeoYun. rev. ed. 2014. (MySELF Bookshelf: Social & Emotional Learning/Social Awareness Ser.). (ENG.). 32p. (J). (gr. k-2). pap. 11.94 *(978-1-60357-658-1(4))*; lib. bdg. 22.60 *(978-1-59953-649-1(8))* Norwood Hse. Pr.

—The Moon Followed Me Home. Bewley, Elizabeth. 2007. (ENG.). 6p. (J). (gr. -1-3). 12.95 *(978-1-58117-598-1(1),* Intervisual/Piggy Toes) Bendon, Inc.

—This Is My Monster. Taplin, Sam. 2008. (Noisy Touchy-Feely Board Bks). 10p. (J). bds. 16.99 *(978-0-7945-2353-4(6),* Usborne) EDC Publishing.

—The Ugly Duckling. (Flip-Up Fairy Tales Ser.). (ENG.). 24p. (J). (gr. -1-2). 2007. *(978-1-84643-095-4(X))*; 2006. pap. *(978-1-84643-022-0(4))* Child's Play International Ltd.

—The Usborne Book of Poems for Little Children. Taplin, Sam. 2007. 47p. (J). 11.99 *(978-0-7945-1426-6(X),* Usborne) EDC Publishing.

Furuya, Michael. The Adventures of Gary & Harry: A Tale of Two Turtles. Matsumoto, Lisa. 2006. (J). 16.95 *(978-0-9647491-4-6(9))* Lehua, Inc.

—Keoni's Special Gift. 2009. (J). *(978-1-56647-915-8(0))* Mutual Publishing LLC.

Furuya, Usamaru. Short Cuts, Vol. 2. Furuya, Usamaru. 2003. (Short Cuts Ser.). (ENG.). 128p. pap. 12.95 *(978-1-59116-069-4(3))* Viz Media.

Futaki, Attila & Gaspar, Tamas. The Sea of Monsters. Riordan, Rick & Venditti, Robert. 2013. (Percy Jackson & the Olympians Ser.). (ENG.). 128p. (J). (gr. 5-9). 19.99 *(978-1-4231-4529-5(1))*; pap. 12.99 *(978-1-4231-4550-9(X))* Hyperion Pr.

Futaki, Attila & Guilhaumond, Gregory. The Titan's Curse. Riordan, Rick & Venditti, Robert. 2013. (Percy Jackson & the Olympians Ser.). (ENG.). 128p. (J). (gr. 5-9). pap. 14.99 *(978-1-4231-4551-6(8))* Hyperion Pr.

—The Titan's Curse. Venditti, Robert & Riordan, Rick. 2013. (Percy Jackson & the Olympians Ser.). (ENG.). 128p. (J). (gr. 5-9). 19.99 *(978-1-4231-4530-1(5))* Disney Pr.

Futaki, Attila & Villarrubia, Jose. The Lightning Thief. Riordan, Rick & Venditti, Robert. 2010. (Percy Jackson & the Olympians Ser.). (ENG.). 128p. (J). (gr. 5-9). 19.99 *(978-1-4231-1696-7(8))*; pap. 12.99 *(978-1-4231-1710-0(7))* Hyperion Pr.

Futran, Eric. A Kiss Means I Love You. Futran, Eric, photos by. Allen, Kathryn Madeline. 2012. (ENG.). 24p. (J). (gr. -1-k). 15.99 *(978-0-8075-4186-9(9))* Whitman, Albert & Co.

Futran, Eric, photos by. Show Me Happy. Allen, Kathryn Madeline. 2015. (ENG., 24p. (J). (gr. -1-k). 15.99 *(978-0-8075-7349-5(3))* Whitman, Albert & Co.

—Somewhere Today: A Book of Peace. Thomas, Shelley Moore. 2004. (ENG., 24p. (J). (gr. k-4). reprint ed. 6.99 *(978-0-8075-7544-4(5))* Whitman, Albert & Co.

Futterer, Ralf. Emile. Futterer, Kurt. Gray, Bronwen et al, trs. from GER. 2004. (ENG.). 32p. (J). *(978-1-931561-95-2(8))* MacAdam/Cage Publishing, Inc.

Fyffe, Brian. Christmas Counting: Count & Create with 42 Holiday Stickers. 2003. 10p. (J). (gr. -1-18). bds. 4.99 *(978-1-57151-722-7(7))* Playhouse Publishing.

—Easter Colors Sticker Book. Mackall, Dandi Daley. 2004. 10p. (J). (gr. -1-18). bds. 4.99 *(978-1-57151-723-4(5))* Playhouse Publishing.

G

G., Ashley R. Mona Whine'ona: (the List) Green, Melissa J. & G., Melissa J. 2007. 20p. per. 24.95 *(978-1-4241-8451-4(7))* PublishAmerica, Inc.

GI, Holly. Best of Sabrina the Teenage Witch. Golliher, Bill. 2011. (Archie & Friends All-Stars Ser.: 15). (ENG.). 128p. (J). (gr. 4-7). pap. 9.95 *(978-1-879794-75-7(6),* Archie Comics) Archie Comic Pubns., Inc.

Gaash, Elisheva. My Middos World: Dina-dee Is a Goody, 4. Beckerman, Menucha. 2003. (My Middos World Ser.: Vol. 4). 24p. (J). (gr. k-5). 11.95 *(978-1-931681-03-2(1))* Israel Bookshop Pubns.

—My Middos World: Dina-dee Loves Shabbos, 5. Beckerman, Menucha. 2003. (My Middos World Ser.: Vol. 5). 24p. (J). (gr. k-5). 11.95 *(978-1-931681-04-9(X))* Israel Bookshop Pubns.

—My Middos World: Why Did Dina-dee's Face Shine, 6. Beckerman, Menucha. 2003. (My Middos World Ser.: Vol. 6). 24p. (J). (gr. k-5). 11.95 *(978-1-931681-05-6(8))* Israel Bookshop Pubns.

Gaban, Jesus. A la Sombra del Maestro. Farias, Juan. 2003. (SPA.). 108p. (J). (gr. 5-8). pap. 9.95 *(978-84-204-4872-5(9))* Santillana USA Publishing Co., Inc.

—No Somos Irrompibles. Bornemann, Elsa. (SPA.). 117p. (YA). (gr. 5-8). pap. *(978-84-207-4249-6(X),* GS5807) Grupo Anaya, S.A. ESP. Dist: Lectorum Pubns., Inc.

—Rafael Alberti para Ninos. Alberti, Rafael. (SPA.). 164p. (J). (gr. 4-6). 20.76 *(978-84-305-9290-6(3),* SU0175) Susaeta Ediciones, S.A. ESP. Dist: Lectorum Pubns., Inc.

—Tiempo de Nubes Negras. Alonso, Manuel L. & Alonso Gómez, Manuel L. 4th ed. 2004.Tr. of Time for Black Clouds. (SPA.). 88p. (J). (gr. 6-8). pap. 12.99 *(978-84-207-7770-2(6))* Grupo Anaya, S.A. ESP. Dist: Lectorum Pubns., Inc.

Gabán, Jesús. Antología. Gabán, Jesús. Fuertes, Gloria. (SPA.). 172p. (J). (gr. 4-5). 20.80 *(978-84-305-9869-4(3),* SU32990) Susaeta Ediciones, S.A. ESP. Dist: Lectorum Pubns., Inc.

Gabán, Jesús. Cuentos de Risa: El Perro Picatoste. Gabán, Jesús, tr. Fuertes, Gloria. 2003. (SPA.). 124p. *(978-84-305-8308-9(4),* SU5206) Susaeta Ediciones, S.A. ESP. Dist: Lectorum Pubns., Inc.

Gabbey, Terry. Daily Life on a Southern Plantation. Slingsby, Miki, photos by. Erickson, Paul. 2006. 48p. (J). (gr. 2-5). reprint ed. pap. 8.00 *(978-1-4223-5727-9(9))* DIANE Publishing Co.

Gabel, Deborah Boudreau. Deep in the Woods. Alossa, Janet M. l.t. ed. 2005. 24p. (J). lib. bdg. 16.95 *(978-0-9769360-0-8(3),* 0503) Adam Hill Pubns.

Gaber, Susan. Angel Coming. Henson, Heather. 2011. (ENG.). 40p. (J). (gr. -1-1). pap. 16.99 *(978-1-4424-3077-8(X),* Atheneum Bks. for Young Readers) Simon & Schuster Children's Publishing.

—The Baker's Dozen. Forest, Heather. 2013. (ENG.). 32p. (J). (gr. -1-3). 8.95 *(978-1-939160-70-6(7))* August Hse. Pubs., Inc.

—The Contest Between the Sun & the Wind: An Aesop's Fable. Forest, Heather. 2013. (ENG.). 32p. (J). (gr. -1-3). pap. 8.95 *(978-1-939160-66-9(9))* August Hse. Pubs., Inc.

—The Finest Horse in Town. Martin, Jacqueline Briggs. 2003. 32p. (J). 17.95 *(978-1-930900-27-1(9))* Purple Hse. Pr.

—The Little Red Hen: An Old Fable. 2006. (ENG.). 32p. (J). (gr. k-3). 16.95 *(978-0-87483-795-7(2))* August Hse. Pubs., Inc.

—Ten Sleepy Sheep. Root, Phyllis. 2009. (ENG.). 12p. (J). (-k). bds. 7.99 *(978-0-7636-4142-9(1))* Candlewick Pr.

—The Very First Thanksgiving Day. Greene, Rhonda Gowler. 2006. (ENG.). 32p. (J). (gr. -1-1). 6.99 *(978-1-4169-1916-2(3),* Atheneum Bks. for Young Readers) Simon & Schuster Children's Publishing.

—Waiting Out the Storm. Macken, JoAnn Early. 2010. (ENG.). 32p. (J). (gr. -1-3). 15.99 *(978-0-7636-3378-3(X))* Candlewick Pr.

—The Woman Who Flummoxed the Fairies. Forest, Heather. 2013. (ENG.). 32p. (J). (gr. -1-3). 8.95 *(978-1-939160-71-3(5))* August Hse. Pubs., Inc.

Gable, Brian. A-B-A-B-A: A Book of Pattern Play. Cleary, Brian P. 2010. (Math Is CATegorical (r) Ser.). (ENG.). 32p. (gr. k-3). lib. bdg. 16.95 *(978-0-8225-7880-2(8))* Lerner Publishing Group.

—A-B-A-B-A-A Book of Pattern Play. Cleary, Brian P. 2012. (Math Is CATegorical (r) Ser.). (ENG.). 32p. (gr. k-3). pap. 6.95 *(978-0-7613-8502-8(9),* Millbrook Pr.) Lerner Publishing Group.

—The Action of Subtraction. Cleary, Brian P. (Math Is CATegorical (r) Ser.). (ENG.). 32p. (gr. k-3). 2008. pap. 6.95 *(978-1-58013-843-7(8),* First Avenue Editions); 2006. lib. bdg. 16.95 *(978-0-7613-9461-7(3),* Millbrook Pr.) Lerner Publishing Group.

—Breezier, Cheesier, Newest, & Bluest: What Are Comparatives & Superlatives? Cleary, Brian P. 2013. (Words Are CATegorical (r) Ser.). (ENG.). 32p. (gr. 2-5). lib. bdg. 16.95 *(978-0-7613-5362-1(3),* Millbrook Pr.) Lerner Publishing Group.

Gable, Brian. Breezier, Cheesier, Newest, & Bluest: What Are Comparatives & Superlatives? Cleary, Brian. 2015. (Words Are CATegorical (r) Ser.). (ENG.). 32p. (gr. 2-5). pap. 6.95 *(978-1-4677-6078-2(1),* Millbrook Pr.) Lerner Publishing Group.

Gable, Brian. But & for, yet & Nor: What Is a Conjunction? Cleary, Brian P. (Words Are CATegorical (r) Ser.). (ENG.). 32p. (gr. 2-5). 2012. pap. 6.95 *(978-0-7613-8503-5(7),* Millbrook Pr.); 2010. pap. 39.62 *(978-0-7613-9205-7(X),* Millbrook Pr.); 2010. lib. bdg. 16.95 *(978-0-8225-9153-5(7))* Lerner Publishing Group.

—Cool! Whoa! Ah & Oh! What Is an Interjection? Cleary, Brian P. (Words Are CATegorical (r) Ser.). (ENG.). 32p. (gr. 2-5). 2013. pap. 6.95 *(978-1-4677-0900-2(X),* Millbrook Pr.); 2011. 16.95 *(978-1-58013-594-8(3))* Lerner Publishing Group.

—Dearly, Nearly, Insincerely: What Is an Adverb? Cleary, Brian P. (Words Are CATegorical (r) Ser.). (ENG.). 32p. (gr. 2-5). 2005. per. 6.95 *(978-1-57505-919-8(3))*; 2003. 16.95 *(978-0-87614-924-9(7))* Lerner Publishing Group.

—Dearly, Nearly, Insincerely: What Is an Adverb? Cleary, Brian P. 2006. (Words Are Categorical Ser.). (gr. k-2). 17.00 *(978-0-7569-6881-6(X))* Perfection Learning Corp.

—A Dollar, a Penny, How Much & How Many? Cleary, Brian P. 2012. (Math Is CATegorical (r) Ser.). (ENG.). 32p. (gr. k-3). lib. bdg. 16.95 *(978-0-8225-7882-6(4),* Millbrook Pr.) Lerner Publishing Group.

—A Dollar, a Penny, How Much & How Many? Cleary, Brian. 2014. (Math Is CATegorical (r) Ser.). 32p. (gr. k-3). pap. 6.95 *(978-1-4677-2629-0(X),* Millbrook Pr.) Lerner Publishing Group.

—Feet & Puppies, Thieves & Guppies: What Are Irregular Plurals? Cleary, Brian P. (Words Are CATegorical (r) Ser.). (ENG.). 32p. (gr. 2-5). 2014. pap. 6.95 *(978-1-4677-2627-6(3))*; 2012. lib. bdg. 16.95 *(978-0-7613-4918-1(9))* Lerner Publishing Group. (Millbrook Pr.).

—A Fraction's Goal: Parts of a Whole. Cleary, Brian P. 2011. (Math Is CATegorical (r) Ser.). (ENG.). 32p. (gr. k-3). lib. bdg. 16.95 *(978-0-8225-7881-9(6),* Millbrook Pr.) Lerner Publishing Group.

—A Fraction's Goal - Parts of a Whole. Cleary, Brian P. 2013. (Math Is CATegorical (r) Ser.). (ENG.). 32p. (gr. k-3). pap. 6.95 *(978-1-4677-1380-1(5),* Millbrook Pr.) Lerner Publishing Group.

—How Long or How Wide? A Measuring Guide. Cleary, Brian P. 2007. (Math Is CATegorical (r) Ser.). (ENG.). 32p. (gr. k-3). lib. bdg. 16.95 *(978-0-8225-6694-6(X),* Millbrook Pr.) Lerner Publishing Group.

—How Long or How Wide? A Measuring Guide. Cleary, Brian. 2009. (Math Is CATegorical (r) Ser.). (ENG.). 32p. (gr. k-3). pap. 6.95 *(978-1-58013-844-4(6),* First Avenue Editions) Lerner Publishing Group.

—How Much Can a Bare Bear Bear? Cleary, Brian P. 2004. (Words Are CATegorical (r) Ser.). (ENG.). (gr. 2-5). pap. 39.62 *(978-0-8225-9899-2(X))* Lerner Publishing Group.

—How Much Can a Bare Bear Bear? What Are Homonyms & Homophones? Cleary, Brian P. (Words Are CATegorical (r) Ser.). (ENG.). 32p. (gr. 2-5). 2007. per. 6.95 *(978-0-8225-6710-3(5),* First Avenue Editions); 2005. lib. bdg. 16.95 *(978-1-57505-824-5(3))* Lerner Publishing Group.

—I & You & Don't Forget Who: What Is a Pronoun? Cleary, Brian P. 2004. (Words Are CATegorical (r) Ser.). (ENG.). 32p. (gr. 2-5). 16.95 *(978-1-57505-596-1(1))* Lerner Publishing Group.

—I & You & Don't Forget Who: What Is a Pronoun? Cleary, Brian P. 2006. (Words Are Categorical Ser.). (gr. 2-4). 17.00 *(978-0-7569-6728-4(7))* Perfection Learning Corp.

—I & You & Don't Forget Who: What Is a Prounoun? Cleary, Brian P. 2006. (Words Are CATegorical (r) Ser.). (ENG.). 32p. (gr. 2-5). per. 6.95 *(978-0-8225-6469-0(6),* First Avenue Editions) Lerner Publishing Group.

—I'm & Won't, They're & Don't: What's a Contraction? Cleary, Brian P. (Words Are CATegorical (r) Ser.). (ENG.). 32p. (gr. 2-5). 2012. pap. 6.95 *(978-0-7613-8504-2(5),* Millbrook Pr.); 2010. lib. bdg. 16.95 *(978-0-8225-9155-9(3))* Lerner Publishing Group.

—Jordan in Pictures. Burns, Diane L. et al. 2nd ed. 2005. (Visual Geography Series, Second Ser.). (ENG.). 80p. (gr. 5-12). 31.93 *(978-0-8225-1173-1(8))* Lerner Publishing Group.

—Lazily, Crazily, Just a Bit Nasally: More about Adverbs. Cleary, Brian P. (Words Are CATegorical (r) Ser.). (ENG.). 32p. (gr. 2-5). 2010. pap. 6.95 *(978-1-58013-937-3(X),* First Avenue Editions); 2008. lib. bdg. 16.95 *(978-0-8225-7848-2(4))* Lerner Publishing Group.

—A Lime, a Mime, a Pool of Slime: More about Nouns. Cleary, Brian. (Words Are CATegorical (r) Ser.). (ENG.). 32p. (gr. 2-5). 2008. pap. 6.95 *(978-1-58013-934-2(5),* First Avenue Editions); 2006. lib. bdg. 16.95 *(978-1-57505-937-2(1),* Millbrook Pr.) Lerner Publishing Group.

G

—Madam & Nun & 1001: What Is a Palindrome? Cleary, Brian P. 2012. (Words Are CATegorical (r) Ser.). (ENG.). 32p. (gr. 2-5). lib. bdg. 16.95 *(978-0-7613-4919-8(7),* Millbrook Pr.) Lerner Publishing Group.

—Madam & Nun And 1001: What Is a Palindrome? Cleary, Brian. 2014. (Words Are CATegorical (r) Ser.). 32p. (gr. 2-5). pap. 6.95 *(978-1-4677-2628-3(1),* Millbrook Pr.) Lerner Publishing Group.

—The Mission of Addition. Cleary, Brian P. (Math Is CATegorical (r) Ser.). (ENG.). 32p. (gr. k-3). 2007. pap. 6.95 *(978-0-8225-6695-3(8),* First Avenue Editions); 2005. lib. bdg. 16.95 *(978-1-57505-859-7(6),* Millbrook Pr.) Lerner Publishing Group.

—On the Scale, a Weighty Tale. Cleary, Brian P. (Math Is CATegorical (r) Ser.). (ENG.). 32p. (gr. k-3). 2010. pap. 6.95 *(978-1-58013-845-1(4),* First Avenue Editions); 2008. 16.95 *(978-0-8225-7851-2(4))* Lerner Publishing Group.

—Pitch & Throw, Grasp & Know: What Is a Synonym? Cleary, Brian P. (Words Are CATegorical (r) Ser.). (ENG.). 32p. (gr. 2-5). 2007. pap. 6.95 *(978-0-8225-6877-3(2),* First Avenue Editions); 2005. 16.95 *(978-1-57505-796-5(4))* Lerner Publishing Group.

—Quirky, Jerky, Extra Perky: More about Adjectives. Cleary, Brian P. (Words Are CATegorical (r) Ser.). (ENG.). 32p. (gr. 2-5). 2009. pap. 6.95 *(978-1-58013-936-6(1),* First Avenue Editions); 2007. lib. bdg. 16.95 *(978-0-8225-6709-7(1),* Millbrook Pr.) Lerner Publishing Group.

—A Second, a Minute, a Week with Days in It: A Book about Time. Cleary, Brian P. 2013. (Math Is CATegorical (r) Ser.). (ENG.). 32p. (gr. k-3). lib. bdg. 16.95 *(978-0-8225-7883-3(2),* Millbrook Pr.) Lerner Publishing Group.

—Skin Like Milk, Hair of Silk: What Are Similes & Metaphors? Cleary, Brian P. (Words Are CATegorical (r) Ser.). (ENG.). (gr. 2-5). 2011. 32p. pap. 6.95 *(978-0-7613-3945-8(0));* 2009. 32p. 16.95 *(978-0-8225-9151-1(0));* 2007. pap. 39.62 *(978-0-7613-8361-1(1))* Lerner Publishing Group. (Millbrook Pr.).

—Slide & Slurp, Scratch & Burp: More about Verbs. Cleary, Brian P. (Words Are CATegorical (r) Ser.). (ENG.). (gr. 2-5). 2007. 32p. lib. bdg. 16.95 *(978-0-8225-6207-8(3),* Millbrook Pr.); 2006. pap. 39.62 *(978-0-7613-4815-3(8))* Lerner Publishing Group.

—Slide & Slurp, Scratch & Burp: More about Verbs. Cleary, Brian. 2009. (Words Are CATegorical (r) Ser.). (ENG.). 32p. (gr. 2-5). pap. 6.95 *(978-1-58013-935-9(3),* First Avenue Editions) Lerner Publishing Group.

—Stop & Go, Yes & No. Cleary, Brian P. 2009. (Words Are CATegorical (r) Ser.). (ENG.). (gr. 2-5). pap. 39.62 *(978-0-8225-9904-3(X))* Lerner Publishing Group.

—Stop & Go, Yes & No: What Is an Antonym? Cleary, Brian P. (Words Are CATegorical (r) Ser.). 32p. (gr. 2-5). 2008. per. 6.95 *(978-0-8225-9025-5(5),* First Avenue Editions); 2006. lib. bdg. 16.95 *(978-1-57505-860-3(X),* Millbrook Pr.) Lerner Publishing Group.

—Straight & Curvy, Meek & Nervy: More about Antonyms. Cleary, Brian P. (Words Are CATegorical (r) Ser.). (ENG.). 32p. (gr. 2-5). 2011. pap. 6.95 *(978-1-58013-939-7(6),* Millbrook Pr.); 2009. 16.95 *(978-0-8225-7878-9(6));* 2008. pap. 39.62 *(978-0-7613-7605-7(4),* Millbrook Pr.) Lerner Publishing Group.

—Stroll & Walk, Babble & Talk: More about Synonyms. Cleary, Brian P. (Words Are CATegorical (r) Ser.). (ENG.). 32p. (gr. 2-5). 2010. pap. 6.95 *(978-1-58013-938-0(8),* First Avenue Editions); 2008. 16.95 *(978-0-8225-7850-5(6))* Lerner Publishing Group.

—Thumbtacks, Earwax, Lipstick, Dipstick: What Is a Compound Word? Cleary, Brian P. (Words Are CATegorical (r) Ser.). (ENG.). 32p. (gr. 2-5). 2013. pap. 6.95 *(978-1-4677-1379-5(1));* 2011. lib. bdg. 16.95 *(978-0-7613-4917-4(0))* Lerner Publishing Group. (Millbrook Pr.).

—Under, over, by the Clover: What Is a Preposition? Cleary, Brian P. 2003. (Words Are CATegorical (r) Ser.). (ENG.). 32p. (gr. 2-5). pap. 6.95 *(978-1-57505-201-4(6))* Lerner Publishing Group.

—Under, over, by the Clover: What Is a Preposition? Cleary, Brian P. 2006. (Words Are Categorical Ser.). (gr. 2-4). 16.95 *(978-0-7569-6885-4(2))* Perfection Learning Corp.

—Windows, Rings, & Grapes: A Look at Different Shapes. Cleary, Brian P. 2009. (Math Is CATegorical (r) Ser.). (ENG.). 32p. (gr. k-3). 16.95 *(978-0-8225-7879-6(4))* Lerner Publishing Group.

—Windows, Rings, & Grapes - A Look at Different Shapes. Cleary, Brian P. 2011. (Math Is CATegorical Ser.). pap. 39.62 *(978-0-7613-8360-4(3));* (ENG.). 32p. pap. 6.95 *(978-1-58013-846-8(2))* Lerner Publishing Group. (Millbrook Pr.).

Gable, Brian, jt. illus. see Goneau, Martin.

Gabler, Michael. The Saint Vincent Coloring Book. Boosel, Brian D. 2005. 36p. (J). 9.99 *(978-0-9708216-7-6(0))* St. Vincent Archabbey Pubns.

Gabriel, Andrea. Grandes Migraciones de la Ballena Gris. 1 vol. Lindsey, Marta. 2014. (SPA.). 32p. (J). (gr. k-3). pap. 9.95 ***(978-1-62855-468-7(1))*** Arbordale Publishing.

Gabriel, Andrea. Little Gray's Great Migration. 1 vol. Lindsey, Marta. 2014. (ENG.). 32p. (J). (gr. k-3). 17.95 *(978-1-62855-452-6(5))* Arbordale Publishing.

—Sequoyah & the Cherokee Alphabet. Townsend, Dana E. 2005. (Voices Reading Ser.). 32p. (J). *(978-0-7367-2953-6(4))* Zaner-Bloser, Inc.

Gabriel, Andrea. Where Do I Sleep? A Pacific Northwest Lullaby. Blomgren, Jennifer. (ENG.). 20p. (— 1). 2015. bds. 9.99 ***(978-1-63217-019-4(1),*** Little Bigfoot); 2008. (J). pap. 10.99 *(978-1-57061-593-1(4))* Sasquatch Bks.

Gabriel, Andrea. Where Would I Be in an Evergreen Tree? Blomgren, Jennifer. 2011. (ENG.). 32p. (J). (gr. -1-2). pap. 10.99 *(978-1-57061-753-9(8))* Sasquatch Bks.

Gabriel, Andrea. Why Do I Sing? Animal Songs of the Pacific Northwest. Blomgren, Jennifer. (ENG.). 2015. 20p. (— 1). bds. 9.99 ***(978-1-63217-020-0(5),*** Little Bigfoot); 2013. 32p. (J). (gr. -1-2). 16.99 *(978-1-57061-845-1(3))* Sasquatch Bks.

Gabriel, Andrea. The Zoopendous Surprise! Hensel, Boots. 2009. (ENG.). 32p. (J). (gr. -1-k). 16.95 *(978-0-9792035-5-8(4))* Pleasant St. Pr.

Gabriel, Andrea. My Favorite Bear. Gabriel, Andrea. 2004. (ENG.). 32p. (J). (-k). pap. 7.95 *(978-1-58089-039-7(3))* Charlesbridge Publishing, Inc.

Gabriel, Evette. Buck's Bad Dreams. Scotto, Michael. 2009. (J). *(978-1-935193-46-3(5))* National Network of Digital Schls.

—Builda the Re-Bicycler. Scotto, Michael. 2009. (J). *(978-1-935193-22-7(8))* National Network of Digital Schls.

Gabriel, Evette, et al. Just Flash. Scotto, Michael. 2009. (J). *(978-1-935193-50-0(3))* National Network of Digital Schls.

Gabriel, Evette. Sweet Tooth Bun. Scotto, Michael. 2009. (J). *(978-1-935193-48-7(1))* National Network of Digital Schls.

Gabrielov, Julia. With You Always. Leibovici, Danielle. l.t. ed. 2012. (ENG.). 62p. pap. 14.95 *(978-1-4565-2627-6(8))* CreateSpace Independent Publishing Platform.

Gabrili, Alexandra. Nicholas Wins the Prize 1: Young Nicholas Experiences the Sacrament of Confession. Iakovos-Dalalakis, Helen. 2003. (ENG.). 24p. (J). (gr. 2-6). 15.95 *(978-1-880971-82-6(8))* Light & Life Publishing Co.

Gaby, Hansen. Are You Ready for Bed. Jane, Johnson. 2010. 24p. bds. 8.95 *(978-1-58925-806-8(1))* Tiger Tales.

Gace, Mariah. Oh, No, Pluto! Bale, Mary. 2011. 33p. (J). pap. 9.95 *(978-1-935086-98-7(7))* Mother's Hse. Publishing.

Gadd, Maxine. Kandide & the Secret of the Mists. Zimmerman, Diana S. 2008. (Calabiyau Chronicles Ser.: Bk. 1). 296p. (YA). (gr. 5-18). 17.99 *(978-0-9794328-3-5(9));*Bk. 1. 289p. (J). (gr. 4-7). pap. 9.99 *(978-0-9794328-2-8(0))* Noesis Publishing.

Gadeselli, Natalie. Curiosity. Philips, Lyn D. 2013. 32p. pap. *(978-1-904928-27-0(7))* Copeland & Wickson.

Gadra, Jessica. Sneaking Treats. McRoberts, Eddison. 2013. 48p. pap. 9.95 *(978-1-62137-298-1(7))* Virtualbookworm.com Publishing, Inc.

—Sneaking Treats: A Halloween Hunt. McRoberts, Eddison. 2012. 48p. 19.95 *(978-1-62137-136-6(0))* Virtualbookworm.com Publishing, Inc.

Gadtan Jean Louis, Rosley. Michael's First Word! Beach, Linda M. 2009. 20p. pap. 12.49 *(978-1-4389-0766-6(4))* AuthorHouse.

Gaffney, Ellen. Wings for a Flower. Gaffney, Ellen. 2013. 32p. 16.95 *(978-0-9882212-6-0(8))* Three Bean Pr.

Gag, Flavia. The Wily Woodchucks. Travers, Georgia. 2009. (Fesler-Lampert Minnesota Heritage Ser.). (ENG.). 32p. 14.95 *(978-0-8166-6548-8(6))* Univ. of Minnesota Pr.

Gág, Wanda. Gone Is Gone: Or the Story of a Man Who Wanted to Do Housework. Gág, Wanda. 2003. (Fesler-Lampert Minnesota Heritage Ser.). 64p. 14.95 *(978-0-8166-4243-4(5))* Univ. of Minnesota Pr.

—Millions of Cats. Gág, Wanda. gif. ed. 2006. (ENG.). 32p. (J). (gr. -1-k). pap. 7.99 *(978-0-14-240708-0(9),* Puffin) Penguin Publishing Group.

—Millions of Cats. Gág, Wanda. 2006. (gr. -1-3). 18.00 *(978-0-7569-6785-7(6))* Perfection Learning Corp.

—More Tales from Grimm. Gág, Wanda. Grimm, Wilhelm K. & Grimm, Jacob. 2006. (Fesler-Lampert Minnesota Heritage Ser.). (ENG.). 272p. (gr. 4-7). per. 16.95 *(978-0-8166-4936-9(3))* Univ. of Minnesota Pr.

Gág, Wanda. Tales from Grimm. Gág, Wanda, tr. Grimm, Wilhelm K. & Grimm, Jacob. 2006. (Fesler-Lampert Minnesota Heritage Ser.). (ENG.). 256p. (gr. 4-7). per. 16.95 *(978-0-8166-4936-5(7))* Univ. of Minnesota Pr.

Gage, Amy Glaser & McIntyre, Connie. Upside Downside Inside Out: Poems about Being a Kid. Gage, Amy Glaser & McIntyre, Connie. 2nd rev. ed. 2003. 49p. (J). per. 9.95 *(978-0-9677685-4-0(3))* Grannie Annie Family Story Celebration, The.

Gage, Christos. Angel & Faith Volume 3: Family Reunion: Family Reunion. Jackson, Dan. Allie, Scott & Hahn, Sierra, eds. 2013. (ENG.). 136p. pap. 17.99 *(978-1-61655-079-0(1))* Dark Horse Comics.

Gage, James. The Children's Hour. Smith, Patty. 2013. (ENG.). 38p. pap. 9.95 *(978-0-615-74446-9(X))* Smith, Patricia.

Gage, Kathryn. Wow, I'm a Big Brother. 2011. 48p. (J). spiral bd. 6.25 net. *(978-1-890703-44-8(3))* Penny Laine Papers, Inc.

—Wow, I'm a Big Sister. 2011. 48p. (J). spiral bd. 6.25 net. *(978-1-890703-45-5(1))* Penny Laine Papers, Inc.

Gaggiotti, Lucia. How Did That Get in My Lunchbox? The Story of Food. Butterworth, Christine. 2011. (ENG.). 32p. (J). (gr. k-3). 12.99 *(978-0-7636-5005-6(6))* Candlewick Pr.

—How Did That Get in My Lunchbox? The Story of Food. Butterworth, Chris. 2013. (ENG.). 32p. (J). (gr. k-3). 5.99 *(978-0-7636-6503-6(7))* Candlewick Pr.

Gaggiotti, Lucia. Where Did My Clothes Come From? Butterworth, Chris. 2015. (ENG.). 32p. (J). (gr. k-3). 12.99 ***(978-0-7636-7750-3(7))*** Candlewick Pr.

Gagliardo, Lucy. Giving Back to the Earth: Teacher's Guide to Project Puffin & Other Seabird Studies. Salmansohn, Pete & Kress, Stephen W. 2010. (National Audubon Society Book). 80p. (Orig.). (gr. 3-6). pap., tchr. ed. 9.95 *(978-0-88448-172-0(7))* Tilbury Hse. Pubs.

Gagnon, Celeste, et al. Franklin & the Cookies. Jennings, Sharon. 2005. 32p. (J). lib. bdg. 15.38 *(978-1-4242-1167-8(0))* Fitzgerald Bks.

—Franklin & the Scooter. Jennings, Sharon. 2004. 32p. (J). lib. bdg. 15.38 *(978-1-4242-1169-2(7))* Fitzgerald Bks.

Gagnon, Céleste. Franklin the Detective. Jennings, Sharon et al. 2004. 32p. (J). pap. *(978-0-439-41822-5(4))* Scholastic, Inc.

Gagnon, Celeste, et al. Franklin the Detective. Jennings, Sharon. 2004. 32p. (J). lib. bdg. 15.38 *(978-1-4242-1171-5(9))* Fitzgerald Bks.

Gagnon, Céleste. Franklin's Library Book. Jennings, Sharon et al. 2005. 32p. (J). *(978-0-439-82297-8(1))* Scholastic, Inc.

Gagnon, Celeste, jt. illus. see Gagnon, Cilleste.

Gagnon, Cileste & Gagnon, Celeste. Knotting: Make Your Own Basketball Nets, Guitar Straps, Sports Bags & More. Sadler, Judy Ann & Sadler, Judy. 2006. (Kids Can Do It Ser.). (ENG.). 40p. (J). (gr. 3-7). 6.95 *(978-1-55337-834-1(2))* Kids Can Pr., Ltd. CAN. Dist: Univ. of Toronto Pr.

Gahng, Hwa-kyeong. I Am a Little Monk: Thailand. Joo, Mi-hwa. Cowley, Joy, ed. 2015. (Global Kids Storybooks Ser.). (ENG.). 32p. (gr. 1-4). 26.65 ***(978-1-925246-06-3(X));*** 26.65 ***(978-1-925246-32-2(9));*** 7.99 ***(978-1-925246-58-2(2))*** ChoiceMaker Pty. Ltd., The AUS. (Big and SMALL). Dist: Lerner Publishing Group.

Gahng, In. Crayon Road: Imagination - Lines. Jeong, Jini. Cowley, Joy, ed. 2015. (Step up - Creative Thinking Ser.). (ENG.). 32p. (gr. -1-2). 26.65 ***(978-1-925246-10-0(8));*** 26.65 ***(978-1-925246-36-0(1));*** 7.99 ***(978-1-925246-62-9(0))*** ChoiceMaker Pty. Ltd., The AUS. (Big and SMALL). Dist: Lerner Publishing Group.

Gaillard, Jason. Running Shoes. Lipp, Frederick. 2008. 32p. (J). (gr. 2-5). 16.95 *(978-1-58089-175-2(6));* pap. 7.95 *(978-1-58089-176-9(4))* Charlesbridge Publishing, Inc.

Gaillard, Jason. Bread Song. Gaillard, Jason, tr. Lipp, Frederick J. 2004. (J). 15.95 *(978-1-59336-000-9(2));* pap. *(978-1-59336-001-6(0))* Mondo Publishing.

Gaisey, Christopher. Pop Goes the Weasel: A Silly Song Book. Auerbach, Annie. 2005. 12p. (J). (gr. -1-3). 12.95 *(978-1-58117-426-7(8),* Intervisual/Piggy Toes) Bendon, Inc.

Gait, Darlene. Secret of the Dance, 1 vol. Spalding, Andrea & Scow, Alfred. 2009. (ENG.). 32p. (J). (gr. -1-3). 9.95 *(978-1-55469-129-6(X))* Orca Bk. Pubs. USA.

—Soapstone Signs, 1 vol. Pinkney, Jeff. 2014. (Orca Echoes Ser.). (ENG.). 64p. (J). (gr. 2-3). pap. 6.95 *(978-1-4598-0400-5(7))* Orca Bk. Pubs. USA.

—Who's in Maxine's Tree?, 1 vol. Léger, Diane Carmel. 2006. (ENG.). 32p. (J). (gr. -1-3). 17.95 *(978-1-55143-346-2(X))* Orca Bk. Pubs. USA.

Gal, Laszlo. Beowulf, 1 vol. Katz, Welwyn Wilton. 2nd ed. 2007. (ENG.). 96p. (J). (gr. 4-7). 17.95 *(978-0-88899-807-1(4))* Groundwood Bks. CAN. Dist: Perseus-PGW.

—Tiktala, 1 vol. Shaw-MacKinnon, Margaret. 2005. (ENG.). 32p. (J). (gr. -1-3). per. 8.95 *(978-1-55005-143-8(1),* 1550051431) Fitzhenry & Whiteside, Ltd. CAN. Dist: Midpoint Trade Bks., Inc.

Gal, Susan. Bella's Fall Coat. Plourde, Lynn. 2016. (J). ***(978-1-4847-2697-6(9))*** Disney Pr.

Gal, Susan. Here Is the World: A Year of Jewish Holidays. Newman, Lesléa. 2014. (ENG.). 48p. (J). (gr. -1-2). 18.95 *(978-1-4197-1185-5(7),* Abrams Bks. for Young Readers) Abrams.

Galan-Robles, Francisco. Wee Dragonslayers. Harrar, Frank W. 2008. 45p. pap. 24.95 *(978-1-60610-851-2(4))* America Star Bks.

Galante, Ashley. There Are Monsters Here! Cimorelli, Amber. 2013. 40p. pap. 24.95 *(978-1-62709-064-3(9))* America Star Bks.

Galante, Studio & Firenze, Inklink. The Great Dinosaur Search. Heywood, Rosie. Wingate, Philippa, ed. rev. ed. 2005. (Great Searches - New Format Ser.). 32p. (J). (gr. -1). pap. 7.99 *(978-0-7945-1046-6(9),* Usborne) EDC Publishing.

Galaska, Taylor, jt. illus. see Paglia, Rhonda.

Galbraith, Alison L. Coco's Vineyard Vacation: Double Fun on Martha's Vineyard. Kelly, Sharon L. C. M. 2005. 40p. (J). 16.95 *(978-0-9766283-0-9(9))* Secret Garden Bookworks.

Galdone, Paul. Anatole. Titus, Eve. 50th ed. 2006. (ENG.). 40p. (J). (gr. k-3). 14.95 *(978-0-375-83901-6(1),* Knopf Bks. for Young Readers) Random Hse. Children's Bks.

Galdone, Paul. The Gingerbread Boy, 1 vol. Galdone, Paul. 2008. (Paul Galdone Classics Ser.). (ENG.). 40p. (J). (gr. -1-3). 10.99 *(978-0-618-89498-7(5))* Houghton Mifflin Harcourt Publishing Co.

—The Little Red Hen. Galdone, Paul. (J). (gr. -1-k). pap. 12.95 incl. audio Weston Woods Studios, Inc.

—The Three Billy Goats Gruff, 1 vol. Galdone, Paul. 2008. (Paul Galdone Classics Ser.). (ENG.). 32p. (J). (gr. -1-3). 10.99 *(978-0-618-89499-4(3))* Houghton Mifflin Harcourt Publishing Co.

—Three Little Kittens, 1 vol. Galdone, Paul. 2007. (Paul Galdone Classics Ser.). (ENG.). 32p. (J). (gr. -1-3). 10.99 *(978-0-618-85285-7(9))* Houghton Mifflin Harcourt Publishing Co.

—The Three Little Pigs, 1 vol. Galdone, Paul. 2006. (Paul Galdone Classics Ser.). (ENG.). 48p. (J). (gr. -1-3). 10.99 *(978-0-618-73277-7(2))* Houghton Mifflin Harcourt Publishing Co.

Gale, Cathy. The Day the Baby Blew Away. Puttock, Simon. 2004. (ENG.). 32p. (J). (gr. k-4). 15.95 *(978-1-84507-046-5(1),* Frances Lincoln) Quarto Publishing Group UK GBR. Dist: Hachette Bk. Group.

—Mary Is Scary. Cottringer, Anne. (Bloomsbury Paperbacks Ser.). (ENG.). 32p. (J). 2007. (gr. k-2). pap. 9.99 *(978-0-7475-7927-4(X));* 2005. (gr. -1-3). 19.99 *(978-0-7475-6464-5(7))* Bloomsbury Publishing Plc GBR. Dist: Independent Pubs. Group.

Galeano, Jose Daniel. The Adventures of Paleta Man. Ramirez, Paul & Ramirez, Matthew. 2010. (ENG.). 48p. pap. 10.99 *(978-1-4563-3701-8(7))* CreateSpace Independent Publishing Platform.

—The Adventures of Paleta Man: Secret of the Gold Medallion. Ramirez, Paul & Ramirez, Matthew. 2011. (ENG.). 52p. pap. 11.99 *(978-1-4610-3244-1(X))* CreateSpace Independent Publishing Platform.

—The Adventures of Paleta Man: Secret of the Gold Medallion Coloring Book. Ramirez, Paul & Ramirez, Matthew. 2011. (ENG.). 28p. pap. 5.38 *(978-1-4635-1158-6(2))* CreateSpace Independent Publishing Platform.

Galeano, Jose Daniel Oviedo. There's an Owl in the Closet. Walchle, Donna Douglas. 2013. (ENG.). 32p. (J). pap. 9.99 *(978-1-4908-0932-8(5),* WestBow Pr.) Author Solutions, Inc.

Galego, Ane M. Leprechaun Magic. Whittle, J. Robert & Sandilands, Joyce. 2004. 64p. (J). *(978-0-9685061-2-7(7))* Whitlands Publishing, Ltd.

Galer, Jeffrey. The Big Red Barn. Galer, Jeffrey. Galer, Christa. 2003. 40p. (J). 11.49 *(978-0-9706491-0-2(X))* Purple Crayon Studios.

Galeron, Henri. Dinosaurs. Prunier, James. 2012. (ENG.). 36p. (J). (gr. -1-k). 12.99 *(978-1-85103-379-9(3))* Moonlight Publishing, Ltd. GBR. Dist: Independent Pubs. Group.

—Dogs. Jeunesse, Gallimard & De Bourgoing, Pascale. 2008. (Scholastic First Discovery Ser.). (ENG.). 24p. (J). (gr. -1-3). pap. 5.99 *(978-0-545-00139-7(0),* Scholastic Reference) Scholastic, Inc.

Galeron, Henri. El Dinosaurio. Galeron, Henri. Prunier, Jameás et al. Prunier, Jameás & Barroso, Paz, trs. 7th ed. (Coleccion Mundo Maravilloso). (SPA.). 40p. (J). (gr. 2-4). *(978-84-348-3725-6(0),* DI9915) SM Ediciones.

—Parrots. Galeron, Henri. 2012. (ENG.). 34p. (J). (gr. k-3). pap. 11.99 *(978-1-85103-370-6(X))* Moonlight Publishing, Ltd. GBR. Dist: Independent Pubs. Group.

Galeron, Henri, jt. illus. see Prunier, James.

Galey, Chuck. A Breath of Hope. Kittinger, Jo S. 2012. (ENG.). 32p. (J). (gr. k-4). 15.95 *(978-1-61438-448-9(7))* American Bar Assn.

—The Cotton Candy Catastrophe at the Texas State Fair, 1 vol. Enderle, Dotti. 2004. (ENG.). 32p. (J). (gr. k-3). 16.99 *(978-1-58980-189-9(X))* Pelican Publishing Co., Inc.

—The Fat Stock Stampede at the Houston Livestock Show & Rodeo, 1 vol. Enderle, Dotti. 2008. (ENG.). 32p. (J). (gr. 1-3). 16.99 *(978-1-58980-443-2(0))* Pelican Publishing Co., Inc.

—Favorite Bible Heroes: Ages 2&3. Pelfrey, Wanda B. & Kuhn, Pamela J. 2005. 96p. (J). pap. 11.95 *(978-0-937282-22-9(7),* RB36196) Rainbow Pubs. & Legacy Pr.

—Favorite Bible Heroes: Ages 4&5. Sanders, Nancy I. & Kuhn, Pamela J. 2005. 96p. (J). (gr. -1-k). pap. 11.95 *(978-0-937282-23-6(5),* RB36197) Rainbow Pubs. & Legacy Pr.

—Favorite Bible Heroes: Grades 1&2. Domeij, Scott & Kuhn, Pamela J. 2005. 96p. (J). (gr. 1-2). pap. 11.95 *(978-0-937282-24-3(3),* RB36198) Rainbow Pubs. & Legacy Pr.

—Favorite Bible Heroes: Grades 3&4. Pearson, Mary R. & Kuhn, Pamela J. 2005. 96p. (J). (gr. 3-4). pap. 11.95 *(978-0-937282-25-0(1),* RB36199) Rainbow Pubs. & Legacy Pr.

—Five-Minute Sunday School Activities for Preschoolers: Bible Adventures. Davis, Mary J. 2005. 96p. (J). pap. 11.95 *(978-1-58411-046-0(5))* Rainbow Pubs. & Legacy Pr.

—Five-Minute Sunday School Activities for Preschoolers: Jesus Shows Me. Davis, Mary J. 2005. 96p. (J). pap. 11.95 *(978-1-58411-047-7(3))* Rainbow Pubs. & Legacy Pr.

—Fun Day in Mrs. Walker's Class. Little, Robert. 2005. 32p. (J). *(978-0-9701863-6-2(3))* Relde Publishing.

—Helping a Hero. Kittinger, Jo S. 2014. (ENG.). 32p. 15.95 *(978-1-62722-195-5(6))* American Bar Assn.

—Jay & the Bounty of Books, 1 vol. Ivey, Randall. 2007. (ENG.). 32p. (J). (gr. k-3). 16.99 *(978-1-58980-372-5(8))* Pelican Publishing Co., Inc.

—My Brother Dan's Delicious, 1 vol. Layne, Steven L. 2003. (ENG.). 32p. (J). (gr. k-3). 16.99 *(978-1-58980-071-7(0))* Pelican Publishing Co., Inc.

—Rock 'n' Roll Dogs, 1 vol. Davis, David. 2006. (ENG.). 32p. (J). (gr. k-3). pap. 16.99 *(978-1-58980-349-7(3))* Pelican Publishing Co., Inc.

Galey, Chuck. Un Aliento de Esperanza. Galey, Chuck. Kittinger, Jo S. & Mlawer, Teresa. 2013. (SPA.). (J). ***(978-1-61438-868-5(7))*** American Bar Assn.

Galey, Chuck & Winn, Chris. Teaching Children Memory Verses: Ages 2&3. Davis, Mary. 2005. 96p. (J). pap. 11.95 *(978-1-58411-063-7(5))* Rainbow Pubs. & Legacy Pr.

—Teaching Children Memory Verses: Grades 1&2. Davis, Mary. 2005. 96p. (J). pap. 11.95 *(978-1-58411-065-1(1))* Rainbow Pubs. & Legacy Pr.

—Teaching Children Memory Verses: Grades 3&4. Davis, Mary. 2005. 96p. (J). pap. 11.95 *(978-1-58411-066-8(X))* Rainbow Pubs. & Legacy Pr.

Galindo, Alejandro. The Party for Papá Luis/La Fiesta para Papá Luis. Bertrand, Diane Gonzales & Ventura, Gabriela Baeza. 2010. (ENG.). 32p. (J). (gr. -1-3). 16.95 *(978-1-55885-532-8(7))* Arte Publico Pr.

Galindo, Felipe. My Teacher Can Teach... Anyone! Nikola-Lisa, W. 2004. (ENG.). 32p. (J). (gr. -1-2). 16.95 *(978-1-58430-163-9(5));* pap. 9.95 *(978-1-60060-276-4(2))* Lee & Low Bks., Inc.

Galindo, Renata. The Cherry Thief. Galindo, Renata. 2014. (Child's Play Library). (ENG.). 32p. (J). *(978-1-84643-652-9(4));* ***(978-1-84643-651-2(6))*** Child's Play International Ltd.

Galkin, Simon. Favorite Russian Fairy Tales. Ransome, Arthur. 2011. (Dover Children's Thrift Classics Ser.). (ENG.). 96p. (J). (gr. 3-8). pap. 4.00 *(978-0-486-28632-7(0))* Dover Pubns., Inc.

Gall, Chris. America the Beautiful. Bates, Katharine Lee. 2010. (ENG.). 32p. (J). (gr. -1-1). pap. 6.99 *(978-0-316-08338-6(0))* Little, Brown Bks. for Young Readers.

—Little Red's Riding 'Hood. Stein, Peter. 2015. (ENG.). 40p. (J). (gr. -1-k). 16.99 *(978-0-545-60969-2(0))* Scholastic, Inc.

Gall, Chris. NanoBots. 2016. (J). ***(978-0-316-37552-8(7))*** Little Brown & Co.

Gall, Chris. Dinotrux. Gall, Chris. 2009. (Dinotrux Ser.: 1). (ENG.). 32p. (J). (gr. -1-1). 16.99 *(978-0-316-02777-9(4))* Little Brown & Co.

Gallagher-Cole, Mernie. Bed, Bats, & Beyond. Holub, Joan. 2010. (Darby Creek Exceptional Titles Ser.). (ENG.). 64p. (J). (gr. 1-3). pap. 6.95 *(978-0-7613-6451-1(X))* Lerner Publishing Group.

—Go Fly a Kite! (and Other Sayings We Don't Really Mean) Klingel, Cynthia Fitterer & Klingel, Cynthia. 2007. (Sayings

The check digit for ISBN-10 appears in parentheses after the full ISBN-13

& Phrases Ser.). (ENG.). 24p. (J). (gr. 2-5). 28.50 *(978-1-59296-904-3(6)*, 200788) Child's World, Inc., The.

—I'm All Thumbs! (and Other Odd Things We Say) Amoroso, Cynthia. 2011. (Sayings & Phrases Ser.). (ENG.). 24p. (J). (gr. 2-5). lib. bdg. 28.50 *(978-1-60253-682-1(1)*, 200781) Child's World, Inc., The.

—It's a Long Shot! (and Other Strange Sayings) Amoroso, Cynthia. 2011. (Sayings & Phrases Ser.). (ENG.). 24p. (J). (gr. 2-5). lib. bdg. 28.50 *(978-1-60253-683-8(X)*, 200782) Child's World, Inc., The.

—El Lugar de Luis, 1 vol. Blackaby, Susan. Ruiz, Carlos, tr. from ENG. 2006. (Read-It! Readers en Español: Story Collection).Tr. of Place for Mike. (SPA.). 24p. (gr. -1-3). 19.99 *(978-1-4048-1688-6(7)*, Easy Readers) Picture Window Bks.

—Max & Buddy Go to the Vet, 1 vol. Klein, Adria F. 2007. (Read-It! Readers: the Life of Max Ser.). (ENG.). 24p. (gr. -1-2). lib. bdg. 19.99 *(978-1-4048-3679-2(9)*, Easy Readers) Picture Window Bks.

—Max & the Adoption Day Party, 1 vol. Klein, Adria F. 2007. (Read-It! Readers: the Life of Max Ser.). (ENG.). 24p. (gr. -1-2). lib. bdg. 19.99 *(978-1-4048-3145-2(2)*, 1265792, Easy Readers) Picture Window Bks.

—Max Aprende la Lengua de Senas, 1 vol. Klein, Adria F. Robledo, Sol, tr. from ENG. 2007. (Read-It! Readers en Español: la Vida de Max Ser.). (SPA.). 24p. (gr. -1-3). lib. bdg. 19.99 *(978-1-4048-3796-6(5)*, Easy Readers) Picture Window Bks.

—Max Celebra el Ano Nuevo Chino, 1 vol. Klein, Adria F. Robledo, Sol, tr. from ENG. 2007. (Read-It! Readers en Español: la Vida de Max Ser.). (SPA.). 24p. (gr. -1-3). lib. bdg. 19.99 *(978-1-4048-3794-2(9)*, Easy Readers) Picture Window Bks.

—Max Celebrates Cinco de Mayo, 1 vol. Worsham, Adria F. 2008. (Read-It! Readers: the Life of Max Ser.). (ENG.). 24p. (gr. -1-2). lib. bdg. 19.99 *(978-1-4048-4759-0(6)*, Easy Readers) Picture Window Bks.

—Max Celebrates Groundhog Day, 1 vol. Worsham, Adria F. 2008. (Read-It! Readers: the Life of Max Ser.). (ENG.). 24p. (gr. -1-2). lib. bdg. 19.99 *(978-1-4048-4760-6(X))* Picture Window Bks.

—Max Celebrates Martin Luther King Jr. Day, 1 vol. Worsham, Adria F. 2008. (Read-It! Readers: the Life of Max Ser.). (ENG.). 24p. (gr. -1-2). lib. bdg. 19.99 *(978-1-4048-4761-3(8)*, Easy Readers) Picture Window Bks.

—Max Celebrates Ramadan, 1 vol. Worsham, Adria F. 2008. (Read-It! Readers: the Life of Max Ser.). (ENG.). 24p. (gr. -1-2). lib. bdg. 19.99 *(978-1-4048-4762-0(6)*, Easy Readers) Picture Window Bks.

—Max Come Al Aire Libre, 1 vol. Klein, Adria F. Robledo, Sol, tr. from ENG. 2007. (Read-It! Readers en Español: la Vida de Max Ser.). (SPA.). 24p. (gr. -1-3). lib. bdg. 19.99 *(978-1-4048-3795-9(7)*, Easy Readers) Picture Window Bks.

—Max Goes Shopping, 1 vol. Klein, Adria F. 2005. (Read-It! Readers: the Life of Max Ser.). (ENG.). 24p. (gr. -1-2). lib. bdg. 19.99 *(978-1-4048-1177-5(X))* Picture Window Bks.

—Max Goes to School. Klein, Adria F. (Read-It! Readers: the Life of Max Ser.). (ENG.). 24p. (gr. -1-2). 2007. per. 3.95 *(978-1-4048-3059-2(6))*; 2005. lib. bdg. 19.99 *(978-1-4048-1179-9(6))* Picture Window Bks. (Easy Readers).

—Max Goes to the Barber. Klein, Adria F. 2007. (Read-It! Readers: the Life of Max Ser.). (ENG.). 24p. (gr. -1-2). per. 3.95 *(978-1-4048-3060-8(X)*, Easy Readers) Picture Window Bks.

—Max Goes to the Dentist. Klein, Adria F. 2007. (Read-It! Readers: the Life of Max Ser.). (ENG.). 24p. (gr. -1-2). per. 3.95 *(978-1-4048-3061-5(8)*, Easy Readers) Picture Window Bks.

—Max Goes to the Doctor, 1 vol. Klein, Adria F. 2007. (Read-It! Readers: the Life of Max Ser.). (ENG.). 24p. (gr. -1-2). lib. bdg. 19.99 *(978-1-4048-3680-8(2))*; per. 3.95 *(978-1-4048-3686-0(1)*, 1274408) Picture Window Bks. (Easy Readers).

—Max Goes to the Farm, 1 vol. Klein, Adria F. 2007. (Read-It! Readers: the Life of Max Ser.). (ENG.). 24p. (gr. -1-2). lib. bdg. 19.99 *(978-1-4048-3678-5(0)*, Easy Readers) Picture Window Bks.

—Max Goes to the Farmers' Market, 1 vol. Klein, Adria F. 2009. (Read-It! Readers: the Life of Max Ser.). (ENG.). 24p. (gr. -1-2). 19.99 *(978-1-4048-5263-1(8)*, Easy Readers) Picture Window Bks.

—Max Goes to the Fire Station, 1 vol. Klein, Adria F. 2009. (Read-It! Readers: the Life of Max Ser.). (ENG.). 24p. (gr. -1-2). 19.99 *(978-1-4048-5266-2(2)*, Easy Readers) Picture Window Bks.

—Max Goes to the Grocery Store, 1 vol. Klein, Adria F. 2007. (Read-It! Readers: the Life of Max Ser.). (ENG.). 24p. (gr. -1-2). lib. bdg. 19.99 *(978-1-4048-3682-2(9)*, Easy Readers) Picture Window Bks.

—Max Goes to the Library. Klein, Adria F. (Read-It! Readers: the Life of Max Ser.). (ENG.). 24p. (gr. -1-2). 2007. per. 3.95 *(978-1-4048-3062-2(6))*; 2005. lib. bdg. 19.99 *(978-1-4048-1182-9(6))* Picture Window Bks. (Easy Readers).

—Max Goes to the Nature Center, 1 vol. Klein, Adria F. 2009. (Read-It! Readers: the Life of Max Ser.). (ENG.). 24p. (gr. -1-2). 19.99 *(978-1-4048-5269-3(7)*, Easy Readers) Picture Window Bks.

—Max Goes to the Playground, 1 vol. Klein, Adria F. 2007. (Read-It! Readers: the Life of Max Ser.). (ENG.). 24p. (gr. -1-2). lib. bdg. 19.99 *(978-1-4048-3681-5(0)*, Easy Readers) Picture Window Bks.

—Max Goes to the Recycling Center, 1 vol. Klein, Adria F. 2009. (Read-It! Readers: the Life of Max Ser.). (ENG.). 24p. (gr. -1-2). 19.99 *(978-1-4048-5272-3(7)*, Easy Readers) Picture Window Bks.

—Max Goes to the Zoo, 1 vol. Klein, Adria F. 2007. (Read-It! Readers: the Life of Max Ser.). (ENG.). 24p. (gr. -1-2). lib. bdg. 19.99 *(978-1-4048-3677-8(2))*; per. 3.95 *(978-1-4048-3683-9(7))* Picture Window Bks. (Easy Readers).

—Max Se Queda a Dormir, 1 vol. Klein, Adria F. Robledo, Sol, tr. from ENG. 2007. (Read-It! Readers en Español: la Vida de Max Ser.). (SPA.). 24p. (gr. -1-3). lib. bdg. 19.99 *(978-1-4048-3797-3(3)*, Easy Readers) Picture Window Bks.

—Max Stays Overnight, 1 vol. Klein, Adria F. 2007. (Read-It! Readers: the Life of Max Ser.). (ENG.). 24p. (gr. -1-2). lib. bdg. 19.99 *(978-1-4048-3149-0(5)*, 1265796, Easy Readers) Picture Window Bks.

—Max Va a la Biblioteca, 1 vol. Klein, Adria F. Lozano, Clara, tr. 2007. (Read-It! Readers en Español: la Vida de Max Ser.). (SPA.). 24p. (gr. -1-3). per. 3.95 *(978-1-4048-3036-3(7)*, Easy Readers) Picture Window Bks.

—Max Va a la Escuela, 1 vol. Klein, Adria F. Lozano, Clara, tr. 2007. (Read-It! Readers en Español: la Vida de Max Ser.). (SPA.). 24p. (gr. -1-3). per. 3.95 *(978-1-4048-3037-0(5)*, Easy Readers) Picture Window Bks.

—Max Va a la Peluqueria, 1 vol. Klein, Adria F. Lozano, Clara, tr. 2007. (Read-It! Readers en Español: la Vida de Max Ser.). (SPA.). 24p. (gr. -1-3). per. 3.95 *(978-1-4048-3038-7(3)*, Easy Readers) Picture Window Bks.

—Max Va Al Dentista, 1 vol. Klein, Adria F. Lozano, Clara, tr. 2007. (Read-It! Readers en Español: la Vida de Max Ser.). (SPA.). 24p. (gr. -1-3). per. 3.95 *(978-1-4048-3039-4(1)*, Easy Readers) Picture Window Bks.

—Max Va Al Doctor. Klein, Adria F. Lozano, Clara, tr. from ENG. 2008. (Read-It! Readers en Español: la Vida de Max Ser.). (SPA.). 24p. (gr. -1-3). per. 3.95 *(978-1-4048-4584-8(4)*, Easy Readers) Picture Window Bks.

—Max Va de Paseo, 1 vol. Klein, Adria F. Robledo, Sol, tr. from ENG. 2007. (Read-It! Readers en Español: la Vida de Max Ser.). (SPA.). 24p. (gr. -1-3). lib. bdg. 19.99 *(978-1-4048-3798-0(1)*, Easy Readers) Picture Window Bks.

—Max y la Fiesta de Adopcion, 1 vol. Klein, Adria F. Robledo, Sol, tr. from ENG. 2007. (Read-It! Readers en Español: la Vida de Max Ser.). (SPA.). 24p. (gr. -1-3). lib. bdg. 19.99 *(978-1-4048-3793-5(0)*, Easy Readers) Picture Window Bks.

—Max's Fun Day, 1 vol. Klein, Adria F. 2007. (Read-It! Readers: the Life of Max Ser.). (ENG.). 24p. (gr. -1-2). lib. bdg. 19.99 *(978-1-4048-3150-6(9)*, 1265797, Easy Readers) Picture Window Bks.

—Mousekin's Special Day: A Book about Special Days. Moncure, Jane Belk. 2013. (Magic Castle Readers: Social Science Ser.). (ENG.). 32p. (J). (gr. -1-2). 25.64 *(978-1-62323-586-4(3)*, 206321) Child's World, Inc., The.

Gallagher-Cole, Mernie. Rev up Your Writing in Blogs. Owings, Lisa. 2015. (Rev up Your Writing Ser.). (ENG.). 24p. (J). (gr. 2-5). 28.50 ***(978-1-63407-061-4(5)***, 208896) Child's World, Inc., The.

—Rev up Your Writing in Fictional Stories. Pearson, Yvonne. 2015. (Rev up Your Writing Ser.). (ENG.). 24p. (J). (gr. 2-5). 28.50 ***(978-1-63407-062-1(3)***, 208897) Child's World, Inc., The.

—Rev up Your Writing in Informational Texts. Garstecki, Julia. 2015. (Rev up Your Writing Ser.). (ENG.). 24p. (J). (gr. 2-5). 28.50 ***(978-1-63407-063-8(1)***, 208898) Child's World, Inc., The.

—Rev up Your Writing in Letters & E-Mails. Simons, Lisa M. Bolt. 2015. (Rev up Your Writing Ser.). (ENG.). 24p. (J). (gr. 2-5). 28.50 ***(978-1-63407-064-5(X)***, 208899) Child's World, Inc., The.

—Rev up Your Writing in Nonfiction Narratives. Garstecki, Julia. 2015. (Rev up Your Writing Ser.). (ENG.). 24p. (J). (gr. 2-5). 28.50 ***(978-1-63407-065-2(8)***, 208900) Child's World, Inc., The.

—Rev up Your Writing in Opinion Pieces. Simons, Lisa M. Bolt. 2015. (Rev up Your Writing Ser.). (ENG.). 24p. (J). (gr. 2-5). 28.50 ***(978-1-63407-066-9(6)***, 208901) Child's World, Inc., The.

—Rev up Your Writing in Procedural Texts. Zee, Amy Van. 2015. (Rev up Your Writing Ser.). (ENG.). 24p. (J). (gr. 2-5). 28.50 ***(978-1-63407-067-6(4)***, 208902) Child's World, Inc., The.

Gallagher-Cole, Mernie. Super Apostrophe Saves the Day! Higgins, Nadia. 2012. (PunctuationBooks Ser.). (ENG.). 24p. (J). (gr. k-3). 27.07 *(978-1-61473-265-5(5)*, 204962) Child's World, Inc., The.

—Super Colon Saves the Day! Lynette, Rachel. 2012. (PunctuationBooks Ser.). (ENG.). 24p. (J). (gr. k-3). 27.07 *(978-1-61473-266-2(3)*, 204963) Child's World, Inc., The.

—Super Comma Saves the Day! Higgins, Nadia. 2012. (PunctuationBooks Ser.). (ENG.). 24p. (J). (gr. k-3). 27.07 *(978-1-61473-267-9(1)*, 204964) Child's World, Inc., The.

—Super Exclamation Point Saves the Day! Higgins, Nadia. 2012. (PunctuationBooks Ser.). (ENG.). 24p. (J). (gr. k-3). 27.07 *(978-1-61473-268-6(X)*, 204965) Child's World, Inc., The.

—Super Parentheses Saves the Day! Lynette, Rachel. 2012. (PunctuationBooks Ser.). (ENG.). 24p. (J). (gr. k-3). 27.07 *(978-1-61473-269-3(8)*, 204966) Child's World, Inc., The.

—Super Period Saves the Day! Higgins, Nadia. 2012. (PunctuationBooks Ser.). (ENG.). 24p. (J). (gr. k-3). 27.07 *(978-1-61473-270-9(1)*, 204967) Child's World, Inc., The.

—Super Question Mark Saves the Day! Higgins, Nadia. 2012. (PunctuationBooks Ser.). (ENG.). 24p. (J). (gr. k-3). 27.07 *(978-1-61473-271-6(X)*, 204968) Child's World, Inc., The.

—Super Quotation Marks Saves the Day! Higgins, Nadia. 2012. (PunctuationBooks Ser.). (ENG.). 24p. (J). (gr. k-3). 27.07 *(978-1-61473-272-3(8)*, 204969) Child's World, Inc., The.

—That's the Last Straw! (And Other Weird Things We Say) Amoroso, Cynthia. 2011. (Sayings & Phrases Ser.). (ENG.). 24p. (J). (gr. 2-5). lib. bdg. 28.50 *(978-1-60954-230-6(4)*, 200783) Child's World, Inc., The.

—Weird-But-True Facts about Scary Things. Coss, Lauren. 2013. (Weird-But-True Facts Ser.). (ENG.). 32p. (J). (gr. 2-5). 28.50 *(978-1-61473-416-1(X)*, 205120) Child's World, Inc., The.

—Weird-But-True Facts about the Human Body. Coss, Lauren. 2013. (Weird-But-True Facts Ser.). (ENG.). 32p. (J). (gr. 2-5). 28.50 *(978-1-61473-419-2(4)*, 205123) Child's World, Inc., The.

—Weird-But-True Facts about U. S. History. Ringstad, Arnold. 2013. (Weird-But-True Facts Ser.). (ENG.). 32p. (J). (gr. 2-5). 28.50 *(978-1-61473-421-5(6)*, 205125) Child's World, Inc., The.

—Weird-But-True Facts about U. S. Presidents. Ringstad, Arnold. 2013. (Weird-But-True Facts Ser.). (ENG.). 32p. (J). (gr. 2-5). 28.50 *(978-1-61473-422-2(4)*, 205126) Child's World, Inc., The.

—Weird-But-True Facts about Weather. Coss, Lauren. 2013. (Weird-But-True Facts Ser.). (ENG.). 32p. (J). (gr. 2-5). 28.50 *(978-1-61473-423-9(2)*, 205127) Child's World, Inc., The.

—What Can We Play Today? A Book about Community Helpers. Moncure, Jane Belk. 2013. (Magic Castle Readers: Social Science Ser.). (ENG.). 32p. (J). (gr. -1-2). 25.64 *(978-1-62323-587-1(1)*, 206322) Child's World, Inc., The.

—What Do You Do with a Grumpy Kangaroo? A Book about Feelings. Moncure, Jane Belk. 2013. (Magic Castle Readers: Social Science Ser.). (ENG.). 32p. (J). (gr. -1-2). 25.64 *(978-1-62323-589-5(8)*, 206324) Child's World, Inc., The.

—What Do You Say When a Monkey Acts This Way? A Book about Manners. Moncure, Jane Belk. 2013. (Magic Castle Readers: Social Science Ser.). (ENG.). 32p. (J). (gr. -1-2). 25.64 *(978-1-62323-590-1(1)*, 206325) Child's World, Inc., The.

Gallagher-Cole, Mernie. Max Va Al Doctor. Gallagher-Cole, Mernie. Klein, Adria F. Lozano, Clara, tr. from ENG. 2008. (Read-It! Readers en Español: la Vida de Max Ser.). (SPA.). 24p. (gr. -1-3). lib. bdg. 19.99 *(978-1-4048-4488-9(0)*, Easy Readers) Picture Window Bks.

—Max Va Al Zoologico. Gallagher-Cole, Mernie. Klein, Adria F. Lozano, Clara, tr. from ENG. 2008. (Read-It! Readers en Español: la Vida de Max Ser.). (SPA.). 24p. (gr. -1-3). lib. bdg. 19.99 *(978-1-4048-4489-6(9)*, Easy Readers) Picture Window Bks.

Gallagher-Cole, Mernie, jt. illus. see Cole, Mernie.

Gallagher, Mary. Families Change: A Book for Children Experiencing Termination of Parental Rights. Nelson, Julie. 2006. (Kids Are Important Ser.). (ENG.). 32p. (J). (gr. -1-5). pap. 9.99 *(978-1-57542-209-1(3))* Free Spirit Publishing, Inc.

—Kids Need to Be Safe: A Book for Children in Foster Care. Nelson, Julie. 2005. (Kids Are Important Ser.). (ENG.). 32p. (J). (gr. -1-5). pap. 9.99 *(978-1-57542-192-6(5))* Free Spirit Publishing, Inc.

Gallagher, S. Saelig. Mama, I'll Give You the World. Schotter, Roni. 2013. (ENG.). 40p. (J). (gr. -1-3). pap. 7.99 *(978-0-449-81142-9(5)*, Dragonfly Bks.) Random Hse. Children's Bks.

Gallardo, Mary. The Tiny Little Raindrop. Gallardo, Mary, as told by. 2007. 32p. (J). 15.99 *(978-0-9779763-0-0(0))* Blue Cat Bks.

Gallas, G. E. Scared Stiff: Everything You Need to Know about 50 Famous Phobias. Latta, Sara. 2014. (ENG.). 224p. (YA). (gr. 5-7). pap. 12.99 *(978-1-936976-49-2(8))* Zest Bks.

Gallego, James, jt. illus. see Laguna, Fabio.

Gallegos, Benito. Diego's Dragon, Book Three: Battle at Tenochtitlan. Gerard, Kevin. Dreadfuls, Penny, ed. 2013. 298p. pap. 14.99 *(978-0-9859802-3-8(0))* Crying Cougar Pr.

Gallegos, Lauren. Kobee Manatee: Heading Home to Florida. Thayer, Robert Scott. Korman, Susan, ed. 2013. (Kobee Manatee Ser.). (ENG.). 32p. (J). (gr. k-2). 16.99 *(978-0-9883269-2-7(2))* Thompson Mill Pr.

—On the Day Love Was Born. Cerrito, Dana. 2011. 24p. (J). pap. 10.95 *(978-0-9835048-0-1(6))* Little Hill Pubs.

Gallegos, Lauren. Vulture Verses: Love Poems for the Unloved. Lang, Diane. 2015. (ENG.). 32p. (J). (gr. -1-2). pap. 9.95 ***(978-1-938849-64-0(7))*** Prospect Park Bks., LLC.

Gallenson, Ann, jt. illus. see Heins, Tanya.

Gallenson, Ann, jt. illus. see Morgan, Mark.

Gallet, Karl. Joe E, 1 vol. Mistretta, Jay. 2009. 19p. pap. 24.95 *(978-1-60749-850-6(2))* America Star Bks.

Gallet, Ryan. The Parkour Code. Mistretta, Jay Francis. Lulu.com, ed. 2012. (ENG.). 114p. pap. 8.98 *(978-1-4537-8833-2(6))* CreateSpace Independent Publishing Platform.

Galli, Stanley W. Kit Carson & the Wild Frontier. Moody, Ralph. 2005. (ENG.). 184p. pap. 13.95 *(978-0-8032-8304-6(0)*, MOOKIX, Bison Bks.) Univ. of Nebraska Pr.

Gallinger, Jared. Life Is Fragile: One Girl's Story of the Bath School Disaster. Spencer, Betty. 2007. 68p. per. 19.95 *(978-1-60441-772-2(2))* America Star Bks.

Gallow, Robyn. Can I Tell You about Selective Mutism? A Guide for Friends, Family & Professionals. Johnson, Maggie & Wintgens, Alison. 2012. (ENG.). 56p. pap. 13.95 *(978-1-84905-289-4(1))* Kingsley, Jessica Ltd.

Galloway, Amy. Tales of Shimmerlee: The MuriMuri. Morton, Machel. 2011. (ENG.). 26p. pap. 9.98 *(978-1-4663-8912-0(5))* CreateSpace Independent Publishing Platform.

Galloway, Fhiona. ABC Alphabet Sticker Book. 2014. (My Little World Ser.). (ENG.). 14p. (J). (gr. -1). pap. 3.99 *(978-1-58925-445-9(7))* Tiger Tales.

—Busy Day Sticker Book. 2014. (My Little World Ser.). (ENG.). 14p. (J). pap. 3.99 *(978-1-58925-446-6(5))* Tiger Tales.

—Hoot: A Hide-And-Seek Book of Counting. Litton, Jonathan. 2014. (My Little World Ser.). 16p. (J). (gr. -1-k). bds. 7.99 *(978-1-58925-595-1(X))* Tiger Tales.

Galloway, Fhiona. I Like to Squeak! How Do You Speak? Litton, Jonathan. 2015. (My Little World Ser.). 10p. bds. 12.99 ***(978-1-68010-505-6(1))*** Tiger Tales.

Galloway, Fhiona. Roar: A Big-Mouthed Book of Sounds! Litton, Jonathan. 2014. 16p. (J). bds. 7.99 *(978-1-58925-593-7(3))* Tiger Tales.

—Snap: A Peek-Through Book of Shapes. Litton, Jonathan. 2014. (My Little World Ser.). 16p. (J). (gr. -1-k). bds. 7.99 *(978-1-58925-566-1(6))* Tiger Tales.

—Surprise: A Book of Christmas Shapes. Litton, Jonathan. 2014. 16p. (J). (gr. -1-k). bds. 7.99 *(978-1-58925-567-8(4))* Tiger Tales.

—Tall & Short: A Peek-Through Book of Opposites. Litton, Jonathan. 2014. (My Little World Ser.). 16p. (J). (gr. -1-k). bds. 7.99 *(978-1-58925-565-4(8))* Tiger Tales.

—123 Counting Sticker Book. 2014. (My Little World Ser.). (ENG.). 14p. (J). (gr. -1). pap. 3.99 *(978-1-58925-444-2(9))* Tiger Tales.

Galloway, Ruth. Fidgety Fish & Friends. Bright, Paul. 2008. (Tiger Tales Ser.). 24p. (J). (gr. -1-2). pap. 6.95 *(978-1-58925-409-1(0))* Tiger Tales.

—How Do You Say That in French? 1000 Words & Phrases for Kids. Delaney, Sally & Richards, Wendy. 2014. (FRE & ENG.). 64p. (J). (gr. 2-6). 12.99 *(978-1-84322-915-5(3)*, Armadillo) Anness Publishing GBR. Dist: National Bk. Network.

Galloway, Ruth. Clumsy Crab. Galloway, Ruth. (Tiger Tales Ser.). 32p. (J). (gr. -1-2). 2007. pap. 6.95 *(978-1-58925-402-2(3))*; 2005. 15.95 *(978-1-58925-050-5(8))* Tiger Tales.

—Fidgety Fish. Galloway, Ruth. (J). 2006. 16p. bds. 6.95 *(978-1-58925-772-6(3))*; 2003. 32p. pap. 6.95 *(978-1-58925-377-3(9))* Tiger Tales.

—Smiley Shark. Galloway, Ruth. 32p. (J). 2005. 6.95 *(978-1-58925-391-9(4))*; 2003. tchr. ed. 15.95 *(978-1-58925-028-4(1))* Tiger Tales.

—Tickly Octopus. Galloway, Ruth. 2007. 15.95 *(978-1-58925-064-2(8))* Tiger Tales.

—The Very Fidgety Fish. Galloway, Ruth. 2014. (My First Storybook Ser.). (ENG.). 32p. (J). (gr. -1-1). 6.99 *(978-1-58925-509-8(7))* Tiger Tales.

Galluzzo, Madeline. The Belly Garden. Story, Rita. 2008. 23p. pap. 24.95 *(978-1-60610-035-6(1))* America Star Bks.

Galouchko, Annouchka. The Walking Stick, 1 vol. Trottier, Maxine. 2012. (ENG.). 32p. (J). pap. 9.95 *(978-1-55455-239-9(7)*, 1554552397) Fitzhenry & Whiteside, Ltd. CAN. Dist: Midpoint Trade Bks., Inc.

Galouchko, Annouchka Gravel & Daigle, Stephan. The Birdman. Charles, Veronika Martenova. 2006. (ENG.). 32p. (J). (gr. k-3). 17.95 *(978-0-88776-740-1(0)*, Tundra Bks.) Tundra Bks. CAN. Dist: Penguin Random Hse., LLC.

Galsterer, Lynne. Making Friends, 2. Haller, Reese. 2nd ed. 2006. (Fred the Mouse Ser.). 112p. (J). per. 4.97 *(978-0-9772321-0-9(7))* Personal Power Pr.

Galvani, Maureen. Make & Play Airplanes. Holzer, David. 2005. (Fun Kits (Top That!) Ser.). 48p. (J). (gr. -1-3). *(978-1-84510-549-5(4))* Top That! Publishing PLC.

Galvez, Daniel. It Doesn't Have to Be This Way. Rodriguez, Luis J. 2013. (ENG & SPA.). 32p. (J). pap. 8.95 *(978-0-89239-203-2(7))* Lee & Low Bks., Inc.

Galvin, Jennifer. My Catholic School Holiday: Reproducible Sheets for Home & School. Galvin, Jennifer. 2005. 32p. act. bk. ed. 6.95 *(978-0-8091-6724-1(7)*, 6724-7) Paulist Pr.

Gam do, Rin Bo. Insects & Spiders. Cowley, Joy, ed. 2015. (Science Storybooks Ser.). (ENG.). 32p. (gr. k-3). 26.65 ***(978-1-925246-23-0(X))*** ChoiceMaker Pty. Ltd., The AUS. Dist: Lerner Publishing Group.

Gama, Esperanza. Abuelo Vivia Solo/Grandpa Used to Live Alone. Costales, Amy. 2010. (ENG.). 32p. (J). (gr. -1-3). 16.95 *(978-1-55885-531-1(9))* Arte Publico Pr.

Gamage, Ken. Fantastically Fun Crosswords for Kids. Payne, Trip. 2006. (Mensa Ser.). (ENG.). 96p. (J). (gr. 3-7). per. 6.95 *(978-1-4027-2163-2(3)*, Puzzlewright) Sterling Publishing Co., Inc.

Gambatesa, Francesca. Hawaii! #6. De Laurentiis, Giada. 2015. (Recipe for Adventure Ser.: 6). (ENG.). 160p. (J). (gr. 2-4). 6.99 *(978-0-448-48391-7(2)*, Grosset & Dunlap) Penguin Publishing Group.

—Hong Kong! #3. De Laurentiis, Giada. 2014. (Recipe for Adventure Ser.: 3). (ENG.). 144p. (J). (gr. 2-5). 6.99 *(978-0-448-46258-5(3))*; 16.99 *(978-0-448-48040-4(9))* Penguin Publishing Group. (Grosset & Dunlap).

—Naples!, No. 1. De Laurentiis, Giada. 2013. (Recipe for Adventure Ser.: 1). (ENG.). 144p. (J). (gr. 2-5). 6.99 *(978-0-448-46256-1(7))*; 16.99 *(978-0-448-47853-1(6))* Penguin Publishing Group. (Grosset & Dunlap).

—New Orleans! #4. De Laurentiis, Giada. 2014. (Recipe for Adventure Ser.: 4). (ENG.). 144p. (J). (gr. 2-5). 6.99 *(978-0-448-46259-2(1)*, Grosset & Dunlap) Penguin Publishing Group.

—Paris!, No. 2. De Laurentiis, Giada. 2013. (Recipe for Adventure Ser.: 2). (ENG.). 144p. (J). (gr. 2-5). 6.99 *(978-0-448-46257-8(5)*, Grosset & Dunlap) Penguin Publishing Group.

—Paris! No. 2. De Laurentiis, Giada. 2013. (Recipe for Adventure Ser.: 2). (ENG.). 144p. (J). (gr. 2-5). 16.99 *(978-0-448-47854-8(4)*, Grosset & Dunlap) Penguin Publishing Group.

—Rio de Janeiro! #5. De Laurentiis, Giada. 2015. (Recipe for Adventure Ser.: 5). (ENG.). 160p. (J). (gr. 2-4). 6.99 *(978-0-448-48204-0(5)*, Grosset & Dunlap) Penguin Publishing Group.

Gambino, Alisha Ann Guadalupe. Sunflowers/Girasoles. Zepeda, Gwendolyn & Ventura, Gabriela Baeza. 2009. (SPA & ENG.). 32p. (J). (gr. -1-2). 16.95 *(978-1-55885-267-9(0)*, Piñata Books) Arte Publico Pr.

Gamble, Gael. Milly Feather. Darragh, Jill. 2013. 64p. pap. *(978-0-473-26560-1(5))* Rangitawa Publishing.

Gamble, Kent. And Nobody Got Hurt! The World's Weirdest, Wackiest True Sports Stories. Berman, Len. 2005. (ENG.). 128p. (J). (gr. 3-7). per. 7.00 *(978-0-316-01029-0(4))* Little, Brown Bks. for Young Readers.

—And Nobody Got Hurt 2! The World's Weirdest, Wackiest Most Amazing True Sports Stories. Berman, Len. rev. ed. 2007. (ENG.). 144p. (J). (gr. 3-7). per. 6.99 *(978-0-316-06705-8(9))* Little, Brown Bks. for Young Readers.

G

Gamble, Kim. The Adventures of Mouse Deer: Favorite Folktales of Southeast Asia. Shepard, Aaron. 2005. 48p. (J). (gr. -1-4). pap. 10.00 *(978-0-938497-32-5(4),* Skyhook Pr.) Shepard Pubns.

—Minton Goes! Underwater & Home at Last. Fienberg, Anna. 2008. (Minton Ser.). (ENG.). 64p. (J). (gr. -1-k). mass mkt. 9.99 *(978-1-74175-429-2(1))* Allen & Unwin AUS. Dist: Independent Pubs. Group.

—Once Tashi Met a Dragon. Fienberg, Anna & Fienberg, Barbara. 2014. (Tashi Ser.). (ENG.). 34p. (J). (gr. k-2). 16.99 *(978-1-74175-887-0(4))* Allen & Unwin AUS. Dist: Independent Pubs. Group.

—Tashi & the Dancing Shoes. Fienberg, Anna & Fienberg, Barbara. 8th ed. 2007. (Tashi Ser.). (ENG.). 64p. (Orig.). (J). (gr. k-2). pap. 8.99 *(978-1-74114-972-2(X))* Allen & Unwin AUS. Dist: Independent Pubs. Group.

—Tashi & the Forbidden Room. Fienberg, Anna & Fienberg, Barbara. 12th ed. 2007. (Tashi Ser.: 12). (ENG.). 64p. (J). (gr. k-2). pap. 8.99 *(978-1-74114-964-7(9))* Allen & Unwin AUS. Dist: Independent Pubs. Group.

—Tashi & the Golem. Fienberg, Anna & Fienberg, Barbara. 2010. (Tashi Ser.: 16). (ENG.). 64p. (J). (gr. k-2). pap. 8.99 *(978-1-74175-792-7(4))* Allen & Unwin AUS. Dist: Independent Pubs. Group.

—Tashi & the Haunted House. Fienberg, Anna & Fienberg, Barbara. 9th ed. 2007. (Tashi Ser.). (ENG.). 64p. (Orig.). (J). (gr. k-2). pap. 8.99 *(978-1-74114-953-1(3))* Allen & Unwin AUS. Dist: Independent Pubs. Group.

—Tashi & the Mixed-up Monster. Fienberg, Anna & Fienberg, Barbara. 2008. (Tashi Ser.: 14). (ENG.). 64p. (Orig.). (J). (gr. k-2). pap. 8.99 *(978-1-74175-191-8(8))* Allen & Unwin AUS. Dist: Independent Pubs. Group.

—Tashi & the Phoenix. Fienberg, Anna & Fienberg, Barbara. 2009. (Tashi Ser.: 15). (ENG.). 64p. (J). (gr. k-2). mass mkt. 8.99 *(978-1-74175-474-2(7))* Allen & Unwin AUS. Dist: Independent Pubs. Group.

—Tashi & the Royal Tomb. Fienberg, Anna & Fienberg, Barbara. 10th ed. 2007. (Tashi Ser.: 10). (ENG.). 64p. (Orig.). (J). (gr. k-2). pap. 8.99 *(978-1-74114-973-9(8))* Allen & Unwin AUS. Dist: Independent Pubs. Group.

—Tashi & the Stolen Bus. Fienberg, Anna & Fienberg, Barbara. 2007. (Tashi Ser.: 13). (ENG.). 64p. (Orig.). (J). (gr. k-2). pap. 8.99 *(978-1-74114-877-0(4))* Allen & Unwin AUS. Dist: Independent Pubs. Group.

—The Tashi Collection, 16 vols. Fienberg, Anna & Fienberg, Barbara. 2013. (Tashi Ser.). (ENG.). 64p. (J). (gr. k-2). 44.99 *(978-1-74237-389-8(5))* Allen & Unwin AUS. Dist: Independent Pubs. Group.

—Tashi Lost in the City. Fienberg, Anna & Fienberg, Barbara. 11th ed. 2007. (Tashi Ser.: 11). (ENG.). 64p. (J). (gr. k-2). pap. 8.99 *(978-1-74114-963-0(0))* Allen & Unwin AUS. Dist: Independent Pubs. Group.

—There Once Was a Boy Called Tashi. Fienberg, Anna & Fienberg, Barbara. 2008. (Tashi Ser.). (ENG.). 32p. (J). (gr. k-2). pap. 11.99 *(978-1-74114-719-3(0))* Allen & Unwin AUS. Dist: Independent Pubs. Group.

Gamble, Penel. Forgetting to Remember. Tayleur, Karen. 2004. iv, 36p. (J). pap. *(978-0-7608-6746-4(1))* Sundance/Newbridge Educational Publishing.

Gamboa, Ricardo. Just One More. Silvano, Wendi. 2007. (ENG.). 36p. (J). reprint ed. pap. 11.95 *(978-0-9744446-5-9(0))* All About Kids Publishing.

Gammage, Dana. Wisdom for Young Hearts Volume 2 - Applications of Wisdom. Delea, Pattie. 2011. 126p. pap. 20.00 *(978-1-61286-058-9(3))* Avid Readers Publishing Group.

Gammel, Stephen. The Frazzle Family Finds a Way. Bonwill, Ann. 2013. (ENG.). 32p. (J). 16.95 *(978-0-8234-2405-4(7))* Holiday Hse., Inc.

Gammelgaard, Leslie. Andi's Fair Surprise, 1 vol. Marlow, Susan K. 2011. (Circle C Beginnings Ser.). 80p. (J). (gr. 1-3). pap. 5.99 *(978-0-8254-4184-4(6))* Kregel Pubns.

—Andi's Indian Summer, 1 vol. Marlow, Susan K. 2010. (Circle C Beginnings Ser.). 80p. (J). (gr. 1-3). pap. 5.99 *(978-0-8254-4182-0(X))* Kregel Pubns.

—Andi's Pony Trouble, 1 vol. Marlow, Susan K. 2010. (Circle C Beginnings Ser.). 80p. (J). (gr. 1-3). pap. 5.99 *(978-0-8254-4181-3(1))* Kregel Pubns.

—Andi's Scary School Days, 1 vol. Marlow, Susan K. 2011. (Circle C Beginnings Ser.). 80p. (J). (gr. 1-3). pap. 5.99 *(978-0-8254-4183-7(8))* Kregel Pubns.

Gammell, Stephen. Humble Pie. Donnelly, Jennifer. 2007. (ENG.). 32p. (J). (gr. -1-2). 13.99 *(978-1-4169-6751-4(6),* Simon & Schuster/Paula Wiseman Bks.) Simon & Schuster/Paula Wiseman Bks.

—I Know an Old Teacher. Bowen, Anne. 2008. (ENG.). 32p. (J). (gr. k-3). 16.95 *(978-0-8225-7984-7(7),* Carolrhoda Bks.) Lerner Publishing Group.

—Laugh-Out-Loud Baby. Johnston, Tony. 2012. (ENG.). 32p. (J). (gr. -1-3). 16.99 *(978-1-4424-1380-1(6),* Simon & Schuster Bks. For Young Readers) Simon & Schuster/Paula Wiseman Bks.

—More Scary Stories to Tell in the Dark. 80p. (J). (gr. 4-6). pap. 4.95 *(978-0-8072-1424-4(8),* Listening Library) Random Hse. Audio Publishing Group.

—My Friend, the Starfinder. Lyon, George Ella. 2008. (ENG.). 40p. (J). (gr. -1-2). 17.99 *(978-1-4169-2738-9(7),* Atheneum/Richard Jackson Bks.) Simon & Schuster Children's Publishing.

—The Old Banjo. Haseley, Dennis. 2013. (ENG.). 32p. (J). (gr. -1-3). 16.99 *(978-1-4424-8879-3(4),* Simon & Schuster Bks. For Young Readers) Simon & Schuster Bks. For Young Readers.

—The Secret Science Project That Almost Ate the School. Sierra, Judy. 2006. (ENG.). 32p. (J). (gr. 1-4). 17.99 *(978-1-4169-1175-3(8),* Simon & Schuster/Paula Wiseman Bks.) Simon & Schuster/Paula Wiseman Bks.

Gammell, Stephen. Song & Dance Man. Ackerman, Karen. 2015. 32p. pap. 8.00 ***(978-1-61003-554-5(2))*** Center for the Collaborative Classroom.

Gammell, Stephen. Song & Dance Man. Ackerman, Karen. 2003. (ENG.). 32p. (J). (gr. -1-2). 15.95 *(978-0-394-89330-3(1),* Knopf Bks. for Young Readers) Random Hse. Children's Bks.

—Thunder at Gettysburg. Gauch, Patricia Lee. 2003. 46p. (J). (gr. -1-3). lib. bdg. 18.75 *(978-0-613-79893-8(7),* Turtleback) Turtleback Bks.

Gammell, Stephen. Mudkin. Gammell, Stephen. 2011. (Carolrhoda Picture Bks). (ENG.). 32p. (J). (gr. k-3). 16.95 *(978-0-7613-5790-2(4),* Carolrhoda Bks.) Lerner Publishing Group.

Gammill, Kerry, et al. Fallen Angels. Duffy, Jo. 2011. (ENG.). 136p. (J). (gr. 4-17). 29.99 *(978-0-7851-5529-4(5))* Marvel Worldwide, Inc.

Gampert, John. We Both Read-President Theodore Roosevelt. McKay, Sindy. 2006. (We Both Read Ser.). (J). (gr. 1-5). 40p. pap. 4.99 *(978-1-891327-68-1(2));* 44p. 7.99 *(978-1-891327-67-4(4))* Treasure Bay, Inc.

Gandy, Meg. The Goblin King. Johnson, Alaya. 2009. (Twisted Journeys (r) Ser.: 10). (ENG.). 112p. (J). (gr. 4-7). pap. 7.95 *(978-0-8225-9259-4(2))* Lerner Publishing Group.

Gandy, Meg & Olson, Meagan. The Goblin King, No. 10. Johnson, Alaya Dawn. 2009. (Twisted Journeys (r) Ser.: 10). (ENG.). 112p. (J). (gr. 4-7). 27.93 *(978-0-8225-9253-2(3),* Graphic Universe) Lerner Publishing Group.

Ganeri, Anita & Forsey, Chris. Ancient Maya. Ganeri, Anita. 2006. (Ancient Civilizations Ser.). (ENG.). 32p. (J). (gr. 4-6). lib. bdg. 29.32 *(978-0-7565-1677-2(3),* CPB Grades 4-8) Compass Point Bks.

Ganeri, Anita, jt. illus. see West, David.

Gang, Jobie. Pookie Lookie: The Pink Spotted Panda Bear. Shealeya, Mildred. 2007. 32p. (J). per. 12.95 *(978-0-9669595-7-4(4))* SMS Cos., Inc.

Gang, MinJeong. Who's Coming Tonight? Choi, JeongIm. rev. ed. 2014. (MySELF Bookshelf: Social & Emotional Learning/Social Awareness Ser.). (ENG.). 32p. (J). (gr. k-2). lib. bdg. 22.60 *(978-1-59953-653-8(6))* Norwood Hse. Pr.

Gangelhoff, Gene. A Walk Through the Minnesota Zoo. Gangelhoff, Jeanne M. & Belk, Bradford. 32p. (J). 9.95 *(978-0-9635006-1-8(9))* G J & B Publishing.

Gangloff, Hope. Rocky Road Trip. Stamper, Judith Bauer. 2004. (Magic School Bus Science Chapter Bks.). 89p. (gr. 2-5). lib. bdg. 15.00 *(978-0-7569-3093-6(6))* Perfection Learning Corp.

—Rocky Road Trip. Stamper, Judith Bauer & Bauer-Stamper, Judith. 2004. (Magic School Bus Ser.: 20). (ENG.). 96p. (J). (gr. 2-5). 4.99 *(978-0-439-56053-5(5),* Scholastic Paperbacks) Scholastic, Inc.

Gannett, Ruth Chrisman. The Dragons of Blueland. Gannett, Ruth Stiles. (Tales of My Father's Dragon Ser.: Bk. 3). 88p. (J). (gr. 3-6). pap. 4.99 incl. audio *(978-0-8072-1287-5(3),* Listening Library) Random Hse. Audio Publishing Group.

—The Dragons of Blueland. Gannett, Ruth Stiles. 2007. (My Father's Dragon Ser.). (ENG.). 112p. (J). (gr. 3-7). 6.99 *(978-0-440-42137-5(3),* Yearling) Random Hse. Children's Bks.

—Elmer & the Dragon. Gannett, Ruth Stiles. (Tales of My Father's Dragon Ser.: Bk. 2). 87p. (J). (gr. 3-6). pap. 4.99 incl. audio *(978-0-8072-1288-2(1),* Listening Library) Random Hse. Audio Publishing Group.

—Elmer & the Dragon. Gannett, Ruth Stiles. 2007. (My Father's Dragon Ser.). (ENG.). 96p. (J). (gr. 3-7). 6.99 *(978-0-440-42136-8(5),* Yearling) Random Hse. Children's Bks.

—My Father's Dragon. Gannett, Ruth Stiles. 2014. (ENG.). 96p. (J). (gr. 2). pap. 5.99 *(978-0-486-49283-4(4))* Dover Pubns., Inc.

—My Father's Dragon. Gannett, Ruth Stiles. 2005. (My Father's Dragon Ser.). (ENG.). 96p. (J). (gr. 3-7). 6.99 *(978-0-440-42121-4(7),* Yearling) Random Hse. Children's Bks.

Gannon, Ned. The Man & the Vine. Meyer, Jane G. 2006. (ENG.). 32p. (J). 18.00 *(978-0-88141-315-1(1))* St. Vladimir's Seminary Pr.

—Time to Pray. Addasi, Maha. Albitar, Nuha, tr. 2010. (ENG & ARA.). 32p. (J). (gr. 2-4). 17.95 *(978-1-59078-611-6(4))* Boyds Mills Pr.

—The White Nights of Ramadan. Addasi, Maha. 2008. (ENG.). 32p. (J). (gr. 2-4). 16.95 *(978-1-59078-523-2(1))* Boyds Mills Pr.

Gannon, Ned, jt. illus. see Meyer, Jane G.

Gant, Linda G. Readers Are Leaders. Gant, Linda G. Date not set. (J). (gr. -1-3). *(978-0-9673625-0-2(4))* Readers Are Leaders.

Gant, Robert. My Big Box of Addition & Subtraction. gif. ed. 2005. 64p. (J). cd-rom 24.95 *(978-1-57791-196-8(2))* Brighter Minds Children's Publishing.

—My Big Box of Letters. gif. ed. 2005. 64p. (J). cd-rom 24.95 *(978-1-57791-193-7(8))* Brighter Minds Children's Publishing.

—My Big Box of Numbers. gif. ed. 2005. 64p. (J). cd-rom 24.95 *(978-1-57791-194-4(6))* Brighter Minds Children's Publishing.

—My Big Box of Reading. gif. ed. 2005. 64p. (J). cd-rom 24.95 *(978-1-57791-195-1(4))* Brighter Minds Children's Publishing.

Gantschev, Ivan. Santa's Favorite Story: Santa Tells the Story of the First Christmas. Aoki, Hisako. 2007. (ENG.). 28p. (J). (gr. -1-3). 9.99 *(978-1-4169-5029-5(X),* Simon & Schuster Bks. For Young Readers) Simon & Schuster Bks. For Young Readers.

—Snow Leopards. Poppenhager, Nicole. James, J. Alison, tr. from GER. 2008. 32p. (J). (gr. -1-3). 6.95 *(978-0-7358-2179-8(8))* North-South Bks., Inc.

Gantt, Amy. Sammy's Big Adventure: Sammy's Super Safari. Mravetz, Pete. 2011. (ENG.). 24p. pap. 9.50 *(978-1-4663-4854-7(2))* CreateSpace Independent Publishing Platform.

Ganz, Cristina Milián. El Alfabeto Cubano. Otero, Eduardo A. 2006. (SPA.). 40p. (J). pap. 16.95 *(978-0-9779124-0-7(X))* Cristal Publishing Co.

Ganzer, Theresa. Llama Tails: Ricky's Adventure. Ganzer, Diane & St. Croix, Sammy. 2008. 172p. pap. 9.99 *(978-0-9801438-7-4(X))* Avid Readers Publishing Group.

Gapaillard, Laurent. The Long Tall Journey. Wahl, Jan. 2015. (ENG.). 48p. (J). (gr. 1-3). 18.99 ***(978-1-56846-230-1(1),*** Creative Editions) Creative Co., The.

Garafalo, Beatrice. Sadie's Wish: Three Little Elves. Addino, Victoria. 2012. 32p. (-18). pap. 24.95 *(978-1-4626-9907-0(3))* America Star Bks.

Garamella, Joyce Orchard. What Makes a Good Teacher? Here's What the Kids Say! Whyte, Donna. 2003. 32p. (J). 6.95 *(978-1-884548-59-8(8),* Crystal Springs Bks.) Staff Development for Educators.

Garay, Luis. Alfredito Flies Home, 1 vol. Argueta, Jorge. Amado, Elisa, tr. from SPA. 2007. (ENG.). 36p. (J). (gr. -1-4). 17.95 *(978-0-88899-585-8(7))* Groundwood Bks. CAN. Dist: Perseus-PGW.

—Alfredito Regresa Volando a Su Casa, 1 vol. Argueta, Jorge. 2007. (SPA.). 36p. (J). (gr. -1-4). 17.95 *(978-0-88899-586-5(5))* Groundwood Bks. CAN. Dist: Perseus-PGW.

—Popol Vuh: A Sacred Book of the Maya, 1 vol. Montejo, Victor. Unger, David, tr. from SPA. 2009. (ENG.). 88p. (J). (gr. 3-18). pap. 14.95 *(978-0-88899-921-4(6))* Groundwood Bks. CAN. Dist: Perseus-PGW.

—Primas, 1 vol. Amado, Elisa. Iribarren, Elena & Iribarren, Leopoldo, trs. from ENG. 2004. (SPA & ENG.). 32p. (J). 16.95 *(978-0-88899-548-3(2))* Groundwood Bks. CAN. Dist: Perseus-PGW.

Garay, Nicole. The Wooden Bowl/El Bol de Madera. Moreno Winner, Ramona. 2009. (ENG & SPA.). (J). (gr. k-3). 15.95 *(978-0-9651174-3-2(X))* BrainStorm 3000.

Garbot, Dave. Easter Bunny on the Loose! Wax, Wendy. 2013. (ENG.). 32p. (J). (gr. -1-3). 7.99 *(978-0-06-223709-5(8))* HarperCollins Pubs.

—First Dog of 1600 Pooch'Lvania Avenue: My First Year in Arf, Arf Office!! Grant, Ron & Ovadia, Ron. 2010. 34p. pap. 13.95 *(978-1-59858-995-5(4))* Dog Ear Publishing, LLC.

—Hurry Up! Murray, Carol. 2003. (Rookie Readers Ser.). (ENG.). 32p. (J). 19.50 *(978-0-516-22585-2(5),* Children's Pr.) Scholastic Library Publishing.

—Map Mania: Discovering Where You Are & Getting to Where You Aren't. Dispenzio, Michael A. 2006. 80p. (J). (gr. 4-8). reprint ed. 20.00 *(978-0-7567-9893-2(0))* DIANE Publishing Co.

—Monsters on the Loose! A Seek & Solve Mystery! Hale, Bruce. 2013. (ENG.). 32p. (J). (gr. -1-3). 7.99 *(978-0-06-223706-4(3))* HarperCollins Pubs.

—Santa on the Loose! Hale, Bruce. 2012. (ENG.). 32p. (J). (gr. -1-3). 7.99 *(978-0-06-202262-2(8))* HarperCollins Pubs.

—Super Science Experiments. Mandell, Muriel. 2005. (No-Sweat Science(r) Ser.). (ENG.). 128p. (J). (gr. 3-7). per. 5.95 *(978-1-4027-2149-6(8))* Sterling Publishing Co., Inc.

Garbowska, Agata. Gandy & Parker Escape the Zoo: An Illustrated Adventure. Garbowska, Agata. Mardon, Austin A. & Mardon, Catherine A. 2013. pap. *(978-1-897472-82-8(X))* Golden Meteorite Pr.].

Garbutt, Chris. Taking Out the Tigers. Moses, Brian. unabr. ed. 2005. (ENG.). 96p. (J). (gr. 1-4). pap. 6.99 *(978-0-330-41797-6(5))* Macmillan Pubs., Ltd. GBR. Dist: Independent Pubs. Group.

Garbutt, Lisa. When I Am an Old Woman: Stationery. Martz, Sandra, ed. 2nd rev. ed. 2006. (C). pap. 7.95 *(978-1-57601-085-3(6),* Papier-Mache Pr.) Moyer Bell.

Garcia, Camille Rose. Alice's Adventures in Wonderland. Carroll, Lewis. 2010. (ENG.). 160p. 16.99 *(978-0-06-188657-7(2),* Collins Design) HarperCollins Pubs.

—Snow White. Brothers Grimm, Becky et al. 2012. (ENG.). 80p. 14.99 *(978-0-06-206446-2(0),* Collins Design) HarperCollins Pubs.

Garcia, Cynthia. Sam & Pam Can & You Can Too! We Can Count. Litz, Amanda. 2011. 32p. (J). pap. 3.99 *(978-0-9841496-3-6(5))* Traveler's Trunk Publishing LLC.

—Sam & Pam Can & You Can Too! We Can Help Our Mom. Litz, Amanda. 2011. 32p. (J). pap. 3.99 *(978-0-9841496-1-2(9))* Traveler's Trunk Publishing LLC.

—Sam & Pam Can & You Can Too! We Can Ride Our Bikes. Litz, Amanda. 2011. 32p. (J). pap. 3.99 *(978-0-9841496-2-9(7))* Traveler's Trunk Publishing LLC.

Garcia, Eduardo. Beastly Basketball, 1 vol. Johnson, Lauren. 2014. (Sports Illustrated Kids Graphic Novels Ser.). (ENG.). 72p. (gr. 2-5). lib. bdg. 25.32 *(978-1-4342-6490-9(4))* Stone Arch Bks.

—Cycling Champion, 1 vol. Maddox, Jake. 2012. (Jake Maddox Sports Stories Ser.). (ENG.). 72p. (gr. 2-3). pap. 5.95 *(978-1-4342-3904-4(7));* lib. bdg. 23.99 *(978-1-4342-3290-8(5))* Stone Arch Bks.

—The Fisherman & the Genie, 1 vol. Fein, Eric. 2010. (Classic Fiction Ser.). (ENG.). 72p. (gr. 2-3). 26.65 *(978-1-4342-2134-6(2));* pap. 7.15 *(978-1-4342-2777-5(4))* Stone Arch Bks. (Graphic Revolve).

—Gold Medal Swim, 1 vol. Maddox, Jake. 2012. (Jake Maddox Sports Stories Ser.). (ENG.). 72p. (gr. 2-3). pap. 5.95 *(978-1-4342-3902-0(0));* lib. bdg. 23.99 *(978-1-4342-3288-5(3))* Stone Arch Bks.

—Julius Caesar, 1 vol. Shakespeare, William. 2011. (Shakespeare Graphics Ser.). (ENG.). 88p. (gr. 2-3). pap. 7.15 *(978-1-4342-3450-6(9));* lib. bdg. 26.65 *(978-1-4342-2631-0(X))* Stone Arch Bks. (Shakespeare Graphics).

—Quarterback Rush, 1 vol. Bowen, Carl. 2014. (Sports Illustrated Kids Graphic Novels Ser.). (ENG.). 72p. (gr. 2-5). 25.32 *(978-1-4342-6489-3(0))* Stone Arch Bks.

—Relay Race Breakdown, 1 vol. Maddox, Jake. 2012. (Jake Maddox Sports Stories Ser.). (ENG.). 72p. (gr. 2-3). pap. 5.95 *(978-1-4342-3903-7(9));* lib. bdg. 23.99 *(978-1-4342-3289-2(1))* Stone Arch Bks.

—Track & Field Takedown, 1 vol. Maddox, Jake. 2012. (Jake Maddox Sports Stories Ser.). (ENG.). 72p. (gr. 2-3). pap. 5.95 *(978-1-4342-3901-3(2));* lib. bdg. 23.99 *(978-1-4342-3287-8(5))* Stone Arch Bks.

Garcia, Eduardo & Ferrara, Eduardo. Caught in a Pickle, 1 vol. Jacobson, Ryan. 2011. (B-Team Ser.). (ENG.). 40p. (gr. 1-3). lib. bdg. 22.65 *(978-1-4342-2606-8(9),* Graphic Sparks) Stone Arch Bks.

Garcia, Geronimo. A Gift from Papa Diego: Un Regalo de Papa Diego. Sáenz, Benjamin Alire. 2008. (Little Diego Book Ser.). (ENG & SPA.). 40p. (J). pap. 10.95 *(978-0-938317-33-3(4))* Cinco Puntos Pr.

—La Perrita Que le Encantaban las Tortillas. Sáenz, Benjamin Alire. 2009. (Little Diego Book Ser.).Tr. of Dog Who Loved Tortillas. (SPA & ENG.). 40p. (J). (gr. 1-4). 17.95 *(978-1-933693-54-5(1))* Cinco Puntos Pr.

Garcia, Helena. A World of Girls. Welsh, Anne Marie & Tuchman, Laura. 2010. 40p. (J). *(978-0-88441-750-7(6))* Girl Scouts of the USA.

—Wow! Wonders of Water. Welsh, Anne Marie & Fenly, Leigh. 2009. 112p. (J). pap. *(978-0-88441-732-3(8))* Girl Scouts of the USA.

Garcia, Humberto. Animales Entreversos. Lozano, Juan Antonio. rev. ed. 2007. (Castillo de la Lectura Blanca Ser.). (SPA & ENG.). 43p. (J). (gr. k). pap. 6.95 *(978-970-20-0341-0(5))* Castillo, Ediciones, S. A. de C. V. MEX. Dist: Macmillan.

Garcia, Juan F. Team 002: The Abduction of the Queen. Hildebrand, Jens. 2013. 224p. pap. *(978-3-929892-46-8(4))* Hildebrand, Jutta Warped Tomato Publishing.

—Team 002 und das Utopia-Element. Hildebrand, Jens. 2013. 270p. pap. *(978-3-929892-39-0(1))* Hildebrand, Jutta Warped Tomato Publishing.

—Team 002 und Die Entführung der Queen. Hildebrand, Jens. 2013. 240p. pap. *(978-3-929892-37-6(5))* Hildebrand, Jutta Warped Tomato Publishing.

Garcia, Manuel. Black Widow: Kiss or Kill. 2011. (ENG.). 96p. (YA). (gr. 8-17). pap. 12.99 *(978-0-7851-4701-5(2))* Marvel Worldwide, Inc.

Garcia, Marc Khayam. The Adventures of Billy Butterfly. Lehnert, R. B. 2003. (J). per. *(978-0-9747628-2-1(2))* BKB Group, Inc., The.

—Color Me & My Pals: The Adventures of Billy Butterfly Coloring Book. 2003. (J). 3.95 *(978-0-9747628-3-8(0))* BKB Group, Inc., The.

GARCIA ORIHUELA, Luis. The Army of Words. Garcia Orihuela, Luis & DIVINCENZO, Sofia & Yoselem. 2012. 24p. pap. 19.99 *(978-1-61196-934-4(4))* Divincenzo, Yoselem G.

Garcia, Patricio. The Eyes of the Weaver: Los Ojos Del Tejedor. Ortega, Cristina. 2006. (ENG.). 64p. (J). 16.95 *(978-0-8263-3990-4(5))* Univ. of New Mexico Pr.

Garcia, Victor Manuel Gut. De la Vez Que Tino Perdio Su Par. Ochoa, Minerva. rev. ed. 2006. (Castillo de la Lectura Blanca Ser.). (SPA & ENG.). 88p. (J). (gr. k-2). pap. 6.95 *(978-970-20-0196-6(X))* Castillo, Ediciones, S. A. de C. V. MEX. Dist: Macmillan.

Garcia, Victor Manuel Gut, jt. illus. see Garcia, Victor Manuel Gutierrez.

Garcia, Victor Manuel Gutierrez & Garcia, Victor Manuel Gut. Espartaco y Yo. Parada, Enrique. rev. ed. 2006. (Castillo de la Lectura Verde Ser.). (SPA & ENG.). 68p. (J). (gr. 2). pap. 7.95 *(978-968-5920-90-2(7))* Castillo, Ediciones, S. A. de C. V. MEX. Dist: Macmillan.

Garden, Jo. Whose Ears? Munro, Fiona. 2011. (ENG.). 10p. (J). (gr. -1-k). bds. 6.99 *(978-0-8431-9814-0(1),* Price Stern Sloan) Penguin Publishing Group.

—Whose Spots? Munro, Fiona. 2011. (ENG.). 10p. (J). (gr. -1-k). bds. 6.99 *(978-0-8431-9813-3(3),* Price Stern Sloan) Penguin Publishing Group.

—Whose Stripes? Munro, Fiona & Phillipson, Fiona. 2011. (ENG.). 10p. (J). (gr. -1-k). bds. 6.99 *(978-0-8431-9812-6(5),* Price Stern Sloan) Penguin Publishing Group.

Gardiner, Lindsey. Abuelita, te Acuerdas? Langston, Laura. 2004.Tr. of Mile High Apple Pie. (SPA.). (J). 18.99 *(978-84-488-1911-8(X))* Beascoa, Ediciones S.A. ESP. Dist: Lectorum Pubns., Inc.

—The Animal Bop Won't Stop! Ormerod, Jan. 2011. (J). *(978-1-4380-8419-0(6))* Barron's Educational Series, Inc.

—The Heffalump Grump. Oram, Hiawyn. 2008. (ENG.). 32p. (J). (gr. k — 1). pap. 9.95 *(978-1-84362-792-0(2))* Hodder & Stoughton GBR. Dist: Independent Pubs. Group.

—If You're Happy & You Know It! Ormerod, Jan. 2003. 32p. (J). (gr. -1-3). 15.95 *(978-1-932065-07-7(5));* pap. 5.95 *(978-1-932065-10-7(5))* Star Bright Bks., Inc.

—Over in the Clover. Ormerod, Jan. 2009. (ENG.). 32p. (J). (gr. -1-k). 9.99 *(978-0-7641-9646-1(4))* Barron's Educational Series, Inc.

—Poppy & Max & the Noisy Night. Grindley, Sally. 2009. (Poppy & Max Ser.: 5). (ENG.). 32p. (J). (gr. k-2). pap. 6.95 *(978-1-84362-409-7(5))* Hodder & Stoughton GBR. Dist: Independent Pubs. Group.

—Poppy & Max & the River Picnic. Grindley, Sally. 2008. (Poppy & Max Ser.: 4). (ENG.). 32p. (J). (gr. k-2). pap. 6.95 *(978-1-84362-395-3(1))* Hodder & Stoughton GBR. Dist: Independent Pubs. Group.

—Trosclair & the Alligator, 1 vol. Huggins, Peter. (ENG.). 32p. (J). 2013. pap. 7.95 *(978-1-59572-640-7(3));* 2005. (gr. -1-3). 15.95 *(978-1-932065-98-5(9))* Star Bright Bks., Inc.

Gardiner, Lisa. The First Boykin Spaniels: The Story of Dumpy & Singo. Kelley, Lynn. 2012. (Distributed for the Author Ser.). (ENG.). 31p. (Orig.). (J). per. 13.50 *(978-0-9761463-0-8(4))* Univ. of South Carolina Pr.

Gardiner, Lisa M. Crazy Critters. Paiva, Johannah Gilman, ed. 2013. (Big Padded Lift-The-Flap Ser.). (ENG.). 20p. (J). (gr. -1-2). 8.99 *(978-1-77093-630-0(0))* Flowerpot Children's Pr. Inc. CAN. Dist: Cardinal Pubs. Group.

Gardiner, Lisa M. Farm Find. Paiva, Johannah Gilman, ed. 2013. 20p. (J). (gr. -1-1). 8.99 ***(978-1-77093-688-1(2))*** Flowerpot Children's Pr. Inc. CAN. Dist: Cardinal Pubs. Group.

Gardiner, Nancy. Tap Shoes & Horse Shoes. Macy, Tana. 2011. 50p. pap. 18.00 *(978-1-60976-086-1(7),* Eloquent Bks.) Strategic Book Publishing & Rights Agency (SBPRA).

Gardner, David. Sarah Gives Thanks: How Thanksgiving Became a National Holiday. Allegra, Mike. 2012. (ENG.). 32p. (J). (gr. 1-4). 16.99 *(978-0-8075-7239-9(X))* Whitman, Albert & Co.

Gardner, Louise. Bear. Powell, Richard. 2014. (Bathing Beauties Ser.). (ENG.). 8p. (J). (gr. -1 — 1). 7.99 *(978-1-4380-7441-2(7))* Barron's Educational Series, Inc.

—Duck. Powell, Richard. 2014. (Bathing Beauties Ser.). (ENG.). 8p. (J). (gr. -1 — 1). 7.99 *(978-1-4380-7442-9(5))* Barron's Educational Series, Inc.

—Five Little Easter Eggs. (ENG.). 10p. (J). 2009. (gr. -1). 5.95 *(978-1-58117-849-4(2))*; 2008. 9.95 *(978-1-58117-682-7(1))* Bendon, Inc. (Intervisual/Piggy Toes).

—Frog. Powell, Richard. 2014. (Bathing Beauties Ser.). (ENG.). 8p. (J). (gr. -1 — 1). 7.99 *(978-1-4380-7443-6(3))* Barron's Educational Series, Inc.

—The Gingerbread Family: A Scratch-and-Sniff Book. Maccarone, Grace. 2010. (ENG.). 14p. (J). (gr. -1-k). 7.99 *(978-1-4424-0678-0(X)*, Little Simon) Little Simon.

—Old MacDonald. 2004. 24p. (J). bds. 6.99 *(978-1-85854-901-9(9))* Brimax Books Ltd. GBR. Dist: Byeway Bks.

Gardner, Louise, et al. Old MacDonald & Other Sing-along Rhymes. 2006. (Mother Goose Ser.). (ENG.). 36p. (J). 12.95 *(978-1-59249-525-2(7)*, 1D028) Soundprints.

Gardner, Louise. Seal. Powell, Richard. 2014. (Bathing Beauties Ser.). (ENG.). 8p. (J). (gr. -1 — 1). 7.99 *(978-1-4380-7444-3(1))* Barron's Educational Series, Inc.

Gardner, Marjory. Hedgeburners: An A-Z PI Mystery. Alexander, Goldie. 2009. 184p. (YA). pap. 13.95 *(978-1-921479-26-7(4)*, IP Kidz) Interactive Pubns. Pty, Ltd. AUS. Dist: CreateSpace Independent Publishing Platform.

—The Present 6 Packs. KinderConcepts. Wallace, Jessica. (Kinderstarters Ser.). 8p. (gr. -1-1). 21.00 *(978-0-7635-8720-8(6))* Rigby Education.

Gardner, Rita. One Day the Animals Talked: Short Stories. MacDonald, Bernell. 2005. (ENG.). 84p. (J). pap. *(978-0-9686034-5-1(9)*, Lion's Head Pr.) Chipmunk Bks.

Gardner, Sally. Polly's Absolutely Worst Birthday Ever. Thomas, Frances. 2012. (ENG.). 96p. (J). (gr. 2-4). pap. 11.99 *(978-1-4088-2516-7(3)*, 127617, Bloomsbury USA Childrens) Bloomsbury USA.

—Polly's Running Away Book. Thomas, Frances. 2012. (ENG.). 96p. (J). (gr. 2-4). pap. 11.99 *(978-1-4088-2515-0(5)*, 127616, Bloomsbury USA Childrens) Bloomsbury USA.

Gardner, Sally. Magical Kids: The Invisible Boy & the Strongest Girl in the World. Gardner, Sally. 2007. (ENG.). 224p. (J). (gr. 3-7). 15.99 *(978-0-8037-3158-5(2)*, Dial) Penguin Publishing Group.

Gardner, Stephen. Childs Play: Positive Affirmations for Children to Sing & Dramatize. Kulsa, Wha. Date not set. 30p. (J). (gr. 1-7). pap. *(978-1-886942-08-0(0))* White Lion Pr.

Gardos, Susan. Stinky, 1 vol. Staunton, Ted. 2003. (Monkey Mountain Ser.). (ENG.). 64p. (J). (gr. 2-5). pap. 6.95 *(978-0-88995-263-8(9))* Red Deer Pr. CAN. Dist: Ingram Pub. Services.

—The Trouble with Girls, 1 vol. Staunton, Ted. 2003. (Monkey Mountain Ser.). (ENG.). 72p. (J). (gr. 2-5). pap. 6.95 *(978-0-88995-264-5(7))* Red Deer Pr. CAN. Dist: Ingram Pub. Services.

Garland, Lynn Rockwell, jt. illus. see Venema, Lisa J.

Garland, Michael. Animal School: What Class Are You? Lord, Michelle. 2014. (ENG.). 32p. (J). (gr. -1-3). 16.95 *(978-0-8234-3045-1(6))* Holiday Hse., Inc.

—The Best Book to Read. Bloom, Susan & Bertram, Debbie. 2008. (Picture Book Ser.). (ENG.). 32p. (J). (gr. -1-2). 14.99 *(978-0-375-84702-8(2)*, Random Hse. Bks. for Young Readers) Random Hse. Children's Bks.

—The Best Book to Read. Bertram, Debbie & Bloom, Susan. 2011. (ENG.). 32p. (J). (gr. -1-2). pap. 7.99 *(978-0-375-87300-3(7)*, Dragonfly Bks.) Random Hse. Children's Bks.

—The Best Place to Read. Bloom, Susan & Bertram, Debbie. 2007. (ENG.). 32p. (J). (gr. -1-2). pap. 6.99 *(978-0-375-83757-9(4)*, Dragonfly Bks.) Random Hse. Children's Bks.

—Casey Jones. York, J. 2012. (American Tall Tales Ser.). (ENG.). 24p. (J). (gr. k-3). 28.50 *(978-1-61473-209-9(4)*, 204903) Child's World, Inc., The.

—I'd Be Your Princess: A Royal Tale of Godly Character. O'Brien, Kathryn. 2007. 28p. (J). (gr. -1-3). 6.99 *(978-0-7847-1964-0(0))* Standard Publishing.

—Joan of Arc: Heroine of France. Tompert, Ann. 2003. (ENG.). 32p. (J). (gr. 1-7). 15.95 *(978-1-59078-009-1(4))* Boyds Mills Pr.

—Johnny Appleseed. York, J. 2012. (American Tall Tales Ser.). (ENG.). 24p. (J). (gr. k-3). 28.50 *(978-1-61473-210-5(8)*, 204904) Child's World, Inc., The.

—The Night Santa Got Lost: How NORAD Saved Christmas. Keane, Michael. 2012. (ENG.). 28p. (J). (gr. -1). 14.95 *(978-1-59698-810-1(X)*, Little Patriot Pr.) Regnery Publishing, Inc., An Eagle Publishing Co.

—Pecos Bill. York, J. 2012. (American Tall Tales Ser.). (ENG.). 24p. (J). (gr. k-3). 28.50 *(978-1-61473-212-9(4)*, 204906) Child's World, Inc., The.

—Pooch on the Loose: A Christmas Adventure, 0 vols. Kroll, Steven. 2013. (ENG.). 32p. (J). (gr. -1-3). pap. 9.99 *(978-0-7614-5443-4(8)*, 9780761454434, Two Lions) Amazon Publishing.

—Pooch on the Loose: A Christmas Adventure, 1 vol. Kroll, Steven & Droll. 2005. (ENG.). 32p. (J). (gr. -1-3). 14.95 *(978-0-7614-5239-3(7))* Marshall Cavendish Corp.

—Saint Nicholas. Tompert, Ann. 2005. (ENG.). 32p. (J). (gr. 1-7). pap. 8.95 *(978-1-59078-336-8(0))* Boyds Mills Pr.

—SantaKid. Patterson, James. 2004. (ENG.). 48p. (J). (gr. -1-1). 14.99 *(978-0-316-00061-1(2))* Little, Brown Bks. for Young Readers.

—That's Good! That's Bad! in Washington, DC. Cuyler, Margery. rev. ed. 2007. (That's Good! That's Bad! Ser.). (ENG.). 32p. (J). (gr. -1-2). 16.95 *(978-0-8050-7727-8(8)*, Holt, Henry & Co. Bks. For Young Readers) Holt, Henry & Co.

Garland, Michael. Car Goes Far. Garland, Michael. 2013. (I Like to Read Ser.). (ENG.). 32p. (J). 14.95 *(978-0-8234-2598-3(3))* Holiday Hse., Inc.

—Car Goes Far. Garland, Michael. 2014. (I Like to Read Ser.). (ENG.). 32p. (J). (gr. -1-3). 6.99 *(978-0-8234-3058-1(8))* Holiday Hse., Inc.

—Fish Had a Wish. Garland, Michael. 2013. (I Like to Read Ser.). (ENG.). 24p. (J). pap. 6.99 *(978-0-8234-2757-4(9))* Holiday Hse., Inc.

—Fish Had a Wish. Garland, Michael. 2012. (I Like to Read Ser.). (ENG.). 24p. (J). 14.95 *(978-0-8234-2394-1(8))* Holiday Hse., Inc.

—Grandpa's Tractor. Garland, Michael. 2011. (ENG.). 32p. (J). (gr. k-1). 16.95 *(978-1-59078-762-5(5))* Boyds Mills Pr.

—Hooray José!, 1 vol. Garland, Michael. 2007. (ENG.). 32p. (J). (gr. -1-3). 16.99 *(978-0-7614-5345-1(8))* Marshall Cavendish Corp.

—King Puck. Garland, Michael. 32p. (J). (gr. -1-3). 2009. (ENG.). pap. 6.99 *(978-0-06-084811-8(1))*; 2007. (ENG.). 16.99 *(978-0-06-084809-5(X))*; 2007. lib. bdg. 18.99 *(978-0-06-084810-1(3))* HarperCollins Pubs.

—Last Night at the Zoo. Garland, Michael. 2003. (ENG.). 32p. (J). (gr. k-2). pap. 10.95 *(978-1-59078-167-8(8))* Boyds Mills Pr.

—Miss Smith & the Haunted Library. Garland, Michael. 2009. (ENG.). 32p. (J). (gr. -1-2). 16.99 *(978-0-525-42139-9(4)*, Dutton Juvenile) Penguin Publishing Group.

—Miss Smith Reads Again! Garland, Michael. (ENG.). 32p. (J). (gr. -1-2). 2008. pap. 6.99 *(978-0-14-241140-7(X)*, Puffin); 2006. 15.99 *(978-0-525-47722-8(5)*, Dutton Juvenile) Penguin Publishing Group.

—Miss Smith under the Ocean. Garland, Michael. 2011. (ENG.). 32p. (J). (gr. -1-2). 16.99 *(978-0-525-42342-3(7)*, Dutton Juvenile) Penguin Publishing Group.

—Miss Smith's Incredible Storybook. Garland, Michael. (ENG.). 32p. (J). (gr. -1-2). 2005. pap. 6.99 *(978-0-14-240282-5(6)*, Puffin); 2003. 16.99 *(978-0-525-47133-2(2)*, Dutton Juvenile) Penguin Publishing Group.

—Oh, What a Christmas! Garland, Michael. 2011. (ENG.). 40p. (J). (gr. -1-3). 16.99 *(978-0-545-24210-3(X)*, Scholastic Pr.) Scholastic, Inc.

—Tugboat. Garland, Michael. 2014. (ENG.). 32p. (J). (gr. -1-3). 16.95 *(978-0-8234-2866-3(4))* Holiday Hse., Inc.

—Where's My Homework? Garland, Michael. 2014. (ENG.). 32p. (J). (gr. -1-k). pap. 6.99 *(978-0-545-43655-7(9)*, Cartwheel Bks.) Scholastic, Inc.

Garland, Nicholas. Mommy Daddy Evan Sage. McHenry, Eric. 2011. (ENG.). 64p. (J). 16.95 *(978-1-904130-45-1(3))* Waywiser Pr., The GBR. Dist: Dufour Editions, Inc.

Garland, Sally Anne. Share. Garland, Sally Anne. 2014. (ENG.). 32p. (J). (gr. -1-2). 17.95 *(978-1-77147-005-6(4)*, Owlkids) Owlkids Bks. Inc. CAN. Dist: Perseus-PGW.

Garland, Sarah. Azzi in Between. 2013. (ENG.). 40p. (J). (gr. 2-6). 17.99 *(978-1-84780-261-3(3)*, Frances Lincoln) Quarto Publishing Group UK GBR. Dist: Hachette Bk. Group.

—Doing Christmas. 2008. (ENG.). 32p. (J). (gr. -1-1). 9.95 *(978-1-84507-724-2(5)*, Frances Lincoln) Quarto Publishing Group UK GBR. Dist: Hachette Bk. Group.

—Eddie's Garden: And How to Make Things Grow. 2009. (ENG.). 40p. (J). (gr. -1-2). pap. 8.95 *(978-1-84507-089-2(5)*, Frances Lincoln) Quarto Publishing Group UK GBR. Dist: Hachette Bk. Group.

—Eddie's Toolbox: And How to Make & Mend Things. 2011. (ENG.). 40p. (J). (gr. -1-2). 17.95 *(978-1-84780-053-4(X)*, Frances Lincoln) Quarto Publishing Group UK GBR. Dist: Perseus-PGW.

Garlick, Mark A. Universe: Journey into Deep Space. Goldsmith, Mike. 2012. (ENG.). 48p. (J). (gr. 3-9). 17.99 *(978-0-7534-6876-0(X)*, Kingfisher) Roaring Brook Pr.

Garlick, Mark A. Astronomy, Set. Garlick, Mark A. 2004. (gr. 9-12). 23.95 *(978-0-86717-676-6(8)*, ES3010, Lifepac) Alpha Omega Pubns., Inc.

Garner, Essex. A Children's Book of Barack Obama Our 44th President. Garner, Lama. 2009.Tr. of Children's Book of Barack Obama Our 44th President. 24p. pap. 7.95 *(978-0-615-31464-8(3))* Art Of Essex Fine Art, The.

Garns, Allen. Parched. Clark, Georgia. 2014. (ENG.). 256p. (J). (gr. 7). 16.95 *(978-0-8234-2949-3(0))* Holiday Hse., Inc.

—The Tomb Robber & King Tut. Gauch, Sarah. 2015. (ENG.). 36p. (J). (gr. k-3). 16.99 *(978-0-670-78452-3(4)*, Viking Juvenile) Penguin Publishing Group.

—Twisters! Penner, Lucille Recht. 2009. (Step into Reading Ser.). (ENG.). 48p. (J). (gr. k-3). pap. 3.99 *(978-0-375-86224-3(2)*, Random Hse. Bks. for Young Readers) Random Hse. Children's Bks.

Garnsey, Wayne. Math 8 X-treme Review: Concise Training for NYS Math Intermediate Assessment. Milanese, Celestine Marie & Peck, Carolyn. Stich, Paul, ed. 2007. 160p. per. 13.95 *(978-0-935487-85-5(9)*, X-treme Reviews) N&N Publishing Co., Inc.

Garnvin, Rebecka. Eli - the Bi-Polar Bear. Liddle, Sharon. Maximilian Press Staff, ed. deluxe ed. 2003. 76p. (J). (gr. 1-4). 29.95 *(978-1-930211-49-0(X))* Maximilian Pr. Pubs.

Garofalo, Gianluca. Hurricane Hunters & Tornado Chasers. Jeffrey, Gary. 2008. (Graphic Careers Ser.). (ENG.). 48p. (gr. 5-8). per. 14.05 *(978-1-4042-1459-0(3))*; (YA). lib. bdg. 31.95 *(978-1-4042-1458-3(5))* Rosen Publishing Group, Inc., The.

Garofoli, Viviana. Are You Living? A Song about Living & Nonliving Things, 1 vol. Salas, Laura Purdie. 2009. (Science Songs Ser.). (ENG.). 24p. (gr. 1-3). lib. bdg. 25.99 *(978-1-4048-5302-7(2)*, Nonfiction Picture Bks.) Picture Window Bks.

—Ducks Go Vroom. Kohuth, Jane. 2011. (Step into Reading Ser.). (ENG.). 32p. (J). (gr. -1-1). pap. 3.99 *(978-0-375-86560-2(8))* Random Hse., Inc.

Garófoli, Viviana. Ducks Go Vroom. Kohuth, Jane. 2011. (Step into Reading Ser.). (ENG.). 32p. (J). (gr. -1-1). lib. bdg. 12.99 *(978-0-375-96567-8(X))* Random Hse., Inc.

Garofoli, Viviana. Firefighters! Speeding! Spraying! Saving!, 0 vols. Hubbell, Patricia. 2012. (ENG.). 32p. (J). (gr. -1-2). pap. 7.99 *(978-0-7614-6245-3(7)*, 9780761462453, Amazon Children's Publishing) Amazon Publishing.

—Firefighters! Speeing! Spraying! Saving!, 0 vols. Hubbell, Patricia. 2009. (ENG.). 32p. (J). (gr. -1-2). bds. 7.99 *(978-0-7614-5615-5(5)*, 9780761456155, Amazon Children's Publishing) Amazon Publishing.

—From Beginning to End: A Song about Life Cycles, 1 vol. Salas, Laura Purdie. 2009. (Science Songs Ser.). (ENG.). 24p. (gr. 1-3). lib. bdg. 25.99 *(978-1-4048-5293-8(X)*, Nonfiction Picture Bks.) Picture Window Bks.

—Halloween Hugs: A HUGS Book. 2014. (Hugs Book Ser.: 6). (ENG.). 10p. (J). (gr. -1-k). bds. 9.99 *(978-0-7944-3240-9(9))* Reader's Digest Assn., Inc., The.

—Home on the Earth: A Song about Earth's Layers, 1 vol. Salas, Laura Purdie. 2009. (Science Songs Ser.). (ENG.). 24p. (gr. 1-3). lib. bdg. 25.99 *(978-1-4048-5296-9(4)*, Nonfiction Picture Bks.) Picture Window Bks.

—I Can Save the Earth! One Little Monster Learns to Reduce, Reuse, & Recycle. Inches, Alison. 2008. (Little Green Bks.). (ENG.). 24p. (J). (gr. -1-1). pap. 3.99 *(978-1-4169-6789-7(3)*, Little Simon) Little Simon.

—I Can Save the Ocean! The Little Green Monster Cleans up the Beach. Inches, Alison. 2010. (Little Green Bks.). (ENG.). 24p. (J). (gr. -1-1). 7.99 *(978-1-4169-9514-2(5)*, Little Simon) Little Simon.

—Ma! There's Nothing to Do Here! A Word from Your Baby-in-Waiting. Park, Barbara. 2008. (Picture Book Ser.). (ENG.). 40p. (J). (gr. -1-2). 15.99 *(978-0-375-83852-1(X))* Random Hse., Inc.

—Meet Einstein. Kleiner, Mariela. 2011. 28p. (J). (gr. -1-1). lib. bdg. *(978-0-615-31579-9(8))* Meet Bks., LLC.

—My Big Rig, 0 vols. London, Jonathan. 2013. (ENG.). 50p. (J). (gr. -1-3). pap. 9.99 *(978-1-4778-1673-8(9)*, 9781477816738, Amazon Children's Publishing) Amazon Publishing.

—My Race into Space! A Water Wonder Book. Auerbach, Annie. 2005. 18p. (J). 9.95 *(978-1-58117-351-2(2)*, Intervisual/Piggy Toes) Bendon, Inc.

—Night Night Sleep Tight. Wolf, Jackie. 2004. 10p. (J). (gr. -1-18). bds. 5.99 *(978-1-57151-734-0(0))* Playhouse Publishing.

Garófoli, Viviana. Ouch Moments: When Words Hurt. Genhart, Michael. 2015. (J). ***(978-1-4338-1961-2(9)***, Magination Pr.) American Psychological Assn.

—Passover Is Coming! Newman, Tracy. 2015. (J). ***(978-1-4677-5242-8(8)***, Kar-Ben Publishing) Lerner Publishing Group.

Garofoli, Viviana. Shabbat Is Coming! Newman, Tracy. 2014. (Shabbat Ser.). (ENG.). 12p. (J). (gr. -1 — 1). bds. 5.95 *(978-1-4677-1367-2(8)*, Kar-Ben Publishing) Lerner Publishing Group.

—The Spooky Smells of Halloween. Man-Kong, Mary. 2005. (Scented Storybook Ser.). (ENG.). 32p. (J). (gr. -1-2). 8.99 *(978-0-375-83285-7(8)*, Golden Bks.) Random Hse. Children's Bks.

Garófoli, Viviana. Tea Time, 0 vols. Rostoker-Gruber, Karen. 2010. (ENG.). 24p. (J). (gr. -1-k). bds. 7.99 *(978-0-7614-5638-4(4)*, 9780761456384, Amazon Children's Publishing) Amazon Publishing.

—What If Your Best Friend Were Blue?, 0 vols. Kochan, Vera. 2011. (ENG.). 24p. (J). (gr. -1-2). 12.99 *(978-0-7614-5897-5(2)*, 9780761458975, Amazon Children's Publishing) Amazon Publishing.

Garofoli, Viviana. Zoom, Zoom, Zoom. Hall, Kirsten. 2004. (My First Reader Ser.). (ENG.). 32p. (J). (gr. k-1). pap. 3.95 *(978-0-516-25509-5(6)*, Children's Pr.) Scholastic Library Publishing.

Garratt, Richard. Agricultural & Urban Areas. Moore, Peter D. 2006. (Biomes of the Earth Ser.). 240p. (gr. 6-12). 39.50 *(978-0-8160-5326-1(X))* Facts On File, Inc.

—Animals. Allaby, Michael. 2010. (Discovering the Earth Ser.). 224p. (C). (gr. 9-18). 39.95 *(978-0-8160-6101-3(7))* Facts On File, Inc.

—Atmosphere: A Scientific History of Air, Weather, & Climate. Allaby, Michael. 2009. (Discovering the Earth Ser.). 256p. (C). (gr. 9-18). 39.95 *(978-0-8160-6098-6(3))* Facts On File, Inc.

—Deserts. Allaby, Michael. 2006. (Biomes of the Earth Ser.). 272p. (gr. 6-12). 39.50 *(978-0-8160-5320-9(0))* Facts On File, Inc.

—Discovering the Earth, 7 vols., Set. Allaby, Michael. 2010. (Discovering the Earth Ser.). 208p. (C). (gr. 9-18). 279.65 *(978-0-8160-6096-2(7))* Facts On File, Inc.

—Earth Science: A Scientific History of the Solid Earth. Allaby, Michael. 2009. (Discovering the Earth Ser.). 240p. (C). (gr. 9-18). 39.95 *(978-0-8160-6097-9(5))* Facts On File, Inc.

—Ecology: Plants, Animals, & the Environment. Allaby, Michael. 2009. (Discovering the Earth Ser.). 240p. (C). (gr. 9-18). 39.95 *(978-0-8160-6100-6(9))* Facts On File, Inc.

—Exploration. Allaby, Michael. 2010. (Discovering the Earth Ser.). 256p. (C). (gr. 9-18). 39.95 *(978-0-8160-6103-7(3))* Facts On File, Inc.

—Grasslands. Allaby, Michael. 2006. (Biomes of the Earth Ser.). 288p. (gr. 6-12). 39.50 *(978-0-8160-5323-0(5))* Facts On File, Inc.

—Lakes & Rivers. Day, Trevor. 2006. (Biomes of the Earth Ser.). 272p. (gr. 6-12). 39.50 *(978-0-8160-5328-5(6))* Facts On File, Inc.

—Oceans. Day, Trevor. 2006. (Biomes of the Earth Ser.). 272p. (gr. 6-12). 39.50 *(978-0-8160-5327-8(8))* Facts On File, Inc.

—Oceans: A Scientific History of Oceans & Marine Life. Allaby, Michael. 2009. (Discovering the Earth Ser.). 224p. (C). (gr. 9-18). 39.95 *(978-0-8160-6099-3(1))* Facts On File, Inc.

—Plants. Allaby, Michael. 2010. (Discovering the Earth Ser.). 240p. (C). (gr. 9-18). 39.95 *(978-0-8160-6102-0(5))* Facts On File, Inc.

—Taiga. Day, Trevor. 2006. (Biomes of the Earth Ser.). 240p. (gr. 6-12). 39.50 *(978-0-8160-5329-2(4))* Facts On File, Inc.

—Temperate Forests. Allaby, Michael. 2006. (Biomes of the Earth Ser.). 288p. (gr. 6-12). 39.50 *(978-0-8160-5321-6(9))* Facts On File, Inc.

—Tropical Forests. Allaby, Michael. 2006. (Biomes of the Earth Ser.). 288p. (gr. 6-12). 39.50 *(978-0-8160-5322-3(7))* Facts On File, Inc.

—Tundra. Moore, Peter D. (Ecosystems Ser.). 2007. 280p. (C). (gr. 9). 70.00 *(978-0-8160-5933-1(0))*; 2006. 240p. (gr. 6-12). 39.50 *(978-0-8160-5325-4(1))* Facts On File, Inc.

—Weather Science: Blizzards. Allaby, Michael. 2011. (Weather Science Ser.). (gr. 9). 40.00 *(978-0-8160-7316-0(3))* Facts On File, Inc.

—Weather Science: Floods. Allaby, Michael. 2011. (Weather Science Ser.). (gr. 9). 40.00 *(978-0-8160-7317-7(1))* Facts On File, Inc.

—Weather Science: Fog. Allaby, Michael. 2011. (Weather Science Ser.). (J). (gr. 9). 40.00 *(978-0-8160-7319-1(8))* Facts On File, Inc.

—Weather Science: Rain & Hail. Allaby, Michael. 2011. (Weather Science Ser.). (gr. 9). 40.00 *(978-0-8160-7318-4(X))* Facts On File, Inc.

—Wetlands. Moore, Peter D. (Biomes of the Earth Ser.). 2006. 240p. (gr. 6-12). 39.50 *(978-0-8160-5324-7(3))*; 2nd rev. ed. 2007. 288p. (C). (gr. 9-12). 70.00 *(978-0-8160-5931-7(4))* Facts On File, Inc.

Garraway, Kym. A Mississippi Summer on Bluebird Hill: A True Story about Our Little Farm in the Hills of Southern Mississippi. Remson, Billie. 2005. (J). pap. 12.95 *(978-1-59571-073-4(6))* Word Association Pubs.

—A Mississippi Winter on Bluebird Hill: A True Story about Our Little Farm in the Hills of Southern Mississippi. Remson, Billie. 2004. (J). per. 12.95 *(978-1-59571-044-4(2))* Word Association Pubs.

Garraway, Kym W. A Mississippi Spring on Bluebird Hill. Remson, Billie. 2004. per. 12.95 *(978-1-59571-004-8(3))* Word Association Pubs.

Garretson, Jerri & Dollar, Diane A. Kansas Tall Tales: Tenth Anniversary Anthology. Garretson, Jerri. 2008. 106p. (J). pap. 19.95 *(978-0-9659712-7-0(9))* Ravenstone Pr.

Garrett, Caroline S. Mushroom's Day Away. Ledbetter, Penny S. 2005. 32p. (J). 9.95 *(978-1-933251-19-6(0))* Parkway Pubs., Inc.

—Sara Bk. 3: A Talking Owl Is Worth a Thousand Words! Hicks, Esther & Hicks, Jerry. 3rd ed. 2008. (ENG.). 240p. per. 16.99 *(978-1-4019-1160-7(9))* Hay Hse., Inc.

—Sara Learns the Secret about the Law of Attraction. Hicks, Esther et al. 2nd ed. 2007. (ENG.). 192p. per. 14.99 *(978-1-4019-1158-4(7))* Hay Hse., Inc.

Garrett, Caroline S. Jeremiah. Garrett, Caroline S., tr. Underhill, Marjorie Fay. 2003. (J). 12.00 *(978-1-887905-75-6(8))* Parkway Pubs., Inc.

Garrett, Jacqueline, photos by. Surviving My Family. Kirst, Kathleen & Kirst, Kat. House, Nancy, ed. 2012. (ENG., 234p. pap. 9.25 *(978-0-615-58633-5(3))* Kat Kirst.

Garrett, Keith. Hooty & Pig: The Missing Christmas Pudding. Williams, Mark. 2013. 24p. pap. *(978-1-78132-133-1(7))* SilverWood Bks.

Garrett, Myers. Meet the Super Sisters. Moore, Mykela. 2013. (J). 9.99 *(978-0-9852746-9-6(7))* Hope of Vision Publishing.

Garrett, Scott. Bookmarks Are People Too! Winkler, Henry & Oliver, Lin. 2014. (Here's Hank Ser.: 1). (ENG.). 128p. (J). (gr. 1-3). 14.99 *(978-0-448-48239-2(8))*;No. 1. 5.99 *(978-0-448-47997-2(4))* Penguin Publishing Group. (Grosset & Dunlap).

—Fake Snakes & Weird Wizards. Winkler, Henry & Oliver, Lin. 2015. (Here's Hank Ser.: No. 4). (ENG.). 128p. (J). (gr. 1-3). 5.99 *(978-0-448-48252-1(5)*, Grosset & Dunlap) Penguin Publishing Group.

—A Short Tale about a Long Dog. Winkler, Henry & Oliver, Lin. 2014. (Here's Hank Ser.: 2). (ENG.). 128p. (J). (gr. 1-3). No. 2. 14.99 *(978-0-448-48240-8(1))*; Vol. 2. 5.99 *(978-0-448-47998-9(2))* Penguin Publishing Group. (Grosset & Dunlap).

—Stop That Frog!, No. 3. Winkler, Henry & Oliver, Lin. 2014. (Here's Hank Ser.: 3). (ENG.). 128p. (J). (gr. 1-3). 5.99 *(978-0-448-48152-4(9))*; 14.99 *(978-0-448-48241-5(X))* Penguin Publishing Group. (Grosset & Dunlap).

Garrett, Scott. There's a Zombie in My Bathtub #5. Oliver, Lin & Winkler, Henry. 2015. (Here's Hank Ser.: 5). (ENG.). 128p. (J). (gr. 1-3). 5.99 ***(978-0-448-48512-6(5)***, Grosset & Dunlap) Penguin Publishing Group.

Garrett, Toni. The Last Voyage of the Dan-D. Alston, E. B. l.t. ed. 2003. 47p. (J). per. 8.00 *(978-0-9747735-0-6(6))* Righter Publishing Co., Inc.

Garrigue, Roland. How to Defeat Dragons. Leblanc, Catherine. 2014. (How to Banish Fears Ser.). (ENG.). 32p. (gr. -1). pap. 8.99 *(978-1-60887-412-5(5))* Insight Editions LP.

—How to Demolish Dinosaurs. Leblanc, Catherine. 2013. (How to Banish Fears Ser.). (ENG.). 32p. (gr. -1). 14.99 *(978-1-60887-191-9(6))* Insight Editions LP.

—How to Get Rid of Ghosts. Leblanc, Catherine. 2013. (How to Banish Fears Ser.). (ENG.). 32p. (gr. -1). 14.99 *(978-1-60887-195-7(9))* Insight Editions LP.

—How to Mash Monsters. Leblanc, Catherine. 2013. (How to Banish Fears Ser.). (ENG.). 32p. (gr. -1). 14.99 *(978-1-60887-190-2(8))* Insight Editions LP.

—How to Outwit Witches. Leblanc, Catherine. 2013. (How to Banish Fears Ser.). (ENG.). 32p. (gr. -1). 14.99 *(978-1-60887-193-3(2))* Insight Editions LP.

—How to Pulverize Pirates. Leblanc, Catherine. 2013. (How to Banish Fears Ser.). (ENG.). 32p. (gr. -1). 14.99 *(978-1-60887-192-6(4))* Insight Editions LP.

—How to Ward off Wolves. Leblanc, Catherine. 2013. (How to Banish Fears Ser.). (ENG.). 32p. (gr. -1). 14.99 *(978-1-60887-194-0(0))* Insight Editions LP.

Garris, Norma. The Story of Christmas. 2013. (Happy Day Ser.). (ENG.). 16p. (J). pap. 2.49 *(978-1-4143-9524-1(8))* Tyndale Hse. Pubs.

Garrison, Barbara. Another Celebrated Dancing Bear. Scheffrin-Falk, Gladys. (J). 2007. 32p. (gr. -1-3). 18.95 *(978-1-930900-35-6(X))*; 20th ed. 2011. 28p. 18.95 *(978-1-930900-50-9(3))* Purple Hse. Pr.

Garrison, Carri. Making the Message Mine. Morgan, Marlo. Grimme, Jeannette, ed. Date not set. 115p. (Orig.). (YA). pap. *(978-1-883473-01-3(2))* MM Co.

Garrison, Ron, jt. illus. see Bohn, Ken.

Garrison, Sue. Willy: The Little Jeep Who Wanted to Be a Fire Truck. Estes, Don. 2003. 46p. (J). lib. bdg. 14.95 *(978-1-883551-47-6(1)*, ASP-471, Attic Studio Pr.) Attic Studio Publishing Hse.

Garrity-Riley, Kelsey. Goldie Takes a Stand! Golda Meir's First Crusade. Krasner, Barbara. 2014. (ENG.). 32p. (J). (gr. k-4). 17.95 *(978-1-4677-1200-2(0))* Lerner Publishing Group.

—Goldie Takes a Stand: Golda Meir's First Crusade. Krasner, Barbara. 2014. 32p. (J). (gr. k-4). 7.95 *(978-1-4677-1201-9(9)*, Kar-Ben Publishing) Lerner Publishing Group.

Garrow, Linda. Planets, Moons, & Stars. Evert, Laura. 2003. (Take along Guides). (ENG.). 48p. (J). (gr. 2-5). pap. 7.95 *(978-1-55971-842-4(0))* Cooper Square Publishing Llc.

Garson, Sarah. Alfie's Angels. Barkow, Henriette. 2004. 32p. (J). (FRE & ENG.). pap. *(978-1-85269-977-2(9))*; (ENG & PAN.). pap. *(978-1-85269-997-0(3))* Mantra Lingua.

—Alfie's Angels: Big Book English Only. Barkow, Henriette. 2004. 30p. (J). *(978-1-84444-119-8(9))* Mantra Lingua.

Garson, Sarah. One, Two, Cockatoo! Garson, Sarah. 2012. (ENG.). 32p. (J). (gr. k — 1). pap. 10.99 *(978-1-84270-944-3(5))* Andersen Pr. GBR. Dist: Independent Pubs. Group.

Gartner, Kathleen. Uncle Willy's Tickles: A Child's Right to Say No. Aboff, Marcie. 2nd ed. 2003. 32p. (J). 14.95 *(978-1-55798-998-7(2))*; pap. 9.95 *(978-1-55798-999-4(0))* American Psychological Assn. (Magination Pr.).

Garton, Michael. Visit to the Dentist. Askew, Amanda & Marleau, Eve. 2009. (My First Ser.). (ENG.). 24p. (J). (gr. -1-17). lib. bdg. 15.99 *(978-1-59566-988-9(4))* QEB Publishing Inc.

—Visit to the Doctor. Marleau, Eve. 2009. (My First Ser.). (ENG.). 24p. (J). (gr. -1-17). lib. bdg. 15.99 *(978-1-59566-987-2(6))* QEB Publishing Inc.

Garton, Sam. I Am Otter. Garton, Sam. 2014. (ENG.). 32p. (J). (gr. -1-3). 16.99 *(978-0-06-224775-9(1))* HarperCollins Pubs.

—Otter in Space. Garton, Sam. 2015. (ENG.). 32p. (J). (gr. -1-3). 16.99 *(978-0-06-224776-6(X))* HarperCollins Pubs.

Garton, Sam. Otter Loves Halloween! Garton, Sam. 2015. (ENG.). 32p. (J). (gr. -1-3). 9.99 ***(978-0-06-236666-5(1)***, Balzer & Bray) HarperCollins Pubs.

Garvey, Brann. Advice about Family: Claudia Cristina Cortez Uncomplicates Your Life. Gallagher, Diana G. 2010. (Claudia Cristina Cortez Ser.). (ENG.). 80p. (gr. 2-3). pap. 6.10 *(978-1-4342-2250-3(0))*; 25.32 *(978-1-4342-1907-7(0))* Stone Arch Bks. (Claudia Cristina Cortez).

—Advice about Friends. Gallagher, Diana G. 2010. (Claudia Cristina Cortez Ser.). (ENG.). 80p. (gr. 2-3). 25.32 *(978-1-4342-1906-0(2)*, Claudia Cristina Cortez) Stone Arch Bks.

—Advice about Friends: Claudia Cristina Cortez Uncomplicates Your Life. Gallagher, Diana G. 2010. (Claudia Cristina Cortez Ser.). (ENG.). 80p. (gr. 2-3). pap. 6.10 *(978-1-4342-2251-0(9)*, Claudia Cristina Cortez) Stone Arch Bks.

—Advice about School: Claudia Cristina Cortez Uncomplicates Your Life. Gallagher, Diana G. 2010. (Claudia Cristina Cortez Ser.). (ENG.). 80p. (gr. 2-3). pap. 6.10 *(978-1-4342-2252-7(7))*; 25.32 *(978-1-4342-1905-3(4))* Stone Arch Bks. (Claudia Cristina Cortez).

—Advice about Work & Play: Claudia Cristina Cortez Uncomplicates Your Life. Gallagher, Diana G. 2010. (Claudia Cristina Cortez Ser.). (ENG.). 80p. (gr. 2-3). pap. 6.10 *(978-1-4342-2253-4(5))*; 25.32 *(978-1-4342-1908-4(9))* Stone Arch Bks. (Claudia Cristina Cortez).

—Bad Luck Bridesmaid: The Complicated Life of Claudia Cristina Cortez, 1 vol. Gallagher, Diana G. 2009. (Claudia Cristina Cortez Ser.). (ENG.). 88p. (gr. 2-3). 25.32 *(978-1-4342-1573-4(3)*, Claudia Cristina Cortez) Stone Arch Bks.

—Beach Blues: The Complicated Life of Claudia Cristina Cortez, 1 vol. Gallagher, Diana G. 2008. (Claudia Cristina Cortez Ser.). (ENG.). 88p. (gr. 2-3). pap. 6.10 *(978-1-4342-0869-9(9))*; lib. bdg. 25.32 *(978-1-4342-0773-9(0))* Stone Arch Bks. (Claudia Cristina Cortez).

—Beware! The Complicated Life of Claudia Cristina Cortez, 1 vol. Gallagher, Diana G. 2009. (Claudia Cristina Cortez Ser.). (ENG.). 88p. (gr. 2-3). 25.32 *(978-1-4342-1575-8(X)*, Claudia Cristina Cortez) Stone Arch Bks.

—Boy Trouble: The Complicated Life of Claudia Cristina Cortez. Gallagher, Diana G. 2009. (Claudia Cristina Cortez Ser.). (ENG.). 88p. (gr. 2-3). 25.32 *(978-1-4342-1576-5(8))*; pap. 6.10 *(978-1-4342-1757-8(4))* Stone Arch Bks. (Claudia Cristina Cortez).

—Camp Can't: The Complicated Life of Claudia Cristina Cortez, 1 vol. Gallagher, Diana G. 2007. (Claudia Cristina Cortez Ser.). (ENG.). 88p. (gr. 2-3). lib. bdg. 25.32 *(978-1-59889-840-8(X))*; per. 6.10 *(978-1-59889-878-1(7))* Stone Arch Bks. (Claudia Cristina Cortez).

—The Curse of the Wendigo: An Agate & Buck Adventure, 1 vol. Welvaert, Scott R. & Jungman, Ann. 2006. (Vortex Bks.). (ENG.). 112p. (gr. 2-3). pap. 7.19 *(978-1-59889-282-6(7)*, Vortex Bks.) Stone Arch Bks.

—The Curse of the Wendigo: An Agate & Buck Adventure, 1 vol. Welvaert, Scott R. 2006. (Agate & Buck Adventure Ser.). (ENG.). 112p. (gr. 2-3). lib. bdg. 25.32 *(978-1-59889-066-2(2)*, Vortex Bks.) Stone Arch Bks.

—Dance Trap: The Complicated Life of Claudia Cristina Cortez, 1 vol. Gallagher, Diana G. 2007. (Claudia Cristina Cortez Ser.). (ENG.). 88p. (gr. 2-3). lib. bdg. 25.32 *(978-1-59889-841-5(8))*; per. 6.10 *(978-1-59889-879-8(5))* Stone Arch Bks. (Claudia Cristina Cortez).

—Excuses! Survive & Succeed with David Mortimore Baxter. Tayleur, Karen. (David Mortimore Baxter Ser.). (ENG.). 88p. (gr. 2-3). 2007. per. 6.05 *(978-1-59889-205-5(3))*; 2006. lib. bdg. 25.32 *(978-1-59889-073-0(5))* Stone Arch Bks. (David Mortimore Baxter).

—Famous (Scholastic) The Awesome Life of David Mortimore Baxter. Tayleur, Karen. 2009. (David Mortimore Baxter Ser.). 88p. pap. 0.80 *(978-1-4342-2503-0(8)*, David Mortimore Baxter) Stone Arch Bks.

—Friends Forever? The Complicated Life of Claudia Cristina Cortez, 1 vol. Gallagher, Diana G. 2008. (Claudia Cristina Cortez Ser.). (ENG.). 88p. (gr. 2-3). pap. 6.10 *(978-1-4342-0868-2(0))*; lib. bdg. 25.32 *(978-1-4342-0772-2(2))* Stone Arch Bks. (Claudia Cristina Cortez).

—Guilty! The Complicated Life of Claudia Cristina Cortez, 1 vol. Gallagher, Diana G. 2007. (Claudia Cristina Cortez Ser.). (ENG.). 88p. (gr. 2-3). lib. bdg. 25.32 *(978-1-59889-838-5(8))*; per. 6.10 *(978-1-59889-881-1(7))* Stone Arch Bks. (Claudia Cristina Cortez).

—Hired or Fired? The Complicated Life of Claudia Cristina Cortez, 1 vol. Gallagher, Diana G. 2009. (Claudia Cristina Cortez Ser.). (ENG.). 88p. (gr. 2-3). 25.32 *(978-1-4342-1574-1(1)*, Claudia Cristina Cortez) Stone Arch Bks.

—Liar! The True Story of David Mortimore Baxter. Tayleur, Karen. (David Mortimore Baxter Ser.). (ENG.). 80p. (gr. 2-3). 2007. per. 6.05 *(978-1-59889-206-2(1))*; 2006. lib. bdg. 25.32 *(978-1-59889-074-7(3))* Stone Arch Bks. (David Mortimore Baxter).

—Manners! Staying Out of Trouble with David Mortimore Baxter. Tayleur, Karen. (David Mortimore Baxter Ser.). (ENG.). 88p. (gr. 2-3). 2007. per. 6.05 *(978-1-59889-207-9(X))*; 2006. lib. bdg. 25.32 *(978-1-59889-075-4(1))* Stone Arch Bks. (David Mortimore Baxter).

—The Mosquito King: An Agate & Buck Adventure, 1 vol. Welvaert, Scott R. 2007. (Agate & Buck Adventure Ser.). (ENG.). 112p. (gr. 2-3). 25.32 *(978-1-59889-857-6(4)*, Vortex Bks.) Stone Arch Bks.

—Party! The Complicated Life of Claudia Cristina Cortez, 1 vol. Gallagher, Diana G. 2008. (Claudia Cristina Cortez Ser.). (ENG.). 88p. (gr. 2-3). pap. 6.10 *(978-1-4342-0867-5(2))*; lib. bdg. 25.32 *(978-1-4342-0771-5(4))* Stone Arch Bks. (Claudia Cristina Cortez).

—The Pirate, Big Fist, & Me, 1 vol. MacPhail, C. & Cosson, M. J. 2006. (Vortex Bks.). (ENG.). 112p. (gr. 2-3). 7.19 *(978-1-59889-279-6(7)*, Vortex Bks.) Stone Arch Bks.

—The Pirate, Big Fist, & Me, 1 vol. Cosson, M. J. 2006. (Vortex Bks.). (ENG.). 112p. (gr. 2-3). 25.32 *(978-1-59889-068-6(9)*, Vortex Bks.) Stone Arch Bks.

—Pool Problem: The Complicated Life of Claudia Cristina Cortez, 1 vol. Gallagher, Diana G. 2009. (Claudia Cristina Cortez Ser.). (ENG.). 88p. (gr. 2-3). 25.32 *(978-1-4342-1577-2(6))*; pap. 6.10 *(978-1-4342-1758-5(2))* Stone Arch Bks. (Claudia Cristina Cortez).

—Promises! Vote for David Mortimore Baxter. Tayleur, Karen. (David Mortimore Baxter Ser.). (ENG.). 96p. (gr. 2-3). 2007. per. 6.05 *(978-1-59889-208-6(8))*; 2006. lib. bdg. 25.32 *(978-1-59889-076-1(X))* Stone Arch Bks. (David Mortimore Baxter).

—Rock Art Rebel, 1 vol. Cosson, M. J. 2006. (Vortex Bks.). (ENG.). 112p. (gr. 2-3). 25.32 *(978-1-59889-070-9(0)*, Vortex Bks.) Stone Arch Bks.

—Secrets! The Secret Life of David Mortimore Baxter, 1 vol. Tayleur, Karen. 2006. (David Mortimore Baxter Ser.). (ENG.). 96p. (gr. 2-3). lib. bdg. 25.32 *(978-1-59889-077-8(8)*, David Mortimore Baxter) Stone Arch Bks.

—Sold! The Complicated Life of Claudia Cristina Cortez, 1 vol. Gallagher, Diana G. 2009. (Claudia Cristina Cortez Ser.). (ENG.). 88p. (gr. 2-3). 25.32 *(978-1-4342-1572-7(5)*, Claudia Cristina Cortez) Stone Arch Bks.

—The Truth! David Mortimore Baxter Comes Clean, 1 vol. Tayleur, Karen. 2006. (David Mortimore Baxter Ser.). (ENG.). 96p. (gr. 2-3). lib. bdg. 25.32 *(978-1-59889-078-5(6)*, David Mortimore Baxter) Stone Arch Bks.

—Vote! The Complicated Life of Claudia Cristina Cortez, 1 vol. Gallagher, Diana G. 2008. (Claudia Cristina Cortez Ser.). (ENG.). 88p. (gr. 2-3). pap. 6.10 *(978-1-4342-0866-8(4))*; lib. bdg. 25.32 *(978-1-4342-0770-8(6))* Stone Arch Bks. (Claudia Cristina Cortez).

—Whatever! The Complicated Life of Claudia Cristina Cortez, 1 vol. Gallagher, Diana G. 2007. (Claudia Cristina Cortez Ser.). (ENG.). 88p. (gr. 2-3). pap. 6.10 *(978-1-59889-880-4(9))*; lib. bdg. 25.32 *(978-1-59889-839-2(6))* Stone Arch Bks. (Claudia Cristina Cortez).

Garvey, Brann & O'Connor, Niamh. The Ghost's Revenge, 1 vol. Peschke, Marci & Townson, H. 2006. (Vortex Bks.). (ENG.). 112p. (gr. 2-3). 7.19 *(978-1-59889-283-3(5)*, Vortex Bks.) Stone Arch Bks.

—The Ghost's Revenge, 1 vol. Peschke, Marci. 2006. (Vortex Bks.). (ENG.). 112p. (gr. 2-3). lib. bdg. 25.32 *(978-1-59889-071-6(9)*, Vortex Bks.) Stone Arch Bks.

Garvin, Elaine. All-Girl Crafts. Ross, Kathy. 2005. (Girl Crafts Ser.). (ENG.). 48p. (gr. 2-5). lib. bdg. 26.60 *(978-0-7613-2776-9(2)*, Millbrook Pr.); per. 7.95 *(978-0-7613-2391-4(0)*, First Avenue Editions) Lerner Publishing Group.

—Babe Ruth & the Ice Cream Mess. Gutman, Dan. 2004. (Ready-To-read COFA Ser.). (ENG.). 32p. (J). (gr. k-2). pap. 3.99 *(978-0-689-85529-0(X)*, Simon Spotlight) Simon Spotlight.

—Jackie Robinson & the Big Game. Gutman, Dan. 2006. 32p. (J). lib. bdg. 15.00 *(978-1-4242-0957-6(9))* Fitzgerald Bks.

—Jackie Robinson & the Big Game. Gutman, Dan. 2006. (Ready-To-read COFA Ser.). (ENG.). 32p. (J). (gr. k-2). pap. 3.99 *(978-0-689-86239-7(3)*, Simon & Schuster/Paula Wiseman Bks.) Simon & Schuster/Paula Wiseman Bks.

—The Little Elephant with the Big Earache. Cowan, Charlotte. 2007. (Dr. Hippo Ser.). (ENG.). 32p. (J). (gr. -1-3). 17.95 *(978-0-9753516-0-4(5))* Hippocratic Pr., The.

—Play Fair, Little Bear. Allan-Meyer, Kathleen. 2003. (Little Bear Adventure Ser.: Vol. 7). 28p. (J). (gr. -1-1). pap. 6.49 *(978-1-57924-887-1(X))* BJU Pr.

—The Story of the Lord's Prayer. Pingry, Patricia A. (ENG.). (J). 2008. 24p. bds. 6.95 *(978-0-8249-6519-8(1))*; 2008. 28p. (gr. -1-k). pap. 3.99 *(978-0-8249-5555-7(2)*, Ideals Children's Bks.); 2005. 26p. (gr. -1-k). 9.95 *(978-0-8249-6637-9(5)*, Candy Cane Pr.) Ideals Pubns.

—Things to Make for Your Doll. Ross, Kathy. 2005. (Girl Crafts Ser.). (ENG.). 48p. (gr. 2-5). lib. bdg. 26.60 *(978-0-7613-2861-2(0)*, Millbrook Pr.) Lerner Publishing Group.

Garvin, Kelly. Caring for Your Dog, 1 vol. Preszler, June. 2006. (Positively Pets Ser.). (ENG.). 24p. (gr. 1-2). 24.65 *(978-0-7368-6385-8(0)*, First Facts) Capstone Pr., Inc.

—Caring for Your Fish, 1 vol. Richardson, Adele & Richardson, Adele D. 2006. (Positively Pets Ser.). (ENG.). 24p. (gr. 1-2). 24.65 *(978-0-7368-6386-5(9)*, First Facts) Capstone Pr., Inc.

—Caring for Your Hamster, 1 vol. Richardson, Adele & Richardson, Adele D. 2006. (Positively Pets Ser.). (ENG.). 24p. (gr. 1-2). 24.65 *(978-0-7368-6387-2(7)*, First Facts) Capstone Pr., Inc.

Garvin, Sheri. Little Rhymes for Quiet Times. Franck, Charlotte. 2006. 29p. per. 15.95 *(978-1-60002-116-9(6)*, 4029) Mountain Valley Publishing, LLC.

Garwood, Gord, jt. illus. see Style Guide Staff.

Gary Cianciarulo, Gary. The Mystery of Rascal Pratt. Scott, Robbie. 2010. (ENG.). 208p. pap. 11.95 *(978-1-4563-1816-1(0))* CreateSpace Independent Publishing Platform.

Gary, Glenn. The Lost Lighthouse. VanRiper, Justin & VanRiper, Gary. 2003. (Adirondack Kids Ser.: Vol. 3). 82p. (J). (gr. 2-7). pap. 9.95 *(978-0-9707044-2-9(9)*, ADK3) Adirondack Kids Pr.

Gary, Ken. The Fire Stealers: A Hopi Story. Gary, Ken, tr. 2003. (J). 15.95 *(978-1-885772-13-8(0))* Kiva Publishing, Inc.

Gary Ripper. Princess Maddy & Her Blankie. Brice, Ginny. 2011. 20p. pap. 24.95 *(978-1-4560-7745-7(7))* America Star Bks.

Garza, Carmen Lomas. Cuadros de Familia.Tr. of Family Pictures. (ENG & SPA.). 32p. (J). (2nd) anniv. ed. 2013. pap. 9.95 *(978-0-89239-207-0(X))*; 15th anniv. ed. 2005. (gr. -1-17). 16.95 *(978-0-89239-206-3(1))* Lee & Low Bks., Inc.

—In My Family. 2013.Tr. of En Mi Familia. (ENG & SPA.). 32p. (J). (gr. 1-4). pap. 9.95 *(978-0-89239-163-9(4))* Lee & Low Bks., Inc.

—Magic Windows: Ventanas Magicas. 2013. (ENG & SPA.). 32p. (J). pap. 9.95 *(978-0-89239-183-7(9)*, Children's Book Press) Lee & Low Bks., Inc.

—Making Magic Windows. 2014. (ENG & SPA.). 32p. (J). (gr. 4-7). pap. 11.95 *(978-0-89239-159-2(6))* Lee & Low Bks., Inc.

Garza, Fabiola. The Story of Saint John Paul II: A Boy Who Became Pope. Garza, Fabiola. 2014. (J). 15.95 *(978-0-8198-9013-9(8))* Pauline Bks. & Media.

Garza, Xavier. The Great & Mighty Nikko. 2015. (ENG.). 32p. (J). pap. 7.95 *(978-1-935955-83-2(7))*; (gr. -1-4). 16.95 *(978-1-935955-82-5(9))* Cinco Puntos Pr.

—Maximilian & the Bingo Rematch: A Lucha Libre Sequel. 2013. (Max's Lucha Libre Adventures Ser.). (ENG.). 208p. (J). 19.95 *(978-1-935955-59-7(4))* Cinco Puntos Pr.

—Maximilian & the Mystery of the Guardian Angel. 2011. (Max's Lucha Libre Adventures Ser.). (SPA & ENG.). 160p. (J). (gr. 5-8). pap. 12.95 *(978-1-933693-98-9(3))* Cinco Puntos Pr.

Garza, Xavier. Lucha Libre: The Man in the Silver Mask - A Bilingual Cuento. Garza, Xavier. 2007. (SPA & ENG.). 40p. (J). (gr. 4-6). pap. 8.95 *(978-1-933693-10-1(X))* Cinco Puntos Pr.

—Lucha Libre: The Man in the Silver Mask - A Bilingual Cuento. Garza, Xavier. Crosthwaite, Luis Humberto, tr. 2005. (ENG & SPA.). 40p. (J). (gr. 4-6). 17.95 *(978-0-938317-92-0(X))* Cinco Puntos Pr.

—Zulema & the Witch Owl/Zulema y la Bruja Lechuza. Garza, Xavier. Villarroel, Carolina. 2009. (SPA & ENG.). 32p. (J). (gr. -1-4). 16.95 *(978-1-55885-515-1(7)*, Piñata Books) Arte Publico Pr.

Gasal, Ben. Boxy: A Tree of the Prairie. Daugherty, Doug. 2008. 24p. pap. 24.95 *(978-1-60610-808-6(5))* PublishAmerica, Inc.

Gascoigne, Martin. The Call of the Wild. Gascoigne, Martin. London, Jack. 2008. (Puffin Classics Ser.). (ENG.). 160p. (J). (gr. 3-7). 5.99 *(978-0-14-132105-9(9)*, Puffin) Penguin Publishing Group.

Gaspar, Tamas, jt. illus. see Futaki, Attila.

Gassler, Stephen, III. Lucy's Family Tree, 1 vol. Schreck, Karen Halvorsen. 2006. (ENG.). 40p. (J). (gr. -1-3). 7.95 *(978-0-88448-292-5(8))* Tilbury Hse. Pubs.

Gast, Linda, photos by. So What, Saw-Whet? Frank, Rochelle. 2004. (J). per. 9.95 *(978-0-9746792-0-4(8))* Hummingbird Mountain Pr.

Gastaldo, Walter. El Cocodrilo Lloron. Barsy, Kalman. 2004. (Yellow Ser.). (SPA.). 31p. (J). (gr. k-3). pap. 5.95 *(978-1-57581-433-9(1))* Santillana USA Publishing Co., Inc.

Gaston, Carter J. How Do You Know When It's Time to Go to Bed? Gaston, P. J. 2008. (ENG.). 28p. (J). 10.00 *(978-0-9675574-2-7(9))* "How Do You Know".

gaston, carter j. How Do You Know When It's Time to Go to Bed? 2008. 28p. (J). pap. 8.00 *(978-0-9675574-3-4(7))* "How Do You Know".

Gaston, Keith A. Call Me Madame President. Pyatt, Sue. 2003. 31p. (J). 17.00 *(978-0-9742575-0-1(8))* Imagination Station Pr.

Gaston, Sierra. Grandma, Do Angels Have Wings?, 1 vol. Wiedeman, Connie. 2010. 40p. 24.95 *(978-1-4512-1054-5(X))* PublishAmerica, Inc.

Gatagan, T. Las Preguntas de Bingo Brown. Byars, Betsy. 2nd ed. 2003. (Espasa Juvenil Ser.: Vol. 15).Tr. of Burning Questions of Bingo Brown. (SPA.). 186p. (J). (gr. 7-18). *(978-84-239-8862-4(7)*, EC4398) Espasa Calpe, S.A. ESP. Dist: Lectorum Pubns., Inc.

Gatagán, Tino. Poesía Española para Niños. Gatagán, Tino, tr. 2nd ed. 2015. (SPA.). 152p. 10.95 ***(978-84-204-4899-2(0))*** Ediciones Alfaguara ESP. Dist: Santillana USA Publishing Co., Inc.

Gateley, Edwina. God Goes on Vacation. Gateley, Edwina. 2009. 32p. (Orig.). (J). pap. 9.95 *(978-0-8091-6747-0(6))* Paulist Pr.

Gateley, Edwina. God Goes to School. Gateley, Edwina, text. 2009. 32p. (J). pap. 9.95 *(978-0-8091-6748-7(4))* Paulist Pr.

Gates, Donald. Hoggle's Christmas. Shelton, Rick. 2007. 80p. (J). pap. 11.95 *(978-1-60306-026-4(X))* NewSouth, Inc.

Gates, Phyllis. My Too Blue Shoes: A Parable about Wearing Your Convictions. Woodruff, Joe. 2011. (ENG.). 24p. pap. 9.95 *(978-1-4611-7792-0(8))* CreateSpace Independent Publishing Platform.

Gathigo, Cyrus Ngatia. Lilana Ageiraŭ. Resman, Michael. Cayetano, Eldred Roy, tr. 2013. 40p. pap. *(978-976-8142-50-4(2))* Producciones de la Hamaca.

—The Villagers. Resman, Michael. Senelwa, Fred, tr. 2012. 40p. pap. *(978-976-8142-41-2(3))* Producciones de la Hamaca.

Gatt, Elizabeth. Sea Otter Pup, 1 vol. Miles, Victoria. 2013. (ENG.). 26p. (J). (gr. -1-k). bds. 9.95 *(978-1-4598-0467-8(8))* Orca Bk. Pubs. USA.

Gatto, Horacio. The Gift. Celcer, Irene. 2009. (J). pap. *(978-0-9755810-6-3(6))* Graphite Pr.

—The Gift of Adoption. Celcer, Irene. 2009. (J). pap. *(978-0-9755810-5-6(8))* Graphite Pr.

—The Gift of Egg Donation. Celcer, Irene. 2007. (Hope & Will Have a Baby Ser.). 32p. (J). (gr. k-3). pap. 19.95 *(978-0-9755810-1-8(5)*, 9780975581018) Graphite Pr.

—The Gift of Embryo Donation. Celcer, Irene. 2007. (Hope & Will Have a Baby Ser.). 32p. (J). (gr. k-3). pap. 19.95 *(978-0-9755810-2-5(3)*, 9780975581025) Graphite Pr.

—The Gift of Sperm Donation. Celcer, Irene. 2007. (Hope & Will Have a Baby Ser.). 32p. (J). (gr. k-3). pap. 19.95 *(978-0-9755810-3-2(1)*, 9780975581032) Graphite Pr.

—The Gift of Surrogacy. Celcer, Irene. 2007. (Hope & Will Have a Baby Ser.). 32p. (J). (gr. k-3). pap. 19.95 *(978-0-9755810-4-9(X)*, 9780975581049) Graphite Pr.

Gatto, Kim. K Is for Kite: God's Springtime Alphabet, 1 vol. Wargin, Kathy-jo. 2010. (ENG.). 40p. (J). (gr. -1-2). 15.99 *(978-0-310-71662-4(4))* Zonderkidz.

Gau Family Studio. The Little Girl Who Lied: The Importance of Honesty. Carty, Amy. Williams, Nancy E., ed. 2013. 40p. (J). pap. 16.98 *(978-1-938526-69-5(4))* Laurus Bks.

Gaudasinska, Elzbieta. The Love for Three Oranges. Prokofiev, Sergei. 2006. (Musical Stories Ser.: Vol. 1). (ENG.). 40p. (J). (gr. 2-4). 16.95 *(978-0-9646010-3-1(6))* Pumpkin Hse., Ltd.

Gaudenzi, Giacinto. Los Caballeros - Internet Linked. Firth, Rachel. 2004. (Titles in Spanish Ser.). (SPA.). 48p. (J). pap. 8.95 *(978-0-7460-5083-5(6)*, Usborne) EDC Publishing.

—Roman Britain: Internet-Linked. Brocklehurst, Ruth. Chisholm, Jane, ed. 2006. (Usborne History of Britain Ser.). 48p. (J). (gr. 4-7). per. 8.99 *(978-0-7945-1232-3(1)*, Usborne) EDC Publishing.

Gaudenzi, Giacinto & Haggerty, Tim. Horses & Ponies. Milbourne, Anna. 2006. (Beginners Nature: Level 1 Ser.). 32p. (J). (gr. k-2). 4.99 *(978-0-7945-1397-9(2)*, Usborne) EDC Publishing.

Gaudenzi, Giacinto & Montgomery, Lee. Knights & Armor. Firth, Rachel. 2006. 95p. (J). (gr. 4-7). 17.99 *(978-0-7945-1279-8(8)*, Usborne) EDC Publishing.

Gaudet, Christine. Donkey Oatie's Field Trip. Rath, Tom H. 2013. 26p. pap. *(978-0-9918033-4-7(5))* Wood Islands Prints.

Gaudiamo, Adi Darda. Berlin Breakout, 1 vol. Avery, Ben & Rogers, Bud. 2008. (Z Graphic Novels / TimeFlyz Ser.). (ENG.). 160p. (J). (gr. 4-7). pap. 6.99 *(978-0-310-71363-0(3))* Zondervan.

—Pyramid Peril, 1 vol. Avery, Ben G. 2007. (Z Graphic Novels / TimeFlyz Ser.). (ENG.). 160p. (J). (gr. 3-7). pap. 6.99 *(978-0-310-71361-6(7))* Zonderkidz.

—Tunnel Twist-Up, 1 vol., Vol. 4. Avery, Ben. 2008. (Z Graphic Novels / TimeFlyz Ser.). (ENG.). 160p. (J). (gr. 4-7). pap. 6.99 *(978-0-310-71364-7(1))* Zondervan.

—Turtle Trouble, 1 vol. Avery, Ben G. 2007. (Z Graphic Novels / TimeFlyz Ser.). (ENG.). 160p. (J). (gr. 3-7). pap. 6.99 *(978-0-310-71362-3(5))* Zonderkidz.

Gauld, Tom. The Three Musketeers. Dumas, Alexandre. Pevear, Richard, tr. 2007. (Penguin Classics Deluxe Edition Ser.). (ENG.). 736p. (gr. 12-18). 16.00 *(978-0-14-310500-8(0)*, Penguin Classics) Penguin Publishing Group.

Gausden, Vicki. Circus Fun! Dale, Elizabeth. 2014. (Green Bananas Ser.). (ENG.). 48p. (J). pap. 7.99 ***(978-1-4052-7069-4(1))*** Egmont Bks., Ltd. GBR. Dist: Independent Pubs. Group.

Gauss, Rose. Callie & the Stepmother. Meyers, Susan A. I.t. ed. 2005. (ENG.). 64p. (J). (gr. -1-3). pap. 6.95 *(978-0-9718348-0-4(6))* Blooming Tree Pr.

Gauthier, Corbert. I Wonder... Did Jesus Have a Pet Lamb? Oke, Janette. 2004. (ENG.). 24p. (J). 9.99 *(978-0-7642-2901-5(X))* Bethany Hse. Pubs.

Gauthier, Elizabeth. A Bald Chimpanzee, an Adventure in ABC's. Gauthier, Elizabeth. 2010. (ENG.). 40p. (J). (gr. -1-4). 16.95 *(978-0-9820812-2-8(7)*, Frog Legs Ink) Gauthier Pubns. Inc.

—Out of the Nursery. Gauthier, Elizabeth. 2013. (ENG.). 30p. pap. 9.99 *(978-0-615-77391-9(5))* Frog Legs Ink.

Gauthier, Elizabeth & Bonney, Joan. A Bald Chimpanzee: An Adventure in ABCs. Gauthier, Elizabeth. 2012. (ENG.). 40p. (J). pap. 12.99 *(978-0-9833593-5-7(0)*, Frog Legs Ink) Gauthier Pubns. Inc.

Gauthier, Glenn G. The A to Z Book. Gauthier, Glenn G. 2006. 32p. (J). 16.95 *(978-1-887542-42-5(6))* Book Pubs. Network.

Gauthier, Manon. Marcel Marceau: Master of Mime. Spielman, Gloria. 2011. (Kar-Ben Biographies Ser.). (ENG.). 32p. (J). (gr. 3-5). pap. 7.95 *(978-0-7613-3962-5(0))*; lib. bdg. 17.95 *(978-0-7613-3961-8(2))* Lerner Publishing Group. (Kar-Ben Publishing).

—The Tooth. Slodovnick, Avi. 2010. (ENG.). 32p. (J). (gr. -1-3). 9.99 *(978-1-935279-72-3(6))* Kane Miller.

Gauthier, Manon & Martz, John. Black & Bittern Was Night. Heidbreder, Robert. 2013. (ENG.). 32p. (J). 16.95 *(978-1-55453-302-2(3))* Kids Can Pr., Ltd. CAN. Dist: Univ. of Toronto Pr.

Gauvin, Matthew. A Cloudy Day. Da Puzzo, Allegra & Da Puzzo, Jackson. 2012. 24p. pap. *(978-0-9843477-5-9(5))* Roxby Media Ltd.

Gavet, Nathalie. Meeting My Cas. Robe, Adam D. Robe, Kim A., ed. 2009. 16p. pap. 11.99 *(978-0-9817403-5-5(9))* Robe Communications, Inc.

—Moving to Another Foster Home. Robe, Adam D. Robe, Kim A., ed. 2009. 16p. pap. 11.99 *(978-0-9817403-4-8(0))* Robe Communications, Inc.

—Robbie's Trail Through Adoption. Robe, Adam D. Robe, Kim A., ed. 2010. 44p. pap. 23.99 *(978-1-935831-03-7(8))* Robe Communications, Inc.

—Robbie's Trail Through Adoption — Activity Book. Robe, Adam D. Robe, Kim A., ed. 2010. 36p. pap. 16.99 *(978-1-935831-04-4(6))* Robe Communications, Inc.

—Robbie's Trail Through Adoption — Adult Guide. Robe, Adam D. Robe, Kim A., ed. 2010. 28p. pap. 16.99 *(978-1-935831-05-1(4))* Robe Communications, Inc.

—Robbie's Trail Through Divorce. Robe, Kim. 2012. 40p. (-18). pap. 23.99 *(978-1-935831-11-2(9))* Robe Communications, Inc.

—Robbie's Trail Through Divorce - Activity Book. Robe, Kim. 2012. 28p. (-18). pap. 16.99 *(978-1-935831-12-9(7))* Robe Communications, Inc.

—Robbie's Trail Through Divorce - Adult Guide. Robe, Kim. 2012. 28p. (-18). pap. 16.99 *(978-1-935831-13-6(5))* Robe Communications, Inc.

—Robbie's Trail Through Foster Care. Robe, Adam D. Robe, Kim A., ed. 2010. 40p. pap. 23.99 *(978-1-935831-00-6(3))* Robe Communications, Inc.

—Robbie's Trail Through Foster Care — Activity Book. Robe, Adam D. Robe, Kim A., ed. 2010. 36p. pap. 16.99 *(978-1-935831-01-3(1))* Robe Communications, Inc.

—Robbie's Trail Through Foster Care — Adult Guide. Robe, Adam D. Robe, Kim A., ed. 2010. 28p. pap. 16.99 *(978-1-935831-02-0(X))* Robe Communications, Inc.

—Robbie's Trail Through Open Adoption. Robe, Adam D. Robe, Kim A., ed. 2010. 44p. pap. 23.99 *(978-1-935831-06-8(2))* Robe Communications, Inc.

—Wanting to Belong. Robe, Adam D. Robe, Kim A., ed. 2009. 16p. pap. 11.99 *(978-0-9817403-6-2(7))* Robe Communications, Inc.

Gavin, Rebecca Thompson. The Adventures of Oakey Dokey Acorn: Oakey & Ivy. Gavin, Rebecca Thompson. 2003. 64p. (J). *(978-1-57579-255-2(9))* Pine Hill Pr.

Gavioli, Gino. Candido, el Limpiador de Chimeneas. Gavioli, Gino. Gavoili, G. Brignole, Giancarla, tr. rev. ed. 2006. (Fabulas De Familia Ser.). (SPA & ENG.). 32p. (J). (gr. k-4). pap. 6.95 *(978-970-20-0264-2(8))* Castillo, Ediciones, S. A. de C. V. MEX. Dist: Macmillan.

Gaviraghi, Giuditta, jt. illus. see Abbot, Judi.

Gavril, David. Chicken Soup. Van Leeuwen, Jean. 2009. (ENG.). 40p. (J). (gr. -1-3). 16.95 *(978-0-8109-8326-7(5),* Abrams Bks. for Young Readers) Abrams.

Gavrilovskiy, Olga. Car Key Elves. Hunter, T. H. 2008. 32p. (J). 16.95 *(978-0-9788085-1-8(7))* Tetoca Pr.

—Elf Night: A Christmas Story. Hunter, Todd H. 2006. 52p. (J). (gr. -1-7). 16.95 *(978-0-9788085-0-1(9))* Tetoca Pr.

Gawron, Gay. The New Hampshire Coloring Book. 2008. 40p. (YA). pap. 8.95 *(978-0-9801672-0-7(5))* Hobblebush Bks.

Gawthrop, Shaughn. Be Happy. D'Arcy, Megan. 2011. 32p. (J). 14.95 *(978-1-879094-95-6(9))* Momentum Bks., LLC.

Gay-Kassel, Doreen. Big Machines. Jones, Melanie Davis. 2003. (Rookie Reader Español Ser.). (ENG.). (J). (gr. k-2). pap. 4.95 *(978-0-516-27829-2(0),* Children's Pr.) Scholastic Library Publishing.

Gay, Maria T. Sweet Little Girl. Hankey, Sandy. 2004. 20p. pap. 24.95 *(978-1-4137-3329-7(8))* PublishAmerica, Inc.

Gay, Marie-Louise. The Christmas Orange, 1 vol. Gilmore, Don. 2003. (ENG.). 32p. (J). pap. 7.95 *(978-1-55005-075-2(3),* 1550050753) Fitzhenry & Whiteside, Ltd. CAN. Dist: Midpoint Trade Bks., Inc.

—The Fabulous Song. Gillmor, Don. 2003. 32p. (J). pap. 7.95 *(978-1-929132-48-5(4))* Kane Miller.

—The Fabulous Song. Gillmor, Don et al. 2006. (ENG.). 44p. (J). (gr. -1-2). 16.95 *(978-2-923163-17-8(6))* La Montagne Secrete CAN. Dist: Independent Pubs. Group.

—Houndsley & Catina. Howe, James. (ENG.). 40p. (J). (gr. k-4). 2013. (Candlewick Sparks Ser.). pap. 3.99 *(978-0-7636-6638-5(6))*; 2006. (Houndsley & Catina Ser.: 1). 15.99 *(978-0-7636-2404-0(7))* Candlewick Pr.

—Houndsley & Catina. Howe, James. 2007. 36p. (J). (gr. k-2). lib. bdg. 12.65 *(978-0-7569-8141-9(7))* Perfection Learning Corp.

—Houndsley & Catina & the Birthday Surprise. Howe, James. (ENG.). 48p. (J). (gr. k-4). 2013. (Candlewick Sparks Ser.). pap. 3.99 *(978-0-7636-6639-2(4))*; 2006. (Houndsley & Catina Ser.: 2). 15.99 *(978-0-7636-2405-7(5))* Candlewick Pr.

—Houndsley & Catina & the Quiet Time. Howe, James. (ENG.). 48p. (J). (gr. k-4). 2013. (Candlewick Sparks Ser.). pap. 3.99 *(978-0-7636-6863-1(X))*; 2008. (Houndsley & Catina Ser.: 3). 15.99 *(978-0-7636-3384-4(4))* Candlewick Pr.

—Houndsley & Catina Plink & Plunk. Howe, James. 2013. (Candlewick Sparks Ser.). (ENG.). 48p. (J). (gr. k-4). pap. 3.99 *(978-0-7636-6640-8(8))* Candlewick Pr.

—Maddie on TV, 1 vol. Leblanc, Louise. Cummins, Sarah, tr. from FRE. 2003. (Formac First Novels Ser.: 48). (ENG.). 64p. (J). (gr. 2-5). 4.95 *(978-0-88780-612-4(0))*; 14.95 *(978-0-88780-613-1(9))* Formac Publishing Co., Ltd. CAN. Dist: Casemate Pubs. & Bk. Distributors, LLC.

—Maddie Stands Tall. Leblanc, Louise. Cummins, Sarah, tr. from FRE. 2005. (Formac First Novels Ser.: 54). (ENG.). 64p. (J). (gr. 2-5). 14.95 *(978-0-88780-683-4(X))* Formac Publishing Co., Ltd. CAN. Dist: Casemate Pubs. & Bk. Distributors, LLC.

—Maddie Stands Tall, 1 vol. Leblanc, Louise. Cummins, Sarah, tr. from FRE. 2005. (Formac First Novels Ser.: 54). (ENG.). 64p. (J). (gr. 2-5). 4.95 *(978-0-88780-682-7(1))* Formac Publishing Co., Ltd. CAN. Dist: Casemate Pubs. & Bk. Distributors, LLC.

—Maddie Surfs for Cyber-Pals. Leblanc, Louise. 2004. 64p. (J). lib. bdg. 12.00 *(978-1-4242-1226-2(X))* Fitzgerald Bks.

—Maddie Surfs for Cyber-Pals. Leblanc, Louise. Cummins, Sarah, tr. from FRE. 2004. (Formac First Novels Ser.: 52). (ENG.). 64p. (gr. 2-5). 14.95 *(978-0-88780-639-1(2))* Formac Publishing Co., Ltd. CAN. Dist: Casemate Pubs. & Bk. Distributors, LLC.

—Maddie Surfs for Cyber Pals, 1 vol. Leblanc, Louise. Cummins, Sarah, tr. from FRE. 2004. (Formac First Novels Ser.: 52). (ENG.). 64p. (J). (gr. 2-5). 4.95 *(978-0-88780-638-4(4))* Formac Publishing Co., Ltd. CAN. Dist: Casemate Pubs. & Bk. Distributors, LLC.

—Maddie's Big Test. Leblanc, Louise. Cummins, Sarah, tr. from FRE. 2006. (Formac First Novels Ser.: 58). (ENG.). 64p. (J). (gr. 2-5). 14.95 *(978-0-88780-718-3(6))* Formac Publishing Co., Ltd. CAN. Dist: Casemate Pubs. & Bk. Distributors, LLC.

—Maddie's Big Test, 1 vol. Leblanc, Louise. Cummins, Sarah, tr. from FRE. 2006. (Formac First Novels Ser.). (ENG.). 64p. (J). (gr. 2-5). 4.95 *(978-0-88780-714-5(3))* Formac Publishing Co., Ltd. CAN. Dist: Casemate Pubs. & Bk. Distributors, LLC.

—On the Road Again! More Travels with My Family. Gay, Homel D. 2008. (ENG.). 144p. (J). (gr. 1-5). 15.95 *(978-0-88899-846-0(5))* Groundwood Bks. CAN. Dist: Perseus-PGW.

—Please, Louise!, 1 vol. Wishinsky, Frieda. 2007. (ENG.). 32p. (J). (gr. k-k). 17.95 *(978-0-88899-796-8(5))* Groundwood Bks. CAN. Dist: Perseus-PGW.

—Plink & Plunk. Howe, James. 2009. (Houndsley & Catina Ser.). (ENG.). 48p. (J). (gr. k-4). 15.99 *(978-0-7636-3385-1(2))* Candlewick Pr.

—Stella, Queen of the Snow. braille ed. 2004. (J). (gr. -1-1). spiral bd. *(978-0-616-08492-2(7))* Canadian National Institute for the Blind/Institut National Canadien pour les Aveugles.

—Yuck, a Love Story. Gillmor, Don. ed. 2004. (J). (gr. k-3). spiral bd. *(978-0-616-07238-7(4))*; spiral bd. *(978-0-616-08494-6(3))* Canadian National Institute for the Blind/Institut National Canadien pour les Aveugles.

—Yuck, a Love Story, 1 vol. Gillmor, Don. 2010. (ENG.). 32p. (J). pap. 9.95 *(978-1-55455-172-9(2))* Fitzhenry & Whiteside, Ltd. CAN. Dist: Midpoint Trade Bks., Inc.

Gay, Marie-Louise. Fat Charlie's Circus, 1 vol. Gay, Marie-Louise. (ENG.). 32p. 6.95 *(978-0-7736-7420-2(9))* Stoddart Kids CAN. Dist: Fitzhenry & Whiteside, Ltd.

—Mademoiselle Moon, 1 vol. Gay, Marie-Louise. 2006. (ENG.). 32p. (J). (gr. -1-3). pap. 7.95 *(978-1-55005-134-6(2),* 1550051342) Fitzhenry & Whiteside, Ltd. CAN. Dist: Midpoint Trade Bks., Inc.

—Rainy Day Magic, 1 vol. Gay, Marie-Louise. (ENG.). 30p. mass mkt. 6.95 *(978-0-7736-7366-3(0))* Stoddart Kids CAN. Dist: Fitzhenry & Whiteside, Ltd.

Gay, Michel. Una Vez Mas. Devernois, Elsa. (SPA.). 32p. (J). 7.16 *(978-84-95150-32-5(8))* Corimbo, Editorial S.L. ESP. Dist: Lectorum Pubns., Inc.

Gayle, Vandercook. Mr. Blair's Labyrinth. Robert, Lytle. 2011. (J). 10.95 *(978-0-9798088-4-5(7))* EDCO Publishing, Inc.

Gazarik, Rebecca Renee. The Caribbean Caribou's Ancient Discovery. Gazarik, Rebecca Renee. Patterson, Aaron James, ed. 2012. 36p. (J). *(978-0-9802258-2-2(5))* Gazarik, Rebecca.

Gazsi, Benjamin. Cats Can't Fly: Teaching Children to Value New Friendships. Neer, P. J. 2012. (Let's Talk Ser.). (ENG.). 48p. (J). (gr. -1-2). pap. 9.95 *(978-0-88282-381-2(7))* New Horizon Pr. Pubs., Inc.

Gazzaneo, Lucia. El Gigante y el Mar. Brignole, Giancarla, tr. (Fabulas De Familia Ser.). (SPA.). 32p. *(978-970-20-0268-0(0))* Castillo, Ediciones, S. A. de C. V.

Gbala, Deswin R. Rock University: A Collection of Short Stories & Poems. Gbala, Deswin R. Date not set. 51p. (Orig.). (J). (gr. 3-10). pap. 8.50 *(978-0-9650629-2-3(9))* Coulee Region Pubns., Inc.

Ge, Tang. The Dragon Emperor: A Chinese Folktale. 2007. (On My Own Folklore Ser.). (ENG.). 48p. (J). (gr. 2-4). lib. bdg. 25.26 *(978-0-8225-6740-0(7),* Millbrook Pr.) Lerner Publishing Group.

Geary, Rick. Great Expectations. Dickens, Charles. abr. ed. 2008. (Classics Illustrated Graphic Novels Ser.: 1). (ENG.). 56p. (J). (gr. 3-9). 9.95 *(978-1-59707-097-3(1))* Papercutz.

Geary, Steve. Beginnings Vol. 2: Tales of the Mandrasaurs, Volume the Second. Everson, Chance. 2004. cd-rom 9.95 *(978-0-9760303-1-7(4))* R.A.R.E. TALES.

—Discoveries: Tales of the Mandrasaurs, Volume the Third. Everson, Chance. 2004. cd-rom 9.95 *(978-0-9760303-2-4(2))* R.A.R.E. TALES.

—Forever & a Day Vol. 1: Tales of the Mandrasaurs, Volume the First. Everson, Chance. 2004. cd-rom 9.95 *(978-0-9760303-0-0(6))* R.A.R.E. TALES.

—Verlin's Magical Blunder: Tales of the Mandrasaurs, Volume the Seventh. Everson, Chance. 2004. cd-rom 9.95 *(978-0-9760303-6-2(5))* R.A.R.E. TALES.

Gebert, Helga. Ten Birds. Amman, Jurg. 2012. (ENG.). 32p. (J). (gr. -1-2). 17.95 *(978-0-7358-4100-0(4))* North-South Bks., Inc.

GEbhard, Andy. Exaggeration Aggravation. BAtey, Kathey. 2006. (J). 8.00 *(978-0-9790017-0-3(6))* Spirited Presentations.

Gebhard, Wilfried. Lo Que Eduardo Sabe Hacer. Gebhard, Wilfried. 2007. (SPA & ENG.). 32p. (J). (gr. -1-k). pap. 7.95 *(978-1-933605-40-1(5),* Libros del Mundo) Kane Miller.

Gebhardt-Gayler, Winnie. The Little Water Sprite. Preussler, Otfried. Bell, Anthea, tr. from GER. 2015. (ENG.). 136p. (J). (gr. k-4). 15.95 ***(978-1-59017-933-8(1),*** NYR Children's Collection) New York Review of Bks., Inc., The.

—The Little Witch. Preussler, Otfried. Bell, Anthea, tr. from GER. 2015. (ENG.). 144p. (J). (gr. k-4). 15.95 ***(978-1-59017-934-5(X),*** NYR Children's Collection) New York Review of Bks., Inc., The.

Gebr, Jaroslav. Jackie Winquackey & Her 43 Cats Go to Hollywood. Frees, Jessie Lynch. 2005. 32p. (J). 14.99 *(978-0-9760553-0-3(9))* Tizbit Books, LLC.

Gecko, Gabriel, et al. Iron Man/War Machine: Hands of the Mandarin. 2013. (ENG.). 280p. (J). (gr. 4-17). pap. 24.99 *(978-0-7851-8428-7(7))* Marvel Worldwide, Inc.

Geddes, Anne, photos by. Opposites. 2010. (ENG., 14p. (J). (gr. k — 1). bds. 5.99 *(978-1-921652-10-3(1))* Geddes, Anne Publishing AUS. Dist: Perseus Distribution.

Geddes, Serena. Blow Me a Kiss. Collum, Karen. 2012. (J). *(978-1-4351-4513-9(5))* Barnes & Noble, Inc.

Geddes, Serena. Buttercup Mystery. Earhart, Kristin. 2015. (Marguerite Henry's Misty Inn Ser.: 2). (ENG.). 128p. (J). (gr. 2-5). pap. 5.99 ***(978-1-4814-1416-6(X),*** Simon & Schuster/Paula Wiseman Bks.) Simon & Schuster/Paula Wiseman Bks.

Geddes, Serena. Lulu Bell & the Birthday Unicorn. Murrell, Belinda. 2014. (Lulu Bell Ser.: 1). (ENG.). 96p. (J). (gr. 1-3). 7.99 *(978-1-74275-875-6(4))* Random Hse. Australia AUS. Dist: Independent Pubs. Group.

Geddes, Serena. Lulu Bell & the Christmas Elf. Murrell, Belinda. 2015. 128p. (J). (gr. 2-4). 11.99 ***(978-0-85798-503-3(5))*** Random Hse. Australia AUS. Dist: Independent Pubs. Group.

Geddes, Serena. Lulu Bell & the Circus Pup. Murrell, Belinda. 2015. (Lulu Bell Ser.: 5). (ENG.). 96p. (J). (gr. 1-3). 7.99 *(978-0-85798-199-8(4))* Random Hse. Australia AUS. Dist: Independent Pubs. Group.

—Lulu Bell & the Cubby Fort. Murrell, Belinda. 2014. (Lulu Bell Ser.: 3). (ENG.). 96p. (J). (gr. 1-3). 7.99 *(978-1-74275-879-4(7))* Random Hse. Australia AUS. Dist: Independent Pubs. Group.

—Lulu Bell & the Fairy Penguin. Murrell, Belinda. 2014. (Lulu Bell Ser.: 2). (ENG.). 96p. (J). (gr. 1-3). 7.99 *(978-1-74275-877-0(0))* Random Hse. Australia AUS. Dist: Independent Pubs. Group.

—Lulu Bell & the Moon Dragon. Murrell, Belinda. 2014. (Lulu Bell Ser.: 4). (ENG.). 96p. (J). (gr. 1-3). 7.99 *(978-1-74275-881-7(9))* Random Hse. Australia AUS. Dist: Independent Pubs. Group.

Geddes, Serena. Lulu Bell & the Pyjama Party. Murrell, Belinda. 2015. 96p. (J). (gr. 2-4). 7.99 ***(978-0-85798-303-9(2))*** Random Hse. Australia AUS. Dist: Independent Pubs. Group.

Geddes, Serena. Lulu Bell & the Sea Turtle. Murrell, Belinda. 2015. (Lulu Bell Ser.: 6). (ENG.). 96p. (J). (gr. 1-3). 7.99 *(978-0-85798-201-8(X))* Random Hse. Australia AUS. Dist: Independent Pubs. Group.

Geddes, Serena. Lulu Bell & the Tiger Cub. Murrell, Belinda. 2015. 95p. (J). (gr. 2-4). 7.99 ***(978-0-85798-301-5(6))*** Random Hse. Australia AUS. Dist: Independent Pubs. Group.

—Welcome Home! Earhart, Kristin. 2015. (Marguerite Henry's Misty Inn Ser.: 1). (ENG.). 128p. (J). (gr. 2-5). 16.99 ***(978-1-4814-1414-2(3),*** Simon & Schuster/Paula Wiseman Bks.) Simon & Schuster/Paula Wiseman Bks.

Geddes, Serena. Why I Love My Mom. Reynolds, Alison. 2015. (ENG.). 22p. (J). (gr. -1-1). 9.99 *(978-1-4998-0020-3(7))* Little Bee Books Inc.

Gedeon, Gloria. In the Hen House. Oppenlander, Meredith. l.t. ed. 2006. (ENG.). 12p. (gr. k-2). pap. 5.95 *(978-1-57874-003-1(7))* Kaeden Corp.

—Little Mouse. Hoenecke, Karen. l.t. ed. 2005. (ENG.). 12p. (gr. k-2). pap. 5.95 *(978-1-57874-023-9(1))* Kaeden Corp.

—Little Rabbit Is Sad. Williams, Deborah. l.t. ed. 2005. (ENG.). 12p. (Orig.). (gr. k-1). pap. 5.95 *(978-1-879835-99-3(1))* Kaeden Corp.

—Moose's Loose Tooth. Spinelle, Nancy Louise. l.t. ed. 2005. (ENG.). 16p. (gr. k-2). pap. 5.95 *(978-1-57874-032-1(0),* Kaeden Bks.) Kaeden Corp.

—Nickels & Pennies. Williams, Deborah. l.t. ed. 2005. (ENG.). 12p. (gr. k-1). pap. 5.95 *(978-1-879835-87-0(8))* Kaeden Corp.

—Rainy Day for Sammy. Urmston, Kathleen & Urmston, Grant. 2004. (ENG.). 20p. (gr. k-2). pap. 5.95 *(978-1-57874-078-9(9))* Kaeden Corp.

—Sammy. Urmston, Kathleen. 2005. (ENG.). 16p. (gr. k-1). pap. 5.95 *(978-1-57874-089-5(4))* Kaeden Corp.

Gedovius, Juan. Ana, Verdad? Hinojosa, Francisco. 2003. (Coleccion Derechos Del Nino Ser.). (SPA.). 32p. (J). (gr. 3-5). pap. 7.95 *(978-84-204-5824-3(4))* Santillana USA Publishing Co., Inc.

—Busca un Magico Lunar. Macias, Elva. 2003. (SPA.). 32p. (J). (gr. k-3). pap. 7.95 *(978-968-19-0744-0(2))* Santillana USA Publishing Co., Inc.

Gedovius, Juan. From the Vine. Gedovius, Juan. 24p. (J). (gr. k-6). 14.95 *(978-968-19-1053-2(2))* Santillana USA Publishing Co., Inc.

—Purple Cubed. Gedovius, Juan. 32p. (J). (gr. k-6). 13.95 *(978-968-19-0751-8(5))* Santillana USA Publishing Co., Inc.

Gedrich, Colleen. A Different Kind of Hero. Evans, Leah Beth. 2007. 40p. (J). per. 14.95 *(978-0-9795045-2-5(X))* Tribute Bks.

—Stanley Seagull. Mazur, Cathy. 2011. 32p. (J). 16.95 *(978-0-9837418-1-7(6))*; pap. 7.95 *(978-0-9837418-0-0(8))* Tribute Bks.

Gedzyk, Emily. Paleo Cooking for Cavekids. 2012. (ENG.). 102p. (J). pap. 19.75 *(978-0-9855541-2-5(6))* Firestorm Editions.

Gee, Bonnie. How to Draw Icky Bugs. Pallotta, Jerry. 2003. (J). mass mkt. *(978-0-439-38916-7(X))* Scholastic, Inc.

Gee, Isybilla. Issy Books Set 1, 5 bks. Calfee, Pat. 2013. 60p. (J). pap. 24.95 *(978-1-938406-13-3(3),* Compass) Raphel Marketing, Inc.

—Issy Books Set 2, 5 bks. Calfee, Pat. 2013. 60p. (J). pap. 24.95 *(978-1-938406-14-0(1),* Compass) Raphel Marketing, Inc.

—Issy Books Set 3, 10 books. Calfee, Pat. 2013. 120p. (J). pap. 39.95 *(978-1-938406-15-7(X),* Compass) Raphel Marketing, Inc.

Geehan, Wayne. Multiplying Menace: The Revenge of Rumpelstiltskin. Calvert, Pam. 2006. (Math Adventures Ser.). (ENG.). 32p. (J). (gr. 2-5). per. 7.95 *(978-1-57091-890-2(2))* Charlesbridge Publishing, Inc.

—The Multiplying Menace Divides! Calvert, Pam. 2011. (ENG.). 32p. (J). (gr. 2-5). pap. 7.95 *(978-1-57091-782-0(5))* Charlesbridge Publishing, Inc.

—Sir Cumference & All the King's Tens. Neuschwander, Cindy. 2009. (ENG.). 32p. (J). (gr. 3-7). 16.95 *(978-1-57091-727-1(2))* Charlesbridge Publishing, Inc.

—Sir Cumference & the Isle of Immeter. Neuschwander, Cindy. 2006. (Math Adventures Ser.). (ENG.). 32p. (J). (gr. 3-7). per. 7.95 *(978-1-57091-681-6(0))* Charlesbridge Publishing, Inc.

—Sir Cumference & the Roundabout Battle. Neuschwander, Cindy. 2015. (ENG.). 32p. (J). (gr. 3-7). lib. bdg. 16.95 *(978-1-57091-765-3(5))* Charlesbridge Publishing, Inc.

—Sir Cumference & the Sword in the Cone. Neuschwander, Cindy. 2003. (Make the Math-Literature Connection Ser.). (ENG.). 32p. (J). (gr. 3-7). pap. 7.95 *(978-1-57091-601-4(2))* Charlesbridge Publishing, Inc.

—Sir Cumference & the Viking's Map. Neuschwander, Cindy. 2012. (ENG.). 32p. (J). (gr. 3-7). 16.95 *(978-1-57091-791-2(4))*; pap. 7.95 *(978-1-57091-792-9(2))* Charlesbridge Publishing, Inc.

—Sir Cumference & the Viking's Map. Neuschwander, Cindy. ed. 2012. (Sir Cumference Ser.). lib. bdg. 18.40 *(978-0-606-26445-7(0),* Turtleback) Turtleback Bks.

Geer, Charles. The Big Chunk of Ice: The Last Known Adventure of the Mad Scientist Club. Brinley, Bertrand R. 2005. (Mad Scientist Club Ser.). 275p. (J). (gr. 3-7). 18.95 *(978-1-930900-29-5(5))* Purple Hse. Pr.

—The Big Kerplop! The Original Adventure of the Mad Scientist's Club. Brinley, Bertrand R. 2003. 238p. (J). 17.95 *(978-1-930900-22-6(8))* Purple Hse. Pr.

—Ginger Box. Foster, Martha S. 2011. 126p. 40.95 *(978-1-258-06588-1(6))* Literary Licensing, LLC.

—Horse Stories: Young Readers. Furman, A. L., ed. 2011. 192p. 42.95 *(978-1-258-09836-0(9))* Literary Licensing, LLC.

—Indian Stories. Furman, A. L., ed. 2011. 190p. 42.95 *(978-1-258-09304-4(9))* Literary Licensing, LLC.

—The Mad Scientists' Club. Brinley, Bertrand R. 50th ed. 2011. (J). 18.95 *(978-1-930900-53-0(8))* Purple Hse. Pr.

—The Mad Scientists' Club Complete Collection. Brinley, Bertrand R. 2010. 619p. (YA). pap. 29.99 *(978-1-930900-51-6(1))* Purple Hse. Pr.

—The Marvelous Inventions of Alvin Fernald. Hicks, Clifford B. 2006. 119p. (J). (gr. 3-7). 16.95 *(978-1-930900-21-9(X))* Purple Hse. Pr.

—Pioneer Stories: Young Readers. Furman, A. L., ed. 2011. 190p. 42.95 *(978-1-258-09907-7(1))* Literary Licensing, LLC.

—Plain Girl. Sorensen, Virginia. 2003. (ENG.). 168p. (J). (gr. 2-5). pap. 6.95 *(978-0-15-204725-2(5))* Houghton Mifflin Harcourt Publishing Co.

—Wild Life Stories: Young Readers. Furman, A. L., ed. 2011. 192p. 42.95 *(978-1-258-10201-2(3))* Literary Licensing, LLC.

—Young Visitor to Mars. Elam Jr., Richard M. 2011. 256p. 47.95 *(978-1-258-09909-1(8))* Literary Licensing, LLC.

Geer, Charles H. Detective Stories: Young Readers. Coombs, Charles. 2011. 194p. 42.95 *(978-1-258-10586-0(1))* Literary Licensing, LLC.

—Indoor Sports Stories. Coombs, Charles Ira. 2011. 190p. 42.95 *(978-1-258-09130-9(5))* Literary Licensing, LLC.

—Railroad Stories: Young Readers. Coombs, Charles. 2011. 194p. 42.95 *(978-1-258-10208-1(0))* Literary Licensing, LLC.

—Young Crow Raider: Young Heroes Library. Kroll, Francis Lynde. 2011. 186p. 42.95 *(978-1-258-09906-0(3))* Literary Licensing, LLC.

—Young Infield Rookie. Coombs, Charles. 2011. 190p. 42.95 *(978-1-258-10529-7(2))* Literary Licensing, LLC.

—Young Sand Hills Cowboy: Young Heroes Library. Kroll, Francis Lynde. 2011. 188p. 42.95 *(978-1-258-09908-4(X))* Literary Licensing, LLC.

—Young Sioux Warrior. Kroll, Francis Lynde. 2011. 188p. 42.95 *(978-1-258-10209-8(9))* Literary Licensing, LLC.

Geer, William J. Nicky Jones & the Roaring Rhinos. Grambling, Lois G. 2004. 32p. (J). 6.95 *(978-1-877810-14-5(2))* Rayve Productions, Inc.

Geeson, Andrew & Veldhoven, Marijke. Save the Orangutan. Eason, Sarah. 2009. (Save the... Ser.). 32p. (J). (gr. 2-5). lib. bdg. 25.25 *(978-1-4358-2811-7(9))* Rosen Publishing Group, Inc., The.

—Save the Panda. Eason, Sarah. 2009. (Save the... Ser.). 32p. (J). (gr. 2-5). lib. bdg. 25.25 *(978-1-4358-2812-4(7))* Rosen Publishing Group, Inc., The.

—Save the Polar Bear. Eason, Sarah. 2009. (Save the... Ser.). 32p. (J). (gr. 2-5). lib. bdg. 25.25 *(978-1-4358-2810-0(0))* Rosen Publishing Group, Inc., The.

—Save the Tiger. Eason, Sarah. 2009. (Save the... Ser.). 32p. (J). (gr. 2-5). lib. bdg. 25.25 *(978-1-4358-2813-1(5))* Rosen Publishing Group, Inc., The.

Gehr, Mary. We're Going to Town! Aldis, Dorothy Keeley. 2011. 58p. 36.95 *(978-1-258-08388-5(4))* Literary Licensing, LLC.

—The Yellow House Mystery. Warner, Gertrude Chandler. 2004. (Boxcar Children Ser.: No. 3). (ENG.). 192p. (YA). (gr. 2-5). reprint ed. mass mkt. 5.99 *(978-0-8075-9366-0(4))* Whitman, Albert & Co.

Gehrmann, Katja. Goose the Bear. 2014. (ENG.). 40p. (J). (gr. -1-3). 16.95 *(978-1-62636-384-7(6),* Sky Pony Pr.) Skyhorse Publishing Co., Inc.

Geiken, Brenda. Free to Be Me: The Eskimo Way. Amundson, Susan. 2003. 56p. lib. bdg. 16.95 *(978-1-883477-65-3(4),* Lone Oak Pr., Ltd.) Finney Co., Inc.

Geiken, Brenda Joy. Three Little Lambs — Somewhere. Amundson, Susan D. 2006. 40p. (J). *(978-1-59984-002-4(2))* Bluedoor, llc.

Geis, Alissa Imre. Our Friendship Rules, 1 vol. Moss, Peggy et al. 2007. (ENG.). 32p. (J). (gr. -1-3). 16.95 *(978-0-88448-291-8(X))* Tilbury Hse. Pubs.

Geis, Jessica. Attack of the Vampire Snowmen. Alano, Benny. 2011. (ENG.). 140p. pap. 9.99 *(978-1-4609-7351-6(8))* CreateSpace Independent Publishing Platform.

—Hand Puppet Horror. Alano, Benny. 2011. (ENG.). 126p. pap. 7.99 *(978-1-4609-3891-1(7))* CreateSpace Independent Publishing Platform.

Geis, Patricia. Néstor Tellini. Geis, Patricia. 2004. (Mi Ciudad Ser.). (SPA & ENG.). 24p. (J). (gr. -1-k). 6.95 *(978-84-7864-798-9(8))* Combel Editorial, S.A. ESP. Dist: Independent Pubs. Group.

—Paca Lamar. Geis, Patricia. 2004. (Mi Ciudad Ser.). (SPA & ENG.). 24p. (J). (gr. -1-k). 6.95 *(978-84-7864-797-2(X))* Combel Editorial, S.A. ESP. Dist: Independent Pubs. Group.

—Pascual Midón. Geis, Patricia. 2004. (Mi Ciudad Ser.). (SPA & ENG.). 24p. (J). (gr. -1-k). 6.95 *(978-84-7864-799-6(6))* Combel Editorial, S.A. ESP. Dist: Independent Pubs. Group.

Geisler, Dagmar. My Body Belongs to Me from My Head to My Toes. International Center for Assault Prevention Staff & Pro Familia, Deutsche Gesellschaft für Sexualberatung und Familienplanung Staff. 2014. (ENG.). 36p. (J). (gr. -1-k). 16.95 *(978-1-62636-345-8(5),* 263345, Sky Pony Pr.) Skyhorse Publishing Co., Inc.

Geist, Hans. And Heaven Stood Silent. Billiot, Christopher. 2009. 36p. pap. 15.49 *(978-1-4389-5894-1(3))* AuthorHouse.

Geister, David. B Is for Battle Cry: A Civil War Alphabet. Bauer, Patricia. 2009. (History Ser.). (ENG.). 40p. (J). (gr. 2-5). 17.95 *(978-1-58536-356-8(1))* Sleeping Bear Pr.

—The Legend of Minnesota. Wargin, Kathy-jo. 2006. (Legend (Sleeping Bear) Ser.). (ENG.). 40p. (J). (gr. 3-7). 17.95 *(978-1-58536-262-2(X))* Sleeping Bear Pr.

—Riding to Washington. Swain, Gwenyth. 2007. (Tales of Young Americans Ser.). (ENG.). 32p. (YA). (gr. 6-12). 17.95 *(978-1-58536-324-7(3))* Sleeping Bear Pr.

—S Is for Scientists: A Discovery Alphabet. Verstraete, Larry. 2010. (Science Alphabet Ser.). (ENG & ABK.). 40p. (J). (gr. 1-4). 16.95 *(978-1-58536-470-1(3),* 202189) Sleeping Bear Pr.

—T Is for Twin Cities: A Minneapolis/St. Paul Alphabet. Carlson, Nancy & McCool, Barry. 2012. (City Alphabet Ser.). (ENG.). 32p. (J). (gr. 1-5). 16.95 *(978-1-58536-583-8(1))* Sleeping Bear Pr.

Geister, David & Van Frankenhuyzen, Gijsbert. The Voyageur's Paddle. Wargin, Kathy-jo. rev. ed. 2007. (ENG.). 40p. (J). (gr. k-6). 17.95 *(978-1-58536-007-9(4))* Sleeping Bear Pr.

Geldart, William. David & the Kittens. Westall, Robert. 2003. (ENG.). 32p. (J). pap. 9.99 *(978-0-340-74380-5(8),* Hodder Children's Books) Hachette Children's Group GBR. Dist: Independent Pubs. Group.

Gelev, Penko. The Odyssey. Homer. 2009. (Graphic Classics Ser.). (ENG.). 48p. (J). (gr. 5-11). pap. 8.99 *(978-0-7641-4276-5(3))* Barron's Educational Series, Inc.

Gelsinger, Dona. All Things Bright & Beautiful. 2007. (ENG.). 10p. bds. 6.99 *(978-1-4037-3411-2(9),* Spirit Pr.) Bendon, Inc.

Gendler, Robert, photos by. The Little Moon Phase Book. Grice, Noreen. 2005. 12p. (J). spiral bd. 23.95 *(978-0-9773285-0-5(3))* Ozone Publishing, Corp.

Gendron, Cathy. The Nutcracker Comes to America: How Three Ballet-Loving Brothers Created a Holiday Tradition. Barton, Chris. 2015. (ENG.). 36p. (J). (gr. 2-5). 19.99 ***(978-1-4677-2151-6(4),*** Millbrook Pr.) Lerner Publishing Group.

Genechten, Guido van. Kangaroo Christine. Genechten, Guido van. 2005. 24p. (J). (gr. 3-7). pap. 6.95 *(978-1-58925-396-4(5))* Tiger Tales.

—Snowy's Special Secret. Genechten, Guido van. 2005. 32p. (J). (gr. -1-2). 15.95 *(978-1-58925-049-9(4))* Tiger Tales.

Genovés, Graciela. Jorge Luis Borges. Genovés, Graciela. Lázaro León, Georgina. 2009. (Cuando los Grandes Eran Pequenos Ser.). (SPA.). 32p. (J). (gr. 4-6). 14.99 *(978-1-933032-40-5(5))* Lectorum Pubns., Inc.

Genovese, Janell. Sienna's Scrapbook: Our African American Heritage Trip. Parker, Toni Trent. 2005. (ENG.). 64p. (J). (gr. 2-7). 15.95 *(978-0-8118-4300-3(9))* Chronicle Bks. LLC.

Genth, Christina. The Messy Monkey Tea Party. Deich, Cheri Bivin. 2007. 32p. (J). (gr. -1-3). 15.95 *(978-1-60108-006-6(9))* Red Cygnet Pr.

Gentieu, Penny. Baby Signs for Animals. Acredolo, Linda & Goodwyn, Susan. 2003. (ENG.). 24p. (J). (gr. -1 — 1). bds. 6.99 *(978-0-06-009075-3(8),* HarperFestival) HarperCollins Pubs.

Gentieu, Penny. Baby! Talk! Gentieu, Penny. 2015. (ENG.). 22p. (J). (— 1). bds. 6.99 *(978-0-517-80079-9(9),* Crown Books For Young Readers) Random Hse. Children's Bks.

Gentieu, Penny, photos by. Knots in My Yo-Yo Strong. Spinelli, Jerry. 2014. 158p. pap. 11.00 *(978-1-61003-375-6(2))* Center for the Collaborative Classroom.

Gentieu, Penny, photos by. You & Me, Baby. Reiser, Lynn. 2008. (ENG., 32p. (J). (— 1). bds. 6.99 *(978-0-375-84420-1(1),* Knopf Bks. for Young Readers) Random Hse. Children's Bks.

Gentile, Christopher. The Little Bitty Story of Austin Q. Peapot, 1 vol. Boie, Kristen. 2009. 20p. pap. 24.95 *(978-1-60749-548-2(1))* America Star Bks.

Gentry, Debra. Jeremy & the Wappo. Elwell, Sharon. 126p. (Orig.). (J). (gr. 3-4). pap. 10.50 *(978-0-9626210-0-0(5))* Rattle OK Pubns.

Gentry, Kyle. The Adventures of Sammy Snowflake, Vol. 1. Becker, Brooke. 2007. (ENG.). 64p. (gr. 4-7). 19.95 *(978-0-9795260-0-8(0))* Courtyard Publishing, LLC.

Gentry, Marita. Beware, Beware of the Big Bad Bear!, 1 vol. Casas, Dianne de Las. 2012. (ENG.). 32p. (J). (gr. k-3). 16.99 *(978-1-4556-1690-9(7))* Pelican Publishing Co., Inc.

—The Cajun Cornbread Boy, 1 vol. de Las Casas, Dianne. 2008. (ENG.). 32p. (J). (gr. k-3). 16.99 *(978-1-58980-224-7(1))* Pelican Publishing Co., Inc.

—Dinosaur Mardi Gras, 1 vol. De Las Casas, Dianne. 2011. (ENG.). 32p. (J). (gr. k-3). 16.99 *(978-1-58980-966-6(1))* Pelican Publishing Co., Inc.

—The Gigantic Sweet Potato, 1 vol. de Las Casas, Dianne. 2010. (ENG.). 32p. (J). (gr. k-3). 16.99 *(978-1-58980-755-6(3))* Pelican Publishing Co., Inc.

—Madame Poulet & Monsieur Roach, 1 vol. de Las Casas, Dianne. 2009. (ENG.). 32p. (J). (gr. k-3). 16.99 *(978-1-58980-686-3(7))* Pelican Publishing Co., Inc.

—There's a Dragon in the Library, 1 vol. De Las Casas, Dianne. 2011. (ENG.). 32p. (J). (gr. k-3). 16.99 *(978-1-58980-844-7(4))* Pelican Publishing Co., Inc.

Gentry, Susana, photos by. What Should I Eat? Sly, Stacey. 2010. 26p. pap. 12.95 *(978-1-60911-432-9(9),* Eloquent Bks.) Strategic Book Publishing & Rights Agency (SBPRA).

Gentry, T. Kyle. Grandpa for Sale. Enderle, Dotti & Sansum, Vicki. 2007. (ENG.). 32p. (J). (gr. k-3). 17.95 *(978-0-9729225-8-6(X))* Flashlight Pr.

—Hidden, 1 vol. Enderle, Dotti. 2007. (ENG.). 104p. (J). (gr. 3-7). per. 8.95 *(978-1-58980-481-4(3))* Pelican Publishing Co., Inc.

—Koala Koala, I'm Not a Bear, I'm a Koala. Earl, David G. 2009. 32p. pap. 12.95 *(978-1-936051-22-9(2))* Peppertree Pr., The.

Genzo, John Paul. Islands of Ice: The Story of a Harp Seal. Hollenbeck, Kathleen M. (Smithsonian Oceanic Collection Ser.). (ENG.). 32p. (J). (gr. -1-3). 2011. 19.95 *(978-1-60727-652-4(6));* 2005. 4.95 *(978-1-56899-966-1(6),* B4071); 2005. 19.95 *(978-1-56899-967-8(4),* BC4021); 2005. 9.95 *(978-1-56899-970-8(4),* PB4071); 2005. 15.95 *(978-1-56899-965-4(8),* B4021) Soundprints.

Geo. Chocolat. Shin, Ji-Sang. (ENG.). (gr. 8-17). Vol. 1B. 2005. 180p. pap. 10.95 *(978-89-527-4453-1(5));* Vol. 2. 2006. 200p. pap. 10.95 *(978-89-527-4472-2(1));* Vol. 3B. 2006. 192p. pap. 11.99 *(978-89-527-4480-7(2))* Yen Pr.

Geoffroi, Remie. The Dreadful Truth: Canadian Crime. Staunton, Ted. 2006. (Dreadful Truth Ser.). (ENG.). 104p. (J). (gr. 3-8). *(978-0-88780-705-3(4))* Formac Publishing Co., Ltd.

—Gold Rush. Staunton, Ted. 2008. (Dreadful Truth Ser.). (ENG.). 104p. (YA). (gr. 3-8). *(978-0-88780-747-3(X))* Formac Publishing Co., Ltd.

—Money: Deal with It or Pay the Price, 1 vol. Mototsune, Kat. 2007. (Lorimer Deal with It Ser.). (ENG.). 32p. (J). (gr. 4-6). pap. 12.95 *(978-1-55028-958-9(6))* Lorimer, James & Co., Ltd., Pubs. CAN. Dist: Casemate Pubs. & Bk. Distributors, LLC.

—Teasing: Before the Joke's on You, 1 vol. Slavens, Elaine & Pitt, Steve. 2010. (Lorimer Deal with It Ser.). (ENG.). 32p. (J). (gr. 4-6). 24.95 *(978-1-55277-497-7(X))* Lorimer, James & Co., Ltd., Pubs. CAN. Dist: Casemate Pubs. & Bk. Distributors, LLC.

—Teasing: Deal with It Before the Joke's on You, 1 vol. Pitt, Steve. 2006. (Lorimer Deal with It Ser.). (ENG.). 32p. (J). (gr. 4-6). pap., instr.'s gde. ed. 12.95 *(978-1-55028-946-6(2))* Lorimer, James & Co., Ltd., Pubs. CAN. Dist: Casemate Pubs. & Bk. Distributors, LLC.

Geoffroi, Remie & Owlkids Books Inc. Staff. The Hilarious Adventures of Mish & Mash: The Story of How Two Monsters - And You - Make the Perfect Joke Book! chickaDEE Magazine Staff. 2008. (ENG.). 160p. (J). (gr. k-3). pap. 9.95 *(978-2-89579-208-6(9))* Owlkids Bks. Inc. CAN. Dist: Perseus-PGW.

George, Audra. Vagabonding. George, Audra. 2006. 32p. (J). (gr. -1-3). 17.95 *(978-1-60108-010-3(7))* Red Cygnet Pr.

George, Boy. I Hear... 2013. (ENG.). 36p. (J). (gr. -1-k). 12.99 *(978-1-908473-07-3(X))* PatrickGeorge GBR. Dist: Independent Pubs. Group.

George, Imelda. The House of Wooden Santas, 1 vol. Pratt, Ned, photos by. Major, Kevin. 2003. (ENG.). 96p. (J). 22.95 *(978-0-88995-166-2(7))* Red Deer Pr. CAN. Dist: Ingram Pub. Services.

George, Jean Craighead. Charlie's Raven. George, Jean Craighead. 2006. (ENG.). 208p. (J). (gr. 5-18). reprint ed. 6.99 *(978-0-14-240547-5(7),* Puffin) Penguin Publishing Group.

George, John, 3rd. Moving Day. Pope, Amy. 2004. (J). bds. 9.99 *(978-1-4183-0010-4(1))* Christ Inspired, Inc.

George, Karen. Freddie & the Fairy, 7. Donaldson, Julia. 4th ed. 2012. (ENG.). 32p. (J). (gr. -1-k). 9.99 *(978-0-330-51118-6(1))* Macmillan Pubs., Ltd. GBR. Dist: Independent Pubs. Group.

George, Leonard, Jr. Eyes, Ears, Nose & Mouth. Olson, Karen W. (ENG.). 20p. 2005. (J). pap. 10.95 *(978-1-894778-34-3(0));* 2009. pap. 9.95 *(978-1-894778-52-7(9))* Theytus Bks., Ltd. CAN. Dist: Univ. of Toronto Pr.

—Living Safe, Playing Safe. Olson, Karen W. 2009. (Caring for Me Ser.). (ENG.). 20p. pap. 9.95 *(978-1-894778-51-0(0))* Theytus Bks., Ltd. CAN. Dist: Univ. of Toronto Pr.

George, Lindsay Barrett. Pick, Pull, Snap! Where Once a Flower Bloomed. Schaefer, Lola M. 2003. (ENG.). 32p. (J). (gr. k-5). 17.99 *(978-0-688-17834-5(0),* Greenwillow Bks.) HarperCollins Pubs.

George, Lindsay Barrett. Alfred Digs. George, Lindsay Barrett. 2008. 40p. (J). (gr. -1-2). 17.89 *(978-0-06-078761-5(9),* Greenwillow Bks.) HarperCollins Pubs.

—Alfred Digs. George, Lindsay Barrett. George, Lindsay B. 2008. (ENG.). 40p. (J). (gr. -1-2). 17.99 *(978-0-06-078760-8(0),* Greenwillow Bks.) HarperCollins Pubs.

—In the Garden: Who's Been Here? George, Lindsay Barrett. George, Lindsay B. 2006. (ENG.). 48p. (J). (gr. -1-3). 17.99 *(978-0-06-078762-2(7),* Greenwillow Bks.) HarperCollins Pubs.

—Inside Mouse, Outside Mouse. George, Lindsay Barrett. 2004. (ENG.). 40p. (J). (gr. -1-3). 17.99 *(978-0-06-000466-8(5),* Greenwillow Bks.) HarperCollins Pubs.

—Inside Mouse, Outside Mouse. George, Lindsay Barrett. George, Lindsay B. 2006. (ENG.). 40p. (J). (gr. -1-3). reprint ed. pap. 6.99 *(978-0-06-000468-2(1),* Greenwillow Bks.) HarperCollins Pubs.

—Maggie's Ball. George, Lindsay Barrett. 2010. (ENG.). 32p. (J). (gr. -1-k). 16.99 *(978-0-06-172166-3(2),* Greenwillow Bks.) HarperCollins Pubs.

—The Secret. George, Lindsay Barrett. 2005. 32p. (J). 16.89 *(978-0-06-029600-1(3))* HarperCollins Pubs.

—That Pup! George, Lindsay Barrett. 2011. (ENG.). 32p. (J). (gr. -1-k). 16.99 *(978-0-06-200413-0(1),* Greenwillow Bks.) HarperCollins Pubs.

George, Patrick. I Taste... George, Patrick. 2013. (ENG.). 36p. (J). (gr. -1-k). 12.99 *(978-1-908473-06-6(1))* PatrickGeorge GBR. Dist: Independent Pubs. Group.

—I Touch .. George, Patrick. 2013. (ENG.). 36p. (J). (gr. -1-k). 12.99 *(978-1-908473-08-0(8))* PatrickGeorge GBR. Dist: Independent Pubs. Group.

George, Peter. Davy Crockett & the Great Mississippi Snag, 1 vol. Meister, Cari. 2014. (American Folk Legends Ser.). (ENG.). 32p. (J). (gr. k-2). lib. bdg. 26.65 *(978-1-4795-5431-7(6))* Picture Window Bks.

Georger, Lucie. Don't Be Afraid to Say No! Lammertink, Ilona. 2013. (ENG.). 32p. (J). (gr. k-2). 15.95 *(978-1-60537-148-1(3))* Clavis Publishing.

Geraci, Drew. Tower of Babel, Vol. 7. Waid, Mark et al. rev. ed. 2005. (Justice League Adventures Ser.: Bk. 7). (ENG.). 160p. (YA). pap. 12.99 *(978-1-56389-727-6(X))* DC Comics.

Geraghty, Paul. Dinosaur in Danger. Geraghty, Paul. 2011. (ENG.). 40p. (J). (gr. k-k). pap. 12.99 *(978-1-84939-072-9(X))* Andersen Pr. GBR. Dist: Independent Pubs. Group.

—Help Me! Geraghty, Paul. 2011. (ENG.). 32p. (J). (gr. -1-k). pap. 8.99 *(978-1-84939-027-9(4))* Andersen Pr. GBR. Dist: Independent Pubs. Group.

—Hoppameleon. Geraghty, Paul. 2014. (ENG.). 32p. (J). (gr. -1-k). pap. 9.99 *(978-1-84939-773-5(2))* Andersen Pr. GBR. Dist: Independent Pubs. Group.

—The Hunter. Geraghty, Paul. 2012. (ENG.). 32p. (J). (gr. k-2). pap. 12.99 *(978-1-84939-376-8(1))* Andersen Pr. GBR. Dist: Independent Pubs. Group.

—Solo. Geraghty, Paul. 2011. (ENG.). 32p. (J). (gr. -1-k). pap. 8.99 *(978-1-84939-244-0(7))* Andersen Pr. GBR. Dist: Independent Pubs. Group.

Geran, Chad. Still a Gorilla. Norman, Kim. 2016. (J). ***(978-0-545-75791-1(6))*** Scholastic, Inc.

Gerard, Justin. Beowulf Bk. 1: Grendel the Ghastly. 2007. 32p. (J). (gr. 4-6). 17.95 *(978-0-9797183-0-4(9))* Portland Studios, Inc.

—Keeping Holiday. Meade, Starr et al. 2008. 192p. (gr. k). pap. 14.99 *(978-1-4335-0142-5(2))* Crossway.

—The Lightlings. 2006. 40p. (J). (gr. -1-3). lib. bdg. *(978-1-56769-078-1(5))* Reformation Pubs.

—The Priest with Dirty Clothes. Sproul, R. C. 2nd ed. 2011. (J). *(978-1-56769-210-5(9))* Reformation Pubs.

—The Prince's Poison Cup. Sproul, R. C. 2008. (J). *(978-1-56769-104-7(8))* Reformation Pubs.

—Secrets of a Christmas Box. Hornby, Steven. 2009. 248p. (J). (gr. 2-5). 18.95 *(978-0-9815883-0-8(1))* Ecky Thump Bks., Inc.

—Through the Skylight. Baucom, Ian. (ENG.). 400p. (J). (gr. 4-8). 2014. pap. 6.99 *(978-1-4424-8167-1(6));* 2013. 17.99 *(978-1-4169-1777-9(2))* Simon & Schuster Children's Publishing. (Atheneum Bks. for Young Readers).

—Twelve Dancing Unicorns. Heyman, Alissa. 2014. (ENG.). 32p. (J). (gr. -1-2). 14.95 *(978-1-4027-8732-4(4))* Sterling Publishing Co., Inc.

Gerard, Justin, jt. illus. see Grosvenor, Charles.

Gerardi, Jan. Fox in Socks, Bricks & Blocks. Seuss, Dr. 2011. (Dr. Seuss Nursery Collection). (ENG.). 14p. (J). (gr. -1 — 1). 7.99 *(978-0-375-87209-9(4),* Random Hse. Bks. for Young Readers) Random Hse. Children's Bks.

—Happy Birthday, Baby! Seuss, Dr. 2009. (Dr. Seuss Nursery Collection). (ENG.). 10p. (J). (— 1). 9.99 *(978-0-375-84621-2(2),* Random Hse. Bks. for Young Readers) Random Hse. Children's Bks.

—In the Deep. Greenburg, J. C. 2004. (Stepping Stone Book Ser.: Bk. 8). (ENG.). 96p. (J). (gr. 1-4). 3.99 *(978-0-375-82526-2(6),* Random Hse. Bks. for Young Readers) Random Hse. Children's Bks.

—In the Desert. Greenburg, J. C. 2008. (Stepping Stone Book Ser.: No. 17). (ENG.). 96p. (J). (gr. 1-4). per. 3.99 *(978-0-375-84667-0(0))* Random Hse., Inc.

—In the Garbage. Greenburg, J. C. 2006. (Stepping Stone Book(TM) Ser.: Bk. 13). (ENG.). 96p. (J). (gr. 1-4). 3.99 *(978-0-375-83562-9(8),* Random Hse. Bks. for Young Readers) Random Hse. Children's Bks.

—In the Ice Age. Greenburg, J. C. 2005. (Stepping Stone Book Ser.: Bk. 12). (ENG.). 96p. (J). (gr. 1-4). 3.99 *(978-0-375-82952-9(0),* Random Hse. Bks. for Young Readers) Random Hse. Children's Bks.

—In Time. Greenburg, J. C. 2004. (Stepping Stone Book(TM) Ser.: Bk. 9). (ENG.). 96p. (J). (gr. 1-4). 3.99 *(978-0-375-82949-9(0),* Random Hse. Bks. for Young Readers) Random Hse. Children's Bks.

—In Uncle Al, No. 16. Greenburg, J. C. 2007. (Stepping Stone Book Ser.: Bk. 16). (ENG.). 96p. (J). (gr. 1-4). 3.99 *(978-0-375-83565-0(2),* Random Hse. Bks. for Young Readers) Random Hse. Children's Bks.

—The Lorax Deluxe Doodle Book. Golden Books Staff. 2013. (Super Coloring Book Ser.). (ENG.). 256p. (J). (gr. -1-2). pap. 9.99 *(978-0-449-81061-3(5),* Golden Bks.) Random Hse. Children's Bks.

—The Lorax Doodle Book. Golden Books Staff. 2012. (Doodle Book Ser.). (ENG.). 128p. (J). (gr. -1-2). pap. 5.99 *(978-0-307-92982-2(5),* Golden Bks.) Random Hse., Inc.

—Oh, Baby! Go, Baby! Seuss, Dr. 2010. (Dr. Seuss Nursery Collection). (ENG.). 14p. (J). (gr. k — 1). 10.99 *(978-0-375-85738-6(9),* Random Hse. Bks. for Young Readers) Random Hse. Children's Bks.

—On Earth. Greenburg, J. C. 10th ed. 2005. (Stepping Stone Book Ser.: Bk. 10). (ENG.). 96p. (J). (gr. 1-4). 3.99 *(978-0-375-82950-5(4),* Random Hse. Bks. for Young Readers) Random Hse. Children's Bks.

—A Tree for Me! Golden Books Staff. 2012. (Stickerific Ser.). (ENG.). 48p. (J). (gr. k — 1). pap. 3.99 *(978-0-307-92981-5(7),* Golden Bks.) Random Hse., Inc.

—With the Bats. Greenburg, J. C. 2006. (Stepping Stone Book Ser.: Bk. 14). (ENG.). 96p. (J). (gr. 1-4). 3.99 *(978-0-375-83563-6(6),* Random Hse. Bks. for Young Readers) Random Hse. Children's Bks.

—With the Dinosaurs. Greenburg, J. C. 2005. (Stepping Stone Book Ser.: Bk. 11). (ENG.). 96p. (J). (gr. 1-4). 3.99 *(978-0-375-82951-2(2),* Random Hse. Bks. for Young Readers) Random Hse. Children's Bks.

—With the Frogs. Greenburg, J. C. 2008. (Stepping Stone Book Ser.: No. 18). (ENG.). 96p. (J). (gr. 1-4). 3.99 *(978-0-375-84668-7(9),* Random Hse. Bks. for Young Readers) Random Hse. Children's Bks.

Gerardi, Jan, jt. illus. see Reed, Mike.

Gerber, Kathryn. Iraq in a Nutshell. Roraback, Amanda. 2003. (Nutshell Notes). 36p. 5.95 *(978-0-9702908-5-4(3))* Enisen Publishing.

Gerber, Mary Jane. A Pioneer Alphabet. Downie, Mary Alice. 2009. (ABC Our Country Ser.). (ENG.). 32p. (J). (gr. k-3). pap. 7.95 *(978-0-88776-961-0(6),* Tundra Bks.) Tundra Bks. CAN. Dist: Penguin Random Hse., LLC.

—Sky, 1 vol. Porter, Pamela. 2005. (ENG.). 104p. (J). (gr. 3-5). pap. 9.95 *(978-0-88899-607-7(1),* Libros Tigrillo) Groundwood Bks. CAN. Dist: Perseus-PGW.

—Tuk & the Whale, 1 vol. Rivera, Raquel. (ENG.). 96p. (J). (gr. 2-5). 2009. pap. 6.95 *(978-0-88899-891-0(0));* 2008. 15.95 *(978-0-88899-689-3(6))* Groundwood Bks. CAN. Dist: Perseus-PGW.

—The Ways I Will Love You, 1 vol. Boehm, Rachel. 2010. (ENG.). 24p. (J). (gr. -1-3). bds. 9.95 *(978-1-55469-187-6(7))* Orca Bk. Pubs. USA.

Gerber, Patric. This Is the Hill. Lasater, Amy. 2005. (J). *(978-1-59156-720-2(3))* Covenant Communications.

Gerber, Pesach. Shadow Play: A True Story of Tefillah. Shollar, Leah Pearl. 2006. 32p. (J). 11.95 *(978-1-929628-21-6(8))* Hachai Publishing.

Gerecke, Bretta. Maximilian's Mistake. Christenson, Jonathan. 2012. (ENG.). 42p. (J). pap. 9.95 *(978-1-897411-35-3(9))* Bayeux Arts, Inc. CAN. Dist: Chicago Distribution Ctr.

Geremia, Daniela & Ecob, Simon. Girls Only: How to Survive Anything! Stride, Lottie & Oliver, Martin. 2012. (Best at Everything Ser.). (ENG.). 64p. (J). (gr. 3-7). pap. 6.99 *(978-0-545-43095-1(X),* Scholastic Paperbacks) Scholastic, Inc.

Gergely, Tibor. Animal Gym. Hoffman, Beth Greiner. 2009. (Little Golden Book Ser.). (ENG.). 24p. (J). (gr. -1-2). 3.99 *(978-0-375-84751-6(0),* Golden Bks.) Random Hse. Children's Bks.

—Daddies. Frank, Janet & Golden Books Staff. 2011. (Little Golden Book Ser.). (ENG.). 24p. (J). (gr. -1-2). 3.99 *(978-0-375-86130-7(0),* Golden Bks.) Random Hse. Children's Bks.

—The Fire Engine Book. Golden Books Staff. 2004. (Little Golden Treasures Ser.). (ENG.). 26p. (J). (gr. k-k). bds. 4.99 *(978-0-375-82841-6(9),* Golden Bks.) Random Hse. Children's Bks.

Gergely, Tibor. The Fire Engine Book. Golden Books. 2015. (Little Golden Board Book Ser.). (ENG.). 26p. (J). (-k). bds. 7.99 ***(978-0-553-52224-2(8),*** Golden Bks.) Random Hse. Children's Bks.

Gergely, Tibor. The Happy Man & His Dump Truck. Golden Books Staff & Miryam. 2005. (Little Golden Book Ser.). (ENG.). 24p. (J). (gr. -1-k). 3.99 *(978-0-375-83207-9(6),* Golden Bks.) Random Hse. Children's Bks.

—The Happy Man & His Dump Truck. Miryam. 2010. (Little Golden Treasures Ser.). (ENG.). 26p. (J). (gr. k — 1). bds. 4.99 *(978-0-375-85517-7(3),* Golden Bks.) Random Hse. Children's Bks.

—The Jolly Barnyard. North Bedford, Annie. 2004. (Little Golden Book Ser.). (ENG.). 24p. (J). (gr. -1-2). 3.99 *(978-0-375-82842-3(7),* Golden Bks.) Random Hse. Children's Bks.

—Little Golden Book Train Stories. Crampton, Gertrude et al. 2014. (Little Golden Book Favorites Ser.). (ENG.). 80p. (J). (-k). 6.99 *(978-0-385-37862-8(9),* Golden Bks.) Random Hse. Children's Bks.

—The Merry Shipwreck. Duplaix, Georges & Golden Books Staff. 2011. (Little Golden Book Ser.). (ENG.). 24p. (J). (gr. -1-2). 3.99 *(978-0-375-86800-9(3),* Golden Bks.) Random Hse. Children's Bks.

—Scuffy the Tugboat. Crampton, Gertrude. deluxe ed. Date not set. (J). (gr. -1-2). reprint ed. *(978-1-929566-59-4(X))* Cronies.

—Scuffy the Tugboat: Classic Edition. Crampton, Gertrude. Date not set. (J). reprint ed. *(978-1-929566-52-5(2))* Cronies.

—Tootle. Golden Books Staff, photos by. deluxe ed. Date not set. (J). (gr. -1-2). reprint ed. *(978-1-929566-58-7(1))* Cronies.

—Tootle: Classic Edition. Crampton, Gertrude. Date not set. 21p. (J). (gr. -1-1). *(978-1-929566-53-2(0))* Cronies.

Gergely, Tibor, jt. illus. see Rojankovsky, Feodor.

Gerhmann, Katja. The Angry Little Knight. Gerhmann, Katja. Langen, Annette. 2013. (ENG.). 32p. (J). (gr. -1-2). 17.95 *(978-0-7358-4110-9(1))* North-South Bks., Inc.

Gerlings, Rebecca. Enormouse! Gerlings, Rebecca. 2011. (ENG.). 32p. (J). (gr. -1-k). pap. 8.99 *(978-1-4052-4832-7(7))* Egmont Bks., Ltd. GBR. Dist: Independent Pubs. Group.

Germain, Daniella. Snap! Holmes, Janet A. 2014. (ENG.). 32p. (J). (gr. -1-k). 16.99 *(978-1-921714-99-3(9))* Little Hare Bks. AUS. Dist: Independent Pubs. Group.

Germain, Philippe. Une Maison dans la Baleine. Hébert, Marie-Francine. 2003. (Premier Roman Ser.). (FRE.). 64p. (J). (gr. 2-5). pap. *(978-2-89021-240-4(8))* Diffusion du livre Mirabel (DLM).

Germano, Nicholas. Dugan Peckles & the Keepers of the Crystal Flame. Pepper, Sly. 2006. 229p. per. 5.99 *(978-0-9747668-1-2(X))* MindMaze Publishing Co.

Gernhart, Carlie. The Adventures of Gertrude Mcduck, Chicken in Charge Vol. 1: The Missing Eggs, 4 vols. Gernhart, Cyndi. l.t. ed. 2005. 32p. (J). 8.00 *(978-0-9778240-1-4(2))* Prairie Winds Publishing.

—The Adventures of Gertrude Mcduck, Chicken in Charge Vol. 2: The Great Crate Mystery, 4 vols. Gernhart, Cyndi. l.t. ed. 2005. 40p. (J). 8.00 *(978-0-9778240-2-1(0))* Prairie Winds Publishing.

—The Adventures of Gertrude Mcduck, Chicken in Charge Vol. 3: The Yellow-Eyed Pond Monster, 4 vols. Gernhart, Cyndi. l.t. ed. 2005. 52p. (J). 8.00 *(978-0-9778240-3-8(9))* Prairie Winds Publishing.

—The Adventures of Gertrude Mcduck, Chicken in Charge Vol. 4: A Midwinter Light's Dream, 4 vols. Gernhart, Cyndi. l.t. ed. 2006. 52p. (J). 8.00 *(978-0-9778240-4-5(7))* Prairie Winds Publishing.

Gernhart, Cyndi, et al. Gertrude Sees... On the Farm. Gernhart, Cyndi. l.t. ed. 2006. 20p. (J). 8.00 *(978-0-9778240-0-7(4))* Prairie Winds Publishing.

Gerrell, Spike. Max Archer, Kid Detective: The Case of the Recurring Stomachaches. Bennett, Howard J. 2012. 48p. (J). 14.95 *(978-1-4338-1130-2(8))*; pap. 9.95 *(978-1-4338-1129-6(4))* American Psychological Assn. (Magination Pr.).

—Max Archer, Kid Detective: The Case of the Wet Bed. Bennett, Howard J. 2011. 48p. (J). (gr. 1-5). 14.95 *(978-1-4338-0953-8(2))*; pap. 9.95 *(978-1-4338-0954-5(0))* American Psychological Assn. (Magination Pr.).

Gerritsen, Paula. The Nothing King. Van Lieshout, Elle & Van Os, Erik. 2004. (ENG.). 32p. (J). (gr. k-3). 15.95 *(978-1-932425-14-7(4))*, Lemniscaat) Boyds Mills Pr.

Gershator, Phillis. Little Lenty. 2014. (J). pap. *(978-1-934370-48-3(7))* Editorial Campana.

Gershman, Jo. Mommy, Daddy, I Had a Bad Dream! Pieper, Martha Heineman. 2012. (ENG.). 32p. (J). 18.99 *(978-0-9838664-0-4(6))* Smart Love Pr., LLC.

—Nutcracker Ballet: A Book, Theater, & Paper Doll Foldout Play Set. Conlon, Mara. 2007. (Foldout Playset Ser.). 30p. (J). 17.99 *(978-1-59359-885-3(8))* Peter Pauper Pr. Inc.

Gershman, Jo, jt. illus. see Chang, Tara Larsen.

Gersing, James & Weaver, Steve. Those Lively Lizards. Gersing, James, photos by. Magellan, Marta. 2008. (Those Amazing Animals Ser.). (ENG.). 55p. (J). (gr. k-4). 14.95 *(978-1-56164-426-1(9))*; pap. 9.95 *(978-1-56164-427-8(7))* Pineapple Pr., Inc.

Gerstein, Mordecai. The Camping Trip That Changed America: Theodore Roosevelt, John Muir, & Our National Parks. Rosenstock, Barb. 2012. (ENG.). 32p. (J). (gr. 1-3). 16.99 *(978-0-8037-3710-5(6)*, Dial) Penguin Publishing Group.

Gerstein, Mordical. Applesauce Season. Lipson, Eden Ross. 2009. (ENG.). 40p. (J). (gr. -1-3). 17.99 *(978-1-59643-216-1(0))* Roaring Brook Pr.

—A Hare-Raising Tale. Levy, Elizabeth. unabr. ed. 2006. (First Chapter Bks.). (J). (gr. 2-4). pap. 17.95 incl. audio *(978-1-59519-704-7(4))*; pap. 20.95 incl. audio compact disk *(978-1-59519-705-4(2))* Live Oak Media.

—I Am Arachne: Fifteen Greek & Roman Myths. Spires, Elizabeth. 2009. (ENG.). 112p. (J). (gr. 3-7). pap. 8.99 *(978-0-312-56125-3(3))* Square Fish.

—The Principal's on the Roof. Levy, Elizabeth. ed. 2005. 74p. (J). lib. bdg. 15.00 *(978-1-59054-912-4(0))* Fitzgerald Bks.

—The Principal's on the Roof. Levy, Elizabeth. unabr. ed. 2006. (First Chapter Bks.). (J). (gr. 2-4). pap. 17.95 incl. audio *(978-1-59519-698-9(6))*; pap. 20.95 incl. audio compact disk *(978-1-59519-699-6(4))* Live Oak Media.

—Three Samurai Cats: A Story from Japan. 2004. (ENG.). 32p. (J). (gr. k-3). 6.95 *(978-0-8234-1877-0(4))* Holiday Hse., Inc.

—Three Samurai Cats: A Story from Japan. 2004. (J). *(978-0-439-69256-4(3))* Scholastic, Inc.

Gerstein, Mordicai. A Book. Gerstein, Mordicai. 2009. (ENG.). 48p. (J). (gr. -1-3). 16.95 *(978-1-59643-251-2(9))* Roaring Brook Pr.

—How to Bicycle to the Moon to Plant Sunflowers: A Simple but Brilliant Plan in 24 Easy Steps. Gerstein, Mordicai. 2013. (ENG.). 40p. (J). (gr. -1-2). 16.99 *(978-1-59643-512-4(7))* Roaring Brook Pr.

—The Man Who Walked Between the Towers. Gerstein, Mordicai. (ENG.). 44p. (J). (gr. k-3). 2007. per. 7.99 *(978-0-312-36878-4(X))*; 2003. 17.95 *(978-0-7613-1791-3(0))* Square Fish.

—Minifred Goes to School. Gerstein, Mordicai. 2009. (ENG.). 32p. (J). (gr. -1-3). 17.99 *(978-0-06-075889-9(9))* HarperCollins Pubs.

—Mountains of Tibet. Gerstein, Mordicai. 2013. (ENG.). 32p. (J). 16.99 *(978-1-78285-047-2(3))* Barefoot Bks., Inc.

—What Charlie Heard. Gerstein, Mordicai. pap. 18.95 incl. audio compact disk *(978-1-59112-277-7(5))*; pap. incl. audio *(978-1-59112-279-1(1))*; pap. 16.95 incl. audio *(978-1-59112-484-9(0))*; pap. incl. audio compact disk *(978-1-59112-525-9(1))* Live Oak Media.

—The White Ram: A Story of Abraham & Isaac. Gerstein, Mordicai. 2006. (ENG.). 32p. (J). (gr. -1-3). 16.95 *(978-0-8234-1897-8(9))* Holiday Hse., Inc.

—You Can't Have Too Many Friends! Gerstein, Mordical. 2014. (ENG.). 32p. (J). (gr. -1-2). 16.95 *(978-0-8234-2393-4(X))* Holiday Hse., Inc.

Gerstein, Mordical & Coville, Katherine. The Dragon of Doom. Levy, Elizabeth & Coville, Bruce. ed. 2005. 71p. (J). lib. bdg. 15.00 *(978-1-59054-903-2(1))* Fitzgerald Bks.

Gerstein, Yoni. Effy Helps Out. Kugel, Bruriah. 2008. 26p. (J). (gr. -1). 14.99 *(978-1-58330-942-1(X))* Feldheim Pubs.

Gerszak, Rafal, photos by. Thunder over Kandahar. McKay, Sharon E. 2010. (ENG., 264p. (YA). (gr. 7-12). pap. 12.95 *(978-1-55451-266-9(2)*, 9781554512669) Annick Pr., Ltd. CAN. Dist: Firefly Bks., Ltd.

Gerth, Melanie, jt. illus. see Diaz, James.

Gervasi, Christine. Poems from the Playground & Other Places. McKenzie, Richard. 2004. (J). 12.00 *(978-0-9725901-0-5(2))* Lekha Pubs., LLC.

Gervasio, et al. Monster Science. Weakland, Mark & Jensen Shaffer, Jody. 2013. (Monster Science Ser.). (ENG.). 32p. (gr. 3-4). pap. 15.90 *(978-1-62065-824-6(0)*, Graphic Library) Capstone Pr., Inc.

—Monster Science. Shaffer, Jody Jensen et al. 2013. (Monster Science Ser.). (ENG.). 32p. (gr. 3-4). lib. bdg. 59.98 *(978-1-4296-9932-7(9)*, Graphic Library) Capstone Pr., Inc.

Gervasio. Vampires & Light, 1 vol. Jensen Shaffer, Jody. 2013. (Monster Science Ser.). (ENG.). 32p. (gr. 3-4). pap. 8.10 *(978-1-62065-820-8(8))*; 47.70 *(978-1-62065-821-5(6))* Capstone Pr., Inc. (Graphic Library).

—Vampires & Light, 1 vol. Shaffer, Jody Jensen. 2013. (Monster Science Ser.). (ENG.). 32p. (gr. 3-4). lib. bdg. 29.99 *(978-1-4296-9928-0(0)*, Graphic Library) Capstone Pr., Inc.

—Zombies & Forces & Motion, 1 vol. Weakland, Mark. 2011. (Monster Science Ser.). (ENG.). 32p. (gr. 3-4). lib. bdg. 29.99 *(978-1-4296-6577-3(7)*, Graphic Library) Capstone Pr., Inc.

Gervasio & Aón, Carlos. Monster Science. Jensen Shaffer, Jody et al. 2013. (Monster Science Ser.). (ENG.). 32p. (gr. 3-4). lib. bdg. 239.92 *(978-1-4296-9933-4(7)*, Graphic Library) Capstone Pr., Inc.

—Monster Science. Weakland, Mark et al. 2013. (Monster Science Ser.). (ENG.). 32p. (gr. 3-4). pap. 381.60 *(978-1-62065-826-0(7)*, Graphic Library) Capstone Pr., Inc.

—Monster Science. Weakland, Mark et al. 2013. (Monster Science Ser.). (ENG.). 32p. (gr. 3-4). pap. 63.60 *(978-1-62065-825-3(9)*, Graphic Library) Capstone Pr., Inc.

Gervasio, jt. illus. see Mallea, Cristian.

Géser, Gretchen. One Bright Ring. Géser, Gretchen. 2013. (ENG.). 32p. (J). (gr. -1-3). 16.99 *(978-0-8050-9279-0(X)*, Holt, Henry & Co. Bks. For Young Readers) Holt, Henry & Co.

Gettys, Katherine. Kavaldo & His Diamond Pills. Ferrier, Paul Eugene. 2013. (ENG.). 72p. pap. 12.99 *(978-1-940395-07-4(0))* Yawn's Bks. & More, Inc.

Gevry, Christine. My Baby. Deprisco Wang, Dorothea. 2007. (Story Book Ser.). 10p. (J). (gr. -1). *(978-1-84666-263-8(X)*, Tide Mill Pr.) Top That! Publishing PLC.

Gévry, Claudine. Baby's Hug-a-Bible. Lloyd-Jones, Sally. 2010. (ENG.). 24p. (J). (gr. -1 — 1). bds. 15.99 *(978-0-06-156621-9(7)*, HarperFestival) HarperCollins Pubs.

—The Big Book of Bible Fish Tales. Finbarr, Desmond. 2003. 10p. (J). bds. 8.99 *(978-0-8254-5514-8(6))* Kregel Pubns.

—Caterpillar Spring, Butterfly Summer. Hood, Susan. 2003. (ENG.). 10p. (J). (gr. k-3). bds. 12.99 *(978-0-7944-0149-8(X))* Reader's Digest Assn., Inc., The.

Gevry, Claudine. Caterpillar Spring, Butterfly Summer: 10th Anniversary Edition. Hood, Susan. 2014. (ENG.). 12p. (J). (gr. -1-k). 12.99 *(978-0-7944-3038-2(4))* Reader's Digest Assn., Inc., The.

—Hippos on Holiday. Mitter, Matt. 2013. (Flap Book Ser.: 1). (ENG.). 20p. (J). (gr. -1-k). 14.99 *(978-0-7944-2863-1(0))* Reader's Digest Assn., Inc., The.

Gévry, Claudine. J Is for Jesus: The Sweetest Story Ever Told, 1 vol. Bowman, Crystal. 2005. (ENG.). 20p. (J). (gr. -1). bds. 6.99 *(978-0-310-70891-9(5))* Zonderkidz.

—Little School of Fish. DePrisco, Dorothea. 2006. 12p. (J). (gr. -1-k). 10.95 *(978-1-58117-485-4(3)*, Intervisual/Piggy Toes) Bendon, Inc.

—One Little Bear & Her Friends. Ranson, Erin. 2007. 10p. (J). (gr. -1-k). bds. *(978-1-84666-354-3(7)*, Tide Mill Pr.) Top That! Publishing PLC.

—One Little Penguin & His Friends: A Pushing, Turning, Counting Book. Top That Publishing Staff, ed. 2007. 10p. (J). (gr. -1-3). bds. *(978-1-84666-268-3(0)*, Tide Mill Pr.) Top That! Publishing PLC.

Gevry, Claudine. One Little Penguin & His Friends: A Pushing, Turning, Counting Book. 2012. (ENG.). 10p. (J). bds. *(978-1-84956-027-6(7))* Top That! Publishing PLC.

Gévry, Claudine. One, Two... Boo! Depken, Kristen & Depken, Kristen L. 2009. (ENG.). 12p. (J). (gr. -1 — 1). bds. 3.99 *(978-0-375-84418-8(X)*, Golden Bks.) Random Hse. Children's Bks.

—Spin & Spell: A Book & Game in One! Perez, Jessica. 2005. 12p. (J). 14.95 *(978-1-58117-332-1(6)*, Intervisual/Piggy Toes) Bendon, Inc.

—Spin the Dreidel! Cooper, Alexandra. 2004. (ENG.). 14p. (J). (gr. -1-2). 7.99 *(978-0-689-86430-8(2)*, Little Simon) Little Simon.

—A Star for Jesus, 1 vol. Bowman, Crystal. 2006. (ENG.). 14p. (J). (gr. -1). bds. 6.99 *(978-0-310-71216-9(5))* Zonderkidz.

—When I Grow Up: A Touch & Feel Book. Wang, Margaret C. 2005. (ENG.). 12p. (J). bds. 10.95 *(978-1-58117-423-6(3)*, Intervisual/Piggy Toes) Bendon, Inc.

—1,2,3 Octopus & Me. Rovetch, L. Bob. 2006. (J). *(978-1-58987-011-6(5))* Kindermusik International.

Geyer, Kim. Go to Sleep, Monty! Geyer, Kim. 2015. (ENG.). 32p. (J). (gr. -1-3). 17.99 ***(978-1-4677-9311-7(6))*** Lerner Publishing Group.

Geyer, Mark Edward. The Inquisitor's Apprentice. Moriarty, Chris. (ENG.). 352p. (gr. 5-7). 2013. (YA). pap. 7.99 *(978-0-547-85084-9(0))*; 2011. (J). 16.99 *(978-0-547-58135-4(1))* Houghton Mifflin Harcourt Publishing Co.

—Secrets of Shakespeare's Grave. Hicks, Deron R. (Shakespeare Mysteries Ser.: 1). (ENG.). (J). (gr. 2-5). 2012. 304p. 16.99 *(978-0-547-84034-5(9))*; Bk. 1. 2013. 320p. pap. 6.99 *(978-0-544-10504-1(4))* Houghton Mifflin Harcourt Publishing Co.

—Tower of the Five Orders. Hicks, Deron R. 2013. (Shakespeare Mysteries Ser.: 2). (ENG.). 320p. (YA). (gr. 5-7). 16.99 *(978-0-547-83953-0(7))* Houghton Mifflin Harcourt Publishing Co.

—Tower of the Five Orders: The Shakespeare Mysteries, Book 2. Hicks, Deron R. 2014. (Shakespeare Mysteries Ser.). (ENG.). 320p. (YA). (gr. 5-7). pap. 6.99 *(978-0-544-33630-8(5))*, HMH Books For Young Readers) Houghton Mifflin Harcourt Publishing Co.

—The Watcher in the Shadows. Moriarty, Chris. (ENG.). 336p. (J). (gr. 5-7). 2014. pap. 7.99 *(978-0-544-22776-7(X)*, HMH Books For Young Readers); 2013. 16.99 *(978-0-547-46632-3(3))* Houghton Mifflin Harcourt Publishing Co.

Geyer, Mark Edward & Harrison, Nancy. Who Was Charles Dickens? Pollack, Pamela D. & Belviso, Meg. 2014. (Who Was... ? Ser.). (ENG.). 112p. (J). (gr. 3-7). pap. 4.99 *(978-0-448-47967-5(2)*, Grosset & Dunlap) Penguin Publishing Group.

Geyer, Mark Edward, jt. illus. see Harrison, Nancy.

Ghahremani, Susie. What Will Hatch? Ward, Jennifer. 2013. (ENG.). 40p. (J). (gr. -1-1). 14.99 *(978-0-8027-2311-6(X)*, Bloomsbury USA Childrens) Bloomsbury USA.

—What Will Hatch? Ward, Jennifer. 2013. (ENG.). 40p. (J). (gr. -1-1). lib. bdg. 13.89 *(978-0-8027-2312-3(8))* Walker & Co.

Ghiuselev, Iassen. Alice's Adventures in Wonderland. Carroll, Lewis. rev. ed. 2012. (ENG.). 120p. (J). (gr. 3). 29.95 *(978-1-897476-42-0(6))* Simply Read Bks. CAN. Dist: Ingram Pub. Services.

—The King of the Golden River. Ruskin, John. 2005. (ENG.). 65p. (J). (gr. k). 19.95 *(978-1-894965-15-6(9))* Simply Read Bks. CAN. Dist: Ingram Pub. Services.

Ghiuselev, Iassen & James, Elizabeth. The Queen Bee. Grimm, Jacob et al. 2003. (ENG.). 24p. (J). 16.95 *(978-0-9688768-4-8(6))* Simply Read Bks. CAN. Dist: Ingram Pub. Services.

Ghosh, Premola. Ten Timeless Tales. 2005. 38p. (J). *(978-81-89013-35-6(1))* Zubaan.

Giacobbe, Beppe. Clang! Clang! Beep! Beep! Listen to the City. Burleigh, Robert. 2009. (ENG.). 32p. (J). (gr. -1-2). 16.99 *(978-1-4169-4052-4(9)*, Simon & Schuster/Paula Wiseman Bks.) Simon & Schuster/Paula Wiseman Bks.

—Nobody's Diggier Than a Dog. Bartoletti, Susan Campbell. 2005. (ENG.). 40p. (J). (gr. -1-17). 15.99 *(978-0-7868-1824-2(7))* Hyperion Pr.

Giacomini, Amanda. Mo Smells Blue: A Scentsational Journey. Hyde, Margaret. 3rd ed. 2010. (Mo's Nose Ser.). (ENG.). 24p. (J). (gr. k-k). 17.95 *(978-0-9816255-4-6(1))* Mo's Nose, LLC.

—Mo Smells Christmas: A Scentsational Journey. Hyde, Margaret. 4th ed. 2010. (Mo's Nose Ser.). (ENG.). 24p. (J). (gr. k-k). 17.95 *(978-0-9816255-6-0(8))* Mo's Nose, LLC.

—Mo Smells Green: A Scentsational Journey. Hyde, Margaret. 2009. (Mo's Nose Ser.). (ENG.). 16p. (J). (gr. k-k). 17.95 *(978-0-9816255-2-2(5))* Mo's Nose, LLC.

—Mo Smells Pink: A Scentsational Journey. Hyde, Margaret. 5th ed. 2011. (Mo's Nose Ser.). (ENG.). 24p. (J). (gr. k-k). 17.95 *(978-0-9816255-5-3(X))* Mo's Nose, LLC.

—Mo Smells the Holidays: A Scentsational Journey. Hyde, Margaret. 2009. (Mo's Nose Ser.). (ENG.). 24p. (J). (gr. k-k). 17.95 *(978-0-9816255-3-9(3))* Mo's Nose, LLC.

Giallongo, Zach. Star Wars Doodles. Giallongo, Zach. 2015. (Doodle Book Ser.). (ENG.). 128p. (J). (gr. 1-3). pap. 12.99 *(978-1-4847-0684-8(6)*, Disney Lucasfilm Press) Disney Publishing Worldwide.

Giallongo, Zack. The Stratford Zoo Midnight Revue Presents Macbeth. Lendler, Ian. 2014. (Stratford Zoo Ser.). (ENG.). 80p. (J). (gr. 2-5). pap. 12.99 *(978-1-59643-915-3(7)*, First Second Bks.) Roaring Brook Pr.

—Tricky Rabbit Tales. Schweizer, Chris. 2011. (Tricky Journeys Ser.: 2). (ENG.). (J). (gr. 2-4). pap. 39.62 *(978-0-7613-8626-1(2))*; 64p. pap. 6.95 *(978-0-7613-7862-4(6))*;No. 2. 64p. lib. bdg. 27.93 *(978-0-7613-6607-2(5))* Lerner Publishing Group. (Graphic Universe).

Giallongo, Zack. Broxo. Giallongo, Zack. 2012. (ENG.). 240p. (J). (gr. 5-9). pap. 16.99 *(978-1-59643-551-3(8)*, First Second Bks.) Roaring Brook Pr.

Giancanelli, Candace. The Adventures of Beezer. Gard, Don. 2006. 100p. per. 12.95 *(978-1-59858-157-7(0))* Dog Ear Publishing, LLC.

Giaquinta, Maria. Forever Friends. Fabbella, Teresa. 2010. 26p. pap. 9.95 *(978-1-60911-366-7(7)*, Eloquent Bks.) Strategic Book Publishing & Rights Agency (SBPRA).

Giarrusso, Chris. Secret Identity Crisis. Bell, Jake. 2010. (Amazing Adventures of Nate Banks Ser.: 1). (ENG.). 176p. (J). (gr. 3-7). mass mkt. 5.99 *(978-0-545-15669-1(6)*, Scholastic Paperbacks) Scholastic, Inc.

Giarrusso, Chris. Mini Marvels: The Complete Collection. Giarrusso, Chris, text. 2013. (ENG.). 216p. (J). (gr. -1-17). pap. 24.99 *(978-0-7851-8490-4(2))* Marvel Worldwide, Inc.

Gibala-Broxholm, Scott. City Witch, Country Switch, 0 vols. Wax, Wendy. 2013. (ENG.). 39p. (J). (gr. -1-3). pap. 9.99 *(978-1-4778-1676-9(3)*, 9781477816769, Amazon Children's Publishing) Amazon Publishing.

Gibala-Broxholm, Scott. Maddie's Monster Dad, 0 vols. Gibala-Broxholm, Scott. 2011. (ENG.). 40p. (J). (gr. -1-3). 16.99 *(978-0-7614-5846-3(8)*, 9780761458463, Amazon Children's Publishing) Amazon Publishing.

Gibb, Sarah. Emily Windsnap & the Monster from the Deep. Kessler, Liz. 2012. (Emily Windsnap Ser.: 2). (ENG.). 240p. (J). (gr. 3-7). pap. 5.99 *(978-0-7636-6018-5(3))* Candlewick Pr.

Gibb, Sarah. Emily Windsnap & the Ship of Lost Souls. Kessler, Liz. 2015. (Emily Windsnap Ser.). (ENG.). 288p. (J). (gr. 3-7). 15.99 ***(978-0-7636-7688-9(8))*** Candlewick Pr.

Gibb, Sarah. Emily Windsnap: Two Magical Mermaid Tales. Kessler, Liz. 2014. (Emily Windsnap Ser.). (ENG.). 464p. (J). (gr. 3-7). pap. 9.99 *(978-0-7636-7452-6(4))* Candlewick Pr.

—Princess Charlotte & the Enchanted Rose. French, Vivian. 2007. (Tiara Club Ser.: No. 7). 80p. (J). (gr. 1-4). pap. 3.99 *(978-0-06-112441-9(9)*, Tegen, Katherine Bks) HarperCollins Pubs.

—Princess Georgia & the Shimmering Pearl. French, Vivian. 2008. (Tiara Club Ser.: No. 3). (ENG.). 80p. (J). (gr. 1-4). pap. 3.99 *(978-0-06-143486-0(8)*, Harper Trophy) HarperCollins Pubs.

—Princess Katie & the Silver Pony. French, Vivian. 2007. (Tiara Club Ser.: No.2). 80p. (J). (gr. 1-4). 15.99 *(978-0-06-112432-7(X)*, Tegen, Katherine Bks) HarperCollins Pubs.

—Princess Parade - Christmas Special 2007. French, Vivian. 2007. (Tiara Club Ser.). (ENG.). 160p. (J). (gr. k-3). pap. 9.99 *(978-1-84616-504-7(0))* Hodder & Stoughton GBR. Dist: Independent Pubs. Group.

—Princess Sarah & the Silver Swan. French, Vivian. 2010. (Tiara Club Ser.: 24). (ENG.). 80p. (J). (gr. k-3). pap. 4.99 *(978-1-84616-503-0(2))* Hodder & Stoughton GBR. Dist: Independent Pubs. Group.

—The Princess Who Had No Kingdom. Jones, Ursula. 2014. (ENG.). 32p. (J). (gr. -1-2). 16.99 *(978-0-8075-6630-5(6))* Whitman, Albert & Co.

—The Tail of Emily Windsnap. Kessler, Liz. 2012. (Emily Windsnap Ser.: 1). (ENG.). 224p. (J). (gr. 3-7). pap. 5.99 *(978-0-7636-6020-8(5))* Candlewick Pr.

Gibb, Sarah. Rapunzel: Based on the Original Story by the Brothers Grimm. Gibb, Sarah. 2011. (ENG.). 32p. (J). (gr. k-6). 16.99 *(978-0-8075-6804-0(X))* Whitman, Albert & Co.

Gibb, Sarah & Ledwidge, Natacha. Emily Windsnap & the Land of the Midnight Sun. Kessler, Liz. 2013. (Emily Windsnap Ser.: 5). (ENG.). 288p. (J). (gr. 3-7). 15.99 *(978-0-7636-5824-3(3))* Candlewick Pr.

—Four Sparkling Underwater Adventures. Kessler, Liz. 2012. (Emily Windsnap Ser.). (ENG.). (J). (gr. 3-7). pap. 23.96 *(978-0-7636-6295-0(X))* Candlewick Pr.

Gibb, Sarah, jt. illus. see Ledwidge, Natacha.

Gibbon, Rebecca. The Bee Who Spoke: The Wonderful World of Belle & the Bee. 2014. (ENG.). 32p. (J). (gr. k-2). 14.95 *(978-0-500-65027-1(6)*, 565027) Thames & Hudson.

—Celebritrees: Historic & Famous Trees of the World. Preus, Margi. 2011. (ENG.). 40p. (J). (gr. 2-4). 16.99 *(978-0-8050-7829-9(0)*, Holt, Henry & Co. Bks. For Young Readers) Holt, Henry & Co.

—Elizabeth Leads the Way: Elizabeth Cady Stanton & the Right to Vote. Stone, Tanya Lee. 2008. (ENG.). 32p. (J). (gr. 1-5). 17.99 *(978-0-8050-7903-6(3)*, Holt, Henry & Co. Bks. For Young Readers) Holt, Henry & Co.

—Elizabeth Leads the Way: Elizabeth Cady Stanton & the Right to Vote. Stone, Tanya Lee. 2010. (ENG.). 32p. (J). (gr. 1-5). pap. 8.99 *(978-0-312-60236-9(7))* Square Fish.

—Papa Is a Poet: A Story about Robert Frost. Bober, Natalie S. 2013. (ENG.). 40p. (J). (gr. -1-3). 17.99 *(978-0-8050-9407-7(5)*, Holt, Henry & Co. Bks. For Young Readers) Holt, Henry & Co.

—Players in Pigtails. Corey, Shana. 2006. 28p. (YA). (gr. 8-11). reprint ed. 17.00 *(978-1-4223-5848-1(8))* DIANE Publishing Co.

—Players in Pigtails. Corey, Shana. 2003. (ENG.). 40p. (J). (gr. -1-3). 19.99 *(978-0-439-18305-5(7))* Scholastic, Inc.

Gibbons, Cassandra. Ride the Potato Train. Selig, Josh. 2013. (Small Potatoes Ser.). (ENG.). 32p. (J). (gr. 1-2). pap. 3.99 *(978-0-448-46365-0(2)*, Warne, Frederick Pubs.) Penguin Bks., Ltd. GBR. Dist: Penguin Publishing Group.

Gibbons, Cassandra. Ride the Potato Train. Selig, Josh. 2013. 30p. (J). ***(978-1-4844-0420-1(3)*** , Planet Dexter) Penguin Publishing Group.

—The Small Potatoes Go Camping. Selig, Josh. 2013. (J). lib. bdg. ***(978-1-4844-0111-8(5)***, Grosset & Dunlap) Penguin Publishing Group.

Gibbons, Dave. All Star Comics, Vol. 3. Thomas, Roy et al. Kahan, Bob, ed. rev. ed. 2005. (DC Archive Editions Ser.). (ENG.). 240p. (YA). 49.99 *(978-1-56389-370-4(3))* DC Comics.

Gibbons, Deanna, jt. illus. see Wilson, Raylene Jenee.

Gibbons, Gail. Alligators & Crocodiles. Gibbons, Gail. (ENG.). 32p. (J). 2011. pap. 7.99 *(978-0-8234-2343-9(3))*; 2010. (gr. -1-3). 17.95 *(978-0-8234-2234-0(8))* Holiday Hse., Inc.

—Beavers. Gibbons, Gail. 2014. (ENG.). 32p. (J). (gr. -1-3). 7.99 *(978-0-8234-3184-7(3))* Holiday Hse., Inc.

—Coral Reefs. Gibbons, Gail. (ENG.). 32p. (J). (gr. -1-3). 2010. pap. 7.99 *(978-0-8234-2278-4(X))*; 2007. 16.95 *(978-0-8234-2080-3(9))* Holiday Hse., Inc.

—Corn. Gibbons, Gail. (ENG.). 32p. (J). (gr. -1-3). 2009. pap. 6.95 *(978-0-8234-2245-6(3))*; 2008. 16.95 *(978-0-8234-2169-5(4))* Holiday Hse., Inc.

—Cowboys & Cowgirls. Gibbons, Gail. 2003. (ENG.). 32p. (J). (gr. 1-4). pap. 8.00 *(978-0-316-16859-5(9))* Little, Brown Bks. for Young Readers.

—Cowboys & Cowgirls. Gibbons, Gail. ed. 2003. (gr. 1-4). 18.45 *(978-0-613-71749-6(X)*, Turtleback) Turtleback Bks.

—Dinosaurs! Gibbons, Gail. 2009. (ENG.). 32p. (J). (gr. -1-1). pap. 7.99 *(978-0-8234-2197-8(X))* Holiday Hse., Inc.

—Elephants of Africa. Gibbons, Gail. (ENG.). 32p. (J). (gr. -1-3). 2010. pap. 7.99 *(978-0-8234-2299-9(2))*; 2008. 16.95 *(978-0-8234-2168-8(6))* Holiday Hse., Inc.

—From Seed to Plant. Gibbons, Gail. 2012. audio compact disk 18.95 *(978-1-4301-1079-8(1))* Live Oak Media.

—Galaxies, Galaxies! Gibbons, Gail. 2008. (ENG.). 32p. (J). (gr. -1-3). pap. 6.95 *(978-0-8234-2192-3(9))* Holiday Hse., Inc.

—Galaxies, Galaxies. Gibbons, Gail. 2006. (ENG.). 32p. (J). (gr. 3-7). 17.95 *(978-0-8234-2002-5(7))* Holiday Hse., Inc.

—Gorillas. Gibbons, Gail. (ENG.). 32p. (J). 2012. pap. 7.95 *(978-0-8234-2433-7(2))*; 2011. (gr. -1-3). 17.95 *(978-0-8234-2236-4(4))* Holiday Hse., Inc.

—Grizzly Bears. Gibbons, Gail. 2003. (ENG.). 32p. (J). (gr. k-3). tchr. ed. 17.95 *(978-0-8234-1793-3(X))* Holiday Hse., Inc.

—Groundhog Day. Gibbons, Gail. 2007. (ENG.). 32p. (J). (gr. -1-3). pap. 7.99 *(978-0-8234-2116-9(3))* Holiday Hse., Inc.

—Horses! Gibbons, Gail. 2005. (ENG.). 32p. (gr. k-3). tchr. ed. 17.95 *(978-0-8234-1703-2(4))* Holiday Hse., Inc.

—Hurricanes! Gibbons, Gail. (ENG.). 32p. (J). (gr. -1-3). 2010. pap. 7.99 *(978-0-8234-2297-5(6))*; 2009. 17.95 *(978-0-8234-2233-3(X))* Holiday Hse., Inc.

—It's Raining! Gibbons, Gail. (ENG.). 32p. (J). (gr. -1-3). 2015. 7.99 *(978-0-8234-3303-2(X))*; 2014. 17.95 *(978-0-8234-2924-0(5))* Holiday Hse., Inc.

—It's Snowing! Gibbons, Gail. (ENG.). 32p. (J). 2012. (gr. 1-4). pap. 7.99 *(978-0-8234-2545-7(2))*; 2011. 17.95 *(978-0-8234-2237-1(2))* Holiday Hse., Inc.

—Ladybugs. Gibbons, Gail. (ENG.). 32p. (J). 2013. pap. 7.99 *(978-0-8234-2760-4(9))*; 2012. 17.95 *(978-0-8234-2368-2(9))* Holiday Hse., Inc.

—Owls. Gibbons, Gail. 2006. (ENG.). 32p. (J). (gr. -1-3). 7.99 *(978-0-8234-2014-8(0))* Holiday Hse., Inc.

—The Planets. Gibbons, Gail. 3rd rev. ed. 2008. (ENG.). 32p. (J). (gr. -1-3). 17.95 *(978-0-8234-2156-5(2))* Holiday Hse., Inc.

—Polar Bears. Gibbons, Gail. 2005. (ENG.). 32p. (J). (gr. k-3). 7.99 *(978-0-8234-1768-1(9))* Holiday Hse., Inc.

—The Quilting Bee. Gibbons, Gail. 2004. (ENG.). 32p. (J). (gr. k-5). 17.99 *(978-0-688-16397-6(1))* HarperCollins Pubs.

—Snakes. Gibbons, Gail. 2010. (ENG.). 32p. (J). (gr. -1-3). pap. 7.99 *(978-0-8234-2300-2(X))* Holiday Hse., Inc.

—Surrounded by Sea: Life on a New England Fishing Island. Gibbons, Gail. (ENG.). 32p. (J). (gr. -1-3). 2006. 6.95 *(978-0-8234-2021-6(3))*; 2005. 17.95 *(978-0-8234-1941-8(X))* Holiday Hse., Inc.

—Tornadoes! Gibbons, Gail. 2010. (ENG.). 32p. (J). (gr. -1-3). pap. 7.99 *(978-0-8234-2274-6(7))* Holiday Hse., Inc.

—Valentine's Day Is... Gibbons, Gail. 2005. (ENG.). 32p. (J). (gr. -1-3). 17.95 *(978-0-8234-1852-7(9))* Holiday Hse., Inc.

—Valentine's Day Is. Gibbons, Gail. 2006. (ENG.). 32p. (J). (gr. k-3). 6.95 *(978-0-8234-2036-0(1))* Holiday Hse., Inc.

Gibbons, Timothy M. Finding Utopia. Sutherland, Paul H. 2006. 44p. (J). (gr. k-7). 20.00 *(978-0-9661060-4-6(0))* Utopia Pr.

—Mani & Pitouee: The True Legend of Sleeping Bear Dunes. Sutherland, Paul H. 2006. 36p. (J). (gr. -1-3). 20.00 *(978-0-9661060-3-9(2))* Utopia Pr.

Gibbons, Tony. The Dodo: Extinct Species. Green, Tamara. 2007. 24p. (J). reprint ed. 15.00 *(978-1-4223-6677-6(4))* DIANE Publishing Co.

Gibbs, Andrew. Pantone: Color Cards: 18 Oversized Flash Cards. Pantone. 2013. (Pantone Ser.). (ENG.). 19p. (J). (gr. -1 — 1). 15.95 *(978-1-4197-0626-4(8)*, Abrams Appleseed) Abrams.

Gibbs, Edward. I Spy in the Sky. Gibbs, Edward. 2014. (ENG.). 32p. (J). (-k). 14.99 *(978-0-7636-6840-2(0)*, Templar) Candlewick Pr.

—I Spy on the Farm. Gibbs, Edward. 2013. (ENG.). 32p. (J). (-k). 14.99 *(978-0-7636-6431-2(6)*, Templar) Candlewick Pr.

—I Spy Pets. Gibbs, Edward. 2013. (ENG.). 32p. (J). (-k). 14.99 *(978-0-7636-6622-4(X)*, Templar) Candlewick Pr.

—I Spy under the Sea. Gibbs, Edward. 2012. (ENG.). 32p. (J). (gr. k-k). 14.99 *(978-0-7636-5952-3(5)*, Templar) Candlewick Pr.

—I Spy with My Little Eye. Gibbs, Edward. 2014. (ENG.). 22p. (J). (-k). bds. 7.99 *(978-0-7636-7163-1(0)*, Templar) Candlewick Pr.

Gibbs, Megan. How the Fox Got His Color. Crouch, Adele. Kim, Seong, tr. ed. 2011. (KOR & ENG.). 60p. pap. 14.95 *(978-1-4637-7705-0(1))* CreateSpace Independent Publishing Platform.

—How the Fox Got His Color Bilingual French English. Crouch, Adele. Rafalli, Yakeen, tr. 2011. (FRE.). 60p. pap. 14.95 *(978-1-4637-9839-0(3))* CreateSpace Independent Publishing Platform.

—How the Fox Got His Color Bilingual German English. Crouch, Adele. Enderle, Evelyn, tr. 2011. (GER.). 60p. pap. 14.95 *(978-1-4636-0751-7(2))* CreateSpace Independent Publishing Platform.

—How the Fox Got His Color Bilingual Greek English. Crouch, Adele. Avrameli, Maria, tr. 2011. (GRE.). 60p. pap. 15.95 *(978-1-4664-6326-4(0))* CreateSpace Independent Publishing Platform.

—How the Fox Got His Color Bilingual Hungarian English. Crouch, Adele. Sholtes, Andrew, tr. 2011. (HUN.). 60p. pap. 14.95 *(978-1-4662-0470-6(2))* CreateSpace Independent Publishing Platform.

—How the Fox Got His Color Bilingual Indonesian English. Crouch, Adele. Mukhid, Abdul, tr. 2011. (IND.). 60p. pap. 15.95 *(978-1-4664-5805-5(4))* CreateSpace Independent Publishing Platform.

—How the Fox Got His Color Bilingual Italian English. Crouch, Adele. Spera, Massimiliano, tr. 2011. (ITA.). 60p. pap. 14.95 *(978-1-4637-9850-5(4))* CreateSpace Independent Publishing Platform.

—How the Fox Got His Color Bilingual Japanese English. Crouch, Adele. Spiller, Yuko & Ikeya, Sarah, trs. 2011. (JPN.). 60p. pap. 14.95 *(978-1-4637-9858-1(X))* CreateSpace Independent Publishing Platform.

—How the Fox Got His Color Bilingual Portuguese English. Crouch, Adele. Kohl, Carly & Clave, Israel, trs. 2011. (POR.). 60p. pap. 14.95 *(978-1-4662-0486-7(9))* CreateSpace Independent Publishing Platform.

—How the Fox Got His Color Bilingual Russian English. Crouch, Adele. Lank, Annytsya, tr. 2011. (RUS.). 60p. pap. 15.95 *(978-1-4664-8166-4(8))* CreateSpace Independent Publishing Platform.

—How the Fox Got His Color Bilingual Spanish English. Crouch, Adele. Retana, Maria, tr. 2011. (SPA.). 60p. pap. 14.95 *(978-1-4662-0439-3(7))* CreateSpace Independent Publishing Platform.

—How the Fox Got His Color Bilingual Vietnamese English. Crouch, Adele. Kha, Dang, tr. 2011. (VIE.). 58p. pap. 14.95 *(978-1-4662-0527-7(X))* CreateSpace Independent Publishing Platform.

—Where Hummingbirds Come from Bilingual Chinese English. Crouch, Adele. Hu, Bin, tr. 2011. (CHI.). 64p. pap. 14.95 *(978-1-4662-0177-4(0))* CreateSpace Independent Publishing Platform.

—Where Hummingbirds Come from Bilingual French English. Crouch, Adele. Rafalli, Yakeen, tr. 2011. (FRE.). 48p. pap. 14.95 *(978-1-4662-0198-9(3))* CreateSpace Independent Publishing Platform.

—Where Hummingbirds Come from Bilingual German English. Crouch, Adele. Enderle, Evelyn, tr. 2011. (GER & ENG.). 48p. pap. 14.95 *(978-1-4637-9826-0(1))* CreateSpace Independent Publishing Platform.

—Where Hummingbirds Come from Bilingual Greek English. Crouch, Adele. Avrameli, Maria, tr. 2011. (GRE.). 48p. pap. 14.95 *(978-1-4664-8126-8(9))* CreateSpace Independent Publishing Platform.

—Where Hummingbirds Come from Bilingual Hungarian English. Crouch, Adele. Sholtes, Andrew, tr. 2011. (HUN.). 48p. pap. 14.95 *(978-1-4662-0448-5(6))* CreateSpace Independent Publishing Platform.

—Where Hummingbirds Come from Bilingual Indonesian English. Crouch, Adele. Mukhid, Abdul, tr. 2011. (IND.). 48p. pap. 14.95 *(978-1-4664-6035-5(0))* CreateSpace Independent Publishing Platform.

—Where Hummingbirds Come from Bilingual Italian English. Crouch, Adele. Spera, Massimiliano, tr. 2011. (ITA.). 48p. pap. 14.95 *(978-1-4662-0205-4(X))* CreateSpace Independent Publishing Platform.

—Where Hummingbirds Come from Bilingual Japanese English. Crouch, Adele. Spiller, Yuko & Ikeya, Sarah, trs. 2011. (JPN.). 48p. pap. 14.95 *(978-1-4662-0275-7(0))* CreateSpace Independent Publishing Platform.

—Where Hummingbirds Come from Bilingual Korean English. Crouch, Adele. Kim, Seong, tr. 2011. (KOR.). 50p. pap. 14.95 *(978-1-4637-9319-7(7))* CreateSpace Independent Publishing Platform.

—Where Hummingbirds Come from Bilingual Portuguese English. Crouch, Adele. Kohl, Carly, tr. 2011. (POR.). 48p. pap. 14.95 *(978-1-4662-0452-2(4))* CreateSpace Independent Publishing Platform.

—Where Hummingbirds Come from Bilingual Russian English. Crouch, Adele. Lank, Annytsya, tr. 2011. (RUS.). 50p. pap. 14.95 *(978-1-4664-9090-1(X))* CreateSpace Independent Publishing Platform.

—Where Hummingbirds Come from Bilingual Spanish English. Crouch, Adele. Retana, Maria, tr. 2011. (SPA.). 48p. pap. 14.95 *(978-1-4662-0277-1(7))* CreateSpace Independent Publishing Platform.

—Where Hummingbirds Come from Bilingual Vietnamese English. Crouch, Adele. Kha, Dang, tr. 2011. (VIE.). 48p. pap. 14.95 *(978-1-4662-0455-3(9))* CreateSpace Independent Publishing Platform.

Gibbs, Tracey. Spider Lies. Banyard, Jen. 2010. (ENG.). 160p. (J). (gr. 4-7). pap. 10.95 *(978-1-921361-51-7(4))* Fremantle Pr. AUS. Dist: Independent Pubs. Group.

Gibbs, Tracy. The Magic Fair. Morgan, Sally. 2010. (Waarda Series for Young Readers Ser.: Bk. 5). (ENG.). 48p. (J). (gr. 2-4). pap. 7.00 *(978-1-921696-12-1(5))* Fremantle Pr. AUS. Dist: Independent Pubs. Group.

Gibert, Jean Claude & Gray, J. M. L. Babar: Four Stories to Read & Share. Weiss, Ellen. 2006. (J). 9.99 *(978-0-8109-9308-2(2)*, Abrams Bks. for Young Readers) Abrams.

Giblin, Sheri, photos by. Grilled Cheese: 50 Recipes to Make You Melt. Spieler, Marlena. 2004. (ENG., 108p. (gr. 8-17). pap. 16.95 *(978-0-8118-4129-0(4))* Chronicle Bks. LLC.

Giblin, Sheri, jt. photos by see Van Vynckt, Virginia.

Gibson, Barbara. Exploring Capitol Hill: A Kid's Guide to the U. S. Capitol & Congress. Dodge, Andrew. Wasniewski, Matthew, ed. 12p. (J). pap. 1.95 *(978-0-916200-25-1(6))* U. S. Capitol Historical Society.

—The Whistling Tree. Penn, Audrey. 2003. 32p. 16.95 *(978-0-87868-852-4(8)*, 8528, Child & Family Pr.) Child Welfare League of America, Inc.

Gibson, Barbara L. Chester Raccoon & the Acorn Full of Memories. Penn, Audrey. 2009. (ENG.). 32p. (J). (gr. -1-3). 16.95 *(978-1-933718-29-3(3))* Tanglewood Pr.

Gibson, Barbara Leonard. Chester the Brave. Penn, Audrey. 2012. (ENG.). 32p. (J). (gr. -1-3). 16.95 *(978-1-933718-79-8(X))* Tanglewood Pr.

—A Color Game for Chester Raccoon. Penn, Audrey. 2012. (ENG.). 14p. (J). (gr. -1-k). bds. 7.95 *(978-1-933718-58-3(7))* Tanglewood Pr.

—The Dragonfly Door. rev. ed. 2007. (ENG.). 40p. (J). (gr. k-5). 17.95 *(978-1-934066-12-6(5))* Feather Rock Bks., Inc.

—A Kiss Goodbye. Penn, Audrey. 2007. (ENG.). 32p. (J). (gr. -1-3). 16.95 *(978-1-933718-04-0(8))* Tanglewood Pr.

—A Kissing Hand for Chester Raccoon. Penn, Audrey. 2014. (ENG.). 14p. (J). (-k). bds. 7.99 *(978-1-933718-77-4(3))* Tanglewood Pr.

—N Is for our Nation's Capital: A Washington, DC Alphabet. Smith, Marie et al. 2005. (Discover America State by State Ser.). (ENG.). 40p. (J). 17.95 *(978-1-58536-148-9(8))* Sleeping Bear Pr.

—A Pocket Full of Kisses. Penn, Audrey. 2004. (New Child & Family Press Titles Ser.). 32p. (gr. -1-1). 16.95 *(978-0-87868-894-4(3)*, 8943, Child & Family Pr.) Child Welfare League of America, Inc.

—A Pocket Full of Kisses. Penn, Audrey. 2006. (ENG.). 32p. (J). (gr. -1-3). 16.95 *(978-1-933718-02-6(1))* Tanglewood Pr.

—The Whistling Tree. Penn, Audrey. 2006. (ENG.). 32p. (J). (gr. -1-3). 16.95 *(978-0-9749303-9-8(3))* Tanglewood Pr.

Gibson, Charles. Donnie Makes New Friends: A Lesson in Eye-to-Eye Contact. Tullgren, Terrence. 2011. (ENG.). 58p. pap. 6.95 *(978-1-4662-8763-1(2))* CreateSpace Independent Publishing Platform.

Gibson, Dave. Davy D's Dog: 3-in-1 Package. Eggleton, Jill. (Sails Literacy Ser.). 24p. (gr. k-18). 57.00 *(978-0-7578-8615-7(9))* Rigby Education.

—Davy D's Dog: 6 Small Books. Eggleton, Jill. (Sails Literacy Ser.). 24p. (gr. k-18). 25.00 *(978-0-7578-7728-5(1))* Rigby Education.

—Davy D's Dog: Big Book Only. Eggleton, Jill. (Sails Literacy Ser.). 24p. (gr. k-18). 27.00 *(978-0-7578-6198-7(9))* Rigby Education.

Gibson, Gregory V. Latawnya the Naughty Horse Two, 1 vol. Gibson, Sylvia Scott & Gibson, James E. 2010. 22p. 24.95 *(978-1-4489-7859-5(9))* PublishAmerica, Inc.

—Ricky the Skating Worm & Friends, 1 vol. Gibson, Sylvia Scott. 2009. 21p. pap. 24.95 *(978-1-60836-473-2(9))* America Star Bks.

—Treetoe the Space Monster, 1 vol. Gibson, James E. & Gibson, Sylvia Scott. 2010. 28p. 24.95 *(978-1-4489-4896-3(7))* PublishAmerica, Inc.

Gibson, James C. Hey, God! Listen! Gibson, Roxie C. 2007. (ENG.). 64p. (J). (gr. -1-3). 7.99 *(978-1-887654-59-3(3))* Premium Pr. America.

—Hey God! What Is Christmas? Gibson, Roxie C. 2007. (ENG.). 64p. (J). (gr. 4-7). 7.99 *(978-1-887654-95-1(X))* Premium Pr. America.

—Hey, God! What Makes You Happy? Gibson, Roxie C. 2007. (ENG.). 64p. (J). 7.99 *(978-1-933725-78-9(8))* Premium Pr. America.

—Hey God, Where Are You? Gibson, Roxie Cawood. 2007. (ENG.). 64p. 7.99 *(978-1-887654-63-0(1))* Premium Pr. America.

Gibson, Jim. Talking with God. Gibson, Roxie. 2007. (ENG.). 24p. (J). (gr. -1-3). 7.99 *(978-1-933725-75-8(3))* Premium Pr. America.

Gibson, Mary. Buried Treasure. 2007. 12p. (J). 5.95 *(978-0-9801269-0-7(8))* Scribe's Closet Pubns., The.

Gibson, Nichoel. Grandma Loves Her Harley Too. Vogl, Nancy & Strange, David. ed. 2006. (J). per. 16.95 *(978-0-9772771-1-7(9))* Cherry Tree Pr. LLC.

Gibson, Sabina. Little Bird, Be Quiet! Hall, Kirsten. 2015. (ENG.). 36p. (J). (gr. -1-3). 14.99 *(978-1-60905-520-2(9))* Blue Apple Bks.

Gibson, Taylor. The Golden Knight #1: The Boy Is Summoned. Clark, Steven & Clark, Justin. 2011. (ENG.). 80p. (J). pap. 5.99 *(978-0-9647933-9-2(3))* New Horizons Pr.

Giddens, Jake. Hoops. Leipold, Judith. 2013. 24p. 23.95 *(978-1-61493-223-9(9))* Peppertree Pr., The.

Giebfried, Rosemary. Sea Soup: Discovering the Watery World of Phytoplankton. Stevens, Betsy T. 2010. 96p. (gr. 3-7). pap., tchr. ed., tchr.'s training gde. ed. 9.95 *(978-0-88448-209-3(X))* Tilbury Hse. Pubs.

—Shelterwood: Discovering the Forest. Markowsky, Judy Kellogg. 2010. 80p. (gr. 3-6). pap., tchr. ed., tchr.'s training gde. ed. 9.95 *(978-0-88448-211-6(1))* Tilbury Hse. Pubs.

Giegreen, Alan, et al. Ramona Empieza el Curso. Cleary, Beverly. Bustelo, Gabriela, tr. 2006. (Ramona Ser.: 6).Tr. of Ramona Quimby, Age 8. (SPA.). 224p. (J). (gr. 3-7). pap. 6.99 *(978-0-688-15487-5(5)*, MR7554, Rayo) HarperCollins Pubs.

Giella, Joe, jt. illus. see Infantino, Carmine.

Giffen, Keith, et al. Rocket Raccoon: Guardian of the Keystone Quadrant. 2011. (ENG.). 120p. (J). (gr. 4-17). 24.99 *(978-0-7851-5527-0(9))* Marvel Worldwide, Inc.

Giffin, Noelle. Courtney Saves Christmas. Chand, Emlyn. 2012. 60p. 21.95 *(978-1-62253-114-1(0))* Evolved Publishing.

—Izzy the Inventor: A Bird Brain Book. Chand, Emlyn. l.t. ed. 2013. 7. (ENG.). 56p. (gr. k-3). 21.95 *(978-1-62253-123-3(X))*; pap. 10.95 *(978-1-62253-122-6(1))* Evolved Publishing.

—Larry the Lonely: A Bird Brain Book. Chand, Emlyn. l.t. ed. 2013. 9. (ENG.). 62p. (gr. k-3). pap. 10.95 *(978-1-62253-128-8(0))* Evolved Publishing.

—Ricky the Runt: A Bird Brain Book. Chand, Emlyn. l.t. ed. 2013. 8. (ENG.). 52p. (gr. k-3). pap. 10.95 *(978-1-62253-125-7(6))* Evolved Publishing.

—Valentina & the Haunted Mansion (Valentina's Spooky Adventures - 1) Verstraete, Majanka. l.t. ed. 2013. (ENG.). 48p. 21.95 *(978-1-62253-057-1(8))*; pap. 10.95 *(978-1-62253-056-4(X))* Evolved Publishing.

—Valentina & the Whackadoodle Witch: Valentina's Spooky Adventures. Verstraete, Majanka. l.t. ed. 2013. 2. (ENG.). 46p. (gr. k-4). pap. 10.95 *(978-1-62253-059-5(4))* Evolved Publishing.

—Vicky Finds a Valentine: Bird Brain Books. Chand, Emlyn. ed. 2013. (ENG.). 50p. (gr. k-1). pap. 10.95 *(978-1-62253-116-5(7))*; 21.95 *(978-1-62253-117-2(5))* Evolved Publishing.

Gifford, Carrie. School of Fear, Vol. 1. Daneshvari, Gitty. 2009. (School of Fear Ser.: 1). (ENG.). 352p. (J). (gr. 3-7). 16.99 *(978-0-316-03326-8(X))* Little, Brown Bks. for Young Readers.

Gil, Rodolpho. Mr. Meme. Goza, Shelly. 2005. (J). bds. 9.99 *(978-1-4183-0077-7(2))* Christ Inspired, Inc.

Gil, Sabina. Macarena la Anguila. Jimenez, Angeles. 2004. 26p. pap. 8.00 *(978-84-931888-0-1(8))* Editorial Brief ESP. Dist: Independent Pubs. Group.

Gilbert, Anne Yvonne. Dracula. Stoker, Bram. 2010. (ENG.). 96p. (YA). (gr. 7-18). 19.99 *(978-0-7636-4793-3(4))* Candlewick Pr.

Gilbert, Anne Yvonne & Andrew, Ian. Children's Stories from the Bible. Pirotta, Saviour. 2009. (ENG.). 304p. (J). (gr. k-12). 19.99 *(978-0-7636-4551-9(6))* Candlewick Pr.

Gilbert, Cecilia. Jammin' Jerone! The lamb who played the Saxaphone. Bey, Angelique. 2008. (ENG.). 34p. pap. 12.99 *(978-1-4196-8093-9(5))* CreateSpace Independent Publishing Platform.

Gilbert, Douglas R., photos by. Bob Dylan: Unscripted. Rojas Cardona, Javier. ed. 2005. 40p. 14.95 *(978-0-9663572-2-6(1))* Tango Latin.

Gilbert, Elizabeth T. Watch Me Draw Tiggerific Tales. 2013. (Watch Me Draw Ser.). 24p. (gr. -1-2). 25.65 *(978-1-936309-87-0(4))* Quarto Publishing Group USA.

Gilbert, Elizabeth T., jt. illus. see Tucker, Marianne.

Gilbert, Rob, jt. illus. see Davenier, Christine.

Gilbert, Yvonne. Goodnight, My Angel: A Lullabye. Joel, Billy. 2004. (J). pap. *(978-0-439-55378-0(4))* Scholastic, Inc.

Gilbert, Yvonne. Off the Page. Picoult, Jodi & van Leer, Samantha. 2015. (YA). lib. bdg. ***(978-0-553-53557-0(9)***, Delacorte Pr); (ENG.). 384p. (gr. 7). 19.99 *(978-0-553-53556-3(0)*, Delacorte Bks. for Young Readers) Random House Publishing Group.

Gilbert, Yvonne. Per & the Dala Horse. Hickox, Rebecca. 2003. 32p. (J). pap. 8.95 *(978-1-57534-034-0(8))* Skandisk, Inc.

—Princess of the Wild Swans. Zahler, Diane. (ENG.). (J). (gr. 3-7). 2013. 240p. pap. 6.99 *(978-0-06-200495-6(6))*; 2012. 224p. 16.99 *(978-0-06-200492-5(1))* HarperCollins Pubs.

—The Thirteenth Princess. Zahler, Diane. 2010. 256p. (J). (gr. 3-7). (ENG.). 15.99 *(978-0-06-182498-2(4))*; lib. bdg. 16.89 *(978-0-06-182499-9(2))* HarperCollins Pubs.

—The Wild Swans. Andersen, Hans Christian. Lewis, Naomi, tr. from DAN. 2005. 48p. (J). 17.99 *(978-1-84148-164-7(5))* Barefoot Bks., Inc.

Gilboa, Rinat. Sing-Along Alef Bet. Thomas, Doni Zasloff & Lindberg, Eric. 2016. (J). ***(978-1-68115-509-8(5))*** Behrman Hse., Inc.

Gilchrist, Jan Spivey. Brothers & Sisters: Family Poems. Greenfield, Eloise. 2008. (ENG.). 32p. (J). (gr. k-4). 17.99 *(978-0-06-056284-7(6)*, Amistad) HarperCollins Pubs.

—The Friendly Four. Greenfield, Eloise. 2006. (ENG.). 48p. (J). (gr. -1-3). 17.99 *(978-0-06-000759-1(1)*, Amistad) HarperCollins Pubs.

—The Great Migration: Journey to the North. Greenfield, Eloise. 2010. (ENG.). 32p. (J). (gr. -1-3). 16.99 *(978-0-06-125921-0(7)*, Amistad) HarperCollins Pubs.

—In the Land of Words: New & Selected Poems. Greenfield, Eloise & Greenfield. 2003. (ENG.). 48p. (J). (gr. -1-3). 17.99 *(978-0-06-028993-5(7)*, Amistad) HarperCollins Pubs.

—Me & Neesie. Greenfield, Eloise. anniv. ed. 2005. (Amistad Ser.). 32p. (J). (gr. -1-3). 15.99 *(978-0-06-000701-0(X)*, Amistad) HarperCollins Pubs.

—Poetry Anthology. Greenfield, Eloise. 2016. 48p. (J). (gr. -1-3). pap. 6.99 *(978-0-06-443692-2(6))* HarperCollins Pubs.

—When the Horses Ride By: Children in the Times of War. Greenfield, Eloise. 2006. (ENG.). (J). 32p. pap. 12.95 *(978-1-60060-454-6(4))*; 40p. (gr. 4-7). 17.95 *(978-1-58430-249-0(6))* Lee & Low Bks., Inc.

—Yafi's Family: An Ethiopian Boy's Journey of Love, Loss, & Adoption. Pettitt, Linda & Darrow, Sharon. 2010. (J). (gr. -1-2). 17.95 *(978-0-9797481-4-1(3))* Amharic Kids.

Gildea, Shir. Loving All the Colors. Gildea, Shir. 2009. 24p. pap. 10.95 *(978-1-4269-0713-5(3))* Trafford Publishing.

Gilderdale, Alan. The Little Yellow Digger Goes to School. Gilderdale, Betty. 2005. 32p. (J). *(978-1-86943-686-5(5))* Scholastic New Zealand Ltd.

Gilders, Michelle, photos by. Why Am I Rare?, 1 vol. Gilders, Michelle. 2003. (ENG.). 32p. (J). (gr. 1-5). 12.95 *(978-0-88995-274-4(4))* Red Deer Pr. CAN. Dist: Ingram Pub. Services.

Giles, Mike. Baby Teeth Fall Out, Big Teeth Grow! 2010. (Yo Gabba Gabba! Ser.). (ENG.). 24p. (J). pap. 3.99 *(978-1-4424-0627-8(5)*, Simon Spotlight) Simon Spotlight.

—Halloween Is Fun! 2009. (Yo Gabba Gabba! Ser.). (ENG.). 16p. (J). (gr. -1-1). pap. 6.99 *(978-1-4169-7824-4(0)*, Simon Spotlight) Simon Spotlight.

—It's Nice to Be Nice! Rao, Lisa & Gallo, Tina. 2009. (Yo Gabba Gabba! Ser.). (ENG.). 24p. (J). (gr. -1-2). pap. 3.99 *(978-1-4169-7866-4(6)*, Simon Spotlight) Simon Spotlight.

—It's Nice to Meet You. Shaw, Natalie. 2010. (Yo Gabba Gabba! Ser.). (ENG.). 24p. (J). (gr. -1-2). pap. 3.99 *(978-1-4169-9721-4(0)*, Simon Spotlight) Simon Spotlight.

—Let's Use Our Imaginations! Kilpatrick, Irene. 2009. (Yo Gabba Gabba! Ser.). (ENG.). 24p. (J). (gr. -1-2). pap. 3.99 *(978-1-4169-7854-1(2)*, Simon Spotlight) Simon Spotlight.

—Sleep & Dream of Happy Things. 2009. (Yo Gabba Gabba! Ser.). (ENG.). 26p. (J). (gr. -1-2). bds. 5.99 *(978-1-4169-7823-7(2)*, Simon Spotlight) Simon Spotlight.

—Spring Showers. Brooke, Samantha. 2010. (Yo Gabba Gabba! Ser.). (ENG.). 24p. (J). (gr. -1-k). pap. 3.99 *(978-1-4169-9078-9(X)*, Simon Spotlight) Simon Spotlight.

—Spring Showers Bring Flowers. 2014. (Yo Gabba Gabba! Ser.). (ENG.). 12p. (J). (gr. -1-k). bds. 5.99 *(978-1-4424-9572-2(3)*, Simon Spotlight) Simon Spotlight.

Giles, Mike & Style Guide Staff. Everyone Is Different. McMahon, Kara. 2010. (Yo Gabba Gabba! Ser.). (ENG.). 24p. (J). (gr. -1-2). bds. 6.99 *(978-1-4169-9936-2(1)*, Simon Spotlight) Simon Spotlight.

Giles, Mike, jt. illus. see Ruiz, Aristides.

Giles, Mike, jt. illus. see Spaziante, Patrick.

Giles, Susan. Caribbean Cats. Giles, Susan. 2003. (Meet the Author Ser.). (ENG.). 16p. (J). pap. 5.75 net. *(978-1-57274-662-6(9)*, 2728, Bks. for Young Learners) Owen, Richard C. Pubs., Inc.

Gilgannon-Collins, Denise. The Rabbit Who Lost His Hop: A Story about Self-Control. Nass, Marcia Shoshana. 2004. (Early Prevention Ser.: 5). (J). per. 19.95 *(978-1-58815-061-5(5)*, 66525) Childswork/Childsplay.

Gilgannon, Denise. Rockhound Science Mysteries: Tenth Anniversary Special Edition. Newhouse, Mark. 2011. (ENG.). 148p. pap. 6.95 *(978-1-4564-9942-6(4))* CreateSpace Independent Publishing Platform.

Gill, Phillida. Cinderella: A Pop-up Book. Gill, Phillida. 2007. 12p. (J). 25.00 *(978-1-4223-9031-3(4))* DIANE Publishing Co.

Gillewe, Unada. God Provides Victory Through Gideon. Bader, Joanne. 2004. (Arch Bks.). 16p. (J). 1.99 *(978-0-7586-0673-0(7))* Concordia Publishing Hse.

Gilkerson, William. Pirate's Passage. Gilkerson, William. 2007. (ENG.). 376p. (J). (gr. 4-7). pap. 14.95 *(978-1-59030-548-5(5)*, Trumpeter) Shambhala Pubns., Inc.

Gill, Bob. A Balloon for a Blunderbuss. Reid, Alastair. 2008. (ENG.). 36p. (J). (gr. -1-3). 14.95 *(978-0-7148-4873-0(5))* Phaidon Pr., Inc.

—Supposing. Reid, Alastair. 2010. (ENG.). 48p. (J). (gr. -1-3). 15.95 *(978-1-59017-369-5(4)*, NYR Children's Collection) New York Review of Bks., Inc., The.

Gill, Deirdre, jt. illus. see Rosenbaum, Andria Warmflash.

Gill, Jacqueline Paske. The Monster in the Basement. Gill, Jacqueline Paske. 2011. 32p. pap. 12.95 *(978-1-61493-003-7(1))* Peppertree Pr., The.

Gill, Joel Christian. Strange Fruit Vol. 1: Uncelebrated Narratives from Black History. 2014. (ENG.). 176p. (gr. 4). pap. 23.95 *(978-1-938486-29-6(3))* Fulcrum Publishing.

Gill, Margery. Dawn of Fear. Cooper, Susan. 2007. (ENG.). 176p. (J). (gr. 5-7). pap. 6.99 *(978-0-15-206106-7(1))* Houghton Mifflin Harcourt Publishing Co.

—Dawn of Fear. Cooper, Susan. 2007. 160p. 15.95 *(978-1-4177-9571-0(9),* Turtleback) Turtleback Bks.

—A Little Princess. Burnett, Frances Hodgson. 2008. (Puffin Classics Ser.). (ENG.). 320p. (J). (gr. 3-7). 4.99 *(978-0-14-132112-7(1),* Puffin) Penguin Publishing Group.

Gill, Tim. Santa's Toys. Williams, Sam. 2003. 14p. bds. *(978-1-85602-274-3(9),* Pavilion Children's Books) Pavilion Bks.

Gillard, Jason. You May Just Be a Dinosaur, 1 vol. Macht, Heather. 2015. (ENG.). 32p. (J). (gr. k-3). 16.99 *(978-1-4556-2040-1(8))* Pelican Publishing Co., Inc.

Gillen, Lisa P. Brians Garden. Williams, Heather L. l.t. ed. 2004. (HRL Little Book Ser.). (J). (gr. -1-1). pap. 10.95 *(978-1-57332-300-0(4));* pap. 10.95 *(978-1-57332-299-7(7))* Carson-Dellosa Publishing, LLC. (HighReach Learning, Incorporated).

—Caillou Finds Colors. Howard-Parham, Pam. l.t. ed. 2005. (HRL Board Book Ser.). (J). (gr. -1-k). bds. 10.95 *(978-1-57332-313-0(6),* HighReach Learning, Incorporated) Carson-Dellosa Publishing, LLC.

—Caillou Finds Shapes. Mullican, Judy & Crowell, Knox. l.t. ed. 2005. (HRL Board Book Ser.). (J). (gr. -1-k). bds. 10.95 *(978-1-57332-312-3(8),* HighReach Learning, Incorporated) Carson-Dellosa Publishing, LLC.

—Caillou Gets in Shape. Howard-Parham, Pam. l.t. ed. 2006. (HRL Board Book Ser.). (J). (gr. k-18). pap. 10.95 *(978-1-57332-331-4(4),* HighReach Learning, Incorporated) Carson-Dellosa Publishing, LLC.

—Caillou's Trip to the Harbor. Hensley, Sarah M. l.t. ed. 2004. (HRL Board Book Ser.). (J). (gr. -1-1). pap. 10.95 *(978-1-57332-290-4(3),* HighReach Learning, Incorporated) Carson-Dellosa Publishing, LLC.

—Let's Take a Ride. Mullican, Judy. l.t. ed. 2004. (HRL Big Book Ser.). (J). (gr. -1-k). pap. 10.95 *(978-1-57332-318-5(7));* pap. 10.95 *(978-1-57332-319-2(5))* Carson-Dellosa Publishing, LLC. (HighReach Learning, Incorporated).

—When I Take a Bath. Parham, Pam H. l.t. ed. 2005. (HRL Board Book Ser.). 12p. (J). (gr. -1-1). pap. 10.95 *(978-1-57332-284-3(9),* HighReach Learning, Incorporated) Carson-Dellosa Publishing, LLC.

—Why Have Rules? Black, Jessica L. l.t. ed. 2003. (HRL Little Book Ser.). 8p. (J). (gr. -1). pap. 10.95 *(978-1-57332-271-3(7));* pap. 10.95 *(978-1-57332-270-6(9))* Carson-Dellosa Publishing, LLC. (HighReach Learning, Incorporated).

Gillen, Lisa P. Spring Time. Gillen, Lisa P. l.t. ed. 2006. 12p. (J). (gr. -1-k). pap. 10.95 *(978-1-57332-351-2(9),* HighReach Learning, Incorporated) Carson-Dellosa Publishing, LLC.

Gillen, Lisa P., jt. illus. see Storch, Ellen N.

Gillen, Rosemarie. Albert & Freddie. Thyroff, Brad. 2013. 24p. pap. 9.99 *(978-1-61286-190-6(3))* Avid Readers Publishing Group.

—Alicia's Blended Family. Powell, Angela. 2013. 24p. pap. 9.99 *(978-1-61286-153-1(9))* Avid Readers Publishing Group.

—Baby & Bunny: Sharing Sign Language with Your Child, 4 vols. Vance, Mimi Brian. 2010. (ENG.). 264p. 9.95 *(978-1-933979-74-8(7),* 14b1df54-c693-4d8d-bb12-9e9482cb3d86) Bright Sky Pr.

—Blessed Jacint: Patron for Children for Tummy Troubles. Lagneau, Mary. 2012. 20p. pap. 7.50 *(978-1-61286-134-0(2))* Avid Readers Publishing Group.

—Boat & Bath: Sharing Sign Language with Your Child, 4 vols. Vance, Mimi Brian. 2010. (ENG.). 24p. 9.95 *(978-1-933979-76-2(3),* 94ee6626-5ed6-49be-be68-5f712fc75b65) Bright Sky Pr.

—The Bonds. Gainey, Gary. 2012. 150p. pap. 9.99 *(978-1-937260-12-5(7))* Sleepytown Pr.

—Book & Bed, 4 vols. Vance, Mimi Brian. 2010. (ENG.). 24p. 9.95 *(978-1-933979-75-5(5),* d897b37d-7f19-420f-b34c-b2edf9914786) Bright Sky Pr.

—Dandylion the Duck. Gober, Thomas. 2012. 26p. (J). 16.95 *(978-1-60131-126-9(5),* Castlebridge Bks.) Big Tent Bks.

—The Haunted House of Riddles. Lee, Vanessa Rose. 2011. 28p. pap. 7.99 *(978-1-61286-053-4(2))* Avid Readers Publishing Group.

—Invisible Isabelle... As Told by Jimmy Pizzelli. Doti Chavez, Caryn. 2013. (ENG.). 24p. pap. 9.75 *(978-0-615-75349-2(3))* Funny Bones Publishing.

—The Lamb Who Counted Clouds. Jolivert, Immaculine. 2013. 24p. pap. 13.75 *(978-1-937260-91-0(7))* Sleepytown Pr.

—Milk & More: Sharing Sign Language with Your Child, 4 vols. Vance, Mimi Brian. 2010. (ENG.). 24p. 9.95 *(978-1-933979-73-1(9),* 21448254-a6c8-4410-bddb-50197780ab0b) Bright Sky Pr.

—Movember with My Doggy. Bucklaschuk, Angela. 2013. 32p. pap. 11.95 *(978-1-61286-188-3(1))* Avid Readers Publishing Group.

—The Queen's Jewels. Carroll, Jacquie Lund. 2013. 26p. pap. 9.99 *(978-1-61286-147-0(4))* Avid Readers Publishing Group.

—Tyler & the Spider. Lancaster, Melinda. 2010. 32p. (J). pap. 9.95 *(978-1-935706-08-3(X))* Wiggles Pr.

—A Voice in the Night. Dail, Ernestine. 2012. 46p. pap. 9.99 *(978-1-61286-099-2(0))* Avid Readers Publishing Group.

—Where Is God, Grandfather. O'Donnell, Candy. 2008. 28p. pap. 12.95 *(978-0-9814532-1-7(X))* Living Waters Publishing Co.

—Words by the Handful Set: Sharing Sign Language with Your Child - Four Stories to Help You & Your Baby Communicate, 4 vols. Vance, Mimi Brian. 2010. (ENG.). 96p. 29.95 *(978-1-933979-72-4(0),* e8ab70da-55c0-42c5-8a85-c405ae9e7bb2) Bright Sky Pr.

Gilles-Gray, Carolyn. Emu Can't Fly. Taylor, Helen. 2013. 24p. pap. *(978-1-921883-39-2(1),* MBS Pr.) Pick-a-Woo Woo Pubs.

Gillespie, Greg G. A Kid's Guide to Being a Winner. Shelton, C. H. & Shelton, C. H. 2011. 38p. (J). (gr. 2-8). 9.99 *(978-0-9841910-4-8(6))* Choice PH.

Gillett, Hallie. Spinner McClock & the Christmas Visit. Dacey, Richard. 2004. 32p. (J). 13.95 *(978-1-929039-24-1(7))* Ambassador Bks., Inc.

Gillette, Henry S. Benjamin Franklin, Man of Science: A First Biography. Eberle, Irmengarde. 2011. 156p. 41.95 *(978-1-258-08044-0(3))* Literary Licensing, LLC.

Gillette, Tim. Baby Bible Board Books Collection No. 1: Stories of Jesus, 4 vols. Bolme, Edward Sarah. l.t. ed. 2003. 20p. (J). bds. 23.99 *(978-0-9725546-4-0(5))* CREST Pubns.

—Jesus Feeds the People. Bolme, Edward Sarah. l.t. ed. 2003. 20p. (J). bds. 6.99 *(978-0-9725546-0-2(2))* CREST Pubns.

—Jesus Heals a Little Girl. Bolme, Edward Sarah. l.t. ed. 2003. 20p. (J). bds. 6.99 *(978-0-9725546-1-9(0))* CREST Pubns.

—Jesus Helps a Blind Man. Bolme, Edward Sarah. l.t. ed. 2003. 20p. (J). bds. 6.99 *(978-0-9725546-2-6(9))* CREST Pubns.

—Jesus Stops a Storm. Bolme, Edward Sarah. l.t. ed. 2003. 20p. (J). bds. 6.99 *(978-0-9725546-3-3(7))* CREST Pubns.

Gilliam, David. Gingertown. Gillam, David. 2012. 216p. (J). 29.99 *(978-1-60131-122-1(2))* Big Tent Bks.

Gillies, Chuck. The Song of the King. Lucado, Max. ed. 2014. 32p. (J). 17.99 *(978-1-4335-4290-9(0))* Crossway.

Gilliland, Jillian Hulme. How the Devil Got His Cat & Other Multicultural Folktales for Children. Downie, Mary Alice & Zola, Mequido. 144p. (J). pap. 16.95 *(978-1-55082-100-0(8))* Quarry Pr. CAN. Dist: LPC/InBook.

Gillingham, Sara. I Am So Brave! Krensky, Stephen. 2014. (Empowerment Ser.). (ENG.). 12p. (J). (gr. -1 — 1). bds. 6.95 *(978-1-4197-0937-1(2),* Abrams Appleseed) Abrams.

—I Can Do It Myself! Krensky, Stephen. 2012. (Empowerment Ser.). (ENG.). 12p. (J). (gr. -1 — 1). bds. 6.95 *(978-1-4197-0400-0(1),* Abrams Appleseed) Abrams.

—I Know a Lot! Krensky, Stephen. 2013. (Empowerment Ser.). (ENG.). 12p. (J). (gr. -1 — 1). bds. 6.95 *(978-1-4197-0938-8(0),* Abrams Appleseed) Abrams.

—Now I Am Big! Krensky, Stephen. 2012. (Empowerment Ser.). (ENG.). 12p. (J). (gr. -1 — 1). bds. 6.95 *(978-1-4197-0416-1(8),* Abrams Appleseed) Abrams.

—Snuggle the Baby. 2014. (ENG.). 12p. (J). (gr. -1 — 1). bds. 12.95 *(978-1-4197-1124-4(5),* Abrams Appleseed) Abrams.

Gillis, Bonnie. Baby Moses. Melania, Mother. 2008. (Old Testament Stories for Children Ser.). 28p. (gr. -1-3). pap. 8.95 *(978-1-888212-97-6(7))* Conciliar Pr.

—The Entrance of the Theotokos into the Temple. Elayne. 2003. (Twelve Great Feasts for Children Ser.). 24p. pap. 5.95 *(978-1-888212-40-2(3))* Conciliar Pr.

Gillis, Jane. Dead End. Frenette, Liza. 2005. x, 65p. (J). *(978-1-59531-001-9(0))* North Country Bks., Inc.

Gillmore, Jean. Dewey Doo-It Feeds a Friend. Wenger, Brahm & Green, Alan. 2004. (J). *(978-0-9745143-0-7(6))* RandallFraser Publishing.

Gilman, Christopher. Ricky Climbs Pikes Peak. Keller, Jeff, Jr. 2006. 36p. (J). pap. 8.95 *(978-0-9773990-9-3(5))* Mother's Hse. Publishing.

Gilman, Sara. Melvin: A True Story with a Happy Ending. Mayfield, Holly. 2013. 38p. pap. 9.99 *(978-0-9892711-9-6(6))* Mindstir Media.

Gilmour, Karen. I Am Your Emotions. McNulty John. 2006. 32p. *(978-0-9769580-4-8(X))* I Am Your Playground LLC.

—I Am Your Imagination. McNulty John. 2006. 32p. *(978-0-9769580-3-1(1))* I Am Your Playground LLC.

—I Am Your Self-Esteem. McNulty John. 2006. 32p. *(978-0-9769580-5-5(8))* I Am Your Playground LLC.

Gilpin, Stephen. Attack of the Growling Eyeballs. Oliver, Lin. 2009. (Who Shrunk Daniel Funk? Ser.: 1). (ENG.). 160p. (J). (gr. 3-7). pap. 6.99 *(978-1-4169-0958-3(3),* Simon & Schuster Bks. For Young Readers) Simon & Schuster Bks. For Young Readers.

—The Big Hairy Secret, 1 vol. Troupe, Thomas Kingsley. 2013. (Furry & Flo Ser.). (ENG.). 128p. (gr. 2-3). 8.95 *(978-1-62370-033-1(7));* lib. bdg. 23.99 *(978-1-4342-3858-0(X))* Stone Arch Bks.

—The Classroom Trick Out My School! Mellom, Robin. 2014. (Classroom Novel Ser.). (ENG.). 288p. (J). (gr. 3-7). 12.99 *(978-1-4231-5065-7(1))* Hyperion Bks. for Children.

—Cronus the Titan Tells All: Tricked by the Kids, 1 vol. Braun, Eric. 2014. (Other Side of the Myth Ser.). (ENG.). 32p. (gr. 2-3). 26.65 *(978-1-4795-2184-5(1))* Picture Window Bks.

—Escape of the Mini-Mummy. Oliver, Lin. 2009. (Who Shrunk Daniel Funk? Ser.: 2). (ENG.). 160p. (J). (gr. 3-7). pap. 8.99 *(978-1-4169-0960-6(5),* Simon & Schuster Bks. For Young Readers) Simon & Schuster Bks. For Young Readers.

—The Extraordinary Adventures of Ordinary Boy. Boniface, William. 2008. (Extraordinary Adventures of Ordinary Boy Ser.: 2). (ENG.). 368p. (J). (gr. 3-7). pap. 6.99 *(978-0-06-077469-1(X))* HarperCollins Pubs.

—The Extraordinary Adventures of Ordinary Boy Bk. 3: The Great Powers Outage. Boniface, William. 2010. (Extraordinary Adventures of Ordinary Boy Ser.: 3). (ENG.). 352p. (J). (gr. 3-7). pap. 7.99 *(978-0-06-077472-1(X))* HarperCollins Pubs.

—Fart Squad. Pilger, Seamus. 2015. (Fart Squad Ser.: 1). (ENG.). 112p. (J). (gr. 1-5). pap. 4.99 *(978-0-06-229045-8(2),* HarperFestival) HarperCollins Pubs.

Gilpin, Stephen. Fart Squad #2: Fartasaurus Rex. Pilger, Seamus. 2015. (Fart Squad Ser.: 2). (ENG.). 112p. (J). (gr. 1-5). 15.99 ***(978-0-06-236632-0(7))*** HarperCollins Pubs.

—Fartasaurus Rex. Pilger, Seamus. 2015. (Fart Squad Ser.: 2). (ENG.). 112p. (J). (gr. 1-5). pap. 4.99 ***(978-0-06-229047-2(9))*** HarperCollins Pubs.

Gilpin, Stephen. Felix Takes the Stage. Lasky, Kathryn. (Deadlies Ser.). (ENG.). 144p. (J). (gr. 2-5). 2011. pap. 5.99 *(978-0-545-11730-2(5),* Scholastic Paperbacks); 2010. 15.99 *(978-0-545-11681-7(3),* Scholastic Pr.) Scholastic, Inc.

—The Gecko & Sticky: the Power Potion. Van Draanen, Wendelin. 2011. (Gecko & Sticky Ser.). (ENG.). 240p. (J). (gr. 3-7). 6.99 *(978-0-440-42245-7(0),* Yearling) Random Hse. Children's Bks.

—The Great Powers Outage. Boniface, William. 2008. (Extraordinary Adventures of Ordinary Boy Ser.: 3). (ENG.). 352p. (J). (gr. 3-7). 16.99 *(978-0-06-077470-7(3))* HarperCollins Pubs.

—The Greatest Power. Van Draanen, Wendelin. 2011. (Gecko & Sticky Ser.: Bk. 1). (ENG.). 208p. (J). (gr. 3-7). 7.99 *(978-0-440-42243-3(4),* Yearling) Random Hse. Children's Bks.

—Helen of Troy Tells All: Blame the Boys, 1 vol. Loewen, Nancy. 2014. (Other Side of the Myth Ser.). (ENG.). 32p. (gr. 2-3). 26.65 *(978-1-4795-2182-1(5))* Picture Window Bks.

—The Hero Revealed. Boniface, William. 2008. (Extraordinary Adventures of Ordinary Boy Ser.: 1). (ENG.). 320p. (J). (gr. 3-7). pap. 6.99 *(978-0-06-077466-0(5))* HarperCollins Pubs.

—Librarian on the Roof! A True Story. King, M. G. 2010. (ENG.). 32p. (J). (gr. 1-3). 16.99 *(978-0-8075-4512-6(0))* Whitman, Albert & Co.

—Librarian on the Roof: A True Story. King, M. G. 2012. (J). *(978-1-61913-147-7(1))* Weigl Pubs., Inc.

—Los Tres Cabritos, 0 vols. Kimmel, Eric A. 2012. (SPA & ENG.). 32p. (J). (gr. k-3). pap. 7.99 *(978-0-7614-5961-3(8),* 9780761459613, Amazon Children's Publishing) Amazon Publishing.

—Medea Tells All: A Mad, Magical Love, 1 vol. Braun, Eric. 2014. (Other Side of the Myth Ser.). (ENG.). 32p. (gr. 2-3). pap. 6.95 *(978-1-4795-2940-7(0))* Picture Window Bks.

—Medusa Tells All: Beauty Missing, Hair Hissing, 1 vol. Fjelland Davis, Rebecca. 2014. (Other Side of the Myth Ser.). (ENG.). 32p. (gr. 2-3). pap. 6.95 *(978-1-4795-2942-1(7))* Picture Window Bks.

—The Misplaced Mummy, 1 vol. Troupe, Thomas Kingsley. 2014. (Furry & Flo Ser.). (ENG.). 128p. (gr. 2-3). 23.99 *(978-1-4342-6396-4(7))* Stone Arch Bks.

—My Daddy Snores. Rothstein, Nancy H. & Rothstein, Nancy. 2007. (ENG.). 32p. (J). (gr. -1-3). pap. 5.99 *(978-0-545-02834-9(5))* Scholastic, Inc.

—One Hundred Snowmen, 0 vols. Arena, Jennifer. 2013. (ENG.). 20p. (J). (gr. k-3). 14.99 *(978-1-4778-4703-9(0),* 9781477847039, Amazon Children's Publishing) Amazon Publishing.

—Pirate Mom. Underwood, Deborah. 2006. (Step into Reading Ser.: Vol. 3). (ENG.). 48p. (J). (gr. k-3). per. 3.99 *(978-0-375-83323-6(4),* Random Hse. Bks. for Young Readers) Random Hse. Children's Bks.

—Pirates, Ho!, 0 vols. Thomson, Sarah L. 2012. (ENG.). 32p. (J). (gr. k-3). pap. 7.99 *(978-0-7614-6247-7(3),* 9780761462477, Amazon Children's Publishing) Amazon Publishing.

—The Problems with Goblins, 1 vol. Troupe, Thomas Kingsley. 2013. (Furry & Flo Ser.). (ENG.). 128p. (gr. 2-3). 8.95 *(978-1-62370-034-8(5));* lib. bdg. 23.99 *(978-1-4342-5042-1(3))* Stone Arch Bks.

—Revenge of the Itty-Bitty Brothers. Oliver, Lin. (Who Shrunk Daniel Funk? Ser.: 3). (ENG.). 176p. (J). (gr. 3-7). 2010. pap. 6.99 *(978-1-4169-0962-0(1));* 2009. 14.99 *(978-1-4169-0961-3(3))* Simon & Schuster Bks. For Young Readers. (Simon & Schuster Bks. For Young Readers).

—Secret of the Super-Small Superstar. Oliver, Lin. 2010. (Who Shrunk Daniel Funk?: 4). (ENG.). 160p. (J). (gr. 3-7). 14.99 *(978-1-4169-0963-7(X),* Simon & Schuster Bks. For Young Readers) Simon & Schuster Bks. For Young Readers.

—Sinister Substitute. Van Draanen, Wendelin. (Gecko & Sticky Ser.: Bk. 3). (ENG.). 224p. (J). (gr. 3-7). 2011. 6.99 *(978-0-440-42244-0(2),* Yearling); 2010. 12.99 *(978-0-375-84378-5(7),* Knopf Bks. for Young Readers) Random Hse. Children's Bks.

—Sir Fartsalot Hunts the Booger. Bolger, Kevin. (ENG.). 224p. (J). (gr. 3-7). 2009. 7.99 *(978-1-59514-284-9(3),* Razorbill); 2008. 12.99 *(978-1-59514-176-7(6))* Penguin Publishing Group.

—The Skeletons in City Park, 1 vol. Troupe, Thomas Kingsley. 2014. (Furry & Flo Ser.). (ENG.). 128p. (gr. 2-3). 23.99 *(978-1-4342-6397-1(5))* Stone Arch Bks.

—The Solemn Golem. Troupe, Thomas Kingsley. 2015. (Furry & Flo Ser.). (ENG.). 128p. (gr. 2-3). 23.99 *(978-1-4342-9646-7(6))* Stone Arch Bks.

—Spiders on the Case. Lasky, Kathryn. (Deadlies Ser.). (ENG.). 176p. (J). (gr. 2-5). 2012. pap. 5.99 *(978-0-545-11731-9(3));* Bk. 2. 2011. 15.99 *(978-0-545-11682-4(1))* Scholastic, Inc. (Scholastic Pr.).

—Student Council Smackdown! Mellom, Robin. 2013. (Classroom Novel Ser.). (ENG.). 288p. (J). (gr. 4-7). 12.99 *(978-1-4231-5064-0(3))* Hyperion Pr.

—The Three Cabritos, 0 vols. Kimmel, Eric A. 2012. (ENG.). 32p. (J). (gr. -1-3). pap. 7.99 *(978-0-7614-6309-2(7),* 9780761463092, Amazon Children's Publishing) Amazon Publishing.

—Uncle Si, the Christmas Elf: Work Hard, Nap Hard. Robertson, Si & Nelson, Ashley Howard. 2014. (ENG.). 48p. (J). (gr. -1-3). 29.99 *(978-1-4814-1821-8(1),* Simon & Schuster Bks. For Young Readers) Simon & Schuster Bks. For Young Readers.

—The Voiceless Vampire. Troupe, Thomas Kingsley. 2015. (Furry & Flo Ser.). (ENG.). 128p. (gr. 2-3). lib. bdg. 23.99 *(978-1-4342-9645-0(8))* Stone Arch Bks.

—What If I Pulled This Thread. Hall, John. 2006. 48p. 12.99 *(978-1-59379-067-7(8))* White Stone Bks.

—What to Do When You're Sent to Your Room. Stott, Ann. 2014. (ENG.). 32p. (J). (gr. -1-3). 15.99 *(978-0-7636-6052-9(3))* Candlewick Pr.

Gilpin, Stephen & Pentney, Ryan. The Other Side of the Myth, 1 vol. Loewen, Nancy et al. 2014. (Other Side of the Myth Ser.). (ENG.). 32p. (gr. 2-3). lib. bdg. 106.60 *(978-1-4795-3336-7(X))* Picture Window Bks.

Gilpin, Stephen, jt. illus. see Basso, Bill.

Gilpin, Stephen, jt. illus. see Blegvad, Erik.

Gilpin, Stephen, jt. illus. see Sisk, Clay.

Gilson, Heather, jt. photos by see Harmon, Heather.

Gilsvik, David. The Complete Book of Trapping. Gilsvik, Bob. 172p. (J). (gr. 7). reprint ed. 14.95 *(978-0-936622-29-3(6))* A.R. Harding Publishing Co.

Gilvan-Cartwright, Chris. Face to Face Safari. Hewitt, Sally. 2003. (ENG.). 12p. (J). (gr. -1-1). 15.95 *(978-0-8109-4261-5(5))* Abrams.

—Who's in the Jungle? DePrisco, Dorothea. 2006. (ENG.). 10p. (J). bds. 4.95 *(978-1-58117-507-3(8),* Intervisual/Piggy Toes) Bendon, Inc.

—Who's in the Jungle? Lift-the-Flap 'n' Learn. Gondek, Heather. 2005. (Fun with Animals Ser.). 10p. (J). 9.95 *(978-1-58117-075-7(0),* Intervisual/Piggy Toes) Bendon, Inc.

—Who's in the Ocean? 2005. (Lift-The-Flap 'n' Learn Ser.). 10p. (J). 9.95 *(978-1-58117-213-3(3),* Intervisual/Piggy Toes) Bendon, Inc.

—Who's in the Ocean? DePrisco, Dorothea. 2006. (ENG.). 10p. (gr. -1-k). bds. 4.95 *(978-1-58117-509-7(4),* Intervisual/Piggy Toes) Bendon, Inc.

—Who's on the Farm? DePrisco, Dorothea. 2006. (ENG.). 10p. (gr. -1-k). bds. 4.95 *(978-1-58117-508-0(6),* Intervisual/Piggy Toes) Bendon, Inc.

—Who's on the Farm? Lift-the-Flap 'n' Learn Book. Gondek, Heather J. 2005. (Fun with Animals Ser.). 10p. (J). (gr. -1-k). act. bk. ed. 9.95 *(978-1-58117-143-3(9),* Intervisual/Piggy Toes) Bendon, Inc.

Gilvan-Cartwright, Christopher. Becoming Me: A Story of Creation. Boroson, Martin & Quarto Generic Staff. 2011. (ENG.). 36p. (J). (gr. 1-4). pap. 8.95 *(978-1-84780-275-0(3),* Frances Lincoln) Quarto Publishing Group UK GBR. Dist: Hachette Bk. Group.

Gimbergsson, Sara. The Rabbit Who Couldn't Find His Daddy. Edvall, Lilian. 2006. 32p. (J). (gr. -1-3). 15.00 *(978-91-29-66429-4(2))* R & S Bks. SWE. Dist: Macmillan.

—The Rabbit Who Didn't Want to Go to Sleep. Edvall, Lilian. Dyssegaard, Elisabeth Kallick, tr. from SWE. 2004. 32p. (J). 15.00 *(978-91-29-66001-2(7))* R & S Bks. SWE. Dist: Macmillan.

Giménez, Paco. ¡¡¡Papááá — !!! Giménez, Paco, tr. Cano, Carles & Cano Peiró, Carles. Cano, Carles, tr. (SPA.). 48p. (J). (gr. k-1). 6.40 *(978-84-207-9236-1(5),* GS0639) Grupo Anaya, S.A. ESP. Dist: Lectorum Pubns., Inc.

Gimlin, Mihaela. The Old Man's Daughter & the Old Woman's Daughter / Fata Babei Si Fata Mosneagului. Creanga, Ion. Todd Kaplan, Delia Angelescu, tr. 2013. 42p. pap. 17.95 *(978-1-936629-30-5(5))* Reflection Publishing.

Ginesin, Zack. Prince Jack, the Little Artist. Ginesin, Lucia. 2009. 28p. pap. 11.99 *(978-1-59858-983-2(0))* Dog Ear Publishing, LLC.

Ginevra, Dante. Arrested for Witchcraft! Nickolas Flux & the Salem Witch Trials, 1 vol. Bolte, Marissa. 2014. (Nickolas Flux History Chronicles Ser.). (ENG.). (gr. 3-4). 40p. pap. 7.95 *(978-1-4765-5151-7(0));* 32p. lib. bdg. 29.99 *(978-1-4765-3947-8(2))* Capstone Pr., Inc.

—Defend until Death! Nickolas Flux & the Battle of the Alamo, 1 vol. Yomtov, Nel. 2014. (Nickolas Flux History Chronicles Ser.). (ENG.). 32p. (gr. 3-4). lib. bdg. 29.99 *(978-1-4765-3945-4(6),* Graphic Library) Capstone Pr., Inc.

—Nickolas Flux History Chronicles, 1 vol. Yomtov, Nel et al. 2014. (Nickolas Flux History Chronicles Ser.). (ENG.). 32p. (gr. 3-4). lib. bdg. 119.96 *(978-1-4765-7310-6(7),* Graphic Library) Capstone Pr., Inc.

—Night of Rebellion! Nickolas Flux & the Boston Tea Party, 1 vol. Yomtov, Nel. 2014. (Nickolas Flux History Chronicles Ser.). (ENG.). 32p. (gr. 3-4). lib. bdg. 29.99 *(978-1-4765-3946-1(4),* Graphic Library) Capstone Pr., Inc.

—Stake a Claim! Nickolas Flux & the California Gold Rush, 1 vol. Collins, Terry. 2014. (Nickolas Flux History Chronicles Ser.). (ENG.). 32p. (gr. 3-4). lib. bdg. 29.99 *(978-1-4765-3944-7(8),* Graphic Library) Capstone Pr., Inc.

—The Sword in the Stone. Hoffman, Mary. 2014. (Collins Big Cat Progress Ser.). (ENG.). 32p. (J). pap. 7.99 *(978-0-00-751935-4(4))* HarperCollins Pubs. Ltd. GBR. Dist: Independent Pubs. Group.

Ginger Illustration. Four Square: The Personal Writing Coach, Grades 4-6. Gould, Judith S. & Burke, Mary F. 2005. 112p. (J). pap. 12.95 *(978-1-57310-447-0(7))* Teaching & Learning Co.

Ginger Illustrations Staff. Discovering Differentiation: Strategies for Success in the Language Arts Classroom. Tuszynski, Kathy & Yarber, Angela. Mitchell, Judy, ed. 2004. 80p. (J). pap. 9.95 *(978-1-57310-423-4(X))* Teaching & Learning Co.

—Storytime Discoveries: Math. Enderle, Dotti. 2004. 64p. (J). pap. 9.95 *(978-1-57310-440-1(X))* Teaching & Learning Co.

Ginnings, Miriam. Wheelie Girl. Ginnings, Miriam. Latimer, Miriam. 2007. (ENG.). 32p. (J). (gr. -1-2). pap. 7.99 *(978-0-340-88416-4(9))* Hodder & Stoughton GBR. Dist: Independent Pubs. Group.

Ginsberg, Dvora. Feivel the Falafel Ball Who Wanted to Do a Mitzvah. Yerushalmi, Miriam. 2007. 28p. (J). 16.50 *(978-0-911643-37-4(0))* Aura Printing, Inc.

Ginukov, Valentin. A Great Time: Children's Poems in Russian & English. Shurin, Masha. Morris, Brian, ed. Barton, Alica, tr. 2007. (RUS & ENG.). 32p. (J). 19.95 *(978-0-9792583-2-9(4))* White Stag Pr.

Giordana, D., et al. Worlds' End, BK. 8. Gaiman, Neil. Kahan, Bob, ed. rev. ed. 2006. (Sandman Ser.: Vol. 8). (ENG.). 168p. pap. 19.99 *(978-1-56389-171-7(9))* DC Comics.

Giordano. A Warm & Fuzzy Christmas. Beilenson, Evelyn. 2013. (ENG.). 80p. 5.95 *(978-1-4413-1358-4(3))* Peter Pauper Pr. Inc.

Giordano, Dick, et al. Beauty & the Beast. Perez, George et al. rev. ed. 2005. (Wonder Woman Ser.). (ENG.). 168p. pap. 19.95 *(978-1-4012-0484-6(8))* DC Comics.

Giordano, Dick. Dracula. 2010. (ENG.). 208p. (gr. 10-17). 19.99 *(978-0-7851-4905-7(8))* Marvel Worldwide, Inc.

Giordano, Dick, jt. illus. see Swan, Curt.

Gioulis, Sue & Anderson, Sue. You're Lovable to Me. Yeh, Kat. 2009. (ENG.). 32p. (J). (gr. -1-2). 15.99 *(978-0-375-86015-7(0))* Random Hse., Inc.

Giovannini, Jody. Grandma Battles the Mouse. Jones, Carroll. 2007. 52p. pap. 16.95 *(978-0-9774260-1-0(7))* Omdee Omnimedia, Inc.

Giovannucci, Sharon. Ivan Icicle's Wedding. Voland, Wanda. 2007. 32p. (J). (gr. -1). per. 10.99 *(978-1-60247-064-4(2))* Tate Publishing & Enterprises, LLC.

Giovine, Sergio. A Bundle of Trouble: A Rebecca Mystery. Reiss, Kathryn. 2011. (ENG.). 192p. (YA). (gr. 4-18). pap. 6.95 *(978-1-59369-754-9(6))* American Girl Publishing, Inc.

—Clue in the Castle Tower: A Samantha Mystery. Buckey, Sarah Masters. Ross, Peg, ed. 2011. (ENG.). 184p. (YA). (gr. 4-18). pap. 6.95 *(978-1-59369-752-5(X))* American Girl Publishing, Inc.

—The Silver Guitar: A Julie Mystery. Reiss, Kathryn. Ansfield, Elizabeth, ed. 2011. (ENG.). 192p. (YA). (gr. 4-18). pap. 6.95 *(978-1-59369-756-3(2))* American Girl Publishing, Inc.

Giraffe, Red. Tonka Construction Zone. Hofer, Charles. 2010. (Tonka Ser.). (ENG.). 12p. (J). (gr. -1-1). bds. 15.99 *(978-0-7944-1972-1(0))* Reader's Digest Assn., Inc., The.

Giraffe, Red & Doughty, Clare. Volcano Alert! Team Mission: A Pop-up Book. Hayler, Kate. 2006. 10p. (J). (gr. k-4). reprint ed. 19.00 *(978-1-4223-5075-1(4))* DIANE Publishing Co.

Girard, Alexander. Alexander Girard Coloring Book. 2014. (ENG.). 30p. pap. 7.95 *(978-1-934429-86-0(4))* AMMO Bks., LLC.

Girard, Philippe. Gustave et le Capitaine Planète. Girard, Philippe. 2004. (Mon Roman Ser.). (FRE.). 96p. (J). (gr. 2). pap. *(978-2-89021-649-5(7))* Diffusion du livre Mirabel (DLM).

—Gustave et les Sosies du Capitaine Planète. Girard, Philippe. 2004. (Mon Roman Ser.). (FRE.). 96p. (J). (gr. 2). pap. *(978-2-89021-707-2(8))* Diffusion du livre Mirabel (DLM).

Girard, Roger. Noah's Bark. Krensky, Stephen. 2010. (ENG.). 32p. (J). (gr. -1-2). lib. bdg. 16.95 *(978-0-8225-7645-7(7))* Lerner Publishing Group.

Girard, Thomas. The Nameless Treasure. Girard, Thomas. 2013. 58p. pap. *(978-0-9918736-0-9(2))* Bric-a-brac Bks.

Girasole, Alessia. The Stinky Giant. Weiss, Ellen & Friedman, Mel. 2012. (Step into Reading Ser.). (ENG.). 48p. (J). (gr. k-3). pap. 3.99 *(978-0-375-86743-9(0))* Random Hse., Inc.

—The Stinky Giant. Weiss, Ellen & Friedman, Mel. ed. 2012. (Step into Reading Level 3 Ser.). lib. bdg. 13.55 *(978-0-606-23858-8(1)*, Turtleback) Turtleback Bks.

—Under the Apple Tree. Metzger, Steve. 2009. (J). *(978-0-545-14200-7(8))* Scholastic, Inc.

Giraud, Teresa, jt. illus. see Allen, Kd.

Giraudon, David. Our Living Earth: A Story of People, Ecology, & Preservation. Arthus-Bertrand, Yann, photos by. 2008. (ENG.). 160p. (J). (gr. 3-9). 24.95 *(978-0-8109-7132-5(1)*, Abrams Bks. for Young Readers) Abrams.

Girel, Stephane. A Bird in Winter: A Children's Book Inspired by Pieter Breugel. 2011. (ENG.). 32p. 14.95 *(978-3-7913-7080-4(4))* Prestel Publishing.

—Where Is the Frog? A Children's Book Inspired by Claude Monet. Elschner, Geraldine. 2013. (ENG.). 32p. 14.95 *(978-3-7913-7139-9(8))* Prestel Publishing.

Girmay, Aracelis. Changing, Changing: Story & Collages. Girmay, Aracelis. 2005. (ENG.). 48p. (gr. 1-17). 19.95 *(978-0-8076-1553-9(6)*, 761553) Braziller, George Inc.

Giron, Elizabeth, jt. illus. see Forcada, Adlela.

Girouard, Patricia L. The Blind Man by the Road. Stockstill, Gloria McQueen. 2003. (Listen! Look! Ser.). 20p. (J). bds. 5.49 *(978-0-7586-0144-5(1))* Concordia Publishing Hse.

Girouard, Patrick. Austin & Alex Learn about Adjectives. Bailer, Darice. 2015. (Language Builders Ser.). (ENG.). 32p. (J). (gr. 2-4). pap. 11.94 *(978-1-60357-703-8(3))*; lib. bdg. 25.27 *(978-1-59953-668-2(4))* Norwood Hse. Pr.

—Basket in the River. Stockstill, Gloria McQueen. 2004. 20p. (J). bds. 5.49 *(978-0-7586-0052-3(6))* Concordia Publishing Hse.

—The Bears Upstairs: A Book of Creative Dramatics. Moncure, Jane Belk. 2013. (Magic Castle Readers: Creative Arts Ser.). (ENG.). 32p. (J). (gr. -1-2). 25.64 *(978-1-62323-564-2(2)*, 206302) Child's World, Inc., The.

—A Color Clown Comes to Town: A Book about Recognizing Colors. Moncure, Jane Belk. 2013. (Magic Castle Readers: Creative Arts Ser.). (ENG.). 32p. (J). (gr. -1-2). 25.64 *(978-1-62323-565-9(0)*, 206299) Child's World, Inc., The.

—Don't Forget the Knight Light. Gagliardi, Tina. 2009. (Carly's Dragon Days Ser.). 32p. (J). (gr. -1-2). 28.50 *(978-1-60270-593-7(3))* ABDO Publishing Co.

—Dragonpox. Gagliardi, Tina. 2009. (Carly's Dragon Days Ser.). 32p. (J). (gr. -1-2). 28.50 *(978-1-60270-594-4(1))* ABDO Publishing Co.

—Drive Along, 1 vol. Crow, Melinda Melton. 2010. (Truck Buddies Ser.). (ENG.). 32p. (gr. -1-1). lib. bdg. 21.32 *(978-1-4342-1866-7(X))*; pap. 6.25 *(978-1-4342-2296-1(9))* Stone Arch Bks.

—Fire-Breathers' Academy. Gagliardi, Tina. 2009. (Carly's Dragon Days Ser.). 32p. (J). (gr. -1-2). 28.50 *(978-1-60270-595-1(X))* ABDO Publishing Co.

—Fire-Breathers' Science Fair. Gagliardi, Tina. 2009. (Carly's Dragon Days Ser.). (ENG.). 32p. (J). (gr. -1-2). 28.50 *(978-1-60270-596-8(8))* ABDO Publishing Co.

—Five Little Monkeys Jumping on the Bed. Thompson, Kim Mitzo. 2010. (Padded Board Book W/CD Ser.). 8p. (J). (gr. k-2). bds. 10.99 incl. audio compact disk *(978-1-59922-581-4(6))* Twin Sisters IP, LLC.

—Getting Ready for Christmas. Browne, Yolanda. 2005. 32p. (gr. -1-3). 7.49 *(978-0-7586-0860-4(8))* Concordia Publishing Hse.

—The Golden Dragon. Gagliardi, Tina. 2009. (Carly's Dragon Days Ser.). (ENG.). 32p. (J). (gr. -1-2). 28.50 *(978-1-60270-597-5(6))* ABDO Publishing Co.

—Hop-Skip-Jump-a-Roo Zoo: A Book about Imitating. Moncure, Jane Belk. 2013. (Magic Castle Readers: Creative Arts Ser.). (ENG.). 32p. (J). (gr. -1-2). 25.64 *(978-1-62323-566-6(9)*, 206300) Child's World, Inc., The.

—The Last One Is a Rotten Egg. Gagliardi, Tina. 2009. (Carly's Dragon Days Ser.). (ENG.). 32p. (J). (gr. -1-2). 28.50 *(978-1-60270-598-2(4))* ABDO Publishing Co.

—Little Wheels, 1 vol. Crow, Melinda Melton. 2010. (Truck Buddies Ser.). (ENG.). 32p. (gr. -1-1). lib. bdg. 21.32 *(978-1-4342-1865-0(1))*; pap. 6.25 *(978-1-4342-2297-8(7))* Stone Arch Bks.

—Nanny Goat's Boat: A Book of Rhyming. Moncure, Jane Belk. 2013. (Magic Castle Readers: Creative Arts Ser.). (ENG.). 32p. (J). (gr. -1-2). 25.64 *(978-1-62323-567-3(7)*, 206301) Child's World, Inc., The.

—Old MacDonald Had a Farm. Thompson, Kim Mitzo. 2010. (Padded Board Book W/CD Ser.). 8p. (J). (gr. k-2). bds. 10.99 incl. audio compact disk *(978-1-59922-579-1(4))* Twin Sisters IP, LLC.

—Ride & Seek, 1 vol. Crow, Melinda Melton. 2010. (Truck Buddies Ser.). (ENG.). 32p. (gr. -1-1). lib. bdg. 21.32 *(978-1-4342-1867-4(8))*; pap. 6.25 *(978-1-4342-2298-5(5))* Stone Arch Bks.

—Teach Me Everyday English V1, 2 bks & 2 cd's, Vol 1. Mahoney, Judy. 2008. (ENG.). 32p. (J). (gr. -1). 19.95 *(978-1-59972-108-8(2))* Teach Me Tapes, Inc.

—Teach Me Everyday French Vol 1, Vol 1. Mahoney, Judy. 2008. (FRE & ENG.). 32p. (J). (gr. -1). 19.95 *(978-1-59972-101-9(5))* Teach Me Tapes, Inc.

—Teach Me Everyday German V. 1, Vol 1. Mahoney, Judy. 2008. (GER & ENG.). 32p. (J). (gr. -1). 19.95 *(978-1-59972-103-3(1))* Teach Me Tapes, Inc.

—Teach Me Everyday Italian: Celebrating the Seasons, 22 vols., Vol. 2. Mahoney, Judy. adapted ed. 2010. (ITA & ENG.). 32p. (J). 19.95 *(978-1-59972-207-8(0)*, 1286051) Teach Me Tapes, Inc.

—Teach Me Everyday Japanese V 1, Vol 1. Mahoney, Judy. 2008. (JPN & ENG.). 32p. (J). (gr. -1). 19.95 *(978-1-59972-104-0(X))* Teach Me Tapes, Inc.

—Teach Me Everyday Spanish: Celebrating the Seasons, 22 vols., Vol. 2. Mahoney, Judy. adapted ed. 2009. (SPA & ENG.). 32p. (J). (gr. -1-2). lib. bdg. 19.95 incl. audio compact disk *(978-1-59972-202-3(X))* Teach Me Tapes, Inc.

—Teach Me Everyday Spanish Vol 1, Volume 1. Mahoney, Judy. 2008. (SPA & ENG.). 32p. (J). (gr. -1). 19.95 *(978-1-59972-102-6(3))* Teach Me Tapes, Inc.

—The Tiger & the General. Millhouse, Jackie. 2007. (J). *(978-1-932911-32-9(4))* World Tribune Pr.

—Tired Trucks, 1 vol. Crow, Melinda Melton. 2010. (Truck Buddies Ser.). (ENG.). 32p. (gr. -1-1). lib. bdg. 21.32 *(978-1-4342-1864-3(3))*; pap. 6.25 *(978-1-4342-2299-2(3))* Stone Arch Bks.

—Yikes-Lice! Caffey, Don. 2003. (ENG.). 24p. (J). (gr. -1-5). reprint ed. pap. 5.95 *(978-0-8075-9375-2(3))* Whitman, Albert & Co.

—5 Steps to Drawing Dinosaurs. Hall, Pamela. 2011. (5 Steps to Drawing Ser.). (ENG.). 32p. (J). (gr. k-3). lib. bdg. 27.07 *(978-1-60973-195-3(6)*, 201102) Child's World, Inc., The.

—5 Steps to Drawing Monsters. StJohn, Amanda. 2011. (5 Steps to Drawing Ser.). (ENG.). 32p. (J). (gr. k-3). lib. bdg. 27.07 *(978-1-60973-202-8(2)*, 201108) Child's World, Inc., The.

Girourard, Patrick. Nina & Nolan Build a Nonsense Poem. Bullard, Lisa. 2011. (Poetry Builders Ser.). 32p. (J). (gr. 2-4). lib. bdg. 25.27 *(978-1-59953-437-4(1))* Norwood Hse. Pr.

Gisser, George H., et al. Happy Kappy-The Flying Kangaroo(Who couldn't hop!) Bk. 1: "Without Our Tails" Gisser, George H. 2011. 30p. (J). pap. 12.99 *(978-0-615-45522-8(0))* Happy Kappy Karacters.

Gist, E. M. More Bones: Scary Stories from Around the World. Olson, Arielle North & Schwartz, Howard. 2008. (ENG.). 176p. (J). (gr. 3-7). 15.99 *(978-0-670-06339-0(8)*, Viking Juvenile) Penguin Publishing Group.

Givens, R. The Eight Ball Bible: A Guide to Bar Table Play. Givens, R. 2004. 288p. (YA). per. 29.95 *(978-0-9747273-7-0(7)*, 415-776-1596) 8-Ball Express, Inc.

Gizicki-Lipson, Coryn. An Angel in the Sky. Gizicki-Lipson, Coryn. Gizicki, Carlie. 2003. (ENG.). 32p. (J). 14.95 *(978-0-9740438-0-7(X))* In the Sky Publishing.

Gladden, Stephanie, et al. Dignifying Science: Stories about Women Scientists. Ottaviani, Jim. 2nd ed. 2006. 144p. (YA). (gr. 4-18). pap. 16.95 *(978-0-9660106-4-0(7))* G T Labs.

Gladfelter, Allen. Cars: Route 66 Dash! Porter, Alan J. 2010. (Cars Ser.). (ENG.). 112p. (J). (gr. 3-6). pap. 9.99 *(978-1-60886-585-7(1))* Boom! Studios.

Gladfelter, Scott, et al. Be the One! The Todd Beamer Story an Adaptation of Let's Roll! by Lisa Beamer & Todd Anderson. 2005. 52p. (J). pap. *(978-1-933206-00-4(4)*, 5010) Bible Visuals International, Inc.

Glanville, Caroline. African & Caribbean Celebrations. Johnson, Gail & Grell, Jane. Green, Toby, ed. 2008. (Crafts, Festivals & Family Activities Ser.). (ENG.). 224p. pap. *(978-1-903458-00-6(5))* Hawthorn Pr. GBR. Dist: SteinerBooks, Inc.

Glanville, Toby, photos by. Breakfast, Lunch, Tea. Carrarini, Rose & Carrarini, Jean Charles. rev. ed. 2006. (ENG., 192p. (gr. 8-17). 29.95 *(978-0-7148-4465-7(9))* Phaidon Pr., Inc.

Glanzman, Louis. The Space Pioneers: A Tom Corbett Space Cadet Adventure. Rockwell, Carey & Ley, Willy. 2011. 220p. 44.95 *(978-1-258-10097-1(5))* Literary Licensing, LLC.

—Treachery in Outer Space: A Tom Corbett Space Cadet Adventure. Rockwell, Carey & Ley, Willy. 2011. 220p. 44.95 *(978-1-258-09685-4(4))* Literary Licensing, LLC.

Glanzman, Louis S. Pippi Longstocking. Lindgren, Astrid. Lamborn, Florence, tr. from SWE. 2005. (Puffin Modern Classics Ser.). (ENG.). 160p. (J). (gr. 3-7). pap. 6.99 *(978-0-14-240249-8(4)*, Puffin) Penguin Publishing Group.

Glanzman, Louis S. The Wish-Tree. Ciardi, John. 2015. (ENG.). 96p. (J). pap. 9.99 ***(978-0-486-79618-5(3))*** Dover Pubns., Inc.

Glasbergen, Randy. Yes, Your Parents Are Crazy! A Teen Survival Handbook. Bradley, Michael J. 2004. (ENG.). 432p. pap. 14.95 *(978-0-936197-48-7(X))* Harbor Pr., Inc.

Glaser, Byron & Higashi, Sandra. Zolocolor! Doodling Between Black & White. Glaser, Byron & Higashi, Sandra. 2011. (ENG.). 96p. (J). 7.99 *(978-1-4424-2261-2(0)*, Little Simon) Little Simon.

—Zolocolor! Christmas Doodling. Glaser, Byron & Higashi, Sandra. 2012. (ENG.). 96p. (J). 7.99 *(978-1-4424-4592-5(0)*, Little Simon) Little Simon.

—Zolocolor! Doodle Canoodle. 2013. (ENG.). 96p. (J). 7.99 *(978-1-4424-6848-1(3)*, Little Simon) Little Simon.

—Zolocolor! Toodle-Oo Doodle-Oo. 2013. (ENG.). 96p. (J). 7.99 *(978-1-4424-6847-4(5)*, Little Simon) Little Simon.

Glaser, Milton. The Alphazeds. Glaser, Shirley. 2005. 32p. (J). (gr. k-4). reprint ed. 20.00 *(978-0-7567-9367-8(X))* DIANE Publishing Co.

Glass, Andrew. The Booford Summer. Smith, Susan Mathias. 2004. (ENG.). 144p. (J). (gr. 5-7). pap. 10.95 *(978-0-618-43245-5(0))* Houghton Mifflin Harcourt Publishing Co.

—Moby Dick: Chasing the Great White Whale. Kimmel, Eric A. 2012. (ENG.). 40p. (J). (gr. k-1). 16.99 *(978-0-312-66297-4(1))* Feiwel & Friends.

—The Tortoise & the Hare Race Again. Bernstein, Dan. 2006. (ENG.). (J). 36p. (gr. -1-3). 6.95 *(978-0-8234-2070-4(1))*; 32p. (gr. 4-8). 16.95 *(978-0-8234-1867-1(7))* Holiday Hse., Inc.

Glass, Andrew. The Wondrous Whirligig: The Wright Brothers¿ First Flying Machine. Glass, Andrew. 2007. 30p. (J). reprint ed. 17.00 *(978-1-4223-6765-0(7))* DIANE Publishing Co.

Glass, Andrew, photos by. Thank You Very Much, Captain Ericsson! Wooldridge, Connie N. & Wooldridge, Connie Nordhielm. 2004. (ENG., 32p. (J). (gr. k-3). tchr. ed. 16.95 *(978-0-8234-1626-4(7))* Holiday Hse., Inc.

Glass, Andrew, jt. illus. see Kimmel, Eric A.

Glass, Eric. Willy & Friends traveling through the Seasons: The continuing story of Willy the little fire Jeep. Estes, Don. 2006. (J). *(978-1-883551-75-9(7)*, Maple Corners Press) Attic Studio Publishing Hse.

Glass, Hilary Ann Love. A Different Kind of Safari. Hipp, Helen C. Diaco, Paula Tedford, ed. 2013. 32p. 17.95 *(978-0-9890134-0-6(5))* WithinU Life Coaching LLC.

Glass House Graphics Staff. Alien Snow, 1 vol. Dahl, Michael. 2011. (Good vs Evil Ser.). (ENG.). 48p. (gr. 1-2). pap. 6.29 *(978-1-4342-3444-5(4)*, Good vs Evil) Stone Arch Bks.

—The Awakening, 1 vol. Lemke, Donald. 2011. (Good vs Evil Ser.). (ENG.). 48p. (gr. 1-2). pap. 5.95 *(978-1-4342-3443-8(6)*, Good vs Evil) Stone Arch Bks.

—Diver Down, 1 vol. Lemke, Donald. 2011. (Good vs Evil Ser.). (ENG.). 48p. (gr. 1-2). pap. 6.29 *(978-1-4342-3446-9(0)*, Good vs Evil) Stone Arch Bks.

Glass, Roger. The M & M's(r) Brand Color Pattern Book. McGrath, Barbara Barbieri. 2004. 32p. (J). 16.95 *(978-1-57091-416-4(8))*; pap. 6.95 *(978-1-57091-417-1(6))* Charlesbridge Publishing, Inc.

—The M & M's(r) Brand Counting Book. McGrath, Barbara Barbieri. rev. ed. 2004. 32p. (J). 16.95 *(978-1-57091-367-9(6))*; pap. 6.95 *(978-1-57091-368-6(4))* Charlesbridge Publishing, Inc.

—Mas Matematicas con los Chocolates de M & M's Brand. McGrath, Barbara Barbieri. Mlawer, Teresa, tr. 2004. (SPA.). 32p. (J). pap. 6.95 *(978-1-57091-481-2(8)*, CH30498) Charlesbridge Publishing, Inc.

Glassby, Cathie. Dads: A Field Guide. Ractliffe, Justin. (ENG.). 32p. (J). (gr. -1-k). 2013. 16.99 *(978-1-74275-549-6(6))*; 2nd ed. 2014. 9.99 *(978-1-74275-551-9(8))* Random Hse. Australia AUS. Dist: Independent Pubs. Group.

Glasser, Robin Preiss. A Is for Abigail: An Almanac of Amazing American Women. Cheney, Lynne. 2003. (ENG.). 48p. (J). (gr. 1-7). 17.99 *(978-0-689-85819-2(1)*, Simon & Schuster Bks. For Young Readers) Simon & Schuster Bks. For Young Readers.

Glasser, Robin Preiss. Alexander, Who's Not (Do You Hear Me? I Mean It!) Going to Move. Viorst, Judith. 2015. 32p. pap. 9.00 ***(978-1-61003-597-2(6))*** Center for the Collaborative Classroom.

Glasser, Robin Preiss. Apples Galore! O'Connor, Jane. 2013. (I Can Read Book 1 Ser.). (ENG.). 32p. (J). (gr. -1-3). 16.99 *(978-0-06-208311-1(2))* HarperCollins Pubs.

—Aspiring Artist. O'Connor, Jane. 2011. (Fancy Nancy Ser.). (ENG.). 32p. (J). (gr. -1-2). 12.99 *(978-0-06-191526-0(2))* HarperCollins Pubs.

—Bonjour, Butterfly. O'Connor, Jane. (Fancy Nancy Ser.). (ENG.). 32p. (J). (gr. -1-2). 2012. 9.99 *(978-0-06-221053-1(X))*; 2008. 17.99 *(978-0-06-123588-7(1))* HarperCollins Pubs.

—Explorer Extraordinaire! O'Connor, Jane. 2009. (Fancy Nancy Ser.). (ENG.). 32p. (J). (gr. -1-2). 12.99 *(978-0-06-168486-9(4))* HarperCollins Pubs.

—Express Yourself! A Doodle & Draw Book. O'Connor, Jane. 2011. (Fancy Nancy Ser.). (ENG.). 64p. (J). (gr. -1-3). pap. 6.99 *(978-0-06-188281-4(X)*, HarperFestival) HarperCollins Pubs.

—Fanciest Doll in the Universe. O'Connor, Jane. 2013. (Fancy Nancy Ser.). 32p. (J). (gr. -1-3). (ENG.). 17.99 *(978-0-06-170384-3(2))*; lib. bdg. 18.89 *(978-0-06-170385-0(0))* HarperCollins Pubs.

—Fancy Day in Room 1-A. O'Connor, Jane. 2012. (I Can Read Book 1 Ser.). (ENG.). 32p. (J). (gr. -1-3). 16.99 *(978-0-06-208305-0(8))*; pap. 3.99 *(978-0-06-208304-3(X))* HarperCollins Pubs.

—Fancy Nancy. O'Connor, Jane. (Fancy Nancy Ser.). 32p. (J). (gr. -1-3). 2009. (ENG.). pap. 24.99 *(978-0-06-171944-8(7)*, HarperFestival); 2005. 17.89 *(978-0-06-054210-8(1))*; 2005. (ENG.). 17.99 *(978-0-06-054209-2(8))* HarperCollins Pubs.

—Fancy Nancy: Bonjour, Butterfly. O'Connor, Jane. 2008. (Fancy Nancy Ser.). (J). 203.88 *(978-0-06-158245-5(X))* HarperCollins Pubs.

—Fancy Nancy: Hair Dos & Hair Don'ts. O'Connor, Jane. 2011. (I Can Read Book 1 Ser.). (ENG.). 32p. (J). (gr. -1-3). 16.99 *(978-0-06-200180-1(9))* HarperCollins Pubs.

Glasser, Robin Preiss, et al. Fancy Nancy: My Family History. O'Connor, Jane. 2010. (I Can Read Book 1 Ser.). (ENG.). 32p. (J). (gr. -1-3). 16.99 *(978-0-06-188270-8(4))* HarperCollins Pubs.

Glasser, Robin Preiss. Fancy Nancy: Our Thanksgiving Banquet. O'Connor, Jane. 2011. (Fancy Nancy Ser.). (ENG.). 24p. (J). (gr. -1-3). pap. 4.99 *(978-0-06-123598-6(9)*, HarperFestival) HarperCollins Pubs.

—Fancy Nancy: Tea for Two. O'Connor, Jane. 2012. (Fancy Nancy Ser.). (ENG.). 24p. (J). (gr. -1-3). pap. 3.99 *(978-0-06-123597-9(0)*, HarperFestival) HarperCollins Pubs.

—Fancy Nancy: Too Many Tutus. O'Connor, Jane. 2012. (I Can Read Book 1 Ser.). (ENG.). 32p. (J). (gr. -1-3). 16.99 *(978-0-06-208308-1(2))* HarperCollins Pubs.

—Fancy Nancy - Apples Galore! O'Connor, Jane. 2013. (I Can Read Book 1 Ser.). (ENG.). 32p. (J). (gr. -1-3). pap. 3.99 *(978-0-06-208310-4(4))* HarperCollins Pubs.

—Fancy Nancy - Budding Ballerina. O'Connor, Jane. 2013. (Fancy Nancy Ser.). (ENG.). 24p. (J). (gr. -1-3). pap. 3.99 *(978-0-06-208628-0(6)*, HarperFestival) HarperCollins Pubs.

—Fancy Nancy - Just My Luck! O'Connor, Jane. 2013. (I Can Read Book 1 Ser.). (ENG.). 32p. (J). (gr. -1-3). pap. 3.99 *(978-0-06-208313-5(9))* HarperCollins Pubs.

—Fancy Nancy - Nancy Clancy Sees the Future. O'Connor, Jane. 2014. (Nancy Clancy Ser.: 3). (ENG.). 144p. (J). (gr. 1-5). pap. 4.99 *(978-0-06-208421-7(6))* HarperCollins Pubs.

Glasser, Robin Preiss. Fancy Nancy - Nancy Clancy's Ultimate Chapter Book Quartet. O'Connor, Jane. 2015. (Nancy Clancy Ser.). (ENG.). 576p. (J). (gr. 1-5). pap. 17.99 ***(978-0-06-242273-6(1))*** HarperCollins Pubs.

Glasser, Robin Preiss. Fancy Nancy - Peanut Butter & Jellyfish. O'Connor, Jane. 2015. (I Can Read Book 1 Ser.). (ENG.). 32p. (J). (gr. -1-3). 16.99 *(978-0-06-226976-8(3))* HarperCollins Pubs.

—Fancy Nancy - Super Secret Surprise Party. O'Connor, Jane. 2015. (I Can Read Book 1 Ser.). (ENG.). 32p. (J). (gr. -1-3). 16.99 *(978-0-06-226979-9(8))* HarperCollins Pubs.

—Fancy Nancy 10th Anniversary Edition. O'Connor, Jane. 2015. (Fancy Nancy Ser.). (ENG.). 40p. (J). (gr. -1-3). 17.99 *(978-0-06-235214-9(8))* HarperCollins Pubs.

—Fancy Nancy & the Fabulous Fashion Boutique. O'Connor, Jane. 2010. (Fancy Nancy Ser.). 32p. (J). (gr. -1-3). (ENG.). 17.99 *(978-0-06-123592-4(X))*; lib. bdg. 18.89 *(978-0-06-123593-1(8))* HarperCollins Pubs.

—Fancy Nancy & the Fall Foliage. O'Connor, Jane. 2014. (Fancy Nancy Ser.). (ENG.). 24p. (J). (gr. -1-3). pap. 4.99 *(978-0-06-208630-3(8)*, HarperFestival) HarperCollins Pubs.

—Fancy Nancy & the Late, Late, Late Night. O'Connor, Jane. 2010. (Fancy Nancy Ser.). (ENG.). 24p. (J). (gr. -1-3). pap. 3.99 *(978-0-06-170377-5(X)*, HarperFestival) HarperCollins Pubs.

—Fancy Nancy & the Mean Girl. O'Connor, Jane. 2011. (I Can Read Book 1 Ser.). (ENG.). 32p. (J). (gr. -1-3). 16.99 *(978-0-06-200178-8(7))*; pap. 3.99 *(978-0-06-200177-1(9))* HarperCollins Pubs.

—Fancy Nancy & the Mermaid Ballet. O'Connor, Jane. 2012. (Fancy Nancy Ser.). 32p. (J). (gr. -1-2). lib. bdg. 18.89 *(978-0-06-170382-9(6))* HarperCollins Pubs.

—Fancy Nancy & the Posh Puppy. O'Connor, Jane. (Fancy Nancy Ser.). 32p. (J). (gr. -1-2). 2012. (ENG.). 9.99 *(978-0-06-221052-4(1))*; 2007. (ENG.). 17.99 *(978-0-06-054213-9(6))*; 2007. lib. bdg. 18.89 *(978-0-06-054215-3(2))* HarperCollins Pubs.

—Fancy Nancy & the Posh Puppy (Nancy la Elegante y la Perrita Popoff) O'Connor, Jane. 2011. (SPA & ENG.). 32p. (J). (gr. -1-3). 16.99 *(978-0-06-179961-7(0)*, Rayo) HarperCollins Pubs.

Glasser, Robin Preiss, et al. Fancy Nancy & the Sensational Babysitter. O'Connor, Jane. 2010. (Fancy Nancy Ser.). (ENG.). 24p. (J). (gr. -1-3). pap. 3.99 *(978-0-06-170378-2(8)*, HarperFestival) HarperCollins Pubs.

Glasser, Robin Preiss. Fancy Nancy & the Wedding of the Century. O'Connor, Jane. 2014. (Fancy Nancy Ser.). 32p. (J). (gr. -1-3). (ENG.). 17.99 *(978-0-06-208319-7(8))*; lib. bdg. 18.89 *(978-0-06-208320-3(1))* HarperCollins Pubs.

—Fancy Nancy at the Museum. O'Connor, Jane & Harper Collins / LeapFrog. 2008. (Fancy Nancy Ser.). (J). 13.99 *(978-1-59319-940-1(6))* LeapFrog Enterprises, Inc.

Glasser, Robin Preiss. Fancy Nancy: Candy Bonanza. O'Connor, Jane. 2015. (Fancy Nancy Ser.). (ENG.). 24p. (J). (gr. -1-3). pap. 4.99 ***(978-0-06-226958-4(5)***, HarperFestival) HarperCollins Pubs.

Glasser, Robin Preiss. Fancy Nancy Collector's Quintet. O'Connor, Jane. 2009. (I Can Read Book 1 Ser.). (J). (gr. k-3). pap. 16.99 *(978-0-06-171905-9(6))* HarperCollins Pubs.

—Fancy Nancy: Nancy Clancy Sees the Future, 3 vols. O'Connor, Jane. 2013. (Fancy Nancy Ser.). (ENG.). 112p. (J). (gr. 1-5). 9.99 *(978-0-06-208297-8(3))* HarperCollins Pubs.

G

Glasser, Robin Preiss. Fancy Nancy: Nancy Clancy, Soccer Mania. O'Connor, Jane. 2015. (Nancy Clancy Ser.: 6). (ENG.). 128p. (J). (gr. 1-5). 9.99 *(978-0-06-226967-6(4))* HarperCollins Pubs.

Glasser, Robin Preiss. Fancy Nancy Petite Library. O'Connor, Jane. 2010. (Fancy Nancy Ser.). (ENG.). 32p. (J). (gr. k-3). 14.99 *(978-0-06-191527-7(0),* HarperFestival) HarperCollins Pubs.

—Fancy Nancy Storybook Treasury. O'Connor, Jane. 2013. (Fancy Nancy Ser.). (ENG.). 192p. (J). (gr. -1-3). 11.99 *(978-0-06-211978-0(8))* HarperCollins Pubs.

—Fancy Nancy's Absolutely Stupendous Sticker Book. O'Connor, Jane. 2009. (Fancy Nancy Ser.). (ENG.). 100p. (J). (gr. -1-2). pap. 12.99 *(978-0-06-172563-0(3),* HarperFestival) HarperCollins Pubs.

—Fancy Nancy's Fabulous Fall Storybook Collection. O'Connor, Jane. 2014. (Fancy Nancy Ser.). (ENG.). 192p. (J). (gr. -1-3). 11.99 *(978-0-06-228884-4(9))* HarperCollins Pubs.

—Fancy Nancy's Fabulously Fancy Treasury. O'Connor, Jane. 2012. (Fancy Nancy Ser.). (ENG.). 25p. (J). (gr. -1-3). 15.99 *(978-0-06-218804-5(6),* HarperFestival) HarperCollins Pubs.

—Fancy Nancy's Fantastic Phonics, 12 vols. O'Connor, Jane. 2013. (My First I Can Read Ser.). (ENG.). 120p. (J). (gr. -1-3). pap. 12.99 *(978-0-06-208633-4(2))* HarperCollins Pubs.

—Fancy Nancy's Favorite Fancy Words: From Accessories to Zany. O'Connor, Jane. 2008. (Fancy Nancy Ser.). (ENG.). 32p. (J). (gr. -1-2). 12.99 *(978-0-06-154923-6(1))* HarperCollins Pubs.

—Fancy Nancy's Marvelous Mother's Day Brunch. O'Connor, Jane. 2011. (Fancy Nancy Ser.). (ENG.). 16p. (J). (gr. -1-3). pap. 6.99 *(978-0-06-170380-5(X),* HarperFestival) HarperCollins Pubs.

—Fancy Nancy's Perfectly Pink Playtime Purse. O'Connor, Jane. 2015. (Fancy Nancy Ser.). (ENG.). 80p. (J). (gr. -1-3). pap. 9.99 *(978-0-06-226962-1(3),* HarperFestival) HarperCollins Pubs.

—Fashionista. O'Connor, Jane. 2011. (Fancy Nancy Ser.). (ENG.). 32p. (J). (gr. -1-3). pap., act. bk. ed. 4.99 *(978-0-06-188266-1(6),* HarperFestival) HarperCollins Pubs.

Glasser, Robin Preiss, et al. Girl on the Go: A Doodle & Draw Book. O'Connor, Jane. 2012. (Fancy Nancy Ser.). (ENG.). 64p. (J). (gr. -1-3). pap. 6.99 *(978-0-06-188282-1(8),* HarperFestival) HarperCollins Pubs.

Glasser, Robin Preiss. Hair Dos & Hair Don'ts. O'Connor, Jane. 2011. (I Can Read Book 1 Ser.). (ENG.). 32p. (J). (gr. -1-3). pap. 3.99 *(978-0-06-200179-5(5))* HarperCollins Pubs.

—Haunted Mansion: A Reusable Sticker Book for Halloween. O'Connor, Jane. 2011. (Fancy Nancy Ser.). (ENG.). 12p. (J). (gr. -1-2). pap. 6.99 *(978-0-06-170388-1(5),* HarperFestival) HarperCollins Pubs.

—Just My Luck! O'Connor, Jane. 2013. (I Can Read Book 1 Ser.). (ENG.). 32p. (J). (gr. -1-3). 16.99 *(978-0-06-208314-2(7))* HarperCollins Pubs.

Glasser, Robin Preiss, et al. My Family History. O'Connor, Jane. 2010. (I Can Read Book 1 Ser.). (ENG.). 32p. (J). (gr. -1-3). pap. 3.99 *(978-0-06-188271-5(2))* HarperCollins Pubs.

Glasser, Robin Preiss. Nancy Clancy: My Secret Diary. O'Connor, Jane. 2015. (Fancy Nancy Ser.). (ENG.). 144p. (J). (gr. 1-5). pap. 11.99 *(978-0-06-234983-5(X))* HarperCollins Pubs.

—Nancy Clancy - Secret of the Silver Key. O'Connor, Jane. 2015. (Nancy Clancy Ser.: 4). (ENG.). 144p. (J). (gr. 1-5). pap. 4.99 *(978-0-06-208422-4(4))* HarperCollins Pubs.

—Nancy Clancy - Super Sleuth. O'Connor, Jane. 2013. (Nancy Clancy Ser.: 1). (ENG.). 144p. (J). (gr. 2-5). pap. 4.99 *(978-0-06-208419-4(4))* HarperCollins Pubs.

—Nancy Clancy, Secret Admirer. O'Connor, Jane. 2013. (Nancy Clancy Ser.: 2). (ENG.). 144p. (J). (gr. 1-5). pap. 4.99 *(978-0-06-208420-0(8))* HarperCollins Pubs.

Glasser, Robin Preiss. Nancy Clancy Sees the Future. O'Connor, Jane. 2015. (Fancy Nancy Ser.). (ENG.). 256p. (J). (gr. 1-5). 12.99 ***(978-0-06-240365-0(6))*** HarperCollins Pubs.

Glasser, Robin Preiss. Nancy Clancy, Star of Stage & Screen. O'Connor, Jane. 2015. (Nancy Clancy Ser.: Bk. 5). (ENG.). 128p. (J). (gr. 1-5). 9.99 *(978-0-06-226964-5(X))* HarperCollins Pubs.

—Nancy Clancy, Super Sleuth, 3 vols. O'Connor, Jane. 2012. (Nancy Clancy Ser.: 1). (ENG.). 128p. (J). (gr. 2-5). 9.99 *(978-0-06-208293-0(0))* HarperCollins Pubs.

—Nancy Clancy's Tres Charming, 3 vols., Set. O'Connor, Jane. 2013. (Nancy Clancy Ser.). (ENG.). 384p. (J). (gr. 1-5). 24.99 *(978-0-06-227793-0(6))* HarperCollins Pubs.

—Nancy la Elegante. O'Connor, Jane. Valenzuela, Liliana, tr. from ENG. 2008. (Fancy Nancy Ser.). (SPA.). 32p. (J). (gr. -1-2). 17.99 *(978-0-06-143528-7(7),* Rayo) HarperCollins Pubs.

—Ooh La La! It's Beauty Day. O'Connor, Jane. 2010. (Fancy Nancy Ser.). (ENG.). 40p. (J). (gr. -1-2). 12.99 *(978-0-06-191525-3(4))* HarperCollins Pubs.

—Our 50 States: A Family Adventure Across America. Cheney, Lynne. 2006. (ENG.). 74p. (J). (gr. 2-5). 19.99 *(978-0-689-86717-0(4),* Simon & Schuster/Paula Wiseman Bks.) Simon & Schuster/Paula Wiseman Bks.

—Peanut Butter & Jellyfish. O'Connor, Jane. 2015. (I Can Read Book 1 Ser.). (ENG.). 32p. (J). (gr. -1-3). pap. 3.99 *(978-0-06-226975-1(5))* HarperCollins Pubs.

—Poet Extraordinaire! O'Connor, Jane. 2010. (Fancy Nancy Ser.). (ENG.). 32p. (J). (gr. -1-2). 12.99 *(978-0-06-189643-9(8))* HarperCollins Pubs.

—Puppy Party. O'Connor, Jane. 2013. (Fancy Nancy Ser.). (ENG.). 24p. (J). (gr. -1-3). pap. 3.99 *(978-0-06-208627-3(8),* HarperFestival) HarperCollins Pubs.

—Puzzle-Palooza. O'Connor, Jane. 2011. (Fancy Nancy Ser.). (ENG.). 32p. (J). (gr. -1-3). pap. 4.99 *(978-0-06-188267-8(4),* HarperFestival) HarperCollins Pubs.

—Sand Castles & Sand Palaces. O'Connor, Jane. 2014. (Fancy Nancy Ser.). (ENG.). 24p. (J). (gr. -1-3). pap. 4.99 *(978-0-06-226954-6(2),* HarperFestival) HarperCollins Pubs.

—Secret Admirer, 3 vols. O'Connor, Jane. 2013. (Fancy Nancy Ser.: Bk. 2). (ENG.). 128p. (J). (gr. 1-5). 9.99 *(978-0-06-208295-4(7))* HarperCollins Pubs.

—The Secret of the Silver Key. O'Connor, Jane. 2014. (Fancy Nancy Ser.). (ENG.). 128p. (J). (gr. 1-5). 9.99 *(978-0-06-208299-2(X))* HarperCollins Pubs.

—A Sock Is a Pocket for Your Toes. Scanlon, Elizabeth Garton & Scanlon, Elizabeth G. 2004. (ENG.). 32p. (J). (gr. -1-2). 16.99 *(978-0-06-029526-4(0))* HarperCollins Pubs.

—Splendid Speller. O'Connor, Jane. 2011. (I Can Read Book 1 Ser.). (ENG.). 32p. (J). (gr. -1-3). 16.99 *(978-0-06-200176-4(0));* pap. 3.99 *(978-0-06-200175-7(2))* HarperCollins Pubs.

—Splendiferous Christmas. O'Connor, Jane. (Fancy Nancy Ser.). 32p. (J). (gr. -1-2). 2011. (ENG.). 17.99 *(978-0-06-123590-0(3));* 2009. lib. bdg. 18.89 *(978-0-06-123591-7(1))* HarperCollins Pubs.

—Spring Fashion Fling. O'Connor, Jane. 2015. (Fancy Nancy Ser.). (ENG.). 24p. (J). (gr. -1-3). pap. 4.99 *(978-0-06-226956-0(9),* HarperFestival) HarperCollins Pubs.

—Stellar Stargazer! O'Connor, Jane. 2011. (Fancy Nancy Ser.). (ENG.). 32p. (J). (gr. -1-2). 12.99 *(978-0-06-191523-9(8))* HarperCollins Pubs.

—Super-Completely & Totally the Messiest. Viorst, Judith. 2004. (ENG.). 32p. (J). (gr. -1-2). 7.99 *(978-0-689-86617-3(8),* Atheneum Bks. for Young Readers) Simon & Schuster Children's Publishing.

—Super-Completely & Totally the Messiest! Viorst, Judith. 2006. (ENG.). 32p. (J). (gr. -1-2). 16.99 *(978-1-4169-4200-9(9),* Atheneum Bks. for Young Readers) Simon & Schuster Children's Publishing.

—Super Secret Surprise Party. O'Connor, Jane. 2015. (I Can Read Book 1 Ser.). (ENG.). 32p. (J). (gr. -1-3). pap. 3.99 *(978-0-06-226978-2(X))* HarperCollins Pubs.

Glasser, Robin Preiss. Super Sleuth. O'Connor, Jane. 2015. (Fancy Nancy Ser.). (ENG.). 256p. (J). (gr. 1-5). 12.99 ***(978-0-06-240364-3(8))*** HarperCollins Pubs.

Glasser, Robin Preiss. Tea for Ruby. Ferguson, Sarah. 2008. (ENG.). 40p. (J). (gr. -1-3). 16.99 *(978-1-4169-5419-4(8),* Simon & Schuster/Paula Wiseman Bks.) Simon & Schuster/Paula Wiseman Bks.

—Tea for Ruby. Ferguson, The Duchess of York, Sarah, The Duchess of York. 2012. (ENG.). 40p. (J). (gr. -1-3). pap. 7.99 *(978-1-4169-5420-0(1),* Simon & Schuster/Paula Wiseman Bks.) Simon & Schuster/Paula Wiseman Bks.

—Tea for Two. O'Connor, Jane. ed. 2012. (Fancy Nancy Picture Bks.). lib. bdg. 13.55 *(978-0-606-23577-8(9),* Turtleback) Turtleback Bks.

—Tea Parties. O'Connor, Jane. 2009. (Fancy Nancy Ser.). (ENG.). 40p. (J). (gr. -1-2). 12.99 *(978-0-06-180174-7(7))* HarperCollins Pubs.

—There's No Day Like a Snow Day. O'Connor, Jane. 2012. (Fancy Nancy Ser.). (ENG.). 24p. (J). (gr. -1-3). pap. 4.99 *(978-0-06-208629-7(4),* HarperFestival) HarperCollins Pubs.

—Too Many Tutus. O'Connor, Jane. 2012. (I Can Read Book 1 Ser.). (ENG.). 32p. (J). (gr. -1-3). pap. 3.99 *(978-0-06-208307-4(4))* HarperCollins Pubs.

Glasser, Robin Preiss & Bracken, Carolyn. Fancy Nancy & the Mermaid Ballet. O'Connor, Jane. 2012. (Fancy Nancy Ser.). (ENG.). 32p. (J). (gr. -1-2). 17.99 *(978-0-06-170381-2(8))* HarperCollins Pubs.

—Fancy Nancy Loves! Loves!! Loves!!! O'Connor, Jane. 2007. (Fancy Nancy Ser.). (ENG.). 12p. (J). (gr. -1-2). pap. 6.99 *(978-0-06-123599-3(7),* HarperFestival) HarperCollins Pubs.

—Fancy Nancy's Fashion Parade! Reusable Sticker Book. O'Connor, Jane. 2008. (Fancy Nancy Ser.). (ENG.). 12p. (J). (gr. -1-2). pap. 6.99 *(978-0-06-123601-3(2),* HarperFestival) HarperCollins Pubs.

—Fancy Nancy's Perfectly Posh Paper Doll Book. O'Connor, Jane. 2009. (Fancy Nancy Ser.). (ENG.). 16p. (J). (gr. -1-3). pap. 6.99 *(978-0-06-187328-7(4),* HarperFestival) HarperCollins Pubs.

—A Flutter of Butterflies. O'Connor, Jane. 2010. (Fancy Nancy Ser.). (ENG.). 12p. (J). (gr. -1-2). pap. 6.99 *(978-0-06-170387-4(7),* HarperFestival) HarperCollins Pubs.

—Halloween... or Bust! O'Connor, Jane. 2009. (Fancy Nancy Ser.). (ENG.). 24p. (J). (gr. -1-3). pap. 4.99 *(978-0-06-123595-5(4),* HarperFestival) HarperCollins Pubs.

—Heart to Heart. O'Connor, Jane. 2009. (Fancy Nancy Ser.). (ENG.). 24p. (J). (gr. -1-3). pap. 4.99 *(978-0-06-123596-2(2),* HarperFestival) HarperCollins Pubs.

Glasser, Robin Preiss & Enik, Ted. The Dazzling Book Report. O'Connor, Jane. 2009. (I Can Read Book 1 Ser.). (ENG.). 32p. (J). (gr. -1-3). pap. 3.99 *(978-0-06-170368-3(0))* HarperCollins Pubs.

—Fancy Nancy: Poison Ivy Expert. O'Connor, Jane. 2008. (I Can Read Book 1 Ser.). (ENG.). 32p. (J). (gr. -1-3). 16.99 *(978-0-06-123614-3(4));* pap. 3.99 *(978-0-06-123613-6(6))* HarperCollins Pubs.

—Fancy Nancy: Poison Ivy Expert. O'Connor, Jane. ed. 2008. (Fancy Nancy: I Can Read! Ser.). 32p. lib. bdg. 13.55 *(978-1-4364-5050-8(0),* Turtleback) Turtleback Bks.

—Fancy Nancy: The Dazzling Book Report. O'Connor, Jane. 2009. (I Can Read Book 1 Ser.). (ENG.). 32p. (J). (gr. -1-3). 16.99 *(978-0-06-170369-0(9))* HarperCollins Pubs.

—Fancy Nancy: The Dazzling Book Report. O'Connor, Jane. 2009. (Fancy Nancy Ser.). 32p. lib. bdg. 14.00 *(978-1-60686-531-6(5))* Perfection Learning Corp.

—Fancy Nancy: The Show Must Go On. O'Connor, Jane. 2009. (I Can Read Book 1 Ser.). (ENG.). 32p. (J). (gr. -1-3). 16.99 *(978-0-06-170373-7(7))* HarperCollins Pubs.

—Fancy Nancy & the Delectable Cupcakes. O'Connor, Jane. 2010. (I Can Read Book 1 Ser.). (ENG.). 32p. (J). (gr. -1-3). 16.99 *(978-0-06-188269-2(0));* pap. 3.99 *(978-0-06-188268-5(2))* HarperCollins Pubs.

—Fancy Nancy & the Too-Loose Tooth. O'Connor, Jane. 2012. (I Can Read Book 1 Ser.). (ENG.). 32p. (J). (gr. -1-3). 16.99 *(978-0-06-208301-2(5));* pap. 3.99 *(978-0-06-208302-9(3))* HarperCollins Pubs.

—Fancy Nancy Sees Stars. O'Connor, Jane. 2008. (I Can Read Book 1 Ser.). (ENG.). 32p. (J). (gr. -1-3). 16.99 *(978-0-06-123612-9(8));* pap. 3.99 *(978-0-06-123611-2(X))* HarperCollins Pubs.

—Fancy Nancy Sees Stars. O'Connor, Jane. 2008. (Fancy Nancy Ser.). 32p. (J). (gr. -1-3). 12.90 *(978-1-4178-2874-6(9),* Turtleback) Turtleback Bks.

—Spectacular Spectacles. O'Connor, Jane. 2010. (I Can Read Book 1 Ser.). (ENG.). 32p. (J). (gr. -1-3). 16.99 *(978-0-06-188263-0(1))* HarperCollins Pubs.

—Spectacular Spectacles, Level 1. O'Connor, Jane. 2010. (I Can Read Book 1 Ser.). (ENG.). 32p. (J). (gr. -1-3). pap. 3.99 *(978-0-06-188264-7(X))* HarperCollins Pubs.

—The 100th Day of School. O'Connor, Jane. 2009. (I Can Read Book 1 Ser.). (ENG.). 32p. (J). (gr. -1-3). 16.99 *(978-0-06-170375-1(3));* pap. 3.99 *(978-0-06-170374-4(5))* HarperCollins Pubs.

Glasser, Robin Preiss & Goode, Diane. President Pennybaker. Feiffer, Kate. 2008. (ENG.). 32p. (J). (gr. -1-3). 16.99 *(978-1-4169-1354-2(8),* Simon & Schuster/Paula Wiseman Bks.) Simon & Schuster/Paula Wiseman Bks.

Glasser, Robin Preiss & Levin, Kate. Fancy Nancy's Gloriously Gigantic Sticker-Tivity Book. O'Connor, Jane. 2010. (Fancy Nancy Ser.). (ENG.). 100p. (J). (gr. -1-2). pap. 12.99 *(978-0-06-197931-6(7),* HarperFestival) HarperCollins Pubs.

Glasser, Robin Preiss, jt. illus. see Bracken, Carolyn.

Glasser, Robin Preiss, jt. illus. see Enik, Ted.

Glastetter, KC & Hollman, Jeremie, photos by. Yellowstone Natl Park Abc Adv. 2010. 64p. (J). pap. 12.00 *(978-0-87842-572-3(1))* Mountain Pr. Publishing Co., Inc.

Glazier, Garth, jt. illus. see Zapater Oliva, Carlos.

Glazunova, Nadezda. The Wonderful Life of Russia's Saint Sergius of Radonezh. Currier, Alvin Alexsi. 2003. 40p. (J). (gr. 3-7). 17.95 *(978-1-888212-24-2(1),* 005131) Conciliar Pr.

Gleason, Anita. Cumberland Island A to Z, a Scrapbook Journal. Barry, Maureen. 2010. (ENG.). 64p. pap. 13.00 *(978-1-4538-6173-8(4))* CreateSpace Independent Publishing Platform.

Gleeson, J. M. & Bransom, Paul. Just So Stories. Kipling, Rudyard. 2009. 208p. pap. 9.95 *(978-1-59915-172-4(3))* Yesterday's Classics.

Gleeson, Joseph M. Just So Stories. 2013. 250p. pap. *(978-1-909302-29-7(5))* Abela Publishing.

Gleich, Jacky. Is Grandpa Wearing a Suit? Fried, Amelie. 2007. (ENG.). 32p. (J). (gr. k-2). 16.95 *(978-0-9787550-4-1(9))* Heryin Publishing Corp.

—Martes Peludo. Pez, Alberto. (SPA.). (J). 8.95 *(978-958-04-5092-4(7))* Norma S.A. COL. Dist: Distribuidora Norma, Inc.

—La Pequena Nina Grande. Orlev, Uri. (Buenas Noches Ser.). (SPA.). (J). 8.95 *(978-958-04-4902-7(3))* Norma S.A. COL. Dist: Distribuidora Norma, Inc.

Glenn, Melissa. Lucky Dog. Ezpeleta, Laurie. 2011. (ENG.). 174p. pap. 8.99 *(978-1-4565-8917-2(2))* CreateSpace Independent Publishing Platform.

Glennon, Michelle. Duncan the Circus Dinosaur. Glennon, Michelle. 2008. 21p. (J). 16.95 *(978-0-9796625-5-3(9))* GDG Publishing.

—My Big Green Teacher: Don't Rock the Boat: Saving Our Oceans. Glennon, Michelle. 2008. 32p. (J). 19.95 *(978-0-9796625-2-2(4))* GDG Publishing.

—My Big Green Teacher: Please Turn off the Lights. Glennon, Michelle. 2008. (ENG.). 32p. (J). 19.95 *(978-0-9796625-3-9(2))* GDG Publishing.

—My Big Green Teacher: Seven Generations from Now. Glennon, Michelle. 2008. (J). 19.95 *(978-0-9797952-1-3(4))* GDG Publishing.

—My Big Green Teacher: Take a Deep Breath: Saving Our Rainforests. Glennon, Michelle. 2008. (ENG.). 32p. (J). 19.95 *(978-0-9797952-0-6(6))* GDG Publishing.

—My Big Green Teacher: Taking the Green Road. Glennon, Michelle. 2008. 32p. (J). 19.95 *(978-0-9796625-7-7(5))* GDG Publishing.

—My Big Green Teacher: Recycling: It's Easy Being Green. Glennon, Michelle. 2007. 32p. (J). 19.95 *(978-0-9796625-6-0(7))* GDG Publishing.

Glick, Nathan. Southern Indian Myths & Legends. Brown, Virginia Pounds & Owens, Laurella, eds. 2014. (ENG.). (J). pap. 19.95 *(978-1-58838-253-5(2),* NewSouth Bks.) NewSouth, Inc.

Glick, Nathan H. The World of the Southern Indians: Tribes, Leaders, & Customs from Prehistoric Times to the Present. Brown, Virginia Pounds & Owens, Laurella. 2010. 176p. (J). 19.95 *(978-1-58838-252-8(4),* NewSouth Bks.) NewSouth, Inc.

Glick, Sharon. ¡Perros! ¡Perros! Guy, Ginger Foglesong & Guy, Ginger F. 2006. (ENG & SPA.). 32p. (J). (gr. -1-3). 16.99 *(978-0-06-083574-3(5),* Greenwillow Bks.) HarperCollins Pubs.

Glick, Shifra. Shikufitsky, Vol. 2. Glick, Shifra. 100p. (J). 19.99 *(978-1-58330-640-6(4))* Feldheim Pubs.

Glicksman, Caroline. Brilliant Billy's Big Book of Dinosaurs. Hutton, Simon. 2008. (ENG.). 80p. (J). (gr. 2-4). pap. 8.95 *(978-1-84270-569-8(5))* Andersen Pr. GBR. Dist: Independent Pubs. Group.

Glienke, Amelie. El Pequeno Vampiro. Sommer-Bodenburg, Angela. 2003. (SPA.). 192p. (J). (gr. 3-5). pap. 11.95 *(978-968-19-0673-3(X))* Santillana USA Publishing Co., Inc.

Gliori, Debi. Amazing Alphabets. Bruce, Lisa. 2003. 24p. (J). pap. 9.95 *(978-0-7112-2129-1(4),* Frances Lincoln) Quarto Publishing Group UK GBR. Dist: Perseus-PGW.

Gliori, Debi. Side by Side. Bright, Rachel. 2015. (ENG.). 32p. (J). (gr. -1-k). 17.99 ***(978-0-545-81326-6(3),*** Scholastic Pr.) Scholastic, Inc.

Gliori, Debi. Tell Me Something Happy Before I Go to Sleep. Dunbar, Joyce. 2013. (ENG.). 24p. (J). (— 1). bds. 11.99 *(978-0-547-94059-5(9))* Houghton Mifflin Harcourt Publishing Co.

Gliori, Debi. Muy Chiquitin. Gliori, Debi. Dunbar, Joyce. 2003.Tr. of Very Small. (SPA.). 32p. (J). (gr. k-2). *(978-84-480-1646-3(7),* TM30375) Timun Mas, Editorial S.A. ESP. Dist: Lectorum Pubns., Inc.

—Stormy Weather. Gliori, Debi. 2009. (ENG.). 32p. (J). (gr. -1-1). 15.99 *(978-0-8027-9419-2(X))* Walker & Co.

—The Trouble with Dragons. Gliori, Debi. 2008. (ENG.). 32p. (J). (gr. -1-1). 16.99 *(978-0-8027-9789-6(X))* Walker & Co.

—Witch Baby & Me on Stage. Gliori, Debi. Hurst, Kelly. 2011. (ENG.). 336p. (J). (gr. 2-4). pap. 7.99 *(978-0-552-55679-8(3))* Transworld Publishers Ltd. GBR. Dist: Independent Pubs. Group.

Gliori, Debi & Bloom, Clive. The Scariest Thing of All. Gliori, Debi. 2012. (ENG.). 32p. (J). (gr. -1-6). 16.99 *(978-0-8027-2391-8(8))* Walker & Co.

Glitschka, Von. Watch Me Go! 8 Amazing Moving Pictures! Young, Rebecca. 2009. (ENG.). 16p. (J). (gr. -1-k). 12.99 *(978-0-545-14699-9(2),* Cartwheel Bks.) Scholastic, Inc.

—Watch Me Hop! 8 Amazing Moving Pictures! Young, Rebecca. 2009. (ENG.). 16p. (J). (gr. -1-k). 12.99 *(978-0-545-14698-2(4),* Cartwheel Bks.) Scholastic, Inc.

Glon, Nancy. Silent Knife, Holy Knife. Magness, Robert. 2003. 345p. 10.00 *(978-0-9774577-0-0(2))* Magness, Robert Pubns., LLC.

Glover, Maria Robinson. Who Do I Want to Be? Contemporary Black Women from A to Z. Glover, Maria Robinson. 2006. (J). 16.95 *(978-0-9787940-0-2(1))* HotComb Pr.

Glover, Robert. A Boy Scout's Handbook of Madcap Tales. Nuttbucket, Oliver S., III. 2003. 48p. (YA). per. 7.95 *(978-0-9741310-0-9(8),* 0-9741310-0-8) Lost Scout Pr.

Glover, Sophie. The Queen's Beasts. Bristow, Sophie. Hiscocks, Dan, ed. 2013. (ENG.). 44p. (J). (gr. k-2). 15.99 *(978-1-903070-84-0(8))* Eye Bks. GBR. Dist: Independent Pubs. Group.

Glyn, Chris. Behind You! Glyn, Chris, tr. Morgan, Ruth. 2003. (ENG.). 48p. pap. 11.95 *(978-1-84323-269-8(3))* Beekman Bks., Inc.

Glynn, Chris. Byd Llawn Hud. Hopwood, Mererid et al. 2005. (WEL.). 32p. pap. 4.99 *(978-1-84323-342-8(8));* pap. 12.99 *(978-1-84323-343-5(6))* Gomer Pr. GBR. Dist: Gomer Pr.

—Dim Mwnci'n y Dosbarth. Lewis, Siân. 2005. (WEL.). 64p. pap. 4.99 *(978-1-84323-427-2(0))* Gomer Pr. GBR. Dist: Gomer Pr.

—One Busy Book. Kay, Francesca. 2004. (ENG.). 32p. pap. 12.95 *(978-1-84323-344-2(4))* Beekman Bks., Inc.

Gnoli, Domenico. Alberic the Wise & Other Journeys. Juster, Norton. 2010. (ENG.). 96p. (J). (gr. 3-7). 5.99 *(978-0-375-86699-9(X),* Yearling) Random Hse. Children's Bks.

Gobble, DeAnna Akers. Plumb Full of History: A Story of Abingdon, Virginia. Warmuth, Donna Akers. 2003. 64p. pap. 9.95 *(978-1-932158-78-6(2))* Ingalls Publishing Group, Inc.

Goble, Faith. Gander Press Review: Fall/Winter 2008. Goble, Faith, ed. Zimny, Stan, photos by. Goble, Brant, ed. 2008. (ENG.). pap. 8.95 *(978-0-9820991-0-0(X))* Loosey Goosey Pr.

Goble, Paul. Mystic Horse. Goble, Paul. 2003. (ENG.). 40p. (J). (gr. k-5). 17.99 *(978-0-06-029813-5(8))* HarperCollins Pubs.

—Song of Creation. Goble, Paul. 2004. 32p. (J). 16.99 *(978-0-8028-5271-7(8))* Eerdmans, William B. Publishing Co.

—Walking Along: Plains Indian Trickster Stories. Goble, Paul. 2011. (J). 19.95 *(978-0-9845041-5-2(X),* South Dakota State Historical Society Pr.) South Dakota State Historical Society Pr.

Goble, Warwick. The Water Babies: A Fairy Tale for a Land-Baby. Kingsley, Charles. 2006. (Dover Children's Classics Ser.). (ENG.). 160p. (J). (gr. 3-6). per. 14.95 *(978-0-486-45000-1(7))* Dover Pubns., Inc.

Godbey, Corey. Sammy & His Shepherd. Hunt, Susan. 2008. (J). *(978-1-56769-109-2(9))* Reformation Pubs.

Godbey, Cory. The Big God Story, 1 vol. Anthony, Michelle. ed. 2010. (ENG.). 36p. (J). 12.99 *(978-1-4347-6454-6(0))* Cook, David C.

—Cinderella. Candau, Brittany. 2015. (ENG.). 40p. (J). (gr. -1-k). 16.99 *(978-1-4847-2360-9(0))* Disney Pr.

—Jamie's Journey: The Savannah. Ebbers, Susan M. 2012. 38p. 17.99 *(978-0-9833971-8-2(X));* pap. 9.99 *(978-0-9833971-9-9(8))* Rowe Publishing and Design.

—That's Where God Is, 1 vol. Morrow, Daniel & Strobel Morrow, Alison. ed. 2010. (ENG.). 36p. (J). 12.99 *(978-1-4347-6434-8(6))* Cook, David C.

Godbout, Geneviève. Joseph Fipps. Robert, Nadine. 2014. (ENG.). 64p. (J). (gr. -1-2). 16.95 *(978-1-59270-117-9(5))* Enchanted Lion Bks., LLC.

—Kindergarten Luck. Borden, Louise. 2015. (ENG.). 32p. (J). (gr. -1-k). 16.99 *(978-1-4521-1394-4(7))* Chronicle Bks. LLC.

Goddard, Brenda & Haskett, Dan. Dora's Christmas Carol (Dora the Explorer) Golden Books. 2012. (Big Golden Book Ser.). (ENG.). 48p. (J). (gr. -1-2). 9.99 *(978-0-307-97592-8(4),* Golden Bks.) Random Hse. Children's Bks.

Goddard, Brenda & Haskett, Dan. Dragon in the School (Dora & Friends) Tillworth, Mary. 2015. (Little Golden Book Ser.). (ENG.). 24p. (J). (gr. -1-2). 4.99 ***(978-0-553-52089-7(X),*** Golden Bks.) Random Hse. Children's Bks.

Goddard, Brenda & Haskett, Dan. Grandma's House (Dora the Explorer) Golden Books Staff & Carbone, Courtney. 2013. (Little Golden Book Ser.). (ENG.). 24p. (J). (-k). 3.99 *(978-0-307-98105-9(3),* Golden Bks.) Random Hse. Children's Bks.

Godeassi, Anna. We Are Brothers. Oh, DaYun. 2015. (MySELF Bookshelf Ser.). (ENG.). 32p. (J). (gr. k-2). pap. 11.94 *(978-1-60357-692-5(4));* lib. bdg. 22.60 *(978-1-59953-657-6(9))* Norwood Hse. Pr.

Godfrey, Arthur Dwayne. Tongue Turning Tales for the Classroom. McCarroll, Barbara. 2008. 36p. pap. 24.95 *(978-1-60703-254-0(6))* America Star Bks.

Godi. Ducoboo: In the Corner! Zidrou. 2007. (ENG.). 48p. (J). (gr. 4-7). pap. 9.99 *(978-1-905460-26-7(0))* CineBook GBR. Dist: National Bk. Network.

—Ducoboo No. 3: Your Answers or Your Life! Zidrou. 2008. (ENG.). 48p. pap. 11.95 *(978-1-905460-28-1(7))* CineBook GBR. Dist: National Bk. Network.

Godi & Grobet, Veronique. Ducoboo: The Class Struggle. Zidrou. Spear, Luke, tr. from FRE. 2010. (ENG.). 46p. (J). (gr. 3-17). pap. 11.95 *(978-1-84918-031-3(8))* CineBook GBR. Dist: National Bk. Network.

Godkin, Celia. Jack: The Story of a Beaver, 1 vol. Woods, Shirley E. 2003. (ENG.). 32p. (J). pap. 7.95 *(978-1-55041-735-7(5)*, 1550417355) Fitzhenry & Whiteside, Ltd. CAN. Dist: Midpoint Trade Bks., Inc.

Godkin, Celia. Skydiver: Saving the Fastest Bird in the World. Godkin, Celia. 2014. (ENG.). 32p. (J). (gr. 1-3). 17.95 *(978-1-927485-61-3(4))* Pajama Pr. CAN. Dist: Ingram Pub. Services.

—When the Giant Stirred: Legend of a Volcanic Island, 1 vol. Godkin, Celia. 2005. (ENG.). 40p. (J). pap. 8.95 *(978-1-55041-965-8(X)*, 155041965X) Fitzhenry & Whiteside, Ltd. CAN. Dist: Midpoint Trade Bks., Inc.

—Wolf Island, 1 vol. Godkin, Celia. 2006. (ENG.). 32p. (J). (gr. 1-4). pap. 9.95 *(978-1-55455-008-1(4)*, 1554550084) Fitzhenry & Whiteside, Ltd. CAN. Dist: Midpoint Trade Bks., Inc.

Godkin, Celia. Amber: The Story of a Fox, 1 vol. Godkin, Celia, tr. Woods, Shirley E. 2005. (ENG.). 96p. pap. *(978-1-55041-810-1(6))* Fitzhenry & Whiteside, Ltd.

Godon, Ingrid. My Daddy Is a Giant: For Everyone Who Has the Best Daddy in the World. Norac, Carl. 2004. 32p. (J). (ENG & GLE.). pap. *(978-1-84444-719-0(7))*; (YOR & ENG.). pap. *(978-1-84444-379-6(5))*; (ENG & VIE.). pap. *(978-1-84444-378-9(7))*; (ENG & URD.). pap. *(978-1-84444-377-2(9))*; (ENG & TWI.). pap. *(978-1-84444-376-5(0))*; (ENG & TGL.). pap. *(978-1-84444-373-4(6))*; (SPA & ENG.). pap. *(978-1-84444-372-7(8))*; (SOM & ENG.). pap. *(978-1-84444-371-0(X))*; (ENG & SNA.). pap. *(978-1-84444-370-3(1))*; (ENG & RUS.). pap. *(978-1-84444-369-7(8))*; (ENG & PAN.). pap. *(978-1-84444-366-6(3))*; (ENG & KUR.). pap. *(978-1-84444-365-9(5))*; (ENG & JPN.). pap. *(978-1-84444-364-2(7))*; (ITA & ENG.). pap. *(978-1-84444-363-5(9))*; (FRE & ENG.). pap. *(978-1-84444-359-8(0))*; (ENG & HRV.). pap. *(978-1-84444-357-4(4))*; (ENG & CHI.). pap. *(978-1-84444-356-7(6))*; (ENG & CHI.). pap. *(978-1-84444-355-0(8))*; (ENG & BUL.). pap. *(978-1-84444-354-3(X))*; (ENG & BEN.). pap. *(978-1-84444-353-6(1))*; (ALB & ENG.). pap. *(978-1-84444-351-2(5))*; (ENG & KOR.). pap. *(978-1-84444-300-0(0))* Mantra Lingua.

—My Daddy Is a Giant: For Everyone Who Has the Best Daddy in the World. Norac, Carl. 2005. (ENG.). 32p. (J). pap. 14.95 *(978-1-4050-2168-5(3)*, Macmillan Children's Bks.) Pan Macmillan GBR. Dist: Trans-Atlantic Pubns., Inc.

—My Mummy Is Magic. Norac, Carl. ed. 2006. (ENG.). 32p. (J). (gr. 3-6). pap. 14.95 *(978-1-4050-9023-0(5)*, Macmillan) Pan Macmillan GBR. Dist: Trans-Atlantic Pubns., Inc.

—Something Big. Neeman, Sylvie. 2013. (ENG.). 40p. (J). (gr. -1-3). 16.95 *(978-1-59270-140-7(X))* Enchanted Lion Bks., LLC.

—What Shall We Do with the Boo Hoo Baby? Cowell, Cressida. 2004. (J). (SER & ENG.). 25p. *(978-1-85269-862-1(4))*; (GER & ENG.). 25p. *(978-1-85269-799-0(7))*; 25p. *(978-1-85269-795-2(4))*; (CZE & ENG.). 25p. *(978-1-85269-794-5(6))*; (ALB & ENG.). 25p. *(978-1-85269-790-7(3))*; 25p. *(978-1-85269-679-5(6))*; 25p. *(978-1-85269-276-6(6))*; 25p. *(978-1-85269-274-2(X))*; (TUR & ENG.). 25p. *(978-1-85269-273-5(1))*; 25p. *(978-1-85269-272-8(3))*; (ENG & SPA.). 25p. *(978-1-85269-271-1(5))*; (SOM & ENG.). 25p. *(978-1-85269-270-4(7))*; (ITA & ENG.). 25p. *(978-1-85269-256-8(1))*; 25p. *(978-1-85269-255-1(3))*; (POR & ENG.). 25p. *(978-1-85269-254-4(5))*; (POL & ENG.). 32p. pap. *(978-1-85269-683-2(4))*; (ENG & PAN.). 32p. pap. *(978-1-85269-258-2(8))*; (ENG & BEN.). 32p. pap. *(978-1-85269-792-1(X))*; (ENG & CHI.). 32p. pap. *(978-1-85269-793-8(8))*; (FRE & ENG.). 32p. pap. *(978-1-85269-796-9(2))*; (ENG & ARA.). 32p. pap. *(978-1-85269-791-4(1))* Mantra Lingua.

Goedde, Steve Diet, photos by. Steve Diet Goedde - Kumi Postcard Collection. 2008. (ENG., 8p. (YA). 10.00 *(978-1-890836-07-8(9))* Steve Diet Goedde.

—Steve Diet Goedde - Masuimi Max Postcard Collection. 2008. (ENG., 10p. (YA). 10.00 *(978-1-890836-00-9(1))* Steve Diet Goedde.

Goede, Irene. Creepy Crawlies. Post, Hans. 2006. (ENG.). 32p. (J). (gr. 4-8). 16.95 *(978-1-932425-65-9(9)*, Lemniscaat) Boyds Mills Pr.

—Sparrows. Post, Hans & Heij, Kees. 2008. (ENG.). 32p. (J). (gr. k-3). 16.95 *(978-1-59078-570-6(3)*, Lemniscaat) Boyds Mills Pr.

Goedeken, Kathy. Fire on Ice: Autobiography of a Champion Figure Skater. Cohen, Sasha & Maciel, Amanda. rev. ed. 2006. (ENG.). 224p. (J). (gr. 3-7). pap. 9.99 *(978-0-06-115385-3(0)*, Collins) HarperCollins Pubs.

—Sasha Cohen: Autobiography of a Champion Figure Skater. Cohen, Sasha. 2005. (ENG.). 192p. (J). (gr. 3-18). pap. 9.99 *(978-0-06-072489-4(7))* HarperCollins Pubs.

Goeke, Mark, photos by. The Path of the Pronghorn. Urbigkit, Cat. 2010. (ENG., 32p. (J). (gr. 2-4). 17.95 *(978-1-59078-756-4(0))* Boyds Mills Pr.

Goembel, Ponder. Castaway Cats. Wheeler, Lisa. 2006. (ENG.). 32p. (J). (gr. -1-2). 17.99 *(978-0-689-86232-8(6)*, Atheneum/Richard Jackson Bks.) Simon & Schuster Children's Publishing.

—Dinosnores. DiPucchio, Kelly. 2005. 32p. (J). (gr. -1 — 1). 17.99 *(978-0-06-051577-5(5))*; lib. bdg. 16.89 *(978-0-06-051578-2(3))* HarperCollins Pubs.

—Give Me Wings. Hopkins, Lee Bennett. 2010. (ENG.). 32p. (J). (gr. -1-3). 16.95 *(978-0-8234-2023-0(X))* Holiday Hse., Inc.

—Mr. Mosquito Put on His Tuxedo. Morrow, Barbara Olenyik. 2009. (ENG.). 32p. (J). (gr. -1-3). 16.95 *(978-0-8234-2072-8(8))* Holiday Hse., Inc.

—Old Cricket. Wheeler, Lisa. 2006. 28p. (gr. -1-1). 18.00 *(978-0-7569-6795-6(3))* Perfection Learning Corp.

—Old Cricket. Wheeler, Lisa. (ENG.). 32p. (J). (gr. -1-1). 2003. 17.99 *(978-0-689-84510-9(3)*, Atheneum/Richard Jackson Bks.); 2006. reprint ed. 7.99 *(978-1-4169-1855-4(8)*, Atheneum Bks. for Young Readers) Simon & Schuster Children's Publishing.

—Swamp Song, 0 vols. Ketteman, Helen. 2009. (ENG.). 32p. (J). (gr. k-4). 17.99 *(978-0-7614-5563-9(9)*, 9780761455639, Amazon Children's Publishing) Amazon Publishing.

Goembel, Ponder. Animal Fair, 0 vols. Goembel, Ponder. (ENG.). 24p. (J). (gr. -1 — 1). 2012. bds. 7.99 *(978-0-7614-6205-7(8)*, 9780761462057); 2010. 12.99 *(978-0-7614-5642-1(2)*, 9780761456421) Amazon Publishing. (Amazon Children's Publishing).

Goettling, Nickalas, jt. illus. see Dabney, Undra.

Goetzl, Robert F. Many Nations. Bruchac, Joseph. 2004. (ENG.). 32p. (J). (gr. 5-9). pap. 6.99 *(978-0-439-63590-5(X))* Scholastic, Inc.

Goff, Brian. The Dreadful Truth: Building the Railway. Staunton, Ted. 2005. (Dreadful Truth Ser.). (ENG.). 80p. (J). (gr. 3-8). *(978-0-88780-690-2(2))* Formac Publishing Co., Ltd.

Goffe, Toni. Big or Little? Stinson, Kathy. 2nd rev. ed. 2009. (ENG.). 32p. (J). (gr. -1-1). 19.95 *(978-1-55451-169-3(0)*, 9781554511693); pap. 6.95 *(978-1-55451-168-6(2)*, 9781554511686) Annick Pr., Ltd. CAN. Dist: Firefly Bks., Ltd.

—The Jesus Book: 40 Bible Stories. Neff, LaVonne. 2004. (Life of Christ for Children Ser.). 84p. (gr. -1-k). 9.95 *(978-0-8294-1373-1(1))* Loyola Pr.

—Knights & Castles. Hindley, Judy. Wheatley, Abigail, ed. 2006. (Time Traveler Ser.). 32p. (J). (gr. 3). lib. bdg. 14.95 *(978-1-58086-554-8(2))* EDC Publishing.

—The Legend of Lightning Larry. Shepard, Aaron. 2005. 48p. (J). pap. 10.00 *(978-0-938497-28-8(6)*, Skyhook Pr.) Shepard Pubns.

—Teach Me to Love. Kid, Penelope. 2004. (Teach Me Ser.). 24p. (gr. -1-2). 6.95 *(978-0-8294-1369-4(3))* Loyola Pr.

—Teach Me to Pray. Kid, Penelope. 2004. (Teach Me Ser.). 24p. (gr. -1-2). 6.95 *(978-0-8294-1368-7(5))* Loyola Pr.

—Where Did Dinosaurs Go? Unwin, Mike. Evans, Cheryl, ed. 2006. (Usborne Starting Point Science Ser.). 24p. (J). (gr. 2). lib. bdg. 12.99 *(978-1-58086-937-9(8)*, Usborne) EDC Publishing.

Gogolewski, Kathe. Tato. 2008. (J). *(978-0-9800064-2-1(2))* Red Engine Pr.

Goh, Tai Hwa. Hello Baldwin! Aryal, Aimee. 2004. 24p. (J). 19.95 *(978-1-932888-13-3(6))* Mascot Bks., Inc.

—Hello, Testudo! Aryal, Aimee. 2004. 24p. (J). 18.95 *(978-0-9743442-1-8(4))* Mascot Bks., Inc.

Gohda, Hiroaki, jt. illus. see Uon, Taraku.

Goins, Heather Lea. Ivy Tales: The First Irish Fairy. Goodnight, Lora. 2012. 28p. pap. 24.95 *(978-1-4626-9484-6(5))* America Star Bks.

Golant, Evgenia. Play Checkers with Me. Golant, Galina & Grant, Lisa. 2003. 32p. (J). pap. 6.95 *(978-1-932133-01-1(1))* Writers' Collective, The.

Gold, Ethel. Outdoor Things. (Picture Bks.: No. S8817-3). 28p. (J). (gr. -1). pap. 3.95 *(978-0-7214-5142-8(X)*, Dutton Juvenile) Penguin Publishing Group.

—Things That Go. (Picture Bks.: No. S8817-1). 28p. (J). (gr. -1). pap. 3.95 *(978-0-7214-5140-4(3)*, Dutton Juvenile) Penguin Publishing Group.

Gold, Michael, photos by. Junk Food. Cobb, Vicki. 2005. (Where's the Science Here? Ser.). (ENG., 48p. (gr. 3-5). 23.93 *(978-0-7613-2773-8(8)*, Millbrook Pr.) Lerner Publishing Group.

—On Stage. Cobb, Vicki. 2005. (Where's the Science Here? Ser.). (ENG., 48p. (gr. 3-5). lib. bdg. 23.93 *(978-0-7613-2774-5(6)*, Millbrook Pr.) Lerner Publishing Group.

Goldacker, "Java John". Bud the Spud. Tritt, Adam Byrn. 2012. (ENG.). 52p. (J). (gr. 3-7). 16.95 *(978-1-60419-062-5(0))* Axios Pr.

Goldberg, Barry. Bubble Blowers, Beware! 2004. (SpongeBob SquarePants Ser.). (ENG.). 24p. (J). pap. 3.99 *(978-0-689-86862-7(6)*, Simon Spotlight/Nickelodeon) Simon Spotlight/Nickelodeon.

—Chew on This! Collins, Terry. 2003. (Adventures of Jimmy Neutron Boy Genius Ser.). 24p. (J). (gr. -1-3). lib. bdg. 11.25 *(978-0-613-58145-5(8)*, Turtleback) Turtleback Bks.

—Halloween Howl. Herman, Gail & Bridwell, Norman. 2004. (Clifford's Puppy Days Ser.). (ENG.). 24p. (J). (gr. -1-k). 3.99 *(978-0-439-58353-4(5)*, Cartwheel Bks.) Scholastic, Inc.

—The Little Blue Easter Egg. Fisch, Sarah & Bridwell, Norman. 2006. (Clifford's Puppy Days Ser.). 23p. (J). *(978-0-439-81617-5(3))* Scholastic, Inc.

—Watch Me Draw SpongeBob's Underwater Escapades. 2012. (J). *(978-1-936309-75-7(0))* Quarto Publishing Group USA.

Goldberg, Stan. Bed Bugged. Salicrup, Jim & Gladir, George. 2012. (Three Stooges Ser.). (ENG.). 64p. (J). (gr. 3-7). pap. 6.99 *(978-1-59707-315-8(6))* Papercutz.

—Ebenezer Stooge. Gladir, George et al. 2012. (Three Stooges Ser.: 2). (ENG.). 64p. (J). (gr. 3-7). 10.99 *(978-1-59707-337-0(7))* Papercutz.

—Nancy Drew & the Clue Crew - Enter the Dragon Mystery. Kinney, Sarah. 2013. (Nancy Drew & the Clue Crew Ser.: 3). (ENG.). 64p. (J). (gr. k-3). pap. 7.99 *(978-1-59707-437-7(3))* Papercutz.

—Nancy Drew & the Clue Crew #3: Enter the Dragon Mystery. Kinney, Sarah. 2013. (Nancy Drew & the Clue Crew Ser.: 3). (ENG.). 64p. (J). (gr. k-3). 11.99 *(978-1-59707-438-4(1))* Papercutz.

—Secret Sand Sleuths. Kinney, Sarah & Petrucha, Stefan. 2013. (Nancy Drew & the Clue Crew Ser.: 2). (ENG.). 64p. (J). (gr. k-3). pap. 7.99 *(978-1-59707-376-9(8))*; Bk. 2. 11.99 *(978-1-59707-377-6(6))* Papercutz.

—Small Volcanoes. Petrucha, Stefan & Kinney, Sarah. 2012. (Nancy Drew & the Clue Crew Ser.: 1). (ENG.). 64p. (J). (gr. 3-7). 10.99 *(978-1-59707-355-4(5))* Papercutz.

—The Three Stooges. Gladir, George et al. 2012. (Three Stooges Ser.: 2). (ENG.). 64p. (J). (gr. 3-7). pap. 6.99 *(978-1-59707-336-3(9))* Papercutz.

—Three Stooges Graphic Novels #1: Bed Bugged. Salicrup, Jim & Gladir, George. 2012. (Three Stooges Ser.). (ENG.). 64p. (J). (gr. 3-7). 10.99 *(978-1-59707-316-5(4))* Papercutz.

Goldberg, Stan. Small Volcanoes, No. 1. Goldberg, Stan. Petrucha, Stefan & Kinney, Sarah. 2012. (Nancy Drew & the Clue Crew Ser.: 1). (ENG.). 64p. (J). (gr. 3-7). pap. 6.99 *(978-1-59707-354-7(7))* Papercutz.

Goldblatt, Rob. The Boy Who Didn't Want to Be Sad. 2004. 32p. (J). 14.95 *(978-1-59147-134-9(6)*, Magination Pr.) American Psychological Assn.

Goldeen, Bill, photos by. Alef-Bet Yoga for Kids. Goldeen, Bill. Goldeen, Ruth. 2009. (Israel Ser.). (ENG., 32p. (J). (gr. -1-2). 15.95 *(978-0-8225-8756-9(4))*; pap. 7.95 *(978-0-7613-4506-0(X))* Lerner Publishing Group. (Kar-Ben Publishing).

Golden Books. Barbie 9 Favorite Fairy Tales (Barbie) 2013. (Little Golden Book Treasury Ser.). (ENG.). 224p. (J). (-k). 10.99 *(978-0-449-81861-9(6)*, Golden Bks.) Random Hse. Children's Bks.

—Barbie Fun & Games (Barbie) Man-Kong, Mary. 2012. (Giant Coloring Book Ser.). (ENG.). 40p. (J). (gr. -1-2). pap. 9.99 *(978-0-307-97678-9(5)*, Golden Bks.) Random Hse. Children's Bks.

—Barbie in the Pink Shoes. Tillworth, Mary. 2013. (Little Golden Book Ser.). (ENG.). 24p. (J). (-k). 3.99 *(978-0-307-98108-0(8)*, Golden Bks.) Random Hse. Children's Bks.

Golden Books. The Big Book of the DC Super Friends. Berrios, Frank. 2015. (Big Golden Book Ser.). (ENG.). 48p. (J). (gr. k-4). 9.99 ***(978-0-553-50773-7(7)***, Golden Bks.) Random Hse. Children's Bks.

Golden Books. Blue Mountain Mystery. Awdry, W. 2012. (Little Golden Book Ser.). (ENG.). 24p. (J). (gr. k-k). 3.99 *(978-0-307-97590-4(8)*, Golden Bks.) Random Hse. Children's Bks.

—Coloring Fun with Pocoyo (Pocoyo) Depken, Kristen L. 2013. (Super Color with Stickers Ser.). (ENG.). 96p. (J). (gr. -1-2). pap. 3.99 *(978-0-307-98162-2(2)*, Golden Bks.) Random Hse. Children's Bks.

—Cranky's Surprise (Thomas & Friends) Awdry, Wilbert V. 2012. (Coloring Book Ser.). (ENG.). 64p. (J). (gr. k-k). pap. 5.99 *(978-0-307-93133-7(1)*, Golden Bks.) Random Hse. Children's Bks.

—DC Super Friends Little Golden Book Favorites (DC Super Friends) 2013. (Little Golden Book Favorites Ser.). (ENG.). 80p. (J). (-k). 6.99 *(978-0-449-81621-9(4)*, Golden Bks.) Random Hse. Children's Bks.

—DC Super Friends Little Golden Book Library (DC Super Friends), 5 vols. 2015. (ENG.). 120p. (J). (-k). 19.95 *(978-0-553-50897-0(0)*, Golden Bks.) Random Hse. Children's Bks.

—Disney Classics Little Golden Book Library, 5 vols. 2013. (ENG.). 24p. (J). (-k). 19.95 *(978-0-7364-3149-1(7)*, Golden/Disney) Random Hse. Children's Bks.

—Disney Junior Little Golden Book Library (Disney Junior), 5 vols. 2013. (ENG.). 120p. (J). (-k). 19.95 *(978-0-7364-3076-0(8)*, Golden/Disney) Random Hse. Children's Bks.

—Dream Dancer. Man-Kong, Mary. 2013. (Color Plus Chunky Crayons Ser.). (ENG.). 48p. (J). (gr. -1-2). pap. 3.99 *(978-0-307-98103-5(7)*, Golden Bks.) Random Hse. Children's Bks.

—Easter Surprises! Man-Kong, Mary. 2015. (Deluxe Coloring Book Ser.). (ENG.). 96p. (J). (gr. -1-2). pap. 3.99 *(978-0-553-50820-8(2)*, Golden Bks.) Random Hse. Children's Bks.

—Frosty the Snowman. Muldrow, Diane. 2013. (Big Golden Board Book Ser.). (ENG.). 22p. (J). (-k). bds. 10.99 *(978-0-385-37870-3(X)*, Golden Bks.) Random Hse. Children's Bks.

—Full Steam Ahead! Awdry, Wilbert V. 2012. (Color Plus Tattoos Ser.). (ENG.). 48p. (J). (gr. -1-2). pap. 3.99 *(978-0-307-93120-7(X)*, Golden Bks.) Random Hse. Children's Bks.

—Happy, Jolly Fun! (Frosty the Snowman) Man-Kong, Mary. 2014. (Color Plus Chunky Crayons Ser.). (ENG.). 48p. (J). (gr. -1-2). pap. 3.99 *(978-0-385-38723-1(7)*, Golden Bks.) Random Hse. Children's Bks.

—Heart of a Hero (DC Super Friends) Carbone, Courtney. 2014. (Color Plus Card Stock Ser.). (ENG.). 48p. (J). (gr. -1-2). pap. 3.99 *(978-0-553-50886-4(5)*, Golden Bks.) Random Hse. Children's Bks.

—Here Come the Heroes! Wrecks, Billy. 2013. (Jumbo Coloring Book Ser.). (ENG.). 224p. (J). (gr. -1-2). pap. 5.99 *(978-0-449-81610-3(9)*, Golden Bks.) Random Hse. Children's Bks.

—Julius Jr. Story Collection. Carbone, Courtney. 2014. (Big Golden Book Ser.). (ENG.). 48p. (J). (gr. -1-2). 9.99 *(978-0-553-49859-2(2)*, Golden Bks.) Random Hse. Children's Bks.

—Julius Jr. Super Deluxe Pictureback (Julius Jr.) Depken, Kristen L. 2014. (Super Deluxe Pictureback Ser.). (ENG.). 24p. (J). (gr. -1-2). 5.99 *(978-0-553-49863-9(0)*, Random Hse. Bks. for Young Readers) Random Hse. Children's Bks.

—Mulan (Disney Princess) Cardona, Jose. 2013. (Little Golden Book Ser.). (ENG.). 24p. (J). (-k). 3.99 *(978-0-7364-3053-1(9)*, Golden/Disney) Random Hse. Children's Bks.

—Nickelodeon Little Golden Book Collection (Nickelodeon) Reisner, Molly et al. 2012. (Little Golden Book Treasury Ser.). (ENG.). 224p. (J). (gr. -1-2). 10.99 *(978-0-375-85120-9(8)*, Golden Bks.) Random Hse. Children's Bks.

—Nickelodeon Little Golden Book Library (Nickelodeon), 5 vols. 2015. (ENG.). 120p. (J). (-k). 19.95 *(978-0-553-50797-3(4)*, Golden Bks.) Random Hse. Children's Bks.

—Nine Classic Tales. 2014. (Little Golden Book Treasury Ser.). (ENG.). 224p. (J). (-k). 11.99 *(978-0-7364-3260-3(4)*, Golden/Disney) Random Hse. Children's Bks.

—Pirate Puzzles! (SpongeBob SquarePants) Berrios, Frank. 2012. (Giant Coloring Book Ser.). (ENG.). 40p. (J). (gr. -1-2). pap. 9.99 *(978-0-307-97612-3(2)*, Golden Bks.) Random Hse. Children's Bks.

—Power-Packed! (DC Super Friends) Carbone, Courtney. 2014. (Deluxe Stickerific Ser.). (ENG.). 64p. (J). (gr. -1-2). pap. 5.99 *(978-0-385-38720-0(2)*, Golden Bks.) Random Hse. Children's Bks.

—Princess & the Popstar. Depken, Kristen L. 2012. (Big Golden Book Ser.). (ENG.). 48p. (J). (gr. -1-2). 9.99 *(978-0-307-97676-5(9)*, Golden Bks.) Random Hse. Children's Bks.

—Purr-Fect Valentine! (Barbie) Man-Kong, Mary. 2012. (Deluxe Paint Box Book Ser.). (ENG.). 128p. (J). (gr. -1-2). pap. 7.99 *(978-0-307-98210-0(6)*, Golden Bks.) Random Hse. Children's Bks.

—Rock & Rule. Tillworth, Mary. 2012. (Color Plus Chunky Crayons Ser.). (ENG.). 48p. (J). (gr. -1-2). pap. 3.99 *(978-0-307-97620-8(3)*, Golden Bks.) Random Hse. Children's Bks.

—Snowman Surprise (Disney Junior: Doc Mcstuffins) Posner-Sanchez, Andrea. 2013. (Little Golden Book Ser.). (ENG.). 24p. (J). (-k). 4.99 *(978-0-7364-3142-2(X)*, Golden/Disney) Random Hse. Children's Bks.

—To the Rescue! (DC Super Friends) Wrecks, Billy. 2012. (3-D Coloring Book Ser.). (ENG.). 32p. (J). (gr. -1-2). pap. 4.99 *(978-0-307-97628-4(9)*, Golden Bks.) Random Hse. Children's Bks.

—Unstoppable! (DC Super Friends) Wrecks, Billy. 2012. (Giant Coloring Book Ser.). (ENG.). 40p. (J). (gr. -1-2). pap. 9.99 *(978-0-307-93049-1(1)*, Golden Bks.) Random Hse. Children's Bks.

—A Very Busy Coloring Book. Miller, Mona. 2013. (Jumbo Coloring Book Ser.). (ENG.). 224p. (J). (gr. -1-2). pap. 5.99 *(978-0-449-81609-7(5)*, Golden Bks.) Random Hse. Children's Bks.

Golden Books. The Art of the Ninja (Teenage Mutant Ninja Turtles) Golden Books. 2014. (Doodle Book Ser.). (ENG.). 128p. (J). (gr. -1-2). pap. 5.99 *(978-0-385-37851-2(3)*, Golden Bks.) Random Hse. Children's Bks.

—Barbie & Ken Vintage Paper Dolls. Golden Books. 50th anniv. ed. 2012. (Paper Doll Book Ser.). (ENG.). 16p. (J). (gr. -1-2). pap. 4.99 *(978-0-307-98091-5(X)*, Golden Bks.) Random Hse. Children's Bks.

Golden Books. The Big Book of Blaze & the Monster Machines. Golden Books. 2015. (Big Golden Book Ser.). (ENG.). 32p. (J). (gr. -1-2). 9.99 ***(978-0-553-52458-1(5)***, Golden Bks.) Random Hse. Children's Bks.

Golden Books. The Big Book of Ninja Turtles (Teenage Mutant Ninja Turtles) Golden Books. 2014. (Big Golden Book Ser.). (ENG.). 48p. (J). (gr. -1-2). 9.99 *(978-0-553-50769-0(9)*, Golden Bks.) Random Hse. Children's Bks.

—The Big Book of Paw Patrol (Paw Patrol) Golden Books. 2014. (Big Golden Book Ser.). (ENG.). 32p. (J). (gr. -1-2). 9.99 *(978-0-553-51276-2(5)*, Golden Bks.) Random Hse. Children's Bks.

—Big City Friends! (Dora & Friends) Golden Books. 2015. (Big Coloring Book Ser.). (ENG.). 48p. (J). (gr. -1-2). pap. 6.99 *(978-0-553-49767-0(7)*, Golden Bks.) Random Hse. Children's Bks.

—Boo Goes There? (SpongeBob SquarePants) Golden Books. 2012. (Glow-In-the-Dark Sticker Book Ser.). (ENG.). 48p. (J). (gr. -1-2). pap. 3.99 *(978-0-307-93102-3(1)*, Golden Bks.) Random Hse. Children's Bks.

—Bubble Bonanza! (Bubble Guppies) Golden Books. 2013. (Color & Paint Plus Stickers Ser.). (ENG.). 128p. (J). (gr. -1-2). pap. 9.99 *(978-0-449-81948-7(5)*, Golden Bks.) Random Hse. Children's Bks.

—Bubble Buddies! (Bubble Guppies) Golden Books. 2014. (Deluxe Stickerific Ser.). (ENG.). 64p. (J). (gr. -1-2). pap. 5.99 *(978-0-385-38434-6(3)*, Golden Bks.) Random Hse. Children's Bks.

Golden Books. Bubble Guppies Little Golden Book Favorites (Bubble Guppies) Golden Books. 2015. (Little Golden Book Favorites Ser.). (ENG.). 80p. (J). (gr. -1-2). 7.99 ***(978-0-553-52115-3(2)***, Golden Bks.) Random Hse. Children's Bks.

Golden Books. Bubble Guppies Magnet Book (Bubble Guppies) Golden Books. 2014. (Magnetic Play Book Ser.). (ENG.). 8p. (J). (— 1). bds. 8.99 *(978-0-385-37527-6(1)*, Golden Bks.) Random Hse. Children's Bks.

—Clash with the Kraang! (Teenage Mutant Ninja Turtles) Golden Books. 2013. (Deluxe Reusable Sticker Book Ser.). (ENG.). 24p. (J). (gr. -1-2). pap. 6.99 *(978-0-449-81883-1(7)*, Golden Bks.) Random Hse. Children's Bks.

—Class Pictures! (Bubble Guppies) Golden Books. 2012. (Big Coloring Book Ser.). (ENG.). 48p. (J). (gr. -1-2). pap. 6.99 *(978-0-307-93137-5(4)*, Golden Bks.) Random Hse. Children's Bks.

—Creature Creations! (Teenage Mutant Ninja Turtles) Golden Books. 2014. (Rub-On Patterns C&a Ser.). (ENG.). 128p. (J). (gr. -1-2). pap. 8.99 *(978-0-449-81886-2(1)*, Golden Bks.) Random Hse. Children's Bks.

—Dora's Sticker Adventure! (Dora the Explorer) Golden Books. 2012. (Deluxe Stickerific Ser.). (ENG.). 64p. (J). (gr. -1-2). pap. 5.99 *(978-0-307-97669-7(6)*, Golden Bks.) Random Hse. Children's Bks.

—Extreme Team! (SpongeBob SquarePants) Golden Books. 2013. (Deluxe Coloring Book Ser.). (ENG.). 96p. (J). (gr. k-3). pap. 3.99 *(978-0-307-98227-8(0)*, Golden Bks.) Random Hse. Children's Bks.

—Fantastic Fairy Fan Book. Golden Books. 2012. (Full-Color Activity Book with Stickers Ser.). (ENG.). 48p. (J). (gr. 2-5). pap. 4.99 *(978-0-307-97996-4(2)*, Golden Bks.) Random Hse. Children's Bks.
—Fearless Firemoose! (Rocky & Bullwinkle) Golden Books. 2014. (Little Golden Book Ser.). (ENG.). 24p. (J). (-k). 3.99 *(978-0-385-37152-0(7)*, Golden Bks.) Random Hse. Children's Bks.
—Field Trip Time! (Bubble Guppies) Golden Books. 2013. (Deluxe Reusable Sticker Book Ser.). (ENG.). 24p. (J). (gr. -1-2). pap. 6.99 *(978-0-449-81884-8(5)*, Golden Bks.) Random Hse. Children's Bks.
Golden Books. Full Speed Ahead! (Blaze & the Monster Machines) Golden Books. 2015. (Color Plus Crayons & Sticker Ser.). (ENG.). 48p. (J). (gr. -1-2). pap. 4.99 ***(978-0-553-52455-0(0)***, Golden Bks.) Random Hse. Children's Bks.
—Giant Adventures. Golden Books. 2015. (Big Coloring Book Ser.). (ENG.). 48p. (J). (gr. -1-2). pap. 6.99 ***(978-0-553-52292-1(2)***, Golden Bks.) Random Hse. Children's Bks.
Golden Books. Guppy Tales (Bubble Guppies) Golden Books. 2012. (Deluxe Chunky Crayon Book Ser.). (ENG.). 128p. (J). (gr. -1-2). pap. 7.99 *(978-0-307-97670-3(X)*, Golden Bks.) Random Hse. Children's Bks.
—Here Comes Peter Cottontail. Golden Books. 2014. (Little Golden Book Ser.). (ENG.). 24p. (J). (-k). 3.99 *(978-0-385-37839-0(4)*, Golden Bks.) Random Hse. Children's Bks.
—Hooray for Dora! (Dora the Explorer) Golden Books. 2012. (Super Jumbo Coloring Book Ser.). (ENG.). 416p. (J). (gr. -1-2). pap. 10.99 *(978-0-307-93093-4(9)*, Golden Bks.) Random Hse. Children's Bks.
—Inventing Time! Golden Books. 2014. (Color & Paint Plus Stickers Ser.). (ENG.). 128p. (J). (gr. -1-2). pap. 9.99 *(978-0-553-49862-2(2)*, Golden Bks.) Random Hse. Children's Bks.
—It's Time for Christmas! (Bubble Guppies) Golden Books. 2014. (Big Coloring Book Ser.). (ENG.). 48p. (J). (gr. -1-2). pap. 6.99 *(978-0-385-38409-4(2)*, Golden Bks.) Random Hse. Children's Bks.
—Join the Team! (Team Umizoomi) Golden Books. 2012. (Big Coloring Book Ser.). (ENG.). 48p. (J). (gr. -1-2). pap. 6.99 *(978-0-307-93138-2(2)*, Golden Bks.) Random Hse. Children's Bks.
Golden Books. Jumbo Coloring Adventures! (Nickelodeon) Golden Books. 2015. (Super Jumbo Coloring Book Ser.). (ENG.). 416p. (J). (gr. -1-2). pap. 10.99 ***(978-0-553-52087-3(3)***, Golden Bks.) Random Hse. Children's Bks.
Golden Books. Jurassic Fun (Dinosaur Train) Golden Books. 2012. (3-D Coloring Book Ser.). (ENG.). 32p. (J). (gr. -1-2). pap. 4.99 *(978-0-307-93104-7(8)*, Golden Bks.) Random Hse. Children's Bks.
Golden Books. Just Yelp for Help! (PAW Patrol) Golden Books. 2015. (Giant Coloring Book Ser.). (ENG.). 40p. (J). (gr. -1-2). pap. 9.99 ***(978-0-553-53386-6(X)***, Golden Bks.) Random Hse. Children's Bks.
Golden Books. Let's Get Epic! (Teenage Mutant Ninja Turtles) Golden Books. 2014. (Big Coloring Book Ser.). (ENG.). 48p. (J). (gr. -1-2). pap. 6.99 *(978-0-385-37849-9(1)*, Golden Bks.) Random Hse. Children's Bks.
—Let's Go, Guppies! (Bubble Guppies) Golden Books. 2013. (Giant Coloring Book Ser.). (ENG.). 40p. (J). (gr. -1-2). pap. 9.99 *(978-0-385-37029-5(6)*, Golden Bks.) Random Hse. Children's Bks.
—Let's Make a Splash! (Bubble Guppies) Golden Books. 2014. (Jumbo Coloring Book Ser.). (ENG.). 224p. (J). (gr. -1-2). pap. 5.99 *(978-0-385-37437-8(2)*, Golden Bks.) Random Hse. Children's Bks.
—Make It Count! (Big Time Rush) Golden Books. 2013. (C & a Digest Ser.). (ENG.). 64p. (J). (gr. 2-5). 2.99 *(978-0-449-81854-1(3)*, Golden Bks.) Random Hse. Children's Bks.
—Mega-Mutations! (Teenage Mutant Ninja Turtles) Golden Books. 2014. (Jumbo Coloring Book Ser.). (ENG.). 224p. (J). (gr. -1-2). pap. 5.99 *(978-0-385-38504-6(8)*, Golden Bks.) Random Hse. Children's Bks.
—Mutants Rule! (Teenage Mutant Ninja Turtles) Golden Books. Berrios, Frank. 2013. (Color & Paint Plus Stickers Ser.). (ENG.). 128p. (J). (gr. -1-2). pap. 9.99 *(978-0-449-81952-4(3)*, Golden Bks.) Random Hse. Children's Bks.
Golden Books. No Job Is Too Big! (Paw Patrol) Golden Books. 2015. (Big Coloring Book Ser.). (ENG.). 48p. (J). (gr. -1-2). pap. 6.99 ***(978-0-553-52276-1(0)***, Golden Bks.) Random Hse. Children's Bks.
Golden Books. The Official Ninja Turtle Handbook (Teenage Mutant Ninja Turtles) Golden Books. 2014. (ENG.). 64p. (J). (gr. 2-4). pap. 6.99 *(978-0-553-50768-3(0)*, Random Hse. Bks. for Young Readers) Random Hse. Children's Bks.
—Once upon a Princess (Dora the Explorer) Golden Books. 2013. (Color & Paint Plus Stickers Ser.). (ENG.). 128p. (J). (gr. -1-2). pap. 9.99 *(978-0-449-81949-4(3)*, Golden Bks.) Random Hse. Children's Bks.
—Painting Pals (Nickelodeon) Golden Books. 2012. (Deluxe Paint Box Book Ser.). (ENG.). 128p. (J). (gr. -1-2). pap. 7.99 *(978-0-307-93136-8(6)*, Golden Bks.) Random Hse. Children's Bks.
—Picture This (Pocoyo) Golden Books. 2012. (Color Plus Chunky Crayons Ser.). (ENG.). 48p. (J). (gr. -1-2). pap. 3.99 *(978-0-307-98035-9(9)*, Golden Bks.) Random Hse. Children's Bks.
Golden Books. Plank-Ton's Big Plan! Golden Books. movie tie-in ed. 2015. (Big Coloring Book Ser.). (ENG.). 48p. (J). (gr. -1-2). pap. 6.99 ***(978-0-553-50827-7(X)***, Golden Bks.) Random Hse. Children's Bks.
Golden Books. Princesses, Mermaids, Fairies & More! Golden Books. 2012. (Super Jumbo Coloring Book Ser.). (ENG.). 416p. (J). (gr. -1-2). pap. 10.99 *(978-0-307-97673-4(4)*, Golden Bks.) Random Hse. Children's Bks.
—Puppy Love! (Bubble Guppies) Golden Books. 2012. (Full-Color Activity Book with Stickers Ser.). (ENG.). 32p. (J). (gr. -1-2). pap. 3.99 *(978-0-307-98197-4(5)*, Golden Bks.) Random Hse. Children's Bks.
—Ready for Battle! (Teenage Mutant Ninja Turtles) Golden Books. 2014. (Color Plus 1,000 Stickers Ser.). (ENG.). 64p. (J). (gr. -1-2). pap. 9.99 *(978-0-385-37529-0(8)*, Golden Bks.) Random Hse. Children's Bks.
—Ready, Set, Explore! (Dora the Explorer) Golden Books. 2013. (Deluxe Reusable Sticker Book Ser.). (ENG.). 24p. (J). (gr. -1-2). pap. 6.99 *(978-0-449-81885-5(3)*, Golden Bks.) Random Hse. Children's Bks.
—Ready to Roll! (Paw Patrol) Golden Books. 2015. (Color Plus 1,000 Stickers Ser.). (ENG.). 64p. (J). (gr. -1-2). pap. 9.99 *(978-0-553-50795-9(8)*, Golden Bks.) Random Hse. Children's Bks.
—Ride the Tide (SpongeBob SquarePants) Golden Books. 2013. (Color & Paint Plus Stickers Ser.). (ENG.). 128p. (J). (gr. -1-2). pap. 9.99 *(978-0-449-81951-7(5)*, Golden Bks.) Random Hse. Children's Bks.
—Rock on! (Julius Jr.) Golden Books. 2015. (Big Coloring Book Ser.). (ENG.). 48p. (J). (gr. -1-2). pap. 6.99 *(978-0-553-50892-5(X)*, Golden Bks.) Random Hse. Children's Bks.
—Ruff-Ruff Rescues! (Paw Patrol) Golden Books. 2015. (Color & Paint Plus Stickers Ser.). (ENG.). 128p. (J). (gr. -1-2). pap. 9.99 *(978-0-553-52080-4(6)*, Golden Bks.) Random Hse. Children's Bks.
—Saved by the Shell! (Teenage Mutant Ninja Turtles) Golden Books. 2012. (Pictureback Series.). (ENG.). 16p. (J). (gr. -1-2). pap. 3.99 *(978-0-307-98071-7(5)*, Random Hse. Bks. for Young Readers) Random Hse. Children's Bks.
—Seafaring Friends (SpongeBob SquarePants) Golden Books. 2013. (Deluxe Reusable Sticker Book Ser.). (ENG.). 24p. (J). (gr. -1-2). pap. 6.99 *(978-0-449-81882-4(9)*, Golden Bks.) Random Hse. Children's Bks.
—Snow Wonder! (Frosty the Snowman) Golden Books. 2013. (Deluxe Paint Box Book Ser.). (ENG.). 128p. (J). (gr. -1-2). pap. 7.99 *(978-0-385-37179-7(9)*, Golden Bks.) Random Hse. Children's Bks.
—Sparkle, Skate, & Spin! (Dora the Explorer) Golden Books. 2013. (Paint Box Book Ser.). (ENG.). 48p. (J). (gr. -1-2). pap. 3.99 *(978-0-385-37920-5(X)*, Golden Bks.) Random Hse. Children's Bks.
—Start Your Engines! (Bubble Guppies) Golden Books. 2015. (Color Plus Crayons & Sticker Ser.). (ENG.). 48p. (J). (gr. -1-2). pap. 4.99 *(978-0-553-49764-9(2)*, Golden Bks.) Random Hse. Children's Bks.
Golden Books. Sticker Celebration! (Nickelodeon) Golden Books. 2015. (Color Plus 1,000 Stickers Ser.). (ENG.). 64p. (J). (gr. -1-2). pap. 9.99 ***(978-0-553-52271-6(X)***, Golden Bks.) Random Hse. Children's Bks.
Golden Books. Sticker Swim-Sation! (Bubble Guppies) Golden Books. 2014. (Color Plus 1,000 Stickers Ser.). (ENG.). 64p. (J). (gr. -1-2). pap. 9.99 *(978-0-385-37510-8(7)*, Golden Bks.) Random Hse. Children's Bks.
—Sticky Situations! (SpongeBob SquarePants) Golden Books. 2012. (Deluxe Stickerific Ser.). (ENG.). 64p. (J). (gr. -1-2). pap. 5.99 *(978-0-307-97668-0(8)*, Golden Bks.) Random Hse. Children's Bks.
—Stroke of Genius (Mr. Peabody & Sherman) Golden Books. 2014. (Deluxe Paint Box Book Ser.). (ENG.). 128p. (J). (gr. -1-2). pap. 7.99 *(978-0-385-37149-0(7)*, Golden Bks.) Random Hse. Children's Bks.
—Teenage Mutant Ninja Turtles. Golden Books. 2014. (Magnetic Play Book Ser.). (ENG.). 8p. (J). (gr. -1-2). bds. 8.99 *(978-0-385-37522-1(0)*, Golden Bks.) Random Hse. Children's Bks.
—Time Wave! (Mr. Peabody & Sherman) Golden Books. 2014. (Color Plus Chunky Crayons Ser.). (ENG.). 48p. (J). (gr. -1-2). pap. 3.99 *(978-0-385-37148-3(9)*, Golden Bks.) Random Hse. Children's Bks.
—Troll Time! Golden Books. 2015. (Color Plus Crayons & Sticker Ser.). (ENG.). 48p. (J). (gr. -1-2). pap. 4.99 *(978-0-385-38769-9(5)*, Golden Bks.) Random Hse. Children's Bks.
—Turtle Power! (Teenage Mutant Ninja Turtles) Golden Books. 2012. (Giant Coloring Book Ser.). (ENG.). 40p. (J). (gr. -1-2). pap. 9.99 *(978-0-449-80992-1(7)*, Golden Bks.) Random Hse. Children's Bks.
—Ultimate Turtles Fan Book (Teenage Mutant Ninja Turtles) Golden Books. 2012. (Full-Color Activity Book with Stickers Ser.). (ENG.). 48p. (J). (gr. 2-5). pap. 4.99 *(978-0-449-80991-4(9)*, Golden Bks.) Random Hse. Children's Bks.
Golden Books. We Can Do It! (Dora & Friends) Golden Books. 2015. (Color & Paint Plus Stickers Ser.). (ENG.). 128p. (J). (gr. -1-2). pap. 9.99 ***(978-0-553-52086-6(5)***, Golden Bks.) Random Hse. Children's Bks.
Golden Books. Wonderful Winx (Winx Club) Golden Books. 2013. (Holographic Sticker Book Ser.). (ENG.). 48p. (J). (gr. -1-2). pap. 3.99 *(978-0-307-98214-8(9)*, Golden Bks.) Random Hse. Children's Bks.
—The World of Barbie. Golden Books. 50th anniv. ed. 2012. (Little Golden Book Ser.). (ENG.). 24p. (J). (gr. -1-2). 3.99 *(978-0-307-98090-8(1)*, Golden Bks.) Random Hse. Children's Bks.
—You Can Count on Us! (Team Umizoomi) Golden Books. 2014. (Deluxe Stickerific Ser.). (ENG.). 64p. (J). (gr. -1-2). pap. 5.99 *(978-0-385-37521-4(2)*, Golden Bks.) Random Hse. Children's Bks.
Golden Books & Aikins, Dave. Good Knight SpongeBob (SpongeBob SquarePants) Golden Books. 2013. (Color Plus Card Stock Ser.). (ENG.). 48p. (J). (gr. -1-2). pap. 3.99 *(978-0-307-98220-9(3)*, Golden Bks.) Random Hse. Children's Bks.
Golden Books & Aikins, David. Umi Egg Hunt (Team Umizoomi) Golden Books. 2013. (Full-Color Activity Book with Stickers Ser.). (ENG.). 32p. (J). (gr. -1-2). pap. 3.99 *(978-0-307-98211-7(4)*, Golden Bks.) Random Hse. Children's Bks.
Golden Books & Meurer, Caleb. SpongeBob Squarepants Movie Tie-In. Golden Books. 2015. (Little Golden Book Ser.). (ENG.). 24p. (J). (-k). 3.99 *(978-0-553-49775-5(8)*, Golden Bks.) Random Hse. Children's Bks.
Golden Books Staff. Barbie: A Fairy Secret. Man-Kong, Mary. 2011. (Little Golden Book Ser.). (ENG.). 24p. (J). (gr. -1-2). 3.99 *(978-0-375-86540-4(3)*, Golden Bks.) Random Hse. Children's Bks.
—Barbie & the Diamond Castle: A Storybook. Man-Kong, Mary. 2008. (Pictureback Ser.). (ENG.). 24p. (J). (gr. -1-2). pap. 3.99 *(978-0-375-87505-2(0)*, Golden Bks.) Random Hse. Children's Bks.
—Barbie in a Mermaid Tale. Man-Kong, Mary. 2010. (Little Golden Book Ser.). (ENG.). (J). (gr. -1-2). 24p. 3.99 *(978-0-375-85733-1(8)*, Golden Bks.); 16p. pap. 3.99 *(978-0-375-85735-5(4)*, Random Hse. Bks. for Young Readers) Random Hse. Children's Bks.
—Barbie in a Mermaid Tale, No. 2. Man-Kong, Mary & Tillworth, Mary. 2012. (Little Golden Book Ser.). (ENG.). 24p. (J). (gr. k-k). 3.99 *(978-0-307-92979-2(5)*, Golden Bks.) Random Hse., Inc.
—Barbie in a Mermaid Tale, No. 2. McGuire, Molly. 2012. (Junior Novel Ser.). (ENG.). 128p. (J). (gr. 3-7). 4.99 *(978-0-307-93024-8(6)*, Random Hse. Bks. for Young Readers) Random Hse. Children's Bks.
—Barbie in a Mermaid Tale 2. Depken, Kristen L. 2012. (Big Golden Book Ser.). (ENG.). 48p. (J). (gr. -1-2). 9.99 *(978-0-307-93036-1(X)*, Golden Bks.) Random Hse., Inc.
—Barbie Little Golden Book Favorites. Man-Kong, Mary. 2010. (Little Golden Book Favorites Ser.). (ENG.). 80p. (J). (gr. -1-2). 6.99 *(978-0-375-85918-2(7)*, Golden Bks.) Random Hse. Children's Bks.
—Barbie Pink Kit. Man-Kong, Mary. 2010. (Fun Kit Ser.). (ENG.). 64p. (J). (gr. -1-2). 9.99 *(978-0-375-85973-1(X)*, Golden Bks.) Random Hse. Children's Bks.
—Big Book of Engines. Awdry, Wilbert V. 2014. (Big Golden Book Ser.). (ENG.). 64p. (J). (gr. -1-2). 9.99 *(978-0-307-93131-3(5)*, Golden Bks.) Random Hse. Children's Bks.
—Big Heroes! (DC Super Friends) Wrecks, Billy. 2011. (Little Golden Book Ser.). (ENG.). 24p. (J). (gr. -1-2). 3.99 *(978-0-375-87237-2(X)*, Golden Bks.) Random Hse. Children's Bks.
—Cosmic Legends (DC Super Friends) Wrecks, Billy. 2012. (Color Plus Gatefold Sticker Ser.). (ENG.). 16p. (J). (gr. -1-2). pap. 3.99 *(978-0-307-93038-5(6)*, Golden Bks.) Random Hse., Inc.
—Danger at the Dieselworks. Awdry, W. 2011. (Pictureback Ser.). (ENG.). 24p. (J). (gr. -1-2). pap. 3.99 *(978-0-375-86799-6(6)*, Random Hse. Bks. for Young Readers) Random Hse. Children's Bks.
—Day of the Diesels. Awdry, Wilbert V. 2012. (Little Golden Book Ser.). (ENG.). 24p. (J). (gr. k-k). 3.99 *(978-0-307-92989-1(2)*, Golden Bks.) Random Hse., Inc.
Golden Books Staff, et al. Dinosaurs A to Z. Posner-Sanchez, Andrea. 2011. (Padded Board Book Ser.). (ENG.). 30p. (J). (gr. -1 — 1). bds. 11.99 *(978-0-375-87143-6(8)*, Golden Bks.) Random Hse. Children's Bks.
Golden Books Staff. Disney-Pixar Little Golden Book Favorites. Saxon, Victoria & Smiley, Ben. 2009. (Little Golden Book Favorites Ser.). (ENG.). 80p. (J). (gr. -1-2). 6.99 *(978-0-7364-2587-2(X)*, Golden/Disney) Random Hse. Children's Bks.
—Dora & the Unicorn Adventure (Dora the Explorer) Reisner, Molly. 2012. (Big Golden Board Book Ser.). (ENG.). 22p. (J). (gr. k-k). bds. 10.99 *(978-0-307-93000-2(9)*, Golden Bks.) Random Hse., Inc.
—Egg in the Hole. Scarry, Richard. 2011. (Shaped Board Book Ser.). (ENG.). 20p. (J). (gr. k — 1). bds. 8.99 *(978-0-375-86291-5(9)*, Golden Bks.) Random Hse. Children's Bks.
—Fairy Surprises! Man-Kong, Mary. 2011. (Hologramatic Sticker Book Ser.). (ENG.). 48p. (J). (gr. -1-2). pap. 3.99 *(978-0-375-86556-5(X)*, Golden Bks.) Random Hse. Children's Bks.
—Favorites: Thomas Breaks a Promise/Thomas & the Big, Big Bridge/May the Best Engine Win! 2009. (Little Golden Book Favorites Ser.). (ENG.). 80p. (J). (gr. -1-2). 6.99 *(978-0-375-85554-2(8)*, Golden Bks.) Random Hse. Children's Bks.
—A Fin-Tastic Journey! Man-Kong, Mary. 2012. (Color Plus Chunky Crayons Ser.). (ENG.). 48p. (J). (gr. k-k). pap. 3.99 *(978-0-307-92978-5(7)*, Golden Bks.) Random Hse., Inc.
—Glimmer, Shimmer, & Shine! Man-Kong, Mary & Hashimoto, Meika. 2010. (Hologramatic Sticker Book Ser.). (ENG.). 48p. (J). (gr. -1-2). pap. 3.99 *(978-0-375-86032-4(0)*, Golden Bks.) Random Hse. Children's Bks.
—Hero of the Rails. Awdry, W. 2010. (Little Golden Book Ser.). (ENG.). 24p. (J). (gr. -1-2). 3.99 *(978-0-375-85950-2(0)*, Golden Bks.) Random Hse. Children's Bks.
—Heroes! Wrecks, Billy. 2011. (Hologramatic Sticker Book Ser.). (ENG.). 48p. (J). (gr. -1-2). pap. 3.99 *(978-0-375-85331-9(6)*, Golden Bks.) Random Hse. Children's Bks.
—Hooting, Tooting Dinosaurs (Dinosaur Train) Posner-Sanchez, Andrea. 2011. (Little Golden Book Ser.). (ENG.). 24p. (J). (gr. -1-2). 3.99 *(978-0-375-86153-6(X)*, Golden Bks.) Random Hse. Children's Bks.
—I Can Be a Dance Star. Man-Kong, Mary. 2010. (Coloring Book Ser.). (ENG.). 64p. (J). (gr. -1-2). pap. 3.29 *(978-0-375-86532-9(2)*, Golden Bks.) Random Hse. Children's Bks.
—I Can Be a Rock Star. Man-Kong, Mary. 2010. (Pictureback Ser.). (ENG.). 16p. (J). (gr. -1-2). pap. 3.99 *(978-0-375-86545-9(4)*, Golden Bks.) Random Hse. Children's Bks.
—Join the Band! (Fresh Beat Band) Berrios, Frank & Mangual, Ines. 2011. (Full-Color Activity Book with Stickers Ser.). (ENG.). 32p. (J). (gr. -1-2). pap. 3.99 *(978-0-375-86120-8(3)*, Golden Bks.) Random Hse. Children's Bks.
—King of the Railway. Awdry, Wilbert V. 2013. (Little Golden Book Ser.). (ENG.). 24p. (J). (gr. -1-1). 3.99 *(978-0-449-81537-3(4)*, Golden Bks.) Random Hse. Children's Bks.
Golden Books Staff, et al. The Lion King. Fontes, Justine & Korman, Justine. 2003. (Little Golden Book Ser.). (ENG.). 24p. (J). (gr. -1-2). 3.99 *(978-0-7364-2095-2(9)*, Golden/Disney) Random Hse. Children's Bks.
Golden Books Staff. Making Tracks! (Thomas & Friends) Awdry, Wilbert V. 2012. (Write-On/Wipe-off Activity Book Ser.). (ENG.). 12p. (J). (gr. -1-2). bds. 9.99 *(978-0-307-93002-6(5)*, Golden Bks.) Random Hse., Inc.
—Mighty & Amazing (DC Super Friends) Wrecks, Billy. 2011. (Deluxe Paint Box Book Ser.). (ENG.). 128p. (J). (gr. -1-2). pap. 7.99 *(978-0-375-85333-3(2)*, Golden Bks.) Random Hse. Children's Bks.
—Misty Island Rescue. Awdry, Wilbert V. 2012. (Big Golden Board Book Ser.). (ENG.). 22p. (J). (gr. k-k). bds. 10.99 *(978-0-307-93001-9(7)*, Golden Bks.) Random Hse., Inc.
—Misty Island Rescue. Awdry, W. 2011. (Little Golden Book Ser.). (ENG.). 24p. (J). (gr. -1-2). 3.99 *(978-0-375-87212-9(4)*, Golden Bks.) Random Hse. Children's Bks.
—My Fabulous Friends! Man-Kong, Mary. 2009. (Pictureback Ser.). (ENG.). 16p. (J). (gr. -1-2). pap. 3.99 *(978-0-375-85789-8(3)*, Golden Bks.) Random Hse. Children's Bks.
—Pat the Bunny. Kunhardt, Dorothy. collector's deluxe ed. 2011. (Touch-And-Feel Ser.). (ENG.). 24p. (J). (gr. -1-2). 14.99 *(978-0-307-20047-1(7)*, Golden Bks.) Random Hse. Children's Bks.
—A Perfect Christmas (Barbie) Man-Kong, Mary & Tillworth, Mary. 2011. (Pictureback Ser.). (ENG.). 16p. (J). (gr. -1-2). pap. 3.99 *(978-0-375-87363-8(5)*, Random Hse. Bks. for Young Readers) Random Hse. Children's Bks.
—A Perfect Christmas Paint. Man-Kong, Mary & Tillworth, Mary. 2011. (Paint Box Book Ser.). (ENG.). 48p. (J). (gr. -1-2). pap. 3.99 *(978-0-375-87364-5(3)*, Golden Bks.) Random Hse. Children's Bks.
—Princess Charm School (Barbie) Man-Kong, Mary & Tillworth, Mary. 2011. (Little Golden Book Ser.). (ENG.). 24p. (J). (gr. -1-2). 3.99 *(978-0-375-87361-4(9)*, Golden Bks.) Random Hse. Children's Bks.
—Princess Charm School (Barbie) Man-Kong, Mary. 2011. (Pictureback Ser.). (ENG.). 16p. (J). (gr. -1-2). pap. 3.99 *(978-0-375-87362-1(7)*, Random Hse. Bks. for Young Readers) Random Hse. Children's Bks.
—Princess in Training (Barbie) Man-Kong, Mary. 2011. (Deluxe Coloring Book Ser.). (ENG.). 96p. (J). (gr. -1-2). pap. 3.99 *(978-0-375-87360-7(0)*, Golden Bks.) Random Hse. Children's Bks.
—Princess Magic (Barbie) Man-Kong, Mary & Tillworth, Mary. 2011. (Color Plus Chunky Crayons Ser.). (ENG.). 48p. (J). (gr. -1-2). pap. 3.99 *(978-0-375-87359-1(7)*, Golden Bks.) Random Hse. Children's Bks.
—Purr-Fect Pets. Man-Kong, Mary. 2012. (3-D Coloring Book Ser.). (ENG.). 32p. (J). (gr. -1-2). pap. 4.99 *(978-0-307-93129-0(3)*, Golden Bks.) Random Hse. Children's Bks.
—Rolling on the Rails. Awdry, Wilbert V. 2011. (Thomas & Friends Ser.). (ENG.). 12p. (J). (gr. k — 1). bds. 8.99 *(978-0-375-87304-1(X)*, Golden Bks.) Random Hse. Children's Bks.
—Sensational Style. Man-Kong, Mary. 2010. (Big Coloring Book Ser.). (ENG.). 48p. (J). (gr. -1-2). pap. 6.99 *(978-0-375-86490-2(3)*, Golden Bks.) Random Hse. Children's Bks.
—Somebunny Special (SpongeBob SquarePants) Carbone, Courtney. 2013. (Holographic Sticker Book Ser.). (ENG.). 48p. (J). (gr. -1-2). pap. 3.99 *(978-0-307-98104-2(5)*, Golden Bks.) Random Hse. Children's Bks.
—Sparkling Style. Man-Kong, Mary. 2010. (Deluxe Coloring Book Ser.). (ENG.). 96p. (J). (gr. -1-2). pap. 3.99 *(978-0-375-86031-7(2)*, Golden Bks.) Random Hse. Children's Bks.
—Spring into Style. Man-Kong, Mary. 2011. (Color Plus Flocked Stickers Ser.). (ENG.). 64p. (J). (gr. -1-2). pap. 4.99 *(978-0-375-86813-9(5)*, Golden Bks.) Random Hse. Children's Bks.
—Steam Work! (Thomas & Friends) Awdry, Wilbert V. 2011. (Giant Paint Box Book Ser.). (ENG.). 40p. (J). (gr. -1-2). pap. 10.99 *(978-0-375-87376-8(7)*, Golden Bks.) Random Hse. Children's Bks.
—Tales of Discovery. Awdry, Wilbert V. 2011. (Padded Board Book Ser.). (ENG.). 30p. (J). (gr. k — 1). bds. 11.99 *(978-0-375-87192-4(6)*, Golden Bks.) Random Hse. Children's Bks.
—Thomas' Colorful Ride (Thomas & Friends) Awdry, Wilbert V. & Awdry, Rev. W. 2011. (Deluxe Chunky Crayon Book Ser.). (ENG.). 128p. (J). (gr. -1-2). pap. 7.99 *(978-0-375-87248-6(5)*, Golden Bks.) Random Hse. Children's Bks.
—Thomas' Super-Jumbo Coloring Book (Thomas & Friends) Awdry, Wilbert V. 2012. (Super Jumbo Coloring Book Ser.). (ENG.). 416p. (J). (gr. -1-2). pap. 10.99 *(978-0-307-93118-4(8)*, Golden Bks.) Random Hse. Children's Bks.
—Thumbelina. Man-Kong, Mary. 2009. (Pictureback Ser.). (ENG.). 16p. (J). (gr. -1-2). pap. 3.99 *(978-0-375-84596-3(8)*, Golden Bks.) Random Hse., Inc.
—Toy Story Little Golden Book Favorites. RH Disney Staff. 2011. (Little Golden Book Favorites Ser.). (ENG.). 80p. (J). (gr. -1-2). 6.99 *(978-0-7364-2752-4(X)*, Golden/Disney) Random Hse. Children's Bks.
—Travel Buddies. Berrios, Frank & RH Disney Staff. 2012. (Little Golden Book Ser.). (ENG.). 24p. (J). (gr. k-k). 3.99 *(978-0-7364-2911-5(5)*, Golden/Disney) Random Hse. Children's Bks.
—Welcome to My Dream House (Barbie) Man-Kong, Mary. 2011. (Giant Coloring Book Ser.). (ENG.). 40p. (J). (gr. -1-2). pap. 9.99 *(978-0-375-87398-0(8)*, Golden Bks.) Random Hse. Children's Bks.
Golden Books Staff. Barbie & the Three Musketeers. Golden Books Staff. 2009. (Pictureback Ser.). (ENG.). 16p. (J). (gr. -1-2). pap. 3.99 *(978-0-375-85446-0(0))* Random Hse. Children's Bks.

—Barbie Loves Ballet/Fashion Show Fun! Golden Books Staff. 2009. (Deluxe Pictureback Ser.). (ENG.). 32p. (J). (gr. -1-2). pap. 4.99 *(978-0-375-85148-3(8)*, Golden Bks.) Random Hse. Children's Bks.
—Beautiful Barbie. Golden Books Staff. 2009. (Super Stickerific Ser.). (ENG.). 64p. (J). (gr. -1-2). pap. 12.99 *(978-0-375-85553-5(X)*, Golden Bks.) Random Hse. Children's Bks.
—The Bengal Tiger Boo-Boo. Golden Books Staff. 2008. (Deluxe Coloring Book Ser.). (ENG.). 96p. (J). (gr. -1-2). pap. 3.99 *(978-0-375-84503-1(8)*, Golden Bks.) Random Hse. Children's Bks.
—Big Coloring Adventures! (Nickelodeon) Golden Books Staff. 2011. (Big Coloring Book Ser.). (ENG.). 48p. (J). (gr. -1-2). pap. 6.99 *(978-0-375-87239-6(6)*, Golden Bks.) Random Hse. Children's Bks.
—Bunny's Fuzzy Christmas. Golden Books Staff. 2010. (ENG.). 12p. (J). (— 1). bds. 6.99 *(978-0-375-86187-1(4)*, Golden Bks.) Random Hse. Children's Bks.
—Bunny's Garden. Golden Books Staff. 2010. (Shaped Board Book Ser.). (ENG.). 12p. (J). (gr. -1 — 1). bds. 7.99 *(978-0-375-85788-1(5)*, Golden Bks.) Random Hse. Children's Bks.
—Cars. Golden Books Staff. 2009. (Make Your Own Little Golden Book Ser.). (ENG.). 16p. (J). (gr. -1-2). 5.99 *(978-0-375-84597-0(6)*, Golden Bks.) Random Hse., Inc.
—Catch a Wave! Golden Books Staff. 2009. (Color Plus Chunky Crayons Ser.). (ENG.). 48p. (J). (gr. -1-2). pap. 3.99 *(978-0-375-85107-0(0)*, Golden Bks.) Random Hse. Children's Bks.
—Dora the Explorer Fun Kit! , Kit. Golden Books Staff. 2010. (Fun Kit Ser.). (ENG.). 64p. (J). (gr. -1-2). 9.99 *(978-0-375-86527-5(6)*, Golden Bks.) Random Hse. Children's Bks.
—Dora's Big Valentine! Golden Books Staff. 2010. (Full-Color Activity Book with Stickers Ser.). (ENG.). 32p. (J). (gr. -1-2). pap. 3.99 *(978-0-375-87321-8(X)*, Golden Bks.) Random Hse. Children's Bks.
—Dora's Super Silly Coloring Book (Dora the Explorer) Golden Books Staff. 2011. (Jumbo Coloring Book Ser.). (ENG.). 224p. (J). (gr. -1-2). pap. 5.99 *(978-0-375-87308-9(2)*, Golden Bks.) Random Hse. Children's Bks.
—Drawing Fiesta! (Dora the Explorer) Golden Books Staff. 2011. (Write-On/Wipe-off Activity Book Ser.). (ENG.). 12p. (J). (gr. k — 1). bds. 9.99 *(978-0-375-87159-7(4)*, Golden Bks.) Random Hse. Children's Bks.
—Easter Deliveries. Golden Books Staff. 2010. (Color Plus Chunky Crayons Ser.). (ENG.). 48p. (J). (gr. -1-2). pap. 3.99 *(978-0-375-85747-8(8)*, Golden Bks.) Random Hse. Children's Bks.
—Explore with Me! Golden Books Staff. 2010. (Reusable Sticker Book Ser.). (ENG & SPA.). 12p. (J). (gr. -1-2). pap. 6.99 *(978-0-375-86520-6(9)*, Golden Bks.) Random Hse. Children's Bks.
—Friends & Flowers (Dora the Explorer) Golden Books Staff. 2011. (Deluxe Chunky Crayon Book Ser.). (ENG.). 128p. (J). (gr. -1-2). pap. 7.99 *(978-0-375-87257-0(4)*, Golden Bks.) Random Hse. Children's Bks.
—In Action! Golden Books Staff. 2009. (Color Plus Chunky Crayons Ser.). (ENG.). 48p. (J). (gr. -1-2). pap. 3.99 *(978-0-375-85329-6(4)*, Golden Bks.) Random Hse. Children's Bks.
—Jumbo Coloring Party. Golden Books Staff. 2010. (Jumbo Coloring Book Ser.). (ENG.). 224p. (J). (gr. -1-2). pap. 5.99 *(978-0-375-86352-3(4)*, Golden Bks.) Random Hse. Children's Bks.
—The Mermaid Princess. Golden Books Staff. 2010. (Color Plus Chunky Crayons Ser.). (ENG.). 48p. (J). (gr. -1-2). pap. 3.99 *(978-0-375-85748-5(6)*, Golden Bks.) Random Hse. Children's Bks.
Golden Books Staff. Mutants in Space! Golden Books Staff. Lewman, David. 2015. (Junior Novel Ser.). (ENG.). 128p. (J). (gr. 3-7). pap. 5.99 ***(978-0-553-52275-4(2)***, Golden Bks.) Random Hse. Children's Bks.
Golden Books Staff. Nickelodeon Little Golden Book Favorites (Nickelodeon) Golden Books Staff. 2011. (Little Golden Book Favorites Ser.). (ENG.). 80p. (J). (gr. -1-2). 6.99 *(978-0-375-87227-3(2)*, Golden Bks.) Random Hse. Children's Bks.
—Paint the Town Pink! Golden Books Staff. 2009. (Deluxe Paint Box Book Ser.). (ENG.). 128p. (J). (gr. -1-2). pap. 7.99 *(978-0-375-85730-0(3)*, Golden Bks.) Random Hse. Children's Bks.
—Princess Dreams. Golden Books Staff. 2010. (Jumbo Coloring Book Ser.). (ENG.). 224p. (J). (gr. -1-2). pap. 5.99 *(978-0-375-85952-6(7)*, Golden Bks.) Random Hse. Children's Bks.
—A Splash of Color! Golden Books Staff. 2009. (Deluxe Paint Box Book Ser.). (ENG.). 128p. (J). (gr. -1-2). pap. 7.99 *(978-0-375-85732-4(X)*, Golden Bks.) Random Hse. Children's Bks.
—SpongeBob SportyPants! (SpongeBob SquarePants) Golden Books Staff. 2012. (Color Plus Stencil Ser.). (ENG.). 64p. (J). (gr. k-k). pap. 5.99 *(978-0-307-93132-0(3)*, Golden Bks.) Random Hse. Children's Bks.
—SpongeBob's Best Days! Golden Books Staff. 2010. (Jumbo Coloring Book Ser.). (ENG.). 224p. (J). (gr. -1-2). pap. 5.99 *(978-0-375-86351-6(6)*, Golden Bks.) Random Hse. Children's Bks.
—Standing Tall! Golden Books Staff. 2010. (Big Coloring Book Ser.). (ENG.). 48p. (J). (gr. -1-2). pap. 6.99 *(978-0-375-85332-6(4)*, Golden Bks.) Random Hse. Children's Bks.
—Super Coloring Adventures! (Nick Jr.) Golden Books Staff. 2012. (Super Jumbo Coloring Book Ser.). (ENG.). 416p. (J). (gr. -1-2). pap. 10.99 *(978-0-307-92991-4(4)*, Golden Bks.) Random Hse., Inc.
—Super Coloring Fiesta! Golden Books Staff. 2006. (Super Stickerific Ser.). (ENG & SPA.). 64p. (J). (gr. -1-2). pap. 12.99 *(978-0-375-84134-7(2)*, Golden Bks.) Random Hse. Children's Bks.
—Trainloads of Fun. Golden Books Staff. 2010. (Jumbo Coloring Book Ser.). (ENG.). 224p. (J). (gr. -1-2). pap. 5.99 *(978-0-375-86363-9(X)*, Golden Bks.) Random Hse. Children's Bks.
—A Very Busy Sticker Book. Golden Books Staff. 2012. (Deluxe Stickerific Ser.). (ENG.). 64p. (J). (gr. -1-2). pap. 5.99 *(978-0-307-93021-7(1)*, Golden Bks.) Random Hse., Inc.
—Winx Forever! (Winx Club) Golden Books Staff. Cartobaleno Staff. 2013. (Color Plus Tattoos Ser.). (ENG.). 48p. (J). (gr. -1-2). pap. 3.99 *(978-0-449-81774-2(1)*, Golden Bks.) Random Hse. Children's Bks.
—Wipe Out! (SpongeBob SquarePants) Golden Books Staff. 2011. (Write-On/Wipe-off Activity Book Ser.). (ENG.). 12p. (J). (gr. k — 1). bds. 9.99 *(978-0-375-87153-5(5)*, Golden Bks.) Random Hse. Children's Bks.
—World of Colors. Golden Books Staff. 2008. (Deluxe Paint Box Book Ser.). (ENG.). 128p. (J). (gr. -1-2). pap. 7.99 *(978-0-375-84293-1(4)*, Golden Bks.) Random Hse., Inc.
Golden Books Staff & Aikins, Dave. King of Karate (SpongeBob SquarePants) Golden Books Staff. 2011. (Paint Box Book Ser.). (ENG.). 48p. (J). (gr. -1-2). pap. 3.99 *(978-0-375-87389-8(9)*, Golden Bks.) Random Hse. Children's Bks.
—Plank-Ton to the Rescue! Golden Books Staff. 2015. (Color Plus Crayons & Sticker Ser.). (ENG.). 48p. (J). (gr. -1-2). pap. 4.99 *(978-0-385-38776-7(8)*, Golden Bks.) Random Hse. Children's Bks.
—SpongeBob for President! (SpongeBob SquarePants) Golden Books Staff. 2012. (Color Plus Chunky Crayons Ser.). (ENG.). 48p. (J). (gr. -1-2). pap. 3.99 *(978-0-307-97634-5(3)*, Golden Bks.) Random Hse. Children's Bks.
Golden Books Staff & An, Jiyoung. I Can Be... a Fashion Designer. Man-Kong, Mary. 2011. (Doodle Book Ser.). (ENG.). 128p. (J). (gr. -1-2). pap. 5.49 *(978-0-375-87259-4(0)*, Golden Bks.) Random Hse. Children's Bks.
—I Can Be... Anything I Want to Be. Man-Kong, Mary. 2011. (Paper Doll Book Ser.). (ENG.). 32p. (J). (gr. -1-2). pap. 5.49 *(978-0-375-87260-0(4)*, Golden Bks.) Random Hse. Children's Bks.
Golden Books Staff & Das Group Staff. Friends, Fashion, & Fun! (Barbie) Man-Kong, Mary. 2012. (Jumbo Coloring Book Ser.). (ENG.). 224p. (J). (gr. -1-2). pap. 5.99 *(978-0-375-87358-4(9)*, Golden Bks.) Random Hse., Inc.
Golden Books Staff & Duarte, Pamela. Pop Star Dreams (Barbie) Man-Kong, Mary. 2013. (Color Plus Tattoos Ser.). (ENG.). 48p. (J). (gr. -1-2). pap. 3.99 *(978-0-449-81611-0(7)*, Golden Bks.) Random Hse. Children's Bks.
—The Sweetest Halloween (Barbie) Man-Kong, Mary. 2012. (Glow-In-the-Dark Sticker Book Ser.). (ENG.). 48p. (J). (gr. -1-2). pap. 3.99 *(978-0-307-93115-3(3)*, Golden Bks.) Random Hse. Children's Bks.
Golden Books Staff & Durk, Jim. Up, up & Away! Awdry, Wilbert V. 2013. (Color Plus Chunky Crayons Ser.). (ENG.). 48p. (J). (gr. -1-1). pap. 3.99 *(978-0-307-98199-8(1)*, Golden Bks.) Random Hse. Children's Bks.
Golden Books Staff & Fruchter, Jason. Brave Knight Dora (Dora the Explorer) Golden Books Staff. 2012. (Holographic Sticker Book Ser.). (ENG.). 48p. (J). (gr. -1-2). pap. 3.99 *(978-0-307-97680-2(7)*, Golden Bks.) Random Hse. Children's Bks.
—Call of the Wild! Miller, Mona. 2011. (Color Plus Chunky Crayons Ser.). (ENG.). 48p. (J). (gr. -1-2). pap. 3.99 *(978-0-375-86158-1(0)*, Golden Bks.) Random Hse. Children's Bks.
—Share a Hug. Golden Books Staff. 2008. (Stickerific Ser.). (ENG.). 32p. (J). (gr. -1-2). pap. 2.99 *(978-0-375-85105-6(4)*, Golden Bks.) Random Hse. Children's Bks.
Golden Books Staff & Hand, Jason. Disney Planes. RH Disney Staff & Hall, Klay. 2013. (Little Golden Book Ser.). (ENG.). 24p. (J). (-k). 3.99 *(978-0-7364-2974-0(3)*, Golden/Disney) Random Hse. Children's Bks.
Golden Books Staff & Jackson, Mike. Ready, Set, Paint! 2012. (Deluxe Paint Box Book Ser.). (ENG.). 128p. (J). (gr. -1-2). pap. 7.99 *(978-0-307-93031-6(9)*, Golden Bks.) Random Hse., Inc.
Golden Books Staff & Lambe, Steve. Follow the Ninja! Golden Books Staff. 2015. (Little Golden Book Ser.). (ENG.). 24p. (J). (-k). 3.99 *(978-0-553-51204-5(8)*, Golden Bks.) Random Hse. Children's Bks.
Golden Books Staff & Lambe, Steve. Green vs. Mean (Teenage Mutant Ninja Turtles) Golden Books Staff & Smith, Geof. 2015. (Little Golden Book Ser.). (ENG.). 24p. (J). (-k). 4.99 ***(978-1-101-93465-4(4)***, Golden Bks.) Random Hse. Children's Bks.
—Mighty Monster Machines (Blaze & the Monster Machines) Golden Books Staff. 2015. (Little Golden Book Ser.). (ENG.). 24p. (J). (-k). 4.99 ***(978-0-553-52456-7(9)***, Golden Bks.) Random Hse. Children's Bks.
Golden Books Staff & Lovett, Nate. All Paws on Deck! (Paw Patrol) Golden Books Staff. 2014. (Deluxe Paint Box Book Ser.). (ENG.). 128p. (J). (gr. -1-2). pap. 7.99 *(978-0-385-38446-9(7)*, Golden Bks.) Random Hse. Children's Bks.
—Puppy Power! (Paw Patrol) Golden Books Staff. 2014. (Color Plus Chunky Crayons Ser.). (ENG.). 48p. (J). (gr. -1-2). pap. 3.99 *(978-0-385-38445-2(9)*, Golden Bks.) Random Hse. Children's Bks.
Golden Books Staff & LV Studio Staff. May I Help You? (Pat the Bunny) Golden Books Staff. 2013. (Little Golden Book Ser.). (ENG.). 24p. (J). (-k). 3.99 *(978-0-449-81736-0(9)*, Golden Bks.) Random Hse. Children's Bks.
Golden Books Staff & Petrossi, Fabrizio. The Itty-Bitty Kitty Rescue (Paw Patrol) Golden Books Staff. 2014. (Little Golden Book Ser.). (ENG.). 24p. (J). (-k). 3.99 *(978-0-553-50884-0(9)*, Golden Bks.) Random Hse. Children's Bks.
Golden Books Staff & Random House Staff. Enter the Lair (Teenage Mutant Ninja Turtles) Golden Books Staff & Random House Staff. 2013. (3-D Pictureback Ser.). (ENG.). 16p. (J). (gr. -1-2). pap. 4.99 *(978-0-449-81385-0(1)*, Golden Bks.) Random Hse. Children's Bks.
Golden Books Staff & Random House Value Publishing Staff. Junior Novelization. Golden Books Staff & Lewman, David. 2015. (Junior Novel Ser.). (ENG.). 128p. (J). (gr. 3-7). 5.99 *(978-0-385-38775-0(X)*, Golden Bks.) Random Hse. Children's Bks.
Golden Books Staff & RH Disney Staff. Cars Little Golden Book Favorites. 2011. (Little Golden Book Favorites Ser.). (ENG.). 80p. (J). (gr. -1-2). 6.99 *(978-0-7364-2751-7(1)*, Golden/Disney) Random Hse. Children's Bks.
Golden Books Staff & Riley, Kellee. Bee Mine. Golden Books Staff. 2010. (Stickerific Ser.). (ENG.). 32p. (J). (gr. -1-2). pap. 2.99 *(978-0-375-86614-2(0)*, Golden Bks.) Random Hse. Children's Bks.
—I Can Be a Teacher (Barbie) Man-Kong, Mary. 2011. (Step into Reading Ser.). (ENG.). 32p. (J). (gr. -1-1). pap. 3.99 *(978-0-375-86927-3(1)*, Random Hse. Bks. for Young Readers) Random Hse. Children's Bks.
Golden Books Staff & Sciarrone, Claudio. Half-Shell Heroes! (Teenage Mutant Ninja Turtles) Carbone, Courtney. 2013. (Color Plus Chunky Crayons Ser.). (ENG.). 48p. (J). (gr. -1-2). pap. 3.99 *(978-0-307-98233-9(5)*, Golden Bks.) Random Hse. Children's Bks.
Golden Books Staff & Spaziante, Patrick. The Big Book of Words (Nickelodeon) Golden Books Staff. 2015. (Big Golden Book Ser.). (ENG.). 48p. (J). (-k). 9.99 *(978-0-553-50877-2(6)*, Golden Bks.) Random Hse. Children's Bks.
Golden Books Staff & Unten, Eren. Julius Jr. - Pirates & Superheroes. Posner-Sanchez, Andrea. 2015. (Little Golden Book Ser.). (ENG.). 24p. (J). (-k). 3.99 *(978-0-553-50861-1(X)*, Golden Bks.) Random Hse. Children's Bks.
Golden Books Staff & Valeri, Jim. Sticker-Tastic! (Julius Jr.) Golden Books Staff. 2015. (Deluxe Stickerific Ser.). (ENG.). 64p. (J). (gr. -1-2). pap. 5.99 *(978-0-553-50976-2(4)*, Golden Bks.) Random Hse. Children's Bks.
Golden Books Staff, jt. illus. see Fruchter, Jason.
Golden Books Staff, jt. illus. see Random House Editors.
Golden Books Staff, jt. illus. see Random House.
Golden Books Staff, jt. illus. see RH Disney Staff.
Golden Books Staff, jt. illus. see Sarl Aky-Aka Creations.
Golden Books Staff, jt. illus. see Scarry, Richard.
Golden Books Staff, jt. illus. see Walt Disney Company Staff.
Golden, Harriet. The Ugly Duckling & Other Fairy Tales. Andersen, Hans Christian. 2012. (Dover Children's Thrift Classics Ser.). (ENG.). 96p. (Orig.). (J). (gr. 3-8). pap. 3.00 *(978-0-486-27081-4(5)*) Dover Pubns., Inc.
Golden, Jess. Snow Dog, Sand Dog. Singleton, Linda Joy. 2014. (ENG.). 32p. (J). (gr. -1-2). 16.99 *(978-0-8075-7536-9(4))* Whitman, Albert & Co.
Golden, John Ashton. Numbering the Crime: Forensic Mathematics, 11 vols. McIntosh, Kenneth. 2007. (Crime Scene Club Ser.). 144p. (YA). (gr. 9-12). lib. bdg. 24.95 *(978-1-4222-0257-9(7))* Mason Crest.
—A Stranger's Voice: Forensic Speech Identification, 9 vols. McIntosh, Kenneth. 2007. (Crime Scene Club Ser.). 144p. (YA). (gr. 9-12). lib. bdg. 24.95 *(978-1-4222-0255-5(0))* Mason Crest.
—Things Fall Apart: Forensic Engineering, 10 vols. McIntosh, Kenneth. 2007. (Crime Scene Club Ser.). 144p. (YA). (gr. 9-12). lib. bdg. 24.95 *(978-1-4222-0256-2(9))* Mason Crest.
Golden, Kathleen M. Cleopatra's Big Birthday BBQ. Golden, Kathleen M. 2003. 18p. (J). (gr. -1-k). mass mkt. 14.95 *(978-0-9726418-0-7(7))* Happyland Media.
Golden, Lilly. See Mom Run. Thom, Kara Douglass. 2003. (ENG.). 32p. (J). 15.00 *(978-1-891369-40-7(7))* Breakaway Bks.
Golden, Michael, et al. The 'Nam, Vol. 3. 2011. (ENG.). 248p. (YA). (gr. 8-17). pap. 29.99 *(978-0-7851-5898-1(7))* Marvel Worldwide, Inc.
Golden, Mike & Vansant, Wayne. The 'Nam, Vol. 1. 2009. (ENG.). 248p. (YA). (gr. 8-17). pap. 29.99 *(978-0-7851-3750-4(5))* Marvel Worldwide, Inc.
Golden, Rayna. Ali & the Magic Ball. Edwards, Wayne. 2009. 24p. pap. 12.50 *(978-1-60860-367-1(9)*, Eloquent Bks.) Strategic Book Publishing & Rights Agency (SBPRA).
Golden Twomey, Emily. Amazing Copycat Coloring Book: Cool Pictures to Copy & Complete. 2015. (ENG.). 48p. (J). (gr. 1-4). pap. 6.99 *(978-1-4380-0635-2(7))* Barron's Educational Series, Inc.
Goldfinger, Jennifer P. I Need Glasses. Thomas, Charlie. 2005. (Rookie Readers Ser.). (ENG.). 32p. (J). (gr. k-2). lib. bdg. 19.50 *(978-0-516-24863-9(4)*, Children's Pr.) Scholastic Library Publishing.
Goldin, David. Baxter, the Pig Who Wanted to Be Kosher. Snyder, Laurel. 2010. (ENG.). 32p. (J). (gr. -1-2). 15.99 *(978-1-58246-315-5(8)*, Tricycle Pr.) Ten Speed Pr.
—Bug Science. Young, Karen Romano. 2009. (Science Fair Winners Ser.). (ENG.). 80p. (J). (gr. 5-9). 24.90 *(978-1-4263-0520-7(6)*, National Geographic Children's Bks.) National Geographic Society.
—Bug Science: 20 Projects & Experiments about Arthropods - Insects, Arachnids, Algae, Worms, & Other Small Creatures. Young, Karen Romano. 2009. (Science Fair Winners Ser.). (ENG.). 80p. (J). (gr. 5-9). pap. 12.95 *(978-1-4263-0519-1(2)*, National Geographic Children's Bks.) National Geographic Society.
—Crime Scene Science. Young, Karen Romano. 2009. (Science Fair Winners Ser.). (ENG.). 80p. (J). (gr. 5-9). 24.90 *(978-1-4263-0522-1(2))*; pap. 12.95 *(978-1-4263-0521-4(4))* National Geographic Society. (National Geographic Children's Bks.).
—Experiments to Do on Your Family. Young, Karen Romano. 2010. (Science Fair Winners Ser.). (ENG.). 80p. (J). (gr. 5-9). 24.90 *(978-1-4263-0692-1(X))*; pap. 12.95 *(978-1-4263-0691-4(1))* National Geographic Society. (National Geographic Children's Bks.).
—Junkyard Science. Young, Karen Romano. 2010. (Science Fair Winners Ser.). (ENG.). 80p. (J). (gr. 5-9). 24.90 *(978-1-4263-0690-7(3))*; pap. 12.95 *(978-1-4263-0689-1(X))* National Geographic Society. (National Geographic Children's Bks.).
Golding, J. C. A Bird's Day at Yaquina Head. Monroe, Guy. Monroe, Karol, ed. 2003. 52p. 7.95 *(978-0-9742443-0-3(9))* Monroe, Guy.
Goldman, Garnet. His Dogness Finds a Blue Heart. Underwood, Ralph Kim. 2004. 32p. (J). 16.95 *(978-0-89587-304-0(4))* Blair, John F. Pub.
—The Wonderful World of Sparkle Girl & Doobins. Underwood, Kim. 2009. 48p. (J). pap. 16.95 *(978-0-89587-373-6(7))* Blair, John F. Pub.
Goldman, Linda Sarah. From Pie Town to Yum Yum: Weird & Wacky Place Names Across the United States. Herman, Debbie. ed. 2011. (ENG.). 120p. (J). pap. 10.99 *(978-1-935279-79-2(3))* Kane Miller.
Goldman, Marcia, photos by. Lola & Tattletale Zeke. 2015. (ENG., 32p. (J). (gr. -1-3). 16.95 *(978-1-939547-16-3(4))* Creston Bks.
—Lola Goes to the Doctor. 2014. (ENG., 32p. (J). (gr. -1-3). 16.95 *(978-1-939547-11-8(3))* Creston Bks.
Goldman, Todd Harris. Boys Are Stupid, Throw Rocks at Them! Goldman, Todd Harris. 2005. (ENG.). 80p. 8.95 *(978-0-7611-3593-7(6)*, 13593) Workman Publishing Co., Inc.
Golds, Alexandra Kimla. I Love My Mommy. Kimla, Lenka J. 2008. 22p. pap. 24.95 *(978-1-60703-126-0(4))* America Star Bks.
Goldsborough, June. Dark As a Shadow. Lowery, Lawrence F. 2014. (ENG.). 36p. (J). pap. 11.95 *(978-1-941316-06-1(9))* National Science Teachers Assn.
Goldsmith, Abby. All I Got for Christmas: Smartboys Club. Shelley, Rebecca. 2011. (ENG.). 108p. pap. 6.99 *(978-1-4664-2804-1(X))* CreateSpace Independent Publishing Platform.
—Bees in My Butt: The Smartboys Club: Book 1. Shelley, Rebecca. 2011. (ENG.). 108p. pap. 6.99 *(978-1-4565-9980-5(1))* CreateSpace Independent Publishing Platform.
—I Lost My Head: Smartboys Club Book 4. Shelley, Rebecca. 2011. (ENG.). 104p. pap. 6.99 *(978-1-4635-6502-2(X))* CreateSpace Independent Publishing Platform.
—I Took a Burp. Shelley, Rebecca. 2011. (ENG.). 108p. pap. 6.99 *(978-1-4611-7678-7(6))* CreateSpace Independent Publishing Platform.
—My Stomach Explodes: The Smartboys Club Book 5. Shelley, Rebecca. 2011. (ENG.). 106p. pap. 6.99 *(978-1-4637-8663-2(8))* CreateSpace Independent Publishing Platform.
Goldsmith, Tom. Ben & Zip: Two Short Friends. Linden, Joanne. 2014. (ENG.). 32p. (J). (gr. -1-k). 16.95 *(978-1-936261-28-4(6))* Flashlight Pr.
—The Pocket Mommy. Eugster, Rachel. 2013. (ENG.). 32p. (J). (gr. -1-1). 16.95 *(978-1-77049-300-1(X))* Tundra Bks. CAN. Dist: Random Hse., Inc.
Goldstein, A. Nancy. Behind the Bedroom Wall. Williams, Laura E. 2005. (Historical Fiction for Young Readers Ser.). (ENG.). 184p. (J). (gr. 3-7). per. 6.95 *(978-1-57131-658-5(2))* Milkweed Editions.
—Behind the Bedroom Wall. Williams, Laura E. 2006. 169p. (gr. -1-7). 17.45 *(978-0-7569-6389-7(3))* Perfection Learning Corp.
Goldstone, Bruce. Great Estimations. Goldstone, Bruce. rev. ed. 2006. (ENG.). 32p. (J). (gr. 2-5). 18.99 *(978-0-8050-7446-8(5)*, Holt, Henry & Co. Bks. For Young Readers) Holt, Henry & Co.
—Great Estimations. Goldstone, Bruce. 2010. (ENG.). 32p. (J). (gr. 2-5). pap. 6.99 *(978-0-312-60887-3(X))* Square Fish.
—Greater Estimations. Goldstone, Bruce. 2008. (ENG.). 32p. (J). (gr. 2-5). 16.95 *(978-0-8050-8315-6(4)*, Holt, Henry & Co. Bks. For Young Readers) Holt, Henry & Co.
—I See a Pattern Here. Goldstone, Bruce. 2015. (ENG.). 32p. (J). (gr. 2-5). 17.99 *(978-0-8050-9209-7(9)*, Holt, Henry & Co. Bks. For Young Readers) Holt, Henry & Co.
—100 Ways to Celebrate 100 Days. Goldstone, Bruce. 2010. (ENG.). 48p. (J). (gr. -1-3). 16.99 *(978-0-8050-8997-4(7)*, Holt, Henry & Co. Bks. For Young Readers) Holt, Henry & Co.
—100 Ways to Celebrate 100 Days. Goldstone, Bruce. 2013. (ENG.). 48p. (J). (gr. -1-3). 7.99 *(978-1-250-03369-7(1))* Square Fish.
Goldstone, Bruce, photos by. Awesome Autumn. Goldstone, Bruce. 2012. (ENG., 48p. (J). (gr. -1-3). 17.99 *(978-0-8050-9210-3(2)*, Holt, Henry & Co. Bks. For Young Readers) Holt, Henry & Co.
Goldstrom, Robert. Dream Away. Durango, Julia & Trupiano, Katie Belle. 2011. (ENG.). 32p. (J). (gr. -1-3). 16.99 *(978-1-4169-8702-4(9)*, Simon & Schuster Bks. For Young Readers) Simon & Schuster Bks. For Young Readers.
Golembe, Carla. Honeybees. Heiligman, Deborah. 2007. (Jump into Science Ser.). (ENG.). 32p. (J). (gr. 1-3). per. 6.95 *(978-1-4263-0157-5(X)*, National Geographic Children's Bks.) National Geographic Society.
—Sun. Tomecek, Steve. 2006. (Jump into Science Ser.). (ENG.). 32p. (J). (gr. -1-3). per. 6.95 *(978-0-7922-5582-6(8))* National Geographic Society.
Golen, Jessica. Smitty Moose, Petey & Me - Episode One, the Witch. Plourde, Paulette. l.t. ed. 2005. 32p. (J). per. 9.95 *(978-1-59879-038-2(2))* Lifevest Publishing, Inc.
Golert, Amanda. Kidpower Safety Comics: An Introduction to "People Safety" for Young Children Ages 3 to 10 & Their Adults. van der Zande, Irene. 2011. 44p. (J). pap. *(978-0-9796191-4-4(9))* van der Zande, Irene.
Goliger, Janet, photos by. I Need to Be SAFE I'm Worth It! How to Protect Your Child from Danger. Goliger, Janet. Bond, Amy, ed. 2006. 144p. (J). per. 19.95 *(978-0-9768273-2-0(8)*, 705-002, CLASS Publications) Children Learning Awareness, Safety & Self-Defense.

Golino, Mirto. The Little Chapel That Stood. Curtiss, A. B. lt. ed. 2005. (ENG.). 36p. (J). (gr. -1-3). 18.95 *(978-0-932529-77-0(1))* Oldcastle Publishing.

Gollan, Stewart. I Want to Be a Cricketer. Carbon, Sally & Langer, Justin. 2008. 32p. (J). pap. 16.95 *(978-1-921361-24-1(7))* Fremantle Pr. AUS. Dist: Independent Pubs. Group.

Golliher, Bill & Vaughan, Jack. Webber Interactive WH Questions Level 2: Whqd22. 2006. (J). cd-rom 49.99 *(978-1-58650-647-6(1))* Super Duper Pubns.

Golliher, Bill, jt. illus. see Ink, Bruce.

Golubeva, Evgenia. Shh..Shh..Shabbat. Marshall, Linda Elovitz. 2016. (J). ***(978-1-4677-5873-4(6)***, Kar-Ben Publishing) Lerner Publishing Group.

Gombert, Bobby. PageLand: A Story about Love & Sharing & Working Together. Hutchens, David. 2004. (gr. 4-8). 14.99 *(978-0-8054-2726-4(0))* B&H Publishing Group.

Gombinski, Rita, jt. illus. see Baker, Syd.

Gomer, William. I am Not a Flying Elephant Fish! A Children's Science Book on the Butterfly. Bronson, Cary. lt. ed. 2004. 32p. (J). lib. bdg. 14.95 *(978-0-9746094-0-9(4))* Connect With Your Kid Bks.

Gomes, Angus. Broken. Pulford, Elizabeth. 2013. (ENG.). 240p. (YA). (gr. 7). pap. 9.95 *(978-0-7624-5004-6(5)*, Running Pr. Kids) Running Pr. Bk. Pubs.

Gomes, John. La Camada con Suerte: Cachorros de Lobo Rescatados de un Incendio Forestal. Curtis, Jennifer Keats. 2015. (ENG & SPA.). 32p. (J). (gr. k-3). pap. 9.95 ***(978-1-62855-720-6(6))*** Arbordale Publishing.

—Kali's Story: an Orphaned Polar Bear Rescue, 1 vol. Keats Curtis, Jennifer. 2014. (SPA.). 32p. (J). (gr. -1-3). pap. 9.95 ***(978-1-62855-226-3(3))*** Arbordale Publishing.

—The Lucky Litter: Wolf Pups Rescued from Wildfire. Curtis, Jennifer Keats. 2015. (ENG.). 32p. (J). (gr. k-3). 17.95 ***(978-1-62855-718-3(4))*** Arbordale Publishing.

Gomes, John, photos by. Kali's Story: An Orphaned Polar Bear Rescue, 1 vol. Curtis, Jennifer Keats. 2014. (ENG., 32p. (J). (gr. -1-3). 17.95 *(978-1-62855-208-9(5))* Arbordale Publishing.

Gomez, Blanca. One Family. Shannon, George. 2015. (ENG.). 32p. (J). (gr. -1-3). 17.99 *(978-0-374-30003-6(8)*, Farrar, Straus & Giroux (BYR)) Farrar, Straus & Giroux.

Gomez, Eddie Martinez. Amigos del Otro Lado. Anza, Ana Luisa. rev. ed. 2004. (Castillo de la Lectura Naranja Ser.). (SPA & ENG.). 136p. (J). pap. 7.95 *(978-970-20-0130-0(7))* Castillo, Ediciones, S. A. de C. V. MEX. Dist: Macmillan.

Gomez, Elena. Creation Song. Scott-Brown, Anna. 2008. 32p. (J). (gr. k-2). 12.99 *(978-0-8254-6263-4(0))* Kregel Pubns.

—Shy Shark. Morgan, Michaela. 2005. (ENG.). 24p. (J). lib. bdg. 23.65 *(978-1-59646-722-4(3))* Dingles & Co.

—Through the Heart of the Jungle. Emmett, Jonathan. 2003. 32p. (J). tchr. ed. 15.95 *(978-1-58925-029-1(X))*; pap. 5.95 *(978-1-58925-380-3(9))* Tiger Tales.

—A World of Prayers. 2004. 32p. (J). (gr. k). 16.00 *(978-0-8028-5285-4(8)*, Eerdmans Bks For Young Readers) Eerdmans, William B. Publishing Co.

Gómez, Elizabeth. Moony Luna. Argueta, Jorge. 2013.Tr. of Luna, Lunita Lunera. (ENG & SPA.). 32p. (J). pap. 8.95 *(978-0-89239-306-0(8)*, Children's Book Press) Lee & Low Bks., Inc.

Gomez, Elizabeth. Moony Luna: Luna, Lunita Lunera. Argueta, Jorge & Alvarez, Cecilia Concepcion. 2005. (ENG & SPA.). 32p. (J). 16.95 *(978-0-89239-205-6(3))* Lee & Low Bks., Inc.

Gómez, Elizabeth. The Upside down Boy. Herrera, Juan Felipe. 2013.Tr. of Nino de Cabeza. (SPA & ENG.). 32p. (J). (gr. k-3). per. 9.95 *(978-0-89239-217-9(7))* Lee & Low Bks., Inc.

Gomez, Elizabeth & Gómez, Elizabeth. Una Pelicula en Mi Almohada. Argueta, Jorge. 2013.Tr. of Movie in My Pillow. (ENG & SPA.). 32p. (J). (gr. k). pap. 8.95 *(978-0-89239-219-3(3))* Lee & Low Bks., Inc.

Gómez, Elizabeth, jt. illus. see Gomez, Elizabeth.

Gomez, Marcela & Silva, David. Celebra el Cinco de Mayo con un Jarabe Tapatio. Flor Ada, Alma. 2006. (Cuentos para Celebrar / Stories to Celebrate Ser.). 30p. (gr. k-6). per. 11.95 *(978-1-59820-118-5(2))* Ediciones Alfaguara ESP. Dist: Santillana USA Publishing Co., Inc.

Gomez, Obed. Mis Papitos: Heroes de la Cosecha. Caraballo, Samuel. 2005. (ENG & SPA.). 32p. (J). (gr. -1-3). 16.95 *(978-1-55885-450-5(9)*, Piñata Books) Arte Publico Pr.

Gomez, Patricio. Gatico-Gatico. Sarduy, Severo. (Literary Encounters Ser.). (SPA.). (J). (gr. 3-5). pap. *(978-968-494-062-8(9)*, CI1124) Centro de Informacion y Desarrollo de la Comunicacion y la Literatura MEX. Dist: Lectorum Pubns., Inc.

Gomez, Patricio & Villagomez, Raul. Me Gusta Jugar Con los Libros. Santirso, Liliana. (SPA.). (J). (gr. k-1). pap. *(978-968-6465-48-8(0))* Casa de Estudios de Literatura y Talleres Artisticos Amaquemecan A.C. MEX. Dist: Lectorum Pubns., Inc.

Gomez, Sergio. Weagol's Big Mess. Torres, Jotam D. 2007. 28p. (J). (gr. -1-3). pap. 12.99 *(978-1-59886-758-9(X))* Tate Publishing & Enterprises, LLC.

Gompper, Gail. Every Day by the Bay. Gompper, Gail. 2011. (ENG.). 24p. (J). bds. 9.95 *(978-0-9726487-7-6(1))* Puddle Jump Pr., Ltd.

Gon, Adriano. The Magic Backpack. Jarman, Julia. 2003. (Flying Foxes Ser.). (ENG.). 48p. (J). lib. bdg. *(978-0-7787-1487-3(X))* Crabtree Publishing Co.

—Number Rhymes to Say & Play! Dunn, Opal. 2005. (ENG.). 32p. (J). (gr. -1 — 1). per. 7.95 *(978-1-84507-441-8(6)*, Frances Lincoln) Quarto Publishing Group UK GBR. Dist: Hachette Bk. Group.

Gonçalves da Silva, Fabio. Ariela Aparecida E O Vale Da Neblina Da Cachoeir. Janesh, Ron. 2012. 56p. pap. 20.50 *(978-1-60976-925-3(2)*, Strategic Bk. Publishing) Strategic Book Publishing & Rights Agency (SBPRA).

Goneau, Martin. Apples, Cherries, Red Raspberries: What Is in the Fruits Group? Cleary, Brian P. 2011. (Food Is CATegorical Ser.). (ENG.). 32p. (gr. k-3). pap. 7.95 *(978-0-7613-6385-9(8)*, Millbrook Pr.) Lerner Publishing Group.

—Apples, Cherries, Red Raspberries: What Is in the Fruits Group? Cleary, Brian P. & Nelson, Jennifer K. 2010. (Food Is CATegorical Ser.). (ENG.). 32p. (gr. k-3). lib. bdg. 25.26 *(978-1-58013-589-4(7))* Lerner Publishing Group.

—A Bat Cannot Bat, a Stair Cannot Stare: More about Homonyms & Homophones. Cleary, Brian P. 2014. (Words Are CATegorical (r) Ser.). (ENG.). 32p. (gr. 2-5). lib. bdg. 16.95 *(978-0-7613-9032-9(4)*, Millbrook Pr.) Lerner Publishing Group.

—Black Beans & Lamb, Poached Eggs & Ham: What Is in the Meat & Beans Group? Cleary, Brian P. 2011. (Food Is CATegorical Ser.). (ENG.). 32p. (gr. k-3). pap. 7.95 *(978-0-7613-6387-3(4)*, Millbrook Pr.) Lerner Publishing Group.

—Black Beans & Lamb, Poached Eggs & Ham: What Is in the Meat & Beans Group? Cleary, Brian P. & Nelson, Jennifer K. 2010. (Food Is CATegorical Ser.). (ENG.). 32p. (gr. k-3). lib. bdg. 25.26 *(978-1-58013-591-7(9))* Lerner Publishing Group.

—Butterfly, Flea, Beetle, & Bee: What Is an Insect? Cleary, Brian P. 2012. (Animal Groups Are CATegorical (tm) Ser.). (ENG.). 32p. (gr. k-3). pap. 7.95 *(978-1-4677-0336-9(2))*; lib. bdg. 26.60 *(978-0-7613-6208-1(8))* Lerner Publishing Group. (Millbrook Pr.).

—Catfish, Cod, Salmon, & Scrod: What Is a Fish? Cleary, Brian P. 2012. (Animal Groups Are CATegorical (tm) Ser.). (ENG.). 32p. (gr. k-3). pap. 7.95 *(978-1-4677-0337-6(0))*; lib. bdg. 26.60 *(978-0-7613-6211-1(8))* Lerner Publishing Group. (Millbrook Pr.).

—Chips & Cheese & Nana's Knees: What Is Alliteration? Cleary, Brian P. 2015. (Words Are CATegorical (r) Ser.). (ENG.). 32p. (gr. 2-5). lib. bdg. 17.95 *(978-1-4677-2649-8(4)*, Millbrook Pr.) Lerner Publishing Group.

—Dolphin, Fox, Hippo, & Ox: What Is a Mammal? Cleary, Brian P. 2012. (Animal Groups Are CATegorical (tm) Ser.). (ENG.). 32p. (gr. k-3). pap. 7.95 *(978-1-4677-0338-3(9))*; lib. bdg. 26.60 *(978-0-7613-6206-7(1))* Lerner Publishing Group. (Millbrook Pr.).

—Ful & -Less, -Er And -Ness: What Is a Suffix? Cleary, Brian P. 2014. (Words Are CATegorical (r) Ser.). (ENG.). 32p. (gr. 2-5). lib. bdg. 16.95 *(978-1-4677-0610-0(8)*, Millbrook Pr.) Lerner Publishing Group.

—Green Beans, Potatoes, & Even Tomatoes: What Is in the Vegetables Group? Cleary, Brian P. 2011. (Food Is CATegorical Ser.). (ENG.). 32p. (gr. k-3). pap. 7.95 *(978-0-7613-6391-0(2)*, Millbrook Pr.) Lerner Publishing Group.

—Green Beans, Potatoes, & Even Tomatoes: What Is in the Vegetables Group? Cleary, Brian P. & Nelson, Jennifer K. 2010. (Food Is CATegorical Ser.). (ENG.). 32p. (gr. k-3). 25.26 *(978-1-58013-588-7(9))* Lerner Publishing Group.

—Macaroni & Rice & Bread by the Slice: What Is in the Grains Group? Cleary, Brian P. 2011. (Food Is CATegorical Ser.). (ENG.). 32p. (gr. k-3). pap. 7.95 *(978-0-7613-6386-6(6)*, Millbrook Pr.) Lerner Publishing Group.

—Macaroni & Rice & Bread by the Slice: What Is in the Grains Group? Cleary, Brian P. & Nelson, Jennifer K. 2010. (Food Is CATegorical Ser.). (ENG.). 32p. (gr. k-3). lib. bdg. 25.26 *(978-1-58013-587-0(0))* Lerner Publishing Group.

—Oils (Just a Bit) to Keep Your Body Fit: What Are Oils? Cleary, Brian P. (Food Is CATegorical Ser.). (ENG.). 32p. (gr. k-3). 2011. pap. 7.95 *(978-0-7613-6389-7(0)*, Millbrook Pr.); 2010. lib. bdg. 25.26 *(978-1-58013-592-4(7))* Lerner Publishing Group.

—Pre- & Re-, Mis- & Dis- What Is a Prefix? Cleary, Brian P. 2013. (Words Are CATegorical (r) Ser.). (ENG.). 32p. (gr. 2-5). lib. bdg. 16.95 *(978-0-7613-9031-2(6)*, Millbrook Pr.) Lerner Publishing Group.

—Run & Hike, Play & Bike: What Is Physical Activity? Cleary, Brian P. 2011. (Food Is CATegorical Ser.). (ENG.). 32p. (gr. k-3). pap. 7.95 *(978-0-7613-6390-3(4)*, Millbrook Pr.) Lerner Publishing Group.

—Salamander, Frog, & Polliwog: What Is an Amphibian? Cleary, Brian P. 2012. (Animal Groups Are CATegorical (tm) Ser.). (ENG.). 32p. (gr. k-3). pap. 7.95 *(978-1-4677-0339-0(7))*; lib. bdg. 26.60 *(978-0-7613-6209-8(6))* Lerner Publishing Group. (Millbrook Pr.).

—Sparrow, Eagle, Penguin, & Seagull: What Is a Bird? Cleary, Brian P. 2012. (Animal Groups Are CATegorical (tm) Ser.). (ENG.). 32p. (gr. k-3). pap. 7.95 *(978-1-4677-0340-6(0))*; lib. bdg. 26.60 *(978-0-7613-6207-4(X))* Lerner Publishing Group. (Millbrook Pr.).

—Tortoise, Tree Snake, Gator, & Sea Snake: What Is a Reptile? Cleary, Brian P. 2012. (Animal Groups Are CATegorical (tm) Ser.). (ENG.). 32p. (gr. k-3). pap. 7.95 *(978-1-4677-0341-3(9))*; lib. bdg. 26.60 *(978-0-7613-6210-4(X))* Lerner Publishing Group. (Millbrook Pr.).

—Yogurt & Cheeses & Ice Cream That Pleases: What Is in the Milk Group? Cleary, Brian P. 2011. (Food Is CATegorical Ser.). (ENG.). 32p. (gr. k-3). pap. 7.95 *(978-0-7613-6388-0(2)*, Millbrook Pr.) Lerner Publishing Group.

—Yogurt & Cheeses & Ice Cream That Pleases: What Is the Milk Group? Cleary, Brian P. & Nelson, Jennifer K. 2010. (Food Is CATegorical Ser.). (ENG.). 32p. (gr. k-3). lib. bdg. 25.26 *(978-1-58013-590-0(0))* Lerner Publishing Group.

Goneau, Martin & Gable, Brian. Run & Hike, Play & Bike: What Is Physical Activity? Cleary, Brian P. 2010. (Food Is CATegorical Ser.). (ENG.). 32p. (gr. k-3). lib. bdg. 25.26 *(978-1-58013-593-1(5))* Lerner Publishing Group.

Gonina, Luba. The Owls of the Enchanted Forest. Harary, Keith. 2008. 52p. (J). pap. 15.88 *(978-0-9799196-8-8(1))* Owl Pals.

—The Owls of the Enchanted Forest - 2007 Special Collector's Edition. Harary, Keith. 2007. 50p. (J). 50.00 incl. DVD *(978-0-9799196-3-3(0))* Owl Pals.

Gonne, Maud. Celtic Wonder-Tales. Young, Ella. 2014. (J). *(978-0-486-78065-8(1))* Dover Pubns., Inc.

Gonsalves, Rob. Imagine a Night. Thomson, Sarah L. 2003. (Imagine A... Ser.). (ENG.). 40p. (J). (gr. -1-3). 19.99 *(978-0-689-85218-3(5)*, Atheneum Bks. for Young Readers) Simon & Schuster Children's Publishing.

—Imagine a Place. Thomson, Sarah L. 2008. (Imagine A... Ser.). (ENG.). 40p. (J). (gr. -1-6). 19.99 *(978-1-4169-6802-3(4)*, Atheneum Bks. for Young Readers) Simon & Schuster Children's Publishing.

Gonsalves, Rob, jt. illus. see Gonsalves, Robert.

Gonsalves, Robert & Gonsalves, Rob. Imagine a Day. Thomson, Sarah L. 2005. (Imagine A... Ser.). (ENG.). 40p. (J). (gr. 1-7). 19.99 *(978-0-689-85219-0(3)*, Atheneum Bks. for Young Readers) Simon & Schuster Children's Publishing.

Gonyea, Mark. A Book about Color: A Clear & Simple Guide for Young Artists. Gonyea, Mark. 2010. (ENG.). 96p. (J). (gr. 4-9). 19.99 *(978-0-8050-9055-0(X)*, Holt, Henry & Co. Bks. For Young Readers) Holt, Henry & Co.

—The Spooky Box. Gonyea, Mark. 2013. (ENG.). 32p. (J). (gr. -1-3). 14.99 *(978-0-8050-8813-7(X)*, Holt, Henry & Co. Bks. For Young Readers) Holt, Henry & Co.

Gonzales, Chuck. The Dwarf in the Drawer: A Mischievous Parody. Van King, L. 2013. (ENG.). 32p. (J). 19.99 *(978-1-250-04143-2(0))* Square Fish.

—Fashionista! Barbo, Maria S. 2009. (ENG.). 128p. (J). (gr. 2-6). pap. 15.99 *(978-0-312-59607-1(3))* Feiwel & Friends.

—The Gigantic, Genuine Genie. Williams, Suzanne. 2007. (Princess Power Ser.: No. 6). 128p. (J). 15.99 *(978-0-06-078309-5(5))* HarperCollins Pubs.

GONZALES, Chuck. Monster High: Ghoul Spirit: A Monster High Doodle Book. Mayer, Kirsten. 2013. (ENG.). 128p. (J). (gr. 1-17). 12.99 *(978-0-316-24655-2(7))* Little, Brown Bks. for Young Readers.

Gonzales, Chuck. The Mysterious, Mournful Maiden. Williams, Suzanne. 2007. 112p. (J). 15.99 *(978-0-06-078305-1(2))* HarperCollins Pubs.

—Rock Star! Barbo, Maria S. 2009. (ENG.). 128p. (J). (gr. 2-6). pap. 15.99 *(978-0-312-59606-4(5))* Feiwel & Friends.

—Survive-O-Pedia. Borgenicht, David et al. ed. 2011. (ENG.). 144p. (J). (gr. 3-17). 16.99 *(978-0-8118-7690-2(X))* Chronicle Bks. LLC.

—The Worst-Case Scenario - Gross. Borgenicht, David et al. 2010. (ENG.). 128p. (J). (gr. 3-17). pap. 10.99 *(978-0-8118-7570-7(9))* Chronicle Bks. LLC.

—The Worst-Case Scenario. Borgenicht, David & Epstein, Robin. 2007. (Worst Case Scenario Ser.: WORS). (ENG.). 128p. (J). (gr. 4-7). pap. 9.95 *(978-0-8118-6065-9(5))* Chronicle Bks. LLC.

Gonzales, Nana. The Sock Thief. Crespo, Ana. 2015. (ENG.). 32p. (J). (gr. -1-2). 16.99 *(978-0-8075-7538-3(0))* Whitman, Albert & Co.

Gonzales, Sharon. Airport Explorers: 2008 Activity Book. 2008. 32p. (J). 6.95 *(978-0-9745294-2-4(7))* San Diego County Regional Airport Authority.

González, Ángel Luis. Mujercitas. González, Ángel Luis, tr. Luna, Sagrario & Alcott, Louisa May. (SPA.). 92p. (J). (gr. 5-8). pap. 9.95 *(978-84-204-5748-2(5))* Santillana USA Publishing Co., Inc.

Gonzalez, Ashley. Magic of Masara. Kagna, Barbara. 2010. 24p. pap. 12.50 *(978-1-4490-5651-3(2))* AuthorHouse.

Gonzalez, Crysol, jt. illus. see Gonzalez, Ricky.

Gonzalez, Francisco. El Coyote Tonto. Garrido, Felipe. 2003. (Infantil Alfaguara Ser.). (SPA.). 60p. (J). (gr. 3-5). pap. 8.95 *(978-968-19-0277-3(7))* Santillana USA Publishing Co., Inc.

Gonzalez, Henry. Aviador Santiago. Nino, Jairo Anibal. 2003. (Literatura Juvenil (Panamericana Editorial) Ser.). (SPA.). 138p. (YA). (gr. -1-7). pap. *(978-958-30-0297-7(6))* Panamericana Editorial.

—La Casa del Abuelo. Buitrago, Fanny. 2003. (Literatura Juvenil (Panamericana Editorial) Ser.). (SPA.). 71p. (YA). (gr. -1-7). per. *(978-958-30-0338-7(7))* Panamericana Editorial.

—La Casa del Arco Iris: Una Novela de la Infancia. Buitrago, Fanny. 2003. (Literatura Juvenil (Panamericana Editorial) Ser.). (SPA.). 186p. (YA). (gr. -1-7). pap. *(978-958-30-0334-9(4))* Panamericana Editorial.

—Las Cosas de la Casa. Roman, Celso. 2003. (Literatura Juvenil (Panamericana Editorial) Ser.). (SPA.). 87p. (YA). (gr. -1-7). per. *(978-958-30-0296-0(8))* Panamericana Editorial.

—El Maravilloso Viaje de Rosendo Bucuru. Roman, Celso. 2003. (Coleccion Corcel Ser.). (SPA.). 109p. (J). (gr. -1-7). pap. *(978-958-30-0343-1(3))* Panamericana Editorial.

—Primitivos Relatos Contados Otra Vez: Heroes y Mitos Amazonicos. Niño, Hugo. 2004. (Literatura Juvenil (Panamericana Editorial) Ser.). (SPA.). 160p. (YA). (gr. 4-7). pap. *(978-958-30-0365-3(4))* Panamericana Editorial.

Gonzalez, Henry & Granada, Nancy. Como el Leopardo Obtuvo Sus Manchas: Y Otros Cuentos de Animales. Kipling, Rudyard. Calderon, Catalina, tr. 2004. (Cajon de Cuentos Ser.). (SPA.). 165p. (J). (gr. -1-7). *(978-958-30-0328-8(X))* Panamericana Editorial.

Gonzalez, Javier A. Friday. Lindeen, Mary. 2008. (Days of the Week Ser.). 24p. (J). (gr. -1-k). 27.07 *(978-1-60270-101-4(6))* Magic Wagon.

—Monday. Lindeen, Mary. 2008. (Days of the Week Ser.). 24p. (J). (gr. -1-k). 27.07 *(978-1-60270-097-0(4))* Magic Wagon.

—Saturday. Lindeen, Mary. 2008. (Days of the Week Ser.). 24p. (J). (gr. -1-k). 27.07 *(978-1-60270-102-1(4))* Magic Wagon.

—Sunday. Lindeen, Mary. 2008. (Days of the Week Ser.). 24p. (J). (gr. -1-k). 27.07 *(978-1-60270-096-3(6))* Magic Wagon.

—Thursday. Lindeen, Mary. 2008. (Days of the Week Ser.). 24p. (J). (gr. -1-k). 27.07 *(978-1-60270-100-7(8))* Magic Wagon.

—Tuesday. Lindeen, Mary. 2008. (Days of the Week Ser.). 24p. (J). (gr. -1-k). 27.07 *(978-1-60270-098-7(2))* Magic Wagon.

—Wednesday. Lindeen, Mary. 2008. (Days of the Week Ser.). 24p. (J). (gr. -1-k). 27.07 *(978-1-60270-099-4(0))* Magic Wagon.

—The Week. Lindeen, Mary. 2008. (Days of the Week Ser.). 24p. (J). (gr. -1-1). 27.07 *(978-1-60270-103-8(2)*, Looking Glass Library- Nonfiction) Magic Wagon.

Gonzalez, Jorge H., photos by. Arte Ruso Sobre Laminas de Aluminio: El Teatro y los Titeres. Neira, Maria Lia. Panamericana Editorial, ed. 2003. (Manos Maestras Ser.). (SPA., 18p. pap. *(978-958-30-1089-7(8))* Panamericana Editorial.

Gonzalez, Jose Antonio, jt. illus. see Andersen, Flemming.

Gonzalez., Jose L. Slinkie the courageous Snail. Adams, Marlene. 2004. 68p. (J). pap. 25.75 *(978-1-4184-8340-1(0))* AuthorHouse.

Gonzalez, Maya Christina. Angels Ride Bikes & Other Fall Poems: Los Angeles Andan Bicicletas y Otros Poemas de Otono. Alarcón, Francisco X. 2013. (ENG & SPA.). 32p. (J). (gr. 1-4). per. 9.95 *(978-0-89239-198-1(7))* Lee & Low Bks., Inc.

—Animal Poems of the Iguazu. Alarcón, Francisco X. 2008. (SPA & ENG.). 32p. (J). (gr. k). 16.95 *(978-0-89239-225-4(8))* Lee & Low Bks., Inc.

—Animal Poems of the Iguazú. Alarcón, Francisco X. 2013.Tr. of Animalario Del Iguazú. (ENG & SPA.). 32p. (J). pap. 9.95 *(978-0-89239-299-5(1)*, Children's Book Press) Lee & Low Bks., Inc.

—Fiesta Femenina. Gerson, Mary-Joan. 2003. (SPA & ENG.). 64p. (J). 19.99 *(978-1-84148-964-3(6))* Barefoot Bks., Inc.

—From the Bellybutton of the Moon & Other Summer Poems (Del Ombligo de la Luna y Otros Poemas de Verano) Alarcón, Francisco X. ed. 2013. (ENG & SPA.). 32p. (J). (gr. 1-4). per. 9.95 *(978-0-89239-201-8(0))* Lee & Low Bks., Inc.

—Iguanas in the Snow & Other Winter Poems. Alarcón, Francisco X. & Alarcon, Francisco. 2004. (ENG & SPA.). 32p. (J). (gr. 1-18). 16.95 *(978-0-89239-168-4(5))* Lee & Low Bks., Inc.

—Iguanas in the Snow & Other Winter Poems: Iguanas en la Nieve y Otros Poemas. Alarcón, Francisco X. 2013. (ENG & SPA.). 32p. (J). (gr. 1-4). per. 8.95 *(978-0-89239-202-5(9))* Lee & Low Bks., Inc.

—Laughing Tomatoes & Other Spring Poems (Jitomates Risueños y Otros Poemas de Primavera) Alarcón, Francisco X. 2013. (ENG & SPA.). 32p. (J). (gr. 1-4). per. 9.95 *(978-0-89239-199-8(5))* Lee & Low Bks., Inc.

—Mi Diario de Aquí Hasta Allá. Pérez, Amada Irma. 2013.Tr. of My Diary from Here to There. (ENG & SPA.). 32p. (J). (gr. k). pap. 9.95 *(978-0-89239-230-8(4))* Lee & Low Bks., Inc.

—Nana, Que Sorpresa! Perez, Amada Irma & Children's Book Press Staff. 2007.Tr. of Nana's Big Surprise. (ENG & SPA.). 32p. (J). (gr. k-2). lib. bdg. 16.95 *(978-0-89239-190-5(1))* Lee & Low Bks., Inc.

—Nana's Big Surprise. Pérez, Amada Irma. 2013.Tr. of Nana, ¡Qué Sorpresa!. (ENG & SPA.). 32p. (J). pap. 8.95 *(978-0-89239-307-7(6)*, Children's Book Press) Lee & Low Bks., Inc.

—Prietita & the Ghost Woman: Prietita y la Llorona. Anzaldúa, Gloria. 2013. (ENG & SPA.). 32p. (J). (gr. 1-18). pap. 9.95 *(978-0-89239-167-7(7))* Lee & Low Bks., Inc.

Gonzalez, Pedro Julio. Turtles. Huelin, Jodi. 2003. (Penguin Young Readers, Level 2 Ser.). (ENG.). 32p. (J). (gr. 1-3). mass mkt. 3.99 *(978-0-448-43117-8(3)*, Warne, Frederick Pubs.) Penguin Bks., Ltd. GBR. Dist: Penguin Random Hse., LLC.

Gonzalez, Ralfka & Ruiz, Ana. Mi Primer Libro de Dichos. 2014.Tr. of My First Book of Proverbs. (SPA & ENG.). 32p. (J). (gr. -1-3). pap. 9.95 *(978-0-89239-200-1(2))* Lee & Low Bks., Inc.

Gonzalez, Ricky & Gonzalez, Crysol. Wiley's Way: El Camino de Wiley. Blumenthal, Bliss & Alarcon, Claudia. 2004. (ENG & SPA.). 96p. mass mkt. 9.95 *(978-0-292-70615-6(4))* Univ. of Texas Pr.

Gonzalez, Santiago, et al. Caminantes del Sol. Iturralde, Edna. 2003. (SPA.). 163p. (J). (gr. 5-8). pap. 14.95 *(978-9978-07-431-2(7))* Santillana USA Publishing Co., Inc.

Gonzalez, Santiago. Un Enano y un Gigante. Delgado, Francisco. 2015. 24p. (J). (gr. -1-2). pap. 12.95 ***(978-9978-07-529-6(1)***, Alfaguara Infantil) Santillana Ecuador ECU. Dist: Santillana USA Publishing Co., Inc.

Gonzalez, Tesa. La Ratita Presumida: Adaptacion Teatral. Ballesteros, Jose Manuel & Manuel, Ballesteros Pastor José.Tr. of Conceited Mouse. (SPA.). 48p. (J). (gr. k-3). 5.56 *(978-84-241-7713-3(4))* Everest Editora ESP. Dist: Lectorum Pubns., Inc.

—Tortuga Numero Cien. Javaloyes, Inigo & Íñigo, Javaloyes. 2006. (Montana Encantada Ser.). (SPA.). 60p. (J). (gr. 3-5). pap. 9.50 *(978-84-241-8047-8(X))* Everest Editora ESP. Dist: Lectorum Pubns., Inc.

Gonzalez, Thomas. Gandhi: The March to the Sea, 0 vols. McGinty, Alice B. 2013. (ENG.). 32p. (J). (gr. 4-7). 17.99 *(978-1-4778-1644-8(5)*, 9781477816448, Amazon Children's Publishing) Amazon Publishing.

—The House on Dirty-Third Street, 1 vol. Kittinger, Jo S. 2012. (ENG.). 32p. (J). 16.95 *(978-1-56145-619-2(5))* Peachtree Pubs.

—Sonia Sotomayor: Jueza de la Corte Suprema, 0 vols. Bernier-Grand, Carmen T. 2010. (SPA & ENG.). 48p. (J). (gr. 3-7). 17.99 *(978-0-7614-5801-2(8)*, 9780761458012, Amazon Children's Publishing) Amazon Publishing.

González, Thomas. Sonia Sotomayor: Supreme Court Justice, 0 vols. Bernier-Grand, Carmen T. 2010. (ENG.). 48p. (J). (gr. 3-7). 17.99 *(978-0-7614-5795-4(X)*, 9780761457954, Amazon Children's Publishing) Amazon Publishing.

Gonzalez, Thomas. Toad Weather, 1 vol. Markle, Sandra. 2015. (ENG.). 32p. (J). (gr. 1-3). 16.95 *(978-1-56145-818-9(X))* Peachtree Pubs.

González, Thomas. 14 Cows for America, 1 vol. Deedy, Carmen Agra. 2009. (ENG.). 36p. (J). (gr. 1-5). 17.95 *(978-1-56145-490-7(7))* Peachtree Pubs.
—14 Vacas para América, 1 vol. Deedy, Carmen Agra. 2010.Tr. of 14 Cows for America. (SPA.). 36p. (J). pap. 8.95 *(978-1-56145-555-3(5))* Peachtree Pubs.
—14 Vacas para América, 1 vol. Deedy, Carmen Agra. De la Torre, Cristina, tr. from ENG. 2010.Tr. of 14 Cows for America. (SPA.). 36p. (J). (gr. 1-5). 17.95 *(978-1-56145-550-8(4))* Peachtree Pubs.
Gonzalez, Tom. Dream of Wings. Gonzalez, Noni. 2013. (ENG.). 40p. (J). pap. 9.99 *(978-1-939337-20-7(8))*; 14.99 *(978-1-939337-71-9(2))* Telemachus Pr., LLC.
—Kubla, a Koi Story. Gonzalez, Noni. 2013. (ENG.). 38p. (J). pap. 9.99 *(978-1-939337-68-9(2))*; 14.99 *(978-1-939337-72-6(0))* Telemachus Pr., LLC.
Gooch, Thelma. Nobody's Girl: Companion Story to Nobody's Boy. Malot, Hector & Crewe-Jones, Florence. 2006. 220p. (J). pap. *(978-1-894666-76-3(3))* Inheritance Pubns.
Gooch, Thelma & Gruelle, Johnny. Nobody's Boy: Companion Story to Nobody's Girl. Malot, Hector & Crewe-Jones, Florence. 2006. 237p. (J). pap. *(978-1-894666-75-6(5))* Inheritance Pubns.
Good, Karen. Change the World Before Bedtime, 1 vol. Moulton, Mark Kimball & Chalmers, Josh. 2012. (ENG.). 32p. (J). 16.99 *(978-0-7643-4238-7(X))* Schiffer Publishing, Ltd.
—Mr Sparrows Merry Fairy Circus. Moulton, Mark. 2004. 24p. 18.00 *(978-0-7412-1940-4(9))* Lang Graphics, Ltd.
Good, Karen H. Miss Sadie Mcgee Who Lived in a Tree. Moulton, Mark Kimball. 2008. (ENG.). 32p. (J). (gr. k-3). 16.95 *(978-0-8249-5152-8(2))*, Ideals Children's Bks.) Ideals Pubns.
—A Royal Wedding. Moulton, Mark K. 2007. (ENG.). 32p. (J). (gr. k-3). 14.99 *(978-0-8249-8677-3(6))* Ideals Pubns.
—Twisted Sistahs. Moulton, Mark Kimball. 2006. (ENG.). 32p. (J). (gr. 2-3). 14.95 *(978-0-8249-8676-6(8))* Ideals Pubns.
Good, Karen Hillard. The Annual Snowman's Ball. Moulton, Mark Kimball. 2007. (ENG.). 32p. (J). (gr. -1-3). 14.99 *(978-0-8249-5564-9(1))*, Ideals Children's Bks.) Ideals Pubns.
—Miss Fiona's Stupendous Pumpkin Pies. Moulton, Mark. 2011. 32p. (J). pap. 7.99 *(978-0-8249-5635-6(4))* Ideals Pubns.
—Reindeer Christmas. Moulton, Mark Kimball. 2008. (ENG.). 40p. (J). (gr. -1-3). 15.99 *(978-1-4169-6108-6(9))*, Simon & Schuster/Paula Wiseman Bks.) Simon & Schuster/Paula Wiseman Bks.
—A Snowgirl Named Just Sue. Moulton, Mark Kimball. 2008. (ENG.). 36p. (J). (gr. -1-3). 14.95 *(978-0-8249-5150-4(6))* Ideals Pubns.
—The Very Best Pumpkin. Moulton, Mark Kimball. 2010. (ENG.). 32p. (J). (gr. -1-3). bds. 12.99 *(978-1-4169-8288-3(4))*, Simon & Schuster/Paula Wiseman Bks.) Simon & Schuster/Paula Wiseman Bks.
Good, Karen Hillard. A Snowman Named Just Bob. Good, Karen Hillard. Moulton, Mark Kimball. ed. 2009. 32p. (J). (gr. -1-3). 18.99 *(978-0-8249-5596-0(X))*, Ideals Children's Bks.) Ideals Pubns.
Goodale, Krystahl. Timothy: A Little Fish with a Big Purpose! Riley, Brad. 2013. 30p. 22.95 *(978-1-62015-341-3(6))*; pap. 14.95 *(978-1-62015-148-8(0))* Booktrope. (Vox Dei).
Goodall, John S. The Christmas Mouse. Read, Miss. (J). lib. bdg. 14.95 *(978-0-8488-1452-6(5))* Amereon LTD.
Goodberry, Jo. Read with Me Jack & the Beanstalk: Sticker Activity Book. Page, Nick & Page, Claire. 2006. (Read with Me (Make Believe Ideas) Ser.). 12p. (J). (gr. k-2). pap. *(978-1-84610-180-9(8))* Make Believe Ideas.
—Ready to Read Jack & the Beanstalk Sticker Activity Workbook. Page, Nick & Page, Claire. 2006. (Ready-to-Read Sticker Ser.). 12p. (J). (gr. -1-3). pap., wbk. ed., act. bk. ed. *(978-1-84610-127-4(1))* Make Believe Ideas.
Goode, Diane. Baby Face: A Book of Love for Baby. Rylant, Cynthia. 2008. (ENG.). 40p. (J). (gr. -1-3). 17.99 *(978-1-4169-4909-1(7))*, Simon & Schuster/Paula Wiseman Bks.) Simon & Schuster/Paula Wiseman Bks.
—Ballerina Rosie. Duchess of York Staff & Ferguson, Sarah. 2012. (ENG.). 32p. (J). (gr. -1-3). 16.99 *(978-1-4424-3066-2(4))*, Simon & Schuster/Paula Wiseman Bks.) Simon & Schuster/Paula Wiseman Bks.
—But I Wanted a Baby Brother! Feiffer, Kate. 2010. (ENG.). 32p. (J). (gr. -1-3). 16.99 *(978-1-4169-3941-2(5))*, Simon & Schuster/Paula Wiseman Bks.) Simon & Schuster/Paula Wiseman Bks.
—Christmas in the Barn. Brown, Margaret Wise. 32p. (J). (gr. -1-3). 2007. (ENG.). per. 6.99 *(978-0-06-052636-8(X))*; 2004. lib. bdg. 16.89 *(978-0-06-052635-1(1))* HarperCollins Pubs.
—Cinderella Smith. Barden, Stephanie. (Cinderella Smith Ser.: 1). (ENG.). (J). 2012. 176p. (gr. 3-7). pap. 5.99 *(978-0-06-196425-1(5))*; 2011. 160p. (gr. 3-7). 16.99 *(978-0-06-196423-7(9))*; Vol. 3. 2013. 144p. (gr. 1-5). 16.99 *(978-0-06-200443-7(3))* HarperCollins Pubs.
—Cinderella Smith: The More the Merrier. Barden, Stephanie. 2013. (Cinderella Smith Ser.: 2). (ENG.). 160p. (J). (gr. 3-7). pap. 5.99 *(978-0-06-200442-0(5))* HarperCollins Pubs.
—Founding Mothers: Remembering the Ladies. Roberts, Cokie. 2014. 40p. (J). (gr. 2-7). (ENG.). 17.99 *(978-0-06-078002-9(9))*; lib. bdg. 18.89 *(978-0-06-078003-6(7))* HarperCollins Pubs.
—Louise the Big Cheese. Primavera, Elise. 2011. (ENG.). 40p. (J). (gr. k-3). 6.99 *(978-1-4424-2066-3(9))*, Simon & Schuster/Paula Wiseman Bks.) Simon & Schuster/Paula Wiseman Bks.
—Louise the Big Cheese: Divine Diva. Primavera, Elise. 2009. (ENG.). 40p. (J). (gr. k-3). 16.99 *(978-1-4169-7180-1(7))*, Simon & Schuster/Paula Wiseman Bks.) Simon & Schuster/Paula Wiseman Bks.
—Louise the Big Cheese & the Back-To-School Smarty-Pants. Primavera, Elise. 2011. (ENG.). 40p. (J). (gr. k-3). 16.99 *(978-1-4424-0600-1(3))*, Simon & Schuster/Paula Wiseman Bks.) Simon & Schuster/Paula Wiseman Bks.
—Louise the Big Cheese & the La-Di-Da Shoes. Primavera, Elise. 2010. (ENG.). 40p. (J). (gr. k-3). 16.99 *(978-1-4169-7181-8(5))*, Simon & Schuster/Paula Wiseman Bks.) Simon & Schuster/Paula Wiseman Bks.
—Louise the Big Cheese & the Ooh-la-La Charm School. Primavera, Elise. 2012. (ENG.). 40p. (J). (gr. k-3). 16.99 *(978-1-4424-0599-8(6))*, Simon & Schuster/Paula Wiseman Bks.) Simon & Schuster/Paula Wiseman Bks.
—The More the Merrier. Barden, Stephanie. 2012. (Cinderella Smith Ser.: 2). (ENG.). 144p. (J). (gr. 3-7). 15.99 *(978-0-06-200440-6(9))* HarperCollins Pubs.
—My Mom Is Trying to Ruin My Life. Feiffer, Kate. 2009. (ENG.). 32p. (J). (gr. -1-3). 16.99 *(978-1-4169-4100-2(2))*, Simon & Schuster/Paula Wiseman Bks.) Simon & Schuster/Paula Wiseman Bks.
—President Pennybaker. Feiffer, Kate. 2012. (ENG.). 32p. (J). (gr. -1-3). 7.99 *(978-1-4169-1355-9(6))*, Simon & Schuster/Paula Wiseman Bks.) Simon & Schuster/Paula Wiseman Bks.
Goode, Diane. The Most Perfect Spot. Goode, Diane. 2006. (ENG.). 32p. (J). (gr. -1-3). 16.99 *(978-0-06-072697-3(0))* HarperCollins Pubs.
—The Story of the Nutcracker Ballet. Goode, Diane. Hautzig, Deborah. 2006. (Pictureback Books Series). (ENG.). 32p. (J). (gr. -1-2). pap. 3.99 *(978-0-394-88178-2(8))*, Random Hse. Bks. for Young Readers) Random Hse. Children's Bks.
—Thanksgiving Is Here! Goode, Diane. 2005. (ENG.). 32p. (J). (gr. -1-3). pap. 6.99 *(978-0-06-051590-4(2))* HarperCollins Pubs.
Goode, Diane & Chambers, Mark. Superlove. Harper, Charise Mericle. 2014. (ENG.). 32p. (J). (gr. k-3). 16.99 *(978-0-375-86923-5(9))*; lib. bdg. 19.99 *(978-0-375-96923-2(3))* Knopf, Alfred A. Inc.
Goode, Diane, jt. illus. see Glasser, Robin Preiss.
Goodell, Jon. Chicks! Horning, Sandra. 2013. (Step into Reading Ser.). (ENG.). 32p. (J). (gr. -1-1). pap. 3.99 *(978-0-307-93221-1(4))*, Random Hse. Bks. for Young Readers) Random Hse. Children's Bks.
—Chicks! Horning, Sandra. 2013. (Step into Reading Ser.). (ENG.). 32p. (J). (gr. -1-1). lib. bdg. 12.99 *(978-0-375-97117-4(3))* Random Hse., Inc.
—The Gold Miner's Daughter: A Melodramatic Fairy Tale, 1 vol. Hopkins, Jackie Mims. 2006. (ENG.). 32p. (J). (gr. k-3). 15.95 *(978-1-56145-362-7(5))* Peachtree Pubs.
—The Racers: A Tale about Fairness. Andersen, Hans Christian. 2007. (J). *(978-1-59939-090-1(6))*, Reader's Digest Young Families, Inc.) Studio Fun International.
—'Twas the Night Before Christmas. Moore, Clement C. 2013. (ENG.). 26p. (J). (gr. -1). bds. 9.99 *(978-1-4494-3557-8(2))* Andrews McMeel Publishing.
—Twas the Night Before Christmas. Andrews McMeel Publishing Staff & Moore, Clement C. deluxe ed. 2009. (ENG.). 26p. (J). (gr. -1-3). 19.99 *(978-0-7407-8432-3(3))* Andrews McMeel Publishing.
Goodell, Jon & Borgo, Deborah Colvin. Mother Goose. Publications International Ltd. Staff, ed. 2010. 10p. (J). bds. 12.98 *(978-0-7853-7395-7(0))* Phoenix International Publications, Inc.
Goodell, Jon & Clar, David Austin. Fairy Tales. Publications International Ltd. Staff, ed. 2010. 10p. (J). bds. 12.98 *(978-0-7853-7394-0(2))* Phoenix International Publications, Inc.
Goodell, Jon, jt. illus. see Dawson, Diane.
Goodell, Mary. The Chicken Pox Puppy: Kate & Jen's Daily Adventures. Goodell, Mary. 2007. 29p. (J). per. 11.99 *(978-1-59879-382-6(9))* Lifevest Publishing, Inc.
Gooderham, Andrew. The True Story of Santa Claus. Walters, Eric & Walters, Christina. 2005. 38p. (J). 9.95 *(978-1-894601-11-5(4))* Chestnut Publishing Group CAN. Dist: Hushion Hse. Publishing, Ltd.
Goodfellow, Dan. Snow White's Seven Patches: A Vitiligo Fairy Tale. Kats, Jewel. 2013. 40p. pap. 14.95 *(978-1-61599-206-5(5))* Loving Healing Pr., Inc.
Goodin, Carolyn M. Candy Land. Goodin, Carolyn M. 2007. 38p. (J). per. 14.99 *(978-0-9797879-1-2(2))* Family Legacy Ministries.
Goodman Koz, Paula. In the Company of Owls. Huggins, Peter. 2008. (J). 15.95 *(978-1-58838-036-4(X))*, Junebug Bks.) NewSouth, Inc.
—Shlemiel Crooks. Olswanger, Anna. 2008. 36p. (J). pap. 11.95 *(978-1-58838-236-8(2))*, Junebug Bks.) NewSouth, Inc.
Goodman, Larry. Grumpy the Grasshopper. Collier, Wayne Evans. 2012. 20p. pap. 24.95 *(978-1-4626-6844-1(5))* America Star Bks.
Goodman, Marlene. German Picture Dictionary. Passport Books Staff, ed. 2003. (Let's Learn... Picture Ser.). (GER.). 72p. (J). (gr. 4-7). pap. 9.95 *(978-0-8442-2167-0(8))*, 21678, Passport Bks.) McGraw-Hill Trade.
—Italian Picture Dictionary. Passport Books Staff, ed. 2003. (Let's Learn... Picture Dictionary Ser.). (ITA.). 72p. (J). (gr. 4-7). pap. 9.95 *(978-0-8442-8065-3(8))*, 80658) McGraw-Hill Trade.
—Japanese Picture Dictionary: Elementary Through Junior High. Passport Books Staff, ed. 2003. (Let's Learn... Picture Dictionary Ser.). (JPN.). 80p. (J). (gr. 4-7). pap. 11.95 *(978-0-8442-8494-1(7))*, 84947) McGraw-Hill Trade.
—Let's Learn American English. Passport Books Staff, ed. 2003. (Let's Learn... Picture Dictionary Ser.). 72p. (J). (gr. 4-7). 9.95 *(978-0-8442-5453-1(3))*, 54533, Passport Bks.) McGraw-Hill Trade.
—Let's Learn Hebrew. Passport Books Staff, ed. 2003. (Let's Learn... Picture Dictionary Ser.). (HEB.). 72p. (J). (gr. 4-7). 11.95 *(978-0-8442-8490-3(4))*, 84904, Passport Bks.) McGraw-Hill Trade.
Goodman, Marlene K. Josh Discovers Passover! Stein, Larry. I.t. ed. 2004. (Josh Discovers Ser.). (ENG.). 32p. (J). (gr. -1-3). pap. 9.95 *(978-0-9669910-1-7(X))* Ruach Publishing.
Goodman, Tama. The Seven Species. Biers-Ariel, Matt. 2003. 48p. 19.95 *(978-0-8074-0852-0(2))*, 161902) URJ Pr.
Goodnow, Patti. I Tell the Truth! Parker, David. 2004. (J). pap. *(978-0-439-62808-2(3))* Scholastic, Inc.
Goodpaster, Nancy. Find Your Magic. Payne, Sandy. 2013. 50p. pap. 12.95 *(978-1-937508-16-6(1))* Bearhead Publishing, LLC.
Goodreau, Sarah. The Hare & the Tortoise Race Across Israel. Gehl, Laura & Aesop. 2015. (ENG.). 32p. (J). (gr. -1-1). lib. bdg. 17.95 *(978-1-4677-2199-8(9))*, Kar-Ben Publishing) Lerner Publishing Group.
—Hare & Tortoise Race Across Israel. Gehl, Laura & Aesop. 2015. (J). *(978-1-4677-6202-1(4))*, Kar-Ben Publishing) Lerner Publishing Group.
Goodrich, Carter. A Creature Was Stirring: One Boy's Night Before Christmas. Goodrich, Carter. Moore, Clement C. 2006. (ENG.). 40p. (J). (gr. -1-3). 17.99 *(978-0-689-86399-8(3))*, Simon & Schuster Bks. For Young Readers) Simon & Schuster Bks. For Young Readers.
—The Hermit Crab. Goodrich, Carter. 2009. (ENG.). 40p. (J). (gr. 1-5). 16.99 *(978-1-4169-3892-7(3))*, Simon & Schuster Bks. For Young Readers) Simon & Schuster Bks. For Young Readers.
—Mister Bud Wears the Cone. Goodrich, Carter. 2014. (ENG.). 48p. (J). (gr. -1-3). 16.99 *(978-1-4424-8088-9(2))*, Simon & Schuster Bks. For Young Readers) Simon & Schuster Bks. For Young Readers.
—Say Hello to Zorro! Goodrich, Carter. 2011. (ENG.). 48p. (J). (gr. -1-3). 15.99 *(978-1-4169-3893-4(1))*, Simon & Schuster Bks. For Young Readers) Simon & Schuster Bks. For Young Readers.
—We Forgot Brock! Goodrich, Carter. 2015. (ENG.). 48p. (J). (gr. -1-3). 17.99 *(978-1-4424-8090-2(4))*, Simon & Schuster Bks. For Young Readers) Simon & Schuster Bks. For Young Readers.
—Zorro Gets an Outfit. Goodrich, Carter. 2012. (ENG.). 48p. (J). (gr. -1-3). 15.99 *(978-1-4424-3535-3(6))*, Simon & Schuster Bks. For Young Readers) Simon & Schuster Bks. For Young Readers.
Goodrow, Carol. Happy Feet, Healthy Food: Your Child's First Journal of Exercise & Healthy Eating. Goodrow, Carol. 2004. (ENG.). 112p. (J). 14.00 *(978-1-891369-46-9(6))* Breakaway Bks.
—The Treasure of Health & Happiness. Goodrow, Carol. 2006. (ENG.). 96p. (J). (gr. 4-7). 14.00 *(978-1-891369-60-5(1))* Consortium Bk. Sales & Distribution.
Goodway, Simon. Leelo. Montreuil, Gaetane. 2013. 50p. pap. *(978-1-926633-67-1(9))* Titles on Demand.
Goodwin, Adrienne Annette. A Day Like Mine. Bridges, Eunice. 2011. 32p. pap. 24.95 *(978-1-4560-5766-4(9))* America Star Bks.
Goodwin, Wendy. Cocoa's Collar, 1 vol. Stalick, Garyanna. 2010. 36p. pap. 24.95 *(978-1-4489-1888-1(X))* America Star Bks.
Goomas, John. Even the Dead Get up for Milk. Holaves, Chris. 2008.Tr. of Hasta los muertos se levantan por Leche. (ENG & SPA.). 64p. (J). lib. bdg. 15.95 *(978-0-9792991-0-0(1))* Astakos Publishing.
—Running with the Bats: Corriendo con los Murcielagos. Holaves, Chris. Medina, Candace, tr. 2009. (ENG & SPA.). 64p. (J). (gr. 4-6). pap. 15.95 *(978-0-9792991-1-7(X))* Astakos Publishing.
Goonack, Katrina, et al. Scaly-Tailed Possum & Echidna. Goonack, Cathy. 2010. (ENG.). 32p. (J). (gr. k). pap. 10.95 *(978-1-921248-16-0(5))* Magabala Bks. AUS. Dist: Independent Pubs. Group.
Goopymart. Mad Tausig vs the Interplanetary Puzzling Peace Patrol. Tausig, Ben. 2007. (ENG.). 94p. (J). (gr. 4-6). per. 7.95 *(978-0-9741319-4-8(6))* 4N Publishing LLC.
Goosens, Philippe. ¡Soy un Dragón! Robberecht, Thierry. 2010. (SPA.). (J). (gr. -1-2). *(978-84-263-7383-0(6))* Vives, Luis Editorial (Edelvives).
Goossens, Philippe. Owl Howl. Friester, Paul. 2014. (ENG.). 32p. (J). 15.95 *(978-0-7358-4188-8(8))* North-South Bks., Inc.
—Superhero School. Robberecht, Thierry. 2012. (ENG.). 30p. (J). (gr. -1-k). 15.95 *(978-1-60537-140-5(8))* Clavis Publishing.
Gorbachev, Kostya. When Someone Is Afraid, 1 vol. Gorbachev, Valeri. (ENG.). 32p. (J). 2012. pap. 6.95 *(978-1-59572-344-4(7))*; 2005. (gr. -1-2). 15.95 *(978-1-932065-99-2(7))* Star Bright Bks., Inc.
Gorbachev, Mikhail, jt. illus. see Gorbachev, Valeri.
Gorbachev, Valeri. All for Pie, Pie for All. Martin, David Lozell. 2008. (ENG.). 32p. (J). (gr. -1-2). pap. 6.99 *(978-0-7636-3891-7(9))* Candlewick Pr.
—The Giant Hug. Horning, Sandra. 2008. (ENG.). 40p. (J). (gr. -1-2). pap. 7.99 *(978-0-553-11262-7(7))*, Dragonfly Bks.) Random Hse. Children's Bks.
—Gobble-Gobble Crash! A Barnyard Counting Bash. Stiegemeyer, Julie. 2008. (ENG.). 32p. (J). (gr. -1-k). 16.99 *(978-0-525-47959-8(7))*, Dutton Juvenile) Penguin Publishing Group.
—Goldilocks & the Three Bears. 2015. (ENG.). 40p. (J). 15.95 *(978-0-7358-4211-3(6))* North-South Bks., Inc.
—Group Soup. Ackerman, Tova. (Orig.). pap. 6.95 *(978-0-9720183-0-2(1))* Puppetry in Practice.
—Little Bunny's Sleepless Night. Roth, Jurgen Philip Philip Philip Kevin Kevin P Geneen Philip Philip Philip Marie, Carol. 2013. (ENG.). 40p. (J). (gr. -1-2). 17.95 *(978-0-7358-4123-9(3))* North-South Bks., Inc.
—Rufus Goes to School. Griswell, Kim T. 2013. (ENG.). 32p. (J). (gr. -1-1). 14.95 *(978-1-4549-0416-8(X))* Sterling Publishing Co., Inc.
—Rufus Goes to Sea. Griswell, Kim T. 2015. (ENG.). 32p. (J). (gr. -1-1). 14.95 *(978-1-4549-1052-7(6))* Sterling Publishing Co., Inc.
—Squirrel's Fun Day. Moser, Lisa. (Candlewick Sparks Ser.). (ENG.). 48p. (J). (gr. k-4). 2015. pap. 3.99 *(978-0-7636-7789-3(2))*; 2013. 14.99 *(978-0-7636-5726-0(3))* Candlewick Pr.
—Squirrel's World. Moser, Lisa. 2013. (Candlewick Sparks Ser.). (ENG.). 48p. (J). (gr. k-4). pap. 3.99 *(978-0-7636-6644-6(0))* Candlewick Pr.
—There Was a Mouse. Blanchard, Patricia & Suhr, Joanne. 2003. (ENG.). 16p. (J). pap. 15.00 *(978-1-57274-702-9(1))*, BB2210, Bks. for Young Learners) Owen, Richard C. Pubs., Inc.
—Where Is Bear? Newman, Lesléa. 2006. (ENG.). 44p. (J). (gr. -1 — 1). pap. 6.99 *(978-0-15-205918-7(0))* Houghton Mifflin Harcourt Publishing Co.
—Who Will Tuck Me in Tonight? Roth, Carol. 2006. (Cheshire Studio Book Ser.). (ENG.). 32p. (J). (gr. -1-1). 6.95 *(978-0-7358-1976-4(9))* North-South Bks., Inc.
Gorbachev, Valeri. The Best Cat. Gorbachev, Valeri. 2010. (ENG.). 32p. (J). (gr. -1-2). 15.99 *(978-0-7636-3675-3(4))* Candlewick Pr.
—The Big Trip. Gorbachev, Valeri. 2004. (ENG.). 32p. (J). (gr. -1-3). 15.99 *(978-0-399-23965-6(0))*, Philomel) Penguin Publishing Group.
—Cats Are Cats. Gorbachev, Valeri. 2014. (ENG.). 32p. (J). (gr. -1-3). 16.95 *(978-0-8234-3052-9(9))* Holiday Hse., Inc.
—Catty Jane Who Hated the Rain. Gorbachev, Valeri. 2012. (ENG.). 32p. (J). (gr. -1-3). 16.95 *(978-1-59078-700-7(5))* Boyds Mills Pr.
—Christopher Counting. Gorbachev, Valeri. 2008. (ENG.). 32p. (J). (gr. -1-3). 16.99 *(978-0-399-24629-6(0))*, Philomel) Penguin Publishing Group.
—Un Dia de lluvia. Gorbachev, Valeri. 2007. (SPA.). 40p. (J). (gr. -1-3). pap. 8.95 *(978-958-04-7074-8(X))* Norma S.A. COL. Dist: Distribuidora Norma, Inc.
—How to Be Friends with a Dragon. Gorbachev, Valeri. 2012. (ENG.). 32p. (J). (gr. -1-2). 16.99 *(978-0-8075-3432-8(3))* Whitman, Albert & Co.
—Me Too! Gorbachev, Valeri. 2014. (ENG.). 32p. (J). (gr. -1-3). 6.99 *(978-0-8234-3179-3(7))* Holiday Hse., Inc.
—Ms. Turtle the Babysitter. Gorbachev, Valeri. 2005. (I Can Read Bks.). 64p. (J). (gr. k-3). (ENG.). 15.99 *(978-0-06-058073-5(9))*; lib. bdg. 16.89 *(978-0-06-058074-2(7))* HarperCollins Pubs.
—That's What Friends Are For. Gorbachev, Valeri. 2005. (ENG.). 32p. (J). (gr. -1-2). 15.99 *(978-0-399-23966-3(9))*, Philomel) Penguin Publishing Group.
—Whose Hat Is It? Gorbachev, Valeri. (My First I Can Read Ser.). 32p. (J). (gr. -1 — 1). 2005. (ENG.). pap. 3.99 *(978-0-06-053436-3(2))*; 2004. (ENG.). 14.99 *(978-0-06-053434-9(6))*; 2004. lib. bdg. 15.89 *(978-0-06-053435-6(4))* HarperCollins Pubs.
Gorbachev, Valeri & Gorbachev, Mikhail. Conejito No Puede Dormir. Roth, Carol. Fernandez, Queta, tr. 2008. (SPA.). 32p. (J). (gr. -1-3). pap. 6.95 *(978-0-7358-2165-9(2))* North-South Bks., Inc.
—Quien Me Arropara Esta Noche? Roth, Carol. Obregon, Jose Maria & Fernandez, Queta, trs. from SPA. 2007. (Cheshire Studio Book Ser.). (SPA.). 32p. (J). (gr. -1-3). pap. 6.95 *(978-0-7358-2107-1(0))* North-South Bks., Inc.
Gorbatov, Vadim. Fidget's Folly. Patterson, Stacey. 2012. 36p. (J). 18.00 *(978-0-87842-594-5(2))* Mountain Pr. Publishing Co., Inc.
Gorbaty, Norman. Sleepy Dog, Wake Up! Ziefert, Harriet. 2015. (Step into Reading Ser.). (ENG.). 32p. (J). (gr. -1-1). lib. bdg. 12.99 *(978-0-375-97360-4(5))*, Random Hse. Bks. for Young Readers) Random Hse. Children's Bks.
Gordan, Gus. My Very First Art Book. Dickens, Rosie & Courtauld, Sarah. ed. 2011. (Art Ser.). 48p. (J). pap. 12.99 *(978-0-7945-3018-1(4))*, Usborne) EDC Publishing.
Gordeev, Denis, jt. illus. see Oberdieck, Bernhard.
Gordo, Aleix. En busca de la Paz. Rodríguez-Nora, Tere. 2005. (SPA & ENG.). 32p. (J). (gr. 2-4). 13.95 *(978-84-96046-51-1(6))* Ediciones Norte, Inc.
Gordon, Andrew. Wave the Flag & Blow the Whistle: A Railway Adventure. Armitage, Ronda. (ENG.). 32p. (J). (gr. -1-k). 2013. pap. 9.99 *(978-1-4052-5340-6(1))*; 2012. 17.99 *(978-1-4052-5339-0(8))* Egmont Bks., Ltd. GBR. Dist: Independent Pubs. Group.
Gordon, Ayala. Happy Purim Night. Simon, Norma. (Festival Series of Picture Storybooks). (J). (gr. -1). vinyl bd. 4.50 *(978-0-8381-0706-5(0))*, 10-706) United Synagogue of America Bk. Service.
Gordon, Carl & Gordon, Mike. Do Princesses Have Best Friends Forever? Coyle, Carmela Lavigna. 2010. (ENG.). 32p. (J). (gr. -1-3). 15.95 *(978-1-58979-542-6(3))* Taylor Trade Publishing.
—Just Me & 6,000 Rats: A Tale of Conjunctions, 1 vol. Walton, Rick. 2011. (ENG.). 36p. (J). pap. 7.99 *(978-1-4236-2076-1(3))* Gibbs Smith, Publisher.
Gordon, Carl, jt. illus. see Gordon, Mike.
Gordon, Danny. The Fall & Rise of Abuse-a-Saurus Rex. Smith-Leckie, Nina. 2003. 28p. (YA). (gr. 5-18). pap. 6.95 *(978-0-9725382-0-6(8))* Prairie Arts, Inc.
Gordon, David. Construction Countdown. Olson, K. C. rev. ed. 2004. (ENG.). 24p. (J). (gr. -1-1). 17.99 *(978-0-8050-6920-4(8))*, Holt, Henry & Co. Bks. For Young Readers) Holt, Henry & Co.
—Dig, Scoop, Ka-Boom! Holub, Joan. 2013. (Step into Reading Ser.). (ENG.). 24p. (J). (gr. -1-1). pap. 3.99 *(978-0-375-86910-5(7))* Random Hse., Inc.
Gordon, David, et al. Dizzy Izzy. Scieszka, Jon. 2010. (Jon Scieszka's Trucktown Ser.). (ENG.). 24p. (J). (gr. -1-1). pap. 3.99 *(978-1-4169-4145-3(2))*, Simon Spotlight) Simon Spotlight.
Gordon, David. Extremely Cute Animals Operating Heavy Machinery. 2016. (J). *(978-1-4169-2441-8(8))*, Simon & Schuster Bks. For Young Readers) Simon & Schuster Bks. For Young Readers.
Gordon, David, et al. Garage Tales. Scieszka, Jon. 2010. (Jon Scieszka's Trucktown Ser.). (ENG.). 80p. (J). (gr. -1-3). pap. 12.99 *(978-1-4424-1196-8(1))*, Simon & Schuster Bks. For Young Readers) Simon & Schuster Bks. For Young Readers.
—Kat's Mystery Gift. Scieszka, Jon. 2009. (Jon Scieszka's Trucktown Ser.). (ENG.). 24p. (J). (gr. -1-1). pap. 3.99 *(978-1-4169-4143-9(6))*, Simon Spotlight) Simon Spotlight.
—Melvin Might? Scieszka, Jon. 2008. (Jon Scieszka's Trucktown Ser.). (ENG.). 40p. (J). (gr. -1-3). 16.99 *(978-1-4169-4134-7(7))*, Simon & Schuster Bks. For Young Readers) Simon & Schuster Bks. For Young Readers.

Gordon, David. The Noisy Airplane Ride. Downs, Mike. 2005. (ENG.). 32p. (J). (gr. -1-2). pap. 6.99 *(978-1-58246-157-1(0),* Tricycle Pr.) Ten Speed Pr.

Gordon, David, et al. Pete's Party. Scieszka, Jon. 2008. (Jon Scieszka's Trucktown Ser.). (ENG.). 24p. (J). (gr. -1-k). lib. bdg. 13.89 *(978-1-4169-4149-1(5));* pap. 3.99 *(978-1-4169-4138-5(X))* Simon Spotlight. (Simon Spotlight).

—Race from A to Z, No. 4. Scieszka, Jon. 2014. (Jon Scieszka's Trucktown Ser.). (ENG.). 48p. (J). (gr. -1-3). 17.99 *(978-1-4169-4136-1(3),* Simon & Schuster Bks. For Young Readers) Simon & Schuster Bks. For Young Readers.

—Shuffle Stories. Ciminera, Siobhan & Testa, Maggie. 2009. (Jon Scieszka's Trucktown Ser.). (ENG.). 50p. (J). pap. 7.99 *(978-1-4169-4189-7(4),* Simon Scribbles) Simon Scribbles.

—Snow Trucking! Scieszka, Jon. 2008. (Jon Scieszka's Trucktown Ser.). (ENG.). 24p. (J). (gr. -1-3). pap. 3.99 *(978-1-4169-4140-8(1),* Simon Spotlight) Simon Spotlight.

—Take a Trip with Trucktown! Jon Scieszkas Trucktown et al. 2011. (Jon Scieszka's Trucktown Ser.). (ENG.). 24p. (J). (gr. -1-3). pap. 3.99 *(978-1-4169-4181-1(9),* Simon & Schuster Bks. For Young Readers) Simon & Schuster Bks. For Young Readers.

—Truckery Rhymes. Scieszka, Jon. 2009. (Jon Scieszka's Trucktown Ser.). (ENG.). 64p. (J). (gr. -1-3). 17.99 *(978-1-4169-4135-4(5),* Simon & Schuster Bks. For Young Readers) Simon & Schuster Bks. For Young Readers.

—Trucks Line Up. Scieszka, Jon. 2011. (Jon Scieszka's Trucktown Ser.). (ENG.). 24p. (J). (gr. -1-1). pap. 3.99 *(978-1-4169-4147-7(9),* Simon Spotlight) Simon Spotlight.

Gordon, David. Smitten. Gordon, David. 2007. (ENG.). 40p. (J). (gr. -1-3). 16.99 *(978-1-4169-2440-1(X),* Atheneum Bks. for Young Readers) Simon & Schuster Children's Publishing.

—The Three Little Rigs. Gordon, David. 2005. (ENG.). 32p. (J). (gr. -1-3). 17.99 *(978-0-06-058118-3(2))* HarperCollins Pubs.

—The Ugly Truckling. Gordon, David. 2004. 32p. (J). (gr. -1-2). lib. bdg. 16.89 *(978-0-06-054601-4(8),* Geringer, Laura Book) HarperCollins Pubs.

Gordon, David George. Motor Dog. Cyrus, Kurt. 2014. (ENG.). 40p. (J). (gr. -1-k). 16.99 *(978-1-4231-6822-5(4))* Hyperion Bks. for Children.

Gordon, Dean, jt. illus. see Tyminski, Lori.

Gordon, Eric A. & Gordon, Steven E. Batman Classic: Dawn of the Dynamic Duo. Sazaklis, John. 2011. (I Can Read Book 2 Ser.). (ENG.). 32p. (J). (gr. -1-3). pap. 3.99 *(978-0-06-188520-4(7))* HarperCollins Pubs.

—Darkseid's Revenge. Aptekar, Devan. 2012. (ENG.). 24p. (J). (gr. -1-3). pap. 3.99 *(978-0-06-188533-4(9),* HarperFestival) HarperCollins Pubs.

—Darkseid's Revenge. Aptekar, Devan. ed. 2012. lib. bdg. 13.55 *(978-0-606-23566-2(3),* Turtleback) Turtleback Bks.

—Going Ape. Sutton, Laurie S. 2012. (I Can Read Book 2 Ser.). (ENG.). 32p. (J). (gr. -1-3). pap. 3.99 *(978-0-06-188522-8(3))* HarperCollins Pubs.

—Justice League: Meet the Justice League. Rosen, Lucy. 2013. (I Can Read Book 2 Ser.). (ENG.). 32p. (J). (gr. -1-3). pap. 3.99 *(978-0-06-221002-9(5))* HarperCollins Pubs.

—Reptile Rampage. Turner, Katharine. 2012. (I Can Read Book 2 Ser.). (ENG.). 32p. (J). (gr. -1-3). pap. 3.99 *(978-0-06-188521-1(5))* HarperCollins Pubs.

Gordon, Eric A., jt. illus. see Gordon, Steven E.

Gordon, F. C. Among the Farmyard People. Pierson, Clara Dillingham. 2008. 176p. pap. 8.95 *(978-1-59915-281-3(9))* Yesterday's Classics.

Gordon, Gus. Basketball Buddies. Arena, Felice & Kettle, Phil. 2004. (J). pap. *(978-1-59336-369-7(9))* Mondo Publishing.

—Battle of the Games. Arena, Felice & Kettle, Phil. 2004. (J). pap. *(978-1-59336-372-7(9))* Mondo Publishing.

—Golf Legends. Arena, Felice & Kettle, Phil. 2004. (J). pap. *(978-1-59336-367-3(2))* Mondo Publishing.

—Halloween Gotcha! Arena, Felice & Kettle, Phil. 2004. (J). pap. *(978-1-59336-373-4(7))* Mondo Publishing.

—I Am Cow, Hear Me Moo! Esbaum, Jill. 2014. (ENG.). 32p. (J). (gr. -1-k). 16.99 *(978-0-8037-3524-8(3),* Dial) Penguin Publishing Group.

—My Life & Other Stuff I Made Up. Bancks, Tristan. (My Life & Other Stuff... Ser.). (ENG.). (J). (gr. 4-7). 2014. 204p. 9.99 *(978-0-85798-319-0(9));* 2011. 208p. 9.99 *(978-1-86471-817-1(X))* Random Hse. Australia AUS. Dist: Independent Pubs. Group.

—My Life & Other Stuff That Went Wrong. Bancks, Tristan. 2014. (My Life & Other Stuff... Ser.). (ENG.). 208p. (J). (gr. 4-7). 9.99 *(978-0-85798-037-3(8))* Random Hse. Australia AUS. Dist: Independent Pubs. Group.

—Park Soccer. Arena, Felice & Kettle, Phil. 2004. (J). *(978-1-59336-366-6(4))* Mondo Publishing.

—Rock Star. Arena, Felice & Kettle, Phil. 2004. (J). pap. *(978-1-59336-368-0(0))* Mondo Publishing.

—So Festy! Mawter, J. A. 2004. 160p. *(978-0-207-19919-6(1))* HarperCollins Pubs. Australia.

—So Grotty! Mawter, J. A. 5th ed. 2004. (So... Ser.: Bk. 5). 160p. (Orig.). (J). *(978-0-207-20007-6(6),* Angus & Robertson) HarperCollins Pubs. Australia.

—So Sick! Mawter, J. A. 2003. 144p. (Orig.). *(978-0-207-19997-4(3))* HarperCollins Pubs. Australia.

—So Stinky! Mawter, J. A. 2005. 160p. (Orig.). *(978-0-207-20008-3(4))* HarperCollins Pubs. Australia.

—To the Moon & Back: The Amazing Australians at the Forefront of Space Travel. Sullivan, Bryan & French, Jackie. 2004. 208p. (Orig.). (J). *(978-0-207-20009-0(2))* HarperCollins Pubs.

Gordon, Gus. Herman & Rosie. Gordon, Gus. 2013. (ENG.). 32p. (J). (gr. 2-5). 17.99 *(978-1-59643-856-9(8))* Roaring Brook Pr.

Gordon, Gus & Vane, Mitch. Battle of the Games. Arena, Felice et al. 2004. 48p. (J). pap. *(978-0-7329-9254-5(0))* Mondo Publishing.

Gordon, John. Meet Teddy Rex! Williams, Bonnie. 2012. (Dino School Ser.). (ENG.). 24p. (J). (gr. -1-1). 15.99 *(978-1-4424-4996-1(9));* pap. 3.99 *(978-1-4424-4995-4(0))* Simon Spotlight. (Simon Spotlight).

—Pete Can Fly! Williams, Bonnie. 2014. (Dino School Ser.). (ENG.). 24p. (J). (gr. -1-1). pap. 3.99 *(978-1-4814-0465-5(2),* Simon Spotlight) Simon Spotlight.

Gordon, Leneé, photos by. I've Got Feelings: An Activity Book for Grinning, Grimacing, & Shouting Out Loud! Grimes-Herbert, Taryn. 2010. (ENG., 40p. pap. 14.95 *(978-1-4515-9102-6(0))* CreateSpace Independent Publishing Platform.

Gordon-Lucas, Bonnie. Fun with My First Words: French-Hebrew Picture Dictionary. Peterseil, Shlomo, ed. 2005. (ENG, FRE & HEB.). 12p. (J). bds. 12.95 *(978-1-930143-24-1(9),* Devora Publishing) Simcha Media Group.

—Fun with My First Words: Hebrew-English - English-Hebrew Dictionary. Peterseil, Shlomo. 2005. (ENG & HEB.). 12p. (J). (gr. -1-1). bds. 12.95 *(978-1-930143-22-7(2),* Devora Publishing) Simcha Media Group.

—Fun with My First Words: Russian-Hebrew Picture Dictionary. Peterseil, Shlomo, ed. 2005. (ENG, HEB & RUS.). 12p. (J). bds. 12.95 *(978-1-930143-26-5(5),* Devora Publishing) Simcha Media Group.

—Fun with My First Words: Spanish-Hebrew Picture Dictionary. Peterseil, Shlomo, ed. 2005. (ENG, HEB & SPA.). 12p. (J). bds. 12.95 *(978-1-930143-23-4(0),* Devora Publishing) Simcha Media Group.

Gordon, Mike. All Wrapped Up. Callahan, Thera S. 2003. (Rookie Readers Ser.). 32p. (J). 19.50 *(978-0-516-22844-0(7),* Children's Pr.) Scholastic Library Publishing.

—Butterfly Garden. McNamara, Margaret. 2012. (Robin Hill School Ser.). (ENG.). 32p. (J). (gr. -1-1). 15.99 *(978-1-4424-3643-5(3));* pap. 3.99 *(978-1-4424-3642-8(5))* Simon Spotlight. (Simon Spotlight).

—The Castle That Jack Built. Sims, Lesley. 2007. (Usborne First Reading: Level 3 Ser.). 48p. (J). (gr. -1-3). 8.99 *(978-0-7945-1599-7(1),* Usborne) EDC Publishing.

—Class Mom. McNamara, Margaret. 2009. (Robin Hill School Ser.). (ENG.). 32p. (J). (gr. -1-1). pap. 3.99 *(978-1-4169-5537-5(2),* Simon Spotlight) Simon Spotlight.

—Class Picture Day. McNamara, Margaret. 2011. (Robin Hill School Ser.). (ENG.). 32p. (J). (gr. -1-1). 15.99 *(978-1-4424-3611-4(5));* pap. 3.99 *(978-1-4169-9173-1(5))* Simon Spotlight. (Simon Spotlight).

—Como Nacen los Bebes? Aprender Sobre Sexualidad. Llewellyn, Claire. (SPA.). (J). (gr. k-2). pap. *(978-950-24-0944-3(2))* Albatros ARG. Dist: Lectorum Pubns., Inc.

—The Counting Race. McNamara, Margaret. ed. 2005. 32p. (J). lib. bdg. 15.00 *(978-1-59054-967-4(8))* Fitzgerald Bks.

—The Counting Race. McNamara, Margaret. 2003. (Robin Hill School Ser.). (ENG.). 32p. (J). (gr. -1-1). pap. 3.99 *(978-0-689-85539-9(7),* Simon Spotlight) Simon Spotlight.

—Croc by the Rock. Robinson, Hilary. 2005. 32p. (J). lib. bdg. 9.00 *(978-1-4242-0885-2(8))* Fitzgerald Bks.

—A Croc Shock! Robinson, Hilary. 2009. (Get Set Readers Ser.). 32p. (J). (gr. -1-2). lib. bdg. 22.60 *(978-1-60754-265-0(X))* Windmill Bks.

—Dad Goes to School. McNamara, Margaret. 2007. (Robin Hill School Ser.). (ENG.). 32p. (J). (gr. -1-1). pap. 3.99 *(978-1-4169-1541-6(9),* Simon Spotlight) Simon Spotlight.

—Do Princesses Make Happy Campers? Coyle, Carmela Lavigna. 2015. (ENG.). 32p. (J). (gr. -1-2). 15.95 *(978-1-63076-054-0(4))* Taylor Trade Publishing.

—Do Superheroes Have Teddy Bears? Coyle, Carmela Lavigna. 2012. (ENG.). 32p. (J). (gr. -1-2). 15.95 *(978-1-58979-693-5(4))* Taylor Trade Publishing.

—Earth Day. McNamara, Margaret. 2009. (Robin Hill School Ser.). (ENG.). 32p. (J). (gr. -1-1). pap. 3.99 *(978-1-4169-5535-1(6),* Simon Spotlight) Simon Spotlight.

—Eating Well. Gogerly, Liz. 2008. (Looking after Me Ser.). (ENG.). 32p. (J). (gr. -1-3). pap. *(978-0-7787-4117-6(6))* Crabtree Publishing Co.

—Election Day. McNamara, Margaret. 2008. (Robin Hill School Ser.). (J). (gr. -1-1). pap. 16.95 *(978-1-4301-0598-5(4))* Live Oak Media.

—Election Day. McNamara, Margaret. 2004. (Robin Hill School Ser.). (ENG.). 32p. (J). (gr. -1-1). pap. 3.99 *(978-0-689-86425-4(6),* Simon Spotlight) Simon Spotlight.

—The Emperor's New Clothes. 2006. 24p. (J). (gr. -1-3). 9.99 *(978-0-7945-1350-4(6),* Usborne) EDC Publishing.

—Estoy Sano? Aprender Sobre Alimentacion y Actividad Fisica. Llewellyn, Claire. (SPA.). (J). (gr. k-2). pap. *(978-950-24-0945-0(0))* Albatros ARG. Dist: Lectorum Pubns., Inc.

—Exercise. Gogerly, Liz. 2008. (Looking after Me Ser.). (ENG.). 32p. (J). (gr. -1-3). pap. *(978-0-7787-4118-3(4))* Crabtree Publishing Co.

—Fall Leaf Project. McNamara, Margaret. 2006. (Robin Hill School Ser.). (ENG.). 32p. (J). (gr. -1-1). pap. 3.99 *(978-1-4169-1537-9(0),* Simon Spotlight) Simon Spotlight.

—Family Photo. Rau, Dana Meachen. 2007. (Rookie Reader Skill Set Ser.). (ENG.). 32p. (J). (gr. k-2). pap. 4.95 *(978-0-531-12492-5(4),* Children's Pr.) Scholastic Library Publishing.

—The First Day of School. McNamara, Margaret. 2008. (Robin Hill School Ser.). (J). (gr. -1-3). pap. 16.95 *(978-1-4301-0604-3(2))* Live Oak Media.

—The First Day of School. McNamara, Margaret. 2005. (Robin Hill School Ser.). (ENG.). 32p. (J). (gr. -1-1). pap. 3.99 *(978-0-689-86914-3(2),* Simon Spotlight) Simon Spotlight.

—First-Grade Bunny. McNamara, Margaret. 2005. (Robin Hill School Ser.). (ENG.). 32p. (J). (gr. -1-1). pap. 3.99 *(978-0-689-86427-8(2),* Simon Spotlight) Simon Spotlight.

—Fred & Finn. Goodey, Madeline. 2014. (ReadZone Picture Bks.). (ENG.). 32p. (J). (gr. k-3). pap. 8.99 *(978-1-78322-421-0(5))* ReadZone Bks. GBR. Dist: Independent Pubs. Group.

—The Frog Prince. rev. ed. 2007. (Young Reading CD Packs Ser.). 48p. (J). (gr. -1-3). 9.99 incl. audio compact disk *(978-0-7945-1868-4(0),* Usborne) EDC Publishing.

—The Garden Project. McNamara, Margaret. 2010. (Robin Hill School Ser.). (ENG.). 32p. (J). (gr. -1-1). pap. 3.99 *(978-1-4169-9171-7(9),* Simon Spotlight) Simon Spotlight.

—Goldilocks & the Three Bears. 2007. (First Reading Level 4 Ser.). 48p. (J). (gr. -1-3). 8.99 *(978-0-7945-1708-3(0),* Usborne) EDC Publishing.

—Groundhog Day. McNamara, Margaret. 2005. (Robin Hill School Ser.). 32p. (J). (gr. -1-3). 11.65 *(978-0-7569-7146-5(2))* Perfection Learning Corp.

—Groundhog Day. McNamara, Margaret. 2006. (Robin Hill School Ser.). (ENG.). 32p. (J). (gr. -1-1). pap. 3.99 *(978-1-4169-0507-3(3),* Simon Spotlight) Simon Spotlight.

—Halloween Fun. McNamara, Margaret. 2008. (Robin Hill School Ser.). (ENG.). 32p. (J). (gr. -1-1). pap. 3.99 *(978-1-4169-3496-7(0),* Simon Spotlight) Simon Spotlight.

—Happy Graduation! McNamara, Margaret. 2008. (Robin Hill School Ser.). (J). (gr. -1-1). pap. 16.95 *(978-1-4301-0610-4(7))* Live Oak Media.

—Happy Graduation! McNamara, Margaret. 2006. (Robin Hill School Ser.). (ENG.). 32p. (J). (gr. -1-1). pap. 3.99 *(978-1-4169-0509-7(X),* Simon Spotlight) Simon Spotlight.

—Happy Thanksgiving. McNamara, Margaret. 2005. (Robin Hill School Ser.). (ENG.). 32p. (J). (gr. -1-1). pap. 3.99 *(978-1-4169-0505-9(7),* Simon Spotlight) Simon Spotlight.

—Keeping Clean. Gogerly, Liz. 2008. (Looking after Me Ser.). (ENG.). 32p. (J). (gr. -1-3). pap. *(978-0-7787-4119-0(2));* lib. bdg. *(978-0-7787-4112-1(5))* Crabtree Publishing Co.

—Last to Finish: A Story about the Smartest Boy in Math Class. Esham, Barbara. 2008. 32p. (J). (gr. k-18). 16.95 *(978-1-60336-456-0(0),* Adventures of Everyday Geniuses, The) Mainstream Connections Publishing.

—Little Red Riding Hood. 2007. (Picture Book Classics Ser.). 24p. (J). (gr. 1-4). 9.99 *(978-0-7945-1787-8(0),* Usborne) EDC Publishing.

—Martin Luther King Jr. Day. McNamara, Margaret. 2007. (Robin Hill School Ser.). (ENG.). 32p. (J). (gr. -1-1). pap. 3.99 *(978-1-4169-3494-3(4),* Simon Spotlight) Simon Spotlight.

—Me Hace Bien o Mal? Aprender Sobre Medicamentos, Drogas y Salud. Llewellyn, Claire. (SPA.). (J). (gr. k-2). pap. *(978-950-24-0946-7(9))* Albatros ARG. Dist: Lectorum Pubns., Inc.

—Mrs. Gorski, I Think I Have the Wiggle Fidgets. Esham, Barbaraa. 2008. (ENG, SPA & FRE.). 32p. (J). (gr. k-18). 16.95 *(978-1-60336-469-0(2),* Adventures of Everyday Geniuses, The) Mainstream Connections Publishing.

—My Best Friend. Namm, Diane. 2004. (My First Reader Ser.). (ENG.). 32p. (J). (gr. k-1). pap. 3.95 *(978-0-516-25504-0(5),* Children's Pr.) Scholastic Library Publishing.

—Once There Was a Caterpillar. Anderson, Judith. 2010. (Nature's Miracles Ser.). (ENG.). 32p. (J). (gr. -1-2). pap. 5.99 *(978-0-7641-4494-3(4))* Barron's Educational Series, Inc.

—Once There Was a Raindrop. Anderson, Judith. 2010. (Nature's Miracles Ser.). (ENG.). 32p. (J). (gr. -1-2). pap. 5.99 *(978-0-7641-4495-0(2))* Barron's Educational Series, Inc.

—Once There Was a Seed. Anderson, Judith. 2010. (Nature's Miracles Ser.). (ENG.). 32p. (J). (gr. -1-2). pap. 5.99 *(978-0-7641-4493-6(6))* Barron's Educational Series, Inc.

—Once There Was a Tadpole. Anderson, Judith. 2010. (Nature's Miracles Ser.). (ENG.). 32p. (J). (gr. -1-2). pap. 5.99 *(978-0-7641-4496-7(0))* Barron's Educational Series, Inc.

—One Hundred Days (Plus One) McNamara, Margaret. 2008. (Robin Hill School Ser.). (J). (gr. -1-3). pap. 16.95 *(978-1-4301-0616-6(6))* Live Oak Media.

—One Hundred Days (Plus One) McNamara, Margaret. 2003. (Ready-to-Read Robin Hill School Ser.). 32p. (J). (gr. -1-3). 11.65 *(978-0-7569-1805-7(7))* Perfection Learning Corp.

—One Hundred Days (Plus One) McNamara, Margaret. 2003. (Robin Hill School Ser.). (ENG.). 32p. (J). (gr. -1-1). pap. 3.99 *(978-0-689-85535-1(4),* Simon Spotlight) Simon Spotlight.

—Picking Apples. McNamara, Margaret. 2009. (Robin Hill School Ser.). (ENG.). 32p. (J). (gr. -1-1). pap. 3.99 *(978-1-4169-5539-9(9),* Simon Spotlight) Simon Spotlight.

—The Playground Problem. McNamara, Margaret. 2004. (Robin Hill School Ser.). (ENG.). 32p. (J). (gr. -1-1). pap. 3.99 *(978-0-689-85876-5(0),* Simon Spotlight) Simon Spotlight.

—Presidents' Day. McNamara, Margaret. 2010. (Robin Hill School Ser.). (ENG.). 32p. (J). (gr. -1-1). pap. 3.99 *(978-1-4169-9170-0(0),* Simon Spotlight) Simon Spotlight.

—The Princess & the Pea. rev. ed. 2007. (Young Reading CD Packs Ser.). 48p. (J). (gr. -1-3). 9.99 incl. audio compact disk *(978-0-7945-1875-2(3),* Usborne) EDC Publishing.

—Princess Handbook. Davidson, Susanna. 2006. 80p. (J). (gr. 3-7). 12.99 *(978-0-7945-1329-0(8),* Usborne) EDC Publishing.

—The Pumpkin Patch. McNamara, Margaret. 2005. (Ready-to-Read Ser.). 32p. (J). lib. bdg. 15.00 *(978-1-59054-932-2(5))* Fitzgerald Bks.

—The Pumpkin Patch. McNamara, Margaret. 2008. (Robin Hill School Ser.). (J). (gr. -1-1). pap. 16.95 *(978-1-4301-0622-7(0))* Live Oak Media.

—Un Regalo Bien Envuelto: All Wrapped Up. Callahan, Thera S. 2003. (Rookie Readers Spanish Ser.). (SPA.). (J). 19.50 *(978-0-516-25885-0(0),* Children's Pr.) Scholastic Library Publishing.

—Safety. Gogerly, Liz. 2008. (Looking after Me Ser.). (ENG.). 32p. (J). (gr. -1-3). pap. *(978-0-7787-4120-6(6));* lib. bdg. *(978-0-7787-4113-8(3))* Crabtree Publishing Co.

—Secret Santa. McNamara, Margaret. 2012. (Robin Hill School Ser.). (ENG.). 32p. (J). (gr. -1-1). 15.99 *(978-1-4424-3649-7(2));* pap. 3.99 *(978-1-4424-3648-0(4))* Simon Spotlight. (Simon Spotlight).

—Snow Day. McNamara, Margaret. 2007. (Robin Hill School Ser.). (ENG.). 32p. (J). (gr. -1-1). pap. 3.99 *(978-1-4169-3493-6(6),* Simon Spotlight) Simon Spotlight.

—Snug as a Bug, 1 vol. Imbody, Amy E. & Imbody, Amy. 2008. (I Can Read! Ser.). (ENG.). 32p. (J). (gr. -1-1). pap. 3.99 *(978-0-310-71575-7(X))* Zondervan.

—Stacey Coolidge's Fancy Smancy Cursive Handwriting. Esham, Barbara. 2008. 32p. (J). (gr. k-18). 16.95 *(978-1-60336-462-1(5),* Adventures of Everyday Geniuses, The) Mainstream Connections Publishing.

—Stories of Princesses. 2006. 144p. (J). (gr. 4-7). 14.99 *(978-0-7945-1385-6(9),* Usborne) EDC Publishing.

—Summer Treasure. McNamara, Margaret. 2012. (Robin Hill School Ser.). (ENG.). 32p. (J). (gr. -1-1). 15.99 *(978-1-4424-3646-6(8));* pap. 3.99 *(978-1-4424-3645-9(X))* Simon Spotlight. (Simon Spotlight).

—Taking Medicine. Gogerly, Liz. 2008. (Looking after Me Ser.). (ENG.). 32p. (J). (gr. -1-3). pap. *(978-0-7787-4121-3(4));* lib. bdg. *(978-0-7787-4114-5(1))* Crabtree Publishing Co.

—Teeth. Gogerly, Liz. 2008. (Looking after Me Ser.). (ENG.). 32p. (J). (gr. -1-3). pap. *(978-0-7787-4122-0(2));* lib. bdg. *(978-0-7787-4115-2(X))* Crabtree Publishing Co.

—Too Many Valentines. McNamara, Margaret. 2003. (Robin Hill School Ser.). (ENG.). 32p. (J). (gr. -1-1). pap. 3.99 *(978-0-689-85537-5(0),* Simon Spotlight) Simon Spotlight.

—Too Many Valentines. McNamara, Margaret. ed. 2003. (Robin Hill School Ready-To-Read Ser.). 32p. (gr. -1-3). lib. bdg. 13.55 *(978-0-613-61592-1(1),* Turtleback) Turtleback Bks.

—A Tooth Story. McNamara, Margaret. 2004. (Robin Hill School Ser.). (ENG.). 32p. (J). (gr. -1-1). pap. 3.99 *(978-0-689-86423-0(X),* Simon Spotlight) Simon Spotlight.

—Wash Your Hands! McNamara, Margaret. 2010. (Robin Hill School Ser.). (ENG.). 32p. (J). (gr. -1-1). pap. 3.99 *(978-1-4169-9172-4(7),* Simon Spotlight) Simon Spotlight.

—Watch Out! Around Town. Llewellyn, Claire. 2006. (Watch Out! Bks.). (ENG.). 32p. (J). (gr. -1-2). pap. 6.99 *(978-0-7641-3326-8(8))* Barron's Educational Series, Inc.

—Watch Out! at Home. Llewellyn, Claire. 2006. (Watch Out! Bks.). (ENG.). 32p. (J). (gr. -1-2). pap. 6.99 *(978-0-7641-3323-7(3))* Barron's Educational Series, Inc.

—Watch Out! on the Road. Llewellyn, Claire. 2006. (Watch Out! Bks.). (ENG.). 32p. (J). (gr. -1-2). pap. 7.99 *(978-0-7641-3324-4(1))* Barron's Educational Series, Inc.

—When the Teacher Isn't Looking: And Other Funny School Poems. Nesbitt, Kenn. 2005. 80p. (J). *(978-0-88166-489-8(8))* Meadowbrook Pr.

—When the Teacher Isn't Looking: And Other Funny School Poems. Nesbitt, Ken. 2010. (Giggle Poetry Ser.). (ENG.). 80p. (J). (gr. 1-6). per. 8.95 *(978-0-684-03128-6(0))* Meadowbrook Pr.

—Why Should I Eat Well? Llewellyn, Claire. 2005. (Why Should I? Bks.). (ENG.). 32p. (J). pap. 7.99 *(978-0-7641-3217-9(2))* Barron's Educational Series, Inc.

—Why Should I Listen? Llewellyn, Claire. 2005. (Why Should I? Bks.). (ENG.). 32p. (J). pap. 7.99 *(978-0-7641-3219-3(9))* Barron's Educational Series, Inc.

—Why Should I Protect Nature? Green, Jen. 2005. (Why Should I? Bks.). (ENG.). 32p. (J). pap. 6.99 *(978-0-7641-3154-7(0))* Barron's Educational Series, Inc.

—Why Should I Recycle? Green, Jen. 2005. (Why Should I? Bks.). (ENG.). 32p. (J). pap. 7.99 *(978-0-7641-3155-4(9))* Barron's Educational Series, Inc.

—Why Should I Save Energy? Green, Jen. 2005. (Why Should I? Bks.). (ENG.). 32p. (J). pap. 6.99 *(978-0-7641-3156-1(7))* Barron's Educational Series, Inc.

—Why Should I Save Water? Green, Jen. 2005. (Why Should I? Bks.). (ENG.). 32p. (J). pap. 6.99 *(978-0-7641-3157-8(5))* Barron's Educational Series, Inc.

—The Wish Fish. 2007. (First Reading Level 1 Ser.). 32p. (J). (gr. -1-3). 8.99 *(978-0-7945-1697-0(1),* Usborne) EDC Publishing.

Gordon, Mike. My Best Friend. Gordon, Mike, tr. Namm, Diane. 2004. (My First Reader Ser.). (ENG.). 31p. (J). 18.50 *(978-0-516-24416-7(7),* Children's Pr.) Scholastic Library Publishing.

Gordon, Mike & Gordon, Carl. Dinner with Dracula. Lansky, Bruce, ed. 2006. 32p. (J). *(978-0-88166-512-3(6))* Meadowbrook Pr.

—Do Princesses Count? Coyle, Carmela Lavigna. 2006. (ENG.). 24p. (J). (gr. -1-3). 6.95 *(978-0-87358-916-1(5))* Cooper Square Publishing Llc.

—Do Princesses Have Best Friends Forever? Coyle, Carmela Lavigna. (J). 2014. (ENG.). 96p. (J). (gr. -1-3). spiral bd. 15.95 *(978-1-58979-947-9(X));* 2010. *(978-1-58979-543-3(1))* Taylor Trade Publishing.

—Do Princesses Really Kiss Frogs? Coyle, Carmela Lavigna. 2005. (ENG.). 32p. (J). (gr. -1-2). 15.95 *(978-0-87358-880-5(0))* Cooper Square Publishing Llc.

—Do Princesses Really Kiss Frogs? Coyle, Carmela Lavigna. 2014. (ENG.). 96p. (J). (gr. -1-2). 15.95 *(978-1-58979-946-2(1))* Taylor Trade Publishing.

—Do Princesses Scrape Their Knees? Keepsake Sticker Doodle Book. Coyle, Carmela Lavigna. 2014. (ENG.). 96p. (J). (gr. -1-2). 15.95 *(978-1-58979-948-6(8))* Taylor Trade Publishing.

—Do Princesses Wear Hiking Boots? Coyle, Carmela Lavigna. 2003. (ENG.). 32p. (J). (gr. -1-2). 15.95 *(978-0-87358-828-7(2))* Cooper Square Publishing Llc.

—Do Princesses Wear Hiking Boots? Coyle, Carmela Lavigna. 2014. (ENG.). 96p. (J). (gr. -1-2). spiral bd. 15.95 *(978-1-58979-945-5(3))* Taylor Trade Publishing.

—I'm Allergic to School: Funny Poems & Songs about School. Pottie, Robert. 2007. 32p. *(978-0-88166-522-2(3))* Meadowbrook Pr.

—Just Me & 6,000 Rats: A Tale of Conjunctions, 1 vol. Walton, Rick. 2007. (ENG.). 32p. (J). (gr. 2-2). 15.95 *(978-1-4236-0219-4(6))* Gibbs Smith, Publisher.

—The Magic Porridge Pot. 2008. (Usborne First Reading: Level 3 Ser.). 48p. (J). (gr. -1-3). 8.99 *(978-0-7945-1883-7(4),* Usborne) EDC Publishing.

—The Musicians of Bremen. Davidson, Susanna. 2007. (Usborne First Reading: Level 3 Ser.). 48p. (J). 8.99 *(978-0-7945-1911-7(3),* Usborne) EDC Publishing.

—Revenge of the Lunch Ladies: The Hilarious Book of School Poetry. Nesbitt, Kenn. 2007. 80p. *(978-0-88166-527-7(4))* Meadowbrook Pr.

Gordon, Mike, jt. illus. see Gordon, Carl.

Gordon-Noy, Aya. Just Like I Wanted. Keller, Elinoar & Peleg-Segal, Naama. 2015. 26p. (J). ***(978-0-8028-5453-7(2),*** Eerdmans Bks For Young Readers) Eerdmans, William B. Publishing Co.

Gordon-Noy, Aya. Nora the Mind Reader. Gidali, Orit. 2012. (ENG.). 32p. (J). (gr. -1-3). 15.95 *(978-1-59270-120-9(5))* Enchanted Lion Bks., LLC.

Gordon, Steven E. Batman: Meet the Super Heroes. Teitelbaum, Michael. 2009. (I Can Read Book 2 Ser.). (ENG.). 32p. (J). (gr. -1-3). pap. 3.99 *(978-0-06-187858-9(8))* HarperCollins Pubs.

—Batman & the Toxic Terror. Huelin, Jodi. 2011. (ENG.). 24p. (J). (gr. -1-3). pap. 3.99 *(978-0-06-188530-3(4),* HarperFestival) HarperCollins Pubs.

—Feline Felonies: With Wonder Woman. Sazaklis, John. 2010. (ENG.). 24p. (J). (gr. -1-3). pap. 3.99 *(978-0-06-188528-0(2),* HarperFestival) HarperCollins Pubs.

—Justice League Classic - I Am the Flash. Sazaklis, John. 2014. (I Can Read Book 2 Ser.). (ENG.). 32p. (J). (gr. -1-3). pap. 3.99 *(978-0-06-221005-0(X))* HarperCollins Pubs.

—Spider-Man 3: Meet the Heroes & Villains. Lime, Harry. 2007. (I Can Read Bks.). 32p. (J). pap. 3.99 *(978-0-06-083721-1(7),* Harper Trophy) HarperCollins Pubs.

—Superman: Escape from the Phantom Zone. Sazaklis, John. 2011. (I Can Read Book 2 Ser.). (ENG.). 32p. (J). (gr. -1-3). pap. 3.99 *(978-0-06-188519-8(3))* HarperCollins Pubs.

—Superman - The Incredible Shrinking Super Hero! With Wonder Woman. Rau, Zachary. 2009. (ENG.). 24p. (J). (gr. -1-3). pap. 3.99 *(978-0-06-187855-8(3),* HarperFestival) HarperCollins Pubs.

—Tools of the Trade. Huelin, Jodi. 2012. (I Can Read Book 2 Ser.). (ENG.). 32p. (J). (gr. k-3). pap. 3.99 *(978-0-06-213223-9(7))* HarperCollins Pubs.

Gordon, Steven E. & Gordon, Eric A. Batman - Who Is Clayface? Lemke, Donald. 2013. (I Can Read Book 2 Ser.). (ENG.). 32p. (J). (gr. -1-3). pap. 3.99 *(978-0-06-188525-9(8))* HarperCollins Pubs.

—Batman - Winter Wasteland. Lemke, Donald. 2014. (I Can Read Book 2 Ser.). (ENG.). 32p. (J). (gr. -1-3). pap. 3.99 *(978-0-06-221004-3(1))* HarperCollins Pubs.

—Batman Classic: Batman Versus the Riddler. Lemke, Donald. 2014. (I Can Read Book 2 Ser.). (ENG.). 32p. (J). (gr. -1-3). pap. 3.99 *(978-0-06-221008-1(4))* HarperCollins Pubs.

—Batman Versus Man-Bat. Bright, J. E. 2012. (I Can Read Book 2 Ser.). (ENG.). 32p. (J). (gr. -1-3). pap. 3.99 *(978-0-06-188523-5(1))* HarperCollins Pubs.

—Fowl Play. Sazaklis, John. 2012. (ENG.). 24p. (J). (gr. -1-3). pap. 3.99 *(978-0-06-188536-5(3),* HarperFestival) HarperCollins Pubs.

—Friends & Foes. Rosen, Lucy. 2013. (I Can Read Book 2 Ser.). (ENG.). 32p. (J). (gr. -1-3). pap. 3.99 *(978-0-06-223595-4(8))* HarperCollins Pubs.

—Justice League Classic: I Am Green Lantern. Santos, Ray. 2013. (I Can Read Book 2 Ser.). (ENG.). 32p. (J). (gr. -1-3). pap. 3.99 *(978-0-06-221006-7(8))* HarperCollins Pubs.

—Parasite City. Rosen, Lucy. 2011. (ENG.). 24p. (J). (gr. -1-3). pap. 3.99 *(978-0-06-188532-7(0),* HarperFestival) HarperCollins Pubs.

Gordon, Steven E., jt. illus. see Gordon, Eric A.

Gordon, Susie. Skipingo Home: A Thoroughbred's Second Chance. Lyons, Jane & Bailey, Karen. 2009. (ENG.). 40p. (J). (gr. -1-3). 16.95 *(978-1-58150-205-3(2),* Eclipse Pr.) Blood-Horse, Inc., The.

Gore, Leonid. And Nick. Gore, Emily. 2015. (ENG.). 40p. (J). (gr. -1-3). 17.99 *(978-1-4169-5506-1(2))* Simon & Schuster Children's Publishing.

—I Am King! Packard, Mary. 2003. (My First Reader Ser.). (ENG.). 32p. (J). 18.50 *(978-0-516-22927-0(3),* Children's Pr.) Scholastic Library Publishing.

—Monarch & Milkweed. Frost, Helen. 2008. (ENG.). 40p. (J). (gr. -1-3). 17.99 *(978-1-4169-0085-6(3),* Atheneum Bks. for Young Readers) Simon & Schuster Children's Publishing.

—The Princess Mouse: A Tale of Finland. Shepard, Aaron. 2008. (ENG.). 40p. (J). (gr. -1-3). 13.99 *(978-1-4169-8969-1(2),* Atheneum Bks. for Young Readers) Simon & Schuster Children's Publishing.

—Saints among the Animals. Zarin, Cynthia. 2012. (ENG.). 96p. (J). (gr. 2-7). pap. 6.99 *(978-1-4424-7296-9(0),* Atheneum Bks. for Young Readers) Simon & Schuster Children's Publishing.

—Voices of the Trojan War. Hovey, Kate. 2012. (ENG.). 128p. (J). (gr. 3-7). pap. 7.99 *(978-1-4424-8880-9(8),* McElderry, Margaret K. Bks.) McElderry, Margaret K. Bks.

Gore, Leonid. Danny's First Snow. Gore, Leonid. 2007. (ENG.). 40p. (J). (gr. -1-2). 16.99 *(978-1-4169-1330-6(0),* Atheneum Bks. for Young Readers) Simon & Schuster Children's Publishing.

—Mommy, Where Are You? Gore, Leonid. 2009. (ENG.). 32p. (J). (gr. -1-2). 16.99 *(978-1-4169-5505-4(4),* Atheneum Bks. for Young Readers) Simon & Schuster Children's Publishing.

—Worms for Lunch? Gore, Leonid. 2011. (ENG.). 32p. (J). (gr. -1-3). 16.99 *(978-0-545-24338-4(6),* Scholastic Pr.) Scholastic, Inc.

Gorelick, Victor. Jughead with Archie in Fool Proof. Ribeiro, Nelson & Spotlight Editors. 2007. (Jughead with Archie Ser.). (ENG.). 80p. (J). (gr. 3-6). 24.21 *(978-1-59961-274-4(7))* Spotlight.

—Jughead with Archie in Power Play. Ribeiro, Nelson. 2007. (Jughead with Archie Ser.). (ENG.). 80p. (J). (gr. 3-6). 24.21 *(978-1-59961-275-1(5))* Spotlight.

—Jughead with Archie in Pup-Ularity Contest. Ribeiro, Nelson & Spotlight Editors. 2007. (Jughead with Archie Ser.). (ENG.). 80p. (J). (gr. 3-6). 24.21 *(978-1-59961-276-8(3))* Spotlight.

—Jughead with Archie in Wish Fulfillment. Ribeiro, Nelson & Spotlight Editors. 2007. (Jughead with Archie Ser.). (ENG.). 80p. (J). (gr. 3-6). 24.21 *(978-1-59961-277-5(1))* Spotlight.

—Laugh with a Test Case. Spotlight Editors. 2007. (Archie Digest Library). (ENG.). 80p. (J). (gr. 3-6). 24.21 *(978-1-59961-284-3(4))* Spotlight.

—Laugh with Mammoth Madness. Ribiero, Nelson & Spotlight Editors. 2007. (Archie Digest Library). (ENG.). 80p. (J). (gr. 3-6). 24.21 *(978-1-59961-281-2(X))* Spotlight.

—Laugh with Snack Swap. Ribiero, Nelson & Spotlight Editors. 2007. (Archie Digest Library). (ENG.). 80p. (J). (gr. 3-6). 24.21 *(978-1-59961-282-9(8))* Spotlight.

—Laugh with Stampede. Ribiero, Nelson & Spotlight Editors. 2007. (Archie Digest Library). (ENG.). 80p. (J). (gr. 3-6). 24.21 *(978-1-59961-283-6(6))* Spotlight.

Gorenman, Marcelo. Little Green. Rudnick, Arnold. 2012. 32p. (J). pap. 9.99 *(978-0-9815879-7-4(6))* Paraphrase, LLC.

Gorey, Edward. The Adventures of Gremlin. Jones, DuPre. 2013. 112p. 17.95 *(978-0-7649-6605-7(7))* Pomegranate Communications, Inc.

—He Was There from the Day We Moved In. Levine, Rhoda. 2012. (ENG.). 32p. (J). (gr. -1-2). 14.95 *(978-1-59017-515-6(8),* NYR Children's Collection) New York Review of Bks., Inc., The.

—The House with a Clock in Its Walls. Bellairs, John. 2004. (Lewis Barnavelt Ser.: Bk. 1). (ENG.). 192p. (J). (gr. 3-7). pap. 5.99 *(978-0-14-240257-3(5),* Puffin) Penguin Publishing Group.

—The Mansion in the Mist. Bellairs, John. 2004. (Anthony Monday Ser.: No. 4). (ENG.). 176p. (J). (gr. 3-7). 6.99 *(978-0-14-240262-7(1),* Puffin) Penguin Publishing Group.

—Men & Gods: Myths & Legends of the Ancient Greeks. Warner, Rex. 2008. (New York Review Books Classics). (ENG.). 288p. 17.95 *(978-1-59017-263-6(9),* NYR Children's Collection) New York Review of Bks., Inc., The.

—Someone Could Win a Polar Bear. Ciardi, John. 2003. 64p. (J). (gr. 2-4). 9.95 *(978-1-59078-012-1(4))* Boyds Mills Pr.

—The Spell of the Sorcerer's Skull. Bellairs, John. 2004. 170p. (J). (gr. 4-7). 13.65 *(978-0-7569-4965-5(3))* Perfection Learning Corp.

—Three Ladies Beside the Sea. Levine, Rhoda. 2010. (ENG.). 40p. (J). (gr. k-4). 14.95 *(978-1-59017-354-1(6),* NYR Children's Collection) New York Review of Bks., Inc., The.

—The War of the Worlds. Wells, H. G. 2005. (New York Review Books Classics). (ENG.). 260p. 17.95 *(978-1-59017-158-5(6),* NYRB Classics) New York Review of Bks., Inc., The.

Gorey, Edward. The Wuggly Ump. Gorey, Edward. 2007. 32p. 12.95 *(978-0-7649-4192-4(5),* A142) Pomegranate Communications, Inc.

Gorey, Edward & Lear, Edward. The Dong with the Luminous Nose. 2010. 48p. 14.95 *(978-0-7649-5427-6(X))* Pomegranate Communications, Inc.

—Jumblies. 2010. 48p. 14.95 *(978-0-7649-5426-9(1))* Pomegranate Communications, Inc.

Goris, Laura. Monkeying Around: Meet Chippey & His Friends. Smith, Kimberly. 2012. 44p. (J). pap. 14.98 *(978-0-9843166-6-3(3))* Artists' Orchard, LLC, The.

Gorissen, Dean. Chaz & the Missing Mayo. Roy, James. 2015. (J). pap. ***(978-1-4966-0245-9(5))*** Capstone Classroom.

—Chaz at the Fish Market. Roy, James. 2015. (J). pap. ***(978-1-4966-0251-0(X))*** Capstone Classroom.

—Chaz, Superbarf Surprise. Roy, James. 2015. (J). pap. ***(978-1-4966-0239-8(0))*** Capstone Classroom.

—Chaz, TV Superstar? Roy, James. 2015. (J). pap. ***(978-1-4966-0257-2(9))*** Capstone Classroom.

—Noob, Amateur Dentist. Bancks, Tristan. 2015. (Legends in Their Own Lunchbox Ser.). (ENG.). 56p. (gr. 2-3). pap. 7.99 ***(978-1-4966-0253-4(6),*** Legends in Their Own Lunchbox) Capstone Classroom.

—Noob & the Librarian Supervillain. Bancks, Tristan. 2015. (Legends in Their Own Lunchbox Ser.). (ENG.). 48p. (gr. 1-2). pap. 7.99 ***(978-1-4966-0247-3(1),*** Legends in Their Own Lunchbox) Capstone Classroom.

—Noob, Crimebuster. Bancks, Tristan. 2015. (Legends in Their Own Lunchbox Ser.). (ENG.). 48p. (gr. 1-2). pap. 7.99 ***(978-1-4966-0241-1(2),*** Legends in Their Own Lunchbox) Capstone Classroom.

—Noob, the Boy Who Could Fly. Bancks, Tristan. 2015. (Legends in Their Own Lunchbox Ser.). (ENG.). 56p. (gr. 2-3). pap. 7.99 ***(978-1-4966-0259-6(5),*** Legends in Their Own Lunchbox) Capstone Classroom.

Gorissen, Dean. Ten Little Elvi. Henson, Laura J. & Grooms, Duffy. 2004. (ENG.). 30p. (J). (gr. -1-2). 12.99 *(978-1-58246-124-3(4),* Tricycle Pr.) Ten Speed Pr.

Gorman, Kyrsten. Alicia & Policia, 1 vol. Gorman, Patrick. 2010. 24p. 24.95 *(978-1-4489-6425-3(3))* PublishAmerica, Inc.

Gorman, Mike. Alien Contact. Service, Pamela F. (Alien Agent Ser.: 5). (ENG.). 144p. (J). (gr. 4-6). 2010. lib. bdg. 16.95 *(978-0-7613-5363-8(1),* Carolrhoda Bks.); No. 5. 2011. pap. 5.95 *(978-0-7613-7297-4(0),* Darby Creek) Lerner Publishing Group.

—Alien Encounter. Service, Pamela F. (Alien Agent Ser.: 4). (ENG.). 152p. (J). (gr. 4-6). 2011. pap. 5.95 *(978-0-7613-5248-8(1));* 2010. 16.95 *(978-0-8225-8873-3(0),* Carolrhoda Bks.) Lerner Publishing Group.

—Alien Envoy. Service, Pamela F. (Alien Agent Ser.). 176p. (J). (gr. 4-6). 2012. pap. 33.92 *(978-0-7613-9208-8(4),* Darby Creek); 2012. (ENG.). pap. 5.95 *(978-0-7613-7298-1(9),* Darby Creek); 2011. (ENG.). 16.95 *(978-0-7613-5364-5(X))* Lerner Publishing Group.

—Alien Expedition. Service, Pamela F. (Alien Agent Ser.: 3). (ENG.). 160p. (J). (gr. 4-6). 2009. 16.95 *(978-0-8225-8870-2(6));* No. 3. 2010. pap. 5.95 *(978-0-7613-5249-5(X))* Lerner Publishing Group. (Carolrhoda Bks.).

—Camp Alien. Service, Pamela F. (Alien Agent Ser.: 2). (ENG.). 160p. (J). (gr. 4-6). 2010. pap. 5.95 *(978-0-7613-5247-1(3));* 2009. 16.95 *(978-0-8225-8656-2(8),* Carolrhoda Bks.) Lerner Publishing Group.

—Escape from Planet Yastol, No. 1. Service, Pamela F. 2011. (Way-Too-Real Aliens Ser.: 1). (ENG.). 112p. (J). (gr. 4-6). 15.95 *(978-0-7613-7918-8(5));* pap. 5.95 *(978-0-7613-7921-8(5))* Lerner Publishing Group. (Darby Creek).

—My Cousin, the Alien. Service, Pamela F. (Alien Agent Ser.: 1). (ENG.). 160p. (J). (gr. 4-6). 2009. pap. 5.95 *(978-0-7613-4964-8(2),* First Avenue Editions); 2008. 16.95 *(978-0-8225-7627-3(9),* Carolrhoda Bks.) Lerner Publishing Group.

—The Not-So-Perfect Planet. Service, Pamela F. 2012. (Way-Too-Real Aliens Ser.: 2). (ENG.). 120p. (J). (gr. 4-6). 15.95 *(978-0-7613-7919-5(3));* pap. 6.95 *(978-0-7613-7923-2(1))* Lerner Publishing Group. (Darby Creek).

—The Wizards of Wyrd World. Service, Pamela F. (Way-Too-Real Aliens Ser.: 3). (ENG.). 112p. (J). (gr. 4-6). 2013. pap. 6.95 *(978-0-7613-7922-5(3),* Darby Creek); 2012. 15.95 *(978-0-7613-7920-1(7))* Lerner Publishing Group.

—#4 Alien Encounter. Service, Pamela F. 2011. (Alien Agent Ser.). 152p. (J). pap. 33.92 *(978-0-7613-7608-8(9),* Darby Creek) Lerner Publishing Group.

—#5 Alien Contact. Service, Pamela F. 2011. (Alien Agent Ser.). pap. 33.92 *(978-0-7613-8347-5(6),* Darby Creek) Lerner Publishing Group.

Gorman, Mike & Görrissen, Janina. I Date Dead People. Kerns, Ann. 2012. (My Boyfriend Is a Monster Ser.: 5). (ENG.). 128p. (YA). (gr. 7-12). pap. 9.95 *(978-0-7613-8549-3(5),* Graphic Universe) Lerner Publishing Group.

Gorman, Stan. Princess Emily & the Secret Library. Balfanz, Mary. 2009. 32p. (J). (gr. -1-3). 16.99 *(978-0-9817636-0-6(X))* Willow Brook Publishing.

Gormley, Julia Ann. Science Projects: Book 1. Project Ideas in the Life Sciences, Vol. 1. Neuhaus, Richard A. 2008. (ENG.). 184p. (YA). pap. 24.95 *(978-0-9794500-1-3(2))* Gormley Publishing.

—Science Projects: Book 2. Project ideas in Chemistry & Biochemistry, Vol. 2. Neuhaus, Richard A. 2008. (ENG.). 196p. (YA). pap. 24.95 *(978-0-9794500-4-4(7))* Gormley Publishing.

—Science Projects: How to Collect, Analyze, & Present Your Data. Neuhaus, Richard A. 2007. (ENG.). 184p. (YA). pap. 24.95 *(978-0-9794500-0-6(4))* Gormley Publishing.

Görrissen, Janina. I Date Dead People. Kerns, Ann. 2012. (My Boyfriend Is a Monster Ser.: 5). (ENG.). 128p. (YA). (gr. 7-12). lib. bdg. 29.27 *(978-0-7613-6007-0(7))* Lerner Publishing Group.

—I Love Him to Pieces. Tsang, Evonne. 2011. (My Boyfriend Is a Monster Ser.: 1). (ENG.). 128p. (YA). (gr. 7-12). 29.27 *(978-0-7613-6004-9(2))* Lerner Publishing Group.

—#01 I Love Him to Pieces. Tsang, Evonne. 2011. (My Boyfriend Is a Monster Ser.). 128p. (YA). pap. 56.72 *(978-0-7613-7602-6(X),* Graphic Universe) Lerner Publishing Group.

Görrissen, Janina, jt. illus. see Gorman, Mike.

Gorsline, Douglas. Captain Waymouth's Indians. Molloy, Anne Stearns Baker. 2011. 204p. 44.95 *(978-1-258-06802-8(8))* Literary Licensing, LLC.

Gorsline, Douglas, jt. illus. see Moore, Clement C.

Gorsline, Douglas W. The Story of Good Queen Bess. Malkus, Alida Sims. Meadowcroft, Enid Lamonte, ed. 2011. 192p. 42.95 *(978-1-258-09564-2(5))* Literary Licensing, LLC.

Gorstein, Mordicai. The Mixed-Up Mask Mystery: A Fletcher Mystery. Levy, Elizabeth. unabr. ed. 2006. (First Chapter Bks.). (J). (gr. 2-4). pap. 17.95 incl. audio *(978-1-59519-710-8(9));* pap. 20.95 incl. audio compact disk *(978-1-59519-711-5(7))* Live Oak Media.

Gorton, Julia. I Face the Wind. Cobb, Vicki. 2003. (Science Play Ser.). (ENG.). 40p. (J). (gr. -1-3). 16.99 *(978-0-688-17840-6(5))* HarperCollins Pubs.

—I Fall Down. Cobb, Vicki. 2004. (Science Play Ser.). 40p. (J). (gr. -1-3). (ENG.). 17.99 *(978-0-688-17842-0(1));* lib. bdg. 18.89 *(978-0-688-17843-7(X))* HarperCollins Pubs.

—Just Like Mama. Newman, Lesléa. 2010. (ENG.). 32p. (J). (gr. -1-3). 15.95 *(978-0-8109-8393-9(1),* Abrams Bks. for Young Readers) Abrams.

—Score! 50 Poems to Motivate & Inspire. Ghigna, Charles. 2008. (ENG.). 48p. (J). (gr. 2-7). 16.95 *(978-0-8109-9488-1(7),* Abrams Bks. for Young Readers) Abrams.

—The Three Little Fish & the Big Bad Shark. Geist, Ken. 2007. (ENG.). 32p. (J). (gr. -1-3). 7.99 *(978-0-439-71962-9(3))* Scholastic, Inc.

Gorton, Steve, jt. illus. see Dann, Geoff.

Goshorn, Shan, jt. illus. see Standingdeer, John, Jr.

Gospodinov, George. Small Enough Tall Enough. Wilson, Barbara E. 2012. 46p. pap. 14.95 *(978-0-9838964-0-1(2))* Simply Silly Stories.

Goss, John. Our Little Norman Cousin of Long Ago. Stein, Evaleen. 2007. 112p. per. 8.95 *(978-1-59915-245-5(2))* Yesterday's Classics.

—The Story of the Red Cross As Told to the Little Colonel. Johnston, Annie Fellows. 2007. 48p. per. *(978-1-4065-3517-4(6))* Dodo Pr.

Goss, Mini. Bendelomena. Wignell, Edel. 2007. (Collins Big Cat Ser.). (ENG.). 24p. (J). pap. 8.99 *(978-0-00-722868-3(6))* HarperCollins Pubs. Ltd. GBR. Dist: Independent Pubs. Group.

—DuckStar & Cyberfarm. Edwards, Hazel & Anketell, Christine. 2010. 96p. (J). pap. *(978-1-921479-57-1(4),* IP Kidz) Interactive Pubns. Pty, Ltd.

—Operatic Duck & Duck on Tour. Edwards, Hazel & Anketell, Christine. 2010. 96p. (J). pap. *(978-1-921479-80-9(9),* IP Kidz) Interactive Pubns. Pty, Ltd.

Got, Yves. Sam's Pop-up Schoolhouse. Got, Yves. 2004. 6p. (J). (gr. k-4). reprint ed. 17.00 *(978-0-7567-8065-4(9))* DIANE Publishing Co.

Gothard, David. Little Lola. Saab, Julie. 2014. (ENG.). 32p. (J). (gr. -1-3). 16.99 *(978-0-06-227457-1(0),* Greenwillow Bks.) HarperCollins Pubs.

Gothard, David. Little Lola Saves the Show. Saab, Julie. 2016. 32p. (J). (gr. -1-3). 17.99 ***(978-0-06-227453-3(8),*** Greenwillow Bks.) HarperCollins Pubs.

Gotlieb, Jules. Fisherman Jody. Olds, Helen Diehl. 2011. 64p. 36.95 *(978-1-258-07129-5(0))* Literary Licensing, LLC.

Goto, Scott. The Enormous Turnip. Tolstoy, Alexei. 2003. (Green Light Readers Level 2 Ser.). (ENG.). 24p. (J). (gr. -1-3). pap. 3.95 *(978-0-15-204843-3(X))* Houghton Mifflin Harcourt Publishing Co.

—Hawai'i. Gill, Shelley. 2006. (ENG.). 32p. (J). (gr. 2-5). lib. bdg. 16.95 *(978-0-88106-296-0(0))* Charlesbridge Publishing, Inc.

—Wordsworth the Poet. Kakugawa, Francis. 2003. 32p. (J). (gr. -1-3). 10.95 *(978-0-9742672-0-3(1))* Watermark Publishing, LLC.

Goto, Scott. Perfect Sword. Goto, Scott. 2010. (ENG.). 48p. (J). (gr. 1-4). pap. 8.95 *(978-1-57091-698-4(5))* Charlesbridge Publishing, Inc.

Gotsubo, Masaru. Samurai Champloo, Vol. 1. Gotsubo, Masaru. Manglobe. 2005. 184p. pap. 9.99 *(978-1-59182-282-0(3))* TOKYOPOP, Inc.

—Samurai Champloo, Vol. 2. Gotsubo, Masaru. Manglobe. 2nd rev. ed. 2006. 184p. per. 9.99 *(978-1-59816-215-8(2))* TOKYOPOP, Inc.

Gott, Barry. The Brotherhood of Rotten Babysitters. Danko, Dan & Mason, Tom. 5th ed. 2005. (ENG.). 144p. (J). (gr. 3-7). pap. 15.99 *(978-0-316-15895-4(X))* Little, Brown Bks. for Young Readers.

—Car Wash Kid. Fishman, Cathy Goldberg. 2003. (Rookie Reader Skill Set Ser.). (ENG.). (J). (gr. k-2). pap. 4.95 *(978-0-516-27811-7(8),* Children's Pr.) Scholastic Library Publishing.

—Carmen's Sticky Scab. Churchill, Ginger. 2007. (ENG.). 32p. (J). (gr. -1-3). 15.95 *(978-1-933718-13-2(7))* Tanglewood Pr.

—Class Pets. 2005. (I'm Going to Read(r) Ser.). (ENG.). 48p. (J). (gr. 2-3). pap. 3.95 *(978-1-4027-2709-2(7))* Sterling Publishing Co., Inc.

—Dino-Baseball. Wheeler, Lisa. 2010. (ENG.). 32p. (J). (gr. k-3). lib. bdg. 16.95 *(978-0-7613-4429-2(2),* Carolrhoda Bks.) Lerner Publishing Group.

—Dino-Basketball. Wheeler, Lisa. 2011. (Carolrhoda Picture Bks). (ENG.). 32p. (J). (gr. k-3). 16.95 *(978-0-7613-6393-4(9),* Carolrhoda Bks.) Lerner Publishing Group.

—Dino-Boarding. Wheeler, Lisa. 2014. (ENG.). 32p. (J). (gr. k-3). lib. bdg. 16.95 *(978-1-4677-0213-3(7),* Carolrhoda Bks.) Lerner Publishing Group.

—Dino-Football. Wheeler, Lisa. 2012. (Carolrhoda Picture Bks). (ENG.). 32p. (J). (gr. k-3). lib. bdg. 16.95 *(978-0-7613-6394-1(7),* Carolrhoda Bks.) Lerner Publishing Group.

—Dino-Hockey. Wheeler, Lisa. 2007. (Carolrhoda Picture Bks.). (ENG.). 32p. (J). (gr. k-3). 16.95 *(978-0-8225-6191-0(3),* Carolrhoda Bks.) Lerner Publishing Group.

—Dino-Soccer. Wheeler, Lisa. 2009. (Carolrhoda Picture Bks). (ENG.). 32p. (J). (gr. k-3). 16.95 *(978-0-8225-9028-6(X),* Carolrhoda Bks.) Lerner Publishing Group.

—Dino-Swimming. Wheeler, Lisa. 2015. (ENG.). 32p. (J). (gr. k-3). lib. bdg. 16.99 *(978-1-4677-0214-0(5),* Carolrhoda Bks.) Lerner Publishing Group.

—Dino-Wrestling. Wheeler, Lisa. 2013. (ENG.). 32p. (J). (gr. k-3). 16.95 *(978-1-4677-0212-6(9),* Carolrhoda Bks.) Lerner Publishing Group.

—Dizzy Dinosaurs: Silly Dino Poems. Hopkins, Lee Bennett. 2011. (I Can Read Book 2 Ser.). (ENG.). 48p. (J). (gr. k-3). 16.99 *(978-0-06-135839-5(8));* pap. 3.99 *(978-0-06-135841-8(X))* HarperCollins Pubs.

—The Great Shape-up. May, Eleanor. 2007. (Science Solves It! Ser.). 32p. (J). (gr. -1-3). pap. 5.95 *(978-1-57565-248-1(X))* Kane Pr., Inc.

—Head, Shoulders, Knees, & Toes. 2006. (J). *(978-1-58987-056-7(5))* Kindermusik International.

—The Invasion of the Shag Carpet Creature. David, Lawrence. 2004. (Horace Splattly Ser.). 151p. (J). (gr. 4-7). 12.65 *(978-0-7569-2818-6(4))* Perfection Learning Corp.

—It Came from Outer Space. Spinner, Stephanie. 2003. (Science Solves It! Ser.). 32p. (J). pap. 5.95 *(978-1-57565-122-4(X))* Kane Pr., Inc.

—The Midnight Kid. Walker, Nan. 2007. (Science Solves It! Ser.). 32p. (J). (gr. -1-3). pap. 5.95 *(978-1-57565-238-2(2))* Kane Pr., Inc.

—El Misterio del Arco Iris. Dussling, Jennifer. Ramirez, Alma B., tr. from ENG. 2009. (Science Solves It! en Espanol Ser.). (SPA.). 32p. (J). (gr. 1-3). pap. 5.95 *(978-1-57565-283-2(8))* Kane Pr., Inc.

—El Misterio Del Arco Iris (the Rainbow Mystery) Dussling, Jennifer. 2009. (Science Solves It! (r) en Espanol Ser.). (SPA.). (gr. 1-3). pap. 33.92 *(978-0-7613-4798-9(4))* Lerner Publishing Group.

—A Moldy Mystery. Knudsen, Michelle. 2006. (Science Solves It! Ser.). 32p. (J). (gr. -1-3). pap. 5.95 *(978-1-57565-167-5(X))* Kane Pr., Inc.

—My New School. Hall, Kirsten. 2004. (My First Reader Ser.). (ENG.). 32p. (J). (gr. k-1). pap. 3.95 *(978-0-516-25505-7(3),* Children's Pr.) Scholastic Library Publishing.

—Patches Lost & Found, 0 vols. Kroll, Steven. 2005. (ENG.). 32p. (J). (gr. k-4). pap. 9.99 *(978-0-7614-5217-1(6),* 9780761452171, Amazon Children's Publishing) Amazon Publishing.

—A Planet Called Home: Eco-Pig's Animal Protection. French, Lisa S. 2009. (Eco-Pig Ser.). 32p. (J). (gr. -1-2). 28.50 *(978-1-60270-662-0(X))* ABDO Publishing Co.

—Que Hacen los Maestros? (Despues de Que Te Vas de la Escuela) Bowen, Anne. 2007. (Ediciones Lerner Single Titles Ser.). (SPA.). 32p. (J). (gr. k-3). 16.95

G

(978-0-8225-6264-1(2), Ediciones Lerner) Lerner Publishing Group.
—The Real Me. May, Eleanor. 2006. (Social Studies Connects). 32p. (J). (gr. k-2). pap. 5.95 (978-1-57565-186-6(6)) Kane Pr., Inc.
—Rock, Brock, & the Savings Shock. 1 vol. Bair, Sheila. 2006. (ENG.). 32p. (J). (gr. 1-5). 16.99 (978-0-8075-7094-4(X)) Whitman, Albert & Co.
—Super Specs. Driscoll, Laura. 2005. (Math Matters Ser.). (ENG.). 32p. (J). (gr. -1-3). pap. 5.95 (978-1-57565-145-3(9)) Kane Pr., Inc.
—The Terrible Trash Trail: Eco-Pig Stops Pollution. French, Lisa S. 2009. (Eco-Pig Ser.). 32p. (J). (gr. -1-2). 28.50 (978-1-60270-663-7(8)) ABDO Publishing Co.
—The Terror of the Pink Dodo Balloons. David, Lawrence. 2003. (Horace Splattly Ser.). 153p. (J). (gr. 4-7). 12.65 (978-0-7569-2816-2(8)) Perfection Learning Corp.
—Vino del Espacio. Barker, Henry. 2008. (Science Solves It! en Espanol Ser.). (SPA.). 32p. (J). (gr. -1-3). pap. 5.95 (978-1-57565-265-8(X)) Kane Pr., Inc.
—Vino Del Espacio (It Came from Outer Space) Barker, Henry. 2009. (Science Solves It! (r) en Espanol Ser.). (SPA.). (gr. 1-3). pap. 33.92 (978-1-58013-771-3(7)) Lerner Publishing Group.
—What Do Teachers Do (after You Leave School)? Bowen, Anne. 2006. (ENG.). 32p. (J). (gr. k-3). 16.95 (978-1-57505-922-8(3), Carolrhoda Bks.) Lerner Publishing Group.
—What Does It Mean to Be Green? Eco-Pig Explains Living Green. French, Lisa S. 2009. (Eco-Pig Ser.). 32p. (J). (gr. -1-2). 28.50 (978-1-60270-665-1(4)) ABDO Publishing Co.
—Who Turned up the Heat? Eco-Pig Explains Global Warming. French, Lisa S. 2009. (Eco-Pig Ser.). 32p. (J). (gr. -1-2). 28.50 (978-1-60270-664-4(6)) ABDO Publishing Co.
—Whoa! UFO! Larsen, Kirsten. 2009. (Science Solves It! Ser.). 32p. (J). (gr. k-2). pap. 5.95 (978-1-57565-280-1(3)) Kane Pr., Inc.
Gottardo, Alessandro. Moon Bear. Lewis, Gill. 2015. (ENG.). 384p. (J). (gr. 3-7). 16.99 (978-1-4814-0094-7(0)) Simon & Schuster Children's Publishing.
Gottesman, Val. Iraq. 2003. Poffenberger, Nancy. 2003. 32p. (YA). per. 9.95 (978-0-938293-11-8(7)) Fun Publishing Co.
Götting, Jean-Claude. The Bible for Young Children. Delval, Marie-Hélène. 2010. 96p. (J). (gr. -1-3). 16.50 (978-0-8028-5383-7(8), Eerdmans Bks For Young Readers) Eerdmans, William B. Publishing Co.
Gottleib, Dale. Are We There Yet?, Level 3. 2005. (I'm Going to Read(r) Ser.). (ENG.). 32p. (J). (gr. 1-2). per. 3.95 (978-1-4027-2713-9(5)) Sterling Publishing Co., Inc.
Gottschalk, Deana. The Three Little Orphan Kittens. Wise, D. Rudd & Wise, Rachel. 2006. (J). 15.95 (978-0-9786276-0-7(1)) Mentzer Printing Ink.
Gotzen-Beek, Betina. Antonia & the Big Competition: The Rosenburg Riding Stables, Volume 2. Zoller, Elisabeth & Kolloch, Brigitte. 2014. (ENG.). 92p. (J). (gr. 2-7). 9.95 (978-1-62873-597-0(X), Sky Pony Pr.) Skyhorse Publishing Co., Inc.
—Antonia, the Horse Whisperer: The Rosenburg Riding Stables, Volume 1. Zöller, Elisabeth & Kolloch, Brigitte. 2014. (ENG.). 96p. (J). (gr. 2-7). 9.95 (978-1-62636-383-0(8), Sky Pony Pr.) Skyhorse Publishing Co., Inc.
Gouge, Angela. Casper & Catherine Move to America: An Immigrant Family's Adventures, 1849-1850. Gouge, Angela, tr. Hasler, Brian. 2003. 32p. 17.95 (978-0-87195-168-7(1)) Indiana Historical Society.
Gough, Bryan. My Friend Isabelle. Gough, Bryan, tr. Woloson, Eliza. 2003. 28p. (J). 14.95 (978-1-890627-50-8(X)) Woodbine Hse.
Gould, Alan, et al. Hot Water & Warm Homes from Sunlight. Sneider, Cary I., photos by. Gould, Alan. rev. ed. 2005. (Great Explorations in Math & Science Ser.). 80p. 13.50 (978-1-931542-04-3(X), GEMS) Univ. of California, Berkeley, Lawrence Hall of Science.
Gould, Jason, photos by. Jinx. Wild, Margaret. 2004. (ENG., 224p. (YA). (gr. 9). reprint ed. pap. 11.95 (978-0-689-86541-1(4), Simon Pulse) Simon Pulse.
Gould, Robert, photos by. Arthur. Duey, Kathleen. 2006. (Time Soldiers Ser.). (ENG., 96p. (gr. -1-4). 24.21 (978-1-59961-224-9(0)) Spotlight.
—Parche, Vol. 3. Big Guy Books Staff & Duey, Kathleen. 2003. (Soldados en el Tiempo: Vol. 3). (SPA & ENG., 48p. (J). (gr. k-4). pap. 8.95 (978-1-929945-37-5(X)) Big Guy Bks., Inc.
Gould, Robert, photos by. Racers. Gould, Robert. 2005. (Big Stuff Ser.). (ENG., 16p. (J). bds. 7.95 (978-1-929945-52-8(3)) Big Guy Bks., Inc.
—Rescue Vehicles. Gould, Robert. 2005. (Big Stuff Ser.). (ENG., 16p. (J). bds. 7.95 (978-1-929945-51-1(5)) Big Guy Bks., Inc.
Gould, Shawn. Giant of the Sea: The Story of a Sperm Whale. Raff, Courtney Granet. 2005. (Smithsonian Oceanic Collection). (ENG.). 32p. (J). (gr. -1-2). 15.95 (978-1-931465-71-7(1), B4023) Soundprints.
Goulding, Celeste. Classic Tales: Thumbelina. Arengo, Sue. 2006. (ENG.). 24p. 5.50 (978-0-19-422537-3(2)) Oxford Univ. Pr., Inc. GBR. Dist: Oxford Univ. Pr., Inc.
Goulding, June. The Great Pirate Adventure: Peek Inside the 3D Windows. Baxter, Nicola. 2012. (ENG.). 12p. (J). (gr. -1-12). 16.99 (978-1-84322-966-7(8)) Anness Publishing GBR. Dist: National Bk. Network.
—The Mystery of the Haunted House: Dare You Peek Through the 3-D Windows? Baxter, Nicola. 2013. (ENG.). 12p. 16.99 (978-1-84322-754-0(1)) Anness Publishing GBR. Dist: National Bk. Network.
—Sunny Bunnies. Blumberg, Margie. 2009. 32p. (gr. -1-k). 15.95 (978-0-9624166-4-4(9)) MB Publishing, LLC.
Goulding, June & Smyth, Iain. Dracula Steps Out. Ratnett, Michael. 2005. 12p. (J). (gr. k-4). reprint ed. 16.00 (978-0-7567-8585-7(5)) DIANE Publishing Co.
Gouldthorpe, Peter. Queenie: One Elephant's Story. King, Corinne & Fenton, Corinne. 2013. (ENG.). 24p. (J). (gr. k-3). 16.99 (978-0-7636-6375-9(1)) Candlewick Pr.
Gourbault, Martine. Once upon a Dragon: Stranger Safety for Kids (and Dragons) Pendziwol, Jean E. & Pendziwol, Jean. 2006. (ENG.). 32p. (J). (gr. -1-2). 7.95 (978-1-55337-969-0(1)); 15.95 (978-1-55337-722-1(2)) Kids Can Pr., Ltd. CAN. Dist: Univ. of Toronto Pr.
—The Tale of Sir Dragon: Dealing with Bullies for Kids (and Dragons) Pendziwol, Jean E. 2007. (ENG.). 32p. (J). (gr. -1-2). 15.95 (978-1-55453-135-6(7)) Kids Can Pr., Ltd. CAN. Dist: Univ. of Toronto Pr.
—A Treasure at Sea for Dragon & Me: Water Safety for Kids (And Dragons) Pendziwol, Jean E. 2005. (ENG.). 32p. (J). (gr. -1-2). 14.95 (978-1-55337-721-4(4)) Kids Can Pr., Ltd. CAN. Dist: Univ. of Toronto Pr.
—A Treasure at Sea for Dragon & Me: Water Safety for Kids (and Dragons) Pendziwol, Jean E. 2005. (ENG.). 32p. (J). (gr. -1-3). 6.95 (978-1-55337-880-8(6)) Kids Can Pr., Ltd. CAN. Dist: Univ. of Toronto Pr.
Gourbault, Martine. The Tale of Sir Dragon: Dealing with Bullies for Kids (and Dragons) Gourbault, Martine. Pendziwol, Jean E. 2007. (ENG.). 32p. (J). (gr. -1-2). pap. 7.95 (978-1-55453-136-3(5)) Kids Can Pr., Ltd. CAN. Dist: Univ. of Toronto Pr.
Gove, Frank Stanley. Bart the Batronaut. Ferris, Margaret Ann. 2011. (ENG.). 32p. (J). pap. 14.95 (978-0-9837470-2-4(4)); pap. (978-0-9832819-8-6(X)) BookCrafters.
Govenar, Alan B., photos by. Extraordinary Ordinary People: Five American Masters of Traditional Arts. Govenar, Alan B. 2006. (ENG., 96p. (J). (gr. 5-7). 22.99 (978-0-7636-2047-9(5)) Candlewick Pr.
Govoni, Dennis, jt. photos by see Maiden, D. W.
Gowen, Fiona. How to Draw Amazing Animals & Incredible Insects. 2015. (How to Draw Ser.). (ENG.). 32p. (J). (gr. 2-6). pap. 4.99 (978-1-4380-0583-6(0)) Barron's Educational Series, Inc.
—How to Draw Awesome Vehicles: Land, Sea, & Air. 2015. (How to Draw Ser.). (ENG.). 32p. (J). (gr. 2-6). pap. 4.99 (978-1-4380-0582-9(2)) Barron's Educational Series, Inc.
—How to Draw Incredible Aliens & Cool Space Stuff. 2015. (How to Draw Ser.). (ENG.). 32p. (J). (gr. 2-6). pap. 4.99 (978-1-4380-0584-3(9)) Barron's Educational Series, Inc.
Gowens, Kyle & Richmond, Bob. Monsters Have Big Feet. Kennis, Don. 2006. (J). per. 8.95 (978-0-9788553-0-7(2)) Guppy Publishing LLC.
Gower, Jeremy & Shields, Chris. Earthquakes & Volcanoes. Watt, Fiona. Stockley, Corinne & Brooks, Felicity, eds. rev. ed. 2007. (Geography Ser.). 32p. (YA). (gr. 8-12). pap. 7.99 (978-0-7945-1531-7(2), Usborne) EDC Publishing.
Gower, Jeremy, jt. illus. see Hewetson, Nicholas J.
Gower, Jim. The Elephants in the City of Light: An Elephant Family Adventure. Eschberger, Beverly. 2010. (J). per. 3.99 (978-1-932926-28-6(3), Kinkajou Pr.) Artemesia Publishing, LLC.
—The Elephants in the Land of Enchantment: An Elephant Family Adventure. Eschberger, Beverly. 2009. 96p. (J). pap. 3.99 (978-1-932926-02-6(X), Kinkajou Pr.) Artemesia Publishing, LLC.
—The Elephants Tour England: An Elephant Family Adventure. Eschberger, Beverly. 2009. 86p. (J). per. 3.99 (978-1-932926-29-3(1), Kinkajou Pr.) Artemesia Publishing, LLC.
—The Elephants Visit London: An Elephant Family Adventure. Eschberger, Beverly. l.t. ed. 2007. 96p. (J). per. 3.99 (978-1-932926-30-9(5), Kinkajou Pr.) Artemesia Publishing, LLC.
Gower, Jim, jt. illus. see Habiger, Geoff.
Gower, Teri. Fairyland Jigsaw Bk. Doherty, Gillian. 2007. 14p. (J). bds. 14.99 (978-0-7945-1430-3(8), Usborne) EDC Publishing.
—Starting Gardening. Allman, Howard, photos by. Johnson, Sue & Evans, Cheryl. 2006. (First Skills Ser.). 32p. (J). (gr. 1). lib. bdg. 12.95 (978-1-58086-543-2(7)) EDC Publishing.
—Stories of Fairies. Lester, Anna. 2006. (Young Reading Series 1 Gift Bks.). 47p. (J). (gr. 2-5). 8.99 (978-0-7945-1326-9(3), Usborne) EDC Publishing.
—The Story of Castles. Sims, Lesley. 2004. (Young Reading Ser.: Vol. 2). 64p. (J). (gr. 2-18). lib. bdg. 13.95 (978-1-58086-701-6(4), Usborne) EDC Publishing.
—The Story of Rome. Dickins, Rosie. 2006. (Usborne Young Reading: Series Two Ser.). 60p. (J). (gr. 2). lib. bdg. 13.99 (978-1-58086-900-3(9), Usborne) EDC Publishing.
—The Usborne Big Book of Things to Spot. Doherty, Gillian et al. 2006. (1001 Things to Spot Ser.). 132p. (J). (gr. 1). lib. bdg. 20.95 (978-1-58086-496-1(1)) EDC Publishing.
—1001 Animals Que Buscar. Brocklehurst, Ruth. 2003. (Facts & Lists Internet-Linked Ser.). (SPA.). 64p. (J). (gr. 4-7). lib. bdg. 14.95 (978-1-58086-493-0(7)) EDC Publishing.
—1001 Bugs to Spot. Helbrough, Emma. 2005. 32p. (J). pap. 6.95 (978-0-7945-1000-8(0), Usborne) EDC Publishing.
—1001 Cosas Que Buscar en el Psia de las Hadas. Doherty, Gillian. 2007. (Titles in Spanish Ser.). 32p. (J). 9.99 (978-0-7460-8346-8(7), Usborne) EDC Publishing.
—1001 Pirate Things to Spot. Jones, Rob Lloyd. 2007. (1001 Things to Spot Ser.). 32p. (J). 9.99 (978-0-7945-1513-3(4), Usborne) EDC Publishing.
—1001 Things to Spot in Fairyland. Doherty, Gillian. 2006. (Usborne 1001 Things to Spot Ser.). 32p. (J). (gr. 1-4). 9.99 (978-0-7945-1220-0(8), Usborne) EDC Publishing.
—1001 Things to Spot in the Sea. Daynes, Katie. 2009. (1001 Things to Spot Ser.). 32p. (J). (gr. 1). 9.99 (978-0-7945-2615-3(2), Usborne) EDC Publishing.
—1001 Things to Spot Long Ago. Doherty, Gillian. Brooks, Felicity, ed. 2006. (Usborne 1001 Things to Spot Ser.). 32p. (J). (gr. 1). lib. bdg. 14.99 (978-1-58086-963-8(7)) EDC Publishing.
—1001 Things to Spot Long Ago. Doherty, Gillian. rev. ed. 2006. (1001 Things to Spot Ser.). 32p. (J). (gr. -1-3). pap. 6.99 (978-0-7945-0716-9(6), Usborne) EDC Publishing.
—1001 Wizard Things to Spot. Doherty, Gillian. 2008. (Usborne 1001 Things to Spot Ser.). 31p. (J). (gr. 4-7). 9.99 (978-0-7945-1860-8(5), Usborne) EDC Publishing.
Gower, Teri, jt. illus. see Lyon, Chris.
Gownley, Jimmy. Her Permanent Record. Gownley, Jimmy. 2012. (Amelia Rules! Ser.). (ENG.). 160p. (J). (gr. 2-7). 19.99 (978-1-4169-8615-7(4)); pap. 10.99 (978-1-4169-8614-0(6)) Simon & Schuster Children's Publishing. (Atheneum Bks. for Young Readers).
—The Meaning of Life ... & Other Stuff. Gownley, Jimmy. 2011. (Amelia Rules! Ser.). (ENG.). 160p. (J). (gr. 2-7). 19.99 (978-1-4169-8613-3(8)); pap. 10.99 (978-1-4169-8612-6(X)) Simon & Schuster Children's Publishing. (Atheneum Bks. for Young Readers).
—Superheroes. Gownley, Jimmy. (Amelia Rules! Ser.). (ENG.). 176p. (J). (gr. 2-7). 2011. 19.99 (978-1-4424-4540-6(8)); 2010. pap. 11.99 (978-1-4169-8606-5(5)) Simon & Schuster Children's Publishing. (Atheneum Bks. for Young Readers).
—True Things: Adults Don't Want Kids to Know. Gownley, Jimmy. 2010. (Amelia Rules! Ser.). (ENG.). 176p. (J). (gr. 2-7). 19.99 (978-1-4169-8611-9(1)); pap. 10.99 (978-1-4169-8609-6(X)) Simon & Schuster Children's Publishing. (Atheneum Bks. for Young Readers).
—The Tweenage Guide to Not Being Unpopular. Gownley, Jimmy. 2010. (Amelia Rules! Ser.). (ENG.). 192p. (J). (gr. 2-7). pap. 10.99 (978-1-4169-8608-9(1), Atheneum Bks. for Young Readers) Simon & Schuster Children's Publishing.
—A Very Ninja Christmas. Gownley, Jimmy. 2009. (Amelia Rules! Ser.). (ENG.). 80p. (J). (gr. 2-7). pap. 7.99 (978-1-4169-8959-2(5), Atheneum Bks. for Young Readers) Simon & Schuster Children's Publishing.
—What Makes You Happy. Gownley, Jimmy. (Amelia Rules! Ser.). (ENG.). (J). (gr. 2-7). 2011. 176p. 19.99 (978-1-4424-4539-0(4)); 2009. 160p. pap. 11.99 (978-1-4169-8605-8(7)) Simon & Schuster Children's Publishing. (Atheneum Bks. for Young Readers).
—When the Past Is a Present. Gownley, Jimmy. (Amelia Rules! Ser.). (ENG.). 176p. (J). (gr. 2-7). 2011. 19.99 (978-1-4424-4541-3(6)); 2010. pap. 12.99 (978-1-4169-8607-2(3)) Simon & Schuster Children's Publishing. (Atheneum Bks. for Young Readers).
—The Whole World's Crazy. Gownley, Jimmy. (Amelia Rules! Ser.). (ENG.). (J). (gr. 2-7). 2011. 176p. 19.99 (978-1-4424-4538-3(6)); 2009. 160p. pap. 11.99 (978-1-4169-8604-1(9)) Simon & Schuster Children's Publishing. (Atheneum Bks. for Young Readers).
Grabas, Peter & Parts, Art. The Homeowner's Handbook: A Guide to Getting Your Act Together & Keeping It That Way. Nosek, Jude. 2003. 124p. (YA). pap. 14.95 (978-0-9726619-6-6(4)) KnackPacks, Inc.
Graber, Jesse. Follow the Leader. Byrne, Marlene. 2009. (ENG.). 39p. (J). 14.99 (978-0-9777135-1-6(2)) Celtic Marketing Inc.
—Ghost in the Graveyard. Byrne, Marlene F. 2010. 57p. (J). pap. 9.99 (978-0-9777135-4-7(7)) Celtic Marketing Inc.
—Kick the Can. Byrne, Marlene. 2009. 61p. pap. 9.99 (978-0-9777135-3-0(9)) Celtic Marketing Inc.
—Treasure Hunt. Byrne, Marlene F. 2009. 36p. (J). 14.99 (978-0-9777135-0-9(4)) Celtic Marketing Inc.
Graber, Lois. A Song in the Storm. 2012. 32p. (J). (978-0-7399-2445-7(1)) Rod & Staff Pubs., Inc.
Graber, Vickie. Great-Grandpa's Chair: A Story about Living & Dying, Shared Between A Great-Grandpa & His 10-year-old Grandson! Bayne, Nancy. l.t. ed. 2005. 22p. (J). per. 9.99 (978-1-59879-046-7(3)) Lifevest Publishing, Inc.
Grablewski, Alexandra, photos by. Sublime Stitching: Hundreds of Hip Embroidery Patterns & How-To. Hart, Jenny. 2006. (ENG., 224p. (gr. 8-17). pap. 22.95 (978-0-8118-5011-7(0)) Chronicle Bks. LLC.
Grabowski, Daniel. No Dinner for Tom. D'Amico, Christy. 2011. (ENG.). 34p. pap. 10.95 (978-1-4679-0683-8(2)) CreateSpace Independent Publishing Platform.
Grace, Bill. Constantine Goes to School. Rogers Yaeger, Nancy. 2006. 60p. (J). (gr. 2-5). (978-1-4050-5714-1(9)) Macmillan Caribbean.
Grace, Sina. Among the Ghosts. Benson, Amber. (ENG.). 256p. (J). (gr. 3-7). 2011. pap. 6.99 (978-1-4169-9426-8(2)); 2010. 15.99 (978-1-4169-9405-3(X)) Simon & Schuster/Paula Wiseman Bks. (Simon & Schuster/Paula Wiseman Bks.).
Gradisher, Martha. Who Spilled the Milk?, Level 1. Linn, Margot. 2005. (I'm Going to Read(r) Ser.). (ENG.). 28p. (J). (gr. -1-k). pap. 3.95 (978-1-4027-2092-5(0)) Sterling Publishing Co., Inc.
Grady, Kit. Bradybug. Shepherd, Donna J. 2010. 20p. pap. 10.95 (978-1-61633-071-2(6)) Guardian Angel Publishing, Inc.
—Flutter Bunnies. McIntyre, Mel. 2008. 24p. pap. 10.95 (978-1-933090-68-5(5)) Guardian Angel Publishing, Inc.
—Flutter Bunnies Fossil of Fortune. McIntyre, Mel & Mcintyre, Mel. 2011. 20p. pap. 9.95 (978-1-61633-170-2(4)) Guardian Angel Publishing, Inc.
—Hamster Holidays: Noun & Adjective Adventures. Reeg, Cynthia. 2009. 24p. pap. 10.95 (978-1-935137-62-7(X)) Guardian Angel Publishing, Inc.
—Humberto, the Bookworm Hamster. Calvani, Mayra. 2009. 20p. pap. 10.95 (978-1-935137-92-4(1)) Guardian Angel Publishing, Inc.
—Rainbow Nights. Harris, Sally M. 2009. 20p. pap. 9.95 (978-1-61633-002-6(3)) Guardian Angel Publishing, Inc.
Graef, Renee. B Is for Badger: A Wisconsin Alphabet. Wargin, Kathy-jo. 2004. (Discover America State by State Ser.). (ENG.). 40p. (J). 17.95 (978-1-58536-135-9(6)) Sleeping Bear Pr.
—B Is for Bookworm: A Library Alphabet. Prieto, Anita C. 2007. (J). (gr. k-7). 16.10 (978-0-7569-6657-7(4)) Perfection Learning Corp.
—B Is for Bookworm: A Library Alphabet. Prieto, Anita C. 2007. (ENG.). 40p. (J). (gr. 1-4). per. 7.95 (978-1-58536-326-1(X), 202290) Sleeping Bear Pr.
—Bedtime in the Southwest. Hodgson, Mona Gansberg. 2004. (ENG.). 32p. (J). (gr. -1-k). 14.95 (978-0-87358-871-3(1)) Cooper Square Publishing Llc.
—Beyond the Heather Hills. Wiley, Melissa. 2003. (Little House Ser.). 189p. (J). (gr. 3-7). 14.65 (978-0-7569-3467-5(2)) Perfection Learning Corp.
Graef, Renée. D Is for Dala Horse: A Nordic Countries Alphabet. Wargin, Kathy-jo. 2010. (Discover the World Ser.). (ENG.). 40p. (J). (gr. 1-3). 17.95 (978-1-58536-510-4(6), 202203) Sleeping Bear Pr.
Graef, Renee. A Girl Named Dan. Mackall, Dandi Daley. 2008. (ENG.). 32p. (J). (gr. k-6). 16.95 (978-1-58536-351-3(0)) Sleeping Bear Pr.
—If Jesus Came to Visit Me. Lord, Jill Roman. (J). 2010. 24p. (gr. -1-1). 8.99 (978-0-8249-5615-8(X), Ideals Children's Bks.); 2008. (ENG.). 28p. bds. 6.95 (978-0-8249-6568-6(X)); 2006. (ENG.). 26p. (gr. -1-k). 12.95 (978-0-8249-6651-5(1), Candy Cane Pr.) Ideals Pubns.
—If Jesus Walked Beside Me. Lord, Jill Roman. 2006. (ENG.). 26p. (J). (gr. -1-3). bds. 6.95 (978-0-8249-6638-6(4), Candy Cane Pr.) Ideals Pubns.
—Kirsten Story Collection. Shaw, Janet. 2008. 380p. 29.95 (978-1-59369-454-8(7)) American Girl Publishing, Inc.
—Lidia's Egg-Citing Farm Adventure. Bastianich, Lidia Matticchio. 2015. (ENG.). 60p. (J). (gr. -1). 16.95 (978-0-7624-5126-5(2), Running Pr. Kids) Running Pr. Bk. Pubs.
—Lidia's Family Kitchen: Nonna's Birthday Surprise. Bastianich, Lidia Matticchio. 2013. (ENG.). 60p. (J). (gr. -1). 16.95 (978-0-7624-4655-1(2), Running Pr. Kids) Running Pr. Bk. Pubs.
—My Favorite Things. Rodgers, Richard & Hammerstein, Oscar, II. 2005. (ENG.). 32p. (J). (gr. -1-3). pap. 6.99 (978-0-06-443627-4(6)) HarperCollins Pubs.
—The Nutcracker: The Untold Story. Schulman, Janet. 2005. 40p. (J). pap. 6.99 (978-0-06-443790-5(6), Harper Trophy) HarperCollins Pubs.
—Prairie Girl: The Life of Laura Ingalls Wilder. Anderson, William T. 2004. (Little House Ser.). 80p. (J). (gr. 2-5). lib. bdg. 13.89 (978-0-06-028974-4(0)) HarperCollins Pubs.
—The Secret of the First One Up. Arno, Iris Hiskey. 2003. (ENG.). 32p. (J). (gr. k-3). 15.95 (978-1-55971-867-7(6)) Cooper Square Publishing Llc.
Graef, Renée. T Is for Time. Smith, Marie & Smith, Roland. 2015. (ENG.). 40p. (J). (gr. 2-5). 16.99 (978-1-58536-512-8(2), 203809) Sleeping Bear Pr.
Graef, Renee. Therese Makes a Tapestry. Hinrichs, Alexandra S. D. 2015. (J). **(978-1-60606-473-3(8)**, J. Paul Getty Museum) Getty Pubns.
Graef, Renee. Who Carved the Mountain? The Story of Mount Rushmore. Patrick, Jean L. S. 2005. 37p. (J). 16.99 (978-0-9752617-4-3(6)) Mount Rushmore Bookstores.
Graef, Renee, jt. illus. see Lewis, Kim.
Graegin, Stephanie. The Art of Flying: A Novel. Hoffman, Judy. 2014. (ENG.). 320p. (J). (gr. 3-7). pap. 7.99 (978-1-4231-5907-0(1)) Hyperion Bks. for Children.
—Don't Feed the Boy. Latham, Irene. 2012. (ENG.). 288p. (J). (gr. 3-7). 17.99 (978-1-59643-755-5(3)) Roaring Brook Pr.
—Don't Feed the Boy. Latham, Irene. 2014. (ENG.). 304p. (J). (gr. 3-7). pap. 7.99 (978-1-250-04428-0(6)) Square Fish.
—Forget Me Not. Van Laan, Nancy. 2014. (ENG.). 40p. (J). (gr. -1-3). 16.99 (978-0-449-81543-4(9), Schwartz & Wade Bks.) Random Hse. Children's Bks.
—Goldilocks & the Three Bears. Namm, Diane. 2013. (Silver Penny Stories Ser.). (ENG.). 40p. (J). (gr. -1-1). 4.95 (978-1-4027-8430-9(9)) Sterling Publishing Co., Inc.
—Hansel & Gretel. McFadden, Deanna. 2012. (Silver Penny Stories Ser.). (ENG.). 40p. (J). (gr. -1-1). 4.95 (978-1-4027-8335-7(3)) Sterling Publishing Co., Inc.
—Happy Birthday, Bunny! Scanlon, Liz Garton. 2013. (ENG.). 32p. (J). (gr. -1-3). 16.99 (978-1-4424-0287-4(3), Beach Lane Bks.) Beach Lane Bks.
—Peace Is an Offering. LeBox, Annette. 2015. (ENG.). 40p. (J). (gr. -1-k). 16.99 (978-0-8037-4091-4(3), Dial) Penguin Publishing Group.
—Sleeping Beauty. McFadden, Deanna et al. 2013. (Silver Penny Stories Ser.). (ENG.). 40p. (J). (gr. -1-1). 4.95 (978-1-4027-8341-8(8)) Sterling Publishing Co., Inc.
—Water in the Park: A Book about Water & the Times of the Day. Jenkins, Emily. 2013. (ENG.). 40p. (J). (gr. -1-2). 16.99 (978-0-375-87002-6(4), Schwartz & Wade Bks.) Random Hse. Children's Bks.
Graf, William. Of Course You Can! Educating Children about Money. Sparks, Candi. 2006. (Can I Have Some Money? Ser.). pap. 11.99 (978-0-9789445-0-6(X)) Sparks Fly.
Grafe, Max. The Bearskinner: A Tale of the Brothers Grimm. Schlitz, Laura Amy. 2007. (ENG.). 40p. (J). (gr. 4-7). 16.99 (978-0-7636-2730-0(5)) Candlewick Pr.
—What the Grizzly Knows. Elliott, David. 2008. (ENG.). 32p. (J). (gr. -1-2). 16.99 (978-0-7636-2778-2(X)) Candlewick Pr.
Graffam, Merle. Boys' Club. Walker, E. G. 2004. (J). (gr. 2-8). pap. 12.95 (978-0-9716071-5-6(X)) Walker, Esther.
Graham, Adele. Missouri Horses Vol. 1: Gift to a Nation. Gilbert, Joan Sewell. 2005. 530p. (gr. 6-18). pap. 23.50 (978-0-9712559-1-3(1)) MoGho Bks., LLC.
—More Missouri Ghosts: Fact, Fiction & Folklore. Gilbert, Joan. 2005. 232p. (gr. 6-18). pap. 14.95 (978-0-615-11888-8(7)) MoGho Bks., LLC.
Graham, Alistair. Full Moon Soup. Graham, Alistair. 2003. (Full Moon Soup & Full Moon Afloat Ser.). 32p. (YA). pap. (978-1-85602-071-8(1), Pavilion Children's Books) Pavilion Bks.
Graham, Andrew S. & Ribeira, Lili. Me Tarzan, You Jane. Graham, Janice Barrett. 2011. 25p. (J). (gr. 1-4). pap. 6.95 (978-0-9724770-8-6(X)) Tidal Wave Bks.
Graham, Bob. I'm Number One. Rosen, Michael. 2009. (ENG.). 32p. (J). (gr. -1-2). 16.99 (978-0-7636-4535-9(4)) Candlewick Pr.
Graham, Bob. Monsieur Albert Rides to Glory. Smith, Peter. 32p. (J). (gr. k-2). 2015. 11.99 **(978-1-74331-842-3(1))**; 2013. (ENG.). 19.99 (978-1-74237-680-6(0)) Allen & Unwin AUS. Dist: Independent Pubs. Group.
Graham, Bob. This Is Our House. Rosen, Michael. 2005. (ENG.). 32p. (J). (gr. -1-2). 7.99 (978-0-7636-2816-1(6)) Candlewick Pr.

—Time to Play! Gray, Nigel. 2008. (ENG.). 24p. (J). (-k). 8.99 *(978-0-7636-4013-2(1))* Candlewick Pr.

Graham, Bob. April & Esme Tooth Fairies. Graham, Bob. (ENG.). 40p. (J). (gr. k-4). 2013. 6.99 *(978-0-7636-6347-6(6))*; 2010. 16.99 *(978-0-7636-4683-7(0))* Candlewick Pr.

—A Bus Called Heaven. Graham, Bob. 2012. (ENG.). 40p. (J). (gr. -1-2). 16.99 *(978-0-7636-5893-9(6))* Candlewick Pr.

Graham, Bob. How the Sun Got to Coco's House. Graham, Bob. 2015. (ENG.). 40p. (J). (gr. -1-1). 17.99 ***(978-0-7636-8109-8(1))*** Candlewick Pr.

Graham, Bob. How to Heal a Broken Wing. Graham, Bob. 2008. (ENG.). 40p. (J). (gr. -1-2). 16.99 *(978-0-7636-3903-7(6))* Candlewick Pr.

—"Let's Get a Pup!" Said Kate. Graham, Bob. 2003. (ENG.). 32p. (J). (gr. -1-2). pap. 6.99 *(978-0-7636-2193-3(5))* Candlewick Pr.

—The Silver Button. Graham, Bob. 2013. (ENG.). 32p. (J). (gr. -1-1). 16.99 *(978-0-7636-6437-4(5))* Candlewick Pr.

—Tales from the Waterhole. Graham, Bob. 2004. (ENG.). 64p. (J). (gr. -1-3). 16.99 *(978-0-7636-2324-1(5))* Candlewick Pr.

—The Trouble with Dogs... Said Dad. Graham, Bob. (ENG.). 32p. (J). (gr. -1-2). 2010. pap. 6.99 *(978-0-7636-4973-9(2))*; 2007. 12.99 *(978-0-7636-3316-5(X))* Candlewick Pr.

—Vanilla Ice Cream. Graham, Bob. 2014. (ENG.). 40p. (J). (gr. -1-1). 16.99 *(978-0-7636-7377-2(3))* Candlewick Pr.

Graham, Brandon. Perverts of the Unknown. Graham, Brandon. 2003. (ENG.). 56p. pap. 10.99 *(978-1-56163-374-6(7)*, Amerotica) NBM Publishing Co.

Graham, C. E. If I Had A Wish. Dukoff, K. D. 2008. 12p. pap. 24.95 *(978-1-60610-241-1(9))* America Star Bks.

Graham, Carl. Tom's Wish. Williams, Paula. 2013. 24p. pap. *(978-1-909740-80-8(2))* Legend Pr.

Graham, Dennis. The Little Clay Jar: La Vasijita de Barro. Ramos, Peregrina. 2006.Tr. of vasijita de Barro. (SPA & ENG.). (J). per. 15.95 *(978-0-9788381-0-2(6))* Word Gift Pubns.

Graham, Earnest. The Unlikely Chosen: A Graphic Novel Translation of the Biblical Books of Jonah, Esther, & Amos. Graham, Shirley Smith. 2008. (ENG.). 125p. pap. 14.00 *(978-1-59627-078-7(0)*, Seabury Bks.) Church Publishing, Inc.

Graham, Georgia. Bibi & the Bull, 1 vol. Vaage, Carol. 2004. (Northern Lights Books for Children Ser.). (ENG.). 30p. (J). (gr. k-2). 6.95 *(978-0-88995-178-5(0))* Red Deer Pr. CAN. Dist: Fitzhenry & Whiteside, Ltd.

—Here Comes Hortense! Hartt-Sussman, Heather. 2012. (ENG.). 32p. (J). (gr. -1-1). 17.95 *(978-1-77049-221-9(6)*, Tundra Bks.) Tundra Bks. CAN. Dist: Penguin Random Hse., LLC.

—Nana's Getting Married. 2010. (ENG.). 32p. (J). (gr. -1-1). 17.95 *(978-0-88776-911-5(X)*, Tundra Bks.) Tundra Bks. CAN. Dist: Penguin Random Hse., LLC.

—Nana's Summer Surprise. Hartt-Sussman, Heather. 2013. (ENG.). 32p. (J). (gr. -1-1). 17.95 *(978-1-77049-324-7(7)*, Tundra Bks.) Tundra Bks. CAN. Dist: Penguin Random Hse., LLC.

—Tiger's New Cowboy Boots, 1 vol. Morck, Irene. 2003. (ENG.). 30p. (J). (gr. -1-4). pap. 9.95 *(978-0-88995-181-5(0))* Red Deer Pr. CAN. Dist: Ingram Pub. Services.

—Wanda & the Frogs. Azore, Barbara. (ENG.). 32p. (J). (gr. -1-1). 2012. pap. 7.95 *(978-1-77049-307-0(7))*; 2007. 18.95 *(978-0-88776-761-6(3))* Tundra Bks. CAN. (Tundra Bks.) Dist: Penguin Random Hse., LLC.

—Wanda & the Wild Hair. Azore, Barbara. 2005. (ENG.). 32p. (J). (gr. -1-2). 15.95 *(978-0-88776-717-3(6)*, Tundra Bks.) Tundra Bks. CAN. Dist: Penguin Random Hse., LLC.

—Wanda & the Wild Hair. Azore, Barbara. 2012. (ENG.). 32p. (J). (gr. -1-2). pap. 7.95 *(978-1-77049-306-3(9)*, Tundra Bks.) Tundra Bks. CAN. Dist: Penguin Random Hse., LLC.

—Wanda's Freckles. Azore, Barbara. (ENG.). 24p. (J). (gr. -1-2). 2012. pap. 7.95 *(978-1-77049-308-7(5))*; 2009. 19.95 *(978-0-88776-862-0(8))* Tundra Bks. CAN. (Tundra Bks.) Dist: Penguin Random Hse., LLC.

Graham, Georgia. A Team Like No Other, 1 vol. Graham, Georgia. 2005. (ENG.). 32p. (J). (gr. 1-3). 18.95 *(978-0-88995-290-4(6))* Red Deer Pr. CAN. Dist: Ingram Pub. Services.

Graham, Heather, jt. illus. see Hotchkiss, Conrad.

Graham, Jack. Coin Collecting for Kids. Otfinoski, Steve. ed. 2007. (ENG.). 12p. (J). (gr. 2-7). spiral bd. 17.99 *(978-1-58476-624-7(7)*, IKIDS) Innovative Kids.

Graham, Jerry L., jt. illus. see Allen, S. Joan.

Graham, Lindsay. The Horse Farm. Workman Publishing Company Staff. 2004. (ENG.). 18p. (J). pap., tchr. ed. 7.95 *(978-1-58017-583-8(X)*, 67583) Storey Publishing, LLC.

Graham, Lorenz. North Town. Graham, Lorenz. 2003. (ENG.). 188p. (J). (gr. 6-9). 16.95 *(978-1-59078-162-3(7))* Boyds Mills Pr.

—Return to South Town. Graham, Lorenz. 2003. (ENG.). 240p. (J). (gr. 6-9). 16.95 *(978-1-59078-164-7(3))* Boyds Mills Pr.

—South Town. Graham, Lorenz. 2003. (ENG.). 188p. (J). (gr. 6-9). 16.95 *(978-1-59078-161-6(9))* Boyds Mills Pr.

—Whose Town? Graham, Lorenz. 2003. (ENG.). 204p. (J). (gr. 6-9). 16.95 *(978-1-59078-163-0(5))* Boyds Mills Pr.

Graham, Margaret Bloy. Harry & the Lady Next Door. Zion, Gene. 2003. (I Can Read Book 1 Ser.). (ENG.). 64p. (J). (gr. k-3). pap. 3.99 *(978-0-06-444008-0(7))* HarperCollins Pubs.

—Harry & the Lady Next Door. Zion, Gene. 2004. (I Can Read Bks.). 64p. (gr. -1-3). 14.00 *(978-0-7569-3087-5(1))* Perfection Learning Corp.

—Harry, el Perrito Sucio. Zion, Gene. Fiol, María A., tr. 2003. (Harper Arco Iris Ser.).Tr. of Harry the Dirty Dog. (SPA.). 32p. (J). (gr. -1-3). pap. 6.99 *(978-0-06-443443-0(5)*, HC0801, Rayo) HarperCollins Pubs.

—Harry the Dirty Dog. Zion, Gene. 50th ed. 2006. (ENG.). (J). (gr. -1-3). 34p. bds. 7.99 *(978-0-06-084244-4(X)*, HarperFestival); 32p. 17.99 *(978-0-06-026865-7(4))* HarperCollins Pubs.

—Harry the Dirty Dog. Zion, Gene & Zion. 50th anniv. ed. 2006. (Trophy Picture Bks.). (ENG.). 32p. (J). (gr. -1-3). pap. 6.99 *(978-0-06-443009-8(X))* HarperCollins Pubs.

Graham, Mark. Murphy & Kate. Howard, Ellen. 2007. (ENG.). 32p. (J). (gr. -1-2). 9.99 *(978-1-4169-6157-4(7)*, Simon & Schuster/Paula Wiseman Bks.) Simon & Schuster/Paula Wiseman Bks.

—My Father's Hands. Ryder, Joanne. 2014. 32p. pap. 8.00 *(978-1-61003-330-5(2))* Center for the Collaborative Classroom.

—Naughty Cherie! Oates, Joyce Carol. 2008. 32p. (J). (gr. -1-3). lib. bdg. 17.89 *(978-0-06-074359-8(X))* HarperCollins Pubs.

—Waiting for Noel: An Advent Story. Dixon, Ann. 2004. 32p. (J). (gr. -1-5). pap. 8.00 *(978-0-8028-5239-7(4))* Eerdmans, William B. Publishing Co.

—Where Is Little Reynard? Oates, Joyce Carol. 2003. 32p. (J). 16.89 *(978-0-06-029583-7(X))* HarperCollins Pubs.

Graham, Michael. The Adventures of Swami Somewhere-the Supermarket. Greene, Reggie. 2011. 32p. (J). 14.95 *(978-1-60131-095-8(1))* Big Tent Bks.

—Allow Me to Introduce Myself. Ramos, Odalys Q. 2012. 24p. (-18). pap. 12.95 *(978-1-61493-121-8(6))* Peppertree Pr., The.

—The Great Inhibinator. 2006. 44p. (J). *(978-0-9772977-0-2(5))* Bio Rx.

—I am Nate. 2007. 40p. (J). *(978-0-9772977-1-9(3))* Bio Rx.

Graham, Michele. Body: An Interactive & 3-D Exploration. Ring, Susan. 2008. (ENG.). 20p. (J). (gr. 2). 19.95 *(978-1-58117-801-2(8)*, Intervisual/Piggy Toes) Bendon, Inc.

Grahame, Kenneth & McKowen, Scott. The Wind in the Willows. Grahame, Kenneth. 2005. (Sterling Unabridged Classics Ser.). (ENG.). 208p. (J). (gr. 5-9). 9.95 *(978-1-4027-2505-0(1))* Sterling Publishing Co., Inc.

Grajczyk, Shane. The Most Important Thing. Roth, Rhonda. 2007. (ENG.). 32p. (J). (gr. -1-3). 16.95 *(978-0-9770141-0-1(X)*, Crossing Guard Bks.) Crossing Guard Bks., LLC.

Gram, Patrick. Stop by a Pond. Nicholas, Melissa. l.t. ed. 2005. (Little Books & Big Bks.: Vol. 3). 8p. (gr. k-2). 23.00 net. *(978-0-8215-7512-3(0))* Sadlier, William H. Inc.

Gramatky, Hardie. Little Toot. Gramatky, Hardie. 2007. (ENG.). 104p. (J). (gr. -1-2). 17.99 *(978-0-399-24713-2(0)*, Putnam Juvenile) Penguin Publishing Group.

Gran, Meredith. Marceline & the Scream Queens. Gran, Meredith. 2013. (Adventure Time Ser.). (ENG.). 128p. (J). (gr. 4). pap. 19.99 *(978-1-60886-313-6(1))* Boom! Studios.

Granada, Nancy, jt. illus. see Gonzalez, Henry.

Granados, Lucia. Bemba's Secret Garden. 2006. (ENG.). 57p. (J). per. 16.95 *(978-0-9790110-0-9(0))* Tpprince Esquire International.

Grand Pre, Mary. The Sorcerer's Stone. Rowling, J. K. 10th anniv. ed. 2008. (Harry Potter Ser.: Year 1). (ENG.). 320p. (J). (gr. 2-5). 30.00 *(978-0-545-06967-0(X)*, Levine, Arthur A. Bks.) Scholastic, Inc.

Grandelis, Leiah. To Be a Bird. Dickson, Vivian. 2013. 24p. pap. *(978-0-9873438-2-6(3))* Link Spots.

Grandfield, Meg & DeMakas, Meg. Captain Jeb, Pirate Cat. Grandfield, Meg & DeMakas, Meg. l.t. ed. 2010. (ENG.). 38p. pap. 10.95 *(978-1-4536-1991-9(7))* CreateSpace Independent Publishing Platform.

Grandits, John. Blue Lipstick: Concrete Poems. Grandits, John. 2007. (ENG.). 48p. (J). (gr. 5-7). 6.99 *(978-0-618-85132-4(1))* Houghton Mifflin Harcourt Publishing Co.

Grandpré, Karen Haus. Misty's Twilight. Henry, Marguerite. 2007. (ENG.). 144p. (J). (gr. 3-7). pap. 6.99 *(978-1-4169-2787-7(5)*, Simon & Schuster/Paula Wiseman Bks.) Simon & Schuster/Paula Wiseman Bks.

GrandPré, Mary. Aunt Claire's Yellow Beehive Hair, 1 vol. Blumenthal, Deborah. 2007. (ENG.). 32p. (J). (gr. k-3). 16.99 *(978-1-58980-491-3(0))* Pelican Publishing Co., Inc.

—The Carnival of the Animals. Prelutsky, Jack. 2010. (Book & CD Ser.). (ENG.). 40p. (J). (gr. k-3). 19.99 *(978-0-375-86458-2(X)*, Knopf Bks. for Young Readers) Random Hse. Children's Bks.

GrandPré, Mary. A Dragon's Guide to Making Your Human Smarter. Yep, Laurence & Ryder, Joanne. 2016. (ENG.). 304p. (J). ***(978-0-385-39232-7(X))*** Bantam Doubleday Dell Large Print Group, Inc.

GrandPré, Mary. A Dragon's Guide to the Care & Feeding of Humans. Yep, Laurence & Ryder, Joanne. 2015. (Dragon's Guide Ser.). (ENG.). 160p. (J). (gr. 3-7). 15.99 *(978-0-385-39228-0(1)*, Crown Books For Young Readers) Random Hse. Children's Bks.

—Harry Potter & the Deathly Hallows. Rowling, J. K. (Harry Potter Ser.: 7). (ENG.). (J). 2009. 784p. (gr. 4-7). pap. 14.99 *(978-0-545-13970-0(8)*, Levine, Arthur A. Bks.); 2007. 784p. (gr. 4-7). 39.99 *(978-0-545-02936-0(8)*, Levine, Arthur A. Bks.); 2007. 784p. (gr. 5-9). 34.99 *(978-0-545-01022-1(5))*; 2007. 816p. (gr. 4-7). 65.00 *(978-0-545-02937-7(6)*, Levine, Arthur A. Bks.) Scholastic, Inc.

—Harry Potter & the Goblet of Fire. Rowling, J. K. l.t. ed. 2003. (Harry Potter Ser.: Vol. 4). (ENG.). 936p. pap. 11.66 *(978-1-59413-003-8(5))* Thorndike Pr.

—Harry Potter & the Half-Blood Prince. Rowling, J. K. 2006. (Harry Potter Ser.: Year 6). 652p. (gr. 4-8). 23.00 *(978-0-7569-6765-9(1))* Perfection Learning Corp.

—Harry Potter & the Half-Blood Prince. Rowling, J. K. (Harry Potter Ser.: 6). (ENG.). (J). 672p. (J). (gr. 4-8). 2005. 34.99 *(978-0-439-78677-5(0))*; 2005. 29.99 *(978-0-439-78454-2(9))*; 2006. reprint ed. per. 12.99 *(978-0-439-78596-9(0))* Scholastic, Inc. (Levine, Arthur A. Bks.).

—Harry Potter & the Order of the Phoenix. Rowling, J. K. (Harry Potter Ser.: 5). (ENG.). (J). (gr. 3-7). 2004. 896p. mass mkt. 12.99 *(978-0-439-35807-1(8)*, Scholastic Paperbacks); 2003. 870p. 29.99 *(978-0-439-35806-4(X))*; 2003. 896p. 60.00 *(978-0-439-56762-6(9))* Scholastic, Inc.

—Harry Potter & the Order of the Phoenix. Rowling, J. K. l.t. ed. 2003. (Thorndike Young Adult Ser.). (ENG.). 1232p. (J). (gr. 4-7). per. 14.95 *(978-1-59413-112-7(0)*, Large Print Pr.) Thorndike Pr.

—How the Leopard Got His Claws. Achebe, Chinua & Iroaganachi, John. 2011. (ENG.). 32p. (J). (gr. 2-5). 16.99 *(978-0-7636-4805-3(1))* Candlewick Pr.

—Nancy & Plum. MacDonald, Betty Bard. 2010. (ENG.). 240p. (J). (gr. 3-7). 15.99 *(978-0-375-86685-2(X))* Knopf, Alfred A. Inc.

—Nancy & Plum. MacDonald, Betty. 2011. (ENG.). 240p. (J). (gr. 3-7). 6.99 *(978-0-375-85986-1(1)*, Yearling) Random Hse. Children's Bks.

—The Noisy Paint Box: The Colors & Sounds of Kandinsky's Abstract Art. Rosenstock, Barb. 2014. (ENG.). 40p. (J). (gr. -1-3). 17.99 *(978-0-307-97848-6(6)*, Knopf Bks. for Young Readers) Random Hse. Children's Bks.

—Plum. Mitton, Tony. 2003. (J). *(978-0-439-36410-2(8)*, Levine, Arthur A. Bks.) Scholastic, Inc.

—The Purple Snerd. Williams, Rozanne Lanczak. 2003. (Green Light Readers Level 2 Ser.). (ENG.). 24p. (J). (gr. -1-3). pap. 3.95 *(978-0-15-204826-6(X))* Houghton Mifflin Harcourt Publishing Co.

—The Tales of Beedle the Bard. Rowling, J. K. 2008. (ENG.). 128p. *(978-0-7475-9987-6(4))* Bloomsbury Publishing Plc.

—The Tales of Beedle the Bard. Rowling, J. K. collector's ed. 2008. 184p. *(978-0-9560109-0-2(3))* Children's High Level Group.

—The Tales of Beedle the Bard. Rowling, J. K. 2008. (Harry Potter Ser.). (ENG.). 128p. (J). (gr. 4-18). 12.99 *(978-0-545-12828-5(5)*, Levine, Arthur A. Bks.) Scholastic, Inc.

—Tickety Tock. Brown, Jason Robert. 2008. 32p. (J). (gr. -1-3). lib. bdg. 18.89 *(978-0-06-078753-0(8)*, Geringer, Laura Book) HarperCollins Pubs.

Grandt, Eve, et al. The Book Bandit: A Mystery with Geometry. Thielbar, Melinda. 2010. (Manga Math Mysteries Ser.: 7). (ENG.). 48p. (gr. 3-5). 29.27 *(978-0-7613-4909-9(X))* Lerner Publishing Group.

Granger, Shane. Psy-Comm. Henderson, Jason. 2005. (Psy-Comm Ser.: Vol. 1). 192p. per. 9.99 *(978-1-59816-269-1(1))* TOKYOPOP, Inc.

Granström, Brita. A Chick Called Saturday. Dunbar, Joyce. 2004. 32p. (J). 16.00 *(978-0-8028-5260-1(2))* Eerdmans, William B. Publishing Co.

—Cock-A-Doodle-Hoooooo!, 1 vol. Manning, Mick. 2007. (ENG.). 28p. (J). (gr. -1-2). pap. 16.95 *(978-1-56148-568-0(3)*, Good Bks.) Skyhorse Publishing Co., Inc.

—Dog Story. Henderson, Kathy. (ENG.). 32p. (J). 2005. pap. 12.99 *(978-0-7475-7133-9(3))*; 2004. 17.95 *(978-0-7475-5071-6(9))* Bloomsbury Publishing Plc GBR. Dist: Independent Pubs. Group.

—Dolphin Baby! Davies, Nicola. 2012. (ENG.). 32p. (J). (gr. k-4). 15.99 *(978-0-7636-5548-8(1))* Candlewick Pr.

—Eyes, Nose, Fingers, & Toes: A First Book All about You. Hindley, Judy. 2004. (ENG.). 24p. (J). (gr. k-k). bds. 6.99 *(978-0-7636-2383-8(0))* Candlewick Pr.

—Mi Primer Libro de Teatro. Manning, Mick & Brita, Granström.Tr. of Drama School. (SPA.). (J). (gr. 3-5). 15.16 *(978-84-241-7922-9(6))* Everest Editora ESP. Dist: Lectorum Pubns., Inc.

—Que Hay Debajo de la Cama? Manning, Mick. Cortes, Eunice, tr. 2003. (Descubriendo Mi Mundo Ser.). (SPA.). 32p. (J). *(978-970-690-588-8(X))* Planeta Mexicana Editorial S. A. de C. V.

—The Secrets of Stonehenge. Manning, Mick. 2013. (ENG.). 32p. (J). (gr. 2-6). 17.99 *(978-1-84780-346-7(6)*, Frances Lincoln) Quarto Publishing Group UK GBR. Dist: Hachette Bk. Group.

—Woolly Mammoth. Manning, Mick. 2011. (ENG.). 32p. (J). (gr. -1-2). pap. 8.95 *(978-1-84780-210-1(9)*, Frances Lincoln) Quarto Publishing Group UK GBR. Dist: Littlehampton Bk Services, Ltd.

Granström, Brita, jt. illus. see Manning, Mick.

Grant, Cheryl. Mitsy & Marty Mouse Visit Grandma. Byers, Marcella. 2014. (Morgan James Kids Ser.). (ENG.). 32p. (gr. -1-2). pap. 8.95 *(978-1-61448-740-1(5)*, 9781614487401) Morgan James Publishing.

Grant, Donald. The Desert. Grant, Donald. 2012. (ENG.). 34p. (J). (gr. k-3). pap. 11.99 *(978-1-85103-299-0(1))* Moonlight Publishing, Ltd. GBR. Dist: Independent Pubs. Group.

—Dinosaurs at Large. Grant, Donald. Delafosse, Claude. 2013. (ENG.). 36p. (J). (gr. -1-k). 12.99 *(978-1-85103-415-4(3))* Moonlight Publishing, Ltd. GBR. Dist: Independent Pubs. Group.

—Flying. Grant, Donald. 2006. (ENG.). 36p. (J). (gr. k-3). pap. 11.99 *(978-1-85103-143-6(X))* Moonlight Publishing, Ltd. GBR. Dist: Independent Pubs. Group.

—Homes. Grant, Donald. 2012. (ENG.). 38p. (J). (gr. -1-k). 12.99 *(978-1-85103-398-0(X))* Moonlight Publishing, Ltd. GBR. Dist: Independent Pubs. Group.

—In the Sky. Grant, Donald. 2013. (ENG.). 36p. (J). (gr. -1-k). 12.99 *(978-1-85103-419-2(6))* Moonlight Publishing, Ltd. GBR. Dist: Independent Pubs. Group.

—Let's Look at Dinosaurs. Grant, Donald. Delafosse, Claude. 2012. (ENG.). 38p. (J). (gr. k-3). pap. 11.99 *(978-1-85103-280-8(0))* Moonlight Publishing, Ltd. GBR. Dist: Independent Pubs. Group.

—Let's Look at the Sky. Grant, Donald. 2006. (ENG.). 38p. (J). (gr. k-3). pap. 11.99 *(978-1-85103-284-6(3))* Moonlight Publishing, Ltd. GBR. Dist: Independent Pubs. Group.

Grant, Donald & Prunier, James. Trains. Prunier, James. 2012. (ENG.). 34p. (J). (gr. -1-k). 12.99 *(978-1-85103-400-0(5))* Moonlight Publishing, Ltd. GBR. Dist: Independent Pubs. Group.

Grant, Douglas. The Tarzan Twins. Burroughs, Edgar Rice. 2011. 126p. 40.95 *(978-1-258-05126-6(5))* Literary Licensing, LLC.

Grant, Leigh & Burke, Jim. Shoeshine Girl. Bulla, Clyde Robert & Bulla. 2004. (Trophy Chapter Bks.). (ENG.). 96p. (J). (gr. 2-5). reprint ed. pap. 4.99 *(978-0-06-440228-6(2))* HarperCollins Pubs.

Grant, Margriet. Baby Moses in a Basket. Mahany, Patricia Shely. 2013. (Happy Day Ser.). (ENG.). 16p. (J). pap. 2.49 *(978-1-4143-9297-4(4))* Tyndale Hse. Pubs.

Grant, Melvyn. The Dragon's Eye. Kingsley, Kaza. 2009. (Erec Rex Ser.: 1). (ENG.). 368p. (J). (gr. 5-9). pap. 9.99 *(978-1-4169-7933-3(6)*, Simon & Schuster Bks. For Young Readers) Simon & Schuster Bks. For Young Readers.

—Erec Rex: The Dragon's Eye. Kingsley, Kaza. Payne, John, ed. 2006. 360p. (J). 17.99 *(978-0-9786555-6-3(7))* Firelight Press, Inc.

—The Monsters of Otherness. Kingsley, Kaza. 2009. (Erec Rex Ser.: 2). (ENG.). 352p. (J). (gr. 5-9). pap. 9.99 *(978-1-4169-7934-0(4)*, Simon & Schuster Bks. For Young Readers) Simon & Schuster Bks. For Young Readers.

Grant, Sarah. Sleeping Bear: The Legend. Lewis, Anne Margaret. 2007. (ENG.). 40p. (J). (gr. -1-2). 16.95 *(978-1-934133-15-6(9)*, Mackinac Island Press, Inc.) Charlesbridge Publishing, Inc.

Grant, Sophia & Noble, Stuart. Eli the Elephant: A Tsunami Story. Donald, Margaret. 2007. (ENG.). 25p. (gr. 3-7). *(978-81-8386-024-6(9))* India Research Pr. IND. Dist: Independent Pubs. Group.

Graphic Manufacture. The Angel with Red Wings. Martinez, Roland. 2008. 27p. pap. 24.95 *(978-1-60672-713-3(3))* America Star Bks.

Graphics Factory. Picture-Word Quizzes Assessment Sheets & Solution Book: For the Children's Picture-Word & Simple Sentence Book. Irving, Harry. 2009. 196p. pap. 17.14 *(978-1-4269-0667-1(6))* Trafford Publishing.

Graphics, Nataly. Jimmy the Squirrel. Taher, Amr. Taher, Layal, ed. 2011. 36p. (J). 14.99 *(978-1-4567-3526-5(8))* AuthorHouse.

Grass, Jeff, photos by. The Emotionally Unavailable Man: A Blueprint for Healing. Henry, Patti. 2008. (ENG., (YA). cd-rom 24.95 *(978-0-9817155-8-2(3))* Henry, Patti.

Grasso, Craig A. & Grasso, Samantha A. Gracie Comes Home: The Adventures of Gracie & Diane. Dike, Diane. 2007. (J). 14.95 *(978-1-932738-45-2(2))* Western Reflections Publishing Co.

Grasso, Samantha A., jt. illus. see Grasso, Craig A.

Graston, Arlene. In Every Moon There Is a Face. Mathes, Charles. 2003. 32p. 15.95 *(978-0-9701907-4-1(3))* Illumination Arts Publishing Co., Inc.

Grater, Lindsay. One Hundred Shining Candles. Lunn, Janet. 2008. (ENG.). 32p. (J). (gr. k-3). 17.95 *(978-0-88776-889-7(X)*, Tundra Bks.) Tundra Bks. CAN. Dist: Penguin Random Hse., LLC.

Gratz, Ali. Rudy Gets A Transplant. 2008. 28p. (J). pap. 10.00 *(978-0-9820983-0-1(8))* Purple Cow Pr.

Grau, Ryon. The ABCs of Frederick Maryland: A Historic Coloring Book. Grau, Maritta, ed. 2007. 32p. 8.95 *(978-0-9772559-0-0(5))* Grau, Ryon.

Graullera, Fabiola. Las Piñatas. Zepeda, Monique.Tr. of Pinatas. (SPA.). 26p. (J). (gr. 3-5). pap. 6.95 *(978-968-19-0612-2(8))* Santillana USA Publishing Co., Inc.

—Poemas de Perros y Gatos. Cordova, Soledad. 2003. (SPA.). 21p. (J). (gr. 3-5). pap. 7.95 *(978-968-19-0987-1(9))* Santillana USA Publishing Co., Inc.

Graullera, Fabiola, jt. illus. see Martinez, Enrique.

Graullera, Fabiolla. I Am Rene, the Boy. Laínez, René Colato. 2005.Tr. of Yo Soy Rene, el Nino. (ENG & SPA.). 32p. (J). (gr. -1-2). 16.95 *(978-1-55885-378-2(2)*, Piñata Books) Arte Publico Pr.

Graullera Ramírez, Fabiola, jt. illus. see Laínez, René Colato.

Graunke, Susan M. Nico & Lola: Kindness Shared Between a Boy & a Dog. Hill, Meggan. 2010. (ENG.). 40p. (J). (gr. -1-3). 16.99 *(978-0-06-199043-4(4))* HarperCollins Pubs.

Graux, Amélie. I Love to Eat. Graux, Amélie. deluxe ed. 2012. (ENG, SPA & FRE.). 12p. (J). (gr. k — 1). bds. 9.99 *(978-0-547-84842-6(0))* Houghton Mifflin Harcourt Publishing Co.

—I Love to Sleep. Graux, Amélie. Dormir, J'aime & Dormir, Me Encanta. deluxe ed. 2012. (ENG, SPA & FRE.). 12p. (J). (gr. k — 1). bds. 9.99 *(978-0-547-84843-3(9))* Houghton Mifflin Harcourt Publishing Co.

Gravel, Élise. The Cranky Ballerina. 2015. (J). ***(978-0-06-235124-1(9))*** HarperCollins Pubs.

Gravel, Elise. A Day in the Office of Doctor Bugspit. 2011. (ENG.). 40p. (J). (gr. 1-4). 11.99 *(978-1-60905-092-4(4))* Blue Apple Bks.

Gravel, Élise. Doodle Journal: My Life in Scribbles. Phillips, Karen. 2010. (ENG.). 76p. (J). (gr. 3-18). 16.95 *(978-1-59174-736-9(8))* Klutz.

—Space Taxi: Archie Takes Flight. Mass, Wendy & Brawer, Michael. 2014. (Space Taxi Ser.: 1). (ENG.). 112p. (J). (gr. 1-5). 15.00 *(978-0-316-24319-3(1))* Little, Brown Bks. for Young Readers.

Gravel, Élise. Jessie Elliot Is a Big Chicken. Gravel, Élise. 2014. (ENG.). 176p. (J). (gr. 5-9). 14.99 *(978-1-59643-741-8(3))* Roaring Brook Pr.

Graves, Dan. Pparcel's Notebook Presents: The Search for the Giant Stone Monkey Head, Truth, Friends & Strange Food. Graves, Dan. 2004. 48p. lib. bdg. 15.00 *(978-0-9744999-0-1(0))* Love Cultivating Editions.

Graves, Dennis. Fun. Yannone, Deborah. Kaeden Corp. Staff, ed. 2003. (ENG.). 12p. (gr. k-1). pap. 5.95 *(978-1-879835-56-6(8))* Kaeden Corp.

—I Have a Watch. Williams, Deborah. l.t. ed. 2003. (ENG.). 12p. (gr. k-1). pap. 5.95 *(978-1-879835-92-4(4))* Kaeden Corp.

—I'll Be a Pirate: World of Discovery II. Eifrig, Kate. l.t. ed. 2006. (SPA & ENG.). 12p. (gr. k-2). pap. 5.95 *(978-1-57874-053-6(3))* Kaeden Corp.

—Scary Monster. Eifrig, Kate. 2003. (ENG.). 8p. (gr. k-1). pap. 4.95 *(978-1-879835-29-0(0)*, Kaeden Bks.) Kaeden Corp.

—Snowflakes. Urmston, Kathleen & Evans, Karen. Kaeden Corp. Staff, ed. 2006. (ENG.). 12p. (gr. k-1). pap. 5.95 *(978-1-879835-01-6(0))* Kaeden Corp.

—Thanksgiving. Evans, Karen & Urmston, Kathleen. Kaeden Corp. Staff, ed. 2006. (ENG.). 12p. (gr. k-2). pap. 5.95 *(978-1-879835-57-3(6))* Kaeden Corp.
—Tree House. Hoenecke, Karen. 2005. (ENG.). 12p. (gr. k-1). pap. 5.95 *(978-1-57874-090-1(8))* Kaeden Corp.
Graves, Emily. A Winter Tale: How Raven Gave Light to the World. Turner, Mark. 2014. (ENG.). 48p. 20.00 *(978-1-62288-032-4(3))* Austin, Stephen F. State Univ. Pr.
Graves, Jeseca. Bessie Coleman: The Story of an Aviation Pioneer. 2007. 24p. (J). *(978-0-9745294-1-7(9))* San Diego County Regional Airport Authority.
Graves, Kassie. Brave Little Sailboat. Graves, Kassie. 2003. 20p. (J). 14.95 *(978-0-9728019-0-4(1))* Bright Eyes Pr.
Graves, Keith. Boo-Hoo Moo. Palatini, Margie. 2009. 32p. (J). (gr. -1-3). lib. bdg. 18.89 *(978-0-06-114376-2(6))* HarperCollins Pubs.
—Clovis Crawfish & His Friends, 1 vol. Fontenot, Mary Alice. 2009. (Clovis Crawfish Ser.). (ENG.). 32p. (J). (gr. k-3). 16.99 *(978-1-58980-762-4(6))* Pelican Publishing Co., Inc.
—Clovis Crawfish & Petit Papillon, 1 vol. Fontenot, Mary Alice. 2009. (Clovis Crawfish Ser.). (ENG.). 32p. (J). (gr. k-3). 16.99 *(978-1-58980-772-3(3))* Pelican Publishing Co., Inc.
—Desert Rose & Her Highfalutin Hog. Jackson, Alison. 2009. (ENG.). 40p. (J). (gr. -1-3). 16.99 *(978-0-8027-9833-6(0))* Walker & Co.
—Moo Who? Palatini, Margie. (ENG.). 40p. (J). (gr. -1-2). 2007. pap. 6.99 *(978-0-06-000107-0(0))*; 2004. 16.99 *(978-0-06-000105-6(4))* HarperCollins Pubs. (Tegen, Katherine Bks).
—Too Many Frogs! Asher, Sandy. 2005. (ENG.). 32p. (J). (gr. -1-k). 16.99 *(978-0-399-23978-6(2)*, Philomel) Penguin Publishing Group.
—The World's Greatest. Lewis, J. Patrick. 2008. (ENG.). 36p. (J). (gr. k-4). 16.99 *(978-0-8118-5130-5(3))* Chronicle Bks. LLC.
Graves, Linda. V Is for Von Trapp: A Musical Family Alphabet. Anderson, William. 2010. (ENG.). 32p. (J). (gr. 1-4). 16.95 *(978-1-58536-531-9(9)*, 202214) Sleeping Bear Pr.
Graves, Linda, jt. illus. see Gruber, Michael.
Graves, Linda, jt. illus. see Linda, Graves.
Graves, Linda Dockey. The Renaissance Kids. Weyn, Suzanne. 2004. 56p. (J). *(978-0-7652-3277-9(4))* Celebration Pr.
Graves, Lisa. History's Witches. Graves, Lisa. 2013. 32p. 19.99 *(978-1-62395-516-8(5))* Xist Publishing.
Graves, Michelle. Henry the Elf. Williams, Hap. 2012. 28p. pap. 24.95 *(978-1-4626-8999-6(X))* America Star Bks.
Gravett, Emily. The Imaginary. Harrold, A. F. 2015. (ENG.). 224p. (J). (gr. 3-6). 16.99 *(978-0-8027-3811-0(7)*, Bloomsbury USA Childrens) Bloomsbury USA.
—Little Mouse's Big Book of Beasts. 2016. (J). *(978-1-4814-3929-9(4)*, Simon & Schuster Bks. For Young Readers) Simon & Schuster Bks. For Young Readers.
Gravett, Emily. Again! Gravett, Emily. 2013. (ENG.). 32p. (J). (gr. -1-3). 17.99 *(978-1-4424-5231-2(5)*, Simon & Schuster Bks. For Young Readers) Simon & Schuster Bks. For Young Readers.
—Bear & Hare Go Fishing. Gravett, Emily. 2015. (Bear & Hare Ser.). (ENG.). 32p. (J). (gr. -1-3). 15.99 *(978-1-4814-2289-5(8)*, Simon & Schuster Bks. For Young Readers) Simon & Schuster Bks. For Young Readers.
—Blue Chameleon. Gravett, Emily. 2011. (ENG.). 32p. (J). (gr. -1-1). 16.99 *(978-1-4424-1958-2(X)*, Simon & Schuster Bks. For Young Readers) Simon & Schuster Bks. For Young Readers.
—Dogs. Gravett, Emily. 2010. (ENG.). 32p. (J). (gr. -1-1). 15.99 *(978-1-4169-8703-1(7)*, Simon & Schuster Bks. For Young Readers) Simon & Schuster Bks. For Young Readers.
—Little Mouse's Big Book of Fears. Gravett, Emily. 2nd rev. ed. 2007. (ENG.). 32p. (J). (gr. k-4). *(978-1-4050-8948-7(2)*, Macmillan Children's Bks.) Pan Macmillan.
—Little Mouse's Big Book of Fears. Gravett, Emily. 2008. (ENG.). 32p. (J). (gr. -1-3). 19.99 *(978-1-4169-5930-4(0)*, Simon & Schuster Bks. For Young Readers) Simon & Schuster Bks. For Young Readers.
—Matilda's Cat. Gravett, Emily. 2014. (ENG.). 32p. (J). (gr. -1-3). 16.99 *(978-1-4424-7527-4(7)*, Simon & Schuster Bks. For Young Readers) Simon & Schuster Bks. For Young Readers.
—Meerkat Mail. Gravett, Emily. 2007. (ENG.). 32p. (J). (gr. -1-3). 17.99 *(978-1-4169-3473-8(1)*, Simon & Schuster Bks. For Young Readers) Simon & Schuster Bks. For Young Readers.
—Monkey & Me. Gravett, Emily. 2008. (ENG.). 32p. (J). (gr. -1-3). 17.99 *(978-1-4169-5457-6(0)*, Simon & Schuster Bks. For Young Readers) Simon & Schuster Bks. For Young Readers.
—The Odd Egg. Gravett, Emily. 2009. (ENG.). 32p. (J). (gr. -1-3). 15.99 *(978-1-4169-6872-6(5)*, Simon & Schuster Bks. For Young Readers) Simon & Schuster Bks. For Young Readers.
—Orange Pear Apple Bear. Gravett, Emily. 2011. (Classic Board Bks.). (ENG.). 24p. (J). (gr. -1 — 1). bds. 7.99 *(978-1-4424-2003-8(0)*, Little Simon) Little Simon.
—Orange Pear Apple Bear. Gravett, Emily. 2007. (ENG.). 32p. (J). (gr. -1 — 1). 12.99 *(978-1-4169-3999-3(7)*, Simon & Schuster Bks. For Young Readers) Simon & Schuster Bks. For Young Readers.
—The Rabbit Problem. Gravett, Emily. 2010. (ENG.). 32p. (J). (gr. -1-3). 17.99 *(978-1-4424-1255-2(0)*, Simon & Schuster Bks. For Young Readers) Simon & Schuster Bks. For Young Readers.
—Spells. Gravett, Emily. 2009. (ENG.). 32p. (J). (gr. -1-3). 16.99 *(978-1-4169-8270-8(1)*, Simon & Schuster Bks. For Young Readers) Simon & Schuster Bks. For Young Readers.
—Wolf Won't Bite! Gravett, Emily. 2012. (ENG.). 32p. (J). (gr. -1-1). 16.99 *(978-1-4424-2763-1(9)*, Simon & Schuster Bks. For Young Readers) Simon & Schuster Bks. For Young Readers.
—Wolves. Gravett, Emily. 2006. (ENG.). 40p. (J). (gr. k-3). 17.99 *(978-1-4169-1491-4(9)*, Simon & Schuster Bks. For Young Readers) Simon & Schuster Bks. For Young Readers.
Gravier, Anne. Prayers Around the Crib. Levivier, Juliette. 2012. (ENG.). 46p. (J). (gr. -1-3). 9.99 *(978-1-58617-773-7(7))* Ignatius Pr.
Gravitt, Bill. Rudee Goes Bananas for Manners. Madore, Michele. 2006. (ENG.). 38p. (J). pap. 6.95 *(978-0-615-17967-4(3))* Manners Toy Co., LLC.
Gray, Angela M. Things I Wonder. Smith, Jennifer Lynne. Perez, Angela J., ed. 2007. 36p. (J). 14.95 *(978-0-9778328-5-9(6))* His Work Christian Publishing.
Gray, Cissy. Wild Beach. Coste, Marion. 2005. 32p. (J). pap. 8.25 *(978-0-89317-062-2(3)*, WW-623); lib. bdg. 17.95 *(978-0-89317-061-5(5)*, WW-0615) Finney Co., Inc. (Windward Publishing).
Gray, Dean. A Moonlight Book: Halloween Hide-And-Seek. Butterfield, Moira & Golding, Elizabeth. 2015. (ENG.). 12p. (J). (gr. -1-3). 10.95 ***(978-0-7624-5846-2(1)***, Running Pr. Kids) Running Pr. Bk. Pubs.
Gray, J. M. L., jt. illus. see Gibert, Jean Claude.
Gray, Jane. Only Tadpoles Have Tails. Clarke, Jane. 2003. (Flying Foxes Ser.). (ENG.). 48p. (J). *(978-0-7787-1530-6(2))*; lib. bdg. *(978-0-7787-1484-2(5))* Crabtree Publishing Co.
Gray, Karen. Pick-a-WooWoo - the Elf That Flew: Love & Joy give you wings to Fly. Mitchell, Lindy. 2011. (ENG.). 28p. pap. *(978-1-921883-07-1(3))* Pick-a-Woo Woo Pubs.
Gray, Leslie. How to Be Nice — & Other Lessons I Didn't Learn. Bowdish, Lynea. 2006. 47p. (J). pap. *(978-1-59336-726-8(0))* Mondo Publishing.
Gray, M. Promethea, Vol. 3. Moore, Alan. 3rd rev. ed. 2003. (Magical Ser.: Bk. 3). (ENG.). 160p. pap. 17.99 *(978-1-4012-0094-7(X))* DC Comics.
Gray, Maureen & Lynch, Josh. The Haunting of Julia, 1 vol. Hooper, M. 2007. (Graphic Quest Ser.). (ENG.). 88p. (gr. 3-3). lib. bdg. 23.99 *(978-1-59889-827-9(2)*, Graphic Quest) Stone Arch Bks.
Gray Mayo, Jo Ann. Love: The Book of Love for Kids. Hawkins Harris, Jennifer. 2003. 20p. (J). per. 7.00 *(978-0-9705458-2-4(7))* Royalty Bks. International, Inc.
Gray, Miranda & Trotter, Stuart. The Usborne Book of Horses & Ponies. Smith, Lucy. 2006. 32p. (J). pap. *(978-0-439-88983-4(9))* Scholastic, Inc.
Gray, Paula. Signing Fun: American Sign Language Vocabulary, Phrases, Games, & Activities. Warner, Penny. 2006. 192p. (gr. 3-7). per. 19.95 *(978-1-56368-292-6(3))* Gallaudet Univ. Pr.
Gray, Sara. If You Were a Capital Letter, 1 vol. Shaskan, Trisha Speed. 2009. (Word Fun Ser.). (ENG.). 24p. (gr. 2-4). pap. 7.95 *(978-1-4048-5694-3(3))*; lib. bdg. 27.32 *(978-1-4048-5515-1(7))* Picture Window Bks. (Nonfiction Picture Bks.).
—If You Were a Comma, 1 vol. Blaisdell, Molly. 2009. (Word Fun Ser.). (ENG.). 24p. (gr. 2-4). pap. 7.95 *(978-1-4048-5321-8(9))*; 27.32 *(978-1-4048-5320-1(0))* Picture Window Bks. (Nonfiction Picture Bks.).
—If You Were a Comma [LTD Commodities]. Blaisdell, Molly. 2010. (Word Fun Ser.). 24p. pap. 3.50 *(978-1-4048-6251-7(X)*, Nonfiction Picture Bks.) Picture Window Bks.
—If You Were a Compound Word, 1 vol. Shaskan, Trisha Speed. 2008. (Word Fun Ser.). (ENG.). 24p. (gr. 2-4). 27.32 *(978-1-4048-4771-2(5))*; pap. 7.95 *(978-1-4048-4776-7(6))* Picture Window Bks. (Nonfiction Picture Bks.).
—If You Were a Conjunction, 1 vol. Loewen, Nancy. 2006. (Word Fun Ser.). (ENG.). 24p. (gr. 2-4). per. 7.95 *(978-1-4048-2389-1(1)*, Nonfiction Picture Bks.) Picture Window Bks.
—If You Were a Contraction, 1 vol. Shaskan, Trisha Speed. 2008. (Word Fun Ser.). (ENG.). 24p. (gr. 2-4). 27.32 *(978-1-4048-4772-9(3))*; pap. 7.95 *(978-1-4048-4775-0(8))* Picture Window Bks. (Nonfiction Picture Bks.).
—If You Were a Homonym or a Homophone, 1 vol. Loewen, Nancy. 2007. (Word Fun Ser.). (ENG.). 24p. (gr. 2-4). lib. bdg. 27.32 *(978-1-4048-3161-2(4))*; per. 7.95 *(978-1-4048-3571-9(7)*, 1265671) Picture Window Bks. (Nonfiction Picture Bks.).
—If You Were a Noun, 1 vol. Dahl, Michael. 2006. (Word Fun Ser.). (ENG.). 24p. (gr. 2-4). 7.95 *(978-1-4048-1980-1(0))*; 27.32 *(978-1-4048-1355-7(1))* Picture Window Bks. (Nonfiction Picture Bks.).
—If You Were a Palindrome, 1 vol. Dahl, Michael. 2007. (Word Fun Ser.). (ENG.). 24p. (gr. 2-4). lib. bdg. 27.32 *(978-1-4048-3162-9(2)*, Nonfiction Picture Bks.) Picture Window Bks.
—If You Were a Palindrome, 1 vol. Dahl, Michael & Loewen, Nancy. 2007. (Word Fun Ser.). (ENG.). 24p. (gr. 2-4). per. 7.95 *(978-1-4048-3573-3(3)*, 1265672, Nonfiction Picture Bks.) Picture Window Bks.
—If You Were a Period, 1 vol. Healy, Nick & Healy, Nicholas M. 2009. (Word Fun Ser.). (ENG.). 24p. (gr. 2-4). lib. bdg. 27.32 *(978-1-4048-5332-4(4)*, Nonfiction Picture Bks.) Picture Window Bks.
—If You Were a Period, 1 vol. Healy, Nicholas M. 2009. (Word Fun Ser.). (ENG.). 24p. pap. 7.95 *(978-1-4048-5333-1(2)*, Nonfiction Picture Bks.) Picture Window Bks.
—If You Were a Period [LTD Commodities]. Healy, Nicholas M. 2010. (Word Fun Ser.). 24p. pap. 3.50 *(978-1-4048-6252-4(8)*, Nonfiction Picture Bks.) Picture Window Bks.
—If You Were a Plural Word, 1 vol. Shaskan, Trisha Speed. 2009. (Word Fun Ser.). (ENG.). 24p. (gr. 2-4). pap. 7.95 *(978-1-4048-5696-7(X))*; lib. bdg. 27.32 *(978-1-4048-5516-8(5))* Picture Window Bks. (Nonfiction Picture Bks.).
—If You Were a Prefix, 1 vol. Aboff, Marcie. 2008. (Word Fun Ser.). (ENG.). 24p. (gr. 2-4). 27.32 *(978-1-4048-4773-6(1))*; pap. 7.95 *(978-1-4048-4777-4(4))* Picture Window Bks. (Nonfiction Picture Bks.).
—If You Were a Preposition. Loewen, Nancy. 2006. (Word Fun Ser.). (ENG.). 24p. (gr. 2-4). lib. bdg. 27.32 *(978-1-4048-2386-0(7))*; per. 7.95 *(978-1-4048-2390-7(5))* Picture Window Bks. (Nonfiction Picture Bks.).
—If You Were a Pronoun, 1 vol. Loewen, Nancy. 2006. (Word Fun Ser.). (ENG.). 24p. (gr. 2-4). per. 7.95 *(978-1-4048-2639-7(4)*, Nonfiction Picture Bks.) Picture Window Bks.
—If You Were a Question Mark, 1 vol. Lyons, Shelly. 2009. (Word Fun Ser.). (ENG.). 24p. (gr. 2-4). pap. 7.95 *(978-1-4048-5324-9(3))*; lib. bdg. 27.32 *(978-1-4048-5323-2(5))* Picture Window Bks. (Nonfiction Picture Bks.).
—If You Were a Question Mark [LTD Commodities]. Lyons, Shelly. 2010. (Word Fun Ser.). 24p. pap. 3.50 *(978-1-4048-6253-1(6)*, Nonfiction Picture Bks.) Picture Window Bks.
—If You Were a Question Mark [Readers World]. Lyons, Shelly. 2010. (Word Fun Ser.). 24p. pap. 2.72 *(978-1-4048-6705-5(8)*, Nonfiction Picture Bks.) Picture Window Bks.
—If You Were a Suffix, 1 vol. Aboff, Marcie. 2008. (Word Fun Ser.). (ENG.). 24p. (gr. 2-4). 27.32 *(978-1-4048-4774-3(X))*; pap. 7.95 *(978-1-4048-4778-1(2))* Picture Window Bks. (Nonfiction Picture Bks.).
—If You Were a Synonym, 1 vol. Dahl, Michael & Picture Window Books Staff. 2007. (Word Fun Ser.). (ENG.). 24p. (gr. 2-4). 27.32 *(978-1-4048-2387-7(5)*, Nonfiction Picture Bks.) Picture Window Bks.
—If You Were a Synonym, 1 vol. Dahl, Michael. 2007. (Word Fun Ser.). (ENG.). 24p. (gr. 2-4). per. 7.95 *(978-1-4048-2391-4(3)*, 1265673, Nonfiction Picture Bks.) Picture Window Bks.
—If You Were a Verb, 1 vol. Dahl, Michael. 2006. (Word Fun Ser.). (ENG.). 24p. (gr. 2-4). 27.32 *(978-1-4048-1354-0(3)*, Nonfiction Picture Bks.) Picture Window Bks.
—If You Were Alliteration. Shaskan, Trisha Speed. 2008. (Word Fun Ser.). (ENG.). 24p. (gr. 2-4). lib. bdg. 27.32 *(978-1-4048-4097-3(4)*, Nonfiction Picture Bks.) Picture Window Bks.
—If You Were an Adjective, 1 vol. Dahl, Michael. 2006. (Word Fun Ser.). (ENG.). 24p. (gr. 2-4). 7.95 *(978-1-4048-1982-5(7))*; 27.32 *(978-1-4048-1356-4(X))* Picture Window Bks. (Nonfiction Picture Bks.).
—If You Were an Adverb, 1 vol. Dahl, Michael. 2006. (Word Fun Ser.). (ENG.). 24p. (gr. 2-4). 27.32 *(978-1-4048-1357-1(8))*; per. 7.95 *(978-1-4048-1983-2(5))* Picture Window Bks. (Nonfiction Picture Bks.).
—If You Were an Antonym, 1 vol. Loewen, Nancy. 2007. (Word Fun Ser.). (ENG.). 24p. (gr. 2-4). lib. bdg. 27.32 *(978-1-4048-2384-6(0)*, Nonfiction Picture Bks.) Picture Window Bks.
—If You Were an Antonym, 1 vol. Loewen, Nancy & Dahl, Michael. 2007. (Word Fun Ser.). (ENG.). 24p. (gr. 2-4). per. 7.95 *(978-1-4048-2388-4(3)*, 1265670, Nonfiction Picture Bks.) Picture Window Bks.
—If You Were an Apostrophe, 1 vol. Blaisdell, Molly & Lyons, Shelly. 2009. (Word Fun Ser.). (ENG.). 24p. (gr. 2-4). lib. bdg. 27.32 *(978-1-4048-5317-1(0)*, Nonfiction Picture Bks.) Picture Window Bks.
—If You Were an Apostrophe, 1 vol. Lyons, Shelly & Blaisdell, Molly. 2009. (Word Fun Ser.). (ENG.). 24p. (gr. 2-4). pap. 7.95 *(978-1-4048-5318-8(9)*, Nonfiction Picture Bks.) Picture Window Bks.
—If You Were an Apostrophe [Readers World]. Lyons, Shelly. 2010. (Word Fun Ser.). 24p. pap. 2.72 *(978-1-4048-6708-6(2)*, Nonfiction Picture Bks.) Picture Window Bks.
—If You Were an Exclamation Point, 1 vol. Lyons, Shelly. 2009. (Word Fun Ser.). (ENG.). 24p. (gr. 2-4). pap. 7.95 *(978-1-4048-5327-0(8))*; lib. bdg. 27.32 *(978-1-4048-5326-3(X))* Picture Window Bks. (Nonfiction Picture Bks.).
—If You Were an Exclamation Point [LTD Commodities]. Lyons, Shelly. 2010. (Word Fun Ser.). 24p. pap. 3.50 *(978-1-4048-6254-8(4)*, Nonfiction Picture Bks.) Picture Window Bks.
—If You Were an Exclamation Point [Readers World]. Lyons, Shelly. 2010. (Word Fun Ser.). 24p. pap. 2.72 *(978-1-4048-6707-9(4)*, Nonfiction Picture Bks.) Picture Window Bks.
—If You Were an Interjection. Loewen, Nancy. 2006. (Word Fun Ser.). (ENG.). 24p. (gr. 2-4). lib. bdg. 27.32 *(978-1-4048-2636-6(X))*; per. 7.95 *(978-1-4048-2638-0(6))* Picture Window Bks. (Nonfiction Picture Bks.).
—If You Were Onomatopoeia. Shaskan, Trisha Speed. 2008. (Word Fun Ser.). (ENG.). 24p. (gr. 2-4). lib. bdg. 27.32 *(978-1-4048-4098-0(2)*, Nonfiction Picture Bks.) Picture Window Bks.
—If You Were Quotation Marks, 1 vol. Blaisdell, Molly. 2009. (Word Fun Ser.). (ENG.). 24p. (gr. 2-4). pap. 7.95 *(978-1-4048-5330-0(8))*; lib. bdg. 27.32 *(978-1-4048-5329-4(4))* Picture Window Bks. (Nonfiction Picture Bks.).
—If You Were Quotation Marks [LTD Commodities]. Blaisdell, Molly. 2010. (Word Fun Ser.). 24p. pap. 3.50 *(978-1-4048-6255-5(2)*, Nonfiction Picture Bks.) Picture Window Bks.
—If You Were Quotation Marks [Readers World]. Blaisdell, Molly. 2010. (Word Fun Ser.). 24p. pap. 2.72 *(978-1-4048-6706-2(6)*, Nonfiction Picture Bks.) Picture Window Bks.
Gray, Stacy A. A Big Mess. Mullican, Judy. l.t. ed. 2003. (HRL Little Book Ser.). 8p. (J). (gr. -1). pap. 10.95 *(978-1-57332-273-7(3)*, HighReach Learning, Incorporated) Carson-Dellosa Publishing, LLC.
—Caillou Is Healthy. Mullican, Judy. l.t. ed. 2004. (HRL Board Book Ser.). (J). (gr. -1-1). pap. 10.95 *(978-1-57332-287-4(3)*, HighReach Learning, Incorporated) Carson-Dellosa Publishing, LLC.
—Fall on the Farm. Mullican, Judy. l.t. ed. 2005. (Hrl Board Book Ser.). (J). (gr. -1-k). pap. 10.95 *(978-1-57332-323-9(3)*, HighReach Learning, Incorporated) Carson-Dellosa Publishing, LLC.
—I Want to Ride. Hensley, Sarah M. l.t. ed. 2004. (HRL Board Book Ser.). 10p. (J). (gr. -1-1). pap. 10.95 *(978-1-57332-282-9(2)*, HighReach Learning, Incorporated) Carson-Dellosa Publishing, LLC.
—May We Go to the Zoo? Mullican, Judy. l.t. ed. 2004. (HRL Little Book Ser.). (J). (gr. -1-1). pap. 10.95 *(978-1-57332-304-8(7))*; pap. 10.95 *(978-1-57332-303-1(9))* Carson-Dellosa Publishing, LLC. (HighReach Learning, Incorporated).
—What Can It Be? Mullican, Jody. l.t. ed. 2006. 12p. (J). (gr. -1-k). pap. 10.95 *(978-1-57332-352-9(7)*, HighReach Learning, Incorporated) Carson-Dellosa Publishing, LLC.
Gray, Steve. Cow Can't Sleep, 0 vols. Baker, Ken. 2012. (ENG.). 24p. (J). (gr. -1-3). 12.99 *(978-0-7614-6198-2(1)*, 9780761461982, Amazon Children's Publishing) Amazon Publishing.
—Un Diente esta Flojo: A Tooth Is Loose. Trumbauer, Lisa. 2005. (Rookie Reader Español Ser.). (SPA & ENG.). 24p. (gr. k-2). 19.50 *(978-0-516-24449-5(3)*, Children's Pr.) Scholastic Library Publishing.
—Farmer McPeepers' Milk Cows. Duffield, Katy. 2003. (ENG.). 32p. (J). (gr. -1-3). 15.95 *(978-0-87358-825-6(8))* Cooper Square Publishing Llc.
Gray, Steve. The Ravenous Raven. Stephenson, Midji. 2015. (J). ***(978-1-934656-70-9(4))*** Grand Canyon Assn.
Gray, Steve. There Was an Old Monkey Who Swallowed a Frog, 0 vols. Ward, Jennifer. 2010. (ENG.). 32p. (J). (gr. k-3). 16.99 *(978-0-7614-5580-6(9)*, 9780761455806, Amazon Children's Publishing) Amazon Publishing.
—A Tooth Is Loose. Trumbauer, Lisa. (Rookie Ready to Learn Ser.). (J). 2011. 32p. pap. 5.95 *(978-0-531-26735-6(0))*; 2011. 32p. (gr. -1-k). lib. bdg. 23.00 *(978-0-531-26503-1(X))*; 2005. (ENG.). 24p. (gr. k-2). pap. 4.95 *(978-0-516-25841-6(9))* Scholastic Library Publishing. (Children's Pr.).
Gray, Steve. Un Diente Está Flojo. Gray, Steve. Trumbauer, Lisa. 2011. (Rookie Ready to Learn Español Ser.). (SPA.). 32p. (J). pap. 5.95 *(978-0-531-26785-1(7))*; lib. bdg. 23.00 *(978-0-531-26117-0(4))* Scholastic Library Publishing. (Children's Pr.).
Gray, Steve, jt. illus. see Sullivan, Mary.
Gray, Susan & Messer, Celia. Colorful Ohio! A Bird's Eye View with Worthington Cardinal, 7 bks. Gray, Susan. 2003. 28p. (J). 4.95 *(978-0-9742862-5-9(7))* Two's Company.
Gray, Virginia. The Great Number Rumble: A Story of Math in Surprising Places. Lee, Cora & O'Reilly, Gillian. 2007. (ENG.). 108p. (J). (gr. 4-6). 24.95 *(978-1-55451-032-0(5)*, 9781554510320); pap. 14.95 *(978-1-55451-031-3(7)*, 9781554510313) Annick Pr., Ltd. CAN. Dist: Firefly Bks., Ltd.
Graybar, Shmuel, jt. illus. see Toron, Eli.
Graybill, Joni. Hello Cocky! Aryal, Aimee. 2004. 24p. (J). 19.95 *(978-1-932888-07-2(1))* Mascot Bks., Inc.
—Hello Tiger! Aryal, Aimee. 2004. 24p. (J). 19.95 *(978-1-932888-25-6(X))* Mascot Bks., Inc.
Grayson, Rick. Captain Jack's Journal. Williams, Rozanne Lanczak. 2006. (Learn to Write Ser.). 16p. (J). (gr. k-2). pap. 2.99 *(978-1-59198-303-3(7)*, 6197) Creative Teaching Pr., Inc.
—Captain Jack's Journal. Williams, Rozanne Lanczak. Maio, Barbara, ed. 2006. (J). per. 8.99 *(978-1-59198-361-3(4))* Creative Teaching Pr., Inc.
—Grammar Minutes: 100 Minutes to Better Basic Skills. Jones, Carmen S. Ly, Dorothy, ed. 2009. 112p. (J). pap. 14.99 *(978-1-60689-123-0(5))* Creative Teaching Pr., Inc.
—Grammar Minutes: 100 Minutes to Better Basic Skills. Hex, Kathleen. Kim, Regina Hurh & Snoddy, Gillian, eds. 2009. 112p. (J). pap. 14.99 *(978-1-60689-124-7(3))* Creative Teaching Pr., Inc.
Grayson, Rick & Iosa, Ann. Reading Comprehension 1-3: Activities for Understanding. Flores, Debra et al. Jennett, Pamela, ed. 2004. 96p. (J). pap. 1.99 *(978-1-59198-045-2(3)*, 3384) Creative Teaching Pr., Inc.
—Reading Comprehension 4-6: Activities for Understanding. Flores, Debra et al. Jennett, Pamela, ed. 2004. 96p. (J). pap. 12.99 *(978-1-59198-046-9(1)*, 3385) Creative Teaching Pr., Inc.
Grayson, Rick, jt. illus. see Armstrong, Beverly.
Grayson, Rick, jt. illus. see Armstrong, Bev.
Grayson, Rick, jt. illus. see Brooks, Nan.
Grayson, Rick, jt. illus. see Campbell, Jenny.
Grayson, Rick, jt. illus. see Hillam, Corbin.
Grayson, Rick, jt. illus. see Iosa, Ann W.
Grayson, Rick, jt. illus. see Rojas, Mary.
Grayson, Rick, jt. illus. see Tom, Darcy.
Graziano, John. Burp! Ripley's Inc. Staff. 2012. (Ripley's Shout Outs Ser.: 4). (ENG.). 96p. (J). (gr. 2-5). pap. 4.99 *(978-0-545-38078-2(2))* Scholastic, Inc.
—Roar! Ripley's Inc. Staff. 2012. (Ripley's Shout Outs Ser.: 1). (ENG.). 96p. (J). (gr. 2-5). pap. 4.99 *(978-0-545-38075-1(8))* Scholastic, Inc.
—Woof! Ripley's Inc. Staff. 2012. (Ripley's Shout Outs Ser.: 3). (ENG.). 96p. (J). (gr. 2-5). pap. 4.99 *(978-0-545-38077-5(4))* Scholastic, Inc.
—Woof! Funny Pet Stories. 2012. 96p. (J). pap. *(978-0-545-38687-6(X))* Ripley Entertainment, Inc.
—Zoom! Ripley's Inc. Staff. 2012. (Ripley's Shout Outs Ser.: 2). (ENG.). 96p. (J). (gr. 2-5). pap. 4.99 *(978-0-545-38076-8(6))* Scholastic, Inc.
Grbich, Aaron. Numeros Importantes. Giganti, Paul. (SPA.). (J). (gr. 1-3). pap. 3.16 net. *(978-0-590-48700-9(0)*, Scholastic Pr.) Scholastic, Inc.
Greathouse, Justin. Gordon Grizwald's Grumpy Goose, 1 vol. Loewen, Nancy. 2008. (Read-It! Readers: Tongue Twisters Ser.). (ENG.). 24p. (gr. k-3). 19.99 *(978-1-4048-4878-8(9)*, Easy Readers) Picture Window Bks.
Greaux, Romea. A Heritage Undone. Quetel, Linda. 33p. (J). (gr. 11). 9.50 *(978-0-9626458-1-5(8))* xbks publishing.
Greban, Quentin. Sarah So Small. Greban, Tanguy. 2004. (ENG.). 32p. (J). (gr. 4-7). 16.95 *(978-1-59687-179-3(2))* IBks., Inc.

—Sarah So Small. Greban, Tanguy. 2004. 32p. (J). 16.95 (978-0-689-03594-4(2), Milk & Cookies) ibooks, Inc.

—Snow White. Grimm, Jacob & Grimm, Wilhelm. 2013. (ENG.). 32p. (J). (gr. -1-3). pap. 7.95 (978-0-7358-4116-1(0)) North-South Bks., Inc.

—We Both Read-Thumbelina (Picture Book) Andersen, Hans Christian. Bell, Elizabeth, tr. from FRE. 2007. (We Both Read Ser.).Tr. of Tommelise. 32p. (J). (gr. -1-3). 14.95 (978-1-60115-007-3(5)) Treasure Bay, Inc.

Greban, Quentin. Mommy, I Love You. Greban, Quentin. 2005. 32p. (978-0-689-03922-5(0), Milk & Cookies) ibooks, Inc.

Greban, Quentin, jt. illus. see Carsey, Alice.

Greco, E. D. Tales & Treasures of California's Missions. Reinstedt, Randall A. 2005. 119p. (YA). reprint ed. 22.00 (978-0-7567-8681-6(9)) DIANE Publishing Co.

Greder, Armin. Great Bear. Gleeson, Libby. 2011. (ENG.). 40p. (J). (gr. k-4). 16.99 (978-0-7636-5136-7(2)) Candlewick Pr.

—I Am Thomas. Gleeson, Libby. 2011. (ENG.). 32p. (J). (gr. 2-4). 22.99 (978-1-74237-333-1(X)) Allen & Unwin AUS. Dist: Independent Pubs. Group.

Greder, Armin. The City. Greder, Armin. 2010. (ENG.). 32p. (J). (gr. 2). 22.99 (978-1-74237-142-9(6)) Allen & Unwin AUS. Dist: Independent Pubs. Group.

—The Island. Greder, Armin. 2008. Orig. Title: Die Insel. (ENG.). 32p. (J). (gr. 2). 23.95 (978-1-74175-266-3(3)) Allen & Unwin AUS. Dist: Independent Pubs. Group.

Green, Babs Brumer. Take Her Back: An Andy-Bear Tale. 2003. 19p. (J). pap. (978-0-9753119-0-5(5)) ATU Golden Pubns.

Green, Barry. Brain Busting Workout. Lambert, Nat. 2015. (Junior Puzzle Book Ser.). (ENG.). 192p. (J). pap. (978-1-78445-271-1(8)) Top That! Publishing PLC.

Green, Barry. Brain Workout. Lambert, Nat. 2014. (ENG.). 192p. (J). (gr. 4-7). pap. (978-1-78244-829-7(2)) Top That! Publishing PLC.

—Funky Junk: Recycle Rubbish into Art! Kings, Gary & Ginger, Richard. 2012. (Dover Children's Activity Bks.). (ENG.). 64p. (J). (gr. 3-5). pap. 9.99 (978-0-486-49022-9(X)) Dover Pubns., Inc.

—I'm Just a Little Sheep. Graham, Oakley. 2014. (ENG.). 12p. (gr. -1). (978-1-78244-591-3(9)) Top That! Publishing PLC.

—Sneaky Snappy Mr Croc. Thompson, Kate. 2013. (Hand Puppet Bks.). (ENG.). 10p. (gr. -1). (978-1-78244-618-7(4)) Top That! Publishing PLC.

—Sneezy Wheezy Mr Shark. Thompson, Kate. 2013. (Hand Puppet Bks.). (ENG.). 10p. (gr. -1). (978-1-78244-619-4(2)) Top That! Publishing PLC.

Green, Burt. Sweet Dreams for Sydney: A Book to Help Dissipate Nightmares, 1 vol. Wiley, Jean. 2009. 25p. pap. 24.95 (978-1-60703-002-7(0)) America Star Bks.

Green, Dan. How to Draw 101 Animals. Green, Barry. 2004. (How to Draw... Ser.). (ENG.). 48p. (J). pap. (978-1-84229-740-7(6)) Top That! Publishing PLC.

—How to Draw 101 Baby Animals. Green, Barry. 2013. (How to Draw 101 Ser.). (ENG.). 48p. (J). (gr. -1). pap. (978-1-78244-611-8(7)) Top That! Publishing PLC.

—How to Draw 101 Dinosaurs. Green, Barry. 2013. (How to Draw 101 Ser.). (ENG.). 48p. (J). (gr. -1). pap. (978-1-78244-612-5(5)) Top That! Publishing PLC.

—How to Draw 101 Funny People. Green, Barry. 2004. (How to Draw... Ser.). (ENG.). 48p. (J). pap. (978-1-84229-739-1(2)) Top That! Publishing PLC.

—How to Draw 101 Monsters. Green, Barry. 2004. (How to Draw... Ser.). (ENG.). 48p. (J). pap. (978-1-84229-742-1(2)) Top That! Publishing PLC.

—How to Draw 101 Spooky Things. Green, Barry. 2013. (How to Draw 101 Ser.). (ENG.). 48p. (J). (gr. -1). pap. (978-1-78244-613-2(3)) Top That! Publishing PLC.

Green, Donna. Merry Christmas: Best - Loved Stories & Carols. Urmy, Deanne, ed. 2004. 90p. (J). (gr. 4-8). reprint ed. 20.00 (978-0-7567-7580-3(9)) DIANE Publishing Co.

Green, Jackie Fourcade. The Queen & I. McMahon, Bea Prior. 2013. (ENG.). 54p. (YA). pap. 19.95 (978-1-4327-4522-6(0)) Outskirts Pr., Inc.

Green, Jedda Ngwarai, et al. Alyawarr Colouring Book. Kunoth, Mark & Turner, Margaret. Turner, Margaret Petyerr, tr. 2006. (ENG.). 24p. (J). (gr. -1). pap. 6.95 (978-1-86465-074-7(5)) IAD Pr. AUS. Dist: Independent Pubs. Group.

Green, Joey. The Jolly President: Or Letters George W. Bush Never Read. Green, Joey. 2006. (ENG.). 36p. 16.95 (978-0-9772590-1-4(3)) Lunatic Pr.

Green, John. The Call of the Wild. London, Jack. abr. ed. 2011. (Dover Children's Thrift Classics Ser.). (ENG.). 64p. (J). (gr. 3-8). pap. 3.00 (978-0-486-40551-3(6)) Dover Pubns., Inc.

—Scottish Fairy Tales. MacKenzie, Donald A. 2011. (Dover Children's Thrift Classics Ser.). (ENG.). 96p. (J). (gr. 3-8). pap. 4.50 (978-0-486-29900-6(7)) Dover Pubns., Inc.

—Teen Boat! Roman, Dave. 2012. (ENG.). 144p. (J). (gr. 7). 14.99 (978-0-547-63669-6(5)) Houghton Mifflin Harcourt Publishing Co.

—The Three Musketeers. Dumas, Alexandre. abr. ed. 2011. (Dover Children's Thrift Classics Ser.). (ENG.). 96p. (J). (gr. 3-8). pap. 3.00 (978-0-486-28326-5(7)) Dover Pubns., Inc.

—Who Lives on the Farm? 2004. (Who Lives... Ser.). 12p. (J). bds. 4.99 (978-1-85854-647-6(8)) Brimax Books Ltd. GBR. Dist: Byeway Bks.

Green, Jonathan. Amadeus, the Leghorn Rooster. 2004. (J). 17.95 (978-0-87844-174-7(3)) Sandlapper Publishing Co., Inc.

—Father & Son. Lauture, Denize. 2009. (ENG.). 30p. (J). (gr. -1-k). bds. 6.99 (978-0-399-25162-7(6), Philomel) Penguin Publishing Group.

Green, Katie May. Stone Angel. Yolen, Jane. 2015. (ENG.). 40p. (J). (gr. k-3). 16.99 (978-0-399-16741-6(2), Philomel) Penguin Publishing Group.

Green, Katie May. Seen & Not Heard. Green, Katie May. 2015. (ENG.). 32p. (J). (gr. k-3). 15.99 (978-0-7636-7612-4(8)) Candlewick Pr.

Green, Lucyna A. M. Love You Little Brother. 2006. (J). (978-1-58669-186-8(4)); (978-1-58669-185-1(6)) Childcraft Education Corp.

Green, Matthew. A Secret Sydney. Valenzuela, Kristine. 2013. 44p. (J). pap. (978-0-9872061-6-9(8)) DoctorZed Publishing.

Green, Megan. The Cookie Man. Bilbrey, Heather. 2008. 20p. pap. 24.95 (978-1-60703-328-8(3)) America Star Bks.

—Myrtle the Turtle, 1 vol. Paige, Nancy. 2009. 19p. pap. 24.95 (978-1-60836-085-7(7)) America Star Bks.

Green, Noel. The Safe Touch Book. Robinson, Beth. 2013. 20p. (J). mass mkt. 8.99 (978-0-9799092-2-1(8)) Robinson, Beth.

—Where Will I Grow Up? Robinson, Beth. 2013. 20p. (J). mass mkt. 8.99 (978-0-9799092-6-9(0)) Robinson, Beth.

Green, Steve. Bad Dreams Are Not Allowed! Pernell, Pasha. 2013. (ENG.). 30p. pap. 14.99 (978-0-615-82699-8(7)) Pernell, Pasha.

Green, Sue. The Little Bear Who Didn't Want to Hibernate. Richter, Bernd & Richter, Susan. 2003. 42p. pap. 9.95 (978-1-931353-10-6(7)) Saddle Pal Creations, Inc.

Green, Timothy. Mystery of Coyote Canyon. Green, Timothy. 2008. (ENG.). 137p. (gr. 8-12). pap. 12.95 (978-0-941270-83-0(1)) Gibbs Smith, Publisher.

Green, Yuko. The Boy Who Drew Cats & Other Japanese Fairy Tales. Hearn, Lafcadio et al. 2012. (Dover Children's Thrift Classics Ser.). (ENG.). 64p. (J). (gr. 3-8). pap. 2.50 (978-0-486-40348-9(3)) Dover Pubns., Inc.

—Winter Is for Whales: A Book of Hawaiian Seasons. Hirschi, Ron. 2007. (ENG.). 36p. (J). (gr. -1-3). (978-1-59700-504-3(5)) Island Heritage Publishing.

Greenagel, Frank L., photos by. Think Like a Photographer! How to Take Better Pictures Than Anyone in Your Family. 2006. (J). (978-1-59336-766-4(X)) Mondo Publishing.

Greenaway, Frank & Burton, Jane, photos by. Hamster. Rayner, Matthew & BVetMed MRCVS Staff. 2004. (I Am Your Pet Ser.). 32p. (gr. k-4). lib. bdg. 26.00 (978-0-8368-4104-6(2), Gareth Stevens Learning Library) Stevens, Gareth Publishing LLLP.

Greenaway, Frank, jt. photos by see Brightling, Geoff.

Greenaway, Frank, jt. photos by see Burton, Jane.

Greenberg, Melanie Hope. Down in the Subway, 1 vol. Cohen, Miriam. 2003. (ENG.). 32p. (J). (gr. k-3). pap. 6.95 (978-1-932065-24-4(5)); 15.95 (978-1-932065-08-4(3)) Star Bright Bks., Inc.

Greenberg, Nicki. The Naughtiest Reindeer. Greenberg, Nicki. 2014. (ENG.). 32p. (J). (gr. -1-k). 14.99 (978-1-74331-304-6(7)) Allen & Unwin AUS. Dist: Independent Pubs. Group.

Greenblatt, C. H. & Reiss, William. Show Me the Bunny! Banks, Steven. 2004. (Spongebob Squarepants Ser.). 32p. (J). 11.65 (978-0-7569-5643-1(9)) Perfection Learning Corp.

—Show Me the Bunny! Banks, Steven & Hillenburg, Stephen. 2004. (SpongeBob SquarePants Ser.: 3). (ENG.). 32p. (J). pap. 3.99 (978-0-689-86485-8(X), Simon Spotlight/Nickelodeon) Simon Spotlight/Nickelodeon.

Greenburg, Nicki & Greenburg, Nicki. An Octopus Has Deadly Spit. Greenburg, Nicki. 2007. (It's True! Ser.). (ENG.). 96p. (J). (gr. 5-8). pap. 5.95 (978-1-55451-077-1(5), 9781554510771) Annick Pr., Ltd. CAN. Dist: Firefly Bks., Ltd.

Greenburg, Nicki, jt. illus. see Greenburg, Nicki.

Greene, Chad Felix. What's That Thing on Your Head? Greene, Chad Felix. 2010. (ENG.). 26p. pap. 9.99 (978-1-4515-7898-0(9)) CreateSpace Independent Publishing Platform.

Greene, Hamilton. Rin Tin Tin & the Lost Indian. Hill, Monica. 2011. 28p. pap. 35.95 (978-1-258-00567-2(0)) Literary Licensing, LLC.

Greene, Judybeth. Mommy, Open up the Secrets of the World. 2005. (J). pap. 9.95 (978-1-932672-76-3(1)) Outskirts Pr., Inc.

Greene, Kelly Evelyn. Oscar, the Inquisitive Spider. Evans, Barbara Greene. 2013. (ENG.). 45p. (J). pap. 24.95 (978-1-4787-1779-9(3)) Outskirts Pr., Inc.

Greene, Sanford. An Army of Frogs. Pryce, Trevor & Naftali, Joel. 2014. (Kulipari Ser.). (ENG.). 304p. (J). (gr. 3-7). pap. 8.95 (978-1-4197-1381-1(7), Amulet Bks.) Abrams.

—An Army of Frogs: A Kulipari Novel. Pryce, Trevor. 2013. (Kulipari Ser.). (ENG.). 288p. (J). (gr. 3-7). 15.95 (978-1-4197-0172-6(X), Amulet Bks.) Abrams.

—The Rainbow Serpent. Pryce, Trevor & Naftali, Joel. 2014. (Kulipari Ser.). (ENG.). 301p. (J). (gr. 3-7). 15.95 (978-1-4197-1309-5(4), Amulet Bks.) Abrams.

Greene, Sanford & Serra, Alexander. Legion of Super-Heroes in the 31st Century: Tomorrow's Heroes. Torres, J. et al. 2008. (ENG.). 144p. (YA). pap. 14.99 (978-1-4012-1668-9(4), DC Kids) DC Comics.

Greene, Tracy. My Uncle's Wedding. Ross, Eric. 2011. (ENG.). 34p. pap. 10.99 (978-1-4565-3103-4(4)) CreateSpace Independent Publishing Platform.

Greeneish, Susan. Animal Baths: Wild & Wonderful Ways Animals Get Clean! Fielding, Beth. 2009. (ENG.). 48p. (J). (gr. -1-3). 14.95 (978-0-9797455-2-2(7)) EarlyLight Bks., Inc.

—Animal Eggs: An Amazing Clutch of Mysteries & Marvels. Cusick, Dawn & O'Sullivan, Joanne. (ENG.). 48p. (J). (gr. -1-3). 2012. pap. 8.95 (978-0-9832014-9-6(8)); 2011. 14.95 (978-0-9797455-3-9(5)) EarlyLight Bks., Inc.

Greenes, Shimra. My Twin Brother. Kleiman, Deanna M. 2012. 24p. pap. 9.13 (978-0-615-35370-8(3)) TwinsBooks.

Greene's 29 after school art students, K. Lemurs! Marino, Angie. 2013. 46p. pap. 11.99 (978-0-9892732-0-6(2)) Illustrate to Educate.

Greenfelder, Jill. A Ride on the Monster's Back. Bogel, Rachel Anne. 2008. 28p. pap. 15.99 (978-1-59858-752-4(8)) Dog Ear Publishing, LLC.

Greengaard, Alex. Itty Bitty Birdie. Lister, Tresina. 2006. 20p. (J). per. 12.95 (978-0-9791171-0-7(0)) Lister, Tresina.

Greenhalgh, Rachel. A Is for Anteater! Cook, Bob. 2011. 36p. pap. 24.95 (978-1-4626-4035-5(4)) America Star Bks.

Greenhead, Bill. A-Hunting We Will Go. Fuerst, Jeffrey B. 2010. (Rising Readers Ser.). (J). 3.49 (978-1-60719-684-6(0)) Newmark Learning LLC.

—Androcles & the Lion: Classic Tales Series. Adams, Alison. 2011. (Classic Tales Ser.). (J). (978-1-936258-60-4(9)) Benchmark Education Co.

—Bingo. Fuerst, Jeffrey B. 2010. (Rising Readers Ser.). (J). 3.49 (978-1-60719-687-7(5)) Newmark Learning LLC.

—Bingo, Come Home! Fuerst, Jeffrey B. 2009. (Reader's Theater Nursery Rhymes & Songs Set B Ser.). 48p. (J). pap. (978-1-60859-151-0(4)) Benchmark Education Co.

—Brer Rabbit Hears a Noise: Classic Tales Series. Adams, Alison. 2011. (Classic Tales Ser.). (J). (978-1-936258-64-2(1)) Benchmark Education Co.

—Chuck, Woodchuck, Chuck! Fuerst, Jeffrey B. 2009. (Reader's Theater Nursery Rhymes & Songs Set B Ser.). 48p. (J). pap. (978-1-60859-152-7(2)) Benchmark Education Co.

—Cinderella: Classic Tales Edition. Smith, Carrie. 2011. (Classic Tales Ser.). (J). (978-1-936258-77-2(3)) Benchmark Education Co.

—The Crow & the Pitcher: Classic Tales Series. Smith, Carrie. 2011. (Classic Tales Ser.). (J). (978-1-936258-73-4(0)) Benchmark Education Co.

—Goldilocks & the Three Bears: Classic Tales Edition. Smith, Carrie. 2011. (Classic Tales Ser.). (J). (978-1-936258-61-1(7)) Benchmark Education Co.

—How the Turtle Cracked Its Shell: Classic Tales Edition. Adams, Alison. 2011. (Classic Tales Ser.). (J). (978-1-936258-58-1(7)) Benchmark Education Co.

—The Lion & the Rabbit: Classic Tales Edition. Smith, Carrie. 2011. (Classic Tales Ser.). (J). (978-1-936258-65-9(X)) Benchmark Education Co.

—Old MacDonald. Fuerst, Jeffrey B. 2010. (Rising Readers Ser.). (J). 3.49 (978-1-60719-694-5(8)) Newmark Learning LLC.

—The Old Woman Who Lived in a Shoe. Fuerst, Jeffrey B. 2010. (Rising Readers Ser.). (J). 3.49 (978-1-60719-703-4(0)) Newmark Learning LLC.

—Peter Pumpkin Eater. Fuerst, Jeffrey B. 2010. (Rising Readers Ser.). (J). 3.49 (978-1-60719-705-8(7)) Newmark Learning LLC.

—Peter Pumpkin Eater Loses His Appetite. Fuerst, Jeffrey B. 2009. (Reader's Theater Nursery Rhymes & Songs Set B Ser.). 48p. (J). pap. (978-1-60859-164-0(6)) Benchmark Education Co.

—The Three Little Pigs: Classic Tales Edition. Adams, Alison. 2011. (Classic Tales Ser.). (J). (978-1-936258-71-0(4)) Benchmark Education Co.

—Why Mosquitoes Buzz in People's Ears: Classic Tales Edition. Adams, Alison. 2011. (Classic Tales Ser.). (J). (978-1-936258-69-7(2)) Benchmark Education Co.

—The Woman Who Lived in a Shoe. Fuerst, Jeffrey B. 2009. (Reader's Theater Nursery Rhymes & Songs Set B Ser.). 48p. (J). pap. (978-1-60859-172-5(7)) Benchmark Education Co.

Greenleaf, Lisa. Women of the Constitution State: 25 Connecticut Women You Should Know. Mayr, Diane & Sisters, Write. 2012. 136p. (J). pap. 16.00 (978-0-9842549-1-0(9)) Apprentice Shop Bks., LLC.

—Women of the Granite State: 25 New Hampshire Women You Should Know. Buell, Janet & Sisters, Write. 2012. 136p. (J). pap. 16.00 (978-0-9842549-8-9(6)) Apprentice Shop Bks., LLC.

—Women of the Green Mountain State: 25 Vermont Women You Should Know. Lyman Schremmer, Patty. 2012. 136p. (J). pap. 16.00 (978-0-9842549-5-8(1)) Apprentice Shop Bks., LLC.

—Women of the Ocean State: 25 Rhode Island Women You Should Know. Brennan, Linda Crotta. 2012. 136p. (J). pap. 16.00 (978-0-9842549-7-2(8)) Apprentice Shop Bks., LLC.

—Women of the Pine Tree State: 25 Maine Women You Should Know. Murphy, Andrea & Ray, Joyce. 2012. 136p. (J). pap. 16.00 (978-0-9842549-6-5(X)) Apprentice Shop Bks., LLC.

—Women of the Prairie State: 25 Illinois Women You Should Know. Darragh, Marty & Pitkin, Jo. 2012. 136p. (J). pap. 16.00 (978-0-9842549-2-7(7)) Apprentice Shop Bks., LLC.

Greenlee, Carolyn Wing. Speaking for Fire. BlueWolf, James Don. 2007. (ENG.). 44p. (gr. 2-7). per. 12.95 (978-1-887400-31-2(1)) Earthen Vessel Production, Inc.

Greenseid, Diane. And Then It Rained ... And Then the Sun Came Out... Dragonwagon, Crescent. 2014. (ENG.). 40p. (J). (gr. -1-3). 19.99 (978-1-4814-2529-2(3), Atheneum Bks. for Young Readers) Simon & Schuster Children's Publishing.

—Barn Storm. Ghigna, Charles & Ghigna, Debra. 2010. (Step into Reading Ser.). (ENG.). 32p. (J). (gr. -1-1). pap. 3.99 (978-0-375-86114-7(9)); lib. bdg. 12.99 (978-0-375-96114-4(3)) Random Hse., Inc.

—Waynetta & the Cornstalk: A Texas Fairy Tale. Ketteman, Helen. 2012. (J). (978-1-61913-152-1(8)) Weigl Pubs., Inc.

—Waynetta & the Cornstalk: A Texas Fairy Tale. Ketteman, Helen. 2012. (ENG.). 32p. (J). (gr. -1-2). pap. 7.99 (978-0-8075-8688-4(9)) Whitman, Albert & Co.

Greenstein, Elaine. The Mitten Tree. Christiansen, Candace. (ENG.). 32p. 2009. (J). (gr. -1-1). pap. 10.95 (978-1-55591-733-3(X)); 2008. pap. 7.95 (978-1-55591-698-5(8)) Fulcrum Publishing.

Greenstein, Susan. A Big Quiet House: A Yiddish Folktale from Eastern Europe. Forest, Heather. 2005. (ENG.). 32p. (J). (gr. k-3). 15.95 (978-0-87483-462-8(7)) August Hse. Pubs., Inc.

—Earthquakes. Prager, Ellen J. 2007. (Jump into Science Ser.). (ENG.). 32p. (J). (gr. -1-3). per. 6.95 (978-1-4263-0090-5(5), National Geographic Children's Bks.) National Geographic Society.

Greenwalt, Mary. Franz Schubert & his Merry Friends. Wheeler, Opal & Deucher, Sybil. 2008. 128p. (J). pap. 13.95 (978-1-933573-13-7(9)) Zeezok Publishing, LLC.

—Handel: at the Court of Kings. Wheeler, Opal. 2006. 166p. per. 13.95 (978-1-933573-03-8(1), 4481) Zeezok Publishing, LLC.

—Joseph Haydn: the Merry Little Peasant. Wheeler, Opal & Deucher, Sybil. 2005. 118p. per. 13.95 (978-1-933573-00-7(7)) Zeezok Publishing, LLC.

—Ludwig Beethoven & the Chiming Tower Bells. Wheeler, Opal. 2005. 166p. per. 13.95 (978-0-9746505-6-2(0)) Zeezok Publishing, LLC.

—Mozart the Wonder Boy. Wheeler, Opal & Deucher, Sybil. 2005. 127p. per. 13.95 (978-0-9746505-3-1(6), 4355) Zeezok Publishing, LLC.

—Sebastian Bach: the Boy from Thuringia. Wheeler, Opal & Deucher, Sybil. l.t. ed. 2005. 126p. per. 13.95 (978-0-9746505-1-7(X), 4354) Zeezok Publishing, LLC.

Greenwood, Marion. Ho Fills the Rice Barrel. Sherer, Mary (Huston). 2012. 128p. 40.95 (978-1-258-25056-0(X)); pap. 25.95 (978-1-258-25732-3(7)) Literary Licensing, LLC.

Greer, Ana. Jules the Lighthouse Dog, 1. Custard, P. T. 2006. (ENG.). 32p. (J). 12.95 (978-0-9785317-0-6(1)) Black Plum Bks.

Greer, Tica. The Lighthouse Summer. Greer, Hannah. 2009. 156p. pap. 24.95 (978-1-60813-493-9(8)) America Star Bks.

Gregeory, Vicki. There's Nothing Wrong with Boys. Stratton, Erin. 2010. 26p. pap. 12.00 (978-1-60911-021-5(8), Eloquent Bks.) Strategic Book Publishing & Rights Agency (SBPRA).

Gregg, Anna, photos by. Glimpse. Williams, Carol Lynch & Gregg, L. B. 2012. (ENG.). 512p. (YA). (gr. 9). pap. 9.99 (978-1-4169-9731-3(8), Simon & Schuster/Paula Wiseman Bks.) Simon & Schuster/Paula Wiseman Bks.

Gregoire, Fabian. Los Ninos de la Mina. Gregoire, Fabian. Malagarriga, Carlos Fanlo, tr. 2006. (SPA.). 45p. (J). (978-84-8470-234-4(0)) Corimbo, Editorial S.L.

Gregor, Terril. Kids from Critter Cove. Dodson, Merilee. 2007. 48p. per. 24.95 (978-1-4137-2644-2(5)) America Star Bks.

Gregori, Anthony. Meet the Itsits. l.t. ed. 2007. 40p. (J). lib. bdg. 9.99 (978-0-9769360-1-5(1)) Adam Hill Pubns.

Gregorio, Giuliana. Counting Rhymes. Brooks, Felicity. 2010. (Look & Say Board Bks). 12p. (J). bds. 8.99 (978-0-7945-2779-2(5), Usborne) EDC Publishing.

—Finger Rhymes. Brooks, Felicity. 2010. (Rhyming Look & Say Ser.). 12p. (J). bds. 8.99 (978-0-7945-2780-8(9), Usborne) EDC Publishing.

Gregory, Dorothy Lake. Jerry & Jean Detectors. Judson, Clara Ingram. 2007. (ENG.). 116p. (J). (gr. 4-7). 34.95 (978-0-548-03300-5(5)) Kessinger Publishing, LLC.

Gregory, Fran. The Return of Gabriel. Armistead, John. 2004. 218p. (gr. 3-8). 17.45 (978-0-7569-3460-6(5)) Perfection Learning Corp.

Gregory, Jenny. Labrador on the Lawn. Baglio, Ben M. & Daniels, Lucy. 2005. (Animal Ark Hauntings Ser.: No. 38). (ENG.). 144p. (J). (gr. 2-5). 3.99 (978-0-439-68488-0(9)) Scholastic, Inc.

Gregory, Jenny, jt. illus. see Baum, Ann.

Gregory, Sally. The Strange Umbrella: And Other Stories. Blyton, Enid. 2013. (ENG.). 192p. (J). 9.95 (978-1-84135-461-3(9)) Award Pubns. Ltd. GBR. Dist: Parkwest Pubns., Inc.

Grejniec, Michael. Buenos Dias, Buenas Noches/Good Morning, Good Night. Grejniec, Michael. Alejandro, Alis, tr. from ENG. 2007. (ENG & SPA.). 32p. (J). (gr. -1-3). pap. 7.95 (978-0-7358-2110-1(0)) North-South Bks., Inc.

—A Taste of the Moon. Grejniec, Michael. Bright Connections Media. 2013. (ENG.). 32p. (J). (gr. -1-k). 15.95 (978-1-62267-024-6(8)) Bright Connections Media.

—What Do You Like? Grejniec, Michael. 2008. (ENG.). 12p. (J). (gr. -1-k). 5.95 (978-0-7358-2214-6(X)) North-South Bks., Inc.

Gremillion, Barry. Finding Rover. Allberti, Frances C. 2006. (J). per. (978-0-9785937-1-1(5)) Open Pages Publishing.

Grenier, Daniel. The World of Penguins. Daigle, Evelyne. Wright, Genevieve, tr. from FRE. 2007. (ENG.). 48p. (J). (gr. 4-7). 18.95 (978-0-88776-799-9(0)) Tundra Bks. CAN. Dist: Random Hse., Inc.

—The World of Penguins. Daigle, Evelyne. Wright, Genevieve, tr. from FRE. 2008. (ENG.). 48p. (J). (gr. 4-7). pap. 12.95 (978-0-88776-947-4(0)) Tundra Bks. CAN. Dist: Random Hse., Inc.

Grepo, Sarah. All the Things You'll Do! Glavin, Kevin. 2012. 80p. 17.95 (978-0-9825466-3-5(7)) Glavin, Kevin.

Gresham, Delia. The Little Brick House. Lael, Anita. 2012. 32p. pap. 24.95 (978-1-4626-9374-0(1)); 30p. 24.95 (978-1-4626-5972-2(1)) America Star Bks.

Greste, Peter. Owen & Mzee: The True Story of a Remarkable Friendship. Hatkoff, Craig et al. 2006. (Owen & Mzee Ser.). (ENG.). 40p. (J). (gr. -1-3). 16.99 (978-0-439-82973-1(9), Scholastic Pr.) Scholastic, Inc.

Greste, Peter, photos by. Owen & Mzee: The Language of Friendship. Hatkoff, Craig et al. 2007. (Owen & Mzee Ser.). (ENG., 40p. (J). (gr. -1-3). 16.99 (978-0-439-89959-8(1), Scholastic Pr.) Scholastic, Inc.

Gretta, J. Clemens. Flying Blackbirds. Burtis, Thomson. 2011. 256p. 47.95 (978-1-258-07554-5(7)) Literary Licensing, LLC.

Gretter, J. Clemens. The Hidden Harbor Mystery, No. 14. Dixon, Franklin W. 2003. (Hardy Boys (Hardcover) Ser.). (ENG.). 228p. (J). (gr. 4-7). 14.95 (978-1-55709-272-4(9)) Applewood Bks.

Gretzer, John. A Touch of Magic. Cavanna, Betty. 2011. 188p. 42.95 (978-1-258-07218-6(1)) Literary Licensing, LLC.

Greve, Hannah K. Move over! Princess Coming Through!, 1 vol. McCusker, Tammy. 2009. 34p. pap. 24.95 (978-1-60749-803-2(0)) America Star Bks.

Greven, Doris. An Unusual Family: A Romani Folktale. Sijercic, Hedina. 2009. 28p. pap. (978-0-9781707-7-6(6)) Magoria Bks.

Grey, Ada. I Love You Just the Way You Are. Salzano, Tammi. 2014. 32p. (J). (gr. -1-3). 16.99 (978-1-58925-161-8(X)) Tiger Tales.

Grey, Andrew. A Rose for My Mother: A Memoir. Canfield, Nancy Lee. 2010. (ENG.). 300p. pap. 21.95 *(978-1-4502-3123-7(3))* iUniverse, Inc.
Grey, Erika. The Alphabet Bears: Spook-Tales Collection. Grey, Erika. 2010. 127p. (YA). pap. 24.95 *(978-0-9790199-3-7(1))* PeDante Pr.
Grey, Mini. The Twin Giants. King-Smith, Dick. 2008. (ENG.). 80p. (J). (gr. 1-4). 16.99 *(978-0-7636-3529-9(4))* Candlewick Pr.
Grey, Mini. Into the Woods. Grey, Mini. Gardner, Lyn. 2009. (ENG.). 448p. (J). (gr. 3-7). 8.99 *(978-0-440-42223-5(X),* Yearling) Random Hse. Children's Bks.
Gribbon, Sean & Jael. A Little Princess: With a Discussion of Generosity. Burnett, Frances Hodgson. Gribbon, Sean & Jael, trs. 2003. (Values in Action Illustrated Classics Ser.). (J). *(978-1-59203-050-7(5))* Learning Challenge, Inc.
Gribel, Christiane & Orlando. No Voy a Dormir/I Am Not Going to Sleep. Gribel, Christiane & Orlando. 2009. (ENG & SPA.). 40p. (J). (gr. -1-1). pap. 7.99 *(978-1-933032-51-1(0))* Lectorum Pubns., Inc.
Grice Lynch, Linda. Thank You God for My Body. Grice Neely, Edwina. 2010. (ENG.). 38p. pap. 15.99 *(978-1-4392-6062-3(1))* CreateSpace Independent Publishing Platform.
Grieb, Wendy. Monster Needs a Christmas Tree. Czajak, Paul. 2014. (Monster & Me Ser.). (ENG.). 32p. (J). (-k). 16.95 *(978-1-938063-46-6(5),* Mighty Media Kids) Mighty Media Pr.
—Monster Needs a Costume. Czajak, Paul. (Monster & Me Ser.). (ENG.). 32p. (J). (-k). 2014. 6.99 *(978-1-938063-38-1(4));* 2013. 16.95 *(978-1-938063-09-1(0))* Mighty Media Pr. (Mighty Media Kids).
—Monster Needs a Party. Czajak, Paul. 2015. (Monster & Me Ser.). (ENG.). 32p. (J). (-k). 16.95 *(978-1-938063-55-8(4),* Mighty Media Kids) Mighty Media Pr.
—Monster Needs His Sleep. Czajak, Paul. 2014. (Monster & Me Ser.). (ENG.). 32p. (J). (-k). 16.95 *(978-1-938063-26-8(0),* Mighty Media Kids) Mighty Media Pr.
Grieb, Wendy. Monster Needs Your Vote. Czajak, Paul. 2015. (Monster & Me Ser.). (ENG.). 32p. (J). (gr. -1-k). 16.95 ***(978-1-938063-63-3(5),*** Mighty Media Kids) Mighty Media Pr.
Griegg, Linda. Do Touch: Instant, Easy, Hands-on Learning Experiences for Young Children. Gilbert, LaBritta. Charner, Kathleen, ed. 2004. 225p. (gr. -1-k). pap. 19.95 *(978-0-87659-118-5(7),* 10010) Gryphon Hse., Inc.
Griego, Tony. AddUps Fun for All Seasons! Tuchman, Gail & Gray, Margaret. 2012. (Dover Little Activity Bks.). (ENG.). 32p. (J). (gr. -1-2). pap. 1.50 *(978-0-486-49860-7(3))* Dover Pubns., Inc.
—AddUps Going Places! Tuchman, Gail & Gray, Margaret. 2012. (Dover Little Activity Bks.). (ENG.). 32p. (J). (gr. -1-2). pap. 1.50 *(978-0-486-49861-4(1))* Dover Pubns., Inc.
—AddUps My Day! Tuchman, Gail & Gray, Margaret. 2012. (Dover Little Activity Bks.). (ENG.). 32p. (J). (gr. -1-2). pap. 1.50 *(978-0-486-49862-1(X))* Dover Pubns., Inc.
—AddUps Things That Go! Tuchman, Gail & Gray, Margaret. 2012. (Dover Little Activity Bks.). (ENG.). 32p. (J). (gr. -1-2). pap. 1.50 *(978-0-486-49859-1(X))* Dover Pubns., Inc.
Grier, Gary. Don't Hit Me! Scholastic, Inc. Staff et al. 2004. (Just for You Ser.). (ENG.). 32p. (gr. k-1). pap. 3.99 *(978-0-439-56860-9(9),* Teaching Resources) Scholastic, Inc.
Grier, Geoffrey. The Shaman's Revenge: Based on the Arctic Diaries of Vilhjalmur Stefansson. Stefansson, Vilhjalmur & Irwin, Violet. 2011. 306p. 48.95 *(978-1-258-05790-9(5))* Literary Licensing, LLC.
Grier, Laura. Flower Girl, 0 vols. Grier, Laura, photos by. Bottner, Barbara. 2012. (ENG.). 32p. (J). (gr. k-3). 16.99 *(978-0-7614-6119-7(1),* 9780761461197, Amazon Children's Publishing) Amazon Publishing.
Grieve, Walter G., jt. illus. see Noble, Edwin.
Grifalconi, Ann. Julio's Magic. Dorros, Arthur. 2005. (ENG.). 32p. (J). (gr. -1-4). 15.99 *(978-0-06-029004-7(8))* HarperCollins Pubs.
—Lubuto Means Light. Williams, Karen Lynn. 2010. (ENG.). 32p. 16.95 *(978-1-59078-716-8(1))* Boyds Mills Pr.
—Patrol: An American Soldier in Vietnam. Myers, Walter Dean. 2005. (ENG.). 40p. (J). (gr. 3-7). pap. 6.99 *(978-0-06-073159-5(1))* HarperCollins Pubs.
Griff. Lilac Peabody & Honeysuckle Hope, No. 4. Dalton, Annie. 2005. (Roaring Good Reads Ser.). (ENG.). 96p. (J). (gr. 2-4). pap. 7.95 *(978-0-00-713774-9(5))* HarperCollins Pubs. Ltd. GBR. Dist: Independent Pubs. Group.
Griffeth, Bunny. Heal of the Hand. Latimer, Kiki. 2012. 44p. (J). pap. 19.50 *(978-1-58432-851-3(7))* Educa Vision.
Griffin, Cheri. Snicker & Snore, 1 vol. Batton, Doris. 2010. 40p. pap. 24.95 *(978-1-4489-6113-9(0))* PublishAmerica, Inc.
Griffin, Don. The Great Pigeon Race. Gail, Ginnie. 2008. 28p. per. 24.95 *(978-1-4241-9457-5(1))* America Star Bks.
Griffin, Georgene. Dinosaurs, Meat-Eaters. 2004. (J). *(978-1-59203-086-6(6))* Learning Challenge, Inc.
—Endangered Mammals. 2004. (J). *(978-1-59203-089-7(0))* Learning Challenge, Inc.
Griffin, Georgene & Jael. Cool Wheels. 2004. (J). *(978-1-59203-087-3(4))* Learning Challenge, Inc.
Griffin, Georgene, jt. illus. see McKee, Karen.
Griffin, Hedley. How to Draw 101 Super Heroes. Top That!, ed. 2005. (ENG.). 48p. (J). per. *(978-1-84510-738-3(1))* Top That! Publishing PLC.
Griffin, Jason. My Name Is Jason. Mine Too: Our Story. Our Way. Griffin, Jason. Reynolds, Jason. 2009. (ENG.). 96p. (J). (gr. 8-18). pap. 12.99 *(978-0-06-154788-1(3),* HarperTeen) HarperCollins Pubs.
Griffin, Jim. Legend of the Christmas Stocking: An Inspirational Story of a Wish Come True, 1 vol. Osborne, Rick. 2004. (ENG.). 32p. (J). 17.99 *(978-0-310-70898-8(2))* Zonderkidz.
Griffin, Lisa M. The Garden in My Mind: Growing Through Positive Choices. McCumbee, Stephie. 2014. 40p. (J). pap. 12.95 *(978-1-934490-54-9(7))* Boys Town Pr.
—The Garden in My Mind Activity Guide: Lessons for Social Skill & Common Core Development. McCumbee, Stephie. 2014. 48p. pap. 20.95 *(978-1-934490-55-6(5))* Boys Town Pr.
Griffin, Lisa M. Spacing Out: Discovering the Importance of Completing Tasks. McCumbee, Stephie. 2015. 32p. (J). pap. 10.95 ***(978-1-934490-77-8(6))*** Boys Town Pr.
Griffin, Marlin. Bucky's Adventures. Cox Gray, Marjorie. 2008. 100p. pap. 28.99 *(978-1-4389-2645-2(6))* AuthorHouse.
Griffin, Paul. Abc, Adoption & Me. Swift, Gayle H. & Swift, Casey Anne. 2013. 36p. pap. 13.99 *(978-0-9856762-8-5(0))* WRB Pub.
Griffin, Rachel. African Tales. Mhlophe, Gcina. 2009. (ENG.). 96p. (J). (gr. 2-9). 19.99 *(978-1-84686-118-5(7))* Barefoot Bks., Inc.
—Celebration Gift Wrap. (J). 4.99 *(978-1-84148-985-8(9))* Barefoot Bks., Inc.
—The Fabrics of Fairytale: Stories Spun from Far & Wide. Batt, Tanya Robyn. 2007. (ENG.). 80p. (J). (gr. -1-3). pap. 16.99 *(978-1-84686-089-8(X))* Barefoot Bks., Inc.
Griffin-Scott, Janet & Sanderson, Ruth. Elska. Hapka, Catherine & Hapka, Cathy. 2009. (Horse Diaries: No. 1). (ENG.). 144p. (J). (gr. 3-7). pap. 5.99 *(978-0-375-84732-5(4),* Random Hse. Bks. for Young Readers) Random Hse. Children's Bks.
Griffith, Andrew. Transformers: Movie Prequel: Foundation: Vol 1: Dark of the Moon. 2012. (Transformers: Dark of the Moon Movie Prequel Ser.). 24p. (J). 24.21 *(978-1-59961-971-2(7),* Graphic Novels) Spotlight.
—Transformers: Movie Prequel: Foundation: Vol 2. 2012. (Transformers: Dark of the Moon Movie Prequel Ser.). 24p. (J). 24.21 *(978-1-59961-972-9(5),* Graphic Novels) Spotlight.
—Transformers: Movie Prequel: Foundation: Vol 3. 2012. (Transformers: Dark of the Moon Movie Prequel Ser.). 24p. (J). 24.21 *(978-1-59961-973-6(3),* Graphic Novels) Spotlight.
—Transformers: Movie Prequel: Foundation: Vol 4. 2012. (Transformers: Dark of the Moon Movie Prequel Ser.). 24p. (J). 24.21 *(978-1-59961-974-3(1),* Graphic Novels) Spotlight.
Griffith, Gershom. The Boston Tea Party, 1 vol. Mortensen, Lori. 2010. (Our American Story Ser.). (ENG.). 32p. (gr. 1-3). lib. bdg. 26.65 *(978-1-4048-5538-0(6),* Nonfiction Picture Bks.) Picture Window Bks.
—Let's Celebrate Martin Luther King, Jr. Day. DeRubertis, Barbara. 2013. (Holidays & Heroes Ser.). 32p. (gr. 1-3). pap. 7.95 *(978-1-57565-638-0(8))* Kane Pr., Inc.
—Let's Celebrate Martin Luther King, Jr. Day. deRubertis, Barbara. 2014. (Holidays & Heroes Ser.). 32p. (gr. 1-3). lib. bdg. 25.26 *(978-1-57565-724-0(4))* Kane Pr., Inc.
—Let's Celebrate Presidents' Day: George Washington & Abraham Lincoln. DeRubertis, Barbara. 2014. (Holidays & Heroes Ser.). 32p. (J). (gr. 1-3). pap. 7.95 *(978-1-57565-649-6(3))* Kane Pr., Inc.
—Rosa Parks: Freedom Rider. Brandt, Keith & Mattern, Joanne. 2006. 54p. (J). pap. *(978-0-439-66045-7(9))* Scholastic, Inc.
Griffith, Indigo, jt. photos by see Bilik-Franklin, MidiAna.
Griffith, John Anthony. The Scientific Golfer: Improving Your Golf Game Through Baselining. 1. Griffith, John Anthony, photos by. 2004. 150p. 39.95 *(978-0-9759331-0-7(8))* Rosetta Stone Communications.
Griffith, Linda Hill. Best Ever Ring Bearer. 2010. (ENG.). 24p. 10.99 *(978-1-4022-3818-5(5))* Sourcebooks, Inc.
—Most Special Flower Girl. 2010. (ENG.). 24p. 10.99 *(978-1-4022-3817-8(7))* Sourcebooks, Inc.
Griffiths, Dean. The Big Tree Gang, 1 vol. Bogart, Jo Ellen. 2005. (Orca Echoes Ser.). (ENG.). 64p. (J). (gr. 2-3). per. 6.95 *(978-1-55143-345-5(1))* Orca Bk. Pubs. USA.
—The Big Tree Gang. Bogart, Jo Ellen. 2005. 60p. (J). lib. bdg. 20.00 *(978-1-4242-1251-4(0))* Fitzgerald Bks.
—La Course-Poursuite des Loups Gris, 1 vol. Brouwer, Sigmund & Gingras, Gaston. 2011. (Loups Gris Ser.). (FRE.). 72p. (J). (gr. 2-3). pap. 6.95 *(978-1-4598-0009-0(5))* Orca Bk. Pubs. USA.
—Le Défi des Loups Gris, 1 vol. Brouwer, Sigmund & Gingras, Gaston. 2011. (Loups Gris Ser.). (FRE.). 72p. (J). (gr. 2-3). pap. 6.95 *(978-1-55469-812-7(X))* Orca Bk. Pubs. USA.
—Les Loups Gris à la Chasse, 1 vol. Brouwer, Sigmund & Gingras, Gaston. 2011. (Loups Gris Ser.). Tr. of Timberwolf Hunt. (FRE.). 72p. (J). (gr. 2-3). pap. 6.95 *(978-1-55469-814-1(6))* Orca Bk. Pubs. USA.
—Maggie Can't Wait, 1 vol. Wishinsky, Frieda. 2009. (ENG.). 32p. (J). (gr. k-3). 17.95 *(978-1-55455-103-3(X),* 155455103X) Fitzhenry & Whiteside, Ltd. CAN. Dist: Midpoint Trade Bks., Inc.
—Only a Cow, 1 vol. Hamilton, Arlene. (ENG.). 32p. (J). (gr. -1-3). 2008. pap. *(978-1-55455-088-3(2));* 2006. *(978-1-55041-871-2(8))* Fitzhenry & Whiteside, Ltd.
—Out & about with the Big Tree Gang, 1 vol. Bogart, Jo Ellen & Bogart, Jill. 2006. (Orca Echoes Ser.). (ENG.). 64p. (J). (gr. 2-3). per. 4.99 *(978-1-55143-603-6(5))* Orca Bk. Pubs. USA.
—Perfect Man, 1 vol. Wilson, Troy. 2005. (ENG.). 32p. (J). (gr. -1-3). per. 9.95 *(978-1-55143-435-3(0))* Orca Bk. Pubs. USA.
—La Revanche des Loups Gris, 1 vol. Brouwer, Sigmund & Gingras, Gaston. 2011. (Loups Gris Ser.). (FRE.). 72p. (J). (gr. 2-3). pap. 6.95 *(978-1-4598-0011-3(7))* Orca Bk. Pubs. USA.
—That's Hockey, 1 vol. Bouchard, David. 2004. (ENG.). 32p. (J). (gr. -1-3). 9.95 *(978-1-55143-348-6(6))* Orca Bk. Pubs. USA.
—Timberwolf Challenge, 1 vol. Brouwer, Sigmund. 2008. (Orca Echoes Ser.). (ENG.). 64p. (J). (gr. 2-3). pap. 6.95 *(978-1-55143-730-9(9))* Orca Bk. Pubs. USA.
—Timberwolf Chase, 1 vol. Brouwer, Sigmund. 2006. (Orca Echoes Ser.). (ENG.). 64p. (J). (gr. 2-3). per. 6.95 *(978-1-55143-548-0(9))* Orca Bk. Pubs. USA.
—Timberwolf Hunt, 1 vol. Brouwer, Sigmund. 2007. (Orca Echoes Ser.). (ENG.). 64p. (J). (gr. 2-3). per. 6.95 *(978-1-55143-726-2(0))* Orca Bk. Pubs. USA.
—Timberwolf Revenge, 1 vol. Brouwer, Sigmund. 2006. (Orca Echoes Ser.). (ENG.). 64p. (J). (gr. 2-3). per. 6.95 *(978-1-55143-544-2(6))* Orca Bk. Pubs. USA.
—Timberwolf Trap, 1 vol. Brouwer, Sigmund. 2007. (Orca Echoes Ser.). (ENG.). 64p. (J). (gr. 2-3). per. 6.95 *(978-1-55143-722-4(8))* Orca Bk. Pubs. USA.
—When Emily Carr Met Woo, 1 vol. Kulling, Monica. 2014. (ENG.). 32p. (J). (gr. k-4). 17.95 *(978-1-927485-40-8(1))* Pajama Pr. CAN. Dist: Ingram Pub. Services.
Griffiths, Dean & Owlkids Books Inc. Staff. Beware, Pirates! Wishinsky, Frieda. 2007. (Canadian Flyer Adventures Ser.: 1). (ENG.). 96p. (J). (gr. 1-4). pap. 7.95 *(978-1-897066-81-2(2),* Maple Tree Pr.) Owlkids Bks. Inc. CAN. Dist: Perseus-PGW.
—Crazy for Gold. Wishinsky, Frieda. 2007. (Canadian Flyer Adventures Ser.: 3). (ENG.). 96p. (J). (gr. 1-4). per. 7.95 *(978-1-897066-93-5(7),* Maple Tree Pr.) Owlkids Bks. Inc. CAN. Dist: Perseus-PGW.
—Danger, Dinosaurs! Wishinsky, Frieda. 2007. (Canadian Flyer Adventures Ser.: 2). (ENG.). 96p. (J). (gr. 1-4). pap. 7.95 *(978-1-897066-82-9(1),* Maple Tree Pr.) Owlkids Bks. Inc. CAN. Dist: Perseus-PGW.
—Flying High! Wishinsky, Frieda. 2007. (Canadian Flyer Adventures Ser.: 5). (ENG.). 96p. (J). (gr. 1-4). per. 7.95 *(978-1-897066-99-7(6),* Maple Tree Pr.) Owlkids Bks. Inc. CAN. Dist: Perseus-PGW.
—Hurry, Freedom. Wishinsky, Frieda. 2008. (Canadian Flyer Adventures Ser.: 7). (ENG.). 96p. (J). (gr. 1-4). per. 9.95 *(978-1-897349-15-1(7),* Maple Tree Pr.) Owlkids Bks. Inc. CAN. Dist: Perseus-PGW.
—Pioneer Kids. Wishinsky, Frieda. 2007. (Canadian Flyer Adventures Ser.: 6). (ENG.). 96p. (J). (gr. 1-4). per. 9.95 *(978-1-897349-05-2(X),* Maple Tree Pr.) Owlkids Bks. Inc. CAN. Dist: Perseus-PGW.
—A Whale Tale. Wishinsky, Frieda. 2008. (Canadian Flyer Adventures Ser.: 8). (ENG.). 96p. (J). (gr. 1-4). pap. 7.95 *(978-1-897349-17-5(3),* Maple Tree Pr.) Owlkids Bks. Inc. CAN. Dist: Perseus-PGW.
—Yikes, Vikings! Wishinsky, Frieda. 2007. (Canadian Flyer Adventures Ser.: 4). (ENG.). 96p. (J). (gr. 1-4). per. 7.95 *(978-1-897066-97-3(X),* Maple Tree Pr.) Owlkids Bks. Inc. CAN. Dist: Perseus-PGW.
Griffiths, Rebecca. Bella's Bubble. Hodgson, Karen J. 2010. (ENG.). 32p. (J). (gr. -1-k). pap. 9.99 ***(978-1-907432-04-0(3))*** Hogs Back Bks. GBR. Dist: Independent Pubs. Group.
Griffo, Daniel. Signing in My World: Sign Language for Kids, 1 vol. Clay, Kathryn. 2013. (Time to Sign Ser.). (ENG.). 32p. (gr. 1-2). 26.65 *(978-1-62065-054-7(1),* Aplus Bks.) Capstone Pr., Inc.
—1-2-3 Va-Va-Vroom! A Counting Book, 0 vols. Lynn, Sarah. 2012. (ENG.). 32p. (J). (gr. -1-3). 16.99 *(978-0-7614-6162-3(0),* 9780761461623, Amazon Children's Publishing) Amazon Publishing.
Griftner, Rebecca. Si Si the Circus Cat. Pruitt, Kat. 2011. (ENG.). 24p. (J). pap. 12.95 *(978-0-9844037-2-1(8))* Pruggus Publishing.
Griggs-Burr, Alexander & Griggs-Burr, Alexander. A Very Small Something. Hickey, David. 2012. (ENG.). 32p. (J). (gr. -1). 15.95 *(978-1-926845-37-1(4))* Biblioasis CAN. Dist: Consortium Bk. Sales & Distribution.
Griggs-Burr, Alexander, jt. illus. see Griggs-Burr, Alexander.
Grill, Gerald. Oh, What a State I'm In: The USA in Rhyme & Riddle, 1 vol. Merrill, Karen Grill. 2010. 48p. pap. 24.95 *(978-1-4489-7979-0(X))* PublishAmerica, Inc.
Grill, William. Shackleton's Journey. 2014. (ENG.). 80p. (J). (gr. -1-2). 24.00 *(978-1-909263-10-9(9))* Flying Eye Bks. GBR. Dist: Consortium Bk. Sales & Distribution.
Grimaldi, Catherine. It's Raining! A Pop-Up Book with Patterns. Grimaldi, Catherine. 2005. (ENG.). 18p. (J). (gr. -1-k). act. bk. ed. 16.99 *(978-1-85707-666-0(4))* Tango Bks. GBR. Dist: Independent Pubs. Group.
Grimard, Gabrielle. The Brave Young Knight, 1 vol. Kingsbury, Karen. 2011. (ENG.). 40p. (J). (gr. -1-2). 15.99 *(978-0-310-71645-7(4))* Zonderkidz.
—La Chasse au Plomb. Pelletier, Maryse. 2004. (Roman Jeunesse Ser.). (FRE.). 96p. (J). (gr. 4-7). pap. *(978-2-89021-692-1(6))* Diffusion du livre Mirabel (DLM).
—The Fabulous World of Mr. Fred, 1 vol. Chartrand, Lili. 2014. (ENG.). 32p. (J). pap. 10.95 *(978-1-55455-346-4(6))* Fitzhenry & Whiteside, Ltd. CAN. Dist: Midpoint Trade Bks., Inc.
—Jesus Gives Us Peace: The Sacrament of Reconciliation. Dumont, Claire & Lacoursiere, Suzanne. Larocque, Gisele, tr. from FRE. 2006. Orig. Title: Conduis Mes Pas Vers la Paix: le Pardon. 48p. pap. 10.95 *(978-0-8198-3984-8(1))* Pauline Bks. & Media.
—Maybe Later, 1 vol. Lee, Ingrid. 2008. (Orca Echoes Ser.). (ENG.). 64p. (J). (gr. 2-3). pap. 6.95 *(978-1-55143-764-4(3))* Orca Bk. Pubs. USA.
—Not My Girl. Jordan-Fenton, Christy & Pokiak-Fenton, Margaret. 2014. (ENG.). 36p. (J). (gr. 1-4). pap. 9.95 *(978-1-55451-624-7(2),* 9781554516247); lib. bdg. 21.95 *(978-1-55451-625-4(0),* 9781554516254) Annick Pr., Ltd. CAN. Dist: Firefly Bks., Ltd.
—The Princess & the Three Knights, 1 vol. Kingsbury, Karen. 2009. (ENG.). 40p. (J). (gr. -1-2). 15.99 *(978-0-310-71641-9(1))* Zondervan.
—Today, Maybe, 1 vol. Demers, Dominique. 2011. (ENG.). 32p. (J). (gr. -1-3). 19.95 *(978-1-55469-400-6(0))* Orca Bk. Pubs. USA.
—When I Was Eight. Jordan-Fenton, Christy & Pokiak-Fenton, Margaret. 2013. (ENG.). 32p. (J). (gr. 1-4). 21.95 *(978-1-55451-491-5(6),* 9781554514915); pap. 9.95 *(978-1-55451-490-8(8),* 9781554514908) Annick Pr., Ltd. CAN. Dist: Firefly Bks., Ltd.
Grimball, Meta. Stories Children Love: a Collection of Stories Arranged for Children. Welsh, Charles, ed. 2007. pap. 36.95 *(978-1-4304-5116-7(5))* Kessinger Publishing, LLC.
Grimes, Cookie. A New Year's Family. Grimes, Cookie. 2007. 32p. (J). (gr. -1-3). 11.99 *(978-1-60247-154-2(1))* Tate Publishing & Enterprises, LLC.
Grimes, Kristopher. Drake the Dragon King. Jones, Brittany. 2013. (ENG.). (J). 14.95 *(978-1-62086-360-2(X))* Mascot Bks., Inc.
Grimly, Gris. Boris & Bella. Crimi, Carolyn. 2006. (ENG.). 32p. (J). (gr. -1-3). reprint ed. pap. 6.00 *(978-0-15-205900-2(8))* Houghton Mifflin Harcourt Publishing Co.
—The Dangerous Alphabet. Gaiman, Neil. (ENG.). 32p. (J). (gr. k). 2010. pap. 6.99 *(978-0-06-078335-8(4));* 2008. 17.99 *(978-0-06-078333-4(8))* HarperCollins Pubs.
—The Death of Yorik Mortwell. Messer, Stephen. 2011. (ENG.). 192p. (J). (gr. 3-7). 18.99 *(978-0-375-96858-7(X))* Random Hse. Children's Bks.
—The Death of Yorik Mortwell. Messer, Stephen. 2012. (ENG.). 192p. (J). (gr. 3-7). 6.99 *(978-0-375-87236-5(1),* Yearling) Random Hse. Children's Bks.
—Edgar Allan Poe's Tales of Death & Dementia. Poe, Edgar Allen. 2009. (ENG.). 144p. (J). (gr. 6-9). 19.99 *(978-1-4169-5025-7(7),* Atheneum Bks. for Young Readers) Simon & Schuster Children's Publishing.
—Edgar Allan Poe's Tales of Mystery & Madness. Poe, Edgar Allen. 2004. (ENG.). 144p. (J). (gr. 5-9). 19.99 *(978-0-689-84837-7(4),* Atheneum Bks. for Young Readers) Simon & Schuster Children's Publishing.
—Grimericks, 0 vols. Pearson, Susan. 2005. (ENG.). 32p. (J). (gr. 1-4). pap. 9.99 *(978-0-7614-5444-1(6),* 9780761454441, Amazon Children's Publishing) Amazon Publishing.
—Gris Grimly's Frankenstein. Shelley, Mary. 2013. (ENG.). 208p. (YA). (gr. 8). 24.99 *(978-0-06-186297-5(5))* HarperCollins Pubs.
—Gris Grimly's Frankenstein. Shelley, Mary. 2015. (ENG.). 208p. (YA). (gr. 8). pap. 16.99 *(978-0-06-186298-4(3))* HarperCollins Pubs.
—Santa Claws. Leuck, Laura. 2006. (ENG.). 32p. (J). (gr. -1-3). 16.95 *(978-0-8118-4992-0(9))* Chronicle Bks. LLC.
—The Tell-Tale Heart & Other Stories. Poe, Edgar Allen. 2011. (ENG.). 144p. (J). (gr. 6-9). pap. 12.99 *(978-1-4169-5026-4(5),* Atheneum Bks. for Young Readers) Simon & Schuster Children's Publishing.
Grimly, Gris. Terrifying Tales. Scieszka, Jon et al. 2015. (Guys Read Ser.: 6). (ENG.). 256p. (J). (gr. 3-7). pap. 6.99 ***(978-0-06-238557-4(7),*** Walden Pond Pr.) HarperCollins Pubs.
Grimly, Gris. Gris Grimly's Wicked Nursery Rhymes. Grimly, Gris. 2003. 32p. 16.95 *(978-0-9729388-7-7(7))* Baby Tattoo Bks.
—Little Jordan Ray's Muddy Spud. Grimly, Gris. 2005. 40p. (J). 19.95 *(978-0-9729388-6-0(9))* Baby Tattoo Bks.
Grimly, Gris, jt. illus. see Hunt, Alfred William.
Grimm, Dave. Mommy, Tell Me a Story about a Car, 2nd Edition. Grimm, Kristi. 2nd ed. 2013. 32p. pap. 13.99 *(978-0-9855699-9-0(9))* Richer Life, LLC.
—Mommy, Tell Me a Story about a Plane, 2nd Edition. Grimm, Kristi. 2nd ed. 2013. 36p. pap. 13.99 *(978-0-9855699-8-3(0))* Richer Life, LLC.
Grimm, Debi & Eadie, Inger Sommer. The Crocodile Song. Siefker, Eunice. 2009. 40p. (J). (gr. -1-3). 19.95 *(978-1-60227-476-1(2))* Above the Clouds Publishing.
Grimwood, Tracie. Maui Tames the Sun Vol. 7: Band 15/Emerald. Trussell-Cullen, Alan. 2007. (Collins Big Cat Ser.). (ENG.). 32p. (J). pap. 8.99 *(978-0-00-722871-3(6))* HarperCollins Pubs. Ltd. GBR. Dist: Independent Pubs. Group.
—Short Pants: Band 14/Ruby. Lock, Kath. 2007. (Collins Big Cat Ser.). (ENG.). 24p. (J). pap. 8.99 *(978-0-00-722865-2(1))* HarperCollins Pubs. Ltd. GBR. Dist: Independent Pubs. Group.
Grindell, Joan & Grindell, Mark. Let's Make Faces. Langeler, Gerard. 2009. (ENG.). 24p. (J). (gr. -1-3). spiral bd. 14.95 *(978-1-932565-63-8(9))* Future Horizons, Inc.
Grindell, Mark, jt. illus. see Grindell, Joan.
Gringhuis, Dirk. Blue Bay Mystery. Warner, Gertrude Chandler. 2004. (Boxcar Children Mysteries Ser.: No. 6). (ENG.). 160p. (J). (gr. 2-5). reprint ed. mass mkt. 5.99 *(978-0-8075-0794-0(6))* Whitman, Albert & Co.
—Mike's Mystery. Warner, Gertrude Chandler. 2004. (Boxcar Children Mysteries Ser.: 5). (ENG.). 128p. (J). (gr. 2-5). reprint ed. mass mkt. 5.99 *(978-0-8075-5141-7(4))* Whitman, Albert & Co.
—Mystery Ranch. Warner, Gertrude Chandler. 2004. (Boxcar Children Ser.: No. 4). (ENG.). 128p. (J). (gr. 2-5). reprint ed. mass mkt. 5.99 *(978-0-8075-5391-6(3))* Whitman, Albert & Co.
Grinvalsky, Peggy. Heartwood. Burns, Mary E. 2003. (ENG.). 144p. (YA). per. 9.95 *(978-0-9656763-4-2(X))* Manitowish River Pr.
Gripe, Harold. Elvis Karlsson. Gripe, Maria. 2003. (SPA.). 148p. (J). (gr. 3-5). pap. 9.95 *(978-958-24-0181-8(8))* Santillana USA Publishing Co., Inc.
Griscom, Laura. The Boy Named 27091: A Teenager's Struggle for Survival during the Holocaust. 2007. (J). lib. bdg. 6.95 *(978-0-9633705-4-9(5))* Share Publishing.
Grisham, Betty. Blue Lewis & Sasha the Great. Newell, Carol Donsky. 2005. (J). per. 6.95 *(978-0-9766199-0-1(3))* Cally Pr.
Grisham, Jason. Benjamin P. Blizzard: Welcome to Christmastown. Nivens, Karen. 2007. 48p. (J). per. *(978-0-9798154-1-6(X))* Living Waters Publishing Co.
Grist, Julie. Flying: Just Plane Fun. Grist, Julie. 2006. 24p. (J). (gr. k-7). pap. 8.95 *(978-0-9725750-2-7(2))* Spoonbender Bks.
Griswold, Earleen. A Caribbean Journey from A to Y: (Read & Discover What Happened to the Z) Picayo, Mario. 2007. (ENG & FRE.). 64p. (J). 19.95 *(978-0-9725611-8-1(8),* Campanita Bks.) Editorial Campana.
Griswold, Phillip. The Circus. Miller, Lindsey Michael. 2005. 32p. (J). (gr. -1-3). 13.95 *(978-0-9709104-8-6(7))* Hickory Tales Publishing.

Gritton, Steve. The Super Dupers. Gritton, Steve. 2013. 30p. pap. 9.29 *(978-0-9795361-8-2(9))* Bad Frog Art/SMG Bks.

Grivas, Vasilis. Cats' Eyes. McRae, J. R. 2014. 108p. pap. 10.99 *(978-1-62563-919-6(8))* Tate Publishing & Enterprises, LLC.

Grobet, Veronique, jt. illus. see Godi.

Grobler, Piet. A Is Amazing: Poems about Feelings. Cooling, Wendy & Quarto Generic Staff. 2013. (ENG.). 48p. (J). (gr. 2-5). 19.99 *(978-1-84780-255-2(9))*, Frances Lincoln Children's Bks.) Quarto Publishing Group UK GBR. Dist: Hachette Bk. Group.

—Aesop's Fables. Naidoo, Beverley. (ENG.). (J). (gr. k-6). 2011. 48p. 18.95 *(978-1-84780-007-7(6))*; 2014. 56p. 19.99 *(978-1-84780-530-0(2))* Quarto Publishing Group UK GBR. (Frances Lincoln). Dist: Hachette Bk. Group.

—All the Wild Wonders: Poems of Our Earth. Cooling, Wendy. 2015. (ENG.). 48p. (J). (gr. 2-5). 18.99 *(978-1-84780-626-0(0))*, Frances Lincoln) Quarto Publishing Group UK GBR. Dist: Hachette Bk. Group.

—All the Wild Wonders: Poems of Our Earth. 2010. (ENG.). 48p. (J). (gr. 2-5). 19.95 *(978-1-84780-073-2(4))*, Frances Lincoln) Quarto Publishing Group UK GBR. Dist: Hachette Bk. Group.

—Carnival of the Animals. De Vos, Philip. 32p. (J). *(978-0-7981-3823-9(8))* Human & Rousseau.

—Colors! / ¡Colores! Luján, Jorge. Simon, John Oliver & Parfitt, Rebecca, trs. 2008.Tr. of Colors!. (SPA & ENG.). 36p. (J). (gr. k-4). 18.95 *(978-0-88899-863-7(5))* Groundwood Bks. CAN. Dist: Perseus-PGW.

—Fussy Freya. Quarmby, Katharine. 2008. (ENG.). 32p. (J). (gr. -1-1). 16.95 *(978-1-84507-511-8(0))*, Frances Lincoln) Quarto Publishing Group UK GBR. Dist: Hachette Bk. Group.

—Little Mouse. Dijkstra, Lida. 2004. (ENG.). 32p. (J). 15.95 *(978-1-932425-06-2(3))*, Lemniscaat) Boyds Mills Pr.

Grobler, Piet, et al. Rights of a Child. 2005. (ENG & MUL.). 28p. 11.95 *(978-0-7957-0162-7(4))* Kwela Bks. ZAF. Dist: Independent Pubs. Group.

Grobler, Piet. Today Is My Day. Ravishankar, Anushka. 2005. (ENG.). 40p. (J). 14.95 *(978-81-86211-76-2(4))* Tara Publishing IND. Dist: Perseus-PGW.

—Who Is King? Naidoo, Beverley. 2015. (ENG.). 72p. (J). (gr. k-4). 22.99 *(978-1-84780-514-0(0))*, Frances Lincoln) Quarto Publishing Group UK GBR. Dist: Hachette Bk. Group.

Grobler, Piet. Little Bird's ABC. Grobler, Piet. 2005. (ENG.). 52p. (J). (gr. -1-3). 8.95 *(978-1-932425-52-9(7))*, Lemniscaat) Boyds Mills Pr.

Grobler, Piet. The Magic Bojabi Tree. Grobler, Piet. Hofmeyr, Dianne. 2014. (ENG.). 32p. (J). (gr. -1-2). pap. 8.99 ***(978-1-84780-586-7(8))***, Frances Lincoln Children's Bks.) Quarto Publishing Group UK GBR. Dist: Hachette Bk. Group.

Groebner, Dominic. El Gran Libro de Los Castillos - Internet Linked. Sims, Lesley. 2004. (Titles in Spanish Ser.). (SPA.). 104p. (J). pap. 14.95 *(978-0-7460-5089-7(5))*, Usborne) EDC Publishing.

—The Usborne Big Book of Picture Puzzles. Khanduri, Kamini et al. 2006. 173p. (J). (gr. 3-7). per. 18.99 *(978-0-7945-1165-4(1))*, Usborne) EDC Publishing.

—The Usborne Castle Jigsaw Book. Pearcey, Alice. Milbourne, Anna, ed. 2006. (Jigsaw Bks.). 14p. (J). (gr. k-3). bds. 14.95 *(978-0-7945-1137-1(6))*, Usborne) EDC Publishing.

Groenewald, Frans. The Mighty Elephant in the Land of Kachoo: The Land of Kachoo Series. Scotford, Groenewald & Scotford, Tina. 2014. (Land of Kachoo Ser.). (ENG.). 32p. (J). (gr. k-2). pap. 10.95 *(978-1-4314-0759-0(3))* Jacana Media ZAF. Dist: Independent Pubs. Group.

—Saving the Rhino in the Land of Kachoo: The Land of Kachoo Series. Scotford, Tina. 2014. (Land of Kachoo Ser.). (ENG.). 32p. (J). (gr. k-2). pap. 10.95 *(978-1-4314-0760-6(7))* Jacana Media ZAF. Dist: Independent Pubs. Group.

Groeninik, Chuck. Dear Daisy Dunnington. Stein, Mathilde. 2012. (ENG.). 32p. (J). (gr. 1). 17.95 *(978-1-935954-18-7(0))*, 9781935954187) Lemniscaat USA.

Groenink, Chuck. The Backwards Birthday Party. Chapin, Tom & Forster, John. 2015. (ENG.). 40p. (J). (gr. -1-3). 17.99 *(978-1-4424-6798-9(3))*, Atheneum Bks. for Young Readers) Simon & Schuster Children's Publishing.

Groenink, Chuck. The Friend Ship. Yeh, Kat. 2016. (J). *(978-1-4847-0726-5(5))* Disney Pr.

Groenink, Chuck. How to Be a Hero. Heide, Florence Parry. 2016. (J). *(978-1-4521-2710-1(7))* Chronicle Bks. LLC.

—Rufus the Writer. Bram, Elizabeth. 2015. (ENG.). 40p. (J). (gr. -1-3). 17.99 *(978-0-385-37853-6(X))*, Schwartz & Wade Bks.) Random Hse. Children's Bks.

—Under a Pig Tree: A History of the Noble Fruit. Palatini, Margie. 2015. (ENG.). 40p. (J). (gr. -1-3). 16.95 *(978-1-4197-1488-7(0))*, Abrams Bks. for Young Readers) Abrams.

Grof, Stanislav. Lillibit's Dream. Sullivan, Melody. 2011. (ENG.). 32p. (J). 19.95 *(978-1-59275-000-9(1))* Hanford Mead Pubs., Inc.

Groff, David. What Was the Alamo? Belviso, Meg & Pollack, Pam. 2013. (What Was... ? Ser.). (ENG.). 112p. (J). (gr. 3-7). 5.99 *(978-0-448-46710-8(0))*, Grosset & Dunlap) Penguin Publishing Group.

—Where Is the White House? Stine, Megan. 2015. (Where Is... ? Ser.). (ENG.). 112p. (J). (gr. 3-7). 5.99 *(978-0-448-48355-9(6))*, Grosset & Dunlap) Penguin Publishing Group.

—Who Was Alexander Graham Bell? Bader, Bonnie. 2013. (Who Was... ? Ser.). (ENG.). 112p. (J). (gr. 3-7). 5.99 *(978-0-448-46460-2(8))*, Grosset & Dunlap) Penguin Publishing Group.

Groff, David. Who Was Clara Barton? Spinner, Stephanie. 2014. 103p. (J). lib. bdg. ***(978-1-4844-3355-3(6))***, Grosset & Dunlap) Penguin Publishing Group.

Groff, David & Colón, Daniel. Where Is the Grand Canyon? O'Connor, Jim. 2015. (Where Is... ? Ser.). (ENG.). 112p. (J). (gr. 3-7). 5.99 *(978-0-448-48357-3(2))*, Grosset & Dunlap) Penguin Publishing Group.

Groff, David & Hinderliter, John. Where Is Mount Rushmore? Kelley, True. 2015. (Where Is... ? Ser.). (ENG.). 112p. (J). (gr. 3-7). 5.99 *(978-0-448-48356-6(4))*, Grosset & Dunlap) Penguin Publishing Group.

Groff, David & Hoare, Jerry. Where Is the Great Wall? Demuth, Patricia Brennan. 2015. (Where Is... ? Ser.). (ENG.). 112p. (J). (gr. 3-7). 5.99 *(978-0-448-48358-0(0))*, Grosset & Dunlap) Penguin Publishing Group.

Groff, David & McVeigh, Kevin. What Was the Hindenburg? Pascal, Janet. 2014. (What Was... ? Ser.). (ENG.). 112p. (J). (gr. 3-7). 5.99 *(978-0-448-48119-7(7))*, Grosset & Dunlap) Penguin Publishing Group.

Groff, David, jt. illus. see Harrison, Nancy.

Groff, David, jt. illus. see Hinderliter, John.

Groff, David, jt. illus. see McVeigh, Kevin.

Groff, David, jt. illus. see ón, Daniel.

Grogan, Patrick. Birding for Children. 2007. 44p. (J). 19.95 *(978-0-615-15948-5(6))* Minton, Art.

Grondel, April. From the Desk of a Three-Year-Old. McNeill, Audrey. 2009. 20p. pap. 24.95 *(978-1-60749-476-8(0))* America Star Bks.

Groome, W. H. C. A Sea-Queen's Sailing. Whistler, Charles W. 2011. 346p. 24.95 *(978-1-934671-42-9(8))* Salem Ridge Press LLC.

Groot, Nicole. The Ants Go Marching One by One. O'Connor, Frankie. 2014. (ENG.). 32p. (J). (gr. -1-3). 7.99 ***(978-1-4867-0004-2(7))*** Flowerpot Children's Pr. Inc. CAN. Dist: Cardinal Pubs. Group.

Groshelle, Dave. Good Night Little Man. Saunders, Helen. 2006. (J). *(978-0-9763143-4-9(7))* Happy Heart Kids Publishing.

Gross-Andrew, Susannah. It's Your Rite: Girls' Coming-of-Age Stories. Coon, Nora E., ed. 2003. 144p. (J). pap. 9.95 *(978-1-58270-074-8(5))* Beyond Words Publishing, Inc.

Gross, Maia. Talitha & the Gnome: The Warg. Sutherland, Rowan. 2011. (ENG.). 46p. pap. 10.18 *(978-1-4565-3353-3(3))* CreateSpace Independent Publishing Platform.

Gross, Margaret. A Visit up & down Wall Street. Gross, Jen & Hoch, Jen. 2005. 32p. (J). 14.95 *(978-0-9760875-0-2(2))* Harry & Stephanie Bks.

Gross, Sanai. The Multiplication Monster. Gross, Kimberley & Gross, Kaiya. 2013. 84p. pap. 10.95 *(978-0-9886402-3-8(6))* Vision Bk. Co.

Gross, Scott. Scooby-Doo! a Number Comparisons Mystery: The Case of the Lunchroom Gobbler, 1 vol. Weakland, Mark. 2014. (Solve It with Scooby-Doo!: Math Ser.). (ENG.). 24p. (gr. k-2). lib. bdg. 27.32 *(978-1-4914-1542-9(8))* Capstone Pr., Inc.

—Scooby-Doo! a Subtraction Mystery: The Case of the Disappearing Doughnuts, 1 vol. Weakland, Mark. 2014. (Solve It with Scooby-Doo!: Math Ser.). (ENG.). 24p. (gr. k-2). lib. bdg. 27.32 *(978-1-4914-1540-5(1))* Capstone Pr., Inc.

—Scooby-Doo! an Addition Mystery: The Case of the Angry Adder, 1 vol. Weakland, Mark. 2014. (Solve It with Scooby-Doo!: Math Ser.). (ENG.). 24p. (gr. k-2). lib. bdg. 27.32 *(978-1-4914-1539-9(8))* Capstone Pr., Inc.

—Scooby-Doo! an Even or Odd Mystery: The Case of the Oddzilla, 1 vol. Weakland, Mark. 2014. (Solve It with Scooby-Doo!: Math Ser.). (ENG.). 24p. (gr. k-2). lib. bdg. 27.32 *(978-1-4914-1541-2(X))* Capstone Pr., Inc.

—Solve It with Scooby-Doo!: Math: Math, 1 vol. Weakland, Mark. 2014. (Solve It with Scooby-Doo!: Math Ser.). (ENG.). 24p. (gr. k-2). 109.28 *(978-1-4914-1543-6(6))* Capstone Pr., Inc.

Gross, Sue. I'm Going to Be a Big Brother! Bercun, Brenda. 2007. (ENG.). 33p. (J). (gr. -1-k). 15.95 *(978-0-9767198-7-8(8))* Nurturing Your Children Pr.

—I'm Going to Be a Big Sister! Bercun, Brenda. 2007. (ENG.). 33p. (J). (gr. -1-k). 15.95 *(978-0-9767198-6-1(X))* Nurturing Your Children Pr.

Gross, Susan. Soul Searching: A Girl's Guide to Finding Herself. Stillman, Sarah. 2012. (ENG.). 176p. (YA). (gr. 7). 17.99 *(978-1-58270-342-8(6))*; pap. 9.99 *(978-1-58270-303-9(5))* Simon Pulse/Beyond Words.

Grosshauser, Peter. Alien Dude! & the Attack of Wormzilla!! Smith, E. K. 2014. (Alien Dude! Ser.). (ENG.). 64p. (J). (gr. 2-4). pap. 4.99 *(978-0-9883792-0-6(1))* Zip Line Publishing.

—Alien Dude! Mr. Evil Potato Man & the Food Fight. Smith, E. K. 2014. (Alien Dude! Ser.). (ENG.). 64p. (J). (gr. 2-4). pap. 4.99 *(978-0-9883792-1-3(X))* Zip Line Publishing.

—My Week. 2010. (My World Ser.). (ENG.). 24p. (J). (gr. -1-1). lib. bdg. 22.60 *(978-1-60754-951-2(4))* Windmill Bks.

—My Week. Wesley, Milliana, ed. 2010. (My World Ser.). (ENG.). 24p. (J). (gr. -1-1). pap. 8.15 *(978-1-61533-035-5(6))* Windmill Bks.

—My Week/Mi Semana. Rosa-Mendoza, Gladys. Wesley, Milliana, ed. 2007. (English Spanish Foundations Ser.). (gr. -1-k). bds. 6.95 *(978-1-931398-25-1(9))* Me+Mi Publishing.

Grosshauser, Peter. The Spark Story Bible: Spark a Journey Through God's Word. Hetherington, Debra Thorpe, ed. 2015. (ENG.). 456p. (J). (gr. -1-2). 22.99 ***(978-1-4514-9978-0(7))***, Sparkhouse Family) Augsburg Fortress, Pubs.

—The Story of Creation: A Spark Bible Story. Smith, Martina. 2015. (Spark Bible Stories Ser.). (ENG.). 32p. (J). (gr. -1-2). 12.99 ***(978-1-4514-9980-3(9))***, Sparkhouse Family) Augsburg Fortress, Pubs.

—The Story of Jesus' Teaching & Healing: A Spark Bible Story. Smith, Martina. 2015. (Spark Bible Stories Ser.). (ENG.). 32p. (J). (gr. -1-2). 12.99 ***(978-1-5064-0228-4(3))***, Sparkhouse Family) Augsburg Fortress, Pubs.

—The Story of Moses & God's Promise: A Spark Bible Story. Smith, Martina. 2015. (Spark Bible Stories Ser.). (ENG.). 32p. (J). (gr. -1-2). 12.99 ***(978-1-4514-9982-7(5))***, Sparkhouse Family) Augsburg Fortress, Pubs.

Grossman, Mendel, photos by. My Secret Camera: Life in the Lodz Ghetto. Smith, Frank Dabba & Quarto Generic Staff. 2008. (ENG.). 40p. (J). (gr. 2-17). pap. 8.99 *(978-1-84507-892-8(6))*, Frances Lincoln) Quarto Publishing Group UK GBR. Dist: Hachette Bk. Group.

Grossman, Nancy. Did You Carry the Flag Today, Charley. Caudill, Rebecca. 2007. 96p. (J). pap. 7.95 *(978-0-8050-8141-1(0))*, Holt, Henry & Co. Bks. For Young Readers) Holt, Henry & Co.

Grossmann, Dan. Bible Stories to Color & Tell, Ages 3-6. Standard Publishing Staff. 2005. (HeartShaper(r) Resources — Early Childhood Ser.). 240p. (J). (gr. -1-3). per. 16.99 *(978-0-7847-1779-0(6))*, 02493) Standard Publishing.

Grossmann-Hensel, Katharina. Papa is a Pirate. Grossmann-Hensel, Katharina. 2009. (ENG.). 32p. (J). (gr. -1-3). 16.95 *(978-0-7358-2237-5(9))* North-South Bks., Inc.

Grosvenor, Charles, et al. A Tale of Dragons. 2014. (How to Train Your Dragon 2 Ser.). (ENG.). 24p. (J). (gr. -1-2). pap. 3.99 *(978-1-4814-0434-1(2))*, Simon Spotlight) Simon Spotlight.

Grosvenor, Charles & Gerard, Justin. Dragon Mountain Adventure. 2014. (How to Train Your Dragon 2 Ser.). (ENG.). 32p. (J). (gr. k-2). pap. 3.99 *(978-1-4814-0440-2(7))*, Simon Spotlight) Simon Spotlight.

—How to Train Your Dragon: Meet the Dragons. Hapka, Catherine. 2010. (I Can Read Book 1 Ser.). 32p. (J). (gr. k-3). pap. 3.99 *(978-0-06-156733-9(7))* HarperCollins Pubs.

Grosvenor, Charles & Roberts, Jeremy. Plants vs. Zombies: Brains & the Beanstalk. Auerbach, Annie & PopCap Games Staff. 2013. (Plants vs. Zombies Ser.). (ENG.). 24p. (J). (gr. -1-3). pap. 4.99 *(978-0-06-222836-9(6))*, HarperFestival) HarperCollins Pubs.

—The Three Little Pigs Fight Back. Auerbach, Annie & PopCap Games Staff. 2013. (Plants vs. Zombies Ser.). (ENG.). 24p. (J). (gr. -1-3). pap. 4.99 *(978-0-06-222838-3(2))*, HarperFestival) HarperCollins Pubs.

Grotke, Christopher A. The Mysterious Jamestown Suitcase: A Bailey Fish Adventure. Salisbury, Linda G. 2006. (Bailey Fish Adventures Ser.). 191p. (J). (gr. 3-7). per. 8.95 *(978-1-881539-43-8(1))* Tabby Hse. Bks.

—No Sisters Sisters Club: A Bailey Fish Adventure. Salisbury, Linda G. 2005. 188p. (J). per. 8.95 *(978-1-881539-40-7(7))* Tabby Hse. Bks.

—The Thief at Keswick Inn: A Bailey Fish Adventure. Salisbury, Linda G. 2006. (Bailey Fish Adventures Ser.). 191p. (J). (gr. 3-7). per. 8.95 *(978-1-881539-41-4(5))* Tabby Hse. Bks.

Grout, Paul A. Pauline Jaricot: Foundress of the Living Rosary & the Society for the Propagation of the Faith. Windeatt, Mary F. 2009. (ENG.). 244p. reprint ed. pap. 15.95 *(978-0-89555-425-3(9))* TAN Bks.

—Saint Louis de Montfort: The Story of Our Lady's Slave. Windeatt, Mary F. 2009. (Stories of the Saints for Young People Ages 10 to 100 Ser.). Orig. Title: Our Lady's Slave: the Story of St. Louis Mary Grignion de Montfort. (ENG.). 211p. (J). (gr. 2-9). reprint ed. pap. 13.95 *(978-0-89555-414-7(3))* TAN Bks.

Grove, Christine. Bounce, Bounce, Baby! Bardaus, Anna W. 2013. (J). ***(978-0-545-61897-7(5))*** Scholastic, Inc.

—Dance, Dance, Baby! Bardaus, Anna W. 2013. (J). ***(978-0-545-61899-1(1))*** Scholastic, Inc.

Grove, Christine. My Mom Has a Job. Snead, Kathi. 2004. (J). *(978-0-9747385-0-5(6))* City of Manassas Department of Social Services.

Grove, Christine. Reach, Reach, Baby! Bardaus, Anna W. 2013. (J). ***(978-0-545-61900-4(9))*** Scholastic, Inc.

—Read, Read, Baby! Bardaus, Anna W. 2013. (J). ***(978-0-545-61898-4(3))*** Scholastic, Inc.

Grove, Gladys. Poudre Canyon. Gonder, Glen W. Gonder, Sharon J., ed. Date not set. (Adventures of Willy Whacker Ser.: Vol. 9). 161p. (YA). (gr. 6-8). lib. bdg. 8.95 *(978-1-58389-004-2(1))* Osage Bend Publishing Co.

Grover, Nina. A Children's Songbook Companion. Graham, Pat et al. 2005. per. 18.95 *(978-0-88290-795-6(6))*, Horizon Pubs.) Cedar Fort, Inc./CFI Distribution.

Grubb, W. B. Quarterback Hothead. Heyliger, William. 2011. 262p. 47.95 *(978-1-258-09738-7(9))* Literary Licensing, LLC.

Gruber, Michael & Graves, Linda. The Legend of the Brog. Gruber, Michael. 2005. (J). per. 9.95 *(978-0-9770413-0-5(1))* Gruber Enterprises.

Grudina, Paola Bertolina. My Baptism Bible Catholic Edition. Godfrey, Jan. 2012. 144p. (J). 16.95 *(978-0-8198-4907-6(3))* Pauline Bks. & Media.

Grudina, Paola Bertolini. The Big Book of Bible Questions. Wright, Sally Ann. 2008. 61p. (gr. -1-3). 15.00 *(978-0-687-65088-0(7))* Abingdon Pr.

—The Christmas Activity Book. Wright, Sally Ann. 2010. 32p. (J). (gr. k-3). 10.95 *(978-0-8198-1584-2(5))* Pauline Bks. & Media.

—The Easter Swallows. Howie, Vicki. 2007. 32p. (J). 10.95 *(978-0-8198-2360-1(0))* Pauline Bks. & Media.

—What Did the Fishermen Catch? And Other Questions. Wright, Sally Ann. 2006. 32p. (J). (gr. -1). 10.95 *(978-0-8091-6732-6(8))*, 6732-8) Paulist Pr.

—Who Built the Ark? And Other Questions. Wright, Sally Ann. 2006. 32p. (J). (gr. -1-3). 10.95 *(978-0-8091-6730-2(1))*, 6730-1) Paulist Pr.

Gruebele, Michelle. Rudy's Incredible Kidney Machine. Waibel, Stacy Raye. 2011. 32p. (J). 10.95 *(978-0-9820983-3-2(2))* Purple Cow Pr.

Gruelle, Johnny. The Complete Fairy Tales of the Brothers Grimm. Grimm, Jacob & Grimm, Wilhelm K. Zipes, Jack D., tr. from GER. 3rd ed. 2003. (Bantam Classics Ser.). (ENG.). 800p. (J). reprint ed. pap. 23.00 *(978-0-553-38216-7(0))*, Bantam) Random House Publishing Group.

Gruelle, Johnny. Raggedy Ann in Cookie Land: (Classic) Gruelle, Johnny. 2010. (Raggedy Ann Ser.). (ENG.). 96p. (J). (gr. k-5). 21.99 *(978-1-4424-2199-8(1))*, Simon & Schuster Bks. For Young Readers) Simon & Schuster Bks. For Young Readers.

Gruelle, Johnny, jt. illus. see Gooch, Thelma.

Gruelle, Justin C. Once Round the Sun. Titchenell, Elsa-Brita. 2011. 62p. 36.95 *(978-1-258-03323-1(2))* Literary Licensing, LLC.

Gruen, Chuck. Little Chief Mischief: From Tales of the Menehune. Salter-Mathieson, Nigel C. S. 2011. 44p. pap. 35.95 *(978-1-258-10135-0(1))* Literary Licensing, LLC.

Gruenfelder, Robin. The Naked Cat With The Velvet Paws. Olek, Lisa B. 2011. 40p. (J). 18.95 *(978-1-60131-092-7(7))* Big Tent Bks.

—Yoshka's Journey to Christmas. Olek, Lisa B. 2012. 70p. (J). 21.95 *(978-1-60131-125-2(7))*, Castlebridge Bks.) Big Tent Bks.

Grummett, Tom. Falcon: Fight or Flight: A Mighty Marvel Chapter Book. Wyatt, Chris. 2015. (Marvel Chapter Book Ser.). (ENG.). 128p. (J). (gr. 3-7). pap. 5.99 *(978-1-4847-1529-1(2))*, Marvel Pr.) Disney Publishing Worldwide.

Grummett, Tom & Disney Storybook Artists Staff. Iron Man: An Origin Story. Thomas, Rich, Jr. 2013. (Origin Story Ser.). (ENG.). 48p. (J). (gr. 1-3). 8.99 *(978-1-4231-7253-6(1))* Marvel Worldwide, Inc.

Grunden, Kimberly. Circle the Moon. Lockhart, Barbara M. 2008. 24p. pap. 10.95 *(978-1-934246-96-2(4))* Peppertree Pr., The.

—I'm a Perfectly Normal Kid Who Happens to Have Diabetes! Morris, Cathy. 2007. 24p. per. 12.95 *(978-1-934246-85-6(9))* Peppertree Pr., The.

Grundy, Jessica. Greystone Valley. Brooks, Charlie. 2013. 166p. 17.99 *(978-1-938821-33-2(5))*; 198p. pap. 9.99 *(978-1-938821-41-7(6))* Grey Gecko Pr.

Grundy, Peter. Information Graphics: Human Body. Rogers, Simon. 2014. (ENG.). 80p. (J). (gr. 1-4). 17.99 *(978-0-7636-7123-5(1))*, Big Picture Press) Candlewick Pr.

Gruszka, Chris A. For the Love of Texas: Tell Me about the Colonists! Christian, Betsy & Christian, George. 2013. Orig. Title: For the Love of Texas: Tell Me about the Colonists!. (ENG.). 112p. (gr. 4-7). 14.99 *(978-1-62619-159-4(X))*, History Pr., The) Arcadia Publishing.

—For the Love of Texas: Tell Me about the Revolution! Christian, Betsy & Christian, George. 2013. Orig. Title: For the Love of Texas: Tell Me about the Revolution!. (ENG.). 128p. (gr. 4-7). 14.99 *(978-1-62619-160-0(3))*, History Pr., The) Arcadia Publishing.

Grutzik, Becky. The Runaway Puppy: A Mystery with Probability. Barriman, Lydia. 2010. (Manga Math Mysteries Ser.: 8). (ENG.). 48p. (gr. 3-5). 29.27 *(978-0-7613-4910-5(3))* Lerner Publishing Group.

—Thr Runaway Puppy: A Mystery with Probability. Barriman, Lydia. 2011. (Manga Math Mysteries Ser.: 8). (ENG.). 48p. (gr. 3-5). pap. 6.95 *(978-0-7613-8137-2(6))*, Graphic Universe) Lerner Publishing Group.

—#8 the Runaway Puppy: A Mystery with Probability. Barriman, Lydia. 2011. (Manga Math Mysteries Set II Ser.). pap. 39.62 *(978-0-7613-8365-9(4))*, Graphic Universe) Lerner Publishing Group.

Grzelak, Kyle. Gravy on My Mashed Potatoes: A Creative Exploration of Special Relationships. Sisler, Stephanie. 2012. 20p. pap. 11.95 *(978-1-61493-123-2(2))* Peppertree Pr., The.

—Matthews Monsters, a Creative Comprehensive Exercise. Sisler, Stephanie. 2011. 32p. pap. 12.95 *(978-1-61493-015-0(5))* Peppertree Pr., The.

—A Peanut Butter & Monster Sandwich. Dooley, Larry. 2013. 24p. pap. 12.95 *(978-1-61493-206-2(9))* Peppertree Pr., The.

Guara, Ig. Avengers vs. Pet Avengers. 2011. (ENG.). 112p. (J). (gr. -1-17). pap. 14.99 *(978-0-7851-5185-2(0))* Marvel Worldwide, Inc.

—The Green Team: Teen Trillionaires, Vol. 1. Baltazar, Art & Franco. 2014. (ENG.). 192p. (YA). pap. 16.99 *(978-1-4012-4641-9(9))* DC Comics.

Guard, Candy. Turning to Jelly, 1. Guard, Candy. unabr. ed. 2014. (ENG.). 224p. (J). (gr. 4-6). pap. 9.99 ***(978-1-4472-5610-6(7))*** Pan Macmillan GBR. Dist: Independent Pubs. Group.

Guarnaccia, Steven. Anansi. Gleeson, Brian. 2005. (Rabbit Ears: A Classic Tale Ser.). 36p. (gr. -1-3). 25.65 *(978-1-59679-342-2(2))* Spotlight.

—I Lie for a Living: Greatest Spies of All Time. Shugaar, Antony & International Spy Museum Staff. 2006. (ENG.). 192p. (J). per. 14.95 *(978-0-7922-5316-7(7))* National Geographic Society.

—Knit Your Bit: A World War I Story. Hopkinson, Deborah. 2013. (ENG.). 32p. (J). (gr. k-3). 16.99 *(978-0-399-25241-9(X))*, Putnam Juvenile) Penguin Publishing Group.

Guarnotta, Lucia. We Are Tigers. 2006. (We Are... Ser.). 40p. (gr. -1-k). bds. *(978-2-7641-1456-6(7))* Tormont Pubns.

Guay, Rebecca. Bad Girls: Sirens, Jezebels, Murderesses, Thieves & Other Female Villains. Yolen, Jane & Stemple, Heidi E. Y. 2013. (ENG.). 172p. (J). (gr. 4-7). lib. bdg. 18.95 *(978-1-58089-185-1(3))* Charlesbridge Publishing, Inc.

—The Barefoot Book Stories from the Ballet. Yolen, Jane et al. 2004. (ENG.). 96p. (J). 19.99 *(978-1-84148-229-3(3))* Barefoot Bks., Inc.

—Goddesses: A World of Myth & Magic. Muten, Burleigh. 2003. (ENG.). 80p. (J). 19.99 *(978-1-84148-075-6(4))* Barefoot Bks., Inc.

—Nellie Bly: A Name to Be Reckoned With. Krensky, Stephen. 2003. (Milestone Ser.). (ENG.). 80p. (J). (gr. 2-5). pap. 5.99 *(978-0-689-85573-3(7))*, Simon & Schuster/Paula Wiseman Bks.) Simon & Schuster/Paula Wiseman Bks.

—A Wizard Named Nell. Koller, Jackie French. 2003. (ENG.). 208p. (J). (gr. 3-7). pap. 11.95 *(978-0-689-85591-7(5))*, Simon & Schuster/Paula Wiseman Bks.) Simon & Schuster/Paula Wiseman Bks.

—The Wizard's Apprentice. Koller, Jackie French. 2003. (ENG.). 208p. (J). (gr. 3-7). pap. 9.99 *(978-0-689-85592-4(3),* Simon & Schuster/Paula Wiseman Bks.) Simon & Schuster/Paula Wiseman Bks.

Guay, Rebecca, jt. illus. see Wilson, Anne.

Gubitosi-D'Aurio, Gina & Gubitosi, Lillian. The Legend of the Rainbow. D'Aurio, Ariana. l.t. ed. 2011. (ENG.). 28p. pap. 9.99 *(978-1-4563-3877-0(3))* CreateSpace Independent Publishing Platform.

Gubitosi, Lillian. A Smickamookum Drinks Belly. Blackman, S. A. 2003. 32p. (J). (gr. -1-k). 16.95 incl. audio *(978-1-929409-02-0(8))* Blade Publishing.

Gubitosi, Lillian, jt. illus. see Gubitosi-D'Aurio, Gina.

Gude, Paul. A Surprise for Giraffe & Elephant. Gude, Paul. 2015. (Giraffe & Elephant Are Friends Ser.). (ENG.). 56p. (J). (gr. -1-k). 16.99 *(978-1-4231-8311-2(8))* Hyperion Bks. for Children.

—When Elephant Met Giraffe. Gude, Paul. 2014. (ENG.). 56p. (J). (gr. -1-k). 16.99 *(978-1-4231-6303-9(6))* Disney Publishing Worldwide.

Gudeon, Adam. Bedtime at Bessie & Lil's. Sternberg, Julie. 2015. (ENG.). 32p. (J). (gr. -1-2). 16.95 *(978-1-59078-934-6(2))* Boyds Mills Pr.

Gudeon, Adam. Me & Meow. Gudeon, Adam. 2011. (ENG.). 32p. (J). (gr. -1-k). 12.99 *(978-0-06-199821-8(4))* HarperCollins Pubs.

—Ping Wants to Play. Gudeon, Adam. 2014. (I Like to Read(r) Ser.). (ENG.). 24p. (J). (gr. -1-3). 14.95 *(978-0-8234-2854-0(0))* Holiday Hse., Inc.

Gudeon, Karla. The Language of Angels: A Story about the Reinvention of Hebrew. Michelson, Richard. 2016. (J). lib. bdg. ***(978-1-58089-636-8(7))*** Charlesbridge Publishing, Inc.

Gudeon, Karla. One Red Apple. Ziefert, Harriet. 2009. 36p. (J). 15.99 *(978-1-934706-46-6(9))* Blue Apple Bks.

—One Red Apple. Ziefert, Harriet. 2009. (ENG.). 36p. (J). (gr. 2-4). 16.99 *(978-1-934706-67-1(1))* Blue Apple Bks.

Guell, Fernanado. Disney Mickey Mouse Clubhouse: Hugs from Mickey: A Hugs Book. Gold, Gina. 2014. (Hugs Book Ser.). (ENG.). 10p. (J). (gr. -1-k). bds. 10.99 *(978-0-7944-3288-1(3))* Studio Fun International.

Guénette, Geneviève. Lucifer, Mon Grand-Père, Tome 1. Rosseau, Paul. 2004. (Mon Roman Ser.). (FRE.). 160p. (J). (gr. 2). pap. *(978-2-89021-650-1(0))* Diffusion du livre Mirabel (DLM).

Guenette, Genevieve. Lucifer, Mon Grand-Pere: Tome 2. Rousseau, Paul. 2004. (Mon Roman Ser.). (FRE.). 184p. (J). (gr. 2). pap. *(978-2-89021-703-4(5))* Diffusion du livre Mirabel (DLM).

Guenther, Kim. My Back Yard: Poems to Read to Your Children. Schiffner, Frederick A. 2004. 32p. (J). 14.95 *(978-0-9765782-0-8(4))* Schiffner, Frederick A.

Guera, R. M. & Jock. Scalped - Indian Country Vol. 1, Vol. 1. Aaron, Jason. rev. ed. 2007. (ENG.). 126p. pap. 14.99 *(978-1-4012-1317-6(0),* Vertigo) DC Comics.

Guerlais, Gérald. A Catfish Tale: A Bayou Story of the Fisherman & His Wife. Stewart, Whitney. 2014. (ENG.). 32p. (J). (gr. -1-2). 16.99 *(978-0-8075-1098-8(X))* Whitman, Albert & Co.

—Honestly, Red Riding Hood Was Rotten! The Story of Little Red Riding Hood As Told by the Wolf, 1 vol. Shaskan, Trisha Speed. 2013. (Other Side of the Story Ser.). (ENG.). 24p. (gr. 2-3). 9.95 *(978-1-4795-1940-8(5))* Picture Window Bks.

—Honestly, Red Riding Hood Was Rotten! The Story of Little Red Riding Hood as Told by the Wolf. Shaskan, Trisha Speed. 2011. (Other Side of the Story Ser.). (ENG.). 24p. (gr. 2-3). pap. 6.95 *(978-1-4048-7046-8(6));* lib. bdg. 26.65 *(978-1-4048-6673-7(6))* Picture Window Bks. (Nonfiction Picture Bks.).

—Seriously, Cinderella Is So Annoying! The Story of Cinderella as Told by the Wicked Stepmother. Shaskan, Trisha Speed. (Other Side of the Story Ser.). (ENG.). 24p. (gr. 2-3). 2013. 9.95 *(978-1-4795-1941-5(3));* 2011. pap. 6.95 *(978-1-4048-7048-2(2),* Nonfiction Picture Bks.); 2011. lib. bdg. 26.65 *(978-1-4048-6674-4(4),* Nonfiction Picture Bks.) Picture Window Bks.

—Seriously, Snow White Was So Forgetful! The Story of Snow White as Told by the Dwarves. Loewen, Nancy. 2013. (Other Side of the Story Ser.). (ENG.). 24p. (gr. 2-3). pap. 6.95 *(978-1-4048-8085-6(2));* lib. bdg. 26.65 *(978-1-4048-7937-9(4))* Picture Window Bks.

—Seriously, Snow White Was SO Forgetful! The Story of Snow White As Told by the Dwarves, 1 vol. Loewen, Nancy. 2013. (Other Side of the Story Ser.). (ENG.). 24p. (gr. 2-3). 9.95 *(978-1-4795-1943-9(X))* Picture Window Bks.

—The Story of Orion: A Roman Constellation Myth, 1 vol. 2012. (Night Sky Stories Ser.). (ENG.). 24p. (gr. 2-3). pap. 7.95 *(978-1-4048-7718-4(5))* Picture Window Bks.

—The Story of Orion: A Roman Constellation Myth, 1 vol. Capstone Press Editors. 2012. (Night Sky Stories Ser.). (ENG.). 24p. (gr. 2-3). lib. bdg. 25.99 *(978-1-4048-7377-3(5))* Picture Window Bks.

—The Story of Ursa Major & Ursa Minor: A Roman Constellation Myth, 1 vol. 2012. (Night Sky Stories Ser.). (ENG.). 24p. (gr. 2-3). pap. 7.95 *(978-1-4048-7720-7(7))* Picture Window Bks.

—The Story of Ursa Major & Ursa Minor: A Roman Constellation Myth, 1 vol. Capstone Press Staff. 2012. (Night Sky Stories Ser.). (ENG.). 24p. (gr. 2-3). lib. bdg. 25.99 *(978-1-4048-7374-2(0))* Picture Window Bks.

Guerlais, Gérald & Bernardini, Cristian. The Other Side of the Story. Loewen, Nancy et al. 2013. (Other Side of the Story Ser.). (ENG.). 24p. (gr. 2-3). pap. 27.80 *(978-1-4795-2006-0(3));* pap. 69.50 *(978-1-4795-2004-6(7));* lib. bdg. 266.50 *(978-1-4048-8079-5(8))* Picture Window Bks.

—The Other Side of the Story. Loewen, Nancy. 2013. (Other Side of the Story Ser.). (ENG.). 24p. (gr. 2-3). pap. 41.70 *(978-1-4048-8088-7(7),* Nonfiction Picture Bks.) Picture Window Bks.

—Trust Me, Jack's Beanstalk Stinks! The Story of Jack & the Beanstalk as Told by the Giant. Loewen, Nancy & Braun, Eric. 2013. (Other Side of the Story Ser.). (ENG.). 24p. (gr. 2-3). 9.95 *(978-1-4795-1942-2(1))* Picture Window Bks.

Guerlais, Gérald, jt. illus. see Bernardini, Cristian.

Guerra, Pia, et al. Girl on Girl, Vol. 6. Vaughan, Brian K. rev. ed. 2005. (Y Ser.: Bk. 6). (ENG.). 128p. pap. 14.99 *(978-1-4012-0501-0(1),* Vertigo) DC Comics.

Guerra, Pia. The Last Man Vol. 4: Safeword, Vol. 4. Vaughan, Brian K. & Marzon, Jose. rev. ed. 2004. (Y Ser.). (ENG.). 144p. pap. 14.99 *(978-1-4012-0232-3(2),* Vertigo) DC Comics.

Guerra, Pia & Marzan, Jose, Jr. Kimono Dragons. Vaughan, Brian K. rev. ed. 2006. (Y Ser.). (ENG.). 144p. pap. 14.99 *(978-1-4012-1010-6(4),* Vertigo) DC Comics.

Guerra, Pia & Marzan, Jose. The Last Man - Ring of Truth, Vol. 5. Vaughan, Brian K. rev. ed. 2005. (Y Ser.: Bk. 5). (ENG.). 192p. pap. 14.99 *(978-1-4012-0487-7(2),* Vertigo) DC Comics.

Guerra, Pia & Marzan, Jose, Jr. One Small Step. Vaughan, Brian K. rev. ed. 2004. (Y Ser.: Vol. 3). (ENG.). 168p. pap. 14.99 *(978-1-4012-0201-9(2),* Vertigo) DC Comics.

Guerra, Pia, jt. illus. see Marzan, Jose, Jr.

Guerrero, Andrés. Los Cazadores de Monstruos. Vallejo-Nagera, Alejandra.Tr. of Monsters Hunters. (SPA.). 31p. (J). (gr. k-1). 8.95 *(978-1-58986-549-5(9))* Santillana USA Publishing Co., Inc.

—Cuando Llegara Mi Cumpleanos? Vallejo-Nagera, Alejandra. (SPA.). 29p. (J). (gr. k-1). 8.95 *(978-1-58986-548-8(0))* Santillana USA Publishing Co., Inc.

—Cuanto me Quieren! Vallejo-Nagera, Alejandra. 2003. (SPA.). 23p. (J). (gr. k-1). 8.95 *(978-84-204-4951-7(2))* Santillana USA Publishing Co., Inc.

—Mira Como He Crecido. Vallejo-Nagera, Alejandra. (SPA.). 31p. (J). (gr. k-1). 8.95 *(978-1-58986-547-1(2))* Santillana USA Publishing Co., Inc.

—No Tengo Sueno! Vallejo-Nagera, Alejandra. (SPA.). 31p. (J). (gr. k-1). 8.95 *(978-1-58986-546-4(4))* Santillana USA Publishing Co., Inc.

Guerrero, Andrés. La Noche. Guerrero, Andrés. 2003. (SPA.). 28p. (J). (gr. k-3). 7.95 *(978-84-204-4321-8(2))* Santillana USA Publishing Co., Inc.

Guest, Peggy. J. Milton Turner; an American Hero. Barile, Mary Collins. 2013. 52p. 24.95 *(978-0-9889643-0-3(9))* MathisJones Communications, LLC.

Guettier, Bénédicte. Dinosaurs. Guettier, Bénédicte. 2005. (ENG.). 14p. (J). (gr. -1-k). 11.95 *(978-1-929132-86-7(7))* Kane Miller.

Guevara, Dennis Villanueva. Pepitina. Iturrondo, Angeles Molina. 2004. (Green Ser.). 24p. (J). *(978-1-57581-435-3(8))* Ediciones Santillana, Inc.

Guevara, Susan. Chato & the Party Animals. Soto, Gary. (Chato Ser.). 25.95 incl. audio *(978-1-59112-460-3(3));* 28.95 incl. audio compact disk *(978-1-59112-920-2(6));* pap. 37.95 incl. audio *(978-1-59112-461-0(1));* pap. 39.95 incl. audio compact disk *(978-1-59112-921-9(4))* Live Oak Media.

—Chato & the Party Animals. Soto, Gary. 2004. (Chato Ser.). (ENG.). 32p. (J). (gr. k-3). reprint ed. pap. 6.99 *(978-0-14-240032-6(7),* Puffin) Penguin Publishing Group.

—Chato & the Party Animals. Soto, Gary. 2004. (Chato Ser.). (gr. -1-3). 17.00 *(978-0-7569-2921-3(0))* Perfection Learning Corp.

—Chato Goes Cruisin' Soto, Gary. 2008. (Chato Ser.). (J). 25.95 incl. audio *(978-1-59519-906-5(3));* pap. 16.95 *(978-1-59519-905-8(5))* Live Oak Media.

—Chato Goes Cruisin' Soto, Gary. 2007. (Chato Ser.). (J). (gr. -1-3). 14.65 *(978-0-7569-8147-1(6))* Perfection Learning Corp.

—Chato y los Amigos Pachangueros. Soto, Gary. 2004.Tr. of Chato & the Party Animals. (SPA & ENG.). 32p. (J). (gr. -1-3). reprint ed. pap. 7.99 *(978-0-14-240033-3(5),* Puffin) Penguin Publishing Group.

—Chato's Kitchen. Soto, Gary. 2003. (Chato Ser.). (J). (gr. -1-2). pap. 39.95 *(978-1-59112-527-3(8))* Live Oak Media.

—Isabel's House of Butterflies. Johnston, Tony. 2005. 32p. pap. 6.95 *(978-1-58685-844-5(0));* (ENG.). (J). (gr. 3-4). per. 7.99 *(978-1-57805-128-1(2))* Gibbs Smith, Publisher.

—The Lady in the Blue Cloak: Legends from the Texas Missions. Kimmel, Eric A. 2006. (ENG.). 40p. (J). (gr. 6-10). 16.95 *(978-0-8234-1738-4(7))* Holiday Hse., Inc.

—Little Roja Riding Hood. Elya, Susan Middleton. 2014. (ENG.). 32p. (J). (gr. k-3). 16.99 *(978-0-399-24767-5(X),* Putnam Juvenile) Penguin Publishing Group.

—Voice from Afar: Poems of Peace. Johnston, Tony. 2008. (ENG.). 32p. (YA). (gr. 5-18). 16.95 *(978-0-8234-2012-4(4))* Holiday Hse., Inc.

Guevara, Susan, jt. illus. see Morgan, Mary.

Gueyfier, Judith. Chandra's Magic Light. Heine, Theresa & Barefoot Books Staff. 2013. (J). 16.99 *(978-1-84686-493-3(3))* Barefoot Bks., Inc.

—Chandra's Magic Light: A Story in Nepal. Heine, Theresa & Barefoot Books Staff. 40p. pap. 8.99 *(978-1-84686-866-5(1))* Barefoot Bks., Inc.

Guggenheim, Jaenet. Grow, Grow, Grow. Riley, Barbara. l.t. ed. 2003. 40p. (J). 19.95 *(978-1-929115-08-2(3))* Azro Pr., Inc.

Guggenheim, Jaenet, photos by. Triassic Hall: Building the Triassic Exhibit from the Ground Up. Guggenheim, Jaenet. Lucas, Spencer G. Lucas, Spencer G., ed. 2011. 130p. 25.00 *(978-1-929115-21-1(0))* Azro Pr., Inc.

Gugu, Abdul M. Juma & Little Sungura. Burgess, Lisa Maria. 2013. 32p. 19.95 *(978-1-939604-06-4(0));* pap. 9.99 *(978-1-939604-02-6(8))* Barranca Pr.

—Juma Cooks Chapati. Burgess, Lisa Maria. 2013. 32p. 19.95 *(978-1-939604-08-8(7));* pap. 9.99 *(978-1-939604-04-0(4))* Barranca Pr.

—Juma on Safari. Burgess, Lisa Maria. 2013. 32p. 19.95 *(978-1-939604-07-1(9));* pap. 9.99 *(978-1-939604-03-3(6))* Barranca Pr.

—Juma's Dhow Race. Burgess, Lisa Maria. 2013. 32p. 19.95 *(978-1-939604-09-5(5));* pap. 9.99 *(978-1-939604-05-7(2))* Barranca Pr.

Guhe, Irmtraud. Understanding Horses with Caddie. von Kessel, Carola. 2004. (ENG.). 32p. (J). (gr. 4). 13.95 *(978-3-86127-948-8(7))* Cadmos Verlag GmbH DEU. Dist: Independent Pubs. Group.

Guiberson, Brenda Z. Disasters: Natural & Man-Made Catastrophes Through the Centuries. Guiberson, Brenda Z. 2010. (ENG.). 240p. (J). (gr. 5-9). 21.99 *(978-0-8050-8170-1(4),* Holt, Henry & Co. Bks. For Young Readers) Holt, Henry & Co.

—Disasters: Natural & Man-Made Catastrophes Through the Centuries. Guiberson, Brenda Z. 2014. (ENG.). 256p. (J). (gr. 5-9). pap. 12.99 *(978-1-250-05066-3(9))* Square Fish.

—Mummy Mysteries: Tales from North America. Guiberson, Brenda Z. 2013. (My Readers Ser.). (ENG.). 48p. (J). (gr. 1-3). 15.99 *(978-0-8050-8976-9(4));* pap. 3.99 *(978-1-250-01047-6(0))* Square Fish.

Guibert, Emmanuel. Alan's War: The Memories of G. I. Alan Cope. Guibert, Emmanuel. 2008. (ENG.). 336p. pap. 24.99 *(978-1-59643-096-9(6),* First Second Bks.) Roaring Brook Pr.

Guibord, Charity. Plug into the Power. Liebenow, Todd et al. 2003. 28p. (YA). spiral bd. 18.00 *(978-1-58302-231-3(7))* One Way St., Inc.

Guicciardini, Desideria. But What If? Graves, Sue. 2013. (Our Emotions & Behavior Ser.). (ENG.). 32p. (J). (gr. -1-3). 12.99 *(978-1-57542-444-6(4))* Free Spirit Publishing, Inc.

—Crabby Gabby. Graves, Sue. 2008. (Tadpoles Ser.). (ENG.). 24p. (J). (gr. -1-3). pap. *(978-0-7787-3883-1(3));* lib. bdg. *(978-0-7787-3852-7(3))* Crabtree Publishing Co.

—Crabby Gabby. Graves, Sue. 2008. (Tadpoles Ser.). 23p. (J). (gr. -1-3). 17.15 *(978-1-4178-0925-7(6),* Turtleback) Turtleback Bks.

—I Hate Everything! Graves, Sue. 2013. (Our Emotions & Behavior Ser.). (ENG.). 32p. (J). (gr. -1-3). 12.99 *(978-1-57542-443-9(6))* Free Spirit Publishing, Inc.

—Max & Millie Start School. Brooks, Felicity. 2013. (Toddler Bks.). (ENG.). 23p. (gr. -1). 7.99 *(978-0-7945-3302-1(7),* Usborne) EDC Publishing.

—Rumpelstiltskin. 2007. (Young Reading Series 1 Gift Bks.). 47p. (J). (gr. -1-3). 8.99 *(978-0-7945-1446-4(4),* Usborne) EDC Publishing.

—Take a Deep Breath. Graves, Sue. 2013. (Our Emotions & Behavior Ser.). (ENG.). 32p. (J). (gr. -1-3). 12.99 *(978-1-57542-446-0(0))* Free Spirit Publishing, Inc.

Guicciardini, Desideria & McNicholas, Shelagh. Hop, Skip & Jump. 2008. (Usborne Baby Board Bks.). 8p. (J). (gr. -1). bds. 15.99 incl. audio compact disk *(978-0-7945-1914-8(8),* Usborne) EDC Publishing.

Guice, Butch, et al. Criminal Intent, Vol. 3. Beatty, Scott. (Ruse Traveler Ser.: Vol. 3). 160p. 2004. (YA). pap. 9.95 *(978-1-59314-060-1(6));* 2003. (gr. 7-18). pap. 15.95 *(978-1-931484-74-9(0))* CrossGeneration Comics, Inc.

—Murder in Mind, Vol. 4. Beatty, Scott. 2004. (Ruse Ser.: Vol. 4). 160p. (YA). pap. 15.95 *(978-1-59314-047-2(9))* CrossGeneration Comics, Inc.

—The Silent Partner, Vol. 2. Waid, Mark & Beatty, Scott. 2003. (Ruse Ser.: Vol. 2). 160p. (YA). (gr. 7-18). 15.95 *(978-1-931484-48-0(1))* CrossGeneration Comics, Inc.

—What If? Vol. 7: Classic. 2011. (ENG.). 304p. (YA). (gr. 8-17). pap. 29.99 *(978-0-7851-5311-5(X))* Marvel Worldwide, Inc.

Guice, Butch & Acuña, Daniel. Captain America: The Trial of Captain America. Brubaker, Ed & Breitweiser, Mitch. 2011. (ENG.). 144p. (YA). (gr. 8-17). pap. 19.99 *(978-0-7851-5120-3(6))* Marvel Worldwide, Inc.

Guice, Butch & Perkins, Mike. Enter the Detective. Waid, Mark. 2003. (Ruse Traveler Ser.: Vol. 1). 192p. (YA). (gr. 7-18). pap. 9.95 *(978-1-59314-012-0(6))* CrossGeneration Comics, Inc.

Guice, Jackson. Albion. Busiek, Kurt et al. 2006. (ENG.). 144p. (YA). pap. 19.99 *(978-1-4012-0994-0(7))* DC Comics.

Guice, Jackson, et al. Captain America. Brubaker, Ed. 2013. (ENG.). 568p. (YA). (gr. 8-17). pap. 39.99 *(978-0-7851-8379-2(5))* Marvel Worldwide, Inc.

Guida, Liisa & Klein, Nancy Spence. Wee Sing Mother Goose, 1 vol. Beall, Pamela Conn & Nipp, Susan Hagen. 2006. (Wee Sing Ser.). (ENG.). 1p. (J). (gr. -1-2). 10.99 *(978-0-8431-0485-1(6),* Price Stern Sloan) Penguin Publishing Group.

Guida, Liisa C. Moon. Tomecek, Steve. 2005. (Jump into Science Ser.). (ENG.). 32p. (J). (gr. -1-3). 25.90 *(978-0-7922-8304-1(X),* National Geographic Children's Bks.) National Geographic Society.

—Stars. Tomecek, Steve. 2003. (Jump into Science Ser.). (J). 16.95 *(978-0-7922-8203-7(5))* CENGAGE Learning.

Guida, Liisa Chauncy. Moon. Tomecek, Steve. (Jump into Science Ser.). (ENG.). 32p. (J). (gr. -1-3). 2008. 6.95 *(978-1-4263-0250-3(9));* 2005. 16.95 *(978-0-7922-5123-1(7))* National Geographic Society. (National Geographic Children's Bks.).

Guida, Liisa Chauncy & Klein, Nancy. Wee Sing & Move. Beall, Pamela Conn & Nipp, Susan Hagen. 2009. (Wee Sing Ser.). (ENG.). 1p. (J). (gr. -1-2). 10.99 *(978-0-8431-8959-9(2),* Price Stern Sloan) Penguin Publishing Group.

Guidera, Daniel. The Deep Dish on Pizza! Krensky, Stephen. 2014. (History of Fun Stuff Ser.). (ENG.). 48p. (J). (gr. 1-3). pap. 3.99 *(978-1-4814-2055-6(0),* Simon Spotlight) Simon Spotlight.

—The Explosive Story of Fireworks! Einhorn, Kama. 2015. (History of Fun Stuff Ser.). (ENG.). 48p. (J). (gr. 1-3). 16.99 *(978-1-4814-3848-3(4))* Simon & Schuster Children's Publishing.

Guidi, Guido. Iron Man: I Am Iron Man! Rao, Lisa. 2008. (I Can Read Bks.). 32p. (J). (gr. -1-2). pap. 3.99 *(978-0-06-082193-7(0),* Harper Trophy) HarperCollins Pubs.

Guile, Gill. Bobby the Bulldozer. 2013. (On the Go! Bks.). (ENG.). 10p. (J). (gr. -1 — 1). bds. 5.99 *(978-0-7641-6602-0(6))* Barron's Educational Series, Inc.

—Danny the Digger. 2013. (On the Go! Bks.). (ENG.). 10p. (J). (gr. -1 — 1). bds. 5.99 *(978-0-7641-6603-7(4))* Barron's Educational Series, Inc.

—Huff & Puff. Rabe, Tish. 2014. (My First I Can Read Ser.). (ENG.). 24p. (J). (gr. -1-3). 16.99 *(978-0-06-230502-2(6));* pap. 3.99 *(978-0-06-230501-5(8))* HarperCollins Pubs.

—Huff & Puff & the New Train. Rabe, Tish. 2014. (My First I Can Read Ser.). (ENG.). 24p. (J). (gr. -1-3). pap. 3.99 *(978-0-06-230503-9(4))* HarperCollins Pubs.

—Huff & Puff Have Too Much Stuff! Rabe, Tish. 2014. (My First I Can Read Ser.). (ENG.). 24p. (J). (gr. -1-3). pap. 3.99 *(978-0-06-230505-3(0))* HarperCollins Pubs.

—In My Garden. 20p. (J). *(978-1-932209-38-9(7))* Bendon, Inc.

—Look & Find Bible: New Testament Stories. B&H Editorial Staff, ed. 2015. (Look & Find Ser.). (ENG.). 24p. (J). (gr. -1-3). 12.99 *(978-1-4336-8598-9(1),* B&H Kids) B&H Publishing Group.

—Look & Find Bible: Old Testament Stories. B&H Editorial Staff, ed. 2015. (Look & Find Ser.). (ENG.). 24p. (J). (gr. -1-3). 12.99 *(978-1-4336-8597-2(3),* B&H Kids) B&H Publishing Group.

—My Nursery Rhyme Pop-up Book. 20p. (J). *(978-1-59394-119-2(6))* Bendon, Inc.

—My Nursery Rhyme Pop-up Book. Davies, Gill. 2005. 20p. (J). (gr. k-4). reprint ed. 20.00 *(978-0-7567-8704-2(1))* DIANE Publishing Co.

—My Very Own Kitten. Hubbard, Ben. 2014. (ENG.). 12p. (J). (gr. -1). *(978-1-78244-602-6(8))* Top That! Publishing PLC.

—My Very Own Puppy. Hubbard, Ben. 2014. (ENG.). 12p. (gr. -1). *(978-1-78244-603-3(6))* Top That! Publishing PLC.

—Silly Tilly Witch: And Other Stories. Jordan, Jennifer. 2004. (Early Learning Ser.). 18p. (J). bds. 2.99 *(978-1-85854-825-8(X))* Brimax Books Ltd. GBR. Dist: Byeway Bks.

—Ten in a Bed: A Pop-up Counting Book. Davies, Gill. 20p. (J). *(978-1-59394-120-8(X))* Bendon, Inc.

—Tiny the Train. 2013. (On the Go! Bks.). (ENG.). 10p. (J). (gr. -1 — 1). bds. 5.99 *(978-0-7641-6604-4(2))* Barron's Educational Series, Inc.

—Tommy the Tractor. 2013. (On the Go! Bks.). (ENG.). 10p. (J). (gr. -1 — 1). bds. 5.99 *(978-0-7641-6605-1(0))* Barron's Educational Series, Inc.

—A Very Merry Christmas. Powell-Tuck, Maudie. 2014. 22p. (J). (gr. -1-k). bds. 8.99 *(978-1-58925-560-9(7))* Tiger Tales.

Guilhaumond, Gregory, jt. illus. see Futaki, Attila.

Guillain, Charlotte & Wildish, Lee. Marshmallows for Martians. Guillain, Adam. 2014. (ENG.). 32p. (J). (-k). pap. 10.99 *(978-1-4052-6681-9(3))* Egmont Bks., Ltd. GBR. Dist: Independent Pubs. Group.

Guille, Rosanne & Mayer, Uwe. Caterpillars & Butterflies. Turnbull, Stephanie. 2007. (Usborne Beginners Ser.). 32p. (J). (gr. -1-3). 4.99 *(978-0-7945-1337-5(9),* Usborne) EDC Publishing.

Guillerey, Aurélie. Tell Me about Colors, Shapes, & Opposites. Badreddine, Delphine. 2012. (ENG.). 72p. (J). (gr. -1-k). 17.95 *(978-1-926973-54-8(2),* Owlkids) Owlkids Bks. Inc. CAN. Dist: Perseus-PGW.

Guillet, Francois. La Puce Cosmique et le Rayon Bleuge. Guillet, Jean-Pierre. 2004. (Des 9 Ans. Ser.). (FRE.). 120p. (J). *(978-2-922565-98-0(X))* Editions de la Paix CAN. Dist: World of Reading, Ltd.

Guillon, Eric. Sleepy Kittens. Paul, Cinco & Daurio, Ken. 2010. (Despicable Me Ser.). (ENG.). 10p. (J). (gr. -1 — 1). bds. 8.99 *(978-0-316-08381-2(X),* L,B Kids) Hachette Bk. Group.

Guillope, Antoine. White Fang. London, Jack. 2013. (ENG.). 40p. (J). (gr. 2). 14.95 *(978-2-7338-2145-9(8))* Auzou, Philippe Editions FRA. Dist: Consortium Bk. Sales & Distribution.

Guilloppé, Antoine. The Arrow Finds Its Mark: A Book of Found Poems. Heard, Georgia. 2012. (ENG.). 48p. (J). (gr. 3-7). 16.99 *(978-1-59643-665-7(4))* Roaring Brook Pr.

Guimarães, Santi Román i. Kikiwi y los desperdicios en el fondo del Mar. Rodriguez-Nora, Tere. 2005. (SPA & ENG.). 32p. (J). (gr. 1). 10.95 *(978-84-96046-36-8(2))* Ediciones Norte, Inc.

Guinan, Paul & Randall, Ron. Proposition Player. Willingham, Bill. rev. ed. 2003. (ENG.). 144p. pap. 14.95 *(978-1-56389-808-2(X))* DC Comics.

Guinard, Geraldine. Dreamstone. Smith, Helene. 2005. 80p. (YA). pap. 13.50 *(978-1-920731-63-2(6))* Fremantle Pr. AUS. Dist: Independent Pubs. Group.

Guion, Melissa. Baby Penguins Everywhere! Guion, Melissa. (ENG.). (J). (gr. -1-k). 2013. 28p. bds. 6.99 *(978-0-399-16516-0(9));* 2012. 32p. 16.99 *(978-0-399-25535-9(4))* Penguin Publishing Group. (Philomel).

—Baby Penguins Love Their Mama. Guion, Melissa. 2014. (ENG.). 32p. (J). (gr. -1-k). 16.99 *(978-0-399-16365-4(4),* Philomel) Penguin Publishing Group.

Guion, Tamara. Hello, Grand Mamoon! Steinmann, Donna. 2005. 32p. (J). 16.95 *(978-0-9663286-4-6(7))* EarthTime Pubns.

Guirao, David. La Biomeaestra. Maestro, Pepe. 2010. (SPA.). 110p. (J). (gr. 4-6). pap. *(978-84-263-7371-7(2))* Vives, Luis Editorial (Edelvives).

Guiza, Vic. Bat in the Bunk: Summer Camp Stories Seires. 2015. (ENG.). 32p. (J). (gr. 1-18). 19.99 ***(978-0-9863743-0-2(X))*** Summer Camp Stories LLC.

Guiza, Victor. Counselor Dynamite: Twas the Day Before Christmas Break. Burgess, Starr. 2012. 28p. (J). 16.95 *(978-1-60131-118-4(4),* Castlebridge Bks.) Big Tent Bks.

—Counselor Dynamite Befuddles the Bullyville Crew. Burgess, Starr. 2013. 52p. (J). 19.95 *(978-1-60131-156-6(7),* Castlebridge Bks.) Big Tent Bks.

—Ms. Irene Is so Demanding. Barret, Marie. 2012. 26p. (J). 14.95 *(978-1-60131-110-8(9))* Big Tent Bks.

—Potato Pie Pirate. Purtle, Louise. 2009. 24p. (J). 15.99 *(978-0-9818145-0-6(6))* Biggaloo Bks.

—Recorder Karate. Shammas, Anna. 2012. 32p. pap. 8.95 *(978-0-9843869-2-5(0),* Castlebridge Bks.) Big Tent Bks.

—The Safety Pin: Summer Camp Stories. Sloyer, Elliot. 2014. (ENG.). 32p. (J). 16.95 *(978-1-60131-182-5(6),* Castlebridge Bks.) Big Tent Bks.

—Treasure Kai & the Lost Gold of Shark Island: Library Version (no chests or Toys) Robertson, Karen. 2008. (ENG.). 28p. (J). *(978-0-9804614-1-1(3))* Treasure Bound Books.
—Treasure Kai & the Lost Gold of Shark Island: Treasure chest & toys Version. Robertson, Karen. 2008. (ENG.). 28p. (J). *(978-0-9804614-0-4(5))* Treasure Bound Books.
Gulacy, Paul. Shang-Chi - Master of Kung Fu Vol. 1: The Hellfire Apocalypse. Moench, Doug. 2003. (Master of Kung Fu Ser.). 144p. pap. 14.99 *(978-0-7851-1124-5(7))* Marvel Worldwide, Inc.
Gulbis, Stephen. A Mom in a Million. Lewis, Jill. 2005. 32p. (J). *(978-1-84458-368-3(6),* Pavilion Children's Books) Pavilion Bks.
—Old MacDonald Had a Barn. 2003. 22p. (YA). *(978-1-85602-453-2(9),* Pavilion Children's Books) Pavilion Bks.
—The Wheels on the Bus. 2003. 22p. (YA). *(978-1-85602-454-9(7),* Pavilion Children's Books) Pavilion Bks.
Guler, Greg & Ulene, Nancy. Learn to Draw Plus Disney Phineas & Ferb. Peterson, Scott. 2012. (J). *(978-1-936309-71-9(8))* Quarto Publishing Group USA.
Gullens, Lee M. Off I Go! Cochran, Jean M. 2008. (ENG.). 32p. (J). (gr. -1-k). 16.95 *(978-0-9792035-1-0(1))* Pleasant St. Pr.
—Your Tummy's Talking! Cochran, Jean M. 2008. (ENG.). 32p. (J). (gr. -1-k). 16.95 *(978-0-9792035-3-4(8))* Pleasant St. Pr.
Gulley, Hardrick M. Buger the Butterfly & the Lion Kitties' First Adventure. Garrett, Diane Marie. 2008. 16p. pap. 24.95 *(978-1-60672-237-4(9))* America Star Bks.
Gulley, Martha. Champlain & the Silent One. Messner, Kate. 2008. (J). *(978-1-59531-050-7(9))* North Country Bks., Inc.
—New York Patriots. Blackman, Dorothy L. 2007. (J). *(978-1-59531-020-0(7))* North Country Bks., Inc.
Gulley SR, Wayne A. Michelangelo Tangelo - a Bully No More. Gulley Sr, Wayne A. Gulley, Robin, ed. 2012. 40p. pap. 13.99 *(978-0-9843505-5-1(1))* Gulley, Wayne.
Gulley Sr, Wayne A. Nick Gets Moving. Prevedel, Brenda. Gulley, Robin R., ed. 2013. 32p. pap. 9.99 *(978-0-9886117-1-9(6))* Gulley, Wayne.
Gulliksen, Eivind. Brains. Lennard, Kate. 2007. (Young Genius Bks.). (ENG.). 32p. (J). (gr. k-3). pap. 6.99 *(978-0-7641-3670-2(4))* Barron's Educational Series, Inc.
Gulliver, Amanda. The Big Mud Puddle, 1 vol. Dale, Jay. 2012. (Engage Literacy Yellow Ser.). (ENG.). 32p. (gr. k-2). pap. 5.99 *(978-1-4296-8956-4(0),* Engage Literacy) Capstone Pr., Inc.
—Colors. 2011. (Baby Rattle Bks.). 12p. (J). (gr. -1-k). 4.99 *(978-0-7641-6391-3(4))* Barron's Educational Series, Inc.
—Dance Just Like Me, 1 vol. Powell, Jillian. 2013. (Start Reading Ser.). (ENG.). 24p. (gr. k-1). pap. 6.99 *(978-1-4765-3188-5(9));* pap. 41.94 *(978-1-4765-3209-7(5))* Capstone Pr., Inc.
—Fun Run. Powell, Jillian. 2013. (Start Reading Ser.). (ENG.). 24p. (gr. k-1). pap. 41.94 *(978-1-4765-3210-3(9));* pap. 6.99 *(978-1-4765-3189-2(7))* Capstone Pr., Inc.
—I Am Big, 1 vol. Dale, Jay. 2012. (Engage Literacy Magenta Ser.). (ENG.). 32p. (gr. k-2). pap. 5.99 *(978-1-4296-8874-1(2),* Engage Literacy) Capstone Pr., Inc.
—I Can See It Too!, 1 vol. Dale, Jay. 2012. (Wonder Words Ser.). (ENG.). 32p. (gr. k-2). pap. 5.99 *(978-1-4296-8896-3(3),* Engage Literacy) Capstone Pr., Inc.
—I Go Up, 1 vol. Dale, Jay. 2012. (Engage Literacy Magenta Ser.). (ENG.). 32p. (gr. k-2). pap. 5.99 *(978-1-4296-8832-1(7),* Engage Literacy) Capstone Pr., Inc.
—Jesus Loves the Little Children. Traditional. 2014. 16p. (J). 12.99 *(978-0-8249-1922-1(X),* Candy Cane Pr.) Ideals Pubns.
—Lea Is Hungry, 1 vol. Dale, Jay. 2012. (Engage Literacy Red Ser.). (ENG.). 32p. (gr. k-2). pap. 5.99 *(978-1-4296-8833-8(5),* Engage Literacy) Capstone Pr., Inc.
—Lea's Birthday, 1 vol. Dale, Jay. 2012. (Engage Literacy Yellow Ser.). (ENG.). 32p. (gr. k-2). pap. 5.99 *(978-1-4296-8964-9(1),* Engage Literacy) Capstone Pr., Inc.
—Oops!, 1 vol. Powell, Jillian. 2013. (Start Reading Ser.). (ENG.). 24p. (gr. k-1). pap. 6.99 *(978-1-4765-3190-8(0));* pap. 41.94 *(978-1-4765-3227-1(3))* Capstone Pr., Inc.
—Pets. 2011. (Baby Rattle Bks.). 12p. (J). (gr. -1-k). 5.99 *(978-0-7641-6392-0(2))* Barron's Educational Series, Inc.
—Underwater. 2011. (Baby Rattle Bks.). 12p. (J). (gr. -1-k). 5.99 *(978-0-7641-6393-7(0))* Barron's Educational Series, Inc.
—Zoo. 2011. (Baby Rattle Bks.). 12p. (J). (gr. -1-k). 6.99 *(978-0-7641-6394-4(9))* Barron's Educational Series, Inc.
Gullotti, Pat. Pig Kissing. LaSala, Paige. 2010. 24p. pap. 12.99 *(978-1-4520-2849-1(4))* AuthorHouse.
Gulzeth, Ray. Warren Is Wonderful. Becklund, Annette L. 2009. 52p. pap. 12.95 *(978-1-4401-2042-8(0))* iUniverse, Inc.
Gumm, Susan Kathleen. Big Mister Little Mister Baby Sister. Piccirillo, Renee. 2006. (J). per. 12.50 *(978-0-9771482-0-2(3),* Ithaca Pr.) Authors & Artists Publishers of New York, Inc.
—God Remembered Us. Lewin, Terry. 2006. 36p. (J). per. 19.00 *(978-0-9771482-1-9(1),* Ithaca Pr.) Authors & Artists Publishers of New York, Inc.
—I Plant a Garden with My Mom. Papazoglu, Paula. 2005. (J). per. 15.00 *(978-0-9754298-9-1(2),* Ithaca Pr.) Authors & Artists Publishers of New York, Inc.
Gundert, Marjorie. D. Q. & the SOOYOO, 1 vol. Gundert, Margaret. 2010. 20p. 24.95 *(978-1-4512-1226-6(7))* PublishAmerica, Inc.
Gunetsreiner, Nina, jt. illus. see Schoene, Kerstin.
Gunn, Linda. Bushed! All in the Woods. Poulter, J. R. 2015. 36p. pap. 19.99 ***(978-1-63418-936-1(1))*** Tate Publishing & Enterprises, LLC.
Gunnell, Beth, jt. illus. see Davies, Hannah.
Gunnella & Gunnella. The Problem with Chickens. McMillan, Bruce. 2005. (ENG.). 32p. (J). (gr. -1-3). 16.00 *(978-0-618-58581-6(8))* Houghton Mifflin Harcourt Publishing Co.
Gunnella, jt. illus. see Gunnella.
Gunson, Dave. Dinosaurs. Martin, Justin McCory. 2008. 32p. *(978-0-545-08456-7(3))* Scholastic, Inc.
Gunther, Richard. The Day the World Went Wacky. Suter, Janine. 2009. 32p. (J). 10.99 *(978-0-89051-575-4(1))* Master Bks.
—Noah's Floating Animal Park. Suter, Janine. 2009. 32p. (J). 10.99 *(978-0-89051-576-1(X))* Master Bks.
—The Not So Super Skyscraper! Suter, Janine. 2009. 32p. (J). 10.99 *(978-0-89051-577-8(8))* Master Bks.
Gupta, Garima. The Mustache Man. Ramanathan, Priya. 2013. (ENG.). 32p. (J). (gr. -1). pap. 9.95 *(978-81-8190-186-6(X))* Karadi Tales Co. Pvt, Ltd. IND. Dist: Consortium Bk. Sales & Distribution.
Gurihiru Staff. Avatar: the Last Airbender: the Rift Part 2. Yang, Gene Luen & DiMartino, Michael Dante. 2014. (Avatar: the Last Airbender Ser.). (ENG.). 80p. pap. 10.99 *(978-1-61655-296-1(4))* Dark Horse Comics.
—Big Trouble at the Big Top! Sumerak, Marc. 2006. (X-Men Power Pack - 4 Titles Ser.). 24p. lib. bdg. 22.78 *(978-1-59961-219-5(4))* Spotlight.
—Costumes On! Sumerak, Marc. 2006. (X-Men Power Pack - 4 Titles Ser.). 24p. lib. bdg. 22.78 *(978-1-59961-220-1(8))* Spotlight.
—Mind over Matter. Sumerak, Marc. 2006. (X-Men Power Pack - 4 Titles Ser.). 24p. lib. bdg. 22.78 *(978-1-59961-222-5(4))* Spotlight.
Gurihiru Staff, jt. illus. see Di Vito, Andrea.
Gurin, Lara. Ella the Baby Elephant: A Baby Elephant's Story. Duey, Kathleen. 2008. (My Animal Family Ser.). (ENG.). 32p. (J). (gr. -1-3). 12.99 *(978-0-8249-5584-7(6),* Ideals Children's Bks.) Ideals Pubns.
—Father & Son Read-Aloud Old Testament Stories. Gould, Robert. 2010. (Father & Son Read-Aloud Stories Ser.). (ENG.). 60p. (J). (gr. -1-k). 14.95 *(978-1-929945-73-3(6))* Big Guy Bks., Inc.
—Father & Son Read-Aloud Stories. Gould, Robert. 2006. (ENG.). 56p. (J). (gr. -1-k). 12.95 *(978-1-929945-67-2(1))* Big Guy Bks., Inc.
—Korow: A Baby Chimpanzee's Story. Duey, Kathleen. 2008. (My Animal Family Ser.). (ENG.). 32p. (J). (gr. -1-3). 12.99 *(978-0-8249-1816-3(9),* Ideals Children's Bks.) Ideals Pubns.
—Leo: A Baby Lion's Story. Duey, Kathleen. 2008. (My Animal Family Ser.). 32p. (J). (gr. -1-3). 12.99 *(978-0-8249-1817-0(7),* Ideals Children's Bks.) Ideals Pubns.
—Nanuq: A Baby Polar Bear's Story. Duey, Kathleen. 2008. (ENG.). 32p. (J). (gr. -1-3). 12.99 *(978-0-8249-1818-7(5),* Ideals Children's Bks.) Ideals Pubns.
—Tahi: A Baby Dolphin's Story. Duey, Kathleen. 2009. (ENG.). 32p. 12.99 *(978-0-8249-1434-9(1),* Candy Cane Pr.) Ideals Pubns.
Gurin, Laura. Leo the Lion - Book & Dvd. Duey, Kathleen. 2007. 32p. 14.99 *(978-0-8249-6724-6(0),* Ideals Children's Bks.) Ideals Pubns.
Guritz, Linda F. The Giving Gnome. Button, Kevin. 2010. 28p. pap. 12.95 *(978-1-936343-22-5(3))* Peppertree Pr., The.
Gurney, James. Dinotopia: Journey to Chandara. Gurney, James. 2007. (ENG.). 160p. (gr. 3-7). 29.95 *(978-0-7407-6431-8(4))* Andrews McMeel Publishing.
—Dinotopia: The World Beneath. Gurney, James. 2003. (Dinotopia Ser.). (ENG.). 160p. (J). pap. 19.99 *(978-0-06-053065-5(0))* HarperCollins Pubs.
Gurney, James & Gurney, James. A Land Apart from Time. Gurney, James & Gurney, James. 2003. (Dinotopia Ser.). (ENG.). 160p. (J). (gr. 3-7). pap. 21.99 *(978-0-06-053064-8(2))* HarperCollins Pubs.
Gurney, James, jt. illus. see Gurney, James.
Gurney, John Steven. The Absent Author. Roy, Ron. unabr. ed. 2004. (A to Z Mysteries Ser.: No. 1). 86p. (J). (gr. k-3). pap. 17.00 incl. audio *(978-0-8072-1703-0(4),* S FTR 269 SP, Listening Library) Random Hse. Audio Publishing Group.
—April Adventure. Roy, Ron. 2010. (Stepping Stone Book(TM) Ser.: No. 4). (ENG.). 80p. (J). (gr. 1-4). 4.99 *(978-0-375-86116-1(5),* Random Hse. Bks. for Young Readers) Random Hse. Children's Bks.
—August Acrobat. Roy, Ron. 2012. (Stepping Stone Book Ser.). (ENG.). 80p. (J). (gr. 1-4). lib. bdg. 12.99 *(978-0-375-96886-0(5),* Random Hse. Bks. for Young Readers) Random Hse. Children's Bks.
—The Bald Bandit. Roy, Ron. unabr. ed. 2004. (A to Z Mysteries Ser.: No. 2). 80p. (J). (gr. k-3). pap. 17.00 incl. audio *(978-0-8072-1704-7(2),* S FTR 270 SP, Listening Library) Random Hse. Audio Publishing Group.
—Bub, Snow, & the Burly Bear Scare. Wallace, Carol & Wallace, Bill. 2003. (ENG.). 128p. (J). (gr. 3-7). pap. 7.99 *(978-0-7434-0640-6(0),* Simon & Schuster/Paula Wiseman Bks.) Simon & Schuster/Paula Wiseman Bks.
—Calendar Mysteries: April Adventure. Roy, Ron. 2010. (Stepping Stone Book(TM) Ser.: No. 4). (ENG.). 80p. (J). (gr. 1-4). lib. bdg. 12.99 *(978-0-375-96116-8(X),* Random Hse. Bks. for Young Readers) Random Hse. Children's Bks.
—Calendar Mysteries #11: November Night. Roy, Ronald. 2014. (Stepping Stone Book(TM) Ser.). (ENG.). 80p. (J). (gr. 1-4). 4.99 *(978-0-385-37165-0(9),* Random Hse. Bks. for Young Readers) Random Hse. Children's Bks.
—Calendar Mysteries #12: December Dog. Roy, Ronald. 2014. (Stepping Stone Book(TM) Ser.). (ENG.). 80p. (J). (gr. 1-4). 4.99 *(978-0-385-37168-1(3),* Random Hse. Bks. for Young Readers) Random Hse. Children's Bks.
—Calendar Mysteries #13: New Year's Eve Thieves. Roy, Ronald. 2014. (Stepping Stone Book(TM) Ser.). (ENG.). 80p. (J). (gr. 1-4). 4.99 *(978-0-385-37171-1(3),* Random Hse. Bks. for Young Readers) Random Hse. Children's Bks.
—Calendar Mysteries #8: August Acrobat. Roy, Ron. 2012. (Stepping Stone Book(TM) Ser.). (ENG.). 80p. (J). (gr. 1-4). 4.99 *(978-0-375-86886-3(0),* Random Hse. Bks. for Young Readers) Random Hse. Children's Bks.
—The Canary Caper. Roy, Ron. unabr. ed. 2004. (A to Z Mysteries Ser.: No. 3). 80p. (J). (gr. k-3). pap. 17.00 incl. audio *(978-0-8072-1705-4(0),* S FTR 271 SP, Listening Library) Random Hse. Audio Publishing Group.
—Chatterbox: The Bird Who Wore Glasses. Uslan, Michael E. 2006. 34p. (J). 17.99 *(978-0-9753843-2-9(5))* ee publishing & productions, inc.
—Detective Camp. Roy, Ron. 2006. (Stepping Stone Book(TM) Ser.: No. 1). (ENG.). 144p. (J). (gr. 1-4). per. 5.99 *(978-0-375-83534-6(2),* Random Hse. Bks. for Young Readers) Random Hse. Children's Bks.
—February Friend. Roy, Ron. 2009. (Stepping Stone Book Ser.: No. 2). (ENG.). 80p. (J). (gr. 1-4). 4.99 *(978-0-375-85662-4(5))* Random Hse., Inc.
—January Joker. Roy, Ron. 2009. (Stepping Stone Book Ser.: No. 1). (ENG.). 96p. (J). (gr. 1-4). 4.99 *(978-0-375-85661-7(7))* Random Hse., Inc.
—July Jitters. Roy, Ron. 2012. (Stepping Stone Book(TM) Ser.). (ENG.). 80p. (J). (gr. 1-4). 4.99 *(978-0-375-86882-5(8))* Random Hse., Children's Bks.
—June Jam. Roy, Ron. 2011. (Stepping Stone Book(TM) Ser.). (ENG.). 80p. (J). (gr. 1-4). 4.99 *(978-0-375-86112-3(2),* Random Hse. Bks. for Young Readers) Random Hse. Children's Bks.
—March Mischief. Roy, Ron. 2010. (Stepping Stone Book Ser.: No. 3). (ENG.). 80p. (J). (gr. 1-4). 4.99 *(978-0-375-85663-1(3));* lib. bdg. 12.99 *(978-0-375-95663-8(8))* Random Hse., Inc.
—May Magic. Roy, Ron. 2011. (Stepping Stone Book Ser.). (ENG.). 80p. (J). (gr. 1-4). 4.99 *(978-0-375-86111-6(4));* lib. bdg. 12.99 *(978-0-375-96111-3(9))* Random Hse. Children's Bks.
—Mayflower Treasure Hunt. Roy, Ron. 2nd ed. 2007. (Stepping Stone Book Ser.: No. 2). (ENG.). 128p. (J). (gr. 1-4). per. 5.99 *(978-0-375-83937-5(2),* Random Hse. Bks. for Young Readers) Random Hse. Children's Bks.
—Mayflower Treasure Hunt. Roy, Ron. ed. 2007. (to Z Mysteries Ser.: 28). 114p. (gr. 4-7). lib. bdg. 16.00 *(978-1-4177-9141-5(1),* Turtleback) Turtleback Bks.
—The Meanest Hound Around. Wallace, Carol & Wallace, Bill. 2004. 149p. (J). (gr. 2-5). 12.65 *(978-0-7569-3960-1(7))* Perfection Learning Corp.
—The Meanest Hound Around. Wallace, Carol & Wallace, Bill. 2004. (ENG.). 160p. (J). (gr. 2-5). pap. 5.99 *(978-0-7434-3786-8(1),* Simon & Schuster/Paula Wiseman Bks.) Simon & Schuster/Paula Wiseman Bks.
—The New Year Dragon Dilemma. Roy, Ron. 2011. (Stepping Stone Book(TM) Ser.). (ENG.). 144p. (J). (gr. 1-4). lib. bdg. 12.99 *(978-0-375-96880-8(6),* Random Hse. Bks. for Young Readers) Random Hse. Children's Bks.
—The New Year Dragon Dilemma. Roy, Ron. 2011. (Stepping Stone Book(TM) Ser.). (ENG.). 144p. (J). (gr. 1-4). 5.99 *(978-0-375-86880-1(1),* Random Hse. Bks. for Young Readers) Random Hse. Children's Bks.
—The Night Before Christmas. Moore, Clement C. & Linz, Peter. 2006. (ENG.). 32p. (J). (gr. -1-3). 18.95 *(978-0-439-89843-0(9))* Scholastic, Inc.
—The Night Before Christmas. Moore, Clement C. 2006. (ENG.). (J). (gr. -1-3). 9.99 *(978-0-439-89557-6(X))* Scholastic, Inc.
—October Ogre. Roy, Ron. 2013. (Stepping Stone Book(TM) Ser.). (ENG.). 80p. (J). (gr. 1-4). 4.99 *(978-0-375-86888-7(7));* lib. bdg. 12.99 *(978-0-375-96888-4(1))* Random Hse., Inc.
Gurney, John Steven. On with the Show! Finch, Kate. 2014. 76p. (J). ***(978-1-4242-5954-0(1))*** Scholastic, Inc.
Gurney, John Steven. Operation Orca. Roy, Ron. 2015. (Stepping Stone Book(TM) Ser.). (ENG.). 144p. (J). (gr. 1-4). 12.99 *(978-0-553-52397-3(X),* Random Hse. Bks. for Young Readers) Random Hse. Children's Bks.
—Roscoe & the Pony Parade. Earhart, Kristin. 2008. (Little Apple Ser.). 88p. (J). *(978-0-545-08094-1(0))* Scholastic, Inc.
—The School Skeleton. Roy, Ron. 2003. (Stepping Stone Book Ser.: No. 19). (ENG.). 96p. (J). (gr. 1-4). pap. 4.99 *(978-0-375-81368-9(3),* Random Hse. Bks. for Young Readers) Random Hse. Children's Bks.
—The School Skeleton. Roy, Ron. ed. 2003. (to Z Mysteries Ser.: 19). (gr. k-3). lib. bdg. 14.75 *(978-0-613-62405-3(X),* Turtleback) Turtleback Bks.
—September Sneakers. Roy, Ron. 2013. (Stepping Stone Book(TM) Ser.). (ENG.). 80p. (J). (gr. 1-4). 4.99 *(978-0-375-86887-0(9))* Random Hse., Inc.
—Sleepy Hollow Sleepover. Roy, Ron. 4th ed. 2010. (Stepping Stone Book(TM) Ser.). (ENG.). 144p. (J). (gr. 1-4). pap. 5.99 *(978-0-375-86669-2(8),* Random Hse. Bks. for Young Readers) Random Hse. Children's Bks.
—Sunny to the Rescue. Dower, Laura. 2013. (Palace Puppies Ser.). (ENG.). 128p. (J). (gr. 1-3). pap. 4.99 *(978-1-4231-6486-9(5))* Disney Pr.
—The Talking T. Rex. Roy, Ron. 2003. (Stepping Stone Book(TM) Ser.: No. 20). (ENG.). 96p. (J). (gr. 1-4). pap. 4.99 *(978-0-375-81369-6(1),* Random Hse. Bks. for Young Readers) Random Hse. Children's Bks.
—The Talking T. Rex. Roy, Ron. ed. 2003. (to Z Mysteries Ser.: 20). (gr. 3-6). lib. bdg. 14.75 *(978-0-613-85127-5(7),* Turtleback) Turtleback Bks.
—A to Z Mysteries Collection, No. 1. Roy, Ron. 2010. (Stepping Stone Book(TM) Ser.: Nos. 1-4). (ENG.). 384p. (J). (gr. 1-4). 9.99 *(978-0-375-85946-5(2),* Random Hse. Bks. for Young Readers) Random Hse. Children's Bks.
—A to Z Mysteries Super Edition #6: the Castle Crime. Roy, Ronald. 2014. (Stepping Stone Book(TM) Ser.). (ENG.). 144p. (J). (gr. 1-4). 5.99 *(978-0-385-37159-9(4),* Random Hse. Bks. for Young Readers) Random Hse. Children's Bks.
—The Unwilling Umpire. Roy, Ron. 2004. (Stepping Stone Book(TM) Ser.: No. 21). (ENG.). 96p. (J). (gr. 1-4). 4.99 *(978-0-375-81370-2(5),* Random Hse. Bks. for Young Readers) Random Hse. Children's Bks.
—The Unwilling Umpire. Roy, Ron. ed. 2004. (to Z Mysteries Ser.: 21). (gr. k-3). lib. bdg. 14.75 *(978-0-613-82496-5(2),* Turtleback) Turtleback Bks.
—The Vampire's Vacation. Roy, Ron. 2004. (Stepping Stone Book(TM) Ser.: No. 22). (ENG.). 96p. (J). (gr. 1-4). pap. 4.99 *(978-0-375-82479-1(0),* Random Hse. Bks. for Young Readers) Random Hse. Children's Bks.
—White House White-Out. Roy, Ron. 2008. (A to Z Mysteries Ser.: No. 3). 124p. (gr. 1-4). 15.00 *(978-0-7569-8799-2(7))* Perfection Learning Corp.
—White House White-Out. Roy, Ron. 2008. (Stepping Stone Book(TM) Ser.: No. 3). (ENG.). 144p. (J). (gr. 1-4). 5.99 *(978-0-375-84721-9(9),* Random Hse. Bks. for Young Readers) Random Hse. Children's Bks.
—The X'ed-Out X-Ray. Roy, Ron. 2005. (Stepping Stone Book(TM) Ser.: No. 24). (ENG.). 96p. (J). (gr. 1-4). 4.99 *(978-0-375-82481-4(2),* Random Hse. Bks. for Young Readers) Random Hse. Children's Bks.
—The Yellow Yacht. Roy, Ron. 2005. (Stepping Stone Book Ser.: No. 25). (ENG.). 96p. (J). (gr. 1-4). pap. 4.99 *(978-0-375-82482-1(0),* Random Hse. Bks. for Young Readers) Random Hse. Children's Bks.
—The Zombie Zone. Roy, Ron. 2005. (Stepping Stone Book Ser.: No. 26). (ENG.). 96p. (J). (gr. 1-4). pap. 4.99 *(978-0-375-82483-8(9),* Random Hse. Bks. for Young Readers) Random Hse. Children's Bks.
Gurney, John Steven. The White Wolf. Gurney, John Steven, tr. Roy, Ron. 2004. (Stepping Stone Book(TM) Ser.: No. 23). (ENG.). 96p. (J). (gr. 1-4). pap. 4.99 *(978-0-375-82480-7(4),* Random Hse. Bks. for Young Readers) Random Hse. Children's Bks.
Gurney, John Steven & Jessell, Tim. Pet Hotel #1: Calling All Pets! Finch, Kate. 2013. (Pet Hotel Ser.: 1). (ENG.). 96p. (J). (gr. 2-5). pap. 4.99 *(978-0-545-50180-4(6),* Scholastic Paperbacks) Scholastic, Inc.
—Pet Hotel #2: a Big Surprise. Finch, Kate. 2013. (Pet Hotel Ser.: 2). (ENG.). 96p. (J). (gr. 2-5). pap. 4.99 *(978-0-545-50182-8(2),* Scholastic Paperbacks) Scholastic, Inc.
—Pet Hotel #3: a Nose for Trouble. Finch, Kate. 2013. (Pet Hotel Ser.: 3). (ENG.). 96p. (J). (gr. 2-5). pap. 4.99 *(978-0-545-50183-5(0),* Scholastic Paperbacks) Scholastic, Inc.
—Pet Hotel #4: on with the Show! Finch, Kate. 2014. (Pet Hotel Ser.: 4). (ENG.). 96p. (J). (gr. 2-5). pap. 4.99 *(978-0-545-50184-2(9),* Scholastic Paperbacks) Scholastic, Inc.
Gurovich, Natalia. Los Numeros Tragaldabas. Robleda, Margarita. 2004. (SPA.). 24p. (J). 12.95 *(978-970-690-807-0(2))* Planeta Mexicana Editorial S. A. de C. V. MEX. Dist: Lectorum Pubns., Inc.
—Quien Soy? Adivinanzas Animales. Robleda, Margarita. 2003. (SPA.). 32p. (J). 12.95 *(978-970-690-805-6(6))* Planeta Mexicana Editorial S. A. de C. V. MEX. Dist: Lectorum Pubns., Inc.
Gurr, Simon. Darwin: A Graphic Biography. Byrne, Eugene. 2013. (ENG.). 100p. (J). (gr. 7). pap. 9.95 *(978-1-58834-352-9(9))* Smithsonian Institution Pr.
Gürth, Per-Henrik. ABC of Canada. Bellefontaine, Kim. (ENG.). (J). 2006. 30p. bds. 8.95 *(978-1-55337-979-9(9));* 2004. 32p. (gr. -1-1). 7.95 *(978-1-55337-685-9(4))* Kids Can Pr., Ltd. CAN. Dist: Univ. of Toronto Pr.
—ABC of Toronto. 2013. (ENG.). 32p. (J). 15.95 *(978-1-77138-037-9(3))* Kids Can Pr., Ltd. CAN. Dist: Univ. of Toronto Pr.
Gurth, Per-Henrik. Canada 123. Bellefontaine, Kim. (ENG.). 24p. (J). 2008. (gr. -1). bds. 8.95 *(978-1-55453-235-3(3));* 2006. 14.95 *(978-1-55337-897-6(0))* Kids Can Pr., Ltd. CAN. Dist: Univ. of Toronto Pr.
—Canada 123. Bellefontaine, Kim. 2011. (ENG.). 24p. (J). 7.95 *(978-1-55453-659-7(6))* Kids Can Pr., Ltd. CAN. Dist: Univ. of Toronto Pr.
—Canada in Colours. Ghione, Yvette. 2008. (ENG.). 24p. (J). (gr. -1). 14.95 *(978-1-55453-240-7(X))* Kids Can Pr., Ltd. CAN. Dist: Univ. of Toronto Pr.
Gürth, Per-Henrik. Hockey Opposites. Ghione, Yvette. 2010. (ENG.). 24p. (J). (gr. -1-1). 15.95 *(978-1-55453-241-4(8))* Kids Can Pr., Ltd. CAN. Dist: Univ. of Toronto Pr.
Gurth, Per-Henrik. Snowy Sports: Ready, Set, Play! 2009. (ENG.). 24p. (J). (gr. -1-2). 14.95 *(978-1-55337-367-4(7))* Kids Can Pr., Ltd. CAN. Dist: Univ. of Toronto Pr.
Gürth, Per-Henrik. Canada in Colours. Gürth, Per-Henrik. 2011. (ENG.). 24p. (J). bds. 8.95 *(978-1-55453-757-0(6))* Kids Can Pr., Ltd. CAN. Dist: Univ. of Toronto Pr.
—Canada in Words. Gürth, Per-Henrik. 2012. (ENG.). 32p. (J). 14.95 *(978-1-55453-710-5(X))* Kids Can Pr., Ltd. CAN. Dist: Univ. of Toronto Pr.
—First Hockey Words. Gürth, Per-Henrik. 2014. (ENG.). 32p. (J). (gr. -1-k). 15.95 *(978-1-77138-114-7(0))* Kids Can Pr., Ltd. CAN. Dist: Univ. of Toronto Pr.
Gurth, Per-Henrik. Oh, Canada! Gurth, Per-Henrik. Ghione, Yvette. 2009. (ENG.). 32p. (J). (gr. -1-2). 14.95 *(978-1-55453-374-9(0))* Kids Can Pr., Ltd. CAN. Dist: Univ. of Toronto Pr.
Gurule, Jennifer. Look at Aunt Clare's Hair. Gurule, Jennifer. ed. 2005. (Daddy's Collection). (J). pap. 11.50 *(978-1-59134-033-1(0))* Maval Publishing, Inc.
Gustafson, Scott. Cuentos y Cantos de Navidad. 2004. (ESP & SPA.). 98p. (YA). 12.98 *(978-1-4127-0628-5(9),* 7137007) Phoenix International Publications, Inc.
Gustafson, Scott. Eddie: The Lost Youth of Edgar Allan Poe. Gustafson, Scott. (ENG.). 208p. (J). (gr. 3-7). 2012. pap. 6.99 *(978-1-4169-9765-8(2));* 2011. 15.99 *(978-1-4169-9764-1(4))* Simon & Schuster Bks. For Young Readers. (Simon & Schuster Bks. For Young Readers).
Gustafson, Troy, jt. illus. see Daly, Dan.
Gustavson, Adam. Better Than You. Ludwig, Trudy. 2011. (ENG.). 32p. (J). (gr. 1-4). 15.99 *(978-1-58246-380-3(8),* Tricycle Pr.) Ten Speed Pr.
—The Blue House Dog, 1 vol. Blumenthal, Deborah. 2010. (ENG.). 32p. (J). (gr. -1-3). 15.95 *(978-1-56145-537-9(7),* Peachtree Junior) Peachtree Pubs.
—Calico Dorsey: Mail Dog of the Mining Camps. Lendroth, Susan. 2010. (ENG.). 32p. (J). (gr. -1-2). 16.99 *(978-1-58246-318-6(2),* Tricycle Pr.) Ten Speed Pr.
—Charlie Bumpers vs. the Really Nice Gnome, 1 vol. Harley, Bill. (Charlie Bumpers Ser.). (ENG.). 160p. (J). (gr. 2-4).

2015. pap. 6.95 *(978-1-56145-831-8(7))*; 2014. 13.95 *(978-1-56145-740-3(X))* Peachtree Pubs.
—Charlie Bumpers vs. the Teacher of the Year, 1 vol. Harley, Bill. (Charlie Bumpers Ser.). (ENG.). 160p. (J). 2014. pap. 6.95 *(978-1-56145-824-0(4))*; 2013. (gr. 2-4). 13.95 *(978-1-56145-732-8(9))* Peachtree Pubs.
—Dirty Rats? Lunde, Darrin. 2015. (ENG.). 32p. (J). (gr. -1-2). 16.95 *(978-1-58089-566-8(2))* Charlesbridge Publishing, Inc.
—Hannah's Way. Glaser, Linda. 2012. (Shabbat Ser.). (ENG.). 32p. (J). (gr. k-3). pap. 7.95 *(978-0-7613-5138-2(8)*, Kar-Ben Publishing) Lerner Publishing Group.
—Jingle Bells: How the Holiday Classic Came to Be, 1 vol. Harris, John. 2011. (ENG.). 32p. (J). 16.95 *(978-1-56145-590-4(3))* Peachtree Pubs.
—The John Hancock Club. Borden, Louise. 2007. (ENG.). 48p. (J). (gr. 2-5). 17.99 *(978-1-4169-1813-4(2)*, McElderry, Margaret K. Bks.) McElderry, Margaret K. Bks.
—Just Kidding. Ludwig, Trudy. 2006. (ENG.). 32p. (J). (gr. 1-4). 15.99 *(978-1-58246-163-2(5)*, Tricycle Pr.) Ten Speed Pr.
—The Last Day of School. Borden, Louise. 2006. (ENG.). 40p. (J). (gr. 2-5). 17.99 *(978-0-689-86869-6(3)*, McElderry, Margaret K. Bks.) McElderry, Margaret K. Bks.
—The Little Rock Nine Stand up for Their Rights. Lucas, Eileen. 2011. (History Speaks: Picture Books Plus Reader's Theater Ser.). (ENG.). 48p. (gr. 2-4). lib. bdg. 27.93 *(978-0-7613-5874-9(9)*, Millbrook Pr.) Lerner Publishing Group.
—Lost & Found, 1 vol. Harley, Bill. 2012. (ENG.). 32p. (J). 16.95 *(978-1-56145-628-4(4))* Peachtree Pubs.
—The Lost-and-Found Tooth. Borden, Louise. 2008. (ENG.). 40p. (J). (gr. 2-5). 16.99 *(978-1-4169-1814-1(0)*, McElderry, Margaret K. Bks.) McElderry, Margaret K. Bks.
—Mind Your Manners, Alice Roosevelt!, 1 vol. Kimmelman, Leslie. 2009. (ENG.). 32p. (J). (gr. -1-3). 16.95 *(978-1-56145-492-1(3))* Peachtree Pubs.
—Rock & Roll Highway: The Robbie Robertson Story. Robertson, Sebastian. 2014. (ENG.). 40p. (J). (gr. 1-4). 17.99 *(978-0-8050-9473-2(3)*, Holt, Henry & Co. Bks. For Young Readers) Holt, Henry & Co.
—Snow Day!, 1 vol. Laminack, Lester L. (ENG.). 32p. (J). 2010. (gr. -1-3). 19.95 *(978-1-56145-554-6(7))*; 2010. (gr. -1-3). pap. 7.95 *(978-1-56145-553-9(9))*; 2007. (gr. k-2). 16.95 *(978-1-56145-418-1(4))* Peachtree Pubs.
—The Trouble with May Amelia. Holm, Jennifer L. (ENG.). 224p. (J). (gr. 3-7). 2012. pap. 5.99 *(978-1-4169-1374-0(2))*; 2011. 15.99 *(978-1-4169-1373-3(4))* Simon & Schuster Children's Publishing. (Atheneum Bks. for Young Readers).
—A Very Improbable Story. Einhorn, Edward. 2008. (ENG.). 32p. (J). (gr. 2-5). pap. 7.95 *(978-1-57091-872-8(4))* Charlesbridge Publishing, Inc.
—The Yankee at the Seder. Weber, Elka. 2009. (ENG.). 40p. (J). (gr. -1-2). 16.99 *(978-1-58246-256-1(9)*, Tricycle Pr.) Ten Speed Pr.
Gustavson, Adam. The A+ Custodian. Gustavson, Adam, tr. Borden, Louise. 2004. (ENG.). 40p. (J). (gr. 2-5). 17.99 *(978-0-689-84995-4(8)*, McElderry, Margaret K. Bks.) McElderry, Margaret K. Bks.
Gustavson, Adam & Schuett, Stacey. Papa's Latkes. Edwards, Michelle. 2004. (ENG.). 32p. (J). (gr. k-4). 15.99 *(978-0-7636-0779-1(7))* Candlewick Pr.
Gusterson, Leigh. Hey Bossie, You're a Spokescow! de Rham, Mickey. 2004. 24p. (J). 9.95 *(978-0-9755216-0-1(8))* Plaidswede Publishing.
Gusti. Los Disfraces de Tento. Alcántara, Ricardo. 2011. (Perrito Tento Ser.). (SPA.). (J). (gr. -1). bds. *(978-84-263-7665-7(7))* Vives, Luis Editorial (Edelvives).
—The Grey Boy. Farre, Lluis. Willis, Judith, tr. from CAT. 2007. (ENG.). 44p. (J). (gr. k-2). 12.95 *(978-1-905341-08-5(3))* WingedChariot Pr. GBR. Dist: Independent Pubs. Group.
—The King & the Magician. Bucay, Jorge. 2014. (ENG.). 52p. (J). (gr. -1). 14.95 *(978-0-7892-1204-7(8)*, Abbeville Kids) Abbeville Pr., Inc.
—¿Quién es Tento? Alcántara, Ricardo. 2011. (SPA.). (J). (gr. -1). bds. *(978-84-263-7663-3(0))* Vives, Luis Editorial (Edelvives).
—Tento Busca su Osito. Alcántara, Ricardo. 2010. (SPA.). (J). (gr. -1). bds. *(978-84-263-7664-0(9))* Vives, Luis Editorial (Edelvives).
—Tento y el Color del Mar. Alcántara, Ricardo. 2011. (SPA.). (J). (gr. -1). bds. *(978-84-263-7666-4(5))* Vives, Luis Editorial (Edelvives).
—Tento y el Diente. Alcántara, Ricardo. (SPA.). 28p. (J). *(978-84-263-4140-2(3))* Vives, Luis Editorial (Edelvives) ESP. Dist: Lectorum Pubns., Inc.
—Tento y el Perro Grandullon. Alcántara, Ricardo. (SPA.). 28p. (J). *(978-84-263-4141-9(1))* Vives, Luis Editorial (Edelvives) ESP. Dist: Lectorum Pubns., Inc.
—Tento y la Tormenta. Alcántara, Ricardo. (SPA.). 28p. (J). *(978-84-263-4144-0(6))* Vives, Luis Editorial (Edelvives) ESP. Dist: Lectorum Pubns., Inc.
—Tento y Su Amigo, Tento and His Friend. Alcántara, Ricardo. 2nd ed. (SPA.). 28p. (J). *(978-84-263-4139-6(X))* Vives, Luis Editorial (Edelvives) ESP. Dist: Lectorum Pubns., Inc.
—Tomas y el Lapiz Magico. Alcantara, Ricardo. 2007. (SPA.). 46p. per. 10.50 *(978-84-263-4829-6(7))* Vives, Luis Editorial (Edelvives) ESP. Dist: Lectorum Pubns., Inc.
—Valentin Se Parece A... Montes, Graciela & Montes, Graciela. 7th ed. (SPA.). 64p. (J). (gr. 2-3). *(978-84-348-3847-5(8))* SM Ediciones.
Gusti. Half of an Elephant. Gusti. 2006. (ENG.). 40p. (J). (gr. -1-3). 10.99 *(978-1-933605-09-8(X))* Kane Miller.
Gustovich, Michael, et al. Heroes Unlimited. Siembieda, Kevin. Marciniszyn, Alex, ed. 2nd rev. ed. 2006. 248p. (YA). (gr. 8-18). pap. 26.95 *(978-1-57457-006-9(4)*, 500) Palladium Bks., Inc.
Guthridge, Bettina. Gigantic Turnip Tug. Walker, Lois. 2007. (Collins Big Cat Ser.). (ENG.). 1p. (J). pap. 7.99 *(978-0-00-722673-7(2))* HarperCollins Pubs. Ltd. GBR. Dist: Independent Pubs. Group.
—Making Sense of Asperger's: A Story for Children. Ende, Debra. 2011. 24p. pap., pap. 29.95 *(978-0-86431-847-3(2))* ACER Pr. AUS. Dist: International Specialized Bk. Services.
—My Mom Tarzan. Shanahan, Lisa. 2008. (ENG.). 32p. (J). (gr. -1-3). *(978-1-59692-239-6(7))* MacAdam/Cage Publishing, Inc.
Guthrie, Lewis. Leah Bug & Her Flying Friends. Satterfield, April. 2011. 20p. pap. 24.95 *(978-1-4560-8422-6(4))* America Star Bks.
Gutierez, Francisco & Renteria, Justin. As I Look in Your Eyes. Dupont, Matthew. 2003. 20p. (YA). pap. 5.99 *(978-0-9728134-0-2(3))* A & E Children's Pr.
Gutierrez, Akemi. I'M a New Big Sister. Gaydos, Nora. 2010. (ENG.). 30p. (J). (gr. -1-17). 6.99 *(978-1-60169-009-8(6))* Innovative Kids.
—I'm Just Like My Mom. Ramos, Jorge. 2008.Tr. of Me Parezco Tanto a mi Papá. (ENG & SPA.). 40p. (J). (gr. -1-1). 16.99 *(978-0-06-123968-7(2)*, Rayo) HarperCollins Pubs.
—Lotsa Matzah. Balsley, Tilda. 2013. (Passover Ser.). (ENG.). 12p. (J). (gr. -1-1). bds. 5.95 *(978-0-7613-6629-4(6)*, Kar-Ben Publishing) Lerner Publishing Group.
—Now I'm Growing! - A Visit to the Doctor. Gaydos, Nora. 2011. (ENG.). 30p. (J). (gr. -1-17). 8.99 *(978-1-60169-153-8(X))* Innovative Kids.
—Now I'm Growing! - First Day of School. Gaydos, Nora. 2011. (ENG.). 30p. (J). (gr. -1-17). 8.99 *(978-1-60169-152-1(1))* Innovative Kids.
—Now I'm Growing! Hands Are Not for Hurting. Gaydos, Nora. 2012. (ENG.). 30p. (J). (gr. -1-17). 8.99 *(978-1-60169-222-1(6))* Innovative Kids.
—Now I'm Growing! Prince of the Potty - Little Steps for Big Kids! Gaydos, Nora. 2011. (ENG.). 30p. (J). (gr. -1-17). 8.99 *(978-1-60169-077-7(0))* Innovative Kids.
—Princess of the Potty - Little Steps for Big Kids! Gaydos, Nora. 2011. (ENG.). 30p. (J). (gr. -1-17). 8.99 *(978-1-60169-076-0(2))* Innovative Kids.
—Three Little Bears Play All Day. Martin, David. 2010. (Brand New Readers Ser.). (ENG.). 48p. (J). (gr. -1-3). pap. 5.99 *(978-0-7636-4230-3(4))* Candlewick Pr.
Gutierrez, Akemia, jt. illus. see Nathan, Cheryl.
Gutierrez, Chris. Jesus, It's Me Nicholas! Sanchez, Elizabeth. 2005. 12p. (J). per. 9.99 *(978-1-59879-062-7(5))* Lifevest Publishing, Inc.
Gutierrez, Rudy. Mama & Me. Dorros, Arthur. 2011. (ENG & SPA.). 32p. (J). (gr. -1-3). 16.99 *(978-0-06-058160-2(3)*, Rayo) HarperCollins Pubs.
—Papá & Me. Dorros, Arthur. 2008. (ENG.). 32p. (J). (gr. -1-3). 16.99 *(978-0-06-058156-5(5)*, Rayo) HarperCollins Pubs.
—Pelé, King of Soccer (Pelé, el Rey del Fútbol) Brown, Monica. Gayesky, Fernando, tr. 2008. (SPA & ENG.). 40p. (J). (gr. -1-3). 17.99 *(978-0-06-122779-0(X)*, Rayo) HarperCollins Pubs.
—Spirit Seeker: John Coltrane's Musical Journey. Golio, Gary. 2012. (ENG.). 48p. (J). (gr. 5-7). 17.99 *(978-0-547-23994-1(7))* Houghton Mifflin Harcourt Publishing Co.
—When I Get Older: The Story Behind Wavin' Flag. Sol & K'naan. 2012. (ENG.). 32p. (J). (gr. 1-4). 17.95 *(978-1-77049-302-5(6))* Tundra Bks. CAN. Dist: Random Hse., Inc.
Guttiere, Benedicte. When Christmas Comes - Welsh Edition. Guttiere, Benedicte. 2011. (Funny Faces Ser.). 14p. bds. *(978-1-84089-711-1(2))* Zero to Ten, Ltd.
Guttormsen, Trygve Lund. The Most Beautiful Dawn. Vars, Elle Márjá. Janda, Laura A., tr. 2013. 80p. (J). pap. 17.99 *(978-0-9772714-6-7(3))* Nordic Studies Pr.
Gutwein, Gwendolyn. Dee Diddly Dragon Is Not a Wimp. Molnar, Cheri Eplin. 2004. 32p. (J). per. 17.95 *(978-0-9746330-3-9(8))* Anton Berkshire Publishing.
—More Than You'll Ever Know. Mustaine Hettinger, Cynthia. 2004. 32p. (J). per. 19.95 *(978-0-9746330-7-7(0))* Anton Berkshire Publishing.
Guy, Robert. Maile. Gilchrist, Reona. 2004. (J). 19.95 *(978-0-9747990-0-1(9))* Gilchrist & Guy Publishing.
Guy, Sue. Four Wheels West: A Wyoming Number Book. Gagliano, Eugene M. 2006. (Count Your Way Across the U. S. A. Ser.). (ENG.). 40p. (J). (gr. -1-3). 17.95 *(978-1-58536-210-3(7))* Sleeping Bear Pr.
Guy, Sue & Guy, Susan. B Is for Buckaroo: A Cowboy Alphabet. Whitney, Gleaves & Whitney, Louise. rev. ed. 2003. (Sports Ser.). (ENG.). 40p. (J). 17.95 *(978-1-58536-139-7(9))* Sleeping Bear Pr.
Guy, Susan. B Is for Buckaroo: A Cowboy Alphabet. Whitney, Gleaves & Whitney, Louise Doak. 2006. (Sleeping Bear Alphabets Ser.). (ENG.). 40p. (J). (gr. -1-3). pap. 7.95 *(978-1-58536-336-0(7))* Sleeping Bear Pr.
—C Is for Cowboy: A Wyoming Alphabet. Gagliano, Eugene. 2003. (Discover America State by State Ser.). (ENG.). 40p. (J). 17.95 *(978-1-58536-097-0(X))* Sleeping Bear Pr.
Guy, Susan, jt. illus. see Guy, Sue.
Guy, Will. Romeo the Rhino's Rocky Romance: A Cautionary Tale about Differences. Ulick, Michael Ackerman. 32p. (J). 15.95 *(978-0-9679813-0-7(1))* Footprints Pr.
Guymon, Jennette King. Daily Discoveries for August. Midgley, Elizabeth Cole. Mitchell, Judith, ed. 2005. 192p. (J). pap. 12.95 *(978-1-57310-452-4(3))* Teaching & Learning Co.
—Daily Discoveries for October. Midgley, Elizabeth Cole. Mitchell, Judith, ed. 2005. 192p. (J). pap. 12.95 *(978-1-57310-454-8(X))* Teaching & Learning Co.
—Daily Discoveries for September. Midgley, Elizabeth Cole. Mitchess, Judith, ed. 2005. 192p. (J). pap. 12.95 *(978-1-57310-453-1(1))* Teaching & Learning Co.
Guymon-King, Jennette. Primary Partners Singing Fun. Ross, Mary H. 2004. *(978-1-59156-793-6(9))* Covenant Communications.
Guyot, Céline. Privacy, Please! Gaining Independence from Your Parents. Amblard, Odile. 2009. (Sunscreen Ser.). (ENG.). 112p. (YA). (gr. 7-11). pap. 10.95 *(978-0-8109-8357-1(5)*, Amulet Bks.) Abrams.
Guze, Tessa. Harry Goes Rowing. Tetlow, Karin. 2013. 32p. pap. 11.95 *(978-0-615-75585-4(2))* Juping Horse Pr.
—Harry the Carousel Horse. Tetlow, Karin. 2012. 32p. pap. 15.96 *(978-0-615-55671-0(X))* Juping Horse Pr.
Guzek, Greta. The Airplane Ride. White, Howard. unabr. ed. 2006. (ENG.). 32p. (J). bds. *(978-0-88971-224-9(7))* Harbour Publishing Co., Ltd.
—Down at the Seaweed Cafe. Perry, Robert. unabr. ed. 2010. (ENG.). 32p. pap. *(978-0-88971-246-1(8))* Nightwood Editions.
—The Golden Pine Cone. Clark, Catherine Anthony. 2nd unabr. ed. (ENG.). 192p. (Orig.). (J). pap. *(978-1-55017-085-6(6))* Harbour Publishing Co., Ltd.
—My Vancouver Sketchbook. Perry, Robert. unabr. ed. 2010. (ENG.). 32p. pap. *(978-0-88971-248-5(4))* Nightwood Editions.
Guzman, Carlos Jose, jt. illus. see Murase, Sho.
Guzman, Jacob. The Adventures of Eliseo & Stefano: My Daddy Can Fly! Guzman, Raquel. 2006. 28p. (J). 16.95 *(978-0-9788332-0-6(1))* Images & Pages.
Guzman, Lula. Sophie Wonders about Marriage. Bradley, Debby. 2013. (Sophie Wonders about the Sacraments Ser.). (ENG.). 31p. (J). pap. 4.99 *(978-0-7648-2351-0(5))* Liguori Pubns.
Guzman, Minerva. The Punctuation Pals Go Snow Skiing. Olker, Constance. 2005. 22p. (J). (gr. -1-3). per. 18.95 *(978-1-933449-14-2(4))* Nightengale Pr.
—The Punctuation Pals Go to the Baseball Park. Olker, Constance. 2005. (Punctuation Pals Ser.). 44p. (J). per. 18.95 *(978-1-933449-15-9(2))* Nightengale Pr.
—The Punctuation Pals Go to the Beach. Olker, Constance. 2005. (Punctuation Pals Ser.). 36p. (J). per. 18.95 *(978-1-933449-12-8(8))* Nightengale Pr.
—The Punctuation Pals Meet at School. Olker, Constance. 2004. (Punctuation Pals Ser.). 24p. (J). (gr. 1-18). 19.95 *(978-0-9743348-6-8(3))* Nightengale Pr.
Gwangjo & Park, Jung-a. Dancing Bear. Subramaniam, Manasi. 2013. (ENG.). 32p. (J). (gr. k). pap. 9.95 *(978-81-8190-200-9(9))* Karadi Tales Co. Pvt, Ltd. IND. Dist: Consortium Bk. Sales & Distribution.
Gwinner, Patricia. Sailor the Cat. Hooker, Adele. 2011. 24p. pap. 24.95 *(978-1-4560-8026-6(1))* America Star Bks.
Gwynne, Fred. The Battle of the Frogs & the Mice. Martin, George W. 2013. (ENG.). 64p. (gr. 12). pap. 18.95 *(978-0-399-16285-5(2)*, Tarcher) Penguin Publishing Group.
Gynux. Digger the Dinosaur. Dotlich, Rebecca Kai. 2013. (My First I Can Read Ser.). (ENG.). 24p. (J). (gr. -1-3). 16.99 *(978-0-06-222222-0(8))*; pap. 3.99 *(978-0-06-222221-3(X))* HarperCollins Pubs.
—Digger the Dinosaur & the Cake Mistake. Dotlich, Rebecca Kai. 2013. (My First I Can Read Ser.). (ENG.). 24p. (J). (gr. -1-3). 16.99 *(978-0-06-222224-4(4))*; pap. 3.99 *(978-0-06-222223-7(6))* HarperCollins Pubs.
—Storm Song, 0 vols. Viau, Nancy & Bolinao, Mela. 2013. (ENG.). (J). (gr. k-3). 12.99 *(978-1-4778-1646-2(1)*, 9781477816462, Amazon Children's Publishing) Amazon Publishing.
—Storm Song. Viau, Nancy. 2013. 24p. pap. 12.99 *(978-1-4778-6646-7(9))* Amazon Publishing.

H

H. J. Ford. The Orange Fairy Book. Andrew Lang, ed. 2010. 260p. pap. 6.89 *(978-1-60386-308-7(7)*, Merchant Bks.) Rough Draft Printing.
—The Pink Fairy Book. Andrew Lang, ed. 2010. 276p. pap. 6.89 *(978-1-60386-291-2(9)*, Merchant Bks.) Rough Draft Printing.
Ha, Ying-Hwa, jt. illus. see Van Wright, Cornelius.
Haag, Bob. A Guide to Cottage Architecture As Seen in Lakeside, Ohio. Haag, Ruth. 2004. 13p. 6.00 *(978-0-9710260-8-7(4))* Haag Pr.
Haake, Martin. Bob the Alien Discovers the Dewey Decimal System, 1 vol. Donovan, Sandy. 2010. (In the Library). (ENG.). 24p. (gr. k-4). lib. bdg. 25.99 *(978-1-4048-5757-5(5)*, Nonfiction Picture Bks.) Picture Window Bks.
Haan, Linda de & Nijland, Stern. King & King. Haan, Linda de & Nijland, Stern. 2003. (ENG.). 32p. (J). (gr. k-3). 15.99 *(978-1-58246-061-1(2)*, Tricycle Pr.) Ten Speed Pr.
Haas, Deborah. Native American Rhymes: The People of the Far North, 9 vols. Rhodes, Sam. Howard, Kimberley, ed. 2003. 92p. (J). (gr. 3-5). mass mkt. 7.50 *(978-0-9743214-0-0(0))* Rhodes Educational Pubns.
Haas, Esti. Smile with Avigayil #1: Avigayil & the Little Student. Fuks, Menuhah & Tager, Gavriella. 2006. 64p. (J). 12.95 *(978-1-932443-60-8(6))* Judaica Pr., Inc., The.
—Smile with Avigayil #2: Avigayil & the Black Cat. Fuks, Menuhah & Tager, Gavriella. 2006. (ENG.). 64p. (J). 12.95 *(978-1-932443-58-5(4))* Judaica Pr., Inc., The.
Haas, Irene. Bess & Bella. Haas, Irene. 2006. (ENG.). 32p. (J). (gr. -1-2). 17.99 *(978-1-4169-0013-9(6)*, McElderry, Margaret K. Bks.) McElderry, Margaret K. Bks.
Haas, Robert. I Dreamed of Flying Like a Bird: My Adventures Photographing Wild Animals from a Helicopter. Haas, Robert. 2010. (ENG.). 64p. (J). (gr. 2-5). 27.90 *(978-1-4263-0694-5(6))*; 17.95 *(978-1-4263-0693-8(8))* National Geographic Society. (National Geographic Children's Bks.).
Haas, Shelly. Thank You, God! A Jewish Child's Book of Prayers. Groner, Judyth & Wikler, Madeline. 2003. (ENG.). 32p. (J). (gr. -1-2). pap. 7.95 *(978-1-58013-101-8(8)*, Kar-Ben Publishing) Lerner Publishing Group.
Haas, Shelly O. ¿Adónde Van Las Personas Cuando Mueren? Portnoy, Mindy Avra. Translations.com Staff, tr. from ENG. 2008. (SPA & ENG.). 24p. (J). (gr. k-3). 15.95 *(978-0-7613-3905-2(1))* Lerner Publishing Group.
—The Schoolchildren's Blizzard. Figley, Marty Rhodes. 2004. (On My Own History Ser.). (ENG.). 48p. (gr. 2-4). pap. 6.95 *(978-1-57505-619-7(4))*; lib. bdg. 25.26 *(978-1-57505-586-2(4)*, Carolrhoda Bks.) Lerner Publishing Group.
Habbas, Frank. Mark Twain at Work! Goldsmith, Howard. ed. 2005. 32p. (J). lib. bdg. 15.00 *(978-1-59054-951-3(1))* Fitzgerald Bks.
—Mark Twain at Work! Goldsmith, Howard. 2003. (Ready-To-read COFA Ser.). (ENG.). 32p. (J). (gr. k-2). pap. 3.99 *(978-0-689-85399-9(8)*, Simon Spotlight) Simon Spotlight.
Habbley, Kathleen. What Is Your Dog Doing? Singer, Marilyn. 2011. (ENG.). 32p. (J). (gr. -1-2). 12.99 *(978-1-4169-7931-9(X)*, Atheneum Bks. for Young Readers) Simon & Schuster Children's Publishing.
Habel, Helen. Puppy Scents: The Kids' Guide to Puppy Care. Kaleta, Don. 2010. (ENG.). 72p. (J). pap. 17.95 *(978-0-615-39881-5(2))* Kaleta Publishing, LLC.
Haber, Jan. The Animals' Vacation. Haber, Shel. 2015. (G&d Vintage Ser.). (ENG.). 24p. (J). (gr. -1-k). 7.99 *(978-0-448-48399-3(8)*, Grosset & Dunlap) Penguin Publishing Group.
Haberstroh, Anne. Ant King. Hanson, Anders. 2007. (Critter Chronicles Ser.). (ENG.). 24p. (J). (gr. k-3). lib. bdg. 24.21 *(978-1-59928-430-9(8)*, SandCastle) ABDO Publishing Co.
—Cow Licks. Scheunemann, Pam. 2006. (Animal Tales Ser.). 24p. (J). (gr. k-3). (ENG.). lib. bdg. 24.21 *(978-1-59679-929-5(3)*, SandCastle); pap. 48.42 *(978-1-59679-930-1(7))* ABDO Publishing Co.
—Crab Cakes. Doudna, Kelly. 2007. (Critter Chronicles Ser.). (ENG.). 24p. (J). (gr. k-3). lib. bdg. 24.21 *(978-1-59928-434-7(0)*, SandCastle) ABDO Publishing Co.
—Doggie Pants. Doudna, Kelly. 2006. (Animal Tales Ser.). 24p. (J). (gr. k-3). (ENG.). lib. bdg. 24.21 *(978-1-59679-931-8(5)*, SandCastle); pap. 48.42 *(978-1-59679-932-5(3))* ABDO Publishing Co.
—Duck Bills. Kompelien, Tracy. 2006. (Animal Tales Ser.). 24p. (J). (gr. k-3). (ENG.). lib. bdg. 24.21 *(978-1-59679-933-2(1)*, SandCastle); pap. 48.42 *(978-1-59679-934-9(X))* ABDO Publishing Co.
—Fly Paper. Kompelien, Tracy. 2007. (Critter Chronicles Ser.). (ENG.). 24p. (J). (gr. k-3). lib. bdg. 24.21 *(978-1-59928-438-5(3)*, SandCastle) ABDO Publishing Co.
Haberstroh, Anne, et al. The Funny Farm: Jokes about Dogs, Cats, Ducks, Snakes, Bears, & Other Animals, 1 vol. Ziegler, Mark & Dahl, Michael. 2010. (Michael Dahl Presents Super Funny Joke Bks.). (ENG.). 80p. (gr. k-3). 23.99 *(978-1-4048-5772-8(9)*, Michael Dahl - Super Funny Joke Bks.) Picture Window Bks.
Haberstroh, Anne. Goat Cheese. Doudna, Kelly. 2006. (Animal Tales Ser.). 24p. (J). (gr. k-3). (ENG.). lib. bdg. 24.21 *(978-1-59679-937-0(4)*, SandCastle); pap. 48.42 *(978-1-59679-938-7(2))* ABDO Publishing Co.
—Goose Down. Doudna, Kelly. 2006. (Animal Tales Ser.). 24p. (J). (gr. k-3). (ENG.). lib. bdg. 24.21 *(978-1-59679-941-7(2)*, SandCastle); pap. 48.42 *(978-1-59679-942-4(0))* ABDO Publishing Co.
—Leap Frog. Kompelien, Tracy. (Critter Chronicles Ser.). 24p. (J). (gr. k-3). 2007. (ENG.). lib. bdg. 24.21 *(978-1-59928-448-4(0)*, SandCastle); 2006. 48.42 *(978-1-59928-449-1(9))* ABDO Publishing Co.
—Lion Manes. Kompelien, Tracy. 2006. (Animal Tales Ser.). (ENG.). 24p. (J). (gr. k-3). lib. bdg. 24.21 *(978-1-59679-949-3(8)*, SandCastle) ABDO Publishing Co.
—Lone Shark. Hanson, Anders. 2007. (Critter Chronicles Ser.). (ENG.). 24p. (J). (gr. k-3). lib. bdg. 24.21 *(978-1-59928-452-1(9)*, SandCastle) ABDO Publishing Co.
—Night Owl. Hanson, Anders. 2006. (Animal Tales Ser.). 24p. (J). (gr. k-3). (ENG.). lib. bdg. 24.21 *(978-1-59679-953-0(6)*, SandCastle); pap. 48.42 *(978-1-59679-954-7(4))* ABDO Publishing Co.
—Parrot Crackers. Doudna, Kelly. 2007. (Critter Chronicles Ser.). (ENG.). 24p. (J). (gr. k-3). lib. bdg. 24.21 *(978-1-59928-458-3(8)*, SandCastle) ABDO Publishing Co.
—El Peinado Del Gallo. Doudna, Kelly. 2007. (Cuentos de Animales Ser.).Tr. of Rooster Combs. (SPA & ENG.). 24p. (J). (gr. k-3). lib. bdg. 24.21 *(978-1-59928-663-1(7)*, SandCastle) ABDO Publishing Co.
—Robin Hoods. Salzmann, Mary Elizabeth. 2007. (Critter Chronicles Ser.). (ENG.). 24p. (J). (gr. k-3). lib. bdg. 24.21 *(978-1-59928-466-8(9)*, SandCastle) ABDO Publishing Co.
—Rooster Combs. Doudna, Kelly. 2006. (Animal Tales Ser.). 24p. (J). (gr. k-3). (ENG.). lib. bdg. 24.21 *(978-1-59679-965-3(X)*, SandCastle); pap. 48.42 *(978-1-59679-966-0(8))* ABDO Publishing Co.
—Spider Web. Kompelien, Tracy. 2007. (Critter Chronicles Ser.). (ENG.). 24p. (J). (gr. k-3). lib. bdg. 24.21 *(978-1-59928-474-3(X)*, SandCastle) ABDO Publishing Co.
Haberstroh, Anne & Reibeling, Brandon. Screaming with Laughter: Jokes about Ghosts, Ghouls, Zombies, Dinosaurs, Bugs, & Other Scary Creatures, 1 vol. Dahl, Michael & Moore, Mark. 2010. (Michael Dahl Presents Super Funny Joke Bks.). (ENG.). 80p. (gr. k-3). 23.99 *(978-1-4048-6101-5(7))*; pap. 6.95 *(978-1-4048-6372-9(9))* Picture Window Bks. (Michael Dahl - Super Funny Joke Bks.).
Habiger, Geoff & Gower, Jim. Dinosaur Learning Activity Book. Habiger, Geoff. 2005. 80p. (J). per. 7.95 *(978-1-932926-96-5(8))* Artemesia Publishing, LLC.
Habinger, Renate. El Viejo John. Härtling, Peter. 2003.Tr. of Old John. (SPA.). 144p. (YA). (gr. 5-8). 12.95 *(978-84-204-4816-9(8))* Ediciones Alfaguara ESP. Dist: Santillana USA Publishing Co., Inc.
—El viejo John. Härtling, Peter. (SPA.). 144p. (J). (gr. 5-8). pap. 9.95 *(978-968-19-0720-4(5))* Santillana USA Publishing Co., Inc.
Habjan, Peter & Duhaney, Rich. REV!-Alation! Diamond, Jeremy. 2010. (Nascar Heroes Ser.: No. 6). 28p. (J). (gr. 4-7). 24.21 *(978-1-59961-667-4(X))* Spotlight.

H

Hacikyan, Talleen. Aesop's Fables, 1 vol. Rosen, Michael. 2013. (ENG.). 32p. (J). (gr. -1-2). 16.95 *(978-1-896580-81-4(5))* Tradewind Bks. CAN. Dist: Orca Bk. Pubs. USA.

Hack, Robert, et al. Diary of a Stinky Dead Kid, No. 8. Gerrold, David et al. 2009. (Tales from the Crypt Graphic Novels Ser.: 8). (ENG.). 96p. (J). (gr. 5-12). 12.95 *(978-1-59707-164-2(1))*; pap. 7.95 *(978-1-59707-163-5(3))* Papercutz.

Hacker, Randy. The Puppy Who Found a Boy, 1 vol. Dean, Sara. 2009. 13p. pap. 24.95 *(978-1-61546-278-0(3))* America Star Bks.

Hackett, Michael. Jesus Returns to Heaven. Baden, Robert. rev. ed. 2004. (ENG.). 16p. (J). 1.99 *(978-0-7586-0407-1(6))* Concordia Publishing Hse.

Hackman, Evelyn. The Rooster's Fate: And Other Stories. Martin, Elaine S. Bowman. 2014. 184p. (J). *(978-0-7399-2481-5(8))* Rod & Staff Pubs., Inc.

Hackmann, Bethany. It Doesn't Have to be Pink. Baliko, Janelle. 2007. 32p. (J). 14.95 *(978-0-9799012-0-1(0))* Baliko, Janelle A.

Hadadi, Hoda. Deep in the Sahara. Cunnane, Kelly. 2013. (ENG.). 40p. (J). (gr. -1-3). 17.99 *(978-0-375-87034-7(2))*, Schwartz & Wade Bks.) Random Hse. Children's Bks.

Haddad-Hamwi, Louise. A Shoulder for Oscar. Craig, Joni. 2013. 40p. pap. 11.95 *(978-0-9887836-6-9(5))* Taylor and Seale Publishing, LLC.

Haefele, Steve. Beach Day. Lee, Quinlan B. 2006. (J). *(978-0-439-81618-2(1))* Scholastic, Inc.

—Clifford's Best School Day. Lee, Quinlan B. & Bridwell, Norman. 2007. (J). *(978-0-545-02844-8(2))* Scholastic, Inc.

—Happy St. Patrick's Day, Clifford! Lee, Quinlan B. & Bridwell, Norman. 2010. (Clifford the Big Red Dog Ser.). (J). *(978-0-545-23401-6(8))* Scholastic, Inc.

—Merry Ham-Ham Christmas. Field, Ellen. 2003. (Hamtaro Ser.). (ENG.). 32p. (J). pap. 3.99 *(978-0-439-54249-4(9))*, Scholastic Paperbacks) Scholastic, Inc.

—Polar Bear Patrol. Stamper, Judith B. 2003. (Magic School Bus Science Chapter Bks.). 91p. (J). (gr. 2-5). 12.65 *(978-0-7569-1577-3(5))* Perfection Learning Corp.

—Polar Bear Patrol. Stamper, Judith. 2010. (Magic School Bus Science Chapter Bks.). (KOR.). 106p. (J). *(978-89-491-5321-6(1))* Biryongso Publishing Co.

—Santa's Big Red Helper. Aboff, Marcie. 2005. (Clifford Ser.). (ENG.). 80p. (J). (gr. k — 1). 2.99 *(978-0-439-79150-2(2))* Scholastic, Inc.

—The Snow Champion. Pugiano-Martin, Carol & Bridwell, Norman. 2006. (Big Red Reader Ser.). (J). *(978-0-439-80845-3(6))* Scholastic, Inc.

—The Snow Dog. Marsoli, Lisa Ann & Bridwell, Norman. 2004. (Big Red Reader Ser.). (J). pap. *(978-0-439-58559-0(7))* Scholastic, Inc.

—Valentine Surprise. Lee, Quinlan B. 2008. (Clifford the Big Red Dog Ser.). (J). *(978-0-545-02845-5(0))* Scholastic, Inc.

—Where Can That Silly Monkey Be? Your Turn, My Turn Reader. Shepherd, Jodie. 2010. (Playskool Ser.). (ENG.). 24p. (J). (gr. -1-k). pap. 3.99 *(978-1-4169-9047-5(X))*, Simon Spotlight) Simon Spotlight.

Haefele, Steve. Polar Bear Patrol. Haefele, Steve. Stamper, Judith Bauer & Bauer-Stamper, Judith. 2003. (Magic School Bus Ser.: No. 13). (ENG.). 96p. (J). (gr. -1-3). pap. 4.99 *(978-0-439-31433-6(X))*, Scholastic Paperbacks) Scholastic, Inc.

Haezer, Jane. Christopher the Choo Choo Train. Kropik, Linda Kristine. 2011. 24p. pap. 11.50 *(978-1-60911-522-7(6))*, Strategic Bk. Publishing) Strategic Book Publishing & Rights Agency (SBPRA).

Hafner, Marylin. Germs Make Me Sick! Berger, Melvin. 2015. (Let's-Read-And-Find-Out Science 2 Ser.). (ENG.). 32p. (J). (gr. -1-3). pap. 6.99 ***(978-0-06-238187-3(3))*** HarperCollins Pubs.

Hafner, Marylin. Hanukkah! Schotter, Roni. 2014. (ENG.). 32p. (J). (gr. -1-1). pap. 5.99 *(978-0-316-37028-8(2))* Little, Brown Bks. for Young Readers.

—It's Christmas! Prelutsky, Jack. 2012. (I Can Read Book 3 Ser.). (ENG.). 48p. (J). (gr. k-3). pap. 3.99 *(978-0-06-053708-1(6))*, Greenwillow Bks.) HarperCollins Pubs.

—It's Thanksgiving. Prelutsky, Jack. 2007. (I Can Read Bks.). 48p. (J). (gr. -1-3). 15.99 *(978-0-06-053710-4(8))*, Greenwillow Bks.) HarperCollins Pubs.

—It's Thanksgiving! Prelutsky, Jack. 2008. (I Can Read Book 3 Ser.). (ENG.). 48p. (J). (gr. k-3). pap. 3.99 *(978-0-06-053711-1(6))* HarperCollins Pubs.

—It's Valentine's Day! Prelutsky, Jack. 2013. (I Can Read Book 3 Ser.). (ENG.). 48p. (J). (gr. -1-3). pap. 3.99 *(978-0-06-053714-2(0))*, Greenwillow Bks.) HarperCollins Pubs.

—Passover Magic, 0 vols. Schotter, Roni. 2011. (ENG.). 32p. (J). (gr. -1-3). pap. 7.99 *(978-0-7614-5842-5(5))*, 9780761458425, Amazon Children's Publishing) Amazon Publishing.

—The Pepins & Their Problems, 1 vol. Horvath, Polly. (ENG.). 192p. pap. 13.95 *(978-0-88899-633-6(0))* Groundwood Bks. CAN. Dist: Perseus-PGW.

—The Pepins & Their Problems. Horvath, Polly. 2008. (ENG.). 208p. (J). (gr. 3-7). per. 9.99 *(978-0-312-37751-9(7))* Square Fish.

—Pocket Poems. Katz, Bobbi. 2013. (ENG.). 32p. (J). (gr. k-3). 6.99 *(978-0-14-750859-1(2))*, Puffin) Penguin Publishing Group.

—Purim Play, 0 vols. Schotter, Roni. 2010. (ENG.). 32p. (J). (gr. -1-2). pap. 6.99 *(978-0-7614-5800-5(X))*, 9780761458005, Amazon Children's Publishing) Amazon Publishing.

—Teacher's Pets. Dodds, Dayle Ann. 2006. (ENG.). 40p. (J). (gr. -1-3). 15.99 *(978-0-7636-2252-7(4))* Candlewick Pr.

—Teacher's Pets. Dodds, Dayle Ann. 2010. (ENG.). 40p. (J). (gr. k-4). pap. 6.99 *(978-0-7636-4631-8(8))* Candlewick Pr.

—Tumble Bunnies. Lasky, Kathryn. 2005. (ENG.). 32p. (J). (gr. k-3). 15.99 *(978-0-7636-2265-7(6))* Candlewick Pr.

Hagan, Donell. These Hands. George, Mindy Lee. 2013. 30p. pap. *(978-0-9878208-4-6(2))* Catching Rainbows.

Hagan, Stacy. Kumi the Bear. Toh, Irene. 2008. (ENG.). 24p. pap. 12.75 *(978-1-4389-1368-1(0))* AuthorHouse.

Hagel, Brooke. Balancing ACT. Gurevich, Margaret. 2015. (Chloe by Design Ser.). (ENG.). 384p. (gr. 5-8). 14.95 ***(978-1-62370-258-8(5))*** Capstone Young Readers.

—Chloe by Design, 4 vols. Gurevich, Margaret. (Chloe by Design Ser.). (ENG.). 96p. (gr. 5-8). 2015. 95.96 ***(978-1-4965-1995-5(7))***; 2014. 95.96 *(978-1-4342-9379-4(3))* Stone Arch Bks.

Hagel, Brooke. Chloe by Design: Making the Cut, 1 vol. Gurevich, Margaret. 2014. (Chloe by Design Ser.). (ENG.). 384p. (gr. 4-8). 14.95 *(978-1-62370-112-3(0))* Capstone Young Readers.

—Design Destiny, 1 vol. Gurevich, Margaret. 2014. (Chloe by Design Ser.). (ENG.). 96p. (gr. 5-8). 23.99 *(978-1-4342-9180-6(4))* Stone Arch Bks.

Hagel, Brooke. Design Disaster. Gurevich, Margaret. 2015. (Chloe by Design Ser.). (ENG.). 96p. (gr. 5-8). 23.99 ***(978-1-4965-0505-7(0))*** Stone Arch Bks.

Hagel, Brooke. Design Diva, 1 vol. Gurevich, Margaret. 2014. (Chloe by Design Ser.). (ENG.). 96p. (gr. 5-8). 23.99 *(978-1-4342-9177-6(4))* Stone Arch Bks.

Hagel, Brooke, et al. Fashion Drawing Studio: A Guide to Sketching Stylish Fashions, 1 vol. Bolte, Marissa. 2013. (Craft It Yourself Ser.). (ENG.). 144p. (gr. 3-4). pap. 14.95 *(978-1-62370-005-8(1))* Capstone Young Readers.

Hagel, Brooke. Fashion Week Finale. Gurevich, Margaret. 2015. (Chloe by Design Ser.). (ENG.). 96p. (gr. 5-8). 23.99 ***(978-1-4965-0507-1(7))*** Stone Arch Bks.

Hagel, Brooke. The First Cut, 1 vol. Gurevich, Margaret. 2014. (Chloe by Design Ser.). (ENG.). 96p. (gr. 5-8). 23.99 *(978-1-4342-9178-3(2))* Stone Arch Bks.

—Girly Girl Style: Fun Fashions You Can Sketch, 1 vol. Bolte, Mari. 2013. (Drawing Fun Fashions Ser.). (ENG.). 32p. (gr. 3-4). lib. bdg. 27.32 *(978-1-62065-035-6(5))*, Snap Bks.) Capstone Pr., Inc.

—Harajuku Style: Fun Fashions You Can Sketch, 1 vol. Bolte, Mari. 2013. (Drawing Fun Fashions Ser.). (ENG.). 32p. (gr. 3-4). lib. bdg. 27.32 *(978-1-62065-034-9(7))*, Snap Bks.) Capstone Pr., Inc.

Hagel, Brooke. Intern Ambition. Gurevich, Margaret. 2015. (Chloe by Design Ser.). (ENG.). 96p. (gr. 5-8). 23.99 ***(978-1-4965-0504-0(2))*** Stone Arch Bks.

Hagel, Brooke. Rosie Wants to Be a Fireman. Klein, Marissa. 2013. 30p. (J). 19.95 *(978-0-9894933-3-8(4))* Rissylyn.

Hagel, Brooke. Runway Rundown. Gurevich, Margaret. 2015. (Chloe by Design Ser.). (ENG.). 96p. (gr. 5-8). 23.99 ***(978-1-4965-0506-4(9))*** Stone Arch Bks.

Hagel, Brooke. Unraveling, 1 vol. Gurevich, Margaret. 2014. (Chloe by Design Ser.). (ENG.). 96p. (gr. 5-8). 23.99 *(978-1-4342-9179-0(0))* Stone Arch Bks.

Hagelberg, Michael. Cheery: The True Adventures of a Chiricahua Leopard Frog. Davidson, Elizabeth W. 2011. (ENG.). 40p. (J). (gr. 3-6). pap. 11.95 *(978-1-58985-025-5(4))* Five Star Pubns., Inc.

Hagelberg, Michael & Jensen, Nathaniel P. Rattlesnake Rules. Storad, Conrad J. 2012. (ENG.). 40p. (J). (gr. 1-4). pap. 7.95 *(978-1-58985-211-2(7))*, Little Five Star) Five Star Pubns., Inc.

Hageman, Erik. Kokopelli & the Island of Change. Sterns, Michael. 2nd ed. 2005. 64p. (J). 17.95 net. *(978-0-615-12724-8(X))* Grasshopper Dream Productions.

Hagen, Stefan. Appetite for Detention. Hagen, Stefan, photos by. Tanen, Sloane. 2008. (ENG.). 80p. (J). (gr. 7-18). 14.99 *(978-1-59990-075-9(0))*, Bloomsbury USA Childrens) Bloomsbury USA.

—Coco All Year Round. Hagen, Stefan, photos by. Tanen, Sloane. 2006. (ENG.). 32p. (J). (gr. -1-3). 15.95 *(978-1-58234-709-7(3))*, Bloomsbury USA Childrens) Bloomsbury USA.

Hager, Christian & Schroeder, Binette. The Frog Prince: Or Iron Henry. Grimm, J. & W. & Grimm, J. 2013. (ENG.). 32p. (J). (gr. -1-3). 17.95 *(978-0-7358-4140-6(3))* North-South Bks., Inc.

Hagerman, Jessica. Even Odder: More Stories to Chill the Heart. Burt, Steve. 2003. 144p. pap. 14.95 *(978-0-9741407-0-4(8))* Burt, Steven E.

—Oddest Yet: Even More Stories to Chill the Heart. Burt, Steve. 2004. 144p. (gr. 5-18). pap. 14.95 *(978-0-9741407-1-1(6))* Burt, Steven E.

—Wicked Odd: Still More Stories to Chill the Heart. Burt, Steve. 2006. 144p. (gr. 5-18). pap. 14.95 *(978-0-9741407-2-8(4))* Burt, Steven E.

Haggerty, Tim. Back off, Sneezy! A Kids' Guide to Staying Well. Kreisman, Rachelle. 2014. (Start Smart: Health Ser.). 32p. (gr. 1-3). pap. 7.95 *(978-1-937529-68-0(1))* Red Chair Pr.

—Start Sweating! A Kids' Guide to Being Active. Kreisman, Rachelle. 2014. (Start Smart: Health Ser.). 32p. (gr. 1-3). pap. 7.95 *(978-1-937529-64-2(9))* Red Chair Pr.

—Wacky Football Facts to Kick Around. Sweeny, Sheila. Saffro, Jill, ed. Date not set. 32p. (Orig.). (J). (gr. k-3). pap. *(978-1-886749-17-7(5))* Sports Illustrated For Kids.

—What's That Smell? A Kids' Guide to Keeping Clean. Kreisman, Rachelle. 2014. (Start Smart: Health Ser.). 32p. (gr. 1-3). pap. 7.95 *(978-1-937529-66-6(5))* Red Chair Pr.

—Why Do We Eat? Turnbull, Stephanie. 2006. (Beginners Science: Level 2 Ser.). 32p. (J). (gr. 1-3). 4.99 *(978-0-7945-1333-7(6))*; (gr. 4-7). lib. bdg. 12.99 *(978-1-58086-933-1(5))* EDC Publishing. (Usborne).

—Why Do We Eat? (Lematha Na'Kol) Turnbull, Stephanie. Ibrahim, Nouran, tr. 2012. (ENG & ARA.). 32p. (J). 6.99 *(978-99921-94-38-6(3))*, 149896) Bloomsbury USA.

—You Want Me to Eat That? A Kids' Guide to Eating Right. Kreisman, Rachelle. 2014. (Start Smart: Health Ser.). 32p. (gr. 1-3). pap. 7.95 *(978-1-937529-70-3(3))* Red Chair Pr.

Haggerty, Tim, jt. illus. see Donaera, Patrizia.

Haggerty, Tim, jt. illus. see Gaudenzi, Giacinto.

Haggerty, Tim, jt. illus. see Pastor, Terry.

Haggerty, Tim, jt. illus. see Tudor, Andy.

Hagin, Sally. A Book of Pacific Lullabies. Duder, Tessa, ed. 2003. 32p. (J). pap. *(978-1-86950-393-2(7))* HarperCollins Pubs. New Zealand.

—Milet Flashwords English. Turhan, Sedat. 2005. (Milet Flashwords Ser.). (ENG.). 60p. (J). (gr. 4-7). 8.95 *(978-1-84059-455-3(1))* Milet Publishing.

Hagin, Sally. Milet Picture Dictionary. Hagin, Sally. Turhan, Sedat. 18th ed. 2003. (Milet Picture Dictionary Ser.). (ENG.). 48p. (J). (gr. -1). 13.95 *(978-1-84059-346-4(6))* Milet Publishing.

Hague, Devon, jt. illus. see Hague, Michael.

Hague, Michael. Little Bitty Mousie. Aylesworth, Jim. 2007. (ENG.). 32p. (J). (gr. -1-1). 16.95 *(978-0-8027-9637-0(0))* Walker & Co.

—Peter Pan. Barrie, J. M. 100th annot. rev. ed. 2003. (ENG.). 176p. (J). (gr. 4-7). 25.00 *(978-0-8050-7245-7(4))*, Holt, Henry & Co. Bks. For Young Readers) Holt, Henry & Co.

—Peter Pan: Lost & Found. Hill, Susan & Barrie, J. M. 2012. (My Readers Ser.). (ENG.). 32p. (J). (gr. k-2). pap. 3.99 *(978-1-250-00459-8(4))* Square Fish.

—The Tale of Peter Rabbit. Potter, Beatrix. 2005. (ENG.). 32p. (J). (gr. -1-3). pap. 6.95 *(978-0-8118-4906-7(6))* Chronicle Bks. LLC.

—The Tale of Peter Rabbit. Potter, Beatrix. 2003. 29p. (J). (gr. 2-5). reprint ed. 16.00 *(978-0-7567-6968-0(X))* DIANE Publishing Co.

—Treasured Classics. 2011. (ENG.). 133p. (J). (gr. -1-17). 19.99 *(978-0-8118-4904-3(X))* Chronicle Bks. LLC.

—The Velveteen Rabbit. Williams, Margery. 2008. (ENG.). 48p. (J). (gr. -1-2). per. 7.99 *(978-0-312-37750-2(9))* Square Fish.

—The Velveteen Rabbit Christmas. Barbo, Maria S. 2013. (My Readers Ser.). (ENG.). 32p. (J). (gr. -1-1). 15.99 *(978-1-250-01768-0(8))*; pap. 3.99 *(978-1-250-01769-7(6))* Square Fish.

—White Christmas. Berlin, Irving. 2010. (ENG.). 32p. (J). 16.99 *(978-0-06-029123-5(0))* HarperCollins Pubs.

Hague, Michael. The Book of Fairies. Hague, Michael. 2006. (ENG.). 128p. (J). (gr. 2-7). pap., pap. 9.99 *(978-0-06-089187-9(4))*, Harper Trophy) HarperCollins Pubs.

—Michael Hague's Magical World of Unicorns. Hague, Michael. 2012. (ENG.). 36p. (J). (gr. -1-3). pap. 17.99 *(978-1-4424-6041-6(5))*, Simon & Schuster Bks. For Young Readers) Simon & Schuster Bks. For Young Readers.

—Michael Hague's Read-To-Me Book of Fairy Tales. Hague, Michael. 2013. (ENG.). 128p. (J). (gr. -1-3). 19.99 *(978-0-688-14010-6(6))* HarperCollins Pubs.

Hague, Michael. A Child's Book of Prayers. Hague, Michael, ed. 2010. (ENG.). 20p. (J). (gr. -1 — 1). bds. 7.99 *(978-0-8050-9094-9(0))*, Holt, Henry & Co. Bks. For Young Readers) Holt, Henry & Co.

—A Child's Book of Prayers, Set. Hague, Michael, ed. unabr. ed. 2010. (ENG.). 32p. (J). (gr. -1-k). 9.99 *(978-1-4272-0991-7(X))* Macmillan Audio.

—A Child's Book of Prayers. Hague, Michael, ed. 2010. (ENG.). 32p. (J). (gr. -1-k). pap. 6.99 *(978-0-312-64576-2(7))* Square Fish.

Hague, Michael & Hague, Devon. The Book of Ghosts. Hague, Michael & Hague, Devon. 2009. (ENG.). 144p. (J). (gr. 1-6). 19.99 *(978-0-688-14008-3(4))* HarperCollins Pubs.

Hahn, Beverly. Twenty Acres of Love: Irrigation Time. Hahn, Beverly. 2003. v, 65p. (J). (gr. -1-6). spiral bd. 12.95 *(978-0-9722494-0-9(0))* Hahn, Beverly.

Hahn, Beverly & Silva, Tom. Twenty Acres of Love: Little Bit, 8 vols. Hahn, Beverly. 2003. (J). (gr. k-6). 12.95 *(978-0-9722494-1-6(9))* Hahn, Beverly.

Hahn, Daniel & Hahn, David. Girls Who Rocked the World: Heroines from Joan of Arc to Mother Teresa. McCann, Michelle Roehm & Welden, Amelie. 2012. (ENG.). 256p. (J). (gr. 3-7). 19.99 *(978-1-58270-361-9(2))*; pap. 10.99 *(978-1-58270-302-2(7))* Aladdin/Beyond Words.

Hahn, David. Boys Who Rocked the World: Heroes from King Tut to Bruce Lee. McCann, Michelle Roehm. 2012. (ENG.). 256p. (J). (gr. 3-7). 18.99 *(978-1-58270-362-6(0))*; pap. 10.99 *(978-1-58270-331-2(0))* Aladdin/Beyond Words.

Hahn, David, jt. illus. see Hahn, Daniel.

Hahn, Marika. Things to Wear. (Picture Bks.: No. S8817-4). 28p. (J). (gr. -1). pap. 3.95 *(978-0-7214-5143-5(8))*, Dutton Juvenile) Penguin Publishing Group.

Hahn, Michael T., photos by. Dad's Deer Tactics 1000: Tom Hahn's Hunting Secrets Revealed by His Son. Hahn, Michael T. unabr. ed. 2003. 295p. (YA). pap. 19.95 *(978-0-9721716-0-1(6))*, 1) In Cider Pr.

Hahner, Chris. Eloise Dresses Up: 50 Reusable Stickers! Cheshire, Marc. 2005. (Eloise Ser.). (ENG.). 12p. (J). (gr. -1-1). pap. 6.99 *(978-0-689-87455-0(3))*, Little Simon) Little Simon.

Hahnl, Olivia. Pocket & Toast, 1 vol. Hahnl, John. 2010. 40p. 24.95 *(978-1-4489-8425-1(4))* PublishAmerica, Inc.

Haidle, David. Journey to the Cross & Victory: The Complete Easter Story of Jesus' Death & Resurrection. Haidle, Helen. 2008. (ENG.). (J). cd-rom 19.99 *(978-1-60101-024-7(9))* Seed Faith Bks.

Haidle, David, jt. illus. see Haidle, Helen.

Haidle, Helen & Haidle, David. Creation Story for Children. Haidle, Helen & Haidle, David. 2009. 32p. (J). 14.99 *(978-0-89051-565-5(4))* Master Bks.

Haight, Joelle. The Journals of Aiden Hunter: The Marakata Shard. Albright, David Edward. 2012. 262p. 24.99 *(978-0-9858325-0-6(9))* Storm Leaf.

Haile, Carol J. Christmas Cows. Haile, Carol J. 2012. (ENG.). 40p. (J). 19.95 *(978-0-9711236-5-6(9))* Firenze Pr.

—Elephant Overboard! Haile, Carol J. 2007. (J). lib. bdg. 19.95 *(978-0-9711236-3-2(2))* Firenze Pr.

Haimura, Kiyotaka. A Certain Magical Index. Kamachi, Kazuma. 2014. (Certain Magical Index Ser.: 1). (ENG.). 224p. (gr. 8-17). 14.00 *(978-0-316-33912-4(1))* Yen Pr.

Haines, Genny. Five Little Puppies. Wang, Margaret. 2006. (ENG.). 12p. (J). (gr. -1-k). 9.95 *(978-1-58117-487-8(X))*, Intervisual/Piggy Toes) Bendon, Inc.

Haines, Geri Berger. The Little Lost Lamb. Haines, Geri Berger. 2009. 40p. (J). (gr. -1-k). 8.95 *(978-0-8198-4528-3(0))* Pauline Bks. & Media.

Hairs, Joya, photos by. Un Barrilete: Para el Día de los Muertos, 1 vol. Amado, Elisa. 2012. (SPA & ENG.). 32p. (J). (gr. k-4). pap. 9.95 *(978-1-55498-112-0(3))* Groundwood Bks. CAN. Dist: Perseus-PGW.

Hairsine, Trevor, jt. illus. see Bagley, Mark.

Haisch, Joshua. Just the Way He Wanted Me to Be. Soske, Becky. 2007. 32p. (J). (gr. -1-3). per. 11.99 *(978-1-59879-339-0(X))* Lifevest Publishing, Inc.

Haith, Sera. The Cows at Honey Hill: Friends for Life. Surratt, Denise. 2014. (ENG.). 14.99 *(978-1-62217-138-5(1))*, Evergreen House Publishing LLC) WaveCloud Corp.

Hajde, Jeremy. Adventures in Puddle Creek: The Value of Teamwork. Peterson, S. L. 2013. (ENG.). 52p. (J). pap. 14.99 *(978-1-62994-370-1(3))* Tate Publishing & Enterprises, LLC.

Hajdinjak-Krec, Marsela & Hansen, Red. Fairies! Redmond, Shirley Raye. 2012. (Step into Reading Ser.). (ENG.). 48p. (J). (gr. k-3). pap. 3.99 *(978-0-375-86561-9(6))* Random Hse., Inc.

Hajdyla, Ken. Men Who Changed the World Vol. I: The Henry Ford Story. Arrathoon, Leigh A. Davio, John, ed. 56p. (J). (gr. 5-6). pap. 5.95 *(978-0-9648564-5-5(X))* Archus Pr., LLC.

—Men Who Changed the World Vol. II: The First Birdmen: Wilbur & Orville Wright. Arrathoon, Leigh A. Davio, John, ed. 56p. (J). (gr. 5-6). pap. 5.95 *(978-0-9648564-6-2(8))* Archus Pr., LLC.

Hakkarainen, Anna-Liisa. Grateful: A Song of Giving Thanks. Bucchino, John. (Julie Andrews Collection). 40p. (J). (gr. -1-3). 2006. pap. 6.99 *(978-0-06-051635-2(6))*, Julie Andrews Collection); 2003. (ENG.). 17.99 *(978-0-06-051633-8(X))* HarperCollins Pubs.

Halasz, Andras, jt. illus. see Horen, Michael.

Halberstadt, Bridget. Jesus in Your Backpack: A Teen's Guide to Spiritual Wisdom. Grimbol, William R. 2007. (ENG.). 256p. (gr. 6-12). per. 14.95 *(978-1-56975-608-9(2))* Ulysses Pr.

Halbower, Susan J. Log Cabin Kitty. Rubin, Donna. 2012. 56p. pap. 20.00 *(978-0-87565-503-1(3))* Texas Christian Univ. Pr.

—Smurglets Are Everywhere. Birkelbach, Alan. 2010. (ENG.). 48p. (J). (gr. -1-6). 19.95 *(978-0-87565-415-7(0))* Texas Christian Univ. Pr.

Hale, Bruce. The Big Nap. Hale, Bruce. 2008. (Chet Gecko Mystery Ser.: No. 4). (ENG.). 128p. (gr. 1-5). 24.21 *(978-1-59961-461-8(8))* Spotlight.

—Farewell, My Lunchbag. Hale, Bruce. 2008. (Chet Gecko Mystery Ser.: No. 3). 128p. (gr. 1-5). 24.21 *(978-1-59961-463-2(4))* Spotlight.

—Hiss Me Deadly. Hale, Bruce. 2009. (Chet Gecko Ser.: 13). (ENG.). 128p. (J). (gr. 2-5). pap. 5.99 *(978-0-15-206424-2(9))* Houghton Mifflin Harcourt Publishing Co.

—Key Lardo: A Chet Gecko Mystery. Hale, Bruce. 2007. (Chet Gecko Ser.: 12). (ENG.). 128p. (J). (gr. 2-5). pap. 5.99 *(978-0-15-205235-5(6))* Houghton Mifflin Harcourt Publishing Co.

—The Malted Falcon. Hale, Bruce. 2008. (Chet Gecko Mystery Ser.: No. 7). (ENG.). 128p. (gr. 1-5). 24.21 *(978-1-59961-467-0(7))* Spotlight.

—Murder, My Tweet. Hale, Bruce. 2008. (Chet Gecko Mystery Ser.: No. 10). (ENG.). 136p. (gr. 1-5). 24.21 *(978-1-59961-468-7(5))* Spotlight.

—The Mystery of Mr. Nice. Hale, Bruce. 2008. (Chet Gecko Ser.: 2). (ENG.). 112p. (J). (gr. 2-5). pap. 5.99 *(978-0-15-202515-1(4))* Houghton Mifflin Harcourt Publishing Co.

—The Mystery of Mr. Nice. Hale, Bruce. 2008. (Chet Gecko Mystery Ser.: No. 2). (ENG.). 112p. (gr. 1-5). 24.21 *(978-1-59961-469-4(3))* Spotlight.

—The Possum Always Rings Twice. Hale, Bruce. 2007. (Chet Gecko Ser.: 11). (ENG.). 128p. (J). (gr. 2-5). pap. 5.99 *(978-0-15-205233-1(X))* Houghton Mifflin Harcourt Publishing Co.

—This Gum for Hire. Hale, Bruce. 2008. (Chet Gecko Mystery Ser.: No. 6). (ENG.). 128p. (gr. 1-5). 24.21 *(978-1-59961-471-7(5))* Spotlight.

—Trouble Is My Beeswax. Hale, Bruce. 2008. (Chet Gecko Mystery Ser.: No. 8). (ENG.). 128p. (gr. 1-5). 24.21 *(978-1-59961-472-4(3))* Spotlight.

Hale, Christy. La Escuela de Elizabeti. Stuve-Bodeen, Stephanie. Sarfatti, Esther, tr. from ENG. 2007. (SPA.). 32p. (J). (gr. -1-2). pap. 9.95 *(978-1-60060-235-1(5))* Lee & Low Bks., Inc.

—Guess Again! Riddle Poems. Morrison, Lillian. 2006. (ENG.). 48p. (J). (gr. 1-4). 16.95 *(978-0-87483-730-8(8))* August Hse. Pubs., Inc.

—La Muneca de Elizabeti. Stuve-Bodeen, Stephanie. Sarfatti, Esther, tr. braille ed. 2004. (SPA.). (J). (gr. k-3). spiral bd. *(978-0-616-08966-8(X))* Canadian National Institute for the Blind/Institut National Canadien pour les Aveugles.

—Sky Dancers, 1 vol. Kirk, Connie Ann. 2013. (ENG.). 32p. (J). (gr. 2-4). pap. 8.95 *(978-1-62014-147-2(7))* Lee & Low Bks., Inc.

Hale, Christy. The East-West House: Noguchi's Childhood in Japan. Hale, Christy. 2012. (ENG.). 32p. (J). (gr. 2-7). 17.95 *(978-1-60060-363-1(7))* Lee & Low Bks., Inc.

Hale, Christy. It Rained All Day That Night: Autograph Album Verses & Inscriptions. Hale, Christy, tr. 2005. (ENG.). 80p. (J). (gr. 3-7). pap. 9.95 *(978-0-87483-726-1(X))* August Hse. Pubs., Inc.

Hale, Christy & Apostolou, Christine Hale. The Forgiveness Garden. Thompson, Lauren. 2012. (ENG.). 32p. (J). (gr. k-1). 16.99 *(978-0-312-62599-3(5))* Feiwel & Friends.

Hale, Cole. Everyone Has Hope. Lynch, Jason. 2011. (J). *(978-0-938467-09-0(3))* Headline Bks., Inc.

Hale, J. P. Dontay's Alphabet Book of Color. Hall, Eve D. 2004. 46p. (J). per. 13.00 *(978-0-9758899-1-6(5))* Imagine Publishing.

Hale, James Graham. From Seed to Pumpkin. Pfeffer, Wendy. (Let's-Read-And-Find-Out Science 1 Ser.). (ENG.). 40p. (J). (gr. -1-3). 2015. pap. 6.99 ***(978-0-06-238185-9(7))***; 2004. 15.99 *(978-0-06-028038-3(7))* HarperCollins Pubs.

—How Mountains Are Made. Zoehfeld, Kathleen Weidner. 2015. (Let's-Read-And-Find-Out Science 2 Ser.). (ENG.). 32p. (J). (gr. -1-3). pap. 6.99 ***(978-0-06-238203-0(9))*** HarperCollins Pubs.

Hale, Jason. Historic Savannah, GA Coloring Book. Lynn, Richard & Nova Blue. Claughton, Dena, ed. 2003. 32p. *(978-0-9725584-0-2(3))* Nova Blue, Inc.

Hale, Jenny. The Big Book of Animals & Bugs. Novick, Mary. (Double Delights Ser.). 32p. (J). pap. *(978-1-877003-38-7(7))* Little Hare Bks. AUS. Dist: HarperCollins Pubs. Australia.

—The Big Book of Nursery Rhymes & Songs. Novick, Mary. 2004. 32p. *(978-1-877003-39-4(5))* Little Hare Bks. AUS. Dist: HarperCollins Pubs. Australia.

—Bugs. Novick, Mary. 2003. 16p. (Orig.). pap. *(978-1-877003-32-5(8))* Little Hare Bks. AUS. Dist: HarperCollins Pubs. Australia.

—Christmas Surprise. Reed, Jonathan. 2011. (ENG.). 16p. (J). (gr. -1-k). 14.99 *(978-1-921714-88-7(3))* Little Hare Bks. AUS. Dist: Independent Pubs. Group.

—Double Delight - Nursery Rhymes. Novick, Mary. 2011. (Double Delight Ser.). (ENG.). 16p. (J). (gr. -1 — 1). pap. 8.99 *(978-1-877003-06-6(9))* Little Hare Bks. AUS. Dist: Independent Pubs. Group.

—Farm. Novick, Mary. 2011. (Double Delight Ser.). (ENG.). 16p. (J). (gr. -1 — 1). pap. 8.99 *(978-1-877003-76-9(X))* Little Hare Bks. AUS. Dist: Independent Pubs. Group.

—Nursery Songs. Novick, Mary. 2003. 16p. (Orig.). pap. *(978-1-877003-33-2(6))* Little Hare Bks. AUS. Dist: HarperCollins Pubs. Australia.

—Shoes. Munro, Maisie. 2009. (ENG.). 9p. (J). (gr. k — 1). bds. 5.95 *(978-1-921272-30-1(9))* Little Hare Bks. AUS. Dist: Independent Pubs. Group.

—Slippers. Munro, Maisie. 2009. (ENG.). 9p. (J). (gr. k — 1). bds. 5.95 *(978-1-921272-31-8(7))* Little Hare Bks. AUS. Dist: Independent Pubs. Group.

—Zoo. Novick, Mary. 2011. (Double Delight Ser.). (ENG.). 16p. (J). (gr. -1 — 1). pap. 8.99 *(978-1-877003-77-6(8))* Little Hare Bks. AUS. Dist: Independent Pubs. Group.

Hale, Nathan. Animal House. Ryan, Candace. 2010. (ENG.). 40p. (J). (gr. -1-3). 16.99 *(978-0-8027-9828-2(4))* Walker & Co.

—The Brave Little Seal. Kipling, Rudyard. 2010. (Easy Reader Classics Ser.: No. 6). (ENG.). 32p. (J). (gr. k-2). pap. 3.95 *(978-1-4027-6724-1(2))* Sterling Publishing Co., Inc.

—Calamity Jack. Hale, Shannon & Hale, Dean. 2010. (ENG.). 144p. (YA). (gr. 6-18). pap. 15.99 *(978-1-59990-373-6(3))*; 19.99 *(978-1-59990-076-6(9))* Bloomsbury USA. (Bloomsbury USA Childrens).

—The Dinosaurs' Night Before Christmas. Muecke, Anne & Moore, Clement C. 2008. (ENG.). 36p. (J). (gr. -1-3). 18.99 *(978-0-8118-6322-3(0))* Chronicle Bks. LLC.

—Frankenstein. Walton, Rick. 2012. (ENG.). 48p. (J). (gr. -1-3). 14.99 *(978-0-312-55366-1(8))* Feiwel & Friends.

—Frankenstein's Fright Before Christmas. Walton, Rick. 2014. (ENG.). 32p. (J). (gr. -1-3). 16.99 *(978-0-312-55367-8(6))* Feiwel & Friends.

—Ghost Mysteries: Unraveling the World's Most Mysterious Hauntings. Zoehfeld, Kathleen Weidner. 2009. (ENG.). 128p. (J). (gr. 4-8). pap. 5.99 *(978-1-4169-6448-3(7)*, Simon & Schuster/Paula Wiseman Bks.) Simon & Schuster/Paula Wiseman Bks.

—Mowgli Knows Best, No. 4. Kipling, Rudyard. 2007. (Easy Reader Classics Ser.). (ENG.). 32p. (J). (gr. k-2). pap. 3.95 *(978-1-4027-4125-8(1))* Sterling Publishing Co., Inc.

—Panic in Pompeii. Peacock, L. A. 2011. 92p. (J). pap. *(978-0-545-34062-5(4))* Scholastic, Inc.

—Rapunzel's Revenge. Hale, Shannon & Hale, Dean. 2008. (ENG.). 144p. (YA). (gr. 5-8). pap. 16.99 *(978-1-59990-288-3(5)*, Bloomsbury USA Childrens) Bloomsbury USA.

—Terror at Troy. Peacock, L. A. 2012. 90p. (J). *(978-0-545-34063-2(2))* Scholastic, Inc.

Hale, Nathan. The Devil You Know. Hale, Nathan. 2005. (ENG.). 32p. (J). (gr. -1-2). 16.95 *(978-0-8027-8981-5(1))* Walker & Co.

—The Twelve Bots of Christmas. Hale, Nathan. (ENG.). 40p. (J). (gr. k-3). 2012. pap. 7.99 *(978-0-8027-3399-3(9))*; 2010. 14.99 *(978-0-8027-2237-9(7))* Walker & Co.

Hale, Pattie. Nathan's Thread. Grabowski, Leo. 2009. 32p. (J). pap. 14.95 *(978-0-9822375-1-9(0))* Relevant Graces Productions.

Hale, Phil. The Drawing of the Three. King, Stephen. rev. ed. 2003. (Dark Tower Ser.: Bk. 2). (ENG.). 432p. (gr. 12-18). pap. 20.00 *(978-0-452-28470-8(8)*, Plume) Penguin Publishing Group.

Hale, Rachael, photos by. Baby Animals. 2009. (Paw Pals Ser.). (ENG., 10p. (J). (gr. -1 — 1). 6.99 *(978-0-316-04129-4(7))* Little, Brown Bks. for Young Readers.

—Bedtime Buddies. 2009. (Paw Pals Ser.). (ENG., 10p. (J). (gr. -1 — 1). 6.99 *(978-0-316-04128-7(9))* Little, Brown Bks. for Young Readers.

Hale, Randy. The Sun & the Wind. Ritz, Lee F. 2013. 62p. 23.99 *(978-1-940840-00-0(7))* Ritz, Lee Pubns.

Hale, Sally. Fixin' Buddy's Little Red Wagon. McGougan, Kathy. 2009. 16p. pap. 9.95 *(978-1-4251-8975-4(X))* Trafford Publishing.

Hales, J. Rulon. When Grandfather Was a Boy. Driggs, Howard R. 2011. 88p. 38.95 *(978-1-258-07716-7(7))* Literary Licensing, LLC.

Haley, Amanda. A Blossom Promise. Byars, Betsy. 4th ed. 2008. (Blossom Family Ser.: Bk. 4). (ENG.). 192p. (J). (gr. 4-7). pap. 6.95 *(978-0-8234-2147-3(3))* Holiday Hse., Inc.

—The Blossoms & the Green Phantom. Byars, Betsy. 2008. (Blossom Family Ser.: Bk. 3). (ENG.). 176p. (J). (gr. 4-7). pap. 6.95 *(978-0-8234-2146-6(5))* Holiday Hse., Inc.

—Dancing Class. Ziefert, Harriet. 2006. (I'm Going to Read(r) Ser.). (ENG.). 32p. (J). (gr. 1-2). pap. 3.95 *(978-1-4027-3427-4(1))* Sterling Publishing Co., Inc.

—Easter Has Eggs. 2008. (I'm Going to Read(r) Ser.). (ENG.). 28p. (J). (gr. -1-k). per. 3.95 *(978-1-4027-5543-9(0))* Sterling Publishing Co., Inc.

—If You're Happy & You Know It, 1 vol. Zondervan Publishing Staff. 2008. (I Can Read! / Song Ser.). (ENG.). 32p. (J). (gr. -1-3). pap. 3.99 *(978-0-310-71621-1(7))* Zondervan.

—Maia & the Monster Baby. Winthrop, Elizabeth. 2012. (ENG.). 32p. (J). 16.95 *(978-0-8234-2518-1(5))* Holiday Hse., Inc.

—Music Class. 2006. (I'm Going to Read(r) Ser.). (ENG.). 32p. (J). (gr. 1-2). pap. 3.95 *(978-1-4027-3081-8(0))* Sterling Publishing Co., Inc.

—The New Baby. Packard, Mary. 2004. (My First Reader Ser.). (ENG.). 32p. (J). (gr. k-1). pap. 3.95 *(978-0-516-25506-4(1)*, Children's Pr.) Scholastic Library Publishing.

—Nora & the Texas Terror. Cox, Judy. 2010. (ENG.). 96p. (J). (gr. 1-5). pap. 15.95 *(978-0-8234-2283-8(6))* Holiday Hse., Inc.

—Pizza & Other Stinky Poems. Linn, Margot. 2005. (I'm Going to Read(r) Ser.: Level 4). (ENG.). 32p. (J). (gr. 2-3). pap. 3.95 *(978-1-4027-2110-6(2))* Sterling Publishing Co., Inc.

—Reading to Peanut. Schubert, Leda. 2011. (ENG.). 32p. (J). 16.95 *(978-0-8234-2339-2(5))* Holiday Hse., Inc.

—Ready, Alice? 2005. (I'm Going to Read(r) Ser.). (ENG.). 32p. (J). (gr. k-1). per. 3.95 *(978-1-4027-2717-7(8))* Sterling Publishing Co., Inc.

—The Secret Chicken Society. Cox, Judy. (ENG.). 96p. (J). 2013. pap. 5.99 *(978-0-8234-2765-9(X))*; 2012. 15.95 *(978-0-8234-2372-9(7))* Holiday Hse., Inc.

—Snowzilla, 0 vols. Lawler, Janet. 2012. (ENG.). 32p. (J). (gr. -1-3). 16.99 *(978-0-7614-6188-3(4)*, 9780761461883, Amazon Children's Publishing) Amazon Publishing.

—Ukulele Hayley. Cox, Judy. (ENG.). 96p. (J). 2014. (gr. 2-5). pap. 5.99 *(978-0-8234-3190-8(8))*; 2013. 16.95 *(978-0-8234-2863-2(X))* Holiday Hse., Inc.

—Wanted... Mud Blossom. Byars, Betsy. 5th ed. 2008. (Blossom Family Ser.: Bk. 5). (ENG.). 192p. (J). (gr. 4-7). pap. 8.95 *(978-0-8234-2148-0(1))* Holiday Hse., Inc.

—Will Princess Isabel Ever Say Please? Metzger, Steve. 2012. (ENG.). 32p. (J). 16.95 *(978-0-8234-2323-1(9))* Holiday Hse., Inc.

—You Can't Build a House If You're a Hippo! Ziefert, Harriet & Ehrlich, Fred. 2014. (You Can't... Ser.). (ENG.). 40p. (J). (gr. -1-2). 16.99 *(978-1-60905-483-0(0))* Blue Apple Bks.

—You Can't Buy a Dinosaur with a Dime. Ziefert, Harriet. 2011. (ENG.). 32p. (J). (gr. k-3). pap. 6.99 *(978-1-60905-146-4(7))* Blue Apple Bks.

—You Can't Ride a Bicycle to the Moon! Ziefert, Harriet. 2014. (ENG.). 40p. (J). (gr. -1-3). 16.99 *(978-1-60905-419-9(9))* Blue Apple Bks.

—You Can't See Your Bones with Binoculars! Ziefert, Harriet. 2014. (ENG.). 40p. (J). (gr. -1-3). 16.99 *(978-1-60905-417-5(2))* Blue Apple Bks.

—You Can't Take Your Body to a Car Mechanic! Ziefert, Harriet & Ehrlich, Fred. 2014. (You Can't... Ser.). (ENG.). 40p. (J). (gr. -1-2). 16.99 *(978-1-60905-452-6(0))* Blue Apple Bks.

—You Can't Taste a Pickle with Your Ear. Ziefert, Harriet. 2014. (ENG.). 40p. (J). (gr. -1-3). 16.99 *(978-1-60905-418-2(0))* Blue Apple Bks.

—You Can't Use Your Brain If You're a Jellyfish! Ziefert, Harriet & Ehrlich, Fred. 2014. (You Can't... Ser.). (ENG.). 40p. (J). (gr. -1-2). 16.99 *(978-1-60905-454-0(7))* Blue Apple Bks.

—40 Uses for a Grandpa. Ziefert, Harriet. 2012. (ENG.). 40p. (J). (gr. k-12). 12.99 *(978-1-60905-276-8(5))* Blue Apple Bks.

—41 Uses for a Grandma. Ziefert, Harriet. 2011. (ENG.). 40p. (J). (gr. -1-3). 12.99 *(978-1-60905-106-8(8))* Blue Apple Bks.

Haley, Gail E. Isabella Propeller & the Magic Beanie. Graves, Jonathan. 2011. (J). 15.95 *(978-1-933251-74-5(3))* Parkway Pubs., Inc.

Haley, Gail E. Kokopelli, Drum in Belly. Haley, Gail E., tr. 2003. (J). pap. 12.95 *(978-0-86541-069-5(0))* Filter Pr., LLC.

Hall, Amanda. The Barefoot Book of Animal Tales. 2004. 80p. (J). pap. 9.99 *(978-1-84148-547-8(0))* Barefoot Bks., Inc.

Hall, Amanda. Brother Giovanni's Little Reward. Smucker, Anna Egan. 2015. 34p. (J). ***(978-0-8028-5420-9(6)***, Eerdmans Bks For Young Readers) Eerdmans, William B. Publishing Co.

Hall, Amanda. The Fantastic Jungles of Henri Rousseau. Markel, Michelle & Rousseau, Henri. 2012. (J). 17.00 *(978-0-8028-5364-6(1)*, Eerdmans Bks For Young Readers) Eerdmans, William B. Publishing Co.

—In Andal's House. 2013. (Tales of the World Ser.). (ENG.). 40p. (J). (gr. 2-5). 17.95 *(978-1-58536-603-3(X)*, 202358) Sleeping Bear Pr.

—Jewish Tales. Gelfand, Shoshana Boyd. 2013. (ENG.). 80p. (J). 19.99 *(978-1-84686-884-9(X))* Barefoot Bks., Inc.

—The Lion Book of Day-by-Day Prayers. Joslin, Mary. 2010. 159p. (J). (gr. k-4). 16.99 *(978-0-8254-7948-9(7))* Kregel Pubns.

—The Lion Classic Aesop's Fables. Aesop. 11th ed. 2012. (ENG.). 128p. (J). (gr. 2-4). 19.99 *(978-0-7459-6200-9(9))* Lion Hudson PLC GBR. Dist: Independent Pubs. Group.

—The Lion Day-by-Day Bible. Joslin, Mary. 2008. (ENG.). 384p. (J). (gr. 2-4). 19.95 *(978-0-7459-6132-3(0))* Lion Hudson PLC GBR. Dist: Independent Pubs. Group.

—The Loyola Treasury of Saints: From the Time of Jesus to the Present Day. Self, David. 2003. (ENG.). 224p. (J). 28.95 *(978-0-8294-1785-2(0))* Loyola Pr.

—Tales from India. Gavin, Jamila. 2011. (ENG.). 96p. (J). (gr. 4-7). 19.99 *(978-0-7636-5564-8(3)*, Templar) Candlewick Pr.

Hall, Amanda. The Stolen Sun. Hall, Amanda. 2004. 32p. (J). (gr. 10-18). 17.00 *(978-0-8028-5225-0(4))* Eerdmans, William B. Publishing Co.

Hall, Amanda. Giant Tales. Hall, Amanda, tr. 2003. 96p. (YA). *(978-1-84365-017-1(7)*, Pavilion Children's Books) Pavilion Bks.

Hall, Arthur. The Adventures of Robin Hood. Green, Roger Lancelyn. 2010. (Puffin Classics Ser.). (ENG.). 334p. (J). (gr. 3-7). pap. 4.99 *(978-0-14-132938-3(6)*, Puffin) Penguin Publishing Group.

Hall, Arthur & Terrazzini, Daniela Jaglenka. Adventures of Robin Hood. Green, Roger Lancelyn & Green, Richard. 2010. (Puffin Classics Ser.). (ENG.). 336p. (J). (gr. 3-7). 16.99 *(978-0-14-133489-9(4)*, Puffin) Penguin Publishing Group.

Hall, August. The Book of Magic, 12 vols., Bk. 12. Barron, T. A. 2011. (Merlin Ser.: 12). (ENG.). 160p. (J). (gr. 5-18). 17.99 *(978-0-399-24741-5(6)*, Philomel) Penguin Publishing Group.

—Keeper. Appelt, Kathi. (ENG.). (J). (gr. 3-7). 2012. 432p. pap. 8.99 *(978-1-4169-5061-5(3))*; 2010. 192p. 17.99 *(978-1-4169-5060-8(5))* Simon & Schuster Children's Publishing. (Atheneum Bks. for Young Readers).

Hall, Beverly H. Take Your Students on a Cruise: Paul's Journeys Lesson Guide. Fisher, Nancy. Witte, Carol, ed. 2004. 40p. (gr. 4-8). wbk. ed. 9.95 *(978-1-890947-00-2(8)*, 308X) Rose Publishing.

Hall, Bob, jt. illus. see Buscema, John.

Hall, Bob, jt. illus. see Liefeld, Rob.

Hall, David, photos by. Octopuses & Squids. Hall, David. Rhodes, Mary Jo. 2006. (Undersea Encounters Ser.). (ENG., 48p. (J). (gr. 3-7). per. 6.95 *(978-0-516-25350-3(6)*, Children's Pr.) Scholastic Library Publishing.

—Partners in the Sea. Hall, David. Rhodes, Mary Jo. 2006. (Undersea Encounters Ser.). (ENG., 48p. (J). (gr. 3-7). per. 6.95 *(978-0-516-25492-0(8)*, Children's Pr.) Scholastic Library Publishing.

—Predators of the Sea. Hall, David. Rhodes, Mary Jo. 2007. (Undersea Encounters Ser.). (ENG., 48p. (J). (gr. 3-7). pap. 6.95 *(978-0-516-25465-4(0)*, Children's Pr.) Scholastic Library Publishing.

—Sea Turtles. Hall, David. Rhodes, Mary Jo. 2006. (Undersea Encounters Ser.). (ENG., 48p. (J). (gr. 3-7). per. 6.95 *(978-0-516-25353-4(0)*, Children's Pr.) Scholastic Library Publishing.

—Seahorses & Sea Dragons. Hall, David. Rhodes, Mary Jo. 2005. (Undersea Encounters Ser.). (ENG., 48p. (J). (gr. 3-7). lib. bdg. 27.00 *(978-0-516-24393-1(4)*, Children's Pr.) Scholastic Library Publishing.

Hall, Dee & Hesselbein, Kent. Can You Imagine? Hall, Dee. 2013. 64p. pap. 8.95 *(978-1-935786-59-7(8))* St. Clair Pubns.

Hall, Dorothy Louise. Forever Friends. Cohen, Barbara S. 2004. 32p. (J). reprint ed. 9.95 *(978-1-931290-54-8(7))* Tallfellow Pr.

Hall, Francois. The Emperor's New Clothes. 2007. (First Fairy Tales Ser.). 32p. (J). (gr. -1-3). lib. bdg. 28.50 *(978-1-59771-071-8(7)*, 1262700) Sea-To-Sea Pubns.

Hall, Francois. Georgie & the Dragon. Graves, Sue. 2008. (Reading Corner Ser.). (ENG.). 24p. (J). (gr. k-2). pap. 6.99 ***(978-0-7496-7700-8(7))*** Hodder & Stoughton GBR. Dist: Independent Pubs. Group.

Hall, Francois. The Pie-Eating Contest. Gowar, Mick. 2013. (Start Reading Ser.). (ENG.). 24p. (gr. k-1). pap. 6.99 *(978-1-4765-4127-3(2))* Capstone Pr., Inc.

—Rodeo Rider, 1 vol. Gowar, Mick. 2013. (Start Reading Ser.). (ENG.). 24p. (gr. k-1). pap. 6.99 *(978-1-4765-4133-4(7))* Capstone Pr., Inc.

Hall, Gladys. Red Riding Hood. 2007. (Shape Bks.). (ENG.). (J). (gr. -1-3). pap. 9.95 *(978-1-59583-133-0(9)*, 9781595831330, Green Tiger Pr.) Laughing Elephant.

Hall, Greg. How Baseball Works. Thomas, Keltie. 2008. (How Sports Work Ser.). (ENG.). 64p. (J). (gr. 3-6). pap. 10.95 *(978-1-897349-21-2(1)*, Maple Tree Pr.) Owlkids Bks. Inc. CAN. Dist: Perseus-PGW.

Hall, Greg & Owlkids Books Inc. Staff. How Basketball Works. Thomas, Keltie. 2005. (How Sports Work Ser.). (ENG.). 64p. (J). (gr. 3-6). pap. 9.95 *(978-1-897066-19-5(8)*, Maple Tree Pr.) Owlkids Bks. Inc. CAN. Dist: Perseus-PGW.

—How Hockey Works. Thomas, Keltie. 2nd ed. 2006. (How Sports Work Ser.). (ENG.). 64p. (J). (gr. 3-6). pap. 10.95 *(978-1-897066-65-2(1)*, Maple Tree Pr.) Owlkids Bks. Inc. CAN. Dist: Perseus-PGW.

Hall, Jean-Blaise, photos by. Paris: Authentic Recipes Celebrating the Foods of the World. Spieler, Marlena & Oxmoor House Staff. rev. ed. 2004. (Williams-Sonoma Foods of the World Ser.). (ENG., 192p. (gr. 12-17). 24.95 *(978-0-8487-2854-0(8)*, 130070) Oxmoor Hse., Inc.

Hall, Lowell. Can Checkers Come Too? Hall, Christina. 2011. 36p. pap. 24.95 *(978-1-4560-7753-2(8))* America Star Bks.

Hall, Marcellus. Because I Am Your Daddy. North, Sherry. 2010. (ENG.). 32p. (J). (gr. -1-1). 16.95 *(978-0-8109-8392-2(3)*, Abrams Bks. for Young Readers) Abrams.

—Because You Are My Baby. North, Sherry. 2008. (ENG.). 32p. (J). (gr. -1-1). 16.95 *(978-0-8109-9482-9(8)*, Abrams Bks. for Young Readers) Abrams.

—City I Love. Hopkins, Lee Bennett. 2009. (ENG.). 32p. (J). (gr. -1-3). 16.95 *(978-0-8109-8327-4(3)*, Abrams Bks. for Young Readers) Abrams.

—The Cow Loves Cookies. Wilson, Karma. 2010. (ENG.). 40p. (J). (gr. -1-3). 17.99 *(978-1-4169-4206-1(8)*, McElderry, Margaret K. Bks.) McElderry, Margaret K. Bks.

—Duddle Puck: The Puddle Duck. Wilson, Karma. 2015. (ENG.). 40p. (J). (gr. -1-3). 17.99 *(978-1-4424-4927-5(6)*, McElderry, Margaret K. Bks.) McElderry, Margaret K. Bks.

—Full Moon & Star. Hopkins, Lee Bennett. 2011. (ENG.). 32p. (J). (gr. -1-2). 16.95 *(978-1-4197-0013-2(8)*, Abrams Bks. for Young Readers) Abrams.

—What's New? the Zoo! A Zippy History of Zoos. Krull, Kathleen. 2014. (ENG.). 40p. (J). (gr. -1-3). 17.99 *(978-0-545-13571-9(0)*, Levine, Arthur A. Bks.) Scholastic, Inc.

Hall, Mary. Amelia the Silver Sister. Castle, Amber. 2012. (ENG.). 160p. (J). (gr. 2-4). pap. 7.99 *(978-0-85707-250-4(1))* Simon & Schuster, Ltd. GBR. Dist: Simon & Schuster, Inc.

—Evie the Swan Sister. Castle, Amber. 2012. (ENG.). 160p. (J). (gr. 2-4). pap. 7.99 *(978-0-85707-252-8(8))* Simon & Schuster, Ltd. GBR. Dist: Simon & Schuster, Inc.

—Grace the Sea Sister. Castle, Amber. 2012. (ENG.). 160p. (J). (gr. 2-4). pap. 5.99 *(978-0-85707-251-1(X))* Simon & Schuster, Ltd. GBR. Dist: Simon & Schuster, Inc.

—Isabella - The Butterfly Sister. Castle, Amber. 2012. (ENG.). 160p. (J). (gr. 2-4). pap. 7.99 *(978-0-85707-249-8(8))* Simon & Schuster, Ltd. GBR. Dist: Simon & Schuster, Inc.

—A Peek-a-Boo Christmas! Oakes, Loretta. 2010. 16p. (J). (gr. -1). pap. 9.95 *(978-0-8091-6754-8(9)*, Ambassador Bks.) Paulist Pr.

—Peek-a-Boo Jesus! Oakes, Loretta. 2010. 16p. (J). (gr. -1). pap. 9.95 *(978-0-8091-6755-5(7)*, Ambassador Bks.) Paulist Pr.

—Sophia the Flame Sister. Castle, Amber. 2012. (ENG.). 160p. (J). (gr. 2-4). pap. 7.99 *(978-0-85707-247-4(1))* Simon & Schuster, Ltd. GBR. Dist: Simon & Schuster, Inc.

—Spell Sisters: Chloe the Storm Sister. Castle, Amber. 2013. (ENG.). 160p. (J). (gr. 2-4). pap. 7.99 *(978-0-85707-254-2(4))* Simon & Schuster, Ltd. GBR. Dist: Simon & Schuster, Inc.

—Spell Sisters: Olivia the Otter Sister. Castle, Amber. 2013. (ENG.). 160p. (J). (gr. 2-4). pap. 7.99 *(978-0-85707-253-5(6))* Simon & Schuster, Ltd. GBR. Dist: Simon & Schuster, Inc.

Hall, Melanie. Born on Christmas Morn. Busch, Melinda Kay. 2003. (Arch Bks.). (ENG.). 16p. (J). (gr. k-4). 1.99 *(978-0-570-07584-4(X))* Concordia Publishing Hse.

—Hanukkah Lights: Holiday Poetry. Hopkins, Lee Bennett. 2004. (I Can Read Bks.). (J). (gr. k-3). 15.99 *(978-0-06-008051-8(5))*; 32p. lib. bdg. 16.89 *(978-0-06-008052-5(3))* HarperCollins Pubs.

—How Did the Animals Help God? Swartz, Nancy Sohn. 2004. (ENG.). 24p. (J). bds. 7.99 *(978-1-59473-044-3(X)*, Skylight Paths Publishing) LongHill Partners, Inc.

—The Littlest Mountain. Rosenstock, Barb. 2011. (ENG.). 24p. (J). (gr. -1-2). 17.95 *(978-0-7613-4495-7(0))*; pap. 7.95 *(978-0-7613-4497-1(7))* Lerner Publishing Group. (Kar-Ben Publishing).

—The Magic Pomegranate. Schram, Peninnah. 2008. (On My Own Folklore Ser.). (ENG.). 48p. (gr. 2-4). pap. 6.95 *(978-0-8225-6746-2(6)*, First Avenue Editions) Lerner Publishing Group.

—The Magic Pomegranate: A Jewish Folktale. Schram, Peninnah. 2007. (On My Own Folklore Ser.). (ENG.). 48p. (gr. 2-4). lib. bdg. 25.26 *(978-0-8225-6742-4(3)*, Millbrook Pr.) Lerner Publishing Group.

—On Sukkot & Simchat Torah. Fishman, Cathy Goldberg. 2006. (ENG.). 32p. (J). (gr. -1-4). lib. bdg. 17.95 *(978-1-58013-165-0(4)*, Kar-Ben Publishing) Lerner Publishing Group.

—Savior of the Nations-Mini BK. Busch, Melinda Kay. 2009. 16p. pap. 2.29 *(978-0-7586-1756-9(9))* Concordia Publishing Hse.

—The Seventh Day. Cohen, Deborah. 2005. (ENG.). 24p. (J). (gr. -1-2). 16.95 *(978-0-929371-24-5(0))*; per. 8.95 *(978-1-58013-125-4(5))* Lerner Publishing Group. (Kar-Ben Publishing).

Hall, Melanie W. Christmas Presents: Holiday Poetry. Hopkins, Lee Bennett. 2004. (I Can Read Bks.). 32p. (J). (gr. k-3). 15.99 *(978-0-06-008054-9(X))*; lib. bdg. 16.89 *(978-0-06-008055-6(8))* HarperCollins Pubs.

—Every Second Something Happens: Poems for the Mind & Senses. Johnson, William. 2009. (ENG.). 48p. (J). (gr. k-2). 17.95 *(978-1-59078-622-2(X)*, Wordsong) Boyds Mills Pr.

—Goodnight Sh'ma. Jules, Jacqueline & Hechtkopf, Jacqueline. 2008. (ENG.). 12p. (J). (gr. -1 — 1). bds. 5.95 *(978-0-8225-8945-7(1)*, Kar-Ben Publishing) Lerner Publishing Group.

—On Hanukkah. Fishman, Cathy Goldberg. 2005. 27p. (J). (gr. k-4). reprint ed. 16.00 *(978-0-7567-9289-3(4))* DIANE Publishing Co.

—Passover Haggadah. Berger, Barry W. 2004. 36p. *(978-0-9674319-3-2(X))* Messianic Perspectives.

Hall, Michael. Cat Tale. Hall, Michael. 2012. (ENG.). 40p. (J). (gr. -1-k). 16.99 *(978-0-06-191516-1(5)*, Greenwillow Bks.) HarperCollins Pubs.

Hall, Michael. Frankencrayon. Hall, Michael. 2016. 32p. (J). (gr. -1-3). 17.99 ***(978-0-06-225211-1(9)***, Greenwillow Bks.) HarperCollins Pubs.

Hall, Michael. It's an Orange Aardvark! Hall, Michael. 2014. (ENG.). 40p. (J). (gr. -1-3). 17.99 *(978-0-06-225206-7(2)*, Greenwillow Bks.) HarperCollins Pubs.

—My Heart Is Like a Zoo. Hall, Michael. (J). (gr. -1-k). 2013. (ENG.). 34p. bds. 7.99 *(978-0-06-191512-3(2))*; 2009. (ENG.). 32p. 16.99 *(978-0-06-191510-9(6))*; 2009. 32p. lib. bdg. 17.89 *(978-0-06-191511-6(4))* HarperCollins Pubs. (Greenwillow Bks.).

—Perfect Square. Hall, Michael. 2011. (ENG.). 40p. (J). (gr. -1-k). 16.99 *(978-0-06-191513-0(0)*, Greenwillow Bks.) HarperCollins Pubs.

—Red: A Crayon's Story. Hall, Michael. 2015. (ENG.). 40p. (J). (gr. -1-3). 17.99 *(978-0-06-225207-4(0)*, Greenwillow Bks.) HarperCollins Pubs.

Hall, Milton. Human Body, Grades 4 - 6: Fun Activities, Experiments, Investigations, & Observations! Carothers, Sue & Henke, Elizabeth. 2003. (Skills for Success Ser.). (ENG.). 128p. (gr. 4-6). pap. 16.99 *(978-0-88724-954-9(X)*, CD-4329) Carson-Dellosa Publishing, LLC.

Hall, Nancy R. My Grandparents Live in an RV. Hall, Nancy R. l.t. ed. 2005. 32p. (J). 16.95 *(978-0-9761759-0-2(8))* Jasnans Publishing Co.

Hall, Norris. The All Animal Band. Moore, Jim. l.t. ed. 2004. 36p. (J). 16.00 *(978-0-9752619-0-3(8))* Animal Band Productions, Inc., The.

—Maggie Mcnair Has Sugar Bugs in There. Booth-Alberstadt, Sheila. 2013. (ENG.). 36p. (J). (gr. -1-1). 14.95 *(978-0-9711404-6-2(4))* SBA Bks., LLC.

—The Silliest Bug & Insect Book Ever. Hensley, Terri Anne. 2007. 28p. per. 6.99 *(978-0-9789057-7-4(6))* Huntington Ludlow Media Group.

—Tobias Andrew Bartholomew. Hensley, Terri Anne. 2007. 32p. per. 8.99 *(978-0-9789057-6-7(8))* Huntington Ludlow Media Group.

—The Two-Tone Frog. Jaques, Jon. 2011. (ENG.). 32p. pap. 9.95 *(978-0-615-56103-5(9))* Skylo, Inc.

Hall, Pat. The Musubi Baby. Takayama, Sandi. 2007. 32p. (J). (gr. -1-3). 10.95 *(978-1-57306-272-5(3))* Bess Pr., Inc.

Hall, Roger & Hobson, Ryan. The Field Guide to Ocean Animals. Perry, Phyllis. 2014. (Field Guides). (ENG.). 32p. (J). (gr. 2). pap. 15.95 *(978-1-62686-006-3(8)*, Silver Dolphin Bks.) Baker & Taylor Publishing Group.

Hall, Ron. Dancing with the Cranes. Armstrong, Jeannette C. 2nd rev. ed. 2009. (ENG.). 24p. pap. 10.95 *(978-1-894778-70-1(7))* Theytus Bks., Ltd. CAN. Dist: Univ. of Toronto Pr.

Hall, Susan. Buenas Noches, Dora! Cuento Para Levantar la Tapita. Ricci, Christine. 2004. (Dora the Explorer Ser.).Tr. of Good Night, Dora!. (SPA.). 16p. (J). pap. 5.99 *(978-0-689-86648-7(8)*, Libros Para Ninos) Libros Para Ninos.

—Dora & the Winter Games (Dora the Explorer) Ottersley, Martha T. 2013. (Pictureback Ser.). (ENG.). 24p. (J). (gr. -1-2). 3.99 *(978-0-385-37930-4(7)*, Random Hse. Bks. for Young Readers) Random Hse. Children's Bks.

—Dora Carryalong Treasury. Koeppel, Ruth. 2010. (Carry along Treasury Ser.). (ENG.). 24p. (J). (gr. -1-1). bds. 14.99 *(978-0-7944-2100-7(8))* Reader's Digest Assn., Inc., The.

—Dora's Book of Manners. Ricci, Christine. ed. 2005. (Dora the Explorer Ser.: No. 7). 22p. (J). lib. bdg. 15.00 *(978-1-59054-793-9(4))* Fitzgerald Bks.

—Dora's Cousin Diego. 2011. (Dora & Diego Ser.). (ENG.). 24p. (J). pap. 3.99 *(978-1-4424-1399-3(9)*, Simon Spotlight/Nickelodeon) Simon Spotlight/Nickelodeon.

—Dora's Picnic. Ricci, Christine. 2003. (Ready-to-Read Ser.: Vol. 1). (ENG.). 24p. (J). pap. 3.99 *(978-0-689-85238-1(X)*, Simon Spotlight/Nickelodeon) Simon Spotlight/Nickelodeon.

—Follow Those Feet! Ricci, Christine. 2003. (Dora the Explorer Ser.: Vol. 2). (ENG.). 24p. (J). pap. 3.99 *(978-0-689-85239-8(8)*, Simon Spotlight/Nickelodeon) Simon Spotlight/Nickelodeon.

—Good Night, Dora! (Dora the Explorer) Random House Staff. 2013. (Pictureback with Flaps Ser.). (ENG.). 16p. (J). (gr. -1-2). 4.99 *(978-0-449-81781-0(4)*, Random Hse. Bks. for Young Readers) Random Hse. Children's Bks.

—Helping Hands. Ricci, Christine. 2007. (J). pap. *(978-1-4127-8921-9(4))* Publications International, Ltd.

—Meet Diego! Valdes, Leslie. ed. 2005. (Dora the Explorer Ser.: No. 4). 22p. (J). lib. bdg. 15.00 *(978-1-59054-799-1(3))* Fitzgerald Bks.

—Mr. Fixit's Lucky Day. 2011. (Busytown Mysteries Ser.). (ENG.). 24p. (J). pap. 3.99 *(978-1-4424-2085-4(5)*, Simon Spotlight) Simon Spotlight.

—Robot Repairman to the Rescue! 2009. (Backyardigans Ser.). (ENG.). 24p. (J). (gr. -1-2). pap. 3.99 *(978-1-4169-9012-3(7)*, Simon Spotlight/Nickelodeon) Simon Spotlight/Nickelodeon.

Hall, Susan & Hall, Susan. Diego Saves the Tree Frogs. 2006. (Go, Diego, Go! Ser.). (ENG.). 24p. (J). (gr. -1-1). pap. 3.99 *(978-1-4169-1574-4(5)*, Simon Spotlight/Nickelodeon) Simon Spotlight/Nickelodeon.

—Dora Explora los Colores. Beinstein, Phoebe. 2007. (Dora la Exploradora Ser.).Tr. of Dora Explores Colors. (SPA & ENG.). 14p. (J). (gr. -1). bds. 4.99 *(978-1-4169-4726-4(4)*, Libros Para Ninos) Libros Para Ninos.

—Hooray for School! Going to School with Nick Jr. Lindner, Brooke. 2008. (ENG.). 16p. (J). (gr. -1-2). pap. 6.99 *(978-1-4169-5861-1(4)*, Simon Spotlight/Nickelodeon) Simon Spotlight/Nickelodeon.

—Surf That Wave! 2006. (Backyardigans Ser.). (ENG.). 24p. (J). (gr. -1-3). pap. 3.99 *(978-1-4169-1482-2(X)*, Simon Spotlight/Nickelodeon) Simon Spotlight/Nickelodeon.

Hall, Susan & Roper, Robert. The Super Soccer Game. Ricci, Christine. 2007. (J). pap. *(978-1-4127-8926-4(5))* Publications International, Ltd.

Hall, Susan, jt. illus. see Hall, Susan.

Hall, Susan T. Presentamos a Diego! 2005. (Dora the Explorer Ser.). Orig. Title: Meet Diego!. (SPA.). 24p. (J). pap. 3.99 *(978-0-689-87749-0(8)*, Libros Para Ninos) Libros Para Ninos.

—Watch Me Draw Diego's Animal Adventures. 2013. (Watch Me Draw Ser.). 24p. (J). (gr. -1-2). 25.65 *(978-1-936309-88-7(2))* Quarto Publishing Group USA.

Hall, Terri L. & Babeaux, Dennis, photos by. Denny & Denise: A Story of Two Ducks: Introducing Pretty Boy & Fella, 1 vol. Hall, Terri L. 2009. 42p. pap. 24.95 *(978-1-60749-609-0(7))* America Star Bks.

Hall, Tracy. Washington Irving. Irving, Washington. 2004. (Great American Short Stories Ser.). 80p. (gr. 4-7). lib. bdg. 24.00 *(978-0-8368-4253-1(7)*, Gareth Stevens Learning Library) Stevens, Gareth Publishing LLLP.

Hall, Wendell E. Buried Treasures of California. Jameson, W. C. 2006. (Buried Treasure Ser.). (ENG.). 175p. (Orig.). (J). (gr. 4-17). pap. 14.95 *(978-0-87483-406-2(6))* August Hse. Pubs., Inc.

—Curing the Cross-Eyed Mule: Appalachian Mountain Humor. Jones, Loyal & Wheeler, Billy Edd. 2005. (ENG.). 212p. (Orig.). (J). (gr. -1-12). pap. 12.95 *(978-0-87483-083-5(4))* August Hse. Pubs., Inc.

—More Laughter in Appalachia: Southern Mountain Humor. Jones, Loyal & Wheeler, Billy Edd. 2005. (American Storytelling Ser.). (ENG.). 218p. (J). (gr. -1-12). pap. 12.95 *(978-0-87483-411-6(2))* August Hse. Pubs., Inc.

—Queen of the Cold-Blooded Tales. Brown, Roberta Simpson. 2005. (American Storytelling Ser.). (ENG.). 175p. (J). (gr. 5-17). pap. 9.95 *(978-0-87483-408-6(2))* August Hse. Pubs., Inc.

—The Stable Boy. Taylor, Shirley A. 2012. (ENG.). 40p. (J). 17.95 *(978-1-935166-79-5(4))* Parkhurst Brothers, Inc., Pubs.

Hallam, Colleen and Peggy. The Adventures of Donny the Doorknob. Ross, Marlene. 2009. 32p. pap. 24.95 *(978-1-61546-539-2(1))* America Star Bks.

Hallam, Serena Sax. The All-Seeing Boy & the Blue Sky of Happiness: A Children's Parable. Kettles, Nick. 2011. (ENG.). 32p. (J). (gr. 1-4). 16.95 *(978-1-55939-371-3(8)*, Snow Lion Publications, Inc.) Shambhala Pubns., Inc.

Hallensleben, Georg. And If the Moon Could Talk. Banks, Kate. 2005. (ENG.). 40p. (J). (gr. -1-1). reprint ed. per. 7.99 *(978-0-374-43558-5(8)*, Sunburst) Farrar, Straus & Giroux.

—The Bear in the Book, 1 vol. Banks, Kate. 2012. (ENG.). 36p. (J). (gr. -1-1). 16.99 *(978-0-374-30591-8(9)*, Farrar, Straus & Giroux (BYR)) Farrar, Straus & Giroux.

—The Cat Who Walked Across France. Banks, Kate. 2004. (ENG.). 40p. (J). (gr. -1-2). 17.99 *(978-0-374-39968-9(9)*, Farrar, Straus & Giroux (BYR)) Farrar, Straus & Giroux.

—Close Your Eyes. Banks, Kate. 2015. (ENG.). 34p. (J). (gr. -1-1). 7.99 *(978-0-374-30101-9(8)*, Farrar, Straus & Giroux (BYR)) Farrar, Straus & Giroux.

—Gaspard & Lisa's Christmas Surprise. Gutman, Anne. 2012. (ENG.). 32p. (J). (gr. k-3). pap. 6.99 *(978-0-449-81013-2(5)*, Dragonfly Bks.) Random Hse. Children's Bks.

—Gaspard & Lisa's Christmas Surprise. Gutman, Anne. ed. 2012. lib. bdg. 17.20 *(978-0-606-26782-3(4)*, Turtleback) Turtleback Bks.

—Lisa's Baby Sister. Gutman, Anne. 2012. (ENG.). 32p. (J). (gr. k-3). pap. 6.99 *(978-0-449-81012-5(7)*, Dragonfly Bks.) Random Hse. Children's Bks.

—The Night Worker. Banks, Kate. 2007. (ENG.). 40p. (J). (gr. -1-1). 8.99 *(978-0-374-40000-2(8))* Square Fish.

Hallensleben, Georg. Baños. Hallensleben, Georg. Gutman, Anne & Gutmann-Hallensleben. 2003. (Coleccion Mira Mira Look Look Ser.). (SPA.). 16p. (J). (gr. -1-k). 9.99 *(978-84-261-3322-9(3))* Juventud, Editorial ESP. Dist: Lectorum Pubns., Inc.

Haller, Reese. Giving & Receiving. Haller, Reese. 2007. (Fred the Mouse Ser.). 104p. (J). (gr. 4-7). per. 4.97 *(978-0-9772321-5-4(8))* Personal Power Pr.

Haller, Thomas. Rescuing Freedom. Haller, Reese. 3rd ed. 2006. (Fred the Mouse Ser.). 112p. (J). (gr. k-4). per. 4.97 *(978-0-9772321-3-0(1))* Personal Power Pr.

Hallett, Joy Davies. Kelly Bear Earth. Davies, Leah. Davies, Leah, ed. 2008. 32p. (J). pap. 5.95 *(978-0-9621054-3-2(0))* Kelly Bear Pr., Inc.

Hallett, Mark. Wild Cats: Past & Present. Becker, John. 2008. (Darby Creek Exceptional Titles Ser.). (ENG.). 80p. (gr. 6-12). 18.95 *(978-1-58196-052-5(2)*, Darby Creek) Lerner Publishing Group.

Halligan, Kelly C., et al. The Smart Princess: And Other Deaf Tales, 1 vol. Carey, Keelin et al. 2007. (ENG.). 148p. (J). (gr. 3-7). per. 9.95 *(978-1-896764-90-0(8))* Second Story Pr. CAN. Dist: Orca Bk. Pubs. USA.

Hallinan, P. K. Brothers Forever. Hallinan, P. K. 2010. 20p. (J). (gr. -1-k). 7.99 *(978-0-8249-1847-7(9)*, Candy Cane Pr.) Ideals Pubns.

—How Do I Love You? Hallinan, P. K. (J). 2014. 24p. bds. 8.99 *(978-0-8249-1944-3(0))*; 2006. (ENG.). 26p. (gr. -1-k). 12.95 *(978-0-8249-6650-8(3))* Ideals Pubns. (Candy Cane Pr.).

—I Know Jesus Loves Me. Hallinan, P. K. 2014. 18p. (J). pap. 6.99 *(978-0-8249-5663-9(X)*, Ideals Children's Bks.) Ideals Pubns.

—Let's Be Happy. Hallinan, P. K. 2005. (ENG.). 26p. (J). (gr. -1-1). bds. 7.95 *(978-0-8249-6588-4(4))* Ideals Pubns.

—Let's Be Helpful. Hallinan, P. K. 2009. (ENG.). 24p. (J). (gr. -1-2). 8.99 *(978-0-8249-5611-0(7)*, Ideals Children's Bks.) Ideals Pubns.

—Let's Be Kind. Hallinan, P. K. 2008. (ENG.). 24p. (J). (gr. -1-2). 8.99 *(978-0-8249-5605-9(2)*, Ideals Children's Bks.) Ideals Pubns.

—Let's Be Thankful. Hallinan, P. K. 2008. (ENG.). 24p. (J). (gr. -1-2). 8.99 *(978-0-8249-5604-2(4)*, Ideals Children's Bks.) Ideals Pubns.

—Let's Share. Hallinan, P. K. 2009. (ENG.). 24p. (J). (gr. -1-2). 8.99 *(978-0-8249-5610-3(9)*, Ideals Children's Bks.) Ideals Pubns.

—Sisters Forever. Hallinan, P. K. 2014. 22p. (J). bds. 7.99 *(978-0-8249-1921-4(1)*, Candy Cane Pr.) Ideals Pubns.

—Today Is Christmas! Hallinan, P. K. 2008. (ENG.). 26p. (J). (gr. -1-k). bds. 6.99 *(978-0-8249-1804-0(5)*, Candy Cane Pr.) Ideals Pubns.

—Today Is Halloween! Hallinan, P. K. 2008. (ENG.). 26p. (J). (gr. -1-k). bds. 6.99 *(978-0-8249-1805-7(3)*, Candy Cane Pr.) Ideals Pubns.

—Today Is Thanksgiving! Hallinan, P. K. 2008. (ENG.). 26p. (J). (gr. -1-k). bds. 6.99 *(978-0-8249-6727-7(5)*, Candy Cane Pr.) Ideals Pubns.

Hallinan, Susan. Sassy the Seahag. Canfield, Andrea. 2003. Orig. Title: Sassy the Seahag. (J). per. *(978-0-9721327-3-2(2))* Studio4264.

Halling, Jonathan. Weird but True: 300 Outrageous Facts. U. S. National Geographic Society Staff & National Geographic Kids Staff. 2009. (ENG.). 208p. (J). (gr. 3-7). pap. 7.95 *(978-1-4263-0594-6(X)*, National Geographic Children's Bks.) National Geographic Society.

—Weird but True! 2: 300 Outrageous Facts. National Geographic Kids Staff. 2010. (ENG.). 208p. (J). (gr. 3-7). pap. 7.95 *(978-1-4263-0688-4(1)*, National Geographic Children's Bks.) National Geographic Society.

Hallmark, Darla. More Dragons: Coloring Book by Darla Hallmark. 2007. 20p. (YA). 10.00 *(978-0-9795206-8-6(1))* Unseen Gallery.

Halperin, Wendy. Planting the Wild Garden, 1 vol. Galbraith, Kathryn O. 2011. (ENG.). 32p. (J). (gr. -1-3). 15.95 *(978-1-56145-563-8(6))* Peachtree Pubs.

Halperin, Wendy Anderson. Let's Go Home: The Wonderful Things about a House. Rylant, Cynthia. 2005. (ENG.). 32p. (J). (gr. -1-3). 7.99 *(978-1-4169-0639-5(0)*, Simon & Schuster Bks. For Young Readers) Simon & Schuster Bks. For Young Readers.

—Love Is ... King James Bible Staff. 2004. (ENG.). 32p. (J). 11.99 *(978-0-689-86675-3(5)*, Simon & Schuster/Paula Wiseman Bks.) Simon & Schuster/Paula Wiseman Bks.

—My Father Is Taller Than a Tree. Bruchac, Joseph. (ENG.). 32p. (J). (gr. -1-k). 2013. pap. 6.99 *(978-0-14-242535-0(4)*, Puffin); 2010. 16.99 *(978-0-8037-3173-8(6)*, Dial) Penguin Publishing Group.

—Nothing to Do. Wood, Douglas. 2006. (ENG.). 32p. (J). (gr. -1-3). 16.99 *(978-0-525-47656-6(3)*, Dutton Juvenile) Penguin Publishing Group.

—The Racketty-Packetty House. Burnett, Frances Hodgson. 100th anniv. ed. 2006. (ENG.). 96p. (J). (gr. 4-7). 19.99 *(978-0-689-86974-7(6)*, Simon & Schuster Bks. For Young Readers) Simon & Schuster Bks. For Young Readers.

—Wedding Flowers. Rylant, Cynthia. 2003. (Cobble Street Cousins Ser.). 72p. (gr. 2-5). 15.00 *(978-0-7569-1476-9(0))* Perfection Learning Corp.

Halperin, Wendy Anderson. Peace. Halperin, Wendy Anderson. Childrens Books Staff & Nash, Scott. 2013. (ENG.). 40p. (J). (gr. -1-3). 17.99 *(978-0-689-82552-1(8)*, Atheneum Bks. for Young Readers) Simon & Schuster Children's Publishing.

Halpern, Chaiky. The Hamentash That Ran Away. (J). (gr. -1-4). 2.95 *(978-0-87306-250-3(7))* Feldheim Pubs.

Halpern, Gina. Where Is Tibet? Halpern, Gina. 2nd ed. 2011. (ENG.). 48p. (J). (gr. -1-2). pap. 14.95 *(978-1-55939-383-6(1)*, Snow Lion Publications, Inc.) Shambhala Pubns., Inc.

Halpern, Shari. Construction Kitties. Sturges, Judy Sue Goodwin. 2013. (ENG.). 28p. (J). (gr. -1-k). 16.99 *(978-0-8050-9105-2(X)*, Holt, Henry & Co. Bks. For Young Readers) Holt, Henry & Co.

—I Love Bugs! Sturges, Philemon. 2005. (ENG.). 32p. (J). (gr. -1-3). 17.99 *(978-0-06-056168-0(8))* HarperCollins Pubs.

—I Love Cranes! Sturges, Philemon. Date not set. 32p. (J). (gr. -1-1). 5.99 *(978-0-06-443666-3(7))* HarperCollins Pubs.

—I Love Planes! Sturges, Philemon. 2003. (ENG.). 32p. (J). (gr. -1-1). 16.99 *(978-0-06-028898-3(1))* HarperCollins Pubs.

—I Love School! Sturges, Philemon. 2014. 32p. pap. 7.00 *(978-1-61003-329-9(9))* Center for the Collaborative Classroom.

—I Love School! Sturges, Philemon. 32p. (J). (gr. -1-1). 2004. lib. bdg. 14.89 *(978-0-06-009285-6(8))*; 2006. (ENG.). reprint ed. pap. 6.99 *(978-0-06-009286-3(6))* HarperCollins Pubs.

—I Love Tools! Sturges, Philemon. 2006. 24p. (J). (gr. -1-1). 14.89 *(978-0-06-009288-7(2))* HarperCollins Pubs.

—I Love Trains! Sturges, Philemon. (ENG.). (J). (gr. -1-1). 2006. 28p. bds. 6.99 *(978-0-06-083774-7(8)*, HarperFestival); 2003. 32p. pap. 6.99 *(978-0-06-443667-0(5))* HarperCollins Pubs.

—I Love Trucks! Sturges, Philemon. 2003. (ENG.). 34p. (J). (gr. -1-3). bds. 7.99 *(978-0-06-052666-5(1)*, HarperFestival) HarperCollins Pubs.

—¡No, Tito, No! - No, No, Titus! Masurel, Claire. Lasconi, Diego, tr. 2006. (SPA.). 32p. (J). (gr. -1-3). 6.95 *(978-0-7358-2075-3(9))* North-South Bks., Inc.

Halpern, Shari. Dinosaur Parade. Halpern, Shari. 2014. (ENG.). 32p. (J). (gr. -1-k). 16.99 *(978-0-8050-9242-4(0)*, Holt, Henry & Co. Bks. For Young Readers) Holt, Henry & Co.

Halperni, Wendy Anderson. Planting the Wild Garden, 1 vol. Galbraith, Kathryn O. 2015. (ENG.). 32p. (J). (gr. 1-3). pap. 7.95 *(978-1-56145-791-5(4))* Peachtree Pubs.

Halpin, Abigail. Bella's Rules. Guest, Elissa Haden. 2013. (ENG.). 32p. (J). (gr. -1-k). 16.99 *(978-0-8037-3393-0(3)*, Dial) Penguin Publishing Group.

—Emma: Lights! Camera! Cupcakes! Simon, Coco. 2014. (Cupcake Diaries: 19). (ENG.). 160p. (J). (gr. 3-7). pap. 5.99 *(978-1-4424-9930-0(3)*, Simon Spotlight) Simon Spotlight.

Halpin, Abigail. Finding Wild. Lloyd, Megan Wagner. 2016. (J). ***(978-1-101-93281-0(3))*** Knopf, Alfred A. Inc.

Halpin, Abigail. The Glitter Trap. Brauner, Barbara & Mattson, James Iver. 2014. (Oh My Godmother Ser.). (ENG.). 256p. (J). (gr. 3-7). pap. 6.99 *(978-1-4231-6474-6(1))* Hyperion Bks. for Children.

—The Grand Plan to Fix Everything. Krishnaswami, Uma. (ENG.). (J). (gr. 3-7). 2013. 288p. pap. 6.99 *(978-1-4169-9590-6(0))*; 2011. 272p. 16.99 *(978-1-4169-9589-0(7))* Simon & Schuster Children's Publishing. (Atheneum Bks. for Young Readers).

—The Magic Mistake. Brauner, Barbara & Mattson, James Iver. 2014. (Oh My Godmother Ser.). (ENG.). 256p. (J). (gr. 3-7). 16.99 *(978-1-4231-6475-3(X))* Hyperion Bks. for Children.

—Maybe Yes, Maybe No, Maybe Maybe. Patron, Susan. 2009. (ENG.). 128p. (J). (gr. 3-5). pap. 5.99 *(978-1-4169-6176-5(3)*, Atheneum Bks. for Young Readers) Simon & Schuster Children's Publishing.

—The Melancholic Mermaid. George, Kallie. 2011. (ENG.). 64p. (J). (gr. k-4). 16.95 *(978-1-897476-53-6(1))* Simply Read Bks. CAN. Dist: Ingram Pub. Services.

—Oh My Godmother the Magic Mistake. Brauner, Barbara & Mattson, James Iver. 2014. (Oh My Godmother Ser.). (ENG.). 272p. (J). (gr. 3-7). pap. 6.99 *(978-1-4231-6479-1(2))* Hyperion Bks. for Children.

—Penny Dreadful. Snyder, Laurel. (ENG.). 320p. (J). (gr. 3-7). 2011. 7.99 *(978-0-375-86169-7(6)*, Yearling); 2010. 16.99 *(978-0-375-86199-4(8)*, Random Hse. Bks. for Young Readers) Random Hse. Children's Bks.

—The Problem with Being Slightly Heroic. Krishnaswami, Uma. (ENG.). 288p. (J). (gr. 3-7). 2014. pap. 6.99 *(978-1-4424-2329-9(3)*, Atheneum Bks. for Young Readers); 2013. 16.99 *(978-1-4424-2328-2(5))* Simon & Schuster Children's Publishing.

—The Spell Bind. Brauner, Barbara & Mattson, James Iver. 2014. (Oh My Godmother Ser.). (ENG.). 256p. (J). (gr. 3-7). 16.99 *(978-1-4231-6476-0(8))* Hyperion Bks. for Children.

—The Year of the Book. Cheng, Andrea. (Anna Wang Novel Ser.: 1). (ENG.). 160p. (J). (gr. 1-4). 2013. pap. 5.99 *(978-0-544-02263-8(7))*; 2012. 15.99 *(978-0-547-68463-5(0))* Houghton Mifflin Harcourt Publishing Co.

Halpin, D. Thomas & Richards, Virginia Helen. Saint Paul. Halpin, D. Thomas & Richards, Virginia Helen. 2008. (COMIColor Saints Ser.: 1). (J). 2.95 *(978-0-8198-7109-1(5))* Pauline Bks. & Media.

Halpin, D. Thomas, jt. illus. see Richards, Virginia Helen.

Halsey, Megan. Backyard Bear. Rockwell, Anne F. 2006. (ENG.). 32p. (J). (gr. -1-2). 15.95 *(978-0-8027-9573-1(0))* Walker & Co.

—Four Seasons Make a Year. Rockwell, Anne F. 2004. (ENG.). 32p. (J). (gr. k-3). 16.99 *(978-0-8027-8883-2(1))* Walker & Co.

—Trucks: Whizz! Zoom! Rumble!, 0 vols. Hubbell, Patricia. 2006. (ENG.). 32p. (J). (gr. -1-1). per. 9.99 *(978-0-7614-5328-4(8)*, 9780761453284, Amazon Children's Publishing) Amazon Publishing.

Halsey, Megan. 3 Pandas Planting, 0 vols. Halsey, Megan. rev. ed. 2011. (ENG.). 32p. (J). (gr. -1-3). pap. 6.99 *(978-0-7614-5844-9(1)*, 9780761458449, Amazon Children's Publishing) Amazon Publishing.

Halsey, Megan & Addy, Sean. Akira to Zoltan: Twenty-Six Men Who Changed the World. Chin-Lee, Cynthia. 2006. (ENG.). 32p. (J). (gr. 3-7). lib. bdg. 15.95 *(978-1-57091-579-6(2))* Charlesbridge Publishing, Inc.

—Amelia to Zora: Twenty-Six Women Who Changed the World. Chin-Lee, Cynthia. 2008. (ENG.). 32p. (J). (gr. 3-7). pap. 7.95 *(978-1-57091-523-9(7))* Charlesbridge Publishing, Inc.

—Boats: Speeding! Sailing! Cruising!, 0 vols. Hubbell, Patricia. 2009. (ENG.). 32p. (J). (gr. -1-1). 17.99 *(978-0-7614-5524-0(8)*, 9780761455240, Amazon Children's Publishing) Amazon Publishing.

—Cars: Rushing! Honking! Zooming!, 0 vols. Hubbell, Patricia. 2010. (ENG.). 32p. (J). (gr. -1-1). pap. 6.99 *(978-0-7614-5616-2(3)*, 9780761456162, Amazon Children's Publishing) Amazon Publishing.

—Cousins of Clouds: Elephant Poems. Zimmer, Tracie Vaughn. 2011. (ENG.). 32p. (J). (gr. -1-3). 16.99 *(978-0-618-90349-8(6))* Houghton Mifflin Harcourt Publishing Co.

—Valentine Be Mine. Farmer, Jacqueline. 2013. (ENG.). 32p. (J). (gr. k-3). pap. 7.95 *(978-1-58089-390-9(2))* Charlesbridge Publishing, Inc.

Halsey, Megan, jt. illus. see Addy, Sean.

Haltermon, Becky. A Rabbit Hash Christmas. Clare, Caitlen. 2012. 36p. (J). 10.00 *(978-0-9816123-9-3(3))* Merlot Group, LLC, The.

Halverson, Lydia. Baby Looney Tunes Visit a Haunted House. Ritchie, Joseph R. 2005. (Baby Looney Tunes Ser.). 14p. (J). (gr. -1-3). bds. 9.95 *(978-0-8249-6609-6(0))* Ideals Pubns.

—An Easter Basket Peek-A-Boo! Ritchie, Joseph R. 2007. (Lift-the-Flap Books (Candycane Press) Ser.). (ENG.). 14p. (J). (gr. -1-1). bds. 7.99 *(978-0-8249-6688-1(0)*, Candy Cane Pr.) Ideals Pubns.

—Frosty the Snowman. Rollins, Jack & Nelson, Steve. 2005. 18p. (J). (gr. -1-k). bds. 9.95 *(978-0-8249-6595-2(7))* Ideals Pubns.

—I Like Noisy, Mom Likes Quiet. Spinelli, Eileen. 2006. (ENG.). 32p. (J). (gr. -1-3). 8.95 *(978-0-8249-5517-5(X)*, 1256103, Ideals Children's Bks.) Ideals Pubns.

—Nursery Rhymes. 2004. (Elements of Reading: Phonics Ser.). 24p. pap. 40.00 *(978-0-7398-9014-1(X))* Houghton Mifflin Harcourt Supplemental Pubs.

—Peek-a-Boo! Ritchie, Joseph R. 2004. (ENG.). 14p. (J). bds. 7.95 *(978-0-8249-6550-1(7))* Ideals Pubns.

—Peek-A-Boo! Valentine. Ritchie, Joseph. 2006. (ENG.). 14p. (J). (gr. -1-k). bds. 7.95 *(978-0-8249-6674-4(0)*, Candy Cane Pr.) Ideals Pubns.

—Peter Cottontail's Busy Day. Ritchie, Joseph R. (J). 2009. 14p. (gr. -1-k). bds. 6.99 *(978-0-8249-1842-2(8)*, Candy Cane Pr.); 2006. (ENG.). 8p. (gr. -1-k). 12.95 *(978-0-8249-6652-2(X)*, Ideals Children's Bks.); 2005. (ENG.). 16p. bds. 9.95 *(978-0-8249-6571-6(X))* Ideals Pubns.

—Peter Cottontail's Easter Surprise. Ritchie, Joseph R. 2006. (ENG.). 18p. (J). (gr. -1-k). bds. 9.95 *(978-0-8249-6627-0(9)*, Candy Cane Pr.) Ideals Pubns.

—The Red Door Detective Club Mysteries, 4 bks., Set. Riehecky, Janet. (J). (gr. 3-6). lib. bdg. 51.80 *(978-1-56674-900-8(X))* Forest Hse. Publishing Co., Inc.

—Trick or Treat! Schaefer, Peggy. 2009. (ENG.). 16p. (J). (gr. -1-k). bds. 12.99 *(978-0-8249-1828-6(2)*, Candy Cane Pr.) Ideals Pubns.

—Where's Santa? Ritchie, Joseph R. 2006. (ENG.). 14p. (J). (gr. -1-k). bds. 7.95 *(978-0-8249-6673-7(2)*, Candy Cane Pr.) Ideals Pubns.

Halverson, Lydia, jt. illus. see Cowdrey, Richard.

Halverson, Tom. The Incredible Rescues. Dunlop, Ed. 2003. 166p. (J). (gr. 4-7). 7.49 *(978-1-59166-012-5(2))* BJU Pr.

—The Search for the Silver Eagle. Dunlop, Ed. 2003. 159p. (J). (gr. 4-7). 7.49 *(978-1-59166-014-9(9))* BJU Pr.

Halvorson, Adeline. La Primera: The Story of Wild Mustangs. Tyson, Ian. 2009. (ENG.). 32p. (J). (gr. 2-4). 20.95 *(978-0-88776-863-7(6)*, Tundra Bks.) Tundra Bks. CAN. Dist: Penguin Random Hse., LLC.

Hamad, Elnour. The Clever Sheikh of the Butana: Sudanese Folk Tales. Harris, Kate W., ed. 2004. (International Folk Tales Ser.). (ENG.). 160p. (gr. 6). pap. 13.95 *(978-1-56656-312-3(7))* Interlink Publishing Group, Inc.

Hamaker, Steve. Bone Handbook. Smith, Jeff. 2010. (Bone Ser.). (ENG.). 128p. (J). (gr. 3-7). pap. 9.99 *(978-0-545-21142-0(5)*, Graphix) Scholastic, Inc.

Hamaker, Steve & Smith, Jeff. Rock Jaw: Master of the Eastern Border. Smith, Jeff. 2007. (Bone Ser.: 5). (ENG.). 128p. (J). (gr. 4-7). 24.99 *(978-0-439-70627-8(0)*, Graphix) Scholastic, Inc.

Hamaker, Steve, jt. illus. see Smith, Jeff.

Hamanaka, Sheila. Grandparents Song. Hamanaka, Sheila. 2003. 32p. (J). 15.99 *(978-0-688-17852-9(9))*; lib. bdg. 16.89 *(978-0-688-17853-6(7))* HarperCollins Pubs.

Hambleton, Laura. American English with Abby & Zak. Traynor, Tracy. 2007. (Abby & Zak Ser.). (ENG.). 48p. (J). (gr. k-2). pap. 16.95 *(978-1-84059-491-1(8))* Milet Publishing.

—Ece Ve Efe İle Türkçe. Erdogan, Fatih. 2007. (Abby & Zak Ser.). (ENG.). 48p. (J). (gr. k-2). pap. 16.95 *(978-1-84059-493-5(4))* Milet Publishing.

—Spanish with Abby & Zak. Traynor, Tracy & Pérez, María. 2008. (Abby & Zak Ser.). (SPA & ENG.). 48p. (J). (gr. k-2). pap. 16.95 *(978-1-84059-515-4(9))* Milet Publishing.

Hambleton, Laura. Telling Tails: Fun with Homonyms. Hambleton, Laura. Turhan, Sedat. 2007. (Milet Wordwise Ser.). (ENG.). 28p. (J). (gr. k-2). pap. 6.95 *(978-1-84059-498-0(5))* Milet Publishing.

Hamblin, George. Nathan & Nicole Learn about Nouns. Malaspina, Ann. 2015. (Language Builders Ser.). (ENG.). 32p. (J). (gr. 2-4). pap. 11.94 *(978-1-60357-701-4(7))*; lib. bdg. 25.27 *(978-1-59953-666-8(8))* Norwood Hse. Pr.

—Teachers' Favorites Fun Activities for Fall! Fort, Holli et al. 2010. 96p. (J). *(978-1-4508-2765-2(9))* Publications International, Ltd.

Hamburger, Carole. The Zippity-Do-Dot: The Dot Who Dared to Pick Her Knows. Hamburger, Carole. 2008. 40p. (J). 16.95 *(978-0-9764921-1-5(3))* Cherry Street Pr.

Hamdan, Noah. Riding on a Beam of Light: Albert Einstein. Dean, Ramsey. 2013. 48p. pap. 10.48 *(978-0-9893372-1-2(9))* Ramsey Dean, Inc.

Hameister, Ann. Enter the Earth. Welles, Lee. (Gaia Girls Ser.: 1). (ENG.). 336p. (YA). (gr. 4-7). 2007. pap. 19.95 *(978-1-933609-01-0(X))*; 2006. 18.95 *(978-1-933609-00-3(1))* Chelsea Green Publishing.

Hamel, Caroline. How to Become a Perfect Knight in Five Days. Dube, Pierrette. 2009. (Rainy Day Readers Ser.). 32p. (J). (gr. -1-3). 22.60 *(978-1-60754-373-2(7))*; pap. 10.55 *(978-1-60754-374-9(5))* Windmill Bks.

Hamelin, Marie-Micheline. Eat, Run & Live Healthy. Olson, Karen. 2nd rev. ed. 2009. (Caring for Me Ser.). (ENG.). 20p. (J). pap. 9.95 *(978-1-894778-50-3(2))* Theytus Bks., Ltd. CAN. Dist: Univ. of Toronto Pr.

—Healthy Choices, Healthy Lives. Olson, Karen W. (ENG.). 20p. 2005. (J). pap. 10.95 *(978-1-894778-31-2(6))*; 2009. pap. 9.95 *(978-1-894778-53-4(7))* Theytus Bks., Ltd. CAN. Dist: Univ. of Toronto Pr.

—Living Safe, Playing Safe. Olson, Karen W. 2005. (Caring for Me Ser.). (ENG.). 20p. (J). pap. 10.95 *(978-1-894778-33-6(2))* Theytus Bks., Ltd. CAN. Dist: Univ. of Toronto Pr.

—Looking after Me. Lecoy, Denise. 2nd rev. ed. 2009. (Caring for Me Ser.). (ENG.). 20p. pap. 9.95 *(978-1-894778-54-1(5))* Theytus Bks., Ltd. CAN. Dist: Univ. of Toronto Pr.

Hamelin, Marie-Micheline, et al. Meshom & the Little One. Wagner, Elaine J. & Wagner, Elaine. ed. 2006. (Meshom & the Little One Ser.). (ENG.). 58p. pap. 12.95 *(978-1-894778-35-0(9))* Theytus Bks., Ltd. CAN. Dist: Univ. of Toronto Pr.

Hamelin, Marie-Micheline. Taking Care of Mother Earth. Kruger, Leanne Flett. 2005. (ENG.). 20p. (J). pap. 10.95 *(978-1-894778-30-5(8))* Theytus Bks., Ltd. CAN. Dist: Univ. of Toronto Pr.

—Taking Care of Mother Earth. Kruger, Leanne Flett. ed. 2009. (Caring for Me Ser.). (ENG.). 20p. pap. 9.95 *(978-1-894778-55-8(3))* Theytus Bks., Ltd. CAN. Dist: Univ. of Toronto Pr.

Hamill, Dion. Amazeing Ruins: Journey Through Lost Civilisations. Hamill, Dion. 2004. 32p. (Orig.). pap., act. bk. ed. *(978-1-877003-69-1(7))* Little Hare Bks. AUS. Dist: HarperCollins Pubs. Australia.

Hamilton, Allen, jt. illus. see Stojic, Manya.

Hamilton, Andrew. Robots. Punter, Russell. 2004. 48p. (J). (gr. 2-18). pap. 5.95 *(978-0-7945-0760-2(3)*, Usborne) EDC Publishing.

Hamilton, Craig, jt. illus. see Lago, Ray.

Hamilton, Dorothy. Magic Snow Bird: And Other Stories. Blyton, Enid. 2013. (ENG.). 192p. (J). 9.95 *(978-1-84135-420-0(1))* Award Pubns. Ltd. GBR. Dist: Parkwest Pubns., Inc.

Hamilton, Helen. The Happy Hollisters & the Indian Treasure. West, Jerry. 2011. (ENG.). 188p. pap. 9.95 *(978-1-4610-9886-7(6))* CreateSpace Independent Publishing Platform.

—The Happy Hollisters at Mystery Mountain. West, Jerry. 2011. (ENG.). 188p. pap. 9.95 *(978-1-4636-5823-6(0))* CreateSpace Independent Publishing Platform.

—The Happy Hollisters at Sea Gull Beach. West, Jerry. 2011. (ENG.). 188p. pap. 9.95 *(978-1-4609-3688-7(4))* CreateSpace Independent Publishing Platform.

—The Happy Hollisters on a River Trip. West, Jerry. 2011. (ENG.). 186p. pap. 9.95 *(978-1-4565-0226-3(3))* CreateSpace Independent Publishing Platform.

Hamilton, James. The Ire of Iron Claw: Gadgets & Gears, Book 2. Hamilton, Kersten. 2015. (Gadgets & Gears Ser.: 2). (ENG.). 176p. (J). (gr. 2-5). 16.99 *(978-0-544-22502-2(3))* Houghton Mifflin Harcourt Publishing Co.

—The Mesmer Menace. Hamilton, Kersten. (Gadgets & Gears Ser.: 1). (ENG.). (J). (gr. 2-5). 2015. 160p. pap. 6.99 *(978-0-544-43934-4(1)*, HMH Books For Young Readers); 2013. 144p. 16.99 *(978-0-547-90568-6(8))* Houghton Mifflin Harcourt Publishing Co.

Hamilton, John C., photos by. Lewis & Clark: An Illustrated Journey. Hamilton, John C. 2003. 192p. (J). 28.00 *(978-0-9719304-2-1(2))* Sparrow Media Group, Inc.

Hamilton, Laurie. Pinocchio. Hillert, Margaret. rev. ed. 2006. (Beginning to Read Ser.). 32p. (J). (gr. -1-3). lib. bdg. 19.93 *(978-1-59953-023-9(6))* Norwood Hse. Pr.

Hamilton, Meredith. A Child's Introduction to the Night Sky: The Story of the Stars, Planets & Constellations - And How You Can Find Them in the Sky. Driscoll, Michael. 2004. (ENG.). 96p. (J). (gr. 3-7). tchr. ed. 19.95 *(978-1-57912-366-6(X)*, 81366, Black Dog & Leventhal Pubs. Inc.) Hachette Bks.

—They're Poets & They Know It! A Collection of 30 Timeless Poems. 2007. 31p. (J). pap. *(978-0-545-03017-5(X))* Scholastic, Inc.

Hamilton, Meredith. A Child's Introduction to Art: The World's Greatest Paintings & Sculptures. Hamilton, Meredith. Alexander, Heather. 2014. (ENG.). 96p. (J). (gr. -1-17). 19.99 *(978-1-57912-956-9(0)*, 81956, Black Dog & Leventhal Pubs. Inc.) Hachette Bks.

Hamilton, Michael. Hands-on English. Hamilton, Fran Santoro. 2nd l.t. ed. 2004. 192p. per. 14.95 *(978-0-9664867-5-9(7))* Portico Bks.

Hamilton, Pamela. Phonics Comics: Pony Tales - Level 1. Gaydos, Nora. 2007. (ENG.). 24p. (J). (gr. 1-17). per. 3.99 *(978-1-58476-553-0(4))* Innovative Kids.

Hamilton, Prissy. A Rainbow Within: An Introduction to the Emotional Energies for Children. Hamilton, Prissy. Hamilton, Prissy, ed. 2005. (J). pap. 14.00 *(978-0-9655933-1-1(2))* IGMI Publishing.

Hamilton, Tim. The Big Fib. Hamilton, Tim. (I Like to Read(r) Ser.). (ENG.). (J). (gr. -1-3). 2015. 24p. 6.99 *(978-0-8234-3312-4(9))*; 2014. 32p. 14.95 *(978-0-8234-2939-4(3))* Holiday Hse., Inc.

—But! Hamilton, Tim. 2014. (ENG.). 32p. (J). (gr. -1-2). 16.95 *(978-0-8234-3046-8(4))* Holiday Hse., Inc.

Hamlin, Janet. The Eyes Have It: The Secrets of Eyes & Seeing. Stewart, Melissa. 2009. (Gross & Goofy Body Ser.). 48p. (gr. 3-4). 29.93 *(978-0-7614-4167-0(0))* Marshall Cavendish Corp.

—It's Spit-Acular! The Secrets of Saliva. Stewart, Melissa. 2009. (Gross & Goofy Body Ser.). 48p. (gr. 3-4). 29.93 *(978-0-7614-4163-2(8))* Marshall Cavendish Corp.

—The Kids' Yoga Book of Feelings, 1 vol. Frost, Michael, photos by. Humphrey, Mary. 2008. (ENG.). 40p. (J). (gr. 3-7). 15.99 *(978-0-7614-5424-3(1))* Marshall Cavendish Corp.

—Musical Genius: A Story about Wolfgang Amadeus Mozart. Allman, Barbara. 2004. (Creative Minds Biographies Ser.). (ENG.). 64p. (gr. 4-8). 22.60 *(978-1-57505-604-3(6))*; per. 8.95 *(978-1-57505-637-1(2))* Lerner Publishing Group.

—Now Hear This! The Secrets of Ears & Hearing. Stewart, Melissa. 2009. (Gross & Goofy Body Ser.). 48p. (gr. 3-4). 29.93 *(978-0-7614-4161-8(1))* Marshall Cavendish Corp.

—Pump It Up! The Secrets of the Heart & Blood. Stewart, Melissa. 2009. (Gross & Goofy Body Ser.). 48p. (gr. 3-4). 29.93 *(978-0-7614-4164-9(6))* Marshall Cavendish Corp.

—Up Your Nose! The Secrets of Schnozes & Snouts. Stewart, Melissa. 2009. (Gross & Goofy Body Ser.). 48p. (gr. 3-4). 29.93 *(978-0-7614-4170-0(0))* Marshall Cavendish Corp.

Hammack, Debi. Eerey Tocsin in the Cryptoid Zoo. Olson, Kevin Noel. 2006. (ENG.). 176p. (YA). per. 15.95 *(978-1-887560-17-7(3)*, Cornerstone Bk. Publishers) Poll, Michael Publishing.

Hammack, Sandra. A Walk with Papa. Zemanick, Patty. 2006. pap. 14.95 *(978-0-9788289-0-5(9))* Dragonfly Ministries.

Hammah, Aisha. A Family Secret. Green, Judith. 2013. 32p. pap. *(978-0-9810759-7-6(5))* WTL International.

Hammah, Aisha. The Image Game. Hammah, Aisha. Stubblefield, Linda, ed. 2013. 192p. pap. *(978-0-9810759-8-3(3))*; pap. *(978-0-9810759-3-8(2))* WTL International.

Hammerquist, Theresa. My Daddy Makes the Best Motorcycles in the Whole Wide World, the Harley-Davidson. Davidson, Jean. 2004. (J). 16.95 *(978-1-930596-26-9(X))* Amherst Pr.

Hammersley, Karen. Sparkles Meets the Easter Bunny: The Adventures of Sparkles. Wellings, Chris R. 2011. 48p. pap. 24.95 *(978-1-4560-7063-2(0))* America Star Bks.

Hammerstrom, Kent. The Adventures of Sunny & the Chocolate Dog: Sunny & the Chocolate Dog Go to the Beach. Neimark, Susie. 2003. per. *(978-0-9725945-1-6(5))* Sunny & The Chocolate Dog, LLC.

—The Adventures of Sunny & the Chocolate Dog: Sunny & the Chocolate Dog Go to the Doctor. Neimark, Susie. 2003. per. *(978-0-9725945-2-3(3))* Sunny & The Chocolate Dog, LLC.

—The Adventures of Sunny & the Chocolate Dog: Sunny Meets Her Baby Sister. Neimark, Susie. 2003. per. *(978-0-9725945-0-9(7))* Sunny & The Chocolate Dog, LLC.

Hammill, Matt. Sir Reginald's Logbook. Hammill, Matt. 2008. (ENG.). 32p. (J). (gr. 4-7). 17.95 *(978-1-55453-202-5(7))* Kids Can Pr., Ltd. CAN. Dist: Univ. of Toronto Pr.

Hammill, Matt & Owlkids Books Inc. Staff. Cryptic Canada: Unsolved Mysteries from Coast to Coast. Hyde, Natalie. 2012. (ENG.). 48p. (J). (gr. 3-7). pap. 12.95 *(978-1-926973-43-2(7)*, Owlkids) Owlkids Bks. Inc. CAN. Dist: Perseus-PGW.

Hammond, Andy. Alf Saves the Day. Peet, Mal. 2004. (ENG.). 24p. (J). lib. bdg. 23.65 *(978-1-59646-692-0(8))* Dingles & Co.

—A Day Out. Owen, Anna. Moon, Cliff, ed. 2005. (Collins Big Cat Ser.). (ENG.). 16p. (J). pap. 5.99 *(978-0-00-718555-9(3))* HarperCollins Pubs. Ltd. GBR. Dist: Independent Pubs. Group.

—Fourth-Grade Fuss. Hurwitz, Johanna. 2004. 144p. (J). lib. bdg. 16.89 *(978-0-06-052344-2(1))*; (ENG.). (gr. 3-7). 16.99 *(978-0-06-052343-5(3))* HarperCollins Pubs.

—The Muffin Man. Blane, Francisco. 2010. (Rising Readers Ser.). (J). 3.49 *(978-1-60719-691-4(3))* Newmark Learning LLC.

Hammond, Barbara. The Duffy Chronicles. Hammond, Barbara, . 2007. 60p. pap. 11.99 *(978-0-9800675-4-5(5))* Mirror Publishing.

Hammond, Gaye. Discovering Sauerkraut. Wolczuk, Alice. unabr. ed. (ENG.). 228p. (J). pap. *(978-0-920576-43-4(5))* Caitlin Pr., Inc.

—Orcas Calling. Smedley, Gord. unabr. ed. (ENG.). 58p. (J). *(978-0-920576-46-5(X))* Caitlin Pr., Inc.

Hammond, Julie. Birds in the Flower Basket. Kelso, Mary Jean. 2012. 26p. 19.95 *(978-1-61633-343-0(X))* Guardian Angel Publishing, Inc.

—Hockey Agony. McDine, Donna M. 2013. 20p. pap. 9.95 *(978-1-61633-360-7(X))* Guardian Angel Publishing, Inc.

—Riley's Heart MacHine. Jones, Lori M. 2012. 16p. pap. 9.95 *(978-1-61633-312-6(X))* Guardian Angel Publishing, Inc.

Hammond, Nancy Robinson. A Snug Little Island, Mara, Sarah Robinson. 2005. 60p. (J). 18.50 *(978-0-9766737-0-5(3))* Pink Granite Pr.

Hammond, Ted. Who Is Richard Branson? Burgan, Michael. 2015. (Who Was... ? Ser.). (ENG.). 112p. (J). (gr. 3-7). 5.99 ***(978-0-448-48315-3(7)***, Grosset & Dunlap) Penguin Publishing Group.

Hammond, Ted. Who Is Wayne Gretzky? Herman, Gail & Harrison, Nancy. 2015. (Who Was... ? Ser.). (ENG.). 112p. (J). (gr. 3-7). 5.99 *(978-0-448-48321-4(1)*, Grosset & Dunlap) Penguin Publishing Group.

Hammond, Ted. Who Was Henry Ford? Burgan, Michael. 2014. 105p. (J). lib. bdg. ***(978-1-4844-3671-4(7)***, Grosset & Dunlap) Penguin Publishing Group.

Hammond, Ted. Who Was Milton Hershey? Buckley, James, Jr. 2013. (Who Was... ? Ser.). (ENG.). 112p. (J). (gr. 3-7). 5.99 *(978-0-448-47936-1(2)*, Grosset & Dunlap) Penguin Publishing Group.

Hammond, Ted & Carbajal, Richard. The Baseball Adventure of Jackie Mitchell, Girl Pitcher vs. Babe Ruth. Patrick, Jean L. S. 2011. (History's Kid Heroes Ser.). 32p. pap. 51.02 *(978-0-7613-7635-4(6))*; (ENG.). (gr. 3-5). pap. 8.95 *(978-0-7613-7072-7(2))* Lerner Publishing Group. (Graphic Universe).

—The Horse-Riding Adventure of Sybil Ludington, Revolutionary War Messenger. Amstel, Marsha. 2011. (History's Kid Heroes Ser.). (ENG.). 32p. (gr. 3-5). 26.60 *(978-0-7613-6181-7(2))*; pap. 8.95 *(978-0-7613-7073-4(0)*, Graphic Universe) Lerner Publishing Group.

—The Prairie Adventure of Sarah & Annie, Blizzard Survivors. Figley, Marty Rhodes. 2011. (History's Kid Heroes Ser.). (ENG.). 32p. (gr. 3-5). lib. bdg. 26.60 *(978-0-7613-7805-1(7))* Lerner Publishing Group.

—The Prison-Ship Adventure of James Forten, Revolutionary War Captive. Figley, Marthy Rhodes & Figley, Marty Rhodes. 2011. (History's Kid Heroes Ser.). (ENG.). 32p. (gr. 3-5). 26.60 *(978-0-7613-6183-1(9))*; pap. 8.95 *(978-0-7613-7075-8(7)*, Graphic Universe) Lerner Publishing Group.

—The Prison-Ship Adventure of James Forten, Revolutionary War Captive. Figley, Marty Rhodes. 2011. (History's Kid Heroes Ser.). 32p. pap. 51.02 *(978-0-7613-7637-8(2)*, Graphic Universe) Lerner Publishing Group.

—The Rescue Adventure of Stenny Green, Hindenburg Crash Eyewitness. Ransom, Candice. 2011. (History's Kid Heroes Ser.). 32p. pap. 51.02 *(978-0-7613-7638-5(0)*, Graphic Universe); (ENG.). (gr. 3-5). 26.60 *(978-0-7613-6178-7(2))*; (ENG.). (gr. 3-5). pap. 8.95 *(978-0-7613-7070-3(6)*, Graphic Universe) Lerner Publishing Group.

—The Rooftop Adventure of Minnie & Tessa, Factory Fire Survivors. Littlefield, Holly. 2011. (History's Kid Heroes Ser.). 32p. pap. 51.02 *(978-0-7613-7639-2(9))*; (ENG.). (gr. 3-5). pap. 8.95 *(978-0-7613-7071-0(4))* Lerner Publishing Group. (Graphic Universe).

—The Underground Adventure of Arly Dunbar, Cave Explorer. Ransom, Candice. 2011. (History's Kid Heroes Ser.). (ENG.). 32p. (gr. 3-5). 26.60 *(978-0-7613-6182-4(0))*; pap. 8.95 *(978-0-7613-7074-1(9)*, Graphic Universe) Lerner Publishing Group.

—The Underground Railroad Adventure of Allen Jay, Antislavery Activist. Brill, Marlene Targ. 2011. (History's Kid Heroes Ser.). (ENG.). 32p. (gr. 3-5). lib. bdg. 26.60 *(978-0-7613-7804-4(9))* Lerner Publishing Group.

Hammond, Ted & Carbajal, Richard Pimentel. The Horse-Riding Adventure of Sybil Ludington, Revolutionary War Messenger. Amstel, Marsha. 2011. (History's Kid Heroes Set III Ser.). pap. 51.02 *(978-0-7613-7636-1(4)*, Graphic Universe) Lerner Publishing Group.

—The Prairie Adventure of Sarah & Annie, Blizzard Survivors. Figley, Marty Rhodes. 2011. (History's Kid Heroes Set III Ser.). pap. 51.02 *(978-0-7613-8621-6(1))*; (ENG.). 32p. (gr. 3-5). pap. 8.95 *(978-0-7613-7808-2(1))* Lerner Publishing Group. (Graphic Universe).

—The Underground Adventure of Arly Dunbar, Cave Explorer. Ransom, Candice. 2011. (History's Kid Heroes Set III Ser.). pap. 51.02 *(978-0-7613-7640-8(2)*, Graphic Universe) Lerner Publishing Group.

—The Underground Railroad Adventure of Allen Jay, Antislavery Activist. Brill, Marlene Targ. 2011. (History's Kid Heroes Set III Ser.). pap. 51.02 *(978-0-7613-8622-3(X))*; (ENG.). 32p. (gr. 3-5). pap. 8.95 *(978-0-7613-7806-8(5))* Lerner Publishing Group. (Graphic Universe).

Hammond, Ted & Harrison, Nancy. Who Is Bill Gates? Brennan, Patricia & Demuth, Patricia Brennan. 2013. (Who Was... ? Ser.). (ENG.). 112p. (J). (gr. 3-7). 14.99 *(978-0-448-46585-2(X)*, Grosset & Dunlap) Penguin Publishing Group.

—Who Is Bill Gates? Demuth, Patricia Brennan. 2013. (Who Was... ? Ser.). (ENG.). 112p. (J). (gr. 3-7). pap. 5.99 *(978-0-448-46332-2(6)*, Grosset & Dunlap) Penguin Publishing Group.

—Who Was Babe Ruth? Holub, Joan. 2012. (Who Was... ? Ser.). (ENG.). 112p. (J). (gr. 3-7). pap. 5.99 *(978-0-448-45586-0(2)*, Grosset & Dunlap) Penguin Publishing Group.

—Who Was Henry Ford? Burgan, Michael. 2014. (Who Was... ? Ser.). (ENG.). 112p. (J). (gr. 3-7). 5.99 *(978-0-448-47957-6(5)*, Grosset & Dunlap) Penguin Publishing Group.

—Who Was Marie Curie? Stine, Megan. 2014. (Who Was... ? Ser.). (ENG.). 112p. (J). (gr. 3-7). 5.99 *(978-0-448-47896-8(X)*, Grosset & Dunlap) Penguin Publishing Group.

—Who Was Roberto Clemente? Buckley, James, Jr. 2014. (Who Was... ? Ser.). (ENG.). 112p. (J). (gr. 3-7). 5.99 *(978-0-448-47961-3(3)*, Grosset & Dunlap) Penguin Publishing Group.

Hammond, Ted & McVeigh, Kevin. Who Is George Lucas? Pollack, Pamela D. & Belviso, Meg. 2014. (Who Was... ? Ser.). (ENG.). 112p. (J). (gr. 3-7). 5.99 *(978-0-448-47947-7(8)*, Grosset & Dunlap) Penguin Publishing Group.

Hammons, Barbara. Alphabetland the Beginning. McAtee, Rick. 2005. 48p. (J). 12.95 *(978-0-9762030-0-1(6))* Turning a New Page.

—Alphabetland the Story of R. McAtee, Rick. ed. 2005. (J). 14.95 *(978-0-9762030-1-8(4)*, 1000) Turning a New Page.

Hammons, Mark. My Grandma Calls Me Lovey. Hartman, Colleen Kelley. 2011. pap. 19.95 *(978-1-934333-26-6(3))* Eagle Bk. Bindery.

Hample, Stoo. The Silly Book. Hample, Stoo. Hample, Stuart E. 2004. (ENG.). 32p. (J). (gr. k-12). 15.99 *(978-0-7636-2256-5(7))* Candlewick Pr.

Hample, Stoo, jt. illus. see Hample, Stuart E.

Hample, Stuart E. & Hample, Stoo. The Silly Book. Hample, Stuart E. & Hample, Stoo. 2010. (ENG.). 32p. (J). (gr. -1-3). 16.99 *(978-0-7636-4124-5(3))* Candlewick Pr.

Hampton, David. Living in India. Thomson, Ruth. 2006. (Living In- Ser.). 32p. (J). (gr. 4-7). lib. bdg. 27.10 *(978-1-59771-046-6(6))* Sea-To-Sea Pubns.

Hampton, David, photos by. Living in Kenya. Thomson, Ruth. 2006. (Living In- Ser.). 32p. (J). (gr. 4-7). lib. bdg. 27.10 *(978-1-59771-044-2(X))* Sea-To-Sea Pubns.

—Living in Spain. Kent, Su. 2006. (Living In- Ser.). 32p. (J). (gr. 4-7). lib. bdg. 27.10 *(978-1-59771-048-0(2))* Sea-To-Sea Pubns.

Hampton, David, photos by. Living in Australia. Hampton, David. 2006. (Living In- Ser.). 32p. (J). (gr. 4-7). lib. bdg. 27.10 *(978-1-59771-041-1(5)*, 1268834) Sea-To-Sea Pubns.

Hampton, John. Gene Autry & the Golden Stallion. Fannin, Cole. 2011. 284p. 48.95 *(978-1-258-02563-2(9))* Literary Licensing, LLC.

Hampton, John W. Gene Autry & Arapaho War Drums. Patten, Lewis B. 2011. 280p. 47.95 *(978-1-258-04495-4(1))* Literary Licensing, LLC.

Hampton, Lin. Bo & the Missing Dogs, 1 vol. Simmons, Lynn Sheffield. 2003. (Bo Ser.). (ENG.). 128p. (J). (gr. 3-6). 8.95 *(978-1-58980-219-3(5))* Pelican Publishing Co., Inc.

—Bo, the Famous Retriever, 1 vol. Simmons, Lynn Sheffield. 2003. (Bo Ser.). (ENG.). 128p. (J). (gr. 3-6). 10.95 *(978-1-58980-217-9(9))* Pelican Publishing Co., Inc.

Hampton, Scott. Black Widow: The Itsy-Bitsy Spider. Grayson, Devin et al. 2011. (ENG.). 152p. (YA). (gr. 8-17). 24.99 *(978-0-7851-5827-1(8))* Marvel Worldwide, Inc.

Hampton, Scott, et al. Devil in the Gateway. Carey, Mike. rev. ed. 2006. (Lucifer Ser.: Bk. 1). (ENG.). 160p. (YA). pap. 14.99 *(978-1-56389-733-7(4)*, Vertigo) DC Comics.

Hampton, Scott. Sky Horizon. Brin, David. 2007. (Colony High Ser.: Bk. 1). 120p. (YA). (gr. 6-18). 35.00 *(978-1-59606-109-5(X))* Subterranean Pr.

Han, Heung-gi. Let's Visit Korea. Han, Suzanne C. rev. ed. 2006. 40p. (J). 18.50 *(978-1-56591-010-2(9))* Hollym International Corp.

Han, Joon-ho. Pinocchio. Collodi, Carlo. Cowley, Joy, ed. 2015. (World Classics Ser.). (ENG.). 32p. (gr. k-4). 26.65 ***(978-1-925246-17-9(5))***; 7.99 ***(978-1-925246-69-8(8))***; 26.65 ***(978-1-925246-43-8(4))*** ChoiceMaker Pty. Ltd., The AUS. (Big and SMALL). Dist: Lerner Publishing Group.

Han, Joy. Little Guy Haiku: Life with Bailey, a Maltese. Han, John J. 2009. 48p. pap. 24.95 *(978-1-61546-044-1(6))* America Star Bks.

Han, Mylene. The Things I See & the Things I Do. Settel, Jim. 2013. 52p. pap. 19.95 *(978-1-4787-0879-7(4))* Outskirts Pr., Inc.

Han, Oki. Basho & the River Stones, 0 vols. Myers, Tim J. 2013. (ENG.). 28p. (J). (gr. 1-4). pap. 9.99 *(978-1-4778-1682-0(8)*, 9781477816820, Amazon Children's Publishing) Amazon Publishing.

Han, Oki S. Basho & Fox, 1 vol. Myers, Tim. 2005. (ENG.). 32p. (J). pap. 5.95 *(978-0-7614-5190-7(0))* Marshall Cavendish Corp.

—K Is for Kabuki: A Japan Alphabet. Whelan, Gloria & Nolan, Jenny. 2009. (Discover the World Ser.). (ENG.). 40p. (J). (gr. 1-3). 17.95 *(978-1-58536-444-2(4)*, 202169) Sleeping Bear Pr.

Han, Soma. Land of Morning Calm: Korean Culture Then & Now. Stickler, John. 2003. (Land of Morning Calm Ser.). 32p. (J). (gr. 4-7). 16.95 *(978-1-885008-22-0(8)*, Shen's Bks.) Lee & Low Bks., Inc.

—Land of Morning Calm: Korean Culture Then & Now. Stickler, John. 2014. (ENG.). 32p. (J). pap. 8.95 *(978-1-885008-47-3(3)*, Shen's Bks.) Lee & Low Bks., Inc.

Han, SooJin. Nicknames. Kim, Cecil. 2015. (MySELF Bookshelf Ser.). (ENG.). 32p. (J). (gr. k-2). pap. 11.94 *(978-1-60357-699-4(1))*; lib. bdg. 22.60 *(978-1-59953-664-4(1))* Norwood Hse. Pr.

Han, Than T. Media Ethics: Ethics, Law & Accountability in the Australian Media. Hendtlass, Jane & Nichols, Alan. 2003. (Ethics in Daily Life Ser.: 3). (ENG.). 80p. (Orig.). (C). pap. *(978-0-908284-45-0(4))* Acorn Press, Ltd.

Han, Xuemei. Brave Little Mongolian Sisters. Han, Xuemei. 2007. (J). pap. 12.99 *(978-0-9763168-7-9(0))* DigitalKu.

—The Radish & the Girl with Long Hair. Han, Xuemei. 2008. (J). per. *(978-0-9763168-6-2(2))* DigitalKu.

Han, Yu-Mei. The Brave Servant: A Tale from China. 2013. (Tales of Honor Ser.). (ENG.). 32p. (J). (gr. 1-4). pap. 8.95 *(978-1-937529-57-4(6))*; lib. bdg. 26.60 *(978-1-937529-73-4(8))* Red Chair Pr.

—Neil & Nan Build Narrative Nonfiction. Pelleschi, Andrea. 2013. (ENG.). 32p. (J). lib. bdg. 25.27 *(978-1-59953-586-9(6))*; (gr. 2-4). pap. 11.94 *(978-1-60357-560-7(X))* Norwood Hse. Pr.

Hanasaki, Akira. Oishinbo: Izakaya — Pub Food: A la Carte. Kariya, Tetsu. 2010. (Oishinbo Ser.: 7). (ENG.). 276p. pap. 12.99 *(978-1-4215-2145-9(8))* Viz Media.

Hanawalt, Josh. Grammy's Curtain Calls, 1 vol. Dierenfeldt, Jane. 2010. 22p. 24.95 *(978-1-4512-1051-4(5))* PublishAmerica, Inc.

—A Time for Everything. Dierenfeldt, Jane. 2012. 36p. 24.95 *(978-1-4626-6146-6(7))* America Star Bks.

Hanawalt, Lisa. Benny's Brigade. Bradford, Arthur. 2012. (ENG.). 48p. 19.95 *(978-1-936365-61-6(8))* McSweeney's Publishing.

Hancock, Anna. Bananas in My Tummy, 1 vol. Dale, Jay. 2012. (Engage Literacy Yellow Ser.). (ENG.). 32p. (gr. k-2). pap. 5.99 *(978-1-4296-8835-2(1)*, Engage Literacy) Capstone Pr., Inc.

—Big Green Crocodile, 1 vol. Dale, Jay. 2012. (Engage Literacy Blue Ser.). (ENG.). 32p. (gr. k-2). pap. 5.99

(978-1-4296-8984-7(6), Engage Literacy) Capstone Pr., Inc.

—In the Water, 1 vol. Giulieri, Anne. 2012. (Engage Literacy Magenta Ser.). (ENG.). 32p. (gr. k-2). pap. 5.99 *(978-1-4296-8854-3(8)*, Engage Literacy) Capstone Pr., Inc.

—Min Monkey, 1 vol. Dale, Jay. 2012. (Engage Literacy Red Ser.). (ENG.). 32p. (gr. k-2). pap. 5.99 *(978-1-4296-8944-1(7)*, Engage Literacy) Capstone Pr., Inc.

—Up Here, 1 vol. Dale, Jay. 2012. (Engage Literacy Magenta Ser.). (ENG.). 32p. (gr. k-2). pap. 5.99 *(978-1-4296-8862-8(9)*, Engage Literacy) Capstone Pr., Inc.

Hancock, David. First Encyclopedia of Dinosaurs - Internet Linked. Taplin, Sam. 2004. (First Encyclopedias Ser.). (ENG.). 64p. (J). (gr. 3-18). pap. 9.99 *(978-0-7945-0696-4(8)*, Usborne) EDC Publishing.

—First Encyclopedia of Dinosaurs & Prehistoric Life: Internet-Linked. Taplin, Sam. 2004. (Usborne First Encyclopedia Library). 64p. (J). (gr. 2-18). lib. bdg. 17.95 *(978-1-58086-657-6(3)*, Usborne) EDC Publishing.

—First Encyclopedia of the Human Body - Internet Linked. Chandler, Fiona. 2004. (First Encyclopedias Ser.). (ENG.). 64p. (J). (gr. 3-18). pap. 9.99 *(978-0-7945-0695-7(X)*, Usborne) EDC Publishing.

—The Great World Search. Khanduri, Kamini. 2007. (Great Searches (EDC Hardcover) Ser.). 48p. (J). (gr. 3). lib. bdg. 16.99 *(978-1-58086-966-9(1)*, Usborne) EDC Publishing.

—See Inside Ancient Egypt. Lloyd Jones, Rob. 2008. (Usborne Flap Book Ser.). 14p. (J). (gr. -1-3). bds. 12.99 *(978-0-7945-2037-3(5)*, Usborne) EDC Publishing.

—See Inside Ancient Rome. Daynes, Katie. 2006. (See Inside Board Bks.). 16p. (J). (gr. 2-5). bds. 12.99 *(978-0-7945-1321-4(2)*, Usborne) EDC Publishing.

—See inside Castles. Daynes, Katie. 2005. 16p. (J). 12.95 *(978-0-7945-1022-0(1)*, Usborne) EDC Publishing.

—The Usborne First Encyclopedia of History. Chandler, Fiona et al. 2005. 64p. (J). *(978-0-439-78717-8(3))* Scholastic, Inc.

—The Usborne Little Encyclopedia of Science: Internet-Linked. Firth, Rachel. 2006. 64p. (J). 6.99 *(978-0-7945-1095-4(7)*, Usborne) EDC Publishing.

—Usborne the Great World Search. Khanduri, Kamini. rev. ed. 2005. (Great Searches (EDC Paperback) Ser.). 48p. (J). (gr. -1). pap. 8.99 *(978-0-7945-1030-5(2)*, Usborne) EDC Publishing.

Hancock, David & Woodcock, John. First Encyclopedia of the Human Body: Internet-Linked. Chandler, Fiona. 2004. (Usborne First Encyclopedia Library). 64p. (J). (gr. 3-18). lib. bdg. 17.95 *(978-1-58086-653-8(0)*, Usborne) EDC Publishing.

—The Usborne Little Encyclopedia of the Human Body: Internet-Linked. Chandler, Fiona. 2006. 64p. (J). (gr. 4-7). 6.99 *(978-0-7945-1094-7(9)*, Usborne) EDC Publishing.

Hancock, David, jt. illus. see Bines, Gary.

Hancock, James Gulliver. Underworld: Exploring the Secret World Beneath Your Feet, 0 vols. Price, Jane. 2014. (ENG.). 96p. (J). 18.95 *(978-1-894786-89-8(0))* Kids Can Pr., Ltd. CAN. Dist: Univ. of Toronto Pr.

Hancock, Stefanie. Indian Legends of the Great Dismal Swamp. Traylor, Waverley. Traylor, Margaret, ed. 2004. 72p. (gr. 8-18). pap. 9.95 *(978-0-9715068-3-1(3))* Traylor, Waverley Publishing.

Hancock, Uyen. Goodnight on the Farm. Hancock, Dennis. 2012. 28p. pap. 24.95 *(978-1-4626-7233-2(7))* America Star Bks.

—The Tree House on the Bluff. Hancock, Dennis & Uyen. 2012. 36p. pap. 24.95 *(978-1-4626-7318-6(X))* America Star Bks.

—What If There Are No Colors. Hancock, Dennis & Hancock, Shawn. 2012. 36p. 24.95 *(978-1-4626-7203-5(5))* America Star Bks.

Hancock, W. Allan. Amazing Animals: The Remarkable Things That Creatures Do. Ruurs, Margriet. 2011. (ENG.). 32p. (J). (gr. 1-4). 17.95 *(978-0-88776-973-3(X)*, Tundra Bks.) Tundra Bks. CAN. Dist: Penguin Random Hse., LLC.

Hancocks, Helen. Penguin in Peril. Hancocks, Helen. 2014. (ENG.). 32p. (J). (gr. -1-2). 15.99 *(978-0-7636-7159-4(2)*, Templar) Candlewick Pr.

Hand, Jason, jt. illus. see Golden Books Staff.

Hand, Terry. Free Passage. McRae, J. R. 2014. 88p. pap. 16.99 *(978-1-62563-910-3(4))* Tate Publishing & Enterprises, LLC.

Hand, Terry. In the Dog House. Poulter, J. R. 2014. pap. 20.99 ***(978-1-63185-049-3(0))*** Tate Publishing & Enterprises, LLC.

Handelman, Dorothy, photos by. Canciones de Monstruos. Eaton, Deborah. Translations.com Staff, tr. from ENG. 2007. (Lecturas para niños de Verdad - Nivel 2 (Real Kids Readers - Level 2) Ser.).Tr. of Monster Songs. (SPA., 32p. (gr. k-3). per. 5.95 *(978-0-8225-7803-1(4)*, Ediciones Lerner) Lerner Publishing Group.

—Lo Haré Después. Tidd, Louise Vitellaro. Translations.com Staff, tr. from ENG. 2007. (Lecturas para niños de Verdad - Nivel 2 (Real Kids Readers - Level 2) Ser.).Tr. of I'll Do It Later. (SPA., 32p. (gr. k-3). per. 5.95 *(978-0-8225-7805-5(0)*, Ediciones Lerner) Lerner Publishing Group.

—Me Gusta el Desorden. Leonard, Marcia. Translations.com Staff, tr. from ENG. 2007. (Lecturas para niños de Verdad - Nivel 1 (Real Kids Readers - Level 1) Ser.).Tr. of I Like Mess. (SPA., 32p. (gr. k-2). per. 5.95 *(978-0-8225-7800-0(X)*, Ediciones Lerner) Lerner Publishing Group.

—Me Gusta Ganar! Simon, Charnan. Translations.com Staff, tr. from ENG. 2007. (Lecturas para niños de Verdad - Nivel 1 (Real Kids Readers - Level 1) Ser.).Tr. of I Like to Win!. (SPA., 32p. (gr. k-2). per. 5.95 *(978-0-8225-7801-7(8)*, Ediciones Lerner) Lerner Publishing Group.

—Mi Dia de Campamento. Leonard, Marcia. Translations.com Staff, tr. from ENG. 2007. (Lecturas para niños de Verdad - Nivel 1 (Real Kids Readers - Level 1) Ser.).Tr. of My Camp-Out. (SPA., 32p. (gr. k-2). per. 5.95 *(978-0-8225-7798-0(4)*, Ediciones Lerner) Lerner Publishing Group.

—Saltar, Brincar, Correr. Leonard, Marcia. Translations.com Staff, tr. from ENG. 2007. (Lecturas para niños de Verdad - Nivel 1 (Real Kids Readers - Level 1) Ser.).Tr. of Hop, Skip, Run. (SPA., 32p. (gr. k-2). per. 5.95 *(978-0-8225-7799-7(2)*, Ediciones Lerner) Lerner Publishing Group.

Handelsman, Valerie. A Coral Reef Neighborhood. Handelsman, Valerie. 2004. 16p. (J). 7.95 *(978-0-9748884-1-5(9))* Little Thoughts For Little Ones Publishing, Inc.

Handelsman, Valerie J. Lobster Monica: Dream, Dream, Dream - Monica Was Always Dreaming. Handelsman, Valerie J. 2004. 31p. (J). pap. 7.95 *(978-0-9748884-0-8(0))* Little Thoughts For Little Ones Publishing, Inc.

Handford, Martin. Where's Waldo Now? 2008. (Where's Waldo? Ser.). 24p. (J). (gr. 4-7). 17.55 *(978-1-4178-2426-7(3)*, Turtleback) Turtleback Bks.

Handford, Martin. The Incredible Paper Chase. Handford, Martin. 2009. (Where's Waldo? Ser.). (ENG.). 24p. (J). (gr. k-4). 14.99 *(978-0-7636-4689-9(X))* Candlewick Pr.

—The Spectacular Poster Book. Handford, Martin. 2010. (Where's Waldo? Ser.). (ENG.). 16p. (J). (gr. k-4). pap. 20.00 *(978-0-7636-4932-6(5))* Candlewick Pr.

—Where's Waldo? Handford, Martin. (Where's Waldo? Ser.). (ENG.). (J). (gr. k-4). 2011. 64p. pap. 9.99 *(978-0-7636-5416-0(7))*; 2nd ed. 2007. 32p. pap. 7.99 *(978-0-7636-3498-8(0))*; 25th anniv. deluxe ed. 2012. 32p. 16.99 *(978-0-7636-4525-0(7))* Candlewick Pr.

—Where's Waldo? in Hollywood. Handford, Martin. (Where's Waldo? Ser.). (ENG.). 32p. (J). (gr. k-4). 2007. pap. 7.99 *(978-0-7636-3501-5(4))*; 2013. 16.99 *(978-0-7636-4527-4(3))* Candlewick Pr.

—Where's Waldo? the Fantastic Journey. Handford, Martin. 2007. (Where's Waldo? Ser.). (ENG.). 32p. (J). (gr. k-4). pap. 7.99 *(978-0-7636-3500-8(6))* Candlewick Pr.

—Where's Waldo? The Fantastic Journey. Handford, Martin. deluxe ed. 2013. (Where's Waldo? Ser.). (ENG.). 32p. (J). (gr. k-12). 16.99 *(978-0-7636-4528-1(1))* Candlewick Pr.

—Where's Waldo? the Great Picture Hunt. Handford, Martin. (Where's Waldo? Ser.). (ENG.). 24p. (J). (gr. k-4). 2010. pap. 7.99 *(978-0-7636-4215-0(0))*; 2006. 14.99 *(978-0-7636-3043-0(8))* Candlewick Pr.

—Where's Waldo? the Magnificent Mini Boxed Set. Handford, Martin. 2013. (Where's Waldo? Ser.). (ENG.). 40p. (J). (gr. k-4). 19.99 *(978-0-7636-4873-2(6))* Candlewick Pr.

—Where's Waldo? the Search for the Lost Things. Handford, Martin. 2012. (Where's Waldo? Ser.). (ENG.). 104p. (J). (gr. 2-5). pap. 12.99 *(978-0-7636-5832-8(4))* Candlewick Pr.

Handford, Martin. Where's Waldo? the Sticker Book! Handford, Martin. 2015. (Where's Waldo? Ser.). (ENG.). 96p. (J). (gr. k-4). pap. 12.99 ***(978-0-7636-8128-9(8))*** Candlewick Pr.

Handford, Martin. Where's Waldo? the Totally Essential Travel Collection. Handford, Martin. 2013. (Where's Waldo? Ser.). (ENG.). 172p. (J). (gr. k-12). 14.99 *(978-0-7636-6178-6(3))* Candlewick Pr.

—Where's Waldo? the Ultimate Travel Collection. Handford, Martin. 2008. (Where's Waldo? Ser.). (ENG.). 152p. (J). (gr. k-12). pap. 12.99 *(978-0-7636-3951-8(6))* Candlewick Pr.

—Where's Waldo? the Wonder Book. Handford, Martin. (Where's Waldo? Ser.). (ENG.). 32p. (J). (gr. k-12). 2014. 16.99 *(978-0-7636-4530-4(3))*; 2007. pap. 7.99 *(978-0-7636-3502-2(2))* Candlewick Pr.

—Where's Waldo Now? Handford, Martin. (Where's Waldo? Ser.). (ENG.). 32p. (J). (gr. k-4). 2007. pap. 7.99 *(978-0-7636-3499-5(9))*; 25th anniv. deluxe ed. 2012. 16.99 *(978-0-7636-4526-7(5))* Candlewick Pr.

—The Wow Collection: Six Amazing Books & a Puzzle. Handford, Martin. 2012. (Where's Waldo? Ser.). (ENG.). (J). (gr. k-4). 49.99 *(978-0-7636-6179-3(1))* Candlewick Pr.

Handley, David, photos by. Ballerina: A Step-by-Step Guide to Ballet. Hackett, Jane & Dorling Kindersley Publishing Staff. 2007. (ENG., 80p. (J). (gr. 3-7). 17.99 *(978-0-7566-2668-6(4))* Dorling Kindersley Publishing, Inc.

Hanes, Don, jt. illus. see Kopervas, Gary.

Hanifin, Laura, photos by. My First Gymnastics Class: A Book with Foldout Pages. Capucilli, Alyssa Satin. 2012. (My First Ser.). (ENG., 14p. (J). (gr. -1-k). 9.99 *(978-1-4424-2749-5(3)*, Little Simon) Little Simon.

Hanke, Karen. Jazz Fly 2: The Jungle Pachanga. Gollub, Matthew. 2010. (J). 32p. (gr. -1-3). 17.95 incl. audio compact disk *(978-1-889910-44-4(9))*; *(978-1-889910-45-1(7))* Tortuga Pr.

—Monkey in the Story Tree. Williams, Rozanne Lanczak. 2006. (Learn to Write Ser.). 8p. (J). (gr. k-2). pap. 3.49 *(978-1-59198-282-1(0)*, 6176) Creative Teaching Pr., Inc.

—Monkey in the Story Tree. Williams, Rozanne Lanczak. Maio, Barbara & Faulkner, Stacey, eds. 2006. (J). per. 6.99 *(978-1-59198-333-0(9))* Creative Teaching Pr., Inc.

—Rhyme Time. Scelsa, Greg. Faulkner, Stacey, ed. 2006. (J). pap. 2.99 *(978-1-59198-323-1(1))* Creative Teaching Pr., Inc.

Hanks, Carol. Emma & Allie. Slaughter, Kristi. 2009. 28p. pap. 12.49 *(978-1-4389-9812-1(0))* AuthorHouse.

Hanley, John. W Is for Wrigley: A Friendly Confines Alphabet. Herzog, Brad. 2013. (ENG.). (J). *(978-1-58536-816-7(4))* Sleeping Bear Pr.

Hanley, Sinéad. Chooky-Doodle-Doo. Whiten, Jan. 2015. (ENG.). 32p. (J). (-k). 12.99 *(978-0-7636-7327-7(7))* Candlewick Pr.

Hanley, Zachary. Ernie the Eagle Goes to Maine. Tata, Cb. 2012. 42p. 24.95 *(978-1-4626-4545-9(3))* America Star Bks.

—Ernie the Eagle Goes to Texas. Tata, Cb. 2012. 44p. 24.95 *(978-1-4626-5374-4(X))* America Star Bks.

Hanlon, Leslie. Traveling with Aunt Patty: Aunt Patty Visits London. Brundige, Patricia. Wright, Cindy, ed. Date not set. (J). (gr. 1-4). 12.95 *(978-0-9659668-0-1(1))* Aunt Patty's Travels-London.

Hanmer, Clayton. The Lowdown on Denim. Kyi, Tanya Lloyd. 2011. (ENG.). 108p. (J). (gr. 3-12). 21.95 *(978-1-55451-355-0(3)*, 9781554513550); pap. 12.95 *(978-1-55451-354-3(5)*, 9781554513543) Annick Pr., Ltd. CAN. Dist: Firefly Bks., Ltd.

Hanmer, Clayton & Owlkids Books Inc. Staff. Not Your Typical Book about the Environment. Kelsey, Elin. 2010. (ENG.). 64p. (J). (gr. 4-7). 22.95 *(978-1-897349-79-3(3))*; pap. 12.95 *(978-1-897349-84-7(X))* Owlkids Bks. Inc. CAN. Dist: Perseus-PGW.

Hanna, Dan. Hide & Seek, Pout-Pout Fish. Diesen, Deborah. 2015. (Pout-Pout Fish Adventure Ser.). (ENG.). 18p. (J). (gr. -1 — 1). bds. 8.99 *(978-1-250-06011-2(7))* Square Fish.

—The Not Very Merry Pout-Pout Fish. Diesen, Deborah. 2015. (Pout-Pout Fish Adventure Ser.). (ENG.). 32p. (J). (gr. -1-1). 16.99 *(978-0-374-35549-4(5)*, Farrar, Straus & Giroux (BYR)) Farrar, Straus & Giroux.

—The Pout-Pout Fish. Diesen, Deborah. (Pout-Pout Fish Adventure Ser.: 1). (ENG.). (J). (gr. -1 — 1). 2013. 36p. bds. 7.99 *(978-0-374-36097-9(9))*; 2008. 32p. 16.99 *(978-0-374-36096-2(0))* Farrar, Straus & Giroux. (Farrar, Straus & Giroux (BYR)).

—The Pout-Pout Fish Goes to School. Diesen, Deborah. 2014. (Pout-Pout Fish Adventure Ser.). (ENG.). 32p. (J). (gr. -1-k). 16.99 *(978-0-374-36095-5(2)*, Farrar, Straus & Giroux (BYR)) Farrar, Straus & Giroux.

—The Pout-Pout Fish in the Big-Big Dark. Diesen, Deborah. (Pout-Pout Fish Adventure Ser.). (ENG.). (J). (gr. -1-1). 2015. 34p. bds. 7.99 *(978-0-374-30189-7(1))*; 2010. 32p. 16.99 *(978-0-374-30798-1(9))* Farrar, Straus & Giroux. (Farrar, Straus & Giroux (BYR)).

—The Pout-Pout Fish Tank. Diesen, Deborah. 2014. (Pout-Pout Fish Adventure Ser.). (ENG.). 32p. (J). (gr. -1-k). 16.99 *(978-0-374-30091-3(7)*, Farrar, Straus & Giroux (BYR)) Farrar, Straus & Giroux.

—Smile, Pout-Pout Fish. Diesen, Deborah. 2014. (Pout-Pout Fish Mini Adventure Ser.). (ENG.). 14p. (J). (gr. -1 — 1). bds. 5.99 *(978-0-374-37084-8(2)*, Farrar, Straus & Giroux (BYR)) Farrar, Straus & Giroux.

Hanna, Gary. Burrow. Spilsbury, Richard. 2013. (Look Inside Ser.). (ENG.). 32p. (gr. 1-3). 26.00 *(978-1-4329-7193-9(X))*; pap. 8.29 *(978-1-4329-7200-4(6))* Heinemann-Raintree. (Heinemann First Library).

—Cave. Spilsbury, Richard. 2013. (Look Inside Ser.). (ENG.). 32p. (gr. 1-3). 26.00 *(978-1-4329-7194-6(8))*; pap. 8.29 *(978-1-4329-7201-1(4))* Heinemann-Raintree. (Heinemann First Library).

—Garbage Can. Spilsbury, Louise. 2013. (Look Inside Ser.). (ENG.). 32p. (gr. 1-3). 26.00 *(978-1-4329-7195-3(6))*; pap. 8.29 *(978-1-4329-7202-8(2))* Heinemann-Raintree. (Heinemann First Library).

—Pond. Spilsbury, Louise. 2013. (Look Inside Ser.). (ENG.). 32p. (gr. 1-3). 26.00 *(978-1-4329-7196-0(4))*; pap. 8.29 *(978-1-4329-7203-5(0))* Heinemann-Raintree. (Heinemann First Library).

—Tide Pool. Spilsbury, Louise. 2013. (Look Inside Ser.). (ENG.). 32p. (gr. 1-3). 26.00 *(978-1-4329-7197-7(2))*; pap. 8.29 *(978-1-4329-7204-2(9))* Heinemann-Raintree. (Heinemann First Library).

—Tree. Spilsbury, Richard. 2013. (Look Inside Ser.). (ENG.). 32p. (gr. 1-3). 26.00 *(978-1-4329-7198-4(0))*; pap. 8.29 *(978-1-4329-7205-9(7))* Heinemann-Raintree. (Heinemann First Library).

Hannah Lane. A Frog Named Dude. 2007. 16p. (J). *(978-0-9800870-0-0(7))* Robillard, Kristy.

Hannah, Wood. This Little Piggy. Tiger Tales Staff, ed. 2010. 24p. (J). (gr. -1-k). bds. 8.95 *(978-1-58925-849-5(5))* Tiger Tales.

Hannan, Peter. Freddy! Deep-Space Food Fighter. Hannan, Peter. 2011. (Freddy! Ser.: 2). (ENG.). 144p. (J). (gr. 2-6). pap. 5.99 *(978-0-06-128468-7(8))* HarperCollins Pubs.

—Freddy! King of Flurb. Hannan, Peter. 2011. (Freddy! Ser.: 1). (ENG.). 160p. (J). (gr. 2-6). pap. 5.99 *(978-0-06-128466-3(1))* HarperCollins Pubs.

—Freddy! Locked in Space. Hannan, Peter. 2011. (Freddy! Ser.: 3). (ENG.). 160p. (J). (gr. 2-6). pap. 5.99 *(978-0-06-128470-0(X))* HarperCollins Pubs.

—The Greatest Snowman in the World! Hannan, Peter. 2010. (ENG.). 32p. (J). (gr. -1-3). 16.99 *(978-0-06-128480-9(7))* HarperCollins Pubs.

—My Big Mouth: 10 Songs I Wrote That Almost Got Me Killed. Hannan, Peter. 2011. (ENG.). 240p. (J). (gr. 3-7). 16.99 *(978-0-545-16210-4(6)*, Scholastic Pr.) Scholastic, Inc.

Hannan, Peter. Petlandia. Hannan, Peter. 2015. (ENG.). 144p. (J). (gr. 2-5). 8.99 ***(978-0-545-16211-1(4)***, Scholastic Pr.) Scholastic, Inc.

Hanner, Albert. Animales del Mar. Brewster, Joy. ed. 2011. (SPA.). 32p. (J). pap. 49.00 net. *(978-1-4108-2337-3(7)*, A23377) Benchmark Education Co.

—From Caves to Canvas & de las cuevas a los Lienzos: 6 English, 6 Spanish Adaptations, 122 vols. Prigioniero, Lily. ed. 2011. (SPA.). (J). instr.'s gde. ed. 89.00 net. *(978-1-4108-2227-7(3)*, 22273) Benchmark Education Co.

—Grandes inventos y cómo Surgieron. Glassman, Jackie. ed. 2011. (SPA.). (J). pap. 45.00 net. *(978-1-4108-2206-2(0)*, 22060) Benchmark Education Co.

—Great Inventions & Where They Came from & Grandes inventos y cómo Surgieron: 6 English, 6 Spanish Adaptations, 122 vols. Glassman, Jackie. ed. 2011. (J). instr.'s gde. ed. 89.00 net. *(978-1-4108-2228-4(1)*, 22281) Benchmark Education Co.

—Human Emotions & Las emociones Humanas: 6 English, 6 Spanish Adaptations, 122 vols., Vol. 2. Smith, Carrie. ed. 2011. (SPA.). (J). instr.'s gde. ed. 97.00 net. *(978-1-4108-2405-9(5)*, 24055) Benchmark Education Co.

—Las emociones Humanas. Smith, Carrie. ed. 2011. (SPA.). 32p. (J). pap. 49.00 net. *(978-1-4108-2345-8(8)*, A23458) Benchmark Education Co.

—Matemáticas en el Jardín. McCay, William. ed. 2011. (SPA.). (J). pap. 45.00 net. *(978-1-4108-2207-9(9)*, 22079) Benchmark Education Co.

—Matemáticas en la Luna. Sullivan, Erin. ed. 2011. (SPA.). (J). pap. 45.00 net. *(978-1-4108-2199-7(4)*, 21994) Benchmark Education Co.

—Math in the Garden & Matemáticas en el Jardín: 6 English, 6 Spanish Adaptations, 122 vols. McCay, William. ed. 2011. (SPA.). (J). instr.'s gde. ed. 89.00 net. *(978-1-4108-2229-1(X)*, 2229X) Benchmark Education Co.

—Math on the Moon & Matemáticas en la Luna: 6 English, 6 Spanish Adaptations, 122 vols., Vol. 2. Sullivan, Erin. ed. 2011. (SPA.). (J). instr.'s gde. ed. 89.00 net. *(978-1-4108-2221-5(4)*, 22214) Benchmark Education Co.

—El mundo bajo las Olas. Brewster, Joy. ed. 2011. (SPA.). 32p. (J). pap. 49.00 net. *(978-1-4108-2339-7(3)*, A23393) Benchmark Education Co.

—Stormy Weather And ¡Tormentas! 6 English, 6 Spanish Adaptations, 122 vols. Lunis, Natalie. ed. 2011. (SPA.). (J). instr.'s gde. ed. 89.00 net. *(978-1-4108-2224-6(9)*, 22249) Benchmark Education Co.

—¡Tormentas! Lunis, Natalie. ed. 2011. (SPA.). (J). pap. 45.00 net. *(978-1-4108-2202-4(8)*, 22028) Benchmark Education Co.

Hanner, Albert & Hortens, Mike. La genética de las Plantas. Cameron, Ken. ed. 2011. (SPA.). 32p. (J). pap. 49.00 net. *(978-1-4108-2341-0(5)*, A23415) Benchmark Education Co.

Hannigan, Katherine. Emmaline & the Bunny. Hannigan, Katherine. 2009. (ENG.). 112p. (J). (gr. 2-7). 14.99 *(978-0-06-162654-8(6)*, Greenwillow Bks.) HarperCollins Pubs.

—Gwendolyn Grace. Hannigan, Katherine. 2015. (ENG.). 32p. (J). (gr. -1-3). 17.99 *(978-0-06-234519-6(2)*, Greenwillow Bks.) HarperCollins Pubs.

Hannon, Holly. The Littlest Candlesticks. Rouss, Sylvia A. 2005. (Littlest Ser.). 32p. (J). 14.95 *(978-1-930143-48-7(6))*; pap. 9.95 *(978-1-930143-49-4(4))* Simcha Media Group. (Devora Publishing).

—The Littlest Frog. Rouss, Sylvia A. 2005. 32p. (J). pap. 9.95 *(978-1-930143-13-5(3))*; (gr. -1-1). 14.95 *(978-1-930143-12-8(5))* Simcha Media Group. (Devora Publishing).

—The Littlest Pair. Rouss, Sylvia A. 2005. 32p. (J). (gr. -1-1). 14.95 *(978-1-930143-17-3(6)*, Devora Publishing) Simcha Media Group.

—The Littlest Pair. Rouss, Sylvia. 2005. 32p. (J). pap. 9.95 *(978-1-930143-18-0(4)*, Devora Publishing) Simcha Media Group.

—Sweet Pea: Escape in the Garden. Meachen Rau, Dana. 2006. (J). *(978-1-58987-200-4(2))* Kindermusik International.

Hannon, Kenneth, photos by. Without a Home. Grantner, Anne M. & Haggart, Gary. 2003. 35p. (YA). (gr. 5-18). pap. 12.95 *(978-0-9740929-0-4(8))* Shelter of Flint, Inc.

Hans, Stephanie. The Magnificent Lizzie Brown & the Fairy Child. Lockwood, Vicki. 2015. (Magnificent Lizzie Brown Ser.). (ENG.). 200p. (gr. 5-9). 10.95 ***(978-1-62370-210-6(0))*** Stone Arch Bks.

—The Magnificent Lizzie Brown & the Ghost Ship. Lockwood, Vicki. 2015. (Magnificent Lizzie Brown Ser.). (ENG.). 200p. (gr. 5-9). lib. bdg. 25.32 ***(978-1-4342-9806-5(X))*** Stone Arch Bks.

Hans, Stephanie. The Magnificent Lizzie Brown & the Mysterious Phantom, 1 vol. Lockwood, Vicki. 2014. (ENG.). 200p. (J). pap. *(978-1-4342-7942-2(1))* Stone Arch Bks.

—The Outlaw of Sherwood Forest, 1 vol. Seven, John. 2014. (Time-Tripping Faradays Ser.). (ENG.). 192p. (gr. 4-5). lib. bdg. 25.32 *(978-1-4342-9174-5(X))* Stone Arch Bks.

—The Terror of the Tengu, 1 vol. Seven, John. 2014. (Time-Tripping Faradays Ser.). (ENG.). 192p. (gr. 4-5). 25.32 *(978-1-4342-9173-8(1))* Stone Arch Bks.

Hansen, Amelia. Are You Ready for Me? Buchwald, Claire. (Sit! Stay! Read! Ser.). (ENG.). 24p. (J). (gr. k-1). 2009. pap. 7.95 *(978-0-940719-08-8(8))*; 2007. 15.95 *(978-0-940719-04-0(5))* Gryphon Pr., The.

—At the Dog Park with Sam & Lucy. Bix, Daisy. 2006. (Sit! Stay! Read! Ser.). (ENG.). 24p. (J). (gr. k-2). 15.95 *(978-0-940719-00-2(2))* Gryphon Pr., The.

—It's Raining Cats & Cats! Prevost, Jeanne. 2008. (ENG.). 24p. (J). (gr. k-2). 16.95 *(978-0-940719-06-4(1))* Gryphon Pr., The.

—It's Raining Pups & Dogs! 2013. (Sit! Stay! Read! Ser.). (ENG.). 24p. (J). (gr. k). 16.95 *(978-0-940719-16-3(9))* Gryphon Pr., The.

Hansen, Angela. Lovely Lily. Holzer, Angela. 2009. (ENG.). 36p. (J). lib. bdg. 8.99 *(978-0-9821563-2-2(4))* Good Sound Publishing.

Hansen, Bjarne. Light Brigade. Tomasi, Peter J. rev. ed. 2005. (ENG.). 200p. pap. 19.99 *(978-1-4012-0795-3(2))* DC Comics.

Hansen, Christine. Watch Me Swim, 6 pack. Holden, Pam. 2009. (Red Rocket Readers Ser.). 16p. (gr. -1-3). pap. *(978-1-877363-31-3(6)*, Red Rocket Readers) Flying Start Bks.

Hansen, Christine. Mira Como Nado. Hansen, Christine. Holden, Pam & Elias, Annette Torres. 2012.Tr. of Watch Me Swim. (SPA.). 16p. (gr. -1-3). pap. ***(978-1-877506-90-1(7)***, Red Rocket Readers) Flying Start Bks.

Hansen, Clint. The Christmas Flower. Ellis, Gwen. 2005. 32p. (J). (gr. -1-3). 9.99 *(978-1-59185-728-0(7))* Charisma Media.

—Dear Mr. Leprechaun: Letters from My First Friendship. Tanner, Dean, photos by. Burton, Martin Nelson. 2003. (ENG.). 32p. (J). 17.00 *(978-0-9666490-0-0(1))* London Town Pr.

—La Flor de Pascua. Ellis, Gwen. 2005. 32p. (J). (gr. -1-3). 8.99 *(978-1-59185-827-0(5)*, Charisma Kids) Charisma Media.
—Fooling the Tooth Fairy. Tanner, Dean, photos by. Burton, Martin Nelson. 2005. (ENG.). 32p. (J). 17.00 *(978-0-9666490-2-4(8))* London Town Pr.
—Fooling the Tooth Fairy. Burton, Martin Nelson. 2005. (J). pap. *(978-0-9666490-3-1(6))* London Town Pr.
Hansen, Doug. Mother Goose in California. 2009. (J). 16.95 *(978-1-59714-101-7(1))* Heyday.
—The Sierra Adventure Coloring Book: Featuring Yosemite National Park. 2013. (ENG.). 24p. (J). (gr. -1-2). pap. 4.95 *(978-1-930238-39-8(8))* Yosemite Assn.
—The Super Silly Yosemite Sticker & Activity Book: Puzzles, Games, Mazes & More! Brumage, Katherine. 2011. (ENG.). 24p. (J). (gr. -1-5). pap. 7.95 *(978-1-59714-155-0(0))* Yosemite Assn.
Hansen, Ernest. The Eagle's Gift: Alaska Eskimo Tales. Rasmussen, Knud. Hutchinson, Isabel, tr. 2011. 258p. 47.95 *(978-1-258-10170-1(X))* Literary Licensing, LLC.
Hansen, Gaby. Are You Ready for Bed? Johnson, Jane. 2004. 32p. (J). tchr. ed. 14.95 *(978-1-58925-017-8(6))* Tiger Tales.
—Big Bears Can! Bedford, David. 2007. (Storytime Board Bks.). 16p. (J). (gr. -1-k). bds. 6.95 *(978-1-58925-826-6(6))* Tiger Tales.
—Little Bear's Special Wish. Lobel, Gill. (Storytime Board Bks.). (J). 2005. 16p. (gr. -1-k). bds. 6.95 *(978-1-58925-769-6(3))*; 2004. 32p. tchr. ed. 16.95 *(978-1-58925-034-5(6))* Tiger Tales.
—Little Bunny's Bedtime. Johnson, Jane. 2006. Orig. Title: Are You Ready for Bed?. 16p. (J). bds. 6.95 *(978-1-58925-773-3(1))* Tiger Tales.
—Molly & the Storm. Leeson, Christine. 2003. 32p. (J). (gr. k-2). tchr. ed. 15.95 *(978-1-58925-027-7(3))* Tiger Tales.
—Oops-a-Daisy! Freedman, Claire. 32p. (J). 2004. tchr. ed. 15.95 *(978-1-58925-037-6(0))*; 2006. reprint ed. 6.95 *(978-1-58925-398-8(1))* Tiger Tales.
—The Very Worried Sparrow. Doney, Meryl. 3rd ed. 2015. (ENG.). 32p. (J). (gr. -1-k). pap. 8.99 *(978-0-7459-6580-2(6))* Lion Hudson PLC GBR. Dist: Independent Pubs. Group.
—The Very Worried Sparrow. Doney, Meryl. 2008. (J). (gr. -1-3). 12.95 *(978-0-8198-8038-3(8))* Pauline Bks. & Media.
Hansen, Jimmy. A Pier Too Far. Abnett, Dan. 2005. (Wallace & Gromit Ser.). (ENG.). 48p. 12.95 *(978-1-84023-953-9(0))* Titan Bks. Ltd. GBR. Dist: Random Hse., Inc.
—The Whippet Vanishes. Rimmer, Ian. 2004. (Wallace & Gromit Ser.). (ENG.). 48p. pap. 8.95 *(978-1-84023-498-5(9))*; 12.95 *(978-1-84023-497-8(0))* Titan Bks. Ltd. GBR. Dist: Random Hse., Inc.
Hansen, Jimmy & Williamson, Brian. The Bootiful Game. Rimmer, Ian. 2005. (Wallace & Gromit Ser.). (ENG.). 48p. pap. 8.95 *(978-1-84023-948-5(4))* Titan Bks. Ltd. GBR. Dist: Random Hse., Inc.
Hansen, Justin LaRocca. Brothers Unite. 2015. (J). ***(978-0-8037-4094-5(8)***, Dial) Penguin Publishing Group.
Hansen, Laurie. A Puppy for the White House. Smith, Kathleen. 2009. 32p. (J). 16.99 *(978-0-615-30165-5(7))* Lollipop Publishing, LLC.
Hansen, Lorie. Can I Have Some Money Please? Prindle, Twyla D. 2004. 20p. (J). (gr. k-4). 7.95 *(978-0-9759527-2-6(2))* Prindle Hse. Publishing Co.
Hansen, Lorie Miller. Can I Have Some Money Please? Prindle, Twyla. 2005. (J). (gr. -1-3). 14.95 *(978-0-9759527-3-3(0)*, Prindle House Publishing Co.) Prindle Hse. Publishing Co.
Hansen, Melissa. Butterflies & Magic Dreams. Henderson, Tim. l.t. ed. 2003. 28p. (J). *(978-0-9728691-0-2(7))* Logan Bks.
Hansen, Paisley. The Popcorn Tree. French, Joyce. 2012. 22p. 15.95 *(978-1-60414-639-4(7))* Fideli Publishing, Inc.
Hansen, Red. The Princess Twins & the Birthday Party, 1 vol. Hodgson, Mona Gansberg. 2012. (I Can Read! / Princess Twins Ser.). (ENG.). 32p. (J). pap. 3.99 *(978-0-310-72707-1(3))* Zonderkidz.
—The Princess Twins & the Puppy, 1 vol. Hodgson, Mona Gansberg. 2011. (I Can Read! / Princess Twins Ser.). (ENG.). 32p. (J). pap. 3.99 *(978-0-310-72709-5(X))* Zonderkidz.
—The Princess Twins & the Tea Party, 1 vol. Hodgson, Mona Gansberg. 2012. (I Can Read! / Princess Twins Ser.). (ENG.). 32p. (J). pap. 3.99 *(978-0-310-72711-8(1))* Zonderkidz.
—The Princess Twins Play in the Garden, 1 vol. Hodgson, Mona Gansberg. ed. 2011. (I Can Read! / Princess Twins Ser.). (ENG.). 32p. (J). pap. 3.99 *(978-0-310-72705-7(7))* Zonderkidz.
—Stay Away from Rat Boy! Lears, Laurie. 2009. (ENG.). 32p. (J). (gr. 2-4). 16.99 *(978-0-8075-6789-0(2))* Whitman, Albert & Co.
Hansen, Red, jt. illus. see Hajdinjak-Krec, Marsela.
Hansen, Red, jt. illus. see Veno, Joe.
Hansen, Thore. The Little Paintbrush. Rorvik, Bjorn F. 2014. (ENG.). 32p. (J). (gr. -1-k). 12.95 *(978-1-62087-996-2(4)*, 620996, Sky Pony Pr.) Skyhorse Publishing Co., Inc.
—Ruffen: The Escape to Loch Ness. Bringsvaerd, Tor Age. 2009. (Ruffen Ser.). 72p. (J). (gr. 1-4). 16.95 *(978-0-9815761-2-1(5))* Mackenzie Smiles, LLC.
—Ruffen: The Sea Serpent Who Couldn't Swim. Bringsvaerd, Tor Age. 2008. (Ruffen Ser.). 64p. (J). (gr. -1-3). 16.95 *(978-0-9790347-9-4(5))* Mackenzie Smiles, LLC.
Hanson, Dana. Terror in the Tetons. Ahlman, Larry. Larsen, Chuck, ed. 2005. (YA). (gr. 9-12). pap. 9.95 *(978-0-9712906-2-4(8))* Ahlman Publishing.
Hanson, Faye. Cinderella's Secret Diary. Hanson, Faye. ed. 2013. (ENG.). 20p. (J). (gr. 1-3). 19.99 *(978-0-230-74204-8(1))* Pan Macmillan GBR. Dist: Independent Pubs. Group.
Hanson, Faye. The Wonder. Hanson, Faye. 2015. (ENG.). 40p. (J). (gr. -1-2). 16.99 ***(978-0-7636-7957-6(7)***, Templar) Candlewick Pr.
Hanson, Lori. Bubblegum Princess. Gribble, Julie. 2013. 32p. (J). 16.99 *(978-0-9890914-0-4(6))* NY Media Works, LLC.
Hanson, Peter E. Botones Para el General Washington. Roop, Peter & Roop, Connie. 2006. (Yo Solo: Historia (on My Own History) Ser.).Tr. of Buttons for General Washington. (SPA.). 48p. (gr. 2-4). lib. bdg. 25.26 *(978-0-8225-6261-0(8)*, Ediciones Lerner) Lerner Publishing Group.
—Buttons for General Washington, 4 bks., Set. Roop, Peter & Roop, Connie. unabr. ed. 2007. (Readalongs for Beginning Readers Ser.). (J). (gr. 2-3). pap. 39.95 incl. audio compact disk *(978-1-59519-935-5(7))* Live Oak Media.
—Manten Las Luces Encendidas, Abbie. Roop, Peter & Roop, Connie. 2005. (Yo Solo: Historia (on My Own History) Ser.). (SPA.). 48p. (gr. 2-4). lib. bdg. 25.26 *(978-0-8225-3098-5(8)*, Ediciones Lerner) Lerner Publishing Group.
Hanson-Roberts, Mary. Cinderella: A Tale of Kindness. 2006. (J). 6.99 *(978-1-59939-001-7(9))* Cornerstone Pr.
Hanson, Sandy & Delage, Kristi. A Camel's Story: A Search for the Messiah. Hanson, Sandy. 2005. 53p. (J). lib. bdg. 21.95 *(978-0-9763271-0-3(4))* MK Publishing.
Hanson, Stephen. Nelly, the Monster Sitter. Gray, Kes. 2009. (ENG.). 272p. (J). (gr. 3-7). 8.99 *(978-1-59514-259-7(2)*, Razorbill) Penguin Publishing Group.
Hanson, Susan Jo. Ivar, the Short, but Brave Viking. Jacobsen, Annie. 2007. (J). lib. bdg. 16.95 *(978-0-9778276-1-9(5))* Pickled Herring Pr.
—The Terrible Troll Cat. Jacobsen, Annie. (J). 2012. 32p. 9.98 *(978-0-9778276-4-0(X))*; 2006. 16.95 *(978-0-9778276-0-2(7))* Pickled Herring Pr.
Hanson, Sydney. Panda Pants. Davies, Jacqueline. 2016. (J). ***(978-0-553-53576-1(5))*** Knopf, Alfred A. Inc.
Hanson, Tippi, jt. illus. see Russell, Lyndsay.
Hanson, Warren. Tell Me What We Did Today. Kupchella, Rick. (ENG.). 32p. (J). 15.95 *(978-0-9726504-0-3(7))* TRISTAN Publishing, Inc.
Hanson, Warren. Kiki's Hats: Our Gifts Live on & On. Hanson, Warren. 2007. (ENG.). 36p. (J). (gr. -1-3). 16.95 *(978-0-931674-94-5(8)*, Waldman House Pr.) TRISTAN Publishing, Inc.
Hanson, Warren, jt. illus. see Hegg, Tom.
Hanstick, Kevin. My Trip to Washington, D. C., 1 vol. Polley, JoAnn. 3rd rev. ed. 2009. (My Trip Ser.). (ENG.). 80p. (J). (gr. 3-7). spiral bd. 16.99 *(978-1-58980-671-9(2))* Pelican Publishing Co., Inc.
Hanstick, Kevin R. My Trip to Gettysburg, 1 vol. Polley, J. Patrick & Polley, JoAnn. Shekerow, Mark D., ed. 2007. (My Trip Ser.). (ENG.). 80p. (J). spiral bd. 14.95 *(978-1-58980-456-2(2))* Pelican Publishing Co., Inc.
Hantel, Johanna. Como Yo. Neasi, Barbara J. 2003. (Rookie Reader Español Ser.).Tr. of Just Like Me. (SPA.). 32p. (J). (gr. k-2). pap. 4.95 *(978-0-516-27795-0(2)*, Children's Pr.) Scholastic Library Publishing.
—I Am Sick. Jensen, Patricia. (My First Reader Ser.). (ENG.). 32p. (J). (gr. k-1). 2006. per. 3.95 *(978-0-516-24970-4(3))*; 2005. lib. bdg. 18.50 *(978-0-516-24878-3(2))* Scholastic Library Publishing. (Children's Pr.).
—I Hate Reading: How to Get Through 20 Minutes of Reading a Day Without Really Reading. Bacon, Arthur & Bacon, Henry. 2008. 20p. (J). (gr. -1-3). 17.95 *(978-1-60213-025-8(6)*, Upstart Bks.) Highsmith Inc.
—Just Like Me. Neasi, Barbara J. 2011. (Rookie Ready to Learn Ser.). 40p. (J). (gr. -1-k). pap. 5.95 *(978-0-531-26676-2(1))*; lib. bdg. 23.00 *(978-0-531-26371-6(1)*, Children's Pr.) Scholastic Library Publishing.
Hantel, Johanna, jt. illus. see Clar, David Austin.
Hanton, Sophie. Hugs: Tuck Each Baby into a Loving Hug. 2010. (ENG.). 12p. (J). (gr. -1 — 1). 9.99 *(978-1-60169-020-3(7))* Innovative Kids.
—Noah & the Animals, 1 vol. Williamson, Karen. 2014. (Candle Tiny Tots Ser.). (ENG.). 16p. (J). 11.99 *(978-1-78128-110-9(6)*, Candle Bks.) Lion Hudson PLC GBR. Dist: Kregel Pubns.
Hantula, Timothy James. The Flower Girl / the Ring Bear. Sharp, N. L. 2009. 40p. (J). 19.95 *(978-0-9759829-3-8(1))* Prairieland Pr.
Happel, Sally. Eve. Golden, Robert Charles. 2012. 32p. 24.95 *(978-1-4626-7621-7(9))* America Star Bks.
Harasimowicz, Ellen. Handle with Care: An Unusual Butterfly Journey. Burns, Loree Griffin. 2014. (ENG.). 32p. (gr. 1-4). lib. bdg. 26.60 *(978-0-7613-9342-9(0)*, Millbrook Pr.) Lerner Publishing Group.
—The Hive Detectives: Chronicle of a Honey Bee Catastrophe. Burns, Loree Griffin. (Scientists in the Field Ser.). (ENG.). 80p. (J). (gr. 5-7). 2013. pap. 9.99 *(978-0-544-00326-2(8))*; 2010. 18.99 *(978-0-547-15231-8(0))* Houghton Mifflin Harcourt Publishing Co.
Harasimowicz, Ellen. Beetle Busters: A Rogue Insect & the People Who Track It. Harasimowicz, Ellen, photos by. Burns, Loree Griffin. 2014. (Scientists in the Field Ser.). (ENG.). 64p. (J). (gr. 5-7). 18.99 *(978-0-547-79267-5(0)*, HMH Books For Young Readers) Houghton Mifflin Harcourt Publishing Co.
Harasimowicz, Ellen, photos by. Citizen Scientists: Be a Part of Scientific Discovery from Your Own Backyard. Burns, Loree Griffin. 2012. (ENG., 80p. (J). (gr. 3-7). 19.99 *(978-0-8050-9062-8(2))*, Holt, Henry & Co. Bks. For Young Readers) Holt, Henry & Co.
—Citizen Scientists: Be a Part of Scientific Discovery from Your Own Backyard. Burns, Loree Griffin. 2012. (ENG., 80p. (J). (gr. 3-7). pap. 12.99 *(978-0-8050-9517-3(9))* Square Fish.
Harber, Hulya. Simon the Policeman on Safari - Claude the Camel. Harber, Chris. 2013. 24p. pap. *(978-0-7552-1552-2(4)*, Bright Pen) Authors OnLine, Ltd.
—Simon the Policeman on the Number Planet. Harber, Chris. 2013. 28p. pap. *(978-0-7552-1560-7(5)*, Bright Pen) Authors OnLine, Ltd.
Harbo, Gary. The Northern Woods Adventure: Advanced Reader, 6 vols. Harbo, Gary. l.t. ed. 2004. (If You Want to Succeed, You Need to Read! Ser.: 6). 33p. (J). per. 10.95 *(978-1-884149-15-3(4))* Kutie Kari Bks., Inc.
—The Northern Woods Adventure: Early Reader. Harbo, Gary. l.t. ed. 2004. (If You Want to Succeed, You Need to Read! Ser.: 6). 33p. (J). 10.95 *(978-1-884149-16-0(2))* Kutie Kari Bks., Inc.
Harbour, Elizabeth. Puppy Love: The Story of Esme & Sam. Shields, Gillian. 2009. (ENG.). 32p. (J). (gr. -1-3). 16.99 *(978-1-4169-8010-0(5)*, Simon & Schuster Bks. For Young Readers) Simon & Schuster Bks. For Young Readers.
Harchy, Atelier Philippe. Chicken Little: A Tale about Common Sense. 2006. (J). 6.99 *(978-1-59939-019-2(1))* Cornerstone Pr.
—Forever Fairytopia. Golden Books Staff. 2007. (Super Stickerific Ser.). (ENG.). 64p. (J). (gr. -1-2). pap. 12.99 *(978-0-375-84717-2(0)*, Golden Bks.) Random Hse. Children's Bks.
—Friends for a Princess. Lagonegro, Melissa & RH Disney Staff. 2004. (Step into Reading Ser.). (ENG.). 32p. (J). (gr. k-3). pap. 3.99 *(978-0-7364-2208-6(0)*, RH/Disney) Random Hse. Children's Bks.
—Glamour Girl. Golden Books Staff. 2004. (Color Plus Lipstick Pen Ser.). (ENG.). 32p. (J). (gr. -1-2). pap. 4.99 *(978-0-375-82811-9(7)*, Golden Bks.) Random Hse. Children's Bks.
—Just Keep Swimming. Lagonegro, Melissa & RH Disney Staff. 2005. (Step into Reading Ser.). (ENG.). 32p. (J). (gr. k-3). pap. 3.99 *(978-0-7364-2319-9(2)*, RH/Disney) Random Hse. Children's Bks.
—A Surprise Garden, 15 vols. Parent, Nancy. 2003. (It's Fun to Learn Ser.). 32p. (J). (gr. -1-3). 3.99 *(978-1-57973-126-7(0))* Advance Pubs. LLC.
—A Tiggeriffic Band, 15 vols. Marsoli, Lisa Ann. 2003. (It's Fun to Learn Ser.). 32p. (J). (gr. -1-3). *(978-1-57973-128-1(7))* Advance Pubs. LLC.
—A Tree for Me, 15 vols. Parent, Nancy. 2003. (It's Fun to Learn Ser.). 32p. (J). (gr. -1-3). 3.99 *(978-1-57973-138-0(4))* Advance Pubs. LLC.
—What Is a Princess? Weinberg, Jennifer Liberts & RH Disney Staff. 2004. (Step into Reading Ser.). (ENG.). 32p. (J). (gr. k-3). pap. 3.99 *(978-0-7364-2238-3(2)*, RH/Disney) Random Hse. Children's Bks.
Harchy, Atelier Philippe, jt. illus. see Harding, Niall.
Hardcastle, Nick. Day of Deliverance. O'Brien, Johnny. 2010. (Jack Christie Adventure Ser.: 2). (ENG.). 192p. (J). (gr. 4-7). 15.99 *(978-0-7636-5075-9(7)*, Templar) Candlewick Pr.
—Day of the Assassins. O'Brien, Johnny. 2010. (Jack Christie Adventure Ser.: 1). (ENG.). 224p. (J). (gr. 4-7). pap. 6.99 *(978-0-7636-4995-1(3)*, Templar) Candlewick Pr.
—Day of the Assassins: A Jack Christie Novel. O'Brien, Johnny. 2009. (Jack Christie Adventure Ser.: 1). (ENG.). 224p. (J). (gr. 4-7). 15.99 *(978-0-7636-4595-3(8))* Candlewick Pr.
Hardcastle, Nick, jt. illus. see Wallis, Diz.
Harder, Rolf. It's Tough to Nap on a Turtle. Harder, Christopher. 2008. (ENG.). 11p. (J). (gr. -1). bds. 5.95 *(978-0-9726614-9-2(2))* Shenanigan Bks.
Hardie, Chris. Bobby & Mandee's Good Touch/Bad Touch: Children's Safety Book. Kahn, doc, Robert. 2011. (ENG.). 25p. pap. 6.95 *(978-1-935274-54-4(6))* Future Horizons, Inc.
Hardin, Teresa. The Tooth Fairy's Quest. Medders, James. 2008. 32p. pap. 24.95 *(978-1-60672-549-8(1))* America Star Bks.
Harding, Niall. Ballerina Princess. Lagonegro, Melissa & RH Disney Staff. 2007. (Step into Reading Ser.). (ENG.). 32p. (J). (gr. k-3). pap. 3.99 *(978-0-7364-2428-8(8)*, RH/Disney) Random Hse. Children's Bks.
—Ten Gifts from Santa Claus: A Counting Book. Bak, Jenny. 2011. (ENG.). 22p. (J). (gr. -1-k). 14.99 *(978-1-4052-5127-3(1))* Egmont Bks., Ltd. GBR. Dist: Independent Pubs. Group.
Harding, Niall & Harchy, Atelier Philippe. Polite as a Princess. Arps, Melissa & Lagonegro, Melissa. 2006. (Pictureback Ser.). (ENG.). 24p. (J). (gr. -1-2). pap. 3.99 *(978-0-7364-2367-0(2)*, RH/Disney) Random Hse. Children's Bks.
Hardison, Brian. ABCs of Character for People Around the World. Mitchell-Tulloss, Delores. 2007. 32p. (J). pap. *(978-0-9670712-6-8(7))* zReyomi Publishing.
Hardison, Buist. God, Do You Love Me? Coffee, Karen Lynn. 2007. 32p. (J). (gr. -1-3). 14.00 *(978-0-687-49270-1(X))* Abingdon Pr.
Hardison, Buist E. 5 Little Shorties. Hardison, Buist E. 2007. 32p. (J). (gr. -1-3). per. 4.95 *(978-0-687-64150-5(0))* Abingdon Pr.
Hardiyono. The Tiny Boy & Other Tales from Indonesia, 1 vol. Bunanta, Murti. 2013. (ENG.). 80p. (J). (gr. 3). 24.95 *(978-1-55498-193-9(X))* Groundwood Bks. CAN. Dist: Perseus-PGW.
Hardwick, Holly. Maine: A Wicked Good Book of Verse: the Way Wildlife Should Be. Pottle, Robert. 2005. 64p. (J). per. 8.95 *(978-0-9709569-3-4(2))* Blue Lobster Pr.
Hardy, Candace J. Cody Knows. Wiesner, Karen Sue. 2012. 16p. pap. 9.95 *(978-1-61633-260-0(3))* Guardian Angel Publishing, Inc.
Hardy, Chris. Miss Tilly's Marching Band. Thompson, Yvonne. 2004. (J). per. 12.95 *(978-0-9749561-1-4(2))* My Sunshine Bks.
Hardy, E. Stuart. The Pigeon Tale. Bennett, Virginia. 2007. 48p. per. *(978-1-4065-4810-5(3))* Dodo Pr.
Hardy, Frank. Ernest's Gift. Windham, Kathryn Tucker. 2004. 20p. 16.95 *(978-1-58838-149-1(8))* NewSouth, Inc.
Hardy, Pris. Austin & Harlow's First Adventure. Jeanne Taylor Thomas Illustrator: Pr. 2011. 28p. pap. 24.95 *(978-1-4560-8383-0(X))* America Star Bks.
Hardy, Sarah Frances. Paint Me! Hardy, Sarah Frances. 2014. (ENG.). 32p. (J). (-k). 14.95 *(978-1-62873-813-1(8)*, Sky Pony Pr.) Skyhorse Publishing Co., Inc.
Hardy, Vincent. Brown Bear, White Bear. Petrovic, Svetlana. 2009. 28p. (J). (gr. -1-3). 17.00 *(978-0-8028-5353-0(6)*, Eerdmans Bks For Young Readers) Eerdmans, William B. Publishing Co.
Hare, John. Great Walker: Ioway Leader. Olson, Greg. 2014. (ENG.). 48p. (J). lib. bdg. 32.00 *(978-1-61248-112-8(4))* Truman State Univ. Pr.
—Helen Stephens: The Fulton Flash. Offutt, Jason. 2014. (ENG.). 48p. (J). lib. bdg. 32.00 *(978-1-61248-114-2(0))* Truman State Univ. Pr.
—Joseph Kinney: Steamboat Captain. McVicker, Maryellen. 2014. (ENG.). 48p. (J). lib. bdg. 32.00 *(978-1-61248-116-6(7))* Truman State Univ. Pr.
—Olive Boone: Frontier Woman. Russell, Greta. 2014. (Notable Missourians Ser.). (ENG.). 48p. (J). lib. bdg. 32.00 *(978-1-61248-118-0(3))* Truman State Univ. Pr.
Hare, Mary Alyce. Cindy's Story, 1 vol. Crosby, Sarah. 2009. 47p. pap. 24.95 *(978-1-60749-608-3(9))* America Star Bks.
Hargens, Charles. Silver Spurs for Cowboy Boots. Garst, Shannon. 2011. 194p. 42.95 *(978-1-258-08454-7(6))* Literary Licensing, LLC.
Hargis, Wes. I Need My Own Country! Walton, Rick. 2012. (ENG.). 40p. (J). (gr. -1-3). 17.89 *(978-1-59990-560-0(4)*, Bloomsbury USA Childrens) Bloomsbury USA.
—I Need My Own Country! Walton, Rick & Kraus, Franz. 2012. (ENG.). 40p. (J). (gr. -1-8). 16.99 *(978-1-59990-559-4(0)*, Bloomsbury USA Childrens) Bloomsbury USA.
—Jackson & Bud's Bumpy Ride: America's First Cross-Country Automobile Trip. Koehler-Pentacoff, Elizabeth. 2009. (Millbrook Picture Bks). (ENG.). 32p. (J). (gr. k-3). lib. bdg. 16.95 *(978-0-8225-7885-7(9))*, Millbrook Pr.) Lerner Publishing Group.
—My New Teacher & Me! Yankovic, Al. 2013. (ENG.). 40p. (J). (gr. -1-3). 17.99 *(978-0-06-219203-5(5))* HarperCollins Pubs.
—When I Grow Up. Yankovic, Al. 2011. (ENG.). 32p. (J). (gr. -1-3). 17.99 *(978-0-06-192691-4(4))* HarperCollins Pubs.
Hargreaves, Adam. Little Miss Splendid & the Princess. Hargreaves, Roger. 2007. (Mr. Men & Little Miss Ser.). (ENG.). 32p. (J). (gr. -1-2). mass mkt. 3.99 *(978-0-8431-2489-7(X)*, Price Stern Sloan) Penguin Publishing Group.
—Mr. Christmas Sticker Activity Book. Hargreaves, Roger. 2010. (Mr. Men & Little Miss Ser.). (ENG.). 24p. (J). (gr. -1-2). act. bk. ed. 4.99 *(978-0-8431-2670-9(1)*, Price Stern Sloan) Penguin Publishing Group.
—Mr. Nobody. Hargreaves, Roger. 2011. (Mr. Men & Little Miss Ser.). (ENG.). 32p. (J). (gr. -1-2). mass mkt. 3.99 *(978-0-8431-9876-8(1)*, Price Stern Sloan) Penguin Publishing Group.
—The Night Before Christmas. Hargreaves, Roger. 2010. (Mr. Men & Little Miss Ser.). (ENG.). 32p. (J). (gr. -1-2). mass mkt. 3.99 *(978-0-8431-9932-1(6)*, Price Stern Sloan) Penguin Publishing Group.
Hargreaves, Adam. Little Miss Birthday. Hargreaves, Adam. Hargreaves, Roger. 2007. (Mr. Men & Little Miss Ser.). (ENG.). 32p. (J). (gr. -1-2). mass mkt. 3.99 *(978-0-8431-2131-5(9)*, Price Stern Sloan) Penguin Publishing Group.
—Little Miss Hug. Hargreaves, Adam. 2014. (Mr. Men & Little Miss Ser.). (ENG.). 32p. (J). (gr. -1-2). 3.99 *(978-0-8431-8059-6(5)*, Price Stern Sloan) Penguin Publishing Group.
—Little Miss Naughty & the Good Fairy. Hargreaves, Adam. Hargreaves, Roger. 2007. (Mr. Men & Little Miss Ser.). (ENG.). 32p. (J). (gr. -1-2). mass mkt. 3.99 *(978-0-8431-2122-3(X)*, Price Stern Sloan) Penguin Publishing Group.
—Little Miss Sunshine & the Wicked Witch. Hargreaves, Adam. Hargreaves, Roger. 2007. (Mr. Men & Little Miss Ser.). (ENG.). 32p. (J). (gr. -1-2). mass mkt. 3.99 *(978-0-8431-2490-3(3)*, Price Stern Sloan) Penguin Publishing Group.
—Little Miss Trouble & the Mermaid. Hargreaves, Adam. Hargreaves, Roger. 2008. (Mr. Men & Little Miss Ser.). (ENG.). 32p. (J). (gr. -1-2). mass mkt. 3.99 *(978-0-8431-3277-9(9)*, Price Stern Sloan) Penguin Publishing Group.
—Mr. Birthday. Hargreaves, Adam. Hargreaves, Roger. 2007. (Mr. Men & Little Miss Ser.). (ENG.). 32p. (J). (gr. -1-2). mass mkt. 3.99 *(978-0-8431-2130-8(0)*, Price Stern Sloan) Penguin Publishing Group.
—Mr. Moustache. Hargreaves, Adam. 2014. (Mr. Men & Little Miss Ser.). (ENG.). 32p. (J). (gr. -1-2). 3.99 *(978-0-8431-8081-7(1)*, Price Stern Sloan) Penguin Publishing Group.
—Mr. Tickle & the Dragon. Hargreaves, Adam. Hargreaves, Roger. 2008. (Mr. Men & Little Miss Ser.). (ENG.). 32p. (J). (gr. -1-2). mass mkt. 3.99 *(978-0-8431-3278-6(7)*, Price Stern Sloan) Penguin Publishing Group.
Hargreaves, Greg, jt. illus. see Sewall, Marcia.
Haring, Keith. Nina's Book of Little Things. Haring, Keith. 2013. (ENG.). 80p. (J). (gr. 1-4). pap. 19.99 *(978-0-7636-6893-8(1)*, Big Picture Press) Candlewick Pr.
Haring, Mary. The Scales of the Silver Fish. Krohn, Gretchen & Johnson, John Norton. 2011. 238p. 46.95 *(978-1-258-08176-8(8))* Literary Licensing, LLC.
Hariton, Anca. A Fruit Is a Suitcase for Seeds. Richards, Jean. 2006. (ENG.). 32p. (J). (gr. -1-3). pap. 6.95 *(978-0-8225-5991-7(9)*, First Avenue Editions) Lerner Publishing Group.
Harker, George A. Stories of the Ancient Greeks. Shaw, Charles D. 2008. 332p. pap. 13.95 *(978-1-59915-269-1(X))* Yesterday's Classics.
Harker, Lesley. Come Home Soon: A First Look at When a Parent Goes to War. Thomas, Pat. 2012. (First Look At... Ser.). (ENG.). 32p. (J). (gr. -1-3). pap. 7.99 *(978-1-4380-0189-0(4))* Barron's Educational Series, Inc.
—Do I Have to Go to the Hospital? A First Look at Going to the Hospital. Thomas, Pat. 2006. (First Look At... Ser.). (ENG.). 32p. (J). (gr. -1-3). pap. 6.99 *(978-0-7641-3215-5(6))* Barron's Educational Series, Inc.

H

—Down to Earth. Hooper, Mary. 2008. (Two Naughty Angels Ser.). (ENG.). 96p. (J). (gr. 2-4). pap. 11.95 *(978-0-7475-9061-3(3))* Bloomsbury Publishing Plc GBR. Dist: Independent Pubs. Group.

—Everyone Matters: A First Look at Respect for Others. Thomas, Pat. 2010. (First Look At... Ser.). (ENG.). 32p. (J). (gr. -1-3). pap. 7.99 *(978-0-7641-4517-9(7))* Barron's Educational Series, Inc.

—The Ghoul at School. Hooper, Mary. 2008. (Two Naughty Angels Ser.). (ENG.). 96p. (J). (gr. 2-4). pap. 11.95 *(978-0-7475-9060-6(5))* Bloomsbury Publishing Plc GBR. Dist: Independent Pubs. Group.

—I Can Be Safe: A First Look at Safety. Thomas, Pat. 2003. (First Look At... Ser.). (ENG.). 32p. (J). pap. 7.99 *(978-0-7641-2460-0(9))* Barron's Educational Series, Inc.

—I Can Do It! A First Look at Not Giving Up. Thomas, Pat. 2010. (First Look At... Ser.). (ENG.). 32p. (J). (gr. -1-3). pap. 6.99 *(978-0-7641-4515-5(0))* Barron's Educational Series, Inc.

—I Can Make a Difference: A First Look at Setting a Good Example. Thomas, Pat. 2010. (First Look At... Ser.). (ENG.). 32p. (J). (gr. -1-3). pap. 6.99 *(978-0-7641-4516-2(9))* Barron's Educational Series, Inc.

—I Miss My Pet: A First Look at When a Pet Dies. Thomas, Pat. 2012. (First Look At... Ser.). (ENG.). 32p. (J). (gr. -1-3). pap. 7.99 *(978-1-4380-0188-3(6))* Barron's Educational Series, Inc.

—Is It Right to Fight? A First Look at Anger. Thomas, Pat. 2003. (First Look At... Ser.). (ENG.). 32p. (J). pap. 7.99 *(978-0-7641-2458-7(7))* Barron's Educational Series, Inc.

—My Manners Matter: A First Look at Being Polite. Thomas, Pat. 2006. (First Look AtÂ... Ser.). (ENG.). 32p. (J). pap. 7.99 *(978-0-7641-3212-4(1))* Barron's Educational Series, Inc.

—My New Family: A First Look at Adoption. Thomas, Pat. 2003. (First Look At... Ser.). (ENG.). 32p. (J). pap. 7.99 *(978-0-7641-2461-7(7))* Barron's Educational Series, Inc.

—Round the Rainbow. Hooper, Mary. 2008. (Two Naughty Angels Ser.). (ENG.). 96p. (J). (gr. 2-4). pap. 11.95 *(978-0-7475-9062-0(1))* Bloomsbury Publishing Plc GBR. Dist: Independent Pubs. Group.

—The Skin I'm In: A First Look at Racism. Thomas, Pat. 2003. (First Look At... Ser.). (ENG.). 32p. (J). pap. 7.99 *(978-0-7641-2459-4(5))* Barron's Educational Series, Inc.

—This Is My Family: A First Look at Same-Sex Parents. Thomas, Pat. 2012. (First Look At... Ser.). (ENG.). 32p. (J). (gr. -1-3). pap. 7.99 *(978-1-4380-0187-6(8))* Barron's Educational Series, Inc.

—Why Do I Feel Scared? A First Look at Being Brave. Thomas, Pat. 2010. (First Look At... Ser.). (ENG.). 32p. (J). (gr. -1-3). pap. 6.99 *(978-0-7641-4514-8(2))* Barron's Educational Series, Inc.

Harkins, Nathan. Miss Lyla's Banana Pancakes to the Rescue! Rossman, Alicia. 2012. 26p. (J). (-18). 19.95 *(978-1-61863-342-2(2))* Bookstand Publishing.

Harland, Jackie. Ding! Dong! Fairley, Melissa. 2011. (ENG.). 12p. (J). (gr. -1-k). 15.95 *(978-1-84898-362-5(X)*, TickTock Books) Octopus Publishing Group GBR. Dist: Independent Pubs. Group.

—Footprints in the Snow, 1 vol. Wallace, Karen. 2013. (Start Reading Ser.). (ENG.). 24p. (gr. k-1). pap. 6.99 *(978-1-4765-4099-3(3))* Capstone Pr., Inc.

—Lost Kittens. Wallace, Karen. 2013. (Start Reading Ser.). (ENG.). 24p. (gr. k-1). pap. 6.99 *(978-1-4765-4115-0(9))* Capstone Pr., Inc.

—Stolen Egg. Wallace, Karen. 2013. (Start Reading Ser.). (ENG.). 24p. (gr. k-1). pap. 6.99 *(978-1-4765-4141-9(8))* Capstone Pr., Inc.

—Treasure Trail, 1 vol. Wallace, Karen. 2013. (Start Reading Ser.). (ENG.). 24p. (gr. k-1). pap. 6.99 *(978-1-4765-4143-3(4))* Capstone Pr., Inc.

Harley, Avis. The Monarch's Progress: Poems with Wings. Harley, Avis. 2008. (ENG.). 32p. (J). (gr. 2-3). 16.95 *(978-1-59078-558-4(4))* Boyds Mills Pr.

Harlin, Greg. We the People: The Story of Our Constitution. Cheney, Lynne. (ENG.). 40p. (J). (gr. k-4). 2012. 7.99 *(978-1-4424-4422-5(3))*; 2008. 17.99 *(978-1-4169-5418-7(X))* Simon & Schuster/Paula Wiseman Bks. (Simon & Schuster/Paula Wiseman Bks.).

Harlin, Greg. Dangerous Crossing: The Revolutionary Voyage of John Quincy Adams. Harlin, Greg, tr. Krensky, Stephen. 2004. (ENG.). 32p. (J). (gr. k-18). 18.99 *(978-0-525-46966-7(4)*, Dutton Juvenile) Penguin Publishing Group.

Harlin, Sybel. The Big Book of Alphabet & Numbers. Novick, Mary. (Double Delights Ser.). 32p. (J). *(978-1-877003-11-0(5))* Little Hare Bks. AUS. Dist: HarperCollins Pubs. Australia.

—Numbers. Novick, Mary & Hale, Jenny. 2010. (Double Delight Ser.). (ENG.). 24p. (J). (gr. -1 — 1). pap. 8.99 *(978-1-877003-57-8(3))* Little Hare Bks. AUS. Dist: Independent Pubs. Group.

—Opposites. Novick, Mary. 2011. (Double Delight Ser.). (ENG.). 16p. (J). (gr. -1 — 1). pap. 8.99 *(978-1-877003-01-1(8))* Little Hare Bks. AUS. Dist: Independent Pubs. Group.

Harlow, Janet. Can You Find Jesus? Introducing Your Child to the Gospels. Gallery, Philip D. 2003. (Search & Learn Book Ser.). 40p. *(978-2-89088-782-4(0))* Novalis Publishing.

Harlow, Janet L. Can You Find Saints? Introducing Your Child to Holy Men & Women. Harlow, Janet L., tr. Gallery, Philip D. 2003. (J). 41p. (gr. 2-4). 16.99 *(978-0-86716-487-9(5))*; 40p. *(978-2-89507-437-3(2))* Franciscan Media.

Harman, Micah. The Blue Baboon. Dwyer, Kevin & Dwyer, Shawnae. 2007. 40p. per. 13.95 *(978-1-59800-247-8(3))* Outskirts Pr., Inc.

Harmer, Sharon. If I Were a Major League Baseball Player. Braun, Eric. 2009. (Dream Big! Ser.). (ENG.). 24p. (gr. k-3). lib. bdg. 25.99 *(978-1-4048-5536-6(X))*; pap. 7.95 *(978-1-4048-5708-7(7))* Picture Window Bks. (Nonfiction Picture Bks.).

—If I Were an Astronaut, 1 vol. Braun, Eric. 2009. (Dream Big! Ser.). (ENG.). 24p. (gr. k-3). lib. bdg. 25.99 *(978-1-4048-5534-2(3))*; pap. 7.95 *(978-1-4048-5710-0(9))* Picture Window Bks. (Nonfiction Picture Bks.).

Harmon, Gedge. Saint Anthony of Padua. Windeatt, Mary F. 2009. (Catholic Story Coloring Bks.). (ENG.). 32p. (J). (gr. k-2). reprint ed. pap., wbk. ed. 4.50 *(978-0-89555-369-0(4))* TAN Bks.

—Saint Francis of Assisi. Windeatt, Mary F. 2009. (Catholic Story Coloring Bks.). (ENG.). 32p. (J). (gr. k-2). reprint ed. pap., stu. ed. 4.50 *(978-0-89555-368-3(6))* TAN Bks.

—Saint Maria Goretti. Windeatt, Mary F. 2009. (Catholic Story Coloring Bks.). (ENG.). 32p. (J). (gr. k-2). reprint ed. pap., stu. ed. 4.50 *(978-0-89555-374-4(0))* TAN Bks.

—Saint Teresa of Avila. Windeatt, Mary F. 2009. (Catholic Story Coloring Bks.). (ENG.). 32p. (J). (gr. k-2). reprint ed. pap., stu. ed. 4.50 *(978-0-89555-372-0(4))* TAN Bks.

Harmon, Glenn. Always the Elf. Jensen, Kimberly. 2007. 38p. (J). (gr. -1-3). 15.99 *(978-1-59955-086-2(5))* Cedar Fort, Inc./CFI Distribution.

—I Am a Child of God. Setzer, Lee Ann. 2007. (Tiny Talks Ser.). 74p. (J). per. 7.99 *(978-1-59955-076-3(8))* Cedar Fort, Inc./CFI Distribution.

—My Wedding Day. Rowley, Deborah Pace. 2007. 24p. (J). (gr. -1-3). 15.99 *(978-1-59955-016-9(4))* Cedar Fort, Inc./CFI Distribution.

—Tiny Talks 2009: My Eternal Family. Setzer, LeeAnn. 2008. 114p. (J). pap. 8.99 *(978-1-59955-210-1(8))* Cedar Fort, Inc./CFI Distribution.

—The Wisemen of Bountiful. Potter, George. 2005. per. 11.99 *(978-1-55517-814-7(6))* Cedar Fort, Inc./CFI Distribution.

Harmon, Heather & Gilson, Heather, photos by. Up to No Good: The Rascally Things Boys Do, as Told by Perfectly Decent Grown Men. Chronicle Books Staff. Harmon, Kitty, ed. 2005. (ENG.). 108p. (gr. 8-17). pap. 9.95 *(978-0-8118-4840-4(X))* Chronicle Bks. LLC.

Harmon, Steve. Papa's New Home. Curtis, Jessica Lynn. 2012. (ENG.). 40p. (J). *(978-0-931674-64-8(6)*, Waldman House Pr.) TRISTAN Publishing, Inc.

Harms, Jeanine. Boss Mouse Coloring Book & Theme Song. 2006. (J). 4.00 *(978-1-4276-0118-6(6))* Aardvark Global Publishing.

Harness, Cheryl. George Washington, Spymaster: How the Americans Outspied the British & Won the Revolutionary War. Allen, Thomas B. 2007. (ENG.). 192p. (J). (gr. 5-7). per. 7.95 *(978-1-4263-0041-7(7)*, National Geographic Children's Bks.) National Geographic Society.

—M Is for Mount Rushmore: A South Dakota Alphabet. Anderson, William. 2005. (Discover America State by State Ser.). (ENG.). 40p. (J). 17.95 *(978-1-58536-141-0(0))* Sleeping Bear Pr.

—Shovelful of Sunshine. Hutton, Stacie Vaughn. 2012. (ENG.). 32p. (J). 16.95 *(978-0-938467-39-7(5))* Headline Bks., Inc.

—Women Daredevils: Thrills, Chills, & Frills. Cummins, Julie & Cummins, Julia. 2008. (ENG.). 48p. (J). (gr. 2-5). 17.99 *(978-0-525-47948-2(1)*, Dutton Juvenile) Penguin Publishing Group.

—Women Explorers. Cummins, Julie. 2012. (ENG.). 48p. (J). (gr. 4-7). 18.99 *(978-0-8037-3713-6(0)*, Dial) Penguin Publishing Group.

Harness, Cheryl. The Adventurous Life of Myles Standish & the Amazing-but-True Survival Story of Plymouth Colony. Harness, Cheryl. 2006. (Cheryl Harness Histories Ser.). (ENG.). 144p. (J). (gr. 5-9). 16.95 *(978-0-7922-5918-3(1))*; lib. bdg. 25.90 *(978-0-7922-5919-0(X))* National Geographic Society. (National Geographic Children's Bks.).

—Flags over America: A Star-Spangled Story. Harness, Cheryl. 2014. (ENG.). 32p. (J). (gr. 2-5). 16.99 *(978-0-8075-2470-1(0))* Whitman, Albert & Co.

—Ghosts of the Civil War. Harness, Cheryl. 2004. (ENG.). 48p. (J). (gr. 2-5). 7.99 *(978-0-689-86992-1(4)*, Simon & Schuster Bks. For Young Readers) Simon & Schuster Bks. For Young Readers.

—Ghosts of the Nile. Harness, Cheryl. 2010. (ENG.). 32p. (J). (gr. 2-5). 13.99 *(978-1-4424-2200-1(9)*, Simon & Schuster Bks. For Young Readers) Simon & Schuster Bks. For Young Readers.

—The Groundbreaking, Chance-Taking Life of George Washington Carver & Science & Invention in America. Harness, Cheryl. 2008. (Cheryl Harness Histories Ser.). (ENG.). 144p. (J). (gr. 3-7). 16.95 *(978-1-4263-0196-4(0))*; lib. bdg. 25.90 *(978-1-4263-0197-1(9))* National Geographic Society. (National Geographic Children's Bks.).

—Our Colonial Year. Harness, Cheryl. 2005. (ENG.). 40p. (J). (gr. -1-3). 16.95 *(978-0-689-83479-0(9)*, Simon & Schuster Bks. For Young Readers) Simon & Schuster Bks. For Young Readers.

—The Remarkable Benjamin Franklin. Harness, Cheryl. 2005. (National Geographic Ser.). (ENG.). 48p. (J). (gr. 2-5). 17.95 *(978-0-7922-7882-5(8))* National Geographic Society.

—Remember the Ladies: 100 Great American Women. Harness, Cheryl. 2003. (ENG.). 64p. (J). (gr. 3-18). pap. 8.99 *(978-0-06-443869-8(4))* HarperCollins Pubs.

—The Tragic Tale of Narcissa Whitman & a Faithful History of the Oregon Trail. Harness, Cheryl. 2006. (Cheryl Harness Histories Ser.). (ENG.). 144p. (J). (gr. 5-9). 16.95 *(978-0-7922-5920-6(3))*; lib. bdg. 25.90 *(978-0-7922-5921-3(1))* National Geographic Society. (National Geographic Children's Bks.).

Harnish, Alexander. The Duck Who Drove a Boat. Harnish, Jeannette. 2008. 31p. pap. 24.95 *(978-1-60610-665-5(1))* America Star Bks.

Harold, Elsie Louise. Stop Bullying: An ABC Guide for Children & the Adults Who Interact with Them. Harold, Elsie Louise. 2004. (J). spiral bd. 14.99 *(978-0-9764644-0-2(3))* Harold, Elsie L.

Harper, Betty. Color My World Vol. 1: Early Elvis (Coloring Book) Harper, Betty. 2004. 32p. (J). 4.95 *(978-0-932117-42-7(2))* Osborne Enterprises Publishing.

Harper, Charise Mericle. Chocolate: A Sweet History. Markle, Sandra. 2004. (Smart about History Ser.). (ENG.). 32p. (J). (gr. k-4). mass mkt. 5.99 *(978-0-448-43480-3(6)*, Grosset & Dunlap) Penguin Publishing Group.

Harper, Charise Mericle. Alien Encounter. Harper, Charise Mericle. 2014. (Sasquatch & Aliens Ser.: 1). (ENG.). 208p. (J). (gr. 2-5). 12.99 *(978-0-8050-9621-7(3)*, Holt, Henry & Co. Bks. For Young Readers) Holt, Henry & Co.

—Cupcake. Harper, Charise Mericle. 2010. (ENG.). 32p. (J). (gr. -1-1). 14.99 *(978-1-4231-1897-8(9))* Hyperion Pr.

—Henry's Heart: A Boy, His Heart, & a New Best Friend. Harper, Charise Mericle. 2011. (ENG.). 40p. (J). (gr. k-3). 17.99 *(978-0-8050-8989-9(6)*, Holt, Henry & Co. Bks. For Young Readers) Holt, Henry & Co.

—Just Grace. Harper, Charise Mericle. 2008. (Just Grace Ser.: 1). (ENG.). 144p. (J). (gr. 1-4). pap. 5.99 *(978-0-547-01440-1(6))* Houghton Mifflin Harcourt Publishing Co.

—Just Grace & the Flower Girl Power. Harper, Charise Mericle. Malk, Steven. (Just Grace Ser.). (ENG.). 208p. (J). (gr. 1-4). 2013. pap. 5.99 *(978-0-544-02283-6(1))*; 2012. 15.99 *(978-0-547-57720-3(6))* Houghton Mifflin Harcourt Publishing Co.

—Just Grace & the Snack Attack. Harper, Charise Mericle. 2009. (Just Grace Ser.: 5). (ENG.). 176p. (J). (gr. 1-4). 15.00 *(978-0-547-15223-3(X))* Houghton Mifflin Harcourt Publishing Co.

—Just Grace Gets Crafty. Harper, Charise Mericle. 2014. (Just Grace Ser.: 12). (ENG.). 192p. (J). (gr. 1-4). 15.99 *(978-0-544-08023-2(8)*, HMH Books For Young Readers) Houghton Mifflin Harcourt Publishing Co.

—Still Just Grace. Harper, Charise Mericle. 2007. (Just Grace Ser.: 2). (ENG.). 160p. (J). (gr. 2-5). 15.99 *(978-0-618-64643-2(4))* Houghton Mifflin Harcourt Publishing Co.

—Super Sasquatch Showdown. Harper, Charise Mericle. 2015. (Sasquatch & Aliens Ser.: 2). (ENG.). 176p. (J). (gr. 2-5). 13.99 *(978-0-8050-9622-4(1)*, Holt, Henry & Co. Bks. For Young Readers) Holt, Henry & Co.

Harper, Charley. Charley Harper Tree of Life. 2013. (ENG.). (J). 7.95 *(978-0-7649-6514-2(X))* Pomegranate Communications, Inc.

—Charley Harper's Birds. 2013. (ENG.). (J). 7.95 *(978-0-7649-6513-5(1))* Pomegranate Communications, Inc.

—Charley Harper's Sticky Birds: An Animal Sticker Kit. 2013. (ENG.). (J). 19.95 *(978-0-7649-6467-1(4))* Pomegranate Communications, Inc.

—Charley Harper's What's in the Rain Forest? A Nature Discovery Book. Burke, Zoe. 2013. 34p. (J). 14.95 *(978-0-7649-6584-5(0))* Pomegranate Communications, Inc.

—Charley Harper's What's in the Woods? A Nature Discovery Book. Burke, Zoe. 2013. (ENG.). 32p. (J). 14.95 *(978-0-7649-6453-4(4))* Pomegranate Communications, Inc.

Harper, Chris. The Dogges of Barkshire - the Grand Kennel. Harper, Chris. 2013. 26p. (J). pap. *(978-1-78222-086-2(0))* Paragon Publishing, Rothersthorpe.

Harper, Clifford. A Little History of the World. Gombrich, E. H. Mustill, Caroline, tr. from GER. 2008. (ENG.). 304p. pap. 15.00 *(978-0-300-14332-4(X))* Yale Univ. Pr.

—A Little History of the World. Gombrich, E. H. Mustill, Caroline, tr. from GER. 2005. (ENG.). 304p. 25.00 *(978-0-300-10883-5(4))* Yale Univ. Pr.

Harper, Fred. Dirtmeister's Nitty Gritty Planet Earth: All about Rocks, Minerals, Fossils, Earthquakes, Volcanoes, & Even Dirt! Tomecek, Steve. 2015. (ENG.). 128p. (J). (gr. 3-7). pap. 12.99 *(978-1-4263-1903-7(7)*, National Geographic Children's Bks.) National Geographic Society.

—George Washington's Rules to Live By: How to Sit, Stand, Smile, & Be Cool! a Good Manners Guide from the Father of Our Country. Washington, George. 2014. (ENG.). 128p. (J). (gr. 3-7). 14.99 *(978-1-4263-1500-8(7)*, National Geographic Children's Bks.) National Geographic Society.

Harper, Fred & Hinderliter, John. What Was Pompeii? O'Connor, Jim. 2014. (What Was... ? Ser.). (ENG.). 112p. (J). (gr. 3-7). 5.99 *(978-0-448-47907-1(9)*, Grosset & Dunlap) Penguin Publishing Group.

Harper, Fred, jt. illus. see Foley, Tim.

Harper, Jamie. Best Friend Emma. Warner, Sally. 2007. (Emma Ser.). (ENG.). 112p. (J). (gr. 3-7). 14.99 *(978-0-670-06173-0(5)*, Viking Juvenile) Penguin Publishing Group.

—EllRay Jakes Is a Rock Star, 2 vols. Warner, Sally. (EllRay Jakes Ser.: 2). (ENG.). (J). (gr. 1-3). 2012. 128p. 5.99 *(978-0-14-241989-2(3)*, Puffin); 2011. 144p. 14.99 *(978-0-670-01158-2(4)*, Viking Juvenile) Penguin Publishing Group.

—EllRay Jakes Is Not a Chicken, 1 vol. Warner, Sally. 2011. (EllRay Jakes Ser.: 1). (ENG.). 144p. (J). (gr. 1-3). 14.99 *(978-0-670-06243-0(X)*, Viking Juvenile) Penguin Publishing Group.

—EllRay Jakes Is Not a Chicken, 1 vol. Warner, Sally. 2012. (EllRay Jakes Ser.: 1). (ENG.). 128p. (J). (gr. 1-3). 5.99 *(978-0-14-241988-5(5)*, Puffin) Penguin Publishing Group.

—Excellent Emma. Warner, Sally. 2010. (Emma Ser.). (ENG.). 144p. (J). (gr. 3-7). 6.99 *(978-0-14-241569-6(3)*, Puffin) Penguin Publishing Group.

—Not-So-Weird Emma. Wallace, Rich & Warner, Sally. 2005. (Emma Ser.). (ENG.). 128p. (J). (gr. 3-7). 14.99 *(978-0-670-06005-4(4)*, Viking Juvenile) Penguin Publishing Group.

—Not-So-Weird Emma. Warner, Sally. 2007. (Emma Ser.). (ENG.). 144p. (J). (gr. 3-7). 6.99 *(978-0-14-240807-0(7)*, Puffin) Penguin Publishing Group.

—Only Emma. Warner, Sally. 2006. (Emma Ser.). (ENG.). 144p. (J). (gr. 3-7). 6.99 *(978-0-14-240711-0(9)*, Puffin) Penguin Publishing Group.

—Super Emma. Warner, Sally. 2008. (Emma Ser.). (ENG.). 112p. (J). (gr. 3-7). 5.99 *(978-0-14-241088-2(8)*, Puffin) Penguin Publishing Group.

—Walks the Plank! Warner, Sally. (EllRay Jakes Ser.: 3). (ENG.). 128p. (J). (gr. 1-3). 2013. pap. 5.99 *(978-0-14-242409-4(9)*, Puffin); 2012. 14.99 *(978-0-670-06306-2(1)*, Viking Juvenile) Penguin Publishing Group.

Harper, Jamie. Excellent Emma. Harper, Jamie. Warner, Sally. 2009. (Emma Ser.). (ENG.). 144p. (J). (gr. 3-7). 14.99 *(978-0-670-06310-9(X)*, Viking Juvenile) Penguin Publishing Group.

—Miles to Go. Harper, Jamie. (ENG.). 32p. (J). (gr. -1-2). 2013. pap. 4.99 *(978-0-7636-6469-5(3))*; 2010. 12.99 *(978-0-7636-3598-5(7))* Candlewick Pr.

—Miss Mingo & the Fire Drill. Harper, Jamie. (ENG.). 40p. (J). (gr. -1-3). 2012. pap. 6.99 *(978-0-7636-6086-4(8))*; 2009. 15.99 *(978-0-7636-3597-8(9))* Candlewick Pr.

—Miss Mingo & the First Day of School. Harper, Jamie. 2009. (ENG.). 32p. (J). (gr. -1-3). pap. 6.99 *(978-0-7636-4134-4(0))* Candlewick Pr.

—Miss Mingo Weathers the Storm. Harper, Jamie. 2012. (ENG.). 40p. (J). (gr. -1-3). 15.99 *(978-0-7636-4931-9(7))* Candlewick Pr.

—Splish Splash, Baby Bundt: A Recipe for Bath Time. Harper, Jamie. 2007. (ENG.). 24p. (J). (— 1). bds. 6.99 *(978-0-7636-3240-3(6))* Candlewick Pr.

Harper, Lee. Looking for the Easy Life. Myers, Walter Dean. 2011. (Looking at Other Countries Ser.). (ENG.). 40p. (J). (gr. -1-3). 16.99 *(978-0-06-054375-4(2))* HarperCollins Pubs.

—Turkey Claus, 0 vols. Silvano, Wendi J. 2012. (ENG.). 32p. (J). (gr. -1-3). 16.99 *(978-0-7614-6239-2(2)*, 9780761462392, Amazon Children's Publishing) Amazon Publishing.

—Woolbur. Helakoski, Leslie. 2008. 32p. (J). (gr. -1-3). 17.89 *(978-0-06-084727-2(1))*; (ENG.). 17.99 *(978-0-06-084726-5(3))* HarperCollins Pubs.

Harper, Lee. Snow! Snow! Snow! Harper, Lee. 2009. (ENG.). 40p. (J). (gr. -1-3). 14.99 *(978-1-4169-8454-2(2)*, Simon & Schuster/Paula Wiseman Bks.) Simon & Schuster/Paula Wiseman Bks.

Harper, Piers. The Young Learner's Bible Storybook: 52 Stories with Activities for Family Fun & Learning. Simon, Mary Manz. 2006. (First Virtues for Toddlers Ser.). 336p. (J). (gr. -1-2). 17.99 *(978-0-7847-1277-1(8)*, 04010) Standard Publishing.

Harper, Ruth E. & James, Robin. Sassafras. Penn, Audrey & Cosgrove, Stephen. 2006. (ENG.). 32p. (J). (gr. -1-3). 16.95 *(978-1-933718-03-3(X))* Tanglewood Pr.

Harper, Ruth E. & Leak, Nancy M. Un Beso en Mi Mano. Penn, Audrey. 2006. (SPA & ENG.). 32p. (J). (gr. -1-3). 16.95 *(978-1-933718-01-9(3))* Tanglewood Pr.

—The Kissing Hand. Penn, Audrey. 2007. (ENG.). 32p. (J). (gr. -1-3). 28.95 *(978-1-933718-07-1(2))*; 12.95 *(978-1-933718-10-1(2))* Tanglewood Pr.

Harper, Suzanne. The Real Spy's Guide to Becoming a Spy. Earnest, Peter. 2009. (ENG.). 144p. (J). (gr. -1-3). 18.95 *(978-0-8109-8329-8(X)*, Abrams Bks. for Young Readers) Abrams.

Harpster, Steve. Ack's New Pet, 1 vol. Hoena, Blake A. 2014. (Eek & Ack Early Chapter Bks.). (ENG.). 32p. (gr. k-2). lib. bdg. 21.32 *(978-1-4342-6406-0(8))* Stone Arch Bks.

—Arnold Gets Angry: An Emotional Literacy Book. 2004. (Emotional Literacy Ser.). 45p. (J). (gr. 2-18). 14.95 *(978-0-9747789-0-7(7)*, 67312) CTC Publishing.

—The Beach Bandit, 1 vol. Yasuda, Anita. 2013. (Dino Detectives Ser.). (ENG.). 32p. (gr. 1-2). pap. 6.25 *(978-1-4342-4830-5(5))*; lib. bdg. 21.32 *(978-1-4342-4154-2(8))* Stone Arch Bks.

—Betty Stops the Bully: An Emotional Literacy Book. 2004. (Emotional Literacy Ser.). 44p. (J). (gr. 2-18). 14.95 *(978-0-9747789-1-4(5)*, 67313) CTC Publishing.

—Beyond the Black Hole. Hoena, Blake A. 2016. (Eek & Ack Ser.). (ENG.). 40p. (gr. 1-3). 22.65 *(978-1-4342-0759-3(5))*; pap. 5.95 *(978-1-4342-0855-2(9))* Stone Arch Bks. (Graphic Sparks).

—Big City Sights, 1 vol. Yasuda, Anita. 2011. (My First Graphic Novel Ser.). (ENG.). 32p. (gr. k-2). pap. 6.25 *(978-1-4342-3060-7(0))*; lib. bdg. 23.32 *(978-1-4342-2515-3(1))* Stone Arch Bks. (My First Graphic Novel).

—The Big Mistake, 1 vol. Hoena, Blake A. 2014. (Eek & Ack Early Chapter Bks.). (ENG.). 32p. (gr. k-2). lib. bdg. 21.32 *(978-1-4342-6408-4(4))* Stone Arch Bks.

—The Black Hole Report, 1 vol. Hoena, Blake A. 2014. (Eek & Ack Early Chapter Bks.). (ENG.). 32p. (gr. k-2). lib. bdg. 21.32 *(978-1-4342-6409-1(2))* Stone Arch Bks.

—Blast to the Past. Nickel, Scott. 2006. (Graphic Sparks Ser.). (ENG.). 40p. (gr. 1-3). 5.95 *(978-1-59889-167-6(7))*; 22.65 *(978-1-59889-033-4(6))* Stone Arch Bks. (Graphic Sparks).

—The Boy Who Burped Too Much, 1 vol. Nickel, Scott. 2006. (Graphic Sparks Ser.). (ENG.). 40p. (gr. 1-3). 22.65 *(978-1-59889-037-2(9)*, Graphic Sparks) Stone Arch Bks.

—The Brave Puffer Fish, 1 vol. Meister, Cari. 2011. (Ocean Tales Ser.). (ENG.). 32p. (gr. 2-3). pap. 6.25 *(978-1-4342-3389-9(8))*; lib. bdg. 21.32 *(978-1-4342-3198-7(4))* Stone Arch Bks.

—Catherine Finds Her Courage: An Emotional Literacy Book. 2004. (Emotional Literacy Ser.). 44p. (J). (gr. 2-18). 14.95 *(978-0-9747789-2-1(3)*, 67314) CTC Publishing.

—Chicken Little: Classic Tales Series. Smith, Carrie. 2011. (Classic Tales Ser.). (J). *(978-1-936258-74-1(9))* Benchmark Education Co.

—Christmas Eve. Torres, J. 2006. (Scribble & Sing Ser.). (ENG.). 80p. (J). 4.99 *(978-1-4169-2731-0(X)*, Simon Scribbles) Simon Scribbles.

—The Clever Dolphin, 1 vol. Meister, Cari. 2012. (Ocean Tales Ser.). (ENG.). 32p. (gr. 2-4). pap. 6.25 *(978-1-4342-4229-7(3))* Stone Arch Bks.

—The Crazy Clues, 1 vol. Yasuda, Anita. 2013. (Dino Detectives Ser.). (ENG.). 32p. (gr. 1-2). lib. bdg. 21.32 *(978-1-4342-5971-4(4))* Stone Arch Bks.

—Crazy Clues. Yasuda, Anita. 2013. (Dino Detectives Ser.). (ENG.). 32p. (gr. 1-2). pap. 5.95 *(978-1-4342-6200-4(6))* Stone Arch Bks.

—Curse of the Red Scorpion, 1 vol. Nickel, Scott. 2006. (Graphic Sparks Ser.). (ENG.). 40p. (gr. 1-3). per. 5.95 *(978-1-59889-169-0(3))*; 22.65 *(978-1-59889-034-1(4))* Stone Arch Bks. (Graphic Sparks).

—The Day Mom Finally Snapped, 1 vol. Temple, Bob. 2006. (Graphic Sparks Ser.). (ENG.). 40p. (gr. 1-3). 22.65 *(978-1-59889-038-9(7)*, Graphic Sparks) Stone Arch Bks.

—Debra Doesn't Take the Dare: An Emotional Literacy Book. 2004. 54p. (J). 14.95 *(978-0-9747789-3-8(1)*, 20705) CTC Publishing.

—Dino Detectives. Yasuda, Anita. 2013. (Dino Detectives Ser.). (ENG.). 32p. (gr. 1-3). pap. 47.60 *(978-1-4342-6221-9(9))*; pap. 23.80 *(978-1-4342-6220-2(0))*; lib. bdg. 170.56 *(978-1-4342-6059-8(3))*; pap. 23.80 *(978-1-4342-3937-2(3))* Stone Arch Bks.

—Dognapped!, 1 vol. Nickel, Scott. 2006. (Jimmy Sniffles Ser.). (ENG.). 40p. (gr. 1-3). lib. bdg. 22.65 *(978-1-59889-053-2(0)*, Graphic Sparks) Stone Arch Bks.

—Dognapped! Jimmy Sniffles. Nickel, Scott. 2006. (Graphic Sparks Ser.). 40p. (gr. 1-3). per. 5.95 *(978-1-59889-226-0(6)*, Graphic Sparks) Stone Arch Bks.

—Double Trouble, 1 vol. Nickel, Scott. 2007. (Jimmy Sniffles Ser.). (ENG.). 40p. (gr. 1-3). lib. bdg. 22.65 *(978-1-59889-314-4(9))*; per. 5.95 *(978-1-59889-411-0(0))* Stone Arch Bks. (Graphic Sparks).

—Down on the Farm, 1 vol. Houts, Amy. 2011. (My First Graphic Novel Ser.). (ENG.). 32p. (gr. k-2). pap. 6.25 *(978-1-4342-3063-8(5))*; lib. bdg. 23.32 *(978-1-4342-2516-0(X))* Stone Arch Bks. (My First Graphic Novel).

—Eek & Ack vs the Wolfman, 1 vol. Hoena, Blake A. 2009. (Eek & Ack Ser.). (ENG.). 40p. (gr. 1-3). lib. bdg. 22.65 *(978-1-4342-1189-7(4)*, Graphic Sparks) Stone Arch Bks.

—Eek Discovers Earth, 1 vol. Hoena, Blake A. 2014. (Eek & Ack Early Chapter Bks.). (ENG.). 32p. (gr. k-2). lib. bdg. 21.32 *(978-1-4342-6407-7(6))* Stone Arch Bks.

—Ethan Has Too Much Energy: An Emotional Literacy Book. Shapiro, Lawrence. 2005. (Emotional Literacy Ser.). 42p. (J). 14.95 *(978-0-9747789-4-5(X)*, 36027) CTC Publishing.

—The Fancy Octopus, 1 vol. Meister, Cari. 2011. (Ocean Tales Ser.). (ENG.). 32p. (gr. 2-3). pap. 6.25 *(978-1-4342-3392-9(8))*; lib. bdg. 21.32 *(978-1-4342-3201-4(8))* Stone Arch Bks.

—First Base Blues, 1 vol. Yasuda, Anita. 2012. (My First Graphic Novel Ser.). (ENG.). 32p. (gr. k-2). pap. 6.25 *(978-1-4342-3863-4(6))*; lib. bdg. 23.32 *(978-1-4342-3279-3(4))* Stone Arch Bks. (My First Graphic Novel).

—First Word Search: Easy First Words. 2011. (First Word Search Ser.). (ENG.). 64p. (J). (gr. -1-1). pap. 4.95 *(978-1-4027-7808-7(2))* Sterling Publishing Co., Inc.

—First Word Search: Fun First Phonics. 2011. (First Word Search Ser.). (ENG.). 64p. (J). pap. 4.95 *(978-1-4027-7806-3(6))* Sterling Publishing Co., Inc.

—First Word Search: Fun First Words. 2011. (First Word Search Ser.). (ENG.). 64p. (J). pap. 4.95 *(978-1-4027-7807-0(4))* Sterling Publishing Co., Inc.

—First Word Search: Reading Made Easy. 2011. (First Word Search Ser.). (ENG.). 64p. (J). (gr. -1-1). pap. 4.95 *(978-1-4027-7802-5(3))* Sterling Publishing Co., Inc.

—The Forest Surprise, 1 vol. Mooney, Carla. 2011. (My First Graphic Novel Ser.). (ENG.). 32p. (gr. k-2). pap. 6.25 *(978-1-4342-3064-5(3))*; lib. bdg. 23.32 *(978-1-4342-2520-7(8))* Stone Arch Bks. (My First Graphic Novel).

—Freddy Fights Fat: An Emotional Literacy Book. Shapiro, Lawrence E. 2004. (Emotional Literacy Ser.). 54p. (J). (gr. 2-18). 14.95 *(978-0-9747789-5-2(8)*, 67873) CTC Publishing.

—Ghost Sounds, 1 vol. Yasuda, Anita. 2013. (Dino Detectives Ser.). (ENG.). 32p. (gr. 1-2). pap. 6.25 *(978-1-4342-4831-2(3))*; lib. bdg. 21.32 *(978-1-4342-4152-8(1))* Stone Arch Bks.

—Growing up Happy: Arnold Gets Angry, Betty Stops the Bully & Catherine Finds Her Courage: the Emotional Literacy Series, 3, 3 vols., Set. 2004. (Emotional Literacy Ser.). 135p. (J). lib. bdg. 52.00 *(978-0-9747789-9-0(0))* CTC Publishing.

—The Grumpy Lobster, 1 vol. Meister, Cari. 2012. (Ocean Tales Ser.). (ENG.). 32p. (gr. 2-4). pap. 6.25 *(978-1-4342-4230-3(7))*; lib. bdg. 21.32 *(978-1-4342-4025-5(8))* Stone Arch Bks.

—The Haunted House, 1 vol. Yasuda, Anita. 2013. (Dino Detectives Ser.). (ENG.). 32p. (gr. 1-2). lib. bdg. 21.32 *(978-1-4342-5970-7(6))* Stone Arch Bks.

—Haunted House. Yasuda, Anita. 2013. (Dino Detectives Ser.). (ENG.). 32p. (gr. 1-2). pap. 5.95 *(978-1-4342-6199-1(9))* Stone Arch Bks.

—The Hiding Eel, 1 vol. Meister, Cari. 2011. (Ocean Tales Ser.). (ENG.). 32p. (gr. 2-3). pap. 6.25 *(978-1-4342-3390-5(1))*; lib. bdg. 21.32 *(978-1-4342-3199-4(2))* Stone Arch Bks.

—Invaders from the Great Goo Galaxy. Hoena, Blake A. 2006. (Eek & Ack Ser.). (ENG.). 40p. (gr. 1-3). lib. bdg. 22.65 *(978-1-59889-052-5(2)*, Graphic Sparks) Stone Arch Bks.

—Jimmy Sniffles vs the Mummy, 1 vol. Nickel, Scott. 2009. (Jimmy Sniffles Ser.). (ENG.). 40p. (gr. 1-3). lib. bdg. 22.65 *(978-1-4342-1190-3(8)*, Graphic Sparks) Stone Arch Bks.

—The Jumping Monkeys. Smith, Carrie. 2009. (Reader's Theater Nursery Rhymes & Songs Set B Ser.). 48p. (J). pap. *(978-1-60859-155-8(7))* Benchmark Education Co.

—The Lucky Manatee, 1 vol. Meister, Cari. 2012. (Ocean Tales Ser.). (ENG.). 32p. (gr. 2-4). pap. 6.25 *(978-1-4342-4231-0(5))*; lib. bdg. 21.32 *(978-1-4342-4028-6(2))* Stone Arch Bks.

—The Missing Trumpet, 1 vol. Yasuda, Anita. 2013. (Dino Detectives Ser.). (ENG.). 32p. (gr. 1-2). pap. 6.25 *(978-1-4342-4832-9(1))*; lib. bdg. 21.32 *(978-1-4342-4155-9(6))* Stone Arch Bks.

—The Mystery Coins, 1 vol. Yasuda, Anita. 2013. (Dino Detectives Ser.). (ENG.). 32p. (gr. 1-2). lib. bdg. 21.32 *(978-1-4342-5972-1(2))* Stone Arch Bks.

—Mystery Coins. Yasuda, Anita. 2013. (Dino Detectives Ser.). (ENG.). 32p. (gr. 1-2). pap. 5.95 *(978-1-4342-6201-1(4))* Stone Arch Bks.

—A Nose for Danger. Temple, Bob. 2006. (Graphic Sparks Ser.). (ENG.). 40p. (gr. 1-3). per. 5.95 *(978-1-59889-171-3(5))*; lib. bdg. 22.65 *(978-1-59889-036-5(0))* Stone Arch Bks. (Graphic Sparks).

—Ocean Tales. Meister, Cari. 2013. (Ocean Tales Ser.). (ENG.). 32p. (gr. -1-3). 149.24 *(978-1-4342-8844-8(7))* Stone Arch Bks.

—Ooze Slingers from Outer Space. Hoena, Blake A. 2007. (Graphic Sparks Ser.). (ENG.). 40p. (gr. 1-3). per. 5.95 *(978-1-59889-410-3(2)*, Graphic Sparks) Stone Arch Bks.

—The Princess & the Pea: Classic Tales Edition. Smith, Carrie. 2011. (Classic Tales Ser.). (J). *(978-1-936258-76-5(5))* Benchmark Education Co.

—The Puzzling Pluto Plot: Eek & Ack, 1 vol. Hoena, Blake A. 2008. (Graphic Sparks Ser.). (ENG.). 40p. (gr. 1-3). pap. 5.95 *(978-1-4342-0502-5(9)*, Graphic Sparks) Stone Arch Bks.

—The Quick Quarterback, 1 vol. Lord, Michelle. 2012. (My First Graphic Novel Ser.). (ENG.). 32p. (gr. k-2). pap. 6.25 *(978-1-4342-3861-0(X))*; lib. bdg. 23.32 *(978-1-4342-3281-6(6))* Stone Arch Bks. (My First Graphic Novel).

—Race on the River, 1 vol. Nickel, Scott. 2011. (My First Graphic Novel Ser.). (ENG.). 32p. (gr. k-2). pap. 6.25 *(978-1-4342-3061-4(9))*; lib. bdg. 23.32 *(978-1-4342-2521-4(6))* Stone Arch Bks. (My First Graphic Novel).

—The Scary Slopes, 1 vol. Pattison, Darcy. 2011. (My First Graphic Novel Ser.). (ENG.). 32p. (gr. k-2). lib. bdg. 23.32 *(978-1-4342-2534-4(8)*, My First Graphic Novel) Stone Arch Bks.

—The Shivery Shark, 1 vol. Meister, Cari. 2011. (Ocean Tales Ser.). (ENG.). 32p. (gr. 2-3). pap. 6.25 *(978-1-4342-3391-2(X))*; lib. bdg. 21.32 *(978-1-4342-3200-7(X))* Stone Arch Bks.

—The Slime Attack, 1 vol. Yasuda, Anita. 2013. (Dino Detectives Ser.). (ENG.). 32p. (gr. 1-2). pap. 6.25 *(978-1-4342-4833-6(X))*; lib. bdg. 21.32 *(978-1-4342-4153-5(X))* Stone Arch Bks.

—The Stranded Orca, 1 vol. Meister, Cari. 2012. (Ocean Tales Ser.). (ENG.). 32p. (gr. 2-4). pap. 6.25 *(978-1-4342-4232-7(3))*; lib. bdg. 21.32 *(978-1-4342-4026-2(6))* Stone Arch Bks.

—The Super-Powered Sneeze. Nickel, Scott. 2007. (Graphic Sparks Ser.). (ENG.). 40p. (gr. 1-3). per. 5.95 *(978-1-59889-409-7(9)*, Graphic Sparks) Stone Arch Bks.

—The Surprise Prize, 1 vol. Yasuda, Anita. 2013. (Dino Detectives Ser.). (ENG.). 32p. (gr. 1-2). lib. bdg. 21.32 *(978-1-4342-5969-1(2))* Stone Arch Bks.

—Surprise Prize. Yasuda, Anita. 2013. (Dino Detectives Ser.). (ENG.). 32p. (gr. 1-2). pap. 5.95 *(978-1-4342-6198-4(0))* Stone Arch Bks.

—The Swim Race, 1 vol. Yasuda, Anita. 2012. (My First Graphic Novel Ser.). (ENG.). 32p. (gr. k-2). pap. 6.25 *(978-1-4342-3864-1(4))*; lib. bdg. 23.32 *(978-1-4342-3280-9(8))* Stone Arch Bks. (My First Graphic Novel).

—The Three Billy Goats Gruff: Classic Tales Edition. Adams, Alison. 2011. (Classic Tales Ser.). (J). *(978-1-936258-62-8(5))* Benchmark Education Co.

—Tide Pool Trouble, 1 vol. Lord, Michelle. 2011. (My First Graphic Novel Ser.). (ENG.). 32p. (gr. k-2). pap. 6.25 *(978-1-4342-3059-1(7))*; lib. bdg. 23.32 *(978-1-4342-2517-7(8))* Stone Arch Bks. (My First Graphic Novel).

—Too Short for the Court, 1 vol. Lemke, Amy J. 2012. (My First Graphic Novel Ser.). (ENG.). 32p. (gr. k-2). pap. 6.25 *(978-1-4342-3862-7(8))*; lib. bdg. 23.32 *(978-1-4342-3282-3(4))* Stone Arch Bks. (My First Graphic Novel).

—Up the President's Nose, 1 vol. Nickel, Scott. 2007. (Jimmy Sniffles Ser.). (ENG.). 40p. (gr. 1-3). lib. bdg. 22.65 *(978-1-59889-837-8(X)*, Graphic Sparks) Stone Arch Bks.

Harr, Alexandra. Make a Stand: When Life Gives You Lemons, Change the World! 2014. (ENG.). (J). (gr. -1-3). 18.99 *(978-0-9911314-0-2(1))* Chocolate Sauce.

Harr, Lynn. The Ice Angel. Spoon, Cynthia. 2006. 24p. (J). (gr. -1-3). per. 8.50 *(978-1-60002-280-7(4)*, 4233) Mountain Valley Publishing, LLC.

Harrad, Matthew. Composting: Nature's Recyclers, 1 vol. Koontz, Robin Michal. 2006. (Amazing Science Ser.). (ENG.). 24p. (gr. k-4). lib. bdg. 25.99 *(978-1-4048-2194-1(5))*; per. 7.95 *(978-1-4048-2200-9(3))* Picture Window Bks. (Nonfiction Picture Bks.).

—Erosion: Changing Earth's Surface, 1 vol. Koontz, Robin Michal. 2006. (Amazing Science Ser.). (ENG.). 24p. (gr. k-4). lib. bdg. 25.99 *(978-1-4048-2195-8(3))*; per. 7.95 *(978-1-4048-2201-6(1))* Picture Window Bks. (Nonfiction Picture Bks.).

Harrald-Pilz, Marilee. Buttercup Hill. Berry, Eileen M. 2006. 39p. (J). (gr. -1-3). pap. *(978-1-59166-667-7(8))* BJU Pr.

—Five Spooky Ghosts Playing Tricks at School. Metzger, Steve. 2005. (J). *(978-0-439-80381-6(0))* Scholastic, Inc.

—Just the Right Home. Schmauss, Judy Kentor. 2006. (Reader's Clubhouse Level 2 Reader Ser.). (ENG.). 24p. (J). (gr. 1-4). pap. 3.99 *(978-0-7641-3299-5(7))* Barron's Educational Series, Inc.

Harrel, Tina. My Blended Family. Picone, Emma Lee. 2012. 32p. pap. 12.95 *(978-0-9829803-9-2(6))* Joshua Tree Publishing.

Harrell, Kim. Perry's Baltimore Adventure: A Bird's-Eye View of Charm City. Dans, Peter E. 2007. (ENG.). 32p. (J). (gr. -1-1). 14.95 *(978-1-933822-08-2(2))* Camino Bks., Inc.

—Perry's Baltimore Adventure: A Bird's-Eye View of Charm City. Dans, Peter E. 2003. 30p. (J). 11.95 *(978-0-87033-540-2(5)*, Cornell Maritime Pr./Tidewater Pubs.) Schiffer Publishing, Ltd.

—While a Tree Grew: The Story of Maryland's Wye Oak. Bachmann, Elaine Rice. 2006. 25p. (J). (gr. -1-3). 10.50 *(978-0-87033-577-8(4)*, Cornell Maritime Pr./Tidewater Pubs.) Schiffer Publishing, Ltd.

Harrell, Maurice. The Boy Who Loved to Be Like Michael Jackson. Yolanda And Reese. 2012. 32p. 24.95 *(978-1-4560-8506-3(9))* America Star Bks.

Harrell, Michael. Busy Bumble Bee Rides the Waves. Moore, Carol Hair. 2009. (I Wish You Ice Cream & Cake Ser.: 2). (ENG.). 32p. (J). lib. bdg. 15.95 *(978-1-935083-06-1(6))* CyPress Pubns.

—Marvin the Magnificent Nubian Goat. Moore, Carol Hair. 2009. (I Wish You Ice Cream & Cake Ser.). 28p. (J). lib. bdg. 15.95 *(978-1-935083-03-0(1))* CyPress Pubns.

Harrell, Micheael. Marvin the Magnificent Nubian Goat. Moore, Carol H. 2006. (J). 20.00 *(978-0-9792019-0-5(X))* iwishyouicecreamandcake.

Harrell, Symear. On Christmas Day. Londa And Pop-Pop. 2011. 16p. pap. 24.95 *(978-1-4560-7078-6(9))* America Star Bks.

Harriet Kasak Portfolio Staff, jt. illus. see Huliska-Beith, Laura.

Harrigan, Mike. Shadow Fox: Sons of Liberty. Hardman, Ron & Hardman, Jessica. Barnecut, Suzanne, ed. 2010. (Shadow Fox Ser.). 186p. (J). (gr. 4-8). 22.99 *(978-0-9819607-1-5(5))* Fox Run Pr., LLC.

—Shadow Fox: Sons of Liberty. Hardman, Ron & Hardman, Jessica. Barnecutt, Suzanne, ed. 2010. (Shadow Fox Ser.). 186p. (J). (gr. 4-8). pap. 11.99 *(978-0-9819607-0-8(7))* Fox Run Pr., LLC.

—Shadow Fox: Sons of Liberty Teacher's Edition. Hardman, Ron & Hardman, Jessica. Barnecutt, Suzanne, ed. 2010. (Shadow Fox Ser.: 1). 186p. (J). 34.99 *(978-0-9819607-2-2(3))* Fox Run Pr., LLC.

Harrill, Cory. One Dream & Collected Stories. Pecora, Bet Shoshannah. 2003. 128p. pap. 10.00 *(978-1-882190-60-7(2))* Polar Bear & Co.

Harriman, Marinell & Harriman, Robert. A Myriad of Minstrels. Harriman, Marinell & Harriman, Robert. 32p. (Orig.). (J). (gr. 5-7). pap. 3.50 *(978-0-940920-00-2(X))* Drollery Pr.

Harriman, Robert, jt. illus. see Harriman, Marinell.

Harrington, David. Amanda's Spider Surprise: A Bible Memory Buddy Book about Being Brave. Duckworth, Liz. 2011. (Bible Memory Buddy Bks.). (J). (gr. -1-3). pap. 4.99 *(978-0-7644-6688-5(7))* Group Publishing, Inc.

—Case of the Bookstore Burglar #3, 3 vols. Rosenberg, Aaron. 2012. (Pete & Penny's Pizza Puzzles Ser.: 3). (ENG.). 64p. (J). (gr. 1-3). pap. 3.99 *(978-0-8431-9809-6(5)*, Price Stern Sloan) Penguin Publishing Group.

—Case of the Secret Sauce, Vol. 1. Rosenberg, Aaron. 2011. (Pete & Penny's Pizza Puzzles Ser.: 1). (ENG.). 64p. (J). (gr. 1-3). pap. 3.99 *(978-0-8431-9928-4(8)*, Price Stern Sloan) Penguin Publishing Group.

—Case of the Topsy-Turvy Toy. Rosenberg, Aaron. 2011. (Pete & Penny's Pizza Puzzles Ser.: 2). (ENG.). 64p. (J). (gr. 1-3). pap. 3.99 *(978-0-8431-9929-1(6)*, Price Stern Sloan) Penguin Publishing Group.

—Chachalaca Chiquita, 1 vol. Chrismer, Melanie. 2012. (ENG.). 32p. (J). (gr. k-3). 16.99 *(978-1-4556-1704-3(0))* Pelican Publishing Co., Inc.

—Charlie's Magical Night. Thomasian, Sara. 2007. (J). per. 11.99 *(978-1-59879-381-9(0))* Lifevest Publishing, Inc.

—Fez & the Big, Bad Bully: A Bible Memory Buddy Book about Standing up to Bullies. Brolsma, Jody. 2011. (Bible Memory Buddy Bks.). (J). (gr. -1-3). pap. 4.99 *(978-0-7644-6689-2(5))* Group Publishing, Inc.

—Griego el Magnifico y la Gotita Verde Golosa Pegajos. Alfaro, Manuel. 2007. (SPA.). 36p. per. 15.50 *(978-1-59858-337-3(9))* Dog Ear Publishing, LLC.

—Lights! Camera! Boomer: A Bible Memory Buddy Book about Being God's Special Creation. Wesemann, Tim. 2011. (Bible Memory Buddy Bks.). (J). (gr. -1-3). pap. 4.99 *(978-0-7644-6687-8(9))* Group Publishing, Inc.

—Lulu on the Loose: A Bible Memory Buddy Book about Self-Control. McGuire, Andy. 2011. (Bible Memory Buddy Bks.). (J). (gr. -1-3). pap. 4.99 *(978-0-7644-6685-4(2))* Group Publishing, Inc.

—Maccabee! The Story of Hanukkah. Balsley, Tilda. 2010. (Hanukkah Ser.). (ENG.). 32p. (J). (gr. -1-2). pap. 7.95 *(978-0-7613-4508-4(6))*; lib. bdg. 7.95 *(978-0-7613-4507-7(8))* Lerner Publishing Group. (Kar-Ben Publishing).

—Mary, Mary, Quite Contrary. Grudzina, Rebecca. 2010. (Rising Readers Ser.). (J). 3.49 *(978-1-60719-704-1(9))* Newmark Learning LLC.

—Olé! Cinco de Mayo!, 1 vol. McManis, Margaret. 2013. (ENG.). 32p. (J). (gr. k-3). 16.99 *(978-1-4556-1754-8(7))* Pelican Publishing Co., Inc.

—Pease Porridge, Please! Grudzina, Rebecca. 2009. (Reader's Theater Nursery Rhymes & Songs Set B Ser.). 48p. (J). pap. *(978-1-60859-163-3(8))* Benchmark Education Co.

—Pecos Bill Invents the Ten-Gallon Hat, 1 vol. Strauss, Kevin. 2012. (ENG.). 32p. (J). (gr. k-3). 16.99 *(978-1-4556-1502-5(1))* Pelican Publishing Co., Inc.

—Pogo's Prank-A-Palooza: A Bible Memory Buddy Book about Respecting Others. Nappa, Mike. 2011. (Bible Memory Buddy Bks.). (J). (gr. -1-3). pap. 1.99 *(978-0-7644-6686-1(0))* Group Publishing, Inc.

—Since We're Friends: An Autism Picture Book. Shally, Celeste. 2007. 32p. (J). (gr. -1-3). per. 8.99 *(978-0-9794713-0-8(3))* Awaken Specialty Pr.

—Since We're Friends: An Autism Picture Book. Shally, Celeste. 2012. (ENG.). 32p. (J). (gr. k-3). 12.95 *(978-1-61608-656-5(4)*, 608656, Sky Pony Pr.) Skyhorse Publishing Co., Inc.

—Spaghetti Smiles, 1 vol. Sorenson, Margo. 2014. (ENG.). 32p. (J). (gr. k-3). 16.99 *(978-1-4556-1922-1(1))* Pelican Publishing Co., Inc.

—Super Griego the Great & the Secret Mission to the Moon. Alfaro, Manuel. 2009. 40p. pap. 15.95 *(978-1-60844-028-3(1))* Dog Ear Publishing, LLC.

—Twinkle, Twinkle, Little Star. Harris, Brooke. 2010. (Rising Readers Ser.). (J). 3.49 *(978-1-60719-697-6(2))* Newmark Learning LLC.

—The Twinkling Stars. Harris, Brooke. 2009. (Reader's Theater Nursery Rhymes & Songs Set B Ser.). 48p. (J). pap. *(978-1-60859-170-1(0))* Benchmark Education Co.

—When Pigs Fly: A Bible Memory Buddy Book. Nappa, Mike. 2012. (ENG.). 32p. (J). (-3). 9.99 *(978-0-7644-8189-5(4))* Group Publishing, Inc.

—Where Has My Dog Gone? Harris, Brooke. 2010. (Rising Readers Ser.). (J). 3.49 *(978-1-60719-693-8(X))* Newmark Learning LLC.

Harrington, David. The Boy Who Wouldn't Read, 1 vol. Harrington, David. McConduit, Denise. 2013. (ENG.). 32p. (J). (gr. k-3). 16.99 *(978-1-4556-1829-3(2))* Pelican Publishing Co., Inc.

Harrington, Glenn. William Shakespeare. Kasten, David Scott & Kastan, Marina, eds. 2008. (Poetry for Young People Ser.). (ENG.). 48p. (J). (gr. 3). pap. 6.95 *(978-1-4027-5478-4(7))* Sterling Publishing Co., Inc.

Harrington, John. Meet Mindy: A Native Girl from the Southwest. Harrington, John, photos by. Secakuku, Susan, photos by. 2013. 48p. (J). *(978-1-933565-20-0(9))* Smithsonian National Museum of the American Indian.

Harrington, John, photos by. Meet Lydia: A Native Girl from Southeast Alaska. Belarde-Lewis, Miranda. 2004. (My World: Young Native Americans Today Ser.). (ENG.). 48p. (J). 15.95 *(978-1-57178-147-5(1))* Council Oak Bks.

—Meet Mindy: A Native Girl from the Southwest. Secakuku, Susan. 2006. (ENG.). 48p. (J). 15.95 *(978-1-57178-148-2(X))* Council Oak Bks.

—Meet Naiche: A Native Boy from the Chesapeake Bay Area. Tayac, Gabrielle. 2007. (My World: Young Native Americans Today Ser.). (ENG.). 48p. (J). (gr. 4-7). 15.95 *(978-1-57178-146-8(3))* Council Oak Bks.

Harrington, Leslie. Conrad Saves Pinger Park. Winans, Carvin. 2010. 32p. (J). (gr. -1-3). 8.95 *(978-1-60349-024-5(8)*, Marimba Bks.) Hudson Publishing Group, The.

—The Remarkable Ronald Reagan: Cowboy & Commander in Chief. Allen, Susan. 2013. (ENG.). 36p. (J). (gr. 1). 16.95 *(978-1-62157-038-7(X))* Regnery Publishing, Inc., An Eagle Publishing Co.

Harrington, Linda. The Voyage of Billy Buckins, 1 vol. Arrington, R. Region. 2009. 73p. pap. 19.95 *(978-1-4489-2083-9(3))* America Star Bks.

Harrington, Rich. The Almost Invisible Cases. Alfonsi, Alice. 2007. 96p. (J). *(978-0-545-01585-1(5))* Scholastic, Inc.

—The Audio Files. West, Tracey. 2006. 96p. (J). pap. *(978-0-439-90719-4(5))* Scholastic, Inc.

—The Clothing Capers. West, Tracey. 2007. 96p. (J). pap. *(978-0-439-91452-9(3))* Scholastic, Inc.

—The Code Red Cases. Alfonsi, Alice. 2006. 96p. (J). *(978-0-439-91447-5(7))* Scholastic, Inc.

—The Fingerprint Files. West, Tracey. 2007. 96p. (J). *(978-0-439-91451-2(5))* Scholastic, Inc.

—The Playing Card Cases. Alfonsi, Alice. 2007. 96p. (J). *(978-0-545-01087-0(X))* Scholastic, Inc.

—The Secret Cipher Cases. West, Tracey. 2006. 96p. (J). *(978-0-439-91448-2(5))* Scholastic, Inc.

—The Teeny Tiny Cases. West, Tracey. 2007. 96p. (J). *(978-0-439-91450-5(7))* Scholastic, Inc.

Harrington, Tim. Nose to Toes, You Are Yummy! Harrington, Tim. 2015. (ENG.). 32p. (J). (gr. -1-3). 17.99 *(978-0-06-232816-8(6))* HarperCollins Pubs.

—This Little Piggy. Harrington, Tim. 2013. (ENG.). 32p. (J). (gr. -1-3). 15.99 *(978-0-06-221808-7(5))* HarperCollins Pubs.

Harris, - Crystal. My Friend Michael: A Short Story about Autism - A Pedro Collection. Saleem-Muhammad, Rasheedah. 2011. 30p. 19.95 *(978-1-4575-0295-8(X))*; pap. 14.95 *(978-1-4575-0037-4(X))* Dog Ear Publishing, LLC.

Harris, Andrew. Tally Cat Keeps Track. Harris, Trudy. 2010. (Math Is Fun! Ser.). (ENG.). 32p. (gr. k-2). lib. bdg. 22.60 *(978-0-7613-4451-3(9)*, Millbrook Pr.) Lerner Publishing Group.

—Your Body Battles a Broken Bone. Cobb, Vicki. 2009. (Body Battles Ser.). (ENG.). 32p. (gr. 2-5). 25.26 *(978-0-8225-7468-2(3))* Lerner Publishing Group.

—Your Body Battles a Cavity. Kunkel, Dennis, photos by. Cobb, Vicki. 2009. (Body Battles Ser.). (ENG.). 32p. (gr. 2-5). 25.26 *(978-0-8225-7469-9(1))* Lerner Publishing Group.

—Your Body Battles a Cold. Kunkel, Dennis, photos by. Cobb, Vicki. 2009. (Body Battles Ser.). (ENG.). 32p. (gr. 2-5). lib. bdg. 25.26 *(978-0-8225-6813-1(6))* Lerner Publishing Group.

—Your Body Battles a Skinned Knee. Kunkel, Dennis, photos by. Cobb, Vicki. 2009. (Body Battles Ser.). (ENG.). 32p. (gr. 2-5). lib. bdg. 25.26 *(978-0-8225-6814-8(4))* Lerner Publishing Group.

—Your Body Battles a Stomachache. Kunkel, Dennis, photos by. Cobb, Vicki. 2009. (Body Battles Ser.). (ENG.). 32p. (gr. 2-5). lib. bdg. 25.26 *(978-0-8225-7166-7(8))* Lerner Publishing Group.

—Your Body Battles an Earache. Kunkel, Dennis, photos by. Cobb, Vicki. 2009. (Body Battles Ser.). (ENG.). 32p. (gr. 2-5). 25.26 *(978-0-8225-6812-4(8))* Lerner Publishing Group.

Harris, Brandy. Freckles from Heaven. Harris, Mary. 2007. 28p. per. 24.95 *(978-1-4241-8647-1(1))* America Star Bks.

Harris, Brian. Watch Me Grow! A Down-to-Earth Guide to Growing Food in the City. Hodge, Deborah. 2011. (ENG.). 32p. (J). (gr. -1-2). 16.95 *(978-1-55453-618-4(9))* Kids Can Pr., Ltd. CAN. Dist: Univ. of Toronto Pr.

Harris, Brian, photos by. Up We Grow! A Year in the Life of a Small, Local Farm. Hodge, Deborah. 2010. (ENG., 32p. (J). (gr. -1-2). 16.95 *(978-1-55453-561-3(1))* Kids Can Pr., Ltd. CAN. Dist: Univ. of Toronto Pr.

Harris, Erin. Elephant on My Roof. Harris, Erin. 2006. 32p. (J). (gr. -1-3). 15.95 *(978-1-60108-002-8(6))* Red Cygnet Pr.

Harris, Jack. Packed with Poison! Deadly Animal Defenses. Souza, D. M. 2006. (On My Own Science Ser.). (ENG.). 48p. (gr. 2-4). lib. bdg. 25.26 *(978-1-57505-877-1(4)*, Millbrook Pr.) Lerner Publishing Group.

H

Harris, Jennifer Beck. Creepy, Crawly Bugs. Williams, Rozanne Lanczak. 2005. (Reading for Fluency Ser.). 8p. (J). pap. 3.49 (978-1-59198-149-7(2), 4249) Creative Teaching Pr., Inc.

—Hog & Dog. Landolf, Diane Wright. 2005. (Step into Reading Ser.: Vol. 1). (ENG.). 32p. (J). (gr. -1-1). per. 3.99 (978-0-375-83165-2(7), Random Hse. Bks. for Young Readers) Random Hse. Children's Bks.

Harris, Jenny B. Tess Builds a Snowman. Williams, Rozanne Lanczak. 2006. (Learn to Write Ser.). 8p. (J). (gr. k-2). pap. 3.49 (978-1-59198-286-9(3), 6180) Creative Teaching Pr., Inc.

—Tess Builds a Snowman. Williams, Rozanne Lanczak. Maio, Barbara & Faulkner, Stacey, eds. 2006. (J). per. 6.99 (978-1-59198-337-8(1)) Creative Teaching Pr., Inc.

Harris, Jim. The Boy & the Dragon, 1 vol. Ode, Eric. 2013. (ENG.). 32p. (J). (gr. k-3). 16.99 (978-1-4556-1813-2(6)) Pelican Publishing Co., Inc.

—Jacques & de Beanstalk. Artell, Mike. 2010. (ENG.). 32p. (J). (gr. k-3). 16.99 (978-0-8037-2816-5(6), Dial) Penguin Publishing Group.

—Librarian's Night Before Christmas, 1 vol. Davis, David. 2007. (Night Before Christmas Ser.). (ENG.). 32p. (J). (gr. k-3). 16.99 (978-1-58980-336-7(1)) Pelican Publishing Co., Inc.

—Petite Rouge. Artell, Mike. 2003. (ENG.). 32p. (J). (gr. k-3). 6.99 (978-0-14-250070-5(4), Puffin) Penguin Publishing Group.

—Ten Little Dinosaurs. Schnetzler, Pattie. 2013. (ENG.). 26p. (J). 12.99 (978-1-4494-4160-9(2)) Andrews McMeel Publishing.

—Ten Little Dinosaurs. Schnetzler, Pattie. 2015. (ENG.). 24p. (J). bds. 9.99 (978-1-4494-6491-2(2)) Andrews McMeel Publishing.

—Ten Little Kittens. Harris, Marian. 2010. (ENG.). 28p. (J). (gr. k). 15.99 (978-0-7407-9197-0(4)) Andrews McMeel Publishing.

—Ten Little Puppies. Harris, Marian. 2009. (ENG.). 26p. (J). (gr. -1-3). 16.99 (978-0-7407-8481-1(1)) Andrews McMeel Publishing.

—Three Little Cajun Pigs. Artell, Mike. 2006. (ENG.). 32p. (J). (gr. k-3). 16.99 (978-0-8037-2815-8(8), Dial) Penguin Publishing Group.

—The Tortoise & the Jackrabbit: La Tortuga y la Liebre. Lowell, Susan. 2004. (New Bilingual Picture Book Ser.). (ENG, SPA & MUL.). 32p. (J). (gr. -1-3). pap. 7.95 (978-0-87358-869-0(X)) Cooper Square Publishing Llc.

—Los Tres Pequenos Jabalies: The Three Little Javelinas. Lowell, Susan. 2004. (SPA, ENG & MUL.). 32p. (J). (gr. -1-3). 15.95 (978-0-87358-661-0(1), NP611) Rowman & Littlefield Publishers, Inc.

—A Very Hairy Christmas. Lowell, Susan. 2012. (J). (978-1-933855-80-6(0)) Rio Nuevo Pubs.

—When You're a Pirate Dog & Other Pirate Poems, 1 vol. Ode, Eric. 2012. (ENG.). 40p. (J). (gr. k-3). 17.99 (978-1-4556-1493-6(9)) Pelican Publishing Co., Inc.

Harris, Jim. Dinosaur's Night Before Christmas, 1 vol. Harris, Jim. 2010. (Night Before Christmas Ser.). (ENG.). 40p. (J). (gr. k-3). 16.99 (978-1-58980-850-8(9)) Pelican Publishing Co., Inc.

Harris, Joe. The Belly Book. Harris, Joe. 2008. (Beginner Books(R) Ser.). (ENG.). 48p. (J). (gr. -1-2). 8.99 (978-0-375-84340-2(X)) Random Hse. Children's Bks.

Harris, Joel & Harris, Sharon. Science Facts. Vecchione, Glen. 2007. (Little Giant Bks.). (ENG.). 352p. (J). (gr. 3-7). pap. 6.95 (978-1-4027-4981-0(3)) Sterling Publishing Co., Inc.

Harris, La Verne Abe. Little Drop & the Healing Place. Carr, Sheryl. 2006. (J). 10.00 (978-0-9791383-0-0(2)) Reliant Energy.

Harris, Lorrayne R. Poodles Tigers Monsters & You. Lewis, L. W. 2004. 64p. kivar 12.95 (978-0-9711572-1-7(9)) Red Pumpkin Pr.

Harris, Miki. Tales of the Monkey King. Jones, Teresa Chin. 2008. (J). (978-1-881896-30-2(7)) Pacific View Pr.

Harris, Nick. Dragon Quest. Dixon, Andy. Brooks, Felicity, ed. rev. ed. 2005. (Usborne Fantasy Puzzle Bks.). 32p. (J). (gr. 3-7). per. 7.99 (978-0-7945-1098-5(1), Usborne) EDC Publishing.

Harris, Nick, et al. Mythology. Evans, Hestia. Steer, Dugald A., ed. 2007. (Ologies Ser.). (ENG.). 32p. (J). (gr. 3-7). 21.99 (978-0-7636-3403-2(4)) Candlewick Pr.

Harris, Nick. Star Quest. Dixon, Andy. Brooks, Felicity, ed. 2006. (Usborne Fantasy Puzzle Bks.). 32p. (YA). (gr. 7). lib. bdg. 15.99 (978-1-58086-906-5(8)); pap. 7.99 (978-0-7945-1099-2(X)) EDC Publishing. (Usborne).

—The Wooden Horse of Troy, 1 vol. 2011. (Greek Myths Ser.). (ENG.). 32p. (gr. 4-5). lib. bdg. 27.99 (978-1-4048-6670-6(1), Nonfiction Picture Bks.) Picture Window Bks.

Harris, Patrick O'Neil. Country Hands. Welch, Michelle Rose. 2013. 24p. pap. 24.95 (978-1-63000-898-7(2)) America Star Bks.

Harris, Phyllis. Easter Surprises. Derico, Laura Ring. 2015. (Faith That Sticks Ser.). (ENG.). 26p. (J). pap. 3.99 (978-1-4964-0311-7(8)) Tyndale Hse. Pubs.

—My Two Holidays - A Hanukkah & Christmas Story. Novack, Danielle. 2010. (My Two Holidays Ser.). (ENG.). 32p. (J). (gr. -1-k). pap. 5.99 (978-0-545-23515-0(4), Cartwheel Bks.) Scholastic, Inc.

—On Christmas Day. Brown, Margaret. 2011. (J). 12.99 (978-1-882077-10-6(5)) WaterMark, Inc.

—Swim, Swam, Swum. Marsaw, Roy. 2007. 32p. (J). pap. 14.95 (978-0-9744446-8-0(5)) All About Kids Publishing.

Harris, Phyllis & Clearwater, Linda. Koala Does His Best. Simon, Mary Manz. 2006. (First Virtuestm for Toddlers Ser.). 20p. (J). 5.99 (978-0-7847-1578-9(5), 04072) Standard Publishing.

—Lamb Is Joyful. Simon, Mary Manz. 2006. (First Virtuestm for Toddlers Ser.). 20p. (J). 5.99 (978-0-7847-1575-8(0), 04069) Standard Publishing.

—Lion Can Share. Simon, Mary Manz. 2006. (First Virtuestm for Toddlers Ser.). 20p. (J). 5.99 (978-0-7847-1576-5(9), 04070) Standard Publishing.

Harris, R. Craig. I'm Walking, I'm Running, I'm Jumping, I'm Hopping. Harris, Richard. 2005. (ENG.). 32p. 16.95 (978-0-9704504-1-8(9)) Hampton Roads Publishing Co., Inc.

Harris, Sharon, jt. illus. see Harris, Joel.

Harris, Steve J. Turtle's Way: Loggy, Greeny & Leather. Hixon, Mara Uman. 2004. 25p. (J). (gr. -1-3). 16.00 (978-1-887774-20-8(3), Wynden) Canmore Pr.

Harris, Steven, et al. Deadpool Classic - Volume 4. Kelly, Joe. 2011. (ENG.). 296p. (YA). (gr. 8-17). pap. 29.99 (978-0-7851-5302-3(0)) Marvel Worldwide, Inc.

Harris, Tiffany. Freddie the Frog & the Bass Clef Monster. Burch, Sharon. 2010. (ENG.). 44p. (gr. -1-4). 24.99 incl. audio compact disk (978-0-9747454-8-0(0), 0974745480) Mystic Publishing.

Harris, Todd. The Hero's Guide to Being an Outlaw. Healy, Christopher. 2014. (Hero's Guide Ser.: 3). (ENG.). 528p. (J). (gr. 3-7). 16.99 (978-0-06-211848-6(X), Walden Pond Pr.) HarperCollins Pubs.

—The Hero's Guide to Saving Your Kingdom. Healy, Christopher. (Hero's Guide Ser.: 1). (ENG.). (J). (gr. 3-7). 2013. 480p. pap. 7.99 (978-0-06-211745-8(9)); 2012. 448p. 16.99 (978-0-06-211743-4(2)) HarperCollins Pubs. (Walden Pond Pr.).

—The Hero's Guide to Storming the Castle. Healy, Christopher. 2013. (Hero's Guide Ser.: 2). (ENG.). 496p. (J). (gr. 3-7). 16.99 (978-0-06-211845-5(5), Walden Pond Pr.) HarperCollins Pubs.

Harris, Tony. The Invincible Iron Man(r): Disassembled. 2007. (ENG.). 144p. (YA). (gr. 8-17). pap. 14.99 (978-0-7851-1653-0(2)) Marvel Worldwide, Inc.

Harris, Wayne. Captain Clawbeak & the Ghostly Galleon. Morgan, Anne. 2007. (Captain Clawbeak Ser.: 3). (ENG.). 144p. (J). (gr. 2-4). pap. 11.99 (978-1-74166-152-1(8)) Random Hse. Australia AUS. Dist: Independent Pubs. Group.

—Captain Clawbeak & the Red Herring. Morgan, Anne. 2006. (Captain Clawbeak Ser.: 1). (ENG.). 144p. (J). (gr. 2-4). pap. 13.99 (978-1-74166-140-8(4)) Random Hse. Australia AUS. Dist: Independent Pubs. Group.

—DragonQuest. Baillie, Allan. 2013. (ENG.). 40p. (J). (gr. k-4). 16.99 (978-0-7636-6617-0(3)) Candlewick Pr.

Harrison, jt. illus. see Harrison, Nancy.

Harrison, Erica. Box of Fairies. 2005. 6p. (J). 11.95 (978-0-7945-1125-8(2), Usborne) EDC Publishing.

—Cowboy Things to Make & Do. Bone, Emily. 2008. (Activity Bks). 34p. (J). (gr. 1). pap. 6.99 (978-0-7945-2077-9(4), Usborne) EDC Publishing.

Harrison, Erica, et al. Monster Things to Make & Do. Allman, Howard, photos by. Gilpin, Rebecca. 2006. (Usborne Activities Ser.). 32p. (J). (gr. -1-3). pap. 6.99 (978-0-7945-1354-2(9), Usborne) EDC Publishing.

Harrison, Erica. The Usborne Book of Drawing, Doodling & Coloring for Christmas. Watt, Fiona. 2010. 96p. (J). (gr. -1-3). pap. 13.99 (978-0-7945-2918-5(6)) EDC Publishing.

—The Usborne Color by Numbers Book. Watt, Fiona. 2014. (ENG.). (J). pap. 5.99 (978-0-7945-3251-2(9), Usborne) EDC Publishing.

Harrison, Erica, et al. The Usborne Little Boys' Activity Book. MacLaine, James & Bowman, Lucy. Watt, Fiona, ed. 2014. (ENG.). 64p. (J). pap. 9.99 (978-0-7945-2888-1(0), Usborne) EDC Publishing.

—The Usborne Little Children's Travel Activity Book. MacLaine, James. Watt, Fiona, ed. 2013. (Activity Books for Little Children Ser.). (ENG.). 63p. (J). pap. 9.99 (978-0-7945-3127-0(X), Usborne) EDC Publishing.

—The Usborne Little Girls' Activity Book. Bowman, Lucy & MacLaine, James. Watt, Fiona, ed. 2014. (ENG.). 64p. (J). pap. 9.99 (978-0-7945-2790-7(6), Usborne) EDC Publishing.

Harrison, Erica. Wizard, Pirate & Princess Things to Make & Do. Gilpin, Rebecca & Brocklehurst, Ruth. 2006. 96p. (J). (gr. 1-4). 14.99 (978-0-7945-1415-0(4), Usborne) EDC Publishing.

—365 Things to Make & Do. Watt, Fiona. 2008. (Usborne Activities Ser.). 127p. (J). (gr. 1). 24.99 (978-0-7945-1954-4(7), Usborne) EDC Publishing.

Harrison, Erica. Monster Snap. Harrison, Erica. 2007. (Card Games Ser.). 52p. (J). 8.99 (978-0-7945-1449-5(9), Usborne) EDC Publishing.

Harrison, Erica & Lovell, Katie. The Usborne Book of Drawing, Doodling & Coloring Book. Watt, Fiona. 2010. 126p. (J). pap. 13.99 (978-0-7945-2788-4(4)) EDC Publishing.

Harrison, Freya. The Owner's Manual for Driving Your Adolescent Brain. Deak, JoAnn & Deak, Terrence. 2013. (ENG.). 72p. (gr. 3-10). pap. 15.95 (978-1-939775-02-3(7), 9781939775023) Little Pickle Press LLC.

Harrison, Hannah E., jt. illus. see Hawkes, Kevin.

Harrison, Harry. A Dirty Story. Brennan, Sarah. 2012. (ENG.). 24p. (J). 21.95 (978-1-937160-26-5(2)) Eliassen Creative.

—An Even Dirtier Story. Brennan, Sarah. 2012. (ENG.). 24p. (J). 21.95 (978-1-937160-27-2(0)) Eliassen Creative.

—Rock Tales. Fletcher, Chris. 2012. (ENG.). 72p. (J). pap., pap. 13.95 (978-1-84771-380-3(7)) Y Lolfa GBR. Dist: Dufour Editions, Inc.

—The Tale of Chester Choi. Brennan, Sarah. 2013. (ENG.). 32p. (J). 24.95 (978-1-937160-16-6(5)) Eliassen Creative.

—The Tale of Oswald Ox. Brennan, Sarah. 2012. (J). (ENG.). 32p. (978-1-937160-24-1(6)); 36p. pap. (978-988-18882-8-0(X)) Auspicious Times.

—The Tale of Pin Yin Panda. Brennan, Sarah. 2012. (ENG.). 32p. (J). 24.95 (978-1-937160-15-9(7)) Eliassen Creative.

—The Tale of Rhonda Rabbit. Brennan, Sarah. 2012. (ENG.). 32p. (J). 24.95 (978-1-937160-22-7(X)) Eliassen Creative.

—The Tale of Run Run Rat. Brennan, Sarah. 2012. (ENG.). 32p. (J). 24.95 (978-1-937160-25-8(4)) Eliassen Creative.

—The Tale of Sybil Snake. Brennan, Sarah. 2012. (ENG.). 32p. (J). (978-1-937160-53-1(X)) Auspicious Times.

—The Tale of Temujin. Brennan, Sarah. 2012. (ENG.). 32p. (J). (978-1-937160-23-4(8)) Auspicious Times.

Harrison, Joanna. Paw Power. Wells, Kitty. 2011. (Pocket Cats Ser.). (ENG.). 208p. (J). (gr. 1-4). lib. bdg. (978-0-385-75202-2(4)) Fickling, David Bks.

Harrison, John. Fergal Onions. Harrison, John. 2004. 36p. (978-0-7022-3448-4(6)) Univ. of Queensland Pr.

Harrison, Kenny. Hide & Seek Harry at the Playground. Harrison, Kenny. 2015. (ENG.). 20p. (J). (-k). bds. 6.99 (978-0-7636-7347-5(1)) Candlewick Pr.

—Hide & Seek Harry on the Farm. Harrison, Kenny. 2015. (ENG.). 20p. (J). (-k). bds. 6.99 (978-0-7636-7370-3(6)) Candlewick Pr.

Harrison, Laura. Sir Cook, the Knight? Mortensen, Erik. 2008. (978-0-9782026-5-1(1)) Crackjaw Publishing.

Harrison-Lever, Brian. In Flanders Fields. Jorgensen, Norman. 2003. (ENG.). 32p. (J). (gr. -1-3). 16.95 (978-1-894965-01-9(9)) Simply Read Bks. CAN. Dist: Ingram Pub. Services.

—In Flanders Fields. Jorgenson, Norman. 2010. (ENG.). 32p. (J). (gr. -1-3). pap. 9.95 (978-1-894965-83-5(3)) Simply Read Bks. CAN. Dist: Ingram Pub. Services.

Harrison, Nancy. Ancient Egypt Dot-to-Dot. Joachim, Jean C. 2006. (Connect the Dots & Color Ser.). (ENG.). 80p. (J). (gr. 1-4). per. 5.95 (978-1-4027-2880-8(8)) Sterling Publishing Co., Inc.

—The Boy Who Cried Wolf. Berendes, Mary & Aesop. 2010. (Aesop's Fables Ser.). (ENG.). 24p. (J). (gr. k-3). 28.50 (978-1-60253-524-4(8), 200028) Child's World, Inc., The.

—The Land of Counterpane. Stevenson, Robert Louis. 2011. (Poetry for Children Ser.). (ENG.). 24p. (J). (gr. k-3). 27.07 (978-1-60973-152-6(2), 201183) Child's World, Inc., The.

—The Maid & the Milk Pail. Berendes, Mary & Aesop. 2010. (Aesop's Fables Ser.). (ENG.). 24p. (J). (gr. k-3). 28.50 (978-1-60253-526-8(4), 200030) Child's World, Inc., The.

—¿Quién Fue Harriet Tubman? (Who Was Harriet Tubman?) McDonough, Yona Zeldis. 2009. (¿Quién Fue... ? / Who Was... ? Ser.). (SPA.). 112p. (gr. 3-5). pap. 9.99 (978-1-60396-423-4(1)) Santillana USA Publishing Co., Inc.

Harrison, Nancy, et al. Who Is Dolly Parton? Kelley, True. 2014. (Who Was... ? Ser.). (ENG.). 112p. (J). (gr. 3-7). 4.99 (978-0-448-47892-0(7), Grosset & Dunlap) Penguin Publishing Group.

Harrison, Nancy. Who Is (Your Name Here)? The Story of My Life. Manzanero, Paula K. 2015. (Who Was... ? Ser.). (ENG.). 112p. (J). (gr. 3-7). 8.99 (978-0-448-48715-1(2), Grosset & Dunlap) Penguin Publishing Group.

Harrison, Nancy. Who Was Anne Frank? Abramson, Ann. 2007. (Who Was... ? Ser.). (ENG.). 112p. (J). (gr. 3-7). pap. 5.99 (978-0-448-44482-6(8), Grosset & Dunlap) Penguin Publishing Group.

—Who Was Anne Frank? Abramson, Ann. 2007. (Who Was... ? Ser.). 103p. (gr. 2-6). 15.00 (978-0-7569-8166-2(2)) Perfection Learning Corp.

—Who Was Anne Frank? Abramson, Ann. ed. 2007. (Who Was... ? Biographies Ser.). 103p. (J). (gr. 4-7). 16.00 (978-1-4177-6854-7(1), Turtleback) Turtleback Bks.

—Who Was Charles Darwin? Hopkinson, Deborah. 2005. (Who Was... ? Ser.). (ENG.). 112p. (J). (gr. 3-7). pap. 5.99 (978-0-448-43764-4(3), Grosset & Dunlap) Penguin Publishing Group.

—Who Was Christopher Columbus? Bader, Bonnie. 2013. (Who Was... ? Ser.). (ENG.). 112p. (J). (gr. 3-7). pap. 5.99 (978-0-448-46333-9(4), Grosset & Dunlap) Penguin Publishing Group.

—Who Was Dr. Seuss? Pascal, Janet. 2011. (Who Was... ? Ser.). (ENG.). 112p. (J). (gr. 3-7). pap. 5.99 (978-0-448-45585-3(4), Grosset & Dunlap) Penguin Publishing Group.

—Who Was Harriet Tubman? McDonough, Yona Zeldis. 2003. (Who Was... ? Ser.). 106p. (gr. 4-7). 15.00 (978-0-7569-1590-2(2)) Perfection Learning Corp.

—Who Was Helen Keller? O'Brien, John A. 2003. (Who Was... ? Ser.). 107p. (J). (gr. 3-7). 12.65 (978-0-7569-1596-4(1)) Perfection Learning Corp.

—Who Was Helen Keller? O'Brien, John A. & Thompson, Gare. ed. 2003. (Who Was... ? Biographies Ser.). 107p. (J). (gr. 3-7). 16.00 (978-0-613-63485-4(3), Turtleback) Turtleback Bks.

—Who Was Jacques Cousteau? Medina, Nico & Putra, Dede. 2015. (Who Was... ? Ser.). (ENG.). 112p. (J). (gr. 3-7). 5.99 (978-0-448-48234-7(7), Grosset & Dunlap) Penguin Publishing Group.

—Who Was Jim Henson? Holub, Joan. 2010. (Who Was... ? Ser.). (ENG.). 112p. (J). (gr. 3-7). pap. 5.99 (978-0-448-45406-1(8), Grosset & Dunlap) Penguin Publishing Group.

—Who Was Mother Teresa? Gigliotti, Jim. 2015. (Who Was... ? Ser.). (ENG.). 112p. (J). (gr. 3-7). 5.99 (978-0-448-48299-6(1), Grosset & Dunlap) Penguin Publishing Group.

Harrison, Nancy, et al. Who Was Steve Jobs? Pollack, Pam et al. 2012. (Who Was... ? Ser.). (ENG.). 112p. (J). (gr. 3-7). pap. 5.99 (978-0-448-46211-0(7), Grosset & Dunlap) Penguin Publishing Group.

Harrison, Nancy. Who Was Walt Disney? Stewart, Whitney. 2009. (Who Was... ? Ser.). (ENG.). 112p. (J). (gr. 3-7). pap. 4.99 (978-0-448-45052-0(6), Grosset & Dunlap) Penguin Publishing Group.

Harrison, Nancy & Copeland, Gregory. Who Was Harriet Beecher Stowe? Rau, Dana Meachen. 2015. (Who Was... ? Ser.). (ENG.). 112p. (J). (gr. 3-7). 5.99 (978-0-448-48301-6(7), Grosset & Dunlap) Penguin Publishing Group.

Harrison, Nancy & Geyer, Mark Edward. Who Was Ulysses S. Grant? Stine, Megan. 2014. (Who Was... ? Ser.). (ENG.). 112p. (J). (gr. 3-7). 5.99 (978-0-448-47894-4(3), Grosset & Dunlap) Penguin Publishing Group.

Harrison, Nancy & Groff, David. Who Was Clara Barton? Spinner, Stephanie. 2014. (Who Was... ? Ser.). (ENG.). 112p. (J). (gr. 3-7). 5.99 (978-0-448-47953-8(2), Grosset & Dunlap) Penguin Publishing Group.

Harrison, Nancy & Harrison. Who Was Queen Elizabeth? Eding, June. 2008. (Who Was... ? Ser.). (ENG.). 112p. (J). (gr. 3-7). pap. 5.99 (978-0-448-44839-8(4), Grosset & Dunlap) Penguin Publishing Group.

Harrison, Nancy & Hergenrother, Max. Who Was Queen Victoria? Gigliotti, Jim. 2014. (Who Was... ? Ser.). (ENG.). 112p. (J). (gr. 3-7). 4.99 (978-0-448-48182-1(0), Grosset & Dunlap) Penguin Publishing Group.

Harrison, Nancy & Hoare, Jerry. Who Was Theodore Roosevelt? Burgan, Michael. 2014. (Who Was... ? Ser.). (ENG.). 112p. (J). (gr. 3-7). 5.99 (978-0-448-47945-3(1), Grosset & Dunlap) Penguin Publishing Group.

Harrison, Nancy & Marchesi, Stephen. Who Was Claude Monet? Waldron, Ann. 2009. (Who Was... ? Ser.). (ENG.). 112p. (J). (gr. 3-7). pap. 5.99 (978-0-448-44985-2(4), Grosset & Dunlap) Penguin Publishing Group.

—Who Was Neil Armstrong? Edwards, Roberta. 2008. (Who Was... ? Ser.). (ENG.). 112p. (J). (gr. 3-7). pap. 5.99 (978-0-448-44907-4(2), Grosset & Dunlap) Penguin Publishing Group.

—Who Was Rosa Parks? McDonough, Yona Zeldis. 2010. (Who Was... ? Ser.). (ENG.). 112p. (J). (gr. 3-7). pap. 4.99 (978-0-448-45442-9(4), Grosset & Dunlap) Penguin Publishing Group.

Harrison, Nancy & O'Brien, John. Who Is Barack Obama? Edwards, Roberta. 2009. (Who Was... ? Ser.). (ENG.). 112p. (J). (gr. 3-7). pap. 4.99 (978-0-448-45330-9(4), Grosset & Dunlap) Penguin Publishing Group.

—Who Is Bob Dylan? O'Connor, Jim. 2013. (Who Was... ? Ser.). (ENG.). 112p. (J). (gr. 3-7). 14.99 (978-0-448-46589-0(2)); pap. 5.99 (978-0-448-46461-9(6)) Penguin Publishing Group. (Grosset & Dunlap).

—Who Was Abraham Lincoln? Pascal, Janet. 2008. (Who Was... ? Ser.). (ENG.). 112p. (J). (gr. 3-7). pap. 4.99 (978-0-448-44886-2(6), Grosset & Dunlap) Penguin Publishing Group.

—Who Was Franklin Roosevelt? Frith, Margaret. 2010. (Who Was... ? Ser.). (ENG.). 112p. (J). (gr. 3-7). pap. 5.99 (978-0-448-45346-0(0), Grosset & Dunlap) Penguin Publishing Group.

—Who Was Jackie Robinson? Herman, Gail. 2010. (Who Was... ? Ser.). (ENG.). 112p. (J). (gr. 3-7). pap. 5.99 (978-0-448-45557-0(9), Grosset & Dunlap) Penguin Publishing Group.

—Who Was Paul Revere? Edwards, Roberta. 2011. (Who Was... ? Ser.). (ENG.). 112p. (J). (gr. 3-7). pap. 5.99 (978-0-448-45715-4(6), Grosset & Dunlap) Penguin Publishing Group.

—Who Was Robert E. Lee? Bader, Bonnie. 2014. (Who Was... ? Ser.). (ENG.). 112p. (J). (gr. 3-7). 5.99 (978-0-448-47909-5(5), Grosset & Dunlap) Penguin Publishing Group.

—Who Was Thomas Jefferson? Fradin, Dennis Brindell. 2003. (Who Was... ? Ser.). (ENG.). 112p. (J). (gr. 3-7). pap. 5.99 (978-0-448-43145-1(9), Grosset & Dunlap) Penguin Publishing Group.

Harrison, Nancy, jt. illus. see Eldridge, Jim.
Harrison, Nancy, jt. illus. see Foley, Tim.
Harrison, Nancy, jt. illus. see Geyer, Mark Edward.
Harrison, Nancy, jt. illus. see Hammond, Ted.
Harrison, Nancy, jt. illus. see Hergenrother, Max.
Harrison, Nancy, jt. illus. see Hoare, Jerry.
Harrison, Nancy, jt. illus. see Kelley, True.
Harrison, Nancy, jt. illus. see Lacey, Mike.
Harrison, Nancy, jt. illus. see Marchesi, Stephen.
Harrison, Nancy, jt. illus. see Mather, Daniel.
Harrison, Nancy, jt. illus. see Moore, Jonathan.
Harrison, Nancy, jt. illus. see O'Brien, John A.
Harrison, Nancy, jt. illus. see O'Brien, John.
Harrison, Nancy, jt. illus. see Putra, Dede.
Harrison, Nancy, jt. illus. see Squier, Robert.
Harrison, Nancy, jt. illus. see Thomson, Andrew.
Harrison, Nancy, jt. illus. see Weber, Jill.
Harrison, Nancy, jt. illus. see Wolf, Elizabeth.

Harrison, Nicholas. Grandma Asks: Were You Good at School Today? Harris, Patrice. 2013. 26p. pap. 10.00 (978-0-9892358-5-3(8)) CLF Publishing.

Harrison, Steve. The Lion Graphic Bible: The Whole Story from Genesis to Revelation. Maddox, Mike & Anderson, Jeff. 2004. (ENG.). 256p. (J). (gr. 5-12). pap. 12.99 (978-0-7459-4923-9(1)) Lion Hudson PLC GBR. Dist: Independent Pubs. Group.

Harrison, T. Latin: A Fresh Approach. Seigel, Mike. 2003. (ENG.). 174p. pap. 19.95 (978-1-898855-27-9(7)) Anthem Pr. GBR. Dist: Books International, Inc.

Harrold, Brian. Catchin' Cooties Consuelo. Thompson, Tolya L. 2004. (Smarties Ser.: 3). (SPA.). (J). 16.00 (978-0-9708296-3-4(9)) Savor Publishing Hse., Inc.

Harry, Rebecca. Foxes in the Snow, 11. Emmett, Jonathan. 3rd ed. 2012. (ENG.). 32p. (J). (gr. -1-k). pap. 9.99 (978-0-230-71229-4(0)) Macmillan Pubs., Ltd. GBR. Dist: Independent Pubs. Group.

—Little Lion. 2007. (Noisy Jungle Babies Ser.). (ENG.). 8p. (J). (gr. -1 — 1). bds. 5.99 (978-0-7641-6036-3(2)) Barron's Educational Series, Inc.

—This Way, Ruby! Emmett, Jonathan. 2010. (ENG.). 32p. (J). (gr. -1-3). pap. 6.99 (978-0-545-16910-3(0), Scholastic Paperbacks) Scholastic, Inc.

Harry, Rebecca. Snow Bunny's Christmas Wish. Harry, Rebecca. 2013. (ENG.). 32p. (J). (gr. -1-3). 16.99 (978-0-545-54103-9(4), Orchard Bks.) Scholastic, Inc.

Harston, David. Michigan Coloring Book. 2005. 24p. (J). pap. (978-1-893624-32-0(3)) Penrod/Hiawatha Co.

—Missy Moo, Where Are You off to? Surfing Adventure. Mindes, Erin. 2011. (J). 14.95 (978-0-9841558-8-0(0)) Tasty Minstrel Games.

Harston, Jerry. Believe & You're There When Ammon Was a Missionary. Johnson, Alice W. & Warner, Allison H. 2010. (J). (978-1-60641-247-3(7)) Deseret Bk. Co.

—Believe & You're There When Lehi Left Jerusalem. Johnson, Alice W. & Warner, Allison H. 2010. (J). (978-1-60641-246-6(9)) Deseret Bk. Co.

—Believe & You're There When the Night Was Bright As Day. Johnson, Alice W. & Warner, Allison H. 2010. viii, 81p. (J). (978-1-60641-249-7(3)) Deseret Bk. Co.

—Believe & You're There When the Prince of Peace Was Born. Johnson, Alice W. & Warner, Allison H. 2009. 74p. (J). (978-1-60641-200-8(0)) Deseret Bk. Co.

—A Child's Collection of Parables. Wach, Randy-Lynne. 2007. 13.95 *(978-1-59038-724-5(4))* Deseret Bk. Co.

—How to Make Snack Mix: Math B. Oppenlander, Meredith. l.t. ed. 2003. (ENG.). 16p. (gr. k-1). pap. 5.95 *(978-1-57874-004-8(5))* Kaeden Corp.

—More of My First Book of Mormon Stories. 2005. 32p. (J). 13.99 *(978-1-59038-402-2(4))* Deseret Bk. Co.

—My First Scripture Stories. Buck, Deanna Draper. 2014. (J). pap. 14.99 *(978-1-60907-948-2(5))* Deseret Bk. Co.

—My First Story of the First Christmas. Buck, Deanna Draper. 2006. 24p. (J). 13.95 *(978-1-59038-635-4(3))* Deseret Bk. Co.

—My Magic Bike. Worthington, Lisa & Moon, Susan. 2006. (ENG.). 16p. (gr. k-2). pap. 5.95 *(978-1-57874-039-0(8))* Kaeden Corp.

—Sleepy Polar Bear. Hiris, Monica. l.t. ed. 2006. (ENG.). 24p. (gr. k-2). pap. 5.95 *(978-1-57874-072-7(X)*, Kaeden Bks.) Kaeden Corp.

—Sneezles & Wheezles. Passey, Marion. 2006. 32p. (J). (gr. -1-3). 15.99 *(978-1-55517-912-0(6))* Cedar Fort, Inc./CFI Distribution.

Hart, James. Academy All-Stars. Loughlin, Patrick. 2015. (Glenn Maxwell Ser.). (ENG.). 192p. (J). (gr. 3). 13.99 ***(978-0-85798-609-2(0))*** Random Hse. Australia AUS. Dist: Independent Pubs. Group.

—State Showdown. Loughlin, Patrick. 2015. (Glenn Maxwell Ser.: 3). (ENG.). 192p. (J). (gr. 4-7). pap. 12.99 ***(978-0-85798-611-5(2))*** Random Hse. Australia AUS. Dist: Independent Pubs. Group.

—World Domination. Loughlin, Patrick. 2015. (Glenn Maxwell Ser.: 4). (ENG.). 192p. (J). (gr. 4-7). pap. 12.99 ***(978-0-85798-613-9(9))*** Random Hse. Australia AUS. Dist: Independent Pubs. Group.

Hart, Jason, jt. illus. see Rosen, Anne.

Hart, Roger. Favourite Maori Legends. Reed, A. W. rev. ed. 2015. 160p. pap. 25.00 ***(978-1-877514-56-2(X))*** Oratia Media NZL. Dist: Casemate Pubs. & Bk. Distributors, LLC.

Hart, Sam & Fujita, Artur. Outlaw: The Legend of Robin Hood. Lee, Tony. 2009. (ENG.). 160p. (J). (gr. 5). 21.99 *(978-0-7636-4399-7(8))*; pap. 12.99 *(978-0-7636-4400-0(5))* Candlewick Pr.

Hart, Sam, jt. illus. see Lee, Tony.

Hartas, Leo. Crypt of the Vampire. Morris, Dave. 2013. 122p. pap. *(978-1-909905-05-4(4))* Fabled Lands Publishing.

Hartelius, Margaret A. & Eagle, Cameron. Zoom! (reissue) The Complete Paper Airplane Kit. Hartelius, Margaret A. ed. 2003. (Trend Friends Ser.). (ENG.). 64p. (J). (gr. -1-3). pap. 8.99 *(978-0-448-43174-1(2)*, Grosset & Dunlap) Penguin Publishing Group.

Harter, Debbie. Bear about Town Gift Wrap. (J). 4.99 *(978-1-84148-622-2(1))* Barefoot Bks., Inc.

—Bear about Town (L'Ours Dans la Ville) Blackstone, Stella. 2010. (ENG & FRE.). 24p. (J). (gr. -1-1). pap. 6.99 *(978-1-84686-376-9(7))* Barefoot Bks., Inc.

—Bear about Town (Oso en las Ciudad) Blackstone, Stella. 2010. (ENG & SPA.). 24p. (J). (gr. -1-1). pap. 6.99 *(978-1-84686-377-6(5))* Barefoot Bks., Inc.

—Bear at Home. Blackstone, Stella. 2003. (Bear Ser.). (ENG.). 24p. (J). (gr. -1). pap. 6.99 *(978-1-84148-701-4(5))* Barefoot Bks., Inc.

—Bear at Home (Oso en Casa) Blackstone, Stella. 2010. (ENG & SPA.). 24p. (J). (gr. -1-1). 6.99 *(978-1-84686-422-3(4))* Barefoot Bks., Inc.

—Bear at Home/L'ours a la Maison. Blackstone, Stella. 2010. (ENG & FRE.). 24p. (J). (gr. -1-1). pap. 6.99 *(978-1-84686-421-6(6))* Barefoot Bks., Inc.

—Bear at Work. Blackstone, Stella. 2011. (ENG.). 24p. (J). (gr. -1-2). bds. 6.99 *(978-1-84686-554-1(9))* Barefoot Bks., Inc.

—Bear in Sunshine. Blackstone, Stella. 2013. (SPA & ENG.). 24p. (J). bds. 7.99 *(978-1-78285-031-1(7))* Barefoot Bks., Inc.

—Bear on a Bike (Oso en Bicicleta) Blackstone, Stella & Barefoot Books. 2014. (ENG & SPA.). 32p. (J). 6.99 *(978-1-78285-079-3(1))* Barefoot Bks., Inc.

—Bear Takes a Trip (Oso Se Va de Viaje) Blackstone, Stella. 2013. (ENG & SPA.). 24p. (J). (gr. k-1). 6.99 *(978-1-84686-945-7(5))* Barefoot Bks., Inc.

—Bear's Birthday. Blackstone, Stella. 2011.Tr. of El Cumpleanos de Oso. (ENG.). 24p. (J). (gr. -1-2). pap. 6.99 *(978-1-84686-515-2(8))*; bds. 6.99 *(978-1-84686-516-9(6))* Barefoot Bks., Inc.

—Bear's Birthday (L'Anniversaire de l'Ours) Blackstone, Stella. 2013. (ENG & FRE.). 24p. (J). (gr. k-1). pap. 6.99 *(978-1-84686-944-0(7))* Barefoot Bks., Inc.

—Bear's Birthday/El Cumpleanos de Oso. Blackstone, Stella. 2013. (ENG & SPA.). 24p. (J). (gr. k-1). 6.99 *(978-1-84686-943-3(9))* Barefoot Bks., Inc.

—Bear's Busy Year. 12p. (J). 12.99 *(978-1-84148-689-5(2))* Barefoot Bks., Inc.

—Bear's School Day. Blackstone, Stella & Barefoot Books Staff. 24p. 6.99 *(978-1-78285-085-4(6))* Barefoot Bks., Inc.

—Creepy Crawly Calypso. Langham, Tony. (ENG.). 32p. (J). 2007. pap. 6.99 *(978-1-84686-133-8(0))*; 2004. 16.99 *(978-1-84148-699-4(X))* Barefoot Bks., Inc.

—A Dragon on the Doorstep. Blackstone, Stella. (ENG.). 32p. (J). 2012. pap. 9.99 *(978-1-84686-826-9(2))*; 2006. pap. 9.99 *(978-1-905236-66-4(2))*; 2006. (gr. -1-k). pap. 6.99 *(978-1-84686-032-4(6))*; 2005. (gr. -1-1). 15.99 *(978-1-84148-227-9(7))* Barefoot Bks., Inc.

—La Familia Activa de Oso. Blackstone, Stella. Sarfatti, Esther, tr. 2003. (Bear Ser.). (SPA.). 24p. (J). pap. 6.99 *(978-1-84148-777-9(5))* Barefoot Bks., Inc.

—Herb, the Vegetarian Dragon. Bass, Jules. 2005. 32p. (J). (gr. 1-5). reprint ed. pap. 6.99 *(978-1-84148-127-2(0))* Barefoot Bks., Inc.

—Herb, the Vegetarian Dragon: Book & Bendo Gift Set. Bass, Jules. 2005. 32p. (J). 14.99 *(978-1-905236-43-5(3))* Barefoot Bks., Inc.

—Herb's Vegetable Patch. (Bear Series Gift Wrap Ser.). (J). 50.00 *(978-1-84148-506-5(3))* Barefoot Bks., Inc.

—L'Ours au Soleil. Blackstone, Stella & Champion, Servane. 2009.Tr. of Bear in Sunshine. (FRE & ENG.). 24p. (J). pap. 6.99 *(978-1-84686-388-2(0))* Barefoot Bks., Inc.

—L'Ours Dans le Carré. Blackstone, Stella & Champion, Servane. 2009.Tr. of Bear in a Square. (FRE & ENG.). 24p. (J). pap. 6.99 *(978-1-84686-386-8(4))* Barefoot Bks., Inc.

—L'Ours Fait un Voyage. Blackstone, Stella & Parker, Elizabeth. 2013.Tr. of Bear Takes a Trip. (FRE & ENG.). 24p. (J). (gr. k-1). pap. 6.99 *(978-1-84686-946-4(3))* Barefoot Bks., Inc.

—Oso Bajo el Sol. Blackstone, Stella & Meza-Riedewald, Leticia. 2009. (SPA & ENG.). 24p. (J). 6.99 *(978-1-84686-389-9(9))* Barefoot Bks., Inc.

—Oso Bajo el Sol. Blackstone, Stella. Sarfatti, Esther, tr. 2003. (Bear Ser.). (SPA.). 24p. (J). pap. 6.99 *(978-1-84148-778-6(3))* Barefoot Bks., Inc.

—Oso en Bicicleta. Blackstone, Stella. Sarfatti, Esther, tr. 2003. (Bear Ser.). (SPA.). 32p. (J). pap. 6.99 *(978-1-84148-775-5(9))* Barefoot Bks., Inc.

—Oso en Casa. Blackstone, Stella. Sarfatti, Esther, tr. 2003. (Bear Ser.). (SPA.). 24p. (J). pap. 6.99 *(978-1-84148-779-3(1))* Barefoot Bks., Inc.

—Oso en la Ciudad. Blackstone, Stella. Sarfatti, Esther, tr. 2003. (Bear Ser.). (SPA.). 24p. (J). pap. 6.99 *(978-1-84148-776-2(7))* Barefoot Bks., Inc.

—Oso en un Cuadrado. Blackstone, Stella. Sarfatti, Esther, tr. 2003. (Bear Ser.). (SPA.). 24p. (J). pap. 6.99 *(978-1-84148-774-8(0))* Barefoot Bks., Inc.

—Oso en un Cuadrado. Blackstone, Stella & Meza-Riedewald, Leticia. ed. 2009. (SPA & ENG.). 24p. (J). 6.99 *(978-1-84686-387-5(2))* Barefoot Bks., Inc.

—Port Side Pirates! Seaworthy, Oscar & Collins, Mark. 2011. (ENG.). 30p. (J). pap. 9.99 *(978-1-84686-667-8(7))* Barefoot Bks., Inc.

—Snow Bear Gift Wrap. (J). 4.99 *(978-1-84148-987-2(5))* Barefoot Bks., Inc.

—Thesaurus Rex. Steinberg, Laya. (ENG.). 24p. (J). 2005. pap. 6.99 *(978-1-84148-180-7(7))*; 2003. 15.99 *(978-1-84148-042-8(8))* Barefoot Bks., Inc.

—Thesaurus Rex Finds a Friend. Steinberg, Laya. 2006. (J). *(978-1-905236-48-0(4))* Barefoot Bks., Inc.

—Walking Through the Jungle. Blackstone, Stella. 2004. (ENG.). 32p. (J). (gr. -1-k). pap. 6.99 *(978-1-84148-548-5(9))* Barefoot Bks., Inc.

—Walking Through the Jungle. 2004. 30p. (J). *(978-1-85269-807-2(1))*; *(978-1-85269-811-9(X))*; *(978-1-85269-826-3(8))*; *(978-1-85269-831-7(4))*; *(978-1-85269-841-6(1))*; *(978-1-85269-846-1(2))*; *(978-1-85269-856-0(X))*; *(978-1-85269-861-4(6))*; *(978-1-85269-866-9(7))*; (ENG & SPA.). *(978-1-85269-871-3(3))*; *(978-1-85269-876-8(4))*; *(978-1-85269-881-2(0))*; *(978-1-85269-886-7(1))* Mantra Lingua.

—Walking Through the Jungle. Blackstone, Stella. 32p. (J). 2006. (ENG.). 9.99 *(978-1-905236-99-2(9))*; 2004. 9.99 *(978-1-84148-182-1(3))* Barefoot Bks., Inc.

—Where's the Cat? Blackstone, Stella. 2003. (ENG.). 24p. (J). (gr. k-2). bds. 6.99 *(978-1-84148-607-9(8))* Barefoot Bks., Inc.

Harter, Debbie. The Animal Boogie. Harter, Debbie. 32p. pap. 6.99 *(978-1-84148-996-4(4))*; 2005. (ENG.). (J). (gr. -1-2). 6.99 *(978-1-905236-60-2(3))* Barefoot Bks., Inc.

—The Animal Boogie Fun Activities. Harter, Debbie. Barefoot College Staff. 2009. (ENG.). 16p. (J). pap. 5.99 *(978-1-84686-285-4(X))* Barefoot Bks., Inc.

—Bear at Work. Harter, Debbie. Blackstone, Stella. 2008. (Bear Ser.). (ENG.). 24p. (J). (gr. -1-k). 6.99 *(978-1-84686-110-9(1))* Barefoot Bks., Inc.

—Bear at Work: Fun Activities. Harter, Debbie. Blackstone, Stella. 2010. (ENG.). 16p. (J). (gr. -1-3). pap. 5.99 *(978-1-84686-444-5(5))* Barefoot Bks., Inc.

—Cha-Cha-Cha en la Selva. Harter, Debbie. Canetti, Yanitzia, tr. 2003.Tr. of Animal Boogie. (SPA.). 32p. (J). pap. 6.99 *(978-1-84148-265-1(X))* Barefoot Bks., Inc.

—Cha-Cha-Cha en la Selva. Harter, Debbie. 2003. (SPA.). 32p. (J). 9.99 *(978-1-84148-913-1(1))* Barefoot Bks., Inc.

—De Paseo Por la Selva. Harter, Debbie. Ugalde, Raquel, tr. 2003. (SPA.). 32p. (J). pap. 6.99 *(978-1-84148-995-7(6))* Barefoot Bks., Inc.

—Mira Quien Toca Calipso! Harter, Debbie. Langham, Tony. 2009. (SPA.). (J). pap. 6.99 *(978-1-84686-281-6(7))* Barefoot Bks., Inc.

—Walking Through the Jungle. Harter, Debbie. 2004. (ENG & PAN.). 32p. (J). pap. *(978-1-85269-851-5(9))* Mantra Lingua.

—Who Are You? Harter, Debbie. Blackstone, Stella. 2003. (ENG.). 24p. (J). (gr. k-2). bds. 6.99 *(978-1-84148-609-3(4))* Barefoot Bks., Inc.

Harter, Debbie. Walking Through the Jungle: Duke Ecur Neper Xhungel. Harter, Debbie, tr. 2004. 30p. (J). *(978-1-85269-806-5(3))* Mantra Lingua.

—Walking Through the Jungle: Marchant a Travers la Jungle. Harter, Debbie, tr. 2004. (ENG & FRE.). 32p. (J). pap. *(978-1-85269-836-2(5))* Mantra Lingua.

Harter, Debbie & Beaton, Clare. A to Z. (Bear Series Gift Wrap Ser.). (J). 4.99 *(978-1-84148-508-9(X))* Barefoot Bks., Inc.

—1 To 20. (Bear Series Gift Wrap Ser.). (J). 4.99 *(978-1-84148-507-2(1))* Barefoot Bks., Inc.

Hartigan, Meg. A Boy & a Bear: The Children's Relaxation Book. Lite, Lori. 2003. 32p. (J). (gr. -1-5). pap. 11.00 *(978-1-886941-07-6(6)*, 0941) Specialty Pr., Inc.

Hartland, Jessie. How the Dinosaur Got to the Museum. 2013. (How the ... Got to the Museum Ser.). (ENG.). 40p. (J). (gr. 1-4). 17.99 *(978-1-60905-090-0(8))* Blue Apple Bks.

—Messing Around on the Monkey Bars: And Other School Poems for Two Voices. Franco, Betsy. 2009. (ENG.). 48p. (J). (gr. 3-7). 18.99 *(978-0-7636-3174-1(4))* Candlewick Pr.

Hartland, Jessie. Bon Appétit! The Delicious Life of Julia Child. Hartland, Jessie. 2012. (ENG.). 48p. (J). (gr. k-12). 17.99 *(978-0-375-86944-0(1))*; 20.99 *(978-0-375-96944-7(6))* Random Hse. Children's Bks. (Schwartz & Wade Bks.).

Hartley, Jill, photos by. Fruits of India. 2010. (ENG., 24p. (J). (gr. k — 1). bds. 7.95 *(978-81-907546-8-2(8))* Tara Publishing IND. Dist: Perseus-PGW.

—Vegetables of India. 2010. (ENG., 24p. (J). (gr. k — 1). bds. 7.95 *(978-81-907546-9-9(6))* Tara Publishing IND. Dist: Perseus-PGW.

Hartley, Joshua. For the Love of My Pet. The Guide Dog, Thelma. 2012. (Morgan James Kids Ser.). (ENG.). 26p. (gr. k-5). pap. 14.95 *(978-1-61448-338-0(8))* Morgan James Publishing.

Hartley, Stephanie Olga. Between Hither & Yon Where Good Things Go On! Hartley, Stephanie Olga. 2004. (J). bds. *(978-0-9676717-5-8(2))* Freet Publishing.

Hartman, Adrienne. The Children's Travel Journal. Banks, Ann. 2nd ed. 2004. (ENG.). 48p. (gr. 1-11). 19.95 *(978-0-9641262-0-6(6))* Little Bookroom.

Hartman, Carrie. The Clock Struck One: A Time-Telling Tale. Harris, Trudy. 2009. (Math Is Fun! Ser.). (ENG.). 32p. (gr. k-2). 16.95 *(978-0-8225-9067-5(0)*, Millbrook Pr.) Lerner Publishing Group.

—Feelings to Share from A to Z. Snow, Todd & Snow, Peggy. 2007. (ENG.). 32p. (J). pap. 9.99 *(978-1-934277-00-3(2))* Marn Green Publishing, Inc.

—It's Hard to Be a Verb! Cook, Julia. 2008. (ENG.). 32p. (J). (gr. 4-7). pap. 9.95 *(978-1-931636-84-1(2))* National Ctr. For Youth Issues.

—Izzy the Whiz & Passover McClean. Mermelstein, Yael. 2012. (Passover Ser.). (ENG.). 32p. (J). (gr. -1-2). lib. bdg. 17.95 *(978-0-7613-5653-0(3)*, Kar-Ben Publishing) Lerner Publishing Group.

—Izzy the Whiz & Passover Mcclean. Mermelstein, Yael. 2012. (Passover Ser.). (ENG.). 32p. (J). (gr. -1-2). pap. 7.95 *(978-0-7613-5654-7(1)*, Kar-Ben Publishing) Lerner Publishing Group.

—Manners Are Important. Snow, Todd. 2007. (ENG.). 24p. (J). (gr. -1-3). bds. 7.99 *(978-1-934277-05-8(3))* Marn Green Publishing, Inc.

—My Mouth Is a Volcano! Cook, Julia. 2008. 32p. (J). (gr. -1-3). pap. 9.95 *(978-1-931636-85-8(0))* National Ctr. For Youth Issues.

—Personal Space Camp. Cook, Julia. 32p. (J). 2009. 15.95 *(978-1-931636-89-6(3))*; 2008. (gr. -1-3). pap. 9.95 *(978-1-931636-87-2(7))* National Ctr. For Youth Issues.

Hartman, Dan. When the Wolves Returned: Restoring Nature's Balance in Yellowstone. Hartman, Cassie, photos by. Patent, Dorothy Hinshaw. 2008. (ENG.). 40p. (J). (gr. 1-4). 19.99 *(978-0-8027-9686-8(9))* Walker & Co.

Hartman, John, jt. illus. see Feldmeier Sims, Julie.

Hartman, Kurt. Life One. Rifkin, L. 2007. (Nine Lives of Romeo Crumb Ser.). 311p. (J). (gr. 6-8). per. 8.95 *(978-0-9743221-3-1(X))* Stratford Road Pr., Ltd.

—Mystery at Manzanar: A WWII Internment Camp Story, 1 vol. Fein, Eric. 2008. (Historical Fiction Ser.). (ENG.). 56p. (gr. 2-3). pap. 6.25 *(978-1-4342-0847-7(8)*, Graphic Flash) Stone Arch Bks.

—The Nine Lives of Romeo Crumb: Life 6. Rifkin, L. 2010. 246p. (YA). pap. 8.95 *(978-0-9743221-8-6(0))* Stratford Road Pr., Ltd.

—The Nine Lives of Romeo Crumb: Life Five. Rifkin, L. (Lauren). 2009. 169p. (YA). pap. 8.95 *(978-0-9743221-7-9(2))* Stratford Road Pr., Ltd.

Hartman, Nancy Lee. I See Without My Eyes. Hayward, Mark Brauner. 2009. 32p. pap. 12.99 *(978-1-4343-3823-5(1))* AuthorHouse.

Hartman, Scott. ABC Dinosaurs. American Museum of Natural History Staff. 2011. (AMNH ABC Board Bks.). (ENG.). 18p. (J). (gr. -1-k). bds. 7.95 *(978-1-4027-7715-8(9))* Sterling Publishing Co., Inc.

Hartmann, April. The Alpha Building Crew. Leman, Nora. 2005. (J). *(978-1-58987-110-6(3))* Kindermusik International.

Hartmann, Dario. A Gallery Girls Collection: Mermaid. 2005. (Gallery Girls Collection). 64p. (YA). per. 9.95 *(978-0-86562-113-8(6))* Diamond Bk. Distributors.

Hartt, Judy. Believe in A Dream: Overcoming Adversity to Make Childhood Dreams Come True. Hartt, Autumn. 2011. (ENG.). 60p. pap. 14.99 *(978-1-4664-1057-2(4))* CreateSpace Independent Publishing Platform.

Hartter, Sean. Three Things about Animals... And Only One of Them's True! Shannon, Jason. 2nd rev. ed. 2008. (J). per. 12.95 *(978-0-9790889-4-0(1))* CatsCurious Pr.

—Three Things about Bugs... And Only One of Them's True! Shannon, Jason. 2008. (J). per. 12.95 *(978-0-9790889-5-7(X))* CatsCurious Pr.

Hartung, Susan Kathleen. Follow Me, Mittens. Schaefer, Lola M. (My First I Can Read Ser.). 32p. (J). (gr. -1 — 1). 2008. (ENG.). pap. 3.99 *(978-0-06-054667-0(0))*; 2007. (ENG.). 15.99 *(978-0-06-054665-6(4))*; 2007. lib. bdg. 16.89 *(978-0-06-054666-3(2))* HarperCollins Pubs.

—Happy Halloween, Mittens. Schaefer, Lola M. 2010. (My First I Can Read Ser.). (ENG.). 32p. (J). (gr. -1-3). 16.99 *(978-0-06-170222-8(6))*; pap. 3.99 *(978-0-06-170221-1(8))* HarperCollins Pubs.

—Little David Sings for the King, 1 vol. Bowman, Crystal. 2010. (I Can Read! / Little David Ser.). (ENG.). 32p. (J). pap. 3.99 *(978-0-310-71711-9(6))* Zonderkidz.

—Mittens. Schaefer, Lola M. 2007. (My First I Can Read Ser.). (ENG.). 32p. (J). (gr. -1-3). pap. 3.99 *(978-0-06-054661-8(1))* HarperCollins Pubs.

—Mittens. Schaefer, Lola M. 2007. (I Can Read Bks.). 25p. (gr. -1-k). 14.00 *(978-0-7569-8104-4(2))* Perfection Learning Corp.

—Mittens at School. Schaefer, Lola M. 2012. (My First I Can Read Ser.). (ENG.). 32p. (J). (gr. -1-3). 16.99 *(978-0-06-170224-2(2))*; pap. 3.99 *(978-0-06-170223-5(4))* HarperCollins Pubs.

—Mittens, Where Is Max? Schaefer, Lola M. 2011. (My First I Can Read Ser.). (ENG.). 32p. (J). (gr. -1 — 1). 16.99 *(978-0-06-170227-3(7))*; pap. 3.99 *(978-0-06-170226-6(9))* HarperCollins Pubs.

—A Mom for Umande. Faulconer, Maria Fasal. 2014. (ENG.). 32p. (J). (gr. -1-3). 16.99 *(978-0-8037-3762-4(9)*, Dial) Penguin Publishing Group.

—One Leaf Rides the Wind. Mannis, Celeste Davidson. 2005. (ENG.). 32p. (J). (gr. k-3). pap. 6.99 *(978-0-14-240195-8(1)*, Puffin) Penguin Publishing Group.

—One Leaf Rides the Wind. Mannis, Celeste Davidson. 2005. (gr. -1-3). 17.00 *(978-0-7569-5213-6(1))* Perfection Learning Corp.

—Three Scoops & a Fig, 1 vol. Akin, Sara Laux. 2010. (ENG.). 32p. (J). (gr. -1-3). 15.95 *(978-1-56145-522-5(9))* Peachtree Pubs.

—What's That, Mittens? Schaefer, Lola M. 2009. (My First I Can Read Ser.). (ENG.). 32p. (J). (gr. -1 — 1). pap. 3.99 *(978-0-06-054664-9(6))* HarperCollins Pubs.

—Where's the Poop? Markes, Julie. 2004. (ENG.). 20p. (J). (gr. -1 — 1). pap. 10.99 *(978-0-06-053089-1(8)*, HarperFestival) HarperCollins Pubs.

—Your Own Big Bed. Bergstein, Rita M. 2008. (ENG.). 36p. (J). (gr. -1-k). 15.99 *(978-0-670-06079-5(8)*, Viking Juvenile) Penguin Publishing Group.

Hartung, Susan Kathleen & Endersly, Frank. Little David & His Best Friend. Bowman, Crystal. 2010. (I Can Read! / Little David Ser.). (ENG.). 32p. (J). pap. 3.99 *(978-0-310-71710-2(8))* Zonderkidz.

—Little David's Brave Day, 1 vol. Bowman, Crystal. 2010. (I Can Read! / Little David Ser.). (ENG.). 32p. (J). pap. 3.99 *(978-0-310-71709-6(4))* Zonderkidz.

Hartzler, Maria. Good Morning Baby! Zimmerman, Mary Joyce. 2013. 48p. (J). pap. ***(978-0-7399-2458-7(3))*** Rod & Staff Pubs., Inc.

Haruta, Nana. Cactus's Secret. Haruta, Nana. 2010. (Cactus's Secret Ser.: 1). (ENG.). 192p. (gr. 8-18). pap. 9.99 *(978-1-4215-3189-2(5))* Viz Media.

Harvancik, Monica. The Little Brown Horse. Revere, John J. 2011. 34p. 17.95 *(978-1-4327-8146-0(4))* Outskirts Pr., Inc.

Harvey, Amanda. Snowed in with Grandmother Silk. Fenner, Carol. 2005. (ENG.). 80p. (J). (gr. 2-5). 6.99 *(978-0-14-240472-0(1)*, Puffin) Penguin Publishing Group.

Harvey, Bob. The Hound of the Baskervilles. Doyle, Arthur. 2004. (Paperback Classics Ser.). 158p. (J). (gr. 5). lib. bdg. 12.95 *(978-1-58086-605-7(0))* EDC Publishing.

—Jane Eyre: From the Story by Charlotte Bronte. Brontë, Charlotte. rev. ed. 2007. (Usborne Classics Retold Ser.). 176p. (J). (gr. 4). per. 4.99 *(978-0-7945-1870-7(2)*, Usborne) EDC Publishing.

—Kidnapped. Stevenson, Robert Louis. 2004. (Paperback Classics Ser.). 144p. (J). pap. 4.95 *(978-0-7945-0659-9(3)*, Usborne) EDC Publishing.

Harvey, Chris. Tales of the Full Moon. Hart, Sue. 2006. (ENG.). 96p. (J). (gr. 3-7). pap. 16.95 *(978-1-55591-582-7(5)*, 800.992.2908) Fulcrum Publishing.

Harvey, Gayle. Ready to Learn Alphabet & Beginning Sounds. Forte, Imogene. Bosarge, Charlotte, ed. 2003. (Ready to Learn Ser.). (ENG.). 64p. (gr. -1-k). per. 8.99 *(978-0-86530-597-7(8))* Incentive Pubns., Inc.

—Ready to Learn Time & Money. Forte, Imogene. 2003. (Ready to Learn Ser.). (ENG.). 64p. (gr. -1-k). per. 8.99 *(978-0-86530-592-2(7))* Incentive Pubns., Inc.

Harvey, Gil. Encyclopedia of Planet Earth: Internet-Linked. Punter, Russell. 2009. (Geography Ser.). 160p. (YA). (gr. 4-18). 9.99 *(978-0-7945-2469-2(9)*, Usborne) EDC Publishing.

Harvey II, Alvin. Bryce & the Blood Ninjas. Weber, Erec-Michael Ollier. 2013. 38p. pap. 20.00 *(978-0-9716481-9-7(0))* Kila Springs Pr.

Harvey, Kathleen. Bubble. Dannenbring-Eichstadt, Lana. 2004. 24p. (J). *(978-1-57579-282-8(6))* Pine Hill Pr.

Harvey, Lisa. Freedom Seeker: A Story about William Penn. Swain, Gwenyth. 2003. (Creative Minds Biographies Ser.). (ENG.). 64p. (gr. 4-8). pap. 8.95 *(978-0-87614-931-7(X)*, Carolrhoda Bks.) Lerner Publishing Group.

Harvey, Martin, photos by. Busy Elephants. Schindel, John. 2011. (Busy Book Ser.). (ENG., 20p. (J). (— 1). bds. 6.99 *(978-1-58246-383-4(2)*, Tricycle Pr.) Ten Speed Pr.

Harvey, Michael C. Bread Garden. Ketchum, Sally. 2008. 164p. pap. 12.95 *(978-0-595-52862-2(7))* iUniverse, Inc.

Harvey, Robin. Exploring Idaho from A to Z. Taylor, Gwen. 2003. (J). pap. *(978-1-930043-35-0(X))* Scott Publishing Co.

Harvey, Roland. The Circus Horse. Lester, Alison. 2009. (ENG.). 64p. (J). (gr. k-3). pap. 4.99 *(978-0-8118-6656-9(4))* Chronicle Bks. LLC.

Harvey, Roland. At the Beach: Postcards from Crabby Spit. Harvey, Roland. 2007. (ENG.). 32p. (J). (gr. -1-k). pap. 11.99 *(978-1-74114-704-9(2))* Allen & Unwin AUS. Dist: Independent Pubs. Group.

—In the Bush: Our Holiday at Wombat Flat. Harvey, Roland. 2008. (ENG.). 32p. (J). (gr. k-2). pap. 12.99 *(978-1-74175-084-3(9))* Allen & Unwin AUS. Dist: Independent Pubs. Group.

—In the City: Our Scrapbook of Souvenirs. Harvey, Roland. 2010. (ENG.). 32p. (J). (gr. 1-4). pap. 11.99 *(978-1-74175-662-3(6))* Allen & Unwin AUS. Dist: Independent Pubs. Group.

—On the Farm: Our Holiday with Uncle Kev. Harvey, Roland. 2013. (ENG.). 32p. (J). (gr. k-2). 19.99 *(978-1-74175-882-5(3))* Allen & Unwin AUS. Dist: Independent Pubs. Group.

—To the Top End: Our Trip Across Australia. Harvey, Roland. 2010. (ENG.). 32p. (J). (gr. 1-4). 19.99 *(978-1-74175-884-9(X))* Allen & Unwin AUS. Dist: Independent Pubs. Group.

Harvey, Ronald. The Wombats Go on Camp. Harvey, Ronald. 2013. 32p. (J). 22.99 *(978-1-74331-504-0(X))* Allen & Unwin AUS. Dist: Independent Pubs. Group.

Harvill, Kitty. Up, up, up! It's Apple-Picking Time. Shapiro, Jody Fickes. 2008. (ENG.). 32p. (J). (gr. -1-3). pap. 6.95 *(978-0-8234-2166-4(X))* Holiday Hse., Inc.

Hascamp, Steve. Eight Silly Monkeys. 2006. (ENG.). 18p. (J). 9.95 (978-1-58117-186-0(2), Intervisual/Piggy Toes) Bendon, Inc.

Hashey, Kim, photos by. I'm A Big Sister. Hashey, Heather. 2010. 16p. 8.49 (978-1-4520-6293-8(5)) AuthorHouse.

Haskamp, Steve. Este Cerdito. 2005.Tr. of This Little Piggy. (SPA & ENG.). 22p. (J). 9.95 (978-1-58117-328-4(8), Intervisual/Piggy Toes) Bendon, Inc.

—Five Silly Monkeys. 2006. (ENG.). 12p. (J). bds. 14.95 (978-1-58117-264-5(8), Intervisual/Piggy Toes) Bendon, Inc.

—Ocho Monitos. 2005.Tr. of Eight Silly Monkeys. (SPA & ENG.). 18p. (J). 9.95 (978-1-58117-334-5(2), Intervisual/Piggy Toes) Bendon, Inc.

—Over, under, in, & Ouch! Harris, Trudy. 2003. (Silly Millies Level 2 Ser.). (ENG.). 32p. (gr. 1-3). lib. bdg. 21.27 (978-0-7613-2912-1(9), Millbrook Pr.) Lerner Publishing Group.

—This Little Piggy. Imperato, Teresa. 2006. (ENG.). 22p. (J). 9.95 (978-1-58117-281-2(8), Intervisual/Piggy Toes) Bendon, Inc.

Haskamp, Steven. Eight Silly Monkeys. 2007. (ENG.). 18p. (J). (gr. -1-3). bds. 15.95 (978-1-58117-577-6(9), Intervisual/Piggy Toes) Bendon, Inc.

—Five Silly Monkeys. 2006. (ENG.). 12p. (J). (gr. -1-k). 12.95 (978-1-58117-460-1(8), Intervisual/Piggy Toes) Bendon, Inc.

Haskett, Dan, jt. illus. see Goddard, Brenda.

Haslam, John. Good Manners at Home. Marsico, Katie. 2009. (Good Manners Matter! Ser.). 32p. (J). (gr. -1-2). 28.50 (978-1-60270-607-1(7)) Magic Wagon.

—Good Manners at School. Marsico, Katie. 2009. (Good Manners Matter! Ser.). 32p. (J). (gr. -1-2). 28.50 (978-1-60270-608-8(5)) Magic Wagon.

—Good Manners in a Restaurant. Marsico, Katie. 2009. (Good Manners Matter! Ser.). 32p. (J). (gr. -1-2). 28.50 (978-1-60270-609-5(3)) Magic Wagon.

—Good Manners in Public. Marsico, Katie. 2009. (Good Manners Matter! Ser.). 32p. (J). (gr. -1-2). 28.50 (978-1-60270-610-1(7)) Magic Wagon.

—Good Manners on the Phone. Marsico, Katie. 2009. (Good Manners Matter! Ser.). 32p. (J). (gr. -1-2). 28.50 (978-1-60270-611-8(5)) Magic Wagon.

—Good Manners on the Playground. Marsico, Katie. 2009. (Good Manners Matter! Ser.). 32p. (J). (gr. -1-2). 28.50 (978-1-60270-612-5(3)) Magic Wagon.

—Tom the Whistling Wonder. Rosselson, Leon. 2005. (ENG.). 24p. (J). lib. bdg. 23.65 (978-1-59646-758-3(4)) Dingles & Co.

Hasler, Ben & Horne, Richard. Deadly Perils: And How to Avoid Them. Turner, Tracey. 2009. (ENG.). 160p. (YA). (gr. 7-18). pap. 11.99 (978-0-8027-8738-5(X)) Walker & Co.

Haspiel, Dean. Mo & Jo: Fighting Together Forever. Lynch, Jay. 2008. (ENG.). 40p. (J). (gr. -1-3). 12.95 (978-0-9799238-5-2(9)) TOON Books / RAW Junior, LLC.

Haspiel, Dean, et al. Scary Summer. Keenan, Sheila & Stine, R. L. 2007. (Goosebumps Graphix Ser.: 3). (ENG.). 144p. (J). (gr. 3-7). pap. 9.99 (978-0-439-85782-6(1)) Scholastic, Inc.

Haspiel, Dean. The Fox - Freak Magnet. Haspiel, Dean. Waid, Mark. 2014. (Fox Ser.). (ENG.). 144p. pap. 14.99 (978-1-936975-93-8(9), Dark Circle Comics) Archie Comic Pubns., Inc.

Haspiel, Dean & Doe, Juan. X-Men: First Class: Class Portraits. 2011. (ENG.). 136p. (J). (gr. 4-17). pap., pap. 14.99 (978-0-7851-5559-1(7)) Marvel Worldwide, Inc.

Hass, Estie. Menucha V'Simcha Series #11: All Aboard! Fuchs, Menucha. 2008. (Menucha V'Simcha Ser.). 20p. (J). 8.95 (978-1-932443-82-0(7), PSHH) Judaica Pr., Inc., The.

Hasselfeldt, Lori. The under the Ocean Alphabet Book. Hasselfeldt, Lori. 2013. 32p. 24.95 (978-1-61493-155-3(0)); pap. 14.95 (978-1-61493-154-6(2)) Peppertree Pr., The.

Hassett, Ann & Hassett, John. Come Back, Ben. Hassett, Ann & Hassett, John. 2014. (ENG.). 32p. (J). (gr. -1-3). pap. 6.99 (978-0-8234-3181-6(9)) Holiday Hse., Inc.

Hassett, John. The Finest Christmas Tree. Hassett, Ann. 2010. (ENG.). 32p. (J). (gr. -1-3). pap. 6.99 (978-0-547-40623-7(1)) Houghton Mifflin Harcourt Publishing Co.

Hassett, John, jt. illus. see Hassett, Ann.

Hastings, Howard L. Hot Dog Partners. Heyliger, William. 2011. 216p. 44.95 (978-1-258-08024-2(9)) Literary Licensing, LLC.

—Sunny Boy in the Far West. White, Ramy Allison. 2011. 216p. 44.95 (978-1-258-09942-8(X)) Literary Licensing, LLC.

Hastings, Ken. Danny the Dump Truck. Creed, Julie. 2003. per. (978-0-9728181-0-0(3)) Creed, Julie.

Hata, Kenjiro. Hayate the Combat Butler. Hata, Kenjiro. 2007. (Hayate Ser.: 4). (ENG.). 200p. pap. 9.99 (978-1-4215-0854-2(0)) Viz Media.

—Hayate the Combat Butler, Vol. 1. Hata, Kenjiro. Hata, Kenjiro & Giambruno, Mark. 2006. (Hayate Ser.). (ENG.). 208p. (gr. 11). pap. 9.99 (978-1-4215-0851-1(6)) Viz Media.

—Hayate the Combat Butler, Vol. 2. Hata, Kenjiro. Giambruno, Mark & Hata, Kenjiro. 2007. (Hayate Ser.). (ENG.). 200p. pap. 9.99 (978-1-4215-0852-8(4)) Viz Media.

—Hayate the Combat Butler, Vol. 3. Hata, Kenjiro. Giambruno, Mark. 2007. (Hayate Ser.). (ENG.). 208p. (gr. 11). pap. 9.99 (978-1-4215-0853-5(2)) Viz Media.

Hata, Kowshiro. On the Seesaw Bridge. Kimura, Yuichi. 2011. (ENG.). 36p. (J). (gr. -1-3). 14.95 (978-1-935654-18-6(7)) Vertical, Inc.

Hatakeyama, Hiroshi. Goodnight, I Wish You Goodnight, Vol. 1. Hood, Karen Jean Matsko. Whispering Pine Press International, Inc. Staff, ed. 2014. (Hood Picture Book Ser.). (ENG.). 44p. (J). 24.95 (978-1-930948-97-6(2)) Whispering Pine Pr. International, Inc.

—Goodnight, I Wish You Goodnight, Bilingual English & Icelandic, Vol. 1. Hood, Karen Jean Matsko. Whispering Pine Press International, ed. ed. 2015. (Hood Picture Book Ser.). (ENG & ICE.). 60p. (J). 94.99 (978-1-930948-83-9(2)); 34.95 (978-1-59649-920-1(6)); pap. 29.95 (978-1-59649-919-5(2)) Whispering Pine Pr. International, Inc.

Hatakeyama, Hiroshi. Adventure Travel Activity & Coloring Book. Hatakeyama, Hiroshi, tr. Hood, Karen Jean Matsko. Whispering Pine Press International, ed. ed. 2014. (Hood Activity & Coloring Book Ser.). (ENG & JPN.). 160p. (J). spiral bd. 19.95 (978-1-59649-334-6(8)); per. 19.95 (978-1-59210-590-8(4)) Whispering Pine Pr. International, Inc.

Hatala, Dan. Daisy on the Farm. O'Donnell, Liam. 2005. (Pet Tales Ser.). (ENG.). 32p. (J). (gr. -1-2). 2.95 (978-1-59249-451-4(X), 1B036) Soundprints.

—Daisy the Farm Pony. O'Donnell, Liam. 2005. (Pet Tales Ser.). (ENG.). 32p. (J). (gr. -1 — 1). 4.95 (978-1-59249-450-7(1), 1B035) Soundprints.

—Patches Finds a Home. Giancamilli, Vanessa. 2006. (Pet Tales Ser.). (ENG.). 32p. (J). (gr. -1-3). 4.95 (978-1-59249-639-6(3)); pap. 2.95 (978-1-59249-640-2(7)) Soundprints.

—Winston in the City. O'Donnell, Liam. 2005. (Pet Tales Ser.). (ENG.). 32p. (J). (gr. -1-2). pap. 2.95 (978-1-59249-448-4(X), 1B032) Soundprints.

—Winston in the City. O'Donnell, Liam. 2005. (Pet Tales Ser.). (ENG.). 32p. (J). (gr. -1 — 1). 4.95 (978-1-59249-447-7(1), 1B031) Soundprints.

Hatam, Samer. Clever Crow. Holden, Pam & Aesop. 24p. (gr. 3-8). pap. **(978-1-927197-34-9(1)**, Red Rocket Readers) Flying Start Bks.

Hatam, Samer. Fire in the Jungle, 6 pack. Holden, Pam. 2009. (Red Rocket Readers Ser.). 16p. (gr. 2-5). pap. (978-1-877363-73-3(1)) Flying Start Bks.

—The Gentle Giant, 6 pack. Holden, Pam. 2009. (Red Rocket Readers Ser.). 16p. (gr. 2-5). pap. (978-1-877363-81-8(2)) Flying Start Bks.

—Too Big & Heavy, 6 pack. Holden, Pam. 2009. (Red Rocket Readers Ser.). 16p. (gr. 2-4). pap. (978-1-877363-70-2(7)) Flying Start Bks.

Hatcher, Bill, photos by. National Geographic Photography Field Guide: Action & Adventure. Hatcher, Bill. 2006. (National Geographic Photography Field Guides). (ENG., 160p. (J). pap. 21.95 (978-0-7922-5315-0(9)) National Geographic Society.

Hatfield, Cynthia. Mosquito Get in Trouble Too. Lewis-Brown, Alscess. 2009. (J). (978-1-934370-09-4(6)) Editorial Campana.

Hatfield, Tommy. Josiah's School Fun Day. Carrier, Therese & Carrier, Stephen. 2007. 29p. (J). 16.95 (978-0-9797648-0-6(7)) Carrier, Therese.

Hatfield, Tyrel. Fix Your Eyes on Jesus. Hatfield, Tyrel. Hatfield, Justin. Hatfield, Lisa & Hatfield, Kari, eds. 2006. (J). cd-rom 99.00 (978-0-9766703-1-5(3)) Little Acorn LLC.

—The Mystery of Christ. Hatfield, Tyrel. Hatfield, Justin. Hatfield, Lisa & Hatfield, Kari, eds. 2006. (J). cd-rom 99.00 (978-0-9766703-2-2(1)) Little Acorn LLC.

—Righteous Roundup: Wanted: Righteous children of God. Hatfield, Tyrel. Hatfield, Justin. 2008. (J). cd-rom 99.00 (978-0-9766703-6-0(4)) Little Acorn LLC.

Hatfield, Tyrel S. Fix your eyes on Jesus. Hatfield, Tyrel S. Hatfield, Justin R. 2005. 108p. (J). spiral bd. 150.00 (978-0-9766703-0-8(5)) Little Acorn LLC.

Hathaway, Karen. Eelfish, a Rock & Roll King. Salton, Liz. 2004. 38p. pap. 24.95 (978-1-4137-1847-8(7)) PublishAmerica, Inc.

Hatke, Ben. Angel in the Waters. Doman, Regina. 2004. 48p. (J). (gr. -1-3). pap. 6.95 (978-1-928832-81-2(4)) Sophia Institute Pr.

—Around the Year Once Upon a Time Saints. Pochocki, Ethel. 2009. 211p. (YA). (gr. 5). pap. 14.95 (978-1-932350-26-5(8)) Bethlehem Bks.

—Can God See Me in the Dark? Lozano, Neal. 2007. (J). (978-1-883551-45-2(5), Maple Corners Press) Attic Studio Publishing Hse.

—Mi Angelito en Las Aguas. Doman, Regina. 2006. (SPA.). 40p. (J). (gr. -1-3). pap. 6.95 (978-1-933184-22-7(1)) Sophia Institute Pr.

—Saint John Vianney: A Priest for All People. DeDomenico, Elizabeth Marie. 2008. (Encounter the Saints Ser.). 122p. (J). (gr. 4-7). pap. 7.95 (978-0-8198-7115-2(X)) Pauline Bks. & Media.

—Will You Bless Me? Lozano, Neal. 2009. (J). lib. bdg. 14.95 (978-1-883551-32-2(3), MCP-323, Maple Corners Press) Attic Studio Publishing Hse.

—The Worm Whisperer. Hicks, Betty. 2013. (ENG.). 192p. (J). (gr. 3-7). 16.99 (978-1-59643-490-5(2)) Roaring Brook Pr.

Hatke, Ben. Julia's House for Lost Creatures. Hatke, Ben. 2014. (ENG.). 40p. (J). (gr. k-3). 17.99 (978-1-59643-866-8(5), First Second Bks.) Roaring Brook Pr.

—Legends of Zita the Spacegirl. Hatke, Ben. 2012. (Zita the Spacegirl Ser.: 2). (ENG.). 224p. (J). (gr. 3-7). 18.99 (978-1-59643-806-4(1)); pap. 12.99 (978-1-59643-447-9(3)) Roaring Brook Pr. (First Second Bks.).

—Zita the Spacegirl. Hatke, Ben. 2011. (Zita the Spacegirl Ser.: 1). (ENG.). 192p. (J). (gr. 3-7). 17.99 (978-1-59643-695-4(6)); pap. 12.99 (978-1-59643-446-2(5)) Roaring Brook Pr. (First Second Bks.).

Hatori, Bisco. Host Club. Hatori, Bisco. (Ouran High School Ser.: 15). (ENG.). 2010. 192p. pap. 9.99 (978-1-4215-3670-5(6)); Vol. 1. 2005. 184p. pap. 9.99 (978-1-59116-915-4(1)); Vol. 2. 2005. 192p. pap. 9.99 (978-1-59116-990-1(9)); Vol. 3. 2005. 192p. pap. 9.99 (978-1-4215-0062-1(0)); Vol. 4. 2006. 200p. pap. 9.99 (978-1-4215-0192-5(9)); Vol. 5. 2006. 176p. pap. 9.99 (978-1-4215-0329-5(8)); Vol. 8. 2007. 184p. pap. 8.99 (978-1-4215-1161-0(4)); Vol. 16. 2011. 192p. pap. 9.99 (978-1-4215-3870-9(9)) Viz Media.

Hattenhauer, Ina. Dollhouse Sticker Book. ed. 2012. (Sticker Activity Book Ser.). 24p. (J). pap. 8.99 (978-0-7945-2944-4(5), Usborne) EDC Publishing.

Hatton, Libby. Pete Puffin's Wild Ride Cruising Alaska's Currents. Hatton, Libby. 2008. (J). pap. 16.95 (978-0-930931-92-6(0)) Alaska Geographic Assn.

Hau, Joseph. I Can Live To 100! Secrets Just for Kids. Hau, Stephanie. 2005. 60p. (J). per. 9.95 (978-0-9767324-0-2(8), Kids Can) Proactive Publishing.

Hauck, Christie. Things I See When I Open My Eyes. Culver, Kathy. 2007. 32p. per. 13.95 (978-1-59858-306-9(9)) Dog Ear Publishing, LLC.

Hauck, Melissa. Der Einsame Drache. Jensen, Elizabeth. Sommerfeld, Monika, tr. l.t. ed. 2013. (GER.). 36p. pap. 9.95 (978-0-615-78027-6(X)) Jensen, Elizabeth.

Hauge, Carl & Hauge, Mary. Thornton Burgess Bedtime Stories: Includes Downloadable MP3s. Burgess, Thornton W. 2013. (Dover Read & Listen Ser.). (ENG.). 112p. (J). (gr. 1). pap. 14.99 (978-0-486-49189-9(7)) Dover Pubns., Inc.

Hauge, Mary, jt. illus. see Hauge, Carl.

Haugen, Ryan. Anthill Home Repair. Stockland, Patricia M. 2008. (Safari Friends Ser.). 32p. (gr. -1-3). 28.50 (978-1-60270-082-6(6), Looking Glass Library) ABDO Publishing Co.

—Back to School, 1 vol. Jones, Christianne C. 2005. (Read-It! Readers Ser.). (ENG.). 24p. (gr. -1-3). lib. bdg. 19.99 (978-1-4048-1166-9(4), Easy Readers) Picture Window Bks.

—The Big Banana Hunt. Stockland, Patricia M. 2008. (Safari Friends Ser.). 32p. (gr. -1-3). 28.50 (978-1-60270-083-3(4), Looking Glass Library) ABDO Publishing Co.

Haugen, Ryan, et al. Chuckle Squad: Jokes about Classrooms, Sports, Food, Teachers, & Other School Subjects, 1 vol. Donahue, Jill L. et al. 2010. (Michael Dahl Presents Super Funny Joke Bks.). (ENG.). 80p. (gr. k-3). 23.99 (978-1-4048-5773-5(7), Michael Dahl - Super Funny Joke Bks.) Picture Window Bks.

Haugen, Ryan. Clean up the Watering Hole! Stockland, Patricia M. 2008. (Safari Friends Ser.). 32p. (gr. -1-3). 28.50 (978-1-60270-084-0(2), Looking Glass Library) ABDO Publishing Co.

—El Cuadro de Mary, 1 vol. Blackaby, Susan & Jones, Christianne C. Ruíz, Carlos, tr. 2006. (Read-It! Readers en Español: Story Collection).Tr. of Mary's Art. (SPA.). 32p. (gr. -1-3). 19.99 (978-1-4048-1649-7(6), Easy Readers) Picture Window Bks.

—De Pesca, 1 vol. Blackaby, Susan. Ruíz, Carlos, tr. 2006. (Read-It! Readers en Español: Story Collection).Tr. of Fishing Trip. (SPA.). 32p. (gr. -1-3). 19.99 (978-1-4048-1684-8(4), Easy Readers) Picture Window Bks.

—Fishing Trip, 1 vol. Blackaby, Susan. 2005. (Read-It! Readers Ser.). (ENG.). 24p. (gr. -1-3). 19.99 (978-1-4048-1004-4(8), Easy Readers) Picture Window Bks.

—El Mejor Futbolista, 1 vol. Blackaby, Susan. Ruíz, Carlos, tr. from ENG. 2006. (Read-It! Readers en Español: Story Collection).Tr. of Best Soccer Player. (SPA.). 24p. (gr. -1-3). 19.99 (978-1-4048-1690-9(9), Easy Readers) Picture Window Bks.

—Moving Day, 1 vol. Blackaby, Susan. 2005. (Read-It! Readers Ser.). (ENG.). 24p. (gr. -1-3). 19.99 (978-1-4048-1006-8(4), Easy Readers) Picture Window Bks.

—Peanut Picking. Stockland, Patricia M. 2008. (Safari Friends Ser.). 32p. (gr. -1-3). 28.50 (978-1-60270-085-7(0), Looking Glass Library) ABDO Publishing Co.

—Stop the Grassfires! Stockland, Patricia M. 2008. (Safari Friends Ser.). 32p. (gr. -1-3). 28.50 (978-1-60270-086-4(9), Looking Glass Library) ABDO Publishing Co.

—There Are Millions of Millionaires: And Other Freaky Facts about Earning, Saving, & Spending, 1 vol. Seuling, Barbara. 2008. (Freaky Facts Ser.). (ENG.). 48p. (gr. 3-5). 25.32 (978-1-4048-4115-4(6), Nonfiction Picture Bks.) Picture Window Bks.

—There are Millions of Millionaires [Scholastic]: And Other Freaky Facts about Earning, Saving, And. Seuling, Barbara. 2010. (Freaky Facts Ser.). 40p. pap. 0.35 (978-1-4048-6550-1(0), Nonfiction Picture Bks.) Picture Window Bks.

—Tiger Toothache. Stockland, Patricia M. 2008. (Safari Friends Ser.). 32p. (gr. -1-3). 28.50 (978-1-60270-087-1(7), Looking Glass Library) ABDO Publishing Co.

Haugen, Ryan, et al. Wise Crackers: Riddles & Jokes about Numbers, Names, Letters, & Silly Words, 1 vol. Dahl, Michael et al. 2010. (Michael Dahl Presents Super Funny Joke Bks.). (ENG.). 80p. (gr. k-3). 23.99 (978-1-4048-6102-2(5), Michael Dahl - Super Funny Joke Bks.) Picture Window Bks.

Haugen, Ryan. You Blink Twelve Times a Minute: And Other Freaky Facts about the Human Body, 1 vol. Seuling, Barbara. 2008. (Freaky Facts Ser.). (ENG.). 40p. (gr. 3-5). pap. 5.29 (978-1-4048-4121-5(0), Nonfiction Picture Bks.) Picture Window Bks.

Haugen, Ryan. Dan Pone la Mesa, 1 vol., Set. Haugen, Ryan. Blackaby, Susan. Ruíz, Carlos, tr. 2006. (Read-It! Readers en Español: Story Collection). (ENG & SPA.). 32p. (gr. -1-3). 19.99 (978-1-4048-1682-4(8), Easy Readers) Picture Window Bks.

Haugen, Ryan & Jensen, Brian. Knock Your Socks Off: A Book of Knock-Knock Jokes, 1 vol. Dahl, Michael. 2010. (Michael Dahl Presents Super Funny Joke Bks.). (ENG.). 80p. (gr. k-3). 23.99 (978-1-4048-5774-2(5), Michael Dahl - Super Funny Joke Bks.) Picture Window Bks.

—Laughs for a Living: Jokes about Doctors, Teachers, Firefighters, & Other People Who Work, 1 vol. Dahl, Michael & Ziegler, Mark. 2010. (Michael Dahl Presents Super Funny Joke Bks.). (ENG.). 80p. (gr. k-3). 23.99 (978-1-4048-5771-1(0)); pap. 6.95 (978-1-4048-6368-2(0)) Picture Window Bks. (Michael Dahl - Super Funny Joke Bks.).

Haugen, Ryan, jt. illus. see Landmark, Ken.

Haughom, Lisa. People, Places & Things. 2010. (J). (978-1-58865-541-7(5)) Kidsbooks, LLC.

—Things That Go! 2010. 16p. (J). (978-1-58865-542-4(3)) Kidsbooks, LLC.

Haughton, Chris. Little Owl Lost. Haughton, Chris. (ENG.). (J). 2013. 30p. (-k). bds. 7.99 (978-0-7636-6750-4(1)); 2010. 32p. (gr. -1-k). 14.99 (978-0-7636-5022-3(6)) Candlewick Pr.

—Oh No, George! Haughton, Chris. (ENG.). 32p. (J). 2015. (-k). bds. 7.99 (978-0-7636-7652-0(7)); 2012. (gr. -1-k). 15.99 (978-0-7636-5546-4(5)) Candlewick Pr.

—Shh! We Have a Plan. Haughton, Chris. (ENG.). 40p. (J). 2015. (-k). bds. 8.99 **(978-0-7636-7977-4(1))**; 2014. (gr. -1-2). 15.99 (978-0-7636-7293-5(9)) Candlewick Pr.

Hauman, Doris, jt. illus. see Hauman, George and Doris.

Hauman, Doris, jt. illus. see Hauman, George.

Hauman, George & Hauman, Doris. The Little Engine That Could. Piper, Watty. deluxe ed. 2009. (Little Engine That Could Ser.). (ENG.). 48p. (J). (gr. -1-2). 17.99 (978-0-448-45257-9(X), Grosset & Dunlap) Penguin Publishing Group.

Hauman, George and Doris & Hauman, Doris. The Little Engine That Could. Piper, Watty. 2015. (Little Engine That Could Ser.). (ENG.). 26p. (J). (gr. -1 — 1). bds. 11.99 (978-0-448-48731-1(4), Grosset & Dunlap) Penguin Publishing Group.

Haus, Estudio. Ancient Myths. 2015. (Ancient Myths Ser.). (ENG.). 32p. (gr. 3-4). lib. bdg. 179.94 **(978-1-4914-2522-0(9)**, Graphic Library) Capstone Pr., Inc.

Haus, Estudio. Build Your Own Fort, Igloo, & Other Hangouts, 1 vol. Enz, Tammy. 2011. (Build It Yourself Ser.). (ENG.). 32p. (gr. 3-4). lib. bdg. 27.32 (978-1-4296-5436-4(8)); pap. 8.29 (978-1-4296-6261-1(1)) Capstone Pr., Inc. (Edge Bks.).

—Cailyn & Chloe Learn about Conjunctions. Atwood, Megan. 2015. (Language Builders Ser.). (ENG.). 32p. (J). (gr. 2-4). pap. 11.94 (978-1-60357-706-9(8)) Norwood Hse. Pr.

—Ghosts & Atoms, 1 vol. Wheeler-Toppen, Jodi. 2011. (Monster Science Ser.). (ENG.). 32p. (gr. 3-4). pap. 8.10 (978-1-4296-7329-7(X)); pap. 47.70 (978-1-4296-7330-3(3)); lib. bdg. 29.99 (978-1-4296-6581-0(5)) Capstone Pr., Inc. (Graphic Library).

Hauser, Bill. Four Secrets. Willey, Margaret. (ENG.). 288p. (YA). (gr. 7-12). 2014. pap. 9.95 (978-1-4677-1626-0(X), Carolrhoda LAB); 2012. 17.95 (978-0-7613-8535-6(5)) Lerner Publishing Group.

—Matzah Meals: A Passover Cookbook for Kids. Tabs, Judy & Steinberg, Barbara. 2004. (Passover Ser.). (ENG.). 64p. (J). (gr. 3-5). pap. 7.95 (978-1-58013-086-8(0), Kar-Ben Publishing) Lerner Publishing Group.

—Mousetraps. Schmatz, Pat. 2008. (ENG.). 192p. (YA). (gr. 7-12). 17.95 (978-0-8225-8657-9(6), Carolrhoda Bks.) Lerner Publishing Group.

Hauser, Salvan. Kindergarten Success. Hauser, Jill Frankel. 2005. (Little Hands! Ser.). 128p. (J). (gr. k-18). pap. 12.95 (978-0-8249-6751-2(8), Williamson Bks.) Ideals Pubns.

Hauser, Savlan. Kindergarten Success: Helping Children Excel Right from the Start. Hauser, Jill Frankel. (ENG.). 128p. (J). (gr. 3-7). 2008. per. 14.25 (978-0-8249-6758-1(5)); 2005. 14.95 (978-0-8249-6777-2(1)) Ideals Pubns. (Williamson Bks.).

Hauser, Sheri, photos by. Crosscurrents. Tolpen, Stanley. 2008. (ENG., 82p. (J). ring bd. 14.95 (978-1-60789-013-3(5)) Glorybound Publishing.

Hausman, Sid. Cactus Critter Bash. Hausman, Sid. 2007. 32p. (J). 21.95 (978-1-929115-15-0(6)) Azro Pr., Inc.

Hausmann, Rex. The Apastron Reports: Quest for Life, 1 vol. Senneff, John A. 2005. 317p. (YA). 22.95 (978-0-9671107-7-6(7)) Quality Pubs.

Hautman, Pete. Invisible. Hautman, Pete. 2006. (ENG.). 160p. (YA). (gr. 7-12). reprint ed. pap. 9.99 (978-0-689-86903-7(7), Simon & Schuster Bks. For Young Readers) Simon & Schuster Bks. For Young Readers.

Hauvette, Marion. A Puzzling Picnic. Knight, Deborah Janet. 2010. 32p. pap. 13.00 (978-1-60860-963-5(4), Eloquent Bks.) Strategic Book Publishing & Rights Agency (SBPRA).

Haverfield, Mary. Johnny Appleseed. Kurtz, Jane. 2004. (Ready-To-Reads Ser.). (ENG.). 32p. (J). (gr. -1-1). pap. 3.99 (978-0-689-85958-8(9), Simon Spotlight) Simon Spotlight.

—Mister Bones: Dinosaur Hunter. Kurtz, Jane. 2004. (Ready-To-Reads Ser.). (ENG.). 32p. (J). (gr. -1-1). pap. 6.99 (978-0-689-85960-1(0), Simon Spotlight) Simon Spotlight.

—Mister Bones Dinosaur Hunter. Kurtz, Jane. ed. 2005. (Ready-to-Read Ser.). 32p. (J). lib. bdg. 15.00 (978-1-59054-929-2(5)) Fitzgerald Bks.

—Sometimes It's Grandmas & Grandpas: Not Mommies & Daddies. Byrne, Gayle. 2009. (ENG.). 32p. (J). (gr. -1-3). 15.95 (978-0-7892-1028-9(2), Abbeville Kids) Abbeville Pr., Inc.

—Sometimes Just One Is Just Right. Byrne, Gayle. 2013. (ENG.). 32p. (J). (gr. k-k). 15.95 (978-0-7892-1129-3(7), Abbeville Kids) Abbeville Pr., Inc.

Havice, Susan. Who Needs Friends? Taylor-Butler, Christine. 2006. (Rookie Readers Ser.). (ENG.). 32p. (J). (gr. k-2). pap. 4.95 (978-0-516-24997-1(5), Children's Pr.) Scholastic Library Publishing.

Haw, Brenda. L' Ile Fantastique: Fantastic Island. Leigh, Susannah. Gemmell, Kathy & Irving, Nicole, eds. (FRE.). 25p. (J). (gr. 2-3). reprint ed. 17.00 (978-0-7881-9300-2(7)) DIANE Publishing Co.

—The Incredible Dinosaur Expedition. Dolby, Karen. 2004. (Puzzle Adventures Ser.). 48p. (J). pap. 4.95 (978-0-7945-0022-1(6), Usborne) EDC Publishing.

—Puzzle Car Race. Heywood, Rosie. 2004. (Young Puzzles Ser.). 32p. (J). pap. 6.95 (978-0-7945-0689-6(5), Usborne) EDC Publishing.

—Puzzle Castle. Leigh, Susannah. Waters, Gaby, ed. 2004. (Usborne Young Puzzles Ser.). 32p. (J). (gr. 1). lib. bdg. 14.95 (978-1-58086-674-3(3)); pap. 6.95 (978-0-7945-0433-5(7)) EDC Publishing. (Usborne).

—Puzzle Dinosaurs. Leigh, Susannah. Tyler, Jenny, ed. 2007. (Young Puzzles Ser.). 32p. (J). pap. 6.99 *(978-0-7945-1778-6(1),* Usborne) EDC Publishing.
—Puzzle Dungeon. Leigh, Susannah. 2004. (Young Puzzles Ser.). 32p. (J). (gr. 1). lib. bdg. 14.95 *(978-1-58086-599-9(2))* EDC Publishing.
—Puzzle Farm. Leigh, Susannah. Waters, Gaby, ed. 2004. (Young Puzzles Ser.). 32p. (J). (gr. 1). lib. bdg. 14.95 *(978-1-58086-627-9(1),* Usborne) EDC Publishing.
—Puzzle Mountain. Leigh, Susannah. Waters, Gaby, ed. 2005. (Usborne Young Puzzles Ser.). 32p. (J). (gr. 1). lib. bdg. 14.95 *(978-1-58086-694-1(8),* Usborne) EDC Publishing.
—Puzzle Mountain. Leigh, Susannah. 2003. 32p. (J). pap. 6.95 *(978-0-7945-0713-8(1),* Usborne) EDC Publishing.
—Puzzle Ocean. Leigh, Susannah. 2006. (Young Puzzles Ser.). 32p. (J). (gr. 1). lib. bdg. 14.95 *(978-1-58086-535-7(6))* EDC Publishing.
—Puzzle Palace. Leigh, Susannah. Tyler, Jenny, ed. 2005. (Usborne Young Puzzles Ser.). 32p. (J). (gr. -1-3). per. 6.95 *(978-0-7945-1120-3(1),* Usborne) EDC Publishing.
—Puzzle Pirates. Leigh, Susannah. 2006. (Usborne Young Puzzles Ser.). 32p. (J). (gr. 1). lib. bdg. 14.99 *(978-1-58086-973-7(4),* Usborne) EDC Publishing.
—Puzzle Pirates. Leigh, Susannah. Tyler, Jenny, ed. 2006. (Usborne Young Puzzles Ser.). 32p. (J). (gr. 1-4). pap. 6.99 *(978-0-7945-1359-7(X),* Usborne) EDC Publishing.
—Puzzle Planet. Leigh, Susannah. Waters, Gaby, ed. 2006. (Young Puzzles Ser.). 32p. (J). (gr. 1). lib. bdg. 14.95 *(978-1-58086-536-4(4))* EDC Publishing.
—Puzzle Pyramid. Leigh, Susannah. 2004. 32p. (J). pap. 6.95 *(978-0-7945-0791-6(3),* Usborne) EDC Publishing.
—Puzzle School. Leigh, Susannah. 2004. (Young Puzzles Ser.). 32p. (Orig.). (J). (gr. 1). lib. bdg. 14.95 *(978-1-58086-600-2(X))* EDC Publishing.
—Puzzle Town. Leigh, Susannah. Waters, Gaby, ed. 2006. (Young Puzzles Ser.). 32p. (J). (gr. 1). lib. bdg. 14.95 *(978-1-58086-537-1(2),* Usborne) EDC Publishing.
—Puzzle Train. Leigh, Susannah. 2004. (Young Puzzles Ser.). 32p. (J). (gr. 1). lib. bdg. 14.95 *(978-1-58086-633-0(6),* Usborne) EDC Publishing.
—Puzzle Train. Leigh, Susannah. Waters, Gaby, ed. 2003. (Young Puzzles Ser.). 32p. (J). pap. 6.95 *(978-0-7945-0683-4(6),* Usborne) EDC Publishing.
—Puzzle World: Combined Volume. Leigh, Susannah. Waters, Gaby, ed. 2004. (Young Puzzles Ser.). 96p. (J). pap. 13.95 *(978-0-7945-0688-9(7),* Usborne) EDC Publishing.
—Travel Puzzles Sticker Book. Heywood, Rosie, ed. rev. ed. 2005. (Travel Puzzles Sticker Book Ser.). 24p. (J). (gr. 1). pap. 6.95 *(978-0-7945-0729-9(8),* Usborne) EDC Publishing.

Haw, Brenda & Dawes, Will. Uncle Pete's Pirate Adventure. Leigh, Susannah. Stowell, Louie, ed. rev. ed. 2007. (Young Puzzle Adventures Ser.). 32p. (J). (gr. -1-3). pap. 4.99 *(978-0-7945-1848-6(6),* Usborne) EDC Publishing.

Hawcock, David. Dinosaurs! Pop-Up Paper Designs. Hawcock, David. 2015. (ENG.). 16p. (J). (gr. -1-k). 14.99 ***(978-1-85707-804-6(7))*** Tango Bks. GBR. Dist: Independent Pubs. Group.

Hawcock, David. Stegosaurus. Hawcock, David. 2003. (Mini Dinosaurs Ser.). (ENG.). 12p. (J). (gr. -1-k). 5.99 *(978-1-85707-019-4(4))* Tango Bks. GBR. Dist: Independent Pubs. Group.
—Triceratops. Hawcock, David. 2003. (Mini Dinosaurs Ser.). (ENG.). 12p. (J). (gr. -1-k). 5.99 *(978-1-85707-021-7(6))* Tango Bks. GBR. Dist: Independent Pubs. Group.

Hawcock, David. Tyrannosaurus. Hawcock, David, tr. 2003. (Mini Dinosaurs Ser.). (ENG.). 12p. (J). (gr. -1-k). 5.99 *(978-1-85707-018-7(6))* Tango Bks. GBR. Dist: Independent Pubs. Group.

Hawcock, David, jt. illus. see Elzbieta.

Hawkes, Kevin. And to Think That We Thought That We'd Never Be Friends. Hoberman, Mary Ann. 2003. (ENG.). 32p. (J). (gr. -1-2). pap. 7.99 *(978-0-440-41776-7(7),* Dragonfly Bks.) Random Hse. Children's Bks.
—A Boy Had a Mother Who Bought Him a Hat. Kuskin, Karla. 2010. (ENG.). 32p. (J). (gr. -1-3). 16.99 *(978-0-06-075330-6(7))* HarperCollins Pubs.
—Brunolandia. Fleischman, Paul. 2003. (SPA.). 16p. (J). *(978-84-348-6640-9(4),* SM30969) SM Ediciones ESP. Dist: Lectorum Pubns., Inc.
—By the Light of the Halloween Moon, 0 vols. Stutson, Caroline. 2012. (ENG.). 32p. (J). (gr. k-4). pap. 7.99 *(978-0-7614-6244-6(9),* 9780761462446, Amazon Children's Publishing) Amazon Publishing.
—Chicken Cheeks. Black, Michael Ian. 2009. (ENG.). 40p. (J). (gr. -1-3). 17.99 *(978-1-4169-4864-3(3),* Simon & Schuster Bks. For Young Readers) Simon & Schuster Bks. For Young Readers.
—¡Compórtate, Pablo Picasso! Winter, Jonah. 2012.Tr. of Just Behave, Pablo Picasso!. (SPA.). 48p. (J). (gr. -1-3). pap. 5.99 *(978-0-545-13294-7(0),* Scholastic en Espanol) Scholastic, Inc.
—Dial-a-Ghost. Ibbotson, Eva. 2003. (ENG.). 224p. (J). (gr. 3-7). pap. 6.99 *(978-0-14-250018-7(6),* Puffin) Penguin Publishing Group.
—Granite Baby. Bertrand, Lynne. 2005. (ENG.). 36p. (J). (gr. -1-3). 18.99 *(978-0-374-32761-3(0),* Farrar, Straus & Giroux (BYR)) Farrar, Straus & Giroux.
—The Great Ghost Rescue. Ibbotson, Eva. 2003. (ENG.). 192p. (J). (gr. 3-7). pap. 6.99 *(978-0-14-250087-3(9),* Puffin) Penguin Publishing Group.
—Handel, Who Knew What He Liked. Anderson, M. T. 2013. (Candlewick Biographies Ser.). (ENG.). 48p. (J). (gr. 3-7). 14.99 *(978-0-7636-6599-9(1));* pap. 4.99 *(978-0-7636-6600-2(9))* Candlewick Pr.
—The Haunting of Granite Falls. Ibbotson, Eva. 2005. (ENG.). 224p. (J). (gr. 3-7). 6.99 *(978-0-14-240371-6(7),* Puffin) Penguin Publishing Group.
—Journey to the River Sea. Ibbotson, Eva. 2003. 298p. (gr. 3-7). 18.00 *(978-0-7569-1552-0(X))* Perfection Learning Corp.
—Journey to the River Sea. Ibbotson, Eva. 2003. (ENG.). 304p. (J). (gr. 3-7). pap. 7.99 *(978-0-14-250184-9(0),* Puffin) Penguin Publishing Group.
—Just Behave, Pablo Picasso! Winter, Jonah. 2012. (ENG.). 48p. (J). (gr. -1-3). 18.99 *(978-0-545-13291-6(6),* Levine, Arthur A. Bks.) Scholastic, Inc.
—Library Lion. Knudsen, Michelle. 2006. (ENG.). 48p. (J). (gr. -1-3). 16.99 *(978-0-7636-2262-6(1))* Candlewick Pr.
—Library Lion. Knudsen, Michelle. 2009. (ENG.). 48p. (J). (gr. -1-3). pap. 6.99 *(978-0-7636-3784-2(X))* Candlewick Pr.
—A Little Bitty Man & Other Poems for the Very Young. Rasmussen, Halfdan Wedel et al. 2011. (ENG.). 32p. (J). (gr. k-12). 15.99 *(978-0-7636-2379-1(2))* Candlewick Pr.
—Me, All Alone, at the End of the World. Anderson, M. T. 2005. (ENG.). 40p. (J). (gr. 1-4). 16.99 *(978-0-7636-1586-4(2))* Candlewick Pr.
—Meanwhile, Back at the Ranch. Isaacs, Anne. 2014. (ENG.). 56p. (J). (gr. k-4). 17.99 *(978-0-375-86745-3(7))* Random Hse., Inc.
—Mountain Manor Mystery. Trumbauer, Lisa. 2006. 96p. (J). pap. *(978-1-59034-810-9(9))* Mondo Publishing.
—My Little Sister Ate One Hare. Grossman, Bill. 2014. 32p. pap. 7.00 *(978-1-61003-374-9(4))* Center for the Collaborative Classroom.
—My Little Sister Hugged an Ape. Grossman, Bill. 2008. (ENG.). 40p. (J). (gr. -1-2). pap. 6.99 *(978-0-385-73660-2(6),* Dragonfly Bks.) Random Hse. Children's Bks.
—A Necklace of Raindrops & Other Stories. Aiken, Joan. 2003. 84p. (J). (gr. 1-5). 13.15 *(978-0-7569-5686-8(2))* Perfection Learning Corp.
—Not Just a Witch. Ibbotson, Eva. 2004. (ENG.). 192p. (J). (gr. 3-7). pap. 5.99 *(978-0-14-240232-0(X),* Puffin) Penguin Publishing Group.
—A Pig Parade Is a Terrible Idea. Black, Michael Ian. 2010. (ENG.). 40p. (J). (gr. -1-3). 16.99 *(978-1-4169-7922-7(0),* Simon & Schuster Bks. For Young Readers) Simon & Schuster Bks. For Young Readers.
—The Road to Oz: Twists, Turns, Bumps, & Triumphs in the Life of L. Frank Baum. Krull, Kathleen. 2008. (ENG.). 48p. (J). (gr. -1-2). 19.99 *(978-0-375-83216-1(5),* Knopf Bks. for Young Readers) Random Hse. Children's Bks.
—Santa from Cincinnati. Barrett, Judi. 2012. (ENG.). 48p. (J). (gr. -1-3). 16.99 *(978-1-4424-2993-2(3),* Atheneum Bks. for Young Readers) Simon & Schuster Children's Publishing.
—Sidewalk Circus. Fleischman, Paul. 2007. (ENG.). 32p. (J). (gr. k-4). 7.99 *(978-0-7636-2795-9(X))* Candlewick Pr.
—Sidewalk Circus. Fleischman, Paul. 2007. (gr. k-4). 18.00 *(978-0-7569-8182-2(4))* Perfection Learning Corp.
—The Star of Kazan. Ibbotson, Eva. 2006. (ENG.). 416p. (J). (gr. 3-7). reprint ed. 8.99 *(978-0-14-240582-6(5),* Puffin) Penguin Publishing Group.
—The Three Mouths of Little Tom Drum. Willard, Nancy. 2015. (ENG.). 48p. (J). (gr. -1-3). 16.99 *(978-0-7636-5476-4(0))* Candlewick Pr.
—Velma Gratch & the Way Cool Butterfly. Madison, Alan. 2007. (ENG.). 40p. (J). (gr. -1-3). 17.99 *(978-0-375-83597-1(0),* Schwartz & Wade Bks.) Random Hse. Children's Bks.
—Velma Gratch & the Way Cool Butterfly. Madison, Alan. 2012. (ENG.). 40p. (J). (gr. -1-3). pap. 7.99 *(978-0-307-97804-2(4),* Dragonfly Bks.) Random Hse. Children's Bks.
—Weslandia. Fleischman, Paul. 2006. (gr. -1-3). 17.00 *(978-0-7569-6566-2(7))* Perfection Learning Corp.
—When Giants Come to Play. Beaty, Andrea. 2006. (ENG.). 32p. (J). (gr. -1-3). 17.95 *(978-0-8109-5759-6(0))* Abrams.
—The Worry Week. Lindbergh, Anne M. 2003. (ENG.). 144p. reprint ed. pap. 12.95 *(978-1-56792-239-4(2))* Godine, David R. Pub.

Hawkes, Kevin & Harrison, Hannah E. Remy & Lulu. Hawkes, Kevin. 2014. (ENG.). 40p. (J). (gr. k-4). 17.99 *(978-0-449-81085-9(2));* lib. bdg. 20.99 *(978-0-449-81087-3(9))* Knopf, Alfred A. Inc.

Hawkes, Spencer. Beagles in My Bed Coloring Book. 2005. 50p. (J). 5.95 *(978-0-9774563-1-4(5))* Ladd, David Pr.

Hawkins, Brett. A Triune Tale of Diminutive Swine. 2012. pap. 15.00 *(978-0-9854699-0-0(0))* Rockshow Comedy, Inc.

Hawkins, Colin, et al. Madcap Book of Laughs. Brandreth, Gyles. 288p. (J). pap. 6.95 *(978-0-233-99569-4(2))* Andre Deutsch GBR. Dist: Trafalgar Square Publishing.
—Pirate Ship: A Pop-up Adventure. Hawkins, Colin. 2006. 28p. (J). (gr. 4-8). reprint ed. 20.00 *(978-0-7567-9827-7(2))* DIANE Publishing Co.

Hawkins, Colin & Hawkins, Jacqui. Pirate Treasure Map: A Fairytale Adventure. Hawkins, Colin & Hawkins, Jacqui. 2006. (ENG.). 40p. (J). (gr. -1-3). 15.99 *(978-0-7636-3205-2(8))* Candlewick Pr.

Hawkins, Jacqui, jt. illus. see Hawkins, Colin.

Hawkins, Jonny. Laugh-Out-Loud Doodles for Boys. Elliott, Rob. 2015. (ENG.). 240p. (J). pap. 8.99 ***(978-0-8007-2236-4(1))*** Revell.
—Laugh-Out-Loud Doodles for Girls. Elliott, Rob. 2015. (ENG.). 240p. (J). pap. 8.99 ***(978-0-8007-2237-1(X))*** Revell.

Hawkins, Jonny. Laugh-Out-Loud Doodles for Kids. Elliott, Rob. 2014. (ENG.). 240p. (J). pap. 8.99 *(978-0-8007-2446-7(1))* Revell.

Hawkins, Kristen. Rollie Pollie Review. Holley, Kim. 2013. 120p. pap. 10.00 *(978-1-939054-22-7(2))* Rowe Publishing and Design.

Hawkins, Linda. The Happy Girl. Heyde, Christiane. 2003. 48p. 14.95 *(978-0-87516-618-6(0),* Devorss Pubns.) DeVorss & Co.

Hawksley, Gerald. Danny Dog's Car: Press Out Parts Make a Car Carrying Danny Dog! 2009. (Toddler Make & Play Ser.). 10p. (J). bds. 6.95 *(978-1-59496-184-7(0))* Teora USA LLC.
—Patty Cow's Tractor: Press Out Parts Make a Tractor Carrying Patty Cow. 2009. (Toddler Make & Play Ser.). 10p. bds. 6.95 *(978-1-59496-182-3(4))* Teora USA LLC.
—Quacky Duck's Plane: Press Out Parts Make an Airplane Carrying Quacky Duck! 2009. (Toddler Make & Play Ser.). 10p. bds. 6.95 *(978-1-59496-185-4(9))* Teora USA LLC.
—Splashy Dolphin's Boat: Press Out Parts Make a Boat Carrying Splashy Dolphin. 2009. (Toddler Make & Play Ser.). 10p. bds. 6.95 *(978-1-59496-183-0(2))* Teora USA LLC.

Hawley, Kelvin. Are You Hungry?, 6 pack. Holden, Pam. 2009. (Red Rocket Readers Ser.). 16p. (gr. -1-3). pap. *(978-1-877363-23-8(5),* Red Rocket Readers) Flying Start Bks.
—The Big Bad Wolf, 6 pack. Holden, Pam. 2009. (Red Rocket Readers Ser.). 16p. (gr. 2-4). pap. *(978-1-877363-56-6(1),* Red Rocket Readers) Flying Start Bks.
—Crumpet, the Cat: 3-in-1 Package. Eggleton, Jill. (Sails Literacy Ser.). 24p. (gr. 1-18). 57.00 *(978-0-7578-8619-5(1))* Rigby Education.
—Crumpet, the Cat: Big Book Only. Eggleton, Jill. (Sails Literacy Ser.). 24p. (gr. 1-18). 27.00 *(978-0-7578-6203-8(9))* Rigby Education.
—Farm Friends, 6 pack. Holden, Pam. 2009. (Red Rocket Readers Ser.). 16p. (gr. -1-2). pap. *(978-1-877363-14-6(6),* Red Rocket Readers) Flying Start Bks.
—The Giant's Ice Cream: 3-in-1 Package. Eggleton, Jill. (Sails Literacy Ser.). 24p. (gr. k-18). 57.00 *(978-0-7578-3195-9(8))* Rigby Education.
—The Giant's Ice Cream: Big Book Only. Eggleton, Jill. (Sails Literacy Ser.). 24p. (gr. k-18). 27.00 *(978-0-7635-6986-0(0))* Rigby Education.
—Going Up, 6 pack. Holden, Pam. 2009. (Red Rocket Readers Ser.). 16p. (gr. -1-2). pap. *(978-1-877363-18-4(9),* Red Rocket Readers) Flying Start Bks.
—Happy Birthday, 6 pack. Holden, Pam. 2009. (Red Rocket Readers Ser.). 16p. (gr. -1-2). pap. *(978-1-877363-03-0(0),* Red Rocket Readers) Flying Start Bks.
—My Hands, 6 pack. Holden, Pam. 2009. (Red Rocket Readers Ser.). 16p. (gr. -1-3). pap. *(978-1-877363-25-2(1),* Red Rocket Readers) Flying Start Bks.
—My Things, 6 Packs. (Sails Literacy Ser.). 16p. (gr. k-18). 27.00 *(978-0-7635-4395-2(0))* Rigby Education.
—The Paper Trail, 6 pack. Holden, Pam. 2009. (Red Rocket Readers Ser.). 16p. (gr. 2-4). pap. *(978-1-877363-69-6(3))* Flying Start Bks.
—Pass It On, 6 pack. Holden, Pam. 2009. (Red Rocket Readers Ser.). 16p. (gr. 2-4). pap. *(978-1-877363-66-5(9),* Red Rocket Readers) Flying Start Bks.
—Pin the Tail on the Donkey, 6 pack. Holden, Pam. 2009. (Red Rocket Readers Ser.). 16p. pap. *(978-1-877363-78-8(2))* Flying Start Bks.
—Presents for Grace, 6 pack. Holden, Pam. 2009. (Red Rocket Readers Ser.). 16p. (gr. 2-4). pap. *(978-1-877363-61-0(8),* Red Rocket Readers) Flying Start Bks.
—Red Riding Hood, 6 pack. Holden, Pam. 2009. (Red Rocket Readers Ser.). 16p. (gr. -1-2). pap. *(978-1-877363-09-2(X),* Red Rocket Readers) Flying Start Bks.
—Stone Soup, 6 pack. Holden, Pam. 2009. (Red Rocket Readers Ser.). 16p. (gr. 2-5). pap. *(978-1-877363-84-9(7))* Flying Start Bks.
—Three Billy Goats Gruff, 6 pack. Holden, Pam. 2009. (Red Rocket Readers Ser.). 16p. (gr. -1-2). pap. *(978-1-877363-10-8(3),* Red Rocket Readers) Flying Start Bks.
—Tin Lizzy, 6 pack. Holden, Pam. 2009. (Red Rocket Readers Ser.). 16p. (gr. 2-5). pap. *(978-1-877363-86-3(3))* Flying Start Bks.
—Tony's Dad. Eggleton, Jill. 2003. (Rigby Sails Sailing Solo Ser.). (ENG.). 24p. (gr. 1-2). pap. 9.05 *(978-0-7578-3975-7(4))* Rigby Education.
—Trip, Trap!, 6 pack. Holden, Pam. 2009. (Red Rocket Readers Ser.). 16p. (gr. 2-4). pap. *(978-1-877363-62-7(6),* Red Rocket Readers) Flying Start Bks.
—The Vacation: Individual Title Six-Packs. (Sails Literacy Ser.). 16p. (gr. k-18). 27.00 *(978-0-7635-4434-8(5))* Rigby Education.

Hawley, Kelvin, jt. illus. see Storey, Jim.

Hawley, R. Spencer. There's a Monster in My Nose. Hawley, Richard And Elizabeth. 2009. 36p. pap. 24.95 *(978-1-61546-177-6(9))* America Star Bks.

Haworth, Hennie. ArtCards: Accessorize. Broom, Jenny. 2013. (ENG.). 72p. (J). (gr. 1-4). pap. 17.99 *(978-0-7636-6892-1(3),* Big Picture Press) Candlewick Pr.
—Artcards: Fashion. Broom, Jenny. 2014. (ENG.). 72p. (J). (gr. 1-4). pap. 17.99 *(978-0-7636-7519-6(9),* Big Picture Press) Candlewick Pr.

Haworth, Margaret, photos by. Jarry, Garry Palas: Cat Tail Stories. Haworth, Margaret. l.t. ed. 2003. (Books That Help Ser.: Vol. 3). 34p. (J). (gr. 1-6). pap. 9.95 *(978-0-9740313-5-4(6))* Haworth, Margaret.
—Oh Holly Dallig: Cat Tail Stories. Haworth, Margaret. l.t. ed. 2003. (Books That Help Ser.: Vol. 3). 34p. (J). (gr. 1-6). pap. 9.95 *(978-0-9740313-4-7(8))* Haworth, Margaret.

Hawthorn, Paul & Hopkins, Simon. Gammy. Helliwell, Sheila. 2nd ed. 2013. 70p. pap. *(978-0-9560331-4-7(8))* Children' Story Pubs.

Hawthorne, Mike. Machine Teen: History101001. 2012. (ENG.). 120p. (J). (gr. 4-17). pap. 14.99 *(978-0-7851-6486-9(3))* Marvel Worldwide, Inc.

Hawyard, Charlie O. Sidecar Scooter. Caldwell, Bruce. 2008. 32p. (J). pap. 9.95 *(978-0-9792612-9-9(5))* Blue Gate Bks.

Haxton-Johns, Rebecca. Grandpa Goes to College. Haxton, Charles. 2004. 14p. (J). 4.95 *(978-1-59466-017-7(4),* Little Ones) Port Town Publishing.

Hay DeSimone, Corkey. Air & Space Activity & Coloring Book: An Early Introduction to the History of Flight. Hay DeSimone, Corkey. 2006. (J). 7.95 *(978-0-9747921-9-4(3))* Gentle Giraffe Pr.
—Dinosaur Explore Activity & Coloring Book: Dinosaurs designed for their littlest Fans. Hay DeSimone, Corkey. 2006. (J). 4.95 *(978-0-9777394-0-0(6))* Gentle Giraffe Pr.
—Future Sports Legend Board Book: An Early Introduction to Sports in Maryland. Hay DeSimone, Corkey. 2006. (J). bds. 4.99 *(978-0-9747921-5-6(2))* Gentle Giraffe Pr.
—Mammal Animal Board Book 2nd Edition. Hay DeSimone, Corkey. 2007. 24p. (J). 7.95 *(978-0-9777394-2-4(2))* Gentle Giraffe Pr.
—Panda Promise Activity & Coloring Book. Hay DeSimone, Corkey. 2006. (J). 4.95 *(978-0-9747921-9-4(5))* Gentle Giraffe Pr.

Hay, Peter. Lesson of the White Eagle. Hay, Barbara. 2012. (ENG.). 144p. (YA). pap. 11.99 *(978-1-937054-01-4(2))* RoadRunner Pr.

Haya, Erwin. Bible Freaks & Geeks, 1 vol. Strauss, Ed. 2007. (2:52 Ser.). (ENG.). 128p. (J). (gr. 3-7). pap. 7.99 *(978-0-310-71309-8(9))* Zonderkidz.
—Grammar Girl Presents the Ultimate Writing Guide for Students. Fogarty, Mignon. 2011. (Quick & Dirty Tips Ser.). (ENG.). 304p. (YA). (gr. 7-12). 19.99 *(978-0-8050-8943-1(8));* pap. 13.99 *(978-0-8050-8944-8(6))* St. Martin's Pr. (St. Martin's Griffin).
—Picture a Home Run: A Baseball Drawing Book, 1 vol. Wacholtz, Anthony. 2013. (Drawing with Sports Illustrated Kids Ser.). (ENG.). 64p. (gr. 5-7). 33.32 *(978-1-4765-3106-9(4))* Capstone Pr., Inc.
—Picture a Slam Dunk: A Basketball Drawing Book, 1 vol. Wacholtz, Anthony. 2013. (Drawing with Sports Illustrated Kids Ser.). (ENG.). 64p. (gr. 5-7). 33.32 *(978-1-4765-3107-6(2))* Capstone Pr., Inc.
—Seriously Sick Bible Stuff, 1 vol. Strauss, Ed. 2007. (2:52 Ser.). (ENG.). 128p. (J). (gr. 3-7). pap. 7.99 *(978-0-310-71310-4(2))* Zonderkidz.

Haya, Erwin & Ray, Mike. Drawing with Sports Illustrated Kids, 1 vol. Wacholtz, Anthony. 2013. (Drawing with Sports Illustrated Kids Ser.). (ENG.). 144p. (gr. 5-7). pap. 14.95 *(978-1-4765-3581-4(7))* Capstone Pr., Inc.

Haya, Erwin, jt. illus. see Jenkins, Ward.

Haya, Erwin, jt. illus. see Ray, Mike.

Hayashi, Nancy. Camp K-9, 1 vol. Rodman, Mary Ann. 2011. (ENG.). 32p. (J). (gr. -1-3). 15.95 *(978-1-56145-561-4(X))* Peachtree Pubs.
—I Can Do It Myself!, 1 vol. Adams, Diane. (ENG.). 32p. (J). (gr. -1-1). 2013. 7.95 *(978-1-56145-725-0(6));* 2009. 15.95 *(978-1-56145-471-6(0))* Peachtree Pubs.
—Raymond & Nelda, 1 vol. Bottner, Barbara. 2007. (ENG.). 32p. (J). (gr. k-3). 15.95 *(978-1-56145-394-8(3))* Peachtree Pubs.
—Teacher's Little Helper, 1 vol. Adams, Diane. 2012. (ENG.). 32p. (J). 15.95 *(978-1-56145-630-7(6))* Peachtree Pubs.

Hayashi, Nancy. I Know It's Autumn. Hayashi, Nancy, tr. Spinelli, Eileen. 2004. 32p. (J). (gr. -1-2). lib. bdg. 17.89 *(978-0-06-029423-6(X))* HarperCollins Pubs.
—I Know It's Autumn. Hayashi, Nancy, tr. Spinelli, Eileen & Spinelli. 2004. (ENG.). 32p. (J). (gr. -1-2). 16.99 *(978-0-06-029422-9(1))* HarperCollins Pubs.

Hayashi, Yoshio. More Japanese Children's Favorite Stories. Sakade, Florence. anniv. ed. 2014. (ENG.). 96p. (J). 17.95 *(978-4-8053-1265-0(3))* Tuttle Publishing.

Hayashida, Q. Dorohedoro. Hayashida, Q. Hayashida, Q. 2010. (Dorohedoro Ser.: 1). (ENG.). 176p. pap. 12.99 *(978-1-4215-3363-6(4))* Viz Media.

Haycraft, Marilynn J. The Cowbears of Texas: The Hero. Edgell, Ernest. 2004. 25p. pap. 24.95 *(978-1-4137-3507-9(X))* PublishAmerica, Inc.

Hayden, Jennifer. Liberty Cafe Is Open. Trimble, Marcia. ed. 2006. (J). pap. 895.00 *(978-1-891577-91-8(3));* 32p. lib. bdg. 15.95 *(978-1-891577-90-1(5))* Images Pr.

Hayden, Jennifer H. Marsby & the Martian Detectives. Trimble, Marcia J. 2004. 56p. (J). per. 9.95 *(978-1-891577-52-9(2),* SAN299-4844) Images Pr.

Hayden, Seito & Chandler, Alton. Beginning Conversations with God: A Prayer & Spiritual Journal for Children. Banks, Calvin J. (J). (gr. -1-3). pap. 14.95 *(978-1-877804-14-4(2))* Chandler/White Publishing Co.

Hayden, Seitu. A Biography of Malcolm X. Gunderson, Jessica. 2011. (American Graphic Ser.). (ENG.). 32p. (gr. 3-4). lib. bdg. 29.99 *(978-1-4296-5471-5(6),* Graphic Library) Capstone Pr., Inc.
—Come to Galapagos at Sea to See. Fogerty, Ramona. 2004. (SPA.). (J). pap. 22.95 *(978-0-9759889-1-6(3))* Potenial Psychotherapy Counseling & Remedial Service.
—Obama: The Historic Election of America's 44th President, 1 vol. Biskup, Agnieszka. 2011. (American Graphic Ser.). (ENG.). 32p. (gr. 3-4). pap. 8.10 *(978-1-4296-7339-6(7));* pap. 47.70 *(978-1-4296-7340-2(0));* lib. bdg. 29.99 *(978-1-4296-6016-7(3))* Capstone Pr., Inc. (Graphic Library).
—X: A Biography of Malcolm X. Gunderson, Jessica. 2011. (American Graphic Ser.). (ENG.). 32p. (gr. 3-4). pap. 8.10 *(978-1-4296-6267-3(0));* pap. 47.70 *(978-1-4296-6438-7(X))* Capstone Pr., Inc. (Graphic Library).

Hayden, Seitu & Kinsella, Pat. American Graphic. Collins, Terry et al. 2012. (American Graphic Ser.). (ENG.). 32p. (gr. 3-4). lib. bdg. 59.98 *(978-1-4296-9162-8(X),* Graphic Library) Capstone Pr., Inc.

Hayden, Seitu, jt. illus. see Still, Wayne A.

Hayes, Betsy. Cozy Clozy: From Fibers to Fabrics. Alford, Douglas. 2004. (J). 6.96 net. *(978-0-9762208-0-0(6))* Mfg Application Konsulting Engineering.

Hayes, Dan. The Thanksgiving. 24p. (J). pap., act. bk. ed. 7.95 *(978-0-8249-5324-9(X))* Ideals Pubns.

Hayes, David, jt. illus. see Hayes, Kathy.

Hayes, Don. The Easter. 24p. (Orig.). (J). pap., act. bk. ed. 4.95 *(978-0-8249-5368-3(1),* Ideals) Ideals Pubns.

Hayes, Fiona. Cuddly Lion. Rivers, Moore Debbie & Henning, Heather. 2009. (Books on the Go! Ser.). (ENG.). 8p. (J). (gr. -1-k). 12.99 *(978-0-7641-4414-1(6))* Barron's Educational Series, Inc.

Hayes, Geoffrey. Jack & the Box. Spiegelman, Art. 2008. (ENG.). 32p. (J). (gr. -1-3). 12.95 *(978-0-9799238-3-8(2))* TOON Books / RAW Junior, LLC.

H

Hayes, Geoffrey. Benny & Penny in Just Pretend. Hayes, Geoffrey. 2008. (Benny & Penny Ser.). (ENG.). 32p. (J). (gr. -1-3). 12.95 *(978-0-9799238-0-7(8))* TOON Books / RAW Junior, LLC.

—Benny & Penny in Just Pretend, Level 2. Hayes, Geoffrey. 2013. (Benny & Penny Ser.). (ENG.). 32p. (J). (gr. -1-3). pap. 4.99 *(978-1-935179-26-9(8))* TOON Books / RAW Junior, LLC.

—A Night-Light for Bunny. Hayes, Geoffrey. 2004. 32p. (J). (gr. -1-3). 14.99 *(978-0-06-029163-1(X))* HarperCollins Pubs.

—Patrick Eats His Peas & Other Stories. Hayes, Geoffrey. 2013. (ENG.). 32p. (J). (gr. -1-3). 12.95 *(978-1-935179-34-4(9))* TOON Books / RAW Junior, LLC.

—A Poor Excuse for a Dragon. Hayes, Geoffrey. 2011. (Step into Reading Ser.). (ENG.). 48p. (J). (gr. 2-4). 12.99 *(978-0-375-87180-1(2),* Random Hse. Bks. for Young Readers) Random Hse. Children's Bks.

Hayes, Karel. Little Loon. Hodgkins, Fran. 2015. (ENG.). 32p. (J). (gr. -1-3). 16.95 *(978-1-60893-372-3(5))* Down East Bks.

—Time for the Fair. Train, Mary. ed. 2005. (ENG.). 28p. (J). (gr. k-17). 15.95 *(978-0-89272-694-3(6))* Down East Bks.

—Who's Been Here? A Tale in Tracks. Hodgkins, Fran. ed. 2008. (ENG.). 32p. (J). (gr. -1-3). 15.95 *(978-0-89272-714-8(4))* Down East Bks.

Hayes, Karel. The Summer Visitors, 10 vols. Hayes, Karel. ed. 2011. (ENG.). 32p. (gr. -1-3). 16.95 *(978-0-89272-918-0(X))* Down East Bks.

Hayes, Kathy & Hayes, David. The Camp Caper: A Shubin Cousins Adventure. Shubin, Masha. 2013. 88p. pap. 6.95 *(978-0-9792145-1-6(3))* Anno Domini.

Hayes, Steve & Cole, Amy. How Maji Gets Mongo off the Couch! Norton, J. Renae. Reed, Cleone, ed. ed. 2012. (Maji & Mongo Bks.: 0). (ENG.). 32p. (J). (gr. k-3). 17.95 *(978-1-934759-60-8(0))* Reed, Robert D. Pubs.

Hayn, Walter. Slovenly Betsy: the American Struwwelpeter: From the Struwwelpeter Library. Hoffmann, Heinrich. 2013. (Dover Children's Classics Ser.). (ENG.). 96p. (J). (gr. 3-8). pap. 12.99 *(978-0-486-49828-7(X))* Dover Pubns., Inc.

Hayne, Mark. The Young Captives: A Story of Judah & Babylon. Jones, Erasmus W. 2007. 200p. per. *(978-1-4065-2718-6(1))* Dodo Pr.

Haynes, Jason & Oke, Rachel. Rudy the Red Pig. Guess, Catherine Ritch. 2006. (ENG.). 32p. (J). 13.95 *(978-1-933341-13-2(0))* CRM.

Haynes, Joyce. The Diary of Marie Landry, Acadian Exile, 1 vol. Albritton, Stacy. 2012. (ENG.). 160p. (J). (gr. 3-7). pap. 14.95 *(978-1-58980-865-2(7))* Pelican Publishing Co., Inc.

—Good Soup Attracts Chairs, 1 vol. Osseo-Asare, Fran. 2006. (ENG.). 160p. (J). (gr. 5-8). pap. 19.95 *(978-1-56554-918-0(X))* Pelican Publishing Co., Inc.

—Jane Wilkinson Long: Texas Pioneer, 1 vol. Petrick, Neila Skinner. 2004. (ENG.). 32p. (J). (gr. k-3). 16.99 *(978-1-58980-147-9(4))* Pelican Publishing Co., Inc.

—Lipstick Like Lindsay's & Other Christmas Stories, 1 vol. Toner, Gerald R. 2005. (ENG.). 112p. per. 14.95 *(978-1-58980-357-2(4))* Pelican Publishing Co., Inc.

Haynes, Penny. Maisie the Animal Minder: Maisie & Ben. Littlefield, Eireann. 2012. 34p. pap. *(978-1-908128-35-5(6))* Spiderwize.

Hays, Ethel. The Town Mouse & the Country Mouse. 2007. (Shape Bks.). (ENG.). 14p. (J). (gr. -1-3). pap. 9.95 *(978-1-59583-192-7(4),* 9781595831927, Green Tiger Pr.) Laughing Elephant.

Hays, Michael. Abiyoyo Returns. Seeger, Pete & Jacobs, Paul DuBois. 2004. (ENG.). 40p. (J). (gr. -1-3). 7.99 *(978-0-689-87054-5(X),* Simon & Schuster/Paula Wiseman Bks.) Simon & Schuster/Paula Wiseman Bks.

—W Is for Windy City: A Chicago City Alphabet. Layne, Steven et al. 2010. (Sleeping Bear City Alphabet Ser.). (ENG.). 40p. (J). 17.95 *(978-1-58536-420-6(7))* Sleeping Bear Pr.

Haysom, John. The Story of Christmas. Jeffs, Stephanie. 2005. 32p. (J). (gr. -1). 15.00 *(978-0-687-05501-2(6))* Abingdon Pr.

—The Story of Easter. Doyle, Christopher. (J). (gr. k-3). 2008. 29p. pap. 7.49 *(978-0-7586-1495-7(0));* 2005. 32p. 13.49 *(978-0-7586-0837-6(3))* Concordia Publishing Hse.

Hayward, Annie. Baba Didi & the Godwits Fly. Muir, Nicola. 2013. (ENG.). 32p. (J). (gr. k-4). 8.95 *(978-1-78026-130-0(6))* New Internationalist Pubns., Ltd. GBR. Dist: Consortium Bk. Sales & Distribution.

Hayward, Roy. The Christmas Elf. Scott, D. P. 2013. 86p. pap. *(978-0-9880635-2-5(2))* Scott, Daren.

Haywood, Ian Benfold. Always by My Side, 1 vol. Kerner, Susan. 2013. (ENG.). 32p. (J). 16.99 *(978-1-59572-336-9(6));* pap. 6.99 *(978-1-59572-337-6(4))* Star Bright Bks., Inc.

—Tim & the Iceberg, 1 vol. Coates, Paul. 2011. (ENG.). 32p. (J). (gr. k-3). 16.95 *(978-1-59572-205-8(X));* pap. 6.95 *(978-1-59572-206-5(8))* Star Bright Bks., Inc.

Hazan, Maurice. Les Animaux et les Verbes. Travis, Joelle & Figueras, Ligaya, eds. 2003. (FRE.). (J). per. 20.00 *(978-1-932770-18-6(6),* FWLB1) Symtalk, Inc.

—Chiffres, Couleurs, Verbes et Phrases. Travis, Joelle & Figueras, Ligaya, eds. 2003. (FRE.). 114p. (J). per. 20.00 *(978-1-932770-19-3(4),* FWLB2) Symtalk, Inc.

—En Plena Vista Level 1. Figueras, Ligaya, ed. 5th ed. 2003. (SPA.). 140p. per. 22.00 *(978-1-932770-98-8(4),* SHB-SM) Symtalk, Inc.

—Le Français en Images, Livre 3. Travis, Joelle & Figueras, Ligaya, eds. 5th ed. 2003. (FRE.). 160p. spiral bd. 22.00 *(978-1-932770-14-8(3),* FB3-SM-0.5) Symtalk, Inc.

—Le Francais en Images, Vol. 3. Travis, Joelle & Figueras, Ligaya, eds. 5th ed. 2003. (FRE.). 160p. tchr. ed., spiral bd. 30.00 *(978-1-932770-15-5(1),* FB3-TG-0.5) Symtalk, Inc.

—French, Bk. 1. 2004. (FRE.). (J). 140.00 *(978-1-932770-30-8(5),* FC-FB1) Symtalk, Inc.

—French Gerard et Ses Copains, Bk. 1. Travis, Joelle & Figueras, Ligaya, eds. 7th ed. 2004. (FRE.). 120p. tchr. ed., spiral bd. 30.00 *(978-1-932770-11-7(9),* FB1-TG) Symtalk, Inc.

—French Gérard et ses Copains. Travis, Joelle & Figueras, Ligaya, eds. (FRE.). Bk. 1. 7th l.t. ed. 2004. 111p. per. 20.00 *(978-1-932770-10-0(0),* FB1-SM); Bk. 2. 6th ed. 2003. 163p. tchr. ed., spiral bd. 30.00 *(978-1-932770-13-1(5),* FB2-TG) Symtalk, Inc.

—French Gérard et Ses Copains, Bk. 2. Travis, Joelle & Figueras, Ligaya, eds. 6th ed. 2003. (FRE.). 163p. spiral bd. 20.00 *(978-1-932770-12-4(7),* FB2-SM) Symtalk, Inc.

—French Junior Book Gérard et ses Copains. Travis, Joelle & Figueras, Ligaya, eds. 5th l.t. ed. 2003. (FRE.). 84p. per. 20.00 *(978-1-932770-08-7(9),* FJRB-SM) Symtalk, Inc.

—French Junior Book Gérard et ses Copains Teacher's Guide. Travis, Joelle & Figueras, Ligaya, eds. 5th ed. 2003. (FRE.). 110p. tchr. ed., spiral bd. 30.00 *(978-1-932770-09-4(7),* FJRB-TG) Symtalk, Inc.

—French Level 1 Assessment with Stickers. Travis, Joelle, ed. 2003. (FRE.). (J). 30.00 *(978-1-932770-23-0(2),* FR LEVEL 1) Symtalk, Inc.

—Los Animales y los Verbos. Travis, Joelle & Figueras, Ligaya, eds. 2003. (SPA.). 89p. (J). per. 20.00 *(978-1-932770-16-2(X),* SWLB1) Symtalk, Inc.

—Numeros, Colores, Verbos y Frases. Travis, Joelle & Figueras, Ligaya, eds. 2003. (SPA.). 112p. (J). per. 20.00 *(978-1-932770-17-9(8),* SWLB2) Symtalk, Inc.

—Spanish Espanol en Imagenes, Vol. 3. Travis, Joelle & Figueras, Ligaya, eds. 6th ed. 2003. (SPA.). 252p. tchr. ed., spiral bd. 30.00 *(978-1-932770-07-0(0),* SB3-TG); 179p. spiral bd. 22.00 *(978-1-932770-06-3(2),* SB3-SM) Symtalk, Inc.

—Spanish Junior Book Pablo y sus Amigos. Travis, Joelle & Figueras, Ligaya, eds. 5th l.t. ed. 2003. (SPA.). 87p. per. 20.00 *(978-1-932770-00-1(3),* SJRB-SM) Symtalk, Inc.

—Spanish Junior Book Pablo y sus amigos Teacher's Guide. Travis, Joelle & Figueras, Ligaya, eds. 5th ed. 2003. (SPA.). 118p. tchr. ed., spiral bd. 30.00 *(978-1-932770-01-8(1),* SJRB-TG) Symtalk, Inc.

—Spanish Level 1 Assessment. Travis, Joelle & Figueras, Ligaya, eds. 2003. (SPA.). (J). 30.00 *(978-1-932770-21-6(6),* SP LEVEL 1) Symtalk, Inc.

—Spanish Pablo y sus amigos, Bk. 1. Travis, Joelle & Figueras, Ligaya, eds. 7th ed. 2004. (SPA.). 156p. tchr. ed., spiral bd. 30.00 *(978-1-932770-03-2(8),* SB1-TG) Symtalk, Inc.

—Spanish Pablo y sus Amigos. Travis, Joelle & Figueras, Ligaya, eds. (SPA.). Bk. 1. 7th l.t. ed. 2004. 111p. per. 20.00 *(978-1-932770-02-5(X),* SB1-SM); Bk. 2. 5th ed. 2003. 131p. per. 20.00 *(978-1-932770-04-9(6),* SB2-SM) Symtalk, Inc.

—Spanish Pablo y sus amigos, Bk. 2. Travis, Joelle & Figueras, Ligaya, eds. 5th ed. 2003. (SPA.). 148p. tchr. ed., spiral bd. 30.00 *(978-1-932770-05-6(4),* SB2-TG) Symtalk, Inc.

Hazan, Maurice. Les Animaux et les verbes flash card Set. Hazan, Maurice, creator. 2003. (FRE.). (J). 95.00 *(978-1-932770-38-4(0),* FC-FWLB1) Symtalk, Inc.

—Chiffres, couleurs, verbes et phrases flash card Set. Hazan, Maurice, creator. 2003. (FRE.). (J). 115.00 *(978-1-932770-39-1(9),* FC-FWLB2) Symtalk, Inc.

—French. Hazan, Maurice, creator. 2004. (FRE.). Bk. 2. (J). 175.00 *(978-1-932770-32-2(1),* FC-FB2); Bk. 3. 199.00 *(978-1-932770-34-6(8),* FC-FB3) Symtalk, Inc.

Hazard, Andrea. Zack Attack! Perez, Angela J. 2007. 36p. (J). 17.95 *(978-0-9778328-9-7(9))* His Work Christian Publishing.

Hazard, John. Joni & the Fallen Star: Helping Children Learn Teamwork. Pilon, Cindy Jett. 2011. (Let's Talk Ser.). (ENG.). 48p. (J). (gr. -1-2). pap. 9.95 *(978-0-88282-353-9(1))* New Horizon Pr. Pubs., Inc.

—Tommy & the T-Tops: Helping Children Overcome Prejudice. Alimonti, Frederick & Tedesco, Ann. 2009. (Let's Talk Ser.). (ENG.). 48p. (J). (gr. -1-4). pap. 8.95 *(978-0-88282-305-8(1))* New Horizon Pr. Pubs., Inc.

Hazel, Andrew. Seeing Red: Story Seeds Vol 1. Hamilton, George. 2008. 20p. pap. 13.99 *(978-1-4343-8004-3(1))* AuthorHouse.

Hazelaar, Cor. The Man Who Lived in a Hollow Tree. Shelby, Anne. 2009. (ENG.). 40p. (J). (gr. -1-2). 17.99 *(978-0-689-86169-7(9),* Atheneum/Richard Jackson Bks.) Simon & Schuster Children's Publishing.

Hazelton, Jack W. Charlie Duck. Hazelton, Jack W. l.t. ed. 2003. 24p. (J). 12.95 *(978-1-928907-54-1(7))* Jack's Bookshelf, Inc.

Hazlegrove, Cary, photos by. Weekends for Two in the Southwest: 50 Romantic Getaways. Gleeson, Bill. 2nd rev. ed. 2005. (ENG., 124p. (gr. 8-17). pap. 18.95 *(978-0-8118-4624-0(5))* Chronicle Bks. LLC.

Head, Mat. Warduff & the Corn Cob Caper. Head, Mat. 2011. (Andersen Press Picture Books Ser.). 16.95 *(978-0-7613-8095-5(7))* Andersen Pr. GBR. Dist: Lerner Publishing Group.

Head, Murray. Frisky Brisky Hippity Hop. Head, Murray, photos by. White, Alexina B. 2012. (ENG.). 32p. (J). 16.95 *(978-0-8234-2410-8(3))* Holiday Hse., Inc.

Head, Murray, photos by. Swim, Duck, Swim! Lurie, Susan. 2014. (ENG., 32p. (J). (gr. -1-2). 16.99 *(978-1-250-04642-0(4))* Feiwel & Friends.

Head, Pat. Hood River Home. Marlow, Herb. 2005. 162p. (YA). per. 18.95 *(978-1-893595-47-7(1));* lib. bdg. 28.95 *(978-1-893595-13-2(7))* Four Seasons Bks., Inc.

—The Lost Kitten. Marlow, Herb. 2003. 16p. (J). 19.95 *(978-1-893595-34-7(X))* Four Seasons Bks., Inc.

—The Tiger's Den. Marlow, Herb. 2003. 22p. (J). 19.95 *(978-1-893595-37-8(4))* Four Seasons Bks., Inc.

Head-Weston, Alex, et al. Know How Know Why Dinosaurs. Matthews, Rupert. 2004. (Know How Know Why Ser.). 48p. (J). (gr. 3-7). pap. *(978-1-84510-031-5(X))* Top That! Publishing PLC.

Headcase Design. For Boys Only: The Biggest, Baddest Book Ever. Aronson, Marc & Newquist, H. P. 2007. (ENG.). 160p. (J). (gr. 5-8). 15.99 *(978-0-312-37706-9(1))* Feiwel & Friends.

Headings, Joseph E. & Headings, Peggy A. Friends for Keeps. Headings, Peggy A. Gordon, Betsy, ed. 2010. (ENG.). 34p. pap. 9.13 *(978-1-4495-8440-5(3))* CreateSpace Independent Publishing Platform.

Headings, Peggy A., jt. illus. see Headings, Joseph E.

Headley, Aaron. Evangel Meets Orsen Whale. Gray, Rick & Gray, Coral. 2007. (ENG.). 32p. (J). (gr. -1-3). 14.95 *(978-0-9790210-1-5(4))* Evening Star Enterprise, Inc.

Heale, Jonathan. Zólw I Zajac: Bajka Ezopa. McAllister, Angela. 2010.Tr. of Tortoise & the Hare/An Aesop's Fablezolw I Zajac. (POL & ENG.). 32p. (J). (gr. -1-1). 17.95 *(978-1-84507-948-2(5),* Frances Lincoln) Quarto Publishing Group UK GBR. Dist: Hachette Bk. Group.

Healy, Jeane. Exploring Art: Create It - Display It. Wilmes, Liz & Wilmes, Dick. 2004. 256p. (J). pap. 19.95 *(978-0-943452-05-0(8),* 20160) Building Blocks, LLC.

Healy, Maggie. A Coming of Winter in the Adirondacks. Heinz, Brian J. 2011. 32p. (J). 19.95 *(978-1-59531-038-5(X))* North Country Bks., Inc.

Heaney Dunn, John. The Little Red House with No Doors & No Windows & A Star Inside. 2011. 25p. (J). pap. 15.95 *(978-1-58909-915-9(X))* Bookstand Publishing.

Heap, Jonathon. Othello. Mulherin, Jennifer & Frost, Abigail. 31p. pap. *(978-1-84234-034-9(4))* Cherrytree Bks.

Heap, Sue. How to Be a Baby: By Me, the Big Sister. Lloyd-Jones, Sally. 2007. (How to Ser.). (ENG.). 40p. (J). (gr. -1-3). 16.99 *(978-0-375-83843-9(0),* Schwartz & Wade Bks.) Random Hse. Children's Bks.

—How to Be a Baby... by Me, the Big Sister. Lloyd-Jones, Sally. 2011. (How to Ser.). (ENG.). 40p. (J). (gr. -1-3). pap. 7.99 *(978-0-375-87388-1(0),* Schwartz & Wade Bks.) Random Hse. Children's Bks.

—How to Get a Job - By Me, the Boss. Lloyd-Jones, Sally. 2011. (How to Ser.). (ENG.). 40p. (J). (gr. -1-3). 17.99 *(978-0-375-86664-7(7),* Schwartz & Wade Bks.) Random Hse. Children's Bks.

—Polly's Pink Pajamas. French, Vivian. 2010. (ENG.). 32p. (J). (gr. -1-2). 14.99 *(978-0-7636-4807-7(8))* Candlewick Pr.

—Very Little Red Riding Hood. Heapy, Teresa. 2014. (Very Little Ser.). (ENG.). 32p. (J). (gr. -1-3). 16.99 *(978-0-544-28000-7(8),* HMH Books For Young Readers) Houghton Mifflin Harcourt Publishing Co.

Heap, Sue. Danny's Drawing Book. Heap, Sue. 2008. (ENG.). 32p. (J). (gr. -1-3). 9.99 *(978-0-7636-3654-8(1))* Candlewick Pr.

—A Fabulous Fairy Feast. Heap, Sue. 2009. (ENG.). 32p. (J). (gr. -1-k). pap. 8.99 *(978-1-4052-3644-7(2))* Egmont Bks., Ltd. GBR. Dist: Independent Pubs. Group.

—Four Friends Together. Heap, Sue. 2003. (ENG.). 32p. (J). (gr. -1-k). 15.99 *(978-0-7636-2111-7(0))* Candlewick Pr.

—Mine! Heap, Sue. 2014. (ENG.). 32p. (J). (-k). 15.99 *(978-0-7636-6888-4(5))* Candlewick Pr.

Heap, Sue, jt. illus. see Sharratt, Nick.

Heap, Will & Dunne, Kevin, photos by. The Kids' Cookbook: Over 50 Fun Recipes for Kids to Cook. Knowlden, Martin. 2006. 128p. *(978-1-85626-626-0(5))* Cathie, Kyle Ltd. GBR. Dist: Independent Pubs. Group.

Heaphy, Paula. Dare!, Bk. 2. Frankel, Erin. (Weird! Ser.). (ENG.). 48p. (J). (gr. k-4). 2013. pap. 9.99 *(978-1-57542-439-2(8));* 2012. 15.99 *(978-1-57542-399-9(5))* Free Spirit Publishing, Inc.

Heaphy, Paula. Nobody! A Story about Overcoming Bullying in Schools. Frankel, Erin. 2015. (ENG.). 48p. (J). (gr. k-4). 15.99 ***(978-1-57542-495-8(9))*** Free Spirit Publishing, Inc.

Heaphy, Paula. Tough!, Bk. 3. Frankel, Erin. 2013. (Weird! Ser.). (ENG.). 48p. (J). (gr. k-4). pap. 9.99 *(978-1-57542-438-5(X))* Free Spirit Publishing, Inc.

—Weird! Frankel, Erin. 2013. (Weird! Ser.). (ENG.). 48p. (J). (gr. k-4). pap. 9.99 *(978-1-57542-437-8(1))* Free Spirit Publishing, Inc.

Hearld, Mark. Outside Your Window: A First Book of Nature. Davies, Nicola. 2012. (ENG.). 108p. (J). (gr. -1-2). 19.99 *(978-0-7636-5549-5(X))* Candlewick Pr.

Hearn, Diane Dawson. Christmas in the Forest. Bauer, Marion Dane. (Holiday House Reader Ser.). (ENG.). 48p. (J). (gr. k-3). tchr. ed. 15.95 *(978-0-8234-1371-3(3))* Holiday Hse., Inc.

—George Washington's First Victory. Krensky, Stephen. 2005. (Ready-To-read COFA Ser.). (ENG.). 32p. (J). (gr. k-2). pap. 3.99 *(978-0-689-85942-7(2),* Simon Spotlight) Simon Spotlight.

—Rain Forests. Levinson, Nancy Smiler. 2008. (Holiday House Readers: Level 2 Ser.). (ENG.). 40p. (J). (gr. 3-7). 15.95 *(978-0-8234-1899-2(5))* Holiday Hse., Inc.

Hearn, Marilyn. My Dear Child, I Have Gone to Heaven Let's Talk: A Child's Recovery Plan, 1 vol. Carson, Shonette. 2010. 36p. 24.95 *(978-1-4489-6341-6(9))* PublishAmerica, Inc.

Hearn, Sam. The Abominators: And My Amazing Panty Wanty Woos! Smith, J. L. 2014. (Abominators Ser.: 1). (ENG.). 144p. (J). (gr. 2-4). pap. 7.99 *(978-1-907411-62-5(3))* Little, Brown Book Group Ltd. GBR. Dist: Independent Pubs. Group.

—The Abominators & the Forces of Evil. Smith, J. L. 2014. (Abominators Ser.: 2). (ENG.). 240p. (J). (gr. 2-4). pap. 7.99 *(978-1-907411-64-9(X))* Little, Brown Book Group Ltd. GBR. Dist: Independent Pubs. Group.

—Ordinary Oscar. Adkins, Laura. 2010. 32p. (J). (gr. -1-2). 15.95 *(978-1-58925-085-7(0));* (gr. k-2). pap. 7.95 *(978-1-58925-418-3(X))* Tiger Tales.

Hearn, Samuel. Cosmo & the Great Witch Escape, 1. Rees, Gwyneth. 2nd unabr. ed. 2006. (Cosmo Ser.: 2). (ENG.). 192p. (J). (gr. 2-4). pap. 9.99 *(978-0-330-43733-2(X))* Macmillan Pubs., Ltd. GBR. Dist: Independent Pubs. Group.

—Cosmo & the Magic Sneeze, 1. Rees, Gwyneth. 3rd unabr. ed. 2005. (Cosmo Ser.: 1). (ENG.). 368p. (J). (gr. 2-4). pap. 8.99 *(978-0-330-43729-5(1))* Macmillan Pubs., Ltd. GBR. Dist: Independent Pubs. Group.

—Cosmo & the Secret Spell, 1. Rees, Gwyneth. unabr. ed. 2010. (Cosmo Ser.: 3). (ENG.). 240p. (J). (gr. 2-4). pap. 7.99 *(978-0-330-44216-9(3))* Macmillan Pubs., Ltd. GBR. Dist: Independent Pubs. Group.

Hearson, Ruth. Leo Loves Baby Time. McQuinn, Anna. 2014. (ENG.). 24p. (J). (— 1). lib. bdg. 9.95 *(978-1-58089-665-8(0))* Charlesbridge Publishing, Inc.

Hearson, Ruth. A Leo le Gusta Bebelandia. Hearson, Ruth. McQuinn, Anna & Miawer, Teresa. 2015. (SPA & ENG.). 24p. (J). (— 1). lib. bdg. 9.95 *(978-1-58089-704-4(5))* Charlesbridge Publishing, Inc.

Heaston, Rebecca J. Before You Were Born. Nixon, Joan Lowery. 2nd sensormatic ed. 2006. 31p. pap. 10.95 *(978-1-59276-219-4(0))* Our Sunday Visitor, Publishing Div.

Heath, Paul Reaves. My Dad Wears Striped Pajamas. DeStout, Carole. 2003. (Children's Outreach Ser.). 38p. (J). pap. 5.00 *(978-1-880994-83-2(6))* Mount Olive College Pr.

Heather, Miss. Creepy Crypt of ABC. Heather, Miss. l.t. ed. 2011. (ENG.). 32p. pap. 10.95 *(978-1-4663-1959-2(3))* CreateSpace Independent Publishing Platform.

Heatley, David. Otis Dooda: Strange but True. Potter, Ellen. 2013. (Otis Dooda Ser.). (ENG.). 240p. (J). (gr. 2-5). 13.99 *(978-1-250-01176-3(0))* Feiwel & Friends.

—Otis Dooda: Downright Dangerous. Potter, Ellen. 2014. (Otis Dooda Ser.). (ENG.). 240p. (J). (gr. 2-5). 13.99 *(978-1-250-01177-0(9))* Feiwel & Friends.

Heaton, Jr. I Just Love You So Much. Hulslander, Dyan. 2009. 28p. pap. 14.49 *(978-1-4490-0454-5(7))* AuthorHouse.

Heaton, Layce. The Weeping Willow Tree. Page, Lawana. Amaya, Laura, tr. 2006. (SPA.). 32p. 10.95 *(978-0-9761128-2-2(5))* KB Bks. & More.

Heaton, Layce D. The Many Tracks of Lap'n Tap, 1. Heaton, Layce D. 2006. 32p. (J). lib. bdg. 18.95 *(978-0-9761128-3-9(3))* KB Bks. & More.

Heavner, Jodi. The Three Wives of Hero the Second. Randall, Marilyn Mae. 2004. (J). per. 14.99 *(978-0-9713589-7-3(4))* Ubavie's Gifts.

Hechter, Janice. Avi's Choice: A Story about Bikur Cholim-Visiting the Sick. Simhaee, Rebeka. 2014. 35p. (J). ***(978-0-8266-0043-1(3))*** Merkos L'Inyonei Chinuch.

Hechter, Janice. The Great Elephant Escape, 1 vol. Townsend, Una Belle. 2012. (ENG.). 32p. (J). (gr. k-3). 16.99 *(978-1-4556-1582-7(X))* Pelican Publishing Co., Inc.

Hechtkopf, H. Chatzkel, Mendel & Me: An adventure Story. Fuchs, Menucha. Daykin, Rachmiel, tr. from HEB. 2005. Orig. Title: Mah Shekarah Ba'Ayarah. 192p. (J). 15.95 *(978-1-932443-39-4(8),* CHMH) Judaica Pr., Inc., The.

Heck, Don, et al. Invaders Classic Vol. 1: The Complete Collection. 2014. (ENG.). 512p. (J). (gr. 4-17). pap. 39.99 *(978-0-7851-9057-8(0))* Marvel Worldwide, Inc.

Heck, Don. Marvel Masterworks: The Avengers - Volume 4. 2012. (ENG.). 224p. (J). (gr. -1-17). pap. 24.99 *(978-0-7851-6360-2(3))* Marvel Worldwide, Inc.

Heck, Don & Byrne, John. Hawkeye. Friedrich, Mike. 2009. (ENG.). 192p. (YA). (gr. 8-17). 24.99 *(978-0-7851-3937-9(0))* Marvel Worldwide, Inc.

Heck, Don, jt. illus. see Colan, Gene.

Heck, Don, jt. illus. see Lieber, Larry.

Hecker, Vera. Fancy the Beautiful Little Dragon: Book Number Two Little One's Series. Banta, Sandra F. l.t. ed. 2006. 45p. per. 11.99 *(978-1-59879-157-0(5))* Lifevest Publishing, Inc.

—A Home for Rainbow. 2007. 32p. (J). *(978-0-9799729-0-4(6))* Banta, Sandra.

—Muffy the Dragon. Banta, Sandra F. l.t. ed. 2005. 19p. (J). per. 9.99 *(978-1-59879-060-3(9))* Lifevest Publishing, Inc.

Hecker, Vera. Mystic World Coloring Book. Hecker, Vera. 2007. (YA). per. *(978-0-9799729-1-1(4))* Banta, Sandra.

Heckman, Mark. Sooper Yooper: Environmental Defender. Newman, Mark. 2010. 48p. (J). 17.95 *(978-1-933272-26-9(0))* Thunder Bay Pr.

Hector, Julian. C. R. Mudgeon. Muir, Leslie. 2012. (ENG.). 32p. (J). (gr. -1-3). 15.99 *(978-1-4169-7906-7(9),* Atheneum Bks. for Young Readers) Simon & Schuster Children's Publishing.

Hector, Julian. Monday Is One Day. Levine, Arthur A. 2015. (ENG.). 32p. (J). (gr. -1-k). 6.99 ***(978-0-439-78925-7(7))*** Scholastic, Inc.

—This Is the Firefighter [Board Book]. Godwin, Laura. 2015. (ENG.). 24p. (J). (gr. -1 — 1). bds. 6.99 ***(978-1-4847-0733-3(8))*** Hyperion Bks. for Children.

Hector, Julian. The Gentleman Bug. Hector, Julian. 2010. (ENG.). 40p. (J). (gr. -1-k). 16.99 *(978-1-4169-9467-1(X),* Atheneum Bks. for Young Readers) Simon & Schuster Children's Publishing.

Hedderich, Tom. Father Like a Tree. Field, Matthew S. 2005. (ENG.). (J). 19.95 *(978-0-9761528-0-4(0))* Matting Leah Publishing Co.

—The Three Pigs, Business School, & Wolf Hash Stew. Field, Matthew S. 2006. (ENG.). (J). 19.95 *(978-0-9761528-1-1(9))* Matting Leah Publishing Co.

Hedderwick, Mairi. Island Stories. Hedderwick, Mairi. ed. 2010. (Katie Morag Ser.: 12). (ENG.). 112p. (J). (gr. k-2). pap. 19.99 *(978-1-84941-088-5(7),* Red Fox) Random House Children's Books GBR. Dist: Independent Pubs. Group.

—Katie Morag & the Big Boy Cousins. Hedderwick, Mairi. 2010. (Katie Morag Ser.: 5). (ENG.). 32p. (J). (gr. k-2). pap. 12.99 *(978-1-84941-089-2(5),* Red Fox) Random House Children's Books GBR. Dist: Independent Pubs. Group.

—Katie Morag & the Birthdays. Hedderwick, Mairi. 2005. (Katie Morag Ser.). (ENG.). 48p. (J). (gr. k-4). per. 14.99 *(978-0-09-946426-6(8),* Red Fox) Random House Children's Books GBR. Dist: Independent Pubs. Group.

—Katie Morag & the Grand Concert. Hedderwick, Mairi. ed. 2010. (Katie Morag Ser.: 6). (ENG.). 32p. (J). (gr. k-2). pap. 12.99 *(978-1-84941-087-8(9),* Red Fox) Random House Children's Books GBR. Dist: Independent Pubs. Group.

—Katie Morag & the Riddles. Hedderwick, Mairi. ed. 2010. (Katie Morag Ser.: 10). (ENG.). 32p. (J). (gr. k-2). pap. 12.99 *(978-1-84941-092-2(5),* Red Fox) Random House Children's Books GBR. Dist: Independent Pubs. Group.

—Katie Morag & the Two Grandmothers. Hedderwick, Mairi. 2010. (Katie Morag Ser.: 2). (ENG.). 32p. (J). (gr. k-2). pap. 12.99 *(978-1-84941-086-1(0),* Red Fox) Random

House Children's Books GBR. Dist: Independent Pubs. Group.
—Katie Morag Delivers the Mail. Hedderwick, Mairi. ed. 2010. (Katie Morag Ser.: 1). (ENG.). 32p. (J). (gr. k-2). pap. 12.99 *(978-1-84941-091-5(7)*, Red Fox) Random House Children's Books GBR. Dist: Independent Pubs. Group.
Heder, Thyra. Penny & Jelly: Slumber under the Stars. Gianferrari, Maria. 2016. (J). ***(978-0-544-28005-2(9))*** Harcourt.
Heder, Thyra. The School Show. Gianferrari, Maria. 2015. (Penny & Jelly Ser.). (ENG.). 32p. (J). (gr. -1-3). 16.99 *(978-0-544-23014-9(0)*, HMH Books For Young Readers) Houghton Mifflin Harcourt Publishing Co.
Hedgecock, Lucie. Peek-A-Boooo Who? A Lift-the-Flap & Sound Book. DePrisco, Dorothea. 2009. 12p. 8.95 *(978-1-58117-952-1(9)*, Intervisual/Piggy Toes) Bendon, Inc.
Hedgecock, Sean. God's Incredible Creatures: The Gift of Sharing. Soleim, Heather. Greisen, Steve, ed. ed. 2005. 24p. (J). bds. 14.95 *(978-0-9707422-9-2(0))* Reel Productions, LLC.
Hedicker, Lisa. Buzz with the Bees. Kenney, Karen Latchana. 2010. (Bug's World Ser.). 32p. 28.50 *(978-1-60270-784-9(7)*, Looking Glass Library- Nonfiction) Magic Wagon.
—Hide with the Ladybugs. Kenney, Karen Latchana. 2010. (Bug's World Ser.). 32p. 28.50 *(978-1-60270-785-6(5)*, Looking Glass Library- Nonfiction) Magic Wagon.
—Hop with the Grasshoppers. Kenney, Karen Latchana. 2010. (Bug's World Ser.). 32p. 28.50 *(978-1-60270-786-3(3)*, Looking Glass Library- Nonfiction) Magic Wagon.
—Hunt with the Fireflies. Kenney, Karen Latchana. 2010. (Bug's World Ser.). 32p. 28.50 *(978-1-60270-787-0(1)*, Looking Glass Library- Nonfiction) Magic Wagon.
—March with the Ants. Kenney, Karen Latchana. 2010. (Bug's World Ser.). 32p. 28.50 *(978-1-60270-788-7(X)*, Looking Glass Library- Nonfiction) Magic Wagon.
—Spin with the Spiders. Kenney, Karen Latchana. 2010. (Bug's World Ser.). 32p. 28.50 *(978-1-60270-789-4(8)*, Looking Glass Library- Nonfiction) Magic Wagon.
Hedrick, David, photos by. BeBe's Merry Christmas... to You. Murray, Libby. 2010. (ENG., 50p. pap. 12.00 *(978-1-4499-4163-5(X))* CreateSpace Independent Publishing Platform.
Hedrick, Mandy. Dylan's Tale. Porter, Harry. 2011. 52p. pap. 10.99 *(978-0-9828346-1-9(6))* 4RV Publishing, LLC.
Hedstrom, Leigh. Becoming God's Friend. Watson, Rhonda. 2006. (J). pap. incl. cd-rom *(978-1-920935-85-6(1))* Anglican Youthworks.
Hee-Joon, Son. PhD Vol. 1: Phantasy Degree. Hee-Joon, Son. 2005. 192p. pap. 9.99 *(978-1-59532-319-4(8))* TOKYOPOP, Inc.
Hee-Joon, Son. PHD: Phantasy Degree, Vol. 2. Hee-Joon, Son, creator. rev. ed. 2005. 192p. (YA). pap. 9.99 *(978-1-59532-320-0(1))* TOKYOPOP, Inc.
—PhD Vol. 1: Phantasy Degree. Hee-Joon, Son, creator. rev. ed. 2005. 184p. pap. 9.99 *(978-1-59532-321-7(X))* TOKYOPOP, Inc.
Heebner, Mary D. A Sacred Geography: Sonnets of the Himalaya & Tibet. Craig, Sienna R. 100th collector's ed. 2005. 24p. bds. 85.00 *(978-0-9766811-0-6(2))* Simplemente Maria Pr.
Heeley, Ted. Hockey Talk: The Language of Hockey from A-Z, 1 vol. Goldner, John. 2010. (ENG.). 96p. (J). (gr. 4-8). pap. *(978-1-55455-092-0(0))* Fitzhenry & Whiteside, Ltd.
Heers, Matt & Heers, Nate. South Dakota: A Journey Through Time Student Workbook. Turnipseed, Susan. 2003. 28p. (J). pap. *(978-1-57579-268-2(0))* Pine Hill Pr.
—South Dakota: A Journey Through Time Student Workbook Answer Key. Turnipseed, Susan. 2003. 28p. (J). pap. *(978-1-57579-269-9(9))* Pine Hill Pr.
Heers, Nate, jt. illus. see Heers, Matt.
Hefferan, Rob. The Bridge Is Up! Hajdusiewicz, Babs Bell. 2006. (J). pap. 7.99 *(978-0-15-365089-5(3))* Houghton Mifflin Harcourt School Pubs.
—Henry's Turn. Fontes, Justine. 2004. (J). *(978-1-59336-004-7(5))*; pap. *(978-1-59336-005-4(3))* Mondo Publishing.
—Little Monster Becomes an Author. Williams, Rozanne Lanczak. 2006. (Learn to Write Ser.). 16p. (J). (gr. k-2). pap. 3.49 *(978-1-59198-300-2(2)*, 6192) Creative Teaching Pr., Inc.
—Little Monster Becomes an Author. Williams, Rozanne Lanczak. Maio, Barbara, ed. 2006. (J). per. 8.99 *(978-1-59198-349-1(5))* Creative Teaching Pr., Inc.
—My Pop-up Nursery Rhymes. 2006. (ENG.). 10p. (J). (gr. -1-3). 4.95 *(978-1-58117-439-7(X)*, Intervisual/Piggy Toes) Bendon, Inc.
—My Sparkling Nursery Rhymes. 2005. (ENG.). 10p. (J). 8.95 *(978-1-58117-295-9(8)*, Intervisual/Piggy Toes) Bendon, Inc.
—Toy Trouble. Fontes, Justine. 2003. 24p. (J). pap. *(978-1-59034-447-7(2))*; 14.95 *(978-1-59034-446-0(4))* Mondo Publishing.
Hefflin, Toby. The Tortoise & the Hairpiece. Winn, Don M. 2009. 20p. pap. 7.99 *(978-0-88144-452-0(9))* Yorkshire Publishing Group.
Heflin, Jenifer, jt. illus. see Thrall, Gordon.
Hegan, Robin. Birds of a Feather. Oelschlager, Vanita. 2011. (ENG.). 32p. (J). (gr. -1-3). pap. 8.95 *(978-0-9826366-1-9(X))* VanitaBooks.
—Birds of a Feather: A Book of Idioms & Silly Pictures. Oelschlager, Vanita. 2009. (ENG.). 32p. (J). (gr. -1-3). 17.95 *(978-0-9800162-8-4(2))* VanitaBooks.
—Mother Goose/Other Goose. Oelschlager, Vanita. 2008. (ENG.). 32p. (J). (gr. -1-3). 17.95 *(978-0-9800162-6-0(6))* VanitaBooks.
—Out of the Blue: A book of color idioms & silly Pictures. Oelschlager, Vanita. 2012. (ENG.). 40p. (J). (gr. -1-3). 15.95 *(978-0-9832904-2-1(3))*; pap. 8.95 *(978-0-9832904-1-4(5))* VanitaBooks.
Hegan, Robin & Blackwood, Kristin. My Grampy Can't Walk. Oelschlager, Vanita. 2008. (ENG.). 36p. (J). (gr. -1-3). 9.95 *(978-0-9800162-0-8(7))* VanitaBooks.
Hegerhorst, Bethany Brady. The Littlest Snowflake. Brady, S. Lamar. 2013. 36p. pap. 24.95 *(978-1-63000-850-5(8))* America Star Bks.
Hegg, Tom & Hanson, Warren. Peef & the Baby Sister. Hegg, Tom & Hanson, Warren. 2006. (ENG.). 36p. (J). (gr. -1-3). 16.95 *(978-0-931674-67-9(0)*, Waldman House Pr.) TRISTAN Publishing, Inc.
Hehenberger, Shelly. The Moment You Were Born: A NICU Story for You & Your Preemie. Lane, Sandra & Miles, Brenda. 2015. (J). ***(978-1-4338-1964-3(3)***, Magination Pr.) American Psychological Assn.
Hehenberger, Shelly. Sanji's Seed: A Story about Honesty. Beinhard, B. J. l.t. ed. 2003. 32p. (J). reprint ed. 13.99 *(978-0-9670843-2-9(6)*, Abiding Life Pr.) Abiding Life Ministries International.
Hehenberger, Shelly. The Shipwrecked Sailor: A Tale from Egypt. Barchers, Suzanne. 2015. (Tales of Honor Ser.). (ENG.). 32p. (gr. 1-3). lib. bdg. 26.60 ***(978-1-939656-86-5(9))*** Red Chair Pr.
Hehenberger, Shelly. Visiting Feelings. Rubenstein, Laurence Z. 2013. 32p. 14.95 *(978-1-4338-1339-9(4))* American Psychological Assn.
—Visiting Feelings. Rubenstein, Lauren. 2014. (J). pap. *(978-1-4338-1340-5(8)*, Magination Pr.) American Psychological Assn.
Heiberg, Anette. I Can Count One Two Three. 2015. (J). ***(978-1-62370-527-5(4))***; ***(978-1-62370-463-6(4))*** Capstone Young Readers.
—I Can See Colors. 2015. (J). ***(978-1-62370-466-7(9))***; ***(978-1-62370-530-5(4))*** Capstone Young Readers.
—I Can Spot Shapes. 2015. (J). ***(978-1-62370-528-2(2))***; ***(978-1-62370-464-3(2))*** Capstone Young Readers.
—I Know My Alphabet. 2015. (J). ***(978-1-62370-465-0(0))*** Capstone Young Readers.
Heid, Karen. Katie's Cabbage. Stagliano, Katie. 2014. (Young Palmetto Bks.). (ENG.). 40p. 19.95 *(978-1-61117-504-2(6))* Univ. of South Carolina Pr.
Heigh, Stephen. Mr. George & the Red Hat. Heigh, Stephen. Burton, Kevin, ed. 2004. 32p. (J). 18.95 *(978-0-9745715-2-2(0))* KRBY Creations, LLC.
—The Snowman in the Moon. Heigh, Stephen. Burton, Kevin, ed. 2005. 28p. (J). (gr. -1-3). 16.95 *(978-0-9745715-5-3(5))* KRBY Creations, LLC.
Height, Ray. Shadowland: Power Man. 2011. (ENG.). 112p. (YA). (gr. 8-17). pap. 15.99 *(978-0-7851-4398-7(X))* Marvel Worldwide, Inc.
Height, Ray-Anthony. Monsuno Combat Chaos. Vol. 3: Rise of the Ocean God. Girner, Sebastian. 2013. (Monsuno Ser.: 3). (ENG.). 64p. (J). pap. 7.99 *(978-1-4215-5728-1(2))* Viz Media.
Heighway-Bury, Robin. Who Built the Pyramid? Hooper, Meredith. 2014. (ENG.). 40p. (J). (gr. 2-5). pap. 7.99 *(978-0-7636-7380-2(3))* Candlewick Pr.
Heike, Mark, jt. illus. see Larson, Scott.
Heilman, Carl, II. Two in the Wilderness. Weber, Sandra. 2005. (ENG.). 48p. (J). (gr. 3). 19.95 *(978-1-59078-182-1(1))* Boyds Mills Pr.
Heimann, Rolf. Brain Busting Bonanza. Heimann, Rolf. 2003. 64p. (Orig.). pap., act. bk. ed. *(978-1-877003-21-9(2))* Little Hare Bks. AUS. Dist: HarperCollins Pubs. Australia.
—Life's Like a Crocodile. Heimann, Rolf. 2004. 108p. *(978-1-877003-55-4(7))* Little Hare Bks. AUS. Dist: HarperCollins Pubs. Australia.
—Puzzle Mazia. Heimann, Rolf. 2004. 32p. pap., act. bk. ed. *(978-1-877003-64-6(6))* Little Hare Bks. AUS. Dist: HarperCollins Pubs. Australia.
Heimerl, Caitlin. Monet Paints a Day. Danneberg, Julie & Monet, Claude. 2012. (J). pap. 15.95 *(978-1-58089-241-4(8))* Charlesbridge Publishing, Inc.
—Monet Paints a Day. Danneberg, Julie. 2012. (ENG.). 32p. (J). (gr. 1-4). 15.95 *(978-1-58089-240-7(X))* Charlesbridge Publishing, Inc.
Hein, Joy Fisher. Bloomin' Tales: Legends of Seven Favorite Texas Wildflowers. Colburn, Cherie Foster. 2012. (ENG.). 64p. (gr. 4-4). 24.95 *(978-1-936474-18-9(2)*, 91c14e7a-1c5d-4381-b022-da21965048db) Bright Sky Pr.
—David Crockett: Creating a Legend. Wade, Mary Dodson. 2009. (ENG.). 24p. (J). (gr. k-2). 16.95 *(978-1-933979-12-0(7)*, 27d688a2-57a1-4d9e-ae27-eac8f57c33d8) Bright Sky Pr.
—Miss Lady Bird's Wildflowers: How a First Lady Changed America. Appelt, Kathi. 2005. 40p. (J). lib. bdg. 17.89 *(978-0-06-001108-6(4))*; (ENG.). (gr. 2-5). 17.99 *(978-0-06-001107-9(6))* HarperCollins Pubs.
Heine, Helme. Ricardo. Heine, Helme. 2003. (la Orilla Del Viento Ser.). (SPA.). 40p. (J). (gr. -1-7). per. 7.50 *(978-968-16-6422-0(1)*, 152) Fondo de Cultura Economica USA.
Heinen, Sandy. Melissa & the Little Red Book. Sanford, Agnes. (J). (gr. 1-6). pap. 3.95 *(978-0-910924-81-8(3))* Macalester Park Publishing Co., Inc.
Heinlen, Marieka. Bedtime. Verdick, Elizabeth. 2010. (Toddler Tools Ser.). (ENG.). 24p. (J). (gr. -1). 7.95 *(978-1-57542-315-9(4))* Free Spirit Publishing, Inc.
—Bye-Bye Time. Verdick, Elizabeth. 2008. (Toddler Tools Ser.). (ENG.). 24p. (J). (gr. k — 1). bds. 7.95 *(978-1-57542-299-2(9))* Free Spirit Publishing, Inc.
—Calm-Down Time. Verdick, Elizabeth. 2010. (Toddler Tools Ser.). (ENG.). 24p. (J). (gr. -1). 7.95 *(978-1-57542-316-6(2))* Free Spirit Publishing, Inc.
—Clean-Up Time. Verdick, Elizabeth. 2008. (Toddler Tools Ser.). (ENG.). 24p. (J). (gr. k — 1). bds. 7.95 *(978-1-57542-298-5(0))* Free Spirit Publishing, Inc.
—Diapers Are Not Forever. Verdick, Elizabeth. (Best Behavior Ser.). (ENG & SPA.). 24p. (J). 2014. bds. 7.95 *(978-1-57542-429-3(0))*; 2008. bds. 7.95 *(978-1-57542-296-1(4))* Free Spirit Publishing, Inc.
—Feet Are Not for Kicking. Verdick, Elizabeth. 2004. (Best Behavior Ser.). (ENG.). 24p. (J). 7.95 *(978-1-57542-158-2(5))* Free Spirit Publishing, Inc.
—Germs Are Not for Sharing. Verdick, Elizabeth. 2006. (Best Behavior Ser.).Tr. of Germenes No Son para Compartir. (ENG.). (J). (gr. -1-2). 24p. 7.95 *(978-1-57542-196-4(8))*; 40p. pap. 11.95 *(978-1-57542-197-1(6))* Free Spirit Publishing, Inc.
—Hands Are Not for Hitting. Agassi, Martine. rev. ed. 2009. (Best Behavior Ser.). (ENG.). 40p. (J). pap. 11.95 *(978-1-57542-308-1(1))* Free Spirit Publishing, Inc.
—Listening Time. Verdick, Elizabeth. 2008. (Toddler Tools Ser.). (ENG.). 24p. (J). (gr. k — 1). bds. 7.95 *(978-1-57542-301-2(4))* Free Spirit Publishing, Inc.
—Manners Time. Verdick, Elizabeth. 2009. (Toddler Tools Ser.). (ENG.). 24p. (J). (gr. -1). 7.95 *(978-1-57542-313-5(8))* Free Spirit Publishing, Inc.
—Las Manos No Son para Pegar. Agassi, Martine & Verdick, Elizabeth. 2009. (Best Behavior Ser.).Tr. of Hands Are Not for Hitting. (SPA & ENG.). 40p. (J). (gr. -1-2). pap. 11.95 *(978-1-57542-310-4(3))* Free Spirit Publishing, Inc.
—Mealtime. Verdick, Elizabeth. 2011. (Toddler Tools Ser.). (ENG.). 24p. (J). (gr. k — 1). 7.95 *(978-1-57542-366-1(9))* Free Spirit Publishing, Inc.
—Naptime. Verdick, Elizabeth. 2008. (Toddler Tools Ser.). (ENG.). 24p. (J). (gr. k — 1). bds. 7.95 *(978-1-57542-300-5(6))* Free Spirit Publishing, Inc.
—Noses Are Not for Picking. Verdick, Elizabeth. 2014. (Best Behavior Ser.). (ENG.). 24p. (J). bds. 7.95 *(978-1-57542-471-2(1))* Free Spirit Publishing, Inc.
—On-the-Go Time. Verdick, Elizabeth. 2011. (Toddler Tools Ser.). (ENG.). 24p. (J). 7.95 *(978-1-57542-379-1(0))* Free Spirit Publishing, Inc.
—Pacifiers Are Not Forever. Verdick, Elizabeth. 2007. (Best Behavior Ser.). (ENG.). 24p. (J). (gr. -1-k). pap. 7.95 *(978-1-57542-257-2(3))* Free Spirit Publishing, Inc.
—Sharing Time. Verdick, Elizabeth. 2009. (Toddler Tools Ser.). (ENG.). 24p. (J). (gr. -1). 7.95 *(978-1-57542-314-2(6))* Free Spirit Publishing, Inc.
—Tails Are Not for Pulling. Verdick, Elizabeth. 2005. (Best Behavior Ser.). (ENG.). (J). 40p. (gr. 4-7). pap. 11.95 *(978-1-57542-181-0(X))*; 24p. (gr. 3-7). 7.95 *(978-1-57542-180-3(1))* Free Spirit Publishing, Inc.
—Teeth Are Not for Biting. Verdick, Elizabeth. 2003. (Best Behavior Ser.). (ENG.). 24p. (J). 7.95 *(978-1-57542-128-5(3))* Free Spirit Publishing, Inc.
Heinlen, Marieka. Voices Are Not for Yelling. Verdick, Elizabeth. 2015. (Best Behavior Ser.). (ENG.). (J). 24p. bds. 7.95 ***(978-1-57542-500-9(9))***; 40p. (gr. -1-2). pap. 11.95 ***(978-1-57542-501-6(7))*** Free Spirit Publishing, Inc.
Heinlen, Marieka. Words Are Not for Hurting. Verdick, Elizabeth. (Best Behavior Ser.). (J). 2009. (SPA & ENG.). 40p. (gr. -1-2). pap. 11.95 *(978-1-57542-312-8(X))*; 2004. (ENG.). 40p. (gr. -1-2). pap. 11.95 *(978-1-57542-156-8(9))*; 2004. (ENG.). 24p. 7.95 *(978-1-57542-155-1(0))* Free Spirit Publishing, Inc.
—Words Are Not for Hurting (Las Palabras No Son para Lastimar) Verdick, Elizabeth & Agassi, Martine. 2009. (Best Behavior Ser.). (SPA & ENG.). 24p. (J). (gr. -1). 7.95 *(978-1-57542-311-1(1))* Free Spirit Publishing, Inc.
Heinlen, Marieka. Las Manos No Son para Pegar. Heinlen, Marieka. Agassi, Martine & Verdick, Elizabeth. 2009. (Best Behavior Ser.).Tr. of Hands Are Not for Hitting. (SPA & ENG.). 24p. (J). (gr. -1). bds. 7.95 *(978-1-57542-309-8(X))* Free Spirit Publishing, Inc.
Heinrich, Christian. The Palace of Versailles. Le Normand, Bruno. 2012. (ENG.). 30p. (J). (gr. 2-6). pap. 11.99 *(978-1-85103-373-7(4))* Moonlight Publishing, Ltd. GBR. Dist: Independent Pubs. Group.
Heinrichs, Jane. How I Learn: A Kid's Guide to Learning Disability. Miles, Brenda & Patterson, Colleen A. 2014. 32p. (J). *(978-1-4338-1660-4(1))*; pap. *(978-1-4338-1661-1(X))* American Psychological Assn.
Heins, Tanya & Gallenson, Ann. Digital Narrative Project for Macromedia Flash MX 2004: Communicating Information & Ideas in Science & Other Disciplines. Dharkar, Anuja & Tapley, Scott. Aho, Kirsti & McCain, Malinda, eds. 2003. 52p. spiral bd. 10.00 *(978-0-9742273-7-5(4)*, Macromedia Education) Macromedia, Inc.
Heinzen, Kory S., jt. illus. see Lorbiecki, Marybeth.
Heiser, Aline. Gotta Have God 2: Ages 10-12. Brewer, Michael. 2005. (Gotta Have God Ser.). 238p. (J). spiral bd. 12.99 *(978-1-58411-059-0(7)*, Legacy Pr.) Rainbow Pubs. & Legacy Pr.
—Gotta Have God 2: Ages 2-5, 3. Klammer, Lynn. 2005. (Gotta Have God Ser.). 238p. (J). spiral bd. 12.99 *(978-1-58411-057-6(0)*, Legacy Pr.) Rainbow Pubs. & Legacy Pr.
—Gotta Have God 2: Ages 6-9. Cory, Diane. 2005. (Gotta Have God Ser.). 238p. (J). spiral bd. 12.99 *(978-1-58411-058-3(9)*, Legacy Pr.) Rainbow Pubs. & Legacy Pr.
Heiser, Aline & DuFalla, Anita. The Christian Girl's Guide to Money. Totilo, Rebecca Park. 2005. 192p. (J). pap. 9.99 *(978-1-58411-067-5(8))* Rainbow Pubs. & Legacy Pr.
Heiser, Aline L. Willie Wonders Why. Patrick, Patsy S. l.t. ed. 2003. 32p. (J). (gr. -1-6). 14.95 *(978-0-9726832-0-3(8))* Lu, Melissa Productions.
Heitz, Tim. Between the Sticks. Wallace, Rich. 2016. (J). ***(978-1-62402-132-9(8))*** Magic Wagon.
—Chasing the Baton. Wallace, Rich. 2016. (J). ***(978-1-62402-133-6(6))*** Magic Wagon.
Heitz, Tim. My Book of Pickles... Oops, I Mean Lists. Oliver, Lin & Winkler, Henry. 2014. (Hank Zipzer Ser.). (ENG.). 144p. (J). (gr. 3-7). 5.99 *(978-0-448-48361-0(0)*, Grosset & Dunlap) Penguin Publishing Group.
Heitz, Tim. No Relief. Wallace, Rich. 2016. (J). ***(978-1-62402-134-3(4))*** Magic Wagon.
—Pressure Point. Wallace, Rich. 2016. (J). ***(978-1-62402-135-0(2))*** Magic Wagon.
Heitz, Tim. The Zippity Zinger, 4 vols. Winkler, Henry & Oliver, Lin. 2004. (Hank Zipzer Ser.: 4). (ENG.). 160p. (J). (gr. 3-7). mass mkt. 5.99 *(978-0-448-43193-2(9)*, Grosset & Dunlap) Penguin Publishing Group.
Heitz, Tim, jt. illus. see Watson, Jesse Joshua.
Helakoski, Leslie. Big Pigs. Helakoski, Leslie. 2014. (ENG.). 32p. (J). (gr. -1-2). 16.95 *(978-1-62091-023-8(3))* Boyds Mills Pr.
—Doggone Feet! Helakoski, Leslie. 2013. (ENG.). 40p. (J). (gr. -1-2). 16.95 *(978-1-59078-933-9(4))* Boyds Mills Pr.
Held, Jean, photos by. Phased: Poems, Etc. Held, George. 2008. (ENG., 34p. pap. 12.00 *(978-0-9817678-0-2(X))* Poets Wear Prada.
Heler, Shraga. Dragonlions & the Spacemen. Halevy, Hanita H. 2012. (ENG.). 140p. (J). pap. 13.00 *(978-965-550-085-1(3))* Contento De Semrik ISR. Dist: AtlasBooks Distribution.
Heliadore. Butterflies. Jeunesse, Gallimard & Delafosse, Claude. 2007. (First Discovery Book Ser.). (ENG.). 24p. (J). (gr. -1-k). 5.99 *(978-0-439-91087-3(0))* Scholastic, Inc.
Heliadore. Animals at Night. Heliadore. 2013. (ENG.). 36p. (J). (gr. -1-k). 12.99 *(978-1-85103-413-0(7))* Moonlight Publishing, Ltd. GBR. Dist: Independent Pubs. Group.
—The Butterfly. Heliadore. 2012. (ENG.). 36p. (J). (gr. -1-k). 12.99 *(978-1-85103-404-8(8))* Moonlight Publishing, Ltd. GBR. Dist: Independent Pubs. Group.
Heliot, Eric. Piano, Piano. Cali, Davide. Rivers, Randi, tr. from FRE. 2007. 28p. (J). (gr. 4-7). 15.95 *(978-1-58089-191-2(8))* Charlesbridge Publishing, Inc.
Heliot, Éric. Santa's Suit. Cali, Davide. 2010.Tr. of coustume de pere Noel. (ENG.). 32p. (J). (gr. k-2). pap. 9.99 *(978-0-9804165-7-2(4))* Wilkins Farago Pty, Ltd. AUS. Dist: Independent Pubs. Group.
Hellard, Sue. Madame Pamplemousse & Her Incredible Edibles. Kingfisher, Rupert. 2008. (ENG.). 144p. (J). (gr. 3-6). 15.99 *(978-1-59990-306-4(7)*, Bloomsbury USA Childrens) Bloomsbury USA.
—Princesses Are Not Just Pretty. Lum, Kate. 2014. (ENG.). 32p. (J). (gr. -1-1). 16.99 *(978-1-59990-778-9(X)*, Bloomsbury USA Childrens) Bloomsbury USA.
—Take a Kiss to School. McAllister, Angela & Hooper, Mary. 2006. (ENG.). 32p. (J). (gr. -1-3). 15.95 *(978-1-58234-702-8(6)*, Bloomsbury USA Childrens) Bloomsbury USA.
Hellard, Sue, jt. illus. see Hellard, Susan.
Hellard, Susan. Blossom & Beany. Dale, Jenny. 2004. 60p. (J). *(978-0-439-66991-7(X))* Scholastic, Inc.
—Bubble & Squeak. Dale, Jenny. 2005. 60p. (J). *(978-0-439-79122-9(7))* Scholastic, Inc.
—The Flying Football. Crebbin, June. 2004. (ENG.). 24p. pap. 6.95 *(978-0-521-75233-6(7))* Cambridge Univ. Pr.
—Please Sit Still. Crebbin, June. 2004. (ENG.). 24p. pap. 7.25 *(978-0-521-75235-0(3))* Cambridge Univ. Pr.
—Poetry & Potatoes. Harrison, Troon. 2003. 32p. (YA). *(978-1-84365-020-1(7)*, Pavilion Children's Books) Pavilion Bks.
—Snowy the Surprise Puppy. Dale, Jenny. 2005. 60p. (J). *(978-0-439-79124-3(3))* Scholastic, Inc.
—Who Loves Mr Tubs? Mooney, Bel. 2006. (Blue Bananas Ser.). (ENG.). 48p. (J). (gr. k-2). pap. 5.99 *(978-1-4052-2304-1(9))* Egmont Bks., Ltd. GBR. Dist: Independent Pubs. Group.
Hellard, Susan & Hellard, Sue. Dilly & the Birthday Treat. Bradman, Tony. 2011. (Blue Bananas Ser.). (ENG.). 48p. (J). (gr. k-2). pap. 5.99 *(978-1-4052-5303-1(7))* Egmont Bks., Ltd. GBR. Dist: Independent Pubs. Group.
Hellberg, Kristian & Hellberg, Madalyn. The Alv. Hellberg, Joanne S. 2010. 68p. pap. 23.49 *(978-1-4490-6868-4(5))* AuthorHouse.
Hellberg, Madalyn, jt. illus. see Hellberg, Kristian.
Helle, Lucy. We Are the Monsters! Williams, Rozanne Lanczak. Hamaguchi, Carla, ed. l.t. ed. 2003. (Sight Word Readers Ser.). (J). (gr. k-2). pap. 3.49 *(978-1-57471-966-6(1)*, 3588) Creative Teaching Pr., Inc.
Hellen, Nancy. A Visit to the Farm: Pop-up. Hellen, Nancy. 2004. 16p. (J). (gr. k-2). reprint ed. 7.00 *(978-0-7567-7063-1(7))* DIANE Publishing Co.
Heller Budnick, Stacy, jt. illus. see Budnick, Stacy Heller.
Heller, Julek. The Last Apprentice: the Spook's Bestiary: The Guide to Creatures of the Dark. Delaney, Joseph. 2014. (Last Apprentice Short Fiction Ser.: 3). (ENG.). 240p. (YA). (gr. 8). pap. 8.99 *(978-0-06-208115-5(2)*, Greenwillow Bks.) HarperCollins Pubs.
—The Spook's Bestiary: The Guide to Creatures of the Dark. Delaney, Joseph. 2011. (Last Apprentice Short Fiction Ser.: 3). (ENG.). 240p. (YA). (gr. 8). 16.99 *(978-0-06-208114-8(4)*, Greenwillow Bks.) HarperCollins Pubs.
Heller, Ruth. King Solomon & the Bee. Renberg, Dalia Hardof. 2010. (ENG.). 32p. (J). (gr. -1-3). pap. 9.95 *(978-1-56656-815-9(3))* Interlink Publishing Group, Inc.
—Merriam-Webster's First Dictionary. Merriam-Webster, Inc. Staff. rev. ed. 2011. (ENG.). 448p. (gr. k-2). 16.95 *(978-0-87779-274-1(7))* Merriam-Webster, Inc.
—Wildflowers. 2011. (Designs for Coloring Ser.). (ENG.). 64p. (J). (gr. 1-4). 6.99 *(978-0-448-45462-7(9)*, Grosset & Dunlap) Penguin Publishing Group.
Heller, Ruth. Galapagos Means Tortoises. Heller, Ruth. ed. 2003. (ENG.). 48p. (J). (gr. k-4). reprint ed. pap. 7.95 *(978-1-57805-101-4(0))* Gibbs Smith, Publisher.
—Sea Life. Heller, Ruth. 2009. (Designs for Coloring Ser.). (ENG.). 64p. (J). (gr. 1-3). 6.99 *(978-0-448-45204-3(9)*, Grosset & Dunlap) Penguin Publishing Group.
—A Sea within a Sea: Secrets of the Sargasso. Heller, Ruth. 2006. 29p. (J). (gr. 4-8). reprint ed. 17.00 *(978-1-4223-5731-6(7))* DIANE Publishing Co.
Hellier, Scott. Can I Tell You about Epilepsy? A Guide for Friends, Family & Professionals. Lambert, Kate. 2012. (ENG.). 48p. pap. *(978-1-84905-309-9(X))* Kingsley, Jessica Ltd.
Helm, Zebedee. Dogs of the World: Ultimate Guide Books to Everything! Helm, Zebedee. Graffito Books Staff. 2012. (ENG.). 32p. (J). (gr. k-2). 14.99 *(978-0-9560284-3-3(8))* Pucci Bks. GBR. Dist: Independent Pubs. Group.
Helmer, Der-Shing. The Great Space Case: A Mystery about Astronomy. Beauregard, Lynda. 2013. (Summer Camp Science Mysteries Ser.: 7). (ENG.). 48p. (gr. 3-6). pap. 6.95 *(978-1-4677-0735-0(X))*; lib. bdg. 29.27 *(978-1-4677-0169-3(6))* Lerner Publishing Group. (Graphic Universe).
—In Search of the Fog Zombie: A Mystery about Matter. Beauregard, Lynda. 2012. (Summer Camp Science Mysteries Ser.: 1). (ENG.). 48p. (gr. 3-6). pap. 39.62 *(978-0-7613-9268-2(8)*, Graphic Universe); pap. 6.95

(978-0-7613-8544-8(4), Graphic Universe); lib. bdg. 29.27 (978-0-7613-5689-9(4)) Lerner Publishing Group.

—The Kung Fu Puzzle: A Mystery with Time & Temperature. Thielbar, Melinda. 2010. (Manga Math Mysteries Ser.: 4). (ENG.). 48p. (gr. 3-5). pap. 6.95 (978-0-7613-5246-4(5), Graphic Universe) Lerner Publishing Group.

—The Missing Cuckoo Clock: A Mystery about Gravity. Beauregard, Lynda. 2013. (Summer Camp Science Mysteries Ser.: 5). (ENG.). 48p. (gr. 3-6). pap. 6.95 (978-1-4677-0733-6(3)); lib. bdg. 29.27 (978-1-4677-0167-9(X)) Lerner Publishing Group. (Graphic Universe).

—The Nighttime Cabin Thief: A Mystery about Light. Beauregard, Lynda. 2012. (Summer Camp Science Mysteries Ser.: 2). (ENG.). 48p. (gr. 3-6). pap. 39.62 (978-0-7613-9269-9(6), Graphic Universe); pap. 6.95 (978-0-7613-8543-1(6), Graphic Universe); lib. bdg. 29.27 (978-0-7613-5692-9(4)) Lerner Publishing Group.

—Summer Camp Science Mysteries. Beauregard, Lynda. 2012. (Summer Camp Science Mysteries Ser.). (ENG.). 48p. (gr. 3-6). pap. 52.82 (978-0-7613-9272-9(6));Pack, Set. pap. 316.92 (978-0-7613-9273-6(4)) Lerner Publishing Group. (Graphic Universe).

Helms, Dana. Future Hope. Bowlby, Linda S. 2008. 298p. (J). (gr. -1-3). pap. 9.95 (978-0-9779993-6-1(X)) Red Earth Publishing.

—How Amazon Got Her Name. Bowlby, Linda S. 2008. 30p. (J). pap. 9.95 (978-0-9779993-7-8(8)) Red Earth Publishing.

—Is That So. Bowlby, Linda S. 2008. 29p. (J). pap. 9.95 (978-0-9779993-5-4(1)) Red Earth Publishing.

—Nasaria's Family/la Familia de Nasaria. Bowlby, Linda S. 2008. 45p. (J). (gr. -1-3). pap. 10.95 (978-0-9779993-9-2(4)) Red Earth Publishing.

—Nentuck's New Family. Bowlby, Linda S. 2008. 30p. (J). (gr. -1-3). pap. 9.95 (978-0-9779993-8-5(6)) Red Earth Publishing.

—The Rock Garden. Bowlby, Linda S. 2008. 29p. (J). (gr. -1-3). pap. 9.95 (978-0-9779993-4-7(3)) Red Earth Publishing.

Helquist, Brett. The Austere Academy. Snicket, Lemony. 2008. (Series of Unfortunate Events Ser.: Bk. 5). (ENG.). 240p. (J). (gr. 5-18). pap. 6.99 (978-0-06-114634-3(X), Harper Trophy) HarperCollins Pubs.

—The Beatrice Letters. Snicket, Lemony. 2006. (Series of Unfortunate Events Ser.). (ENG.). 72p. (J). (gr. 5-7). 19.99 (978-0-06-058658-4(3)) HarperCollins Pubs.

—Bud Barkin, Private Eye. Howe, James. (Tales from the House of Bunnicula Ser.: 5). (ENG.). (J). (gr. 2-5). 2004. 112p. pap. 5.99 (978-0-689-86989-1(4)); 2003. 96p. 13.99 (978-0-689-85632-7(6)) Simon & Schuster Children's Publishing. (Atheneum Bks. for Young Readers).

—The Calder Game. Balliett, Blue. (ENG.). (J). (gr. 3-7). 2010. 416p. 7.99 (978-0-439-85208-1(0), Scholastic Paperbacks); 2008. 400p. 17.99 (978-0-439-85207-4(2), Scholastic Pr.) Scholastic, Inc.

—Chasing Vermeer. Balliett, Blue. (ENG.). (J). (gr. 3-7). 2004. 320p. 18.99 (978-0-439-37294-7(1)); 2005. 288p. reprint ed. pap. 7.99 (978-0-439-37297-8(6)) Scholastic, Inc.

—A Christmas Carol. Dickens, Charles. 2009. (ENG.). 40p. (Orig.). (J). (gr. k). 17.99 (978-0-06-165099-4(4)) HarperCollins Pubs.

—The Complete Wreck, Bks. 1-13. Snicket, Lemony. 2006. (Series of Unfortunate Events Ser.: Bks. 1-13). (J). (gr. 5). 165.00 (978-0-06-111906-4(7)) HarperCollins Pubs.

—The Dilemma Deepens, 3 vols. Snicket, Lemony. 2003. (Series of Unfortunate Events Ser.: Bks. 7-9). (J). (gr. 5-6). 38.99 (978-0-06-055620-4(X)) HarperCollins Pubs.

—The Doll People Set Sail. Martin, Ann M. & Godwin, Laura. 2014. (Doll People Ser.: Bk. 4). (ENG.). 304p. (J). (gr. 3-7). 17.99 (978-1-4231-3683-5(7)) Hyperion Bks. for Children.

—The End. Snicket, Lemony. 2006. (Series of Unfortunate Events Ser.: Bk. 13). 368p. (J). lib. bdg. 15.89 (978-0-06-029644-5(5)) HarperCollins Pubs.

—The Fort That Jack Built. Ashburn, Boni. 2013. (ENG.). 32p. (J). (gr. -1-3). 18.95 (978-1-4197-0795-7(7), Abrams Bks. for Young Readers) Abrams.

—The Gloom Looms, Bks. 10-12. Snicket, Lemony. 2005. (Series of Unfortunate Events Ser.: Bks. 10-12). (J). (gr. 5). 38.99 (978-0-06-083909-3(0)) HarperCollins Pubs.

—The Grim Grotto. Snicket, Lemony. 2004. (Series of Unfortunate Events Ser.: Bk. 11). 352p. (J). (gr. 3-6). lib. bdg. 15.89 (978-0-06-029642-1(9)) HarperCollins Pubs.

—The Grimjinx Rebellion. Farrey, Brian. 2014. (Vengekeep Prophecies Ser.: 3). (ENG.). 432p. (J). (gr. 3-7). 16.99 (978-0-06-204934-6(8)) HarperCollins Pubs.

—Guys Read: Thriller. Scieszka, Jon. 2011. (Guys Read Ser.: 2). (ENG.). 288p. (J). (gr. 3-7). pap. 6.99 (978-0-06-196375-9(5), Waldon Pond Pr.) HarperCollins Pubs.

—Howie Monroe & the Doghouse of Doom. Howe, James. 2003. (Tales from the House of Bunnicula Ser.: 3). (ENG.). 112p. (J). (gr. 2-4). pap. 5.99 (978-0-689-83952-8(9), Atheneum Bks. for Young Readers) Simon & Schuster Children's Publishing.

—Invasion of the Mind Swappers from Asteroid 6! Howe, James. 2003. (Tales from the House of Bunnicula Ser.). 89p. (J). (gr. 2-5). 11.65 (978-0-7569-2814-8(1)) Perfection Learning Corp.

—Invasion of the Mind Swappers from Asteroid 6! Howe, James. 2003. (Tales from the House of Bunnicula Ser.: 2). (ENG.). 112p. (J). (gr. 2-5). pap. 5.99 (978-0-689-83950-4(2), Simon & Schuster/Paula Wiseman Bks.) Simon & Schuster/Paula Wiseman Bks.

—It Came from Beneath the Bed! Howe, James. 2003. (Tales from the House of Bunnicula Ser.: 1). (ENG.). 112p. (J). (gr. 2-4). pap. 6.99 (978-0-689-83948-1(0), Atheneum Bks. for Young Readers) Simon & Schuster Children's Publishing.

—The League of Seven. Gratz, Alan. (League of Seven Ser.: 1). (ENG.). 352p. (J). (gr. 5-9). 2015. pap. 9.99 (978-0-7653-3825-9(4)); 2014. 16.99 (978-0-7653-3822-8(X)) Doherty, Tom Assocs., LLC. (Starscape).

—Lemony Snicket: The Unauthorized Autobiography. Snicket, Lemony. 2003. (Series of Unfortunate Events Ser.). (ENG.). 240p. (J). (gr. 5-6). pap. 6.99 (978-0-06-056225-0(0)) HarperCollins Pubs.

—The Loathsome Library, Bks. 1-6. Snicket, Lemony. 2005. (Series of Unfortunate Events Ser.: Bks. 1-6). (J). (gr. 5). 65.00 (978-0-06-083353-4(X)) HarperCollins Pubs.

—The Lump of Coal. Snicket, Lemony. 2008. 40p. (J). (gr. -1). lib. bdg. 14.89 (978-0-06-157425-2(2)); (ENG.). 12.99 (978-0-06-157428-3(7)) HarperCollins Pubs.

—Milly & the Macy's Parade. Corey, Shana. 2006. 38p. (J). (gr. 4-8). reprint ed. 17.00 (978-1-4223-5174-1(2)) DIANE Publishing Co.

—Milly & the Macy's Parade. Corey, Shana. 2006. (Scholastic Bookshelf Ser.). (ENG.). 40p. (J). (gr. -1-3). pap. 6.99 (978-0-439-29755-4(9)) Scholastic, Inc.

—The Miserable Mill, 13 vols. Snicket, Lemony. 2008. (Series of Unfortunate Events Ser.: Bk. 4). (ENG.). 208p. (J). (gr. 5-18). pap. 6.99 (978-0-06-114632-9(3), Harper Trophy) HarperCollins Pubs.

—More Scary Stories to Tell in the Dark. Schwartz, Alvin. 2010. (Scary Stories Ser.). (ENG.). 128p. (J). (gr. 4-18). 16.99 (978-0-06-083521-7(4)); pap. 5.99 (978-0-06-083522-4(2)) HarperCollins Pubs.

—Odd & the Frost Giants. Gaiman, Neil. 128p. (J). 2009. (ENG.). (gr. 3-18). 14.99 (978-0-06-167173-9(8)); 2008. lib. bdg. 15.89 (978-0-06-167175-3(4)) HarperCollins Pubs.

—The Odorous Adventures of Stinky Dog. Howe, James. 2003. (Tales from the House of Bunnicula Ser.: 6). (ENG.). 112p. (J). (gr. 2-5). 13.99 (978-0-689-85633-4(4), Atheneum Bks. for Young Readers) Simon & Schuster Children's Publishing.

—The Odorous Adventures of Stinky Dog. Howe, James. 2004. (Tales from the House of Bunnicula Ser.: 6). (ENG.). 112p. (J). (gr. 2-5). pap. 6.99 (978-0-689-87412-3(X), Simon & Schuster/Paula Wiseman Bks.) Simon & Schuster/Paula Wiseman Bks.

—The Rise & Fall of Mount Majestic. Trafton, Jennifer. 2011. (ENG.). 352p. (J). (gr. 3-7). 6.99 (978-0-14-241934-2(6), Puffin) Penguin Publishing Group.

—Scary Stories 3: More Tales to Chill Your Bones. Schwartz, Alvin. 2011. (Scary Stories Ser.). (ENG.). 128p. (J). (gr. 4-18). 16.99 (978-0-06-083523-1(0)); pap. 5.99 (978-0-06-083524-8(9)) HarperCollins Pubs.

Helquist, Brett. Scary Stories 3: More Tales to Chill Your Bones. 2011. 109p. (J). pap. (978-0-545-38507-7(5)) Scholastic, Inc.

Helquist, Brett. Scary Stories Box Set, 3 vols. Schwartz, Alvin. 2011. (Scary Stories Ser.). (ENG.). 128p. (J). (gr. 4). pap. 14.99 (978-0-06-198093-0(5)) HarperCollins Pubs.

—Scary Stories to Tell in the Dark. Schwartz, Alvin. 2010. (Scary Stories Ser.). (ENG.). 128p. (J). (gr. 4-18). 16.99 (978-0-06-083519-4(2)); pap. 5.99 (978-0-06-083520-0(6)) HarperCollins Pubs.

—Screaming Mummies of the Pharaoh's Tomb II. Howe, James. (Tales from the House of Bunnicula Ser.: 4). (ENG.). 112p. (J). (gr. 2-5). 2004. pap. 5.99 (978-0-689-83954-2(5)); 2003. 13.99 (978-0-689-83953-5(7)) Simon & Schuster Children's Publishing. (Atheneum Bks. for Young Readers).

—A Series of Unfortunate Events: The Bad Beginning; The Reptile Room; The Wide Window. Snicket, Lemony. 2004. (Series of Unfortunate Events Ser.: Bks. 1-3). (ENG.). 624p. (J). 24.99 (978-0-06-055621-1(8)) HarperCollins Pubs.

—The Shadowhand Covenant. Farrey, Brian. (Vengekeep Prophecies Ser.: 2). (ENG.). (J). (gr. 3-7). 2014. 400p. pap. 7.99 (978-0-06-204932-2(1)); 2013. 384p. 16.99 (978-0-06-204931-5(3)) HarperCollins Pubs.

—The Slippery Slope. Snicket, Lemony. 2003. (Series of Unfortunate Events Ser.: Bk. 10). (YA). (gr. 5-18). 197.82 (978-0-06-057743-8(6)); 352p. (J). (gr. 3-6). lib. bdg. 15.89 (978-0-06-029641-4(0)) HarperCollins Pubs.

—The Storm Makers. Smith, Jennifer E. 2013. (ENG.). 384p. (J). (gr. 3-7). pap. 8.00 (978-0-316-17959-1(0)) Little, Brown Bks. for Young Readers.

—The Three Musketeers. Dumas, Alexandre. ed. 2011. (ENG.). 384p. (J). (gr. 5). pap. 6.99 (978-0-06-206013-6(9)) HarperCollins Pubs.

—Thriller. Scieszka, Jon. 2011. (Guys Read Ser.: 2). (ENG.). 288p. (J). (gr. 3-7). 16.99 (978-0-06-196376-6(3), Waldon Pond Pr.) HarperCollins Pubs.

—The Trouble Begins. Snicket, Lemony. movie tie-in ed. 2004. (Series of Unfortunate Events Ser.: Bks. 1-3). (J). 35.99 (978-0-06-075773-1(6)) HarperCollins Pubs.

—The Vengekeep Prophecies. Farrey, Brian. (Vengekeep Prophecies Ser.: 1). (ENG.). (J). (gr. 3-7). 2013. 416p. pap. 7.99 (978-0-06-204929-2(1)); 2012. 400p. 16.99 (978-0-06-204928-5(3)) HarperCollins Pubs.

—The Wright 3. Balliett, Blue. 2008. 318p. (gr. 4-7). 18.00 (978-0-7569-8942-2(6)) Perfection Learning Corp.

—The Wright 3. Balliett, Blue. 2007. (ENG.). 352p. (J). (gr. 3-7). pap. 7.99 (978-0-439-69368-4(3), Scholastic Paperbacks) Scholastic, Inc.

Helquist, Brett. Bedtime for Bear. Helquist, Brett. 2010. (ENG.). 32p. (J). (gr. -1-2). 16.99 (978-0-06-050205-8(3)) HarperCollins Pubs.

—Grumpy Goat. Helquist, Brett. 2013. (ENG.). 40p. (J). (gr. -1-3). 17.99 (978-0-06-113953-6(X)) HarperCollins Pubs.

—Roger: The Jolly Pirate. Helquist, Brett. Helquist. 2004. (ENG.). 40p. (J). (gr. -1-3). 16.99 (978-0-06-623805-0(6)) HarperCollins Pubs.

—Roger, the Jolly Pirate. Helquist, Brett. Helquist. 2007. (ENG.). 40p. (J). (gr. -1-2). pap. 6.99 (978-0-06-443851-3(1)) HarperCollins Pubs.

—Roger, the Jolly Pirate. Helquist, Brett. 2004. 40p. (J). (gr. -1-3). lib. bdg. 17.89 (978-0-06-623806-7(4)) HarperCollins Pubs.

Helquist, Brett & Kupperman, Michael. The Bad Beginning No. 1: Or, Orphans! Snicket, Lemony. 2007. (Series of Unfortunate Events Ser.: 1). (ENG.). 176p. (J). (gr. 5-9). pap. 6.99 (978-0-06-114630-5(7)) HarperCollins Pubs.

—The End. Snicket, Lemony. 2006. (Series of Unfortunate Events Ser.: 13). (ENG.). 368p. (J). (gr. 5-18). 12.99 (978-0-06-441016-8(1)) HarperCollins Pubs.

—The Grim Grotto. Snicket, Lemony. 2004. (Series of Unfortunate Events Ser.: 11). (ENG.). 352p. (J). (gr. 5-6). 12.99 (978-0-06-441014-4(5)) HarperCollins Pubs.

—The Penultimate Peril. Snicket, Lemony. 2005. (Series of Unfortunate Events Ser.: 12). (ENG.). 368p. (J). (gr. 5). 12.99 (978-0-06-441015-1(3)) HarperCollins Pubs.

—The Reptile Room: Or, Murder! Snicket, Lemony. 2007. (Series of Unfortunate Events Ser.: 2). (ENG.). 192p. (J). (gr. 5-9). pap. 6.99 (978-0-06-114631-2(5)) HarperCollins Pubs.

—The Slippery Slope. Snicket, Lemony. 2003. (Series of Unfortunate Events Ser.: 10). (ENG.). 352p. (J). (gr. 5-6). 12.99 (978-0-06-441013-7(7)) HarperCollins Pubs.

—The Wide Window - Or, Disappearance! Snicket, Lemony. 2007. (Series of Unfortunate Events Ser.: 3). (ENG.). 208p. (J). (gr. 5). pap. 6.99 (978-0-06-114633-6(1)) HarperCollins Pubs.

Helsom, Geoff. Ella's Joy: Signs of Joy. Dykema, Marjorie. 2009. (ENG.). 32p. 16.95 (978-0-615-31066-4(4)) One Coin Publishing, LLC.

Helson, Rachel Annette. Philanthropy: A Big Word for Big Hearted People. Helson, Rachel Annette. Helson, Jan. 2010. 32p. (J). (gr. 3-5). 16.99 (978-1-935497-20-2(0)) Butler Bk. Publishing.

Helton, David. Come to School, Dear Dragon. Hillert, Margaret. rev. ed. 2006. (Beginning to Read Ser.). 32p. (J). (gr. -1-3). lib. bdg. 19.93 (978-1-59953-017-8(1)) Norwood Hse. Pr.

—A Friend for Dear Dragon. Hillert, Margaret. rev. ed. 2006. (Beginning to Read Ser.). 32p. (J). (gr. -1-3). lib. bdg. 19.93 (978-1-59953-016-1(3)) Norwood Hse. Pr.

—Go to Sleep, Dear Dragon. Hillert, Margaret. rev. ed. 2006. (Beginning to Read Ser.). 32p. (J). (gr. -1-3). lib. bdg. 19.93 (978-1-59953-018-5(X)) Norwood Hse. Pr.

—Help for Dear Dragon. Hillert, Margaret. rev. ed. 2006. (Beginning to Read Ser.). 32p. (J). (gr. -1-3). lib. bdg. 19.93 (978-1-59953-019-2(8)) Norwood Hse. Pr.

—I Need You, Dear Dragon. Hillert, Margaret. rev. exp. ed. 2006. (Beginning to Read Ser.). 32p. (J). (gr. -1-3). lib. bdg. 14.95 (978-1-59953-039-0(2)) Norwood Hse. Pr.

—It's Circus Time, Dear Dragon. Hillert, Margaret. rev. exp. ed. 2006. (Beginning to Read Ser.). 32p. (J). (gr. -1-3). lib. bdg. 14.95 (978-1-59953-040-6(6)) Norwood Hse. Pr.

Helvey, Rebecca. Greta's Purpose. Helvey, Rebecca. 2008. 68p. (J). pap. 14.95 (978-0-9774754-7-6(6)) Spiritbuilding.

Helweg, Hans & Crawford, Mel. Roy Rogers & the New Cowboy. Bedford, Annie North. 2011. 30p. 35.95 (978-1-258-03516-7(2)) Literary Licensing, LLC.

Hemby, Margaret. How Much Do I Love You? Shaw, Wendy M. 2006. (J). 14.95 (978-0-9788398-1-9(1)) Jostens Bks.

Heming, Leah-Ellen. Humpty Dumpty's Great Fall. Durant, Alan. 2012. (ENG.). 32p. (J). (978-0-7787-8028-1(7)); pap. (978-0-7787-8039-7(2)) Crabtree Publishing Co.

—Little Bo-Peep's Missing Sheep. Durant, Alan. 2012. (ENG.). 32p. (J). (978-0-7787-8029-8(5)); pap. (978-0-7787-8040-3(6)) Crabtree Publishing Co.

—Little Miss Muffet's Big Scare. Durant, Alan. 2012. (ENG.). 32p. (J). (978-0-7787-8030-4(9)); pap. (978-0-7787-8041-0(4)) Crabtree Publishing Co.

—Old Mother Hubbard's Stolen Bone. Durant, Alan. 2012. (ENG.). 32p. (J). (978-0-7787-8031-1(7)); pap. (978-0-7787-8042-7(2)) Crabtree Publishing Co.

Hemingway, Edward. Tiny Pie. Bailey, Mark & Oatman, Michael. 2013. (ENG.). 32p. (J). (gr. -1-3). 15.95 (978-0-7624-4482-3(7), Running Pr. Kids) Running Pr. Bk. Pubs.

Hemingway, Edward. Bad Apple: A Tale of Friendship. Hemingway, Edward. 2012. (ENG.). 32p. (J). (gr. -1-k). 16.99 (978-0-399-25191-7(X), Putnam Juvenile) Penguin Publishing Group.

—Bad Apple's Perfect Day. Hemingway, Edward. 2014. (ENG.). 32p. (J). (gr. -1-k). 16.99 (978-0-399-16036-3(1), Putnam Juvenile) Penguin Publishing Group.

Hemmingson, Nancy S. Lazy Hero Cat of Egypt. Crow, Stanford. 2013. 24p. 24.00 (978-1-940021-01-0(4)) Bliss Group.

Hemphill, Rick. The Adventures of Kirra & Rincon: Li'l Kids, Big Waves. 2005. 32p. (J). 17.99 (978-0-9766408-0-6(5)) Kerr, Justin & Shelley.

Henaff, Carole. The Arabian Nights. Tarnowska, Wafa'. 2010. (ENG.). 128p. (J). (gr. 3-18). 24.99 (978-1-84686-122-2(5)) Barefoot Bks., Inc.

Hénaff, Carole. The Arabian Nights Chapter. Tarnowska, Wafa'. 2011. (ENG.). (J). pap. 12.99 (978-1-84686-568-8(9)) Barefoot Bks., Inc.

—Demeter & Persephone. Lupton, Hugh. 2013. (Greek Myths Ser.: 1). (ENG.). 40p. (J). (gr. 3-6). pap. 7.99 (978-1-84686-834-4(3)) Barefoot Bks., Inc.

—Orpheus & Eurydice. Lupton, Hugh. 2013. (Greek Myths Ser.: 3). (ENG.). 40p. (J). (gr. 3-6). pap. 7.99 (978-1-84686-784-2(3)) Barefoot Bks., Inc.

—Theseus & the Minotaur. Lupton, Hugh. 2013. (Greek Myths Ser.: 2). (ENG.). 64p. (J). (gr. 3-6). pap. 7.99 (978-1-84686-782-8(7)) Barefoot Bks., Inc.

Henaff, Carole. The Adventures of Achilles. Henaff, Carole. Lupton, Hugh & Morden, Daniel. 2012. (ENG.). 96p. (J). (gr. 6-9). 23.99 (978-1-84686-420-9(8)); pap. 12.99 (978-1-84686-800-9(9)) Barefoot Bks., Inc.

Henderson, Cecil. Zoo 1000 Miles. Alexander, Carmen. 2005. 42p. (J). (gr. -1-5). pap. 9.99 (978-1-886383-57-9(X)) Blue Forge Pr.

Henderson, Dana. Isabelle's Dream: A Story & Activity Book for a Child's Grief Journey. Arenella, Betsy Bottino. 2007. 64p. (gr. -1-3). per. 7.95 (978-0-9675532-9-0(6)) Quality of Life Publishing Co.

Henderson, Dave. A Story of Three Trees: And the miracle of Prayer. 2005. (ENG.). 12p. (J). bds. 5.99 (978-1-4037-1197-7(6), Spirit Pr.) Bendon, Inc.

Henderson, Kathy. And the Good Brown Earth. Henderson, Kathy. 2008. (ENG.). 40p. (J). (gr. -1-2). per. 6.99 (978-0-7636-3841-2(2)) Candlewick Pr.

Henderson, Ken. Once upon a Family: A Son's Journey of Love, Loss, & Hope. Adams, Pamela L. I.t. ed. 2003. 116p. per. (978-1-891029-35-6(5)) Henderson Publishing.

Henderson, Liz. Bible Folks Shape Books. Gray, Charlotte. 2003. (J). spiral bd. 14.99 (978-0-89098-267-9(8)) Twentieth Century Christian Bks.

—My Bible Box in Color. Gray, Charlotte. 2003. (J). spiral bd. 24.99 (978-0-89098-266-2(X)) Twentieth Century Christian Bks.

—Traveling Through the Bible with Bible Folks. Gray, Charlotte. (J). spiral bd. 14.99 (978-0-89098-265-5(1)) Twentieth Century Christian Bks.

Henderson, McDavid. The Jacket. Clements, Andrew. 2003. (ENG.). 96p. (J). (gr. 3-7). pap. 6.99 (978-0-689-86010-2(2), Atheneum Bks. for Young Readers) Simon & Schuster Children's Publishing.

Henderson, Meryl. Alligators & Crocodiles! Pringle, Laurence. 2009. (Strange & Wonderful Ser.). (ENG.). 32p. (J). (gr. 2-4). 16.95 (978-1-59078-256-9(9)) Boyds Mills Pr.

—Andrew Jackson: Young Patriot. Stanley, George Edward. 2003. (Childhood of Famous Americans Ser.). (ENG.). 192p. (J). (gr. 3-7). pap. 9.99 (978-0-689-85744-7(6), Simon & Schuster/Paula Wiseman Bks.) Simon & Schuster/Paula Wiseman Bks.

—Arthur Ashe: Young Tennis Champion. Mantell, Paul. 2006. (Childhood of Famous Americans Ser.). 213p. (J). 13.65 (978-0-7569-6387-3(7)) Perfection Learning Corp.

—Arthur Ashe: Young Tennis Champion. Mantell, Paul. 2006. (Childhood of Famous Americans Ser.). (ENG.). 224p. (J). (gr. 3-7). pap. 10.99 (978-0-689-87346-1(8), Simon & Schuster/Paula Wiseman Bks.) Simon & Schuster/Paula Wiseman Bks.

—Bats! Strange & Wonderful. Pringle, Laurence. 2009. (Strange & Wonderful Ser.). (ENG.). 32p. (J). (gr. 1-4). pap. 9.95 (978-1-59078-781-6(1)) Boyds Mills Pr.

—Crazy Horse: Young War Chief. Stanley, George E. 2005. (Childhood of Famous Americans Ser.). (ENG.). 208p. (J). (gr. 3-7). pap. 6.99 (978-0-689-85746-1(2), Simon & Schuster/Paula Wiseman Bks.) Simon & Schuster/Paula Wiseman Bks.

—Dale Earnhardt: Young Race Car Driver. Mantell, Paul. 2006. 216p. (J). lib. bdg. 18.46 (978-1-4242-2205-6(2)) Fitzgerald Bks.

—Dr. Seuss: Young Author & Artist. Kudlinski, Kathleen. 2005. 184p. (J). lib. bdg. 18.46 (978-1-4242-2201-8(X)) Fitzgerald Bks.

—Dr. Seuss: Young Author & Artist. Kudlinski, Kathleen. 2005. (Childhood of Famous Americans Ser.). (ENG.). 192p. (J). (gr. 3-7). pap. 6.99 (978-0-689-87347-8(6), Simon & Schuster/Paula Wiseman Bks.) Simon & Schuster/Paula Wiseman Bks.

—Franklin Delano Roosevelt: Champion of Freedom. Kudlinski, Kathleen. 2003. (Childhood of Famous Americans Ser.). (ENG.). 192p. (J). (gr. 3-7). pap. 6.99 (978-0-689-85745-4(4), Simon & Schuster/Paula Wiseman Bks.) Simon & Schuster/Paula Wiseman Bks.

—Frederick Douglass: Abolitionist Hero. Stanley, George E. 2008. (Childhood of Famous Americans Ser.). (ENG.). 208p. (J). (gr. 3-7). pap. 6.99 (978-1-4169-5547-4(X), Simon & Schuster/Paula Wiseman Bks.) Simon & Schuster/Paula Wiseman Bks.

—Frogs! Strange & Wonderful. Pringle, Laurence. 2012. (Strange & Wonderful Ser.). (ENG.). 32p. (J). (gr. 1-4). 16.95 (978-1-59078-371-9(9)) Boyds Mills Pr.

—George S. Patton: War Hero. Stanley, George E. 2007. (Childhood of Famous Americans Ser.). (ENG.). 192p. (J). (gr. 3-7). pap. 5.99 (978-1-4169-1547-8(8), Simon & Schuster/Paula Wiseman Bks.) Simon & Schuster/Paula Wiseman Bks.

—Harry S. Truman: Thirty-Third President of the United States. Stanley, George E. 2004. (Childhood of Famous Americans Ser.). (ENG.). 256p. (J). (gr. 3-7). pap. 12.99 (978-0-689-86247-2(4), Simon & Schuster/Paula Wiseman Bks.) Simon & Schuster/Paula Wiseman Bks.

—Jackie Robinson. Dunn, Herb. 2014. (History's All-Stars Ser.). (ENG.). 192p. (J). (gr. 3-7). pap. 6.99 (978-1-4814-1380-0(5), Simon & Schuster/Paula Wiseman Bks.) Simon & Schuster/Paula Wiseman Bks.

—Jesse Owens: Young Record Breaker. Eboch, M. M. 2008. (Childhood of Famous Americans Ser.). (ENG.). 208p. (J). (gr. 3-7). pap. 6.99 (978-1-4169-3922-1(9), Simon & Schuster/Paula Wiseman Bks.) Simon & Schuster/Paula Wiseman Bks.

—Mickey Mantle: All-Star Athlete. Jackson, Max. 2009. (Childhood of Famous Americans Ser.). (ENG.). 224p. (J). pap. 5.99 (978-1-4169-7472-7(5), Simon & Schuster/Paula Wiseman Bks.) Simon & Schuster/Paula Wiseman Bks.

—Milton Hershey: Young Chocolatier. Eboch, M. M. 2008. (Childhood of Famous Americans Ser.). (ENG.). 224p. (J). (gr. 3-7). pap. 6.99 (978-1-4169-5569-6(0), Simon & Schuster/Paula Wiseman Bks.) Simon & Schuster/Paula Wiseman Bks.

—Mr. Rogers: Young Friend & Neighbor. Stanley, George E. 2004. (Childhood of Famous Americans Ser.). (ENG.). 208p. (J). (gr. 3-7). mass mkt. 10.99 (978-0-689-87186-3(4), Simon & Schuster/Paula Wiseman Bks.) Simon & Schuster/Paula Wiseman Bks.

—Octopuses! Strange & Wonderful. Pringle, Laurence. 2015. (ENG.). 32p. (J). (gr. 1-4). 16.95 (978-1-59078-928-5(8)) Boyds Mills Pr.

—Penguins! Strange & Wonderful. Pringle, Laurence. 2013. (Strange & Wonderful Ser.). (ENG.). 32p. (J). (gr. 3-5). pap. 7.95 (978-1-62091-591-2(X)) Boyds Mills Pr.

—Penguins! Strange & Wonderful. Pringle, Laurence. 2007. (Strange & Wonderful Ser.). (ENG.). 32p. (J). (gr. 2-8). 16.95 (978-1-59078-090-9(6)) Boyds Mills Pr.

—Ray Charles: Young Musician. Sloate, Susan. 2007. (Childhood of Famous Americans Ser.). (ENG.). 176p. (J). (gr. 3-7). pap. 5.99 (978-1-4169-1437-2(4), Simon & Schuster/Paula Wiseman Bks.) Simon & Schuster/Paula Wiseman Bks.

—Scorpions! Strange & Wonderful. Pringle, Laurence. 2013. (Strange & Wonderful Ser.). (ENG.). 32p. (J). (gr. 3-5). 16.95 (978-1-59078-473-0(1)) Boyds Mills Pr.

—Sharks! Strange & Wonderful. Pringle, Laurence. 2008. (Strange & Wonderful Ser.). (ENG.). 32p. (J). (gr. 2-4). pap. 9.95 *(978-1-59078-571-3(1))* Boyds Mills Pr.
—Snakes! Strange & Wonderful. Pringle, Laurence. 2009. (Strange & Wonderful Ser.). (ENG.). 32p. (J). (gr. 2-4). pap. 9.95 *(978-1-59078-744-1(7))* Boyds Mills Pr.
—Things to Play With. (Picture Bks.: No. S8817-5). 28p. (J). (gr. -1). pap. 3.95 *(978-0-7214-5144-2(6)*, Dutton Juvenile) Penguin Publishing Group.
—Whales! Strange & Wonderful. Pringle, Laurence. 2012. (Strange & Wonderful Ser.). (ENG.). 32p. (J). (gr. 2-4). pap. 9.95 *(978-1-59078-917-9(2))* Boyds Mills Pr.
—Wilma Rudolph: Olympic Runner. Harper, Jo. 2004. (Childhood of Famous Americans Ser.). (ENG.). 192p. (J). (gr. 3-7). pap. 5.99 *(978-0-689-85873-4(6)*, Simon & Schuster/Paula Wiseman Bks.) Simon & Schuster/Paula Wiseman Bks.
Henderson, Meryl, jt. illus. see Madsen, Jim.
Henderson, Meryle. Cicadas! Strange & Wonderful. Pringle, Laurence. unabr. ed. 2010. (Strange & Wonderful Ser.). (ENG.). 32p. (J). (gr. 2-4). 16.95 *(978-1-59078-673-4(4))* Boyds Mills Pr.
Henderson, Sara & Zenz, Aaron. Howie Goes Shopping(Fido Va de Compras), 1 vol. Henderson, Sara & Zenz, Aaron. ed. 2009. (I Can Read! / Howie Series / ¡Yo Sé Leer! / Serie: Fido Ser.). (ENG.). 32p. (J). pap. 3.99 *(978-0-310-71874-1(0))* Zonderkidz.
—Howie Wants to Play, 1 vol. Henderson, Sara & Zenz, Aaron. ed. 2009. (I Can Read! / Howie Series / ¡Yo Sé Leer! / Serie: Fido Ser.). (ENG.). 32p. (J). pap. 3.99 *(978-0-310-71875-8(9))* Zonderkidz.
Henderson, Scott B. The Ballad of Nancy April: Shawnadithit. Robertson, David. 2014. (Tales from Big Spirit Ser.: 6). (ENG.). 32p. pap. ***(978-1-55379-477-6(X)***, 7a5bbbca-e620-446e-8c13-29bf73a0b984, HighWater Pr.) Portage & Main Pr.
—Betty: The Helen Betty Osborne Story. Robertson, David. 2015. (ENG.). 32p. (YA). pap. ***(978-1-55379-544-5(X)***, 155379544X, HighWater Pr.) Portage & Main Pr.
Henderson, Scott B. Ends/Begins. Robertson, David Alexander. 2010. (7 Generations Ser.: 3). (ENG.). 32p. pap. *(978-1-55379-262-8(9)*, 72bc3568-4f12-4574-9f82-146597fa1b3a, HighWater Pr.) Portage & Main Pr.
—The Pact. Robertson, David Alexander. 2011. (7 Generations Ser.: 4). (ENG.). 32p. pap. *(978-1-55379-230-7(0)*, 9781553792307, HighWater Pr.) Portage & Main Pr.
Henderson, Scott B. The Poet: Pauline Johnson. Robertson, David. 2014. (Tales from Big Spirit Ser.: 6). (ENG.). 32p. pap. ***(978-1-55379-481-3(8)***, ab04cc8e-58f6-479c-9f04-879c4a722ff3, HighWater Pr.) Portage & Main Pr.
Henderson, Scott B. Scars. Robertson, David Alexander. 2010. (7 Generations Ser.: 2). (ENG.). 32p. pap. *(978-1-55379-228-4(9)*, 4ae83eb9-baca-4c13-a381-ea5771ba95b7, HighWater Pr.) Portage & Main Pr.
Henderson, Scott B. The Scout: Tommy Prince. Robertson, David. 2014. (Tales from Big Spirit Ser.: 6). (ENG.). 32p. pap. ***(978-1-55379-478-3(8)***, 78912685-2d85-4153-9f88-b7d8feb31ffe, HighWater Pr.) Portage & Main Pr.
Henderson, Scott B. Stone. Robertson, David Alexander. 2010. (7 Generations Ser.: 1). (ENG.). 32p. pap. *(978-1-55379-227-7(0)*, 4ae83eb9-baca-4c13-a381-ea5771ba95b7, HighWater Pr.) Portage & Main Pr.
—Sugar Falls: A Residential School Story. Robertson, David Alexander. 2012. (ENG.). 40p. (YA). pap. *(978-1-55379-334-2(X)*, 9781553793342, HighWater Pr.) Portage & Main Pr.
Henderson, Scott B. 7 Generations: A Plains Cree Saga. Robertson, David. 2012. (ENG.). 136p. (YA). pap. ***(978-1-55379-355-7(2)***, 9781553793557, HighWater Pr.) Portage & Main Pr.
Hendley, Tess. Stump. Hendley, Jeff. 2007. (J). pap. *(978-0-9762014-7-2(X))* L'Edge Pr.
Hendra, Sue. Buddy to the Rescue. Kertell, Lynn Maslen. 2012. (Scholastic Reader Level 1 Ser.). (ENG.). 32p. (J). (gr. -1-2). pap. 3.99 *(978-0-545-38273-1(4))* Scholastic, Inc.
—Cupcake Surprise! Kertell, Lynn Maslen. 2012. (Scholastic Reader Level 1 Ser.). (ENG.). 32p. (J). (gr. -1-3). pap. 3.99 *(978-0-545-38269-4(6))* Scholastic, Inc.
—Dragon Jelly. Freedman, Claire. 2015. (ENG.). 32p. (J). (gr. k-3). 14.99 *(978-1-61963-682-8(4)*, Bloomsbury USA Childrens) Bloomsbury USA.
—I Can Ride! Kertell, Lynn Maslen. 2012. (Scholastic Reader Level 1 Ser.). (ENG.). 32p. (J). (gr. -1-3). pap. 3.99 *(978-0-545-38272-4(6))* Scholastic, Inc.
—Monsters Don't Eat Broccoli. Hicks, Barbara Jean. 2009. (ENG.). 40p. (J). (gr. -1-2). 16.99 *(978-0-375-85686-0(2))* Knopf, Alfred A. Inc.
—Monsters Don't Eat Broccoli. Hicks, Barbara Jean. 2014. (ENG.). 40p. (J). (gr. -1-2). 7.99 *(978-0-385-75521-4(X)*, Dragonfly Bks.) Random Hse. Children's Bks.
—My School Trip. Kertell, Lynn Maslen. 2012. (Scholastic Reader Level 1 Ser.). (ENG.). 32p. (J). (gr. -1-3). pap. 3.99 *(978-0-545-38270-0(X))* Scholastic, Inc.
—Quiet as a Mouse: A Moving Picture Storybook. Powell, Richard. 2003. 16p. (J). 7.95 *(978-1-58925-678-1(6))* Tiger Tales.
—Spider Sandwiches. Freedman, Claire. 2014. (ENG.). 32p. (J). (gr. k-3). 14.99 *(978-1-61963-364-3(7)*, Bloomsbury USA Childrens) Bloomsbury USA.
—Under the Sea. Mayfield, Sue. 2013. (Green Bananas Ser.). (ENG.). 48p. (J). (gr. 1-2). pap. 5.99 *(978-1-4052-5676-6(1))* Egmont Bks., Ltd. GBR. Dist: Independent Pubs. Group.
Hendra, Sue & Maslen, John R. Pre-Reading Skills. Kertell, Lynn Maslen. 2008. (Bob Bks.). (ENG.). 144p. (J). (gr. -1-k). 16.99 *(978-0-545-01922-4(2)*, Cartwheel Bks.) Scholastic, Inc.
Hendra, Sue, jt. illus. see Maslen, John R.
Hendra, Sue, jt. illus. see Maslen, John.
Hendrick, Betty Acey. No Half, No Step, Just a Whole. Furcron, Bertha Phillips. 2003. Orig. Title: Yes. 32p. (J). (gr. 1-3). lib. bdg. 15.95 *(978-1-884242-55-7(3))*; pap. 7.95 *(978-1-884242-57-1(X))* Multicultural Pubns.
Hendricks, Brenda K. The German Girl. Lickel, Lisa J. 2013. 38p. pap. 5.95 *(978-0-9856215-4-4(0))* Fox Ridge Pubns.
—The Potawatomi Boy. Lickel, Lisa J. 2013. 34p. pap. 5.95 *(978-0-9856215-2-0(4))* Fox Ridge Pubns.
Hendricks, Brenda K. Much More to Christmas. Hendricks, Brenda K. 2013. 30p. pap. 9.99 *(978-0-9826582-5-3(7))* Two Small Fish Pubns.
—What's Better Than That, Seren Dippity? Hendricks, Brenda K. 2013. 32p. pap. 9.99 *(978-0-9826582-4-6(9))* Two Small Fish Pubns.
—What's the Buzz, Bumbly Bee? Hendricks, Brenda K. 2013. 30p. pap. 9.99 *(978-0-9826582-3-9(0))* Two Small Fish Pubns.
Hendricks, Sandy. T-Bear the Most Special Bear. Mason, Bonita. 2008. 26p. (J). 19.95 *(978-0-9798718-0-1(8))* Encore Pubns.
Hendricks, Tracey. Wake up & Recognize: Life of a Stepdaughter. Robbins-Turner, Darlene. Date not set. (YA). 16.95 *(978-1-889506-09-8(5))* Kendar Publishing, Inc.
Hendrix, Bryan. 100 Monsters in My School. Bader, Bonnie. 2003. (All Aboard Math Reader Ser.). 48p. (gr. -1-3). 14.00 *(978-0-7569-1648-0(8))* Perfection Learning Corp.
Hendrix, Bryan & Bryan, Hendrix. Max's 4 Questions. Bader, Bonnie. 2006. (Reading Railroad Ser.). (ENG.). 24p. (J). (gr. -1-k). mass mkt. 4.99 *(978-0-448-44121-4(7)*, Grosset & Dunlap) Penguin Publishing Group.
Hendrix, John. Abe Lincoln Crosses a Creek: A Tall, Thin Tale (Introducing His Forgotten Frontier Friend) Hopkinson, Deborah. 2008. (ENG.). 40p. (J). (gr. -1-3). 17.99 *(978-0-375-83768-5(X)*, Schwartz & Wade Bks.) Random Hse. Children's Bks.
—A Boy Called Dickens. Hopkinson, Deborah. 2012. (ENG.). 40p. (J). (gr. -1-3). 17.99 *(978-0-375-86732-3(5)*, Schwartz & Wade Bks.) Random Hse. Children's Bks.
—The Giant Rat of Sumatra. Fleischman, Sid. 208p. (J). (gr. 5-18). 2005. 15.99 *(978-0-06-074238-6(0))*; 2005. lib. bdg. 16.89 *(978-0-06-074239-3(9)*, Greenwillow Bks.); 2006. (ENG.). reprint ed. pap. 6.99 *(978-0-06-074240-9(2)*, Greenwillow Bks.) HarperCollins Pubs.
Hendrix, John. Hook's Revenge. Schulz, Heidi. (Hook's Revenge Ser.: Bk. 1). (ENG.). (J). (gr. 3-7). 2015. 310p. pap. 7.99 ***(978-1-4847-1188-0(2))***; 2015. 352p. 16.99 ***(978-1-4847-1717-2(1))***; 2014. 296p. 16.99 *(978-1-4231-9867-3(0))* Hyperion Bks. for Children.
Hendrix, John. Ice Whale. George, Jean Craighead. (ENG.). (J). (gr. 4-7). 2015. 224p. 7.99 *(978-0-14-242741-5(1)*, Puffin); 2014. 208p. 17.99 *(978-0-8037-3745-7(9)*, Dial) Penguin Publishing Group.
Hendrix, John. McToad Mows Tiny Island. Angleberger, Tom. 2015. (ENG.). 40p. (J). (gr. -1-3). 16.95 ***(978-1-4197-1650-8(6)***, Abrams Bks. for Young Readers) Abrams.
Hendrix, John. Nurse, Soldier, Spy: The Story of Sarah Edmonds, a Civil War Hero. Moss, Marissa. 2011. (ENG.). 48p. (J). (gr. 3-7). 19.95 *(978-0-8109-9735-6(5)*, Abrams Bks. for Young Readers) Abrams.
—Rutherford B., Who Was He? Poems about Our Presidents. Singer, Marilyn. 2013. (ENG.). 56p. (YA). (gr. 1-3). 17.99 *(978-1-4231-7100-3(4))* Hyperion Pr.
—Shooting at the Stars: The Christmas Truce of 1914. 2014. (ENG.). 40p. (J). (gr. 3-7). 18.95 *(978-1-4197-1175-6(X)*, Abrams Bks. for Young Readers) Abrams.
Hendry, Linda. Benny Bensky & the Parrot-Napper. Borsky, Mary. 2008. (ENG.). 128p. (J). (gr. 4-7). pap. 9.95 *(978-0-88776-840-8(7))* Tundra Bks. CAN. Dist: Random Hse., Inc.
—How to Make Super Pop-Ups. Irvine, Joan. 2008. (Dover Origami Papercraft Ser.). (ENG.). 96p. (gr. 3-7). per. 8.95 *(978-0-486-46589-0(6))* Dover Pubns., Inc.
—Jocelyn & the Ballerina, 1 vol. Hartry, Nancy. 2nd ed. 2003. (ENG.). 32p. (J). pap. 8.95 *(978-1-55041-803-3(3)*, 1550418033) Fitzhenry & Whiteside, Ltd. CAN. Dist: Midpoint Trade Bks., Inc.
—The Kids Can Press French & English Phrase Book. Kenny, Chantal Lacourcière. 2004. (ENG.). 40p. (J). 7.95 *(978-1-55337-650-7(1))* Kids Can Pr., Ltd. CAN. Dist: Univ. of Toronto Pr.
—No Frogs for Dinner, 1 vol. Wishinsky, Frieda. 2012. (ENG.). 32p. (J). pap. 6.95 *(978-1-55455-189-7(7)*, 1554551897) Fitzhenry & Whiteside, Ltd. CAN. Dist: Midpoint Trade Bks., Inc.
—Pup & Hound. Hood, Susan. 2004. (Kids Can Read Ser.). (ENG.). 32p. (J). (gr. k-1). 3.95 *(978-1-55337-673-6(0))*; 14.95 *(978-1-55337-572-2(6))* Kids Can Pr., Ltd. CAN. Dist: Univ. of Toronto Pr.
—Pup & Hound at Sea. Hood, Susan. 2006. (Kids Can Read Ser.). (ENG.). 32p. (J). (gr. k-1). 3.95 *(978-1-55337-805-1(9))*; 14.95 *(978-1-55337-804-4(0))* Kids Can Pr., Ltd. CAN. Dist: Univ. of Toronto Pr.
—Pup & Hound Catch a Thief. Hood, Susan. 2007. (Kids Can Read Ser.). (ENG.). 32p. (J). (gr. k-1). 3.95 *(978-1-55337-973-7(X))* Kids Can Pr., Ltd. CAN. Dist: Univ. of Toronto Pr.
—Pup & Hound Hatch an Egg. Hood, Susan. 2007. (Kids Can Read! Ser.). (ENG.). 32p. (J). (gr. k-1). 3.95 *(978-1-55337-975-1(6))* Kids Can Pr., Ltd. CAN. Dist: Univ. of Toronto Pr.
—Pup & Hound in Trouble. Hood, Susan. 2005. (Kids Can Read Ser.). (ENG.). 32p. (J). (gr. k-1). 3.95 *(978-1-55337-677-4(3))* Kids Can Pr., Ltd. CAN. Dist: Univ. of Toronto Pr.
—Pup & Hound Lost & Found. Hood, Susan. 2006. (ENG.). 32p. (J). (gr. k-1). 14.95 *(978-1-55337-806-8(7))* Kids Can Pr., Ltd. CAN. Dist: Univ. of Toronto Pr.
—Pup & Hound Move In. Hood, Susan. 2004. (Kids Can Read Ser.). (ENG.). 32p. (J). (gr. k-1). 3.95 *(978-1-55337-675-0(7))*; 14.95 *(978-1-55337-674-3(9))* Kids Can Pr., Ltd. CAN. Dist: Univ. of Toronto Pr.
—Pup & Hound Play Copycats. Hood, Susan. 2007. (Kids Can Read Ser.). (ENG.). 32p. (J). (gr. k-3). 3.95 *(978-1-55453-145-5(4))* Kids Can Pr., Ltd. CAN. Dist: Univ. of Toronto Pr.
—Pup & Hound Scare a Ghost. Hood, Susan. 2007. (Kids Can Read Ser.). (ENG.). 32p. (J). (gr. k-3). 3.95 *(978-1-55453-143-1(8))* Kids Can Pr., Ltd. CAN. Dist: Univ. of Toronto Pr.
—Pup & Hound Stay up Late. Hood, Susan. 2005. (Kids Can Read Ser.). (ENG.). 32p. (J). (gr. k-1). 3.95 *(978-1-55337-679-8(X))*; 14.95 *(978-1-55337-678-1(1))* Kids Can Pr., Ltd. CAN. Dist: Univ. of Toronto Pr.
—Room 207. Tokio, Marnelle. 2006. (ENG.). 120p. (J). (gr. 4-7). pap. 8.95 *(978-0-88776-695-4(1))* Tundra Bks. CAN. Dist: Random Hse., Inc.
Hendry, Linda. Horse Crafts. Hendry, Linda. 2006. (Kids Can Do It Ser.). (ENG.). 40p. (J). (gr. 3-7). 6.95 *(978-1-55337-647-7(1))* Kids Can Pr., Ltd. CAN. Dist: Univ. of Toronto Pr.
—Outside the Box! Creative Activities for Ecology-Minded Kids. Hendry, Linda. Irvine, Joan. 2009. (Dover Children's Activity Bks.). (ENG.). 96p. (J). (gr. 2-5). pap. 8.99 *(978-0-486-47000-9(8))* Dover Pubns., Inc.
—Pup & Hound. Hendry, Linda. Hood, Susan. 2012. (ENG.). 32p. (J). bds. 7.95 *(978-1-55453-818-8(1))* Kids Can Pr., Ltd. CAN. Dist: Univ. of Toronto Pr.
Heney, Clare, jt. illus. see Hunter, Carl.
Henkel, D. B., VIII. Painted Treasures or the Original 288 Tree Gnomes. Henkel, Donald G. 2006. (J). mass mkt. 20.50 *(978-0-9673504-1-7(7))* Quillpen.
Henkel, Vernon, et al. Eternity Vol. 45: New Testament, Revelation Part 4: the Lord Reigns Forever. Greiner, Ruth B. et al. 2005. 36p. (J). pap. *(978-1-932381-31-3(7)*, 1045) Bible Visuals International, Inc.
—Fellowship, Enjoying God Vol. 41: New Testament Volume 41: 1, 2 & 3 John & Jude. Kiefer, Velma et al. 2004. (ENG.). 36p. (J). pap. *(978-1-932381-00-9(7)*, 1041) Bible Visuals International, Inc.
Henkel, Vernon & Tweed, Sean. Esther Vol. 28: Old Testament Volume 28: Esther. 2003. (ENG.). 30p. (J). pap. *(978-1-932381-01-6(5)*, 2028) Bible Visuals International, Inc.
Henkes, Kevin. All Alone. Henkes, Kevin. 2003. (ENG.). 40p. (J). (gr. -1-3). 16.99 *(978-0-06-054115-6(6)*, Greenwillow Bks.) HarperCollins Pubs.
—A Box Full of Lilly: Lilly's Big Day. Henkes, Kevin. 2006. (J). (gr. -1-4). 27.99 *(978-0-06-112852-3(X)*, Greenwillow Bks.) HarperCollins Pubs.
—A Box of Treats: Five Little Picture Books about Lilly & Her Friends. Henkes, Kevin. 2004. (ENG.). (J). (gr. -1-k). pap. 14.99 *(978-0-06-073211-0(3)*, Greenwillow Bks.) HarperCollins Pubs.
—Chrysanthemum. Henkes, Kevin. (ENG.). 32p. (J). (gr. -1-3). 2008. pap. 6.99 *(978-0-688-14732-7(1))*; 2007. pap. 24.99 *(978-0-06-111974-3(1))* HarperCollins Pubs. (Greenwillow Bks.).
—A Good Day. Henkes, Kevin. 2007. (ENG.). 32p. (gr. -1-3). 16.99 *(978-0-06-114018-1(X)*, Greenwillow Bks.) HarperCollins Pubs.
—A Good Day Board Book. Henkes, Kevin. 2010. (ENG.). 28p. (J). (gr. -1 — 1). bds. 7.99 *(978-0-06-185778-2(5)*, Greenwillow Bks.) HarperCollins Pubs.
—El Gran Dia de Lily. Henkes, Kevin. Posada, Maria Candelaria, tr. from ENG. 2008. (SPA.). 40p. (J). (gr. -1-3). 17.99 *(978-0-06-136316-0(2)*, Greenwillow Bks.) HarperCollins Pubs.
—Julius, the Baby of the World. Henkes, Kevin. 2003. (J). 25.95 incl. audio *(978-1-59112-250-0(3))*; 28.95 incl. audio compact disk *(978-1-59112-518-1(9))*; pap. 33.95 incl. audio *(978-1-59112-251-7(1))*; pap. 35.95 incl. audio compact disk *(978-1-59112-523-5(5))* Live Oak Media.
—Julius's Candy Corn. Henkes, Kevin. 2003. (ENG.). 24p. (J). (gr. -1-k). bds. 6.99 *(978-0-06-053789-0(2)*, Greenwillow Bks.) HarperCollins Pubs.
—Junonia. Henkes, Kevin. 192p. (J). (gr. 3-7). 2012. (ENG.). pap. 6.99 *(978-0-06-196419-0(0))*; 2011. (ENG.). 15.99 *(978-0-06-196417-6(4))*; 2011. lib. bdg. 16.89 *(978-0-06-196418-3(2))* HarperCollins Pubs. (Greenwillow Bks.).
—Kitten's First Full Moon. Henkes, Kevin. 2004. (ENG.). 40p. (J). (gr. -1-3). 17.99 *(978-0-06-058828-1(4)*, Greenwillow Bks.) HarperCollins Pubs.
Henkes, Kevin. Kitten's First Full Moon Board Book. Henkes, Kevin. 2015. (ENG.). 34p. (J). (gr. -1 — 1). bds. 8.99 ***(978-0-06-241710-7(X)***, Greenwillow Bks.) HarperCollins Pubs.
Henkes, Kevin. Lilly's Big Day. Henkes, Kevin. 40p. (J). (gr. -1-3). 2014. (ENG.). pap. 6.99 *(978-0-06-231358-4(4))*; 2006. (ENG.). 17.99 *(978-0-06-074236-2(4))*; 2006. lib. bdg. 18.89 *(978-0-06-074237-9(2))* HarperCollins Pubs. (Greenwillow Bks.).
—Lilly's Chocolate Heart. Henkes, Kevin. 2003. (ENG.). 24p. (J). (gr. -1-k). bds. 6.99 *(978-0-06-056066-9(5)*, Greenwillow Bks.) HarperCollins Pubs.
—Lilly's Purple Plastic Purse. Henkes, Kevin. 10th anniv. ed. 2006. (ENG.). 40p. (J). (gr. -1-4). 17.99 *(978-0-688-12897-5(1)*, Greenwillow Bks.) HarperCollins Pubs.
—Lilly's Purple Plastic Purse. Henkes, Kevin. pap. 16.95 incl. audio *(978-0-87499-686-9(4))*; pap. incl. audio *(978-0-87499-688-3(0))*; pap. 18.95 incl. audio compact disk *(978-1-59112-347-7(X))*; pap. incl. audio compact disk *(978-1-59112-557-0(X))* Live Oak Media.
—Little White Rabbit. Henkes, Kevin. 2011. 40p. (J). (gr. -1-3). (ENG.). 16.99 *(978-0-06-200642-4(8))*; 17.89 *(978-0-06-200643-1(6))* HarperCollins Pubs. (Greenwillow Bks.).
—Little White Rabbit Board Book. Henkes, Kevin. 2014. (ENG.). 34p. (J). (gr. -1-3). bds. 7.99 *(978-0-06-231409-3(2)*, Greenwillow Bks.) HarperCollins Pubs.
—My Garden. Henkes, Kevin. 2010. 40p. (J). (gr. -1-2). (ENG.). 17.99 *(978-0-06-171517-4(4))*; lib. bdg. 18.89 *(978-0-06-171518-1(2))* HarperCollins Pubs. (Greenwillow Bks.).
—Old Bear. Henkes, Kevin. 2008. 32p. (J). (gr. -1-5). (ENG.). 17.99 *(978-0-06-155205-2(4))*; lib. bdg. 18.89 *(978-0-06-155206-9(2))* HarperCollins Pubs. (Greenwillow Bks.).
—Old Bear Board Book. Henkes, Kevin. 2011. (ENG.). 28p. (J). (gr. -1 — 1). bds. 7.99 *(978-0-06-208963-2(3)*, Greenwillow Bks.) HarperCollins Pubs.
—Penny & Her Doll. Henkes, Kevin. 2012. 32p. (J). (gr. -1-3). (ENG.). 12.99 *(978-0-06-208199-5(3))*; lib. bdg. 14.89 *(978-0-06-208200-8(0))* HarperCollins Pubs. (Greenwillow Bks.).
—Penny & Her Marble. Henkes, Kevin. 2013. (I Can Read Book 1 Ser.). 48p. (J). (gr. -1-3). (ENG.). pap. 3.99 *(978-0-06-208205-3(1))*; (ENG.). 12.99 *(978-0-06-208203-9(5))*; 14.89 *(978-0-06-208204-6(3))* HarperCollins Pubs. (Greenwillow Bks.).
—Penny & Her Song. Henkes, Kevin. 2012. (I Can Read Book 1 Ser.). 32p. (J). (gr. -1-3). (ENG.). pap. 3.99 *(978-0-06-208197-1(7))*; (ENG.). 12.99 *(978-0-06-208195-7(0))*; lib. bdg. 14.89 *(978-0-06-208196-4(9))* HarperCollins Pubs. (Greenwillow Bks.).
—La Primera Luna Llena de Gatita. Henkes, Kevin. 2006. Orig. Title: Kitten's First Full Moon. (SPA.). 40p. (J). (gr. -1-2). 17.99 *(978-0-06-087223-6(3)*, Greenwillow Bks.) HarperCollins Pubs.
—Sheila Rae, the Brave. Henkes, Kevin. 9.95 *(978-1-59112-865-6(X))* Live Oak Media.
—Two under Par. Henkes, Kevin. 2005. (ENG.). 128p. (J). (gr. 3-7). pap. 4.99 *(978-0-06-075695-6(0)*, Greenwillow Bks.) HarperCollins Pubs.
—Waiting. Henkes, Kevin. 2015. 32p. (J). (gr. -1-3). (ENG.). 17.99 *(978-0-06-236843-0(5)*, Collins Design); lib. bdg. 18.89 ***(978-0-06-236844-7(3)***, Greenwillow Bks.) HarperCollins Pubs.
—Wemberly Worried. Henkes, Kevin. 2010. (ENG.). 32p. (J). (gr. -1-4). pap. 6.99 *(978-0-06-185776-8(9)*, Greenwillow Bks.) HarperCollins Pubs.
—Wemberly Worried. Henkes, Kevin. pap. 16.95 incl. audio *(978-0-87499-806-1(9))*; pap. incl. audio *(978-0-87499-808-5(5))*; pap. 18.95 incl. audio compact disk *(978-1-59112-359-0(3))*; pap. 39.95 incl. audio compact disk *(978-1-59112-561-7(8))* Live Oak Media.
—Wemberly's Ice-Cream Star. Henkes, Kevin. 2003. (ENG.). 24p. (J). (gr. -1-k). bds. 6.99 *(978-0-06-050405-2(6)*, Greenwillow Bks.) HarperCollins Pubs.
—The Year of Billy Miller. Henkes, Kevin. 2013. 240p. (J). (gr. 3-7). (ENG.). 16.99 *(978-0-06-226812-9(0))*; lib. bdg. 17.89 *(978-0-06-226813-6(9))* HarperCollins Pubs. (Greenwillow Bks.).
Henley, Claire. In My Little Blue Bed. Top That Publishing Staff, ed. 2007. 11p. (J). (gr. -1-k). bds. *(978-1-84666-280-5(X)*, Tide Mill Pr.) Top That! Publishing PLC.
—In My Little Pink Bed: A Counting Book. Top That Publishing Staff, ed. 2007. (In My Bed Book Ser.). 11p. (J). (gr. -1-k). bds. *(978-1-84666-285-0(0)*, Tide Mill Pr.) Top That! Publishing PLC.
Henn, Astrid, jt. illus. see Weigelt, Udo.
Henn, Sophy. Where Bear? Henn, Sophy. 2015. (ENG.). 32p. (J). (gr. k-3). 16.99 *(978-0-399-17158-1(4))* Penguin Publishing Group.
Henneberger, Robert. The Lucky Baseball Bat. Christopher, Matt. 2005. 123p. (gr. -1-3). 16.00 *(978-0-7569-4890-0(8))* Perfection Learning Corp.
—The Lucky Baseball Bat: 50th Anniversary Commemorative Edition. Christopher, Matt. anniv. ed. 2004. (ENG.). 128p. (J). (gr. -1-17). pap. 5.99 *(978-0-316-01012-2(X))* Little, Brown Bks. for Young Readers.
Henninger, Michelle. Bradford Street Buddies: Backyard Camp-Out. Nolen, Jerdine et al. 2015. (Green Light Readers Level 3 Ser.). (ENG.). 48p. (J). (gr. 1-4). pap. 3.99 *(978-0-544-36844-6(4)*, HMH Books For Young Readers) Houghton Mifflin Harcourt Publishing Co.
—Bradford Street Buddies: Block Party Surprise. Nolen, Jerdine. 2015. (Green Light Readers Level 3 Ser.). (ENG.). 48p. (J). (gr. 1-4). pap. 3.99 *(978-0-544-35863-8(5)*, HMH Books For Young Readers) Houghton Mifflin Harcourt Publishing Co.
—Princess & the Frog: A Readers' Theater Script & Guide. Wallace, Nancy K. 2013. (Readers' Theater: How to Put on a Production Ser.). 32p. (J). (gr. 2-6). lib. bdg. 28.50 *(978-1-61641-989-9(X)*, Looking Glass Library-Nonfiction) Magic Wagon.
Henny, Rose. Teddy Finds His Way: A Teddy Tale. Henny, Rose. l.t. ed. 2005. 22p. (J). per. 17.95 *(978-0-9705458-7-9(8))* Royalty Bks. International, Inc.
Henriksen, Rebecca. With Butterfly Eyes. Harrold, Yvette. 2009. 36p. pap. 15.49 *(978-1-4490-0946-5(8))* AuthorHouse.
Henrique, Paulo. Break-Up! Conway, Gerry. 2011. (Hardy Boys the New Case Files Ser.: 2). (ENG.). (J). (gr. 3-7). 64p. 10.99 *(978-1-59707-243-4(5))*; 96p. pap. 6.99 *(978-1-59707-242-7(7))* Papercutz.
—The Challenge of Samukai. Farshtey, Greg. 2011. (Ninjago Ser.: 1). (ENG.). 64p. (J). (gr. 1-6). 10.99 *(978-1-59707-298-4(2))*; pap. 6.99 *(978-1-59707-297-7(4))* Papercutz.
—Crawling with Zombies. Conway, Gerry. 2010. (Hardy Boys the New Case Files Ser.: 1). (ENG.). 64p. (J). (gr. 3-7). pap. 6.99 *(978-1-59707-219-9(2))* Papercutz.
—The Deadliest Stunt. Lobdell, Scott. 2008. (Hardy Boys Graphic Novels Ser.: 13). (ENG.). 112p. (J). (gr. 3-7). pap. 7.95 *(978-1-59707-102-4(1))* Papercutz.
—Deadly Strategy, No. 20. Lobdell, Scott. 2010. (Hardy Boys Graphic Novels Ser.: 20). (ENG.). 96p. (J). (gr. 3-7). pap. 8.99 *(978-1-59707-182-6(X))* Papercutz.
—Dude Ranch O' Death! Lobdell, Scott. 12th ed. 2008. (Hardy Boys Graphic Novels Ser.: 12). (ENG.). 112p. (J). (gr. 3-7). pap. 7.95 *(978-1-59707-088-1(2))* Papercutz.
—Haley Danelle's Top Eight! Lobdell, Scott. 2008. (Hardy Boys Graphic Novels Ser.: 14). (ENG.). 96p. (J). (gr. 3-7). pap. 7.95 *(978-1-59707-113-0(7))* Papercutz.
—Hardy Boys #18: D. A. N. G. E. R. Spells the Hangman! Lobdell, Scott. 2009. (Hardy Boys Graphic Novels Ser.:

H

18). (ENG.). 96p. (J). (gr. 3-7). 12.95 *(978-1-59707-161-1(7))*; pap. 7.95 *(978-1-59707-160-4(9))* Papercutz.

—Hardy Boys #19: Chaos at 30,000 Feet! Lobdell, Scott. 2010. (Hardy Boys Graphic Novels Ser.: 19). (ENG.). 96p. (J). (gr. 3-7). pap. 7.95 *(978-1-59707-169-7(2))* Papercutz.

—Live Free, Die Hardy!, No. 15. Lobdell, Scott. 2008. (Hardy Boys Graphic Novels Ser.: 15). (ENG.). 96p. (J). (gr. 3-7). pap. 7.95 *(978-1-59707-123-9(4))* Papercutz.

—"Mask of the Sensei" Farshtey, Greg. 2012. (Ninjago Ser.: 2). (ENG.). 64p. (J). (gr. 1-6). 10.99 *(978-1-59707-311-0(3))* Papercutz.

—Mask of the Sensei. Farshtey, Greg. 2012. (Ninjago Ser.: 2). (ENG.). 64p. (J). (gr. 1-6). pap. 6.99 *(978-1-59707-310-3(5))* Papercutz.

—Power Rangers Megaforce. Petrucha, Stefan. 2013. (Power Rangers Ser.: 4). (ENG.). 64p. (J). (gr. k-5). pap. 7.99 *(978-1-59707-392-9(X))* Papercutz.

—Power Rangers Megaforce - Broken World. Petrucha, Stefan. 2013. (Power Rangers Ser.: 4). (ENG.). 64p. (J). (gr. k-5). 11.99 *(978-1-59707-393-6(8))* Papercutz.

—Shhhhhh! Lobdell, Scott. 16th ed. 2009. (Hardy Boys Graphic Novels Ser.: 16). (ENG.). 96p. (J). (gr. 3-7). pap. 7.95 *(978-1-59707-138-3(2))* Papercutz.

—Super Samurai - Terrible Toys. Petrucha, Stefan. 2012. (Power Rangers Ser.: 2). (ENG.). 64p. (J). (gr. 1-5). pap. 6.99 *(978-1-59707-338-7(5))* Papercutz.

—Terrible Toys. Petrucha, Stefan. 2012. (Power Rangers Ser.: 2). (ENG.). 64p. (J). (gr. 1-5). 10.99 *(978-1-59707-339-4(3))* Papercutz.

—Word Up! Lobdell, Scott. 2009. (Hardy Boys Graphic Novels Ser.: 17). (ENG.). 96p. (J). (gr. 3-7). pap. 7.95 *(978-1-59707-147-5(1))* Papercutz.

Henrique, Paulo & Lee, Paul. Rise of the Serpentine. Farshtey, Greg. 2012. (Ninjago Ser.: 3). (ENG.). 64p. (J). (gr. 1-6). 10.99 *(978-1-59707-326-4(1))*; pap. 6.99 *(978-1-59707-325-7(3))* Papercutz.

Henrique, Paulo & Yates, Jolyon. Tomb of the Fangpyre. Farshtey, Greg. 2012. (Ninjago Ser.: 4). (ENG.). 64p. (J). (gr. 1-6). 10.99 *(978-1-59707-330-1(X))*; pap. 6.99 *(978-1-59707-329-5(6))* Papercutz.

Henriquez, Cesar. Jonathan's Colorful Campus Tour - University of Connecticut A-Z. 2004. (J). 9.99 *(978-1-933069-06-7(6))* Odd Duck Ink, Inc.

—Sebastian's Colorful Campus Tour - University of Miami A-Z. 2004. (J). 9.99 *(978-1-933069-05-0(8))* Odd Duck Ink, Inc.

Henriquez, Emile. The Battle of New Orleans: The Drummer's Story, 1 vol. Williams Evans, Freddi & Evans, Freddi Williams. 2005. (ENG.). 32p. (J). (gr. k-3). 16.99 *(978-1-58980-300-8(0))* Pelican Publishing Co., Inc.

—The Oklahoma Land Run, 1 vol. Townsend, Una Belle. 2008. (ENG.). 32p. (J). (gr. k-3). 16.99 *(978-1-58980-566-8(6))* Pelican Publishing Co., Inc.

—Toby Belfer Learns about Heroes & Martyrs, 1 vol. Pushker, Gloria Teles & Tarman, Mel. 2009. (Toby Belfer Ser.). (ENG.). 128p. (J). (gr. 3-7). 14.95 *(978-1-58980-647-4(6))* Pelican Publishing Co., Inc.

Henriquez, Emile F. D. J. & the Debutante Ball, 1 vol. McConduit, Denise Walter. 2004. (D. J. Ser.). (ENG.). 32p. (J). (gr. k-3). 16.99 *(978-1-58980-173-8(3))* Pelican Publishing Co., Inc.

Henry, Blake. Chronal Engine. Smith, Greg Leitich. (ENG.). 192p. (gr. 5-7). 2012. (J). 16.99 *(978-0-547-60849-5(7))*; 2013. (YA). pap. 5.99 *(978-0-544-02277-5(7))* Houghton Mifflin Harcourt Publishing Co.

Henry, Heather French. Claire's Magic Sades. Henry, Heather French. 2004. (Claire's Everyday Adventures Ser.). 32p. (J). (gr. k-4). pap. 8.95 *(978-0-9706341-7-7(X)*, 1231609) Cubbie Blue Publishing.

—Claire's Magic Shoes. Henry, Heather French. 2004. (Claire's Everyday Adventures Ser.). (ENG.). 32p. (J). (gr. k-4). 15.95 *(978-0-9706341-3-9(7)*, 1231609) Cubbie Blue Publishing.

—Flying Away. Henry, Heather French. 2004. (Claire's Everyday Adventures Ser.). 32p. (J). (gr. k-4). pap. 8.95 *(978-0-9706341-8-4(8)*, 1231610); (ENG.). 15.95 *(978-0-9706341-4-6(5)*, 1231610) Cubbie Blue Publishing.

—Pepper's Purple Heart: A Veteran's Day Story. Henry, Heather French. 2004. (Claire's Holiday Adventures Ser.: Vol. 1). 32p. (J). (gr. k-4). pap. 8.95 *(978-0-9706341-1-5(0))* Cubbie Blue Publishing.

—What Freedom Means to Me: A Flag Day Story. Henry, Heather French. 2004. (Claire's Holiday Adventures Ser.). 32p. (J). (gr. k-4). (ENG.). 15.95 *(978-0-9706341-2-2(9)*, 1231611); pap. 8.95 *(978-0-9706341-9-1(6))* Cubbie Blue Publishing.

Henry, Henther French. Life, Liberty & the Pursuit of Jellybeans: A Fourth of July Story. Henry, Henther French. 2004. (Claire's Holiday Adventures Ser.). (ENG.). 32p. (J). (gr. k-4). 15.95 *(978-0-9706341-6-0(1))* Cubbie Blue Publishing.

—Life, Liberty & the Pursuit of Jellybeans: An Independence Day Story. Henry, Henther French. 2004. (Claire's Holiday Adventures Ser.). (ENG.). 32p. (J). (gr. k-4). 16.95 *(978-0-9706341-5-3(3))* Cubbie Blue Publishing.

Henry, J. The Rulers of the Lakes: A Story of George & Champlain. Altsheler, Joseph A. 2007. (French & Indian War Ser.: Vol. 3). 214p. (J). reprint ed. pap. 20.99 *(978-1-4264-8272-4(8))* BiblioBazaar.

Henry, Jed. Friends of a Feather. Myracle, Lauren. 2015. (Life of Ty Ser.: 3). (ENG.). 144p. (J). (gr. 1-4). 12.99 *(978-0-525-42288-4(9)*, Dutton Juvenile) Penguin Publishing Group.

—I Love You near & Far. Parker, Marjorie Blain. 2015. (Snuggle Time Stories Ser.). (ENG.). 24p. (J). (gr. -1-1). 9.95 *(978-1-4549-0507-3(7))* Sterling Publishing Co., Inc.

—Just Say Boo! Hood, Susan. 2012. (ENG.). 32p. (J). (gr. -1-3). 12.99 *(978-0-06-201029-2(8))* HarperCollins Pubs.

—The Life of Ty: Penguin Problems. Myracle, Lauren. 2013. (Life of Ty Ser.: 1). (ENG.). 128p. (J). (gr. 1-4). 12.99 *(978-0-525-42264-8(1)*, Dutton Juvenile) Penguin Publishing Group.

—The Life of Ty - Non-Random Acts of Kindness. Myracle, Lauren. 2015. (Life of Ty Ser.: 2). (ENG.). 128p. (J). (gr. 1-4). 5.99 *(978-0-14-242319-6(X)*, Puffin) Penguin Publishing Group.

—Love You More Than Anything. Harber Freeman, Anna. 2014. (Snuggle Time Stories Ser.). (ENG.). 24p. (J). (gr. -1-k). 9.95 *(978-1-4549-0021-4(0))* Sterling Publishing Co., Inc.

—My Dream Playground. Becker, Kate M. 2013. (ENG.). 32p. (J). (gr. -1-3). 15.99 *(978-0-7636-5531-0(7))* Candlewick Pr.

—Non-Random Acts of Kindness. Myracle, Lauren. 2014. (Life of Ty Ser.: 2). (ENG.). 128p. (J). (gr. 1-4). 12.99 *(978-0-525-42266-2(8)*, Dutton Juvenile) Penguin Publishing Group.

—El Perro en Sombrero: A Bilingual Doggy Tale. Taylor Kent, Derek. ed. 2015. (ENG & SPA.). 40p. (J). (gr. -1-2). 17.99 *(978-0-8050-9989-8(1)*, Holt, Henry & Co. Bks. For Young Readers) Holt, Henry & Co.

—Pick a Pup. Chall, Marsha Wilson. 2011. (ENG.). 32p. (J). (gr. -1-k). 16.99 *(978-1-4169-7961-6(1)*, McElderry, Margaret K. Bks.) McElderry, Margaret K. Bks.

Henry, Jed. Time for Cranberries. Detlefsen, Lisl H. 2015. (ENG.). 32p. (J). (gr. -1-2). 17.99 ***(978-1-62672-098-5(3))*** Roaring Brook Pr.

Henry, Jed. Cheer up, Mouse! Henry, Jed. 2013. (ENG.). 32p. (J). (gr. -1-3). 12.99 *(978-0-547-68107-8(0))* Houghton Mifflin Harcourt Publishing Co.

—Good Night, Mouse! Henry, Jed. 2013. (ENG.). 32p. (J). (gr. -1-3). 16.99 *(978-0-547-98156-7(2))* Houghton Mifflin Harcourt Publishing Co.

Henry, Maggie. Forest Green: A Walk Through the Adirondack Seasons. Mahoney, Liana. 2014. (J). *(978-1-59531-047-7(9))* North Country Bks., Inc.

Henry, Marilyn. Marilyn Monroe Paper Dolls. Henry, Marilyn. 2007. (ENG.). 16p. pap. 12.00 *(978-0-9790668-8-7(3))* Paper Studio Pr.

Henry, Mike. Cuzzies Find the Rainbow's End. Kapai, Tommy. 2004. (Cuzzies Adventures Ser.). (MAO & ENG.). 32p. (J). (gr. -1-3). pap. 9.00 *(978-0-9582517-0-9(3)*, Kina) Huia Pubs. NZL. Dist: Univ. of Hawaii Pr.

—Cuzzies Meet the Motuhoa Shark. Kapai, Tommy. 2006. (Cuzzies Adventures Ser.). (MAO & ENG.). 32p. (J). (gr. -1-3). pap. 9.00 *(978-1-86969-100-4(8))* Huia Pubs. NZL. Dist: Univ. of Hawaii Pr.

Henry, Steve. Happy Cat. Henry, Steve. 2014. (ENG.). 32p. (J). (gr. -1-3). 6.99 *(978-0-8234-3177-9(0))* Holiday Hse., Inc.

Henry, Steven. It's Raining Bats & Frogs. Colby, Rebecca. 2015. (ENG.). 40p. (J). (gr. -1-k). 16.99 *(978-1-250-04992-6(X))* Feiwel & Friends.

Henry, Thomas. Just Jimmy Again. Crompton, Richmal. 2003. (ENG.). 256p. (J). 16.95 *(978-0-333-71231-3(5))* Macmillan Pubs., Ltd. GBR. Dist: Trafalgar Square Publishing.

—More William. Crompton, Richmal. 2008. 196p. pap. *(978-1-4099-4227-6(9))* Dodo Pr.

Henson, Brooke. Counting in the Crazy Garden. Burnette, Margarette. 2008. (Chipper Kids Ser.). 30p. (J). (gr. -1-2). 15.95 *(978-0-9653791-3-7(2))* JenPrint Pubns., LLC.

Henson, Gaby. We Love Animals on the Farm. Baxter, Nicola. 2013. (ENG.). 12p. (J). (gr. -1-12). 9.99 *(978-1-84322-693-2(6)*, Armadillo) Anness Publishing GBR. Dist: National Bk. Network.

Henterly, Jamichael. Forest Bright, Forest Night. Ward, Jennifer. (Simply Nature Book Ser.). (J). 2007. 26p. (gr. -1 — 1). bds. 7.95 *(978-1-58469-089-4(5))*; 2005. 32p. (gr. k-3). 16.95 *(978-1-58469-066-5(6))*; 2005. 32p. (gr. k-3). pap. 8.95 *(978-1-58469-067-2(4))* Dawn Pubns.

Hentzell, Brittany. Annie & Amie's Arduous Afternoon. 2005. spiral bd. 12.95 *(978-0-9773550-0-6(4))* Smartypants Bks.

Heo, Yumi. Flabbersmashed about You. Vail, Rachel. 2012. (ENG.). 32p. (J). (gr. -1-3). 16.99 *(978-0-312-61345-7(8))* Feiwel & Friends.

—Pirican Pic & Pirican Mor. Lupton, Hugh. 2003. (ENG.). 40p. (J). (gr. 1-3). 16.99 *(978-1-84148-070-1(3))* Barefoot Bks., Inc.

—Sometimes I'm Bombaloo. Vail, Rachel. 2005. (Bookshelf Ser.). (ENG.). 32p. (J). (gr. -1-3). pap. 6.99 *(978-0-439-66941-2(3))* Scholastic, Inc.

Heo, Yumi. Sun & Moon Have a Tea Party. 2016. (J). ***(978-0-385-39033-0(5)***, Schwartz & Wade Bks.) Random Hse. Children's Bks.

Heo, Yumi. Uncle Peter's Amazing Chinese Wedding. Look, Lenore. 2006. (ENG.). 40p. (J). (gr. -1-3). 17.99 *(978-0-689-84458-4(1)*, Atheneum Bks. for Young Readers) Simon & Schuster Children's Publishing.

Heo, Yumi. Lady Hahn & Her Seven Friends. Heo, Yumi. MacDonald, George. rev. ed. 2012. (ENG.). 32p. (J). (gr. -1-2). 16.99 *(978-0-8050-4127-9(3)*, Holt, Henry & Co. Bks. For Young Readers) Holt, Henry & Co.

Heo, Yumi. Red Light, Green Light. Heo, Yumi. 2015. (ENG.). 20p. (J). (gr. -1-k). bds. 6.99 ***(978-0-545-74463-8(6)***, Cartwheel Bks.) Scholastic, Inc.

Heo, Yumi. Ten Days & Nine Nights: An Adoption Story. Heo, Yumi. 2009. (ENG.). 40p. (J). (gr. -1-3). 17.99 *(978-0-375-84718-9(9)*, Schwartz & Wade Bks.) Random Hse. Children's Bks.

Hepburn, C J. Reading & Language Arts: Level J. 2003. (Test Best for Success Ser.). 63p. (gr. 9-12). per. *(978-0-7398-6714-3(5))* Steck-Vaughn.

Heran, Michelle, jt. illus. see Rogers, Melissa.

Herbert, Frances. Fran's Van & the Magic Box. Herbert, Frances. 2013. 24p. pap. *(978-1-78222-085-5(2))* Paragon Publishing, Rothersthorpe.

—Fran's Van & the Naughty Terrier. Herbert, Frances. 2013. 32p. pap. *(978-1-78222-164-7(6))* Paragon Publishing, Rothersthorpe.

Herbert, Jennifer. What Am I? Granfield, Linda. 2007. (ENG.). 32p. (J). (gr. k-k). 15.95 *(978-0-88776-812-5(1)*, Tundra Bks.) Tundra Bks. CAN. Dist: Penguin Random Hse., LLC.

—What Will We Do with the Baby-O? Heras, Theo. 2004. (ENG.). 32p. (J). (gr. k-k). 12.95 *(978-0-88776-689-3(7)*, Tundra Bks.) Tundra Bks. CAN. Dist: Penguin Random Hse., LLC.

Herbstritt, T. J. God Loves You More Than Rainbows & Butterflies! Herbstritt, Rj. 2011. 40p. pap. 24.95 *(978-1-4560-6735-9(4))* America Star Bks.

Hergenroeder, Ernie. Daddy Got His Orders. Mitchell, Kathy. 2004. 16p. (J). pap. 14.95 *(978-0-9760811-0-4(5))* T.J. Publishing.

—The Hamburger Tree. Pacheco, Maria & Garcia-Martinez, Julia. 2006. 24p. (J). *(978-0-9776835-0-5(8))* Run With Me Publishing.

—Little Drop of Water. 2007. 24p. (J). 15.00 *(978-0-9724272-4-1(4))* Katydid Publishing LLC.

Hergenrother, Max. Tomorrow Is the First Day of School. MacDowell, Maureen. 2007. 32p. (J). 15.95 *(978-0-9791463-0-5(5))* Wading River Bks., LLC.

—Who Was Ernest Shackleton? Buckley, James, Jr. 2013. (Who Was... ? Ser.). (ENG.). 112p. (J). (gr. 3-7). 5.99 *(978-0-448-47931-6(1)*, Grosset & Dunlap) Penguin Publishing Group.

Hergenrother, Max & Harrison, Nancy. Who Is Gloria Steinem? Fabiny, Sarah. 2014. (Who Was... ? Ser.). (ENG.). 112p. (J). (gr. 3-7). 4.99 *(978-0-448-48238-5(X)*, Grosset & Dunlap) Penguin Publishing Group.

Hergenrother, Max, jt. illus. see Harrison, Nancy.

Herges, Connie. Grandma Lucy Feeds the Birds, 1 vol. Simonson, Lona Marie. 2009. 44p. pap. 24.95 *(978-1-60836-732-0(0))* America Star Bks.

—Noodles by Mcnoodle. Simonson, Lona. 2008. 28p. pap. 24.95 *(978-1-60441-644-2(0))* America Star Bks.

Herkert, Barbara. Birds in Your Backyard. 2004. (Sharing Nature with Children Book Ser.). 36p. (J). pap. 8.95 *(978-1-58469-025-2(9))*; 17.95 *(978-1-58469-026-9(7))* Dawn Pubns.

Herman, Scott. Wisdom for Young Hearts Volume 1 Wisdom's Foundation. Delea, Pattie. DeLea, Ray and Daniella, ed. 2011. 114p. pap. 20.00 *(978-1-61286-030-5(3))* Avid Readers Publishing Group.

Hermans, Rene. Shaka, Warrior King of the Zulu. Hall, Lynn Bradford. 2006. 32p. (J). (gr. 4-7). per. 11.00 *(978-1-86825-418-7(6))* Struik Pubs. ZAF. Dist: International Publishers Marketing.

Hermanson, Kyle. Chicken Little, 1 vol. Jones, Christianne C. (My First Classic Story Ser.). (ENG.). 32p. (gr. k-3). 2011. pap. 7.10 *(978-1-4048-7355-1(4))*; 2010. lib. bdg. 21.32 *(978-1-4048-6072-8(X))* Picture Window Bks. (My First Classic Story).

—Pollita Pequeñita, 1 vol. Jones, Christianne C. Abello, Patricia, tr. from ENG. 2006. (Read-It! Readers en Español: Cuentos Folclóricos Ser.).Tr. of Chicken Little. (SPA.). 32p. (gr. k-3). 19.99 *(978-1-4048-1646-6(1)*, Easy Readers) Picture Window Bks.

Hermes, Mary Sue. The 'Fridge Games. Harvey, Ken. 2003. (Life in the 'Fridge Ser.). (J). *(978-1-930093-20-1(9))* Brookfield Reader, Inc., The.

—The Leftovers. Harvey, Ken. 2003. (Life in the 'Fridge Ser.). (J). *(978-1-930093-21-8(7))* Brookfield Reader, Inc., The.

Hernandez, Bibi. Mary's Gift. Shaw, Sandra Anne. Rosales, Mary, tr. 2011. 12p. (J). (gr. k-3). pap. 1.00 *(978-0-946889-14-3(7))*; (gr. 1-6). mass mkt. 2.50 *(978-0-9668891-4-7(2))* Teach My Children Pubns.

Hernandez, Gabriel, et al. Creepy Creatures. Stine, R. L. 2006. (Goosebumps Graphix Ser.: 1). (ENG.). 144p. (J). (gr. 3-7). pap. 9.99 *(978-0-439-84125-2(9)*, Graphix) Scholastic, Inc.

Hernández, Gabriel. El País de Juan. Andruetto, María Teresa. 2009. (SPA.). 80p. (J). (gr. 4-6). pap. 12.99 *(978-84-667-2644-3(6))* Grupo Anaya, S.A. ESP. Dist: Lectorum Pubns., Inc.

Hernandez, Gilbert & Mazzucchellil, David. Fairy Tale Comics: Classic Tales Told by Extraordinary Cartoonists. Various Authors. Duffy, Chris, ed. 2013. (ENG.). 128p. (J). (gr. 1-7). 19.99 *(978-1-59643-823-1(1)*, First Second Bks.) Roaring Brook Pr.

Hernandez, Lea. Teen Titans Go!, Vol. 1. Fisch, Sholly. 2015. (ENG.). 128p. (gr. 2-5). pap. 12.99 *(978-1-4012-5242-7(0))* DC Comics.

Hernandez, Leeza. Bored Bella Learns about Fiction & Nonfiction, 1 vol. Donovan, Sandy. 2010. (In the Library). (ENG.). 24p. (gr. k-4). lib. bdg. 25.99 *(978-1-4048-5758-2(3))*; pap. 7.29 *(978-1-4048-6105-3(X))* Picture Window Bks. (Nonfiction Picture Bks.).

—Eat Your Math Homework: Recipes for Hungry Minds. McCallum, Ann. 2011. (Eat Your Homework Ser.). (ENG.). 48p. (J). (gr. 2-5). pap. 7.95 *(978-1-57091-780-6(9))* Charlesbridge Publishing, Inc.

—Eat Your Science Homework: Recipes for Inquiring Minds. McCallum, Ann. 2014. (Eat Your Homework Ser.). (ENG.). 48p. (J). (gr. 2-5). 16.95 *(978-1-57091-298-6(X))* Charlesbridge Publishing, Inc.

—Never Play Music Right Next to the Zoo. Lithgow, John. 2013. (ENG.). 40p. (J). (gr. -1-1). 17.99 *(978-1-4424-6743-9(6)*, Simon & Schuster Bks. For Young Readers) Simon & Schuster Bks. For Young Readers.

Hernandez, Leeza. Cat Napped. Hernandez, Leeza. 2014. (ENG.). 32p. (J). (gr. -1-k). 15.99 *(978-0-399-16438-5(3)*, Putnam Juvenile) Penguin Publishing Group.

—Dog Gone! Hernandez, Leeza. 2012. (ENG.). 40p. (J). (gr. -1-k). 15.99 *(978-0-399-25447-5(1)*, Putnam Juvenile) Penguin Publishing Group.

Hernández, René Mario. Vidas Desesperadas. Mederos, Miriam. 2004. (SPA.). 106p. (YA). pap. 15.00 *(978-1-931481-39-7(3))* LiArt-Literature & Art.

Hernandez, Stacy. Welcome to Humming Meadow Ranch. Hernandez, Elaine. 2005. 28p. (J). lib. bdg. 16.95 *(978-0-9766431-0-4(3))* Humming Meadow Ranch.

Hernandez, Stephanie. The Turtle & the Universe. Whitt, Stephen. 2008. (ENG.). 86p. (J). (gr. 3-7). pap. 14.99 *(978-1-59102-626-6(1))* Prometheus Bks., Pubs.

Hernandez, Steven. City Dancin' Dancin' at Peppy's. Berton, Judy. 2004. 36p. (J). per. 16.95 *(978-0-9761051-0-7(1))* Kidrich Corp.

Hernandez, Tino Santanach. Uncle Scrooge #355. Korhonen, Kari et al. Clark, John, ed. 2006. (Walt Disney's Uncle Scrooge Ser.). 64p. pap. 6.95 *(978-1-888472-24-0(3))* Gemstone Publishing, Inc.

Hernandez Walta, Gabriel, et al. X-Men - Curse of the Mutants: Mutants vs. Vampires. Kim, Chuck et al. 2011. (ENG.). 192p. (gr. 10-17). pap. 19.99 *(978-0-7851-5229-3(6))* Marvel Worldwide, Inc.

Herndon, Christopher. Terra Tempo: The Four Corners of Time. Shapiro, David R. 2013. (Terra Tempo Ser.). (ENG.). 264p. (J). pap. 17.99 *(978-0-9844422-6-3(X))* Craigmore Creations.

—Terra Tempo Vol. 3: The Academy of Planetary Evolution. Shapiro, David R. 2014. (Terra Tempo Ser.). (ENG.). 182p. (J). (gr. 2-4). pap. 17.99 *(978-1-940052-09-0(2))* Craigmore Creations.

Heroldt, Richard. He's Risen! He's Alive! Bader, Joanne. 2003. (Arch Bks.). (ENG.). 16p. (J). 1.99 *(978-0-570-07583-7(1))* Concordia Publishing Hse.

Herpin, K. K. Katrina & the Rinky-Dink Sewing Machine. Riebel, Jessica Mire. 2008. 32p. pap. 24.95 *(978-1-60813-545-5(4))* America Star Bks.

Herr, Tad. Germs. Oetting, Judy. (Rookie Ready to Learn Ser.). (J). 2011. 40p. (gr. -1-k). pap. 5.95 *(978-0-531-26732-5(6))*; 2011. 40p. (gr. -1-k). lib. bdg. 23.00 *(978-0-531-26500-0(5)*, Children's Pr.); 2006. (ENG.). 32p. (gr. k-2). pap. 4.95 *(978-0-516-24995-7(9))* Scholastic Library Publishing.

Herrbach, Stéphanie & Owlkids Books Inc. Staff. Animal Babies: Lift the Flap & Learn. Hédelin, Pascale. 2010. (Lift the Flap & Learn Ser.). (ENG.). 38p. (J). (gr. -1). spiral bd. 19.95 *(978-1-897349-90-8(4))* Owlkids Bks. Inc. CAN. Dist: Perseus-PGW.

Herrera, Aaron Jeremiah, jt. illus. see McGhee, Katie Mariah.

Herrera, Francisco, et al. Venom by Daniel Way Ultimate Collection. Way, Daniel & Medina, Paco. 2011. (ENG.). 424p. (YA). (gr. 8-17). pap., pap. 34.99 *(978-0-7851-5704-5(2))* Marvel Worldwide, Inc.

Herrera, Juan Felipe & Cuevas, Ernesto. Featherless. ed. 2013.Tr. of Desplumado. (SPA & ENG.). 32p. (J). pap. 8.95 ***(978-0-89239-303-9(3))*** Lee & Low Bks., Inc.

Herrera, Velino. In My Mother's House. Clark, Ann Nolan. 2004. 56p. (J). (gr. k-3). reprint ed. pap. 14.00 *(978-0-7567-7104-1(8))* DIANE Publishing Co.

Herrick, Mark. Buck Wilder's Animal Wisdom. Smith, Tim. 2006. 32p. (J). (gr. 3-7). *(978-1-934133-02-6(7)*, Mackinac Island Press, Inc.) Charlesbridge Publishing, Inc.

Herrick, Mark J. Core Democratic Values with Rock U. S. A. Stephens, Edna Cucksey. 2004. (Connect-It Ser.). 62p. (J). (gr. -1-3). pap. 24.95 *(978-0-9749412-0-2(4))* EDCO Publishing, Inc.

—Lost in the Woods: A Photographic Fantasy. Sams, Carl R., II & Stoick, Jean. 2005. (Connect-It Ser.). 68p. (J). (gr. -1-3). pap. 24.95 *(978-0-9749412-2-6(0))* EDCO Publishing, Inc.

—Rock U. S. A. & the American Way! A Freedom Handbook. Stephens, Edna Cucksey. 2004. (Connect-It Ser.). 124p. (J). (gr. -1-3). pap. 29.95 *(978-0-9749412-1-9(2))* EDCO Publishing, Inc.

Herridge, Debbie. Milly's Magic Play House: The Hospital, 1 vol. Wakem, Samantha. 2010. 20p. 24.95 *(978-1-4489-5114-7(3))* PublishAmerica, Inc.

Herring, Aimée, photos by. Holiday Crafting & Baking with Kids: Gifts, Sweets, & Treats for the Whole Family! Strand, Jessica. 2011. (ENG., 128p. (gr. 13-17). pap. 19.95 *(978-1-4521-0109-5(4))* Chronicle Bks. LLC.

Herring, Kip. Lady Bug. Stone, Jodi. 2005. 36p. (J). per. 15.00 *(978-0-9754298-7-7(6)*, Ithaca Pr.) Authors & Artists Publishers of New York, Inc.

Herring, M. L. Ellie's Log: Exploring the Forest Where the Great Tree Fell. Li, Judith L. 2013. (ENG.). 112p. (J). (gr. 3-6). pap. 16.95 *(978-0-87071-696-6(4))* Oregon State Univ. Pr.

Herrod, Mike. Comics to Go! 19 Stories for You to Finish! And More... 2008. (ENG.). 64p. (J). (gr. 2-5). spiral bd. 12.95 *(978-1-934706-38-1(8))* Blue Apple Bks.

—Doggie Dreams. 2011. (ENG.). 40p. (J). (gr. 1-4). 10.99 *(978-1-60905-065-8(7))* Blue Apple Bks.

—Hiccup! 2012. (ENG.). 40p. (J). (gr. 1-4). 11.99 *(978-1-60905-255-3(2))* Blue Apple Bks.

Herron, Carolivia, photos by. Little Georgia & the Apples: A Retelling of Aunt Georgia's First Catalpa Tale, Herron, Carolivia, told to. l.t. ed. 2004. 33p. (J). 10.00 *(978-0-9760222-0-6(6)*, Catalpa01) Epicenter Literary Software.

Herron, Dorothy. The Butterfly Adventure. Lorraine, Nancy. 2nd ed. 2013. 50p. 22.50 *(978-0-9886194-9-4(0))* ProsePress.

—Tatty, the Lonely Monarch. Lorraine, Nancy. 2013. 48p. pap. 17.50 *(978-0-9893063-8-6(0))* ProsePress.

Herron, Edwin. Rocks, Rivers & the Changing Earth: A First Book about Geology. Schneider, Herman & Schneider, Nina. 2014. (ENG.). 192p. (J). (gr. 3-8). pap. 6.99 *(978-0-486-78201-0(8))* Dover Pubns., Inc.

Herron, Mark. Balancing the Energy Equation: One Step at a Time! Lombardo, Michelle. 2003. (J). lib. bdg. 17.95 *(978-1-931212-51-9(1))* OrganWise Guys Inc., The.

—The OrganWise Guys Pepto's Place Activity Book. Lombardo, Michelle. 2003. (J). pap., act. bk. ed. 4.95 *(978-1-931212-52-6(X))* OrganWise Guys Inc., The.

—Pepto's Place: Where Every Portion Size Is OrganWise! Lombardo, Michelle. 2003. 32p. (J). lib. bdg. 17.95 *(978-1-931212-50-2(3))* OrganWise Guys Inc., The.

Hersey, Bob. Birds of Prey. Legg, Gerald. 2004. (Scary Creatures Ser.). (ENG.). 32p. (J). (gr. 2-4). pap. 6.95 *(978-0-531-16747-2(X)*, Watts, Franklin) Scholastic Library Publishing.

—Little Red Riding Hood. Skevington, Andrea. 2003. 48p. (J). *(978-0-439-57189-0(8))* Scholastic, Inc.

—Norman Rockwell: A Pop-Up Art Experience. 2004. 6p. (J). (gr. k-4). reprint ed. 19.00 *(978-0-7567-7642-8(2))* DIANE Publishing Co.

—Wolves. Clarke, Penny. 2004. (Scary Creatures Ser.). (ENG.). 32p. (J). (gr. 2-4). pap. 6.95

(978-0-531-16749-6(6), Watts, Franklin) Scholastic Library Publishing.
Hershenson, Ken, jt. photos by see Shepherd, Wendy.
Hertling, Heiner. A Pirate's Quest: For His Family Heirloom Peg Leg. Sams, Laura & Sams, Robert. 2008. 48p. (J). 19.95 (978-0-9770108-7-5(2)) Sams, II, Carl R. Photography, Inc.
Hertzler, Frances, et al. No Darkness at All: An Adaptation of Patricia St. John's Star of Light. St. John, Patricia et al. 2005. 56p. (J). pap. (978-1-933206-14-1(4), 5340) Bible Visuals International, Inc.
Hertzler, Frances & Olson, Ed. The Inspiration of the Scriptures: New Testament Volume 33: 1 & 2 Timothy, Titus, Philemon. Lyster, R. Iona et al. 2004. 34p. (J). pap. (978-1-932381-05-4(8), 1033) Bible Visuals International, Inc.
Hertzler, Frances B. & Ober, Jonathan. The Eternal God Vol. 1: New Testament. 2004. 36p. (J). pap. (978-1-932381-03-0(1), 1001) Bible Visuals International, Inc.
Hertzler, Frances H.. Doming the Popsicle Boy: A Story of the Philippines. Carvin, Rose-Mae. 2010. (ENG.). 68p. (J). spiral bd. (978-1-932381-11-5(2), 5100) Bible Visuals International, Inc.
Hertzler, Frances H.., et al. Faith Volume 5: New Testament. Greiner, Ruth B. 2004. 36p. (J). pap. (978-1-932381-36-8(8)) Bible Visuals International, Inc.
—The Saviour Vol. 3: New Testament Volume 3: the Life of Christ Part 3: Everybody Needs Jesus. Greiner, Ruth B. 2004. (ENG.). 36p. (J). pap. (978-1-932381-02-3(3), 1003) Bible Visuals International, Inc.
—Sin Vol. 4: New Testament Volume 4, Life of Christ, Part 4. Greiner, Ruth B. et al. 2005. 36p. (J). pap. (978-1-932381-23-8(6), 1004) Bible Visuals International, Inc.
Hertzler, Frances H.. & Olson, Ed. GOD His Son, His Book, His Home: New Testament Introductory Volume. Greiner, Ruth B. et al. 2004. 32p. (J). pap. (978-1-932381-35-1(X), 1000) Bible Visuals International, Inc.
Herxheimer, Sophie. Tales Told in Tents: Stories from Central Asia. Clayton, Sally. 2004. (ENG.). 64p. (J). (gr. 2-5). 17.95 (978-1-84507-066-3(6), Frances Lincoln) Quarto Publishing Group UK GBR. Dist: Hachette Bk. Group.
Herz, Irene & Herz, Irene L. Paul Harris, Grow Up! A Book for Children about the Founder of Rotary. Herz, Irene. 2010. (ENG.). 64p. pap. 7.99 (978-1-4515-0824-6(7)) CreateSpace Independent Publishing Platform.
Herz, Irene L., jt. illus. see Herz, Irene.
Herzog, Inge. Animal Island. Shue, Jenna. 2005. 27p. (J). (gr. -1-3). per. 14.95 (978-1-4259-0039-7(9)) AuthorHouse.
Heschke, Elena. Hair Care Tips & Tricks. Hunt, Sara R. & Kenney, Karen Latchana. 2015. (ENG.). 32p. (J). (gr. 4-8). lib. bdg. 26.65 (978-1-4677-5218-3(5), Lerner Pubns.) Lerner Publishing Group.
—Jewelry Tips & Tricks. Berne, Emma Carlson. 2015. (ENG.). 32p. (J). (gr. 4-8). lib. bdg. 26.65 (978-1-4677-5220-6(7), Lerner Pubns.) Lerner Publishing Group.
—Nail Care Tips & Tricks. Berne, Emma Carlson. 2015. (ENG.). 32p. (J). (gr. 4-8). lib. bdg. 26.65 (978-1-4677-5221-3(5), Lerner Pubns.) Lerner Publishing Group.
—Skin Care & Makeup Tips & Tricks. Kenney, Karen Latchana. 2015. (ENG.). 32p. (J). (gr. 4-8). lib. bdg. 26.65 (978-1-4677-5219-0(3), Lerner Pubns.) Lerner Publishing Group.
Heshka, Ryan. Welcome to Robot Town. Heshka, Ryan. 2013. (ENG.). 32p. (J). (gr. -1-2). 16.99 (978-0-8050-8874-8(1), Ottaviano, Christy Bks.) Holt, Henry & Co.
Hess, Erwin L. Convoy Patrol: A Thrilling Story of the U. S. Navy. Winterbotham, R. R. 2011. 426p. 56.95 (978-1-258-01444-5(0)) Literary Licensing, LLC.
—Roy Rogers: Robin Hood of the Range. Gruskin, Edward I. 2011. 420p. 54.95 (978-1-258-04369-8(5)) Literary Licensing, LLC.
Hess, Harvalee. Whitepaws Fabio Giorgio Don Gato Hess. Hess, Kathryn. l.t. ed. 2011. (ENG.). 32p. pap. 9.99 (978-1-4637-3447-3(6)) CreateSpace Independent Publishing Platform.
Hess, Ingrid. The Family Song. Peifer, Jane Hoober. 2008. 64p. (J). (gr. -1-3). pap. 18.99 incl. audio compact disk (978-0-8361-9414-2(4)) Herald Pr.
—Praying with Our Feet. Weaver, Lisa D. 2005. 40p. (J). pap. 12.99 (978-0-8361-9306-0(7)) Herald Pr.
Hess, Mark. When Mr. Jefferson Came to Philadelphia: What I Learned of Freedom 1776. Turner, Ann Warren. 2004. 32p. (J). (gr. -1-3). 15.99 (978-0-06-027579-2(0)) HarperCollins Pubs.
Hess, Paul. Amethyst. Lisle, Rebecca. 2007. (ENG.). 176p. (J). (gr. 4-7). per. 8.99 (978-1-84270-541-4(5)) Andersen Pr. GBR. Dist: Independent Pubs. Group.
—The Cow on the Roof. Maddern, Eric. 2006. (ENG.). 32p. (J). (gr. k-3). 15.95 (978-1-84507-374-9(6), Frances Lincoln) Quarto Publishing Group UK GBR. Dist: Hachette Bk. Group.
—Death in a Nut. Maddern, Eric & Williamson, Duncan. 2005. (ENG.). 32p. (J). 15.95 (978-1-84507-081-6(X), Frances Lincoln) Quarto Publishing Group UK GBR. Dist: Perseus-PGW.
—Hidden Tales from Eastern Europe. Barber, Antonia & Quarto Generic Staff. Guild, Shena, ed. 2004. (ENG.). 48p. (J). (gr. 2-17). 9.99 (978-1-84507-147-9(6), Frances Lincoln) Quarto Publishing Group UK GBR. Dist: Hachette Bk. Group.
—The King & the Seed. Maddern, Eric. 2009. (ENG.). 32p. (J). (gr. k-3). 16.95 (978-1-84507-926-0(4), Frances Lincoln) Quarto Publishing Group UK GBR. Dist: Perseus-PGW.
—The King with Horse's Ears. Maddern, Eric. 2003. 36p. (J). 14.95 (978-0-7112-1957-1(5), Frances Lincoln) Quarto Publishing Group UK GBR. Dist: Perseus-PGW.
—The Pig in a Wig. MacDonald, Alan. 2003. 32p. (J). (gr. k-3). pap. 6.95 (978-1-56145-299-6(8), Q32523) Peachtree Pubs.
—Rainforest Animals. 2003. (Animals Ser.). 24p. (J). pap. (978-1-84089-172-0(6)) Zero to Ten, Ltd.
—The Stone of Destiny: Tales from Turkey. Tavaci, Elspeth & Quarto Generic Staff. 2013. (ENG.). 144p. (J). (gr. 3-6). pap. 8.99 (978-1-84780-279-8(6), Frances Lincoln) Quarto Publishing Group UK GBR. Dist: Hachette Bk. Group.
—Troll Wood. Cave, Kathryn & Quarto Generic Staff. 2013. (ENG.). 32p. (J). (gr. -1-2). 17.99 (978-1-84780-238-5(9), Frances Lincoln) Quarto Publishing Group UK GBR. Dist: Hachette Bk. Group.
Hess, Paul. Farmyard Animals. Hess, Paul. 2009. (Animal Verse Ser.). (ENG.). 24p. (J). (gr. -1-k). pap. (978-1-84089-559-9(4)) Zero to Ten, Ltd.
—Polar Animals. Hess, Paul. 2009. (Animal Verse Ser.). (ENG.). 24p. (J). (gr. -1-k). pap. (978-1-84089-561-2(6)) Zero to Ten, Ltd.
—Rainforest Animals. Hess, Paul. 2009. (Animal Verse Ser.). (ENG.). 24p. (J). (gr. -1-k). pap. (978-1-84089-560-5(8)) Zero to Ten, Ltd.
—Safari Animals. Hess, Paul. 2009. (Animal Verse Ser.). (ENG.). 24p. (J). (gr. -1-k). pap. (978-1-84089-562-9(4)) Zero to Ten, Ltd.
Hesselbein, Kent, jt. illus. see Hall, Dee.
Heston, Charles. The True Book of Indians. Martini, Teri. 2011. 48p. 35.95 (978-1-258-05468-7(X)) Literary Licensing, LLC.
Hetherington, Jan. Where's Pa? Hetherington, Sally. 2013. 28p. pap. 15.97 (978-1-62516-299-1(5), Strategic Bk. Publishing) Strategic Book Publishing & Rights Agency (SBPRA).
Hetland, Beth. Backyard Biology: Investigate Habitats Outside Your Door with 25 Projects. Latham, Donna. 2013. (Build It Yourself Ser.). (ENG.). 128p. (J). (gr. 3-7). 21.95 (978-1-61930-152-8(0)); pap. 15.95 (978-1-61930-151-1(2)) Nomad Pr.
—Garbage: Investigate What Happens When You Throw It Out with 25 Projects. Latham, Donna. 2011. (Build It Yourself Ser.). (ENG.). 128p. (J). (gr. 3-7). 21.95 (978-1-936313-47-1(2)) Nomad Pr.
—Mapping & Navigation: Explore the History & Science of Finding Your Way with 20 Projects. Brown, Cynthia Light & McGinty, Patrick. 2013. (Build It Yourself Ser.). (ENG.). 128p. (J). (gr. 3-7). 21.95 (978-1-61930-194-8(6)); pap. 16.95 (978-1-61930-198-6(9)) Nomad Pr.
—Native Americans: Discover the History & Cultures of the First Americans with 15 Projects. Kavin, Kim. 2013. (Build It Yourself Ser.). (ENG.). 128p. (J). (gr. 3-7). 21.95 (978-1-61930-175-7(X)); pap. 16.95 (978-1-61930-170-2(9)) Nomad Pr.
Heuer, Christoph. Lola & Fred & Tom. 2007. (Lola & Fred Ser.). (ENG.). 48p. (J). (gr. -1-3). 15.95 (978-0-9741319-9-3(7)) 4N Publishing LLC.
Heuninck, Ronald. Rain or Shine. Heuninck, Ronald. Orig. Title: Buiten Spelen. 12p. (J). pap. 5.50 (978-0-86315-089-0(6), 20269) Floris Bks. GBR. Dist: Gryphon Hse., Inc.
Heuvel, Eric. A Family Secret. Heuvel, Eric. Miller, Lorraine T. Miller, Lorraine T., tr. from DUT. 2009. (ENG.). 64p. (J). (gr. 5-9). pap. 10.99 (978-0-374-42265-3(6)) Square Fish.
—The Search. Heuvel, Eric. van der Rol, Ruud et al. Miller, Lorraine T., tr. from DUT. 2009. (ENG.). 64p. (J). (gr. 4-8). pap. 14.99 (978-0-374-46455-4(3), Farrar, Straus & Giroux (BYR)) Farrar, Straus & Giroux.
Hewetson, Nicholas. How to Be a Roman Soldier. MacDonald, Fiona. 2005. (How to Be Ser.). (ENG.). 32p. (J). (gr. 3-7). 21.90 (978-0-7922-3631-3(9), National Geographic Children's Bks.) National Geographic Society.
Hewetson, Nicholas J. How to Be a Roman Soldier. MacDonald, Fiona. (How to Be Ser.). (ENG.). 32p. (J). (gr. 3-7). 2008. pap. 5.95 (978-1-4263-0169-8(3)); 2005. 14.95 (978-0-7922-3616-0(5)) National Geographic Society. (National Geographic Children's Bks.).
—How to Be an Egyptian Princess. Morley, Jacqueline. 2006. (How to Be (National Geographic) Ser.). 32p. (gr. 3-7). lib. bdg. 21.90 (978-0-7922-7548-0(9)) CENGAGE Learning.
—How to Be an Egyptian Princess. Morley, Jacqueline. (How to Be Ser.). (ENG.). 32p. (J). 2008. (gr. 3-7). pap. 5.95 (978-1-4263-0246-6(0)); 2006. (gr. 4-7). 14.95 (978-0-7922-7494-0(6)) National Geographic Society. (National Geographic Children's Bks.).
—The Usborne Book of World Religions. Meredith, Susan. Evans, Cheryl, ed. 2006. (World Religions (Usborne) Ser.). 64p. (J). (gr. 5). lib. bdg. 17.99 (978-1-58086-908-9(4), Usborne) EDC Publishing.
Hewetson, Nicholas J. & Gower, Jeremy. The Usborne Book of World Religions. Meredith, Susan. Evans, Cheryl, ed. rev. ed. 2006. (World Cultures Ser.). 64p. (J). (gr. 5). pap. 9.99 (978-0-7945-1027-5(2)) EDC Publishing.
Hewetson, Nick. Dinosaurs. Stewart, David. 2013. (World of Wonder Ser.). (ENG.). 32p. (J). (gr. 4-7). lib. bdg. (978-1-908973-98-6(6)) Book Hse.
—Dinosaurs. Stewart, David. 2008. (World of Wonder Ser.). (ENG.). 32p. (J). (gr. 1-4). 29.00 (978-0-531-20450-4(2), Children's Pr.) Scholastic Library Publishing.
Hewett, Angela, et al. Animals: Touch & Trace Early Learning Fun! Award, Anna. 2014. (ENG.). 26p. (J). pap. 13.50 (978-1-84135-944-1(0)) Award Pubns. Ltd. GBR. Dist: Parkwest Pubns., Inc.
—A B C: Touch & Trace Early Learning Fun! Award, Anna. 2014. (ENG.). 26p. (J). 13.50 (978-1-84135-942-7(4)) Award Pubns. Ltd. GBR. Dist: Parkwest Pubns., Inc.
Hewett, Angela. Bedtime. Pitchall, Chez. 2015. (ENG.). 10p. (J). 11.99 **(978-1-909763-43-2(8))** Award Pubns. Ltd. GBR. Dist: Parkwest Pubns., Inc.
Hewett, Angela. Bumper Junior Art: Colour by Numbers. 2013. (ENG.). 64p. (J). (gr. -1-3). pap. 8.50 (978-1-84135-998-4(X)) Parkwest Pubns., Inc.
Hewett, Angela, jt. illus. see Peters, Andy.
Hewins, Shirley. No Bulley Destroy's Chloe's Hairdo. Hawkins-Rodgers, Donzella. 2003. 32p. (J). (gr. 3-18). lib. bdg. 16.95 (978-1-884242-56-4(1)) Multicultural Pubns.
—Rainy Brown & the Seven Midgets. l.t. ed. 2006. (J). (gr. k-3). pap. 11.95 (978-1-884242-24-3(3), RB1STED); 44p. lib. bdg. 19.95 (978-1-884242-25-0(1), RB1STED) Multicultural Pubns.
Hewitt, Elizabeth. How Full Is Sophia's Backpack? Jacobs, Karen & Miller, Leah. 2012. 40p. pap. 11.95 (978-0-9850440-0-8(4)) Jacobs, Karen.
Hewitt, Kathryn. Flower Garden. Bunting, Eve. 2004. 28p. (gr. -1-2). 17.00 (978-0-7569-4113-0(X)) Perfection Learning Corp.
Hewitt, Kathryn. Jamaica Tag-Along. Bunting, Eve. 2015. 32p. pap. 7.00 **(978-1-61003-504-0(6))** Center for the Collaborative Classroom.
Hewitt, Kathryn. Lives of the Artists: Masterpieces, Messes (and What the Neighbors Thought) Krull, Kathleen. 2014. (Lives Of ... Ser.). (ENG.). 96p. (J). (gr. 5-7). pap. 8.99 (978-0-544-25223-3(3), HMH Books For Young Readers) Houghton Mifflin Harcourt Publishing Co.
—Lives of the Athletes: Thrills, Spills (and What the Neighbors Thought) Krull, Kathleen. 2013. (Lives Of ... Ser.). (ENG.). 96p. (J). (gr. 5-7). pap. 8.99 (978-0-544-24760-4(4)) Houghton Mifflin Harcourt Publishing Co.
—Lives of the Explorers: Discoveries, Disasters (and What the Neighbors Thought) Krull, Kathleen. 2014. (ENG.). 96p. (J). (gr. 5-7). 20.99 (978-0-15-205910-1(5), HMH Books For Young Readers) Houghton Mifflin Harcourt Publishing Co.
—Lives of the Musicians: Good Times, Bad Times (and What the Neighbors Thought) Krull, Kathleen. 2013. (Lives Of ... Ser.). (ENG.). 96p. (J). (gr. 5-7). pap. 8.99 (978-0-544-23806-0(0)) Houghton Mifflin Harcourt Publishing Co.
—Lives of the Pirates: Swashbucklers, Scoundrels (Neighbors Beware!) Krull, Kathleen. 2013. (Lives Of ... Ser.). (ENG.). 96p. (J). (gr. 5-7). pap. 8.99 (978-0-544-10495-2(1)) Houghton Mifflin Harcourt Publishing Co.
—Lives of the Presidents: Fame, Shame (And What the Neighbors Thought) Krull, Kathleen. 2011. (Lives Of ... Ser.). (ENG.). 104p. (YA). (gr. 5-7). 21.00 (978-0-547-49809-6(8)) Houghton Mifflin Harcourt Publishing Co.
—Lives of the Scientists: Experiments, Explosions (And What the Neighbors Thought) Krull, Kathleen. 2013. (ENG.). 96p. (J). (gr. 5-7). 20.99 (978-0-15-205909-5(1)) Houghton Mifflin Harcourt Publishing Co.
—Uncle Sam's America. Hewitt, David. 2011. (ENG.). 40p. (J). (gr. 2-5). pap. 19.99 (978-1-4424-3092-1(3)) Simon & Schuster Children's Publishing.
Heyer, Carol. The Christmas Story. (J). 6.95 (978-0-8249-5347-8(9)) Ideals Pubns.
—The Crow & the Pitcher: A Tale about Problem Solving. Aesop. 2006. (J). (978-1-59939-096-3(5), Reader's Digest Young Families, Inc.) Studio Fun International.
—Day of the Iguana, 3 vols. Winkler, Henry & Oliver, Lin. 2003. (Hank Zipzer Ser.: 3). (ENG.). 160p. (J). (gr. 3-7). 13.99 (978-0-448-43288-5(9), Grosset & Dunlap) Penguin Publishing Group.
—The First Easter. 2003. (ENG.). 32p. (J). 14.95 (978-0-8249-5463-5(7)) Ideals Pubns.
Heyer, Carol, et al. Holy Enchilada! Winkler, Henry & Oliver, Lin. 2004. (Hank Zipzer Ser.: 6). (ENG.). 160p. (J). (gr. 3-7). pap. 5.99 (978-0-448-43353-0(2), Grosset & Dunlap) Penguin Publishing Group.
Heyer, Carol. Let's Read About — George W. Bush. Fry, Sonali. 2003. (Scholastic First Biographies Ser.). (J). pap. (978-0-439-45953-2(2)) Scholastic, Inc.
Heyer, Carol, et al. Summer School! What Genius Thought That Up?, 8 vols. Winkler, Henry & Oliver, Lin. 2005. (Hank Zipzer Ser.: 8). (ENG.). 160p. (J). (gr. 3-7). mass mkt. 5.99 (978-0-448-43739-2(2), Grosset & Dunlap) Penguin Publishing Group.
Heyer, Carol. Summer School! What Genius Thought That Up?, 8 vols. Winkler, Henry & Oliver, Lin. 2005. (Hank Zipzer Ser.: 8). (ENG.). 160p. (J). (gr. 3-7). 14.99 (978-0-448-43740-8(6), Grosset & Dunlap) Penguin Publishing Group.
Heyer, Carol. The First Christmas. Heyer, Carol. 2007. (ENG.). 32p. (J). (gr. k-3). 8.99 (978-0-8249-5566-3(8), Ideals Children's Bks.) Ideals Pubns.
—The First Easter. Heyer, Carol. 2008. (ENG.). 28p. (J). (gr. -1-3). 8.99 (978-0-8249-5576-2(5), Ideals Children's Bks.) Ideals Pubns.
—Humphrey's First Christmas. Heyer, Carol. 2008. (ENG.). 32p. (J). (gr. -1-3). 14.99 (978-0-8249-5559-5(5), Ideals Children's Bks.) Ideals Pubns.
—Humphrey's First Palm Sunday. Heyer, Carol. 2012. 32p. (J). 14.99 (978-0-8249-5636-3(2), Ideals Children's Bks.) Ideals Pubns.
Heyer, Carol. The Easter Story. Heyer, Carol, retold by. 32p. (J). 12.95 (978-0-8249-5363-8(0), Ideals) Ideals Pubns.
—Excalibur. Heyer, Carol, retold by. (978-1-59093-022-9(3), Eager Minds Pr.) Warehousing & Fulfillment Specialists, LLC (WFS, LLC).
Heyer, Carol & Watson, Jesse Joshua. My Secret Life as a Ping-Pong Wizard, 9 vols. Winkler, Henry & Oliver, Lin. 2005. (Hank Zipzer Ser.: 9). (ENG.). 160p. (J). (gr. 3-7). pap. 5.99 (978-0-448-43749-1(X), Grosset & Dunlap) Penguin Publishing Group.
Heyer, Carol & White, Charlotte L. Tommy Wilson, Junior Veterinarian: The Case of the Orphaned Bobcat. Smith, Maggie Caldwell. 2006. (J). per. 7.95 (978-0-9788391-1-6(0)) Magpie Pr., Pine Mountain Club, CA.
Heyes, Jane. Candle Day by Day Bible, 1 vol. David, Juliet. 2014. (ENG.). 400p. (J). 16.99 (978-1-85985-824-0(4), Candle Bks.) Lion Hudson PLC GBR. Dist: Kregel Pubns.
Heyman, Ken, photos by. On the Go. Morris, Ann. 2015. 32p. pap. 7.00 **(978-1-61003-611-5(5))** Center for the Collaborative Classroom.
—Tools. Morris, Ann. 2015. 32p. pap. 7.00 **(978-1-61003-622-1(0))** Center for the Collaborative Classroom.
Heyworth, Heather. Dress-Up Day, 1 vol. Dale, Jay. 2012. (Engage Literacy Green Ser.). (ENG.). 32p. (gr. k-2). pap. 5.99 (978-1-4296-9003-4(8), Engage Literacy) Capstone Pr., Inc.
—Goal! Matthew, Anna. 2013. (Start Reading Ser.). (ENG.). 24p. (gr. k-1). pap. 41.94 (978-1-4765-3215-8(X)); pap. 6.99 (978-1-4765-3203-5(6)) Capstone Pr., Inc.
—Hide & Seek. Matthew, Anna. 2013. (Start Reading Ser.). (ENG.). 24p. (gr. k-1). pap. 41.94 (978-1-4765-3217-2(6)); pap. 6.99 (978-1-4765-3204-2(4)) Capstone Pr., Inc.
—Hopscotch. Matthew, Anna. 2013. (Start Reading Ser.). (ENG.). 24p. (gr. k-1). pap. 41.94 (978-1-4765-3218-9(4)); pap. 6.99 (978-1-4765-3205-9(2)) Capstone Pr., Inc.
—If I Were a Ballerina, 1 vol. Troupe, Thomas Kingsley. 2009. (Dream Big! Ser.). (ENG.). 24p. (gr. k-3). lib. bdg. 25.99 (978-1-4048-5532-8(7)); pap. 7.95 (978-1-4048-5706-3(0)) Picture Window Bks. (Nonfiction Picture Bks.).
—If I Were the President, 1 vol. Troupe, Thomas Kingsley. 2009. (Dream Big! Ser.). (ENG.). 24p. (gr. k-3). lib. bdg. 25.99 (978-1-4048-5533-5(5)); pap. 7.95 (978-1-4048-5712-4(5)) Picture Window Bks. (Nonfiction Picture Bks.).
—If I Were the President [Scholastic]. Troupe, Thomas Kingsley. 2010. (Dream Big! Ser.). 24p. pap. 0.62 (978-1-4048-6196-1(3), Nonfiction Picture Bks.) Picture Window Bks.
—Jumping Rope! Matthew, Anna. 2013. (Start Reading Ser.). (ENG.). 24p. (gr. k-1). pap. 41.94 (978-1-4765-3222-6(2)); pap. 6.99 (978-1-4765-3206-6(0)) Capstone Pr., Inc.
—My Princesses Learn to Be Brave. Rische, Stephanie. 2014. (ENG.). 24p. (J). 6.99 (978-1-4143-9661-3(9)) Tyndale Hse. Pubs.
—My Princesses Learn to Share. Carlson, Amie. 2014. (ENG.). 24p. (J). 6.99 (978-1-4143-9662-0(7)) Tyndale Hse. Pubs.
Hezlep, Amber. It Could Happen... on the Bus. Higbee, Heidi. 2012. 32p. (J). pap. 16.95 (978-0-9882940-0-4(1)) Bryson Taylor Publishing.
Hibbert, Hollie. Echo's Lucky Charm. Hapka, Cathy. 2015. 92p. (J). **(978-0-545-75025-7(3))** Scholastic, Inc.
Hibbert, Hollie. The Three Bears ABC. Maccarone, Grace. ed. 2013. (ENG.). 32p. (J). (gr. -1-2). 16.99 (978-0-8075-7904-6(1)) Whitman, Albert & Co.
Hibbert, Rhonda. Share Day, 1 vol. Hibbert, Dee. 2009. 31p. pap. 24.95 (978-1-60813-294-2(3)) America Star Bks.
Hibbs, Gillian. Tilly's at Home Holiday. Hibbs, Gillian. 2014. (Child's Play Library). (ENG.). 32p. (J). (978-1-84643-601-7(X)) Child's Play International Ltd.
Hickerson, Joel. ImagineLand's Bubble Gum Trouble, Vol. 1. l.t. ed. 2004. 32p. (J). (978-0-9765038-0-4(8)) Imagineland, Ltd.
Hickey, Brenda. Applejack. Curnow, Bobby. 2015. (J). **(978-1-61479-331-1(X))** Spotlight.
Hickey, Josh. Betsy Beansprout Camping Guide. Elmore, Amber. 2013. 50p. pap. 13.99 (978-1-937331-37-5(7)) ShadeTree Publishing, LLC.
Hickman, Paula. Tiberius Meets Sneaky Cat. Harvey, Keith. 2010. (Tiberius Tales Ser.). 24p. (J). (gr. -1-2). pap. 8.15 (978-1-60754-835-5(6)); lib. bdg. 22.60 (978-1-60754-831-7(3)) Windmill Bks.
Hickman, Paula, jt. illus. see Brown, Kate.
Hicks, Alan and Aaron. Twin Hicks Noah's Ark. Richardson, Robert. 2008. 36p. pap. 16.95 (978-1-4389-1809-9(7)) AuthorHouse.
Hicks, Angela, jt. illus. see Burton, Terry.
Hicks, Angie. Alien. 2012. (ENG.). 24p. (J). 4.95 (978-1-84135-585-6(2)) Award Pubns. Ltd. GBR. Dist: Parkwest Pubns., Inc.
—Butterfly. 2012. (ENG.). 24p. (J). 4.95 (978-1-84135-582-5(8)) Award Pubns. Ltd. GBR. Dist: Parkwest Pubns., Inc.
—Colour by Numbers. 2012. (ENG.). 16p. (J). 3.25 (978-1-84135-860-4(6)) Award Pubns. Ltd. GBR. Dist: Parkwest Pubns., Inc.
—Colour by Numbers - Pirate. 2012. (ENG.). 16p. (J). 3.25 (978-1-84135-857-4(6)) Award Pubns. Ltd. GBR. Dist: Parkwest Pubns., Inc.
—The Fairy Horse. 2012. (ENG.). 24p. (J). 9.95 (978-1-84135-834-5(7)) Award Pubns. Ltd. GBR. Dist: Parkwest Pubns., Inc.
—Fish. 2012. (ENG.). 24p. (J). 4.95 (978-1-84135-584-9(4)) Award Pubns. Ltd. GBR. Dist: Parkwest Pubns., Inc.
—Mermaid. 2012. (ENG.). 16p. (J). 3.25 (978-1-84135-859-8(2)) Award Pubns. Ltd. GBR. Dist: Parkwest Pubns., Inc.
—Moonlight & the Mermaid. 2012. (ENG.). 24p. (J). 9.95 (978-1-84135-833-8(9)) Award Pubns. Ltd. GBR. Dist: Parkwest Pubns., Inc.
—Pirate. 2012. (ENG.). 24p. (J). 4.95 (978-1-84135-583-2(6)) Award Pubns. Ltd. GBR. Dist: Parkwest Pubns., Inc.
—Shark. 2012. (ENG.). 16p. (J). 3.25 (978-1-84135-858-1(4)) Award Pubns. Ltd. GBR. Dist: Parkwest Pubns., Inc.
—Sparkle the Seahorse. King, Karen. 2012. (ENG.). 24p. (J). 9.95 (978-1-84135-879-6(7)) Award Pubns. Ltd. GBR. Dist: Parkwest Pubns., Inc.
—Unicorn Magic. King, Karen. 2012. (ENG.). 24p. 9.95 (978-1-84135-832-1(0)) Award Pubns. Ltd. GBR. Dist: Parkwest Pubns., Inc.
Hicks, Bob. Cornelius, the Little Dragon Book. Hicks, Bob. 2004. (J). ring bd. incl. audio compact disk (978-0-9722036-5-4(6)) T. E. Publishing, Inc.
Hicks, Faith. Nellie in the News. Kelly, Claire. 2007. 48p. (J). lib. bdg. 23.08 (978-1-4242-1631-4(1)) Fitzgerald Bks.
Hicks, Faith Erin. Brain Camp. Kim, Susan & Klavan, Laurence. 2010. (ENG.). 160p. (J). (gr. 6-9). pap. 17.99 (978-1-59643-366-3(3), First Second Bks.) Roaring Brook Pr.
—Into the Woods. Torres, J. 2012. (Bigfoot Boy Ser.: 1). (ENG.). 100p. (J). 17.95 (978-1-55453-711-2(8)); pap. 9.95 (978-1-55453-712-9(6)) Kids Can Pr., Ltd. CAN. Dist: Univ. of Toronto Pr.
—Nothing Can Possibly Go Wrong. Shen, Prudence. 2013. (ENG.). 288p. (YA). (gr. 7). pap. 16.99 (978-1-59643-659-6(X), First Second Bks.) Roaring Brook Pr.
—The Unkindness of Ravens. Torres, J. 2013. (Bigfoot Boy Ser.). (ENG.). 100p. (J). 17.95 (978-1-55453-713-6(4)) Kids Can Pr., Ltd. CAN. Dist: Univ. of Toronto Pr.
Hicks, Faith Erin. The Adventures of Superhero Girl. Hicks, Faith Erin. Edidin, Rachel, ed. 2013. (ENG.). 112p. (gr. 5). 16.99 (978-1-61655-084-4(8)) Dark Horse Comics.

H

—Friends with Boys. Hicks, Faith Erin. 2012. (ENG.). 224p. (YA). (gr. 7-11). pap. 16.99 *(978-1-59643-556-8(9)*, First Second Bks.) Roaring Brook Pr.

Hicks, Kaylee. I'm So Cute, You Can't Be Mad. Bruton, Seth. 2012. 24p. pap. 13.97 *(978-1-61204-897-0(8)*, Strategic Bk. Publishing) Strategic Book Publishing & Rights Agency (SBPRA).

Hicks, Rebecca. Little Vampires. Hicks, Rebecca. 2007. 56p. per. 8.95 *(978-0-9799290-0-7(8))* Lunasea Studios.

Hief, Gina. The Garden Adventures: The Mishaps of Martha & Matilda. Rothchild, Erik. 2013. 44p. *(978-0-9883568-5-6(6))* Inkwell Productions, LLC.

Hierlmaier, Joy. Green Yellow Go! Nat Knows Bananas. Hierlmaier Nelson, Christine M. 2004. 26p. (J). spiral bd. 14.95 *(978-0-9759362-0-7(4))* Expressive Ink.

Hiers, Christopher. Rush Revere & the American Revolution. Limbaugh, Rush H., III & Limbaugh, Kathryn Adams. 2014. (J). pap. *(978-1-4767-8989-7(4)*, Threshold Editions) Threshold Editions.

Hierstein, Judith. The American Revolution from A to Z, 1 vol. Crawford, Laura. 2009. (ENG.). 32p. (J). (gr. k-3). 16.99 *(978-1-58980-515-6(1))* Pelican Publishing Co., Inc.

—Benjamin Franklin from A to Z, 1 vol. Crawford, Laura. 2013. (ENG.). 32p. (J). (gr. k-3). 16.99 *(978-1-4556-1713-5(X))* Pelican Publishing Co., Inc.

—Jim Limber Davis: A Black Orphan in the Confederate White House, 1 vol. Pittman, Rickey. 2007. (ENG.). 32p. (J). (gr. k-3). 16.99 *(978-1-58980-435-7(X))* Pelican Publishing Co., Inc.

—Nathan's Hanukkah Bargain, 1 vol. Greene, Jacqueline. 2008. (ENG.). 32p. (J). (gr. 1-3). 16.99 *(978-1-58980-454-8(6))* Pelican Publishing Co., Inc.

—The Pilgrims' Thanksgiving from A to Z, 1 vol. Crawford, Laura. 2005. (ENG.). 32p. (J). (gr. k-3). per. 8.99 *(978-1-58980-238-4(1))* Pelican Publishing Co., Inc.

—Toby Belfer Visits Ellis Island, 1 vol. Pushker, Gloria Teles. 2003. (Toby Belfer Ser.). (ENG.). 32p. (J). (gr. k-3). 16.99 *(978-1-58980-117-2(2))* Pelican Publishing Co., Inc.

—Two Sides to Every Story. Lipson, Greta Barclay. 2004. 128p. (J). pap. 14.95 *(978-1-57310-439-5(6))* Teaching & Learning Co.

—Voices of Gettysburg, 1 vol. Garland, Sherry. 2010. (Voices of History Ser.). (ENG.). 40p. (J). (gr. 3-3). 17.99 *(978-1-58980-653-5(0))* Pelican Publishing Co., Inc.

—Voices of the Dust Bowl, 1 vol. Garland, Sherry. 2012. (Voices of History Ser.). (ENG.). 40p. (J). (gr. 3-3). 17.99 *(978-1-58980-964-2(5))* Pelican Publishing Co., Inc.

Hierstein, Judy & Boyer, Lyn. The Ultimate Book of Second Grade Skills: Grade 2. Fetty, Margaret, ed. 2009. (Ultimate Book of Skills Ser.). 224p. pap. 16.99 *(978-1-4190-9953-3(1))* Steck-Vaughn.

Higashi, Sandra, jt. illus. see Glaser, Byron.

Higgie, Will K., jt. illus. see Vincent, Andrew M.

Higgins, Anne Keenan. Blowout, No. 1. Morris, Taylor. 2011. (Hello, Gorgeous! Ser.: 1). (ENG.). 224p. (J). (gr. 3-7). pap. 6.99 *(978-0-448-45526-6(9)*, Grosset & Dunlap) Penguin Publishing Group.

—Fashionably Me: A Journal That's Just My Style. Phillips, Karen. 2013. (ENG.). 100p. (J). (gr. 3). 16.99 *(978-0-545-56165-5(5))* Klutz.

—Foiled #2. Morris, Taylor. 2011. (Hello, Gorgeous! Ser.: 2). (ENG.). 224p. (J). (gr. 3-7). pap. 6.99 *(978-0-448-45527-3(7)*, Grosset & Dunlap) Penguin Publishing Group.

—Starring Jules (As Herself) Ain, Beth. 2013. (Starring Jules Ser.: No. 1). (ENG.). 160p. (J). (gr. 2-5). 14.99 *(978-0-545-44352-4(0)*, Scholastic Pr.) Scholastic, Inc.

—Starring Jules (in Drama-Rama) Ain, Beth. 2013. (Starring Jules Ser.: No. 2). (ENG.). 176p. (J). (gr. 2-5). 14.99 *(978-0-545-44354-8(7)*, Scholastic Pr.) Scholastic, Inc.

Higgins, Anne Keenan. I Love It When... Higgins, Anne Keenan. 2009. (Sticker Stories Ser.). (ENG.). 16p. (J). (gr. -1-2). pap. 5.99 *(978-0-448-45245-6(6)*, Grosset & Dunlap) Penguin Publishing Group.

Higgins, Clark L. We've Seen Sant. Higgins, Tiffany A. 2011. 26p. pap. 12.27 *(978-1-61204-267-1(8)*, Eloquent Bks.) Strategic Book Publishing & Rights Agency (SBPRA).

Higgins, Dusty. Attack of the Alien Horde. Venditti, Robert. 2015. (Miles Taylor & the Golden Cape Ser.: 1). (ENG.). 304p. (J). (gr. 4-7). 16.99 *(978-1-4814-0542-3(X))* Simon & Schuster, Inc.

Higgins, Krystal. Hello Smokey! Aryal, Aimee. 2004. 22p. (J). 19.95 *(978-1-932888-09-6(8))* Mascot Bks., Inc.

Higgins, Quentin R. Hippity Has a Hot Idea. Higgins, Quentin R. 2003. 30p. (J). *(978-1-929204-11-3(6))* Dryden Publishing.

Higgins, Ryan. Wilfred. Higgins, Ryan. 2013. (ENG.). 40p. (J). (gr. -1-k). 16.99 *(978-0-8037-3732-7(7)*, Dial) Penguin Publishing Group.

Higham, Amanda. Our Cat Cuddles. Phinn, Gervase. 2006. (Child's Play Library). (ENG.). 32p. (J). *(978-1-84643-027-5(5))* Child's Play International Ltd.

Hight, Lloyd R. 44 Animals of the Bible. Johnson, Nancy Pelander. 2014. (ENG.). 44p. (J). (gr. -1-3). 9.99 *(978-0-89051-843-4(2))* Master Bks.

Hight, Michael. Flamingo Bendalingo: Poems from the Zoo. Green, Paula. 2006. (ENG.). 100p. (gr. 4-7). 24.95 *(978-1-86940-353-9(3))* Auckland Univ. Pr. NZL. Dist: Independent Pubs. Group.

Higuchi, Daisuke. Re-Start, Vol. 4. Higuchi, Daisuke. 2005. (Whistle! Ser.). (ENG.). 200p. pap. 7.99 *(978-1-59116-727-3(2))* Viz Media.

—Whistle! Higuchi, Daisuke. Kokubo, Naomi, tr. from JPN. 2005. (Whistle! Ser.: Vol. 6). (ENG.). 200p. pap. 7.99 *(978-1-59116-836-2(8))* Viz Media.

—Whistle! Higuchi, Daisuke. 2004. (Whistle! Ser.: Vol. 2). (ENG.). 208p. pap. 7.99 *(978-1-59116-686-3(1))* Viz Media.

—Whistle!, Vol. I. Higuchi, Daisuke. Moyoco, Anno. 2004. (Whistle! Ser.). (ENG.). 208p. pap. 7.99 *(978-1-59116-685-6(3))* Viz Media.

—Whistle! Higuchi, Daisuke. 2005. (Whistle! Ser.). (ENG.). Vol. 3. 208p. pap. 7.99 *(978-1-59116-692-4(6))*; Vol. 5. 192p. (gr. -1-13). pap. 7.99 *(978-1-59116-789-1(2))* Viz Media.

—Whistle!, Vol. 7. Higuchi, Daisuke. Daisuke, Higuchi. 2005. (Whistle! Ser.). (ENG.). 200p. pap. 7.99 *(978-1-59116-973-4(9))* Viz Media.

—Whistle! Higuchi, Daisuke. (Whistle! Ser.). (ENG.). Vol. 8. 2005. 200p. pap. 7.99 *(978-1-4215-0068-3(X))*; Vol. 9. 2006. 200p. pap. 7.99 *(978-1-4215-0206-9(2))*; Vol. 10. 2006. 208p. pap. 7.99 *(978-1-4215-0340-0(9))*; Vol. 12. 2006. 208p. pap. 7.99 *(978-1-4215-0686-9(6))*; Vol. 15. 2007. 208p. pap. 7.99 *(978-1-4215-0689-0(0))* Viz Media.

Hiiragi, Aoi. The Cat Returns Picture Book. Morita, Hiroyuki. Searleman, Eric, ed. 2007. (Cat Returns Ser.: 1). (ENG.). 112p. (gr. -1). pap. 14.99 *(978-1-4215-1498-7(2))* Viz Media.

Hiiragi, Aoi. Baron: The Cat Returns. Hiiragi, Aoi. 2005. (Baron Ser.). (ENG.). 224p. pap. 9.99 *(978-1-59116-956-7(9))* Viz Media.

Hijioka, Makoto. Giratina & the Sky Warrior! Hijioka, Makoto. 2009. (Pokemon Ser.). (ENG.). 192p. (J). pap. 7.99 *(978-1-4215-2701-7(4))* Viz Media.

Hikadova, Katerina, et al. World Atlas. Dusek, Jiri et al. 2014. (ENG.). 42p. (J). (gr. 3-5). 16.95 *(978-1-4549-1235-4(9))* Sterling Publishing Co., Inc.

Hikawa, Kyoko. From Far Away. Hikawa, Kyoko. (From Far Away Ser.). (ENG.). Vol. 2. 2005. 184p. (YA). pap. 9.99 *(978-1-59116-601-6(2))*; Vol. 4. 2005. 192p. (YA). pap. 9.99 *(978-1-59116-770-9(1))*; Vol. 11. 2006. 208p. pap. 9.99 *(978-1-4215-0538-1(X))* Viz Media.

Hilb, Nora. Itsy Bitsy Spider. (Classic Books with Holes Ser.). (ENG.). (J). 2015. 16p. ***(978-1-84643-676-5(1))***; 2012. 14p. bds. *(978-1-84643-509-6(9))*; 2012. 16p. pap. *(978-1-84643-498-3(X))* Child's Play International Ltd.

Hilb, Nora. Kids Do, Animals Too: A Book of Playground Opposites. Pearson, Debora. 2005. (ENG.). 24p. (J). (gr. -1 — 1). 17.95 *(978-1-55037-923-5(2)*, 9781550379235) Annick Pr., Ltd. CAN. Dist: Firefly Bks., Ltd.

—Leo's Tree. Pearson, Debora. 2004. (ENG.). 24p. (J). (gr. -1-1). 19.95 *(978-1-55037-845-0(7)*, 9781550378450) Annick Pr., Ltd. CAN. Dist: Firefly Bks., Ltd.

—Una Montana para Pancho. Maine, Margarita. (SPA.). 32p. (J). *(978-84-236-4740-8(4))* Edebé ESP. Dist: Lectorum Pubns., Inc.

—Nora's Ark, 1 vol. Spinelli, Eileen. 2013. (ENG.). 32p. (J). 16.99 *(978-0-310-72006-5(0))* Zonderkidz.

—Sophie's Wheels. Pearson, Debora. 2006. (ENG.). 24p. (J). (gr. -1-1). pap. 6.95 *(978-1-55451-037-5(6)*, 9781554510375) Annick Pr., Ltd. CAN. Dist: Firefly Bks., Ltd.

HildaRose. Baby's Lullaby, 1 vol. Barber, Jill. ed. 2011. (ENG.). 16p. (J). (gr. -1-k). bds. 8.95 *(978-1-55109-795-4(8))* Nimbus Publishing, Ltd. CAN. Dist: Orca Bk. Pubs. USA.

—Kisses Kisses Baby-O!, 1 vol. Fitch, Sheree. 2008. (ENG.). 12p. (J). (gr. -1-2). bds. 6.50 *(978-1-55109-646-9(3))* Nimbus Publishing, Ltd. CAN. Dist: Orca Bk. Pubs. USA.

Hildebrandt, Lowell. Darza the Little Dragon. Kaneko, Amanda Bullard. 2010. 28p. 13.99 *(978-1-4520-4198-8(9))* AuthorHouse.

—Salma & the Christmas Star. Torres, Christopher S. 2010. 24p. 12.99 *(978-1-4490-8981-8(X))* AuthorHouse.

Hilder, Rowland. The Midnight Folk. Masefield, John. 2008. (ENG.). 256p. (J). (gr. 4-7). 16.95 *(978-1-59017-290-2(6)*, NYR Children's Collection) New York Review of Bks., Inc., The.

Hilinski, Clint. Ali Baba: Fooling the Forty Thieves [an Arabian Tale]. Croall, Marie. 2009. (Graphic Myths & Legends Ser.). (ENG.). 48p. (gr. 4-8). pap. 8.95 *(978-1-58013-887-1(X))* Lerner Publishing Group.

—Sinbad: Sailing into Peril. Croall, Marie. 2007. (Graphic Myths & Legends Ser.). (ENG.). 48p. (gr. 4-8). lib. bdg. 27.93 *(978-0-8225-6375-4(4))* Lerner Publishing Group.

—Sinbad: Sailing into Peril. Croall, Marie P. 2008. (Graphic Myths & Legends Ser.). (ENG.). 48p. (gr. 4-8). pap. 8.95 *(978-0-8225-8516-9(2))* Lerner Publishing Group.

—The Treasure of Mount Fate. Limke, Jeff. 2007. (Twisted Journeys (r) Ser.: 4). (ENG.). (J). (gr. 4-7). pap. 45.32 *(978-0-8225-9468-0(4))*; 112p. lib. bdg. 27.93 *(978-0-8225-6205-4(7)*, Graphic Universe); 112p. per. 7.95 *(978-0-8225-6206-1(5))* Lerner Publishing Group.

Hill, Beth. Pup & Pokey. Kantner, Seth. 2014. 48p. pap. 14.95 *(978-1-60223-241-9(5))* Univ. of Alaska Pr.

Hill, Bethanne. Why the Oyster Has the Pearl, 1 vol. Downing, Johnette. 2011. (ENG.). 32p. (J). (gr. k-3). 16.99 *(978-1-4556-1460-8(2))* Pelican Publishing Co., Inc.

Hill, Bodhi. Littering Is for Losers. Dunn, Jill. 2012. 64p. (J). 21.99 *(978-0-9852146-2-3(7))* AuthorMike Ink.

Hill, Chris. What Does It Mean to Be Global? Little Pickle Press & DiOrio, Rana. ed. 2009. (What Does It Mean to Be... ? Ser.). (ENG.). 32p. (J). (gr. -1-2). 17.95 *(978-0-9840806-0-1(0))* Little Pickle Press LLC.

Hill, Dave. Daddy. Daddy There's a Mouse in the House. Sanna, Charles A. 2006. (J). 10.00 *(978-0-9762839-1-1(3))* Elizabooks.

—The Pentecost Story. Jaeger, Elizabeth. 2014. (Arch Bks.). (ENG.). 16p. (J). pap. 2.49 *(978-0-7586-4604-0(6))* Concordia Publishing Hse.

—Princess Polly & the Pony. Davidson, Susanna. 2007. (First Reading Level 4 Ser.). 48p. (J). 8.99 *(978-0-7945-1756-4(0)*, Usborne) EDC Publishing.

—What Happened to Merry Christmas? Baker, Robert C. 2007. 32p. (J). (gr. -1-3). 13.49 *(978-0-7586-1346-2(6))* Concordia Publishing Hse.

—The Wonder of Christmas. Mackall, Dandi Daley. 2008. 32p. (J). (gr. -1-3). 13.49 *(978-0-7586-1499-5(3))* Concordia Publishing Hse.

Hill, David. Hildegard's Gift. Hoyt, Megan. 2014. (ENG.). 32p. (J). pap. 15.99 *(978-1-61261-358-1(6))* Paraclete Pr., Inc.

—Sharing God's Love: The Jesus Creed for Chldren. McKnight, Scot & McKnight Barringer, Laura. 2014. (ENG.). 32p. (J). pap. 15.99 *(978-1-61261-581-3(3))* Paraclete Pr., Inc.

Hill, Eric. First Christmas. Hill, Eric. 2004. (Spot Ser.). (ENG.). 20p. (J). (gr. -1-k). 6.99 *(978-0-14-240202-3(8)*, Warne) Penguin Publishing Group.

—Good Night, Spot. Hill, Eric. 2004. (Spot Ser.). (ENG.). 16p. (J). (gr. -1 — 1). bds. 4.99 *(978-0-399-24319-6(4)*, Warne) Penguin Publishing Group.

—Hide & Seek. Hill, Eric. 2010. (Spot Ser.). (ENG.). 10p. (J). (gr. -1 — 1). bds. 5.99 *(978-0-399-25475-8(7)*, Warne) Penguin Publishing Group.

—Night-Night, Spot. Hill, Eric. 2005. (Spot Ser.). (ENG.). 32p. (J). (gr. -1-k). pap. 3.99 *(978-0-448-43810-8(0)*, Warne) Penguin Publishing Group.

—Spot Bakes a Cake. Hill, Eric. (Spot Ser.). (ENG.). (J). 2005. 20p. (gr. k — 1). 6.99 *(978-0-14-240329-7(6)*, Warne); 2003. 22p. (gr. -1-1). bds. 7.99 *(978-0-399-24013-3(6))* Penguin Publishing Group.

—Spot Can Count. Hill, Eric. (ENG.). (J). (gr. -1-1). 2005. 22p. bds. 7.99 *(978-0-399-24361-5(5))*; 2003. 24p. 6.99 *(978-0-14-250121-4(2)*, Warne) Penguin Publishing Group.

—Spot Goes Shopping. Hill, Eric. 2014. (Spot Ser.). (ENG.). 12p. (J). (gr. -1-k). bds. 5.99 *(978-0-7232-8997-5(2)*, Warne) Penguin Publishing Group.

—Spot Goes to School. Hill, Eric. 2004. (Spot Ser.). (ENG.). 24p. (J). (gr. -1-k). 6.99 *(978-0-14-240167-5(6)*, Warne) Penguin Publishing Group.

—Spot Goes to the Farm. Hill, Eric. 2003. (Spot Ser.). (ENG.). 24p. (J). (gr. -1-k). 7.99 *(978-0-14-250123-8(9)*, Warne) Penguin Publishing Group.

—Spot Goes to the Park. Hill, Eric. 2005. (Spot Ser.). (ENG.). 12p. (J). (gr. -1 — 1). bds. 7.99 *(978-0-399-24363-9(1)*, Putnam Juvenile) Penguin Publishing Group.

—Spot Loves His Daddy. Hill, Eric. 2005. (Spot Ser.). (ENG.). 12p. (J). (gr. -1 — 1). bds. 5.99 *(978-0-399-24351-6(8)*, Warne) Penguin Publishing Group.

—Spot Loves His Friends. Hill, Eric. 2010. (Spot Ser.). (ENG.). 12p. (J). (gr. -1 — 1). bds. 5.99 *(978-0-399-25450-5(1)*, Warne) Penguin Publishing Group.

—Spot Loves His Grandma. Hill, Eric. 2008. (Spot Ser.). (ENG.). 12p. (J). (gr. -1 — 1). bds. 5.99 *(978-0-399-24728-6(9)*, Warne) Penguin Publishing Group.

—Spot Loves His Grandpa. Hill, Eric. 2008. (Spot Ser.). (ENG.). 12p. (J). (gr. -1 — 1). bds. 5.99 *(978-0-399-24729-3(7)*, Warne) Penguin Publishing Group.

—Spot Loves His Mommy. Hill, Eric. 2006. (Spot Ser.). (ENG.). 12p. (J). (gr. -1 — 1). bds. 5.99 *(978-0-399-24511-4(1)*, Warne) Penguin Publishing Group.

—Spot Loves School. Hill, Eric. 2015. (Spot Ser.). (ENG.). 10p. (J). (gr. -1-k). bds. 5.99 *(978-0-14-135654-9(5)*, Warne) Penguin Publishing Group.

—Spot Loves Sports. Hill, Eric. 2012. (Spot Ser.). (ENG.). 12p. (J). (gr. -1 — 1). bds. 5.99 *(978-0-399-25775-9(6)*, Warne) Penguin Publishing Group.

—Spot on the Move. Hill, Eric. 2014. (Spot Ser.). (ENG.). 10p. (J). (gr. -1-k). bds. 12.99 *(978-0-7232-8169-6(6)*, Warne) Penguin Publishing Group.

—Spot Says Please. Hill, Eric. 2013. (Spot Ser.). (ENG.). 12p. (J). (gr. -1-k). bds. 5.99 *(978-0-7232-7832-0(6)*, Warne) Penguin Publishing Group.

—Spot's Baby Sister. Hill, Eric. 2004. (Spot Ser.). (ENG.). 24p. (J). (gr. -1-k). 7.99 *(978-0-14-240169-9(2)*, Warne) Penguin Publishing Group.

—Spot's Balloon. Hill, Eric. 2010. (Spot Ser.). (ENG.). 12p. (J). (gr. -1 — 1). bds. 9.99 *(978-0-399-25531-1(1)*, Warne) Penguin Publishing Group.

—Spot's Birthday Party. Hill, Eric. 2007. (Spot Ser.). (ENG.). 12p. (J). (gr. -1 — 1). bds. 7.99 *(978-0-399-24770-5(X)*, Putnam Juvenile) Penguin Publishing Group.

—Spot's Christmas. Hill, Eric. 2004. (Spot Ser.). (ENG.). 12p. (J). (gr. -1 — 1). bds. 5.99 *(978-0-399-24320-2(8)*, Warne) Penguin Publishing Group.

—Spot's Christmas Plush Doll. Hill, Eric. 2005. (J). 11.00 *(978-0-399-24472-8(7)*, Putnam Juvenile) Penguin Publishing Group.

—Spot's Easter Surprise. Hill, Eric. 2007. (Spot Ser.). (ENG.). 10p. (J). (gr. -1-k). bds. 5.99 *(978-0-399-24743-9(2)*, Warne) Penguin Publishing Group.

—Spot's Favorite Shapes. Hill, Eric. 2015. (Spot Ser.). (ENG.). 10p. (J). (gr. -1-k). bds. 6.99 *(978-0-7232-9638-6(3)*, Warne) Penguin Publishing Group.

—Spot's Favorite Things. Hill, Eric. 2012. (Spot Ser.). (ENG.). 12p. (J). (gr. -1 — 1). bds. 8.99 *(978-0-399-25758-2(6)*, Warne) Penguin Publishing Group.

—Spot's First Colors. Hill, Eric. 2011. (Spot Ser.). (ENG.). 12p. (J). (gr. -1 — 1). bds. 7.99 *(978-0-399-25630-1(X)*, Warne) Penguin Publishing Group.

—Spot's First Numbers. Hill, Eric. 2010. (Spot Ser.). (ENG.). 12p. (J). (gr. -1 — 1). bds. 7.99 *(978-0-399-25533-5(8)*, Warne) Penguin Publishing Group.

—Spot's First Shapes. Hill, Eric. 2011. (Spot Ser.). (ENG.). 12p. (J). (gr. -1 — 1). bds. 7.99 *(978-0-399-25631-8(8)*, Warne) Penguin Publishing Group.

—Spot's First Walk. Hill, Eric. (Spot Ser.). (ENG.). 24p. (J). (gr. -1 — 1). 2005. bds. 7.99 *(978-0-399-24482-7(4)*, Putnam Juvenile); 2004. 7.99 *(978-0-14-240085-2(8)*, Warne) Penguin Publishing Group.

—Spot's First Words. Hill, Eric. 2010. (Spot Ser.). (ENG.). 12p. (J). (gr. -1 — 1). bds. 7.99 *(978-0-399-25532-8(X)*, Warne) Penguin Publishing Group.

—Spot's Fun First Words. Hill, Eric. 2012. (Spot Ser.). (ENG.). 12p. (J). (gr. -1 — 1). bds. 8.99 *(978-0-399-25766-7(7)*, Warne) Penguin Publishing Group.

—Spot's Halloween. Hill, Eric. 2003. (Spot Ser.). (ENG.). 10p. (J). (gr. -1 — 1). bds. 5.99 *(978-0-399-24185-7(X)*, Putnam Juvenile) Penguin Publishing Group.

—Spot's Toys. Hill, Eric. 2011. (Spot Ser.). (ENG.). 12p. (J). (gr. -1 — 1). bds. 5.99 *(978-0-399-25637-0(7)*, Warne) Penguin Publishing Group.

—What Do You See, Spot? Hill, Eric. 2012. (Spot Ser.). (ENG.). 10p. (J). bds. 8.99 *(978-0-399-26010-0(2)*, Warne) Penguin Publishing Group.

—Where's Spot? Hill, Eric. 2003. (Spot Ser.). (J). (gr. -1 — 1). (SPA & ENG.). 12p. bds. 7.99 *(978-0-399-24046-1(2)*, 53517281, Putnam Juvenile); (ENG.). 24p. 7.99 *(978-0-14-250126-9(3)*, Warne) Penguin Publishing Group.

—Where's Spot? Hill, Eric. 2007. (Spot Ser.). (ENG.). 18.00 *(978-0-7569-7965-2(X))* Perfection Learning Corp.

Hill, Heather C. & Roush, April. Picture Me Christmas Princess. Hapka, Cathy. 2003. (Picture Me Holiday Ser.). 10p. (J). (gr. -1-18). bds. 6.99 *(978-1-57151-571-1(2))* Playhouse Publishing.

Hill, Isabel T., photos by. Urban Animals, 1 vol. Hill, Isabel T. 2009. (ENG., 32p. (J). (gr. 2-7). 17.95 *(978-1-59572-209-6(2))*; pap. 7.95 *(978-1-59572-210-2(6))* Star Bright Bks., Inc.

Hill, Jen. Percy & TumTum: A Tale of Two Dogs. 2012. (ENG.). 32p. (J). 15.95 *(978-0-7624-4429-8(0))* Running Pr. Bk. Pubs.

Hill, Jenn. The Boy with Pink Hair. Hilton, Perez. 2011. (ENG.). 32p. (J). (gr. -1-k). 17.99 *(978-0-451-23420-9(0)*, Celebra) Penguin Publishing Group.

Hill, Jessie. No Ordinary Princess. Johnson, Rachel N. 2012. 32p. pap. 16.97 *(978-1-61204-993-9(1)*, Strategic Bk. Publishing) Strategic Book Publishing & Rights Agency (SBPRA).

Hill, Jonathan David. Americus. Reed, M. K. 2011. (ENG.). 224p. (YA). (gr. 7). 18.99 *(978-1-59643-768-5(5))*; pap. 14.99 *(978-1-59643-601-5(8))* Roaring Brook Pr. (First Second Bks.).

Hill, Kevin. Me & My Big Career, , Byrd-Hill, Ida. Hill, Karen, ed. 2010. (ENG.). 24p. (J). 14.95 *(978-0-9829610-0-1(6))* Upheaval Media, Inc.

Hill, Lynn. Old Woman's Garbage. Pyatt, A. K. 2003. *(978-0-9718431-3-4(9))* M.O.T.H.E.R. Publishing Co., Inc., The.

Hill, Malissa. A Ladybug's Defense: Part One of the Fascinating Bug's Series. Healan, Tammy. 2011. 24p. pap. 24.95 *(978-1-4626-4459-9(7))* America Star Bks.

Hill, Nicolas. Jane's Adventures: Jane's Adventures in & Out of the Book; Jane's Adventures on the Island of Peeg; Jane's Adventures in a Balloon. Gathorne-Hardy, Jonathan. 2006. (ENG.). 588p. (gr. 4-13). 27.95 *(978-1-58567-798-6(1)*, 856798) Overlook Pr., The.

Hill-Peterson, Jodi. Cartwheeling. Given, Cate. 2006. (J). *(978-0-9790057-1-8(X))* Paws In the Sand Publishing.

—The Great Pogo Stick. Given, Cate. 2006. (J). *(978-0-9790057-0-1(1))* Paws In the Sand Publishing.

Hill, Prescott. Lalaloopsy: Christmas Magic. Cecil, Lauren. 2012. (Lalaloopsy Ser.). (ENG.). 24p. (J). (gr. -1-3). pap. 4.99 *(978-0-545-46756-8(X))* Scholastic, Inc.

—Lalaloopsy: Cinder Slippers & the Grand Ball. Cecil, Lauren. 2013. (Lalaloopsy Ser.). (ENG.). 24p. (J). (gr. -1-3). pap. 3.99 *(978-0-545-47769-7(7))* Scholastic, Inc.

—Lalaloopsy: Easter Eggs-Travaganza. Simon, Jenne. 2014. (ENG.). 24p. (J). (gr. -1-3). pap. 4.99 *(978-0-545-60802-2(3))* Scholastic, Inc.

—Lalaloopsy: Here Come the Little Sisters! Cecil, Lauren. 2013. (Lalaloopsy Ser.). (ENG.). 5p. (J). (gr. -1-k). bds. 9.99 *(978-0-545-44266-4(4))* Scholastic, Inc.

—Lalaloopsy: School Day! Simon, Jenne. 2012. (Lalaloopsy Ser.). (ENG.). 32p. (J). (gr. -1-3). pap. 3.99 *(978-0-545-40321-4(9))* Scholastic, Inc.

—Let's Pick Apples. Simon, Jenne. 2013. (Lalaloopsy Ser.). (ENG.). 32p. (J). (gr. -1-3). pap. 3.99 *(978-0-545-53182-5(9))* Scholastic, Inc.

—Party Time! Cecil, Lauren & Scholastic, Inc. Staff. 2011. (Lalaloopsy Ser.: 2). (ENG.). 24p. (J). (gr. -1-3). pap. 3.99 *(978-0-545-37998-4(9))* Scholastic, Inc.

—Snow Day!, Level 2. Simon, Jenne. 2013. (Lalaloopsy Ser.). (ENG.). 32p. (J). (gr. -1-3). pap. 3.99 *(978-0-545-58123-3(0))* Scholastic, Inc.

Hill, Ros. Shamooo: A Whale of a Cow. Hill, Ros. 2005. 32p. (J). 15.95 *(978-0-689-04634-6(0)*, Milk & Cookies) ibooks, Inc.

Hill, Shannon. Sammie the Lil' Dog on the Porch. Owens, Wanda. 2011. 20p. pap. 24.95 *(978-1-4560-5736-7(7))* America Star Bks.

Hill, Stephanie. God Deserves Your Best. Hill, Clarissa. 2005. (ENG.). 20p. (J). pap. 11.00 *(978-0-9785539-0-6(X))* Hill, Stephanie & Clarissa.

Hill, Steve. The Bear Man. Scott, Keith. 2010. 32p. (J). pap. 5.95 *(978-0-88839-655-6(4))* Hancock Hse. Pubs.

Hill, T. J. Stuart the Donkey: A Tale of His Tail. Hipp, Diane. 2010. 52p. pap. 21.99 *(978-1-4520-3420-1(6))* AuthorHouse.

Hill, Tracy. It All Began with a Bean. Mcky, Katie. 2004. (ENG.). 32p. (J). (gr. -1-3). 14.95 *(978-0-9749303-0-5(X))* Tanglewood Pr.

—It All Began with a Bean: The True Story of the World's Biggest Fart. McKy, Katie. 2011. (ENG.). 32p. (J). (gr. -1-3). pap. 8.95 *(978-1-933718-23-1(4))* Tanglewood Pr.

Hill, Trish. Lulu. Zail, Suzy. 2004. iv, 36p. (J). pap. *(978-0-7608-6741-9(0))* Sundance/Newbridge Educational Publishing.

Hill, Vicki Trego & Pennypacker, Mona. La Llorona - The Weeping Woman: An Hispanic Legend Told in Spanish & English. Hayes, Joe. (ENG & SPA.). 32p. (J). (gr. 4-6). 2006. pap. 7.95 *(978-0-938317-39-5(3))*; 3rd ed. 2004. 16.95 *(978-0-938317-86-9(5))* Cinco Puntos Pr.

Hillam, Corbin. Ancient China. Sylvester, Diane. 2006. (Museum Ser.). 64p. (J). (gr. 5-8). per. 13.99 *(978-0-88160-389-7(9)*, LW444, Learning Works, The) Creative Teaching Pr., Inc.

—Ancient Rome. Sylvester, Diane. 2006. (Museum Ser.). 64p. (J). (gr. 5-8). pap. 13.99 *(978-0-88160-390-3(2)*, LW445, Learning Works, The) Creative Teaching Pr., Inc.

—The Complete Book of Multiplication & Division: Grades 2-3. Kim, Hy. Applebaum, Teri L. & Rous, Sheri, eds. 2004. 144p. per. 16.99 *(978-1-59198-034-6(8)*, CTP 2571) Creative Teaching Pr., Inc.

—I Have, Who Has? Language Arts, Grades 3-4: 38 Interactive Card Games, Vol. 2206. Callella, Trisha. Hamaguchi, Carla, ed. 2006. (I Have, Who Has? Ser.). 204p. (J). (gr. 3-4). per. 19.99 *(978-1-59198-228-9(6)*, 2206) Creative Teaching Pr., Inc.

—I Have, Who Has? Language Arts, Grades 5-6: 38 Interactive Card Games. Callella, Trisha. Hamaguchi, Carla, ed. 2006. (I Have, Who Has? Ser.). 204p. (J). (gr. 5-6). per. 19.99 *(978-1-59198-229-6(4))* Creative Teaching Pr., Inc.

—I Have, Who Has? Math, Grades 3-4: 38 Interactive Card Games. Callella, Trisha. Hamaguchi, Carla, ed. 2006. (I Have, Who Has? Ser.). 204p. (J). (gr. 3-4). per. 19.99 *(978-1-59198-230-2(8),* 2208) Creative Teaching Pr., Inc.

—More Greek & Latin Roots: Teaching Vocabulary to Improve Reading Comprehension. Callella, Trisha. Faulkner, Stacey, ed. 2006. (J). pap. 18.99 *(978-1-59198-328-6(2))* Creative Teaching Pr., Inc.

—Passport to Genre: A Literature Enrichment Guide. Connolly, Debbie & Danley, Laurie. Mitchell, Judy, ed. 2006. 64p. (J). pap. 9.95 *(978-1-57310-488-3(4))* Teaching & Learning Co.

Hillam, Corbin & Ciccarelli, Gary. Ancient Greece. Sylvester, Diane. VanBlaricum, Pam, ed. 2006. (Museum Ser.). 64p. pap. 13.99 *(978-0-88160-387-3(2),* LW441, Learning Works, The) Creative Teaching Pr., Inc.

Hillam, Corbin & Grayson, Rick. Electing Our President: The Process to Elect the Nation's Leader. Jennett, Pamela & Marchant, Sherry. Jennett, Pamela, ed. 2004. 48p. pap. 8.99 *(978-0-88160-379-8(1),* LW-436) Creative Teaching Pr., Inc.

Hillam, Corbin & Vangsgard, Amy. American History Reader's Theater Vol. 2244: Develop Reading Fluency & Text Comprehension Skills. Hults, Alaska, ed. 2004. 96p. (J). pap. 14.99 *(978-1-59198-039-1(9),* 2244) Creative Teaching Pr., Inc.

—Ancient Civilizations Reader's Theater Vol. 2246: Develop Reading Fluency & Text Comprehension Skills. Ellermeyer, Deborah & Rowell, Judy. Hults, Alaska, ed. 2004. 96p. (J). pap. 12.99 *(978-1-59198-041-4(0),* 2246) Creative Teaching Pr., Inc.

—Fables & Folklore Reader's Theater: Develop Reading Fluency & Text Comprehension Skills. Allen, Margaret. Hults, Alaska, ed. 2004. 96p. (J). (gr. 1-2). pap. 14.99 *(978-1-59198-037-7(2),* 2242) Creative Teaching Pr., Inc.

—Fairy Tales Reader's Theater: Develop Reading Fluency & Text Comprehension Skills. Allen, Margaret. Hults, Alaska, ed. 2004. 96p. (J). pap. 14.99 *(978-1-59198-036-0(4))* Creative Teaching Pr., Inc.

—Philosophers to Astronauts Reader's Theater Vol. 2243: Develop Reading Fluency & Text Comprehension Skills. Hults, Alaska, ed. 2004. 96p. (J). pap. 12.99 *(978-1-59198-038-4(0),* 2243) Creative Teaching Pr., Inc.

Hillard Good, Karen. A Snowman Named Just Bob. Moulton, Mark Kimball. 2006. (ENG.). 16p. (J). (gr. k-3). 14.95 *(978-0-8249-1707-4(3))* Ideals Pubns.

Hillenbrand, Will. Andy & Tamika. Adler, David A. 2005. (Andy Russell Ser.: 2). (ENG.). 144p. (J). (gr. 1-4). pap. 5.99 *(978-0-15-205446-5(4))* Houghton Mifflin Harcourt Publishing Co.

—Andy & Tamika. Adler, David A. 2005. (Andy Russell Ser.: Bk. 2). 129p. 16.00 *(978-0-7569-4898-6(3))* Perfection Learning Corp.

—Bear in Love. Pinkwater, Daniel M. 2012. (ENG.). 40p. (J). (gr. k-k). 15.99 *(978-0-7636-4569-4(9))* Candlewick Pr.

—The Biggest, Best Snowman. Cuyler, Margery. 2007. (ENG.). (J). (gr. -1-k). 9.95 *(978-0-545-01484-7(0))* Scholastic, Inc.

—Calendar. Livingston, Myra Cohn. 2007. (ENG.). 32p. (J). (gr. -1-3). 16.95 *(978-0-8234-1725-4(5))* Holiday Hse., Inc.

—Down on the Farm. Kutner, Merrily. (ENG.). (J). (gr. -1). 2008. 24p. bds. 7.95 *(978-0-8234-2177-0(5));* 2005. 32p. pap. 7.99 *(978-0-8234-1985-2(1))* Holiday Hse., Inc.

—The Journey of the One & Only Declaration of Independence. St. George, Judith. (ENG.). 48p. (J). (gr. 2-5). 2014. 8.99 *(978-0-14-751164-5(X),* Puffin); 2005. 17.99 *(978-0-399-23738-6(0),* Philomel) Penguin Publishing Group.

—The Journey of the One & Only Declaration of Independence. St. George, Judith. 2011. (J). (gr. 1-7). 29.95 *(978-0-439-02760-1(8),* WHCD806) Weston Woods Studios, Inc.

—Kiss the Cow! Root, Phyllis. 2003. (ENG.). 32p. (J). (gr. -1-3). pap. 6.99 *(978-0-7636-2003-5(3))* Candlewick Pr.

—Look Out, Jack! the Giant Is Back! ed. 2003. (ENG.). 32p. (J). (gr. -1-3). 6.95 *(978-0-8234-1776-6(X))* Holiday Hse., Inc.

—The Many Troubles of Andy Russell. Adler, David A. 2005. (Andy Russell Ser.: 1). (ENG.). 144p. (J). (gr. 1-4). pap. 6.99 *(978-0-15-205440-3(5))* Houghton Mifflin Harcourt Publishing Co.

—One Fine Trade. Miller, Bobbi. 2009. (ENG.). 32p. (J). (gr. -1-3). 16.95 *(978-0-8234-1836-7(7))* Holiday Hse., Inc.

—Please Say Please! Penguin's Guide to Manners. Cuyler, Margery. 2005. (J). *(978-0-439-67874-2(9))* Scholastic, Inc.

—School Trouble for Andy Russell. Adler, David A. 2005. (Andy Russell Ser.: Bk. 3). (ENG.). 128p. (J). (gr. 1-4). pap. 9.95 *(978-0-15-205428-1(6))* Houghton Mifflin Harcourt Publishing Co.

—School Trouble for Andy Russell. Adler, David A. 2007. (Andy Russell Ser.: Bk. 3). 118p. pap. 6.60 *(978-1-4189-5227-3(3))* Houghton Mifflin Harcourt Supplemental Pubs.

—School Trouble for Andy Russell. Adler, David A. 2008. (Andy Russell Ser.: Bk. 3). (J). (gr. 2-5). pap. 28.95 incl. audio compact disk *(978-1-4301-0484-1(8));* pap. 24.95 incl. audio *(978-1-4301-0483-4(X))* Live Oak Media.

—Sleep, Big Bear, Sleep!, 0 vols. Wright, Maureen. 2009. (ENG.). 32p. (J). (gr. -1-3). 16.99 *(978-0-7614-5560-8(4),* 9780761455608, Amazon Children's Publishing) Amazon Publishing.

—Smash! Mash! Crash! There Goes the Trash! Odanaka, Barbara. 2006. (ENG.). 32p. (J). (gr. -1-3). 17.99 *(978-0-689-85160-5(X),* McElderry, Margaret K. Bks.) McElderry, Margaret K. Bks.

—Sneeze, Big Bear, Sneeze!, 0 vols. Wright, Maureen. 2011. (ENG.). 32p. (J). (gr. -1-3). 16.99 *(978-0-7614-5959-0(6),* 9780761459590, Amazon Children's Publishing) Amazon Publishing.

—What a Treasure! Hillenbrand, Jane. (ENG.). 24p. (J). (gr. -1-3). 2007. pap. 6.95 *(978-0-8234-2077-3(9));* 2006. 16.95 *(978-0-8234-1896-1(0))* Holiday Hse., Inc.

—Whopper Cake. Wilson, Karma. 2007. (ENG.). 32p. (J). (gr. -1-3). 17.99 *(978-0-689-83844-6(1),* McElderry, Margaret K. Bks.) McElderry, Margaret K. Bks.

Hillenbrand, Will. Kite Day: A Bear & Mole Story. Hillenbrand, Will. (ENG.). 32p. (J). 2013. pap. 6.99 *(978-0-8234-2758-1(7));* 2012. 17.95 *(978-0-8234-1603-5(8))* Holiday Hse., Inc.

—Mother Goose Picture Puzzles, 0 vols. Hillenbrand, Will. 2011. (ENG.). 40p. (J). (gr. k-3). 17.99 *(978-0-7614-5808-1(5),* 9780761458081, Amazon Children's Publishing) Amazon Publishing.

—Off We Go! A Bear & Mole Story. Hillenbrand, Will. 2014. (ENG.). 32p. (J). (gr. -1-1). pap. 6.99 *(978-0-8234-3172-4(X))* Holiday Hse., Inc.

—Spring Is Here! Hillenbrand, Will. 2011. (ENG.). 32p. (J). (gr. -1-1). 16.95 *(978-0-8234-1602-8(X))* Holiday Hse., Inc.

—Spring Is Here. Hillenbrand, Will. 2012. (ENG.). 32p. (J). pap. 7.99 *(978-0-8234-2431-3(6))* Holiday Hse., Inc.

Hilley, Thomas. Billy Black Ant's Exciting Adventures. Danley, Jerry J. 2012. 56p. pap. 12.99 *(978-0-9885180-5-6(8))* Mindstir Media.

Hilliam, Corbin & Ellithorpe, Chris. Math Graphic Organizers 1-2: Simple & Effective Strategies for Solving Math Word Problems. Harding, Davilla. Hults, Alaska, ed. 2003. (Math Graphic Organizers Ser.). 112p. (J). pap. 13.99 *(978-1-57471-979-6(3),* 2573) Creative Teaching Pr., Inc.

—Math Graphic Organizers 3-5: Simple & Effective Strategies for Solving Math Word Problems. Harding, Davilla. Hults, Alaska, ed. 2003. (Math Graphic Organizers Ser.). 112p. (J). (gr. 2-7). pap. 13.99 *(978-1-57471-980-2(7),* 2574) Creative Teaching Pr., Inc.

Hilliam, Corbin & Vangsgard, Amy. Discoverers & Inventors Reader's Theater Vol. 2245: Develop Reading Fluency & Test Comprehension Skills. Jennett, Pamela. Hults, Alaska, ed. 2004. 96p. (J). pap. 12.99 *(978-1-59198-040-7(2),* 2245) Creative Teaching Pr., Inc.

Hilliard, Carol. I Like Dogs. Cheehy, Debra/Ilene. 2009. 52p. (J). 16.95 *(978-0-9820817-0-9(7))* Four Foot Pr. LLC.

Hilliard, Richard. Mammoth Bones & Broken Stones: The Mystery of North America's First People. Harrison, David L. 2010. (ENG.). 48p. (J). (gr. 4-6). 18.95 *(978-1-59078-561-4(4))* Boyds Mills Pr.

Hilliker, Phillip. I Dare You! Brezenoff, Steve. 2008. (Vortex Bks.). (ENG.). 112p. (gr. 2-3). 25.32 *(978-1-4342-0798-2(6),* Vortex Bks.) Stone Arch Bks.

—The Runaway Skeleton. Muldoon, Kathleen M. 2008. (Vortex Bks.). (ENG.). 112p. (gr. 2-3). 25.32 *(978-1-4342-0800-2(1),* Vortex Bks.) Stone Arch Bks.

Hillman, Shane. Fat Cat of Underwhere. Hale, Bruce. 2009. (Underwhere Ser.). 176p. (J). pap. 5.99 *(978-0-06-085135-4(X))* HarperCollins Pubs.

—Mole Men of Underwhere. Hale, Bruce. 2009. (Underwhere Ser.). 160p. (J). 15.99 *(978-0-06-085136-1(8))* HarperCollins Pubs.

—Pirates of Underwhere. Hale, Bruce. (Underwhere Ser.: 2). (J). (gr. 3-7). 2009. (ENG.). 176p. pap. 5.99 *(978-0-06-085129-3(5));* 2008. 164p. lib. bdg. 16.89 *(978-0-06-085128-6(7))* HarperCollins Pubs.

—Prince of Underwhere. Hale, Bruce. (Underwhere Ser.: 1). (ENG.). 176p. (J). (gr. 3-7). 2009. pap. 5.99 *(978-0-06-085126-2(0));* 2007. 15.99 *(978-0-06-085124-8(4))* HarperCollins Pubs.

Hillmann, Joe & Cox, Chad. Snort, Wheeze, Rattle & Grunt. Reich, J. J. 2006. (J). 8.99 *(978-0-9762971-1-6(6))* Outdoor Originals LLC.

Hills, Alan & Brightling, Geoff, photos by. Eyewitness Travel Guide - Ancient China. Cotterell, Arthur et al. 2005. (DK Eyewitness Bks.). (ENG.). 72p. (J). (gr. 3-7). 16.99 *(978-0-7566-1382-2(5))* Dorling Kindersley Publishing, Inc.

Hills, Jodi. Believe. Hills, Jodi. 2003. (ENG.). 48p. (J). 39.95 *(978-0-931674-52-5(2),* Waldman House Pr.) TRISTAN Publishing, Inc.

Hills, Laila. Elephant. ed. 2014. (Squirty Bath Bks.). (ENG.). 8p. (J). (— 1). 8.99 *(978-1-4472-6818-5(0))* Pan Macmillan GBR. Dist: Independent Pubs. Group.

—Squirty Bath Books - Duck. ed. 2014. (Squirty Bath Bks.). (ENG.). 8p. (J). (— 1). 8.99 *(978-1-4472-6816-1(4))* Pan Macmillan GBR. Dist: Independent Pubs. Group.

—Sword to Words. Su, Tami. 2010. 36p. pap. 14.99 *(978-1-60844-524-0(0))* Dog Ear Publishing, LLC.

Hills, Tad. Duck & Goose. Hills, Tad. 2006. (Duck & Goose Ser.). (ENG.). 40p. (J). (gr. -1-2). 17.99 *(978-0-375-83611-4(X),* Schwartz & Wade Bks.) Random Hse. Children's Bks.

—Duck & Goose: How Are You Feeling? Hills, Tad. 2009. (Duck & Goose Ser.). (ENG.). 22p. (J). (gr. -1 — 1). bds. 6.99 *(978-0-375-84629-8(8),* Schwartz & Wade Bks.) Random Hse. Children's Bks.

—Duck & Goose, 1, 2, 3. Hills, Tad. 2008. (Duck & Goose Ser.). (ENG.). 22p. (J). (gr. k — 1). bds. 6.99 *(978-0-375-85621-1(8),* Schwartz & Wade Bks.) Random Hse. Children's Bks.

—Duck & Goose Colors. Hills, Tad. 2015. (Duck & Goose Ser.). (ENG.). 22p. (J). (— 1). bds. 6.99 *(978-0-553-50806-2(7),* Schwartz & Wade Bks.) Random Hse. Children's Bks.

—Duck & Goose, Goose Needs a Hug. Hills, Tad. 2012. (Duck & Goose Ser.). (ENG.). 22p. (J). (-k). bds. 6.99 *(978-0-307-98293-3(9),* Schwartz & Wade Bks.) Random Hse. Children's Bks.

—Duck & Goose, Here Comes the Easter Bunny! Hills, Tad. 2012. (Duck & Goose Ser.). (ENG.). 22p. (J). (gr. k-k). bds. 6.99 *(978-0-375-87280-8(9),* Schwartz & Wade Bks.) Random Hse. Children's Bks.

—Duck, Duck, Goose. Hills, Tad. 2007. (Duck & Goose Ser.). (ENG.). 40p. (J). (gr. -1-2). 17.99 *(978-0-375-84068-5(0),* Schwartz & Wade Bks.) Random Hse. Children's Bks.

—Find a Pumpkin. Hills, Tad. (Duck & Goose Ser.). (ENG.). 22p. (J). (gr. k-k). 2012. bds. 10.99 *(978-0-307-98155-4(X));* 2009. bds. 6.99 *(978-0-375-85813-0(X))* Random Hse. Children's Bks. (Schwartz & Wade Bks.).

—How Rocket Learned to Read. Hills, Tad. 2010. (ENG.). 40p. (J). (gr. -1-2). 17.99 *(978-0-375-85899-4(7));* lib. bdg. 20.99 *(978-0-375-95899-1(1))* Random Hse. Children's Bks. (Schwartz & Wade Bks.).

—It's Time for Christmas! Hills, Tad. (Duck & Goose Ser.). (ENG.). 22p. (J). 2011. (gr. -1 — 1). bds. 10.99 *(978-0-375-87112-2(8));* 2010. (gr. k — 1). bds. 7.99 *(978-0-375-86484-1(9),* Schwartz & Wade Bks.) Random Hse. Children's Bks.

—Rocket Writes a Story. Hills, Tad. 2012. (ENG.). 40p. (J). (gr. -1-3). 17.99 *(978-0-375-87086-6(5),* Schwartz & Wade Bks.) Random Hse. Children's Bks.

—Rocket's Learning Box, 2 vols. Hills, Tad. 2012. (ENG.). 40p. (J). (gr. -1-3). 35.98 *(978-0-307-98235-3(1),* Schwartz & Wade Bks.) Random Hse. Children's Bks.

—What's up, Duck? A Book of Opposites. Hills, Tad. 2008. (Duck & Goose Ser.). (ENG.). 22p. (J). (gr. k — 1). bds. 6.99 *(978-0-375-84738-7(3))* Random Hse. Children's Bks.

Hilmer, Evelyn. Nanook the Penguin. Counter, Marlow & Counter, Marlow. 2011. (ENG.). 32p. pap. 9.95 *(978-1-4664-2879-9(1))* CreateSpace Independent Publishing Platform.

Hilts, Ben. Seaver the Weaver. Czajak, Paul & Brothers Hilts Staff. 2015. (ENG.). 32p. (J). (-k). 15.95 *(978-1-938063-57-2(0),* Mighty Media Kids) Mighty Media Pr.

Hilty, Bertha. The Adventures of Clever Coyote. Brown, W. C. 2011. (ENG.). 32p. pap. 14.99 *(978-1-4636-0747-0(4))* CreateSpace Independent Publishing Platform.

Himekawa, Akira. Four Swords, Vol. 6, Pt. 1. Himekawa, Akira. 2009. (Legend of Zelda Ser.: 6). (ENG.). 192p. (J). pap. 9.99 *(978-1-4215-2332-3(9))* Viz Media.

—Four Swords Pt. 2, Vol. 7, Pt. 2. Himekawa, Akira. 2009. (Legend of Zelda Ser.: 7). (ENG.). 176p. (J). pap. 9.99 *(978-1-4215-2333-0(7))* Viz Media.

—The Legend of Zelda: Hyrule Historia. Himekawa, Akira. Miyamoto, Shigeru & Aonuma, Eiji. Thorpe, Patrick, ed. 2013. (ENG.). 276p. 34.99 *(978-1-61655-041-7(4))* Dark Horse Comics.

—The Legend of Zelda: Phantom Hourglass. Himekawa, Akira. 2010. (Legend of Zelda Ser.: 10). (ENG.). 200p. (J). (gr. 2-5). pap. 9.99 *(978-1-4215-3724-5(9))* Viz Media.

—A Link to the Past. Himekawa, Akira. 2010. (Legend of Zelda Ser.: 9). (ENG.). 192p. (YA). pap. 9.99 *(978-1-4215-2335-4(3))* Viz Media.

—Majora's Mask. Himekawa, Akira. 2009. (Legend of Zelda Ser.: 3). (ENG.). 216p. (J). pap. 9.99 *(978-1-4215-2329-3(9))* Viz Media.

—The Minish Cap. Himekawa, Akira. 2009. (Legend of Zelda Ser.: 8). (ENG.). 192p. (J). pap. 9.99 *(978-1-4215-2334-7(5))* Viz Media.

—Ocarina of Time. Himekawa, Akira. 2008. (Legend of Zelda Ser.: 1). (ENG.). 200p. (J). (gr. 1). Vol. 1. pap. 9.99 *(978-1-4215-2327-9(2));* Vol. 2. pap. 9.99 *(978-1-4215-2328-6(0))* Viz Media.

—Oracle of Ages, Vol. 5. Himekawa, Akira. 2009. (Legend of Zelda Ser.: 5). (ENG.). 200p. (J). pap. 9.99 *(978-1-4215-2331-6(0))* Viz Media.

Himler, Ronald. Always with You. Vander Zee, Ruth. 2008. 32p. (J). (gr. -1-3). 17.00 *(978-0-8028-5295-3(5),* Eerdmans Bks For Young Readers) Eerdmans, William B. Publishing Co.

—Anna & Natalie, 1 vol. Cole, Barbara. 2007. (ENG.). 32p. (J). 16.95 *(978-1-59572-105-1(3))* Star Bright Bks., Inc.

—Anna & Natalie, 1 vol. Cole, Barbara H. 2010. (ENG.). 32p. (J). pap. 6.95 *(978-1-59572-211-9(4))* Star Bright Bks., Inc.

—Bee My Valentine!, 1 vol. Cohen, Miriam. 2008. (ENG.). 32p. (J). (gr. k-3). 15.95 *(978-1-59572-085-6(5))* Star Bright Bks., Inc.

—The Best Cat in the World. Newman, Lesléa. 2004. 32p. (J). (gr. 1-4). 16.00 *(978-0-8028-5252-6(1));* (gr. -1-3). 8.00 *(978-0-8028-5294-6(7),* Eerdmans Bks For Young Readers) Eerdmans, William B. Publishing Co.

—The Best Horse Ever. DeLaCroix, Alice. 2010. (ENG.). 80p. (J). (gr. 1-5). pap. 16.95 *(978-0-8234-2254-8(2))* Holiday Hse., Inc.

—The Blizzard. Wright, Betty Ren. (ENG.). 32p. (J). 2005. pap. 7.95 *(978-0-8234-1981-4(9));* 2003. 17.95 *(978-0-8234-1656-1(9))* Holiday Hse., Inc.

—The Buffalo Soldier, 1 vol. Garland, Sherry. 2006. (ENG.). 32p. (J). (gr. k-3). 16.99 *(978-1-58980-391-6(4))* Pelican Publishing Co., Inc.

—First Grade Takes a Test, 1 vol. Cohen, Miriam. 2006. (ENG.). 32p. (J). (gr. -1-3). 15.95 *(978-1-59572-054-2(5));* (gr. k-3). pap. 5.95 *(978-1-59572-055-9(3))* Star Bright Bks., Inc.

—First Grade Takes a Test (Spanish/English), 1 vol. Cohen, Miriam. 2008. (ENG & SPA.). 32p. (J). (gr. k-3). 15.95 *(978-1-59572-150-1(9));* pap. 5.95 *(978-1-59572-151-8(7))* Star Bright Bks., Inc.

—I Wonder As I Wander. Swain, Gwenyth. 2004. 32p. (J). (gr. 2-5). 16.00 *(978-0-8028-5214-4(9))* Eerdmans, William B. Publishing Co.

—I Wonder as I Wander. Swain, Gwenyth. 2005. 32p. (J). (gr. k-3). pap. 8.00 *(978-0-8028-5298-4(X),* Eerdmans Bks For Young Readers) Eerdmans, William B. Publishing Co.

—Janey. Zolotow, Charlotte. Date not set. 32p. (J). (gr. -1-3). 15.89 *(978-0-06-027872-4(2))* HarperCollins Pubs.

—Jim's Dog Muffins, 1 vol. Cohen, Miriam. 2008. 32p. (J). (ENG.). 15.95 *(978-1-59572-099-3(5));* (gr. -1-3). pap. 5.95 *(978-1-59572-100-6(2))* Star Bright Bks., Inc.

—Layla's Head Scarf, 1 vol. Cohen, Miriam. 2009. (ENG.). 32p. (J). (gr. -1-3). 15.95 *(978-1-59572-177-8(0));* pap. 5.95 *(978-1-59572-178-5(9))* Star Bright Bks., Inc.

—Liar, Liar, Pants on Fire!, 1 vol. Cohen, Miriam. 2008. (ENG.). 32p. (J). (gr. -1-3). 15.95 *(978-1-59572-077-1(4));* pap. 5.95 *(978-1-59572-078-8(2))* Star Bright Bks., Inc.

—The Log Cabin Wedding. Howard, Ellen. 2006. (ENG.). 64p. (J). (gr. -1-3). 15.95 *(978-0-8234-1989-0(4))* Holiday Hse., Inc.

—My Big Brother, 1 vol. Cohen, Miriam. 2005. (ENG.). 32p. (J). 15.95 *(978-1-59572-007-8(3));* pap. 6.95 *(978-1-59572-158-7(4))* Star Bright Bks., Inc.

—My Big Brother (Spanish/English), 1 vol. Cohen, Miriam. 2008. (ABK, SPA & ENG.). 32p. (J). (gr. -1-3). pap. 5.95 *(978-1-59572-037-5(5))* Star Bright Bks., Inc.

—A Picture Book of Dolley & James Madison. Adler, David A. & Adler, Michael S. 2009. (ENG.). 32p. (J). (gr. -1-3). 17.95 *(978-0-8234-2009-4(4))* Holiday Hse., Inc.

—A Picture Book of John & Abigail Adams. Adler, David A. & Adler, Michael S. 2007. (ENG.). 32p. (J). (gr. -1-3). 17.95 *(978-0-8234-2007-0(8))* Holiday Hse., Inc.

—A Picture Book of John Hancock. Adler, David A. & Adler, Michael S. 2007. (ENG.). 32p. (J). (gr. -1-3). 16.95 *(978-0-8234-2005-6(1))* Holiday Hse., Inc.

—A Picture Book of Lewis & Clark. Adler, David A. 2003. (ENG.). 32p. (J). (gr. k-3). tchr. ed. 17.95 *(978-0-8234-1735-3(2))* Holiday Hse., Inc.

—A Picture Book of Samuel Adams. Adler, David A. & Adler, Michael S. 2005. (ENG.). 32p. (J). 16.95 *(978-0-8234-1846-6(4))* Holiday Hse., Inc.

—Prairie Christmas. Van Steenwyk, Elizabeth. 2006. 32p. (J). (gr. k). 17.00 *(978-0-8028-5280-9(7),* Eerdmans Bks For Young Readers) Eerdmans, William B. Publishing Co.

—The Roses in My Carpets, 1 vol. Khan, Rukhsana. 2004. (ENG.). 32p. (J). pap. 9.95 *(978-1-55005-069-1(9),* 1550050699) Fitzhenry & Whiteside, Ltd. CAN. Dist: Midpoint Trade Bks., Inc.

—Rudi's Pond. Bunting, Eve. 2004. (ENG.). 32p. (J). (gr. -1-3). pap. 6.99 *(978-0-618-48604-5(6))* Houghton Mifflin Harcourt Publishing Co.

—Sadako & the Thousand Paper Cranes. Coerr, Eleanor. 2004. (Puffin Modern Classics Ser.). (ENG.). 80p. (J). (gr. 3-7). pap. 6.99 *(978-0-14-240113-2(7),* Puffin) Penguin Publishing Group.

—Tough Jim, 1 vol. Cohen, Miriam. (ENG.). 32p. (J). (gr. -1-3). 2008. 15.95 *(978-1-59572-071-9(5));* 2007. pap. 5.95 *(978-1-59572-072-6(3))* Star Bright Bks., Inc.

—Train to Somewhere. Bunting, Eve. 2004. 32p. (gr. -1-3). 18.00 *(978-0-7569-4260-1(8))* Perfection Learning Corp.

—Voices of the Alamo, 1 vol. Garland, Sherry. 2004. (Voices of History Ser.). (ENG.). 40p. (J). (gr. 3-3). 17.99 *(978-1-58980-222-3(5))* Pelican Publishing Co., Inc.

—Wash Day, 1 vol. Cole, Barbara H. 2004. (ENG.). 32p. (J). 15.95 *(978-1-932065-36-7(9),* 7187849112) Star Bright Bks., Inc.

—Will I Have a Friend?, 1 vol. Cohen, Miriam. 2008. (ENG.). 32p. (J). (gr. k-3). 15.95 *(978-1-59572-069-6(3))* Star Bright Bks., Inc.

Himler, Ronald. Dancing Boy, 1 vol. Himler, Ronald. 2005. (ENG.). 32p. (J). (gr. -1-k). 15.95 *(978-1-59572-020-7(0))* Star Bright Bks., Inc.

—El examen de primer Grado, 1 vol. Himler, Ronald. Cohen, Miriam. 2006.Tr. of First Grade Takes a Test. (SPA.). 32p. (J). (gr. k-3). 15.95 *(978-1-59572-153-2(3));* pap. 5.95 *(978-1-59572-152-5(5))* Star Bright Bks., Inc.

—The Girl on the Yellow Giraffe, 1 vol. Himler, Ronald. 2004. (ENG.). 32p. (J). 15.95 *(978-1-932065-93-0(8))* Star Bright Bks., Inc.

Himmelman, Jeff, jt. illus. see Howell, Troy.

Himmelman, John. A Daddy Longlegs Isn't a Spider. Stewart, Melissa. 2009. 32p. (J). (gr. 1-7). pap. 8.95 *(978-0-89317-069-1(0),* Windward Publishing) Finney Co., Inc.

Himmelman, John. Chickens to the Rescue. Himmelman, John. 2006. (Barnyard Rescue Ser.). (ENG.). 32p. (J). (gr. -1-3). 17.99 *(978-0-8050-7951-7(3),* Holt, Henry & Co. Bks. For Young Readers) Holt, Henry & Co.

—Cows to the Rescue. Himmelman, John. 2011. (Barnyard Rescue Ser.). (ENG.). 32p. (J). (gr. -1-3). 17.99 *(978-0-8050-9249-3(8),* Holt, Henry & Co. Bks. For Young Readers) Holt, Henry & Co.

—Duck to the Rescue. Himmelman, John. 2014. (Barnyard Rescue Ser.). (ENG.). 32p. (J). (gr. -1-3). 16.99 *(978-0-8050-9485-5(7),* Holt, Henry & Co. Bks. For Young Readers) Holt, Henry & Co.

—Frog in a Bog. Himmelman, John. 2004. (ENG.). 32p. (J). (gr. -1-2). pap. 7.95 *(978-1-57091-518-5(0))* Charlesbridge Publishing, Inc.

—Katie & the Puppy Next Door. Himmelman, John. 2013. (ENG.). 32p. (J). (gr. -1-1). 16.99 *(978-0-8050-9484-8(9),* Holt, Henry & Co. Bks. For Young Readers) Holt, Henry & Co.

—Katie Loves the Kittens. Himmelman, John. 2008. (ENG.). 32p. (J). (gr. -1-3). 17.99 *(978-0-8050-8682-9(X),* Holt, Henry & Co. Bks. For Young Readers) Holt, Henry & Co.

—Noisy Bird Sing-Along. Himmelman, John. 2015. (ENG.). 32p. (J). (gr. -1-4). pap. 8.95 *(978-1-58469-514-1(5))* Dawn Pubns.

—Noisy Bug Sing-Along. Himmelman, John. 2013. (ENG.). 32p. (J). (gr. -1-4). 16.95 *(978-1-58469-191-4(3));* pap. 8.95 *(978-1-58469-192-1(1))* Dawn Pubns.

—Noisy Frog Sing-Along. Himmelman, John. 2013. (ENG.). 32p. (J). (gr. -1-4). 16.95 *(978-1-58469-339-0(8));* pap. 8.95 *(978-1-58469-340-6(1))* Dawn Pubns.

—Pigs to the Rescue. Himmelman, John. 2010. (ENG.). 32p. (J). (gr. -1-3). 16.99 *(978-0-8050-8683-6(8),* Holt, Henry & Co. Bks. For Young Readers) Holt, Henry & Co.

—Tales of Bunjitsu Bunny. Himmelman, John. 2014. (Bunjitsu Bunny Ser.). (ENG.). 128p. (J). (gr. 1-3). 13.99 *(978-0-8050-9970-6(0),* Holt, Henry & Co. Bks. For Young Readers) Holt, Henry & Co.

—Tudley Didn't Know, 1 vol. Himmelman, John. 2006. (ENG.). 32p. (J). (gr. -1-3). 15.95 *(978-0-9764943-6-2(1));* pap. 8.95 *(978-1-934359-04-4(1))* Arbordale Publishing.

Himmler, Ronald. Bee My Valentine, 1 vol. Cohen, Miriam. 2009. (ENG.). 32p. (J). (gr. k-3). pap. 5.95 *(978-1-59572-086-3(3))* Star Bright Bks., Inc.

Hinckley, Greg. An Ancient Tale of Rags & Riches. Cahn, Yehudah. 126p. (J). (gr. 5-8). 12.95 *(978-1-56062-073-0(0),* CJR119H); pap. 9.95 *(978-1-56062-074-7(9),* CJR119S) C I S Communications, Inc.

Hinder, Sara Jane. Good Night Yoga: A Pose-By-Pose Bedtime Story, 1 vol. Gates, Mariam. 2015. 32p. (J). 17.95 *(978-1-62203-466-6(X),* 162203466X) Sounds True, Inc.

Hinder, Sarah Jane. Zen & Bodhi's Snowy Day. Brown, Gina Bates. 2014. (ENG.). 24p. (J). 15.95 *(978-1-61429-165-7(9))* Wisdom Pubns.

Hinderliter, John. Who Is Jeff Kinney? Kinney, Patrick. 2015. (Who Was... ? Ser.). (ENG.). 112p. (J). (gr. 3-7). 5.99 ***(978-0-448-48677-2(6)***, Grosset & Dunlap) Penguin Publishing Group.

Hinderliter, John, et al. Who Was Bruce Lee? Gigliotti, Jim. 2014. (Who Was... ? Ser.). (ENG.). 112p. (J). (gr. 3-7). 5.99 *(978-0-448-47949-1(4)*, Grosset & Dunlap) Penguin Publishing Group.

Hinderliter, John & Groff, David. Where Is Mount Everest? Medina, Nico. 2015. (Where Is... ? Ser.). (ENG.). 112p. (J). (gr. 3-7). 5.99 *(978-0-448-48408-2(0)*, Grosset & Dunlap) Penguin Publishing Group.

Hinderliter, John & McVeigh, Kevin. What Was Hurricane Katrina? Koontz, Robin. 2015. (What Was... ? Ser.). (ENG.). 112p. (J). (gr. 3-7). 5.99 ***(978-0-448-48662-8(8)***, Grosset & Dunlap) Penguin Publishing Group.

Hinderliter, John, jt. illus. see Groff, David.

Hinderliter, John, jt. illus. see Harper, Fred.

Hindle, James K. The Mothman's Curse. Hayes, Christine. 2015. (ENG.). 320p. (J). (gr. 3-7). 15.99 *(978-1-62672-027-5(4))* Roaring Brook Pr.

Hindley, Kate. How to Wash a Woolly Mammoth. Robinson, Michelle. 2014. (ENG.). 32p. (J). (gr. -1-3). 16.99 *(978-0-8050-9966-9(2)*, Holt, Henry & Co. Bks. For Young Readers) Holt, Henry & Co.

—Smashie Mcperter & the Mystery of Room 11. Griffin, N. 2015. (ENG.). 256p. (J). (gr. 2-5). 15.99 *(978-0-7636-6145-8(7))* Candlewick Pr.

—Worst in Show. Bee, William. 2015. (ENG.). 40p. (J). (gr. -1-2). 15.99 *(978-0-7636-7318-5(8))* Candlewick Pr.

Hinds, Gareth. Gifts from the Gods: Ancient Words & Wisdom from Greek & Roman Mythology. Lunge-Larsen, Lise. 2011. (ENG.). 96p. (J). (gr. 5-7). 18.99 *(978-0-547-15229-5(9))* Houghton Mifflin Harcourt Publishing Co.

Hinds, Gareth. Beowulf. Hinds, Gareth, adapted by. 2007. (ENG.). 128p. (J). (gr. 5-12). pap. 12.99 *(978-0-7636-3023-2(3))* Candlewick Pr.

Hinds, Gareth. Macbeth. Hinds, Gareth. 2015. (ENG.). 152p. (J). (gr. 7). 21.99 *(978-0-7636-6943-0(1))* Candlewick Pr.

—The Merchant of Venice. Hinds, Gareth. 2008. (ENG.). 80p. (J). (gr. 7-12). pap. 12.99 *(978-0-7636-3025-6(X))* Candlewick Pr.

—The Merchant of Venice. Hinds, Gareth. Shakespeare, William. 2008. (ENG.). 80p. (J). (gr. 7-12). 21.99 *(978-0-7636-3024-9(1))* Candlewick Pr.

—The Odyssey. Hinds, Gareth. 2010. (ENG.). 256p. (YA). (gr. 7-18). 24.99 *(978-0-7636-4266-2(5))*; pap. 14.99 *(978-0-7636-4268-6(1))* Candlewick Pr.

—Romeo & Juliet. Hinds, Gareth. 2013. (ENG.). 144p. (gr. 7). (J). 21.99 *(978-0-7636-5948-6(7))*; (YA). pap. 12.99 *(978-0-7636-6807-5(9))* Candlewick Pr.

Hine, Eileen. Desert Opposites. 2005. (ENG.). 12p. (J). (gr. -1 — 1). 5.95 *(978-0-87358-890-4(8))* Cooper Square Publishing Llc.

Hines, Anna Grossnickle. Curious George at the Aquarium. Rey, H. A. & Rey, Margret. 2007. (Curious George Ser.). (ENG.). 24p. (J). (gr. -1-3). 13.99 *(978-0-618-80067-4(0))* Houghton Mifflin Harcourt Publishing Co.

—Curious George at the Baseball Game. Driscoll, Laura & Rey, H. A. 2006. (Curious George Ser.). (ENG.). 24p. (J). (gr. -1-3). pap. 3.99 *(978-0-618-66375-0(4))* Houghton Mifflin Harcourt Publishing Co.

—Curious George at the Baseball Game. Driscoll, Laura et al. 2006. (Curious George Ser.). (ENG.). 24p. (J). (gr. -1-3). 13.99 *(978-0-618-66374-3(6))* Houghton Mifflin Harcourt Publishing Co.

—Curious George's Dinosaur Discovery. Hapka, Catherine & Rey, H. A. 2006. (Curious George Ser.). (ENG.). 24p. (J). (gr. -1-3). pap. 3.95 *(978-0-618-66377-4(0))* Houghton Mifflin Harcourt Publishing Co.

—Curious George's First Day of School. Rey, Margret & Rey, H. A. 2005. (Curious George Ser.). (ENG.). 24p. (J). (gr. -1-3). 13.99 *(978-0-618-60563-7(0))*; pap. 3.95 *(978-0-618-60564-4(9))* Houghton Mifflin Harcourt Publishing Co.

—Dinosaur Discovery, 2 vols. Hapka, Catherine et al. 2006. (Curious George Ser.). (ENG.). 24p. (J). (gr. -1-3). 10.99 *(978-0-618-68945-3(1))* Houghton Mifflin Harcourt Publishing Co.

—Learns to Count from 1 to 100: Counting, Grouping, Mapping, & More! Rey, H. A. 2005. (Curious George Ser.). (ENG.). 64p. (J). (gr. -1-3). 16.99 *(978-0-618-47602-2(4))* Houghton Mifflin Harcourt Publishing Co.

—Whistling. 2003. 40p. (J). 16.89 *(978-0-06-050236-2(3))* HarperCollins Pubs.

Hines, Anna Grossnickle. I Am a Tyrannosaurus. Hines, Anna Grossnickle. 2011. (ENG.). 40p. (J). (gr. -1-2). 12.99 *(978-1-58246-413-8(8)*, Tricycle Pr.) Ten Speed Pr.

—Peaceful Pieces: Poems & Quilts about Peace. Hines, Anna Grossnickle. 2011. (ENG.). 32p. (J). (gr. -1-3). 17.99 *(978-0-8050-8996-7(9)*, Holt, Henry & Co. Bks. For Young Readers) Holt, Henry & Co.

—Pieces: A Year in Poems & Quilts. Hines, Anna Grossnickle. 2003. (ENG.). 32p. (J). (gr. k-5). pap. 6.99 *(978-0-06-055960-1(8)*, Greenwillow Bks.) HarperCollins Pubs.

—Winter Lights: A Season in Poems & Quilts. Hines, Anna Grossnickle. 2005. 32p. (J). lib. bdg. 17.89 *(978-0-06-000818-5(0))* HarperCollins Pubs.

Hines, Anna Grossnickle, jt. illus. see Paprocki, Greg.

Hines, Irene. Baa. Arnold, Shauna. 2004. 19p. (J). (gr. -1-3). 12.00 *(978-0-9743669-0-6(0))* Trinity Bks.

Hines, Laura Freeman. L Is for Liberty. Lewison, Wendy Cheyette. 2003. (Reading Railroad Ser.). (ENG.). 24p. (J). (gr. -1-3). mass mkt. 3.99 *(978-0-448-43228-1(5)*, Grosset & Dunlap) Penguin Publishing Group.

Hines, Marcel. Santana's Harrowing Halloween. Dunagan, Jennifer. 2012. 26p. pap. 12.95 *(978-1-60911-977-5(0)*, Strategic Bk. Publishing) Strategic Book Publishing & Rights Agency (SBPRA).

Hines, Thomas. The Bubble Machine. l.t. ed. 2003. 26p. (J). per. *(978-1-887636-02-5(1))* Creative Writing & Publishing Co.

Hinlicky, Gregg. Moving Again Mom! Sportelli-Rehak, Angela. (J). 2004. (Uncle Sam's Kids Ser.: Bk. 2). 40p. (gr. -1-7). pap. 7.95 *(978-0-9714515-0-6(8))*; 2003. (gr. k-7). pap. *(978-0-9714515-3-7(2))* Abidenme Bks.

—Uncle Sam's Kids: Moving Again Mom. Sportelli-Rehak, Angela. 2004. (Uncle Sam's Kids Ser.: Bk. 2). 40p. (gr. k-6). 16.95 *(978-0-9714515-2-0(4))* Abidenme Bks.

—Uncle Sam's Kids: When Duty Calls. Sportelli-Rehak, Angela. 2004. (Uncle Sam's Kids Ser.: Bk. 1). 40p. (gr. k-6). 15.95 *(978-0-9714515-1-3(6))* Abidenme Bks.

Hino, Hideshi. The Bug Boy No. 2: Hino Horror: A Graphic Novel. Hino, Hideshi. 2005. 204p. (YA). (gr. 4-9). reprint ed. pap. 10.00 *(978-0-7567-9709-6(8))* DIANE Publishing Co.

Hino, Matsuri. Captive Hearts. Hino, Matsuri. 2008. (Captive Hearts Ser.: 1). (ENG.). 194p. (gr. 8-18). pap. 8.99 *(978-1-4215-1932-6(1))* Viz Media.

—MeruPuri. Hino, Matsuri. (MeruPuri Ser.: Vol. 4). (ENG.). 2006. 208p. pap. 8.99 *(978-1-4215-0399-8(9))*; Vol. 1. 2005. 192p. pap. 9.99 *(978-1-4215-0120-8(1))*; Vol. 2. 2005. 200p. pap. 8.99 *(978-1-4215-0121-5(X))*; Vol. 3. 2006. 192p. (gr. 8). pap. 9.99 *(978-1-4215-0221-2(6))* Viz Media.

—Vampire Knight. Hino, Matsuri. Kimura, Tomo. 2008. (Vampire Knight Ser.: 4). (ENG.). 208p. pap. 9.99 *(978-1-4215-1563-2(6))* Viz Media.

—Vampire Knight. Hino, Matsuri. Bates, Megan, ed. 2007. (Vampire Knight Ser.: 3). (ENG.). 200p. pap. 9.99 *(978-1-4215-1324-9(2))* Viz Media.

—Vampire Knight. Hino, Matsuri. 2007. (Vampire Knight Ser.: 2). (ENG.). 200p. (gr. 11-18). pap. 9.99 *(978-1-4215-1130-6(4))*; Vol. 1. pap. 9.99 *(978-1-4215-0822-1(2))* Viz Media.

Hinojosa, Francisco. Yanka, Yanka. Hinojosa, Francisco. 2003. (SPA.). 44p. (J). (gr. k-3). pap. 10.95 *(978-968-19-0440-1(0))* Santillana USA Publishing Co., Inc.

Hinrichsen, Natalie. Something to Do. Walton, Ann. 2010. (ENG.). 24p. (J). (gr. k-2). pap. 6.00 *(978-1-77009-706-3(6))* Jacana Media ZAF. Dist: Independent Pubs. Group.

—The Ugly Duckling. Magona, Sindiwe. 2011. (Best Loved Tales for Africa Ser.). (ENG.). 32p. (J). (gr. k-2). pap. 10.95 *(978-1-77009-823-7(2))* Jacana Media ZAF. Dist: Independent Pubs. Group.

Hinrichsen, Tamsin. The Tale of Sun & Moon. Walton, Ann. 2010. (ENG.). 32p. (J). (gr. k-2). 11.95 *(978-1-77009-705-6(8))* Jacana Media ZAF. Dist: Independent Pubs. Group.

Hinton, Sophie. Peekaboo! Sea. Hinton, Sophie. 2014. (Animaru Ser.). (ENG.). 12p. (J). (— 1). bds. 9.99 *(978-1-4052-6778-6(X))* Egmont Bks., Ltd. GBR. Dist: Independent Pubs. Group.

—Peekaboo! Snow. Hinton, Sophie. 2014. (Animaru Ser.). (ENG.). 12p. (J). (— 1). bds. 9.99 *(978-1-4052-6775-5(5))* Egmont Bks., Ltd. GBR. Dist: Independent Pubs. Group.

Hinton, Stephanie. Busy Book for Boys: 550 Things to Find. 2014. (J). ***(978-1-4351-5358-5(8))*** Barnes & Noble, Inc.

—A Trip to Busy Town: A Pull-The-Tab Book. Hopgood, Sally. 2014. (J). ***(978-1-4351-5690-6(0))*** Barnes & Noble, Inc.

Hintz, Amy. Once upon a Time: An Adoption Story. Bigler, Ashley Hansen. 2010. (J). pap. 12.99 *(978-1-59955-310-8(4))* Cedar Fort, Inc./CFI Distribution.

Hintze, Amy. I'm So Glad When Daddy Comes Home. 2006. 16p. (J). 5.99 *(978-1-59156-562-8(6))* Covenant Communications, Inc.

Hipp, Ryan, jt. illus. see Kammeraad, Kevin.

Hirao, Amiko. How the Fisherman Tricked the Genie. Sunami, Kitoba & Sunami, Christopher. 2007. (ENG.). 40p. (J). (gr. k-3). 14.99 *(978-1-4169-6137-6(2)*, Simon & Schuster/Paula Wiseman Bks.) Simon & Schuster/Paula Wiseman Bks.

—Take Me Out to the Ball Game. Norworth, Jack & Simon, Carly. 2011. (ENG.). 26p. (J). (gr. k-12). 17.95 *(978-1-936140-26-8(8))* Charlesbridge Publishing, Inc.

Hirashima, Jean. Hello Kitty, Hello Fall! Sanrio Company, Ltd Staff. 2013. (ENG.). 14p. (J). (gr. -1 — 1). bds. 7.95 *(978-1-4197-0799-5(X)*, Abrams Appleseed) Abrams.

—Hello Kitty, Hello New York! Sanrio Company, Ltd Staff. 2014. (ENG.). 16p. (J). (gr. -1 — 1). bds. 7.95 *(978-1-4197-1096-4(6)*, Abrams Appleseed) Abrams.

—Hello Kitty, Hello Winter! Sanrio Company, LTD. 2013. (ENG.). 14p. (J). (gr. -1 — 1). bds. 7.95 *(978-1-4197-0797-1(3)*, Abrams Appleseed) Abrams.

—A Home for Little Fish. Ferrier, Charlotte. 2005. (J). *(978-1-890647-16-2(0))* TOMY International, Inc.

Hires, Josh. A Stone in the Soup. Gilmore, Dorina Lazo. 2006. 39p. per. 15.00 *(978-0-938911-29-6(5))* Individualized Education Systems/Poppy Lane Publishing.

Hires, Josh, photos by. Children of the San Joaquin Valley. Lazo, Dorina. 2005. 35p. (YA). (gr. 7-12). pap. 15.00 *(978-0-938911-28-9(7))* Individualized Education Systems/Poppy Lane Publishing.

Hirose, George, photos by. I Catch My Moment: Art & Writing by Children on the Life of Play. 2008. 56p. (J). (gr. -1-3). pap. 10.00 *(978-1-929299-06-5(0))* Touchstone Ctr. Pubns.

Hirsch, Charmaine. Walter's Discovery. Magers, Ramona Hirsch. 2008. 26p. pap. 24.95 *(978-1-60563-623-8(1))* America Star Bks.

Hirsch, Kerry. Whiskers. Silk, Max V. 2004. (J). pap. 12.00 *(978-0-9748524-6-1(5))* Biblio Bks. International.

Hirschmann, Kris & Langdo, Bryan. We're Going on a Ghost Hunt. 2011. (J). *(978-0-545-34173-8(6))* Scholastic, Inc.

Hirsh, Alice. The Wonder of Light: A Picture Story of How & Why We See. Ruchlis, Hyman. 2011. 160p. 41.95 *(978-1-258-09816-2(4))* Literary Licensing, LLC.

Hirsh, Marilyn. House on the Roof. Adler, David A. 2009. (ENG.). 32p. (J). (gr. -1-3). pap. 7.95 *(978-0-8234-2232-6(1))* Holiday Hse., Inc.

Hirsheimer, Christopher, photos by. The New Irish Table: 70 Contemporary Recipes. Johnson, Margaret M. 2003. (ENG., 168p. (gr. 8-17). pap. 24.95 *(978-0-8118-3387-5(9))* Chronicle Bks. LLC.

Hirsheimer, Christopher, photos by. The San Francisco Ferry Plaza Farmers' Market Cookbook: A Comprehensive Guide to Impeccable Produce Plus 130 Seasonal Recipes. Hirsheimer, Christopher. Knickerbocker, Peggy. 2006. (ENG., 288p. (gr. 8-17). pap. 22.95 *(978-0-8118-4462-8(5))* Chronicle Bks. LLC.

Hirst, Damien. Don't Be So... Fryer, Paul. 2004. 168p. 39.95 *(978-0-9542079-1-5(2))* Trolley GBR. Dist: D.A.P./Distributed Art Pubs.

Hische, Jessica. Five Children & It. Nesbit, E. 2013. (Penguin Drop Caps Ser.). (ENG.). 256p. (gr. 12). 23.00 *(978-0-14-312466-5(8))* Penguin Publishing Group.

Hiscock, Bruce. Turtle Tide: The Ways of Sea Turtles. Swinburne, Stephen R. 2010. (ENG.). 32p. (J). (gr. 2-4). pap. 11.95 *(978-1-59078-827-1(3))* Boyds Mills Pr.

Hiscock, Bruce. Armadillo Trail: The Northward Journey of the Armadillo. Hiscock, Bruce. Swinburne, Stephen R. 2009. (ENG.). 32p. (J). (gr. 2-4). 16.95 *(978-1-59078-463-1(4))* Boyds Mills Pr.

—The Big Caribou Herd: Life in the Arctic National Wildlife Refuge. Hiscock, Bruce. 2003. (ENG.). 32p. (J). (gr. 2-4). 16.95 *(978-1-59078-010-7(8))* Boyds Mills Pr.

—The Big Tree. Hiscock, Bruce. 2003. (ENG.). 32p. (YA). (gr. 2-4). pap. 9.95 *(978-1-56397-810-4(5))* Boyds Mills Pr.

HIT Entertainment, H. I. T. Evie the Knight. 2015. (Mike the Knight Ser.). (ENG.). 24p. (J). (gr. -1-2). pap. 3.99 *(978-1-4814-2758-6(X)*, Simon Spotlight) Simon Spotlight.

—The Fireless Dragon. 2015. (Mike the Knight Ser.). (ENG.). 16p. (J). (gr. -1-2). pap. 5.99 *(978-1-4814-2869-9(1)*, Simon Spotlight) Simon Spotlight.

HIT Entertainment, H. I. T. Mike & the Invisible Monster. HIT Entertainment, H. I. T., adapted by. 2014. (Mike the Knight Ser.). (ENG.). 24p. (J). (gr. -1-2). pap. 3.99 *(978-1-4814-0371-9(0)*, Simon Spotlight) Simon Spotlight.

HIT Entertainment Staff. The Amazing Egg. 2014. (Mike the Knight Ser.). (ENG.). 16p. (J). (gr. -1-2). pap. 6.99 *(978-1-4424-9549-4(9)*, Simon Spotlight) Simon Spotlight.

—Christmas in Glendragon. Evans, Cordelia. 2013. (Mike the Knight Ser.). (ENG.). 32p. (J). (gr. -1-2). 4.99 *(978-1-4424-8651-5(1)*, Simon Scribbles) Simon Scribbles.

Hit Entertainment Staff. Friends from Sodor. Golden Books Staff. 2008. (Deluxe Paint Box Book Ser.). (ENG.). 128p. (J). (gr. -1-2). pap. 7.99 *(978-0-375-84292-4(6)*, Golden Bks.) Random Hse., Inc.

HIT Entertainment Staff. The Great Mom Rescue. 2014. (Mike the Knight Ser.). (ENG.). 24p. (J). (gr. -1-2). pap. 3.99 *(978-1-4424-9605-7(3)*, Simon Spotlight) Simon Spotlight.

—Huzzah for Spring! Gallo, Tina. 2014. (Mike the Knight Ser.). (ENG.). 32p. (J). (gr. -1-2). 4.99 *(978-1-4424-9614-9(2)*, Simon Scribbles) Simon Scribbles.

—Journey to Dragon Mountain. 2014. (Mike the Knight Ser.). (ENG.). 24p. (J). (gr. -1-2). pap. 3.99 *(978-1-4814-1989-5(7)*, Simon Spotlight) Simon Spotlight.

—Mike the Knight & Sir Trollee. 2014. (Mike the Knight Ser.). (ENG.). 14p. (J). (gr. -1-2). bds. 5.99 *(978-1-4424-9662-0(2)*, Simon Spotlight) Simon Spotlight.

—On the Go in Glendragon. Pendergrass, Daphne. 2014. (Mike the Knight Ser.). (ENG.). 96p. (J). (gr. -1-2). 3.99 *(978-1-4814-0428-0(8)*, Simon Scribbles) Simon Scribbles.

—Thomas & Friends Movie Theater. Reader's Digest Staff. 2010. (Movie Theater Ser.). (ENG.). 48p. (J). (gr. -1-2). bds. 19.99 *(978-0-7944-2002-4(8))* Reader's Digest Assn., Inc., The.

—The Tricky Trail. 2014. (Mike the Knight Ser.). (ENG.). 24p. (J). (gr. -1-1). 16.99 *(978-1-4424-9545-6(6)*, Simon Spotlight) Simon Spotlight.

Hitch, Bryan. Gods & Monsters, Vol. 1. 2006. (ENG.). 152p. (gr. 10-17). pap. 15.99 *(978-0-7851-1093-4(3))* Marvel Worldwide, Inc.

—Homeland Security Vol. 2. 2006. (ENG.). 200p. (gr. 10-17). pap. 17.99 *(978-0-7851-1078-1(X))* Marvel Worldwide, Inc.

Hitch, David. One of a Kind. Winter, Ariel S. 2012. (ENG.). 32p. (J). (gr. -1-2). 15.99 *(978-1-4424-2016-8(2)*, Simon & Schuster/Paula Wiseman Bks.) Simon & Schuster/Paula Wiseman Bks.

Hites, Kati. Winnie & Waldorf. Hites, Kati. 2015. (ENG.). 40p. (J). (gr. -1-3). 17.99 *(978-0-06-231161-0(1))* HarperCollins Pubs.

Hiti, Sam. The Chinese: Life in China's Golden Age. Doeden, Matt. 2009. (Life in Ancient Civilizations Ser.). (ENG.). 48p. (gr. 3-6). lib. bdg. 29.27 *(978-0-8225-8681-4(9)*, Millbrook Pr.) Lerner Publishing Group.

Hiti, Samuel. Addition. Midthun, Joseph. 2013. (Building Blocks of Mathematics Ser.). 32p. pap. 169.00 *(978-0-7166-1432-6(4))* World Bk., Inc.

—The Aztecs: Life in Tenochtitlan. Doeden, Matt. 2009. (Life in Ancient Civilizations Ser.). (ENG.). 48p. (gr. 3-6). lib. bdg. 29.27 *(978-0-8225-8684-5(3)*, Millbrook Pr.) Lerner Publishing Group.

—Division. Midthun, Joseph. 2013. (Building Blocks of Mathematics Ser.). 32p. pap. 169.00 *(978-0-7166-1433-3(2))* World Bk., Inc.

—Fractions. Midthun, Joseph. 2013. (Building Blocks of Mathematics Ser.). 32p. pap. 169.00 *(978-0-7166-1435-7(9))* World Bk., Inc.

—The Greeks: Life in Ancient Greece. Levine, Michelle. 2009. (Life in Ancient Civilizations Ser.). (ENG.). 48p. (gr. 3-6). lib. bdg. 29.27 *(978-0-8225-8680-7(0)*, Lerner Pubns.) Lerner Publishing Group.

—Multiplication. Midthun, Joseph. 2013. (Building Blocks of Mathematics Ser.). 32p. pap. 169.00 *(978-0-7166-1437-1(5))* World Bk., Inc.

—The Romans: Life in Ancient Rome. Sonnebom, Liz. 2009. (Life in Ancient Civilizations Ser.). (ENG.). 48p. (gr. 3-6). lib. bdg. 29.27 *(978-0-8225-8679-1(7)*, Millbrook Pr.) Lerner Publishing Group.

Hiti, Samuel. Waga's Big Scare. Hiti, Samuel. 2012. (Carolrhoda Picture Bks). (ENG.). 32p. (J). (gr. k-3). lib. bdg. 16.95 *(978-0-7613-5622-6(3)*, Carolrhoda Bks.) Lerner Publishing Group.

Hitschler, Cynthia. Gleb... the Terrible! 2004. 36p. pap. *(978-0-9761041-1-7(3)*, 1239008) Celstumo Publishing.

—The Perils of Pink Cat. 2004. 36p. (J). pap. *(978-0-9761041-2-4(1)*, 1239009) Celstumo Publishing.

—The World of Jacky Blue & Other Cats. 2004. 40p. (J). pap. *(978-0-9761041-0-0(5)*, 1239007) Celstumo Publishing.

Hitz, Dustin. The Puppy Twins, Backyard Colors. Rex, Judith. l.t. ed. 2010. (ENG.). 28p. pap. 13.99 *(978-1-4563-4781-9(0))* CreateSpace Independent Publishing Platform.

Hiwatari, Saki. Please Save My Earth. Hiwatari, Saki. (Please Save My Earth Ser.). (ENG.). Vol. 3. 2004. 192p. pap. 9.95 *(978-1-59116-142-4(8))*; Vol. 5. 2004. 208p. pap. 9.95 *(978-1-59116-268-1(8))*; Vol. 6. 2004. 200p. pap. 9.99 *(978-1-59116-269-8(6))*; Vol. 8. 2004. 200p. pap. 9.99 *(978-1-59116-271-1(8))*; Vol. 10. 2005. 208p. pap. 9.99 *(978-1-59116-273-5(4))*; Vol. 11. 2005. 208p. pap. 9.99 *(978-1-59116-846-1(5))*; Vol. 12. 2005. 184p. pap. 9.99 *(978-1-59116-987-1(9))*; Vol. 14. 2006. 192p. (gr. 11). pap. 9.99 *(978-1-4215-0193-2(7))*; Vol. 15. 2006. 208p. (gr. 11). pap. 9.99 *(978-1-4215-0326-4(3))*; Vol. 17. 2006. 208p. pap. 9.99 *(978-1-4215-0550-3(9))*; Vol. 18. 2006. 208p. pap. 9.99 *(978-1-4215-0551-0(7))* Viz Media.

Hixson, Bryce. Dig It! DeWitt, Lockwood. 2003. (J). per. 14.95 *(978-1-931801-02-7(9))* Loose In The Lab.

Hixson, Bryce. Anatomy Academy. Hixson, Bryce. 2003. (J). per. 14.95 *(978-1-931801-03-4(7))* Loose In The Lab.

—Digits, Midgets, & Degrees Kelvin. Hixson, Bryce. 2003. (J). per. 9.95 *(978-1-931801-04-1(5))* Loose In The Lab.

—Galactic Cookie Dough. Hixson, Bryce. 2003. (J). per. 14.95 *(978-1-931801-06-5(1))* Loose In The Lab.

—Get Your Poop in a Group. Hixson, Bryce. 2003. (J). per. 9.95 *(978-1-931801-01-0(0))* Loose In The Lab.

—Great Graphs in Ten Days. Hixson, Bryce. 2003. (J). 6.95 *(978-1-931801-18-8(5))* Loose In The Lab.

—Newton Take 3. Hixson, Bryce. 2003. (J). per. 14.95 *(978-0-9660965-3-8(3))* Loose In The Lab.

—The Original World Wide Web. Hixson, Bryce. 2003. (J). per. 12.95 *(978-1-931801-07-2(X))* Loose In The Lab.

—Plant Stigmas & Other Botanical Concerns. Hixson, Bryce. 2003. (J). per. 12.95 *(978-1-931801-09-6(6))* Loose In The Lab.

—What's Up? Hixson, Bryce. 2003. (J). per. 14.95 *(978-1-931801-05-8(3))* Loose In The Lab.

HL Studios, H. L. Shhh! Listen!: Hearing Sounds, 1 vol. Spilsbury, Louise & Spilsbury, Richard. 2014. (Exploring Sound Ser.). (ENG.). 32p. (gr. 2-4). lib. bdg. 29.99 *(978-1-4109-6002-3(1)*, Raintree Perspectives) Heinemann-Raintree.

HL Studios Staff. Caves. Claybourne, Anna. 2013. (Explorer Travel Guides). (ENG.). 48p. (gr. 3-6). 29.00 *(978-1-4109-5428-2(5))*; pap. 7.99 *(978-1-4109-5435-0(8))* Heinemann-Raintree.

—Deserts: An Explorer Travel Guide, 1 vol. Hunter, Nick. 2013. (Explorer Travel Guides). (ENG.). 48p. (gr. 3-6). 29.00 *(978-1-4109-5429-9(3))*; pap. 7.99 *(978-1-4109-5436-7(6))* Heinemann-Raintree. (NA-r).

—John F. Kennedy, 1 vol. Burgan, Michael. 2013. (ENG.). 56p. (gr. 4-8). 32.65 *(978-1-4329-8096-2(3))*; pap. 9.99 *(978-1-4329-8097-9(1))* Heinemann-Raintree.

—Polar Scientist: The Coolest Jobs on the Planet, 1 vol. Shuckburgh, Emily & Chambers, Catherine. 2014. (Coolest Jobs on the Planet Ser.). (ENG.). 48p. (gr. 6-6). 32.00 *(978-1-4109-6642-1(9))*; pap. 8.99 *(978-1-4109-6648-3(8))* Heinemann-Raintree.

—Turn It up!; Turn It down!: Volume, 1 vol. Spilsbury, Louise & Spilsbury, Richard. 2014. (Exploring Sound Ser.). (ENG.). 32p. (gr. 2-4). lib. bdg. 29.99 *(978-1-4109-6001-6(3)*, Raintree Perspectives) Heinemann-Raintree.

—Volcanologist: The Coolest Jobs on the Planet, 1 vol. Tuffen, Hugh & Waldron, Melanie. 2014. (Coolest Jobs on the Planet Ser.). (ENG.). 48p. (gr. 6-6). 32.00 *(978-1-4109-6643-8(7))*; pap. 8.99 *(978-1-4109-6649-0(6))* Heinemann-Raintree.

—Who Journeyed on the Mayflower?, 1 vol. Barber, Nicola. 2014. (Primary Source Detectives Ser.). (ENG.). 64p. (gr. 7-8). lib. bdg. 35.00 *(978-1-4329-9602-4(9))* Heinemann-Raintree.

—Who Marched for Civil Rights?, 1 vol. Spilsbury, Richard. 2014. (Primary Source Detectives Ser.). (ENG.). 64p. (gr. 7-8). lib. bdg. 35.00 *(978-1-4329-9604-8(5))* Heinemann-Raintree.

—Why Can't I Hear That?: Pitch & Frequency, 1 vol. Spilsbury, Louise & Spilsbury, Richard. 2014. (Exploring Sound Ser.). (ENG.). 32p. (gr. 2-4). lib. bdg. 29.99 *(978-1-4109-6000-9(5)*, Raintree Perspectives) Heinemann-Raintree.

Hnatiuk, Charlie. A Hero's Worth. Ouellet, Debbie. 120p. *(978-1-897039-47-2(6))* High Interest Publishing (HIP).

Hnatov, Catherine. Valentino Finds a Home, 1 vol. Whiteside, Andy. 2012. (ENG.). 32p. (J). 15.95 *(978-1-59572-284-3(X))*; pap. 5.95 *(978-1-59572-286-7(6))* Star Bright Bks., Inc.

Ho, David. Dragon Games. Catanese, P. W. (Books of Umber Ser.: 2). (ENG.). (J). (gr. 3-7). 2011. 400p. pap. 7.99 *(978-1-4169-5383-8(3))*; 2010. 304p. 17.99 *(978-1-4169-7521-2(7))* Simon & Schuster/Paula Wiseman Bks. (Simon & Schuster/Paula Wiseman Bks.).

—The End of Time. Catanese, P. W. (Books of Umber Ser.: 3). (ENG.). 432p. (J). (gr. 3-7). 2012. pap. 6.99 *(978-1-4169-5384-5(1))*; 2011. 16.99 *(978-1-4169-7520-5(9))* Simon & Schuster/Paula Wiseman Bks. (Simon & Schuster/Paula Wiseman Bks.).

Ho, Jannie. Bunny & Bird Are Best Friends: Making New Friends. Dinardo, Jeff. 2014. (Funny Bone Readers: Being a Friend Ser.). 24p. (gr. -1-1). pap. 4.99 *(978-1-939656-02-5(8))* Red Chair Pr.

Ho, Jannie. Christmas. Dahl, Michael. 2015. (Baby Face Ser.). (ENG.). 10p. (gr. -1 — 1). bds. 9.99 ***(978-1-62370-292-2(5))*** Capstone Young Readers.

Ho, Jannie. Cutie Pie Looks for the Easter Bunny: A Tiny Tab Book. Nosy Crow. 2015. (ENG.). 8p. (J). (— 1). bds. 7.99 *(978-0-7636-7599-8(7),* Nosy Crow) Candlewick Pr.

—The Great Reindeer Rebellion. Trumbauer, Lisa. 2014. (ENG.). 32p. (J). (gr. -1). pap. 6.95 *(978-1-4549-1356-6(8))* Sterling Publishing Co., Inc.

Ho, Jannie. Halloween. Dahl, Michael. 2015. (Baby Face Ser.). (ENG.). 10p. (gr. -1 — 1). bds. 9.99 ***(978-1-62370-293-9(3))*** Capstone Young Readers.

Ho, Jannie. Halloween Howlers: Frightfully Funny Knock-Knock Jokes. Teitelbaum, Michael. 2011. (ENG.). 16p. (J). (gr. k-3). pap. 6.99 *(978-0-06-180891-3(1),* HarperFestival) HarperCollins Pubs.

—Light the Menorah. 2009. (ENG.). 12p. (J). (gr. -1-k). 6.99 *(978-0-8431-8954-4(1),* Price Stern Sloan) Penguin Publishing Group.

—Lily's Lucky Leotard, 1 vol. Meister, Cari. 2009. (My First Graphic Novel Ser.). (ENG.). 32p. (gr. k-2). pap. 6.25 *(978-1-4342-1411-9(7));* lib. bdg. 23.32 *(978-1-4342-1296-2(3))* Stone Arch Bks. (My First Graphic Novel).

—Little Bubba Looks for His Elephant. Nosy Crow. 2014. (ENG.). 8p. (J). (— 1). bds. 7.99 *(978-0-7636-7401-4(X),* Nosy Crow) Candlewick Pr.

—The Mixed-Up Alphabet. Metzger, Steve. 2007. (J). *(978-0-545-00098-7(X))* Scholastic, Inc.

—Muddle Zoo. 2013. (Muddle Bks.). 8p. (J). (gr. -1 — 1). 10.99 *(978-0-7641-6623-5(9))* Barron's Educational Series, Inc.

Ho, Jannie. Pirate. Dahl, Michael. 2015. (Baby Face Ser.). (ENG.). 10p. (gr. -1 — 1). bds. 9.99 ***(978-1-62370-294-6(1))*** Capstone Young Readers.

Ho, Jannie. Pookie Pop Plays Hide-And-Seek: A Tiny Tab Book. Nosy Crow. 2015. (ENG.). 8p. (J). (— 1). bds. 7.99 *(978-0-7636-7600-1(4),* Nosy Crow) Candlewick Pr.

Ho, Jannie. Princess. Dahl, Michael. 2015. (Baby Face Ser.). (ENG.). 10p. (gr. -1 — 1). bds. 9.99 ***(978-1-62370-295-3(X))*** Capstone Young Readers.

Ho, Jannie. T-Ball Trouble, 1 vol. Meister, Cari. 2009. (My First Graphic Novel Ser.). (ENG.). 32p. (gr. k-2). pap. 6.25 *(978-1-4342-1413-3(3));* lib. bdg. 23.32 *(978-1-4342-1300-6(5))* Stone Arch Bks. (My First Graphic Novel).

—Teeny Weeny Looks for His Mommy: A Tiny Tab Book. Crow, Nosy. 2014. (ENG.). 8p. (J). (— 1). bds. 7.99 *(978-0-7636-7273-7(4),* Nosy Crow) Candlewick Pr.

—Wickle Woo Has a Halloween Party. Nosy Crow. 2014. (ENG.). 8p. (J). (— 1). bds. 7.99 *(978-0-7636-7400-7(1),* Nosy Crow) Candlewick Pr.

Ho, Jannie. The Great Matzoh Hunt. Ho, Jannie. 2010. (ENG.). 12p. (J). (gr. -1-k). bds. 6.99 *(978-0-8431-8969-8(X),* Price Stern Sloan) Penguin Publishing Group.

—Guess Who? Ho, Jannie. 2013. (ENG.). 8p. (J). (gr. -1 — 1). bds. 7.99 *(978-0-545-49331-4(5),* Cartwheel Bks.) Scholastic, Inc.

—You Can Draw Monsters & Other Scary Things, 1 vol. Ho, Jannie. Bruning, Matt. 2011. (You Can Draw Ser.). (ENG.). 24p. (gr. 1-2). lib. bdg. 25.99 *(978-1-4048-6276-0(5),* Nonfiction Picture Bks.) Picture Window Bks.

—You Can Draw Zoo Animals, 1 vol. Ho, Jannie. Bruning, Matt. 2011. (You Can Draw Ser.). (ENG.). 24p. (gr. 1-2). lib. bdg. 25.99 *(978-1-4048-6275-3(7),* Nonfiction Picture Bks.) Picture Window Bks.

Ho, Jannie & Sexton, Brenda. Easy to Draw Animals, 1 vol. Ho, Jannie & Sexton, Brenda. Capstone Press Staff. 2011. (You Can Draw Ser.). (ENG.). 48p. (gr. 1-2). pap. 5.19 *(978-1-4048-6760-4(0),* Nonfiction Picture Bks.) Picture Window Bks.

Ho, Jannie, jt. illus. see Cerato, Mattia.

Ho, Jannie, jt. illus. see Sexton, Brenda.

Ho, Jason. Frankenstein. Shelley, Mary. 2007. (Graphic Horror Ser.). 32p. (gr. 4-7). 28.50 *(978-1-60270-059-8(1),* Graphic Planet- Fiction) ABDO Publishing Co.

Ho, Louise. One Magical Morning. Freeman, Claire. 2005. (ENG.). 26p. (J). pap. 16.00 *(978-1-56148-472-0(5),* Good Bks.) Skyhorse Publishing Co., Inc.

—The Sea Mice & the Stars, 1 vol. Steven, Kenneth. 2005. (ENG.). 28p. (J). pap. 16.00 *(978-1-56148-490-4(3),* Good Bks.) Skyhorse Publishing Co., Inc.

Ho, Winnie & Egan, Caroline LaVelle. I Love School! Glass, Calliope & Disney Book Group Staff. 2012. (ENG.). 24p. (J). (gr. -1-k). pap. 3.99 *(978-1-4231-6231-5(5))* Disney Pr.

Hoar, Gail. Grandmother's Guest: The Blue Lady of Wilton. Schoen, Robin. 2013. 32p. 16.95 *(978-0-615-89154-5(3))* Hobby Horse Publishing, LLC.

Hoard, Angela. Did the Aardvarks Say "No Ark"? Coburn, Claudia. 2004. 32p. (J). *(978-0-9759343-1-9(7))* Purfect Promises.

Hoare, Jerry. George Ferris, What a Wheel! Lowell, Barbara. 2014. (Penguin Core Concepts Ser.). (ENG.). 32p. (J). (gr. -1-k). 3.99 *(978-0-448-47925-5(7),* Grosset & Dunlap) Penguin Publishing Group.

Hoare, Jerry. Where Are the Great Pyramids? Hoobler, Dorothy & Hoobler, Thomas. 2015. (Where Is...? Ser.). (ENG.). 112p. (J). (gr. 3-7). 5.99 ***(978-0-448-48409-9(9)),*** Grosset & Dunlap) Penguin Publishing Group.

Hoare, Jerry. Who Was Frida Kahlo? Fabiny, Sarah. 2013. (Who Was...? Ser.). (ENG.). 112p. (J). (gr. 3-7). 5.99 *(978-0-448-47938-5(9),* Grosset & Dunlap) Penguin Publishing Group.

Hoare, Jerry & Harrison, Nancy. Who Was Gandhi? Rau, Dana Meachen. 2014. (Who Was...? Ser.). (ENG.). 112p. (J). (gr. 3-7). pap. 5.99 *(978-0-448-48235-4(5),* Grosset & Dunlap) Penguin Publishing Group.

—Who Was Winston Churchill? Labrecque, Ellen. 2015. (Who Was...? Ser.). (ENG.). 112p. (J). (gr. 3-7). 5.99 *(978-0-448-48300-9(9),* Grosset & Dunlap) Penguin Publishing Group.

Hoare, Jerry, jt. illus. see Groff, David.

Hoare, Jerry, jt. illus. see Harrison, Nancy.

Hoban, Lillian. A Baby Sister for Frances. Hoban, Russell. 2011. (I Can Read Book 2 Ser.). (ENG.). 48p. (J). (gr. k-3). 16.99 *(978-0-06-083804-1(3));* pap. 3.99 *(978-0-06-083806-5(X))* HarperCollins Pubs.

—A Bargain for Frances. Hoban, Russell. Lt. ed. 2003. (I Can Read Book 2 Ser.). (ENG.). 64p. (J). (gr. k-3). pap. 3.99 *(978-0-06-444001-1(X))* HarperCollins Pubs.

—Best Friends for Frances. Hoban, Russell. 2009. (I Can Read Book 2 Ser.). 48p. (J). (gr. -1-3). 16.99 *(978-0-06-083801-0(9));* (ENG.). (gr. k-3). pap. 3.99 *(978-0-06-083803-4(5))* HarperCollins Pubs.

—A Birthday for Frances. Hoban, Russell. 2012. (I Can Read Book 2 Ser.). (ENG.). 48p. (J). (gr. k-3). 16.99 *(978-0-06-083795-2(0));* pap. 3.99 *(978-0-06-083797-6(7))* HarperCollins Pubs.

—Bread & Jam for Frances. Hoban, Russell. 2008. (I Can Read Book 2 Ser.). (ENG.). 48p. (J). (gr. k-3). 16.99 *(978-0-06-083798-3(5));* pap. 3.99 *(978-0-06-083800-3(0))* HarperCollins Pubs.

—The Little Brute Family. Hoban, Russell. 2011. (My Readers Ser.). (ENG.). 40p. (J). (gr. k-2). pap. 3.99 *(978-0-312-56373-8(6))* Square Fish.

—The Sorely Trying Day. Hoban, Russell. 2010. (ENG.). 48p. (J). (gr. -1-3). 14.95 *(978-1-59017-343-5(0),* NYR Children's Collection) New York Review of Bks., Inc., The.

Hoban, Tana. Black & White. Hoban, Tana. 2007. (ENG.). 16p. (J). (gr. -1 — 1). bds. 7.99 *(978-0-06-117211-3(1),* Greenwillow Bks.) HarperCollins Pubs.

—Over, under & Through. Hoban, Tana. 2008. (ENG.). 32p. (J). (gr. -1-2). 8.99 *(978-1-4169-7541-0(1),* Simon & Schuster/Paula Wiseman Bks.) Simon & Schuster/Paula Wiseman Bks.

Hobbie, Holly. Charming Opal. Hobbie, Holly. 2003. (Toot & Puddle Ser.: 7). (ENG.). 32p. (J). (gr. -1-1). 16.99 *(978-0-316-36633-5(1))* Little, Brown Bks. for Young Readers.

—Toot & Puddle. Hobbie, Holly. 2007. (Toot & Puddle Ser.: 1). (ENG.). 32p. (J). (gr. -1-1). 17.00 *(978-0-316-16702-4(9))* Little, Brown Bks. for Young Readers.

Hobbie, Jocelyn. Priscilla & the Great Santa Search. Hobbie, Nathaniel. 2008. (ENG.). 32p. (J). (gr. -1-1). 16.99 *(978-0-316-11331-1(X))* Little, Brown Bks. for Young Readers.

—Priscilla & the Pink Planet. Hobbie, Nathaniel. 2008. (ENG.). 32p. (J). (gr. -1-1). 7.00 *(978-0-316-11349-6(2))* Little, Brown Bks. for Young Readers.

—Priscilla & the Pixie Princess. Hobbie, Nathaniel. 2011. (ENG.). 32p. (J). (gr. -1-1). pap. 6.99 *(978-0-316-08349-2(6))* Little, Brown Bks. for Young Readers.

Hobbs, Leigh. Stew a Cockatoo: My Aussie Cookbook. May, Ruthie. 2010. (ENG.). (J). 40p. (gr. k-2). 22.95 *(978-1-921541-51-3(2));* 48p. (gr. 1-7). pap. 15.99 *(978-1-921714-52-8(2))* Little Hare Bks. AUS. Dist: Independent Pubs. Group.

—Your Hair Is Dead. Lawrenson, Diana. 2006. (It's True! Ser.). (ENG.). 96p. (J). (gr. 5-8). 19.95 *(978-1-55451-024-5(4),* 9781554510245); pap. 5.95 *(978-1-55451-023-8(6),* 9781554510238) Annick Pr., Ltd. CAN. Dist: Firefly Bks., Ltd.

Hobbs, Leigh. Hooray for Horrible Harriet. Hobbs, Leigh. 2013. (Horrible Harriet Ser.). (ENG.). 32p. (J). (gr. k-2). mass mkt. 11.99 *(978-1-74114-703-2(4))* Allen & Unwin AUS. Dist: Independent Pubs. Group.

—Horrible Harriet. Hobbs, Leigh. 2013. (Horrible Harriet Ser.). (ENG.). 32p. (J). (gr. k-2). mass mkt. 11.99 *(978-1-86508-440-4(9))* Allen & Unwin AUS. Dist: Independent Pubs. Group.

—Mr Badger & the Magic Mirror. Hobbs, Leigh. 2013. (Mr Badger Ser.: 4). (ENG.). 80p. (J). (gr. 2-4). 10.99 *(978-1-74237-420-8(4))* Allen & Unwin AUS. Dist: Independent Pubs. Group.

—Old Tom, Man of Mystery, 1 vol. Hobbs, Leigh. 2005. (ENG.). 32p. (J). (gr. -1-3). 16.95 *(978-1-56145-346-7(3))* Peachtree Pubs.

—Old Tom's Holiday. Hobbs, Leigh. 2004. (ENG.). 32p. (J). 16.95 *(978-1-56145-316-0(1))* Peachtree Pubs.

Hobson, Charles. The Wolf Who Ate the Sky. Hobson, Mary Daniel & Rauh, Anna Isabel. 2015. (J). *(978-1-59714-298-4(0))* Heyday.

Hobson, Ryan, jt. illus. see Dando, Marc.

Hobson, Ryan, jt. illus. see Hall, Roger.

Hoch, Doug. Beaser the Bear's Rocky Mountain Christmas. Derrick Patricia. 2007. 32p. (J). (gr. -1-3). 18.95 incl. audio compact disk *(978-1-933818-09-2(3))* Animalations.

Hoch, Kevin. The Squirrel Who Was Afraid to Climb Trees. Simpson, Richard. 2003. 55p. (J). pap. 9.95 *(978-0-7414-1825-8(8))* Infinity Publishing.

Hochain, Serge. Building Liberty: A Statue Is Born. Hochain, Serge. 2006. 46p. (J). (gr. 4-8). reprint ed. 25.00 *(978-1-4223-5181-9(5))* DIANE Publishing Co.

Hochstatter, Daniel J. Italian. 2003. (Just Look 'n Learn Picture Dictionary Ser.). (ITA & ENG.). 96p. (J). (gr. 4-7). pap. 11.95 *(978-0-8442-8057-8(7),* 80577) McGraw-Hill Trade.

Hock, Dan. The Birthday Bash 2 vols. An Iggy & Igor Mystery (#2) Hock, Dan. Lt. ed. 2004. 51p. (J). per. 4.99 *(978-0-9754046-1-4(X))* Anticipation Pr.

Hockerman, Dennis. The Big Hungry Bear. Williams, Rozanne Lanczak. 2005. (Reading for Fluency Ser.). 8p. (J). pap. 3.49 *(978-1-59198-146-6(8),* 4246) Creative Teaching Pr., Inc.

—The Country Mouse & the City Mouse: A Tale of Tolerance. 2006. (J). 6.99 *(978-1-59939-003-1(5))* Cornerstone Pr.

Hockerman, Dennis, et al. Folktales from Ecosystems Around the World. 2009. (Steck-Vaughn Pair-It Books Proficiency Stage 6 Ser.). (ENG.). 48p. (gr. 5-5). pap. 9.65 *(978-0-7398-6171-4(9))* Houghton Mifflin Harcourt Publishing Co.

Hockerman, Dennis. Good Night, Little Kitten. Christensen-Hall, Nancy. 2004. (My First Reader Ser.). (ENG.). 32p. (J). (gr. k-1). pap. 3.95 *(978-0-516-24628-4(3),* Children's Pr.) Scholastic Library Publishing.

—The Grasshopper & the Ant: A Tale about Planning. Aesop. 2006. (J). *(978-1-59939-082-6(5),* Reader's Digest Young Families, Inc.) Studio Fun International.

—Lights! Action! California! Wilsdon, Christina. 2006. 28p. (J). 7.99 *(978-1-59939-009-3(4))* Cornerstone Pr.

—The Lion & the Mouse: A Tale about Being Helpful. 2006. (J). 6.99 *(978-1-59939-007-9(8))* Cornerstone Pr.

—The Little Seed: A Tale about Integrity. 2006. (J). *(978-1-59939-094-9(9),* Reader's Digest Young Families, Inc.) Studio Fun International.

—A New York Sailing Adventure. Wilsdon, Christina. 2006. 26p. (J). 7.99 *(978-1-59939-014-7(0))* Cornerstone Pr.

—A School Year of Poems: 180 Favorites from Highlights. Barbe, Walter B. 2005. (ENG.). 116p. (J). (gr. 2-4). pap. 11.95 *(978-1-59078-395-5(6))* Boyds Mills Pr.

—Tom Thumb. Hillert, Margaret. rev. ed. 2006. (Beginning to Read Ser.). 32p. (J). (gr. -1-3). lib. bdg. 19.93 *(978-1-59953-028-4(7))* Norwood Hse. Pr.

Hocking, Deborah. The Family Dam. Markle, Sandra. 2016. (J). ***(978-1-4677-4900-8(1),*** Millbrook Pr.) Lerner Publishing Group.

Hocking, Geoff. Jamie Wins Again. Marwood, Lorraine. 2004. iv, 36p. (J). pap. *(978-0-7608-6743-3(7))* Sundance/Newbridge Educational Publishing.

Hoda, Rubina. Diwali: A Cultural Adventure. Sood, Sana Hoda. 2013. (ENG.). (J). (gr. -1-3). 14.95 *(978-1-62086-396-1(0))* Mascot Bks., Inc.

Hodes, Loren. Who Would Have Guessed? It's All for the Best! Hodes, Loren. 2006. 32p. (J). (gr. -1-3). 13.95 *(978-1-932443-48-6(7))* Judaica Pr., Inc., The.

Hodges, Benjamin. Wandihnu & the Old Dugong. Wymarra, Elizabeth & Wymarra, Wandihnu. 2007. (ENG.). 28p. (J). (gr. k-7). pap. 13.95 *(978-1-921248-18-4(1))* Magabala Bks. AUS. Dist: Independent Pubs. Group.

Hodgkinson, Jo. A Big Day for Migs. Hodgkinson, Jo. 2014. (ENG.). 32p. (J). (gr. -1-3). 16.95 *(978-1-4677-5014-1(X))* Lerner Publishing Group.

—The Talent Show. Hodgkinson, Jo. 2011. (ENG.). 32p. (J). (gr. -1-3). 16.95 *(978-0-7613-7487-9(6))* Lerner Publishing Group.

Hodgkinson, Leigh. Don't Put Your Pants on Your Head, Fred! Hart, Caryl. 2012. (ENG.). 32p. (J). (gr. -1-k). pap. 11.95 *(978-1-4083-0917-9(3))* Hodder & Stoughton GBR. Dist: Independent Pubs. Group.

—Magical Mix-Ups: Birthdays & Bridesmaids. Edwards, Marnie. 2012. (Mega Mix-Ups Ser.). (ENG.). 96p. (J). (gr. 2-5). pap. 6.99 *(978-0-7636-6272-1(0),* Nosy Crow) Candlewick Pr.

—Magical Mix-Ups: Friends & Fashion. Edwards, Marnie. 2012. (Mega Mix-Ups Ser.). (ENG.). 96p. (J). (gr. 2-5). pap. 6.99 *(978-0-7636-6166-3(X),* Nosy Crow) Candlewick Pr.

—Magical Mix-Ups: Spells & Surprises. Edwards, Marnie. 2014. (Mega Mix-Ups Ser.). (ENG.). (J). (gr. 2-5). pap. 6.99 *(978-0-7636-6610-1(6),* Nosy Crow) Candlewick Pr.

—Pets & Parties. Edwards, Marnie. 2013. (Mega Mix-Ups Ser.). (ENG.). 96p. (J). (gr. 2-5). pap. 6.99 *(978-0-7636-6371-1(9),* Nosy Crow) Candlewick Pr.

Hodgkinson, Leigh. Boris & the Snoozebox. Hodgkinson, Leigh. 2008. (Tiger Tales Ser.). 40p. (J). (gr. -1-3). 15.95 *(978-1-58925-071-0(0))* Tiger Tales.

—Boris & the Wrong Shadow. Hodgkinson, Leigh. 2009. 32p. (J). (gr. -1-2). 15.95 *(978-1-58925-082-6(6))* Tiger Tales.

—Goldilocks & Just One Bear. Hodgkinson, Leigh. 2012. (ENG.). 32p. (J). (gr. -1-2). 15.99 *(978-0-7636-6172-4(4),* Nosy Crow) Candlewick Pr.

—Limelight Larry. Hodgkinson, Leigh. 2011. 32p. (J). *(978-1-58925-102-1(4))* Tiger Tales.

—Smile! Hodgkinson, Leigh. 2009. (ENG.). 32p. (J). (gr. -1-1). 16.99 *(978-0-06-185269-5(4))* HarperCollins Pubs.

—Troll Swap. Hodgkinson, Leigh. 2014. (ENG.). 32p. (J). (gr. -1-2). 15.99 *(978-0-7636-7101-3(0),* Nosy Crow) Candlewick Pr.

Hodgman, Ann, photos by. How to Die of Embarrassment Every Day. Hodgman, Ann. 2011. (ENG.). 224p. (J). (gr. 3-7). 24.99 *(978-0-8050-8705-5(2),* Holt, Henry & Co. Bks. For Young Readers) Holt, Henry & Co.

Hodnefjeld, Hilde. Elephant Man. Di Fiore, Mariangela. 2015. (ENG.). 52p. (J). (gr. 3-6). 19.95 ***(978-1-55451-778-7(8),*** 9781554517787) Annick Pr., Ltd. CAN. Dist: Firefly Bks., Ltd.

Hodson, Ben. Captain Jake, 1 vol. Stewart, Shannon. 2008. (Orca Echoes Ser.). (ENG.). 64p. (J). (gr. 2-3). pap. 6.95 *(978-1-55143-896-2(8))* Orca Bk. Pubs. USA.

—Gran on a Fan. Bolger, Kevin. 2015. (ENG.). 40p. (J). (gr. -1-3). 7.99 *(978-0-06-228596-6(3))* HarperCollins Pubs.

—Hear My Roar: A Story of Family Violence. Watts, Gillian. 2009. (ENG.). 56p. (J). (gr. 1-4). 19.95 *(978-1-55451-202-7(6),* 9781554512027); pap. 9.95 *(978-1-55451-201-0(8),* 9781554512010) Annick Pr., Ltd. CAN. Dist: Firefly Bks., Ltd.

—How the Moon Regained Her Shape, 1 vol. Heller, Janet Ruth. 2006. (ENG.). 32p. (J). (gr. 1-5). 15.95 *(978-0-9764943-4-8(5))* Arbordale Publishing.

—I Love Yoga: A Source Book for Teens. Schwartz, Ellen. 2003. (ENG.). 128p. (J). (gr. 5-18). pap. 9.95 *(978-0-88776-598-8(X))* Tundra Bks. CAN. Dist: Random Hse., Inc.

—In Arctic Waters, 1 vol. Crawford, Laura. 2007. (ENG.). 32p. (J). (gr. -1-2). 15.95 *(978-0-9768823-4-3(5))* Arbordale Publishing.

—Jeffrey & Sloth, 1 vol. Winters, Kari-Lynn. 2008. (ENG.). 32p. (J). (gr. -1-3). per. 9.95 *(978-1-55143-974-7(3))* Orca Bk. Pubs. USA.

—Lazy Bear, Crazy Bear. Bolger, Kevin. 2015. (ENG.). 40p. (J). (gr. -1-3). 7.99 *(978-0-06-228598-0(X))* HarperCollins Pubs.

—Pigs Aren't Dirty, Bears Aren't Slow: And Other Truths about Misunderstood Animals. Boutilier, Joanna. 2005. (ENG.). 40p. (J). (gr. 2-4). 19.95 *(978-1-55037-849-8(X),* 9781550378498) Annick Pr., Ltd. CAN. Dist: Firefly Bks., Ltd.

—Richard Was a Picker, 1 vol. Beck, Carolyn. 2010. (ENG.). 32p. (J). (gr. -1-3). 19.95 *(978-1-55469-088-6(9))* Orca Bk. Pubs. USA.

—'Twas the Day Before Zoo Day, 1 vol. Ipcizade, Catherine. 2008. (ENG.). 32p. (J). (gr. -1-2). 17.95 *(978-1-60718-585-7(7))* Arbordale Publishing.

Hodson, Jewel. White Dresses: A Baptism Keepsake for Girls. Rowley, Deborah Pace. 2006. 32p. (J). 16.99 *(978-1-59038-632-3(9))* Deseret Bk. Co.

Hoedl, Lee, photos by. Jesse the Wait of the Wood. Hoedl, Lee. 2006. 30p. (J). per. 12.95 *(978-1-59879-139-6(7))* Lifevest Publishing, Inc.

Hoeffner, Deb. Andi's Choice. Messer, Celeste M. 2004. 82-92p. 4.95 *(978-0-9702171-6-5(1))* AshleyAlan Enterprises.

—The Boy Who Cried Wolf. Messer, Celeste M. 2004. 82-92p. 4.95 *(978-0-9702171-9-6(6))* AshleyAlan Enterprises.

—The Broken Wing: The Adventures of Andi O'Malley. Messer, Celeste M. 2004. (Adventures of Andi O'Malley Ser.). 82-92p. (J). (gr. 4-7). 4.95 *(978-0-9702171-1-0(0))* AshleyAlan Enterprises.

—Forever & Always. Messer, Celeste M. 2004. 82-92p. 4.95 *(978-0-9710145-0-3(7))* AshleyAlan Enterprises.

—Forever Home: Tales of Four Lucky Dogs. Whitman, Lynn. 2012. 32p. (J). 14.95 *(978-0-9860222-0-3(9))* Becklyns, LLC.

—The Ghost of Piper's Landing. Messer, Celeste M. 2004. 82-92p. 4.95 *(978-0-9702171-7-2(X))* AshleyAlan Enterprises.

—A Message from Teddy. Messer, Celeste M. 2004. 82-92p. 4.95 *(978-0-9702171-5-8(3))* AshleyAlan Enterprises.

—When Eagles Fly. Messer, Celeste M. 2004. 82-92p. 4.95 *(978-0-9702171-8-9(8))* AshleyAlan Enterprises.

Hoefler, Kate & Bean, Jonathan. Real Cowboys. Hoefler, Kate & Bean, Jonathan. 2016. (J). ***(978-0-544-14892-5(4))*** Harcourt.

Hofer, Ernst & Hofer, Nelly. The Wild Swans. 2003. (ENG.). 40p. (J). (gr. 2-5). 17.95 *(978-0-88776-615-2(3))* Tundra Bks. CAN. Dist: Random Hse., Inc.

Hofer, Nelly, jt. illus. see Hofer, Ernst.

Hoff, Syd. Danny & the Dinosaur. Hoff, Syd. 50th anniv. ed. 2008. (I Can Read Book 1 Ser.). (J). (ENG.). 64p. (gr. -1-3). pap. 3.99 *(978-0-06-444002-8(8));*Set. (gr. k-3). pap. 11.99 *(978-0-06-143083-1(8))* HarperCollins Pubs.

—The Littlest Leaguer. Hoff, Syd. 2008. (I Can Read Book 1 Ser.). (ENG.). 48p. (J). (gr. -1-3). pap. 3.99 *(978-0-06-053774-6(4))* HarperCollins Pubs.

Hoffbauer, Wyng, jt. illus. see Eakins, Bonny Mae.

Hoffman, Isobel. It's Not Easy Being a Pelican. Dabritz, Evelyn. 2012. 32p. (J). *(978-1-930401-87-7(6))* Central Coast Pr.

Hoffman, Kimberly. Tito, the Firefighter/Tito, el Bombero. Hoppey, Tim. de la Vega, Eida, tr. 2005. Tr. of Tito, el Bombero. (SPA & ENG.). 32p. (J). (gr. -1-3). 16.95 *(978-0-9724973-3-6(1),* 626999, Raven Tree Pr.,Csi) Continental Sales, Inc.

Hoffman, Mary Hramiec. Lolek the Boy Who Became Pope John Paul II. Hoffman, Mary Hramiec. 2008. 56p. (J). 18.95 *(978-0-9746901-1-7(2))* Hramiec Hoffman Publishing.

Hoffman, Paul G. Spooky Texas: Tales of Hauntings, Strange Happenings, & Other Local Lore. Schlosser, S. E. 2008. (Spooky Ser.). (ENG.). 200p. pap. 14.95 *(978-0-7627-4853-2(2))* Globe Pequot Pr., The.

—Tales with a Texas Twist: Original Stories & Enduring Folklore from the Lone Star State. Ingham, Donna. 2005. (ENG.). 160p. (gr. -1-7). per. 12.95 *(978-0-7627-3899-1(5))* Globe Pequot Pr., The.

Hoffman, Rosekrans. Pignic: An Alphabet Book in Rhyme. Miranda, Anne. 2004. (ENG.). 32p. (J). (gr. -1-1). pap. 8.95 *(978-1-59078-328-3(X))* Boyds Mills Pr.

Hoffman, Sanford. Joke & Riddle Bonanza. Pellowski, Michael J. 2012. (ENG.). 96p. (J). (gr. 1-4). pap. 4.95 *(978-1-4027-8837-6(1))* Sterling Publishing Co., Inc.

—Jokes. Rosenbloom, Joseph. 2007. (Little Giant Bks.). (ENG.). 360p. (J). (gr. 2-5). pap. 6.95 *(978-1-4027-4973-5(2))* Sterling Publishing Co., Inc.

—Knock-Knocks. Keller, Charles. 2007. (Little Giant Bks.). (ENG.). 360p. (J). (gr. 2-5). pap. 6.95 *(978-1-4027-4970-4(8))* Sterling Publishing Co., Inc.

—Riddles. Rosenbloom, Joseph. 2007. (Little Giant Bks.). (ENG.). 352p. (J). (gr. 2-5). pap. 6.95 *(978-1-4027-4972-8(4))* Sterling Publishing Co., Inc.

—Take My Picture. Linn, Margot. 2005. (I'm Going to Read(r) Ser.: Level 2). (ENG.). 28p. (J). (gr. -1-1). pap. 3.95 *(978-1-4027-2096-3(3))* Sterling Publishing Co., Inc.

—Wackiest Jokes in the World. Pellowski, Michael J. 2012. (ENG.). 96p. (J). (gr. 1-4). pap. 4.95 *(978-1-4027-8835-2(5))* Sterling Publishing Co., Inc.

Hoffman, Steve. 'Twas the Night Before Christ. Roberts, Tom. 2003rd ed. 2004. (J). per. *(978-0-9723868-1-4(5))* T & T Roberts Publishing.

Hoffmann, Eric. DNA: The Master Molecule of Life, 1 vol. Stille, Darlene R. 2006. (Exploring Science: Life Science Ser.). (ENG.). 48p. (gr. 6-7). 28.65 *(978-0-7565-1617-6(X));* per. 8.29 *(978-0-7565-1762-5(1))* Compass Point Bks. (Exploring Science).

Hoffmann, Eric & Hossain, Farhana. Human Body Systems: Maintaining the Body's Functions, 1 vol. Cooper, Sharon Katz & Compass Point Books Staff. 2007. (Exploring Science: Life Science Ser.). (ENG.). 48p. (gr. 6-7). 28.65 *(978-0-7565-1958-2(6),* Exploring Science) Compass Point Bks.

Hoffmann, Erich. Great Shakes: The Science of Earthquakes, 1 vol. Stille, Darlene R. 2008. (Headline Science Ser.). (ENG.). 48p. (gr. 7-8). lib. bdg. 28.65 *(978-0-7565-3947-4(1),* Headline Science) Compass Point Bks.

Hoffmann, Heinrich. Struwwelpeter: Or Pretty Stories & Funny Pictures. Hoffmann, Heinrich. 2010. (ENG.). 48p. (J). (gr. 2-7). 14.99 *(978-1-84365-153-6(X),* Pavilion Children's Books) Pavilion Bks. GBR. Dist: Independent Pubs. Group.

Hoffmann, Omer. Leopardpox! Sadie Is Having the Funniest Sick Day Ever! Landau, Orna. 2015. (ENG.). 40p. (J). (gr. -1-3). 16.99 *(978-0-544-29001-3(1))* Houghton Mifflin Harcourt Publishing Co.

H

Hoffmire, A. B. The Ogre Bully. Hoffmire, A. B., as told by. 2007. (Story Cove Ser.). (ENG.). 32p. (J). (gr. -1-3). 3.95 *(978-0-87483-803-9(7))* August Hse. Pubs., Inc.

Hoffmire, Baird. Anansi & the Pot of Beans. Norfolk, Bobby & Norfolk, Sherry. 2006. (Story Cove Ser.). (ENG.). 32p. (J). (gr. -1-3). 4.95 *(978-0-87483-811-4(8))* August Hse. Pubs., Inc.

—Anansi & the Sky Kingdom. Norfolk, Bobby & Norfolk, Sherry. 2008. (Story Cove Ser.). (ENG.). 32p. (J). (gr. -1-3). pap. 3.95 *(978-0-87483-881-7(9))* August Hse. Pubs., Inc.

—Anansi & the Tug O' War. 2007. (Story Cove Ser.). (ENG.). 32p. (J). (gr. -1-3). pap. 4.95 *(978-0-87483-825-1(8))* August Hse. Pubs., Inc.

—Anansi & Turtle Go to Dinner. Norfolk, Bobby & Norfolk, Sherry. 2007. (Story Cove Ser.). (ENG.). 32p. (J). (gr. -1-3). pap. 3.95 *(978-0-87483-856-5(8))* August Hse. Pubs., Inc.

—Anansi Goes to Lunch. Norfolk, Bobby & Norfolk, Sherry. 2007. (Story Cove Ser.). (ENG.). 32p. (J). (gr. -1-3). pap. 3.95 *(978-0-87483-852-7(5))* August Hse. Pubs., Inc.

—The Archer & the Sun: A Tale from China. Cleveland, Rob. 2007. (Story Cove Ser.). (ENG.). 24p. (J). (gr. -1-3). pap. 3.95 *(978-0-87483-878-7(9))* August Hse. Pubs., Inc.

—The Bear, the Bat & the Dove: Three Stories from Aesop. Cleveland, Rob. 2006. (Story Cove Ser.). (ENG.). 32p. (J). (gr. -1-3). pap. 3.95 *(978-0-87483-810-7(X))* August Hse. Pubs., Inc.

—The Big Wide-Mouth Frog. 2009. (J). pap. *(978-0-87483-890-9(8),* August House Story Cove) August Hse. Pubs., Inc.

—Billy Brown & the Belly Button Beastie. Norfolk, Bobby & Norfolk, Sherry. 2007. (ENG.). 32p. (J). (gr. -1-3). 16.95 *(978-0-87483-831-2(2))* August Hse. Pubs., Inc.

—The Clever Monkey: A Folktale from West Africa. Cleveland, Rob. 2006. (Story Cove Ser.). (ENG.). 32p. (J). (gr. -1-3). pap. 4.95 *(978-0-87483-801-5(0))* August Hse. Pubs., Inc.

—How Tiger Got His Stripes: A Folktale from Vietnam. 2006. (Story Cove Ser.). (ENG.). 32p. (J). (gr. -1-3). pap. 4.95 *(978-0-87483-799-5(5))* August Hse. Pubs., Inc.

—The Magic Apple: A Middle Eastern Folktale. Cleveland, Rob. 2006. (Story Cove Ser.). (ENG.). 32p. (J). (gr. -1-3). pap. 4.95 *(978-0-87483-800-8(2))* August Hse. Pubs., Inc.

—Rooster's Night Out. Weiss, Mitch & Hamilton, Martha. 2007. (Story Cove Ser.). (ENG.). 32p. (J). (gr. -1-3). pap. 3.95 *(978-0-87483-826-8(6))* August Hse. Pubs., Inc.

Hofher, Cathy. Take a Deep Breath: Little Lessons from Flowers for a Happier World. Stoutland, Allison. l.t. ed. 2003. 32p. 14.95 *(978-0-9670941-2-0(7))* Inch By Inch Pubns., LLC.

—What Day Is Today? Parker, Sandy. l.t. ed. 2003. 24p. (gr. k-1). 13.95 *(978-0-9643462-3-9(0),* 10, Just Think Bks.) Canary Connect Pubns.

—What Month Is It? Parker, Sandy. l.t. ed. 2004. 32p. 15.95 *(978-0-9643462-5-3(7),* Just Think Bks.) Canary Connect Pubns.

Hofmann, Ginnie. Who Wants an Old Teddy Bear?, 5 vols. Hofmann, Ginnie. 2003. 32p. (J). pap. 5.95 *(978-1-932485-00-4(7))* Reverie Publishing Co.

Hofmann, Ginnie, jt. illus. see Bart, Kathleen.

Hofmann-Maniyar, Ariane. Ice in the Jungle. 2015. (Child's Play Library). (ENG.). 32p. (J). pap. ***(978-1-84643-730-4(X))*** Child's Play International Ltd.

Hofner, Cathy. What Can I Do Today? To Make This World a Happier Place. Stoutland, Allison. 2005. 32p. (J). (gr. -1-3). 16.95 *(978-0-9670941-3-7(5))* Inch By Inch Pubns., LLC.

Hogan, Eric. Tea Parties with Grandm. McNair, Barbara. 2009. 48p. pap. 24.95 *(978-1-60749-617-5(8))* America Star Bks.

Hogan, Jamie. Here Come the Humpbacks! Sayre, April Pulley. 2013. (ENG.). 40p. (J). (gr. -1-3). pap. 7.95 *(978-1-58089-406-7(2))*; lib. bdg. 17.95 *(978-1-58089-405-0(4))* Charlesbridge Publishing, Inc.

—Ice Harbor Mittens. Hansen, Robin. ed. 2010. (ENG.). 32p. (J). (gr. -1-3). 16.95 *(978-0-89272-905-0(8))* Down East Bks.

—John Muir Wrestles a Waterfall. Danneberg, Julie. 2015. (ENG.). 32p. (J). (gr. -1-3). lib. bdg. 16.95 *(978-1-58089-586-6(7))* Charlesbridge Publishing, Inc.

—Nest, Nook & Cranny. Blackaby, Susan. 2010. (ENG.). 60p. (J). (gr. 4-7). 15.95 *(978-1-58089-350-3(3))* Charlesbridge Publishing, Inc.

—Rickshaw Girl. Perkins, Mitali. (ENG.). 96p. (J). (gr. 2-5). 2008. pap. 6.95 *(978-1-58089-309-1(0))*; 2007. 14.95 *(978-1-58089-308-4(2))* Charlesbridge Publishing, Inc.

—Tiger Boy. Perkins, Mitali. 2015. (ENG.). 144p. (J). (gr. 2-5). lib. bdg. 14.95 *(978-1-58089-660-3(X))* Charlesbridge Publishing, Inc.

—A Warmer World. Arnold, Caroline. 2012. (ENG.). 32p. (J). (gr. 2-5). pap. 7.95 *(978-1-58089-267-4(1))* Charlesbridge Publishing, Inc.

Hogan, Jamie. Seven Days of Daisy, 1 vol. Hogan, Jamie. ed. 2011. (ENG.). 32p. (J). (gr. -1-3). 14.95 *(978-0-89272-919-7(8))* Down East Bks.

Hogan, Sophie, photos by. Where's Mom's Hair? A Family's Journey Through Cancer, 1 vol. Watters, Debbie et al. 2005. (ENG., 32p. (J). (gr. -1-5). per. 14.95 *(978-1-896764-94-8(0))* Second Story Pr. CAN. Dist: Orca Bk. Pubs. USA.

Hogan, Tom, jt. illus. see Hogan, Wes.

Hogan, Wes & Hogan, Tom. Balloons. Hogan, Wes. 2008. 24p. pap. 13.99 *(978-1-4389-0206-7(9))* AuthorHouse.

Hoggatt, Pamla. You Did It All for Me. Hoggatt, Pamla. l.t. ed. 2011. (ENG.). 32p. pap. 10.95 *(978-1-4610-1677-9(0))* CreateSpace Independent Publishing Platform.

Hoglund, Anna. Can You Whistle, Johanna? A Boy's Search for a Grandfather. Stark, Ulf. Segerberg, Ebba, tr. from SWE. 2004. 48p. (gr. 2-5). 16.95 *(978-1-57143-057-1(1))* RDR Bks.

Hogner, Nils. Our American Horse. Hogner, Dorothy Childs. 2015. (ENG.). 128p. (J). (gr. 3-12). pap. 5.99 *(978-0-486-78441-0(X))* Dover Pubns., Inc.

Hogrogian, Nonny. Come Back, Moon. Kherdian, David. 2013. (ENG.). 32p. (J). (gr. -1-3). pap. 16.99 *(978-1-4424-5887-1(9),* Beach Lane Bks.) Beach Lane Bks.

Hogrogian, Nonny. One Fine Day. Hogrogian, Nonny. 2nd ed. 2005. (Stories to Go! Ser.). (ENG.). 32p. (J). 4.99 *(978-1-4169-0312-3(7),* Simon & Schuster/Paula Wiseman Bks.) Simon & Schuster/Paula Wiseman Bks.

Hohn, David. Addie, the Playful Pekingese. Howell, Trisha Adelena. 2005. 128p. (YA). pap. 11.95 *(978-1-931210-27-0(6))* Howell Canyon Pr.

—A Gaggle of Geese & a Clutter of Cats. Mackall, Dandi Daley. 2007. (Dandilion Rhymes Ser.). (ENG.). 40p. (J). (gr. -1-3). 9.99 *(978-1-4000-7204-0(2),* WaterBrook Pr.) Doubleday Religious Publishing Group, The.

—Talia & the Great Sapphire of Knowledge. Howell, Trisha Adelena. 2005. 128p. (J). pap. 11.95 *(978-1-931210-11-9(X))* Howell Canyon Pr.

Hohn, David & Clark, David. Zachary Zormer - Shape Transformer. Reisberg, Joanne. 2006. (Math Adventures Ser.). (ENG.). 32p. (J). (gr. 2-5). per. 7.95 *(978-1-57091-876-6(7))* Charlesbridge Publishing, Inc.

Hohn, Tracy. Heroes Need Practice, Too! Durden, Angela K. 2006. (J). 11.95 *(978-0-9701356-1-2(0))* WRITER for HIRE!.

—Painless Junior: Grammar. McClamon, Marciann. Oliverio, Donna Christina, ed. 2007. (Painless Junior Ser.). (ENG.). 168p. (gr. 3-7). per. 8.99 *(978-0-7641-3561-3(9))* Barron's Educational Series, Inc.

Hohnstadt, Cedric. Big Shark's Valentine Surprise. Metzger, Steve. 2007. (J). pap. *(978-0-439-92251-7(8))* Scholastic, Inc.

—Day of the Field Trip Zombies, 1 vol. Nickel, Scott. 2007. (School Zombies Ser.). (ENG.). 40p. (gr. 1-3). lib. bdg. 22.65 *(978-1-59889-834-7(5))*; per. 5.95 *(978-1-59889-890-3(6),* 1271403) Stone Arch Bks. (Graphic Sparks).

—The Purple Cow. Harris, Brooke. 2009. (Reader's Theater Nursery Rhymes & Songs Set B Ser.). 48p. (J). pap. *(978-1-60859-166-4(2))* Benchmark Education Co.

—Scratch & Sniff. Comfort, Ray. 2007. (Creation for Kids Ser.). 24p. (gr. -1-5). 14.99 *(978-0-88270-328-2(5))* Bridge-Logos Foundation.

—What Your Nose Shows. Comfort, Ray. 2007. (Creation for Kids Ser.). 24p. (gr. -1-5). bds. 14.99 *(978-0-88270-326-8(9))* Bridge-Logos Foundation.

Holt, Richard. Katie Did It. McDaniel, Becky Bring. rev. ed. 2003. (Rookie Reader Español Ser.). (ENG.). (J). (gr. k-2). pap. 4.95 *(978-0-516-27832-2(0),* Children's Pr.) Scholastic Library Publishing.

—Knock, Knock!, 6 pack. Holden, Pam. 2009. (Red Rocket Readers Ser.). 16p. (gr. 2-4). pap. *(978-1-877363-60-3(X),* Red Rocket Readers) Flying Start Bks.

—Naughty Goldilocks, 6 pack. Holden, Pam. 2009. (Red Rocket Readers Ser.). 16p. (gr. -1-2). pap. *(978-1-877363-08-5(1),* Red Rocket Readers) Flying Start Bks.

—Saturday Morning Soccer. Smith, Annette. 2009. 16p. pap. 10.67 *(978-1-4190-5503-4(8))* Rigby Education.

—The Surprise Visitor, 6 pack. Holden, Pam. 2009. (Red Rocket Readers Ser.). 16p. (gr. 2-5). pap. *(978-1-877363-85-6(5))* Flying Start Bks.

Hokanson, Lars, jt. illus. see Hokanson, Lois.

Hokanson, Lois & Hokanson, Lars. Remember Not to Forget: A Memory of the Holocaust. Finkelstein, Norman H. 2004. (ENG.). 32p. pap. 9.95 *(978-0-8276-0770-5(9))* Jewish Pubn. Society.

Hoke, Jason. Sam Loses His Sneaker. Dara Cicciarelli. 2011. 20p. pap. 24.95 *(978-1-4560-9178-1(6))* America Star Bks.

Hoke, Jeenhyun. My Lemonade Stand Can't Stand Me. Thomas, Mark Lawton. 114p. 2013. pap. 9.99 *(978-1-935711-23-0(7))*; 2012. (ENG.). (J). pap. 9.99 *(978-1-935711-22-3(9))* Peak City Publishing, LLC.

Hokie. The Life & Adventures of Santa Claus (Yesterday's Classics) Houghton, Amelia C. 2006. (J). per. 8.95 *(978-1-59915-191-5(X))* Yesterday's Classics.

Holbert, Raymond. The Barber's Cutting Edge. Battle-Lavert, Gwendolyn. 2004. (ENG.). 32p. (J). pap. 7.95 *(978-0-89239-196-7(0))* Lee & Low Bks., Inc.

Holcomb, Michele. What Would You Be? MacMillan, Lesley. 2006. 21p. (J). (gr. -1-3). per. 12.99 *(978-1-59879-228-7(8))* Lifevest Publishing, Inc.

Holcomb, Nicholas. One Bright Monster. Sisler, Stephanie. 2012. 36p. pap. 12.95 *(978-1-61493-124-9(0))* Peppertree Pr., The.

Holcomb, Sue A. Tex R Masaur: Down in the Dump. Holcomb, Sue A. Holcomb, J. Paul. (Tex R Masaur, Dinodillo Bks.). 32p. (Orig.). (J). (gr. k-3). pap. 3.95 *(978-0-9636122-2-9(0))* Post Oak Hill.

Holcroft, John. The Story of Flight: Panorama Pops. Candlewick Press, Candlewick. 2015. (ENG.). 30p. (J). (gr. k-4). 8.99 *(978-0-7636-7700-8(0))* Candlewick Pr.

Holcroft, John. Space Exploration: Panorama Pops. Holcroft, John. Candlewick Press Staff. 2015. (ENG.). 30p. (J). (gr. k-4). 8.99 *(978-0-7636-7699-5(3))* Candlewick Pr.

Holdcroft, Tina. Aztec. Scandiffio, Laura. 2009. (Kids at the Crossroads Ser.). (ENG.). 80p. (J). (gr. 4-6). pap. 14.95 *(978-1-55451-176-1(3),* 9781554511761) Annick Pr., Ltd. CAN. Dist: Firefly Bks., Ltd.

—What the Snakes Wrote. Hutchins, Hazel. 2013. (ENG.). 32p. (J). (gr. k-3). 21.95 *(978-1-55451-473-1(8),* 9781554514731); pap. 9.95 *(978-1-55451-472-4(X),* 9781554514724) Annick Pr., Ltd. CAN. Dist: Firefly Bks., Ltd.

Holdcroft, Tina. Hidden Depths: Amazing Underwater Discoveries. Holdcroft, Tina. 2004. (Hidden! Ser.). (ENG.). 32p. (J). (gr. 1-6). 19.95 *(978-1-55037-863-4(5),* 9781550378634) Annick Pr., Ltd. CAN. Dist: Firefly Bks., Ltd.

—Hidden Treasures: Amazing Stories of Discovery. Holdcroft, Tina. 2003. (Hidden! Ser.). (ENG.). 32p. (J). (gr. 2-5). pap. 6.95 *(978-1-55037-802-3(3),* 9781550378023) Annick Pr., Ltd. CAN. Dist: Firefly Bks., Ltd.

Holdcroft, Tina, jt. illus. see Mantha, John.

Holdeen, Bonnie, jt. illus. see Boynton, Jeannette.

Holden, Anthony. The Shivering. Bondor-Stone, Annabeth & White, Connor. 2016. (Shivers! Ser.: 2). 208p. (J). (gr. 3-7). 12.99 ***(978-0-06-231389-8(4))*** HarperCollins Pubs.

Holden, Anthony. Shivers! - The Pirate Who's Afraid of Everything. Bondor-Stone, Annabeth & White, Connor. 2015. (Shivers! Ser.: 1). (ENG.). 192p. (J). (gr. 3-7). 12.99 *(978-0-06-231387-4(8))* HarperCollins Pubs.

Holden, Chanler. On the Flippy Side. Mese, John R. & Kelsey, Dawn M. 2009. 30p. (J). 10.95 *(978-0-9725853-1-6(1))* Mosscovered Gumbo Barn.

Holder, Jimmy. Avast, Ye Dog Thief! Higgins, Nadia. 2008. (Barnacle Barb & Her Pirate Crew Ser.). 32p. (gr. -1-3). 28.50 *(978-1-60270-089-5(3),* Looking Glass Library) ABDO Publishing Co.

—Aye, My Eye! Higgins, Nadia. 2008. (Barnacle Barb & Her Pirate Crew Ser.). 32p. (gr. -1-3). 28.50 *(978-1-60270-090-1(7),* Looking Glass Library) ABDO Publishing Co.

—The Ball Hogs, No. 1. Wallace, Rich. 2011. (Kickers Ser.: Bk. 1). (ENG.). 128p. (J). (gr. 1-4). 5.99 *(978-0-375-85092-9(9),* Yearling) Random Hse. Children's Bks.

—Benched. Wallace, Rich. 2010. (Kickers Ser.: Bk. 3). (ENG.). 128p. (J). (gr. 1-4). 12.99 *(978-0-375-85756-0(7))* Knopf, Alfred A. Inc.

—Blimey, That's Slimy! Higgins, Nadia. 2008. (Barnacle Barb & Her Pirate Crew Ser.). 32p. (gr. -1-3). 28.50 *(978-1-60270-091-8(5),* Looking Glass Library) ABDO Publishing Co.

—Break a Sea Leg, Shrimp-Breath! Higgins, Nadia. 2008. (Barnacle Barb & Her Pirate Crew Ser.). 32p. (gr. -1-3). 28.50 *(978-1-60270-092-5(3),* Looking Glass Library) ABDO Publishing Co.

—Fake Out. Wallace, Rich. 2011. (Kickers Ser.: Bk. 2). (ENG.). 128p. (J). (gr. 1-4). 5.99 *(978-0-375-85093-6(7),* Yearling) Random Hse. Children's Bks.

—Game-Day Jitters. Wallace, Rich. 2012. (Kickers Ser.). (ENG.). 128p. (J). (gr. 2-5). 5.99 *(978-0-375-85095-0(3),* Yearling) Random Hse. Children's Bks.

—Isle Be Seeing You. Beech, Sandy. 2005. (Castaways Ser.: 3). (ENG.). 192p. (J). (gr. 3-7). mass mkt. 9.99 *(978-0-689-87598-4(3),* Simon & Schuster/Paula Wiseman Bks.) Simon & Schuster/Paula Wiseman Bks.

—Kickers #3: Benched. Wallace, Rich. 2011. (Kickers Ser.). (ENG.). 128p. (J). (gr. 1-4). 5.99 *(978-0-375-85094-3(5),* Yearling) Random Hse. Children's Bks.

—Pegleg Gets Stumped. Higgins, Nadia. 2008. (Barnacle Barb & Her Pirate Crew Ser.). 32p. (gr. -1-3). 28.50 *(978-1-60270-093-2(1),* Looking Glass Library) ABDO Publishing Co.

—Pig Pigger Piggest. Walton, Rick. ed. 2003. (ENG.). 32p. (J). (gr. 1). reprint ed. pap. 6.99 *(978-1-58685-318-1(X))* Gibbs Smith, Publisher.

—Walk the Plank, Plankton. Higgins, Nadia. 2008. (Barnacle Barb & Her Pirate Crew Ser.). 32p. (gr. -1-3). 28.50 *(978-1-60270-094-9(X),* Looking Glass Library) ABDO Publishing Co.

—Worst Class Trip Ever. Beech, Sandy. 2005. (Castaways Ser.: 1). (ENG.). 176p. (J). (gr. 3-7). pap. 9.99 *(978-0-689-87596-0(7),* Simon & Schuster/Paula Wiseman Bks.) Simon & Schuster/Paula Wiseman Bks.

Holder, John, jt. illus. see Fricker, Steve.

Holderness, Grizelda. The Story of Queen Esther. Koralek, Jenny. 2009. 28p. (J). (gr. -1-3). 17.50 *(978-0-8028-5348-6(X),* Eerdmans Bks For Young Readers) Eerdmans, William B. Publishing Co.

Holdredge, Jon, jt. illus. see Calafiore, Jim.

Holdren, Maria K. Pack Your Bags.... Go U. S. A. Weaver, Kimberley & Murphy, Allyson. 2005. (J). 15.99 *(978-0-9767351-0-6(5))* Sorella Bks.

Holdsworth, Henry, photos by. Moose Family Close Up. Krauskopf, Sharma. 2007. 28p. per. *(978-0-9543367-4-5(7))* Scottish Radiance Pubns.

Hole, Stian. Garmann's Secret. Hole, Stian. 2012. (J). 17.00 *(978-0-8028-5400-1(1),* Eerdmans Bks For Young Readers) Eerdmans, William B. Publishing Co.

—Garmann's Summer. Hole, Stian. Bartlett, Don, tr. from NOR. 2008. 42p. (J). (gr. k-3). 17.50 *(978-0-8028-5339-4(0))* Eerdmans, William B. Publishing Co.

Holgate, Doug. Evil Twins. Savage, J. Scott. (Case File 13 Ser.: No. 3). (ENG.). (J). (gr. 3-7). 2015. 288p. pap. 6.99 *(978-0-06-213338-0(1))*; 2014. 272p. 14.99 *(978-0-06-213337-3(3))* HarperCollins Pubs.

—Making the Team. Savage, J. Scott. (Case File 13 Ser.: No. 2). (ENG.). (J). (gr. 3-7). 2015. 288p. pap. 6.99 *(978-0-06-213335-9(7))*; 2013. 272p. 14.99 *(978-0-06-213331-1(4))* HarperCollins Pubs.

—Planet Tad. Carvell, Tim. (Planet Tad Ser.: 1). 256p. (J). (gr. 3-7). 2014. (ENG.). pap. 6.99 *(978-0-06-193438-4(0))*; 2012. (ENG.). 12.99 *(978-0-06-193436-0(4))*; 2012. lib. bdg. 14.89 *(978-0-06-193437-7(2))* HarperCollins Pubs.

—Super-Dragon, 0 vols. Kroll, Steven. 2011. (ENG.). 32p. (J). (gr. -1-2). 16.99 *(978-0-7614-5819-7(0),* 9780761458197, Amazon Children's Publishing) Amazon Publishing.

—Zombie Kid. Savage, J. Scott. (Case File 13 Ser.: No. 1). (ENG.). (J). (gr. 3-7). 2013. 304p. pap. 6.99 *(978-0-06-213327-4(6))*; 2012. 288p. 14.99 *(978-0-06-213325-0(X))* HarperCollins Pubs.

Holgate, Douglas. The Adventures of Commander Zack Proton & the Red Giant. Anderson, Brian. 2006. (Adventures of Commander Zack Proton Ser.: 1). (ENG.). 128p. (J). (gr. 2-5). pap. 5.99 *(978-1-4169-1364-1(5),* Simon & Schuster/Paula Wiseman Bks.) Simon & Schuster/Paula Wiseman Bks.

—The Adventures of Commander Zack Proton & the Warlords of Nibblecheese. Anderson, Brian. 2006. (Adventures of Commander Zack Proton Ser.: 2). (ENG.). 112p. (J). (gr. 2-5). pap. 4.99 *(978-1-4169-1365-8(3),* Simon & Schuster/Paula Wiseman Bks.) Simon & Schuster/Paula Wiseman Bks.

—The Adventures of Commander Zack Proton & the Wrong Planet. Anderson, Brian. 2007. (Adventures of Commander Zack Proton Ser.: 3). (ENG.). 128p. (J). (gr. 2-5). pap. 4.99 *(978-1-4169-1366-5(1),* Simon & Schuster/Paula Wiseman Bks.) Simon & Schuster/Paula Wiseman Bks.

—Cheesie Mack Is Not Exactly Famous. Cotler, Steve. 2014. (Cheesie Mack Ser.). (ENG.). 256p. (J). (gr. 3-7). 15.99 *(978-0-385-36984-8(0),* Random Hse. Bks. for Young Readers) Random Hse. Children's Bks.

—Cheesie Mack Is Running Like Crazy! Cotler, Steve. (Cheesie Mack Ser.). (ENG.). 256p. (J). (gr. 3-7). 2014. pap. 6.99 *(978-0-307-97716-8(1))*; 2013. 15.99 *(978-0-307-97713-7(7))* Random Hse., Inc.

—Cheesie Mack Is Sort of Freaked Out. Cotler, Steve. 2014. (Cheesie Mack Ser.). (ENG.). 256p. (J). (gr. 3-7). 15.99 *(978-0-385-36988-6(3),* Random Hse. Bks. for Young Readers) Random Hse. Children's Bks.

—Coldfinger, 1 vol. Lemke, Donald B. 2009. (Zinc Alloy Ser.). (ENG.). 40p. (gr. 1-3). lib. bdg. 22.65 *(978-1-4342-1586-4(5),* Graphic Sparks) Stone Arch Bks.

—Coldfinger: Zinc Alloy. Lemke, Donald. 2010. (Graphic Sparks Ser.). (ENG.). 40p. (gr. 1-3). pap. 5.95 *(978-1-4342-2314-2(0),* Graphic Sparks) Stone Arch Bks.

—Laff-O-Tronic Joke Books. Dahl, Michael & Collins, Daryll. 2013. (Laff-O-Tronic Joke Books! Ser.). (ENG.). 96p. (gr. k-3). 95.96 *(978-1-4342-6325-4(8))* Stone Arch Bks.

—Revealed!, 1 vol. Lemke, Donald. 2008. (Zinc Alloy Ser.). (ENG.). 40p. (gr. 1-3). 22.65 *(978-1-4342-0763-0(3),* Graphic Sparks) Stone Arch Bks.

—Revealed! Zinc Alloy, 1 vol. Lemke, Donald. 2008. (Graphic Sparks Ser.). (ENG.). 40p. (gr. 1-3). pap. 5.95 *(978-1-4342-0859-0(1),* Graphic Sparks) Stone Arch Bks.

—School Shake-Up: Hidden Picture Puzzles, 1 vol. Kalz, Jill. 2012. (Seek It Out Ser.). (ENG.). 32p. (gr. 1-2). 9.95 *(978-1-4048-7726-9(6))*; lib. bdg. 25.99 *(978-1-4048-7496-1(8))* Picture Window Bks.

—Spokes on the Water, 1 vol. Lemke, Donald B. 2011. (Bike Rider Ser.). (ENG.). 40p. (gr. 1-3). lib. bdg. 22.65 *(978-1-4342-2537-5(2),* Graphic Sparks) Stone Arch Bks.

—Super Zero, 1 vol. Lemke, Donald. 2008. (Zinc Alloy Ser.). (ENG.). 40p. (gr. 1-3). 22.65 *(978-1-4342-0762-3(5))*; pap. 5.95 *(978-1-4342-0858-3(3))* Stone Arch Bks. (Graphic Sparks).

—There's a Worm on My Eyeball: The Alien Zoo of Germs, Worms & Lurgies That Could Be Living Inside You. Taor, Adam. 2009. (ENG.). 192p. (J). (gr. 4-7). pap. 7.99 *(978-1-74166-213-9(3))* Random Hse. Australia AUS. Dist: Independent Pubs. Group.

—Wheelies of Justice, 1 vol. Lemke, Donald B. 2010. (Bike Rider Ser.). (ENG.). 40p. (gr. 1-3). lib. bdg. 22.65 *(978-1-4342-1892-6(9),* Graphic Sparks) Stone Arch Bks.

—Zinc Alloy vs Frankenstein, 1 vol. Lemke, Donald B. (Graphic Sparks Ser.). (ENG.). 40p. (gr. 1-3). 2010. pap. 5.95 *(978-1-4342-1391-4(9))*; 2009. lib. bdg. 22.65 *(978-1-4342-1188-0(6))* Stone Arch Bks. (Graphic Sparks).

Holgate, Douglas & Collins, Daryll. Laff-O-Tronic Animal Jokes! Dahl, Michael. 2013. (Laff-O-Tronic Joke Books! Ser.). (ENG.). 96p. (gr. k-3). pap. 29.70 *(978-1-4342-6238-7(3))* Stone Arch Bks.

—Laff-O-Tronic School Jokes! Dahl, Michael. 2013. (Laff-O-Tronic Joke Books! Ser.). (ENG.). 96p. (gr. k-3). pap. 29.70 *(978-1-4342-6240-0(5))* Stone Arch Bks.

—Laff-O-Tronic Sports Jokes! Dahl, Michael. 2013. (Laff-O-Tronic Joke Books! Ser.). (ENG.). 96p. (gr. k-3). pap. 29.70 *(978-1-4342-6241-7(3))* Stone Arch Bks.

Holgate, Douglas, jt. illus. see Collins, Daryll.

Holgren, Anna C. Where's My Face? A Simon-the-Cat Tale. Collins, C. B. 2008. 36p. pap. 24.95 *(978-1-60441-009-9(4))* America Star Bks.

Holiday, J. D. Janoose the Goose. Holiday, J. D. 2008. 24p. (J). 10.00 *(978-0-9818614-0-1(7))* Bk. Garden Publishing.

Holifield, Vicky. Hiking the Benton MacKaye Trail, 1 vol. Homan, Tim. 2004. (ENG.). 272p. pap. 15.95 *(978-1-56145-311-5(0))* Peachtree Pubs.

Holinaty, Josh. It's Catching: The Infectious World of Germs & Microbes. Gardy, Jennifer. 2014. (ENG.). 64p. (J). (gr. 3-7). 18.95 *(978-1-77147-001-8(1))*; pap. 13.95 *(978-1-77147-053-7(4))* Owlkids Bks. Inc. CAN. (Owlkids). Dist: Perseus-PGW.

—You Just Can't Help It! Your Guide to the Wild & Wacky World of Human Behavior. Szpirglas, Jeff. 2011. (ENG.). 64p. (J). (gr. 4-6). pap. 10.95 *(978-1-926818-08-5(3),* Maple Tree Pr.) Owlkids Bks. Inc. CAN. Dist: Perseus-PGW.

Holladay, Reggie. The Little Red Hen (La Gallinita Roja), Grades PK - 3. Ottolenghi, Carol. 2007. (Keepsake Stories Ser.). (ENG & SPA.). 32p. (gr. -1-3). pap. 3.99 *(978-0-7696-5417-1(7))* Carson-Dellosa Publishing, LLC.

Holland, Gay W. Dream Catcher. Kavasch, E. Barrie. 2003. (Books for Young Learners). (ENG.). 16p. (J). 5.75 net. *(978-1-57274-257-4(7),* 2733, Bks. for Young Learners) Owen, Richard C. Pubs., Inc.

—Hello, Squirrels! Scampering Through the Seasons. Glaser, Linda. 2006. (Linda Glaser's Classic Creatures Ser.). (ENG.). 32p. (gr. k-3). 22.60 *(978-0-7613-2887-2(4),* Millbrook Pr.) Lerner Publishing Group.

Holland, Joe. Monsoon Murder: Forensic Meteorology, 12 vols. McIntosh, Kenneth. 2007. (Crime Scene Club Ser.). 144p. (YA). (gr. 9-12). lib. bdg. 24.95 *(978-1-4222-0258-6(5))* Mason Crest.

Holland, Kathy. Sam Snake Says. Dunlap, Jim. 2008. 35p. pap. 24.95 *(978-1-60672-709-6(5))* America Star Bks.

Holland, Lisa Tomms. Baxter & the Sidewalk Alligator. Engram, Teta. 2009. 32p. pap. 12.99 *(978-1-4389-9367-6(6))* AuthorHouse.

Holland, Mary, photos by. The Beavers' Busy Year, 1 vol. Holland, Mary. 2014. (ENG., 32p. (J). (gr. -1-3). pap. 9.95 *(978-1-62855-213-3(1))* Arbordale Publishing.

—Milkweed Visitors. Holland, Mary. 2006. 32p. (J). per. 10.95 *(978-0-9657472-4-0(7))* Bas Relief, LLC.

Holland, Richard. Ali Baba & the Forty Thieves. Clynes, Kate et al. 2005. (ENG & BEN.). 32p. (J). pap. *(978-1-84444-402-1(3))*; pap. *(978-1-84444-411-3(2))*; pap. *(978-1-84444-414-4(7))*; pap. *(978-1-84444-415-1(5))*; pap. *(978-1-84444-424-3(4))* Mantra Lingua.
—Ali Baba & the Forty Thieves. Attard, Enebor. 32p. (J). 2005. pap. *(978-1-84444-526-4(7))*; 2004. (CHI & ENG.). bds. *(978-1-84444-530-1(5))* Mantra Lingua.
—Happy Harry's Cafe. Rosen, Michael. 2012. (ENG.). 32p. (J). (gr. -1-2). 16.99 *(978-0-7636-6239-4(9))* Candlewick Pr.
—Mary's Penny. Landman, Tanya. 2010. (ENG.). 40p. (J). (gr. k-3). 15.99 *(978-0-7636-4768-1(3))* Candlewick Pr.
—The Museum Book: A Guide to Strange & Wonderful Collections. Mark, Jan. (ENG.). 56p. (J). 2014. (gr. 2-5). 8.99 *(978-0-7636-7500-4(8))*; 2007. (gr. 3-7). 18.99 *(978-0-7636-3370-7(4))* Candlewick Pr.
Holland, Rick. Tales of the Rainbow Forest. Willis, McKenzie. 2012. 58p. pap. 14.00 *(978-0-615-73173-5(2))* McKenzie's Expressions.
Holland, Ruth. The Night of the Round Stable. Wrench, Peter. 2012. 174p. pap. *(978-1-908895-49-3(7))* FeedARead.com.
Hollander, Sarah. I Paint a Rainbow. Plummer, David & Archambault, John. 2007. (J). *(978-1-58669-228-5(3))*; *(978-1-58669-227-8(5))* Childcraft Education Corp.
—The Twelve Days of Christmas in Washington, D. C. Ransom, Candice. 2010. (Twelve Days of Christmas in America Ser.). (ENG.). 32p. (J). (gr. k). 12.95 *(978-1-4027-6394-6(8))* Sterling Publishing Co., Inc.
—Two Birds SAT upon a Stone. Archambault, John & Plummer, David. 2006. (J). pap. *(978-1-58669-187-5(2))* Childcraft Education Corp.
Holley, Vanessa. My Shoelaces Are Hard to Tie! Scholastic, Inc. Staff & Roberson, Karla. 2004. (Just for You Ser.). (ENG.). 32p. pap. 3.99 *(978-0-439-56869-2(2),* Teaching Resources) Scholastic, Inc.
Holliday, Holly. Ellie's Big Day. Keithley, Laura Lee. 2008. 40p. pap. 24.95 *(978-1-60672-474-3(6))* America Star Bks.
Holliday, Reggie. Test Prep with a Twist Grade 2, 3 vols., 2253. Jacks, Cyndie & Lewis, Dawn. Rous, Sheri, ed. 2003. 64p. pap. 9.99 *(978-1-57471-974-1(2))* Creative Teaching Pr., Inc.
Hollinger, Deanne. They Led the Way: 14 American Women. Johnston, Johanna. 2004. (ENG.). 128p. (J). (gr. 3-7). 5.99 *(978-0-14-240057-9(2))* Penguin Publishing Group.
Hollinger, Valerie Bunch. Gift/ Book Combo. O'Connor, Crystal Ball. 2005. (J). 25.00 *(978-0-9774038-0-6(7))* Monarch Pubs.
—Jake & the Migration of the Monarch. O'Connor, Crystal Ball. 2005. 32p. (J). 17.95 *(978-0-615-12659-3(6))* Monarch Pubs.
—Jake & the Migration of the Monarch with CD. O'Connor, Crystal Ball. 2005. (J). audio compact disk 18.95 *(978-0-9774038-3-7(1))* Monarch Pubs.
—Jake y la Migraci'on de la Monarca. O'Connor, Crystal Ball. Brenes-Sotela, Guillermo J. & Quave, Gloria Martinez, trs. from ENG. 2005. (SPA.). (J). 17.95 *(978-0-9774038-2-0(3))* Monarch Pubs.
Hollinrake, Chriss. Jasmin & the Nature Fairies. Apted, Violet. 2012. 16p. pap. 10.00 *(978-1-61897-806-6(3),* Strategic Bk. Publishing) Strategic Book Publishing & Rights Agency (SBPRA).
Hollis, Michael. You'll See, Little Tree. Trembley, Skip & Ochs, Susan A. 2003. (J). pap. 7.95 *(978-0-9643452-2-5(6))* Graphics North.
Hollis, Tyler. Do Snakes Wear Shoes? Gaddy, Kathi. 2011. (ENG.). 24p. pap. 10.99 *(978-1-4610-5444-3(3))* CreateSpace Independent Publishing Platform.
—Kevin & the Magic Skateboard. Tuttle, Brad. 2011. (ENG.). 30p. pap. 10.17 *(978-1-4609-5714-1(8))* CreateSpace Independent Publishing Platform.
Hollman, Jeremie, jt. photos by see Glastetter, KC.
Holly, Davison. Jack's Cap: More Short Vowel Stories. Sylvia, Davison. 2003. 96p. (gr. 1-18). spiral bd. 17.00 *(978-0-9726479-4-6(5))* Foundations for Learning, LLC.
—Noses & Roses: More Long Vowel Stories. Sylvia, Davison. 2003. 64p. (gr. 1-18). spiral bd. 12.00 *(978-0-9726479-5-3(3))* Foundations for Learning, LLC.
Holly, Julia. Mrs Winkler's Cure. Holly, Julia. 2010. 214p. pap. 19.99 *(978-1-883376-45-1(9))* Stellium Pr.
Holm, Jennifer L. & Holm, Matt. Bad Babysitter. Holm, Jennifer L. & Holm, Matt. 2015. (Babymouse Ser.: No. 19). (ENG.). 96p. (J). (gr. 2-5). pap. 6.99 *(978-0-307-93162-7(5),* Random Hse. Bks. for Young Readers) Random Hse. Children's Bks.
—Captain Disaster. Holm, Jennifer L. & Holm, Matt. 2012. (Squish Ser.: No. 4). (ENG.). 96p. (J). (gr. 2-5). pap. 6.99 *(978-0-375-84392-1(2))*; lib. bdg. 12.99 *(978-0-375-93786-6(2))* Random Hse. Children's Bks. (Random Hse. Bks. for Young Readers).
—Extreme Babymouse. Holm, Jennifer L. & Holm, Matt. 2013. (Babymouse Ser.: Bk. 17). (ENG.). 96p. (J). (gr. 2-5). pap. 6.99 *(978-0-307-93160-3(9))*; lib. bdg. 12.99 *(978-0-375-97096-2(7))* Random Hse. Children's Bks. (Random Hse. Bks. for Young Readers).
—The Power of the Parasite. Holm, Jennifer L. & Holm, Matt. 2012. (Squish Ser.: No. 3). (ENG.). 96p. (J). (gr. 2-5). pap. 6.99 *(978-0-375-84391-4(4))*; lib. bdg. 12.99 *(978-0-375-93785-9(4))* Random Hse. Children's Bks. (Random Hse. Bks. for Young Readers).
Holm, Jennifer L. & Holm, Matthew. Babymouse for President. Holm, Jennifer L. & Holm, Matthew. 2012. (Babymouse Ser.: No. 16). (ENG.). 96p. (J). (gr. 2-5). 12.99 *(978-0-375-96780-1(6))*; pap. 6.99 *(978-0-375-86780-4(5))* Random Hse., Inc.
—Brave New Pond. Holm, Jennifer L. & Holm, Matthew. 2011. (Squish Ser.: No. 2). (ENG.). 96p. (J). (gr. 3-7). 12.99 *(978-0-375-93784-2(6))*; pap. 6.99 *(978-0-375-84390-7(6))* Random Hse. Children's Bks. (Random Hse. Bks. for Young Readers).
—Burns Rubber. Holm, Jennifer L. & Holm, Matthew. 2010. (Babymouse Ser.: No. 12). (ENG.). 96p. (J). (gr. 2-5). pap. 6.99 *(978-0-375-85713-3(3))*; lib. bdg. 12.99 *(978-0-375-95713-0(8))* Random Hse. Children's Bks. (Random Hse. Bks. for Young Readers).
—Cupcake Tycoon. Holm, Jennifer L. & Holm, Matthew. 2010. (Babymouse Ser.: No. 13). (ENG.). 96p. (J). (gr. 2-5). pap. 6.99 *(978-0-375-86573-2(X))*; lib. bdg. 12.99 *(978-0-375-96573-9(4))* Random Hse. Children's Bks.
Holm, Jennifer L. & Holm, Matthew. Deadly Disease of Doom. Holm, Jennifer L. & Holm, Matthew. 2015. (Squish Ser.). (ENG.). 96p. (J). (gr. 2-5). lib. bdg. 12.99 *(978-0-307-98306-0(4),* Random Hse. Bks. for Young Readers) Random Hse. Children's Bks.
Holm, Jennifer L. & Holm, Matthew. Dragonslayer. Holm, Jennifer L. & Holm, Matthew. 2009. (Babymouse Ser.: No. 11). (ENG.). 96p. (J). (gr. 2-5). pap. 6.99 *(978-0-375-85712-6(5))*; lib. bdg. 12.99 *(978-0-375-95712-3(X))* Random Hse. Children's Bks. (Random Hse. Bks. for Young Readers).
—Fear the Amoeba. Holm, Jennifer L. & Holm, Matthew. 2014. (Squish Ser.: No. 6). (ENG.). 96p. (J). (gr. 2-5). 12.99 *(978-0-307-98303-9(X))*; No. 6. pap. 6.99 *(978-0-307-98302-2(1))* Random Hse., Inc.
—Game On! Holm, Jennifer L. & Holm, Matthew. 2013. (Squish Ser.: No. 5). (ENG.). 96p. (J). (gr. 2-5). pap. 6.99 *(978-0-307-98299-5(8))*; lib. bdg. 12.99 *(978-0-307-98300-8(5))* Random Hse., Inc.
—Happy Birthday, Babymouse! Holm, Jennifer L. & Holm, Matthew. 2014. (Babymouse Ser.: No. 18). (ENG.). 96p. (J). (gr. 2-5). 12.99 *(978-0-375-97097-9(5))*; pap. 6.99 *(978-0-307-93161-0(7))* Random Hse., Inc.
—Mad Scientist. Holm, Jennifer L. & Holm, Matthew. 2011. (Babymouse Ser.: No. 14). (ENG.). 96p. (J). (gr. 2-5). pap. 6.99 *(978-0-375-86574-9(8))*; lib. bdg. 12.99 *(978-0-375-96574-6(2))* Random Hse., Inc.
—Monster Mash. Holm, Jennifer L. & Holm, Matthew. 2008. (Babymouse Ser.: No. 9). (ENG.). 96p. (J). (gr. 2-5). pap. 6.99 *(978-0-375-84387-7(6))*; lib. bdg. 12.99 *(978-0-375-93789-7(7))* Random Hse. Children's Bks. (Random Hse. Bks. for Young Readers).
—The Musical. Holm, Jennifer L. & Holm, Matthew. 2009. (Babymouse Ser.: No. 10). (ENG.). 96p. (J). (gr. 2-5). pap. 6.99 *(978-0-375-84388-4(4))*; lib. bdg. 12.99 *(978-0-375-93791-0(9))* Random Hse. Children's Bks. (Random Hse. Bks. for Young Readers).
—Super Amoeba. Holm, Jennifer L. & Holm, Matthew. 2011. (Squish Ser.: No. 1). (ENG.). 96p. (J). (gr. 3-7). pap. 6.99 *(978-0-375-84389-1(2))*; lib. bdg. 12.99 *(978-0-375-93783-5(8))* Random Hse., Inc.
—A Very Babymouse Christmas. Holm, Jennifer L. & Holm, Matthew. 2011. (Babymouse Ser.: No. 15). (ENG.). 96p. (J). (gr. 2-5). 12.99 *(978-0-375-96779-5(6))*; pap. 6.99 *(978-0-375-86779-8(1))* Random Hse. Children's Bks. (Random Hse. Bks. for Young Readers).
Holm, Matt, jt. illus. see Holm, Jennifer L.
Holm, Matthew, jt. illus. see Holm, Jennifer L.
Holm, Sharon. All Week at School. Williams, Rozanne Lanczak. Hamaguchi, Carla, ed. 2003. (Sight Word Readers Ser.). 16p. (J). (gr. k-2). pap. 3.49 *(978-1-57471-962-8(9),* 3584) Creative Teaching Pr., Inc.
—Balancing Bears: Comparing Numbers. Atwood, Megan. 2012. (Count the Critters Ser.). 24p. (J). (gr. k-3). 27.07 *(978-1-61641-851-9(6))* Magic Wagon.
—Busy Beavers: Counting By 5s. Atwood, Megan. 2012. (Count the Critters Ser.). 24p. (J). (gr. k-3). 27.07 *(978-1-61641-852-6(4))* Magic Wagon.
—Circles. Lorbiecki, Marybeth. 2007. (Shapes Ser.). 24p. (gr. -1-2). 27.07 *(978-1-60270-043-7(5),* Looking Glass Library- Nonfiction) Magic Wagon.
—Crescents. Vogel, Julia. 2007. (Shapes Ser.). 24p. (gr. -1-2). 27.07 *(978-1-60270-044-4(3),* Looking Glass Library- Nonfiction) Magic Wagon.
—Cuddly Kittens: Discovering Fractions. Atwood, Megan. 2012. (Count the Critters Ser.). 24p. (J). (gr. k-3). 27.07 *(978-1-61641-853-3(2))* Magic Wagon.
—Monarch Migration: Counting by 10s. Atwood, Megan. 2012. (Count the Critters Ser.). 24p. (J). (gr. k-3). 27.07 *(978-1-61641-854-0(0))* Magic Wagon.
—Ovals. Vogel, Julia. 2007. (Shapes Ser.). 24p. (gr. -1-2). 27.07 *(978-1-60270-045-1(1),* Looking Glass Library- Nonfiction) Magic Wagon.
—Piglets Playing: Counting from 11 To 20. Atwood, Megan. 2012. (Count the Critters Ser.). 24p. (J). (gr. k-3). 27.07 *(978-1-61641-855-7(9))* Magic Wagon.
—Rectangles. Hall, Pamela. 2007. (Shapes Ser.). 24p. (gr. -1-2). 27.07 *(978-1-60270-046-8(X),* Looking Glass Library- Nonfiction) Magic Wagon.
—Sparrows Singing: Discovering Addition & Subtraction. Atwood, Megan. 2012. (Count the Critters Ser.). 24p. (J). (gr. k-3). 27.07 *(978-1-61641-856-4(7))* Magic Wagon.
—Squares. Hall, Pamela. 2007. (Shapes Ser.). 24p. (gr. -1-2). 27.07 *(978-1-60270-047-5(8),* Looking Glass Library- Nonfiction) Magic Wagon.
—Triangles. Lorbiecki, Marybeth. 2007. (Shapes Ser.). 24p. (gr. -1-2). 27.07 *(978-1-60270-048-2(6),* Looking Glass Library- Nonfiction) Magic Wagon.
—101 Questions about Reproduction: Or How 1 + 1 = 3 or 4 or More. Brynie, Faith Hickman. 2005. (101 Questions... Ser.). (ENG.). 176p. (gr. 7-12). 30.60 *(978-0-7613-2311-2(2))* Lerner Publishing Group.
—101 Questions about Sex & Sexuality: With Answers for the Curious, Cautious, & Confused. Brynie, Faith Hickman. 2003. (101 Questions... Ser.). (ENG.). 176p. (gr. 7-12). lib. bdg. 30.60 *(978-0-7613-2310-5(4),* Twenty-First Century Bks.) Lerner Publishing Group.
—101 Questions about Sleep & Dreams: That Kept You Awake Nights... until Now. Brynie, Faith Hickman. 2006. (101 Questions... Ser.). (ENG.). 176p. (gr. 7-12). lib. bdg. 30.60 *(978-0-7613-2312-9(0))* Lerner Publishing Group.
Holm, Sharon, jt. illus. see Leonard, Barbara.
Holm, Sharon Lane. All New Crafts for Earth Day. Ross, Kathy. 2006. (All New Holiday Crafts for Kids Ser.). (ENG.). 48p. (gr. k-3). lib. bdg. 25.26 *(978-0-7613-3400-2(9),* Millbrook Pr.); per. 7.95 *(978-0-8225-5976-4(5),* First Avenue Editions) Lerner Publishing Group.
—All New Crafts for Mother's Day & Father's Day. Ross, Kathy. 2007. (All New Holiday Crafts for Kids Ser.). (ENG.). 48p. (gr. k-3). per. 7.95 *(978-0-8225-6368-6(1),* First Avenue Editions) Lerner Publishing Group.
—All New Crafts for Thanksgiving. Ross, Kathy. 2005. (All New Holiday Crafts for Kids Ser.). (ENG.). 48p. (gr. k-3). lib. bdg. 25.26 *(978-0-7613-2922-0(6),* Millbrook Pr.) Lerner Publishing Group.
—All New Holiday Crafts for Mother's & Father's Day. Ross, Kathy. 2007. (All New Holiday Crafts for Kids Ser.). (ENG.). 48p. (gr. k-3). lib. bdg. 25.26 *(978-0-8225-6367-9(3),* Millbrook Pr.) Lerner Publishing Group.
—Buzzing Bees: Discovering Odd Numbers. Tourville, Amanda Doering. 2008. (Count the Critters Ser.). 24p. (J). (gr. k-3). 27.07 *(978-1-60270-262-2(4))* Magic Wagon.
—Hiding Hippos: Counting from 1 To 10. Tourville, Amanda Doering. 2008. (Count the Critters Ser.). 24p. (J). (gr. k-3). 27.07 *(978-1-60270-263-9(2))* Magic Wagon.
—Jenna & the Three R's, 1 vol. Blackaby, Susan. 2009. (Read-It! Readers: Science Ser.). (ENG.). 32p. (gr. k-2). 19.99 *(978-1-4048-5257-0(3),* Easy Readers) Picture Window Bks.
—Lions Leaving: Counting from 10 To 1. Tourville, Amanda Doering. 2008. (Count the Critters Ser.). 24p. (J). (gr. k-3). 27.07 *(978-1-60270-264-6(0))* Magic Wagon.
—More of the Best Holiday Crafts Ever! Ross, Kathy. 2005. 160p. (J). (gr. k-4). bds. 19.95 *(978-0-7613-2345-7(7))* Lerner Publishing Group.
—Penguin Pairs: Counting By 2s. Tourville, Amanda Doering. 2008. (Count the Critters Ser.). 24p. (J). (gr. k-3). 27.07 *(978-1-60270-265-3(9))* Magic Wagon.
—Prairie Dogs Perching: Counting By 3s. Tourville, Amanda Doering. 2008. (Count the Critters Ser.). 24p. (J). (gr. k-3). 27.07 *(978-1-60270-266-0(7))* Magic Wagon.
—Sunning Sea Lions: Discovering Even Numbers. Tourville, Amanda Doering. 2008. (Count the Critters Ser.). 24p. (J). (gr. k-3). 27.07 *(978-1-60270-267-7(5))* Magic Wagon.
—Twinkle, Twinkle, Little Star. Taylor, Jane. 2010. (Favorite Children's Songs Ser.). (ENG.). 16p. (J). (gr. -1-2). 25.64 *(978-1-60253-533-6(7),* 200115) Child's World, Inc., The.
—The Wheels on the Bus. Thompson, Kim Mitzo. 2010. (Padded Board Book W/CD Ser.). 8p. (J). (gr. k-2). bds. 10.99 incl. audio compact disk *(978-1-59922-580-7(8))* Twin Sisters IP, LLC.
Holm, Sharon Lane. Zoe's Hats: A Book of Colors & Patterns. Holm, Sharon Lane. 2009. (ENG.). 32p. (J). (gr. -1-k). pap. 8.95 *(978-1-59078-748-9(X))* Boyds Mills Pr.
Holm, Sharon Lane. All New Crafts for Easter. Holm, Sharon Lane, tr. Ross, Kathy. 2005. (All New Holiday Crafts for Kids Ser.). (ENG.). 48p. (gr. k-3). pap. 7.95 *(978-0-7613-2392-1(9))*; lib. bdg. 25.26 *(978-0-7613-2921-3(8))* Lerner Publishing Group. (Millbrook Pr.).
Holman, Karen. Primary Numbers: A New Hampshire Numbers Book. Harris, Marie. 2004. (Count Your Way Across the U. S. A. Ser.). (ENG.). 40p. (J). 16.95 *(978-1-58536-192-2(5))* Sleeping Bear Pr.
Holman, Karen Busch. Minn from Minnesota. Wargin, Kathy-jo. 2006. (ENG.). 144p. (J). (gr. k-7). 14.95 *(978-1-58726-304-0(1),* Mitten Pr.) Ann Arbor Editions LLC.
—Mitt & Minn at the Wisconsin Cheese Jamboree. Wargin, Kathy-jo. 2007. (ENG.). 144p. (J). (gr. k-7). 14.95 *(978-1-58726-305-7(X),* Mitten Pr.) Ann Arbor Editions LLC.
—Mitt & Minn's Illinois Adventure. Wargin, Kathy-jo. 2007. (ENG.). 144p. (J). (gr. k-7). 14.95 *(978-1-58726-306-4(8),* Mitten Pr.) Ann Arbor Editions LLC.
—Nicholas: A New Hampshire Tale. Arenstam, Peter. 2009. (ENG.). 144p. (J). (gr. k-7). 14.95 *(978-1-58726-521-1(4),* Mitten Pr.) Ann Arbor Editions LLC.
—Nicholas: A Vermont Tale. Arenstam, Peter. 2010. (ENG.). 144p. (J). (gr. k-7). 14.95 *(978-1-58726-522-8(2),* Mitten Pr.) Ann Arbor Editions LLC.
—Nicholas Bk. 2: A Maine Tale. Arenstam, Peter. 2008. (ENG.). 144p. (J). (gr. k-7). 14.95 *(978-1-58726-520-4(6),* Mitten Pr.) Ann Arbor Editions LLC.
Holmberg, Ansgar & Connelly, Gwen. Days of Faith: Assignment Book & Student Planner/Intermediate Grades 2005-2006. Fischer, Carl. 2005. 108p. (J). spiral bd. 4.99 *(978-1-933178-03-5(5),* 9807) Pflaum Publishing Group.
Holmberg, Ansgar, jt. illus. see Connelly, Gwen.
Holme, Sharon. Meg Sale a Pasear, 1 vol. Blackaby, Susan. Ruiz, Carlos, tr. from ENG. 2006. (Read-It! Readers en Español: Story Collection).Tr. of Meg Takes a Walk. (SPA.). 24p. (gr. -1-3). 19.99 *(978-1-4048-1685-5(2),* Easy Readers) Picture Window Bks.
Holmes, Denise. If I Wrote a Book about You. Aulenback, Stephany. 2014. (ENG.). 32p. (J). (gr. -1-3). 16.95 *(978-1-927018-46-0(3),* 9781927018460) Simply Read Bks. CAN. Dist: Ingram Pub. Services.
—The Yoga Game by the Sea. Beliveau, Kathy. 2015. (Yoga Game Ser.: 1). (ENG.). 32p. (J). 16.95 *(978-1-927018-49-1(8))* Simply Read Bks. CAN. Dist: Ingram Pub. Services.
Holmes, Ekua. Voice of Freedom - Fannie Lou Hamer: The Spirit of the Civil Rights Movement. Weatherford, Carole Boston. 2015. (ENG.). 56p. (J). (gr. 4-7). 17.99 *(978-0-7636-6531-9(2))* Candlewick Pr.
Holmes, Fay. The Happy Little Ghost: A Halloween Tale. Holmes, Fay. 2003. 20p. (J). (gr. 1-3). pap. 5.00 *(978-0-9674241-4-9(3))* IZA Publishing Co.
Holmes, Gerald L. The Big Question. Erickson, John R. 2012. 128p. (J). pap. *(978-1-59188-160-5(9))* Maverick Bks.
—The Big Question. Erickson, John R. 2012. (Hank the Cowdog Ser.: Vol. 60). (ENG.). 128p. (J). (gr. 3-6). 15.99 *(978-1-59188-260-2(5))* Maverick Bks., Inc.
—The Case of the Black-Hooded Hangmans. Erickson, John R. 2011. (Hank the Cowdog Ser.). (ENG.). 113p. (J). (gr. 3-6). pap. 5.99 *(978-1-59188-124-7(2))* Maverick Bks., Inc.
—The Case of the Blazing Sky. Erickson, John R. 2011. (Hank the Cowdog Ser.). (ENG.). 129p. (J). (gr. 3-6). pap. 5.99 *(978-1-59188-151-3(X))* Maverick Bks., Inc.
—The Case of the Booby-Trapped Pickup. Erickson, John R. 2011. (Hank the Cowdog Ser.). (ENG.). 129p. (J). (gr. 3-6). pap. 5.99 *(978-1-59188-149-0(8))* Maverick Bks., Inc.
—The Case of the Burrowing Robot. Erickson, John R. 2011. (Hank the Cowdog Ser.). (ENG.). 125p. (J). (gr. 3-6). pap. 5.99 *(978-1-59188-142-1(0))* Maverick Bks., Inc.
—The Case of the Car-Barkaholic Dog. Erickson, John R. 2011. (Hank the Cowdog Ser.: No. 22). (ENG.). 115p. (J). (gr. 3-6). pap. 5.99 *(978-1-59188-117-9(X))* Maverick Bks., Inc.
—The Case of the Coyote Invasion. Erickson, John R. 2011. (Hank the Cowdog Ser.: No. 56). (ENG.). 132p. (J). (gr. 3-6). pap. 5.99 *(978-1-59188-156-8(0))* Maverick Bks., Inc.
—The Case of the Deadly Ha-Ha Game. Erickson, John R. 2011. (Hank the Cowdog Ser.). (ENG.). 128p. (J). (gr. 3-6). pap. 5.99 *(978-1-59188-137-7(4))* Maverick Bks., Inc.
—The Case of the Dinosaur Birds. Erickson, John R. 2011. (Hank the Cowdog Ser.). (ENG.). 125p. (J). (gr. 3-6). pap. 5.99 *(978-1-59188-154-4(4))* Maverick Bks., Inc.
—The Case of the Double Bumblebee Sting. Erickson, John R. 2011. (Hank the Cowdog Ser.: No. 22). (ENG.). 114p. (J). (gr. 3-6). pap. 5.99 *(978-1-59188-122-3(6))* Maverick Bks., Inc.
—The Case of the Falling Sky. Erickson, John R. 2011. (Hank the Cowdog Ser.: No. 45). (ENG.). 129p. (J). (gr. 3-6). pap. 5.99 *(978-1-59188-145-2(5))* Maverick Bks., Inc.
—The Case of the Fiddle-Playing Fox. Erickson, John R. 2011. (Hank the Cowdog Ser.: No. 12). (ENG.). 118p. (J). (gr. 3-6). pap. 5.99 *(978-1-59188-112-4(9))* Maverick Bks., Inc.
—The Case of the Halloween Ghost. Erickson, John R. 2011. (Hank the Cowdog Ser.). (ENG.). 123p. (J). (gr. 3-6). pap. 5.99 *(978-1-59188-109-4(9))* Maverick Bks., Inc.
—The Case of the Haystack Kitties. Erickson, John R. 2011. (Hank the Cowdog Ser.). (ENG.). 123p. (J). (gr. 3-6). pap. 5.99 *(978-1-59188-130-8(7))* Maverick Bks., Inc.
—The Case of the Hooking Bull. Erickson, John R. 2011. (Hank the Cowdog Ser.). (ENG.). 119p. (J). (gr. 3-6). pap. 5.99 *(978-1-59188-118-6(8))* Maverick Bks., Inc.
—The Case of the Kidnapped Collie. Erickson, John R. 2011. (Hank the Cowdog Ser.). (ENG.). 113p. (J). (gr. 3-6). pap. 5.99 *(978-1-59188-126-1(9))* Maverick Bks., Inc.
—The Case of the Measled Cowboy. Erickson, John R. 2011. (Hank the Cowdog Ser.: No. 33). (ENG.). 126p. (J). (gr. 3-6). pap. 5.99 *(978-1-59188-133-9(1))* Maverick Bks., Inc.
—The Case of the Midnight Rustler. Erickson, John R. 2011. (Hank the Cowdog Ser.: No. 19). (ENG.). 113p. (J). (gr. 3-6). pap. 5.99 *(978-1-59188-119-3(6))* Maverick Bks., Inc.
—The Case of the Missing Bird Dog. Erickson, John R. 2011. (Hank the Cowdog Ser.: No. 40). (ENG.). 126p. (J). (gr. 3-6). pap. 5.99 *(978-1-59188-140-7(4))* Maverick Bks., Inc.
—The Case of the Missing Cat. Erickson, John R. 2011. (Hank the Cowdog Ser.: No. 15). (ENG.). 114p. (J). (gr. 3-6). pap. 5.99 *(978-1-59188-115-5(3))* Maverick Bks., Inc.
—The Case of the Monkey Burglar. Erickson, John R. 2011. (Hank the Cowdog Ser.: No. 48). (ENG.). 129p. (J). (gr. 3-6). pap. 5.99 *(978-1-59188-148-3(X))* Maverick Bks., Inc.
—The Case of the Most Ancient Bone. Erickson, John R. 2011. (Hank the Cowdog Ser.). (ENG.). 239p. (J). (gr. 3-6). pap. 5.99 *(978-1-59188-150-6(1))* Maverick Bks., Inc.
—The Case of the Mysterious Voice. Erickson, John R. 2012. (Hank the Cowdog (Quality) Ser.: Vol. 58). (ENG.). 123p. (J). (gr. 3-6). pap. 5.99 *(978-1-59188-158-2(7))* Maverick Bks., Inc.
—The Case of the Night-Stalking Bone Monster. Erickson, John R. 2011. (Hank the Cowdog Ser.). (ENG.). 115p. (J). (gr. 3-6). pap. 5.99 *(978-1-59188-127-8(7))* Maverick Bks., Inc.
—The Case of the One-Eyed Killer Stud Horse. Erickson, John R. 2011. (Hank the Cowdog Ser.: No. 8). (ENG.). 120p. (J). (gr. 3-6). pap. 5.99 *(978-1-59188-108-7(0))* Maverick Bks., Inc.
—The Case of the Perfect Dog. Erickson, John R. 2012. 127p. (J). *(978-1-59188-259-6(1))* Maverick Bks.
—The Case of the Perfect Dog. Erickson, John R. 2012. (Hank the Cowdog (Quality) Ser.). (ENG.). 127p. (J). (gr. 3-6). pap. 5.99 *(978-1-59188-159-9(5))* Maverick Bks., Inc.
—The Case of the Raging Rottweiler. Erickson, John R. 2011. (Hank the Cowdog Ser.). (ENG.). 131p. (J). (gr. 3-6). pap. 5.99 *(978-1-59188-136-0(6))* Maverick Bks., Inc.
—The Case of the Saddle House Robbery. Erickson, John R. 2011. (Hank the Cowdog Ser.: No. 35). (ENG.). 125p. (J). (gr. 3-6). pap. 5.99 *(978-1-59188-135-3(8))* Maverick Bks., Inc.
—The Case of the Secret Weapon. Erickson, John R. 2011. (Hank the Cowdog Ser.). (ENG.). 125p. (J). (gr. 3-6). pap. 5.99 *(978-1-59188-155-1(2))* Maverick Bks., Inc.
—The Case of the Shipwrecked Tree. Erickson, John R. 2011. (Hank the Cowdog Ser.: No. 41). (ENG.). 119p. (J). (gr. 3-6). pap. 5.99 *(978-1-59188-141-4(2))* Maverick Bks., Inc.
—The Case of the Swirling Killer Tornado. Erickson, John R. 2011. (Hank the Cowdog Ser.). (ENG.). 112p. (J). (gr. 3-6). pap. 5.99 *(978-1-59188-125-4(0))* Maverick Bks., Inc.
—The Case of the Tender Cheeping Chickies. Erickson, John R. 2011. (Hank the Cowdog Ser.). (ENG.). 129p. (J). (gr. 3-6). pap. 5.99 *(978-1-59188-147-6(1))* Maverick Bks., Inc.
Holmes, Gerald L. The Case of the Three Rings. Erickson, John R. 2014. 124p. (J). pap. *(978-1-59188-164-3(1))* Maverick Bks., Inc.

H

Holmes, Gerald L. The Case of the Tricky Trap. Erickson, John R. 2011. (Hank the Cowdog Ser.). (ENG.). 126p. (J). (gr. 3-6). pap. 5.99 *(978-1-59188-146-9(3))* Maverick Bks., Inc.

—The Case of the Twisted Kitty. Erickson, John R. 2004. (Hank the Cowdog Ser.: No. 43). 131p. (J). lib. bdg. 17.00 *(978-1-4242-1600-0(1))* Fitzgerald Bks.

—The Case of the Twisted Kitty. Erickson, John R. 2011. (Hank the Cowdog Ser.). (ENG.). 131p. (J). (gr. 3-6). pap. 5.99 *(978-1-59188-143-8(9))* Maverick Bks., Inc.

—The Case of the Vampire Cat. Erickson, John R. 2011. (Hank the Cowdog Ser.). (ENG.). 115p. (J). (gr. 3-6). pap. 5.99 *(978-1-59188-121-6(8))* Maverick Bks., Inc.

—The Case of the Vampire Vacuum Sweeper. Erickson, John R. 2011. (Hank the Cowdog Ser.). (ENG.). 119p. (J). (gr. 3-6). pap. 5.99 *(978-1-59188-129-2(3))* Maverick Bks., Inc.

—The Case of the Vanishing Fishhook. Erickson, John R. 2011. (Hank the Cowdog Ser.: No. 31). (ENG.). 124p. (J). (gr. 3-6). pap. 5.99 *(978-1-59188-131-5(5))* Maverick Bks., Inc.

—The Curse of the Incredible Priceless Corncob. Erickson, John R. 2011. (Hank the Cowdog Ser.: No. 7). (ENG.). 127p. (J). (gr. 3-6). pap. 5.99 *(978-1-59188-107-0(2))* Maverick Bks., Inc.

—The Disappearance of Drover. Erickson, John R. 2011. (Hank the Cowdog Ser.). (ENG.). 122p. (J). (gr. 3-6). pap. 5.99 *(978-1-59188-157-5(9))* Maverick Bks., Inc.

—Drover's Secret Life. Erickson, John R. 2011. (Hank the Cowdog Ser.). (ENG.). 118p. (J). (gr. 3-6). pap. 5.99 *(978-1-59188-153-7(6))* Maverick Bks., Inc.

—The Dungeon of Doom. Erickson, John R. 2004. (Hank the Cowdog Ser.: No. 44). 122p. (J). lib. bdg. 17.00 *(978-1-4242-1601-7(X))* Fitzgerald Bks.

—The Dungeon of Doom. Erickson, John R. 2011. (Hank the Cowdog Ser.). (ENG.). 122p. (J). (gr. 3-6). pap. 5.99 *(978-1-59188-144-5(7))* Maverick Bks., Inc.

—Every Dog Has His Day. Erickson, John R. 2011. (Hank the Cowdog Ser.). (ENG.). 118p. (J). (gr. 3-6). pap. 5.99 *(978-1-59188-110-0(2))* Maverick Bks., Inc.

—Faded Love. Erickson, John R. 2011. (Hank the Cowdog Ser.: No. 5). (ENG.). 125p. (J). (gr. 3-6). pap. 5.99 *(978-1-59188-105-6(6))* Maverick Bks., Inc.

—The Fling. Erickson, John R. 2011. (Hank the Cowdog Ser.). (ENG.). 126p. (J). (gr. 3-6). pap. 5.99 *(978-1-59188-138-4(2))* Maverick Bks., Inc.

—The Garbage Monster from Outer Space. Erickson, John R. 2011. (Hank the Cowdog Ser.). (ENG.). 126p. (J). (gr. 3-6). pap. 5.99 *(978-1-59188-132-2(3))* Maverick Bks., Inc.

—The Ghost of Rabbits Past. Erickson, John R. 2013. 128p. (J). pap. 5.99 *(978-1-59188-162-9(5))* Maverick Bks., Inc.

—Hank Cowdog 50. Erickson, John R. 2007. 256p. 16.99 *(978-0-670-62249-8(4),* Viking Adult) Penguin Publishing Group.

—Hank the Cowdog & Monkey Business. Erickson, John R. 2011. (Hank the Cowdog Ser.). (ENG.). 110p. (J). (gr. 3-6). pap. 5.99 *(978-1-59188-114-8(5))* Maverick Bks., Inc.

—It's a Dog's Life. Erickson, John R. (Hank the Cowdog Ser.: No. 3). (J). 100p. (gr. 2-5). 9.95 *(978-0-916941-04-8(3));* 2011. (ENG.). 127p. (gr. 3-6). pap. 5.99 *(978-1-59188-103-2(X))* Maverick Bks., Inc.

—Let Sleeping Dogs Lie. Erickson, John R. 2011. (Hank the Cowdog Ser.: No. 6). (ENG.). 129p. (J). (gr. 3-6). pap. 5.99 *(978-1-59188-106-3(4))* Maverick Bks., Inc.

—Lost in the Blinded Blizzard. Erickson, John R. 2011. (Hank the Cowdog Ser.). (ENG.). 115p. (J). (gr. 3-6). pap. 5.99 *(978-1-59188-116-2(1))* Maverick Bks., Inc.

—Lost in the Dark Unchanted Forest. Erickson, John R. 2011. (Hank the Cowdog Ser.). (ENG.). 124p. (J). (gr. 3-6). pap. 5.99 *(978-1-59188-111-7(0))* Maverick Bks., Inc.

—Moonlight Madness. Erickson, John R. 2011. (Hank the Cowdog Ser.: No. 23). (ENG.). 114p. (J). (gr. 3-6). pap. 5.99 *(978-1-59188-123-0(4))* Maverick Bks., Inc.

—The Mopwater Files. Erickson, John R. 2011. (Hank the Cowdog Ser.). (ENG.). 111p. (J). (gr. 3-6). pap. 5.99 *(978-1-59188-128-5(5))* Maverick Bks., Inc.

—Murder in the Middle Pasture. Erickson, John R. 2011. (Hank the Cowdog Ser.). (ENG.). 120p. (J). (gr. 3-6). pap. 5.99 *(978-1-59188-104-9(8))* Maverick Bks., Inc.

—The Original Adventures of Hank the Cowdog. Erickson, John R. (ENG.). 127p. (J). (gr. 3-6). 2012. (Hank the Cowdog Ser.: Vol. 1). 15.99 *(978-1-59188-201-5(X));* 2011. (Hank the Cowdog Ser.: No. 1). pap. 5.99 *(978-1-59188-101-8(3))* Maverick Bks., Inc.

—The Phantom in the Mirror. Erickson, John R. 2011. (Hank the Cowdog Ser.: No. 20). (ENG.). 114p. (J). (gr. 3-6). pap. 5.99 *(978-1-59188-120-9(X))* Maverick Bks., Inc.

—The Quest for the Great White Quail. Erickson, John R. 2011. (Hank the Cowdog Ser.). (ENG.). 123p. (J). (gr. 3-6). pap. 5.99 *(978-1-59188-152-0(8))* Maverick Bks., Inc.

—The Return of the Charlie Monsters. Erickson, John R. 2014. 128p. (J). pap. *(978-1-59188-163-6(3))* Maverick Bks., Inc.

—The Secret Laundry Monster Files. Erickson, John R. 2011. (Hank the Cowdog Ser.). (ENG.). 128p. (J). (gr. 3-6). pap. 5.99 *(978-1-59188-139-1(0))* Maverick Bks., Inc.

—Slim's Good-Bye. Erickson, John R. 2011. (Hank the Cowdog Ser.). (ENG.). 132p. (J). (gr. 3-6). pap. 5.99 *(978-1-59188-134-6(X))* Maverick Bks., Inc.

—The Wounded Buzzard on Christmas Eve. Erickson, John R. 2011. (Hank the Cowdog Ser.: No. 13). (ENG.). 112p. (J). (gr. 3-6). pap. 5.99 *(978-1-59188-113-1(7))* Maverick Bks., Inc.

Holmes, Gerald L., jt. illus. see Erickson, John R.

Holmes, Helen. Magic of the Mabinogion. Ifans, Rhiannon. 2006. (ENG.). 112p. (J). pap. 9.95 *(978-0-86243-174-7(3))* Y Lolfa GBR. Dist: Dufour Editions, Inc.

—Tales from Wales. Ifans, Rhiannon. 2009. (ENG.). 112p. (J). pap. 8.95 *(978-0-86243-182-2(4))* Y Lolfa GBR. Dist: Dufour Editions, Inc.

Holmes, Jeremy. Great Ball of Light. Kuhlman, Evan. 2015. (ENG.). 304p. (J). (gr. 5-9). 16.99 *(978-1-4169-6461-2(4))* Simon & Schuster Children's Publishing.

—Make a Scene, Bk. 2. Weiner, Ellis. 2013. (Templeton Twins Ser.). (ENG.). 261p. (J). (gr. 3-7). 16.99 *(978-1-4521-1184-1(7))* Chronicle Bks. LLC.

—Poem-Mobiles: Crazy Car Poems. Lewis, J. Patrick & Florian, Douglas. 2014. (ENG.). 40p. (J). (gr. -1-3). 17.99 *(978-0-375-86690-6(0));* 20.99 *(978-0-375-96690-3(0))* Random Hse. Children's Bks. (Schwartz & Wade Bks.).

—The Templeton Twins Have an Idea. Weiner, Ellis. 2012. (ENG.). 232p. (J). (gr. 4-7). 16.99 *(978-0-8118-6679-8(3))* Chronicle Bks. LLC.

—The Templeton Twins Have an Idea: Book 1. Weiner, Ellis. 2013. (Templeton Twins Ser.). (ENG.). 240p. (J). (gr. 3-7). pap. 6.99 *(978-1-4521-2704-0(2))* Chronicle Bks. LLC.

—The Templeton Twins Make a Scene: Book 2. Weiner, Ellis. 2014. (ENG.). 272p. (J). (gr. 3-7). pap. 6.99 *(978-1-4521-2872-6(3))* Chronicle Bks. LLC.

Holmes, Joshua D. The Raindrop. Firely, G. M. 2004. 21p. pap. 24.95 *(978-1-4137-3388-4(3))* PublishAmerica, Inc.

Holmes, Matthew. The Pizza Counting. Dobson, Christina. 2003. (ENG.). 32p. (J). (gr. 1-4). pap. 7.95 *(978-0-88106-339-4(8))* Charlesbridge Publishing, Inc.

Holmes, Mike. Secret Coders. Yang, Gene Luen. 2015. (Secret Coders Ser.: 1). (ENG.). 96p. (J). (gr. 3-7). 17.99 ***(978-1-62672-276-7(5))***; pap. 9.99 ***(978-1-62672-075-6(4))*** Roaring Brook Pr. (First Second Bks.).

Holmes, Mike. Bravest Warriors, Vol. 2. Holmes, Mike. Comeau, Joey. 2014. (Bravest Warriors Ser.: 2). (ENG.). 128p. (J). (gr. 4). pap. 14.99 *(978-1-60886-352-5(2))* Boom! Studios.

Holmes, Rebecca. Little Shoko & the Crocodile. Sithole, Thelma. 2007. 36p. per. 12.00 *(978-1-59858-330-4(1))* Dog Ear Publishing, LLC.

Holmes, Robert & Mills, Dan, photos by. The Heirloom Tomato Cookbook. Luebbermann, Mimi. 2006. (ENG.). 132p. (gr. 8-17). pap. 16.95 *(978-0-8118-5355-2(1))* Chronicle Bks. LLC.

Holmes, Stephen. Tom's Big Nap. Graves, Sue. 2010. (Reading Corner Phonics Ser.). (ENG.). 24p. (J). (gr. k-2). pap. 7.99 ***(978-0-7496-9158-5(1))*** Hodder & Stoughton GBR. Dist: Independent Pubs. Group.

Holmes, Stephen, jt. illus. see Faulkner, Keith.

Holmes, Steve. Animales Marinos: Mezcla y Diviertete. 2005. (Mezcla y Diviertete Ser.). (SPA.). 5p. (J). (gr. -1-7). *(978-970-718-291-2(1),* Silver Dolphin en Español) Advanced Marketing, S. de R. L. de C. V.

—Nature's Neighborhoods. Hilton, Samantha. 2004. (Interfact Ladders Ser.). (ENG.). 48p. (J). (gr. -1-2). 14.95 *(978-1-58728-420-5(0))* Cooper Square Publishing Llc.

—Rain Forest Animals. Wilkes, Angela et al. rev. ed. 2004. (Ladders Ser.). 32p. (J). (gr. -1-3). 12.95 *(978-1-58728-606-3(8),* Two-Can Publishing) T&N Children's Publishing.

—World of Insects. Hilton, Samantha. 2004. (Interfact Ladders Ser.). (ENG.). 48p. (J). (gr. -1-2). 14.95 *(978-1-58728-419-9(7))* Cooper Square Publishing Llc.

Holmlund, Heather D. As Long As the Rivers Flow, 1 vol. Loyie, Larry & Brissenden, Constance. 2005. (ENG.). 48p. (J). (gr. 4-7). pap. 9.95 *(978-0-88899-696-1(9))* Groundwood Bks. CAN. Dist: Perseus-PGW.

Holob, Victoria. Arco Iris Del Sr. Paloma: The Spanish Edition. Holob, Victoria. l.t. ed. 2011. (SPA.). 32p. pap. 10.00 *(978-1-4609-6232-9(X))* CreateSpace Independent Publishing Platform.

—Miss Stella, the Child Care Magician. Holob, Victoria. l.t. ed. 2011. (ENG.). 30p. pap. 10.00 *(978-1-4565-5325-8(9))* CreateSpace Independent Publishing Platform.

—Mr. Dove's Rainbow. Holob, Victoria. l.t. ed. 2011. (ENG.). 54p. pap. 11.58 *(978-1-4565-7883-1(9))* CreateSpace Independent Publishing Platform.

Holob, Victoria. The Indiana Birdman: Grandpa Bud Aviation Stories, the Complete Collection. Holob, Victoria, photos by. 2011. (ENG.). 96p. pap. 19.00 *(978-1-4609-1002-3(8))* CreateSpace Independent Publishing Platform.

Holob, Victoria, photos by. Trilogy: Three Airplane Stories for Children. Holob, Victoria. l.t. ed. 2011. (ENG., 60p. pap. 13.00 *(978-1-4564-5390-9(4))* CreateSpace Independent Publishing Platform.

Holoska, Jiri, photos by. Kirigami Greeting Cards: The Art of Paper Cutting & Folding. Krcmár, Karol. Simekova, Jela, ed. Chorvathova, Michaela, tr. 2005. (Kirigami Craft Books Ser.). 80p. (J). pap. 14.95 *(978-0-9715411-7-7(5))* Kotzig Publishing, Inc.

—Kirigami Paper Kingdom: The Art of Paper Cutting & Folding. Krcmár, Karol. Simekova, Jela, ed. Kovac, Stefan Patrik, tr. 2005. (Kirigami Craft Books Ser.). 112p. (J). pap. 14.95 *(978-0-9715411-6-0(7))* Kotzig Publishing, Inc.

Holroyd, Geraldine. Caught in the Net. Pavese, Candace. 2013. 84p. pap. 9.95 *(978-1-937449-19-3(X))* YAV.

Holsather, Bill. Henry of York: The Secret of Juan de Vega. Holsather, Kent. 2003. 176p. (YA). (gr. 5-18). 22.95 *(978-0-9729101-0-1(7));* 2nd ed. per. 12.95 *(978-0-9729101-1-8(5))* Lonejack Mountain Pr.

Holsinger, Carol. Abadaba Alphabet: Learning Letter Sounds. Moore, Sheila. 2006. 31p. (gr. -1-3). 19.95 *(978-0-9789473-0-9(4))* Abadaba Reading LLC.

Holstad, Kathy, photos by. Tillamook Cheese Cookbook: Celebrating 100 Years of Excellence. Holstad, Kathy. Tillamook County Creamery Association. 2008. (ENG., 196p. 24.95 *(978-0-9801942-4-1(5))* ACS, LLC Amica Creative Services.

Holt Ayriss, Linda. E Is for Evergreen: A Washington State Alphabet. Smith, Roland & Smith, Marie. 2004. (State Ser.). (ENG.). 40p. (J). 17.95 *(978-1-58536-143-4(7))* Sleeping Bear Pr.

Holt, Lindsey. Harold's Adventures. Love, Makada H. 2008. 92p. pap. 10.99 *(978-1-4343-6875-1(0))* AuthorHouse.

Holt, Steven. Busy Piggies. Holt, Steven, photos by. Schindel, John. 2006. (Busy Book Ser.). (ENG.). 20p. (J). (gr. k — 1). bds. 6.99 *(978-1-58246-169-4(4),* Tricycle Pr.) Ten Speed Pr.

Holt, Steven, photos by. Busy Barnyard. Schindel, John. 2006. (Busy Book Ser.). (ENG., 20p. (J). (— 1). bds. 6.99 *(978-1-58246-168-7(6),* Tricycle Pr.) Ten Speed Pr.

—Busy Birdies. Schindel, John. 2010. (Busy Book Ser.). (ENG., 20p. (J). (gr. -1 — 1). bds. 6.99 *(978-1-58246-317-9(4),* Tricycle Pr.) Ten Speed Pr.

—Busy Bunnies. Schindel, John. 2008. (Busy Book Ser.). (ENG., 20p. (J). (— 1). bds. 6.99 *(978-1-58246-242-4(9),* Tricycle Pr.) Ten Speed Pr.

Holt, Steven, photos by. Busy Chickens. Holt, Steven. Schindel, John. 2009. (Busy Book Ser.). (ENG., 20p. (J). (gr. -1 — 1). bds. 6.99 *(978-1-58246-275-2(5),* Tricycle Pr.) Ten Speed Pr.

Holtsclaw, Josh, jt. illus. see RH Disney Staff.

Holub, Joan. All about You with Inspector McQ. Mullins, Patty Rutland. 2004. (Treasure Tree Ser.). 32p. (J). *(978-0-7166-1646-7(7))* World Bk., Inc.

—Hot Cha-Cha!, Nobisso, Josephine. 2009. (ENG.). 32p. (J). (gr. k-2). 16.95 *(978-0-940112-18-6(3))* Gingerbread Hse.

—I'm Not Scared. Hall, Kirsten. 2003. (My First Reader Ser.). (ENG.). 32p. (J). 18.50 *(978-0-516-22929-4(X),* Children's Pr.) Scholastic Library Publishing.

—My First Book of Sign Language. Scholastic, Inc. Staff. 2004. (ENG.). 32p. (J). (gr. 3-7). pap. 3.99 *(978-0-439-63582-0(9))* Scholastic, Inc.

Holub, Joan & Fisher, Cynthia. Deena y su centavo de la Suerte. deRubertis, Barbara. 2007. (Math Matters Ser.). (SPA.). 32p. (J). (gr. -1-3). pap. 5.95 *(978-1-57565-249-8(8))* Kane Pr., Inc.

Holyfield, John. Belle, the Last Mule at Gee's Bend: A Civil Rights Story. Stroud, Bettye & Ramsey, Calvin Alexander. 2011. (ENG.). 32p. (J). (gr. k-3). 16.99 *(978-0-7636-4058-3(1))* Candlewick Pr.

—Bessie Smith & the Night Riders. Stauffacher, Sue. 2006. (ENG.). 32p. (J). (gr. -1-3). 16.99 *(978-0-399-24237-3(6),* Putnam Juvenile) Penguin Publishing Group.

—The Hallelujah Flight. Bildner, Phil. 2010. (ENG.). 32p. (J). (gr. k-3). 16.99 *(978-0-399-24789-7(0),* Putnam Juvenile) Penguin Publishing Group.

—Hard-Times Jar. Smothers, Ethel Footman & Smothers, Ethel F. 2003. (ENG.). 32p. (J). (gr. k-3). 18.99 *(978-0-374-32852-8(8),* Farrar, Straus & Giroux (BYR)) Farrar, Straus & Giroux.

—Mahalia Jackson: Walking with Kings & Queens. Nolan, Nina. 2015. (ENG.). 32p. (J). (gr. -1-3). 17.99 *(978-0-06-087944-0(0))* HarperCollins Pubs.

Holzmann, Angela. The First Good Shepherd: Psalm 23 for Children. Steinkühler, Martina. 2015. 28p. 12.95 ***(978-0-8091-6774-6(3))*** Paulist Pr.

Hom, John. Diego & Papi to the Rescue. Wax, Wendy. 2007. (Go, Diego, Go! Ser.: 3). (ENG.). 24p. (J). pap. 3.99 *(978-1-4169-2781-5(6),* Simon Spotlight/Nickelodeon) Simon Spotlight/Nickelodeon.

—Diego y Papi al Rescate. Wax, Wendy. Ziegler, Argentina Palacios, tr. 2008. (Go, Diego, Go! Ser.).Tr. of Diego & Papi to the Rescue. (SPA.). 24p. (J). (gr. -1-2). pap. 3.99 *(978-1-4169-5044-8(3),* Libros Para Ninos) Libros Para Ninos.

Hom, Nancy. Nine-In-One:Grr! Grr! Spagnoli, Cathy. 2013. (ENG.). 32p. (J). (gr. -1-5). pap. 9.95 *(978-0-89239-048-9(4))* Lee & Low Bks., Inc.

Homberg, Ansgar. Days of Faith Assignment Book & Student Planner. Fischer, Carl. 2003. 108p. (J). spiral bd. 4.99 *(978-0-89837-232-8(1),* 9804) Pflaum Publishing Group.

Homfray, Nick. The Adventures of Eric Seagull. Greenham, Caz. 2013. 40p. pap. *(978-1-78132-093-8(4))* SilverWood Bks.

—The Adventures of Eric Seagull 'Story-Teller' Book 2 a Fairy's Wish. Greenham, Caz. 2013. 48p. pap. *(978-1-78132-110-2(8))* SilverWood Bks.

Hondel, Gary. Pudgee Woodchuck. Hondel, Gary. 2007. 36p. per. 14.95 *(978-1-59858-323-6(9))* Dog Ear Publishing, LLC.

Hondru, Ovi. Robert Louis Stevenson's Treasure Island: My Sea Adventure Israel Hands. Fuerst, Jeffrey B. & Benchmark Education Co., LLC. 2014. (Text Connections Ser.). (J). (gr. 3). *(978-1-4509-9652-5(3))* Benchmark Education Co.

Honey, Elizabeth. Asmir No Quiere Pistolas. Mattingley, Christobel. Balseiro, Maria Luisa, tr.Tr. of No Gun for Asmir. (SPA.). 129p. (J). (gr. 5-8). pap. 9.95 *(978-84-204-4891-6(5))* Santillana USA Publishing Co., Inc.

Honey, Elizabeth. That's Not a Daffodil! Honey, Elizabeth. 2011. (ENG.). 32p. (J). (gr. -1-k). 19.99 *(978-1-74237-248-8(1))* Allen & Unwin AUS. Dist: Independent Pubs. Group.

—To the Boy in Berlin. Honey, Elizabeth. Brandt, Heike. 2007. (ENG.). 288p. (J). (gr. 5-9). 12.99 *(978-1-74175-004-1(0))* Allen & Unwin AUS. Dist: Independent Pubs. Group.

Honey, Elizabeth & Johnson, Sue. I'm Still Awake, Still! Honey, Elizabeth. 2009. (ENG.). 32p. (J). (gr. k-1). 19.99 *(978-1-74175-321-9(X))* Allen & Unwin AUS. Dist: Independent Pubs. Group.

Hong, Denise, jt. illus. see Lopez, Paul.

Hong, Lily T. El Senor Sol y el Senor Mar, Level 3. Butler, Andrea. Flor Ada, Alma, tr. 2003. (Dejame Leer Ser.). (SPA.). 16p. (J). (gr. -1-3). 6.50 *(978-0-673-36302-2(3),* Good Year Bks.) Celebration Pr.

Hong, Lily Toy. Two of Everything. Hong, Lily Toy, retold by. 2012. (J). *(978-1-61913-138-5(2))* Weigl Pubs., Inc.

Hong, Lily Toy & Lin, Grace. The Seven Chinese Sisters, Bk. 2. Tucker, Kathy & Hong, Lily Toy. 2010. (Book & DVD Packages with Nutmeg Media Ser.). (ENG.). 4p. (J). (gr. -1-3). 69.95 *(978-0-8075-9984-6(0))* Whitman, Albert & Co.

Hong, Richard. The Book of Bad Habits for Young (and Not So Young!) Men & Women: How to Chuck the Worst & Turn the Rest to Your Advantage. Hawkins, Frank C. & Laube, Greta L. B. 2010. (ENG.). 148p. (J). (gr. 7). pap. 12.95 *(978-0-9793219-3-1(X))* Big Book Pr., LLC.

Honsinger, Alise. Leonard Lou: Beautiful, Brave, Strong, & True. Honsinger, Linda. 2012. 38p. 24.95 *(978-1-4626-6872-4(0))* America Star Bks.

Hoobler, David. Zonk & the Secret Lagoon: The Further Adventures of Zonk the Dreaming Tortoise. Hoobler, David. l.t. ed. 2005. 32p. (J). lib. bdg. 18.95 *(978-0-9706537-1-0(9))* Zonk Galleries and Pubns.

Hood, George W. The Chinese Fairy Book. Wilhelm, Richard, ed. Martens, Frederick H., tr. from CHI. 2008. (Dover Children's Classics Ser.). (ENG.). 224p. (J). (gr. 4-7). pap. 10.95 *(978-0-486-45435-1(5))* Dover Pubns., Inc.

Hood, Jack B. The Legend of Holly Boy. rev. ed. 38p. (J). (gr. -1-12). pap. 3.95 *(978-0-9640474-2-6(X))* Latino, Frank Publishing Co.

Hood, Joyce. Lightning Bugs. Ketch, Ann. 2003. (ENG.). 12p. (gr. k-1). pap. 5.95 *(978-1-57874-038-3(X))* Kaeden Corp.

Hood, Philip, jt. illus. see Rane, Walter.

Hooff Andreozzi, Mareml. I. M. Green. Hooff, Gudren. 2011. 32p. (J). pap. 12.00 *(978-0-9825922-6-7(4))* Commonwealth Books of Virginia, LLC.

Hoofnagle, Therese. Bug, Bug, Where's the Bug? Dawson, J. M. 2008. 26p. pap. 24.95 *(978-1-60474-365-4(4))* America Star Bks.

Hoogstad, Alice. How Much Does the Gray in an Elephant Weigh? Van Os, Erik & Van Lieshout, Elle. 2013. (ENG.). 32p. (J). (gr. -1). 17.95 *(978-1-935954-27-9(X),* 9781935954279) Lemniscaat USA.

Hook, Adam. Ancient Greece Health & Disease, 1 vol. Dargie, Richard & Compass Point Books Staff. 2007. (Changing Times: Ancient Greece Ser.). (ENG.). 32p. (gr. 4-6). 29.32 *(978-0-7565-2087-8(8),* CPB Grades 4-8) Compass Point Bks.

Hook, Christa. British Infantryman in South Africa 1877-81. Castle, Ian. 2003. (Warrior Ser.: 83). (ENG.). 64p. pap. *(978-1-84176-555-6(4),* Osprey Publishing) Bloomsbury Publishing Plc.

Hook, Frances, jt. illus. see Hook, Richard.

Hook, Richard. Martin Luther: Hero of Faith. Nohl, Frederick. 2003. 160p. (YA). pap. 9.99 *(978-0-7586-0592-4(7))* Concordia Publishing Hse.

—Where's the Dragon? Hook, Jason. 2004. (Where's The ... ? Ser.). (ENG.). 26p. (J). (gr. -1-2). 14.95 *(978-1-4027-1624-9(9))* Sterling Publishing Co., Inc.

Hook, Richard & Hook, Frances. Jesus the Friend of Children. 6th ed. 2006. (David C Cook Read to Me Bible Stories Ser.). 112p. (J). (gr. 3-7). 14.99 *(978-0-7814-4390-6(3))* Cook, David C.

Hooper, Hadley. Here Come the Girl Scouts! Corey, Shana. 2012. (ENG.). 40p. (J). (gr. -1-3). 17.99 *(978-0-545-34278-0(3),* Scholastic Pr.) Scholastic, Inc.

—How I Discovered Poetry. Nelson, Marilyn. 2014. (ENG.). 112p. (YA). (gr. 7). 17.99 *(978-0-8037-3304-6(6),* Dial) Penguin Publishing Group.

—The Iridescence of Birds: A Book about Henri Matisse. MacLachlan, Patricia. 2014. (ENG.). 40p. (J). (gr. -1-3). 17.99 *(978-1-59643-948-1(3))* Roaring Brook Pr.

Hooper, Hadley & Stryk, Suzanne. Sow What? Person, Naomi et al. 2009. 94p. (YA). pap. *(978-0-88441-735-4(2))* Girl Scouts of the USA.

Hoover, Charity. Grandma's Goose. Martin, Mary. 2012. 188p. *(978-0-7399-2452-5(4))* Rod & Staff Pubs., Inc.

Hoover, Dave. Fighting Chance - Denial, Vol. 1. 2009. (ENG.). 160p. (J). (gr. 4-17). pap. 19.99 *(978-0-7851-3738-2(6))* Marvel Worldwide, Inc.

Hoover, Dave, et al. Levi Strauss & Blue Jeans, 1 vol. Olson, Nathan. 2006. (Inventions & Discovery Ser.). (ENG.). 32p. (gr. 3-4). 29.99 *(978-0-7368-6484-8(9),* Graphic Library) Capstone Pr., Inc.

—Shackleton & the Lost Antarctic Expedition, 1 vol. Hoena, Blake A. & Hoena, B. A. 2006. (Disasters in History Ser.). (ENG.). 32p. (gr. 3-4). 29.99 *(978-0-7368-5482-5(7),* Graphic Library) Capstone Pr., Inc.

Hoover, Dave & Anderson, Bill. Harriet Tubman & the Underground Railroad, 1 vol. Martin, Michael & Martin, Michael J. 2005. (Graphic History Ser.). (ENG.). 32p. (gr. 3-4). 29.99 *(978-0-7368-3829-0(5),* Graphic Library) Capstone Pr., Inc.

—Harriet Tubman & the Underground Railroad, 1 vol. Martin, Michael J. 2005. (Graphic History Ser.). (ENG.). 32p. (gr. 3-4). per. 8.10 *(978-0-7368-5245-6(X),* Graphic Library) Capstone Pr., Inc.

Hoover, Dave, jt. illus. see Barnett, Charles, III.

Hoover, Dave, jt. illus. see Barnett III, Charles.

Hop, Nguyen Thi, jt. illus. see Ames, Philippe.

Hope, Bill. Buzzbomb: Adventures in the Forbidden Zone. Matheson, Jason. 2013. 80p. (J). pap. *(978-1-925011-26-5(7))* Australian Self Publishing Group/ Inspiring Pubs.

Hope, Michelle. When Bees Win. Galjanic, Lisa. 2007. (J). 9.95 *(978-1-933532-04-2(1))* LSG Pubns.

—When Caterpillars Grow Up. Galjanic, Lisa. 2007. (J). 9.95 *(978-1-933532-03-5(3))* LSG Pubns.

—When Fish Are Mean. Galjanic, Lisa. 2007. (J). 9.95 *(978-1-933532-01-1(7))* LSG Pubns.

—When Flowers Dance. Galjanic, Lisa. 2007. (J). 9.95 *(978-1-933532-05-9(X))* LSG Pubns.

—When Leaves Die. Galjanic, Lisa. 2007. (J). 9.95 *(978-1-933532-00-4(9))* LSG Pubns.

—When Squirrels Try. Galjanic, Lisa. 2007. (J). 9.95 *(978-1-933532-02-8(5))* LSG Pubns.

Hopgood, Andrew. Let's Grow a Garden. Reynolds, Alison. 2009. (Save Our Planet! Ser.). 12p. (J). (gr. -1-3). bds. 11.40 *(978-1-60754-412-8(1))* Windmill Bks.

—Let's Save Water. Reynolds, Alison. 2009. (Save Our Planet! Ser.). 12p. (J). (gr. -1-3). bds. 11.40 *(978-1-60754-413-5(X))* Windmill Bks.

—Let's Turn It Off. Reynolds, Alison. 2009. (Save Our Planet! Ser.). 12p. (J). (gr. -1-3). bds. 11.40 *(978-1-60754-414-2(8))* Windmill Bks.

—Let's Use It Again. Reynolds, Alison. 2009. (Save Our Planet! Ser.). 12p. (J). (gr. -1-3). bds. 11.40 *(978-1-60754-415-9(6))* Windmill Bks.

Hopgood, Andrew. Riley & the Fantastic Plan. Condon, Bill. 2015. (Legends in Their Own Lunchbox Ser.). (ENG.). 56p. (gr. 2-3). pap. 7.99 ***(978-1-4966-0252-7(8),*** Legends in Their Own Lunchbox) Capstone Classroom.

—Riley & the Treasure. Condon, Bill. 2015. (Legends in Their Own Lunchbox Ser.). (ENG.). 56p. (gr. 2-3). pap. 7.99

(978-1-4966-0258-9(7), Legends in Their Own Lunchbox) Capstone Classroom.
—Riley Clowns Around. Condon, Bill. 2015. (Legends in Their Own Lunchbox Ser.). (ENG.). 48p. (gr. 1-2). pap. 7.99 *(978-1-4966-0240-4(4)*, Legends in Their Own Lunchbox) Capstone Classroom.
—Riley Versus the Giant Banana. Condon, Bill. 2015. (Legends in Their Own Lunchbox Ser.). (ENG.). 48p. (gr. 1-2). pap. 7.99 *(978-1-4966-0246-6(3)*, Legends in Their Own Lunchbox) Capstone Classroom.
Hopgood, Kevin. The Shocking Story of Electricity. Claybourne, Anna. 2006. (Young Reading Series 2 Ser.). 63p. (J). (gr. 2-5). pap. 5.99 *(978-0-7945-1248-4(8)*, Usborne) EDC Publishing.
Hopgood, Tim. What a Wonderful World. Thiele, Bob & Weiss, George David. 2014. (ENG.). 32p. (J). (gr. -1-k). 17.99 *(978-1-62779-254-7(6)*, Holt, Henry & Co. Bks. For Young Readers) Holt, Henry & Co.
Hopgood, Tim. Wow! Said the Owl. Hopgood, Tim. 2009. (ENG.). 28p. (J). (gr. -1-k). 16.99 *(978-0-374-38518-7(1)*, Farrar, Straus & Giroux (BYR)) Farrar, Straus & Giroux.
Hopkins, Emily. Alphabear. Willeford, Tammy Jean. 2013. 32p. pap. 8.00 *(978-1-62080-998-3(2))* Hopkins Publishing.
Hopkins, Jeff. The Only One Club. Naliboff, Jane. 2013. (ENG.). 32p. (J). (gr. k-2). 6.95 *(978-1-936261-30-7(8))* Flashlight Pr.
Hopkins, Simon, jt. illus. see Farrelly, Linda.
Hopkins, Simon, jt. illus. see Hawthorn, Paul.
Hopkinson, Deborah. Independence Cake: A Revolutionary Confection Inspired by Amelia Simmons, Whose True History Is Unfortunately Unknown, Embellished with Scrumptious Illustrations. 2016. (J). *(978-0-385-39017-0(3)*, Schwartz & Wade Bks.) Random Hse. Children's Bks.
Hopman, Philip. Mikis & the Donkey. Tak, Bibi Dumon. 2014. 89p. (J). 13.00 *(978-0-8028-5430-8(3))* Eerdmans, William B. Publishing Co.
—Soldier Bear. Tak, Bibi Dumon & Dumon Tak, Bibi. 2011. 144p. (J). 13.00 *(978-0-8028-5375-2(7)*, Eerdmans Bks For Young Readers) Eerdmans, William B. Publishing Co.
—Spider Mcdrew & the Egyptians: Band 12. Durant, Alan. 2007. (Collins Big Cat Ser.). (ENG.). 32p. (J). pap. 7.99 *(978-0-00-723076-1(1))* HarperCollins Pubs. Ltd. GBR. Dist: Independent Pubs. Group.
—Spider's Big Match. Durant, Alan. 2007. (Collins Big Cat Ser.). (ENG.). 32p. (J). pap. 8.99 *(978-0-00-723081-5(8))* HarperCollins Pubs. Ltd. GBR. Dist: Independent Pubs. Group.
—Tom the Tamer. Veldkamp, Tjibbe. 2011. (ENG.). 32p. (J). (gr. -1). 16.95 *(978-1-935954-05-7(9)*, 9781935954057) Lemniscaat USA.
—Uncle Gus's Magic Box. van Lieshout, Ted. Sideri, Simona, tr. from DUT. 2005. (ENG.). 60p. (J). (gr. 2-4). pap. 5.95 *(978-1-55037-934-1(8)*, 9781550379341) Annick Pr., Ltd. CAN. Dist: Firefly Bks., Ltd.
—The Usborne First Book of Art. Dickins, Rosie. 2008. (Usborne First Book Ser.). 62p. (J). (gr. -1-3). 18.99 *(978-0-7945-2035-9(9)*, Usborne) EDC Publishing.
Hoppe, Paul. Can I See Your I.D.? True Stories of False Identities. Barton, Chris. 2011. (ENG.). 144p. (YA). (gr. 7-18). 16.99 *(978-0-8037-3310-7(0)*, Dial) Penguin Publishing Group.
—Last-But-Not-Least Lola & the Wild Chicken. Pakkala, Christine. 2014. (Last-But-Not-Least Lola Ser.). (ENG.). 216p. (J). (gr. 2-5). 15.95 *(978-1-59078-983-4(0))* Boyds Mills Pr.
—Last-but-Not-Least Lola Going Green. Pakkala, Christine. 2013. (Last-But-Not-Least Lola Ser.). (ENG.). 192p. (J). (gr. 2-5). 15.95 *(978-1-59078-935-3(0))* Boyds Mills Pr.
—Last-But-Not-Least Lola Going Green. Pakkala, Christine. 2014. (Last-But-Not-Least Lola Ser.). (ENG.). 192p. (J). (gr. 2-5). pap. 7.95 *(978-1-62979-113-5(X))* Boyds Mills Pr.
—Metal Man. Reynolds, Aaron. 2010. (ENG.). 32p. (J). (gr. k-3). pap. 7.95 *(978-1-58089-151-6(9))* Charlesbridge Publishing, Inc.
—Peanut. Halliday, Ayun. 2012. (ENG.). 216p. (J). (gr. 5-9). 18.99 *(978-0-375-96590-6(4))*; pap. 15.99 *(978-0-375-86590-9(X))* Random Hse. Children's Bks. (Schwartz & Wade Bks.).
Hoppe, Paul. Hat. Hoppe, Paul. 2009. (ENG.). 32p. (J). (gr. -1-1). 14.99 *(978-1-59990-247-0(8)*, Bloomsbury USA Childrens) Bloomsbury USA.
Hopper, Andy Lee. Bleep the Purple Bear. Hopper, Bobby E. 2009. 36p. pap. 18.99 *(978-1-4389-1908-9(5))* AuthorHouse.
Hopper, Billy. The Dynamic Dinosaur of Faith's History Vol. I: From Christ to 1000 AD. Bertch, David P. & Bertch, Barbara A. Martin, Terry & Martin, Dyna, eds. (Roots of the Past Ser.: Bk. 1). 150p. (J). (gr. 6). stu. ed. 9.95 *(978-0-9634472-4-1(6))* Good Works Pr.
Hopper, Pegge. Clever Dog. Finney, Jefferson. 2007. 32p. (J). pap. 15.95 *(978-1-56647-845-8(6))* Mutual Publishing LLC.
Horacek, Judy. Good Night, Sleep Tight. Fox, Mem. 2013. (ENG.). 32p. (J). (gr. -1-k). 16.99 *(978-0-545-53370-6(8)*, Orchard Bks.) Scholastic, Inc.
Horacek, Judy. The Story of Growl. Horacek, Judy. 2008. (ENG.). 32p. (J). (gr. -1-3). 10.99 *(978-1-933605-80-7(4))* Kane Miller.
—Where Is the Green Sheep? Big Book. Horacek, Judy. Fox, Mem. 2010. (ENG.). 32p. (J). (gr. -1-3). 26.99 *(978-0-547-32856-0(7))* Houghton Mifflin Harcourt Publishing Co.
—Where Is the Green Sheep? (¿Dónde Está la Oveja Verde?) Horacek, Judy. Fox, Mem. 2010. (SPA & ENG.). 32p. (J). (gr. k — 1). bds. 4.99 *(978-0-547-39694-1(5))* Houghton Mifflin Harcourt Publishing Co.
—Yellow Is My Color Star. Horacek, Judy. 2014. (ENG.). 32p. (J). (gr. -1-3). 16.99 *(978-1-4424-9299-8(6)*, Beach Lane Bks.) Beach Lane Bks.
Horácek, Petr. Little Moon's Christmas: Imagination - Objects. Kim, Cecil. Cowley, Joy, ed. 2015. (Step up - Creative Thinking Ser.). (ENG.). 32p. (gr. -1-2). 26.65 *(978-1-925246-11-7(6))*; 7.99 *(978-1-925246-63-6(9))*; 26.65 *(978-1-925246-37-7(X))* ChoiceMaker Pty. Ltd., The AUS. (Big and SMALL). Dist: Lerner Publishing Group.
Horácek, Petr. Animal Opposites. Horácek, Petr. 2013. (ENG.). 20p. (J). (gr. -1-2). 15.99 *(978-0-7636-6776-4(5))* Candlewick Pr.
—Beep Beep. Horácek, Petr. 2008. (ENG.). 16p. (J). (gr. k-k). bds. 5.99 *(978-0-7636-3482-7(4))* Candlewick Pr.
—Butterfly Butterfly: A Book of Colors. Horácek, Petr. 2007. (ENG.). 16p. (J). (gr. -1-2). 15.99 *(978-0-7636-3343-1(7))* Candlewick Pr.
—Choo Choo. Horácek, Petr. 2008. (ENG.). 16p. (J). (gr. k-k). bds. 5.99 *(978-0-7636-3477-3(8))* Candlewick Pr.
—The Fly. Horácek, Petr. 2015. (ENG.). 32p. (J). (gr. -1-2). 14.99 *(978-0-7636-7480-9(X))* Candlewick Pr.
—Honk, Honk! Baa, Baa! Horácek, Petr. 2014. (ENG.). 16p. (J). (— 1). bds. 7.99 *(978-0-7636-6780-1(3))* Candlewick Pr.
—Las Fresas Son Rojas. Horácek, Petr. 2014. (ENG.). 16p. (J). (-k). bds. 5.99 *(978-0-7636-7393-2(5))* Candlewick Pr.
—Look Out, Suzy Goose. Horácek, Petr. 2008. (ENG.). 32p. (J). (gr. k-k). 14.99 *(978-0-7636-3803-0(X))* Candlewick Pr.
—The Mouse Who Ate the Moon. Horácek, Petr. 2014. (ENG.). 32p. (J). (gr. -1-2). 15.99 *(978-0-7636-7059-7(6))* Candlewick Pr.
—My Elephant. Horácek, Petr. 2009. (ENG.). 40p. (J). (gr. -1-2). 15.99 *(978-0-7636-4566-3(4))* Candlewick Pr.
—Puffin Peter. Horácek, Petr. 2013. (ENG.). 40p. (J). (gr. -1-2). 16.99 *(978-0-7636-6572-2(X))* Candlewick Pr.
—Silly Suzy Goose. Horácek, Petr. 2009. (ENG.). 32p. (J). (— 1). bds. 7.99 *(978-0-7636-4141-2(3))* Candlewick Pr.
Horácek, Petr. A Surprise for Tiny Mouse. Horácek, Petr. 2015. (ENG.). 16p. (J). (— 1). bds. 8.99 *(978-0-7636-7967-5(4))* Candlewick Pr.
Horácek, Petr. Suzy Goose & the Christmas Star. Horácek, Petr. 2009. (ENG.). 32p. (J). (gr. -1-2). 15.99 *(978-0-7636-4487-1(0))* Candlewick Pr.
—Suzy Goose & the Christmas Star: Midi Edition. Horácek, Petr. 2010. (ENG.). 32p. (J). (gr. -1-2). 7.99 *(978-0-7636-5000-1(5))* Candlewick Pr.
—Time for Bed. Horácek, Petr. 2014. (ENG.). 16p. (J). (— 1). bds. 7.99 *(978-0-7636-6779-5(X))* Candlewick Pr.
Horak, Mila. Fearless John: The Legend of John Beargrease. Rauzi, Kelly Emerling. 2006. 32p. 19.95 *(978-0-9774831-3-6(4))* Singing River Pubns.
Horen, Michael. My Blessings for Food. 2003. (ArtScroll Ser.). (ENG, ARC & HEB.). (J). 49.99 *(978-0-89906-702-5(6)*, TCH3) Mesorah Pubns., Ltd.
Horen, Michael & Halasz, Andras. Pirkei Avos, Vol. 2. Gold, Avie. (J). pap. 12.99 *(978-0-89906-199-3(0)*, PIYP) Mesorah Pubns., Ltd.
Hori, Hatsuki. A Snowflake Fell: Poems about Winter. Whipple, Laura. 2003. 40p. (J). 16.99 *(978-1-84148-033-6(9))* Barefoot Bks., Inc.
Hormeo, Marielo Gil. Besitos de Chocolate: El Valle de la Ternura. Perez Saez, Lucrecia et al. 2005. (SPA.). 90p. (J). 23.00 incl. audio compact disk *(978-84-7669-724-5(4))* El Aleph Editores, S.A. ESP. Dist: Ediciones Universal.
Hornbeck, Ken. The Time of His Life. Graham, J. 2011. (ENG.). 194p. pap. 8.95 *(978-1-4662-6186-8(3))* CreateSpace Independent Publishing Platform.
Horne, Diantha W. Mildred's Inheritance, Just Her Way & Ann's Own Way. Johnston, Annie Fellows. 2007. 48p. per. *(978-1-4065-3515-0(X))* Dodo Pr.
—The Sandman: His Sea Stories (Yesterday's Classics) Hopkins, William J. 2009. 188p. pap. 9.95 *(978-1-59915-303-2(3))* Yesterday's Classics.
—The Sandman: His Ship Stories (Yesterday's Classics) Hopkins, William J. 2009. 174p. pap. 9.95 *(978-1-59915-302-5(5))* Yesterday's Classics.
Horne, Doug. Big Bad Bible Bullies. Hagan, Scott. 2005. 24p. (J). (gr. -1-3). 9.99 *(978-1-59185-604-7(3))* Charisma Media.
—Los Buscapleitos de la Biblia. Hagan, Scott. 2005. 22p. (J). (gr. 1-3). 8.99 *(978-1-59185-482-1(2)*, Charisma Kids) Charisma Media.
Horne, Grace. Greedy Pigeon the Hungry Porcupine & Friends. Rossitter, Derek. 2004. 60p. pap. *(978-0-7552-0142-6(6))* Authors OnLine, Ltd.
Horne, J. My Pretty Pink School Purse. Bugbird, T. 2010. 16p. (J). 12.99 *(978-1-84879-379-8(0))* Make Believe Ideas GBR. Dist: Nelson, Thomas Inc.
Horne, Nathan. Poppy. Booth, Sara. 2012. 28p. pap. 12.50 *(978-1-61897-666-6(4)*, Strategic Bk. Publishing) Strategic Book Publishing & Rights Agency (SBPRA).
Horne, Philip & Loter, John. Fish School. Mackerel, Seymour & RH Disney Staff. 2003. (Pictureback(R) Ser.). (ENG.). 24p. (J). (gr. -1-2). pap. 3.99 *(978-0-7364-2127-0(0)*, RH/Disney) Random Hse. Children's Bks.
Horne, Richard. 101 Things to Do Before You're Old & Boring. Horne, Richard. Szirtes, Helen. 2006. (101 Things Ser.). (ENG.). 224p. (J). (gr. 5-12). pap. 12.99 *(978-0-8027-7745-4(7))* Walker & Co.
Horne, Richard, jt. illus. see Hasler, Ben.
Horne, Sarah. Dead or Alive? Gifford, Clive. 2015. (ENG.). 48p. (J). (gr. 2-4). 14.99 *(978-1-4052-6858-5(1))* Egmont Bks., Ltd. GBR. Dist: Independent Pubs. Group.
—Gargoyles Gone AWOL. Beauvais, Clémentine. 2015. (Sesame Seade Ser.: 2). (ENG.). 208p. (J). (gr. 2-6). 16.95 *(978-0-8234-3205-9(X))* Holiday Hse., Inc.
—Guinea Pigs Online: Furry Towers. Gray, Jennifer & Swift, Amanda. 2014. (Guinea Pigs Online Ser.: 2). (ENG.). 128p. (J). (gr. 1-4). 12.99 *(978-1-62365-116-9(6)*, Quercus) Quercus NA.
—Horror Holiday. Saddlewick, A. B. 2013. (Monstrous Maud Ser.: 5). (ENG.). 128p. (J). (gr. k-2). pap. 6.99 *(978-1-78055-172-2(X))* O'Mara, Michael Bks., Ltd. GBR. Dist: Independent Pubs. Group.
—Mission 1: Flying Solo. Coburn, Ann. 2006. (Dream Team Ser.: Vol. 1). 80p. (J). pap. *(978-1-84428-118-3(3))* Walker & Co.
—Monstrous Maud: Freaky Sleepover. Saddlewick, A. B. 2013. (Monstrous Maud Ser.: 3). (ENG.). 128p. (J). (gr. k-2). pap. 6.99 *(978-1-78055-074-9(X))* O'Mara, Michael Bks., Ltd. GBR. Dist: Independent Pubs. Group.
—Monstrous Maud: Scary Show. Saddlewick, A. B. 2013. (Monstrous Maud Ser.: 6). (ENG.). 128p. (J). (gr. k-2). pap. 6.99 *(978-1-78055-173-9(8))* O'Mara, Michael Bks., Ltd. GBR. Dist: Independent Pubs. Group.
—Monstrous Maud: School Scare. Saddlewick, A. B. 2013. (Monstrous Maud Ser.: 4). (ENG.). 128p. (J). (gr. k-2). pap. 6.99 *(978-1-78055-075-6(8))* O'Mara, Michael Bks., Ltd. GBR. Dist: Independent Pubs. Group.
—Monstrous Maud - Big Fright. Saddlewick, A. B. 2013. (Monstrous Maud Ser.: 1). (ENG.). 128p. (J). (gr. k-2). pap. 6.99 *(978-1-78055-072-5(3))* O'Mara, Michael Bks., Ltd. GBR. Dist: Independent Pubs. Group.
—Nana Cracks the Case! Lane, Kathleen et al. 2009. (ENG.). 112p. (J). (gr. -1-7). 14.99 *(978-0-8118-6258-5(5))* Chronicle Bks. LLC.
—Nana Takes the Reins, Bk. 2. Lane, Kathleen. 2011. (ENG.). 142p. (J). (gr. -1-7). 14.99 *(978-0-8118-6260-8(7))* Chronicle Bks. LLC.
—Old Woman Who Swallowed a Fly. Davies, Kate, ed. 2009. (First Reading Level 3 Ser.). 48p. (J). (gr. 2). 6.99 *(978-0-7945-2267-4(X)*, Usborne) EDC Publishing.
—Rhino? What Rhino? Hart, Caryl. 2012. (ENG.). 32p. (J). (gr. -1-k). pap. 8.99 *(978-0-340-98140-5(7))* Hodder & Stoughton GBR. Dist: Independent Pubs. Group.
—Showtime. Coburn, Ann. 2006. (Dream Team Mission Ser.: Vol. 2). 80p. (J). pap. *(978-1-84428-071-1(3))* Walker Bks., Ltd.
—Sleuth on Skates. Beauvais, Clémentine. 2014. (Sesame Seade Ser.: 1). (ENG.). 128p. (J). (gr. 2-6). 16.95 *(978-0-8234-3197-7(5))* Holiday Hse., Inc.
—Spike & Ali Enson. Stanley, Malaika Rose. 2010. (ENG.). 128p. (J). (gr. 2-4). pap. 8.99 *(978-1-84853-023-2(4))* Transworld Publishers Ltd. GBR. Dist: Independent Pubs. Group.
—Thirty Days Has September: Cool Ways to Remember Stuff. Scholastic, Inc. Staff & Stevens, Chris. 2008. (Best at Everything Ser.). (ENG.). 128p. (J). (gr. 3-7). 9.99 *(978-0-545-10740-2(7)*, Scholastic Nonfiction) Scholastic, Inc.
—Thumbelina: The Graphic Novel, 1 vol. Andersen, Hans Christian & Sandoval, Gerardo. 2009. (Graphic Spin Ser.). (ENG.). 40p. (gr. 1-3). pap. 5.95 *(978-1-4342-1741-7(8))*; lib. bdg. 23.99 *(978-1-4342-1592-5(X))* Stone Arch Bks. (Graphic Revolve).
—Vile: A Cautionary Tale for Little Monsters. Robinson, Mark. 2011. (ENG.). 32p. (J). (gr. k-2). 14.99 *(978-0-7459-6254-2(8))* Lion Hudson PLC GBR. Dist: Independent Pubs. Group.
—You Can Save the Planet: 50 Ways You Can Make a Difference. Wines, Jacquie. 2008. (ENG.). 112p. (J). (gr. 3-7). pap. 4.99 *(978-0-545-05332-7(3)*, Scholastic Reference) Scholastic, Inc.
—You Can Save the Planet: 50 Ways You Can Make a Difference. Wines, Jacquie. 2008. 111p. (J). (gr. 4-7). 14.05 *(978-1-4178-0836-6(5)*, Turtleback) Turtleback Bks.
—You Get What You Get, 1 vol. Gassman, Julie A. (Little Boost Ser.). (ENG.). 32p. (gr. k-3). 2013. 14.95 *(978-1-4795-2157-9(4))*; 2012. lib. bdg. 22.65 *(978-1-4048-6794-9(5))* Picture Window Bks. (Little Boost).
Horne, Sarah & Barker, Vicky. The Usborne Animal Alphabet Activity Book. MacKinnon, Mairi. 2014. (ENG.). (J). pap. 9.99 *(978-0-7945-3274-1(8)*, Usborne) EDC Publishing.
Horner, Doogie. Kid Presidents: True Tales of Childhood from America's Presidents. Stabler, David. 2014. (Kid Legends Ser.: 1). (ENG.). 224p. (J). (gr. 4-7). 13.95 *(978-1-59474-731-1(8))* Quirk Bks.
Hornung, Phyllis. A Place for Zero. LoPresti, Angeline Sparagna. alt. ed. 2003. (Math Adventures Ser.). (ENG.). 32p. (J). (gr. 1-4). pap. 7.95 *(978-1-57091-196-5(7))* Charlesbridge Publishing, Inc.
—What's Your Angle, Pythagoras? Ellis, Julie. 2004. (Math Adventures Ser.). (ENG.). 32p. (J). (gr. 2-5). pap. 7.95 *(978-1-57091-150-7(9))* Charlesbridge Publishing, Inc.
Hornung, Phyllis. Simon Can't Say Hippopotamus. Hornung, Phyllis, tr. Taylor, Bonnie Highsmith. 2003. 24p. (J). 14.95 *(978-1-59336-017-7(7))*; pap. *(978-1-59336-018-4(5))* Mondo Publishing.
Horowitz, Alena Netia & De La Fuente, Mary. The Tlytlettlym Tree. Horowitz, Alena Netia. I.t. ed. 2003. 64p. (J). per. 12.95 *(978-0-923550-42-4(9))* Tetrahedron Publishing LLC.
Horowitz, Dave. Duck Duck Moose. Horowitz, Dave. 2009. (ENG.). 32p. (J). (gr. k-3). 16.99 *(978-0-399-24782-8(3)*, Putnam Juvenile) Penguin Publishing Group.
—Five Little Gefiltes. Horowitz, Dave. 2007. (ENG.). 32p. (J). (gr. -1-3). 15.99 *(978-0-399-24608-1(8)*, Putnam Juvenile) Penguin Publishing Group.
—Humpty Dumpty Climbs Again. Horowitz, Dave. 2011. (ENG.). 32p. (J). (gr. -1-k). pap. 6.99 *(978-0-14-241932-8(X)*, Puffin) Penguin Publishing Group.
—A Monkey among Us. Horowitz, Dave. 2004. 40p. (J). (gr. -1-1). 14.99 *(978-0-06-054335-8(3)*, HarperFestival) HarperCollins Pubs.
—Twenty-Six Pirates: An Alphabet Book. Horowitz, Dave. 2013. (ENG.). 32p. (J). (gr. -1-k). 16.99 *(978-0-399-25777-3(2))* Penguin Publishing Group.
—Twenty-Six Princesses. Horowitz, Dave. 2008. (ENG.). 32p. (J). (gr. -1-k). 15.99 *(978-0-399-24607-4(X)*, Putnam Juvenile) Penguin Publishing Group.
—Twenty-Six Princesses: An Alphabet Story. Horowitz, Dave. 2011. (ENG.). 32p. (J). (gr. -1-k). pap. 6.99 *(978-0-14-241536-8(7)*, Puffin) Penguin Publishing Group.
—The Ugly Pumpkin. Horowitz, Dave. 2008. (ENG.). 40p. (J). (gr. -1-k). pap. 6.99 *(978-0-14-241145-2(0)*, Puffin) Penguin Publishing Group.
Horrell, Charles. Etheldreda the Ready. Vaizey, George de Horne. 2007. 200p. per. *(978-1-4065-4688-0(7))* Dodo Pr.
Horrocks, Savannah. Protecting the Prairie, 1 vol. Temple, Bob. 2008. (Read-It! Chapter Books: Science Tales: Biome Battles Ser.). (ENG.). 64p. (gr. 2-4). lib. bdg. 21.32 *(978-1-4048-3651-8(9)*, Chapter Readers) Picture Window Bks.
—Taking Back the Tundra, 1 vol. Temple, Bob. 2008. (Read-It! Chapter Books: Science Tales: Biome Battles Ser.). (ENG.). 64p. (gr. 2-4). lib. bdg. 21.32 *(978-1-4048-3648-8(9)*, Chapter Readers) Picture Window Bks.
—War over the Wetlands, 1 vol. Temple, Bob. 2008. (Read-It! Chapter Books: Science Tales: Biome Battles Ser.). (ENG.). 64p. (gr. 2-4). lib. bdg. 21.32 *(978-1-4048-3649-5(7)*, Chapter Readers) Picture Window Bks.
Horrocks, Steve. Gulliver's Travels. Matthews, Andrew. 2014. (Collins Big Cat Progress Ser.). (ENG.). 32p. (J). pap. 7.99 *(978-0-00-751937-8(0))* HarperCollins Pubs. Ltd. GBR. Dist: Independent Pubs. Group.
Horse, Harry. The Last Castaways. Horse, Harry. 2009. (ENG.). 128p. (J). (gr. 1-5). 12.95 *(978-1-56145-439-6(7))* Peachtree Pubs.
—The Last Cowboys. Horse, Harry. 2008. (ENG.). 128p. (J). (gr. 1-5). 12.95 *(978-1-56145-451-8(6)*, Peachtree Junior) Peachtree Pubs.
—The Last Gold Diggers: Being as It Were, an Account of a Small Dog's Adventures, down Under. Horse, Harry. 2008. (ENG.). 128p. (J). (gr. 1-5). 12.95 *(978-1-56145-435-8(4))* Peachtree Pubs.
—The Last Polar Bears. Horse, Harry. 2007. (ENG.). 128p. (J). (gr. 1-5). 12.95 *(978-1-56145-379-5(X)*, Peachtree Junior) Peachtree Pubs.
—Little Rabbit Goes to School. Horse, Harry. (Little Rabbit Ser.). 32p. (J). 2011. (gr. -1-1). pap. 7.95 *(978-1-56145-574-4(1))*; 2004. (ENG.). (gr. k-1). 15.95 *(978-1-56145-320-7(X))* Peachtree Pubs.
—Little Rabbit Lost. Horse, Harry. 2005. (ENG.). 32p. (J). (gr. k-1). bds. 9.95 *(978-1-56145-345-0(5))* Peachtree Pubs.
—Little Rabbit Runaway. Horse, Harry. 2005. (ENG.). 32p. (J). (gr. k-1). 15.95 *(978-1-56145-343-6(9))* Peachtree Pubs.
—Little Rabbit's Christmas. Horse, Harry. 32p. (J). 2010. (gr. -1-1). pap. 7.95 *(978-1-56145-557-7(1))*; 2007. (gr. k-3). 15.95 *(978-1-56145-419-8(2))* Peachtree Pubs.
—Little Rabbit's New Baby. Horse, Harry. 2008. (Little Rabbit Ser.). 32p. (J). (gr. k-1). 16.95 *(978-1-56145-431-0(1))* Peachtree Pubs.
Horsfall, Kyla May & Horsfall, Kyla May. As an International Super Spy. Horsfall, Kyla May & May, Kyla. 2006. (Kyla May Miss. Behaves Ser.). (ENG.). 64p. (J). (gr. 2-5). pap. 5.99 *(978-0-8431-1397-6(9)*, Price Stern Sloan) Penguin Publishing Group.
Horsfall, Kyla May, jt. illus. see Horsfall, Kyla May.
Horst, Melisa. The Daudyhouse. Bowman, Silas. 2012. 51p. (J). *(978-0-7399-2450-1(8))* Rod & Staff Pubs., Inc.
Horsted, Paul, photos by. Custer State Park: From the Mountains to the Plains. Horsted, Paul. 2004. 96p. 19.95 *(978-0-9718053-2-3(6))* Golden Valley Pr.
Horstman, Lisa. One Baby Mountain Goat. Ketel, Debbie M. 2005. (J). bds. 6.99 *(978-0-9752617-3-6(8))* Mount Rushmore Bookstores.
Horstman, Lisa. Smoky Mountain Wee Ones. Horstman, Lisa. Kemp, Steve, ed. 2003. 16p. (J). bds. 6.99 *(978-0-937207-41-3(1))* Great Smoky Mountains Assn.
Hortens, Mike, jt. illus. see Hanner, Albert.
Horton, Lori. Whose Hat Is That? Opheim, Sandra. 2004. (J). 5.95 *(978-0-9758958-0-1(X))* Better Than One Publishing.
Horvath, Ferdinand H. Golden Tusk. Slaughter, Charles E. 2011. 180p. 42.95 *(978-1-258-09834-6(2))* Literary Licensing, LLC.
Horvath, James. Build, Dogs, Build: A Tall Tail. Horvath, James. 2013. (ENG.). 40p. (J). (gr. -1-3). 15.99 *(978-0-06-218967-7(0))* HarperCollins Pubs.
—Dig, Dogs, Dig: A Construction Tail. Horvath, James. 2013. (ENG.). 40p. (J). (gr. -1-3). 15.99 *(978-0-06-218964-6(6))* HarperCollins Pubs.
—Work, Dogs, Work: A Highway Tail. Horvath, James. 2014. (ENG.). 40p. (J). (gr. -1-3). 15.99 *(978-0-06-218970-7(0))* HarperCollins Pubs.
Hose, Ryan. Bobby & Buddy Friends for Life. Edward, J. P. 2011. 16p. pap. 24.95 *(978-1-4560-7520-0(9))* America Star Bks.
Hosegood, Lynn. Stonewall Jackson's Black Sunday School, 1 vol. Pittman, Rickey E. 2010. (ENG.). 32p. (J). (gr. k-3). 16.99 *(978-1-58980-713-6(8))* Pelican Publishing Co., Inc.
Hoseley, Rantz. Rich Dad's Escape from the Rat Race: How to Become a Rich Kid by Following Rich Dad's Advice. Kiyosaki, Robert T. & Lechter, Sharon L. 2005. (ENG.). 64p. (J). (gr. 3-7). pap. 9.99 *(978-0-316-00047-5(7))* Little, Brown Bks. for Young Readers.
Hosemann, Theodor. Slovenly Kate & Other Stories: From the Struwwelpeter Library. Hoffmann, Heinrich. 2012. (Dover Children's Classics Ser.). (ENG.). 96p. (J). (gr. 3-5). pap. 12.99 *(978-0-486-49032-8(7))* Dover Pubns., Inc.
Hosford, Eric. The Princess Fables. Clark, Marc. 2013. 114p. pap. 5.99 *(978-0-9910345-0-5(3))* Seven C's Productions, Inc.
Hosford, William. ABalloonC. Hosford, William. 2007. 32p. (J). per. 10.00 *(978-0-9776562-1-9(7))* WGH Arts LLC.
Hosford, William G. Geo the Geode. Hosford, William G. 2006. 32p. (J). lib. bdg. 19.95 *(978-0-9776562-0-2(9)*, CN0601) WGH Arts LLC.
Hoshine, Ken. Macbeth. SparkNotes Staff. 2008. (No Fear Shakespeare Illustrated Ser.). (ENG.). 208p. (gr. 5-7). per. 9.95 *(978-1-4114-9871-6(2)*, Spark Notes) Sterling Publishing Co., Inc.
Hoshino, Felicia. Juna's Jar. Bahk, Jane. 2015. (ENG.). 32p. (J). 17.95 *(978-1-60060-853-7(1)*, 9781600000000) Lee & Low Bks., Inc.

H

—A Place Where Sunflowers Grow. Lee-Tai, Amy. 2012. (ENG & JPN.). pap. 9.95 ***(978-0-89239-274-2(6)***, Children's Book Press); 2006. (JPN & ENG.). 32p. (J). 17.95 *(978-0-89239-215-5(0))* Lee & Low Bks., Inc.

Hoshino, Katsura. D. Gray-Man. Hoshino, Katsura. 2008. (D. Gray-Man Ser.: 10). (ENG.). 200p. pap. 9.99 *(978-1-4215-1937-1(2))* Viz Media.

—D. Gray-Man. Hoshino, Katsura. Katsura, Hoshino. (D. Gray-Man Ser.: 9). (ENG.). 200p. 2008. pap. 9.99 *(978-1-4215-1610-3(1))*; Vol. 4. 2007. pap. 9.99 *(978-1-4215-1052-1(9))* Viz Media.

Hosler, Danamarie. The Different Dragon. Bryan, Jennifer Liu. 2006. (J). pap. 12.95 *(978-0-9674468-6-8(4))* Two Lives Publishing.

—El Dragón Diferente. Bryan, Jennifer. 2nd ed. 2015.Tr. of Different Dragon. (SPA.). 36p. (Orig.). (J). pap. 12.95 *(978-0-9674468-9-9(9))* Two Lives Publishing.

Hosoe, Eikoh, photos by. Taka-Chan & I: A Dog's Journey to Japan by Runcible. Lifton, Betty Jean. 2012. (ENG., 64p. (J). (gr. k-4). 16.95 *(978-1-59017-502-6(6)*, NYR Children's Collection) New York Review of Bks., Inc., The.

Hossain, Farhana. Atoms & Molecules: Building Blocks of the Universe, 1 vol. Stille, Darlene R. & Compass Point Books Staff. 2007. (Exploring Science: Physical Science Ser.). (ENG.). 48p. (gr. 6-7). 28.65 *(978-0-7565-1960-5(8)*, Exploring Science) Compass Point Bks.

—Invisible Exposure: The Science of Ultraviolet Rays, 1 vol. Stille, Darlene R. 2010. (Headline Science Ser.). (ENG.). 48p. (gr. 7-8). lib. bdg. 28.65 *(978-0-7565-4215-3(4)*, Headline Science) Compass Point Bks.

—Manipulating Light: Reflection, Refraction, & Absorption, 1 vol. Stille, Darlene R. 2005. (Exploring Science: Physical Science Ser.). (ENG.). 48p. (gr. 6-7). lib. bdg. 28.65 *(978-0-7565-1258-3(1)*, Exploring Science) Compass Point Bks.

—Minerals: From Apatite to Zinc, 1 vol. Stille, Darlene R. 2005. (Exploring Science: Earth Science Ser.). (ENG.). 48p. (gr. 6-7). 28.65 *(978-0-7565-0855-5(X)*, Exploring Science) Compass Point Bks.

—Natural Resources: Using & Protecting Earth's Supplies, 1 vol. Stille, Darlene R. 2005. (Exploring Science: Earth Science Ser.). (ENG.). 48p. (gr. 6-7). 28.65 *(978-0-7565-0856-2(8)*, Exploring Science) Compass Point Bks.

—The Periodic Table: Mapping the Elements, 1 vol. Cooper, Sharon Katz & Compass Point Books Staff. 2007. (Exploring Science: Physical Science Ser.). (ENG.). 48p. (gr. 6-7). 28.65 *(978-0-7565-1961-2(6)*, Exploring Science) Compass Point Bks.

—Physical Change: Reshaping Matter, 1 vol. Stille, Darlene R. 2005. (Exploring Science: Physical Science Ser.). (ENG.). 48p. (gr. 6-7). lib. bdg. 28.65 *(978-0-7565-1257-6(3)*, Exploring Science) Compass Point Bks.

—Soil: Digging into Earth's Vital Resource, 1 vol. Stille, Darlene R. 2005. (Exploring Science: Earth Science Ser.). (ENG.). 48p. (gr. 6-7). 28.65 *(978-0-7565-0857-9(6)*, Exploring Science) Compass Point Bks.

Hossain, Farhana & Schultz, Ashlee. Kinetic Energy: The Energy of Motion, 1 vol. Nardo, Don. 2007. (Exploring Science: Physical Science Ser.). (ENG.). 48p. (gr. 6-7). lib. bdg. 28.65 *(978-0-7565-3378-6(3)*, Exploring Science) Compass Point Bks.

Hossain, Farhana, jt. illus. see Hoffmann, Eric.

Hosselkus, Devin. The Apple Tree's Secret, 1 vol. Gates, Pat. 2009. 47p. pap. 24.95 *(978-1-60836-637-8(5))* America Star Bks.

Hosta, Dar. I Love the Night. Hosta, Dar. l.t. ed. 2003. 32p. (J). (gr. k-3). 16.95 *(978-0-9721967-0-3(6))* Brown Dog Bks.

Hoston, Jim. Shop Talk. Scholastic, Inc. Staff & Ford, Juwanda G. 2004. (Just for You Ser.). (ENG.). 32p. (gr. k-3). pap. 3.99 *(978-0-439-56873-9(0)*, Teaching Resources) Scholastic, Inc.

—Shop Talk. Ford, Juwanda G. 2004. 32p. (J). lib. bdg. 15.00 *(978-1-4242-0236-2(1))* Fitzgerald Bks.

Hotchkiss, Conrad & Graham, Heather. I Have Been in Danger, 1 vol. Foggo, Cheryl. 2005. (In the Same Boat Ser.: No. 3). (ENG.). 184p. (J). (gr. 4-6). pap. 7.95 *(978-1-55050-185-8(2))* Coteau Bks. CAN. Dist: Fitzhenry & Whiteside, Ltd.

Hotta, Yumi & Obata, Takeshi. Hikaru No Go, Vol. 3. Hotta, Yumi. 2005. (Hikaru No Go Ser.). (ENG.). 208p. pap. 7.95 *(978-1-59116-687-0(X))* Viz Media.

Houbre, Gilbert. On the Seashore. De Bourgoing, Pascale et al. 2006. (ENG.). 38p. (J). (gr. k-3). pap. 11.99 *(978-1-85103-131-3(6))* Moonlight Publishing, Ltd. GBR. Dist: Independent Pubs. Group.

Houbre, Gilbert. Light. Houbre, Gilbert. 2012. (ENG.). 36p. (J). (gr. -1-k). 12.99 *(978-1-85103-405-5(6))* Moonlight Publishing, Ltd. GBR. Dist: Independent Pubs. Group.

—Vegetables. Houbre, Gilbert. 2012. (ENG.). 36p. (J). (gr. -1-k). 12.99 *(978-1-85103-402-4(1))* Moonlight Publishing, Ltd. GBR. Dist: Independent Pubs. Group.

Houdeshell, Jennifer T. Ebeneezer's Cousin. Zajac, Kristen J. 2010. 20p. pap. 10.95 *(978-1-61633-045-3(7))* Guardian Angel Publishing, Inc.

Houdeshell, Jennifer Thomas. Ebeneezer's Cousin. Zajac, Kristen K. 2013. 24p. 19.95 *(978-1-61633-440-6(1))* Guardian Angel Publishing, Inc.

—El Primo de Ebeneezer. Zajac, Kristen K. 2011. 20p. pap. 10.95 *(978-1-61633-164-1(X))* Guardian Angel Publishing, Inc.

—That's a Lot of Love. Reed, Jennifer Bond. 2011. 16p. pap. 9.95 *(978-1-61633-172-6(0))* Guardian Angel Publishing, Inc.

Hough, Charlotte. Black Beauty. Sewell, Anna. 2008. (Puffin Classics Ser.). (ENG.). 288p. (J). (gr. 3-7). 4.99 *(978-0-14-132103-5(2)*, Puffin) Penguin Publishing Group.

Hough, Hannah Bliss. See with Me. Lewis, Joan Lane. 2011. 32p. pap. 24.95 *(978-1-4626-2347-1(6))* America Star Bks.

Houghton, Chris & Morrison, Jeff. Jeff Gordon. Carney, Larry. PC Treasures Staff, ed. 2009. (Nascar Drivers Coloring/Sticker Book Ser.). (ENG.). 96p. (J). pap. 6.95 *(978-1-60072-162-5(1))* PC Treasures, Inc.

Houghton, Christopher. Epic Tales from Adventure Time: Queen of Rogues. MacDangereuse, T. T. 2014. (Adventure Time Ser.). (ENG.). 144p. (J). (gr. 3-7). 6.99 *(978-0-8431-8035-0(8)*, Price Stern Sloan) Penguin Publishing Group.

—Epic Tales from Adventure Time: the Untamed Scoundrel. MacDangereuse, T. T. 2014. (Adventure Time Ser.). (ENG.). 144p. (J). (gr. 3-7). 6.99 *(978-0-8431-8032-9(3)*, Price Stern Sloan) Penguin Publishing Group.

Houghton, Diane R. Helpin' Bugs. Lonborg, Rosemary. 2006. 32p. (J). (gr. -1-3). reprint ed. pap. 7.00 *(978-1-4223-5405-6(9))* DIANE Publishing Co.

—My Little Friend Goes to a Baseball Game. Finnegan, Evelyn M. 2006. 32p. (J). (gr. -1-3). reprint ed. pap. 7.00 *(978-1-4223-5403-2(2))* DIANE Publishing Co.

—My Little Friend Goes to the Dentist. Finnegan, Evelyn M. 2006. 32p. (J). (gr. -1-3). reprint ed. pap. 7.00 *(978-1-4223-5404-9(0))* DIANE Publishing Co.

Houghton, Roswitha. City Zoo Blizzard Revue. Crispin, Barbara. 2003. 40p. 14.95 *(978-0-9716346-1-9(0))* Dancing Words Pr., Inc.

Housley, Cathren. The Christmas Cats, 1 vol. Wallace, Nancy. 2011. (ENG.). 32p. (J). (gr. k-3). 16.99 *(978-1-58980-979-6(3))* Pelican Publishing Co., Inc.

Housman, Clemence. Moonshine & Clover. Housman, Laurence, ed. 2013. 236p. (J). pap. *(978-1-909302-25-9(2))* Abela Publishing.

Houssais, Emmanuelle. Hot Air. Roy, Sandrine Dumas. Ardizzone, Sarah, tr. from FRE. 2013. (ENG.). 32p. (J). (gr. 2-6). pap. 11.99 *(978-1-907912-22-1(3))* Phoenix Yard Bks. GBR. Dist: Independent Pubs. Group.

Houston, Bronwyn. Loongie, the Greedy Crocodile. Dann, Lucy & Dann, Kiefer. 2010. (ENG.). 24p. (J). (gr. k-2). pap. 12.95 *(978-1-921248-54-2(8))* Magabala Bks. AUS. Dist: Independent Pubs. Group.

Houston, Lauren, jt. illus. see Disney Storybook Art Team.

Houston, Melissa. Is the Moon God's? Jordan, Stephanie. 2005. (J). bds. 9.99 *(978-1-4183-0062-3(4))* Christ Inspired, Inc.

Houx, Emily Marie Cornell du. The Adventures of Sir Goblin, the Feline Knight. Moss, Barbara E. 2009. 336p. pap. 15.95 *(978-1-882190-03-4(3))* Polar Bear & Co.

Hovell, John. Jenny Found a Penny. Harris, Trudy. 2007. (Math Is Fun! Ser.). (ENG.). 32p. (gr. k-3). lib. bdg. 23.93 *(978-0-8225-6725-7(3)*, Millbrook Pr.) Lerner Publishing Group.

Hovemann, Anisa Claire. Earth Heroes, Champions of the Wilderness. Malnor, Bruce & Malnor, Carol. 2009. 144p. (J). (gr. 5-9). pap. 11.95 *(978-1-58469-116-7(6))* Dawn Pubns.

—Earth Heroes, Champions of Wild Animals. Malnor, Carol L. & Malnor, Bruce. 2010. 144p. (J). pap. 11.95 *(978-1-58469-123-5(9))* Dawn Pubns.

—Eliza & the Dragonfly. Rinehart, Susie Caldwell. 2004. (Sharing Nature with Children Book Ser.). 32p. (J). 16.95 *(978-1-58469-060-3(7))*; 8.95 *(978-1-58469-059-7(3))* Dawn Pubns.

—If You Give a T-Rex a Bone. Myers, Tim. 2007. (Sharing Nature with Children Book Ser.). 32p. (J). (gr. -1-5). 16.95 *(978-1-58469-097-9(6))*; 8.95 *(978-1-58469-098-6(4))* Dawn Pubns.

Hovhannisyan, Nune. A Bike of Bees. Velikanje, Kathryn. 2013. 58p. (J). pap. 12.28 *(978-1-939896-03-2(7))* Levity Pr.

—Zebras Paint Themselves Rainbow. Velikanje, Kathryn. 2013. 58p. pap. 12.28 *(978-1-939896-02-5(9))* Levity Pr.

Hovland, Gary. The Goldfish in the Chandelier. Kesterson, Casie. 2012. (ENG.). 32p. 17.95 *(978-1-60606-094-0(5)*, J. Paul Getty Museum) Getty Pubns.

—If the Walls Could Talk: Family Life at the White House. O'Connor, Jane. 2004. (ENG.). 48p. (J). (gr. 1-4). 17.99 *(978-0-689-86863-4(4)*, Simon & Schuster/Paula Wiseman Bks.) Simon & Schuster/Paula Wiseman Bks.

Hovland, Oivind. Vampires. Orme, David. 2010. (Fact to Fiction Grafx Ser.). 36p. pap. 7.45 *(978-0-7891-7999-9(7))* Perfection Learning Corp.

Howard, Arthur. Bubba & Beau, Best Friends. Appelt, Kathi. 2006. (Bubba & Beau Ser.). (ENG.). 32p. (J). (gr. -1-3). pap. 6.99 *(978-0-15-205580-6(0))* Houghton Mifflin Harcourt Publishing Co.

—Bullies Never Win. Cuyler, Margery. 2009. (ENG.). 32p. (J). (gr. k-3). 17.99 *(978-0-689-86187-1(7)*, Simon & Schuster Bks. For Young Readers) Simon & Schuster Bks. For Young Readers.

—Friendship Stories You Can Share. Lobel, Arnold & Rylant, Cynthia. 2004. 64p. (J). (gr. 1-4). reprint ed. 15.00 *(978-0-7567-7149-2(8))* DIANE Publishing Co.

—Goatilocks & the Three Bears. Perl, Erica S. 2014. (ENG.). 40p. (J). (gr. -1-3). 17.99 *(978-1-4424-0168-6(0)*, Beach Lane Bks.) Beach Lane Bks.

—Gooseberry Park. Rylant, Cynthia. 2007. (ENG.). 144p. (J). (gr. 2-5). pap. 6.99 *(978-0-15-206159-3(2))* Houghton Mifflin Harcourt Publishing Co.

—Gooseberry Park & the Master Plan. Rylant, Cynthia. 2015. (ENG.). 128p. (J). (gr. 3-7). 16.99 *(978-1-4814-0449-5(0)*, Beach Lane Bks.) Beach Lane Bks.

—Hooray for Reading Day! Cuyler, Margery. 2008. (Jessica Worries Ser.). (ENG.). 32p. (J). (gr. k-3). 17.99 *(978-0-689-86188-8(5)*, Simon & Schuster Bks. For Young Readers) Simon & Schuster Bks. For Young Readers.

—Hooray for Reading Day! Cuyler, Margery. 2008. (J). (gr. k-1). 27.95 incl. audio *(978-0-8045-6969-9(X))*; 29.95 incl. audio compact disk *(978-0-8045-4194-7(9))* Spoken Arts, Inc.

—I Repeat, Don't Cheat! Cuyler, Margery. 2010. (ENG.). 32p. (J). (gr. k-3). 15.99 *(978-1-4169-7167-2(X)*, Simon & Schuster Bks. For Young Readers) Simon & Schuster Bks. For Young Readers.

—Life As We Knew It. Pfeffer, Susan Beth. 2006. (Life As We Knew It Ser.: 1). (ENG.). 352p. (YA). (gr. 7-12). 17.99 *(978-0-15-205826-5(5))* Houghton Mifflin Harcourt Publishing Co.

—Mr. Putter & Tabby Catch the Cold. Rylant, Cynthia. 2007. (Mr. Putter & Tabby Ser.). pap. 7.93 *(978-1-4189-5220-4(6))* Houghton Mifflin Harcourt Trade & Reference Pubs.

—Mr. Putter & Tabby Catch the Cold. Rylant, Cynthia. 2003. (Mr. Putter & Tabby Ser.). (gr. 1-4). 16.00 *(978-0-7569-1514-8(7))* Perfection Learning Corp.

—Mr. Putter & Tabby Clear the Decks. Rylant, Cynthia. (Mr. Putter & Tabby Ser.: 19). (ENG.). 44p. (J). (gr. 1-4). 2010. 15.00 *(978-0-15-206715-1(9))*; 2011. pap. 5.99 *(978-0-547-57695-4(1))* Houghton Mifflin Harcourt Publishing Co.

—Mr. Putter & Tabby Dance the Dance. Rylant, Cynthia. 2012. (Mr. Putter & Tabby Ser.: 21). (ENG.). 40p. (J). (gr. 1-4). 14.99 *(978-0-15-206415-0(X))* Houghton Mifflin Harcourt Publishing Co.

—Mr. Putter & Tabby Drop the Ball. Rylant, Cynthia. (Mr. Putter & Tabby Ser.). (ENG.). 44p. (J). (gr. 1-4). 2014. pap. 5.99 *(978-0-544-34115-9(5)*, HMH Books For Young Readers); 2013. 14.99 *(978-0-15-205072-6(8))* Houghton Mifflin Harcourt Publishing Co.

—Mr. Putter & Tabby Feed the Fish. Rylant, Cynthia. 2007. (Mr. Putter & Tabby Ser.). pap. 7.93 *(978-1-4189-5238-9(9))* Houghton Mifflin Harcourt Supplemental Pubs.

—Mr. Putter & Tabby Make a Wish. Rylant, Cynthia. 2006. (Mr. Putter & Tabby Ser.). (ENG.). 44p. (J). (gr. -1-3). pap. 5.99 *(978-0-15-205443-4(X))* Houghton Mifflin Harcourt Publishing Co.

—Mr. Putter & Tabby Make a Wish. Rylant, Cynthia. 2006. (Mr. Putter & Tabby Ser.). (gr. 1-4). 16.00 *(978-0-7569-6892-2(5))* Perfection Learning Corp.

—Mr. Putter & Tabby Ring the Bell. Rylant, Cynthia. (Mr. Putter & Tabby Ser.). (ENG.). 44p. (J). (gr. 1-4). 2012. pap. 5.99 *(978-0-547-85075-7(1))*; 2011. 14.99 *(978-0-15-205071-9(X))* Houghton Mifflin Harcourt Publishing Co.

—Mr. Putter & Tabby Ring the Bell. Rylant, Cynthia. ed. 2012. (Mr. Putter & Tabby Ser.). lib. bdg. 16.00 *(978-0-606-26614-7(3)*, Turtleback) Turtleback Bks.

—Mr. Putter & Tabby Run the Race. Rylant, Cynthia. 2010. (Mr. Putter & Tabby Ser.). (ENG.). 44p. (J). (gr. 1-4). pap. 5.99 *(978-0-547-24824-0(5))* Houghton Mifflin Harcourt Publishing Co.

—Mr. Putter & Tabby See the Stars. Rylant, Cynthia. 2008. (Mr. Putter & Tabby Ser.). (ENG.). 44p. (J). (gr. 1-4). pap. 5.99 *(978-0-15-206366-5(8))* Houghton Mifflin Harcourt Publishing Co.

Howard, Arthur. Mr. Putter & Tabby Smell the Roses. Rylant, Cynthia. 2015. (ENG.). 40p. (J). ***(978-0-15-206081-7(2))*** Harcourt.

Howard, Arthur. Mr. Putter & Tabby Spill the Beans. Rylant, Cynthia. (Mr. Putter & Tabby Ser.). (ENG.). 44p. (J). (gr. 1-4). 2010. pap. 5.99 *(978-0-547-41433-1(1))*; 2009. 15.00 *(978-0-15-205070-2(1))* Houghton Mifflin Harcourt Publishing Co.

—Mr. Putter & Tabby Spin the Yarn. Rylant, Cynthia. 2007. (Mr. Putter & Tabby Ser.). (ENG.). 44p. (J). (gr. 1-4). pap. 5.99 *(978-0-15-206095-4(2))* Houghton Mifflin Harcourt Publishing Co.

—Mr. Putter & Tabby Spin the Yarn. Rylant, Cynthia. 2007. (Mr. Putter & Tabby Ser.). (gr. 1-4). lib. bdg. 16.00 *(978-0-7569-8062-7(3))* Perfection Learning Corp.

—Mr. Putter & Tabby Stir the Soup. Rylant, Cynthia. 2004. (Mr. Putter & Tabby Ser.). (ENG.). 44p. (J). (gr. 1-4). pap. 5.99 *(978-0-15-205058-0(2))* Houghton Mifflin Harcourt Publishing Co.

—Mr. Putter & Tabby Stir the Soup. Rylant, Cynthia. 2004. (Mr. Putter & Tabby Ser.). (gr. 1-4). 16.00 *(978-0-7569-3915-1(1))* Perfection Learning Corp.

—Mr. Putter & Tabby Turn the Page. Rylant, Cynthia. 2014. (Mr. Putter & Tabby Ser.: 23). (ENG.). 40p. (J). (gr. 1-4). 14.99 *(978-0-15-206063-3(4)*, HMH Books For Young Readers) Houghton Mifflin Harcourt Publishing Co.

—Mr. Putter & Tabby Walk the Dog. Rylant, Cynthia. 2007. (Mr. Putter & Tabby Ser.). pap. 7.93 *(978-1-4189-5209-9(5))* Houghton Mifflin Harcourt Trade & Reference Pubs.

—Mr. Putter & Tabby Write the Book. Rylant, Cynthia. ed. 2005. (Mr. Putter & Tabby Ser.). (ENG.). 44p. (J). (gr. 1-4). pap. 5.99 *(978-0-15-200242-8(1))* Houghton Mifflin Harcourt Publishing Co.

—Mr. Putter & Tabby Write the Book. Rylant, Cynthia. 2005. (Mr. Putter & Tabby Ser.). 36p. (J). (gr. 1-4). 13.60 *(978-0-7569-5446-8(0))* Perfection Learning Corp.

—Noodle & Lou. Scanlon, Liz Garton. 2011. (ENG.). 32p. (J). (gr. -1-1). 15.99 *(978-1-4424-0288-1(1)*, Beach Lane Bks.) Beach Lane Bks.

—Stop Drop & Roll. Cuyler, Margery. 25.95 incl. audio *(978-1-59112-976-9(1))*; 28.95 incl. audio compact disk *(978-1-59112-980-6(X))*; pap. 16.95 incl. audio *(978-1-59112-975-2(3))*; pap. incl. audio *(978-1-59112-977-6(X))*; pap. 18.95 incl. audio compact disk *(978-1-59112-979-0(6))*; pap. incl. audio compact disk *(978-1-59112-981-3(8))* Live Oak Media.

—100th Day Worries. Cuyler, Margery. 2006. (ENG.). 32p. (J). (gr. k-3). reprint ed. 7.99 *(978-1-4169-0789-3(0)*, Simon & Schuster Bks. For Young Readers) Simon & Schuster Bks. For Young Readers.

Howard, Arthur. Mr. Putter & Tabby Catch the Cold. Howard, Arthur. Rylant, Cynthia. 2003. (Mr. Putter & Tabby Ser.). (ENG.). 44p. (J). (gr. 1-4). pap. 5.99 *(978-0-15-204760-3(3))* Houghton Mifflin Harcourt Publishing Co.

—Mr. Putter & Tabby Dance the Dance. Howard, Arthur. Rylant, Cynthia. 2013. (Mr. Putter & Tabby Ser.). (ENG.). 40p. (J). (gr. 1-4). pap. 5.99 *(978-0-544-10496-9(X))* Houghton Mifflin Harcourt Publishing Co.

Howard, Becky L. Harrison Goes Camping. Howard, Becky L. Pine, Margherita N., ed. 2nd ed. 2012. 26p. (-18). pap. 11.98 *(978-0-9848782-1-5(1))* Palmetto Street Publishing.

Howard, Colin. Drawing Fascinating Animals. Colich, Abby. 2015. (Drawing Amazing Animals Ser.). (ENG.). 32p. (gr. 3-4). 27.32 *(978-1-4914-2133-8(9))* Capstone Pr., Inc.

—The Ultimate Girls' Guide to Drawing: Puppies, Polar Bears, & Other Adorable Animals. Colich, Abby. 2015. (ENG.). 144p. (gr. 3-4). pap. 14.95 *(978-1-62370-229-8(1))* Capstone Young Readers.

—Wolves. Black, Robyn Hood. 2008. (ENG.). 24p. (J). (gr. 3-18). 19.95 *(978-1-58117-817-3(4)*, Intervisual/Piggy Toes) Bendon, Inc.

Howard, Colin, jt. illus. see Calle, Juan.

Howard, Dave. Lady's Day to Play. Howard, Dave. 2011. (ENG.). 32p. (J). (gr. -1-3). pap. 14.95 *(978-0-938467-25-0(5))* Headline Bks., Inc.

Howard, Devon, photos by. Surfboards: From Start to Finish. Smith, Ryan A. 2006. (Made in the U. S. A. Ser.). (ENG., 32p. (J). (gr. 3-7). lib. bdg. 25.65 *(978-1-4103-0728-6(X)*, Blackbirch Pr., Inc.) Cengage Gale.

Howard, Ellie Nothaus. Daddies Don't Get Snow Days. Ball, S. N. 2013. (ENG.). 28p. (J). pap. 13.95 *(978-1-4787-1188-9(4))* Outskirts Pr., Inc.

Howard, Josh. Dead@17: Blood of Saints. Howard, Josh. 2004. 112p. (YA). per. 14.95 *(978-0-9754193-1-1(5))* Viper Comics.

—Dead@17: The Complete First Series. Howard, Josh. 2004. (YA). per. 14.95 *(978-0-9754193-0-4(7))* Viper Comics.

Howard, Juliet. My Very Own Dreidel: A Pop-up Hanakkah Celebration! Kollin, Dani. 2007. (ENG.). 12p. 10.95 *(978-1-58117-592-9(2)*, Intervisual/Piggy Toes) Bendon, Inc.

Howard, Linda & Dockray, Tracy Arah. Mi Gran Libro de Palabras Play-Doh. 2006. (SPA.). 10p. (J). (gr. -1-4). reprint ed. 10.00 *(978-1-4223-5586-2(1))* DIANE Publishing Co.

Howard, Megz. Fiona Faintly: A Goats Tale. Bristol, P. L. & Branda, Barnabus. 2011. 32p. pap. 24.95 *(978-1-4626-3362-3(5))* America Star Bks.

Howard, Monique. The Moon Creeper (Simplified Chinese & English) Howard, Monique. Li, Helen, tr. 2010. (CHI & ENG.). 40p. (YA). pap. 7.95 *(978-1-935706-24-3(1))* Wiggles Pr.

Howard, Norma. Walking the Choctaw Road: Stories from Red People Memory. Tingle, Tim. 2003. (ENG.). 128p. (J). (gr. 7-9). 16.95 *(978-0-938317-74-6(1))* Cinco Puntos Pr.

Howard, Pam. Alex & the Amazing Lemonade Stand. Scott, Liz et al. 2005. 32p. (gr. -1-5). 15.95 *(978-0-9753200-0-6(9))* PAJE Publishing Co.

Howard, Patricia. Live! From the Classroom! It's Mythology! Five Read-Aloud Plays Based on Hero Myths from Around the World. Thurston, Cheryl Miller & Etzel, Laurie Hopkins. 2003. (ENG.). 82p. per. 16.95 *(978-1-877673-59-7(5)*, MYTH-BWK03) Cottonwood Pr., Inc.

Howard, Paul. The Cat Who Wanted to Go Home. Tomlinson, Jill. 2014. (ENG.). 96p. (J). (gr. -1-2). pap. 9.99 *(978-1-4052-7196-7(5))* Egmont Bks., Ltd. GBR. Dist: Independent Pubs. Group.

—Classic Poetry. Rosen, Michael, ed. 2009. (Candlewick Illustrated Classic Ser.). (ENG.). 160p. (J). (gr. 5-7). pap. 12.99 *(978-0-7636-4210-5(X))* Candlewick Pr.

—Full, Full, Full of Love. Cooke, Trish. 2008. (ENG.). 32p. (J). (gr. -1-k). pap. 3.99 *(978-0-7636-3883-2(8))* Candlewick Pr.

—The Gorilla Who Wanted to Grow Up. Tomlinson, Jill. 2014. (ENG.). 112p. (J). (gr. -1-2). pap. 9.99 *(978-1-4052-7195-0(7))* Egmont Bks., Ltd. GBR. Dist: Independent Pubs. Group.

—The Hen Who Wouldn't Give Up. Tomlinson, Jill. 2014. (ENG.). 112p. (J). (gr. -1-2). pap. 9.99 *(978-1-4052-7193-6(0))* Egmont Bks., Ltd. GBR. Dist: Independent Pubs. Group.

—Look at You! A Baby Body Book. Henderson, Kathy. 2007. (ENG.). 40p. (J). (-k). 15.99 *(978-0-7636-2745-4(3))* Candlewick Pr.

—The Otter Who Wanted to Know. Tomlinson, Jill. (ENG.). 96p. (J). (gr. -1-2). 2014. pap. 8.99 *(978-1-4052-7194-3(9))*; 2004. reprint ed. pap. 8.99 *(978-1-4052-1082-9(6))* Egmont Bks., Ltd. GBR. Dist: Independent Pubs. Group.

—The Owl Who Was Afraid of the Dark. Tomlinson, Jill. 2014. (ENG.). 112p. (J). (gr. -1-2). pap. 9.99 *(978-1-4052-7197-4(3))* Egmont Bks., Ltd. GBR. Dist: Independent Pubs. Group.

Howard, Paul. The Owl Who Was Afraid of the Dark, Pack. Tomlinson, Jill. 2015. (ENG.). 32p. (J). (gr. -1-2). 19.99 ***(978-1-4052-7554-5(5))*** Egmont Bks., Ltd. GBR. Dist: Independent Pubs. Group.

Howard, Paul. The Penguin Who Wanted to Find Out. Tomlinson, Jill. 2014. (ENG.). 96p. (J). (gr. -1-2). pap. 9.99 *(978-1-4052-7191-2(4))* Egmont Bks., Ltd. GBR. Dist: Independent Pubs. Group.

—Stomp! Willis, Jeanne. 2012. (ENG.). 32p. (J). (gr. -1-k). pap. 9.99 *(978-1-84616-795-9(7))* Hodder & Stoughton GBR. Dist: Independent Pubs. Group.

—Three Favourite Animal Stories. Tomlinson, Jill. 2014. (ENG.). 304p. (J). (gr. k). pap. 12.99 *(978-1-4052-7192-9(2))* Egmont Bks., Ltd. GBR. Dist: Independent Pubs. Group.

Howard, Pauline Rodriguez. Icy Watermelon/Sandia Fria: CD & Book Set. 2008. (ENG & SPA.). 32p. (J). 23.95 *(978-0-9815686-0-7(2))* Lorito Bks., Inc.

Howard, Pauline Rodriguez, jt. illus. see Rodriguez Howard, Pauline.

Howard, Philip & Miller, Josh. Mystery at Blackbeard's Cove. Penn, Audrey. 2004. (ENG.). 200p. (J). (gr. 3-7). 14.95 *(978-0-9749303-1-2(8))* Tanglewood Pr.

Howard, Philip & Miller, Joshua. Mystery at Blackbeard's Cove. Penn, Audrey. 2004. (ENG.). 263p. (J). (gr. 2-7). per. 7.95 *(978-1-933718-09-5(9))* Tanglewood Pr.

Howard, Rebecca. Flagtastic Flags. 2006. (ENG.). 32p. (J). (gr. -1-3). 14.95 *(978-0-7145-3305-6(X))* Boyars, Marion Pubs., Inc.

Howard, Rushton. Sebastian Reckless. Howard, Rushton. 2005. 263p. (J). per. 8.99 (978-0-9768088-0-0(3)) Abdiel Productions.
Howard, Virginia. Timothy Hubble & the King Cake Party, 1 vol. Prieto, Anita C. 2008. (ENG.). 32p. (J). (gr. k-3). 16.99 (978-1-58980-584-2(4)) Pelican Publishing Co., Inc.
Howard, Zachariah. The Shroud of A'Ranka. Sniegoski, Thomas E. 2008. (Brimstone Network Ser.: 2). (ENG.). 288p. (J). (gr. 4-8). pap. 5.99 (978-1-4169-5105-6(9), Simon & Schuster/Paula Wiseman Bks.) Simon & Schuster/Paula Wiseman Bks.
Howarth, Craig. Dirkle Smat Inside Mount Flatbottom. Garthwaite, Lynn D. 2006. 48p. (J). pap. 9.95 (978-1-59663-512-8(6), Castle Keep Pr.) Rock, James A. & Co. Pubs.
—Michael's Safari. Francis, JennaKay. 2013. 12p. pap. 8.95 (978-1-61633-411-6(8)) Guardian Angel Publishing, Inc.
—That's Not A Pickle! Kruse, Donald W. 2008. (ENG.). 40p. (J). pap. 12.95 (978-1-59663-560-9(6), Castle Keep Pr.) Rock, James A. & Co. Pubs.
—That's Not a Pickle! Part 2 Pt. 2. Kruse, Donald W. 2010. 44p. (J). pap. 12.95 (978-1-59663-686-6(6), Castle Keep Pr.) Rock, James A. & Co. Pubs.
Howarth, Craigh. The Perfect Gift. Mair, J. Samia. 2010. (ENG.). 29p. (J). (gr. k-2). 8.95 (978-0-86037-438-1(6)) Kube Publishing Ltd. GBR. Dist: Consortium Bk. Sales & Distribution.
Howarth, Daniel. The Big Fuzzy. Castle, Caroline. 2007. (Storytime Ser.). (ENG.). 24p. (J). (gr. -1-17). lib. bdg. 15.99 (978-1-59566-368-9(1)) QEB Publishing Inc.
—'Cause I Love You. Carr, Jan. 2011. (ENG.). 22p. (J). (gr. k — 1). bds. 8.99 (978-0-439-87278-2(2), Cartwheel Bks.) Scholastic, Inc.
—Daisy Dinosaur Gets Lost. Smallman, Steve. 2010. (Storytime Ser.). (ENG.). 24p. (J). (gr. -1-1). lib. bdg. 15.99 (978-1-59566-858-5(6)) QEB Publishing Inc.
—Good Night Little Moo. Cabral, Jeane. 2007. (Night Light Book Ser.). 10p. (gr. -1-k). (978-1-84666-128-0(5), Tide Mill Pr.) Top That! Publishing PLC.
—Good Night Little Piggy. Williams, Becky. 2007. (Night Light Book Ser.). 10p. (gr. -1-k). bds. (978-1-84666-129-7(3), Tide Mill Pr.) Top That! Publishing PLC.
—The Goose That Laid the Golden Eggs. 2006. (First Reading Level 3 Ser.). 48p. (J). (gr. 1-4). 8.99 (978-0-7945-1378-8(6), Usborne) EDC Publishing.
—The Hare & the Tortoise. MacKinnon, Mairi, ed. 2007. (First Reading Level 4 Ser.). 48p. (J). (gr. -1-3). 8.99 (978-0-7945-1612-3(2), Usborne) EDC Publishing.
—Hoppy Hanukkah!, 1 vol. Glaser, Linda. 2009. (ENG.). 24p. (J). (gr. -1-k). 15.99 (978-0-8075-3378-9(5)) Whitman, Albert & Co.
—How to Catch a Falling Star. Howarth, Heidi. 2010. (Storytime Ser.). (ENG.). 24p. (J). (gr. -1-1). lib. bdg. 15.99 (978-1-59566-835-6(7)) QEB Publishing Inc.
—I Am a Mole, & I Live in a Hole. Conchie, Kathryn. Top That Publishing Staff, ed. 2008. (Story Book Ser.). 12p. (J). (gr. -1). (978-1-84666-575-2(2), Tide Mill Pr.) Top That! Publishing PLC.
—Land of the lost Teddies. Fischel, Emma. rev. ed. 2003. 32p. (J). (gr. 2-18). pap. 4.95 (978-0-7945-0402-1(7), Usborne) EDC Publishing.
—Mouse's Summer Muddle. Loughrey, Anita. 2012. (Animal Seasons Ser.). (ENG.). 24p. (J). (gr. -1-1). 15.99 (978-1-60992-226-9(3)) QEB Publishing Inc.
Howarth, Daniel. The Otter Who Loved to Hold Hands. Howarth, Heidi. 2014. (J). (978-1-4351-5537-4(8)) Barnes & Noble, Inc.
Howarth, Daniel. Owl's Winter Rescue. Loughrey, Anita. 2012. (Animal Seasons Ser.). (ENG.). 24p. (J). (gr. -1-1). 15.99 (978-1-60992-224-5(7)) QEB Publishing Inc.
—Paddywack. Spinner, Stephanie. 2010. (Step into Reading Ser.). (ENG.). 48p. (J). (gr. k-3). pap. 3.99 (978-0-375-86186-4(6)) Random Hse., Inc.
—Polar Bears: Internet-Referenced. Mason, Conrad. 2009. (First Reading Level 4 Ser.). 48p. (J). 6.99 (978-0-7945-2457-9(5), Usborne) EDC Publishing.
—Rabbit's Spring Adventure. Loughrey, Anita. 2012. (Animal Seasons Ser.). (ENG.). 24p. (J). (gr. -1-1). 15.99 (978-1-60992-225-2(5)) QEB Publishing Inc.
—Santa's Little Helper. McAllister, Angela & Scholastic, Inc. Staff. 2008. (ENG.). 32p. (J). (gr. -1-k). 14.99 (978-0-545-09444-3(5), Orchard Bks.) Scholastic, Inc.
—Who's Been Eating My Porridge? Butler, M. Christina. 2004. 32p. (J). (gr. -1). tchr. ed. 15.95 (978-1-58925-040-6(0)) Tiger Tales.
—A Wild Day with Dad. Callahan, Sean. 2012. (ENG.). 18p. (J). (gr. -1-k). bds. 7.99 (978-0-8075-2295-0(3)) Whitman, Albert & Co.
Howe, Cindy T. From Bullies to Friends. Nikolet, C. T. 2008. 25p. pap. 24.95 (978-1-60610-121-6(8)) America Star Bks.
Howe, John. Literary Lessons from The Lord of the Rings. Harper, Amelia. 2004. 622p. (YA). (gr. 7-12). stu. ed., spiral bd. 50.00 (978-0-9754934-1-0(8), Literary Lessons) HomeScholar Bks.
Howe, Kim. American Life Series: Family, Teacher, Friend, 3 books. 2006. 80p. 19.95 (978-1-59971-554-4(6)) Aardvark Global Publishing.
Howe, Norma. Crocodile Tours. Tye, Peter. 2012. 80p. pap. (978-1-78176-536-4(7)) FeedARead.com.
Howe, Philip. Kailey. Koss, Amy Goldman. 2003. (American Girl of Today Ser.). (ENG.). 160p. (J). pap. 6.95 (978-1-58485-591-0(6)) American Girl Publishing, Inc.
Howe, Tina Field. Snailsworth, a slow ittle Story. Howe, Tina Field. 2007. 24p. (J). per. 12.95 (978-0-9768585-3-9(3)) Howe, Tina Field.
Howell, Corin. The Great Core Caper. Wyatt, Chris "Doc". 2014. (Bravest Warriors Ser.: 1). (ENG.). 112p. (J). pap. 7.99 (978-1-4215-7539-1(6)) Viz Media.
Howell, Jason W. Remember Me Always: A Remembrance Scrapbook. Crain, Suzanne L. 2004. 52p. spiral bd. (978-0-9763254-0-6(3)) Crain, Suzanne.
Howell, Richard, jt. illus. see Milgrom, Al.
Howell, Troy. First Prayers: A Celebration of Faith & Love. 2012. (ENG.). 32p. (J). 12.95 (978-1-4027-6454-7(5)) Sterling Publishing Co., Inc.
—Goliath: Hero of the Great Baltimore Fire. Friddell, Claudia. 2010. (True Stories Ser.). (ENG.). 32p. (J). 17.95 (978-1-58536-455-8(X)) Sleeping Bear Pr.
—The Last of the Mohicans. Cooper, James Fenimore. 2008. (Classic Starts(tm) Ser.). (ENG.). 160p. (J). (gr. 2-4). 6.95 (978-1-4027-4577-5(X)) Sterling Publishing Co., Inc.
—Little Lord Fauntleroy. Burnett, Frances Hodgson. 2008. (Classic Starts(tm) Ser.). (ENG.). 160p. (J). (gr. 2-4). 5.95 (978-1-4027-4578-2(8)) Sterling Publishing Co., Inc.
—The Man in the Iron Mask. Dumas, Alexandre. 2008. (Classic Starts(tm) Ser.). (ENG.). 160p. (J). (gr. 2-4). 6.95 (978-1-4027-4579-9(6)) Sterling Publishing Co., Inc.
—O Is for Old Dominion: A Virginia Alphabet. Edwards, Pamela Duncan. 2005. (State Ser.). (ENG.). 40p. (J). (gr. -1-3). 17.95 (978-1-58536-161-8(5)) Sleeping Bear Pr.
—The Phantom of the Opera. Leroux, Gaston. 2008. (Classic Starts(tm) Ser.). (ENG.). 160p. (J). (gr. 2-4). 6.95 (978-1-4027-4580-5(X)) Sterling Publishing Co., Inc.
—The Time Machine. Wells, H. G. 2008. (Classic Starts(tm) Ser.). (ENG.). 160p. (J). (gr. 2-4). 6.95 (978-1-4027-4582-9(6)) Sterling Publishing Co., Inc.
Howell, Troy & Himmelman, Jeff. Jean Laffite: The Pirate Who Saved America. Rubin, Susan Goldman. 2012. (ENG.). 48p. (J). (gr. 1-4). 19.95 (978-0-8109-9733-2(9), Abrams Bks. for Young Readers) Abrams.
Howell, Troy, jt. illus. see Minor, Wendell.
Howells, Graham. The Children's Book of Myths & Legends. Randall, Ronne. 2012. (ENG.). 128p. (J). (gr. 2-7). pap. 11.99 (978-1-84322-819-6(X)) Anness Publishing GBR. Dist: National Bk. Network.
—Creu Brawddegau. Meek, Elin. ed. 2005. (Helpwch Eich Plentyn / Help Your Child Ser.).Tr. of Forming Sentences. (WEL & ENG.). 48p. pap. 4.99 (978-1-84323-354-1(1)) Gomer Pr. GBR. Dist: Gomer Pr.
—Dragon Masters #1: Rise of the Earth Dragon (a Branches Book) West, Tracey. 2014. (Dragon Masters Ser.: 1). (ENG.). 96p. (J). (gr. 1-3). pap. 4.99 (978-0-545-64623-9(5)) Scholastic, Inc.
—Dragon Masters #1: Rise of the Earth Dragon (a Branches Book) - Library Edition. West, Tracey. 2014. (Dragon Masters Ser.: 1). (ENG.). 96p. (J). (gr. 1-3). 15.99 (978-0-545-64624-6(3)) Scholastic, Inc.
—Dragon Masters #2: Saving the Sun Dragon (a Branches Book) West, Tracey. 2014. (Dragon Masters Ser.: 2). (ENG.). 96p. (J). (gr. 1-3). pap. 4.99 (978-0-545-64625-3(1)) Scholastic, Inc.
Howells, Graham. Power of the Fire Dragon. West, Tracey. 2015. (Dragon Masters Ser.: No. 4). (ENG.). 96p. (J). (gr. 1-3). pap. 4.99 (978-0-545-64631-4(6)) Scholastic, Inc.
Howells, Graham. Saving the Sun Dragon. West, Tracey. 2014. (Dragon Masters Ser.: 2). (ENG.). 96p. (J). (gr. 1-3). 15.99 (978-0-545-64626-0(X)) Scholastic, Inc.
—Secret of the Water Dragon. West, Tracey. 2015. (Dragon Masters Ser.: 3). (ENG.). 96p. (J). (gr. 1-3). pap. 4.99 (978-0-545-64628-4(6)) Scholastic, Inc.
—Tales of King Arthur: Ten Legendary Stories of the Knights of the Round Table. Randall, Daniel & Randall, Ronne. 2013. (ENG.). 80p. pap. 9.99 (978-1-84322-922-3(6)) Anness Publishing GBR. Dist: National Bk. Network.
Howells, Tania. Berkeley's Barn Owl Dance. Johnson, Tera. 2008. (ENG.). 32p. (J). (gr. -1-2). 16.95 (978-1-55453-263-6(9)) Kids Can Pr., Ltd. CAN. Dist: Univ. of Toronto Pr.
—Willow Finds a Way. Button, Lana. 2013. (ENG.). 32p. (J). 16.95 (978-1-55453-842-3(4)) Kids Can Pr., Ltd. CAN. Dist: Univ. of Toronto Pr.
—Willow's Whispers, 0 vols. Button, Lana. (ENG.). 32p. (J). 2014. pap. 7.95 (978-1-55453-744-0(4)); 2010. (gr. -1-2). 16.95 (978-1-55453-280-3(9)) Kids Can Pr., Ltd. CAN. Dist: Univ. of Toronto Pr.
Howes, Bryan Arthur. The Purple Scarf. Coughlin, Jennie Rose. 2008. 20p. per. 24.95 (978-1-60441-733-3(1)) America Star Bks.
Howland, Naomi. The Nutcracker. Dewhurst, Carin. 2006. 24p. (J). (gr. 4-8). reprint ed. 20.00 (978-1-4223-5524-4(1)) DIANE Publishing Co.
Howland, Naomi. The Mystery Bear: A Purim Story. Howland, Naomi, tr. Adelson, Leone. 2004. 32p. (J). (gr. -1-2). 15.00 (978-0-618-33727-9(X), Clarion Bks.) Houghton Mifflin Harcourt Trade & Reference Pubs.
Howling, Adam. Plants vs. Zombies: Official Guide to Protecting Your Brains. Swatman, Simon. 2013. (Plants vs. Zombies Ser.). (ENG.). 176p. (J). (gr. 1-5). pap. 7.99 (978-0-06-222855-0(2), HarperFestival) HarperCollins Pubs.
Hoyes, Kerry. What You Eat It's up to You. Yanisko, Thomas. 2012. 36p. pap. 9.99 (978-1-937260-26-2(7)) Sleepytown Pr.
Hoyt, Ard. Alice from Dallas. Sadler, Marilyn. 2014. (ENG.). 40p. (J). (gr. -1-3). 16.95 (978-1-4197-0790-2(6), Abrams Bks. for Young Readers) Abrams.
—Chasing George Washington. Kidd, Ronald et al. 2009. (ENG.). 80p. (J). (gr. 2-5). 12.99 (978-1-4169-4858-2(9), Simon & Schuster Bks. For Young Readers) Simon & Schuster Bks. For Young Readers.
—Chasing George Washington. Kennedy Center Staff. 2011. (ENG.). 80p. (J). (gr. 2-5). pap. 5.99 (978-1-4169-4861-2(9), Simon & Schuster Bks. For Young Readers) Simon & Schuster Bks. For Young Readers.
—Daniel Boone's Great Escape. Spradlin, Michael P. 2008. (ENG.). 32p. (J). (gr. k-3). 16.95 (978-0-8027-9581-6(1)) Walker & Co.
—The Day Dirk Yeller Came to Town. Casanova, Mary. 2011. (ENG.). 36p. (J). (gr. -1-3). 16.99 (978-0-374-31742-3(9), Farrar, Straus & Giroux (BYR)) Farrar, Straus & Giroux.
—The Hair of Zoe Fleefenbacher Goes to School. Anderson, Laurie Halse. 2009. (ENG.). 32p. (J). (gr. 1-5). 17.99 (978-0-689-85809-3(4), Simon & Schuster Bks. For Young Readers) Simon & Schuster Bks. For Young Readers.
—I'm a Manatee. Lithgow, John. 2007. (ENG.). 32p. (J). (gr. -1-3). 9.99 (978-0-689-85452-1(8), Little Simon) Little Simon.
—I'm a Manatee. Lithgow, John. 2003. (ENG.). 32p. (J). (gr. -1-3). 18.99 (978-0-689-85427-9(7), Simon & Schuster Bks. For Young Readers) Simon & Schuster Bks. For Young Readers.
—The Impossible Patriotism Project. Skeers, Linda. 2009. (ENG.). 32p. (J). (gr. -1-1). pap. 6.99 (978-0-14-241391-3(7), Puffin) Penguin Publishing Group.
—Love the Baby, 1 vol. Layne, Steven L. 2007. (ENG.). 32p. (J). (gr. k-k). 16.99 (978-1-58980-392-3(2)) Pelican Publishing Co., Inc.
—One-Dog Canoe. Casanova, Mary. 2003. (ENG.). 32p. (J). (gr. -1-1). 18.99 (978-0-374-35638-5(6), Farrar, Straus & Giroux (BYR)) Farrar, Straus & Giroux.
—One-Dog Canoe. Casanova, Mary. 2009. (ENG.). 32p. (J). (gr. -1-1). pap. 7.99 (978-0-312-56118-5(0)) Square Fish.
—One-Dog Sleigh. Casanova, Mary. 2013. (ENG.). 32p. (J). (gr. k-3). 16.99 (978-0-374-35639-2(4), Farrar, Straus & Giroux (BYR)) Farrar, Straus & Giroux.
—Piggies in Pajamas. Meadows, Michelle. 2013. (ENG.). 32p. (J). (gr. -1-2). 15.99 (978-1-4169-4982-4(8), Simon & Schuster Bks. For Young Readers) Simon & Schuster Bks. For Young Readers.
—Piggies in the Kitchen. Meadows, Michelle. 2011. (ENG.). 32p. (J). (gr. -1-2). 14.99 (978-1-4169-3787-6(0), Simon & Schuster Bks. For Young Readers) Simon & Schuster Bks. For Young Readers.
—Saying Goodbye to Lulu. Demas, Corinne. 2009. (ENG.). 32p. (J). (gr. -1-1). pap. 7.00 (978-0-316-04749-4(X)) Little, Brown Bks. for Young Readers.
—Share with Brother, 1 vol. Layne, Steven L. 2010. (ENG.). 32p. (J). (gr. k-3). 16.99 (978-1-58980-860-7(6)) Pelican Publishing Co., Inc.
—Some Cat! Casanova, Mary. 2012. (ENG.). 40p. (J). (gr. -1-k). 17.99 (978-0-374-37123-4(7), Farrar, Straus & Giroux (BYR)) Farrar, Straus & Giroux.
—Some Dog! Casanova, Mary. 2007. (ENG.). 40p. (J). (gr. -1-1). 17.99 (978-0-374-37133-3(4), Farrar, Straus & Giroux (BYR)) Farrar, Straus & Giroux.
—Stay with Sister, 1 vol. Layne, Steven L. 2012. (ENG.). 32p. (J). (gr. k-3). 16.99 (978-1-4556-1523-0(4)) Pelican Publishing Co., Inc.
—Teachers' Night Before Halloween, 1 vol. Layne, Steven L. 2008. (ENG.). 32p. (gr. k-3). 16.99 (978-1-58980-585-9(2)) Pelican Publishing Co., Inc.
—Teddy Roosevelt & the Treasure of Ursa Major. Kennedy Center Staff. 2011. (ENG.). 128p. (J). (gr. 2-5). pap. 5.99 (978-1-4169-4860-5(0), Simon & Schuster Bks. For Young Readers) Simon & Schuster Bks. For Young Readers.
—Tilly the Trickster. Shannon, Molly. 2011. (ENG.). 32p. (J). (gr. -1-3). 16.95 (978-1-4197-0030-9(8), Abrams Bks. for Young Readers) Abrams.
—Unleashed: The Lives of White House Pets. Kennedy Center Staff. 2011. (ENG.). 112p. (J). (gr. 2-5). pap. 5.99 (978-1-4169-4862-9(7), Simon & Schuster Bks. For Young Readers) Simon & Schuster Bks. For Young Readers.
—Utterly Otterly Day. Casanova, Mary. 2008. (ENG.). 40p. (J). (gr. -1-3). 17.99 (978-1-4169-0868-5(4), Simon & Schuster Bks. For Young Readers) Simon & Schuster Bks. For Young Readers.
—Utterly Otterly Night. Casanova, Mary. 2011. (ENG.). 40p. (J). (gr. -1-1). 16.99 (978-1-4169-7562-5(4), Simon & Schuster Bks. For Young Readers) Simon & Schuster Bks. For Young Readers.
—When the Cows Got Loose. Weis, Carol. 2006. (ENG.). 40p. (J). (gr. -1-1). 17.99 (978-0-689-85166-7(9), Simon & Schuster Bks. For Young Readers) Simon & Schuster Bks. For Young Readers.
—Winnie Finn, Worm Farmer. Brendler, Carol & Brendler, Carol H. 2009. (ENG.). 32p. (J). (gr. -1-3). 17.99 (978-0-374-38440-1(1), Farrar, Straus & Giroux (BYR)) Farrar, Straus & Giroux.
Hoyt, Richard, photos by. Living with a Star: From Sunscreen to Space Weather. Glaser, David et al. 2004. (Great Explorations in Math & Science Ser.). 176p. (YA). (gr. 6-8). pap. 28.00 incl. cd-rom (978-0-924886-73-7(0), GEMS) Univ. of California, Berkeley, Lawrence Hall of Science.
Hranilovich, Barbara. Pretty Little Lilly & the Land of Sweet Dreams (Hard Bound) Hornsby, Ashley Brooke. 2007. (J). 15.95 (978-0-9777241-2-3(3)) Cepia LLC.
—Pretty Little Lilly & the Land of Sweet Dreams (Paperback) Hornsby, Ashley Brooke. 2007. (J). (978-0-9777241-3-0(1)) Cepia LLC.
—Skimper-Scamper. Newell, Jeff. 2005. (Green Light Readers Level 2 Ser.). (J). (gr. k-2). 11.60 (978-0-7569-5244-0(1)) Perfection Learning Corp.
Hruby, Patrick. Counting in the Garden. Hruby, Emily. 2013. (ENG.). 58p. (J). 16.95 (978-1-62326-005-7(1)) AMMO Bks., LLC.
Hsu, Florence. Perfect Solution. Keay, Ben. 2009. (YA). (978-1-933791-09-8(8)) Finial Publishing.
Hsu, Jack. Poppie's Adventures: Serpents in Paradise. Yeh, Julie. 2003. 48p. (J). per. (978-0-9742386-0-9(0)) Way Out Comics.
Hu, Caroline. The Elephant Dancer: A Story of Ancient India, 1 vol. Gunderson, Jessica. 2009. (Read-It! Chapter Books: Historical Tales Ser.). (ENG.). 64p. (gr. 2-4). 21.32 (978-1-4048-5219-8(0), Chapter Readers) Picture Window Bks.
—The Horse on the Hill: A Story of Ancient India, 1 vol. Gunderson, Jessica. 2009. (Read-It! Chapter Books: Historical Tales Ser.). (ENG.). 64p. (gr. 2-4). 21.32 (978-1-4048-5222-8(0), Chapter Readers) Picture Window Bks.
—The King's Warrior: A Story of Ancient India, 1 vol. Gunderson, Jessica. 2009. (Read-It! Chapter Books: Historical Tales Ser.). (ENG.). 64p. (gr. 2-4). 21.32 (978-1-4048-5228-0(X), Chapter Readers) Picture Window Bks.
—Olivia & Oscar Build an Opinion Piece. Pelleschi, Andrea. 2013. (ENG.). 32p. (J). lib. bdg. 25.27 (978-1-59953-582-1(3)); (gr. 2-4). pap. 11.94 (978-1-60357-556-0(1)) Norwood Hse. Pr.
—Phillip & Penny Learn about Pronouns. Robinson, Joanna Jarc. 2015. (Language Builders Ser.). (ENG.). 32p. (J). (gr. 2-4). pap. 11.94 (978-1-60357-705-2(X)); lib. bdg. 25.27 (978-1-59953-670-5(6)) Norwood Hse. Pr.
—The Servant & the Water Princess: A Story of Ancient India, 1 vol. Gunderson, Jessica. 2009. (Read-It! Chapter Books: Historical Tales Ser.). (ENG.). 64p. (gr. 2-4). 21.32 (978-1-4048-5225-9(5), Chapter Readers) Picture Window Bks.
—Stranger on the Silk Road: A Story of Ancient China, 1 vol. Gunderson, Jessica. 2008. (Read-It! Chapter Books: Historical Tales Ser.). (ENG.). 64p. (gr. 2-4). lib. bdg. 21.32 (978-1-4048-4736-1(7), Chapter Readers) Picture Window Bks.
Hu, Ying-Hwa. The Three Billy Goats Gruff, 1 vol. Wright, Rebecca Hu-Van & Asbjørnsen, Peter Christen. 2014. (ENG.). 32p. (J). (978-1-59572-666-0(5)); pap. (978-1-59572-667-4(5)) Star Bright Bks., Inc.
Hu, Ying-Hwa & Van Wright, Cornelius. Alicia's Happy Day, 1 vol. Starr, Meg. 2003. (ENG.). 32p. (J). (gr. -1-3). 15.95 (978-1-887734-85-1(6)) Star Bright Bks., Inc.
—Jumping the Broom. Scholastic, Inc. Staff & Black, Sonia. 2004. (Just for You Ser.). (ENG.). 32p. pap. 3.99 (978-0-439-56878-4(1), Teaching Resources) Scholastic, Inc.
—Singing for Dr. King. Medearis, Angela Shelf. 2004. 32p. (J). lib. bdg. 15.00 (978-1-4242-0237-9(X)) Fitzgerald Bks.
—Snow in Jerusalem. da Costa, Deborah. 2008. (ENG.). 32p. (J). (gr. 1-5). 6.99 (978-0-8075-7525-3(9)) Whitman, Albert & Co.
Hu, Ying-Hwa, jt. illus. see Van Wright, Cornelius.
Huadi. Leyendas, Mitos, Cuentos y Otros Relatos de las Praderas Norteamericanas. Sugobono, Nahuel. 2003. (SPA.). 96p. pap. 11.95 (978-987-550-278-9(2)) Longseller S.A. ARG. Dist: Bilingual Pubns. Co., The.
—Leyendas, Mitos, Cuentos y Otros Relatos Tobas. Sugobono, Nahuel. 2003. (SPA.). 86p. pap. 11.95 (978-987-550-296-3(0)) Longseller S.A. ARG. Dist: Bilingual Pubns. Co., The.
Huadi. Tinke Tinke. Bornemann, Elsa. 2015. 152p. (J). (gr. 4-8). pap. 10.95 (978-968-19-1518-6(6)) Aguilar, Altea, Taurus, Alfaguara, S.A. de C.V MEX. Dist: Santillana USA Publishing Co., Inc.
Huang, Benrei. The Bedtime Rhyme. Wangerin, Walter, Jr. 2008. (ENG.). 32p. (J). (gr. -1-3). 16.95 (978-1-55725-467-2(2)) Paraclete Pr., Inc.
—Chinese New Year. Heinrichs, Ann. 2013. (Holidays & Celebrations Ser.). (ENG.). 32p. (J). (gr. k-3). 27.07 (978-1-62323-504-8(9), 206275) Child's World, Inc., The.
—Dragon Dance: A Chinese New Year. Holub, Joan. 2003. (Lift-The-Flap, Puffin Ser.). (ENG.). 16p. (J). (gr. -1-k). pap. 6.99 (978-0-14-240000-5(9), Puffin) Penguin Publishing Group.
—Easter. Trueit, Trudi Strain. 2013. (Holidays & Celebrations Ser.). (ENG.). 32p. (J). (gr. k-3). 27.07 (978-1-62323-515-4(4), 206278) Child's World, Inc., The.
—Fiona's Fairy Magic. Imperato, Teresa. 2005. 14p. (J). 10.95 (978-1-58117-322-2(9), Intervisual/Piggy Toes) Bendon, Inc.
—Las Gallinas de la Senora Sato, Level 1. Min, Laura. Flor Ada, Alma, tr. 2003. (Dejame Leer Ser.). (SPA.). 8p. (J). (gr. -1-3). 6.50 (978-0-673-36298-8(1), Good Year Bks.) Celebration Pr.
—Hunting the Daddyosaurus. Bateman, Teresa. 2004. 29p. (J). (gr. k-4). reprint ed. 16.00 (978-0-7567-7796-8(8)) DIANE Publishing Co.
—The Kite. Packard, Mary. 2003. (My First Reader Ser.). (ENG.). 32p. (J). 18.50 (978-0-516-22930-0(3), Children's Pr.) Scholastic Library Publishing.
—Luna the Wake-Up Cat. Simon, Charnan. 2011. (Rookie Ready to Learn Ser.). 40p. (J). pap. 5.95 (978-0-531-26695-3(8)); (gr. -1-k). lib. bdg. 23.00 (978-0-531-26414-0(9)) Scholastic Library Publishing. (Children's Pr.).
—Oh, Come, Little Children. Stohs, Anita Reith. 2006. 22p. (J). (gr. -1-3). 14.99 (978-0-7586-1215-1(X)) Concordia Publishing Hse.
—Surprise! Packard, Mary. 2003. (My First Reader Ser.). (ENG.). 32p. (J). 18.50 (978-0-516-22937-9(0), Children's Pr.) Scholastic Library Publishing.
Huang, H Y, jt. illus. see Yang, A.
Huang, Kathryn. Lost Tales of Ga'Hoole. Lasky, Kathryn. 2010. (Guardians of Ga'hoole Ser.). (ENG.). 192p. (J). (gr. 3-7). 6.99 (978-0-545-10244-5(8), Scholastic Paperbacks) Scholastic, Inc.
Huang, Yu-Hsuan. Baby Bear: Finger Puppet Book. 2016. (ENG.). 12p. (J). bds. (978-1-4521-4235-7(1)) Chronicle Bks. LLC.
—Baby Elephant: Finger Puppet Book. 2016. (J). (978-1-4521-4237-1(8)) Chronicle Bks. LLC.
—Baby Reindeer: Finger Puppet Book. 2016. (J). (978-1-4521-4661-4(6)) Chronicle Bks. LLC.
—Baby Tiger: Finger Puppet Book. 2016. (ENG.). 12p. (J). bds. (978-1-4521-4236-4(X)) Chronicle Bks. LLC.
Huat, Tan Eng & Pearson, Jason. Punisher. 2010. (ENG.). 168p. (gr. 10-17). pap. 16.99 (978-0-7851-4162-4(6)) Marvel Worldwide, Inc.
Hubbard, Suzanna. The Lady Who Lived in a Car. Hubbard, Suzanna. 2007. (ENG.). 24p. (J). (gr. k-2). pap. 6.99 (978-1-84458-055-2(5)) Pavilion Bks. GBR. Dist: Independent Pubs. Group.
Hubbell, Will. Apples Here! 2015. (J). (978-1-4896-3846-5(6)) Weigl Pubs., Inc.
Hubenthal, Dayna. The Last Goose Concert. Fey, Jaki. 2012. 126p. pap. 12.99 (978-1-938282-02-7(7)) Koho Pono, LLC.
Huber, Becca & Pope, Lauren. Erin & Katrina. Sugg, Nan. 2007. 32p. (J). 19.90 (978-0-9788889-0-9(1)) Acorn Hill Pr.

H

Huber, Jim. Beamer Visits the Emergency Room. Chambers, Cindy & Demme, Tina. 2012. 32p. pap. 14.95 *(978-1-4575-1289-6(0))* Dog Ear Publishing, LLC.

Huber, Joyce. Porridge Poetry, Lofting, Hugh. 2nd collector's rev. l.t. ed. 2005. (ENG.). 54p. (J). lib. bdg. 7.95 *(978-0-9643844-8-4(5),* sku PP1, Doctor Dolittle's Library) PhotoGraphics Publishing.

Huber, June. The Gumboot Geese. Cameron, Anne. unabr. ed. (ENG.). 26p. (Orig.). (J). *(978-1-55017-063-4(5))* Harbour Publishing Co., Ltd.

Hubert, Marie-Luce & Klein, Jean-Louis, photos by. Face-to-Face with the Dog: Loyal Companion. Tracqui, Valérie. Laird, Lisa, tr. from FRE. 2004. (Face-to-Face Ser.). 28p. (J). (gr. 2-4). 9.95 *(978-1-57091-452-2(4))* Charlesbridge Publishing, Inc.

Hubert, Marie-Luce, jt. illus. see Klein, Jean-Louis.

Huckin, J. J., photos by. Inspire. Huckin, J. J. 2005. 164p. (YA). per. 39.99 net. *(978-0-9765700-1-1(7))* WayaMedia.

Huddleston, Courtney. Decoy. Williams, Eli & Jensen, Donald D. 112p. pap. 15.95 *(978-0-9673683-2-0(4))* Penny-Farthing Pr., Inc.

—Decoy: Storm of the Century. Scalera, Buddy. 2003. 160p. pap. 17.95 *(978-0-9719012-0-9(1))* Penny-Farthing Pr., Inc.

—Horror in Space. Young, J. E. 2011. (Twisted Journeys (r) Ser.: 18). (ENG.). 112p. (J). (gr. 4-7). pap. 7.95 *(978-0-8225-9273-0(8));* pap. 45.32 *(978-0-7613-7614-9(3));* lib. bdg. 27.93 *(978-0-8225-9265-5(7))* Lerner Publishing Group. (Graphic Universe).

—Jam-Bo, Litta-Girl, & the Bullies. Ford, Adam B. 2013. 44p. pap. 12.95 *(978-0-9794104-9-9(5))* H Bar Pr.

—Shipwrecked on Mad Island. Jolley, Dan. 2009. (Twisted Journeys (r) Ser.: 11). (ENG.). 112p. (J). (gr. 4-7). pap. 7.95 *(978-0-8225-8875-7(7),* Carolrhoda Bks.);No. 11. 27.93 *(978-0-8225-7911-3(1),* Graphic Universe) Lerner Publishing Group.

—Tricky Spider Tales. Schweizer, Chris. 2011. (Tricky Journeys Ser.: 5). (ENG.). (J). (gr. 2-4). pap. 39.62 *(978-0-7613-8629-2(7));* 64p. pap. 6.95 *(978-0-7613-7864-8(2));*No. 5. 64p. lib. bdg. 27.93 *(978-0-7613-6609-6(1))* Lerner Publishing Group. (Graphic Universe).

Huddleston, Courtney. A Bit Haywire. Huddleston, Courtney. Zirkel, Scott. 2006. 112p. per. 11.95 *(978-0-9777863-5-4(0))* Viper Comics.

Hudecki, Peter. City Dogs, 1 vol. Goertzen, Glenda. 2007. (ENG.). 133p. (J). (gr. 4-7). pap. *(978-1-55455-005-0(X))* Fitzhenry & Whiteside, Ltd.

Hudgens, Melica. Flim Flam & Other Such Gobbledygook. 2015. (J). 14.99 ***(978-1-4621-1684-3(1))*** Cedar Fort, Inc./CFI Distribution.

Hudgins, Tim. The Town of Nowhere, 1 vol. Hudgins, Mary Jane. 2009. 17p. pap. 24.95 *(978-1-60672-544-3(0))* America Star Bks.

Hudnall, Ken, photos by. Spirits of the Border: The History & Mystery of Fort Bliss, 2 vols. Hudnall, Ken. 2003. (Spirits of the Border Ser.: 2). 208p. per. 16.95 *(978-0-9626087-4-2(2))* Omega Pr.

Hudon-Verrelli, Jacqueline. Charlie's Dirt Day, 1 vol. Larsen, Andrew. 2014. (Tell-Me-More Storybook Ser.). (ENG.). 32p. (J). 17.95 *(978-1-55455-334-1(2))* Fitzhenry & Whiteside, Ltd. CAN. Dist: Midpoint Trade Bks., Inc.

Hudrisier, Cecile. We Both Read-the Horse Lover's Book. Ledu, Stephanie. 2009. 44p. (J). 9.95 *(978-1-60115-019-6(9))* Treasure Bay, Inc.

—We Both Read-The Horse Lover's Book. Ledu, Stéphanie. 2009. 44p. (J). pap. 5.99 *(978-1-60115-020-2(2))* Treasure Bay, Inc.

Hudson, Annabel. Lift-the-Flap. Goodings, Christina. 2009. (ENG.). 24p. (J). (gr. -1-k). 12.95 *(978-0-7459-6091-3(X))* Lion Hudson PLC GBR. Dist: Independent Pubs. Group.

—Lift-the-Flap Christmas Stories. Goodings, Christina. 2010. (ENG.). 16p. (J). (gr. -1-k). 12.99 *(978-0-7459-6203-0(3))* Lion Hudson PLC GBR. Dist: Independent Pubs. Group.

—My Look & Point Bible. Goodings, Christina. 2012. (ENG.). 224p. (J). (gr. -1-k). 16.99 *(978-0-7459-6206-1(8))* Lion Hudson PLC GBR. Dist: Independent Pubs. Group.

—My Look & Point First Easter. Goodings, Christina. 2015. (ENG.). 16p. (J). (gr. -1-k). 6.99 *(978-0-7459-6453-9(2))* Lion Hudson PLC GBR. Dist: Independent Pubs. Group.

—My Look & Point in the Beginning Stick-A-Story Book. Goodings, Christina. 2015. (ENG.). 16p. (J). (gr. -1-k). 6.99 *(978-0-7459-6540-6(7))* Lion Hudson PLC GBR. Dist: Independent Pubs. Group.

—My Look & Point Jonah & the Whale Stick-a-Story Book. Goodings, Christina. 2014. (ENG.). 16p. (J). (gr. -1-k). 6.99 *(978-0-7459-6454-6(0))* Lion Hudson PLC GBR. Dist: Independent Pubs. Group.

—My Look & Point Story of Jesus Stick-A-Story Book. Goodings, Christina. 2015. (ENG.). 16p. (J). (gr. -1-k). 6.99 *(978-0-7459-6539-0(3))* Lion Hudson PLC GBR. Dist: Independent Pubs. Group.

Hudson, Brett. Copy Cat. George, Olivia. 2004. (My First Reader Ser.). (J). 18.50 *(978-0-516-24679-6(8),* Children's Pr.) Scholastic Library Publishing.

—The Noisy Stable & Other Christmas Stories. Hartman, Bob. 2004. (Storyteller Tales Ser.). (ENG.). 64p. (J). (gr. k-4). pap. 6.99 *(978-0-7459-4824-9(3),* Lion Bks.) Lion Hudson PLC GBR. Dist: Independent Pubs. Group.

—Stories from the Stable. Hartman, Bob. 2010. (ENG.). 128p. (J). (gr. k-2). pap. 6.99 *(978-0-7459-6109-5(6))* Lion Hudson PLC GBR. Dist: Independent Pubs. Group.

Hudson, Cullan. Strange State: Mysteries & legends of Oklahoma. Centennial edition, expanded & Revised, 1. Hudson, Cullan. rev. exp. ed. 2007. (ENG.). 222p. (YA). per. 24.00 *(978-0-9778850-8-4(9),* 20071, WhorlBooks Thumbprints) Whorl Bks.

Hudson, David W., photos by. A Spiritual Trilogy. Ume, Anne. 2003. (ENG., 352p. (YA). pap. 21.00 *(978-0-9727967-0-5(3),* 77707) Bois Pubns.

Hudson, Don. Escape from the Forest. Hunter, Erin & Jolley, Dan. 2008. (Warriors Manga Ser.: 2). (ENG.). 112p. (J). (gr. 3-7). pap. 6.99 *(978-0-06-154793-5(X))* HarperCollins Pubs.

—Into the Woods. Hunter, Erin. 2008. (Warriors Manga Ser.: 1). (ENG.). 112p. (J). (gr. 3-7). pap. 6.99 *(978-0-06-154792-8(1))* HarperCollins Pubs.

—Return to the Clans. Hunter, Erin. 2009. (Warriors Manga Ser.: 3). (ENG.). 112p. (J). (gr. 3-7). pap. 6.99 *(978-0-06-154794-2(8))* HarperCollins Pubs.

Hudson, Katy. Bear & Duck. Hudson, Katy. 2015. (ENG.). 32p. (J). (gr. -1-3). 17.99 *(978-0-06-232051-3(3))* HarperCollins Pubs.

Hudson, Katy, jt. illus. see O'Byrne, Nicola.

Hudson, Stephan, photos by. Langston's Legacy: 101 Ways to Celebrate the Life & Work of Langston Hughes. Hudson, Katura J. & Hudson, Cheryl Willis. 2004. 48p. (J). (gr. 4-18). pap. 7.95 *(978-0-940975-99-6(8),* Sankofa Bks.) Just Us Bks., Inc.

Hudson, Stephen J. The Pioneers. Hudson, Wade. 2004. (Poetry from the Masters Ser.). 88p. (J). pap. 9.95 *(978-0-940975-96-5(3),* Sankofa Bks.) Just Us Bks., Inc.

Hudson, Ted. Keep Your Computer Alive - Coloring Book. Uitti, Dan. 2011. (ENG.). 32p. pap. 5.99 *(978-1-4662-8526-2(5))* CreateSpace Independent Publishing Platform.

Huebsch, Rand. The Telling Pool. Clement-Davies, David. 2007. (ENG.). 382p. (YA). (gr. 7-17). per. 8.95 *(978-0-8109-9257-3(4))* Abrams.

Huerta, Catherine. Hoppy Goes to School. Bentley, Dawn. 2006. (ENG.). 32p. (J). pap. 9.95 *(978-1-59249-559-7(1));* (gr. -1-3). 4.95 *(978-1-59249-556-6(7))* Soundprints.

—Hoppy Goes to School. Bentley, Catherine & Bentley, Dawn. 2006. (Pet Tales Ser.). (ENG.). 32p. (J). 2.95 *(978-1-59249-558-0(3))* Soundprints.

—Me, Minerva & the Flying Flora. Emmer, E. R. 2nd rev. ed. 2003. (Going to Ser.). Orig. Title: Me, Minera & the Flying Car. (ENG.). 133p. (J). (gr. 4-8). pap. 6.95 *(978-1-893577-10-7(4))* Four Corners Publishing.

—Princess: A Lucky Kitten. Schwaeber, Barbie Heit. 2007. (Pet Tales Ser.). (ENG.). 32p. (J). 4.95 *(978-1-59249-675-4(X))* Soundprints.

—Princess: A Lucky Kitten. Schwaeber, Barbie H. 2007. (Pet Tales Ser.). (ENG.). 32p. (J). per. 2.95 *(978-1-59249-676-1(8))* Soundprints.

—Princess a Lucky Kitten. Schwaeber, Barbie Heit. 2007. (ENG.). 32p. (J). 9.95 *(978-1-59249-677-8(6))* Soundprints.

—Scout Hits the Trail. O'Donnell, Liam. 2007. (ENG.). 32p. (J). 2.95 *(978-1-59249-741-6(1))* Soundprints.

—Scout Hits the Trail. O'Donnel, Liam. (Pet Tales Ser.). (ENG.). 32p. (J). (gr. -1-3). 2008. 4.95 *(978-1-59249-740-9(3));* 2007. 9.95 *(978-1-59249-742-3(X))* Soundprints.

—Speechless in New York. Dreyer, Ellen. 2nd rev. ed. 2003. (Going to Ser.). (ENG.). 129p. (J). (gr. 4-8). pap. 6.95 *(978-1-893577-09-1(0))* Four Corners Publishing.

Huey, Debbie & Viray, Sherwin. Little Laura & the Birthday Surprise. Lee, Laura. 2011. (ENG.). 32p. (J). (gr. -1-k). 17.95 *(978-0-9845226-0-6(3))* Little Laura Music, LLC.

Huff, Ariella. Tanny's Meow. Ferro, Ursula. 2005. 51p. (J). pap. 12.95 *(978-0-9766006-0-2(9))* Marti Bks.

Huff, Jeane. Amy Armadillo: Mind Your Mama, 15 vols. Sargent, Dave & Sargent, Pat. 2003. (Animal Pride Ser.: 15). 42p. (J). pap. 6.95 *(978-1-56763-788-5(4));* lib. bdg. 20.95 *(978-1-56763-787-8(6))* Ozark Publishing.

—Bandit: I Help Others, 56 vols., Vol. 14. Sargent, Dave & Sargent, Pat. 2003. (Animal Pride Ser.: 14). 42p. (J). lib. bdg. 20.95 *(978-1-56763-785-4(X));* 2nd rev. ed. pap. 10.95 *(978-1-56763-786-1(8))* Ozark Publishing.

—Big Jake: I'm Very Curious, 56 vols., Vol. 12. Sargent, Dave & Sargent, Pat. 2nd rev. ed. 2003. (Animal Pride Ser.: 12). 42p. (J). lib. bdg. 20.95 *(978-1-56763-781-6(7))* Ozark Publishing.

—Billy Beaver: A New Beginning, 15 vols., Vol. 2. Sargent, Dave & Sargent, Pat. 2nd rev. ed. 2003. (Animal Pride Ser.: 2). 42p. (J). pap. 6.95 *(978-1-56763-762-5(0));* lib. bdg. 20.95 *(978-1-56763-761-8(2))* Ozark Publishing.

—Bobby Bobcat: Be a Friend, 15 vols., Vol. 10. Sargent, Dave & Sargent, Pat. 2nd rev. ed. 2003. (Animal Pride Ser.: No. 10). 42p. (J). pap. 6.95 *(978-1-56763-778-6(7));* lib. bdg. 20.95 *(978-1-56763-777-9(9))* Ozark Publishing.

—Brutus the Bear: Show Respect, 15 vols., Vol. 4. Sargent, Dave & Sargent, Pat. 2nd rev. ed. 2003. (Animal Pride Ser.: 4). 42p. (J). pap. 6.95 *(978-1-56763-766-3(3));* lib. bdg. 20.95 *(978-1-56763-765-6(5))* Ozark Publishing.

—Buddy Badger: I'm a Little Bully, 15 vols., Vol. 17. Sargent, Dave & Sargent, Pat. 2nd rev. ed. 2003. (Animal Pride Ser.: 17). 42p. (J). pap. 10.95 *(978-1-56763-792-2(2));* lib. bdg. 20.95 *(978-1-56763-791-5(4))* Ozark Publishing.

—Chrissy Cottontail: Mind Your Mama, 15 bks. Sargent, Dave & Sargent, Pat. 2nd rev. ed. 2003. (Animal Pride Ser.: 7). 42p. (J). 7. pap. 6.95 *(978-1-56763-772-4(8));* Vol. 7. lib. bdg. 20.95 *(978-1-56763-771-7(X))* Ozark Publishing.

—Dawn the Deer: Family & Friends, 56 vols., Vol. 8. Sargent, Dave & Sargent, Pat. 2nd rev. ed. 2003. (Animal Pride Ser.: Vol. 8). 42p. (J). lib. bdg. 20.95 *(978-1-56763-773-1(6))* Ozark Publishing.

—Dike the Wolf: Teamwork, 56 vols., Vol. 5. Sargent, Dave & Sargent, Pat. 2nd rev. ed. 2003. (Animal Pride Ser.: Vol. 15). 42p. (J). lib. bdg. 20.95 *(978-1-56763-767-0(1))* Ozark Publishing.

—Emma! Sargent, David M. 2004. (Doggie Tails Ser.). (J). *(978-1-56763-851-6(1));* pap. *(978-1-56763-852-3(X))* Ozark Publishing.

—Greta Groundhog: I'm Special!, 20 vols., Vol. 20. Sargent, Dave & Sargent, Pat. 2nd rev. ed. 2003. (Animal Pride Ser.: 20). 42p. (J). pap. 10.95 *(978-1-56763-798-4(1));* lib. bdg. 20.95 *(978-1-56763-797-7(3))* Ozark Publishing.

—Mad Jack: I Throw Fits, 15 vols., Vol. 16. Sargent, Dave & Sargent, Pat. 2nd rev. ed. 2003. (Animal Pride Ser.: 16). 42p. (J). pap. 10.95 *(978-1-56763-790-8(6));* lib. bdg. 20.95 *(978-1-56763-789-2(2))* Ozark Publishing.

—Molly's Journey: I'm Getting Older, 15 vols., Vol. 19. Sargent, Dave & Sargent, Pat. 2nd rev. ed. 2003. (Animal Pride Ser.: 19). 42p. (J). pap. 10.95 *(978-1-56763-796-0(5));* lib. bdg. 20.95 *(978-1-56763-795-3(7))* Ozark Publishing.

—Peggy Porcupine: Don't Wander Off, 15 vols., Vol. 13. Sargent, Dave & Sargent, Pat. 2nd rev. ed. 2003. (Animal Pride Ser.: 13). 42p. (J). (AFA.). pap. 10.95 *(978-1-56763-784-7(1));* lib. bdg. 20.95 *(978-1-56763-783-0(3))* Ozark Publishing.

—Pokey Opossum: I'm Kinda Slow, 15 vols., Vol. 18. Sargent, Dave & Sargent, Pat. 2nd rev. ed. 2003. (Animal Pride Ser.: 18). 42p. (J). pap. 10.95 *(978-1-56763-794-6(9));* lib. bdg. 20.95 *(978-1-56763-793-9(0))* Ozark Publishing.

—Redi Fox: Friendship, 15 vols., Vol. 3. Sargent, Dave & Sargent, Pat. 2nd rev. ed. 2003. (Animal Pride Ser.: 3). 42p. (J). pap. 10.95 *(978-1-56763-764-9(7));* lib. bdg. 20.95 *(978-1-56763-763-2(9))* Ozark Publishing.

—Roy Raccoon: I Love Adventure, 15 vols., Vol. 1. Sargent, Dave & Sargent, Pat. 2nd rev. ed. 2003. (Animal Pride Ser.: 1). 42p. (J). pap. 10.95 *(978-1-56763-760-1(4));* lib. bdg. 20.95 *(978-1-56763-759-5(0))* Ozark Publishing.

—Sammy Skunk: I'm a Little Stinker, 56 vols., Vol. 9. Sargent, Dave & Sargent, Pat. 2nd rev. ed. 2003. (Animal Pride Ser.: 9). 42p. (J). lib. bdg. 20.95 *(978-1-56763-775-5(2))* Ozark Publishing.

—Tunnel King: I Work Hard, 15 vols., Vol. 11. Sargent, Dave & Sargent, Pat. 2nd rev. ed. 2003. (Animal Pride Ser.: No. 11). 42p. (J). pap. 10.95 *(978-1-56763-780-9(9));* lib. bdg. 20.95 *(978-1-56763-779-3(5))* Ozark Publishing.

—White Thunder: I'm a Leader, 56 vols., Vol. 6. Sargent, Dave & Sargent, Pat. 2nd rev. ed. 2003. (Animal Pride Ser.: 6). 42p. (J). lib. bdg. 20.95 *(978-1-56763-769-4(8))* Ozark Publishing.

Huff, Jeane Lirley. Autumn's Emergency. Sargent, David M., Jr. 2003. (Doggie Tails Ser.). 32p. (J). pap. 10.95 *(978-1-56763-846-2(5));* lib. bdg. 19.95 *(978-1-56763-845-5(7))* Ozark Publishing.

—Buffy's Revenge. Sargent, David M., Jr. 2003. (Doggie Tails Ser.). 32p. (J). pap. 10.95 *(978-1-56763-844-8(9));* lib. bdg. 20.95 *(978-1-56763-843-1(0))* Ozark Publishing.

—Guard Dog Mary, 9 vols. Sargent, David M., Jr. 2003. (Doggie Tails Ser.). 32p. (J). pap. 10.95 *(978-1-56763-850-9(3))* Ozark Publishing.

—Portia's Prank, 9 vols. Sargent, David M., Jr. 2003. (Doggie Tails Ser.). 32p. (J). pap. 10.95 *(978-1-56763-848-6(1));* lib. bdg. 20.95 *(978-1-56763-847-9(3))* Ozark Publishing.

—Vicious Vera, 9 vols. Sargent, Dave M., Jr. 2004. (Doggie Tails Ser.: 9). (J). pap. 10.95 *(978-1-56763-854-7(6))* Ozark Publishing.

Huff, Tim. The Cardboard Shack Beneath the Bridge. 2007. 31p. *(978-1-897186-09-1(6))* Castle Quay Bks. Canada.

—It's Hard Not to Stare: Helping Children Understand Disabilities. Fukumoto, Jan. 2013. pap. *(978-1-927355-28-2(1))* BayRidge Bks.

Huffine, Erik. Signs of Wisdom: Expressing God's Wisdom in Sign Language. Sewell, James C. 2005. (Signing God's Word Ser.). (ENG.). 64p. (J). (gr. k-4). per. 8.99 *(978-1-59441-080-2(1),* CD-204007) Carson-Dellosa Publishing, LLC.

Huffman, Jared & Rampley, Leigh. The Lost Piece. Huffman, Jared. 2011. 36p. pap. 24.95 *(978-1-4626-1784-5(0))* America Star Bks.

Huffman, Tom. The Dove Dove: Funny Homograph Riddles. Terban, Marvin. 2008. (ENG.). 64p. (J). (gr. 5-7). pap. 6.95 *(978-0-547-03186-6(6))* Houghton Mifflin Harcourt Publishing Co.

Huffmaster, Elizabeth. Chelsea's Healthy Secrets. Schiavi, Sherry. 2004. (J). per. 14.95 *(978-0-9746378-0-8(7))* Celltrition.

Huggens, Karin. School Is Cool. Rainey. 2004. (J). *(978-0-9666199-9-7(4))* DreamDog Pr.

Huggins, Carl. The Lion & the Man: A Fable. Baron, Lindamichelle. 2009. 72p. pap. 15.95 *(978-0-940938-25-0(1))* Harlin Jacque Pubns.

Hughes, Arthur. The Princess & the Goblin. MacDonald, George. 2003. 136p. pap. 12.99 *(978-1-57646-633-9(7))* Quiet Vision Publishing.

—The Princess & the Goblin. MacDonald, George. 2010. (Looking Glass Library). (ENG.). 272p. (J). (gr. 3-7). 9.99 *(978-0-375-86338-7(9))* Random Hse., Inc.

—Princess & the Goblin. MacDonald, George. 2nd ed. 2011. (Puffin Classics Ser.). (ENG.). 262p. (J). (gr. 3-7). 4.99 *(978-0-14-133248-2(4),* Puffin) Penguin Publishing Group.

Hughes, Arthur, jt. illus. see Kirk, Maria L.

Hughes, Brooke Boynton. Baby Love. DiTerlizzi, Angela. 2015. (ENG.). 32p. (J). (gr. -1-3). 17.99 *(978-1-4424-3392-2(2),* Beach Lane Bks.) Beach Lane Bks.

—Cupcake Cousins. Hannigan, Kate. 2014. (Cupcake Cousins Ser.: Bk. 1). (ENG.). 288p. (J). (gr. 3-7). 16.99 *(978-1-4231-7830-9(0))* Hyperion Bks. for Children.

Hughes, Brooke Boynton. Summer Showers, Bk. 2. Hannigan, Kate. 2015. (Cupcake Cousins Ser.: Bk. 2). (ENG.). 240p. (J). (gr. 3-7). 16.99 ***(978-1-4847-1662-5(0))*** Hyperion Bks. for Children.

Hughes, Cathy. Ben Bunny Is Very Hungry. Alligator Books Staff & Fabiny, Sarah. 2012. (Squeaky Board Bks.). (ENG.). 18p. (J). bds. 4.99 *(978-0-7641-6479-8(1))* Barron's Educational Series, Inc.

—Katie Kitten Finds a Friend. Alligator Books Staff & Fabiny, Sarah. 2012. (Squeaky Board Bks.). (ENG.). 20p. (J). bds. 4.99 *(978-0-7641-6481-1(3))* Barron's Educational Series, Inc.

—My Carry-Along Noah: Activity Book with Stickers. Miller, Jocelyn. 2014. (ENG.). 32p. (J). (gr. k-2). pap. 9.99 *(978-0-7459-6939-8(9))* Lion Hudson PLC GBR. Dist: Independent Pubs. Group.

—My Carry-Along Santa Activity Book: Christmas Fun with Stickers. Miller, Jocelyn. 2013. (ENG.). 32p. (J). (gr. k-2). pap. 9.99 *(978-0-7459-6419-5(2))* Lion Hudson PLC GBR. Dist: Independent Pubs. Group.

—Pip Puppy Looks for Mom. Alligator Books Staff & Fabiny, Sarah. 2012. (Squeaky Board Bks.). (ENG.). 18p. (J). bds. 4.99 *(978-0-7641-6482-8(1))* Barron's Educational Series, Inc.

Hughes, Emily. Brilliant. Doyle, Roddy. 2015. (ENG.). 192p. (J). (gr. 3-7). 16.95 ***(978-1-4197-1479-5(1),*** Amulet Bks.) Abrams.

Hughes, Emily. The Little Gardener. 2015. (ENG.). 40p. (J). (gr. -1-2). 17.95 *(978-1-909263-43-7(5))* Flying Eye Bks. GBR. Dist: Consortium Bk. Sales & Distribution.

—Wild. 2013. (ENG.). 32p. (J). (gr. -1-2). 16.95 *(978-1-909263-08-6(7))* Flying Eye Bks. GBR. Dist: Consortium Bk. Sales & Distribution.

Hughes, Evan. The Quest for Comfort: The Story of the Heidelberg Catechism. Boekestein, William. 2011. 32p. (J). pap. 10.00 *(978-1-60178-152-9(0))* Reformation Heritage Bks.

Hughes, Fox Carlton. Rainbow Rhino. Hughes, Fox Carlton. 2007. (ENG.). 36p. (J). (gr. -1-3). 16.95 *(978-0-9790275-3-6(5))* Ovation Bks.

Hughes, George. Help! I'm a Prisoner in the Library. Clifford, Eth. 2004. (Jo-Beth & Mary Rose Mystery Ser.). (ENG.). 112p. (J). (gr. 2-5). pap. 6.99 *(978-0-618-49482-8(0))* Houghton Mifflin Harcourt Publishing Co.

Hughes, Greg. The Shapes & Colors Bible. Hughes, Greg. 2004. 80p. (J). 7.99 *(978-0-9741091-3-8(4),* 7002) smart Life Ministries, Inc., The.

Hughes, Janet. The Life Story of TV Star Herman the Worm. Sroda, George. 199p. (Orig.). (J). (gr. 3-18). 10.95 *(978-0-9604486-2-3(4))* Sroda, George.

Hughes, Jon. Allosaurus. Frost, Helen. 2005. (Dinosaurs & Prehistoric Animals Ser.). (ENG.). 24p. (gr. k-1). per. 7.29 *(978-0-7368-5104-6(6));* 24.65 *(978-0-7368-3646-3(2))* Capstone Pr., Inc. (Pebble Plus).

—Apatosaurus, 1 vol. Lindeen, Carol K. & Lugtu, Carol J. 2005. (Dinosaurs & Prehistoric Animals Ser.). (ENG.). 24p. (gr. k-1). 24.65 *(978-0-7368-4256-3(X),* Pebble Plus) Capstone Pr., Inc.

—Brachiosaurus, 1 vol. Lindeen, Carol K. 2005. (Dinosaurs & Prehistoric Animals Ser.). (ENG.). 24p. (gr. k-1). 24.65 *(978-0-7368-4257-0(8),* Pebble Plus) Capstone Pr., Inc.

—Braquiosaurio/Brachiosaurus, 1 vol. Lindeen, Carol K. et al. Saunders-Smith, Gail, ed. Ferrer, Martin Luis Guzman, tr. from ENG. 2007. (Dinosaurios y Animales Prehistoricos/Dinosaurs & Prehistoric Animals Ser.). (MUL & SPA.). 24p. (gr. k-1). 24.65 *(978-0-7368-7636-0(7))* Capstone Pr., Inc.

—Diplodocus/Diplodocus, 1 vol. Riehecky, Janet & Capstone Press Staff. Saunders-Smith, Gail, ed. Ferrer, Martin Luis Guzman, tr. 2007. (Dinosaurios y Animales Prehistoricos/Dinosaurs & Prehistoric Animals Ser.). (MUL & SPA.). 24p. (gr. k-1). 24.65 *(978-0-7368-7637-7(5))* Capstone Pr., Inc.

—Pteranodonte/Pteranodon, 1 vol. Riehecky, Janet & Capstone Press Staff. Saunders-Smith, Gail, ed. Ferrer, Martin Luis Guzman, tr. from ENG. 2007. (Dinosaurios y Animales Prehistoricos/Dinosaurs & Prehistoric Animals Ser.). (MUL & SPA.). 24p. (gr. k-1). 24.65 *(978-0-7368-7640-7(5))* Capstone Pr., Inc.

—Sabertooth Cat. Frost, Helen. 2005. (Dinosaurs & Prehistoric Animals Ser.). (ENG.). 24p. (gr. k-1). per. 7.29 *(978-0-7368-5105-3(4));* 24.65 *(978-0-7368-3648-7(9))* Capstone Pr., Inc. (Pebble Plus).

—Sabertooth Cat [Scholastic]. Frost, Helen. 2009. (Dinosaurs & Prehistoric Animals Ser.). 24p. (gr. k-1). pap. 1.00 *(978-1-4296-4249-1(1),* Pebble Plus) Capstone Pr., Inc.

—Stegosaurus, 1 vol. Frost, Helen. 2005. (Dinosaurs & Prehistoric Animals Ser.). (ENG.). 24p. (gr. k-1). 24.65 *(978-0-7368-3647-0(0),* Pebble Plus) Capstone Pr., Inc.

—Tiranosaurio Rex. Frost, Helen. 2006. (Dinosaurios y Animales Prehistoricos/Dinosaurs & Prehistoric Animals Ser.).Tr. of Tyrannosaurus Rex. (SPA, ENG & MUL.). 24p. (gr. k-1). 24.65 *(978-0-7368-6688-0(4))* Capstone Pr., Inc.

—Triceratops, 1 vol. Frost, Helen. 2005. (Dinosaurs & Prehistoric Animals Ser.). (ENG.). 24p. (gr. k-1). 24.65 *(978-0-7368-3650-0(0),* Pebble Plus) Capstone Pr., Inc.

—Tyrannosaurus Rex, 1 vol. Frost, Helen. Saunders-Smith, Gail, ed. 2005. (Dinosaurs & Prehistoric Animals Ser.). (ENG.). 24p. (gr. k-1). 24.65 *(978-0-7368-3651-7(9),* Pebble Plus) Capstone Pr., Inc.

—Velociraptor. Lindeen, Carol K. & Capstone Press Staff. Saunders-Smith, Gail, ed. Ferrer, Martin Luis Guzman, tr. from ENG. 2007. (Dinosaurios y Animales Prehistoricos/Dinosaurs & Prehistoric Animals Ser.). (MUL & SPA.). 24p. (gr. k-1). 24.65 *(978-0-7368-7641-4(3))* Capstone Pr., Inc.

—Velociraptor, 1 vol. Lindeen, Carol K. & Lugtu, Carol J. 2005. (Dinosaurs & Prehistoric Animals Ser.). (ENG.). 24p. (gr. k-1). 24.65 *(978-0-7368-4258-7(6),* Pebble Plus) Capstone Pr., Inc.

—Velociraptor [Scholastic]. Lindeen, Carol K. 2009. (Dinosaurs & Prehistoric Animals Ser.). 24p. (gr. k-1). pap. 1.00 *(978-1-4296-4247-7(5),* Pebble Plus) Capstone Pr., Inc.

—Woolly Mammoth. Frost, Helen. 2005. (Dinosaurs & Prehistoric Animals Ser.). (ENG.). 24p. (gr. k-1). per. 7.29 *(978-0-7368-5109-1(7));* 24.65 *(978-0-7368-3649-4(7))* Capstone Pr., Inc. (Pebble Plus).

—Woolly Mammoth [Scholastic]. Frost, Helen. 2009. (Dinosaurs & Prehistoric Animals Ser.). 24p. (gr. k-1). pap. 1.00 *(978-1-4296-4250-7(5),* Pebble Plus) Capstone Pr., Inc.

Hughes, Jon. What Happened to Dinosaurs? Band 13. Hughes, Jon. 2007. (Collins Big Cat Ser.). (ENG.). 32p. (J). pap. 8.99 *(978-0-00-723084-6(2))* HarperCollins Pubs. Ltd. GBR. Dist: Independent Pubs. Group.

Hughes, Laura. The Eighth Menorah. Wohl, Lauren L. 2013. (ENG.). 32p. (J). (gr. -1-2). 16.99 *(978-0-8075-1892-2(1))* Whitman, Albert & Co.

Hughes-Odgers, Kyle. Ten Tiny Things. McKinlay, Meg. 2012. (ENG.). 36p. (J). (gr. -1-k). 18.00 *(978-1-921888-94-6(5))* Fremantle Pr. AUS. Dist: Independent Pubs. Group.

Hughes, Sarah Anne. Butterflies. Pyle, Robert Michael & Peterson, Roger Tory. Peterson, Roger Tory, ed. 2nd ed. 2013. (Peterson Field Guide Color-In Bks.). (ENG.). 64p. (J). 8.95 *(978-0-544-03339-9(6))* Houghton Mifflin Harcourt Publishing Co.

Hughes, Sarah Anne. Reptiles & Amphibians. Hughes, Sarah Anne. Peterson, Roger Tory, ed. 2nd ed. 2013. (Peterson Field Guide Color-In Bks.). (ENG.). 64p. (J). 8.95 *(978-0-544-02695-7(0))* Houghton Mifflin Harcourt Publishing Co.

Hughes, Serifati. I Can Paint a Rainbow of Words. Salardino, Nicholas. 2010. (ENG.). 30p. pap. 9.99 *(978-1-4499-0954-3(X))* CreateSpace Independent Publishing Platform.

Hughes, Shirley. The Bell Family. Streatfeild, Noel. 2015. (ENG.). 368p. (J). (gr. 4-6). 12.99 *(978-0-09-958336-3(4))* Random Hse. GBR. Dist: Independent Pubs. Group.

—More Naughty Little Sister Stories. Edwards, Dorothy. 2010. (My Naughty Little Sister Ser.). (ENG.). 144p. (J). (gr. -1-2). pap. 9.99 *(978-1-4052-5338-3(X))* Egmont Bks., Ltd. GBR. Dist: Independent Pubs. Group.

—My Naughty Little Sister. Edwards, Dorothy. 2010. (My Naughty Little Sister Ser.: 1). (ENG.). 192p. (gr. -1-2). pap. 9.99 *(978-1-4052-5334-5(7))* Egmont Bks., Ltd. GBR. Dist: Independent Pubs. Group.

—My Naughty Little Sister's Friends. Edwards, Dorothy. 2010. (My Naughty Little Sister Ser.). (ENG.). 160p. (J). (gr. -1-2). pap. 9.99 *(978-1-4052-5335-2(5))* Egmont Bks., Ltd. GBR. Dist: Independent Pubs. Group.

—When My Naughty Little Sister Was Good. Edwards, Dorothy. 2010. (My Naughty Little Sister Ser.). (ENG.). 96p. (J). (gr. -1-2). pap. 9.99 *(978-1-4052-5337-6(1))* Egmont Bks., Ltd. GBR. Dist: Independent Pubs. Group.

Hughes, Shirley. Alfie & the Big Boys. Hughes, Shirley. 2009. (Alfie Ser.). (ENG.). 32p. (J). (gr. -1-k). pap. 9.99 *(978-0-09-948844-6(2),* Red Fox) Random House Children's Books GBR. Dist: Independent Pubs. Group.

—Alfie & the Birthday Surprise. Hughes, Shirley. ed. 2009. (Alfie Ser.). (ENG.). 32p. (J). (gr. -1-k). pap. 11.99 *(978-1-86230-787-2(3),* Red Fox) Random House Children's Books GBR. Dist: Independent Pubs. Group.

—Alfie Gets in First. Hughes, Shirley. ed. 2009. (Alfie Ser.). (ENG.). 32p. (J). (gr. -1-k). pap. 9.99 *(978-1-86230-783-4(0),* Red Fox) Random House Children's Books GBR. Dist: Independent Pubs. Group.

—Alfie Gives a Hand. Hughes, Shirley. ed. 2009. (Alfie Ser.). (ENG.). 32p. (J). (gr. -1-k). pap. 9.99 *(978-1-86230-785-8(7),* Red Fox) Random House Children's Books GBR. Dist: Independent Pubs. Group.

—Alfie Weather. Hughes, Shirley. 2007. (Alfie Ser.). (ENG.). 48p. (J). (gr. -1-k). pap. 9.99 *(978-0-09-940425-5(7),* Red Fox) Random House Children's Books GBR. Dist: Independent Pubs. Group.

—Alfie Wins a Prize. Hughes, Shirley. rev. ed. 2010. (Alfie Ser.). (ENG.). 32p. (J). (gr. -1-k). pap. 9.99 *(978-1-86230-788-9(1),* Red Fox) Random House Children's Books GBR. Dist: Independent Pubs. Group.

—Alfie's Feet. Hughes, Shirley. ed. 2009. (Alfie Ser.). (ENG.). 32p. (J). (gr. -1-k). pap. 9.99 *(978-1-86230-784-1(9),* Red Fox) Random House Children's Books GBR. Dist: Independent Pubs. Group.

—The Big Alfie & Annie Rose. Hughes, Shirley. 2007. (Alfie Ser.). (ENG.). 64p. (J). (gr. -1-k). pap. 14.99 *(978-0-09-975030-7(9),* Red Fox) Random House Children's Books GBR. Dist: Independent Pubs. Group.

—The Big Alfie Out of Doors Storybook. Hughes, Shirley. 2007. (Alfie Ser.). (ENG.). 64p. (J). (gr. -1-k). 15.95 *(978-0-09-925891-9(9),* Red Fox) Random House Children's Books GBR. Dist: Independent Pubs. Group.

—Bobbo Goes to School. Hughes, Shirley. 2013. (ENG.). 32p. (J). (gr. -1-2). 16.99 *(978-0-7636-6524-1(X))* Candlewick Pr.

—The Christmas Eve Ghost. Hughes, Shirley. 2010. (ENG.). 32p. (J). (gr. -1-3). 15.99 *(978-0-7636-4472-7(2))* Candlewick Pr.

—Daisy Saves the Day. Hughes, Shirley. 2015. (ENG.). 32p. (J). (gr. k-4). 16.99 *(978-0-7636-7323-9(4))* Candlewick Pr.

—Dogger, 1 vol. Hughes, Shirley. (ENG.). 32p. (J). (gr. k-k). 2009. pap. 14.99 *(978-1-86230-593-9(5));* 2010. pap. 9.99 *(978-1-86230-805-3(5))* Random House Children's Books GBR. (Red Fox). Dist: Independent Pubs. Group.

—Don't Want to Go! Hughes, Shirley. 2010. (ENG.). 32p. (J). (gr. -1-2). 16.99 *(978-0-7636-5091-9(9))* Candlewick Pr.

—An Evening at Alfie's. Hughes, Shirley. ed. 2009. (Alfie Ser.). (ENG.). 32p. (J). (gr. k-k). pap. 9.99 *(978-1-86230-786-5(5),* Red Fox) Random House Children's Books GBR. Dist: Independent Pubs. Group.

—Jonadab & Rita. Hughes, Shirley. 2010. (Alfie Ser.). (ENG.). 32p. (J). (gr. -1-k). pap. 11.99 *(978-1-86230-313-3(4),* Red Fox) Random House Children's Books GBR. Dist: Independent Pubs. Group.

—Out & About: A First Book of Poems. Hughes, Shirley. 2015. (ENG.). 56p. (J). (-k). 16.99 *(978-0-7636-7644-5(6))* Candlewick Pr.

—Stories by Firelight. Hughes, Shirley. 2007. (ENG.). 64p. (J). (gr. -1-k). pap. 13.95 *(978-0-09-918611-3(X),* Red Fox) Random House Children's Books GBR. Dist: Independent Pubs. Group.

Hughes, Steven. Tru Detective, 1 vol. McClintock, Norah. 2015. (ENG.). 128p. (YA). (gr. 10-12). pap. 19.95 *(978-1-4598-0379-4(5))* Orca Bk. Pubs. USA.

Hughes, Ted. Timmy the Tug. Hughes, Ted. Downer, Jim. 2010. (ENG.). 40p. 19.95 *(978-0-500-51496-2(8),* 551496) Thames & Hudson.

Hughey, Sue C. Herby's Secret Formula. Hughey, Sue C. 2013. 232p. pap. 11.95 *(978-0-9840358-1-6(8))* Associated Arts Pub.

Hugo, Pierre de. Let's Look at the Hedge. Allaire, Caroline & Krawczyk, Sabine. 2012. (ENG.). 38p. (J). (gr. 1-4). pap. 11.99 *(978-1-85103-339-3(4))* Moonlight Publishing, Ltd. GBR. Dist: Independent Pubs. Group.

—The Seashore. 2012. (ENG.). 38p. (J). (gr. -1-k). 12.99 *(978-1-85103-394-2(7))* Moonlight Publishing, Ltd. GBR. Dist: Independent Pubs. Group.

Hui-Jin, Park. Chronicles of Cursed Sword, Vol. 10. Beop-Ryong, Yeo. rev. ed. 2005. 192p. (YA). pap. 9.99 *(978-1-59532-387-3(2))* TOKYOPOP, Inc.

—Chronicles of the Cursed Sword, 10 vols. Beop-Ryong, Yuy. 2004. 176p. Vol. 4. rev. ed. pap. 9.99 *(978-1-59182-421-3(4));* Vol. 5. 5th rev. ed. pap. 9.99 *(978-1-59182-422-0(2))* TOKYOPOP, Inc.

—Chronicles of the Cursed Sword, 12 vols. Yeo, Beop-Ryong. 2004. Vol. 8. 8th rev. ed. 168p. pap. 9.99 *(978-1-59182-425-1(7));* Vol. 9. 9th rev. ed. 176p. pap. 9.99 *(978-1-59182-426-8(5))* TOKYOPOP, Inc.

—Chronicles of the Cursed Sword, Vol. 11. rev. ed. 2005. 192p. pap. 9.99 *(978-1-59532-388-0(0))* TOKYOPOP, Inc.

—Chronicles of the Cursed Sword. Beop-Ryong, Yeo. (Chronicles of the Cursed Sword Ser.). 192p. Vol. 12. rev. ed. 2005. pap. 9.99 *(978-1-59532-389-7(9));* Vol. 13. 13th rev. ed. 2005. per. 9.99 *(978-1-59532-645-4(6));* Vol. 14. rev. ed. 2006. per. 9.99 *(978-1-59532-646-1(4))* TOKYOPOP, Inc.

Huiett, William, jt. illus. see Denman, Michael.

Huiett, William J. & Denman, Michael L. An Elephant Grows Up, 1 vol. Suen, Anastasia. 2005. (Wild Animals Ser.). (ENG.). 24p. (gr. k-2). lib. bdg. 25.99 *(978-1-4048-0984-0(8),* Nonfiction Picture Bks.) Picture Window Bks.

—A Kangaroo Grows Up, 1 vol. Tourville, Amanda Doering. 2007. (Wild Animals Ser.). (ENG.). 24p. (gr. k-2). lib. bdg. 25.99 *(978-1-4048-3160-5(6),* 1265742, Nonfiction Picture Bks.) Picture Window Bks.

Huiett, William J., jt. illus. see Denman, Michael L.

Huiett, William J., jt. illus. see Denman, Michael.

Huismann, Duane. Nobody's Lion. Fisher, Barbara. 2004. (J). per. 16.95 *(978-1-59571-049-9(3))* Word Association Pubs.

Huling, Phil. Cactus Soup, 0 vols. Kimmel, Eric A. 2011. (ENG.). 32p. (J). (gr. -1-3). pap. 9.99 *(978-0-7614-5832-6(8),* 9780761458326, Amazon Children's Publishing) Amazon Publishing.

—Puss in Cowboy Boots. Huling, Jan. 2007. (ENG.). 40p. (J). (gr. 1-4). 11.99 *(978-1-4169-6749-1(4),* Simon & Schuster/Paula Wiseman Bks.) Simon & Schuster/Paula Wiseman Bks.

Huliska-Beith, Laura. Adventures of Granny Clearwater & Little Critter. Holt, Kimberly Willis. 2010. (ENG.). 32p. (J). (gr. k-4). 16.99 *(978-0-8050-7899-2(1),* Holt, Henry & Co. Bks. For Young Readers) Holt, Henry & Co.

—Cinco Pequenas Mariquitas. 2005.Tr. of Five Little Ladybugs. (SPA & ENG.). 12p. (J). 4.95 *(978-1-58117-333-8(4),* Intervisual/Piggy Toes) Bendon, Inc.

—Diez Pequeñas Mariquitas. Gerth, Melanie. 2005. Orig. Title: Ten Little Ladybugs. (SPA & ENG.). 22p. (J). (gr. -1). 10.95 *(978-1-58117-006-1(8),* Intervisual/Piggy Toes) Bendon, Inc.

—A Farmer's Life for Me. Dobbins, Jan. 2013. (ENG.). 24p. (J). (gr. k-3). 16.99 *(978-1-84686-790-3(8));* pap. 9.99 *(978-1-84686-791-0(6));* pap. 6.99 *(978-1-84686-939-6(0))* Barefoot Bks., Inc.

—Five Little Ladybugs. Gerth, Melanie. 2006. 12p. (J). bds. 14.95 *(978-1-58117-218-8(4),* Intervisual/Piggy Toes) Bendon, Inc.

—The Goodnight Train. Sobel, June. 2006. (ENG.). 32p. (J). (gr. -1-3). 16.99 *(978-0-15-205436-6(7))* Houghton Mifflin Harcourt Publishing Co.

—Little Red Hot, 0 vols. Kimmel, Eric A. 2013. (ENG.). (J). (gr. -1-3). 17.99 *(978-1-4778-1638-7(0),* 9781477816387, Amazon Children's Publishing) Amazon Publishing.

—Mary Had a Little Lamb, 0 vols. Hale, Sarah Josepha. 2011. (ENG.). 24p. (J). (gr. -1-2). 12.99 *(978-0-7614-5824-1(7),* 9780761458241, Amazon Children's Publishing) Amazon Publishing.

—Poetry for Young People: Edward Lear. Mendelson, Edward, ed. 2010. (Poetry for Young People Ser.). (ENG.). 48p. (J). (gr. 3). pap. 6.95 *(978-1-4027-7294-8(7))* Sterling Publishing Co., Inc.

—Ten Little Ladybugs. Gerth, Melanie. 2007. (ENG.). 22p. (J). (gr. -1-3). bds. 15.95 *(978-1-58117-578-3(7),* Intervisual/Piggy Toes) Bendon, Inc.

—Vivamos la Granja! Dobbins, Jan & Bernal, Natalia. 2013. (SPA.). 24p. (J). (gr. k-3). pap. 9.99 *(978-1-84686-860-3(2))* Barefoot Bks., Inc.

—The Wild, Wild Inside: A View from Mommy's Tummy! Feiffer, Kate. 2010. (ENG.). 32p. (J). (gr. -1-3). 15.99 *(978-1-4169-4099-9(5),* Simon & Schuster/Paula Wiseman Bks.) Simon & Schuster/Paula Wiseman Bks.

Huliska-Beith, Laura & Harriet Kasak Portfolio Staff. Bubble Gum, Bubble Gum. Wheeler, Lisa. 2004. (ENG.). 32p. (J). (gr. -1-1). 17.00 *(978-0-316-98894-0(4))* Little, Brown Bks. for Young Readers.

Huliska-Beith, Laura & Laura, Huliska-beith. Violet's Music. Johnson, Angela. 2004. (ENG.). 32p. (J). (gr. -1-3). 16.99 *(978-0-8037-2740-3(2),* Dial) Penguin Publishing Group.

Hull, Biz. Starlight Surprise. Chapman, Linda. 2003. (My Secret Unicorn Ser.). 130p. (J). *(978-0-439-65275-9(8))* Scholastic, Inc.

Hull, Biz & Farley, Andrew. Flying High. Chapman, Linda. 2004. (My Secret Unicorn Ser.). 118p. (J). *(978-0-439-65273-5(1))* Scholastic, Inc.

Hull, Jim. Casey at the Bat. Thayer, Ernest L. & Gardner, Martin. 2012. (Dover Children's Classics Ser.). (ENG.). 72p. (J). (gr. 2-5). pap. 6.99 *(978-0-486-48510-2(2))* Dover Pubns., Inc.

Hullinger, C. D. The Weather. Rosa-Mendoza, Gladys. Cifuentes, Carolina, ed. 2004. (English-Spanish Foundations Ser.: Vol. 6). Orig. Title: El Tiempo. (ENG & SPA.). 20p. (J). (gr. -1-4). bds. 6.95 *(978-0-9679748-5-9(2))* Me+Mi Publishing.

—The Weather. Cifuentes, Carolina. 2010. (My World Ser.). Orig. Title: El Tiempo. (ENG.). 24p. (J). (gr. -1-1). lib. bdg. 22.60 *(978-1-60754-955-0(7))* Windmill Bks.

—The Weather. Cifuentes, Carolina, ed. 2010. (My World Ser.). Orig. Title: El Tiempo. (ENG.). 24p. (J). (gr. -1-1). pap. 8.15 *(978-1-61533-043-0(7))* Windmill Bks.

Hulse, Gillian. Rainforest. Morris, Ting & Morris, Neil. 2006. (Sticky Fingers Ser.). 32p. (J). lib. bdg. 28.50 *(978-1-59771-028-2(8))* Sea-To-Sea Pubns.

Hulse, Kris. A Cowhand Christmas. Hulse, Kris. 2006. 32p. (J). lib. bdg. 21.95 *(978-0-9761128-6-0(8))* KB Bks. & More.

Hulst, W. G. van de & Hulst, Willem G. van de. Annie & the Goat. 2014. (J). *(978-1-928136-06-4(0))* Inheritance Pubns.

—The Basket. 2014. (J). *(978-1-928136-04-0(4))* Inheritance Pubns.

—The Black Kitten. 2014. (J). *(978-1-928136-07-1(9))* Inheritance Pubns.

—Bruno the Bear. 2014. (J). *(978-1-928136-03-3(6))* Inheritance Pubns.

—Footprints in the Snow. 2014. (J). *(978-1-928136-13-2(3))* Inheritance Pubns.

—Herbie, the Runaway Duck. 2014. (J). *(978-1-928136-19-4(2))* Inheritance Pubns.

—Kittens, Kittens Everywhere. 2014. (J). *(978-1-928136-20-0(6))* Inheritance Pubns.

—The Little Wooden Shoe. 2014. (J). *(978-1-928136-01-9(X))* Inheritance Pubns.

—The Pig under the Pew. 2014. (J). *(978-1-928136-10-1(9))* Inheritance Pubns.

—The Rockity Rowboat. 2014. (J). *(978-1-928136-18-7(4))* Inheritance Pubns.

—The Search for Christmas. 2014. (J). *(978-1-928136-12-5(5))* Inheritance Pubns.

—The Secret Hiding Place. 2014. (J). *(978-1-928136-16-3(8))* Inheritance Pubns.

—The Secret in the Box. 2014. (J). *(978-1-928136-17-0(6))* Inheritance Pubns.

—Three Foolish Sisters. 2014. (J). *(978-1-928136-15-6(X))* Inheritance Pubns.

—Through the Thunderstorm. 2014. (J). *(978-1-928136-02-6(8))* Inheritance Pubns.

—The Woods Beyond the Wall. 2017. (J). *(978-1-928136-08-8(7))* Inheritance Pubns.

Hulst, Willem G. van de, jt. illus. see Hulst, W. G. van de.

Hume, Jeff. The Shining Thing, 1 vol. Ballard, John. 2009. 35p. pap. 19.95 *(978-1-61546-655-9(X))* PublishAmerica, Inc.

Hume, John. My Florida Alphabet. Johnson, Annie P. & Johnson, Russell. 2014. (ENG.). 64p. (J). pap. 15.95 *(978-1-56164-729-3(2))* Pineapple Pr., Inc.

Hummel, Jim. Help! Mom! There Are Liberals under My Bed! DeBrecht, Katharine. 2005. (ENG.). 54p. pap. 15.95 *(978-0-9767269-0-6(4),* Kids Ahead Bks.) WND Bks, Inc.

Hummingbird, Jesse T. Native American Night Before Christmas. Robinson, Gary. 2007. 40p. (J). *(978-1-57416-093-2(1))* Clear Light Pubs.

—Native American Twelve Days of Christmas. Robinson, Gary. 2011. (ENG.). 32p. (J). 19.95 *(978-1-57416-105-2(9))* Clear Light Pubs.

Humphrey, Bobby, photos by. Rules of the Game. Nixon, James. 2011. (Soccer File Ser.). 32p. (YA). (gr. 3-6). lib. bdg. 28.50 *(978-1-59920-529-8(7))* Black Rabbit Bks.

Humphrey Williams, Ann. The Journey Through Middle School Math. Crews, Elizabeth, photos by. Mayfield-Ingram, Karen. 2005. (Equals Ser.). 140p. pap. 18.95 *(978-0-912511-31-3(1),* EQUALS) Univ. of California, Berkeley, Lawrence Hall of Science.

—El Viaje-Por la matematica de la escuela Secundaria. Ramirez, Alma. 2005. (Equals Ser.). (SPA.). (J). pap. 18.95 *(978-0-912511-32-0(X),* EQUALS) Univ. of California, Berkeley, Lawrence Hall of Science.

Humphreys, David, photos by. Holly Clegg's Trim & Terrific Freezer Friendly Meals: Quick & Healthy Recipes You Can Make in Advance. Clegg, Holly. 2006. (ENG.). 304p. 19.95 *(978-0-7624-2597-6(0))* Running Pr. Bk. Pubs.

Humphreys, Dolores. The Adventures of J. G. & Echo: The Land of All Creatures & the Swamp Creature. 1. 2003. 81p. (J). per. 16.00 *(978-0-9727415-2-1(6))* Cuccia, Louis.

Humphreys, Graham. Jason & the Argonauts. Brooks, Felicity. 2005. 144p. (J). pap. 4.95 *(978-0-7945-0275-1(X),* Usborne) EDC Publishing.

Humphries, Tudor. Are You a Butterfly? Allen, Judy. 2003. (Backyard Bks.). (ENG.). 28p. (J). (gr. k-3). pap. 6.99 *(978-0-7534-5608-8(7),* Kingfisher) Roaring Brook Pr.

—Are You a Dragonfly? Allen, Judy. 2004. (Backyard Bks.). (ENG.). 32p. (J). (gr. k-3). pap. 6.99 *(978-0-7534-5805-1(5),* Kingfisher) Roaring Brook Pr.

—Are You a Grasshopper? Allen, Judy. 2004. (Backyard Bks.). (ENG.). 32p. (J). (gr. k-3). pap. 6.99 *(978-0-7534-5806-8(3),* Kingfisher) Roaring Brook Pr.

—Are You a Ladybug? Allen, Judy. 2003. (Backyard Bks.). (ENG.). 31p. (J). (gr. k-3). pap. 6.99 *(978-0-7534-5603-3(6),* Kingfisher) Roaring Brook Pr.

—Are You a Snail? Allen, Judy. 2003. (Backyard Bks.). (ENG.). 31p. (J). (gr. k-3). pap. 6.99 *(978-0-7534-5604-0(4),* Kingfisher) Roaring Brook Pr.

—Are You a Spider? Allen, Judy. 2003. (Backyard Bks.). (ENG.). 31p. (J). (gr. k-3). pap. 6.99 *(978-0-7534-5609-5(5),* Kingfisher) Roaring Brook Pr.

—Are You an Ant? Allen, Judy. 2004. (Backyard Bks.). (ENG.). 32p. (J). (gr. k-3). pap. 6.99 *(978-0-7534-5803-7(9),* Kingfisher) Roaring Brook Pr.

—Creepy-Crawlies. Wallace, Karen. 2012. (Flip the Flaps Ser.). (ENG.). 32p. (J). (gr. -1-1). pap. 6.99 *(978-0-7534-6739-8(9),* Kingfisher) Roaring Brook Pr.

—Flip the Flaps: Dinosaurs. Allen, Judy. 2011. (Flip the Flaps Ser.). (ENG.). 32p. (J). (gr. -1-1). pap. 6.99 *(978-0-7534-6496-0(9),* Kingfisher) Roaring Brook Pr.

—Flip the Flaps: Things That Go! Ganeri, Anita. 2014. (Flip the Flaps Ser.). (ENG.). 32p. (J). (gr. -1-1). pap. 6.99 *(978-0-7534-7133-3(7),* Kingfisher) Roaring Brook Pr.

—The Giant Surprise: A Narnia Story. Oram, Hiawyn. 2005. (Step into Narnia Ser.). 40p. (J). (gr. -1-2). lib. bdg. 16.89 *(978-0-06-001360-8(5))* HarperCollins Pubs.

—The Lion, the Witch & the Wardrobe. Lewis, C. S. 2004. (Chronicles of Narnia Ser.). 48p. (J). (gr. -1-2). lib. bdg. 17.89 *(978-0-06-055651-8(X))* HarperCollins Pubs.

—The Lion, the Witch & the Wardrobe. Lewis, C. S. & Orem, Hiawyn. 2004. (Chronicles of Narnia Ser.). (ENG.). 48p. (J). (gr. -1-2). 16.99 *(978-0-06-055650-1(1))* HarperCollins Pubs.

Humphries, Tudor, jt. illus. see Allen, Judy.

Humphrys-Bajaj, Holly. Tails of Sweetbrier. Humphrys-Dunne, Deanie. 2013. 82p. pap. 9.95 *(978-1-61286-182-1(2))* Avid Readers Publishing Group.

Huna Smith, Ryan. The Three Little Sheep/Dibe Yazhi Taa'go Baa Hane' Yazzie, Seraphine G. Thomas, Peter A., tr. 2006. (ENG & NAV.). 32p. (J). (gr. 4-7). 12.95 *(978-1-893354-09-8(1))* Salina Bookshelf Inc.

Hund, Marjolein. Pirates. Boshouwers, Suzan. 2012. (Want to Know Ser.). (ENG.). 30p. (J). (gr. -1-2). 16.95 *(978-1-60537-135-1(1))* Clavis Publishing.

Hundley, Sam. Our Fantasy Island: An Interactive Book. Suhay, Lisa. 2006. 30p. (J). pap. 8.00 *(978-0-9766628-0-8(9))* Fantasy Island Pr.

Huneck, Stephen. Sally Gets a Job. Huneck, Stephen. 2008. (ENG.). 32p. (J). (gr. 1-4). 16.95 *(978-0-8109-9493-5(3),* Abrams Bks. for Young Readers) Abrams.

—Sally Goes to the Vet. Huneck, Stephen. 2004. (ENG.). 32p. (J). (gr. -1-3). 19.95 *(978-0-8109-4813-6(3))* Abrams.

—Sally's Snow Adventure. Huneck, Stephen. 2006. (ENG.). 32p. (J). (gr. -1-3). 15.95 *(978-0-8109-7061-8(9))* Abrams.

Hunkel, Cary. Discovering Wolves. Field, Nancy & Karasov, Corliss. 2011. (Discovering Nature Library). (ENG.). 40p. (J). (gr. 3-8). pap. 6.95 *(978-0-941042-39-0(1))* Dog-Eared Pubns.

Hunner, Trina L. Green Bean! Green Bean! Thomas, Patricia. 2016. 32p. (J). (gr. k-4). 16.95 ***(978-1-58469-543-1(9))*** Dawn Pubns.

Hunner, Trina L. On Kiki's Reef. Malnor, Carol L. 2014. (ENG.). 32p. (J). (gr. k-4). 16.95 *(978-1-58469-476-2(9))* Dawn Pubns.

Hunner, Trina L. Molly's Organic Farm. Hunner, Trina L. Malnor, Carol L. 2012. (ENG.). 32p. (J). (gr. k-4). 16.95 *(978-1-58469-166-2(2));* pap. 8.95 *(978-1-58469-167-9(0))* Dawn Pubns.

Hunt, Alfred William & Grimly, Gris. Gris Grimly's Tales from the Brothers Grimm: Being a Selection from the Household Stories Collected by Jacob & Wilhelm Grimm. Grimm, Jacob et al. 2016. (J). 17.99 ***(978-0-06-235233-0(4),*** Balzer & Bray) HarperCollins Pubs.

Hunt, Craig J. S. The Dinosaur Who Loved to Bake & Eat Cakes. Hunt, Debbie Colleen. 2012. 32p. 24.95 *(978-1-4626-3213-8(0))* America Star Bks.

Hunt, E. Marlene. Every Apple. Hunt, E. Marlene. l.t. ed. 2003. 12p. pap. 10.00 *(978-1-893555-45-7(3))* Grace Publishing.

Hunt, Jane. There's Something in My Sandwich. Ayers, Linda. 50p. (J). 2006. 13.95 *(978-0-9760505-7-5(9));* 2005. per. 6.95 *(978-0-9760505-5-1(2))* Blue Thistle Pr.

—Tiger Does the Write Thing. Ayers, Linda. l.t. ed. 2005. 35p. (J). per. 7.95 *(978-0-9760505-4-4(4))* Blue Thistle Pr.

—Tiger Goes Collecting. Ayers, Linda. l.t. ed. 2004. 55p. (J). per. 7.95 *(978-0-9760505-2-0(8))* Blue Thistle Pr.

Hunt, Jim. Baby Kong. Stroud, Scott. 2006. (J). 8.95 *(978-1-60131-001-9(3),* Castlebridge Bks.) Big Tent Bks.

—Boomer Explores Annapolis, 1 vol. Clarke, Angelique. 2012. (ENG.). 32p. (J). 12.99 *(978-0-7643-4008-6(5))* Schiffer Publishing, Ltd.

—Grumpy Mr. Grady. Stroud, Scott. 2007. 24p. (J). 8.95 *(978-1-60131-008-8(0),* Castlebridge Bks.) Big Tent Bks.

—My Loveable Little Monster. Lara, Sahai. 2011. 22p. (J). pap. 5.99 *(978-0-615-48221-7(X))* SNL Publishing.

Hunt, John, jt. illus. see Barry, James L.

Hunt, Judith. Animals under Our Feet. McKay, Sindy. 2007. 40p. (J). *(978-1-891327-97-1(6));* pap. *(978-1-891327-98-8(4))* Treasure Bay, Inc.

—Half & Half-Earthquake! Hodgkins, Fran. 2011. (ENG.). 52p. (J). 9.95 *(978-1-60115-217-6(5));* pap. 4.99 *(978-1-60115-218-3(3))* Treasure Bay, Inc.

—Prunes & Rupe. Griffin, Lydia. 2007. 32p. (J). 16.00 *(978-0-86541-086-2(0))* Filter Pr., LLC.

—We Both Read-Animals under Our Feet. McKay, Sindy. 2007. (We Both Read Ser.). 40p. (J). (gr. -1-3). 9.95 *(978-1-60115-003-5(2));* pap. 5.99 *(978-1-60115-004-2(0))* Treasure Bay, Inc.

Hunt, Judith & Smith, Wendy. We Both Read-Sharks! McKay, Sindy. 2012. 44p. (J). 9.95 *(978-1-60115-261-9(2));* pap. 5.99 *(978-1-60115-262-6(0))* Treasure Bay, Inc.

Hunt, Judith A. The Bald Eagle. Kenney, Karen Latchana. 2011. (Our Nation's Pride Set 2 Ser.). 32p. (J). (gr. 1-4). 28.50 *(978-1-61641-149-7(X))* Magic Wagon.

—Ellis Island. Kenney, Karen Latchana. 2011. (Our Nation's Pride Set 2 Ser.). 32p. (J). (gr. 1-4). 28.50 *(978-1-61641-150-3(3))* Magic Wagon.

—The Lincoln Memorial. Kenney, Karen Latchana. 2011. (Our Nation's Pride Set 2 Ser.). 32p. (J). (gr. 1-4). 28.50 *(978-1-61641-151-0(1))* Magic Wagon.

—Memorial Day. Kenney, Karen Latchana. 2011. (Our Nation's Pride Set 2 Ser.). 32p. (J). (gr. 1-4). 28.50 *(978-1-61641-152-7(X))* Magic Wagon.

—Mount Rushmore. Kenney, Karen Latchana. 2011. (Our Nation's Pride Set 2 Ser.). 32p. (J). (gr. 1-4). 28.50 *(978-1-61641-153-4(8))* Magic Wagon.

—The White House. Kenney, Karen Latchana. 2011. (Our Nation's Pride Set 2 Ser.). 32p. (J). (gr. 1-4). 28.50 *(978-1-61641-154-1(6))* Magic Wagon.

Hunt, Lisa. Manners Matter in the Classroom, 1 vol. Mortensen, Lori. 2011. (First Graphics: Manners Matter Ser.). (ENG.). 24p. (gr. 1-2). lib. bdg. 23.32 *(978-1-4296-5333-6(7));* pap. 35.70 *(978-1-4296-6392-2(8))* Capstone Pr., Inc.

—Manners Matter in the Library, 1 vol. Mortensen, Lori. 2011. (First Graphics: Manners Matter Ser.). (ENG.). 24p. (gr. 1-2). lib. bdg. 23.32 *(978-1-4296-5330-5(2));* pap. 6.29 *(978-1-4296-6224-6(7));* pap. 35.70 *(978-1-4296-6393-9(6))* Capstone Pr., Inc.

—Manners Matter on a Field Trip, 1 vol. Mortensen, Lori. 2011. (First Graphics: Manners Matter Ser.). (ENG.). 24p. (gr. 1-2). lib. bdg. 23.32 *(978-1-4296-5331-2(0));* pap. 35.70 *(978-1-4296-6394-6(4))* Capstone Pr., Inc.

—Manners Matter on the Playground, 1 vol. Mortensen, Lori. 2011. (First Graphics: Manners Matter Ser.). (ENG.). 24p. (gr. 1-2). lib. bdg. 23.32 *(978-1-4296-5332-9(9));* pap. 35.70 *(978-1-4296-6395-3(2))* Capstone Pr., Inc.

Hunt, Matt. Lady Liberty's Holiday. Arena, Jen. 2016. (ENG.). 40p. (J). ***(978-0-553-52067-5(9))*** Knopf, Alfred A. Inc.

H

Hunt, Meg. Interstellar Cinderella. 2015. (ENG.). 40p. (J). (gr. -1-k). 16.99 *(978-1-4521-2532-9(5))* Chronicle Bks. LLC.
Hunt, Miguel, photos by. Berlin. Garner, Simon. 2007. (Global Cities Ser.). 64p. (gr. 5-8). lib. bdg. 30.00 *(978-0-7910-8846-3(4),* Chelsea Hse.) Facts On File, Inc.
Hunt, Paul. Rodeo Rocky. Oldfield, Jenny. 2009. (J). Non-ISBN Publisher.
—Wild Horses. Oldfield, Jenny. 2009. (J). Non-ISBN Publisher.
Hunt, Robert. Julie Story Collection. McDonald, Megan. 2007. 472p. pap. 29.95 *(978-1-59369-450-0(4))* American Girl Publishing, Inc.
—Rebecca Story Collection. Greene, Jacqueline. Hirsch, Jennifer, ed. 2009. (ENG.). 456p. (YA). (gr. 3-18). 29.95 *(978-1-59369-626-9(4))* American Girl Publishing, Inc.
—Rocket Man: The Mercury Adventure of John Glenn, 1 vol. Ashby, Ruth. 2004. (ENG.). 144p. (J). (gr. 2-5). 12.95 *(978-1-56145-323-8(4))* Peachtree Pubs.
—Swiss Family Robinson. Wyss, Johann David. 2006. (Stepping Stone Book Ser.). (ENG.). 112p. (J). (gr. 1-4). per. 3.99 *(978-0-375-87525-0(5),* Random Hse. Bks. for Young Readers) Random Hse. Children's Bks.
—What Was America's Deadliest War? And Other Questions about the Civil War. Sandler, Martin W. 2014. (Good Question! Ser.). (ENG.). 32p. (J). pap. 5.95 *(978-1-4027-9046-1(5))* Sterling Publishing Co., Inc.
Hunt, Robert, jt. illus. see Elliott, Mark.
Hunt, Robert, jt. illus. see McAliley, Susan.
Hunt, Scott. Becoming Joe Dimaggio. Testa, Maria. 2005. (ENG.). 64p. (J). (gr. 5-9). reprint ed. pap. 6.99 *(978-0-7636-2444-6(6))* Candlewick Pr.
—Becoming Joe Dimaggio. Testa, Maria. 2006. 51p. (gr. 5-9). 17.00 *(978-0-7569-6576-1(4))* Perfection Learning Corp.
Hunter, Anne. Who Would Like a Christmas Tree? A Tree for All Seasons. Obed, Ellen Bryan. 2009. (ENG.). 32p. (J). (gr. -1-3). 16.00 *(978-0-547-04625-9(1))* Houghton Mifflin Harcourt Publishing Co.
Hunter, Carl & Heney, Clare. The Unforgotten Coat. Hunter, Carl & Heney, Clare, photos by. Boyce, Frank Cottrell. 2011. (ENG.). 112p. (J). (gr. 3-7). 15.99 *(978-0-7636-5729-1(8))* Candlewick Pr.
Hunter, Charlene. See You in Heaven. Stripling, Joe. Carroll, Joan, ed. Date not set. (Sunday School Two Thousand Ser.). 38p. (J). pap. 12.95 *(978-1-881223-07-8(8))* Zulema Enterprises Publishing.
Hunter, Erin E. A Day in the Deep, 1 vol. Kurtz, Kevin. 2013. (ENG.). 32p. (J). (gr. -1-4). 17.95 *(978-1-60718-617-5(9));* pap. 9.95 *(978-1-60718-629-8(2))* Arbordale Publishing.
—A Day on the Mountain, 1 vol. Kurtz, Kevin. 2010. (ENG.). 32p. (J). (gr. -1-4). 16.95 *(978-1-60718-073-9(1))* Arbordale Publishing.
—Un Día en la Profundidad, 1 vol. Kurtz, Kevin. 2013. (SPA.). 32p. (J). (gr. -1-4). 17.95 *(978-1-60718-715-8(9))* Arbordale Publishing.
—The Great Divide, 1 vol. Slade, Suzanne. 2012. (ENG.). 32p. (J). (gr. -1-4). 17.95 *(978-1-60718-521-5(0));* pap. 9.95 *(978-1-60718-530-7(X))* Arbordale Publishing.
—Multiply on the Fly, 1 vol. Slade, Suzanne. 2011. (ENG.). 32p. (J). (gr. -1-4). 16.95 *(978-1-60718-128-6(2));* pap. 8.95 *(978-1-60718-138-5(X))* Arbordale Publishing.
Hunter, Gerald. Miss B's First Cookbook: Twenty Family-Sized Recipes for for the Youngest Cook. Hoffmann, Peggy. 2011. 48p. pap. 35.95 *(978-1-258-06433-2(3))* Literary Licensing, LLC.
Hunter, Llyn. A Little Book of Magical Beings. Hunter, Llyn. 2008. 32p. (J). 7.95 *(978-0-9776419-1-8(0))* Bobcat Publishing.
—A Little Book of Monsters. Hunter, Llyn. 2007. 32p. (J). 7.95 *(978-0-9776419-0-1(2),* 0-9776419-0-2) Bobcat Publishing.
Hunter, R. The Adventures of Pillow Head: The Fallen Star. Ruzycki, Dandan. 2010. (ENG.). 24p. pap. 9.95 *(978-1-4538-3167-0(3))* CreateSpace Independent Publishing Platform.
Hunter, R. Chase. The Adventures of Pillow Head & the Bubble Boys. Ruzycki, Dan Dan. 2010. (ENG.). 26p. pap. 9.95 *(978-1-4564-5513-2(3))* CreateSpace Independent Publishing Platform.
Hunter, Robbie Chase. The Adventures of Pillow Head: The Fallen Star. Ruzycki, Dan Dan. 2012. 26p. (J). 13.95 *(978-0-9834315-5-8(8))* Dan Dan Fantasy.
Huntington, Amy. Adding with Sebastian Pig & Friends at the Circus. Anderson, Jill. 2009. (Math Fun with Sebastian Pig & Friends! Ser.). 32p. (J). (gr. k-3). lib. bdg. 23.94 *(978-0-7660-3360-3(0))* Enslow Pubs., Inc.
—Counting with Sebastian Pig & Friends on the Farm. Anderson, Jill. 2009. (Math Fun with Sebastian Pig & Friends! Ser.). 32p. (J). (gr. k-3). lib. bdg. 23.94 *(978-0-7660-3359-7(7))* Enslow Pubs., Inc.
—Finding Shapes with Sebastian Pig & Friends at the Museum. Anderson, Jill. 2009. (Math Fun with Sebastian Pig & Friends! Ser.). 32p. (J). (gr. k-3). lib. bdg. 23.94 *(978-0-7660-3363-4(5))* Enslow Pubs., Inc.
—Grandma Drove the Garbage Truck. Clark, Katie. 2006. (ENG.). 32p. (J). (gr. -1-17). 15.95 *(978-0-89272-698-1(9))* Down East Bks.
—Grandma Drove the Lobsterboat, 1 vol. Clark, Katie. 2012. (ENG.). 32p. (J). (gr. -1-1). 16.95 *(978-1-60893-004-3(1))* Down East Bks.
—Matthew & Tall Rabbit Go Camping. Meyer, Susan. ed. 2008. (ENG.). 32p. (J). (gr. -1-3). 15.95 *(978-0-89272-769-8(1))* Down East Bks.
—Measuring with Sebastian Pig & Friends on a Road Trip. Anderson, Jill. 2009. (Math Fun with Sebastian Pig & Friends! Ser.). 32p. (J). (gr. k-3). lib. bdg. 23.94 *(978-0-7660-3362-7(7))* Enslow Pubs., Inc.
—Money Math with Sebastian Pig & Friends at the Farmer's Market. Anderson, Jill. 2009. (Math Fun with Sebastian Pig & Friends! Ser.). 32p. (J). (gr. k-3). lib. bdg. 23.94 *(978-0-7660-3364-1(3))* Enslow Pubs., Inc.
—Moose Power! Muskeg Saves the Day. Beckhorn, Susan Williams. ed. 2010. (ENG.). 40p. (J). (gr. -1-3). 16.95 *(978-0-89272-762-9(4))* Down East Bks.
—Penelope & Pip Build a Prose Poem. Heiden, Pete. 2011. (Poetry Builders Ser.). 32p. (J). (gr. 2-4). lib. bdg. 25.27 *(978-1-59953-438-1(X))* Norwood Hse. Pr.
—Seagull Sam. Clark, Katherine. ed. 2007. (ENG.). 32p. (J). (gr. -1-3). 15.95 *(978-0-89272-715-5(2))* Down East Bks.
—Subtracting with Sebastian Pig & Friends on a Camping Trip. Anderson, Jill. 2009. (Math Fun with Sebastian Pig & Friends! Ser.). 32p. (J). (gr. k-3). lib. bdg. 23.94 *(978-0-7660-3361-0(9))* Enslow Pubs., Inc.
—Take Me Out to the Ball Game. Norworth, Jack. 2011. (Favorite Children's Songs Ser.). (ENG.). 16p. (J). (gr. -1-2). lib. bdg. 25.64 *(978-1-60954-294-8(0),* 200098) Child's World, Inc., The.
Huntley, Doris. I'm Da Muva, Said Miss Bossy. Dowell, Vivian "Vee". 2008. 32p. pap. 24.95 *(978-1-60610-045-5(9))* America Star Bks.
Hupf, Zetta. Detective Buddy & the Case of the Missing Football, 1 vol. Hupf, Zetta. Hupf, Mitchellx. 2009. 23p. pap. 19.95 *(978-1-61582-312-3(3))* PublishAmerica, Inc.
—Henry Goes to the Park, 1 vol. Hupf, Zetta. Hupf, Mitchell. 2009. 33p. pap. 24.95 *(978-1-61546-279-7(1))* America Star Bks.
Huras, Lynne. Ned: The Story of Bear Six Nine Three, 1 vol. Pavelka, Joe. 2007. (ENG.). 32p. (J). (gr. -1-1). *(978-1-894765-95-4(8))* Rocky Mountain Bks.
Hurd, Clement. A Baby's Gift: Goodnight Moon & the Runaway Bunny, 2 vols. Brown, Margaret Wise. 2014. 70p. (J). (gr. -1 — 1). pap. 15.99 *(978-0-694-01638-9(1),* HarperFestival) HarperCollins Pubs.
—Buenas Noches, Luna. Brown, Margaret Wise. Mlawer, Teresa, tr. from ENG. 2006.Tr. of Goodnight Moon. (SPA.). 32p. (J). (gr. -1-3). 17.99 *(978-0-06-026214-3(1),* HC0528, Rayo) HarperCollins Pubs.
—Buenas Noches, Luna. Brown, Margaret Wise & Brown, Wise M. Mlawer, Teresa, tr. from ENG. ed. 2006. (Trophy Picture Bks.).Tr. of Goodnight Moon. (SPA.). 32p. (J). (gr. -1-3). pap. 6.99 *(978-0-06-443416-4(8),* HC0527, Rayo) HarperCollins Pubs.
—El Conejito Andarín. Brown, Margaret Wise. Marcuse, Aida E., tr. 2006. (SPA.). 48p. (J). (gr. -1-2). pap. 6.99 *(978-0-06-077694-7(3),* Rayo) HarperCollins Pubs.
—Goodnight Moon. Brown, Margaret Wise. (J). (gr. -1 — 1). 2012. (ENG.). 8p. pap. 14.99 *(978-0-06-076224-7(1),* HarperFestival); 2007. (ENG.). 32p. pap. 24.99 *(978-0-06-111977-4(6),* HarperFestival); 2005. 32p. lib. bdg. 18.89 *(978-0-06-077586-5(6));* 60th anniv. ed. 2007. (ENG.). 34p. bds. 8.99 *(978-0-694-00361-7(1),* HarperFestival); 60th anniv. ed. 2007. (ENG.). 32p. 18.99 *(978-0-06-077585-8(8));* 60th anniv. ed. 2007. (ENG.). 32p. pap. 6.99 *(978-0-06-443017-3(0))* HarperCollins Pubs.
—Goodnight Moon. Brown, Margaret Wise. (J). pap. 32.75 incl. audio. (gr. -1-3). 24.95 incl. audio Weston Woods Studios, Inc.
—Goodnight Moon 1 2 3: A Counting Book. Brown, Margaret Wise. 2008. (ENG.). 30p. (J). (gr. -1-k). bds. 8.99 *(978-0-06-112597-3(0),* HarperFestival) HarperCollins Pubs.
—Goodnight Moon 123: A Counting Book. Brown, Margaret Wise. (J). 2013. (ENG.). 30p. (gr. -1-k). bds. 9.99 *(978-0-06-224405-5(1),* HarperFestival); 2007. (ENG.). 32p. (gr. -1-k). 16.99 *(978-0-06-112593-5(8));* 2007. 32p. (gr. -1-k). lib. bdg. 17.89 *(978-0-06-112594-2(6));* 2007. *(978-1-4287-4853-8(9))* HarperCollins Pubs.
—Goodnight Moon 123 Lap Edition. Brown, Margaret Wise. 2008. (ENG.). 30p. (J). (gr. -1 — 1). pap. 12.99 *(978-0-06-166755-8(2),* HarperFestival) HarperCollins Pubs.
—Goodnight Moon 123/Buenas Noches, Luna 123: A Counting Book/un Libro para Contar. Brown, Margaret Wise. 2007. (ENG & SPA.). 32p. (J). (gr. -1-k). 16.99 *(978-0-06-117325-7(8),* Rayo) HarperCollins Pubs.
—Goodnight Moon ABC: An Alphabet Book. Brown, Margaret Wise. 2010. (ENG.). (J). (gr. -1-k). 30p. bds. 8.99 *(978-0-06-189490-9(7),* HarperFestival); 32p. 16.99 *(978-0-06-189484-8(2))* HarperCollins Pubs.
—Goodnight Moon ABC Padded Board Book: An Alphabet Book. Brown, Margaret Wise. 2013. (ENG.). 30p. (J). (gr. -1-k). bds. 9.99 *(978-0-06-224404-8(3),* HarperFestival) HarperCollins Pubs.
—Goodnight Moon Board Book & Bunny. Brown, Margaret Wise. 2005. (ENG.). 34p. (J). (gr. -1 — 1). bds. 16.99 *(978-0-06-076027-4(3),* HarperFestival) HarperCollins Pubs.
—Goodnight Moon Classic Library: Contains Goodnight Moon, the Runaway Bunny, & My World. Brown, Margaret Wise. 2011. (ENG.). 32p. (J). (gr. -1-1). 14.99 *(978-0-06-199823-2(0))* HarperCollins Pubs.
—Goodnight Moon Cloth Book Box. Brown, Margaret Wise. 2012. (ENG.). 8p. (J). (gr. -1 — 1). pap. 14.99 *(978-0-06-223589-3(3),* HarperFestival) HarperCollins Pubs.
—Goodnight Moon/Buenas Noches, Luna. Brown, Margaret Wise. 2014. (ENG.). 34p. (J). (gr. -1-3). bds. 8.99 *(978-0-06-236791-4(9))* HarperCollins Pubs.
—My World. Brown, Margaret Wise. 2004. (J). (gr. -1-3). lib. bdg. 14.15 *(978-0-613-83488-9(7),* Turtleback) Turtleback Bks.
—My World: A Companion to Goodnight Moon. Brown, Margaret Wise. (ENG.). (J). (gr. -1 — 1). 2004. 32p. pap. 6.99 *(978-0-694-01660-0(8));* 2003. 36p. bds. 8.99 *(978-0-694-00862-9(1),* HarperFestival) HarperCollins Pubs.
—Over the Moon: Goodnight Moon, the Runaway Bunny, & My World. Brown, Margaret Wise. 2006. (ENG.). 108p. (J). (gr. -1-1). 19.99 *(978-0-06-076162-2(8))* HarperCollins Pubs.
—The Runaway Bunny. Brown, Margaret Wise. (Trophy Picture Bks.). 48p. (J). (gr. -1-1). 2006. (ENG.). pap. 6.99 *(978-0-06-443018-0(9));* 2005. (ENG.). 17.99 *(978-0-06-077582-7(3));* 2005. lib. bdg. 18.89 *(978-0-06-077583-4(1))* HarperCollins Pubs.
—The World Is Round. Stein, Gertrude & Hurd, Thacher. 75th ed. 2013. (ENG.). 128p. 19.99 *(978-0-06-220307-6(X),* Collins Design) HarperCollins Pubs.
Hurd, Thacher. The Pea Patch Jig. rev. ed. 2015. (ENG.). 40p. (J). (gr. -1). 16.95 ***(978-1-939547-21-7(0))*** Creston Bks.
Hurd, Thacher. Art Dog. Hurd, Thacher. Hurd. 2004. (ENG.). 32p. (J). (gr. -1-3). 18.99 *(978-0-06-024424-8(0))* HarperCollins Pubs.
—Bad Frogs. Hurd, Thacher. 2009. (ENG.). 40p. (J). (gr. -1-2). 15.99 *(978-0-7636-3253-3(8))* Candlewick Pr.
—Mama Don't Allow. Hurd, Thacher. Hurd. 25th anniv. ed. 2008. (Trophy Picture Bks.). (ENG.). 40p. (J). (gr. -1-3). pap. 6.99 *(978-0-06-443078-4(2))* HarperCollins Pubs.
—Mystery on the Docks. Hurd, Thacher. Hurd, Thacher. 25th anniv. ed. 2008. (Trophy Picture Bks.). (ENG.). 32p. (J). (gr. -1-3). pap. 8.99 *(978-0-06-443058-6(8))* HarperCollins Pubs.
Hurd, Thacher, photos by. Mama Don't Allow. Hurd, T. ed. 2006. (gr. -1-2). 17.20 *(978-0-8085-3698-7(2),* Turtleback) Turtleback Bks.
Hurley, Jorey. Fetch. Hurley, Jorey. 2015. (ENG.). 40p. (J). (gr. -1-2). 17.99 *(978-1-4424-8969-1(3),* Simon & Schuster Bks. For Young Readers) Simon & Schuster Bks. For Young Readers.
—Nest. Hurley, Jorey. 2014. (ENG.). 40p. (J). (gr. -1-2). 16.99 *(978-1-4424-8971-4(5),* Simon & Schuster/Paula Wiseman Bks.) Simon & Schuster/Paula Wiseman Bks.
Hurst, Ceri, jt. illus. see Mitchell, Joanne.
Hurst, Debbie. About Gossip: What Would Jesus Do, 1 vol. Gould, M. & Gould, R. 2009. 28p. pap. 24.95 *(978-1-60749-680-9(1))* America Star Bks.
—The Bleeks: The Bleek Family's First Christmas, 1 vol. Gould, M&R. 2010. 30p. pap. 24.95 *(978-1-4489-2770-8(6))* PublishAmerica, Inc.
Hurst, Elise. The Twin Competition. Trussell-Cullen, Alan. 2009. (Rigby PM Stars Bridge Bks.). (ENG.). 16p. (gr. 2-3). pap. 8.70 *(978-1-4190-5510-2(0))* Rigby Education.
Hurst, Margaret. The First Days of the Dinosaurs: Text Edition. Gabriele, Joseph. 32p. (Orig.). (J). (gr. 1-3). pap. 1.95 *(978-0-911211-55-9(1))* Penny Lane Pubns., Inc.
Hurst, Oliver. Finn at Clee Point. Knight, Richard et al. 2012. (ENG.). 128p. (J). pap. 12.99 *(978-1-84686-401-8(1))* Barefoot Bks., Inc.
—Stubby the Dog Soldier: World War I Hero, 1 vol. Hoena, Blake. 2014. (Animal Heroes Ser.). (ENG.). 32p. (gr. k-2). 27.99 *(978-1-4795-5461-4(8))* Picture Window Bks.
Hurt, Barbara. Dragons & Dragoons. Hurt, Barbara. 2010. (ENG.). 82p. pap. 16.99 *(978-1-4537-2959-5(3))* CreateSpace Independent Publishing Platform.
Husar, Lisa & Husar, Mike, photos by. Bobcat Babies. 2013. 26p. (J). 8.95 *(978-1-56037-133-5(1))* Farcountry Pr.
—Busy Bear Cubs. Schindel, John. 2009. (Busy Book Ser.). (ENG., 20p. (J). (gr. k — 1). bds. 6.99 *(978-1-58246-302-5(6))* Ten Speed Pr.
—Busy Pandas. Schindel, John. 2008. (Busy Book Ser.). (ENG., 20p. (J). (gr. k — 1). bds. 6.99 *(978-1-58246-259-2(3),* Tricycle Pr.) Ten Speed Pr.
Husar, Mike, jt. photos by see Husar, Lisa.
Husband, Amy. The Story of Life: A First Book about Evolution. Barr, Catherine & Williams, Steve. 2015. (ENG.). 40p. (J). (gr. k-3). 18.99 *(978-1-84780-485-3(3),* Frances Lincoln) Quarto Publishing Group UK GBR. Dist: Hachette Bk. Group.
Husband, Ron. Steamboat School. Hopkinson, Deborah. 2016. (J). ***(978-1-4231-2196-1(1))*** Disney Pr.
Husberg, Rob. Better Than a Lemonade Stand! Small Business Ideas for Kids. Bernstein, Daryl. 2012. (ENG.). 224p. (J). (gr. 4-9). 19.99 *(978-1-58270-360-2(4));* pap. 10.99 *(978-1-58270-330-5(2))* Aladdin/Beyond Words.
Huseman, Ryan. Peter's Purpose. Oramas, Jennifer. 2012. 34p. 24.95 *(978-1-4626-6585-3(3))* America Star Bks.
Huskins, Suzanne Hallier. No Matter What! 2004. (J). *(978-1-887905-93-0(6))* Parkway Pubs., Inc.
—Sunbeam. Wyont, Wanda. 2006. 32p. (J). 12.50 *(978-1-933251-07-3(7))* Parkway Pubs., Inc.
Huss, Sally. Lara Takes Charge: For Kids with Diabetes, Their Friends, & Siblings, 2 bks, Book 1. Lang, Rocky. 2nd ed. 2012. 28p. (J). 12.95 *(978-1-934980-05-7(6))* Cable Publishing.
Hussain, Nelupa, jt. illus. see Fearn, Katrina.
Hussey, Lorna. Nonsense Verse. Carroll, Lewis. 2004. (ENG.). 32p. (J). (gr. 4). pap. 12.99 *(978-0-7475-5019-8(0))* Bloomsbury Publishing Plc GBR. Dist: Independent Pubs. Group.
—Not This Bear: A First Day of School Story. Capucilli, Alyssa Satin. 2015. (ENG.). 32p. (J). (gr. -1-1). 16.99 *(978-0-8050-9896-9(8),* Holt, Henry & Co. Bks. For Young Readers) Holt, Henry & Co.
—Owls: Internet-Referenced. Courtauld, Sarah. 2009. (First Reading Level 3 Ser.). 48p. (J). (gr. 2). 6.99 *(978-0-7945-2502-6(4),* Usborne) EDC Publishing.
Husted, Marty. We Share One World. Hoffelt, Jane. 2004. 32p. (J). per. 15.95 *(978-0-9701907-8-9(6))* Illumination Arts Publishing Co., Inc.
Hustins, Shelley. No Room: A Read-Aloud Story of Christmas. Riddle, Peter H. 2009. 40p. (J). pap. *(978-1-926585-43-7(7),* CCB Publishing) CCB Publishing.
Huston, Kyle, jt. illus. see Leon, Loni.
Huszar, Susan, photos by. Grandma & Grandpa. Bailey, Debbie. 2010. (Annikins Ser.). (ENG., 32p. (J). (gr. -1-k). pap. 1.99 *(978-1-55451-270-6(0),* 9781554512706) Annick Pr., Ltd. CAN. Dist: Firefly Bks., Ltd.
—Mi Animalito. Bailey, Debbie. 2003. (Hablemos Ser.).Tr. of My Pet. (SPA., 14p. (J). (gr. -1 — 1). bds. 5.95 *(978-1-55037-826-9(0),* 9781550378269) Annick Pr., Ltd. CAN. Dist: Firefly Bks., Ltd.
—Mis Amigos. Bailey, Debbie. 2003. (Hablemos Ser.).Tr. of My Friends. (SPA., 14p. (J). (gr. -1 — 1). bds. 5.95 *(978-1-55037-827-6(9),* 9781550378276) Annick Pr., Ltd. CAN. Dist: Firefly Bks., Ltd.
—My Friends. Bailey, Debbie. 2003. (Talk-About-Bks.: 17). (ENG., 14p. (J). (gr. -1 — 1). bds. 6.95 *(978-1-55037-817-7(1),* 9781550378177) Annick Pr., Ltd. CAN. Dist: Firefly Bks., Ltd.
—My Mom & My Dad. Bailey, Debbie. 2010. (Annikins Ser.). (ENG., 32p. (J). (gr. -1-k). pap. 1.99 *(978-1-55451-268-3(9),* 9781554512683) Annick Pr., Ltd. CAN. Dist: Firefly Bks., Ltd.
—My Pet. Bailey, Debbie. 2003. (Talk-About-Bks.: 18). (ENG., 14p. (J). (gr. -1 — 1). bds. 6.95 *(978-1-55037-816-0(3),* 9781550378160) Annick Pr., Ltd. CAN. Dist: Firefly Bks., Ltd.
—Sisters & Brothers. Bailey, Debbie. 2010. (Annikins Ser.). (ENG., 32p. (J). (gr. -1-k). pap. 1.99 *(978-1-55451-269-0(7),* 9781554512690) Annick Pr., Ltd. CAN. Dist: Firefly Bks., Ltd.
Hutchcraft, Steve, photos by. B Is for Bufflehead: Flying Through the ABC's with Fun Feathered Friends. Hutchcraft, Steve. 2009. 80p. (J). (gr. -1-4). 19.95 *(978-0-9824925-0-5(2))* PhotoHutch.
Hutcherson, Darren. Papa Golley's Journey Home. Norton, George. Date not set. 14.95 *(978-1-889506-06-7(0))* Kendar Publishing, Inc.
—Ten Buttermilk Pancakes. Norton, George. Date not set. (J). 9.95 *(978-1-889506-10-4(9))* Kendar Publishing, Inc.
Hutchings, Tony. Okomi & the Tickling Game, Vol. 2. Dorman, Helen & Dorman, Clive. 2004. (Sharing Nature with Children Book Ser.: 2). 24p. (J). pap. 4.95 *(978-1-58469-046-7(1))* Dawn Pubns.
—Okomi Climbs a Tree, Vol. 4. Dorman, Helen & Dorman, Clive. 2004. (Sharing Nature with Children Book Ser.: 4). 24p. (J). pap. 4.95 *(978-1-58469-045-0(3))* Dawn Pubns.
—Okomi Enjoys His Outings, Vol. 5. Dorman, Clive & Dorman, Helen. 2004. (Okomi Stories Ser.). 24p. (J). pap. 4.95 *(978-1-58469-055-9(0))* Dawn Pubns.
—Okomi Goes Fishing, Vol. 7. Dorman, Clive & Dorman, Helen. 2004. (Okomi Stories Ser.). 24p. (J). pap. 4.95 *(978-1-58469-057-3(7))* Dawn Pubns.
—Okomi Plays in the Leaves, Vol. 3. Dorman, Helen & Dorman, Clive. 2004. (Sharing Nature with Children Book Ser.: 3). 24p. (J). pap. 4.95 *(978-1-58469-047-4(X))* Dawn Pubns.
—Okomi, the New Baby. Dorman, Helen & Dorman, Clive. 2004. (Sharing Nature with Children Book Ser.: 1). 24p. (J). pap. 4.95 *(978-1-58469-044-3(5))* Dawn Pubns.
—Okomi Wakes up Early, Vol. 6. Dorman, Clive & Dorman, Helen. 2004. (Okomi Stories Ser.). 24p. (J). pap. 4.95 *(978-1-58469-056-6(9))* Dawn Pubns.
—Okomi Wanders Too Far, Vol. 8. Dorman, Clive & Dorman, Helen. 2004. (Okomi Stories Ser.). 24p. (J). pap. 4.95 *(978-1-58469-058-0(5))* Dawn Pubns.
—A Week at the Seaside. 2014. (J). *(978-1-4351-5464-3(9))* Barnes & Noble, Inc.
Hutchins, Annie H. Barnyard Buddies II. Brown, Pamela. 2004. 90p. (J). pap. 16.00 *(978-1-928589-21-1(9))* Gival Pr., LLC.
Hutchins, Laurence. I'm the King of the Castle! And Other Plays for Children. Hutchins, Laurence. 2005. (ENG.). 107p. per. 16.95 *(978-1-84002-486-9(0))* Theatre Communications Group, Inc.
Hutchins, Pat. Barn Dance! Hutchins, Pat. 2007. 32p. (J). (gr. -1-k). lib. bdg. 17.89 *(978-0-06-089122-0(X),* Greenwillow Bks.) HarperCollins Pubs.
Hutchinson, David. Macbeth. Dunn, Joeming. 2008. (Graphic Shakespeare Ser.). 48p. (gr. 5-10). 29.93 *(978-1-60270-190-8(3),* Graphic Planet- Fiction) ABDO Publishing Co.
Hutchinson, Joy. Gifts for a King. Aston, Al. 2005. 16p. pap. 2.00 *(978-1-84427-179-5(X))* Scripture Union GBR. Dist: Send The Light Distribution LLC.
—A Message for Mary. Aston, Al. 2005. 16p. 2.00 *(978-1-84427-176-4(5))* Scripture Union GBR. Dist: Send The Light Distribution LLC.
—The Shepherds' Surprise. Aston, Al. 2005. 16p. pap., pap. 2.00 *(978-1-84427-178-8(1))* Scripture Union GBR. Dist: Send The Light Distribution LLC.
Hutchinson, Michelle. Malcolm Dooswaddles Good Day. Ten Hagen, Evelyn. 2013. 82p. pap. 12.95 *(978-1-59930-415-1(5))* TAG Publishing, LLC.
Hutchinson, Tim. Alien Adventure: Peek Inside the Pop-Up Windows! Taylor, Dereen. 2015. (ENG.). 12p. 16.99 *(978-1-86147-487-2(3),* Armadillo) Anness Publishing GBR. Dist: National Bk. Network.
—A Cool Kid's Field Guide to Weather. Regan, Lisa. 2009. (Cool Kid's Field Guide Ser.). 26p. (J). (gr. 1-3). spiral bd. 6.99 *(978-0-8416-7147-8(8))* Hammond World Atlas Corp.
—The Dragon's Magic Wish. Taylor, Dereen. 2012. (ENG.). 12p. (J). (gr. 1-6). 16.99 *(978-1-84322-856-1(4))* Anness Publishing GBR. Dist: National Bk. Network.
—Find Out about China: Learn Chinese Words & Phrases & about Life in China. Qing, Zheng. 2006. (Find Out about Bks.). (ENG.). 64p. (J). (gr. 3-18). 14.99 *(978-0-7641-5952-7(6))* Barron's Educational Series, Inc.
—Find Out about France: Learn French Words & Phrases & about Life in France. Crosbie, Duncan. 2006. (Find Out about Bks.). (ENG.). 64p. (J). (gr. 3-18). 13.99 *(978-0-7641-5953-4(4))* Barron's Educational Series, Inc.
—Life in a Castle. Tango Books Staff. 2011. (3 Dimensional Carousel Book Ser.). (ENG.). 1p. (J). (gr. -1-2). 24.99 *(978-1-85707-708-7(3))* Tango Bks. GBR. Dist: Independent Pubs. Group.
—Life in a Watermill. Cheshire, Gerard & Tango Books Staff. 2011. (3 Dimensional Carousel Book Ser.). (ENG.). 1p. (J). (gr. -1-2). 34.99 *(978-1-85707-737-7(7))* Tango Bks. GBR. Dist: Independent Pubs. Group.
—The Lost Treasure of the Jungle Temple: Peek Inside the 3D Windows! Taylor, Dereen. 2013. (ENG.). 12p. (J). (gr. 1-8). 16.99 *(978-1-84322-822-6(X),* Armadillo) Anness Publishing GBR. Dist: National Bk. Network.
—Paulo & the Football Thieves: Peek Inside the Pop-Up Windows! Taylor, Dereen. 2014. (ENG.). 12p. 16.99 *(978-1-86147-409-4(1),* Armadillo) Anness Publishing GBR. Dist: National Bk. Network.
—Robo-Pup to the Rescue! Taylor, Dereen. 2013. (ENG.). 12p. (J). (gr. 1-8). 16.99 *(978-1-84322-821-9(1),* Armadillo) Anness Publishing GBR. Dist: National Bk. Network.
Hutchinson, William. The Tinker's Armor: The Story of John Bunyan. Barr, Gladys H. 2011. 176p. 42.95 *(978-1-258-05498-4(1))* Literary Licensing, LLC.

Hutchison, D. C. The Eyes of the Woods: A Story of the Ancient Wilderness. Altsheler, Joseph A. 2008. (Young Trailers Ser.: Vol. 4). 256p. (J). reprint ed. pap. *(978-1-4065-4512-8(0))* Dodo Pr.

Hutto, Victoria. Hello, Bunny! Hirschmann, Kris. 2010. (Paint Me Pals Ser.). (ENG.). 24p. (J). 9.99 *(978-1-4169-7903-6(4),* Simon Scribbles) Simon Scribbles.

—The Twelve Days of Christmas in Oklahoma. Sauer, Tammi. 2012. (Twelve Days of Christmas in America Ser.). (ENG.). 32p. (J). (gr. k-3). 12.95 *(978-1-4027-9224-3(7))* Sterling Publishing Co., Inc.

Hutton, Jason. Dream, Dream, Little Sweet Pea. Pettitt, Emily. 2012. (ENG.). 20p. (J). (gr. -1-3). pap. 9.99 *(978-1-62024-736-5(4))* Tate Publishing & Enterprises, LLC.

Huxley, Dee. Look See, Look at Me! Norrington, Leonie. 2010. (ENG.). 32p. (J). (gr. -1-k). 19.99 *(978-1-74175-883-2(1))* Allen & Unwin AUS. Dist: Independent Pubs. Group.

Huxtable, John. Bubble Party! (Bubble Guppies) Golden Books. 2013. (Color Plus Stencil Ser.). (ENG.). 64p. (J). (gr. -1-2). pap. 5.99 *(978-0-307-98205-6(X),* Golden Bks.) Random Hse. Children's Bks.

—Giddy-Up, Guppies! (Bubble Guppies) Nagaraj, Josephine. 2014. (Step into Reading Ser.). (ENG.). 32p. (J). (gr. -1-1). 3.99 *(978-0-385-36974-9(3),* Random Hse. Bks. for Young Readers) Random Hse. Children's Bks.

—Ho-Ho Holidays! (Bubble Guppies) Golden Books. 2013. (Paint Box Book Ser.). (ENG.). 48p. (J). (gr. -1-2). pap. 3.99 *(978-0-449-81767-4(9),* Golden Bks.) Random Hse. Children's Bks.

Huxtable, John, jt. illus. see Huxtable, Tonja.

Huxtable, Tonja & Huxtable, John. Rapunzel. Bryant, Megan E. 2007. (Berry Fairy Tales Ser.). (J). *(978-1-4287-4159-1(3),* Grosset & Dunlap) Penguin Publishing Group.

Huyck, David. Nine Words Max. Bar-el, Dan. 2014. (ENG.). 32p. (J). (gr. k-4). 17.99 *(978-1-77049-562-3(2))* Tundra Bks. CAN. Dist: Random Hse., Inc.

—That One Spooky Night. Bar-el, Dan. 2012. (ENG.). 80p. (J). 8.95 *(978-1-55453-752-5(5));* 16.95 *(978-1-55453-751-8(7))* Kids Can Pr., Ltd. CAN. Dist: Univ. of Toronto Pr.

Hwang, Jung Sun. Fights, Flights, & the Chosen Ones, 1 vol. Lee, Young Shin & Rogers, Buddy. Burner, Brett & Earls, J. S., eds. 2008. (Z Graphic Novels / Manga Bible Ser.). (ENG.). 160p. (J). (gr. 4-7). pap. 6.99 *(978-0-310-71289-3(0))* Zondervan.

—Trips, Ships, & the Ultimate Vision Pt. 2: Acts, 1 vol. Rogers, Bud & Lee, Young Shin. Burner, Brett & Earls, J. S., eds. 2012. (Z Graphic Novels / Manga Bible Ser.: Vol. 8). (ENG.). 176p. (J). pap. 6.99 *(978-0-310-71294-7(7))* Zondervan.

Hwang, YoSeob. The Wise Boy. Kim, JiYu. 2015. (MySELF Bookshelf Ser.). (ENG.). 32p. (J). (gr. k-2). pap. 11.94 *(978-1-60357-690-1(8));* lib. bdg. 22.60 *(978-1-59953-655-2(2))* Norwood Hse. Pr.

Hyatt, Joe. Buddy Unchained. Bix, Daisy. 2006. (Sit! Stay! Read! Ser.). (ENG.). 24p. (J). (gr. k-2). 15.95 *(978-0-940719-01-9(0))* Gryphon Pr., The.

Hyatt, Sean. Naja Plays Hide-Go-Seek, 1 vol. White. 2010. 28p. pap. 24.95 *(978-1-4489-8842-6(X))* America Star Bks.

Hyatt, Sean & McGrath, Michael. Naja Learns to Ride. White. 2011. 32p. pap. 24.95 *(978-1-4489-8369-8(X))* America Star Bks.

Hyde, Catherine. Firebird. Pirotta, Saviour. 2010. (ENG.). 40p. (J). (gr. k-3). 18.99 *(978-0-7636-5076-6(5),* Templar) Candlewick Pr.

—Little Evie in the Wild Wood. Morris, Jackie. 2013. (ENG.). 40p. (J). (gr. -1-2). 18.99 *(978-1-84780-371-9(7),* Frances Lincoln) Quarto Publishing Group UK GBR. Dist: Hachette Bk. Group.

Hyde, Catherine Ryan. The Princess's Blankets. Duffy, Carol Ann. 2009. (ENG.). 40p. (J). (gr. k-3). 18.99 *(978-0-7636-4547-2(8))* Candlewick Pr.

Hyde, Maureen. Francis Woke up Early. Nobisso, Josephine. 2011. (ENG.). 32p. (J). (gr. k-2). 17.95 *(978-0-940112-20-9(5));* pap. 9.95 *(978-0-940112-22-3(1))* Gingerbread Hse.

Hyde, Michelle Hazelwood. Night Night, Birmingham. 2011. (J). *(978-1-59421-074-7(8))* Seacoast Publishing, Inc.

Hyland, Greg. Save the Galaxy! Landers, Ace & Doodle Pictures Studio Staff. 2011. (Lego Star Wars Ser.). (ENG.). 7p. (J). (gr. -1-3). bds. 9.99 *(978-0-545-30101-5(7))* Scholastic, Inc.

Hyman, Miles & Allbert, Eric. Half & Half-Giants of the Ocean: Great Story & Cool Facts. Craipeau, Jean-Lou & Dutrieux, Julien. 2009. 56p. (J). 9.95 *(978-1-60115-211-4(6))* Treasure Bay, Inc.

—Half & Half-Giants of the Ocean: Great Story & Cool Facts. Craipeau, Jean-Lou & Dutrieux, Brigitte. 2009. 56p. (J). pap. 4.99 *(978-1-60115-212-1(4))* Treasure Bay, Inc.

Hyman, Trina Schart. Changing Woman & Her Sisters: Stories of Goddesses from Around the World. Tchana, Katrin Hyman. 2006. (ENG.). 80p. (gr. 4-18). 18.95 *(978-0-8234-1999-9(1))* Holiday Hse., Inc.

—Children of the Dragon: Selected Tales from Vietnam, 1 vol. Garland, Sherry. 2012. (ENG.). 32p. (J). (gr. 3-7). 16.99 *(978-1-4556-1709-8(1))* Pelican Publishing Co., Inc.

—A Child's Calendar, 4 bks. Updike, John. 2004. (J). (gr. k-4). pap. 37.95 incl. audio *(978-1-59112-473-3(5));* 25.95 incl. audio *(978-1-59112-472-6(7))* Live Oak Media.

—Hershel & the Hanukkah Goblins. 25th anniv. ed. 2014. (ENG.). 32p. (J). (gr. -1-3). 7.99 *(978-0-8234-3194-6(0))* Holiday Hse., Inc.

—Hershel & the Hanukkah Goblins. Kimmel, Eric A. 25th anniv. ed. 2014. (ENG.). 32p. (J). (gr. -1-3). 17.95 *(978-0-8234-3164-9(9))* Holiday Hse., Inc.

—Let's Steal the Moon: Jewish Tales, Ancient & Recent. Serwer-Berstein, Blanche. 2005. 96p. 14.95 *(978-1-56171-896-2(3))* SPI Bks.

—Star Mother's Youngest Child. Moeri, Louise. 30th ed. 2005. (ENG.). 48p. (J). (gr. -1-3). 8.95 *(978-0-618-61509-4(1))* Houghton Mifflin Harcourt Publishing Co.

—Will You Sign Here, John Hancock? Fritz, Jean. 2005. (J). (gr. 2-7). 29.95 *(978-0-439-76750-7(4),* WHCD480) Weston Woods Studios, Inc.

Hyman, Trina Schart. Merlin & the Making of the King. Hyman, Trina Schart, tr. Hodges, Margaret & Malory, Thomas. 2004. (ENG.). 40p. (J). (gr. 4-6). tchr. ed. 16.95 *(978-0-8234-1647-9(X))* Holiday Hse., Inc.

Hyman, Trina Schart, jt. illus. see Updike, John.

Hymas, Anna. The Boy Who Harnessed the Wind. Mealer, Bryan & Kamkwamba, William. 2015. (ENG.). 304p. (J). (gr. 5). 16.99 *(978-0-8037-4080-8(8),* Dial) Penguin Publishing Group.

Hymper, W. & Stacey, W. S. Cassy. Stretton, Hesba. 2006. (Golden Inheritance Ser.: Vol. 9). 117p. (J). pap. *(978-0-921100-94-2(9))* Inheritance Pubns.

Hynes, Robert. Animal Families, Animal Friends. Woelfle, Gretchen. 2005. (ENG.). 32p. (J). (gr. k-3). 15.95 *(978-1-55971-901-8(X))* Cooper Square Publishing Llc.

—Baxter Needs a Home. O'Donnell, Liam. 2005. (Pet Tales Ser.). (ENG.). 32p. (J). (gr. -1-2). 2.95 *(978-1-59249-298-5(3),* 1B015); 9.95 *(978-1-59249-320-3(3),* 1B016) Soundprints.

—Baxter Needs a Home. O'Donnell, Liam. 2004. (ENG.). 32p. (J). (gr. -1-2). 4.95 *(978-1-59249-297-8(5),* 1B013) Soundprints.

—Duncan: A Brave Rescue. O'Donnell, Liam & O'Donnell, Laura. 2004. (Pet Tales Ser.). (ENG.). 32p. (J). (gr. -1-3). 4.95 *(978-1-59249-291-6(6),* 1B001) Soundprints.

—Duncan: A Brave Rescue. O'Donnell, Liam & O'Donnell, Laura. 2005. (Pet Tales Ser.). (ENG.). 32p. (J). (gr. -1-2). 2.95 *(978-1-59249-292-3(4),* 1B003) Soundprints.

—Duncan: A Brave Rescue. O'Donnell, Liam. 2004. (ENG.). 32p. (J). (gr. -1-2). 9.95 *(978-1-59249-317-3(3),* 1B004) Soundprints.

—Gray Wolf Pup's Adventure. Smith, Stephanie & Smith, Stephanie A. 2nd ed. 2003. (ENG.). 32p. (J). (gr. 1-3). 12.95 *(978-1-931465-43-4(6),* PS2077) Soundprints.

—Hedgehog Haven: The Story of an English Hedgerow Community. Dennard, Deborah. 2005. (ENG.). (J). (gr. 1-4). 32p. 19.95 *(978-1-56899-989-0(5),* BC7020); 36p. 15.95 *(978-1-56899-987-6(9),* B7020); 36p. pap. 6.95 *(978-1-56899-988-3(7),* S7020) Soundprints.

—Hurry up, Hedgehog! Dennard, Deborah. 2003. (Soundprints' Read-and-Discover Ser.). (ENG.). 32p. (gr. -1-1). 12.95 *(978-1-59249-150-6(2),* PS2012) Soundprints.

—Hurry up, Hedgehog! Dennard, Deborah. 2003. (Amazing Animal Adventures Ser.). (ENG.). 32p. (J). (gr. -1-3). per. 3.95 *(978-1-59249-149-0(9),* S2012) Soundprints.

—Lucy & the Busy Boat. O'Donnell, Liam. (Pet Tales Ser.). (ENG.). 32p. (J). (gr. -1-2). 2005. 2.95 *(978-1-59249-296-1(7),* 1B021); 2004. 4.95 *(978-1-59249-295-4(9),* 1B019); 2004. 9.95 *(978-1-59249-319-7(X),* 1B022) Soundprints.

—Muskrat Will Be Swimming, 1 vol. Savageau, Cheryl. 2010. (ENG.). 32p. (J). (gr. 3-7). 7.95 *(978-0-88448-280-2(4))* Tilbury Hse. Pubs.

—Snowshoe Hare's Family. Smith, Stephanie. 2nd ed. 2007. (Soundprints' Read-and-Discover Ser.). (ENG.). (J). (gr. 1-3). 32p. 12.95 *(978-1-931465-44-1(4),* PS2053); 48p. pap. 3.95 *(978-1-931465-15-1(0),* S2003) Soundprints.

—Tracker on the Job. O'Donnell, Liam. (Pet Tales Ser.). (ENG.). 32p. (J). (gr. -1-2). 2005. 2.95 *(978-1-59249-294-7(0),* 1B009); 2004. 9.95 *(978-1-59249-318-0(1),* 1B010) Soundprints.

—Tracker on the Job. O'Donnell, Liam. 2004. (Pet Tales Ser.). (ENG.). 32p. (J). (gr. -1-2). 4.95 *(978-1-59249-293-0(2),* 1B007) Soundprints.

Hyun, Jinsun. Doodle Bug: Digging to Reach the Top. Cordell, Greg. 2004. (J). *(978-0-9759699-0-8(0))* Greenville Family Partnership.

Hyun, You. Faeries' Landing. Hyun, You. rev. ed. 2006. (Faeries' Landing Ser.: Vol. 12). 192p. per. 9.99 *(978-1-59532-400-9(3));* Vol. 13. pap. 9.99 *(978-1-59532-401-6(1))* TOKYOPOP, Inc.

Hyun, You. Faeries' Landing, Vol. 8. Hyun, You, creator. rev. ed. 2005. 192p. pap. 9.99 *(978-1-59532-396-5(1))* TOKYOPOP, Inc.

Hyung Kim, Tae. Planet Blood, Vol. 2. Hyung Kim, Tae, creator. rev. ed. 2005. 200p. pap. 9.99 *(978-1-59532-538-9(7))* TOKYOPOP, Inc.

Hyung, Min-Woo. Justice N Mercy, Vol. 1. 2005. 120p. pap. 39.99 *(978-1-59532-980-6(3))* TOKYOPOP, Inc.

Hyung, Min-Woo. Priest, 9 vols., Vol 4. Hyung, Min-Woo. Kim, Jessica, tr. from JPN. rev. ed. 2003. 208p. (gr. 11-18). pap. 9.99 *(978-1-59182-088-8(X))* TOKYOPOP, Inc.

—Priest, 9 vols. Hyung, Min-Woo. Vol. 8. rev. ed. 2003. 192p. (YA). pap. 9.99 *(978-1-59182-204-2(1));* Vol. 9. 9th rev. ed. 2003. 176p. pap. 9.99 *(978-1-59182-205-9(X));* Vol. 10. rev. ed. 2004. 192p. pap. 9.99 *(978-1-59182-511-1(3))* TOKYOPOP, Inc.

I

Iacopo, Bruno & Bruno, Iacopo. The Soprano's Last Song, 1 vol. Adler, Irene. 2014. (Sherlock, Lupin, & Me Ser.). (ENG.). 240p. (gr. 4-8). lib. bdg. 25.32 *(978-1-4342-6522-7(6))* Stone Arch Bks.

Iacovello, Dick, photos by. Grasshopper on the Moon. Iacovello, Dick. Iacovello, Dick. 2011. (ENG., 44p. pap. 9.99 *(978-0-615-45131-2(4))* Iacovello, Dick.

Ian, Crowe. The Birth of Tragedy. Nietzsche, Friedrich. Ian, Johnston, tr. 2009. 145p. (YA). pap. 13.95 *(978-0-9797571-3-6(4))* Richer Resources Pubns.

Ian, Shickle. The Other Side of the Window. Cameron, Kristy. 2013. 28p. pap. *(978-0-9859790-2-7(X))* LP Publishing.

Iantorno, Danlyn. Books for Children of the World: The Story of Jella Lepman, 1 vol. Pearl, Sydelle. 2007. (ENG.). 32p. (J). (gr. k-3). 16.99 *(978-1-58980-438-8(4))* Pelican Publishing Co., Inc.

Ibarra, Rosa. Soledad Sigh-Sighs. Gonzalez, Rigoberto & González, Rigoberto. 2013.Tr. of Soledad Suspiros. (ENG.). 32p. (J). pap. 8.95 *(978-0-89239-309-1(2),* Children's Book Press) Lee & Low Bks., Inc.

Ibatoulline, Bagram. The Animal Hedge. Fleischman, Paul. 2008. (ENG.). 48p. (J). (gr. 1-4). pap. 7.99 *(978-0-7636-3842-9(0))* Candlewick Pr.

—Bella at Midnight. Stanley, Diane. (J). 2007. (ENG.). 304p. (gr. 3-7). pap. 7.99 *(978-0-06-077575-9(0));* 2006. 288p. (gr. 5-9). lib. bdg. 17.89 *(978-0-06-077574-2(2))* HarperCollins Pubs.

—Boom Boom Go Away! Bass, L. G. & Geringer, Laura. 2010. (ENG.). 40p. (J). (gr. -1-1). 15.99 *(978-0-689-85093-6(X),* Atheneum Bks. for Young Readers) Simon & Schuster Children's Publishing.

—Crossing. Booth, Philip. 2013. (ENG.). 40p. (J). (gr. k-4). pap. 6.99 *(978-0-7636-6664-4(5))* Candlewick Pr.

—Crow Call. Lowry, Lois. 2009. (ENG.). 32p. (J). (gr. 3-7). 18.99 *(978-0-545-03035-9(8),* Scholastic Pr.) Scholastic, Inc.

—The Giver. Lowry, Lois. gif. ed. 2011. (Giver Quartet Ser.: 1). (ENG.). 208p. (J). (gr. 7). 19.99 *(978-0-547-42477-4(9))* Houghton Mifflin Harcourt Publishing Co.

—The Granddaughter Necklace. Wyeth, Sharon Dennis. (J). 2013. (ENG.). 32p. (gr. -1-3). 16.99 *(978-0-545-08125-2(4));* 2012. pap. *(978-0-545-23983-7(4))* Scholastic, Inc. (Levine, Arthur A. Bks.).

—Graven Images. Fleischman, Paul. (ENG.). 128p. (YA). 2005. (gr. 5-9). per. 6.99 *(978-0-7636-2984-7(7));* 2006. (gr. 7-9). reprint ed. 16.99 *(978-0-7636-2775-1(5))* Candlewick Pr.

—Great Joy. DiCamillo, Kate. (ENG.). 32p. (J). (gr. -1-3). 2010. 8.99 *(978-0-7636-4996-8(1));* 2007. 16.99 *(978-0-7636-2920-5(0))* Candlewick Pr.

—A Little Women Christmas. Frederick, Heather Vogel. 2014. (ENG.). 32p. (J). (gr. -1-3). 17.99 *(978-1-4424-1359-7(X),* Simon & Schuster Bks. For Young Readers) Simon & Schuster Bks. For Young Readers.

—The Matchbox Diary. Fleischman, Paul. 2013. (ENG.). 40p. (J). (gr. 1-4). 16.99 *(978-0-7636-4601-1(6))* Candlewick Pr.

—The Miraculous Journey of Edward Tulane. DiCamillo, Kate. (ENG.). (J). 2009. 228p. (gr. 2-5). pap. 11.99 *(978-0-7636-4783-4(7));* 2009. 224p. (gr. 2-5). 6.99 *(978-0-7636-4367-6(X));* 2006. 228p. (gr. 1-4). 19.99 *(978-0-7636-2589-4(2))* Candlewick Pr.

—The Miraculous Journey of Edward Tulane. DiCamillo, Kate. ed. 2007. 198p. (gr. 8-12). 23.30 *(978-1-4178-0763-5(6),* Turtleback) Turtleback Bks.

—Mr. Lincoln's Boys. Rabin, Staton. 2008. (ENG.). 36p. (J). (gr. k-3). 16.99 *(978-0-670-06169-3(7),* Viking Juvenile) Penguin Publishing Group.

—On the Blue Comet. Wells, Rosemary. (ENG.). 336p. (J). (gr. 5). 2012. pap. 8.99 *(978-0-7636-5815-1(4));* 2010. 16.99 *(978-0-7636-3722-4(X))* Candlewick Pr.

—The Scarecrow's Dance. Yolen, Jane. 2009. (ENG.). 32p. (J). (gr. -1-3). 16.99 *(978-1-4169-3770-8(6),* Simon & Schuster Bks. For Young Readers) Simon & Schuster Bks. For Young Readers.

—The Snow Queen. Andersen, Hans Christian. 2013. (ENG.). 40p. (J). (gr. -1-3). 17.99 *(978-0-06-220950-4(7))* HarperCollins Pubs.

—Stand There! She Shouted: The Invincible Photographer Julia Margaret Cameron. Rubin, Susan Goldman. 2014. (ENG.). 80p. (J). (gr. 3-7). 16.99 *(978-0-7636-5753-6(0))* Candlewick Pr.

—The Third Gift. Park, Linda Sue. 2011. (ENG.). 32p. (J). (gr. 1-4). 16.99 *(978-0-547-20195-5(8))* Houghton Mifflin Harcourt Publishing Co.

—Thumbelina. Andersen, Hans Christian. 2009. (ENG.). 40p. (J). (gr. -1-3). 17.99 *(978-0-7636-2079-0(3))* Candlewick Pr.

Ibelings, Anne. From Mud Huts to Skyscrapers. Paxmann, Christine. 2012. (ENG.). 64p. 19.95 *(978-3-7913-7113-9(4))* Prestel Publishing.

Ibsen, Henrik. The Wild Duck. Landes, William-Alan, ed. 2003. 85p. (YA). (gr. 8-12). pap. 8.00 *(978-0-88734-747-4(9))* Players Pr., Inc.

Ice, D. C. Acrylics, 1 vol. Bolte, Mari. 2013. (Paint It Ser.). (ENG.). 32p. (gr. 3-4). 27.32 *(978-1-4765-3109-0(9),* Snap Bks.) Capstone Pr., Inc.

—The Legend of the Loch Ness Monster, 1 vol. Troupe, Thomas Kingsley. 2011. (Legend Has It Ser.). (ENG.). 32p. (gr. 2-4). lib. bdg. 26.65 *(978-1-4048-6659-1(0),* Nonfiction Picture Bks.) Picture Window Bks.

—The Legend of the Werewolf, 1 vol. Troupe, Thomas Kingsley. 2010. (Legend Has It Ser.). (ENG.). 32p. (gr. 2-4). lib. bdg. 26.65 *(978-1-4048-6033-9(9),* Nonfiction Picture Bks.) Picture Window Bks.

—Paint It: The Art of Acrylics, Oils, Pastels, & Watercolors, 1 vol. Bolte, Mari. 2013. (Craft It Yourself Ser.). (ENG.). 144p. (gr. 3-4). pap. 14.95 *(978-1-62370-009-6(4))* Capstone Young Readers.

—Watercolors, 1 vol. Bolte, Mari. 2013. (Paint It Ser.). (ENG.). 32p. (gr. 3-4). 27.32 *(978-1-4765-3108-3(0),* Snap Bks.) Capstone Pr., Inc.

Ichikawa, Santomi. Grandpa's Soup. Kadono, Eiko. 2009. 40p. (J). (gr. -1-3). pap. 8.50 *(978-0-8028-5347-9(1),* Eerdmans Bks For Young Readers) Eerdmans, William B. Publishing Co.

Ichikawa, Satomi. Tanya entre Bastidores. Gauch, Patricia Lee & GAUCH, PATRICIA LEE. 2004.Tr. of Tanya & the Magic Wardrobe. (SPA.). (J). 16.99 *(978-84-8488-083-7(4))* Serres, Ediciones, S. L. ESP. Dist: Lectorum Pubns., Inc.

—Tú Eres Mi Te Quiero. Love, Maryann Cusimano. 2012.Tr. of You Are My I Love You. (SPA & ENG.). 28p. (J). (gr. -1 — 1). bds. 6.99 *(978-0-399-24396-7(8),* Philomel) Penguin Publishing Group.

—You Are My I Love You. Love, Maryann Cusimano. (Little Letters Ser.). (ENG.). (J). (gr. -1-k). 2012. 32p. 4.99 *(978-0-448-46307-0(5),* Grosset & Dunlap); 2010. 30p. bds. 6.99 *(978-0-399-24395-0(X),* Philomel) Penguin Publishing Group.

—You Are My Miracle. Love, Maryann Cusimano. (ENG.). (J). (gr. -1 — 1). 2012. 28p. bds. 6.99 *(978-0-399-25791-9(8));* 2005. 32p. 16.99 *(978-0-399-24037-9(3))* Penguin Publishing Group. (Philomel).

Ichikawa, Satomi. Come Fly with Me. Ichikawa, Satomi. 2008. (ENG.). 40p. (J). (gr. -1-3). 15.99 *(978-0-399-24679-1(7),* Philomel) Penguin Publishing Group.

—My Little Train. Ichikawa, Satomi. 2010. (ENG.). 36p. (J). (gr. -1-k). 15.99 *(978-0-399-25453-6(6),* Philomel) Penguin Publishing Group.

Ichikawa, Satomi & Lewin, Ted. You Are My Wonders. Love, Maryann Cusimano. 2012. (ENG.). 32p. (J). (gr. -1-2). 16.99 *(978-0-399-25293-8(2),* Philomel) Penguin Publishing Group.

Idle, Molly. Flora & the Flamingo. 2013. (ENG.). 44p. (J). (gr. -1-1). 16.99 *(978-1-4521-1006-6(9))* Chronicle Bks. LLC.

—He's Got the Whole World in His Hands, 1 vol. Zondervan Publishing Staff. 2008. (I Can Read! / Song Ser.). (ENG.). 32p. (J). (gr. -1-3). pap. 3.99 *(978-0-310-71622-8(5))* Zondervan.

—My Shadow. Stevenson, Robert Louis. 2011. (Poetry for Children Ser.). (ENG.). 24p. (J). (gr. k-3). 27.07 *(978-1-60973-154-0(9),* 201181) Child's World, Inc., The.

—Santa's Workshop: A Mini Animotion Book. Accord Publishing Staff. 2011. (ENG.). 12p. (J). 9.99 *(978-1-4494-0834-3(6))* Andrews McMeel Publishing.

—Zombelina. Crow, Kristyn. 2013. (ENG.). 32p. (J). (gr. -1-3). 16.99 *(978-0-8027-2803-6(0),* Bloomsbury USA Childrens) Bloomsbury USA.

—Zombelina. Crow, Kristyn. 2013. (ENG.). 32p. (J). (gr. -1-3). 17.89 *(978-0-8027-2804-3(9))* Walker & Co.

Idle, Molly. Zombelina Dances the Nutcracker. Crow, Kristyn. 2015. (ENG.). 40p. (J). (gr. -1-3). 16.99 ***(978-1-61963-640-8(9)***, Bloomsbury USA Childrens) Bloomsbury USA.

Idle, Molly. Camp Rex. Idle, Molly. 2014. (ENG.). 40p. (J). (gr. -1-k). 16.99 *(978-0-670-78573-5(3),* Viking Juvenile) Penguin Publishing Group.

—Sea Rex. Idle, Molly. 2015. (ENG.). 40p. (J). (-k). 16.99 *(978-0-670-78574-2(1),* Viking Juvenile) Penguin Publishing Group.

Idumi, Rei. Hack//Ai Buster, 2 vols. Hamazaki, Tatsuya & Tatsuya, Hamazaki. 2006. (Hack//AI Buster Ser.: Vol. 2). 192p. pap. 7.99 *(978-1-59816-407-7(4))* TOKYOPOP, Inc.

Iglesias, Álvaro. Sgt. Reckless - The War Horse: Korean War Hero. Higgins, Melissa. 2014. (Animal Heroes Ser.). (ENG.). 32p. (gr. k-2). 27.99 *(978-1-4795-5462-1(6))* Picture Window Bks.

Ihara, Shigekatsu. Diamond & Pearl Adventure! Ihara, Shigekatsu. (Pokemon Ser.: 6). (ENG.). (J). 2010. 192p. pap. 7.99 *(978-1-4215-3170-0(4));* 2009. 200p. pap. 9.99 *(978-1-4215-2923-3(8));* Vol. 1. 2008. 208p. (gr. k). pap. 9.99 *(978-1-4215-2286-9(1));* Vol. 2. 2008. 192p. (gr. 1). pap. 9.99 *(978-1-4215-2287-6(X));* Vol. 3. 2009. 200p. pap. 7.99 *(978-1-4215-2574-7(7));* Vol. 7. 2010. 200p. pap. 9.99 *(978-1-4215-3491-6(6))* Viz Media.

—Pokeman - Diamond & Pearl Adventure! Ihara, Shigekatsu. 2009. (Pokemon Ser.: 4). (ENG.). 192p. (J). pap. 7.99 *(978-1-4215-2674-4(3))* Viz Media.

—Pokémon Diamond & Pearl Adventure! Ihara, Shigekatsu. 2010. (Pokemon Ser.: 8). (ENG.). 192p. (J). pap. 7.99 *(978-1-4215-3671-2(4))* Viz Media.

Iida, Haruko. Crescent Moon, Vol. 5. Iida, Haruko, creator. rev. ed. 2005. 176p. pap. 9.99 *(978-1-59182-952-2(6),* Tokyopop Adult) TOKYOPOP, Inc.

Iida, Toshitsugu. Wolf's Rain. Nobumoto, Keiko. (YA). 14.95 *(978-1-59116-791-4(4))* Viz Media.

Ikala Aten, Dayle Marc, jt. illus. see Castulo Aten, Vicky Talaro.

Ikeda, Akihisa. Rosario+Vampire - Season II. Ikeda, Akihisa. 2011. (ROSARIO & VAMPIRE Ser.: 4). (ENG.). 182p. pap. 9.99 *(978-1-4215-3544-9(0))* Viz Media.

—Rosario+Vampire - Season II Vol. 1, 2 vols. in 1. Ikeda, Akihisa. 2010. (ROSARIO & VAMPIRE Ser.: 1). (ENG.). 184p. pap. 9.99 *(978-1-4215-3136-6(4))* Viz Media.

Ikonen, Jani. The School of Possibilities. Parkkola, Seita. Silver, Annira & Gass, Marja, trs. from FIN. 2010. (ENG.). 368p. (J). (gr. 4-7). 12.99 *(978-1-4022-1835-4(4),* Sourcebooks Jabberwocky) Sourcebooks, Inc.

Ikumi, Mia. Tokyo Mew Mew a la Mode, 2 vols., Vol. 1. Kodansha. 2005. (Tokyo Mew-Mew a la Mode Ser.). 192p. (J). pap. 14.99 *(978-1-59532-789-5(4),* Tokyopop Kids) TOKYOPOP, Inc.

Ilka, Benjamin Alexander. A Boy & His Shadow. Ilka, Benjamin Alexander. (YA). Pt. 1. 2005. per. 4.95 net. *(978-0-9779504-0-9(9));* Pt. 2. 2006. 3.95 net. *(978-0-9779504-1-6(7))* Hogan Publishing LLC.

Ill, Noel. Teo in Palo Verde/Teo en Palo Verde. Del Rio, Adam. 2008. (ENG & SPA.). (J). (gr. k-3). 28p. 15.95 *(978-1-60448-000-9(9));* 32p. pap. 8.95 *(978-1-60448-001-6(7))* Lectura Bks.

Illingworth, Sasha, photos by. First Love. Patterson, James & Raymond, Emily. 2014. (ENG., 288p. (YA). 26.00 *(978-0-316-20704-1(7))* Little Brown & Co.

Illustrated by: Charles Duke. Nosey Rosey. Carr, Suzanna & Crutchfield, Tylicia. 2011. 44p. pap. 24.95 *(978-1-4560-7939-0(5))* America Star Bks.

Illustrations byVoigt, Karen S. Spike the Sewer Cat. Hansen, Kate. 2008. 27p. pap. 24.95 *(978-1-60474-094-3(9))* America Star Bks.

Ilya. King Lear. Shakespeare, William. 2009. (Manga Shakespeare Ser.). (ENG.). 208p. (YA). (gr. 7-11). pap. 12.95 *(978-0-8109-4222-6(4),* Amulet Bks.) Abrams.

Imai, Ayano. The 108th Sheep. Imai, Ayano. 2007. 32p. (gr. -1-2). 15.95 *(978-1-58925-063-5(X))* Tiger Tales.

I

Imai, Yasue. B. B. Explosion. Imai, Yasue. 2004. (B. B. Explosion Ser.). (ENG.). 192p. Vol. 2. pap. 9.95 *(978-1-59116-385-5(4))*; Vol. 3. pap. 9.95 *(978-1-59116-386-2(2))*; Vol. 4. (YA). pap. 9.95 *(978-1-59116-387-9(0))* Viz Media.

—B. B. Explosion, Vol. 5. Imai, Yasue. Anzai, Nobuyuki. 2005. (B. B. Explosion Ser.). (ENG.). 192p. (YA). pap. 9.95 *(978-1-59116-388-6(9))* Viz Media.

Imai, Yasue & Imai, Yasue. B. B. Explosion, Vol. 1. Imai, Yasue. 2004. (B. B. Explosion Ser.). (ENG.). 192p. pap. 9.95 *(978-1-59116-384-8(6))* Viz Media.

Imai, Yasue, jt. illus. see Imai, Yasue.

Immelman, Sarita. African Dream. Wyss, Tyan. 2006. 48p. (J). pap. 15.95 *(978-1-58939-915-0(3))* Virtualbookworm.com Publishing, Inc.

—Night Flyer. Wyss, Tyan. 2006. 40p. (J). per. 14.95 *(978-1-58939-916-7(1))* Virtualbookworm.com Publishing, Inc.

Immonen, Stuart. Magnetic North. 2006. (ENG.). 128p. (YA). (gr. 8-17). pap. 12.99 *(978-0-7851-1906-7(X))* Marvel Worldwide, Inc.

Immonen, Stuart, et al. Ultimatum Companion. 2011. (ENG.). 488p. (YA). (gr. 8-17). 49.99 *(978-0-7851-5507-2(4))* Marvel Worldwide, Inc.

Imodraj. Baa, Baa, Black Sheep. Everett, Melissa. 2013. (ENG.). 20p. (J). (gr. -1-3). 8.99 *(978-1-77093-537-2(1))* Flowerpot Children's Pr. Inc. CAN. Dist: Cardinal Pubs. Group.

Imodraj. The Brave Little Tailor. 2014. (ENG.). 16p. (J). (gr. -1-3). 7.99 ***(978-1-4867-0016-5(0))*** Flowerpot Children's Pr. Inc. CAN. Dist: Cardinal Pubs. Group.

Imodraj. Diddle Diddle Dumpling. Everett, Melissa. 2013. (ENG.). 20p. (J). (gr. -1-1). 8.99 *(978-1-77093-522-8(3))* Flowerpot Children's Pr. Inc. CAN. Dist: Cardinal Pubs. Group.

Imodraj. Jack & Jill. Everett, Melissa. 2014. (ENG.). 20p. (J). (gr. -1-1). 8.99 ***(978-1-77093-843-4(5))*** Flowerpot Children's Pr. Inc. CAN. Dist: Cardinal Pubs. Group.

Impey, Allison & Phillips, Craig. Ghostgirl. Hurley, Tonya. Frieyro, Alicia, tr. 2009. (SPA.). 1200p. (YA). (gr. 8-12). pap. 19.99 *(978-607-11-0185-3(9)*, Alfaguara Juvenil) Santillana USA Publishing Co., Inc.

Impey, Martin. At the End of the Garden. Dolan, Penny. 2008. (Tadpoles Ser.). 23p. (J). (gr. -1-3). 17.15 *(978-1-4178-0923-3(X)*, Turtleback) Turtleback Bks.

—Hetty's New Hat. Nash, Margaret. 2005. (Reading Corner Ser.). 24p. (J). (gr. k-3). lib. bdg. 22.80 *(978-1-59771-007-7(5))* Sea-To-Sea Pubns.

—Rapunzel. 2006. (First Fairy Tales Ser.). 31p. (J). (gr. -1-3). lib. bdg. 28.50 *(978-1-59771-076-3(8))* Sea-To-Sea Pubns.

In Den Bosch, Nicole. Creative Kitchen Crafts. Ross, Kathy. 2010. (Girl Crafts Ser.). (ENG.). 48p. (gr. 2-5). pap. 7.95 *(978-1-58013-886-4(1)*, First Avenue Editions) Lerner Publishing Group.

—Fairy World Crafts. Ross, Kathy. 2008. (Girl Crafts Ser.). (ENG.). 48p. (gr. 2-5). per. 7.95 *(978-0-8225-9024-8(7)*, First Avenue Editions) Lerner Publishing Group.

—Girlfriends' Get-Together Craft Book. Ross, Kathy. 2007. (Girl Crafts Ser.). (ENG.). 48p. (gr. 2-5). lib. bdg. 26.60 *(978-0-7613-3408-8(4)*, Millbrook Pr.) Lerner Publishing Group.

In-Soo, Ra. King of Hell, 6 vols., Vol. 6. Jae-Hwan, Kim. Na, Lauren, tr. from KOR. rev. ed. 2004. 192p. pap. 9.99 *(978-1-59182-484-8(2))* TOKYOPOP, Inc.

Inada, Koji. Beet the Vandal Buster, Vol. 5. Sanjo, Riku. 2005. (Beet the Vandel Buster Ser.). (ENG.). 208p. (YA). pap. 7.99 *(978-1-59116-806-5(6))* Viz Media.

—Beet the Vandel Buster. Sanjo, Riku. (Beet the Vandel Buster Ser.). (ENG.). 2005. 208p. (YA). pap. 7.99 *(978-1-59116-750-1(7))*; 2004. 200p. (YA). pap. 7.99 *(978-1-59116-690-0(X))*; Vol. 6. 2005. 216p. pap. 7.99 *(978-1-59116-871-3(6))* Viz Media.

—Beet the Vandel Buster, Vol. 7. Sanjo, Riku. 2005. (Beet the Vandel Buster Ser.). (ENG.). 200p. pap. 7.99 *(978-1-4215-0076-8(0))* Viz Media.

Inada, Koji. Beet the Vandel Buster, Vol. 3. Inada, Koji. 2005. (Beet the Vandel Buster Ser.). (ENG.). 216p. (YA). pap. 7.99 *(978-1-59116-693-1(4))* Viz Media.

Inagaki, Riichiro & Toriyama, Akira. Dragon Ball Z, Vol. 19. Inagaki, Riichiro & Toriyama, Akira. 2005. (Dragon Ball Z Ser.: 19). (ENG.). 184p. (gr. -1-13). pap. 9.99 *(978-1-59116-751-8(5))* Viz Media.

Incrocci, Rick. Bible Stories for Tiny Tots. Larsen, Carolyn. 2008. 35p. (J). bds. *(978-1-86920-241-5(4))* Christian Art Pubs.

—Little Angels Bible Storybook. Larsen, Carolyn. 2012. (ENG.). 432p. (J). 16.99 *(978-1-4143-7022-4(9))* Tyndale Hse. Pubs.

—My Bedtime Bible. Larsen, Carolyn & Baker Publishing Group Staff. 2003. 381p. (J). 19.99 *(978-1-932587-15-9(2))* Baker Publishing Group.

—Psalms for Toddlers. 2012. 32p. (J). pap. 12.00 *(978-1-935014-43-0(9))* Hutchings, John Pubs.

—See It/Say It Bible Storybook. Adams, Anne. 2006. 191p. 12.99 *(978-0-7814-4403-3(9))* Cook, David C.

—Stories about Jesus for Little Ones. Larsen, Carolyn. 2008. 35p. (gr. -1-k). bds. *(978-1-86920-173-9(6))* Christian Art Pubs.

—What Does the Bible Say about That? Larsen, Carolyn. 2009. 352p. (J). (gr. 3-7). pap. 17.99 *(978-1-4335-0213-2(5))* Crossway.

Infante, Francesc. El Pastorcito Mentiroso. Bailer, Darice et al. 2007. (SPA & ENG.). 28p. (J). *(978-0-545-02960-5(0))* Scholastic, Inc.

—Rumpelstiltskin. Carrasco, Xavier. 2007. (Bilingual Fairy Tales Ser.: BILI). (ENG & SPA.). 32p. (J). (gr. -1-3). 14.95 *(978-0-8118-5971-4(1))* Chronicle Bks. LLC.

Infantino, Carmine & Giella, Joe. The Elongated Man. Fox, Gardner & Broome, John. rev. ed. 2006. (Showcase Presents Ser.: Vol. 1). (ENG.). 560p. (YA). pap. 16.99 *(978-1-4012-1042-7(2))* DC Comics.

—The Flash. Kanigher, Robert & Broome, John. rev. ed. 2007. (Showcase Presents Ser.). (ENG.). 552p. (YA). (gr. 11-18). pap. 16.99 *(978-1-4012-1327-5(8))* DC Comics.

Infurnari, Joe. Marathon. Yakin, Boaz. 2012. (ENG.). 192p. (YA). (gr. 7-12). pap. 16.99 *(978-1-59643-680-0(8)*, First Second Bks.) Roaring Brook Pr.

Ingham, Julie. Design by Me Wings: Fancy Art & Fun Display Ideas! Magruder, Trula & American Girl Editors, eds. 2011. (ENG.). 32p. (J). spiral bd. 14.95 *(978-1-59369-897-3(6))* American Girl Publishing, Inc.

—Sweet Treats. Eliot, Hannah. 2014. (Dream Doodle Draw! Ser.). (ENG.). 96p. (J). (gr. -1-2). pap. 7.99 *(978-1-4814-0452-5(0)*, Little Simon) Little Simon.

Inglese, Judith. I See the Sun in Afghanistan. King, Dedie. Vahidi, Mohd, tr. 2011. (I See the Sun In ... Ser.: 0). (PER & ENG.). 40p. (J). (gr. k). pap. 12.95 *(978-0-9818720-8-7(5))* Satya Hse. Pubns.

—I See the Sun in Mexico, 1 vol. King, Dedie. ed. 2012. (I See the Sun Ser.: 5). (ENG.). 40p. (J). pap. 12.95 *(978-1-935874-14-0(4))* Satya Hse. Pubns.

—I See the Sun in Russia. King, Dedie. Ossipova, Irina, tr. ed. 2012. (I See the Sun Ser.: 0). (RUS & ENG.). 40p. (J). 12.95 *(978-1-935874-08-9(X))* Satya Hse. Pubns.

Inglese, Judith. I Have a Friend. Inglese, Judith. ed. 2014. (ENG.). 40p. (J). 17.95 *(978-1-935874-22-5(5))* Satya Hse. Pubns.

Ingman, Bruce. Double Pink. Feiffer, Kate. (ENG.). 32p. (J). (gr. -1-1). 2013. 7.99 *(978-1-4424-6033-1(4))*; 2005. 17.99 *(978-0-689-87190-0(2))* Simon & Schuster/Paula Wiseman Bks. (Simon & Schuster/Paula Wiseman Bks.).

—Everybody Was a Baby Once: And Other Poems. Ahlberg, Allan. 2010. (ENG.). 64p. (J). (gr. -1-k). 15.99 *(978-0-7636-4682-0(2))* Candlewick Pr.

—Hooray for Bread. Ahlberg, Allan. 2013. (ENG.). 32p. (J). (gr. -1-2). 15.99 *(978-0-7636-6311-7(5))* Candlewick Pr.

—The Pencil. Ahlberg, Allan. 2012. (ENG.). 48p. (J). (gr. -1-3). pap. 6.99 *(978-0-7636-6088-8(4))* Candlewick Pr.

—The Pencil. Ahlberg, Allan. ed. 2012. lib. bdg. 17.20 *(978-0-606-26942-1(8)*, Turtleback) Turtleback Bks.

—Previously. Ahlberg, Allan. 2011. (ENG.). 32p. (J). (gr. -1-3). pap. 6.99 *(978-0-7636-5304-0(7))* Candlewick Pr.

Ingman, Bruce. The Runaway Dinner. Ingman, Bruce. Ahlberg, Allan. 2008. (ENG.). 40p. (J). (gr. -1-3). pap. 6.99 *(978-0-7636-3893-1(5))* Candlewick Pr.

Ingpen, Robert R. The Adventures of Tom Sawyer. Twain, Mark. 2010. (Sterling Illustrated Classics Ser.). (ENG.). 240p. (J). (gr. 5-18). 19.95 *(978-1-4027-6762-3(5))* Sterling Publishing Co., Inc.

—Alice's Adventures in Wonderland. Carroll, Lewis. 2009. (Sterling Illustrated Classics Ser.). (ENG.). 192p. (J). (gr. 5-18). 19.95 *(978-1-4027-6835-4(4))* Sterling Publishing Co., Inc.

—Around the World in Eighty Days. Verne, Jules. 2012.Tr. of Tour du Monde en Quatre-Vingts Jours. (ENG.). 224p. (J). (gr. 4-7). 19.99 *(978-0-9564942-5-2(0))* Palazzo Editions, Ltd. GBR. Dist: Independent Pubs. Group.

—Broken Beaks. Lachenmeyer, Nathaniel. 2005. 32p. (J). 15.95 *(978-0-85572-335-4(1))* Warwick Publishing CAN. Dist: Perseus Distribution.

—Dickens: His Work & His World. Rosen, Michael. 2005. (ENG.). 96p. (J). (gr. 7-11). 19.99 *(978-0-7636-2752-2(6))* Candlewick Pr.

—The Jungle Book. Kipling, Rudyard. 2012. (Sterling Illustrated Classics Ser.). (ENG.). 192p. (J). (gr. 5-8). 19.95 *(978-1-4027-8284-8(5))* Sterling Publishing Co., Inc.

—Just So Stories. Kipling, Rudyard. 2013. (ENG.). 192p. (J). (gr. 4-7). 22.99 *(978-0-9571483-1-4(3))* Palazzo Editions, Ltd. GBR. Dist: Independent Pubs. Group.

—Peter Pan & Wendy: Centenary Edition. Barrie, J. M. 2004. (ENG.). 216p. (J). *(978-1-897035-12-2(8)*, Blue Heron Bks.) Raincoast Bk. Distribution.

—Peter Pan & Wendy: Centenary Edition. Barrie, J. M. 2010. (Sterling Illustrated Classics Ser.). (ENG.). 216p. (J). (gr. 5-18). 19.95 *(978-1-4027-2868-6(9))* Sterling Publishing Co., Inc.

—Scott y Amundsen: La Conquista del Polo Sur. Hao, K. T. & Fulla, Monserrat. 2006.Tr. of Scott & Amundsen, The Conquest of the South Pole. (SPA.). (J). (gr. 6-8). 9.60 *(978-84-316-7172-3(6)*, W32815) Vicens-Vives, Editorial, S.A. ESP. Dist: Lectorum Pubns., Inc.

—The Secret Garden. Burnett, Frances Hodgson. 2011. (Sterling Illustrated Classics Ser.). (ENG.). 240p. (J). (gr. 5-18). 19.95 *(978-1-4027-7872-8(4))* Sterling Publishing Co., Inc.

—Shakespeare: His Work & His World. Rosen, Michael. 2006. (ENG.). 96p. (J). (gr. 7-11). pap. 10.99 *(978-0-7636-3201-4(5))* Candlewick Pr.

—Storm Boy. Thiele, Colin. 2006. (ENG.). 1p. (J). (gr. -1-3). 7.95 *(978-1-74110-187-4(5))*; 40th anniv. ed. pap. 7.95 *(978-1-86436-804-8(7))* New Holland Pubs. Pty, Ltd. AUS. Dist: Tuttle Publishing.

—Treasure Island. Stevenson, Robert Louis. 2006. (ENG.). 192p. (J). *(978-1-897035-30-6(6)*, Blue Heron Bks.) Raincoast Bk. Distribution.

—The Wind in the Willows. Grahame, Kenneth. 2012. (Sterling Illustrated Classics Ser.). (ENG.). 224p. (J). (gr. 2-8). 19.95 *(978-1-4027-8283-1(7))* Sterling Publishing Co., Inc.

Ingram, Anne. A Visit to Hawaii. Holm, Barbara. 2005. 32p. (J). pap. 5.95 *(978-0-9772200-0-7(1))* Visit to Hawaii, A.

Ingram, Charles. Seven Spectral: The Orange World Outlaw. Wicks, Valerie. Lang, Leslie, ed. 2013. 342p. pap. 12.99 *(978-0-9912594-0-3(8))* Wicks, Valerie.

Ingram, Chris. Superhighway. Oldman, James. 2012. 184p. pap. *(978-1-78176-206-6(6))* FeedARead.com.

Ingram, Glenda Brown. Uga Hunkers down in Athens Town. Weaver, Jack. 2004. (J). *(978-0-9773370-0-2(6))* Weaver, Jack R. Company.

Ingram, Jan. Purple Frogs & Pumpkin Seeds. Lovvorn, Ann R. 2008. 44p. per. 24.95 *(978-1-4241-8734-8(6))* America Star Bks.

Ings, William. Great Global Puzzle Challenge with Google Earth. Gifford, Clive. 2011. (ENG.). 32p. (J). (gr. 3). 15.99 *(978-0-7534-6721-3(6)*, Kingfisher) Roaring Brook Pr.

Ink, Bruce. Party Pups: The Game of Prepositional Fun! Webber, Sharon et al. 2011. (J). 39.95 net. *(978-1-60723-002-1(X))* Super Duper Pubns.

Ink, Bruce & Golliher, Bill. Webber HearBuilder Following Directions Fun Sheets: Hbbk55. Holland, Beth. 2011. 216p. (J). spiral bd. 34.95 net. *(978-1-58650-992-7(6))* Super Duper Pubns.

Ink, Bruce & Schwartz, Marty. Early Articulation Roundup! Bk305. Foster, Beverly & Foster, Stacy Lynn. 2003. (J). per. 34.95 *(978-1-58650-284-3(0))* Super Duper Pubns.

Ink, Lancman. Chaucha y Palito. Walsh, Maria Elena. 2003. (SPA.). 134p. (J). (gr. 5-8). pap. 11.95 *(978-950-511-615-7(2))* Santillana USA Publishing Co., Inc.

—Hotel Pioho's Palace. 2003. (SPA.). 164p. (J). (gr. 5-8). pap. 12.95 *(978-950-511-781-9(7))* Santillana USA Publishing Co., Inc.

Inklink Staff. Uncover Nature. Brookes, Olivia. 2009. (Hide-and-Seek Visual Adventures Ser.). 24p. (J). (gr. 2-5). lib. bdg. 22.60 *(978-1-60754-655-9(8))* Windmill Bks.

Inklink, Studio. The Human Body in Action. Gallavotti, Barbara. Shapiro, Brett, tr. from ITA. 2004. 123p. (J). (gr. 4-8). reprint ed. pap. 9.00 *(978-0-7567-8334-1(8))* DIANE Publishing Co.

Inkpen, Mick. The House on the Rock. Butterworth, Nick. 2008. (ENG.). 32p. pap. *(978-1-85985-749-6(3)*, Candle Bks.) Lion Hudson PLC.

Inkpen, Mick. Kipper's Toybox. Inkpen, Mick. 2008. (Kipper Ser.). (ENG.). 32p. (J). (-k). pap. 10.99 ***(978-0-340-93207-0(4))*** Hodder & Stoughton GBR. Dist: Independent Pubs. Group.

Inkpen, Mick. Lullabyhullaballoo! Inkpen, Mick. 2009. (ENG.). 32p. (J). (gr. k-2). pap. 10.95 *(978-0-340-93108-0(6))* Hodder & Stoughton GBR. Dist: Independent Pubs. Group.

—Rollo & Ruff & the Little Fluffy Bird. Inkpen, Mick. 2012. (ENG.). 32p. (J). (gr. -1-k). pap. 9.99 *(978-0-340-98959-3(9))* Hodder & Stoughton GBR. Dist: Independent Pubs. Group.

—This Is My Book. Inkpen, Mick. 2012. (ENG.). 32p. (J). (gr. -1-k). pap. 10.99 *(978-0-340-98963-0(7))* Hodder & Stoughton GBR. Dist: Independent Pubs. Group.

Innerst, Stacy. The Beatles Were Fab (and They Were Funny) Krull, Kathleen & Brewer, Paul. 2013. (ENG.). 40p. (J). (gr. 1-4). lib. bdg. 16.99 *(978-0-547-50991-4(X))* Houghton Mifflin Harcourt Publishing Co.

—Levi Strauss Gets a Bright Idea: A Fairly Fabricated Story of a Pair of Pants. Johnston, Tony. 2011. (ENG.). 32p. (J). (gr. -1-3). 16.99 *(978-0-15-206145-6(2))* Houghton Mifflin Harcourt Publishing Co.

—Lincoln Tells a Joke: How Laughter Saved the President (and the Country) Krull, Kathleen & Brewer, Paul. 2010. (ENG.). 40p. (J). (gr. 1-4). 17.99 *(978-0-15-206639-0(X))* Houghton Mifflin Harcourt Publishing Co.

—M Is for Music. Krull, Kathleen. 2003. (ENG.). 56p. (J). (gr. -1-3). 17.00 *(978-0-15-201438-4(1))* Houghton Mifflin Harcourt Publishing Co.

—M Is for Music. Krull, Kathleen. 2009. (ENG.). 48p. (J). (gr. -1-3). pap. 6.99 *(978-0-15-206479-2(6))* Houghton Mifflin Harcourt Publishing Co.

Innes, Calvin. Mini Mysteries & Kooky Spookies. Nass, Marcia & Campisi, Stephanie. 2007. 176p. per. 6.99 *(978-0-9795364-2-7(1))* Chowder Bay Bks.

Innes, Sue. The Pact of the Wolves. Blazon, Nina. 2008. (ENG.). 224p. (YA). (gr. 8-12). 19.95 *(978-1-55451-124-2(0)*, 9781554511242); pap. 10.95 *(978-1-55451-135-8(6)*, 9781554511358) Annick Pr., Ltd. CAN. Dist: Firefly Bks., Ltd.

Innocenti, Roberto. Christmas Carol. Dickens, Charles. 2005. 152p. (J). (gr. 4-6). 35.00 *(978-1-56846-182-3(8))* Creative Co., The.

—Cinderella. Perrault, Charles. 2013. (ENG.). 32p. (J). (gr. 1-17). pap. 7.99 *(978-0-89812-828-4(5)*, Creative Paperbacks) Creative Co., The.

—Erika's Story. Vander Zee, Ruth. (ENG.). 24p. (J). (gr. 1-3). 2013. pap. 10.99 *(978-0-89812-891-8(9)*, Creative Paperbacks); 2003. 19.99 *(978-1-56846-176-2(3))* Creative Co., The.

—The House. Lewis, J. Patrick. 2009. (ENG.). 64p. (J). (gr. 4-7). 19.95 *(978-1-56846-201-1(8)*, 1300178, Creative Editions) Creative Co., The.

—The Last Resort. Lewis, J. Patrick. 2003. (ENG.). 48p. (J). (gr. 1-3). 24.99 *(978-1-56846-172-4(0)*, Creative Editions) Creative Co., The.

—Rose Blanche. Gallaz, Christophe. 2011. (ENG.). 32p. (J). (gr. 5-17). pap. 10.99 *(978-0-89812-385-2(2))* Creative Co., The.

Innocenti, Roberto, jt. illus. see Staino, Franco.

Inoue, Kazurou. Midori Days. Inoue, Kazurou. 2006. (Midori Days Ser.). (ENG.). 208p. Vol. 4. pap. 9.99 *(978-1-4215-0254-0(2))*; Vol. 5. pap. 9.99 *(978-1-4215-0287-8(9))*; Vol. 6. pap. 9.99 *(978-1-4215-0495-7(2))*; Vol. 7. pap. 9.99 *(978-1-4215-0496-4(0))* Viz Media.

Inoue, Kazurou & Inoue, Kazurou. Midori Days, Vol. 1. Inoue, Kazurou. 2005. (Midori Days Ser.). (ENG.). 200p. pap. 9.99 *(978-1-59116-905-5(4))* Viz Media.

Inoue, Kazurou, jt. illus. see Inoue, Kazurou.

Inoue, Momota. Genesect & the Legend Awakened. Inoue, Momota. 2013. (Pokemon Ser.). (ENG.). 192p. (J). pap. 9.99 *(978-1-4215-6804-1(7))* Viz Media.

Inoue, Takehiko. Slam Dunk. Inoue, Takehiko. (Slam Dunk Ser.: 8). (ENG.). (gr. 8-18). 2010. 196p. pap. 9.99 *(978-1-4215-2863-2(0))*; 2008. 208p. pap. 9.99 *(978-1-4215-0679-1(3))* Viz Media.

—Slam Dunk, Vol. 23. Inoue, Takehiko. 2012. (Slam Dunk Ser.: 23). (ENG.). 192p. pap. 9.99 *(978-1-4215-3330-8(8))* Viz Media.

—Vagabond Vol. 14: The Letter. Inoue, Takehiko. 2004. (Vagabond Ser.). (ENG.). 200p. pap. 9.95 *(978-1-59116-452-4(4))* Viz Media.

Inoue, Takehiko, jt. illus. see Yoshikawa, Eiji.

Inouye, Carol. Anthony Best: A Picture Book about Asperger's. Fahy, Davene & Mueller, Dagmar H. 2013. (ENG.). 32p. (J). (gr. -1-3). 16.95 *(978-1-61608-961-0(X)*, 608961, Sky Pony Pr.) Skyhorse Publishing Co., Inc.

—Charlie, Who Couldn't Say His Name. Fahy, Davene. 2004. 32p. (J). per. 12.95 *(978-0-9746589-0-2(1))* Limerock Bks.

—Kids Cooking Without a Stove: A Cookbook for Young Children. Paul, Aileen. rev. ed. 2005. 64p. (J). pap. 10.95 *(978-0-86534-060-2(9))* Sunstone Pr.

Intrater, Roberta Grobel, photos by. Peek-a-Boo, You! Intrater, Roberta Grobel. 2nd rev. l.t. ed. 2005. 14p. (J). 14.99 *(978-0-9764985-0-6(2))* 1212 Pr.

Intriago, Patricia. Dot. Intriago, Patricia. 2011. (ENG.). 36p. (J). (gr. -1-1). 14.99 *(978-0-374-31835-2(2)*, Farrar, Straus & Giroux (BYR)) Farrar, Straus & Giroux.

Inui, Sekihiko. Comic Party, Vol. 4. Inui, Sekihiko, creator. rev. ed. 2004. 192p. pap. 14.99 *(978-1-59532-584-6(0)*, Tokyopop Adult) TOKYOPOP, Inc.

Iosa, Ann. I Need a Little Help. Schulz, Kathy. 2011. (Rookie Ready to Learn - All about Me! Ser.). 32p. (J). (gr. -1-k). lib. bdg. 23.00 *(978-0-531-26526-0(9)*, Children's Pr.) Scholastic Library Publishing.

—Jobs Around My Neighborhood/Oficios en Mi Vecindario. Rosa-Mendoza, Gladys. 2007. (English Spanish Foundations Ser.). 20p. (gr. -1-k). pap. 19.95 *(978-1-931398-81-7(X))* Me+Mi Publishing.

—Jobs in My Neighborhood. 2010. (My World Ser.). (ENG.). 24p. (J). (gr. -1-1). pap. 8.15 *(978-1-61533-037-9(2))*; lib. bdg. 22.60 *(978-1-60754-952-9(2))* Windmill Bks.

—Necesito una Ayudita. Schulz, Kathy. 2011. (Rookie Ready to Learn Español Ser.). (SPA.). 32p. (J). pap. 5.95 *(978-0-531-26782-0(2))*; lib. bdg. 23.00 *(978-0-531-26114-9(X))* Scholastic Library Publishing. (Children's Pr.).

—The Open Road. Grahame, Kenneth. 2003. 32p. (J). *(978-0-7607-3215-1(9))* Barnes & Noble, Inc.

—Reading Fluency: Using Modeled Reading, Phrasing, & Repeated Oral Reading. Callella, Trisha. Hults, Alaska, ed. 2004. (J). Vol. 2232. 96p. (gr. 5-18). pap. 12.99 *(978-1-59198-065-0(8)*, 2232); Vol. 2233. (gr. 6-8). pap. 12.99 *(978-1-59198-066-7(6)*, 2233) Creative Teaching Pr., Inc.

—A Watermelon in the Sukkah. Rouss, Sylvia A. & Rouss, Shannan. 2013. 24p. 17.95 *(978-1-4677-1642-0(1))*; (ENG.). (J). (gr. -1-2). 16.95 *(978-0-7613-8118-1(X)*, Kar-Ben Publishing); (ENG.). (J). (gr. -1-2). 7.95 *(978-0-7613-8119-8(8)*, Kar-Ben Publishing) Lerner Publishing Group.

—The Wind in the Willows. Grahame, Kenneth. 2003. 32p. (J). *(978-0-7607-3214-4(0))* Barnes & Noble, Inc.

Iosa, Ann, jt. illus. see Grayson, Rick.

Iosa, Ann W. Developing Reading Fluency, Grade 2: Using Modeled Reading, Phrasing, & Repeated Oral Reading. Callella, Trisha. Fisch, Teri L., ed. 2003. (Developing Reading Fluency Ser.). 96p. (J). (gr. 2-3). pap. 14.99 *(978-1-57471-995-6(5)*, 2248) Creative Teaching Pr., Inc.

—Developing Reading Fluency, Grade 4: Using Modeled Reading, Phrasing, & Repeated Oral Reading. Callella, Trisha. Fisch, Teri L., ed. 2003. (Developing Reading Fluency Ser.). 96p. (J). (gr. 4-5). pap. 14.99 *(978-1-57471-997-0(1)*, 2250) Creative Teaching Pr., Inc.

Iosa, Ann W. & Grayson, Rick. Math Tub Topics: Math Instruction Through Discovery. Morton, Debra & Stover, Elizabeth. Jennett, Pamela, ed. 2003. 128p. (J). (gr. k-3). pap. 13.99 *(978-1-57471-954-3(8)*, 2812) Creative Teaching Pr., Inc.

Ipcar, Dahlov. Black & White. 2015. (Dahlov Ipcar Collection). (ENG.). 40p. (J). (gr. -1-2). 17.95 *(978-1-909263-44-4(3))* Flying Eye Bks. GBR. Dist: Consortium Bk. Sales & Distribution.

—I Like Animals. 2014. (Dahlov Ipcar Collection). (ENG.). 40p. (J). (gr. -1-2). 17.95 *(978-1-909263-25-3(7))* Flying Eye Bks. GBR. Dist: Consortium Bk. Sales & Distribution.

—The Wonderful Egg. 2014. (Dahlov Ipcar Collection). (ENG.). 48p. (J). (gr. -1-2). 19.95 *(978-1-909263-28-4(1))* Flying Eye Bks. GBR. Dist: Consortium Bk. Sales & Distribution.

Ipcar, Dahlov. One Horse Farm, 1 vol. Ipcar, Dahlov. ed. 2011. (ENG.). 36p. (J). 17.95 *(978-1-934031-39-1(9)*, f72697cf-1ee4-41bd-94d7-a193b2391a9b) Islandport Pr., Inc.

Ippolito, Eva Marie. The Donkey's Tale. Ippolito, Eva Marie. 2003. III, 15p. (J). (gr. -1-3). pap. 1.95 *(978-0-9705350-3-0(1))* Ippolito, Eva Marie.

—Hear, O Lord. Ippolito, Eva Marie. l.t. ed. 2009. 72p. (YA). (gr. 7-12). pap. 13.69 *(978-1-4389-2422-9(4))* AuthorHouse.

Irish, Leigh Ann. I Love You, Baby Deer. Gilleland, Linda. 2012. 56p. 19.99 *(978-1-61254-025-2(2))* Brown Bks. Publishing Group.

Irish, Martin. Flip-Flap Math: Flip the Flpas to Check Your Answers! Faulkner, Keith. 2005. 12 p.p. (J). *(978-0-439-78578-5(2))* Scholastic, Inc.

Irvin, Feliza. Idaly's Learning Chest, Series 1: Learning Body Parts. Irvin, Feliza. Soto, Jasmine, photos by. irvin, Feliza. Vigil, Sabrina, ed. 2010. (ENG.). 38p. pap. 10.92 *(978-1-4536-5750-8(9))* CreateSpace Independent Publishing Platform.

Irvin, Frank. Walt Disney. Hammontree, Marie. 2014. (History's All-Stars Ser.). (ENG.). 208p. (J). (gr. 3-7). pap. 6.99 *(978-1-4814-1374-9(0)*, Simon & Schuster/Paula Wiseman Bks.) Simon & Schuster/Paula Wiseman Bks.

Irvin, Sioux. Rusty, the Rainbow Trout: Moving Day. Irvin, David. 2007. 24p. per. 24.95 *(978-1-4241-8455-2(X))* America Star Bks.

Irvine, Wil. Butterflies Don't Crawl. Grateful Steps Publishing & Tipton, Angela. 2009. 32p. (J). 16.95 *(978-1-935130-14-7(5))* Grateful Steps.

Irving, Frazer. Frankenstein. Shelley, Mary. 2005. 176p. (gr. 3-7). 21.00 *(978-0-7569-5809-1(1))* Perfection Learning Corp.

—Puffin Graphics: Frankenstein. Reed, Gary & Shelley, Mary. 2005. (ENG.). 352p. (J). (gr. 3-7). 10.99 *(978-0-14-240407-2(1)*, Puffin) Penguin Publishing Group.

Irving, Frazier, jt. illus. see Bachalo, Chris.

Irving, George S. Historias de Miedo. Schwartz, Alvin & Alvin, Schwartz. 2003. (Historias de Miedo Scary Stories to Tell in the Dark Ser.). (SPA.). 120p. (YA). (gr. 5-8). pap. 11.99 *(978-84-241-8662-3(1))* Everest Editora ESP. Dist: Lectorum Pubns., Inc.

—Historias de Miedo 2: Relatos Espeluznantes para No Dejarte Dormir. Schwartz, Alvin & Alvin, Schwartz. 2003. (Historias de Miedo Scary Stories to Tell in the Dark Ser.).Tr. of More Scary Stories to Tell in the Dark. (SPA.). 112p. (YA). (gr. 5-8). pap. 11.99 *(978-84-241-8663-0(X))* Everest Editora ESP. Dist: Lectorum Pubns., Inc.

—Historias de Miedo 3: Relatos Aterradores para Helarte la Sangre. Schwartz, Alvin & Alvin, Schwartz. 2003. (Historias de Miedo Scary Stories to Tell in the Dark Ser.).Tr. of Scary Stories 3: More Tales to Chill Your Bones. (SPA.). 128p. (YA). (gr. 5-8). pap. 11.99 *(978-84-241-8664-7(8))* Everest Editora ESP. Dist: Lectorum Pubns., Inc.

Irwin, April. Daisy. Clark, Danell. 2008. 28p. pap. 11.95 *(978-1-59858-642-8(4))* Dog Ear Publishing, LLC.

Irwin, Dana. Grandpa & the Truck Book One. Mellor, Colleen Kelly. 2012. 34p. pap. 9.99 *(978-0-9856770-0-8(7))* truckerkidzPr.

Irwin, Dana M. Grandpa & the Truck Book 2. Mellor, Colleen Kelly. 2012. 34p. pap. 9.99 *(978-0-9856770-2-2(3))* truckerkidzPr.

Irwin, Kendra. Catching Fireflies: Family Night Devotional Fun. Lyttle, Marcy. 2007. 273p. 12.99 *(978-1-932307-77-1(X)*, Ambassador International) Emerald Hse. Group, Inc.

Isaac, W. Smiley. If Daddy Can, I Can. Arceneaux, Kitty. 2012. 24p. 24.95 *(978-1-4626-4945-7(9))*; pap. 12.99 *(978-1-4626-7852-5(1))* America Star Bks.

Isaacs, Rebekah & Timmons, Jonathan. Los Hermanos Wright. Mayo, Gretchen Will & O'Hern, Kerri. 2007. (Biografias Graficas (Graphic Biographies) Ser.). (SPA.). 32p. (gr. 5-8). lib. bdg. 27.00 *(978-0-8368-7883-7(3))* Stevens, Gareth Publishing LLLP.

—The Wright Brothers. Mayo, Gretchen Will & O'Hern, Kerri. 2006. (Graphic Biographies Ser.). 32p. (gr. 5-8). lib. bdg. 27.00 *(978-0-8368-6199-0(X))* Stevens, Gareth Publishing LLLP.

Isabel, Michelle & Thomas, Franselica. Murtle the Sea Turtle. Isabel, Michelle. 2011. 24p. pap. 24.95 *(978-1-4626-0114-1(6))* America Star Bks.

Isabelle, Decenciere. It's Me! Drachman, Eric. 2005. (ENG.). 32p. (J). (gr. -1-2). 18.95 *(978-0-9703809-2-0(5))* Kidwick Bks.

Isadora, Rachel. In the Small, Small Night. Kurtz, Jane. 2005. (Amistad Ser.). 32p. (J). (gr. k-5). (ENG.). 17.99 *(978-0-06-623814-2(5))*; lib. bdg. 17.89 *(978-0-06-623813-5(7))* HarperCollins Pubs. (Greenwillow Bks.).

—Invitation to Ballet: A Celebration of Dance & Degas. Vaughan, Carolyn. 2012. (ENG.). 32p. (J). (gr. 1-4). 16.95 *(978-1-4197-0260-0(2)*, Abrams Bks. for Young Readers) Abrams.

Isadora, Rachel. Bea at Ballet. Isadora, Rachel. (ENG.). 32p. (J). (gr. -1 — 1). 2014. bds. 7.99 *(978-0-399-16844-4(3))*; 2012. 12.99 *(978-0-399-25409-3(9))* Penguin Publishing Group. (Nancy Paulsen Bks.).

—The Fisherman & His Wife. Isadora, Rachel. Brothers Grimm, Becky. 2008. (ENG.). 32p. (J). (gr. -1-3). 16.99 *(978-0-399-24771-2(8)*, Putnam Juvenile) Penguin Publishing Group.

—Hansel & Gretel. Isadora, Rachel. 2009. (ENG.). 32p. (J). (gr. 1-3). 16.99 *(978-0-399-25028-6(X)*, Putnam Juvenile) Penguin Publishing Group.

—Happy Belly, Happy Smile. Isadora, Rachel. 2009. (ENG.). 32p. (J). (gr. -1-3). 16.00 *(978-0-15-206546-1(6))* Houghton Mifflin Harcourt Publishing Co.

—Jake at Gymnastics. Isadora, Rachel. 2014. (ENG.). 32p. (J). (gr. -1-k). 14.99 *(978-0-399-16048-6(5)*, Nancy Paulsen Bks.) Penguin Publishing Group.

—Nick Plays Baseball. Isadora, Rachel. 2003. (ENG.). 32p. (J). (gr. k-4). pap. 6.99 *(978-0-698-11989-5(4)*, Puffin) Penguin Publishing Group.

—The Night Before Christmas. Isadora, Rachel. 2012. (ENG.). 32p. (J). (gr. k-3). mass mkt. 7.99 *(978-0-14-242339-4(4)*, Puffin) Penguin Publishing Group.

—Old Mikamba Had a Farm. Isadora, Rachel. 2013. (ENG.). 40p. (J). (gr. -1-k). 17.99 *(978-0-399-25740-7(3)*, Nancy Paulsen Bks.) Penguin Publishing Group.

—Peekaboo Morning. Isadora, Rachel. 2008. (ENG.). 24p. (J). (gr. -1 — 1). bds. 7.99 *(978-0-399-25153-5(7)*, Putnam Juvenile) Penguin Publishing Group.

—Say Hello! Isadora, Rachel. 2010. (ENG.). 32p. (J). (gr. -1-k). 16.99 *(978-0-399-25230-3(4)*, Putnam Juvenile) Penguin Publishing Group.

—There Was a Tree. Isadora, Rachel. 2012. (ENG.). 32p. (J). (gr. -1-k). 16.99 *(978-0-399-25741-4(1)*, Nancy Paulsen Bks.) Penguin Publishing Group.

—The Twelve Dancing Princesses. Isadora, Rachel. 2009. (ENG.). 32p. (J). (gr. k-3). pap. 6.99 *(978-0-14-241450-7(6)*, Puffin) Penguin Publishing Group.

Isaksen, Lisa A. Nazi Zombies. Bozanich, Tony L. & Wight, Joe. Isaksen, Patricia, ed. 2013. 112p. (gr. -1-4). pap. 14.95 *(978-0-930655-00-6(1))* Antarctic Pr., Inc.

Isaza, Juanita. Conjuros y Sortilegios. Vasco, Irene. 2004. (SPA.). 29p. (J). (gr. -1-7). pap. *(978-958-30-0522-0(3))* Panamericana Editorial.

—Historias Inmorales. Quiroga, Horacio. 2004. (Cajon de Cuentos Ser.). (SPA.). 246p. (J). (gr. 8-12). *(978-958-30-0457-5(X))* Panamericana Editorial.

—El Quinto Viaje y Otras Historias del Nuevo Mundo. Nino, Jairo Anibal. 2004. (Literatura Juvenil (Panamericana Editorial) Ser.). (SPA.). 153p. (J). (gr. 4-7). pap. *(978-958-30-0573-2(8)*, PV4381) Centro de Informacion y Desarrollo de la Comunicacion y la Literatura MEX. Dist: Lectorum Pubns., Inc.

Isbell, Toby. Silly Rules: Jokes for Kids. Campbell, Anna. 2008. (ENG.). 100p. (J). pap. 4.99 *(978-0-9801861-3-0(7))* Summerhill Pr.

Ische, Bryan. On Your Own: A College Readiness Guide for Teens with ADHD/LD. Quinn, Patricia O. & Maitland, Theresa E. Laurie. 2011. 112p. (YA). (gr. 9-18). pap. 14.95 *(978-1-4338-0955-2(9)*, Magination Pr.) American Psychological Assn.

Isely, Chad. The Power of Bystanders: Willie Bohanon & Friends Learn to Handle Bullying Like a B. O. S. S. Jones, Kip. 2015. 40p. (J). pap. 10.95 ***(978-1-934490-79-2(2))*** Boys Town Pr.

Isely, Chad. The Power of Self-D: Willie Bohanon & Friends Learn the Power of Self-Determination. Jones, Kip. 2014. 32p. (J). pap. 10.95 *(978-1-934490-66-2(0))* Boys Town Pr.

Iseminger, Jonathan, jt. illus. see Sjostrom, Nicole.

Iseminger, Jonathon, jt. illus. see Sjostrom, Nicole.

Ishe, Bryan. Type 1 Teens: A Guide to Managing Your Diabetes. Hood, Korey K. 2010. 112p. (YA). (gr. 7-18). pap. 14.95 *(978-1-4338-0788-6(2)*, Magination Pr.) American Psychological Assn.

Isherwood, Matthew. Baby Animals Sticker Activities. Litton, Jonathan. 2014. (My First Sticker Activity Book Ser.). (ENG.). 77p. (J). (gr. -1-3). pap. 9.99 *(978-1-58925-302-5(7))* Tiger Tales.

Ishibash, Toshiharu, jt. illus. see Mizuno, Junko.

Ishida, Jui. Animal Stories: Heartwarming True Tales from the Animal Kingdom. Yolen, Jane. 2014. (ENG.). 160p. (J). (gr. k-12). 24.99 *(978-1-4263-1725-5(5)*, National Geographic Children's Bks.) National Geographic Society.

—Goodnight Little One: Bedtime Around the World. Matsuda, Christine. 2008. (J). 15.95 *(978-0-87358-925-3(4)*, Rising Moon Bks. for Young Readers) Northland Publishing.

—The Silver Moon: Lullabies & Cradle Songs. Prelutsky, Jack. 2013. (ENG.). 48p. (J). (gr. -1-3). 17.99 *(978-0-06-201467-2(6)*, Greenwillow Bks.) HarperCollins Pubs.

—Who Says Baa? A Touch & Feel Board Book. 2005. (Board Books). 16p. (J). bds. 6.95 *(978-1-58117-177-8(3)*, Intervisual/Piggy Toes) Bendon, Inc.

—Who Says Moo? A Touch & Feel Board Book. 2005. 16p. (J). bds. 6.95 *(978-1-58117-178-5(1)*, Intervisual/Piggy Toes) Bendon, Inc.

Ishii, Minako, photos by. Girls' Day/Boys' Day. Ishii, Minako. 2007. 64p. (J). (gr. 4-7). 16.95 *(978-1-57306-274-9(X))* Bess Pr., Inc.

Isik, Sernur. Australia. Ganeri, Anita. 2015. (Country Guides, with Benjamin Blog & His Inquisitive Dog Ser.). (ENG.). 32p. (gr. 1-3). 29.32 *(978-1-4109-6846-3(4))* Heinemann-Raintree.

—Brazil: A Benjamin Blog & His Inquisitive Dog Guide, 1 vol. Ganeri, Anita. 2014. (Country Guides, with Benjamin Blog & His Inquisitive Dog Ser.). (ENG.). 32p. (gr. 1-3). pap. 7.99 *(978-1-4109-6674-2(7)*, Read Me!) Heinemann-Raintree.

—Canada. Ganeri, Anita. 2015. (Country Guides, with Benjamin Blog & His Inquisitive Dog Ser.). (ENG.). 32p. (gr. 1-3). 29.32 *(978-1-4109-6847-0(2))* Heinemann-Raintree.

—China: A Benjamin Blog & His Inquisitive Dog Guide, 1 vol. Ganeri, Anita. 2014. (Country Guides, with Benjamin Blog & His Inquisitive Dog Ser.). (ENG.). 32p. (gr. 1-3). pap. 7.99 *(978-1-4109-6670-4(4)*, Read Me!) Heinemann-Raintree.

—Country Guides, with Benjamin Blog & His Inquisitive Dog, 1 vol. Ganeri, Anita. 2014. (Country Guides, with Benjamin Blog & His Inquisitive Dog Ser.). (ENG.). 32p. (gr. 1-3). 234.56 *(978-1-4109-6669-8(0)*, Read Me!) Heinemann-Raintree.

—Dream Birthday, 1 vol. Phillips, Ruby Ann. 2014. (Krystal Ball Ser.). (ENG.). 112p. (gr. 2-3). 23.99 *(978-1-4795-2178-4(7))* Picture Window Bks.

—Egypt: A Benjamin Blog & His Inquisitive Dog Guide, 1 vol. Ganeri, Anita. 2014. (Country Guides, with Benjamin Blog & His Inquisitive Dog Ser.). (ENG.). 32p. (gr. 1-3). pap. 7.99 *(978-1-4109-6672-8(0)*, Read Me!) Heinemann-Raintree.

—England. Ganeri, Anita. 2015. (Country Guides, with Benjamin Blog & His Inquisitive Dog Ser.). (ENG.). 32p. (gr. 1-3). 29.32 *(978-1-4109-6848-7(0))* Heinemann-Raintree.

—Fortune Cookie Fiasco. Phillips, Ruby Ann. 2015. (Krystal Ball Ser.). (ENG.). 112p. (gr. 2-3). lib. bdg. 23.99 *(978-1-4795-5874-2(5))* Picture Window Bks.

—France: A Benjamin Blog & His Inquisitive Dog Guide, 1 vol. Ganeri, Anita. 2014. (Country Guides, with Benjamin Blog & His Inquisitive Dog Ser.). (ENG.). 32p. (gr. 1-3). pap. 7.99 *(978-1-4109-6676-6(3)*, Read Me!) Heinemann-Raintree.

Isik, Sernur. Germany. Ganeri, Anita. 2015. (Country Guides, with Benjamin Blog & His Inquisitive Dog Ser.). (ENG.). 32p. (gr. 1-3). 29.32 ***(978-1-4109-7994-0(6))*** Heinemann-Raintree.

Isik, Sernur. The Great & Powerful, 1 vol. Phillips, Ruby Ann. 2014. (Krystal Ball Ser.). (ENG.). 112p. (gr. 2-3). 23.99 *(978-1-4795-2179-1(5))* Picture Window Bks.

—India: A Benjamin Blog & His Inquisitive Dog Guide, 1 vol. Ganeri, Anita. 2014. (Country Guides, with Benjamin Blog & His Inquisitive Dog Ser.). (ENG.). 32p. (gr. 1-3). pap. 7.99 *(978-1-4109-6671-1(2)*, Read Me!) Heinemann-Raintree.

Isik, Sernur. Italy. Ganeri, Anita. 2015. (Country Guides, with Benjamin Blog & His Inquisitive Dog Ser.). (ENG.). 32p. (gr. 1-3). 29.32 ***(978-1-4109-7995-7(4))*** Heinemann-Raintree.

Isik, Sernur. Japan: A Benjamin Blog & His Inquisitive Dog Guide, 1 vol. Ganeri, Anita. 2014. (Country Guides, with Benjamin Blog & His Inquisitive Dog Ser.). (ENG.). 32p. (gr. 1-3). 29.32 *(978-1-4109-6666-7(6)*, Read Me!) Heinemann-Raintree.

—Mexico: A Benjamin Blog & His Inquisitive Dog Guide, 1 vol. Ganeri, Anita. 2014. (Country Guides, with Benjamin Blog & His Inquisitive Dog Ser.). (ENG.). 32p. (gr. 1-3). 29.32 *(978-1-4109-6664-3(X)*, Read Me!) Heinemann-Raintree.

—Pet Psychic. Phillips, Ruby Ann. 2015. (Krystal Ball Ser.). (ENG.). 112p. (gr. 2-3). lib. bdg. 23.99 *(978-1-4795-5875-9(3))* Picture Window Bks.

—Republic of Ireland. Ganeri, Anita. 2015. (Country Guides, with Benjamin Blog & His Inquisitive Dog Ser.). (ENG.). 32p. (gr. 1-3). 29.32 *(978-1-4109-6849-4(9))* Heinemann-Raintree.

Isik, Sernur. Russia. Ganeri, Anita. 2015. (Country Guides, with Benjamin Blog & His Inquisitive Dog Ser.). (ENG.). 32p. (gr. 1-3). 29.32 ***(978-1-4109-7997-1(0))*** Heinemann-Raintree.

Isik, Sernur. Scotland. Ganeri, Anita. 2015. (Country Guides, with Benjamin Blog & His Inquisitive Dog Ser.). (ENG.). 32p. (gr. 1-3). 29.32 *(978-1-4109-6850-0(2))* Heinemann-Raintree.

—South Africa: A Benjamin Blog & His Inquisitive Dog Guide, 1 vol. Ganeri, Anita. 2014. (Country Guides, with Benjamin Blog & His Inquisitive Dog Ser.). (ENG.). 32p. (gr. 1-3). 29.32 *(978-1-4109-6668-1(2))*; pap. 7.99 *(978-1-4109-6677-3(1))* Heinemann-Raintree.

Isik, Sernur. Spain. Ganeri, Anita. 2015. (Country Guides, with Benjamin Blog & His Inquisitive Dog Ser.). (ENG.). 32p. (gr. 1-3). 29.32 ***(978-1-4109-7996-4(2))*** Heinemann-Raintree.

Isik, Sernur. Uncle Eli's Wedding. Newman, Tracy. 2015. (ENG.). 32p. (J). (gr. -1-2). 16.99 *(978-0-8075-8293-0(X))* Whitman, Albert & Co.

—United States of America. Ganeri, Anita. 2015. (Country Guides, with Benjamin Blog & His Inquisitive Dog Ser.). (ENG.). 32p. (gr. 1-3). 29.32 *(978-1-4109-6851-7(0))* Heinemann-Raintree.

Isings, J. H. Bible Stories for Our Little Ones. Hulst, W. G. van de. 2004. 262p. *(978-1-894666-69-5(0))* Inheritance Pubns.

Iskowitz, Joel. Rebekkah's Journey: A World War II Refugee Story. Burg, Ann. 2006. (Tales of Young Americans Ser.). (ENG.). 32p. (J). (gr. 3-7). 17.95 *(978-1-58536-275-2(1))* Sleeping Bear Pr.

Ismail, Yasmeen. Inside, Outside, Upside Down. 2013. (ENG.). 56p. (J). (gr. -1-3). pap. 9.99 *(978-1-60905-404-5(0))* Blue Apple Bks.

—One Word from Sophia. Averbeck, Jim. 2015. (ENG.). 40p. (J). (gr. -1-3). 17.99 *(978-1-4814-0514-0(4))* Simon & Schuster Children's Publishing.

Isol. Doggy Slippers, 1 vol. Luján, Jorge. Amado, Elisa, tr. from SPA. 2010. (ENG.). 32p. (J). (gr. k-k). 18.95 *(978-0-88899-983-2(6))* Groundwood Bks. CAN. Dist: Perseus-PGW.

—Habia una Vez una Llave. Montes, Graciela. 2005. (Pictocuentos Ser.). (SPA.). 24p. (J). 8.95 *(978-1-59820-213-7(8)*, Alfaguara) Santillana USA Publishing Co., Inc.

Isol. Regalo Sorpresa. Isol. 2nd ed. 2007. (la Orilla del Viento Ser.). (SPA.). 33p. (J). (gr. 1-2). pap. *(978-968-16-6151-9(6)*, FC33641) Fondo de Cultura Economica.

Isol Staff. Numeralia, 1 vol. Luján, Jorge. Ouriou, Susan, tr. from SPA. 2014. (ENG.). 32p. (J). (gr. -1). 18.95 *(978-1-55498-444-2(0))* Groundwood Bks. CAN. Dist: Perseus-PGW.

Israel, David, et al, photos by. Offerings of the Spirit: Tributes to Brother Thomas. Gressler, Jeanne, ed. 2003. 88p. 35.00 *(978-1-879985-09-4(8)*, Pucker Art Pubns.) Pucker Gallery.

Ito, Akihiro. Geobreeders 1, Vol. 1. Ito, Akihiro. 2004. 224p. pap. 9.99 *(978-1-58664-929-6(9)*, CMX 61501MM, CPM Comics) Central Park Media Corp.

Ito, Akira. Yu-Gi-Oh! R. Ito, Akira. Takahashi, Kazuki. 2010. (Yu-Gi-Oh! R Ser.: 4). (ENG.). 200p. (gr. 8-18). pap. 9.99 *(978-1-4215-3009-3(0))*; Vol. 3. 216p. pap. 9.99 *(978-1-4215-3008-6(2))* Viz Media.

—Yu-Gi-Oh! R, Vol. 5. Ito, Akira. Takahashi, Kazuki. 2010. (Yu-Gi-Oh! R Ser.: 5). (ENG.). 296p. pap. 9.99 *(978-1-4215-3010-9(4))* Viz Media.

Ito, Joel & Kemly, Kathleen. The Human Body. Bruhn, Aron. 2010. (Inside Ser.). (ENG.). 48p. (gr. 4-6). pap. 9.95 *(978-1-4027-7779-0(5))* Sterling Publishing Co., Inc.

Ito, Joel & Kemly, Kathleen Hadam. Inside Human Body. Bruhn, Aron. 2010. (Inside Ser.). (ENG.). 48p. (gr. 4-6). 16.95 *(978-1-4027-7091-3(X))* Sterling Publishing Co., Inc.

Ito, Leonardo. Amplified, Vol. 5. Hoena, Blake A. & Tortosa, Wilson. 2012. (Tony Hawk's 900 Revolution Ser.). (ENG.). 128p. (gr. 3-4). pap. 7.19 *(978-1-4342-3887-0(3))*; lib. bdg. 25.32 *(978-1-4342-3311-0(1))* Stone Arch Bks. (Tony Hawk's 900 Revolution).

—Exiled, Vol. 7. Terrell, Brandon & Tortosa, Wilson. 2012. (Tony Hawk's 900 Revolution Ser.). (ENG.). 128p. (gr. 3-4). pap. 7.19 *(978-1-4342-3889-4(X))*; lib. bdg. 25.32 *(978-1-4342-3313-4(8))* Stone Arch Bks. (Tony Hawk's 900 Revolution).

—Lockdown, Vol. 8. Manning, Matthew K. & Majado, Caio. 2012. (Tony Hawk's 900 Revolution Ser.). (ENG.). 128p. (gr. 3-4). pap. 7.19 *(978-1-4342-3890-0(3))*; lib. bdg. 25.32 *(978-1-4342-3314-1(6))* Stone Arch Bks. (Tony Hawk's 900 Revolution).

—Tunnel Vision, Vol. 6. Terrell, Brandon & Majado, Caio. 2012. (Tony Hawk's 900 Revolution Ser.). (ENG.). 128p. (gr. 3-4). pap. 7.19 *(978-1-4342-3888-7(1))*; lib. bdg. 25.32 *(978-1-4342-3312-7(X))* Stone Arch Bks. (Tony Hawk's 900 Revolution).

Ito, Willie. A Boy of Heart Mountain. Bazaldua, Barbara. 2010. (J). pap. *(978-0-578-05342-4(X))* Yabitoon Bks.

Ivan & Moxo, jt. illus. see Redondo, Jesus.

Ivanke. Sparkling Easter Eggs: A Glittery Counting Book. 2008. (ENG.). 10p. (J). bds. 7.95 *(978-1-58117-685-8(6)*, Intervisual/Piggy Toes) Bendon, Inc.

Ivanke, jt. illus. see Lola.

Ivanke & Lola, jt. illus. see Lola.

Ivanov, A. & Ivanov, O. Adventures of MIA. Farley, Robin. 2013. 158p. (J). *(978-1-4351-5061-4(9))* Barnes & Noble, Inc.

Ivanov, Aleksey. Boomer to the Rescue. Parente, Peter. I.t. ed. 2005. 28p. 15.95 *(978-0-9745052-3-7(4)*, Peeper & Friends) Tree Of Life Publishing.

Ivanov, Aleksey, et al. Every Day Is Earth Day. O'Connor, Jane. 2010. (I Can Read Book 1 Ser.). (ENG.). 32p. (J). (gr. -1-3). 16.99 *(978-0-06-187327-0(6))*; pap. 3.99 *(978-0-06-187326-3(8))* HarperCollins Pubs.

—Harry Cat & Tucker Mouse: Starring Harry. Feldman, Thea et al. 2011. (My Readers Ser.). (ENG.). 32p. (J). (gr. k-2). pap. 3.99 *(978-0-312-68169-2(0))* Square Fish.

Ivanov, Aleksey & Ivanov, Olga. Because of Shoe & Other Dog Stories. Martin, Ann M., ed. 2012. (ENG.). 272p. (J). (gr. 3-7). 15.99 *(978-0-8050-9314-8(1)*, Holt, Henry & Co. Bks. For Young Readers) Holt, Henry & Co.

—Dios es Bueno Todo el Tiempo. McCombs, Margi. 2012. (SPA.). 20p. (J). (gr. -1-k). bds. 9.99 *(978-0-545-45618-0(5)*, Scholastic en Espanol) Scholastic, Inc.

—Flappy & Scrappy. Yorinks, Arthur. 2010. (I Can Read Book 2 Ser.). (ENG.). 48p. (J). (gr. k-3). pap. 3.99 *(978-0-06-205913-0(0))* HarperCollins Pubs.

—God Is Good... All the Time. McCombs, Margi. 2012. (ENG.). 20p. (J). (gr. -1-k). bds. 9.99 *(978-0-545-45415-5(8))* Scholastic, Inc.

—Harry Cat & Tucker Mouse: Tucker's Beetle Band. Feldman, Thea et al. Selden, George et al. 2011. (My Readers Ser.). (ENG.). 32p. (J). (gr. k-2). pap. 3.99 *(978-0-312-62576-4(6))* Square Fish.

—Mia & the Tiny Toe Shoes. Farley, Robin. 2012. (My First I Can Read Ser.). (ENG.). 32p. (J). (gr. -1-3). 16.99 *(978-0-06-208683-9(9))*; pap. 3.99 *(978-0-06-208682-2(0))* HarperCollins Pubs.

—Mia & the Too Big Tutu. Farley, Robin. 2010. (My First I Can Read Ser.). (ENG.). 32p. (J). (gr. -1-3). 16.99 *(978-0-06-173302-4(4))*; pap. 3.99 *(978-0-06-173301-7(6))* HarperCollins Pubs.

—Mountain Dog. Engle, Margarita. 2013. (ENG.). 224p. (J). (gr. 3-7). 17.99 *(978-0-8050-9516-6(0)*, Holt, Henry & Co. Bks. For Young Readers) Holt, Henry & Co.

—Mountain Dog. Engle, Margarita. 2014. (ENG.). 240p. (J). (gr. 3-7). pap. 7.99 *(978-1-250-04424-2(3))* Square Fish.

—Revenge of Superstition Mountain. Broach, Elise. 2014. (Superstition Mountain Mysteries Ser.: 3). (ENG.). 304p. (J). (gr. 3-7). 16.99 *(978-0-8050-8909-7(8)*, Holt, Henry & Co. Bks. For Young Readers) Holt, Henry & Co.

—The Sweetest Valentine. Farley, Robin. 2012. (Mia Ser.). (ENG.). 24p. (J). (gr. -1-3). pap. 4.99 *(978-0-06-210012-2(2)*, HarperFestival) HarperCollins Pubs.

—The Tall Book of Mother Goose. Domain Public Staff. 2006. (Harper Tall Book Ser.). (ENG.). 80p. (J). (gr. -1-2). 6.99 *(978-0-06-054373-0(6)*, HarperFestival) HarperCollins Pubs.

Ivanov, Aleksey, jt. illus. see Ivanov, Olga.

Ivanov, Alex, photos by. The Complete Visual Dictionary. Reynolds, David West et al. 2006. (ENG., 272p. (J). (gr. 5-12). 40.00 *(978-0-7566-2238-1(7))* Dorling Kindersley Publishing, Inc.

Ivanov, Alexsey & Ivanov, Olga. Cake: Love, Chickens, & a Taste of Peculiar, 1 vol. Magnin, Joyce. 2013. (ENG.). 224p. (J). 14.99 *(978-0-310-73333-1(2))* Zondervan.

Ivanov, Evgueni. Bursunsul & Paskualina. Tavadze, Olesya. 2007. (POL & ENG.). 32p. (J). pap. 16.95 *(978-1-60195-095-6(0))* International Step by Step Assn.

Ivanov, O., jt. illus. see Ivanov, A.

Ivanov, Olga & Ivanov, Aleksey. Because of Shoe & Other Dog Stories. Martin, Ann M., ed. 2013. (ENG.). 288p. (J). (gr. 3-7). pap. 6.99 *(978-1-250-02728-3(4))* Square Fish.

—Flappy & Scrappy. Yorinks, Arthur. 2010. (I Can Read Book 2 Ser.). (ENG.). 48p. (J). (gr. k-3). 16.99 *(978-0-06-205117-2(2))* HarperCollins Pubs.

—Mia - The Snow Day Ballet. Farley, Robin. 2014. (Mia Ser.). (ENG.). 24p. (J). (gr. -1-k). pap. 4.99 *(978-0-06-210015-3(7)*, HarperFestival) HarperCollins Pubs.

—Mia & the Big Sister Ballet. Farley, Robin. 2012. (My First I Can Read Ser.). (ENG.). 32p. (J). (gr. -1-3). 16.99 *(978-0-06-173308-6(3))*; pap. 3.99 *(978-0-06-173307-9(5))* HarperCollins Pubs.

—Mia & the Daisy Dance. Farley, Robin. 2012. (My First I Can Read Ser.). (ENG.). 32p. (J). (gr. -1-3). 16.99 *(978-0-06-173306-2(7))*; pap. 3.99 *(978-0-06-173305-5(9))* HarperCollins Pubs.

—Mia & the Dance for Two. Farley, Robin. 2011. (My First I Can Read Ser.). (ENG.). 32p. (J). (gr. -1-3). 16.99 *(978-0-06-173304-8(0))*; pap. 3.99 *(978-0-06-173303-1(2))* HarperCollins Pubs.

—Mia & the Girl with a Twirl. Farley, Robin. 2013. (My First I Can Read Ser.). (ENG.). 32p. (J). (gr. -1-3). 16.99 *(978-0-06-208689-1(8))*; pap. 3.99 *(978-0-06-208688-4(X))* HarperCollins Pubs.

—Mia Dances Back to School! Farley, Robin. 2013. (Mia Ser.). (ENG.). 24p. (J). (gr. -1-3). pap. 4.99 *(978-0-06-210014-6(9)*, HarperFestival) HarperCollins Pubs.

—Mia Jazzes It Up! Farley, Robin. 2013. (My First I Can Read Ser.). (ENG.). 32p. (J). (gr. -1-3). 16.99 *(978-0-06-208692-1(8))*; pap. 3.99 *(978-0-06-208691-4(X))* HarperCollins Pubs.

—Mia Sets the Stage. Farley, Robin. 2013. (My First I Can Read Ser.). (ENG.). 32p. (J). (gr. -1-3). 16.99 *(978-0-06-208686-0(3))*; pap. 3.99 *(978-0-06-208685-3(5))* HarperCollins Pubs.

—Mia's Nutcracker Ballet. Farley, Robin. 2013. (Mia Ser.). (ENG.). 32p. (J). (gr. -1-3). 9.99 *(978-0-06-223830-6(2))* HarperCollins Pubs.

—Revenge of Superstition Mountain. Broach, Elise. 2015. (Superstition Mountain Mysteries Ser.: 3). (ENG.). 320p. (J). (gr. 3-7). pap. 8.99 *(978-1-250-05686-3(1))* Square Fish.

—Time to Trick or Treat! Farley, Robin. 2012. (Mia Ser.). (ENG.). 24p. (J). (gr. -1-3). pap. 4.99 *(978-0-06-210011-5(4)*, HarperFestival) HarperCollins Pubs.

Ivanov, Olga, jt. illus. see Ivanov, Aleksey.

Ivanov, Olga, jt. illus. see Ivanov, Alexsey.

Iversen, Portia. The Magic Nutcracker. Hillert, Margaret. 2008. (Beginning-to-Read Bks.). 32p. (J). (gr. -1-2). lib. bdg. 19.93 *(978-1-59953-190-8(9))* Norwood Hse. Pr.

Iverson, Diane. The DesertAlphabet Encyclopedia. Allred, Sylvester. 2006. 50p. (YA). pap. 7.95 *(978-0-88045-168-0(8)*, NaturEncyclopedia) Stemmer Hse. Pubs.

I

—The ForestAlphabet: Encyclopedia. Allred, Sylvester. unabr. ed. 2005. (Naturencyclopedia Ser.). 48p. (J). (gr. k-3). pap. 24.95 *(978-0-88045-155-0(6))* Stemmer Hse. Pubs.

—The Freshwater Alphabet. Allred, Sylvester. 2009. 48p. (J). (gr. 4-7). pap. 8.95 *(978-0-916144-48-7(8))* Stemmer Hse. Pubs.

—Rascal, the Tassel-Eared Squirrel. Allred, Sylvester. 2007. (ENG.). 64p. 16.95 *(978-0-938216-88-9(0))* Grand Canyon Assn.

—We Like to Help Cook: Nos Gusta Ayudar a Cocinar. Allsop, Marcus. 2007. 32p. (J). (gr. -1-1). pap. 9.95 *(978-1-890772-70-3(4))* Hohm Pr.

—We Like to Help Cook: Nos Gusta Ayudar a Cocinar. Allsop, Marcus. (We Like To Ser.). 32p. 2011. (SPA & ENG.). pap. 9.95 *(978-1-935826-00-2(X))*; 2011th alt. ed. 2012. (ENG.). pap. 9.95 *(978-1-935826-05-7(0))* Kalindi Pr.

Iverson, Diane. Nos Gusta Ayudar a Cocinar: We Like to Help Cook. Iverson, Diane. Allsop, Marcus. 2009. (SPA & ENG.). (J). pap. *(978-1-890772-97-0(6))* Hohm Pr.

—Nos Gusta Movernos: El Ejercicio Es Divertido = We Like to Move: Exercise Is Fun. Iverson, Diane. April, Elyse & Ryan, Regina Sara. 2009. (SPA & ENG.). (J). pap. *(978-1-890772-95-6(X))* Hohm Pr.

Ives, Penny. Five Little Ducks. (Classic Books with Holes 8x8 Ser.). (ENG.). 16p. (J). 2005. pap. *(978-0-85953-447-5(2))*; 2004. bds. *(978-0-85953-204-4(6))* Child's Play International Ltd.

—I'll Always Love You. Lewis, Paeony. (J). 2013. pap. ***(978-1-58925-441-1(4))***; 2008. 12p. (gr. -1-3). bds. 7.95 *(978-1-58925-833-4(9))*; 2004. 32p. pap. 5.95 *(978-1-58925-360-5(4))* Tiger Tales.

Ives, Penny. Rabbit Pie. Ives, Penny. 2012. (Child's Play Library). (ENG.). 22p. (J). bds. *(978-1-84643-513-3(7))* Child's Play International Ltd.

Ives, Sarah Noble. Mother Stories. Lindsay, Maud. 2008. 160p. pap. 9.95 *(978-1-59915-167-0(7))* Yesterday's Classics.

Ivie, Emily & Parker, Buzz. The Battle of the Bands. Reger, Rob & Huehner, Mariah. Gibbons, Jim, ed. 2014. (Emily & the Strangers Ser.: Vol. 1). (ENG.). 80p. (gr. 5). 12.99 *(978-1-61655-323-4(5))* Dark Horse Comics.

Ivy, Elena T. Learn About... Texas Birds. Lockwood, Mark W. 2007. (ENG.). 52p. (J). (gr. 1-7). pap. 10.95 *(978-0-292-71685-8(0))* Univ. of Texas Pr.

—Texas Indians. Zappler, Georg. 2007. (ENG.). 48p. (J). (gr. 1-7). pap. 10.95 *(978-0-292-71684-1(2))* Univ. of Texas Pr.

Iwai, Melissa. B Is for Bulldozer: A Construction ABC. Sobel, June. 2006. 28p. (gr. -1-k). 17.00 *(978-0-7569-7037-6(7))* Perfection Learning Corp.

—B Is for Bulldozer: A Construction ABC. Sobel, June. 2006. (ENG.). 32p. (J). (gr. -1-3). pap. 6.99 *(978-0-15-205774-9(9))* Houghton Mifflin Harcourt Publishing Co.

—Before We Eat: A Thank You Prayer. Jules, Jacqueline. 2010. (ENG.). 12p. (J). (gr. -1-1). bds. 5.95 *(978-0-7613-3954-0(X),* Kar-Ben Publishing) Lerner Publishing Group.

—Bim & Bom: A Shabbat Tale. Swartz, Daniel J. rev. ed. 2011. (Shabbat Ser.). (ENG.). 24p. (J). (gr. -1-1). pap. 8.95 *(978-0-7613-6717-8(9),* Kar-Ben Publishing) Lerner Publishing Group.

—Chanukah Lights Everywhere. Rosen, Michael J. 2006. (ENG.). 32p. (J). (gr. -1-3). pap. 7.00 *(978-0-15-205675-9(0))* Houghton Mifflin Harcourt Publishing Co.

—Corn Aplenty. Rau, Dana Meachen. 2009. (Step into Reading Ser.). (ENG.). 32p. (J). (gr. -1-1). 3.99 *(978-0-375-85575-7(0))* Random Hse. Children's Bks.

—Eight Chanukah Lights. Auerbach, Annie. 2005. (ENG.). 18p. (J). 10.95 *(978-1-58117-326-0(1),* Intervisual/Piggy Toes) Bendon, Inc.

—Hush, Little Monster. Markell, Denis. 2012. (ENG.). 32p. (J). (gr. -1-1). 9.99 *(978-1-4424-4195-8(X),* Little Simon) Little Simon.

Iwai, Melissa. Just Because I Am: A Child's Book of Affirmation. Payne, Lauren Murphy. 2nd rev. ed. 2015. (ENG.). 36p. (J). (gr. -1-2). 14.99 ***(978-1-63198-051-0(3))*** Free Spirit Publishing, Inc.

Iwai, Melissa. One Is Enough. Cook, Julie Kidd. 2005. (Rookie Reader Skill Set Ser.). (ENG.). 24p. (J). (gr. 1-2). per. 4.95 *(978-0-516-25283-4(6),* Children's Pr.) Scholastic Library Publishing.

Iwai, Melissa. We Can Get Along: A Child's Book of Choices. Payne, Lauren Murphy. 2nd rev. ed. 2015. (ENG.). 40p. (Orig.). (J). (gr. -1-2). pap. 9.99 ***(978-1-63198-027-5(0))*** Free Spirit Publishing, Inc.

Iwai, Melissa. B Is for Bulldozer: A Construction ABC. Iwai, Melissa. Sobel, June. 2013. (ENG.). 32p. (J). (— 1). bds. 7.99 *(978-0-544-10808-0(6))* Houghton Mifflin Harcourt Publishing Co.

—Soup Day. Iwai, Melissa. 2010. (ENG.). 32p. (J). (gr. -1-k). 14.99 *(978-0-8050-9004-8(5),* Holt, Henry & Co. Bks. For Young Readers) Holt, Henry & Co.

Iwamuara, Kazuo. Hooray for Fall! Iwamuara, Kazuo. 2009. (ENG.). 32p. (J). (gr. -1-3). 16.95 *(978-0-7358-2252-8(2))* North-South Bks., Inc.

Iwamura, Kazuo. Hooray for Snow! Iwamura, Kazuo. 2009. (ENG.). 24p. (J). (gr. -1-3). 16.95 *(978-0-7358-2219-1(0))* North-South Bks., Inc.

—Hooray for Spring! Iwamura, Kazuo. 2009. (ENG.). 32p. (J). (gr. -1-3). 16.95 *(978-0-7358-2228-3(X))* North-South Bks., Inc.

Iwanaga, Kent. The Girl & Her Cat. Squadrito, Vanessa. 2011. 24p. 12.56 *(978-1-4269-5531-0(6))* Trafford Publishing.

Iwasaki, Glen. Nikkei Donburi: A Japanese American Cultural Survival Guide. Aihara, Chris. 2004. 124p. (J). (gr. 1-4). pap. 18.95 *(978-1-879965-18-6(8))* Polychrome Publishing Corp.

Iwasaki, Masakazu. Popo Can, Vol. 3. Iwasaki, Masakazu. 2005. (Po Po Tan Ser.: Vol. 3). 208p. (YA). per. 9.95 *(978-1-59697-113-4(4))* Infinity Studios LLC.

Iyengar, Malathi. Dance & Devotion: A Hand Book on 'Bharatanatyam' Dance & Traditional Prayers for Students Pursuing Indian Classical Dance. Iyengar, Malathi, compiled by. 2004. (SAN, ENG & HIN.). 184p. 20.00 *(978-0-9753912-0-4(8))* Iyengar, Malathi.

Iyengar, Uma. The Shoshan. Iyengar, Uma. 2005. (ESP.). 228p. (YA). *(978-0-9771184-0-3(1))* Infobus, Inc.

Izenwata, Chinwendu. Why, Oh Why, Why Must I Be So Shy!?!, 1 vol. Ajiri, Ijeoma. 2010. 16p. 24.95 *(978-1-4512-0928-0(2))* PublishAmerica, Inc.

Izu, Kenro, photos by. Passage to Angkor. 2nd ed. 2006. 144p. (YA). 59.95 *(978-0-9653574-7-0(3))* Friends Without a Border.

Izumi, Kaneyoshi. Doubt!, Vol. 1. Izumi, Kaneyoshi. 2005. (Doubt Ser.). (ENG.). 192p. (YA). pap. 9.99 *(978-1-59116-908-6(9))* Viz Media.

—Doubt!!, Vol. 2. Izumi, Kaneyoshi. 2005. (Doubt Ser.). (ENG.). 184p. (YA). pap. 9.99 *(978-1-59116-909-3(7))* Viz Media.

—Doubt!!TM. Izumi, Kaneyoshi. Kokubo, Naomi, tr. 2005. (Doubt Ser.: Vol. 3). (ENG.). 200p. (YA). pap. 9.99 *(978-1-59116-910-9(0))* Viz Media.

—Seiho Boys' High School!, Vol. 3. Izumi, Kaneyoshi. 2010. (Seiho Boys' High School! Ser.: 3). (ENG.). 200p. pap. 9.99 *(978-1-4215-3733-7(8))* Viz Media.

Izumi, Rei. .Hack: //Legend of the Twilight, 3 vols. Hamazaki, Tatsuya. Kokubo, Naomi, tr. from JPN. 2003. 192p. (YA). (gr. 4-12). pap. 9.99 *(978-1-59182-414-5(1))* TOKYOPOP, Inc.

—. hack //Legend of the Twilight, Volume 1: Kaplan SAT/ACT Vocabulary-Building Manga. Hamazaki, Tatsuya. 2007. (Kaplan SAT/ACT Score-Raising Manga Ser.). 192p. pap. 9.99 *(978-1-4277-5497-4(7))* Kaplan Publishing.

—. Hack//Ai Buster. 2005. 192p. pap. 7.99 *(978-1-59532-869-4(6))* TOKYOPOP, Inc.

—Legend of the Twilight Bracelet, 3 vols. Hamazaki, Tatsuya. rev. ed. 192p. Vol. 2. 2003. pap. 9.99 *(978-1-59182-415-2(X))*; Vol. 3. 2004. (YA). pap. 9.99 *(978-1-59532-369-9(4))* TOKYOPOP, Inc.

J

Jabar, Cynthia. Hello, My New Baby... With Love from Your Big Brother or Big Sister. Kimmelman, Leslie. 2012. (ENG.). 48p. (J). (gr. k-12). 9.99 *(978-1-60905-266-9(8))* Blue Apple Bks.

—One Frog Sang. Parenteau, Shirley. 2007. (ENG.). 32p. (J). (gr. -1-2). 15.99 *(978-0-7636-2394-4(6))* Candlewick Pr.

—The Scrubbly-Bubbly Car Wash. O'Garden, Irene. 2003. (ENG.). 32p. (J). (gr. -1-1). 15.99 *(978-0-694-00871-1(0))* HarperCollins Pubs.

—Tally O'Malley. Murphy, Stuart J. 2004. (MathStart Ser.). 40p. (J). (gr. 1-18). 15.99 *(978-0-06-053162-1(2))*; (ENG.). pap. 5.99 *(978-0-06-053164-5(9))* HarperCollins Pubs.

Jacana Agency, photos by. The Wolf: Night Howler. Havard, Christian. 2006. (Animal Close-Ups Ser.). 28p. (Orig.). (J). (gr. -1-3). pap. 6.95 *(978-1-57091-630-4(6))* Charlesbridge Publishing, Inc.

Jack, Colin. Drake Makes a Splash! O'Ryan, Ray. 2014. (Galaxy Zack Ser.: 8). (ENG.). 128p. (J). (gr. k-2). pap. 4.99 *(978-1-4424-9360-5(7),* Little Simon) Little Simon.

—Eureka! Lachenmeyer, Nathaniel. 2013. (J). *(978-0-8037-3514-9(6),* Dial) Penguin Publishing Group.

—A Galactic Easter! O'Ryan, Ray. 2014. (Galaxy Zack Ser.: 7). (ENG.). 128p. (J). (gr. k-4). pap. 5.99 *(978-1-4424-9357-5(7),* Little Simon) Little Simon.

—Galaxy Zack 3-Pack: Hello, Nebulon!; Journey to Juno; the Prehistoric Planet. O'Ryan, Ray. 2014. (Galaxy Zack Ser.). (ENG.). 384p. (J). (gr. k-4). pap. 14.97 *(978-1-4814-2844-6(6),* Little Simon) Little Simon.

—A Green Christmas! O'Ryan, Ray. 2013. (Galaxy Zack Ser.: 6). (ENG.). 128p. (J). (gr. k-2). 16.99 *(978-1-4424-8225-8(7))*; pap. 4.99 *(978-1-4424-8224-1(9))* Little Simon. (Little Simon).

—Hello, Nebulon! O'Ryan, Ray. 2013. (Galaxy Zack Ser.: 1). (ENG.). 128p. (J). (gr. k-2). 15.99 *(978-1-4424-5387-6(7))*; pap. 5.99 *(978-1-4424-5386-9(9))* Little Simon. (Little Simon).

—If You Happen to Have a Dinosaur. Bailey, Linda. 2014. (ENG.). 40p. (J). (gr. -1-2). 17.99 *(978-1-77049-568-5(1))* Tundra Bks. CAN. Dist: Penguin Random Hse., LLC.

Jack, Colin. Jack & Jill Flip-Side Rhymes. Harbo, Christopher L. 2015. (Flip-Side Nursery Rhymes Ser.). (ENG.). 24p. (gr. -1-2). lib. bdg. 26.65 ***(978-1-4795-5988-6(1))*** Picture Window Bks.

Jack, Colin. Journey to Juno. O'Ryan, Ray. 2013. (Galaxy Zack Ser.: 2). (ENG.). 128p. (J). (gr. k-4). 16.99 *(978-1-4424-5391-3(5))*; pap. 5.99 *(978-1-4424-5390-6(7))* Little Simon. (Little Simon).

Jack, Colin. Little Miss Muffet Flip-Side Rhymes. Harbo, Christopher L. 2015. (Flip-Side Nursery Rhymes Ser.). (ENG.). 24p. (gr. -1-2). lib. bdg. 26.65 ***(978-1-4795-5987-9(3))*** Picture Window Bks.

Jack, Colin. Monsters in Space! O'Ryan, Ray. 2013. (Galaxy Zack Ser.: 4). (ENG.). 128p. (J). (gr. k-2). 15.99 *(978-1-4424-6721-7(5))*; pap. 5.99 *(978-1-4424-6718-7(5))* Little Simon. (Little Simon).

—The Prehistoric Planet. O'Ryan, Ray. 2013. (Galaxy Zack Ser.: 3). (ENG.). 128p. (J). (gr. k-2). pap. 5.99 *(978-1-4424-6715-6(0))*; 16.99 *(978-1-4424-6716-3(9))* Little Simon. (Little Simon).

—Three's a Crowd! O'Ryan, Ray. 2013. (Galaxy Zack Ser.: 5). (ENG.). 128p. (J). (gr. k-2). 15.99 *(978-1-4424-8222-7(2))*; pap. 5.99 *(978-1-4424-8221-0(4))* Little Simon. (Little Simon).

—Toads on Toast. Bailey, Linda. 2012. (ENG.). 32p. (J). 16.95 *(978-1-55453-662-7(6))* Kids Can Pr., Ltd. CAN. Dist: Univ. of Toronto Pr.

Jack, Colin. Unlike Other Monsters. Vernick, Audrey. 2016. (J). ***(978-1-4231-9959-5(6))*** Disney Pr.

Jack, Colin. 1 Zany Zoo. Degman, Lori. 2010. (ENG.). 32p. (J). (gr. -1-2). 15.99 *(978-1-4169-8990-5(0),* Simon & Schuster Bks. For Young Readers) Simon & Schuster Bks. For Young Readers.

Jack, Colin & Chatzikonstantinou, Danny. Flip-Side Nursery Rhymes. Harbo, Christopher. 2015. (Flip-Side Nursery Rhymes Ser.). (ENG.). 24p. (gr. -1-2). lib. bdg. 106.60 ***(978-1-4795-6022-6(7))*** Picture Window Bks.

Jack, Tickle. Very Greedy Bee. Steve, Smallman. 2010. 32p. pap. 7.95 *(978-1-58925-422-0(8))* Tiger Tales.

Jackowski, Amelie. The Bad Mood! Petz, Moritz. 2006. (ENG.). 32p. (J). pap. 6.95 *(978-0-7358-2035-7(X))* North-South Bks., Inc.

Jackowski, Amélie. The Bad Mood! Petz, Moritz. 2008. (ENG.). 24p. (J). (gr. -1-k). bds. 7.95 *(978-0-7358-2212-2(3))* North-South Bks., Inc.

—The Day Everything Went Wrong. Petz, Moritz. 2015. (ENG.). 32p. (J). 17.95 *(978-0-7358-4209-0(4))* North-South Bks., Inc.

Jackson, Anthony B. Oliver Vance Pull up Your Pants! McBride, Maurice & Wallace, Jessica K. 2011. 32p. (J). 13.95 *(978-1-935802-06-8(2))* Father & Son Publishing.

Jackson, April Eley & DeShazo, Sharon B. Carpentry & Woodworking Tools of Hope Plantation. Jones, Alice Eley. 2004. 100p. (YA). (gr. 4-18). pap. 20.00 *(978-0-9727480-4-9(0))* Minnie Troy Pubs.

Jackson, Barry. John Henry. Kessler, Brad. 2005. (Rabbit Ears-A Classic Tale Ser.). 36p. (J). (gr. k-5). 25.65 *(978-1-59197-764-3(9))* Spotlight.

Jackson, Barry E. Danny Diamondback. Jackson, Barry E. 2008. 40p. (J). (gr. k-2). lib. bdg. 17.89 *(978-0-06-113185-1(7))* HarperCollins Pubs.

Jackson, Brittany Janay. Tim the Cat. Hansen, Roland. 2008. (ARA.). 28p. per. 8.85 *(978-0-9814650-0-5(5))* G Publishing LLC.

Jackson-Carter, Stuart. Lifesize: Ocean. Ganeri, Anita. 2014. (ENG.). 32p. (J). (gr. k-4). 16.99 *(978-0-7534-7096-1(9),* Kingfisher) Roaring Brook Pr.

—Lifesize: Rainforest: See Rainforest Creatures at Their Actual Size. Ganeri, Anita. 2014. (Lifesize Ser.). (ENG.). 32p. (J). (gr. k-5). 16.99 *(978-0-7534-7190-6(6),* Kingfisher) Roaring Brook Pr.

Jackson, Helen. Ben & the Big Balloon. Graves, Sue. 2008. (Tadpoles Ser.). (ENG.). 24p. (J). (gr. -1-3). lib. bdg. *(978-0-7787-3860-2(4))* Crabtree Publishing Co.

Jackson, Helston & Anderson, Betheny. Pepere's Little Girl. Jackson, Penny. 2008. 27p. pap. 24.95 *(978-1-60441-881-1(8))* America Star Bks.

Jackson, Ian. Baby Animals. Parker, Steve. 2010. (I Love Animals Ser.). (ENG.). 24p. (J). (gr. 1-5). pap. 8.15 *(978-1-61533-231-1(6))*; lib. bdg. 22.60 *(978-1-61533-225-0(1))* Windmill Bks.

—Big Bug Search. Young, Caroline. rev. ed. 2005. 32p. (J). pap. 7.99 *(978-0-7945-1045-9(0),* Usborne) EDC Publishing.

—Big Cats. Parker, Steve. 2010. (I Love Animals Ser.). (ENG.). 24p. (J). (gr. 1-5). pap. 8.15 *(978-1-61533-251-9(0))*; lib. bdg. 22.60 *(978-1-61533-245-8(6))* Windmill Bks.

—The Great Animal Search. Young, Caroline. 2006. (Great Searches New Format Ser.). 48p. (J). (gr. 3). lib. bdg. 15.99 *(978-1-58086-965-2(3))*; (gr. -1-3). pap. 8.99 *(978-0-7945-1028-2(0),* Usborne) EDC Publishing.

—Great Planet Earth Search. Helbrough, Emma. Milbourne, Anna, ed. 2005. (Great Searches Ser.). 32p. (J). (gr. 3). lib. bdg. 15.95 *(978-1-58086-827-3(4))* EDC Publishing.

—Great Planet Earth Search. Helbrough, Emma. 2006. 32p. (J). *(978-0-439-83402-5(3))* Scholastic, Inc.

—Great Prehistoric Search. Bingham, Jane. 2004. (Great Searches Ser.). 32p. (J). pap. 8.95 *(978-0-7945-0663-6(1),* Usborne) EDC Publishing.

—Great Wildlife Search: Big Bug Search, Great Animal Search & Great Undersea Search. Young, Caroline & Needham, Kate. 2004. (Great Searches Ser.). 112p. (J). pap. 15.99 *(978-0-7945-0892-0(8),* Usborne) EDC Publishing.

—Greeks. Peach, Susan & Millard, Anne. 2004. (Illustrated World History Ser.). 96p. (J). (gr. 6). lib. bdg. 20.95 *(978-1-58086-631-6(X),* Usborne) EDC Publishing.

—Horses. Regan, Lisa. 2010. (I Love Animals Ser.). (ENG.). 24p. (J). (gr. 1-5). pap. 8.15 *(978-1-61533-234-2(0))*; lib. bdg. 22.60 *(978-1-61533-228-1(6))* Windmill Bks.

—Usborne the Great Undersea Search. Needham, Kate. Brooks, Felicity, ed. rev. ed. 2006. (Great Searches Ser.). 32p. (J). (gr. -1-3). per. 7.99 *(978-0-7945-1228-6(3),* Usborne) EDC Publishing.

—The Young Naturalist. Mitchell, Andrew. Jacquemier, Sue & Bramwell, Martyn, eds. 2008. (Hobby Guides Ser.). 32p. (J). (gr. 5-9). pap. 6.99 *(978-0-7945-2219-3(X),* Usborne) EDC Publishing.

—10 Things You Should Know about Big Cats. Parker, Steve. Borton, Paula, ed. 2004. (Things You Should Know about Ser.). 24p. (J). 6.99 *(978-1-84236-119-1(8))* Miles Kelly Publishing, Ltd. GBR. Dist: Independent Pubs. Group.

—50 Horses & Ponies to Spot. Kahn, Sarah, ed. 2009. (Spotter's Cards Ser.). 52p. (J). 9.99 *(978-0-7945-2171-4(1),* Usborne) EDC Publishing.

Jackson, Ian & Suttie, Alan. Rocks & Fossils. Bramwell, Martyn. Bramwell, Martyn, ed. rev. ed. 2007. (Hobby Guides). 31p. (J). pap. 6.99 *(978-0-7945-1526-3(6),* Usborne) EDC Publishing.

Jackson, Ian & Wood, Gerald. Romans. Marks, Anthony & Tingay, Graham. 2005. (Illustrated World History Ser.). 96p. (J). (gr. 6-12). lib. bdg. 20.95 *(978-1-58086-782-5(0),* Usborne) EDC Publishing.

Jackson, Ian, jt. illus. see McGregor, Malcolm.

Jackson, Ian, jt. illus. see Montgomery, Lee.

Jackson, Jack. New Texas History Movies. Jackson, Jack. Magruder, Jana. 2007. (ENG.). 66p. pap. 19.95 *(978-0-87611-231-1(9))* Texas State Historical Assn.

Jackson, James. Dancing with David. Date not set. 24p. (J). *(978-1-887399-02-9(X))* Colbert Hse., LLC, The.

Jackson, Jeannie. Squizzy the Black Squirrel: A Fabulous Fable of Friendship. Jackson, Jeannie, tr. Stone, Chuck. 2003. 30p. (J). 16.95 *(978-0-940880-71-9(7))* Open Hand Publishing, LLC.

Jackson, Jeff. Me & My Feelings: What Emotions Are & How We Can Manage Them. Guarino, Robert. 2010. 168p. (YA). (gr. 7-18). pap. 15.99 *(978-1-933779-71-3(3),* Hoopoe Bks.) I S H K.

—The Silly Chicken. Shah, Idries. 2005. 32p. (J). pap., pap. 6.99 *(978-1-883536-50-3(2),* Hoopoe Bks.) I S H K.

—The Silly Chicken/el Pollo Bobo. Shah, Idries. Wirkala, Rita, tr. 2005. 32p. (J). (gr. -1-3). 18.00 *(978-1-883536-37-4(5),* Hoopoe Bks.) I S H K.

—What's the Catch: How to Avoid Getting Hooked & Manipulated. Sobel, David S. 2010. 144p. (YA). (gr. 7-18). pap. 15.99 *(978-1-933779-78-2(0),* Hoopoe Bks.) I S H K.

Jackson, Katy. Little Sam, 1 vol. Dale, Jay. 2012. (Wonder Words Ser.). (ENG.). 32p. (gr. k-2). pap. 5.99 *(978-1-4296-8900-7(5),* Engage Literacy) Capstone Pr., Inc.

—Pretty Fashions: Beautiful Fashions to Color! 2014. (ENG.). 96p. (J). (gr. -1-2). 7.99 *(978-1-4424-8386-6(5),* Little Simon) Little Simon.

—Shopping for Socks, 1 vol. Dale, Jay. 2012. (Engage Literacy Red Ser.). (ENG.). 32p. (gr. k-2). pap. 5.99 *(978-1-4296-8942-7(0),* Engage Literacy) Capstone Pr., Inc.

—Where Is Molly's Teddy?, 1 vol. Dale, Jay. 2012. (Wonder Words Ser.). (ENG.). 32p. (gr. k-2). pap. 5.99 *(978-1-4296-8914-4(5),* Engage Literacy) Capstone Pr., Inc.

Jackson, Kay. Shag Finds a Home. Whisler, Barbara. 2008. 24p. pap. 24.95 *(978-1-60703-730-9(0))* America Star Bks.

Jackson, Kay Whytock. Adventures with Mama Scottie & the Kids. Scott, Elizabeth M. 2008. 60p. pap. 8.95 *(978-0-595-51760-2(9))* iUniverse, Inc.

Jackson, Lance. Twice Just to Be Sure: A Musicky Tale for Imaginative People. Pea, Uncle & Pomerantz, Joel. 2011. (ENG.). 48p. pap. 18.95 *(978-1-4636-4971-5(1))* CreateSpace Independent Publishing Platform.

Jackson, Lisa. Best-Loved Irish Legends: Mini Edition. Massey, Eithne. 2012. (ENG.). 64p. (J). 8.95 *(978-1-84717-237-2(7))* O'Brien Pr., Ltd., The IRL. Dist: Dufour Editions, Inc.

Jackson, Lisa, jt. illus. see Ryan, Nellie.

Jackson, Mark. Bilby: Secrets of an Australian Marsupial. Wignell, Edel. 2015. (ENG.). 32p. (J). (gr. k-4). 16.99 *(978-0-7636-6759-7(5))* Candlewick Pr.

—Python. Cheng, Christopher. 2013. (ENG.). 32p. (J). (gr. k-3). 15.99 *(978-0-7636-6396-4(4))* Candlewick Pr.

Jackson, Mike. The Big Magic Show! (Bubble Guppies) Nagaraj, Josephine. 2015. (Step into Reading Ser.). (ENG.). 24p. (J). (gr. -1-1). 4.99 *(978-0-385-38457-5(2),* Random Hse. Bks. for Young Readers) Random Hse. Children's Bks.

—Big Truck Show! Random House Staff. 2013. (Step into Reading Ser.). (ENG.). 32p. (J). (gr. -1-1). 3.99 *(978-0-449-81896-1(9))*; lib. bdg. 12.99 *(978-0-449-81897-8(7))* Random Hse. Children's Bks. (Random Hse. Bks. for Young Readers).

—Dinosaur Dig! (Bubble Guppies) Golden Books. 2013. (Paint Box Book Ser.). (ENG.). 48p. (J). (gr. -1-2). pap. 3.99 *(978-0-307-98166-0(5),* Golden Bks.) Random Hse. Children's Bks.

—A Fairytale Adventure (Dora the Explorer) Tillworth, Mary. 2014. (Pictureback Series.). (ENG.). 24p. (J). (gr. -1-2). 3.99 *(978-0-385-37443-9(7),* Random Hse. Bks. for Young Readers) Random Hse. Children's Bks.

—Happy Holidays, Bubble Guppies! (Bubble Guppies) Tillworth, Mary. 2013. (Pictureback with Flaps Ser.). (ENG.). 16p. (J). (gr. -1-2). 4.99 *(978-0-449-81779-7(2),* Random Hse. Bks. for Young Readers) Random Hse. Children's Bks.

Jackson, Mike. Ice Team (Paw Patrol) Random House. 2015. (Glitter Picturebook Ser.). (ENG.). 16p. (J). (gr. -1-1). 5.99 ***(978-0-553-52281-5(7),*** Random Hse. Bks. for Young Readers) Random Hse. Children's Bks.

Jackson, Mike. Let's Find Adventure! (Paw Patrol) Random House. 2015. (Nifty Lift-And-Look Ser.). (ENG.). 12p. (J). (-k). bds. 5.99 *(978-0-553-51027-0(4),* Random Hse. Bks. for Young Readers) Random Hse. Children's Bks.

—On the Farm (Bubble Guppies) Golden Books. 2012. (Super Color with Stickers Ser.). (ENG.). 96p. (J). (gr. -1-2). pap. 3.99 *(978-0-307-93096-5(3),* Golden Bks.) Random Hse. Children's Bks.

—Pit Crew Pups. Depken, Kristen L. 2015. (Step into Reading Ser.). (ENG.). 24p. (J). (gr. -1-1). 4.99 *(978-0-553-50853-6(9),* Random Hse. Bks. for Young Readers) Random Hse. Children's Bks.

Jackson, Mike. Rubble to the Rescue! (Paw Patrol) Depken, Kristen L. 2015. (Step into Reading Ser.). (ENG.). 24p. (J). (gr. -1-1). 4.99 ***(978-0-553-52290-7(6),*** Random Hse. Bks. for Young Readers) Random Hse. Children's Bks.

Jackson, Mike. We Totally Rock! (Bubble Guppies) Golden Books. 2012. (Hologramatic Sticker Book Ser.). (ENG.). 48p. (J). (gr. -1-2). pap. 3.99 *(978-0-307-93095-8(5),* Golden Bks.) Random Hse. Children's Bks.

Jackson, Mike, jt. illus. see Golden Books Staff.

Jackson, Mike, jt. illus. see Random House Staff.

Jackson, Shelley. The Chicken-Chasing Queen of Lamar County. Harrington, Janice N. 2007. (ENG.). 40p. (J). (gr. -1-3). 17.99 *(978-0-374-31251-0(6),* Farrar, Straus & Giroux (BYR)) Farrar, Straus & Giroux.

Jackson, Shelley & Crosby, Jeff. Ten Texas Babies, 1 vol. Davis, David. 2014. (ENG.). 32p. (J). (gr. k-3). 16.99 *(978-1-4556-1874-3(8))* Pelican Publishing Co., Inc.

Jackson, Shelley Ann & Crosby, Jeff. Harness Horses, Bucking Broncos & Pit Ponies: A History of Horse Breeds. Jackson, Shelley Ann & Crosby, Jeff. 2011. (ENG.). 72p. (J). (gr. k-12). 19.95 *(978-0-88776-986-3(1))* Tundra Bks. CAN. Dist: Random Hse., Inc.

Jackson, Shelley Ann, jt. illus. see Crosby, Jeff.

Jackson, Vicky. Poepal's Purpose. l.t. ed. 2005. 20p. (J). 7.95 *(978-0-9718741-0-7(7))* Tawa Productions.

Jacob, Murv. The Boy Who Lived with the Bears: And Other Iroquois Stories. Bruchac, Joseph. 2003. (Storytime Ser.). 63p. (J). (gr. k-5). pap. 11.95 *(978-0-930407-61-2(X))* Parabola Bks.

—How Medicine Came to the People: A Tale of the Ancient Cherokees. Duvall, Deborah L. (Grandmother Stories Ser.). (ENG.). 32p. (J). 2012. pap. 18.95 *(978-0-8263-3008-6(8))*; 2003. 16.95 *(978-0-8263-3007-9(X))* Univ. of New Mexico Pr.

—How Rabbit Lost His Tail: A Traditional Cherokee Legend. Duvall, Deborah L. 2003. (Grandmother Stories Ser.: Vol. 3). (ENG.). 32p. (J). 16.95 *(978-0-8263-3010-9(X))* Univ. of New Mexico Pr.

—How Rabbit Tricked Otter: And Other Cherokee Trickster Stories. Ross, Gayle. 2003. (Storytime Ser.). 78p. (J). (gr. k-6). per. 12.95 *(978-0-930407-60-5(1))* Parabola Bks.

—Rabbit & the Fingerbone Necklace. Duvall, Deborah L. 2009. (ENG.). 32p. (J). (gr. 1). 19.95 *(978-0-8263-4723-7(1))* Univ. of New Mexico Pr.

—Rabbit & the Wolves. Duvall, Deborah L. 2005. (Grandmother Stories Ser.). (ENG.). 32p. (J). (gr. 3-7). 16.95 *(978-0-8263-3563-0(2))* Univ. of New Mexico Pr.

—Rabbit Goes Duck Hunting: A Traditional Cherokee Legend. Duvall, Deborah L. 2004. (Grandmother Stories, 5 Ser.). (ENG.). 32p. (J). 16.95 *(978-0-8263-3336-0(2))* Univ. of New Mexico Pr.

—Rabbit Goes to Kansas. Duvall, Deborah L. 2007. (ENG.). 32p. (J). (gr. 1-18). 16.95 *(978-0-8263-4181-5(0))* Univ. of New Mexico Pr.

—Rabbit Plants the Forest. Duvall, Deborah L. 2006. (ENG.). 32p. (J). (gr. 3-7). 18.95 *(978-0-8263-3691-0(4))* Univ. of New Mexico Pr.

Jacob, Sona &. Grandma Birdie's Red String. Dekel, Amir. 2010. (ENG.). 26p. pap. 12.95 *(978-1-4499-6417-7(6))* CreateSpace Independent Publishing Platform.

Jacobs, D. K. Jinja of the Munjyburr. Thomas, Kerrie Annette. 2011. 34p. pap. 13.50 *(978-1-61204-421-7(2))*, Eloquent Bks.) Strategic Book Publishing & Rights Agency (SBPRA).

Jacobs, Joyce M. Moxie. Connelly, Claire K. 2010. 84p. pap. 10.49 *(978-1-4520-7634-8(0))* AuthorHouse.

Jacobs, Nadine. Un Bebe Caido del Cielo. Jacobs, Nadine. Hellings, Collete. 2003. (SPA.). 32p. (J). (gr. k-1). 16.95 *(978-84-95150-10-3(7)*, COR4033) Corimbo, Editorial S.L. ESP. Dist: Distribooks, Inc.

—Zefir, la Cebrita en Peligro. Jacobs, Nadine. Vicens, Paula, tr. 2004. (SPA.). 32p. (J). 15.99 *(978-84-8470-108-8(5))* Corimbo, Editorial S.L. ESP. Dist: Lectorum Pubns., Inc.

Jacobs, Parker. Goon Holler: Goon Fishin' Jacobs, Christian. 2015. (ENG.). 48p. (J). (gr. 1-4). 15.00 ***(978-0-316-40552-2(3))*** Little, Brown Bks. for Young Readers.

Jacobs, Parker. Super Gabba Friends! 2013. (Yo Gabba Gabba! Ser.). (ENG.). 24p. (J). (gr. -1-k). pap. 3.99 *(978-1-4424-6184-0(5)*, Simon Spotlight) Simon Spotlight.

—Welcome to Goon Holler. Jacobs, Christian. 2014. (ENG.). 48p. (J). (gr. -1-3). 15.00 *(978-0-316-40550-8(7))* Little, Brown Bks. for Young Readers.

Jacobsen, Amie. Spenser Goes to el Paso. Brooks, Melanie & Spenser and Mom Staff. 2010. (SpenserNation Ser.). 32p. (J). 14.95 *(978-0-9817598-3-8(1))* Simple Fish Bk. Co., LLC.

—Spenser Goes to Portland. Spenser & Mom. 2008. 32p. 14.95 *(978-0-9817598-0-7(7))* Simple Fish Bk. Co., LLC.

—Spenser Via a el Paso. Spenser & Brooks, Melanie. 2010. (SpenserNation Ser.). (SPA.). 32p. (J). 14.95 *(978-0-9817598-5-2(8))* Simple Fish Bk. Co., LLC.

Jacobsen, Laura. Animal Mischief. Jackson, Rob. 2006. (ENG.). 32p. (J). (gr. k-7). 15.95 *(978-1-59078-254-5(2)*, Wordsong) Boyds Mills Pr.

—The Best Eid Ever. Mobin-Uddin, Asma. 2007. (ENG.). 32p. (J). (gr. 2-4). 16.95 *(978-1-59078-431-0(6))* Boyds Mills Pr.

—The Boy & the North Wind: A Tale from Norway. 2013. (Tales of Honor Ser.). (ENG.). 32p. (J). (gr. 1-4). pap. 8.95 *(978-1-937529-56-7(8))* Red Chair Pr.

Jacobsen, Laura. Exploring the West: Tales of Courage on the Lewis & Clark Expedition. Mead, Maggie. 2015. (Setting the Stage for Fluency Ser.). (ENG.). 40p. (gr. 3-5). lib. bdg. 27.93 ***(978-1-939656-65-0(6))*** Red Chair Pr.

Jacobsen, Laura. My Muslim Friend: A Young Catholic Learns about Islam. Kemmetmueller, Donna Jean. 2006. 47p. (J). 15.95 *(978-0-8198-4844-4(1))* Pauline Bks. & Media.

—A Party in Ramadan. Mobin-Uddin, Asma. 2009. (ENG.). 34p. (J). (gr. 2-4). 16.95 *(978-1-59078-604-8(1))* Boyds Mills Pr.

Jacobsen, Laura. The Boy & the North Wind: A Tale from Norway. Jacobsen, Laura, retold by. 2013. (Tales of Honor (Red Chair Press) Ser.). (ENG.). 32p. (J). (gr. 1-4). lib. bdg. 26.60 *(978-1-937529-72-7(X))* Red Chair Pr.

Jacobsen, Terry. The Littlest Cowboy's Christmas, 2 vols. Chandler, Michael. 2006. (ENG.). 32p. (J). (gr. k-3). 17.95 *(978-1-58980-381-7(7))* Pelican Publishing Co., Inc.

Jacobson, David. The Big Red Blanket. Linn, Margot. 2005. (I'm Going to Read(r) Ser.: Level 1). (ENG.). 28p. (J). (gr. -1-k). pap. 3.95 *(978-1-4027-2091-8(2))* Sterling Publishing Co., Inc.

Jacobson, Jim, photos by. Pika: Life in the Rocks. Bill, Tannis. 2010. (ENG., 32p. (J). (gr. k-2). 18.95 *(978-1-59078-803-5(6))* Boyds Mills Pr.

Jacobson, Judith. El Vuelo de los Colibries. Flor Ada, Alma. 32p. (J). (gr. 3-6). pap. 9.95 *(978-1-56492-211-3(1))* Laredo Publishing Co., Inc.

Jacobson, Rick & Fernandez, Laura. The Mona Lisa Caper. Jacobson, Rick. 2005. (ENG.). 24p. (J). (gr. k-3). 15.95 *(978-0-88776-726-5(5)*, Tundra Bks.) Tundra Bks. CAN. Dist: Penguin Random Hse., LLC.

—Picasso: Soul on Fire. Jacobson, Rick. (ENG.). 32p. (J). (gr. 5-18). 2011. pap. 8.95 *(978-1-77049-263-9(1))*; 2004. 15.95 *(978-0-88776-599-5(8))* Tundra Bks. CAN. (Tundra Bks.). Dist: Penguin Random Hse., LLC.

Jacobson, Rick, jt. illus. see Fernandez, Laura.

Jacobus, Tim. The Search for Truth. Kingsley, Kaza. (Erec Rex Ser.: 3). (ENG.). 352p. (J). (gr. 5-9). 2010. pap. 9.99 *(978-1-4169-7989-0(1))*; 2009. 17.99 *(978-1-4169-7988-3(3))* Simon & Schuster Bks. For Young Readers. (Simon & Schuster Bks. For Young Readers).

Jacoby, Nickolina Dye. Little Miss Neat-As-A-Pin. Eberhard, Phyllis Lunde Brees. 2007. (J). *(978-0-9722741-7-3(0))* Publishing Factory, The.

Jacome, Mauricio. El Pais de Los Juguetes. Garcia, Edgar Allan. 2015. 24p. (J). (gr. -1-2). pap. 12.95 ***(978-9942-05-066-3(3)***, Alfaguara Infantil) Santillana Ecuador ECU. Dist: Santillana USA Publishing Co., Inc.

Jacquemain, Patti. Journey of the Great Bear: Through California's Golden Past. Jacquemain, Patti. 2006. (J). *(978-0-929702-10-0(7))* Mission Creek Studios.

Jacques, Faith. Charlie y el Gran Ascensor de Cristal. Dahl, Roald. 2003.Tr. of Charlie & the Great Glass Elevator. (SPA.). 164p. (J). (gr. 5-8). pap. 12.95 *(978-968-19-0988-8(7))* Santillana USA Publishing Co., Inc.

—Charlie y la Fabrica de Chocolate. Dahl, Roald. 2003.Tr. of Charlie & the Chocolate Factory. (FRE & SPA.). 176p. (J). (gr. 4-7). *(978-84-204-4771-1(4)*, AF0153) Ediciones Alfaguara.

Jacques Huiswood. Nandi & Masani. Mineuittie, Abike. 2011. 40p. pap. 24.95 *(978-1-4560-2700-1(X))* America Star Bks.

Jacques, Laura. Baby Owl's Rescue, 1 vol. Curtis, Jennifer Keats. 2009. (ENG.). 32p. (J). (gr. -1-3). 16.95 *(978-1-934359-95-2(5))* Arbordale Publishing.

—For the Birds: The Life of Roger Tory Peterson. Thomas, Peggy. 2011. (ENG.). 40p. (J). (gr. 3). 16.95 *(978-1-59078-764-9(1)*, Calkins Creek) Boyds Mills Pr.

—Los Más Peligrosos, 1 vol. Fields, Terri. 2012. (SPA.). 32p. (J). (gr. -1-3). 17.95 *(978-1-60718-677-9(2))* Arbordale Publishing.

Jacques, Laura. The Most Dangerous, 1 vol. Fields, Terri. 32p. (J). (gr. -1-3). 2014. (SPA.). pap. 9.95 ***(978-1-62855-424-3(X))***; 2012. (ENG.). 17.95 *(978-1-60718-526-0(1))* Arbordale Publishing.

Jacques, Laura. Squirrel Rescue, 1 vol. Curtis, Jennifer Keats. 2012. (ENG.). 32p. (J). 16.99 *(978-0-7643-4246-2(0))* Schiffer Publishing, Ltd.

—Whistling Wings, 1 vol. Goering, Laura. 2008. (ENG.). 32p. (J). (gr. -1-3). 16.95 *(978-1-934359-12-9(2))*; pap. 8.95 *(978-1-934359-30-3(0))* Arbordale Publishing.

Jae-Hwan, Kim. Dragon Hunt: World of Warcraft, Vol. 1. 2005. (Sunwell Trilogy: Vol. 1). 176p. (YA). pap. 9.99 *(978-1-59532-712-3(6))* TOKYOPOP, Inc.

—King of Hell, 13 vols. In-Soo, Ra & Ra, In-Soo. 12th rev. ed. 2006. (King of Hell Ser.: Vol. 12). 192p. (gr. 8-12). pap. 9.99 *(978-1-59816-060-4(5))* TOKYOPOP, Inc.

—King of Hell, Vol. 2. Na, In-Soo. rev. ed. 2003.Tr. of Ma-Je. 216p. (YA). (gr. 8-18). pap. 9.99 *(978-1-59182-188-5(6))* TOKYOPOP, Inc.

—King of Hell, 5 vols., Vol. 4. In-Soo, Na. rev. ed. 2004. 192p. pap. 9.99 *(978-1-59182-482-4(6))* TOKYOPOP, Inc.

—King of Hell, 8 vols., Vol. 7. Ra, In-Soo. 7th rev. ed. 2004. 200p. pap. 9.99 *(978-1-59182-867-9(8))* TOKYOPOP, Inc.

—King of Hell, 8 vols. In-Soo, Ra. rev. ed. 2005. Vol. 8. 200p. pap. 9.99 *(978-1-59182-914-0(3))*; Vol. 9. 192p. pap. 9.99 *(978-1-59532-597-6(2))* TOKYOPOP, Inc.

—King of Hell, Vol. 10. rev. ed. 2005. 192p. (YA). pap. 9.99 *(978-1-59532-598-3(0))* TOKYOPOP, Inc.

—King of Hell, Vol. 11. In-Soo, Ra. 11th rev. ed. 2005. (King of Hell Ser.). 192p. per. 9.99 *(978-1-59816-059-8(1))* TOKYOPOP, Inc.

Jae-Hwan, Na. King of Hell, 3 vols., Vol. 3. In-Soo, Na. rev. ed. 2003. 192p. (YA). pap. 9.99 *(978-1-59182-189-2(4))* TOKYOPOP, Inc.

Jaeggi, Yoshiko. I Am Tama, Lucky Cat: A Japanese Legend, 1 vol. Henrichs, Wendy. 2011. (ENG.). 32p. (J). (gr. k-4). 16.95 *(978-1-56145-589-8(X)*, Peachtree Junior) Peachtree Pubs.

—Monsoon Afternoon, 1 vol. Sheth, Kashmira. 2008. (ENG.). 32p. (J). (gr. k-3). 16.95 *(978-1-56145-455-6(9)*, Peachtree Junior) Peachtree Pubs.

—My Dadima Wears a Sari, 1 vol. Sheth, Kashmira. 2007. (ENG.). 32p. (J). (gr. k-3). 16.95 *(978-1-56145-392-4(7))* Peachtree Pubs.

—Saving the Griffin, 1 vol. Nitz, Kristin Wolden. 2007. (ENG.). 192p. (J). (gr. 3-7). 14.95 *(978-1-56145-380-1(3))* Peachtree Pubs.

Jaeggi, Yoshiko. Sona & the Wedding Game, 1 vol. Sheth, Kashmira. 2015. (ENG.). 32p. (J). (gr. 1-3). 16.95 ***(978-1-56145-735-9(3))*** Peachtree Pubs.

Jaekel, Susan. Marie Curie: Prize-Winning Scientist, 1 vol. Mortensen, Lori. 2008. (Biographies Ser.). (ENG.). 24p. (gr. k-3). lib. bdg. 25.99 *(978-1-4048-3731-7(0)*, Nonfiction Picture Bks.) Picture Window Bks.

—The Tortoise & the Hare: A Tale about Determination. 2006. (J). 6.99 *(978-1-59939-015-4(9))* Cornerstone Pr.

—A Wild Ride in Texas. Wilsdon, Christina. 2006. 26p. (J). 7.99 *(978-1-59939-011-6(6))* Cornerstone Pr.

Jaekel, Susan M. The Gift of the Magi: A Story about Giving. Henry, O. 2006. (J). *(978-1-59939-084-0(1)*, Reader's Digest Young Families, Inc.) Studio Fun International.

—Stone Soup: A Tale about Sharing. 2006. (J). *(978-1-59939-080-2(9)*, Reader's Digest Young Families, Inc.) Studio Fun International.

—Tug of War: A Tale about Being Resourceful. 2006. (J). *(978-1-59939-091-8(4)*, Reader's Digest Young Families, Inc.) Studio Fun International.

Jael, jt. illus. see Gribbon, Sean.

Jael, jt. illus. see Griffin, Georgene.

Jäger, Jan. My First Book of Knots. Jäger, Jan. Sundsten, Berndt et al. 2009. (ENG.). 48p. (J). (gr. 1-3). 12.95 *(978-1-60239-623-4(X)*, 239623) Skyhorse Publishing Co., Inc.

Jager, Korin Elizabeth. Introducing Myself. Jager, Phyllis. 2005. (J). 9.95 *(978-1-59571-080-2(9))* Word Association Pubs.

Jago. Ali Baba & the Forty Thieves. 2004. (ITA & ENG.). 31p. (J). *(978-1-84444-543-1(7))* Mantra Lingua.

—Ali Baba & the Forty Thieves. Gregory, Manju. 2004. (J). *(978-1-84444-544-8(5))* Mantra Lingua.

—An Ambush of Tigers: A Wild Gathering of Collective Nouns. Rosenthal, Betsy R. 2015. (ENG.). 32p. (J). (gr. k-3). lib. bdg. 19.99 *(978-1-4677-1464-8(X)*, Millbrook Pr.) Lerner Publishing Group.

—The Jesus Storybook Bible: Every Story Whispers His Name, 1 vol. Lloyd-Jones, Sally. (ENG.). 352p. (J). (gr. -1-3). 2007. 16.99 *(978-0-310-70825-4(7))*; 2009. 24.99 *(978-0-310-71878-9(3))* Zonderkidz.

—Little Red Hen & the Grains of Wheat. Johnson, Richard & Barkow, Henriette. 2005. 32p. (J). (KOR & ENG.). pap. *(978-1-84444-210-2(1))*; (ENG & BEN.). pap. *(978-1-84444-200-3(4))*; (ENG & CHI.). pap. *(978-1-84444-201-0(2))*; (FRE & ENG.). pap. *(978-1-84444-205-8(5))*; (ENG & HIN.). pap. *(978-1-84444-208-9(X))*; (PAN & ENG.). pap. *(978-1-84444-211-9(X))*; (ENG & POR.). pap. *(978-1-84444-212-6(8))*; (ENG & URD.). pap. *(978-1-84444-217-1(9))*; (POL & ENG.). pap. *(978-1-84444-394-9(9))*; (ENG & TGL.). pap. *(978-1-84444-395-6(7))*; (ENG & RUS.). pap. *(978-1-84444-398-7(1))* Mantra Lingua.

—Mr Aesop's Story Shop. Hartman, Bob. 2012. (ENG.). 48p. (J). (gr. 2-4). pap. 10.99 *(978-0-7459-6298-6(X))* Lion Hudson PLC GBR. Dist: Independent Pubs. Group.

—Nachshon, Who Was Afraid to Swim: A Passover Story. Cohen, Deborah Bodin. 2009. (Passover Ser.). (ENG.). 32p. (J). (gr. -1-2). pap. 8.95 *(978-0-8225-8765-1(3)*, Kar-Ben Publishing) Lerner Publishing Group.

—Thank You, God. Wigger, J. Bradley. 2014. (J). 16.00 *(978-0-8028-5424-7(9)*, Eerdmans Bks For Young Readers) Eerdmans, William B. Publishing Co.

Jago & Moxley, Sheila. Grandpa's Garden. Fry, Stella. 2012. (ENG.). 40p. (J). 16.99 *(978-1-84686-053-9(9))* Barefoot Bks., Inc.

Jagodits, Carolyn Lee. Angel of the Poor: A Story of Mother Emmelie Gamelin. Ernest, Brother. 2011. 96p. 38.95 *(978-1-258-06652-9(1))* Literary Licensing, LLC.

—Don't Push! a Story of Cesar Franck. Roberto, Brother. 2011. 94p. 38.95 *(978-1-258-07305-3(6))* Literary Licensing, LLC.

—A Dream Come True: A Story of St. Isaac Jogues. Pelous, Donald. 2011. 94p. 38.95 *(978-1-258-06266-8(6))* Literary Licensing, LLC.

—Father of the American Cavalry: A Story of Brigadier General Casimir Pulaski. Flavius, Brother. 2011. 96p. 38.95 *(978-1-258-07161-5(4))* Literary Licensing, LLC.

—Music for Millions: A Story of Ignace Paderewski. Roberto, Brother. 2011. 94p. 38.95 *(978-1-258-09336-5(7))* Literary Licensing, LLC.

Jagucki, Marek. Fins of Fury. O'Hara, Mo. 2015. (My Big Fat Zombie Goldfish Ser.: Bk. 3). (ENG.). 224p. (J). (gr. 2-5). 12.99 *(978-1-250-02921-8(X))* Feiwel & Friends.

Jagucki, Marek. Language on the Loose, 4 vols. Meister, Cari & Loewen, Nancy. 2015. (Language on the Loose Ser.). (ENG.). 24p. (gr. 2-4). 109.28 ***(978-1-4795-8021-7(X))*** Picture Window Bks.

Jagucki, Marek. My Big Fat Zombie Goldfish. O'Hara, Mo. 2014. (My Big Fat Zombie Goldfish Ser.: 1). (ENG.). 208p. (J). (gr. 2-5). pap. 6.99 *(978-1-250-05215-5(7))* Square Fish.

—The Sea-Quel. O'Hara, Mo. 2014. (My Big Fat Zombie Goldfish Ser.: 2). (ENG.). 208p. (J). (gr. 2-5). 12.99 *(978-1-250-02920-1(1))* Feiwel & Friends.

Jagucki, Marek. They're up to Something in There: Understanding There, Their, & They're. Meister, Cari. 2015. (Language on the Loose Ser.). (ENG.). 24p. (gr. 2-4). pap. 7.95 ***(978-1-4795-6971-7(2))*** Picture Window Bks.

Jagucki, Marek. When & Why Did the Horse Fly? Knowing & Using Question Words, 1 vol. Meister, Cari. 2013. (Language on the Loose Ser.). (ENG.). 24p. (gr. 2-4). lib. bdg. 27.32 *(978-1-4048-8319-2(3))* Capstone Pr., Inc.

—When & Why Did the Horse Fly? Knowing & Using Question Words, 1 vol. Meister, Cari. 2013. (Language on the Loose Ser.). (ENG.). 24p. (gr. 2-4). pap. 7.95 *(978-1-4795-1918-7(9))* Picture Window Bks.

Jahier, Milena. Thank You God for Rain, 1 vol. Hodgson, Mona. 2008. (I Can Read! / Desert Critters Ser.). (ENG.). 32p. (J). pap. 3.99 *(978-0-310-71741-6(8))* Zonderkidz.

Jahn-Clough, Lisa. Felicity & Cordelia: A Tale of Two Bunnies. Jahn-Clough, Lisa. 2011. (ENG.). 40p. (J). (gr. -1-3). 16.99 *(978-0-374-32300-4(3)*, Farrar, Straus & Giroux (BYR)) Farrar, Straus & Giroux.

Jaime, Daniel, jt. illus. see Torres, Nora Estela.

Jain, Priti. The Efelant Hunters Part One: Shipwreck! Marsh, Mike. 2013. 28p. pap. *(978-1-927506-21-9(2))* Yellow Toadstool Pr.

—The Grumblies Set a Trap. Marsh, Mike. 2012. 24p. pap. *(978-0-9878019-2-0(9))* Yellow Toadstool Pr.

—The Skyrats Capture the Grumblies! Marsh, Mike. 2012. 28p. pap. *(978-1-927506-01-1(8))* Yellow Toadstool Pr.

Jainschigg, Nicholas. Ethan of Athos. Bujold, Lois McMaster. Lewis, Suford, ed. 2003. (Vorkosigan Ser.). 23.00 *(978-1-886778-39-9(6))* New England Science Fiction Assn., Inc.

Jakesevic, Nenad. Walk Across the Sea. Fletcher, Susan. 2003. (ENG.). 224p. (J). (gr. 4-8). pap. 11.95 *(978-0-689-85707-2(1)*, Atheneum Bks. for Young Readers) Simon & Schuster Children's Publishing.

Jakobsen, Kathy. My New York. Jakobsen, Kathy. anniv. rev. ed. 2005. 54p. (J). (gr. k-4). 19.00 *(978-0-7567-8588-8(X))* DIANE Publishing Co.

—My New York. Jakobsen, Kathy. anniv. ed. 2003. (ENG.). 48p. (J). (gr. -1-1). 20.00 *(978-0-316-92711-6(2))* Little, Brown Bks. for Young Readers.

Jakobsen, Lars. The Mysterious Manuscript. Jakobsen, Lars. 2012. (Mortensen's Escapades Ser.: 1). (ENG.). 48p. (gr. 6-12). pap. 6.95 *(978-0-8225-9409-3(9))*; lib. bdg. 27.93 *(978-0-7613-7883-9(9))* Lerner Publishing Group. (Graphic Universe).

—The Red Ruby. Jakobsen, Lars. 2013. (Mortensen's Escapades Ser.: 3). (ENG.). 48p. (gr. 6-12). pap. 6.95 *(978-1-4677-0729-9(5)*, Graphic Universe) Lerner Publishing Group.

—The Red Ruby. Jakobsen, Lars. Chapman, Robyn. 2013. (Mortensen's Escapades Ser.: 3). (ENG.). 48p. (gr. 6-12). lib. bdg. 27.93 *(978-0-7613-7914-0(2)*, Graphic Universe) Lerner Publishing Group.

—The Santa Fe Jail. Jakobsen, Lars. 2012. (Mortensen's Escapades Ser.: 2). (ENG.). 48p. (gr. 6-12). pap. 6.95 *(978-0-8225-9421-5(8))*; lib. bdg. 27.93 *(978-0-7613-7886-0(3))* Lerner Publishing Group. (Graphic Universe).

—The Secret Mummy. Jakobsen, Lars. 2013. (Mortensen's Escapades Ser.: 4). (ENG.). 48p. (gr. 6-12). pap. 6.95 *(978-1-4677-0730-5(9))*; lib. bdg. 27.93 *(978-0-7613-7915-7(0))* Lerner Publishing Group. (Graphic Universe).

Jakson, Helen. Ben & the Big Balloon. Graves, Sue. 2008. (Tadpoles Ser.). (ENG.). 24p. (J). (gr. -1-3). pap. *(978-0-7787-3891-6(4))* Crabtree Publishing Co.

J.A.M.A.D. Punchkinhead, the Never-Give-Up Boy. Washburn, Patrik. 2010. (ENG.). 40p. pap. 12.00 *(978-1-4538-8151-4(4))* CreateSpace Independent Publishing Platform.

Jamaldinian, Joe. Bob Winging It. Jamaldinian, Joe. 2005. 32p. (J). 14.00 *(978-0-9766657-0-0(0))* Jamaldinian, Yousef.

Jamana, Pharida & Zaman, Farida. The Remarkable Journey of Josh's Kippah. Savedoff, Barbara E. & Elissa, Barbara. 2010. (ENG.). 24p. (J). (gr. -1-2). lib. bdg. 7.95 *(978-0-8225-9911-1(2)*, Kar-Ben Publishing) Lerner Publishing Group.

James, Ann. Audrey Goes to Town. Harris, Christine. (Audrey Ser.: 2). (ENG.). (J). (gr. 2-4). 2014. 176p. pap. 8.99 *(978-1-74297-796-6(0))*; 2009. 192p. pap. 7.99 *(978-1-921272-67-7(8))* Little Hare Bks. AUS. Dist: Independent Pubs. Group.

—Audrey of the Outback. Harris, Christine. 2015. (Audrey Ser.: 1). (ENG.). 176p. (J). (gr. 2-4). pap. 8.99 *(978-1-74297-795-9(2))* Little Hare Bks. AUS. Dist: Independent Pubs. Group.

—The Audrey of the Outback Collection. Harris, Christine. collector's ed. 2012. (Audrey Ser.). (ENG.). 522p. (J). (gr. 2-4). 19.99 *(978-1-921714-21-4(2))* Little Hare Bks. AUS. Dist: Independent Pubs. Group.

—Audrey's Big Secret. Harris, Christine. (Audrey Ser.: 3). (ENG.). (J). 2015. 176p. (gr. 2-4). pap. 8.99 *(978-1-74297-797-3(9))*; 2010. 192p. (gr. 1-5). 7.99 *(978-1-921272-53-0(8))* Little Hare Bks. AUS. Dist: Independent Pubs. Group.

—A Coat of Cats. Kroll, Jeri. 32p. pap. *(978-0-7344-0118-2(3)*, Lothian Children's Bks.) Hachette Australia.

—Go Baby Go! Rippin, Sally. 2009. (ENG.). 12p. (J). (gr. k — 1). bds. 7.99 *(978-1-74175-388-2(0))* Allen & Unwin AUS. Dist: Independent Pubs. Group.

—I'm a Dirty Dinosaur. Brian, Janeen. 2014. (ENG.). 22p. (J). 11.99 *(978-1-61067-296-2(8))* Kane Miller.

—It's a Miroocool! Harris, Christine. 2012. (ENG.). 32p. (J). (gr. -1). 22.99 *(978-1-921541-01-8(6))* Little Hare Bks. AUS. Dist: Independent Pubs. Group.

—Lucy Goosey. Wild, Margaret. 2014. (ENG.). 32p. (J). (gr. -1-k). pap. 9.99 *(978-1-74297-552-8(6))* Little Hare Bks. AUS. Dist: Independent Pubs. Group.

—Madeline the Mermaid. Fienberg, Anna. 2011. (ENG.). 80p. (J). (gr. 2-4). 10.99 *(978-1-74237-228-0(7))* Allen & Unwin AUS. Dist: Independent Pubs. Group.

—Sadie & Ratz. Hartnett, Sonya. (ENG.). 64p. (J). (gr. k-3). 2013. pap. 5.99 *(978-0-7636-6461-9(8))*; 2012. 14.99 *(978-0-7636-5315-6(2))* Candlewick Pr.

—There Was an Old Lady Who Swallowed a Fly. Carthew, Mark & Rosen, Michael. 2007. (Collins Big Cat Ser.). (ENG.). 16p. (J). pap. 7.99 *(978-0-00-722872-0(4))* HarperCollins Pubs. Ltd. GBR. Dist: Independent Pubs. Group.

—The Way I Love You. Bedford, David. (ENG.). 24p. (J). (gr. -1-k). 2015. bds. 9.99 ***(978-1-76012-395-6(1))***; 2008. pap. 7.95 *(978-1-877003-81-3(6))* Little Hare Bks. AUS. Dist: Independent Pubs. Group.

James, Ann. Bird & Bear. James, Ann. 2015. (ENG.). 40p. (J). (gr. -1-2). 16.99 *(978-1-4998-0037-1(1))* Little Bee Books Inc.

James, Annie. The Adventures of Elbert & Leopoldina. Kubik, Dorothy. 2006. 104p. (J). per. 15.00 *(978-0-9790775-1-7(6))* Touchstone Communications.

James, Ben. Los Tres Reyes Magos, the Three Wise Men. 2006. (J). bds. *(978-0-9786863-2-1(2))* ITRON Publishing.

James, Betsy. Listening at the Gate. James, Betsy. 2007. (Seeker Chronicles Ser.). (ENG.). 512p. (YA). (gr. 7-12). pap. 22.99 *(978-0-689-85069-1(7)*, Atheneum Bks. for Young Readers) Simon & Schuster Children's Publishing.

James, Cate. Breaking the Spell: Stories of Magic & Mystery from Scotland. James, Cate. Don, Lari. 2014. (ENG.). 72p. (J). (gr. 2-5). 19.99 *(978-1-84780-342-9(3)*, Frances Lincoln) Quarto Publishing Group UK GBR. Dist: Hachette Bk. Group.

James, Diane. Watch It Cook. Bulloch, Ivan. 2004. (I Can Do It Ser.). 32p. (J). (gr. 2-5). 12.95 *(978-1-58728-510-3(X)*, Two-Can Publishing) T&N Children's Publishing.

James, Elizabeth, jt. illus. see Ghiuselev, Iassen.

James, Emma J. A Surprise for Santa. James, Emma J. 32p. (Orig.). (J). (gr. -1-3). pap. *(978-1-885935-02-1(1))* Appalachian Log Publishing Co., The.

James, Eric. Celebrate My Hopi Name. Poleahla, Anita. 2013. (CAI & ENG.). (J). ***(978-1-893354-65-4(2))*** Salina Bookshelf Inc.

James, Estes. Octavus Octopus. Rose, Williams. 2008. (LAT & ENG.). 20p. (J). pap. 10.00 *(978-0-86516-698-1(6))* Bolchazy-Carducci Pubs.

—Rena Rhinoceros. Rose, Williams. 2008. (LAT & ENG.). 20p. (J). pap. 10.00 *(978-0-86516-699-8(4))* Bolchazy-Carducci Pubs.

—Taurus Rex. Rose, Williams. 2008. (LAT & ENG.). 20p. (J). pap. 10.00 *(978-0-86516-700-1(1))* Bolchazy-Carducci Pubs.

J

—Ursus et Porcus. Rose, Williams. 2008. (LAT & ENG.). 20p. (J). pap. 10.00 *(978-0-86516-701-8(X))* Bolchazy-Carducci Pubs.

James, Gordon, jt. illus. see James, Gordon C.

James, Gordon C. Abby Takes a Stand. McKissack, Patricia C. 2007. 104p. (J). *(978-0-439-02797-7(7))* Scholastic, Inc.

James, Gordon C., et al. Abby Takes a Stand. McKissack, Patricia C. 2006. (Scraps of Time Ser.). (ENG.). 112p. (J). (gr. 3-7). 4.99 *(978-0-14-240687-8(2),* Puffin) Penguin Publishing Group.

James, Gordon C. & James, Gordon. Away West. McKissack, Patricia C. 2006. (Scraps of Time Ser.). (ENG.). 128p. (J). (gr. 3-7). 4.99 *(978-0-14-240688-5(0),* Puffin) Penguin Publishing Group.

James, Helen. Fall. Butterworth Moira. 2005. (Seasons (Smart Apple Media) Ser.). 32p. (YA). (gr. 2-4). lib. bdg. 27.10 *(978-1-58340-616-8(6))* Black Rabbit Bks.

—Spring. Butterfield, Moira. 2005. (Seasons (Smart Apple Media) Ser.). 32p. (YA). (gr. 2-4). lib. bdg. 27.10 *(978-1-58340-614-4(X))* Black Rabbit Bks.

—Summer. Butterworth Moira. 2005. (Seasons (Smart Apple Media) Ser.). 32p. (YA). (gr. 2-4). lib. bdg. 27.10 *(978-1-58340-615-1(8))* Black Rabbit Bks.

—Winter. Butterworth Moira. 2005. (Seasons (Smart Apple Media) Ser.). 32p. (YA). (gr. 2-4). lib. bdg. 27.10 *(978-1-58340-617-5(4))* Black Rabbit Bks.

James, John. How to Be a Revolutionary War Soldier. Ratliff, Thomas. 2006. (How to Be Ser.). (ENG.). 32p. (J). (gr. 4-7). 14.95 *(978-0-7922-7489-6(X))*; lib. bdg. 21.90 *(978-0-7922-7546-6(2))* National Geographic Society. (National Geographic Children's Bks.).

—How to Be a Samurai Warrior. MacDonald, Fiona & Donnelly, S. E. 2005. (How to Be Ser.). (ENG.). 32p. (J). (gr. 3-7). 14.95 *(978-0-7922-3618-4(1))* CENGAGE Learning.

—How to Be a Samurai Warrior. MacDonald, Fiona. (How to Be Ser.). (ENG.). 32p. (J). (gr. 3-7). 2007. pap. 5.95 *(978-1-4263-0135-3(9))*; 2005. lib. bdg. 21.90 *(978-0-7922-3633-7(5))* National Geographic Society. (National Geographic Children's Bks.).

James, John, et al. Inside Ancient Rome. Stewart, David. 2005. (Inside... Ser.). 48p. (J). (gr. 5). lib. bdg. 19.95 *(978-1-59270-045-5(4))* Enchanted Lion Bks., LLC.

James, John. Inside the Tomb of Tutankhamun. Morley, Jacqueline. 2005. (ENG.). 48p. (J). (gr. 3-7). 19.95 *(978-1-59270-042-4(X))* Enchanted Lion Bks., LLC.

—Real Knights: Over 20 True Stories of Chivalrous Deeds. Gravett, Christopher. 2005. (ENG.). 48p. (J). (gr. 3-9). 15.95 *(978-1-59270-034-9(9))* Enchanted Lion Bks., LLC.

—Real Pirates. Hibbert, Clare. 2003. (ENG.). 48p. (J). (gr. 3). 15.95 *(978-1-59270-018-9(7))* Enchanted Lion Bks., LLC.

James, Kennon. Abraham Lincoln: Will You Ever Give Up?, 1bk. Uglow, Loyd. 2003. (Another Great Achiever Ser.). (J). lib. bdg. 23.95 incl. audio *(978-1-57537-790-2(X))*; 48p. (YA). 16.95 incl. audio compact disk *(978-1-57537-540-3(0))*; (ENG.). 48p. (YA). lib. bdg. 23.95 incl. audio compact disk *(978-1-57537-740-7(3))* Advance Publishing, Inc.

—George Washington Carver: What Do You See?, 1bk. Benge, Janet. 2003. (Another Great Achiever Ser.). (J). lib. bdg. 23.95 incl. audio *(978-1-57537-792-6(6))* Advance Publishing, Inc.

—Helen Keller: Facing Her Challenges - Challenging the World, 1 bk. Benge, Janet. 2003. (Another Great Achiever Ser.). (J). lib. bdg. 23.95 incl. audio *(978-1-57537-793-3(4))* Advance Publishing, Inc.

—If Only I Were. . . Sommer, Carl. 2003. (Another Sommer-Time Story Ser.). (ENG.). 48p. (J). 16.95 incl. audio compact disk *(978-1-57537-502-1(8))* Advance Publishing, Inc.

—If Only I Were... Sommer, Carl. 2003. (Another Sommer-Time Story Ser.). (ENG.). 48p. (J). (gr. k-4). lib. bdg. 23.95 incl. audio compact disk *(978-1-57537-702-5(0))* Advance Publishing, Inc.

James, Kennon. If Only I Were- Sommer, Carl. 2014. (J). pap. ***(978-1-57537-954-8(6))*** Advance Publishing, Inc.

James, Kennon. If Only I Were...(Si Yo Fuese...) Sommer, Carl. ed. 2009. (Another Sommer-Time Story Bilingual Ser.). (SPA & ENG.). 48p. (J). lib. bdg. 16.95 *(978-1-57537-154-2(5))* Advance Publishing, Inc.

James, Kennon. Light Your Candle. Sommer, Carl. (J). 2014. pap. ***(978-1-57537-957-9(0))***; 2003. (ENG.). 48p. 16.95 incl. audio compact disk *(978-1-57537-518-2(4))*; 2003. 48p. lib. bdg. 23.95 incl. audio compact disk *(978-1-57537-718-6(7))* Advance Publishing, Inc.

James, Kennon. Light Your Candle(Enciende Tu Vela) Sommer, Carl. ed. 2009. (Another Sommer-Time Story Bilingual Ser.). (SPA & ENG.). 48p. (J). lib. bdg. 16.95 *(978-1-57537-157-3(X))* Advance Publishing, Inc.

James, Kennon. The Little Red Train. Sommer, Carl. (J). 2014. pap. ***(978-1-57537-958-6(9))***; 2003. (ENG.). 48p. 16.95 incl. audio compact disk *(978-1-57537-014-9(X))*; 2003. (ENG.). 48p. lib. bdg. 23.95 incl. audio compact disk *(978-1-57537-714-8(4))* Advance Publishing, Inc.

James, Kennon. The Little Red Train(El Trenecito Rojo) Sommer, Carl. ed. 2009. (Another Sommer-Time Story Bilingual Ser.). (SPA & ENG.). 48p. (J). lib. bdg. 16.95 *(978-1-57537-158-0(8))* Advance Publishing, Inc.

James, Kennon. No Longer a Dilly Dally. Sommer, Carl. (J). 2014. pap. ***(978-1-57537-961-6(9))***; 2003. (ENG.). 48p. (gr. 1-4). 16.95 incl. audio compact disk *(978-1-57537-501-4(X))* Advance Publishing, Inc.

James, Kennon. No Longer a Dilly Dally Read-Along. Sommer, Carl. 2003. (Another Sommer-Time Story Ser.). (ENG.). 48p. (J). lib. bdg. 23.95 incl. audio compact disk *(978-1-57537-701-8(2))* Advance Publishing, Inc.

—No Longer a Dilly Dally(iNunca Mas a Troche y Moche) Sommer, Carl. ed. 2009. (Another Sommer-Time Story Bilingual Ser.). (SPA & ENG.). 48p. (J). lib. bdg. 16.95 *(978-1-57537-162-7(6))* Advance Publishing, Inc.

James, Kennon. Noise! Noise! Noise! Sommer, Carl. (J). 2014. pap. ***(978-1-57537-963-0(5))***; 2003. (ENG.). 48p. 9.95 *(978-1-57537-020-0(4))*; 2003. (ENG.). 48p. lib. bdg. 16.95 *(978-1-57537-069-9(7))*; 2003. (ENG.). 48p. lib. bdg. 23.95 incl. audio compact disk *(978-1-57537-719-3(5))*; 2003. (ENG.). 48p. (gr. 1-4). 16.95 incl. audio compact disk *(978-1-57537-519-9(2))* Advance Publishing, Inc.

James, Kennon. Noise! Noise! Noise!(Ruido! Ruido! Ruido!) Sommer, Carl. ed. 2009. (Another Sommer-Time Story Bilingual Ser.). (SPA & ENG.). 48p. (J). lib. bdg. 16.95 *(978-1-57537-161-0(8))* Advance Publishing, Inc.

James, Kennon. The Sly Fox & the Chicks. Sommer, Carl. (J). 2014. pap. ***(978-1-57537-966-1(X))***; 2003. (ENG.). 48p. 16.95 incl. audio compact disk *(978-1-57537-504-5(4))* Advance Publishing, Inc.

James, Kennon. The Sly Fox & the Chicks Read-along. Sommer, Carl. 2003. (Another Sommer-Time Story Ser.). (ENG.). 48p. (J). lib. bdg. 23.95 incl. audio compact disk *(978-1-57537-704-9(7))* Advance Publishing, Inc.

—The Sly Fox & the Chicks(El Zorro Astuto y los Pollitos) Sommer, Carl. ed. 2009. (Another Sommer-Time Story Bilingual Ser.). (SPA & ENG.). 48p. (J). lib. bdg. 16.95 *(978-1-57537-166-5(9))* Advance Publishing, Inc.

James, Kennon. You Move You Lose. Sommer, Carl. (J). 2014. pap. ***(978-1-57537-972-2(4))***; 2003. (ENG.). 48p. lib. bdg. 23.95 incl. audio compact disk *(978-1-57537-705-6(5))*; 2003. (ENG.). 48p. (gr. 1-4). 16.95 incl. audio compact disk *(978-1-57537-505-2(2))* Advance Publishing, Inc.

James, Kennon. You Move You Lose(El Que Se Mueva, Pierde) Sommer, Carl. ed. 2009. (Another Sommer-Time Story Bilingual Ser.). (SPA & ENG.). 48p. (J). lib. bdg. 16.95 *(978-1-57537-172-6(3))* Advance Publishing, Inc.

James, Kennon. Your Job Is Easy. Sommer, Carl. (J). 2014. pap. ***(978-1-57537-973-9(2))***; 2003. (ENG.). 48p. (gr. -1-4). 9.95 *(978-1-57537-018-7(2))*; 2003. (ENG.). 48p. (gr. 1-4). 16.95 incl. audio compact disk *(978-1-57537-517-5(6))*; 2003. (ENG.). 48p. (gr. 2-4). lib. bdg. 16.95 *(978-1-57537-067-5(0))* Advance Publishing, Inc.

James, Kennon. Your Job Is Easy Read-along. Sommer, Carl. 2003. (Another Sommer-Time Story Ser.). (ENG.). 48p. (J). lib. bdg. 23.95 incl. audio compact disk *(978-1-57537-717-9(9))* Advance Publishing, Inc.

—Your Job Is Easy(Tu Trabajo Es Facil) Sommer, Carl. ed. 2009. (Another Sommer-Time Story Bilingual Ser.). (SPA & ENG.). 48p. (J). lib. bdg. 16.95 *(978-1-57537-173-3(1))* Advance Publishing, Inc.

James, Larry W. & Freshman, Floris R. Captain Petey: An Adventure at Sea. James, Larry W. Ramos, Violet M., ed. 2003. 28p. pap. 6.99 *(978-0-9742154-0-2(6))* Cross Pointe Printing.

James, Laura. Anna Carries Water, 1 vol. Senior, Olive. 2014. (ENG.). 40p. (J). (gr. k-3). 18.95 *(978-1-896580-60-9(2))* Tradewind Bks. CAN. Dist: Orca Bk. Pubs. USA.

James, Margaret Ray. Thank You, God. Lundy, Charlotte. Waldrep, Evelyn L., ed. 2004. 32p. (J). (gr. k-3). 15.95 *(978-0-9670280-9-5(4))* Bay Light Publishing.

James, Martin, et al. How to Draw the Craziest, Creepiest Characters, 1 vol. Singh, Asavari. 2011. (Drawing Ser.). (ENG.). 48p. (gr. 3-4). lib. bdg. 31.32 *(978-1-4296-6595-7(5))* Capstone Pr., Inc.

—How to Draw the Fastest, Coolest Cars, 1 vol. Singh, Asavari. 2011. (Drawing Ser.). (ENG.). 48p. (gr. 3-4). lib. bdg. 31.32 *(978-1-4296-6596-4(3))* Capstone Pr., Inc.

—How to Draw the Most Exciting, Awesome Manga, 1 vol. Singh, Asavari. 2011. (Drawing Ser.). (ENG.). 48p. (gr. 3-4). lib. bdg. 31.32 *(978-1-4296-6593-3(9))* Capstone Pr., Inc.

James, Martin, jt. illus. see Ahmad, Aadil.

James, Matt. From There to Here, 1 vol. Croza, Laurel. 2014. (ENG.). 36p. (J). (gr. -1-2). 18.95 *(978-1-55498-365-0(7))* Groundwood Bks. CAN. Dist: Perseus-PGW.

—Northwest Passage, 1 vol. Rogers, Stan. 2013. (ENG.). 56p. (J). (gr. k). 24.95 *(978-1-55498-153-3(0))* Groundwood Bks. CAN. Dist: Perseus-PGW.

—Yellow Moon, Apple Moon, 1 vol. Porter, Pamela. 2008. (ENG.). 32p. (J). (gr. k — 1). 17.95 *(978-0-88899-809-5(0))* Groundwood Bks. CAN. Dist: Perseus-PGW.

James, McKelvy Walker. My Way: The Memoirs of Coach Larry Folloni. Folloni, Larry. Michael, Folloni, ed. 2003. per. 19.95 *(978-0-9740480-0-0(3))* Light Energy Bks.

James, Melody. White Fire, the Indian Boy. Ballard, George Anne. 2012. 24p. pap. 12.00 *(978-0-9855312-3-2(1))* Bolton Publishing LLC.

James, Melody A. & Arelys, Aguilar. Read to Me! Ballard, George Anne. 2013. 60p. pap. 10.00 *(978-0-9855312-8-7(2))* Bolton Publishing LLC.

James, Rhian Nest. Owl Ninja. Fussell, Sandy. 2011. (Samurai Kids Ser.: 2). (ENG.). 272p. (J). (gr. 4-7). 15.99 *(978-0-7636-5003-2(X))* Candlewick Pr.

—Samurai Kids #1: White Crane. Fussell, Sandy. 2011. (Samurai Kids Ser.: 1). (ENG.). 256p. (J). (gr. 4-7). pap. 6.99 *(978-0-7636-5346-0(2))* Candlewick Pr.

—Samurai Kids #2: Owl Ninja. Fussell, Sandy. 2011. (Samurai Kids Ser.: 2). (ENG.). 272p. (J). (gr. 4-7). pap. 6.99 *(978-0-7636-5772-7(7))* Candlewick Pr.

—Samurai Kids #4: Monkey Fist. Fussell, Sandy. 2012. (Samurai Kids Ser.: 4). (ENG.). 272p. (J). (gr. 4-7). pap. 6.99 *(978-0-7636-5827-4(8))* Candlewick Pr.

—Shaolin Tiger. Fussell, Sandy. 2011. (Samurai Kids Ser.: 3). (ENG.). 272p. (J). (gr. 4-7). pap. 6.99 *(978-0-7636-5702-4(6))* Candlewick Pr.

—Toppling. Murphy, Sally. 2012. (ENG.). 128p. (J). (gr. 3-7). 15.99 *(978-0-7636-5921-9(5))* Candlewick Pr.

—White Crane. Fussell, Sandy. 2010. (Samurai Kids Ser.: 1). (ENG.). 256p. (J). (gr. 4-7). 15.99 *(978-0-7636-4503-8(6))* Candlewick Pr.

James, Robin. Alaska's Dog Heroes: True Stories of Remarkable Canines. Gill, Shelley. 2014. (ENG.). 32p. (J). (gr. 1-4). pap. 10.99 *(978-1-57061-909-0(3))* Sasquatch Bks.

—Buttermilk. Cosgrove, Stephen. 2013. (Serendipity Ser.: 2). (ENG.). 32p. (J). (gr. k-4). pap. 7.95 *(978-1-939011-52-7(3))* Heritage Builders, LLC.

—Creole. Cosgrove, Stephen. 2013. (Serendipity Ser.: 3). (ENG.). 32p. (J). (gr. k-4). pap. 7.95 *(978-1-939011-53-4(1))* Heritage Builders, LLC.

—Fanny. Cosgrove, Stephen. 2013. (Serendipity Ser.: 4). (ENG.). 32p. (J). (gr. k-4). pap. 7.95 *(978-1-939011-54-1(X))* Heritage Builders, LLC.

—Flutterby. Cosgrove, Stephen. 2013. (Serendipity Ser.: 5). (ENG.). 32p. (J). (gr. k-4). pap. 7.95 *(978-1-939011-55-8(8))* Heritage Builders, LLC.

—Gnome from Nome. Cosgrove, Stephen. 2012. (Paws IV Ser.). (ENG.). 32p. (J). (gr. -1-2). pap. 10.99 *(978-1-57061-777-5(5))* Sasquatch Bks.

—The Grumpling. Cosgrove, Stephen. 2003. (Serendipity Bks.). (Orig.). (J). (gr. k-4). 12.65 *(978-0-7569-5259-4(X))* Perfection Learning Corp.

—Leo the Lop. Cosgrove, Stephen. 2013. (Serendipity Ser.: 6). (ENG.). 32p. (J). (gr. k-4). pap. 7.95 *(978-1-939011-56-5(6))* Heritage Builders, LLC.

—Morgan & Me. Cosgrove, Stephen. 2013. (Serendipity Ser.: 7). (ENG.). 32p. (J). (gr. k-4). pap. 7.95 *(978-1-939011-57-2(4))* Heritage Builders, LLC.

—The Muffin Dragon. Cosgrove, Stephen. 2013. (Serendipity Ser.: 8). (ENG.). 32p. (J). (gr. k-4). pap. 7.95 *(978-1-939011-59-6(0))* Heritage Builders, LLC.

—Pickles & the P-Flock Bullies. Cosgrove, Stephen. 2014. (ENG.). 32p. (J). (gr. k-3). 16.99 *(978-1-57061-887-1(9))* Sasquatch Bks.

—Sniffles. Cosgrove, Stephen. 2013. (Serendipity Ser.: 1). (ENG.). 32p. (J). (gr. k-4). pap. 7.95 *(978-1-939011-58-9(2))* Heritage Builders, LLC.

—Wheedle & the Noodle. Cosgrove, Stephen. 2011. (ENG.). 32p. (J). (gr. -1-2). 16.99 *(978-1-57061-730-0(9))* Sasquatch Bks.

—Wheedle on the Needle. Cosgrove, Stephen. 2009. (ENG.). 32p. (J). (gr. -1-2). 16.99 *(978-1-57061-628-0(0))* Sasquatch Bks.

James, Robin, jt. illus. see Harper, Ruth E.

James, Simon. Baby Brains: The Smartest Baby in the Whole World. James, Simon. (ENG.). 32p. (J). 2008. (Candlewick Storybook Animation Ser.). (gr. k-k). 14.99 *(978-0-7636-4024-8(7))*; 2007. (Baby Brains Ser.: 1). (gr. -1-3). pap. 6.99 *(978-0-7636-3682-1(7))* Candlewick Pr.

—Little One Step. James, Simon. 2007. (ENG.). 24p. (J). (— 1). bds. 6.99 *(978-0-7636-3520-6(0))* Candlewick Pr.

James, Simon. Days Like This: A Collection of Small Poems. James, Simon, compiled by. 2005. (ENG.). 48p. (J). (gr. 1-4). reprint ed. pap. 6.99 *(978-0-7636-2314-2(8))* Candlewick Pr.

James, Steve. The Demigod Files. Riordan, Rick. 2009. (ENG.). 160p. (J). (gr. 5-6). 12.95 *(978-1-4231-2166-4(X))* Hyperion Pr.

—Dewey: There's a Cat in the Library! Myron, Vicki & Witter, Bret. 2009. (ENG.). 40p. (J). (gr. -1-1). 16.99 *(978-0-316-06874-1(8))* Little, Brown Bks. for Young Readers.

—The Walnut Cup. Carman, Patrick. 2009. (Elliot's Park Ser.: Bk. 3). 80p. (J). (gr. 1-5). 8.99 *(978-0-545-01932-3(X),* Orchard Bks.) Scholastic, Inc.

James, Steven. Heart on Fire: Susan B. Anthony Votes for President. Malaspina, Ann. 2012. (ENG.). 32p. (J). (gr. 1-4). 16.99 *(978-0-8075-3188-4(X))* Whitman, Albert & Co.

James, Will. The Dark Horse, Vol. 1. James, Will. rev. ed. 288p. (J). (gr. 4). pap. *(978-0-87842-486-3(5),* 817) Mountain Pr. Publishing Co., Inc.

Jamieson, Eden, jt. illus. see Levy, Shaun.

Jamieson, Sandy. Adam Cox Meets the CrackleCrunch for Lunch. Benesch, Walter. 2004. 32p. (J). 24.95 *(978-1-932053-09-8(3))* Nonetheless Pr.

Jamieson, Victoria. The Gollywhopper Games. Feldman, Jody. (Gollywhopper Games Ser.: 1). (J). (gr. 3-7). 2013. (ENG.). 336p. pap. 6.99 *(978-0-06-121452-3(3))*; 2008. (ENG.). 320p. 16.99 *(978-0-06-121450-9(7))*; 2008. 320p. lib. bdg. 17.89 *(978-0-06-121451-6(5))* HarperCollins Pubs. (Greenwillow Bks.).

—The Gollywhopper Games: The New Champion. Feldman, Jody. 2014. (Gollywhopper Games Ser.: 2). (ENG.). 400p. (J). (gr. 3-7). 16.99 *(978-0-06-221125-5(0),* Greenwillow Bks.) HarperCollins Pubs.

—The Gollywhopper Games - Friend or Foe. Feldman, Jody. 2015. (Gollywhopper Games Ser.: 3). (ENG.). 432p. (J). (gr. 3-7). 16.99 *(978-0-06-221128-6(5),* Greenwillow Bks.) HarperCollins Pubs.

—The Gollywhopper Games - The New Champion. Feldman, Jody. 2015. (Gollywhopper Games Ser.: 2). (ENG.). 400p. (J). (gr. 3-7). pap. 6.99 *(978-0-06-221126-2(9),* Greenwillow Bks.) HarperCollins Pubs.

—Grandpa, What's That Sound in the Middle of the Night? Singlehurst, Naomi. Ellen Koski, Rachel, ed. 2008. (ENG.). 32p. (J). (gr. k-2). 14.95 *(978-1-930650-24-4(8))* mTrellis Publishing, Inc.

—The Lightning Catcher. Cameron, Anne. (Lightning Catcher Ser.). (ENG.). (J). (gr. 3-7). 2075. 368p. 7.99 *(978-0-06-211277-4(5))*; 2013. 432p. 16.99 *(978-0-06-211276-7(7))* HarperCollins Pubs. (Greenwillow Bks.).

—Lightning Catcher: The Storm Tower Thief. Cameron, Anne. 2014. (Lightning Catcher Ser.: 2). (ENG.). 432p. (J). (gr. 3-7). 16.99 *(978-0-06-211279-8(1),* Greenwillow Bks.) HarperCollins Pubs.

—The Lightning Catcher - The Secrets of the Storm Vortex. Cameron, Anne. 2015. (Lightning Catcher Ser.: 3). (ENG.). 464p. (J). (gr. 3-7). 16.99 *(978-0-06-211283-5(X),* Greenwillow Bks.) HarperCollins Pubs.

—Where Triplets Go, Trouble Follows. Poploff, Michelle. 2015. (ENG.). 96p. (J). (gr. 2-6). 16.95 *(978-0-8234-3289-9(0))* Holiday Hse., Inc.

Jamison, Sharon. Lacey's Legacy: Stretch's Story. Goril, Cindy. 2013. 28p. (J). pap. 12.95 *(978-1-935188-56-8(9))* Star Publish LLC.

Jan, R. R. Piko the Penguinaut. Abraham, M. K. 2012. 112p. (J). 12.95 *(978-1-937489-00-7(0))* StoryRobin Co.

Jan, Stephanie Liu, photos by. Martin Yan Quick & Easy. Yan, Martin. 2004. (ENG., 224p. (gr. 8-17). pap. 24.95 *(978-0-8118-4447-5(1))* Chronicle Bks. LLC.

Janco, Tania. El Tejon de la Barca: Y Otras Historias. Howker, Janni. Tovar Cross, Juan Elias, tr. 2003. (la Orilla del Viento Ser.). (SPA.). 160p. (J). per. *(978-968-16-6282-0(2))* Fondo de Cultura Economica.

Jane, Fred T. Tsar Wars Episode One: Angel of the Revolution. Griffith, George. Rowland, Marcus L., ed. 2003. Orig. Title: The Angel of the Revolution. 275p. per. 14.95 *(978-1-930658-16-5(8),* HEL 5816) Heliograph, Inc.

—Tsar Wars Episode Two: Syren of the Skies. Griffith, George. Rowland, Marcus L., ed. 2003. Orig. Title: Olga Romanoff or Syren of the Skies. 274p. per. 14.95 *(978-1-930658-17-2(6),* HEL 5817) Heliograph, Inc.

Jane, Mary & Auch, Herm. Poultrygeist. Auch, Mary Jane. 2004. (ENG.). 32p. (J). (gr. k-3). reprint ed. 6.95 *(978-0-8234-1876-3(6))* Holiday Hse., Inc.

Jane, Nance'. If I Had a Daddy. Sullivan, Mary M. 2008. 28p. pap. 24.95 *(978-1-60610-555-9(8))* America Star Bks.

Jane, Pamela & Manning, Jane. Little Goblins Ten. Jane, Pamela. 2011. (ENG.). 32p. (J). (gr. -1-3). 16.99 *(978-0-06-176798-2(0))* HarperCollins Pubs.

Janes, Andy. Shaun the Sheep: the Beast of Soggy Moor. Howard, Martin. 2015. (Tales from Mossy Bottom Farm Ser.). (ENG.). (J). (gr. k-3). pap. 4.99 *(978-0-7636-7586-8(5))* Candlewick Pr.

—Shaun the Sheep: the Flock Factor. Howard, Martin. 2014. (Tales from Mossy Bottom Farm Ser.). (ENG.). 96p. (J). (gr. k-3). pap. 4.99 *(978-0-7636-7535-6(0))* Candlewick Pr.

Jang, EunJoo. The Chirping Band. Lee, WonKyeong. 2015. (MySELF Bookshelf Ser.). (ENG.). 32p. (J). (gr. k-2). pap. 11.94 *(978-1-60357-698-7(3))*; lib. bdg. 22.60 *(978-1-59953-663-7(3))* Norwood Hse. Pr.

Jang, Yeong-seon. Peter Pan. Barrie, J. M. Cowley, Joy, ed. 2015. (World Classics Ser.). (ENG.). 32p. (gr. k-4). 26.65 ***(978-1-925246-19-3(1))***; 7.99 ***(978-1-925246-71-1(X))*** ChoiceMaker Pty. Ltd., The AUS. (Big and SMALL). Dist: Lerner Publishing Group.

Jang, Yeong-seon. Peter Pan. Barrie, James Matthew. Cowley, Joy, ed. 2015. (World Classics Ser.). (ENG.). 32p. (gr. k-4). 26.65 ***(978-1-925246-45-2(0),*** Big and SMALL) ChoiceMaker Pty. Ltd., The AUS. Dist: Lerner Publishing Group.

Jang, Yeong-seon. Peter Pan. Barrie, James Matthew. Cowley, Joy, ed. 2015. (World Classics Ser.). (ENG.). 32p. (J). (gr. k-4). 26.65 *(978-1-925186-71-0(7))*; pap. 7.99 *(978-1-925186-65-9(2))* Lerner Publishing Group.

Janguay, Patricia. There's A Giant in the Garden. Stuefloten, Helen. l.t. ed. 2006. 35p. (J). per. 11.99 *(978-1-59879-161-7(3))* Lifevest Publishing, Inc.

Janicke, Gregory. The Conquerors, 1 vol. Janicke, Gregory. 2008. (Outcasts Ser.: Bk. 4). (ENG.). 328p. (YA). (gr. 5-18). pap. 7.99 *(978-0-7614-5442-7(X))* Marshall Cavendish Corp.

—The Shadow Beasts, 1 vol. Janicke, Gregory. 2007. (Outcasts Ser.: Bk. 1). (ENG.). 276p. (YA). (gr. 8-12). pap. 6.99 *(978-0-7614-5364-2(4))* Marshall Cavendish Corp.

Jankowski, Dan. Up Close & Gross. Hall, Kirsten. 2009. 64p. (J). *(978-0-545-13583-2(4))* Scholastic, Inc.

—What's a Jaybird to Do? Sauer, Cat. l.t. ed. 2003. (Brown Bag Bedtime Bks.: 1). 31p. (YA). spiral bd. 16.95 *(978-0-9704460-8-4(X))* Writer's Ink. Studios, Inc.

Jankowski, Daniel. Flip Flop & Hoot. Sauer, Cat. l.t. ed. 2006. (Brown Bag Bedtime Bks.: 1). 35p. (J). (gr. -1-2). 16.95 incl. audio compact disk *(978-0-9704460-6-0(3))* Writer's Ink. Studios, Inc.

—Gwendolyn the Ghost. Sauer, Cat. l.t. ed. 2006. (Brown Bag Bedtime Bks.: 1). 29p. (J). (gr. -1-2). 16.95 incl. audio compact disk *(978-0-9704460-9-1(8))* Writer's Ink. Studios, Inc.

—A Possum in the Roses. Sauer, Cat. l.t. ed. 2006. (Brown Bag Bedtime Bks.: 1). 27p. (J). (gr. -1-2). 16.95 incl. audio compact disk *(978-0-9704460-7-7(1))* Writer's Ink. Studios, Inc.

—Rocks, Minerals, & Gemstones. Salzano, Tammi J. 2009. 24p. (J). pap. *(978-0-545-19868-4(2))* Scholastic, Inc.

Janosch. Yo Te Curare, Dijo el Pequeno Oso. Janosch. 2003. (SPA.). 48p. (J). (gr. k-3). pap. 8.95 *(978-958-24-0110-8(9))* Santillana USA Publishing Co., Inc.

Janovitz, Marilyn. Airplane Adventure, 1 vol. Meister, Cari. 2010. (My First Graphic Novel Ser.). 32p. (gr. k-2). (ENG.). pap. 6.25 *(978-1-4342-2286-2(1))*; pap. 4.95 *(978-1-4342-3602-9(1))* Stone Arch Bks. (My First Graphic Novel).

—Innovative Kids Readers: Milly's Silly Suitcase - Level 1. Rabe, Tish. 2006. (J). (gr. -1-1). 6.99 *(978-1-58476-493-9(7))* Innovative Kids.

—Pirate Pickle & the White Balloon. Burg, Ann E. 2007. (Rookie Reader Skill Set Ser.). (ENG.). 32p. (J). (gr. -1-3). pap. 4.95 *(978-0-531-17778-5(5),* Children's Pr.) Scholastic Library Publishing.

—Train Trip, 1 vol. Meister, Cari & Stone Arch Books Staff. 2010. (My First Graphic Novel Ser.). (ENG.). 32p. (gr. k-2). pap. 6.25 *(978-1-4342-2289-3(6),* My First Graphic Novel) Stone Arch Bks.

—Train Trip, 1 vol. Meister, Cari. 2009. (My First Graphic Novel Ser.). (ENG.). 32p. (gr. k-2). 23.32 *(978-1-4342-1616-8(0),* My First Graphic Novel) Stone Arch Bks.

Janovitz, Marilyn. I Will Try. Janovitz, Marilyn. (I Like to Read Ser.). (ENG.). 24p. (J). 2013. pap. 6.99 *(978-0-8234-2756-7(0))*; 2012. 14.95 *(978-0-8234-2399-6(9))* Holiday Hse., Inc.

—Te Puedo Ayudar?/Can I Help? Janovitz, Marilyn. Fernandez, Queta, tr. 2008. (SPA.). 32p. (J). (gr. -1-3). 6.95 *(978-0-7358-2184-2(4))* North-South Bks., Inc.

—We Love School! Janovitz, Marilyn. 2007. (We Love Ser.). (ENG.). 24p. (J). (gr. -1-k). 9.95 *(978-0-7358-2112-5(7))* North-South Bks., Inc.

—We Love School (¡Nos Encanta la Escuela!) Janovitz, Marilyn. 2009. (ENG & SPA.). 32p. (J). (gr. -1-k). 7.95 *(978-0-7358-2246-7(8))* North-South Bks., Inc.

Janry. Adventure down Under, Vol. 1. Tome. Saincantin, Jerome, tr. from FRE. 2010. (ENG.). 46p. (J). (gr. 4-7). pap. 11.95 *(978-1-84918-011-5(3))* CineBook GBR. Dist: National Bk. Network.
—Spirou & Fantasio in New York. Tome. 2011. (ENG.). 48p. (J). (gr. 3-17). pap. 11.95 *(978-1-84918-054-2(7))* CineBook GBR. Dist: National Bk. Network.
—Spirou & Fantasio Vol. 4: Valley of the Exiles. 2013. (ENG.). 48p. pap. 11.95 *(978-1-84918-157-0(8))* CineBook GBR. Dist: National Bk. Network.
Jansdotter, Lotta. Simple Sewing: Patterns & How-To for 24 Fresh & Easy Projects. Jansdotter, Lotta. Arquillos, Meiko, photos by. 2007. (ENG.). 144p. (gr. 8-17). 24.95 *(978-0-8118-5267-9(1))* Chronicle Bks. LLC.
Janson, Klaus. Gambit Classic - Volume 2. Mackie, Howard & Kavanagh, Terry. 2013. (ENG.). 208p. (J). (gr. 4-17). pap. 29.99 *(978-0-7851-6790-7(0))* Marvel Worldwide, Inc.
Janson, Klaus & Sienkiewicz, Bill. Daredevil: End of Days. Mack, David. 2013. (ENG.). 216p. (YA). (gr. 8-17). 39.99 *(978-0-7851-2420-7(9))* Marvel Worldwide, Inc.
Janssen, Mark. Fairy Marie's New Home. Rieu, Jean-Philippe. 2012. (Marie Ser.). (ENG.). 30p. (J). (gr. -1-k). 19.95 *(978-1-60537-133-7(5))* Clavis Publishing.
Jansson, Alexander. The Cabinet of Curiosities: 36 Tales Brief & Sinister. Bachmann, Stefan et al. 2014. (ENG.). 496p. (J). (gr. 3-7). 16.99 *(978-0-06-233105-2(1))*; pap. 6.99 *(978-0-06-231314-0(2))* HarperCollins Pubs. (Greenwillow Bks.).
—The Mad Apprentice. Wexler, Django. 2015. (Forbidden Library). (ENG.). 352p. (J). (gr. 5). 16.99 *(978-0-8037-3976-5(1)*, Dawson, Kathy Bks.) Penguin Publishing Group.
Jansson, Tove. Comet in Moominland. Jansson, Tove. Portch, Elizabeth, tr. 2010. (Moomins Ser.: 1). (ENG.). 192p. (J). (gr. 4-7). pap. 7.99 *(978-0-312-60888-0(8))* Square Fish.
—Finn Family Moomintroll. Jansson, Tove. Portch, Elizabeth, tr. from SWE. 2010. (Moomins Ser.: 2). (ENG.). 176p. (J). (gr. 4-7). pap. 7.99 *(978-0-312-60889-7(6))* Square Fish.
—Moomin & the Birthday Button. Jansson, Tove. 2011. (Moomins Ser.). (ENG.). 32p. (J). (gr. -1-1). 12.99 *(978-0-374-35050-5(7)*, Farrar, Straus & Giroux (BYR)) Farrar, Straus & Giroux.
—Moominland Midwinter. Jansson, Tove. Warburton, Thomas, tr. 2010. (Moomins Ser.: 5). (ENG.). 160p. (J). (gr. 4-7). pap. 7.99 *(978-0-312-62541-2(3))* Square Fish.
—Moominpappa at Sea. Jansson, Tove. Hart, Kingsley, tr. 2010. (Moomins Ser.: 7). (ENG.). 240p. (J). (gr. 4-7). pap. 7.99 *(978-0-312-60892-7(6))* Square Fish.
—Moominpappa's Memoirs. Jansson, Tove. Warburton, Thomas, tr. 2010. (Moomins Ser.: 3). (ENG.). 192p. (J). (gr. 4-7). pap. 7.99 *(978-0-312-62543-6(X))* Square Fish.
—Moominsummer Madness. Jansson, Tove. Warburton, Thomas, tr. 2010. (Moomins Ser.: 4). (ENG.). 176p. (J). (gr. 4-7). pap. 7.99 *(978-0-312-60891-0(8))* Square Fish.
—Moominvalley in November. Jansson, Tove. Hart, Kingsley, tr. 2010. (Moomins Ser.: 8). (ENG.). 208p. (J). (gr. 4-7). pap. 7.99 *(978-0-312-62544-3(8))* Square Fish.
—Tales from Moominvalley. Jansson, Tove. Warburton, Thomas, tr. 2010. (Moomins Ser.: 6).Tr. of Osynliga Barnet. (ENG.). 192p. (J). (gr. 4-7). pap. 7.99 *(978-0-312-62542-9(1))* Square Fish.
Jantner, Janos. Drawing Fantasy Monsters. 2013. (How to Draw Monsters Ser.). (ENG.). 32p. (J). (gr. 3-6). pap. 11.75 *(978-1-4777-0344-1(6))*; lib. bdg. 26.50 *(978-1-4777-0311-3(X))* Rosen Publishing Group, Inc., The. (PowerKids Pr.).
—Drawing Horror-Movie Monsters. 2013. (How to Draw Monsters Ser.). (ENG.). 32p. (J). (gr. 3-6). 26.50 *(978-1-4777-0308-3(X))*; pap. 11.75 *(978-1-4777-0338-0(1))* Rosen Publishing Group, Inc., The. (PowerKids Pr.).
—Drawing Monsters from Great Books. 2013. (How to Draw Monsters Ser.). (ENG.). 32p. (J). (gr. 3-6). pap. 11.75 *(978-1-4777-0348-9(9))*; lib. bdg. 26.50 *(978-1-4777-0313-7(6))* Rosen Publishing Group, Inc., The. (PowerKids Pr.).
—Drawing Mythological Monsters. 2013. (How to Draw Monsters Ser.). (ENG.). 32p. (J). (gr. 3-6). pap. 11.75 *(978-1-4777-0340-3(3))*; lib. bdg. 26.50 *(978-1-4777-0309-0(8))* Rosen Publishing Group, Inc., The. (PowerKids Pr.).
—Drawing Science-Fiction Monsters. 2013. (How to Draw Monsters Ser.). (ENG.). 32p. (J). (gr. 3-6). pap. 11.75 *(978-1-4777-0342-7(X))*; lib. bdg. 26.50 *(978-1-4777-0310-6(1))* Rosen Publishing Group, Inc., The. (PowerKids Pr.).
—Drawing Unexplained-Mystery Monsters. 2013. (How to Draw Monsters Ser.). (ENG.). 32p. (J). (gr. 3-6). pap. 11.75 *(978-1-4777-0346-5(2))*; lib. bdg. 26.50 *(978-1-4777-0312-0(8))* Rosen Publishing Group, Inc., The. (PowerKids Pr.).
January, Stella. Come Out to the Garden. January, Rick. 2012. (ENG.). 30p. (J). pap. 12.95 *(978-1-937084-66-0(3)*, BQB Publishing) Boutique of Quality Books Publishing Co.
Janus Kahn, Katherine. Sammy Spider's First Mitzvah. Rouss, Sylvia. 2014. 24p. (J). (gr. -1-3). 17.95 *(978-1-4677-1947-6(1)*, Kar-Ben Publishing) Lerner Publishing Group.
Jaques, Laura. The Most Dangerous, 1 vol. Fields, Terri. 2012. (ENG.). 32p. (J). (gr. -1-3). pap. 9.95 *(978-1-60718-535-2(0))* Arbordale Publishing.
Jaquith, A. The Bee in the Yellow Jacket. Jaquith, A. Jaquith, A. l.t. ed. 2011. (ENG.). 28p. pap. 12.00 *(978-1-4662-2079-9(1))* CreateSpace Independent Publishing Platform.
Jara, Jose. The Stranger & the Red Rooster: El Forastero y el Gallo Rojo. Villasenor, Victor. Ventura, Gabriela Baeza, tr. 2005. (ENG & SPA.). 26p. (J). (gr. -1-2). 16.95 *(978-1-55885-420-8(7)*, Piñata Books) Arte Publico Pr.
Jaraiz, David. Storytime with Paige. Friden, Chris & Rodriguez Braojos, Alberto. 2008. (J). *(978-0-9758785-8-3(1))*; *(978-0-9801849-4-5(0))* Haydenburri Lane.
Jaramillo, Raquel. The Handiest Things in the World. Clements, Andrew. 2010. (ENG.). 48p. (J). (gr. -1-3). 16.99 *(978-1-4169-6166-6(6)*, Atheneum Bks. for Young Readers) Simon & Schuster Children's Publishing.
Jaramillo, Raquel. Peter Pan: The Original Tale of Neverland. Jaramillo, Raquel, photos by. Barrie, J. M. unabr. ed. 2003. 135p. (YA). (gr. 5-8). reprint ed. 25.00 *(978-0-7567-6883-6(7))* DIANE Publishing Co.
Jardine, David. There's a Cow under My Bed, 1 vol. Sherrard, Valerie. 2008. (ENG.). 32p. (J). (gr. 1-8). 10.95 *(978-1-897174-34-0(9))* Creative Bk. Publishing CAN. Dist: Orca Bk. Pubs. USA.
—There's a Goldfish in My Shoe!, 1 vol. Sherrard, Valerie. 2009. (ENG.). 32p. (J). (gr. 1-7). 12.95 *(978-1-897174-47-0(0)*, Tuckamore Bks) Creative Bk. Publishing CAN. Dist: Orca Bk. Pubs. USA.
Jarkins, Sheila. Mr. Bee Man: Story of Lorenzo Lorraine Langstroth Father of American Beekeeping. Gabbert, Rosalie M. 2013. (ENG.). 40p. (J). 28.95 *(978-1-4787-1080-6(2))*; pap. 19.95 *(978-1-4787-1243-5(0))* Outskirts Pr., Inc.
Jarkins, Sheila. Adv Marco Flamingo Under Sea. Jarkins, Sheila. 2010. (ENG.). 32p. (J). (gr. -1-12). pap. 7.95 *(978-1-934960-69-1(1)*, Raven Tree Pr.,Csi) Continental Sales, Inc.
—The Adventures of Marco Flamingo in the Jungle. Jarkins, Sheila. 2011. (ENG.). 32p. (gr. -1-3). lib. bdg. 16.95 *(978-1-936299-22-5(4)*, Raven Tree Pr.,Csi) Continental Sales, Inc.
—The Adventures of Marco Flamingo in the Jungle. Jarkins, Sheila. 2012. 32p. (J). 1.99 *(978-1-936299-31-7(3)*, Raven Tree Pr.) Delta Systems Company, Inc.
—Marco Flamenco. Jarkins, Sheila. de la Vega, Eida, tr. 2008. (SPA & ENG.). 32p. (J). (gr. -1-3). 16.95 *(978-0-9794462-7-6(9)*, Raven Tree Pr.,Csi) Continental Sales, Inc.
—Marco Flamingo/Marco Flamenco. Jarkins, Sheila. de la Vega, Eida, tr. 2008. (ENG & SPA.). 32p. (J). (gr. -1-3). pap. 7.95 *(978-0-9794462-6-9(0)*, Raven Tree Pr.,Csi) Continental Sales, Inc.
Jarman, Brandy S. The Halloween Chase. Hooley, Rachelle B. & Butler, Mackay M. 2012. 36p. 24.95 *(978-1-4626-7160-1(8))* America Star Bks.
Jaroszko, Mike. Away in a Manger. 2008. 32p. (J). (gr. -1). 13.49 *(978-0-7586-1496-4(9))* Concordia Publishing Hse.
—Away in a Manger Devotional. 2008. pap. 2.29 *(978-0-7586-1449-0(7))* Concordia Publishing Hse.
Jarret, Judy. Every Day & Sunday, Too. Ramshaw, Gail. 2004. 44p. 15.99 *(978-0-8066-2334-4(9)*, 10-23349, Augsburg Bks.) Augsburg Fortress, Pubs.
Jarrett, Michael. Adding. Jarrett, Michael, photos by. Williams, Rozanne Lanczak. 2004. (I Can Do Math Ser.). 24p. (gr. k-3). lib. bdg. 22.00 *(978-0-8368-4108-4(5)*, Gareth Stevens Learning Library) Stevens, Gareth Publishing LLLP.
—Crayola Counting. Jarrett, Michael, photos by. Williams, Rozanne Lanczak. 2004. (I Can Do Math Ser.). 24p. (gr. k-3). lib. bdg. 22.00 *(978-0-8368-4109-1(3)*, Gareth Stevens Learning Library) Stevens, Gareth Publishing LLLP.
Jarrett, Michael, photos by. I Can Share with Others. Burch, Regina G. & Donovan Guntly, Jenette. 2004. (Doing the Right Thing Ser.). 16p. (gr. -1-2). lib. bdg. 20.00 *(978-0-8368-4246-3(4)*, Gareth Stevens Learning Library) Stevens, Gareth Publishing LLLP.
—I Can Show I Care. Burch, Regina G. & Donovan Guntly, Jenette. 2004. (Doing the Right Thing Ser.). 16p. (gr. -1-2). lib. bdg. 20.00 *(978-0-8368-4247-0(2)*, Gareth Stevens Learning Library) Stevens, Gareth Publishing LLLP.
—Learning about Coins. Williams, Rozanne Lanczak. 2004. (I Can Do Math Ser.). 24p. (gr. k-3). lib. bdg. 22.00 *(978-0-8368-4110-7(7)*, Gareth Stevens Learning Library) Stevens, Gareth Publishing LLLP.
—My Favorites, Your Favorites. Williams, Rozanne Lanczak. Hamaguchi, Carla, ed. 2003. (Sight Word Readers Ser.). 16p. (J). (gr. k-2). pap. 3.49 *(978-1-57471-964-2(5)*, 3586) Creative Teaching Pr., Inc.
—Subtracting. Williams, Rozanne Lanczak. 2004. (I Can Do Math Ser.). 24p. (gr. k-3). lib. bdg. 22.00 *(978-0-8368-4113-8(1)*, Gareth Stevens Learning Library) Stevens, Gareth Publishing LLLP.
Jarrett, Sandra. Who Is He in Yonder Stall? Neal, Sharon, ed. 2008. (ENG.). 24p. (J). pap. *(978-1-932381-21-4(X)*, 6500) Bible Visuals International, Inc.
Jarvis. Pig & Pug. Marchesani, Laura & Medina, Zenaides A., Jr. 2015. (Penguin Young Readers, Level 2 Ser.). (ENG.). 32p. (J). (gr. 1-2). pap. 3.99 *(978-0-448-48342-9(4)*, Warne, Frederick Pubs.) Penguin Bks., Ltd. GBR. Dist: Penguin Random Hse., LLC.
Jarvis. Lazy Dave. Jarvis. 2015. (ENG.). 32p. (J). (gr. -1-3). 17.99 ***(978-0-06-235598-0(8))*** HarperCollins Pubs.
Jarvis, James. Vortigem's Machine: And the Great Sage of Wisdom. Jarvis, James. Waterman, Russell. 2006. 48p. per. 24.00 *(978-3-89955-098-6(6))* Die Gestalten Verlag DEU. Dist: Prestel Publishing.
Jarzabek, Ela. Guess Who Noah's Boat, 1 vol. Mitter, Matt. 2014. 10p. (J). 11.99 *(978-0-8254-4205-6(2))* Kregel Pubns.
Jasinski, Aaron. Fall Leaves. Curry, Don L. (Rookie Reader Skill Set Ser.). (J). (gr. k-2). 2005. (ENG.). 24p. pap. 4.95 *(978-0-516-26831-6(7))*; 2004. 23p. 19.50 *(978-0-516-25904-8(0))* Scholastic Library Publishing. (Children's Pr.).
—The Golem's Latkes, 0 vols. Kimmel, Eric A. 2011. (ENG.). 40p. (J). (gr. k-3). 17.99 *(978-0-7614-5904-0(9)*, 9780761459040, Amazon Children's Publishing) Amazon Publishing.
Jaskiel, Stan. Dumplings Are Delicious. Capone, Deb. 2006. 24p. (J). (gr. -1-3). 16.95 *(978-0-9728666-4-4(7))* As Simple As That Publishing.
—The Great Pirate Christmas Battle, 1 vol. Lewis, Michael. 2014. (ENG.). 32p. (J). (gr. k-3). 16.99 *(978-1-4556-1934-4(5))* Pelican Publishing Co., Inc.
Jasmin, Lynn. Birdies' Seaside Gym. Handelsman, Valerie. 2005. (ENG.). 32p. (J). 7.95 *(978-0-9748884-2-2(7))* Little Thoughts For Little Ones Publishing, Inc.
Jasnoch, Dorothy. The Adventures of Oskar: Oskar's New School. Saldivar, Jose A. Nilsson, Janet Busbey, ed. 2013. 32p. pap. 13.99 *(978-1-937752-14-9(3))*; (ENG.). pap. 13.99 *(978-1-937752-07-1(0))* Owl About Bks. Pub., Inc.
Jasnoch, Dorothy. Adventure of Little Mouse Maggie. Jasnoch, Dorothy. Kern, Kimberly, ed. 2012. (ENG.). 36p. pap. 14.99 *(978-1-937752-06-4(2))* Owl About Bks. Pub., Inc.
—The Adventures of Oskar: Oskar's New School. Jasnoch, Dorothy. Korzeniowski, Samson O., ed. 2013. 32p. 18.99 *(978-1-937752-27-9(5))* Owl About Bks. Pub., Inc.
—Frankie the Bunny: Helping the Birds. Jasnoch, Dorothy. Korzeniowski, Samson O., ed. 2013. 28p. 17.99 *(978-1-937752-20-0(8))* Owl About Bks. Pub., Inc.
—Frankie the Bunny: Mystery in the Forest. Jasnoch, Dorothy. Korzeniowski, Samson O., ed. 2013. 32p. 17.99 *(978-1-937752-16-3(X))* Owl About Bks. Pub., Inc.
—Frankie the Bunny: Newfound Friends. Jasnoch, Dorothy. Korzeniowski, Samson O., ed. 2013. 28p. 17.99 *(978-1-937752-15-6(1))* Owl About Bks. Pub., Inc.
—Frankie the Bunny: The Fall Scramble Begins. Jasnoch, Dorothy. Korzeniowski, Samson O., ed. 2013. 28p. 17.99 *(978-1-937752-19-4(4))* Owl About Bks. Pub., Inc.
—Frankie the Bunny: Wheels of Fortune. Jasnoch, Dorothy. Korzeniowski, Samson O., ed. 2013. 28p. 17.99 *(978-1-937752-17-0(8))* Owl About Bks. Pub., Inc.
—Frankie the Bunny: Woodland Warning. Jasnoch, Dorothy. Korzeniowski, Samson O., ed. 2013. 28p. 17.99 *(978-1-937752-18-7(6))* Owl About Bks. Pub., Inc.
—Frankie the Bunny: Woodland Warning. Jasnoch, Dorothy. Korzeniowski, Samson, ed. 2012. 28p. pap. 12.99 *(978-1-937752-03-3(8))* Owl About Bks. Pub., Inc.
—Frankie the Bunny Helping the Birds. Jasnoch, Dorothy. Korzeniowski, Samson, ed. 2012. (ENG.). 28p. pap. 12.99 *(978-1-937752-05-7(4))* Owl About Bks. Pub., Inc.
—Frankie the Bunny the Fall Scramble Begins. Jasnoch, Dorothy. Korzeniowski, Samson, ed. 2012. 28p. pap. 12.99 *(978-1-937752-04-0(6))* Owl About Bks. Pub., Inc.
Jasper, Mark. Good Night North Pole. Gamble, Adam. 2012. (Good Night Our World Ser.). (ENG.). 28p. (J). (gr. k — 1). bds. 9.95 *(978-1-60219-071-9(2))* Our World of Books.
—Good Night Ohio. Gamble, Adam. 2013. (Good Night Our World Ser.). (ENG.). 20p. (J). (— 1). bds. 9.95 *(978-1-60219-076-4(3))* Our World of Books.
Jasper, Mark. Good Night Delaware. Jasper, Mark. Gamble, Adam. 2012. (Good Night Our World Ser.). (ENG.). 20p. (J). (gr. k — 1). bds. 9.95 *(978-1-60219-066-5(6))* Our World of Books.
—Good Night New York State. Jasper, Mark. Gamble, Jasper & Gamble, Adam. 2012. (Good Night Our World Ser.). (ENG.). 20p. (J). (gr. k — 1). bds. 9.95 *(978-1-60219-063-4(1))* Our World of Books.
Jasper, Mark & Kelly, Cooper. Good Night Wisconsin. Gamble, Jasper et al. 2012. (Good Night Our World Ser.). (ENG.). 20p. (J). (gr. k — 1). bds. 9.95 *(978-1-60219-064-1(X))* Our World of Books.
Jasper, Mark, jt. illus. see Rosen, Anne.
Jasper, Mark, jt. illus. see Veno, Joe.
Jastrzebski, Brandy. Brayden & Ryan's Summer Vacation. Reimiller, Diane. 2012. 24p. pap. 24.95 *(978-1-4626-7792-4(4))* America Star Bks.
—A Duck Named Quackers, 1 vol. Reimiller, Diane L. 2009. 12p. pap. 24.95 *(978-1-60836-771-9(1))* America Star Bks.
—Ike & Jamie. Reimiller, Diane L. 2008. 32p. pap. 24.95 *(978-1-60610-227-5(3))* America Star Bks.
Jasuna, Aija. The Bee in Bonnie Bondelle's Bow. Sauers, Charlotte. 2008. (J). 16.95 *(978-1-60131-014-9(5))* Big Tent Bks.
—Casey & Bella Go to New York. Lovascio, Jane. 2008. 24p. (J). 14.95 *(978-1-60131-007-1(2))* Big Tent Bks.
—Clean Clara. Oltchick, Peter. 2012. 34p. (J). (-18). 16.95 *(978-1-60131-127-6(3)*, Castlebridge Bks.) Big Tent Bks.
—One Step at a Time. Sax, Anita. 2013. 24p. (J). 17.95 *(978-1-60131-152-8(4)*, Castlebridge Bks.) Big Tent Bks.
—Oscar & the Zoo. Sax, Anita. 2013. 32p. (J). 14.95 *(978-1-60131-174-0(5))* Big Tent Bks.
—The River of Glass. Corwin, Katherine. 2009. 24p. (J). 14.95 *(978-1-60131-002-6(1)*, Castlebridge Bks.) Big Tent Bks.
Jatkowska, Ag. The Alphabet Parade. Ghigna, Charles. 2014. 24p. (J). pap. ***(978-1-4795-1930-9(8))*** Picture Window Bks.
Jatkowska, Ag. Alphabet Parade. Ghigna, Charles. 2013. (Learning Parade Ser.). (ENG.). (gr. -1-2). 20p. bds. 7.99 *(978-1-4048-8314-7(2))*; 24p. 21.32 *(978-1-4048-8310-9(X))* Picture Window Bks.
—The Christmas Treasure Hunt. ed. 2014. (ENG.). 10p. (J). (gr. -1-k). 15.99 *(978-0-230-76863-5(6))* Pan Macmillan GBR. Dist: Independent Pubs. Group.
—Grandma Rose's Magic. Marshall, Linda Elovitz. 2012. (Shabbat Ser.). (ENG.). 32p. (J). (gr. -1-2). pap. 7.95 *(978-0-7613-5216-7(3)*, Kar-Ben Publishing) Lerner Publishing Group.
—Grandma Rose's Magic/By Linda Elovitz Marshall; Illustrated by Ag Jatkowska. Marshall, Linda Elovitz. 2012. (Shabbat Ser.). (ENG.). 32p. (J). (gr. -1-2). lib. bdg. 17.95 *(978-0-7613-5215-0(5)*, Kar-Ben Publishing) Lerner Publishing Group.
—I Love You Too. Marley, Ziggy. 2014. (ENG.). 48p. (J). (-2). 15.95 *(978-1-61775-310-7(6))* Akashic Bks.
—I See Fall, 1 vol. Ghigna, Charles. 2011. (I See Ser.). (ENG.). 24p. (gr. -1 — 1). pap. 6.10 *(978-1-4048-6851-9(8))*; lib. bdg. 21.32 *(978-1-4048-6589-1(6))* Picture Window Bks. (I See).
—I See Spring, 1 vol. Ghigna, Charles. 2011. (I See Ser.). (ENG.). 24p. (gr. -1 — 1). pap. 6.10 *(978-1-4048-6849-6(6))*; lib. bdg. 21.32 *(978-1-4048-6587-7(X))* Picture Window Bks. (I See).
—I See Summer, 1 vol. Ghigna, Charles. 2011. (I See Ser.). (ENG.). 24p. (gr. -1 — 1). pap. 6.10 *(978-1-4048-6852-6(6))*; lib. bdg. 21.32 *(978-1-4048-6590-7(X))* Picture Window Bks. (I See).
—I See Winter, 1 vol. Ghigna, Charles. 2011. (I See Ser.). (ENG.). 24p. (gr. -1 — 1). pap. 6.10 *(978-1-4048-6850-2(X))*; lib. bdg. 21.32 *(978-1-4048-6588-4(8))* Picture Window Bks. (I See).
—Inch & Roly & the Sunny Day Scare. Wiley, Melissa. 2014. (Ready-To-Reads Ser.). (ENG.). 24p. (J). (gr. -1-1). 16.99 *(978-1-4424-9072-7(1)*, Simon Spotlight) Simon Spotlight.
—Inch & Roly & the Very Small Hiding Place. Wiley, Melissa. 2013. (Ready-To-Reads Ser.). (ENG.). 24p. (J). (gr. -1-1). 16.99 *(978-1-4424-5281-7(1))*; pap. 3.99 *(978-1-4424-5279-4(X))* Simon Spotlight. (Simon Spotlight).
—Inch & Roly Make a Wish. Wiley, Melissa. 2012. (Ready-To-Reads Ser.). (ENG.). 24p. (J). (gr. -1-1). 15.99 *(978-1-4424-5277-0(3))*; pap. 3.99 *(978-1-4424-5276-3(5))* Simon Spotlight. (Simon Spotlight).
—Learning Parade. Ghigna, Charles. 2013. (Learning Parade Ser.). (ENG.). 20p. (gr. -1-2). bds. 31.96 *(978-1-4048-8144-0(1))* Picture Window Bks.
—Learning Parade [10 X 10]. Ghigna, Charles. 2014. (Learning Parade Ser.). (ENG.). 20p. (gr. -1-2). bds. 51.96 *(978-1-4914-1900-7(8))* Picture Window Bks.
—Little Seeds, 1 vol. Ghigna, Charles. 2012. (My Little Planet Ser.). (ENG.). 24p. (gr. -1 — 1). 6.95 *(978-1-4048-7226-4(4))*; lib. bdg. 21.32 *(978-1-4048-6790-1(2)*, My Little Planet) Picture Window Bks.
—My Little School House. Ghigna, Charles. 2013. (My Little School House Ser.). (ENG.). 24p. (gr. -1-2). lib. bdg. 85.28 *(978-1-4048-8143-3(3))* Picture Window Bks.
—My Name Is Aviva. Newman, Lesléa. 2015. (ENG.). 32p. (J). (gr. -1-2). lib. bdg. 17.99 *(978-1-4677-2654-2(0)*, Kar-Ben Publishing) Lerner Publishing Group.
—Numbers at the Park: 1-10, 1 vol. Ghigna, Charles. 2013. (My Little School House Ser.). (ENG.). 24p. (gr. -1-2). 21.32 *(978-1-4048-8308-6(8))* Picture Window Bks.
—Numbers at the Park: 1 2 3 4 5 6 7 8 9 10. Ghigna, Charles. 2013. (Learning Parade Ser.). (ENG.). 20p. (gr. -1-2). bds. 7.99 *(978-1-4048-8312-3(6))* Picture Window Bks.
Jatkowska, Ag, et al. The Other Side of the Story. Loewen, Nancy & Speed Shaskan, Trisha. 2013. (Other Side of the Story Ser.). (ENG.). 24p. (gr. 2-3). lib. bdg. 53.30 *(978-1-4048-7255-4(8)*, Nonfiction Picture Bks.) Picture Window Bks.
Jatkowska, Ag. Pick up the Park, 1 vol. Ghigna, Charles. 2012. (My Little Planet Ser.). (ENG.). 24p. (gr. -1 — 1). 6.95 *(978-1-4048-7228-8(0))*; lib. bdg. 21.32 *(978-1-4048-6793-2(7)*, My Little Planet) Picture Window Bks.
—Recycling Is Fun, 1 vol. Ghigna, Charles. 2012. (My Little Planet Ser.). (ENG.). 24p. (gr. -1 — 1). 6.95 *(978-1-4048-7229-5(9))*; lib. bdg. 21.32 *(978-1-4048-6791-8(0)*, My Little Planet) Picture Window Bks.
—Shapes Are Everywhere! Ghigna, Charles. 2013. (Learning Parade Ser.). (ENG.). 20p. (gr. -1-2). bds. 7.99 *(978-1-4048-8313-0(4))*; 24p. (J). pap. *(978-1-4795-1929-3(4))*; (ENG.). 24p. (gr. -1-2). lib. bdg. 21.32 *(978-1-4048-8309-3(6))* Picture Window Bks.
—Veo el Invierno. Ghigna, Charles. 2012. (Bilingual I See Ser.).Tr. of I See Winter. (ENG, SPA & MUL.). 24p. (gr. -1 — 1). lib. bdg. 21.32 *(978-1-4048-7310-0(4))* Picture Window Bks.
—Veo el Otoño. Ghigna, Charles. 2012. (Bilingual I See Ser.).Tr. of I See Fall. (ENG, SPA & MUL.). 24p. (gr. -1 — 1). lib. bdg. 21.32 *(978-1-4048-7307-0(4))* Picture Window Bks.
—Veo el Verano. Ghigna, Charles. 2012. (Bilingual I See Ser.).Tr. of I See Summer. (ENG, SPA & MUL.). 24p. (gr. -1 — 1). lib. bdg. 21.32 *(978-1-4048-7309-4(0))* Picture Window Bks.
—Veo la Primavera. Ghigna, Charles. 2012. (Bilingual I See Ser.).Tr. of I See Spring. (ENG, SPA & MUL.). 24p. (gr. -1 — 1). lib. bdg. 21.32 *(978-1-4048-7308-7(2))* Picture Window Bks.
—We Need Water, 1 vol. Ghigna, Charles. 2012. (My Little Planet Ser.). (ENG.). 24p. (gr. -1 — 1). 6.95 *(978-1-4048-7227-1(2))*; lib. bdg. 21.32 *(978-1-4048-6792-5(9)*, My Little Planet) Picture Window Bks.
—Wonders of the Color Wheel. Ghigna, Charles. 2013. (Learning Parade Ser.). (ENG.). (gr. -1-2). 20p. bds. 7.99 *(978-1-4048-8311-6(8))*; 24p. 21.32 *(978-1-4048-8307-9(X))* Picture Window Bks.
Jatkowska, Ag. The Wonders of the Color Wheel. Ghigna, Charles. 2014. 24p. (J). pap. ***(978-1-4795-1927-9(8))*** Picture Window Bks.
Jaunn, Adele. Baby Bilby's Question. Morgan, Sally. 2013. (ENG.). 32p. (J). (gr. -1-k). pap. 9.99 *(978-1-74297-553-5(4))* Little Hare Bks. AUS. Dist: Independent Pubs. Group.
—Puppy Playtime 1, 2, 3. Walters, Celeste. 2013. (ENG.). 24p. (J). (-k). pap. 12.99 *(978-1-74297-716-4(2))* Little Hare Bks. AUS. Dist: Independent Pubs. Group.
Jauss, Anne Marie. The Storks of Lillegaard. Frisch, Wilhelmine. 2011. 230p. 46.95 *(978-1-258-08105-8(9))* Literary Licensing, LLC.
—Turn Here for Strawberry Roam. Myers, Byrona. 2011. 134p. 40.95 *(978-1-258-08195-9(4))* Literary Licensing, LLC.
—Yo Ho for Strawberry Roam! Myers, Byrona. 2011. 154p. 41.95 *(978-1-258-08204-8(7))* Literary Licensing, LLC.
Javier, Emmanuel Xerx & Burton, Daniel. The Women's Rights Movement. Glenn, Avery et al. 2007. (Jt Am Hist Graph Novel Ser.). (ENG.). 24p. (gr. 6-12). pap. 11.40 *(978-0-07-878025-7(X)*, 007878025X) McGraw-Hill Cos., The.

J

Jawa, Sadhvi. An Elephant in My Backyard. Viswanath, Shobha. 2013. (ENG.). 28p. (J). (gr. -1). 11.95 (978-81-8190-240-5(8)) Karadi Tales Co. Pvt. Ltd. IND. Dist: Consortium Bk. Sales & Distribution.

Jax, T. L. Fraidy-Frieda's Light Show. Jax, T. L. l.t. ed. 2004. 30p. (J). 9.95 (978-0-9743890-2-8(1)) Flaxenfluff Pr., LLC.

Jay, Alison. A Child's First Book of Prayers. Rock, Lois. 2012. (ENG.). 224p. (J). (gr. k-2). 12.99 (978-0-7459-4474-6(4)) Lion Hudson PLC GBR. Dist: Independent Pubs. Group.

—The Cloud Spinner. Catchpool, Michael. 2012. (ENG.). 32p. (J). (gr. k-3). 16.99 (978-0-375-87011-8(3), Knopf Bks. for Young Readers) Random Hse. Children's Bks.

—A Gift for Mama. Lodding, Linda Ravin. 2014. (ENG.). 32p. (J). (gr. -1-3). 17.99 (978-0-385-75331-9(4), Knopf Bks. for Young Readers) Random Hse. Children's Bks.

—I Took the Moon for a Walk. Curtis, Carolyn. (ENG.). 32p. (J). 2012. pap. 7.99 (978-1-84148-803-5(8)); 2004. 16.99 (978-1-84148-611-6(6)) Barefoot Bks., Inc.

—If Kisses Were Colors. Lawler, Janet. (ENG.). (J). (gr. -1 — 1). 2010. 22p. bds. 6.99 (978-0-8037-3530-9(8)); 2003. 32p. 16.99 (978-0-8037-2617-8(1)) Penguin Publishing Group. (Dial).

—Listen, Listen. Gershator, Phillis. 2007. (ENG.). 32p. (J). (gr. -1-3). 16.99 (978-1-84686-084-3(9)) Barefoot Bks., Inc.

—The Nutcracker. Harris, Annmarie. 2010. (ENG.). 40p. (J). (gr. -1-k). 16.99 (978-0-8037-3285-8(6), Dial) Penguin Publishing Group.

Jay, Alison. ABC: A Child's First Alphabet Book. Jay, Alison. 2005. (ENG.). 32p. (J). (gr. -1 — 1). bds. 10.99 (978-0-525-47524-8(9), Dutton Juvenile) Penguin Publishing Group.

—Lleve a la Luna a Pasear. Jay, Alison. Curtis, Carolyn & Barefoot Books. 2014. (SPA.). 32p. (J). 7.99 (978-1-78285-084-7(8)) Barefoot Bks., Inc.

Jay, Alison, jt. illus. see Allison, Jay.

Jay, Leisten, jt. illus. see Land, Greg.

Jazvic, Beryl. After the Storm. Hall, Rose. 2005. (J). bds. 19.95 (978-0-9770503-0-7(0)) Institute For Behavior Change Incorporated The.

Jean, David. Rainbow Crow, 1 vol. Bouchard, David. 2012. (ENG & OJI.). 32p. (J). 24.95 (978-0-88995-458-8(5)) Red Deer Pr. CAN. Dist: Ingram Pub. Services.

Jean-P, Tibbles. Spy on the Home Front. Alison, Hart. 2005. (American Girls Collection). (ENG.). 176p. (J). 10.95 (978-1-58485-996-3(2), American Girl) American Girl Publishing, Inc.

Jean, S. L. Alana's Prince. Pierce, Darlene. 2011. (ENG.). 24p. pap. 10.15 (978-1-4662-2898-6(9)) CreateSpace Independent Publishing Platform.

—A Bear of Another Color. Pierce, Darlene. 2011. (ENG.). 26p. pap. 9.15 (978-1-4662-2902-0(0)) CreateSpace Independent Publishing Platform.

—Drummer. Pierce, Darlene. 2011. (ENG.). 24p. pap. 10.15 (978-1-4662-2891-7(1)) CreateSpace Independent Publishing Platform.

Jean, Texier. Alfie Green & the Magical Gift. Joe, O'Brien. 2007. (Alfie Green Ser.). (ENG.). 80p. (J). pap. 10.95 (978-1-84717-041-5(2)) O'Brien Pr., Ltd., The IRL. Dist: Dufour Editions, Inc.

Jeanette, Canyon. Over in the Jungle: A Rainforest Rhyme. Marianne, Berkes. 2008. 26p. (J). (gr. -1). bds. 7.95 (978-1-58469-108-2(5)) Dawn Pubns.

Jeanne, Arnold. Carlos Digs to China Carlos Excava Hasta la China. Jan, Romero Stevens. 2004. (Carlos Digs to China / Carlos Excava Hasta la China Ser.). (SPA, MUL & ENG.). 32p. (J). (gr. k-3). pap. 7.95 (978-0-87358-870-6(3)) Cooper Square Publishing Llc.

Jeanne, Miss. The Wise Mullet of Cook Bayou. Weeks, Timothy. rev. ed. 2006. 48p. (J). per. 14.99 (978-0-9779928-0-5(2)) Foolosophy Media.

Jeannotte, Lawrence. The Black Cherry Forest: Storybook 1. Utsler, Elaine. Wendle, Stan, ed. 2nd ed. 2003. 48p. (J). per. 6.95 (978-0-9727787-1-8(3), BCF1B) EV Publishing Corp.

Jeanty, Georges. Weapon X: The Underground, Vol. 2. Tieri, Frank. Youngquist, Jeff, ed. 2004. (X-Men Ser.). 184p. pap. 19.99 (978-0-7851-1253-2(7)) Marvel Worldwide, Inc.

Jeanty, Georges, et al. Wolves at the Gate, 8 vols., Vol. 2. Goddard, Drew & Jeanty, Georges. Vaughan, Brian K. 2008. (Buffy the Vampire Slayer Ser.). (ENG.). 320p. pap. 15.99 (978-1-59307-963-5(X)) Dark Horse Comics.

Jeanty, Georges & Leon, John Paul. Weapon X: Defection, Vol. 3. Tieri, Frank. Youngquist, Jeff, ed. 2004. (X-Men Ser.). 120p. pap. 13.99 (978-0-7851-1407-9(6)) Marvel Worldwide, Inc.

Jeanty, Georges & Madsen, Michelle. Predators & Prey, 8 vols., Vol. 5. Espenson, Jane et al. 2009. (ENG.). 144p. pap. 15.99 (978-1-59582-342-7(5)) Dark Horse Comics.

Jecan, Gavriel. Hide & Seek: Nature's Best Vanishing Acts. Helman, Andrea. 2008. (ENG.). 40p. (J). (gr. 1-4). 16.95 (978-0-8027-9690-5(7)) Walker & Co.

Jecan, Gavriel, photos by. Alaska Animal Babies. Vanasse, Deb. 2005. (ENG.). 32p. (J). (gr. -1-2). pap. 10.99 (978-1-57061-433-0(4)) Sasquatch Bks.

—Southwest Colors. Helman, Andrea. 2011. 24p. (J). 12.95 (978-1-933855-64-6(9)) Rio Nuevo Pubs.

Jedele, Christie. Andrea's Fiddle. Klippenstein, Blaine. 2008. (J). incl. audio compact disk (978-1-896201-82-5(2)) Loon Bks. Pub.

Jeevan, Dhamindra. Mars Colony. Cutting, Robert. 2007. 48p. (J). lib. bdg. 23.08 (978-1-4242-1630-7(3)) Fitzgerald Bks.

Jeff Albrecht Studios Staff. Historical Animals. Moberg, Julia. 2015. (ENG.). 96p. (J). (gr. 3-7). 15.95 (978-1-62354-048-7(8), Imagine Publishing) Charlesbridge Publishing, Inc.

Jeff Albrecht Studios Staff, jt. illus. see Albrecht, Jeff.

Jeff, Marsh & Povenmire, Dan. Phineas & Ferb: Lights, Camera, Perry? O'Ryan, Ellie. 2014. (World of Reading Level 3 Ser.). (ENG.). 48p. (J). (gr. 6-9). lib. bdg. 24.21 (978-1-61479-268-0(2)) Spotlight.

Jeffers, Oliver. The Boy Who Swam with Piranhas. Almond, David. (ENG.). 256p. (J). (gr. 4-7). 2015. pap. 7.99 (978-0-7636-7680-3(2)); 2013. 15.99 (978-0-7636-6169-4(4)) Candlewick Pr.

Jeffers, Oliver. The Day the Crayons Came Home. Daywalt, Drew. 2015. (ENG.). 48p. (J). (gr. k-3). 18.99 (978-0-399-17275-5(0), Philomel) Penguin Publishing Group.

Jeffers, Oliver. The Day the Crayons Quit. Daywalt, Drew. 2013. (ENG.). 40p. (J). (gr. -1-2). 17.99 (978-0-399-25537-3(0), Philomel) Penguin Publishing Group.

Jeffers, Oliver. Imaginary Fred. Colfer, Eoin. 2015. (ENG.). 48p. (J). (gr. -1-3). 18.99 (978-0-06-237955-9(0)) HarperCollins Pubs.

Jeffers, Oliver. Noah Barleywater Runs Away. Boyne, John. 2011. (ENG.). 240p. (J). (gr. 3-7). (978-0-385-75246-6(6)) Fickling, David Bks.

—Noah Barleywater Runs Away. Boyne, John. 2012. (ENG.). 240p. (J). (gr. 3-7). 7.99 (978-0-385-75264-0(4), Yearling) Random Hse. Children's Bks.

—Noah Barleywater Runs Away. Boyne, John. ed. 2012. lib. bdg. 18.40 (978-0-606-26408-2(6), Turtleback) Turtleback Bks.

—Stay Where You Are & Then Leave. Boyne, John. 2014. (ENG.). 256p. (J). (gr. 4-7). 16.99 (978-1-62779-031-4(4), Holt, Henry & Co. Bks. For Young Readers) Holt, Henry & Co.

—The Terrible Thing That Happened to Barnaby Brocket. Boyne, John. (ENG.). 288p. (J). (gr. 3-7). 2014. 6.99 (978-0-307-97765-6(X), Yearling); 2013. 16.99 (978-0-307-97762-5(5), Knopf Bks. for Young Readers) Random Hse. Children's Bks.

Jeffers, Oliver. Cómo Atrapar una Estrella. Jeffers, Oliver. Lujan, Jorge, tr. 2005. (Los Especiales de A la Orilla del Viento Ser.). (SPA.). 32p. (J). (gr. -1-3). (978-968-16-7758-9(7)) Fondo de Cultura Economica.

—The Great Paper Caper. Jeffers, Oliver. 2009. (ENG.). 40p. (J). (gr. -1-k). 17.99 (978-0-399-25097-2(2), Philomel) Penguin Publishing Group.

—The Heart & the Bottle. Jeffers, Oliver. 2010. (ENG.). 32p. (J). (gr. -1-3). 17.99 (978-0-399-25452-9(8), Philomel) Penguin Publishing Group.

—How to Catch a Star. Jeffers, Oliver. 2004. (ENG.). 32p. (J). (gr. -1-2). 17.99 (978-0-399-24286-1(4), Philomel) Penguin Publishing Group.

—The Incredible Book Eating Boy. Jeffers, Oliver. (ENG.). 32p. pap. (978-0-00-718231-2(7), HarperCollins Children's Bks.) HarperCollins Pubs. Ltd.

—The Incredible Book Eating Boy. Jeffers, Oliver. 2007. (ENG.). 32p. (J). (gr. -1-3). 17.99 (978-0-399-24749-1(1), Philomel) Penguin Publishing Group.

—It Wasn't Me. Jeffers, Oliver. 2014. (Hueys Ser.: 2). (ENG.). 32p. (J). (gr. -1-k). 17.99 (978-0-399-25768-1(3), Philomel) Penguin Publishing Group.

—Lost & Found. Jeffers, Oliver. 2005. (ENG.). 32p. (J). (gr. -1-2). 17.99 (978-0-399-24503-9(0), Philomel) Penguin Publishing Group.

—The New Sweater. Jeffers, Oliver. 2012. (Hueys Ser.: 1). (ENG.). 32p. (J). (gr. -1-2). 17.99 (978-0-399-25767-4(5), Philomel) Penguin Publishing Group.

—The New Sweater: The Hueys, Book 1. Jeffers, Oliver. 2015. (Hueys Ser.: 1). (ENG.). 24p. (J). (gr. -1-k). bds. 6.99 (978-0-399-17391-2(9), Philomel) Penguin Publishing Group.

—None the Number. Jeffers, Oliver. 2014. (Hueys Ser.: 3). (ENG.). 32p. (J). (gr. -1-k). 17.99 (978-0-399-25769-8(1), Philomel) Penguin Publishing Group.

—None the Number: A Hueys Book. Jeffers, Oliver. 2015. (Hueys Ser.: 3). (ENG.). 24p. (J). (gr. -1-k). bds. 6.99 (978-0-399-17416-2(8), Philomel) Penguin Publishing Group.

—Once upon an Alphabet: Short Stories for All the Letters. Jeffers, Oliver. 2014. (ENG.). 112p. (J). (gr. -1-k). 26.99 (978-0-399-16791-1(9), Philomel) Penguin Publishing Group.

—Stuck. Jeffers, Oliver. 2011. (ENG.). 32p. (J). (gr. -1-2). 17.99 (978-0-399-25737-7(3), Philomel) Penguin Publishing Group.

—This Moose Belongs to Me. Jeffers, Oliver. 2012. (ENG.). 32p. (J). (gr. -1-2). 16.99 (978-0-399-16103-2(1), Philomel) Penguin Publishing Group.

—Up & Down. Jeffers, Oliver. 2010. (ENG.). 40p. (J). (gr. -1-2). 17.99 (978-0-399-25545-8(1), Philomel) Penguin Publishing Group.

—The Way Back Home. Jeffers, Oliver. 2008. (ENG.). 32p. (J). (gr. -1-3). 17.99 (978-0-399-25074-3(3), Philomel) Penguin Publishing Group.

Jeffers, Susan. Black Beauty. Lerner, Sharon & Sewell, Anna. 2009. (ENG.). 40p. (J). (gr. k-4). 16.99 (978-0-375-85892-5(X)) Random Hse., Inc.

—McDuff Comes Home. Wells, Rosemary. 2007. 24p. (J). pap. 4.99 (978-0-7868-1192-2(7)) Hyperion Paperbacks for Children.

—McDuff Comes Home. Wells, Rosemary. rev. ed. 2006. (ENG.). 32p. (gr. -1-k). 9.99 (978-0-7868-3833-2(7)) Hyperion Pr.

—Stopping by Woods on a Snowy Evening. Frost, Robert. 2004. 27p. (J). (gr. k-4). 16.00 (978-0-7567-7973-3(1)) DIANE Publishing Co.

—The Twelve Days of Christmas. 2013. (J). (978-0-06-206616-9(1)) Harper & Row Ltd.

—The Wild Swans. Ehrlich, Amy. 2008. (ENG.). 32p. (J). (gr. -1-3). 17.99 (978-0-525-47914-7(7), Dutton Juvenile) Penguin Publishing Group.

Jeffers, Susan. Cinderella. Jeffers, Susan. Ehrlich, Amy. Battcock, Gregory, ed. 2004. (ENG.). 32p. (J). (gr. -1-3). 18.99 (978-0-525-47345-9(9), Dutton Juvenile) Penguin Publishing Group.

—My Pony. Jeffers, Susan. 2008. (ENG.). 32p. (J). (gr. -1-3). 6.99 (978-1-4231-1295-2(4)) Hyperion Pr.

—The Nutcracker. Jeffers, Susan. 2007. 40p. (J). (gr. -1-3). 17.89 (978-0-06-074387-1(5)); (ENG.). 16.99 (978-0-06-074386-4(7)) HarperCollins Pubs.

—The Twelve Days of Christmas. Jeffers, Susan. 2013. (ENG.). 40p. (J). (gr. -1-3). 17.99 (978-0-06-206615-2(3)) HarperCollins Pubs.

Jefferson, Daniel E. The Luck of the Dragonfly. Jefferson, Barbara. 2008. 31p. pap. 24.95 (978-1-60672-283-1(2)) America Star Bks.

Jefferson Elementary Art Club. Domino. 2007. 32p. (J). 15.00 (978-0-9767244-2-1(1)) SkyMacSyd Publishing.

Jefferson, Patti Brassard. How Long Will You Love Me? Jefferson, Patti Brassard. 2013. 28p. pap. 12.95 (978-1-61244-178-8(5)) Halo Publishing International.

Jefferson, Robert Louis. Road Map to Wholeness. Cretan, Gladys Yessayan. 145.00 (978-0-687-02526-8(5)) Abingdon Pr.

Jeffery, Megan E., jt. illus. see Barr, Marilynn G.

Jeffirs, Matt. Sharks. Kasso, Martin. 2008. (ENG.). 24p. (J). (gr. 3-18). 19.95 (978-1-58117-797-8(6), Intervisual/Piggy Toes) Bendon, Inc.

Jeffrey, Gary. Defying Death in the Desert. 2010. (Graphic Survival Stories Ser.). 48p. (YA). (gr. 5-8). lib. bdg. 31.95 (978-1-4358-3528-3(X), Rosen Reference) Rosen Publishing Group, Inc., The.

—Defying Death in the Jungle. 2010. (Graphic Survival Stories Ser.). 48p. (YA). (gr. 5-8). lib. bdg. 31.95 (978-1-4358-3529-0(8)) Rosen Publishing Group, Inc., The.

—Tsunamis & Floods. 2007. (Graphic Natural Disasters Ser.). (ENG.). 48p. (J). (gr. 5-9). lib. bdg. 31.95 (978-1-4042-1990-8(0)) Rosen Publishing Group, Inc., The.

Jeffrey, Gary & Riley, Terry. The Cuban Missile Crisis. 2013. (ENG.). 48p. (J). (978-0-7787-1233-6(8)); pap. (978-0-7787-1237-4(0)) Crabtree Publishing Co.

—The Korean War. 2013. (ENG.). 48p. (J). (978-0-7787-1234-3(6)); pap. (978-0-7787-1238-1(9)) Crabtree Publishing Co.

Jeffrey, Gary & Spender, Nik. The Vietnam War. 2013. (ENG.). 48p. (J). (978-0-7787-1236-7(2)); pap. (978-0-7787-1240-4(0)) Crabtree Publishing Co.

Jeffrey, Megan. What Is the Lord's Prayer? Learning about the Lord's Prayer. Reed, G L. 2006. (What Is? Ser.). 32p. (J). (gr. 4-7). pap. 3.99 (978-0-687-49347-0(1)) Abingdon Pr.

Jeffrey, Sean, et al. Franklin Stays Up. Jennings, Sharon. 2003. 32p. (J). pap. (978-0-439-41815-7(1)) Scholastic, Inc.

—Franklin's Trading Cards. Jennings, Sharon & Bourgeois, Paulette. 2004. (Franklin Ser.). 32p. (gr. 1-2). 13.95 (978-0-7569-4402-5(3)) Perfection Learning Corp.

—Franklin's Trading Cards. Jennings, Sharon. 2003. 32p. (J). (978-0-439-41816-4(X)) Scholastic, Inc.

Jellett, Tom. Little Piggy's Got No Moves. Gwynne, Phillip & McCann, Eliza. 2015. (ENG.). 32p. (J). (gr. -1-1). 17.99 (978-1-921894-25-1(3)) Little Hare Bks. AUS. Dist: Independent Pubs. Group.

Jellett, Tom. My Dad Thinks He's Funny. Germein, Katrina. 2013. (ENG.). 32p. (J). (gr. k-3). 14.99 (978-0-7636-6522-7(3)) Candlewick Pr.

Jellett, Tom. Quiz Champs. Halliday, Susan. l.t. ed. 2014. 44p. pap. (978-1-4596-7622-0(X)) ReadHowYouWant.com, Ltd.

—Santa's Outback Secret. Dumbleton, Mike. 2015. 32p. (J). (-k). 17.99 (978-0-85798-225-4(7)) Random Hse. Australia AUS. Dist: Independent Pubs. Group.

Jellett, Tom. Santa's Secret. Dumbleton, Mike. (ENG.). 32p. (J). (gr. -1-k). 2014. 9.99 (978-1-74275-240-2(3)); 2012. 17.99 (978-1-74275-239-6(X)) Random Hse. Australia AUS. Dist: Independent Pubs. Group.

—Seadog. Saxby, Claire. (ENG.). 32p. (J). (gr. -1-k). 2014. 11.99 (978-1-74275-651-6(4)); 2013. 17.99 (978-1-74275-650-9(6)) Random Hse. Australia AUS. Dist: Independent Pubs. Group.

Jellett, Tom. Stories for Eight Year Olds. Knight, Linsay, ed. 2015. (ENG.). 208p. (Orig.). (J). (gr. 2-4). 9.99 (978-0-85798-475-3(6)) Random Hse. Australia AUS. Dist: Independent Pubs. Group.

—Stories for Nine Year Olds. Knight, Linsay, ed. 2015. (ENG.). 208p. (Orig.). (J). (gr. 3-5). 9.99 (978-0-85798-477-7(2)) Random Hse. Australia AUS. Dist: Independent Pubs. Group.

—Stories for Seven Year Olds. Knight, Linsay, ed. 2015. (ENG.). 208p. (Orig.). (J). (gr. 1-3). 9.99 (978-0-85798-479-1(9)) Random Hse. Australia AUS. Dist: Independent Pubs. Group.

—Stories for Six Year Olds. Knight, Linsay, ed. 2015. (ENG.). 208p. (Orig.). (J). (gr. k-2). 9.99 (978-0-85798-481-4(0)) Random Hse. Australia AUS. Dist: Independent Pubs. Group.

Jellett, Tom. Two Tough Crocs. Bedford, David. 2014. (ENG.). 24p. (J). (gr. -1-3). 16.95 (978-0-8234-3048-2(0)) Holiday Hse., Inc.

Jen, Kallin, photos by. He's My God!-(Book 2) Knowing God Through His Names - a Childrens' Devotional. Joanna, Harris. 2012. 48p. (J). 7.99 (978-1-930547-78-0(1)) Deeper Roots Pubns. & Media.

Jenkins, C. S. The Bears & the Baby. McLean, P. J. 2012. 44p. pap. 17.44 (978-1-4669-1335-6(5)) Trafford Publishing.

Jenkins, Debra Reid. Glory. Carlstrom, Nancy White. 2004. 32p. (J). (gr. -1-3). 17.00 (978-0-8028-5143-7(6)) Eerdmans, William B. Publishing Co.

—I See the Moon. Appelt, Kathi. 2004. 24p. (J). (gr. -1-2). 15.00 (978-0-8028-5118-5(5)); pap. 8.00 (978-0-8028-5226-7(2)) Eerdmans, William B. Publishing Co.

—I Wanted to Know All about God. Kroll, Virginia. 2010. 12p. (J). (gr. -1). 7.99 (978-0-8028-5380-6(3)) Eerdmans, William B. Publishing Co.

—My Freedom Trip: A Child's Escape from North Korea. Park, Frances & Park, Ginger. 2010. (ENG.). 32p. (J). pap. 11.95 (978-1-59078-826-4(5)) Boyds Mills Pr.

Jenkins, Delores. Preep II: More Tales of Early Texas. Jackson, Sarah. 2007. 48p. (J). 19.95 (978-1-931823-52-4(9)) Halcyon Pr., Ltd.

—Preep of Old Washington Square: A Collection of East Texas Tales. Jackson, Sarah. l.t. ed. 2005. 48p. (J). 16.95 (978-1-931823-25-8(1)) Halcyon Pr., Ltd.

Jenkins, Emily. That New Animal. Jenkins, Emily. 2006. (J). (gr. -1-4). 29.95 (978-0-439-84925-8(X), WHCD687) Weston Woods Studios, Inc.

Jenkins, Jacqueline. Faith's Star. Kauffman, Christopher G. 2011. 32p. pap. 24.95 (978-1-4560-9584-0(6)) America Star Bks.

Jenkins, Leonard. The Best Beekeeper of Lalibela: A Tale from Africa. Kessler, Cristina. 2006. (ENG.). 32p. (J). (gr. -1-3). 16.95 (978-0-8234-1858-9(8)) Holiday Hse., Inc.

—A Good Night for Freedom. Morrow, Barbara Olenyik. 2003. (ENG.). 32p. (J). (gr. k-3). tchr. ed. 17.95 (978-0-8234-1709-4(3)) Holiday Hse., Inc.

—I've Already Forgotten Your Name, Philip Hall! Greene, Bette. 2004. 176p. (J). (gr. 5-18). 15.99 (978-0-06-051835-6(9)) HarperCollins Pubs.

—I've Seen the Promised Land: The Life of Dr. Martin Luther King, Jr. Myers, Walter Dean. 2012. (ENG.). 40p. (J). (gr. -1-3). pap. 6.99 (978-0-06-225002-5(7), Amistad) HarperCollins Pubs.

—Malcolm X: A Fire Burning Brightly. Myers, Walter Dean. 2003. (ENG.). 40p. (J). (gr. k-3). pap. 6.99 (978-0-06-056201-4(3), Amistad) HarperCollins Pubs.

—Motorcycle Song. Siebert, Diane. Date not set. 32p. (J). (gr. -1-3). 5.99 (978-0-06-443632-8(2)) HarperCollins Pubs.

—Sweet Land of Liberty, 1 vol. Hopkinson, Deborah. 2007. (ENG.). 32p. (J). (gr. 1-5). 16.95 (978-1-56145-395-5(1)) Peachtree Pubs.

Jenkins, Leonard. I've Seen the Promised Land: The Life of Dr. Martin Luther King, Jr. Jenkins, Leonard, tr. Myers, Walter Dean. 2003. (ENG.). 40p. (J). (gr. -1-3). 17.99 (978-0-06-027703-1(3), Amistad) HarperCollins Pubs.

Jenkins, Reid Debra. I See the Moon. Appelt, Kathi. 2009. 12p. (J). (gr. -1). bds. 8.00 (978-0-8028-5358-5(7), Eerdmans Bks For Young Readers) Eerdmans, William B. Publishing Co.

Jenkins, Sandra. When Father Christmas Resigned. Jenkins, Peter. 2012. 36p. pap. (978-1-908775-94-8(7)) Legend Pr.

Jenkins, Sharon I. Remember the Ten Commandments with Jam & Jean Jellybean. Jenkins, Sharon I. l.t. ed. 2006. 32p. (J). (gr. -1-3). per. 10.99 (978-1-59879-240-9(7)) Lifevest Publishing, Inc.

Jenkins, Simon. Being Confirmed. Aiken, Nick. 2004. 160p. pap. (978-0-281-05631-6(5)) SPCK Publishing.

Jenkins, Steve. Animal Poems. Worth, Valerie. 2007. (ENG.). 48p. (J). (gr. -1-3). 17.99 (978-0-374-38057-1(0), Farrar, Straus & Giroux (BYR)) Farrar, Straus & Giroux.

—Bees, Snails, & Peacock Tails: Patterns & Shapes... Naturally. Franco, Betsy. 2008. (ENG.). 40p. (J). (gr. -1-3). 17.99 (978-1-4169-0386-4(0), McElderry, Margaret K. Bks.) McElderry, Margaret K. Bks.

—Billions of Years, Amazing Changes: The Story of Evolution. Pringle, Laurence. 2011. (ENG.). 112p. (J). (gr. 3). 17.95 (978-1-59078-723-6(4)) Boyds Mills Pr.

—Birdsongs. Franco, Betsy & Franco-Feeney, Betsy. 2007. (ENG.). 40p. (J). (gr. -1-3). 17.99 (978-0-689-87777-3(3), McElderry, Margaret K. Bks.) McElderry, Margaret K. Bks.

Jenkins, Steve. Bugs Are Insects. Rockwell, Anne. 2015. (Let's-Read-And-Find-Out Science 1 Ser.). (ENG.). 40p. (J). (gr. -1-3). pap. 6.99 (978-0-06-238182-8(2)) HarperCollins Pubs.

Jenkins, Steve. Eat Like a Bear. Sayre, April Pulley. 2013. (ENG.). 32p. (J). (gr. -1-3). 16.99 (978-0-8050-9039-0(8), Holt, Henry & Co. Bks. For Young Readers) Holt, Henry & Co.

—Hello Baby! Fox, Mem. 2009. (ENG.). 32p. (J). (gr. -1-k). 17.99 (978-1-4169-8513-6(1), Beach Lane Bks.) Beach Lane Bks.

—Life in a Coral Reef. Pfeffer, Wendy. 2009. (Let's-Read-And-Find-Out Science 2 Ser.). (ENG.). 40p. (J). (gr. 1-4). pap. 5.99 (978-0-06-445222-9(0), Collins) HarperCollins Pubs.

—Mama Built a Little Nest. Ward, Jennifer. 2014. (ENG.). 40p. (J). (gr. -1-3). 17.99 (978-1-4424-2116-5(9), Beach Lane Bks.) Beach Lane Bks.

—Move! Page, Robin. 2006. (ENG.). 32p. (J). (gr. -1-3). 16.99 (978-0-618-64637-1(X)) Houghton Mifflin Harcourt Publishing Co.

—Pug: And Other Animal Poems. Worth, Valerie. 2013. (ENG.). 40p. (J). (gr. -1-1). 16.99 (978-0-374-35024-6(8), Farrar, Straus & Giroux (BYR)) Farrar, Straus & Giroux.

—Vulture View. Sayre, April Pulley. rev. ed. 2007. (ENG.). 32p. (J). (gr. k-3). 16.95 (978-0-8050-7557-1(7), Holt, Henry & Co. Bks. For Young Readers) Holt, Henry & Co.

—What Do You Do with a Tail Like This? Page, Robin. 2011. (J). (gr. -1-3). 29.95 (978-0-545-10698-6(2)) Weston Woods Studios, Inc.

—Wiggling Worms at Work. Pfeffer, Wendy. 2003. (Let's-Read-And-Find-Out Science 2 Ser.). (ENG.). 40p. (J). (gr. k-4). 16.99 (978-0-06-028448-0(X), Collins) HarperCollins Pubs.

—Wiggling Worms at Work. Pfeffer, Wendy & Pfeffer. 2003. (Let's-Read-And-Find-Out Science 2 Ser.). (ENG.). 40p. (J). (gr. k-4). pap. 5.99 (978-0-06-445199-4(2), Collins) HarperCollins Pubs.

—Wiggling Worms at Work. Pfeffer, Wendy. 2004. (Let's-Read-and-Find-Out Science Ser.). 31p. (gr. -1-3). 16.00 (978-0-7569-3095-0(2)) Perfection Learning Corp.

—Woodpecker Wham! Sayre, April Pulley. 2015. (ENG.). 40p. (J). (gr. -1-3). 17.99 (978-0-8050-8842-7(3), Holt, Henry & Co. Bks. For Young Readers) Holt, Henry & Co.

Jenkins, Steve. Almost Gone: The World's Rarest Animals. Jenkins, Steve. 2006. (Let's-Read-And-Find-Out Science 2 Ser.). (ENG.). 40p. (J). (gr. k-4). 16.99 (978-0-06-053598-8(9)); pap. 5.99 (978-0-06-053600-8(4)) HarperCollins Pubs. (Collins).

—The Animal Book: A Collection of the Fastest, Fiercest, Toughest, Cleverest, Shyest - And Most Surprising - Animals on Earth. Jenkins, Steve. 2013. (ENG.). 208p. (J). (gr. 1-4). 21.99 (978-0-547-55799-1(X)) Houghton Mifflin Harcourt Publishing Co.

—Animals in Flight. Jenkins, Steve. Page, Robin. 2005. (ENG.). 32p. (J). (gr. -1-3). pap. 6.99 *(978-0-618-54882-8(3))* Houghton Mifflin Harcourt Publishing Co.

—Animals Upside Down: A Pull, Pop, Lift & Learn Book! Jenkins, Steve. Page, Robin. 2013. (ENG.). 24p. (J). (gr. -1-3). 24.99 *(978-0-547-34127-9(X))* Houghton Mifflin Harcourt Publishing Co.

—The Beetle Book. Jenkins, Steve. 2012. (ENG.). 40p. (J). (gr. -1-3). 17.99 *(978-0-547-68084-2(8))* Houghton Mifflin Harcourt Publishing Co.

—Bones: Skeletons & How They Work. Jenkins, Steve. 2010. (ENG.). 48p. (J). (gr. 2-5). 17.99 *(978-0-545-04651-0(3),* Scholastic Reference) Scholastic, Inc.

—Creature Features: Twenty-Five Animals Explain Why They Look the Way They Do. Jenkins, Steve. Page, Robin. 2014. (ENG.). 32p. (J). (gr. -1-3). 17.99 *(978-0-544-23351-5(4),* HMH Books For Young Readers) Houghton Mifflin Harcourt Publishing Co.

—Down, down, Down: A Journey to the Bottom of the Sea. Jenkins, Steve. 2009. (ENG.). 40p. (J). (gr. -1-3). 17.99 *(978-0-618-96636-3(6))* Houghton Mifflin Harcourt Publishing Co.

—How Many Ways Can You Catch a Fly? Jenkins, Steve. Page, Robin. 2008. (ENG.). 32p. (J). (gr. -1-3). 16.00 *(978-0-618-96634-9(X))* Houghton Mifflin Harcourt Publishing Co.

—How to Clean a Hippopotamus: A Look at Unusual Animal Partnerships. Jenkins, Steve. Page, Robin. (ENG.). 32p. (J). (gr. 1-4). 2013. pap. 6.99 *(978-0-547-99484-0(2));* 2010. 16.99 *(978-0-547-24515-7(7))* Houghton Mifflin Harcourt Publishing Co.

Jenkins, Steve. How to Swallow a Pig: Step-By-Step Advice from the Animal Kingdom. Jenkins, Steve. Page, Robin. 2015. (ENG.). 32p. (J). (gr. 1-4). 17.99 ***(978-0-544-31365-1(8),*** HMH Books For Young Readers) Houghton Mifflin Harcourt Publishing Co.

Jenkins, Steve. Living Color. Jenkins, Steve. 2007. (ENG.). 32p. (J). (gr. 2-5). 17.00 *(978-0-618-70897-0(9))* Houghton Mifflin Harcourt Publishing Co.

—My First Day: What Animals Do on Day One. Jenkins, Steve. Page, Robin. 2013. (ENG.). 32p. (J). (gr. -1-3). 17.99 *(978-0-547-73851-2(X))* Houghton Mifflin Harcourt Publishing Co.

—Never Smile at a Monkey: And 17 Other Important Things to Remember. Jenkins, Steve. 2009. (ENG.). 32p. (J). (gr. -1-3). 17.99 *(978-0-618-96620-2(X))* Houghton Mifflin Harcourt Publishing Co.

—Sisters & Brothers: Sibling Relationships in the Animal World. Jenkins, Steve. Page, Robin. 2008. (ENG.). 32p. (J). (gr. -1-3). 16.00 *(978-0-618-37596-7(1))* Houghton Mifflin Harcourt Publishing Co.

—Time for a Bath. Jenkins, Steve. Page, Robin. (ENG.). 24p. (J). (gr. -1-3). 2014. 26.99 *(978-0-544-23779-7(X),* HMH Books For Young Readers); 2011. 12.99 *(978-0-547-25037-3(1))* Houghton Mifflin Harcourt Publishing Co.

—Time to Eat. Jenkins, Steve. Page, Robin. (ENG.). 24p. (J). (gr. -1-3). 2014. 26.99 *(978-0-544-23753-7(6),* HMH Books For Young Readers); 2011. 12.99 *(978-0-547-25032-8(0))* Houghton Mifflin Harcourt Publishing Co.

—Time to Sleep. Jenkins, Steve. Page, Robin. (ENG.). 24p. (J). (gr. -1-3). 2014. 26.99 *(978-0-544-23757-5(9),* HMH Books For Young Readers); 2011. 12.99 *(978-0-547-25040-3(1))* Houghton Mifflin Harcourt Publishing Co.

Jenkins, Steve & Rodriguez, Edel. The Mystery of Darwin's Frog. Crump, Marty. 2013. (ENG.). 40p. (J). (gr. 2-5). 16.95 *(978-1-59078-864-6(8))* Boyds Mills Pr.

Jenkins, Steven. Move! Page, Robin. 2009. (ENG.). 28p. (J). (gr. k — 1). bds. 7.99 *(978-0-547-24000-8(7))* Houghton Mifflin Harcourt Publishing Co.

Jenkins, Ward. Chicks Run Wild. Bardhan-Quallen, Sudipta. 2011. (ENG.). 32p. (J). (gr. -1-1). 15.99 *(978-1-4424-0673-5(9),* Simon & Schuster Bks. For Young Readers) Simon & Schuster Bks. For Young Readers.

—How to Train with a T. Rex & Win 8 Gold Medals. Phelps, Michael & Abrahamson, Alan. 2009. (ENG.). 32p. (J). (gr. -1-3). 17.99 *(978-1-4169-8669-0(3),* Simon & Schuster Bks. For Young Readers) Simon & Schuster Bks. For Young Readers.

—New York, Baby! Chronicle Books Staff. 2012. (ENG.). 24p. (J). (gr. -1 — 1). 12.99 *(978-1-4521-0619-9(3))* Chronicle Bks. LLC.

—San Francisco, Baby! Chronicle Books Staff. 2012. (ENG.). 24p. (J). (gr. -1 — 1). 12.99 *(978-1-4521-0620-5(7))* Chronicle Bks. LLC.

Jenkins, Ward & Haya, Erwin. Not Your Parents' Money Book: Making, Saving, & Spending Your Own Money. Chatzky, Jean. 2010. (ENG.). 176p. (J). (gr. 5-9). pap. 12.99 *(978-1-4169-9472-5(6),* Simon & Schuster Bks. For Young Readers) Simon & Schuster Bks. For Young Readers.

Jenne, Ed, jt. illus. see Siple, Greg.

Jennenga, John. The Attack of Mr. Crohn's. Albers, Megan & Albers, Christine. Albers, Randy, ed. 2008. 71p. (YA). pap. 8.00 *(978-0-615-19666-4(7))* Albers, Christine.

Jenner, Lorelai. Castlecliff & the Fossil Princess. Pulford, Elizabeth. 2007. pap. *(978-1-921150-11-1(4))* Walker Bks. Australia Pty. Ltd.

Jennewein, Daniel. Chick-O-Saurus Rex. Jennewein, Lenore. 2013. (ENG.). 32p. (J). (gr. -1-3). 16.99 *(978-1-4424-5186-5(6),* Simon & Schuster Bks. For Young Readers) Simon & Schuster Bks. For Young Readers.

—Is Your Buffalo Ready for Kindergarten? Vernick, Audrey. 2010. (ENG.). 32p. (J). (gr. -1-3). 16.99 *(978-0-06-176275-8(X))* HarperCollins Pubs.

—Teach Your Buffalo to Play Drums. Vernick, Audrey. 2011. (ENG.). 32p. (J). (gr. -1-3). 16.99 *(978-0-06-176253-6(9))* HarperCollins Pubs.

Jennings, C. S. The Dozer Strikes! Dahl, Michael & Nickel, Scott. 2010. (Incredible Rockhead Ser.). (ENG.). 40p. (gr. 1-3). lib. bdg. 22.65 *(978-1-4342-1894-0(5),* Graphic Sparks) Stone Arch Bks.

—The Incredible Rockhead, 1 vol. Nickel, Scott. 2009. (Incredible Rockhead Ser.). (ENG.). 40p. (gr. 1-3). lib. bdg. 22.65 *(978-1-4342-1591-8(1),* Graphic Sparks) Stone Arch Bks.

—The Incredible Rockhead & the Spectacular Scissorlegz, 1 vol. Nickel, Scott et al. 2010. (Incredible Rockhead Ser.). (ENG.). 40p. (gr. 1-3). 22.65 *(978-1-4342-2127-8(X),* Graphic Sparks) Stone Arch Bks.

—The Incredible Rockhead vs Papercut!, 1 vol. Nickel, Scott. 2010. (Incredible Rockhead Ser.). (ENG.). 40p. (gr. 1-3). 22.65 *(978-1-4342-1976-3(3),* Graphic Sparks) Stone Arch Bks.

—Rock, Paper, Scissorlegz. Nickel, Scott. 2012. (Incredible Rockhead Ser.). (ENG.). 128p. (gr. 1-3). pap. 8.95 *(978-1-4342-4596-0(9))* Stone Arch Bks.

—A Serious Case of the Sillies. Hirschmann, Kris. 2013. 32p. (J). pap. *(978-0-545-56765-7(3))* Scholastic, Inc.

—Teeny Genie. Katschke, Judy. 2009. (ENG.). 24p. (J). (gr. 1-17). pap. 3.99 *(978-1-58476-813-5(4))* Innovative Kids.

Jennings, R. W. The Burksfield Bike Club, Book 2: Lost & Found. Finkelstein, Chaim. 2007. 224p. (J). 15.95 *(978-1-932443-69-1(X),* BBC1H) Judaica Pr., Inc., The.

Jennings, Randy. Don't You Wish Your Momma Could Cook Like Mine? Blake, Colleen H. Robley. 2012. 40p. pap. 16.97 *(978-1-61204-876-5(5),* Strategic Bk. Publishing) Strategic Book Publishing & Rights Agency (SBPRA).

—Maggiemoosetracks: Making Friends. Campbell, Mari. Katsumoto, Sayaka, tr. 2013. 108p. pap. 21.99 *(978-0-9895205-6-0(0))* MaggieMooseTracks.

—Maggiemoosetracks: Making Friends. Campbell, Mari. 2013. 84p. pap. 21.00 *(978-0-9895205-0-8(1))* MaggieMooseTracks.

—Maggiemoosetracks: Wolf Pack. Campbell, Mari. 2013. 106p. pap. 21.00 *(978-0-9895205-5-3(2))* MaggieMooseTracks.

—"What Are Parents?" Fox-Lee, Susan & Fox-Lee, Kyme. 2005. 32p. (J). 15.95 *(978-0-9753699-0-6(3))* StoryTyme Publishing.

—What Are Parents? Fox-Lee, Kyme & Fox-Lee, Susan. 2007. 32p. (J). 15.95 *(978-0-9753699-1-3(1))* StoryTyme Publishing.

—Where Is My Money? Prindle, Twyla. 2007. (J). bds. 14.95 *(978-0-9759527-8-8(1),* 1000, Prindle House Publishing Co.) Prindle Hse. Publishing Co.

—Who Stole Pop Pop's Underwear? Greenberg, Carmel. 2009. (ENG.). 46p. (J). 16.99 *(978-0-615-20924-1(6))* Kicks and Giggles Today.

Jenny, Christine. Turtle's Party in the Clouds. Birch, Beverley. 2015. (Collins Big Cat Ser.). (ENG.). 24p. pap. 6.95 ***(978-0-00-759106-0(3))*** HarperCollins Pubs. Ltd. GBR. Dist: Independent Pubs. Group.

Jenny, Lindley, jt. photos by see Reuben, Borgen.

Jensema, Marissa. ASL Songs for Kids - 1: With Songs in American Sign Language. 2003. (J). cd-rom 29.95 *(978-0-9752933-1-7(1))* Institute for Disabilities Research & Training, Inc.

Jensen, Astrid & Teo, Ali. Oh Hogwash, Sweet Pea! Gabel, Ngareta. Rainforth, Hannah, tr. 2007.Tr. of Tekiteora, Kei Hea o Hu?. 32p. (J). (gr. 4-8). pap. 12.00 *(978-1-877283-96-3(7))* Huia Pubs. NZL. Dist: Univ. of Hawaii Pr.

Jensen, Brian. Fast, Faster, Fastest: Animals That Move at Great Speeds, 1 vol. Dahl, Michael. 2005. (Animal Extremes Ser.). (ENG.). 24p. (gr. k-2). lib. bdg. 25.99 *(978-1-4048-1172-0(9),* Nonfiction Picture Bks.) Picture Window Bks.

—Hot, Hotter, Hottest: Animals That Adapt to Great Heat. Dahl, Michael. 2005. (Animal Extremes Ser.). (ENG.). 24p. (gr. k-2). lib. bdg. 25.99 *(978-1-4048-1017-4(X),* Nonfiction Picture Bks.) Picture Window Bks.

—Let's Trade: A Book about Bartering. Loewen, Nancy. 2005. (Money Matters Ser.). (ENG.). 24p. (gr. 1-3). lib. bdg. 25.99 *(978-1-4048-1157-7(5),* Nonfiction Picture Bks.) Picture Window Bks.

—Old, Older, Oldest: Animals That Live Long Lives, 1 vol. Dahl, Michael. 2005. (Animal Extremes Ser.). (ENG.). 24p. (gr. k-2). lib. bdg. 25.99 *(978-1-4048-1173-7(7),* Nonfiction Picture Bks.) Picture Window Bks.

Jensen, Brian, jt. illus. see Dahl, Michael.

Jensen, Brian, jt. illus. see Fitzpatrick, Brad.

Jensen, Brian, jt. illus. see Haugen, Ryan.

Jensen, Hans. Rescue Vehicles. Somerville, Louisa. (J). mass mkt. 8.99 *(978-0-590-24557-9(0))* Scholastic, Inc.

Jensen, Jakob Hjort. The Mystery Hat. Bennicke, Rune Brandt. 2014. (ENG.). 32p. (J). (gr. -1-k). 16.95 *(978-1-62914-621-8(8),* Sky Pony Pr.) Skyhorse Publishing Co., Inc.

Jensen, Leyah. My First Ballet Class: A Book with Foldout Pages. Jensen, Leyah, photos by. Capucilli, Alyssa Satin. 2011. (My First Ser.). (ENG.). 14p. (J). (gr. -1-k). 9.99 *(978-1-4424-0895-1(2),* Little Simon) Little Simon.

Jensen, Leyah, photos by. My First Karate Class: A Book with Foldout Pages. Capucilli, Alyssa Satin. 2012. (My First Ser.). (ENG.). 14p. (J). (gr. -1-k). 9.99 *(978-1-4424-2748-8(5),* Little Simon) Little Simon.

—My First Soccer Game: A Book with Foldout Pages. Capucilli, Alyssa Satin. 2011. (My First Ser.). (ENG.). 14p. (J). (gr. -1-k). 9.99 *(978-1-4424-2747-1(7),* Little Simon) Little Simon.

Jensen, Lisa. If My Hair Were Like Spagetti. Jensen, Lisa. Date not set. (J). (gr. -1-3). mass mkt. 15.95 *(978-0-9666973-0-8(8))* Jensen, Lissa.

Jensen, Nathaniel P. Burton the Kind Scarecrow. Boehlt, V. A. Christensen, Jennifer Steele, ed. 2012. (Burton the Scarecrow — Friendship Tales from the Farm Ser.: 1). (ENG.). 36p. (J). pap. 11.95 *(978-1-58985-202-0(8),* Little Five Star) Five Star Pubns., Inc.

—Burton's Friendship Garden. Boehlt, V. A. 2013. (Burton the Scarecrow áe Friendship Tales from the Farm Ser.: 2). (ENG.). 36p. (J). pap. 11.95 *(978-1-58985-210-5(9),* Little Five Star) Five Star Pubns., Inc.

—Desert Night Shift: A Pack Rat Story. Storad, Conrad J. 2006. 48p. (J). (gr. -1-3). 15.95 *(978-1-891795-16-9(3))* RGU Group, The.

—Don't Ever Cross That Road! An Armadillo Story. Storad, Conrad J. 2006. (Sonoran Desert Tails Ser.). 32p. (J). (gr. k-4). 15.95 *(978-1-891795-08-4(2))* RGU Group, The.

—Large Sitting Armadillo Character. Storad, Conrad J. (J). 10.95 *(978-1-891795-12-1(0),* 652910 177077) RGU Group, The.

—Small Standing Armadillo Character. Storad, Conrad J. (J). 3.95 *(978-1-891795-13-8(9),* 652910 176070) RGU Group, The.

Jensen, Nathaniel P., jt. illus. see Hagelberg, Michael.

Jensen, Rebecca Ridges. My Heavenly Father Loves Me. 2015. (J). 10.99 ***(978-1-4621-1564-8(0),*** Horizon Pubs.) Cedar Fort, Inc./CFI Distribution.

Jensz, Penny. The Brementown Musicians Vol. 1: Band 13/Topaz. Boylan, Eleanor. 2007. (Collins Big Cat Ser.). (ENG.). 224p. (J). pap. 8.99 *(978-0-00-722864-5(3))* HarperCollins Pubs. Ltd. GBR. Dist: Independent Pubs. Group.

Jentsch, Joyce Harp. Froggy & Friends Go to the Creek, 1 vol. Jentsch, R. D. 2009. 41p. pap. 24.95 *(978-1-60836-966-9(8))* America Star Bks.

Jeong, HaJin. Friendship Quilt. Kim, Cecil. rev. ed. 2014. (MySELF Bookshelf: Social & Emotional Learning/Social Awareness Ser.). (ENG.). 32p. (J). (gr. k-2). pap. 11.94 *(978-1-60357-659-8(2));* lib. bdg. 22.60 *(978-1-59953-650-7(1))* Norwood Hse. Pr.

Jeppesen, Ryan. Bible Ites: An Illustrated Guide to the People in the Holy Bible. Butler, David. 2015. (J). 19.99 ***(978-1-62972-108-8(5))*** Deseret Bk. Co.

Jepson, Beth. The Tooth Fairy's Guide to Lost Teeth: A Fortune for Every Day a Tooth Is Lost. Caldwell, J. Lynn. 2005. (J). per. 11.95 *(978-0-9774463-0-8(1))* Caldwell, Judy.

Jeralds, Scott. Scooby-Doo Animal Jokes. Dahl, Michael. 2015. (Scooby-Doo Joke Bks.). (ENG.). 64p. (gr. 2-3). lib. bdg. 21.32 *(978-1-4342-9683-2(0))* Stone Arch Bks.

—Scooby-Doo! Food Jokes! Dahl, Michael. 2015. (Scooby-Doo Joke Bks.). (ENG.). 64p. (gr. 2-3). lib. bdg. 21.32 *(978-1-4342-9682-5(2))* Stone Arch Bks.

Jeralds, Scott. Scooby Doo Joke Books. Dahl, Michael. 2015. (Scooby-Doo Joke Bks.). (ENG.). 64p. (gr. 2-3). lib. bdg. 85.28 ***(978-1-4965-0300-8(7),*** Scooby-Doo) Stone Arch Bks.

Jeralds, Scott. Scooby-Doo Monster Jokes. Dahl, Michael. 2015. (Scooby-Doo Joke Bks.). (ENG.). 64p. (gr. 2-3). lib. bdg. 21.32 *(978-1-4342-9681-8(4))* Stone Arch Bks.

—Scooby-Doo on the Go Jokes. Dahl, Michael. 2015. (Scooby-Doo Joke Bks.). (ENG.). 64p. (gr. 2-3). lib. bdg. 21.32 *(978-1-4342-9684-9(9))* Stone Arch Bks.

—Scooby-Doo's Laugh-Out-Loud Jokes! Dahl, Michael. 2015. (Scooby-Doo Joke Bks.). (ENG.). 64p. (gr. 2-3). pap. 9.95 *(978-1-62370-182-6(1))* Capstone Young Readers.

Jeram, Anita. All Pigs Are Beautiful. King-Smith, Dick. 2008. (Read, Listen, & Wonder Ser.). (ENG.). 32p. (J). (gr. -1-3). pap. 8.99 *(978-0-7636-3866-5(8))* Candlewick Pr.

—Un Beso de Buenas Noches. Hest, Amy. Rubio, Esther, tr. (SPA.). (J). 16.00 *(978-1-930332-04-1(1),* LC3294) Lectorum Pubns., Inc.

—Colors Everywhere. McBratney, Sam. 2007. (Guess How Much I Love You Ser.). (ENG.). 24p. (J). (-k). bds. 7.99 *(978-0-7636-3545-9(6))* Candlewick Pr.

—Don't You Feel Well, Sam? Hest, Amy. 2007. (Sam Bks.). (ENG.). 32p. (J). (gr. -1-k). 4.99 *(978-0-7636-2408-8(X))* Candlewick Pr.

—Guess How Much I Love You. McBratney, Sam. 2005. 34p. (J). bds. 19.95 *(978-0-9769313-1-7(1))* BrailleInk.

—Guess How Much I Love You. McBratney, Sam. (Guess How Much I Love You Ser.). (J). 2014. (ENG.). 30p. (gr. k-4). 9.99 *(978-0-7636-7446-5(X));* 2011. (ENG.). 16p. (gr. -1-2). 19.99 *(978-0-7636-5378-1(0));* 2011. (ENG.). (gr. k — 1). bds. 9.99 *(978-0-7636-4976-0(7));* 2006. 32p. (gr. -1-3). 15.99 *(978-0-7636-3503-9(0))* Candlewick Pr.

—Guess How Much I Love You. McBratney, Sam. 2008. (Guess How Much I Love You Ser.). (ENG.). 24p. (J). (— 1). bds. 7.99 *(978-0-7636-4264-8(9))* Candlewick Pr.

—Guess How Much I Love You 20th Anniversary Edition. McBratney, Sam. 2014. (Guess How Much I Love You Ser.). (ENG.). 40p. (J). (gr. k-12). 16.99 *(978-0-7636-7448-9(6))* Candlewick Pr.

—Guess How Much I Love You All Year Round. McBratney, Sam. 2010. (Guess How Much I Love You Ser.). (ENG.). 72p. (J). (gr. -1-2). 16.99 *(978-0-7636-4654-7(7))* Candlewick Pr.

—Guess How Much I Love You: Baby Book. McBratney, Sam. 2014. (Guess How Much I Love You Ser.). (ENG.). 64p. (J). (gr. k-12). 14.99 *(978-0-7636-7023-8(5))* Candlewick Pr.

—Guess How Much I Love You: Colors. McBratney, Sam. 2013. (Guess How Much I Love You Ser.). (ENG.). 14p. (J). (— 1). bds. 4.99 *(978-0-7636-6476-3(6))* Candlewick Pr.

—Guess How Much I Love You Lap-Size Board Book. McBratney, Sam. 2013. (Guess How Much I Love You Ser.). (ENG.). 24p. (J). (— 1). bds. 12.99 *(978-0-7636-7006-1(5))* Candlewick Pr.

—Guess How Much I Love You: Look What I Can Do: A First Concepts Book. McBratney, Sam. 2014. (Guess How Much I Love You Ser.). (ENG.). 16p. (J). (— 1). bds. 9.99 *(978-0-7636-7064-1(2))* Candlewick Pr.

—Guess How Much I Love You Sweetheart Edition. McBratney, Sam. 2009. (Guess How Much I Love You Ser.). (ENG.). 32p. (J). (gr. k-12). 12.00 *(978-0-7636-4913-5(9))* Candlewick Pr.

—Kiss Good Night. Hest, Amy. (Sam Bks.). (ENG.). (J). (gr. k-12). 2006. 32p. pap. 4.99 *(978-0-7636-2114-8(5));* 2004. 30p. bds. 6.99 *(978-0-7636-2094-3(7))* Candlewick Pr.

—Kiss Good Night: Book & Toy Gift Set. Hest, Amy. gif. ed. 2004. (Sam Bks.). (ENG.). 30p. (J). (gr. k-12). bds. 14.99 *(978-0-7636-2524-5(8))* Candlewick Pr.

—Kiss Good Night Lap-Size Board Book. Hest, Amy. 2014. (Sam Bks.). (ENG.). 32p. (J). (— 1). bds. 12.99 *(978-0-7636-4748-3(9))* Candlewick Pr.

—Let's Play in the Snow. McBratney, Sam. 2012. (Guess How Much I Love You Ser.). (ENG.). 24p. (J). (gr. k — 1). bds. 4.99 *(978-0-7636-6121-2(X))* Candlewick Pr.

—Little Chick. Hest, Amy. 2009. (ENG.). 56p. (J). (gr. -1-k). 17.99 *(978-0-7636-2890-1(5))* Candlewick Pr.

—The Nutbrown Hare Storybook Pair. McBratney, Sam. 2008. (Guess How Much I Love You Ser.). (ENG.). 48p. (J). (gr. k-k). bds. 14.99 *(978-0-7636-4265-5(7))* Candlewick Pr.

—A Surprise for the Nutbrown Hares. McBratney, Sam. 2009. (J). *(978-0-7636-4903-6(1))* Candlewick Pr.

—A Surprise for the Nutbrown Hares: A Guess How Much I Love You Storybook. McBratney, Sam. 2009. (Guess How Much I Love You Ser.). (ENG.). 24p. (J). (gr. -1-k). bds. 7.99 *(978-0-7636-4163-4(4))* Candlewick Pr.

—Todos Son Mis Favoritos. McBratney, Sam. 2004.Tr. of You're All My Favorites. (SPA.). 32p. (J). 16.99 *(978-84-88342-67-6(5))* S.A. Kokinos ESP. Dist: Lectorum Pubns., Inc.

—Tomhais Méid Mo Ghrá Duit (Guess How Much I Love You in Irish) McBratney, Sam. 2013. (Guess How Much I Love You Ser.). (ENG & GLE.). 32p. (J). (gr. -1-2). 9.99 *(978-0-7636-6570-8(3))* Candlewick Pr.

—Tu Puedes Hacerlo, Sam. Hest, Amy. 2004.Tr. of You Can Do It, Sam. (SPA.). (J). 16.00 *(978-1-930332-53-9(X))* Lectorum Pubns., Inc.

—You Can Do It, Sam. Hest, Amy. 2007. (Sam Bks.). (ENG.). 32p. (J). (gr. -1-k). pap. 4.99 *(978-0-7636-3688-3(6))* Candlewick Pr.

—You're All My Favorites. McBratney, Sam. 2008. (ENG.). 32p. (J). (gr. k-k). bds. 7.99 *(978-0-7636-4297-6(5));* (gr. -1-k). 14.99 *(978-0-7636-4045-3(X))* Candlewick Pr.

—You're All My Favorites with Audio. McBratney, Sam. 2011. (Candlewick Storybook Audio Ser.). (ENG.). 32p. (J). (gr. k-k). pap. 9.99 *(978-0-7636-5158-9(3))* Candlewick Pr.

Jeram, Anita. Bunny My Honey. Jeram, Anita. 2009. (ENG.). 22p. (J). (gr. k-k). bds. 7.99 *(978-0-7636-4645-5(8))* Candlewick Pr.

—I Love My Little Storybook. Jeram, Anita. 2010. (ENG.). 32p. (J). (-k). 7.99 *(978-0-7636-4806-0(X))* Candlewick Pr.

Jerde, Susan. Inuit Tales: Read Well Level K Unit 10 Storybook. Gunn, Barbara. 2003. (Read Well Level K Ser.). 20p. (J). *(978-1-57035-681-0(5))* Cambium Education, Inc.

—Rhyming Fun: Read Well Level K Unit 6 Storybook. Sprick, Marilyn et al. 2003. (Read Well Level K Ser.). 20p. (J). *(978-1-57035-678-0(5))* Cambium Education, Inc.

—Shells on the Shore: Read Well Level K Unit 14 Storybook. Jones, Shelley V. & Gunn, Barbara. 2003. (Read Well Level K Ser.). 20p. (J). *(978-1-57035-685-8(8),* 55546) Cambium Education, Inc.

Jeremiah. Tanner's Turtle. Labadie, Sally. 2012. 32p. pap. 12.95 *(978-1-61244-085-9(1))* Halo Publishing International.

Jermann, David. The Secret of the Lost Kingdom. Bolton, Michael. 2004. 36p. (J). (gr. k-4). reprint ed. *(978-0-7567-7849-1(2))* DIANE Publishing Co.

—El Secreto del Reino Perdido. Bolton, Michael. (Buenas Noches Ser.). (SPA.). (J). (gr. 3). pap. 7.16 *(978-958-04-4904-1(X))* Norma S.A. COL. Dist: Lectorum Pubns., Inc.

Jerome, Barb. Solomon & Lily. Schield, Allie Schield. 2003. 34p. (J). per. 11.99 *(978-0-9743948-0-0(7))* One Little Miracle.

Jerome, Elaine. Sundays on Fourth Street/Los Domingos en la Calle Cuatro. Costales, Amy. 2009. (SPA & ENG.). 32p. (J). (gr. -1-3). 16.95 *(978-1-55885-520-5(3))* Arte Publico Pr.

—The Woodcutter's Gift/el Regalo del Lenador. Ruiz-Flores, Lupe. Ventura, Gabriela Baeza, tr. from ENG. 2007. (SPA & ENG.). 32p. (J). (gr. -1-2). 16.95 *(978-1-55885-489-5(4),* Piñata Books) Arte Publico Pr.

Jerome, Karen A. If Nathan Were Here. Bahr, Mary. 2004. 32p. (J). (gr. -1-4). pap. 8.00 *(978-0-8028-5235-9(1));* (gr. 1-7). 16.00 *(978-0-8028-5187-1(8))* Eerdmans, William B. Publishing Co.

—Just Add One Chinese Sister: An Adoption Story. McMahon, Patricia & McCarthy, Conor Clarke. 2005. (ENG.). 32p. (J). (gr. k-3). 17.95 *(978-1-56397-989-7(6))* Boyds Mills Pr.

—Sometimes Smart Is Good/A Veces Es Bueno Ser Listo. Luchsinger, Dena. 2007. (SPA & ENG.). 32p. (J). (gr. -1). 16.00 *(978-0-8028-5215-1(7),* Eerdmans Bks For Young Readers) Eerdmans, William B. Publishing Co.

Jeschke, Stefanie. I Wish I Were A... Holzwarth, Werner. 2013. (ENG.). 40p. (J). (gr. -1-k). 16.95 *(978-1-62087-993-1(X),* 620993, Sky Pony Pr.) Skyhorse Publishing Co., Inc.

Jesner, Alois. 101 Life Skills Games for Children: Learning, Growing, Getting along (Ages 6-12) Badegruber, Bernie. 2005. (SmartFun Activity Bks.). (ENG.). 160p. per. 14.95 *(978-0-89793-441-1(5),* 1251580, Hunter Hse.) Turner Publishing Co.

Jess Golden, Jess. Lana's World - Let's Go Fishing! Silverman, Erica & Rucker, Justin. 2015. (Green Light Readers Level 2 Ser.). (ENG.). 32p. (J). (gr. 1-4). 12.99 *(978-0-544-10652-9(0),* HMH Books For Young Readers) Houghton Mifflin Harcourt Publishing Co.

—Lana's World - Let's Have a Parade! Silverman, Erica. 2015. (Green Light Readers Level 2 Ser.). (ENG.). 32p. (J). (gr. 1-4). 12.99 *(978-0-544-10677-2(6),* HMH Books For Young Readers) Houghton Mifflin Harcourt Publishing Co.

Jessa, Azra. Ramadhan & Eid-Ul-Fitr. Jessa, Azra. 2008. (ENG.). 16p. (J). (gr. -1). 12.95 *(978-1-879402-23-2(8))* Tahrike Tarsile Quran, Inc.

Jessee, Diana. Lawyer Will: The Story of an Appalachian Lawyer. Cooper, Ann Goode & Bowlin, William Harrison. 2004. 36p. (J). 12.95 *(978-1-887905-90-9(1))* Parkway Pubs., Inc.

—Zebordee Goes to the Races. Cooper, Ann Goode. 2005. 32p. (J). (gr. -1-3). *(978-1-933251-01-1(8))* Parkway Pubs., Inc.

J

Jessell, Tim. Babe Ruth & the Baseball Curse. Kelly, David A. 2009. (Stepping Stone Book(TM) Ser.). (ENG.). 112p. (J). (gr. 2-5). 4.99 (978-0-375-85603-7(X)) Random Hse., Inc.

—The Boxcar Children. 2013. (Boxcar Children Mysteries Ser.). (ENG.). 538p. (J). (gr. 2-5). 45.00 (978-0-8075-0864-0(0)) Whitman, Albert & Co.

—The Boxcar Children Beginning: The Aldens of Fair Meadow Farm. MacLachlan, Patricia. 2012. (Boxcar Children Mysteries Ser.). (ENG.). 144p. (J). (gr. 2-5). 16.99 (978-0-8075-6616-9(0)) Whitman, Albert & Co.

—The Boxcar Children Beginning - The Aldens of Fair Meadow Farm. MacLachlan, Patricia. 2013. (Boxcar Children Mysteries Ser.). (ENG.). 144p. (J). (gr. 2-5). 5.99 (978-0-8075-6617-6(9)) Whitman, Albert & Co.

—City in the Clouds. Abbott, Tony. 2004. (Secrets of Droon Ser.: No. 4). 88p. 15.00 (978-0-7569-3930-4(5)) Perfection Learning Corp.

—Dog Diaries No. 4: Togo. Klimo, Kate. 2014. (Dog Diaries). (ENG.). 176p. (J). (gr. 2-5). pap. 7.99 (978-0-385-37335-7(X), Random Hse. Bks. for Young Readers) Random Hse. Children's Bks.

—Dog Diaries #2: Buddy. Ingle, Annie & Klimo, Kate. 2013. (Dog Diaries). (ENG.). 160p. (J). (gr. 2-5). pap. 6.99 (978-0-307-97904-9(0), Random Hse. Bks. for Young Readers) Random Hse. Children's Bks.

—Dog Diaries #3: Barry. Klimo, Kate. 2013. (Dog Diaries). (ENG.). 160p. (J). (gr. 2-5). pap. 7.99 (978-0-449-81280-8(4), Random Hse. Bks. for Young Readers) Random Hse. Children's Bks.

—Dog Diaries #5: Dash. Klimo, Kate. 2014. (Dog Diaries). (ENG.). 160p. (J). (gr. 2-5). pap. 7.99 (978-0-385-37338-8(4), Random Hse. Bks. for Young Readers) Random Hse. Children's Bks.

—A Dog's Way Home. Pyron, Bobbie. 2011. (ENG.). 336p. (J). (gr. 3-7). 16.99 (978-0-06-198674-1(7), Tegen, Katherine Bks) HarperCollins Pubs.

—Double Team. Stoudemire, Amar'e. 2012. (STAT: Standing Tall & Talented Ser.: No. 2). (ENG.). 144p. (J). (gr. 3-7). pap. 5.99 (978-0-545-38760-6(4), Scholastic Paperbacks) Scholastic, Inc.

—Double Team. Stoudemire, Amar'e. ed. 2012. (STAT: Standing Tall & Talented Ser.: 2). lib. bdg. 16.00 (978-0-606-26762-5(X), Turtleback) Turtleback Bks.

—Flight of the Genie. Abbott, Tony. 2004. (Secrets of Droon Ser.: No. 21). 122p. (J). lib. bdg. 15.38 (978-1-4242-0314-7(7)) Fitzgerald Bks.

—Ginger. Worth, Bonnie & Klimo, Kate. 2013. (Dog Diaries). (ENG.). 160p. (J). (gr. 2-5). pap. 7.99 (978-0-307-97899-8(0)) Random Hse., Inc.

—The Hidden Stairs & the Magic Carpet. Abbott, Tony. 2004. (Secrets of Droon Ser.: No. 1). 80p. (gr. 2-5). 15.00 (978-0-7569-3939-7(9)) Perfection Learning Corp.

—Home Court. Stoudemire, Amar'e. 2012. (STAT: Standing Tall & Talented Ser.: 1). (ENG.). 144p. (J). (gr. 3-7). pap. 5.99 (978-0-545-38759-0(0), Scholastic Pr.) Scholastic, Inc.

—The Magic Escapes. Abbott, Tony. 2004. (Secrets of Droon Ser.: No. 1). 161p. (gr. 2-5). 16.00 (978-0-7569-3944-1(5)) Perfection Learning Corp.

—The Moon Scroll. Abbott, Tony. 2004. (Secrets of Droon Ser.: No. 15). 129p. (gr. 2-5). 15.00 (978-0-7569-3946-5(1)) Perfection Learning Corp.

—Mystery of the Fallen Treasure. 2013. (Boxcar Children Mysteries Ser.: #132). (ENG.). 128p. (J). (gr. 2-5). 5.99 (978-0-8075-5506-4(1)); 15.99 (978-0-8075-5508-8(8)) Whitman, Albert & Co.

—Racing the Moon. Armstrong, Alan W. 2013. (ENG.). 224p. (J). (gr. 3-7). pap. 6.99 (978-0-375-85890-1(3)) Random Hse., Inc.

—Raleigh's Page. Armstrong, Alan. 2009. (ENG.). 336p. (J). (gr. 3-7). 7.99 (978-0-375-83320-5(X), Yearling) Random Hse. Children's Bks.

—The Return of the Graveyard Ghost. 2013. (Boxcar Children Mysteries Ser.: #133). (ENG.). 128p. (J). (gr. 2-5). 15.99 (978-0-8075-6935-1(6)); 5.99 (978-0-8075-6936-8(4)) Whitman, Albert & Co.

—Slam Dunk: Standing Tall & Talented. Stoudemire, Amar'e. 2013. (Stat Ser.: 3). (ENG.). 144p. (J). (gr. 3-7). pap. 5.99 (978-0-545-38761-3(2), Scholastic Paperbacks) Scholastic, Inc.

—Stubby. Klimo, Kate. 2015. (Dog Diaries: 7). (ENG.). 160p. (J). (gr. 2-5). lib. bdg. 12.99 (978-0-385-39244-0(3)) Random Hse., Inc.

—Superhero Christmas. Lee, Stan. 2004. 32p. (J). (gr. -1-2). 16.89 (978-0-06-056560-2(8)) HarperCollins Pubs.

—Sweetie, No. 6. Klimo, Kate. 2015. (Dog Diaries). (ENG.). 160p. (J). (gr. 2-5). pap. 6.99 (978-0-385-39240-2(0)) Random Hse., Inc.

—Two Hot Dogs with Everything. Haven, Paul. 2007. (ENG.). 320p. (J). (gr. 3-7). per. 7.99 (978-0-375-83349-6(8), Yearling) Random Hse. Children's Bks.

Jessell, Tim, jt. illus. see Adams, Gil.

Jessell, Tim, jt. illus. see Gurney, John Steven.

Jesset, Aurore & Korthues, Barbara. Loopy. Jesset, Aurore. 2009. (ENG.). 32p. (J). (gr. -1-3). 7.95 (978-0-7358-2261-0(1)) North-South Bks., Inc.

JessT, Grant, jt. illus. see Scott, Peter.

Jevons, Chris. Hansel & Gretel & the Green Witch. North, Laura. 2015. (ENG.). 32p. (J). **(978-0-7787-1928-1(6))** Crabtree Publishing Co.

Jewett, Anne. The Warmest Place of All. Rando, Licia. 2009. (ENG.). 32p. (J). (gr. -1-k). 16.95 (978-0-9792035-8-9(9)) Pleasant St. Pr.

Jeyaveeran, Ruth. El árbol Más Feliz: Un Cuento Sobre Yoga. Krishnaswami, Uma. 2008.Tr. of Happiest Tree: a Yoga Story. (SPA.). 32p. (J). pap. 9.95 (978-1-62014-149-6(3)) Lee & Low Bks., Inc.

Jeyaveeran, Ruth & Akib, Jamel. Bringing Asha Home, 1 vol. Krishnaswami, Uma. 2006. (ENG.). 32p. (J). (gr. -1-3). 16.95 (978-1-58430-259-9(3)) Lee & Low Bks., Inc.

Ji, Zhaohua & Xu, Cui. No! That's Wrong! Ji, Zhaohua & Xu, Cui. 2008. (ENG.). 32p. (J). (gr. -1-3). 10.99 (978-1-933605-66-1(9)) Kane Miller.

Jian, Li. The Little Monkey King's Journey: Retold in English & Chinese. Wert, Yijin, tr. 2012. (ENG & CHI.). 48p. (J). (gr. -1-2). 16.95 (978-1-60220-981-7(2)) BetterLink Pr., Inc.

Jim Connelly. The Mouse Who Lived in Fenway Park. Bradford James Nolan. 2009. 36p. pap. 19.99 (978-1-4389-4491-3(8)) AuthorHouse.

Jimena Pinto-Krowjiline. Quirky Kids Zoo. Brannon, Pat. 2011. 32p. pap. 11.99 (978-1-933300-83-2(3)) Wandering Sage Pubns., LLC.

Jimenez, Leticia Serrano. DOS Casos de Casas y Algunas Otras Cosas. Avila, Juan Casas. rev. ed. 2006. (Castillo de la Lectura Verde Ser.). (SPA & ENG.). 72p. (J). (gr. 2-4). pap. 7.95 (978-970-20-0175-1(7)) Castillo, Ediciones, S. A. de C. V. MEX. Dist: Macmillan.

Jimenez, Resu. Amigos en el Bosque. Lopez, Minia. 2006. (SPA.). (J). 8.00 (978-0-9773531-3-2(3)) Charming Pubns.

—Friends in the Forest. Lopez, Minia. 2006. (J). 8.00 (978-0-9773531-4-9(1)) Charming Pubns.

Jimenz, Jim & Calero, Dennis. The Fall of the House of Usher, 1 vol. Manning, Matthew K. & Poe, Edgar Allen. 2013. (Edgar Allan Poe Graphic Novels Ser.). (ENG.). 72p. (gr. 2-3). 26.65 (978-1-4342-3024-9(4)); pap. 6.10 (978-1-4342-4258-7(7)) Stone Arch Bks.

Jin, Katherine. Sam & Nate. Collins, P. J. Sarah. 2005. 60p. (J). lib. bdg. 20.00 (978-1-4242-1261-3(8)) Fitzgerald Bks.

—Sam & Nate, 1 vol. Collins, P. J. Sarah. 2005. (Orca Echoes Ser.). (ENG.). 64p. (J). (gr. 2-3). per. 6.95 (978-1-55143-334-9(6)) Orca Bk. Pubs. USA.

Jin, Susie Lee. It's Bedtime for Little Monkeys. 2010. 5p. (J). 5.99 (978-0-7369-2832-8(4)) Harvest Hse. Pubs.

Jinshan Painting Academy. We See the Moon. Kitze, Carrie A. I.t. ed. 2003. 32p. (J). (gr. -1-3). 16.95 (978-0-9726244-0-4(6)) EMK Pr.

Jirak, Tracey. Our Cool School Zoo Revue. Berthiaume, Donna M. 2008. 36p. pap. 24.95 (978-1-60672-672-3(2)) America Star Bks.

Jirankova-Limbrick, Martina. Name That Dinosaur. Edwards, Amelia. 2009. (ENG.). 40p. (J). (gr. -1-3). 17.99 (978-0-7636-3473-5(5)) Candlewick Pr.

JiSeung, Kook. Ouch! It Stings! JiSeung, Kook. rev. ed. 2014. (MySELF Bookshelf: Social & Emotional Learning/Self-Worth Ser.). (ENG.). 32p. (J). (gr. k-2). pap. 11.94 (978-1-60357-653-6(3)); lib. bdg. 22.60 (978-1-59953-644-6(7)) Norwood Hse. Pr.

Jo, Eun-hwa. What Does the Bee See? Observation - Parts & Whole. Kim, Soo-hyeon. Cowley, Joy, ed. 2015. (Step up - Creative Thinking Ser.). (ENG.). 32p. (gr. -1-2). 26.65 **(978-1-925246-08-7(6))**; 26.65 **(978-1-925246-34-6(5))**; 7.99 **(978-1-925246-60-5(4))** ChoiceMaker Pty. Ltd., The AUS. (Big and SMALL). Dist: Lerner Publishing Group.

—What Does the Bee See? Observation - Parts & Whole. Kim, Soo-hyeon. Cowley, Joy, ed. 2015. (Step up - Creative Thinking Ser.). (ENG.). 32p. (J). (gr. -1-2). 7.99 **(978-1-925186-54-3(7))** Lerner Publishing Group.

Jo, Hyeon-suk. Hansel & Gretel. Brothers Grimm. Cowley, Joy, ed. 2015. (World Classics Ser.). (ENG.). 32p. (gr. k-4). 26.65 **(978-1-925246-40-7(X)**, Big and SMALL) ChoiceMaker Pty. Ltd., The AUS. Dist: Lerner Publishing Group.

—Hansel & Gretel. Brothers Grimm Staff. Cowley, Joy, ed. 2015. (World Classics Ser.). (ENG.). 32p. (gr. k-4). 26.65 **(978-1-925246-14-8(0))**; 7.99 **(978-1-925246-66-7(3))** ChoiceMaker Pty. Ltd., The AUS. (Big and SMALL). Dist: Lerner Publishing Group.

Jo, Sinae. Song of the Mekong River: Vietnam. Choi, Na-mi. Cowley, Joy, ed. 2015. (Global Kids Storybooks Ser.). (ENG.). 32p. (gr. 1-4). 26.65 **(978-1-925246-01-8(9))**; 26.65 **(978-1-925246-27-8(2))**; 7.99 **(978-1-925246-53-7(1))** ChoiceMaker Pty. Ltd., The AUS. (Big and SMALL). Dist: Lerner Publishing Group.

Joan, Pere. The Three Little Pigs/Los Tres Cerditos. Bas, Mercè Escardó I. 2006. (Bilingual Fairy Tales Ser.: BILI). (ENG & SPA.). 32p. (J). (gr. -1-7). pap. 6.99 (978-0-8118-5064-3(1)) Chronicle Bks. LLC.

—Los Tres Cerditos. Escardo Bas, Mercè. 2003. (SPA.). 24p. (978-84-246-1939-8(0), GL30510) La Galera, S.A. Editorial ESP. Dist: Lectorum Pubns., Inc.

Joane', E'nea. Momzilla, 1 vol. Keonna-E'nea. 2009. 18p. pap. 24.95 (978-1-60749-607-6(0)) America Star Bks.

Jobling, Curtis. The Skeleton in the Closet. Schertle, Alice. 2003. (ENG.). 32p. (J). (gr. 1-18). 15.99 (978-0-688-17738-6(7)) HarperCollins Pubs.

Jobling, Curtis. My Daddy. Jobling, Curtis. 2007. (ENG.). 32p. (J). (gr. -1-k). 9.99 (978-0-00-722164-6(9), HarperCollins Children's Bks.) HarperCollins Pubs. Ltd. GBR. Dist: Independent Pubs. Group.

Jocelyn, Marthe. Time Is When. Gleick, Beth. 2008. (ENG.). 32p. (J). (gr. -1-2). 15.95 (978-0-88776-870-5(9), Tundra Bks.) Tundra Bks. CAN. Dist: Penguin Random Hse., LLC.

Jocelyn, Marthe. A Day with Nellie. Jocelyn, Marthe. 2008. (ENG.). 16p. (J). (gr. k-k). bds. 7.95 (978-0-88776-869-9(5), Tundra Bks.) Tundra Bks. CAN. Dist: Penguin Random Hse., LLC.

—Sneaky Art: Crafty Surprises to Hide in Plain Sight. Jocelyn, Marthe. 2013. (ENG.). 64p. (J). (gr. 3-7). 12.99 (978-0-7636-5648-5(8)) Candlewick Pr.

Jocelyn, Sawyer & Liza, Behles. Petunia Patch Pockets & the Golden Locket. Lorenzen, Margaret Brownell. 2005. 76p. (J). per. 12.50 (978-0-9724922-7-0(5)) Authors & Artists Publishers of New York, Inc.

Jock, jt. illus. see Guera, R. M.

Jodie, Dias & Wendy, Watson. Lexi & Hippocrates: Find Trouble at the Olympics. Keen, Marian. 2014. (ENG.). 92p. pap. (978-1-77141-026-7(4), Influence Publishing) Lean Marketing Pr.

Joe Kent. The Beginning of People's Chicken. Delena Deatherage. 2009. 40p. pap. 18.95 (978-1-4208-9094-5(8)) AuthorHouse.

Joe, Staton, et al. Crossovers, Vol. 2. 2004. (Crossovers Ser.). 160p. (YA). pap. 9.95 (978-1-59314-051-9(7)) CrossGeneration Comics, Inc.

Johannes, Shelley. Feelings Only I Know: Mom & Dad Are Getting Divorced. McKenna, Susan. 2007. 24p. (J). 14.95 (978-0-9789965-0-5(X)) Wayfarer Pr., LLC.

—More Feelings Only I Know: Divorce & Fighting Are Hurting My Heart. McKenna, Susan. 2007. 24p. (J). 14.95 (978-0-9789965-1-2(8)) Wayfarer Pr., LLC.

—Sleep Sweet, My Little One. Clairmont, Patsy. 2014. (ENG.). 24p. (J). pap. 12.99 (978-1-4003-2401-9(7)) Nelson, Thomas Inc.

—Super Luke Faces His Bully: GiggleHeart Adventures #2. Cogswell, Jackie Chirco. 2011. 224p. (J). 14.99 (978-0-9820490-2-0(1)); pap. 9.99 (978-0-9820490-1-3(3)) Divine Inspiration Publishing, LLC.

Johansen, Tesia, jt. illus. see Johnson, Gary.

Johanson, Anna. There's a Frog Trapped in the Bathroom. Snyder, Susan. 2005. 23p. (J). (gr. 1-3). 9.95 (978-0-9715411-0-8(8)) Kotzig Publishing, Inc.

—The Very Stubborn Centipede. Snyder, Susan. 2005. 24p. (J). (gr. 2-4). 9.95 (978-0-9767163-0-3(5)) Kotzig Publishing, Inc.

Johansson, Anna. The Peaceable Forest: India's Tale of Kindness to Animals. Ely, Kosa. 2012. (ENG.). 32p. (J). (gr. k). 16.99 (978-1-60887-115-5(0)) Mandala Publishing.

Johansson, Cecilia. Digger Dog. Bee, William. 2014. (ENG.). 36p. (J). (gr. -1-2). 14.99 (978-0-7636-6162-5(7), Nosy Crow) Candlewick Pr.

—The Haunted Shipwreck. McKain, Kelly. 2004. (Mermaid Rock Ser.). 48p. (J). (978-0-439-62647-7(1)) Scholastic, Inc.

—Just Like Mommy. 2006. (ENG.). 16p. (J). (gr. -1 — 1). bds. 7.99 (978-1-4169-1218-7(5), Little Simon) Little Simon.

—Zoo (First Sticker Book) Taplin, Sam. ed. 2011. (First Sticker Book Ser.). 24p. (J). pap. 6.99 (978-0-7945-2927-7(5), Usborne) EDC Publishing.

Johari, Harish & Weltevrede, Pieter. Ganga: The River That Flows from Heaven to Earth. Sperling, Vatsala. 2008. (ENG.). 32p. (J). (gr. -1-6). 15.95 (978-1-59143-089-6(5)) Bear & Co.

Johari, Sandeep. Hanuman's Journey to the Medicine Mountain. Sperling, Vatsala. 2006. (ENG.). 32p. (J). (gr. -1-6). 15.95 (978-1-59143-063-6(1)) Inner Traditions International, Ltd.

—Karna: The Greatest Archer in the World. Sperling, Vatsala. 2007. (ENG.). 32p. (J). (gr. -1-6). 15.95 (978-1-59143-073-5(9), Bear Cub Bks.) Bear & Co.

John & Wendy. Free the Worms! Krulik, Nancy. 2008. (Katie Kazoo, Switcheroo Ser.). 78p. (J). 11.65 (978-0-7569-8807-4(1)) Perfection Learning Corp.

—Something's Fishy. Krulik, Nancy E. 2008. (Katie Kazoo, Switcheroo Ser.). 76p. 14.00 (978-0-7569-8348-2(7)) Perfection Learning Corp.

John and Wendy. Cat Days. Andrews, Alexa. 2012. (Penguin Young Readers, Level 1 Ser.). (ENG.). 32p. (J). (gr. k-1). pap. 3.99 (978-0-448-46305-6(9), Warne, Frederick Pubs.) Penguin Bks., Ltd. GBR. Dist: Penguin Random Hse., LLC.

—A Collection of Katie: Books 1-4. Krulik, Nancy. 2012. (Katie Kazoo, Switcheroo Ser.). (ENG.). 320p. (J). (gr. 2-4). pap. 7.99 (978-0-448-46304-9(0), Grosset & Dunlap) Penguin Publishing Group.

—Katie Kazoo, Switcheroo: A Collection of Katie. Krulik, Nancy. 2008. (Katie Kazoo, Switcheroo Ser.: Bks. 1-4). (ENG.). 320p. (J). (gr. 2-4). 10.99 (978-0-448-44910-4(2), Grosset & Dunlap) Penguin Publishing Group.

—Witch Switch. Krulik, Nancy. 2006. (Katie Kazoo, Switcheroo Ser.: No. 4). (ENG.). 160p. (J). (gr. 2-4). pap. 4.99 (978-0-448-44330-0(9), Grosset & Dunlap) Penguin Publishing Group.

John and Wendy Staff. All's Fair. Krulik, Nancy. 2013. (Katie Kazoo, Switcheroo Ser.). (ENG.). 144p. (J). (gr. 2-4). pap. 4.99 (978-0-448-45682-9(6), Grosset & Dunlap) Penguin Publishing Group.

—Any Way You Slice It. Krulik, Nancy. 9th ed. 2003. (Katie Kazoo, Switcheroo Ser.: 9). (ENG.). 80p. (J). (gr. 2-4). pap. 3.99 (978-0-448-43204-5(8), Grosset & Dunlap) Penguin Publishing Group.

—Bad Rap, 16 vols. Krulik, Nancy. 2005. (Katie Kazoo, Switcheroo Ser.: 16). (ENG.). 80p. (J). (gr. 2-4). pap. 3.99 (978-0-448-43741-5(4), Grosset & Dunlap) Penguin Publishing Group.

—Be Nice to Mice!, No. 20. Krulik, Nancy. 2006. (Katie Kazoo, Switcheroo Ser.: 20). (ENG.). 80p. (J). (gr. 2-4). pap. 3.99 (978-0-448-44132-0(2), Grosset & Dunlap) Penguin Publishing Group.

—Camp Rules! Krulik, Nancy. 2007. (Katie Kazoo, Switcheroo Ser.: No. 5). (ENG.). 160p. (J). (gr. 2-4). pap. 4.99 (978-0-448-44542-7(5), Grosset & Dunlap) Penguin Publishing Group.

—Doggone It!, 8 vols. Krulik, Nancy. 8th ed. 2006. (Katie Kazoo, Switcheroo Ser.: 8). (ENG.). 80p. (J). (gr. 2-4). pap. 3.99 (978-0-448-43172-7(6), Grosset & Dunlap) Penguin Publishing Group.

—Don't Be Such a Turkey! Krulik, Nancy. 2010. (Katie Kazoo, Switcheroo Ser.). (ENG.). 160p. (J). (gr. 2-4). pap. 4.99 (978-0-448-45448-1(3), Grosset & Dunlap) Penguin Publishing Group.

—Flower Power, 27 vols. Krulik, Nancy. 2008. (Katie Kazoo, Switcheroo Ser.: 27). (ENG.). 80p. (J). (gr. 2-4). pap. 3.99 (978-0-448-44674-5(X), Grosset & Dunlap) Penguin Publishing Group.

—Flower Power. Krulik, Nancy E. 2008. (Katie Kazoo, Switcheroo Ser.). 78p. (gr. 2-5). 14.00 (978-0-7569-8806-7(3)) Perfection Learning Corp.

—Free the Worms! Krulik, Nancy. 2008. (Katie Kazoo, Switcheroo Ser.: 28). (ENG.). 80p. (J). (gr. 2-4). pap. 3.99 (978-0-448-44675-2(8), Grosset & Dunlap) Penguin Publishing Group.

—Friends for Never, 14 vols. Krulik, Nancy. 2004. (Katie Kazoo, Switcheroo Ser.: 14). (ENG.). 80p. (J). (gr. 2-4). pap. 3.99 (978-0-448-43606-7(X), Grosset & Dunlap) Penguin Publishing Group.

—Get Lost!, 6 vols. Krulik, Nancy. 2006. (Katie Kazoo, Switcheroo Ser.: 6). (ENG.). 80p. (J). (gr. 2-4). pap. 3.99 (978-0-448-43101-7(7), Grosset & Dunlap) Penguin Publishing Group.

—Girls Don't Have Cooties, 4 vols. Krulik, Nancy. 2005. (Katie Kazoo, Switcheroo Ser.: 4). (ENG.). 80p. (J). (gr. 2-4). mass mkt. 3.99 (978-0-448-42705-8(2), Grosset & Dunlap) Penguin Publishing Group.

—Going Batty. Krulik, Nancy. 2009. (Katie Kazoo, Switcheroo Ser.: 32). (ENG.). 80p. (J). (gr. 2-4). pap. 3.99 (978-0-448-45042-1(9), Grosset & Dunlap) Penguin Publishing Group.

—Going Overboard! Krulik, Nancy. 2012. (Katie Kazoo, Switcheroo Ser.: No. 9). (ENG.). 144p. (J). (gr. 2-4). pap. 4.99 (978-0-448-45681-2(8), Grosset & Dunlap) Penguin Publishing Group.

—Gotcha! Gotcha Back! Krulik, Nancy. 2006. (Katie Kazoo, Switcheroo Ser.: 19). (ENG.). 80p. (J). (gr. 2-4). pap. 3.99 (978-0-448-43768-2(6), Grosset & Dunlap) Penguin Publishing Group.

—Hair Today, Gone Tomorrow!, 34 vols., No. 34. Krulik, Nancy. 2010. (Katie Kazoo, Switcheroo Ser.: 34). (ENG.). 80p. (J). (gr. 2-4). pap. 3.99 (978-0-448-45231-9(6), Grosset & Dunlap) Penguin Publishing Group.

—Holly's Jolly Christmas. Krulik, Nancy. 2009. (Katie Kazoo, Switcheroo Ser.: No. 8). (ENG.). 160p. (J). (gr. 2-4). pap. 4.99 (978-0-448-45218-0(9), Grosset & Dunlap) Penguin Publishing Group.

—Horsing Around, 30 vols. Krulik, Nancy. 2009. (Katie Kazoo, Switcheroo Ser.: 30). (ENG.). 80p. (J). (gr. 2-4). pap. 3.99 (978-0-448-44677-6(4), Grosset & Dunlap) Penguin Publishing Group.

—I Hate Rules!, 5 vols. Krulik, Nancy. 2006. (Katie Kazoo, Switcheroo Ser.: 5). (ENG.). 80p. (J). (gr. 2-4). pap. 3.99 (978-0-448-43100-0(9), Grosset & Dunlap) Penguin Publishing Group.

—I'm Game!, No. 21. Krulik, Nancy. 2006. (Katie Kazoo, Switcheroo Ser.: 21). (ENG.). 80p. (J). (gr. 2-4). pap. 3.99 (978-0-448-44133-7(0), Grosset & Dunlap) Penguin Publishing Group.

—It's Snow Joke. Krulik, Nancy. 2006. (Katie Kazoo, Switcheroo Ser.: 22). (ENG.). 80p. (J). (gr. 2-4). pap. 3.99 (978-0-448-44396-6(1), Grosset & Dunlap) Penguin Publishing Group.

—Karate Katie, 18 vols. Krulik, Nancy. 2006. (Katie Kazoo, Switcheroo Ser.: 18). (ENG.). 80p. (J). (gr. 2-4). pap. 3.99 (978-0-448-43767-5(8), Grosset & Dunlap) Penguin Publishing Group.

—A Katie Kazoo Christmas. Krulik, Nancy. 2005. (Katie Kazoo, Switcheroo Ser.). (ENG.). 240p. (J). (gr. 2-4). pap. 6.99 (978-0-448-43970-9(0), Grosset & Dunlap) Penguin Publishing Group.

—Love Stinks!, 15 vols., Vol. 15. Krulik, Nancy. 2004. (Katie Kazoo, Switcheroo Ser.: 15). (ENG.). 80p. (J). (gr. 2-4). pap. 3.99 (978-0-448-43640-1(X), Grosset & Dunlap) Penguin Publishing Group.

—Major League Mess-Up. Krulik, Nancy. 2008. (Katie Kazoo, Switcheroo Ser.: 29). (ENG.). 80p. (J). (gr. 2-4). pap. 3.99 (978-0-448-44676-9(6), Grosset & Dunlap) Penguin Publishing Group.

—My Pops Is Tops!, 25 vols. Krulik, Nancy. 2007. (Katie Kazoo, Switcheroo Ser.: 25). (ENG.). 80p. (J). (gr. 2-4). pap. 3.99 (978-0-448-44441-3(0), Grosset & Dunlap) Penguin Publishing Group.

—No Biz Like Show Biz, Vol. 24. Krulik, Nancy. 2007. (Katie Kazoo, Switcheroo Ser.: 24). (ENG.). 80p. (J). (gr. 2-4). pap. 3.99 (978-0-448-44440-6(2), Grosset & Dunlap) Penguin Publishing Group.

—No Bones about It. Krulik, Nancy. 12th ed. 2004. (Katie Kazoo, Switcheroo Ser.: 12). (ENG.). 80p. (J). (gr. 2-4). pap. 3.99 (978-0-448-43358-5(3), Grosset & Dunlap) Penguin Publishing Group.

—No Messin' with My Lesson. Krulik, Nancy. 11th ed. 2004. (Katie Kazoo, Switcheroo Ser.: 11). (ENG.). 80p. (J). (gr. 2-4). pap. 3.99 (978-0-448-43357-8(5), Grosset & Dunlap) Penguin Publishing Group.

—Oh, Baby!, 3 vols., No. 3. Krulik, Nancy. 2005. (Katie Kazoo, Switcheroo Ser.: 3). (ENG.). 80p. (J). (gr. 2-4). pap. 3.99 (978-0-448-42704-1(4), Grosset & Dunlap) Penguin Publishing Group.

—On Thin Ice. Krulik, Nancy. 2007. (Katie Kazoo, Switcheroo Ser.: No. 6). (ENG.). 160p. (J). (gr. 2-4). pap. 5.99 (978-0-448-44447-5(X), Grosset & Dunlap) Penguin Publishing Group.

—On Your Mark, Get Set, Laugh!, 13 vols. Krulik, Nancy. 2004. (Katie Kazoo, Switcheroo Ser.: 13). (ENG.). 80p. (J). (gr. 2-4). pap. 3.99 (978-0-448-43605-0(1), Grosset & Dunlap) Penguin Publishing Group.

—Open Wide, 23 vols. Krulik, Nancy. 2007. (Katie Kazoo, Switcheroo Ser.: 23). (ENG.). 80p. (J). (gr. 2-4). pap. 3.99 (978-0-448-44439-0(9), Grosset & Dunlap) Penguin Publishing Group.

—Quiet on the Set! Krulik, Nancy. 10th ed. 2003. (Katie Kazoo, Switcheroo Ser.: 10). (ENG.). 80p. (J). (gr. 2-4). pap. 3.99 (978-0-448-43214-4(5), Grosset & Dunlap) Penguin Publishing Group.

—Red, White, & - Achoo! Krulik, Nancy. 2010. (Katie Kazoo, Switcheroo Ser.: 33). (ENG.). 80p. (J). (gr. 2-4). pap. 3.99 (978-0-448-45230-2(8), Grosset & Dunlap) Penguin Publishing Group.

—Something's Fishy, No. 26. Krulik, Nancy. 2007. (Katie Kazoo, Switcheroo Ser.: 26). (ENG.). 80p. (J). (gr. 2-4). pap. 3.99 (978-0-448-44442-0(9), Grosset & Dunlap) Penguin Publishing Group.

—Three Cheers For... Who? Krulik, Nancy. 2011. (Katie Kazoo, Switcheroo Ser.: 35). (ENG.). 80p. (J). (gr. 2-4). pap. 3.99 (978-0-448-45449-8(1), Grosset & Dunlap) Penguin Publishing Group.

—Tip-Top Tappin' Mom!, 31 vols. Krulik, Nancy. 2009. (Katie Kazoo, Switcheroo Ser.: 31). (ENG.). 80p. (J). (gr. 2-4). pap. 3.99 (978-0-448-45041-4(0), Grosset & Dunlap) Penguin Publishing Group.

—Vote for Suzanne. Krulik, Nancy. 2008. (Katie Kazoo, Switcheroo Ser.: No. 7). (ENG.). 160p. (J). (gr. 2-4). pap. 4.99 (978-0-448-44678-3(2), Grosset & Dunlap) Penguin Publishing Group.

—A Whirlwind Vacation. Krulik, Nancy. 2005. (Katie Kazoo, Switcheroo Ser.: No. 2). (ENG.). 160p. (J). (gr. 2-4). mass mkt. 4.99 *(978-0-448-43748-4(1))*, Grosset & Dunlap) Penguin Publishing Group.

—Who's Afraid of Fourth Grade? Krulik, Nancy. 2004. (Katie Kazoo, Switcheroo Ser.: No. 1). (ENG.). 160p. (J). (gr. 2-4). mass mkt. 4.99 *(978-0-448-43555-8(1))*, Grosset & Dunlap) Penguin Publishing Group.

—Write On!, 17 vols. Krulik, Nancy. 2005. (Katie Kazoo, Switcheroo Ser.: 17). (ENG.). 80p. (J). (gr. 2-4). pap. 3.99 *(978-0-448-43742-2(2))*, Grosset & Dunlap) Penguin Publishing Group.

John, Matthew. El Agua: Arriba, Abajo y en Todos Lados, 1 vol. Rosinsky, Natalie M. Robledo, Sol, tr. from ENG. 2007. (Ciencia Asombrosa Ser.). (SPA.). 24p. (gr. k-4). lib. bdg. 25.99 *(978-1-4048-3238-1(6))* Picture Window Bks.

—Las Rocas: Duras, Blandas, Lisas y Ásperas. Rosinsky, Natalie M. & Picture Window Books Staff. Robledo, Sol, tr. from ENG. 2007. (Ciencia Asombrosa Ser.). (SPA.). 24p. (gr. k-4). 25.99 *(978-1-4048-3225-1(4))* Picture Window Bks.

—El Sonido: Fuerte, Suave, Alto y Bajo, 1 vol. Rosinsky, Natalie M. & Picture Window Books Staff. Robledo, Sol, tr. from ENG. 2007. (Ciencia Asombrosa Ser.). (SPA.). 24p. (gr. k-4). 25.99 *(978-1-4048-3229-9(7))* Picture Window Bks.

—El Sonido: Fuerte, Suave, Alto y Bajo, 1 vol. Rosinsky, Natalie M. Robledo, Sol, tr. from ENG. 2007. (Ciencia Asombrosa Ser.). (SPA.). 24p. (gr. k-4). per. 8.19 *(978-1-4048-2493-5(6))* Picture Window Bks.

John R Neill. Glinda of Oz. Baum, L. Frank. 2010. 144p. pap. 5.88 *(978-1-60386-310-0(9))*, Merchant Bks.) Rough Draft Printing.

Johnathan, Kuehl. Deer Dad: Kampp Tales Outdoor Adventures. Reich, J. J. 2006. (BAT.). 32p. (J). *(978-0-9762971-0-9(8))* Outdoor Originals LLC.

—Snort, Wheeze, Rattle & Grunt: Kampp Tales Outdoor Adventures. Reich, J. J. 2006. 64p. (J). *(978-0-9762971-2-3(4))* Outdoor Originals LLC.

Johns, Ann. Beth & the Bugs. Hay, Sam. 2011. (My Phonics Readers: Level 2 Ser.). 24p. (J). (gr. -1-1). 24.25 *(978-1-84898-511-7(8))* Sea-To-Sea Pubns.

—Chuck & Duck. Hay, Sam. 2011. (My Phonics Readers: Level 2 Ser.). 24p. (J). (gr. -1-1). 24.25 *(978-1-84898-509-4(6))* Sea-To-Sea Pubns.

Johns, Dick. Sammy Squirrel & the Sunflower Seeds. Mayer, Marvin S. 2008. 73p. pap. 19.95 *(978-1-60672-193-3(3))* America Star Bks.

Johnson, Amber W. Sam the Walrus: A Grumpy Day to Play. Adams, Tonya. 2008. 28p. pap. 24.95 *(978-1-60672-861-1(X))* America Star Bks.

Johnson, Andi. Ali in Egypt. Popper, Garry. 2004. 36p. (gr. -1-7). 4.00 *(978-1-84161-078-8(X))* Ravette Publishing, Ltd. GBR. Dist: Parkwest Pubns., Inc.

—Big World. Popper, Garry. 2004. 36p. (gr. -1-7). 4.00 *(978-1-84161-052-8(6))* Ravette Publishing, Ltd. GBR. Dist: Parkwest Pubns., Inc.

—Big World Activity Sticker Book. Popper, Garry & Volke, Gordon. 2004. 16p. 6.00 *(978-1-84161-082-5(8))* Ravette Publishing, Ltd. GBR. Dist: Parkwest Pubns., Inc.

—Billy Joe in the U. S. A. Popper, Garry. 2004. 36p. (gr. -1-7). 4.00 *(978-1-84161-053-5(4))* Ravette Publishing, Ltd. GBR. Dist: Parkwest Pubns., Inc.

—James & Jemma in Great Britain. Popper, Garry. 2004. 36p. (gr. -1-7). 4.00 *(978-1-84161-054-2(2))* Ravette Publishing, Ltd. GBR. Dist: Parkwest Pubns., Inc.

—Keito in Japan. Popper, Garry. 2004. 36p. (gr. -1-7). 4.00 *(978-1-84161-058-0(5))* Ravette Publishing, Ltd. GBR. Dist: Parkwest Pubns., Inc.

—Kez in Australia. Popper, Garry. 2004. 36p. (gr. -1-7). 4.00 *(978-1-84161-055-9(0))* Ravette Publishing, Ltd. GBR. Dist: Parkwest Pubns., Inc.

—Lena & Peter in Germany. Popper, Garry. 2004. 36p. (gr. -1-7). 4.00 *(978-1-84161-060-3(7))* Ravette Publishing, Ltd. GBR. Dist: Parkwest Pubns., Inc.

—Li & Lilly May in China. Popper, Garry. 2004. 36p. (gr. -1-7). 4.00 *(978-1-84161-057-3(7))* Ravette Publishing, Ltd. GBR. Dist: Parkwest Pubns., Inc.

—Mario in Italy. Popper, Garry. 2004. 36p. (gr. -1-7). 4.00 *(978-1-84161-059-7(3))* Ravette Publishing, Ltd. GBR. Dist: Parkwest Pubns., Inc.

—Mina in India. Popper, Garry. 2004. 36p. (gr. -1-7). 4.00 *(978-1-84161-079-5(8))* Ravette Publishing, Ltd. GBR. Dist: Parkwest Pubns., Inc.

—Paul in France. Popper, Garry. 2004. 36p. (gr. -1-7). 4.00 *(978-1-84161-056-6(9))* Ravette Publishing, Ltd. GBR. Dist: Parkwest Pubns., Inc.

—Winston in the Caribbean. Popper, Garry. 2004. 36p. (gr. -1-7). 4.00 *(978-1-84161-061-0(5))* Ravette Publishing, Ltd. GBR. Dist: Parkwest Pubns., Inc.

Johnson, Andrew. Alice in Verse the Lost Rhymes of Wonderland: The Lost Rhymes of Wonderland. Holden, J. T. 2011. (ENG.). 112p. (J). 14.99 *(978-0-9825089-9-2(9))* Candleshoe Bks.

Johnson, Arden. Wherever Bears Be. Alderson, Sue Ann. 2003. 32p. (J). (gr. -1-3). 14.95 *(978-1-883672-77-5(5))*, Tricycle Pr.) Ten Speed Pr.

Johnson, Bee. On the Train: Shine-A-Light. Brown, Carron. 2015. (ENG.). 36p. (J). 12.99 *(978-1-61067-365-5(4))* Kane Miller.

Johnson, Betsy & Thompson, Betsy. Eggs 1 2 3: Who Will the Babies Be? Halfmann, Janet. 2012. (ENG.). 32p. (J). (gr. k-k). 17.99 *(978-1-60905-191-4(2))* Blue Apple Bks.

Johnson, Bill. Monster Cheese. Wolfson, Steve. 2013. 34p. pap. 10.95 *(978-0-9798324-3-7(8))* Argami Productions, LLC.

Johnson, Bill, photos by. Minnesota Bug Hunt. Giebink, Bruce. 2013. (ENG., 32p. (J). (gr. -1-2). 16.95 *(978-0-87351-865-9(9))* Minnesota Historical Society Pr.

Johnson, Bob. The Lost Mine of the Mechanical Spider. Johnson, Bob. 2006. (Squatland Chronicles Ser.). 53p. (J). (gr. -1-3). per. 11.00 *(978-1-60002-185-5(9))*, 3977) Mountain Valley Publishing, LLC.

Johnson, Brandon. Life on Peavine Creek: Sam's Story. Bonner, Gayle. 2008. 33p. pap. 24.95 *(978-1-60610-624-2(4))* America Star Bks.

Johnson, Britt. Legend of the Blue Unicorn: Return of the Dragons, 3 vols. Johnson, Britt. Durant, Sybrina & Johnson, Sandi. I.t. ed. 2003. (ENG.). 25p. (J). (gr. k-5). spiral bd. 8.99 *(978-1-929063-93-2(8))*, 331) Moons & Stars Publishing For Children.

Johnson, Bruce. Hey Latrell, 1 vol. Benson, Linda Sue. 2009. 48p. pap. 16.95 *(978-1-60813-961-3(1))* America Star Bks.

Johnson, Bruce & Johnson, Meredith. A Day at the Zoo. 2012. 27p. (J). ***(978-1-60115-595-5(6))*** Treasure Bay, Inc.

Johnson, Bryant. Bone Wars: The Game of Ruthless Paleontology. 2005. (YA). 19.95 *(978-0-9770419-0-9(5))* Zygote Games LLC.

Johnson Cadwell, Warwick. No 1 Car Spotter & the Firebird. Atinuke. ed. 2012. (Fiction Ser.). (ENG.). 112p. (J). pap. 4.99 *(978-1-61067-052-4(3))* Kane Miller.

Johnson, Carol Ann. The Magic Shark Learns to Cook. Laird, Donivee Martin. 2004. 48p. (J). 9.95 *(978-1-57306-233-6(2))* Bess Pr., Inc.

Johnson, Catherine LeAnn. The Bus Trip, 1 vol. DeMico, Judy. 2010. 26p. pap. 24.95 *(978-1-4489-2767-8(6))* PublishAmerica, Inc.

Johnson, Cathy Ann. The Girls in the Circle. Scholastic, Inc. Staff & Giovanni, Nikki. 2004. (Just for You Ser.). (ENG.). 32p. pap. 3.99 *(978-0-439-56861-6(7))*, Teaching Resources) Scholastic, Inc.

Johnson, Celeste. T Is for Tortilla: A Southwestern Alphabet Book. Alpers, Jody. 2006. (J). (gr. -1-3). *(978-1-929115-14-3(8))* Azro Pr., Inc.

Johnson, Charles. The Adventures of Emery Jones, Boy Science Wonder: Bending Time. Johnson, Charles. Johnson, Elisheba. 2013. 110p. pap. 9.99 *(978-1-62015-181-5(2))*, Booktrope Editions) Booktrope.

Johnson, Chelsea. A House for Wally & Me. Stelten, Gene. 2009. 32p. (J). 13.95 *(978-1-935130-13-0(7))* Grateful Steps.

Johnson, Craig. Harry the Woodpecker's Search for a Home. Johnson, Joy. 2013. 28p. (J). pap. 9.95 *(978-0-9785191-7-9(5))* Orange Spot Publishing.

Johnson, Crockett. The Carrot Seed. Krauss, Ruth. 60th anniv. ed. 2004. (ENG.). 32p. (J). (gr. -1-1). 16.99 *(978-0-06-023350-1(8))* HarperCollins Pubs.

—The Carrot Seed. Krauss, Ruth & Krauss. 60th anniv. ed. 2004. (Trophy Picture Bks.). (ENG.). 32p. (J). (gr. -1-3). pap. 6.99 *(978-0-06-443210-8(6))* HarperCollins Pubs.

—The Carrot Seed. Krauss, Ruth. 60th anniv. ed. 2004. 32p. (J). (gr. -1-3). lib. bdg. 17.89 *(978-0-06-023351-8(6))* HarperCollins Pubs.

—The Happy Egg. Krauss, Ruth. 2005. (ENG.). 32p. (J). (gr. -1-3). 12.99 *(978-0-06-076005-2(2))* HarperCollins Pubs.

—Harold et le Crayon Violet: The French Edition of Harold & the Purple Crayon. 2013. (FRE & ENG.). 64p. (J). (gr. -1-3). 10.00 *(978-1-61243-164-2(X))* Ulysses Pr.

—The Little Fish That Got Away. Cook, Bernadine. 2005. 64p. (J). (gr. -1-3). lib. bdg. 15.89 *(978-0-06-055714-0(1))* HarperCollins Pubs.

Johnson, Crockett. Harold & the Purple Crayon. Johnson, Crockett. 50th anniv. ed. 2015. (ENG.). 64p. (J). (gr. -1-3). pap. 6.99 *(978-0-06-443022-7(7))*; 16.99 *(978-0-06-022935-1(7))* HarperCollins Pubs.

—Harold & the Purple Crayon Board Book. Johnson, Crockett. 2015. (ENG.). 34p. (J). (gr. -1-3). bds. 7.99 *(978-0-06-208652-5(9))*, HarperFestival) HarperCollins Pubs.

Johnson, Crockett. Harold at the North Pole. Johnson, Crockett. 2015. (ENG.). 48p. (J). (gr. -1-3). 16.99 ***(978-0-06-242861-5(6))*** HarperCollins Pubs.

—Harold's ABC Board Book. Johnson, Crockett. 2015. (ENG.). 34p. (J). (gr. -1-3). bds. 7.99 ***(978-0-06-242731-1(8))***, HarperFestival) HarperCollins Pubs.

Johnson, Curtis, photos by. BrainerdBound: Landmarks to the Lakes. Rustad, Mark & Utter, Mark. 2004. 224p. (YA). 27.95 *(978-0-9726738-0-8(6))* Landmark Publishing Inc.

Johnson, D. B. Four Legs Bad, Two Legs Good! 2007. (J). *(978-1-4287-6423-1(2))* Houghton Mifflin Harcourt Publishing Co.

Johnson, D. B. Bear's Picture. Johnson, D. B. Pinkwater, Daniel M. 2008. (ENG.). 32p. (J). (gr. -1-3). 16.00 *(978-0-618-75923-1(9))* Houghton Mifflin Harcourt Publishing Co.

—Henry Hikes to Fitchburg. Johnson, D. B. 2006. (gr. -1-3). 16.95 *(978-0-7569-6798-7(8))* Perfection Learning Corp.

—Magritte's Marvelous Hat. Johnson, D. B. 2012. (ENG.). 32p. (J). (gr. -1-3). 17.99 *(978-0-547-55864-6(3))* Houghton Mifflin Harcourt Publishing Co.

Johnson, D. C. & Johnson, Darnell. Let's Be Friends. Johnson, D. C. & Turner, Sandra. 2007. (J). per. 9.95 *(978-1-933556-66-6(8))* Publishers' Graphics, L.L.C.

Johnson, Darnell, jt. illus. see Johnson, D. C.

Johnson, David. Call Me Marianne. Bryant, Jen. 2006. 32p. (J). (gr. 1-4). 16.00 *(978-0-8028-5242-7(4))*, Eerdmans Bks For Young Readers) Eerdmans, William B. Publishing Co.

—Thumbelina. Andersen, Hans Christian. 2005. (Rabbit Ears-A Classic Tale Set 2 Ser.). 28p. (gr. k-5). 25.65 *(978-1-59197-756-8(8))* Spotlight.

—When No One Is Watching. Spinelli, Eileen. 2013. (J). 16.00 *(978-0-8028-5303-5(X))*, Eerdmans Bks For Young Readers) Eerdmans, William B. Publishing Co.

Johnson, David. The Boy Who Drew Cats. Johnson, David. 2007. (Rabbit Ears: A Classic Tale Ser.). 36p. (gr. -1-3). 25.65 *(978-1-59961-305-5(0))* Spotlight.

Johnson, David A. Attack of the Turtle. Carlson, Drew. 2008. 149p. (J). (gr. 4-9). per. 8.00 *(978-0-8028-5338-7(2))* Eerdmans, William B. Publishing Co.

Johnson, Deacon. The Unprincess: A Bedtime Story for Kids. Johnson, Deacon. Johnson, Deacon. I.t. ed. 2011. (ENG.). 24p. pap. 9.99 *(978-1-4609-2914-8(4))* CreateSpace Independent Publishing Platform.

Johnson, Deborah C. Boo's Bad Day. Lockwood, Penny. 2013. 32p. pap. 11.99 *(978-0-9852661-5-8(5))* 4RV Publishing, LLC.

—My Cat. Lopresti, Tony. 2012. 24p. pap. 13.99 *(978-0-9838018-6-3(X))* 4RV Publishing, LLC.

Johnson, Dell. Rite of Passage. Peterson, Brandon. 2003. (Mystic Traveler Ser.: Vol. 1). 160p. (YA). (gr. 7-18). pap. 9.95 *(978-1-59314-015-1(0))* CrossGeneration Comics, Inc.

Johnson, Dirk. Purdue University Coloring & Activity Adventure Book. 2007. 52p. (J). pap. *(978-0-9790923-0-5(2))* DirkDesigns, LLC.

Johnson, Dolores. Entrepreneurial Kids' Books: Books That Inspire, Teach & Entertain, 4 vols. Linderman, Dianne. 128p. (J). 24.00 *(978-0-9704876-6-7(5))* First Mom's Club, The.

—My Cookie Business. Linderman, Dianne. 2005. 32p. (J). 8.95 *(978-0-9704876-0-5(6))* First Mom's Club, The.

—My Fishing Business. Linderman, Dianne. 2005. 32p. (J). 8.95 *(978-0-9704876-2-9(2))* First Mom's Club, The.

—My Pony Ride Business. Linderman, Dianne. 2005. 32p. (J). 8.95 *(978-0-9704876-1-2(4))* First Mom's Club, The.

Johnson, Dolores Uselman. Animal Adventures at the Farm. Rosie, Maura & Gavlik, Sherry. 32p. (J). 8.95 *(978-0-9764557-0-7(6))* First Mom's Club, The.

—Great American Pony Ride. Boyer, Melody. 32p. (J). 2.00 *(978-0-9704876-3-6(0))* First Mom's Club, The.

Johnson, Donna T. What God Has Made! Gibbons, Joyce. 2004. 36p. 24.95 *(978-1-4137-3566-6(5))* PublishAmerica, Inc.

Johnson, Drew & Raiz, James. Eyes of the Gorgon. Ruka, Greg. rev. ed. 2005. (Wonder Woman Ser.). (ENG.). 144p. (YA). pap. 19.99 *(978-1-4012-0797-7(9))* DC Comics.

Johnson, E. Harper. Clara Barton: Soldier of Mercy. Rose, Mary Catherine. 2011. 80p. 37.95 *(978-1-258-07364-0(1))* Literary Licensing, LLC.

Johnson, Earl L., photos by. The Best of the West, Vol. 6. Johnson, Earl L. Hawkins, Grace M., ed. 2005. (World's Greatest Working Trucks Ser.). 104p. (YA). (gr. 8-12). pap. 19.95 *(978-0-9649645-2-5(X))* Johnson, Earl Photography.

Johnson, Elijah. Little Edward Pumpernickel. Jordan, Pasquel. 2007. (J). *(978-0-9795586-0-3(3))* Journique Publishing Group, Inc.

Johnson, Emily. The Story of the Little Red Leaf. Johnson, Donna. I.t. ed. 2006. (ENG.). 22p. (J). 25.00 *(978-0-9778774-0-9(X))* Choice Point Editions.

Johnson, Eric. Phoebe's Sweater. Johnson, Joanna. 2010. (ENG.). 38p. (J). 18.95 *(978-0-578-04697-6(0))* Slate Falls Pr., LLC.

Johnson, Fiona. Illustrated Dictionary of Chemistry. Wertheim, Jane et al. Rogers, Kirsteen, ed. 2008. (Illustrated Dictionaries Ser.). 128p. (YA). (gr. 7). pap. 12.99 *(978-0-7945-1560-7(6))*, Usborne) EDC Publishing.

—Illustrated Dictionary of Physics. Stockley, Corinne et al. 2007. (Illustrated Dictionaries Ser.). 128p. (J). (gr. 4-7). pap. 12.99 *(978-0-7945-1561-4(4))*, Usborne) EDC Publishing.

Johnson, Gary & Johansen, Tesia. The Christmas Secret. Johansen, Tesia. 2011. 28p. pap. 24.95 *(978-1-4626-3242-8(4))* America Star Bks.

Johnson, Gary M. The Adventures of MolarMan: Oral Health Bilingual (English/Spanish) Coloring Workbook. 2006. (ENG & SPA.). (J). *(978-0-9791794-1-9(6))* Johnson, Gary.

Johnson, Gary R. Deep in Alaska. Johnson, Christine. 2013. 42p. pap. 12.95 *(978-1-60223-215-0(6))* Univ. of Alaska Pr.

Johnson, Gee. Bald Eagles. Fleischer, Jayson. 2011. (2G Predator Animals Ser.). (ENG.). 32p. (J). (gr. k-2). pap. 8.50 *(978-1-61541-492-5(4))* American Reading Co.

Johnson, Gee. The Octopus. Johnson, Gee. 2010. (Marine Life Ser.). (ENG.). 20p. (J). (gr. k-2). pap. 7.50 *(978-1-61541-221-1(2))* American Reading Co.

—Polar Bears. Johnson, Gee. 2011. (1-3Y Marine Life Exploration Ser.). (ENG.). 16p. (J). (gr. k-2). pap. 6.50 *(978-1-61541-481-9(9))* American Reading Co.

Johnson, George Ann. Portraits of the Music Masters. Persons, Marjorie Kiel. I.t. ed. 2005. 102p. (J). per. 11.95 *(978-0-9675997-7-9(6))* Classical Magic, Inc.

Johnson, George Ann, jt. illus. see Nellis, Philip.

Johnson, Gillian. Bun Bun's Birthday. Scrimger, Richard. 2003. (ENG.). 24p. (J). (gr. -1-2). pap. 6.95 *(978-0-88776-637-4(4))*, Tundra Bks.) Tundra Bks. CAN. Dist: Penguin Random Hse., LLC.

—Eugene's Story. Scrimger, Richard. 2003. (ENG.). 24p. (J). (gr. -1-2). 15.95 *(978-0-88776-544-5(0))*, Tundra Bks.) Tundra Bks. CAN. Dist: Penguin Random Hse., LLC.

—James the Dancing Dog. Maybarduk, Linda. 2004. (ENG.). 24p. (J). (gr. -1-2). 15.95 *(978-0-88776-619-0(6))*, Tundra Bks.) Tundra Bks. CAN. Dist: Penguin Random Hse., LLC.

—Melonhead. Kelly, Katy. 2010. (Melonhead Ser.). (ENG.). 240p. (J). (gr. 3-7). 6.99 *(978-0-440-42187-0(X))*, Yearling) Random Hse. Children's Bks.

—Melonhead & the Big Stink. Kelly, Katy. 2010. (Melonhead Ser.). (ENG.). 224p. (J). (gr. 3-7). 14.99 *(978-0-385-73658-9(4))*, Delacorte Pr) Random House Publishing Group.

—Melonhead & the Undercover Operation. Kelly, Katy. 2012. (Melonhead Ser.). (ENG.). 256p. (J). (gr. 3-7). 6.99 *(978-0-375-84528-4(3))*, Yearling) Random Hse. Children's Bks.

—Melonhead & the Vegalicious Disaster. Kelly, Katy. 2013. (Melonhead Ser.). (ENG.). 224p. (J). (gr. 3-7). 6.99 *(978-0-307-92969-3(8))*, Yearling) Random Hse. Children's Bks.

—Melonhead & the We-Fix-It Company. Kelly, Katy. 2014. (Melonhead Ser.). (ENG.). 240p. (J). (gr. 3-7). 6.99 *(978-0-307-92970-9(1))*, Yearling) Random Hse. Children's Bks.

Johnson, Gillian. Thora. Johnson, Gillian. 2003. 128p. *(978-0-207-19815-1(2))* HarperCollins Pubs. Australia.

—Thora: A Half-Mermaid Tale. Johnson, Gillian. 2005. 256p. (J). (gr. 3-7). lib. bdg. 15.89 *(978-0-06-074379-6(4))*, Tegen, Katherine Bks) HarperCollins Pubs.

—Thora & the Green Sea-Unicorn. Johnson, Gillian. 2005. 272p. *(978-0-207-20016-8(5))* HarperCollins Pubs. Australia.

Johnson, Gretchen. Gracie, the Glass Tree Frog. Sandusky, Thomas & Hill, Kathy. 2008. 24p. pap. 12.95 *(978-0-9820479-2-7(4))* Peppertree Pr., The.

—Peter the Poison Dart Frog, Stories of the Rainforest. Sandusky, Thomas & Hill, Kathy. 2011. 24p. pap. 12.95 *(978-1-936343-85-0(1))* Peppertree Pr., The.

—Spidy the Spider Monkey. Sandusky, Thomas & Hill, Kathy. 2009. 32p. pap. 12.95 *(978-0-9823002-5-1(5))* Peppertree Pr., The.

Johnson, Gwen. Diggin' the Big'un. Johnson, Gwen. Johnson, Carl. 2007. 16p. (YA). 14.95 *(978-0-9795860-1-9(1))* Fish Tales Publishing.

—Dreamland Friends. Johnson, Gwen. Johnson, Carl. 2007.Tr. of Amigos del Tierra del Sue#324;os. (ENG & SPA.). 18p. (J). 5.95 *(978-0-9795860-7-1(0))* Fish Tales Publishing.

Johnson, Howard David. Seven Wonders of the Ancient World: A MyReportLinks.com Book. Laliberte, Michelle. 2005. (Seven Wonders of the World Ser.). 48p. (J). (gr. 4-10). lib. bdg. 26.60 *(978-0-7660-5293-2(1))*, MyReportLinks.com Bks.) Enslow Pubs., Inc.

Johnson-Isaacs, Cally. Elephantantrum! Shields, Gillian. 2013. (ENG.). 32p. (J). (gr. -1-3). 14.99 *(978-1-58925-126-7(1))* Tiger Tales.

Johnson, Jake. Gingerbread Land. Grim, Katie. 2007. (ENG.). 24p. (J). (gr. 1-18). 19.95 *(978-1-58117-635-3(X))*, Intervisual/Piggy Toes) Bendon, Inc.

Johnson, Jane. La Princesa y el Pintor. Johnson, Jane. 2003.Tr. of Princess & the Painter. (SPA.). 32p. (J). (gr. -1-3). pap. 14.95 *(978-1-56014-618-6(4))*, SAN6184) Santillana USA Publishing Co., Inc.

Johnson, Jared. One Day at the North Pole. Hurst, Joshua. 2008. 44p. pap. 24.95 *(978-1-60703-327-1(5))* America Star Bks.

Johnson, Jay. Graduation Day. Denega, Danielle. 2007. (J). pap. *(978-0-439-90900-6(7))* Scholastic, Inc.

—My Santa Claus. Karr, Lily. 2012. (ENG.). 12p. (J). (gr. -1-k). bds. 4.99 *(978-0-545-43649-6(4))* Scholastic, Inc.

—Ten Grouchy Groundhogs. Heling, Kathryn & Hembrook, Deborah. 2009. (ENG.). 24p. (J). (gr. -1-k). pap. 3.99 *(978-0-545-13414-9(5))*, Cartwheel Bks.) Scholastic, Inc.

—Ten Little Pumpkins. 2012. (J). *(978-0-545-46862-6(0))* Scholastic, Inc.

—Ten Lucky Leprechauns. Heling, Kathryn & Hembrook, Deborah. 2013. (ENG.). 24p. (J). (gr. -1-k). pap. 3.99 *(978-0-545-43648-9(6))*, Cartwheel Bks.) Scholastic, Inc.

Johnson, Jay B. Lots of Love. Fisch, Sarah & Bridwell, Norman. 2008. (J). *(978-0-545-02843-1(4))* Scholastic, Inc.

—My Easter Bunny! Karr, Lily. 2012. (ENG.). 12p. (J). (gr. -1-k). bds. 4.99 *(978-0-545-37117-9(1))*, Cartwheel Bks.) Scholastic, Inc.

Johnson, Jeff, et al. The Dragon's Wake, Vol. 2. Dixon, Chuck. 2003. (Way of the Rat Ser.: Vol. 2). 160p. (YA). (gr. 7-18). pap. 15.95 *(978-1-931484-77-0(5))* CrossGeneration Comics, Inc.

—Haunted Zhumar, Vol. 3. Dixon, Chuck. 2004. (Way of the Rat Ser.: Vol. 3). 160p. (YA). pap. 15.95 *(978-1-59314-042-7(8))* CrossGeneration Comics, Inc.

—The Walls of Zhumar. Dixon, Chuck. 2003. (Way of the Rat Ser.: Vol. 1). 160p. (YA). (gr. 7-18). pap. 9.95 *(978-1-931484-51-0(1))* CrossGeneration Comics, Inc.

Johnson, Jennifer. ABC Science Riddles. Saffer, Barbara. 2004. (ABC Riddles Ser.). 32p. (J). (gr. -1-3). 13.95 *(978-0-939217-55-7(4))* Peel Productions, Inc.

Johnson, Jerome A. The Mouse That Went to Find Christmas. Mitchell, Gloria. (J). pap. *(978-0-9706186-0-3(3))* Fourth Generation Pubs.

Johnson, Jessica. Robbie & the Dolphins. D'Ath, Justin. 2006. (Making Tracks Ser.). (ENG.). 64p. (J). (gr. 2-4). pap. 9.95 *(978-1-876944-42-1(0))* National Museum of Australia AUS. Dist: Independent Pubs. Group.

Johnson, Jim. 4 - Dorp the Scottish Dragon Bk. 4: New York Christmas. Johnson, Sandi. Durant, Sybrina, ed. 2014. (Little Choo-Choo Bks.). 46p. (J). (gr. -1-6). pap. 14.99 *(978-1-929063-03-1(2))*, 104) Moons & Stars Publishing For Children.

Johnson, Jim, jt. illus. see Krittendon, Kim.

Johnson, Jim, jt. illus. see Trevino, Juan.

Johnson, John. Blue Wise. Douglas, Babette. 2006. (Kiss a Me Teacher Creature Stories Ser.). 62p. (J). (gr. -1-3). *(978-1-890343-07-1(2))* Kiss A Me Productions, Inc.

—Falcon Eddie. Douglas, Babette. 2006. (Kiss a Me Teacher Creature Stories Ser.). (J). (gr. -1-3). 9.99 *(978-1-890343-21-7(8))* Kiss A Me Productions, Inc.

—Larkspur: And His Wooden Nose. Douglas, Babette. 2006. (Kiss a Me Teacher Creature Stories Ser.). (J). (gr. -1-3). 9.99 *(978-1-890343-23-1(4))* Kiss A Me Productions, Inc.

—The Lyon Bear. Douglas, Babette. 2006. (Kiss a Me Teacher Creature Stories Ser.). (J). (gr. -1-3). 9.99 *(978-1-890343-18-7(8))* Kiss A Me Productions, Inc.

—Miss Evonne: And the Mice of Nice! Douglas, Babette. 2006. (Kiss a Me Teacher Creature Stories Ser.). (J). (gr. -1-3). 9.99 *(978-1-890343-19-4(6))* Kiss A Me Productions, Inc.

—Noreen: The Real King of the Jungle. Douglas, Babette. 2006. (Kiss a Me Teacher Creature Stories Ser.). 20p. (J). (gr. -1-3). 9.99 *(978-1-890343-25-5(0))* Kiss A Me Productions, Inc.

Johnson, Karen. Activities to Share with Your Grandchild. Gordon, Lynn. 2004. (52 Ser.: 52SE). (ENG.). 54p. (gr. 8-17). 6.95 *(978-0-8118-4125-2(1))* Chronicle Bks. LLC.

—52 Activities for Jewish Holidays. Gordon, Lynn. 2004. (52 Ser.: 52SE). (ENG.). 52p. (J). (gr. k-4). 6.95 *(978-0-8118-4124-5(3))* Chronicle Bks. LLC.

—52 Activities for You & Your Baby. Gordon, Lynn. 2003. (52 Ser.: 52SE). (ENG.). 54p. (gr. 8-17). 6.95 *(978-0-8118-3629-6(0))* Chronicle Bks. LLC.

J

—52 Adventures in San Francisco. Gordon, Lynn. rev. ed. 2006. (52 Ser.: 52SE). (ENG.). (gr. 8-17). 6.95 *(978-0-8118-5179-4(6))* Chronicle Bks. LLC.
—52 Boredom Busters for Kids! Gordon, Lynn. 2008. (ENG.). 54p. (gr. -1-17). 6.95 *(978-0-8118-6219-6(4))* Chronicle Bks. LLC.
—52 Christmas Activities. Gordon, Lynn. 2004. (52 Ser.: 52SE). (ENG.). 52p. (J). (gr. k-4). 6.95 *(978-0-8118-4123-8(5))* Chronicle Bks. LLC.
—52 Great Family Films. Gordon, Lynn. 2003. (52 Ser.: 52SE). (ENG.). 52p. (gr. 8-17). 6.95 *(978-0-8118-3630-2(4))* Chronicle Bks. LLC.
Johnson, Karen & Synarski, Susan. 52 Fun Things to Do in the Car. Gordon, Lynn. rev. ed. 2009. (ENG.). 54p. (J). (gr. -1-17). 6.95 *(978-0-8118-6371-1(9))* Chronicle Bks. LLC.
—52 Fun Things to Do on the Plane. Gordon, Lynn. rev. ed. 2009. (ENG.). 54p. (J). (gr. -1-17). 6.95 *(978-0-8118-6372-8(7))* Chronicle Bks. LLC.
Johnson, Karen, jt. illus. see Synarski, Susan.
Johnson, Kenny Ray. Charly's Adventure, 1 vol. Hughes, Donna L. 2009. 14p. pap. 24.95 *(978-1-4489-1822-5(7))* America Star Bks.
Johnson, Kim. Prom! The Complete Guide to a Truly Spectacular Night. Krulik, Nancy. 2003. 96p. (YA). 8.00 *(978-0-7567-9038-7(7))* DIANE Publishing Co.
Johnson, Kimberli Anne. My Grandma Mary. Webster, Raelyn & Rasmussen, Kenneth L. 2013. 38p. 22.95 *(978-1-940379-00-5(8))* Telling Family Tales.
Johnson, Kris, photos by. Childsplay: A Collection of Scenes & Monologues for Children, 1 vol. Muir, Kerry. 2004. (ENG., 286p. (Orig.). (gr. -1-18). pap. 16.99 *(978-0-87910-188-6(1),* 0879101881, Limelight Editions) Leonard, Hal Corp.
Johnson, Krista M. Slangalicious: Where We Got That Crazy Lingo. O'Reilly, Gillian. 2004. (ENG.). 88p. (J). (gr. 5-18). 24.95 *(978-1-55037-765-1(5),* 9781550377651); pap. 14.95 *(978-1-55037-764-4(7),* 9781550377644) Annick Pr., Ltd. CAN. Dist: Firefly Bks., Ltd.
Johnson, Larry. Alec's Primer. Walter, Mildred Pitts. 2005. (Family Heritage Ser.). (ENG.). 32p. (J). (gr. -1-3). 15.95 *(978-0-916718-20-6(4))* Vermont Folklife Ctr.
—Daisy & the Doll. Medearis, Michael & Medearis, Angela Shelf. 2005. (Vermont Folklife Center Children's Book Ser.). (ENG.). 32p. (J). (gr. -1-3). reprint ed. pap. 7.95 *(978-0-916718-23-7(9))* Vermont Folklife Ctr.
—Heinrich Melchior Muhlenberg. Hovland, Stephenie M. 2012. (Hero of Faith Ser.). (ENG.). 58p. (J). pap. 7.99 *(978-0-7586-3076-6(X))* Concordia Publishing Hse.
—A Hunger for Learning: A Story about Booker T. Washington. Swain, Gwenyth. (Creative Minds Biographies Ser.). (ENG.). 64p. (gr. 4-8). 2006. pap. 8.95 *(978-0-8225-3090-9(2));* 2005. lib. bdg. 22.60 *(978-1-57505-754-5(9))* Lerner Publishing Group.
—Wilma Rudolph. Sherrow, Victoria. Translations.com Staff, tr. 2006. (Yo Solo: Biografías (on My Own Biographies) Ser.). (SPA.). 48p. (gr. 2-4). pap. 6.95 *(978-0-8225-6623-6(0),* Ediciones Lerner) Lerner Publishing Group.
Johnson, Lauren. The Raggedy Beggar. Goyer, Deb. 2008. 19p. pap. 24.95 *(978-1-60703-698-2(3))* America Star Bks.
Johnson, Layne. Christmas Kitten, Home at Last, 1 vol. Pulver, Robin. 2010. (ENG.). 32p. (J). (gr. k-3). 16.99 *(978-0-8075-1157-2(9))* Whitman, Albert & Co.
—The Declaration of Independence from A to Z, 1 vol. Osornio, Catherine L. 2010. (ENG.). 32p. (J). (gr. 1-7). 16.99 *(978-1-58980-676-4(X))* Pelican Publishing Co., Inc.
—Farmer George Plants a Nation. Thomas, Peggy. (ENG.). 40p. (J). (gr. 4-6). 2013. pap. 7.95 *(978-1-62091-029-0(2));* 2008. 17.95 *(978-1-59078-460-0(X))* Boyds Mills Pr. (Calkins Creek).
—Grandparent Poems. 2004. (ENG.). 32p. (J). (gr. 1-7). 15.95 *(978-1-56397-900-2(4))* Boyds Mills Pr.
—Off Like the Wind! The First Ride of the Pony Express. Spradlin, Michael P. 2010. (ENG.). 40p. (J). (gr. 2-5). 17.99 *(978-0-8027-9652-3(4));* 18.89 *(978-0-8027-9653-0(2))* Walker & Co.
—The Poppy Lady: Moina Belle Michael & Her Tribute to Veterans. Walsh, Barbara. 2012. (ENG.). 40p. (J). (gr. 2-4). 16.95 *(978-1-59078-754-0(4),* Calkins Creek) Boyds Mills Pr.
—Race the Wild Wind: A Story of the Sable Island Horses. Markle, Sandra. 2011. (ENG.). 40p. (J). 17.99 *(978-0-8027-9766-7(0))* Walker & Co.
—Voices of Pearl Harbor, 1 vol. Garland, Sherry. 2013. (ENG.). 40p. (J). (gr. 3-3). 17.99 *(978-1-4556-1609-1(5))* Pelican Publishing Co., Inc.
—A Young Man's Dance. Knowlton, Laurie Lazzaro. 2006. (ENG.). 32p. (J). (gr. 1). 15.95 *(978-1-59078-259-0(3))* Boyds Mills Pr.
Johnson, Marcella. Kingdom's Reign, 4 bks. Black, Chuck. Black, Andrea & Black, Brittney, eds. 2004. 160p. (YA). per. 9.95 *(978-0-9679240-3-8(0))* Perfect Praise Publishing.
Johnson, Meredith. Accept & Value Each Person. Meiners, Cheri J. 2006. (Learning to Get Along(r) Ser.). (ENG.). 40p. (J). (gr. 3-7). pap. 10.95 *(978-1-57542-203-9(4))* Free Spirit Publishing, Inc.
—Baby Elephant. Shively, Julie. 2005. (ENG.). 24p. (J). bds. 6.95 *(978-0-8249-6577-8(9))* Ideals Pubns.
—Baby Orangutan. Shively, Julie. 2005. (San Diego Zoo Animal Library: Vol. 9). (ENG.). 24p. (J). bds. 6.95 *(978-0-8249-6578-5(7))* Ideals Pubns.
—Baby Polar Bear. Shively, Julie. 2005. (ENG.). 24p. (J). bds. 6.95 *(978-0-8249-6576-1(0))* Ideals Pubns.
—Be Careful & Stay Safe. Meiners, Cheri J. 2006. (Learning to Get Along(r) Ser.). (ENG.). 40p. (J). (gr. -1-3). pap. 10.95 *(978-1-57542-211-4(5))* Free Spirit Publishing, Inc.
—Be Honest & Tell the Truth. Meiners, Cheri J. 2007. (Learning to Get Along(r) Ser.). (ENG.). 40p. (gr. -1-3). pap. 10.95 *(978-1-57542-258-9(1))* Free Spirit Publishing, Inc.
—The Christmas Star. Raum, Elizabeth. (ENG.). (J). (gr. -1-k). 2008. 32p. per. 3.99 *(978-0-8249-5567-0(6),* Ideals Children's Bks.); 2005. 28p. bds. 7.95 *(978-0-8249-6620-1(1))* Ideals Pubns.
—Discover Thomas Jefferson: Architect, Inventor, President. Pingry, Patricia A. 2005. (Discovery Readers Ser.). (ENG.). 32p. (J). (gr. 1-2). pap. 4.35 *(978-0-8249-5510-6(2))* Ideals Pubns.
—Do Not Wake Jake. Willson, Sarah. 2006. (Step-By-Step Readers Ser.). (J). *(978-1-59939-059-8(0),* Reader's Digest Young Families, Inc.) Studio Fun International.
—Genevieve & the Moon. Ryan, Karlene Kay. 2013. 34p. pap. 9.99 *(978-0-9888843-3-5(X))* Ryan, Karlene Kay Author.
—Genevieve Goes to School. Ryan, Karlene Kay. 2013. 34p. pap. 9.99 *(978-0-9888843-2-8(1))* Ryan, Karlene Kay Author.
—Gigi, God's Little Princess, 1 vol. Walsh, Sheila. 2005. (Gigi, God's Little Princess Ser.: 1). (ENG.). 32p. 14.99 *(978-1-4003-0529-2(2))* Nelson, Thomas Inc.
—God's Little Princess Treasury, 1 vol. Walsh, Sheila. 2009. (ENG.). 128p. (gr. -1-2). 19.99 *(978-1-4003-1472-0(0))* Nelson, Thomas Inc.
—Ha! Ha! Halloween. Adams, Michelle Medlock. 2005. 30p. (J). (gr. 3-7). 12.95 *(978-0-8249-5508-3(0))* Ideals Pubns.
—The Hut in the Forest: A Tale about Being Kind to Animals. Lang, Andrew. 2006. (J). *(978-1-59939-083-3(3),* Reader's Digest Young Families, Inc.) Studio Fun International.
—I'm Glad I'm Your Grandma. Horlacher, Kathy & Horlacher, Bill. 2014. (Happy Day Ser.). (ENG.). 16p. (J). pap. 2.49 *(978-1-4143-9408-4(X))* Tyndale Hse. Pubs.
—I'm Glad I'm Your Mother. Horlacher, Bill & Horlacher, Kathy. 2013. (Happy Day Ser.). (ENG.). 16p. (J). pap. 2.49 *(978-1-4143-9292-9(3))* Tyndale Hse. Pubs.
Johnson, Meredith. Know & Follow Rules. Meiners, Cheri J. (Learning to Get Along(r) Ser.). (ENG & SPA.). (J). (gr. -1-3). 2015. 48p. pap. 12.45 ***(978-1-57542-498-9(3));*** 2005. 40p. pap. 10.95 *(978-1-57542-130-8(5))* Free Spirit Publishing, Inc.
Johnson, Meredith. The Learning to Get along Series Interactive Software. Meiners, Cheri J. 2008. (Learning to Get Along Ser.). (ENG.). 24p. (gr. k-3). cd-rom 99.99 *(978-1-57542-281-7(6))* Free Spirit Publishing, Inc.
—Los dos leemos-Fiebre de Beisbol: Nivel 1-2. McKay, Sindy. 2006. (We Both Read Ser.). (SPA.). 48p. (J). (gr. k-4). 7.99 *(978-1-891327-83-4(6));* pap. 3.99 *(978-1-891327-84-1(4))* Treasure Bay, Inc.
—Los dos leemos-Mi Dia. McKay, Sindy. Canetti, Yanitzia James, tr. 2006. (We Both Read Ser.). (SPA.). 48p. (J). (gr. -1-2). pap. 3.99 *(978-1-891327-76-6(3))* Treasure Bay, Inc.
—Los dos leemos-Mi Dia: Nivel K. McKay, Sindy. 2006. (We Both Read Ser.). (SPA.). 48p. (J). (gr. -1-2). 7.99 *(978-1-891327-75-9(5))* Treasure Bay, Inc.
—Meet Robert E. Lee. Pingry, Patricia A. 2004. (J). 9.95 *(978-0-8249-5465-9(3),* Ideals Pr.) Ideals Pubns.
—Merrilee Mannerly & Her Magnificent Manners. Cashman, Mary & Whipple, Cynthia. 2010. (J). 16.99 *(978-0-615-36448-3(9))* Pink&Brown Publishing, LLP.
Johnson, Meredith. The Missing Christmas Treasure. Sears, Gale. 2012. (J). ***(978-1-60861-283-3(X))*** Covenant Communications, Inc.
Johnson, Meredith. My Funny Valentine. Adams, Michelle Medlock. 2005. (ENG.). 32p. (J). 12.95 *(978-0-8249-5487-1(4))* Ideals Pubns.
—On Easter Sunday. Pingry, Patricia A. 2007. (ENG.). 26p. (J). (gr. -1-3). bds. 6.99 *(978-0-8249-6692-8(9),* Candy Cane Pr.) Ideals Pubns.
—The Perfect Christmas Gift, 1 vol. Walsh, Sheila. 2006. (Gigi, God's Little Princess Ser.: 3). (ENG.). 32p. (gr. -1-2). 14.99 *(978-1-4003-0801-9(1))* Nelson, Thomas Inc.
—Reach Out & Give. Meiners, Cheri J. 2006. (Learning to Get Along(r) Ser.). (ENG.). 40p. (J). (gr. 3-7). pap. 10.95 *(978-1-57542-204-6(2))* Free Spirit Publishing, Inc.
—Respect & Take Care of Things. Meiners, Cheri J. 2004. (Learning to Get Along(r) Ser.). (ENG.). 40p. (J). (gr. -1-3). pap. 10.95 *(978-1-57542-160-5(7))* Free Spirit Publishing, Inc.
—Share & Take Turns. Meiners, Cheri J. 2003. (Learning to Get Along Ser.). 35p. (J). (gr. -1-3). 21.00 *(978-0-613-97123-2(X),* Turtleback) Turtleback Bks.
—Stella Brite & the Dark Matter Mystery. Latta, Sara L. 2006. (ENG.). 32p. (J). (gr. 2-5). 16.95 *(978-1-57091-883-4(X))* Charlesbridge Publishing, Inc.
—The Story of Robert E. Lee. Pingry, Patricia A. 2004. (ENG.). 26p. (J). (gr. -1-k). bds. 6.95 *(978-0-8249-6501-3(9))* Ideals Pubns.
—The Story of the Wright Brothers. Burke, Michelle Prater. 2008. (ENG.). 26p. (J). (gr. -1-3). bds. 6.99 *(978-0-8249-6729-1(1),* Candy Cane Pr.) Ideals Pubns.
—The Story of Thomas Jefferson. Pingry, Patricia A. 2003. (ENG.). 26p. (J). (gr. -1-k). bds. 7.69 *(978-0-8249-6502-0(7))* Ideals Pubns.
—Talk & Work It Out. Meiners, Cheri J. 2005. (Learning to Get Along(r) Ser.). (ENG.). 40p. (J). (gr. -1-3). pap. 10.95 *(978-1-57542-176-6(3))* Free Spirit Publishing, Inc.
Johnson, Meredith. Talk & Work It Out / Hablar y Resolver. Meiners, Cheri J. 2015. (Learning to Get Along(r) Ser.). (ENG & SPA.). 48p. (J). (gr. -1-3). pap. 12.45 ***(978-1-57542-497-2(5))*** Free Spirit Publishing, Inc.
Johnson, Meredith. Try & Stick with It. Meiners, Cheri J. 2004. (Learning to Get Along(r) Ser.). (ENG.). 40p. (J). (gr. -1-3). pap. 10.95 *(978-1-57542-159-9(3))* Free Spirit Publishing, Inc.
—We Both Read-A Pony Named Peanut. McKay, Sindy. 2008. (We Both Read Ser.). 44p. (J). (gr. 1-4). pap. 5.99 *(978-1-60115-016-5(4))* Treasure Bay, Inc.
—We Both Read Bilingual Edition-Too Many Cats/Demasiados Gatos. McKay, Sindy. ed. 2011. (ENG & SPA.). 44p. (J). pap. 5.99 *(978-1-60115-040-0(7))* Treasure Bay, Inc.
—We Both Read-My Car Trip. McKay, Sindy. 2005. (We Both Read Ser.). 48p. (J). (gr. -1-2). lib. bdg. 7.99 *(978-1-891327-63-6(1));* per. 5.99 *(978-1-891327-64-3(X))* Treasure Bay, Inc.
—We Both Read-My Day Big Book. McKay, Sindy. 2006. (We Both Read Ser.). 40p. (J). (gr. -1-4). pap. 29.95 *(978-1-891327-93-3(3))* Treasure Bay, Inc.
—We Both Read-My Day (Picture Book) McKay, Sindy. 2007. (We Both Read Ser.). 44p. (J). (gr. -1-2). lib. bdg. 14.95 *(978-1-60115-005-9(9))* Treasure Bay, Inc.
—We Both Read-My Town. McKay, Sindy. 2007. (We Both Read Ser.). 44p. (J). (gr. -1-2). 7.99 *(978-1-60115-001-1(6));* pap. 5.99 *(978-1-60115-002-8(4))* Treasure Bay, Inc.
—We Both Read-Oh No! We're Doing a Show! Ross, Dev. 2011. 44p. (J). 9.95 *(978-1-60115-255-8(8));* pap. 4.99 *(978-1-60115-256-5(6))* Treasure Bay, Inc.
—We Both Read-The Ruby Rose Show. McKay, Sindy. 2010. (We Both Read Ser.). 44p. (J). (gr. k-3). pap. 4.99 *(978-1-60115-246-6(9))* Treasure Bay, Inc.
—We Both Read-Too Many Cats. McKay, Sindy. 2003. (We Both Read Ser.). 44p. (J). (gr. k-18). 7.99 *(978-1-891327-49-0(6));* pap. 5.99 *(978-1-891327-50-6(X))* Treasure Bay, Inc.
Johnson, Meredith. We Both Read-Zoo Day. Johnson, Bruce & McKay, Sindy. 2015. (We Both Read - Level 1 (Quality) Ser.). (ENG.). 44p. (J). (gr. k-2). pap. 5.99 ***(978-1-60115-274-9(4))*** Treasure Bay, Inc.
Johnson, Meredith. We Read Phonics-A Day at the Zoo. Johnson, Bruce. 2012. 32p. (J). 9.95 *(978-1-60115-349-4(X));* pap. 4.99 *(978-1-60115-350-0(3))* Treasure Bay, Inc.
—We Read Phonics-If I Had a Snake. McGuire, Leslie. 2010. (We Read Phonics Ser.). 32p. (J). (gr. 1-5). 9.95 *(978-1-60115-333-3(3));* pap. 4.99 *(978-1-60115-334-0(1))* Treasure Bay, Inc.
—We Read Phonics-Magic Tricks. McKay, Sindy. 2011. (We Read Phonics Ser.). 32p. (J). (gr. 1-3). 9.95 *(978-1-60115-337-1(6));* pap. 4.99 *(978-1-60115-338-8(4))* Treasure Bay, Inc.
—We Read Phonics-Pat, Cat, & Rat. McKay, Sindy. 2010. 32p. (J). 9.95 *(978-1-60115-311-1(2));* pap. 4.99 *(978-1-60115-312-8(0))* Treasure Bay, Inc.
—We Read Phonics-the Garden Crew. McKay, Sindy. 2011. 32p. (J). 9.95 *(978-1-60115-345-6(7));* pap. 4.99 *(978-1-60115-346-3(5))* Treasure Bay, Inc.
—When Daddy Needs a Timeout. Pearce, Valarie. 2012. 28p. pap. 10.99 *(978-0-9843111-4-9(9))* ImaRa Publishing.
—When Mommy Needs a Timeout. Pearce, Valarie. 2012. 26p. pap. 10.99 *(978-0-9843111-5-6(7))* ImaRa Publishing.
—Will, God's Mighty Warrior, 1 vol. Walsh, Sheila. 2006. (Will, God's Mighty Warrior Ser.: 1). (ENG.). 32p. (gr. -1-3). 14.99 *(978-1-4003-0805-7(4))* Nelson, Thomas Inc.
Johnson, Meredith. Meet Thomas Jefferson. Johnson, Meredith, ed. Pingry, Patricia A. 2003. 32p. (J). 9.95 *(978-0-8249-5459-8(9))* Ideals Pubns.
—Milo & the Flapjack Fiasco! Johnson, Meredith, ed. Jane, Pamela. 2004. 32p. (J). 13.95 *(978-1-59336-113-6(0));* pap. *(978-1-59336-114-3(9))* Mondo Publishing.
Johnson, Meredith, jt. illus. see Johnson, Bruce.
Johnson, Michael. Workaholism: Getting a Life in the Killing Fields of Work. Johnson, Michael. Thorne, Paul. 2005. 138p. (YA). reprint ed. pap. 18.00 *(978-0-7567-9220-6(7))* DIANE Publishing Co.
Johnson, Mike, et al. Kindergarten: Ages 5-6. Carder, Ken & LaRoy, Sue. 2005. 95p. (J). (gr. -1-3). pap. 12.99 incl. audio compact disk *(978-1-57583-818-2(4))* Twin Sisters IP, LLC.
Johnson, Milton. Little Fishes. Haugaard, Erik Christian. 2008. (J). (gr. 4-7). 23.00 *(978-0-8446-6245-9(3))* Smith, Peter Pub., Inc.
Johnson, Nancy Jo, photos by. Our Journey from Tibet. Dolphin, Laurie. 2006. 40p. (J). (gr. k-4). 16.00 *(978-0-7567-9812-3(4))* DIANE Publishing Co.
Johnson, Nick. Homophobia: Deal with It & Turn Prejudice into Pride, 1 vol. Solomon, Steven. 2013. (Lorimer Deal with It Ser.). (ENG.). 32p. (J). (gr. 4-6). 24.95 *(978-1-4594-0441-0(6));* pap. 12.95 *(978-1-4594-0442-7(4))* Lorimer, James & Co., Ltd., Pubs. CAN. Dist: Casemate Pubs. & Bk. Distributors, LLC.
Johnson, Nikki. Agate: What Good Is a Moose? Dey, Joy M. 2007. 32p. (J). (gr. -1-3). 17.95 *(978-0-942235-73-9(8))* Lake Superior Port Cities, Inc.
—Nightlight. Anderson, Jeannine. 2004. 32p. (J). pap. 7.95 *(978-0-89317-057-8(7),* WW-0577); lib. bdg. 16.95 *(978-0-89317-056-1(9),* WW-0569) Finney Co., Inc. (Windward Publishing).
Johnson, Pamela. The Birth of a Humpback Whale. Matero, Robert. 2014. (ENG.). 64p. (J). (gr. 3-7). 13.99 *(978-1-4814-4460-6(3),* Simon & Schuster Bks. For Young Readers) Simon & Schuster Bks. For Young Readers.
Johnson, Pamela. David & Goliath. 2015. (ENG.). 24p. pap. 6.50 ***(978-1-84135-949-6(1))*** Award Pubns. Ltd. GBR. Dist: Parkwest Pubns., Inc.
Johnson, Pamela. Giant Squid: Mystery of the Deep. Dussling, Jennifer. 2004. (American Museum of Natural History Ser.). 48p. (gr. 1-3). 14.00 *(978-0-7569-1981-8(9))* Perfection Learning Corp.
—If You Lived When There Was Slavery in America. Kamma, Anne. 2004. (If You Lived Ser.). 63p. (J). 14.65 *(978-0-7569-3016-5(2))* Perfection Learning Corp.
—If You Lived When There Was Slavery in America. Kamma, Anne. 2004. (If You... Ser.). (ENG.). 64p. (J). (gr. 2-5). pap. 6.99 *(978-0-439-56706-0(8))* Scholastic, Inc.
—If You Lived When Women Won Their Rights. Kamma, Anne. 2008. (If You... Ser.). (ENG.). 64p. (J). (gr. 2-5). pap. 6.99 *(978-0-439-74869-8(0),* Scholastic Reference) Scholastic, Inc.
Johnson, Pamela. Jonah & the Whale. 2015. (ENG.). 24p. pap. 6.50 ***(978-1-84135-950-2(5))*** Award Pubns. Ltd. GBR. Dist: Parkwest Pubns., Inc.
—Joseph & His Brothers. 2015. (ENG.). 24p. pap. 6.50 ***(978-1-84135-952-6(1))*** Award Pubns. Ltd. GBR. Dist: Parkwest Pubns., Inc.
Johnson, Pamela. Kenya's Song. Trice, Linda. 2013. (ENG.). 32p. (J). (gr. -1-3). pap. 7.95 *(978-1-57091-847-6(3));* lib. bdg. 17.95 *(978-1-57091-846-9(5))* Charlesbridge Publishing, Inc.
—Polar Bears: In Danger. Edwards, Roberta. 2008. (Penguin Young Readers, Level 3 Ser.). (ENG.). 48p. (J). (gr. 1-3). mass mkt. 3.99 *(978-0-448-44924-1(2),* Grosset & Dunlap) Penguin Publishing Group.
Johnson, Pamela & Squier, Robert. The Good Samaritan. Berendes, Mary. 2011. (Parables Ser.). (ENG.). 24p. (J). (gr. k-3). lib. bdg. 28.50 *(978-1-60954-391-4(2),* 201186) Child's World, Inc., The.
Johnson, Pamela Ford. If You Lived at the Time of Squanto. Kamma, Anne. 2006. 63p. (J). pap. *(978-0-439-87628-5(1))* Scholastic, Inc.
Johnson, Pamela G. Outside My Window. Rappoport, Bernice. 2004. (Treasure Tree Ser.). 32p. (J). *(978-0-7166-1622-1(X))* World Bk., Inc.
Johnson, Patrick. I Shook up the World: The Incredible Life of Muhammad Ali. Ali, Maryum. 2004. (ENG.). 32p. (J). (gr. 1-5). 16.95 *(978-1-58270-090-8(7))* Aladdin/Beyond Words.
Johnson, Patrick Henry. Feeling Great with Jasper State: Eat Your Green Things Every Day. Johnson, Judith Margaret. 2011. 32p. 14.95 *(978-0-9820228-5-6(9))* Jasper State Brand, Inc.
Johnson, Paul. Bible Story Hidden Pictures: Coloring & Activity Book. Fogle, Robin. 2006. 16p. (J). (gr. 1-5). 1.79 *(978-1-59317-160-5(9))* Warner Pr. Pubs.
Johnson, Paul Brett. Jack Outwits the Giants. Johnson, Paul Brett, adapted by. 2008. (ENG.). 36p. (J). (gr. -1-3). 11.99 *(978-1-4169-7861-9(5),* Simon & Schuster/Paula Wiseman Bks.) Simon & Schuster/Paula Wiseman Bks.
Johnson, Paul Brett. Fearless Jack. Johnson, Paul Brett. 2007. (ENG.). 32p. (J). (gr. -1-3). 10.99 *(978-1-4169-6833-7(4),* Simon & Schuster/Paula Wiseman Bks.) Simon & Schuster/Paula Wiseman Bks.
Johnson-Petrov, Arden. Farmer's Dog Goes to the Forest: Rhymes for Two Voices. Harrison, David L. 2005. (ENG.). 32p. (J). (gr. k-3). 15.95 *(978-1-59078-242-2(9))* Boyds Mills Pr.
—Farmer's Garden: Rhymes for Two Voices. Harrison, David L. 2003. (ENG.). 32p. (J). (gr. k-2). pap. 10.95 *(978-1-59078-177-7(5))* Boyds Mills Pr.
Johnson, R. Kikuo, jt. illus. see Loeffler, Trade.
Johnson, Regan. Kichi in Jungle Jeopardy. Guzman, Lila. (J). 2007. (ENG.). 135p. (gr. 2-7). pap. 8.95 *(978-0-9769417-2-9(4));* 2006. 144p. 13.95 *(978-0-9769417-1-2(6))* Blooming Tree Pr.
Johnson, Regan. Hold on to Your Tail: Letters from Camp Lizard. Johnson, Regan. 2008. (Letters From Camp Lizard Ser.). (ENG.). 112p. (J). (gr. 1-5). pap. 7.95 *(978-1-933831-04-6(9))* Blooming Tree Pr.
—Little Bunny Kung Fu. Johnson, Regan. 2005. (ENG.). 32p. (J). (gr. -1 — 1). 14.95 *(978-0-9769417-8-1(3))* Blooming Tree Pr.
Johnson, Richard. Aesop's Fables. Pirotta, Saviour. 2007. (ENG.). 80p. (J). (gr. -1-3). pap. 9.99 *(978-0-7534-6133-4(1),* Kingfisher) Roaring Brook Pr.
—Don't Cry, Sly! 2004. 32p. (J). (SPA & ENG.). pap. *(978-1-85269-662-7(1));* (ENG & POR.). pap. *(978-1-85269-659-7(1));* (ENG & PER.). pap. *(978-1-85269-653-5(2));* (ENG, ARA & BEN.). pap. *(978-1-85269-649-8(4))* Mantra Lingua.
—Don't Cry, Sly! Barkow, Henriette. 2004. 32p. (J). (ENG & CZE.). pap. *(978-1-85269-652-8(4));* (ENG & CHI.). pap. *(978-1-85269-651-1(6));* (GER & ENG.). pap. *(978-1-85269-655-9(9));* (ENG & GUJ.). pap. *(978-1-85269-656-6(7));* (ENG & ITA.). pap. *(978-1-85269-657-3(5));* (ENG & PAN.). pap. *(978-1-85269-658-0(3));* (ENG & BEN.). pap. *(978-1-85269-650-4(8));* (ENG.). pap. *(978-1-85269-660-3(5));* (ENG & SOM.). pap. *(978-1-85269-661-0(3));* (ENG & TAM.). pap. *(978-1-85269-663-4(X));* (ENG & TUR.). pap. *(978-1-85269-670-2(2));* (ENG & URD.). pap. *(978-1-85269-671-9(0));* (ENG & VIE.). pap. *(978-1-85269-672-6(9));* (ENG & POL.). pap. *(978-1-85269-813-3(6))* Mantra Lingua.
—Don't Cry Sly: Big Book English Only. Barkaw, Henniette. 2004. (J). *(978-1-85269-999-4(X))* Mantra Lingua.
—Don't Cry, Sly! Ne Pleure Pas Sly! Barkow, Henriette. 2004. (ENG & FRE.). 32p. (J). pap. *(978-1-85269-654-2(0))* Mantra Lingua.
—Easter Egg Hunt. Wang, Margaret. 2005. (ENG.). 10p. (J). bds. 9.95 *(978-1-58117-375-8(X),* Intervisual/Piggy Toes) Bendon, Inc.
—The Fourth Wise Man. Joslin, Mary. 2007. 28p. (J). (gr. -1-2). 14.99 *(978-0-7814-4545-0(0))* Cook, David C.
—The Giant Turnip. 2004. (J). 24p. *(978-1-85269-789-1(X));* 24p. *(978-1-85269-749-5(0));* 24p. *(978-1-85269-748-8(2));* 24p. *(978-1-85269-747-1(4));* 24p. *(978-1-85269-746-4(6));* 24p. *(978-1-85269-745-7(8));* 24p. *(978-1-85269-741-9(5));* 24p. *(978-1-85269-740-2(7));* 24p. *(978-1-85269-739-6(3));* 24p. *(978-1-85269-737-2(7));* 24p. *(978-1-85269-736-5(9));* 24p. *(978-1-85269-735-8(0));* 24p. *(978-1-85269-733-4(4));* (ENG & RUS.). 32p. pap. *(978-1-85269-788-4(1))* Mantra Lingua.
—The Giant Turnip. Barkow, Henriette. 2004. 32p. (J). (ENG & PAN.). pap. *(978-1-85269-742-6(3));* (POL & ENG.). pap. *(978-1-85269-743-3(1));* (ENG & POR.). pap. *(978-1-85269-744-0(X));* (ENG & BEN.). pap. *(978-1-85269-734-1(2));* (ENG & URD.). pap. *(978-1-85269-750-1(4))* Mantra Lingua.
—Giant Turnip. 2004. (J). E-Book incl. cd-rom *(978-1-84444-459-5(7))* Mantra Lingua.
—The Giant Turnip: Le Navet Geant. Barkow, Henriette. 2004. (ENG & FRE.). 32p. (J). pap. *(978-1-85269-738-9(5))* Mantra Lingua.
—Giant Turnip - Big Book. Barkow, Henriette. 2004. (ENG & MAY.). 23p. (J). *(978-1-85269-896-6(9))* Mantra Lingua.
—A Is for Acadia: Mount Desert Island from A to Z. Grierson, Ruth. 2007. (ENG.). 32p. (J). 15.95

(978-1-934031-03-2(8), 5605501a-a510-48b1-a5fb-bed4fcf85688) Islandport Pr., Inc.

—It's Tu B'Shevat. Zolkower, Edie Stoltz. 2005. (Very First Board Bks.). (ENG.). 12p. (J). (gr. -1 — 1). bds. 5.95 (978-1-58013-127-8(1), Kar-Ben Publishing) Lerner Publishing Group.

—The Lion Book of Five-Minute Bible Stories. 2013. (ENG.). 96p. (J). (gr. k-2). pap. 10.99 (978-0-7459-4984-0(3)) Lion Hudson PLC GBR. Dist: Independent Pubs. Group.

—The Lion Book of Five-Minute Christmas Stories. Goodwin, John. 2008. (ENG.). 48p. (J). (gr. k-2). 16.95 (978-0-7459-4943-7(6)) Lion Hudson PLC GBR. Dist: Independent Pubs. Group.

—Three Billy Goats Gruff. Barkow, Henriette. 2004. (J). (SER & ENG.). 24p. (978-1-85269-620-7(6)); (ENG & ALB.). 32p. pap. (978-1-85269-611-5(7)); (ARA & ENG.). 32p. pap. (978-1-85269-612-2(5)); (ENG & PER.). 32p. pap. (978-1-85269-615-3(X)); (FRE & ENG.). 32p. pap. (978-1-85269-616-0(8)); (ENG & GUJ.). 32p. pap. (978-1-85269-617-7(6)); (ENG & PAN.). 32p. pap. (978-1-85269-618-4(4)); (ENG & POR.). 32p. pap. (978-1-85269-619-1(2)); (ENG & SOM.). 32p. pap. (978-1-85269-621-4(4)); (ENG & SPA.). 32p. pap. (978-1-85269-622-1(2)); (ENG & TAM.). 32p. pap. (978-1-85269-623-8(0)); (ENG & TUR.). 32p. pap. (978-1-85269-624-5(9)); (ENG & URD.). 32p. pap. (978-1-85269-625-2(7)); (ENG & CZE.). 32p. pap. (978-1-85269-627-6(3)); (GER & ENG.). 32p. pap. (978-1-85269-785-3(7)); (ITA & ENG.). 32p. pap. (978-1-85269-786-0(5)) Mantra Lingua.

—Three Billy Goats Gruff: English Big Book. Barkow, Henriette. 2004. (ENG.). 32p. (J). pap. (978-1-85269-784-6(9)) Mantra Lingua.

—Three Little Pigs. (Classic Fairy Tales Ser.). (ENG.). 24p. (J). 2011. (978-1-84643-457-0(2)); 2007. (gr. -1-2). (978-1-84643-087-9(9)); 2005. pap. (978-1-904550-21-1(5)) Child's Play International Ltd.

—Winter Shadow. Knight, Richard John & Walker, Richard. 2009. (ENG.). 80p. (J). (gr. 3-9). pap. 16.99 (978-1-84686-116-1(0)) Barefoot Bks., Inc.

—Winter Shadow. Knight, Richard. 2011. (ENG.). 30p. (J). 9.99 (978-1-84686-624-1(3)) Barefoot Bks., Inc.

Johnson, Richard. Jack & the Beanstalk. Johnson, Richard, tr. 2004. 31p. (J). (978-1-84444-108-2(3)) Mantra Lingua.

Johnson, Richard, jt. illus. see Barkow, Henriette.

Johnson, Richard A. The Lion Book of Five-Minute Christmas Stories. Goodwin, John. 2014. (ENG.). 48p. (J). (gr. k-2). pap. 12.99 (978-0-7459-6926-8(7)) Lion Hudson PLC GBR. Dist: Independent Pubs. Group.

Johnson, Richard G. S Is for Snowman, 1 vol. Wargin, Kathy-jo. 2011. (ENG.). 40p. (J). 15.99 (978-0-310-71661-7(6)) Zonderkidz.

—The Story of the Resurrection Eggs, 1 vol. Bowman, Crystal. 2013. (ENG.). 40p. (J). 7.99 (978-0-310-72595-4(X)) Zonderkidz.

Johnson, Rick. The Legend of the Sand Dollar: An Inspirational Story of Hope for Easter, 1 vol. Auer, Chris. 2005. (ENG.). 32p. (J). 16.99 (978-0-310-70780-6(3)) Zonderkidz.

Johnson, Robyn. The Enchanted Dolls' House. Johnson, Robyn. 2006. (ENG.). 32p. (J). (gr. -1-7). 27.99 (978-1-59354-182-8(1), Handprint Bks.) Chronicle Bks. LLC.

Johnson, Shane. OLIVIA Paints a Mural. 2011. (Olivia TV Tie-In Ser.). (ENG.). 12p. (J). (gr. -1-1). bds. 5.99 (978-1-4424-1674-1(2), Simon Spotlight) Simon Spotlight.

Johnson, Shane L. Be the Brush Doodle Book. Snider, Brandon T. 2014. (Amazing World of Gumball Ser.). (ENG.). 128p. (J). (gr. 3-7). 12.99 (978-0-8431-8101-2(X), Price Stern Sloan) Penguin Publishing Group.

—The Chickens & the Eggs. 2014. (Rabbids Invasion Ser.). (ENG.). 40p. (J). (gr. 1-3). pap. 3.99 (978-1-4814-0042-8(8), Simon Spotlight) Simon Spotlight.

—Destination: Ooo: Land of Ooo in under 20 Snails a Day. Black, Jake. 2013. (Adventure Time Ser.). (ENG.). 160p. (J). (gr. 3-7). pap. 9.99 (978-0-8431-7328-4(9), Price Stern Sloan) Penguin Publishing Group.

—Fashion Face-off. Black, Allyson. 2011. (Scarlett & Crimson Ser.). (ENG.). 112p. (J). (gr. 3-7). pap. 6.99 (978-1-4169-5937-3(8), Simon Spotlight) Simon Spotlight.

—The Need for Speed. 2014. (Rabbids Invasion Ser.). (ENG.). 40p. (J). (gr. 1-3). 16.99 (978-1-4814-2292-5(8)); pap. 3.99 (978-1-4814-2291-8(X)) Simon Spotlight. (Simon Spotlight).

—Olivia & Grandma's Visit. Evans, Cordelia. 2013. (Olivia TV Tie-In Ser.). (ENG.). 24p. (J). (gr. -1-2). pap. 3.99 (978-1-4424-4586-4(6), Simon Spotlight) Simon Spotlight.

—Olivia & Her Ducklings. 2010. (Olivia TV Tie-In Ser.). (ENG.). 24p. (J). (gr. -1-1). 15.99 (978-1-4424-1382-5(4), Simon Spotlight) Simon Spotlight.

—Olivia & Her Ducklings. Hiranandani, Veera. 2010. (Olivia TV Tie-In Ser.). (ENG.). 24p. (J). (gr. -1-1). pap. 3.99 (978-1-4169-9079-6(8), Simon Spotlight) Simon Spotlight.

—OLIVIA & the Best Teacher Ever. Oliver, Ilanit. 2012. (Olivia TV Tie-In Ser.). (ENG.). 24p. (J). (gr. -1-2). pap. 3.99 (978-1-4424-3599-5(2), Simon Spotlight) Simon Spotlight.

—OLIVIA & the Christmas Present. 2011. (Olivia TV Tie-In Ser.). (ENG.). 24p. (J). (gr. -1-2). 9.99 (978-1-4424-3624-4(7), Simon Spotlight) Simon Spotlight.

—OLIVIA & the Dog Wash. 2012. (Olivia TV Tie-In Ser.). (ENG.). 16p. (J). (gr. -1-1). pap. 5.99 (978-1-4424-4638-0(2), Simon Spotlight) Simon Spotlight.

—OLIVIA & the Easter Egg Hunt. 2013. (Olivia TV Tie-In Ser.). (ENG.). 24p. (J). (gr. -1-2). pap. 4.99 (978-1-4424-6022-5(9), Simon Spotlight) Simon Spotlight.

—OLIVIA & the Fancy Party. Evans, Cordelia. 2014. (Olivia TV Tie-In Ser.). (ENG.). 24p. (J). (gr. -1-2). pap. 3.99 (978-1-4814-0364-1(8), Simon Spotlight) Simon Spotlight.

—Olivia & the Ice Show: A Lift-The-Flap Story. 2013. (Olivia TV Tie-In Ser.). (ENG.). 16p. (J). (gr. -1-2). pap. 6.99 (978-1-4424-2083-0(9), Simon Spotlight) Simon Spotlight.

—OLIVIA & the Perfect Valentine. Shaw, Natalie. 2013. (Olivia TV Tie-In Ser.). (ENG.). 24p. (J). (gr. -1-2). pap. 4.99 (978-1-4424-8484-9(5), Simon Spotlight) Simon Spotlight.

—OLIVIA & the Snow Day. 2010. (Olivia TV Tie-In Ser.). (ENG.). 24p. (J). (gr. -1-1). 15.99 (978-1-4423-3638-4(2), Simon Spotlight) Simon Spotlight.

—OLIVIA Builds a House. 2012. (Olivia TV Tie-In Ser.). (ENG.). 24p. (J). (gr. -1-1). 15.99 (978-1-4424-5323-4(0)); pap. 3.99 (978-1-4424-5322-7(2)) Simon Spotlight. (Simon Spotlight).

—OLIVIA Counts down to Christmas. Testa, Maggie. 2012. (Olivia TV Tie-In Ser.). (ENG.). 16p. (J). (gr. -1-1). pap. 6.99 (978-1-4424-5747-8(3), Simon Spotlight) Simon Spotlight.

—OLIVIA la Princesa. 2011. (Olivia TV Tie-In Ser.). (ENG & SPA.). 24p. (J). (gr. -1-2). pap. 3.99 (978-1-4424-4640-3(4), Libros Para Ninos) Libros Para Ninos.

—OLIVIA Leads a Parade. 2011. (Olivia TV Tie-In Ser.). (ENG.). 24p. (J). (gr. -1-2). pap. 3.99 (978-1-4424-2137-0(1), Simon Spotlight) Simon Spotlight.

—Olivia the Princess. 2011. (Olivia TV Tie-In Ser.). (ENG.). 24p. (J). (gr. -1-2). pap. 3.99 (978-1-4424-3033-4(8), Simon Spotlight) Simon Spotlight.

—OLIVIA Trains Her Cat. (Olivia TV Tie-In Ser.). (ENG.). 24p. (J). (gr. -1-1). 2010. 16.99 (978-1-4424-1383-2(2)); 2009. pap. 3.99 (978-1-4169-8296-8(5)) Simon Spotlight. (Simon Spotlight).

—Olivia y el Regalo de Navidad. Romay, Alexis, tr. 2012. (Olivia TV Tie-In Ser.). (SPA.). 24p. (J). (gr. -1-2). pap. 5.99 (978-1-4424-6568-8(9), Libros Para Ninos) Libros Para Ninos.

—Once upon a Time in Elmore: When Gumball Met Penny. Stuart, Wrigley. 2015. (Amazing World of Gumball Ser.). (ENG.). 80p. (J). (gr. 3-7). 5.99 (978-0-8431-8257-6(1), Price Stern Sloan) Penguin Publishing Group.

—Princess for a Day: A Pop-Up Storybook. 2011. (Olivia TV Tie-In Ser.). (ENG.). 12p. (J). (gr. -1-1). 17.99 (978-1-4424-3141-6(5), Simon Spotlight) Simon Spotlight.

—A Special Day with Dad. Shaw, Natalie. 2014. (Olivia TV Tie-In Ser.). (ENG.). 24p. (J). (gr. -1-2). pap. 4.99 (978-1-4424-9751-1(3), Simon Spotlight) Simon Spotlight.

—Star of the Show. 2014. (Olivia TV Tie-In Ser.). (ENG.). 24p. (J). (gr. -1-2). 7.99 (978-1-4424-9860-0(9), Simon Spotlight) Simon Spotlight.

—Turtles to the Rescue! (Teenage Mutant Ninja Turtles) Golden Books. 2012. (Color Plus Tattoos Ser.). (ENG.). 48p. (J). (gr. -1-2). pap. 3.99 (978-0-307-98069-4(3), Golden Bks.) Random Hse. Children's Bks.

Johnson, Shane L. & Mawhinney, Art. The Deep Freeze. 2014. (Rabbids Invasion Ser.). (ENG.). 40p. (J). (gr. 1-3). pap. 3.99 (978-1-4814-0045-9(2), Simon Spotlight) Simon Spotlight.

Johnson, Shane L., jt. illus. see Mawhinney, Art.

Johnson, Shane L., jt. illus. see Osterhold, Jared.

Johnson, Sharon. Spinman, Katydid & Bump: A Spider Vane Collection. Nash, Myrna Lee. 2003. 48p. (YA). (gr. 4-10). 11.95 (978-0-9724549-0-2(X)) Chapter & Verse Pr.

Johnson, Sidra. Mesha's Great Big World. Johnson, Sidra. 2011. (ENG.). 34p. pap. 9.50 (978-1-4664-7977-7(9)) CreateSpace Independent Publishing Platform.

Johnson, Staz, et al. Dracula. Stoker, Bram. Bryant, Clive, ed. 2012. (ENG.). 144p. (gr. 6). pap. 16.95 (978-1-906332-68-6(1)); pap. 16.95 (978-1-906332-67-9(3)) Classical Comics GBR. (Classical Comics, Ltd.). Dist: Perseus-PGW.

Johnson, Staz. Special Forces. Brook, Henry. Frith, Alex, ed. 2014. (ENG.). 80p. (J). pap. 8.99 (978-0-7945-3337-3(X), Usborne) EDC Publishing.

Johnson, Staz & Roots, Adrian. Spying. Brook, Henry. Frith, Alex, ed. 2014. (ENG.). 80p. (J). (gr. 4-7). pap. 8.99 (978-0-7945-2809-6(0), Usborne) EDC Publishing.

Johnson, Stephen T. A Is for Art: An Abstract Alphabet. Johnson, Stephen T. 2008. (ENG.). 40p. (J). (gr. k-4). 17.99 (978-0-689-86301-1(2), Simon & Schuster/Paula Wiseman Bks.) Simon & Schuster/Paula Wiseman Bks.

Johnson, Stephen T. Alphabet School. Johnson, Stephen T. 2015. (ENG.). 32p. (J). (gr. -1-3). 17.99 **(978-1-4169-2521-7(X),** Simon & Schuster Bks. For Young Readers) Simon & Schuster Bks. For Young Readers.

Johnson, Stephen T. City by Numbers. Johnson, Stephen T. Johnson, Stephen. 2003. (ENG.). 32p. (J). (gr. k-3). 6.99 (978-0-14-056636-9(8), Puffin) Penguin Publishing Group.

—My Little Blue Robot. Johnson, Stephen T. 2012. (ENG.). 16p. (J). (gr. -1-3). 19.99 (978-1-4424-5416-3(4), Simon & Schuster/Paula Wiseman Bks.) Simon & Schuster/Paula Wiseman Bks.

—My Little Pink Princess Purse. Johnson, Stephen T. 2010. (ENG.). 16p. (J). (gr. -1-3). 19.99 (978-1-4169-7979-1(4), Simon & Schuster/Paula Wiseman Bks.) Simon & Schuster/Paula Wiseman Bks.

—My Little Red Fire Truck. Johnson, Stephen T. 2009. (ENG.). 16p. (J). (gr. -1-2). 19.99 (978-1-4169-2522-4(8), Simon & Schuster/Paula Wiseman Bks.) Simon & Schuster/Paula Wiseman Bks.

Johnson, Steve, et al. Amazing Peace: A Christmas Poem, 1 vol. Angelou, Maya. 2008. (ENG.). 40p. (J). (gr. k-12). 18.99 (978-0-375-84150-7(4), Schwartz & Wade Bks.) Random Hse. Children's Bks.

—Casey Back at Bat. Gutman, Dan. 2009. (ENG.). 32p. (J). (gr. -1-3). pap. 6.99 (978-0-06-056027-0(4)) HarperCollins Pubs.

Johnson, Steve. The Frog Prince. Scieszka, Jon. 2014. 32p. pap. 7.00 (978-1-61003-314-5(0)) Center for the Collaborative Classroom.

—The Frog Prince, Continued. Scieszka, Jon. 2003. pap. 39.95 incl. audio compact disk (978-1-59112-522-8(7)) Live Oak Media.

Johnson, Steve & Fancher, Lou. The Bebop Express. Panahi, H. L. 2005. (ENG.). 32p. (J). (gr. -1-3). 16.99 (978-0-06-057190-0(X)) HarperCollins Pubs.

—A Boy Named FDR: How Franklin D. Roosevelt Grew up to Change America. Krull, Kathleen. 2010. (ENG.). 48p. (J). (gr. 1-4). 17.99 (978-0-375-85716-4(8)) Knopf, Alfred A. Inc.

—The Boy on Fairfield Street: How Ted Geisel Grew up to Become Dr. Seuss. Krull, Kathleen. 2010. (ENG.). 48p. (J). (gr. k-4). pap. 7.99 (978-0-375-85550-4(5), Dragonfly Bks.) Random Hse. Children's Bks.

—Bugtown Boogie. Hanson, Warren. 2008. 32p. (J). (gr. -1-3). 17.89 (978-0-06-059938-6(3), Geringer, Laura Book) HarperCollins Pubs.

—Cat, You Better Come Home. Keillor, Garrison. 2010. (ENG.). 32p. (J). (gr. -1-k). 16.99 (978-0-670-01277-0(7), Viking Juvenile) Penguin Publishing Group.

—The Cheese. Palatini, Margie. 2007. (ENG.). 32p. (J). (gr. -1-2). 17.99 (978-0-06-052630-6(0), Tegen, Katherine Bks) HarperCollins Pubs.

—La Hermosa Señora: Nuestra Señora de Guadalupe. Mora, Pat & Johnson, Steve. Fancher, Lou & Dominguez, Adriana. 2012. (SPA & ENG.). 40p. (J). (gr. k-3). pap. 8.99 (978-0-375-86840-5(2), Dragonfly Bks.) Random Hse. Children's Bks.

—Jim Henson: the Guy Who Played with Puppets. Krull, Kathleen. 2011. (ENG.). 40p. (J). (gr. k-4). 16.99 (978-0-375-85721-8(4), Random Hse. Bks. for Young Readers) Random Hse. Children's Bks.

—The King's Taster. Oppel, Kenneth. 2009. 32p. (J). (gr. -1-1). (ENG.). 17.99 (978-0-06-075372-6(2)); lib. bdg. 18.89 (978-0-06-075373-3(0)) HarperCollins Pubs.

—New York's Bravest. Osborne, Mary Pope. 2006. (ENG.). 32p. (J). (gr. -1-2). 6.99 (978-0-375-83841-5(4), Dragonfly Bks.) Random Hse. Children's Bks.

—No Star Nights. Smucker, Anna. 2012. 40p. (J). pap. 8.95 (978-1-891852-82-4(5)) Quarrier Pr.

—One Frozen Lake. Larson, Deborah Jo. 2012. (ENG.). 32p. (J). 16.95 (978-0-87351-866-6(7)) Minnesota Historical Society Pr.

—A Special Gift for Grammy. George, Jean Craighead. 2013. (ENG.). 32p. (J). (gr. -1-3). 17.99 (978-0-06-053176-8(2)) HarperCollins Pubs.

Johnson, Steve, jt. illus. see Cowdrey, Richard.

Johnson, Steve, jt. illus. see Fancher, Lou.

Johnson, Sue, jt. illus. see Honey, Elizabeth.

Johnson, Tamaris. Seaweed, the Purrfect Cat. Williams, Lee. 2013. 36p. (J). 9.99 (978-1-937493-47-9(4)) Dancing Moon Pr.

—Twin Dragons. Williams, Lee. 2012. 32p. (J). 8.99 (978-1-937493-18-9(0)) Dancing Moon Pr.

Johnson, Tucker. All Hallows' Eve: The Story of the Halloween Fairy. Johnson, Lisa. l.t. ed. 2005. 32p. (J). 12.95 (978-0-9773096-0-3(6)) Positive Spin Pr.

Johnson, Vickie. Time for Bed - The Secret of Shadows: Shadow Theater Inside. Allen, Lisa & Sharp, Julis. 26p. (J). (gr. -1-2). pap. (978-1-56021-355-0(8), 206) W.J. Fantasy, Inc.

—The Troll of MacKinac. Thorne, K. C. 2010. 32p. pap. 13.00 (978-1-60911-178-6(8), Eloquent Bks.) Strategic Book Publishing & Rights Agency (SBPRA).

Johnson, Virginia. Don't, 1 vol. 2014. (ENG.). 24p. (J). (— 1). bds. 9.95 (978-1-55498-355-1(X)) Groundwood Bks. CAN. Dist: Perseus-PGW.

—This New Baby. Jam, Teddy. 2011. (ENG.). 22p. (J). (gr. k — 1). bds. 8.95 (978-1-55498-088-8(7)) Groundwood Bks. CAN. Dist: Perseus-PGW.

Johnston, Jillian S. In That Land There Are Giants. Powell, Gary Allison. 2011. 38p. pap. 14.50 (978-1-60860-891-1(3), Eloquent Bks.) Strategic Book Publishing & Rights Agency (SBPRA).

Johnston, Joe. Snag & Me - Christmas Miracle in Blanchard Forks. Johnston, Joe. 2004. (YA). per. 10.00 (978-1-932496-15-4(7)) Penman Publishing, Inc.

Johnston, Lisa Harp. Mason's Mashed Potato Tree. Waszak, Madonna. 2011. 34p. pap. 14.95 (978-1-4575-0159-3(7)) Dog Ear Publishing, LLC.

Johnston, Phillip. Nathan Meets His Monsters. Kropp, Joseph P. 2012. 34p. 16.95 (978-1-890905-59-0(3)); pap. 9.95 (978-1-890905-58-3(5)) Day to Day Enterprises.

Johnstone, Anne Grahame. The Water Babies. Kingsley, Charles. 2012. (ENG.). 32p. 9.95 (978-1-84135-236-7(5)) Award Pubns. Ltd. GBR. Dist: Parkwest Pubns., Inc.

Johri, Shaan Mohammad. The Snackman & His Son, 1 vol. Johri, Subia Ali. 2010. 28p. 24.95 (978-1-4512-0978-5(9)) America Star Bks.

Joiner, D. Wayne, Sr. Dudley Gloworm & the Saving Light. Joiner, D. Wayne, Sr. 2006. (J). 25.00 (978-0-9785103-0-5(5)) Willy Waw wees, LLC.

Jok. Vampires & Cells. Biskup, Agnieszka. 2011. (Monster Science Ser.). (ENG.). 32p. (gr. 3-4). pap. 47.70 (978-1-4296-7332-7(X), Graphic Library) Capstone Pr., Inc.

—Zombies & Electricity, 6 vols. Weakland, Mark. 2013. (Monster Science Ser.). (ENG.). 32p. (gr. 3-4). 47.70 (978-1-62065-823-9(2), Graphic Library) Capstone Pr., Inc.

Jok, Diego. Vampires & Cells, 1 vol. Biskup, Agnieszka. 2011. (Monster Science Ser.). (ENG.). 32p. (gr. 3-4). pap. 8.10 (978-1-4296-7331-0(1)); lib. bdg. 29.99 (978-1-4296-6582-7(3)) Capstone Pr., Inc. (Graphic Library).

—Zombies & Electricity, 1 vol. Weakland, Mark. 2013. (Monster Science Ser.). (ENG.). 32p. (gr. 3-4). pap. 8.10 (978-1-62065-822-2(4), Graphic Library); lib. bdg. 29.99 (978-1-4296-9929-7(9)) Capstone Pr., Inc.

Jolby. Monsters under Bridges. 2013. (ENG.). 32p. (J). (gr. -1-3). 16.99 (978-1-57061-856-7(9)) Sasquatch Bks.

Jolet, Stefan. Cinderellaphant, 1 vol. De Las Casas, Dianne. 2014. (ENG.). 32p. (J). (gr. k-3). 16.99 (978-1-4556-1900-9(0)) Pelican Publishing Co., Inc.

Jolivet, Joelle. In This Book. Marceau, Fani. 2014. (ENG.). 64p. (J). (gr. -1 — 1). 17.99 (978-1-4521-2588-6(0)) Chronicle Bks. LLC.

Jolivet, Joëlle. Oops! Fromental, Jean-Luc. Connors, Thomas, tr. from FRE. 2010. (ENG.). 42p. (J). (gr. -1-3). 17.95 (978-0-8109-8749-4(X)) Abrams.

—Panorama: A Foldout Book. Marceau, Fani. 2009. (ENG.). 32p. (J). (gr. -1-7). 21.95 (978-0-8109-8332-8(X), Abrams Bks. for Young Readers) Abrams.

—Rapido's Next Stop. Fromental, Jean-Luc. 2012. (ENG.). 20p. (J). (gr. -1-3). 17.95 (978-1-4197-0195-5(9), Abrams Bks. for Young Readers) Abrams.

—Tales from Shakespeare. Lamb, Charles & Lamb, Mary. 2007. (ENG.). 180p. (gr. 8-17). 21.95 (978-0-8109-9453-9(4), Abrams Image) Abrams.

—10 Little Penguins. 2010. (ENG.). 24p. (J). (gr. -1-17). 18.95 (978-0-8109-9582-6(4), Abrams Bks. for Young Readers) Abrams.

—365 Penguins. Fromental, Jean-Luc. 2006. (ENG.). 48p. (J). (gr. -1-3). 19.95 (978-0-8109-4460-2(X), Abrams Bks. for Young Readers) Abrams.

Jolivet, Joelle. Almost Everything. Jolivet, Joelle. Siegel, Alexis, tr. from FRE. 2005. (ENG.). 40p. (J). (gr. -1-3). 29.99 (978-1-59643-090-7(7)) Roaring Brook Pr.

—Zoo - Ology. Jolivet, Joelle. rev. ed. 2003. (ENG.). 40p. (J). (gr. -1-3). 29.99 (978-0-7613-1894-1(1)) Roaring Brook Pr.

Jolley, Mack. I Can't Go to Church. Brown, Toni Sorenson. 2005. (J). (978-1-59156-270-2(8)) Covenant Communications.

Jolliffe, Angela. Fun with Action Rhymes & Poems. Williams, Brenda. 2004. 108p. pap. (978-1-903853-50-4(8)) Brilliant Pubns.

Jolliffe, Angela. Noah. Clayden, Julie. 2005. (First Word Heroes Ser.). (ENG.). 12p. (J). (gr. 3-5). bds. 7.99 (978-1-904637-11-0(6), 1904637116) Authentic Media GBR. Dist: EMI CMG Distribution.

Jolliffe, Susan Rennick. The Twelve Days of Summer, 1 vol. Andrews, Jan. 2007. (ENG.). 32p. (J). (gr. -1-3). per. 8.95 (978-1-55143-735-4(X)) Orca Bk. Pubs. USA.

Joma. Rapunzel: A Bilingual Book. Bofill, Francesc. 2006. (Bilingual Fairy Tales Ser.: BILI). (ENG.). 32p. (J). (gr. -1-7). 14.95 (978-0-8118-5059-9(5)) Chronicle Bks. LLC.

—Rapunzel/Rapunzel. Bofill, Francesc. 2006. (Bilingual Fairy Tales Ser.: BILI). (CAT & ENG.). 32p. (J). (gr. -1-7). per. 6.99 (978-0-8118-5060-5(9)) Chronicle Bks. LLC.

Jonas, Ann. Stars Beneath Your Bed: The Surprising Story of Dust. Sayre, April Pulley. 2005. 32p. (J). lib. bdg. 17.89 (978-0-06-057189-4(6)); (ENG.). 17.99 (978-0-06-057188-7(8), Greenwillow Bks.) HarperCollins Pubs.

Jonason, Dave. Midge & Max's Scavenger Hunt. Ellis, Libby. 2005. 12p. (J). (gr. -1-3). act. bk. ed. 14.95 (978-1-58117-109-9(9), Intervisual/Piggy Toes) Bendon, Inc.

Jonathan Siruno. Moxie Day the Prankster: Another Laugh & Learn Book of Poetry. Pottle, Robert. 2004. 64p. (J). per. 8.95 (978-0-9709569-2-7(4), MDTP) Blue Lobster Pr.

Jones, Aaron. Please Be Quiet! Drake, Karen. 2011. (ENG.). 46p. pap. 14.95 (978-1-4610-6925-6(4)) CreateSpace Independent Publishing Platform.

Jones., Amber. Ollie & Grampa Go to the Zoo: How the Polar Bear Got to the Zoo. Ken Lindstrom To Ken Lindstrom. 2011. 28p. pap. 12.49 (978-1-4520-1529-3(5)) AuthorHouse.

Jones, Ann. Granny's Clan: A Tale of Wild Orcas. Hodson, Sally. 2012. (ENG.). 32p. (J). (gr. k-4). 16.95 (978-1-58469-171-6(9)); pap. 8.95 (978-1-58469-172-3(7)) Dawn Pubns.

Jones, Anna. Dinosaur Disasters. Agnew, Kate. 2010. (Green Bananas Ser.). (ENG.). 48p. (J). (gr. k-2). pap. 5.99 (978-1-4052-4778-8(9)) Egmont Bks., Ltd. GBR. Dist: Independent Pubs. Group.

—Goodnight, Mouse: A Peek-A-Boo Adventure. 2012. (J). (978-1-4351-4387-6(6)) Barnes & Noble, Inc.

—Ho! Ho! Ho! Reasoner, Charles. 2013. (Charles Reasoner Holiday Bks.). (ENG.). 10p. (gr. -1 — 1). bds. 9.99 (978-1-4048-7913-3(7)) Picture Window Bks.

—Let It Snow. Reasoner, Charles. 2013. (Charles Reasoner Holiday Bks.). (ENG.). 10p. (gr. -1 — 1). bds. 9.99 (978-1-4048-8147-1(6)) Picture Window Bks.

Jones, Anna. My First Bedtime Bible Stories. Froeb, Lori C., ed. 2015. (ENG.). 10p. (J). (gr. -1-k). bds. 8.99 **(978-0-7944-3474-8(6))** Studio Fun International.

Jones, Anna. Red Nose Go! Reasoner, Charles. 2013. (Charles Reasoner Holiday Bks.). (ENG.). 10p. (gr. -1 — 1). bds. 9.99 (978-1-4048-8146-4(8)) Picture Window Bks.

—Scrub-A-Dub Ducky: Bath Mitt & Bath Book Set. Rivers-Moore, Debbie. 2014. (ENG.). 8p. (J). (gr. -1 — 1). 9.99 (978-1-4380-7530-3(8)) Barron's Educational Series, Inc.

—Scrub-a-Dub Froggy: Bath Mitt & Book Set. 2013. (ENG.). 8p. (J). (gr. -1 — 1). 9.99 (978-1-4380-7439-9(5)) Barron's Educational Series, Inc.

—Winter Friends. Reasoner, Charles. 2013. (Charles Reasoner Holiday Bks.). (ENG.). 10p. (gr. -1 — 1). bds. 9.99 (978-1-4048-8148-8(4)) Picture Window Bks.

Jones, Anna & Le Ray, Marina. Humpty Dumpty, 1 vol. Reasoner, Charles. 2013. (Charles Reasoner Nursery Rhymes Ser.). (ENG.). 10p. (gr. -1 — 1). bds. 9.99 (978-1-4048-8172-3(7)) Picture Window Bks.

—Itsy Bitsy Spider, 1 vol. Reasoner, Charles. 2013. (Charles Reasoner Nursery Rhymes Ser.). (ENG.). 10p. (gr. -1 — 1). bds. 9.99 (978-1-4048-8173-0(5)) Picture Window Bks.

—This Little Piggy, 1 vol. Reasoner, Charles. 2013. (Charles Reasoner Nursery Rhymes Ser.). (ENG.). 10p. (gr. -1 — 1). bds. 9.99 (978-1-4048-8174-7(3)) Picture Window Bks.

—Twinkle, Twinkle, Little Star, 1 vol. Reasoner, Charles & Taylor, Jane. 2013. (Charles Reasoner Nursery Rhymes Ser.). (ENG.). 10p. (gr. -1 — 1). bds. 9.99 (978-1-4048-8175-4(1)) Picture Window Bks.

Jones, Anna, jt. illus. see Dreidemy, Joëlle.

Jones, Anna, jt. illus. see Le Ray, Marina.

Jones, Anna, jt. illus. see Reasoner, Charles.

Jones, Ayanna. Friends Will Be There Forever. Walter-Goodspeed, Dee Dee. 2012. 26p. (J). (-18). pap. 15.99 (978-1-933846-36-1(4)) Fairwood Pr.

Jones, Barry. Dracula. Stoker, Bram. 2004. (Paperback Classics Ser.). 144p. (J). pap. 4.95 (978-0-7945-0089-4(7), Usborne) EDC Publishing.

J

—Frankenstein. Shelley, Mary & Shelley, Mary. 2004. (Paperback Classics Ser.). 144p. (J). pap. 4.95 *(978-0-7945-0090-0(0),* Usborne) EDC Publishing.

—Tales of Mystery & Imagination. Poe, Edgar Allen. 2004. (Paperback Classics Ser.). 144p. (J). pap. 4.95 *(978-0-7945-0186-0(9),* Usborne) EDC Publishing.

Jones, Bill. Five-Minute Halloween Mysteries. Weber, Ken. De la Hoz, Cindy, ed. 2007. (ENG.). 128p. 5.95 *(978-0-7624-3076-5(1))* Running Pr. Bk. Pubs.

Jones, Bill, jt. illus. see Fasbinder, George.

Jones, Bob. Pinuccio. Dioma, Joseph. 2009. 24p. pap. 14.99 *(978-1-60844-036-8(2))* Dog Ear Publishing, LLC.

Jones, Branson & Mikle, Toby. Alphabet Anatomy: Meet the Capital Letters. Jones, Linda. 2012. 32p. pap. *(978-1-4602-0047-6(0))* FriesenPress.

Jones, Brenda. Born: A Foal, Five Kittens & Confederation, 1 vol. Kessler, Deirdre. 2015. (ENG.). 48p. (J). (gr. k-2). pap. 12.95 ***(978-1-927502-33-4(0))*** Acorn Pr., The CAN. Dist: Orca Bk. Pubs. USA.

Jones, Brenda. Bubba Begonia, You'll Be Sorry. O'Brien, Gerry. ed. 2006. (ENG.). 80p. (J). per. 6.95 *(978-1-894838-23-8(8))* Acorn Pr., The CAN. Dist: Univ. of Toronto Pr.

—Hockey Night Tonight, 1 vol. Connors, Stompin' Tom. ed. 2010. (ENG.). 24p. (J). (gr. -1-k). bds. 12.95 *(978-1-55109-733-6(8))* Nimbus Publishing, Ltd. CAN. Dist: Orca Bk. Pubs. USA.

—I Is for Island: A Prince Edward Island Alphabet. MacDonald, Hugh. 2012. (ENG.). 40p. (J). (gr. 1-5). 16.95 *(978-1-58536-367-4(7))* Sleeping Bear Pr.

—Lobster Fishing on the Sea, 1 vol. Hull, Maureen. ed. 2010. (ENG.). 32p. (J). (gr. -1-3). pap. 8.95 *(978-1-55109-754-1(0))* Nimbus Publishing, Ltd. CAN. Dist: Orca Bk. Pubs. USA.

—Lobster in My Pocket, 1 vol. Kessler, Deirdre. 2nd ed. 2010. (ENG.). 32p. (J). (gr. -1-3). pap. 8.95 *(978-1-55109-767-1(2))* Nimbus Publishing, Ltd. CAN. Dist: Orca Bk. Pubs. USA.

—Simon & Catapult Man's Perilous Playground Adventure, 1 vol. Smiley, Norene. ed. 2009. (ENG.). 32p. (J). (gr. -1-2). pap. 8.95 *(978-1-55109-714-5(1))* Nimbus Publishing, Ltd. CAN. Dist: Orca Bk. Pubs. USA.

—Skunks for Breakfast, 1 vol. Choyce, Lesley. 2007. (ENG.). 32p. (J). (gr. -1-2). pap. 8.95 *(978-1-55109-586-8(6))* Nimbus Publishing, Ltd. CAN. Dist: Orca Bk. Pubs. USA.

Jones, Brian T. Quackenstein Hatches a Family. Bardhan-Quallen, Sudipta. 2010. (ENG.). 32p. (J). (gr. -1-3). 15.95 *(978-0-8109-8973-3(5),* Abrams Bks. for Young Readers) Abrams.

—You Can't Milk a Dancing Cow. Dunsmuir, Tom. 2005. (ENG.). 24p. (J). (gr. -1-3). 14.95 *(978-0-9749303-3-6(4))* Tanglewood Pr.

Jones, Bruce Patrick. Action Stars Paper Dolls. Jones, Bruce Patrick. 2010. (Dover Celebrity Paper Dolls Ser.). (ENG.). 32p. (J). (gr. 3-5). pap. 9.99 *(978-0-486-47606-3(5))* Dover Pubns., Inc.

Jones, Buck. The Great Treasure Quest. McDowell, Josh & Johnson, Kevin. 2006. 103p. (J). (gr. 3-7). per. 10.99 *(978-1-932587-85-2(3))* Practical Christianity Foundation.

—Greatest Goofiest Jokes. Pierce, Terry. 2010. (ENG.). 96p. (J). pap. 4.95 *(978-1-4027-7847-6(3))* Sterling Publishing Co., Inc.

—Kids' Silliest Jokes. Horsfall, Jacqueline. 2003. (ENG.). 96p. (J). pap. 4.95 *(978-1-4027-0598-4(0))* Sterling Publishing Co., Inc.

—Obesity. Moore, Arden. 2005. (Simple Solutions Ser.). (ENG.). 64p. per. 6.95 *(978-1-931993-62-3(9))* i-5 Publishing LLC.

—Ridiculous Tongue Twisters. Tait, Chris. 2010. (ENG.). 96p. (J). pap. 4.95 *(978-1-4027-7854-4(6))* Sterling Publishing Co., Inc.

—Ten-Second Tongue Twisters. Artell, Mike. 2010. (ENG.). 96p. (J). pap. 4.95 *(978-1-4027-7858-2(9))* Sterling Publishing Co., Inc.

Jones, C. Denise West & Darby, Stephania Pierce. Koko & Friends: Born to Play-Destined to Win! Jones, C. Denise West & Darby, Stephania Pierce. (J). *(978-1-892313-00-3(6))* D. W. Ink.

Jones, Casey, jt. illus. see Wieringo, Mike.

Jones, Chamira. Where Do Crickets Go When Winter Comes? Russell-Gilmer, Phyllis A. 2009. 32p. (J). 16.95 *(978-1-934363-10-2(3))* Zoe Life Publishing.

Jones, Channing. Sounds in the House! A Mystery. Beckstrand, Karl. 2004.Tr. of Sonidos en la Casa. (ENG.). 24p. (J). per. 4.00 *(978-0-9672012-5-2(X))* Premio Publishing & Gozo Bks., LLC.

Jones, Chris B. First Graphics: Body Systems. Kolpin, Molly et al. 2012. (First Graphics: Body Systems Ser.). (ENG.). 24p. (gr. 1-2). pap. 178.50 *(978-1-4296-9333-2(9))*; pap. 29.75 *(978-1-4296-9332-5(0))*; lib. bdg. 93.28 *(978-1-4296-9158-1(1))* Capstone Pr., Inc.

Jones, Chris B. Jim Nasium Is a Basket Case. McKnight, Marty. 2015. (Jim Nasium Ser.). (ENG.). 88p. (gr. 2-3). pap. 5.95 ***(978-1-4965-0526-2(3))*** Stone Arch Bks.

—Jim Nasium Is a Football Fumbler. McKnight, Marty. 2015. (Jim Nasium Ser.). (ENG.). 88p. (gr. 2-3). lib. bdg. 23.99 ***(978-1-4965-0522-4(0))*** Stone Arch Bks.

—Jim Nasium Is a Hockey Hazard. McKnight, Marty. 2015. (Jim Nasium Ser.). (ENG.). 88p. (gr. 2-3). pap. 5.95 ***(978-1-4965-0524-8(7))*** Stone Arch Bks.

—Jim Nasium Is a Soccer Goofball. McKnight, Marty. 2015. (Jim Nasium Ser.). (ENG.). 88p. (gr. 2-3). pap. 5.95 ***(978-1-4965-0525-5(5))*** Stone Arch Bks.

Jones, Chris B. A Tour of Your Circulatory System, 1 vol. Ballen, Karen. 2012. (First Graphics: Body Systems Ser.). (ENG.). 24p. (gr. 1-2). pap. 6.29 *(978-1-4296-9322-6(3))*; pap. 35.70 *(978-1-4296-9323-3(1))* Capstone Pr., Inc.

—A Tour of Your Digestive System, 1 vol. Kolpin, Molly Erin. 2012. (First Graphics: Body Systems Ser.). (ENG.). 24p. (gr. 1-2). pap. 6.29 *(978-1-4296-9324-0(X))* Capstone Pr., Inc.

—A Tour of Your Digestive System. Kolpin, Molly. 2012. (First Graphics: Body Systems Ser.). (ENG.). 24p. (gr. 1-2). pap. 35.70 *(978-1-4296-9325-7(8))* Capstone Pr., Inc.

—A Tour of Your Muscular & Skeletal Systems, 1 vol. Clark, Katie Lea. 2012. (First Graphics: Body Systems Ser.). (ENG.). 24p. (gr. 1-2). pap. 6.29 *(978-1-4296-9326-4(6))* Capstone Pr., Inc.

—A Tour of Your Muscular & Skeletal Systems. Clark, Katie. 2012. (First Graphics: Body Systems Ser.). (ENG.). 24p. (gr. 1-2). pap. 35.70 *(978-1-4296-9327-1(4))*; lib. bdg. 23.32 *(978-1-4296-8605-1(7))* Capstone Pr., Inc.

—A Tour of Your Nervous System, 1 vol. Kolpin, Molly Erin. 2012. (First Graphics: Body Systems Ser.). (ENG.). 24p. (gr. 1-2). pap. 6.29 *(978-1-4296-9328-8(2))* Capstone Pr., Inc.

—A Tour of Your Nervous System. Kolpin, Molly. 2012. (First Graphics: Body Systems Ser.). (ENG.). 24p. (gr. 1-2). pap. 35.70 *(978-1-4296-9329-5(0))*; lib. bdg. 23.32 *(978-1-4296-8739-3(8))* Capstone Pr., Inc.

—A Tour of Your Respiratory System, 1 vol. Reina, Mary. 2012. (First Graphics: Body Systems Ser.). (ENG.). 24p. (gr. 1-2). pap. 6.29 *(978-1-4296-9330-1(4))*; pap. 35.70 *(978-1-4296-9331-8(2))*; lib. bdg. 23.32 *(978-1-4296-8652-5(9))* Capstone Pr., Inc.

Jones, Christopher. Fears, 1 vol. Baltazar, Art et al. 2013. (Young Justice Ser.). (ENG.). 32p. (gr. 2-3). 21.27 *(978-1-4342-6038-3(0))* Stone Arch Bks.

—Wonderland, 1 vol. Weisman, Greg et al. 2013. (Young Justice Ser.). (ENG.). 32p. (gr. 2-3). 21.27 *(978-1-4342-6040-6(2))* Stone Arch Bks.

Jones, Chuck. Rikki-Tikki-Tavi. Kipling, Rudyard. 2006. (ENG.). 32p. (J). (gr. -1-3). 8.95 *(978-0-8249-6597-6(3),* Ideals Children's Bks.) Ideals Pubns.

—The White Seal. Kipling, Rudyard. 2006. (ENG.). 32p. (J). (gr. -1-3). 8.95 *(978-0-8249-6598-3(1),* Ideals Children's Bks.) Ideals Pubns.

Jones, Cory. The Donkey & Jesus. Schmidt, Troy. 2015. (Their Side of the Story Ser.). (ENG.). 32p. (J). (gr. -1-3). pap. 3.99 ***(978-1-4336-8719-8(4),*** B&H Kids) B&H Publishing Group.

Jones, Cory. The Donkey Tells His Side of the Story: Hey God, I'm Sorry to Be Stubborn, but I Just Don't Like Anyone Riding on My Back! Schmidt, Troy. 2014. (ENG.). 32p. (gr. -1-3). 9.99 *(978-1-4336-8309-1(1),* B&H Kids) B&H Publishing Group.

Jones, Cory. The Frog & the Plagues. Schmidt, Troy. 2015. (Their Side of the Story Ser.). (ENG.). 32p. (J). (gr. -1-3). pap. 3.99 ***(978-1-4336-8720-4(8),*** B&H Kids) B&H Publishing Group.

—The Lion & Daniel. Schmidt, Troy. 2015. (Their Side of the Story Ser.). (ENG.). 32p. (J). (gr. -1-3). pap. 3.99 ***(978-1-4336-8721-1(6),*** B&H Kids) B&H Publishing Group.

Jones, Cory. The Lion Tells His Side of the Story: Hey God, I'm Starving in This Den So Why Won't You Let Me Eat This Guy Named Daniel?! Schmidt, Troy. 2014. (ENG.). 32p. (gr. -1-3). 9.99 *(978-1-4336-8310-7(5),* B&H Kids) B&H Publishing Group.

Jones, Cory. The Raven & Noah's Ark. Schmidt, Troy. 2015. (Their Side of the Story Ser.). (ENG.). 32p. (J). (gr. -1-3). pap. 3.99 ***(978-1-4336-8722-8(4),*** B&H Kids) B&H Publishing Group.

Jones, Cory. VeggieTales SuperComics: Vol 1. Big Idea Entertainment, LLC. 2015. (VeggieTales Super Comics Ser.: 1). (ENG.). 104p. (J). (gr. -1-3). pap. 12.99 *(978-1-4336-8534-7(5),* B&H Kids) B&H Publishing Group.

—VeggieTales SuperComics: Vol 2. Big Idea Entertainment, LLC. 2015. (VeggieTales Super Comics Ser.). (ENG.). 104p. (J). (gr. -1-3). pap. 12.99 *(978-1-4336-8535-4(3),* B&H Kids) B&H Publishing Group.

Jones, Cory. The Whale & Jonah. Schmidt, Troy. 2015. (Their Side of the Story Ser.). (ENG.). 32p. (J). (gr. -1-3). pap. 3.99 ***(978-1-4336-8723-5(2),*** B&H Kids) B&H Publishing Group.

Jones, Dani. The Best Mariachi in the World/El Mejor Mariachi del Mundo. Smith, J. D. de la Vega, Eida, tr. 2008. (ENG & SPA.). 32p. (J). (gr. 4-7). lib. bdg. 16.95 *(978-0-9770906-1-7(2),* Raven Tree Pr.,Csi) Continental Sales, Inc.

—The One-Eyed People Eater: The Story of Cyclops. Holub, Joan. 2014. (Ready-To-Reads Ser.). (ENG.). 48p. (J). (gr. 1-3). pap. 3.99 *(978-1-4424-8500-6(0),* Simon Spotlight) Simon Spotlight.

—Surprise, Trojans! The Story of the Trojan Horse. Holub, Joan. 2014. (Ready-To-Reads Ser.). (ENG.). 32p. (J). (gr. k-2). 16.99 *(978-1-4814-2087-7(9))*; pap. 3.99 *(978-1-4814-2086-0(0))* Simon Spotlight. (Simon Spotlight).

—What If You Get Lost?, 1 vol. Guard, Anara. 2011. (Danger Zone Ser.). (ENG.). 24p. (gr. 1-2). pap. 7.49 *(978-1-4048-7035-2(0))*; lib. bdg. 25.32 *(978-1-4048-6684-3(1))* Picture Window Bks. (Nonfiction Picture Bks.).

Jones, Davy. In a Dark, Dark House. Dussling, Jennifer. Date not set. (All Aboard Reading Ser.). 32p. (J). (gr. -1-k). pap. *(978-0-448-40974-0(7),* Grosset & Dunlap) Penguin Publishing Group.

Jones, Davy. Ruedas! Jones, Davy. Cobb, Annie. 2003. (Road to Reading Ser.). (J). lib. bdg. 11.99 *(978-0-375-91500-0(1),* Golden Bks.) Random Hse. Children's Bks.

Jones, Deborah. The Starlight Ballerina. Baxter, Nicola. 2014. 14p. (J). bds. 9.99 *(978-1-84322-885-1(8))* Anness Publishing.

Jones, Denise West & Darby, Stephania Pierce. Koko & Friends: Friends? Oh, Really!!! Jones, Denise West & Darby, Stephania Pierce. (J). *(978-1-892313-01-0(4))* D. W. Ink.

Jones, Dennis. Adam & Eve, God's First People, 1 vol. Zondervan Publishing Staff. 2010. (I Can Read! / Dennis Jones Ser.). (ENG.). 32p. (J). (gr. -1-2). pap. 3.99 *(978-0-310-71883-3(X))* Zonderkidz.

—Daniel God's Faithful Follower, 1 vol. Zondervan Publishing Staff. 2010. (I Can Read! / Dennis Jones Ser.). (ENG.). 32p. (J). (gr. -1-2). pap. 3.99 *(978-0-310-71834-5(1))* Zonderkidz.

—David & God's Giant Victory: Biblical Values, 1 vol. Zondervan Publishing Staff. 2010. (I Can Read! / Dennis Jones Ser.). (ENG.). 32p. (J). (gr. -1-2). pap. 3.99 *(978-0-310-71879-6(1))* Zonderkidz.

—The First Christmas Ever, 1 vol. Zondervan, A. 2014. (ENG.). 32p. (J). pap. 1.99 *(978-0-310-74083-4(5))* Zonderkidz.

—The First Easter Ever, 1 vol. Zondervan Publishing Staff. 2015. (ENG.). 32p. (J). pap. 1.99 *(978-0-310-74084-1(3))* Zonderkidz.

—Jesus God's Only Son, 1 vol. Zondervan Publishing Staff. 2010. (I Can Read! / Dennis Jones Ser.). (ENG.). 32p. (J). (gr. -1-2). pap. 3.99 *(978-0-310-71880-2(5))* Zonderkidz.

—Jonah, God's Messenger, 1 vol. Zondervan Bibles Staff. 2011. (I Can Read! / Dennis Jones Ser.). (ENG.). 32p. (J). pap. 3.99 *(978-0-310-71835-2(X))* Zonderkidz.

—Noah & God's Great Promise, 1 vol. Zondervan Publishing Staff. 2010. (I Can Read! / Dennis Jones Ser.). (ENG.). 32p. (J). (gr. -1-2). pap. 3.99 *(978-0-310-71884-0(8))* Zonderkidz.

Jones, Dennis G. Jesus God's Great Gift, 1 vol. Zondervan Publishing Staff. 2010. (I Can Read! / Dennis Jones Ser.). (ENG.). 32p. (J). (gr. -1-2). pap. 3.99 *(978-0-310-71881-9(3))* Zonderkidz.

—Moses, God's Brave Servant, 1 vol. Zondervan Publishing Staff. 2010. (I Can Read! / Dennis Jones Ser.). (ENG.). 32p. (J). (gr. -1-2). pap. 3.99 *(978-0-310-71882-6(1))* Zonderkidz.

Jones, Diana Wynne & Miyazaki, Hayao. Howl's Moving Castle. Miyazaki, Hayao. 2005. (Howl's Moving Castle Ser.). (ENG.). 176p. pap. 9.99 *(978-1-4215-0093-5(0))*; Vol. 1. pap. 9.99 *(978-1-4215-0091-1(4))* Viz Media.

Jones, Don. What You Can See, You Can Be! Anderson, David A. 2003. 48p. (gr. 3-8). 13.95 *(978-0-87516-603-2(2),* Devorss Pubns.) DeVorss & Co.

Jones, Donald M., photos by. Buffalo Country: America's National Bison Range. 2005. 72p. per. 14.95 *(978-1-931832-56-4(0),* 8667872363) Riverbend Publishing.

Jones, Doug. Crazy Buildings. Rosen, Michael J. & Kassoy, Ben. 2013. (No Way! Ser.). (ENG.). 32p. (gr. 3-5). lib. bdg. 26.60 *(978-0-7613-8986-6(5),* Millbrook Pr.) Lerner Publishing Group.

—The Itchy-Scratchy Caterpillar. Tomblin, Mark. 2010. 16p. (J). *(978-0-545-24822-8(1))* Scholastic, Inc.

—Strange Foods. Rosen, Michael J. & Kassoy, Ben. 2013. (No Way! Ser.). (ENG.). 32p. (gr. 3-5). lib. bdg. 26.60 *(978-0-7613-8984-2(9),* Millbrook Pr.) Lerner Publishing Group.

—Three Bouncing Balls. Charlesworth, Liza. 2005. (Number Tales Ser.). (ENG.). 16p. (J). (gr. -1-1). pap. 2.99 *(978-0-439-68999-1(6))* Scholastic, Inc.

—Totally Lent! A Teen's Journey to Easter 2004. Broslavick, Chris & Pichler, Tony. Cannizzo, Karen, ed. 2003. 64p. (J). 5.95 *(978-0-89837-233-5(X),* 3564) Pflaum Publishing Group.

—Totally Lent! A Teen's Journey to Lent 2005. Broslavick, Chris & Pichler, Tony. Cannizzo, Karen, ed. 2004. 64p. (YA). 5.95 *(978-0-89837-247-2(X),* 3565) Pflaum Publishing Group.

—Two Bunny Slippers. Charlesworth, Liza. 2005. (Number Tales Ser.). (ENG.). 16p. (J). (gr. -1-1). pap. 2.99 *(978-0-439-68998-4(8))* Scholastic, Inc.

—Wacky Sports. Rosen, Michael J. & Kassoy, Ben. 2013. (No Way! Ser.). (ENG.). 32p. (gr. 3-5). lib. bdg. 26.60 *(978-0-7613-8982-8(2),* Millbrook Pr.) Lerner Publishing Group.

—Zero Spots. Charlesworth, Liza. 2005. (Number Tales Ser.). (ENG.). 16p. (J). (gr. -1-1). pap. 2.99 *(978-0-439-69022-5(6))* Scholastic, Inc.

Jones, Douglas B. Madam President: The Extraordinary, True (and Evolving) Story of Women in Politics. Thimmesh, Catherine. 2008. (ENG.). 80p. (J). (gr. 1-4). pap. 8.95 *(978-0-618-97143-5(2))* Houghton Mifflin Harcourt Publishing Co.

—The Milkman. Cordsen, Carol Foskett. 2007. (gr. -1-3). 17.00 *(978-0-7569-8148-8(4))* Perfection Learning Corp.

Jones, Elizabeth Orton. Oración para los Niños. Field, Rachel. Romay, Alexis, tr. 2011.Tr. of Prayer for a Child. (SPA.). 32p. (J). (gr. -1-2). bds. 6.99 *(978-1-4424-1350-4(6),* Libros Para Ninos) Libros Para Ninos.

—The Peddler's Clock. Hunt, Mabel Leigh. 2011. 30p. 35.95 *(978-1-258-09998-5(5))* Literary Licensing, LLC.

—Prayer for a Child. Field, Rachel. 2005. (ENG.). 30p. (J). (gr. -1-k). 7.99 *(978-0-689-87886-2(9),* Little Simon) Little Simon.

—Prayer for a Child. Field, Rachel. 100th anniv. ed. 2004. (ENG.). 32p. (J). (gr. -1-2). 12.99 *(978-0-689-87356-0(5),* Simon & Schuster Bks. For Young Readers) Simon & Schuster Bks. For Young Readers.

—Prayer for a Child: Lap Edition. Field, Rachel. 2013. (ENG.). 32p. (J). (gr. -1-2). bds. 12.99 *(978-1-4424-7659-2(1),* Little Simon) Little Simon.

Jones, Emily. Face 2 Face. Ster, Caroline Rose. 2011. 110p. (J). pap. 16.95 *(978-1-61660-002-0(0))* Reflections Publishing, Inc.

Jones, Eric. Evil in a Skirt! #5, 1 vol. Walker, Landry Q. & Mason, Joey. 2013. (Supergirl: Cosmic Adventures in the 8th Grade Ser.). (ENG.). 32p. (gr. 2-3). 21.27 *(978-1-4342-6045-1(3))* Stone Arch Bks.

—Her First Extra-Ordinary Adventure! #1, 1 vol. Walker, Landry Q. & Mason, Joey. 2013. (Supergirl: Cosmic Adventures in the 8th Grade Ser.). (ENG.). 32p. (gr. 2-3). 21.27 *(978-1-4342-4717-9(1))* Stone Arch Bks.

—My Own Best Frenemy: #2, 1 vol. Walker, Landry Q. & Mason, Joey. 2013. (Supergirl: Cosmic Adventures in the 8th Grade Ser.). (ENG.). 32p. (gr. 2-3). 21.27 *(978-1-4342-4718-6(X))* Stone Arch Bks.

—Off to Save the Day..., No. 6. Walker, Landry Q. & Mason, Joey. 2013. (Supergirl: Cosmic Adventures in the 8th Grade Ser.). (ENG.). 32p. (gr. 2-3). 21.27 *(978-1-4342-6046-8(1))* Stone Arch Bks.

—Secret Entity! #4, 1 vol. Walker, Landry Q. 2013. (Supergirl: Cosmic Adventures in the 8th Grade Ser.). (ENG.). 32p. (gr. 2-3). 21.27 *(978-1-4342-4720-9(1))* Stone Arch Bks.

—Super Hero School: #3, 1 vol. Walker, Landry Q. 2013. (Supergirl: Cosmic Adventures in the 8th Grade Ser.). (ENG.). 32p. (gr. 2-3). 21.27 *(978-1-4342-4719-3(8))* Stone Arch Bks.

—Supergirl: Cosmic Adventures in the 8th Grade. Walker, Landry Q. 2013. (Supergirl: Cosmic Adventures in the 8th Grade Ser.). (ENG.). 32p. (gr. 2-3). lib. bdg. 42.54 *(978-1-4342-8831-8(5))*; lib. bdg. 127.62 *(978-1-4342-8830-1(7))*; lib. bdg. 85.08 *(978-1-4342-4367-6(2))* Stone Arch Bks.

Jones, Erik. God Is in the Refrigerator. 2006. 38p. (J). 18.95 *(978-0-9771936-4-6(0))* InterWeave Corp.

—God Is in the Window. King, Kimberly. 2007. 37p. (J). 18.95 *(978-0-9771936-6-0(7))* InterWeave Corp.

Jones, Ernest. The Great Mix Up. 2005. (ENG.). 42p. (J). 17.99 *(978-0-9772282-0-1(7))* B. T. Brooks.

Jones, Gregory Burgess. Brady Needs a Nightlight. Barlics, Brian. 2013. (ENG.). 32p. (J). pap. 18.95 *(978-1-61296-195-8(9))* Black Rose Writing.

Jones, Helen. Spectacular Spain, 1 vol. Thompson, Lisa. 2006. (Read-It! Chapter Books: SWAT Ser.). (ENG.). 80p. (gr. 2-4). 21.32 *(978-1-4048-1675-6(5),* Chapter Readers) Picture Window Bks.

Jones, Henrietta. Amish Moving Day. Seyfert, Ella Maie. 2011. 132p. 40.95 *(978-1-258-01315-8(0))* Literary Licensing, LLC.

Jones, Jac. A Nod from Nelson. Weston, Simon. 2008. (ENG.). 48p. (J). (gr. 2-4). 17.99 ***(978-1-84323-813-3(6))*** Gomer Pr. GBR. Dist: Independent Pubs. Group.

Jones, Jac. In Chatter Wood. Jones, Jac. 2004. (ENG.). 40p. pap. 13.95 *(978-1-84323-290-2(1))* Beekman Bks., Inc.

Jones, Jac. Weird Tales from the Storyteller. Jones, Jac, tr. Morden, Daniel. 2003. (ENG.). 63p. (J). (gr. 2-4). pap. 9.99 *(978-1-84323-210-0(3))* Gomer Pr. GBR. Dist: Independent Pubs. Group.

Jones, Jan. The Secret of the Dragonfly: A Story of Hope & Promise. Cramer, Gayle Shaw. 2006. (YA). pap. 19.95 *(978-0-9729346-7-1(7))* Ambrosia Press LLC.

Jones, Jan Naimo. The Apple Bandit. Keene, Carolyn. 2005. (Nancy Drew Notebooks). 74p. (J). (gr. 1-4). 11.65 *(978-0-7569-6505-1(5))* Perfection Learning Corp.

—The Apple Bandit. Frost, Michael, photos by. Keene, Carolyn. 68th ed. 2005. (Nancy Drew Notebooks Ser.: 68). (ENG.). 80p. (J). (gr. 1-4). pap. 4.99 *(978-1-4169-0829-6(3),* Simon & Schuster/Paula Wiseman Bks.) Simon & Schuster/Paula Wiseman Bks.

—The Bunny-Hop Hoax. Keene, Carolyn. 2005. (Nancy Drew Notebooks). 70p. (J). (gr. 1-4). 11.65 *(978-0-7569-5884-8(9))* Perfection Learning Corp.

—The Bunny-Hop Hoax. Frost, Michael, photos by. Keene, Carolyn. 64th ed. 2005. (Nancy Drew Notebooks Ser.: 64). (ENG.). 80p. (J). (gr. 1-4). pap. 3.99 *(978-0-689-87754-4(4),* Simon & Schuster/Paula Wiseman Bks.) Simon & Schuster/Paula Wiseman Bks.

—Candy Is Dandy. Keene, Carolyn. 2004. (Nancy Drew Notebooks). 74p. (gr. 2-4). 17.00 *(978-0-7569-3437-8(0))* Perfection Learning Corp.

—The Dollhouse Mystery. Keene, Carolyn. 2004. (Nancy Drew Notebooks). 68p. (J). (gr. 1-4). 12.65 *(978-0-7569-5524-3(6))* Perfection Learning Corp.

—The Dollhouse Mystery. Keene, Carolyn. 58th ed. 2004. (Nancy Drew Notebooks Ser.: 58). (ENG.). 80p. (J). (gr. 1-4). pap. 4.99 *(978-0-689-86534-3(1),* Simon & Schuster/Paula Wiseman Bks.) Simon & Schuster/Paula Wiseman Bks.

—Farmland Innovator: A Story about Cyrus Mccormick. Welch, Catherine A. 2007. (Creative Minds Biographies Ser.). (ENG.). 64p. (gr. 4-8). lib. bdg. 22.60 *(978-0-8225-5988-7(9))* Lerner Publishing Group.

—The Kitten Caper. Frost, Michael, photos by. Keene, Carolyn. 69th ed. 2005. (Nancy Drew Notebooks Ser.: 69). (ENG.). 80p. (J). (gr. 1-4). pap. 4.99 *(978-1-4169-0830-2(7),* Simon & Schuster/Paula Wiseman Bks.) Simon & Schuster/Paula Wiseman Bks.

—The Singing Suspects. Keene, Carolyn. 2005. (Nancy Drew Notebooks). 69p. (J). (gr. 1-4). 11.65 *(978-0-7569-5952-4(7))* Perfection Learning Corp.

—The Singing Suspects. Frost, Michael, photos by. Keene, Carolyn. 67th ed. 2005. (Nancy Drew Notebooks Ser.: 67). (ENG.). 80p. (J). (gr. 1-4). pap. 4.99 *(978-1-4169-0087-0(X),* Simon & Schuster/Paula Wiseman Bks.) Simon & Schuster/Paula Wiseman Bks.

Jones, Jan Naimo. Maker of Machines: A Story about Eli Whitney. Jones, Jan Naimo, tr. Mitchell, Barbara. 2004. (Creative Minds Biographies Ser.). (ENG.). 64p. (gr. 4-8). 22.60 *(978-1-57505-603-6(8),* Carolrhoda Bks.); pap. 8.95 *(978-1-57505-634-0(8))* Lerner Publishing Group.

Jones, Jennie. Surgeon - Craftsman: Laurence Knight Groves, M.D. 1922-2007. Jones, Jennie, . 2008. (ENG.). 78p. (YA). pap. 35.00 net. *(978-0-9617637-8-7(7))* Cleveland Stock Images.

Jones, Joëlle. The Girl Who Owned a City: The Graphic Novel. Jolley, Dan & Nelson, O. T. 2012. (Single Titles Ser.). (ENG.). 128p. (YA). (gr. 5-12). pap. 9.95 *(978-0-7613-5634-9(7),* Graphic Universe) Lerner Publishing Group.

Jones, Joff. Hit Em' with Words, 1 vol. Nettles Jr, J. H. 2010. 22p. 24.95 *(978-1-4489-4102-5(4))* PublishAmerica, Inc.

Jones, John R. Dinosaur Hunters. McMullan, Kate. 2005. (Step into Reading Ser.: No. 5). (ENG.). 48p. (J). (gr. 2-4). per. 3.99 *(978-0-375-82450-0(2),* Random Hse. Bks. for Young Readers) Random Hse. Children's Bks.

Jones, Juan Luis. A La Rueda, Rueda: Traditional Latin American Folk Songs for Children. Cabrera, Mima Y. & Esquenazi, Martha E., eds. 2010. (LAT & ENG.). 64p. pap. 29.99 incl. audio compact disk *(978-1-4234-7797-6(9),* 1423477979) Leonard, Hal Corp.

Jones, Julie. The Problem at Pepperpine Zoo. Jones, Julie. l.t. ed. 2004. 24p. (J). pap. 7.95 *(978-0-9745553-0-0(4))* Greenwood Street Publishing. GSP.

Jones, Julienne. Makimba's Animal World. Jackson, Bobby L. 2nd rev. l.t. ed. 2004. 32p. (J). (gr. k-4). 19.95 *(978-1-884242-00-7(6),* MAW2NED); pap. 11.95 *(978-1-884242-01-4(4),* MAW2NED) Multicultural Pubns.

Jones, K. L. The Land That Time Forgot: Graphic Novel. Burroughs, Edgar Rice. 2011. (Campfire Graphic Novels Ser.). (ENG.). 72p. (gr. 3-7). pap. 9.99 *(978-93-80028-38-5(5)*, Campfire) Kalyani Navyug Media Pty. Ltd. IND. Dist: Random Hse., Inc.

—Space Race. Welsh, C. E. L. 2011. (Campfire Graphic Novels Ser.). (ENG.). 68p. (gr. 3-7). pap. 9.99 *(978-93-80028-62-0(8)*, Campfire) Kalyani Navyug Media Pty. Ltd. IND. Dist: Random Hse., Inc.

Jones, K. L. & Manikandan. Abraham Lincoln: From the Log Cabin to the White House - Campfire Heroes Line. Helfand, Lewis. 2013. (Campfire Graphic Novels Ser.). (ENG.). 108p. (gr. 3-7). pap. 12.99 *(978-93-80741-21-5(9)*, Campfire) Kalyani Navyug Media Pty. Ltd. IND. Dist: Random Hse., Inc.

Jones, Kelley. Disney Comics Tomorrowland. Disney Book Group Staff & Miller, Bryan Q. 2014. (Disney Original Graphic Novel Ser.: 1). (ENG.). 176p. (J). (gr. 3-7). pap. 12.99 *(978-1-4231-6229-2(3))* Disney Pr.

Jones, Kirk. Lisa the Ministering Mole: Meet the Mole. Jones, Kirk. 2004. 24p. (J). bds. 5.00 net. *(978-0-9759688-0-2(7))* Jones, Kirk.

Jones, Lara. Baby Bear's Birthday Hiccups! Little, Penny. ed. 2008. (ENG.). 32p. (J). (gr. 2-4). 24.50 *(978-0-230-53029-4(X)*, Macmillan) Pan Macmillan GBR. Dist: Trans-Atlantic Pubns., Inc.

—Poppy Cat's Garden. Finch, Keith. ed. 2008. (ENG.). 8p. (J). (gr. 3-6). bds. 16.95 *(978-0-230-01715-3(0)*, Macmillan) Pan Macmillan GBR. Dist: Trans-Atlantic Pubns., Inc.

Jones, Margaret. King Arthur. Thomas, Gwyn. 2006. (ENG.). 144p. (J). pap. 21.95 *(978-0-86243-798-5(9))* Y Lolfa GBR. Dist: Dufour Editions, Inc.

—Owain Glyndwr: Prince of Wales. Ifans, Rhiannon. 2003. (WEL & ENG.). 96p. (J). pap. 13.95 *(978-0-86243-544-8(7))* Y Lolfa GBR. Dist: Dufour Editions, Inc.

—Story of Dafydd AP Gwilym. Thomas, Gwyn. 2004. (ENG.). 108p. (J). pap. 13.95 *(978-0-86243-712-1(1))* Y Lolfa GBR. Dist: Dufour Editions, Inc.

—Tales from the Celtic Countries. Ifans, Rhiannon. 2005. (ENG.). 96p. (J). pap. 13.95 *(978-0-86243-501-1(3))* Y Lolfa GBR. Dist: Dufour Editions, Inc.

Jones, Mark. Janjak & Freda Go to the Iron Market. Turnbull, Elizabeth J. Turnbull, Wally R., tr. 2013. 36p. pap. 12.95 *(978-1-61153-062-9(8))* Light Messages Publishing.

—Janjak & Freda Go to the Iron Market. Turnbull, Elizabeth. Turnbull, Wally, tr. 2013. 36p. 18.95 *(978-1-61153-072-8(5))* Light Messages Publishing.

—Snuggle Time Devotions That End with a Hug! Elkins, Stephen. 2015. (Share-A-Hug! Ser.). (ENG.). 168p. (J). 14.99 *(978-1-4143-9948-5(0))* Tyndale Hse. Pubs.

Jones, Mary Noble. Itsy Rabbit & Friends: Itsy's First Adventure. Jones, Mary Noble. 2007. 28p. (J). per. 15.00 *(978-0-9796209-8-0(8))* Righter Publishing Co., Inc.

Jones, Nathan. Gotta See Nathan! Gray, Susannah. 2012. 20p. pap. 15.00 *(978-1-4575-1315-2(3))* Dog Ear Publishing, LLC.

Jones, Noah. Here Comes Trouble! Demas, Corinne. 2013. (J). *(978-0-545-55449-7(7)*, Scholastic Pr.) Scholastic, Inc.

—Poem Runs: Baseball Poems & Paintings. Florian, Douglas. 2012. (ENG.). 32p. (J). (gr. 1-4). 16.99 *(978-0-547-68838-1(5))* Houghton Mifflin Harcourt Publishing Co.

—Those Shoes. Boelts, Maribeth. 2007. (J). *(978-1-4287-6554-2(9))* Candlewick Pr.

Jones, Noah Z. Always in Trouble. Demas, Corinne. 2009. (ENG.). 40p. (J). (gr. -1-3). 17.99 *(978-0-545-02453-2(6)*, Scholastic Pr.) Scholastic, Inc.

—Duck, Duck, Moose! Bardhan-Quallen, Sudipta. 2014. (ENG.). 32p. (J). (gr. -1-k). 16.99 *(978-1-4231-7110-2(1))* Hyperion Bks. for Children.

—Here Comes Trouble! Demas, Corinne. 2013. (ENG.). 40p. (J). (gr. -1-3). 16.99 *(978-0-545-35906-1(6)*, Scholastic Pr.) Scholastic, Inc.

—Little Sweet Potato. Bloom, Amy Beth. 2012. (ENG.). 32p. (J). (gr. -1-2). 16.99 *(978-0-06-180439-7(8)*, Tegen, Katherine Bks) HarperCollins Pubs.

—Magic at the Bed & Biscuit. Carris, Joan. 2012. (ENG.). 112p. (J). (gr. 1-4). pap. 5.99 *(978-0-7636-5849-6(9))* Candlewick Pr.

—The Monster in the Backpack. Moser, Lisa. 2013. (Candlewick Sparks Ser.). (ENG.). 40p. (J). (gr. k-4). pap. 3.99 *(978-0-7636-6643-9(2))* Candlewick Pr.

—Not Norman: A Goldfish Story. Bennett, Kelly. (ENG.). 32p. (J). (gr. -1-3). 2008. pap. 6.99 *(978-0-7636-2763-8(1))*; 2005. 16.99 *(978-0-7636-2384-5(9))* Candlewick Pr.

—Stuff. Palatini, Margie. 2011. (ENG.). 32p. (J). (gr. -1-2). 16.99 *(978-0-06-171921-9(8)*, Tegen, Katherine Bks) HarperCollins Pubs.

—The Superheroes Employment Agency. Singer, Marilyn. 2012. (ENG.). 40p. (J). (gr. 1-4). 16.99 *(978-0-547-43559-6(2))* Houghton Mifflin Harcourt Publishing Co.

—Those Shoes. Boelts, Maribeth. 2009. (ENG.). 40p. (J). (gr. k-3). pap. 6.99 *(978-0-7636-4284-6(3))* Candlewick Pr.

—Welcome to the Bed & Biscuit. Carris, Joan. 2009. (ENG.). 128p. (J). (gr. 1-4). 5.99 *(978-0-7636-4621-9(0))* Candlewick Pr.

—Wild Times at the Bed & Biscuit. Carris, Joan. (ENG.). 128p. (J). (gr. 1-4). 2011. pap. 5.99 *(978-0-7636-5294-4(6)*, Nosy Crow); 2009. 15.99 *(978-0-7636-3705-7(X))* Candlewick Pr.

Jones, Noah Z. Moldylocks & the Three Beards. Jones, Noah Z. 2014. (Princess Pink & the Land of Fake-Believe Ser.: 1). (ENG.). 80p. (J). (gr. k-2). pap. 4.99 *(978-0-545-63839-5(9))* Scholastic, Inc.

—Princess Pink & the Land of Fake-Believe #2: Little Red Quacking Hood (a Branches Book) Jones, Noah Z. Jones, Noah Z. 2014. (ENG.). 80p. (J). (gr. k-2). pap. 4.99 *(978-0-545-63841-8(0))* Scholastic, Inc.

Jones, Noah Z., jt. illus. see Meserve, Jessica.

Jones, Paul, jt. illus. see Takhar, Jodi.

Jones, Penny & Norris, Aaron. Bangu the Flying Fox: A Dreamtime Story of the Yuin People of Wallaga Lake. 2nd ed. 2011. (ENG.). 24p. (J). (gr. -1-k). pap. 17.95 *(978-0-85575-700-7(0))* Aboriginal Studies Pr. AUS. Dist: Independent Pubs. Group.

Jones, Phil. Airport Mouse. Clark, Ruth E. 2008. (ENG.). 32p. (J). (gr. -1-3). 15.95 *(978-0-9792963-2-1(3))* Hibiscus Publishing.

—Airport Mouse Activity Fun Book 1. Clark, Ruth E. 2010. 16p. (J). pap. 5.99 *(978-0-9792963-6-9(6))* Hibiscus Publishing.

—Airport Mouse Becomes a VIP/VIM World Traveler. Clark, Ruth E. 2009. 32p. (J). 15.95 *(978-0-9792963-5-2(8))* Hibiscus Publishing.

—Airport Mouse Becomes a VIP/VIM World Traveler Activity Fun Book 4. Clark, Ruth E. 2010. 16p. (J). pap. 5.99 *(978-0-9792963-9-0(0))* Hibiscus Publishing.

—Airport Mouse Explores on Opening Day Activity Fun Book 3. Clark, Ruth E. 2010. 16p. (J). pap. 5.99 *(978-0-9792963-8-3(2))* Hibiscus Publishing.

—Airport Mouse Works the Night Shift Activity Fun Book 2. Clark, Ruth E. 2010. 16p. (J). pap. 5.99 *(978-0-9792963-7-6(4))* Hibiscus Publishing.

Jones, Randy. Places in Time: A New Atlas of American History. Leacock, Elspeth & Buckley, Susan. 2006. 48p. (J). (gr. 4-8). reprint ed. 15.00 *(978-1-4223-5555-8(1))* DIANE Publishing Co.

Jones, Richard. Chrissa Stands Strong, Bks. 2. Casanova, Mary. England, Tamara, ed. 2009. (ENG.). 130p. (YA). (gr. 3-18). pap. 6.95 *(978-1-59369-567-5(5)*, American Girl) American Girl Publishing, Inc.

Jones, Rob. Burly & Grum & the Birthday Surprise. Tenbeth, Kate. 2012. 108p. pap. *(978-0-9572119-9-5(6))* Magic Toy Bks.

—Burly & Grum & the Secret City. Tenbeth, Kate. 2012. 108p. pap. *(978-0-9572119-5-7(3))* Magic Toy Bks.

—Burly & Grum & the Tiger's Tale. Tenbeth, Kate. 2013. 36p. pap. *(978-0-9572119-7-1(X))* Magic Toy Bks.

Jones, Robert S. More Sign & Say. Flegal, Daphna, ed. 2004. 48p. (gr. -1-18). 13.00 *(978-0-687-01457-6(3))* Abingdon Pr.

—Sing & Say Bible Verses for Children. Flegal, Daphna & Smith, Betsi H. 2004. 48p. (gr. -1-3). 13.00 *(978-0-687-07442-6(8))* Abingdon Pr.

Jones, Ryan. Too Much Picnic. Honigsberg, Peter John. 2006. 32p. (J). 16.95 *(978-1-57143-154-7(3))* RDR Bks.

Jones, Seth. The Man in the Clouds, 1 vol. Stamey, Marsha. 2009. 21p. pap. 24.95 *(978-1-60836-730-6(4))* PublishAmerica, Inc.

Jones, Sherilyn. Can't Keep up with the Joneses: Created to Be. Jones, Sherilyn. 2015. (ENG.). (J). pap. 9.99 ***(978-0-9864191-0-2(9))*** Concept Media Group, LLC, The.

Jones, Stephanie. Bedtime. 2007. (Luxury Look & Say Board Bks.). 12p. (J). (gr. -1-k). bds. 12.99 *(978-0-7945-1461-7(8)*, Usborne) EDC Publishing.

—123. Allman, Howard & MMStudios, photos by. Litchfield, Jo & Sanchez Gallego, Maria Isabel. 2007. (Dime lo Que Ves Ser.). 22p. (J). bds. 14.99 *(978-0-7460-8354-3(8)*, Usborne) EDC Publishing.

Jones, Stephanie, jt. illus. see Durber, Matt.

Jones, Stephanie, jt. illus. see Litchfield, Jo.

Jones, Steven E., Jr. The Ballad of Blue Eagle. Jones, Steven E. 2011. (Blue Eagle Ser.). (ENG.). 48p. (J). (gr. -1-2). 18.95 *(978-0-9794655-1-2(6))* Blue Eagle Bks., Inc.

—Blue Eagle Meets Double Trouble. Jones, Steven E. 2008. (Blue Eagle Ser.). (ENG.). 40p. (J). (gr. -1-2). 15.95 *(978-0-9794655-0-5(8))* Blue Eagle Bks., Inc.

Jones, Terry & Foreman, Michael. Fairy Tales & Fantastic Stories. Jones, Terry & Foreman, Michael, trs. 10th anniv. ed. 2003. 256p. (YA). *(978-1-84365-055-3(X)*, Pavilion Children's Books) Pavilion Bks.

Jones, Tim. Carlos Escribe Su Nombre! Murphy, Stuart J. & Mlawer, Teresa. 2014. (Isil Ser.). (SPA.). 32p. (J). (-k). 14.95 *(978-1-58089-496-8(8))*; pap. 6.95 *(978-1-58089-497-5(6))* Charlesbridge Publishing, Inc.

—En Busca de Freda. Murphy, Stuart J. Mlawer, Teresa, tr. from ENG. 2012. (Isil Ser.). (SPA & ENG.). 32p. (J). (-k). 14.95 *(978-1-58089-494-4(1))*; pap. 6.95 *(978-1-58089-495-1(X))* Charlesbridge Publishing, Inc.

—Freda Says Please. Murphy, Stuart J. 2013. (Isil Ser.). (ENG.). 32p. (J). (-k). pap. 6.95 *(978-1-58089-475-3(5))* Charlesbridge Publishing, Inc.

—Freda Says Please. Murphy, Stuart J. 2013. (Isil Ser.). (ENG.). 32p. (J). (-k). lib. bdg. 14.95 *(978-1-58089-474-6(7))* Charlesbridge Publishing, Inc.

—Freda Stops a Bully. Murphy, Stuart J. 2012. (Isil Ser.). (ENG.). 32p. (J). (-k). 14.95 *(978-1-58089-466-1(6))*; pap. 6.95 *(978-1-58089-467-8(4))* Charlesbridge Publishing, Inc.

—Scrubba Dub, Carlos. Murphy, Stuart J. 2013. (Isil Ser.). (ENG.). 32p. (J). (-k). 14.95 *(978-1-58089-478-4(X))*; pap. 6.95 *(978-1-58089-479-1(8))* Charlesbridge Publishing, Inc.

—Write on, Carlos! Murphy, Stuart J. 2011. (Isil Ser.). (ENG.). 32p. (J). (-k). 14.95 *(978-1-58089-464-7(X))*; pap. 6.95 *(978-1-58089-465-4(8))* Charlesbridge Publishing, Inc.

Jones, Tina C. & Balogh, Jared. Mothballs, Mothballs All in the Hall: Memories of a Great World War II Hero. Jones, Tina C. 2012. 48p. pap. 24.95 *(978-1-4560-7483-8(0))* America Star Bks.

Jones, Val. Who Wants Broccoli? Jones, Val. 2015. (ENG.). 40p. (J). (gr. -1-3). 17.99 *(978-0-06-230351-6(1))* HarperCollins Pubs.

Jones, Zach. Alligators Coming! Gray, Susannah. 2012. 20p. pap. 15.00 *(978-1-4575-1316-9(1))* Dog Ear Publishing, LLC.

Joni, Rasa. Ziggy's Big Idea. Long, Ilana. 2014. (Kar-Ben Favorites Ser.). (ENG.). 32p. (J). (gr. -1-4). 17.95 *(978-0-7613-9053-4(7))*; 7.95 *(978-0-7613-9054-1(5))* Lerner Publishing Group. (Kar-Ben Publishing).

Jonke, Tim. Los Tres Árboles: Cento Tradicional. Hunt, Angela Elwell. ed. 2010. Orig. Title: The Tale of Three Trees - A Traditional Folktale. (SPA & ENG.). 32p. (J). 5.99 *(978-1-4143-3737-1(X))* Tyndale Hse. Pubs.

Jonniaux, Isabelle. Mi Primer Baul de Palabras. Girard, Franck. 2005. (Baúl de Palabras Ser.). (SPA & ENG.). 120p. (J). (gr. k-2). 19.95 *(978-84-7864-788-0(0))* Combel Editorial, S.A. ESP. Dist: Independent Pubs. Group.

Jonsdottir, Aslaug. The Story of the Blue Planet. Magnason, Andri Snaer. D'Arcy, Julian Meldon, tr. (ENG.). (J). (gr. 2-5). 2013. 136p. pap. 9.95 *(978-1-60980-506-7(2))*; 2012. 96p. 12.99 *(978-1-60980-428-2(7))* Seven Stories Pr.

Jönsson, Maria. Astrid the Fly. Jönsson, Maria. Reiss, Christina, tr. from SWE. 2015. (ENG.). 32p. (J). (gr. -1-1). 16.95 *(978-0-8234-3200-4(9))* Holiday Hse., Inc.

Joo, Soon-kyo. Dad's Favorite Cookie: Japan. Jeong, Gu-mi. Cowley, Joy, ed. 2015. (Global Kids Storybooks Ser.). (ENG.). 32p. (gr. 1-4). 26.65 ***(978-1-925246-00-1(0))***; 26.65 ***(978-1-925246-26-1(4))***; 7.99 ***(978-1-925246-52-0(3))*** ChoiceMaker Pty. Ltd., The AUS. (Big and SMALL). Dist: Lerner Publishing Group.

Joost, Trudy. Cassandra's Angel, Set. Otto, Gina. 2003. 32p. (J). 34.99 *(978-0-9740454-3-6(8))* Gina's Ink.

Jordan, Carol. I Know You Won't Forget. Truly Blessed Ink. 2007. (ENG.). 40p. (J). 16.95 *(978-0-9789066-1-0(6))* Square Circle Pr. LLC.

Jordan, Carrie. America the Beautiful: A Pop-up Book about the Famous Song by Katharine Lee Bates. Lee Bates, Katharine & Garnwell, Calvert. 2006. 16p. (J). (gr. 4-8). reprint ed. 17.00 *(978-1-4223-5447-6(4))* DIANE Publishing Co.

Jordan, Charles. Daniel el Descortes: Rude Ralph. Fontes, Justine. 2005. (Rookie Reader Español Ser.). 32p. (gr. k-2). 19.50 *(978-0-516-24444-0(2)*, Children's Pr.) Scholastic Library Publishing.

—Rude Ralph: A Rookie Reader. Fontes, Justine. 2011. (Rookie Ready to Learn Ser.). 40p. (J). pap. 5.95 *(978-0-531-26711-0(3))*; (gr. -1-k). lib. bdg. 23.00 *(978-0-531-26529-1(3))* Scholastic Library Publishing. (Children's Pr.).

—Thanksgiving. Heinrichs, Ann. 2013. (Holidays & Celebrations Ser.). (ENG.). 32p. (J). (gr. k-3). 27.07 *(978-1-62323-513-0(8)*, 206286) Child's World, Inc., The.

Jordan, Charles. Daniel el Descortés. Jordan, Charles. Fontes, Justine. 2011. (Rookie Ready to Learn Español Ser.). (SPA.). 40p. (J). pap. 5.95 *(978-0-531-26790-5(3))*; lib. bdg. 23.00 *(978-0-531-26122-4(0))* Scholastic Library Publishing. (Children's Pr.).

Jordan, Sid. Little Puff. Hillert, Margaret. 2008. 32p. (J). lib. bdg. 19.93 *(978-1-59953-185-4(2))* Norwood Hse. Pr.

Jorge, Gutiérrez Sahagún. Dicionario Inicial Everest. Equipo Staff. (SPA.). 336p. *(978-84-241-1013-0(7))* Everest Editora ESP. Dist: Lectorum Pubns., Inc.

Jorgensen, David. The Steadfast Tin Soldier. Andersen, Hans Christian. 2005. (Rabbit Ears: A Classic Tale Ser.).Tr. of Standhaftige Tinsoldat. 42p. (gr. -1-3). 25.65 *(978-1-59679-346-0(5))* Spotlight.

—The Tailor of Gloucester. Potter, Beatrix. 2007. (Rabbit Ears: A Classic Tale Ser.). 44p. (gr. -1-3). 25.65 *(978-1-59961-312-3(3))* Spotlight.

—The Tale of Mr. Jeremy Fisher. Potter, Beatrix. 2005. (Rabbit Ears: A Classic Tale Ser.). 28p. (gr. 2-7). 25.65 *(978-1-59197-753-7(3))* Spotlight.

—The Tale of Peter Rabbit. Potter, Beatrix. 2007. (Rabbit Ears: A Classic Tale Ser.). 36p. (gr. -1-3). 25.65 *(978-1-59961-313-0(1))* Spotlight.

—The Three Billy Goats Gruff. Roberts, Tom & Asbjørnsen, Peter Christen. 2005. (Rabbit Ears-A Classic Tale Set 2 Ser.). 28p. (gr. k-5). 25.65 *(978-1-59197-754-4(1))* Spotlight.

—The Three Little Pigs. 2005. (Rabbit Ears-A Classic Tale Set 2 Ser.). 28p. (gr. k-5). 25.65 *(978-1-59197-755-1(X))* Spotlight.

—The Velveteen Rabbit. Williams, Margery. 2005. (Rabbit Ears: A Classic Tale Ser.). 42p. (gr. 2-7). 25.65 *(978-1-59197-757-5(6))* Spotlight.

Jorisch, Stéphane. Betty Bunny Didn't Do It. Kaplan, Michael B. 2013. (Betty Bunny Ser.). (ENG.). 32p. (J). (gr. -1-k). 16.99 *(978-0-8037-3858-4(7)*, Dial) Penguin Publishing Group.

—Betty Bunny Loves Chocolate Cake. Kaplan, Michael B. 2011. (Betty Bunny Ser.). (ENG.). 32p. (J). (gr. -1-k). 16.99 *(978-0-8037-3407-4(7)*, Dial) Penguin Publishing Group.

—Betty Bunny Loves Easter. Kaplan, Michael B. 2015. (Betty Bunny Ser.). (ENG.). 32p. (J). (gr. -1-k). 16.99 *(978-0-8037-4061-7(1)*, Dial) Penguin Publishing Group.

—Betty Bunny Wants a Goal. Kaplan, Michael B. 2014. (Betty Bunny Ser.). (ENG.). 32p. (J). (gr. -1-k). 16.99 *(978-0-8037-3859-1(5)*, Dial) Penguin Publishing Group.

—Betty Bunny Wants Everything. Kaplan, Michael B. 2012. (Betty Bunny Ser.). (ENG.). 32p. (J). (gr. -1-k). 16.99 *(978-0-8037-3408-1(5)*, Dial) Penguin Publishing Group.

—La Boite a Bonheur. Gingras, Charlotte. 2004. (Mon Roman Ser.). (FRE.). 64p. (J). (gr. 2). pap. *(978-2-89021-668-6(3))* Diffusion du livre Mirabel (DLM).

—Un Cadeau Pour Sophie: Conte et Chansons. Vigneault, Gilles. 2013. (FRE.). 40p. (J). (gr. k-2). 16.95 *(978-2-923163-38-3(9))* La Montagne Secrete CAN. Dist: Independent Pubs. Group.

—Footwork: The Story of Fred & Adele Astaire. Orgill, Roxane. 2013. (Candlewick Biographies Ser.). (ENG.). 48p. (J). (gr. 3-7). pap. 4.99 *(978-0-7636-6215-8(1))* Candlewick Pr.

—Footwork: The Story of Fred & Adele Astaire. Orgill, Roxane. 2013. (Candlewick Biographies Ser.). (ENG.). 48p. (J). (gr. 3-7). 14.99 *(978-0-7636-6460-2(X))* Candlewick Pr.

—Le Gardien du Sommeil. Tibo, Gilles. 2004. (Mon Roman Ser.). (FRE.). 64p. (J). (gr. 2). pap. *(978-2-89021-691-4(8))* Diffusion du livre Mirabel (DLM).

—A Gift for Sophie. Vigneault, Gilles. 2013. (ENG.). 44p. (J). (gr. k-2). 16.95 *(978-2-923163-98-7(2))* La Montagne Secrete CAN. Dist: Independent Pubs. Group.

—Jabberwocky. Carroll, Lewis. 2008. (Visions in Poetry Ser.). (ENG.). 40p. (YA). (gr. 5-9). pap. 9.95 *(978-1-55453-266-7(3))* Kids Can Pr., Ltd. CAN. Dist: Univ. of Toronto Pr.

—Lulu's Pajamas. Papineau, Lucie. 2009. (ENG.). 24p. (J). (gr. -1-1). 16.95 *(978-1-55453-371-8(6))* Kids Can Pr., Ltd. CAN. Dist: Univ. of Toronto Pr.

—My Father Knows the Names of Things. Yolen, Jane. 2010. (ENG.). 32p. (J). (gr. -1-3). 17.99 *(978-1-4169-4895-7(3)*, Simon & Schuster Bks. For Young Readers) Simon & Schuster Bks. For Young Readers.

—My Name Is Chicken Joe. Trout Fishing in America Staff et al. 2009. (ENG.). 50p. (J). (gr. -1-2). 16.95 *(978-2-923163-49-9(4))* La Montagne Secrete CAN. Dist: Independent Pubs. Group.

—New Year at the Pier: A Rosh Hashanah Story. Wayland, April Halprin. 2009. (J). 352p. *(978-0-8037-3110-3(8))*; (ENG.). 32p. 16.99 *(978-0-8037-3279-7(1))* Penguin Publishing Group. (Dial).

—The Owl & the Pussycat. Lear, Edward. 2007. (Visions in Poetry Ser.). (ENG.). 48p. (YA). (gr. 5-18). pap. 9.95 *(978-1-55453-232-2(9))* Kids Can Pr., Ltd. CAN. Dist: Univ. of Toronto Pr.

Jorisch, Stephane. The Owl & the Pussycat. Lear, Edward. 2007. (Visions in Poetry Ser.). (ENG.). 48p. (YA). (gr. -1-3). 17.95 *(978-1-55337-828-0(8))* Kids Can Pr., Ltd. CAN. Dist: Univ. of Toronto Pr.

Jorisch, Stéphane. El Principe y el Mendigo. Bourgeois, Paulette & Paulette, Bourgeois. 2003.Tr. of Oma's Quilt. (SPA.). 32p. (J). (gr. k-2). 14.99 *(978-84-241-8644-9(3))* Everest Editora ESP. Dist: Lectorum Pubns., Inc.

—The Real Story of Stone Soup. Compestine, Ying Chang. 2007. (ENG.). 32p. (J). (gr. k-3). 16.99 *(978-0-525-47493-7(5)*, Dutton Juvenile) Penguin Publishing Group.

—Rosie & Buttercup. Uegaki, Chieri. 2008. (ENG.). 32p. (J). (gr. -1-2). 18.95 *(978-1-55337-997-3(7))* Kids Can Pr., Ltd. CAN. Dist: Univ. of Toronto Pr.

Jorisch, Stephane. Suki's Kimono. Uegaki, Chieri. 2005. (ENG.). 32p. (J). (gr. 3). pap. 8.95 *(978-1-55337-752-8(4))* Kids Can Pr., Ltd. CAN. Dist: Univ. of Toronto Pr.

Jorisch, Stéphane. Les Tenebres Piegees, Vol. RJ 65. Gauthier, Bertrand. 2003. (Roman Jeunesse Ser.). (FRE.). 96p. (YA). (gr. 4-7). pap. *(978-2-89021-292-3(0))* Diffusion du livre Mirabel (DLM).

—A Treasure in My Garden. Vigneault, Gilles. 2007. (ENG & FRE.). 36p. (J). (gr. -1-2). 16.95 *(978-2-923163-14-7(1))* La Montagne Secrete CAN. Dist: Independent Pubs. Group.

—What to Expect When You're Expecting Hatchlings: A Guide for Crocodilian Parents (and Curious Kids) Heos, Bridget. 2012. (Expecting Animal Babies Ser.). (ENG.). 32p. (gr. 2-5). lib. bdg. 25.26 *(978-0-7613-5860-2(9))* Lerner Publishing Group.

—What to Expect When You're Expecting Joeys: A Guide for Marsupial Parents (And Curious Kids) Heos, Bridget. 2011. (Expecting Animal Babies Ser.: 2). (ENG.). 32p. (gr. 2-5). lib. bdg. 25.26 *(978-0-7613-5859-6(5))* Lerner Publishing Group.

—What to Expect When You're Expecting Larvae: A Guide for Insect Parents (And Curious Kids) Heos, Bridget. 2011. (Expecting Animal Babies Ser.). (ENG.). 32p. (gr. 2-5). 25.26 *(978-0-7613-5858-9(7))* Lerner Publishing Group.

Jorisch, Stéphane, jt. illus. see Trout Fishing in America Staff.

Jos, Luis Telleria. Mis Primeros Relatos de Miedo. Maneru, Maria et al. 2004. 312p. (J). *(978-968-13-3782-7(4))* Editorial Diana, S.A. MEX. Dist: Lectorum Pubns., Inc.

Joseph, Albert. The Magic Log. Mesibere, Ellen. Naime, Sophie, ed. 2012. 24p. pap. *(978-9980-945-68-6(0))* University of Papua New Guinea Press.

Joseph, Debbie, jt. illus. see Auld, Francis.

Joseph, Patricia. Daddy's Number One Little Girl. Cooper, Glenessa. 2008. 10p. pap. 24.95 *(978-1-60563-983-3(4))* America Star Bks.

Joseph, Patrick. Mouse's Hide-and-Seek Words. Heling, Kathryn & Hembrook, Deborah. 2003. (Step into Reading Ser.: Vol. 1). (ENG.). 32p. (J). (gr. -1-1). pap. 3.99 *(978-0-375-82185-1(6)*, Random Hse. Bks. for Young Readers) Random Hse. Children's Bks.

Joseph, Robin & Campbell, Scott. Zombie in Love. DiPucchio, Kelly. 2011. (ENG.). 32p. (J). (gr. -1-3). 14.99 *(978-1-4424-0270-6(9)*, Atheneum Bks. for Young Readers) Simon & Schuster Children's Publishing.

Josephine, Wall. Scented Adventures of the Bouquet Sisters in Fairyland. Hall, Susan Liberty. 2011. 85p. (YA). pap. 21.50 *(978-0-9833247-6-8(X))* Inkwell Productions, LLC.

Josephs, Alison. Custard & Mustard: Carlos in Coney Island. Sullivan, Maureen. 2009. 32p. 17.95 *(978-0-9820381-1-6(9))* MoJo InkWorks.

Josephs, Alison. Ankle Soup: A Thanksgiving Story. Josephs, Alison. Sullivan, Maureen. 2008. 32p. 17.95 *(978-0-9820381-0-9(0))* MoJo InkWorks.

Josh Green. My Sanctuary: A Place I Call Home - Keepers of the Wild. Ingram, Doreen. 2013. 54p. pap. 17.50 *(978-1-62516-273-1(1)*, Strategic Bk. Publishing) Strategic Book Publishing & Rights Agency (SBPRA).

Joshi, Jagdish. The Ramayana in Pictures. Dayal, Mala. 2006. 64p. (J). *(978-81-291-0896-8(8))* Rupa & Co.

Joshua, Aaron. There Was a Man & He Was Mad. 2008. (First Steps in Music Ser.). (ENG.). 24p. (J). (gr. -1-k). 16.95 *(978-1-57999-681-9(7))* G I A Pubns., Inc.

Joshua, Benson Benson Joshua. Who Were the Magi. Benson, Lyn. 2007. 56p. pap. 23.99 *(978-0-615-13524-3(2))* Benson, Lyn.

Josie, Melinda. Powwow Counting in Cree. Thomas, Penny. 2013. (CRE & ENG.). 24p. (J). *(978-1-55379-392-2(7)*, 9781553793922, HighWater Pr.) Portage & Main Pr.

Joslin, Irene. Never Too Big for Monkey Hugs. Neely, Judith. 2009. 16p. pap. 8.49 *(978-1-4389-7289-3(X))* AuthorHouse.

—What If Marshmallows Fell from the Sky. Becker, Michele Joy. 2009. 32p. pap. 12.99 *(978-1-4389-0152-7(6))* AuthorHouse.

—When I Grow Up. Eisenberg, Kristy. 2009. 28p. pap. 12.49 *(978-1-4389-0183-1(6))* AuthorHouse.

Josse, Annabelle. Noah's Garden: When Someone You Love Is in the Hospital. Johnson, Mo. 2010. (ENG.). 32p. (J). (gr. -1-2). 15.99 (978-0-7636-4782-7(9)) Candlewick Pr.

Jossem, Carol. Ula Li'i & the Magic Shark. Laird, Donivee M. 2003. 49p. (J). (gr. k-3). 9.95 (978-0-940350-23-6(8)) Barnaby Bks., Inc.

—Wili Wai Kula & the Three Mongooses. Laird, Donivee M. 2003. 41p. (J). (gr. k-3). 9.95 (978-0-940350-24-3(6)) Barnaby Bks., Inc.

Jotave, Jazmin Velasco. Confidencias de un Superhéroe. Sandoval, Jaime Alfonso et al. rev. ed. 2004. (Castillo de la Lectura Roja Ser.). (SPA & ENG.). 232p. (J). pap. 8.95 (978-970-20-0180-5(3)) Castillo, Ediciones, S. A. de C. V. MEX. Dist: Macmillan.

Joubert, Beverly, photos by. Face to Face with Elephants. Joubert, Dereck. 2008. (Face to Face with Animals Ser.). (ENG., 32p. (J). (gr. 2-5). 16.95 (978-1-4263-0325-8(4)); 25.90 (978-1-4263-0326-5(2)) National Geographic Society.

—Face to Face with Lions. Joubert, Dereck. 2008. (Face to Face with Animals Ser.). (ENG., 32p. (J). (gr. 1-4). 16.95 (978-1-4263-0207-7(X)); (gr. 2-5). lib. bdg. 25.90 (978-1-4263-0208-4(8)) National Geographic Society.

Jougla, Karina. Tricked on Halloween: Rina & Jax's Stories. Jougla, Frederic. l.t. ed. 2004. 36p. (J). bds. 14.99 (978-0-9754287-0-2(5)) Imagery Pr.

Jourdenais-Martin, Norma Jean. Make Your Own Puppets & Puppet Theaters. Carreiro, Carolyn. 2005. (ENG.). 64p. (YA). 10.95 (978-0-8249-6776-5(3), 1249275); per. 10.95 (978-0-8249-6770-3(4), 1249275) Ideals Pubns. (Williamson Bks.).

Jourdenais, Norma Jean. The Kids' Multicultural Craft Book: 35 Crafts from Around the World. Gould, Roberta. 2004. (Williamson Multicultural Kids Can! Book Ser.). (ENG.). 128p. (J). pap. 14.29 (978-1-885593-91-7(0), Williamson Bks.) Ideals Pubns.

Jovanovic, Vanja Vuleta & Second Story Press Staff. Violet, 1 vol. Stehlik, Tania Duprey. 2009. (ENG.). 24p. (J). (gr. k-3). 14.95 (978-1-897187-60-9(2)) Second Story Pr. CAN. Dist: Orca Bk. Pubs. USA.

Joven, John. Worm & Farmer Maguire: Teamwork/Working Together. Dinardo, Jeff. 2014. (Funny Bone Readers: Being a Friend Ser.). 24p. (gr. -1-1). pap. 4.99 (978-1-939656-07-0(9)) Red Chair Pr.

—The Wounded Lion: A Tale from Spain. 2013. (Tales of Honor (Red Chair Press) Ser.). (ENG.). 32p. (J). (gr. 1-4). lib. bdg. 26.60 (978-1-937529-79-6(7)) Red Chair Pr.

—The Wounded Lion: A Tale from Spain. Barchers, Suzanne I. 2013. (Tales of Honor Ser.). 32p. (gr. 1-3). pap. 8.95 (978-1-937529-63-5(0)) Red Chair Pr.

Joy, Delgado. Zooprise Party / Fiesta Zoorpresa Activity Book / Actividades. Joy, Delgado. 2008. (ENG & SPA.). 20p. (J). 4.95 (978-0-9755454-2-3(6), Laughing Zebra - Bks. for Children) J.O.Y. Publishing.

Joy, Elvis. Knock Knock... ... Is My Father Here? The Pursuit of a Baby Sheep. Cherian, Raichel & Cherian, Raichel. 2011. (ENG.). 28p. pap. 12.99 (978-1-4679-2467-2(9)) CreateSpace Independent Publishing Platform.

Joyart, B. Gossip Queen. Hope, Rinnah Y. 2012. (ENG.). 28p. (J). (gr. 3-7). pap. 19.99 (978-1-62147-097-7(0)) Tate Publishing & Enterprises, LLC.

Joyce, John. Black John the Bogus Pirate - Cartoon Workbook of Marine Beasts. Joyce, John. 2012. (ENG.). 20p. (J). (978-0-9557637-8-6(9)) Sprindrift Pr.

Joyce, Peter. The Once upon a Time Map Book: Take a Tour of Six Enchanted Lands. Hennessy, Barbara G. 2013. (ENG.). 16p. (J). (gr. 1-4). 24.99 (978-0-7636-6475-6(8)) Candlewick Pr.

—The Once upon a Time Map Book: Take a Tour of Six Enchanted Lands. Hennessy, B. G. 2010. (ENG.). 16p. (J). (gr. 1-4). pap. 8.99 (978-0-7636-2682-2(1)) Candlewick Pr.

Joyce, Sophie. Glow-Worm Who Lost Her Glow. Bedford, William. 2004. (Blue Bananas Ser.). (ENG.). 48p. (J). (gr. k-2). pap. 5.99 (978-1-4052-0976-2(3)) Egmont Bks., Ltd. GBR. Dist: Independent Pubs. Group.

—The Glowworm Who Lost Her Glow. Bedford, William. 2005. (Blue Go Bananas Ser.). (ENG.). 48p. (J). (gr. 1-2). (978-0-7787-2652-4(5)); lib. bdg. (978-0-7787-2630-2(4)) Crabtree Publishing Co.

Joyce, William. Big Time Olie. Joyce, William. 2006. (Rolie Polie Olie Ser.). (ENG.). 40p. (J). (gr. -1-3). pap. 6.99 (978-0-06-008812-5(5), Harper Trophy) HarperCollins Pubs.

—Billy's Booger. Joyce, William. 2015. (ENG.). 40p. (J). (gr. -1-3). 17.99 (978-1-4424-7351-5(7)) Simon & Schuster Children's Publishing.

—A Day with Wilbur Robinson. Joyce, William. 2006. (ENG.). 40p. (J). (gr. -1-3). 16.99 (978-0-06-089098-8(3)) HarperCollins Pubs.

—E. Aster Bunnymund & the Warrior Eggs at the Earth's Core!, Bk. 2. Joyce, William. 2012. (Guardians Ser.: 2). (ENG.). 272p. (J). (gr. 2-6). 15.99 (978-1-4424-3050-1(8), Atheneum Bks. for Young Readers) Simon & Schuster Children's Publishing.

—George Shrinks. Joyce, William. 2003. (Trophy Picture Bks.). (ENG.). 40p. (J). (gr. -1-2). reprint ed. pap. 6.99 (978-0-06-443129-3(0)) HarperCollins Pubs.

—The Man in the Moon. Joyce, William. 2011. (Guardians of Childhood Ser.). (ENG.). 56p. (J). (gr. -1-3). 17.99 (978-1-4424-3041-9(9)); 200.00 (978-1-4424-4357-0(X)) Simon & Schuster Children's Publishing. (Atheneum Bks. for Young Readers).

—Nicholas St. North & the Battle of the Nightmare King, Bk. 1. Joyce, William. Geringer, Laura. 2011. (Guardians Ser.: 1). (ENG.). 240p. (J). (gr. 2-6). 15.99 (978-1-4424-3048-8(6), Atheneum Bks. for Young Readers) Simon & Schuster Children's Publishing.

—The Sandman. Joyce, William. 2012. (Guardians of Childhood Ser.). (ENG.). 48p. (J). (gr. -1-3). 17.99 (978-1-4424-3042-6(7), Atheneum Bks. for Young Readers) Simon & Schuster Children's Publishing.

—The Sandman & the War of Dreams. Joyce, William. 2013. (Guardians Ser.: 4). (ENG.). 240p. (J). (gr. 2-6). 15.99 (978-1-4424-3054-9(0), Atheneum Bks. for Young Readers) Simon & Schuster Children's Publishing.

—Toothiana Bk. 3: Queen of the Tooth Fairy Armies. Joyce, William. 2012. (Guardians Ser.: 3). (ENG.). 240p. (J). (gr. 2-6). 15.99 (978-1-4424-3052-5(4), Atheneum Bks. for Young Readers) Simon & Schuster Children's Publishing.

Joyce, William & Bluhm, Joe. The Fantastic Flying Books of Mr. Morris Lessmore. Joyce, William. 2012. (ENG.). 56p. (J). (gr. -1-3). 18.99 (978-1-4424-5702-7(3), Atheneum Bks. for Young Readers) Simon & Schuster Children's Publishing.

Joyce, William & Callicutt, Kenny. A Bean, a Stalk & a Boy Named Jack. Joyce, William. 2014. (ENG.). 56p. (J). (gr. -1-1). 17.99 (978-1-4424-7349-2(5), Atheneum Bks. for Young Readers) Simon & Schuster Children's Publishing.

Joyce, William & Ellis, Christina. The Numberlys. Joyce, William. 2014. (ENG.). 56p. (J). (gr. -1-2). 17.99 (978-1-4424-7343-0(6), Atheneum Bks. for Young Readers) Simon & Schuster Children's Publishing.

Joyce, William, jt. illus. see Moonbot.

Joyner, Andrew. The Baby Swap. Ormerod, Jan. 2015. (ENG.). 32p. (J). (gr. -1-1). 16.99 (978-1-4814-1914-7(5), Little Simon) Little Simon.

—The Terrible Plop. Dubosarsky, Ursula. 2009. (ENG.). 40p. (J). (gr. -1-1). 17.99 (978-0-374-37428-0(7), Farrar, Straus & Giroux (BYR)) Farrar, Straus & Giroux.

—What's the Matter, Aunty May? Friend, Peter. 2013. (ENG.). 32p. (J). (gr. -1-k). 17.99 (978-1-921714-53-5(0)) Little Hare Bks. AUS. Dist: Independent Pubs. Group.

Joyner, Andrew & Joyner, Louise. Yobbos Do Yoga. Gwynne, Phillip. 2013. (ENG.). 32p. (J). (gr. -1-k). 22.99 (978-1-921714-83-2(2)) Little Hare Bks. AUS. Dist: Independent Pubs. Group.

Joyner, Louise, jt. illus. see Joyner, Andrew.

Joynes, Gary, jt. illus. see Escott, Ian.

JoySoul Corporation. God Is for Every Day(r) - Horse Dreams: Teach-A-Child Companion Book with VCD, 2 vols., Vol. 2. Monson, Lois, photos by. Monson, Lois. 2006. 24p. (J). spiral bd. 14.95 (978-0-9727786-9-5(1)) JoySoul Corp.

Ju-Yeon, Rhim. President Dad. Ju-Yeon, Rhim. (President Dad Ser.). Vol. 4. 4th rev. ed. 2005. 192p. per. 9.99 (978-1-59532-237-1(X)); Vol. 5. 5th rev. ed. 2006. 208p. per. 9.99 (978-1-59532-238-8(8)) TOKYOPOP, Inc.

Ju-Young Im, Joy & Da-Young Im, Linda. Mr Otagiri's Promise. Roberts, Deborah. 2012. 40p. pap. (978-1-77067-719-7(4)) FriesenPress.

Juan, Ana. The Boy Who Lost Fairyland. Valente, Catherynne M. 2015. (Fairyland Ser.: 4). (ENG.). 240p. (J). (gr. 5-9). 16.99 (978-1-250-02349-0(1)) Feiwel & Friends.

—Elena's Serenade. Geeslin, Campbell. 2004. (ENG.). 40p. (J). (gr. -1-2). 19.99 (978-0-689-84908-4(7), Atheneum Bks. for Young Readers) Simon & Schuster Children's Publishing.

—For You Are a Kenyan Child. Cunnane, Kelly. 2006. (ENG.). 40p. (J). (gr. -1-3). 17.99 (978-0-689-86194-9(X), Atheneum Bks. for Young Readers) Simon & Schuster Children's Publishing.

—The Girl Who Circumnavigated Fairyland in a Ship of Her Own Making. Valente, Catherynne M. 2011. (Fairyland Ser.: 1). (ENG.). 256p. (J). (gr. 5-9). 16.99 (978-0-312-64961-6(4)) Feiwel & Friends.

—The Girl Who Circumnavigated Fairyland in a Ship of Her Own Making. Valente, Catherynne M. 2012. (Fairyland Ser.: 1). (ENG.). 288p. (J). (gr. 5-9). pap. 7.99 (978-1-250-01019-3(5)) Square Fish.

—The Girl Who Circumnavigated Fairyland in a Ship of Her Own Making. Valente, Catherynne M. ed. 2012. lib. bdg. 18.40 (978-0-606-26128-9(1), Turtleback) Turtleback Bks.

—The Girl Who Fell Beneath Fairyland & Led the Revels There. Valente, Catherynne M. 2013. (Fairyland Ser.: 2). (ENG.). 304p. (J). (gr. 5-9). pap. 7.99 (978-1-250-03412-0(4)) Square Fish.

—The Girl Who Soared over Fairyland & Cut the Moon in Two. Valente, Catherynne M. 2013. (Fairyland Ser.: 3). (ENG.). 256p. (J). (gr. 5-9). 16.99 (978-1-250-02350-6(5)) Feiwel & Friends.

Juan, Ana. The Pet Shop Revolution. Juan, Ana. 2011. (ENG.). 40p. (J). (gr. -1-3). 17.99 (978-0-545-12810-0(2), Levine, Arthur A. Bks.) Scholastic, Inc.

Juarez, Adriana & Puglisi, Adriana. The Doggone Dog, 1 vol. Gallagher, Diana G. 2013. (Pet Friends Forever Ser.). (ENG.). 88p. (gr. 1-3). pap. 5.95 (978-1-4795-1865-4(4)); lib. bdg. 23.99 (978-1-4048-7502-9(6)) Picture Window Bks.

—The Great Kitten Challenge, 1 vol. Gallagher, Diana G. 2013. (Pet Friends Forever Ser.). (ENG.). 88p. (gr. 1-3). pap. 5.95 (978-1-4795-1864-7(6)); lib. bdg. 23.99 (978-1-4048-7501-2(8)) Picture Window Bks.

—Mice Capades, 1 vol. Gallagher, Diana G. 2013. (Pet Friends Forever Ser.). (ENG.). 88p. (gr. 1-3). pap. 5.95 (978-1-4795-1863-0(8)); lib. bdg. 23.99 (978-1-4048-7500-5(X)) Picture Window Bks.

—A No-Sneeze Pet, 1 vol. Gallagher, Diana G. 2013. (Pet Friends Forever Ser.). (ENG.). 88p. (gr. 1-3). pap. 5.95 (978-1-4795-1862-3(X)); lib. bdg. 23.99 (978-1-4048-7499-2(2)) Picture Window Bks.

Juarez, Fernando. Phonics Comics: Twisted Tales - Level 3, Level 3. Richards, Kitty. 2006. (ENG.). 24p. (J). (gr. 1-17). per. 3.99 (978-1-58476-514-1(3), IKIDS) Innovative Kids.

Jubb, Kendahl Jan. Flashy Fantastic Rain Forest Frogs. Patent, Dorothy Hinshaw. 2015. 32p. pap. 8.00 (978-1-61003-544-6(5)) Center for the Collaborative Classroom.

Jubb, Kendahl Jan. Slinky, Scaly, Slithery Snakes. Patent, Dorothy Hinshaw. 2003. (ENG.). 32p. (J). (gr. 1-5). pap. 7.99 (978-0-8027-7652-5(3)) Walker & Co.

Judah, Nathan. Mrs. Kisses. Fanning, Meghan. 2013. 28p. pap. 9.99 (978-1-61225-227-8(3)) Mirror Publishing.

Judah, Susan. Anansi & the Alligator Eggs y Los Huevos Del Caimán. Sherlock, Philip. Rickham, Elethia, tr. 2nd ed. 2013. 42p. pap. 15.00 (978-976-95510-6-0(6)) Minna Pr.

Judal. Vampire Game, Vol. 11. Coffman, Patrick, tr. from JPN. rev. ed. 2005. 192p. pap. 9.99 (978-1-59532-441-2(0)) TOKYOPOP, Inc.

Judal, et al. Vampire Game, Vol. 12. Judal & Judal. 12th rev. ed. 2005. (Vampire Game Ser.). 192p. per. 9.99 (978-1-59532-442-9(9)) TOKYOPOP, Inc.

Judal. Vampire Game. Judal. Judal. 14th rev. ed. 2006. (Vampire Game Ser.: Vol. 14). 192p. per. 9.99 (978-1-59532-444-3(5)) TOKYOPOP, Inc.

—Vampire Game, Vol. 10. Judal. Coffman, Patrick, tr. from JPN. rev. ed. 2005. 192p. (YA). pap. 9.99 (978-1-59532-440-5(2)) TOKYOPOP, Inc.

Judal & Judal. Vampire Game. Judal & Judal. 13th rev. ed. 2005. (Vampire Game Ser.: Vol. 13). 192p. per. 9.99 (978-1-59532-443-6(7)) TOKYOPOP, Inc.

Judal, jt. illus. see Judal.

Jude, Connie & Dobson, Phil. Banana Splits: Ways into Part-Singing. Sanderson, Ana. 2004. (ENG.). 80p. 16.95 (978-0-7136-4196-7(7), 93402, A & C Black) Bloomsbury Publishing Plc GBR. Dist: Consortium Bk. Sales & Distribution.

Jude, Conny. Acting & Theatre. Putsman, Helen, photos by. Evans, Cheryl & Smith, Lucy. Evans, Cheryl, ed. 2008. (Acting & Theatre Ser.). 64p. (J). pap. 8.99 (978-0-7945-2216-2(5), Usborne) EDC Publishing.

Judge, Chris. The Lonely Beast. Judge, Chris. 2011. (Andersen Press Picture Books Ser.). 32p. (J). (gr. -1-4). 16.95 (978-0-7613-8097-9(3)) Andersen Pr. GBR. Dist: Lerner Publishing Group.

—Tin. Judge, Chris. 2014. (ENG.). 32p. (J). (gr. -1-3). 16.95 (978-1-4677-5013-4(1)) Lerner Publishing Group.

Judge, Kathleen. Growing up in Slavery: Stories of Young Slaves as Told by Themselves. Taylor, Yuval, ed. 2007. (ENG.). 256p. (J). (gr. 9). pap. 11.95 (978-1-55652-635-0(0), Hill, Lawrence Bks.) Chicago Review Pr., Inc.

Judge, Lita. S Is for S'Mores: A Camping Alphabet. James, Helen Foster. rev. ed. 2007. (ENG.). 40p. (J). (gr. k-6). 17.95 (978-1-58536-302-5(2)) Sleeping Bear Pr.

Judge, Lita. Bird Talk: What Birds Are Saying & Why. Judge, Lita. 2012. (ENG.). 48p. (J). (gr. 1-4). 18.99 (978-1-59643-646-5(6)) Roaring Brook Pr.

—Born in the Wild: Baby Mammals & Their Parents. Judge, Lita. 2014. (ENG.). 48p. (J). (gr. k-3). 18.99 (978-1-59643-925-2(4)) Roaring Brook Pr.

—Born to Be Giants: How Baby Dinosaurs Grew to Rule the World. Judge, Lita. 2010. (ENG.). 48p. (J). (gr. 1-4). 17.99 (978-1-59643-443-1(0)) Roaring Brook Pr.

—D Is for Dinosaur: A Prehistoric Alphabet. Judge, Lita. Chapman, Todd. 2007. (Science Ser.). (ENG.). 40p. (J). (gr. 1-7). 17.95 (978-1-58536-242-4(5)) Sleeping Bear Pr.

—Flight School. Judge, Lita. 2014. (ENG.). 40p. (J). (gr. -1-3). 17.99 (978-1-4424-8177-0(3), Atheneum Bks. for Young Readers) Simon & Schuster Children's Publishing.

—Good Morning to Me! Judge, Lita. 2015. (ENG.). 40p. (J). (gr. -1-3). 17.99 (978-1-4814-0369-6(9)) Simon & Schuster Children's Publishing.

—How Big Were Dinosaurs? Judge, Lita. 2013. (ENG.). 40p. (J). (gr. 1-4). 17.99 (978-1-59643-719-7(7)) Roaring Brook Pr.

—Red Hat. Judge, Lita. 2013. (ENG.). 40p. (J). (gr. -1-k). 16.99 (978-1-4424-4232-0(8), Atheneum Bks. for Young Readers) Simon & Schuster Children's Publishing.

—Red Sled. Judge, Lita. 2011. (ENG.). 40p. (J). (gr. -1-3). 17.99 (978-1-4424-2007-6(3), Atheneum Bks. for Young Readers) Simon & Schuster Children's Publishing.

Judowitz, Chani. Baruch & His Disappearing Yarmulke. Gerstenblit, Rivke. 2014. 32p. (J). (978-1-4226-1530-0(8)) Mesorah Pubns., Ltd.

Judowitz, Yoel. Middos Man Book & CD. Ornstein, Esther. 2013. 33p. 19.95 (978-1-60091-257-3(5)) Israel Bookshop Pubns.

Juhasz, Brenda. Posey & Mosey Go Camping. Juhasz, Mike. 2008. 16p. pap. 24.95 (978-1-60610-258-9(3)) America Star Bks.

Juhasz, George. Henry Chow & Other Stories, 1 vol. Miles, Victoria et al. 2010. (ENG.). 134p. (YA). (gr. 8-11). pap. 12.95 (978-1-896580-33-3(5)) Tradewind Bks. CAN. Dist: Orca Bk. Pubs. USA.

—Pacific Tree Frogs, 1 vol. Owen, Leslie E. 2003. (ENG.). 32p. (J). (gr. 2-5). pap. 7.95 (978-1-896580-42-5(4)) Tradewind Bks. CAN. Dist: Orca Bk. Pubs. USA.

—Rescuing Einstein's Compass. Oppenheim, Shulamith. 2003. (ENG.). 32p. (J). (gr. k-3). 15.95 (978-1-56656-507-3(3), Interlink Bks.) Interlink Publishing Group, Inc.

Juhasz, Victor. D Is for Democracy: A Citizen's Alphabet. Grodin, Elissa. (ENG.). 40p. (J). (gr. 1-4). 2006. per. 7.95 (978-1-58536-328-5(6), 203807); 2004. 16.95 (978-1-58536-234-9(4), 202059) Sleeping Bear Pr.

—Everyone Counts: A Citizens' Number Book. Elissa Grodin. rev. ed. 2006. (Count Your Way Across the U. S. A. Ser.). (ENG.). 40p. (J). (gr. -1-3). 17.95 (978-1-58536-295-0(6)) Sleeping Bear Pr.

—G Is for Gladiators: An Ancient Rome Alphabet. Shoulders, Debbie & Shoulders, Michael. 2010. (Sleeping Bear Alphabets Ser.). (ENG.). 40p. (J). 17.95 (978-1-58536-457-2(6)) Sleeping Bear Pr.

—H Is for Honor: A Military Family Alphabet. Scillian, Devin. 2006. (ENG.). 40p. (J). (gr. k-6). 17.95 (978-1-58536-292-9(1)) Sleeping Bear Pr.

—Hot Dog! Eleanor Roosevelt Throws a Picnic. Kimmelman, Leslie. 2014. (ENG.). 40p. (J). (gr. 3-6). 16.99 (978-1-58536-830-3(X), 203013) Sleeping Bear Pr.

—R Is for Rhyme: A Poetry Alphabet. Young, Judy & A12. 2010. (ENG.). 48p. (J). pap. 7.95 (978-1-58536-519-7(X)) Sleeping Bear Pr.

—R Is for Rhyme: A Poetry Alphabet. Young, Judy. rev. ed. 2006. (Art & Culture Ser.). (ENG.). 40p. (J). (gr. -1-3). 17.95 (978-1-58536-240-0(9)) Sleeping Bear Pr.

—Z Is for Zeus: A Greek Mythology Alphabet. Wilbur, Helen L. rev. ed. 2008. (Art & Culture Ser.). (ENG.). 40p. (J). (gr. 1-7). 17.95 (978-1-58536-341-4(3)) Sleeping Bear Pr.

Juillard, André. The Sarcophagi of the Sixth Coninent, Pt. 1, Vol. 9. Sente, Yves. 2011. (ENG.). 64p. (gr. 5-17). pap. 15.95 (978-1-84918-067-2(9)) CineBook GBR. Dist: National Bk. Network.

Jules, Prud'homme, jt. illus. see Prud'homme, Jules.

Julian, Alison. The Nutcracker. Hoffmann, E. T. A. 2005. (J). (978-0-7607-6690-3(8)) Barnes & Noble, Inc.

—The 12 Days of Christmas. 2005. (J). (978-1-74157-281-0(9)) Hinkler Bks. Pty, Ltd.

Julian, Russell. Bouncy Bouncy Bedtime. Bedford, David. 2011. (ENG.). 32p. (J). (gr. -1-k). pap. 8.99 (978-1-4052-5742-8(3)) Egmont Bks., Ltd. GBR. Dist: Independent Pubs. Group.

—Goat & Donkey in Strawberry Sunglasses, 1 vol. Puttock, Simon. 2007. (ENG.). 28p. (J). (gr. -1-2). pap. 16.00 (978-1-56148-572-7(1), Good Bks.) Skyhorse Publishing Co., Inc.

—The Magic Footprints. Balfour, Melissa. 2005. (Green Bananas Ser.). (ENG.). 48p. (J). lib. bdg. (978-0-7787-1023-3(8)) Crabtree Publishing Co.

—The Monster of the Woods! Freedman, Claire. 2013. (ENG.). 32p. (J). pap. (978-0-545-51571-9(8), Cartwheel Bks.) Scholastic, Inc.

—The Monster of the Woods!/By Claire Freedman & Russell Julian. Freedman, Claire. 2013. (J). (978-0-545-56837-1(4), Cartwheel Bks.) Scholastic, Inc.

—Splitting the Herd: A Corral of Odds & Evens. Harris, Trudy. 2008. (Math Is Fun! Ser.). (ENG.). 32p. (J). (gr. k-2). 16.95 (978-0-8225-7466-8(7), Millbrook Pr.) Lerner Publishing Group.

—What Can You See? On Christmas Night. Tebbs, Victoria. 2010. (ENG.). 32p. (J). (gr. -1-k). 9.99 (978-0-7459-6142-2(8)) Lion Hudson PLC GBR. Dist: Independent Pubs. Group.

Julian, Sean. Five Little Ducklings Go to Bed. Roth, Carol. 2014. (ENG.). 32p. (J). (gr. k-3). 17.95 (978-0-7358-4128-4(4)) North-South Bks., Inc.

Julian, Sean. Five Little Ducklings Go to School. Roth, Carol. 2015. (ENG.). 32p. (J). 17.95 (978-0-7358-4132-1(2)) North-South Bks., Inc.

Julian, Sean. Muffin. Rooney, Anne. 2009. (Go! Readers Ser.). 48p. (J). (gr. 2-5). pap. 12.85 (978-1-60754-270-4(6)); lib. bdg. 29.25 (978-1-60754-269-8(2)) Windmill Bks.

—Where's My Mommy? Roth, Carol. 2012. (ENG.). 32p. (J). 17.95 (978-0-7358-4032-4(6)) North-South Bks., Inc.

Julich, Jenniffer. Bows, Does & Bucks! An Introduction to Archery Deer Hunting. DiLorenzo, Michael A. 2010. 88p. (J). 19.95 (978-0-9777210-2-3(7)) Running Moose Publications.

—Cole Family Christmas. Bryan, Jennifer Liu & Kendle, Hazel Cole. 2008. 80p. (J). (gr. 4-7). 17.95 (978-0-9816265-0-5(5)) Next Chapter Pr.

—Encounter at Ogre Island. Greene, John McBride. 2006. 96p. pap. 9.50 (978-0-9772809-0-2(X)) Comprecom.

—Nonnie, What's God? Lile, Linda L. 2008. 16p. (J). 13.95 (978-0-9817092-0-8(6)) A-Lu Publishing.

—The Player Piano Mouse. Dachman, Adam. 2008. 32p. (J). 14.99 (978-0-9797794-0-4(5)) Player Piano Mouse Productions (PPMP).

—Walter's Pond: The True Story of Three Brothers Who Went Fishing for Trouble. Farrell, Bill. 2008. 16p. 8.95 (978-0-9797790-0-8(6)) Lower Lane Publishing LLC.

—Yolandababy: A Pooch Finds Her Purpose! an Adventure in Self-Esteem. Bennett-Boltinghouse, Jo Ann. 2007. (YolandaBaby Ser.). 28p. (J). (gr. -1-3). 16.00 (978-0-9785151-0-2(2)) Ginger Pr., The.

Julie, jt. illus. see Fil.

Julien, Terry. Brave & Beautiful Queen Esther. Holder, Jennifer. 2014. (Happy Day Ser.). (ENG.). 16p. (J). pap. 2.49 (978-1-4143-9474-9(8)) Tyndale Hse. Pubs.

Julien, Terry. Brave & Beautiful Queen Esther. Holder, Jennifer. 2015. (Faith That Sticks Ser.). (ENG.). 30p. (J). pap. 3.99 (978-1-4964-0314-8(2)) Tyndale Hse. Pubs.

Julien, Terry. Daniel & His Faithful Friends. Holder, Jennifer. 2014. (Faith That Sticks Ser.). (ENG.). 27p. (J). pap. 3.99 (978-1-4143-9827-3(1)) Tyndale Hse. Pubs.

Julien, Terry, jt. illus. see Marlin, Kathryn.

Julieta, Irla. Entre Suenos. Garza, Ben. rev. ed. 2007. (Castillo de la Lectura Roja Ser.). (SPA & ENG.). 108p. (YA). (gr. 7). pap. 8.95 (978-970-20-0199-7(4)) Castillo, Ediciones, S. A. de C. V. MEX. Dist: Macmillan.

Julings, Emma, jt. photos by see Freeman, Mike.

Jullien, Jean. Hoot Owl, Master of Disguise. Taylor, Sean. 2015. (ENG.). 48p. (J). (gr. -1-2). 15.99 (978-0-7636-7578-3(4)) Candlewick Pr.

Junaid, Bushra. Nana's Cold Days, 1 vol. Badoe, Adwoa. 2009. (ENG.). 32p. (J). (gr. k-k). pap. 6.95 (978-0-88899-937-5(2)) Groundwood Bks. CAN. Dist: Perseus-PGW.

Junaid, Bushra, jt. illus. see Rudnicki, Richard.

June, Cathy. We Eat Food That's Fresh. Russ-Ayon, Angela. 2009. 32p. (J). (gr. -1-2). 11.99 (978-1-934214-09-1(4)) OurRainbow Pr., LLC.

Jung, Shirley. Ten Spunky Monkeys. Phillips, Clifton. 2007. 32p. (J). 8.99 (978-0-9797106-4-3(2)) Avid Readers Publishing Group.

Jung, Wook Jin. Go Bot, Robot! Rau, Dana Meachen. 2013. 32p. (J). (978-0-449-81429-1(7)); (ENG.). (gr. -1-1). 3.99 (978-0-375-87083-5(0)) Random Hse., Inc.

Jungle Factor Staff. The Complete Pokémon Pocket Guide, Vol. 2. VIZ Media Staff. 2008. (Pokemon Ser.: 2). (ENG.). 256p. (J). (gr. 1). pap. 10.99 (978-1-4215-2326-2(4)) Viz Media.

Jungle Factor Staff. The Complete Pokémon, Vol. 1. Jungle Factor Staff. Media Staff. 2008. (Pokemon Ser.: 1). (ENG.). 256p. (J). (gr. 1). pap. 10.99 (978-1-4215-2325-5(6)) Viz Media.

Junjie, Cheng. Chinese Fables & Folktales (III) Li, Ma et al. 2010. (ENG.). 48p. (J). (gr. -1-2). 16.95 (978-1-60220-964-0(2)) BetterLink Pr., Inc.

Jupin, David Perez. Love. 2013. 20p. pap. 11.95 (978-1-937504-67-0(0)) Worthy Shorts.

Jurevicius, Nathan. Lookout London, 1 vol. Thompson, Lisa. 2006. (Read-It! Chapter Books: SWAT Ser.). (ENG.). 80p. (gr. 2-4). 21.32 (978-1-4048-1672-5(0), Chapter Readers) Picture Window Bks.

Jurinich, Anna. Where Do the Balloons Go? Davis, Elena. 2006. (ENG.). 32p. (J). (gr. -1-3). 16.95 (978-0-9714372-3-4(8)) Red Rock Pr., Inc.

Just, John. The Amazing Tale of Archie the Alligator. Kick, J. D. 2nd ed. 2003. (J). per. 12.95 *(978-1-929424-14-6(0),* Owl Creek Farm Bks.) Owl Tree Pr.

—A Goose Tale — Downside up. Kick, J. D. 2nd l.t. ed. 2003. 80p. (J). per. 16.95 *(978-1-929424-13-9(2),* Owl Creek Farm Bks.) Owl Tree Pr.

Justin McGovern. Be Kind to the Earth: A Little Kid's Guide to Reducing your Carbon Footprint. Kelly McGovern Lu. 2009. 28p. pap. 14.99 *(978-1-4389-7356-2(X))* AuthorHouse.

Justine, Torode, jt. illus. see Scott, Peter.

Justinen, Kim. Shoebox Kids Bible Stories, Vol. 5. Thomas, Jerry D. 2003. 128p. (J). 7.99 *(978-0-8163-1971-8(5))* Pacific Pr. Publishing Assn.

Juta, Jason. Drawing Wild Animals. Colich, Abby. 2015. (Drawing Amazing Animals Ser.). (ENG.). 32p. (gr. 3-4). 27.32 *(978-1-4914-2132-1(0))* Capstone Pr., Inc.

—A Field Guide to Griffins, Unicorns, & Other Mythical Beasts, 1 vol. Sautter, A. J. 2014. (Fantasy Field Guides). (ENG.). 32p. (gr. 3-4). lib. bdg. 27.32 *(978-1-4914-0690-8(9))* Capstone Pr., Inc.

Juta, Jason, jt. illus. see McGrath, Tom.

Jutte, Jan. Roawr! Joosse, Barbara M. 2009. (ENG.). 40p. (J). (gr. 1-3). 16.99 *(978-0-399-24777-4(7),* Philomel) Penguin Publishing Group.

—Sleepover at Gramma's House. Joosse, Barbara M. 2010. (ENG.). 40p. (J). (gr. -1-k). 17.99 *(978-0-399-25261-7(4),* Philomel) Penguin Publishing Group.

—The Swan's Child. Kuyper, Sjoerd. 2005. (ENG.). 128p. (J). (gr. 5-9). 16.95 *(978-0-8234-1861-9(8))* Holiday Hse., Inc.

K

K, Mark. Larry Bendeco Johannes Von Sloop. V, Larry. 2014. (ENG.). 32p. (J). (gr. k-5). 7.99 ***(978-1-4867-0000-4(4))*** Flowerpot Children's Pr. Inc. CAN. Dist: Cardinal Pubs. Group.

Kaaris. Legend: the Graphic Novel. Lu, Marie. 2015. (Legend Ser.). (ENG.). 160p. (YA). (gr. 7). pap. 14.99 *(978-0-399-17189-5(4),* Putnam Juvenile) Penguin Publishing Group.

Kaback, Suzy. The Back to School Book. Kaback, Suzy. Power, Brenda et al. 2003. (ENG.). 128p. pap. 15.95 *(978-0-439-36599-4(6))* Scholastic, Inc.

Kacer, Stephen. The Harry Bear Story. Painter, Grace. 2011. 28p. pap. 24.95 *(978-1-4626-3327-2(7))* America Star Bks.

Kadair, Deborah. I Spy in the Louisiana Sky, 1 vol. Kadair, Deborah. 2011. (ENG.). 32p. (J). (gr. k-3). 16.99 *(978-1-58980-885-0(1))* Pelican Publishing Co., Inc.

Kadair, Deborah Ousley. Grandma's Gumbo, 1 vol. Kadair, Deborah Ousley. 2003. (ENG.). 32p. (J). (gr. k-3). 16.99 *(978-1-58980-133-2(4))* Pelican Publishing Co., Inc.

—I Spy in the Texas Sky, 1 vol. Kadair, Deborah Ousley. 2009. (ENG.). 32p. (J). (gr. k-3). 16.99 *(978-1-58980-654-2(9))* Pelican Publishing Co., Inc.

Kadmon, Christina. Hide Easter Bunny Hide. Weigelt, Udo. 2010. (ENG.). 32p. (J). (gr. -1-3). pap. 7.95 *(978-0-7358-2264-1(6))* North-South Bks., Inc.

Kadmon, Cristina. The Best Father of All. Horn, Peter. James, J. Alison, tr. from GER. 2005. (ENG.). 32p. (J). (gr. -1). pap. 6.95 *(978-0-7358-1977-1(7))* North-South Bks., Inc.

—When I Grow Up... Horn, Peter. 2014. 32p. pap. 8.00 *(978-1-61003-370-1(1))* Center for the Collaborative Classroom.

Kaergel, Julia. Luisa Quiere Ser Princesa. Dorrie, Doris & Dörrie, Doris. 2005. (SPA.). (J). (gr. 1-3). 16.80 *(978-84-89804-70-8(2),* LG32983) Lóguez Ediciones ESP. Dist: Lectorum Pubns., Inc.

Kaeser, Gigi, photos by. Nothing to Hide: Mental Illness in the Family. Beard, Jean J. & Gillespie, Peggy, eds. 2005. 296p. (YA). reprint ed. pap. 30.00 *(978-0-7567-9382-1(3))* DIANE Publishing Co.

Kageyama, Naoyuki. The Semifinals Begin!, 9 vols., Vol. 4. Kageyama, Naoyuki. Takahashi, Kazuki. 2010. (Yu-Gi-Oh! GX Ser.: 4). (ENG.). 216p. pap. 9.99 *(978-1-4215-3173-1(9))* Viz Media.

—Yu-Gi-Oh! GX, 9 vols., Vol. 1. Kageyama, Naoyuki. Takahashi, Kazuki. 2007. (Yu-Gi-oh!: Gx Ser.: 1). (ENG.). 224p. (gr. 2-18). pap. 9.99 *(978-1-4215-1378-2(1))* Viz Media.

Kahlo, Frida. Frida: Viva la Vida! - Long Live Life!, 0 vols. Bernier-Grand, Carmen T. 2007. (ENG.). 64p. (YA). (gr. 7-11). lib. bdg. 18.99 *(978-0-7614-5336-9(9),* 9780761453369, Amazon Children's Publishing) Amazon Publishing.

Kahn, Katherine. Sammy Spider's First Book of Jewish Holidays. Rouss, Sylvia A. 2013. (ENG.). 12p. (J). (gr. -1 — 1). bds. 5.95 *(978-1-4677-1916-2(1),* Kar-Ben Publishing) Lerner Publishing Group.

—Sammy Spider's First Day of School. Rouss, Sylvia A. 2009. (Kar-Ben Favorites Ser.). (ENG.). 32p. (J). (gr. -1-2). 16.95 *(978-0-8225-8583-1(9),* Kar-Ben Publishing) Lerner Publishing Group.

—Sammy Spider's First Haggadah. Rouss, Sylvia. 2007. (Passover Ser.). (ENG.). 32p. (J). (gr. -1-3). per. 6.95 *(978-1-58013-230-5(8),* Kar-Ben Publishing) Lerner Publishing Group.

—Sammy Spider's First Simchat Torah. Rouss, Sylvia A. 2010. (Sukkot & Simchat Torah Ser.). (ENG.). 32p. (J). (gr. -1-2). lib. bdg. 15.95 *(978-0-7613-3965-6(5),* Kar-Ben Publishing) Lerner Publishing Group.

—Sammy Spider's First Yom Kippur. Rouss, Sylvia A. 2013. (High Holidays Ser.). (ENG.). 32p. (J). (gr. -1-3). lib. bdg. 16.95 *(978-0-7613-9195-1(9),* Kar-Ben Publishing) Lerner Publishing Group.

Kahn, Katherine Janus. Noah & the Ziz. Jules, Jacqueline & Hechtkopf, Jacqueline. 2005. (ENG.). 32p. (gr. -1-2). 9.95 *(978-0-929371-01-6(1),* Kar-Ben Publishing) Lerner Publishing Group.

—Noah & the Ziz. Jules, Jacqueline. 2005. (ENG.). 32p. (J). (gr. -1-2). per. 10.95 *(978-1-58013-121-6(2),* Kar-Ben Publishing) Lerner Publishing Group.

—The Princess & the Ziz. Jules, Jacqueline. 2008. (ENG.). 32p. (J). (gr. -1-1). pap. 7.95 *(978-0-8225-7382-1(2),* Kar-Ben Publishing) Lerner Publishing Group.

—Sammy Spider's First Day of School. Rouss, Sylvia A. 2009. (Kar-Ben Favorites Ser.). (ENG.). 32p. (J). (gr. -1-2). pap. 7.95 *(978-0-8225-8584-8(7),* Kar-Ben Publishing) Lerner Publishing Group.

—Sammy Spider's First Haggadah. Rouss, Sylvia A. 2007. (Sammy Spider's First Bks.). (J). (gr. -1-3). 15.20 *(978-1-4177-7156-1(9),* Turtleback) Turtleback Bks.

—Sammy Spider's First Shavuot. Rouss, Sylvia A. 2008. (Sammy Spider's First Bks.). (ENG.). 32p. (J). (gr. -1-3). lib. bdg. 15.95 *(978-0-8225-7224-4(9));* per. 7.95 *(978-0-8225-7225-1(7))* Lerner Publishing Group. (Kar-Ben Publishing).

—Sammy Spider's First Simchat Torah. Rouss, Sylvia A. 2010. (Sukkot & Simchat Torah Ser.). (ENG.). 32p. (J). (gr. -1-2). pap. 7.95 *(978-0-7613-3966-3(3),* Kar-Ben Publishing) Lerner Publishing Group.

—Sammy Spider's First Sukkot. Rouss, Sylvia A. 2004. (ENG.). 32p. (J). (gr. -1-3). 17.95 *(978-1-58013-142-1(5));* pap. 7.95 *(978-1-58013-083-7(6))* Lerner Publishing Group. (Kar-Ben Publishing).

—Sammy Spider's First Taste of Hanukkah: A Cookbook. Rouss, Sylvia A. & Turndorf, Genene Levy. 2015. (ENG.). 32p. (J). (gr. -1-3). 16.99 *(978-1-4677-5237-4(1),* Kar-Ben Publishing) Lerner Publishing Group.

—Sammy Spider's First Yom Kippur. Rouss, Sylvia A. 2013. (High Holidays Ser.). (ENG.). 32p. (J). (gr. -1-3). 7.95 *(978-0-7613-9196-8(7),* Kar-Ben Publishing) Lerner Publishing Group.

—Sammy Spider's Shabbat Fun Book. Rouss, Sylvia. 2006. (Sammy Spider Set Ser.). (ENG.). 24p. (J). (gr. -1-3). pap. 4.95 *(978-1-58013-147-6(6),* Kar-Ben Publishing) Lerner Publishing Group.

—Tamar's Sukkah. Gellman, Ellie B. rev. ed. 2015. (ENG.). 32p. (J). (gr. -1-2). lib. bdg. 17.99 *(978-1-4677-5636-5(9));* pap. 7.99 ***(978-1-4677-5637-2(7))*** Lerner Publishing Group. (Kar-Ben Publishing).

—Tasty Bible Stories: A Menu of Tales & Matching Recipes. Lehman-Wilzig, Tami. 2003. (ENG.). 64p. (J). (gr. 3-5). pap. 10.95 *(978-1-58013-080-6(1),* Kar-Ben Publishing) Lerner Publishing Group.

—The Ziz & the Hanukkah Miracle. Jules, Jacqueline & Hechtkopf, Jacqueline. 2006. (ENG.). 32p. (J). (gr. -1-2). lib. bdg. 17.95 *(978-1-58013-160-5(3),* Kar-Ben Publishing) Lerner Publishing Group.

—The Ziz & the Hanukkah Miracle. Jules, Jacqueline. 2006. (ENG.). 32p. (J). (gr. -1-2). per. 9.95 *(978-1-58013-164-3(6),* Kar-Ben Publishing) Lerner Publishing Group.

Kahn, Katherine Janus & Redenbaugh, Vicki Jo. Lots of Latkes: A Hanukkah Story. Rouss, Sylvia A. & Lanton, Sandy. 2003. (ENG.). 32p. (J). (gr. -1-3). pap. 6.95 *(978-1-58013-061-5(5),* Kar-Ben Publishing) Lerner Publishing Group.

Kai. Peter Wanted a Pet. Summers, Terry. 2012. 26p. 24.95 *(978-1-4626-6120-6(3))* America Star Bks.

Kaida, Garrett. Fire Truck! Ulz, Ivan. 2013. 36p. 19.00 *(978-0-9896231-0-0(6))* Temple Street Pr.

Kain, Bob & Owlkids Books Inc. Staff. The Chirp Book. Kain, Bob. 10th anniv. ed. 2007. (ENG.). 112p. (J). (gr. -1-1). 14.95 *(978-2-89579-162-1(7))* Owlkids Bks. Inc. CAN. Dist: Perseus-PGW.

—Joking Around with Chirp: More Than 130 Feather-Ruffling Jokes, Riddles, & Tongue Twisters! Chirp Magazine Editors. 2013. (ENG.). 96p. (J). (gr. -1-1). pap. 8.95 *(978-1-926973-65-4(8))* Owlkids Bks. Inc. CAN. Dist: Perseus-PGW.

—Laugh with Chirp: Jokes, Riddles, Tongue Twisters, & More! Kain, Bob. 2005. (ENG.). 24p. (J). (gr. -1-1). 9.95 *(978-2-89579-111-9(2));* pap. 4.95 *(978-2-89579-071-6(X))* Owlkids Bks. Inc. CAN. Dist: Perseus-PGW.

—Play with Chirp: Puzzles, Mazes, Games, & More! Kain, Bob. 2006. (ENG.). 24p. (J). (gr. -1-1). pap. 4.95 *(978-2-89579-113-3(9))* Owlkids Bks. Inc. CAN. Dist: Perseus-PGW.

—Read with Chirp: Read along with Pictures. Kain, Bob. 2006. (ENG.). 24p. (J). (gr. -1-1). pap. 4.95 *(978-2-89579-082-2(5))* Owlkids Bks. Inc. CAN. Dist: Perseus-PGW.

—Read with Chirp: Read along with Pictures. Kain, Bob & Becker, Helaine. 2006. (ENG.). 24p. (J). (gr. -1-1). 9.95 *(978-2-89579-110-2(4))* Owlkids Bks. Inc. CAN. Dist: Perseus-PGW.

—Travel with Chirp: Comics, Jokes, Games, & More Travelling Fun! Kain, Bob. 2007. (ENG.). 24p. (J). (gr. -1-1). 4.95 *(978-2-89579-139-3(2))* Owlkids Bks. Inc. CAN. Dist: Perseus-PGW.

Kaino, Kim, jt. illus. see Youso, Justin.

Kaiser, Lisa. A Little Story, about the Biggest thing that Ever Happened. Dalton, William. 2006. per. *(978-0-9764395-0-9(6))* Dalton, William.

Kaiser, Lori. Florence Flamingo Gets the Flu. Kaiser, Lori. 2012. 30p. pap. *(978-0-9836651-5-1(X))* Roxby Media Ltd.

—George Washington. Kaiser, Lori. 2012. 26p. pap. *(978-0-9836651-7-5(6))* Roxby Media Ltd.

—Gigi the Greedy Giraffe. Kaiser, Lori. 2012. 28p. pap. *(978-0-9836651-8-2(4))* Roxby Media Ltd.

—Megan the Moody Moose. Kaiser, Lori. 2013. 26p. pap. *(978-0-9883770-5-9(5))* Roxby Media Ltd.

Kako, Franco. Encountering Ghosts: Eyewitness Accounts, 1 vol. Bolte, Mari. 2014. (Eyewitness to the Unexplained Ser.). (ENG.). 32p. (gr. 3-4). 29.99 *(978-1-4914-0245-0(8))* Capstone Pr., Inc.

Kako, Satoshi. Where Is Little Toko? Matsuoka, Kyoko. 2006. 32p. (J). 11.95 *(978-1-74126-022-9(1))* R.I.C. Pubns. AUS. Dist: SCB Distributors.

Kalafatis, John, jt. illus. see Smith, Jacquelyn.

Kalahele, Imaikalani. Breaking the Blood. Eyre, David. 2008. 40p. 14.95 *(978-0-87336-162-0(8))* Kamehameha Publishing.

—Lumpy Poi & Twisting Eels. Eyre, David. 2007. 32p. 14.95 *(978-0-87336-154-5(7))* Kamehameha Publishing.

—Sacred Awa Piercing Spears. Eyre, David. 2009. 31p. 14.95 *(978-0-87336-217-7(9))* Kamehameha Publishing.

Kalal, Dan. Rosa Parks & the Montgomery Bus Boycott, 1 vol. Miller, Connie Colwell. 2006. (Graphic History Ser.). (ENG.). 32p. (gr. 3-4). 29.99 *(978-0-7368-6495-4(4),* Graphic Library) Capstone Pr., Inc.

—Rosa Parks & the Montgomery Bus Boycott, 1 vol. Miller, Connie Colwell. 2006. (Graphic History Ser.). (ENG.). 32p. (gr. 3-4). per. 8.10 *(978-0-7368-9658-0(9),* Graphic Library) Capstone Pr., Inc.

Kalanovic, Dubravka. Wake up, Sleepyhead! Early Morning Poems. Ross, Mandy. 2004. (Poems for the Young Ser.). (ENG.). 32p. (J). (gr. -1). pap. *(978-1-904550-33-4(9))* Child's Play International Ltd.

Kalasea. What Might I Find in a Geyser. Declus, Jennifer. 2004. (J). *(978-0-9743690-0-6(4))* Britt Allcroft Productions.

—What Might I Find in a Rainforest. Declus, Jennifer. 2004. (ENG.). (J). *(978-0-9743690-1-3(2))* Britt Allcroft Productions.

—What Might I Find in a Swamp. Declus, Jennifer. 2004. (J). *(978-0-9743690-3-7(9))* Britt Allcroft Productions.

—What Might I Find in a Tidepool. Declus, Jennifer. 2004. (J). *(978-0-9743690-4-4(7))* Britt Allcroft Productions.

—What Might I Find on a Pond. Declus, Jennifer. 2004. (J). *(978-0-9743690-2-0(0))* Britt Allcroft Productions.

Kalb, Chris. Rachael Ray's 30-Minute Meals for Kids: Cooking Rocks! Ray, Rachael. 2004. (ENG.). 192p. spiral bd. 16.95 *(978-1-891105-15-9(9))* Lake Isle Pr., Inc.

Kalda, Sam. The Great Gatsby. Fitzgerald, F. Scott. adapted ed. 2014. (American Classics Ser.). (ENG.). 64p. pap. 6.95 *(978-1-906230-74-6(9))* Real Reads Ltd. GBR. Dist: International Publishers Marketing.

Kale, Ann Stephanian. Artie - The Ugly Frog. Kale, Ann Stephanian. 2004. 20p. (J). pap. 10.00 *(978-0-9704131-6-1(5))* Abril BookStore & Publishing.

—Marco & Princess Gina. Kale, Ann Stephanian. 2003. 24p. (J). (gr. k-3). pap. 10.00 *(978-0-9704131-5-4(7))* Abril BookStore & Publishing.

Kalender, Oznur. Animal Wonders of the Sky. Kaplan, Osman. 2009. (Amazing Animals Ser.). (ENG.). 56p. (J). (gr. 2-4). 9.95 *(978-1-59784-201-3(X))* Tughra Bks.

—Animal Wonders of the Water. Kaplan, Osman. 2009. (Amazing Animals Ser.). (ENG.). 56p. (J). (gr. 2-4). 9.95 *(978-1-59784-200-6(1))* Tughra Bks.

—Giants of the World. Kaplan, Osman. 2008. (Amazing Animals Ser.). (ENG.). 56p. (J). (gr. 2-4). pap. 9.95 *(978-1-59784-139-9(0))* Tughra Bks.

—Wonders of the Land. Kaplan, Osman. 2008. (Amazing Animals Ser.). (ENG.). 56p. (J). (gr. -1-3). pap. 9.95 *(978-1-59784-145-0(5))* Tughra Bks.

Kalis, Jennifer. The BFF Journal, 1 vol. Wood, Anita. 2011. (ENG.). 144p. (J). (gr. 1). spiral bd. 12.99 *(978-1-4236-1814-0(9))* Gibbs Smith, Publisher.

—The Big Book of Girl Stuff, 1 vol. King, Bart. 2014. (ENG.). 320p. pap. 19.99 *(978-1-4236-3762-2(3))* Gibbs Smith, Publisher.

—Campfire Mallory. Friedman, Laurie. (Mallory Ser.: 9). (ENG.). 176p. (J). (gr. 2-5). 2009. pap. 5.95 *(978-1-58013-841-3(1),* First Avenue Editions); 2008. lib. bdg. 15.95 *(978-0-8225-7657-0(0),* Carolrhoda Bks.) Lerner Publishing Group.

—Change Is in the Air, Mallory. Friedman, Laurie B. 2015. (ENG.). 160p. (J). (gr. 2-5). 15.95 *(978-1-4677-0924-8(7))* Lerner Publishing Group.

—Doodle Your Day, 1 vol. Wood, Anita. 2013. (ENG.). 224p. (J). pap. 16.99 *(978-1-4236-2368-7(1))* Gibbs Smith, Publisher.

—Fairy Doodles, 1 vol. Wood, Anita. 2014. (ENG.). 240p. (J). pap. 9.99 *(978-1-4236-3606-9(6))* Gibbs Smith, Publisher.

—Fashion Doodles, 1 vol. Wood, Anita. 2014. (ENG.). 240p. pap. 16.99 *(978-1-4236-3607-6(4))* Gibbs Smith, Publisher.

—Game Time, Mallory! Friedman, Laurie B. 2015. (J). *(978-1-4677-6188-8(5))* Lerner Publishing Group.

—Happy New Year, Mallory! Friedman, Laurie. (Mallory Ser.: 12). (ENG.). 176p. (J). (gr. 2-5). 2010. pap. 5.95 *(978-0-7613-3947-2(7));* 2009. 15.95 *(978-0-8225-8883-2(8))* Lerner Publishing Group. (Carolrhoda Bks.).

—Made with Love for Mom. Ikids Staff. 2008. (ENG.). 24p. (J). (gr. 1-17). 7.99 *(978-1-58476-660-5(3),* IKIDS) Innovative Kids.

—Mallory & Mary Ann Take New York. Friedman, Laurie. (Mallory Ser.: 19). (ENG.). 160p. (J). (gr. 2-5). 2014. pap. 5.95 *(978-1-4677-0935-4(2),* Darby Creek); 2013. 15.95 *(978-0-7613-6074-2(3))* Lerner Publishing Group.

—Mallory Goes Green! Friedman, Laurie. (Mallory Ser.). 160p. (J). 2011. pap. 33.92 *(978-0-7613-7606-4(2),* Darby Creek); 2011. (ENG.). (gr. 2-5). pap. 5.95 *(978-0-7613-3949-6(3));* 2010. (ENG.). (gr. 2-5). 15.95 *(978-0-8225-8885-6(4),* Carolrhoda Bks.) Lerner Publishing Group.

—Mallory in the Spotlight. Friedman, Laurie. (Mallory Ser.). 2011. pap. 33.92 *(978-0-7613-8359-8(X),* Darby Creek); 2011. (ENG.). 160p. (J). (gr. 2-5). pap. 5.95 *(978-0-7613-3948-9(5),* Darby Creek); 2010. (ENG.). 160p. (J). (gr. 2-5). 15.95 *(978-0-8225-8884-9(6),* Carolrhoda Bks.) Lerner Publishing Group.

—Mallory McDonald, Baby Expert. Friedman, Laurie B. 2014. (Mallory Ser.: 22). (ENG.). 152p. (J). (gr. 2-5). 15.95 *(978-1-4677-0922-4(0))* Lerner Publishing Group.

—Mallory McDonald, Super Snoop. Friedman, Laurie. (Mallory Ser.: 18). (ENG.). 152p. (J). (gr. 2-5). 2013. pap. 5.95 *(978-1-4677-0929-3(8),* Darby Creek); 2012. 15.95 *(978-0-7613-6073-5(5))* Lerner Publishing Group.

—Mallory's Guide to Boys, Brothers, Dads, & Dogs. Friedman, Laurie. (Mallory Ser.). 160p. (J). (gr. 2-5). 2012. pap. 33.92 *(978-0-7613-9206-4(8),* Darby Creek); 2012. (ENG.). pap. 5.95 *(978-0-7613-5250-1(3),* Darby Creek); 2011. (ENG.). 15.95 *(978-0-8225-8886-3(2),* Carolrhoda Bks.) Lerner Publishing Group.

—Mallory's Super Sleepover. Friedman, Laurie. (Mallory Ser.: 16). (ENG.). 160p. (J). (gr. 2-5). 2012. pap. 5.95 *(978-1-4677-0209-6(9));* No. 16. 2011. 15.95 *(978-0-8225-8887-0(0))* Lerner Publishing Group. (Darby Creek).

—Mama's Many Hats. Erhard, Lorie. 2014. (ENG.). 32p. (J). 18.99 *(978-0-9914701-4-3(1))* Bumble Bee Bks.

—Mary Cassatt: Family Pictures. O'Connor, Jane. 2003. (Smart about Art Ser.). (ENG.). 32p. (J). (gr. k-4). mass mkt. 5.99 *(978-0-448-43152-9(1),* Grosset & Dunlap) Penguin Publishing Group.

—Oh Boy, Mallory. Friedman, Laurie. (Mallory Ser.: 17). (ENG.). 160p. (J). (gr. 2-5). 2013. pap. 5.95 *(978-1-4677-0863-0(1));* 2012. 15.95 *(978-0-7613-6072-8(7),* Darby Creek) Lerner Publishing Group.

—Play It Again, Mallory. Friedman, Laurie. (Mallory Ser.: 20). 160p. (J). (gr. 2-5). 2014. pap. 5.95 *(978-1-4677-0936-1(0));* 2013. (ENG.). 15.95 *(978-0-7613-6075-9(1))* Lerner Publishing Group. (Darby Creek).

—Pocketdoodles for Girls, 1 vol. Wood, Anita. 2010. (ENG.). 272p. (J). (gr. 1). 9.99 *(978-1-4236-0755-7(4))* Gibbs Smith, Publisher.

—Pocketdoodles for Princesses, 1 vol. Wood, Anita. 2011. (ENG.). 272p. (J). (gr. 3). 9.99 *(978-1-4236-1877-5(7))* Gibbs Smith, Publisher.

—Red, White, & True Blue Mallory. Friedman, Laurie. (Mallory Ser.: 11). (ENG.). 184p. (J). (gr. 2-5). 2010. pap. 5.95 *(978-0-7613-3946-5(9));* 2009. 15.95 *(978-0-8225-8882-5(X))* Lerner Publishing Group. (Carolrhoda Bks.).

—Step Fourth, Mallory! Friedman, Laurie. (Mallory Ser.: 10). (ENG.). 176p. (J). (gr. 2-5). 2009. pap. 5.95 *(978-1-58013-842-0(X),* First Avenue Editions); 2008. 15.95 *(978-0-8225-8881-8(1),* Carolrhoda Bks.) Lerner Publishing Group.

—Three's Company, Mallory! Friedman, Laurie. 2014. (Mallory Ser.: 21). (ENG.). 160p. (J). (gr. 2-5). 15.95 *(978-1-4677-0921-7(2),* Darby Creek) Lerner Publishing Group.

—Welcome to the Daisy Flower Garden. Tuchman, Laura. 2008. 88p. (J). *(978-0-88441-709-5(3))* Girl Scouts of the USA.

Kallai, Kriszta Nagy. Silent Night. Howie, Vicki. 2009. 32p. (J). (gr. -1). pap. 13.49 *(978-0-7586-1779-8(8))* Concordia Publishing Hse.

Kallai, Nagy. Animal Lullabies. Ross, Mandy. 2007. (Poems for the Young Ser.). (ENG.). 32p. (J). *(978-1-84643-052-7(6))* Child's Play International Ltd.

Kallai Nagy, Krisztina. Animal Lullabies. Ross, Mandy. 2005. (Poems for the Young Ser.). (ENG.). 32p. (J). *(978-1-904550-93-8(2))* Child's Play International Ltd.

—The Lion Storyteller Bible, 4 vols. Hartman, Bob. 2014. (ENG.). 160p. (J). (gr. k-2). 22.99 *(978-0-7459-6433-1(8))* Lion Hudson PLC GBR. Dist: Independent Pubs. Group.

—My Advent Calendar Christmas Book. Jackson, Antonia. 2014. (ENG.). 32p. (J). (-2). 9.99 *(978-0-7459-6392-1(7))* Lion Hudson PLC GBR. Dist: Independent Pubs. Group.

Kallanovic, Dubravka. My First Big Book Shapes & Colors. Poitier, Anton. ed. 2012. (Novelty Ser.). (ENG.). 16p. (J). 9.99 *(978-1-61067-089-0(2))* Kane Miller.

Kalman, Lola. Bullies to Buddies - How to Turn Your Enemies into Friends! How to Turn Your Enemies into Friends! Kalman, Izzy C. 2005. (ENG.). 128p. (YA). per. 15.00 *(978-0-9706482-1-1(9))* The Wisdom Pages, Inc.

Kalman, Maira. Girls Standing on Lawns. Handler, Daniel. 2014. (ENG.). 64p. (gr. 3-7). 14.95 *(978-0-87070-908-1(9))* Museum of Modern Art.

—Why We Broke Up. Handler, Daniel. (ENG.). 368p. (YA). (gr. 10-17). 2013. pap. 15.00 *(978-0-316-12726-4(4));* 2011. 20.00 *(978-0-316-12725-7(6))* Little, Brown Bks. for Young Readers.

—13 Words. Snicket, Lemony. (ENG.). 40p. (J). (gr. -1-3). 2014. pap. 6.99 *(978-0-06-166467-0(7));* 2010. 16.99 *(978-0-06-166465-6(0))* HarperCollins Pubs.

Kalman, Maira. Fireboat: The Heroic Adventures of the John J. Harvey. Kalman, Maira. 2005. (ENG.). 48p. (J). (gr. -1-3). reprint ed. pap. 6.99 *(978-0-14-240362-4(8),* Puffin) Penguin Publishing Group.

—Looking at Lincoln. Kalman, Maira. 2012. (ENG.). 32p. (J). (gr. k-3). 17.99 *(978-0-399-24039-3(X),* Nancy Paulsen Bks.) Penguin Publishing Group.

—Smartypants (Pete in School) Kalman, Maira. 2003. (ENG.). 32p. (J). (gr. k-3). 17.99 *(978-0-399-23478-1(0),* Putnam Juvenile) Penguin Publishing Group.

—Thomas Jefferson: Life, Liberty & the Pursuit of Everything. Kalman, Maira. 2014. (ENG.). 40p. (J). (gr. k-3). 17.99 *(978-0-399-24040-9(3),* Nancy Paulsen Bks.) Penguin Publishing Group.

Kalmenoff, Matthew. Charles John Seghers: Pioneer in Alaska. Bosco, Antoinette. 2011. 194p. 42.95 *(978-1-258-01868-9(3))* Literary Licensing, LLC.

—In the Steps of the Great American Herpetologist. Wright, A. Gilbert. 2014. (ENG.). 128p. (J). (gr. 2-6). pap. 11.95 *(978-1-59077-360-4(8))* Evans, M. & Co., Inc.

Kalpart. Remy's First Day of School. Davis, Melissa. 2013. 20p. pap. 10.95 *(978-1-62212-480-0(4),* Strategic Bk. Publishing) Strategic Book Publishing & Rights Agency (SBPRA).

—Seven Cats & the Big Gray Fence. Risselada, Melissa. 2013. 28p. pap. 12.50 *(978-1-62516-777-4(6),* Strategic Bk. Publishing) Strategic Book Publishing & Rights Agency (SBPRA).

—The Tiny Tomato & His Terrific Manners. Prignano, Barbara. 2013. 32p. pap. 12.95 *(978-1-62857-080-9(6),* Strategic Bk. Publishing) Strategic Book Publishing & Rights Agency (SBPRA).

K

Kalpart Designs. The Big Squeal: A True Story about a Homeless Pig's Search for Life, Liberty & the Pursuit of Happiness. Alexander, Carol. 2012. (ENG.). 24p. (J). 24.00 *(978-1-61009-036-0(5),* Acorn) Oak Tree Publishing.

Kaltenborn, Karl. Ikky Dikky Dak: Magical Adventures with Googler! Book Two. McGee, Helen. 2011. pap. 21.95 *(978-1-60494-573-7(7))* Wheatmark.

Kalthoff, Robert. Viking Life. 2005. spiral bd. 20.00 net. *(978-0-9762042-4-4(X))* Hubbell, Gerald.

Kalvoda, LeAnn. Lost & Found Teaching Unit. Holmes, Wayne & Pelletier, Christine. rev. ed. 2003. 96p. (J). ring bd. 35.00 *(978-1-58302-232-0(5))* One Way St., Inc.

Kalyan, Srivi. Jungu, the Baiga Princess. Rajan, Vithal. 2015. 112p. pap. 12.00 *(978-93-83074-05-1(1))* 'Zubaan Bks. IND. Dist: Chicago Distribution Ctr.

Kam, Kathleen. The Legend of Kuamo'o Mo'okini & Hamumu the Great Whale. Lum, Leimomi o. Kamahae Kuamoo Mookini. 2004. 24p. (J). 12.95 *(978-1-58178-036-9(2))* Bishop Museum Pr.

Kambadais, George. Rudolph the Red-Nosed Reindeer: the Island of Misfit Toys. Deneen, Brendan. 2014. (Rudolph the Red-Nosed Reindeer Ser.: 1). (ENG.). 80p. (J). (gr. 2-7). pap. 9.99 *(978-1-250-05063-2(4))* Square Fish.

Kamerer, Justin & Bascle, Brian. The Salem Witch Trials, 1 vol. Martin, Michael & Martin, Michael J. 2005. (Graphic History Ser.). (ENG.). 32p. (gr. 3-4). 29.99 *(978-0-7368-3847-4(3),* Graphic Library) Capstone Pr., Inc.

Kami, Y. Z. The Sun, the Moon, & the Gardener's Son. Bronn, Charles Heil. 2006. 30p. (J). (gr. 4-12). reprint ed. 16.00 *(978-1-4223-5222-9(6))* DIANE Publishing Co.

Kamijyo, Akimine. Samurai Deeper Kyo, 18 vols. Kamijyo, Akimine. rev. ed. (YA). Vol. 4. 2003. 192p. pap. 14.99 *(978-1-59182-249-3(1));* Vol. 11. 2005. 200p. pap. 14.99 *(978-1-59532-451-1(8))* TOKYOPOP, Inc. (Tokyopop Adult).

Kamijyo, Akimine. Samurai Deeper Kyo, Vol. 10. Kamijyo, Akimine, creator. rev. ed. 2004. 208p. (YA). pap. 14.99 *(978-1-59532-450-4(X),* Tokyopop Adult) TOKYOPOP, Inc.

Kaminski, Karol. Every Body Is a Gift: God Made Us to Love. Ashour, Monica. 2015. (J). 12.95 *(978-0-8198-2376-2(7))* Pauline Bks. & Media.

—Every Body Is Smart: God Helps Me Listen & Choose. Ashour, Monica. 2015. (J). 12.95 *(978-0-8198-2372-4(4))* Pauline Bks. & Media.

—Everybody Has a Body: God Made Boys & Girls. Ashour, Monica. 2015. (J). 12.95 *(978-0-8198-2368-7(6))* Pauline Bks. & Media.

—God Made Wonderful Me! Monchamp, Genny. 2008. 14p. (J). (gr. -1). 8.95 *(978-0-8198-3108-8(5))* Pauline Bks. & Media.

—Shine: Choices to Make God Smile. Monchamp, Genny. 2011. (J). 10.95 *(978-0-8198-7149-7(4))* Pauline Bks. & Media.

—Too, Too Hot! Schmauss, Judy Kentor. 2006. (Reader's Clubhouse Level 1 Reader Ser.). (ENG.). 24p. (J). (gr. 1-4). pap. 3.99 *(978-0-7641-3285-8(7))* Barron's Educational Series, Inc.

Kaminski, Karol, jt. illus. see Williams, Ted.

Kaminsky, Jef. Dear Santasaurus. McAnulty, Stacy. 2013. (ENG.). 32p. (J). (gr. k-3). 15.95 *(978-1-59078-876-9(1))* Boyds Mills Pr.

—Monstergarten. Mahoney, Daniel J. 2013. (ENG.). 40p. (J). (gr. -1-k). 16.99 *(978-1-250-01441-2(7))* Feiwel & Friends.

Kamio, Yoko. Boys over Flowers. Kamio, Yoko. (Boys over Flowers Ser.). (ENG.). Vol. 11. 2005. 184p. (YA). pap. 9.99 *(978-1-59116-747-1(7));* Vol. 14. 2005. 192p. pap. 9.99 *(978-1-4215-0018-8(3));* Vol. 18. 2006. 208p. pap. 9.99 *(978-1-4215-0532-9(0))* Viz Media.

—Boys over Flowers: Volume 4. Kamio, Yoko. 2004. (Boys over Flowers: Hana Yori Dango Ser.). 190p. (YA). (gr. 7-12). lib. bdg. 18.75 *(978-0-613-83674-6(X),* Turtleback) Turtleback Bks.

—Hana Yori Dango. Kamio, Yoko. 2004. (Boys over Flowers Ser.). (ENG.). 200p. Vol. 7. pap. 9.95 *(978-1-59116-370-1(6));* Vol. 8. pap. 9.95 *(978-1-59116-371-8(4))* Viz Media.

Kammeraad, Kevin & Hipp, Ryan. A Curious Glimpse of Michigan. Kammeraad, Kevin & Kammeraad, Stephanie. 32p. (J). 2006. (gr. 4-7). pap. 9.95 *(978-0-9749412-9-5(8));* 2004. (gr. 3-7). 19.95 *(978-0-9712692-9-3(7))* EDCO Publishing, Inc.

Kanae, Billy. Hanauma Bay. Markrich, Mike & Bourke, Bob. (J). pap. 5.95 *(978-0-9643421-0-1(3))* Ecology Comics.

Kanagy, Audrey Ann Zimmerman, jt. illus. see Zimmerman, Edith Fay Martin.

Kanako & Yuzuru. Skeleton Key. Horowitz, Anthony. 2009. (Alex Rider Ser.: Bk. 3). (ENG.). 128p. (J). (gr. 5-18). pap. 14.99 *(978-0-399-25418-5(8),* Philomel) Penguin Publishing Group.

Kanako, jt. illus. see Yuzuru.

Kanarek, Michael. I Wanna Be Purr-Fect! ShowCat. Corrado, Diane. 2006. 48p. (J). 14.95 incl. audio compact disk *(978-0-9795049-2-1(9))* Kidz Entertainment, Inc.

Kane, Barry, photos by. Fairy Houses & Beyond! Kane, Tracy. 2008. (Fairy Houses Series(r) Ser.). (ENG.). 62p. (J). (gr. -1-k). 15.95 *(978-0-9708104-6-5(6))* Light-Beams Publishing.

Kane, Brenden. Abby's Adventures: Abby the Pirate. Hartley, Susan. 2005. 37p. pap. 24.95 *(978-1-4137-4491-0(5))* PublishAmerica, Inc.

Kane, Gil, et al. The Incredible Hulk Vol. 2, Vol. 2. Lee, Stan. 2012. (ENG.). 256p. (J). (gr. -1-17). pap. 24.99 *(978-0-7851-5883-7(9))* Marvel Worldwide, Inc.

—Thor Epic Collection: A Kingdom Lost. 2014. (ENG.). 480p. (J). (gr. 4-17). pap. 34.99 *(978-0-7851-8862-9(2))* Marvel Worldwide, Inc.

Kane, Gil, jt. illus. see Andru, Ross.

Kane, Herb K., jt. illus. see Feher, Joseph.

Kane, John, photos by. The Human Alphabet. Pilobolus. Pilobolus. 2003. 40p. (J). *(978-1-58717-225-0(9));* lib. bdg. *(978-1-58717-226-7(7))* Chronicle Bks. LLC. (SeaStar Bks.).

Kane, Sharon. Kitty & Me. Kane, Sharon. 2014. (ENG.). 32p. (J). (gr. -1-2). 15.99 *(978-0-8050-9705-4(8),* Holt, Henry & Co. Bks. For Young Readers) Holt, Henry & Co.

—Little Mommy. Kane, Sharon. 2008. (Little Golden Book Ser.). (ENG.). 24p. (J). (gr. -1-2). 3.99 *(978-0-375-84820-9(7),* Golden Bks.) Random Hse. Children's Bks.

Kane, Tracy. The Magic of Color. Kane, Tracy. l.t. ed. 2005. (ENG.). 40p. (J). (gr. -1-k). 17.95 *(978-0-9766289-0-3(2))* Light-Beams Publishing.

Kaneda, Mario. Girls Bravo, Vol. 2. Kaneda, Mario. 2nd rev. ed. 2005. (Girls Bravo Ser.). 192p. pap. 9.99 *(978-1-59816-041-3(9),* Tokyopop Adult) TOKYOPOP, Inc.

Kaneko, Shinya. Culdcept, Vol. 4. Kaneko, Shinya. rev. ed. 2005. 234p. pap. 14.99 *(978-1-59532-447-4(X),* Tokyopop Adult) TOKYOPOP, Inc.

Kanekuni, Daniel. Okazu at the Zoo. Ide, Laurie Shimizu. 2006. (J). 12.95 *(978-1-56647-776-5(X))* Mutual Publishing LLC.

Kanemoto, Dan. Happy Easter, Sprinkles! Silverhardt, Lauryn. 2008. (Blue's Clues Ser.). (ENG.). 12p. (J). (gr. -1-k). bds. 5.99 *(978-1-4169-4775-2(2),* Simon Spotlight/Nickelodeon) Simon Spotlight/Nickelodeon.

Kanesata, Yukio. Kamikaze Girls. Takemoto, Novala. 2006. (Kamikaza Girls Ser.). (ENG.). 208p. pap. 8.99 *(978-1-4215-0268-7(2))* Viz Media.

Kaneshiro, Scott. Limu: The Blue Turtle & His Hawaiian Garden. Armitage, Kimo. 2004. 28p. (J). 11.95 *(978-0-931548-64-2(0))* Island Heritage Publishing.

Kaneyoshi, Izumi. Doubt!! Kaneyoshi, Izumi. 2005. (Doubt Ser.). (ENG.). 192p. Vol. 4. pap. 9.99 *(978-1-59116-984-0(4));* Vol. 5. pap. 9.99 *(978-1-4215-0055-3(8))* Viz Media.

Kang, Andrea. Ball: Baby Unplugged. Hutton, John. Hutton, John, ed. 2012. (Baby Unplugged Ser.). (ENG.). 14p. (J). (— 1). bds. 7.99 *(978-1-936669-05-9(6))* Blue Manatee Press.

—Beach: Baby Unplugged. Hutton, John. 2012. (Baby Unplugged Ser.). (ENG.). 14p. (J). (— 1). bds. 7.99 *(978-1-936669-07-3(2))* Blue Manatee Press.

—Blanket: Baby Unplugged. Hutton, John. 2011. (Baby Unplugged Ser.). (ENG.). 14p. (J). (— 1). bds. 7.99 *(978-1-936669-00-4(5))* Blue Manatee Press.

—Blocks: Baby Unplugged. Hutton, John. Hutton, John, ed. 2013. (Baby Unplugged Ser.). (ENG.). 14p. (J). (— 1). bds. 7.99 *(978-1-936669-13-4(7))* Blue Manatee Press.

—Book: Baby Unplugged. Hutton, John. Hutton, John, ed. 2012. (Baby Unplugged Ser.). (ENG.). 14p. (J). (— 1). bds. 7.99 *(978-1-936669-06-6(4))* Blue Manatee Press.

—Box: Baby Unplugged. Hutton, John. 2012. (Baby Unplugged Ser.). (ENG.). 14p. (J). (— 1). bds. 7.99 *(978-1-936669-08-0(0))* Blue Manatee Press.

—Pets: Baby Unplugged. Hutton, John. 2011. (Baby Unplugged Ser.). (ENG.). 14p. (J). (— 1). bds. 7.99 *(978-1-936669-02-8(1))* Blue Manatee Press.

—Wet: Baby Unplugged. Hutton, John. Hutton, John, ed. 2013. (Baby Unplugged Ser.). (ENG.). 14p. (J). (— 1). bds. 7.99 *(978-1-936669-14-1(5))* Blue Manatee Press.

—Yard: Baby Unplugged. Hutton, John. 2011. (Baby Unplugged Ser.). (ENG.). 14p. (J). (— 1). bds. 7.99 *(978-1-936669-01-1(3))* Blue Manatee Press.

Kang, Mi-Sun. The Lazy Man/the Spring of Youth. 2008. (Korean Folk Tales for Children Ser.: Vol. 3). (ENG & KOR.). 45p. (J). (gr. 2-5). lib. bdg. 14.50 *(978-0-930878-73-3(6))* Hollym International Corp.

—The Snail Lady/the Magic Vase. 2008. (Korean Folk Tales for Children Ser.: Vol. 6). (ENG & KOR.). 45p. (J). (gr. 2-5). lib. bdg. 14.50 *(978-0-930878-89-4(2))* Hollym International Corp.

Kang, Mi-Sun & Kim, Yon-Kyong. Brave Hong Gil-Dong/the Man Who Bought the Shade of a Tree. 2008. (Korean Folk Tales for Children Ser.: Vol. 8). (ENG & KOR.). 45p. (J). (gr. 2-5). lib. bdg. 14.50 *(978-0-930878-91-7(4))* Hollym International Corp.

—The Faithful Daughter Sim Cheong/the Little Frog Who Never Listened. 2008. (Korean Folk Tales for Children Ser.: Vol. 9). (ENG & KOR.). 43p. (J). (gr. 2-5). lib. bdg. 14.50 *(978-0-930878-92-4(2))* Hollym International Corp.

Kang, Mi-Sun, jt. illus. see Kim, Yon-Kyong.

Kang Won, Kim. The Queen's Knight, 15 vols. Kang Won, Kim. 5th rev. ed. 2006. (Queen's Knight Ser.: Vol. 5). 192p. per. 9.99 *(978-1-59532-261-6(2))* TOKYOPOP, Inc.

Kang Won, Kim. The Queen's Knight. Kang Won, Kim, creator. 2005. Vol. 3. 3rd rev. ed. 208p. pap. 9.99 *(978-1-59532-259-3(0));* Vol. 4. rev. ed. 192p. pap. 9.99 *(978-1-59532-260-9(4))* TOKYOPOP, Inc.

Kania, Matt. Texas. Peterson, Sheryl. 2009. (This Land Called America Ser.). 32p. (YA). (gr. 3-6). 19.95 *(978-1-58341-796-6(6))* Creative Co., The.

Kanitsch, Christine. Harry the Hopetown Hermit Crab. Williams, Jonnie. Date not set. (Abaco Ser.). (J). (gr. -1-3). pap. 5.97 *(978-0-9657849-1-7(6))* Island Ink.

Kann, Victoria. Aqualicious. Kann, Victoria. 2015. (ENG.). 40p. (J). (gr. -1-3). 17.99 *(978-0-06-233016-1(0))* HarperCollins Pubs.

—Cherry Blossom. Kann, Victoria. 2015. (I Can Read Book 1 Ser.). (ENG.). 32p. (J). (gr. -1-3). pap. 3.99 *(978-0-06-224594-6(5))* HarperCollins Pubs.

—Emeraldalicious. Kann, Victoria. 2013. 40p. (J). (gr. -1-3). (ENG.). 17.99 *(978-0-06-178126-1(6));* lib. bdg. 18.89 *(978-0-06-178127-8(4))* HarperCollins Pubs.

—Fairy House. Kann, Victoria. 2013. (I Can Read Book 1 Ser.). (ENG.). 32p. (J). (gr. -1-3). 16.99 *(978-0-06-218783-3(X))* HarperCollins Pubs.

—Flower Girl. Kann, Victoria. 2013. (Pinkalicious Ser.). (ENG.). 24p. (J). (gr. -1-3). pap. 3.99 *(978-0-06-218766-6(X),* HarperFestival) HarperCollins Pubs.

—Goldidoodles. Kann, Victoria. 2013. (Pinkalicious Ser.). (ENG.). 128p. (J). (gr. -1-3). pap. 12.99 *(978-0-06-223334-9(3),* HarperFestival) HarperCollins Pubs.

—Goldilicious. Kann, Victoria. 2009. 40p. (J). (gr. k-3). (ENG.). 17.99 *(978-0-06-124408-7(2));* lib. bdg. 18.89 *(978-0-06-124409-4(0))* HarperCollins Pubs.

—Love, Pinkalicious. Kann, Victoria. 2009. (Pinkalicious Ser.). (ENG.). 12p. (J). (gr. -1-2). pap. 6.99 *(978-0-06-192731-7(7),* HarperFestival) HarperCollins Pubs.

—Merry Pinkmas! Kann, Victoria. 2013. (Pinkalicious Ser.). (ENG.). 24p. (J). (gr. -1-3). pap. 6.99 *(978-0-06-218912-7(3),* HarperFestival) HarperCollins Pubs.

—Mother's Day Surprise. Kann, Victoria. 2015. (Pinkalicious Ser.). (ENG.). 24p. (J). (gr. -1-3). pap. 6.99 *(978-0-06-224587-8(2),* HarperFestival) HarperCollins Pubs.

—The Perfectly Pink Collection. Kann, Victoria. 2010. (Pinkalicious Ser.). (ENG.). 100p. (J). (gr. k-3). 15.99 *(978-0-06-199048-9(5),* HarperFestival) HarperCollins Pubs.

—Pink-a-Rama. Kann, Victoria. 2012. (I Can Read Book 1 Ser.). (ENG.). 96p. (J). (gr. k-3). pap. 16.99 *(978-0-06-198966-7(5))* HarperCollins Pubs.

—Pink of Hearts. Kann, Victoria. 2011. (Pinkalicious Ser.). (ENG.). 24p. (J). (gr. -1-2). pap. 6.99 *(978-0-06-198923-0(1),* HarperFestival) HarperCollins Pubs.

—Pink or Treat! Kann, Victoria. 2013. (Pinkalicious Ser.). (ENG.). 24p. (J). (gr. -1-3). pap. 4.99 *(978-0-06-218770-3(8),* HarperFestival) HarperCollins Pubs.

—Pinkadoodles. Kann, Victoria. 2011. (Pinkalicious Ser.). (ENG.). 128p. (J). (gr. -1-7). pap. 12.99 *(978-0-06-202265-3(2),* HarperFestival) HarperCollins Pubs.

—Pinkafy Your World. Kann, Victoria. 2013. (Pinkalicious Ser.). (ENG.). 12p. (J). (gr. -1-3). pap. 6.99 *(978-0-06-223333-2(5),* HarperFestival) HarperCollins Pubs.

—Pinkalicious. Kann, Victoria. 2013. (Pinkalicious Ser.). (ENG.). 192p. (J). (gr. -1-3). 11.99 *(978-0-06-218800-7(3))* HarperCollins Pubs.

—Pinkalicious. Kann, Victoria. Kann, Elizabeth. (Pinkalicious Ser.). 40p. (J). 2011. (SPA.). (gr. k-3). 17.99 *(978-0-06-179959-4(9),* Rayo); 2006. (ENG.). (gr. -1-3). 17.99 *(978-0-06-077639-8(0));* 2006. (gr. -1-3). lib. bdg. 17.89 *(978-0-06-077640-4(4))* HarperCollins Pubs.

—Pinkalicious: Crazy Hair Day. Kann, Victoria. 2014. (Pinkalicious Ser.). (ENG.). 24p. (J). (gr. -1-3). pap. 3.99 *(978-0-06-218768-0(6),* HarperFestival) HarperCollins Pubs.

—Pinkalicious: Pink Around the Rink. Kann, Victoria. 2010. (I Can Read Book 1 Ser.). (ENG.). 32p. (J). (gr. -1-3). 16.99 *(978-0-06-192880-2(1));* pap. 3.99 *(978-0-06-192879-6(8))* HarperCollins Pubs.

—Pinkalicious: Pinkie Promise. Kann, Victoria. 2011. (I Can Read Book 1 Ser.). (ENG.). 32p. (J). (gr. -1-3). pap. 3.99 *(978-0-06-192887-1(9))* HarperCollins Pubs.

—Pinkalicious: School Rules! Kann, Victoria. 2010. (I Can Read Book 1 Ser.). (ENG.). 32p. (J). (gr. -1-3). 16.99 *(978-0-06-192886-4(0))* HarperCollins Pubs.

—Pinkalicious: The Royal Tea Party. Kann, Victoria. 2014. (I Can Read Book 1 Ser.). (ENG.). 32p. (J). (gr. -1-3). pap. 3.99 *(978-0-06-218791-8(0))* HarperCollins Pubs.

—Pinkalicious - Cherry Blossom. Kann, Victoria. 2015. (I Can Read Book 1 Ser.). (ENG.). 32p. (J). (gr. -1-3). 16.99 *(978-0-06-224593-9(7))* HarperCollins Pubs.

—Pinkalicious - Eggstraordinary Easter. Kann, Victoria. 2014. (Pinkalicious Ser.). (ENG.). 24p. (J). (gr. -1-3). pap. 4.99 *(978-0-06-218772-7(4),* HarperFestival) HarperCollins Pubs.

—Pinkalicious - Puptastic! Kann, Victoria. 2013. (I Can Read Book 1 Ser.). (ENG.). 32p. (J). (gr. -1-3). pap. 3.99 *(978-0-06-218785-7(6))* HarperCollins Pubs.

—Pinkalicious - Soccer Star. Kann, Victoria. 2012. (I Can Read Book 1 Ser.). (ENG.). 32p. (J). (gr. -1-3). pap. 3.99 *(978-0-06-198964-3(9))* HarperCollins Pubs.

—Pinkalicious - Thanksgiving Helper. Kann, Victoria. 2014. (Pinkalicious Ser.). (ENG.). 24p. (J). (gr. -1-3). pap. 6.99 *(978-0-06-218774-1(0),* HarperFestival) HarperCollins Pubs.

—Pinkalicious - Tutu-Rrific! Kann, Victoria. 2014. (I Can Read Book 1 Ser.). (ENG.). 32p. (J). (gr. -1-3). pap. 3.99 *(978-0-06-218795-6(3))* HarperCollins Pubs.

—Pinkalicious & the Cupcake Calamity. Kann, Victoria. 2013. (I Can Read Book 1 Ser.). (ENG.). 32p. (J). (gr. -1-3). 16.99 *(978-0-06-218777-2(5));* pap. 3.99 *(978-0-06-218776-5(7))* HarperCollins Pubs.

—Pinkalicious & the New Teacher. Kann, Victoria. 2014. (Pinkalicious Ser.). (ENG.). 24p. (J). (gr. -1-3). pap. 6.99 *(978-0-06-218913-4(1),* HarperFestival) HarperCollins Pubs.

—Pinkalicious & the Perfect Present. Kann, Victoria. 2014. (I Can Read Book 1 Ser.). (ENG.). 32p. (J). (gr. -1-3). 16.99 *(978-0-06-218789-5(9));* pap. 3.99 *(978-0-06-218788-8(0))* HarperCollins Pubs.

—Pinkalicious & the Pink Drink. Kann, Victoria. 2010. (Pinkalicious Ser.). (ENG.). 24p. (J). (gr. -1-3). pap. 3.99 *(978-0-06-192732-4(5),* HarperFestival) HarperCollins Pubs.

—Pinkalicious & the Pink Hat Parade. Kann, Victoria. 2012. (Pinkalicious Ser.). (ENG.). 24p. (J). (gr. -1-2). pap. 6.99 *(978-0-06-198960-5(6),* HarperFestival) HarperCollins Pubs.

—Pinkalicious & the Pink Parakeet. Kann, Victoria. 2015. (I Can Read Book 1 Ser.). (ENG.). 32p. (J). (gr. -1-3). 16.99 *(978-0-06-224596-0(1))* HarperCollins Pubs.

—Pinkalicious & the Pink Pumpkin. Kann, Victoria. 2011. (Pinkalicious Ser.). (ENG.). 16p. (J). (gr. -1-2). pap. 6.99 *(978-0-06-198961-2(4),* HarperFestival) HarperCollins Pubs.

—Pinkalicious & the Pinkatastic Zoo Day. Kann, Victoria. 2012. (I Can Read Book 1 Ser.). (ENG.). 32p. (J). (gr. -1-3). 16.99 *(978-0-06-218780-2(5));* pap. 3.99 *(978-0-06-218779-6(1))* HarperCollins Pubs.

Kann, Victoria. Pinkalicious & the Sick Day. Kann, Victoria. 2015. (I Can Read Book 1 Ser.). (ENG.). 32p. (J). (gr. -1-3). 16.99 ***(978-0-06-224599-1(6))*** HarperCollins Pubs.

—Pinkalicious & the Snow Globe. Kann, Victoria. 2015. (Pinkalicious Ser.). (ENG.). 24p. (J). (gr. -1-3). pap. 4.99 ***(978-0-06-224588-5(0),*** HarperFestival) HarperCollins Pubs.

Kann, Victoria. Pinkalicious Cupcake Cookbook. Kann, Victoria. 2013. (Pinkalicious Ser.). (ENG.). 64p. (J). (gr. 1-5). 14.99 *(978-0-06-202357-5(8),* HarperFestival) HarperCollins Pubs.

Kann, Victoria. The Pinkalicious Take-Along Storybook Set. Kann, Victoria. 2015. (Pinkalicious Ser.). (ENG.). 120p. (J). (gr. -1-3). pap. 11.99 ***(978-0-06-241080-1(6),*** HarperFestival) HarperCollins Pubs.

Kann, Victoria. The Pinkatastic Giant Sticker Book. Kann, Victoria. 2011. (Pinkalicious Ser.). (ENG.). 100p. (J). (gr. -1-2). pap. 12.99 *(978-0-06-192889-5(5),* HarperFestival) HarperCollins Pubs.

—The Pinkerrific Playdate. Kann, Victoria. 2011. (I Can Read Book 1 Ser.). (ENG.). 32p. (J). (gr. -1-3). 16.99 *(978-0-06-192884-0(4));* pap. 3.99 *(978-0-06-192883-3(6))* HarperCollins Pubs.

—Pinkie Promise. Kann, Victoria. 2011. (I Can Read Book 1 Ser.). (ENG.). 32p. (J). (gr. -1-3). 16.99 *(978-0-06-192888-8(7))* HarperCollins Pubs.

—The Princess of Pink Slumber Party. Kann, Victoria. 2012. (I Can Read Book 1 Ser.). (ENG.). 32p. (J). (gr. -1-3). 16.99 *(978-0-06-198963-6(0));* pap. 3.99 *(978-0-06-198962-9(2))* HarperCollins Pubs.

—The Princess of Pink Treasury. Kann, Victoria. 2011. (Pinkalicious Ser.). (ENG.). 208p. (J). (gr. -1-3). 19.99 *(978-0-06-210236-2(2))* HarperCollins Pubs.

—Puptastic! Kann, Victoria. 2013. (I Can Read Book 1 Ser.). (ENG.). 32p. (J). (gr. -1-3). 16.99 *(978-0-06-218786-4(4))* HarperCollins Pubs.

—Purpledoodles. Kann, Victoria. 2012. (Pinkalicious Ser.). (ENG.). 128p. (J). (gr. -1-7). pap. 12.99 *(978-0-06-208586-3(7),* HarperFestival) HarperCollins Pubs.

—Purplicious. Kann, Victoria. Kann, Elizabeth. 2007. 40p. (J). (gr. k-3). (ENG.). 17.99 *(978-0-06-124405-6(8));* lib. bdg. 17.89 *(978-0-06-124406-3(6))* HarperCollins Pubs.

—School Lunch. Kann, Victoria. 2015. (Pinkalicious Ser.). (ENG.). 24p. (J). (gr. -1-3). pap. 4.99 *(978-0-06-224590-8(2),* HarperFestival) HarperCollins Pubs.

—School Rules! Kann, Victoria. 2010. (I Can Read Book 1 Ser.). (ENG.). 32p. (J). (gr. -1-3). pap. 3.99 *(978-0-06-192885-7(2))* HarperCollins Pubs.

—Silverlicious. Kann, Victoria. 2011. 40p. (J). (gr. k-3). (ENG.). 17.99 *(978-0-06-178123-0(1));* lib. bdg. 18.89 *(978-0-06-178124-7(X))* HarperCollins Pubs.

—Soccer Star. Kann, Victoria. 2012. (I Can Read Book 1 Ser.). (ENG.). 32p. (J). (gr. -1-3). 16.99 *(978-0-06-198965-0(7))* HarperCollins Pubs.

—Tickled Pink. Kann, Victoria. 2010. (Pinkalicious Ser.). (ENG.). 24p. (J). (gr. -1-3). pap. 3.99 *(978-0-06-192877-2(1),* HarperFestival) HarperCollins Pubs.

—Tickled Pink. Kann, Victoria. ed. 2010. (Pinkalicious Ser.). lib. bdg. 13.55 *(978-0-606-14869-6(8),* Turtleback) Turtleback Bks.

Kanno, Aya. Otomen. Kanno, Aya. (Otomen Ser.: 8). (ENG.). 2010. 200p. pap. 9.99 *(978-1-4215-3591-3(2));* 2010. 192p. (gr. 8-18). pap. 9.99 *(978-1-4215-2737-6(5));* 2009. 208p. (gr. 8-18). pap. 9.99 *(978-1-4215-2186-2(5));* Vol. 7. 2010. 200p. pap. 9.99 *(978-1-4215-3236-3(0))* Viz Media.

Kano & Lieber, Steve. Dead Robin. Rucka, Greg & Brubaker, Ed. rev. ed. 2007. (Gotham Central Ser.). (ENG.). 168p. (YA). pap. 17.99 *(978-1-4012-1329-9(4))* DC Comics.

Kano & Olivetti, Ariel. Asymmetry. Spencer, Nick. 2012. (ENG.). 128p. (YA). (gr. 8-17). pap. 14.99 *(978-0-7851-4751-0(9))* Marvel Worldwide, Inc.

Kano, Shiuko. Yakuza in Love, 3 vols., Vol. 3. Kano, Shiuko. Weber, Adrienne & Behrens, H. Ryland. 2008. 224p. pap. 12.95 *(978-1-934496-31-2(6))* Aurora Publishing, Inc.

Kano, Yasuhiro. Pretty Face, Vol. 2. Kano, Yasuhiro. 2007. (Pretty Face Ser.: 2). (ENG.). 200p. pap. 7.99 *(978-1-4215-1369-0(2))* Viz Media.

Kantjas, Linda. Wild Colt, 1 vol. Szymanski, Lois. 2012. (ENG.). 40p. (J). 16.99 *(978-0-7643-3975-2(3))* Schiffer Publishing, Ltd.

Kantjas, Linda, photos by. Chincoteague Pony Identification Cards, 1 vol. Szymanski, Lois. 2013. (ENG., 75p. (J). 19.99 *(978-0-7643-4453-4(6))* Schiffer Publishing, Ltd.

Kantorovitz, Sylvie. The Very Tiny Baby. Kantorovitz, Sylvie. 2014. (ENG.). 32p. (J). (gr. -1-2). lib. bdg. 14.95 *(978-1-58089-445-6(3))* Charlesbridge Publishing, Inc.

Kantorovitz, Sylvie & Wickstrom, Sylvie. Smarty Sara. Hays, Anna Jane. 2008. (Step into Reading Ser.). (ENG.). 32p. (J). (gr. -1-1). pap. 3.99 *(978-0-375-83512-4(1),* Random Hse. Bks. for Young Readers) Random Hse. Children's Bks.

Kantrowitz, David. Mission to California. Pillsbury, Samuel H. 2003. (Planet Wampetter Adventure Ser.). 140p. (J). pap. 8.95 *(978-1-930085-03-9(6))* Perspective Publishing, Inc.

Kantz, Bill. Miss Molly's Adventure at the Beach: Another Great Adventure Brought to You by Miss Molly & Her Dog Reyburn, 10 vols. Tompkins, Robyn Lee. 2004. (J). per. *(978-0-9741647-5-5(5))* NRG Pubns.

Kantz, John. Chibi. Acosta, Robert. 2005. (How to Draw Manga Ser.). 144p. (YA). pap. 19.95 *(978-1-932453-88-1(1))* Antarctic Pr., Inc.

Kanuit, Larry. Alaska's Fun Bears: Coloring & Activity Book, Vol. 1. Kanuit, Larry. rev. ed. 2004. (ENG.). 94p. pap. *(978-0-9709537-2-8(0))* Paper Talk.

Kanzler, John. Animal Talk. Lofting, Hugh. 2006. (Easy Reader Classics Ser.). (ENG.). 32p. (J). (gr. k-2). pap. 3.95 *(978-1-4027-3291-1(0))* Sterling Publishing Co., Inc.

—Battle in a Bottle. Asch, Frank. 2014. (Class Pets Ser.). (ENG.). 96p. (J). (gr. 2-6). pap. 13.99 *(978-1-4814-3625-0(2),* Simon & Schuster/Paula Wiseman Bks.) Simon & Schuster/Paula Wiseman Bks.

—The Christmas Pups. Bateman, Teresa. 2012. (J). *(978-1-61913-112-5(9))* Weigl Pubs., Inc.

—The Christmas Pups. Bateman, Teresa. 2011. (ENG.). 32p. (J). (gr. -1-3). 16.99 *(978-0-8075-1160-2(9))* Whitman, Albert & Co.
—Doctor Dolittle's Magical Cure. Lofting, Hugh. 2007. (Easy Reader Classics Ser.: Bk. 4). (ENG.). 32p. (J). (gr. k-2). pap. 3.95 *(978-1-4027-4123-4(5))* Sterling Publishing Co., Inc.
—The Ghost of P. S. 42. Asch, Frank. 2014. (Class Pets Ser.). (ENG.). 96p. (J). (gr. 2-5). pap. 13.99 *(978-1-4814-3624-3(4),* Simon & Schuster/Paula Wiseman Bks.) Simon & Schuster/Paula Wiseman Bks.
—Hush Little One: A Lullaby for God's Children. Stohs, Anita Reith. 2006. 20p. (J). (gr. -1). bds. 5.49 *(978-0-7586-0861-1(6))* Concordia Publishing Hse.
—Little Lucy. Cooper, Ilene. 2011. (Step into Reading Ser.). (ENG.). 48p. (J). (gr. k-3). pap. 3.99 *(978-0-375-86760-6(0));* lib. bdg. 12.99 *(978-0-375-96760-3(5))* Random Hse. Children's Bks. (Random Hse. Bks. for Young Readers).
—Paul Bunyan: My Story. Harrison, David L. 2008. (Step into Reading Ser.). (ENG.). 48p. (J). (gr. k-3). 3.99 *(978-0-375-84688-5(3),* Random Hse. Bks. for Young Readers) Random Hse. Children's Bks.
—Priceless Gifts: A Tale from Italy. Hamilton, Martha & Weiss, Mitch. 2006. (ENG.). 32p. (J). (gr. k-3). 16.95 *(978-0-87483-788-9(X))* August Hse. Pubs., Inc.
—The Story of Doctor Dolittle: Animal Talk. Lofting, Hugh. 2008. (Easy Reader Classics Ser.). (ENG.). 32p. (gr. 3-7). lib. bdg. 24.21 *(978-1-59961-338-3(7))* Spotlight.
—The Story of Doctor Dolittle: The Circus Crocodile. Lofting, Hugh. 2008. (Easy Reader Classics Ser.). (ENG.). 32p. (gr. 3-7). lib. bdg. 24.21 *(978-1-59961-339-0(5))* Spotlight.
—Survival School. Asch, Frank & Asch, Frank. 2004. (Class Pets Ser.: No. 3). (ENG.). 96p. (J). (gr. 2-6). pap. 6.99 *(978-0-689-84656-4(8),* Simon & Schuster/Paula Wiseman Bks.) Simon & Schuster/Paula Wiseman Bks.
—Survival School. Asch, Frank. 2014. (Class Pets Ser.). (ENG.). 96p. (J). (gr. 2-6). pap. 13.99 *(978-1-4814-3627-4(9),* Simon & Schuster/Paula Wiseman Bks.) Simon & Schuster/Paula Wiseman Bks.
Kanzler, John. Rock-a -Bye Baby. Kanzler, John. Tiger Tales Staff, ed. 2011. 24p. (J). (gr. -1-k). bds. 8.95 *(978-1-58925-853-2(3))* Tiger Tales.
Kanzler, John. The Big Rock Candy Mountain. Kanzler, John, tr. 2004. 24p. (J). 15.95 *(978-1-59336-062-7(2));* pap. *(978-1-59336-063-4(0))* Mondo Publishing.
—Hush, Little One: A Lullaby for God's Children. Kanzler, John, tr. Stohs, Anita Reith. 2004. 32p. (J). 12.99 *(978-0-570-07144-0(5))* Concordia Publishing Hse.
—Whose Feet? Kanzler, John, tr. Hess, Nina. 2004. (Step into Reading Ser.). (ENG.). 32p. (J). (gr. -1-1). pap. 3.99 *(978-0-375-82623-8(8),* Random Hse. Bks. for Young Readers) Random Hse. Children's Bks.
Kao, Sleepless. Emilie & the Mighty Om. Lolley, Sarah. 2014. (ENG.). 40p. (J). (gr. -1-3). 16.95 *(978-1-897476-35-2(3))* Simply Read Bks. CAN. Dist: Ingram Pub. Services.
Kapart. It's Turtle Time. Howard, Cheryl L. 2011. 28p. pap. 24.95 *(978-1-4560-6676-5(5))* America Star Bks.
Kapatos, Elizabeth. The Adventures of Exokid & the Teachings of Money. Outram, Richard. 2009. 36p. pap. 12.95 *(978-1-59858-898-9(2))* Dog Ear Publishing, LLC.
Kaplan, Bruce Eric. Cousin Irv from Mars. Kaplan, Bruce Eric. 2013. (ENG.). 40p. (J). (gr. -1-3). 16.99 *(978-1-4424-4923-7(3),* Simon & Schuster Bks. For Young Readers) Simon & Schuster Bks. For Young Readers.
—Meaniehead. Kaplan, Bruce Eric. 2014. (ENG.). 40p. (J). (gr. -1-3). 17.99 *(978-1-4424-8542-6(6),* Simon & Schuster Bks. For Young Readers) Simon & Schuster Bks. For Young Readers.
—Monsters Eat Whiny Children. Kaplan, Bruce Eric. 2010. (ENG.). 40p. (J). (gr. -1-3). 17.99 *(978-1-4169-8689-8(8),* Simon & Schuster Bks. For Young Readers) Simon & Schuster Bks. For Young Readers.
Kaposy, Jeremy. Are You Afraid Yet? The Science Behind Scary Stuff. O'Meara, Stephen James. 2009. (ENG.). 80p. (J). (gr. 4-7). 17.95 *(978-1-55453-294-0(9));* pap. 9.95 *(978-1-55453-295-7(7))* Kids Can Pr., Ltd. CAN. Dist: Univ. of Toronto Pr.
Kara, György. Demon Diary. Hyong, Lee Chi. 2003. 192p. (gr. 8-18). pap. 9.99 *(978-1-59182-154-0(1))* TOKYOPOP, Inc.
—Demon Diary, Vol. 3. Hee, Lee Yun. Na, Lauren, tr. from KOR. rev. ed. 2003. 192p. pap. 9.99 *(978-1-59182-156-4(8))* TOKYOPOP, Inc.
Karakida, Toshihiko & Murakami, Yoshiko. My Book of Mazes Around the World. Kumon Staff. 2007. 80p. (J). (gr. -1-3). pap. 7.95 *(978-1-933241-40-1(3))* Kumon Publishing North America, Inc.
Karanja, Geoffrey Gacheru. My Sister's Wedding: A Story of Kenya. Mbuthia, Waithira. 2005. (Make Friends Around the World Ser.). (ENG.). 32p. (J). (gr. k-3). 19.95 *(978-1-56899-898-5(8),* BC8006); 15.95 *(978-1-56899-896-1(1),* B8006) Soundprints.
Karas, G., jt. illus. see Karas, G. Brian.
Karas, G. Brian. Ant & Honey Bee: A Pair of Friends at Halloween. McDonald, Megan. 2013. (Candlewick Sparks Ser.). (ENG.). 48p. (J). (gr. k-4). pap. 3.99 *(978-0-7636-6864-8(8))* Candlewick Pr.
—Ant & Honey Bee: A Pair of Friends in Winter. McDonald, Megan. 2014. (Candlewick Sparks Ser.). (ENG.). 64p. (J). (gr. k-4). pap. 3.99 *(978-0-7636-6862-4(1))* Candlewick Pr.
—The Apple Orchard Riddle. McNamara, Margaret. 2013. (Mr. Tiffin's Classroom Ser.). (ENG.). 40p. (J). (gr. -1-3). 15.99 *(978-0-375-84744-8(8));* 18.99 *(978-0-375-95744-4(8))* Random Hse., Inc.
—Best Friends. Michaels, Anna. 2004. 24p. (J). lib. bdg. 10.00 *(978-1-4242-0217-1(5))* Fitzgerald Bks.
—Best Friends. Michaels, Anna. 2004. (Green Light Readers Level 1 Ser.). (ENG.). 32p. (J). (gr. -1-3). pap. 3.95 *(978-0-15-205133-4(3))* Houghton Mifflin Harcourt Publishing Co.
—Best Friends. Michaels, Anna. 2004. (Green Light Readers Level 1 Ser.). (gr. -1-1). 13.95 *(978-0-7569-4282-3(9))* Perfection Learning Corp.
—Big Bad Bunny. Billingsley, Franny. 2008. (ENG.). 40p. (J). (gr. k-3). 17.99 *(978-1-4169-0601-8(0),* Atheneum/Richard Jackson Bks.) Simon & Schuster Children's Publishing.
—The Case of the Baffled Bear. Rylant, Cynthia. 2006. (I Can Read Book 2 Ser.: No. 7). (ENG.). 48p. (J). (gr. k-3). per. 3.99 *(978-0-06-053450-9(8),* Greenwillow Bks.) HarperCollins Pubs.
—The Case of the Climbing Cat. Rylant, Cynthia. 2003. (High-Rise Private Eyes Ser.: No. 2). (J). (gr. -1-3). 25.96 incl. audio *(978-1-59112-190-9(6));* (gr. -1-3). pap. 29.95 incl. audio *(978-1-59112-191-6(4));* (gr. k-3). 28.95 incl. audio compact disk *(978-1-59112-611-9(8))* Live Oak Media.
—The Case of the Desperate Duck. Rylant, Cynthia. (I Can Read Book 2 Ser.: No. 8). 48p. (J). (gr. k-3). 2006. (ENG.). pap. 3.99 *(978-0-06-053453-0(2),* Greenwillow Bks.); 2005. 14.99 *(978-0-06-053451-6(6));* 2005. lib. bdg. 15.89 *(978-0-06-053452-3(4))* HarperCollins Pubs.
—The Case of the Desperate Duck. Rylant, Cynthia. 2006. (High-Rise Private Eyes Ser.). 48p. (gr. -1-3). 14.00 *(978-0-7569-6958-5(1))* Perfection Learning Corp.
—The Case of the Fidgety Fox. Rylant, Cynthia. unabr. ed. 2005. (High-Rise Private Eyes Ser.: No. 6). (J). (gr. k-4). 25.95 incl. audio *(978-1-59519-405-3(3));*Set. pap. 29.95 incl. audio *(978-1-59519-406-0(1));*Set. pap. 31.95 incl. audio compact disk *(978-1-59519-410-7(X))* Live Oak Media.
—The Case of the Fidgety Fox. Rylant, Cynthia. 2004. (High-Rise Private Eyes Ser.). 58p. (J). (gr. 1-3). 11.65 *(978-0-7569-3210-7(6))* Perfection Learning Corp.
—The Case of the Missing Monkey. Rylant, Cynthia. 2003. (I Can Read Book 2 Ser.: No. 1). (ENG.). 48p. (J). (gr. k-3). pap. 3.99 *(978-0-06-444306-7(X),* Greenwillow Bks.) HarperCollins Pubs.
—The Case of the Missing Monkey. Rylant, Cynthia. 2003. (High-Rise Private Eyes Ser.: No. 1). 28.95 incl. audio compact disk *(978-1-59112-615-7(0));* (J). 25.95 incl. audio *(978-1-59112-194-7(9));* (J). pap. 29.95 incl. audio *(978-1-59112-195-4(7))* Live Oak Media.
—The Case of the Missing Monkey. 2004. (High-Rise Private Eyes Ser.: No. 1). (J). (gr. -1-2). pap. 31.95 incl. audio compact disk *(978-1-59112-616-4(9))* Live Oak Media.
—The Case of the Puzzling Possum. Rylant, Cynthia. 2003. (High-Rise Private Eyes Ser.: No. 3). (J). (gr. -1-3). 25.95 incl. audio *(978-1-59112-198-5(1));* (gr. k-3). 28.95 incl. audio compact disk *(978-1-59112-619-5(3));* (gr. k-3). pap. 29.95 incl. audio *(978-1-59112-199-2(X))* Live Oak Media.
—The Case of the Puzzling Possum. 2004. (High-Rise Private Eyes Ser.: No. 3). (J). (gr. -1-2). pap. 31.95 incl. audio compact disk *(978-1-59112-620-1(7))* Live Oak Media.
—The Case of the Sleepy Sloth. Rylant, Cynthia. unabr. ed. 2005. (High-Rise Private Eyes Ser.: No. 5). (J). (gr. k-4). 29.95 incl. audio *(978-1-59519-413-8(4));* 28.95 incl. audio compact disk *(978-1-59519-417-6(7));*Set. pap. 29.95 incl. audio *(978-1-59519-414-5(2));*Set. pap. 31.95 incl. audio compact disk *(978-1-59519-418-3(5))* Live Oak Media.
—Clever Jack Takes the Cake. Fleming, Candace. 2010. (ENG.). 40p. (J). (gr. -1-3). 17.99 *(978-0-375-84979-4(3),* Schwartz & Wade Bks.) Random Hse. Children's Bks.
—Daniel y Su Mascota. Flor Ada, Alma. 2008. (Green Light Readers Level 1 Ser.).Tr. of Daniel's Pet. (SPA & ENG.). 28p. (J). (gr. -1-3). pap. 3.95 *(978-0-15-206243-9(2))* Houghton Mifflin Harcourt Publishing Co.
—Daniel's Mystery Egg. Flor Ada, Alma. 2003. (Green Light Readers Level 2 Ser.). (ENG.). 24p. (J). (gr. -1-3). pap. 3.95 *(978-0-15-204845-7(6))* Houghton Mifflin Harcourt Publishing Co.
—Daniel's Mystery Egg. Flor Ada, Alma. ed. 2003. (Green Light Readers — Level 2 Ser.). 32p. (gr. -1-3). lib. bdg. 13.50 *(978-0-613-64169-2(8),* Turtleback) Turtleback Bks.
—Daniel's Pet. Flor Ada, Alma. 2003. (Green Light Readers Level 1 Ser.). 24p. (J). (gr. -1-3). pap. 3.95 *(978-0-15-204865-5(0))* Houghton Mifflin Harcourt Publishing Co.
—Fractions = Trouble! Mills, Claudia. 2011. (ENG.). 128p. (J). (gr. 2-5). 15.99 *(978-0-374-36716-9(7),* Farrar, Straus & Giroux (BYR)) Farrar, Straus & Giroux.
—The High-Rise Private Eye: The\Case of the Troublesome Turtle. Rylant, Cynthia. 2003. (High-Rise Private Eyes Ser.: No. 4). (J). (gr. k-3). 25.95 incl. audio *(978-1-59112-202-9(3));* 28.95 incl. audio compact disk *(978-1-59112-623-2(1));* pap. 29.95 incl. audio *(978-1-59112-203-6(1));* pap. 31.95 incl. audio compact disk *(978-1-59112-624-9(X))* Live Oak Media.
—The High-Rise Private Eyes Series. Rylant, Cynthia. 2003. pap. 61.95 incl. audio *(978-1-59112-430-6(1));* pap. 68.95 incl. audio compact disk *(978-1-59112-858-8(7))* Live Oak Media.
—How Many Seeds in a Pumpkin? McNamara, Margaret. 2007. (Mr. Tiffin's Classroom Ser.). (ENG.). 40p. (J). (gr. -1-2). 17.99 *(978-0-375-84014-2(1),* Schwartz & Wade Bks.) Random Hse. Children's Bks.
—If It Weren't for You. Zolotow, Charlotte. 2006. 32p. (J). (gr. -1-3). 16.89 *(978-0-06-027876-2(5))* HarperCollins Pubs.
—Incredible Me! Appelt, Kathi. 2003. 32p. (J). (gr. -1-1). lib. bdg. 16.89 *(978-0-06-028623-1(7));* (ENG.). 16.99 *(978-0-06-028622-4(9))* HarperCollins Pubs.
—Ivan: the Remarkable True Story of the Shopping Mall Gorilla. Applegate, Katherine. 2014. (ENG.). 40p. (J). (gr. -1-3). 17.99 *(978-0-544-25230-1(6))* Houghton Mifflin Harcourt Publishing Co.
—Lemonade in Winter: A Book about Two Kids Counting Money. Jenkins, Emily. 2012. (ENG.). 40p. (J). (gr. -1-2). 16.99 *(978-0-375-85883-3(0));* 18.99 *(978-0-375-95883-0(5))* Random Hse. Children's Bks. (Schwartz & Wade Bks.).
—El Misterioso Huevo de Daniel. Flor Ada, Alma. Flor Ada, Alma, tr. from ENM. 2007. (Green Light Readers Level 2 Ser.).Tr. of Daniel's Mystery Egg. (SPA & ENG.). 28p. (J). (gr. 1-4). pap. 3.95 *(978-0-15-205971-2(7))* Houghton Mifflin Harcourt Publishing Co.
—Muncha! Muncha! Muncha! Fleming, Candace. pap. 16.95 incl. audio *(978-1-59112-463-4(8));* pap. incl. audio *(978-1-59112-465-8(4));* pap. 18.95 incl. audio compact disk *(978-1-59112-923-3(0));* pap. incl. audio compact disk *(978-1-59112-925-7(7))* Live Oak Media.
—My Wild Woolly. Eaton, Deborah J. 2005. (Green Light Readers Level 2 Ser.). (ENG.). 24p. (J). (gr. -1-3). pap. 3.95 *(978-0-15-205147-1(3))* Houghton Mifflin Harcourt Publishing Co.
—My Wild Woolly. Eaton, Deborah J. 2005. (Green Light Readers Level 2 Ser.). (gr. k-2). 13.95 *(978-0-7569-5445-1(2))* Perfection Learning Corp.
—Nam! Nam! Nam! Fleming, Candace. Schmidt, Alejandra, tr. from ENG. 2007. (SPA.). 32p. (J). (gr. -1-2). 15.95 *(978-1-933032-35-1(9))* Lectorum Pubns., Inc.
—Neville. Juster, Norton. 2011. (ENG.). 32p. (J). (gr. -1-3). 17.99 *(978-0-375-86765-1(1),* Schwartz & Wade Bks.) Random Hse. Children's Bks.
—Oh No, Gotta Go! Elya, Susan Middleton. 2005. 29p. (J). (gr. k-4). reprint ed. 15.00 *(978-0-7567-8946-6(X))* DIANE Publishing Co.
—Oh No, Gotta Go! Elya, Susan Middleton. 2003. (SPA & ENG.). 32p. (J). (gr. -1-2). 15.99 *(978-0-399-23493-4(4),* Putnam Juvenile) Penguin Publishing Group.
—Pair of Friends in Winter. McDonald, Megan. 2013. (ENG.). 64p. (J). (gr. k-4). 14.99 *(978-0-7636-5712-3(3))* Candlewick Pr.
—A Place Called Kindergarten. Harper, Jessica. 2008. (ENG.). 32p. (J). (gr. -1-k). pap. 6.99 *(978-0-14-241174-2(4),* Puffin) Penguin Publishing Group.
—A Poem in Your Pocket. McNamara, Margaret. 2015. (Mr. Tiffin's Classroom Ser.). (ENG.). 40p. (J). (gr. -1-3). 16.99 *(978-0-307-97947-6(4),* Schwartz & Wade Bks.) Random Hse. Children's Bks.
—Raising Sweetness, 4 bks. Stanley, Diane. 2004. (J). pap. 39.95 incl. audio compact disk *(978-1-59112-524-2(3))* Live Oak Media.
—The Seals on the Bus. Hort, Lenny. rev. ed. 2003. (ENG.). 32p. (J). (gr. -1-k). pap. 7.99 *(978-0-8050-7263-1(2))* Square Fish.
—Sweetness Series. Stanley, Diane. 2003. pap. 30.95 incl. audio *(978-1-59112-847-2(1));* pap. 34.95 incl. audio compact disk *(978-1-59112-860-1(9))* Live Oak Media.
—Switching on the Moon: A Very First Book of Bedtime Poems. 2010. (ENG.). 96p. (J). (gr. k-12). 21.99 *(978-0-7636-4249-5(5))* Candlewick Pr.
—Tap Tap Boom Boom. Bluemle, Elizabeth. 2014. (ENG.). 32p. (J). (gr. -1-2). 16.99 *(978-0-7636-5696-6(8))* Candlewick Pr.
Karas, G. Brian. Throw Your Tooth on the Roof. Beeler, Selby B. 2015. 32p. pap. 7.00 ***(978-1-61003-501-9(1))*** Center for the Collaborative Classroom.
Karas, G. Brian. Tippy-Tippy-Tippy, Hide! Fleming, Candace. 2007. (ENG.). 40p. (J). (gr. -1-3). 17.99 *(978-0-689-87479-6(0),* Atheneum Bks. for Young Readers) Simon & Schuster Children's Publishing.
—Tippy-Tippy-Tippy, Splash! Fleming, Candace. 2014. (ENG.). 40p. (J). (gr. -1-3). 16.99 *(978-1-4169-5403-3(1),* Atheneum Bks. for Young Readers) Simon & Schuster Children's Publishing.
—Whale Trails, Before & Now. Cline-Ransome, Lesa. 2015. (ENG.). 40p. (J). (gr. k-4). 17.99 *(978-0-8050-9642-2(6),* Holt, Henry & Co. Bks. For Young Readers) Holt, Henry & Co.
—7 X 9 = Trouble! Mills, Claudia. 2004. 103p. (J). (gr. 2-5). 13.60 *(978-0-7569-3397-5(8))* Perfection Learning Corp.
—7 X 9 = Trouble! Mills, Claudia. 2004. (ENG.). 112p. (J). (gr. 2-5). pap. 6.99 *(978-0-374-46452-3(9))* Square Fish.
Karas, G. Brian. As an Oak Tree Grows. Karas, G. Brian. 2014. (ENG.). 32p. (J). (gr. k-3). 17.99 *(978-0-399-25233-4(9),* Nancy Paulsen Bks.) Penguin Publishing Group.
—Atlantic. Karas, G. Brian. 2004. (ENG.). 32p. (J). (gr. -1-3). reprint ed. pap. 6.99 *(978-0-14-240027-2(0),* Puffin) Penguin Publishing Group.
—On Earth. Karas, G. Brian. (ENG.). 32p. (J). (gr. k-3). 2008. pap. 7.99 *(978-0-14-241063-9(2),* Puffin); 2005. 16.99 *(978-0-399-24025-6(X),* Putnam Juvenile) Penguin Publishing Group.
—On Earth. Karas, G. Brian. 2008. (gr. k-3). 18.00 *(978-0-7569-8926-2(4))* Perfection Learning Corp.
Karas, G. Brian & Karas, G. Seals on the Bus. Hort, Lenny. 2008. (ENG.). 32p. (J). (gr. -1-k). pap. 26.99 *(978-0-8050-8678-2(1),* Holt, Henry & Co. Bks. For Young Readers) Holt, Henry & Co.
Karas, Roma. Mural on Second Avenue & Other City Poems. Moore, Lilian. (ENG.). 32p. (J). (gr. k-4). 2013. pap. 6.99 *(978-0-7636-6349-0(2));* 2005. 16.99 *(978-0-7636-1987-9(6))* Candlewick Pr.
Karcz, Katherine. Paddle, the Extraordinary Duck. Craig, Deborah Anne. Glueck, Michael Wells, ed. 2011. 42p. pap. 19.95 *(978-1-4583-6916-1(1))* Lulu Enterprises Inc.
—Weighty Words, Too. Levitt, Paul M. et al. 2009. (ENG.). 96p. (J). (gr. 4-18). 21.95 *(978-0-8263-4558-5(1))* Univ. of New Mexico Pr.
Karim, Joseph & Karim, Silvana. What Does Happy Look Like? Karim, Joseph & Karim, Silvana. 2009. 47p. (J). pap. 18.95 *(978-1-934575-54-3(2))* Autism Asperger Publishing Co.
Karim, Silvana, jt. illus. see Karim, Joseph.
Karl, Linda. Cabbage Patch Kids: We Are All Best Friends. Masino, Brian. 2006. (J). pap. *(978-0-439-76820-7(9))* Scholastic, Inc.
—Easter Stencil Fun! (Peter Cottontail) Man-Kong, Mary. 2014. (Color Plus Stencil Ser.). (ENG.). 64p. (J). (gr. -1-2). pap. 5.99 *(978-0-385-37442-2(9),* Golden Bks.) Random Hse. Children's Bks.
—Here Comes Peter Cottontail (Peter Cottontail) Depken, Kristen L. 2012. (Step into Reading Ser.). (ENG.). 32p. (J). (gr. -1-1). pap. 3.99 *(978-0-307-93032-3(7),* Random Hse. Bks. for Young Readers) Random Hse. Children's Bks.
—Hoppy Easter! (Peter Cottontail) Man-Kong, Mary. 2013. (Full-Color Activity Book with Stickers Ser.). (ENG.). 32p. (J). (gr. -1-2). pap. 3.99 *(978-0-307-98230-8(0),* Golden Bks.) Random Hse. Children's Bks.
—My Easter Basket. Golden Books Staff. 2011. (Golden Go-Along Book Ser.). (ENG.). 12p. (J). (— 1). bds. 4.99 *(978-0-375-86816-0(X),* Golden Bks.) Random Hse. Children's Bks.
—Rudolph the Red-Nosed Reindeer. Depken, Kristen L. 2014. (My Readers Ser.). (ENG.). 32p. (J). (gr. k-2). 15.99 *(978-1-250-05044-1(8))* Square Fish.
Karl, Therese. A Buddy in Winter: Lost & Found. Karl, Mary Eileen. 2010. 44p. pap. 15.50 *(978-1-60911-424-4(8),* Eloquent Bks.) Strategic Book Publishing & Rights Agency (SBPRA).
Karla, Nicolee. Rossi & Lucy Go to the Beach. Bonacci, Ross. 2013. 38p. pap. *(978-0-9873831-2-9(4))* Bonacci Publishing.
Karmaga, Ramanda. Psy-Comm, Vol. 2. Henderson, Jason & Salvaggio, Tony. 2007. (Psy-Comm Ser.). 192p. per. 9.99 *(978-1-59816-270-7(5))* TOKYOPOP, Inc.
Karn, Mike. Lighten up Lenny. Snyder, Vicki & West, Lois. 2005. (J). *(978-0-9773187-0-4(2))* Snyder, Vicki.
Karp, Cindy. Sharing Our Homeland: Palestinian & Jewish Children at Summer Peace Camp, 1 vol. Marx, Trish. 2010. (ENG.). 48p. (J). (gr. 1-6). 19.95 *(978-1-58430-260-5(7))* Lee & Low Bks., Inc.
Karp, Cindy. Everglades Forever: Restoring America's Great Wetland, 1 vol. Karp, Cindy, photos by. Marx, Trish. 2004. (ENG.). 40p. (J). 17.95 *(978-1-58430-164-6(3))* Lee & Low Bks., Inc.
Karp, Ken. Will You Wear a Blue Hat? 2009. (Rookie Toddler: Sing along Toddler Ser.). (ENG.). 12p. (J). (gr. -1). bds. 6.95 *(978-0-531-24549-1(7))* Scholastic Library Publishing.
Karp, Ken, photos by. Petting Farm. Set. Ackerman, Jill & Bryan, Beth. 2007. (Little Scholastic Ser.). (ENG.). 12p. (J). (gr. k — 1). 12.99 *(978-0-439-88558-4(2),* Cartwheel Bks.) Scholastic, Inc.
Karsky, A. K. Dreams of the Super Bowl. Wojciechowska, Maia. (Dreams of...Ser.). 80p. (J). 14.50 *(978-1-883740-20-7(7))* Pebble Beach Pr., Ltd.
Kasko, John, photos by. Breaking Benjamin: The Road to Platinum. Kasko, John. Fabbri, Freddie. 2005. (YA). 19.95 *(978-0-9767234-0-0(9))* On Tour Publishing.
Kasner, Kurt. Beyond the Hole in the Universe: Crisis in the World Next Door. Kasner, Kurt. 2011. (ENG.). 242p. pap. 10.98 *(978-1-4565-0348-2(0))* CreateSpace Independent Publishing Platform.
Kasparavicius, Kestutis. El Viaje de Lisa. Maar, Paul. 2008. (la Orilla del Viento Ser.). (SPA.). 28p. (J). (gr. -1-3). 12.99 *(978-968-16-7452-6(9))* Fondo de Cultura Economica USA.
Kassab, Selena. Mommy & Daddy Are Going on a Trip. Asher, Penny & Booker, Ricki. 2006. 32p. (J). 12.95 *(978-0-9755902-1-8(9))* Change Is Strange, Inc.
—My First Day of School. Asher, Penny & Booker, Ricki. 2006. 32p. (J). 12.95 *(978-0-9755902-2-5(7))* Change Is Strange, Inc.
—No More Pacifier. Asher, Penny & Booker, Ricki. 2006. 32p. (J). 12.95 *(978-0-9755902-3-2(5))* Change Is Strange, Inc.
—We're Having a Baby. Asher, Penny & Booker, Ricki. 2006. 32p. 12.95 *(978-0-9755902-0-1(0))* Change Is Strange, Inc.
Kassian, Olena. What Kind of Seeds Are These? Roemer, Heidi. 2006. (ENG.). 32p. (J). (gr. k-1). 16.95 *(978-1-55971-955-1(9))* Cooper Square Publishing Llc.
Kastan, Bill. Dragon in My Pocket. Coughlin, Denise. 2005. (J). *(978-0-9765905-0-7(6))* Rose Valley Publishing.
Kasten, Nancy. First Feather. 2003. 70p. (J). pap. 9.99 *(978-0-9744863-0-7(2))* Paulus Publishing.
Kastl, Christine. When the Earth Lost Its Shapes. Viswanath, Shobha. 2013. (ENG.). 36p. (J). (gr. -1). pap. 9.95 *(978-81-8190-192-7(4))* Karadi Tales Co. Pvt. Ltd. IND. Dist: Consortium Bk. Sales & Distribution.
Kastner, Jill. Beardream. Hobbs, Will. 2014. 32p. pap. 8.00 *(978-1-61003-340-4(X))* Center for the Collaborative Classroom.
—In November. Rylant, Cynthia. 2014. 32p. pap. 7.00 *(978-1-61003-180-6(6))* Center for the Collaborative Classroom.
—In November. Rylant, Cynthia. 2008. (ENG.). 32p. (J). (gr. -1-3). pap. 6.99 *(978-0-15-206342-9(0))* Houghton Mifflin Harcourt Publishing Co.
—The Lizard Man of Crabtree County, 1 vol. Nolan, Lucy. 2003. (ENG.). 32p. (J). (gr. 1-4). pap. 5.95 *(978-0-7614-5144-0(7))* Marshall Cavendish Corp.
Kasun, Mike. Charlie Canoe & Other Boats, Too. Tuzee, John & Tuzee, Diane. 2006. (J). *(978-0-9755348-2-3(3))* Kids Life Pr.
Kasunick, Heather & Reusch, Mister. Unbored: The Essential Field Guide to Serious Fun. Larsen, Elizabeth Foy & Glenn, Joshua. 2012. (ENG.). 352p. 25.00 *(978-1-60819-641-8(0))* Bloomsbury USA.
—Unbored Games: Serious Fun for Everyone. Glenn, Joshua & Larsen, Elizabeth Foy. 2014. (ENG.). 176p. pap. 16.00 *(978-1-62040-706-6(X))* Bloomsbury USA.
Kasy, Frank. Blue: The Luckiest Dog in the World. Liepelt, Juanita. 2008. 48p. 19.95 *(978-0-9791317-0-7(7),* Realitylis Bks.) RealitylsBooks.com, Inc.
Kasza, Keiko. Badger's Fancy Meal. Kasza, Keiko. 2007. (ENG.). 32p. (J). (gr. -1-3). 16.99 *(978-0-399-24603-6(7),* Putnam Juvenile) Penguin Publishing Group.
—The Dog Who Cried Wolf. Kasza, Keiko. (ENG.). 32p. (J). (gr. -1-2). 2009. pap. 6.99 *(978-0-14-241305-0(4),* Puffin); 2005. 16.99 *(978-0-399-24247-2(3),* Putnam Juvenile) Penguin Publishing Group.
—Finders Keepers. Kasza, Keiko. 2015. (ENG.). 32p. (J). (gr. -1-k). 16.99 *(978-0-399-16898-7(2),* Putnam Adult) Penguin Publishing Group.
—My Lucky Birthday. Kasza, Keiko. 2013. (ENG.). 32p. (J). (gr. -1-k). 16.99 *(978-0-399-25763-6(2),* Putnam Juvenile) Penguin Publishing Group.

K

—My Lucky Day. Kasza, Keiko. (ENG.). (J). (gr. -1-3). 2005. 30p. pap. 5.99 *(978-0-14-240456-0(X)*, Puffin); 2003. 32p. 16.99 *(978-0-399-23874-1(3)*, Putnam Juvenile) Penguin Publishing Group.
—My Lucky Day. Kasza, Keiko. 2005. (gr. -1-3). lib. bdg. 16.00 *(978-0-7569-5492-5(4))* Perfection Learning Corp.
—Ready for Anything! Kasza, Keiko. 2009. (ENG.). 32p. (J). (gr. -1-k). 16.99 *(978-0-399-25235-8(5)*, Putnam Juvenile) Penguin Publishing Group.
—Silly Goose's Big Story. Kasza, Keiko. 2012. (ENG.). 32p. (J). (gr. -1-k). 16.99 *(978-0-399-25542-7(7)*, Putnam Juvenile) Penguin Publishing Group.
—When the Elephant Walks. Kasza, Keiko. 2004. (ENG.). 30p. (J). (gr. -1 — 1). bds. 6.99 *(978-0-399-24261-8(9)*, Putnam Juvenile) Penguin Publishing Group.
Kaszonyi, Janet. Racin' Jason. Wagner, Elaine. ed. 2009. (Racin' Jason Ser.). (ENG.). 52p. (gr. 2-3). pap. 10.95 *(978-1-894778-73-2(1))* Theytus Bks., Ltd. CAN. Dist: Univ. of Toronto Pr.
Katayama, Mits. What about Me? 12 Ways to Get Your Parents' Attention. Parenting Press & Kennedy-Moore, Eileen. 2005. (ENG.). 32p. (J). (gr. -1-3). 14.95 *(978-1-884734-86-1(3))* Parenting Pr., Inc.
Kate Greenaway. The Queen of the Pirate Isle. Bret Harte, Harte & Bret Harte. 2010. 56p. pap. 3.49 *(978-1-60386-381-0(8)*, Watchmaker Publishing) Wexford College Pr.
Kate Smith Designs. Who's Playing on the Farm? 2011. (Magic Bath Bks.). (ENG.). 8p. (J). (gr. -1-3). 4.99 *(978-1-4380-7179-4(5))* Barron's Educational Series, Inc.
—Who's Playing Outdoors? 2011. (Magic Bath Bks.). (ENG.). 8p. (J). (gr. -1-3). 5.99 *(978-1-4380-7178-7(7))* Barron's Educational Series, Inc.
Kath, Katie. Annie. Meehan, Thomas. 2015. (Penguin Young Readers, Level 3 Ser.). (ENG.). 48p. (J). (gr. 1-3). pap. 3.99 *(978-0-448-48223-1(1)*, Warne, Frederick Pubs.) Penguin Bks., Ltd. GBR. Dist: Penguin Random Hse., LLC.
Kath, Katie. Penelope Perfect: A Tale of Perfectionism Gone Wild. Anderson, Shannon. 2015. (ENG.). 48p. (gr. k-3). 15.99 ***(978-1-63198-019-0(X))*** Free Spirit Publishing, Inc.
—The Trouble with Ants. Mills, Claudia. 2015. (Nora Notebooks Ser.: 1). (ENG.). 176p. (J). (gr. 2-5). lib. bdg. 17.99 ***(978-0-385-39162-7(5)***, Knopf Bks. for Young Readers) Random Hse. Children's Bks.
Kath, Katie. Unusual Chickens for the Exceptional Poultry Farmer. Jones, Kelly. 2015. (ENG.). 224p. (J). (gr. 3-7). 16.99 *(978-0-385-75552-8(X))* Knopf, Alfred A. Inc.
Kath, Katie, jt. illus. see Wesson, Andrea.
Kathie, Gabriel. Grandma's Roses. Hawkesworth, Asha. 2006. (J). per. *(978-0-9738442-9-0(9))* Avatar Pubns., Inc. CAN. Dist: NACSCORP, Inc.
Kaths, Kathy. The Last Eagle. Hoover, T. A. 2004. 38p. (J). 16.00 *(978-0-9702216-3-6(0))* Sport Story Publishing.
Kathuria, Rohit. Children Ask Kalam. Abdul Kalam, A. P. J. 2006. 109p. (J). *(978-81-7758-245-1(3))* Pearson Education.
Kathy, Newell-Worby. When Horses Could Fly: And Other Fantastic Tales. Sharon, Janusz. 2007. 80p. (J). pap. 19.95 *(978-0-9658533-6-1(5))* Amigo Pubns., Inc.
Kato, Gary. Barry Baskerville Solves a Case. Kellogg, Richard. 2013. (ENG.). 28p. pap. 9.99 *(978-0-615-79715-1(6))* Airship 27.
Kato, Haruhi. Panda Man & the Treasure Hunt. Makura, Sho. 2011. (Adventures of Panda Man Ser.). (ENG.). 96p. (J). (gr. 1-4). pap. 7.99 *(978-1-4215-3521-0(1))* Viz Media.
—Panda Man to the Rescue! Makura, Sho. 2010. (Adventures of Panda Man Ser.). (ENG.). 96p. (J). pap. 7.99 *(978-1-4215-3520-3(3))* Viz Media.
—Panda Man vs. Chiwanda. Makura, Sho. 2011. (Adventures of Panda Man Ser.). (ENG.). 96p. (J). (gr. 1-4). pap. 7.99 *(978-1-4215-3522-7(X))* Viz Media.
Katsura, Masakazu. Bitter Summer. Katsura, Masakazu. 2005. (Is Ser.: Vol. 3). (ENG.). 184p. pap. 7.99 *(978-1-59116-969-7(0))* Viz Media.
—Close-Up, Vol. 12. Katsura, Masakazu. 2005. (Video Girl Ai Ser.). (ENG.). 192p. pap. 9.99 *(978-1-59116-307-7(2))* Viz Media.
—Cut Scenes, Vol. 9. Katsura, Masakazu. 2004. (Video Girl Ai Ser.). (ENG.). 200p. pap. 9.99 *(978-1-59116-304-6(8))* Viz Media.
—Fade Out, Vol. 13. Katsura, Masakazu. 2005. (Video Girl Ai Ser.). (ENG.). 192p. pap. 9.99 *(978-1-59116-308-4(0))* Viz Media.
—IS, Vol. 4. Katsura, Masakazu. 2005. (Is Ser.). (ENG.). 200p. pap. 7.99 *(978-1-4215-0054-6(X))* Viz Media.
—IS, Vol. 6. Katsura, Masakazu. Masakazu Staff. 2006. (I S Ser.). (ENG.). 208p. pap. 7.99 *(978-1-4215-0333-2(6))* Viz Media.
—IS, Vol. 8. Katsura, Masakazu. 2006. (I S Ser.). (ENG.). 208p. pap. 7.99 *(978-1-4215-0649-4(1))* Viz Media.
—I's Vol. 1: Iori. Katsura, Masakazu. 2005. (I S Ser.). (ENG.). 192p. pap. 9.99 *(978-1-59116-952-9(6))* Viz Media.
—I's Vol. 2: Itsuki. Katsura, Masakazu. 2005. (Is Ser.). (ENG.). 200p. (YA). pap. 7.99 *(978-1-59116-953-6(4))* Viz Media.
—Mix Down, Vol. 2. Katsura, Masakazu. 2nd ed. 2004. (Video Girl Ai Ser.). (ENG.). 200p. pap. 9.99 *(978-1-59116-075-5(8))* Viz Media.
—Off-Line. Katsura, Masakazu. 2nd ed. 2004. (Video Girl Ai Ser.). (ENG.). 200p. pap. 9.99 *(978-1-59116-104-2(5))* Viz Media.
—Preproduction. Katsura, Masakazu. 2nd ed. 2004. (Video Girl Ai Ser.: Vol. 1). (ENG.). 192p. pap. 9.99 *(978-1-59116-074-8(X))* Viz Media.
—Recall Vol. 3. Katsura, Masakazu. 2nd ed. 2004. (Video Girl Ai Ser.). (ENG.). 184p. pap. 9.99 *(978-1-59116-103-5(7))* Viz Media.
—Rough Cut, Vol. 10. Katsura, Masakazu. 2004. (Video Girl Ai Ser.). (ENG.). 200p. (YA). pap. 9.99 *(978-1-59116-305-3(6))* Viz Media.
—Spinoff, Vol. 5. Katsura, Masakazu. 2004. (Video Girl Ai Ser.). (ENG.). 200p. (YA). pap. 9.99 *(978-1-59116-146-2(0))* Viz Media.
—Video Girl Ai, Vol. 15. Katsura, Masakazu. 2006. (Video Girl Ai Ser.). (ENG.). 208p. pap. 9.99 *(978-1-4215-0295-3(X))* Viz Media.
—Video Girl Ai: Cutting Room, Vol. 6. Katsura, Masakazu. 2005. (Video Girl Ai Ser.). (ENG.). 200p. (YA). pap. 9.99 *(978-1-59116-607-8(1))* Viz Media.
—Video Girl Ai: Farewell Scene, Vol. 11. Katsura, Masakazu. 2005. (Video Girl Ai Ser.). (ENG.). 192p. (YA). pap. 9.99 *(978-1-59116-306-0(4))* Viz Media.
—Video Girl Ai: Retake, Vol. 7. Katsura, Masakazu. 2005. (Video Girl Ai Ser.). (ENG.). 192p. pap. 9.99 *(978-1-59116-748-8(5))* Viz Media.
Katsura, Masakazu & Oshii, Mamoru. Ghost in the Shell 2: Innocence, 4 vols. Katsura, Masakazu & Oshii, Mamoru. 2005. (Ghost in the Shell 2 Ani-Manga Ser.). (ENG.). 200p. pap. 39.99 *(978-1-59116-829-4(5))* Viz Media.
Katz, Avi. The Adventures of Jeremy & Heddy Levi. Ganz, Yaffa. 2005. 204p. (J). 16.95 *(978-1-930143-50-0(8)*, 3508); pap. 12.95 *(978-1-930143-51-7(6)*, 3516) Simcha Media Group. (Devora Publishing).
—The Boy from Seville. Orgad, Dorit. Silverston, Sondra, tr. from HEB. 2007. (Kar-Ben for Older Readers Ser.). (ENG.). 200p. (J). (gr. 5-7). lib. bdg. 16.95 *(978-1-58013-253-4(7)*, Kar-Ben Publishing) Lerner Publishing Group.
—The Boy in the Invisible Box. Reiss, I. 2007. 24p. per. 9.95 *(978-965-7344-30-9(1))* Mazo Pubs.
—The Burning Light. Ramsay, Elizabeth. 2005. 144p. (J). (gr. 4-9). 14.95 *(978-1-930143-43-2(5))*; pap. 9.95 *(978-1-930143-44-9(3))* Simcha Media Group. (Devora Publishing).
—A Day Full of Mitzvos. Seltzer, Sara Leah. 2009. 26p. (J). *(978-1-4226-0949-1(9))* Mesorah Pubns., Ltd.
Katz, Avi. In My Family. Perlowitz, Rebecca & Becky, Morah. 2014. (ENG.). 32p. (J). (gr. k-2). pap. 10.95 ***(978-965-7514-10-8(X))*** Urim Pubns. ISR. Dist: Independent Pubs. Group.
Katz, Avi. The Little Peninsula. Dran, Ruth. 2011. 264p. (YA). pap. 18.95 *(978-1-936778-87-4(4))* Mazo Pubs.
—Shemot Muzarim. Greenspan, Shari Dash. 2005.Tr. of Strange Names. (HEB.). 32p. 14.00 *(978-965-7108-58-1(6))* Urim Pubns. ISR. Dist: Coronet Bks.
—The Stupendous Adventures of Shragi & Shia. Mermelstein, Yael. 2008. 93p. (J). pap. *(978-1-4226-0865-4(4))* Mesorah Pubns., Ltd.
—A Verseful of Jewish Holidays. Gordon, Ellen. 2008. 24p. pap. 9.95 *(978-965-7344-47-7(6))* Mazo Pubs.
Katz, Avi, jt. illus. see Reilly, Joan.
Katz, David. Electricity & You: Be Smart, Be Safe. Friend, Robyn & Cohen, Judith. l.t. ed. 2012. (ENG.). 40p. (J). pap. 7.00 *(978-1-935999-02-7(8))* Cascade Pass, Inc.
katz, david A. A Clean Planet: The Solar Power Story. friend, robyn C. & cohen, Judith Love. 2009. 48p. (J). pap. 7.00 *(978-1-880599-86-0(4))* Cascade Pass, Inc.
Katz, David A. A Clean Planet: The Solar Power Story. friend, robyn C. & Cohen, Judith Love. 2009. 48p. (J). 13.95 *(978-1-880599-87-7(2))* Cascade Pass, Inc.
—A Clean Sky: The Global Warming Story. Cohen, Judith Love & Friend, Robyn C. 2007. (J). (gr. 4-8). 46p. pap. 7.00 *(978-1-880599-81-5(3))*; 42p. 13.95 *(978-1-880599-82-2(1))* Cascade Pass, Inc.
katz, david A. Future Engineering: The Clean Water Challenge. cohen, judith L. & friend, robyn. 2015. 44p. (J). pap. 7.00 *(978-1-935999-08-9(7))* Cascade Pass, Inc.
Katz, David A. You Can Be A Chemist. Cohen, Judith Love. l.t. ed. 2005. Orig. Title: You Can Be A Woman Chemist. 40p. (J). per. 7.00 *(978-1-880599-71-6(6))* Cascade Pass, Inc.
—You Can Be A Woman Chemist. Cohen, Judith Love. l.t. ed. 2005. 40p. (J). 13.95 *(978-1-880599-72-3(4))* Cascade Pass, Inc.
Katz, David Arthur. A Cleaner Port; A Brighter Future: The Greening of the Port of Los Angeles. Friend, Robyn C. & Cohen, Judith Love. 2011. 46p. (J). 13.95 *(978-1-935999-01-0(X))*; pap. 7.00 *(978-1-935999-00-3(1))* Cascade Pass, Inc.
—The Women of Apollo. Friend, Robyn C. l.t. ed. 2006. 80p. (J). 17.95 *(978-1-880599-80-8(5))*; pap. 12.95 *(978-1-880599-79-2(1))* Cascade Pass, Inc.
—You Can Be A Woman Astronomer. Ghez, Andrea Mia & Cohen, Judith Love. l.t. ed. 40p. (J). 2006. pap. 12.95 incl. DVD *(978-1-880599-77-8(5))*; 2005. 17.95 incl. DVD *(978-1-880599-78-5(3))* Cascade Pass, Inc.
—You Can Be a Woman Botanist. Bozak, Kristin & Cohen, Judith Love. Date not set. 40p. (J). (gr. 3-6). 13.95 *(978-1-880599-41-9(4))*; pap. 12.95 *(978-1-880599-42-6(2))* Cascade Pass, Inc.
—You Can Be A Woman Oceanographer. Franks, Sharon E. & Cohen, Judith Love. 2004. (J). 40p. 19.95 incl. DVD *(978-1-880599-67-9(8))*; pap. 13.95 incl. DVD *(978-1-880599-66-2(X))* Cascade Pass, Inc.
Katz, Jon, photos by. Lenore Finds a Friend: A True Story from Bedlam Farm. Katz, Jon. 2012. (ENG., 32p. (J). (gr. -1-3). 15.99 *(978-0-8050-9220-2(X)*, Holt, Henry & Co. Bks. For Young Readers) Holt, Henry & Co.
—Lenore Finds a Friend: A True Story from Bedlam Farm. Katz, Jon. 2014. (My Readers Ser.). (ENG., 32p. (J). (gr. -1-3). 15.99 *(978-1-250-03432-8(9))* Square Fish.
—Meet the Dogs of Bedlam Farm. Katz, Jon. 2011. (ENG., 32p. (J). (gr. -1-3). 17.99 *(978-0-8050-9219-6(6)*, Holt, Henry & Co. Bks. For Young Readers) Holt, Henry & Co.
Katz, Karen. A Child's Good Morning Book. Brown, Margaret Wise. 2009. 32p. (J). (gr. -1-3). lib. bdg. 18.89 *(978-0-06-128861-6(6))* HarperCollins Pubs.
—In Grandma's Arms. Shelton, Jayne C. 2008. (ENG.). 24p. (J). (gr. -1-k). bds. 6.99 *(978-0-545-06868-0(1))* Scholastic, Inc.
—Sleepy ABC. Brown, Margaret Wise. 2009. (ENG.). 40p. (J). (gr. -1-3). 16.99 *(978-0-06-128863-0(2))* HarperCollins Pubs.
—Subway. Suen, Anastasia. (ENG.). (J). (gr. -1-k). 2008. 24p. bds. 6.99 *(978-0-670-01109-4(6))*; 2004. 40p. 15.99 *(978-0-670-03622-6(6))* Penguin Publishing Group. (Viking Juvenile).
—Toes, Ears, & Nose! Bauer, Marion Dane. 2003. (ENG.). 16p. (J). (gr. -1 — 1). 6.99 *(978-0-689-84712-7(2)*, Little Simon) Little Simon.
Katz, Karen. The Babies on the Bus. Katz, Karen. (ENG.). (J). (gr. -1-k). 2013. 28p. bds. 7.99 *(978-0-8050-9779-5(1))*; 2011. 32p. 14.99 *(978-0-8050-9011-6(8))* Holt, Henry & Co. (Holt, Henry & Co. Bks. For Young Readers).
—Baby at the Farm. Katz, Karen. 2009. (ENG.). 12p. (J). (gr. -1 — 1). bds. 7.99 *(978-1-4169-8568-6(9)*, Little Simon) Little Simon.
—Baby Loves Fall! A Karen Katz Lift-The-Flap Book. Katz, Karen. 2013. (ENG.). 14p. (J). (gr. -1 — 1). bds. 6.99 *(978-1-4424-5209-1(9)*, Little Simon) Little Simon.
—Baby Loves Spring! Katz, Karen. 2012. (ENG.). 14p. (J). (gr. -1 — 1). bds. 6.99 *(978-1-4424-2745-7(0)*, Little Simon) Little Simon.
—Baby Loves Summer! Katz, Karen. 2012. (ENG.). 14p. (J). (gr. -1 — 1). bds. 6.99 *(978-1-4424-2746-4(9)*, Little Simon) Little Simon.
—Baby Loves Winter! A Karen Katz Lift-The-Flap Book. Katz, Karen. 2013. (ENG.). 14p. (J). (gr. -1 — 1). bds. 6.99 *(978-1-4424-5213-8(7)*, Little Simon) Little Simon.
—Baby's Box of Family Fun!, Set. Katz, Karen. gif. ed. 2006. (ENG.). 56p. (J). (gr. -1 — 1). bds. 27.99 *(978-1-4169-2795-2(6)*, Little Simon) Little Simon.
—Baby's Box of Fun! A Karen Katz Lift-the-Flap Gift Set - Where Is Baby's Bellybutton? - Where Is Baby's Mommy? - Toes, Ears, & Nose! Katz, Karen. Bauer, Marion Dane. gif. ed. 2004. (ENG.). 44p. (J). (gr. -1 — 1). bds. 17.99 *(978-0-689-03862-4(3)*, Little Simon) Little Simon.
—Baby's Colors. Katz, Karen. 2010. (ENG.). 14p. (J). (gr. -1 — 1). bds. 5.99 *(978-1-4169-9821-1(7)*, Little Simon) Little Simon.
—Baby's Day. Katz, Karen. 2007. (ENG.). 10p. (J). (gr. -1 — 1). 15.99 *(978-1-4169-3580-3(0)*, Little Simon) Little Simon.
—Baby's Numbers. Katz, Karen. 2010. (ENG.). 14p. (J). (gr. -1 — 1). 5.99 *(978-1-4424-0827-2(8)*, Little Simon) Little Simon.
—Baby's Shapes. Katz, Karen. 2010. (ENG.). 14p. (J). (gr. -1 — 1). bds. 5.99 *(978-1-4169-9824-2(1)*, Little Simon) Little Simon.
—Beddy-Bye, Baby. Katz, Karen. 2009. (ENG.). 12p. (J). (gr. -1 — 1). 7.99 *(978-1-4169-8048-3(2)*, Little Simon) Little Simon.
—Buzz, Buzz, Baby! Katz, Karen. 2014. (ENG.). 14p. (J). (gr. -1 — 1). bds. 6.99 *(978-1-4424-9313-1(5)*, Little Simon) Little Simon.
—Can You Say Peace? Katz, Karen. 2006. (ENG.). 32p. (J). (gr. -1-2). 18.99 *(978-0-8050-7893-0(2)*, Holt, Henry & Co. Bks. For Young Readers) Holt, Henry & Co.
—The Colors of Us. Katz, Karen. 2007. (ENG.). 32p. (J). (gr. -1-3). pap. 26.99 *(978-0-8050-8118-3(6)*, Holt, Henry & Co. Bks. For Young Readers) Holt, Henry & Co.
—Counting Christmas. Katz, Karen. 2007. (Classic Board Bks.). (ENG.). 32p. (J). (gr. -1-1). bds. 7.99 *(978-1-4169-3624-4(6)*, Little Simon) Little Simon.
—Counting Christmas. Katz, Karen. 2003. (ENG.). 32p. (J). (gr. -1-1). 16.99 *(978-0-689-84925-1(7)*, McElderry, Margaret K. Bks.) McElderry, Margaret K. Bks.
—Counting Kisses. Katz, Karen. 2003. (Classic Board Bks.). (ENG.). 32p. (J). (gr. -1-k). bds., bds. 7.99 *(978-0-689-85658-7(X)*, Little Simon) Little Simon.
—Counting Kisses: Lap Edition. Katz, Karen. 2010. (ENG.). 26p. (J). (gr. -1 — 1). 12.99 *(978-1-4424-0792-3(1)*, Little Simon) Little Simon.
—¡Cu-Cú, Bebé! Katz, Karen. 2009. (SPA.). 14p. (J). (gr. -1 — 1). bds. 7.99 *(978-1-4169-7938-8(7)*, Libros Para Ninos) Libros Para Ninos.
—Daddy & Me. Katz, Karen. 2003. (ENG.). 14p. (J). (gr. -1-k). 6.99 *(978-0-689-84906-0(0)*, Little Simon) Little Simon.
—Daddy Hugs. Katz, Karen. 2007. (Classic Board Bks.). (ENG.). 32p. (J). (gr. -1 — 1). 7.99 *(978-1-4169-4120-0(7)*, Little Simon) Little Simon.
—Daddy Hugs 1 2 3. Katz, Karen. 2005. (ENG.). 32p. (J). (gr. -1-1). 17.99 *(978-0-689-87771-1(4)*, McElderry, Margaret K. Bks.) McElderry, Margaret K. Bks.
—¿Dónde Está el Ombliguito? Katz, Karen. Ziegler, Argentina Palacios, tr. 2004. (SPA.). 14p. (J). (gr. -1-1). bds. 6.99 *(978-0-689-86977-8(0)*, Libros Para Ninos) Libros Para Ninos.
—Grandpa & Me. Katz, Karen. 2004. (ENG.). 14p. (J). (gr. -1-k). 6.99 *(978-0-689-86644-9(5)*, Little Simon) Little Simon.
—How Does Baby Feel? A Karen Katz Lift-The-Flap Book. Katz, Karen. 2013. (ENG.). 14p. (J). (gr. -1 — 1). bds. 6.99 *(978-1-4424-5204-6(8)*, Little Simon) Little Simon.
—I Can Share. Katz, Karen. 2004. (ENG.). 14p. (J). (gr. -1-k). 5.99 *(978-0-448-43611-1(6)*, Grosset & Dunlap) Penguin Publishing Group.
—Mommy Hugs. Katz, Karen. 2007. (Classic Board Bks.). (ENG.). 32p. (J). (gr. -1 — 1). bds. 7.99 *(978-1-4169-4121-7(5)*, Little Simon) Little Simon.
—Mommy Hugs. Katz, Karen. 2006. (ENG.). 32p. (J). (gr. -1-3). 17.99 *(978-0-689-87772-8(2)*, McElderry, Margaret K. Bks.) McElderry, Margaret K. Bks.
—Mommy Hugs: Lap Edition. Katz, Karen. 2010. (ENG.). 26p. (J). (gr. -1 — 1). bds. 12.99 *(978-1-4424-0791-6(3)*, Little Simon) Little Simon.
—My First Chinese New Year. Katz, Karen. rev. ed. 2005. (My First Holiday Ser.). (ENG.). 32p. (J). (gr. -1-k). 16.99 *(978-0-8050-7076-7(1)*, Holt, Henry & Co. Bks. For Young Readers) Holt, Henry & Co.
—My First Chinese New Year. Katz, Karen. 2012. (My First Holiday Ser.). (ENG.). 32p. (J). (gr. -1-k). 6.99 *(978-1-250-01868-7(4))* Square Fish.
—My First Kwanzaa. Katz, Karen. rev. ed. 2003. (My First Holiday Ser.). (ENG.). 28p. (J). (gr. -1-k). 14.95 *(978-0-8050-7077-4(X)*, Holt, Henry & Co. Bks. For Young Readers) Holt, Henry & Co.
—My First Kwanzaa. Katz, Karen. 2014. (My First Holiday Ser.). (ENG.). 32p. (J). (gr. -1-k). 6.99 *(978-1-250-05046-5(4))* Square Fish.
—No Hitting! Katz, Karen. 2004. (ENG.). 14p. (J). (gr. -1-k). 5.99 *(978-0-448-43612-8(4)*, Grosset & Dunlap) Penguin Publishing Group.
—Now I'm Big! Katz, Karen. 2013. (ENG.). 32p. (J). (gr. -1-k). 15.99 *(978-1-4169-3547-6(9)*, McElderry, Margaret K. Bks.) McElderry, Margaret K. Bks.
—Peek-a-Baby. Katz, Karen. (ENG.). 14p. (J). (gr. -1 — 1). 2010. bds. 11.99 *(978-1-4424-0790-9(5))*; 2007. 6.99 *(978-1-4169-3622-0(X))* Little Simon. (Little Simon).
—A Potty for Me! Katz, Karen. 2005. (ENG.). 28p. (J). (gr. -1-k). tchr. ed. 7.99 *(978-0-689-87423-9(5)*, Little Simon) Little Simon.
—Princess Baby. Katz, Karen. (Princess Baby Ser.). (ENG.). (J). (gr. k-k). 2012. 30p. bds. 6.99 *(978-0-307-93146-7(3))*; 2008. 32p. 14.99 *(978-0-375-84119-4(9))* Random Hse. Children's Bks. (Schwartz & Wade Bks.).
—Princess Baby, Night-Night. Katz, Karen. 2014. (Princess Baby Ser.). (ENG.). 28p. (J). (— 1). bds. 6.99 *(978-0-385-37848-2(3)*, Schwartz & Wade Bks.) Random Hse. Children's Bks.
—Princess Baby on the Go. Katz, Karen. 2010. (Princess Baby Ser.). (ENG.). 14p. (J). (— 1). 7.99 *(978-0-375-85664-8(1)*, Schwartz & Wade Bks.) Random Hse. Children's Bks.
—Roar, Roar, Baby! Katz, Karen. 2015. (ENG.). 14p. (J). (gr. -1 — 1). bds. 6.99 *(978-1-4814-1788-4(6)*, Little Simon) Little Simon.
—Shake It up, Baby! Katz, Karen. 2009. (ENG.). 14p. (J). (gr. -1 — 1). 7.99 *(978-1-4169-6737-8(0)*, Little Simon) Little Simon.
—Ten Tiny Babies. Katz, Karen. 2011. (Classic Board Bks.). (ENG.). 32p. (J). (gr. -1-k). bds. 7.99 *(978-1-4424-1394-8(8)*, Little Simon) Little Simon.
—Ten Tiny Babies. Katz, Karen. 2008. (ENG.). 32p. (J). (gr. -1-k). 17.99 *(978-1-4169-3546-9(0)*, McElderry, Margaret K. Bks.) McElderry, Margaret K. Bks.
—Ten Tiny Tickles. Katz, Karen. 2008. (Classic Board Bks.). (ACE & ENG.). 32p. (J). (gr. -1-k). bds. 7.99 *(978-1-4169-5101-8(6)*, Little Simon) Little Simon.
—Ten Tiny Tickles. Katz, Karen. 2005. (ENG.). 32p. (J). (gr. -1-k). 15.99 *(978-0-689-85976-2(7)*, McElderry, Margaret K. Bks.) McElderry, Margaret K. Bks.
—What Does Baby Say? Katz, Karen. 2004. (ENG.). 16p. (J). (gr. -1-k). 6.99 *(978-0-689-86645-6(3)*, Little Simon) Little Simon.
—Where Are Baby's Easter Eggs? Katz, Karen. 2008. (ENG.). 14p. (J). (gr. -1 — 1). bds. 7.99 *(978-1-4169-4924-4(0)*, Little Simon) Little Simon.
—Where Is Baby's Beach Ball? Katz, Karen. 2009. (ENG.). 14p. (J). (gr. -1 — 1). 6.99 *(978-1-4169-4962-6(3)*, Little Simon) Little Simon.
—Where Is Baby's Belly Button? Katz, Karen. anniv. ed. 2009. (ENG.). 14p. (J). (gr. -1 — 1). bds. 12.99 *(978-1-4169-8733-8(9)*, Little Simon) Little Simon.
—Where Is Baby's Birthday Cake? Katz, Karen. 2008. (ENG.). 14p. (J). (gr. -1 — 1). 6.99 *(978-1-4169-5817-8(7)*, Little Simon) Little Simon.
—Where Is Baby's Christmas Present? Katz, Karen. 2009. (ENG.). 14p. (J). (gr. -1 — 1). bds. 7.99 *(978-1-4169-7145-0(9)*, Little Simon) Little Simon.
—Where Is Baby's Dreidel? Katz, Karen. 2007. (ENG.). 14p. (J). (gr. -1 — 1). bds. 6.99 *(978-1-4169-3623-7(8)*, Little Simon) Little Simon.
—Where Is Baby's Pumpkin? Katz, Karen. 2006. (ENG.). 14p. (J). (gr. -1 — 1). 7.99 *(978-1-4169-0970-5(2)*, Little Simon) Little Simon.
—Where Is Baby's Puppy? Katz, Karen. 2011. (ENG.). 14p. (J). (gr. -1 — 1). 6.99 *(978-1-4169-8684-3(7)*, Little Simon) Little Simon.
—Where Is Baby's Valentine? Katz, Karen. 2006. (ENG.). 14p. (J). (gr. -1 — 1). bds. 7.99 *(978-1-4169-0971-2(0)*, Little Simon) Little Simon.
—Where Is Baby's Yummy Tummy? Katz, Karen. 2011. (ENG.). 14p. (J). (gr. -1 — 1). bds. 6.99 *(978-1-4424-2165-3(7)*, Little Simon) Little Simon.
—Wiggle Your Toes: A Karen Katz Book to Pull, Fluff, & Wiggle. Katz, Karen. 2006. (ENG.). 14p. (J). (gr. -1-k). bds. 8.99 *(978-1-4169-0365-9(8)*, Little Simon) Little Simon.
—Zoom, Zoom, Baby! A Karen Katz Lift-The-Flap Book. Katz, Karen. 2014. (ENG.). 14p. (J). (gr. -1 — 1). bds. 6.99 *(978-1-4424-9314-8(3)*, Little Simon) Little Simon.
Katz, Nevin. Constructing the Earth: Middle & High School. Katz, Nevin. Norris, Jill, ed. 2009. (Dr. Birdley Teaches Science Ser.). (ENG.). 96p. (gr. 5-9). pap. 12.99 *(978-0-86530-542-7(0))* Incentive Pubns., Inc.
Katz, Tova. The Adventures of Aliza & Dovid: Holidays at the Farm. Blitz, Shmuel. 2005. (ArtScroll Youth Ser.). 48p. (J). *(978-1-4226-0021-4(1))* Mesorah Pubns., Ltd.
Katz, Tova. ArtScroll Children's Book of Berachos: [Sefer Ha-Berakhot Sheli]. Blitz, Shmuel. 2011. (ENG & HEB.). 48p. (J). ***(978-1-4226-1170-8(1))*** Mesorah Pubns., Ltd.
Katz, Tova. Every Story Has a Soul. Blitz, Shmuel. 2006. 47p. (J). 15.99 *(978-1-4226-0224-9(9))* Mesorah Pubns., Ltd.
—[ha-Tehilim Ha-Rishon]: ArtScroll Children's Tehillim. Blitz, Shmuel. 2008. (Artscroll Youth Ser.). 96p. (J). *(978-1-4226-0751-0(8))* Mesorah Pubns., Ltd.
—Megilat Ester: The ArtScroll Children's Megillah. Blitz, Shmuel. 2003. (ArtScroll Ser.). (ENG & HEB.). 79p. (J). 16.99 *(978-1-57819-708-8(2)*, MCHH); pap. 10.99 *(978-1-57819-709-5(0)*, MCHP) Mesorah Pubns., Ltd.
—[Megilat Rut]: The Artscroll Children's Book of Ruth. Blitz, Shmuel. 2005. (ArtScroll Youth Ser.). 48p. (J). *(978-1-57819-069-0(X))*; pap. *(978-1-57819-070-6(3))* Mesorah Pubns., Ltd.
—[Sefer Yonah]: The Artscroll Children's Book of Jonah. Blitz, Shmuel. 2006. 48p. (J). *(978-1-4226-0130-3(7))*; pap. *(978-1-4226-0131-0(5))* Mesorah Pubns., Ltd.
—Stories for a Child's Heart. Pruzansky, Binyomin. 2009. 48p. (J). *(978-1-4226-0915-6(4))* Mesorah Pubns., Ltd.
—The Story of Chanukah. Leon, Sarah & Eisikowitz, Michal. 2008. 63p. (J). *(978-1-4226-0875-3(1))* Mesorah Pubns., Ltd.

Katzen, Mollie. The Vegetable Dishes I Can't Live Without. Katzen, Mollie. rev. ed. 2007. (ENG.). 160p. (gr. 8-17). 24.00 *(978-1-4013-2232-8(8))* Hyperion Pr.

Katzenstein, Jason A. Kitai's Journal. Peymani, Christine. 2013. (ENG.). 144p. (J). (gr. 3-7). pap. 5.99 *(978-0-06-226857-0(0))* HarperCollins Pubs.

Kauenhofen, Jessica. My First A B C Book. Kauenhofen, Jessica. 2007. (Little Jewel Book Ser.). 24p. (J). (gr. 2). pap. 2.70 *(978-0-7399-2385-6(4))* Rod & Staff Pubs., Inc.

Kauffin, Karlynn. Anit: The Chef. Gaskins, Melda. 2011. 24p. pap. 24.95 *(978-1-4626-4485-8(6))* America Star Bks.

Kauffman, Margaret, jt. illus. see Peggykauffman.com Staff.

Kaufman, Angelika. Piruleta. Nöstlinger, Christine. 2003. (SPA.). 132p. (gr. 3-5). pap. 9.95 *(978-968-19-0983-3(6))* Santillana USA Publishing Co., Inc.

Kaufman, Elliott, photos by. Alphabet Everywhere. 2012. (ENG., 60p. (J). (gr. -1). 14.95 *(978-0-7892-1115-6(7)*, Abbeville Kids) Abbeville Pr., Inc.

—Numbers Everywhere. 2013. (ENG., 32p. (J). (gr. -1). 12.95 *(978-0-7892-1157-6(2)*, Abbeville Kids) Abbeville Pr., Inc.

Kaufman, Mary Bee. The Journey of Perm. Peterson, Sara Budinger. 2004. 96p. pap. 11.95 *(978-0-9665282-3-7(9))* Saranjon Publishing.

Kaufman, Yaki. The Ant & the Wheat Kernel: For Young Readers. Penina, M. 2012. 24p. 19.75 net. *(978-1-60046-090-6(9))* Yofi Bk. Publishing, Inc.

—Dove Builds a Nest: For Young Readers. Penina, M. 2012. 22p. 19.75 net. *(978-1-60046-091-3(7))* Yofi Bk. Publishing, Inc.

Kaufmann, Angelika. Hoppelpopp & the Best Bunny. Lobe, Mira & Kovacs, Cécilie. 2015. (ENG.). 32p. (J). (gr. -1-3). 16.95 *(978-0-8234-3287-5(4))* Holiday Hse., Inc.

—Piruleta. Nöstlinger, Christine. 2003. (SPA.). 136p. (J). (gr. 3-5). 9.95 *(978-84-204-4777-3(3))* Ediciones Alfaguara ESP. Dist: Santillana USA Publishing Co., Inc.

Kaulbach, Kathy, jt. illus. see MacDonald, Clarke.

Kaulbach, Kathy R. Healing the Bruises, 1 vol. Morgan, Lori. 2013. (ENG.). 32p. (J). (gr. 1-4). 16.95 *(978-1-4595-0283-3(3))* Formac Publishing Co., Ltd. CAN. Dist: Casemate Pubs. & Bk. Distributors, LLC.

Kaur, Bal. The Homcastles & the Magnopeus Medicine. Kaur, K. S. 2012. 154p. pap. *(978-1-78148-023-6(0))* Grosvenor Hse. Publishing Ltd.

Kavanagh, Peter. Annie to the Rescue. Lindsay, Elizabeth. 2003. 94p. (J). *(978-0-439-56006-1(3))* Scholastic, Inc.

—Beauty & the Beast. Wilson, Jacqueline. 2012. *(978-0-88734-073-4(3))* Players Pr., Inc.

Kavanagh, Peter. The Frankenstein Teacher. Bradman, Tony. 2014. (Colour First Reader Ser.). (ENG.). 80p. (J). (gr. k-2). pap. 9.99 ***(978-0-552-56899-9(6))*** Transworld Publishers Ltd. GBR. Dist: Independent Pubs. Group.

Kavanagh, Peter. The Ghost Teacher. Bradman, Tony. 2012. (ENG.). 64p. (J). (gr. -1-2). pap. 8.99 *(978-0-552-56580-6(6))* Transworld Publishers Ltd. GBR. Dist: Independent Pubs. Group.

—Journey to the World of the Dinosaurs: Peek Inside the Pop-Up Windows! Taylor, Dereen. 2014. (ENG.). 12p. (J). (gr. 2-7). 16.99 *(978-1-86147-319-6(2)*, Armadillo) Anness Publishing GBR. Dist: National Bk. Network.

—The Knight's First Tournament. Taylor, Dereen. 2012. (ENG.). 12p. (J). (gr. 1-6). 16.99 *(978-1-84322-760-1(6))* Anness Publishing GBR. Dist: National Bk. Network.

—The Soft-Hearted Sheepdog. Green, Sylvia. 2003. 144p. (J). *(978-0-439-62569-2(6))* Scholastic, Inc.

Kawa, Cosei. Feeding the Flying Fanellis: And Other Poems from a Circus Chef. Hosford, Kate. 2015. (ENG.). 32p. (J). (gr. 1-3). 17.99 *(978-1-4677-7511-3(8))*; lib. bdg. 17.99 *(978-1-4677-3905-4(7))* Lerner Publishing Group. (Carolrhoda Bks.).

—Rifka Takes a Bow. Perlov, Betty Rosenberg. 2013. (ENG.). 32p. (J). (gr. k-3). 17.95 *(978-0-7613-8127-3(9))*; 7.95 *(978-0-7613-8128-0(7))* Lerner Publishing Group. (Kar-Ben Publishing).

Kawahara, Yumiko. Dolls. Kawahara, Yumiko. (Dolls Ser.). (ENG.). 1. 2004. 200p. (YA). pap. 9.99 *(978-1-59116-508-8(3))*; Vol. 2. 2005. 216p. (YA). pap. 9.99 *(978-1-59116-670-2(5))*; Vol. 3. 2005. 200p. pap. 9.99 *(978-1-59116-769-3(8))*; Vol. 4. 2005. 224p. pap. 9.99 *(978-1-59116-866-9(X))* Viz Media.

Kawai, Ritsuko. Balloon Adventure. Kawai, Ritsuko. 2003. (Hamtaro Ser.: Vol. 2). (ENG.). 16p. (J). pap. 7.95 *(978-1-56931-815-7(8))* Viz Media.

—Ham-Ham Party Vol. 1. Kawai, Ritsuko. 2003. (Hamtaro Ser.). (ENG.). 16p. (J). pap. 7.95 *(978-1-56931-814-0(X))* Viz Media.

—Hamtaro Gets Lost & Other Stories. Kawai, Ritsuko. 2003. (Adventures of Hamtaro Ser.: Vol. 2). (ENG.). 92p. (J). (gr. 1-3). 9.95 *(978-1-56931-817-1(4))* Viz Media.

—Hamtaro Pop-Up Playset. Kawai, Ritsuko. 2003. (Hamtaro Ser.). (ENG.). 20p. (J). pap. 16.95 *(978-1-56931-846-1(8))* Viz Media.

—Hamtaro Postcard Book. Kawai, Ritsuko. 2003. (Hamtaro Ser.). (ENG.). 24p. (J). pap. 7.95 *(978-1-56931-845-4(X))* Viz Media.

—Let's Play! Vol. 4: A Playground for Ham-Ham. Kawai, Ritsuko. 2003. (Hamtaro Ser.). (ENG.). 16p. (J). (gr. 1-3). pap. 7.95 *(978-1-56931-821-8(2))* Viz Media.

—The Little Lost Caterpillar, Vol. 3. Kawai, Ritsuko. 2003. (Hamtaro Ser.). (ENG.). 16p. (J). pap. 7.95 *(978-1-56931-816-4(6))* Viz Media.

Kawaiae, Aaron A. Kohala Kuamoo. Kawaiae, Kekaulelenaeole A. 2010. 32p. 16.00 *(978-0-87336-232-0(2))* Kamehameha Publishing.

Kawanishi, Mikio. Creating Stories. Sugamoto, Junichi. 2007. (How to Draw Manga Ser.: Vol. 39). 140p. (YA). per. 19.99 *(978-4-7661-1330-3(6))* Graphic-Sha JPN. Dist: Diamond Bk. Distributors.

Kawasaki, Shauna Mooney. Christmas in Idaho. Carabine, Sue & Adams, Jennifer. ed. 2004. (ENG.). 64p. (J). 5.99 *(978-1-58685-451-5(8))* Gibbs Smith, Publisher.

—My Family Can Be Forever: Sharing Time Activities. 2003. 62p. (J). pap. *(978-1-59038-232-5(3))* Deseret Bk. Co.

—The Night Before Christmas in Michigan. Carabine, Sue & Smith, Johanna. ed. 2004. (ENG.). 64p. (J). 5.99 *(978-1-58685-452-2(6))* Gibbs Smith, Publisher.

Kay, Jim. Bugs: A Stunning Pop-Up Look at Insects, Spiders, & Other Creepy-Crawlies. McGavin, George. 2013. (ENG.). 12p. (J). (gr. 2-5). 19.99 *(978-0-7636-6762-7(5))* Candlewick Pr.

—The Great War: Stories Inspired by Items from the First World War. Almond, David et al. 2015. (ENG.). 304p. (J). (gr. 5). 19.99 *(978-0-7636-7554-7(7))* Candlewick Pr.

—A Monster Calls: Inspired by an Idea from Siobhan Dowd. Ness, Patrick. (ENG.). 224p. (J). (gr. 7). 2013. pap. 9.99 *(978-0-7636-6065-9(5))*; 2011. 16.99 *(978-0-7636-5559-4(7))* Candlewick Pr.

Kaye, Donna M. Jewish Holiday Adventures. Stein, Ethel. 2010. 52p. 25.00 *(978-1-4349-9618-3(2)*, RoseDog Bks.) Dorrance Publishing Co., Inc.

Kaye, Rosalind Charney. Chanukah on the Prairie. Schuman, Burt E. 2004. (gr. k-3). 13.95 *(978-0-8074-0814-8(X)*, 381780) URJ Pr.

—Come, Let Us Be Joyful! The Story of Hava Nagila. Manushkin, Fran. 2004. (gr. k-3). 13.95 *(978-0-8074-0731-8(3)*, 101073) URJ Pr.

—Hello, Hello, Are You There, God? Cone, Molly. rev. ed. 2004. viii, 55p. (gr. k-3). pap. 13.95 *(978-0-8074-0648-9(1)*, 102553) URJ Pr.

—Hello, Hello, Are You There God?, Grades Preschool-3. Cone, Molly. 2004. (gr. k-3). pap., tchr. ed. 14.95 *(978-0-8074-0655-7(4)*, 208048) URJ Pr.

—Sophie & the Shofar. Manushkin, Fran. 2004. (J). (gr. k-3). 13.95 *(978-0-8074-0751-6(8)*, 101078) URJ Pr.

Kayganich, Bob. Flight of the Butterflies. Edwards, Roberta. 2010. (Penguin Young Readers, Level 3 Ser.). (ENG.). 48p. (J). (gr. 1-3). mass mkt. 3.99 *(978-0-448-45396-5(7)*, Grosset & Dunlap) Penguin Publishing Group.

—Titanic: The Story Lives On! Driscoll, Laura. 2012. (Penguin Young Readers, Level 4 Ser.). (ENG.). 48p. (J). (gr. 3-4). 14.99 *(978-0-448-45902-8(7))*; mass mkt. 3.99 *(978-0-448-45757-4(1))* Penguin Bks., Ltd. GBR. (Warne, Frederick Pubs.). Dist: Penguin Random Hse., LLC.

Kaylor, Emiko, jt. illus. see Muronaka, Michael.

Kazui, Kazumi. Yami No Matsuei. Katayama, Kyoichi. 2005. (Socrates in Love Ser.: Vol. 1). (ENG.). 192p. pap. 8.99 *(978-1-4215-0199-4(6))* Viz Media.

Kazuko. What Will the Weather Be Like Today? Rogers, Paul. 2011. (Houghton Mifflin Reading Ser.). 38p. (J). pap. 61.35 *(978-0-618-03420-8(X))* Houghton Mifflin Harcourt Trade & Reference Pubs.

Keaggy, Sarah. The Abcs of Making Good Choices. Young, Dawn. 2013. 34p. 17.00 *(978-0-9860244-8-1(1))* O'More Publishing.

—Little Blue, Little Gray. Gentry, Nancy. 2012. 56p. pap. 10.00 *(978-0-9846244-9-2(X))* O'More Publishing.

—Skyler & the Se. Rogers, Lauren. Sexton, Jessa, ed. 2012. 36p. pap. 8.00 *(978-0-9860150-1-4(6))* O'More Publishing.

—The Sneaky Shoe Bug. Robertson, Robbin Davis. Sexton, Jessa R., ed. 2012. 44p. 16.00 *(978-0-9860150-4-5(0))* O'More Publishing.

Keane, Dave. First Day Frights. Keane, Dave. 2012. (I Can Read Book 2 Ser.). (ENG.). 32p. (J). (gr. -1-3). pap. 3.99 *(978-0-06-085475-1(8))* HarperCollins Pubs.

—The Haunted Toolshed. Keane, Dave. 2006. (Joe Sherlock, Kid Detective Ser.: 1). (ENG.). 128p. (J). (gr. 2-5). pap. 3.99 *(978-0-06-076188-2(1))* HarperCollins Pubs.

—Monster School: First Day Frights. Keane, Dave. 2012. (I Can Read Book 2 Ser.). (ENG.). 32p. (J). (gr. -1-3). 16.99 *(978-0-06-085476-8(6))* HarperCollins Pubs.

—Monster School: The Spooky Sleepover. Keane, Dave. 2014. (I Can Read Book 2 Ser.). (ENG.). 32p. (J). (gr. -1-3). pap. 3.99 *(978-0-06-085477-5(4))* HarperCollins Pubs.

Kearney, Brendan. Flying Machines. Candlewick Press Staff & Arnold, Nick. 2014. (ENG.). (J). (gr. 3-7). 19.99 *(978-0-7636-7107-5(X))* Candlewick Pr.

Kearney, Jennifer. The Sunflower. King, Ken. 2008. 24p. (J). pap. 14.99 *(978-1-4343-8463-8(2))* AuthorHouse.

Keates, Colin, photos by. Crystal & Gem: Eyewitness Books. Symes, R. F. & Harding, Robert. 2004. 63p. (J). (gr. 4-8). reprint ed. 19.00 *(978-0-7567-7687-9(2))* DIANE Publishing Co.

Keating, Nancy. The Colours of My Home: A Portrait of Newfoundland & Labrador, 1 vol. Pynn, Susan. 2007. (ENG.). 32p. (J). (gr. -1-2). pap. 8.95 *(978-1-897174-06-7(3))* Creative Bk. Publishing CAN. Dist: Orca Bk. Pubs. USA.

—Find Scruncheon & Touton 2: All Around Newfoundland, 1 vol. Keating, Laurel. 2012. (ENG.). 32p. (J). (gr. k-3). pap. 10.95 *(978-1-897174-89-0(6)*, Tuckamore Bks) Creative Bk. Publishing CAN. Dist: Orca Bk. Pubs. USA.

—Forget-Me-Not, 1 vol. Trottier, Maxine. 2008. (ENG.). 32p. (J). (gr. 1-8). pap. 10.95 *(978-1-897174-24-1(1)*, Tuckamore Bks) Creative Bk. Publishing CAN. Dist: Orca Bk. Pubs. USA.

—The Land of a Thousand Whales, 1 vol. Browne, Susan Chalker. 2007. (ENG.). 32p. (J). (gr. 3-7). pap. 8.95 *(978-1-897174-08-1(X))* Creative Bk. Publishing CAN. Dist: Orca Bk. Pubs. USA.

—A Puppy Story, 1 vol. Pynn, Susan. 2007. (ENG.). 32p. (J). (gr. -1-3). pap. 8.95 *(978-1-897174-18-0(7))* Creative Bk. Publishing CAN. Dist: Orca Bk. Pubs. USA.

—Rebecca's Ducks, 1 vol. Moore, Angela. 2007. (ENG.). 32p. (J). (gr. -1-2). pap. 8.95 *(978-1-897174-00-5(4)*, Tuckamore Bks) Creative Bk. Publishing CAN. Dist: Orca Bk. Pubs. USA.

—Search for Scruncheon & Touton, 1 vol. Keating, Laurel. 2012. (ENG.). 32p. (J). (gr. -1-3). 10.95 *(978-1-897174-69-2(1)*, Tuckamore Bks) Creative Bk. Publishing CAN. Dist: Orca Bk. Pubs. USA.

Keaton, Pam. Burton the Sneezing Cow. Hall, Lisa. 2012. 28p. (-18). pap. 9.95 *(978-1-939289-06-3(8)*, Little Creek Bks.) Jan-Carol Publishing, INC.

Keats, Ezra Jack. Jennie's Hat. Keats, Ezra Jack. 2003. (ENG.). 32p. (J). (gr. -1-2). 6.99 *(978-0-14-250035-4(6)*, Puffin) Penguin Publishing Group.

—Louie. Keats, Ezra Jack. 2004. (ENG.). 40p. (J). (gr. -1-2). pap. 6.99 *(978-0-14-240080-7(7)*, Puffin) Penguin Publishing Group.

—Peter's Chair. Keats, Ezra Jack. 2006. (ENG.). 32p. (J). (gr. -1 — 1). bds. 6.99 *(978-0-670-06190-7(5)*, Viking Juvenile) Penguin Publishing Group.

Keay, Claire. Bumblebee Bike. Levins, Sandra. 2014. (J). *(978-1-4338-1645-1(8))*; 32p. pap. *(978-1-4338-1646-8(6))* American Psychological Assn. (Magination Pr.).

—I Love You All Year Long. Metzger, Steve. 2009. 20p. (J). (gr. -1-k). 8.95 *(978-1-58925-847-1(9))* Tiger Tales.

—The Littlest Levine. Lanton, Sandy. 2014. (Passover Ser.). (ENG.). 24p. (J). (gr. -1-2). 17.95 *(978-0-7613-9045-9(6))*; 7.95 *(978-0-7613-9046-6(4))* Lerner Publishing Group. (Kar-Ben Publishing).

Keay, Claire. Somebody Cares: A Guide for Kids Who Have Experienced Neglect. Straus, Susan Farber. 2016. (J). ***(978-1-4338-2109-7(5)**,* Magination Pr.) American Psychological Assn.

Keay, Claire. 1-2-3 a Calmer Me. Patterson, Colleen A. & Miles, Brenda. 2015. (J). *(978-1-4338-1931-5(7))* American Psychological Assn.

Keba, Jamila. Beautiful Wild Rose Girl. Magnolia, B. Hugel, William K., ed. 2012. 34p. pap. 7.95 *(978-0-9854289-0-7(2))* Mystic World Pr.

Kecskés, Anna. Danny Strikes Out in Americ: A R. E. A. d Book. Judybee. 2013. 32p. pap. *(978-1-78092-335-2(X))* MX Publishing, Ltd.

—Story Time for Kids with Nlp by the English Sisters: The Little Grasshopper & the Big Ball of Dung. Zuggo, Violeta & Zuggo, Jutka. 2013. 24p. pap. *(978-1-78092-493-9(3))* MX Publishing, Ltd.

KecskTs, Anna. Leah - the Fairy of the Lime Tree. Kisson, Nisha. 2008. 36p. pap. *(978-1-904312-39-0(X))* MX Publishing, Ltd.

Keddy, Brian. Emily to the Rescue. Williamson, Liza. 2011. 28p. pap. 24.95 *(978-1-4626-3342-5(0))* America Star Bks.

Keeble, Susan. Halimah & the Snake & Other Omani Folktales. Tondino-Gonguet, Grace. 2008. (ENG.). 56p. (J). 16.95 *(978-1-905299-63-8(X)*, Stacey International) Stacey Publishing GBR. Dist: Casemate Academic.

—Tina the Turtle. Todino, Grace. 2013. (ENG.). 58p. (J). (gr. k). 19.95 *(978-1-908531-00-1(2))* Gilgamesh Publishing GBR. Dist: Consortium Bk. Sales & Distribution.

Keegan, Charles. The Hunt Begins. Jordan, Robert. 2004. (Wheel of Time (Starscape) Ser.: 2). (ENG.). 432p. (YA). (gr. 7-12). mass mkt. 5.99 *(978-0-7653-4843-2(8)*, Starscape) Doherty, Tom Assocs., LLC.

—The Hunt Begins. Jordan, Robert. 2005. (Great Hunt Ser.: Bk. 1). 397p. (gr. 5-9). 16.00 *(978-0-7569-5065-1(1))* Perfection Learning Corp.

Keegan, Coral. Who Is Baby Hoo Hoo? Keegan, Orsolya. 2011. (ENG.). 34p. pap. 12.95 *(978-1-4565-5671-6(1))* CreateSpace Independent Publishing Platform.

Keegan, Jonathan. The Lambkins. Bunting, Eve. 2005. 192p. (J). (gr. 5-18). (ENG.). 15.99 *(978-0-06-059906-5(5))*; lib. bdg. 16.89 *(978-0-06-059907-2(3))* HarperCollins Pubs. (Cotler, Joanna Books).

Keeler, Patricia. Thank You, Angels! Virtue, Doreen. 2007. (ENG.). 32p. (gr. -1-3). 15.95 *(978-1-4019-1846-0(8))* Hay Hse., Inc.

Keeler, Patricia A. Drumbeat in Our Feet, 1 vol. Keeler, Patricia A. Leitão, Júlio T. 2012. (ENG.). 32p. (J). (gr. 1-6). lib. bdg. 16.95 *(978-1-58430-264-3(X))* Lee & Low Bks., Inc.

Keeler, Renee. Seasons. 2006. (Learn to Write Ser.). 8p. (J). (gr. k-2). pap. 3.49 *(978-1-59198-291-3(X)*, 6185) Creative Teaching Pr., Inc.

Keely, Jack. Animal Grossology: The Science of Creatures Gross & Disgusting. Branzei, Sylvia. 2004. (Grossology Ser.). (ENG.). 80p. (J). (gr. 3-7). reprint ed. mass mkt. 9.99 *(978-0-8431-1011-1(2)*, Price Stern Sloan) Penguin Publishing Group.

—Hands-On Grossology: Really Gross Science Experiments. Branzei, Sylvia. 2003. (Grossology Ser.). (ENG.). 80p. (J). (gr. 3-7). mass mkt. 6.99 *(978-0-8431-0305-2(1)*, Price Stern Sloan) Penguin Publishing Group.

—The History of Vampires & Other Real Blood Drinkers. Branzei, Sylvia. 2009. (All Aboard Reading Ser.). (ENG.). 48p. (J). (gr. 1-3). mass mkt. 3.99 *(978-0-448-45032-2(1)*, Grosset & Dunlap) Penguin Publishing Group.

—Ickstory - Unraveling the History of Mummies Around the World. Branzei, Sylvia. 2009. (Penguin Young Readers, Level 4 Ser.). (ENG.). 48p. (J). (gr. 3-4). mass mkt. 3.99 *(978-0-448-45033-9(X)*, Warne, Frederick Pubs.) Penguin Bks., Ltd. GBR. Dist: Penguin Random Hse., LLC.

Keen, Sophie. My Favorite Michael. Heiman, Laura. 2009. (J). (gr. -1-2). 32p. 15.95 *(978-1-58925-086-4(9))*; 24p. pap. 7.95 *(978-1-58925-419-0(8))* Tiger Tales.

—Selkie Child. Howell, Gill. 2005. (ENG.). 24p. (J). lib. bdg. 23.65 *(978-1-59646-750-7(9))* Dingles & Co.

Keenan, Brona. Kangaroo Christmas. Rose, M. E. 2007. (ENG.). 140p. (YA). 10.95 *(978-1-896209-89-0(0))* Bayeux Arts, Inc. CAN. Dist: Chicago Distribution Ctr.

Keep, Richard. Clatter Bash! A Day of the Dead Celebration, 1 vol. Keep, Richard. (ENG.). 32p. (J). (gr. k-3). 2008. pap. 7.95 *(978-1-56145-461-7(3))*; 2004. 15.95 *(978-1-56145-322-1(6))* Peachtree Pubs.

—A Thump from Upstairs: Starring Mr. Boo & Max, 1 vol. Keep, Richard. 2005. (ENG.). 36p. (J). (gr. -1-3). 15.95 *(978-1-56145-348-1(X))* Peachtree Pubs.

Keep, Virginia. The April fool Doll. Gates, Josephine Scribner. 2007. 152p. (J). lib. bdg. 59.00 *(978-1-60304-009-9(9))* Dollworks.

—The dolls in Fairyland. Gates, Josephine Scribner. 2007. 136p. (J). lib. bdg. 59.00 *(978-1-60304-013-6(7))* Dollworks.

—Little girl Blue: Lives in the woods till she learns to say Please. Gates, Josephine Scribner. 2007. 54p. (J). lib. bdg. 59.00 *(978-1-60304-012-9(9))* Dollworks.

—Little red white & Blue. Gates, Josephine Scribner. 2007. 118p. (J). lib. bdg. 59.00 *(978-1-60304-006-8(4))* Dollworks.

—The live dolls' busy Days. Gates, Josephine Scribner. 2007. 106p. (J). lib. bdg. 59.00 *(978-1-60304-007-5(2))* Dollworks.

—The live dolls' house Party. Gates, Josephine Scribner. 2007. 104p. (J). lib. bdg. 59.00 *(978-1-60304-005-1(6))* Dollworks.

—The live dolls in Wonderland. Gates, Josephine Scribner. 2007. 150p. (J). lib. bdg. 59.00 *(978-1-60304-015-0(3))* Dollworks.

—The live dolls' play Days. Gates, Josephine Scribner. 2007. 110p. (J). lib. bdg. 59.00 *(978-1-60304-008-2(0))* Dollworks.

—More about live Dolls. Gates, Josephine Scribner. 2007. 106p. (J). lib. bdg. 59.00 *(978-1-60304-002-0(1))* Dollworks.

—The Story of Live Dolls: Being an account by Josephine Scribner Gates of how, on a certian June morning, all of the dolls in the Cloverdale came Alive. Gates, Josephine Scribner. 2007. 102p. (J). lib. bdg. 59.00 *(978-1-60304-001-3(3))* Dollworks.

—The story of the lost Doll. Gates, Josephine Scribner. 2007. 108p. (J). lib. bdg. 59.00 *(978-1-60304-003-7(X))* Dollworks.

—The Story of the three Dolls. Gates, Josephine Scribner. 2007. 148p. (J). lib. bdg. 59.00 *(978-1-60304-004-4(8))* Dollworks.

Keeping, Charles. God Beneath the Sea. Garfield, Leon & Blishen, Edward. 2015. (ENG.). 224p. (J). (gr. 4-6). 19.99 ***(978-0-85753-311-1(8))*** Transworld Publishers Ltd. GBR. Dist: Independent Pubs. Group.

Keeping, Charles. The Highwayman. Noyes, Alfred. ed. 2015. (ENG.). 32p. pap. 12.95 *(978-0-19-279442-0(6))* Oxford Univ. Pr., Inc.

Keeshig-Tobias, Polly. Emma & the Trees. Keeshig-Tobias, Lenore. Date not set. 78p. pap. *(978-0-920813-11-9(9))* Sister Vision Pr.

Keesler, Karen. I Love You More. Duksta, Laura. (ENG.). (J). 2009. 24p. bds. 6.99 *(978-1-4022-2460-7(5))*; 2007. 34p. 16.99 *(978-1-4022-1126-3(0))* Sourcebooks, Inc. (Sourcebooks Jabberwocky).

—I Love You More Padded Board Book. Duksta, Laura. 2013. (ENG.). 24p. (J). bds. 8.99 *(978-1-4022-9250-7(3)*, Sourcebooks Jabberwocky) Sourcebooks, Inc.

—Te Quiero Más. Duksta, Laura. 2013. (ENG & SPA.). 24p. (J). bds. 6.99 *(978-1-4022-8177-8(3)*, Sourcebooks Jabberwocky) Sourcebooks, Inc.

Keeter, Susan. An Apple for Harriet Tubman. Turner, Glennette Tilley. 2006. (ENG.). 24p. (J). (gr. 1-4). lib. bdg. 15.95 *(978-0-8075-0395-9(9))* Whitman, Albert & Co.

—Honey Baby Sugar Child. Duncan, Alice Faye. 2005. (ENG.). 32p. (J). (gr. -1-1). 17.99 *(978-0-689-84678-6(9)*, Simon & Schuster Bks. For Young Readers) Simon & Schuster Bks. For Young Readers.

—El Leon Ruge. Merlo, Maria. 2012. (SPA.). 16p. (J). pap. 54.70 *(978-0-663-62198-9(4))* Silver, Burdett & Ginn, Inc.

—Phillis Sings Out Freedom: The Story of George Washington & Phillis Wheatley. Malaspina, Ann. 2012. (J). 34.28 *(978-1-61913-149-1(8))* Weigl Pubs., Inc.

—Phillis Sings Out Freedom: The Story of George Washington & Phillis Wheatley. Malaspina, Ann. 2010. (ENG.). 32p. (J). (gr. 2-5). 16.99 *(978-0-8075-6545-2(8))* Whitman, Albert & Co.

—Tippy Lemmey. McKissack, Patricia C. 2003. (Ready-for-Chapters Ser.). 59p. (gr. 2-5). lib. bdg. 15.00 *(978-0-7569-1432-5(9))* Perfection Learning Corp.

—Tippy Lemmey. McKissack, Patricia C. 2003. (Ready-For-Chapters Ser.). (ENG.). 64p. (J). (gr. 2-5). pap. 5.99 *(978-0-689-85019-6(0)*, Simon & Schuster/Paula Wiseman Bks.) Simon & Schuster/Paula Wiseman Bks.

—Waiting for Benjamin: A Story about Autism. Altman, Alexandra Jessup. 2008. (ENG.). 32p. (J). (gr. 2-4). lib. bdg. 16.99 *(978-0-8075-7364-8(7))* Whitman, Albert & Co.

Kehl, Drusilla. Shoshana & the Native Rose. Levinson, Robin K. 2006. 103p. (J). (gr. 3-5). per. 12.00 *(978-0-9773673-2-0(0))* Gali Girls, Inc.

Kehn, Regina. El Largo Camino Hacia Santa Cruz. Ende, Michael & Michael, Ende. (SPA.). 64p. (J). (gr. 3-5). 6.95 *(978-84-241-3354-2(4)*, EV3073) Everest Editora ESP. Dist: Lectorum Pubns., Inc.

—El Largo Camino Hacia Santa Cruz. Ende, Michael & Michael, Ende. 2003.Tr. of Lange Weg nach Santa Cruz. (SPA.). 63p. (gr. 2-3). 14.99 *(978-84-241-3348-1(X)*, EV0114) Everest Editora ESP. Dist: Lectorum Pubns., Inc.

Kehoe, Lindy. Home on a Giggle. 2004. (J). *(978-0-9752801-0-2(4))* Beres, Nancy.

Keimig, Candice. At the Beach. Andrews, Alexa. 2013. (Penguin Young Readers, Level 1 Ser.). (ENG.). 32p. (J). (gr. k-1). 14.99 *(978-0-448-46570-8(1))*; pap. 3.99 *(978-0-448-46471-8(3))* Penguin Bks., Ltd. GBR. (Warne, Frederick Pubs.). Dist: Penguin Random Hse., LLC.

—Bears: Level 1. Gunderson, Megan M. 2014. (Magic Readers Ser.). (ENG.). 24p. (J). (gr. 5-9). 24.21 *(978-1-62402-057-5(7))* ABDO Publishing Co.

—Bears Eat & Grow: Level 2. Gunderson, Megan M. 2014. (Magic Readers Ser.). (ENG.). 24p. (J). (gr. 5-9). 24.21 *(978-1-62402-058-2(5))* ABDO Publishing Co.

—Bears in the Mountains: Level 3. Gunderson, Megan M. 2014. (Magic Readers Ser.). (ENG.). 24p. (J). (gr. 5-9). 24.21 *(978-1-62402-059-9(3))* ABDO Publishing Co.

—Buffaloes: Level 1. Elston, Heidi M. D. 2014. (Magic Readers Ser.). (ENG.). 24p. (J). (gr. 5-9). 24.21 *(978-1-62402-060-5(7))* ABDO Publishing Co.

—Buffaloes Eat & Grow: Level 2. Elston, Heidi M. D. 2014. (Magic Readers Ser.). (ENG.). 24p. (J). (gr. 5-9). 24.21 *(978-1-62402-061-2(5))* ABDO Publishing Co.

—Buffaloes on the Prairie: Level 3. Elston, Heidi M. D. 2014. (Magic Readers Ser.). (ENG.). 24p. (J). (gr. 5-9). 24.21 *(978-1-62402-062-9(3))* ABDO Publishing Co.

—Deer: Level 1. O'Brien, Bridget. 2014. (Magic Readers Ser.). (ENG.). 24p. (J). (gr. 5-9). 24.21 *(978-1-62402-063-6(1))* ABDO Publishing Co.

—Deer Eat & Grow: Level 2. O'Brien, Bridget. 2014. (Magic Readers Ser.). (ENG.). 24p. (J). (gr. 5-9). 24.21 *(978-1-62402-064-3(X))* ABDO Publishing Co.

—Deer in the Woods: Level 3. O'Brien, Bridget. 2014. (Magic Readers Ser.). (ENG.). 24p. (J). (gr. 5-9). 24.21 *(978-1-62402-065-0(8))* ABDO Publishing Co.

—Dolphins Eat & Grow: Level 2. Baltzer, Rochelle. 2014. (Magic Readers Ser.). (ENG.). 24p. (J). (gr. 5-9). 24.21 *(978-1-62402-067-4(4))* ABDO Publishing Co.

—Dolphins in the Ocean: Level 3. Baltzer, Rochelle. 2014. (Magic Readers Ser.). (ENG.). 24p. (J). (gr. 5-9). 24.21 *(978-1-62402-068-1(2))* ABDO Publishing Co.

—In the Forest. Andrews, Alexa. 2013. (Penguin Young Readers, Level 1 Ser.). (ENG.). 32p. (J). (gr. k-1). 14.99 *(978-0-448-46720-7(8))*; pap. 3.99 *(978-0-448-46719-1(4))* Penguin Bks., Ltd. GBR. (Warne, Frederick Pubs.). Dist: Penguin Random Hse., LLC.

—On a Farm. Andrews, Alexa. 2013. (Penguin Young Readers, Level 1 Ser.). (ENG.). 32p. (J). (gr. k-1). 14.99 *(978-0-448-46505-0(1))*; mass mkt. 3.99 *(978-0-448-46376-6(8))* Penguin Bks., Ltd. GBR. (Warne, Frederick Pubs.). Dist: Penguin Random Hse., LLC.

Keino. Homeroom Diaries. Patterson, James & Papademetriou, Lisa. 2014. (ENG.). 272p. (YA). (gr. 7-17). 18.00 *(978-0-316-20762-1(4))* Little Brown & Co.

—How Big? Wacky Ways to Compare Size, 1 vol. Gunderson, Jessica. 2013. (Wacky Comparisons Ser.). (ENG.). 24p. (gr. -1-2). 27.32 *(978-1-4048-8325-3(8))*; pap. 7.95 *(978-1-4795-1915-6(4))* Picture Window Bks.

Keiser, Hugh M. Annie the River Otter: The Adventures of Pelican Pete. Keiser, Frances R. l.t. ed. 2006. (ENG.). 32p. (J). 17.00 *(978-0-9668845-4-8(X))* Sagaponack Bks.

Keiser, Paige. How Much Does God Love You? Adams, Michelle Medlock. 2010. 22p. (J). (gr. -1-k). 6.99 *(978-0-8249-1848-4(7))*, Candy Cane Pr.) Ideals Pubns.

—The Little Green Pea. Barber, Alison. 2009. (ENG.). 28p. (J). (gr. k-6). 15.95 *(978-1-58536-448-0(7))* Sleeping Bear Pr.

—Raj the Bookstore Tiger. Pelley, Kathleen T. 2011. (ENG.). 32p. (J). (gr. -1-3). 15.95 *(978-1-58089-230-8(2))* Charlesbridge Publishing, Inc.

Keiser, Paige, jt. illus. see Davis, Jon.

Keiser, Tammy L. The Perfect Prayer. Rossoff, Donald. 2003. (gr. k-3). 13.95 *(978-0-8074-0853-7(0)*, 164005) URJ Pr.

—The Purim Costume. Schram, Peninnah. 2004. 13.95 *(978-0-8074-0874-2(3)*, 101312) URJ Pr.

—A Year of Jewish Stories: 52 Tales for Children & Their Families. Maisel, Grace Ragues & Shubert, Samantha. (gr. k-3). 29.95 *(978-0-8074-0895-7(6)*, 101071) URJ Pr.

Keister, Douglas, photos by. El Regalo de Fernando. Keister, Douglas. 2004.Tr. of Fernando's Gift. (SPA., 32p. (J). (gr. 3-3). reprint ed. 16.95 *(978-0-87156-414-6(9))* Sierra Club Bks. for Children.

Keith, Barbara Benson. Mosaic Zoo: An ABC Book. Keith, Barbara Benson. 2008. 32p. (J). per. 8.99 *(978-0-9789688-1-6(6))* Brownian Bee Pr.

Keith, Barbara Benson. The Girls & Boys of Mother Goose. Keith, Barbara Benson, compiled by. 2006. 32p. (J). per. 7.99 *(978-0-9789688-0-9(8))* Brownian Bee Pr.

Keith, Doug. B Is for Baseball: Alphabet Cards. 2011. (ENG.). 26p. (J). 12.95 *(978-1-897476-55-0(8))* Simply Read Bks. CAN. Dist: Ingram Pub. Services.

—Dear Ichiro. Okimoto, Jean Davies. 2006. 29p. (J). (gr. 4-8). reprint ed. 17.00 *(978-1-4223-5803-0(8))* DIANE Publishing Co.

—The Errant Knight. Tompert, Ann. 2003. 32p. 15.95 *(978-0-9701907-6-5(X))* Illumination Arts Publishing Co., Inc.

—Something Special. Cohlene, Terri. 2005. 32p. (J). (gr. -1-k). 15.95 *(978-0-9740190-1-7(1))* Illumination Arts Publishing Co., Inc.

—Wild Waters: The Continuing Adventures of Farley & Breezy. Adler, Kathy. 2008. 64p. (J). pap. 5.99 *(978-0-9768816-2-9(4))* Beachfront Bks.

Keith, Patty J., photos by. I Wish I Was a Mallard but God Made Me a Pekin Instead. Keith, Patty J. 2013. 32p. pap. 12.95 *(978-0-9893303-0-5(3))* Patty's Blooming Words.

—Will You Be My Friend? Even If I Am Different from You. Keith, Patty J. 2013. 36p. pap. 12.95 *(978-0-615-78050-4(4))* Patty's Blooming Words.

Keithline, Brian. A Story from Graandfather Tree. Redwine, Connie. 2005. 25p. (J). (gr. k-2). pap. 7.95 *(978-0-88100-135-8(X))* National Writers Pr., The.

Keitzmueller, Christian. Uncover a T. Rex: Take a Three-Dimensional Look Inside a T. Rex! Schatz, Dennis & Bonadonna, Davide. 2003. (Uncover Bks.). (ENG.). 16p. (J). 18.95 *(978-1-57145-790-5(9))* Baker & Taylor Publishing Group.

Keleher, Fran. Game Face. Kantar, Andrew. 2013. 160p. pap. 12.95 *(978-1-61160-566-2(0))* Whiskey Creek Restorations.

Kell, Harley. Pearls of Wisdom; Pearl Makes Pono. Kell, Nancy. l.t. ed. 2011. (ENG.). 48p. pap. 12.95 *(978-1-4663-8389-0(5))* CreateSpace Independent Publishing Platform.

Kelleher, Kathie. Buon Natale: Learning Songs & Traditions in Italian. Rossi, Sophia. 2007. (Teach Me Ser.). (ITA & SPA.). 32p. (J). (gr. -1-3). 19.95 *(978-1-59972-067-8(1))* Teach Me Tapes, Inc.

—Orangutan Houdini. Neme, Laurel. 2014. (ENG.). 32p. (J). (gr. 1-2). 17.95 *(978-1-59373-153-3(1))* Bunker Hill Publishing, Inc.

—Willow's Walkabout: A Children's Guide to Boston. Cunningham, Sheila S. 2012. (ENG.). 32p. (J). (gr. 1-3). 17.95 *(978-1-59373-096-3(9))* Bunker Hill Publishing, Inc.

Kelleher, Michael, jt. illus. see Massey, Mitch.

Kellem-Kellner, Blynda. There Are No Blankets on the Moon. Miller-Gill, Angela. 2004. 32p. (J). 16.00 *(978-0-9716442-2-9(5))* Jackson Publishing.

Keller, Dick. Santa Visits the Thingumajigs. Keller, Irene. 2005. (ENG.). 28p. (J). (gr. -1-k). bds. 7.95 *(978-0-8249-6619-5(8))* Ideals Pubns.

—Thingamajig Book of Manners. Keller, Irene. 2005. (ENG.). 30p. (J). bds. 7.95 *(978-0-8249-6590-7(6))* Ideals Pubns.

—Thingamajig Books of Do's & Don'ts. Keller, Irene. 2005. (ENG.). 30p. (J). bds. 7.95 *(978-0-8249-6591-4(4))* Ideals Pubns.

Keller, Holly. From Tadpole to Frog. Pfeffer, Wendy. 2015. (Let's-Read-And-Find-Out Science 1 Ser.). (ENG.). 32p. (J). (gr. -1-3). pap. 6.99 ***(978-0-06-238186-6(5))*** HarperCollins Pubs.

—What's It Like to Be a Fish? Pfeffer, Wendy. 2015. (Let's-Read-And-Find-Out Science 1 Ser.). (ENG.). 32p. (J). (gr. -1-3). pap. 6.99 ***(978-0-06-238199-6(7))*** HarperCollins Pubs.

Keller, Holly. Farfallina & Marcel. Keller, Holly. 2005. (ENG.). 32p. (J). (gr. -1-4). reprint ed. pap. 6.99 *(978-0-06-443872-8(4)*, Greenwillow Bks.) HarperCollins Pubs.

—Farfallina & Marcel. Keller, Holly. 2005. (gr. -1-3). 17.00 *(978-0-7569-5785-8(0))* Perfection Learning Corp.

—The Hat. Keller, Holly. 2005. (Green Light Readers Level 1 Ser.). (gr. -1-1). 13.95 *(978-0-7569-5241-9(7))* Perfection Learning Corp.

—Help! A Story of Friendship. Keller, Holly. 2007. (ENG.). 40p. (J). (gr. -1-3). 16.99 *(978-0-06-123913-7(5)*, Greenwillow Bks.) HarperCollins Pubs.

—Miranda's Beach Day. Keller, Holly. 2009. 32p. (J). (gr. -1). lib. bdg. 18.89 *(978-0-06-158300-1(6))*; (ENG.). 17.99 *(978-0-06-158298-1(0))* HarperCollins Pubs. (Greenwillow Bks.).

—Pearl's New Skates. Keller, Holly. 2005. 24p. (J). lib. bdg. 17.89 *(978-0-06-056281-6(1))* HarperCollins Pubs.

—Sophie's Window. Keller, Holly. 2005. 32p. (J). 16.89 *(978-0-06-056283-0(8))* HarperCollins Pubs.

Keller, Jennifer. The Roaring Twenties: Discover the Era of Prohibition, Flappers, & Jazz. Amidon Lusted, Marcia. 2014. (Inquire & Investigate Ser.). (ENG.). 128p. (J). (gr. 6-10). 22.95 *(978-1-61930-260-0(8))* Nomad Pr.

Keller, Jennifer K. Explore Native American Cultures! With 25 Great Projects. Yasuda, Anita. 2013. (Explore Your World Ser.). (ENG.). 96p. (J). (gr. k-4). pap. 12.95 *(978-1-61930-160-3(1))* Nomad Pr.

Keller, Laurie. Toys! Wulffson, Don. 2014. (ENG.). 208p. (J). (gr. 3-7). pap. 9.99 *(978-1-250-03409-0(4))* Square Fish.

Keller, Laurie. Arnie - The Doughnut. Keller, Laurie. rev. ed. 2003. (Adventures of Arnie the Doughnut Ser.: 1). (ENG.). 40p. (J). (gr. -1-3). 17.95 *(978-0-8050-6283-0(1)*, Holt, Henry & Co. Bks. For Young Readers) Holt, Henry & Co.

—Arnie the Doughnut. Keller, Laurie. 2005. (J). (gr. k-4). 29.95 *(978-0-439-76641-8(9)*, WHCD649) Weston Woods Studios, Inc.

—Birdy's Smile Book. Keller, Laurie. 2010. (ENG.). 40p. (J). (gr. k-3). 16.99 *(978-0-8050-8883-0(0))*, Holt, Henry & Co. Bks. For Young Readers) Holt, Henry & Co.

—Bowling Alley Bandit. Keller, Laurie. 2013. (Adventures of Arnie the Doughnut Ser.: 1). (ENG.). 128p. (J). (gr. 2-5). 13.99 *(978-0-8050-9076-5(2)*, Ottaviano, Christy Bks.) Holt, Henry & Co.

—Do unto Otters: A Book about Manners. Keller, Laurie. 2007. (ENG.). 40p. (J). (gr. k-3). 17.99 *(978-0-8050-7996-8(3)*, Holt, Henry & Co. Bks. For Young Readers) Holt, Henry & Co.

—Do unto Otters: A Book about Manners. Keller, Laurie. 2009. (ENG.). 40p. (J). (gr. k-3). pap. 7.99 *(978-0-312-58140-4(8))* Square Fish.

—Invasion of the Ufonuts. Keller, Laurie. 2014. (Adventures of Arnie the Doughnut Ser.: 2). (ENG.). 128p. (J). (gr. 2-5). 12.99 *(978-0-8050-9075-8(4)*, Holt, Henry & Co. Bks. For Young Readers) Holt, Henry & Co.

—Open Wide: Tooth School Inside. Keller, Laurie. rev. ed. 2003. (ENG.). 40p. (J). (gr. k-3). pap. 7.99 *(978-0-8050-7268-6(3))* Square Fish.

—Open Wide: Tooth School Inside. Keller, Laurie. unabr. ed. 2006. (J). (gr. k-5). 18.95 *(978-0-439-84920-3(9)*, WPCD650); 29.95 *(978-0-439-84918-0(7)*, WHCD650) Weston Woods Studios, Inc.

—The Scrambled States of America. Keller, Laurie. 2nd rev. ed. 2008. (ENG.). 40p. (J). (gr. 2-5). 16.95 *(978-0-8050-7997-5(1)*, Holt, Henry & Co. Bks. For Young Readers) Holt, Henry & Co.

—The Scrambled States of America Talent Show. Keller, Laurie. 2010. (ENG.). 40p. (J). (gr. 2-5). pap. 6.99 *(978-0-312-62824-6(2))* Square Fish.

Keller, Matt. Matthew's Bible Stories: Esther Is Brave. Burkum, Rachel. 2011. 52p. (J). 10.00 *(978-1-59799-083-7(3))* Deaf Missions.

Keller, Matthew M. The Whirl Story Bible: Lively Bible Stories to Inspire Faith. Gibbons, Erin, ed. 2015. (ENG.). 416p. (J). (gr. -1-5). 22.99 ***(978-1-5064-0000-6(0)***, Sparkhouse Family) Augsburg Fortress, Pubs.

Keller-Miller, LeAnn Marie. When I Grow Up: An A-Z Poem Book for Children & Their Dreams. 2005. *(978-0-9711480-4-8(X))* ICanPublish.

Kelley, D. G., et al. An Illustrated Guide to Common Rocks & Their Minerals. Allan, David & Brown, Vinson. rev. ed. 2003. 60p. (Orig.). pap. 4.95 *(978-0-87961-054-8(9))* Naturegraph Pubs., Inc.

Kelley, Gary. And the Soldiers Sang. Lewis, J. Patrick. (ENG.). 32p. (J). (gr. 1-3). pap. 9.99 *(978-0-89812-975-5(3)*, Creative Paperbacks); 2011. (gr. 4-7). 19.99 *(978-1-56846-220-2(4)*, Creative Editions) Creative Co., The.

—Dark Fiddler: The Life & Legend of Nicolo Paganini. Frisch, Aaron. 2008. (ENG.). 32p. (J). (gr. 1-3). 17.95 *(978-1-56846-200-4(X)*, Creative Editions) Creative Co., The.

Kelley, Gary. Edgar Allan Poe. Frisch, Aaron. 2014. (Voices in Poetry Ser.). 47p. lib. bdg. 35.65 ***(978-1-60818-324-1(6)***, Creative Education) Creative Co., The.

Kelley, Gary. Eleanor, Quiet No More. Rappaport, Doreen. 2009. (ENG.). 48p. (J). (gr. 1-3). 16.99 *(978-0-7868-5141-6(4))* Hyperion Pr.

—Harlem Hellfighters. Lewis, J. Patrick. 2014. (ENG.). 32p. (J). (gr. 4-7). 19.99 *(978-1-56846-246-2(8)*, Creative Editions) Creative Co., The.

—The Necklace. de Maupassant, Guy. 2004. (ENG.). 48p. (J). (gr. 4-7). 19.95 *(978-1-56846-193-9(3))* Creative Co., The.

—The Stolen Smile. Lewis, J. Patrick. 2nd ed. 2015. (ENG.). 40p. (J). (gr. 2-4). 16.99 *(978-1-56846-281-3(6)*, Creative Editions) Creative Co., The.

Kelley, Gary & Nelson, Kadir. Abe's Honest Words: The Life of Abraham Lincoln. Rappaport, Doreen. 2008. (Big Words Ser.). (ENG.). 48p. (J). (gr. 3-7). 16.99 *(978-1-4231-0408-7(0))* Hyperion Pr.

Kelley, Gerald. A Is for America: A Patriotic Alphabet Book. Stone, Tanya Lee. 2011. (ENG.). 24p. (J). (gr. -1-k). mass mkt. 4.99 *(978-0-8431-9877-5(X)*, Price Stern Sloan) Penguin Publishing Group.

—Amazing Out-of-Body Experiences. Green, Carl R. & Sanford, William R. 2011. (Investigating the Unknown Ser.). 48p. (J). (gr. 5-18). pap. 8.95 *(978-1-59845-307-2(6))*; lib. bdg. 25.27 *(978-0-7660-3822-6(X))* Enslow Pubs., Inc.

—Astonishing Mind Powers. Green, Carl R. & Sanford, William R. 2011. (Investigating the Unknown Ser.). 48p. (J). (gr. 5-18). pap. 8.95 *(978-1-59845-305-8(X))*; lib. bdg. 25.27 *(978-0-7660-3820-2(3))* Enslow Pubs., Inc.

—Boas & Pythons: Cool Pets! Silverstein, Alvin et al. 2012. (Far-Out & Unusual Pets Ser.). 48p. (J). (gr. 3-4). pap. 8.95 *(978-1-4644-0129-9(2)*, Enslow Elementary) Enslow Pubs., Inc.

—Boas & Pythons: Cool Pets! Silverstein, Alvin et al. 2012. (Far-Out & Unusual Pets Ser.). 48p. (J). (gr. 3-4). 25.27 *(978-0-7660-3878-3(5)*, Enslow Elementary) Enslow Pubs., Inc.

—The Boy Who Cried Wolf: Classic Tales Edition. Smith, Carrie. 2011. (Classic Tales Ser.). (J). *(978-1-936258-59-8(5))* Benchmark Education Co.

—Chocolate Ants, Maggot Cheese, & More: The Yucky Food Book. Silverstein, Alvin et al. 2010. (Yucky Science Ser.). 48p. (J). (gr. 5-9). 25.27 *(978-0-7660-3315-3(5))* Enslow Pubs., Inc.

—Creepy, Crawly Jokes about Spiders & Other Bugs: Laugh & Learn about Science. Stewart, Melissa. 2012. (Super Silly Science Jokes Ser.). 48p. (J). (gr. 3-4). pap. 8.95 *(978-1-4644-0167-1(5))*; 25.27 *(978-0-7660-3966-7(8))* Enslow Pubs., Inc. (Enslow Elementary).

—Dino-Mite Jokes about Prehistoric Life: Laugh & Learn about Science. Stewart, Melissa. 2012. (Super Silly Science Jokes Ser.). 48p. (J). (gr. 3-4). pap. 8.95 *(978-1-4644-0164-0(0)*, Enslow Elementary); (gr. 3-4). 25.27 *(978-0-7660-3968-1(4)*, Enslow Elementary); E-Book *(978-1-4645-1071-7(7))* Enslow Pubs., Inc.

—Discovering Past Lives. Green, Carl R. & Sanford, William R. 2011. (Investigating the Unknown Ser.). 48p. (J). (gr. 5-18). pap. 8.95 *(978-1-59845-308-9(4))*; lib. bdg. 25.27 *(978-0-7660-3818-9(1))* Enslow Pubs., Inc.

—Don't Let the Barber Pull Your Teeth: Could You Survive Medieval Medicine? Bredeson, Carmen. 2011. (Ye Yucky Middle Ages Ser.). 48p. (J). (gr. 5-18). pap. 8.95 *(978-1-59845-373-7(4))*; (gr. 7-12). lib. bdg. 25.27 *(978-0-7660-3693-2(6))* Enslow Pubs., Inc.

—Dung Beetles, Slugs, Leeches, & More: The Yucky Animal Book. Silverstein, Alvin et al. 2010. (Yucky Science Ser.). 48p. (J). (gr. 5-9). 25.27 *(978-0-7660-3317-7(1))* Enslow Pubs., Inc.

—Ferrets: Cool Pets! Silverstein, Alvin et al. 2011. (Far-Out & Unusual Pets Ser.). 48p. (J). (gr. 2-5). lib. bdg. 25.27 *(978-0-7660-3683-3(9))* Enslow Pubs., Inc.

—Hairless Cats: Cool Pets! Silverstein, Alvin et al. 2011. (Far-Out & Unusual Pets Ser.). 48p. (J). (gr. 3-5). lib. bdg. 25.27 *(978-0-7660-3688-8(X)*, Enslow Elementary) Enslow Pubs., Inc.

—Hermit Crabs: Cool Pets! Silverstein, Alvin et al. 2011. (Far-Out & Unusual Pets Ser.). 48p. (J). (gr. 2-5). lib. bdg. 25.27 *(978-0-7660-3684-0(7))* Enslow Pubs., Inc.

—Hissing Cockroaches: Cool Pets! Silverstein, Alvin et al. 2011. (Far-Out & Unusual Pets Ser.). 48p. (J). (gr. 2-5). lib. bdg. 25.27 *(978-0-7660-3685-7(5))* Enslow Pubs., Inc.

—Iguanas: Cool Pets! Silverstein, Alvin et al. 2011. (Far-Out & Unusual Pets Ser.). 48p. (J). (gr. 2-5). lib. bdg. 25.27 *(978-0-7660-3686-4(3))* Enslow Pubs., Inc.

—Lazy Mary. Fuerst, Jeffrey B. 2010. (Rising Readers Ser.). (J). 3.49 *(978-1-60719-699-0(9))* Newmark Learning LLC.

—Lazy Mary Gets Up. Fuerst, Jeffrey B. 2009. (Reader's Theater Nursery Rhymes & Songs Set B Ser.). 48p. (J). pap. *(978-1-60859-156-5(5))* Benchmark Education Co.

—The Little Girl with Curl. Blane, Francisco. 2009. (Reader's Theater Nursery Rhymes & Songs Set B Ser.). 48p. (J). pap. *(978-1-60859-157-2(3))* Benchmark Education Co.

—Little Red Riding Hood: Classic Tales Edition. Smith, Carrie. 2011. (Classic Tales Ser.). (J). *(978-1-936258-75-8(7))* Benchmark Education Co.

—Miniature Horses: Cool Pets! Silverstein, Alvin et al. 2012. (Far-Out & Unusual Pets Ser.). 48p. (J). (gr. 3-4). pap. 8.95 *(978-1-4644-0125-1(X)*, Enslow Elementary) Enslow Pubs., Inc.

—Miniature Horses: Cool Pets! Silverstein, Alvin et al. 2012. (Far-Out & Unusual Pets Ser.). 48p. (J). (gr. 3-4). 25.27 *(978-0-7660-3880-6(7)*, Enslow Elementary) Enslow Pubs., Inc.

—Mountains of Jokes about Rocks, Minerals, & Soil: Laugh & Learn about Science. Stewart, Melissa. 2012. (Super Silly Science Jokes Ser.). 48p. (J). (gr. 3-4). pap. 8.95 *(978-1-4644-0165-7(9))*; 25.27 *(978-0-7660-3969-8(2))* Enslow Pubs., Inc. (Enslow Elementary).

—The Mysterious Secrets of Dreams. Green, Carl R. & Sanford, William R. 2011. (Investigating the Unknown Ser.). 48p. (J). (gr. 5-18). pap. 8.95 *(978-1-59845-306-5(8))*; lib. bdg. 25.27 *(978-0-7660-3821-9(1))* Enslow Pubs., Inc.

—The Mystery of Fortune-Telling. Green, Carl R. & Sanford, William R. 2011. (Investigating the Unknown Ser.). 48p. (J). (gr. 5-18). pap. 8.95 *(978-1-59845-304-1(1))*; lib. bdg. 25.27 *(978-0-7660-3819-6(X))* Enslow Pubs., Inc.

—Out of This World Jokes about the Solar System: Laugh & Learn about Science. Stewart, Melissa. 2012. (Super Silly Science Jokes Ser.). 48p. (J). (gr. 3-4). pap. 8.95 *(978-1-4644-0166-4(7))*; 25.27 *(978-0-7660-3970-4(6))* Enslow Pubs., Inc. (Enslow Elementary).

—Poison Dart Frogs: Cool Pets! Silverstein, Alvin et al. 2012. (Far-Out & Unusual Pets Ser.). 48p. (J). (gr. 3-4). pap. 8.95 *(978-1-4644-0126-8(8)*, Enslow Elementary) Enslow Pubs., Inc.

—Poison Dart Frogs: Cool Pets! Silverstein, Alvin et al. 2012. (Far-Out & Unusual Pets Ser.). 48p. (J). (gr. 3-4). 25.27 *(978-0-7660-3881-3(5)*, Enslow Elementary) Enslow Pubs., Inc.

—Poop Collectors, Armpit Sniffers, & More: The Yucky Jobs Book. Silverstein, Alvin et al. 2010. (Yucky Science Ser.). 48p. (J). 25.27 *(978-0-7660-3316-0(3))* Enslow Pubs., Inc.

—Potbellied Pigs: Cool Pets! Silverstein, Alvin et al. 2011. (Far-Out & Unusual Pets Ser.). 48p. (J). (gr. 2-5). lib. bdg. 25.27 *(978-0-7660-3687-1(1))* Enslow Pubs., Inc.

—Rats: Cool Pets! Silverstein, Alvin et al. 2012. (Far-Out & Unusual Pets Ser.). 48p. (J). (gr. 3-4). pap. 8.95 *(978-1-4644-0127-5(6)*, Enslow Elementary) Enslow Pubs., Inc.

—Rats: Cool Pets! Silverstein, Alvin et al. 2012. (Far-Out & Unusual Pets Ser.). 48p. (J). (gr. 3-4). 25.27 *(978-0-7660-3882-0(3)*, Enslow Elementary) Enslow Pubs., Inc.

—Row, Row, Row Your Boat. Blane, Francisco. 2010. (Rising Readers Ser.). (J). 3.49 *(978-1-60719-695-2(6))* Newmark Learning LLC.

—Sensing the Unknown. Green, Carl R. & Sanford, William R. 2011. (Investigating the Unknown Ser.). 48p. (J). (gr. 5-18). pap. 8.95 *(978-1-59845-303-4(3))*; 25.27 *(978-0-7660-3823-3(8))* Enslow Pubs., Inc.

—Shockingly Silly Jokes about Electricity & Magnetism: Laugh & Learn about Science. Stewart, Melissa. 2012. (Super Silly Science Jokes Ser.). 48p. (J). (gr. 3-4). pap. 8.95 *(978-1-4644-0163-3(2)*, Enslow Elementary); (J). (gr. 3-4). 25.27 *(978-0-7660-3967-4(6)*, Enslow Elementary); E-Book *(978-1-4645-1070-0(9))* Enslow Pubs., Inc.

—Smog, Oil Spills, Sewage, & More: The Yucky Pollution Book. Silverstein, Alvin et al. 2010. (Yucky Science Ser.). 48p. (J). (gr. 5-9). 25.27 *(978-0-7660-3313-9(9))* Enslow Pubs., Inc.

—Snot, Poop, Vomit, & More: The Yucky Body Book. Silverstein, Alvin et al. 2010. (Yucky Science Ser.). 48p. (J). (gr. 5-9). 25.27 *(978-0-7660-3318-4(X))* Enslow Pubs., Inc.

—Sparky & Tidbit. Galbraith, Kathryn O. 2015. (Ready-To-Reads Ser.). (ENG.). 40p. (J). (gr. 1-3). pap. 3.99 *(978-1-4814-0424-2(5)*, Simon Spotlight) Simon Spotlight.

—Sweaty Suits of Armor: Could You Survive Being a Knight? Stiefel, Chana. 2011. (Ye Yucky Middle Ages Ser.). 48p. (J). (gr. 5-18). pap. 8.95 *(978-1-59845-376-8(9))*; (gr. 7-12). lib. bdg. 25.27 *(978-0-7660-3784-7(3))* Enslow Pubs., Inc.

—T Is for Turkey: A True Thanksgiving Story. Stone, Tanya Lee. 2009. (ENG.). 24p. (J). (gr. -1-k). mass mkt. 4.99 *(978-0-8431-2570-2(5)*, Price Stern Sloan) Penguin Publishing Group.

—Tapeworms, Foot Fungus, Lice, & More: The Yucky Disease Book. Silverstein, Alvin et al. 2010. (Yucky Science Ser.). 48p. (J). (gr. 5-9). 25.27 *(978-0-7660-3314-6(7))* Enslow Pubs., Inc.

—Tarantulas: Cool Pets! Silverstein, Alvin et al. 2012. (Far-Out & Unusual Pets Ser.). 48p. (J). (gr. 3-4). pap. 8.95 *(978-1-4644-0128-2(4)*, Enslow Elementary) Enslow Pubs., Inc.

—Tarantulas: Cool Pets! Silverstein, Alvin et al. 2012. (Far-Out & Unusual Pets Ser.). 48p. (J). (gr. 3-4). 25.27 *(978-0-7660-3883-7(1)*, Enslow Elementary) Enslow Pubs., Inc.

—There's a Rat in My Soup: Could You Survive Medieval Food? Stiefel, Chana. 2011. (Ye Yucky Middle Ages Ser.). 48p. (J). (gr. 5-18). pap. 8.95 *(978-1-59845-375-1(0))*; (gr. 7-12). lib. bdg. 25.27 *(978-0-7660-3785-4(1))* Enslow Pubs., Inc.

—Wacky Weather & Silly Season Jokes: Laugh & Learn about Science. Stewart, Melissa. 2012. (Super Silly Science Jokes Ser.). 48p. (J). (gr. 3-4). pap. 8.95 *(978-1-4644-0168-8(3))*; 25.27 *(978-0-7660-3971-1(4))* Enslow Pubs., Inc. (Enslow Elementary).

—When I Grow Up - Abraham Lincoln. Anderson, AnnMarie. 2014. (Scholastic Reader Level 3 Ser.). (ENG.). 32p. (J). (gr. 1-2). pap. 3.99 *(978-0-545-60979-1(8)*, Scholastic Paperbacks) Scholastic, Inc.

—When I Grow up - Sally Ride. Anderson, AnnMarie. 2015. (Scholastic Reader Level 3 Ser.). (ENG.). 32p. (J). (gr. 1-2). pap. 3.99 *(978-0-545-60983-8(6)*, Scholastic Paperbacks) Scholastic, Inc.

—Ye Castle Stinketh: Could You Survive Living in a Castle? Stiefel, Chana. 2011. (Ye Yucky Middle Ages Ser.). 48p. (J). (gr. 5-18). pap. 8.95 *(978-1-59845-374-4(2))*; (gr. 7-12). lib. bdg. 25.27 *(978-0-7660-3786-1(X))* Enslow Pubs., Inc.

Kelley, Maria Felicia. Buz Words: Discovering Words in Pairs. Kelley, Maria Felicia. 2007. (J). (gr. -1-3). 32p. 14.95 *(978-0-9650918-1-7(3))*; 29p. per. 7.95 *(978-0-9650918-2-4(1))* April Arts Press & Productions.

Kelley, Marty. Crustacean Vacation, 1 vol. Benoit, Brian. 2012. (ENG.). 36p. (J). 17.95 *(978-1-934031-95-7(X)*, 14581bf9-2b61-42b1-8413-13cac209cd63) Islandport Pr., Inc.

—Spring Goes Squish: A Vibrant Volume of Vociferous Vernal Verse. 2008. (J). (gr. k-2). 14.95 *(978-1-55933-315-3(4))* Zino Pr. Children's Bks.

—Winter Woes. 2003. 32p. (J). 12.95 *(978-1-55933-306-1(5))* Zino Pr. Children's Bks.

Kelley, Marty. Fame, Fortune, & the Bran Muffins of Doom. Kelley, Marty. 2012. (ENG.). 144p. (J). 16.95 *(978-0-8234-2606-5(8))* Holiday Hse., Inc.

Kelley, Patrick. And God Blessed the Irish: The Story of Patrick. Driscoll, Christ. 2007. 59p. (J). (gr. 3-7). 14.95 *(978-1-929039-40-1(9))* Ambassador Bks., Inc.

—Dorothy Day: Champion of the Poor. Stone, Elaine Murray. 2004. 128p. 9.95 *(978-0-8091-6719-7(0)*, 6719-0) Paulist Pr.

—Jake's First Word. Luongo, Jane. 2003. (Books for Young Learners). 16p. (J). 5.75 net. *(978-1-57274-258-1(5)*, 2456, Bks. for Young Learners) Owen, Richard C. Pubs., Inc.

Kelley, True. How People Learned to Fly. Hodgkins, Fran & Hodgkins. 2007. (Let's-Read-And-Find-Out Science 2 Ser.). (ENG.). 40p. (J). (gr. k-4). 16.99 *(978-0-06-029558-5(9),* Collins) HarperCollins Pubs.
—How People Learned to Fly. Hodgkins, Fran. 2007. (Let's-Read-And-Find-Out Science 2 Ser.). (ENG.). 40p. (J). (gr. k-4). pap. 5.99 *(978-0-06-445221-2(2),* Collins) HarperCollins Pubs.
—How People Learned to Fly. Hodgkins, Fran. 2007. (Let's-Read-and-Find-Out Science Ser.). 33p. (gr. k-4). 16.00 *(978-0-7569-8101-3(8))* Perfection Learning Corp.
—In the Doghouse: An Emma & Bo Story. Kimmelman, Leslie. 2006. (Holiday House Reader Ser.: Level 2). (ENG.). 32p. (J). (gr. 5-8). 14.95 *(978-0-8234-1882-4(0))* Holiday Hse., Inc.
—Lots & Lots of Coins. Reid, Margarette S. 2011. (ENG.). 32p. (J). (gr. 1-3). 16.99 *(978-0-525-47879-9(5),* Dutton Juvenile) Penguin Publishing Group.
—No Sword Fighting in the House. Hill, Susanna Leonard. (Holiday House Reader Ser.: Level 2). (ENG.). 32p. (J). (gr. k-3). 14.95 *(978-0-8234-1916-6(9))* Holiday Hse., Inc.
—¿Quién Fue el Rey Tut? (Who Was King Tut?) Edwards, Roberta. 2009. (¿Quién Fue... ? / Who Was... ? Ser.). (SPA.). 112p. (gr. 3-5). pap. 9.99 *(978-1-60396-422-7(3))* Santillana USA Publishing Co., Inc.
—Who Was Leonardo da Vinci? Edwards, Roberta. 2005. (Who Was... ? Ser.). (ENG.). 112p. (J). (gr. 3-7). pap. 5.99 *(978-0-448-44301-0(5),* Grosset & Dunlap) Penguin Publishing Group.
—Who Was Leonardo da Vinci? Edwards, Roberta. 2005. (Who Was... ? Ser.). 106p. (J). (gr. 2-6). 12.65 *(978-0-7569-6971-4(9))* Perfection Learning Corp.
Kelley, True. The Dog Who Saved Santa. Kelley, True. 2008. (ENG.). 32p. (J). (gr. -1-3). 16.95 *(978-0-8234-2120-6(1))* Holiday Hse., Inc.
—School Lunch. Kelley, True. 2005. (ENG.). 32p. (J). (gr. -1-3). 16.95 *(978-0-8234-1894-7(4))* Holiday Hse., Inc.
Kelley, True & Harrison, Nancy. Quién Fue Pablo Picasso? Kelley, True. 2012. (Who Was... ? Ser.). (ENG & SPA.). 112p. (J). (gr. 3-7). pap. 7.99 *(978-0-448-46175-5(7),* Grosset & Dunlap) Penguin Publishing Group.
—Who Was George Washington? Edwards, Roberta. 2009. (Who Was... ? Ser.). (ENG.). 112p. (J). (gr. 3-7). pap. 5.99 *(978-0-448-44892-3(0),* Grosset & Dunlap) Penguin Publishing Group.
—Who Was Pablo Picasso? Kelley, True. 2009. (Who Was... ? Ser.). (ENG.). 112p. (J). (gr. 3-7). pap. 5.99 *(978-0-448-44987-6(0),* Grosset & Dunlap) Penguin Publishing Group.
Kellogg, Steven. The Baby Beebee Bird. Massie, Diane Redfield. 2003. (ENG.). 32p. (J). (gr. -1-1). pap. 6.99 *(978-0-06-051784-7(0))* HarperCollins Pubs.
—Clorinda. Kinerk, Robert. 2007. (ENG.). 40p. (J). (gr. -1-3). 7.99 *(978-1-4169-3964-1(4),* Simon & Schuster/Paula Wiseman Bks.) Simon & Schuster/Paula Wiseman Bks.
—Clorinda Plays Baseball! Kinerk, Robert. 2012. (ENG.). 40p. (J). (gr. -1-3). 16.99 *(978-0-689-86865-8(0),* Simon & Schuster/Paula Wiseman Bks.) Simon & Schuster/Paula Wiseman Bks.
—Clorinda Takes Flight. Kinerk, Robert. 2007. (ENG.). 40p. (J). (gr. -1-3). 17.99 *(978-0-689-86864-1(2),* Simon & Schuster/Paula Wiseman Bks.) Simon & Schuster/Paula Wiseman Bks.
—Come Back, Cat. Nodset, Joan L. 2008. 40p. (J). (gr. -1-3). lib. bdg. 17.89 *(978-0-06-028082-6(4))* HarperCollins Pubs.
—Cuanto Es un Millon? Schwartz, David M. 2003. (SPA.). (J). (gr. k-3). pap. 3.96 net. *(978-0-590-47393-4(X),* SO30942) Scholastic, Inc.
—Farty Marty. Ward, B. J. 2013. (ENG.). 32p. (J). (gr. -1-3). 16.99 *(978-1-4424-3901-6(7),* Simon & Schuster Bks. For Young Readers) Simon & Schuster Bks. For Young Readers.
—The Green Bath. Mahy, Margaret. 2013. (J). pap. *(978-0-545-20668-6(5));* (ENG.). 40p. (gr. -1-3). 16.99 *(978-0-545-20667-9(7))* Scholastic, Inc. (Levine, Arthur A. Bks.).
—How Much Is a Million? Schwartz, David M. 20th anniv. ed. 2004. (Reading Rainbow Bks.). (ENG.). 40p. (J). (gr. -1-3). pap. 6.99 *(978-0-688-09933-6(5))* HarperCollins Pubs.
—If You Decide to Go to the Moon. McNulty, Faith. 2005. (ENG.). 48p. (J). (gr. -1-3). 18.99 *(978-0-590-48359-9(5))* Scholastic, Inc.
—The Invisible Moose. Haseley, Dennis. 2008. (ENG.). 40p. (J). (gr. -1-3). pap. 6.99 *(978-0-14-241066-0(7),* Puffin) Penguin Publishing Group.
—Is Your Mama a Llama? Guarino, Deborah. (ENG.). (J). (gr. -1-3). 2006. 18.95 incl. audio compact disk *(978-0-439-87594-3(3));* 2004. 32p. pap. 6.99 *(978-0-439-59842-2(7),* Scholastic Paperbacks); 2006. 9.99 *(978-0-439-87588-2(9))* Scholastic, Inc.
—Jimmy's Boa & the Bungee Jump Slam Dunk. Noble, Trinka Hakes. 2005. 28p. (gr. -1-3). 16.00 *(978-0-7569-5765-0(6))* Perfection Learning Corp.
—Millions to Measure. Schwartz, David M. 2003. 40p. (J). lib. bdg. 18.89 *(978-0-06-623784-8(X))* HarperCollins Pubs.
—Millions to Measure. Schwartz, David M. & Schwartz, David. 2003. (ENG.). 40p. (J). (gr. k-7). 17.99 *(978-0-688-12916-3(1))* HarperCollins Pubs.
—Millions to Measure. Schwartz, David M. 2006. (ENG.). 40p. (J). (gr. k-7). reprint ed. pap. 6.99 *(978-0-06-084806-4(5))* HarperCollins Pubs.
—Santa Claus Is Comin' to Town. Coots, J. Fred. 2004. 40p. (J). (gr. -1-3). 16.89 *(978-0-06-623849-4(8))* HarperCollins Pubs.
—Snowflakes Fall. MacLachlan, Patricia. 2013. (ENG.). 32p. (J). (gr. -1-2). 17.99 *(978-0-385-37693-8(6),* Random Hse. Bks. for Young Readers) Random Hse. Children's Bks.
Kellogg, Steven. Clorinda. Kellogg, Steven. Kinerk, Robert. 2003. (ENG.). 40p. (J). (gr. -1-3). 17.99 *(978-0-689-86449-0(3),* Simon & Schuster/Paula Wiseman Bks.) Simon & Schuster/Paula Wiseman Bks.
—Johnny Appleseed. Kellogg, Steven. Cohn, Amy, ed. 2008. (ENG.). 48p. (J). (gr. -1-3). reprint ed. pap. 6.99 *(978-0-688-14025-0(4))* HarperCollins Pubs.
—The Missing Mitten Mystery. Kellogg, Steven. 2004. (Picture Puffins Ser.). (gr. -1-3). 17.00 *(978-0-7569-2581-9(9))* Perfection Learning Corp.
—The Mysterious Tadpole. Kellogg, Steven. 25th anniv. ed. 2004. (ENG.). 40p. (J). (gr. k-3). reprint ed. pap. 6.99 *(978-0-14-240140-8(4),* Puffin) Penguin Publishing Group.
—Paul Bunyan. Kellogg, Steven. 20th anniv. ed. 2004. (ENG.). 48p. (J). (gr. -1-3). pap. 6.99 *(978-0-688-05800-5(0))* HarperCollins Pubs.
—The Pied Piper's Magic. Kellogg, Steven. 2009. (ENG.). 40p. (J). (gr. -1-3). 16.99 *(978-0-8037-2818-9(2),* Dial) Penguin Publishing Group.
Kellogg, Steven. Santa Claus Is Comin' to Town. Kellogg, Steven, tr. Gillespie, Haven & Coots, J. Fred. 2004. (ENG.). 40p. (J). (gr. -1-3). 15.99 *(978-0-688-14938-3(3))* HarperCollins Pubs.
Kelly, Becky. Heavenly Skies & Lullabies: Illustrated Songbook & CD. Fallon, Kathy Reilly & Pellegrino, Frank. 2006. (J). (gr. -1-3). 29.95 incl. audio compact disk *(978-1-933626-06-2(2),* Llumina Pr.) Aeon Publishing Inc.
Kelly, Cathy. The Blue Number Counting Book. Gould, Ellen. 13p. (J). (gr. -1-2). pap. 6.00 *(978-0-938017-01-1(2))* Learning Tools Co.
Kelly, Cooper. Buenas Noches, California. Gamble, Adam. 2012. (Good Night Our World Ser.). (SPA & ENG.). 24p. (J). (gr. k — 1). bds. 9.95 *(978-1-60219-070-2(4))* Our World of Books.
—Good Night Alaska. Gamble, Adam & Jasper, Mark. 2015. (ENG.). 20p. (J). (— 1). bds. 9.95 *(978-1-60219-219-5(7))* Our World of Books.
—Good Night Beach. Gamble, Adam. 2007. (Good Night Our World Ser.). (ENG.). 20p. (J). (gr. k — 1). bds. 9.95 *(978-1-60219-002-3(X))* Our World of Books.
—Good Night California. Gamble, Adam. 2008. (Good Night Our World Ser.). (ENG.). 26p. (J). (gr. k — 1). bds. 9.95 *(978-1-60219-021-4(6))* Our World of Books.
—Good Night Canada. Gamble, Adam & Adams, David J. 2010. (Good Night Our World Ser.). (ENG.). 28p. (J). (gr. k — 1). bds. 9.95 *(978-1-60219-038-2(0))* Our World of Books.
—Good Night Charleston. Jasper, Mark. 2007. (Good Night Our World Ser.). (ENG.). 20p. (J). (gr. k — 1). bds. 9.95 *(978-1-60219-022-1(4))* Our World of Books.
—Good Night Christmas. Gamble, Adam & Jasper, Mark. 2015. (ENG.). 20p. (J). (-k). bds. 9.95 *(978-1-60219-197-6(2))* Our World of Books.
Kelly, Cooper. Good Night Daddy. Gamble, Adam & Jasper, Mark. 2015. (ENG.). 20p. (J). (— 1). bds. 9.95 ***(978-1-60219-229-4(4))*** Our World of Books.
Kelly, Cooper. Good Night Dinosaur. Gamble, Adam & Jasper, Mark. 2013. (Good Night Our World Ser.). (ENG.). 28p. (J). (— 1). bds. 9.95 *(978-1-60219-078-8(X))* Our World of Books.
—Good Night Galaxy. Jasper, Mark & Gamble, Adam. 2012. (Good Night Our World Ser.). (ENG.). 28p. (J). (gr. k — 1). bds. 9.95 *(978-1-60219-065-8(8))* Our World of Books.
—Good Night Lake. Gamble, Adam. 2008. (Good Night Our World Ser.). (ENG.). 28p. (J). (gr. k — 1). bds. 9.95 *(978-1-60219-028-3(3))* Our World of Books.
—Good Night Los Angeles. Gamble, Adam. 2007. (Good Night Our World Ser.). (ENG.). 20p. (J). (gr. k — 1). bds. 9.95 *(978-1-60219-009-2(7))* Our World of Books.
—Good Night Montreal. Gamble, Adam. 2007. (Good Night Our World Ser.). (ENG.). 20p. (J). (gr. k — 1). bds. 9.95 *(978-1-60219-012-2(7))* Our World of Books.
—Good Night New Orleans. Gamble, Adam et al. 2012. (Good Night Our World Ser.). (ENG.). 20p. (J). (gr. k — 1). bds. 9.95 *(978-1-60219-061-0(5))* Our World of Books.
—Good Night Philadelphia. Gamble, Adam. 2006. (Good Night Our World Ser.). (ENG.). 20p. (J). (gr. k — 1). bds. 9.95 *(978-0-9777979-4-3(5))* Our World of Books.
—Good Night Pirate Ship. Gamble, Adam & Jasper, Mark. 2015. (ENG.). 26p. (J). (— 1). bds. 9.95 *(978-1-60219-217-1(0))* Our World of Books.
—Good Night Planes. Gamble, Adam & Jasper, Mark. 2015. (ENG.). 26p. (J). (— 1). bds. 9.95 *(978-1-60219-218-8(9))* Our World of Books.
—Good Night San Diego. Gamble, Adam. 2006. (Good Night Our World Ser.). (ENG.). 20p. (J). (gr. k — 1). bds. 9.95 *(978-0-9777979-6-7(1))* Our World of Books.
—Good Night Vermont. Tougias, Michael et al. 2007. (Good Night Our World Ser.). (ENG.). 20p. (J). (gr. k — 1). bds. 9.95 *(978-1-60219-017-7(8))* Our World of Books.
—Good Night World. Gamble, Adam. 2009. (Good Night Our World Ser.). (ENG.). 28p. (J). (gr. k — 1). bds. 9.95 *(978-1-60219-030-6(5))* Our World of Books.
—Good Night Yellowstone. Gamble, Adam & Jasper, Mark. 2013. (Good Night Our World Ser.). (ENG.). 20p. (J). (— 1). bds. 9.95 *(978-1-60219-079-5(8))* Our World of Books.
—Good Night Zoo. Gamble, Adam. 2007. (Good Night Our World Ser.). (ENG.). 20p. (J). (gr. k — 1). bds. 9.95 *(978-1-60219-018-4(6))* Our World of Books.
Kelly, Cooper. Good Night Farm. Kelly, Cooper. Gamble, Adam. 2009. (Good Night Our World Ser.). (ENG.). 28p. (J). (gr. k — 1). bds. 9.95 *(978-1-60219-029-0(1))* Our World of Books.
Kelly, Cooper, jt. illus. see Jasper, Mark.
Kelly, Cooper, jt. illus. see Veno, Joe.
Kelly, Geoff. Paul Needs Specs. Cohen, Bernard. 2004. (ENG.). 32p. (J). 9.99 *(978-1-929132-61-4(1))* Kane Miller.
Kelly, Irene. Even an Octopus Needs a Home. Kelly, Irene. 2011. (ENG.). 32p. (J). 16.95 *(978-0-8234-2235-7(6))* Holiday Hse., Inc.
Kelly, Jo'Anne. Som See & the Magic Elephant. Oliviero, Jamie. 2005. 27p. (J). (gr. -1-2). reprint ed. 17.00 *(978-0-7567-8929-9(X))* DIANE Publishing Co.
Kelly, John. Amazing Things for Boys to Make & Do. Tincknell, Cathy. 2013. (Dover Children's Activity Bks.). (ENG.). 32p. (J). (gr. 3-5). 6.99 *(978-0-486-49723-5(2))* Dover Pubns., Inc.
—Amazing Things for Girls to Make & Do. Tincknell, Cathy. 2013. (Dover Children's Activity Bks.). (ENG.). 32p. (J). (gr. 3-5). 6.99 *(978-0-486-49722-8(4))* Dover Pubns., Inc.
—Jack's Tractor. Taylor, Thomas. 2010. (ENG.). 32p. (J). (gr. -1-k). pap. 10.99 *(978-0-340-95707-3(7))* Hodder & Stoughton GBR. Dist: Independent Pubs. Group.
—Plagues, Pox, & Pestilence. Platt, Richard. 2011. (ENG.). 48p. (J). (gr. 2-7). 15.99 *(978-0-7534-6687-2(2),* Kingfisher) Roaring Brook Pr.
—Slow Magic. Goodhart, Pippa. (Flying Foxes Ser.). (J). 2015. (ENG.). 32p. *(978-0-7787-1535-1(3));* 2003. *(978-0-7787-1489-7(6))* Crabtree Publishing Co.
—Slow Magic. Goodhart, Pippa & Goodheart, Pippa. 2003. (Flying Foxes Ser.). (ENG.). 48p. (J). *(978-0-7787-1528-3(0));* lib. bdg. *(978-0-7787-1482-8(9))* Crabtree Publishing Co.
Kelly, Joseph. Blazing Ahead! Kerrin, Jessica Scott. 2006. (Martin Bridge Ser.). (ENG.). 112p. (J). (gr. 2-5). 6.95 *(978-1-55337-962-1(4))* Kids Can Pr., Ltd. CAN. Dist: Univ. of Toronto Pr.
—In High Gear! Kerrin, Jessica Scott. 2008. (Martin Bridge Ser.). (ENG.). 112p. (J). (gr. 2-5). pap. 6.95 *(978-1-55453-157-8(8))* Kids Can Pr., Ltd. CAN. Dist: Univ. of Toronto Pr.
—Martin Bridge: On the Lookout! Kerrin, Jessica Scott & Kerrin, Jessica. 2005. (ENG.). 144p. (J). (gr. 2-5). 6.95 *(978-1-55337-773-3(7))* Kids Can Pr., Ltd. CAN. Dist: Univ. of Toronto Pr.
—Martin Bridge: Onwards & Upwards! Kerrin, Jessica Scott. 2009. (Martin Bridge Ser.). (ENG.). 112p. (J). (gr. 2-5). 6.95 *(978-1-55453-161-5(6))* Kids Can Pr., Ltd. CAN. Dist: Univ. of Toronto Pr.
—Out of Orbit! Kerrin, Jessica Scott. 2007. (Martin Bridge Ser.). (ENG.). 112p. (J). (gr. 2-5). 6.95 *(978-1-55453-149-3(7))* Kids Can Pr., Ltd. CAN. Dist: Univ. of Toronto Pr.
—A Paddling of Ducks: Animals in Groups from A to Z. Parker, Marjorie Blain. 2010. (ENG.). 32p. (J). (gr. -1-2). 16.95 *(978-1-55337-682-8(X))* Kids Can Pr., Ltd. CAN. Dist: Univ. of Toronto Pr.
—Ready for Takeoff! Kerrin, Jessica Scott & Kerrin, Jessica. 2005. (Martin Bridge Ser.). (ENG.). 120p. (J). (gr. 2-5). 6.95 *(978-1-55337-772-6(9))* Kids Can Pr., Ltd. CAN. Dist: Univ. of Toronto Pr.
—The Sky's the Limit! Kerrin, Jessica Scott. 2008. (Martin Bridge Ser.). (ENG.). 112p. (J). (gr. 2-5). pap. 6.95 *(978-1-55453-159-2(4))* Kids Can Pr., Ltd. CAN. Dist: Univ. of Toronto Pr.
—Sound the Alarm! Kerrin, Jessica Scott. 2007. (Martin Bridge Ser.). (ENG.). 112p. (J). (gr. 2-5). 6.95 *(978-1-55337-977-5(2))* Kids Can Pr., Ltd. CAN. Dist: Univ. of Toronto Pr.
Kelly, Judy. Rosie Robin: The Bird Who Loved People, 1 vol. Everson, Hobart G. 2010. 22p. 24.95 *(978-1-4489-4095-0(8))* PublishAmerica, Inc.
Kelly, Julia. Corky's Humane Tail Tale. Brenner, Harriett A. 2006. 32p. (J). bds. 16.95 *(978-0-9768667-0-1(6))* M & D Publishing, Inc.
Kelly, Keith. Peace Comes to Ajani. Kelly, Keith. 2009. 56p. (J). pap. 9.95 *(978-0-932112-59-0(5))* Carolina Wren Pr.
Kelly, Leslie A. Les Kelly. Anderson, William. Date not set. (J). (gr. 3-7). Vol. 1. 9.99 *(978-0-06-440851-6(5));* Vol. 2. 9.99 *(978-0-06-440850-9(7))* HarperCollins Pubs.
—The Little House Guidebook. Anderson, William. 2007. (Little House Ser.). (ENG.). 96p. (J). (gr. 3-7). pap. 9.99 *(978-0-06-125512-0(2),* Collins) HarperCollins Pubs.
Kelly, Lucas. Shining Scars. Leonard, Krystian. 2013. (ENG.). 31p. (J). 16.95 *(978-0-938467-72-4(7))* Headline Bks., Inc.
Kelly, Maeve. Drochla Gruaige. Doolan, Catherine. 2004. (Sraith Sos Ser.: 09). (IRI, ENG & GLE.). 64p. (J). pap. 9.95 *(978-0-86278-866-7(8))* O'Brien Pr., Ltd., The IRL. Dist: Dufour Editions, Inc.
Kelly, Mary B. For the Love of Strangers. Horsfall, Jacqueline. 2011. 292p. (YA). (gr. 6-9). pap. 14.99 *(978-1-61603-003-2(8))* Leap Bks.
Kelly, Robert. Does Noah's Kitten Have Autism Too? Boehm, Patricia. 2013. 16p. pap. 24.95 *(978-1-62709-877-9(1))* America Star Bks.
Kelly, Ryan. Lucifer, Vol. 7. Carey, Mike. rev. ed. 2005. (ENG.). 168p. pap. 14.99 *(978-1-4012-0491-4(0),* Vertigo) DC Comics.
Kelly, Susan, photos by. Jimmy the Joey: The True Story of an Amazing Koala Rescue. Kelly, Susan. Rose, Deborah Lee. 2013. (ENG.). 32p. (J). (gr. -1-3). 16.95 *(978-1-4263-1371-4(3));* lib. bdg. 25.90 *(978-1-4263-1372-1(1))* National Geographic Society. (National Geographic Children's Bks.).
Kelsey, Amanda. Berlina's Quest. Hartley, James. Legge, Barbara, ed. 2013. 146p. (J). pap. 17.99 *(978-1-61572-948-7(8))* Damnation Bks.
—Weather. Winter, Isobelle. Odgers, Sally, ed. 2013. 236p. (J). pap. 23.25 *(978-1-61572-946-3(1))* Damnation Bks.
Kelsey, Avonelle. Grandma Says, 4 bks., Set. Kelsey, Avonelle. (Series of Short Stories). 200p. (J). *(978-0-9640610-1-9(5))* Cheval International.
—Iroquois Medicine Woman. Kelsey, Avonelle. 300p. (Orig.). (YA). *(978-0-9640610-5-7(8))* Cheval International.
Kelsey-Livin, Barbara. Big Fish. Kelsey, Linda J. 2012. 28p. pap. 24.95 *(978-1-4626-6887-8(9))* America Star Bks.
Kelson, Ellen & Cecil, Jennifer. Let's Build a Playground. Rosen, Michael J. & Kaboom! Staff. 2013. (ENG.). 32p. (J). (gr. 1-4). 15.99 *(978-0-7636-5532-7(5))* Candlewick Pr.
Kemarskaya, Oksana. The Legend of the Vampire, 1 vol. Troupe, Thomas Kingsley. 2010. (Legend Has It Ser.). (ENG.). 32p. (gr. 2-4). lib. bdg. 26.65 *(978-1-4048-6031-5(2),* Nonfiction Picture Bks.) Picture Window Bks.
—The Patchwork Garden. De Anda, Diane. Ventura, Gabriela Baeza, tr. 2013.Tr. of Pedacitos de Huerto. (ENG & SPA.). 32p. (J). 16.95 *(978-1-55885-763-6(X),* Piñata Books) Arte Publico Pr.
—The Secret Lives of Plants!, 1 vol. Slingerland, Janet. 2012. (Adventures in Science Ser.). (ENG.). 32p. (gr. 3-4). pap. 8.10 *(978-1-4296-7989-3(1));* pap. 47.70 *(978-1-4296-8467-5(4));* lib. bdg. 29.99 *(978-1-4296-7686-1(8))* Capstone Pr., Inc. (Graphic Library).
Kemble, Mai S. I Can Speak Bully. Morrison, Kevin. 2009. 32p. (J). 14.95 *(978-0-8091-6744-9(1),* Ambassador Bks.) Paulist Pr.
—I'm So Not Wearing a Dress! 2010. (ENG.). 32p. (J). 11.99 *(978-1-935703-05-1(6))* Downtown Bookworks.
—Lou Lou. Guerras Safia. 2013. (ENG.). 24p. (J). pap. 16.95 *(978-1-4787-2359-2(9))* Outskirts Pr., Inc.
—The Moon & the Night Sweeper. 2007. 30p. (J). (gr. -1-2). 15.95 *(978-1-60108-013-4(1))* Red Cygnet Pr.
—Polka-Dot Fixes Kindergarten. Urdahl, Catherine. 2011. (ENG.). 32p. (J). (gr. -1-3). 16.95 *(978-1-57091-737-0(X));* pap. 7.95 *(978-1-57091-738-7(8))* Charlesbridge Publishing, Inc.
—Taylor's Birthday Party. Khan, Hana. 2008. (J). *(978-1-60108-048-6(4))* Red Cygnet Pr.
Kemble, Mai S. The Moon & the Night Sweeper. Kemble, Mai S. 2008. (J). pap. 6.95 *(978-1-60108-023-3(9))* Red Cygnet Pr.
Kemly, Kathleen. Benjamin Brown & the Great Steamboat Race. Jordan, Shirley. 2011. (History Speaks: Picture Books Plus Reader's Theater Ser.). 48p. pap. 56.72 *(978-0-7613-7630-9(5));* (ENG.). (gr. 2-4). pap. 9.95 *(978-0-7613-6133-6(2))* Lerner Publishing Group.
—Dios Lo Hizo para Ti! La Historia de la Creacion. Lehmann, Charles. 2009. (SPA.). 32p. (J). (gr. k). pap. 7.99 *(978-0-7586-1751-4(8))* Concordia Publishing Hse.
—A Fishing Surprise. McDonald, Rae A. 2007. (ENG.). 32p. (J). (gr. -1-3). 16.95 *(978-1-55971-977-3(X))* Cooper Square Publishing Llc.
—God Made It for You! The Story of Creation. Lehmann, Charles. 2007. 32p. (J). (gr. -1-3). 14.99 *(978-0-7586-1287-8(7))* Concordia Publishing Hse.
—Golden Delicious: A Cinderella Apple Story. Smucker, Anna Egan. 2008. (ENG.). 32p. (J). (gr. 1-3). 16.99 *(978-0-8075-2987-4(7))* Whitman, Albert & Co.
—Molly, by Golly! The Legend of Molly Williams, America's First Female Firefighter. Ochiltree, Dianne. 2012. (ENG.). 32p. (J). (gr. 2-4). 16.95 *(978-1-59078-721-2(8),* Calkins Creek) Boyds Mills Pr.
—Shannon & the World's Tallest Leprechaun. Callahan, Sean. 2008. (ENG.). 32p. (J). (gr. 2-4). lib. bdg. 15.95 *(978-0-8075-7326-6(4))* Whitman, Albert & Co.
Kemly, Kathleen, jt. illus. see Chayka, Doug.
Kemly, Kathleen, jt. illus. see Ito, Joel.
Kemly, Kathleen Hadam, jt. illus. see Ito, Joel.
Kemp, Kathie. Boundary Waters ABC, 1 vol. Erwin, Wesley. 2014. 64p. (gr. -1-k). 12.95 *(978-1-59193-498-1(2))* Adventure Pubns., Inc.
Kemp, Loraine. Tabasco the Saucy Raccoon, 1 vol. Hancock, Lyn. 2006. (ENG.). 168p. (J). (gr. 4-7). per. 10.95 *(978-1-55039-156-5(9))* Sono Nis Pr. CAN. Dist: Orca Bk. Pubs. USA.
Kemp, Moira. Cachorro. Price, Mathew. Goldman, Judy, tr. 2010. (SPA & ENG.). 10p. bds. 5.99 *(978-1-935021-64-3(8))* Price, Mathew Ltd.
—Gatito. Price, Mathew. Goldman, Judy, tr. 2010. (SPA & ENG.). 10p. bds. 5.99 *(978-1-935021-99-5(0))* Price, Mathew Ltd.
—Pollito. Price, Mathew. Goldman, Judy, tr. 2010. (SPA & ENG.). 10p. bds. 5.99 *(978-1-935021-59-9(1))* Price, Mathew Ltd.
Kemp, Moira. Hey Diddle Diddle. Kemp, Moira. 2009. (Favorite Mother Goose Rhymes Ser.). (ENG.). 16p. (J). (gr. -1-2). 25.64 *(978-1-60253-289-2(3),* 200245) Child's World, Inc., The.
—I'm a Little Teapot. Kemp, Moira. 2009. (Favorite Children's Songs Ser.). (ENG.). 16p. (J). (gr. -1-2). 25.64 *(978-1-60253-192-5(7),* 200103) Child's World, Inc., The.
—Knock at the Door. Kemp, Moira. 2009. (Favorite Children's Songs Ser.). (ENG.). 16p. (J). (gr. -1-2). 25.64 *(978-1-60253-193-2(5),* 200104) Child's World, Inc., The.
—Pat-a-Cake, Pat-a-Cake. Kemp, Moira. 2009. (Favorite Children's Songs Ser.). (ENG.). 16p. (J). (gr. -1-2). 25.64 *(978-1-60253-194-9(3),* 200105) Child's World, Inc., The.
—Round & Round the Garden. Kemp, Moira. 2009. (Favorite Children's Songs Ser.). (ENG.). 16p. (J). (gr. -1-2). 25.64 *(978-1-60253-195-6(1),* 200106) Child's World, Inc., The.
Ken, Akamatsu. Love Hina, 14 vols., Vol. 14. Ken, Akamatsu. Rymer, Nan, tr. from JPN. rev. ed. 2003. 200p. pap. 14.99 *(978-1-59182-120-5(7),* Tokyopop Adult) TOKYOPOP, Inc.
Kendall, Bradford. Blood in the Library, 1 vol. Dahl, Michael. 2011. (Return to the Library of Doom Ser.). (ENG.). 72p. (gr. 1-3). lib. bdg. 22.65 *(978-1-4342-3228-1(X),* Zone Bks.) Stone Arch Bks.
—The Book That Ate My Brother, 1 vol. Dahl, Michael. 2010. (Return to the Library of Doom Ser.). (ENG.). 72p. (gr. 1-3). lib. bdg. 22.65 *(978-1-4342-2144-5(X),* Zone Bks.) Stone Arch Bks.
—The Book That Dripped Blood, 1 vol. Dahl, Michael. 2007. (Library of Doom Ser.). (ENG.). 40p. (gr. 1-3). lib. bdg. 22.65 *(978-1-59889-324-3(6));* per. 6.25 *(978-1-59889-419-6(6))* Stone Arch Bks. (Zone Bks.).
—Carnival of Horrors, 1 vol. Preece, Philip. 2009. (Shade Bks.). (ENG.). 80p. (gr. 2-3). lib. bdg. 23.99 *(978-1-4342-1615-1(2),* Shade Bks.) Stone Arch Bks.
—Cave of the Bookworms, 1 vol. Dahl, Michael. 2008. (Library of Doom Ser.). (ENG.). 40p. (gr. 1-3). pap. 6.25 *(978-1-4342-0549-0(5));* lib. bdg. 22.65 *(978-1-4342-0489-9(8))* Stone Arch Bks. (Zone Bks.).
—The Creeping Bookends, 1 vol. Dahl, Michael. 2008. (Library of Doom Ser.). (ENG.). 40p. (gr. 1-3). pap. 6.25 *(978-1-4342-0546-9(0));* lib. bdg. 22.65 *(978-1-4342-0486-8(3))* Stone Arch Bks. (Zone Bks.).
—Dictionary of 1,000 Rooms, 1 vol. Dahl, Michael. 2011. (Return to the Library of Doom Ser.). (ENG.). 72p. (gr. 1-3). lib. bdg. 22.65 *(978-1-4342-3229-8(8),* Zone Bks.) Stone Arch Bks.
—Escape from the Pop-Up Prison. Dahl, Michael. 2008. (Library of Doom Ser.). (ENG.). 40p. (gr. 1-3). pap. 6.25

K

(978-1-4342-0550-6(9)); lib. bdg. 22.65 (978-1-4342-0490-5(1)) Stone Arch Bks. (Zone Bks.).
—Ghost Writer, 1 vol. Dahl, Michael. 2011. (Return to the Library of Doom Ser.). (ENG.). 72p. (gr. 1-3). lib. bdg. 22.65 (978-1-4342-3230-4(1), Zone Bks.) Stone Arch Bks.
—Inkfoot, 1 vol. Dahl, Michael. 2010. (Return to the Library of Doom Ser.). (ENG.). 72p. (gr. 1-3). 22.65 (978-1-4342-2146-9(6), Zone Bks.) Stone Arch Bks.
—Killer App, 1 vol. Dahl, Michael. 2011. (Return to the Library of Doom Ser.). (ENG.). 72p. (gr. 1-3). lib. bdg. 22.65 (978-1-4342-3231-1(X), Zone Bks.) Stone Arch Bks.
—Rats on the Page, 1 vol. Dahl, Michael. 2010. (Return to the Library of Doom Ser.). (ENG.). 72p. (gr. 1-3). lib. bdg. 22.65 (978-1-4342-2147-6(4), Zone Bks.) Stone Arch Bks.
—The Sea of Lost Books, 1 vol. Dahl, Michael. 2010. (Return to the Library of Doom Ser.). (ENG.). 72p. (gr. 1-3). lib. bdg. 22.65 (978-1-4342-2142-1(3), Zone Bks.) Stone Arch Bks.
—The Smashing Scroll, 1 vol. Dahl, Michael. 2007. (Library of Doom Ser.). (ENG.). 40p. (gr. 1-3). lib. bdg. 22.65 (978-1-59889-326-7(2)); per. 6.25 (978-1-59889-421-9(8)) Stone Arch Bks. (Zone Bks.).
—The Twister Trap, 1 vol. Dahl, Michael. 2008. (Library of Doom Ser.). (ENG.). 40p. (gr. 1-3). pap. 6.25 (978-1-4342-0548-3(7)); lib. bdg. 22.65 (978-1-4342-0488-2(X)) Stone Arch Bks. (Zone Bks.).
—The Vampire Chapter, 1 vol. Dahl, Michael. 2010. (Return to the Library of Doom Ser.). (ENG.). 72p. (gr. 1-3). 22.65 (978-1-4342-2143-8(1), Zone Bks.) Stone Arch Bks.
—The Word Eater, 1 vol. Dahl, Michael. 2008. (Library of Doom Ser.). (ENG.). 40p. (gr. 1-3). lib. bdg. 22.65 (978-1-4342-0491-2(X)); per. 6.25 (978-1-4342-0551-3(7)) Stone Arch Bks. (Zone Bks.).
—Zombie in the Library, 1 vol. Dahl, Michael. 2010. (Return to the Library of Doom Ser.). (ENG.). 72p. (gr. 1-3). lib. bdg. 22.65 (978-1-4342-2145-2(8), Zone Bks.) Stone Arch Bks.
Kendall, Bradford, jt. illus. see Evergreen, Nelson.
Kendall, Gideon. Dino Pets. Plourde, Lynn. 2007. (ENG.). 32p. (J). (gr. -1-18). 15.99 (978-0-525-47778-5(0), Dutton Juvenile) Penguin Publishing Group.
—Dinosaurs. Ring, Susan. 2008. (ENG.). 10p. (J). (gr. -1-1). 15.99 (978-1-58476-730-5(8)) Innovative Kids.
—Elliot & the Last Underworld War. Nielsen, Jennifer A. 2012. (Underworld Chronicles: Bk. 3). (ENG.). 208p. (J). (gr. 3-8). 12.99 (978-1-4022-4021-8(X), Sourcebooks Jabberwocky) Sourcebooks, Inc.
—Elliot & the Pixie Plot. Nielsen, Jennifer A. 2011. (Underworld Chronicles: Bk. 2). (ENG.). 208p. (J). (gr. 3-8). 12.99 (978-1-4022-4020-1(1), Sourcebooks Jabberwocky) Sourcebooks, Inc.
—Rabbits Rabbits Everywhere: A Fibonacci Tale. McCallum, Ann. (ENG.). 32p. (J). (gr. 1-4). 2008. 16.95 (978-1-57091-895-7(3)); 2007. per. 7.95 (978-1-57091-896-4(1)) Charlesbridge Publishing, Inc.
—Los Seems: Un Segundo Perdido. Hulme, John & Wexler, Michael. Vidal, Jordi, tr. 2009. (SPA.). 306p. (YA). (gr. 5-8). 19.95 (978-84-666-4122-7(X)) Ediciones B ESP. Dist: Spanish Pubs., LLC.
Kendall, Jane. The Alligator in the Closet: And Other Poems Around the House. Harrison, David L. 2003. (ENG.). 48p. (J). (gr. 1-5). 16.95 (978-1-56397-994-1(2)) Boyds Mills Pr.
Kendall, Monica. Hattie, Get a Haircut! Glatzer, Jenna. 2005. (ENG.). 32p. (J). (gr. -1-3). lib. bdg. 19.95 (978-0-9724853-0-2(9)) Keene Publishing.
Kendall, Peter. A Sausage Went for a Walk. Majid, Ellisha. 2008. 20p. (J). bds. 12.95 (978-1-921361-38-8(7)) Fremantle Pr. AUS. Dist: Independent Pubs. Group.
Kendall, Russell. A Day in the Life of a Pilgrim Girl. Waters, Kate. 2008. (Sarah Morton's Day Ser.). (ENG.). 32p. (J). (gr. -1-3). pap. 6.99 (978-0-439-81220-7(8), Scholastic Paperbacks) Scholastic, Inc.
Kendree, McLean. Pandora's Vase, 1 vol. 2011. (Greek Myths Ser.). (ENG.). 32p. (gr. 4-5). lib. bdg. 27.99 (978-1-4048-6668-3(X), Nonfiction Picture Bks.) Picture Window Bks.
—Vampires vs. Werewolves: Battle of the Bloodthirsty Beasts. O'Hearn, Michael. 2011. (Monster Wars Ser.). (ENG.). 32p. (gr. 3-4). pap. 47.70 (978-1-4296-7266-5(8)); lib. bdg. 27.32 (978-1-4296-6521-6(1)) Capstone Pr., Inc. (Edge Bks.).
Kendrick, D. Seymour Simon's Silly Riddles & Jokes Coloring Book. Simon, Seymour. 2013. (Dover Coloring Bks.). (ENG.). 48p. (J). (gr. 2-5). pap. 4.99 (978-0-486-48045-9(3)) Dover Pubns., Inc.
Kendrick, D., jt. illus. see Artell, Mike.
Kendrick-TaZiyah, Brandi. Little Lily Mays & the Daddy Dilemma. Lollino, Jessica. 2006. (Little Lily Mays Ser.: vol. 1). 32p. (J). per. 20.00 (978-0-9712383-1-2(6)) Culturatti Ink.
Kenison, Misti. Egypt - The Tiny Traveler: A Book of Shapes. 2015. (ENG.). 24p. (J). (— 1). bds. 5.95 (978-1-62914-607-2(2), Sky Pony Pr.) Skyhorse Publishing Co., Inc.
—France - The Tiny Traveler: A Book of Colors. 2015. (ENG.). 24p. (J). (— 1). bds. 5.95 (978-1-62914-609-6(9), Sky Pony Pr.) Skyhorse Publishing Co., Inc.
Kenna, Diane. A Lucky Dog: Owney, U.S. Rail Mail Mascot. Wales, Dirk. 2003. 32p. (J). 15.95 (978-0-9632459-0-8(2)) Great Plains Pr.
—Penny House. Wales, Dirk. 2005. 32p. (J). (gr. -1). 16.95 (978-0-9632459-1-5(0)) Great Plains Pr.
Kenna, Kara. Counting Bunnies. Boyd, Michele. 2013. (Play-Doh First Concepts Ser.). (ENG.). 14p. (J). (gr. -1). bds. 6.95 (978-1-60710-769-9(4), Silver Dolphin Bks.) Baker & Taylor Publishing Group.
—Making Shapes with Monkey. Boyd, Michele. 2013. (Play-Doh First Concepts Ser.). (ENG.). 14p. (J). (gr. -1). bds. 6.95 (978-1-60710-811-5(9), Silver Dolphin Bks.) Baker & Taylor Publishing Group.
—Mama's Little Ducklings. Boyd, Michele. 2013. (ENG.). 12p. (J). (gr. -1). bds. 6.95 (978-1-60710-771-2(6), Silver Dolphin Bks.) Baker & Taylor Publishing Group.
—PLAY-DOH: Old MacDonald Had a Farm. 2014. (PLAY-DOH Sound Ser.). (ENG.). 14p. (J). bds. 14.95 (978-1-60710-919-8(0), Silver Dolphin Bks.) Baker & Taylor Publishing Group.
—PLAY-DOH: the Wheels on the Bus. 2014. (PLAY-DOH Sound Ser.). (ENG.). 14p. (J). bds. 14.95 (978-1-60710-920-4(4), Silver Dolphin Bks.) Baker & Taylor Publishing Group.
—Rainbow Butterflies. Boyd, Michele. 2013. (Play-Doh First Concepts Ser.). (ENG.). 14p. (J). (gr. -1). bds. 6.95 (978-1-60710-770-5(8), Silver Dolphin Bks.) Baker & Taylor Publishing Group.
Kenna, Kara. PLAY-DOH: Twinkle, Twinkle, Little Star. Kenna, Kara. 2014. (ENG.). 14p. (J). bds. 14.95 (978-1-60710-918-1(2), Silver Dolphin Bks.) Baker & Taylor Publishing Group.
Kennard, Michaela. What Shall I Paint? Gibson, Ray. Everett, Felicity, ed. 2006. (What Shall I Do Today? Ser.). 32p. (J). (gr. 2). lib. bdg. 15.95 (978-1-58086-549-4(6)) EDC Publishing.
Kennard, Thomas, jt. illus. see Armour, Steven.
Kennaway, Adrienne. Awkward Aardvark. Kennaway, Mwalimu & Hadithi, Mwenye. 2nd ed. 2005. (African Animal Tales Ser.). (ENG.). 32p. (J). (gr. k-3). pap. 10.99 (978-0-340-52581-4(9), Hodder Children's Books) Hachette Children's Group GBR. Dist: Independent Pubs. Group.
—Bumping Buffalo. Hadithi, Mwenye. 2012. (African Animal Tales Ser.). (ENG.). 32p. (J). (gr. k-3). pap. 9.99 (978-0-340-98936-4(X)) Hodder & Stoughton GBR. Dist: Independent Pubs. Group.
—Cross Crocodile. Hadithi, Mwenye. 2010. (African Animal Tales Ser.). (ENG.). 32p. (J). (gr. k-3). pap. 10.99 (978-0-340-97033-1(2)) Hodder & Stoughton GBR. Dist: Independent Pubs. Group.
—Running Rhino. Hadithi, Mwenye. 2012. (African Animal Tales Ser.). (ENG.). 32p. (J). (gr. k-3). pap. 10.99 (978-0-340-98938-8(6)) Hodder & Stoughton GBR. Dist: Independent Pubs. Group.
—This Is the Oasis. Moss, Miriam. 2005. 32p. (J). (gr. -1-3). 12.99 (978-1-929132-76-8(X)) Kane Miller.
—This Is the Tree. Moss, Miriam. 2005. 32p. (J). pap. 7.99 (978-1-929132-77-5(8)) Kane Miller.
Kennedy, Allan. Inferences for Young Audiences. Milligan, Jean F. 2004. 96p. (J). (gr. 3-7). 14.95 (978-0-9637825-2-6(5)) Autumn Hse. Publishing.
Kennedy, Anne. At the Show. Hapka, Catherine. 2011. (I Can Read Book 2 Ser.). (ENG.). 32p. (J). (gr. -1-3). 16.99 (978-0-06-125542-7(4)); pap. 3.99 (978-0-06-125544-1(0)) HarperCollins Pubs.
—Back in the Saddle. Hapka, Catherine. 2011. (I Can Read Book 2 Ser.). (ENG.). 32p. (J). (gr. k-3). 16.99 (978-0-06-125539-7(4)); pap. 3.99 (978-0-06-125541-0(6)) HarperCollins Pubs.
—Blue Ribbon Day. Hapka, Catherine. 2013. (I Can Read Book 2 Ser.). (ENG.). 32p. (J). (gr. -1-3). 16.99 (978-0-06-208677-8(4)); pap. 3.99 (978-0-06-208676-1(6)) HarperCollins Pubs.
—Callie Cat, Ice Skater. Spinelli, Eileen. 2012. (ENG.). 32p. (J). (gr. 1-4). pap. 7.99 (978-0-8075-1043-8(2)) Whitman, Albert & Co.
—Hedgehog Goes to Kindergarten. Marie, Lynne. 2011. (J). pap. (978-0-545-29874-2(1)) Scholastic, Inc.
—The Hug Book. Fliess, Sue. 2014. (Little Golden Book Ser.). (ENG.). 24p. (J). (-k). 3.99 (978-0-385-37907-6(2), Golden Bks.) Random Hse. Children's Bks.
—Miss Fox's Class Earns a Field Trip. Spinelli, Eileen. 2012. (J). (978-1-61913-122-4(6)) Weigl Pubs., Inc.
—Miss Fox's Class Earns a Field Trip, 1 vol. Spinelli, Eileen. 2010. (ENG.). 32p. (J). (gr. 1-3). 16.99 (978-0-8075-5169-1(4)) Whitman, Albert & Co.
—Miss Fox's Class Gets It Wrong. Spinelli, Eileen. 2012. (ENG.). 32p. (J). (gr. -1-2). 16.99 (978-0-8075-5165-3(1)) Whitman, Albert & Co.
—Miss Fox's Class Goes Green. Spinelli, Eileen. 2012. (J). 34.28 (978-1-61913-123-1(4)) Weigl Pubs., Inc.
—Miss Fox's Class Goes Green. Spinelli, Eileen. 2011. (ENG.). 32p. (J). (gr. 1-3). 6.99 (978-0-8075-5167-7(8)) Whitman, Albert & Co.
—Miss Fox's Class Shapes Up. Spinelli, Eileen. 2011. (ENG.). 32p. (J). (gr. 1-3). 16.99 (978-0-8075-5171-4(6)) Whitman, Albert & Co.
—The New Pony. Hapka, Catherine. 2013. (I Can Read Book 2 Ser.). (ENG.). 32p. (J). (gr. -1-3). 16.99 (978-0-06-208645-7(X)) HarperCollins Pubs.
—One Little, Two Little, Three Little Apples. Ringler, Matt. 2005. (J). pap. (978-0-439-77500-7(0)) Scholastic, Inc.
—Peace Week in Miss Fox's Class. Spinelli, Eileen. 2012. (J). (978-1-61913-155-2(2)) Weigl Pubs., Inc.
—Peace Week in Miss Fox's Class. Spinelli, Eileen. 2009. (ENG.). 32p. (J). (gr. k-3). 16.99 (978-0-8075-6379-3(X)) Whitman, Albert & Co.
—Pony Crazy. Hapka, Catherine. (I Can Read Book 2 Ser.). (ENG.). 32p. (J). (gr. -1-3). 2010. pap. 3.99 (978-0-06-125535-9(1)); 2009. 16.99 (978-0-06-125533-5(5)) HarperCollins Pubs.
—Pony Scouts - Pony Party. Hapka, Catherine. 2013. (I Can Read Book 2 Ser.). (ENG.). 32p. (J). (gr. -1-3). 16.99 (978-0-06-208680-8(4)); pap. 3.99 (978-0-06-208679-2(0)) HarperCollins Pubs.
—Pony Scouts - The Camping Trip. Hapka, Catherine. 2014. (I Can Read Book 2 Ser.). (ENG.). 32p. (J). (gr. -1-3). pap. 3.99 (978-0-06-208663-1(4)) HarperCollins Pubs.
—Pony Scouts: the Camping Trip. Hapka, Catherine. 2014. (I Can Read Book 2 Ser.). (ENG.). 32p. (J). (gr. -1-3). 16.99 (978-0-06-208665-5(0)) HarperCollins Pubs.
—Really Riding! Hapka, Catherine. (I Can Read Book 2 Ser.). 32p. (J). (gr. -1-3). 2010. (ENG.). pap. 3.99 (978-0-06-125538-0(8)); 2009. 16.99 (978-0-06-125536-6(X)) HarperCollins Pubs.
—Riff Raff Sails the High Cheese. Schade, Susan. 2014. (I Can Read Book 2 Ser.). (ENG.). 24p. (J). (gr. -1-3). pap. 3.99 (978-0-06-230509-1(3)) HarperCollins Pubs.
—Riff Raff the Mouse Pirate. Schade, Susan. 2014. (I Can Read Book 2 Ser.). (ENG.). 24p. (J). (gr. -1-3). pap. 3.99 (978-0-06-230507-7(7)) HarperCollins Pubs.
—Runaway Ponies! Hapka, Catherine. 2012. (I Can Read Book 2 Ser.). (ENG.). 32p. (J). (gr. -1-3). 16.99 (978-0-06-208669-3(3)); pap. 3.99 (978-0-06-208667-9(7)) HarperCollins Pubs.
—Ten Fingers Can! Charlesworth, Liza & Scholastic, Inc. Staff. 2005. (Number Tales Ser.). (ENG.). 16p. (J). (gr. -1-1). pap. 2.99 (978-0-439-69021-8(8)) Scholastic, Inc.
—The Trail Ride. Hapka, Catherine. 2012. (I Can Read Book 2 Ser.). (ENG.). 32p. (J). (gr. -1-3). 16.99 (978-0-06-208671-6(5)); pap. 3.99 (978-0-06-208670-9(7)) HarperCollins Pubs.
—The Trail Ride. Hapka, Catherine. ed. 2012. (Pony Scouts: I Can Read! Ser.). lib. bdg. 13.55 (978-0-606-26285-9(7), Turtleback) Turtleback Bks.
—Where Do Giggles Come From? Muldrow, Diane & Golden Books Staff. 2011. (Little Golden Book Ser.). (ENG.). 24p. (J). (gr. -1-2). 3.99 (978-0-375-86133-8(5), Golden Bks.) Random Hse. Children's Bks.
—The Zoo Is Closed Today! Beilenson, Evelyn. 2014. (ENG.). 32p. (J). 16.99 (978-1-4413-1526-7(8), 9781441315267) Peter Pauper Pr. Inc.
Kennedy, Anne Vittur. The Farmer's Away! Baa! Neigh! Kennedy, Anne Vittur. 2014. (ENG.). 32p. (J). (-k). 15.99 (978-0-7636-6679-8(3)) Candlewick Pr.
Kennedy, Anne Vittur. Ragweed's Farm Dog Handbook. Kennedy, Anne Vittur. 2015. (ENG.). 32p. (J). (gr. -1-2). 15.99 **(978-0-7636-7417-5(6))** Candlewick Pr.
Kennedy, Annie. We All Fall for Apples. Herman, Emmi S. 2003. (Hello Reader Ser.). 32p. (J). pap. (978-0-439-57396-2(3)) Scholastic, Inc.
Kennedy, Cam. Kidnapped. Stevenson, Robert Louis. 2007. (ENG.). 64p. (YA). (gr. 5). pap. 11.95 (978-0-88776-843-9(1)) Tundra Bks. CAN. Dist: Random Hse., Inc.
—Strange Case of Dr. Jekyll & Mr. Hyde. Stevenson, Robert Louis. 2008. (ENG.). 48p. (YA). (gr. 5). pap. 11.95 (978-0-88776-882-8(2)) Tundra Bks. CAN. Dist: Random Hse., Inc.
Kennedy, Catherine. Swimming Along. Herbertson, Lisa. 2011. 26p. pap. 12.00 (978-1-60976-293-3(2), Eloquent Bks.) Strategic Book Publishing & Rights Agency (SBPRA).
Kennedy, Debi. The Angry Monster Book. Kennedy, Debi. 2005. 30p. (J). 8.99 (978-0-9769959-0-6(5)) nJoy Bks.
Kennedy, Doug. Pirate Pete's Talk Like a Pirate. Kennedy, Kim. 2007. (ENG.). 40p. (J). (gr. k-17). 16.95 (978-0-8109-9348-8(1), Abrams Bks. for Young Readers) Abrams.
—Six Foolish Fishermen, 1 vol. San Souci, Robert D. 2011. (ENG.). 32p. (J). (gr. k-3). 16.99 (978-1-4556-1473-8(4)) Pelican Publishing Co., Inc.
Kennedy, Doug & Kennedy, Roy D. Pirate Pete. Kennedy, Kim. ed. 2010. (ENG.). 40p. (J). (gr. 1-4). pap. 8.95 (978-0-8109-8923-8(9)) Abrams.
—The Ugly Duckling Dinosaur: A Prehistoric Tale. Bardoe, Cheryl. 2011. (ENG.). 32p. (J). (gr. -1-3). 16.95 (978-0-8109-9739-4(8), Abrams Bks. for Young Readers) Abrams.
Kennedy, Graham. African Myths. Morris, Neil. 2009. (Myths from Many Lands Ser.). 48p. (YA). (gr. 2-6). pap. 12.85 (978-1-60754-216-2(1)) Windmill Bks.
—Chinese Myths. Bingham, Jane & Sansom, Fiona. 2009. (Myths from Many Lands Ser.). 48p. (YA). (gr. 2-6). pap. 12.85 (978-1-60754-219-3(6)); (gr. 4-7). 29.25 (978-1-60754-218-6(8)) Windmill Bks.
—Moses the Child: Kept by God. Mackenzie, Carine. 2008. (Bible Alive Ser.). (ENG.). 24p. 3.99 (978-1-84550-330-7(9)) Christian Focus Pubns. GBR. Dist: Send The Light Distribution LLC.
—Moses the Leader: Used by God. MacKenzie, Carine. 2008. (Bible Alive Ser.). (ENG.). 24p. 3.99 (978-1-84550-332-1(5)) Christian Focus Pubns. GBR. Dist: Send The Light Distribution LLC.
—Moses the Shepherd: Chosen by God. Mackenzie, Carine. 2008. (Bible Alive Ser.). (ENG.). 24p. 3.99 (978-1-84550-331-4(7)) Christian Focus Pubns. GBR. Dist: Send The Light Distribution LLC.
—Moses the Traveller: Guided by God. Mackenzie, Carine. 2008. (Bible Alive Ser.). (ENG.). 24p. 3.99 (978-1-84550-333-8(3)) Christian Focus Pubns. GBR. Dist: Send The Light Distribution LLC.
Kennedy, Graham, jt. illus. see Sansom, Fiona.
Kennedy, Kelly. Chicken in the City. Fleming, Maria & Charlesworth, Liza. 2004. (Grammar Tales Ser.). (ENG.). 16p. (J). (gr. 3-7). pap. 3.25 (978-0-439-45816-0(1)) Scholastic, Inc.
—A Dog Named Opposite. Teagarden, Janine. 2010. 16p. (J). (978-0-545-24821-1(3)) Scholastic, Inc.
Kennedy, Kelly. The Emperor's New Uniform. Haselhurst, Maureen. 2015. (ENG.). 32p. (J). **(978-0-7787-1933-5(2))** Crabtree Publishing Co.
Kennedy, Kelly. Four Fiddlers. Slater, Teddy. 2005. (Number Tales Ser.). (ENG.). 16p. (J). (gr. -1-1). pap. 2.99 (978-0-439-69008-9(0)) Scholastic, Inc.
—How to Master the School Universe: Homework, Teachers, Tests, Bullies, & Other Ways to Survive the Classroom. Whitney, Brooks. 2004. 80p. (J). pap. (978-0-439-57902-5(3)) Scholastic, Inc.
—The Mystery of the Missing Socks. Martin, Justin McCory. 2004. (Grammar Tales Ser.). (ENG.). 16p. (J). (gr. 3-7). pap. 3.25 (978-0-439-45823-8(4)) Scholastic, Inc.
—One Little Egg. Lucero, Jaime. 2005. (Number Tales Ser.). (ENG.). 16p. (J). (gr. -1-1). pap. 2.99 (978-0-439-68997-7(X)) Scholastic, Inc.
—Operation Fowl Play. Menotti, Andrea. 2004. (Spy Five Ser.). 92p. (J). (978-0-439-70349-9(2)) Scholastic, Inc.
—Operation Master Mole. Menotti, Andrea. 2004. (Spy Five Ser.). 93p. (J). (978-0-439-70351-2(4)) Scholastic, Inc.
—Science Quiz Whiz. Schwartz, Linda. Larson, Eric, ed. 2003. 128p. (YA). (gr. 5-8). pap. 13.99 (978-0-88160-342-2(2), LW-416) Creative Teaching Pr., Inc.
—Social Studies Quiz Whiz. Schwartz, Linda. Larson, Eric, ed. 2003. 128p. (YA). (gr. 5-8). pap. 13.99 (978-0-88160-343-9(0), LW-417) Creative Teaching Pr., Inc.
—Who's There? 501 Side-Splitting Knock-Knock Jokes from Highlights. 2012. (Laugh Attack! Ser.). (ENG.). 256p. (J). (gr. k). pap. 5.95 (978-1-59078-918-6(0)) Boyds Mills Pr.
—100 Wacky Wishes. Charlesworth, Liza & Scholastic, Inc. Staff. 2005. (Number Tales Ser.). (ENG.). 16p. (J). (gr. -1-1). pap. 2.99 (978-0-439-69030-0(7)) Scholastic, Inc.
Kennedy, Kelly & Downey, Dagney. The Innings & Outs of Baseball. Brown, Jordan D. 2015. (Science of Fun Stuff Ser.). (ENG.). 48p. (J). (gr. 1-3). 16.99 (978-1-4814-2862-0(4)); pap. 3.99 (978-1-4814-2861-3(6)) Simon Spotlight. (Simon Spotlight).
Kennedy, Richard. The Kingdom of Carbonel. Sleigh, Barbara. 2009. (ENG.). 240p. (J). (gr. 4-7). 17.95 (978-1-59017-315-2(5), NYR Children's Collection) New York Review of Bks., Inc., The.
—The Lost Island. Dillon, Eilis. 2006. (New York Review Children's Collection). (ENG.). 208p. (J). (gr. 4-7). 17.95 (978-1-59017-205-6(1), NYR Children's Collection) New York Review of Bks., Inc., The.
Kennedy, Roy D., jt. illus. see Kennedy, Doug.
Kennedy, Sam, jt. illus. see Le Feyer, Diane.
Kennedy, Seamus, jt. illus. see Martin, Laura.
Kennedy, Victor. Willy the Scrub. McEwan, Jamie. 2004. (Junior Library Guild Selection Ser.). (ENG.). 64p. (J). (gr. 2-5). 11.95 (978-1-58196-010-5(7), Darby Creek) Lerner Publishing Group.
Kennell, Julie. Sparkles Goes Home for the Holidays. Wellings, Chris R. 2011. 40p. pap. 24.95 (978-1-4560-4120-5(7)) America Star Bks.
Kennett, Chris. Star Wars: the Empire Strikes Back (Star Wars) Smith, Geof. 2015. (Little Golden Book Ser.). (ENG.). 24p. (J). (-k). 4.99 **(978-0-7364-3544-4(1),** Golden Bks.) Random Hse. Children's Bks.
Kenney, Sean. Amazing ABC: An Alphabet Book of Lego Creations. Kenney, Sean. 2012. (ENG.). 30p. (J). (gr. -1-k). bds. 7.99 (978-0-8050-9464-0(4), Holt, Henry & Co. Bks. For Young Readers) Holt, Henry & Co.
—Cool Cars & Trucks. Kenney, Sean. Barrett, John E., photos by. 2009. (ENG.). 32p. (J). (gr. -1-3). 12.99 (978-0-8050-8761-1(3), Holt, Henry & Co. Bks. For Young Readers) Holt, Henry & Co.
—Cool City. Kenney, Sean. 2011. (ENG.). 32p. (J). (gr. -1-3). 12.99 (978-0-8050-8762-8(1), Holt, Henry & Co. Bks. For Young Readers) Holt, Henry & Co.
—Cool Creations in 101 Pieces. Kenney, Sean. 2014. (ENG.). 32p. (J). (gr. -1-4). 14.99 (978-1-62779-017-8(9), Holt, Henry & Co. Bks. For Young Readers) Holt, Henry & Co.
—Cool Creations in 35 Pieces. Kenney, Sean. 2013. (ENG.). 32p. (J). (gr. -1-3). 12.99 (978-0-8050-9692-7(2), Holt, Henry & Co. Bks. For Young Readers) Holt, Henry & Co.
—Cool Robots. Kenney, Sean. 2010. (ENG.). 32p. (J). (gr. -1-3). 12.99 (978-0-8050-8763-5(X), Holt, Henry & Co. Bks. For Young Readers) Holt, Henry & Co.
—Totally Cool Creations. Kenney, Sean. 2013. (ENG.). 128p. (J). (gr. -1-3). pap. 19.99 (978-1-250-03110-5(9)) Square Fish.
Kent, Jack. Q Is for Duck: An Alphabet Guessing Game. Folsom, Michael & Elting, Mary. 2005. (ENG.). 64p. (J). (gr. -1-3). pap. 6.95 (978-0-618-57412-4(3)) Houghton Mifflin Harcourt Publishing Co.
—Q Is for Duck: An Alphabet Guessing Game. Folsom, Michael & Elting, Mary. 2007. 60p. (gr. -1-k). 16.95 (978-0-7569-7871-6(8)) Perfection Learning Corp.
—There's No Such Thing as a Dragon. 2009. (ENG.). 32p. (J). (gr. -1-2). pap. 7.99 (978-0-375-85137-7(2), Dragonfly Bks.) Random Hse. Children's Bks.
Kent, Lorna. At the Beach. 2004. 8p. (J). bds. 3.99 (978-1-85854-087-0(9)) Brimax Books Ltd. GBR. Dist: Byeway Bks.
—At the Zoo. 2004. 8p. (J). bds. 3.99 (978-1-85854-084-9(4)) Brimax Books Ltd. GBR. Dist: Byeway Bks.
—Baby's First ABC Book. 2004. 12p. (J). bds. 7.99 (978-1-85854-659-9(1)) Brimax Books Ltd. GBR. Dist: Byeway Bks.
—Baby's First Animal Book. 2004. 12p. (J). bds. 7.99 (978-1-85854-884-5(5)) Brimax Books Ltd. GBR. Dist: Byeway Bks.
—Baby's First Board Books: On the Move; Animals; My Home; Playtime. 2004. (Baby's First Board Books Gift Set Ser.). 12p. (J). bds. 12.99 (978-1-85854-694-0(X)) Brimax Books Ltd. GBR. Dist: Byeway Bks.
—Baby's First Counting Book. 2004. 12p. (J). bds. 7.99 (978-1-85854-616-2(8)) Brimax Books Ltd. GBR. Dist: Byeway Bks.
—Baby's First Toys Book. 2004. 10p. (J). bds. 7.99 (978-1-85854-882-1(9)) Brimax Books Ltd. GBR. Dist: Byeway Bks.
—Baby's First Word Book. 2004. 12p. (J). bds. 7.99 (978-1-85854-478-6(5)) Brimax Books Ltd. GBR. Dist: Byeway Bks.
—In My House. 2004. 8p. (J). bds. 3.99 (978-1-85854-086-3(0)) Brimax Books Ltd. GBR. Dist: Byeway Bks.
—In the Garden. 2004. 8p. (J). bds. 3.99 (978-1-85854-088-7(7)) Brimax Books Ltd. GBR. Dist: Byeway Bks.
—In the Park. 2004. 8p. (J). bds. 3.99 (978-1-85854-097-9(6)) Brimax Books Ltd. GBR. Dist: Byeway Bks.
—On the Move. 2004. 8p. (J). bds. 3.99 (978-1-85854-089-4(5)) Brimax Books Ltd. GBR. Dist: Byeway Bks.
—Word Magic: Magnetic Sentence Builder. 8p. (J). bds. (978-1-58048-382-7(8)) Sandvik Publishing.
Kent, Peter. Jesus Detective: A Puzzle Search Book. Martin, Peter. 2014. (ENG.). 48p. (J). (gr. 2-4). 14.99 (978-0-7459-6444-7(3)) Lion Hudson PLC GBR. Dist: Independent Pubs. Group.

—Uncover History. Brookes, Olivia. 2009. (Hide-and-Seek Visual Adventures Ser.). 24p. (J). (gr. 2-5). lib. bdg. 22.60 *(978-1-60754-653-5(1))* Windmill Bks.

—Uncover Technology. Brookes, Olivia. 2009. (Hide-and-Seek Visual Adventures Ser.). 24p. (J). (gr. 2-5). lib. bdg. 22.60 *(978-1-60754-658-0(2))* Windmill Bks.

Kent, Rockwell. Paul Bunyan. Shephard, Esther. 2006. (ENG.). 256p. (J). (gr. 5-7). pap. 15.95 *(978-0-15-205857-9(5))* Houghton Mifflin Harcourt Publishing Co.

Kenyon, David Grayson & Anderson, Scott. What Was D-Day? Demuth, Patricia Brennan. 2015. (What Was... ? Ser.). (ENG.). 112p. (J). (gr. 3-7). 5.99 *(978-0-448-48407-5(2),* Grosset & Dunlap) Penguin Publishing Group.

Kenyon, Tony. Floppy Ears. Symes, Ruth Louise. 2005. 32p. (J). *(978-1-84255-264-3(3),* Orion Children's Bks.) Hachette Children's Group.

—Old Mcdonald-San's Farm. Schmicker, Michael. 2004. 19p. (J). (gr. -1-5). pap. 13.95 incl. audio *(978-0-9631154-4-7(8))* Watermark Publishing, LLC.

Kerber, Kathy. The Backpack Bears' Adventure: No Bullies Allowed. Nelson, Sheila K. 2010. 24p. pap. 14.99 *(978-1-4490-9726-4(X))* AuthorHouse.

Kerby, Johanna, photos by. Little Pink Pup. Kerby, Johanna. 2010. (ENG., 32p. (J). (gr. -1-k). 16.99 *(978-0-399-25435-2(8),* Putnam Juvenile) Penguin Publishing Group.

Kerchner, Janet Hall. 'Cuz That's Just My Way. RAZ. 2005. 32p. (J). bds. 15.95 *(978-0-9712070-4-2(6))* B2Z Publishing, Inc.

Keren Weaver Graphics. Luke & Lori's Musical Journey: Learning the Basic Elements of Music. Price, Melissa. 2003. 48p. (J). spiral bd. *(978-0-9747792-0-1(2))* Luke & Lori Bks.

Kerins, Tony. Before I Go to Sleep. Randall, Ronne. 2010. (Picture Books Ser.). (J). (gr. -1-k). bds. *(978-1-4075-8756-1(0))* Parragon, Inc.

Kern, Adrienne. The Midnight Ghosts. Fischel, Emma. 2005. (Young Reading Ser.: Vol. 2). 64p. (J). (gr. 2-18). lib. bdg. 13.95 *(978-1-58086-777-1(4),* Usborne) EDC Publishing.

Kern, Corbyn. Picture Prompts for Writing. Schwartz, Linda. Larson, Eric, ed. 2003. 80p. (YA). (gr. 5-8). pap. 10.99 *(978-0-88160-335-4(X),* LW-409) Creative Teaching Pr., Inc.

Kern, Debb. The Little Red Frog. Williams, Noele. 2012. 54p. pap. 14.99 *(978-1-61807-066-1(5),* Little Blue Flower Pr.) Grey Gate Media, LLC.

Kern, Donna. Animal Alphabet. Kern, Donna. 60.00 *(978-1-57281-296-3(6),* DAA12) U.S. Games Systems, Inc.

—Kern Alphabet Card Games. Kern, Donna. 5.00 *(978-1-57281-092-1(0),* AZ54) U.S. Games Systems, Inc.

Kern, Shelly. Laci the Ladybug. Adams, Wayne. 2012. 16p. pap. 24.95 *(978-1-4626-7615-6(4))* America Star Bks.

Kernen, Steven. The Legend of Papa Balloon, 1 vol. McClure, C. R. 2013. (ENG.). 40p. (J). 16.99 *(978-0-7643-4410-7(2))* Schiffer Publishing, Ltd.

Kerr, George. Mother West Wind's Children. Burgess, Thornton W. 2013. (Dover Children's Classics Ser.). (ENG.). 144p. (J). (gr. 1-5). pap. 3.00 *(978-0-486-49724-2(0))* Dover Pubns., Inc.

—Old Mother West Wind. Burgess, Thornton W. annot. ed. 2011. (Dover Children's Classics Ser.). (ENG.). 336p. (J). (gr. 1-5). 20.00 *(978-0-486-48051-0(8))* Dover Pubns., Inc.

Kerr, George & Stewart, Pat. Mother West Wind's Neighbors. Burgess, Thornton W. 2003. (Dover Children's Thrift Classics Ser.). (ENG.). 96p. (J). (gr. 3-8). pap. 2.50 *(978-0-486-42846-8(X))* Dover Pubns., Inc.

Kerr, George & Stewart, Pat Ronson. Mother West Wind's Animal Friends. Burgess, Thornton W. Kerr, George, tr. 2003. (Dover Children's Thrift Classics Ser.). (ENG.). 128p. (J). (gr. 3-8). pap. 3.50 *(978-0-486-43030-0(8))* Dover Pubns., Inc.

Kerr, Judith. Goodbye Mog. Kerr, Judith. 2003. (ENG.). 32p. (J). (gr. k-2). pap. 9.99 *(978-0-00-714969-8(7),* HarperCollins Children's Bks.) HarperCollins Pubs. Ltd. GBR. Dist: HarperCollins Pubs.

—Goose in a Hole. Kerr, Judith. 2006. (ENG.). 40p. (J). (gr. k-2). pap. 9.99 *(978-0-00-720794-7(8),* HarperCollins Children's Bks.) HarperCollins Pubs. Ltd. GBR. Dist: Independent Pubs. Group.

—Mog & Bunny. Kerr, Judith. ed. 2005. (Mog Ser.). (ENG.). 32p. (J). (gr. k-2). pap. 10.99 *(978-0-00-717130-9(7))* HarperCollins Pubs. Ltd. GBR. Dist: Independent Pubs. Group.

—Mog & the Baby. Kerr, Judith. ed. 2005. (ENG.). 32p. (J). (gr. k-2). pap. 11.95 *(978-0-00-717132-3(3),* HarperCollins Children's Bks.) HarperCollins Pubs. Ltd. GBR. Dist: HarperCollins Pubs.

—MOG & the V. E. T. Kerr, Judith. ed. 2005. (ENG.). 32p. (J). (gr. k-2). pap. 9.99 *(978-0-00-717128-6(5),* HarperCollins Children's Bks.) HarperCollins Pubs. Ltd. GBR. Dist: HarperCollins Pubs.

—Mog in the Dark. Kerr, Judith. ed. 2006. (ENG.). 48p. (J). (gr. k-2). pap. 9.99 *(978-0-00-717133-0(1),* HarperCollins Children's Bks.) HarperCollins Pubs. Ltd. GBR. Dist: HarperCollins Pubs.

—Mog on Fox Night. Kerr, Judith. ed. 2004. (ENG.). 32p. (J). (gr. k-2). pap. 12.95 *(978-0-00-717136-1(6),* HarperCollins Children's Bks.) HarperCollins Pubs. Ltd. GBR. Dist: HarperCollins Pubs.

—Mog the Forgetful Cat. Kerr, Judith. (ENG.). 40p. (J). 2006. (gr. -1-2). bds. 7.99 *(978-0-00-722895-9(3));* 2005. (gr. k-2). pap. 9.99 *(978-0-00-717134-7(X))* HarperCollins Pubs. Ltd. GBR. (HarperCollins Children's Bks.). Dist: HarperCollins Pubs.

—Mog's Amazing Birthday Caper. Kerr, Judith. ed. 2005. (ENG.). 48p. (J). (gr. -1-k). pap. 8.99 *(978-0-00-717131-6(5),* HarperCollins Children's Bks.) HarperCollins Pubs. Ltd. GBR. Dist: HarperCollins Pubs.

—One Night in the Zoo. Kerr, Judith. 2010. 32p. (J). (gr. -1-3). 10.99 *(978-1-935279-37-2(8))* Kane Miller.

—The Tiger Who Came to Tea. Kerr, Judith. 2009. (ENG.). 32p. (J). (gr. -1-2). 17.99 *(978-0-7636-4563-2(X))* Candlewick Pr.

—Twinkles, Arthur & Puss. Kerr, Judith. 2008. (ENG.). 40p. (J). (gr. k-2). pap. 9.95 *(978-0-00-725447-7(4))* HarperCollins Pubs. Ltd. GBR. Dist: Independent Pubs. Group.

Kerrigan, Brooke. Bullying: Deal with It Before Push Comes to Shove. Slavens, Elaine. 3rd ed. 2014. (Lorimer Deal with It Ser.). (ENG.). 32p. (J). (gr. 4-6). pap. 12.95 *(978-1-4594-0653-7(2))* Lorimer, James & Co., Ltd., Pubs. CAN. Dist: Casemate Pubs. & Bk. Distributors, LLC.

—Dog Breath, 1 vol. Beck, Carolyn. 2011. (ENG.). 32p. (J). 18.95 *(978-1-55455-180-4(3))* Fitzhenry & Whiteside, Ltd. CAN. Dist: Midpoint Trade Bks., Inc.

—Kiss Me! (I'M a Prince), 1 vol. McLeod, Heather. 2010. (ENG.). 32p. (J). (gr. k-2). 18.95 *(978-1-55455-161-3(7))* Fitzhenry & Whiteside, Ltd. CAN. Dist: Midpoint Trade Bks., Inc.

—Wellington's Rainy Day, 1 vol. Beck, Carolyn. 2011. (ENG.). 32p. (J). (gr. -1-3). 19.95 *(978-1-55469-284-2(9))* Orca Bk. Pubs. USA.

Kershaw, Linda. Alberta Wayside Wildflowers. Kershaw, Linda. rev. ed. 2003. (ENG.). 160p. (J). (gr. 4). pap. *(978-1-55105-350-9(0))* Lone Pine Publishing USA.

Kershner, Gerry. Lancaster Landmarks Coloring Book. Kershner, Gerry. 2006. 25p. (J). 4.50 *(978-1-60126-010-9(5))* Masthof Pr.

Kesel, Karl. History of the DC Universe. Wolfman, Marv. rev. ed. 2009. (ENG.). 104p. (YA). pap. 12.99 *(978-1-56389-798-6(9))* DC Comics.

Kesler, Matt. The Night Before Christmas. Moore, Clement C. 2012. 16p. (J). 29.95 *(978-1-59530-407-0(X))* Hallmark Card, Inc.

Kessel, Margaret May. Mama Is A Mammal. Kessel, Quinta Cattell. 2005. 80p. (J). 16.95 *(978-0-9725027-3-3(4))* Vernissage Pr., LLC.

Kessler, Leonard P. Mr. Pine's Purple House. Kessler, Leonard P. 40th anniv. ed. 2005. 64p. (J). 16.00 *(978-1-930900-32-5(5))* Purple Hse. Pr.

—Mrs. Pine Takes a Trip. Kessler, Leonard P. 2005. (J). 16.00 *(978-1-930900-25-7(2))* Purple Hse. Pr.

Kessler, Mario. Moaning Morris. Hubner, Franz. 2004. 32p. (J). pap. *(978-81-87649-93-9(3))* Katha.

Kessler, Siglint. El Verano de los Animales. Fiedler, Christamaria. 2003. (SPA.). 155p. (J). (gr. 5-8). 9.95 *(978-968-19-0706-8(X))* Aguilar, Altea, Taurus, Alfaguara, S.A. de C.V MEX. Dist: Santillana USA Publishing Co., Inc.

Kest, Kristin. Alphabet of Animals. Galvin, Laura Gates. (Alphabet Bks.). (ENG.). 40p. 2011. (J). (gr. -1-3). 9.95 *(978-1-60727-443-8(4));* 2009. 9.95 *(978-1-59249-991-5(0));* 2006. (J). (gr. -1-k). 15.95 *(978-1-59249-655-6(5))* Soundprints.

—Amphibians: Water-to-Land Animals. Salas, Laura Purdie. 2009. (Amazing Science: Animal Classification Ser.). (ENG.). 24p. (gr. k-3). lib. bdg. 25.32 *(978-1-4048-5521-2(1),* Nonfiction Picture Bks.) Picture Window Bks.

—Animals A to Z. Galvin, Laura Gates & Soundprints Editorial Staff. Schwaeber, Barbie H. & Williams, Tracee, eds. 2008. (ENG.). 36p. (J). (gr. 3-7). 12.99 *(978-1-59069-672-9(7))* Studio Mouse LLC.

—Badger at Sandy Ridge Road. Diaz, Katacha. 2005. (Smithsonian's Backyard Ser.). (ENG.). 32p. (J). (gr. -1-2). 15.95 *(978-1-59249-420-0(X),* B5028); 4.95 *(978-1-59249-421-7(8),* B5078); pap. 6.95 *(978-1-59249-422-4(6),* S5028) Soundprints.

—Badger at Sandy Ridge Road. Diaz, Katacha. 2005. (Smith Sonian's Backyard Ser.). (ENG.). 32p. (J). (gr. 2-2). 19.95 *(978-1-59249-424-8(2),* BC5028); (gr. 2-2). 8.95 *(978-1-59249-423-1(4),* SC5028); (gr. -1-2). 9.95 *(978-1-59249-425-5(0),* PB5078) Soundprints.

—Birds: Winged & Feathered Animals, 1 vol. Slade, Suzanne. 2009. (Amazing Science: Animal Classification Ser.). (ENG.). 24p. (gr. k-3). lib. bdg. 25.32 *(978-1-4048-5522-9(X),* Nonfiction Picture Bks.) Picture Window Bks.

—Bullfrog at Magnolia Circle. Dennard, Deborah. 2005. (Smithsonian's Backyard Ser.). (ENG.). 32p. (J). (gr. -1-2). 9.95 *(978-1-931465-09-0(6),* PB5072); pap. 6.95 *(978-1-931465-39-7(8),* S5022); 15.95 *(978-1-931465-04-5(5),* B5022) Soundprints.

—Bumblebee at Apple Tree Lane. Galvin, Laura Gates. 2005. (Smithsonian's Backyard Ser.). (ENG.). 32p. (J). (gr. -1-2). pap. 6.95 *(978-1-931465-41-0(X),* S5019) Soundprints.

—Bumblee at Apple Tree Lane. Galvin, Laura Gates. 2005. (Smithsonian's Backyard Ser.: Vol. 19). (ENG.). 32p. (J). (gr. -1-2). 15.95 *(978-1-56899-820-6(1),* B5019) Soundprints.

—Gecko Gathering. Giancamilli, Vanessa. 2005. (Amazing Animal Adventures Ser.). (ENG.). (J). (gr. -1-2). 36p. 2.95 *(978-1-59249-289-3(4),* S7157); 32p. 9.95 *(978-1-59249-323-4(8),* PS7157); 36p. 15.95 *(978-1-59249-288-6(6),* B7107); 36p. pap. 6.95 *(978-1-59249-290-9(8),* S7107); 32p. 19.95 *(978-1-59249-321-0(1),* BC7107) Soundprints.

—How Do You Sleep?, 1 vol. Bonnett-Rampersaud, Louise. 2008. (ENG.). 34p. (J). (gr. -1). 6.99 *(978-0-7614-5449-6(7))* Marshall Cavendish Corp.

—Lemur Landing: A Story of a Madagascan Dry Tropical Forest. Dennard, Deborah. 2005. (Wild Habitats Ser.). (ENG.). 32p. (J). (gr. 1-4). 19.95 *(978-1-56899-980-7(1))* Soundprints.

—The Peregrine's Journey: A Story of Migration. Dunphy, Madeleine. 2008. (ENG.). 32p. (J). (gr. k-4). 16.95 *(978-0-9777539-3-2(X));* per. 9.95 *(978-0-9777539-2-5(1))* Web of Life Children's Bks.

—500 Palabras Nuevas Para Ti. Random House Staff. 2005. (Pictureback Ser.). (ENG & SPA.). 32p. (J). (gr. -1-2). pap. 3.99 *(978-0-375-83308-3(0),* Random House Para Ninos) Random Hse. Children's Bks.

—500 Words to Grow On. Random House Staff. 2005. (Pictureback(R) Ser.). (ENG.). 32p. (J). (gr. -1-k). pap. 3.99 *(978-0-375-83307-6(2),* Random Hse. Bks. for Young Readers) Random Hse. Children's Bks.

Ketchum, Ron. Rochestrivia: 2,000 Amazing questions & answers all about Rochester NY, it's people & surrounding Towns. l.t. ed. 2005. 250p. per. 19.95 *(978-0-930249-01-4(1))* Big Kids Productions (Publishing).

Kewley, Ken. Mama. Jones, Kelly. 2004. 32p. (J). *(978-0-9745930-0-5(1))* Stunt Publishing.

Key, Pamela. The Cat Who Slept All Day: What Happens While the Cat Sleeps. Coniglio, John. 2006. 24p. (J). per. 2.99 *(978-1-59958-004-3(7))* Journey Stone Creations, LLC.

—The Plight of the Queen Bee. Fairchild, Simone. 2006. 34p. (J). per. 17.95 *(978-0-9767732-3-8(6))* Better Be Write Pub., A.

Key, Pamela Marie. Queen Bee's Midnight Caper, 3 vols. Fairchild, Simone. 2006. 33p. (J). (gr. -1-3). per. 17.95 *(978-0-9771971-4-9(X))* Better Be Write Pub., A.

Keyama, Hiroshi Hata. Adventures of My Dentist & Tooth Fairy Activity & Coloring Book: Activity & Coloring Book. Keyama, Hiroshi Hata, tr. Hood, Karen Jean Matsko. Whispering Pine Press International, Inc. Staff, ed. 2010. (ENG.). 160p. (J). pap. 9.95 *(978-1-930948-76-1(X))* Whispering Pine Pr. International, Inc.

Keyes, Tina Misrasi. The Little Black Hen. Hege, Lynnita. 2013. 208p. (J). ***(978-0-7399-2465-5(6))*** Rod & Staff Pubs., Inc.

Keylock, Andy & Veres, Laszlo. Football Spy. Waddell, Martin. 2007. (Collins Big Cat Ser.). (ENG.). 80p. (J). pap. 8.99 *(978-0-00-723086-0(9))* HarperCollins Pubs. Ltd. GBR. Dist: Independent Pubs. Group.

Keylon, Joe. The Drummer Who Lost His Beat. Bloom, Stephanie. 2005. 40p. (J). lib. bdg. 16.95 *(978-1-931969-47-5(7))* Bloom & Grow Bks.

Keys, Larry. A Fabumouse Vacation for Geronimo. Stilton, Geronimo. 2004. (Geronimo Stilton Ser.: 9). (ENG.). 128p. (J). (gr. 2-5). pap. 6.99 *(978-0-439-55971-3(5),* Scholastic Paperbacks) Scholastic, Inc.

Keys, Larry, et al. Field Trip to Niagara Falls. Stilton, Geronimo. 2005. (Geronimo Stilton Ser.: No. 24). 121p. (J). lib. bdg. 18.46 *(978-1-4242-0293-5(0))* Fitzgerald Bks.

—Valentine's Day Disaster. Stilton, Geronimo. 2006. (Geronimo Stilton Ser.: No. 23). 122p. (J). lib. bdg. 18.46 *(978-1-4242-0292-8(2))* Fitzgerald Bks.

Keys, Larry, jt. illus. see Wolf, Matt.

Khan, Aziz. Dictionary of horses & ponies - internet Linked. Reid, Struan. rev. ed. 2004. 128p. (J). pap. 14.95 *(978-0-7945-0843-2(X),* Usborne) EDC Publishing.

Khan, Sophie. Can I Tell You about Stammering? A Guide for Friends, Family & Professionals. Cottrell, Sue. 2013. (Can I Tell You About...? Ser.). (ENG.). 48p. pap. *(978-1-84905-415-7(0))* Kingsley, Jessica Ltd.

—Can I Tell You about Stuttering? A Guide for Friends, Family, & Professionals. Cottrell, Sue. 2013. (Can I Tell You About...? Ser.). (ENG.). 48p. pap. *(978-1-84905-435-5(5))* Kingsley, Jessica Ltd.

Kheiriyeh, Rashin. There Was an Old Lady Who Swallowed a Fly. 2014. (ENG.). 32p. (J). 17.95 *(978-0-7358-4183-3(7))* North-South Bks., Inc.

—Tortoise & Hare. Kim, YeShil. 2015. (MySELF Bookshelf Ser.). (ENG.). 32p. (J). (gr. k-2). pap. 11.94 *(978-1-60357-700-7(9));* lib. bdg. 22.60 *(978-1-59953-665-1(X))* Norwood Hse. Pr.

Khory, Emil. Gemini Cricket: John Glenn - First Person to Orbit the Earth. Crotts, Barbara. 2011. 56p. pap. 10.03 *(978-1-4269-6213-4(4))* Trafford Publishing.

Kiaulevicius, Rolandas. Zoolidays. Glassman, Bruce. 2006. 32p. (J). (gr. -1-3). 15.95 *(978-1-60108-011-0(5))* Red Cygnet Pr.

Kibuishi, Kazu. Daisy Kutter: The Last Train. Kibuishi, Kazu. 2005. 192p. (YA). per. 10.95 *(978-0-9754193-2-8(3))* Viper Comics.

Kickingbird, Samantha. Hailey Ann Lindsey Heath. Chovanetz, Tabatha Moran. 2012. (ENG.). 24p. (J). (gr. -1-3). pap. 8.99 *(978-1-62147-132-5(2))* Tate Publishing & Enterprises, LLC.

Kicksee, John & Owlkids Books Inc. Staff. Inside Hockey! The Legends, Facts, & Feats That Made the Game. Thomas, Keltie. 2008. (ENG.). 64p. (J). (gr. 3-6). pap. 10.95 *(978-1-897349-29-8(7),* Maple Tree Pr.) Owlkids Bks. Inc. CAN. Dist: Perseus-PGW.

Kidd, Diane. Pluto's Secret: An Icy World's Tale of Discovery. Weitekamp, Margaret. 2013. (ENG.). 40p. (J). (gr. k-4). 16.95 *(978-1-4197-0423-9(0),* Abrams Bks. for Young Readers) Abrams.

—Pluto's Secret: An Icy World's Tale of Discovery. Weitekamp, Margaret A. & DeVorkin, David. 2015. (ENG.). 40p. (J). (gr. k-4). pap. 9.95 *(978-1-4197-1526-6(7),* Abrams Bks. for Young Readers) Abrams.

Kidd, Tom. Stonefather. Card, Orson Scott. 2008. 112p. 35.00 *(978-1-59606-194-1(4))* Subterranean Pr.

Kido, Yukiko. Crab Cab: Flip-a-Word. Ziefert, Harriet. 2014. (ENG.). 36p. (J). (gr. -1-1). 12.99 *(978-1-60905-430-4(X))* Blue Apple Bks.

—Draw + Learn - Faces Everywhere! Ziefert, Harriet. 2013. (ENG.). 80p. (J). (gr. -1-2). pap. 9.99 *(978-1-60905-339-0(7))* Blue Apple Bks.

—Frog Jog. Ziefert, Harriet. 2014. (Flip-A-Word Ser.). (ENG.). 36p. (J). (gr. -1-k). 12.99 *(978-1-60905-432-8(6))* Blue Apple Bks.

—Fun Land Fun! Ziefert, Harriet. 2006. (I'm Going to Read(r) Ser.). (ENG.). 32p. (J). (gr. k-1). pap. 3.95 *(978-1-4027-3416-8(6))* Sterling Publishing Co., Inc.

—Ice Mice. Ziefert, Harriet. 2013. (Flip-A-Word Ser.). (ENG.). 36p. (J). (gr. -1-1). 12.99 *(978-1-60905-410-6(5))* Blue Apple Bks.

—Lower-Case Letters. Ziefert, Harriet. 2007. (I'm Going to Read(r) Ser.). (ENG.). 64p. (J). (gr. -1-1). pap. 5.95 *(978-1-4027-5055-7(2))* Sterling Publishing Co., Inc.

—Posey Paints Princess. Ziefert, Harriet. 2013. (Posey Ser.). (ENG.). 32p. (J). (-k). pap. 5.99 *(978-1-60905-369-7(9))* Blue Apple Bks.

—Posey Plans a Party. Ziefert, Harriet. 2013. (Posey Ser.). (ENG.). 32p. (J). (-k). pap. 5.99 *(978-1-60905-368-0(0))* Blue Apple Bks.

—Posey Prefers Pink. Ziefert, Harriet. 2013. (Posey Ser.). (ENG.). 32p. (J). (-k). pap. 5.99 *(978-1-60905-367-3(2))* Blue Apple Bks.

—Quack Shack. Ziefert, Harriet. 2014. (ENG.). 36p. (J). (gr. -1-1). 12.99 *(978-1-60905-431-1(8))* Blue Apple Bks.

—Read + Write - Rhyming Words. Ziefert, Harriet. 2013. (ENG.). 80p. (J). (gr. -1-1). pap. 9.99 *(978-1-60905-335-2(4))* Blue Apple Bks.

—Rhyming Words. Ziefert, Harriet. 2007. (I'm Going to Read(r) Ser.). (ENG.). 64p. (J). (gr. -1-1). pap. 5.95 *(978-1-4027-5059-5(5))* Sterling Publishing Co., Inc.

—Snow Bow: Flip-a-Word. Ziefert, Harriet. 2014. (ENG.). 36p. (J). (gr. -1-1). 12.99 *(978-1-60905-429-8(6))* Blue Apple Bks.

—Stop Pop. Ziefert, Harriet. 2013. (Flip-A-Word Ser.). (ENG.). 36p. (J). (gr. -1-1). 12.99 *(978-1-60905-409-0(1))* Blue Apple Bks.

—Upper-Case Letters. Ziefert, Harriet. 2007. (I'm Going to Read(r) Ser.). (ENG.). 64p. (J). (gr. -1-1). pap. 5.95 *(978-1-4027-5054-0(4))* Sterling Publishing Co., Inc.

Kiedrowski, Steve. Guess Who Saves the Rain Forest? Hoch, Jeff. Hoch, Jeff, ed. Date not set. 39p. (J). (gr. k-5). pap. 7.00 *(978-0-9650629-3-0(7))* Coulee Region Pubns., Inc.

Kiefer, Karen. Kamehameha: The Warrior King of Hawai'i. Kiefer, Karen, tr. Morrison, Susan. 2003. (Latitude 20 Bks.). 104p. pap. 15.00 *(978-0-8248-2700-7(7),* Latitude 20 Bks.) Univ. of Hawaii Pr.

Kiefer, Katja. Wir Gehen in Die Bibliothek - A Visit to the Library: Deutsch-Englische Ausgabe. Mörchen, Roland. 2010. (ENG.). 40p. (J). (gr. 3-7). 19.99 *(978-3-487-08843-3(6))* Olms, Georg Verlag AG DEU. Dist: Independent Pubs. Group.

—Wir Gehen Ins Fernsehstudio. Mörchen, Roland. 2010. (ENG.). 40p. (J). (gr. 3-7). 19.99 *(978-3-487-08836-5(3))* Olms, Georg Verlag AG DEU. Dist: Independent Pubs. Group.

Kiejna, Magdalenea. Christmas Lost & Found. Martini, T. J. 2007. (J). per. 15.99 *(978-0-9705018-7-5(0))* Wings, Inc.

Kiel, Casey K. Andrew Goes to the Chiropractor. Carlson, Geri L. 2007. (J). 21.99 *(978-1-59879-432-8(9));* per. 15.99 *(978-1-59879-467-0(1))* Lifevest Publishing, Inc. (Lifevest).

Kiel, Casey Kizer. Maggie Seeks the Kingdom of God. Moore, Angela Hays. 2007. 32p. (J). 19.99 *(978-1-59879-323-9(3))* Lifevest Publishing, Inc.

Kieley, Rob. The Amazing Machine. Eggleton, Jill. (Sails Literacy Ser.). 24p. (gr. 3-18). 27.00 *(978-0-7578-6979-2(3));*Pack. 57.00 *(978-0-7578-6995-2(5))* Rigby Education.

—The Amazing Machine: 6 Small Books. Eggleton, Jill. (Sails Literacy Ser.). 24p. (gr. 3-18). 25.00 *(978-0-7578-6987-7(4))* Rigby Education.

Kiely, Orla. Shapes. 2014. (Orla Kiely Ser.). (ENG.). 20p. (J). (— 1). bds. 12.99 *(978-1-4052-6206-4(0))* Egmont Bks., Ltd. GBR. Dist: Independent Pubs. Group.

Kiely, Orla. Colors. Kiely, Orla. 2012. (ENG.). 20p. (J). (gr. -1 — 1). bds. 12.99 *(978-0-8050-9491-6(1),* Holt, Henry & Co. Bks. For Young Readers) Holt, Henry & Co.

—Numbers. Kiely, Orla. 2012. (ENG.). 20p. (J). (gr. -1 — 1). bds. 12.99 *(978-0-8050-9492-3(X),* Holt, Henry & Co. Bks. For Young Readers) Holt, Henry & Co.

Kiely, Rob. Dinosaurs. Hinkler Books Staff. rev. ed. 2006. (ENG.). 6p. (J). (gr. 2-5). 9.95 *(978-1-74157-725-9(X))* Hinkler Bks. Pty. Ltd. AUS. Dist: Penton Overseas, Inc.

Kiernan, Kenny. Detective Chase McCain - Stop That Heist! Scholastic, Inc. Staff & King, Trey. 2013. (Lego City Ser.). (ENG.). 32p. (J). (gr. -1-3). pap. 3.99 *(978-0-545-49596-7(2))* Scholastic, Inc.

—The Last Laugh! King, Trey. 2013. (LEGO DC Superheroes Ser.). (ENG.). 32p. (J). (gr. -1-3). pap. 3.99 *(978-0-545-48029-1(9))* Scholastic, Inc.

—The Lego Movie. Salane, Jeffrey. 2013. (ENG.). 64p. (J). (gr. 2-5). pap. 5.99 *(978-0-545-62462-6(2))* Scholastic, Inc.

—Look Out Below! Steele, Michael Anthony. 2012. (Lego City Ser.). (ENG.). 32p. (J). (gr. -1-3). pap. 3.99 *(978-0-545-41555-2(1))* Scholastic, Inc.

—Look Out Below! Steele, Michael Anthony. ed. 2012. (Lego City Scholastic Readers Level 1 Ser.). lib. bdg. 13.55 *(978-0-606-26236-1(9),* Turtleback) Turtleback Bks.

—Save the Day! King, Trey. 2013. (LEGO DC Superheroes Ser.). (ENG.). 32p. (J). (gr. -1-3). pap. 3.99 *(978-0-545-48028-4(0))* Scholastic, Inc.

—Save the Day! 2013. (J). *(978-1-4844-0146-0(8))* Scholastic, Inc.

Kiesler, Kate. Crab Moon. Horowitz, Ruth. 2004. (Read & Wonder Ser.). (ENG.). 32p. (J). (gr. -1-3). pap. 6.99 *(978-0-7636-2313-5(X))* Candlewick Pr.

—The Great Frog Race: And Other Poems. George, Kristine O'Connell. 2005. (ENG.). 48p. (J). (gr. -1-3). reprint ed. 6.99 *(978-0-618-60478-4(2))* Houghton Mifflin Harcourt Publishing Co.

—Hello, Harvest Moon. Fletcher, Ralph J. & Fletcher, Ralph. 2003. (ENG.). 32p. (J). (gr. -1-3). 17.99 *(978-0-618-16451-6(0))* Houghton Mifflin Harcourt Publishing Co.

—Old Elm Speaks. George, Kristine O'Connell. 2007. (ENG.). 48p. (J). (gr. -1-3). 5.95 *(978-0-618-75242-3(0))* Houghton Mifflin Harcourt Publishing Co.

Kightley, Rosalinda. Big Hug for Little Cub. Grover, Lorie Ann. 2014. (ENG.). 18p. (J). (— 1). bds. 7.99 *(978-0-545-53091-0(1),* Cartwheel Bks.) Scholastic, Inc.

—I'm a Big Brother. Cole, Joanna. 2010. (ENG.). 32p. (J). (gr. -1-3). 6.99 *(978-0-06-190065-5(6),* HarperFestival) HarperCollins Pubs.

—I'm a Big Sister. Cole, Joanna. 2010. (ENG.). 32p. (J). (gr. -1-3). 6.99 *(978-0-06-190062-4(1),* HarperFestival) HarperCollins Pubs.

—Soy un Hermano Mayor. Cole, Joanna. 2010. (SPA & ENG.). 32p. (J). (gr. -1-k). 6.99 *(978-0-06-190066-2(4),* Rayo) HarperCollins Pubs.

K

—Soy una Hermana Mayor. Cole, Joanna. 2010.Tr. of I am a Big Sister. (SPA.). 32p. (J). (gr. -1-k). 6.99 *(978-0-06-190063-1(X)*, Rayo) HarperCollins Pubs.

—Sparkly Christmas Angel. Watt, Fiona. 2007. (Luxury Touchy-Feely Board Bks.). 10p. (J). (gr. -1-k). bds. 15.99 *(978-0-7945-1477-8(4)*, Usborne) EDC Publishing.

Kightly, Rosalinda. The Right Shoes for Me! Wang, Margaret. 2006. (ENG.). 12p. (J). (gr. -1-k). bds. 9.95 *(978-1-58117-494-6(2)*, Intervisual/Piggy Toes) Bendon, Inc.

Kilby, Don. One Christmas in Lunenburg, 1 vol. Bennet, Amy. 2004. (ENG.). 24p. (J). (gr. -1-3). 16.95 *(978-1-55028-868-1(7))* Lorimer, James & Co., Ltd., Pubs. CAN. Dist: Casemate Pubs. & Bk. Distributors, LLC.

Kilby, Don. At a Construction Site. Kilby, Don. 2006. (Wheels at Work Ser.). (ENG.). 24p. (J). (gr. -1-3). 6.95 *(978-1-55337-987-4(X))* Kids Can Pr., Ltd. CAN. Dist: Univ. of Toronto Pr.

—In the City. Kilby, Don. 2006. (Wheels at Work Ser.). (ENG.). 24p. (J). (gr. -1-3). 5.95 *(978-1-55337-984-3(5))* Kids Can Pr., Ltd. CAN. Dist: Univ. of Toronto Pr.

—In the Country. Kilby, Don. 2006. (Wheels at Work Ser.). (ENG.). 24p. (J). (gr. -1-3). 5.95 *(978-1-55337-985-0(3))* Kids Can Pr., Ltd. CAN. Dist: Univ. of Toronto Pr.

—On the Road. Kilby, Don. 2006. (Wheels at Work Ser.). (ENG.). 24p. (J). (gr. -1-3). 5.95 *(978-1-55337-986-7(1))* Kids Can Pr., Ltd. CAN. Dist: Univ. of Toronto Pr.

Kilby, Jak. Keystones: Hindu Mandir. A&C Black Staff & Ganeri, Anita. 2004. (ENG.). 32p. pap. *(978-0-7136-5495-0(3)*, A & C Black) Bloomsbury Publishing Plc.

Killaire, B. M. The Adventures of Betty & Bo-Bob: A Tale of One & a Half Frogs. Killaire, B. M. Kwik, Penny Shannon, ed. 2012. 32p. pap. 24.95 *(978-1-4626-6621-8(3))* America Star Bks.

Kille, Steve. Boris the Dog. Soling, Cevin. 2015. (ENG.). 44p. 14.95 *(978-0-9767771-6-8(9))* Spectacle Films, Inc.

Killen, Nicola. Animal Numbers. 2014. (Nicola Killen Animals Ser.). (ENG.). 10p. (J). (— 1). bds. 8.99 *(978-1-4052-6277-4(X))* Egmont Bks., Ltd. GBR. Dist: Independent Pubs. Group.

Killian, Sue. Once upon a Peanut: A true Story... Whelahan, Marlene. 2009. 24p. pap. 12.99 *(978-1-4389-5925-2(7))* AuthorHouse.

Killpack, David C. North American Box Turtles: Natural History & Captive Maintenance. Franklin, Carl J. 2003. (YA). 24.99 *(978-0-9741381-0-7(X))* Illumination Studios.

Kilmer, Nidra N. And So You Were Born. Parsa, Mona. 2013. (ENG.). 32p. (J). (gr. -1-k). 12.00 *(978-0-9839047-0-0(7))* Twin Peacocks Publishing.

Kim, Alex. Explore Ancient Egypt! 25 Great Projects, Activities, Experiments. Van Vleet, Carmella. 2006. (Explore Your World Ser.). (ENG.). 96p. (J). (gr. k-4). pap. 12.95 *(978-0-9792268-3-0(X))* Nomad Pr.

—Explore Ancient Rome! 25 Great Projects, Activities, Experiments. Van Vleet, Carmella. 2008. (Explore Your World Ser.). (ENG.). 96p. (J). (gr. k-4). pap. 12.95 *(978-0-9792268-4-7(8))* Nomad Pr.

Kim, Alex & Stone, Bryan. Explore the Wild West! With 25 Great Projects. Yasuda, Anita. 2012. (Explore Your World Ser.). (ENG.). 96p. (J). (gr. k-4). pap. 12.95 *(978-1-936749-71-3(8))* Nomad Pr.

Kim, Alex, jt. illus. see Shedd, Blair.

Kim, Bo Young. The Shark That Taught Me English/El Tiburon Que Me Enseno Ingles. Markel, Michelle. 2008. 28p. (J). pap. 8.95 *(978-1-60448-003-0(3))* Lectura Bks.

—The Shark That Taught Me English/El Tiburon Que Me Enseno Ingles. Markel, Michelle. Guerrero, Ernesto, tr. 2008. (ENG & SPA.). 28p. (J). (gr. 1-2). 15.95 *(978-1-60448-002-3(5))* Lectura Bks.

Kim, Boo Young, et al. Stone Age Santa. O'Donnell, Kevin & Gon, Zang Sung. 2007. (ENG.). 184p. (J). (gr. 4-7). per. 11.95 *(978-1-58818-153-4(7))* Hill Street Pr., LLC.

Kim, Cecil & Kim, Joo-Kyung. A Happy Hat. 2014. (J). *(978-1-4338-1337-5(8)*, Magination Pr.) American Psychological Assn.

Kim, Derek Kirk. The Eternal Smile. Yang, Gene Luen. 2009. (ENG.). 176p. (YA). (gr. 9-12). pap. 17.99 *(978-1-59643-156-0(3)*, First Second Bks.) Roaring Brook Pr.

Kim, Derek Kirk. Vanishing Point. Kim, Derek Kirk. 2012. (Tune Ser.: 1). (ENG.). 160p. pap. 17.99 *(978-1-59643-516-2(X)*, First Second Bks.) Roaring Brook Pr.

Kim, Dong-soo. Twinkle Twinkle: Insect Life Cycle. Lee, Mi-Ae. Cowley, Joy, ed. 2015. (Science Storybooks Ser.). (ENG.). 32p. (gr. k-3). 7.99 ***(978-1-925246-76-6(0))***; 26.65 ***(978-1-925246-24-7(8))***; 26.65 ***(978-1-925246-50-6(7))*** ChoiceMaker Pty. Ltd., The AUS. (Big and SMALL). Dist: Lerner Publishing Group.

Kim, Glenn. When the Sky Fell. Lynch, Mike & Barr, Brandon. 2009. (Sky Chronicles: 1). (ENG.). 368p. (YA). 18.95 *(978-0-9787782-3-1(5))* Silver Leaf Bks., LLC.

Kim, IhHyeon. Ida's Present. Lee, HaeDa. 2015. (MySELF Bookshelf Ser.). (ENG.). 32p. (J). (gr. k-2). pap. 11.94 *(978-1-60357-694-9(0))*; lib. bdg. 22.60 *(978-1-59953-659-0(5))* Norwood Hse. Pr.

Kim, Intae, photos by. Wind Drawing. 2003. 126p. pap. 50.00 *(978-0-9741052-0-8(1))* I-Mar.

Kim, Isabel Joy. Tangled in Beauty: Contemplative Nature Poems. Kim, Isabel Joy. Prasad, Siona. 2013. 74p. pap. 7.99 *(978-0-9912472-0-2(5))* Philokalos Pr.

Kim, Jay Jiyeon. Meet Arzeen, Citizen of the World. Shariati, Karen Allison. 2006. 45p. (J). *(978-0-9770475-0-5(4))* Arzana, Inc.

Kim, Jeehyun. Worth the Wait. Cook, William. 2007. 32p. (J). per. 15.00 *(978-0-9791387-0-6(1))*; per. 15.00 *(978-0-9791387-1-3(X))* Yadda Yadda Pr.

Kim, Ji-Hyuk. The Forget-Me-Not Summer. Howland, Leila. 2015. (Silver Sisters Ser.: 1). (ENG.). 352p. (J). (gr. 3-7). 16.99 *(978-0-06-231869-5(1))* HarperCollins Pubs.

Kim, Ji-yeon. All Kinds of Nests: Birds. Choi, Eun-gyu. Cowley, Joy, ed. 2015. (Science Storybooks Ser.). (ENG.). 32p. (gr. k-3). 26.65 ***(978-1-925246-22-3(1))***; 7.99 ***(978-1-925246-74-2(4))***; 26.65 ***(978-1-925246-48-3(5))*** ChoiceMaker Pty. Ltd., The AUS. (Big and SMALL). Dist: Lerner Publishing Group.

Kim, Jin-Woo. The Little Match Girl. Olmstead, Kathleen & Andersen, Hans Christian. 2014. (J). *(978-1-4027-8348-7(5))* Sterling Publishing Co., Inc.

Kim, Joo-Kyung, jt. illus. see Kim, Cecil.

Kim, Joung Un. Hen Hears Gossip. McDonald, Megan. 2008. 32p. (J). (gr. -1-k). lib. bdg. 17.89 *(978-0-06-113877-5(0))*; (ENG.). 17.99 *(978-0-06-113876-8(2))* HarperCollins Pubs. (Greenwillow Bks.).

—Neighbors: The Yard Critters Too. Held, George. 2013. (ENG.). 32p. 20.00 *(978-0-916754-26-6(X))* Filsinger & Co., Ltd.

—Sid's Surprise. Carter, Candace. 2005. (Green Light Readers Level 1 Ser.). (ENG.). 32p. (J). (gr. -1-3). pap. 3.95 *(978-0-15-205182-2(1))* Houghton Mifflin Harcourt Publishing Co.

—Sid's Surprise. Carter, Candace. 2005. (Green Light Readers Level 1 Ser.). (gr. -1-3). 13.95 *(978-0-7569-5242-6(5))* Perfection Learning Corp.

—Why the Frog Has Big Eyes. Franco, Betsy & Franco-Feeney, Betsy. 2003. (Green Light Readers Level 2 Ser.). (ENG.). 24p. (J). (gr. -1-3). pap. 3.95 *(978-0-15-204834-1(0))* Houghton Mifflin Harcourt Publishing Co.

Kim, Julie. Sweety, Vol. 3. Kim, Ju-Ri. 2008. (Sweety Ser.: Vol. 3). 196p. (YA). pap. 9.95 *(978-1-59697-233-9(5))* Infinity Studios LLC.

—Sweety, Vol. 4. Park, Je-Sung. 2007. (Sweety Ser.: Vol. 4). 200p. (YA). per. 9.95 *(978-1-59697-234-6(3))* Infinity Studios LLC.

—Sweety, Vol. 5. Park, Se-Jung. 2007. (Sweety Ser.: Vol. 5). 200p. (YA). per. 9.95 *(978-1-59697-235-3(1))* Infinity Studios LLC.

—Sweety. Park, Je-Sung. 2007. (Sweety Ser.: Vol. 7). 200p. (YA). Vol. 6. per. 9.95 *(978-1-59697-236-0(X))*; Vol. 7. per. 9.95 *(978-1-59697-237-7(8))* Infinity Studios LLC.

Kim, Julie J. Mi Lugar Preferido: My Special Space. Meachen Rau, Dana. 2005. (Rookie Reader Español Ser.). 32p. (gr. k-2). 19.50 *(978-0-516-25250-6(X)*, Children's Pr.) Scholastic Library Publishing.

—My Special Space. Meachen Rau, Dana. 2003. (Rookie Readers Ser.). 32p. (J). 19.50 *(978-0-516-22881-5(1)*, Children's Pr.) Scholastic Library Publishing.

—Mysterious Spinners. Pfeffer, Wendy. 2005. 48p. (J). *(978-1-59336-315-4(X))*; pap. *(978-1-59336-316-1(8))* Mondo Publishing.

Kim, Julie J. Rhymitis. Kim, Julie J., tr. Bramwell, Wendie & Normand, Bridgid. 2003. 32p. (J). pap. *(978-0-9741388-8-6(6))* Committee for Children.

Kim, Kang Won. INVU, 4 vols., Vol. 4. Kim, Kang Won. 2003. 192p. (YA). 9.99 *(978-1-59182-175-5(4))* TOKYOPOP, Inc.

Kim, KyeMahn. Brown Bear's Dream. Kim, YunYeong. rev. ed. 2014. (MySELF Bookshelf: Social & Emotional Learning/Self-Worth Ser.). (ENG.). 32p. (J). (gr. k-2). pap. 11.94 *(978-1-60357-655-0(X))*; lib. bdg. 22.60 *(978-1-59953-646-0(3))* Norwood Hse. Pr.

Kim, Lindsey. A Tiny Bud. Kim, Aerim. 2008. 80p. (J). 29.95 *(978-0-9789624-0-1(0))* Blue Lotus Wave.

Kim, Nicole. American History, Vol. 1. Kim, Allen. 2005. (ENG.). 160p. (J). (gr. 3-8). per. 12.95 *(978-981-05-2765-5(9))* Youngjin (Singapore) Pte Ltd. SGP. Dist: Independent Pubs. Group.

Kim, Sarah. Little Belly Monster Makes French Toast. John, Margaret. 2012. 40p. pap. *(978-0-9869424-2-6(1))* Belly Productions, Inc.

Kim, So-yeong. Sleeping Beauty. Perrault, Charles. Cowley, Joy, ed. 2015. (World Classics Ser.). (ENG.). 32p. (gr. k-4). 26.65 ***(978-1-925246-18-6(3))***; 7.99 ***(978-1-925246-70-4(1))***; 26.65 ***(978-1-925246-44-5(2))*** ChoiceMaker Pty. Ltd., The AUS. (Big and SMALL). Dist: Lerner Publishing Group.

Kim, SookKyeong. Kanga & Anger. Kim, HoJeong. rev. ed. 2014. (MySELF Bookshelf: Social & Emotional Learning/Self-Worth Ser.). (ENG.). 32p. (J). (gr. k-2). pap. 11.94 *(978-1-60357-652-9(5))*; lib. bdg. 22.60 *(978-1-59953-643-9(9))* Norwood Hse. Pr.

Kim, Soyeon. Wild Ideas. Kelsey, Elin. 2015. (ENG.). 32p. (J). (gr. k). 18.95 *(978-1-77147-062-9(3))* Owlkids Bks. Inc. CAN. Dist: Perseus-PGW.

—You Are Stardust. Kelsey, Elin. 2012. (ENG.). 32p. (J). (gr. -1). 18.95 *(978-1-926973-35-7(6))* Owlkids Bks. Inc. CAN. Dist: Perseus-PGW.

Kim, Soyeon & Owlkids Books Inc. Staff. Is This Panama? A Migration Story. Thornhill, Jan. 2013. (ENG.). 40p. (J). (gr. k-3). 16.95 *(978-1-926973-88-3(7)*, Owlkids) Owlkids Bks. Inc. CAN. Dist: Perseus-PGW.

Kim, Sung-Min. The Toad Bridegroom & Other Fantastic Tales Retold. Seo & So, Chong-O. 2008. 125p. (J). *(978-0-9768086-7-1(6))* Rienner, Lynne Pubs.

Kim, Tong-Song, jt. illus. see Dong-Seong, Kim.

Kim, Violet. Earth Day, Birthday!, 0 vols. Wright, Maureen. 2012. (ENG.). 32p. (J). (gr. k-3). 17.99 *(978-0-7614-6109-8(4)*, 9780761461098, Amazon Children's Publishing) Amazon Publishing.

—The Little Gray Bunny. McGrath, Barbara Barbieri. 2013. (ENG.). 32p. (J). (gr. -1-2). 16.95 *(978-1-58089-394-7(5))*; pap. 7.95 *(978-1-58089-395-4(3))* Charlesbridge Publishing, Inc.

Kim, Yon-Kyong. Mr. Moon & Miss Sun/the Herdsman & the Weaver. 2008. (Korean Folk Tales for Children Ser.: Vol. 2). (ENG & KOR.). 45p. (J). (gr. 2-5). lib. bdg. 14.50 *(978-0-930878-72-6(8))* Hollym International Corp.

—The Ogres' Magic Clubs - the Tiger & the Dried Persimmons. 2008. (Korean Folk Tales for Children Ser.: Vol. 5). (ENG & KOR.). 45p. (J). (gr. 2-5). lib. bdg. 14.50 *(978-0-930878-88-7(4))* Hollym International Corp.

—The Woodcutter & the Heavenly Maiden & the Fire Dogs. 2008. (Korean Folk Tales for Children Ser.: Vol. 1.). (ENG & KOR.). 45p. (J). (gr. 2-5). lib. bdg. 14.50 *(978-0-930878-71-9(X))* Hollym International Corp.

Kim, Yon-Kyong & Kang, Mi-Sun. The Son of the Cinnamon Tree/the Donkey's Egg. 2006. (Korean Folk Tales for Children Ser.: Vol. 10). (ENG.). 45p. (J). (gr. 2-5). lib. bdg. 14.50 *(978-0-930878-93-1(0))* Hollym International Corp.

Kim, Yon-Kyong, jt. illus. see Kang, Mi-Sun.

Kim, Yon-Kyong, jt. illus. see Pak, Mi-Son.

Kim, Yoon-Kyung. iD_eNTITY, Vol. 1. 2005. 200p. pap. 9.99 *(978-1-59532-345-3(7))* TOKYOPOP, Inc.

—Id_Entity, Vol. 2. rev. ed. 2005. 192p. pap. 9.99 *(978-1-59532-346-0(5))* TOKYOPOP, Inc.

—iD_eNTITY, Vol. 3. Son, Hee-Joon. 3rd rev. ed. 2005. 192p. pap. 9.99 *(978-1-59532-347-7(3))* TOKYOPOP, Inc.

Kim, Youn-Kyung. iD_eNTITY, 13 vols. Son, Hee-Joon. (Id_entity Ser.: Vol. 5). 192p. 5th rev. ed. 2006. per. 9.99 *(978-1-59532-349-1(X))*; Vol. 4. 4th rev. ed. 2005. pap. 9.99 *(978-1-59532-348-4(1))* TOKYOPOP, Inc.

Kim, Young. Crepúsculo, Vol. 1. Meyer, Stephenie. 2010.Tr. of Twilight. (SPA.). 216p. (gr. 8-12). pap. 19.99 *(978-607-11-0482-3(3)*, Alfaguara Juvenil) Santillana USA Publishing Co., Inc.

Kim, Youngsun. The Truth about Princesses, 1 vol. Allen, Nancy Kelly. 2010. (Fairy-Tale Superstars Ser.). (ENG.). 32p. (gr. 1-3). lib. bdg. 26.65 *(978-1-4048-5747-6(8)*, Nonfiction Picture Bks.) Picture Window Bks.

Kimber, Murray. Ancient Voices. Hovey, Kate. 2007. (ENG.). 40p. (J). (gr. 3-7). 11.99 *(978-1-4169-6818-4(0)*, Simon & Schuster/Paula Wiseman Bks.) Simon & Schuster/Paula Wiseman Bks.

—The Highwayman. Noyes, Alfred. (Visions in Poetry Ser.). (ENG.). 48p. (YA). (gr. 5-18). 2009. 9.95 *(978-1-55453-384-8(8))*; 2005. 17.95 *(978-1-55337-425-1(8))* Kids Can Pr., Ltd. CAN. Dist: Univ. of Toronto Pr.

Kimmel, Eric A. Wonders & Miracles: A Passover Companion. Kimmel, Eric A. 2004. (Wonders & Miracles Ser.). (ENG.). 144p. (J). 21.99 *(978-0-439-07175-8(5))* Scholastic, Inc.

Kimmel, Eric A. & Glass, Andrew. Lavender. Hesse, Karen. 2010. (ENG.). 48p. (J). (gr. 2-5). pap. 9.99 *(978-0-312-37609-3(X))* Square Fish.

Kimura, ken, jt. illus. see Murakami, Yasanuri.

Kinard, Brandi. I Just Want to Be Liked. Kay, Regina. 2013. (J). 19.95 *(978-1-56411-592-8(5)*, CB Publishing & Design) UBUS Communications Systems.

Kinarney, Tom. Little Book of Saints. Wallace, Susan Helen. 2010. 24p. (J). (gr. 1-3). Vol. 5. 4.95 *(978-0-8198-4530-6(2))*; Vol. 6. 4.95 *(978-0-8198-4531-3(0))* Pauline Bks. & Media.

—Little Book of Saints: Volume 4, 4. Wallace, Susan Helen. 2009. (J). 4.95 *(978-0-8198-4527-6(2))* Pauline Bks. & Media.

Kinarney, Tom, jt. illus. see Mattozzi, Patricia R.

Kincaid, Angela. Mythical Creatures: Sticker Book. Reed, Natasha. 2005. (Stickertastic Ser.). 24p. (J). (gr. -1-7). pap. *(978-1-84510-119-0(7))* Top That! Publishing PLC.

Kincannon, Karla M. Creativity & Divine Surprise: Finding the Place of Your Resurrection. Kincannon, Karla M. 2005. 221p. per. 17.00 *(978-0-8358-9812-6(1))* Upper Room Bks.

Kindberg, Sally. Dreadful Fates: What a Shocking Way to Go! Turner, Tracey. 2011. (ENG.). 112p. (J). (gr. 3-7). 14.95 *(978-1-55453-644-3(8))* Kids Can Pr., Ltd. CAN. Dist: Univ. of Toronto Pr.

Kindersley, Anabel, jt. photos by see Kindersley, Barnabas.

Kindersley, Barnabas & Kindersley, Anabel, photos by. Celebraciones. 2005.Tr. of Celebrations. (SPA., (J). (gr. 1-4). 18.95 *(978-0-9628720-5-1(9))* Iaconi, Mariuccia Bk. Imports.

Kindert, Jennifer. Mommy's Bed. Scholastic, Inc. Staff & Black, Sonia. 2004. (Just for You Ser.). (ENG.). 32p. pap. 3.99 *(978-0-439-56857-9(9)*, Teaching Resources) Scholastic, Inc.

Kindert, Jennifer C. Hurry Up! Ford, Bernette G. 2004. (Just for You Ser.). (ENG.). 32p. (gr. k-1). pap. 3.99 *(978-0-439-56849-4(8)*, Teaching Resources) Scholastic, Inc.

—Three Years & Eight Months. Smith, Icy. 2013. (J). *(978-0-9856237-8-4(0))* East West Discovery Pr.

Kindt, Kathleen G. J Is for Jupiter: A-Z of People, Places & Things in Jupiter, Florida. Brasch, Pamela. 2011. 52p. (J). pap. 19.95 *(978-0-9846071-7-4(X))* Middle River Pr.

Kindt, Matt. Be Confident in Who You Are, Vol. 1. Fox, Annie. 2008. (Middle School Confidential Ser.: Bk. 1). (ENG.). 96p. (YA). (gr. 6-18). pap. 9.99 *(978-1-57542-302-9(2)*, 1285958) Free Spirit Publishing, Inc.

—Real Friends vs. the Other Kind. Fox, Annie. 2009. (Middle School Confidential Ser.). (ENG.). 96p. (YA). (gr. 6-9). pap. 9.99 *(978-1-57542-319-7(7))* Free Spirit Publishing, Inc.

Kindt, Rita. Aunt Tami's Strawberry Farm. Ward, Terri & Ward, Tom. 2010. 38p. pap. 14.50 *(978-1-60693-935-2(1)*, Eloquent Bks.) Strategic Book Publishing & Rights Agency (SBPRA).

King, Andy, photos by. El Calor. Walker, Sally M. Translations.com Staff, tr. from ENG. 2007. (Libros de Energía para Madrugadores (Early Bird Energy) Ser.). (SPA., 48p. (gr. 2-5). lib. bdg. 26.60 *(978-0-8225-7718-8(6)*, Ediciones Lerner) Lerner Publishing Group.

—Electricity. Walker, Sally M. 2005. (Early Bird Energy Ser.). (ENG., 48p. (gr. 2-5). lib. bdg. 26.60 *(978-0-8225-2919-4(X)*, Lerner Pubns.) Lerner Publishing Group.

—Heat. Walker, Sally M. 2005. (Early Bird Energy Ser.). (ENG., 48p. (gr. 2-5). lib. bdg. 26.60 *(978-0-8225-2459-5(7)*, Lerner Pubns.) Lerner Publishing Group.

—Light. Walker, Sally M. 2005. (Early Bird Energy Ser.). (ENG., 48p. (gr. 2-5). lib. bdg. 26.60 *(978-0-8225-2925-5(4)*, Lerner Pubns.) Lerner Publishing Group.

—La Luz. Walker, Sally M. Translations.com Staff, tr. from ENG. 2007. (Libros de Energía para Madrugadores (Early Bird Energy) Ser.). (SPA., 48p. (gr. 2-5). lib. bdg. 26.60 *(978-0-8225-7719-5(4)*, Ediciones Lerner) Lerner Publishing Group.

—Magnetism. Walker, Sally M. 2005. (Early Bird Energy Ser.). (ENG., 48p. (gr. 2-5). lib. bdg. 26.60 *(978-0-8225-2932-3(7)*, Lerner Pubns.) Lerner Publishing Group.

—El Magnetismo. Walker, Sally M. Translations.com Staff, tr. from ENG. 2007. (Libros de Energía para Madrugadores (Early Bird Energy) Ser.). (SPA., 48p. (gr. 2-5). lib. bdg. 26.60 *(978-0-8225-7720-1(8)*, Ediciones Lerner) Lerner Publishing Group.

—La Materia. Walker, Sally M. Translations.com Staff, tr. from ENG. 2007. (Libros de Energía para Madrugadores (Early Bird Energy) Ser.). (SPA., 48p. (gr. 2-5). lib. bdg. 26.60 *(978-0-8225-7721-8(6)*, Ediciones Lerner) Lerner Publishing Group.

—Planos Inclinados. Walker, Sally M. & Feldmann, Roseann. 2005. (Libros de Física para Madrugadores (Early Bird Physics) Ser.). (SPA & ENG., 48p. (gr. 3-6). lib. bdg. 26.60 *(978-0-8225-2970-5(X)*, Ediciones Lerner) Lerner Publishing Group.

—Poleas. Walker, Sally M. & Feldmann, Roseann. 2005. (Libros de Física para Madrugadores (Early Bird Physics) Ser.). (SPA & ENG., 48p. (gr. 3-6). lib. bdg. 26.60 *(978-0-8225-2980-4(7)*, Ediciones Lerner) Lerner Publishing Group.

—Ruedas y Ejes. Walker, Sally M. & Feldmann, Roseann. 2005. (Libros de Física para Madrugadores (Early Bird Physics) Ser.). (SPA & ENG., 48p. (gr. 3-6). lib. bdg. 26.60 *(978-0-8225-2982-8(3)*, Ediciones Lerner) Lerner Publishing Group.

—El Sonido. Walker, Sally M. Translations.com Staff, tr. from ENG. 2007. (Libros de Energía para Madrugadores (Early Bird Energy) Ser.). (SPA., 48p. (gr. 2-5). lib. bdg. 26.60 *(978-0-8225-7722-5(4)*, Ediciones Lerner) Lerner Publishing Group.

—Tornillos. Walker, Sally M. & Feldmann, Roseann. 2005. (Libros de Física para Madrugadores (Early Bird Physics) Ser.). (SPA & ENG., 48p. (gr. 3-6). lib. bdg. 26.60 *(978-0-8225-2974-3(2)*, Ediciones Lerner) Lerner Publishing Group.

—Trabajo. Walker, Sally M. & Feldmann, Roseann. 2005. (Libros de Física para Madrugadores (Early Bird Physics) Ser.). (SPA & ENG., 48p. (gr. 3-6). lib. bdg. 26.60 *(978-0-8225-2984-2(X)*, Ediciones Lerner) Lerner Publishing Group.

King, Cheryl. Alexee's Animals from A-Z, 1 vol. Eagan, Mary. 2010. 30p. 24.95 *(978-1-4489-3967-1(4))* PublishAmerica, Inc.

King, Chris. Aliens & UFOs. Hile, Lori. 2013. (Solving Mysteries with Science Ser.). (ENG.). 48p. (gr. 3-6). pap. 9.25 *(978-1-4109-5504-3(4))* Heinemann-Raintree.

—Bigfoot & the Yeti, 1 vol. Colson, Mary. 2013. (Solving Mysteries with Science Ser.). (ENG.). 48p. (gr. 3-6). pap. 9.25 *(978-1-4109-5505-0(2))* Heinemann-Raintree.

—Ghosts & Haunted Houses, 1 vol. Bingham, Jane. 2013. (Solving Mysteries with Science Ser.). (ENG.). 48p. (gr. 3-6). pap. 9.25 *(978-1-4109-5506-7(0))* Heinemann-Raintree.

—Vampires & Werewolves, 1 vol. Bingham, Jane. 2013. (Solving Mysteries with Science Ser.). (ENG.). 48p. (gr. 3-6). pap. 9.25 *(978-1-4109-5507-4(9))* Heinemann-Raintree.

King, Chris, jt. illus. see Deverell, Richard.

King, Colin. Amazing Dragons: Fiendish Tales of Dastardly Deeds. Baxter, Nicola. 2012. (ENG.). 80p. (J). (gr. k-4). pap. 9.99 *(978-1-84322-836-3(X))* Anness Publishing GBR. Dist: National Bk. Network.

—Castles: Information for Young Readers - Level 1. Turnbull, Stephanie. 2007. (Usborne Beginners Ser.). 32p. (J). 4.99 *(978-0-7945-1335-1(2)*, Usborne) EDC Publishing.

—Egyptians. Turnbull, Stephanie. 2007. (Usborne Beginners Ser.). 32p. (J). 4.99 *(978-0-7945-1344-3(1)*, Usborne) EDC Publishing.

—Egyptians Kid Kit. Turnbull, Stephanie. 2005. 32p. (J). 9.99 *(978-1-58086-844-0(4)*, Usborne) EDC Publishing.

—Elizabeth I Internet Referenced. Turnbull, Stephanie. 2004. 32p. (J). (gr. 1-18). pap. 4.95 *(978-0-7945-0808-1(1)*, Usborne) EDC Publishing.

—Jigsaw Atlas of North America. 2006. (Usborne Jigsaw Bks.). 14p. (J). (gr. k-3). bds. 14.99 *(978-0-7945-1242-2(9)*, Usborne) EDC Publishing.

—The Perils of Pirates & Other Dastardly Deeds: A Compendium of Swashbuckling Pirate Adventure Stories. Baxter, Nicola. 2012. (ENG.). 80p. (J). (gr. k-4). pap. 9.99 *(978-1-84322-802-8(5))* Anness Publishing GBR. Dist: National Bk. Network.

—See Inside Ships. Mason, Conrad. ed. 2011. (See Inside Board Books Ser.). 16p. (J). ring bd. 12.99 *(978-0-7945-3005-1(2)*, Usborne) EDC Publishing.

—See Inside Your Body. Daynes, Katie. 2006. 15p. (J). (gr. -1-3). bds. 12.99 *(978-0-7945-1233-0(X)*, Usborne) EDC Publishing.

—Ships. Bingham, Jane. 2004. (Young Reading Ser.). 64p. (J). (gr. 2-18). pap. 5.95 *(978-0-7945-0730-5(1)*, Usborne) EDC Publishing.

—Ships. Bone, Emily. 2009. (Beginner's Science Ser.). 32p. (J). 4.99 *(978-0-7945-2507-1(5)*, Usborne) EDC Publishing.

—The Story of Ships. Bingham, Jane. 2004. (Young Reading Ser.: Vol. 2). 62p. (J). (gr. 2-18). lib. bdg. 13.95 *(978-1-58086-700-9(6)*, Usborne) EDC Publishing.

—The Story of Trains. Bingham, Jane. 2004. 64p. (J). (gr. 2-18). (Young Reading Series Two Ser.). pap. 5.95 *(978-0-7945-0737-4(9))*; (Young Reading Ser.: Vol. 2). lib. bdg. 13.95 *(978-1-58086-702-3(2))* EDC Publishing. (Usborne).

—The Usborne Book of KnowHow. Amery, Heather et al. 2008. (Usborne Book Of... Ser.). 127p. (J). (gr. 4-7). 19.99 *(978-0-7945-2040-3(5)*, Usborne) EDC Publishing.

King, Colin. Planes. King, Colin. Patchett, F. 2004. (Beginners Ser.). (ENG.). 32p. (J). (gr. 1-18). pap. 4.95 *(978-0-7945-0319-2(5),* Usborne) EDC Publishing.

King, Dave, photos by. Baby Loves Peekaboo! Dorling Kindersley Publishing Staff. Quasha, Jennifer, ed. 2008. (ENG., 12p. (J). (gr. -1-k). bds. 6.99 *(978-0-7566-3486-5(5))* Dorling Kindersley Publishing, Inc.

—Beep! Beep! Peekaboo! Sirett, Dawn & Dorling Kindersley Publishing Staff. Quasha, Jennifer, ed. 2008. (ENG., 12p. (J). (gr. -1-k). bds. 6.99 *(978-0-7566-3487-2(3))* Dorling Kindersley Publishing, Inc.

—Counting Book. Whittington, Melanie & Holtz, Lara Tankel, eds. 2003. 32p. (J). *(978-0-681-62667-6(4))* Dorling Kindersley.

—Farm Peekaboo! Gardner, Charlie & Dorling Kindersley Publishing Staff. 2007. (ENG., 12p. (J). (gr. -1-k). bds. 6.99 *(978-0-7566-3104-8(1))* Dorling Kindersley Publishing, Inc.

King, Dave, jt. photos by see Burton, Jane.

King, Elizabeth, photos by. Quinceanera: Celebrating Fifteen. King, Elizabeth. 2006. 40p. (YA). (gr. 8-11). reprint ed. 17.00 *(978-1-4223-5728-6(7))* DIANE Publishing Co.

King, Janet. Bluey, the Little Drip. King, Philip. 2011. 40p. pap. 14.95 *(978-1-60976-661-0(X),* Eloquent Bks.) Strategic Book Publishing & Rights Agency (SBPRA).

King, Jerry. God Made the Skunk: And Other Animal Poems. Lewis, J. Patrick. 2005. 60p. (J). 14.95 *(978-0-9722820-1-7(7))* Doggerel Daze.

King, Jessie Marion. A House of Pomegranates. Wilde, Oscar. 2011. (Calla Editions Ser.). (ENG.). 208p. (J). (gr. 5). 35.00 *(978-1-60660-021-4(4))* Dover Pubns., Inc.

King, Joseph. Granny & the Tractor. Menges, Thais D. 2012. 36p. pap. 10.95 *(978-1-60920-047-3(0))* Ajoyin Publishing, Inc.

King, Judy. When Summer Comes Again. King, Judy. 2013. 160p. (J). pap. *(978-1-884377-20-4(3))* Green Pastures Pr.

King, Sally. Desert Blooms. 2007. 39p. pap. 7.95 *(978-1-55566-405-3(9))* Johnson Bks.

King, Stephen Michael. The Big Big Book of Gibblewort the Goblin, 7 bks. in 1. Kelleher, Victor. 2009. (Gibblewort the Goblin Ser.). (ENG.). 528p. (J). (gr. 2-4). pap. 18.99 *(978-1-74166-315-0(6))* Random Hse. Australia AUS. Dist: Independent Pubs. Group.

—Figaro & Rumba & the Crocodile Cafe. Fienberg, Anna. 2014. (ENG.). 96p. (J). (gr. k-3). 14.99 *(978-1-74237-311-9(9))* Allen & Unwin AUS. Dist: Independent Pubs. Group.

—Gibblewort the Goblin, 3 Bks. Kelleher, Victor. 2005. (Gibblewort the Goblin Ser.). (ENG.). 224p. (J). (gr. 2-4). pap. 14.99 *(978-1-74166-005-0(X))* Random Hse. Australia AUS. Dist: Independent Pubs. Group.

—Goblin at the Beach. Kelleher, Victor. 2011. (Gibblewort the Goblin Ser.). (ENG.). 80p. (Orig.). (J). (gr. 2-4). pap. 6.99 *(978-1-86471-955-0(9))* Random Hse. Australia AUS. Dist: Independent Pubs. Group.

—Goblin at the Zoo. Kelleher, Victor. (Gibblewort the Goblin Ser.). (ENG.). 80p. (J). (gr. 2-4). 2011. 6.99 *(978-1-86471-953-6(2));* 2005. pap. 5.99 *(978-0-7593-2100-7(0))* Random Hse. Australia AUS. Dist: Independent Pubs. Group.

—Goblin in the Bush. Kelleher, Victor. 2010. (Gibblewort the Goblin Ser.). (ENG.). 80p. (Orig.). (J). (gr. 2-4). 6.99 *(978-1-86471-949-9(4))* Random Hse. Australia AUS. Dist: Independent Pubs. Group.

—Goblin in the City. Kelleher, Victor. 2010. (Gibblewort the Goblin Ser.). (ENG.). 80p. (J). (gr. 2-4). pap. 6.99 *(978-1-86471-951-2(6))* Random Hse. Australia AUS. Dist: Independent Pubs. Group.

—Goblin in the Snow. Kelleher, Victor. 2010. (Gibblewort the Goblin Ser.). (ENG.). 80p. (J). (gr. 2-4). pap. 6.99 *(978-1-86471-954-3(0))* Random Hse. Australia AUS. Dist: Independent Pubs. Group.

—Goblin on the Reef. Kelleher, Victor. (Gibblewort the Goblin Ser.). (ENG.). 80p. (Orig.). (J). (gr. 2-4). 2010. pap. 6.99 *(978-1-86471-950-5(8));* 2003. pap. 5.99 ***(978-1-74051-855-0(1))*** Random Hse. Australia AUS. Dist: Independent Pubs. Group.

—My Dad the Dragon. French, Jackie. 2004. 128p. *(978-0-207-19950-9(7))* HarperCollins Pubs. Australia.

—My Dog the Dinosaur. French, Jackie. 2006. (Wacky Families Ser.). (ENG.). 112p. *(978-0-207-19941-7(8))* HarperCollins Pubs. Australia.

—My Gran the Gorilla. French, Jackie. 2005. 112p. *(978-0-207-20012-0(2))* HarperCollins Pubs. Australia.

—My Mum the Pirate. French, Jackie. 2006. (Wacky Families Ser.). (ENG.). 112p. *(978-0-207-19949-3(3))* HarperCollins Pubs. Australia.

—My Uncle Gus the Garden Gnome. French, Jackie. 2004. 128p. (Orig.). *(978-0-207-19958-5(2))* HarperCollins Pubs. Australia.

—Piglet & Granny. Wild, Margaret. 2009. (ENG.). 32p. (J). (gr. -1-1). 15.95 *(978-0-8109-4063-5(9),* Abrams Bks. for Young Readers) Abrams.

—Piglet & Mama. Wild, Margaret. 2005. (ENG.). 32p. (J). (gr. -1-1). 15.95 *(978-0-8109-5869-2(4))* Abrams.

—Prudence Wants a Pet. Daly, Cathleen. 2011. (ENG.). 32p. (J). (gr. -1-2). 17.99 *(978-1-59643-468-4(6))* Roaring Brook Pr.

—The Return of Gibblewort the Goblin, 3 bks. in 1. Kelleher, Victor. 2007. (Gibblewort the Goblin Ser.). (ENG.). 224p. (J). (gr. 2-4). pap. 14.99 *(978-1-74166-185-9(4))* Random Hse. Australia AUS. Dist: Independent Pubs. Group.

King, Stephen Michael. Mutt Dog! King, Stephen Michael. 2005. 32p. (J). *(978-1-86504-636-5(1));* pap. *(978-1-86504-637-2(X))* Scholastic, Inc. (Scholastic Pr.).

—You: A Story of Love & Friendship. King, Stephen Michael. 2011. 32p. (J). 14.99 *(978-0-06-206014-3(7),* Greenwillow Bks.) HarperCollins Pubs.

King, Steve. Molly's Sweet Shop. Canning, Laura A. 2012. 48p. pap. *(978-1-78148-772-3(3))* Grosvenor Hse. Publishing Ltd.

King, Sue. Tractors. Watt, Fiona. 2009. (Luxury Touchy-Feely Board Bks). 10p. (J). bds. 15.99 *(978-0-7945-2432-6(X),* Usborne) EDC Publishing.

King, Sue, jt. illus. see Cooper, Jenny.

King, Tara Calahan. Pastel para Enemigos. Munson, Derek. 2004.Tr. of Enemy Pie. (SPA.). 40p. (J). (gr. k-2). pap. 9.99 *(978-84-261-3378-6(9))* Juventud, Editorial ESP. Dist: Lectorum Pubns., Inc.

King, Travis. Old MacDonald's Farm. Ikids Staff. 2010. (ENG.). 20p. (J). (gr. -1-k). 14.99 *(978-1-60169-024-1(X))* Innovative Kids.

—10 Little Monkeys. Ikids Staff. 2009. (ENG.). 20p. (J). (gr. -1-k). 14.99 *(978-1-58476-938-5(6))* Innovative Kids.

King, W. B. Tom Cardiff's Circus. Garis, Howard Roger. 2005. reprint ed. pap. 28.95 *(978-1-4179-3393-8(3))* Kessinger Publishing, LLC.

Kingsley, Linda Kurtz. Bringing up Sophie. Kingsley, Linda Kurtz. 2010. 32p. (J). lib. bdg. 15.95 *(978-0-944727-25-6(5),* Turtle Bks.) Jason & Nordic Pubs.

—Signs of Jays. Kingsley, Linda Kurtz. 2008. 32p. (J). (ENG.). lib. bdg. 15.95 *(978-0-944727-23-2(9));* pap. 9.95 *(978-0-944727-22-5(0))* Jason & Nordic Pubs. (Turtle Bks.).

Kini, Kanyika. The Rumor. Ravishankar, Anushka. 2012. (ENG.). 32p. (J). (gr. -1-1). 17.95 *(978-1-77049-280-6(1),* Tundra Bks.) Tundra Bks. CAN. Dist: Penguin Random Hse., LLC.

Kinkade, Thomas. Away in a Manger. Public Domain Staff. 2009. (ENG.). 32p. (J). (gr. -1-3). pap. 7.99 *(978-0-06-078734-9(1))* HarperCollins Pubs.

—Away in a Manger. 2005. 32p. (J). lib. bdg. 17.89 *(978-0-06-078733-2(3))* HarperCollins Pubs.

—Away in a Manger. 2005. 32p. (J). 16.99 *(978-0-06-078730-1(9))* Zonderkidz.

Kinnaird, Ross. It's a Feudal, Feudal World: A Different Medieval History. Shapiro, Stephen. 2013. (ENG.). 48p. (J). (gr. 4-8). pap. 14.95 *(978-1-55451-552-3(1),* 9781554515523); lib. bdg. 24.95 *(978-1-55451-553-0(X),* 9781554515530) Annick Pr., Ltd. CAN. Dist: Firefly Bks., Ltd.

—The Make Your Own Joke Book. Holt, Sharon. 2009. (ENG.). 96p. (J). (gr. 4-7). 7.99 *(978-1-74175-582-4(4))* Allen & Unwin AUS. Dist: Independent Pubs. Group.

Kinnaird, Ross. Woolly Wally. McMillan, Dawn. 2014. 32p. pap. 16.95 ***(978-1-877514-49-4(7))*** Oratia Media NZL. Dist: International Publishers Marketing.

Kinnaird, Ross. 50 Body Questions: A Book That Spills Its Guts. Kyi, Tanya Lloyd. 2014. (50 Questions Ser.). (ENG.). 108p. (J). (gr. 4-6). 22.95 *(978-1-55451-613-1(7),* 9781554516131); pap. 14.95 *(978-1-55451-612-4(9),* 9781554516124) Annick Pr., Ltd. CAN. Dist: Firefly Bks., Ltd.

—50 Burning Questions: A Sizzling History of Fire. Kyi, Tanya Lloyd. 2010. (50 Questions Ser.). (ENG.). 104p. (J). (gr. 3-18). 21.95 *(978-1-55451-221-8(2),* 9781554512218); pap. 12.95 *(978-1-55451-220-1(4),* 9781554512201) Annick Pr., Ltd. CAN. Dist: Firefly Bks., Ltd.

—50 Poisonous Questions: A Book with Bite. Kyi, Tanya Lloyd. 2011. (50 Questions Ser.). (ENG.). 110p. (J). (gr. 3-18). 21.95 *(978-1-55451-281-2(6),* 9781554512812); pap. 12.95 *(978-1-55451-280-5(8),* 9781554512805) Annick Pr., Ltd. CAN. Dist: Firefly Bks., Ltd.

—50 Underwear Questions: A Bare-All History. Kyi, Tanya Lloyd. 2011. (50 Questions Ser.). (ENG.). 116p. (J). (gr. 3-18). 21.95 *(978-1-55451-353-6(7),* 9781554513536); pap. 12.95 *(978-1-55451-352-9(9),* 9781554513529) Annick Pr., Ltd. CAN. Dist: Firefly Bks., Ltd.

Kinneman, D. Michael. The Adventures of Jilly & Brad: Noises in the Attic. Hees, Miriam. 2003. 128p. (J). pap. 5.95 *(978-0-9718348-4-2(9))* Blooming Tree Pr.

Kinney, Jeff. The Long Haul. Kinney, Jeff. 2014. (Diary of a Wimpy Kid Ser.: Bk. 9). (ENG.). 224p. (J). (gr. 3-7). 13.95 *(978-1-4197-1189-3(X),* Amulet Bks.) Abrams.

Kinney, Jo Hannah. When George Stopped Talking. Enos, Barbara. 2011. 20p. pap. 24.95 *(978-1-4626-4254-0(3))* America Star Bks.

Kinra, Richa. The Alley that Wanted to be a Street: Kirkland Morris. Morris, Kirkland. 2012. (ENG.). 27p. (J). pap. 11.95 *(978-1-4327-7844-6(7))* Outskirts Pr., Inc.

—Annabelle's Secret. Barth, Amy. 2009. (J). pap. 12.95 *(978-1-932690-95-8(6))* Loving Healing Pr., Inc.

—Annabelle's Secret: A Story about Sexual Abuse. Barth, Amy. 2011. 24p. (gr. 3-7). 28.95 *(978-1-61599-099-3(2))* Loving Healing Pr., Inc.

—Cinderella's Magical Wheelchair: An Empowering Fairy Tale. Kats, Jewel. 2012. (J). 24p. 29.95 *(978-1-61599-113-6(1));* 20p. pap. 16.95 *(978-1-61599-112-9(3))* Loving Healing Pr., Inc.

—The Flip Flop Family. Vance, Colleen. 2013. (ENG.). (J). (gr. -1-3). 14.95 *(978-1-62086-275-9(1))* Mascot Bks., Inc.

—Jiali's Traveling Heart. MacLean, Betty. 2013. 34p. (J). 17.95 *(978-1-60131-157-3(5),* Castlebridge Bks.) Big Tent Bks.

—Moongi & Mohan: A Story from India As Told to Me by My Mother. Singal, Sudesh. 2011. (ENG.). 32p. pap. 11.99 *(978-1-4565-4120-0(X))* CreateSpace Independent Publishing Platform.

—The Princess & the Ruby: An Autism Fairy Tale. Kats, Jewel. 2013. 42p. 26.95 *(978-1-61599-193-8(X));* (gr. 3-7). pap. 16.95 *(978-1-61599-175-4(1))* Loving Healing Pr., Inc.

—The Princess Panda Tea Party: A Cerebral Palsy Fairy Tale. 2014. (J). pap. 14.95 *(978-1-61599-219-5(7))* Loving Healing Pr., Inc.

—The Soap Bubble Frog. Lawson, Brandi. 2012. 32p. pap. 14.50 *(978-1-61897-784-7(9),* Strategic Bk. Publishing) Strategic Book Publishing & Rights Agency (SBPRA).

—Will Was All Boy: A Story about Sexual Abuse. Barth, Amy. 2009. (J). pap. *(978-1-61599-000-9(3))* Loving Healing Pr., Inc.

Kinsella, Pat. Houdini: The Life of the Great Escape Artist, 1 vol. Biskup, Agnieszka. 2011. (American Graphic Ser.). (ENG.). 32p. (gr. 3-4). pap. 8.10 *(978-1-4296-6268-0(9));* pap. 47.70 *(978-1-4296-6435-6(5))* Capstone Pr., Inc. (Graphic Library).

—Jay-Z: Hip-Hop Icon, 1 vol. Gunderson, Jessica. 2012. (American Graphic Ser.). (ENG.). 32p. (gr. 3-4). pap. 8.10 *(978-1-4296-7993-0(X));* pap. 47.70 *(978-1-4296-8475-0(5));* lib. bdg. 29.99 *(978-1-4296-6017-4(1))* Capstone Pr., Inc. (Graphic Library).

—True Stories of the Revolutionary War, 1 vol. Raum, Elizabeth. 2012. (Stories of War Ser.). (ENG.). 32p. (gr. 3-4). 29.99 *(978-1-4296-8674-7(X));* pap. 8.10 *(978-1-4296-9342-4(8));* pap. 47.70 *(978-1-4296-9343-1(6),* Graphic Library) Capstone Pr., Inc.

—True Stories of World War II, 1 vol. Collins, Terry. 2012. (Stories of War Ser.). (ENG.). 32p. (gr. 3-4). pap. 8.10 *(978-1-4296-9346-2(0));* pap. 47.70 *(978-1-4296-9347-9(9),* Graphic Library); lib. bdg. 29.99 *(978-1-4296-8623-5(5))* Capstone Pr., Inc.

Kinsella, Pat, et al. True War Stories: Personal Accounts of History's Greatest Conflicts. Raum, Elizabeth et al. 2017. (J). *(978-1-4914-1965-6(2))* Capstone Pr., Inc.

Kinsella, Pat & Byers, Michael. American Graphic. Gunderson, Jessica & Collins, Terry. 2012. (American Graphic Ser.). (ENG.). 32p. (gr. 3-4). pap. 15.90 *(978-1-4296-9505-3(6));* pap. 477.00 *(978-1-4296-8478-1(X));* pap. 79.50 *(978-1-4296-8477-4(1));* lib. bdg. 269.91 *(978-1-4296-8179-7(9));* lib. bdg. 59.98 *(978-1-4296-8178-0(0))* Capstone Pr., Inc. (Graphic Library).

Kinsella, Pat, jt. illus. see Hayden, Seitu.

Kinsella, Sophie, pseud. Tizzy Blenkinsop. Oliver, A. J. 2013. (ENG.). 24p. 9.99 *(978-1-62884-784-0(0))* Speedy Publishing LLC.

Kinsley, Sean. Pick Me, Pick Me. Horton, Elizabeth. ed. 2008. (ENG.). 32p. (J). 16.95 *(978-0-9797460-0-0(0))* Lerue Pr., LLC.

Kinstle Nocera, Suzanne. A Day with Little Duke. Rode, Maureen. 2012. (J). *(978-0-9786675-1-1(4))* Gerardian Inkspot & Paint Society.

Kipling, John Lockwood, jt. illus. see Kipling, Rudyard.

Kipling, Rudyard & Kipling, John Lockwood. The Jungle Book. 2014. (J). *(978-1-4677-5836-9(1),* First Avenue Editions) Lerner Publishing Group.

Kiplinger Pandy, Lori. Another Way of Life. Collins, Arda. l.t. ed. 2005. 30p. (J). (gr. -1-3). per. 9.99 *(978-1-59879-023-8(4))* Lifevest Publishing, Inc.

—Besos y Abrazos Al Aire. Sample, Jewel. Tenorio-Gavin, Lucero, tr. l.t. ed. 2006. (SPA.). 30p. (J). 23.95 *(978-1-59879-291-1(1))* Lifevest Publishing, Inc.

—Flying Hugs & Kisses. l.t. ed. 2006. 32p. (J). 15.95 *(978-1-59879-119-8(2))* Lifevest Publishing, Inc.

—Flying Hugs & Kisses Activity Book. Sample, Jewel. 2007. 68p. (J). (gr. -1-3). per. 13.99 *(978-1-59879-377-2(2))* Lifevest Publishing, Inc.

—Goose Dreams. McWilliams Pittard, Irene. 2005. (J). 10.00 *(978-1-59971-142-3(7))* Aardvark Global Publishing.

Kirby, Jack, et al. Captain America vs. the Red Skull. 2011. (ENG.). 264p. (J). (gr. -1-17). pap. 24.99 *(978-0-7851-5096-1(X))* Marvel Worldwide, Inc.

Kirby, Jack. Essential Fantastic Four, Vol. 4. rev. ed. 2006. (ENG.). 536p. (J). (gr. 4-17). pap. 19.99 *(978-0-7851-1484-0(X))* Marvel Worldwide, Inc.

Kirby, Jack, et al. Ka-Zar. Lee, Stan et al. 2013. (ENG.). 312p. (J). (gr. -1-17). 69.99 *(978-0-7851-5957-5(6))* Marvel Worldwide, Inc.

Kirby, Jack & Ditko, Steve. The Incredible Hulk, Vol. 1. 2009. (ENG.). 176p. (J). (gr. -1-17). pap. 24.99 *(978-0-7851-3714-6(9))* Marvel Worldwide, Inc.

Kirby, Jack, jt. illus. see Molina, Jorge.

Kirby, Pamela F., photos by. What Bluebirds Do. Kirby, Pamela F. 2013. (ENG., 48p. (J). (gr. k-2). pap. 6.95 *(978-1-62091-593-6(6))* Boyds Mills Pr.

Kirchhoff, Art. The Adventures of Martin Luther. Bergt, Carolyn. 16p. (gr. -1-k). 20.00 *(978-0-570-00643-5(0),* 22-2808) Concordia Publishing Hse.

—Behold the Lamb: An Introduction to the Signs & Symbols of the Church. Nielsen, Pamela & Luhmann, Edward Q. 2010. 48p. (J). 9.99 *(978-0-7586-1550-3(7))* Concordia Publishing Hse.

Kirchhoff, Arthur. Worshiping with Angels & Archangels: An Introduction to the Divine Service. Kinnaman, Scott A. 2005. 48p. 7.99 *(978-0-7586-1206-9(0))* Concordia Publishing Hse.

Kirchmeier, Jenn-Ann. The Tails of Brinkley the Berner: The Beginning. 2008. 32p. (J). 16.95 *(978-0-9793288-0-0(2))* Brinkley Bks., Inc.

Kirchoff, Arthur. The Adventures of Billie & Annie — Baby Bison. Meyer, Kay L. l.t. ed. 2004. 32p. (J). 6.00 *(978-0-9744536-0-6(9),* 9780974453606) Meyer, Tjaden.

Kirk, Andrea Cope. Beating the Bully. McLelland, Michael J. 2007. 16p. (J). 15.99 *(978-1-59955-006-0(7))* Cedar Fort, Inc./CFI Distribution.

Kirk, Daniel. Block City. Stevenson, Robert Louis. 2005. (ENG.). 32p. (J). (gr. -1-3). 17.99 *(978-0-689-86964-8(9),* Simon & Schuster Bks. For Young Readers) Simon & Schuster Bks. For Young Readers.

—Dinosaur, Dinosaur. Lewis, Kevin. 2006. (J). *(978-0-439-78228-9(7),* Orchard Bks.) Scholastic, Inc.

—Hello, Hello! Schlein, Miriam. 2011. (ENG.). 32p. (J). (gr. -1-1). pap. 16.99 *(978-1-4424-5229-9(3),* Simon & Schuster Bks. For Young Readers) Simon & Schuster Bks. For Young Readers.

—Tugga-Tugga Tugboat. Lewis, Kevin. 2006. (ENG.). 32p. (J). (gr. -1-k). 15.99 *(978-0-7868-5615-2(7))* Hyperion Pr.

Kirk, Daniel. Honk Honk! Beep Beep! Kirk, Daniel. 2014. (ENG.). 32p. (J). (gr. -1-k). bds. 6.99 *(978-1-4231-8041-8(0))* Hyperion Bks. for Children.

—My Truck Is Stuck! Kirk, Daniel. Lewis, Kevin. 2006. (ENG.). 30p. (J). (gr. -1 — 1). bds. 7.99 *(978-0-7868-3739-7(X))* Hyperion Pr.

—Ten Thank-You Letters. Kirk, Daniel. 2014. (ENG.). 32p. (J). (gr. k-3). 16.99 *(978-0-399-16937-3(7),* Nancy Paulsen Bks.) Penguin Publishing Group.

—Ten Things I Love about You. Kirk, Daniel. 2012. (ENG.). 36p. (J). (gr. k-3). 16.99 *(978-0-399-25288-4(6))* Penguin Publishing Group.

Kirk, David. Oh So Brave Dragon. Kirk, David. 2014. (ENG.). 40p. (J). (gr. -1-1). 17.99 *(978-1-250-01689-8(4))* Feiwel & Friends.

—Oh So Tiny Bunny. Kirk, David. 2013. (ENG.). 36p. (J). (gr. -1-1). 16.99 *(978-1-250-01688-1(6))* Feiwel & Friends.

Kirk, Heather. My First Picture Numbers. 2012. (ENG.). 24p. (J). 9.95 *(978-1-84135-795-9(2))* Award Pubns. Ltd. GBR. Dist: Parkwest Pubns., Inc.

—Tiberius & the Chocolate Cake. Harvey, Keith. 2010. (Tiberius Tales Ser.). 24p. (J). (gr. -1-2). pap. 8.15 *(978-1-60754-836-2(4));* lib. bdg. 22.60 *(978-1-60754-832-4(1))* Windmill Bks.

—Tiberius & the Friendly Dragon. Harvey, Keith. 2010. (Tiberius Tales Ser.). 24p. (J). (gr. -1-2). pap. 8.15 *(978-1-60754-834-8(8));* lib. bdg. 22.60 *(978-1-60754-830-0(5))* Windmill Bks.

Kirk, Jacqueline. The Ant in the Cellar. Rosenblatt, Danielle. 2008. (J). per. 16.95 *(978-0-9801555-5-6(X))* Argus Enterprises International, Inc.

—The Ant in the Cellar. Rosenblatt, Danielle. 2008. 127p. per. 19.95 *(978-0-9788985-3-3(2))* Better Be Write Pub., A.

Kirk, Janice. The Christmas Redwood. Kirk, Janice. 2007. 56p. per. 18.95 *(978-1-60290-147-6(3))* OakTara Publishing Group LLC.

Kirk, Leonard. Attack of 50 Foot Girl! Parker, Jeff. 2014. (Avengers Set 4 Ser.). (ENG.). 24p. (J). (gr. 9-14). lib. bdg. 24.21 *(978-1-61479-293-2(3))* Spotlight.

—Avenging Seven. Parker, Jeff. 2014. (Avengers Set 4 Ser.). (ENG.). 24p. (J). (gr. 9-14). lib. bdg. 24.21 *(978-1-61479-294-9(1))* Spotlight.

Kirk, Maria L. Heidi. Spyri, Johanna & Stork, Elisabeth P. 2014. (J). *(978-1-4677-5846-8(9),* First Avenue Editions) Lerner Publishing Group.

Kirk, Maria L. & Hughes, Arthur. The Princess & Curdie. MacDonald, George, ed. 2011. 260p. pap. 10.95 *(978-1-59915-251-6(7))* Yesterday's Classics.

—The Princess & the Goblin. MacDonald, George. 2011. 260p. pap. 10.95 *(978-1-59915-250-9(9))* Yesterday's Classics.

Kirk, Tim. Muggles & Magic: An Unofficial Guide to J. K. Rowling & the Harry Potter Phenomenon. Beahm, George. 2005. (J). lib. bdg. 19.95 *(978-1-57174-480-7(0))* Hampton Roads Publishing Co., Inc.

—Muggles & Magic: J.K. Rowling & the Harry Potter Phenomenon. Beahm, George. 2004. 416p. pap. 16.95 *(978-1-57174-412-8(6))* Hampton Roads Publishing Co., Inc.

—Passport to Narnia: A Newcomer's Guide. Beahm, George. 2005. (ENG.). 200p. (YA). (gr. 8-12). per. 12.95 *(978-1-57174-465-4(7))* Hampton Roads Publishing Co., Inc.

—Passport to Narnia: The Unofficial Guide. Beahm, George. 2005. (J). lib. bdg. 15.95 *(978-1-57174-481-4(9))* Hampton Roads Publishing Co., Inc.

—Twinkle: The Only Firefly Who Couldn't Light Up. Black, Cassandra. 3rd ed. 2012. (ENG.). 111p. (J). (gr. 4-7). pap. 12.99 *(978-0-9742739-3-8(7))* Lavender Bks.

Kirkby, Joanne & Cooper, Sharon. Mosaic Picture Sticker Book. 2015. (Mosaic Sticker Bks.). (ENG.). 24+12p. (J). (gr. k-5). pap. 10.99 ***(978-0-7945-3015-0(X),*** Usborne) EDC Publishing.

Kirkland, Katherine. The Bears Go to School. Winters, Kay. 2013. (Pete & Gabby Book Ser.). (ENG.). 32p. (J). (gr. -1-2). 16.99 *(978-0-8075-0592-2(7))* Whitman, Albert & Co.

—Grandma Loves You! Hallinan, P. K. 2014. 22p. (J). bds. 8.99 *(978-0-8249-1931-3(9),* Candy Cane Pr.) Ideals Pubns.

—Grandpa Loves You! Hallinan, P. K. 2014. 22p. (J). bds. 8.99 *(978-0-8249-1932-0(7),* Candy Cane Pr.) Ideals Pubns.

—My Grandma & Me: Rhyming Devotions for You & Your Grandchild. Bowman, Crystal. 2012. (ENG.). 68p. (J). 14.99 *(978-1-4143-7170-2(5),* Tyndale Kids) Tyndale Hse. Pubs.

Kirkman, Kelly. Catherine the Great & Her Teatime Tagalongs, 1 vol. Swensen, Karen & Ronquillo, Karen. 2005. (ENG.). 32p. (J). (gr. k-3). 16.99 *(978-1-58980-343-5(4))* Pelican Publishing Co., Inc.

Kirkova, Milena. Lights Out, Night's Out. Boniface, William. (ENG.). 24p. (J). 2011. pap. 6.99 *(978-1-4494-0236-5(4));* 2009. (gr. -1-3). 17.99 *(978-0-7407-8431-6(5))* Andrews McMeel Publishing.

K

—Where Does Love Come From? Accord Publishing Staff. 2011. (ENG.). 18p. (J). 9.99 *(978-1-4494-0839-8(7))* Andrews McMeel Publishing.

—Where Does Love Come From? Accord Publishing Staff. 2012. (ENG.). 18p. (J). bds. 5.99 *(978-1-4494-2884-6(3))* Andrews McMeel Publishing.

Kirkpatrick, Karen. The Boy Who Captured the Sun. Rodenbur, Susan. 2007. 32p. per. 12.95 *(978-1-59858-515-5(0))* Dog Ear Publishing, LLC.

Kirkpatrick, Katrina. Night Work. Gifune, Greg F. 2003. (ENG.). 278p. pap. 14.99 *(978-1-58124-094-8(5))* Fiction Works, The.

Kirmse, Marguerite. Alfred Ollivant's Bob, Son of Battle: The Last Gray Dog of Kenmuir. Davis, Lydia & Ollivant, Alfred. 2014. (ENG.). 320p. (J). (gr. 3-7). 17.95 *(978-1-59017-729-7(0),* NYR Children's Collection) New York Review of Bks., Inc., The.

—Lassie Come-Home. Knight, Eric. rev. ed. 2003. (ENG.). 256p. (J). (gr. 3-7). 24.99 *(978-0-8050-7206-8(3),* Holt, Henry & Co. Bks. For Young Readers) Holt, Henry & Co.

—Lassie Come-Home. Knight, Eric. 2007. (ENG.). 256p. (J). (gr. 3-7). per. 7.99 *(978-0-312-37131-9(4))* Square Fish.

Kirsch, Vincent X. Gingerbread for Liberty! How a German Baker Helped Win the American Revolution. Rockliff, Mara. 2015. (ENG.). 32p. (J). (gr. 1-4). 17.99 *(978-0-544-13001-2(4),* HMH Books For Young Readers) Houghton Mifflin Harcourt Publishing Co.

—Noah Webster & His Words. Ferris, Jeri Chase. 2012. (ENG.). 32p. (J). (gr. -1-3). 16.99 *(978-0-547-39055-0(6))* Houghton Mifflin Harcourt Publishing Co.

Kirsch, Vincent X. The Whole Story of the Doughnut. Miller, Pat. 2016. (J). *(978-0-544-31961-5(3))* Harcourt.

Kirsch, Vincent X. Freddie & Gingersnap. Kirsch, Vincent X. 2014. (Freddie & Gingersnap Ser.). (ENG.). 40p. (J). (gr. -1-k). 16.99 *(978-1-4231-5958-2(6))* Hyperion Pr.

—Freddie & Gingersnap Find a Cloud to Keep. Kirsch, Vincent X. 2015. (Freddie & Gingersnap Ser.). (ENG.). 40p. (J). (gr. -1-k). 16.99 *(978-1-4231-5976-6(4))* Hyperion Bks. for Children.

Kirton, Pamela T. Dino the Dog & His Day in the Country. Garr, Hillary. Date not set. 15.95 *(978-0-9637143-3-6(3))* Amicus Pr.

Kirwan, Wednesday. The Night Dad Went to Jail: What to Expect When Someone You Love Goes to Jail, 1 vol. Higgins, Melissa. 2011. (Life's Challenges Ser.). (ENG.). 24p. (gr. 2-3). lib. bdg. 25.32 *(978-1-4048-6679-9(5),* Nonfiction Picture Bks.) Picture Window Bks.

—Night Dad Went to Jail: What to Expect When Someone You Love Goes to Jail. Higgins, Melissa. 2013. (Life's Challenges Ser.). (ENG.). 24p. (gr. 2-3). 8.99 *(978-1-4795-2142-5(6))* Picture Window Bks.

—Santa Claus Is Green! How to Have an Eco-Friendly Christmas. Inches, Alison. 2009. (Little Green Bks.). (ENG.). 24p. (J). (gr. -1-1). pap. 5.99 *(978-1-4169-7223-5(4),* Little Simon) Little Simon.

—Weekends with Dad: What to Expect When Your Parents Divorce, 1 vol. Higgins, Melissa. 2011. (Life's Challenges Ser.). (ENG.). 24p. (gr. 2-3). lib. bdg. 25.32 *(978-1-4048-6678-2(7),* Nonfiction Picture Bks.) Picture Window Bks.

—Yeti, Turn Out the Light! Long, Greg & Edmundson, Chris. 2013. (ENG.). 36p. (J). (gr. -1-k). 12.99 *(978-1-4521-1158-2(8))* Chronicle Bks. LLC.

Kirwan, Wednesday. Baby Loves to Boogie! Kirwan, Wednesday. 2014. (ENG.). 30p. (J). (gr. -1 — 1). bds. 5.99 *(978-1-4814-0383-2(4),* Little Simon) Little Simon.

—Baby Loves to Rock! Kirwan, Wednesday. 2013. (ENG.). 28p. (J). (gr. -1 — 1). bds. 5.99 *(978-1-4424-5989-2(1),* Little Simon) Little Simon.

—Baby Loves to Rock! & Baby Loves to Boogie! 2-Pack. Kirwan, Wednesday. 2014. (ENG.). 58p. (J). (gr. -1 — 1). bds. 11.98 *(978-1-4814-2924-5(8),* Little Simon) Little Simon.

Kiryakova, Niya. Calico Bear: A Story about Unchanging Love. Hunt, Angela. 2013. (ENG.). 34p. pap. 11.99 *(978-0-615-84497-8(9))* Hunthaven Pr.

Kishimoto, Jon Wayne. Kids Like Me... Learn ABCs. Ronay, Laura. 2008. 26p. (J). (gr. -1-1). bds. 12.95 *(978-1-60613-000-1(5))* Woodbine Hse.

—Kids Like Me... Learn Colors. Ronay, Laura. 2008. 14p. (J). (gr. -1-1). 11.95 *(978-1-60613-001-8(3))* Woodbine Hse.

Kishimoto, Masashi. The Art of Naruto: Uzumaki. Kishimoto, Masashi. Wall, Frances, ed. 2007. (Naruto Ser.: 1). (ENG.). 148p. (gr. 8-18). pap. 24.99 *(978-1-4215-1407-9(9))* Viz Media.

—Beauty Is the Beast. Kishimoto, Masashi. 2010. (Naruto Ser.: 13). (ENG.). 80p. (J). pap. 4.99 *(978-1-4215-3043-7(0))* Viz Media.

—The Boy Ninja, Vol. 1. Kishimoto, Masashi. 2008. (Naruto Ser.: 1). (ENG.). 80p. (J). (gr. 1-5). pap. 4.99 *(978-1-4215-2056-8(7))* Viz Media.

—Bridge of Courage. Kishimoto, Masashi. 2009. (Naruto Ser.: 5). (ENG.). 80p. (J). (gr. 1). pap. 4.99 *(978-1-4215-2315-6(9))* Viz Media.

—Cell Seven Reunion. Kishimoto, Masashi. 2011. (Naruto Ser.: 52). (ENG.). 192p. pap. 9.99 *(978-1-4215-3957-7(8))* Viz Media.

—Coward. Kishimoto, Masashi. 2010. (Naruto Ser.: 12). (ENG.). 80p. (J). pap. 4.99 *(978-1-4215-3042-0(2))* Viz Media.

—The Last Chance, Bk. 15. Kishimoto, Masashi. 2010. (Naruto Ser.). (ENG.). 80p. (J). (gr. 1-4). pap. 4.99 *(978-1-4215-3045-1(7))* Viz Media.

—Naruto. Kishimoto, Masashi. (ENG.). 2010. (Naruto Ser.: 47). 192p. (gr. 8-18). pap. 9.99 *(978-1-4215-3305-6(7));* 2009. (Naruto Ser.: 46). 192p. pap. 9.99 *(978-1-4215-3304-9(9));* 2009. (Naruto Ser.: 7). 80p. (J). pap. 4.99 *(978-1-4215-2317-0(5));* 2009. (Naruto Ser.: 6). 80p. (J). pap. 4.99 *(978-1-4215-2316-3(7));* 2007. (Naruto Ser.: 22). 200p. (gr. 8). pap. 9.99 *(978-1-4215-1858-9(9));* 2007. (Naruto Ser.: 23). 200p. (gr. 8). pap. 9.99 *(978-1-4215-1859-6(7));* 2005. (Naruto Ser.: Vol. 8). 192p. pap. 9.99 *(978-1-4215-0124-6(4));* 3rd ed. 2011. (Naruto 3-in-1 Ser.: 1). 600p. pap. 14.99 *(978-1-4215-3989-8(6));* Vol. 1. 2003. (Naruto Ser.). 192p. pap. 9.99 *(978-1-56931-900-0(6));* Vol. 2. 2003. (Naruto Ser.). 216p. pap. 9.99 *(978-1-59116-178-3(9));* Vol. 3. 2004. (Naruto Ser.). 208p. pap. 9.99 *(978-1-59116-187-5(8));* Vol. 4. 2004. (Naruto Ser.). 184p. pap. 9.99 *(978-1-59116-358-9(7));* Vol. 5. 2004. (Naruto Ser.). 184p. pap. 9.99 *(978-1-59116-359-6(5));* Vol. 7. 2005. (Naruto Ser.). 192p. pap. 9.99 *(978-1-59116-875-1(9));* Vol. 9. 2006. (Naruto Ser.). 184p. pap. 9.99 *(978-1-4215-0239-7(9))* Viz Media.

—Naruto: The First Test. Kishimoto, Masashi. 2009. (Naruto Ser.: 10). (ENG.). 80p. (J). pap. 4.99 *(978-1-4215-2320-0(5))* Viz Media.

—Naruto: The Forest of Death. Kishimoto, Masashi. 2005. (Naruto Ser.: Vol. 6). (ENG.). 192p. pap. 9.99 *(978-1-59116-739-6(6))* Viz Media.

—Naruto Vol. 14. Kishimoto, Masashi. 2010. (Naruto Ser.). (ENG.). 80p. (J). pap. 4.99 *(978-1-4215-3044-4(9))* Viz Media.

—Naruto Vol. 64. Kishimoto, Masashi. 2014. (Naruto Ser.: Vol. 64). (ENG.). 192p. (YA). pap. 9.99 *(978-1-4215-6139-4(5))* Viz Media.

—Naruto 28. Kishimoto, Masashi. ed. 2008. (Naruto Ser.: 28). 189p. 20.85 *(978-1-4178-1760-3(7),* Turtleback) Turtleback Bks.

—Naruto: Chapter Book , Vol. 16: Trapped. Kishimoto, Masashi. 2010. (Naruto Ser.: 16). (ENG.). 80p. (J). pap. 4.99 *(978-1-4215-3046-8(5))* Viz Media.

—Naruto Illustration Book. Kishimoto, Masashi. 2010. (Naruto Ser.). (ENG.). 148p. pap. 19.99 *(978-1-4215-3869-3(5))* Viz Media.

—The Official Character Data Book. Kishimoto, Masashi. 2012. (Naruto Ser.). (ENG.). 360p. pap. 16.99 *(978-1-4215-4125-9(4))* Viz Media.

—The Secret Plan. Kishimoto, Masashi. 2008. (Naruto Ser.: 4). (ENG.). 80p. (J). (gr. 1-5). pap. 4.99 *(978-1-4215-2314-9(0))* Viz Media.

—The Tenth Question, Vol. 11. Kishimoto, Masashi. 2010. (Naruto Ser.: 11). (ENG.). 80p. (J). pap. 4.99 *(978-1-4215-3041-3(4))* Viz Media.

—The Tests of a Ninja. Kishimoto, Masashi. 2008. (Naruto Ser.: 2). (ENG.). 80p. (J). (gr. 1-5). pap. 4.99 *(978-1-4215-2213-5(6))* Viz Media.

—The Worst Job, Vol. 3. Kishimoto, Masashi. 2008. (Naruto Ser.: 3). (ENG.). 80p. (J). (gr. 1-5). pap. 4.99 *(978-1-4215-2214-2(4))* Viz Media.

Kishimoto, Seishi. O-Parts Hunter. Kishimoto, Seishi. 2007. (O-Parts Hunter Ser.). (ENG.). 200p. Vol. 2. pap. 9.99 *(978-1-4215-0856-6(7));* Vol. 3. pap. 9.99 *(978-1-4215-0857-3(5))* Viz Media.

Kishimoto, Yuko. God Will Take Care of You. 2007. (ENG.). 16p. (J). pap. *(978-1-932381-18-4(X),* 6160) Bible Visuals International, Inc.

Kishiro, Yukito. Angel of Victory, Vol. 4. Kishiro, Yukito. 2nd ed. 2004. (Battle Angel Alita Ser.). (ENG.). 216p. pap. 9.95 *(978-1-59116-275-9(0))* Viz Media.

—Battle Angel Alita, Vol. 1. Kishiro, Yukito. 2nd ed. 2003. (Battle Angel Alita Ser.: Vol. 1). (ENG.). 224p. (Orig.). pap. 9.95 *(978-1-56931-945-1(6))* Viz Media.

—Battle Angel Alita - Last Order, Vol. 12. Kishiro, Yukito. 2009. (Battle Angel Alita Last Order Ser.). (ENG.). 216p. pap. 9.99 *(978-1-4215-2918-9(1))* Viz Media.

—Battle Angel Alita Last Order Vol. 4: Angel of Protest. Kishiro, Yukito. 2004. (Battle Angel Alita Last Order Ser.: Vol. 4). (ENG.). 200p. (YA). pap. 9.95 *(978-1-59116-281-0(5))* Viz Media.

—Fallen Angel, Vol. 8, Kishiro, Yukito. 2nd ed. 2005. (Battle Angel Alita Ser.). (ENG.). 232p. pap. 9.95 *(978-1-59116-279-7(3))* Viz Media.

—Killing Angel, Vol. 3. Kishiro, Yukito. 2nd ed. 2004. (Battle Angel Alita Ser.). (ENG.). 208p. pap. 9.95 *(978-1-59116-274-2(2))* Viz Media.

Kiss, Andrew. Cool Woods: A Trip Around the World's Boreal Forest. Drake, Jane & Love, Ann. 2003. (ENG.). 80p. (J). (gr. 4-7). 19.95 *(978-0-88776-608-4(0))* Tundra Bks. CAN. Dist: Random Hse., Inc.

—A Mountain Alphabet. Ruurs, Margriet. 2009. (ABC Our Country Ser.). (ENG.). 32p. (J). (gr. 1-4). pap. 7.95 *(978-0-88776-940-5(3),* Tundra Bks.) Tundra Bks. CAN. Dist: Penguin Random Hse., LLC.

—When We Go Camping. Ruurs, Margriet. 2004. (ENG.). 32p. (J). (gr. 1-4). pap. 8.95 *(978-0-88776-685-5(4),* Tundra Bks.) Tundra Bks. CAN. Dist: Penguin Random Hse., LLC.

—Wild Babies. Ruurs, Margriet. 2003. (ENG.). 32p. (J). (gr. -1-3). 14.95 *(978-0-88776-627-5(7),* Tundra Bks.) Tundra Bks. CAN. Dist: Penguin Random Hse., LLC.

Kiss, Gergely. Animals in the Outhouse. Frohlich, Anja. 2012. (ENG.). 28p. (J). (gr. k-3). 16.95 *(978-1-61608-659-6(9),* 608659, Sky Pony Pr.) Skyhorse Publishing Co., Inc.

Kiste, Tori Lynn. Billy's Wish. Barnett, Wm. 2008. 28p. pap. 24.95 *(978-1-60563-330-5(5))* America Star Bks.

Kitamura, Satoshi. Beetle & Bug & the Grissel Hunt. Oram, Hiawyn. 2014. (ENG.). 40p. (J). (gr. -1-k). 19.95 *(978-1-84939-625-7(6))* Andersen Pr. GBR. Dist: Independent Pubs. Group.

—Goldilocks on CCTV. Agard, John. 2014. (ENG.). 64p. (J). (gr. 6-9). pap. 12.99 *(978-1-84780-499-0(3),* Frances Lincoln) Quarto Publishing Group UK GBR. Dist: Hachette Bk. Group.

—Goldilocks on CCTV. Agard, John & Quarto Generic Staff. 2012. (ENG.). 64p. (J). (gr. 6-9). 19.99 *(978-1-84780-183-8(8),* Frances Lincoln Children's Bks.) Quarto Publishing Group UK GBR. Dist: Hachette Bk. Group.

—Hello H2O. Agard, John. 2014. (ENG.). 96p. (J). (gr. 2-4). pap. 10.99 *(978-1-4449-1772-7(2))* Hodder & Stoughton GBR. Dist: Independent Pubs. Group.

—The History of Money: From Bartering to Banking. Jenkins, Martin. 2014. (ENG.). 64p. (J). (gr. 4-7). 16.99 *(978-0-7636-6763-4(3))* Candlewick Pr.

—In the Attic. Oram, Hiawyn. 2012. (ENG.). 32p. (J). (gr. -1-k). pap. 12.99 *(978-1-84939-298-3(6))* Andersen Pr. GBR. Dist: Independent Pubs. Group.

—Ned & the Joybaloo. Oram, Hiawyn. 2012. (ENG.). 32p. (J). (gr. -1-k). pap. 10.99 *(978-1-84270-605-3(5))* Andersen Pr. GBR. Dist: Independent Pubs. Group.

—The Yes. Bee, Sarah. 2015. (J). 16.00 *(978-0-8028-5449-0(4),* Eerdmans Bks For Young Readers) Eerdmans, William B. Publishing Co.

—The Young Inferno. Agard, John. 2009. (ENG.). 80p. (J). (gr. 6-8). 19.95 *(978-1-84507-769-3(5),* Frances Lincoln) Quarto Publishing Group UK GBR. Dist: Hachette Bk. Group.

Kitamura, Satoshi. Colours. Kitamura, Satoshi. 2007. (Collins Big Cat Ser.). (ENG.). 48p. (J). pap. 5.99 *(978-0-00-718663-1(0))* HarperCollins Pubs. Ltd. GBR. Dist: Independent Pubs. Group.

—Comic Adventures of Boots. Kitamura, Satoshi. 2012. (ENG.). 32p. (J). (gr. k-4). pap. 10.99 *(978-1-84270-908-5(9))* Andersen Pr. GBR. Dist: Independent Pubs. Group.

—Cuando los Borregos No Pueden Dormir. Kitamura, Satoshi. 2nd ed. 2003. (Picture Books Collection). (SPA.). 26p. (J). (gr. k-3). pap. 12.95 *(978-84-372-2182-3(X))* Santillana USA Publishing Co., Inc.

—Me & My Cat? Kitamura, Satoshi. 2009. (ENG.). 32p. (J). (gr. k-k). pap. 12.95 *(978-1-84270-775-3(2))* Andersen Pr. GBR. Dist: Independent Pubs. Group.

—Por el Hilo se Saca el Ovillo. Kitamura, Satoshi. 2003. (Picture Books Collection). (SPA.). 32p. (J). (gr. k-3). 14.95 *(978-84-372-2357-5(1))* Altea, Ediciones, S.A. - Grupo Santillana ESP. Dist: Santillana USA Publishing Co., Inc.

—Pot-San's Tabletop Tales. Kitamura, Satoshi. 2013. (ENG.). 32p. (J). (gr. -1-k). 16.99 *(978-1-84939-378-2(8))* Andersen Pr. GBR. Dist: Independent Pubs. Group.

—UFO Diary. Kitamura, Satoshi. 2007. (ENG.). 32p. (J). (gr. k-2). 12.99 *(978-1-84270-591-9(1))* Andersen Pr. GBR. Dist: Independent Pubs. Group.

Kitchel, JoAnn E. Bach's Goldberg Variations. Celenza, Anna Harwell. 2016. (J). lib. bdg. ***(978-1-58089-529-3(8))*** Charlesbridge Publishing, Inc.

Kitchel, JoAnn E. Barabbas Goes Free. Rottmann, Erik. 2003. (Arch Bks.). (ENG.). 16p. (J). 1.99 *(978-0-570-07582-0(3))* Concordia Publishing Hse.

Kitchel, JoAnn E. Beethoven's Heroic Symphony. Celenza, Anna Harwell. 2016. (J). lib. bdg. ***(978-1-58089-530-9(1))*** Charlesbridge Publishing, Inc.

Kitchel, JoAnn E. Saint-Saëns's Danse Macabre. Celenza, Anna Harwell. 2013. (ENG.). 32p. (J). (gr. 1-4). 19.95 *(978-1-57091-348-8(X))* Charlesbridge Publishing, Inc.

Kitchell, Joann E. Gershwin's Rhapsody in Blue. Celenza, Anna Harwell. 2006. (ENG.). 32p. (J). (gr. 1-4). 21.95 *(978-1-57091-556-7(3))* Charlesbridge Publishing, Inc.

Kitchen, Bert. Tom Crean's Rabbit: A True Story from Scott's Last Voyage. Hooper, Meredith. 2005. (ENG.). 32p. (J). (gr. -1-3). pap. 8.99 *(978-1-84507-393-0(2),* Frances Lincoln) Quarto Publishing Group UK GBR. Dist: Hachette Bk. Group.

—Whoo Goes There? Ericsson, Jennifer A. 2009. (ENG.). 40p. (J). (gr. -1-1). 17.99 *(978-1-59643-371-7(X))* Roaring Brook Pr.

Kitching, Laura. Underwood. Henry, A. 2011. (ENG.). 288p. pap. 10.75 *(978-1-4636-9537-8(3))* CreateSpace Independent Publishing Platform.

Kitora, Tetsuo. La Rama. Paz Lozano, Octavio. 2005.Tr. of Branch. (SPA.). (J). (gr. k-2). pap. 10.95 *(978-968-494-046-8(7))* Centro de Informacion y Desarrollo de la Comunicacion y la Literatura MEX. Dist: Iaconi, Mariuccia Bk. Imports.

Kitson, Barry. Palmer Addley Is Dead. Spencer, Nick. 2011. (ENG.). 176p. (YA). (gr. 8-17). pap. 16.99 *(978-0-7851-4749-7(7))* Marvel Worldwide, Inc.

Kittell DiOrio, Kathy. No More Garbage. Gilkey, Gail. Gilkey, Gail, ed. 2003. 32p. (J). (gr. k-2). lib. bdg. 14.95 *(978-0-9662983-4-5(9))* Windy Hill Pr.

Kitzmüller, Christian, jt. illus. see Bonadonna, Davide.

Kiuchi, Tatsuro. The Lotus Seed. Garland, Sherry. 2014. 32p. pap. 7.00 *(978-1-61003-219-3(5))* Center for the Collaborative Classroom.

Kiwak, Barbara. Bold Composer: A Story about Ludwig Van Beethoven. Josephson, Judith Pinkerton. 2007. (Creative Minds Biographies Ser.). (ENG.). 64p. (gr. 4-8). lib. bdg. 22.60 *(978-0-8225-5987-0(0))* Lerner Publishing Group.

—Jazz Age Poet: A Story about Langston Hughes. Jones, Veda Boyd. (Creative Minds Biographies Ser.). (ENG.). 64p. (gr. 4-8). 2006. per. 8.95 *(978-0-8225-3092-3(9));* 2005. lib. bdg. 22.60 *(978-1-57505-757-6(3),* Carolrhoda Bks.) Lerner Publishing Group.

—My Name Is Bilal. Mobin-Uddin, Asma. 2005. (ENG.). 32p. (J). (gr. 1-7). 15.95 *(978-1-59078-175-3(9))* Boyds Mills Pr.

—Saint Andre Bessette: Miracles in Montreal. Jablonski, Patricia Edward. 2010. (J). (gr. 4-7). pap. 7.95 *(978-0-8198-7140-4(0))* Pauline Bks. & Media.

—Saint Frances Xavier Cabrini: Cecchina's Dream. Dority, Victoria & Andes, Mary Lou. 2005. (Encounter the Saints Ser.: No. 20). 109p. (J). (gr. 3-7). per. 7.95 *(978-0-8198-7092-6(7))* Pauline Bks. & Media.

—Saint Katharine Drexel: The Total Gift. Wallace, Susan Helen. 2003. (Encounter the Saints Ser.: Vol. 15). 144p. (J). pap. 5.95 *(978-0-8198-7068-1(4),* 332-365) Pauline Bks. & Media.

—Saint Teresa of Avila: Joyful in the Lord. Wallace, Susan Helen. 2008. (Encounter the Saints Ser.: No. 24). 106p. (J). (gr. 4-7). pap. 7.95 *(978-0-8198-7116-9(8))* Pauline Bks. & Media.

Kiwak, Barbara. Blessed Teresa of Calcutta: Missionary of Charity. Kiwak, Barbara, tr. Glavich, Mary Kathleen. 2003. (Encounter the Saints Ser.: Vol. 17). 136p. (J). pap. 7.95 *(978-0-8198-1160-8(2),* 332-024) Pauline Bks. & Media.

Kizer, Fran. Playing: A Kid's Curriculum. Stone, Sandra J. 2nd ed. 2005. 234p. (Orig.). per. 18.95 *(978-1-59647-003-3(8))* Good Year Bks.

Kizlauskas, Diana. Jorge from Argentina: The Story of Pope Francis for Children. Monge, Marlyn & Wolfe, Jaymie Stuart. 2013. 64p. (J). pap. 8.95 *(978-0-8198-4006-6(8))* Pauline Bks. & Media.

KJA Artists Staff. Creepy-Crawlies: a 3D Pocket Guide. Candlewick Press Staff. 2013. (Panorama Pops Ser.). (ENG.). 30p. (J). (gr. -1-2). 8.99 *(978-0-7636-6662-0(9))* Candlewick Pr.

—Dinosaurs: a 3D Pocket Guide. Candlewick Press Staff. 2013. (Panorama Pops Ser.). (ENG.). 30p. (J). (gr. -1-2). 8.99 *(978-0-7636-6235-6(6))* Candlewick Pr.

—Mapping Earth from Space, 1 vol. Graf, Mike & Snedden, Robert. 2010. (Science Missions Ser.). (ENG.). 56p. (gr. 6-6). 33.99 *(978-1-4109-3826-8(3),* Raintree Freestyle) Heinemann-Raintree.

Kjartansson, Stefan. Sometimes I Work in Atlanta: What I Do When I'm Not with You. 2004. 16p. (J). 10.95 *(978-0-9760259-0-0(6),* SIWI-ATL-01) Relevant Ventures, LLC.

Klanot, Makenna Karen. The Blue Penguin. Pimot, Karen Hutchins. 2008. 44p. pap. 14.95 *(978-1-934246-79-5(4))* Peppertree Pr., The.

Klanot, Sameon Clay. The Colors of Myself. Pimot, Dr Karen Hutchins & Pimot, Karen Hutchins. 2010. 20p. pap. 12.95 *(978-1-936051-96-0(6))* Peppertree Pr., The.

Klanot, Taryn Lane. A Colorful Day. Pimot, Karen Hutchins. 2008. 28p. pap. 12.95 *(978-0-9814894-9-0(4))* Peppertree Pr., The.

Klassen, Jon. Cats' Night Out. Stutson, Caroline. 2010. (ENG.). 32p. (J). (gr. -1-3). 15.99 *(978-1-4169-4005-0(7),* Simon & Schuster/Paula Wiseman Bks.) Simon & Schuster/Paula Wiseman Bks.

—The Dark. Snicket, Lemony. 2013. (ENG.). 40p. (J). (gr. -1-1). 16.99 *(978-0-316-18748-0(8))* Little, Brown Bks. for Young Readers.

—Extra Yarn. Barnett, Mac. 2012. (ENG.). 40p. (J). (gr. -1-3). 16.99 *(978-0-06-195338-5(5))* HarperCollins Pubs.

—The Hidden Gallery. Wood, Maryrose. (J). (gr. 3-7). 2015. (Incorrigible Children of Ashton Place Ser.: 2). (ENG.). 336p. pap. 6.99 *(978-0-06-236694-8(7));* 2011. (Incorrigible Children of Ashton Place Ser.: 2). (ENG.). 320p. 16.99 *(978-0-06-179112-3(1));* 2011. (Incorrigible Children of Ashton Place Ser.: Bk. 2). 16.89 *(978-0-06-179114-7(8));* Bk. 2. 2012. (Incorrigible Children of Ashton Place Ser.: Bk. 2). (ENG.). 320p. pap. 6.99 *(978-0-06-179113-0(X))* HarperCollins Pubs.

—House Held up by Trees. Kooser, Ted. 2012. (ENG.). 32p. (J). (gr. -1-3). 16.99 *(978-0-7636-5107-7(9))* Candlewick Pr.

—The Mysterious Howling. Wood, Maryrose. (ENG.). (J). (gr. 3-7). 2015. (Incorrigible Children of Ashton Place Ser.: 1). 288p. pap. 6.99 *(978-0-06-236693-1(9));* 2011. (Incorrigible Children of Ashton Place Ser.: Bk. 1). 288p. pap. 6.99 *(978-0-06-179110-9(5));* Bk. I. 2010. (Incorrigible Children of Ashton Place Ser.: 1). 272p. 16.99 *(978-0-06-179105-5(9))* HarperCollins Pubs.

—Sam & Dave Dig a Hole. Barnett, Mac. 2014. (ENG.). 40p. (J). (gr. -1-3). 16.99 *(978-0-7636-6229-5(1))* Candlewick Pr.

—The Unseen Guest. Wood, Maryrose. (Incorrigible Children of Ashton Place Ser.: 3). (ENG.). 352p. (J). (gr. 3-7). 2015. pap. 6.99 *(978-0-06-236695-5(5));* 2012. 16.99 *(978-0-06-179118-5(0))* HarperCollins Pubs.

Klassen, Jon. I Want My Hat Back. Klassen, Jon. 2011. (ENG.). 40p. (J). (gr. -1-3). 15.99 *(978-0-7636-5598-3(8))* Candlewick Pr.

—This Is Not My Hat. Klassen, Jon. 2012. (ENG.). 40p. (J). (gr. -1-3). 15.99 *(978-0-7636-5599-0(6))* Candlewick Pr.

Klaus, Machelle. Winston Wonders about Capacity: A mathematical Story. Jones, Dee. 2010. 36p. pap. 14.95 *(978-1-60844-181-5(4))* Dog Ear Publishing, LLC.

Klauss, Anja. The Little Hippo: A Children's Book Inspired by Egyptian Art. Elschner, Geraldine. 2014. (ENG.). 32p. 14.95 *(978-3-7913-7167-2(3))* Prestel Publishing.

Klco, Gene, photos by. Loon Chick's First Flight. Klco, Gene. 2015. (ENG., 32p. (J). 17.95 ***(978-1-933272-51-1(1))*** Thunder Bay Pr.

Kleback, Amanda & Kleback, Brian. Hoo Hoo's Song. Kleback, Amanda. 2009. 24p. pap. 12.00 *(978-1-4389-1322-3(2))* AuthorHouse.

Kleback, Brian, jt. illus. see Kleback, Amanda.

Kleid, Neil. Xander Nash, Vol. 3. Talen, Hunter. 2010. (Xander Nash Ser.). (ENG.). 96p. (J). pap. 6.99 *(978-0-9826077-6-7(7))* Creation By Design.

Kleiman, Zalman. 5 Novelettes by Marcus Lehman Slipcased: Adopted Princess, Bustenai, Out of the Depths, Rabenu Gershom & Unpaid Ransom. Lehman, Marcus. Mindel, Nissan, tr. from GER. 2012. (ENG.). (YA). 64.95 *(978-0-8266-0033-2(6))* Kehot Pubn. Society.

Klein, David, et al. Doom 2099: The Complete Collection by Warren Ellis. Ellis, Warren. 2013. (ENG.). 424p. (J). (gr. 4-17). pap. 39.99 *(978-0-7851-6754-9(4),* Marvel Pr.) Disney Publishing Worldwide.

Klein, Ellen Marie. I Have a Chuck. Johnson, Dawn M. 2013. 28p. pap. 24.95 *(978-1-62709-628-7(0))* America Star Bks.

Klein, Jean-Louis & Hubert, Marie-Luce. Face-to-Face with the Cat. Frattini, Stephane. 2004. (Face to Face Ser.). 28p. (J). 9.95 *(978-1-57091-454-6(0))* Charlesbridge Publishing, Inc.

Klein, Jean-Louis, jt. photos by see Hubert, Marie-Luce.

Klein, Laurie. The Buttermilk Biscuit Boy, 1 vol. Nelson, Amanda. 2014. (ENG.). 32p. (J). (gr. k-3). 16.99 *(978-1-4556-1970-2(1))* Pelican Publishing Co., Inc.

Klein, Laurie Allen. Conoce Los Planetas, 1 vol. McGranaghan, John. 2014. (SPA.). 32p. (J). (gr. k-5). pap. 9.95 ***(978-1-62855-411-3(8))*** Arbordale Publishing.

Klein, Laurie Allen. Fur & Feathers, 1 vol. Halfmann, Janet. 2010. (ENG.). 32p. (J). (gr. -1-4). 16.95 *(978-1-60718-075-3(8));* pap. 8.95 *(978-1-60718-086-9(3))* Arbordale Publishing.

—The Ghost of Donley Farm, 1 vol. Johnson, Jaime Gardner. 2015. (ENG.). 32p. (J). (gr. k-3). 17.95 *(978-1-62855-451-9(7));* pap. 9.95 *(978-1-62855-459-5(2))* Arbordale Publishing.

—If a Dolphin Were a Fish, 1 vol. Wlodarski, Loran. 2006. (ENG.). 32p. (J). (gr. -1-2). 15.95 *(978-0-9768823-2-9(9))* Arbordale Publishing.

—Little Skink's Tail, 1 vol. Halfmann, Janet. 2007. (ENG.). 32p. (J). (gr. -1-3). 15.95 *(978-0-9768823-8-1(8))* Arbordale Publishing.

—Meet the Planets, 1 vol. McGranaghan, John. 2011. (ENG.). 32p. (J). (gr. k-5). 16.95 *(978-1-60718-123-1(1));* pap. 9.95 *(978-1-60718-869-8(4))* Arbordale Publishing.

—El Pronóstico Del Sistema Solar, 1 vol. Whitt, Kelly Kizer. 2012. (SPA & ENG.). 32p. (J). (gr. -1-4). 17.95 *(978-1-60718-678-6(0))* Arbordale Publishing.

—Solar System Forecast, 1 vol. Whitt, Kelly Kizer. 2012. (ENG & SPA.). 32p. (J). (gr. -1-4). 17.95 *(978-1-60718-523-9(7))* Arbordale Publishing.

—Solar System Forecast, 1 vol. Whit, Kelly. 2012. (SPA & ENG.). 32p. (J). (gr. -1-4). pap. 9.95 *(978-1-60718-532-1(6))* Arbordale Publishing.

Klein, Laurie Allen. They Just Know: Animal Instincts, 1 vol. Yardi, Robin. 2015. (ENG.). 32p. (J). (gr. k-3). 17.95 ***(978-1-62855-634-6(X))*** Arbordale Publishing.

—They Just Know - Animal Instincts. Yardi, Robin. 2015. (SPA & ENG.). 32p. (J). (gr. k-3). pap. 9.95 ***(978-1-62855-644-5(7))*** Arbordale Publishing.

Klein, Laurie Allen. Where Should Turtle Be?, 1 vol. Ring, Susan. 2009. (ENG.). 32p. (J). (gr. -1-3). 16.95 *(978-1-934359-89-1(0))* Arbordale Publishing.

Klein, Nancy, jt. illus. see Guida, Lisa Chauncy.

Klein, Nancy Spence, jt. illus. see Guida, Lisa.

Klein, Nic, jt. illus. see Alixe, Pascal.

Klein, Nic, jt. illus. see Pacheco, Carlos.

Kleinman, Andi. Zip & Zap Take a Nap. Gowey, Christine Ann. 2014. (Morgan James Kids Ser.). (ENG.). 36p. (gr. -1-6). pap. 9.95 *(978-1-61448-788-3(X))* Morgan James Publishing.

Kleinova, Pavla. Maya, Aztecs & Incas. Ruzicka, Oldrich. 2011. (Shape Bks.). (ENG.). 30p. (J). (gr. 1-18). bds., bds. 16.95 *(978-1-55407-933-9(0)*, 9781554079339) Firefly Bks., Ltd.

Klemek, Ryan. Bedtime Stories. Gavin, Fred. Date not set. 64p. (J). (gr. k-3). pap. *(978-0-935668-00-1(4))* Gavin, Fred Enterprises.

Kleven, Dean. Little Einsteins. 2007. (Look & Find Ser.). (J). (gr. -1-3). 7.98 *(978-1-4127-7424-6(1))* Publications International, Ltd.

Kleven, Elisa. Angels Watching over Me. Durango, Julia. 2007. (ENG.). 32p. (J). (gr. -1-3). 18.99 *(978-0-689-86252-6(0)*, Simon & Schuster Bks. For Young Readers) Simon & Schuster Bks. For Young Readers.

—City of Angels: In & Around Los Angeles. Jaskol, Julie & Lewis, Brian. 2008. (J). *(978-1-883318-85-7(8))* Angel City Pr.

—One Little Chicken. Weber, Elka. 2011. (ENG.). 32p. (J). (gr. -1-2). 16.99 *(978-1-58246-374-2(3)*, Tricycle Pr.) Ten Speed Pr.

—Wish: Wishing Traditions Around the World. Chronicle Books Staff & Thong, Roseanne. 2008. (ENG.). 44p. (J). (gr. -1-3). 16.99 *(978-0-8118-5716-1(6))* Chronicle Bks. LLC.

Kleven, Elisa. The Puddle Pail. Kleven, Elisa. 2007. (ENG.). 32p. (J). (gr. -1-2). pap. 6.99 *(978-1-58246-206-6(2)*, Tricycle Pr.) Ten Speed Pr.

—Welcome Home, Mouse. Kleven, Elisa. 2010. (ENG.). 32p. (J). (gr. -1-2). 15.99 *(978-1-58246-277-6(1)*, Tricycle Pr.) Ten Speed Pr.

Klick, Gloria. The Adventure of Mookin Munchkin. Wood, Barbie. 2013. 32p. pap. 24.95 *(978-1-63004-041-3(X))* America Star Bks.

Kligge, Elizabeth. Tae Kwon Do Classic Forms: 21 Hyung — Novice White Belt Through Advanced Black Belt. Hillson, Ted. 2003. 232p. (YA). spiral bd. 22.50 *(978-0-9729293-0-1(4))* Double Dagger Pr.

Klimes, Jan. Time Traveler Inventions. Ruzicka, Oldrich & Sanza, Silvie. 2015. (Time Traveler Ser.). (ENG.). 40p. (J). (gr. 1-3). 16.95 ***(978-1-63322-006-5(0))*** Quarto Publishing Group USA.

—Time Traveler Prehistory. Ruzicka, Oldrich. 2015. (Time Traveler Ser.). (ENG.). 40p. (J). (gr. 1-3). 16.95 ***(978-1-63322-005-8(2))*** Quarto Publishing Group USA.

Klimko, Andrew. Bungalow 29. Ross, Jay. 2005. 125p. pap. 12.95 *(978-0-9771994-0-2(1))* Visor Bks.

Kline, Michael. Creating Clever Castles & Cars (from Boxes & Other Stuff) Kids Ages 3-8 Make Their Own Pretend Play Spaces. Mitchell, Mari Rutz. 2006. (Williamson Little Hands Book Ser.). (ENG.). 128p. (J). (gr. -1-3). 14.95 *(978-0-8249-6783-3(6)*, 1256115); (gr. 3-7). pap. 12.95 *(978-0-8249-6782-6(8)*, 1256115) Ideals Pubns. (Williamson Bks.).

—The Doodles of Sam Dibble. Press, J. 2013. (Doodles of Sam Dibble Ser.: 1). (ENG.). 128p. (J). (gr. 1-3). pap. 4.99 *(978-0-448-46107-6(2))*;No. 4. 4.99 *(978-0-448-46110-6(2))* Penguin Publishing Group. (Grosset & Dunlap).

—Double Trouble #2. Press, J. 2013. (Doodles of Sam Dibble Ser.: 2). (ENG.). 128p. (J). (gr. 1-3). pap. 4.99 *(978-0-448-46108-3(0)*, Grosset & Dunlap) Penguin Publishing Group.

—Kids Care! 75 Ways to Make a Difference for People, Animals & the Environment. Olien, Rebecca. (ENG.). 128p. (J). (gr. 3-7). 2008. pap. 12.99 *(978-0-8249-6792-5(5))*; 2007. 16.99 *(978-0-8249-6793-2(3))* Ideals Pubns. (Williamson Bks.).

—The Kid's Guide to Becoming the Best You Can Be! Developing 5 Traits You Need to Achieve Your Personal Best. Hauser, Jill Frankel. (ENG.). 128p. (J). (gr. 3-7). 2008. pap. 14.25 *(978-0-8249-6788-8(7))*; 2006. 16.95 *(978-0-8249-6789-5(5))* Ideals Pubns. (Williamson Bks.).

—Kids Write: Fantasy & Sci Fi, Mystery, Autobiography, Adventure & More! Olien, Rebecca. 2005. (ENG.). 128p. (J). (gr. 4-7). per. 14.25 *(978-0-8249-6771-0(2))*; (YA). (gr. 7-14). 14.95 *(978-0-8249-6775-8(5))* Ideals Pubns. (Williamson Bks.).

—Lighthouses of North America! Exploring Their History, Lore & Science. Trumbauer, Lisa. 2007. (Kaleidoscope Kids Bks.). (ENG.). 96p. (J). (gr. 3-7). 16.99 *(978-0-8249-6791-8(7))*; pap. 12.99 *(978-0-8249-6790-1(9))* Ideals Pubns. (Williamson Bks.).

—Little Hands Celebrate America: Learning about the U. S. A. through Crafts & Activities. Hauser, Jill Frankel. 2012. (Little Hands! Book Ser.). 128p. (J). pap. 12.99 *(978-0-8249-6836-6(0)*, Williamson Bks.) Ideals Pubns.

—Peanut-Free Tea for Three. Mehra, Heather & McManama, Kerry. 2009. (J). *(978-0-9822150-1-2(0))* Parent Perks, Inc.

—Robots Don't Clean Toilets. Press, J. 2013. (Doodles of Sam Dibble Ser.: 3). (ENG.). 128p. (J). (gr. 1-3). pap. 4.99 *(978-0-448-46109-0(9)*, Grosset & Dunlap) Penguin Publishing Group.

—Science Play. Hauser, Jill Frankel. 2008. (ENG.). 144p. (J). (gr. 4-7). pap. 12.99 *(978-0-8249-6798-7(4)*, Williamson Bks.) Ideals Pubns.

—Science Play: Beginning Discoveries for 2 to 6 Year Olds. Hauser, Jill Frankel. 2007. (Williamson Little Hands Book Ser.). (ENG.). 144p. (J). (gr. 4-7). 16.99 *(978-0-8249-6799-4(2)*, Williamson Bks.) Ideals Pubns.

Kline, Michael, et al. Sea Life Games & Puzzles: 100 Brainteasers, Word Games, Jokes & Riddles, Picture Puzzles, Matches & Logic Tests. Littlefield, Cindy A. 2006. (ENG.). 144p. (J). pap. 9.95 *(978-1-58017-624-8(0)*, 67624) Storey Publishing, LLC.

Kline, Michael. Super Science Concoctions. Hauser, Jill Frankel. 2008. (ENG.). 160p. (J). (gr. 1-7). 16.99 *(978-0-8249-6802-1(6)*, Williamson Bks.) Ideals Pubns.

Kline, Michael. The Kids' Book of Weather Forecasting. Kline, Michael. Friestad, Kathleen M. et al. 2008. 160p. (J). 16.99 *(978-0-8249-6822-9(0)*, Williamson Bks.) Ideals Pubns.

—Wordplay Cafe: Cool Codes, Priceless Punzles & Phantastic Phonetic Phun. Kline, Michael. 2008. (ENG.). 128p. (J). (gr. 4-7). per. 12.95 *(978-0-8249-6753-6(4)*, Williamson Bks.) Ideals Pubns.

Kline, Michael, jt. illus. see Friestad, Kathleen M.

Kline, Michael P. In the Days of Dinosaurs: A Rhyming Romp Through Dino History. Temperley, Howard. 2004. (J). pap. 9.95 *(978-1-885593-81-8(3)*, Williamson Bks.) Ideals Pubns.

—In The Days of the Dinosaurs. Temperley, Howard. 2008. (ENG.). 64p. (J). pap. 9.95 *(978-0-8249-6759-8(3)*, Williamson Bks.) Ideals Pubns.

—The Kids' Multicultural Cookbook: Food & Fun Around the World. Cook, Deanna F. 2008. (ENG.). 160p. (J). (gr. k). per. 12.99 *(978-0-8249-6818-2(2))*; 16.99 *(978-0-8249-6817-5(4))* Ideals Pubns. (Williamson Bks.).

—Wordplay Cafe. 2006. (ENG.). 128p. (J). 14.95 *(978-0-8249-6773-4(9)*, Williamson Bks.) Ideals Pubns.

Klineman, Harvey. Four in One: Four Favorites. Ganz, Yaffa. 2008. 24.99 *(978-1-59826-183-7(5))* Feldheim Pubs.

—Raise a Rabbit, Grow a Goose. Ganz, Yaffa. 2008. 30p. 14.99 *(978-1-59826-235-3(1))* Feldheim Pubs.

—Thirty-One Cakes: A Hashvas Aveida Adventure. Hodes, Loren. Rosenfeld, Devorah Leah, ed. 2003. (J). 10.95 *(978-1-929628-13-1(7))* Hachai Publishing.

Kling, Leslie. The Reindeer That Couldn't Fly. Chandler, Bill & Chandler, Marie. 2009. 48p. pap. 19.99 *(978-1-933817-40-8(2))* Profits Publishing.

Klingbeil, Kendall. GUARDIAN of DREAMS (1st Edition), Torrel, Wendy. I.t. ed. 2004. 32p. (J). 14.95 *(978-0-9746890-0-5(9))*; pap. 10.95 *(978-0-9746890-1-2(7))* White Tulip Publishing.

Klinting, Lars. Beaver the Tailor: A How-to Picture Book. Klinting, Lars. 2004. Orig. Title: Castor Syr.. 32p. (J). (gr. k-3). reprint ed. 17.00 *(978-0-7567-7213-0(3))* DIANE Publishing Co.

Kliros, Thea. Dracula. Stoker, Bram. 2011. (Dover Children's Thrift Classics Ser.). (ENG.). 96p. (J). (gr. 3-8). reprint ed. pap. 4.00 *(978-0-486-29567-1(2))* Dover Pubns., Inc.

—Favorite Uncle Wiggily Animal Bedtime Stories. Garis, Howard Roger. unabr. ed. 2011. (Dover Children's Thrift Classics Ser.). (ENG.). 64p. (J). (gr. 3-8). pap. 2.50 *(978-0-486-40101-0(4))* Dover Pubns., Inc.

—Heidi: Adapted for Young Readers. Spyri, Johanna & Blaisdell, Robert. 2011. (Dover Children's Thrift Classics Ser.). (ENG.). 80p. (J). (gr. 3-8). pap. 2.50 *(978-0-486-40166-9(9))* Dover Pubns., Inc.

—Kidnapped: Adapted for Young Readers. Stevenson, Robert Louis. abr. ed. 2011. (Dover Children's Thrift Classics Ser.). (ENG.). 96p. (J). (gr. 3-8). reprint ed. pap. 4.00 *(978-0-486-29354-7(8))* Dover Pubns., Inc.

—Listen & Color: Favorite Poems for Children. Dover Staff. 2004. (Dover Coloring Bks.). (ENG.). 48p. (J). (gr. -1-5). pap. 6.95 *(978-0-486-43891-7(0))* Dover Pubns., Inc.

—The Little Mermaid & Other Fairy Tales. Andersen, Hans Christian. 2011. (Dover Children's Thrift Classics Ser.). (ENG.). 96p. (J). (gr. 3-8). reprint ed. pap. 3.50 *(978-0-486-27816-2(6))* Dover Pubns., Inc.

—A Little Princess. Burnett, Frances Hodgson. abr. ed. 2012. (Dover Children's Thrift Classics Ser.). (ENG.). 96p. (J). (gr. 3-8). pap. 3.00 *(978-0-486-29171-0(5))* Dover Pubns., Inc.

—A Little Princess Coloring Book. Burnett, Frances Hodgson. abr. ed. 2013. (Dover Coloring Bks.). (ENG.). 48p. (J). (gr. 1-5). pap. 4.99 *(978-0-486-40561-2(3))* Dover Pubns., Inc.

—The Nutcracker. Hoffmann, E. T. A. 2003. 22p. (J). (gr. -1-1). 5.99 *(978-0-06-052745-7(5)*, HarperFestival) HarperCollins Pubs.

—The Prince & the Pauper. Twain, Mark et al. abr. ed. 2011. (Dover Children's Thrift Classics Ser.). (ENG.). 112p. (J). (gr. 3-8). reprint ed. pap. 3.00 *(978-0-486-29383-7(1))* Dover Pubns., Inc.

—The Secret Garden Coloring Book. Burnett, Frances Hodgson. 2014. (ENG.). 48p. (J). (gr. 4-7). pap. 4.99 *(978-0-486-27680-9(5))* Dover Pubns., Inc.

—Three Billy Goats Gruff. Domain Public Staff. 2003. (Once upon a Time Ser.). (ENG.). 20p. (J). (gr. -1-3). bds. 6.99 *(978-0-06-008237-6(2)*, HarperFestival) HarperCollins Pubs.

—Three Little Pigs. Domain Public Staff. 2003. (Once upon a Time Ser.). (ENG.). 20p. (J). (gr. -1-1). bds. 6.99 *(978-0-06-008236-9(4)*, HarperFestival) HarperCollins Pubs.

—Uncle Wiggily Bedtime Stories: In Easy-to-Read Type. Garis, Howard Roger. unabr. ed. 2011. (Dover Children's Thrift Classics Ser.). (ENG.). 80p. (J). (gr. 3-8). pap. 2.50 *(978-0-486-29372-1(6))* Dover Pubns., Inc.

—The Velveteen Rabbit. Williams, Margery. 2004. (ENG.). 22p. (J). (gr. -1-1). bds. 5.99 *(978-0-06-052746-4(3)*, HarperFestival) HarperCollins Pubs.

—The Velveteen Rabbit Coloring Book. Williams, Margery. 2013. (ENG.). 48p. (J). (gr. 2-5). pap. 4.99 *(978-0-486-25924-6(2))* Dover Pubns., Inc.

—The Wind in the Willows. Grahame, Kenneth. 2011. (Dover Children's Thrift Classics Ser.). (ENG.). 96p. (J). (gr. 3-8). pap. 4.00 *(978-0-486-28600-6(2))* Dover Pubns., Inc.

Klise, Kate & Klise, M. Sarah. Grammy Lamby & the Secret Handshake. Klise, Kate. 2012. (ENG.). 32p. (J). (gr. -1-3). 17.99 *(978-0-8050-9313-1(3)*, Holt, Henry & Co. Bks. For Young Readers) Holt, Henry & Co.

—Regarding the Bathrooms: A Privy to the Past. Klise, Kate. 2008. (Regarding The ... Ser.: Bk. 4). (ENG.). 160p. (J). (gr. 2-5). pap. 6.99 *(978-0-15-206261-3(0))* Houghton Mifflin Harcourt Publishing Co.

—Till Death Do Us Bark. Klise, Kate & Klise, M. Sarah. 2011. (43 Old Cemetery Road Ser.: 3). (ENG.). 144p. (J). (gr. 2-5). 16.99 *(978-0-547-40036-5(5))* Houghton Mifflin Harcourt Publishing Co.

Klise, M. Sarah. The Circus Goes to Sea. Klise, Kate. (Three-Ring Rascals Ser.). (ENG.). 160p. (J). 2015. (gr. 2-5). pap. 5.95 *(978-1-61620-481-5(8))*; 2014. 15.95 *(978-1-61620-365-8(X)*, 73365) Algonquin Bks. of Chapel Hill.

—Dying to Meet You. Klise, Kate. (43 Old Cemetery Road Ser.: Bk. 1). (ENG.). 160p. (J). (gr. 2-5). 2010. pap. 5.99 *(978-0-547-39848-8(4))*; 2009. 15.99 *(978-0-15-205727-5(7))* Houghton Mifflin Harcourt Publishing Co.

—Greetings from the Graveyard. Klise, Kate. 2014. (43 Old Cemetery Road Ser.: 6). (ENG.). 160p. (J). (gr. 2-5). 15.99 *(978-0-544-10567-6(2)*, HMH Books For Young Readers) Houghton Mifflin Harcourt Publishing Co.

—Hollywood, Dead Ahead. Klise, Kate. (43 Old Cemetery Road Ser.: 5). (ENG.). 144p. (J). (gr. 2-5). 2014. pap. 6.99 *(978-0-544-33661-2(5)*, HMH Books For Young Readers); 2013. 15.99 *(978-0-547-85283-6(5))* Houghton Mifflin Harcourt Publishing Co.

—Little Rabbit & the Meanest Mother on Earth. Klise, Kate. (ENG.). 32p. (J). (gr. -1-3). 2015. 6.99 *(978-0-544-45611-2(4)*, HMH Books For Young Readers); 2010. 17.00 *(978-0-15-206201-9(7))* Houghton Mifflin Harcourt Publishing Co.

—Over My Dead Body. Klise, Kate. (43 Old Cemetery Road Ser.: Bk. 2). (ENG.). 128p. (J). (gr. 2-5). 2011. pap. 5.99 *(978-0-547-57713-5(3))*; 2009. 15.99 *(978-0-15-205734-3(X))* Houghton Mifflin Harcourt Publishing Co.

—The Phantom of the Post Office. Klise, Kate. (43 Old Cemetery Road Ser.: 4). (ENG.). 160p. (J). (gr. 2-5). 2013. pap. 5.99 *(978-0-544-02281-2(5))*; 2012. 15.99 *(978-0-547-51974-6(5))* Houghton Mifflin Harcourt Publishing Co.

—Pop Goes the Circus! Klise, Kate. 2015. (Three-Ring Rascals Ser.: 4). (ENG.). 144p. (J). (gr. 2-5). 15.95 *(978-1-61620-464-8(8))* Algonquin Bks. of Chapel Hill.

—Regarding the Bees: A Lesson, in Letters, on Honey, Dating, & Other Sticky Subjects. Klise, Kate & Klise, Kate. 2009. (Regarding The ... Ser.: Bk. 5). (ENG.). 144p. (J). (gr. 2-5). pap. 6.99 *(978-0-15-206668-0(3))* Houghton Mifflin Harcourt Publishing Co.

—Regarding the Sink: Where, Oh Where, Did Waters Go? Klise, Kate. 2006. (Regarding The ... Ser.: Bk. 2). (ENG.). 144p. (J). (gr. 2-5). pap. 6.99 *(978-0-15-205544-8(4))* Houghton Mifflin Harcourt Publishing Co.

—Shall I Knit You a Hat? A Christmas Yarn. Klise, Kate. 2007. (ENG.). 32p. (J). (gr. -1-2). per. 7.99 *(978-0-312-37139-5(X))* Square Fish.

—Stand Straight, Ella Kate: The True Story of a Real Giant. Klise, Kate. 2010. (ENG.). 32p. (J). (gr. 1-3). 16.99 *(978-0-8037-3404-3(2)*, Dial) Penguin Publishing Group.

—Till Death Do Us Bark. Klise, Kate. 2012. (43 Old Cemetery Road Ser.: 3). (ENG.). 144p. (J). (gr. 2-5). pap. 6.99 *(978-0-547-85081-8(6))* Houghton Mifflin Harcourt Publishing Co.

—Why Do You Cry? Not a Sob Story. Klise, Kate. rev. ed. 2006. (ENG.). 32p. (J). (gr. -1-2). 18.99 *(978-0-8050-7319-5(1)*, Holt, Henry & Co. Bks. For Young Readers) Holt, Henry & Co.

Klise, M. Sarah. The Greatest Star on Earth. Klise, M. Sarah. Klise, Kate. 2014. (Three-Ring Rascals Ser.: 2). (ENG.). 144p. (J). (gr. 2-5). 15.95 *(978-1-61620-245-3(9)*, 73245) Algonquin Bks. of Chapel Hill.

—The Loch Ness Punster. Klise, M. Sarah. Klise, Kate. 2015. (43 Old Cemetery Road Ser.: 7). (ENG.). 144p. (J). (gr. 2-5). 15.99 *(978-0-544-31337-8(2)*, HMH Books For Young Readers) Houghton Mifflin Harcourt Publishing Co.

Klise, M. Sarah, jt. illus. see Klise, Kate.

Klock, Kimberly. Jason, Lizzy & the Snowman Village. Kountz, Charity. 2013. 132p. 24.99 *(978-0-9859601-1-7(6))* Kountz Marketing Group.

Klofkorn, Lisa. Convection: A Current Event. Hoyt, Richard, photos by. Gould, Alan. rev. ed. 2005. (Great Explorations in Math & Science Ser.). 60p. (J). reprint ed. pap. 10.50 *(978-1-931542-05-0(8)*, GEMS) Univ. of California, Berkeley, Lawrence Hall of Science.

—Crime Lab Chemistry: Solving Mysteries with Chromatography. Beals, Kevin, photos by. Barber, Jacqueline et al. 2004. (Great Explorations in Math & Science Ser.). 104p. (J). pap. 10.50 *(978-0-924886-90-4(0)*, GEMS) Univ. of California, Berkeley, Lawrence Hall of Science.

—Early Adventures in Algebra: Featuring Zero the Hero. Krauss, Dan, photos by. Kopp, Jaine. 2004. (GEMS Guides Ser.). 132p. (J). pap. 16.00 *(978-0-924886-77-5(3)*, GEMS) Univ. of California, Berkeley, Lawrence Hall of Science.

—Moons of Jupiter. Hoyt, Richard & Bergman Publishing Co. Staff, photos by. Sutter, Debra et al. 2003. (Great Explorations in Math & Science Ser.). 116p. (J). pap., tchr. ed. 16.00 *(978-0-924886-87-4(0)*, GEMS) Univ. of California, Berkeley, Lawrence Hall of Science.

Klofkorn, Lisa, jt. illus. see Bevilacqua, Carol.

Klofkorn, Lisa, jt. illus. see Erickson, John.

Klossner, John & Ricceri, David. Judaism's Great Debates. Schwartz, Barry L. & Levine, Mark H. 2012. (J). pap. *(978-0-87441-852-1(6))* Behrman Hse., Inc.

Klotz, Bryan. Lucy's Hero: Remembering Paul Wellstone. Shragg, Karen I. 2010. (ENG.). 32p. (J). (gr. 2-3). 18.95 *(978-0-9801045-7-8(2))*; pap. 12.95 *(978-0-9801045-8-5(0))* Raven Productions, Inc.

Klubien, Jorgen. Frankenweenie: a Graphic Novel. Burton, Tim & Disney Book Group Staff. 2014. (ENG.). 72p. (J). (gr. 5-9). pap. 14.99 *(978-1-4231-7658-9(8))* Disney Pr.

Klug, Dave. See for Yourself! More Than 100 Amazing Experiments for Science Fairs & School Projects. Cobb, Vicki. 2nd ed. 2010. (ENG.). 192p. (J). (gr. 1-3). pap. 14.95 *(978-1-61608-083-9(3)*, 608083) Skyhorse Publishing Co., Inc.

—Space Station Science. Dyson, Marianne J. 2nd ed. 2004. 128p. (J). pap. 11.95 *(978-0-89317-059-2(3)*, WW-0593, Windward Publishing) Finney Co., Inc.

Klug, David. Brainiac's Go Green! Activity Book. Conlon, Mara. 2008. (Activity Book Ser.). 127p. (J). (gr. k-5). 12.99 *(978-1-59359-806-8(8))* Peter Pauper Pr. Inc.

—Mega Magna Forms Safari Adventure. Bryan, Sarah Jane & Bellenson, Suzanne. 2008. (Activity Book Ser.). 48p. (J). (gr. -1-3). spiral bd. 19.95 *(978-1-59359-809-9(2))* Peter Pauper Pr. Inc.

Klug, Eric. The Monster in My Closet. Klug, Eric. 2007. 32p. (J). (gr. -1-3). 15.95 *(978-1-60108-007-3(7))* Red Cygnet Pr.

Klug, Frances Marie. Stories from Heaven, Vol. 33. Klug, Frances Marie, photos by. I.t. ed. 2004. (gr. 7-18). pap. 15.95 *(978-1-892957-33-7(7))* City of God, St. Joseph's Hill of Hope.

Klug, Leigh A. & Bryant, Carol W. Hamilton Troll Meets Chatterton Squirrel. Shields, Kathleen J. 4th ed. 2013. 42p. 14.00 *(978-0-9882745-3-2(1))* Erin Go Bragh Publishing.

—Hamilton Troll Meets Dinosaurs. Shields, Kathleen J. 6th ed. 2013. 36p. 14.00 *(978-0-9882745-5-6(8))* Erin Go Bragh Publishing.

—Hamilton Troll Meets Elwood Woodpecker. Shields, Kathleen J. 5th ed. 2013. 36p. 14.00 *(978-0-9882745-4-9(X))* Erin Go Bragh Publishing.

Klund, Barbara. Tattoo You! Color & Make Your Own Temporary Tattoo Designs. Glossop, Jennifer. 2004. 30p. (J). (gr. k-4). reprint ed. pap. 8.00 *(978-0-7567-8260-3(0))* DIANE Publishing Co.

Klusza, Maureen. Handy Stories to Read & Sign. Napoli, Donna Jo & DeLuca, Doreen. 2009. (ENG.). 56p. (gr. k-3). pap. 19.95 *(978-1-56368-407-4(1))* Gallaudet Univ. Pr.

Knapp, Cheryl. Walking with God: The Young Person's Prayer Diary. Drake, Michelle. 2005. (ENG.). 224p. per. 12.99 *(978-0-927545-79-2(9))* YWAM Publishing.

Knapp, Vincent, photos by. Kelly Hoppen Home: From Concept to Reality. Hoppen, Kelly. rev. ed. 2007. (ENG.). 192p. 40.00 *(978-0-316-11428-8(6))* Little Brown & Co.

Knaupp, Andrew & Koford, Adam. Heavenly Fathers Plan of Salvation Coloring Book. Rich, J. Milton. 2003. 108p. (J). per. 7.95 *(978-0-9726670-2-9(4))* Rich Publishing.

Kneen, Maggie. The Christmas Hat. Wood, A. J. 2004. (ENG.). 24p. (J). *(978-1-55168-267-9(2))* Fenn, H. B. & Co., Ltd.

—Cockcrow to Starlight: A Day Full of Poetry. Godden, Rumer. 2003. (ENG.). 144p. (J). pap. 13.99 *(978-0-330-34302-2(5)*, Pan) Pan Macmillan GBR. Dist: Trafalgar Square Publishing.

—The Owl Keeper. Brodien-Jones, Christine. 2011. (ENG.). 320p. (J). (gr. 3-7). 8.99 *(978-0-385-73815-6(3)*, Yearling) Random Hse. Children's Bks.

—Some Pig! A Charlotte's Web Picture Book. 2006. (Charlotte's Web Ser.). 32p. (J). (gr. k-2). 17.89 *(978-0-06-078162-0(9))* HarperCollins Pubs.

—Summer at Forsaken Lake. Beil, Michael D. 2013. (ENG.). 336p. (J). (gr. 5). pap. 7.99 *(978-0-375-86496-4(2)*, Knopf Bks. for Young Readers) Random Hse. Children's Bks.

—Thimbleberry Stories. Rylant, Cynthia. 2006. (ENG.). 64p. (J). (gr. -1-3). reprint ed. pap. 8.99 *(978-0-15-205645-2(9))* Houghton Mifflin Harcourt Publishing Co.

—Wilbur's Adventure: A Charlotte's Web Picture Book. White, E. B. 2008. (Charlotte's Web Ser.). 32p. (J). (gr. k-2). lib. bdg. 17.89 *(978-0-06-078165-1(3))* HarperCollins Pubs.

Kneen, Maggie. Christmas in the Mouse House. Kneen, Maggie. Wood, Amanda. 2011. (ENG.). 16p. (J). (gr. -1-2). 14.99 *(978-0-7636-5287-6(3)*, Templar) Candlewick Pr.

—The Christmas Surprise. Kneen, Maggie. 2006. 18p. (J). (gr. k-4). reprint ed. 16.00 *(978-0-7567-9837-6(X))* DIANE Publishing Co.

Kneep, Maggie. The Hanukkah Mice. Randall, Ronne. ed. 2010. (ENG.). 18p. (J). (gr. -1-1). 9.99 *(978-0-8118-7663-6(2))* Chronicle Bks. LLC.

Kneupper, Setch. All in a Night's Work. Specter, Baron. 2012. (Graveyard Diaries Ser.). 128p. (J). (gr. 3-8). 27.07 *(978-1-61641-903-5(2))* Magic Wagon.

—Approaching the Undead. Spector, Baron. 2012. (Graveyard Diaries Ser.). 128p. (J). (gr. 3-8). lib. bdg. 27.07 *(978-1-61641-899-1(0)*, Calico Chapter Bks) Magic Wagon.

—How Not to Be Killed by a Zombie. Specter, Baron. 2012. (Graveyard Diaries Ser.). 128p. (J). (gr. 3-8). 27.07 *(978-1-61641-900-4(8))* Magic Wagon.

—To Werewolf or Not to Werewolf. Specter, Baron. 2012. (Graveyard Diaries Ser.). 128p. (J). (gr. 3-8). 27.07 *(978-1-61641-901-1(6))* Magic Wagon.

—Tracking Your Nightmare. Spector, Baron. 2012. (Graveyard Diaries Ser.). 128p. (J). (gr. 3-8). lib. bdg. 27.07 *(978-1-61641-898-4(2)*, Calico Chapter Bks) Magic Wagon.

—Vampires Are Not Your Friends. Specter, Baron. 2012. (Graveyard Diaries Ser.). 128p. (J). (gr. 3-8). 27.07 *(978-1-61641-902-8(4))* Magic Wagon.

Knight, C. R. The World of the Great Forest: How Animals, Birds, Reptiles & Insects Talk, Think, Work & Live. Du Chaillu, Paul. 2004. reprint ed. pap. 31.95 *(978-1-4179-0914-8(5))* Kessinger Publishing, LLC.

Knight, Christopher G., photos by. Interrupted Journey: Saving Endangered Sea Turtles. Lasky, Kathryn. 2006. (ENG., 48p. (J). (gr. 1-4). 6.99 *(978-0-7636-2883-3(2))* Candlewick Pr.

Knight, Georgia. The Little House Mouse. Knight, Georgia. 2011. (ENG.). 42p. (J). pap. 6.99 *(978-0-9832355-1-4(1))* Grandfeather Pr.

Knight, Hilary. Kay Thompson's Eloise: The Absolutely Essential 50th Anniversary Edition: A Book for Precocious Grown-Ups. Thompson, Kay & Brenner, Marie. 2007. 84p. (J). reprint ed. 20.00 *(978-1-4223-6789-6(4))* DIANE Publishing Co.

Knight, Hilary. A Firefly in a Fir Tree: A Carol for Mice. Knight, Hilary. 2004. 32p. (J). (gr. -1-3). lib. bdg. 15.89 *(978-0-06-000992-2(6)*, Tegen, Katherine Bks) HarperCollins Pubs.

K

Knight, Hilary & Boiger, Alexandra. Hello, Mrs. Piggle-Wiggle. MacDonald, Betty. 2007. (ENG.). 176p. (J). (gr. 3-7). 16.99 *(978-0-397-31715-8(8))*; pap. 5.99 *(978-0-06-440149-4(9))* HarperCollins Pubs.

—Mrs. Piggle-Wiggle. MacDonald, Betty. rev. ed. 2007. (ENG.). 144p. (J). (gr. 3-7). 16.99 *(978-0-397-31712-7(3))* HarperCollins Pubs.

—Mrs. Piggle-Wiggle's Magic. MacDonald, Betty. 2007. (Trophy Bk.). (ENG.). 192p. (J). (gr. 3-7). pap. 5.99 *(978-0-06-440151-7(0))* HarperCollins Pubs.

Knight, Michael T. Because Daddy's Coming Home Today. Chatlos, Timothy J. 2012. 24p. (J). pap. 12.99 *(978-1-59755-300-1(X)*, Advantage Childrens) Advantage Bks.

Knight, Paula. Alphabet. Law, Felicia. 2015. (Patchwork Ser.). (ENG.). 24p. (J). (gr. k-3). pap. 10.60 ***(978-1-60357-805-9(6))***; lib. bdg. 22.60 ***(978-1-59953-715-3(X))*** Norwood Hse. Pr.

Knight, Paula. Busy Bee. Brown, J. A. 2003. (Funny Faces Ser.). 10p. (J). bds. 3.95 *(978-1-58925-715-3(4))* Tiger Tales.

Knight, Paula. Colors. Law, Felicia. 2015. (Patchwork Ser.). (ENG.). 24p. (J). (gr. k-3). pap. 10.60 ***(978-1-60357-799-1(8))***; lib. bdg. 22.60 ***(978-1-59953-709-2(5))*** Norwood Hse. Pr.

—Family. Law, Felicia. 2015. (Patchwork Ser.). (ENG.). 24p. (J). (gr. k-3). pap. 10.60 ***(978-1-60357-801-1(3))***; lib. bdg. 22.60 ***(978-1-59953-711-5(7))*** Norwood Hse. Pr.

—Feelings. Law, Felicia. 2015. (Patchwork Ser.). (ENG.). 24p. (J). (gr. k-3). pap. 10.60 ***(978-1-60357-802-8(1))***; lib. bdg. 22.60 ***(978-1-59953-712-2(5))*** Norwood Hse. Pr.

Knight, Paula. Lion's Mane. Brown, J. A. 2003. (Funny Faces Ser.). 10p. (J). 3.95 *(978-1-58925-718-4(9))* Tiger Tales.

Knight, Paula. Numbers. Law, Felicia. 2015. (Patchwork Ser.). (ENG.). 24p. (J). (gr. k-3). pap. 10.60 ***(978-1-60357-800-4(5))***; lib. bdg. 22.60 ***(978-1-59953-710-8(9))*** Norwood Hse. Pr.

Knight, Paula. Scaredy Duck. Brown, J. A. 2004. (Funny Faces Ser.). 10p. (J). 3.95 *(978-1-58925-716-0(2))* Tiger Tales.

Knight, Paula. Shapes. Law, Felicia. 2015. (Patchwork Ser.). (ENG.). 24p. (J). (gr. k-3). pap. 10.60 ***(978-1-60357-804-2(8))***; lib. bdg. 22.60 ***(978-1-59953-714-6(1))*** Norwood Hse. Pr.

—Size. Law, Felicia. 2015. (Patchwork Ser.). (ENG.). 24p. (J). (gr. k-3). pap. 10.60 ***(978-1-60357-803-5(X))***; lib. bdg. 22.60 ***(978-1-59953-713-9(3))*** Norwood Hse. Pr.

Knight, Tom. Little Red Riding Hood. 2013. (Story House Book Ser.). (ENG.). 32p. (J). (gr. -1-k). 16.95 *(978-1-907967-38-2(9))* Boxer Bks., Ltd. GBR. Dist: Sterling Publishing Co., Inc.

Knight, Vanessa. Christmas Tails. Miller, Jennifer. 2009. 56p. pap. 17.26 *(978-1-4251-8987-7(3))* Trafford Publishing.

—Roger's Lion. De Charleroy, Charles, Jr. 2005. 20p. (J). (gr. -1-3). pap. 12.50 *(978-1-4120-7206-9(9))* Trafford Publishing.

—Tell Me, Tell Me, What You See. Howard, Jim & Welsh-Howard, Paula. 2009. 24p. (J). pap. *(978-1-926585-65-9(8)*, CCB Publishing) CCB Publishing.

—Wuffy the Wonder Dog. Morgan, Margaret. 2005. 60p. (J). per. 9.95 *(978-1-59594-034-6(0)*, Wingspan Pr.) WingSpan Publishing.

Knipping, Jutta. Dime Dónde Crece la Pimienta: Culturas Exóticas Explicadas a Los Niños. Schultze, Miriam. (SPA.). 117p. *(978-84-9754-098-8(0)*, (87909)) Ediciones Oniro S.A.

Kniss, Michelle. If Every Day Was a Summer Day. Kniss, Michelle. 2010. (ENG.). 46p. pap. 10.99 *(978-1-4537-9247-6(3))* CreateSpace Independent Publishing Platform.

Knoblock, Julie. The Thirsty Flowers. Wilson, Tony. 2013. (ENG.). 40p. (J). (gr. -1-1). 12.99 *(978-1-74297-699-0(9))* Hardie Grant Egmont Pty, Ltd. AUS. Dist: Independent Pubs. Group.

Knold, Nijlon. The Adventures of Chickolet Pigolet: The Bribe of Frankenbeans. Branning, Debe. 2008. 48p. pap. 7.95 *(978-1-935137-40-5(9))* Guardian Angel Publishing, Inc.

Knopf, Heather. The Cow in Patrick o'Shanahan's Kitchen. Prichard, Diana. 2013. (ENG.). 32p. (J). (gr. -1-2). 17.95 *(978-1-939775-01-6(9))* Little Pickle Press LLC.

Knorr, Laura. A Isn't for Fox: An Isn't Alphabet. Ulmer, Wendy. rev. ed. 2007. (ENG.). 32p. (J). (gr. k-6). 16.95 *(978-1-58536-319-3(7))* Sleeping Bear Pr.

—K Is for Keystone: A Pennsylvania Alphabet. Kane, Kristen. 2003. (Discover America State by State Ser.). (ENG.). 40p. (J). 17.95 *(978-1-58536-104-5(6))* Sleeping Bear Pr.

—The Legend of Papa Noel: A Cajun Christmas Story. Dunham, Terri Hoover. 2006. (Legends Ser.). (ENG.). 32p. (J). (gr. -1-3). 17.95 *(978-1-58536-256-1(5))* Sleeping Bear Pr.

—Little Georgia. Crane, Carol. 2013. (Little State Ser.). (ENG.). 20p. (J). (gr. -1-k). 9.95 *(978-1-58536-203-5(4)*, 202355) Sleeping Bear Pr.

—Little Louisiana. Prieto, Anita C. 2011. (My Little State Ser.). (ENG.). 20p. 9.95 *(978-1-58536-184-7(4))* Sleeping Bear Pr.

—P Is for Pelican: A Louisiana Alphabet. Prieto, Anita C. 2004. (Discover America State by State Ser.). (ENG.). 40p. (J). 17.95 *(978-1-58536-137-3(2))* Sleeping Bear Pr.

—Zero, Zilch, Nada: Counting to None. Ulmer, Wendy K. 2010. (ENG.). 32p. (J). (gr. -1-3). 16.95 *(978-1-58536-461-9(4))* Sleeping Bear Pr.

Knott, Simon. Newton's Wildlife Adventures: The Old Mill Pond. Correll, Stephanie. 2013. 24p. pap. *(978-1-910053-64-5(3))* Legend Pr.

Knott, Stephen. The Kitten Tales of Pumpkin & Parsnip 'Fairy Fields. Allman-Varty, Faye. 2008. 20p. pap. *(978-1-905553-28-0(5))* BookPublishingWorld.

Knotz, Sarah. Goodnight Miami. Baloyra, Patricia. 2012. (ENG.). 28p. (J). (gr. -1-3). 17.95 *(978-1-4507-9592-0(7))* Ampersand, Inc.

Knowelden, Martin. Life-Size Sharks & Other Underwater Creatures. Gilpin, Daniel. 2005. (Life-Size Ser.). (ENG.). 28p. (J). (gr. 2-7). 9.95 *(978-1-4027-2537-1(X))* Sterling Publishing Co., Inc.

Knowles, Kent. Lucius & the Storm. Knowles, Kent. 2007. 32p. (J). (gr. -1-3). 15.95 *(978-1-60108-005-9(0))* Red Cygnet Pr.

Knowlton, Charlotte & Coates, Kathy. Cowgirl Alphabet, 1 vol. Knowlton, Laurie Lazzaro. 2011. (ENG.). 32p. (J). (gr. k-3). 16.99 *(978-1-58980-669-6(7))* Pelican Publishing Co., Inc.

Knowlton, Dwight. The Little Red Racing Car: A Father/Son/Car Story. Knowlton, Dwight. 2013. (ENG.). (J). 21.99 *(978-0-9892949-0-4(0))* Carpe Viam Productions, LLC.

Knox, Anna Mae. Frank the Colorful Frog. Hutton, Gaila. 2011. 28p. pap. 24.95 *(978-1-4560-5607-0(7))* America Star Bks.

Knox, E. C. Don't Call Me Honey! Call Me Cherry Pie. Knox, E. C. 2011. 38p. pap. 14.50 *(978-1-60976-192-9(8)*, Eloquent Bks.) Strategic Book Publishing & Rights Agency (SBPRA).

Knox, Susi Grell. Free As a Butterfly. Boone, Sheila. 2003. 32p. (J). (gr. -1-3). pap. 7.95 *(978-1-891577-80-2(8))* Image Pr., Inc.

Knudson, Dana. Archibald My Pet Pig. Griner, Jack. 2011. pap. 8.95 *(978-0-9836081-1-0(3))* Canoed Sun Publishing, LLC.

Knudson, Jason. Pirate Gear: Cannons, Swords, & the Jolly Roger, 1 vol. O'Donnell, Liam. 2006. (Real World of Pirates Ser.). (ENG.). 32p. (gr. 3-4). 27.32 *(978-0-7368-6425-1(3)*, Edge Bks.) Capstone Pr., Inc.

Knudtsen, Ken. Crowpsey / Rufus & Cleveland. Ferrara, Brian. 2005. (YA). per. 6.95 *(978-0-9753683-1-2(1))* Terminal Pr., LLC.

Knutson, Barbara. The Color of Me. McDunn, Linda L. 2004. (ENG.). 32p. 16.95 *(978-0-8146-2952-9(0))* Liturgical Pr.

—Day of the Dead. Lowery, Linda. 2003. (On My Own Holidays Ser.). (ENG.). 48p. (gr. 2-4). pap. 6.95 *(978-1-57505-581-7(3))*; lib. bdg. 25.26 *(978-0-87614-914-0(X))* Lerner Publishing Group.

—El Día de los Muertos. Lowery, Linda. Translations.com Staff, tr. 2005. (Yo Solo: Festividades (on My Own Holidays) Ser.).Tr. of Day of the Dead. (SPA & ENG.). 48p. (gr. 2-4). lib. bdg. 25.26 *(978-0-8225-3122-7(4)*, Ediciones Lerner) Lerner Publishing Group.

Knutson, Barbara. Love & Roast Chicken: A Trickster Tale from the Andes Mountains. Knutson, Barbara. 2004. (Carolrhoda Picture Books Ser.). (ENG.). 40p. (J). (gr. k-3). 17.95 *(978-1-57505-657-9(7))* Lerner Publishing Group.

Knuvers, Onno. At the Comma Store. Fuerst, Jeffrey B. 2013. (Reader's Theater Word Plays Ser.). (J). (gr. 1-2). *(978-1-4509-8921-3(7))* Benchmark Education Co.

Kobak, Carrie. Tyrone: A Turtle Tale. Foley, Sue. 2010. (ENG.). 32p. (gr. -1-5). 14.95 *(978-1-885003-88-1(9))* Reed, Robert D. Pubs.

Kobasic, Kevin, et al. Green Goblin: A Lighter Shade of Green. Defalco, Tom & McDaniel, Scott. 2011. (ENG.). 392p. (J). (gr. 4-17). pap. 39.99 *(978-0-7851-5757-1(3))* Marvel Worldwide, Inc.

Kobasic, Kevin. Ready to Race! (Blaze & the Monster Machines) Random House. 2015. (Step into Reading Ser.). (ENG.). 24p. (J). (gr. -1-1). 4.99 ***(978-0-553-52460-4(7)***, Random Hse. Bks. for Young Readers) Random Hse. Children's Bks.

Kobayashi, Gavin. Whose Slippers Are Those? Kahalewai, Marilyn. 2005. 24p. (J). (gr. -1-3). 10.95 *(978-1-57306-238-1(3))* Bess Pr., Inc.

Kobayashi, Tatsuyoshi. Leonardo Da Vinci: The Life of a Genius. Sugaya, Atsuo. 2012. (Biographical Comic Ser.). (ENG.). 152p. (J). (gr. 3-6). 18.99 *(978-1-4215-4975-0(1))*; pap. 9.99 *(978-1-4215-4976-7(X))* Shogakukan JPN. Dist: Simon & Schuster, Inc.

—Thomas Edison: Genius of the Electric Age. 2011. (Biographical Comic Ser.). (ENG.). 152p. (J). (gr. 2-6). 18.99 *(978-1-4215-4236-2(6))* Shogakukan JPN. Dist: Simon & Schuster, Inc.

—Thomas Edison: Genius of the Electric Age. Kurosawa, Tetsuya. 2011. (Biographical Comic Ser.). (ENG.). 152p. (J). (gr. 2-6). pap. 9.99 *(978-1-4215-4237-9(4))* Shogakukan JPN. Dist: Simon & Schuster, Inc.

Kober, Shahar. Dreidel, Dreidel, Dreidel. 2014. (ENG.). 12p. (J). (gr. -1 — 1). bds. 4.99 *(978-0-545-53364-5(3)*, Cartwheel Bks.) Scholastic, Inc.

—Engineer Ari & the Hanukkah Mishap. Cohen, Deborah Bodin. 2011. (Hanukkah Ser.). (ENG.). 32p. (J). (gr. k-3). pap. 7.95 *(978-0-7613-5146-7(9))*; lib. bdg. 17.95 *(978-0-7613-5145-0(0))* Lerner Publishing Group. (Kar-Ben Publishing).

—Engineer Ari & the Passover Rush. Cohen, Deborah Bodin. 2015. (J). *(978-1-4677-6201-4(6))*; (ENG.). 32p. lib. bdg. 17.95 *(978-1-4677-3470-7(5))* Lerner Publishing Group. (Kar-Ben Publishing).

—Engineer Ari & the Rosh Hashanah Ride. Cohen, Deborah Bodin. 2008. (ENG.). 32p. (J). (gr. k-3). pap. 7.95 *(978-0-8225-8650-0(9)*, Kar-Ben Publishing) Lerner Publishing Group.

—Engineer Ari & the Sukkah Express. Cohen, Deborah Bodin. 2010. (Sukkot & Simchat Torah Ser.). (ENG.). 32p. (J). (gr. k-3). pap. 7.95 *(978-0-7613-5128-3(0))*; lib. bdg. 17.95 *(978-0-7613-5126-9(4))* Lerner Publishing Group. (Kar-Ben Publishing).

Koch, Carla. Karol from Poland: The Life of Pope John Paul II for Children. Wilson, M. Leonora. rev. ed. 2006. 38p. (J). pap. 7.95 *(978-0-8198-4209-1(5))* Pauline Bks. & Media.

Koch-Gotha, Fritz. Rabbit School: A Light-Hearted Tale. Sixtus, Albert. Freischlad, Roland, tr. from GER. 2009. (ENG.). 32p. (J). (gr. -1-2). 14.95 *(978-1-56792-383-4(6))* Godine, David R. Pub.

Koch, Miriam. Digby Differs. Koch, Miriam. Garlid, Ann, tr. from GER. 2013. 40p. 17.99 *(978-1-4413-1306-5(0))* Peter Pauper Pr. Inc.

Koch, Nobu & Rizal, Clarissa. Mary's Wild Winter Feast. Lindoff, Hannah. 2014. 40p. pap. 14.95 *(978-1-60223-232-7(6))* Univ. of Alaska Pr.

Kochalka, James. The Cute Manifesto. 2005. (ENG.). 168p. (gr. 8). pap. 19.95 *(978-1-891867-73-6(3))* Alternative Comics.

Kochalka, James. The Glorkian Warrior Delivers a Pizza. Kochalka, James. 2014. (Glorkian Warrior Ser.: 1). (ENG.). 112p. (J). (gr. k-4). pap. 12.99 *(978-1-59643-917-7(3)*, First Second Bks.) Roaring Brook Pr.

Kochnevitz, Jane, jt. illus. see Kochnez, Jane.

Kochnez, Jane & Kochnevitz, Jane. Stories from the Bible Vol. 2: With Over 50 Flaps to Open, 1 vol., 2. Dowley, Tim. 2007. 16p. (J). (gr. -1-3). bds. 12.99 *(978-0-8254-7348-7(9)*, Candle Bks.) Lion Hudson PLC GBR. Dist: Kregel Pubns.

Koci, Rudin. Glenn Gould: Sketches of Solitude. Kaufmann, Anne. 2013. *(978-0-9868657-9-4(6))* Brownridge Publishing.

Kock, Carl. Happy Birthday, Dear Dragon. Hillert, Margaret. rev. exp. ed. 2006. (Beginning to Read Ser.). 32p. (J). (gr. -1-3). lib. bdg. 14.95 *(978-1-59953-037-6(6))* Norwood Hse. Pr.

—Happy Easter, Dear Dragon. Hillert, Margaret. rev. exp. ed. 2006. (Beginning to Read Ser.). 32p. (J). (gr. -1-3). lib. bdg. 19.93 *(978-1-59953-038-3(4))* Norwood Hse. Pr.

—I Love You, Dear Dragon. Hillert, Margaret. rev. ed. 2006. (Beginning to Read Ser.). 32p. (J). (gr. -1-3). lib. bdg. 19.93 *(978-1-59953-020-8(1))* Norwood Hse. Pr.

—It's Halloween, Dear Dragon. Hillert, Margaret. rev. exp. ed. 2006. (Beginning to Read Ser.). 32p. (J). (gr. -1-3). lib. bdg. 14.95 *(978-1-59953-041-3(4))* Norwood Hse. Pr.

—Let's Go, Dear Dragon. Hillert, Margaret. rev. ed. 2006. (Beginning to Read Ser.). 32p. (J). (gr. -1-3). lib. bdg. 19.93 *(978-1-59953-021-5(X))* Norwood Hse. Pr.

—Merry Christmas, Dear Dragon. Hillert, Margaret. rev. exp. ed. 2006. (Beginning to Read Ser.). 32p. (J). (gr. -1-3). lib. bdg. 14.95 *(978-1-59953-042-0(2))* Norwood Hse. Pr.

Kocsis, J. C. As If Being 12 3/4 Isn't Bad Enough, My Mother Is Running for President! Gephart, Donna. 2010. (ENG.). 240p. (J). (gr. 3-7). pap. 7.99 *(978-0-440-42211-2(6)*, Yearling) Random Hse. Children's Bks.

Kodaira, Machiyo. Hachiko Waits. Newman, Lesléa. 2008. (ENG.). 96p. (J). (gr. 3-5). pap. 7.99 *(978-0-312-55806-2(6))* Square Fish.

Kodera, Craig. Chester Nimitz & the Sea, 1 vol. Sutcliffe, Jane. 2013. (ENG.). 32p. (J). (gr. k-3). 16.99 *(978-1-4556-1796-8(2))* Pelican Publishing Co., Inc.

—A Dream of Pilots, 1 vol. Handleman, Philip. 2009. (ENG.). 128p. (J). (gr. 3-7). 14.95 *(978-1-58980-570-5(4))* Pelican Publishing Co., Inc.

Kodman, Stanislawa. Grow, 1 vol. Havill, Juanita. 2008. (ENG.). 144p. (J). (gr. 3-7). 14.95 *(978-1-56145-441-9(9))* Peachtree Pubs.

Kodman, Stansislawa. Grow, 1 vol. Havill, Juanita. 2011. (ENG.). 160p. (J). (gr. 3-7). pap. 7.95 *(978-1-56145-575-1(X))* Peachtree Pubs.

Koefler, Leatha. Churchmouse Tales: Puppet Book, 10 vols. Toler, Violet M. rev. ed. 2004. Orig. Title: Charlie Church Mouse. (J). (gr. -1-6). pap. 10.95 *(978-0-9749749-0-3(0))* Wayside Pubns.

—Churchmouse Tales: Puppet Plays, 10 vols., Vol. 2. Toler, Violet M. 2nd rev. ed. 2004. Orig. Title: "Puppet Plays, Adventures of Charlie & His Friends". (J). (gr. -1-6). pap. 10.95 *(978-0-9749749-1-0(9))* Wayside Pubns.

Koehler, Ed. Bible Puzzlers. Molski, Carol. 2007. (CPH Teaching Resource Ser.). (ENG.). 63p. (J). (gr. 4-7). per. 10.99 *(978-0-7586-1332-5(6))* Concordia Publishing Hse.

—Bible Word Suduko. Molski, Carol. 2007. (CPH Teaching Resource Ser.). (ENG.). 64p. pap. 10.99 *(978-0-7586-1344-8(X))* Concordia Publishing Hse.

—The Fiery Furnace. Busch, Melinda Kay. 2004. (Arch Bks.). 16p. (J). (gr. k-4). 1.99 *(978-0-7586-0479-8(3))* Concordia Publishing Hse.

—Manualidades Faciles con Vasos de Papel. Stohs, Anita Reight. Beckmann, Ewaldo, tr. 2008. 64p. (J). pap. 9.99 *(978-0-7586-1586-2(8))* Concordia Publishing Hse.

—Mary Magdalene's Easter Story. Hartman, Sara. 2005. (ENG.). 16p. (J). 1.99 *(978-0-7586-0722-5(9))* Concordia Publishing Hse.

—The Mystery of the Moving Hand. Burgdorf, Larry. 2014. (Arch Bks.). (ENG.). 16p. (J). pap. 2.49 *(978-0-7586-4603-3(8))* Concordia Publishing Hse.

—Praise God with Paper Cups: 45 Easy Bible Crafts; Grades 1-5. Stohs, Anita Reith. 2005. (CPH Teaching Resource Ser.). 64p. pap. 10.99 *(978-0-7586-0842-0(X))* Concordia Publishing Hse.

Koehler, Ed, jt. illus. see Marxhausen, Benjamin.

Koehler, Ed, jt. illus. see Marxhausen, Ben.

Koehler, Mary. The Children are Happy Story CD with Animals from the Southwest. 2003. (J). cd-rom 5.00 *(978-0-9744005-1-8(3))* In the Desert.

Koeller, Carol. Ah-Choo. Taylor-Butler, Christine. 2005. (My First Reader Ser.). (ENG.). 32p. (J). (gr. k-1). 18.50 *(978-0-516-25175-2(9)*, Children's Pr.) Scholastic Library Publishing.

—Camino al Primer Grado. Cleveland, Alexandra et al. Franco, Sharon, tr. from ENG. 2004. (SPA.). 128p. (Orig.). (J). pap. 14.95 *(978-0-943452-35-7(X))* Building Blocks, LLC.

—Easel Art. Wilmes, Liz & Wilmes, Dick. 2004. 128p. (J). pap. 12.95 *(978-0-943452-25-8(2))* Building Blocks, LLC.

—Nick Is Sick. Riggs, Sandy. 2006. (Reader's Clubhouse Level 1 Reader Ser.). (ENG.). 24p. (J). (gr. 1-4). pap. 3.99 *(978-0-7641-3284-1(9))* Barron's Educational Series, Inc.

—Why I Thank You, God. Adams, Michelle Medlock. 2006. 20p. (J). (gr. -1). bds. 5.49 *(978-0-7586-0911-3(6))* Concordia Publishing Hse.

Koeller, Carol. All about Adoption: How Families Are Made & How Kids Feel about It. Koeller, Carol, tr. Nemiroff, Marc A. & Annunziata, Jane. 2003. 48p. (J). (gr. k-3). 14.95 *(978-1-59147-058-8(7))*; pap. 9.95 *(978-1-59147-059-5(5))* American Psychological Assn. (Magination Pr.).

Koelsch, Michael. Into the Danger Zone. Christopher, Matt. 6th ed. 2004. (ENG.). 64p. (J). (gr. 1-4). pap. 10.99 *(978-0-316-76267-0(9)*, Tingley, Megan Bks.) Little, Brown Bks. for Young Readers.

—Listos para Leer. Wells, Rosemary & Rosemary, Wells. Fernandez, Leire Amigo, tr. 2004. (SPA.). 32p. (J). (gr. k-1). 14.99 *(978-84-241-8712-5(1))* Everest Editora ESP. Dist: Lectorum Pubns., Inc.

—El Mundo Que Nos Rodea. Wells, Rosemary & Rosemary, Wells. Fernandez, Leire Amigo, tr. 2004. (SPA.). 32p. (J). (gr. -1-1). 14.99 *(978-84-241-8711-8(3))* Everest Editora ESP. Dist: Lectorum Pubns., Inc.

—On Thin Ice. Christopher, Matt. 4th ed. 2004. (ENG.). 64p. (J). (gr. 1-4). pap. 10.99 *(978-0-316-73739-5(9))* Little, Brown Bks. for Young Readers.

—One Smooth Move. Christopher, Matt. 2004. (ENG.). 64p. (J). (gr. 1-4). pap. 10.99 *(978-0-316-73749-4(6))* Little, Brown Bks. for Young Readers.

—Rock On. Christopher, Matt. 5th ed. 2004. (ENG.). 64p. (J). (gr. 1-4). pap. 10.99 *(978-0-316-76265-6(2))* Little, Brown Bks. for Young Readers.

—Wild Ride. Christopher, Matt. 7th ed. 2005. (ENG.). 64p. (J). (gr. 1-4). pap. 10.99 *(978-0-316-76263-2(6))* Little, Brown Bks. for Young Readers.

Koelsch, Michael. Roller Hockey Rumble. Koelsch, Michael, tr. Christopher, Matt. 3rd ed. 2004. (ENG.). 64p. (J). (gr. 1-4). pap. 10.99 *(978-0-316-73755-5(0))* Little, Brown Bks. for Young Readers.

Koelsch, Michael, jt. illus. see Cowdrey, Richard.

Koff, Deborah. Marissa the Tooth Fairy. Andersdatter, Karla Margaret. 2nd ed. 2005. (J). *(978-0-9717611-2-4(4))* Depot Bks.

Koffsky, Ann. The Sun's Special Blessing: Happens Only Once in 28 Years - French Flap. Wasserman, Sand. 2009. 36p. 12.95 *(978-1-934440-76-6(0)*, Pitspopany Pr.) Simcha Media Group.

—The Sun's Special Blessing: Happens Only Once in 28 Years - HC. Wasserman, Sand. 2009. 36p. 17.95 *(978-1-934440-92-6(2)*, Pitspopany Pr.) Simcha Media Group.

Koffsky, Ann D. Kayla & Kugel. 2015. (J). ***(978-0-87441-898-9(4)); (978-1-68115-502-9(8))*** Behrman Hse., Inc.

—Kayla & Kugel's Almost-Perfect Passover. 2016. (J). ***(978-1-68115-508-1(7))*** Behrman Hse., Inc.

Koffsky, Ann D. My Cousin Tamar Lives in Israel. Abraham, Michelle Shapiro. 2006. 14p. (J). (gr. -1). pap. 6.95 *(978-0-8074-0989-3(8))* URJ Pr.

—Shabbat Shalom, Hey! 2015. (J). (ENG.). 24p. (gr. -1-k). lib. bdg. 16.95 *(978-1-4677-4917-6(6))*; *(978-1-4677-6208-3(3))* Lerner Publishing Group. (Kar-Ben Publishing).

—Teacher's Guide for to Learn Is to Do: A Tikkun Olam Roadmap. Halper, Sharon D. 2003. 46p. (gr. 4-6). pap., tchr. ed., tchr.'s training gde. ed. 12.00 *(978-0-8074-0730-1(5)*, 208051) URJ Pr.

—To Learn Is to Do: A Tikkun Olam Road Map. Halper, Sharon. 2004. vi, 56p. (gr. 4-6). pap. 11.95 *(978-0-8074-0729-5(1)*, 123935) URJ Pr.

Koford, Adam. The Book of Mormon on Trial Activity Learning Book. Koford, Adam, compiled by. 2003. 123p. (J). per. 14.95 *(978-0-9726670-3-6(2))* Rich Publishing.

Koford, Adam, jt. illus. see Knaupp, Andrew.

Kofsky, Ann. Reaching Godward: Voices from Jewish Spiritual Guidance. Ochs, Carol. 2004. 250p. pap. 14.95 *(978-0-8074-0866-7(2)*, 142612) URJ Pr.

Kofsky, Kristen. Coral Reefs A to Z Coloring Book. Pierce, Terry. 2003. 32p. 4.95 *(978-1-57306-122-3(0))* Bess Pr., Inc.

—Father Damien. Williams, Laura E. 2009. (ENG.). 60p. (J). (gr. 4). pap. *(978-1-59700-757-3(9))* Island Heritage Publishing.

—Surfing A to Z Coloring Book. Pierce, Terry. 2004. 24p. pap. 4.95 *(978-1-57306-178-0(6))* Bess Pr., Inc.

Koge-Donbo. Pita-Ten Official Fan Book. Koge-Donbo. (Pita-Ten Ser.). 176p. Vol. 1. 2005. pap. 9.99 *(978-1-59816-106-9(7))*; Vol. 2. 2nd rev. ed. 2006. per. 9.99 *(978-1-59816-107-6(5))* TOKYOPOP, Inc.

Kogo, Yoshi. Big Al & Shrimpy. Clements, Andrew. 2005. (ENG.). 40p. (J). (gr. -1-3). reprint ed. 6.99 *(978-1-4169-0366-6(6)*, Atheneum Bks. for Young Readers) Simon & Schuster Children's Publishing.

Kohara, Kazuno. Ghosts in the House! Kohara, Kazuno. 2012. (ENG.). 26p. (J). (gr. -1 — 1). bds. 7.99 *(978-1-59643-725-8(1))* Roaring Brook Pr.

—Ghosts in the House! Kohara, Kazuno. 2010. (ENG.). 32p. (J). (gr. -1-1). pap. 7.99 *(978-0-312-60886-6(1))* Square Fish.

—Here Comes Jack Frost. Kohara, Kazuno. 2009. (ENG.). 32p. (J). (gr. -1-1). 12.99 *(978-1-59643-442-4(2))* Roaring Brook Pr.

—Here Comes Jack Frost. Kohara, Kazuno. 2011. (ENG.). 32p. (J). (gr. -1-1). pap. 7.99 *(978-0-312-60446-2(7))* Square Fish.

—The Midnight Library. Kohara, Kazuno. 2014. (ENG.). 32p. (J). (gr. -1-1). 16.99 *(978-1-59643-985-6(8))* Roaring Brook Pr.

Kohler, Michelle. Santa Horse. Tapler, Judy. 2008. 36p. pap. 16.99 *(978-1-4389-2290-4(6))* AuthorHouse.

Kohler, Ursula. The Dolls Nose. Haxhia, Miranda. 2007. 32p. (J). (POL & ENG.). pap. 16.95 *(978-1-60195-097-0(7))*; (ARA & ENG.). pap. 16.95 *(978-1-60195-087-1(X))* International Step by Step Assn.

Kohn, Arnie. Dinosaurs. Spizzirri, Linda, ed. 32p. (J). (gr. 1-8). pap. 4.98 incl. audio *(978-0-86545-019-6(6))* Spizzirri Pr., Inc.

—Prehistoric Sea Life. Spizzirri, Linda, ed. 32p. (J). (gr. 1-8). pap. 4.98 incl. audio *(978-0-86545-020-2(X))* Spizzirri Pr., Inc.

Kohner, Elaine. Guided Meditations for Youth on Sacramental Life. Arsenault, Jane & Cedor, Jean. Stamschror, Robert P., ed. unabr. ed. 2003. (Quiet Place Apart Ser.). 40p. (YA). (gr. 9-12). pap. 9.95 incl. audio *(978-0-88489-308-0(1))* St. Mary's Pr. of MN.

Koji, Jeanette. A Really, Really, Scary Monster Story! Blume, Rebecca. l.t. ed. 2006. 32p. (J). 24.95 *(978-0-9785427-0-2(3))* Liberty Artists Management.

Koka. The Adventures of Popoki: The Curious Kitten with a Crooked Tail. Koka. 2011. (ENG.). 124p. pap. 6.99 *(978-1-4636-7974-3(2))* CreateSpace Independent Publishing Platform.

The check digit for ISBN-10 appears in parentheses after the full ISBN-13

Kolanovic, Dubravka. Baby Bear & the Big, Wide World. Patterson, Ellie. 2013. (J). *(978-1-4351-4929-8(7))* Barnes & Noble, Inc.

—Bible Stories for Little Angels. Dodd, Sarah J. 2011. (Little Angels Ser.). (ENG.). 48p. (J). (gr. -1-k). 12.99 *(978-0-7459-6209-2(2))* Lion Hudson PLC GBR. Dist: Independent Pubs. Group.

—Christmas Stories for Little Angels. Dodd, Sarah J. 2010. (Little Angels Ser.). (ENG.). 32p. (J). (gr. -1-k). 12.99 *(978-0-7459-6917-6(8))* Lion Hudson PLC GBR. Dist: Independent Pubs. Group.

—Count My Blessing 1 to 10. Cabral, Jeane. 2007. (Magnetic Counting Book Ser.). 10p. *(978-1-84666-360-4(1),* Tide Mill Pr.) Top That! Publishing PLC.

—Ituku's Christmas Journey. 1 vol. Pasquali, Elena. 2005. (ENG.). 32p. (J). (gr. -1-3). pap. 16.00 *(978-1-56148-495-9(4),* Good Bks.) Skyhorse Publishing Co., Inc.

—The Lion Book of Nursery Fables. Piper, Sophie. 2014. (ENG.). 128p. (J). (gr. -1 — 1). 17.99 *(978-0-7459-6466-9(4))* Lion Hudson PLC GBR. Dist: Independent Pubs. Group.

—Little Bear's Special Friend. Freedman, Claire. 2007. (J). *(978-0-545-06757-7(X))* Scholastic, Inc.

—The Little Raindrop. Gray, Joanna. 2014. (J). *(978-1-4351-5254-0(9))* Barnes & Noble, Inc.

—The Little Raindrop. Gray, Joanna. 2014. (ENG.). 32p. (J). (gr. -1-k). 16.95 *(978-1-62873-821-6(9),* Sky Pony Pr.) Skyhorse Publishing Co., Inc.

—My Baptism Book. Piper, Sophie. 2007. (ENG.). 64p. (J). (gr. -1-1). 14.95 *(978-1-55725-535-8(0))* Paraclete Pr., Inc.

—Nursery Rhyme Treasury. Davidson, Susanna. 2006. 96p. (J). 19.99 *(978-0-7945-1281-1(X),* Usborne) EDC Publishing.

Kolanovic, Dubravka. The Princess & the Pea. Andersen, Hans Christian. 2014. (J). ***(978-1-4723-5207-1(6))*** Parragon Bk. Service Ltd.

Kolanovic, Dubravka. Safe This Night: A Book of Bedtime Prayers. Pasquali, Elena. 2013. (ENG.). 64p. (J). (gr. k-2). 12.99 *(978-0-7459-6378-5(1))* Lion Hudson PLC GBR. Dist: Independent Pubs. Group.

—Safely Through the Night. Pasquali, Elena. 2008. (ENG.). 32p. (J). (gr. k-k). 16.95 *(978-0-7459-6048-7(0))* Lion Hudson PLC GBR. Dist: Independent Pubs. Group.

—Shine Moon Shine. Conway, David. 2008. 32p. (J). (gr. -1-2). 15.95 *(978-1-58925-073-4(7))* Tiger Tales.

—What Bear Likes Best! Ritchie, Alison. 2005. (ENG.). 26p. (J). pap. 16.00 *(978-1-56148-473-7(3),* Good Bks.) Skyhorse Publishing Co., Inc.

Kolanovic, Dubravka. Wipe-Clean Colours. Kolanovic, Dubravka. ed. 2009. (Honey Hill Ser.). (ENG.). 12p. (J). (gr. -1-k). bds. 9.99 *(978-0-230-70915-7(X))* Macmillan Pubs., Ltd. GBR. Dist: Independent Pubs. Group.

Kolar, Bob. Alpha Oops! The Day Z Went First. Kontis, Alethea. (ENG.). 48p. (J). (gr. -1-3). 2012. pap. 6.99 *(978-0-7636-6084-0(1));* 2006. 15.99 *(978-0-7636-2728-7(3))* Candlewick Pr.

—Alpha Oops! The Day Z Went First. Kontis, Alethea. ed. 2012. lib. bdg. 17.20 *(978-0-606-26928-5(2),* Turtleback) Turtleback Bks.

—Alphaoops! H Is for Halloween. Kontis, Alethea. (ENG.). 40p. (J). (gr. -1-3). 2010. 15.99 *(978-0-7636-3966-2(4));* 2011. 7.99 *(978-0-7636-5686-7(0))* Candlewick Pr.

—The Boy & the Book. Slater, David Michael. 2015. (ENG.). 32p. (J). (-k). lib. bdg. 16.95 *(978-1-58089-562-0(X))* Charlesbridge Publishing, Inc.

—A Cat & a Dog. Masurel, Claire. (ENG.). (gr. -1). 2008. 24p. bds. 6.95 *(978-0-7358-2177-4(1));* 2003. 32p. (J). 7.95 *(978-0-7358-1780-7(4))* North-South Bks., Inc.

—The Little Dump Truck. Cuyler, Margery. (ENG.). (J). (gr. -1-1). 2014. 24p. 7.99 *(978-0-8050-9990-4(5));* 2009. 32p. 13.99 *(978-0-8050-8281-4(6))* Holt, Henry & Co. (Holt, Henry & Co. Bks. For Young Readers).

—The Little School Bus. Cuyler, Margery. 2014. (ENG.). 32p. (J). (gr. -1-1). 12.99 *(978-0-8050-9435-0(0),* Holt, Henry & Co. Bks. For Young Readers) Holt, Henry & Co.

—Nothing Like a Puffin. Soltis, Sue. 2011. (ENG.). 40p. (J). (gr. -1-1). 15.99 *(978-0-7636-3617-3(7))* Candlewick Pr.

Kolar, Bob. Big Kicks. Kolar, Bob. (ENG.). (J). (gr. -1-1). 2010. 32p. pap. 6.99 *(978-0-7636-4912-8(0));* 2008. 40p. 16.99 *(978-0-7636-3390-5(9))* Candlewick Pr.

Kolb, Andrew. Edmund Unravels. Kolb, Andrew. 2015. (ENG.). 34p. (J). (gr. k-3). 16.99 *(978-0-399-16914-4(8),* Nancy Paulsen Bks.) Penguin Publishing Group.

Kolding, Richard Max. Waking Up. Seese, Ellen. 2004. (ENG.). 24p. (gr. k-2). pap. 5.95 *(978-1-57874-041-3(X))* Kaeden Corp.

—What Is Faith? Mueller, Virginia. 2013. (Happy Day Ser.). (ENG.). 16p. (J). pap. 2.49 *(978-1-4143-9293-6(1))* Tyndale Hse. Pubs.

Kole, Nicholas, jt. illus. see Disney Storybook Artists Staff.

Kolins, Scott. Excalibur Visionaries, Vol. 3. 2011. (ENG.). 216p. (J). (gr. 4-17). pap. 24.99 *(978-0-7851-5543-0(0))* Marvel Worldwide, Inc.

Kolitsky, Joy. Escapade Johnson & Mayhem at Mount Moosilauke. Sullivan, Michael. 2007. (Escapade Johnson Ser.). (ENG.). 96p. (J). (gr. 2-4). per. 3.95 *(978-1-929945-70-2(1))* Big Guy Bks., Inc.

—Escapade Johnson & the Witches of Belknap County. Sullivan, Michael. 2008. (Escapade Johnson Ser.). (ENG.). 99p. (J). (gr. 2-4). pap. 3.95 *(978-1-929945-90-0(6))* Big Guy Bks., Inc.

Kollman, Carrie. Grand Entry. Compton, Dawn. 2004. 64p. pap. 12.95 *(978-1-932196-45-0(5))* WordWright.biz, Inc.

Kolnik, Paul, photos by. Dancing to America. Morris, Ann. 2004. 40p. (YA). (gr. 7-10). 16.00 *(978-0-7567-7577-3(9))* DIANE Publishing Co.

Koltun, Amy. Meet Julius Carmichael: First Day Blues. Carroll, Jonathan. 2003. 96p. (J). (gr. 3-6). pap. 6.95 *(978-0-9724935-0-5(6))* Striking Presence Pubns.

Kolvanovic, Dubravka. Jingle Bells: A Collection of Songs & Carols. Tiger Tales, ed. 2014. 22p. (J). (gr. -1-k). bds. 8.99 *(978-1-58925-568-5(2))* Tiger Tales.

—This Little Light of Mine. Tiger Tales, ed. 2014. 22p. (J). (gr. -1-k). bds. 8.99 *(978-1-58925-569-2(0))* Tiger Tales.

Komai, Asuka. October Moon. 2009. (J). *(978-1-60108-017-2(4))* Red Cygnet Pr.

Komarck, Michael. Baby's Fraction Lunch. Hunt, Darleen L. 2003. (Sherman's Math Corner Ser.). (J). (gr. -1-3). *(978-1-929591-07-7(1))* Reading Rock, Inc.

—Bob's Busy Year: Months of the Year. Hunt, Darleen L. 2003. (Sherman's Math Corner Ser.). (J). (gr. -1-3). *(978-1-929591-03-9(9))* Reading Rock, Inc.

—Dad's Pancakes: Number Reduction. Hunt, Darleen L. 2003. (Sherman's Math Corner Ser.). (J). (gr. -1-3). *(978-1-929591-04-6(7))* Reading Rock, Inc.

—Dog & Cat Compare: Comparing Amounts. Hunt, Darleen L. 2003. (Sherman's Math Corner Ser.). (J). (gr. -1-3). *(978-1-929591-09-1(8))* Reading Rock, Inc.

—Dog's Dollars: Patterns. Hunt, Darleen L. 2003. (Sherman's Math Corner Ser.). (J). (gr. -1-3). *(978-1-929591-08-4(X))* Reading Rock, Inc.

—Ellen Elizabeth's Peanut Butter Jar: Counting. Hunt, Darleen L. 2003. (Sherman's Math Corner Ser.). (J). (gr. -1-3). *(978-1-929591-11-4(X))* Reading Rock, Inc.

—Harvey T. Crow Puts It All Together: Addition. Hunt, Darleen L. 2003. (Sherman's Math Corner Ser.). (J). (gr. -1-3). *(978-1-929591-02-2(0))* Reading Rock, Inc.

—Lyle & Mildred Are a Pair: Counting by 2's. Hunt, Darleen L. 2003. (Sherman's Math Corner Ser.). (J). (gr. -1-3). *(978-1-929591-00-8(4))* Reading Rock, Inc.

—Mr. Reed's Class Estimates: Estimating. Hunt, Darleen L. 2003. (Sherman's Math Corner Ser.). (J). (gr. -1-3). *(978-1-929591-06-0(3))* Reading Rock, Inc.

—Samanta Uses Patterns: Patterns. Hunt, Darleen L. 2003. (Sherman's Math Corner Ser.). (J). (gr. -1-3). *(978-1-929591-10-7(1))* Reading Rock, Inc.

—Samantha Visits Grandpa Geo: Shapes. Hunt, Darleen L. 2003. (Sherman's Math Corner Ser.). (J). (gr. -1-3). *(978-1-929591-01-5(2))* Reading Rock, Inc.

—Spider Inventories: Count & Record. Hunt, Darleen L. 2003. (Sherman's Math Corner Ser.). (J). (gr. -1-3). *(978-1-929591-05-3(5))* Reading Rock, Inc.

Komarudin. The Golden Feather: A Jataka Tale: A Story & Coloring Book. 2012. (J). *(978-1-60103-008-5(8))* Buddhist Text Translation Society.

Komatsu, Eiko, jt. illus. see Nishiyama, Akira.

Komorova, Nadia. GQ GQ. Where Are You? Adventures of a Gambel's Quail. Ritt, Sharon I. 2013. (ENG.). 40p. (J). (gr. 2). pap. 14.95 *(978-1-58985-223-5(0))* Five Star Pubns., Inc.

Komura, Ayumi. Mixed Vegetables. Komura, Ayumi. (Mixed Vegetables Ser.: 7). (ENG.). 2010. 200p. (gr. 8-18). pap. 9.99 *(978-1-4215-3199-1(2));* 2009. 192p. pap. 9.99 *(978-1-4215-1982-1(8));* 2008. 208p. (gr. 8-18). pap. 8.99 *(978-1-4215-1967-8(4))* Viz Media.

—Mixed Vegetables, Vol. 8. Komura, Ayumi. 2010. (Mixed Vegetables Ser.: 8). (ENG.). 208p. pap. 9.99 *(978-1-4215-3235-6(2))* Viz Media.

Konatich, James. Twelve Treasures of the East: Legends & Folk Tales from Asia. Dutta-Yean, Tutu & Maire, Lucy Bedoya. Dutta-Yean, Tutu, ed. ed. 2005. (J). per. *(978-0-9768436-0-3(9),* 20) Maire, Lucy Bedoya.

Kondeatis, Christos. Scenes from the Life of Jesus Christ: A Three-Dimensional Bible Storybook. Kondeatis, Christos. 2006. 10p. (J). (gr. k-4). reprint ed. 20.00 *(978-0-7567-9826-0(4))* DIANE Publishing Co.

Konecny, John. The Book Monster. Waisanen, Emily. 2012. 24p. pap. 8.99 *(978-1-937165-25-3(6))* Orange Hat Publishing.

—Dogs Don't Have Pockets. Raffaelli, Sean & Dreske, Erin. 2013. 24p. pap. 9.99 *(978-1-937165-55-0(8))* Orange Hat Publishing.

—Miller: The Mostly Misunderstood Mischief-Maker Who Went Missing. Thieme-Baeseman, Rebecca. 2012. 24p. pap. 9.99 *(978-1-937165-32-1(9))* Orange Hat Publishing.

—What If the Rain Were Bugs? Dewane, Patrick Ryan. 2013. 24p. 14.99 *(978-1-937165-39-0(6))* Orange Hat Publishing.

—Work Your Body Grow Your Brain. Boodey, Erin. 2012. 26p. 13.99 *(978-1-937165-23-9(X))* Orange Hat Publishing.

Kong, Emilie, jt. illus. see McCue, Lisa.

Konigsburg, E. L. About the B'nai Bagels. Konigsburg, E. L. 2008. (ENG.). 208p. (J). (gr. 3-7). pap. 6.99 *(978-1-4169-5798-0(7),* Atheneum Bks. for Young Readers) Simon & Schuster Children's Publishing.

—George. Konigsburg, E. L. 2007. (ENG.). 176p. (J). (gr. 3-7). pap. 9.99 *(978-1-4169-4957-2(7),* Atheneum Bks. for Young Readers) Simon & Schuster Children's Publishing.

Koniver, Laura. From the Ground Up. Koniver, Laura. 2012. 44p. pap. 16.99 *(978-1-937848-03-3(5))* Do Life Right, Inc.

Könnecke, Ole. Anton Can Do Magic. Könnecke, Ole. Chidgey, Catherine. 2011. (Gecko Press Titles Ser.). 32p. 17.95 *(978-1-877467-37-0(5))* Gecko Pr. NZL. Dist: Lerner Publishing Group.

Könnecke, Ole. The Big Book of Animals of the World. Könnecke, Ole. 2015. (ENG.). 20p. (J). (gr. -1-k). bds. 14.99 ***(978-1-77657-012-6(X))*** Gecko Pr. NZL. Dist: Lerner Publishing Group.

Könnecke, Ole. The Big Book of Words & Pictures. Könnecke, Ole. 2012. (Gecko Press Titles Ser.). 22p. (J). (gr. -1-k). bds. 14.95 *(978-1-877579-05-9(X))* Gecko Pr. NZL. Dist: Lerner Publishing Group.

Kono, Erin Eitter. A Bit Is a Bite. Brimner, Larry Dane. 2007. (Rookie Reader Skill Set Ser.). (ENG.). 32p. (J). (gr. -1-3). pap. 4.95 *(978-0-531-17780-8(7),* Children's Pr.) Scholastic Library Publishing.

—The Twelve Days of Christmas in Wisconsin. 2007. (Twelve Days of Christmas in America Ser.). (ENG.). 32p. (J). (gr. -1-3). 12.95 *(978-1-4027-3815-9(3))* Sterling Publishing Co., Inc.

Konomi, Takeshi. The Prince of Tennis. Konomi, Takeshi. (Prince of Tennis Ser.: 31). (ENG.). 2009. 184p. pap. 7.95 *(978-1-4215-2432-0(5));* 2009. 192p. pap. 7.95 *(978-1-4215-2431-3(7));* 2009. 210p. pap. 7.95 *(978-1-4215-1651-6(9));* 2008. 210p. pap. 7.95 *(978-1-4215-1650-9(0));* 2008. 189p. pap. 7.95 *(978-1-4215-1649-3(7));* 2008. 189p. pap. 7.95 *(978-1-4215-1648-6(9));* 2008. 200p. pap. 7.95 *(978-1-4215-1647-9(0));* 2008. 200p. pap. 7.95 *(978-1-4215-1646-2(2))* Viz Media.

—The Prince of Tennis. Konomi, Takeshi. Brown, Urian, ed. 2008. (Prince of Tennis Ser.: 23). (ENG.). 200p. (gr. 4). pap. 7.95 *(978-1-4215-1473-4(7))* Viz Media.

—The Prince of Tennis. Konomi, Takeshi. (Prince of Tennis Ser.: 20). (ENG.). 2007. 192p. pap. 7.95 *(978-1-4215-1096-5(0));* 2006. 208p. pap. 7.95 *(978-1-4215-0668-5(8));* 2005. 184p. pap. 7.95 *(978-1-59116-995-6(X));* 2005. 200p. pap. 7.95 *(978-1-59116-440-1(0));* Vol. 1. 2004. 192p. pap. 9.99 *(978-1-59116-435-7(4));* Vol. 2. 2004. 200p. pap. 7.95 *(978-1-59116-436-4(2));* Vol. 4. 2004. 200p. pap. 7.95 *(978-1-59116-438-8(9));* Vol. 5. 2004. 200p. pap. 7.95 *(978-1-59116-439-5(7));* Vol. 7. 2005. 192p. pap. 7.95 *(978-1-59116-787-7(6));* Vol. 8. 2005. 184p. pap. 9.99 *(978-1-59116-853-9(8))* Viz Media.

—Prince of Tennis, Vol. 10. Konomi, Takeshi. 2005. (Prince of Tennis Ser.). (ENG.). 184p. pap. 7.95 *(978-1-4215-0070-6(1))* Viz Media.

—The Prince of Tennis. Konomi, Takeshi. (Prince of Tennis Ser.). (ENG.). Vol. 11. 2006. 176p. pap. 7.95 *(978-1-4215-0201-4(1));* Vol. 12. 2006. 208p. pap. 7.95 *(978-1-4215-0337-0(9));* Vol. 13. 2006. 200p. pap. 7.95 *(978-1-4215-0666-1(1));* Vol. 14. 2006. 208p. pap. 7.95 *(978-1-4215-0667-8(X));* Vol. 17. 2007. 208p. pap. 7.95 *(978-1-4215-0670-8(X));* Vol. 19. 2007. 200p. pap. 7.95 *(978-1-4215-1095-8(2));* Vol. 21. 2007. 192p. pap. 7.95 *(978-1-4215-1097-2(9))* Viz Media.

—The Prince of TennisTM, Vol. 3. Konomi, Takeshi. Yamazaki, Joe, tr. from JPN. 2004. (Prince of Tennis Ser.). (ENG.). 200p. pap. 7.95 *(978-1-59116-437-1(0))* Viz Media.

Konopka, Jan. Alex & the Archangel. Williams, Rachel. 2005. (ENG.). 56p. pap. *(978-1-84401-614-3(5))* Athena Pr.

Konstantinov, Vitali. Loyola Kids Book of Heroes: Stories of Catholic Heroes & Saints Throughout History. Welborn, Amy. 2003. (ENG.). 208p. (J). (gr. 3-7). 15.95 *(978-0-8294-1584-1(X))* Loyola Pr.

Kontzias, Bill, photos by. Look & See: A What's-Not-The-Same-Game. Kontzias, Bill. 2014. (ENG.). 32p. (J). (gr. -1-3). 16.95 *(978-0-8234-2860-1(5))* Holiday Hse., Inc.

Konye, Paul. Rosie & the Audition. Rushby, Pamela. 2009. 24p. pap. 10.67 *(978-1-4190-5524-9(0))* Rigby Education.

—Rosie Goes Home. Rushby, Pamela. 2009. (Rigby PM Stars Bridge Bks.). (ENG.). 24p. (gr. 2-3). pap. 8.70 *(978-1-4190-5529-4(1))* Rigby Education.

—Zap! Fab Things to Draw. Ashforth, Kate. 2014. (ENG.). (J). (gr. 4-7). pap. *(978-1-74363-385-4(8))* Hinkler Bks. Pty. Ltd.

Koo, Rob. Great Buddhist Stories. 2011. (J). pap. *(978-1-935523-22-2(8))* World Tribune Pr.

—More Great Buddhist Stories. 2012. (J). pap. *(978-1-935523-48-2(1))* World Tribune Pr.

Kooistra, Alex. Yoga Games for Children: Fun & Fitness with Postures, Movements & Breath. Bersma, Danielle & Visscher, Marjoke. Evans, Amina Marix, tr. from DUT. 2003. (SmartFun Activity Bks.). (ENG.). 160p. (J). pap. 14.95 *(978-0-89793-389-6(3),* Hunter Hse.) Turner Publishing Co.

Koon, Cheng Puay. Secrets of the Swamp. Humphreys, Neil. 2014. (ENG.). 72p. pap. 11.90 *(978-981-4484-16-9(4))* Marshall Cavendish International (Asia) Private Ltd. SGP. Dist: National Bk. Network.

Koon-Chiu, Lo. Favorite Children's Stories from China & Tibet. Hume, Lotta Carswell & Lo, Koon-Chiu. 2004. (ENG.). 112p. (J). (gr. k-8). 18.95 *(978-0-8048-3586-2(1))* Tuttle Publishing.

Koontz, Robin. Cinderella Zelda. Koontz, Robin. ed. 2011. (ENG.). 24p. (gr. 2-3). pap. 7.95 *(978-1-61236-027-0(0))* Rourke Educational Media.

—Paul Bunyan. Koontz, Robin. 2012. (ENG.). 24p. (gr. 2-3). pap. 7.95 *(978-1-61810-326-0(1));* lib. bdg. 28.50 *(978-1-61810-193-8(5))* Rourke Educational Media.

—Robin Hood. Koontz, Robin. 2012. (ENG.). 24p. (gr. 2-3). lib. bdg. 28.50 *(978-1-61810-192-1(7))* Rourke Educational Media.

—Rumpelstiltskin. Koontz, Robin. 2012. (ENG.). 24p. (gr. 2-3). pap. 7.95 *(978-1-61810-327-7(X));* lib. bdg. 28.50 *(978-1-61810-194-5(3))* Rourke Educational Media.

—Run... It's a Bee! Koontz, Robin. 2012. (ENG.). 24p. (gr. 2-3). pap. 7.95 *(978-1-61810-333-8(4));* lib. bdg. 28.50 *(978-1-61810-200-3(1))* Rourke Educational Media.

—The Three Billy Goats & Gruff. Koontz, Robin. ed. 2011. (ENG.). 24p. (gr. 2-3). pap. 7.95 *(978-1-61236-030-0(0))* Rourke Educational Media.

Koontz, Robin Michal. Whales: Read Well Level K Unit 18 Storybook. Dunn, Richard & Sprick, Jessica. 2003. (Read Well Level K Ser.). 20p. (J). *(978-1-57035-689-6(0),* 55589) Cambium Education, Inc.

Koontz, Robin Michal. The King's New Clothes. Koontz, Robin Michal. ed. 2011. (ENG.). 24p. (gr. 2-3). pap. 7.95 *(978-1-61236-028-7(9))* Rourke Educational Media.

—Lizzie Little, the Sky Is Falling! Koontz, Robin Michal. ed. 2011. (ENG.). 24p. (gr. 2-3). pap. 7.95 *(978-1-61236-029-4(7))* Rourke Educational Media.

—Robin Hood. Koontz, Robin Michal. 2012. (ENG.). 24p. (gr. 2-3). pap. 7.95 *(978-1-61810-325-3(3))* Rourke Educational Media.

Koopmans, Loek. Stella & the Berry Thief. 1 vol. Koopmans, Loek. tr. Mason, Jane B. 2004. (ENG.). 32p. (J). 16.95 *(978-0-7614-5123-5(4))* Marshall Cavendish Corp.

Koorang, Mundara. Little Platypus & the Fire Spirit. Koorang, Mundara. 2nd ed. 2011. (ENG.). 32p. (J). (gr. -1-k). pap. 17.95 *(978-0-85575-701-4(9))* Aboriginal Studies Pr. AUS. Dist: Independent Pubs. Group.

Kopald, Sue-Anne. Hey, Look at Me! Baby Days. Thomasson, Merry F. (Hey, Look at Me! Ser.). (J). *(978-1-882607-06-8(6))* Merrybooks & More.

Kopelke, Lisa. Super Oscar. De La Hoya, Oscar. Montejo, Andrea, tr. 2012. (ENG & SPA.). 32p. (J). (gr. -1-3). 6.99 *(978-1-4169-0612-4(6),* Simon & Schuster Bks. For Young Readers) Simon & Schuster Bks. For Young Readers.

Kopelke, Lisa. The Younger Brother's Survival Guide. Kopelke, Lisa. 2006. (ENG.). 32p. (J). (gr. -1-3). 17.99 *(978-0-689-86249-6(0),* Simon & Schuster Bks. For Young Readers) Simon & Schuster Bks. For Young Readers.

Kopervas, Gary & Hanes, Don. AbuLLard's ABC's of Branding: 26 Concepts That Capture the Essence of Good Brand Management. Wilcox, Jean K. & Cameron, E. Jane. unabr. ed. 2003. 64p. 19.95 *(978-0-9745612-0-2(7),* CPN-BMS-001) CattLeLogos Brand Management Systems.

Kopler, Joe. Lennie's Pennies. Garrett, Kelsey. 2012. (ENG.). 64p. pap. 19.95 *(978-1-4327-9606-8(2))* Outskirts Pr., Inc.

Kopper, Lisa. Sleep Tight. Hallworth, Grace. 2004. (ENG.). 24p. per. 7.25 *(978-0-521-75249-7(3))* Cambridge Univ. Pr.

Kopper, Lisa. Stories from the Ballet. Kopper, Lisa, tr. Greaves, Margaret. 2003. 72p. (J). pap. 12.95 *(978-0-7112-2162-8(6),* Frances Lincoln) Quarto Publishing Group UK GBR. Dist: Perseus-PGW.

Korda, Lerryn. Into the Wild. Korda, Lerryn. 2010. (Playtime with Little Nye Ser.). (ENG.). 26p. (J). (gr. -1 — 1). 8.99 *(978-0-7636-4812-1(4))* Candlewick Pr.

—It's Vacation Time. Korda, Lerryn. 2010. (Playtime with Little Nye Ser.). (ENG.). 26p. (J). (— 1). 8.99 *(978-0-7636-4813-8(2))* Candlewick Pr.

—Millions of Snow. Korda, Lerryn. 2010. (Playtime with Little Nye Ser.). (ENG.). 32p. (J). (— 1). 8.99 *(978-0-7636-4651-6(2))* Candlewick Pr.

—So Cozy. Korda, Lerryn. 2015. (ENG.). 32p. (J). (— 1). 15.99 *(978-0-7636-7373-4(0))* Candlewick Pr.

Korda, Lerryn & Korda, Lerryn. Rocket to the Moon. Korda, Lerryn & Korda, Lerryn. 2010. (Playtime with Little Nye Ser.). (ENG.). 32p. (J). (— 1). 8.99 *(978-0-7636-4652-3(0))* Candlewick Pr.

Korda, Lerryn, jt. illus. see Korda, Lerryn.

Kordey, Igor. Soldier X. Macan, Darko. 2003. 144p. (YA). pap. 12.99 *(978-0-7851-1013-2(5))* Marvel Worldwide, Inc.

Kordich, Melinda. Bella-Blue Butterfly's Purple Surprise. Baumann, Jessica. 2013. 30p. pap. 9.99 *(978-1-937165-38-3(8))* Orange Hat Publishing.

Koren, Edward. Oops! Katz, Alan. 2008. (ENG.). 144p. (J). (gr. 2-5). 19.99 *(978-1-4169-0204-1(X),* McElderry, Margaret K. Bks.) McElderry, Margaret K. Bks.

—Poems I Wrote When No One Was Looking. Katz, Alan. 2011. (ENG.). 176p. (J). (gr. 2-5). 17.99 *(978-1-4169-3518-6(5),* McElderry, Margaret K. Bks.) McElderry, Margaret K. Bks.

Koren, Edward. Very Hairy Harry. Koren, Edward. 2003. *(978-0-06-057744-5(4));* (J). *(978-0-06-056868-9(2))* HarperCollins Pubs.

Korkos, Alain. Be Your Own Rock & Mineral Expert. Pinet, Michele. Greenbaum, Fay, tr. from FRE. 2003. 40p. (J). (gr. 5-7). 14.95 *(978-0-8069-9580-9(7))* Sterling Publishing Co., Inc.

Korman, Justine. The Poky Little Puppy's First Christmas. Korman, Justine. 2014. (Little Golden Board Book Ser.). (ENG.). 26p. (J). (-k). bds. 7.99 *(978-0-385-38473-5(4),* Golden Bks.) Random Hse. Children's Bks.

Kornacki, Christine. The Sparkle Box: The Story of a Very Special Christmas Gift. Hardie, Jill. 2012. 32p. (J). 19.99 *(978-0-8249-5647-9(8),* Ideals Children's Bks.) Ideals Pubns.

—The Sparkle Egg. Hardie, Jill. 2014. 32p. (J). 16.99 *(978-0-8249-5664-6(8),* Ideals Children's Bks.) Ideals Pubns.

Kornell, Max. Bear with Me. Kornell, Max. 2011. (ENG.). 32p. (J). (gr. -1-k). 15.99 *(978-0-399-25257-0(6),* Putnam Juvenile) Penguin Publishing Group.

—Me First. Kornell, Max. 2014. (ENG.). 32p. (J). (gr. k-3). 16.99 *(978-0-399-15997-8(5),* Nancy Paulsen Bks.) Penguin Publishing Group.

Korobkina, Katya. Green Smoothie Magic. Boutenko, Victoria. 2013. (ENG.). 56p. (J). (gr. -1-3). 12.95 *(978-1-58394-601-5(2))* North Atlantic Bks.

Korrow, Chris. The Organic Bug Book. Korrow, Chris. 2013. (ENG.). 44p. (J). pap. 11.95 *(978-1-58420-145-8(2),* Lindisfarne Bks.) SteinerBooks, Inc.

Korthues, Barbara. The Advent Elf. Stalder, Päivi. 2010. (ENG.). 32p. (J). (gr. -1-3). 16.95 *(978-0-7358-2335-8(9))* North-South Bks., Inc.

—Loopy. Jesset, Aurore. 2008. (ENG.). 32p. (J). (gr. -1-3). 16.95 *(978-0-7358-2175-0(5))* North-South Bks., Inc.

—Loquillo. Jesset, Aurore. 2009. (SPA & ENG.). 32p. (J). (gr. -1-3). 7.95 *(978-0-7358-2262-7(X))* North-South Bks., Inc.

Korthues, Barbara, jt. illus. see Jesset, Aurore.

Kosaka, Fumi. Be Mine, Be Mine, Sweet Valentine. Weeks, Sarah. 2005. (ENG.). 20p. (J). (gr. -1-k). 9.99 *(978-0-694-01514-6(8),* HarperFestival) HarperCollins Pubs.

—If You'll Be My Valentine. Rylant, Cynthia. 2005. (ENG.). 32p. (J). (gr. -1-3). pap. 6.99 *(978-0-06-009271-9(8))* HarperCollins Pubs.

Koshi, Rikdo. Excel Saga. Koshi, Rikdo. (Excel Saga Ser.). (ENG.). Vol. 1. 2003. 200p. (YA). pap. 9.95 *(978-1-56931-988-8(X));* Vol. 2. 2003. 208p. (YA). pap. 9.95 *(978-1-56931-989-5(8));* Vol. 3. 2003. 208p. (YA). pap. 9.95 *(978-1-56931-990-1(1));* Vol. 9. 2004. 208p. (YA). pap. 9.95 *(978-1-59116-234-6(3));* Vol. 10. 2005. 200p. (YA). pap. 9.99 *(978-1-59116-644-3(6));* Vol. 11. 2005. 208p. (YA). pap. 9.99 *(978-1-59116-722-8(1));* Vol. 12. 2005. 208p. (YA). pap. 9.99 *(978-1-59116-775-4(2));* Vol. 13. 2005. 208p. pap. 9.99 *(978-1-4215-0143-7(0));* Vol. 14. 2006. 208p. pap. 9.99 *(978-1-4215-0481-0(2));* Vol. 16. 2007. 192p. pap. 9.99 *(978-1-4215-1347-8(1))* Viz Media.

Koshiba, Tetsuya. Remote, 3 vols., Vol. 1. Amagi, Seimaru. 2004. 192p. pap. 14.99 *(978-1-59182-740-5(X)*, Tokyopop Adult) TOKYOPOP, Inc.
—Remote. rev. ed. 2005. Vol. 5. 216p. pap. 14.99 *(978-1-59532-032-2(6))*; Vol. 6. 192p. pap. 14.99 *(978-1-59532-033-9(4))* TOKYOPOP, Inc. (Tokyopop Adult).
—Remote, Vol. 7. Amagi, Seimaru. 7th rev. ed. 2005. (Remote Ser.). 190p. (YA). per. 14.99 *(978-1-59532-810-6(6)*, Tokyopop Adult) TOKYOPOP, Inc.
Kosir, Ana. The Pirate Kitty. Glover, Darryl. Austin, Britta, ed. 2008. 24p. (J). 16.95 *(978-0-9821387-0-0(9))* MagicStar Inc.
Kosits, Andrew. Tea Party at Chestertown. Maxson, H. A. & Young, Claudia H. 2003. (Magical History Tours Ser.). 55p. (J). per. 8.95 *(978-0-9741713-0-2(1))* Bay Oak Pubs., Ltd.
Koski, Rozanne. Enemy Cat: A Companion to the Growing Erbs Series. Erb, Diane. 2010. (ENG.). 52p. pap. 20.00 *(978-1-4563-0177-4(2))* CreateSpace Independent Publishing Platform.
—Time to Go: The Growing Erb Series. Caza, Sheila. 2010. (ENG.). 160p. pap. 17.00 *(978-1-4538-8728-8(8))* CreateSpace Independent Publishing Platform.
Kostecke, Nancy, jt. illus. see Fenton, Mary Frances.
Kostecki-Shaw, Jenny Sue. Luna & Me: The True Story of a Girl Who Lived in a Tree to Save a Forest. Kostecki-Shaw, Jenny Sue. 2015. (ENG.). 40p. (J). (gr. k-4). 18.99 *(978-0-8050-9976-8(X)*, Holt, Henry & Co. Bks. For Young Readers) Holt, Henry & Co.
—My Travelin' Eye. Kostecki-Shaw, Jenny Sue. 2008. (ENG.). 40p. (J). (gr. -1-2). 18.99 *(978-0-8050-8169-5(0)*, Holt, Henry & Co. Bks. For Young Readers) Holt, Henry & Co.
—Same, Same but Different. Kostecki-Shaw, Jenny Sue. 2011. (ENG.). 40p. (J). (gr. -1-2). 17.99 *(978-0-8050-8946-2(2)*, Holt, Henry & Co. Bks. For Young Readers) Holt, Henry & Co.
Kostelyk, Jason. Bubba: A True Story about an Amazing Alligator. Nesci, Andrea Lynn & Nesci, Jim. l.t. ed. 2003. 24p. (J). pap. 12.50 *(978-0-9713197-6-9(6))* ECO Herpetological Pub. & Dist.
Kostic, Dimitri. Fight for Rights. Winter, Barbara. 2007. 48p. (J). lib. bdg. 23.08 *(978-1-4242-1636-9(2))* Fitzgerald Bks.
Koszowski, Allen, jt. illus. see Clark, Alan M.
Kote, Geneviève. Crushes, Codas, & Corsages, No. 4. Schusterman, Michelle. 2014. (I Heart Band Ser.: 4). (ENG.). 208p. (J). (gr. 3-7). 6.99 *(978-0-448-45686-7(9)*, Grosset & Dunlap) Penguin Publishing Group.
Kote, Genevieve. Friends, Fugues, & Fortune Cookies. Schusterman, Michelle. 2014. (I Heart Band Ser.: 2). (ENG.). 208p. (J). (gr. 3-7). 6.99 *(978-0-448-45684-3(2)*, Grosset & Dunlap) Penguin Publishing Group.
—I Heart Band #1. Schusterman, Michelle. 2014. (I Heart Band Ser.: 1). (ENG.). 208p. (J). (gr. 3-7). 6.99 *(978-0-448-45683-6(4)*, Grosset & Dunlap) Penguin Publishing Group.
Kotler, Arkady & Kotler, Elina. Seder in Herlin: And Other Stories. Kranzler, Gershon. 2003. 108p. (gr. 5-9). reprint ed. 13.95 *(978-0-8266-0343-2(2))* Merkos L'Inyonei Chinuch.
Kotler, Elina, jt. illus. see Kotler, Arkady.
Kotoyoshi, Yumisuke. Saber Marionette J, 3 vols., Vol. 2. Akahori, Satoru. 2nd rev. ed. 2003. 192p. 9.99 *(978-1-59182-387-2(0))* TOKYOPOP, Inc.
—Saber Marionette J, 3 vols., Vol. 3. Akahori, Satoru. Fukami, Yuko, tr. from JPN. rev. ed. 2003. 192p. 9.99 *(978-1-59182-388-9(9))* TOKYOPOP, Inc.
—Saber Marionette J, 5 vols. Akahori, Satoru. 2004. Vol. 4. 4th rev. ed. 168p. 9.99 *(978-1-59182-539-5(3))*; Vol. 5. rev. ed. 208p. 9.99 *(978-1-59182-540-1(7))* TOKYOPOP, Inc.
Kotrous, Chad. Jayhawk Adventures, a Day at the Zoo. Goode, Teresa. 2006. 29p. (J). (gr. 1-3). pap. 5.95 *(978-0-9646898-5-5(5))* Leathers Publishing.
—Jayhawk Adventures, Jed's Birthday Surprise. Goode, Teresa. 2006. 27p. (J). (gr. 1-3). pap. 5.95 *(978-0-9646898-6-2(3))* Leathers Publishing.
—Wildcat Adventures: A Vacation in the Big Apple. Goode, Teresa. 2006. 31p. (J). pap. 5.95 *(978-1-890622-13-8(3))* Leathers Publishing.
Kouga, Yun. Earthian. Kouga, Yun. 2005. (Earthian Ser.). 408p. (YA). per. 14.99 *(978-1-59816-006-2(0)*, TOKYOPOP Manga) TOKYOPOP, Inc.
—Loveless, 5 vols. Kouga, Yun. 2006. (Loveless (Tokyopop) Ser.: Vol. 1). 200p. pap. 9.99 *(978-1-59816-221-9(7))* TOKYOPOP, Inc.
Kouse, Patrick. Megan Has to Move, 1 vol. Wolfe, Jacqueline A. 2006. (Read-It! Readers Ser.). (ENG.). 32p. (gr. -1-3). 19.99 *(978-1-4048-1613-8(5)*, Easy Readers) Picture Window Bks.
Kousky, Vern. Otto the Owl Who Loved Poetry. Kousky, Vern. 2015. (ENG.). 32p. (J). (gr. k-3). 16.99 *(978-0-399-16440-8(5)*, Nancy Paulsen Bks.) Penguin Publishing Group.
Koutsky, Jan Dale. My Grandma, My Pen Pal. Koutsky, Jan Dale. 2003. (ENG.). 32p. (J). (gr. k-2). 15.95 *(978-1-56397-118-1(6))* Boyds Mills Pr.
Kovalcik, Terry. Cats! Cats! Cats!, 2. Evans, Mary. l.t. ed. 2005. (Sadlier Phonics Reading Program). 8p. (gr. -1-1). 23.00 net. *(978-0-8215-7348-8(9))* Sadlier, William H. Inc.
Kovalski, Maryann. Omar on Board, 1 vol. Kovalski, Maryann. 2005. (ENG.). 32p. (J). 9.95 *(978-1-55041-918-4(8)*, 1550419188) Fitzhenry & Whiteside, Ltd. CAN. Dist: Midpoint Trade Bks., Inc.
Kovar, Ben. Dark Tower Rising, 1 vol. Dahl, Michael. 2012. (Troll Hunters Ser.). (ENG.). 112p. (gr. 2-3). lib. bdg. 23.99 *(978-1-4342-3308-0(1)*, Troll Hunters) Stone Arch Bks.
—Fallen Star, 1 vol. Dahl, Michael. 2012. (Troll Hunters Ser.). (ENG.). 112p. (gr. 2-3). lib. bdg. 23.99 *(978-1-4342-3310-3(3)*, Troll Hunters) Stone Arch Bks.
—The Lava Crown, 1 vol. Dahl, Michael. 2012. (Troll Hunters Ser.). (ENG.). 112p. (gr. 2-3). lib. bdg. 23.99 *(978-1-4342-3309-7(X)*, Troll Hunters) Stone Arch Bks.
—Skyfall, 1 vol. Dahl, Michael. 2012. (Troll Hunters Ser.). (ENG.). 112p. (gr. 2-3). lib. bdg. 23.99 *(978-1-4342-3307-3(3)*, Troll Hunters) Stone Arch Bks.
—Troll Hunters, 1 vol. Dahl, Michael. 2012. (Troll Hunters Ser.). (ENG.). 320p. (gr. 4-4). 12.95 *(978-1-4342-4590-8(X))* Stone Arch Bks.
Kove, Torill. John Jensen Feels Different. Hovland, Henrik & Bartlett, Don. 2012. (J). 16.00 *(978-0-8028-5399-8(4)*, Eerdmans Bks For Young Readers) Eerdmans, William B. Publishing Co.
Kowitt, Holly. The Loser List. 2011. 213p. (J). pap. *(978-0-545-32900-2(0)*, Scholastic Pr.) Scholastic, Inc.
—Revenge of the Loser. 2012. 233p. (J). *(978-0-545-42611-4(1)*, Scholastic Pr.) Scholastic, Inc.
Koyose, Junji. Who Made This Cake? Nakagawa, Chihiro. 2008. (ENG.). 32p. (J). (gr. -1-2). 16.95 *(978-1-59078-595-9(9)*, Front Street) Boyds Mills Pr.
Koz, Paula Goodman. Shlemiel Crooks. Olswanger, Anna. 2005. 36p. (J). (gr. 2-4). 15.95 *(978-1-58838-165-1(X))* NewSouth, Inc.
Koziara, Colleen. Thirteen Silver Moons. Koziara, Colleen. 2004. (J). per. *(978-0-9763205-0-0(9))* Mystical Willow Productions.
Kozjan, Drazen. Julia Gillian - And the Art of Knowing. McGhee, Alison. 2009. (Julia Gillian Ser.). (ENG.). 304p. (J). (gr. 3-7). 6.99 *(978-0-545-03349-7(7)*, Scholastic Paperbacks) Scholastic, Inc.
—Julia Gillian (and the Dream of the Dog) McGhee, Alison. (Julia Gillian Ser.). (ENG.). 336p. (J). (gr. 3-7). 2011. pap. 6.99 *(978-0-545-03353-4(5))*; 2010. 16.99 *(978-0-545-03351-0(9))* Scholastic, Inc. (Scholastic Pr.).
—Julia Gillian (and the Quest for Joy) McGhee, Alison. 2010. (Julia Gillian Ser.). (ENG.). 320p. (J). (gr. 3-7). 6.99 *(978-0-545-03352-7(7)*, Scholastic Pr.) Scholastic, Inc.
—Oh, How Sylvester Can Pester! And Other Poems More or Less about Manners. Kinerk, Robert. 2011. (ENG.). 32p. (J). (gr. -1-3). 16.99 *(978-1-4169-3362-5(X)*, Simon & Schuster/Paula Wiseman Bks.) Simon & Schuster/Paula Wiseman Bks.
—Revolutionary Friends: General George Washington & the Marquis de Lafayette. Castrovilla, Selene. 2013. (ENG.). 40p. (J). (gr. 3). 16.95 *(978-1-59078-880-6(X)*, Calkins Creek) Boyds Mills Pr.
Kozlowski, Tomasz. The Beast in My Belly. Kasdepke, Grzegorz. 2015. (ENG.). 48p. (J). (gr. k-4). 16.95 *(978-1-59270-160-5(4))* Enchanted Lion Bks., LLC.
Krackow, Eric T. Lobsters on the Loose, 1 vol. Ginn, Jennifer. 2011. (ENG.). 48p. (J). 16.99 *(978-0-7643-3826-7(9)*, Schiffer Publishing Ltd) Schiffer Publishing, Ltd.
Kraegel, Kenneth. King Arthur's Very Great Grandson. Kraegel, Kenneth. 2012. (ENG.). 40p. (J). (gr. k-3). 15.99 *(978-0-7636-5311-8(X))* Candlewick Pr.
—The Song of Delphine. Kraegel, Kenneth. 2015. (ENG.). 40p. (J). (gr. k-3). 15.99 *(978-0-7636-7001-6(4))* Candlewick Pr.
Kraft, Erik P. Lenny & Mel. Kraft, Erik P. 2012. (Ready-For-Chapters Ser.). (ENG.). 64p. (J). (gr. 2-5). pap. 6.99 *(978-0-689-85891-8(4)*, Simon & Schuster/Paula Wiseman Bks.) Simon & Schuster/Paula Wiseman Bks.
—Lenny & Mel after-School Confidential. Kraft, Erik P. 2012. (Lenny & Mel Ser.). (ENG.). 64p. (J). (gr. 2-5). pap. 6.99 *(978-1-4424-6314-1(7)*, Simon & Schuster/Paula Wiseman Bks.) Simon & Schuster/Paula Wiseman Bks.
—Lenny & Mel's Summer Vacation. Kraft, Erik P. 2012. (Ready-For-Chapters Ser.). (ENG.). 64p. (J). (gr. 2-5). pap. 6.99 *(978-0-689-86874-0(X)*, Simon & Schuster/Paula Wiseman Bks.) Simon & Schuster/Paula Wiseman Bks.
Kraft, Jason. A Haunted Halloween. O'Ryan, Ray. 2015. (Galaxy Zack Ser.: 11). (ENG.). 128p. (J). (gr. k-4). 16.99 *(978-1-4814-3491-1(6)*, Little Simon) Little Simon.
Kraft, Jason. Operation Twin Trouble. O'Ryan, Ray. 2015. (Galaxy Zack Ser.: 12). (ENG.). 128p. (J). (gr. k-4). pap. 5.99 ***(978-1-4814-4399-9(2)***, Little Simon) Little Simon.
Kraft, Jason. Return to Earth! O'Ryan, Ray. 2015. (Galaxy Zack Ser.: 10). (ENG.). 128p. (J). (gr. k-4). pap. 5.99 *(978-1-4814-2181-2(6)*, Little Simon) Little Simon.
Kraft, Jason, jt. illus. see Leyssenne, Mathieu.
Kraft, Joe. Gracie Blue Knows a Secret, 1 vol. Kraft, Andrea. 2009. 23p. pap. 19.95 *(978-1-61582-554-7(1))* PublishAmerica, Inc.
Kraft, Lauri. The Peaceful Lion. Johnson, Sandi. Johnson, Britt, ed. l.t. ed. 2014. (ENG.). 28p. (J). (gr. k-5). pap. 12.99 *(978-1-929063-95-6(4)*, 325) Moons & Stars Publishing For Children.
Krahulik, Mike. Attack of the Bacon Robots! Holkins, Jerry. 2006. (Penny Arcade Ser.). (ENG.). 168p. pap. 12.95 *(978-1-59307-444-9(1))* Dark Horse Comics.
Krajenbrink Hulin, Yvonne. Gretchen & the Gremlins. Holst, Jerome Alphonse. 2012. 48p. pap. 15.95 *(978-0-9794133-5-3(4))* TV Acres Bks.
Kralapp, Karl E. Fish Food. Kralapp, Karl E. 2013. 28p. pap. 9.99 *(978-1-937165-62-8(0))* Orange Hat Publishing.
Krall, Dan. Oh, Nuts! Sauer, Tammi. 2012. (ENG.). 32p. (J). 17.89 *(978-1-59990-467-2(5))*; (gr. -1-6). 16.99 *(978-1-59990-466-5(7)*, 244271) Bloomsbury USA. (Bloomsbury USA Childrens).
—Skeleton Cat. Crow, Kristyn. 2012. (ENG.). 32p. (J). (gr. -1-3). pap. 6.99 *(978-0-545-15385-0(9)*, Scholastic Pr.) Scholastic, Inc.
Krall, Dan. The Great Lollipop Caper. Krall, Dan. 2013. (ENG.). 48p. (J). (gr. -1-3). 16.99 *(978-1-4424-4460-7(6)*, Simon & Schuster Bks. For Young Readers) Simon & Schuster Bks. For Young Readers.
—Sick Simon. Krall, Dan. 2015. (ENG.). 48p. (J). (gr. -1-3). 17.99 *(978-1-4424-9097-0(7)*, Simon & Schuster Bks. For Young Readers) Simon & Schuster Bks. For Young Readers.
Kralovansky, Susan. Twelve Cowboys Ropin', 1 vol. Kralovansky, Susan. 2015. (ENG.). 32p. (J). (gr. k-3). 16.99 ***(978-1-4556-2081-4(5))*** Pelican Publishing Co., Inc.
Kramek, Oren & Walker, Steve. The Sons of Liberty, No. 1. Lagos, Alexander & Lagos, Joseph. 2010. (ENG.). 176p. (J). (gr. 3-7). 18.99 *(978-0-375-85670-9(6)*, Random Hse. Bks. for Young Readers) Random Hse. Children's Bks.
Kramek, Oren, jt. illus. see Walker, Steve.
Kramer, Berri, photos by. Mbali: A story from South Africa. Kramer, Berri, text. 2nd ed. 2006. (J). per. *(978-0-9706901-1-1(8))* Rotaplast Pr.
Kramer, Brandie. Footlights & Fairy Dust: Matt & Maria Go to the Theatre. Tirabassi, Maren C. 2007. (ENG.). 48p. (J). (gr. 2-7). pap. 14.95 *(978-1-933002-26-2(3))* PublishingWorks.
Kramer, Connie, photos by. Cupcakes! A Sweet Treat with More Than 200 Stickers. Cooke, Brandy. 2011. (ENG., 18p. (J). (gr. -1-k). bds. 6.99 *(978-1-4424-2825-6(2)*, Little Simon) Little Simon.
Kramer, David. Monkey of the Month, 1 vol. Kramer, Adam. 2012. (ENG.). 40p. (J). 16.99 *(978-0-7643-4156-4(1))* Schiffer Publishing, Ltd.
—My Father Flies, 1 vol. Ginn, Jennifer. 2013. (ENG.). 32p. (J). 16.99 *(978-0-7643-4385-8(8))* Schiffer Publishing, Ltd.
Kramer, Jaap. The Mystery of the Abandoned Mill. Prins, Piet. 2006. 127p. (J). pap. *(978-1-894666-48-0(8))* Inheritance Pubns.
—One Day at a Time, Margreet. Vogelaar, Alie. VanBrugge, Jeanne, tr. from DUT. 2004. Orig. Title: Elke Dag Genoeg, Margreet. 124p. *(978-0-9670728-6-9(7))* Early Foundations Pubs.
—The Sailing Sleuths. Prins, Piet. 2006. 137p. (J). pap. *(978-1-894666-46-6(1))* Inheritance Pubns.
—The Search for Sheltie. Prins, Piet. 2006. 137p. (J). pap. *(978-1-894666-43-5(7))* Inheritance Pubns.
—The Treasure of Rodensteyn Castle. Prins, Piet. 2006. 132p. (J). pap. *(978-1-894666-47-3(X))* Inheritance Pubns.
Kramer, Pat, photos by. Totem Poles for Kids: A Kids Own SuperGuide. Kramer, Pat. 48p. (J). pap. *(978-1-55153-626-2(9))* Altitude Publishing Canada Ltd.
Kramin, Valerie. Into the Forest & down the Tower. Bugg, Ann T. 2012. 136p. pap. *(978-1-927044-24-7(3))* Writers AMuse Me.
Krassa, Victoria. Grandma, How Do You Say I Love You? Unobagha, Uzo. 2007. 28p. (J). 16.95 *(978-0-9773180-0-1(1))* Adonoke Inc.
Krasulja, Zorica. Kelly's Cabin, 1 vol. Smith, Linda. 2006. (Orca Echoes Ser.). (ENG.). 64p. (J). (gr. 2-3). per. 6.95 *(978-1-55143-408-7(3))* Orca Bk. Pubs. USA.
Kratter, Paul. A Tiger Tale. Nagda, Ann Whitehead. (Soundprints' Amazing Animal Adventures! Ser.). (ENG.). 36p. (J). 2005. (gr. -1-2). 2.95 *(978-1-59249-044-8(1)*, S7151); 2005. (gr. -1-2). 15.95 *(978-1-59249-042-4(5)*, B7101); 2005. (gr. -1-2). pap. 6.95 *(978-1-59249-043-1(3)*, S7101); 2005. (gr. -1-2). 19.95 *(978-1-59249-388-3(2)*, BC7101); 2005. (gr. 2-2). 8.95 *(978-1-59249-389-0(0)*, SC7101); 2003. (gr. -1-3). 9.95 *(978-1-59249-057-8(3)*, PS7151) Soundprints.
—World above the Clouds: A Story of a Himalayan Ecosystem. Nagda, Ann Whitehead. 2005. (Wild Habitats Ser.: Vol. 18). (ENG.). 36p. (J). (gr. 1-4). 19.95 *(978-1-56899-880-0(5)*, BC7017); 15.95 *(978-1-56899-878-7(3)*, B7017); pap. 6.95 *(978-1-56899-879-4(1)*, S7017) Soundprints.
Kratter, Paul. The Living Rain Forest: An Animal Alphabet. Kratter, Paul. rev. ed. 2010. (ENG.). 32p. (J). (gr. 1-4). pap. 7.95 *(978-1-58089-393-0(7))* Charlesbridge Publishing, Inc.
Kraulis, Julie. Whimsy's Heavy Things. Kraulis, Julie. 2013. (ENG.). 32p. (J). (gr. -1-1). 17.95 *(978-1-77049-403-9(0))* Tundra Bks. CAN. Dist: Random Hse., Inc.
Krause, George, photos by. Chicken Boy. Dowell, Frances O'Roark. 2007. (ENG., 224p. (J). (gr. 5-9). pap. 6.99 *(978-1-4169-3482-0(0)*, Atheneum Bks. for Young Readers) Simon & Schuster Children's Publishing.
Krauss, Trisha. France. Candlewick Press, Candlewick. 2015. (Panorama Pops Ser.). (ENG.). 30p. (J). (gr. k-4). 8.99 ***(978-0-7636-7836-4(8))*** Candlewick Pr.
Krauss, Trisha. Maude: The Not-So-Noticeable Shrimpton. Child, Lauren. 2013. (ENG.). 32p. (J). (gr. k-3). 16.99 *(978-0-7636-6515-9(0))* Candlewick Pr.
—Rio de Janeiro: a 3D Keepsake Cityscape. Candlewick Press Staff. 2014. (Panorama Pops Ser.). (ENG.). 30p. (J). (gr. k-4). 8.99 *(978-0-7636-7029-0(4))* Candlewick Pr.
Kravanek, J. Elise. Holly the Christmas Collie. Draper, Melissa J. 2004. 63p. (J). *(978-0-9741081-3-1(8))* Acres Publishing.
Krawczyk, Sabine. Fish. Krawczyk, Sabine. Biard, Philippe et al. 2006. (ENG.). 36p. (J). (gr. k-3). pap. 11.99 *(978-1-85103-365-2(3))* Moonlight Publishing, Ltd. GBR. Dist: Independent Pubs. Group.
—Insects. Krawczyk, Sabine. Sautai, Raoul. 2012. (ENG.). 36p. (J). (gr. -1-k). 12.99 *(978-1-85103-411-6(0))* Moonlight Publishing, Ltd. GBR. Dist: Independent Pubs. Group.
—Let's Look at Insects. Krawczyk, Sabine. Delafosse, Claude. 2012. (ENG.). 38p. (J). (gr. k-3). pap. 11.99 *(978-1-85103-279-2(7))* Moonlight Publishing, Ltd. GBR. Dist: Independent Pubs. Group.
—Let's Look at the Circus. Krawczyk, Sabine. Delafosse, Claude. 2012. (ENG.). 38p. (J). (gr. k-3). pap. 11.99 *(978-1-85103-367-6(X))* Moonlight Publishing, Ltd. GBR. Dist: Independent Pubs. Group.
—Let's Look at the Zoo at Night. Krawczyk, Sabine. Delafosse, Claude. 2012. (ENG.). 38p. (J). (gr. k-3). pap. 11.99 *(978-1-85103-333-1(5))* Moonlight Publishing, Ltd. GBR. Dist: Independent Pubs. Group.
—Let's Look under the Stone. Krawczyk, Sabine. Allaire, Caroline. 2013. (ENG.). 36p. (J). (gr. 1-4). pap. 11.99 *(978-1-85103-353-9(X))* Moonlight Publishing, Ltd. GBR. Dist: Independent Pubs. Group.
—Plantas. Krawczyk, Sabine. Delafosse, Claude. Barroso, Paz, tr. (Coleccion Mundo Maravilloso).Tr. of Plants. (SPA.). (J). (gr. 3-5). *(978-84-348-4501-5(6))* SM Ediciones.
Kray, Robert C. Bugs & Bugsicles: Insects in the Winter. Hansen, Amy S. 2010. (ENG.). 32p. (J). (gr. 2-4). pap. 11.95 *(978-1-59078-763-2(3))*; 17.95 *(978-1-59078-269-9(0))* Boyds Mills Pr.
Kraynak, George. Akio & the Moon Goddess. Falk, Elsa. 2011. 158p. 41.95 *(978-1-258-06311-5(5))* Literary Licensing, LLC.
Krebs, Patricia. On Your Mark, Get Set, Go! 2009. 32p. (J). 16.95 *(978-0-9796380-1-5(1))* Three Wishes Publishing Co.
—Zee: Adventure One: Borrowing China. Gilbert, Marcie. l.t. ed. 2006. 48p. (J). per. 16.99 *(978-0-9771566-0-3(5))* Librujas.
Krecskay, Stephen. Miss Tilly's Party. Thompson, Yvonne. 2004. (J). per. *(978-0-9749561-0-7(4))* My Sunshine Bks.
Kredel, Fritz. Slovenly Peter. Twain, Mark, tr. from GER. 2013. (Calla Editions Ser.). (ENG.). 48p. (gr. 5). 20.00 *(978-1-60660-048-1(6))* Dover Pubns., Inc.
—The Story of Beethoven. Kaufmann, Helen L. Meadowcroft, Enid Lamonte, ed. 2011. 192p. 42.95 *(978-1-258-10000-1(2))* Literary Licensing, LLC.
Krehbiel, Angie. Sierra, the Black Lab Who Loved to Eat: (a True Story) Unruh, Cindy. 2012. 32p. pap. 24.95 *(978-1-4626-5537-3(8))* America Star Bks.
Kreinberg, Sylvia. Volcano Bubbles, 1 vol. Giulieri, Anne. 2012. (Engage Literacy Blue Ser.). (ENG.). 32p. (gr. k-2). pap. 5.99 *(978-1-4296-8978-6(1)*, Engage Literacy) Capstone Pr., Inc.
Kreinberg, Sylvia, photos by. The Castle, 1 vol. Giulieri, Anne. 2012. (Engage Literacy Magenta Ser.). (ENG., 32p. (gr. k-2). pap. 5.99 *(978-1-4296-8872-7(6)*, Engage Literacy) Capstone Pr., Inc.
—Chocolate Banana Pops, 1 vol. Giulieri, Anne. 2012. (Engage Literacy Yellow Ser.). (ENG., 32p. (gr. k-2). pap. 5.99 *(978-1-4296-8836-9(X)*, Engage Literacy) Capstone Pr., Inc.
—Here Is a Robot, 1 vol. Giulieri, Anne. 2012. (Engage Literacy Magenta Ser.). (ENG., 32p. (gr. k-2). pap. 5.99 *(978-1-4296-8848-2(3)*, Engage Literacy) Capstone Pr., Inc.
—In My Car, 1 vol. Dale, Jay. 2012. (Engage Literacy Magenta Ser.). (ENG., 32p. (gr. k-2). pap. 5.99 *(978-1-4296-8850-5(5)*, Engage Literacy) Capstone Pr., Inc.
—Look at the Picture, 1 vol. Giulieri, Anne. 2012. (Engage Literacy Magenta Ser.). (ENG., 32p. (gr. k-2). pap. 5.99 *(978-1-4296-8858-1(0)*, Engage Literacy) Capstone Pr., Inc.
—Make a Monkey, 1 vol. Dale, Jay. 2012. (Engage Literacy Red Ser.). (ENG., 32p. (gr. k-2). pap. 5.99 *(978-1-4296-8946-5(3)*, Engage Literacy) Capstone Pr., Inc.
—Make Two Crocodiles, 1 vol. Giulieri, Anne. 2012. (Engage Literacy Blue Ser.). (ENG., 32p. (gr. k-2). pap. 5.99 *(978-1-4296-8986-1(2)*, Engage Literacy) Capstone Pr., Inc.
—My Birthday, 1 vol. Giulieri, Anne. 2012. (Engage Literacy Magenta Ser.). (ENG., 32p. (gr. k-2). pap. 5.99 *(978-1-4296-8868-0(8)*, Engage Literacy) Capstone Pr., Inc.
—My Toy Box, 1 vol. Dale, Jay. 2012. (Engage Literacy Magenta Ser.). (ENG., 32p. (gr. k-2). pap. 5.99 *(978-1-4296-8860-4(2)*, Engage Literacy) Capstone Pr., Inc.
Krejca, Gary. Generous Me. Pearson, Mary E. 2011. (Rookie Ready to Learn Ser.). 40p. (J). pap. 5.95 *(978-0-531-26652-6(4))*; (gr. -1-k). lib. bdg. 23.00 *(978-0-531-26427-0(0))* Scholastic Library Publishing. (Children's Pr.).
—Two Nice Mice. Gillis, Jennifer Blizin. 2006. (Reader's Clubhouse Level 2 Reader Ser.). (ENG.). 24p. (J). (gr. 1-4). pap. 3.99 *(978-0-7641-3295-7(4))* Barron's Educational Series, Inc.
Krejcova, Zdenka. Adventures of Saint Paul. Selucky, Oldrich. Trouve, Marianne Lorraine, tr. from CZE. 2008. Orig. Title: Pavel, dobrudruh Viry. 96p. (J). (gr. 1-3). pap. *(978-0-8198-0786-1(9))* Pauline Bks. & Media.
Kreloff, Elliot. Counting Duckies. 2010. 16p. (J). bds. *(978-1-60906-007-7(5))* Begin Smart LLC.
—Grandma Is an Author. Conroy, Melissa. 2011. (ENG.). 36p. (J). (gr. 1-4). 11.99 *(978-1-60905-039-9(8))* Blue Apple Bks.
—It's a Seashell Day. Ochiltree, Dianne. 2015. (ENG.). 32p. (J). (gr. -1-2). 12.99 *(978-1-60905-530-1(6))* Blue Apple Bks.
—Lights on Broadway: A Theatrical Tour from A to Z. Ziefert, Harriet & Nagel, Karen. 2009. (ENG.). 48p. (J). (gr. -1-3). 19.99 *(978-1-934706-68-8(X))* Blue Apple Bks.
—Matching Puzzle Cards - Numbers. 2012. (ENG.). 36p. (J). (gr. k-12). 9.99 *(978-1-60905-221-8(8))* Blue Apple Bks.
—My Little Baby. 2010. 12p. (J). bds. *(978-1-60906-008-4(3))* Begin Smart LLC.
—No More TV, Sleepy Cat. 2005. (I'm Going to Read(r) Ser.). (ENG.). 28p. (J). (gr. -1-k). pap. 3.95 *(978-1-4027-2508-1(6))* Sterling Publishing Co., Inc.
—Sleepy Barker. Ziefert, Harriet & Johnston, Jan. 2015. (¡Hola, English! Ser.). (ENG & SPA.). 28p. (J). (gr. -1-3). 12.99 *(978-1-60905-509-7(8))* Blue Apple Bks.
—Splish-Splash, into the Bath! Danis, Naomi. 2007. 16p. (J). *(978-1-59354-609-0(2))* Handprint Bks.
—Tic & Tac. Ziefert, Harriet. 2006. (I'm Going to Read(r) Ser.). (ENG.). 48p. (J). (gr. k-1). pap. 3.95 *(978-1-4027-3432-8(8))* Sterling Publishing Co., Inc.
—Tic & Tac Clean Up. 2007. (I'm Going to Read(r) Ser.). (ENG.). 32p. (J). (gr. k-1). pap. 3.95 *(978-1-4027-4243-9(6))* Sterling Publishing Co., Inc.
—Where's Your Nose. 2010. 24p. (J). bds. *(978-1-60906-004-6(0))* Begin Smart LLC.
—10 Little Fish. Ziefert, Harriet. 2015. (¡Hola, English! Ser.). (ENG & SPA.). 28p. (J). (gr. -1-3). 12.99 *(978-1-60905-510-3(1))* Blue Apple Bks.
Kreloff, Elliot & Lee, Huy Voun. Animals. Ziefert, Harriet. 2013. (ENG.). 30p. (J). (-k). 14.99 *(978-1-60905-272-0(2))* Blue Apple Bks.

Krementz, Jill, photos by. A Very Young Rider. Krementz, Jill. ed. 2006. 124p. (gr. 4-7). 24.95 *(978-0-9755516-2-2(0))* DreamHse. Publishing Inc.

Kremsner, Cynthia. My Puppy Gave to Me, 1 vol. Dannenbring, Cheryl. 2014. (ENG.). 32p. (J). (gr. k-3). 16.99 *(978-1-4556-1943-6(4))* Pelican Publishing Co., Inc.

Krenina, Katya. The Birds' Gift: A Ukrainian Easter Story. 32p. (J). (gr. k-3). tchr. ed. 16.95 *(978-0-8234-1384-3(5))* Holiday Hse., Inc.

—The Castle of Cats: A Story from Ukraine. Kimmel, Eric A. 2004. (ENG.). 32p. (J). (gr. k-3). tchr. ed. 16.95 *(978-0-8234-1565-6(1))* Holiday Hse., Inc.

—The Mysterious Guests: A Sukkot Story. Kimmel, Eric A. 2008. (ENG.). 32p. (J). (gr. 1-5). 16.95 *(978-0-8234-1893-0(6))* Holiday Hse., Inc.

—The Spider's Gift: A Ukrainian Christmas Story. 2005. (ENG.). 32p. (J). (gr. -1-3). 16.95 *(978-0-8234-1743-8(3))* Holiday Hse., Inc.

Kress, Camille. The High Holy Days. Kress, Camille. 2004. bds. 6.25 *(978-0-8074-0776-9(3)*, 241856) URJ Pr.

—Purim! Kress, Camille. 2004. 10p. (gr. -1-k). bds. 5.95 *(978-0-8074-0654-0(6)*, 102555) URJ Pr.

—A Tree Trunk Seder. Kress, Camille. 2004. (Camille Kress Library: Vol. 4). 7p. (gr. -1-k). bds. 6.25 *(978-0-8074-0735-6(6)*, 101252) URJ Pr.

Krietzman, Ariel. Fashion 101: A Crash Course in Clothing. Stalder, Erika. 2008. (ENG.). 128p. (YA). (gr. 7). pap. 18.99 *(978-0-9790173-4-6(3))* Zest Bks.

Krilanovich, Nadia. Chicken, Chicken, Duck! Krilanovich, Nadia. 2011. (ENG.). 32p. (J). (gr. -1-2). 14.99 *(978-1-58246-385-8(9)*, Tricycle Pr.) Ten Speed Pr.

Krings, Antoon. Duendecillo Membrillo. Krings, Antoon. 2005. (Bichitos Curiosos Ser.). (SPA & ENG.). 32p. (J). (gr. -1-k). 5.95 *(978-84-932442-6-2(0))* Blume ESP. Dist: Independent Pubs. Group.

—Ursula Libelula. Krings, Antoon. 2010. (Bichitos Curiosos Ser.). (SPA.). 32p. (J). (gr. -1-k). 5.95 *(978-84-9801-407-5(7))* Blume ESP. Dist: Independent Pubs. Group.

Krishnaswamy, Uma. Out of the Way! Out of the Way!, 1 vol. Krishnaswami, Uma. 2012. (ENG.). 28p. (J). (gr. -1-2). 17.95 *(978-1-55498-130-4(1))* Groundwood Bks. CAN. Dist: Perseus-PGW.

Kristen, Mantooth. Danny Goes to the Doctor. Kristen, Mantooth. 2007. 24p. (J). 10.00 *(978-0-9800580-0-0(7))* Ballyhoo Printing.

Kristiansen, Teddy. M Is for Magic. Gaiman, Neil. 272p. (J). (gr. 5-9). 2008. (ENG.). pap. 6.99 *(978-0-06-118647-9(3))*; 2007. 16.99 *(978-0-06-118642-4(2))* HarperCollins Pubs.

Kristie Kryssing. Bath Time Bears Have So Much Fun. Jennie Lyon Wood. 2009. 24p. pap. 12.99 *(978-1-4389-4420-3(9))* AuthorHouse.

Kristof Pincheira, Kyra. Where's Leon? Storybook & Reader's Guide CD-ROM, 1. Cassell, Jody. l.t. ed. 2006. 48p. (J). lib. bdg. 17.95 *(978-1-59494-013-2(4))* CPCC Pr.

Krit, Joey. Hooty & the Magic Power. Kamon. 2011. 36p. pap. 14.39 *(978-1-4634-1042-1(5))* AuthorHouse.

—Playtoon & the Antpod. Kamon. 2012. 28p. pap. 24.95 *(978-1-4626-7346-9(5))* PublishAmerica, Inc.

Krittendon, Kim & Johnson, Jim. Legend of the Blue Unicorn: Land of OSM. Johnson, Sandi et al. Johnson, Britt, ed. 2014. (Little Choo-Choo Bks.). (ENG.). 40p. (J). (gr. -1-6). 14.99 *(978-1-929063-09-3(1)*, 109) Moons & Stars Publishing For Children.

Krizmanic, Tatjana. Ilian. Fordham, Walter. 2012. 42p. pap. *(978-0-9813889-5-3(7))* Publish Yourself.

—Stories to Nourish the Hearts of Our Children. Simms, Laura. 2013. 100p. pap. 19.99 *(978-0-9911692-1-4(2))* Simms, Laura Storyteller.

Krock, Libby Carruth. The Legend of OinkADoodleMoo. St. Jean, Alan. St. Jean, Alan, ed. 2013. 32p. 19.95 *(978-0-9777272-9-2(7))* Oren Village, LLC.

Kroeger, Vanesa. Dios Me Escucha: Oraciones en Rima para Ninos. Fernandez, Cecilia Fau. 2007. 48p. (J). lib. bdg. 8.99 *(978-0-7586-1248-9(6))* Concordia Publishing Hse.

Krome, Mike. Christmas/Easter Flip-Over Book. Kovacs, Victoria. 2015. (Little Bible Heroes(tm) Ser.). (ENG.). 32p. (J). (gr. k-2). pap. 3.99 ***(978-1-4336-8711-2(9)***, B&H Kids) B&H Publishing Group.

—Creation/Noah Flip-Over Book. Kovacs, Victoria. 2015. (Little Bible Heroes(tm) Ser.). (ENG.). 32p. (J). (gr. k-2). pap. 3.99 ***(978-1-4336-8712-9(7)***, B&H Kids) B&H Publishing Group.

—David/Esther Flip-Over Book. Kovacs, Victoria. 2015. (Little Bible Heroes(tm) Ser.). (ENG.). 32p. (J). (gr. k-2). pap. 3.99 ***(978-1-4336-8713-6(5)***, B&H Kids) B&H Publishing Group.

—Joseph/the Good Samaritan Flip-Over Book. Kovacs, Victoria. 2015. (Little Bible Heroes(tm) Ser.). (ENG.). 32p. (J). (gr. k-2). pap. 3.99 ***(978-1-4336-8715-0(1)***, B&H Kids) B&H Publishing Group.

—Samuel/the Little Maid Flip-Over Book. Kovacs, Victoria. 2015. (Little Bible Heroes(tm) Ser.). (ENG.). 32p. (J). (gr. k-2). pap. 3.99 ***(978-1-4336-8718-1(6)***, B&H Kids) B&H Publishing Group.

Krome, Mike & Ryley, David. Jesus' Miracles/Martha Flip-Over Book. Kovacs, Victoria. 2015. (Little Bible Heroes(tm) Ser.). (ENG.). 32p. (J). (gr. k-2). pap. 3.99 ***(978-1-4336-8714-3(3)***, B&H Kids) B&H Publishing Group.

—Miriam/Daniel Flip-Over Book. Kovacs, Victoria. 2015. (Little Bible Heroes(tm) Ser.). (ENG.). 32p. (J). (gr. k-2). pap. 3.99 ***(978-1-4336-8717-4(8)***, B&H Kids) B&H Publishing Group.

Krömer, Christiane. Anh's Anger. Silver, Gail. 2009. (ENG.). 40p. (J). (gr. -1-2). 16.95 *(978-1-888375-94-7(9)*, Plum Blossom Bks.) Parallax Pr.

Kromer, Christiane. Anh's Anger. Silver, Gail. 2011. (J). *(978-1-935209-65-2(5)*, Plum Blossom Bks.) Parallax Pr.

—Flower Girl Butterflies. Howard, Elizabeth Fitzgerald. 2004. 32p. (J). 16.89 *(978-0-688-17810-9(3))* HarperCollins Pubs.

Krömer, Christiane. Steps & Stones: An Anh's Anger Story. Silver, Gail. 2011. (ENG.). 40p. (J). (gr. -1-5). 16.95 *(978-1-935209-87-4(6)*, Plum Blossom Bks.) Parallax Pr.

Krommes, Beth. Blue on Blue. White, Dianne. 2014. (ENG.). 48p. (J). (gr. k-3). 17.99 *(978-1-4424-1267-5(4)*, Beach Lane Bks.) Beach Lane Bks.

—Butterfly Eyes & Other Secrets of the Meadow. Sidman, Joyce. 2006. (ENG.). 48p. (J). (gr. 2-5). 17.99 *(978-0-618-56313-5(X))* Houghton Mifflin Harcourt Publishing Co.

—The House in the Night. Swanson, Susan Marie. (ENG.). (J). 2011. 36p. (gr. k — 1). bds. 7.99 *(978-0-547-57769-2(9))*; 2008. 40p. (gr. -1-3). 17.99 *(978-0-618-86244-3(7))* Houghton Mifflin Harcourt Publishing Co.

—The Lamp, the Ice, & the Boat Called Fish: Based on a True Story. Martin, Jacqueline Briggs. 2005. (ENG.). 48p. (J). (gr. -1-3). 6.95 *(978-0-618-54895-8(5))* Houghton Mifflin Harcourt Publishing Co.

—The Sun in Me: Poems about the Planet. Nicholls, Judith. 2008. (ENG.). 40p. (J). (gr. -1). 12.99 *(978-1-84686-161-1(6))* Barefoot Bks., Inc.

—The Sun in Me: Poems about the Planet. Nicholls, Judith. ed. 2003. 40p. (J). pap. 16.99 *(978-1-84148-058-9(4))* Barefoot Bks., Inc.

—Swirl by Swirl: Spirals in Nature. Sidman, Joyce. 2011. (ENG.). 40p. (J). (gr. -1-3). 17.99 *(978-0-547-31583-6(X))* Houghton Mifflin Harcourt Publishing Co.

Krone, Mike. Let's Be Friends. Sperry, Amanda. 2004. (Elements of Reading: Phonics Ser.). 8p. pap. 40.00 *(978-0-7398-9008-0(5))* Houghton Mifflin Harcourt Supplemental Pubs.

Kroneberger, Abigail Grace. The Sensory Room Kids Get in Sync. Kroneberger, Abigail Grace. 2008. 24p. per. 12.95 *(978-1-934246-98-6(0))* Peppertree Pr., The.

Kronheimer, Ann. The Golden Goose. King-Smith, Dick. 2006. (ENG.). 128p. (J). (gr. 3-7). 5.99 *(978-0-440-42030-9(X)*, Yearling) Random Hse. Children's Bks.

—Pretty Princesses: Beautiful Princesses to Color! 2014. (ENG.). 96p. (J). (gr. -1-2). 7.99 *(978-1-4424-8385-9(7)*, Little Simon) Little Simon.

—Pride & Prejudice. Austen, Jane. 2013. (Jane Austen Ser.). (ENG.). 64p. pap. 6.95 *(978-1-906230-06-7(4))* Real Reads Ltd. GBR. Dist: International Publishers Marketing.

—Sense & Sensibility. Austen, Jane. 2013. (Jane Austen Ser.). (ENG.). 64p. pap. 6.95 *(978-1-906230-11-1(0))* Real Reads Ltd. GBR. Dist: International Publishers Marketing.

—Twilight Magic. Chapman, Linda. 2008. 149p. (J). pap. *(978-0-545-03160-8(5))* Scholastic, Inc.

Krosoczka, Jarrett J. Chew, Chew, Gulp! Thompson, Lauren. 2011. (ENG.). 32p. (J). (gr. -1-k). 14.99 *(978-1-4169-9744-3(X)*, McElderry, Margaret K. Bks.) McElderry, Margaret K. Bks.

—Hop, Hop, Jump! Thompson, Lauren. 2012. (ENG.). 32p. (J). (gr. -1-k). 14.99 *(978-1-4169-9745-0(8)*, McElderry, Margaret K. Bks.) McElderry, Margaret K. Bks.

—Must. Push. Buttons! Good, Jason. 2015. (ENG.). 32p. (J). (gr. -1-1). 16.99 *(978-1-61963-095-6(8))* Bloomsbury USA Childrens) Bloomsbury USA.

Krosoczka, Jarrett J. Totally Tardy Marty. Perl, Erica S. 2015. (ENG.). 32p. (J). 16.95 ***(978-1-4197-1661-4(1)***, Abrams Bks. for Young Readers) Abrams.

Krosoczka, Jarrett J. Baghead. Krosoczka, Jarrett J. 2004. (ENG.). 40p. (J). (gr. -1-2). reprint ed. pap. 7.99 *(978-0-553-11172-9(8)*, Dragonfly Bks.) Random Hse. Children's Bks.

—The Frog Who Croaked. Krosoczka, Jarrett J. 2013. (Platypus Police Squad Ser.: 1). (ENG.). 240p. (J). (gr. 3-7). 12.99 *(978-0-06-207164-4(5)*, Waldon Pond Pr.) HarperCollins Pubs.

—Good Night, Monkey Boy. Krosoczka, Jarrett J. (ENG.). (J). 2013. 32p. (-k). bds. 6.99 *(978-0-449-81323-2(1)*, Knopf Bks. for Young Readers); 2003. 40p. (gr. -1-2). pap. 7.99 *(978-0-440-41798-9(8)*, Dragonfly Bks.) Random Hse. Children's Bks.

—Platypus Police Squad: Last Panda Standing. Krosoczka, Jarrett J. 2015. (Platypus Police Squad Ser.: 3). (ENG.). 256p. (J). (gr. 3-7). 12.99 *(978-0-06-207168-2(8)*, Waldon Pond Pr.) HarperCollins Pubs.

—Platypus Police Squad: The Ostrich Conspiracy. Krosoczka, Jarrett J. 2014. (Platypus Police Squad Ser.: 2). (ENG.). 240p. (J). (gr. 3-7). 12.99 *(978-0-06-207166-8(1)*, Waldon Pond Pr.) HarperCollins Pubs.

Krovatin, Dan. A Matter of Conscience: The Trial of Anne Hutchinson. Nichols, Joan K. 2009. (Steck-Vaughn Stories of America Ser.). (ENG.). 112p. (gr. 3-8). pap. 14.20 *(978-0-8114-8073-4(9))* Houghton Mifflin Harcourt Publishing Co.

Krudop, Walter Lyon. At Ellis Island: A History in Many Voices. Peacock, Louise. 2007. (ENG.). 48p. (J). (gr. 2-5). 19.99 *(978-0-689-83026-6(2)*, Atheneum Bks. for Young Readers) Simon & Schuster Children's Publishing.

—Black Whiteness: Admiral Byrd Alone in the Antarctic. Burleigh, Robert. 2011. (ENG.). 40p. (J). (gr. 2-5). pap. 19.99 *(978-1-4424-5334-0(6)*, Atheneum Bks. for Young Readers) Simon & Schuster Children's Publishing.

—Crossing the Delaware: A History in Many Voices. Peacock, Louise. 2007. (ENG.). 48p. (J). (gr. 3-7). 12.99 *(978-1-4169-5890-1(8)*, Simon & Schuster/Paula Wiseman Bks.) Simon & Schuster/Paula Wiseman Bks.

Krueger, Diane & Westenbroek, Ken. Blessly's Carrotnog Christmas Book & Coloring Book. Krueger, Diane. 2004. 14.99 *(978-0-9763695-1-6(6))* Hope Harvest Publishing.

Krug, Ken. No, Silly! Krug, Ken. 2015. (ENG.). 40p. (J). (gr. -1-3). 17.99 *(978-1-4814-0066-4(5)*, Beach Lane Bks.) Beach Lane Bks.

Krum, Ronda. Jesus Lives! the Easter Story. Derico, Laura Ring. 2014. (Happy Day Ser.). (ENG.). 16p. (J). pap. 2.49 *(978-1-4143-9415-2(2))* Tyndale Hse. Pubs.

Krupin, Connie G. The Jewish Pope: A Yiddish Tale. Mark, Yudel. Goodman, Ruth Fisher, tr. from YID. 2006. 127p. per. 10.00 *(978-1-56474-459-3(0)*, Fithian Pr) Daniel & Daniel, Pubs., Inc.

Krupinski, Loretta. Cómo Crece una Semilla. Jordan, Helene J. Fiol, Maria A., tr. 2006. (Let's-Read-And-Find-Out Science 1 Ser.). Tr. of How a Seed Grows. (SPA.). 32p. (J). (gr. -1-3). pap. 6.99 *(978-0-06-088716-2(8)*, Rayo) HarperCollins Pubs.

Krupinski, Loretta. How a Seed Grows. Jordan, Helene J. 2015. (Let's-Read-And-Find-Out Science 1 Ser.). (ENG.). 32p. (J). (gr. -1-3). pap. 6.99 ***(978-0-06-238188-0(1))*** HarperCollins Pubs.

—Why Do Leaves Change Color? Maestro, Betsy. 2015. (Let's-Read-And-Find-Out Science 2 Ser.). (ENG.). 32p. (J). (gr. -1-3). pap. 6.99 ***(978-0-06-238201-6(2))*** HarperCollins Pubs.

Krupnek, Joann J. Sandbox Sandshoes. Eddy, Catherine J. 2009. 38p. pap. 10.95 *(978-0-9818488-5-3(0))* Ajoyin Publishing, Inc.

Krupp, Marian N. No-No & the Secret Touch: The Gentle Story of a Little Seal Who Learns to Stay Safe, Say "No" & Tell! Patterson, Sherri et al. unabr. ed. 70p. (J). (gr. 1-6). pap. 14.95 incl. audio *(978-0-9632276-2-1(9))* National Self-Esteem Resources & Development Ctr.

Kruse, Jason T. Arctic Attack. Greenberger, Robert & Loughridge, Lee. (Batman Ser.). (ENG.). 56p. (gr. 2-3). 2013. pap. 4.95 *(978-1-4342-1728-8(0))*; 2009. 25.32 *(978-1-4342-1561-1(X))* Stone Arch Bks. (DC Super Heroes).

Krush, Beth, et al. Emily's Runaway Imagination. Cleary, Beverly. 2008. (Cleary Reissue Ser.). (ENG.). 288p. (J). (gr. 3-7). pap. 6.99 *(978-0-380-70923-6(6))* HarperCollins Pubs.

Krush, Beth. Senior Year. Emery, Anne. 2006. (YA). per. 11.95 *(978-1-59511-005-3(4))* Image Cascade Publishing.

Krush, Beth & Krush, Joe. The Borrowers. Norton, Mary. 2003. (Borrowers Ser.: 1). (ENG.). 192p. (YA). (gr. 2-5). pap. 6.99 *(978-0-15-204737-5(9))* Houghton Mifflin Harcourt Publishing Co.

—The Borrowers. Norton, Mary. l.t. ed. 2005. 215p. (J). (gr. 3). per. 10.95 *(978-0-7862-7954-8(0))* Thorndike Pr.

—The Borrowers. Norton, Mary. ed. 2003. (Odyssey Classic Ser.). 180p. (gr. 4-7). 17.20 *(978-0-613-63581-3(7)*, Turtleback) Turtleback Bks.

—The Borrowers Afield. Norton, Mary. 50th anniv. ed. 2003. (Borrowers Ser.: 2). (ENG.). 228p. (J). (gr. 2-5). pap. 6.99 *(978-0-15-204732-0(8))* Houghton Mifflin Harcourt Publishing Co.

—The Borrowers Afloat. Norton, Mary. 2003. (Borrowers Ser.: 3). (ENG.). 192p. (J). (gr. 2-5). pap. 6.99 *(978-0-15-204733-7(6))* Houghton Mifflin Harcourt Publishing Co.

—The Borrowers Aloft: Plus the Short Tale Poor Stainless. Norton, Mary. 50th anniv. ed. 2003. (Borrowers Ser.: 4). (ENG.). 228p. (J). (gr. 2-5). pap. 6.99 *(978-0-15-204734-4(4))* Houghton Mifflin Harcourt Publishing Co.

—Gone-Away Lake. Enright, Elizabeth. 2006. 256p. (J). (gr. 4-8). reprint ed. pap. 6.00 *(978-1-4223-5436-0(9))* DIANE Publishing Co.

Krush, Beth, jt. illus. see Krush, Joe.

Krush, Joe, et al. The Borrowers Avenged. Norton, Mary. 50th anniv. ed. 2003. (Borrowers Ser.: 5). (ENG.). 312p. (J). (gr. 2-5). pap. 6.99 *(978-0-15-204731-3(X))* Houghton Mifflin Harcourt Publishing Co.

Krush, Joe & Krush, Beth. Miracles on Maple Hill. Sorensen, Virginia. 2003. (ENG.). 256p. (J). (gr. 2-5). pap. 7.99 *(978-0-15-204718-4(2))* Houghton Mifflin Harcourt Publishing Co.

Krush, Joe, jt. illus. see Krush, Beth.

Krutop, Lee. Ocean Creatures. 2008. (Jigsaw Bks.). 12p. (J). (gr. -1-3). bds. *(978-1-86503-923-7(3))* Five Mile Pr. Pty Ltd. The.

Krygsman, Joan. Rosa Rose. Priest, Robert. 2013. (ENG.). 50p. pap. 10.00 *(978-1-894987-73-8(X))* Wolsak & Wynn Pubs., Ltd. CAN. Dist: Independent Pubs. Group.

Krykorka, Vladyana. A Grain of Sand, 1 vol. Page, P. K. 2003. (ENG.). 28p. (J). *(978-1-55041-801-9(7))* Fitzhenry & Whiteside, Ltd.

—The Littlest Sled Dog, 1 vol. Kusugak, Michael. (ENG.). 32p. (J). (gr. -1-3). 2010. pap. 9.95 *(978-1-55469-174-6(5))*; 2008. 19.95 *(978-1-55143-752-1(X))* Orca Bk. Pubs. USA.

—Orphans in the Sky, 1 vol. Bushey, Jeanne. 2005. (ENG.). 32p. (J). (gr. 1-3). 9.95 *(978-0-88995-291-1(4))* Red Deer Pr. CAN. Dist: Ingram Pub. Services.

Krykorka, Vladyana & Ohi, Ruth. Next Stop!, 1 vol. Page, P. K. & Ellis, Sarah. 2005. (ENG.). 32p. (J). pap. 6.95 *(978-1-55041-809-5(2)*, 1550418092) Fitzhenry & Whiteside, Ltd. CAN. Dist: Midpoint Trade Bks., Inc.

Krykorka, Vladyana, jt. illus. see Krykorka, Vladyana Langer.

Krykorka, Vladyana Langer & Krykorka, Vladyana. My Arctic 1, 2, 3. Kusugak, Michael Arvaarluk & Kusugak, Michael. 2005. (ENG.). 24p. (J). (gr. -1-1). 18.95 *(978-1-55037-505-3(9)*, 9781550375053); pap. 7.95 *(978-1-55037-504-6(0)*, 9781550375046) Annick Pr., Ltd. CAN. Dist: Firefly Bks., Ltd.

Krystoforski, Andrej. Alexander Graham Bell. MacLeod, Elizabeth. 2007. (ENG.). 32p. (J). (gr. -1-3). 3.95 *(978-1-55453-002-1(4))*; 14.95 *(978-1-55453-001-4(6))* Kids Can Pr., Ltd. CAN. Dist: Univ. of Toronto Pr.

—The Boy Who Loved Bananas. Elliott, George. 2005. 32p. (J). (gr. -1-2). 15.95 *(978-1-55337-744-3(3))* Kids Can Pr., Ltd. CAN. Dist: Univ. of Toronto Pr.

—From Then to Now: A Short History of the World. Moore, Christopher. 2011. (ENG.). 192p. (J). (gr. 5-18). 25.95 *(978-0-88776-540-7(8))* Tundra Bks. CAN. Dist: Random Hse., Inc.

—Helen Keller. MacLeod, Elizabeth. 2007. (Kids Can Read Ser.). (ENG.). 32p. (J). (gr. -1-3). 3.95 *(978-1-55453-000-7(8))*; 14.95 *(978-1-55337-999-7(3))* Kids Can Pr., Ltd. CAN. Dist: Univ. of Toronto Pr.

—In the Land of the Jaguar: South America & Its People. Gorrell, Gena K. 2007. (ENG.). 160p. (J). (gr. 4-7). 22.95 *(978-0-88776-756-2(7))* Tundra Bks. CAN. Dist: Random Hse., Inc.

—Mystery of the Lake. Thomas, Cameron. 2004. (Jungle of Utt Ser.). 40p. (J). 16.95 *(978-0-921800-02-6(9))* MGT Developments, Ltd. CAN. Dist: Independent Pubs. Group.

—Shipwrecked on the Island of Skree. Thomas, Cameron. 2004. (Jungle of Utt Ser.). 48p. (J). 16.95 *(978-0-921800-01-9(0))* MGT Developments, Ltd. CAN. Dist: Independent Pubs. Group.

—Thomas Edison. MacLeod, Elizabeth. 2008. (ENG.). 32p. (J). (gr. 1-3). 14.95 *(978-1-55453-057-1(1))*; pap. 3.95 *(978-1-55453-058-8(X))* Kids Can Pr., Ltd. CAN. Dist: Univ. of Toronto Pr.

—The Utt Jungle Airline: The Jungle of Utt. Thomas, Cameron. 2004. (Jungle of Utt Ser.). 48p. (J). 16.95 *(978-0-921800-03-3(7))* MGT Developments, Ltd. CAN. Dist: Independent Pubs. Group.

—The Wright Brothers. MacLeod, Elizabeth. 2008. (Kids Can Read Ser.). (ENG.). 32p. (J). (gr. 1-3). 14.95 *(978-1-55453-053-3(9))*; pap. 3.95 *(978-1-55453-054-0(7))* Kids Can Pr., Ltd. CAN. Dist: Univ. of Toronto Pr.

Ku, Min Sung. Batman Origami: Amazing Folding Projects for the Dark Knight. Montroll, John. 2015. (DC Origami Ser.). (ENG.). 48p. (gr. 4-5). lib. bdg. 27.32 ***(978-1-4914-1786-7(2))*** Capstone Pr., Inc.

—DC Origami. Montroll, John. 2015. (DC Origami Ser.). (ENG.). 48p. (gr. 4-5). 109.28 ***(978-1-4914-1790-4(0)***, DC Super Heroes) Stone Arch Bks.

—DC Super Heroes Origami: 46 Folding Projects for Batman, Superman, Wonder Woman, & More! Montroll, John. 2015. (DC Super Heroes Ser.). (ENG.). 448p. (gr. 4-5). pap. 14.95 ***(978-1-62370-217-5(8))*** Capstone Young Readers.

—Justice League Origami: Amazing Folding Projects for the JLA. Montroll, John. 2015. (DC Origami Ser.). (ENG.). 48p. (gr. 4-5). lib. bdg. 27.32 ***(978-1-4914-1789-8(7))*** Capstone Pr., Inc.

Ku, Min Sung. The Kid Who Saved Superman, 1 vol. Kupperberg, Paul & Loughridge, Lee. (Superman Ser.). (ENG.). 56p. (gr. 2-3). 2013. pap. 4.95 *(978-1-4342-1937-4(2))*; 2009. lib. bdg. 25.32 *(978-1-4342-1936-7(4))* Stone Arch Bks. (DC Super Heroes).

—LEGO Friends: Andrea's New Horse. Simon, Jenne. 2014. (LEGO Friends Ser.). (ENG.). 24p. (J). (gr. -1-3). pap. 3.99 *(978-0-545-78391-0(7))* Scholastic, Inc.

—Superman. Lemke, Donald B. 2014. (DC Super Friends Word Adventures Ser.). (ENG.). 12p. (gr. -1 — 1). bds. 6.99 *(978-1-4795-5243-6(7))* Picture Window Bks.

Ku, Min Sung. Superman Origami: Amazing Folding Projects for the Man of Steel. Montroll, John. 2015. (DC Origami Ser.). (ENG.). 48p. (gr. 4-5). lib. bdg. 27.32 ***(978-1-4914-1787-4(0))*** Capstone Pr., Inc.

Ku, Min Sung. Wonder Woman. Lemke, Donald B. 2014. (DC Super Friends Word Adventures Ser.). (ENG.). 12p. (gr. -1 — 1). bds. 6.99 *(978-1-4795-5244-3(5))* Picture Window Bks.

Ku, Min Sung. Wonder Woman Origami: Amazing Folding Projects for the Warrior Princess. Montroll, John. 2015. (DC Origami Ser.). (ENG.). 48p. (gr. 4-5). lib. bdg. 27.32 ***(978-1-4914-1788-1(9))*** Capstone Pr., Inc.

Kuang, Miao. Jug-a-Ro-Mack-a-la-Lulu-e-Quack-a-la-Lulu-e-Zack-a-la-Lulu-O-Pippin & the Bullies of Badgersville. Jay, Eric. 2011. (ENG.). 40p. pap. 11.99 *(978-1-4499-8058-0(9))* CreateSpace Independent Publishing Platform.

Kubasta, Vojtech. Once upon a Time: Folk & Fairy Tales of the World. Green, Roger Lancelyn, ed. 2011. 140p. 40.95 *(978-1-258-03324-8(0))* Literary Licensing, LLC.

Kubert, Adam, et al. Hellfire & Brimstone, 4 vols. 2006. (ENG.). 144p. (J). (gr. -1-17). pap. 12.99 *(978-0-7851-1089-7(5))* Marvel Worldwide, Inc.

Kubert, Adam. Return to Weapon X, Vol. 2. 2006. (ENG.). 144p. (J). (gr. -1-17). pap. 14.95 *(978-0-7851-0868-9(8))* Marvel Worldwide, Inc.

—Ultimate Fantastic Four - The Fantastic, Vol. 1. Youngquist, Jeff, ed. 2007. (ENG.). 144p. (J). (gr. -1-17). pap. 12.99 *(978-0-7851-1393-5(2))* Marvel Worldwide, Inc.

Kubert, Adam, et al. Ultimate X-Men, 2 vols., Vol. 2. Millar, Mark & Austen, Chuck. 2003. (Ultimate X-Men Ser.). 336p. (YA). 29.99 *(978-0-7851-1130-6(1))* Marvel Worldwide, Inc.

Kubert, Adam & Bachalo, Chris. World Tour. 2006. (ENG.). 192p. (J). (gr. -1-17). pap. 17.99 *(978-0-7851-0961-7(7))* Marvel Worldwide, Inc.

Kubert, Adam & Finch, David. Return of the King, 7 vols. 2006. (ENG.). 192p. (YA). (gr. 8-17). pap. 16.99 *(978-0-7851-1091-0(7))* Marvel Worldwide, Inc.

Kubert, Adam & Kubert, Andy. Tomorrow People, Vol. 1. 2006. (ENG.). 160p. (J). (gr. 4-17). pap. 14.99 *(978-0-7851-0788-0(6))* Marvel Worldwide, Inc.

Kubert, Andy, et al. Captain America: Land of the Free. 2013. (ENG.). 160p. (J). (gr. 4-17). pap. 19.99 *(978-0-7851-6753-2(6))* Marvel Worldwide, Inc.

Kubert, Andy & Ferry, Pasqual. Ultimate Comics Iron Man Ultimate Collection. 2010. (ENG.). 256p. (gr. 10-17). pap. 29.99 *(978-0-7851-4641-4(5))* Marvel Worldwide, Inc.

Kubert, Andy, jt. illus. see Kubert, Adam.

Kubert, Andy, jt. illus. see Quesada, Joe.

Kubic, Ginger. Just in Time. Butler, Dori Hillestad. Trissler, Rebecca Johns, ed. (Adventures of Storydog Ser.). (J). pap. *(978-0-9722690-2-5(9)*, 1002) Storydog, Inc.

—Subway Crush. Bonk, John J. Trissler, Rebecca Johns, ed. (Adventures of Storydog Ser.). 75p. (J). pap. *(978-0-9722690-1-8(0)*, 1001) Storydog, Inc.

Kubick, Dana. I Love You, Grandpa. French, Vivian. 2006. (ENG.). 32p. (J). (gr. -1-2). 5.99 *(978-0-7636-2748-5(8))* Candlewick Pr.

—A Present for Santa Claus. Wood, David. 2008. (ENG.). 24p. (J). (gr. -1-3). 16.99 *(978-0-7636-3858-0(7))* Candlewick Pr.

Kubinyi, Laszlo. Dig It! Riggs, Kate. 2013. (ENG.). 14p. (J). (gr. -1-k). bds. 7.99 *(978-1-56846-237-0(9)*, Creative Editions) Creative Co., The.

K

—Goldilocks. Roberts, Tom. 2005. (Rabbit Ears: A Classic Tale Ser.). 28p. (gr. 2-7). 25.65 (978-1-59197-748-3(7)) Spotlight.

—Red Riding Hood. Roberts, Tom. 2005. (Rabbit Ears: A Classic Tale Ser.). 28p. (gr. 2-7). 25.65 (978-1-59197-752-0(5)) Spotlight.

—Skywriting: Poems to Fly. Lewis, J. Patrick. 2010. (ENG.). 32p. (J). (gr. 4-7). 17.95 (978-1-56846-203-5(4), Creative Editions) Creative Co., The.

Kubinyi, Laszlo. Survivors: the Gathering Darkness #1: a Pack Divided. Hunter, Erin. 2015. (Survivors: the Gathering Darkness Ser.: 1). (ENG.). 288p. (J). (gr. 3-7). 16.99 **(978-0-06-234333-8(5))** HarperCollins Pubs.

Kubinyi, Laszlo, jt. illus. see Dogi, Fiammetta.

Kubler, Annie. Baa, Baa, Black Sheep! 2005. (ENG.). 12p. (J). bds. (978-1-904550-01-3(0)) Child's Play International Ltd.

—Dive in, Ducky! 2009. (Chatterboox Ser.). (ENG.). 12p. (J). (gr. -1). bds. (978-1-84643-290-3(1)) Child's Play International Ltd.

—Dress Up! 2012. (Mix & Match Babies Ser.). (ENG.). 12p. (J). bds. (978-1-84643-485-3(8)) Child's Play International Ltd.

—Hickory Dickory Dock. 2014. (Classic Books with Holes Big Book Ser.). (ENG.). 16p. (J). (978-1-84643-667-3(2)) Child's Play International Ltd.

—Hop a Little, Jump a Little! 2010. (Baby Board Bks.). (ENG.). 12p. (J). bds. (978-1-84643-341-2(X)) Child's Play International Ltd.

—Humpty Dumpty. 2010. (Baby Board Bks.). (ENG.). 12p. (J). bds. (978-1-84643-339-9(8)) Child's Play International Ltd.

—Incey Wincey Spider. 2005. (ENG.). 12p. (J). bds. (978-1-904550-03-7(7)) Child's Play International Ltd.

—Itsy Bitsy Spider. 2014. (Classic Books with Holes Big Book Ser.). (ENG.). 16p. (J). (978-1-84643-666-6(4)) Child's Play International Ltd.

—Mary Had a Little Lamb. 2014. (Classic Books with Holes Big Book Ser.). (ENG.). 16p. (J). (978-1-84643-669-7(9)) Child's Play International Ltd.

—The Mixed up Caterpillar. 2006. (Finger Puppet Bks.). (ENG.). 24p. (J). (978-1-84643-026-8(7)) Child's Play International Ltd.

—My First Signs. 2005. (Baby Signing Ser.). (ENG.). 12p. (J). (gr. -1). bds. (978-1-904550-39-6(8)); bds. (978-1-904550-04-4(5)) Child's Play International Ltd.

—Pat-A-Cake! 2010. (Baby Board Bks.). (ENG.). 12p. (J). bds. (978-1-84643-338-2(X)) Child's Play International Ltd.

—Pat-A-Cake! Nursery Rhymes. 2005. (Nursery Time Ser.). (ENG.). 12p. (J). (gr. -1-k). bds. (978-1-904550-82-2(7)) Child's Play International Ltd.

—Peek-A-Boo! Nursery Games. 2005. (Nursery Time Ser.). (ENG.). 12p. (J). (gr. -1-k). bds. (978-1-904550-83-9(5)) Child's Play International Ltd.

—Pinocchio. 2014. (Flip-Up Fairy Tales Ser.). (ENG.). 24p. (J). (978-1-84643-653-6(2)) Child's Play International Ltd.

—Play Time, Puppy! 2009. (Chatterboox Ser.). (ENG.). 12p. (J). (gr. -1). bds. (978-1-84643-289-7(8)) Child's Play International Ltd.

—Pussy Cat, Pussy Cat. 2010. (Baby Board Bks.). (ENG.). 12p. (J). bds. (978-1-84643-340-5(1)) Child's Play International Ltd.

—Ride On! 2012. (Mix & Match Babies Ser.). (ENG.). 12p. (J). bds. (978-1-84643-483-9(1)) Child's Play International Ltd.

—See Saw! Nursery Songs. 2005. (Nursery Time Ser.). (ENG.). 12p. (J). (gr. -1-k). bds. (978-1-904550-81-5(9)) Child's Play International Ltd.

—Sleep Tight, Teddy! 2009. (Chatterboox Ser.). (ENG.). 12p. (J). (gr. -1). bds. (978-1-84643-291-0(X)) Child's Play International Ltd.

—Teddy Bear, Teddy Bear. 2005. (Sign & Singalong Ser.). (ENG.). 12p. (J). (gr. -1). bds. (978-1-904550-40-2(1)) Child's Play International Ltd.

—Twinkle, Twinkle, Little Star. 2005. (Sign & Singalong Ser.). (ENG.). 12p. (J). (gr. -1). bds. (978-1-904550-42-6(8)); bds. (978-1-904550-02-0(9)) Child's Play International Ltd.

—What Can I Feel? 2011. (Small Senses Ser.). (ENG.). 12p. (J). bds. (978-1-84643-374-0(6)) Child's Play International Ltd.

—What Can I Hear? 2011. (Small Senses Ser.). (ENG.). 12p. (J). bds. (978-1-84643-377-1(0)) Child's Play International Ltd.

—What Can I Look? 2011. (Small Senses Ser.). (ENG.). 12p. (J). bds. (978-1-84643-378-8(9)) Child's Play International Ltd.

—What Can I Smell? 2011. (Small Senses Ser.). (ENG.). 12p. (J). bds. (978-1-84643-376-4(2)) Child's Play International Ltd.

—What Can I Taste? 2011. (Small Senses Ser.). (ENG.). 12p. (J). bds. (978-1-84643-375-7(4)) Child's Play International Ltd.

Kubler, Annie. What Do I Feel? / ¿Qué Siento? Mlawer, Teresa, tr. ed. 2015. (Small Senses Bilingual Ser.: 5). (ENG & SPA.). 12p. (J). bds. **(978-1-84643-721-2(0))** Child's Play International Ltd.

—What Do I Hear? / ¿Qué Oigo? Mlawer, Teresa, tr. ed. 2015. (Small Senses Bilingual Ser.: 5). (ENG & SPA.). 12p. (J). bds. **(978-1-84643-724-3(5))** Child's Play International Ltd.

—What Do I See? / ¿Qué Veo? Mlawer, Teresa, tr. ed. 2015. (Small Senses Bilingual Ser.: 5). (ENG & SPA.). 12p. (J). bds. **(978-1-84643-725-0(3))** Child's Play International Ltd.

—What Do I Smell? / ¿Qué Huelo? Mlawer, Teresa, tr. ed. 2015. (Small Senses Bilingual Ser.: 5). (ENG & SPA.). 12p. (J). bds. **(978-1-84643-723-6(7))** Child's Play International Ltd.

—What Do I Taste? / ¿Qué Saboreo? Mlawer, Teresa, tr. ed. 2015. (Small Senses Bilingual Ser.: 5). (ENG & SPA.). 12p. (J). bds. **(978-1-84643-722-9(9))** Child's Play International Ltd.

Kubler, Annie. What's the Time, Mr. Wolf? 2003. (Finger Puppet Bks.). (ENG.). 24p. (J). (gr. -1-1). (978-0-85953-944-9(X)) Child's Play International Ltd.

—The Wheels on the Bus: Go Round & Round. 2007. (Classic Books with Holes 8x8 with CD Ser.). (ENG.). 16p. (J). (gr. -1-1). (978-1-904550-66-2(5)) Child's Play International Ltd.

—Work Out! 2012. (Mix & Match Babies Ser.). (ENG.). 12p. (J). bds. (978-1-84643-484-6(X)) Child's Play International Ltd.

Kubler, Annie. Wheels on the Bus, 15 vols. Kubler, Annie. 2005. 14p. (J). (ARA, ENG & MUL.). bds. (978-1-84444-970-5(X)); (BEN, ENG & MUL.). bds. (978-1-84444-971-2(8)); (ENG, CHI & MUL.). bds. (978-1-84444-972-9(6)); (CHI, ENG & MUL.). bds. (978-1-84444-973-6(4)); (ENG, FRE & MUL.). bds. (978-1-84444-974-3(2)); (ENG, HIN & MUL.). bds. (978-1-84444-975-0(0)); (ENG, SOM & MUL.). bds. (978-1-84444-978-1(5)); (ENG, TUR & MUL.). bds. (978-1-84444-980-4(7)); (URD, ENG & MUL.). bds. (978-1-84444-981-1(5)) Mantra Lingua.

—The Wheels on the Bus, 15 vols. Kubler, Annie. 14p. (J). 2005. (ENG, PER & MUL.). bds. (978-1-84444-532-5(1)); 2005. (SWA, ENG & MUL.). bds. (978-1-84444-533-2(X)); 2004. (ENG, TGL & MUL.). bds. (978-1-84444-534-9(8)) Mantra Lingua.

Kubler, Annie. The Wheels on the Bus Go Round & Round. Kubler, Annie, tr. 2003. (Classic Books with Holes 8x8 Ser.). (ENG.). 16p. (J). (978-0-85953-136-8(8)) Child's Play International Ltd.

Kubler, Annie & Nascimbeni, Barbara. Little Miss Muffet. 2014. (Classic Books with Holes Big Book Ser.). (ENG.). 16p. (J). (978-1-84643-668-0(0)) Child's Play International Ltd.

Kubley, Ashley Newsome. Boho Fashion. Kenney, Karen Latchana. 2014. (What's Your Style? Ser.). (ENG.). 48p. (gr. 5-8). lib. bdg. 30.60 (978-1-4677-1470-9(4), Lerner Pubns.) Lerner Publishing Group.

—Streetwear Fashion. Watson, Stephanie. 2014. (What's Your Style? Ser.). (ENG.). 48p. (gr. 5-8). lib. bdg. 30.60 (978-1-4677-1471-6(2), Lerner Pubns.) Lerner Publishing Group.

Kubo, Tite. Bleach. Kubo, Tite. (Bleach Ser.: 30). (ENG.). (gr. 8-18). 2010. 192p. pap. 9.99 (978-1-4215-2388-0(4)); 2009. 216p. pap. 7.95 (978-1-4215-2384-2(1)) Viz Media.

—Bleach. Kubo, Tite. Wall, Frances, ed. 2007. (Bleach Ser.: 21). (ENG.). 200p. (gr. 8-13). pap. 9.99 (978-1-4215-1165-8(7)) Viz Media.

—Bleach. Kubo, Tite. Caselman, Lance. (Bleach Ser.: Vol. 20). (ENG.). 2007. 216p. pap. 9.99 (978-1-4215-1044-6(8)); 2007. 216p. pap. 9.99 (978-1-4215-1043-9(X)); 2007. 216p. pap. 9.99 (978-1-4215-1042-2(1)); 2006. 208p. pap. 9.99 (978-1-4215-0612-8(2)); 2006. 192p. pap. 9.99 (978-1-4215-0611-1(4)); 2006. 208p. pap. 9.99 (978-1-4215-0403-2(0)); 2006. 208p. pap. 9.99 (978-1-4215-0271-7(2)); 2005. 200p. pap. 9.99 (978-1-4215-0081-2(7)); 2005. 200p. pap. 9.99 (978-1-59116-924-6(0)); 2005. 200p. pap. 9.99 (978-1-59116-872-0(4)); 2005. 200p. (gr. 8-13). pap. 9.99 (978-1-59116-728-0(0)); 2005. 192p. pap. 9.99 (978-1-59116-445-6(1)); 2004. 192p. pap. 9.99 (978-1-59116-444-9(3)); 2004. 192p. pap. 9.99 (978-1-59116-443-2(5)); 2004. 192p. pap. 9.99 (978-1-59116-442-5(7)); 2004. 192p. pap. 9.99 (978-1-59116-441-8(9)) Viz Media.

—The Broken Coda. Kubo, Tite. Caselman, Lance. 2005. (Bleach Ser.: Vol. 7). (ENG.). 200p. pap. 9.99 (978-1-59116-807-2(4)) Viz Media.

—Zombie Powder. Kubo, Tite. 2007. (Zombie Powder Ser.: Vol. 4). (ENG.). 200p. pap. 7.99 (978-1-4215-1122-1(3)); 208p. pap. 7.99 (978-1-4215-1121-4(5)) Viz Media.

Kucharik, Elena. Bed Time Blessings. Mackall, Dandi Daley. 2012. (Little Blessings Ser.). (ENG.). 32p. (J). pap. 3.99 (978-1-4143-7528-1(X)) Tyndale Hse. Pubs.

—Bedtime Stories & Prayers. Mackall, Dandi Daley & Bostrom, Kathleen Long. 2013. (Little Blessings Ser.). (ENG.). 128p. (J). 14.99 (978-1-4143-8111-4(5)) Tyndale Hse. Pubs.

—Easter Stories & Prayers. Bostrom, Kathleen Long. 2015. (Little Blessings Ser.). (ENG.). 144p. (J). 7.99 (978-1-4964-0280-6(4)) Tyndale Hse. Pubs.

—Is God Always with Me? Bowman, Crystal. 2005. (Little Blessings Ser.). (ENG.). 64p. (J). 9.99 (978-1-4143-0287-4(8)) Tyndale Hse. Pubs.

—No, No Noah!, 1 vol. Mackall, Dandi Daley. 2007. (ENG.). 26p. (gr. -1-k). bds. 6.99 (978-1-4003-1007-4(5)) Nelson, Thomas Inc.

—The One Year Devotions for Preschoolers. Bowman, Crystal. 2004. (Little Blessings Ser.). (ENG.). 384p. (J). 14.99 (978-0-8423-8940-2(7), Tyndale Kids) Tyndale Hse. Pubs.

—The One Year Devotions for Preschoolers 2. Barnhill, Carla. 2009. (Little Blessings Ser.). (ENG.). 384p. (J). 14.99 (978-1-4143-3445-5(1), Tyndale Kids) Tyndale Hse. Pubs.

—Questions from Little Hearts. Bostrom, Kathleen Long. 2009. (Little Blessings Ser.). (ENG.). 288p. (J). (gr. -1-k). 14.99 (978-1-4143-2998-7(9)) Tyndale Hse. Pubs.

—What about Heaven? Bostrom, Kathleen Long. 2012. (Little Blessings Ser.). (ENG.). 32p. (J). pap. 3.99 (978-1-4143-7510-6(7)) Tyndale Hse. Pubs.

—Who Made the World? Bostrom, Kathleen Long. 2009. (Little Blessings Ser.). (ENG.). 80p. (J). (gr. -1-1). 9.99 (978-1-4143-2011-3(6), Tyndale Kids) Tyndale Hse. Pubs.

—Why Is There a Cross? Bostrom, Kathleen Long. 2005. (Little Blessings Ser.). (ENG.). 64p. (J). (gr. 4-7). 9.99 (978-1-4143-0288-1(6)) Tyndale Hse. Pubs.

Kuefler, Joseph. Beyond the Pond. Kuefler, Joseph. 2015. (ENG.). 40p. (J). (gr. -1-3). 17.99 **(978-0-06-236427-2(8))** HarperCollins Pubs.

Kueker, Donald. The Easter Story According to Matthew. 2007. 32p. (J). per. 7.49 (978-0-7586-1008-9(4)) Concordia Publishing Hse.

Kuerner, Karl J., jt. illus. see Wyeth, Andrew N.

Kuga, Cain. Cowboy Bebop, 2 vols. Yadate, Hajime. 2003. pap. 44.99 (978-1-59182-590-6(3)) TOKYOPOP, Inc.

Kuga, Cain. Cowboy Bebop: Shooting Star, 2 vols., Vol. 2. Kuga, Cain. Nakamura, Yuki, tr. from JPN. rev. ed. 2003. 192p. (gr. 8-18). pap. 9.99 (978-1-59182-298-1(X)) TOKYOPOP, Inc.

—Cowboy Bebop Shooting Star, 2, 1. Kuga, Cain. 2003. 192p. (gr. 8-18). pap. 9.99 (978-1-59182-297-4(1)) TOKYOPOP, Inc.

Kügler, Carson, jt. illus. see Kügler, Tina.

Kügler, Tina. The Change Your Name Store. Shirtliffe, Leanne. 2014. (ENG.). 32p. (J). (gr. -1-k). 16.95 (978-1-62873-608-3(9), Sky Pony Pr.) Skyhorse Publishing Co., Inc.

Kügler, Tina & Kügler, Carson. In Mary's Garden. Kügler, Tina & Kügler, Carson. 2015. (ENG.). 32p. (J). (gr. 1-4). 16.99 (978-0-544-27220-0(X), HMH Books For Young Readers) Houghton Mifflin Harcourt Publishing Co.

Kügler, Tina & Kügler, Carson. Snail & Worm: Meet My Friend. 2016. (J). **(978-0-544-49412-1(1))** Harcourt.

Kuhn, Andy. Michelangelo. Lynch, Brian. 2015. (J). **(978-1-61479-340-3(9))** Spotlight.

Kuhn, Douglas W. Little Chick: Learns to Trust in the Lord, 1 vol. Kuhn, Tom B. 2009. 23p. pap. 24.95 (978-1-60836-929-4(3)) America Star Bks.

Kuhn, Douglas Wolcik. Uncle Kyle's Magic Kite. Kuhn, Douglas Wolcik. 2012. 28p. pap. 24.95 (978-1-4626-9699-4(6)) America Star Bks.

Kuhn, Dwight. Bugs. Kuhn, Dwight, photos by. Pascoe, Elaine. 2003. 48p. (J). 23.70 (978-1-56711-458-4(X), Blackbirch Pr., Inc.) Cengage Gale.

—Where Else in the Wild? Kuhn, Dwight, photos by. Schwartz, David M. & Schy, Yael. 2009. (ENG.). 50p. (J). (gr. -1-2). 16.99 (978-1-58246-283-7(6), Tricycle Pr.) Ten Speed Pr.

Kuhn, Dwight, photos by. Animal Noses. Schwartz, David M. (Plants & Animals Ser.). 16p. (J). (gr. 1-3). pap. 2.99 (978-1-57471-321-3(3), 3030) Creative Teaching Pr., Inc.

—Bean. Schwartz, David M. (Life Cycles Ser.). 16p. (J). (gr. 1-3). pap. 2.99 (978-1-57471-580-4(1), 3060) Creative Teaching Pr., Inc.

—Fighting Fish. Schwartz, David M. (Life Cycles Ser.). 16p. (J). (gr. 1-3). pap. 2.99 (978-1-57471-560-6(7), 3070) Creative Teaching Pr., Inc.

—Green Snake. Schwartz, David M. (Life Cycles Ser.). 16p. (J). (gr. 1-3). pap. 2.99 (978-1-57471-557-6(7), 3067) Creative Teaching Pr., Inc.

—Look Once Look Again Collection Box Set. Schwartz, David M. 2005. (Look Once, Look Again! Ser.). (J). pap. 549.00 incl. audio compact disk (978-1-59198-170-1(0), CTP 3269) Creative Teaching Pr., Inc.

—What in the Wild? Mysteries of Nature Concealed... And Revealed. Schy, Yael & Schwartz, David. 2010. (ENG., 44p. (J). (gr. 1-4). 16.99 (978-1-58246-310-0(7), Tricycle Pr.) Ten Speed Pr.

—Where in the Wild? Camouflaged Creatures Concealed... & Revealed. Schwartz, David M. & Schy, Yael. 2011. (ENG., 44p. (J). (gr. -1-2). pap. 8.99 (978-1-58246-399-5(9), Tricycle Pr.) Ten Speed Pr.

Kuhn, Dwight, photos by. Where in the Wild? Camouflaged Creatures Concealed... & Revealed. Kuhn, Dwight. Schwartz, David M. & Schy, Yael. 2007. (ENG., 44p. (J). (gr. -1-2). 16.99 (978-1-58246-207-3(0), Tricycle Pr.) Ten Speed Pr.

Kuhn, Jesse. Andy Acid, 26 vols. Cook, Sherry & Johnson, Terri. l.t. ed. 2006. (Quirkles — Exploring Phonics through Science Ser.: 1). 32p. (J). 7.99 (978-1-933815-00-8(0), Quirkles, The) Creative 3, LLC.

—Botanist Bert, 26 vols. Cook, Sherry & Johnson, Terri. l.t. ed. 2006. (Quirkles — Exploring Phonics through Science Ser.: 2). 32p. (J). 7.99 (978-1-933815-01-5(9), Quirkles, The) Creative 3, LLC.

—Colorful Caroline, 26 vols. Cook, Sherry & Johnson, Terri. l.t. ed. 2006. (Quirkles — Exploring Phonics through Science Ser.: 3). 32p. (J). 7.99 (978-1-933815-02-2(7), Quirkles, The) Creative 3, LLC.

—Density Dan, 26 vols. Cook, Sherry & Johnson, Terri. l.t. ed. 2006. (Quirkles — Exploring Phonics through Science Ser.: 4). 32p. (J). 7.99 (978-1-933815-03-9(5), Quirkles, The) Creative 3, LLC.

—Ellie Electricity, 26 vols. Cook, Sherry & Johnson, Terri. l.t. ed. 2006. (Quirkles — Exploring Phonics through Science Ser.: 5). 32p. (J). 7.99 (978-1-933815-04-6(3), Quirkles, The) Creative 3, LLC.

—Friction Fred, 26 vols. Cook, Sherry & Johnson, Terri. l.t. ed. 2006. (Quirkles — Exploring Phonics through Science Ser.: 6). 32p. (J). 7.99 (978-1-933815-05-3(1), Quirkles, The) Creative 3, LLC.

—Gilbert Gas, 26 vols. Cook, Sherry & Johnson, Terri. l.t. ed. 2006. (Quirkles — Exploring Phonics through Science Ser.: 7). 32p. (J). 7.99 (978-1-933815-06-0(X), Quirkles, The) Creative 3, LLC.

—Hallie Heat, 26 vols. Cook, Sherry & Johnson, Terri. l.t. ed. 2006. (Quirkles — Exploring Phonics through Science Ser.: 8). 32p. (J). 7.99 (978-1-933815-07-7(8), Quirkles, The) Creative 3, LLC.

—Inquisitive Inman, 26 vols. Cook, Sherry & Johnson, Terri. l.t. ed. 2006. (Quirkles — Exploring Phonics through Science Ser.: 9). 32p. (J). 7.99 (978-1-933815-08-4(6), Quirkles, The) Creative 3, LLC.

—Jazzy Jet, 26 vols. Cook, Sherry & Johnson, Terri. l.t. ed. 2006. (Quirkles — Exploring Phonics through Science Ser.: 10). 32p. (J). 7.99 (978-1-933815-09-1(4), Quirkles, The) Creative 3, LLC.

—Kitchen Chemistry Kal, 26 vols. Cook, Sherry & Johnson, Terri. l.t. ed. 2006. (Quirkles — Exploring Phonics through Science Ser.: 11). 32p. (J). 7.99 (978-1-933815-10-7(8), Quirkles, The) Creative 3, LLC.

—Mary Motion, 26 vols. Cook, Sherry & Johnson, Terri. l.t. ed. 2006. (Quirkles — Exploring Phonics through Science Ser.: 13). 32p. (J). 7.99 (978-1-933815-12-1(4), Quirkles, The) Creative 3, LLC.

—Nosey Nina, 26 vols. Cook, Sherry & Johnson, Terri. l.t. ed. 2006. (Quirkles — Exploring Phonics through Science Ser.: 14). 32p. (J). 7.99 (978-1-933815-13-8(2), Quirkles, The) Creative 3, LLC.

—Ollie Oxygen, 26 vols. Cook, Sherry & Johnson, Terri. l.t. ed. 2006. (Quirkles — Exploring Phonics through Science Ser.: 15). 32p. (J). 7.99 (978-1-933815-14-5(0), Quirkles, The) Creative 3, LLC.

—Pressure Pete, 26 vols. Cook, Sherry & Johnson, Terri. l.t. ed. 2006. (Quirkles — Exploring Phonics through Science Ser.: 16). 32p. (J). 7.99 (978-1-933815-15-2(9), Quirkles, The) Creative 3, LLC.

—Quincy Quake, 26. Cook, Sherry & Johnson, Terri. l.t. ed. 2006. (Quirkles — Exploring Phonics through Science Ser.: 17). 32p. (J). 7.99 (978-1-933815-16-9(7), Quirkles, The) Creative 3, LLC.

—Ronnie Rock, 26. Cook, Sherry & Johnson, Terri. l.t. ed. 2006. (Quirkles — Exploring Phonics through Science Ser.: 18). 32p. (J). 7.99 (978-1-933815-17-6(5), Quirkles, The) Creative 3, LLC.

—Susie Sound, 26. Cook, Sherry & Johnson, Terri. l.t. ed. 2006. 32p. (J). 7.99 (978-1-933815-18-3(3), Quirkles, The) Creative 3, LLC.

—Timothy Tornado, 26. Cook, Sherry & Johnson, Terri. l.t. ed. 2006. (Quirkles — Exploring Phonics through Science Ser.: 20). 32p. 7.99 (978-1-933815-19-0(1), Quirkles, The) Creative 3, LLC.

—Underwater Utley, 26. Cook, Sherry & Johnson, Martin. l.t. ed. 2006. (Quirkles — Exploring Phonics through Science Ser.: 21). 32p. (J). 7.99 (978-1-933815-20-6(5), Quirkles, The) Creative 3, LLC.

—Vinnie Volcano, 26. Cook, Sherry & Johnson, Terri. l.t. ed. 2006. (Quirkles — Exploring Phonics through Science Ser.: 22). 32p. (J). 7.99 (978-1-933815-21-3(3), Quirkles, The) Creative 3, LLC.

—Watery William, 26. Cook, Sherry & Johnson, Terri. l.t. ed. 2006. (Quirkles — Exploring Phonics through Science Ser.: 23). 32p. (J). 7.99 (978-1-933815-22-0(1), Quirkles, The) Creative 3, LLC.

—X. E. Ecology, 26. Cook, Sherry & Johnson, Terri. l.t. ed. 2006. (Quirkles — Exploring Phonics through Science Ser.: 24). 32p. (J). 7.99 (978-1-933815-23-7(X), Quirkles, The) Creative 3, LLC.

—Zany Science Zeke, 26. Cook, Sherry & Johnson, Terri. l.t. ed. 2006. (Quirkles — Exploring Phonics through Science Ser.: 26). 32p. (J). 7.99 (978-1-933815-25-1(6), Quirkles, The) Creative 3, LLC.

Kujiradov, Misaho. Princess Ai: Lumination, 3 vols., Vol. 2. Kujiradov, Misaho. Milky, D. J. Fujikawa, Kimiko & Johnson, Yuki N., trs. from JPN. 2005. 192p. (YA). pap. 9.99 (978-1-59182-670-5(5)) TOKYOPOP, Inc.

Kukahiko, Puni. Kou Lima. Honda, Liana. 2010. 22p. 8.00 (978-0-87336-236-8(5)) Kamehameha Publishing.

—Kou Wawae. Honda, Liana. 2010. 22p. 8.00 (978-0-87336-237-5(3)) Kamehameha Publishing.

Kuklin, Susan, photos by. Beyond Magenta: Transgender Teens Speak Out. Kuklin, Susan. 2015. (ENG., 192p. (YA). (gr. 9). pap. 12.99 (978-0-7636-7368-0(4)) Candlewick Pr.

Kukreja, Julie. Jesus, I Believe. Harrah, Judith. 2012. 34p. (J). pap. 10.99 (978-1-937331-10-8(5)) ShadeTree Publishing, LLC.

Kulak, Jeff & Owlkids Books Inc. Staff. Learn to Speak Dance: A Guide to Creating, Performing & Promoting Your Moves. Williams, Ann-Marie. 2011. (Learn to Speak Ser.). (ENG.). 96p. (J). (gr. 4-7). pap. 14.95 (978-1-926818-89-4(X)) Owlkids Bks. Inc. CAN. Dist: Perseus-PGW.

—Learn to Speak Fashion: A Guide to Creating, Showcasing, & Promoting Your Style. deCarufel, Laura. 2012. (Learn to Speak Ser.). (ENG.). 96p. (J). (gr. 4-8). pap. 14.95 (978-1-926973-42-5(9), Owlkids) Owlkids Bks. Inc. CAN. Dist: Perseus-PGW.

—Learn to Speak Film: A Guide to Creating, Promoting & Screening Your Movies. Glassbourg, Michael. 2013. (Learn to Speak Ser.). (ENG.). 96p. (J). (gr. 4-8). pap. 14.95 (978-1-926973-85-2(2), Maple Tree Pr.) Owlkids Bks. Inc. CAN. Dist: Perseus-PGW.

—Learn to Speak Music: A Guide to Creating, Performing, & Promoting Your Songs. Crossingham, John. 2009. (Learn to Speak Ser.). (ENG.). 96p. (J). (gr. 4-7). pap. 17.95 (978-1-897349-65-6(3)) Owlkids Bks. Inc. CAN. Dist: Perseus-PGW.

—Starting from Scratch: What You Should Know about Food & Cooking, 0 vols. Elton, Sarah. 2014. (ENG.). 96p. (J). (gr. 5). 18.95 (978-1-926973-96-8(8), Owlkids) Owlkids Bks. Inc. CAN. Dist: Perseus-PGW.

Kulihin, Vic. Super Hockey Infographics. Savage, Jeff. 2015. (Super Sports Infographics Ser.). (ENG.). 32p. (gr. 3-5). pap. 8.99 (978-1-4677-7577-9(0), Lerner Pubns.) Lerner Publishing Group.

—US Culture Through Infographics. Higgins, Nadia. 2014. (Super Social Studies Infographics Ser.). 32p. (gr. 3-5). pap. 8.95 (978-1-4677-4565-9(0)) Lerner Publishing Group.

Kulihin, Vic, jt. illus. see Thompson, Bryon.

Kulikov, Boris. Albert Einstein. Krull, Kathleen. (Giants of Science Ser.). (ENG.). 144p. (J). (gr. 3-7). 2015. 7.99 (978-0-14-751464-6(9), Puffin); 2009. 15.99 (978-0-670-06332-1(0), Viking Juvenile) Penguin Publishing Group.

—Barnum's Bones: How Barnum Brown Discovered the Most Famous Dinosaur in the World, 1 vol. Fern, Tracey E. 2012. (ENG.). 36p. (J). (gr. k-4). 17.99 (978-0-374-30516-1(1), Farrar, Straus & Giroux (BYR)) Farrar, Straus & Giroux.

—Benjamin Franklin. Krull, Kathleen. (Giants of Science Ser.). (ENG.). 128p. (J). (gr. 3-7). 2014. pap. 7.99 (978-0-14-751178-2(X), Puffin); 2013. 15.99 (978-0-670-01287-9(4), Viking Juvenile) Penguin Publishing Group.

—The Boy Who Cried Wolf. Hennessy, B. G. 2006. (ENG.). 40p. (J). (gr. -1-3). 17.99 (978-0-689-87433-8(2), Simon & Schuster Bks. For Young Readers) Simon & Schuster Bks. For Young Readers.

—The Boy Who Cried Wolf. Hennessy, B. G. 2011. (J). (gr. -1-2). 29.95 (978-0-545-09452-8(6)) Weston Woods Studios, Inc.

—The Carnival of the Animals. Lithgow, John. 2004. (ENG.). 40p. (J). (gr. -1-3). 19.99 *(978-0-689-86721-7(2)*, Simon & Schuster Bks. For Young Readers) Simon & Schuster Bks. For Young Readers.
—Carnival of the Animals. Lithgow, John. 2007. (ENG.). 40p. (J). (gr. -1-3). 7.99 *(978-0-689-87343-0(3)*, Simon & Schuster Bks. For Young Readers) Simon & Schuster Bks. For Young Readers.
—The Castle on Hester Street. Heller, Linda. 2007. (ENG.). 40p. (J). (gr. -1-3). 17.99 *(978-0-689-87434-5(0)*, Simon & Schuster Bks. For Young Readers) Simon & Schuster Bks. For Young Readers.
—Charles Darwin. Krull, Kathleen. (Giants of Science Ser.). (ENG.). 144p. (J). (gr. 3-7). 2015. 7.99 *(978-0-14-751463-9(0)*, Puffin); 2010. 15.99 *(978-0-670-06335-2(5)*, Viking Juvenile) Penguin Publishing Group.
Kulikov, Boris. Come Home, Angus. Downes, Patrick. 2016. (J). ***(978-0-545-59768-5(4))*** Scholastic, Inc.
Kulikov, Boris. The Eraserheads. Banks, Kate. 2010. (ENG.). 40p. (J). (gr. -1-3). 16.99 *(978-0-374-39920-7(4)*, Farrar, Straus & Giroux (BYR)) Farrar, Straus & Giroux.
—Fartiste. Krull, Kathleen & Brewer, Paul. 2008. (ENG.). 40p. (J). (gr. -1-3). 17.99 *(978-1-4169-2828-7(6)*, Simon & Schuster Bks. For Young Readers) Simon & Schuster Bks. For Young Readers.
—Isaac Newton. Krull, Kathleen. 2008. (Giants of Science Ser.). (ENG.). 128p. (J). (gr. 3-7). 7.99 *(978-0-14-240820-9(4)*, Puffin) Penguin Publishing Group.
—Leonardo Da Vinci. Krull, Kathleen. 2008. (Giants of Science Ser.). (ENG.). 128p. (J). (gr. 3-7). 7.99 *(978-0-14-240821-6(2)*, Puffin) Penguin Publishing Group.
—Max's Castle. Banks, Kate. 2011. (Max's Words Ser.: 3). (ENG.). 40p. (J). (gr. -1-3). 16.99 *(978-0-374-39919-1(0)*, Farrar, Straus & Giroux (BYR)) Farrar, Straus & Giroux.
—Max's Dragon. Banks, Kate. 2008. (Max's Words Ser.: 2). (ENG.). 32p. (J). (gr. -1-3). 17.99 *(978-0-374-39921-4(2)*, Farrar, Straus & Giroux (BYR)) Farrar, Straus & Giroux.
—Max's Math. Banks, Kate. 2015. (Max's Words Ser.: 4). (ENG.). 40p. (J). (gr. -1-3). 17.99 *(978-0-374-34875-5(8)*, Farrar, Straus & Giroux (BYR)) Farrar, Straus & Giroux.
—Max's Words. Banks, Kate. 2006. (Max's Words Ser.: 1). (ENG.). 32p. (J). (gr. -1-3). 17.99 *(978-0-374-39949-8(2)*, Farrar, Straus & Giroux (BYR)) Farrar, Straus & Giroux.
—Papa's Mechanical Fish. Fleming, Candace. 2013. (ENG.). 40p. (J). (gr. k-3). 16.99 *(978-0-374-39908-5(5)*, Farrar, Straus & Giroux (BYR)) Farrar, Straus & Giroux.
—Sandy's Circus: A Story about Alexander Calder. Stone, Tanya Lee. 2008. (ENG.). 40p. (J). (gr. 1-3). 16.99 *(978-0-670-06268-3(5)*, Viking Juvenile) Penguin Publishing Group.
Kulikov, Boris. Six Dots: A Story of Young Louis Braille. Bryant, Jennifer. 2016. (J). ***(978-0-449-81337-9(1))*** Knopf, Alfred A. Inc.
Kulikovsky-Romanoff, Grand Duchess Olga Alexandrovna. The Adventures of Three White Bears. 2011. 26p. (J). pap. *(978-0-9716365-2-1(4)*, St. Nicholas Pr.) CrossBearers Publishing.
Kulka, Joe. Gingerbread Man Superhero!, 1 vol. Enderle, Dotti. 2009. (ENG.). 32p. (J). (gr. k-3). 16.99 *(978-1-58980-521-7(6))* Pelican Publishing Co., Inc.
—Granny Gert & the Bunion Brothers, 1 vol. Enderle, Dotti. 2006. (ENG.). 32p. (J). (gr. k-3). 16.99 *(978-1-58980-373-2(6))* Pelican Publishing Co., Inc.
—Monkey Math. Brimner, Larry Dane. 2007. (Rookie Reader Skill Set Ser.). (ENG.). 32p. (J). (gr. k-2). pap. 4.95 *(978-0-531-13850-2(X))* Scholastic Library Publishing.
—My Crocodile Does Not Bite. 2013. (ENG.). 32p. (J). (gr. k-3). lib. bdg. 16.95 *(978-0-7613-8937-8(7)*, Carolrhoda Bks.) Lerner Publishing Group.
—The Spitting Twins. Jones, Andrea. 2004. 32p. (J). *(978-1-58394-095-2(2)*, Frog Ltd.) North Atlantic Bks.
—Storytime Stickers: Cowboy Dreams. Plourde, Lynn. 2010. (Storytime Stickers Ser.). (ENG.). 16p. (J). (gr. k-2). pap. 5.95 *(978-1-4027-7128-6(2))* Sterling Publishing Co., Inc.
—We Both Read-Just Five More Minutes! Brown, Marcy & Haley, Dennis. 2008. (We Both Read Ser.). 44p. (J). (gr. -1-3). 7.99 *(978-1-60115-013-4(X))*; pap. 3.99 *(978-1-60115-014-1(8))* Treasure Bay, Inc.
—We Read Phonics-Talent Night. Orshoski, Paul. 2011. (We Read Phonics Ser.). 32p. (J). (gr. 1-3). 9.95 *(978-1-60115-339-5(2))*; pap. 4.99 *(978-1-60115-340-1(6))* Treasure Bay, Inc.
Kulka, Joe. Christmas Coal Man. Kulka, Joe. 2015. (ENG.). 32p. (J). (gr. k-3). lib. bdg. 17.99 ***(978-1-4677-1607-9(3)***, Carolrhoda Bks.) Lerner Publishing Group.
Kulka, Joe. Vacation's Over! Return of the Dinosaurs. Kulka, Joe. 2010. (Carolrhoda Picture Bks). (ENG.). 32p. (J). (gr. k-3). lib. bdg. 17.95 *(978-0-7613-5212-9(0)*, Carolrhoda Bks.) Lerner Publishing Group.
—Wolf's Coming! Kulka, Joe. 2007. (ENG.). 32p. (J). (gr. -1-3). lib. bdg. 16.95 *(978-1-57505-930-3(4)*, Carolrhoda Bks.) Lerner Publishing Group.
Kulp, Jodee. S. M. A. R. T. Pre-K: Program Guide: Get to the CORE of Readiness. Smythe, Cheryl et al. 2011. (ENG.). 136p. pap. 24.95 *(978-1-4635-5705-8(1))* CreateSpace Independent Publishing Platform.
Kumakura, Yuichi. Jing Twilight Tales: King of Bandits, 6 vols. Kirsch, Alexis, tr. from JPN. rev. ed. 2005. 196p. pap. 14.99 *(978-1-59182-471-8(0)*, Tokyopop Kids) TOKYOPOP, Inc.
Kumakura, Yuichi. Jing Vol. 6: King of Bandits, 7 vols. Kumakura, Yuichi. rev. ed. 2004. Vol. 4. 216p. pap. 14.99 *(978-1-59182-179-3(7))*; Vol. 5. 192p. pap. 14.99 *(978-1-59182-466-4(4))* TOKYOPOP, Inc. (Tokyopop Kids).
—Jing: Kind of Bandits Twilight Tales, 6 vols., Vol. 4. Kumakura, Yuichi. rev. ed. 2005. (Jing: King of Bandits-Twilight Tales Ser.). 192p. pap. 14.99 *(978-1-59532-417-7(8)*, Tokyopop Kids) TOKYOPOP, Inc.
—Jing, King of Bandits, 7 vols., Vol. 3. Kumakura, Yuichi. 3rd rev. ed. 2003. 216p. pap. 14.99 *(978-1-59182-178-6(9)*, Tokyopop Kids) TOKYOPOP, Inc.
—Jing, King of Bandits: Twilight Tales, 6 vols. Kumakura, Yuichi. 6th rev. ed. 2005. (Jing: King of Bandits-Twilight Tales Ser.). 171p. pap. 14.99 *(978-1-59532-419-1(4)*, Tokyopop Kids) TOKYOPOP, Inc.
Kumar, Naresh. The Dusk Society. 2011. (Campfire Graphic Novels Ser.). (ENG.). 88p. (gr. 3-7). pap. 11.99 *(978-93-80028-63-7(6)*, Campfire) Kalyani Navyug Media Pty. Ltd. IND. Dist: Random Hse., Inc.
—Kidnapped. Stevenson, Robert Louis. 2011. (Campfire Graphic Novels Ser.). (ENG.). 72p. (gr. 3-7). pap. 9.99 *(978-93-80028-52-1(0)*, Campfire) Kalyani Navyug Media Pty. Ltd. IND. Dist: Random Hse., Inc.
—They Changed the World: Bell, Edison & Tesla. Helfand, Lewis. 2014. (Campfire Graphic Novels Ser.). (ENG.). 102p. (J). (gr. 7). pap. 12.99 *(978-93-80741-87-1(1)*, Campfire) Kalyani Navyug Media Pty. Ltd. IND. Dist: Random Hse., Inc.
Kumar, Vinay. Wash & Dry. Holland, Trish. 2010. (J). *(978-1-60617-119-6(4))* Teaching Strategies, Inc.
Kumar, Vinod. The Hound of the Baskervilles. Doyle, Arthur. 2011. (Campfire Graphic Novels Ser.). (ENG.). 72p. (gr. 3-7). pap. 9.99 *(978-93-80028-44-6(X)*, Campfire) Kalyani Navyug Media Pty. Ltd. IND. Dist: Random Hse., Inc.
—A Journey to the Center of the Earth. Verne, Jules. 2011. (Campfire Graphic Novels Ser.). (ENG.). 72p. (gr. 3-7). pap. 9.99 *(978-93-80028-40-8(7)*, Campfire) Kalyani Navyug Media Pty. Ltd. IND. Dist: Random Hse., Inc.
Kumata, Michelle Reiko. Flowers from Mariko. Noguchi, Rick & Jenks, Deneen. 2013. (ENG.). 32p. (J). (gr. 1-18). 16.95 *(978-1-58430-032-8(9))* Lee & Low Bks., Inc.
Kummer, Mark. I Am So Awesome. Fitzpatrick, Joe. 2014. (ENG.). 32p. (J). (gr. k-4). 7.99 ***(978-1-4867-0005-9(5))*** Flowerpot Children's Pr. Inc. CAN. Dist: Cardinal Pubs. Group.
—The Owl & the Kitty Cat. Everett, Melissa. 2013. (ENG.). 20p. (J). (gr. -1-3). 8.99 ***(978-1-77093-535-8(5))*** Flowerpot Children's Pr. Inc. CAN. Dist: Cardinal Pubs. Group.
Kummer, Mark. Pat-A-Cake. Everett, Melissa. 2013. (ENG.). 20p. (J). (gr. -1-1). 8.99 *(978-1-77093-521-1(5))* Flowerpot Children's Pr. Inc. CAN. Dist: Cardinal Pubs. Group.
Kun Rong, Yap. It Screams at Night, 1 vol. Dahl, Michael. 2009. (Dragonblood Ser.). (ENG.). 40p. (gr. 1-3). 22.65 *(978-1-4342-1261-0(0)*, Zone Bks.) Stone Arch Bks.
Kun Rong, Yap, jt. illus. see Evans, Mark.
Kun Rong, Yap, jt. illus. see Rong, Yap Kun.
Kunardi, Marco. Rick & Bobo: Two Brothers. One a Genius. One Not, 4 vols. Ventrillo, James & Ventrillo, Nick. 2009. 332p. (YA). pap. 13.95 *(978-0-615-28865-9(0))* Vanir Bks.
Kunda, Shmuel. Boruch Learns His Brochos. Kunda, Shmuel. 2005. 40p. (J). 17.95 *(978-1-932443-41-7(X))* Judaica Pr., Inc., The.
Kundalic, Damir. Ferdinand Fox's Big Sleep Colouring Book. Inglis, Karen. 2013. 32p. pap. *(978-0-9569323-4-1(7))* Well Said Pr.
Kundiger, Marion S. Izzie of Fergus Falls: A Minnesota Childhood in The 1880s. Kundiger, Marion S. 2008. (ENG.). 56p. (J). 29.95 *(978-0-9659712-8-7(7))* Ravenstone Pr.
Kung, Isabella. Sammy Experiences Jesus. Blackaby, Tom & Osborne, Rick. 2014. (Experiencing God at Home Ser.). (ENG.). 32p. (J). (gr. -1-3). 14.99 *(978-1-4336-7981-0(7)*, B&H Kids) B&H Publishing Group.
Kunhardt, Dorothy. Junket Is Nice. Kunhardt, Dorothy. 2013. (ENG.). 72p. (J). (gr. -1-2). 16.95 *(978-1-59017-628-3(6)*, NYR Children's Collection) New York Review of Bks., Inc., The.
—Now Open the Box. Kunhardt, Dorothy. 2013. (ENG.). 72p. (J). (gr. -1-2). 16.95 *(978-1-59017-708-2(8)*, NYR Children's Collection) New York Review of Bks., Inc., The.
Kunkel, Dennis. Bug Shots: The Good, the Bad, & the Bugly. Siy, Alexandra, photos by. Siy, Alexandra. 2011. (ENG.). 32p. (J). 16.95 *(978-0-8234-2286-9(0))* Holiday Hse., Inc.
—Mosquito Bite. Siy, Alexandra. (ENG.). 32p. (J). (gr. 2-5). 2006. pap. 7.95 *(978-1-57091-592-5(X))*; 2005. 16.95 *(978-1-57091-591-8(1))* Charlesbridge Publishing, Inc.
Kunkel, Dennis, photos by. The Good, the Bad, the Slimy: The Secret Life of Microbes. Latta, Sara L. 2006. (Prime (Middle/Senior) Ser.). 128p. (J). (gr. 4-9). lib. bdg. 33.27 *(978-0-7660-1294-3(8))* Enslow Pubs., Inc.
—Hidden Worlds: Looking Through a Scientist's Microscope. Kramer, Stephen. 2003. (Scientists in the Field Ser.). (ENG., 64p. (J). (gr. 5-7). pap. 9.99 *(978-0-618-35405-4(0))* Houghton Mifflin Harcourt Publishing Co.
—Hidden Worlds: Looking Through a Scientist's Microscope. Kramer, Stephen. 2005. 57p. (gr. 4-7). 20.00 *(978-0-7569-5188-7(7))* Perfection Learning Corp.
—Spidermania: Friends on the Web. Siy, Alexandra. 2015. (ENG., 48p. (J). (gr. 1-5). 17.95 *(978-0-8234-2871-7(0))* Holiday Hse., Inc.
Kunkel, Mike. Billy Batson & the Magic. Kunkel, Mike. 2015. (Billy Batson & the Magic of Shazam! Ser.). (ENG.). 32p. (gr. 2-3). 212.70 ***(978-1-4965-0290-2(6))*** Stone Arch Bks.
Kunkel, Mike. Billy Batson & the Magic of Shazam!, 1 vol. Kunkel, Mike. 2014. (Billy Batson & the Magic of Shazam! Ser.). (ENG.). 32p. (gr. 2-3). 85.08 *(978-1-4342-9524-8(9))* Stone Arch Bks.
—Brother vs. Brother!, 1 vol. Kunkel, Mike. 2014. (Billy Batson & the Magic of Shazam! Ser.). (ENG.). 32p. (gr. 2-3). 21.27 *(978-1-4342-9228-5(2))* Stone Arch Bks.
—Herobear & the Kid Vol. 1 the Inheritance. Kunkel, Mike. 2014. (Herobear & the Kid Ser.: 1). (ENG.). 128p. (J). (gr. 3). pap. 19.99 *(978-1-60886-366-2(2))* Boom! Studios.
—Magic Words!, 1 vol. Kunkel, Mike. 2014. (Billy Batson & the Magic of Shazam! Ser.). (ENG.). 32p. (gr. 2-3). 21.27 *(978-1-4342-9209-4(6))* Stone Arch Bks.
—Perilous Peril!, 1 vol. Kunkel, Mike. 2014. (Billy Batson & the Magic of Shazam! Ser.). (ENG.). 32p. (gr. 2-3). 21.27 *(978-1-4342-9227-8(4))* Stone Arch Bks.
—The World's Mightiest Mortal!, 1 vol. Kunkel, Mike. 2014. (Billy Batson & the Magic of Shazam! Ser.). (ENG.). 32p. (gr. 2-3). 21.27 *(978-1-4342-9226-1(6))* Stone Arch Bks.
Kunoth, Joanne Kamara, et al. Eastern Anmatyerr Colouring Book. Kunoth, Mark. Purvis, Jedda Ngwarai & Purvis, Joy Pitjara, trs. 2006. (ENG.). 24p. (J). (gr. -1). pap. 6.95 *(978-1-86465-073-0(7))* IAD Pr. AUS. Dist: Independent Pubs. Group.
Kunz, Robert & Kunz, Stephanie. The Childe. Kunz, C. A. 2011. (ENG.). 412p. pap. 14.99 *(978-0-615-43574-9(2))* Kunz, C.A.
Kunz, Stephanie, jt. illus. see Kunz, Robert.
Kuo, Julia. Daisy & Josephine. Gilbert, Melissa. 2014. (ENG.). 32p. (J). (gr. -1-3). 17.99 *(978-1-4424-4578-9(5)*, Simon & Schuster/Paula Wiseman Bks.) Simon & Schuster/Paula Wiseman Bks.
—The Sound of Silence. Grigg-Saito, Katrina. 2016. (J). *(978-0-316-20337-1(8))* Little Brown & Co.
—The Thing about Luck. Kadohata, Cynthia. (ENG.). (J). (gr. 5-9). 2014. 304p. pap. 7.99 *(978-1-4424-7465-9(3)*, Atheneum Bks. for Young Readers); 2013. 288p. 16.99 *(978-1-4169-1882-0(5))* Simon & Schuster Children's Publishing.
Kuo, Julia. Everyone Eats. Kuo, Julia. 2012. (ENG.). 22p. (J). (gr. -1). 9.95 *(978-1-897476-74-1(4))* Simply Read Bks. CAN. Dist: Ingram Pub. Services.
Kuon, Vuthy. The Adventures of Roopster Roux: That's Not Punny, 1 vol. Lavette, Lavaille. Nguyen, Duke, ed. 2007. (Roopster Roux Ser.: Vol. 5). (ENG.). 32p. (J). (gr. 3-7). 16.95 *(978-1-58980-483-8(X))* Pelican Publishing Co., Inc.
—Adventures of Roopster Roux: You're So Victor Vain, 1 vol. Lavette, Lavaille. 2007. (Roopster Roux Ser.). (ENG.). 32p. (J). (gr. 3-7). 16.95 *(978-1-58980-484-5(8))* Pelican Publishing Co., Inc.
—The Rolling Stone: And Other Read Aloud Stories. Kimmel, Eric A. & Kang, Setha. 2004. 36p. (J). (gr. k-6). 15.95 *(978-0-9651661-2-6(0))* Providence Publishing.
Kuon, Vuthy & Nguyen, Duke. Herbert Hilligan & His Magical Adventure. Epner, Paul. 2003. 32p. (J). 15.95 *(978-0-9743335-0-2(6))* Imaginative Publishing, Ltd.
—Herbert Hilligan & His Magical Lunchbox. Epner, Paul. rev. ed. (Herbert Hilligan Ser.). 15.95 *(978-1-57168-549-0(9))* Eakin Pr.
—Herbert Hilligan's Lone Star Adventure. Epner, Paul. 2003. 32p. (J). 15.95 *(978-0-9743335-3-3(0))* Imaginative Publishing, Ltd.
—Herbert Hilligan's Prehistoric Adventure. Epner, Paul. 2003. 32p. (J). 15.95 *(978-0-9743335-1-9(4))* Imaginative Publishing, Ltd.
—Herbert Hilligan's Tropical Adventure. Epner, Paul. 2003. 32p. (J). 15.95 *(978-0-9743335-2-6(2))* Imaginative Publishing, Ltd.
Kupesic, Rajka. The Nutcracker. Kain, Karen. 2005. (ENG.). 32p. (J). (gr. k-12). 18.95 *(978-0-88776-696-1(X)*, Tundra Bks.) Tundra Bks. CAN. Dist: Penguin Random Hse., LLC.
Kupesic, Rajka. The White Ballets. Kupesic, Rajka, retold by. 2011. (ENG.). 40p. (J). (gr. k-12). 19.95 *(978-0-88776-923-8(3)*, Tundra Bks.) Tundra Bks. CAN. Dist: Penguin Random Hse., LLC.
Kupperberg, Alan, et al. Essential Defenders - Volume 7. 2013. (ENG.). 528p. (J). (gr. 4-17). pap. 19.99 *(978-0-7851-8405-8(8))* Marvel Worldwide, Inc.
Kupperman, Michael, jt. illus. see Helquist, Brett.
Kurelek, William. They Sought a New World: The Story of European Immigration to North America. Kurelek, William. Engelhart, Margaret S. 2005. 48p. (J). (gr. 4-8). reprint ed. 20.00 *(978-0-7567-8682-3(7))* DIANE Publishing Co.
Kuricheva, Natasha. The Nutcracker. Regan, Patrick. 2012. (ENG.). 28p. (J). (-4). 19.99 *(978-1-4494-2166-3(0))* Andrews McMeel Publishing.
Kurihashi, Shinsuke. Record of the Last Hero, Vol. 3. Kurihashi, Shinsuke. Asamiya, Kia. 2007. (Junk Ser.). (ENG.). 200p. (YA). pap. 9.95 *(978-1-59796-109-7(4))* DrMaster Pubns. Inc.
Kurilla, Renee. Be Aware! My Tips for Personal Safety. Bellisario, Gina. 2014. (Cloverleaf Books — My Healthy Habits Ser.). (ENG.). 24p. (gr. k-2). lib. bdg. 23.93 *(978-1-4677-1351-1(1)*, Millbrook Pr.) Lerner Publishing Group.
Kurilla, Renee. Blizzard! A Bel the Weather Girl Book. Jensen, Belinda. 2015. (J). ***(978-1-4677-7961-6(X)***, Millbrook Pr.) Lerner Publishing Group.
—Clouds! A Bel the Weather Girl Book. Jensen, Belinda. 2015. (J). ***(978-1-4677-7963-0(6)***, Millbrook Pr.) Lerner Publishing Group.
—Hail! A Bel the Weather Girl Book. Jensen, Belinda. 2015. (J). ***(978-1-4677-7958-6(X)***, Millbrook Pr.) Lerner Publishing Group.
—Hurricane! A Bel the Weather Girl Book. Jensen, Belinda. 2015. (J). ***(978-1-4677-7962-3(8)***, Millbrook Pr.) Lerner Publishing Group.
Kurilla, Renee. I'M All Wrapped Up! - Meet a Mummy. Knudsen, Shannon. 2014. (Monster Buddies Ser.). (ENG.). 24p. (gr. k-2). lib. bdg. 23.93 *(978-0-7613-9188-3(6)*, Millbrook Pr.) Lerner Publishing Group.
—Keep Calm! My Stress-Busting Tips. Bellisario, Gina. 2014. (Cloverleaf Books — My Healthy Habits Ser.). (ENG.). 24p. (gr. k-2). lib. bdg. 23.93 *(978-1-4677-1354-2(6)*, Millbrook Pr.) Lerner Publishing Group.
—Move Your Body! My Exercise Tips. Bellisario, Gina. 2014. (Cloverleaf Books — My Healthy Habits Ser.). (ENG.). 24p. (gr. k-2). lib. bdg. 23.93 *(978-1-4677-1349-8(X)*, Millbrook Pr.) Lerner Publishing Group.
Kurilla, Renee. My Clothes, Your Clothes. Bullard, Lisa. 2015. (Cloverleaf Books (tm) — Alike & Different Ser.). (ENG.). 24p. (gr. k-2). pap. 6.99 ***(978-1-4677-6030-0(7)***, Millbrook Pr.) Lerner Publishing Group.
Kurilla, Renee. Orangutanka. Engle, Margarita. 2015. (ENG.). 40p. (J). (gr. -1-3). 17.99 *(978-0-8050-9839-6(9)*, Holt, Henry & Co. Bks. For Young Readers) Holt, Henry & Co.
Kurilla, Renee. Thunderstorms: A Bel the Weather Girl Book. Jensen, Belinda. 2015. (J). ***(978-1-4677-7959-3(8)***, Millbrook Pr.) Lerner Publishing Group.
—Tornadoes: A Bel the Weather Girl Book. Jensen, Belinda. 2015. (J). ***(978-1-4677-7960-9(1)***, Millbrook Pr.) Lerner Publishing Group.
Kurilla, Renee, jt. illus. see Reynolds, Peter H.
Kurisu, Jane. Eco-Fun: Projects, Experiments & Games for a Greener Earth. Suzuki, David & Vanderlinden, Kathy. 2003. (ENG.). 128p. (J). (gr. 3-6). pap. 14.95 *(978-1-55054-823-5(9))* Greystone Books Ltd. CAN. Dist: Perseus-PGW.
—Fantastic Feats & Failures. Yes Magazine Editors. 2004. (ENG.). 52p. (J). (gr. 3-7). 9.95 *(978-1-55337-634-7(X))* Kids Can Pr., Ltd. CAN. Dist: Univ. of Toronto Pr.
—Funtime Riddles. Helmer, Marilyn. 2004. 31p. (J). lib. bdg. 15.38 *(978-1-4242-1184-5(0))* Fitzgerald Bks.
—Junk Drawer Jewelry. Warwick, Ellen & Di Salle, Rachel. 2006. (Kids Can Do It Ser.). (ENG.). 40p. (J). (gr. 3-7). 6.95 *(978-1-55337-966-9(7))* Kids Can Pr., Ltd. CAN. Dist: Univ. of Toronto Pr.
—Mathemagic! Number Tricks. Colgan, Lynda. 2011. (ENG.). 40p. (J). (gr. 5-9). 16.95 *(978-1-55453-425-8(9))* Kids Can Pr., Ltd. CAN. Dist: Univ. of Toronto Pr.
—My Pet Puppy. Baillie, Marilyn. 2005. (ENG.). 32p. (J). (gr. k-3). 6.95 *(978-1-55337-651-4(X))* Kids Can Pr., Ltd. CAN. Dist: Univ. of Toronto Pr.
—Simply Sewing. Sadler, Judy Ann & Sadler, Judy. 2004. (Kids Can Do It Ser.). (ENG.). 48p. (J). (gr. 3-18). pap. 7.95 *(978-1-55337-660-6(9))* Kids Can Pr., Ltd. CAN. Dist: Univ. of Toronto Pr.
Kurisu, Jane. The Jumbo Book of Drama. Kurisu, Jane, tr. Dunleavy, Deborah. 2004. (Jumbo Bks.). (ENG.). 208p. (J). (gr. 4-6). 14.95 *(978-1-55337-008-6(2))* Kids Can Pr., Ltd. CAN. Dist: Univ. of Toronto Pr.
Kurkela, Cassidy S. Lilies on the Moon. Kurkela, Robert W. 2005. 32p. (J). 16.95 *(978-0-9760220-0-8(1))* Kidzpoetz Publishing.
Kurkoski, Bettina. The Rise of Scourge. Jolley, Dan & Hunter, Erin. ed. 2008. (Warriors Manga Readers Ser.: No. 3). 82p. (gr. 3-7). lib. bdg. 17.20 *(978-1-4178-3120-3(0)*, Turtleback) Turtleback Bks.
Kurkoski, Bettina M. Kallik's Adventure. Hunter, Erin. 2011. (Seekers Manga Ser.). (ENG.). 112p. (J). (gr. 3-7). pap. 6.99 *(978-0-06-172383-4(5))* HarperCollins Pubs.
—The Rise of Scourge. Hunter, Erin. 2008. (Warriors Manga Ser.: No. 3). (ENG.). 112p. (J). (gr. 3-7). pap. 6.99 *(978-0-06-147867-3(9))* HarperCollins Pubs.
—Toklo's Story. Hunter, Erin. 2010. (Seekers Manga Ser.). (ENG.). 112p. (J). (gr. 3-7). pap. 6.99 *(978-0-06-172380-3(0))* HarperCollins Pubs.
Kurlansky, Mark. The Girl Who Swam to Euskadi: Euskadiraino Igerian Joan Zen Neska. Kurlansky, Mark. 2005. (ENG & BAQ.). 32p. (J). (gr. -1-3). 18.95 *(978-1-877802-54-6(9))* Ctr. for Basque Studies.
Kurosaki, Yoshisuke. Japanese Children's Favorite Stories. Sakade, Florence. anniv. ed. 2014. (ENG.). 112p. (J). 17.95 *(978-4-8053-1260-5(2))* Tuttle Publishing.
—Urashima Taro & Other Japanese Children's Favorite Stories. Sakade, Florence & Hayashi, Yoshio. 2008. (ENG.). 48p. (J). (gr. -1-2). 12.95 *(978-4-8053-0997-1(0))* Tuttle Publishing.
Kurt D Williams and Jeff Baker. The Little Lost Allygator. Knapp, Rene & Berger, Marjorie B. 2012. 44p. pap. 24.95 *(978-1-4626-8155-6(7))* America Star Bks.
Kurth, Steve. Hercules: The Twelve Labors - A Greek Myth. Storrie, Paul D. 2007. (Graphic Myths & Legends Ser.). (ENG.). 48p. (gr. 4-8). per. 8.95 *(978-0-8225-6485-0(8))* Lerner Publishing Group.
—Iron Man: Armor Wars. Ellis, Warren. 2010. (ENG.). 112p. (YA). (gr. 8-17). pap. 14.99 *(978-0-7851-4430-4(7))* Marvel Worldwide, Inc.
—Iron Man: War of the Iron Man. 2010. (ENG.). 144p. (YA). (gr. 8-17). 19.99 *(978-0-7851-4729-9(2))* Marvel Worldwide, Inc.
—Iron Man: War of the Iron Men. 2011. (ENG.). 136p. (YA). (gr. 8-17). pap., pap. 16.99 *(978-0-7851-4730-5(6))* Marvel Worldwide, Inc.
Kurth, Steve & Schulz, Barbara. Demeter & Persephone: Spring Held Hostage. Fontes, Justine & Fontes, Ron. 2008. (Graphic Myths & Legends Ser.). (ENG.). 48p. (gr. 4-8). per. 8.95 *(978-0-8225-6570-3(6))* Lerner Publishing Group.
Kurth, Steve, jt. illus. see Schulz, Barbara.
Kurtz, Barbara, photos by. Sebastian's Neighborhood: A Hummingbird's Story. Kurtz, Barbara. Naughton, Christine, ed. 2011. (ENG., 28p. pap. 11.00 *(978-1-4611-9033-2(9))* CreateSpace Independent Publishing Platform.
Kurtz, John. Christmas Angel. Lee, Quinlan B. 2006. (Clifford's Puppy Days Ser.). (ENG.). 24p. (J). (gr. -1-k). pap. 3.99 *(978-0-439-75533-7(6))* Scholastic, Inc.
—Disney Princess: Look & Find. 2004. (Disney Princess Ser.). 24p. (J). 7.98 *(978-0-7853-7918-8(5)*, 7179200) Phoenix International Publications, Inc.
—What Belongs? Shively, Julie. 2004. (Baby Looney Toons Ser.). (ENG.). 16p. (J). 6.95 *(978-0-8249-6561-7(2))* Ideals Pubns.
—Winnie the Pooh's Many Adventures, Set. Marshall, Hallie. 2003. 176p. (J). 15.99 *(978-0-7868-3440-2(4))* Disney Pr.
Kurtz, John. JATS Fairytale Classics - Goldilocks & the Three Bears. Kurtz, John. 2004. 24p. (J). lib. bdg. 8.00 *(978-1-4242-0635-3(9))* Fitzgerald Bks.
—JATS Fairytale Classics - Jack & the Beanstalk. Kurtz, John. 2004. 24p. (J). lib. bdg. 8.00 *(978-1-4242-0636-0(7))* Fitzgerald Bks.
Kurtz, John & Lo Raso, Carlo. Fly, Dumbo, Fly! Weinberg, Jennifer Liberts. 2012. (Step into Reading Ser.). (ENG.). 32p. (J). (gr. -1-1). pap. 3.99 *(978-0-7364-2044-0(4)*, Random Hse. Bks. for Young Readers) Random Hse. Children's Bks.
Kurumada, Masami. Knights of the Zodiac. Kurumada, Masami. (Knights of the Zodiac Ser.). (ENG.). 200p. 2004. (YA). pap. 7.95 *(978-1-59116-525-5(3))*; Vol. 5. 2004. pap. 7.95 *(978-1-59116-470-8(2))*; Vol. 7. 2005. (YA). pap. 7.95 *(978-1-59116-616-0(0))* Viz Media.
—Knights of the Zodiac (Saint Seiya) Kurumada, Masami. (Knights of the Zodiac Ser.: Vol. 4). (ENG.). Vol. 4. 2004.

K

192p. pap. 7.95 (978-1-59116-335-0(8)); Vol. 11. 2005. 184p. pap. 7.95 (978-1-59116-993-2(3)) Viz Media.

Kurup, Prakash. A-B-C in Action. Mehta, Poonam V. 2012. 36p. pap. 22.12 (978-1-4669-2687-5(2)) Trafford Publishing.

Kuryla, Mary, jt. illus. see Yelchin, Eugene.

Kurzyca, Krystyna Emilia. Adventures with Bingo Borden. Anderson, Al. Agora Publications Staff, tr. 2010. 77p. (J). pap. 9.50 (978-1-887250-46-7(8)) Agora Pubns., Inc.

—The Wise Enchanter: A Journey through the Alphabet. Davidow, Shelley. 2005. 159p. (J). (gr. 3-7). per. 17.95 (978-0-88010-562-0(3)) SteinerBooks, Inc.

Kusaka, Hidenori. Pokémon Adventures. Kusaka, Hidenori. 2010. (Pokemon Ser.: 10). (ENG.). (J). 200p. pap. 9.99 (978-1-4215-3063-5(5)); 224p. pap. 9.99 (978-1-4215-3062-8(7)) Viz Media.

—Pokemon Adventures. Kusaka, Hidenori. 2010. (Pokemon Ser.: 8). (ENG.). 232p. (J). pap. 9.99 (978-1-4215-3061-1(9)) Viz Media.

—Pokémon Adventures. Kusaka, Hidenori. 2nd ed. (Pokemon Ser.: 6). (ENG.). (J). 2010. 208p. pap. 9.99 (978-1-4215-3059-8(7)); 2009. 200p. pap. 9.99 (978-1-4215-3054-3(6)) Viz Media.

—Pokemon Adventures. Kusaka, Hidenori. 2nd ed. 2010. (Pokemon Ser.: 7). (ENG.). 224p. (J). pap. 9.99 (978-1-4215-3060-4(0)) Viz Media.

—Pokémon Adventures, Vol. 2. Kusaka, Hidenori. 2nd ed. 2009. (Pokemon Ser.: 2). (ENG.). 200p. (J). pap. 9.99 (978-1-4215-3055-0(4)) Viz Media.

—Pokemon Adventures, Vol. 3. Kusaka, Hidenori. 2nd ed. 2009. (Pokemon Ser.: 3). (ENG.). 240p. (J). pap. 9.99 (978-1-4215-3056-7(2)) Viz Media.

—Pokémon Adventures, Vol. 4. Kusaka, Hidenori. 2nd ed. 2009. (Pokemon Ser.: 4). (ENG.). 216p. (J). pap. 9.99 (978-1-4215-3057-4(0)) Viz Media.

—Pokemon Adventures, Vol. 5. Kusaka, Hidenori. 2nd ed. 2010. (Pokemon Ser.: 5). (ENG.). 216p. (J). pap. 9.99 (978-1-4215-3058-1(9)) Viz Media.

Kushii, Tetsuo. Dinosaurs. Turnbull, Stephanie. 2006. (Usborne Beginners Ser.). 32p. (J). (gr. 2). lib. bdg. 12.99 (978-1-58086-929-4(7), Usborne) EDC Publishing.

Kushii, Tetsuo, et al. Spiders. Gilpin, Rebecca. 2006. (Beginners Nature: Level 1 Ser.). 32p. (J). (gr. k-2). 4.99 (978-0-7945-1398-6(0), Usborne) EDC Publishing.

Kushii, Tetsuo. Under the Sea. Patchett, Fiona. 2006. (Usborne Beginners Ser.). 32p. (J). (gr. 1). lib. bdg. 12.99 (978-1-58086-931-7(9), Usborne) EDC Publishing.

—Usborne Dinosaur Stencil Book. Pearcey, Alice. 2006. 14p. (J). (gr. -1-3). bds. 12.99 (978-0-7945-1138-8(4), Usborne) EDC Publishing.

Kushii, Tetsuo & Larkum, Adam. Bears. Helbrough, Emma. 2006. (Beginners Nature: Level 1 Ser.). 32p. (J). (gr. k-2). 4.99 (978-0-7945-1393-1(X)); (gr. 1). lib. bdg. 12.99 (978-1-58086-941-6(6)) EDC Publishing. (Usborne).

Kushii, Tetsuo & Wray, Zoe. Eggs & Chicks. Patchett, Fiona. 2007. (Usborne Beginners Ser.). 32p. (J). (gr. -1). 4.99 (978-0-7945-1342-9(5), Usborne) EDC Publishing.

—Under the Sea. Patchett, Fiona. Ibrahim, Nouran, tr. from ARA. 2013. (ENG.). 32p. (J). 6.99 (978-99921-94-36-2(7), 149894) Bloomsbury USA.

—Under the Sea. Patchett, Fiona. 2006. (Beginners Nature: Level 1 Ser.). 32p. (J). (gr. k-2). 4.99 (978-0-7945-1336-8(0), Usborne) EDC Publishing.

Kushii, Tetsuo & Wright, David. Spiders. Gilpin, Rebecca. 2006. (Usborne Beginners Ser.). 32p. (J). (gr. 1). lib. bdg. 12.99 (978-1-58086-946-1(7), Usborne) EDC Publishing.

Kushii, Tetsuo, jt. illus. see Wray, Zoe.

Kushner, Sarah. What You Have Now What Your Mommy Had Then. Shoemaker, Craig. 2004. 32p. 15.95 (978-0-9713454-2-3(2)) Bennett/Novak & Co., Inc.

Kusinitz, Nat. Sometimes the Spoon Runs Away with Another Spoon Coloring Book. Bunnell, Jacinta. 2010. (Reach & Teach Ser.). (ENG.). 32p. pap. 10.00 (978-1-60486-329-1(3)) PM Pr.

Kuskin, Karla. Traces. Fox, Paula. 2011. (ENG.). 32p. (J). (gr. 2-4). pap. 9.95 (978-1-59078-870-7(2)) Boyds Mills Pr.

Kusunoki, Kei. Sengoku Nights, Vol. 1. Ohashi, Kaoru. 2006. 208p. pap. 9.99 (978-1-59532-945-5(5)) TOKYOPOP, Inc.

Kutschbach, Doris. Claude Monet. Aston, Paul, tr. 2006. (ENG.). 32p. 8.95 (978-3-7913-3713-5(0)) Prestel Publishing.

—Coloring Book: Wassily Kandinsky. Aston, Paul, tr. 2006. (ENG.). 32p. 8.95 (978-3-7913-3712-8(2)) Prestel Publishing.

Kutsuwada, Chie. As You Like It. Shakespeare, William. 2009. (Manga Shakespeare Ser.). (ENG.). 208p. (YA). (gr. 7-11). pap. 10.95 (978-0-8109-8351-9(6), Amulet Bks.) Abrams.

—Hagakure: The Code of the Samurai. Tsunetomo, Yamamoto & Wilson, William Scott. 2011. (ENG.). 144p. pap. 14.95 (978-4-7700-3120-4(3)) Kodansha America, Inc.

Kuumba, Mshindo. A Day at the Four Seasons: "Finding the Ingredients" Pitt, Roosevelt, Jr. 2005. (Food Adventures with Charles the Chef Ser.). (J). per. 12.95 (978-0-9760745-0-2(8)) AMARA Entertainment.

Kuyper, Tony, photos by. Sand to Stone: And Back Again. Flood, Nancy Bo. 2009. (ENG.). 32p. (J). (gr. -1-5). pap. 9.95 (978-1-55591-657-2(0)) Fulcrum Publishing.

Kuzma, Jakub. Alena & the Favorite Thing. Anderson, Eric B. 2008. 36p. (J). (ENG.). 18.95 (978-0-9798659-2-3(1)); pap. 13.95 (978-0-9798659-3-0(X)) Edgecliff Pr. LLC.

Kvasnosky, Laura McGee. The Big Picture. Kvasnosky, Laura McGee. 2010. (Zelda & Ivy Ser.). (ENG.). 48p. (J). (gr. k-4). 14.99 (978-0-7636-4180-1(4)) Candlewick Pr.

—Keeping Secrets. Kvasnosky, Laura McGee. 2009. (Zelda & Ivy Ser.). (ENG.). 48p. (J). (gr. k-4). 15.99 (978-0-7636-4179-5(0)) Candlewick Pr.

—Really Truly Bingo. Kvasnosky, Laura McGee. 2008. (ENG.). 32p. (J). (gr. k-k). 15.99 (978-0-7636-3210-6(4)) Candlewick Pr.

—The Runaways. Kvasnosky, Laura McGee. 2006. (Zelda & Ivy Ser.). (ENG.). 48p. (J). (gr. k-4). 14.99 (978-0-7636-2689-1(9)) Candlewick Pr.

—Zelda & Ivy - Big Picture. Kvasnosky, Laura McGee. 2013. (Candlewick Sparks Ser.). (ENG.). 48p. (J). (gr. k-4). pap. 3.99 (978-0-7636-6637-8(8)) Candlewick Pr.

—Zelda & Ivy - Keeping Secrets. Kvasnosky, Laura McGee. 2013. (Candlewick Sparks Ser.). (ENG.). 48p. (J). (gr. k-4). pap. 3.99 (978-0-7636-6636-1(X)) Candlewick Pr.

—Zelda & Ivy - The Runaways. Kvasnosky, Laura McGee. 2013. (Candlewick Sparks Ser.). (ENG.). 48p. (J). (gr. k-4). pap. 3.99 (978-0-7636-6635-4(1)) Candlewick Pr.

—Zelda & Ivy & the Boy Next Door. Kvasnosky, Laura McGee. (Candlewick Sparks Ser.). (ENG.). 40p. (J). (gr. k-4). 2014. pap. 3.99 (978-0-7636-7182-2(7)); 2008. 15.99 (978-0-7636-4004-0(2)) Candlewick Pr.

—Zelda & Ivy One Christmas. Kvasnosky, Laura McGee. 2013. (Candlewick Sparks Ser.). (ENG.). 40p. (J). (gr. k-4). pap. 3.99 (978-0-7636-6865-5(6)) Candlewick Pr.

Kveta. Smoke: A Wolf's Story, 1 vol. Kveta, tr. Banner, Melanie Jane. 2003. (ENG.). 160p. pap. (978-1-55041-322-9(8)) Fitzhenry & Whiteside, Ltd.

Kwag, Jin-yeong. Typhoon Holidays: Taiwan. Hsu, Yi Ling. Cowley, Joy, ed. 2015. (Global Kids Storybooks Ser.). (ENG.). 32p. (gr. 1-4). 26.65 (978-1-925246-04-9(3)); 26.65 (978-1-925246-30-8(2)); 7.99 (978-1-925246-56-8(6)) ChoiceMaker Pty. Ltd., The AUS. (Big and SMALL). Dist: Lerner Publishing Group.

Kwakkenbos, Frans. Unlocking the Secret of Otherland: A Story & Activity Book for Children Living Abroad. Janssen-Mathes, Mieke M. E. 2007. 96p. pap. 34.95 (978-90-6832-587-4(6)) Royal Tropical Institute Pr. (KIT (Koninklijk Instituut voor de Tropen) NLD. Dist: Stylus Publishing, LLC.

Kwas, Susan Estelle. Wild Birds. Ryder, Joanne. 2003. 40p. (J). (gr. -1-2). 16.99 (978-0-06-027738-3(6)) HarperCollins Pubs.

Kwasney, Karl, et al. Clara Barton - Angel of the Battlefield. Hood, Ann. 2012. (Treasure Chest Ser.: 1). (ENG.). 208p. (J). (gr. 3-7). pap. 6.99 (978-0-448-45467-2(X), Grosset & Dunlap) Penguin Publishing Group.

—Little Lion, 2 vols. Hood, Ann. 2012. (Treasure Chest Ser.: 2). (ENG.). 192p. (J). (gr. 3-7). 15.99 (978-0-448-45472-6(6), Grosset & Dunlap) Penguin Publishing Group.

Kwasney, Karl & Zilber, Denis. Alexander Hamilton - Little Lion, 2 vols. Hood, Ann & Altmann, Scott. 2012. (Treasure Chest Ser.: 2). (ENG.). 224p. (J). (gr. 3-7). pap. 6.99 (978-0-448-45468-9(8), Grosset & Dunlap) Penguin Publishing Group.

—Angel of the Battlefield. Hood, Ann & Altmann, Scott. 2012. (Treasure Chest Ser.: 1). (ENG.). 208p. (J). (gr. 3-7). 15.99 (978-0-448-45471-9(8), Grosset & Dunlap) Penguin Publishing Group.

Kwasny, Karl, et al. Jewel of the East. Hood, Ann. 2012. (Treasure Chest Ser.: 3). (ENG.). 208p. (J). (gr. 3-7). 15.99 (978-0-448-45473-3(4)); pap. 6.99 (978-0-448-45469-6(6)) Penguin Publishing Group. (Grosset & Dunlap).

Kwasny, Karl. Nightmares! Segel, Jason & Miller, Kirsten. (ENG.). (J). (gr. 3-7). 2015. 400p. 7.99 (978-0-385-74426-3(9), Yearling); 2014. 368p. 16.99 (978-0-385-74425-6(0), Delacorte Bks. for Young Readers); 2014. 368p. lib. bdg. 19.99 (978-0-375-99157-8(3), Delacorte Bks. for Young Readers) Random Hse. Children's Bks.

Kwasny, Karl. The Year of Shadows. Legrand, Claire. 2013. (ENG.). 416p. (J). (gr. 3-7). 16.99 (978-1-4424-4294-8(8), Simon & Schuster Bks. For Young Readers) Simon & Schuster Bks. For Young Readers.

Kwaymullina, Ambelin. Bush Bash. Morgan, Sally. 2013. (ENG.). 24p. (J). (gr. -1). 22.99 (978-1-921714-77-1(8)) Little Hare Bks. AUS. Dist: Independent Pubs. Group.

Kwiat, Ernie. Abby Cadabby up & Down: Brand New Readers. Sesame Workshop. 2013. (Sesame Street Bks.). (ENG.). (J). (gr. -1-3). 48p. 14.99 (978-0-7636-6652-1(1)); pap. 5.99 (978-0-7636-6653-8(X)) Candlewick Pr.

—Abby Caddaby up & Down. 2013. (J). (978-0-7636-6741-2(2)) Candlewick Pr.

—Bert & Ernie Go Camping: Brand New Readers. Sesame Workshop. 2012. (Sesame Street Bks.). (ENG.). (J). (gr. -1-3). 48p. 14.99 (978-0-7636-5750-5(6)); pap. 5.99 (978-0-7636-5793-2(X)) Candlewick Pr.

—Big Bird at Home: Brand New Readers. Sesame Workshop Staff. 2011. (Sesame Street Bks.). (ENG.). (J). (gr. -1-3). 48p. 14.99 (978-0-7636-5067-4(6)); pap. 5.99 (978-0-7636-5148-0(6)) Candlewick Pr.

—Cookie Monster's Busy Day: Brand New Readers. Sesame Workshop. 2012. (Sesame Street Bks.). (ENG.). (J). (gr. -1-3). 48p. 14.99 (978-0-7636-5732-1(8)); pap. 5.99 (978-0-7636-5777-2(8)) Candlewick Pr.

—Here Comes Super Grover! Brand New Readers. Sesame Workshop. 2013. (Sesame Street Bks.). (ENG.). (J). (gr. -1-3). 48p. 14.99 (978-0-7636-6655-2(6)); pap. 5.99 (978-0-7636-6654-5(8)) Candlewick Pr.

Kwiat, Ernie. Sesame Street Boo! Guess Who, Elmo! 2015. (Guess Who! Book Ser.). (ENG.). 10p. (J). (gr. -1-k). bds. 10.99 (978-0-7944-3475-5(4)) Studio Fun International.

Kwon, Elisa & Rem. Vampire Kisses - Blood Relatives, Vol. 3. Schreiber, Ellen. 2009. (Vampire Kisses: Blood Relatives Ser.: Vol. 3). (ENG.). 192p. (YA). (gr. 8-18). pap. 9.99 (978-0-06-134083-3(9), Tegen, Katherine Bks) HarperCollins Pubs.

Kwon, Min. Snow Biz, Vol. 5. 2006. (Serenity Ser.: Vol. 5). 96p. (YA). (gr. 7-12). per. 7.97 (978-1-59310-874-8(5), Barbour Bks.) Barbour Publishing, Inc.

Kwon, Yeong-mook. Ah I'm Full: Food Chain. Jo, Eun-sook. Cowley, Joy, ed. 2015. (Science Storybooks Ser.). (ENG.). 32p. (gr. k-3). 26.65 (978-1-925246-21-6(3)); 7.99 (978-1-925246-73-5(6)); 26.65 (978-1-925246-47-6(7)) ChoiceMaker Pty. Ltd., The AUS. (Big and SMALL). Dist: Lerner Publishing Group.

Kwon, Yoon-duck. My Cat Copies Me. Kwon, Yoon-duck. 2007. (ENG.). 32p. (J). (gr. -1-1). 11.99 (978-1-933605-26-5(X)) Kane Miller.

Kwong, Alvina. My Imagination. Estes-Hill, Katrina. 2007. 32p. (J). (gr. -1-2). 15.95 (978-0-9745715-6-0(3)) KRBY Creations, LLC.

Kyle, Margaret. The Bible in the Hunger Games: A "Bibleizing" Study Guide. Chapman, Patricia. 2012. (ENG.). 52p. (J). (gr. 17-17). pap. 9.95 (978-1-77064-565-3(9)) Wood Lake Publishing, Inc. CAN. Dist: Westminster John Knox Pr.

Kyle, Margaret. 52 More Crafts: For the Church Year. Payne-Krzyzanowski, Anna et al. 2008. (ENG.). 64p. pap. 16.95 (978-1-55145-570-9(6)) Wood Lake Publishing, Inc. CAN. Dist: Westminster John Knox Pr.

Kyong-Nan, Nani. Korean Children's Day. Suyenaga, Ruth et al. 2005. (Multicultural Celebrations Ser.). 32p. (J). 4.95 (978-1-59373-011-6(X)) Bunker Hill Publishing, Inc.

—Korean Children's Day. Suyenaga, Ruth. 2004. 23p. (J). (gr. 4-8). reprint ed. pap. 15.00 (978-0-7567-7068-6(8)) DIANE Publishing Co.

Kyoung-Sim, Jeong. The Tigers of the Kumgang Mountains: A Korean Folktale. So-Un, Kim. 2005. (ENG.). 1p. (J). (gr. 4-11). 16.95 (978-0-8048-3653-1(1)) Tuttle Publishing.

Kypta, Judith. Abby Ding Glove & ... Friends. Kypta, Judith. 2010. (ENG.). 56p. pap. 12.99 (978-1-4563-6855-5(9)) CreateSpace Independent Publishing Platform.

Kyung-ah, Choi. Snow Drop. Kyung-ah, Choi, creator. 2005. Vol. 8. rev. ed. 208p. pap. 9.99 (978-1-59532-044-5(X)); Vol. 9. 9th rev. ed. 192p. pap. 9.99 (978-1-59532-045-2(8)) TOKYOPOP, Inc.

L

L, Joe. Times Three. May, Maggie. 2011. 36p. pap. 24.95 (978-1-4626-2504-8(5)) America Star Bks.

La Beree, Brian. Herbert the Tadpole in the Big Change. Bodrogi, Michael. 2003. 48p. (J). (gr. -1-4). 15.95 (978-1-878398-61-1(X), Blue Note Bks.) Blue Note Pubns.

—Herbert the Tadpole in the Big Change: Color-Me Version. 2007. 48p. (J). 6.95 (978-0-9800736-0-7(X)) Sophrose Entertainment Inc.

La Fave, Kim. Bear Stories. Evans, Hubert. (ENG.). 32p. (Orig.). (J). (978-0-88971-153-2(4)) Harbour Publishing Co., Ltd.

—Paul Bunyan on the West Coast. Henry, Tom. unabr. ed. (ENG.). 56p. (Orig.). (J). pap. (978-1-55017-109-9(7)) Harbour Publishing Co., Ltd.

—Silversides: The Life of a Sockeye. Evans, Hubert. (ENG.). 32p. (Orig.). (J). (978-0-88971-152-5(6)) Harbour Publishing Co., Ltd.

La Grange, Myrtle. Bogwaddle Pond. Jordan, Annie Laurie. 2004. 25p. pap. 24.95 (978-1-4137-2013-6(7)) PublishAmerica, Inc.

La Ray, Marina. A Halloween Scare in Alabama. James, Eric. 2015. (ENG.). 32p. (J). (-5). 9.99 (978-1-4926-2359-5(8), Sourcebooks Jabberwocky) Sourcebooks, Inc.

—A Halloween Scare in Alaska. James, Eric. 2015. (ENG.). 32p. (J). (-5). 9.99 (978-1-4926-2360-1(1), Sourcebooks Jabberwocky) Sourcebooks, Inc.

—A Halloween Scare in Albuquerque. James, Eric. 2015. (ENG.). 32p. (J). (-5). 9.99 (978-1-4926-2361-8(X), Sourcebooks Jabberwocky) Sourcebooks, Inc.

—A Halloween Scare in Arizona. James, Eric. 2015. (ENG.). 32p. (J). (-5). 9.99 (978-1-4926-2362-5(8), Sourcebooks Jabberwocky) Sourcebooks, Inc.

—A Halloween Scare in Arkansas. James, Eric. 2015. (ENG.). 32p. (J). (-5). 9.99 (978-1-4926-2363-2(6), Sourcebooks Jabberwocky) Sourcebooks, Inc.

—A Halloween Scare in Bentonville. James, Eric. 2015. (ENG.). 32p. (J). (-5). 9.99 (978-1-4926-2364-9(4), Sourcebooks Jabberwocky) Sourcebooks, Inc.

—A Halloween Scare in Boise. James, Eric. 2015. (ENG.). 32p. (J). (-5). 9.99 (978-1-4926-2365-6(2), Sourcebooks Jabberwocky) Sourcebooks, Inc.

—A Halloween Scare in Boston. James, Eric. 2015. (ENG.). 32p. (J). (-5). 9.99 (978-1-4926-2366-3(0), Sourcebooks Jabberwocky) Sourcebooks, Inc.

—A Halloween Scare in Calgary. James, Eric. 2015. (ENG.). 32p. (J). (-5). 11.99 (978-1-4926-2367-0(9), Sourcebooks Jabberwocky) Sourcebooks, Inc.

—A Halloween Scare in Charleston. James, Eric. 2015. (ENG.). 32p. (J). (-5). 9.99 (978-1-4926-2368-7(7), Sourcebooks Jabberwocky) Sourcebooks, Inc.

—A Halloween Scare in Cincinnati. James, Eric. 2015. (ENG.). 32p. (J). (-5). 9.99 (978-1-4926-2369-4(5), Sourcebooks Jabberwocky) Sourcebooks, Inc.

—A Halloween Scare in Connecticut. James, Eric. 2015. (ENG.). 32p. (J). (-5). 9.99 (978-1-4926-2370-0(9), Sourcebooks Jabberwocky) Sourcebooks, Inc.

—A Halloween Scare in Delaware. James, Eric. 2015. (ENG.). 32p. (J). (-5). 9.99 (978-1-4926-2371-7(7), Sourcebooks Jabberwocky) Sourcebooks, Inc.

—A Halloween Scare in Edmonton. James, Eric. 2015. (ENG.). 32p. (J). (-5). 11.99 (978-1-4926-2372-4(5), Sourcebooks Jabberwocky) Sourcebooks, Inc.

—A Halloween Scare in Hawaii. James, Eric. 2015. (ENG.). 32p. (J). (-5). 9.99 (978-1-4926-2373-1(3), Sourcebooks Jabberwocky) Sourcebooks, Inc.

—A Halloween Scare in Idaho. James, Eric. 2015. (ENG.). 32p. (J). (-5). 9.99 (978-1-4926-2374-8(1), Sourcebooks Jabberwocky) Sourcebooks, Inc.

—A Halloween Scare in Illinois. James, Eric. 2015. (ENG.). 32p. (J). (-5). 9.99 (978-1-4926-2375-5(X), Sourcebooks Jabberwocky) Sourcebooks, Inc.

—A Halloween Scare in Kansas. James, Eric. 2015. (ENG.). 32p. (J). (-5). 9.99 (978-1-4926-2376-2(8), Sourcebooks Jabberwocky) Sourcebooks, Inc.

—A Halloween Scare in Kansas City. James, Eric. 2015. (ENG.). 32p. (J). (-5). 9.99 (978-1-4926-2377-9(6), Sourcebooks Jabberwocky) Sourcebooks, Inc.

—A Halloween Scare in Las Vegas. James, Eric. 2015. (ENG.). 32p. (J). (-5). 9.99 (978-1-4926-2378-6(4), Sourcebooks Jabberwocky) Sourcebooks, Inc.

—A Halloween Scare in Los Angeles. James, Eric. 2015. (ENG.). 32p. (J). (-5). 9.99 (978-1-4926-2379-3(2), Sourcebooks Jabberwocky) Sourcebooks, Inc.

—A Halloween Scare in Maine. James, Eric. 2015. (ENG.). 32p. (J). (-5). 9.99 (978-1-4926-2380-9(6), Sourcebooks Jabberwocky) Sourcebooks, Inc.

—A Halloween Scare in Massachusetts. James, Eric. 2015. (ENG.). 32p. (J). (-5). 9.99 (978-1-4926-2381-6(4), Sourcebooks Jabberwocky) Sourcebooks, Inc.

—A Halloween Scare in Mississippi. James, Eric. 2015. (ENG.). 32p. (J). (-5). 9.99 (978-1-4926-2382-3(2), Sourcebooks Jabberwocky) Sourcebooks, Inc.

—A Halloween Scare in Missouri. James, Eric. 2015. (ENG.). 32p. (J). (-5). 9.99 (978-1-4926-2383-0(0), Sourcebooks Jabberwocky) Sourcebooks, Inc.

—A Halloween Scare in Montana. James, Eric. 2015. (ENG.). 32p. (J). (-5). 9.99 (978-1-4926-2384-7(9), Sourcebooks Jabberwocky) Sourcebooks, Inc.

—A Halloween Scare in Nebraska. James, Eric. 2015. (ENG.). 32p. (J). (-5). 9.99 (978-1-4926-2385-4(7), Sourcebooks Jabberwocky) Sourcebooks, Inc.

—A Halloween Scare in Nevada. James, Eric. 2015. (ENG.). 32p. (J). (-5). 9.99 (978-1-4926-2386-1(5), Sourcebooks Jabberwocky) Sourcebooks, Inc.

—A Halloween Scare in New Hampshire. James, Eric. 2015. (ENG.). 32p. (J). (-5). 9.99 (978-1-4926-2387-8(3), Sourcebooks Jabberwocky) Sourcebooks, Inc.

—A Halloween Scare in New Mexico. James, Eric. 2015. (ENG.). 32p. (J). (-5). 9.99 (978-1-4926-2388-5(1), Sourcebooks Jabberwocky) Sourcebooks, Inc.

—A Halloween Scare in New York City. James, Eric. 2015. (ENG.). 32p. (J). (-5). 9.99 (978-1-4926-2389-2(X), Sourcebooks Jabberwocky) Sourcebooks, Inc.

—A Halloween Scare in North Carolina. James, Eric. 2015. (ENG.). 32p. (J). (-5). 9.99 (978-1-4926-2855-2(7), Sourcebooks Jabberwocky) Sourcebooks, Inc.

—A Halloween Scare in North Dakota. James, Eric. 2015. (ENG.). 32p. (J). (-5). 9.99 (978-1-4926-2390-8(3), Sourcebooks Jabberwocky) Sourcebooks, Inc.

—A Halloween Scare in Oklahoma. James, Eric. 2015. (ENG.). 32p. (J). (-5). 9.99 (978-1-4926-2391-5(1), Sourcebooks Jabberwocky) Sourcebooks, Inc.

—A Halloween Scare in Omaha. James, Eric. 2015. (ENG.). 32p. (J). (-5). 9.99 (978-1-4926-2392-2(X), Sourcebooks Jabberwocky) Sourcebooks, Inc.

—A Halloween Scare in Oregon. James, Eric. 2015. (ENG.). 32p. (J). (-5). 9.99 (978-1-4926-2393-9(8), Sourcebooks Jabberwocky) Sourcebooks, Inc.

—A Halloween Scare in Ottawa. James, Eric. 2015. (ENG.). 32p. (J). (-5). 11.99 (978-1-4926-2394-6(6), Sourcebooks Jabberwocky) Sourcebooks, Inc.

—A Halloween Scare in Philadelphia. James, Eric. 2015. (ENG.). 32p. (J). (-5). 9.99 (978-1-4926-2395-3(4), Sourcebooks Jabberwocky) Sourcebooks, Inc.

—A Halloween Scare in Pittsburgh. James, Eric. 2015. (ENG.). 32p. (J). (-5). 9.99 (978-1-4926-2396-0(2), Sourcebooks Jabberwocky) Sourcebooks, Inc.

—A Halloween Scare in Portland. James, Eric. 2015. (ENG.). 32p. (J). (-5). 9.99 (978-1-4926-2397-7(0), Sourcebooks Jabberwocky) Sourcebooks, Inc.

—A Halloween Scare in Rhode Island. James, Eric. 2015. (ENG.). 32p. (J). (-5). 9.99 (978-1-4926-2398-4(9), Sourcebooks Jabberwocky) Sourcebooks, Inc.

—A Halloween Scare in San Francisco. James, Eric. 2015. (ENG.). 32p. (J). (-5). 9.99 (978-1-4926-2399-1(7), Sourcebooks Jabberwocky) Sourcebooks, Inc.

—A Halloween Scare in South Carolina. James, Eric. 2015. (ENG.). 32p. (J). (-5). 9.99 (978-1-4926-2860-6(3), Sourcebooks Jabberwocky) Sourcebooks, Inc.

—A Halloween Scare in South Dakota. James, Eric. 2015. (ENG.). 32p. (J). (-5). 9.99 (978-1-4926-2400-4(4), Sourcebooks Jabberwocky) Sourcebooks, Inc.

—A Halloween Scare in St. Louis. James, Eric. 2015. (ENG.). 32p. (J). (-5). 9.99 (978-1-4926-2401-1(2), Sourcebooks Jabberwocky) Sourcebooks, Inc.

—A Halloween Scare in Tampa Bay. James, Eric. 2015. (ENG.). 32p. (J). (-5). 9.99 (978-1-4926-2402-8(0), Sourcebooks Jabberwocky) Sourcebooks, Inc.

—A Halloween Scare in Toronto. James, Eric. 2015. (ENG.). 32p. (J). (-5). 11.99 (978-1-4926-2403-5(9), Sourcebooks Jabberwocky) Sourcebooks, Inc.

—A Halloween Scare in Tulsa. James, Eric. 2015. (ENG.). 32p. (J). (-5). 9.99 (978-1-4926-2404-2(7), Sourcebooks Jabberwocky) Sourcebooks, Inc.

—A Halloween Scare in Utah. James, Eric. 2015. (ENG.). 32p. (J). (-5). 9.99 (978-1-4926-2405-9(5), Sourcebooks Jabberwocky) Sourcebooks, Inc.

—A Halloween Scare in Vancouver. James, Eric. 2015. (ENG.). 32p. (J). (-5). 11.99 (978-1-4926-2406-6(3), Sourcebooks Jabberwocky) Sourcebooks, Inc.

—A Halloween Scare in Vermont. James, Eric. 2015. (ENG.). 32p. (J). (-5). 9.99 (978-1-4926-2407-3(1), Sourcebooks Jabberwocky) Sourcebooks, Inc.

—A Halloween Scare in Washington, DC. James, Eric. 2015. (ENG.). 32p. (J). (-5). 9.99 (978-1-4926-2408-0(X), Sourcebooks Jabberwocky) Sourcebooks, Inc.

—A Halloween Scare in West Virginia. James, Eric. 2015. (ENG.). 32p. (J). (-5). 9.99 (978-1-4926-2409-7(8), Sourcebooks Jabberwocky) Sourcebooks, Inc.

—A Halloween Scare in Wyoming. James, Eric. 2015. (ENG.). 32p. (J). (-5). 9.99 (978-1-4926-2410-3(1), Sourcebooks Jabberwocky) Sourcebooks, Inc.

Laaker, Terry. Charlie & the Rodent Queen. Goody, C. A. I. t. ed. 2003. (Charlie's Great Adventures: No. 3). 88p. per. 5.95 (978-0-9702546-2-7(8), 623-876-1518) GoodyGoody Bks.

—Charlie the Spy: Charlie's Great Adventure #6. 2008. 104p. (J). pap. 5.95 (978-0-9702546-7-2(9)) GoodyGoody Bks.

LaBaff, Stephanie. Genetics & Evolution Science Fair Projects, Revised & Expanded Using the Scientific Method. Gardner, Robert. 2010. (Biology Science Projects Using the Scientific Method Ser.). 160p. (J). (gr. 5-18). 35.94 *(978-0-7660-3422-8(4))* Enslow Pubs., Inc.

—Science Fair Projects about the Properties of Matter, Revised & Expanded Using the Scientific Method. Gardner, Robert. 2010. (Physics Science Projects Using the Scientific Method Ser.). 160p. (J). (gr. 5-18). 35.94 *(978-0-7660-3417-4(8))* Enslow Pubs., Inc.

LaBaff, Stephanie & LaBaff, Tom. Earth Science Fair Projects, Revised & Expanded Using the Scientific Method. Calhoun, Yael. 2010. (Earth Science Projects Using the Scientific Method Ser.). 160p. (J). (gr. 5-18). 35.94 *(978-0-7660-3425-9(9))* Enslow Pubs., Inc.

—Electricity & Magnetism Science Fair Projects, Revised & Expanded Using the Scientific Method. Gardner, Robert. 2010. (Physics Science Projects Using the Scientific Method Ser.). 160p. (J). (gr. 5-18). 35.94 *(978-0-7660-3418-1(6))* Enslow Pubs., Inc.

—Planet Earth Science Fair Projects, Revised & Expanded Using the Scientific Method. Gardner, Robert. 2010. (Earth Science Projects Using the Scientific Method Ser.). 160p. (J). (gr. 5-18). 35.94 *(978-0-7660-3423-5(2))* Enslow Pubs., Inc.

LaBaff, Stephanie, jt. illus. see LaBaff, Tom.

LaBaff, Tom. Addition Made Easy. Wingard-Nelson, Rebecca. 2005. (Making Math Easy Ser.). 48p. (J). (gr. 2-4). lib. bdg. 25.27 *(978-0-7660-2508-0(X),* Enslow Elementary) Enslow Pubs., Inc.

—Animal Word Problems Starring Addition & Subtraction. Wingard-Nelson, Rebecca. 2009. (Math Word Problems Solved Ser.). 48p. (J). (gr. 2-5). lib. bdg. 25.27 *(978-0-7660-2917-0(4))* Enslow Pubs., Inc.

—Awesome Animal Science Projects. Benbow, Ann & Mably, Colin. 2009. (Real Life Science Experiments Ser.). 48p. (J). (gr. 2-5). lib. bdg. 25.27 *(978-0-7660-3148-7(9))* Enslow Pubs., Inc.

—Dazzling Science Projects with Light & Color. Gardner, Robert. 2006. (Fantastic Physical Science Experiments Ser.). 48p. (J). (gr. 3-7). lib. bdg. 25.27 *(978-0-7660-2587-5(X),* Enslow Elementary) Enslow Pubs., Inc.

—Division Made Easy. Wingard-Nelson, Rebecca. 2005. (Making Math Easy Ser.). 48p. (J). (gr. 2-4). lib. bdg. 25.27 *(978-0-7660-2511-0(X),* Enslow Elementary) Enslow Pubs., Inc.

—Draw Aliens & Space Objects in 4 Easy Steps: Then Write a Story. LaBaff, Stephanie. 2012. (Drawing in 4 Easy Steps Ser.). 48p. (J). (gr. 3-18). lib. bdg. 25.27 *(978-0-7660-3841-7(6))* Enslow Pubs., Inc.

—Draw Aliens & Space Objects in 4 Easy Steps: Then Write a Story. Labaff, Stephanie. 2012. (Drawing in 4 Easy Steps Ser.). 48p. (J). (gr. 3-18). pap. 8.95 *(978-1-4644-0014-8(8),* Enslow Elementary) Enslow Pubs., Inc.

—Draw Animals in 4 Easy Steps: Then Write a Story. LaBaff, Stephanie. 2012. (Drawing in 4 Easy Steps Ser.). 48p. (J). (gr. 3-18). 25.27 *(978-0-7660-3840-0(8))* Enslow Pubs., Inc.

—Draw Animals in 4 Easy Steps: Then Write a Story. Labaff, Stephanie. 2012. (Drawing in 4 Easy Steps Ser.). 48p. (J). (gr. 3-18). pap. 8.95 *(978-1-4644-0013-1(X),* Enslow Elementary) Enslow Pubs., Inc.

—Draw Cartoon People in 4 Easy Steps: Then Write a Story. LaBaff, Stephanie. 2012. (Drawing in 4 Easy Steps Ser.). 48p. (J). (gr. 3-18). 25.27 *(978-0-7660-3843-1(2))* Enslow Pubs., Inc.

—Draw Cartoon People in 4 Easy Steps: Then Write a Story. Labaff, Stephanie. 2012. (Drawing in 4 Easy Steps Ser.). 48p. (J). (gr. 3-18). pap. 8.95 *(978-1-4644-0016-2(4),* Enslow Elementary) Enslow Pubs., Inc.

—Draw Pirates in 4 Easy Steps: Then Write a Story. LaBaff, Stephanie. 2012. (Drawing in 4 Easy Steps Ser.). 48p. (J). (gr. 3-18). pap. 8.95 *(978-1-4644-0012-4(1),* Enslow Elementary); 25.27 *(978-0-7660-3839-4(4))* Enslow Pubs., Inc.

—Draw Princesses in 4 Easy Steps: Then Write a Story. LaBaff, Stephanie. 2012. (Drawing in 4 Easy Steps Ser.). 48p. (J). (gr. 3-18). 25.27 *(978-0-7660-3838-7(6))* Enslow Pubs., Inc.

—Draw Princesses in 4 Easy Steps: Then Write a Story. Labaff, Stephanie. 2012. (Drawing in 4 Easy Steps Ser.). 48p. (J). (gr. 3-18). pap. 8.95 *(978-1-4644-0011-7(3),* Enslow Elementary) Enslow Pubs., Inc.

—Draw Superheroes in 4 Easy Steps: Then Write a Story. LaBaff, Stephanie. 2012. (Drawing in 4 Easy Steps Ser.). 48p. (J). (gr. 3-18). pap. 8.95 *(978-1-4644-0015-5(6),* Enslow Elementary); 25.27 *(978-0-7660-3842-4(4))* Enslow Pubs., Inc.

—Earth-Shaking Science Projects about Planet Earth. Gardner, Robert. 2007. (Rockin' Earth Science Experiments Ser.). 48p. (J). (gr. 3-4). lib. bdg. 25.27 *(978-0-7660-2733-6(3),* Enslow Elementary) Enslow Pubs., Inc.

—Energizing Science Projects with Electricity & Magnetism. Gardner, Robert. 2006. (Fantastic Physical Science Experiments Ser.). 48p. (J). (gr. 4-7). lib. bdg. 25.27 *(978-0-7660-2584-4(5),* Enslow Elementary) Enslow Pubs., Inc.

—Far-Out Science Projects about Earth's Sun & Moon. Gardner, Robert. 2007. (Rockin' Earth Science Experiments Ser.). 48p. (J). (gr. 3-4). lib. bdg. 25.27 *(978-0-7660-2736-7(8),* Enslow Elementary) Enslow Pubs., Inc.

—Jazzy Science Projects with Sound & Music. Gardner, Robert. 2006. (Fantastic Physical Science Experiments Ser.). 48p. (J). (gr. 4-7). lib. bdg. 25.27 *(978-0-7660-2588-2(8),* Enslow Elementary) Enslow Pubs., Inc.

—Master the Scientific Method with Fun Life Science Projects. Benbow, Ann & Mably, Colin. 2009. (Real Life Science Experiments Ser.). 48p. (J). (gr. 2-5). lib. bdg. 25.27 *(978-0-7660-3151-7(9))* Enslow Pubs., Inc.

—Multiplication Made Easy. Wingard-Nelson, Rebecca. 2005. (Making Math Easy Ser.). 48p. (J). (gr. 2-4). lib. bdg. 25.27 *(978-0-7660-2510-3(1),* Enslow Elementary) Enslow Pubs., Inc.

—Nature's Secret Habitats Science Projects. Benbow, Ann & Mably, Colin. 2009. (Real Life Science Experiments Ser.). 48p. (J). (gr. 2-5). lib. bdg. 25.27 *(978-0-7660-3150-0(0))* Enslow Pubs., Inc.

—Never Eat Soggy Waffles: Fun Mnemonic Memory Tricks. Murphy, Patricia J. 2009. (Prime (Elementary) Ser.). 48p. (J). (gr. 2-5). lib. bdg. 25.27 *(978-0-7660-2710-7(4))* Enslow Pubs., Inc.

—Ready for Addition. Wingard-Nelson, Rebecca. 2014. (Ready for Math Ser.). 48p. (J). pap. 8.95 *(978-1-4644-0433-7(X),* Enslow Elementary) Enslow Pubs., Inc.

—Ready for Division. Wingard-Nelson, Rebecca. 2014. (Ready for Math Ser.). 48p. (J). (gr. 3-18). lib. bdg. 25.27 *(978-0-7660-4249-0(9),* Enslow Elementary) Enslow Pubs., Inc.

—Ready for Fractions & Decimals. Wingard-Nelson, Rebecca. 2014. (Ready for Math Ser.). 48p. (J). pap. 8.95 *(978-1-4644-0437-5(2),* Enslow Elementary); (gr. 3-18). 25.27 *(978-0-7660-4247-6(2))* Enslow Pubs., Inc.

—Ready for Multiplication. Wingard-Nelson, Rebecca. 2014. (Ready for Math Ser.). 48p. (J). pap. 8.95 *(978-1-4644-0439-9(9),* Enslow Elementary); (gr. 3-18). 25.27 *(978-0-7660-4248-3(0))* Enslow Pubs., Inc.

—Ready for Subtraction. Wingard-Nelson, Rebecca. 2014. (Ready for Math Ser.). 48p. (J). (gr. 3-18). lib. bdg. 25.27 *(978-0-7660-4246-9(4),* Enslow Elementary) Enslow Pubs., Inc.

—Ready for Word Problems & Problem Solving. Wingard-Nelson, Rebecca. 2014. (Ready for Math Ser.). 48p. (J). pap. 8.95 *(978-1-4644-0443-6(7),* Enslow Elementary); (gr. 3-18). 25.27 *(978-0-7660-4250-6(2))* Enslow Pubs., Inc.

—Sensational Human Body Science Projects. Benbow, Ann & Mably, Colin. 2009. (Real Life Science Experiments Ser.). 48p. (J). (gr. 2-5). lib. bdg. 25.27 *(978-0-7660-3149-4(7))* Enslow Pubs., Inc.

—Sensational Science Projects with Simple Machines. Gardner, Robert. 2006. (Fantastic Physical Science Experiments Ser.). 48p. (J). (gr. 3-4). lib. bdg. 25.27 *(978-0-7660-2585-1(3),* Enslow Elementary) Enslow Pubs., Inc.

—Sizzling Science Projects with Heat & Energy. Gardner, Robert. 2006. (Fantastic Physical Science Experiments Ser.). 48p. (J). (gr. 3-4). lib. bdg. 25.27 *(978-0-7660-2586-8(1),* Enslow Elementary) Enslow Pubs., Inc.

—Smashing Science Projects about Earth's Rocks & Minerals. Gardner, Robert. 2007. (Rockin' Earth Science Experiments Ser.). 48p. (J). (gr. 3-4). lib. bdg. 25.27 *(978-0-7660-2731-2(7),* Enslow Elementary) Enslow Pubs., Inc.

Labaff, Tom. Sprouting Seed Science Projects. Benbow, Ann & Mably, Colin. 2009. (Real Life Science Experiments Ser.). 48p. (J). (gr. 2-5). lib. bdg. 25.27 *(978-0-7660-3147-0(0))* Enslow Pubs., Inc.

LaBaff, Tom. Stellar Science Projects about Earth's Sky. Gardner, Robert. 2007. (Rockin' Earth Science Experiments Ser.). 48p. (J). (gr. 3-4). lib. bdg. 25.27 *(978-0-7660-2732-9(5),* Enslow Elementary) Enslow Pubs., Inc.

—Subtraction Made Easy. Wingard-Nelson, Rebecca. 2005. (Making Math Easy Ser.). 48p. (J). (gr. 2-4). lib. bdg. 25.27 *(978-0-7660-2509-7(8),* Enslow Elementary) Enslow Pubs., Inc.

—Super Science Projects about Earth's Soil & Water. Gardner, Robert. 2007. (Rockin' Earth Science Experiments Ser.). 48p. (J). (gr. 3-4). lib. bdg. 25.27 *(978-0-7660-2735-0(X),* Enslow Elementary) Enslow Pubs., Inc.

—Weather Science Fair Projects, Revised & Expanded Using the Scientific Method. Gardner, Robert. 2010. (Earth Science Projects Using the Scientific Method Ser.). 160p. (J). (gr. 5-18). 35.94 *(978-0-7660-3424-2(0))* Enslow Pubs., Inc.

—Wild Science Projects about Earth's Weather. Gardner, Robert. 2007. (Rockin' Earth Science Experiments Ser.). 48p. (J). (gr. 3-4). lib. bdg. 25.27 *(978-0-7660-2734-3(1),* Enslow Elementary) Enslow Pubs., Inc.

—Word Problems Made Easy. Wingard-Nelson, Rebecca. 2005. (Making Math Easy Ser.). 48p. (J). (gr. 2-4). lib. bdg. 25.27 *(978-0-7660-2512-7(8),* Enslow Elementary) Enslow Pubs., Inc.

LaBaff, Tom & LaBaff, Stephanie. Chemistry Science Fair Projects Using Inorganic Stuff. Gardner, Robert. rev. exp. ed. 2010. (Chemistry Science Projects Using the Scientific Method Ser.). 160p. (J). (gr. 5-18). 35.94 *(978-0-7660-3413-6(5))* Enslow Pubs., Inc.

—Environmental Science Fair Projects, Revised & Expanded Using the Scientific Method. Rybolt, Thomas R. & Mebane, Robert C. 2010. (Earth Science Projects Using the Scientific Method Ser.). 160p. (J). (gr. 5-18). 35.94 *(978-0-7660-3426-6(7))* Enslow Pubs., Inc.

—Forces & Motion Science Fair Projects, Revised & Expanded Using the Scientific Method. Gardner, Robert. 2010. (Physics Science Projects Using the Scientific Method Ser.). 160p. (J). (gr. 5-18). 35.94 *(978-0-7660-3415-0(1))* Enslow Pubs., Inc.

—Organic Chemistry Science Fair Projects, Revised & Expanded Using the Scientific Method. Gardner, Robert & Conklin, Barbara Gardner. 2010. (Chemistry Science Projects Using the Scientific Method Ser.). 160p. (J). (gr. 5-18). 35.94 *(978-0-7660-3414-3(3))* Enslow Pubs., Inc.

—Plastics & Polymers Science Fair Projects. Goodstein, Madeline P. rev. exp. ed. 2010. (Chemistry Science Projects Using the Scientific Method Ser.). 160p. (J). (gr. 5-18). 35.94 *(978-0-7660-3412-9(7))* Enslow Pubs., Inc.

—Water Science Fair Projects, Revised & Expanded Using the Scientific Method. Goodstein, Madeline P. 2010. (Chemistry Science Projects Using the Scientific Method Ser.). 160p. (J). (gr. 5-18). 35.94 *(978-0-7660-3411-2(9))* Enslow Pubs., Inc.

Labaff, Tom & LaBaff, Tom. Lively Plant Science Projects. Benbow, Ann & Mably, Colin. 2009. (Real Life Science Experiments Ser.). 48p. (J). (gr. 2-5). lib. bdg. 25.27 *(978-0-7660-3146-3(2))* Enslow Pubs., Inc.

LaBaff, Tom, jt. illus. see LaBaff, Stephanie.

LaBaff, Tom, jt. illus. see Labaff, Tom.

Labat, Yancey. Amazon: You Decide Now to Survive! Borgenicht, David & Khan, Hena. 2012. (Worst Case Scenario Ser.: WORS). (ENG.). 208p. (J). (gr. 4-7). 12.99 *(978-1-4521-0795-0(5))* Chronicle Bks. LLC.

—Deadly Seas: You Decide How to Survive! Borgenicht, David & Lurie, Alexander. 2012. (ENG.). 208p. (J). (gr. 3-7). 12.99 *(978-1-4521-0917-6(6))* Chronicle Bks. LLC.

—How Many Jelly Beans? A Giant Book of Giant Numbers! Menotti, Andrea. 2012. (ENG.). 28p. (J). (gr. -1-1). 18.99 *(978-1-4521-0206-1(6))* Chronicle Bks. LLC.

—Mars: You Decide How to Survive! Borgenicht, David & Khan, Hena. 2011. (Worst Case Scenario Ser.: WORS). (ENG.). 208p. (J). (gr. 4-7). 12.99 *(978-0-8118-7124-2(X))* Chronicle Bks. LLC.

—The Worst-Case Scenario: Everest - You Decide How to Survive! Borgenicht, David et al. 2011. (ENG.). 208p. (J). (gr. 4-5). 12.99 *(978-0-8118-7123-5(1))* Chronicle Bks. LLC.

Labat, Yancey C. Fun Foods for Holidays! 2007. 56p. (J). *(978-0-439-83229-8(2))* Scholastic, Inc.

—It's Party Time! 2006. 56p. (J). *(978-0-439-83227-4(6))* Scholastic, Inc.

—Let's Have a Cookout! 2007. 56p. (J). *(978-0-439-83228-1(4))* Scholastic, Inc.

—Make, Draw, & Design Your Own Book. Gaylord, Susan Kapuscinski & Jabbour, Joyce. 2006. 48p. (J). *(978-0-439-81339-6(5))* Scholastic, Inc.

—Pizza-Zazz & Lotsa Pasta. 2006. 56p. (J). *(978-0-439-83187-1(3))* Scholastic, Inc.

—Rise & Shine! It's Breakfast Time! 2006. 56p. (J). *(978-0-439-83223-6(3))* Scholastic, Inc.

—S'mores, Shakes & Chocolate Cakes: Chocolate, Chocolate All Day Long. 2006. 56p. (J). *(978-0-439-83226-7(8))* Scholastic, Inc.

—The Space Explorer's Guide to the Universe. Doyle, Bill. 2003. (Space University Ser.). 48p. (J). *(978-0-439-55739-9(9))* Scholastic, Inc.

Labbé, Jesse. Glubbery Gray, the Knight-Eating Beast, 1 vol. Kander, Beth & Kenyon, Bret. 2010. (ENG.). 40p. (J). (gr. k-3). 17.99 *(978-1-58980-867-6(3))* Pelican Publishing Co., Inc.

Labbe, Jesse & Coffey, Anthony. Fight for Amity. Labbe, Jesse & Coffey, Anthony. Morrissey, Paul, ed. 2011. (Berona's War Ser.: 1). (ENG.). 144p. (YA). (gr. 2). 19.95 *(978-1-936393-16-9(6))* Boom Entertainment, Inc.

Labeda, Patricia R. Miko & the Mystery Friend. Labeda, Patricia R. 2007. 73p. (J). (gr. 4-7). per. 10.99 *(978-1-59879-415-1(9),* Lifevest) Lifevest Publishing, Inc.

Labrecque, Candida & Labrecque, Candida. A Riverside Walk with Grandma. Labrecque, Candida. l.t. ed. 2006. 23p. (J). per. 11.95 *(978-1-59879-137-2(0))* Lifevest Publishing, Inc.

Labrecque, Candida, jt. illus. see Labrecque, Candida.

Lacámara, Laura. Alicia's Fruity Drinks / Las Aguas Frescas de Alicia. Ruiz-Flores, Lupe. Baeza Ventura, Gabriela, tr. from ENG. 2012. (SPA & ENG.). (J). 17.95 *(978-1-55885-705-6(2),* Piñata Books) Arte Publico Pr.

—The Runaway Piggy/El Cochinito Fugitivo. Luna, James & Villarroel, Carolina. 2010. (SPA.). 32p. (J). (gr. -1-3). 16.95 *(978-1-55885-586-1(6),* Piñata Books) Arte Publico Pr.

Lacamara, Laura. Dalia's Wondrous Hair / el Maravilloso Cabello de Dalia. Lacamara, Laura. Baeza Ventura, Gabriela, tr. from SPA. 2014. (ENG & SPA.). (J). 17.95 *(978-1-55885-789-6(3),* Piñata Books) Arte Publico Pr.

Lacapa, Michael. The Good Rainbow Road. Ortiz, Simon J. 2010. (ENG.). 80p. pap. 9.95 *(978-0-8165-2935-3(3))* University of Arizona Pr.

Lacey, Mike. Abraham Lincoln: The Life of America's Sixteenth President. Jeffery, Gary & Petty, Kate. 2005. (Graphic Biographies Ser.). (ENG.). 48p. (gr. 5-8). pap. 14.05 *(978-1-4042-5164-9(2))* Rosen Publishing Group, Inc., The.

—The Bermuda Triangle: Strange Happenings at Sea. West, David. 2006. (Graphic Mysteries Ser.). (ENG.). 48p. (gr. 5-8). pap. 14.05 *(978-1-4042-0806-3(2));* (YA). lib. bdg. 31.95 *(978-1-4042-0795-0(3))* Rosen Publishing Group, Inc., The.

—Hurricanes. Jeffrey, Gary. 2007. (Graphic Natural Disasters Ser.). (ENG.). 48p. (J). (gr. 5-9). lib. bdg. 31.95 *(978-1-4042-1991-5(9))* Rosen Publishing Group, Inc., The.

—Incredible Space Missions. Jeffrey, Gary. 2008. (Graphic Discoveries Ser.). (ENG.). 48p. (J). (gr. 5-9). lib. bdg. 31.95 *(978-1-4042-1090-5(3))* Rosen Publishing Group, Inc., The.

—Incredible Space Missions: By Gary Jeffrey: Illustrated by Mike Lacey. Jeffrey, Gary. 2008. (Graphic Nonfiction Ser.). (ENG.). 48p. (gr. 3-8). pap. 14.05 *(978-1-4042-9595-7(X))* Rosen Publishing Group, Inc., The.

Lacey, Mike & Harrison, Nancy. Who Was Beatrix Potter? Fabiny, Sarah. 2015. (Who Was... ? Ser.). (ENG.). 112p. (J). (gr. 3-7). 5.99 ***(978-0-448-48305-4(X),*** Grosset & Dunlap) Penguin Publishing Group.

Lacey, Mike & Harrison, Nancy. Who Was Susan B. Anthony? Pollack, Pamela D. & Belviso, Meg. 2014. (Who Was... ? Ser.). (ENG.). 112p. (J). (gr. 3-7). 5.99 *(978-0-448-47963-7(X),* Grosset & Dunlap) Penguin Publishing Group.

Lachuk, Dani. Saint Thomas More: Courage, Conscience, & the King. Wallace, Susan Helen & Jablonski, Patricia E. 2014. (ENG.). 144p. (J). pap. 8.95 *(978-0-8198-9021-4(9))* Pauline Bks. & Media.

Lacombe, Benjamin. Lin Yi's Lantern: A Moon Festival Tale. Williams, Brenda. 2009. (ENG.). 32p. (J). (gr. -1-5). 16.99 *(978-1-84686-147-5(0))* Barefoot Bks., Inc.

Lacombe, Benjamin. The Shrunken Head. Oliver, Lauren & Chester, H. C. 2015. (Curiosity House Ser.: 1). (ENG.). 368p. (J). (gr. 3-7). 16.99 ***(978-0-06-227081-8(8))*** HarperCollins Pubs.

Lacombe, Benjamin. Genealogía de una Bruja. Lacombe, Benjamin. Krahe, Elena Gallo, tr. 2009. (SPA.). 120p. (J). (gr. 4-6). *(978-84-263-7247-5(3))* Vives, Luis Editorial (Edelvives).

—Lin Yi's Lantern. Lacombe, Benjamin. Williams, Brenda. 2012. (ENG.). 32p. (J). (gr. -1-4). pap. 7.99 *(978-1-84686-793-4(2))* Barefoot Bks., Inc.

Lacome, Julie. Walking Through the Jungle Big Book. Lacome, Julie. 2004. (Big Books! Ser.). (ENG.). 32p. (J). (gr. k-k). pap. 24.99 *(978-0-7636-2471-2(3))* Candlewick Pr.

Lacome, Susie. Teddy Bear's Fun to Learn First 1000 Words. Baxter, Nicola. 2013. (ENG.). 96p. (J). (gr. -1-k). 12.99 *(978-1-84322-955-1(2))* Anness Publishing GBR. Dist: National Bk. Network.

—1000 First Words in French. Dopffer, Guillaume. 2013. (ENG & FRE.). 96p. (J). (gr. k-4). 12.99 *(978-1-84322-957-5(9))* Anness Publishing GBR. Dist: National Bk. Network.

—1000 First Words in German. Kenkmann, Andrea. 2013. (ENG & GER.). 96p. (J). (gr. k-4). 12.99 *(978-1-84322-958-2(7))* Anness Publishing GBR. Dist: National Bk. Network.

—1000 First Words in Italian. Campaniello, Don. 2013. (ENG & ITA.). 96p. (J). (gr. k-4). 12.99 *(978-1-84322-956-8(0))* Anness Publishing GBR. Dist: National Bk. Network.

—1000 First Words in Spanish. Budds, Sam. 2013. (ENG & SPA.). 96p. (J). (gr. k-4). 12.99 *(978-1-84322-959-9(5))* Anness Publishing GBR. Dist: National Bk. Network.

LaCoste, Gary. First Word Search: Phonics Word Search. 2011. (First Word Search Ser.). (ENG.). 64p. (J). (gr. -1-1). pap. 4.95 *(978-1-4027-7801-8(5))* Sterling Publishing Co., Inc.

—First Word Search: Words to Learn. 2011. (First Word Search Ser.). (ENG.). 64p. (J). (gr. -1-1). pap. 4.95 *(978-1-4027-7809-4(0))* Sterling Publishing Co., Inc.

—Phonics Fun. 2011. (First Word Search Ser.). (ENG.). 64p. (J). (gr. -1-1). pap. 4.95 *(978-1-4027-8391-3(4))* Sterling Publishing Co., Inc.

LaCoste, Gary. Poems from under My Bed: LOL Halloween Rhymes. Katz, Alan. 2013. 47p. (J). pap. ***(978-0-545-48295-0(X))*** Scholastic, Inc.

LaCoste, Gary. Sharks at Sea. Murray, Carol. 2008. (Storytime Stickers Ser.). (ENG.). 16p. (J). (gr. k-2). pap. 5.95 *(978-1-4027-4660-4(1))* Sterling Publishing Co., Inc.

—TJ Zaps a Nightmare: Stopping Blackmail Bullying #5. Mullarkey, Lisa. 2012. (TJ Trapper, Bully Zapper Ser.). 80p. (J). (gr. 2-5). lib. bdg. 27.07 *(978-1-61641-909-7(1),* Calico Chapter Bks) Magic Wagon.

—TJ Zaps the Freeze Out: Stopping the Silent Treatment #3. Mullarkey, Lisa. 2012. (TJ Trapper, Bully Zapper Ser.). 80p. (J). (gr. 2-5). lib. bdg. 27.07 *(978-1-61641-907-3(5),* Calico Chapter Bks) Magic Wagon.

—TJ Zaps the New Kid: Stopping a Social Bully #1. Mullarkey, Lisa. 2012. (TJ Trapper, Bully Zapper Ser.). 80p. (J). (gr. 2-5). lib. bdg. 27.07 *(978-1-61641-905-9(9),* Calico Chapter Bks) Magic Wagon.

—TJ Zaps the One-Upper: Stopping One-Upping & Cell Phone Bullying #2. Mullarkey, Lisa. 2012. (TJ Trapper, Bully Zapper Ser.). 80p. (J). (gr. 2-5). lib. bdg. 27.07 *(978-1-61641-906-6(7),* Calico Chapter Bks) Magic Wagon.

—TJ Zaps the Rumor Mill: Stopping Gossip #4. Mullarkey, Lisa. 2012. (TJ Trapper, Bully Zapper Ser.). 80p. (J). (gr. 2-5). lib. bdg. 27.07 *(978-1-61641-908-0(3),* Calico Chapter Bks) Magic Wagon.

—TJ Zaps the Smackdown: Stopping a Physical Bully #6. Mullarkey, Lisa. 2012. (TJ Trapper, Bully Zapper Ser.). 80p. (J). (gr. 2-5). lib. bdg. 27.07 *(978-1-61641-910-3(5),* Calico Chapter Bks) Magic Wagon.

—Ultimate Puzzle Challenge: Head Twisters. Hovanec, Helene. 2010. (ENG.). 96p. (J). (gr. 2-5). pap. 5.95 *(978-1-4027-6206-2(2))* Sterling Publishing Co., Inc.

Lacy, Lauren. Chocolate Cupcake: Celebrating Our Sweetness. Chocolate Cupcake Staff. 2010. (ENG.). 60p. pap. 15.00 *(978-1-4505-8529-3(9))* CreateSpace Independent Publishing Platform.

Ladd, London. Lend a Hand: Poems About Giving. Frank, John. 2014. (ENG.). 32p. (J). 17.95 *(978-1-60060-970-1(8))* Lee & Low Bks., Inc.

—March On! The Day My Brother Martin Changed the World. Farris, Christine King. 2011. (J). (gr. 2-7). 29.95 *(978-0-545-10689-4(3))* Weston Woods Studios, Inc.

—Under the Freedom Tree. Vanhecke, Susan. 2014. (J). pap. *(978-1-58089-551-4(4))* Charlesbridge Publishing, Inc.

—Under the Freedom Tree. VanHecke, Susan. 2014. (ENG.). 32p. (J). (gr. 1-4). lib. bdg. 16.95 *(978-1-58089-550-7(6))* Charlesbridge Publishing, Inc.

Ladecka, Anna. Mommy & Daddy Love You. Kim, Cecil. 2015. (MySELF Bookshelf Ser.). (ENG.). 32p. (J). (gr. k-2). pap. 11.94 *(978-1-60357-691-8(6));* lib. bdg. 22.60 *(978-1-59953-656-9(0))* Norwood Hse. Pr.

Laden, Nina. The Blues of Flats Brown. Myers, Walter Dean. 2005. (ENG.). 32p. (J). (gr. k-3). pap. 7.95 *(978-0-8234-1679-0(8))* Holiday Hse., Inc.

LaDuca, Michael. Can You Imagine? Seidler, Rena. 2011. (ENG.). 24p. pap. 14.99 *(978-1-4611-7114-0(8))* CreateSpace Independent Publishing Platform.

—The Don't-Give-Up Kid: And Learning Disabilities. Gehret, Jeanne. 4th ed. 2009. (Coping Ser.). (ENG.). 32p. (J). (gr. 1-3). 17.95 *(978-0-9821982-0-9(5))* Verbal Images Pr.

—Eagle Eyes: A Child's Guide to Paying Attention. Gehret, Jeanne. 4th ed. 2009. (Coping Ser.). (ENG.). 32p. (J). (gr. 1-3). 17.95 *(978-0-9821982-1-6(3))* Verbal Images Pr.

Ladwig, Tim. The Beatitudes: From Slavery to Civil Rights. Weatherford, Carole Boston. 2009. 36p. (J). (gr. 3-7). 16.99 *(978-0-8028-5352-3(8),* Eerdmans Bks For Young Readers) Eerdmans, William B. Publishing Co.

—The Delany Sisters Reach High. Hearth, Amy Hill. 2004. 32p. 17.00 *(978-0-687-03074-3(9))* Abingdon Pr.

L

—Especially Heroes. Kroll, Virginia L. 2004. 32p. (J). 16.00 *(978-0-8028-5221-2(1))* Eerdmans, William B. Publishing Co.

—Good King Wenceslas. Neale, J. M. 2005. 32p. (J). (gr. k-17). 16.99 *(978-0-8028-5209-0(2)*, Eerdmans Bks For Young Readers) Eerdmans, William B. Publishing Co.

—The Lord's Prayer. 2004. 32p. pap. 8.50 *(978-0-8028-5238-0(6))*; (J). (gr. -1-3). 17.00 *(978-0-8028-5180-2(0))* Eerdmans, William B. Publishing Co.

—Probity Jones & the Fear Not Angel. Wangerin, Walter, Jr. 2005. 32p. (J). (gr. 1-4). 16.95 *(978-1-55725-457-3(5))* Paraclete Pr., Inc.

—Tonight You Are My Baby: Mary's Christmas Gift. Norris, Jeannine Q. 2010. (HarperBlessings Ser.). (ENG.). 30p. (J). (gr. -1-k). bds. 7.99 *(978-0-06-147999-1(3)*, HarperFestival) HarperCollins Pubs.

—What Does the Sky Say? Carlstrom, Nancy White. 2004. 32p. (J). (gr. -1-3). 17.00 *(978-0-8028-5208-3(4))* Eerdmans, William B. Publishing Co.

—When Daddy Prays. Grimes, Nikki. 2004. 32p. (J). pap. 8.00 *(978-0-8028-5266-3(1))*; 16.00 *(978-0-8028-5152-9(5))* Eerdmans, William B. Publishing Co.

Lady Josephine. Madeline & Friends: Fruits & Veggies vs Candy. Hassan, Masood. 2010. *(978-0-9812600-6-8(3))* Sapphira Pubns.

Ladybird Books Staff. Peppa Pig & the Lost Christmas List. Candlewick Press Staff. 2012. (Peppa Pig Ser.). (ENG.). 32p. (J). (gr. k-k). 12.99 *(978-0-7636-6276-9(3))* Candlewick Pr.

Ladybird Books Staff. Peppa Pig & the Muddy Puddles. Ladybird Books Staff. Candlewick Press Staff. 2013. (Peppa Pig Ser.). (ENG.). 32p. (J). (-k). 12.99 *(978-0-7636-6523-4(1))* Candlewick Pr.

Ladybird Books Staff, jt. illus. see Candlewick Press, Candlewick.

Lafan, Algie. The Infinite Odyssey. Dingler, Jay. 2004. 540p. (YA). pap. 25.00 *(978-0-9754539-0-2(4))* Gray Jay Bks.

Lafarge, Kelly. An Ugly Black Bird, 1 vol. Lawson, Barbara. 2009. 35p. pap. 24.95 *(978-1-61546-656-6(8))* America Star Bks.

Lafave, Kim. Amos's Sweater, 1 vol. Lunn, Janet. 2nd ed. 2007. (ENG.). 32p. (J). (gr. -1-k). pap. 6.95 *(978-0-88899-845-3(7))* Groundwood Bks. CAN. Dist: Perseus-PGW.

LaFave, Kim. Angels Inc., 1 vol. McBay, Bruce. 2008. (ENG.). 72p. (J). (gr. 1-3). pap. 7.95 *(978-1-896580-30-2(0))* Tradewind Bks. CAN. Dist: Orca Bk. Pubs. USA.

—At the Circus, 1 vol. McFarlane, Sheryl. 2006. (What's That Sound? Ser.). (ENG.). 20p. (J). (gr. -1-k). bds. 6.95 *(978-1-55041-959-7(5)*, 1550419595) Fitzhenry & Whiteside, Ltd. CAN. Dist: Midpoint Trade Bks., Inc.

—Ben over Night, 1 vol. Ellis, Sarah. 2005. (ENG.). 32p. (J). 10.95 *(978-1-55041-807-1(6)*, 1550418076) Fitzhenry & Whiteside, Ltd. CAN. Dist: Midpoint Trade Bks., Inc.

—Big Ben. Ellis, Sarah. ed. 2004. (J). (gr. -1-1). spiral bd. *(978-0-616-11108-6(8))*; spiral bd. *(978-0-616-11109-3(6))* Canadian National Institute for the Blind/Institut National Canadien pour les Aveugles.

—A Bumblebee Sweater, 1 vol. Waterton, Betty. 2007. (ENG.). 32p. (J). (gr. -1-3). *(978-1-55455-028-9(9))* Fitzhenry & Whiteside, Ltd.

—Fire Fighters. Bourgeois, Paulette. 2005. 32p. (J). lib. bdg. 15.38 *(978-1-4242-1189-0(1))* Fitzgerald Bks.

—Firefighters. Bourgeois, Paulette & Bourgeois, Paulette. 2005. (Kids Can Read Ser.). (ENG.). 32p. (J). (gr. 1-3). 3.95 *(978-1-55337-751-1(6))* Kids Can Pr., Ltd. CAN. Dist: Univ. of Toronto Pr.

—Garbage Collectors. Bourgeois, Paulette. 2004. 32p. (J). lib. bdg. 15.38 *(978-1-4242-1190-6(5))* Fitzgerald Bks.

—Un Perro Muy Diferente. Harris, Dorothy Joan. Rioja, Alberto Jimenez, tr. from ENG. 2006. (SPA.). 28p. (J). (gr. 5-6). pap. 5.99 *(978-1-933032-04-7(9))* Lectorum Pubns., Inc.

—Police Workers. Bourgeois, Paulette. 2004. 32p. (J). lib. bdg. 15.38 *(978-1-4242-1191-3(3))* Fitzgerald Bks.

—Postal Workers. Bourgeois, Paulette. 2005. 32p. (J). lib. bdg. 15.38 *(978-1-4242-1192-0(1))* Fitzgerald Bks.

—Postal Workers. Bourgeois, Paulette & Bourgeois, Paulette. 2005. (Kids Can Read Ser.). (ENG.). 32p. (J). (gr. 1-3). 3.95 *(978-1-55337-747-4(8))* Kids Can Pr., Ltd. CAN. Dist: Univ. of Toronto Pr.

—Shi-Shi-Etko, 1 vol. Campbell, Nicola. 2005. (ENG.). 32p. (J). (gr. -1-2). 18.95 *(978-0-88899-659-6(4))* Groundwood Bks. CAN. Dist: Perseus-PGW.

Lafave, Kim. Shin-Chi's Canoe. Campbell, Nicola I. 2008. (ENG.). 40p. (J). (gr. -1-2). 18.95 *(978-0-88899-857-6(0))* Groundwood Bks. CAN. Dist: Perseus-PGW.

LaFave, Kim. We'll All Go Exploring, 1 vol. Thompson, Richard & Spicer, Maggee. 2003. (ENG.). 32p. (J). 5.95 *(978-1-55041-732-6(0)*, 1550417320) Fitzhenry & Whiteside, Ltd. CAN. Dist: Midpoint Trade Bks., Inc.

LaFerriere, Suzanne. Gracey's Desire. Castle, Jan And Kare. 2008. 28p. pap. 17.99 *(978-1-4389-2433-5(5))* AuthorHouse.

LaFever, Greg. The Legend of Ohio. Mackall, Dandi Daley. 2005. (Legend Ser.). (ENG.). 40p. (J). (gr. k-5). 17.95 *(978-1-58536-244-8(1))* Sleeping Bear Pr.

LaFleur, David. Stop That Bull, Theseus! McMullan, Kate. 2003. (Myth-o-Mania Ser.: Bk. 5). (ENG.). 160p. (J). (gr. 3-7). 9.99 *(978-0-7868-0861-8(6))* Hyperion Bks. for Children.

Lafrance, Daniel. War Brothers: The Graphic Novel. Lafrance, Daniel. McKay, Sharon E. 2013. (ENG.). 176p. (YA). (gr. 9-12). 27.95 *(978-1-55451-489-2(4)*, 9781554514892); pap. 18.95 *(978-1-55451-488-5(6)*, 9781554514885) Annick Pr., Ltd. CAN. Dist: Firefly Bks., Ltd.

Lafrance, David. L' Oiseau Tatoué. Chiasson, Herménégilde. 2004. (Poetry Ser.). (FRE.). 36p. (J). (gr. 7). pap. *(978-2-89021-675-4(6))* Diffusion du livre Mirabel (DLM).

LaFrance, Debbie. Elf Dog. Redmond, Pamela Woods. 2005. 44p. (J). 15.95 *(978-0-9760767-0-4(5))* Redmond, Pamela.

Lafrance, Marie. The Firehouse Light. Nolan, Janet. 2010. (ENG.). 32p. (J). (gr. k-3). 15.99 *(978-1-58246-298-1(4)*, Tricycle Pr.) Ten Speed Pr.

—The First Gift. Gadot, A. S. 2006. (ENG.). 24p. (J). (gr. -1-3). lib. bdg. 15.95 *(978-1-58013-146-9(8)*, Kar-Ben Publishing) Lerner Publishing Group.

Lafrance, Marie. Oscar Lives Next Door: A Story Inspired by Oscar Peterson's Childhood. Farmer, Bonnie. 2015. (ENG.). 32p. (J). (gr. k-3). 16.95 ***(978-1-77147-104-6(2)***, Owlkids) Owlkids Bks. Inc. CAN. Dist: Perseus-PGW.

Lafrance, Marie. The Princess & the Giant: A Tale from Scotland. 2013. (Tales of Honor (Red Chair Press) Ser.). (ENG.). 32p. (J). (gr. 1-4). lib. bdg. 26.60 *(978-1-937529-77-2(0))* Red Chair Pr.

—The Princess & the Giant: A Tale from Scotland. Barchers, Suzanne I. 2013. (Tales of Honor Ser.). 32p. (gr. 1-3). pap. 8.95 *(978-1-937529-61-1(4))* Red Chair Pr.

—Who Likes the Rain? Kaner, Etta. 2007. (Exploring the Elements Ser.). (ENG.). 32p. (J). (gr. -1-2). 14.95 *(978-1-55337-841-9(5))* Kids Can Pr., Ltd. CAN. Dist: Univ. of Toronto Pr.

—Who Likes the Snow? Kaner, Etta. 2006. (Exploring the Elements Ser.). (ENG.). 32p. (J). (gr. -1-2). 14.95 *(978-1-55337-842-6(3))* Kids Can Pr., Ltd. CAN. Dist: Univ. of Toronto Pr.

—Who Likes the Sun? Kaner, Etta. 2007. (Exploring the Elements Ser.). (ENG.). 32p. (J). (gr. -1-2). 14.95 *(978-1-55337-840-2(7))* Kids Can Pr., Ltd. CAN. Dist: Univ. of Toronto Pr.

—Who Likes the Wind? Kaner, Etta. 2006. (Exploring the Elements Ser.). (ENG.). 32p. (J). (gr. -1-2). 14.95 *(978-1-55337-839-6(3))* Kids Can Pr., Ltd. CAN. Dist: Univ. of Toronto Pr.

Lagares, Luciano. But It's True. Gemmen, Heather. 2004. (Tough Stuff for Kids Ser.). 36p. (J). (gr. 4-7). pap., pap. 5.99 *(978-0-7814-4033-2(5)*, 0781440335) Cook, David C.

Lagarrigue, Jerome. Freedom on the Menu: The Greensboro Sit-Ins. Weatherford, Carole Boston. 2004. (ENG.). 32p. (J). (gr. -1-3). 17.99 *(978-0-8037-2860-8(3)*, Dial) Penguin Publishing Group.

—Freedom on the Menu: The Greensboro Sit-Ins. Weatherford, Carole Boston. 2007. (gr. 4-7). 16.00 *(978-0-7569-8160-0(3))* Perfection Learning Corp.

—Freedom Summer. Wiles, Deborah. 50th anniv. ed. 2014. (ENG.). 32p. (J). (gr. -1-3). 17.99 *(978-1-4814-2298-7(7)*, Atheneum Bks. for Young Readers) Simon & Schuster Children's Publishing.

—Freedom Summer. Wiles, Deborah. 2005. (ENG.). 32p. (J). (gr. -1-3). reprint ed. 7.99 *(978-0-689-87829-9(X)*, Simon & Schuster/Paula Wiseman Bks.) Simon & Schuster/Paula Wiseman Bks.

—Going North. Harrington, Janice N. 2004. (ENG.). 40p. (J). (gr. k-3). 17.99 *(978-0-374-32681-4(9)*, Farrar, Straus & Giroux (BYR)) Farrar, Straus & Giroux.

Lagarrigue, Jerome. My Man Blue. Grimes, Nikki. 2015. 32p. pap. 7.00 ***(978-1-61003-533-0(X))*** Center for the Collaborative Classroom.

Lagarrigue, Jerome. Poetry for Young People: Maya Angelou. Wilson, Edwin Graves, ed. 2013. (Poetry for Young People Ser.). (ENG.). 48p. (J). (gr. 3). 14.95 *(978-1-4549-0329-1(5))* Sterling Publishing Co., Inc.

Lagarrigue, Jerome Lagarrigue. Freedom on the Menu: The Greensboro Sit-Ins. Weatherford, Carole Boston. 2007. (ENG.). 32p. (J). (gr. -1-3). pap. 5.99 *(978-0-14-240894-0(8)*, Puffin) Penguin Publishing Group.

Lago, Alexis. Mi Isla y Yo: La Naturaleza de Cuba. Silva Lee, Alfonso. Hayskar, Bonnie J., ed. 2010. (SPA.). 32p. (J). pap. 9.95 *(978-1-929165-22-3(6))* PANGAEA.

—Mi Isla y Yo: La Naturaleza de Puerto Rico. Silva Lee, Alfonso. Hayskar, Bonnie J., ed. 2007. (SPA.). 32p. (J). pap. 8.95 *(978-1-929165-19-3(6))* PANGAEA.

—Mi Isla y Yo: La Naturaleza de Republica Dominicana. Silva Lee, Alfonso. Hayskar, Bonnie, ed. 2010. (SPA.). 32p. (J). pap. 9.95 *(978-1-929165-25-4(0))* PANGAEA.

—Mi isla y yo/My Island & I: La naturaleza de Puerto Rico/The Nature of Puerto Rico. Silva Lee, Alfonso. Hayskar, Bonnie J., ed. 2003. (SPA & ENG.). 32p. (J). pap. 9.95 *(978-1-929165-12-4(9))* PANGAEA.

—Mon Ile et Moi: La Nature d'Haiti: Lanati an Ayti: Peyin Avem. Silva Lee, Alfonso. Hayskar, Bonnie, ed. Hilaire, Jean Vilmond, tr. 2010. (FRE & CRP.). 32p. (J). pap. 9.95 *(978-1-929165-28-5(5))* PANGAEA.

—My Island & I: The Nature of the Caribbean. Silva Lee, Alfonso. Hayskar, Bonnie J., ed. 2010. 32p. (J). pap. 9.95 *(978-1-929165-14-8(5))* PANGAEA.

Lago, Angela. El Cuento del Joven Marinero. Dinesen, Isak. 2008. (Coleccion Clasicos Ser.). Tr. of Skibsdrengens Fortlling. (SPA.). 26p. (J). (gr. 4-7). 12.99 *(978-968-16-8075-6(8))* Fondo de Cultura Economica USA.

Lago, Ray. Ivanhoe. Scott, Walter. 2011. (Classics Illustrated Graphic Novels Ser.: 13). (ENG.). 56p. (J). (gr. 3-9). 9.99 *(978-1-59707-248-9(6))* Papercutz.

Lago, Ray & Hamilton, Craig. Marwe: Into the Land of the Dead - An East African Folktale. Croall, Marie P. 2008. (Graphic Myths & Legends Ser.). (ENG.). 48p. (gr. 4-8). 27.93 *(978-0-8225-7134-6(X)*, Graphic Universe) Lerner Publishing Group.

—Marwe: Into the Land of the Dead [an East African Legend]. Croall, Marie P. 2009. (Graphic Myths & Legends Ser.). (ENG.). 48p. (gr. 4-8). pap. 8.95 *(978-0-8225-8514-5(6))* Lerner Publishing Group.

LaGrange, Tiffany. The Adventure of a Lifetime! Medley, Shari. 2009. 24p. pap. 10.95 *(978-1-936051-20-5(6))* Peppertree Pr., The.

—Animals & Stuff. Shaber, Mark. 2008. 32p. pap. 12.95 *(978-1-934246-10-8(7))* Peppertree Pr., The.

—Bunko's Journey. Bender, Randy L. 2008. 44p. pap. 13.95 *(978-0-9818683-2-5(0))* Peppertree Pr., The.

—Camp Charlie, the Adventures of Grandma Lipstick. Snyder, Karen. 2013. 20p. pap. 12.95 *(978-1-61493-218-5(2))* Peppertree Pr., The.

—Just Molly & Me & Nikki Make Three. Tarsy, Jean. 2008. 36p. pap. 12.95 *(978-0-9820479-6-5(7))* Peppertree Pr., The.

—Making Beautiful Music. Stilwell, Norma Minturn. 2011. 28p. pap. 14.95 *(978-1-936343-92-8(4))* Peppertree Pr., The.

—Mona Lisa's Makeover. Snyder, Karen. 2010. 24p. pap. 12.95 *(978-1-936343-15-7(0))* Peppertree Pr., The.

—Mrs Owl's Nest of Rhymes. Howell, Julie Ann. 2008. 24p. pap. 12.95 *(978-0-9818683-8-7(X))* Peppertree Pr., The.

—My Abc Blue Book. Lagrange, Tiffany. 2008. 32p. pap. 12.95 *(978-1-934246-38-2(7))* Peppertree Pr., The.

—My Abc Pink Book. Lagrange, Tiffany. 2008. 32p. pap. 12.95 *(978-0-9814894-3-8(5))* Peppertree Pr., The.

—Numbers All in a Row. Reeves, Pamela. 2008. 24p. pap. 12.95 *(978-0-9820479-5-8(9))* Peppertree Pr., The.

—The Pepper Tree, How the Seeds Were Planted! Howell, Julie. 2007. 28p. per. 12.95 *(978-1-934246-51-1(4))* Peppertree Pr., The.

—The Pepper Tree, How the Seeds Were Planted! Howell, Julie Ann. 2008. 28p. pap. 12.95 *(978-0-9820479-0-3(8))* Peppertree Pr., The.

—The Pepper Tree, How the Seeds Were Planted. Howell, Julie Ann. 2012. 28p. 24.95 *(978-1-61493-059-4(7))* Peppertree Pr., The.

—Safari Smooches. Snyder, Karen. 2011. 24p. pap. 12.95 *(978-1-936343-95-9(9))* Peppertree Pr., The.

—Talking to the Moon. Bootsma, Verner. 2007. 32p. per. 12.95 *(978-1-934246-70-2(0))* Peppertree Pr., The.

—United We Stand, a Story about Two Bullies. Reeves, Pamela. 2009. 24p. pap. 12.95 *(978-1-936051-36-6(2))* Peppertree Pr., The.

—Weather or Not? Falcon, David. 2009. 28p. pap. 12.95 *(978-1-936051-24-3(9))* Peppertree Pr., The.

Laguna, Fabio. Fang-Tastic! (Disney Junior: Henry Hugglemonster) Posner-Sanchez, Andrea. 2015. (Little Golden Book Ser.). (ENG.). 24p. (J). (-k). 3.99 *(978-0-7364-3348-8(1)*, Golden/Disney) Random Hse. Children's Bks.

—Sherman's Awesome Adventure. 2014. (Golden First Chapters Ser.). (ENG.). 80p. (J). (gr. 1-4). 4.99 *(978-0-385-37145-2(4)*, Golden Bks.) Random Hse. Children's Bks.

Laguna, Fabio & Cagol, Andrea. A Cake to Bake (Disney Princess) Jordan, Apple. 2014. (Step into Reading Ser.). (ENG.). 32p. (J). (gr. -1-1). 3.99 *(978-0-7364-3215-3(9)*, RH/Disney) Random Hse. Children's Bks.

—Frosty the Snowman Big Golden Book (Frosty the Snowman) Capozzi, Suzy. 2014. (Big Golden Book Ser.). (ENG.). 48p. (J). (gr. -1-2). 9.99 *(978-0-385-38877-1(2)*, Golden Bks.) Random Hse. Children's Bks.

Laguna, Fabio & Gallego, James. The Hugglefish (Disney Junior: Henry Hugglemonster) Posner-Sanchez, Andrea. 2015. (Little Golden Book Ser.). (ENG.). 24p. (J). (-k). 4.99 ***(978-0-7364-3360-0(0)***, Golden/Disney) Random Hse. Children's Bks.

Laguna, Fabio & Gallego, James. Let Them Eat Cake! (Mr. Peabody & Sherman) Random House. 2014. (Pictureback Series.). (ENG.). 24p. (J). (gr. -1-2). 3.99 *(978-0-385-37147-6(0)*, Random Hse. Bks. for Young Readers) Random Hse. Children's Bks.

Laguna, Fabio & Spaziante, Patrick. Mr. Peabody & Sherman Big Golden Book (Mr. Peabody & Sherman) David, Erica. 2014. (Big Golden Book Ser.). (ENG.). 48p. (J). (gr. k-4). 9.99 *(978-0-385-37142-1(X)*, Golden Bks.) Random Hse. Children's Bks.

Laguna, Fabio, jt. illus. see Dalton, Alex.

Laguna, Fabio, jt. illus. see RH Disney Staff.

Lahdensuo, Debbie. I Wish I Was... Teys, Jo-Anne. 2005. 36p. (J). pap. *(978-0-9757001-1-2(1))* Love Song Publishing.

Lai, Ben, et al. Sigil: Out of Time. Waid, Mark et al. 2011. (ENG.). 96p. (YA). (gr. 8-17). pap. 14.99 *(978-0-7851-5622-2(4))* Marvel Worldwide, Inc.

Lai, Hsin-Shih. The Bremen Town Musicians. Bell, Anthea, ed. Bell, Anthea, tr. 2007. 32p. (J). (gr. -1-3). 17.95 *(978-0-88010-583-5(6)*, Bell Pond Bks.) SteinerBooks, Inc.

—Thumbelina. Andersen, Hans Christian. 2008.Tr. of Tommelise. 56p. (J). 19.95 *(978-0-88010-592-7(5)*, Bell Pond Bks.) SteinerBooks, Inc.

Lai-Ma. The Monster of Palapala Mountain. Lai-Ma. Lai-Ma. 2006. (ENG.). 44p. (J). (gr. -1-k). 17.95 *(978-0-9762056-5-4(3))* Heryin Publishing Corp.

Laidley, Victoria, jt. illus. see Antonello, Marisa.

Lailah, Daniel, photos by. Kids Cooking Made Easy. Schapira, Leah & Dwek, Victoria. 2013. (ENG.). 144p. (J). pap. 15.99 *(978-1-4226-1435-8(2))* Mesorah Pubns., Ltd.

Lainez, René Colato & Graullera Ramirez, Fabiola. René Has Two Last Names/René Tiene Dos Apellidos. Lainez, René Colato. 2009. (SPA & ENG.). 32p. (J). (gr. -1-3). 16.95 *(978-1-55885-530-4(0))* Arte Publico Pr.

Laing, Sarah. The Curioseum: Collected Stories of the Odd & Marvellous. Jansen, Adrienne, ed. 2014. (ENG.). 160p. (J). (gr. 4-7). pap. 24.99 *(978-1-877385-92-6(1))* Te Papa Pr. NZL. Dist: Independent Pubs. Group.

Laiug, Naucie, jt. illus. see Walker, John.

Lajeunesse, Nicolas. Silent Words. Fournier, Chantal. deluxe ed. 2013. (ENG.). 52p. 26.95 *(978-1-62253-096-0(9))*; pap. 10.95 *(978-1-62253-098-4(5))* Evolved Publishing.

Lajic, Maïté, jt. illus. see Buffiere, Mélanie.

Lake, Oliver. Beauty & the Beast: Les Petits Fairytales. Belle, Trixie & Caruso-Scott, Melissa. 2013. (Petits Fairytales Ser.). (ENG.). 26p. (J). (gr. -1 — 1). bds. 7.99 *(978-0-8050-9788-7(0)*, Holt, Henry & Co. Bks. For Young Readers) Holt, Henry & Co.

—Cinderella: Les Petits Fairytales. Mack, Tracy et al. 2012. (Petits Fairytales Ser.). (ENG.). 24p. (J). (gr. -1 — 1). bds. 7.99 *(978-0-8050-9624-8(8)*, Holt, Henry & Co. Bks. For Young Readers) Holt, Henry & Co.

—Goldilocks & the Three Bears: Les Petits Fairytales. Belle, Trixie & Caruso-Scott, Melissa. 2014. (Petits Fairytales Ser.). (ENG.). 26p. (J). (gr. -1 — 1). bds. 7.99 *(978-0-8050-9912-6(3)*, Holt, Henry & Co. Bks. For Young Readers) Holt, Henry & Co.

—The Little Mermaid: Les Petits Fairytales. Belle, Trixie & Caruso-Scott, Melissa. 2013. (Petits Fairytales Ser.). (ENG.). 26p. (J). (gr. -1 — 1). bds. 7.99 *(978-0-8050-9789-4(9)*, Holt, Henry & Co. Bks. For Young Readers) Holt, Henry & Co.

—Little Red Riding Hood: Les Petits Fairytales. Belle, Trixie & Caruso-Scott, Melissa. 2014. (Petits Fairytales Ser.). (ENG.). 26p. (J). (gr. -1 — 1). bds. 7.99 *(978-0-8050-9905-8(0)*, Holt, Henry & Co. Bks. For Young Readers) Holt, Henry & Co.

—Rapunzel. Belle, Trixie & Caruso-Scott, Melissa. 2013. (Petits Fairytales Ser.). (ENG.). 26p. (J). (gr. -1 — 1). bds. 7.99 *(978-0-8050-9790-0(2)*, Holt, Henry & Co. Bks. For Young Readers) Holt, Henry & Co.

—Sleeping Beauty: Les Petits Fairytales. Belle, Trixie & Caruso-Scott, Melissa. 2013. (Petits Fairytales Ser.). (ENG.). 26p. (J). (gr. -1 — 1). bds. 7.99 *(978-0-8050-9791-7(0)*, Holt, Henry & Co. Bks. For Young Readers) Holt, Henry & Co.

—Snow White: Les Petits Fairytales. Mack, Tracy et al. 2012. (Petits Fairytales Ser.). (ENG.). 26p. (J). (gr. -1 — 1). bds. 7.99 *(978-0-8050-9623-1(X)*, Holt, Henry & Co. Bks. For Young Readers) Holt, Henry & Co.

Lakes, Lofton & Metu. The Dream Team. 2007. 48p. (YA). pap. *(978-0-9799320-0-7(9))* Pinkney, Gail.

Laliberete, Louise-Andree. Dimples Delight. Wishinsky, Frieda. 2005. (SPA.). 61p. (J). lib. bdg. 20.00 *(978-1-4242-1252-1(9))* Fitzgerald Bks.

Laliberté, Louise-Andrée. A Bee in Your Ear, 1 vol. Wishinsky, Frieda. 2004. (Orca Echoes Ser.). (ENG.). 64p. (J). (gr. 2-3). pap. 6.95 *(978-1-55143-324-0(9))* Orca Bk. Pubs. USA.

Laliberte, Louise-Andree. A Bee in Your Ear. Wishinsky, Frieda. 2004. 64p. (J). lib. bdg. 20.00 *(978-1-4242-1255-2(3))* Fitzgerald Bks.

Laliberté, Louise-Andrée. Dimples Delight, 1 vol. Wishinsky, Frieda. 2005. (Orca Echoes Ser.). (ENG.). 64p. (J). (gr. 2-3). per. 6.95 *(978-1-55143-362-2(1))* Orca Bk. Pubs. USA.

—A Frog in My Throat, 1 vol. Wishinsky, Frieda. 2008. (Orca Echoes Ser.). (ENG.). 64p. (J). (gr. 2-3). pap. 6.95 *(978-1-55143-632-6(9))* Orca Bk. Pubs. USA.

—A Noodle up Your Nose, 1 vol. Wishinsky, Frieda. 2004. (Orca Echoes Ser.). (ENG.). 64p. (J). (gr. 2-3). pap. 6.95 *(978-1-55143-294-6(3))* Orca Bk. Pubs. USA.

Laliberte, Mario. Match, Sort & Play. 2007. (Hands-on Bks.). 48p. (J). (gr. -1-k). spiral bd. *(978-2-7641-1936-5(4))* Tormont Pubns.

Lalla, Christine, photos by. This Is My Digger. Oxlade, Chris. 2008. (Mega Machine Drivers Ser.). 30p. (J). (gr. k). lib. bdg. 28.50 *(978-1-59771-104-3(7))* Sea-To-Sea Pubns.

—This Is My Tractor. Oxlade, Chris. 2008. (Mega Machine Drivers Ser.). 30p. (J). (gr. k). lib. bdg. 28.50 *(978-1-59771-106-7(3))* Sea-To-Sea Pubns.

Lally, Cory. The Adventures of Pea-Shooter: Into the Forbidden Forest. Serino, Robert. 2012. 32p. pap. 24.95 *(978-1-4626-8019-1(4))* America Star Bks.

LaLonde, Deanna L. The Golden Metis. Ell, Flynn J. 2004. 352p. (J). pap. *(978-1-894717-20-5(1)*, Spotlight Poets) Pemmican Pubns., Inc.

Lalonde, Johnathan. Hide Tommy Turkey. Lalonde, Carolyn. 2005. 20p. (J). 9.60 *(978-1-4120-4893-4(1))* Trafford Publishing.

Lam, Maple. Two Girls Want a Puppy. Cordell, Ryan & Cordell, Evie. 2015. (ENG.). 32p. (J). (gr. -1-3). 17.99 *(978-0-06-229261-2(7))* HarperCollins Pubs.

Laman, Tim, photos by. Rain Forest Colors. Lawler, Janet. 2014. (ENG., 32p. (J). (-k). 16.99 *(978-1-4263-1733-0(6)*, National Geographic Children's Bks.) National Geographic Society.

Lamanna, Paolo, jt. illus. see Rigano, Giovanni.

LaMarca, Luke. The Curious Demise of a Contrary Cat. Berry, Lynne. 2006. (ENG.). 40p. (J). (gr. -1-3). 17.99 *(978-1-4169-0211-9(2)*, Simon & Schuster Bks. For Young Readers) Simon & Schuster Bks. For Young Readers.

—The Day Ray Got Away. Johnson, Angela. 2010. (ENG.). 40p. (J). (gr. k-3). 16.99 *(978-0-689-87375-1(1)*, Simon & Schuster Bks. For Young Readers) Simon & Schuster Bks. For Young Readers.

LaMarche, Jim. Albert. Napoli, Donna Jo. 2005. (ENG.). 32p. (J). (gr. -1-3). reprint ed. pap. 7.00 *(978-0-15-205249-2(6))* Houghton Mifflin Harcourt Publishing Co.

—The Carpenter's Gift: A Christmas Tale about the Rockefeller Center Tree. Rubel, David. 2011. (ENG.). 48p. (J). (gr. k-4). 17.99 *(978-0-375-86922-8(0))* Random Hse., Inc.

—Ivy Takes Care. Wells, Rosemary. (ENG.). 208p. (J). (gr. 3-7). 2015. pap. 6.99 *(978-0-7636-7660-5(8))*; 2013. 15.99 *(978-0-7636-5352-1(7))* Candlewick Pr.

—The Little Fir Tree. Brown, Margaret Wise. 32p. (J). (gr. -1-1). 2009. (ENG.). pap. 6.99 *(978-0-06-443529-1(6))*; 2005. lib. bdg. 16.89 *(978-0-06-028190-8(1))*; 2005. (ENG.). 15.99 *(978-0-06-028189-2(8))* HarperCollins Pubs.

—The Rainbabies. Melmed, Laura Krauss. 2004. (ENG.). 32p. (J). (gr. -1-3). pap. 6.99 *(978-0-688-15113-3(2))* HarperCollins Pubs.

—Sea of Sleep. Hanson, Warren. 2010. (ENG.). 32p. (J). (gr. -1-3). 16.99 *(978-0-439-69735-4(2)*, Scholastic Pr.) Scholastic, Inc.

—Winter Is Coming. Johnston, Tony. 2014. (ENG.). 40p. (J). (gr. -1-3). 17.99 *(978-1-4424-7251-8(0)*, Simon & Schuster Bks. For Young Readers) Simon & Schuster Bks. For Young Readers.

LaMarche, Jim & Andreasen, Dan. The Map Trap. Clements, Andrew. 2014. (ENG.). 144p. (J). (gr. 3-7). 16.99 *(978-1-4169-9727-6(X)*, Atheneum Bks. for Young Readers) Simon & Schuster Children's Publishing.

Lamb, Braden, jt. illus. see Paroline, Shelli.

Lamb, Branden, jt. illus. see Paroline, Shelli.

Lamb, Janie. Around Our Feeder with George the Groundhog & Friends. Renshaw, Douglas. 2008. 48p. pap. 24.95 *(978-1-60610-657-0(0))* America Star Bks.

Lamb, Karen. The Music Handbook - Level 3: A Handbook for Teaching Key Music Skills (Inc. 7 Audio CDs) Rowsell, Cyrilla & Vinden, David. 2011. 212p. spiral bd. 59.95 (978-1-84414-265-1(5)) Jolly Learning, Ltd. GBR. Dist: American International Distribution Corp.
Lamb, Melody. Thomas & Autumn. Laiz, Jana. 2013. 40p. (J). 14.95 (978-0-9814910-9-7(X)) Crow Flies Pr.
Lamb, Michael. Ace Canary & Dud Clutch. Lamb, Phillip C. 2011. 40p. pap. 24.95 (978-1-4626-0401-2(3)) America Star Bks.
Lamb, Rosy. Paul Meets Bernadette. Lamb, Rosy. 2013. (ENG.). 40p. (J). (gr. -1-3). 14.00 (978-0-7636-6130-4(9)) Candlewick Pr.
Lamb, Sally Ann. Best of Friends! Roddie, Shen & Quarto Generic Staff. 2004. (ENG.). 25p. (J). (gr. -1-17). pap. 7.95 (978-1-84507-172-1(7), Frances Lincoln) Quarto Publishing Group UK GBR. Dist: Hachette Bk. Group.
Lamb, Sandra. Je Suis Ballerine! Coulman, Valerie. Duchesne, Christiane, tr. from ENG. (FRE.). 32p. (J). pap. 6.95 (978-2-922435-05-4(9)) Editions Homard CAN. Dist: Univ. of Toronto Pr.
Lamb, Stacey. ABC. 2009. (Sticker Bks). 24p. (J). pap. 6.99 (978-0-7945-2362-6(5), Usborne) EDC Publishing.
—Dinosaurs. Taplin, Sam. ed. 2011. (First Sticker Books Ser.). 16p. (J). pap. 6.99 (978-0-7945-2994-9(1), Usborne) EDC Publishing.
—My ABC Bible, 1 vol. Bowman, Crystal. 2012. (ENG.). 56p. (J). 5.99 (978-0-310-73037-8(6)) Zonderkidz.
—My ABC Prayers, 1 vol. Bowman, Crystal. 2012. (ENG.). 56p. (J). 5.99 (978-0-310-73039-2(2)) Zonderkidz.
Lamb, Stacey, et al. My First Christmas Activity Book. 2013. (ENG.). 50p. (J). pap. 11.99 (978-0-7945-3182-9(2), Usborne) EDC Publishing.
Lamb, Stacey. Wipe Clean 123 Book. ed. 2011. (Wipe-Clean Bks). 20p. (J). pap. 7.99 (978-0-7945-3075-4(3), Usborne) EDC Publishing.
—Wipe Clean Alphabet Book. ed. 2011. (Wipe-Clean Bks). 20p. (J). pap. 7.99 (978-0-7945-3099-0(0), Usborne) EDC Publishing.
—Wipe-Clean Doodles. ed. 2013. (Wipe-Clean Bks). 20p. (J). pap. 7.99 (978-0-7945-3312-0(4), Usborne) EDC Publishing.
—Wipe-Clean Dot-To-Dot. ed. 2013. (Wipe-Clean Bks). 20p. (J). pap. 7.99 (978-0-7945-3278-9(0), Usborne) EDC Publishing.
—Wipe Clean First Letters. ed. 2011. (Wipe-Clean Bks). 20p. (J). pap. 7.99 (978-0-7945-3100-3(8), Usborne) EDC Publishing.
—Wipe-Clean Mazes. ed. 2012. (Wipe-Clean Bks). 20p. (J). pap. 7.99 (978-0-7945-3257-4(8), Usborne) EDC Publishing.
—Wipe Clean Ready for Writing. ed. 2011. (Wipe-Clean Bks). 20p. (J). pap. 7.99 (978-0-7945-3076-1(1), Usborne) EDC Publishing.
—123 Sticker Book. 2009. (Sticker Bks). 24p. (J). pap. 6.99 (978-0-7945-2361-9(7), Usborne) EDC Publishing.
Lamb, Stacey. Shapes Sticker Book. Lamb, Stacey. 2009. (Sticker Bks). 16p. (J). pap. 6.99 (978-0-7945-2501-9(6), Usborne) EDC Publishing.
Lamb, Stacy. First Puzzles. 2014. (Usborne Wipe-Clean Ser.). (ENG.). 22p. (J). pap. 7.99 (978-0-7945-2524-8(5), Usborne) EDC Publishing.
Lamb, Susan Condie. Miss Dorothy & Her Bookmobile. Houston, Gloria M. 2011. (ENG.). 32p. (J). (gr. 1-4). 16.99 (978-0-06-029155-6(9)) HarperCollins Pubs.
—Prairie Primer: A to Z. Stutson, Caroline. 2006. 29p. (J). (gr. -1-2). reprint ed. 16.00 (978-1-4223-5585-5(3)) DIANE Publishing Co.
Lamb, T. S. Asim the Awesome Possum: Asim Gets His Awesome. Oddo, Jennifer M. 2012. 36p. 16.95 (978-0-9855906-2-8(9)) Pie Plate Publishing Co.
Lambdin, Victor R. Viking Tales (Yesterday's Classics) Hall, Jennie. 2005. 168p. (J). per. 8.95 (978-1-59915-004-8(2)) Yesterday's Classics.
Lambe, Steve. Green vs. Mean (Teenage Mutant Ninja Turtles) Golden Books Staff & Smith, Geof. 2013. (Little Golden Book Ser.). (ENG.). 24p. (J). (-k). 3.99 (978-0-449-81765-0(2), Golden Bks.) Random Hse. Children's Bks.
Lambe, Steve, jt. illus. see Golden Books Staff.
Lambert, Angela. Animals. 2004. (All Change! Ser.). (ENG.). 12p. (J). (gr. -1-k). bds. (978-1-904550-16-7(9)) Child's Play International Ltd.
Lambert, Celeste. 8 Boys & 8 Beasts, 1 vol. Lambert, George J. 2010. 24p. 24.95 (978-1-4489-5901-3(2)) PublishAmerica, Inc.
Lambert, Jonathan. Charlie Chimp's Christmas: A Pop-up Extravaganza of Festive Friends. Faulkner, Keith. 2006. 12p. (J). (gr. -1-3). reprint ed. 10.00 (978-1-4223-5446-9(6)) DIANE Publishing Co.
—Cuddly Koala. Goldhawk, Emma. 2015. (Snuggle Puppet Ser.). (ENG.). 10p. bds. 14.95 (978-1-62686-328-6(8), Silver Dolphin Bks.) Baker & Taylor Publishing Group.
—Little Lamb. Goldhawk, Emma. 2014. (Snuggle Puppet Ser.). (ENG.). 10p. (J). (gr. -1). bds. 14.95 (978-1-62686-014-8(9), Silver Dolphin Bks.) Baker & Taylor Publishing Group.
—Snuggle Bunny. Goldhawk, Emma. 2015. (Snuggle Puppet Ser.). (ENG.). 10p. (J). bds. 14.95 (978-1-62686-327-9(X), Silver Dolphin Bks.) Baker & Taylor Publishing Group.
Lambert, Sally Anne. Gator Gumbo: A Spicy-Hot Tale. Fleming, Candace. 2004. (ENG.). 32p. (J). (gr. -1-3). 18.99 (978-0-374-38050-2(3), Farrar, Straus & Giroux (BYR)) Farrar, Straus & Giroux.
—The Story of the Easter Bunny. Tegen, Katherine. 40p. (J). (gr. -1-3). 2007. (ENG.). pap. 6.99 (978-0-06-058781-9(4)); 2005. (ENG.). 12.99 (978-0-06-050711-4(X)); 2005. lib. bdg. 14.89 (978-0-06-050712-1(8)) HarperCollins Pubs.
—The Story of the Leprechaun. Tegen, Katherine Brown. 2011. (J). lib. bdg. 14.89 (978-0-06-143085-5(4)); (ENG.). 40p. (gr. -1-3). 12.99 (978-0-06-143086-2(2)) HarperCollins Pubs.
—The Yippy, Yappy Yorkie in the Green Doggy Sweater. Macomber, Debbie & Carney, Mary Lou. 2011. (ENG.). 32p. (J). (gr. -1-2). 16.99 (978-0-06-165096-3(X)) HarperCollins Pubs.
Lambert, Stephen. Christmas Is Coming! Wood, A. J. 2009. (ENG.). 12p. (J). (gr. -1-3). 16.95 (978-0-8109-3898-4(7), Abrams Bks. for Young Readers) Abrams.
—Little Book of Horses & Ponies. Khan, Sarah. 2010. (Miniature Editions Ser.). 64p. (YA). (gr. 3-18). 6.99 (978-0-7945-2791-4(4), Usborne) EDC Publishing.
—El Reloj de Mi Abuela. MacCaughrean, Geraldine et al. 2003. (SPA.). 32p. (J). (gr. k-2). 14.99 (978-84-241-8643-2(5)) Everest Editora ESP. Dist: Lectorum Pubns., Inc.
—Shakespeare's Tales. Birch, Beverley. 2003. 128p. pap. (978-0-340-79891-1(2), Hodder Children's Books) Hachette Children's Group.
—El Viaje en Tren. Crebbin, June. Rubio, Esther, tr. 2004. (SPA.). (J). 7.95 (978-1-930332-76-8(9)) Lectorum Pubns., Inc.
Lambiase, Lauren. Glove of Their Own. Conkling, Keri. 2008. 32p. 15.95 (978-0-9760469-5-0(4)) Franklin Mason Pr.
Lambil, Willy. Bluecoats - Greenhorn, Vol. 4. Cauvin, Raoul. 4th ed. 2011. (ENG.). 48p. (gr. 3-17). pap. 11.95 (978-1-84918-066-5(0)) CineBook GBR. Dist: National Bk. Network.
—Bluecoats the, Vol. 6: Bronco Benny. Cauvin, Raoul. 2013. (ENG.). 48p. pap. 11.95 (978-1-84918-146-4(2)) CineBook GBR. Dist: National Bk. Network.
—The Navy Blues. Cauvin, Raoul. 2009. (ENG.). 46p. (J). (gr. 4-7). pap. 11.95 (978-1-905460-82-3(1)) CineBook GBR. Dist: National Bk. Network.
—Robertsonville Prison, Vol. 1. Cauvin, Raoul. 2009. (ENG.). 46p. (J). (gr. -1-17). pap. 11.95 (978-1-905460-71-7(6)) CineBook GBR. Dist: National Bk. Network.
—Rumberley. Cauvin, Raoul. 2012. (ENG.). 48p. (J). (gr. 3-8). pap. 11.95 (978-1-84918-108-2(X)) CineBook GBR. Dist: National Bk. Network.
Lambo, Don. Magic Fingers. Mulcahy, Lucille. 2012. 124p. 40.95 (978-1-258-23435-5(1)); pap. 25.95 (978-1-258-24669-3(4)) Literary Licensing, LLC.
Lambson, Elizabeth. Just Like You. Gill, Janie S. Date not set. 5.95 (978-0-89868-430-8(7)); pap. 3.95 (978-0-89868-429-2(3)) ARO Publishing Co.
—Socks. Spaht-Gill, Janie. (J). 5.95 (978-0-89868-301-1(7)) ARO Publishing Co.
Lamere, Jill. Upside Down. Lamere, Jill. 2005. (J). bds. 12.95 (978-0-9772320-0-0(X)) Minikin Pr.
Lammle, Leslie. Pajama Pirates. Kramer, Andrew. 2010. (ENG.). 40p. (J). (gr. k-3). 16.99 (978-0-06-125194-8(1)) HarperCollins Pubs.
Lammle, Leslie. Once upon a Saturday. Lammle, Leslie. 2009. 32p. (J). (gr. k-2). lib. bdg. 18.89 (978-0-06-125191-7(7)); (ENG.). 17.99 (978-0-06-125190-0(9)) HarperCollins Pubs.
—Princess Wannabe. Lammle, Leslie. 2014. (ENG.). 40p. (J). (gr. -1-3). 17.99 (978-0-06-125197-9(6)) HarperCollins Pubs.
Lamont, Priscilla. All Kinds of Kisses. Dowdy, Linda Cress. 2010. (ENG.). 24p. (J). (gr. -1-k). bds. 8.99 (978-0-545-14599-2(6), Cartwheel Bks.) Scholastic, Inc.
—Animal Rescue Team: Gator on the Loose! Stauffacher, Sue. 2011. (Animal Rescue Team Ser.). (ENG.). 160p. (J). (gr. 3-7). 5.99 (978-0-375-85131-5(3), Yearling) Random Hse. Children's Bks.
—Animal Rescue Team: Hide & Seek. Stauffacher, Sue. 2011. (Animal Rescue Team Ser.). (ENG.). 160p. (J). (gr. 3-7). 5.99 (978-0-375-85133-9(X), Yearling) Random Hse. Children's Bks.
—Animal Rescue Team: Show Time. Stauffacher, Sue. 2011. (Animal Rescue Team Ser.). (ENG.). 160p. (J). (gr. 3-7). 5.99 (978-0-375-85134-6(8), Yearling) Random Hse. Children's Bks.
—Animal Rescue Team: Special Delivery! Stauffacher, Sue. 2011. (Animal Rescue Team Ser.). (ENG.). 176p. (J). (gr. 3-7). 5.99 (978-0-375-85132-2(1), Yearling) Random Hse. Children's Bks.
—Gator on the Loose! Stauffacher, Sue. 2010. (Animal Rescue Team Ser.). (ENG.). 160p. (J). (gr. 3-7). 12.99 (978-0-375-85847-5(4), Knopf Bks. for Young Readers) Random Hse. Children's Bks.
—Goose & Duck. George, Jean Craighead. 2008. (I Can Read Book 2 Ser.). (ENG.). 48p. (J). (gr. k-3). 16.99 (978-0-06-117076-8(3)) HarperCollins Pubs.
—The Lion Nursery Bible. Pasquali, Elena. 2014. (ENG.). 192p. (J). (gr. -1 — 1). 14.99 (978-0-7459-6399-0(4)) Lion Hudson PLC GBR. Dist: Independent Pubs. Group.
—Lovely Old Roly. Rosen, Michael & Quarto Generic Staff. 2004. (ENG.). 32p. (J). (gr. -1-2). pap. 7.95 (978-1-84507-144-8(1), Frances Lincoln) Quarto Publishing Group UK GBR. Dist: Hachette Bk. Group.
—Lulu & the Cat in the Bag. McKay, Hilary. (Lulu Ser.: 3). (ENG.). 112p. (J). (gr. 2-5). 2014. pap. 4.99 (978-0-8075-4805-9(7)); 2013. 13.99 (978-0-8075-4804-2(9)) Whitman, Albert & Co.
—Lulu & the Dog from the Sea. McKay, Hilary. 2013. (Lulu Ser.: Book 2). (ENG.). 112p. (J). (gr. 2-5). 13.99 (978-0-8075-4820-2(0)) Whitman, Albert & Co.
—Lulu & the Duck in the Park. McKay, Hilary. (Lulu Ser.: Book 1). (ENG.). (J). (gr. 2-5). 2012. 104p. 13.99 (978-0-8075-4808-0(1)); Bk. 1. 2014. 112p. 4.99 (978-0-8075-4809-7(X)) Whitman, Albert & Co.
—Lulu & the Hamster in the Night. McKay, Hilary. 2015. (Lulu Ser.: 6). (ENG.). 112p. (J). (gr. 2-5). 13.99 (978-0-8075-4824-0(3)) Whitman, Albert & Co.
—Lulu & the Hedgehog in the Rain. McKay, Hilary. 2014. (Lulu Ser.: 5). (ENG.). 112p. (J). (gr. 2-5). 13.99 (978-0-8075-4812-7(X)) Whitman, Albert & Co.
—Secrets of the Garden: Food Chains & the Food Web in Our Backyard. Zoehfeld, Kathleen Weidner. (ENG.). 40p. (J). (gr. k-3). 2014. 7.99 (978-0-385-75364-7(0), Dragonfly Bks.); 2012. 16.99 (978-0-517-70990-0(2), Random Hse. Bks. for Young Readers) Random Hse. Children's Bks.
—Show Time. Stauffacher, Sue. 2011. (Animal Rescue Team Ser.). (ENG.). 160p. (J). (gr. 3-7). 12.99 (978-0-375-85850-5(4)) Knopf, Alfred A. Inc.
—Special Delivery! Stauffacher, Sue. 2010. (Animal Rescue Team Ser.: No. 2). (ENG.). 176p. (J). (gr. 3-7). 12.99 (978-0-375-85848-2(2)) Knopf, Alfred A. Inc.
—Tom & Sofia Start School. Barkow, Henriette. 2004. (J). (BEN, ENG & MAL.). (978-1-84444-573-8(9)); (MAL & ENG.). 32p. pap. (978-1-84444-587-5(9)); (SPA & ENG.). 32p. pap. (978-1-84444-586-8(0)); (SOM & ENG.). 32p. pap. (978-1-84444-585-1(2)); (ENG & VIE.). 32p. pap. (978-1-84444-584-4(4)); (URD & ENG.). 32p. pap. (978-1-84444-583-7(6)); (ENG & TUR.). 32p. pap. (978-1-84444-582-0(8)); (TAM & ENG.). 32p. pap. (978-1-84444-581-3(X)); (ENG & TGL.). 32p. pap. (978-1-84444-580-6(1)); (ENG & RUS.). 32p. pap. (978-1-84444-579-0(8)); (ENG & POR.). 32p. pap. (978-1-84444-577-6(1)); (ENG & POL.). 32p. pap. (978-1-84444-576-9(3)); (ENG & PAN.). 32p. pap. (978-1-84444-575-2(5)); (ENG & KUR.). 32p. pap. (978-1-84444-574-5(7)); (ENG & JPN.). 32p. pap. (978-1-84444-572-1(0)); (ENG & ITA.). 32p. pap. (978-1-84444-571-4(2)); (ENG & HIN.). 32p. pap. (978-1-84444-570-7(4)); (ENG & GUJ.). 32p. pap. (978-1-84444-569-1(0)); (ENG & GRE.). 32p. pap. (978-1-84444-568-4(2)); (ENG & GER.). 32p. pap. (978-1-84444-567-7(4)); (FRE & ENG.). 32p. pap. (978-1-84444-566-0(6)); (ENG & PER.). 32p. pap. (978-1-84444-565-3(8)); (ENG & CHI.). 32p. pap. (978-1-84444-564-6(X)); (CHI & ENG.). 32p. pap. (978-1-84444-563-9(1)); (ENG & BEN.). 32p. pap. (978-1-84444-562-2(3)); (ENG & ARA.). 32p. pap. (978-1-84444-561-5(5)); (ENG & ALB.). 32p. pap. (978-1-84444-560-8(7)) Mantra Lingua.
Lamoreaux, M. A. The Princess & the Pea: The Graphic Novel, 1 vol. Andersen, Hans Christian. 2009. (Graphic Spin Ser.). (ENG.). 40p. (gr. 1-3). pap. 5.95 (978-1-4342-1743-1(4), Graphic Revolve) Stone Arch Bks.
Lamoreaux, M. A. & Lamoreaux, Michelle. The Legend of Johnny Appleseed. Stone Arch Books Staff. 2010. (Graphic Spin Ser.). (ENG.). 40p. (gr. 1-3). pap. 5.95 (978-1-4342-2266-4(7), Graphic Revolve) Stone Arch Bks.
—The Princess & the Pea: The Graphic Novel, 1 vol. Andersen, Hans Christian. 2009. (Graphic Spin Ser.). (ENG.). 40p. (gr. 1-3). lib. bdg. 23.99 (978-1-4342-1594-9(6), Graphic Revolve) Stone Arch Bks.
Lamoreaux, Michelle. Beauty & the Basement, 1 vol. Snowe, Olivia. 2014. (Twicetold Tales Ser.). (ENG.). 128p. (gr. 3-4). 8.95 (978-1-4342-9830-0(2)) Stone Arch Bks.
—Cassie & the Woolf, 1 vol. Snowe, Olivia. 2013. (Twicetold Tales Ser.). (ENG.). 128p. (gr. 3-4). lib. bdg. 23.99 (978-1-4342-3786-6(9)) Stone Arch Bks.
—Dandelion & the Witch, 1 vol. Snowe, Olivia. 2014. (Twicetold Tales Ser.). (ENG.). 128p. (gr. 3-4). 23.99 (978-1-4342-9147-9(2)) Stone Arch Bks.
Lamoreaux, Michelle. The Girl & the Seven Thieves, 1 vol. Snowe, Olivia. (Twicetold Tales Ser.). (ENG.). 128p. (gr. 3-4). 2014. pap. 5.95 (978-1-4342-9555-2(9)); 2013. 8.95 (978-1-4342-6280-6(4)); 2013. lib. bdg. 23.99 (978-1-4342-6018-5(6)) Stone Arch Bks.
Lamoreaux, Michelle. The Glass Voice, 1 vol. Snowe, Olivia. 2014. (Twicetold Tales Ser.). (ENG.). 128p. (gr. 3-4). 23.99 (978-1-4342-9148-6(0)) Stone Arch Bks.
—Hansen & Gracie, 1 vol. Snowe, Olivia. 2014. (Twicetold Tales Ser.). (ENG.). 128p. (gr. 3-4). pap. 5.95 (978-1-4342-9150-9(2)) Stone Arch Bks.
Lamoreaux, Michelle. A Home in the Sky, 1 vol. Snowe, Olivia. (Twicetold Tales Ser.). (ENG.). 128p. (gr. 3-4). 2014. pap. 5.95 (978-1-4342-9554-5(0)); 2013. 8.95 (978-1-4342-6279-0(0)); 2013. lib. bdg. 23.99 (978-1-4342-5041-4(5)) Stone Arch Bks.
Lamoreaux, Michelle. The Legend of Johnny Appleseed. Capstone Press Staff. 2010. (Graphic Spin Ser.). (ENG.). 40p. (gr. 1-3). lib. bdg. 23.99 (978-1-4342-1895-7(3), Graphic Revolve) Stone Arch Bks.
—Made You Look: How Advertising Works & Why You Should Know. Graydon, Shari. 2nd rev. ed. 2013. (ENG.). 160p. (J). (gr. 6-12). 26.95 (978-1-55451-561-5(0), 9781554515615); pap. 16.95 (978-1-55451-560-8(2), 9781554515608) Annick Pr., Ltd. CAN. Dist: Firefly Bks., Ltd.
Lamoreaux, Michelle. The Sealed-Up House, 1 vol. Snowe, Olivia. (Twicetold Tales Ser.). (ENG.). 128p. (gr. 3-4). 2014. pap. 5.95 (978-1-4342-9556-9(7)); 2013. 8.95 (978-1-4342-6281-3(2)); 2013. lib. bdg. 23.99 (978-1-4342-6019-2(4)) Stone Arch Bks.
Lamoreaux, Michelle. Twicetold Tales, 1 vol. Snowe, Olivia. (Twicetold Tales Ser.). (ENG.). 128p. (gr. 3-4). 2014. 95.96 (978-1-4342-9469-2(2)); 2013. 95.96 (978-1-4342-6355-1(X)) Stone Arch Bks.
Lamoreaux, Michelle, jt. illus. see Lamoreaux, M. A.
Lamut, Sonja. Papa's Pastries, 1 vol. Toscano, Charles. 2010. (ENG.). 32p. (J). (gr. -1-2). 15.99 (978-0-310-71602-0(0)) Zonderkidz.
Lanan, Jessica. Good Fortune in a Wrapping Cloth. Schoettler, Joan. 2011. (ENG.). (J). 17.95 (978-1-885008-40-4(6), Shen's Bks.) Lee & Low Bks., Inc.
Lancaster, Derek. Cock-a-Doodle-Doo, I Love You. Wixom, Jason Kay & Wixom, Tedi Tuttle. 2nd ed. 2003. (Ralph Rooster Ser.: Vol. 1). 16p. (J). (gr. -1-2). 6.95 (978-1-885227-05-8(1)) TNT Bks.
Lance, Charlotte. A Really Super Hero. Lance, Charlotte. 2013. (ENG.). 24p. (J). (gr. -1-2). 18.99 (978-1-74331-302-2(0)) Allen & Unwin AUS. Dist: Independent Pubs. Group.
Land Eagle. The Storyteller. Packard, Mary. 2009. 196p. (J). (978-1-4351-1557-6(0)) Metro Bks.
Land, Fiona. Colors. Ackerman, Jill & Smith, Justine. 2007. (Little Scholastic Ser.). (ENG.). 5p. (J). (gr. k — 1). bds. 4.99 (978-0-439-02145-6(6)) Scholastic, Inc.
—Go! Go! Go! Bird, Nicola. 2012. (ENG.). 10p. (J). (— 1). bds. 10.99 (978-0-545-42545-2(X)) Scholastic, Inc.
—Peek-a-Zoo. Ackerman, Jill. 2007. (Little Scholastic Ser.). (ENG.). 5p. (J). (gr. k — 1). bds. 10.99 (978-0-439-02154-8(5)) Scholastic, Inc.
—Playtime. Smith, Justine & Ackerman, Jill. Scholastic, Inc. Staff, ed. 2008. (Little Scholastic Ser.). (ENG.). 10p. (J). (gr. k — 1). 12.99 (978-0-545-08579-3(9)) Scholastic, Inc.
—Shapes. Ackerman, Jill & Smith, Justine. 2007. (Little Scholastic Ser.). (ENG.). 5p. (J). (gr. k — 1). bds. 4.99 (978-0-439-02146-3(4)) Scholastic, Inc.
Land, Greg. Crossover. 2006. (ENG.). 144p. (YA). (gr. 8-17). pap. 12.99 (978-0-7851-1802-2(0)) Marvel Worldwide, Inc.
Land, Greg, et al. Sojourn, Vol. 4. Marz, Ron. 2003. (Sojourn Ser.: Vol. 4). 160p. (YA). pap. 15.95 (978-1-931484-91-6(0)) CrossGeneration Comics, Inc.
—Sojourn: The Sorcerer's Tale, Vol. 5. Edginton, Ian. 2004. (Sojourn Ser.). 160p. (YA). pap. 15.95 (978-1-59314-038-0(X)) CrossGeneration Comics, Inc.
—The Warrior's Tale, Vol. 3. Marz, Ron. (Sojourn Traveler Ser.: Vol. 3). 160p. (YA). 2004. pap. 9.95 (978-1-59314-043-4(6)); 2003. (gr. 7-18). pap. 15.95 (978-1-931484-65-7(1)) CrossGeneration Comics, Inc.
Land, Greg & Eaglesham, Dale. No Man's Land. Rucka, Greg et al. rev. ed. 2005. (Batman Ser.: Vol. 5). (ENG.). 208p. (YA). pap. 17.99 (978-1-56389-709-2(1)) DC Comics.
Land, Greg & Jay, Leisten. From the Ashes. Marz, Ron. 2003. (Sojourn Traveler Ser.: Vol. 1). 192p. (YA). (gr. 7-18). pap. 9.95 (978-1-59314-013-7(4)) CrossGeneration Comics, Inc.
Land, Greg, jt. illus. see Dodson, Terry.
Land of Milk and Honey Staff. ABC God Loves Me. 2007. 5p. (J). 5.99 (978-0-7369-2095-7(1)) Harvest Hse. Pubs.
Landau, Donna. Round & Round the Garden, Finger Games in English & Spanish. MansBach, Sara. Arroyave, Heidy, tr. 2007. 42p. spiral bd. (978-0-9785477-2-1(1)) BladeRunner Publishing.
Landau, Elaine. Tyrannosaurus Rex. Landau, Elaine. rev. ed. 2007. (True Bks.). (ENG.). 48p. (J). (gr. 3-5). pap. 6.95 (978-0-531-15472-4(6), Children's Pr.) Scholastic Library Publishing.
—Velociraptor. Landau, Elaine. rev. ed. 2007. (True Bks.). (ENG.). 48p. (J). (gr. 3-5). pap. 6.95 (978-0-531-15473-1(4), Children's Pr.) Scholastic Library Publishing.
—Your Pet Cat. Landau, Elaine. rev. ed. 2007. (True Bks.). (ENG.). 48p. (J). (gr. 3-5). pap. 6.95 (978-0-531-15464-9(5), Children's Pr.) Scholastic Library Publishing.
Landau, Helena Von & Meister, Charles. Our Little Frankish Cousin of Long Ago. Stein, Evaleen. 2007. 92p. per. 8.95 (978-1-59915-244-8(4)) Yesterday's Classics.
Landau, Natasha. Misha Loves to Sing. 2004. (J). (978-0-615-12595-4(6)) Tikva Corp.
Landers, Jeri. The Journey of Bushky Bushybottom. Landers, Jeri. 2008. 40p. (J). 21.00 (978-0-9765303-1-2(7)) Ocher Moon Pr.
Landes, William-Alan, photos by. Assignments in Musical Theatre: Acting & Directing. Landes, William-Alan, ed. Wheeler, Jacque & Laughlin, Haller. unabr. ed. 2003. (Musical Theatre Ser.). 192p. (Orig.). (YA). (gr. 8-12). pap. 28.00 (978-0-88734-676-7(6)) Players Pr., Inc.
Landgraf, Kenneth. Robinson Crusoe: With a Discussion of Resourcefulness. Defoe, Daniel. 2003. (Values in Action Illustrated Classics Ser.). 190p. (J). (978-1-59203-035-4(1)) Learning Challenge, Inc.
Landinez, Jairo Linares. El Globito Azul. Arrieta, Luisa Noguera. 2003. (Coleccion OA Infantil Ser.). (SPA.). 69p. (J). (gr. -1-7). pap. (978-958-30-0878-8(8)) Panamericana Editorial.
—Un Pescado en la Olla! Silva, Luna. 2003. (Primer Acto: Teatro Infantil y Juvenil Ser.). (SPA.). 54p. (J). (gr. -1-7). pap. (978-958-30-0996-9(2)) Panamericana Editorial.
Landmann, Bimba. Clare & Francis. Visconti, Guido. 2004. 40p. 20.00 (978-0-8028-5269-4(6)) Eerdmans, William B. Publishing Co.
—The Genius of Leonardo. (J). 12.99 (978-1-84148-482-2(2)) Barefoot Bks., Inc.
—In Search of the Little Prince: The Story of Antoine de Saint-Exupéry. 2014. (J). 17.00 (978-0-8028-5435-3(4), Eerdmans Bks For Young Readers) Eerdmans, William B. Publishing Co.
Landmann, Bimba. I Am Marc Chagall. Landmann, Bimba. 2005. (Eerdmans Books for Young Readers). 40p. (J). (gr. 2). 18.00 (978-0-8028-5305-9(6), Eerdmans Bks For Young Readers) Eerdmans, William B. Publishing Co.
Landmark, Ken & Haugen, Ryan. Bell Buzzers: A Book of Knock-Knock Jokes, 1 vol. Dahl, Michael. 2003. (Read-It! Joke Bks.). (ENG.). 24p. (gr. k-3). 19.99 (978-1-4048-0236-0(3), Easy Readers) Picture Window Bks.
Landolt, Gredna. Carolina's Gift: A Story of Peru. Diaz, Katacha. (ENG.). 32p. (J). (gr. k-3). 2005. 8.95 (978-1-56899-699-8(3), SC8005); 2003. 15.95 (978-1-56899-695-0(0), B8005) Soundprints.
Landowne, Youme. Selavi, That Is Life: A Haitian Story of Hope. Landowne, Youme. (ENG.). 40p. (J). (gr. k-2). 2005. pap. 8.95 (978-0-938317-95-1(4)); 2004. 17.95 (978-0-938317-84-5(9)) Cinco Puntos Pr.
Landry, Douglas. Maggie Mae Moose. Maxfield, Deanna. 2011. 28p. (J). pap. 8.95 (978-0-9743407-0-8(7)) ASMedia Publishing.
Landry, Leo. Emily's Magic Words: Please, Thank You, & More. Post, Peggy et al. 2007. (ENG.). 32p. (J). (gr. -1-1). 15.99 (978-0-06-111680-3(7), Collins) HarperCollins Pubs.
—Let's Sign, Baby! A Fun & Easy Way to Talk with Baby. Ault, Kelly. abr. ed. 2010. (ENG.). 40p. (J). (gr. k — 1). bds. 7.99 (978-0-547-31596-6(1)) Houghton Mifflin Harcourt Publishing Co.
Landry, Leo. Grin & Bear It. Landry, Leo. (ENG.). 48p. (J). (gr. k-3). 2014. pap. 5.95 (978-1-57091-746-2(9)); 2011. 12.95 (978-1-57091-745-5(0)) Charlesbridge Publishing, Inc.

L

—Space Boy. Landry, Leo. 2007. (ENG.). 32p. (J). (gr. -1-3). 16.99 *(978-0-618-60568-2(1))* Houghton Mifflin Harcourt Publishing Co.

Landstrom, Olaf. Benito y el Chupon. Lindgren, Barbro. rev. ed. 2006. (Castillo de la Lectura Preschool Ser.). (ENG.). 40p. (J). (gr. -1-k). pap. 6.95 *(978-970-20-0847-7(6))* Castillo, Ediciones, S. A. de C. V. MEX. Dist: Macmillan.

Landstrom, Olof. Benny's Had Enough! Lindgren, Barbro. Dyssegaard, Elisabeth Kallick, tr. from SWE. 2005. 28p. (J). (gr. -1-1). reprint ed. 6.95 *(978-91-29-66338-9(5))* R & S Bks. SWE. Dist: Macmillan.

—Boris's Glasses. Cohen, Peter. Sandin, Joan, tr. from SWE. 2003. 28p. (J). (gr. k-3). 15.00 *(978-91-29-65942-9(6))* R & S Bks. SWE. Dist: Macmillan.

—Four Hens & a Rooster. Landstrom, Lena. Sandin, Joan, tr. from SWE. 2005. 28p. (J). (gr. -1-3). 16.00 *(978-91-29-66336-5(9))* R & S Bks. SWE. Dist: Macmillan.

—Oink, Oink Benny. Lindgren, Barbro & Lindgren, B. L. Dyssegaard, Elisabeth Kallick, tr. from SWE. 2008. 28p. (J). (gr. -1-1). 16.00 *(978-91-29-66855-1(7))* R & S Bks. SWE. Dist: Macmillan.

—Wallace's Lists. Bottner, Barbara & Kruglik, Gerald. 2011. (J). (gr. 1-3). 29.95 *(978-0-545-04275-8(5))* Weston Woods Studios, Inc.

Landstrom, Olof. Wallace's Lists. Landstrom, Olof, tr. Bottner, Barbara & Kruglik, Gerald. 2004. (ENG.). 40p. (J). (gr. -1-2). 16.99 *(978-0-06-000224-4(7))*, Tegen, Katherine Bks) HarperCollins Pubs.

Lane, Chris. Harry Houdini: The Legend of the World's Greatest Escape Artist. Weaver, Janice. 2011. (ENG.). 48p. (J). (gr. 3-7). 19.95 *(978-1-4197-0014-9(6)*, Abrams Bks. for Young Readers) Abrams.

Lane, Cody R. Frantic the Frog. Johnson, Cindy B. 2004. 27p. pap. 24.95 *(978-1-4137-2954-2(1))* America Star Bks.

Lane, Dakota. Gothic Lolita: A Mystical Thriller. Lane, Dakota. 2008. (ENG.). 208p. (YA). (gr. 7-18). 17.99 *(978-1-4169-1396-2(3)*, Atheneum Bks. for Young Readers) Simon & Schuster Children's Publishing.

Lane Holm, Sharon. 5 Steps to Drawing Farm Animals. Hall, Pamela. 2011. (5 Steps to Drawing Ser.). (ENG.). 32p. (J). (gr. k-3). lib. bdg. 27.07 *(978-1-60973-199-1(9)*, 201105) Child's World, Inc., The.

Lane, Kim. The Complete Book of the Microscope. Rogers, Kirsteen. Dowswell, Paul, ed. rev. ed. 2005. (Complete Bks.). 96p. (J). pap. 14.99 *(978-0-7945-1558-4(4)*, Usborne) EDC Publishing.

—Pasta & Pizza: For Beginners. Allman, Howard, photos by. Watt, Fiona. rev. ed. 2004. (Cooking School Ser.). 48p. (J). (gr. 5). lib. bdg. 15.95 *(978-1-58086-567-8(4))* EDC Publishing.

—What Shall I Grow? Allman, Howard, photos by. Gibson, Ray. Watt, Fiona, ed. 2006. (What Shall I Do Today? Ser.). 32p. (J). (gr. 2). lib. bdg. 15.95 *(978-1-58086-548-7(8))* EDC Publishing.

Lane, Nancy. Call the Horse Lucky. Havill, Juanita. 2010. (ENG.). 24p. (J). (gr. k-3). 16.95 *(978-0-940719-10-1(X))* Gryphon Pr., The.

—Finding Chance. Benson, Linda. 2006. 112p. (J). *(978-1-59336-696-4(5))* Mondo Publishing.

—KokoCat, Inside & Out. Graham-Barber, Lynda. 2012. (ENG.). 24p. (J). (gr. k). 16.95 *(978-0-940719-12-5(6))* Gryphon Pr., The.

—Rembrandt & the Boy Who Drew Dogs: A Story about Rembrandt van Rijn. Blaisdell, Molly. 2008. (ENG.). 32p. (J). (gr. k-3). 14.99 *(978-0-7641-6097-4(4))* Barron's Educational Series, Inc.

—Renoir & the Boy with Long Hair: A Story about Pierre-Auguste Renoir. Wax, Wendy. 2007. (ENG.). 32p. (J). (gr. -1-3). 14.99 *(978-0-7641-6041-7(9))* Barron's Educational Series, Inc.

Lane, Queen. It's Christmas Time (BABYTOWN Storybook) Lane, Queen, creator. 2005. (BABYTOWN Ser.: Bk. 4). 36p. (J). spiral bd. 15.00 *(978-0-9772738-1-2(4))* Quebla.

Lane, Queen & Boykin, Brian. No No Baby (Babytown Storybook) 2005. (BABYTOWN Ser.: Bk. 1). 30p. (J). spiral bd. 15.00 *(978-0-9772738-0-5(6))* Quebla.

Lane, Ranae. Follow God. Comley, Kathryn. 2004. (J). bds. 9.99 *(978-1-4183-0009-8(8))* Christ Inspired, Inc.

—Know & Remember all These Things. Comley, Kathryn. 2004. (J). bds. *(978-1-4183-0011-1(X))* Christ Inspired, Inc.

—That's How I Found God. Comley, Kathryn. 2004. (J). bds. 9.99 *(978-1-4183-0014-2(4))* Christ Inspired, Inc.

Lang, Allison. Ashie: Lost in the Hurricane. Cohen, Pamela June. 2008. 40p. pap. 24.95 *(978-1-60474-961-8(X))* America Star Bks.

Lang, Carole. The Adventures of Willy & Billy Bk. 1: The Lake Lure Chronicles - Book 1. Klett, David. l.t. ed. 2006. 32p. (J). lib. bdg. 17.95 *(978-0-9779325-0-4(8))* Five Oaks Pr.

Lang, Cecily. Una Cesta de Cumpleanos para Tia Abuela. Mora, Pat. (SPA.). (J). (gr. k-2). pap. 3.16 net. *(978-0-395-78817-2(X)*, HMS088) Houghton Mifflin Harcourt Publishing Co.

Lang, Gary. The Glass Heart. Killion, Kathleen. 2005. 19.95 *(978-0-9723067-2-0(2))* Imagine That Enterprises.

Lang, Glenna. The Children's Hour. Longfellow, Henry Wadsworth. 2008. (ENG.). 32p. (YA). (gr. 8-12). pap. 9.95 *(978-1-56792-344-5(5))* Godine, David R. Pub.

—The Runaway. Frost, Robert. Date not set. (ENG.). 32p. pap. 9.95 *(978-1-56792-243-1(0))* Godine, David R. Pub.

Lang, Glenna. Looking Out for Sarah. Lang, Glenna. 2003. (ENG.). 32p. (J). (gr. -1-3). pap. 7.95 *(978-1-57091-607-6(1))* Charlesbridge Publishing, Inc.

Lang, Mark. Capturing Joy: The Story of Maud Lewis. Bogart, Jo Ellen. 2011. (ENG.). 32p. (J). (gr. 3-7). pap. 8.95 *(978-1-77049-262-2(3)*, Tundra Bks.) Tundra Bks. CAN. Dist: Penguin Random Hse., LLC.

—Tales of Court & Castle. Bodger, Joan. 2003. (ENG.). 96p. (J). (gr. 3-7). pap. 9.95 *(978-0-88776-614-5(5))* Tundra Bks. CAN. Dist: Random Hse., Inc.

Lang, Max. Families, Families, Families! Lang, Suzanne. 2015. (ENG.). 32p. (J). (gr. -1-2). 19.99 *(978-0-375-97426-7(1))* Random Hse., Inc.

Langan, Bob. Destiny, Valor & a Lizard Named Louie. Ambrosio, Michael. 2004. 128p. pap. 5.95 *(978-0-9716085-3-5(9))* LionX Publishing.

Langcaon, Jeff. My Grandpa's Battleship Missouri Tour. 2007. (J). 14.95 *(978-1-56647-831-1(6))* Mutual Publishing LLC.

Langdo, Bryan. Cat & Dog. Minarik, Else Holmelund. 2005. (My First I Can Read Ser.). (ENG.). 32p. (J). (gr. -1 — 1). 16.99 *(978-0-06-074247-8(X))* HarperCollins Pubs.

—Do You Sing Twinkle? A Story about Remarriage & New Family. Levins, Sandra. 2009. 32p. (J). (gr. -1-3). 14.95 *(978-1-4338-0539-4(1))*; pap. 9.95 *(978-1-4338-0551-6(0))* American Psychological Assn. (Magination Pr.).

—Hero Dad, 0 vols. Hardin, Melinda. 2010. (ENG.). 24p. (J). (gr. -1-3). 12.99 *(978-0-7614-5713-8(5)*, 9780761457138, Amazon Children's Publishing) Amazon Publishing.

—Hero Mom, 0 vols. Hardin, Melinda. 2013. 24p. (ENG.). (J). (gr. -1-3). 12.99 *(978-1-4778-1645-5(3)*, 9781477816455, Amazon Children's Publishing); pap. 12.99 *(978-1-4778-6645-0(0))* Amazon Publishing.

—The Leaf That Wouldn't Leave. Trinco, Trish. 2008. (ENG.). 32p. (J). 16.95 *(978-0-931674-90-7(5)*, Waldman House Pr.) TRISTAN Publishing, Inc.

—The Miracle of Easter. Malone, Jean M. 2010. (Penguin Young Readers, Level 3 Ser.). (ENG.). 48p. (J). (gr. 1-3). pap. 3.99 *(978-0-448-45265-4(0)*, Warne, Frederick Pubs.) Penguin Bks., Ltd. GBR. Dist: Penguin Random Hse., LLC.

—Mummy Math: An Adventure in Geometry. Neuschwander, Cindy. 2009. (ENG.). 32p. (J). (gr. 2-5). pap. 7.99 *(978-0-312-56117-8(2))* Square Fish.

—No Room at the Inn: The Nativity Story. Malone, Jean M. 2009. (Penguin Young Readers, Level 3 Ser.). (ENG.). 48p. (J). (gr. 1-3). mass mkt. 3.99 *(978-0-448-45217-3(0)*, Grosset & Dunlap) Penguin Publishing Group.

—Pastry School in Paris: An Adventure in Capacity. Neuschwander, Cindy. 2009. (ENG.). 32p. (J). (gr. 2-6). 18.99 *(978-0-8050-8314-9(6)*, Holt, Henry & Co. Bks. For Young Readers) Holt, Henry & Co.

—Sometimes I'm Scared. Annunziata, Jane & Nemiroff, Marc. 2009. 32p. pap. 9.95 *(978-1-4338-0550-9(2))*; (J). (gr. -1-3). 14.95 *(978-1-4338-0449-6(2))* American Psychological Assn. (Magination Pr.).

—Was It the Chocolate Pudding? A Story for Little Kids about Divorce. Levins, Sandra. 2005. 40p. (J). 14.95 *(978-1-59147-308-4(X))*; (gr. -1-3). per. 9.95 *(978-1-59147-309-1(8))* American Psychological Assn. (Magination Pr.).

Langdo, Bryan, jt. illus. see Hirschmann, Kris.

Langelier-Lebeda, Suzanne. Green Golly & Her Golden Flute. Torgan, Keith & Siesel, Barbara. 2013. 58p. pap. 19.99 *(978-1-936172-61-0(5))* Elfrig Publishing.

Langford, Alton. Seagull by the Shore: The Story of a Herring Gull. Birch, Vanessa Giancamilli. (Smithsonian Oceanic Collection Ser.). (ENG.). (J). (gr. -1-3). 2011. 31p. pap. 4.95 *(978-1-60727-540-4(6))*; 2010. 32p. 16.95 *(978-1-60727-089-8(7))*; 2010. 32p. pap. 6.95 *(978-1-60727-090-4(0))* Soundprints.

Langille, Elaine. Down in the Tropics. Hann, Harry Henry & Johnson, Nancy. 2013. 48p. pap. 14.99 *(978-0-9891323-0-5(7))* Goin' Native, Inc.

Langille, Rob. There Is a Boy on Top of My Bed. Stewart, Andrew. 2011. (ENG.). 34p. pap. 9.99 *(978-1-4611-3720-7(9))* CreateSpace Independent Publishing Platform.

Langley, Andrew. September 11: Attack on America, 1 vol. Langley, Andrew. 2006. (Snapshots in History Ser.). (ENG.). 96p. (gr. 7-8). lib. bdg. 33.99 *(978-0-7565-1620-8(X)*, Snapshots in History) Compass Point Bks.

Langley, Bill & Dias, Ron. 101 Dalmatians. Korman, Justine. 2007. (Little Golden Book Ser.). (ENG.). 24p. (J). (gr. -1-2). 3.99 *(978-0-7364-2420-2(2)*, Golden/Disney) Random Hse. Children's Bks.

Langley, Bill, jt. illus. see Wakeman, Bill.

Langley, Gene. The Return of the Alaskan: Mailboat in the Outpost. Herron, Edward A. 2011. 190p. 42.95 *(978-1-258-09093-7(7))* Literary Licensing, LLC.

Langley, Jonathan. Farmyard Read & Play Set, 3 vols. Rosen, Michael. 2008. (ENG.). 96p. (J). (gr. -1-k). bds. 19.95 *(978-0-00-725969-4(7))* HarperCollins Pubs. Ltd. GBR. Dist: Independent Pubs. Group.

—I Very Really Miss You. Walters, Clare & Kemp, Jane. 2006. (ENG.). 32p. (J). (gr. -1-1). 15.95 *(978-1-84507-260-5(X)*, Frances Lincoln) Quarto Publishing Group UK GBR. Dist: Hachette Bk. Group.

—Ronquidos! Rosen, Michael.Tr. of Snore!. (SPA.). (J). (gr. 1-3). *(978-958-04-4646-0(6))* Norma S.A.

—Snore! Rosen, Michael. ed. 2003. (ENG.). 32p. (J). (gr. -1-k). pap. 10.99 *(978-0-00-716031-0(3)*, HarperCollins Children's Bks.) HarperCollins Pubs. Ltd. GBR. Dist: HarperCollins Pubs.

Langlois, Florence. The Extraordinary Gift. Langlois, Florence. Goodman, John, tr. from FRE. 2005. 48p. (J). (gr. -1-2). reprint ed. 15.00 *(978-0-7567-8942-8(7))* DIANE Publishing Co.

Langlois, Suzane. Smarty pants. Sydor, Colleen. 2nd rev. ed. 2003. 32p. (J). (gr. 1-5). *(978-1-894222-62-4(8))* Lobster Pr.

Langridge, Roger. Meet the Muppets. Langridge, Roger. 2009. (Muppet Show Ser.). (ENG.). 112p. (J). 24.99 *(978-1-60886-527-7(4))* Boom! Studios.

—The Muppet Show Comic Book: The Treasure of Peg-Leg Wilson. Langridge, Roger. 2010. (Muppet Show Ser.). (ENG.). 112p. (J). 24.99 *(978-1-60886-530-7(4))*; (gr. 4-7). pap. 9.99 *(978-1-60886-504-8(5))* Boom! Studios.

—The Muppet Show Comic Book - Muppet Mash. Langridge, Roger. 2011. (Muppet Show Ser.). 128p. pap. 9.99 *(978-1-60886-611-3(4))* Boom! Studios.

—On the Road. Langridge, Roger. 2010. (Muppet Show Ser.). (ENG.). 112p. (J). pap. 9.99 *(978-1-60886-516-1(9))* Boom! Studios.

—Ships & Sealing Wax. Langridge, Roger. 2012. (Snarked Ser.). (ENG.). 112p. (J). (gr. 4). pap. 14.99 *(978-1-60886-276-4(3))* Boom! Studios.

Langridge, Roger & Mebberson, Amy. Family Reunion. Langridge, Roger. 2010. (Muppet Show Ser.). (ENG.). 112p. (J). pap. 9.99 *(978-1-60886-587-1(8))* Boom! Studios.

Langrish, Bob, et al, photos by. Dream Horses. 2004. (ENG., 64p. (J). pap. 10.95 *(978-1-58017-574-6(0)*, 67574) Storey Publishing, LLC.

Langrish, Bob, photos by. The Foaling Primer: A Step-By-Step Guide to Raising a Healthy Foal. McFarland, Cynthia. 2005. (ENG., 160p. pap. 19.95 *(978-1-58017-608-8(9)*, 67608) Storey Publishing, LLC.

Langton, Bruce. Count on Us: A Tennessee Number Book. Shoulders, Michael. 2003. (Count Your Way Across the U. S. A. Ser.). (ENG.). 40p. (J). 16.95 *(978-1-58536-131-1(3))* Sleeping Bear Pr.

—Discover Ohio, 2 bks. Schonberg, Marcia. 2003. (ENG.). 40p. (J). 27.95 *(978-1-58536-225-7(5))* Sleeping Bear Pr.

—Discover Tennessee: Count on Us; V is for Volunteer, 2 bks. Shoulders, Michael. 2003. (ENG.). 40p. (J). 27.95 *(978-1-58536-228-8(X))* Sleeping Bear Pr.

—Full Count: A Baseball Number Book. Herzog, Brad. 2009. (ENG.). 40p. (J). (gr. k-6). 17.95 *(978-1-58536-429-9(0))* Sleeping Bear Pr.

—Hands as Warm as Toast. Hilme, Lisa. 2006. 32p. (J). (gr. -1-3). 17.95 *(978-1-58726-298-2(3)*, Mitten Pr.) Ann Arbor Editions LLC.

—P Is for Putt: A Golf Alphabet. Herzog, Brad. (Alphabet-Sports Ser.). (ENG.). 40p. 2009. (gr. k-6). pap. 7.95 *(978-1-58536-476-3(2))*; 2005. (J). (gr. -1-5). 16.95 *(978-1-58536-252-3(2))* Sleeping Bear Pr.

—Win One for the Gipper: America's Football Hero. Wargin, Kathy-jo. 2004. (ENG.). 40p. (J). (gr. k-6). 16.95 *(978-1-58536-221-9(2))* Sleeping Bear Pr.

Langton, Bruce. H Is for Hawkeye: An Iowa Alphabet. Langton, Bruce, tr. Pierce, Patricia A. 2003. (Discover America State by State Ser.). (ENG.). 40p. (J). 17.95 *(978-1-58536-114-4(3))* Sleeping Bear Pr.

Langton, Bruce, jt. illus. see Larson, Katherine.

Langton, Roger. The Bible in Pictures for Toddlers. Lindvall, Ella K. adapted ed. 2003. (Leading Young Hearts & Minds to God Ser.). (ENG.). 144p. (J). 9.99 *(978-0-8024-3058-8(9))* Moody Pubs.

—Classic Folk Tales: 80 Traditional Stories from Around the World. Baxter, Nicola. 2013. (ENG.). 96p. (J). (gr. 7-12). pap. 9.99 *(978-1-84322-855-4(6))* Anness Publishing GBR. Dist: National Bk. Network.

—My First Story Bible, 1 vol. Dowley, Tim. 2010. (ENG.). 138p. (J). (gr. -1-2). 13.99 *(978-1-85985-774-8(4)*, Candle Bks.) Lion Hudson PLC GBR. Dist: Kregel Pubns.

—My First Story of Christmas. Dowley, Tim. ed. 2004. (My First Story Ser.). (ENG.). 24p. (J). 7.99 *(978-0-8024-1758-9(2))* Moody Pubs.

—My First Story of Easter. Dowley, Tim. ed. 2005. (My First Story Ser.). (ENG.). 24p. (J). 7.99 *(978-0-8024-1767-1(1))* Moody Pubs.

—My First Story of Jesus. Dowley, Tim. ed. 2007. (My First Story Ser.). (ENG.). 28p. 7.99 *(978-0-8024-1776-3(0))* Moody Pubs.

Langton, Roger. Children's Stories from the Bible: A Collection of over 20 Tales from the Old & New Testaments, Retold for Younger Readers. Langton, Roger. Baxter, Nicola. 2013. (ENG.). 80p. (J). (gr. 5-12). pap. 9.99 *(978-1-84322-982-7(X)*, Armadillo) Anness Publishing GBR. Dist: National Bk. Network.

Langton, Roger W. A Little Life of Jesus - To Read & Treasure. Rock, Lois. 2nd ed. 2015. (ENG.). 352p. (J). (gr. -1-k). pap. 8.99 *(978-0-7459-6567-3(9))* Lion Hudson PLC GBR. Dist: Independent Pubs. Group.

Lanino, Deborah. Maria's Comet. Hopkinson, Deborah. 2003. (ENG.). 32p. (J). (gr. -1-3). 8.99 *(978-0-689-85678-5(4)*, Simon & Schuster/Paula Wiseman Bks.) Simon & Schuster/Paula Wiseman Bks.

Lanning, Andrea J. The Imposturous Egg. Lanning, Andrea J. Corcacas, Maria, photos by. 2012. 32p. *(978-0-9571677-0-4(9))*; pap. *(978-0-9571677-4-2(1))* Ginnal Creatives Ltd.

Lanphear, Dave, jt. illus. see Cariello, Sergio.

Lanquetin, Anne-Sophie. Not All Princesses Dress in Pink. Yolen, Jane & Stemple, Heidi E. Y. 2010. (ENG.). 32p. (J). (gr. -1-3). 17.99 *(978-1-4169-8018-6(0)*, Simon & Schuster Bks. For Young Readers) Simon & Schuster Bks. For Young Readers.

Lanting, Frans. Animal Groups. Esbaum, Jill. 2015. (ENG.). 32p. (J). (gr. -1-3). 16.99 ***(978-1-4263-2060-6(4)***, National Geographic Children's Bks.) National Geographic Society.

Lanza, Barbara. Time to Fly: A Fairy Lane Book. Lanza, Barbara. 2005. (ENG.). 32p. (J). (gr. 4-7). 19.95 *(978-0-9724853-7-1(6))* Keene Publishing.

Lanza, Marco, photos by. The Kids' Cookbook: Recipes from Around the World. Gioffre, Rosalba et al. Wilson, Alison & Farrell, Helen, eds. 2008. (ENG., 120p. (J). (gr. 2-18). 19.95 *(978-88-88166-96-4(3))* McRae Bks. Srl ITA. Dist: Independent Pubs. Group.

Lanzrein, Helen. All Things Bright & Beautiful: A Collection of Prayer & Verse. 2007. (Padded Board Bks.). 24p. (J). (gr. -1). bds. 7.95 *(978-1-58925-799-3(5))* Tiger Tales.

LaPadula, Thomas. My Big Dump Truck. Lovitt, Chip. 2011. (Diecut Vehicles Ser.). (ENG.). 12p. (J). (gr. -1-1). bds. 5.99 *(978-0-7944-2272-1(1))* Reader's Digest Assn., Inc., The.

—My Giant Tractor. 2014. (ENG.). 12p. (J). (gr. -1 — 1). bds. 10.99 *(978-0-7944-3012-2(0))* Reader's Digest Assn., Inc., The.

—My Red Fire Truck. Lovitt, Chip. 2011. (My Truckology Ser.). (ENG.). 12p. (J). (gr. -1-1). bds. 5.99 *(978-0-7944-2271-4(3))* Reader's Digest Assn., Inc., The.

Lapadula, Thomas. Santa's Little Engine (Thomas & Friends) Awdry, W. 2014. (Step into Reading Ser.). (ENG.). 32p. (J). (gr. -1-1). lib. bdg. 12.99 *(978-0-375-97210-2(2)*, Random Hse. Bks. for Young Readers) Random Hse. Children's Bks.

—Thomas & the Dinosaur (Thomas & Friends) Golden Books. 2015. (Little Golden Book Ser.). (ENG.). 24p. (J). (-k). 3.99 *(978-0-553-49681-9(6)*, Golden Bks.) Random Hse. Children's Bks.

—Thomas at the Animal Park (Thomas & Friends) Random House. 2014. (ENG.). 10p. (J). (— 1). 10.99 *(978-0-385-38469-8(6)*, Random Hse. Bks. for Young Readers) Random Hse. Children's Bks.

LaPadula, Tom. Clifford for President. McVeigh, Mark et al. 2004. (Clifford's Big Red Reader Ser.). (ENG.). 32p. (J). (gr. -1-3). pap. 3.99 *(978-0-439-69391-2(8))* Scholastic, Inc.

LaPadula, Tom. Learn to Draw Planes, Choppers & Watercraft. 2013. 40p. (J). ***(978-1-936309-82-5(3))*** Quarto Publishing Group USA.

LaPadula, Tom. No More Mr. Smart Guy. Beechen, Adam. 2003. (Adventures of Jimmy Neutron Boy Genius Ser.). 32p. (J). (gr. 4-7). lib. bdg. 11.80 *(978-0-613-66370-0(5)*, Turtleback) Turtleback Bks.

—Thanks a Lot, Robo-Turkey! Banks, Steven. ed. 2005. (Adventures of Jimmy Neutron Ser.: 10). 24p. (J). lib. bdg. 15.00 *(978-1-59054-787-8(X))* Fitzgerald Bks.

Lapadula, Tom. Tough Trucks. 2013. (ENG.). 10p. (J). (gr. -1-k). bds. 7.99 *(978-0-545-56651-3(7))* Scholastic, Inc.

LaPadula, Tom & Shellly, Jeff. All about Drawing: Cool Cars, Fast Planes & Military Machines. 2014. (All about Drawing Ser.). (ENG.). 80p. (J). (gr. 3-7). lib. bdg. 34.60 *(978-1-939581-09-9(5))* Quarto Publishing Group USA.

LaPadula, Tom & Shelly, Jeff. Learn to Draw Cars, Planes & Moving Machines: Step-By-Step Instructions for More Than 25 High-Powered Vehicles. Walter Foster Creative Team. 2015. (Learn to Draw: Expanded Edition Ser.). (ENG.). 64p. (J). (gr. 3-5). 33.32 ***(978-1-939581-69-3(9))*** Quarto Publishing Group USA.

LaPierre, Karina. Nugri90, 0 vols. Dellasega, Cheryl. 2007. (Bloggrls Ser.: 1). (ENG.). 200p. (YA). (gr. 7-11). pap. 6.99 *(978-0-7614-5396-3(2)*, 9780761453963, Amazon Children's Publishing) Amazon Publishing.

Lapointe, Claude. Un Ordenador Nada Ordinario. Lapointe, Claude, tr. Kahn, Michaèle. Trapero, Florentino, tr. 2003. (SPA.). 124p. (J). (gr. 3-5). pap. 10.95 *(978-84-204-4767-4(6))* Santillana USA Publishing Co., Inc.

Lara, David. La Gran Rata de Sumatra. Fleischman, Sid. rev. ed. 2006. (Castillo de la Lectura Roja Ser.). 152p. (YA). (gr. 7). pap. 8.95 *(978-970-20-0855-2(7))* Castillo, Ediciones, S. A. de C. V. MEX. Dist: Macmillan.

Larade, April. Pilot, Swaydy & Friends. May, Maggie. 2011. 30p. pap. 24.95 *(978-1-4560-8499-8(2))* America Star Bks.

Larcenet, Manu. A Dungeon Too Many. Sfar, Joann & Trondheim, Lewis. 2007. (Dungeon Ser.: 1). (ENG.). 60p. (gr. 8-18). pap. 9.95 *(978-1-56163-495-8(6))* NBM Publishing Co.

Lard, Mary Anne. Thank God for Rocks. Bender, Esther. 2003. (ENG.). 32p. 15.00 *(978-0-8192-1902-2(9)*, Morehouse Publishing) Church Publishing, Inc.

Lardot, Christopher. Clothes & Fashion Sticker Book IR. Brocklehurst, Ruth. ed. 2013. (Clothes & Fashion Sticker Book Ser.). 31p. (J). pap. 9.99 *(978-0-7945-3235-2(7)*, Usborne) EDC Publishing.

Lardy, Philippe. A Wreath for Emmett Till. Nelson, Marilyn. 2009. (ENG.). 48p. (YA). (gr. 7). pap. 7.99 *(978-0-547-07636-2(3))* Houghton Mifflin Harcourt Publishing Co.

LaReau, Jenna. Rocko & Spanky Call It Quits. LaReau, Kara. 2008. (Rocko & Spanky Ser.). 40p. (J). 16.00 *(978-0-15-216611-3(4))* Harcourt Children's Bks.

—Top Secret: A Handbook of Codes, Ciphers & Secret Writing. Janeczko, Paul B., ed. 2006. (ENG.). 144p. (J). (gr. 4-7). per. 7.99 *(978-0-7636-2972-4(3))* Candlewick Pr.

LaRiccia, Mike. Harvey's Woods: the Royal Adventures. Dauer, Marty. 2007. 52p. per. 16.95 *(978-1-4241-7924-4(6))* America Star Bks.

Lark, Casi, photos by. Busy Horsies. Schindel, John. 2007. (Busy Book Ser.). (ENG., 20p. (J). (gr. k — 1). bds. 6.99 *(978-1-58246-223-3(2)*, Tricycle Pr.) Ten Speed Pr.

Larkin, Catherine. Harry Scores A Hat Trick, Pawns, Pucks, & Scoliosis: The Sequel to Stand Tall, Harry. Mahony, Mary. Pasternack, Susan, ed. 2003. 130p. (YA). (gr. 5-8). per. 14.95 *(978-0-9658879-3-9(6))* Redding Pr.

Larkin, Eric. Farmer Will Allen & the Growing Table. Martin, Jacqueline Briggs. 2013. (ENG.). 32p. (J). (gr. k). 17.95 *(978-0-9836615-3-5(7))* READERS to EATERS.

Larkin, Paige A. Pearlie. Stroud-Peace, Glenda. 2009. 48p. pap. 16.95 *(978-1-60844-033-7(8))* Dog Ear Publishing, LLC.

Larkins, Mona. Dear Grandchild, When You Come for a Visit. Robinson, Linda M. 2005. 37p. (J). (gr. -1-4). 15.99 *(978-0-9740841-4-5(X))* K&B Products.

—Mother Duck Knows the Way. Thomas, Kate. 2005. 32p. (J). 8.95 *(978-1-58374-122-1(4))* Chicago Spectrum Pr.

Larkins, Mona & Anderson, Jan. Bullies Beware! Day-Bivins, Pat. 2006. (ENG.). 32p. (J). (gr. -1). 16.95 *(978-0-9742806-5-3(8))* Heart to Heart Publishing, Inc.

Larkum, A. Cars. Daynes, Katie. 2005. 64p. (J). (gr. 2-18). pap. 5.95 *(978-0-7945-0999-6(1)*, Usborne) EDC Publishing.

Larkum, Adam. Chocolate. Daynes, Katie. 2004. 48p. (J). (gr. 2-18). pap. 5.95 *(978-0-7945-0759-6(X)*, Usborne) EDC Publishing.

—The Story of Toilets, Telephones & Other Useful Inventions. Daynes, Katie. 2005. (Usborne Young Reading: Series One Ser.). 48p. (J). (gr. 2). lib. bdg. 13.95 *(978-1-58086-983-6(1)*, Usborne) EDC Publishing.

—Vikings. Turnbull, Stephanie. 2006. (Beginners Social Studies: Level 2 Ser.). 32p. (J). (gr. 1-3). 4.99 *(978-0-7945-1254-5(2)*, Usborne) EDC Publishing.

—What's Happening to Me? Firth, Alex. Meredith, Susan, ed. 2007. 48p. (J). (gr. 4-7). pap. 6.99 *(978-0-7945-1514-0(2)*, Usborne) EDC Publishing.

—Why Shouldn't I Eat Junk Food? Knighton, Kate. 2008. (Usborne Ser.). 48p. (J). (gr. 4-7). pap. 6.99 *(978-0-7945-1953-7(9)*, Usborne) EDC Publishing.

—World History Sticker Atlas. Dalby, Elizabeth. 2006. (Sticker Atlases Ser.). 24p. (J). (gr. -1-4). pap. 8.99 *(978-0-7945-1244-6(5)*, Usborne) EDC Publishing.

—Your Body (Jismok) Turnbull, Stephanie. Ibrahim, Nouran, tr. 2013. (ENG & ARA.). 32p. (J). 6.99 *(978-99921-94-39-3(1)*, 149897) Bloomsbury USA.

Larkum, Adam, jt. illus. see Donaera, Patrizia.

Larkum, Adam, jt. illus. see Kushii, Tetsuo.

Larkum, Adam, jt. illus. see Sage, Molly.

Larned, Phillip. The Magic Muffin, 1 vol. Larned, S. 2010. 22p. pap. 24.95 *(978-1-4489-8138-0(7))* PublishAmerica, Inc.

Laroche, Bridget. Thunder & the Pirates. Valeska, Jon & Fripp, Jean. Fripp, Jean, ed. 2004. 32p. (J). (gr. k-4). 5.99 *(978-0-9701008-9-4(2))* Bicast, Inc.

Laroche, Giles. ¿Qué Hacen las Ruedas Todo el Día? Prince, April Jones. 2013.Tr. of What Do Wheels Do All Day. (SPA & ENG.). 32p. (J). (— 1). bds. 4.99 *(978-0-547-99625-7(X))* Houghton Mifflin Harcourt Publishing Co.

—What Do Wheels Do All Day? Prince, April Jones. 2006. (ENG.). 32p. (J). (gr. -1-3). 16.99 *(978-0-618-56307-4(5))* Houghton Mifflin Harcourt Publishing Co.

LaRoe, Misty Bailey. Oops Was Bullied? Hey, Why Did You Hurt Me That Way? King, Sharon. 2013. (ENG.). 32p. (J). pap. 16.95 *(978-1-4787-1364-7(X))* Outskirts Pr., Inc.

Laronde, Gary. Hector Saves the Moon, Vol. 2. Bauld, Jane Scoggins. 2003. (Hector's Escapades Ser.). 34p. (J). (gr. -1-3). per. 7.95 *(978-1-57168-312-0(7))* Eakin Pr.

—Hector Visits His Country Cousin, Vol. 3. Bauld, Jane Scoggins. 2003. (Hector's Escapades Ser.). 25p. (gr. -1). per. 7.95 *(978-1-57168-676-3(2))* Eakin Pr.

Larosa, Lewis. In the Beginning. 2006. (ENG.). 144p. (gr. 13-17). pap. 14.99 *(978-0-7851-1391-1(6))* Marvel Worldwide, Inc.

Larranaga, Ana. Little Turtles. Ikids Staff. 2008. (iBaby Float-Alongs Ser.). (ENG.). 6p. (J). (gr. -1). 12.99 *(978-1-58476-808-1(8))* Innovative Kids.

—Matching Puzzle Cards - Animals. 2012. (ENG.). 36p. (J). (gr. k-12). 9.99 *(978-1-60905-225-6(0))* Blue Apple Bks.

—Tiny Tugboats. Ikids Staff. 2008. (iBaby Float-Alongs Ser.). (ENG.). 6p. (J). (gr. -1). 12.99 *(978-1-58476-807-4(X))* Innovative Kids.

—Wiggle My Ears. Powell, Richard. 2004. (Wrigglers Ser.). 8p. (J). bds. 5.95 *(978-1-58925-692-7(1))* Tiger Tales.

—Zoo Faces. Schultz, Lucy & Shultz, Lucy. 2007. (ENG.). 12p. (J). (gr. -1 — 1). bds. 6.99 *(978-1-58476-556-1(9)*, IKIDS) Innovative Kids.

Larrañaga, Ana Martín. Airplane Flight! Hill, Susanna Leonard. 2009. (ENG.). 12p. (J). (gr. -1-k). bds. 7.99 *(978-1-4169-7832-9(1)*, Little Simon) Little Simon.

Larranaga, Ana Martin. Baby Dolphins. Jugran, Jan. 2006. (ENG.). 6p. (J). (gr. -1 — 1). 14.99 *(978-1-58476-490-8(2)*, IKIDS) Innovative Kids.

—Chupi: El Binky Que Regresó a Su Hogar. Thalia. 2013. (SPA & ENG.). 32p. (J). (gr. -1 — 1). 16.99 *(978-0-451-41606-3(6)*, Celebra) Penguin Publishing Group.

—Chupie: The Binky That Returned Home. Thalia. 2013. (ENG.). 32p. (J). (gr. -1 — 1). 16.99 *(978-0-451-41605-6(8)*, Celebra) Penguin Publishing Group.

Larrañaga, Ana Martín. Colors - E-Z Page Turners. Page, Liza & Innovative Kids Staff. 2008. (ENG.). 12p. (J). (gr. -1 — 1). bds. 5.99 *(978-1-58476-655-1(7))* Innovative Kids.

Larranaga, Ana Martin. Counting. ed. 2013. (Pull & Play Ser.). (ENG.). 10p. (J). (— 1). bds. 7.99 *(978-0-230-75038-8(9))* Pan Macmillan GBR. Dist: Independent Pubs. Group.

Larrañaga, Ana Martín. Counting: E-Z Page Turners. Innovative Kids Staff. 2008. (ENG.). 12p. (J). (gr. -1 — 1). bds. 5.99 *(978-1-58476-657-5(3))* Innovative Kids.

Larranaga, Ana Martin. Farm Faces: A Book of Masks. Ikids Staff. 2006. (ENG.). 12p. (J). (gr. -1 — 1). bds. 6.99 *(978-1-58476-471-7(6)*, IKIDS) Innovative Kids.

Larrañaga, Ana Martín. Freight Train Trip! A Lift-the-Flap Adventure. Hill, Susanna Leonard. 2009. (ENG.). 12p. (J). (gr. -1-k). bds. 7.99 *(978-1-4169-7833-6(X)*, Little Simon) Little Simon.

Larranaga, Ana Martin. Goodnight Faces: A Book of Masks. Jugran, Jan. 2007. (ENG.). 12p. (J). (gr. -1 — 1). bds. 6.99 *(978-1-58476-672-8(7)*, IKIDS) Innovative Kids.

—Hugs. Jugran, Jan. 2007. (ENG.). 12p. (J). (gr. -1 — 1). 9.99 *(978-1-58476-620-9(4)*, IKIDS) Innovative Kids.

Larrañaga, Ana Martín. I Love You All Day Long. 2012. (ENG.). 12p. (J). (gr. -1 — 1). 9.99 *(978-1-60169-269-6(2))* Innovative Kids.

Larranaga, Ana Martin. Ibaby - Goodnight, Baby: Tuck All the Babies into Their Beds. Ikids Staff. 2006. (ENG.). 12p. (J). (gr. -1 — 1). 9.99 *(978-1-58476-482-3(1)*, IKIDS) Innovative Kids.

—Ibaby - Rub-a-Dub-Dub. Jugran, Jan. 2007. (ENG.). 6p. (J). (gr. -1 — 1). 14.99 *(978-1-58476-555-4(0)*, IKIDS) Innovative Kids.

Larrañaga, Ana Martín. Mommies & Babies. Page, Liza & Innovative Kids Staff. 2008. (ENG.). 12p. (J). (gr. -1 — 1). bds. 5.99 *(978-1-58476-656-8(5))* Innovative Kids.

Larrañaga, Ana Martín. Opposites. Page, Liza & Innovative Kids Staff. 2008. (ENG.). 12p. (J). (gr. -1 — 1). bds. 5.99 *(978-1-58476-654-4(9))* Innovative Kids.

Larranaga, Ana Martin. Owl. Rivers-Moore, Debbie. 2012. (Come Out & Play Bks.). (ENG.). 10p. (J). bds. 2.99 *(978-0-7641-6518-4(6))* Barron's Educational Series, Inc.

—Pig. Rivers-Moore, Debbie. 2012. (Come Out & Play Bks.). (ENG.). 10p. (J). bds. 2.99 *(978-0-7641-6519-1(4))* Barron's Educational Series, Inc.

—Pony. Rivers-Moore, Debbie. 2012. (Come Out & Play Bks.). (ENG.). 10p. (J). bds. 2.99 *(978-0-7641-6520-7(8))* Barron's Educational Series, Inc.

—Puppy. Rivers-Moore, Debbie. 2012. (Come Out & Play Bks.). (ENG.). 10p. (J). bds. 2.99 *(978-0-7641-6521-4(6))* Barron's Educational Series, Inc.

—Shapes. Ikids Staff. 2009. (ENG.). 12p. (J). (gr. -1 — 1). bds. 5.99 *(978-1-58476-937-8(8))* Innovative Kids.

—Trucks. Ikids Staff. 2009. (ENG.). 12p. (J). (gr. -1 — 1). bds. 5.99 *(978-1-58476-936-1(X))* Innovative Kids.

Larrañaga, Ana Martín. Who Said Boo? A Lift-the-Flap Book. Root, Phyllis. 2005. (ENG.). 14p. (J). (gr. -1-k). bds. 5.99 *(978-0-689-85408-8(0)*, Little Simon) Little Simon.

Larranaga, Ana Martin. Noisy Beach. Larranaga, Ana Martin. 2011. (Rattle Buggy Buddies Ser.). (ENG.). 12p. (J). (gr. k — 1). bds. 7.99 *(978-0-230-70622-4(3))* Macmillan Pubs., Ltd. GBR. Dist: Independent Pubs. Group.

—Noisy Park. Larranaga, Ana Martin. 2nd ed. 2011. (Rattle Buggy Buddies Ser.). (ENG.). 12p. (J). (gr. k — 1). bds. 7.99 *(978-0-230-70623-1(1))* Macmillan Pubs., Ltd. GBR. Dist: Independent Pubs. Group.

Larranaga, Ana Martin, jt. illus. see Parsons, Jackie.

Larroca, Salvador. House of M. Peyer, Tom. 2006. (ENG.). 120p. (J). (gr. 4-17). pap. 13.99 *(978-0-7851-1753-7(9))* Marvel Worldwide, Inc.

—Namor: Sea & Sand. Jemas, Bill & Watson, Andi. 2004. (Marvel Heroes Ser.). 144p. (YA). pap. 12.99 *(978-0-7851-1241-9(3))* Marvel Worldwide, Inc.

Larsen, Alison. My Turtle. Larsen, Alison. 2006. 24p. (J). (gr. -1-3). per. 11.95 *(978-1-60002-095-7(X)*, 3963) Mountain Valley Publishing, LLC.

—What Makes You Smile? Larsen, Alison. 2006. 23p. (J). (gr. -1-3). per. 13.95 *(978-1-60002-094-0(1))* Mountain Valley Publishing, LLC.

Larsen, Angela Sage. Petalwink Learns to Fly. Larsen, Angela Sage. 2010. 32p. (J). lib. bdg. 12.95 *(978-1-936086-20-7(4))* Rising Star Studios, LLC.

Larsen, Dan. Return to Winterville. Wood, Francis Eugene. Pickett, Elizabeth & Dean, Tina, eds. 2004. 96p. (YA). per. 14.95 net. *(978-0-9746372-1-1(1))* Tip-Of-The-Moon Publishing Co.

—The SnowPeople. Wood, Francis. 2003. 96p. (YA). per. 14.95 *(978-0-9746372-0-4(3))* Tip-Of-The-Moon Publishing Co.

Larsen, Eric, et al. Powerless! Kavanagh, Terry & Harris, Joseph. 2010. (ENG.). 144p. (YA). (gr. 8-17). pap. 16.99 *(978-0-7851-4677-3(6))* Marvel Worldwide, Inc.

Larsen, Eric, jt. illus. see Michael, Joan.

Larsen, Erik, et al. Spider-Man: The Vengeance of Venom. 2011. (ENG.). 304p. (J). (gr. 4-17). pap. 34.99 *(978-0-7851-5760-1(3))* Marvel Worldwide, Inc.

Larsen, Ramonita. Yes, I Can Do It/Sí, lo Puedo Hacer. Larsen, Ramonita. l.t. ed. 2006. 18p. (J). per. 10.99 *(978-1-59879-292-8(X))* Lifevest Publishing, Inc.

Larson, Abigail. Monster Goose Nursery Rhymes, 1 vol. Herz, Henry et al. 2015. (ENG.). 32p. (J). (gr. k-3). 16.99 *(978-1-4556-2032-6(7))* Pelican Publishing Co., Inc.

Larson, Amanda. The Adventures of Baylee Beagle — Annabelle Beagle. Gildea, Kathy. 2005. 28p. (J). 7.95 *(978-0-9767096-1-9(9))* Maxim Pr.

—The Adventures of Baylee Beagle — Hurricane Hound. Gildea, Kathy. 2005. 28p. (J). 7.95 *(978-0-9767096-2-6(7))* Maxim Pr.

Larson, Caleb A. It's Your Ball after All. Larson, Melissa J. 2007. 20p. per. 24.95 *(978-1-4241-9046-1(0))* America Star Bks.

Larson, D. J. Pigsley Brew. Larson, D. J. 2003. 39p. (J). (gr. k-2). pap. 5.95 *(978-0-9728234-0-1(9))* Don't Look Publishing.

Larson, Hope. A Wrinkle in Time. L'Engle, Madeleine. 2012. (ENG.). 392p. (J). (gr. 5-9). 19.99 *(978-0-374-38615-3(3)*, Farrar, Straus & Giroux (BYR)) Farrar, Straus & Giroux.

Larson, Hope. Chiggers. Larson, Hope. 2008. (ENG.). 176p. (J). (gr. 5-9). pap. 11.99 *(978-1-4169-3587-2(8)*, Simon & Schuster/Paula Wiseman Bks.) Simon & Schuster Children's Publishing.

—Mercury. Larson, Hope. 2010. (ENG.). 240p. (YA). (gr. 7-18). 19.99 *(978-1-4169-3585-8(1))*; pap. 12.99 *(978-1-4169-3588-9(6))* Simon & Schuster Children's Publishing. (Atheneum Bks. for Young Readers).

Larson, J. E. Hades Speaks! A Guide to the Underworld by the Greek God of the Dead. Shecter, Vicky Alvear. 2014. (Secrets of the Ancient Gods Ser.). (ENG.). 128p. (J). (gr. 4-7). 16.95 *(978-1-62091-598-1(7))* Boyds Mills Pr.

Larson, Jennifer S., photos by. The Nitty-Gritty Gardening Book: Fun Projects for All Seasons. Cornell, Kari A. 2015. (ENG., 48p. (J). (gr. 4-8). lib. bdg. 26.65 *(978-1-4677-2647-4(8)*, Millbrook Pr.) Lerner Publishing Group.

Larson, Joan. Yetsa's Sweater, 1 vol. Olsen, Sylvia. 2007. (ENG.). 40p. (J). (gr. -1-5). 19.95 *(978-1-55039-155-8(0))* Sono Nis Pr. CAN. Dist: Orca Bk. Pubs. USA.

—Yetsa's Sweater, 1 vol. Olsen, Sylvia. 2013. (ENG.). 40p. (J). (gr. -1-5). 9.95 *(978-1-55039-202-9(6))* Sono Nis Pr. CAN. Dist: Orca Bk. Pubs. USA.

Larson, Katherine. Break-in at the Basilica: Adventures with Sister Philomena, Special Agent to the Pope. Ahern, Dianne. 2006. (J). *(978-0-9679437-8-7(7))* Aunt Dee's Attic, Inc.

—Lost in Peter's Tomb: Adventures with Sister Philomena, Special Agent to the Pope. Ahern, Dianne. 2006. (J). pap. *(978-0-9679437-9-4(5))* Aunt Dee's Attic, Inc.

—M Is for Melody: A Music Alphabet. Wargin, Kathy-jo. rev. ed. 2006. (Art & Culture Ser.). (ENG.). 40p. (J). (gr. 1-4). pap. 7.95 *(978-1-58536-332-2(4)*, 202295) Sleeping Bear Pr.

—Today I Made My First Reconciliation. Ahern, Dianne. 2004. 56p. 19.95 *(978-0-9679437-3-2(6))* Aunt Dee's Attic, Inc.

Larson, Katherine & Langton, Bruce. A Is for Arches: A Utah Alphabet. Hall, Rebecca. 2003. (Discover America State by State Ser.). (ENG.). 40p. (J). (gr. 1-3). 17.95 *(978-1-58536-096-3(1)*, 201976) Sleeping Bear Pr.

Larson, Lisa K. Claudius Saves the Pumpkin Patch. Kirby, Ruth M. 2008. 20p. pap. 24.95 *(978-1-60703-827-6(7))* America Star Bks.

Larson, Maria Burgaleta. The ABC's of Fruits & Vegetables & Beyond: Delicious Alphabet Poems Plus Food, Facts & Fun for Everyone. Charney, Steve & Goldbeck, David. 2007. 112p. (J). (gr. -1-4). per. 16.95 *(978-1-886101-07-4(8))* Ceres Pr.

Larson, Scott & Heike, Mark. Marie Curie & Radioactivity, 1 vol. Miller, Connie Colwell. 2006. (Inventions & Discovery Ser.). (ENG.). 32p. (gr. 3-4). 29.99 *(978-0-7368-6486-2(5)*, Graphic Library) Capstone Pr., Inc.

Larter, John & Bianco, Mike. Penguin Brothers, Vol. 1. Blaylock, Josh. 2005. 144p. (YA). pap. 10.95 *(978-1-932796-20-9(7))* Devil's Due Publishing, Inc.

LaRue, Athena Mariah. Danny the Fisherman, 1 vol. Stanley, Dan. 2010. 46p. 24.95 *(978-1-4512-9695-2(9))* PublishAmerica, Inc.

Lasalle, Janet. Cinderella at the Ball. Hillert, Margaret. rev. exp. ed. 2006. (Beginning to Read Ser.). 32p. (J). (gr. -1-3). lib. bdg. 14.95 *(978-1-59953-046-8(5))* Norwood Hse. Pr.

Lasher, Mary Ann, jt. illus. see Baum, Ann.

Lashley, Ken & Pichelli, Sara. Women of Marvel. 2011. (ENG.). 352p. (YA). (gr. 8-17). pap. 24.99 *(978-0-7851-4953-8(8))* Marvel Worldwide, Inc.

Laskey, Shannon. All about You Quiz Book: Discover More about Yourself & How to Be Your Best! Madison, Lynda. 2009. (ENG.). 64p. (YA). (gr. 3-18). spiral bd. 9.95 *(978-1-59369-598-9(5))* American Girl Publishing, Inc.

—Go for It! Start Smart, Have Fun, & Stay Inspired in Any Activity. Anton, Carrie, ed. 2008. (American Girl Library). (ENG.). 64p. (YA). (gr. 3-18). pap. 9.95 *(978-1-59369-423-4(7))* American Girl Publishing, Inc.

—A Smart Girl's Guide to Style: How to Have Fun with Fashion, Shop Smart, & Let Your Personal Style Shine Through. Cindrich, Sharon. 2010. (ENG.). 120p. (J). (gr. 4-7). pap. 9.95 *(978-1-59369-648-1(5))* American Girl Publishing, Inc.

—3-D Studio. Falligant, Erin, ed. 2008. 48p. (J). 17.95 *(978-1-59369-414-2(8))* American Girl Publishing, Inc.

Lasky, David. El Deafo. Bell, Cece. 2014. (ENG.). 248p. (J). (gr. 3-7). 21.95 *(978-1-4197-1020-9(6))*; pap. 10.95 *(978-1-4197-1217-3(9))* Abrams. (Amulet Bks.).

—Oregon Trail: The Road to Destiny. Young, Frank. 2011. (ENG.). 128p. (J). (gr. 4-7). pap. 14.95 *(978-1-57061-649-5(3))* Sasquatch Bks.

Lasley, Tony. April's Journal: A Journal for Children. Reinoso, Marta. 13.95 incl. audio *(978-0-9676203-0-5(9))* Reinoso, Marta.

Lassen, Christian R. Ocean Friends. Book Company Staff. 2003. (Puzzles Ser.). (J). bds. 14.95 *(978-1-74047-381-1(7))* Book Co. Publishing Pty, Ltd., The AUS. Dist: Penton Overseas, Inc.

—Treasures of the Sea: Birthday & Address Book. Book Company Staff. 2003. (Stationery Ser.). (J). 14.95 *(978-1-86309-793-2(7))* Book Co. Publishing Pty, Ltd., The AUS. Dist: Penton Overseas, Inc.

Lassen, Christian Riese. Moon Dance. 2005. 16p. (J). (gr. -1-3). bds. 8.95 *(978-1-74047-591-4(7)*, Penton Kids) Penton Overseas, Inc.

Lasson, Matt. Santa Heads South: Casey's Christmas Surprise. Jordan, L. W. 2008. 40p. per. 24.95 *(978-1-60441-374-8(3))* America Star Bks.

Last, Ian & Smith, Diana. How to Draw. 2005. (Art Tricks Ser.). 48p. (J). (gr. 4-7). *(978-1-84510-676-8(8))* Top That! Publishing PLC.

Laster, Brenda. The Valley of the Christmas Trees: A Legend. Rucker, David. 2007. 41p. (J). (gr. -1-3). 14.95 *(978-1-931643-94-8(6))* Seven Locks Pr.

Lat. Kampung Boy. Lat. rev. ed. 2006. Orig. Title: The Kampung Boy. (ENG.). 144p. (YA). (gr. 7-8). pap. 18.99 *(978-1-59643-121-8(0)*, First Second Bks.) Roaring Brook Pr.

Latham, Karen & Latham, Rebecca. V Is for Viking: A Minnesota Alphabet. Wargin, Kathy-jo. 2003. (Discover America State by State Ser.). (ENG.). 40p. (J). 17.95 *(978-1-58536-125-0(9))* Sleeping Bear Pr.

Latham, Rebecca, jt. illus. see Latham, Karen.

Latham, Sarah. The Day an Angel Ran into My Room. Valenzuela, Anabelle. 2012. 56p. 30.50 *(978-1-61897-794-6(6)*, Strategic Bk. Publishing) Strategic Book Publishing & Rights Agency (SBPRA).

Lathrop, Dorothy P. The Three Mulla-Mulgars (the Three Royal Monkeys) Mare, Walter de La. 2013. (ENG.). 288p. (J). (gr. 3-6). pap. 12.95 *(978-0-486-49380-0(6))* Dover Pubns., Inc.

Latimer, Alex. The Baseball Player & the Walrus. Loory, Ben. 2015. (ENG.). 32p. (J). (gr. k-3). 16.99 *(978-0-8037-3951-2(6)*, Dial) Penguin Publishing Group.

—Just So Stories. Kipling, Rudyard. 2008. (ENG.). 240p. (J). (gr. 5-6). 4.99 *(978-0-14-132162-2(8)*, Puffin) Penguin Publishing Group.

—Penguin's Hidden Talent, 1 vol. 2012. (ENG.). 32p. (J). 15.95 *(978-1-56145-629-1(2))* Peachtree Pubs.

Latimer, Alex. The Boy Who Cried Ninja, 1 vol. Latimer, Alex. 2011. (ENG.). 32p. (J). (gr. -1-3). 15.95 *(978-1-56145-579-9(2))* Peachtree Pubs.

—Lion vs Rabbit, 1 vol. Latimer, Alex. 2013. (ENG.). 32p. (J). (gr. -1-3). 15.95 *(978-1-56145-709-0(4))* Peachtree Pubs.

Latimer, Miriam. Choose to Recycle. Bewley, Elizabeth. 2009. 10p. 7.95 *(978-1-58117-904-0(9)*, Intervisual/Piggy Toes) Bendon, Inc.

—Dayenu! A Favorite Passover Song. Traditional Staff. 2012. (ENG.). 12p. (J). (gr. -1-k). bds. 7.99 *(978-0-545-31236-3(1)*, Cartwheel Bks.) Scholastic, Inc.

—El Desayuno Del Principe. Oppenheim, Joanne F. & Barefoot Books. 32p. pap. 7.99 *(978-1-78285-076-2(7))* Barefoot Bks., Inc.

—El Hermanito de Ruby. White, Kathryn. 2013. (SPA.). 32p. (J). pap. 7.99 *(978-1-78285-026-7(0))* Barefoot Bks., Inc.

—The Prince's Bedtime. Oppenheim, Joanne F. (ENG.). 32p. (J). (gr. -1-3). 2007. pap. 7.99 *(978-1-84686-106-2(3))*; 2006. 16.99 *(978-1-84148-597-3(7))* Barefoot Bks., Inc.

—The Prince's Breakfast. Oppenheim, Joanne F. & Barefoot Books Staff. 32p. 16.99 *(978-1-78285-074-8(0))*; pap. 9.99 *(978-1-78285-075-5(9))* Barefoot Bks., Inc.

—El Principe No Duerme. Oppenheim, Joanne F. & Barefoot Books Staff. 32p. pap. 7.99 *(978-1-78285-077-9(5))* Barefoot Bks., Inc.

—Ruby's Baby Brother. White, Kathryn. 2013. (ENG.). 32p. (J). 16.99 *(978-1-84686-864-1(5))*; pap. 7.99 *(978-1-84686-950-1(1))* Barefoot Bks., Inc.

—Ruby's School Walk. White, Kathryn. (ENG.). 32p. (J). (gr. -1-2). 2012. pap. 7.99 *(978-1-84686-786-6(X))*; 2010. 16.99 *(978-1-84686-275-5(2))* Barefoot Bks., Inc.

—Ruby's Sleepover. White, Kathryn. 2012. (ENG.). 32p. (J). 16.99 *(978-1-84686-593-0(X))*; pap. 7.99 *(978-1-84686-758-3(4))* Barefoot Bks., Inc.

—Shopping with Dad. Harvey, Matt. 2008. (ENG.). 32p. (J). (gr. -1-3). 16.99 *(978-1-84686-172-7(1))* Barefoot Bks., Inc.

—The Sunflower Sword. Sperring, Mark. 2011. (Andersen Press Picture Bks). (ENG.). 32p. (J). (gr. -1-3). 16.95 *(978-0-7613-7486-2(8))* Lerner Publishing Group.

Latimer, Miriam. Shopping with Dad. Latimer, Miriam. Harvey, Matt. 2010. (ENG.). 32p. (J). pap. 7.99 *(978-1-84686-449-0(6))* Barefoot Bks., Inc.

—Shrinking Sam. Latimer, Miriam. 2007. (ENG.). 32p. (J). (gr. -1-3). 16.99 *(978-1-84686-038-6(5))* Barefoot Bks., Inc.

Latimer, Muriam. The Prince's Bedtime. Latimer, Muriam. Oppenheim, Joanne F. 2007. (ENG.). 32p. (J). pap. 9.99 *(978-1-84686-096-6(2))* Barefoot Bks., Inc.

Latimor, Miriam. Emily's Tiger. Latimor, Miriam. 2011. (ENG.). 80p. (J). pap. 7.99 *(978-1-84686-594-7(8))* Barefoot Bks., Inc.

Latorre, Adolfo. Cornbread Runs for Class President. Taylor, Vincent. Griffin, Kasana & Griggs, Charles, eds. 2004. (Cornbread Ser.: 1). 96p. (J). per. 4.99 *(978-0-9704512-4-8(5))* TriEclipse, Inc.

Lätti, Leo. Cristoforo Colombo e la Pasta Al Pomodoro - Christopher Columbus & the Pasta with Tomato Sauce: A Bilingual Picture Book (Italian-English Text) Bach, Nancy. 2013. 30p. pap. *(978-1-938712-06-7(4))* Roxby Media Ltd.

—Galileo Galilei e la Torre Di Pisa - Galileo Galilei & the Pisa Tower: A Bilingual Picture Book about the Italian Astronomer (Italian-English Text) Bach, Nancy. 2013. 26p. pap. *(978-1-938712-07-4(2))* Roxby Media Ltd.

—Giuseppe Verdi, Compositore d'Opera Italiano - Giuseppe Verdi, Italian Opera Composer: A Bilingual Picture Book (Italian-English Text) Bach, Nancy. 2013. 28p. pap. *(978-1-938712-12-8(9))* Roxby Media Ltd.

—Maria Montessori & Her Quiet Revolution: A Picture Book about Maria Montessori & Her School Method. Bach, Nancy. 2013. 24p. pap. *(978-1-938712-10-4(2))* Roxby Media Ltd.

—Ottavia e I Gatti Di Roma - Octavia & the Cats of Rome: A Bilingual Picture Book in Italian & English. Cerulli, Claudia. 2013. 40p. pap. *(978-1-938712-11-1(0))* Roxby Media Ltd.

Lattimore, Eleanor Frances. Little Pear. Lattimore, Eleanor Frances. 2006. (Odyssey Classics Ser.). (ENG.). 128p. (J). (gr. 1-4). pap. 5.95 *(978-0-15-205502-8(9))* Houghton Mifflin Harcourt Publishing Co.

—Little Pear & His Friends. Lattimore, Eleanor Frances. 2006. (Odyssey Classics Ser.). (ENG.). 144p. (J). (gr. 1-4). pap. 10.95 *(978-0-15-205490-8(1))* Houghton Mifflin Harcourt Publishing Co.

Latushkin, Valentin. The Picture Book Dictionary: The Essential Source for Bilingual Families, English-Spanish Edition. Laud, Valerie. l.t. ed. 2005. (ENG & SPA.). 96p. (J). *(978-0-9747387-0-3(0))* EKADOO Publishing Group.

Latyk, Olivier. Jeannette Claus Saves Christmas. Rees, Douglas. 2010. (ENG.). 40p. (J). (gr. k-3). 16.99 *(978-1-4169-2686-3(0)*, McElderry, Margaret K. Bks.) McElderry, Margaret K. Bks.

—The Little Boy Star: An Allegory of the Holocaust. Hausfater, Rachel. Zimmerman, Joelle, tr. from FRE. 2006. (ENG.). 32p. (J). (gr. 4-7). 16.95 *(978-1-59687-172-4(5))* IBks., Inc.

—El Nino Estrella. Hausfater-Douieb, Rachel. 2005. (SPA.). 32p. (J). 20.99 *(978-84-263-5007-7(0))* Vives, Luis Editorial (Edelvives) ESP. Dist: Lectorum Pubns., Inc.

Lau, Benny. Socks Heaven. Benny. 2003. (ENG.). 32p. (J). (-k). 15.50 *(978-962-86816-5-5(6))* Zephyr Pr.

Lau, Kevin. Sunn. Roman, Steven A. Preiss, Byron, ed. 2003. 192p. pap. 9.95 *(978-0-7434-7504-4(6))* ibooks, Inc.

Laub, Frima & Uhlig, Elizabeth. Between the Shadows. Laub, Frima. 2009. 81p. (J). pap. 12.95 *(978-0-9815345-2-7(X))* Marble Hse. Editions.

Laubscher, André, jt. illus. see Lomofsky, Lynne.

Laud, Julia. Eighth Grade Bites. Brewer, Heather. 2013. (Chronicles of Vladimir Tod Ser.: 1). (ENG.). 144p. (YA). (gr. 7). pap. 12.99 *(978-0-8037-3811-9(0)*, Dial) Penguin Publishing Group.

Laudec. Cedric Vol. 4: Hot & Cold. Cauvin, Raoul. 2013. (ENG.). 48p. pap. 11.95 *(978-1-84918-158-7(6))* CineBook GBR. Dist: National Bk. Network.

—What Got into Him?, Vol. Cauvin, Raoul. 2011. (ENG.). 48p. (gr. 3-17). pap. 11.95 *(978-1-84918-081-8(4))* CineBook GBR. Dist: National Bk. Network.

Laudec, Calvinaoul. Cedric 1 - High-Risk Class. Cauvin, Raoul. 2008. (ENG.). 48p. pap. 11.95 *(978-1-905460-68-7(6))* CineBook GBR. Dist: National Bk. Network.

Lauffray, Mathieu. The Emerald Maze, Vol. 3. Dorison, Xavier. 2012. (ENG.). 56p. pap. 13.95 *(978-1-84918-105-1(5))* CineBook GBR. Dist: National Bk. Network.

—Lady Vivian Hastings. Dorison, Xavier. Saincantin, Jerome, tr. from FRE. 2011. (ENG.). 56p. pap. 13.95 *(978-1-84918-062-7(8))* CineBook GBR. Dist: National Bk. Network.

—Long John Silver Vol. 4: Guiana-Capac. Dorison, Xavier. 2014. (ENG.). 64p. pap. 15.95 *(978-1-84918-175-4(6))* CineBook GBR. Dist: National Bk. Network.

—Neptune Vol. 2: Long John Silver. Dorison, Xavier. 2011. (ENG.). 56p. pap. 13.95 *(978-1-84918-072-6(5))* CineBook GBR. Dist: National Bk. Network.

Laugesen, Malene R. Flying Solo: How Ruth Elder Soared into America's Heart. Cummins, Julie. 2013. (ENG.). 32p. (J). (gr. 1-3). 17.99 *(978-1-59643-509-4(7))* Roaring Brook Pr.

Laughbaum, Steve & Crutchfield, Jim. Tennessee Trailblazers. Sparkman, Winette. 56p. (J). pap., wbk. ed., act. bk. ed. 6.95 *(978-0-9634824-1-9(6))* March Media, Inc.

L

Laughead, Mike. The Big Catch: A Robot & Rico Story, 1 vol. Suen, Anastasia. 2009. (Robot & Rico Ser.). (ENG.). 32p. (gr. 1-2). 21.32 *(978-1-4342-1626-7(8))*; pap. 6.25 *(978-1-4342-1751-6(5))* Stone Arch Bks.

—The Comet of Doom. Perritano, John. 2014. (Kid Squad Saves the World Ser.). (ENG.). 112p. (J). (gr. 8-12). 27.07 *(978-1-62402-038-4(0))* Magic Wagon.

—Dino Hunt: A Robot & Rico Story. Suen, Anastasia. 2010. (Robot & Rico Ser.). (ENG.). 32p. (gr. 1-2). pap. 6.25 *(978-1-4342-2300-5(0))* Stone Arch Bks.

—A Dress for Me!, 0 vols. Fliess, Sue. 2012. (ENG.). 24p. (J). (gr. k-3). 12.99 *(978-0-7614-6148-7(5))*, 9780761461487, Amazon Children's Publishing) Amazon Publishing.

—The Egyptian Prophecy. Perritano, John. 2014. (Kid Squad Saves the World Ser.). (ENG.). 112p. (J). (gr. 8-12). 27.07 *(978-1-62402-039-1(9))* Magic Wagon.

—La Gran Pesca. Suen, Anastasia & Heck, Claudia M. 2012. (Robot y Rico/Robot & Rico Ser.).Tr. of Big Catch. (MUL & SPA.). 32p. (gr. 1-2). pap. 5.05 *(978-1-4342-3920-4(9))*; lib. bdg. 21.32 *(978-1-4342-3781-1(8))* Stone Arch Bks. (Bilingual Stone Arch Readers).

—La Noche de Terror. Suen, Anastasia. Heck, Claudia M., tr. from ENG. 2012. (Robot y Rico/Robot & Rico Ser.).Tr. of Scary Night. (MUL & SPA.). 32p. (gr. 1-2). pap. 5.05 *(978-1-4342-3918-1(7))*; lib. bdg. 21.32 *(978-1-4342-3779-8(6))* Stone Arch Bks. (Bilingual Stone Arch Readers).

—The Pirate Map: A Robot & Rico Story. Suen, Anastasia. 2010. (Robot & Rico Ser.). (ENG.). 32p. (gr. 1-2). pap. 6.25 *(978-1-4342-2301-2(9))*; lib. bdg. 21.32 *(978-1-4342-1871-1(6))* Stone Arch Bks.

—Un Premio Adentro. Suen, Anastasia. Heck, Claudia M., tr. from ENG. 2012. (Robot y Rico/Robot & Rico Ser.).Tr. of Prize Inside. (MUL & SPA.). 32p. (gr. 1-2). pap. 5.05 *(978-1-4342-3919-8(5))*; lib. bdg. 21.32 *(978-1-4342-3780-4(X))* Stone Arch Bks. (Bilingual Stone Arch Readers).

—A Prize Inside: A Robot & Rico Story, 1 vol. Suen, Anastasia. 2009. (Robot & Rico Ser.). (ENG.). 32p. (gr. 1-2). 21.32 *(978-1-4342-1627-4(6))*; pap. 6.25 *(978-1-4342-1749-3(3))* Stone Arch Bks.

—The Scary Night: A Robot & Rico Story, 1 vol. Suen, Anastasia. 2009. (Robot & Rico Ser.). (ENG.). 32p. (gr. 1-2). 21.32 *(978-1-4342-1628-1(4))*; pap. 6.25 *(978-1-4342-1752-3(3))* Stone Arch Bks.

—Shoes for Me!, 0 vols. Fliess, Sue. 2011. (ENG.). 24p. (J). (gr. -1-3). 12.99 *(978-0-7614-5825-8(5))*, 9780761458258, Amazon Children's Publishing) Amazon Publishing.

—Skate Trick: A Robot & Rico Story, 1 vol. Suen, Anastasia. 2009. (Robot & Rico Ser.). (ENG.). 32p. (gr. 1-2). pap. 6.25 *(978-1-4342-1750-9(7))* Stone Arch Bks.

—The Snickerblooms & the Age Bug. Perritano, John. 2014. (Kid Squad Saves the World Ser.). (ENG.). 112p. (J). (gr. 8-12). 27.07 *(978-1-62402-041-4(0))* Magic Wagon.

—Snow Games: A Robot & Rico Story. Suen, Anastasia. 2010. (Robot & Rico Ser.). (ENG.). 32p. (gr. 1-2). pap. 6.25 *(978-1-4342-2302-9(7))*; lib. bdg. 21.32 *(978-1-4342-1869-8(4))* Stone Arch Bks.

—Test Drive: A Robot & Rico Story. Suen, Anastasia. 2010. (Robot & Rico Ser.). (ENG.). 32p. (gr. 1-2). pap. 6.25 *(978-1-4342-2303-6(5))*; lib. bdg. 21.32 *(978-1-4342-1868-1(6))* Stone Arch Bks.

—Trucos en la Patineta. Suen, Anastasia. Heck, Claudia M., tr. from ENG. 2012. (Robot y Rico/Robot & Rico Ser.).Tr. of Skate Trick. (MUL & SPA.). 32p. (gr. 1-2). pap. 5.05 *(978-1-4342-3917-4(9))*; lib. bdg. 21.32 *(978-1-4342-3778-1(8))* Stone Arch Bks. (Bilingual Stone Arch Readers).

—What If You Need to Call 911?, 1 vol. Guard, Anara. 2011. (Danger Zone Ser.). (ENG.). 24p. (gr. 1-2). pap. 7.49 *(978-1-4048-7037-6(7))*; lib. bdg. 25.32 *(978-1-4048-6682-9(5))* Picture Window Bks. (Nonfiction Picture Bks.).

Laughing Gravy Design Staff. Computers: A Magic Mouse Guide. Ward-Johnson, Chris. 2003. (Magic Mouse Guides). 32p. (J). lib. bdg. 22.60 *(978-0-7660-2263-8(3))* Enslow Pubs., Inc.

—E-Mail: A Magic Mouse Guide. Ward-Johnson, Chris. 2003. (Magic Mouse Guides). 32p. (J). lib. bdg. 23.94 *(978-0-7660-2261-4(7))* Enslow Pubs., Inc.

—Internet: A Magic Mouse Guide. Ward-Johnson, Chris. 2003. (Magic Mouse Guides). 32p. (J). lib. bdg. 22.60 *(978-0-7660-2260-7(9))* Enslow Pubs., Inc.

—The Magic Mouse Dictionary of Computers & Information Technology. Ward-Johnson, Chris & Gould, William. 2003. (Magic Mouse Guides). 64p. (J). lib. bdg. 29.27 *(978-0-7660-2264-5(1))* Enslow Pubs., Inc.

—World Wide Web: A Magic Mouse Guide. Ward-Johnson, Chris. 2003. (Magic Mouse Guides). 32p. (J). lib. bdg. 23.94 *(978-0-7660-2262-1(5))* Enslow Pubs., Inc.

Launay, Melissa. My Mama Earth. Katz, Susan B. 2012. (ENG.). 24p. (J). 16.99 *(978-1-84686-419-6(6))* Barefoot Bks., Inc.

Laune, Paul. A Figure in Hiding, No. 16. Dixon, Franklin W. 2005. (Hardy Boys (Hardcover) Ser.). (ENG.). 228p. (J). (gr. 3-9). 17.95 *(978-1-55709-274-8(5))* Applewood Bks.

—The Lone Ranger Traps the Smugglers. Striker, Fran. 2011. 224p. 44.95 *(978-1-258-09845-2(8))* Literary Licensing, LLC.

—Wilbur & Orville Wright: Boys with Wings. Stevenson, Augusta. 2011. 192p. (gr. 2-5). 42.95 *(978-1-258-07857-7(0))* Literary Licensing, LLC.

—William Henry Harrison, Young Tippecanoe: Childhood of Famous Americans Series. Peckham, Howard Henry. 2011. 190p. 42.95 *(978-1-258-07766-2(3))* Literary Licensing, LLC.

—A Yankee Flier in the Far East. Avery, Al. 2011. 224p. 44.95 *(978-1-258-06349-8(2))* Literary Licensing, LLC.

Laura, Huliska-beith, jt. illus. see Huliska-Beith, Laura.

Laura Lee, Cundiff. The Last Little Polar Bear: A Global Change Adventure Story. Foresman, Timothy. 2007. 60p. (J). per. 19.95 *(978-0-9776906-2-6(8))* Blueline Publishing.

Laurel, Hylton. The Cowboy Frog. Laurel, Hylton. 2003. (ENG.). 24p. (J). (gr. k-5). pap. 5.95 *(978-1-875641-85-7(8))* Magabala Bks. AUS. Dist: Independent Pubs. Group.

Laurence, Laurence. Ella & the Balloons in the Sky. Appleby, Danny & Pirie, Lauren. 2013. (ENG.). 32p. (J). (gr. k-4). 15.95 *(978-1-77049-528-9(2))* Tundra Bks. CAN. Dist: Random Hse., Inc.

Laurente, Lourdes. The Faraway Kingdom of Oop Loop la Pink. Bradley, Adrian. 2013. 36p. pap. 10.95 *(978-0-9910180-0-0(1))* Someday Ranch.

Laurie, Caple. Fiddleheads to Fir Trees: Leaves in All Seasons. Linden, Joanne. 2013. 32p. (J). 12.00 *(978-0-87842-606-5(X))* Mountain Pr. Publishing Co., Inc.

Laurie, Cook. Amelia Asks Why. 2007. (J). 3.99 *(978-0-9726075-4-4(4))* EPI Bks.

Laurie, Jane. Twisted Fairy Tales. McHugh, Maura. 2013. (ENG.). 144p. (J). (gr. 6-11). 19.99 *(978-0-7641-6588-7(7))* Barron's Educational Series, Inc.

Lauritano, Michael. Snowmobile: Bombardier's Dream Machine. Older, Jules. 2012. (ENG.). 64p. (J). (gr. 3-7). 14.95 *(978-1-58089-334-3(1))*; pap. 6.95 *(978-1-58089-335-0(X))* Charlesbridge Publishing, Inc.

Lauso, Judith. Maz, You're Up! Mazeroski, Kelly. 2010. 24p. (J). pap. 12.95 *(978-0-936340-18-0(5))* Historical Society of Western Pennsylvania.

Lauter, Richard. Little Women. (Young Collector's Illustrated Classics Ser.). 192p. (J). 9.95 *(978-1-56156-371-5(4))* Kidsbooks, LLC.

—Little Women: With a Discussion of Family. Alcott, Louisa May. 2003. (Values in Action Illustrated Classics Ser.). 191p. (J). *(978-1-59203-032-3(7))* Learning Challenge, Inc.

—The Secret Garden: With a Discussion of Compassion. Burnett, Frances Hodgson. 2003. (Values in Action Illustrated Classics Ser.). 191p. (J). *(978-1-59203-037-8(8))* Learning Challenge, Inc.

Lauter, Richard. The Adventures of Huckleberry Finn: With a Discussion of Friendship. Lauter, Richard, tr. Twain, Mark. 2003. (Values in Action Illustrated Classics Ser.). (J). *(978-1-59203-042-2(4))* Learning Challenge, Inc.

Lauve, Celia & Shepherd, Rosalie M. Clarence Thomas: Fighter with Words, 1 vol. Collins, David R. 2003. (ENG.). 32p. (J). (gr. 1-3). 16.99 *(978-1-56554-862-6(0))* Pelican Publishing Co., Inc.

Lavallee, Barbara. All You Need for a Snowman. Schertle, Alice. 2007. (ENG.). 32p. (J). (gr. -1-3). pap. 6.99 *(978-0-15-206115-9(0))* Houghton Mifflin Harcourt Publishing Co.

—Groucho's Eyebrows: An Alaskan Cat Tale. Brown, Tricia. 2012. (ENG.). 32p. (J). (gr. -1-1). pap. 9.99 *(978-0-88240-892-7(5))*, Alaska Northwest Bks.) Graphic Arts Ctr. Publishing Co.

—The Sourdough Man: An Alaska Folktale. Stihler, Cherie B. 2010. (ENG.). 32p. (J). (gr. -1-2). pap. 10.99 *(978-1-57061-594-8(2))* Sasquatch Bks.

—This Place Is Cold. Cobb, Vicki. 2013. (Imagine Living Here Ser.). (ENG.). 32p. (J). (gr. k-4). pap. 8.99 *(978-0-8027-3401-3(4)*, 226322) Walker & Co.

—This Place Is Wet. Cobb, Vicki. 2013. (Imagine Living Here Ser.). (ENG.). 32p. (J). (gr. k-3). pap. 8.99 *(978-0-8027-3400-6(6)*, 226321) Walker & Co.

Lavallee, Barbara. Papa, Do You Love Me? Lavallee, Barbara. Joosse, Barbara M. 2005. (Mama Ser.: MAMA). (ENG.). 36p. (J). (gr. -1-7). 15.99 *(978-0-8118-4265-5(7))* Chronicle Bks. LLC.

Lavandeira, Sandra. Celebra el Dia De3 San Patricio con Samantha y Lola. Flor Ada, Alma. 2006. (Cuentos para Celebrar / Stories to Celebrate Ser.). (SPA.). 30p. (gr. k-6). per. 11.95 *(978-1-59820-117-8(4)*, Alfaguara) Santillana USA Publishing Co., Inc.

—Cuentopos de Gulubu. Walsh, Maria Elena. 2003. (SPA.). 120p. (J). (gr. 3-5). 14.95 *(978-950-511-630-0(6))* Alfaguara S.A. de Ediciones ARG. Dist: Santillana USA Publishing Co., Inc.

—Dailan Kifki. Walsh, Maria Elena. 2003. (SPA.). 248p. (YA). (gr. 5-8). 18.95 *(978-950-511-629-4(2))* Alfaguara S.A. de Ediciones ARG. Dist: Santillana USA Publishing Co., Inc.

—Mi Dia de la A a la Z. Campoy, F. Isabel. 2009. (SPA.). 32p. (gr. -1-2). pap. 14.95 *(978-1-59820-942-6(6)*, Alfaguara) Santillana USA Publishing Co., Inc.

—No Necesito Paraguas. White, Amy. Kratky, Lada J., tr. 2009. (Colección Fácil de Leer Ser.). (SPA.). 16p. (gr. k-2). pap. 5.99 *(978-1-60396-419-7(3))* Ediciones Alfaguara ESP. Dist: Santillana USA Publishing Co., Inc.

Lavar, Vanda. Tucker's Tale. Walsh, Christopher. 2009. 28p. pap. 11.95 *(978-1-935137-21-4(2))* Guardian Angel Publishing, Inc.

Lavarello, Jose Maria. Aquello Que Tanto Queria Susana. Ramon, Elisa. 2004.Tr. of What Susana Loved Dearly. (SPA.). (J). pap. 7.99 *(978-84-236-6702-4(2))* Edebé ESP. Dist: Lectorum Pubns., Inc.

—Cuentame un Cuento, No. 2. (SPA.). 366p. (J). (gr. k-3). *(978-84-480-1124-6(4)*, TM2346) Timun Mas, Editorial S.A. ESP. Dist: Lectorum Pubns., Inc.

—Que Llueva, Que Llueva. Zubizarreta, Paxti. 2nd ed. (SPA.). 31p. (J). pap. 7.99 *(978-84-236-3678-5(X))* Edebé ESP. Dist: Lectorum Pubns., Inc.

Lavender, Todd. Creak in the Night - Mystery of the Crypts. Freeman, J. Miller. 2012. 74p. pap. 9.99 *(978-0-9850410-1-4(3))* Akmaeon Publishing, LLC.

Lavender, Todd. Farmer Fred & His Hen So Red. Lavender, Todd. 2012. 48p. pap. 9.99 *(978-0-9850410-0-7(5))* Akmaeon Publishing, LLC.

Laver, Sarah, 8th. Where's Jesus. Jeffs, Stephanie. 2004. 32p. 13.95 *(978-0-8294-1728-9(1))* Loyola Pr.

Lavers, Ralph. Redskin Morning & Other Stories. Grant, Joan Marshall. 2010. (J). pap. *(978-1-59731-555-5(9))* Perennis, Sophia.

—Scarlet Fish & Other Stories. Grant, Joan Marshall. 2010. (J). pap. *(978-1-59731-554-8(0))* Perennis, Sophia.

Lavis, Steve. Mrs. Noah's Vegetable Ark. Dickson, John & Pasquali, Elena. 2011. (ENG.). 32p. (J). (gr. k-2). 14.99 *(978-0-7459-6253-5(X))* Lion Hudson PLC GBR. Dist: Independent Pubs. Group.

—You're Too Small! Roddie, Shen. 2004. 32p. (J). 6.95 *(978-1-58925-385-8(X))*; tchr. ed. 15.95 *(978-1-58925-038-3(9))* Tiger Tales.

Lavreys, Debbie. Cinderella. Grimm, Jacob et al. 2010. (ENG.). 24p. (J). (gr. k-2). 16.95 *(978-1-60537-063-7(0))* Clavis Publishing.

—The Little Hamster. Van Der Linden, Elly. 2007. 12p. (gr. -1-k). *(978-0-86315-605-2(3))* Floris Bks.

—The Prickly Hedgehog. Van Der Linden, Elly. 2007. 12p. (J). (gr. -1-k). *(978-0-86315-603-8(7))* Floris Bks.

—The Woolly Sheep. Van Der Linden, Elly. 2007. 12p. (gr. -1-k). *(978-0-86315-604-5(5))* Floris Bks.

Law, Felicia, et al. Castaway Code: Sequencing in Action. Law, Felicia & Way, Steve. 2010. (Mandrill Mountain Math Mysteries Ser.). 32p. (J). (gr. 2-6). 22.60 *(978-1-60754-817-1(8))*; pap. 10.55 *(978-1-60754-822-5(4))* Windmill Bks.

Law, Jenny. Penny & the Punctuation Bee, 1 vol. Donohue, Moira Rose. 2010. (ENG.). 32p. (J). (gr. 1-4). pap. 6.99 *(978-0-8075-6478-3(8))* Whitman, Albert & Co.

Law, Stephanie Pui-Mun. The Hotel under the Sand. Baker, Kage. 2009. (ENG.). 179p. (J). (gr. 2-7). pap. 8.00 *(978-1-892391-89-6(9))* Tachyon Pubns.

Lawn, John. Abraham Lincoln: Road to the White House. Brandt, Keith & Macken, JoAnn Early. 2007. 53p. (J). *(978-0-439-88005-3(X))* Scholastic, Inc.

—Daniel Boone: Frontier Explorer. Brandt, Keith & Macken, JoAnn Early. 2008. 55p. (J). pap. *(978-0-439-02020-6(4))* Scholastic, Inc.

Lawrason, June. The Birthday Girl. Little, Jean. 2004. 64p. (J). lib. bdg. 20.00 *(978-1-4242-1256-9(1))* Fitzgerald Bks.

Lawrence, C. H. Aladdin or, the Wonderful Lamp. 2012. (Shape Bks.). (ENG.). 16p. pap. 9.95 *(978-1-59583-454-6(0))*, 9781595834546, Green Tiger Pr.) Laughing Elephant.

Lawrence, C. H., jt. illus. see Adams, Frank.

Lawrence, David. The Egyptians. Platt, Richard. 2011. (How They Made Things Work! Ser.). 32p. (J). (gr. 2-5). lib. bdg. 28.50 *(978-1-59771-287-3(6))* Sea-To-Sea Pubns.

—The Greeks. Platt, Richard. 2011. (How They Made Things Work! Ser.). 32p. (J). (gr. 2-5). lib. bdg. 28.50 *(978-1-59771-288-0(4))* Sea-To-Sea Pubns.

—In the Renaissance. Platt, Richard. 2011. (How They Made Things Work! Ser.). 32p. (YA). (gr. 2-5). lib. bdg. 28.50 *(978-1-59771-289-7(2))* Sea-To-Sea Pubns.

Lawrence, George. The Voyage of the Beetle: A Journey Around the World with Charles Darwin & the Search for the Solution to the Mystery of Mysteries, as Narrated by Rosie, an Articulate Beetle. Weaver, Anne H. 2007. (ENG.). 80p. (J). (gr. 5-8). 18.95 *(978-0-8263-4304-8(X))* Univ. of New Mexico Pr.

Lawrence, Jack. The Ice Castle. Titan Comics, Titan. 2015. (Riders of Berk Ser.). (ENG.). 64p. (J). (gr. 3-7). pap. 6.99 *(978-1-78276-078-8(4)*, Titan Comics) Titan Bks. Ltd. GBR. Dist: Random Hse., Inc.

Lawrence, Jim, et al. Captain Britain: Siege of Camelot. Lieber, Larry & Parkhouse, Steve. 2011. (ENG.). 376p. (J). (gr. 4-17). 39.99 *(978-0-7851-5753-3(0))* Marvel Worldwide, Inc.

Lawrence, John. Lyra's Oxford. Pullman, Philip. 2006. (His Dark Materials Ser.). 49p. (YA). reprint ed. 11.00 *(978-1-4223-5410-0(5))* DIANE Publishing Co.

—Lyra's Oxford. Pullman, Philip. (His Dark Materials Ser.). (ENG.). 64p. (YA). (gr. 5-12). 2007. per. 6.99 *(978-0-375-84369-3(8))*; 2003. 12.99 *(978-0-375-82819-5(2))* Random Hse. Children's Bks. (Knopf Bks. for Young Readers).

—Once upon a Time in the North. Pullman, Philip. 2008. (His Dark Materials Ser.). (ENG.). 112p. (J). (gr. 5-12). 12.99 *(978-0-375-84510-9(0))* Random Hse. Children's Bks.

—Sea Horse: The Shyest Fish in the Sea. Butterworth, Christine. 2010. (Read, Listen, & Wonder Ser.). (ENG.). 32p. (J). (gr. -1-3). pap. 9.99 *(978-0-7636-4868-8(X))*; pap. 8.99 *(978-0-7636-4650-9(4))* Candlewick Pr.

—Sea Horse: The Shyest Fish in the Sea. Butterworth, Christine. 2009. (Read & Wonder Ser.). (ENG.). 32p. (J). (gr. -1-3). pap. 6.99 *(978-0-7636-4140-5(5))* Candlewick Pr.

—Tiny's Big Adventure. Waddell, Martin. 2004. (ENG.). 32p. (J). (gr. -1-2). 15.99 *(978-0-7636-2170-4(6))* Candlewick Pr.

—Treasure Island. Stevenson, Robert Louis. 2009. (Candlewick Illustrated Classic Ser.). (ENG.). 272p. (J). (gr. 4-7). 24.99 *(978-0-7636-4445-1(5))* Candlewick Pr.

Lawrence, John. This Little Chick. Lawrence, John. 2013. (ENG.). 32p. (J). (gr. -1-k). 4.99 *(978-0-7636-6350-6(6))* Candlewick Pr.

Lawrence, Mike. Muddy Max: The Mystery of Marsh Creek. Rusch, Elizabeth. 2014. (ENG.). 224p. (J). pap. 9.99 *(978-1-4494-3561-5(0))* Andrews McMeel Publishing.

Lawrence, Muriel. Miguel & the Pirates: A Tale of Mission Santa Cruz. Roberts, Helen M. 2011. 28p. 35.95 *(978-1-258-02882-4(4))* Literary Licensing, LLC.

Lawrey, Derek. Oscar & Willie: Silly Oscar's Days of the Week. Hetherington, Lisa. 2012. (ENG.). 26p. (J). pap. 9.99 *(978-0-9839963-0-9(X))* Hetherington Hall.

Lawrie, Chris, jt. illus. see Lawrie, Robin.

Lawrie, Robin. Cuda of the Cells. Ashe, Susan. 2005. (Yellow Go Bananas Ser.). (ENG.). 48p. (J). (gr. 3-4). lib. bdg. *(978-0-7787-2720-0(3))* Crabtree Publishing Co.

—Great Irish Legends for Children. 2005. (ENG.). 64p. (J). 20.95 *(978-0-7171-3872-2(0))* Gill & MacMillan, Ltd. IRL. Dist: Dufour Editions, Inc.

—Great Irish Legends for Children, 1 vol. Carroll, Yvonne. 2005. (ENG.). 64p. (J). (gr. k-3). 18.99 *(978-1-58980-345-9(0))* Pelican Publishing Co., Inc.

—Nid Fy Mai I. Huws, Emily. 2005. (WEL.). 64p. pap. *(978-1-84512-025-2(6))* Cymdeithas Lyfrau Ceredigion.

—The Secret Garden. Burnett, Frances Hodgson. 2008. (Puffin Classics Ser.). (ENG.). 368p. (J). (gr. 3-7). 5.99 *(978-0-14-132106-6(7)*, Puffin) Penguin Publishing Group.

Lawrie, Robin & Lawrie, Chris. Chain Reaction. 32p. pap. *(978-0-237-52110-3(5))* Evans Brothers, Ltd.

—Fear 3.1. 32p. (J). pap. *(978-0-237-52107-3(5))* Evans Brothers, Ltd.

—Muddy Mayhem. 32p. (J). pap. *(978-0-237-52105-9(9))* Evans Brothers, Ltd.

—Winged Avenger. 32p. pap. *(978-0-237-52106-6(7))* Evans Brothers, Ltd.

Lawson, Devin. Digibots Classroom Adventures. Holmes, Kimberly. 2004. (J). *(978-0-9755725-0-4(4)*, 1238415) Digibots Corp.

Lawson, Greg, photos by. Natural States. ltd. ed. 2005. 208p. (ENG., 135.00 *(978-0-9762197-6-7(X))*; 135.00 *(978-0-9762197-7-4(8))* Oakana Hse.

Lawson, J. Chip the Buffalo: Based on a True Story. Beemtsen, Tammy, photos by. Lawson, Cheri. 2006. 32p. (J). lib. bdg. 14.95 *(978-1-930580-61-9(4)*, Luminary Media Group) Pine Orchard, Inc.

Lawson, Keri, photos by. Randy Grows a Garden for Julia. Taylor, "Grandma" Mary. 2005. (J). 12.50 *(978-1-58597-321-7(1))* Leathers Publishing.

Lawson, Peter. Fire Engine. Goldsack, Gaby. 2009. (Turn the Wheel Ser.). (ENG.). 10p. (J). (gr. -1-k). bds. 5.95 *(978-0-7892-1022-7(3)*, Abbeville Kids) Abbeville Pr., Inc.

—Fishing Boat. Goldsack, Gaby. 2009. (Turn the Wheel Ser.). (ENG.). 10p. (J). (gr. -1-k). bds. 5.95 *(978-0-7892-1025-8(8)*, Abbeville Kids) Abbeville Pr., Inc.

—My Pumpkin. Noonan, Julia. 2005. (My First Reader Ser.). (ENG.). 32p. (J). (gr. k-1). lib. bdg. 18.50 *(978-0-516-24876-9(6)*, Children's Pr.) Scholastic Library Publishing.

—Noah's Ark: My Little Bible Book. Goldsack, Gaby & Dawson, Peter. 2003. 12p. (J). bds. 10.99 *(978-0-8254-7266-4(0)*, Candle Bks.) Lion Hudson PLC GBR. Dist: Kregel Pubns.

—Pull the Lever: Who's at Nursery? Baxter, Nicola. 2014. (ENG.). 8p. (J). (gr. -1-1). bds. 6.99 *(978-1-86147-393-6(1)*, Armadillo) Anness Publishing GBR. Dist: National Bk. Network.

—Who's on the Farm? Wolfe, Jane & Baxter, Nicola. 2013. (ENG.). 8p. bds. 6.99 *(978-1-84322-652-9(9)*, Armadillo) Anness Publishing GBR. Dist: National Bk. Network.

Lawson, Rob. Duke Finds a Home. 2006. (Duke's Tails Ser.). 32p. (J). *(978-0-9779308-0-7(7))* Bush Brothers & Co.

Lawson, Robert. Adam of the Road. Gray, Elizabeth Janet. 2006. (Puffin Modern Classics Ser.). (ENG.). 320p. (J). (gr. 3-7). 6.99 *(978-0-14-240659-5(7)*, Puffin) Penguin Publishing Group.

—Just for Fun: A Collection of Stories & Verses. 2013. (Dover Children's Classics Ser.). (ENG.). 72p. (gr. 2-5). pap. 6.99 *(978-0-486-49720-4(8))* Dover Pubns., Inc.

—The Little Woman Wanted Noise. Teal, Val. 2013. (ENG.). 48p. (J). (gr. -1-2). 14.95 *(978-1-59017-711-2(8)*, NYR Children's Collection) New York Review of Bks., Inc., The.

—The Story of Ferdinand. Leaf, Munro. (ENG.). (J). (gr. -1-k). 2011. 32p. pap. 3.99 *(978-0-448-45694-2(X)*, Grosset & Dunlap); 2007. 15p. 9.99 *(978-0-14-240952-7(9)*, Puffin) Penguin Publishing Group.

—Wee Gillis. Leaf, Munro. ed. 2006. (New York Review Children's Collection). (ENG.). 80p. (J). (gr. -1-2). 15.95 *(978-1-59017-206-3(X)*, NYR Children's Collection) New York Review of Bks., Inc., The.

Lawson, Robert. The Great Wheel. Lawson, Robert. 2004. (ENG.). 192p. (J). (gr. 5). pap. 9.99 *(978-0-8027-7705-8(8))* Walker & Co.

—Rabbit Hill. Lawson, Robert. 2007. (Puffin Modern Classics Ser.). (ENG.). 128p. (J). (gr. 3-7). 6.99 *(978-0-14-240796-7(8)*, Puffin) Penguin Publishing Group.

Lawson, Robert & Spatrisano, Kimberly. Road Wrangler: Cowboys on Wheels. Novara, Joe. 2007. 112p. (J). pap. 8.95 *(978-1-58980-507-1(0))* Pelican Publishing Co., Inc.

—Wa-Tonka! Camp Cowboys, 1 vol. Novara, Joe. 2006. (ENG.). 120p. (J). (gr. 3-6). per. 8.95 *(978-1-58980-354-1(X))* Pelican Publishing Co., Inc.

Lawton, Natasha. IF: A Treasury of Poems for Almost Every Possibility. Esiri, Allie & Kelly, Rachel, eds. 2013. (ENG.). 288p. (J). (gr. 4). 27.99 *(978-0-85786-557-1(9))* Canongate Bks. GBR. Dist: Independent Pubs. Group.

Lawton, Val. Emily's Magical Journey with Toothena the Tooth Fairy. Clark, CoraMarie. 2007. (ENG.). 32p. (J). *(978-0-9783779-0-8(7))* Strategix Ltd.

Layne, Deborah, jt. illus. see Ettlinger, Doris.

Layton, Neal. Deadly! The Truth about the Most Dangerous Creatures on Earth. Davies, Nicola. (Animal Science Ser.). (ENG.). 64p. (J). (gr. 3-7). 2015. pap. 7.99 ***(978-0-7636-7971-2(2))***; 2013. 14.99 *(978-0-7636-6231-8(3))* Candlewick Pr.

Layton, Neal. Don't Make Me Laugh, Liam. Oldfield, Jenny. (ENG.). 128p. (J). pap. 8.95 *(978-0-340-85107-4(4))* Macmillan Pubs., Ltd. GBR. Dist: Trafalgar Square Publishing.

—Drop Dead, Danielle. Oldfield, Jenny. (ENG.). 112p. mass mkt. *(978-0-340-85106-7(6)*, Coronet) Hodder & Stoughton.

—Emily Brown & the Elephant Emergency. Cowell, Cressida. 2010. (Emily Brown Ser.: 3). (ENG.). 32p. (J). (gr. -1-k). pap. 10.99 *(978-1-4083-0203-3(9))* Hodder & Stoughton GBR. Dist: Independent Pubs. Group.

—Extreme Animals: The Toughest Creatures on Earth. Davies, Nicola. 2009. (Animal Science Ser.). (ENG.). 64p. (J). (gr. 3-7). pap. 7.99 *(978-0-7636-4127-6(8))* Candlewick Pr.

—Get Lost, Lola. Oldfield, Jenny. (ENG.). 112p. mass mkt. 7.99 *(978-0-340-85104-3(X)*, Coronet) Hodder & Stoughton GBR. Dist: Trafalgar Square Publishing.

—Just the Right Size: Why Big Animals Are Big & Little Animals Are Little. Davies, Nicola. 2011. (Animal Science Ser.). (ENG.). 64p. (J). (gr. 3-7). pap. 7.99 *(978-0-7636-5300-2(4))* Candlewick Pr.

—Poop: A Natural History of the Unmentionable. Davies, Nicola. 2011. (Animal Science Ser.). (ENG.). 64p. (J). (gr. 3-7). pap. 7.99 *(978-0-7636-4128-3(6))* Candlewick Pr.

—Stanley's Stick. Hegley, John. 2012. (ENG.). 32p. (J). (gr. -1-k). pap. 11.99 *(978-0-340-98819-0(3))* Hodder & Stoughton GBR. Dist: Independent Pubs. Group.

—That Rabbit Belongs to Emily Brown. Cowell, Cressida. 2007. (ENG.). 40p. (gr. -1-3). 16.99 *(978-1-4231-0645-6(8))* Hyperion Pr.
—What's Eating You? Parasites — the Inside Story. Davies, Nicola. 2009. (Animal Science Ser.). (ENG.). 64p. (J). (gr. 3-7). pap. 7.99 *(978-0-7636-4521-2(4))* Candlewick Pr.
—Wicked Poems. McGough, Roger. 2004. (ENG.). 208p. (gr. 2-4). pap. 15.00 *(978-0-7475-6195-8(8))* Bloomsbury Publishing Plc GBR. Dist: Independent Pubs. Group.
Layton, Neal. Hot Hot Hot. Layton, Neal. 2004. (ENG.). 32p. (J). (gr. -1-3). 15.99 *(978-0-7636-2148-3(X))* Candlewick Pr.
Layton, Neal. Rainbow Soup: Adventures in Poetry. Layton, Neal, tr. Cleary, Brian P. 2004. (ENG.). 88p. (gr. 3-6). 26.60 *(978-1-57505-597-8(X))* Lerner Publishing Group.
Lazar, Ligia. Coloring Book Happy Vegetables. Tudosa-Fundureanu, Lucia. Chabvepi-Tudosa, Patricia, tr. 2012. 50p. pap. 11.95 *(978-1-936629-17-6(8))* Reflection Publishing.
Lazewnik, Sara. Guess-the-Ending Mitzvah Book. Finkelstein, Ruth. 2004. 26p. (J). (gr. k-3). 9.95 *(978-0-9628157-4-4(8))* Finkelstein, Ruth.
Laznicka, Mike, et al. Who Is Stan Lee? Edgers, Geoff. 2014. (Who Was...? Ser.). (ENG.). 112p. (J). (gr. 3-7). pap. 5.99 *(978-0-448-48236-1(3),* Grosset & Dunlap) Penguin Publishing Group.
Lazzati, Laura & Aón, Carlos. The Lonely Existence of Asteroids & Comets, 1 vol. Weakland, Mark. 2012. (Adventures in Science Ser.). (ENG.). 32p. (gr. 3-4). pap. 8.10 *(978-1-4296-7987-9(5),* Graphic Library) Capstone Pr., Inc.
Lazzati, Laura, jt. illus. see Aón, Carlos.
Lazzell, R. H. It's Go Time! McCormick, Scott. 2014. (Mr. Pants Ser.: 1). (ENG.). 128p. (J). (gr. 1-3). 14.99 *(978-0-8037-4007-5(7),* Dial) Penguin Publishing Group.
Lazzell, R. H. Mr. Pants: It's Go Time! Mccormick, Scott. 2015. (Mr. Pants Ser.: 1). (ENG.). 128p. (J). (gr. 1-3). pap. 7.99 ***(978-0-14-751710-4(9)***, Puffin) Penguin Publishing Group.
—Mr. Pants: Slacks, Camera, Action! Mccormick, Scott. 2015. (Mr. Pants Ser.: 2). (ENG.). 128p. (J). (gr. k-3). pap. 7.99 ***(978-0-14-751711-1(7)***, Puffin) Penguin Publishing Group.
Lazzell, R. H. Slacks, Camera, Action! McCormick, Scott. 2015. (Mr. Pants Ser.: 2). (ENG.). 128p. (J). (gr. k-3). 14.99 *(978-0-8037-4009-9(3),* Dial) Penguin Publishing Group.
Lazzell, R. H. Trick or Feet! McCormick, Scott. 2015. (Mr. Pants Ser.: 3). (ENG.). 128p. (J). (gr. k-3). 12.99 ***(978-0-525-42811-4(9)***, Dial) Penguin Publishing Group.
Lê, Christine & Lê, Michel. The Hawai'i Snowman. 2008. (J). 14.95 *(978-1-56647-879-3(0))* Mutual Publishing LLC.
Le Fevebvre, Severine. Tom Sawyer. Twain, Mark. 4th ed. 2009. (Classics Illustrated Deluxe Graphic Nove Ser.: 4). (ENG.). 144p. (YA). (gr. 3-9). pap. 13.95 *(978-1-59707-153-6(6))* Papercutz.
Le Feyer, Diane. Avalanche Alert, 1 vol. Burchett, Jan & Vogler, Sara. (Wild Rescue Ser.). (ENG.). 152p. (gr. 3-6). 2013. 9.95 *(978-1-4342-4893-0(3))*; 2012. 23.99 *(978-1-4342-3772-9(9))* Stone Arch Bks.
Le Feyer, Diane. Be a Star! Alexander, Heather. 2015. (Amazing Stardust Friends Ser.: 2). (ENG.). 96p. (J). (gr. 1-3). pap. 4.99 ***(978-0-545-75754-6(1))*** Scholastic, Inc.
Le Feyer, Diane. Desert Danger, 1 vol. Burchett, Jan & Vogler, Sara. 2013. (Wild Rescue Ser.). (ENG.). 152p. (gr. 3-6). 9.95 *(978-1-4342-4892-3(5))* Stone Arch Bks.
—Earthquake Escape, 1 vol. Burchett, Jan & Vogler, Sara. 2012. (Wild Rescue Ser.). (ENG.). 152p. (gr. 3-6). lib. bdg. 23.99 *(978-1-4048-6891-5(7))* Picture Window Bks.
—Ocean S. O. S. Burchett, Jan & Vogler, Sara. 2013. (Wild Rescue Ser.). (ENG.). 152p. (gr. 3-6). 9.95 *(978-1-4342-4891-6(7))* Stone Arch Bks.
—Poacher Panic, 1 vol. Burchett, Jan & Vogler, Sara. 2012. (Wild Rescue Ser.). (ENG.). 152p. (gr. 3-6). 9.95 *(978-1-4342-4593-9(4))*; lib. bdg. 23.99 *(978-1-4342-3286-1(7))* Stone Arch Bks.
—Polar Meltdown, 1 vol. Burchett, Jan & Vogler, Sara. 2012. (Wild Rescue Ser.). (ENG.). 152p. (gr. 3-6). 9.95 *(978-1-4342-4594-6(2))*; lib. bdg. 23.99 *(978-1-4342-3769-9(9))* Stone Arch Bks.
—Rainforest Rescue, 1 vol. Burchett, Jan & Vogler, Sara. 2012. (Wild Rescue Ser.). (ENG.). 152p. (gr. 3-6). 9.95 *(978-1-4342-4595-3(0))*; lib. bdg. 23.99 *(978-1-4342-3768-2(0))* Stone Arch Bks.
—Safari Survival, 1 vol. Burchett, Jan & Vogler, Sara. 2013. (Wild Rescue Ser.). (ENG.). 152p. (gr. 3-6). 9.95 *(978-1-4342-4890-9(9))* Stone Arch Bks.
—Step into the Spotlight! Alexander, Heather. 2015. (Amazing Stardust Friends Ser.: 1). (ENG.). 96p. (J). (gr. 1-3). pap. 4.99 *(978-0-545-75752-2(5))* Scholastic, Inc.
Le Feyer, Diane & Kennedy, Sam. Desert Danger, 1 vol. Burchett, Jan & Vogler, Sara. 2012. (Wild Rescue Ser.). (ENG.). 152p. (gr. 3-6). lib. bdg. 23.99 *(978-1-4342-3773-6(7))* Stone Arch Bks.
—Ocean S. O. S. Burchett, Jan & Vogler, Sara. 2012. (Wild Rescue Ser.). (ENG.). 152p. (gr. 3-6). lib. bdg. 23.99 *(978-1-4342-3771-2(0))* Stone Arch Bks.
—Safari Survival, 1 vol. Burchett, Jan & Vogler, Sara. 2012. (Wild Rescue Ser.). (ENG.). 152p. (gr. 3-6). lib. bdg. 23.99 *(978-1-4342-3770-5(2))* Stone Arch Bks.
Le Grand, Claire. Paolo from Rome. Husar, Stephane. 2014. (AV2 Fiction Readalong Ser.: Vol. 134). (ENG.). 32p. (J). (gr. -1-3). lib. bdg. 34.28 *(978-1-4896-2274-7(6),* AV2 by Weigl) Weigl Pubs., Inc.
Le, Guo. The Dragon's Tears. 2004. (ENG & POR.). 24p. (J). pap. *(978-1-85269-693-1(1))*; pap. *(978-1-85269-700-6(8))* Mantra Lingua.
—The Dragon's Tears. Gregory, Manju. 2004. (ENG & ARA.). 24p. (J). pap. *(978-1-85269-686-3(9))*; pap. *(978-1-85269-687-0(7))*; pap. *(978-1-85269-688-7(5))*; pap. *(978-1-85269-691-7(5))*; pap. *(978-1-85269-692-4(3))*; pap. *(978-1-85269-694-8(X))*; pap. *(978-1-85269-695-5(8))*; pap. *(978-1-85269-696-2(6))*; pap. *(978-1-85269-697-9(4))*; pap. *(978-1-85269-698-6(2))*; pap. *(978-1-85269-699-3(0))*; pap. *(978-1-85269-787-7(3))*; pap. *(978-1-85269-805-8(5))*; pap. *(978-1-85269-810-2(1))* Mantra Lingua.
—Dragon's Tears. Gregory, Manju. 2004. (ENG & CHI.). 24p. (J). pap. *(978-1-84444-477-9(5))* Mantra Lingua.
—The Dragon's Tears: Les Larmes du Dragon. Gregory, Manju. 2004. (ENG & FRE.). 24p. (J). pap. *(978-1-85269-689-4(3))* Mantra Lingua.
—The Dragon's Tears: Lotet e Kucedres. Gregory, Manju. 2004. (ENG & ALB.). 24p. (J). pap. *(978-1-85269-685-6(0))* Mantra Lingua.
Le Huche, Magali. City Kitty Cat. Webb, Steve. 2015. (ENG.). 32p. (J). (gr. -1-3). 17.99 *(978-1-4814-4331-9(3),* Simon & Schuster Bks. For Young Readers) Simon & Schuster Bks. For Young Readers.
Le Huche, Magali. Happy Zappa Cat. Webb, Steve. 2014. (ENG.). 32p. 15.99 ***(978-0-85707-620-5(5)***, Simon & Schuster Children's) Simon & Schuster, Ltd. GBR. Dist: Simon & Schuster, Inc.
Le, Leonard Rolland. Second world war - internet Linked. Dowswell, Paul. 2005. 128p. (J). 19.99 *(978-0-7945-1044-2(2),* Usborne) EDC Publishing.
Le, Loanne. The Fake Doughnut. Chedekel, Evelyn. 2013. 24p. 16.95 *(978-0-9888974-0-3(7))* BugaBk. llc.
Le Mair, Henriette Willebeek. A Gallery of Children. Milne, A. A. 2006. 79p. (J). (gr. k-4). reprint ed. 20.00 *(978-1-4223-5106-2(8))* DIANE Publishing Co.
Lê, Michel, jt. illus. see Lê, Christine.
Le Pere, Leslie. B Is for Beer. Robbins, Tom. 2009. (ENG.). 128p. 17.95 *(978-0-06-168727-3(8),* Ecco) HarperCollins Pubs.
Le Ray, Marina. A Halloween Scare at My House. James, Eric. 2014. (ENG.). 32p. (J). (-5). 9.99 *(978-1-4926-0612-3(X),* Sourcebooks Jabberwocky) Sourcebooks, Inc.
—A Halloween Scare in California. James, Eric. 2014. (ENG.). 32p. (J). (-5). 9.99 *(978-1-4926-0570-6(0),* Sourcebooks Jabberwocky) Sourcebooks, Inc.
—A Halloween Scare in Canada. James, Eric. 2014. (ENG.). 32p. (J). (-5). 9.99 *(978-1-4926-0573-7(5),* Sourcebooks Jabberwocky) Sourcebooks, Inc.
—A Halloween Scare in Chicago. James, Eric. 2014. (ENG.). 32p. (J). (-5). 9.99 *(978-1-4926-0579-9(4),* Sourcebooks Jabberwocky) Sourcebooks, Inc.
—A Halloween Scare in Colorado. James, Eric. 2014. (ENG.). 32p. (J). (-5). 9.99 *(978-1-4926-0582-9(4),* Sourcebooks Jabberwocky) Sourcebooks, Inc.
—A Halloween Scare in Florida. James, Eric. 2014. (ENG.). 32p. (J). (-5). 9.99 *(978-1-4926-0585-0(9),* Sourcebooks Jabberwocky) Sourcebooks, Inc.
—A Halloween Scare in Georgia. James, Eric. 2014. (ENG.). 32p. (J). (-5). 9.99 *(978-1-4926-0588-1(3),* Sourcebooks Jabberwocky) Sourcebooks, Inc.
—A Halloween Scare in Indiana. James, Eric. 2014. (ENG.). 32p. (J). (-5). 9.99 *(978-1-4926-0591-1(3),* Sourcebooks Jabberwocky) Sourcebooks, Inc.
—A Halloween Scare in Iowa. James, Eric. 2014. (ENG.). 32p. (J). (-5). 9.99 *(978-1-4926-0594-2(8),* Sourcebooks Jabberwocky) Sourcebooks, Inc.
—A Halloween Scare in Kentucky. James, Eric. 2014. (ENG.). 32p. (J). (-5). 9.99 *(978-1-4926-0597-3(2),* Sourcebooks Jabberwocky) Sourcebooks, Inc.
—A Halloween Scare in Louisiana. James, Eric. 2014. (ENG.). 32p. (J). (-5). 9.99 *(978-1-4926-0600-0(6),* Sourcebooks Jabberwocky) Sourcebooks, Inc.
—A Halloween Scare in Maryland. James, Eric. 2014. (ENG.). 32p. (J). (-5). 9.99 *(978-1-4926-0603-1(0),* Sourcebooks Jabberwocky) Sourcebooks, Inc.
—A Halloween Scare in Michigan. James, Eric. 2014. (ENG.). 32p. (J). (-5). 9.99 *(978-1-4926-0606-2(5),* Sourcebooks Jabberwocky) Sourcebooks, Inc.
—A Halloween Scare in Minnesota. James, Eric. 2014. (ENG.). 32p. (J). (-5). 9.99 *(978-1-4926-0609-3(X),* Sourcebooks Jabberwocky) Sourcebooks, Inc.
—A Halloween Scare in New England. James, Eric. 2014. (ENG.). 32p. (J). (-5). 9.99 *(978-1-4926-0615-4(4),* Sourcebooks Jabberwocky) Sourcebooks, Inc.
—A Halloween Scare in New Jersey. James, Eric. 2014. (ENG.). 32p. (J). (-5). 9.99 *(978-1-4926-0618-5(9),* Sourcebooks Jabberwocky) Sourcebooks, Inc.
—A Halloween Scare in New York. James, Eric. 2014. (ENG.). 32p. (J). (-5). 9.99 *(978-1-4926-0621-5(9),* Sourcebooks Jabberwocky) Sourcebooks, Inc.
—A Halloween Scare in Ohio. James, Eric. 2014. (ENG.). 32p. (J). (-5). 9.99 *(978-1-4926-0624-6(3),* Sourcebooks Jabberwocky) Sourcebooks, Inc.
—A Halloween Scare in Pennsylvania. James, Eric. 2014. (ENG.). 32p. (J). (-5). 9.99 *(978-1-4926-0627-7(8),* Sourcebooks Jabberwocky) Sourcebooks, Inc.
—A Halloween Scare in Tennessee. James, Eric. 2014. (ENG.). 32p. (J). (-5). 9.99 *(978-1-4926-0630-7(8),* Sourcebooks Jabberwocky) Sourcebooks, Inc.
—A Halloween Scare in Texas. James, Eric. 2014. (ENG.). 32p. (J). (-5). 9.99 *(978-1-4926-0633-8(2),* Sourcebooks Jabberwocky) Sourcebooks, Inc.
—A Halloween Scare in the Carolinas. James, Eric. 2014. (ENG.). 32p. (J). (-5). 9.99 *(978-1-4926-0576-8(X),* Sourcebooks Jabberwocky) Sourcebooks, Inc.
—A Halloween Scare in Virginia. James, Eric. 2014. (ENG.). 32p. (J). (-5). 9.99 *(978-1-4926-0636-9(7),* Sourcebooks Jabberwocky) Sourcebooks, Inc.
—A Halloween Scare in Washington. James, Eric. 2014. (ENG.). 32p. (J). (-5). 9.99 *(978-1-4926-0639-0(1),* Sourcebooks Jabberwocky) Sourcebooks, Inc.
—A Halloween Scare in Wisconsin. James, Eric. 2014. (ENG.). 32p. (J). (-5). 9.99 *(978-1-4926-0642-0(1),* Sourcebooks Jabberwocky) Sourcebooks, Inc.
—Hey, Diddle, Diddle, 1 vol. Reasoner, Charles. 2014. (Charles Reasoner Nursery Rhymes Ser.). (ENG.). 10p. (gr. -1 — 1). bds. 4.99 *(978-1-4795-3807-2(8))* Picture Window Bks.
—Hickory, Dickory, Dock. Reasoner, Charles. 2014. (Charles Reasoner Nursery Rhymes Ser.). (ENG.). 10p. (gr. -1 — 1). bds. 4.99 *(978-1-4795-3805-8(1))* Picture Window Bks.
—Hide-And-Ghost Seek... Matthews, Rupert. 2013. (J). *(978-1-4351-4895-6(9))* Barnes & Noble, Inc.
—Humpty Dumpty, 1 vol. Reasoner, Charles. 2013. (Charles Reasoner Nursery Rhymes Ser.). (ENG.). 10p. (gr. -1 — 1). bds. 4.99 *(978-1-4795-1690-2(2))* Picture Window Bks.
—Itsy Bitsy Spider, 1 vol. Reasoner, Charles. 2013. (Charles Reasoner Nursery Rhymes Ser.). (ENG.). 10p. (gr. -1 — 1). bds. 4.99 *(978-1-4795-1691-9(0))* Picture Window Bks.
—Jack & Jill, 1 vol. Reasoner, Charles. 2014. (Charles Reasoner Nursery Rhymes Ser.). (ENG.). 10p. (gr. -1 — 1). bds. 4.99 *(978-1-4795-3806-5(X))* Picture Window Bks.
—Little Bo Peep, 1 vol. Reasoner, Charles. 2014. (Charles Reasoner Nursery Rhymes Ser.). (ENG.). 10p. (gr. -1 — 1). bds. 4.99 *(978-1-4795-3804-1(3))* Picture Window Bks.
—Peek-a-Boo Dinosaurs. Reasoner, Charles. 2013. (Charles Reasoner Peek-A-Boo Bks.). (ENG.). 10p. (gr. -1 — 1). bds. 9.99 *(978-1-4795-2171-5(X))* Picture Window Bks.
—Peek-A-Boo Dinosaurs, 1 vol. Reasoner, Charles. 2013. (Charles Reasoner Peek-A-Boo Bks.). (ENG.). 10p. (gr. -1 — 1). bds. 4.99 *(978-1-4795-2316-0(X))* Picture Window Bks.
—Peek-a-Boo Fairies. Reasoner, Charles. 2013. (Charles Reasoner Peek-A-Boo Bks.). (ENG.). 10p. (gr. -1 — 1). bds. 9.99 *(978-1-4795-2173-9(6))* Picture Window Bks.
—Peek-A-Boo Fairies, 1 vol. Reasoner, Charles. 2013. (Charles Reasoner Peek-A-Boo Bks.). (ENG.). 10p. (gr. -1 — 1). bds. 4.99 *(978-1-4795-2318-4(6))* Picture Window Bks.
—Peek-a-Boo Monsters. Reasoner, Charles. 2013. (Charles Reasoner Peek-A-Boo Bks.). (ENG.). 10p. (gr. -1 — 1). bds. 9.99 *(978-1-4795-2170-8(1))* Picture Window Bks.
—Peek-A-Boo Monsters, 1 vol. Reasoner, Charles. 2013. (Charles Reasoner Peek-A-Boo Bks.). (ENG.). 10p. (gr. -1 — 1). bds. 4.99 *(978-1-4795-2315-3(1))* Picture Window Bks.
—Peek-a-Boo Pirates. Reasoner, Charles. 2013. (Charles Reasoner Peek-A-Boo Bks.). (ENG.). 10p. (gr. -1 — 1). bds. 9.99 *(978-1-4795-2172-2(8))* Picture Window Bks.
—Peek-A-Boo Pirates, 1 vol. Reasoner, Charles. 2013. (Charles Reasoner Peek-A-Boo Bks.). (ENG.). 10p. (gr. -1 — 1). bds. 4.99 *(978-1-4795-2317-7(8))* Picture Window Bks.
—Row, Row, Row Your Boat; and, Ride, Ride, Ride Your Bike. 2013. (ENG.). 24p. (J). *(978-0-7787-1149-0(8))* Crabtree Publishing Co.
—This Little Piggy, 1 vol. Reasoner, Charles. 2013. (Charles Reasoner Nursery Rhymes Ser.). (ENG.). 10p. (gr. -1 — 1). bds. 4.99 *(978-1-4795-1692-6(9))* Picture Window Bks.
—Twinkle, Twinkle, Little Star, 1 vol. Reasoner, Charles. 2013. (Charles Reasoner Nursery Rhymes Ser.). (ENG.). 10p. (gr. -1 — 1). bds. 4.99 *(978-1-4795-1693-3(7))* Picture Window Bks.
Le Ray, Marina & Jones, Anna. Peek-A-Boo Ghosts. Reasoner, Charles. 2013. (Charles Reasoner Peek-A-Boo Bks.). (ENG.). 10p. (gr. -1 — 1). bds. 9.99 *(978-1-4795-2359-7(3))*; bds. 4.99 *(978-1-4795-2360-3(7))* Picture Window Bks.
Le Ray, Marina, jt. illus. see Jones, Anna.
Le Rolland, Leonard. The Complete Book of Chess. Dalby, Elizabeth. 2006. (Chess Guides). 96p. (J). (gr. 5). lib. bdg., act. bk. ed. 25.95 *(978-1-58086-517-3(8))* EDC Publishing.
—Martin Luther King Jr. Jones, Rob Lloyd. 2006. (Usborne Famous Lives Gift Bks.). 64p. (J). (gr. 2-5). 8.99 *(978-0-7945-1260-6(7),* Usborne) EDC Publishing.
—Seas & Oceans Sticker Atlas. Clarke, Phillip. 2006. 24p. (J). pap. 8.95 *(978-0-7945-1218-7(6),* Usborne) EDC Publishing.
—The Usborne Book of Really Awful Jokes: About School & Other Stuff. Howell, Laura, ed. 2005. (Usborne Ser.). 288p. (J). (gr. -1-7). per. 10.95 *(978-0-7945-0578-3(3),* Usborne) EDC Publishing.
—The Usborne Book of Silly Jokes. Howell, Laura, ed. 2003. (Jokes Ser.). 96p. (J). (gr. 4-7). pap. 6.95 *(978-0-7945-0395-6(0),* Usborne) EDC Publishing.
Le-Tan, Pierre. Puss in Boots. Metaxas, Eric. 2007. (Rabbit Ears: A Classic Tale Ser.). 36p. (gr. -1-3). 25.65 *(978-1-59961-311-6(5))* Spotlight.
—What the Dormouse Said: Lessons for Grown-Ups from Children's Books. Gash, Amy. 2004. (ENG.). 160p. (J). pap. 9.95 *(978-1-56512-451-6(0),* 72451) Algonquin Bks. of Chapel Hill.
Le Tord, Bijou. A Bird or Two: A Story about Henri Matisse. Le Tord, Bijou. 2004. 32p. (gr. 2-7). 18.00 *(978-0-8028-5184-0(3))* Eerdmans, William B. Publishing Co.
—A Mountain Is to Climb. Le Tord, Bijou. Date not set. 40p. (J). 5.99 *(978-0-06-443591-8(1))* HarperCollins Pubs.
Lea, Corinne. Goobadabers. Powell, Gregg E. 2011. 24p. pap. 24.95 *(978-1-4626-0734-1(9))* America Star Bks.
Leach, Emma. Santa. Child, Jeremy. 2010. (Snow Shakers Ser.). (ENG.). 8p. (J). (gr. -1-k). bds. 4.99 *(978-0-7641-6384-5(1))* Barron's Educational Series, Inc.
Leader, Christine. You Can't Make a Dinosaur Out of Three Dead Horses. Leader, Christine. 2011. (ENG.). 30p. pap. 12.95 *(978-1-4565-9945-4(3))* CreateSpace Independent Publishing Platform.
Leadlove, Ben. Louie the Loon & the Moon. Lowe, Tom. 2011. 28p. pap. 11.00 *(978-1-61170-030-5(2))* Robertson Publishing.
Leak, Nancy M., jt. illus. see Harper, Ruth E.
Leake, Kate. Smelly Feet Sandwich: And Other Silly Poems. Zobel-Nolan, Allia. 2008. 22p. (J). (gr. -1-2). 7.95 *(978-1-58925-836-5(3))* Tiger Tales.
Lear, Edward, jt. illus. see Gorey, Edward.
Lear, John. The King Nobody Wanted. Langford, Norman F. 2007. (ENG.). 142p. pap. 18.99 *(978-1-4264-9571-7(4))*; 154p. pap. 21.99 *(978-1-4264-9952-4(3))* BiblioBazaar.
Lear, Ruth. Boing-Boing the Bionic Cat & the Jewel Thief. Hench, Larry. Steed, Tobias, ed. 2004. (Boing-Boing the Bionic Cat Ser.: 2). (ENG.). 60p. (J). (gr. 2-4). pap. 7.99 *(978-1-904872-01-6(8),* Can of Worms Kids Pr.) Can of Worms Pr. GBR. Dist: Independent Pubs. Group.
Learner, Vickie. Harriet Higby. Howard-Hess, Susan. 2006. (ENG.). 20p. (gr. k-2). pap. 5.95 *(978-1-57874-093-2(2))* Kaeden Corp.
Leary, Catherine. Are We There Yet? Williams, Rozanne Lanczak. 2005. (Science Mini Units Ser.). 8p. (J). pap. 2.49 *(978-1-59198-151-0(4),* 4251) Creative Teaching Pr., Inc.
—Cat Can't Write: A Cat & Dog Story. Williams, Rozanne Lanczak. (Learn to Write Ser.). 16p. (J). 2007. (gr. -1-3). pap. 8.99 *(978-1-59198-344-6(4))*; 2006. (gr. k-2). pap. 3.49 *(978-1-59198-293-7(6),* 6187) Creative Teaching Pr., Inc.
—Cat's Fairy Tale: A Cat & Dog Story. Williams, Rozanne Lanczak. 2006. (Learn to Write Ser.). 16p. (J). (gr. k-2). pap. 3.49 *(978-1-59198-294-4(4),* 6191) Creative Teaching Pr., Inc.
—Cat's Fairy Tale: A Cat & Dog Story. Williams, Rozanne Lanczak. Maio, Barbara, ed. 2006. (J). per. 8.99 *(978-1-59198-348-4(7))* Creative Teaching Pr., Inc.
—Granny's Coming 'Round the Mountain' Scelsa, Greg. Faulkner, Stacey, ed. 2006. (J). pap. 2.99 *(978-1-59198-350-7(9))* Creative Teaching Pr., Inc.
Leary, Catherine, jt. illus. see Christensen, David.
Lease, Janice m. Rudy the Roadrunner. Lease, Janice M. 2009. 48p. pap. 19.95 *(978-0-9800762-3-3(4))* Cinnamon Ridge Publishing.
Leasman, Nancy Packard. A Kitty Named Indra/Una Gata Llamada Indra. Tanner, Dawn Leasman. l.t. ed. 2003. (SPA & ENG.). 36p. (J). per. 6.95 *(978-0-9741725-0-7(2))* Leatherwood Publishing.
Leatham, Marc Vincent. The Story of the Five Squirrels. Leatham, Marc Vincent. 2007. (J). (gr. -1-3). per. 15.99 *(978-1-59879-275-1(X))* Lifevest Publishing, Inc.
Leathers, Philippa. The Black Rabbit. Leathers, Philippa. 2013. (ENG.). 40p. (J). (gr. -1-2). 14.00 *(978-0-7636-5714-7(X))* Candlewick Pr.
—How to Catch a Mouse. Leathers, Philippa. 2015. (ENG.). 40p. (J). (gr. -1-2). 15.99 *(978-0-7636-6912-6(1))* Candlewick Pr.
LeBar, Anna. Terry the Tiny Parrot My Granny & Me. LeBar, Stephen. l.t. ed. 2011. (ENG.). 26p. pap. 12.95 *(978-1-4505-9278-9(3))* CreateSpace Independent Publishing Platform.
Lebedev, Aleksandr. Bible Stories. 2006. (Play & Learn Puzzle Bks.). 12p. (J). 12.95 *(978-0-88271-385-4(X))* Regina Pr., Malhame & Co.
—Life of Jesus Puzzle Book. Brierley, Jane. 2006. (Play & Learn Puzzle Bks.). (J). 12.95 *(978-0-88271-854-5(1))* Regina Pr., Malhame & Co.
Lebedev, Vladimir. The Circus & Other Stories. Marshak, Samuil. Capus, Stephen, tr. from RUS. 2013. (ENG.). 76p. (J). (gr. 7-17). 26.95 *(978-1-84976-102-4(7))* Tate Publishing, Ltd. GBR. Dist: Abrams.
LeBlanc, Andre. La Biblia Ilustrada. Hoth, Iva. 2012.Tr. of Picture Bible. (SPA.). 800p. (J). 19.99 *(978-1-4143-6307-3(9))* Tyndale Hse. Pubs.
LeBlanc, Giselle, jt. illus. see Collier, Kevin Scott.
LeBlanc, Marc. The Angel Who Didn't Fit In. Rogers-Busboom, Kimberly. 2010. 32p. (J). lib. bdg. 16.99 *(978-0-9823145-3-1(1))* Dirks Publishing, LLC.
LeBlanc, Nancy. The Santa Beacon. Gardner, Graham. 2012. 40p. (J). 19.95 *(978-0-9859358-0-1(4),* Belle Isle Bks.) Brandylane Pubs., Inc.
LeBreton, Zachary. Rhyming with the Little Ones, 1 vol. LeBreton, Heather. 2009. 31p. pap. 24.95 *(978-1-60749-114-9(1))* America Star Bks.
Lechler, Louan. When the Bear Came Back: The Whole Story. Wooten, Terry. 2006. (J). per. 9.49 *(978-1-893972-27-8(5))* Wordsmith Pr.
Lechner, John. The Clever Stick. Lechner, John. 2009. (ENG.). 40p. (J). (gr. k-3). 14.99 *(978-0-7636-3950-1(8))* Candlewick Pr.
—Sticky Burr: Adventures in Burrwood Forest. Lechner, John. 2008. (ENG.). 56p. (J). (gr. 1-4). pap. 7.99 *(978-0-7636-3567-1(7))* Candlewick Pr.
Lechon, Daniel. The Desert Is My Mother/el Desierto Es Mi Madre. Mora, Pat. 97th ed. 2008. (SPA & ENG.). 32p. (J). (gr. -1-2). pap. 7.95 *(978-1-55885-158-0(5),* Piñata Books) Arte Publico Pr.
—The Desert Is My Mother/El Desierto Es Mi Madre: CD & Book Set. Mora, Pat. 2008. 32p. (J). pap. 18.95 *(978-0-9815686-2-1(9))* Lorito Bks., Inc.
Lechón, Daniel. Kikiriki / Quiquiriquí. De Anda, Diane. Hernández, Karina, tr. from ENG. 2004. (ENG & SPA.). 32p. 16.95 *(978-1-55885-382-9(0),* Piñata Books) Arte Publico Pr.
Lechon, Daniel. My Tata's Guitar / la guitarra de mi Tata. Brammer, Ethriam Cash. (ENG & SPA.). 32p. (J). 16.95 *(978-1-55885-369-0(3),* Piñata Books) Arte Publico Pr.
Lecia, Balian, jt. illus. see Lorna, Balian.
Ledbetter, John'el. The Tickle Man. Curry, Cicero. 2013. 44p. 24.95 *(978-1-63004-279-0(X))*; pap. 24.95 *(978-1-63000-015-8(9))* America Star Bks.
Lederhos, Anne. Kitten up a Tree. Abel, Melanie. 2008. 24p. (J). pap. 15.95 *(978-0-9791606-4-6(2))* E & E Publishing.
Lederman, Marsha. Virginia: An Alphabetical Journey Through History. Shepard, Betty Bruce. 2007. 32p. (J). (gr. -1-3). 17.95 *(978-1-893622-14-2(2),* VSP Bks.) Vacation Spot Publishing.
Lederman, Todd. Notch Ear's Sacrifice. Lederman, Todd. 2010. (ENG.). 172p. pap. 7.99 *(978-1-4505-0713-4(1))* CreateSpace Independent Publishing Platform.
Ledger, Bill. Pies for Simple Simon. Fuerst, Jeffrey B. 2009. (Reader's Theater Nursery Rhymes & Songs Set B Ser.). 48p. (J). pap. *(978-1-60859-165-7(4))* Benchmark Education Co.
—Red Roses, Blue Violets, And... ? Grudzina, Rebecca. 2009. (Reader's Theater Nursery Rhymes & Songs Set B Ser.). 48p. (J). pap. *(978-1-60859-167-1(0))* Benchmark Education Co.

L

—Simple Simon. Fuerst, Jeffrey B. 2010. (Rising Readers Ser.). (J). 3.49 (978-1-60719-706-5(5)) Newmark Learning LLC.

—This Little Piggy. Harris, Brooke. 2010. (Rising Readers Ser.). (J). 3.49 (978-1-60719-696-9(4)) Newmark Learning LLC.

Ledger, Faye. Buggy Buggy. Hall, Shirley. 2010. 20p. 12.00 (978-1-4520-6787-2(2)) AuthorHouse.

Ledwidge, Natacha. Emily Windsnap & the Castle in the Mist. Kessler, Liz. 2012. (Emily Windsnap Ser.: 3). (ENG.). 208p. (J). (gr. 3-7). pap. 5.99 (978-0-7636-6017-8(5)) Candlewick Pr.

Ledwidge, Natacha & Gibb, Sarah. Emily Windsnap & the Castle in the Mist. Kessler, Liz. 2007. (Emily Windsnap Ser.: 3). (ENG.). 208p. (J). (gr. 3-7). 15.99 (978-0-7636-3330-1(5)) Candlewick Pr.

Ledwidge, Natacha, jt. illus. see Gibb, Sarah.

Ledwon, Peter & Mets, Marilyn. Mia's Secret. Ledwon, Peter. 2006. (ENG.). 24p. (J). (gr. -1-3). pap. 7.95 (978-0-88776-801-9(6), Anchor) Tundra Bks. CAN. Dist: Penguin Random Hse., LLC.

Ledwon, Peter, jt. illus. see Mets, Marilyn.

Ledyard, Addie. What Katy Did. Coolidge, Susan. 2013. 132p. pap. (978-1-909735-03-3(5)) Aziloth Bks.

—What Katy Did. Coolidge, Susan. 284p. 2010. 35.16 (978-1-163-85079-4(9)); 2010. pap. 23.16 (978-1-163-77965-1(2)); 2007. 43.95 (978-0-548-53870-8(0)); 2007. per. 28.95 (978-0-548-48700-6(6)) Kessinger Publishing, LLC.

Lee, Hye Ran . El jardín secreto. Burnett, Frances Hodgson. 2014. (SPA.). 360p. (J). pap. 16.99 (978-607-01-1877-7(4)) Santillana Ediciones Generales, S.A. de C.V. MEX. Dist: Santillana USA Publishing Co., Inc.

Lee, Alan. The Iliad. Sutcliff, Rosemary. rev. ed. 2014. (Classics Ser.). (ENG.). 136p. (J). (gr. 3-6). 19.99 (978-1-84780-528-7(0), Frances Lincoln) Quarto Publishing Group UK GBR. Dist: Hachette Bk. Group.

Lee, Alan & Sutcliff, Rosemary. The Odyssey. Sutcliff, Rosemary. rev. ed. 2014. (Classics Ser.). (ENG.). 128p. (J). (gr. 4-6). 19.99 (978-1-84780-529-4(9), Frances Lincoln) Quarto Publishing Group UK GBR. Dist: Hachette Bk. Group.

Lee, Anais. A Hat for Melinda: Fighting Leukemia Together. Tucker, Seletha Marie Head. 2013. (978-1-62086-164-6(X)) Mascot Bks., Inc.

—The Toy-Gobbling Monster. V, Vasanthi. 2013. (ENG.). (J). 14.95 (978-1-62086-330-5(8)) Mascot Bks., Inc.

Lee, Anne. Old Abe, Eagle Hero: The Civil War's Most Famous Mascot. Young, Patrick. 2010. (ENG.). 48p. (J). (gr. k-4). 11.99 (978-1-935279-23-5(8)) Kane Miller.

Lee, Anne. When You Are Camping. Lee, Anne. ed. 2012. (Picture Bks). (ENG.). 32p. (J). 10.99 (978-1-61067-064-7(7)) Kane Miller.

Lee, Bill. Ko'eku Tohi Lau Fika. Thompson, Richard & Thompson, Ofa. l.t. ed. 2003. (TON.). 24p. (J). (gr. -1-18). 5.00 (978-0-9678979-1-2(2)) Friendly Isles Pr.

Lee, Bin. Together at Christmas. Spinelli, Eileen. 2012. (ENG.). 24p. (J). (gr. -1-2). 15.99 (978-0-8075-8010-3(4)) Whitman, Albert & Co.

Lee, Bowen Lyam. The Shining Light In My Cat's Eye. Lee, Bowen Lyam. 2010. (ENG.). 94p. pap. 6.99 (978-1-4499-7907-2(6)) CreateSpace Independent Publishing Platform.

Lee, Brian. A Castle. 2005. (What's Inside? Ser.). (J). (978-0-7607-6568-5(5)) backpackbooks.

—A Construction Site. 2005. (What's Inside Ser.). (J). (978-0-7607-6570-8(7)) backpackbook.

—Let's Explore a Castle. Harris, Nicholas. 2010. 36p. (J). (gr. k-3). 13.99 (978-0-8437-1395-4(X)) Hammond World Atlas Corp.

—Let's Explore a Pirate Ship. Harris, Nicholas. 2010. 36p. (J). 13.99 (978-0-8437-1378-7(X)) Hammond World Atlas Corp.

—A Pirate Ship. 2005. (What's Inside? Ser.). (978-0-7607-6809-9(9)) backpackbook.

—The World of Dinosaurs. 2005. (J). (978-0-7607-6569-2(3)) backpackbook.

Lee, Britney, jt. illus. see Disney Storybook Artists Staff.

Lee, Brittney. Loser/Queen. Anderson, Jodi Lynn. 2010. (ENG.). 272p. (YA). (gr. 7-18). pap. 9.99 (978-1-4169-9646-0(X), Simon & Schuster Bks. For Young Readers) Simon & Schuster Bks. For Young Readers.

Lee, Chi-ching. Romance of the Three Kingdoms Manga: The Oath in the Peach Orchard, 23 vols., Vol. 1. Ahlstrom, Peter, ed. Kirsch, Alexis, tr. from CHI. 2003. (YA). pap. 9.95 (978-1-932592-00-9(8), ROM1101) Romancing Cathay.

Lee, David. Danny & the Portal of the World: Danny Falls into a Portal, Meets His Relatives & Returns Home Again. Lee, David. 2011. (ENG.). 58p. pap. 10.00 (978-1-4635-7223-5(9)) CreateSpace Independent Publishing Platform.

—Danny & the Trip to Outer Space: This Book Is Written & Illustrated by 8 Year Old Author, David T. Lee. It Contains 16 Chapters, 6,500 Words & 6 Full Color Illustrations. It Is the Sequel of Danny & the Portal of the World. Lee, David. 2012. (Adventures of Danny Hoopenbiller Ser.). (ENG.). 64p. pap. 15.00 (978-1-4782-9451-1(5)) CreateSpace Independent Publishing Platform.

Lee, Dom. Baseball Saved Us. Mochizuki, Ken. (Picture Book Readalong Ser.). pap. 39.95 incl. audio compact disk (978-1-59112-917-2(6)); 2004. (J). (gr. -1-2). 25.95 incl. audio (978-1-59112-456-6(5)) Live Oak Media.

—Sixteen Years in Sixteen Seconds: The Sammy Lee Story, 1 vol. Yoo, Paula. 2005. (ENG.). 32p. (J). (gr. 1-5). 16.95 (978-1-58430-247-6(X)) Lee & Low Bks., Inc.

Lee, Ella Dolbear. The Wonderful Story of Jesus. 2004. reprint ed. pap. 20.95 (978-1-4179-3177-4(9)) Kessinger Publishing, LLC.

Lee, Fran. My Vacation Album: Includes: Reusable Camera, Film, Batteries & Glue Stick. Elton, Candice & Elton, Richard. 2003. 28p. (J). spiral bd. 19.95 (978-1-58685-280-1(9)) Gibbs Smith, Publisher.

—Riding on a Range: Western Activities for Kids. Drinkard, Lawson. ed. 2003. (ENG.). 64p. (YA). pap. 9.99 (978-1-58685-036-4(9)) Gibbs Smith, Publisher.

Lee, Fran. Backyard Birding for Kids, 1 vol. Lee, Fran. 2005. (ENG.). 64p. (J). pap. 9.99 (978-1-58685-411-9(9)) Gibbs Smith, Publisher.

Lee, Frances Cook. Sliding in the Snow: Winter Activities for Kids, 1 vol. Dymock, Melissa. 2015. (ENG.). 64p. pap. 9.99 (978-1-4236-3893-3(X)) Gibbs Smith, Publisher.

Lee, Frank. Steve Longenecker's Wilderness Emergency Medical Aid Book for Kids & Their Adults. Longnecker, Steve. 2005. 176p. (YA). (gr. 5-18). pap. 16.95 (978-1-889596-18-1(3)) Milestone Pr., Inc.

Lee, Gail. Prayer of the Child Mystic. Lazdowski, Ken. 2006. (ENG.). 59p. 28.00 (978-0-9777612-0-3(7), PCM-2006-1) Contemplative Pubns.

Lee, George Douglas. Oppy Stops the Hopping Popper. Lee, George Douglas. Lee, Brenda Donaloio, ed. 2012. 30p. pap. 10.95 (978-0-9848486-1-4(4)) Electric Theatre Radio Hour.

—Twyla the Truffle Pig. Lee, George Douglas. Lee, Brenda Donaloio, ed. 2012. 34p. pap. 10.95 (978-0-9848486-0-7(6)) Electric Theatre Radio Hour.

—The Wolf Who Cried Boy. Lee, George Douglas. Lee, Brenda Donaloio, ed. 2012. 46p. pap. 15.95 (978-0-9848486-2-1(2)) Electric Theatre Radio Hour.

Lee, George T. Petie the Parrot's Amazing Adventures: P. D. Q., 1 vol. Hannaford, Linda S. 2010. 16p. pap. 24.95 (978-1-61582-767-1(6)) PublishAmerica, Inc.

Lee, Grace. Sofia the First. Disney Book Group Staff & Hapka, Catherine. 2012. (ENG.). 40p. (J). (gr. -1-k). 15.99 (978-1-4231-6986-4(7)) Disney Pr.

—Sofia the First: a Royal Mouse in the House. Disney Book Group Staff & Scollon, Bill. 2015. (ENG.). 40p. (J). (gr. -1-k). 8.99 (978-1-4847-0643-5(9)) Disney Pr.

—Sofia the First the Curse of Princess Ivy: Purchase Includes Disney EBook! Disney Book Group Staff et al. 2014. (ENG.). 40p. (J). (gr. -1-k). 16.99 (978-1-4231-8655-7(9)) Disney Pr.

—Sofia the First the Floating Palace. Hapka, Catherine & Disney Book Group Staff. 2013. (ENG.). 40p. (J). (gr. -1-k). 15.99 (978-1-4231-6390-9(7)) Disney Pr.

Lee, Grace & Cagol, Andrea. Frozen (Disney Frozen) Saxon, Victoria. 2015. (Little Golden Book Ser.). (ENG.). 24p. (J). (-k). 4.99 (978-0-7364-3471-3(2), Golden/Disney) Random Hse. Children's Bks.

Lee, Grace & Disney Storybook Artists. Sofia the First Little Golden Book Favorites (Disney Junior: Sofia the First) Posner-Sanchez, Andrea. 2015. (Little Golden Book Favorites Ser.). (ENG.). 80p. (J). (-k). 7.99 (978-0-7364-3406-5(2), Golden/Disney) Random Hse. Children's Bks.

Lee, Grace & Disney Storybook Artists Staff. Sofia's Royal World (Disney Junior: Sofia the First) Posner-Sanchez, Andrea. 2014. (Big Golden Book Ser.). (ENG.). 64p. (J). (gr. -1-2). 9.99 (978-0-7364-3262-7(0), Golden/Disney) Random Hse. Children's Bks.

Lee, Grace, jt. illus. see Disney Storybook Artists Staff.

Lee, Han & Wu, Stacie. My New School: Blonde Boy. Anderson, Pamela. 2004. (J). 12.95 (978-1-932555-05-9(6)) Watch Me Grow Kids.

—My New School: Blonde Girl. Anderson, Pamela. 2004. (J). 12.95 (978-1-932555-04-2(8)) Watch Me Grow Kids.

—My New School: Brunette Boy. Anderson, Pamela. 2004. (J). 12.95 (978-1-932555-07-3(2)) Watch Me Grow Kids.

—My New School: Brunette Girl. Anderson, Pamela. 2004. (J). 12.95 (978-1-932555-06-6(4)) Watch Me Grow Kids.

Lee, Hanlim & WU, Stacie. My New School: Afro Boy. Anderson, Pamela Dell. 2003. 24p. (J). 12.95 (978-1-932555-01-1(3)) Watch Me Grow Kids.

—My New School: Afro Girl. Anderson, Pamela Dell. 2003. 24p. (J). 12.95 (978-1-932555-00-4(5)) Watch Me Grow Kids.

—My New School: Asian/Latin Boy. Anderson, Pamela Dell. 2003. 24p. (J). 12.95 (978-1-932555-03-5(X)) Watch Me Grow Kids.

—My New School: Latin/Asian Girl. Anderson, Pamela Dell. 2003. 24p. (J). 12.95 (978-1-932555-02-8(1)) Watch Me Grow Kids.

Lee, Haylen. Planet of Success: An Inspirational Book about Attitude Adn Character. Woods, Shirley. 2006. 41p. (J). per. 9.95 (978-1-60002-183-1(2), 4207) Mountain Valley Publishing, LLC.

Lee, Ho Baek. Bee-Bim Bop! Park, Linda Sue. (ENG.). 32p. (J). (gr. -1-3). 2008. pap. 6.99 (978-0-547-07671-3(1)); 2005. 16.99 (978-0-618-26511-4(2)) Houghton Mifflin Harcourt Publishing Co.

Lee, Ho Baek. While We Were Out. Lee, Ho Baek. 2006. (ENG.). 32p. (J). (gr. -1-1). 10.99 (978-1-929132-44-7(1)) Kane Miller.

Lee, Huy Voun. Fire Drill. Jacobs, Paul DuBois & Swender, Jennifer. 2010. (ENG.). 32p. (J). (gr. -1-2). 16.99 (978-0-8050-8953-0(5), Holt, Henry & Co. Bks. For Young Readers) Holt, Henry & Co.

—Honk, Honk, Goose! Canada Geese Start a Family. Sayre, April Pulley. 2009. (ENG.). 32p. (J). (gr. -1-3). 16.95 (978-0-8050-7103-0(2), Holt, Henry & Co. Bks. For Young Readers) Holt, Henry & Co.

—Red, White, & Boom! Wardlaw, Lee. 2012. (ENG.). 32p. (J). (gr. -1-2). 16.99 (978-0-8050-9065-9(7), Holt, Henry & Co. Bks. For Young Readers) Holt, Henry & Co.

Lee, Huy Voun, jt. illus. see Kreloff, Elliot.

Lee, Hye-Seong. The Call of Samuel: From 1 Samuel 3:1-10. 2003. 29p. (J). 13.50 (978-0-9659164-9-3(9)) Fountain Publishing.

Lee, Hyeon-joo. There It Is! Observation - Objects. Kim, Soo-hyeon. Cowley, Joy, ed. 2015. (Step up - Creative Thinking Ser.). (ENG.). 32p. (gr. -1-2). 26.65 (978-1-925246-09-4(4)); 26.65 (978-1-925246-35-3(3)); 7.99 (978-1-925246-61-2(2)) ChoiceMaker Pty. Ltd., The AUS. (Big and SMALL). Dist: Lerner Publishing Group.

Lee, Hyeongjin. Shooting Stars Soccer Team. Kim, YoeongAh. rev. ed. 2014. (MySELF Bookshelf: Social & Emotional Learning/Social Awareness Ser.). (ENG.). 32p. (J). (gr. k-2). pap. 11.94 (978-1-60357-657-4(6)) Norwood Hse. Pr.

—The Shooting Stars Soccer Team. Kim, YoeongAh. rev. ed. 2014. (MySELF Bookshelf: Social & Emotional Learning/Social Awareness Ser.). (ENG.). 32p. (J). (gr. k-2). lib. bdg. 22.60 (978-1-59953-648-4(X)) Norwood Hse. Pr.

Lee, Hyun Young. Something for School. Lee, Hyun Young. 2008. (ENG.). 32p. (J). (gr. -1-1). 10.99 (978-1-933605-85-2(5)) Kane Miller.

Lee, Imani K. Clever! Clever! & the Book of Forever. 2005. 17p. (YA). per. 9.99 (978-0-9768429-2-7(0)) Genius In A Bottle Technology Corp.

—The Origin of the Forever Four! F4 Clever! Clever! Lee, Glenn E. 2005. (YA). per. 19.99 (978-0-9768429-4-1(7)) Genius In A Bottle Technology Corp.

Lee, Ioe. Power Reading: Comic Book/Treasure Island. Cole, Bob. 2005. 70p. (J). (gr. 4-6). vinyl bd. (978-1-883186-78-4(1), PPCLC3) National Reading Styles Institute, Inc.

Lee, Jack. Three Dogs & a Horse Named Blue. Lee, Patty. 2009. 80p. pap. 10.49 (978-1-4389-9685-1(3)) AuthorHouse.

—Wild Animals: What Is That I Ask? Lee, Patty. 2013. 30p. pap. 14.00 (978-1-4349-3518-2(3), RoseDog Bks.) Dorrance Publishing Co., Inc.

Lee, Jacqui. Murilla Gorilla & the Hammock Problem. Lloyd, Jennifer. 2014. (ENG.). 42p. (J). (gr. -1-3). 9.95 (978-1-927018-47-7(1)) Simply Read Bks. CAN. Dist: Ingram Pub. Services.

—Murilla Gorilla & the Lost Parasol. Lloyd, Jennifer. 2013. (ENG.). 42p. (J). (gr. -1-3). 9.95 (978-1-927018-23-1(4)) Simply Read Bks. CAN. Dist: Ingram Pub. Services.

—Murilla Gorilla, Jungle Detective. Lloyd, Jennifer. George, Kallie, ed. 2013. (Murilla Gorilla Ser.: 1). (ENG.). 42p. (J). (gr. -1-3). 9.95 (978-1-927018-15-6(3)) Simply Read Bks. CAN. Dist: Ingram Pub. Services.

—Taffy Time. Lloyd, Jennifer. 2015. (ENG.). 40p. (J). (gr. -1-3). 16.95 (978-1-927018-62-0(5)) Simply Read Bks. CAN. Dist: Ingram Pub. Services.

Lee, Jae. Fantastic Four: 1234. 2011. (ENG.). 120p. (YA). (gr. 8-17). 19.99 (978-0-7851-5896-7(0)) Marvel Worldwide, Inc.

Lee, Janet. Emma. 2011. (ENG.). 120p. (YA). (gr. 8-17). 19.99 (978-0-7851-5685-7(2)) Marvel Worldwide, Inc.

Lee, Janet K. The Wonderland Alphabet: Alice's Adventures Through the ABCs & What She Found There. Carroll, Lewis & Kontis, Alethea. 2012. (ENG.). 30p. (J). (gr. -1). 11.95 (978-1-936393-86-2(7)) Boom Entertainment, Inc.

Lee, Jared. April Fools' Day from the Black Lagoon. Thaler, Mike. 2008. (J). (978-0-545-01767-1(X)) Scholastic, Inc.

—The Art Teacher from the Black Lagoon. Thaler, Mike. 2012. (Black Lagoon Set 2 Ser.: No. 2). (ENG.). 32p. (J). (gr. 1-4). lib. bdg. 24.21 (978-1-59961-952-1(0)) Spotlight.

—Believe It! Bible Basics That Won't Break Your Brain. James, Steven. 2006. 76p. (YA). pap. 11.99 (978-0-7847-1393-8(6), 42171) Standard Publishing.

—Bible Knock Knock Jokes from the Back Pew, 1 vol. Thaler, Mike. 2010. (Tales from the Back Pew Ser.). (ENG.). 32p. (J). pap. 4.99 (978-0-310-71598-6(9)) Zonderkidz.

—The Big Foot in the End Zone. Doyle, Bill. 2012. (Scream Team Ser.). (ENG.). 96p. (J). (gr. 2-5). pap. 4.99 (978-0-545-47977-6(0), Scholastic Paperbacks) Scholastic, Inc.

—The Big Foot in the End Zone. Doyle, Bill. ed. 2012. (Scream Team Ser.: 3). lib. bdg. 14.75 (978-0-606-31560-9(8), Turtleback) Turtleback Bks.

—The Book Fair from the Black Lagoon. Thaler, Mike. 2006. pap. (978-0-439-88348-1(2)) Scholastic, Inc.

—The Bully from the Black Lagoon. Thaler, Mike. 2008. (From the Black Lagoon Ser.). (gr. -1-3). 14.00 (978-0-7569-8834-0(9)) Perfection Learning Corp.

—The Bully from the Black Lagoon. Thaler, Mike. (Black Lagoon Adventures Ser.). (J). 2008. (ENG.). 32p. (gr. -1-3). pap. 3.99 (978-0-545-06521-4(6), Cartwheel Bks.); 2004. (978-0-439-68072-1(7)) Scholastic, Inc.

—The Bully from the Black Lagoon. Thaler, Mike. 2012. (Black Lagoon Set 2 Ser.: No. 2). (ENG.). 32p. (J). (gr. 1-4). lib. bdg. 24.21 (978-1-59961-953-8(9)) Spotlight.

—The Cafeteria Lady from the Black Lagoon. Thaler, Mike. 2012. (Black Lagoon Set 2 Ser.: No. 2). (ENG.). 32p. (J). (gr. 1-4). lib. bdg. 24.21 (978-1-59961-954-5(7)) Spotlight.

—The Christmas Party from the Black Lagoon. Thaler, Mike. 2006. 64p. (J). pap. (978-0-439-87160-0(3)) Scholastic, Inc.

—Church Harvest Mess-Tivall, 1 vol. Thaler, Mike. 2010. (Tales from the Back Pew Ser.). (ENG.). 32p. (J). pap. 4.99 (978-0-310-71595-5(4)) Zondervan.

—Church Summer Cramp, 1 vol. Thaler, Mike. 2009. (Tales from the Back Pew Ser.). (ENG.). 32p. (J). (gr. 1-4). pap. 4.99 (978-0-310-71592-4(X)) Zonderkidz.

—The Class Election from the Black Lagoon. Thaler, Mike. 2004. (Black Lagoon Adventures Ser.: Vol. 3). (ENG.). 64p. (J). (gr. 2-5). 4.99 (978-0-439-55716-0(X), Scholastic Paperbacks) Scholastic, Inc.

—The Class Pet from the Black Lagoon. Thaler, Mike. 2008. (Black Lagoon Adventures Ser.). (ENG.). 32p. (J). (gr. -1-3). pap. 3.99 (978-0-545-06930-4(0), Cartwheel Bks.) Scholastic, Inc.

—The Class Trip from the Black Lagoon. Thaler, Mike. 2004. (Black Lagoon Adventures Ser.: 1). (ENG.). 64p. (J). (gr. 2-5). pap. 3.99 (978-0-439-42927-6(7), Scholastic Paperbacks) Scholastic, Inc.

—The Computer Teacher from the Black Lagoon. Thaler, Mike. 2007. (J). (978-0-439-87133-4(6)) Scholastic, Inc.

—The Computer Teacher from the Black Lagoon. Thaler, Mike. 2012. (Black Lagoon Set 2 Ser.: No. 2). (ENG.). 32p. (J). (gr. 1-4). lib. bdg. 24.21 (978-1-59961-955-2(5)) Spotlight.

—El Dia Que Jordan Se Enfermo: Jordan's Silly Sick Day. Fontes, Justine. 2005. (Rookie Reader Español Ser.). 32p. (gr. k-2). 19.50 (978-0-516-24445-7(0), Children's Pr.) Scholastic Library Publishing.

—Easter Egg Haunt, 1 vol. Thaler, Mike. 2009. (Tales from the Back Pew Ser.). (ENG.). 32p. (J). (gr. 1-4). pap. 4.99 (978-0-310-71591-7(1)) Zonderkidz.

—The Field Day from the Black Lagoon. Thaler, Mike. 2008. (From the Black Lagoon Ser.). 64p. (gr. 2-5). 14.00 (978-0-7569-8801-2(2)) Perfection Learning Corp.

—The Field Day from the Black Lagoon. Thaler, Mike. 2008. (Black Lagoon Adventures Ser.: 6). (ENG.). 64p. (J). (gr. 2-5). pap. 4.99 (978-0-439-68076-9(X)) Scholastic, Inc.

Lee, Jared. Groundhog Day from Black Lagoon. Thaler, Mike. 2015. 64p. (J). (978-0-545-78520-4(0)) Scholastic, Inc.

Lee, Jared. The Gym Teacher from the Black Lagoon. Thaler, Mike. 2011. (Black Lagoon Set 1 Ser.: No. 1). (ENG.). 32p. (J). (gr. -1-2). lib. bdg. 24.21 (978-1-59961-794-7(3)) Spotlight.

—The Gym Teacher from the Black Lagoon. Thaler, Mike. (J). (gr. -1-3). 2009. pap. 18.95 incl. audio compact disk (978-0-545-19706-9(6)); 2008. (ENG.). 32p. pap. 3.99 (978-0-545-06931-1(9)) Weston Woods Studios, Inc.

—In the Big Inning Bible Riddles from the Back Pew. Thaler, Mike. 2010. (Tales from the Back Pew Ser.). (ENG.). 32p. (J). pap. 4.99 (978-0-310-71597-9(0)) Zonderkidz.

—The Librarian from the Black Lagoon. Thaler, Mike. unabr. ed. 2007. (J). (gr. k-2). pap. 14.95 incl. audio (978-0-439-02773-1(X)) Scholastic, Inc.

—The Librarian from the Black Lagoon. Thaler, Mike. 2011. (Black Lagoon Set 1 Ser.: No. 1). (ENG.). 32p. (gr. -1-2). lib. bdg. 24.21 (978-1-59961-795-4(1)) Spotlight.

—The Music Teacher from the Black Lagoon. Thaler, Mike. 2011. (Black Lagoon Set 1 Ser.: No. 1). (ENG.). 32p. (gr. -1-2). lib. bdg. 24.21 (978-1-59961-796-1(X)) Spotlight.

—The New Kid from the Black Lagoon. Thaler, Mike. 2012. (Black Lagoon Set 2 Ser.: No. 2). (ENG.). 32p. (J). (gr. 1-4). lib. bdg. 24.21 (978-1-59961-956-9(3)) Spotlight.

—The Planet Without Pronouns. Martin, Justin McCory. 2004. (Grammar Tales Ser.). (ENG.). 16p. (J). (gr. 3-7). pap. 3.25 (978-0-439-45820-7(X)) Scholastic, Inc.

—Pluto Visits Earth! Metzger, Steve. 2012. (ENG.). 32p. (J). (gr. -1-3). 16.99 (978-0-545-24934-8(1), Orchard Bks.) Scholastic, Inc.

—Preacher Creature Strikes on Sunday, 1 vol. Thaler, Mike. 2009. (Tales from the Back Pew Ser.). (ENG.). 32p. (J). (gr. 1-4). pap. 4.99 (978-0-310-71589-4(X)) Zonderkidz.

—The Principal from the Black Lagoon. Thaler, Mike. 2009. (From the Black Lagoon Ser.). 14.00 (978-1-60686-507-1(2)) Perfection Learning Corp.

—The Principal from the Black Lagoon. Thaler, Mike. 2008. (Black Lagoon Adventures Ser.). (ENG.). 32p. (J). (gr. -1-3). pap. 3.99 (978-0-545-06932-8(7), Cartwheel Bks.) Scholastic, Inc.

—The Principal from the Black Lagoon. Thaler, Mike. 2011. (Black Lagoon Set 1 Ser.: No. 1). (ENG.). 32p. (gr. -1-2). lib. bdg. 24.21 (978-1-59961-797-8(8)) Spotlight.

—The School Bus Driver from the Black Lagoon. Thaler, Mike. 2012. (Black Lagoon Set 2 Ser.: No. 2). (ENG.). 32p. (J). (gr. 1-4). lib. bdg. 24.21 (978-1-59961-957-6(1)) Spotlight.

—The School Carnival from the Black Lagoon. Thaler, Mike. 2005. 64p. (J). pap. (978-0-439-80075-4(7)) Scholastic, Inc.

—The School Nurse from the Black Lagoon. Thaler, Mike. 2011. (Black Lagoon Set 1 Ser.: No. 1). (ENG.). 32p. (gr. -1-2). lib. bdg. 24.21 (978-1-59961-798-5(6)) Spotlight.

—School Riddles from the Black Lagoon. Thaler, Mike. 2007. (J). pap. (978-0-545-01758-9(0)) Scholastic, Inc.

—The School Secretary from the Black Lagoon. Thaler, Mike. 2006. (J). (978-0-439-80077-8(3)) Scholastic, Inc.

—The Science Fair from the Black Lagoon. Thaler, Mike. 2005. (Black Lagoon Adventures Ser.: 4). (ENG.). 64p. (J). (gr. 2-5). pap. 3.99 (978-0-439-55717-7(8), Scholastic Paperbacks) Scholastic, Inc.

—The Snow Day from the Black Lagoon. Thaler, Mike. 2008. 63p. (J). pap. (978-0-545-01766-4(1)) Scholastic, Inc.

—The Spring Dance from the Black Lagoon. Thaler, Mike. 2009. 62p. (J). (978-0-545-07223-6(9)) Scholastic, Inc.

—St. Patrick's Day from the Black Lagoon. Thaler, Mike. 2011. 61p. (J). (978-0-545-27328-2(5)) Scholastic, Inc.

—The Talent Show from the Black Lagoon. Thaler, Mike. 2004. (Black Lagoon Adventures Ser.: 2). (ENG.). 64p. (J). (gr. 2-5). 4.99 (978-0-439-43894-0(2), Scholastic Paperbacks) Scholastic, Inc.

—The Teacher from the Black Lagoon. Thaler, Mike. 2008. (From the Black Lagoon Ser.). (gr. -1-3). 14.00 (978-0-7569-8779-4(2)) Perfection Learning Corp.

—The Teacher from the Black Lagoon. Thaler, Mike. unabr. ed. 2006. (ENG.). (J). (gr. -1-3). 9.99 (978-0-439-87590-5(0)) Scholastic, Inc.

—The Teacher from the Black Lagoon. Thaler, Mike. 2011. (Black Lagoon Set 1 Ser.: No. 1). (ENG.). 32p. (gr. -1-2). lib. bdg. 24.21 (978-1-59961-799-2(4)) Spotlight.

—The Teacher from the Black Lagoon. Thaler, Mike. 2004. (J). (gr. k-3). 18.95 (978-1-55592-495-9(6)) Weston Woods Studios, Inc.

—The Thanksgiving Day from the Black Lagoon. Thaler, Mike. 2009. 64p. (J). (978-0-545-16812-0(0)) Scholastic, Inc.

—There Was a Cold Lady Who Swallowed Some Snow! Colandro, Lucille. (J). 2006. (ENG.). (gr. -1-3). 18.95 (978-0-439-89841-6(2)); 2003. (ENG.). 32p. (gr. -1-3). pap. 6.99 (978-0-439-56703-9(3), Cartwheel Bks.); 2003. 32p. (gr. k-3). pap. 5.95 (978-0-439-47109-1(5), Cartwheel Bks.); 2006. (ENG.). (gr. -1-3). 9.95 (978-0-439-89556-9(1)) Scholastic, Inc.

—There Was an Old Lady Who Swallowed a Bat! Colandro, Lucille. 2005. (ENG.). 32p. (J). (gr. -1-3). pap. 6.99 (978-0-439-73766-1(4), Cartwheel Bks.) Scholastic, Inc.

—There Was an Old Lady Who Swallowed a Bell! Colandro, Lucille. 2008. (ENG.). (J). (gr. -1-3). 32p. pap. 6.99 (978-0-545-04361-8(1), Cartwheel Bks.); 9.95 (978-0-545-09238-8(8)) Scholastic, Inc.

—There Was an Old Lady Who Swallowed a Chick! Colandro, Lucille. (ENG.). (J). (gr. -1-k). 2011. 9.99 (978-0-545-27367-1(6)); 2011. pap. 18.99 incl. audio compact disk (978-0-545-27369-5(2)); 2010. 32p. pap.

6.99 *(978-0-545-16181-7(9)*, Cartwheel Bks.) Scholastic, Inc.

—There Was an Old Lady Who Swallowed a Chick! Colandro, Lucille. ed. 2010. (There Was an Old Lady... Ser.). lib. bdg. 17.20 *(978-0-606-06821-5(X)*, Turtleback) Turtleback Bks.

—There Was an Old Lady Who Swallowed a Clover. Colandro, Lucille. 2012. (There Was an Old Lady Ser.). (ENG.). 32p. (J). (gr. -1-k). pap. 6.99 *(978-0-545-35222-2(3)*, Cartwheel Bks.) Scholastic, Inc.

—There Was an Old Lady Who Swallowed a Rose! Colandro, Lucille. 2012. (There Was an Old Lad Ser.). (ENG.). 32p. (J). (gr. -1-k). pap. 6.99 *(978-0-545-35223-9(1))* Scholastic, Inc.

—There Was an Old Lady Who Swallowed a Rose! Colandro, Lucille. ed. 2012. (There Was an Old Lady... Ser.). lib. bdg. 17.20 *(978-0-606-26734-2(4)*, Turtleback) Turtleback Bks.

—There Was an Old Lady Who Swallowed a Shell! Colandro, Lucille. (J). 2008. (ENG.). 32p. (gr. -1-3). pap. 6.99 *(978-0-439-87380-2(0)*, Cartwheel Bks.); 2006. *(978-0-439-81536-9(3))* Scholastic, Inc.

—There Was an Old Lady Who Swallowed Some Books! Colandro, Lucille. 2012. (ENG.). 32p. (J). (gr. -1-k). 6.99 *(978-0-545-40287-3(5)*, Cartwheel Bks.) Scholastic, Inc.

—There Was an Old Lady Who Swallowed Some Books! Colandro, Lucille. ed. 2012. (There Was an Old Lady... Ser.). lib. bdg. 17.20 *(978-0-606-26208-8(3)*, Turtleback) Turtleback Bks.

—There Was an Old Lady Who Swallowed Some Leaves! Colandro, Lucille. 2010. (ENG.). 32p. (J). (gr. -1-k). pap. 6.99 *(978-0-545-24198-4(7)*, Cartwheel Bks.) Scholastic, Inc.

—The Three Wise Guys, 1 vol. Thaler, Mike. 2010. (Tales from the Back Pew Ser.). (ENG.). 32p. (J). (gr. 1-4). pap. 4.99 *(978-0-310-71593-1(8))* Zonderkidz.

—Vacation Bible Snooze, 1 vol. Thaler, Mike. 2010. (Tales from the Back Pew Ser.). (ENG.). 32p. (J). (gr. 1-4). pap. 4.99 *(978-0-310-71596-2(2))* Zondervan.

—The Vice Principal from the Black Lagoon. Thaler, Mike. 2007. (J). pap. *(978-0-439-87132-7(8))* Scholastic, Inc.

—Walking the Plank to the Baptism Tank, 1 vol. Thaler, Mike. 2009. (Tales from the Back Pew Ser.). (ENG.). 32p. (J). (gr. 1-4). pap. 4.99 *(978-0-310-71594-8(6))* Zonderkidz.

—You're Different & That's Super. Kressley, Carson. 2005. (ENG.). 64p. (J). (gr. -1-3). 14.99 *(978-1-4169-0070-2(5)*, Simon & Schuster Bks. For Young Readers) Simon & Schuster Bks. For Young Readers.

—The Zombie at the Finish Line. Doyle, Bill. 2013. (Scream Team Ser.). (ENG.). 96p. (J). (gr. 2-5). pap. 4.99 *(978-0-545-47978-3(9)*, Scholastic Paperbacks) Scholastic, Inc.

—The 100th Day of School from the Black Lagoon. Thaler, Mike. 2012. 64p. (J). pap. *(978-0-545-37325-8(5))* Scholastic, Inc.

Lee, Jared. Jordan's Silly Sick Day. Lee, Jared, tr. Fontes, Justine. 2004. (Rookie Readers Ser.). 31p. (J). 19.50 *(978-0-516-25897-3(4)*, Children's Pr.) Scholastic Library Publishing.

Lee, Jared D. The Amusement Park from the Black Lagoon. Thaler, Mike. 2014. 64p. (J). ***(978-0-545-61641-6(7))*** Scholastic, Inc.

—The Big Game from the Black Lagoon. Thaler, Mike. 2013. 63p. (J). pap. ***(978-0-545-61639-3(5))*** Scholastic, Inc.

Lee, Jared D. The Class Picture Day from the Black Lagoon. Thaler, Mike. 2012. 64p. (J). pap. *(978-0-545-47666-9(6))* Scholastic, Inc.

—The Dentist from the Black Lagoon. 2014. (ENG.). (J). 24.21 *(978-1-61479-197-3(X))* Spotlight.

—Earth Day from the Black Lagoon. Thaler, Mike. 2013. 64p. (J). *(978-0-545-47669-0(0))* Scholastic, Inc.

—The Little League Team from the Black Lagoon. Thaler, Mike. 2009. (Black Lagoon Adventures Ser.: 10). (ENG.). 64p. (J). (gr. 2-5). 4.99 *(978-0-439-87162-4(X)*, Scholastic Paperbacks) Scholastic, Inc.

—Meatloaf Monster from the School Cafeteria. Thaler, Mike. 2012. (J). pap. *(978-0-545-48570-8(3))* Scholastic, Inc.

Lee, Jared D. The Reading Challenge from the Black Lagoon. Thaler, Mike. 2015. 64p. (J). pap. ***(978-0-545-78521-1(9))*** Scholastic, Inc.

—The Secret Santa from the Black Lagoon. Thaler, Mike. 2014. 64p. (J). ***(978-0-545-78519-8(7))*** Scholastic, Inc.

Lee, Jared D. The Summer Vacation from the Black Lagoon. Thaler, Mike. 2010. 62p. (J). *(978-0-545-07224-3(7))* Scholastic, Inc.

—The Teacher from the Black Lagoon. Thaler, Mike. 2008. (Black Lagoon Adventures Ser.). (ENG.). 32p. (J). (gr. -1-3). pap. 3.99 *(978-0-545-06522-1(4)*, Cartwheel Bks.) Scholastic, Inc.

—There Was an Old Lady Who Swallowed a Bat! Colandro, Lucille. 2009. (ENG.). (J). (gr. -1-3). 9.99 *(978-0-545-16353-8(6))* Scholastic, Inc.

—There Was an Old Lady Who Swallowed a Fly! Colandro, Lucille. 2014. (There Was an Old Lad Ser.). (ENG.). 32p. (J). (gr. -1-k). 6.99 *(978-0-545-68292-3(4)*, Cartwheel Bks.) Scholastic, Inc.

—There Was an Old Lady Who Swallowed a Frog! Colandro, Lucille. 2014. (There Was an Old Lad Ser.). (ENG.). 32p. (J). (gr. k-2). pap. 6.99 *(978-0-545-69138-3(9)*, Cartwheel Bks.) Scholastic, Inc.

—There Was an Old Lady Who Swallowed a Sticker Book! Colandro, Lucille. 2014. (ENG.). 16p. (J). (gr. -1-k). 6.99 *(978-0-545-61308-8(6)*, Cartwheel Bks.) Scholastic, Inc.

—There Was an Old Lady Who Swallowed Some Books! Colandro, Lucille. 2012. (J). *(978-0-545-48186-1(4))* Scholastic, Inc.

Lee, Jared D. This Is the House That Monsters Built. Metzger, Steve. 2016. (J). ***(978-0-545-61112-1(1))*** Scholastic, Inc.

Lee, Jared D. The Werewolf at Home Plate. Doyle, Bill. 2012. (Scream Team Ser.: 1). (ENG.). 96p. (J). (gr. 2-5). pap. 4.99 *(978-0-545-34198-1(1)*, Scholastic Paperbacks) Scholastic, Inc.

Lee, Jeannie, jt. illus. see Whitten, Samantha.

Lee, Jenn Manley & Chow, Candice. The Book Bandit No. 7: A Mystery with Geometry. Thielbar, Melinda. 2011. (Manga Math Mysteries Ser.: 7). (ENG.). 48p. (gr. 3-5). pap. 6.95 *(978-0-7613-8136-5(8)*, Graphic Universe) Lerner Publishing Group.

—#7 the Book Bandit: A Mystery with Geometry. Thielbar, Melinda. 2011. (Manga Math Mysteries Set II Ser.). pap. 39.62 *(978-0-7613-8364-2(6)*, Graphic Universe) Lerner Publishing Group.

Lee, Jim. Absolute Sandman, 4 vols., Vol. 1. Azzarello, Brian et al. rev. ed. 2006. (Absolute Ser.: Vol. 1). (ENG.). 612p. 99.99 *(978-1-4012-1082-3(1)*, Vertigo) DC Comics.

Lee, Jim, et al. X-Tinction Agenda. Claremont, Chris & Simonson, Louise. 2011. (ENG.). 304p. (J). (gr. 4-17). 49.99 *(978-0-7851-5531-7(7))* Marvel Worldwide, Inc.

Lee, Jisun. Dad's Shirt, 1 vol. Donahue, Jill Lynn. 2007. (Read-It! Readers Ser.). (ENG.). 32p. (gr. -1-3). lib. bdg. 19.99 *(978-1-4048-3163-6(0)*, Easy Readers) Picture Window Bks.

—Groceries for Grandpa, 1 vol. Blackaby, Susan. 2007. (Read-It! Readers: Social Studies). (ENG.). 32p. (gr. k-2). lib. bdg. 19.99 *(978-1-4048-2334-1(4)*, Easy Readers) Picture Window Bks.

Lee, Joe. The Day My Peanut Butter Lost Its Stick. Tait, Elena. 2008. 24p. pap. 12.99 *(978-1-4389-1936-2(0))* AuthorHouse.

—I'm with Poppy!! Markette, Paul Scott. 2010. 24p. pap. 12.99 *(978-1-4520-6276-1(5))* AuthorHouse.

—Megan's Monster. Harris, M. S. Ed Rebecca a. & Harris, M. S. Ed. 2009. 28p. pap. 15.00 *(978-1-4490-2822-0(5))* AuthorHouse.

—Power Reading: Classics/Treasure Island. Cole, Bob. 2004. 94p. (J). (gr. 5-6). vinyl bd. 39.95 *(978-1-883186-59-3(5)*, PPCL3) National Reading Styles Institute, Inc.

—Putting on the Brakes: Understanding & Taking Control of Your ADD or ADHD. Quinn, Patricia O. & Stern, Judith M. 2nd ed. 2008. 80p. (J). (gr. 3-7). pap. 12.95 *(978-1-4338-0387-1(9))*; 16.95 *(978-1-4338-0386-4(0))* American Psychological Assn. (Magination Pr.).

—Putting on the Brakes Activity Book for Kids with ADD or ADHD. Quinn, Patricia O. & Stern, Judith M. 2nd ed. 2009. 96p. (J). (gr. 3-8). pap. 14.95 *(978-1-4338-0441-0(7)*, Magination Pr.) American Psychological Assn.

Lee, Jumin. Mermaids. Heinrichs, Cynthia. 2011. (ENG.). 32p. (J). (gr. -1-3). 16.95 *(978-1-897476-37-6(X))* Simply Read Bks. CAN. Dist: Ingram Pub. Services.

Lee, Jung Hwa. Adrenalin, 4 vols. Lee, Jung Hwa. (Adrenalin Ser.: Vol. 2). 192p. (YA). Vol. 2. 2006. per. 9.95 *(978-1-59697-001-4(4))*; Vol. 3. 2007. per. 9.95 *(978-1-59697-002-1(2))*; Vol. 4. 2007. per. 9.99 *(978-1-59697-003-8(0))* Infinity Studios LLC.

Lee, Kang-Woo. Rebirth, 11 vols., Vol. 5. Lee, Kang-Woo. 5th rev. ed. 2003. 184p. pap. 9.99 *(978-1-59182-220-2(3))* TOKYOPOP, Inc.

—Rebirth, Vol. 14. Lee, Kang-Woo. Woo & Yi, Kang-u. rev. ed. 2005. 192p. pap. 9.99 *(978-1-59532-029-2(6))* TOKYOPOP, Inc.

—Rebirth, Vol. 15. Lee, Kang-Woo. 15th rev. ed. 2005. (Rebirth Ser.). 200p. per. 9.99 *(978-1-59532-030-8(X))* TOKYOPOP, Inc.

Lee, Karen. Un día Non, 1 vol. Fisher, Doris & Sneed, Dani. 2012. (SPA.). 32p. (J). (gr. -1-3). 17.95 *(978-1-60718-694-6(2))* Arbordale Publishing.

—Mi día Par, 1 vol. Fisher, Doris & Sneed, Dani. 2012. (SPA & ENG.). 32p. (J). (gr. -1-3). 17.95 *(978-1-60718-692-2(6))* Arbordale Publishing.

—My Even Day, 1 vol. Fisher, Doris & Sneed, Dani. 2007. (ENG.). 32p. (J). (gr. -1-3). pap. 8.95 *(978-1-934359-22-8(X))*; Vol. 2. 15.95 *(978-0-9777423-3-2(4))* Arbordale Publishing.

—My Half Day, 1 vol. Sneed, Dani & Fisher, Doris. 2008. (ENG.). 32p. (J). (gr. -1-3). 16.95 *(978-1-934359-14-3(9))*; pap. 8.95 *(978-1-934359-29-7(7))* Arbordale Publishing.

—One Odd Day, 1 vol. Fisher, Doris & Sneed, Dani. 2006. (ENG.). 32p. (J). (gr. -1-3). 15.95 *(978-0-9768823-3-6(7))*; Vol. 1. pap. 8.95 *(978-1-934359-33-4(5))* Arbordale Publishing.

—Seth & Savannah Build a Speech. Ingalls, Ann. 2012. 32p. (J). lib. bdg. 25.27 *(978-1-59953-511-1(4))* Norwood Hse. Pr.

Lee, Karen. ABC Safari, 1 vol. Lee, Karen. 2007. (ENG.). 32p. (J). (gr. -1-3). 15.95 *(978-0-9777423-0-1(X))*; pap. 8.95 *(978-0-9777423-6-3(9))* Arbordale Publishing.

—Mushy Mashed Bananas. Lee, Karen. 2012. 24p. pap. *(978-1-4602-0136-7(1))* FriesenPress.

Lee, Kary. Dizzy. Nyikos, Stacy. l.t. ed. 2006. 32p. (J). (gr. -1-3). 15.95 *(978-0-9764199-2-1(0)*, 888-867-1927) Stonehorse Publishing, LLC.

Lee, Katie. Monarch Butterfly of Aster Way. Ring, Elizabeth. (ENG.). 32p. (J). (gr. -1-2). 2005. pap. 7.65 *(978-1-931465-40-3(1)*, S5017); Incl. toy. 2003. 9.95 *(978-1-56899-573-1(3)*, PB5067) Soundprints.

—Orca Song. Armour, Michael C. (ENG.). 32p. (J). (gr. -1-2). pap. 6.95 *(978-1-59249-479-8(X)*, S4004) Soundprints.

—Sea Turtle Journey: The Story of a Loggerhead Turtle. Jay, Lorraine A. 2011. (Smithsonian Oceanic Collection Ser.). (ENG.). 32p. (J). (gr. -1-3). 19.95 *(978-1-60727-660-9(7))* Soundprints.

Lee, Kim. The Magic in Believing: The Tooth Fairies. Webb, Carla. (Magic in Believing Ser.). 36p. (J). (gr. k-5). *(978-0-9705726-0-8(3))* Ageless Treasures.

Lee, Kong. Hiss! Pop! Boom! Celebrating Chinese New Year. Morrissey, Tricia. 2006. (ENG.). 32p. (J). (gr. -1-3). 12.95 *(978-0-9715940-7-4(4))* ThingsAsian Pr.

Lee, Leslie W., jt. illus. see Lee, Melicent Humason.

Lee, Linda. Pat, the Cat. Strong, Frances Dinkins. 2003. 24p. (J). pap. *(978-0-9720267-1-0(1))* Learning Abilities Bks.

Lee, Martin. 40 Elaboration Activities That Take Writing from Bland to Brilliant! Lee, Martin. Miller, Marcia & Miller, Marcia K. 2007. (40 Elaboration Activities That Take Writing from Bland to Brilliant! Ser.). (ENG.). 80p. pap. 12.99 *(978-0-439-55434-3(9)*, Teaching Resources) Scholastic, Inc.

Lee, Maxine. Pi-Rat! Lee, Maxine. 2013. (ENG.). 32p. (J). (gr. -1-k). 14.99 *(978-1-58925-143-4(1))* Tiger Tales.

Lee, Maxine & Enright, Amanda. Fairy Magic! Wharton, Ellie. 2014. (Magnetic Play Bks.). (ENG.). 10p. (J). (gr. -1-3). *(978-1-78244-827-3(6))* Top That! Publishing PLC.

Lee, Maxine, jt. illus. see Enright, Amanda.

Lee, Melicent Humason & Lee, Leslie W. Indians of the Oaks. 2nd ed. 2007. xiv, 244p. (J). pap. *(978-0-937808-50-4(4))* San Diego Museum of Man.

Lee, Myung Jin. Ragnarok, 10 vols., Vol. 9. Lee, Myung Jin. rev. ed. 2004. 192p. pap. 9.99 *(978-1-59182-208-0(4))* TOKYOPOP, Inc.

Lee, Myung Jin. Lights Out, Vol. 2. Lee, Myung Jin, creator. 2nd rev. ed. 2006. 192p. pap. 14.99 *(978-1-59532-361-3(9)*, Tokyopop Adult) TOKYOPOP, Inc.

Lee, Na Hyeon. Traveler of the Moon, 3 vols. Lee, Na Hyeon. (Traveler of the Moon Ser.: Vol. 2). 176p. Vol. 2. 2005. pap. 9.95 *(978-1-59697-062-5(6))*; Vol. 3. 2007. pap. 9.95 *(978-1-59697-063-2(4))* Infinity Studios LLC.

Lee, Nikita. Bessie Bump Gets a New Family. Meredith, Amberley. 2010. 26p. pap. 13.95 *(978-1-60911-901-0(0)*, Eloquent Bks.) Strategic Book Publishing & Rights Agency (SBPRA).

Lee, Paul. Hank Aaron: Brave in Every Way. Golenbock, Peter. 2005. (ENG.). 32p. (J). (gr. -1-3). reprint ed. pap. 6.99 *(978-0-15-205250-8(X))* Houghton Mifflin Harcourt Publishing Co.

—A Voice of Her Own: The Story of Phillis Wheatley, Slave Poet. Lasky, Kathryn. 2012. (Candlewick Biographies Ser.). (ENG.). 48p. (J). (gr. 3-7). 14.99 *(978-0-7636-6427-5(8))*; pap. 4.99 *(978-0-7636-6091-8(4))* Candlewick Pr.

Lee, Paul & Yates, Jolyon. Kingdom of the Snakes. Farshtey, Greg. 2012. (Ninjago Ser.: 5). (ENG.). 64p. (J). (gr. 1-6). pap. 6.99 *(978-1-59707-356-1(3))* Papercutz.

—"Kingdom of the Snakes" Farshtey, Greg. 2012. (Ninjago Ser.: 5). (ENG.). 64p. (J). (gr. 1-6). 10.99 *(978-1-59707-357-8(1))* Papercutz.

Lee, Paul, jt. illus. see Henrique, Paulo.

Lee, Roslyn. Pick-a-WooWoo- Grandma's Great Advice: The Art of Listening, 16 vols., Vol. 4. Harper, Julie-Ann. 2009. 32p. pap. *(978-0-9803669-3-8(3))* Pick-a-Woo Woo Pubs.

Lee, Ru. Witch Class, Vol. 3. Lee, Ru. 2006. (Witch Class Ser.: Vol. 3). 192p. (YA). per. 9.95 *(978-1-59697-083-0(9))* Infinity Studios LLC.

Lee, Sarah Ann. The Buggy That Boogied Away. Lee, Betsy B. 2006. 24p. (J). pap. 6.95 *(978-0-9720267-7-2(0))* Learning Abilities Bks.

Lee, So-Young. Arcana. Lee, So-Young. 3rd rev. ed. 2005. (Arcana (Tokyopop) Ser.: Vol. 3). 192p. pap. 9.99 *(978-1-59532-483-2(6))* TOKYOPOP, Inc.

Lee, So-Young. Arcana, Vol. 1. Lee, So-Young, creator. 2005. 208p. pap. 9.99 *(978-1-59532-481-8(X))* TOKYOPOP, Inc.

Lee, Soo. Enter the Dumpling, Vol. 1. Goh, Colin & Woo, Yen Yen. 2013. 144p. (J). pap. 12.99 *(978-0-9881899-0-4(9))* Yumcha Studios LLC.

Lee, Susan. How the Winter Frog Came to Was: Or, How to Get a Nice Surprise on Thanksgiving! Hurley, Wes. 2007. 36p. per. 24.95 *(978-1-4241-8395-1(2))* America Star Bks.

Lee, Suzy. Ask Me. Waber, Bernard. 2015. (ENG.). 40p. (J). (gr. -1-3). 16.99 *(978-0-547-73394-4(1)*, HMH Books For Young Readers) Houghton Mifflin Harcourt Publishing Co.

—Open This Little Book. Klausmeier, Jesse. 2013. (ENG.). 40p. (J). (gr. -1-3). 16.99 *(978-0-8118-6783-2(8))* Chronicle Bks. LLC.

Lee, Suzy. The Zoo. Lee, Suzy. 2007. (ENG.). 32p. (J). (gr. -1-1). 9.99 *(978-1-933605-28-9(6)*, 05289) Kane Miller.

Lee, Tae E. A Medieval Tale. Pulido, Brian. 2003. (Lady Death Ser.: Vol. 1). 160p. (YA). (gr. 7-18). pap. 9.95 *(978-1-931484-72-5(4))* CrossGeneration Comics, Inc.

Lee, Tony & Hart, Sam. Excalibur: The Legend of King Arthur. Lee, Tony. 2011. (ENG.). 144p. (J). (gr. 5-18). 21.99 *(978-0-7636-4644-8(X))* Candlewick Pr.

Lee, Tricia Ting. The Adventures of Henry Hamper & the Flying Fish. Libby, Lori Ann. 2010. 34p. pap. 13.95 *(978-1-60911-493-0(0)*, Eloquent Bks.) Strategic Book Publishing & Rights Agency (SBPRA).

Lee, Virginia. Persephone. Clayton, Sally Pomme. 2009. 28p. (J). (gr. 2-5). 18.00 *(978-0-8028-5349-3(8)*, Eerdmans Bks For Young Readers) Eerdmans, William B. Publishing Co.

Lee, Wei-Chun. Little Lotus & the Loving-Kindness Cup. Tidwell, Susan. 2012. 77p. (J). 6.95 *(978-1-932293-72-2(8))* Buddha's Light Publishing.

Lee, Wendy W. The Apple Tree's Discovery. Schram, Peninnah & Davis, Rachayl Eckstein. 2012. (Kar-Ben Favorites Ser.). (ENG.). 24p. (J). (gr. -1-2). pap. 7.95 *(978-0-7613-5132-0(9))*; lib. bdg. 16.95 *(978-0-7613-5130-6(2))* Lerner Publishing Group. (Kar-Ben Publishing).

Lee, Williams. The Adventures of Old Henry: Nobody Cares. Brouillette, Peter. 2004. (J). per. 19.99 *(978-0-9760419-3-1(6))* ThatsMyLife Co.

Lee, Xiongpao. The African Interior Mission. Allen, C. William. 2006. 232p. (J). pap. 20.00 *(978-0-9653308-5-5(0))* Africana Homestead Legacy Pubs., Inc.

Lee, Y. J. The Little Moon Princess. Lee, Y. J. 2010. (ENG.). 32p. (J). (gr. -1-3). 16.99 *(978-0-06-154736-2(0))* HarperCollins Pubs.

Lee, Yuan. The Parthenon: The Height of Greek Civilization. Mann, Elizabeth. 2006. (Wonders of the World Book Ser.). (ENG.). 48p. (J). (gr. 4-8). 22.95 *(978-1-931414-15-9(7)*, 9781931414159) Mikaya Pr.

Leech, Jacob. It's Me, Penny! The Hot Air Balloon Adventure. Guerrero, Rhonda. 2011. 28p. pap. 24.95 *(978-1-4489-7070-4(9))* America Star Bks.

Leech, John. The Annotated Christmas Carol: A Christmas Carol in Prose. Dickens, Charles. annot. ed. 2004. (Annotated Bks.). (ENG.). 288p. 29.95 *(978-0-393-05158-2(7)*, 5158) Norton, W. W. & Co., Inc.

Leeds, Marjorie M. The Adventures of Giggles & Owen: Adventure Three - Unlimited Pawsibilities. Terrill Holdman, Shirley. 2013. 50p. pap. 17.95 *(978-1-4575-2175-1(X))* Dog Ear Publishing, LLC.

Leedy, Loreen. Crazy Like a Fox. Leedy, Loreen. 2009. (ENG.). 32p. (J). (gr. -1-3). 7.99 *(978-0-8234-2248-7(8))* Holiday Hse., Inc.

—The Edible Pyramid: Good Eating Every Day. Leedy, Loreen. rev. ed. 2007. (ENG.). 32p. (J). (gr. -1-3). 17.95 *(978-0-8234-2074-2(4))*; 6.95 *(978-0-8234-2075-9(2))* Holiday Hse., Inc.

—The Great Graph Contest. Leedy, Loreen. (ENG.). 32p. (J). (gr. -1-3). 2006. 7.99 *(978-0-8234-2029-2(9))*; 2005. 17.95 *(978-0-8234-1710-0(7))* Holiday Hse., Inc.

—It's Probably Penny. Leedy, Loreen. rev. ed. 2007. (Penny Ser.). (ENG.). 32p. (J). (gr. k-3). 17.99 *(978-0-8050-7389-8(2)*, Holt, Henry & Co. Bks. For Young Readers) Holt, Henry & Co.

—Mapping Penny's World. Leedy, Loreen. rev. ed. 2003. (Penny Ser.). (ENG.). 32p. (J). (gr. k-3). pap. 7.99 *(978-0-8050-7262-4(4))* Square Fish.

—Messages from Mars. Leedy, Loreen. Schuerger, Andrew. 2006. (ENG.). 40p. (J). (gr. 3-7). 16.95 *(978-0-8234-1954-8(1))* Holiday Hse., Inc.

—The Monster Money Book. Leedy, Loreen. 2005. (ENG.). 32p. (J). (gr. k-3). pap. 6.95 *(978-0-8234-1558-8(9))* Holiday Hse., Inc.

—Seeing Symmetry. Leedy, Loreen. (ENG.). 32p. (J). 2013. pap. 7.99 *(978-0-8234-2762-8(5))*; 2012. 17.95 *(978-0-8234-2360-6(3))* Holiday Hse., Inc.

—The Shocking Truth about Energy. Leedy, Loreen. 2010. (ENG.). 32p. (J). (gr. k-3). 17.95 *(978-0-8234-2220-3(8))* Holiday Hse., Inc.

—Shocking Truth about Energy. Leedy, Loreen. 2011. (ENG.). 32p. (J). pap. 7.95 *(978-0-8234-2388-0(3))* Holiday Hse., Inc.

—Subtraction Action. Leedy, Loreen. 2005. (ENG.). 32p. (J). (gr. k-3). 8.95 *(978-0-8234-1764-3(6))* Holiday Hse., Inc.

—There's a Frog in My Throat! 440 Animal Sayings a Little Bird Told Me. Leedy, Loreen. Street, Pat. 2003. (Ala Notable Book Ser.). (ENG.). 48p. (J). (gr. k-3). tchr. ed. 17.95 *(978-0-8234-1774-2(3))*; reprint ed. pap. 8.99 *(978-0-8234-1819-0(7))* Holiday Hse., Inc.

Leeflang-Oudenarden, C. Tina's Island Home. Van Walsum-Quispel, J. M. 36p. (J). (gr. k-5). 12.95 *(978-0-87592-053-5(5))* Scroll Pr., Inc.

Leek, Kenny. How to Be a Human Bean. Markels, Bobby. Date not set. 24p. (J). (gr. 3-18). reprint ed. pap. 4.50 *(978-1-880991-01-5(2))* Stone Publishing Co.

Leeks, David. Big Book of Science. Cullen, Dave. 2004. 48p. (J). 7.99 *(978-1-85854-532-5(3))* Brimax Books Ltd. GBR. Dist: Byeway Bks.

—Big Book of Transport. Richard, John. 2004. 48p. (J). 7.99 *(978-1-85854-550-9(1))* Brimax Books Ltd. GBR. Dist: Byeway Bks.

—My First Atlas. Cullen, Dave & Williams, Simon. 2004. 48p. (J). 5.99 *(978-1-85854-709-1(1))* Brimax Books Ltd. GBR. Dist: Byeway Bks.

—My First Atlas. Cullen, Dave. 2004. 48p. (J). 7.99 *(978-1-85854-425-0(4))* Brimax Books Ltd. GBR. Dist: Byeway Bks.

Leeper, Chris & Leeper, Chris. Jeshi the Gorilla. Grey, Chelsea Gillian. (Internet Interactive Ser.). (ENG.). 36p. (J). (gr. -1-2). 8.95 *(978-1-59249-417-0(X)*, SD6504) Soundprints.

Leeper, Chris, jt. illus. see Leeper, Chris.

Leeper, Christopher. Ema the Rhinoceros. Shriver, Chelsea & Grey, Chelsea Gillian. 2005. (African Wildlife Foundation Kids Ser.). (ENG.). 36p. (J). (gr. -1-2). 9.95 *(978-1-59249-180-3(4)*, PS6550) Soundprints.

—Norman the Lion. Galvin, Laura Gates. (African Wildlife Foundation Ser.). (ENG.). 36p. (J). (gr. -1-2). 2005. 2.95 *(978-1-59249-191-9(X)*, S6553); 2004. 8.95 *(978-1-59249-208-4(8)*, SD6503); 2004. 9.95 *(978-1-59249-192-6(8)*, PS6553) Soundprints.

—River Otter at Autumn Lane. Galvin, Laura Gates. 2005. (Smithsonian's Backyard Ser.). (ENG.). 32p. (J). (gr. -1-2). 19.95 *(978-1-931465-63-2(0)*, BC5023); 15.95 *(978-1-931465-61-8(4)*, B5023) Soundprints.

—River Otter at Autumn Lane. Galvin, Laura. 2003. (ENG.). 32p. (J). (gr. -1-3). 9.95 *(978-1-931465-66-3(5)*, PB5073) Soundprints.

Leeper, Christopher J., et al. Alphabet of African Animals. Galvin, Laura Gates. 2011. (Alphabet Bks.). (ENG.). 40p. (J). (gr. -1-3). 17.95 *(978-1-60727-574-9(0))* Soundprints.

Leeper, Christopher J. Jeshi the Gorilla. Grey, Chelsea Gillian. 2005. (Meet Africa's Animals Ser.). (ENG.). 32p. (J). (gr. -1-2). 2.95 *(978-1-59249-418-7(8)*, S6554) Soundprints.

—River Otter at Autumn Lane. Galvin, Laura Gates. 2011. (Smithsonian's Backyard Ser.). (ENG.). 32p. (J). (gr. -1-3). 8.95 *(978-1-60727-642-5(9))*; 19.95 *(978-1-60727-641-8(0))* Soundprints.

Leeper, Christopher J. Ema the Rhinoceros. Leeper, Christopher J., tr. Shriver, Chelsea & Grey, Chelsea Gillian. 2005. (African Wildlife Foundation Ser.). (ENG.). 36p. (J). (gr. -1-2). 14.95 *(978-1-59249-177-3(4)*, H6500); pap. 6.95 *(978-1-59249-178-0(2)*, S6500) Soundprints.

—Norman the Lion. Leeper, Christopher J., tr. Galvin, Laura Gates. 2005. (African Wildlife Foundation Ser.). (ENG.). 36p. (J). (gr. -1-2). 14.95 *(978-1-59249-189-6(8)*, H6503); pap. 6.95 *(978-1-59249-190-2(1)*, S6503) Soundprints.

Leer, Rebecca. A Spoon for Every Bite. Hayes, Joe. 2005. (SPA & ENG.). 32p. (J). (gr. 1-4). reprint ed. pap. 8.95 *(978-0-938317-93-7(8))* Cinco Puntos Pr.

Lees, Harry H. John Wanamaker: Boy Merchant. Burt, Olive Woolley. 2011. 192p. 42.95 *(978-1-258-08290-1(X))* Literary Licensing, LLC.

Leeson, Tom and Pat, et al, photos by. Cascade Babies. 2013. 26p. (J). 8.95 *(978-1-56037-330-8(X))* Farcountry Pr.

Leeuwen, Joke van. Eep! Leeuwen, Joke van. Leeuwen, Joke Van. 2012. (Gecko Press Titles Ser.). 152p. (J). (gr. 2-5). pap. 7.95 *(978-1-877579-07-3(6))* Gecko Pr. NZL. Dist: Lerner Publishing Group.

L

Lefebure, Ingrid. Ella & the Worry Doll. Canale, Allison. 2013. (ENG.). (J). (gr. -1-3). 14.95 *(978-1-62086-332-9(4))* Mascot Bks., Inc.

Lefebvre, Patrick, photos by. Cool in School Communication Game: Gb362. Eisenberg, Rebecca & Kjesbo, Rynette. 2011. (J). 64.95 net. *(978-1-58650-994-1(2))* Super Duper Pubns.

Leff, Tova. Azoi Vi Ess Past Fahr a Princessen (Fit for a Princess) Rotman, Risa. Fiohr, Perel, tr. 2012.Tr. of Fit for a Princess. 32p. (J). 10.95 *(978-1-929628-66-7(8))* Hachai Publishing.

—Big Small or Just One Wall: A Book about Shuls. Fajnland, Leibel. Rosenfeld, D. L., ed. 2011. 36p. (J). 12.95 *(978-1-929628-59-9(5))* Hachai Publishing.

—On This Night: The Steps of the Seder in Rhyme. Steiner, Nancy. 2013. 32p. (J). 10.95 *(978-1-929628-51-3(X))* Hachai Publishing.

—Ten Tzedakah Pennies. Klein-Higger, Joni. 2005. 30p. (J). 10.95 *(978-1-929628-19-3(6))* Hachai Publishing.

—What Did Pinny Do? An Upsherin Story. Sitner, Nechama. 2013. 36p. (J). 12.95 *(978-1-929628-72-8(2))* Hachai Publishing.

Leffler, Silke. Andersen's Fairy Tales. 2007. (ENG.). 92p. (J). (gr. -1-3). 19.95 *(978-0-7358-2141-5(0))* North-South Bks., Inc.

—Emma in Buttonland. Rylance, Ulrike. Morby, Connie Stradling, tr. from GER. 2013. (ENG.). 120p. (J). (gr. 2-5). 12.95 *(978-1-62087-992-4(1)*, 620992, Sky Pony Pr.) Skyhorse Publishing Co., Inc.

—The Flower Ball. Laube, Sigrid. Boehm, Philip, tr. from GER. 2006. Orig. Title: Der Blumenball. (ENG.). 30p. (J). (gr. 1-4). 15.95 *(978-0-9646010-2-4(8))* Pumpkin Hse., Ltd.

Leffler, Silke. "I Have a Little Problem," Said the Bear. Leffler, Silke. Janisch, Heinz. 2009. (ENG.). 24p. (J). (gr. -1-3). 17.95 *(978-0-7358-2235-1(2))* North-South Bks., Inc.

Leftheri, Eleftheria-Garyfallia. Mom's Robot, 1 vol. Atkins, Jill. 2013. (Start Reading Ser.). (ENG.). 24p. (gr. k-1). pap. 6.99 *(978-1-4765-4119-8(1))* Capstone Pr., Inc.

Legendre, Philippe. Animals Around the World. Osle, Janessa. 2015. (I Can Draw Ser.). (ENG.). 48p. (J). (gr. -1-3). 30.65 *(978-1-939581-56-3(7))* Quarto Publishing Group USA.

—Favorite Pets. Osle, Janessa. 2015. (I Can Draw Ser.). (ENG.). 48p. (J). (gr. -1-3). 30.65 *(978-1-939581-55-6(9))* Quarto Publishing Group USA.

—Planes, Trains & Moving Machines. Osle, Janessa. 2015. (I Can Draw Ser.). (ENG.). 48p. (J). (gr. -1-3). 30.65 *(978-1-939581-58-7(3))* Quarto Publishing Group USA.

—Princesses, Fairies & Fairy Tales. Osle, Janessa. 2015. (I Can Draw Ser.). (ENG.). 48p. (J). (gr. -1-3). 30.65 *(978-1-939581-59-4(1))* Quarto Publishing Group USA.

—Sea Creatures & Other Favorite Animals. Osle, Janessa. 2015. (I Can Draw Ser.). (ENG.). 48p. (J). (gr. -1-3). 30.65 *(978-1-939581-57-0(5))* Quarto Publishing Group USA.

leger, Jarett & Mayeaux, Alicia. Courage in the Swamp. Leleux, Skip. 2011. (ENG.). 38p. pap. 12.00 *(978-0-615-46654-5(0))* Leger, Jarett.

Léger, Michael. Emily Carr's Attic, 1 vol. Léger, Diane Carmel. 2008. (ENG.). 32p. (J). (gr. -1-3). pap. 9.95 *(978-1-55143-958-7(1))* Orca Bk. Pubs. USA.

Legg, Barbara. Born under a Star, 1 vol. Buchholz, Erwin. 2009. 44p. pap. 24.95 *(978-1-61546-130-1(2))* America Star Bks.

Legge, David. Kisses for Daddy. Watts, Frances. 2008. 24p. (J). bds. *(978-1-921272-56-1(2))*; (ENG.). 22.95 *(978-1-877003-78-3(6))* Little Hare Bks. AUS. Dist: HarperCollins Pubs. Australia, Independent Pubs. Group.

—Kisses for Daddy. Watts, Frances. 2010. (ENG.). 26p. (J). (gr. -1-k). bds. 7.99 *(978-1-4169-8721-5(5)*, Little Simon) Little Simon.

—Kisses for Daddy Gift Pack: Book & Soft Toy. Watts, Frances. 2007. 22p. *(978-1-921049-48-4(0))* Little Hare Bks. AUS. Dist: HarperCollins Pubs. Australia.

Leggitt, Marjorie. Arches & Canyonlands National Parks - In the Land of Standing Rocks. Graf, Mike. 2012. (Adventures with the Parkers Ser.: 10). (ENG.). 112p. pap. 12.95 *(978-0-7627-7962-8(4)*, Falcon Guides) Globe Pequot Pr., The.

—Bryce Canyon & Zion National Parks: Danger in the Narrows. Graf, Mike. 2012. (Adventures with the Parkers Ser.: 1). (ENG.). 96p. pap. 12.95 *(978-0-7627-7974-1(8)*, Falcon Guides) Globe Pequot Pr., The.

—Glacier National Park: Going to the Sun. Graf, Mike. 2012. (Adventures with the Parkers Ser.: 7). (ENG.). 96p. pap. 12.95 *(978-0-7627-7964-2(0)*, Falcon Guides) Globe Pequot Pr., The.

—Grand Canyon National Park: Tail of the Scorpion. Graf, Mike. 2012. (Adventures with the Parkers Ser.: 2). (ENG.). 96p. pap. 12.95 *(978-0-7627-7965-9(9)*, Falcon Guides) Globe Pequot Pr., The.

—Great Smokies National Park: Ridge Runner Rescue. Graf, Mike. 2012. (Adventures with the Parkers Ser.: 6). (ENG.). 96p. pap. 12.95 *(978-0-7627-7966-6(7)*, Falcon Guides) Globe Pequot Pr., The.

—Kupe & the Corals. Padilla-Gamino, Jacqueline L. 2014. (Long Term Ecological Research Ser.). (ENG.). 32p. (J). (gr. 3-7). 15.95 *(978-1-58979-753-6(1))* Taylor Trade Publishing.

—Mount Rushmore, Badlands, Wind Cave: Going Underground. Graf, Mike. 2012. (Adventures with the Parkers Ser.: 9). (ENG.). 96p. pap. 12.95 *(978-0-7627-7968-0(3)*, Falcon Guides) Globe Pequot Pr., The.

—Yellowstone National Park: Eye of the Grizzly. Graf, Mike. 2012. (Adventures with the Parkers Ser.: 4). (ENG.). 96p. pap. 12.95 *(978-0-7627-7972-7(1)*, Falcon Guides) Globe Pequot Pr., The.

—Yosemite National Park: Harrowing Ascent of Half Dome. Graf, Mike. 2012. (Adventures with the Parkers Ser.: 3). (ENG.). 96p. pap. 12.95 *(978-0-7627-7973-4(X)*, Falcon Guides) Globe Pequot Pr., The.

Legnazzi, Claudia. Habia una Vez una Nube. Montes, Graciela. 2006. 23p. (J). (gr. -1-3). 8.95 *(978-1-59820-214-4(6)*, Alfaguara) Santillana USA Publishing Co., Inc.

Legramandi, Francesco. Bizarro Day! (DC Super Friends) Wrecks, Billy. 2013. (Step into Reading Ser.). (ENG.). 32p. (J). (gr. k-3). pap. 3.99 *(978-0-307-98119-6(3)*, Random Hse. Bks. for Young Readers) Random Hse. Children's Bks.

—A Fairy-Tale Fall. Jordan, Apple. 2010. (Step into Reading Ser.). (ENG.). 32p. (J). (gr. k-3). pap. 3.99 *(978-0-7364-2674-9(4)*, RH/Disney) Random Hse. Children's Bks.

—Glamorous Gowns & Terrific Tiaras (Disney Princess) Posner-Sanchez, Andrea. 2011. (Paper Doll Book Ser.). (ENG.). 32p. (J). (gr. -1-2). pap. 5.49 *(978-0-7364-2815-6(1)*, Golden/Disney) Random Hse. Children's Bks.

—Jailbreak! (DC Super Friends) Wrecks, Billy. 2014. (Pictureback Series.). (ENG.). 16p. (J). (gr. -1-2). 4.99 *(978-0-385-37398-2(8)*, Random Hse. Bks. for Young Readers) Random Hse. Children's Bks.

—Princess Big Lift-And-Look Book. Posner-Sanchez, Andrea. 2011. (Big Lift-And-Look Book Ser.). (ENG.). 12p. (J). (— 1). bds. 11.99 *(978-0-7364-2834-7(8)*, RH/Disney) Random Hse. Children's Bks.

—Princess Surprises. Posner-Sanchez, Andrea. 2011. (ENG.). 8p. (J). (— 1). bds. 7.99 *(978-0-7364-2753-1(8)*, RH/Disney) Random Hse. Children's Bks.

Legramandi, Francesco & Disney Storybook Artists Staff. Heart to Heart. RH Disney Staff. 2006. (Holographic Sticker Book Ser.). (ENG.). 32p. (J). (gr. -1-2). pap. 3.99 *(978-0-7364-2361-8(3)*, Golden/Disney) Random Hse. Children's Bks.

Legramandi, Francesco & Matta, Gabriella. All Dressed Up. RH Disney Staff. 2008. (Paper Doll Book Ser.). (ENG.). 64p. (J). (gr. -1-2). pap. 8.99 *(978-0-7364-2551-3(9)*, RH/Disney) Random Hse. Children's Bks.

—Christmas in the Castle (Disney Princess) RH Disney Staff. 2013. (Pictureback with Flaps Ser.). (ENG.). 16p. (J). (gr. -1-2). 4.99 *(978-0-7364-2991-7(3)*, RH/Disney) Random Hse. Children's Bks.

—Good Night, Princess! (Disney Princess) Posner-Sanchez, Andrea. 2012. (Pictureback with Flaps Ser.). (ENG.). 16p. (J). (gr. -1-2). pap. 4.99 *(978-0-7364-2851-4(8)*, RH/Disney) Random Hse. Children's Bks.

—The Princess Word Book. RH Disney Staff. 2010. (ENG.). 30p. (J). (gr. -1 — 1). bds. 11.99 *(978-0-7364-2747-0(3)*, RH/Disney) Random Hse. Children's Bks.

—Princesses & Puppies (Disney Princess) Weinberg, Jennifer Liberts. 2013. (Step into Reading Ser.). (ENG.). 32p. (J). (gr. -1-1). 3.99 *(978-0-7364-3104-0(7))*; lib. bdg. 12.99 *(978-0-7364-8133-5(8))* Random Hse. Children's Bks. (RH/Disney).

—Teacup: Belle's Star Pup (Disney Princess: Palace Pets) Random House Disney Staff & Redbank, Tennant. 2015. (Stepping Stone Book(TM) Ser.). (ENG.). 64p. (J). (gr. 1-4). 5.99 *(978-0-7364-3345-7(7)*, RH/Disney) Random Hse. Children's Bks.

Legramandi, Francesco & Matta, Gabriella. Three Royal Birthdays! (Disney Princess) Posner-Sanchez, Andrea. 2015. (Super Deluxe Pictureback Ser.). (ENG.). 24p. (J). (gr. -1-2). 5.99 *(978-0-7364-3403-4(8)*, RH/Disney) Random Hse. Children's Bks.

Legramandi, Francesco, jt. illus. see Disney Storybook Artists Staff.

Legramandi, Francesco, jt. illus. see Matta, Gabriella.

Legramandi, Francesco, jt. illus. see RH Disney Staff.

Legramandi, Francesco, jt. illus. see Robinson, William.

Lehman, A. C. Girl Scouts in Arizona & New Mexico. Roy, Lillian Elizabeth. 2011. 250p. 46.95 *(978-1-258-05940-8(1))* Literary Licensing, LLC.

Lehman, Barbara. Say Boo! Graham-Barber, Lynda. 2006. (ENG.). 24p. (J). (gr. -1-2). pap. 3.99 *(978-0-7636-2911-3(1))* Candlewick Pr.

Lehman, Barbara. The Red Book. Lehman, Barbara. 2004. (ENG.). 32p. (J). (gr. -1-3). 16.99 *(978-0-618-42858-8(5))* Houghton Mifflin Harcourt Publishing Co.

Lehman, Denise. Before I Knew You. Lee, Shelley R. Lee, Shelley R., ed. 2006. (J). lib. bdg. 20.00 *(978-0-9786757-0-7(3))* Lee, Shelley.

Lehmkuhl, Pat. Miranda & Starlight: (the Starlight Books, 1) Revised Edition, 6 vols. Hill, Janet Muirhead. 2nd rev. ed. 2003. (Starlight Bks.: 1). 168p. (J). (gr. 3-7). per. 9.00 *(978-0-9714161-4-7(1))* Raven Publishing Inc. of Montana.

—Starlight, Star Bright: (the Starlight Books, 3), 6 vols. 2003. (Starlight Bks.: Bk. 3). 192p. (J). (gr. 3-7). per. 12.00 *(978-0-9714161-2-3(5))* Raven Publishing Inc. of Montana.

Lehner-Rhoades, Shirley. Can I Have Some Cake Too? Nazareth, Melanie. 2013. 32p. pap. 14.95 *(978-1-935914-28-0(6))* River Sanctuary Publishing.

Lehto, Christine. I'm Only a Little Bunny. Jenks, Patricia. 2013. 34p. 15.99 *(978-1-937165-48-2(5))* Orange Hat Publishing.

Leialoha, Steve. Fables: Homelands, Vol. 6. Willingham, Bill. rev. ed. 2005. (Fables Ser.: Vol. 6). (ENG.). 192p. pap. 17.99 *(978-1-4012-0500-3(3)*, Vertigo) DC Comics.

Leialoha, Steve, et al. Sons of Empire. Willingham, Bill & Jean, James. rev. ed. 2007. (Fables Ser.: Vol. 9). (ENG.). 200p. pap. 17.99 *(978-1-4012-1316-9(2)*, Vertigo) DC Comics.

Leib, Michael S. What Were They Thinking?!, Vol.1. Giffen, Keith. 2008. (ENG.). 128p. pap. 14.99 *(978-1-934506-07-3(9))* Boom! Studios.

Leick, Bonnie. Alien Invaders. Cooper, Lynne. 2010. (ENG.). 32p. (J). (gr. 4-7). 16.95 *(978-1-934960-83-7(7)*, Raven Tree Pr.,Csi) Continental Sales, Inc.

—Alien Invaders/Invasores Extraterrestres. Huggins-Cooper, Lynn. de la Vega, Eida, tr. from ENG. 2005.Tr. of Invasores Extraterrestres. (SPA & ENG.). 32p. (J). (gr. 4-7). 16.95 *(978-0-9724973-9-8(0)*, 626999, Raven Tree Pr.,Csi) Continental Sales, Inc.

—Baby Bear Eats the Night, 0 vols. Pearson, Anthony. 2012. (ENG.). 32p. (J). (gr. k-3). 16.99 *(978-0-7614-6103-6(5)*, 9780761461036, Amazon Children's Publishing) Amazon Publishing.

—Beautiful Moon. Jeffers, Dawn. (ENG.). 32p. (J). (gr. -1-3). 2010. pap. 7.95 *(978-1-934960-06-6(3))*; 2009. 16.95 *(978-1-934960-05-9(5))* Continental Sales, Inc. (Raven Tree Pr.,Csi).

—Beautiful Moon/Bella Luna. Jeffers, Dawn. Del Risco, Eida, tr. 2009. 32p. (J). (gr. -1-3). (SPA & ENG.). 16.95 *(978-1-932748-87-1(3))*; (ENG & SPA.). pap. 7.95 *(978-1-932748-86-4(5))* Continental Sales, Inc. (Raven Tree Pr.,Csi).

—Goodnight, Little Monster, 0 vols. Ketteman, Helen. 2010. (ENG.). 32p. (J). (gr. -1-3). 16.99 *(978-0-7614-5683-4(X)*, 9780761456834, Amazon Children's Publishing) Amazon Publishing.

—Impetuous R. , Secret Agent. Conly, Jane Leslie. 2008. (ENG.). 240p. (gr. 3-7). 16.99 *(978-1-4231-0418-6(8))* Hyperion Pr.

—Where the Mild Things Are: A Very Meek Parody. Send-up, Maurice. 2009. (ENG.). 40p. (J). (gr. -1-3). 16.99 *(978-1-4169-9551-7(X)*, Simon & Schuster Bks. For Young Readers) Simon & Schuster Bks. For Young Readers.

—Wolf Camp. McKy, Katie. 2009. (ENG.). 32p. (J). (gr. -1-3). 15.95 *(978-1-933718-21-7(8))*; pap. 8.95 *(978-1-933718-25-5(0))* Tanglewood Pr.

—47 Strings: Tessa's Special Code. Carey, Becky. Stidwell O'Boyle, Carrie, ed. 2012. (ENG.). 36p. 16.95 *(978-0-9849245-6-1(6))* Little Creek Press.

Leidemer, Adam. The Puppy Who Wasn't. Ritner, Amelia. 2012. 24p. 24.95 *(978-1-4626-6221-0(8))* America Star Bks.

Leigh, Rob, jt. illus. see Research & Education Association Editors.

Leigh, Tom. Angus & Sadie. Voigt, Cynthia. (ENG.). 208p. (J). (gr. 3-7). 2008. pap. 6.99 *(978-0-06-074584-4(3))*; 2005. 16.99 *(978-0-06-074582-0(7))* HarperCollins Pubs.

—The Count's Hanukkah Countdown. Balsley, Tilda & Fischer, Ellen. 2012. (Hanukkah Ser.). 24p. (J). (gr. -1-1). (SPA & ENG.). 6.95 *(978-0-7613-7557-9(0))*; (ENG.). lib. bdg. 16.95 *(978-0-7613-7556-2(2))* Lerner Publishing Group. (Kar-Ben Publishing).

—Elmo Says... Albee, Sarah. 2009. (Big Bird's Favorites Board Bks.). (ENG.). 24p. (J). (gr. k — 1). bds. 4.99 *(978-0-375-84540-6(2)*, Random Hse. Bks. for Young Readers) Random Hse. Children's Bks.

—Grover & Big Bird's Passover Celebration. Balsley, Tilda & Fischer, Ellen. 2013. (Passover Ser.). (ENG.). 24p. (J). (gr. -1-1). 6.95 *(978-0-7613-8492-2(8)*, Kar-Ben Publishing) Lerner Publishing Group.

—Grover & Big Bird's Passover Journey. Balsley, Tilda & Fischer, Ellen. 2013. (Passover Ser.). (ENG.). 24p. (J). (gr. -1-1). lib. bdg. 16.95 *(978-0-7613-8491-5(X)*, Kar-Ben Publishing) Lerner Publishing Group.

—Hello, Cat, Hello, Dog. Albee, Sarah. 2006. (Step-By-Step Readers Ser.). (J). pap. *(978-1-59939-054-3(X)*, Reader's Digest Young Families, Inc.) Studio Fun International.

—I'm Sorry, Grover! A Rosh Hashanah Tale. Balsley, Tilda & Fischer, Ellen. 2013. (High Holidays Ser.). (ENG.). 24p. (J). (gr. -1-k). lib. bdg. 16.95 *(978-0-7613-7560-9(0)*, Kar-Ben Publishing) Lerner Publishing Group.

—I'm Sorry, Grover: A Rosh Hashanah Tale. Balsley, Tilda & Fischer, Ellen. 2013. (High Holidays Ser.). (ENG.). 24p. (J). (gr. -1-k). 6.95 *(978-0-7613-7561-6(9)*, Kar-Ben Publishing) Lerner Publishing Group.

—It's a Mitzvah, Grover! Balsley, Tilda & Fischer, Ellen. 2013. (ENG.). 24p. (J). (gr. -1-1). 6.95 *(978-0-7613-7563-0(5))*; lib. bdg. 16.95 *(978-0-7613-7562-3(7))* Lerner Publishing Group. (Kar-Ben Publishing).

—Off to the Moon! Marbury, Stephanie. 2006. 20p. (J). *(978-1-59939-100-7(7)*, Reader's Digest Young Families, Inc.) Studio Fun International.

—Pinocchio: A Tale of Honesty. 2006. (J). 6.99 *(978-1-59939-005-5(1))* Cornerstone Pr.

Leigh, Tom. Shalom Everybodeee! Balsley, Tilda & Fischer, Ellen. 2015. (J). *(978-0-7613-7558-6(9)*, Kar-Ben Publishing) Lerner Publishing Group.

Leigh, Tom, jt. illus. see Swanson, Maggie.

Leighton, Robert. Bugged: How Insects Changed History. Albee, Sarah. 2014. (ENG.). 176p. (J). (gr. 3-6). pap. 17.99 *(978-0-8027-3422-8(7)*, Bloomsbury USA Childrens) Bloomsbury USA.

—Poop Happened! A History of the World from the Bottom Up. Albee, Sarah. 2010. (ENG.). 176p. (J). (gr. 5-9). pap. 17.99 *(978-0-8027-2077-1(3))* Walker & Co.

Leijs, Tommie. Playtime Adventures. Vinsh, Aara J. 2011. 48p. pap. 24.95 *(978-1-4560-9982-4(5))* America Star Bks.

Leijten, Aileen. Bella & Bean. Dotlich, Rebecca Kai. 2009. (ENG.). 40p. (J). (gr. -1-3). 17.99 *(978-0-689-85616-7(4)*, Atheneum Bks. for Young Readers) Simon & Schuster Children's Publishing.

—City Hall: The Heart of Los Angeles. Bloom, Susan & Bertram, Debbie. 2003. 32p. (J). 9.95 *(978-1-931290-24-1(5)*, Smallfellow Pr.) Tallfellow Pr.

—Leaping Lily: A Ballet Story. Marsoli, Lisa Ann. 2005. (J). bds. 14.99 *(978-0-9767325-3-2(X))* Toy Quest.

Leiper, Esther M. An Odd Fable. Sundberg, Norma J. 2007. 32p. (J). pap. 13.95 *(978-0-9776958-5-0(9))* CyPress Pubns.

Leipsic, Regina. Zane & the Armadillo. Knesek, Marian. 2012. 26p. 24.95 *(978-1-4626-6685-0(X))* America Star Bks.

Leist, Christina. Jack the Bear. 2009. (ENG.). 40p. (J). (gr. -1-3). 16.95 *(978-1-894965-97-2(3))* Simply Read Bks. CAN. Dist: Ingram Pub. Services.

—Nutz!, 1 vol. Schwartz, Virginia Frances. 2012. (ENG.). 152p. (J). (gr. 3-6). pap. 12.95 *(978-1-896580-87-6(4))* Tradewind Bks. CAN. Dist: Orca Bk. Pubs. USA.

—On My Walk, 1 vol. Winters, Kari-Lynn. 2010. (ENG.). 32p. (J). (gr. k-1). 16.95 *(978-1-896580-61-6(0))* Tradewind Bks. CAN. Dist: Orca Bk. Pubs. USA.

Leist, Kara Suzanne. The Littlest Star. Kieffer, Elise Lael. 2005. (J). 14.99 *(978-1-59971-086-0(2))* Aardvark Global Publishing.

Leith, Marcus & Dunkley, Andrew, photos by. Peter Blake's ABC. Blake, Peter. 2010. (ENG., 64p. (J). (gr. -1-3). 13.50 *(978-1-85437-816-3(3))* Tate Publishing, Ltd. GBR. Dist: Abrams.

Lekander, Lance. Dr. Knucklehead's Knock-Knocks. Tait, Chris. 2010. (ENG.). 96p. (J). pap. 4.95 *(978-1-4027-7845-2(7))* Sterling Publishing Co., Inc.

Leland, Toni M. Christa Joins a Horse Club: Second in Christa Duncan Series. Leland, Toni M. 2004. Orig. Title: Christa Joins 4-H. (J). pap. 6.95 *(978-1-887932-49-3(6)*, SmallHorse Pr.) Equine Graphics Publishing Group.

Leloup, Geneviève. Too Pickley! Reidy, Jean. (Too! Bks.). (ENG.). (J). (gr. -1 — 1). 2012. 26p. bds. 7.99 *(978-1-59990-680-5(5))*; 2010. 32p. 11.99 *(978-1-59990-309-5(1))* Bloomsbury USA. (Bloomsbury USA Childrens).

—Too Princessy! Reidy, Jean. (Too! Bks.). (ENG.). (J). (gr. -1 — 1). 2013. 26p. bds. 7.99 *(978-1-59990-955-4(3))*; 2012. 32p. 12.99 *(978-1-59990-722-2(4))* Bloomsbury USA. (Bloomsbury USA Childrens).

—Too Purpley! Reidy, Jean. (Too! Bks.). (ENG.). (J). (gr. -1 — 1). 2011. 26p. bds. 7.99 *(978-1-59990-679-9(1))*; 2010. 32p. 11.99 *(978-1-59990-307-1(5))* Bloomsbury USA. (Bloomsbury USA Childrens).

Lemaire, Bonnie. When Jungle Jim Comes to Visit Fred the Snake. Cotton, Peter B. 2013. 48p. 24.95 *(978-0-9883370-4-6(5))* Fig & The Vine, LLC, The.

LeMaistre, Gretchen, photos by. Boo ABC: A to Z with the World's Cutest Dog. 2013. (ENG., 32p. (J). (gr. -1-1). 12.99 *(978-1-4521-0919-0(2))* Chronicle Bks. LLC.

Lemaitre, Pascal. Always. McGhee, Alison. 2009. (ENG.). 40p. (J). (gr. -1-3). 15.99 *(978-1-4169-7481-9(4)*, Simon & Schuster/Paula Wiseman Bks.) Simon & Schuster/Paula Wiseman Bks.

LeMaitre, Pascal. The Amazing Adventures of Supercat! Making the World Safe for Blankies. McMullan, Kate. 2011. (ENG.). 40p. (J). (gr. k — 1). 7.95 *(978-0-7611-6320-6(4)*, 16320) Workman Publishing Co., Inc.

Lemaitre, Pascal. Artist Ted. Beaty, Andrea. 2012. (ENG.). 32p. (J). (gr. -1-3). 16.99 *(978-1-4169-5374-6(4)*, McElderry, Margaret K. Bks.) McElderry, Margaret K. Bks.

—Bulldog's Big Day. McMullan, Kate. 2011. (J). *(978-0-545-17156-4(3)*, Orchard Bks.) Scholastic, Inc.

—Do Not Open This Book. Muntean, Michaela. 2006. (ENG.). 40p. (J). (gr. -1-3). 17.99 *(978-0-439-69839-9(1)*, Scholastic Pr.) Scholastic, Inc.

—Doctor Ted. Beaty, Andrea. 2008. (ENG.). 32p. (J). (gr. -1-3). 17.99 *(978-1-4169-2820-1(0)*, McElderry, Margaret K. Bks.) McElderry, Margaret K. Bks.

—Firefighter Ted. Beaty, Andrea. 2009. (ENG.). 32p. (J). (gr. -1-3). 17.99 *(978-1-4169-2821-8(9)*, McElderry, Margaret K. Bks.) McElderry, Margaret K. Bks.

—Goodnight, Dragons [padded Board Book]. Roth, Judith. 2015. (ENG.). 32p. (J). (gr. -1-k). bds. 8.99 *(978-1-4847-2190-2(X))* Hyperion Bks. for Children.

—Hush, Baby Ghostling. Beaty, Andrea. 2009. (ENG.). 32p. (J). (gr. -1-3). 14.99 *(978-1-4169-2545-3(7)*, McElderry, Margaret K. Bks.) McElderry, Margaret K. Bks.

—Let's Get a Checkup! Katz, Alan. 2010. (ENG.). 16p. (J). (gr. -1-1). 7.99 *(978-1-4169-8992-9(7)*, Little Simon) Little Simon.

—The Lion or the Mouse? Morrison, Toni & Morrison, Slade. 2014. (Who's Got Game? Ser.: 2). (ENG.). 36p. pap. 13.99 *(978-1-4767-9268-2(2)*, Scribner) Scribner.

—Me! Me! Mine! Katz, Alan. 2011. (ENG.). 16p. (J). (gr. -1-1). bds. 7.99 *(978-1-4169-8993-6(5)*, Little Simon) Little Simon.

—A Pet Named Sneaker. Heilbroner, Joan. 2013. (Beginner Books Ser.). (ENG.). 48p. (J). (gr. k-3). 8.99 *(978-0-307-97580-5(0))* Random Hse. Children's Bks.

LeMaitre, Pascal. Pinocchio. 2014. (Cartoon Classics Ser.). (ENG.). 144p. (J). (gr. 2-5). 12.99 *(978-0-8050-9699-6(X)*, Holt, Henry & Co. Bks. For Young Readers) Holt, Henry & Co.

Lemaitre, Pascal. Squirrels on Skis. Ray, J. Hamilton. 2013. (Beginners Books Ser.). (ENG.). 64p. (J). (gr. k-3). 8.99 *(978-0-449-81081-1(X))*; lib. bdg. 12.99 *(978-0-375-97152-5(1))* Random Hse. Children's Bks. (Random Hse. Bks. for Young Readers).

—You Are the Pea, & I Am the Carrot. Elkins, J. Theron. 2013. (ENG.). 32p. (J). (gr. -1-2). 16.95 *(978-1-4197-0850-3(3)*, Abrams Bks. for Young Readers) Abrams.

Lemanski, Mike. Design Line - Planes, Trains, & Automobiles. Oxlade, Chris. 2014. (ENG.). 16p. (J). (gr. k-12). 17.99 *(978-0-7636-7121-1(5)*, Big Picture Press) Candlewick Pr.

Lemaster, Michael. Corn for Tomorrow: A Story from Glengary. Lemaster, Kevin. 2009. 28p. pap. 13.99 *(978-1-4343-8548-2(5))* AuthorHouse.

LeMay, Meagan. Emma's First Agate, 1 vol. Magnuson, James. 2014. 32p. (gr. 1-2). pap. 7.95 *(978-1-59193-443-1(5))* Adventure Pubns., Inc.

Lemay, Violet. Doodle New York: Create. Imagine. Draw Your Way Through the Big Apple. Puck. 2012. (ENG.). 120p. (J). (gr. k-2). pap. 12.95 *(978-0-9838121-3-5(6))* Duo Pr. LLC.

—Doodle Texas: Create Imagine Draw Your Way Through the Lone Star State. Puck & Pohlen, Jerome. 2013. (ENG.). 120p. (J). (gr. k-2). pap. 12.95 *(978-1-938093-05-0(4))* Duo Pr. LLC.

—I Am Daisy. Froeb, Lori. 2015. (ENG.). 32p. (J). (gr. 1-3). pap. 3.99 *(978-0-7944-3311-6(1))* Studio Fun International.

—I Am Daisy, Level 2. Froeb, Lori. 2015. (Rescue Readers Ser.: 2). (ENG.). 32p. (J). (gr. k-3). lib. bdg. 16.99 *(978-0-7944-3350-5(2))* Studio Fun International.

—My Foodie ABC: A Little Gourmet's Guide. Puck. 2010. (ENG.). 22p. (J). (gr. -1-k). bds. 8.95 *(978-0-9825295-2-2(X))* Duo Pr. LLC.

—New York Baby. Puck. 2012. (Local Baby Bks.). (ENG.). 22p. (J). (gr. k — 1). bds. 8.95 *(978-0-9838121-4-2(4))* Duo Pr. LLC.

—San Francisco Baby: A Local Baby Book. Shea, Tess & Pohlen, Jerome. 2013. (Local Baby Bks.). (ENG.). 22p. (— 1). bds. 8.95 *(978-1-938093-16-6(X))* Duo Pr. LLC.
—100 Pablo Picassos. 2015. (ENG.). 32p. (J). (gr. k-5). 14.99 *(978-1-938093-32-6(1))* Duo Pr. LLC.
Lemay, Violet. Southern Baby. Lemay, Violet. 2015. (ENG.). 22p. (gr. k — 1). bds. 8.95 ***(978-1-938093-45-6(3)***, Duo Pr. Llc (US)) Duo Pr. LLC.
Lember, Barbara Hirsch, photos by. If You Find a Rock. Christian, Peggy. 2008. (ENG., 32p. (J). (gr. -1-3). pap. 6.99 *(978-0-15-206354-2(4))* Houghton Mifflin Harcourt Publishing Co.
Lemire, Jeff. Tales from the Farm. Lemire, Jeff. 2007. (Essex County Ser.). 19.85 *(978-1-4178-0691-1(5)*, Turtleback) Turtleback Bks.
Lemke, Horst. Around the World in Eighty Dishes. Van der Linde, Polly & Van der Linde, Tasha. 88p. (J). (gr. k-7). 12.95 *(978-0-87592-007-8(1))* Scroll Pr., Inc.
—Places & Faces. 32p. (J). (gr. -1). 14.95 *(978-0-87592-041-2(1))* Scroll Pr., Inc.
—Ride with Me Through ABC. Bond, Susan. 32p. (J). (gr. -1). 14.95 *(978-0-87592-043-6(8))* Scroll Pr., Inc.
Lemoine, Georges. Lullaby. Le Clézio, J. M. G. 2007. (FRE.). 72p. (J). (gr. 5-10). pap. *(978-2-07-061258-1(9))* Gallimard, Editions.
Lemus, Kristina. Catch me if you Can. Mau, Connie. l.t. ed. 2006. 28p. (J). 14.95 *(978-0-9778843-0-8(9))* Mau, C. Publishing Co.
Lenart, Claudia. Hansel & Gretel: A Fairy Tale with a down Syndrome Twist. Kats, Jewel. 2014. 37p. (J). *(978-1-61599-251-5(0))* Loving Healing Pr., Inc.
Lendway, Andy. From A to Zamboni, the Alphabet Hockey Style! Flyers Edition. Grocki, Jennifer. 2007. 32p. (J). 16.95 *(978-0-9793833-0-4(7))* Team Kidz, Inc.
Lenehan, Mary & Weber, Rich. Flight: First Vehicles. Mott, Professor. 8p. (J). (gr. -1-3). 14.99 *(978-1-890647-36-0(5))* TOMY International, Inc.
Leng, Qin. The Best Thing about Kindergarten. Lloyd, Jennifer. 2013. (ENG.). 36p. (J). (gr. -1-1). 16.95 *(978-1-897476-82-6(5))* Simply Read Bks. CAN. Dist: Ingram Pub. Services.
—A Flock of Shoes. Tsiang, Sarah. 2010. (ENG.). 32p. (J). (gr. -1-k). 19.95 *(978-1-55451-249-2(2)*, 9781554512492); pap. 8.95 *(978-1-55451-248-5(4)*, 9781554512485) Annick Pr., Ltd. CAN. Dist: Firefly Bks., Ltd.
—Kamik: An Inuit Puppy Story, 1 vol. Uluadluak, Donald. 2013. (ENG.). 32p. (J). (gr. 1-3). 10.95 *(978-1-927095-11-9(5))* Inhabit Media Inc. CAN. Dist: Independent Pubs. Group.
Leng, Qin. Kamik's First Sled, 1 vol. Sulurayok, Matilda. 2015. (ENG.). 32p. (J). (gr. k-2). 10.95 ***(978-1-77227-020-4(2))*** Inhabit Media Inc. CAN. Dist: Independent Pubs. Group.
Leng, Qin. Nala's Magical Mitsiaq: A Story of Inuit Adoption, 1 vol. Noah, Jennifer. 2013. (ENG.). 32p. (J). (gr. 1-3). 10.95 *(978-1-927095-26-3(3))* Inhabit Media Inc. CAN. Dist: Independent Pubs. Group.
Leng, Qin. Never Give Up: A Story about Self-Esteem, 1 vol. Cole, Kathryn. 2015. (I'm a Great Little Kid Ser.). (ENG.). 24p. (J). (gr. 1-3). 15.95 ***(978-1-927583-60-9(8))*** Second Story Pr. CAN. Dist: Orca Bk. Pubs. USA.
Leng, Qin. Not Just Another Princess Story. 2015. (ENG.). 62p. (J). 16.95 *(978-1-927018-57-6(9))* Simply Read Bks. CAN. Dist: Ingram Pub. Services.
—Piper Green & the Fairy Tree. Potter, Ellen. 2015. (Piper Green & the Fairy Tree Ser.). (ENG.). 112p. (J). (gr. 2-4). pap. 5.99 *(978-0-553-49926-1(2)*, Yearling) Random Hse. Children's Bks.
Leng, Qin. Piper Green & the Fairy Tree: Too Much Good Luck. Potter, Ellen. 2015. (Piper Green & the Fairy Tree Ser.). (ENG.). 128p. (J). (gr. 2-4). 14.99 ***(978-0-553-49927-8(0)***, Knopf Bks. for Young Readers) Random Hse. Children's Bks.
—Reptile Flu: A Story about Communication, 1 vol. Cole, Kathryn. 2015. (I'm a Great Little Kid Ser.). (ENG.). 24p. (J). (gr. 1-3). 15.95 ***(978-1-927583-61-6(6))*** Second Story Pr. CAN. Dist: Orca Bk. Pubs. USA.
Leng, Qin. Smudge's Mark. Lloyd, Jennifer & Osmond, Claudia. 2nd ed. 2015. (ENG.). 356p. (J). pap. 9.95 *(978-1-897476-78-9(7))* Simply Read Bks. CAN. Dist: Ingram Pub. Services.
—A Walk on the Tundra, 1 vol. Hainnu, Rebecca & Ziegler, Anna. 2011. (ENG.). 40p. (J). (gr. 1-3). 13.95 *(978-1-926569-43-7(1))* Inhabit Media Inc. CAN. Dist: Independent Pubs. Group.
Leng, Qin. A History of Just about Everything: 180 Events, People & Inventions That Changed the World. Leng, Qin. MacLeod, Elizabeth & Wishinsky, Frieda. 2013. (ENG.). 124p. (J). 21.95 *(978-1-55453-775-4(4))* Kids Can Pr., Ltd. CAN. Dist: Univ. of Toronto Pr.
Leng, Qin & Second Story Press Staff. Dear Baobab, 1 vol. Foggo, Cheryl. 2011. (ENG.). 24p. (J). (gr. 1-3). 15.95 *(978-1-897187-91-3(2))* Second Story Pr. CAN. Dist: Orca Bk. Pubs. USA.
Lenkiewicz, Isaac. Triassic Terrors. Crumpton, Nick. 2013. (ENG.). 32p. (J). (gr. k). pap. 13.95 *(978-1-909263-05-5(2))* Flying Eye Bks. GBR. Dist: Consortium Bk. Sales & Distribution.
Lenman, Jamie. Daring, Deadly, Brilliant, Brave: History's Toughest People. Turner, Tracey. 2012. 110p. (J). *(978-1-4351-4760-7(X))* Barnes & Noble, Inc.
Lenman, Jamie. Hard As Nails in Ancient Egypt. Turner, Tracey. 2015. (ENG.). 64p. (J). ***(978-0-7787-1511-5(6))*** Crabtree Publishing Co.
—Hard As Nails in Ancient Greece. Turner, Tracey. 2015. (ENG.). 64p. (J). ***(978-0-7787-1512-2(4))*** Crabtree Publishing Co.
—Hard As Nails in Ancient Rome. Turner, Tracey. 2015. (ENG.). 64p. (J). ***(978-0-7787-1513-9(2))*** Crabtree Publishing Co.
—Hard As Nails in Wars & Battles. Turner, Tracey. 2015. (ENG.). 64p. (J). pap. ***(978-0-7787-1526-9(4))*** Crabtree Publishing Co.
—Hard as Nails Warriors. Turner, Tracey. 2015. (ENG.). 64p. (J). pap. ***(978-0-7787-1517-7(5))*** Crabtree Publishing Co.
Lennhoff, Andrew. I Love You Every Minute. Stone, Amy Wingrove. 2006. pap. 18.00 *(978-0-8059-9119-2(0)*, RoseDog Bks.) Dorrance Publishing Co., Inc.
Lennicx, Michael. The Big Day at School. Fremont, Eleanor. 2003. (Little Bill Ser.). 24p. (J). (gr. -1-3). 11.65 *(978-1-4176-0109-7(4)*, Turtleback) Turtleback Bks.
Lenoir, Jane. Alaska: Be Brave, 4 vols. Sargent, Daina. l.t. ed. 2004. (Double Trouble Ser.: 4). 48p. (J). pap. 10.95 *(978-1-59381-121-1(7))*; lib. bdg. 23.60 *(978-1-59381-120-4(9))* Ozark Publishing.
—Arkansas: Dream Big. Sargent, Daina. l.t. ed. 2004. (Double Trouble Ser.). 48p. (J). pap. 10.95 *(978-1-59381-123-5(3))*; lib. bdg. *(978-1-59381-122-8(5))* Ozark Publishing.
—Baldy Eagle: Honor. Sargent, Dave. 2003. (Feather Tales Ser.: 1). 42p. (J). pap. 6.95 *(978-1-56763-720-5(5))* Ozark Publishing.
—Bashful: (Dusty Dun) Be Brave. Sargent, Dave & Sargent, Pat. 2003. (Saddle up Ser.: Vol. 1). 42p. (J). pap. 10.95 *(978-1-56763-684-0(5))*; lib. bdg. 23.60 *(978-1-56763-683-3(7))* Ozark Publishing.
—Berry Picking Time Vol. 3: (Apache) Be Brave, 20 vols. Sargent, Dave et al. l.t. ed. 2003. (Story Keeper Ser.: 3). 42p. (J). Vol. 3. lib. bdg. 23.60 *(978-1-56763-907-0(0)*, 1228136); vol. 3. pap. 6.95 *(978-1-56763-908-7(9)*, 1228136) Ozark Publishing.
—The Black Panther, 6 vols., Vol. 2. Sargent, Pat. 2003. (Barney the Bear Killer Ser.: Vol. 2). 137p. (J). pap. 10.95 *(978-1-56763-966-7(6))*; lib. bdg. 26.25 *(978-1-56763-965-0(8))* Ozark Publishing.
—Blackie Crow: Tell the Truth, 20 vols. Sargent, Dave. 2003. (Feather Tales Ser.: No. 2). 42p. (J). Vol. 2. lib. bdg. 20.95 *(978-1-56763-721-2(3))*; vol. 2. pap. 6.95 *(978-1-56763-722-9(1))* Ozark Publishing.
—Bo: (Linebacked Orange Dun) Be Happy, 30 vols., Vol. 4. Sargent, Dave & Sargent, Pat. 2003. (Saddle up Ser.: Vol. 4). 42p. (J). lib. bdg. 23.60 *(978-1-56763-685-7(3))*; mass mkt. 10.95 *(978-1-56763-686-4(1))* Ozark Publishing.
—Bob White: Use Good Judgement, 20 vols., Vol. 3. Sargent, David M. 2003. (Feather Tales Ser.: No. 3). 42p. (J). lib. bdg. 20.95 *(978-1-56763-723-6(X))* Ozark Publishing.
—Bob White: Use Good Judgement, 20 vols., Vol. 3. Sargent, Dave & Sargent, David M. 2003. (Feather Tales Ser.: No. 3). 42p. (J). pap. 10.95 *(978-1-56763-724-3(8))* Ozark Publishing.
—The Bobcat, 6 vols., Vol. 5. Sargent, Pat. 2003. (Barney the Bear Killer Ser.: Vol. 5). 136p. (J). pap. 10.95 *(978-1-56763-972-8(0))*; lib. bdg. 26.25 *(978-1-56763-971-1(2))* Ozark Publishing.
—Bogart Blue Jay: Be Thoughtful, 19, vol. 4. Sargent, Dave. 2003. (Feather Tales Ser.: 4). 42p. (J). pap. *(978-1-56763-726-7(4))* Ozark Publishing.
—Bogart Blue Jay: Be Thoughtful, 20 vols., Vol. 4. Sargent, Dave & Sargent, David M. 2nd ed. 2003. (Feather Tales Ser.: 3). 42p. (J). lib. bdg. 20.95 *(978-1-56763-725-0(6))* Ozark Publishing.
—Brandy: (Blue Roan) Beauty Is Inside, 30 vols., Vol. 5. Sargent, Dave & Sargent, Pat. 2003. (Saddle up Ser.: Vol. 5). 42p. (J). lib. bdg. 23.60 *(978-1-56763-799-1(X))*; mass mkt. 10.95 *(978-1-56763-800-4(7))* Ozark Publishing.
—The Bundle Keeper: (Pawnee) Be Responsible, 20 vols., Vol. 18. Sargent, Dave et al. l.t. ed. 2004. (Story Keeper Ser.: 18). 48p. (J). pap. 10.95 *(978-1-56763-938-4(0))* Ozark Publishing.
—Buttons: (Muddy Dun) Have Courage, Vol. 9. Sargent, Dave & Sargent, Pat. 2003. (Saddle up Ser.: Vol. 9). 42p. (J). pap. 10.95 *(978-1-56763-688-8(8))*; lib. bdg. 23.60 *(978-1-56763-687-1(X))* Ozark Publishing.
—Buzz Buzzard: Obey the Rules, 19 vols., Vol. 5. Sargent, Dave & Sargent, David M. 2003. (Feather Tales Ser.: 5). 42p. (J). pap. 10.95 *(978-1-56763-728-1(0))*; 2nd ed. lib. bdg. 20.95 *(978-1-56763-727-4(2))* Ozark Publishing.
—The Cheetah, 6 vols., Vol. 6. Sargent, Pat L. l.t. ed. 2004. (Barney the Bear Killer Ser.: No. 6). 146p. (YA). pap. 10.95 *(978-1-56763-974-2(7))* Ozark Publishing.
—Chick: (Chocolate Chestnut) Be Loyal, 30 vols., Vol. 16. Sargent, Dave & Sargent, Pat. 2003. (Saddle up Ser.: Vol. 16). 42p. (J). pap. 10.95 *(978-1-56763-678-9(0))*; lib. bdg. 23.60 *(978-1-56763-677-2(2))* Ozark Publishing.
—The Chuck Wagon: Don't Be Stubborn, 10 vols., Vol. 7. Sargent, Dave & Sargent, Pat. 2005. (Colorado Cowboys Ser.: 10). 32p. (J). pap. 10.95 *(978-1-59381-099-3(7))*; lib. bdg. 23.60 *(978-1-59381-098-6(9))* Ozark Publishing.
—Cindy Sparrow: Respect the Property of Others, 19 vols., Vol. 6. Sargent, Dave & Sargent, David M. 2003. (Feather Tales Ser.: 6). 42p. (J). pap. 10.95 *(978-1-56763-730-4(2))*; 2nd ed. lib. bdg. 20.95 *(978-1-56763-729-8(9))* Ozark Publishing.
—The Colorado Blizzard: Be Determined, 10 vols., Vol. 8. Sargent, Dave & Sargent, Pat. (Colorado Cowboys Ser.: 10). 32p. (J). 2005. pap. 10.95 *(978-1-59381-027-6(X))*; 2004. (gr. 3-8). lib. bdg. 23.60 *(978-1-59381-026-9(1))* Ozark Publishing.
—Colors & the Number 1, 11 vols. Sargent, Daina. (Learn to Read Ser.: 11). 24p. (J). 2005. pap. 10.95 *(978-1-59381-031-3(8))*; 2004. lib. bdg. 20.95 *(978-1-59381-030-6(X))* Ozark Publishing.
—Colors & the Number 10, 11 vols. Sargent, Daina. 2004. (Learn to Read Ser.: 11). 24p. (J). pap. 10.95 *(978-1-59381-049-6(0))*; per. 9.95 *(978-1-59381-527-1(1))*; lib. bdg. 20.95 *(978-1-59381-048-1(2))* Ozark Publishing.
—Colors & the Number 10/Los Colores y el Número 10, 11 vols. Sargent, Daina. 2005. (Learn to Read Ser.: 11). (ENG & SPA.). 24p. (J). pap. 10.95 *(978-1-59381-147-1(0))*; lib. bdg. 20.95 *(978-1-59381-146-4(2))* Ozark Publishing.
—Colors & the Number 1/Los Colores y el Número 1, 11 vols. Sargent, Daina. 2004. (Learn to Read Ser.: 11). (SPA & ENG.). 24p. (J). pap. 10.95 *(978-1-59381-129-7(2))* Ozark Publishing.
—Colors & the Number 2, 11 vols. Sargent, Daina. 2004. (Learn to Read Ser.: 11). 24p. (J). pap. 10.95 *(978-1-59381-033-7(4))*; per. 10.95 *(978-1-59381-529-5(8))*; lib. bdg. 20.95 *(978-1-59381-032-0(6))* Ozark Publishing.
—Colors & the Number 2/Los Colores y el Número 2, 11 vols. Sargent, Daina. 2004. (Learn to Read Ser.: 11).Tr. of Los colores y el Número 2. (SPA & ENG.). 24p. (J). pap. 10.95 *(978-1-59381-131-0(4))*; lib. bdg. 20.95 *(978-1-59381-130-3(6))* Ozark Publishing.
—Colors & the Number 3, 11 vols. Sargent, Daina. 2004. (Learn to Read Ser.: 11). 24p. (J). pap. 10.95 *(978-1-59381-035-1(0))*; pap. 10.95 *(978-1-59381-530-1(1))* Ozark Publishing.
—Colors & the Number 3/Los Colores y el Número 3, 11 vols. Sargent, Daina. 2004. (Learn to Read Ser.: 11).Tr. of Los colores y el el Número 3. (SPA & ENG.). 24p. (J). pap. 10.95 *(978-1-59381-133-4(0))*; lib. bdg. 20.95 *(978-1-59381-132-7(2))* Ozark Publishing.
—Colors & the Number 4, 11 vols. Sargent, Daina. (Learn to Read Ser.). 24p. (J). 2005. pap. 10.95 *(978-1-59381-037-5(7))*; 2004. per. 10.95 *(978-1-59381-531-8(X))* Ozark Publishing.
—Colors & the Number 4/Los colores y el Número 4, 11 vols. Sargent, Daina. 2004. (Learn to Read Ser.: 11).Tr. of Los colores y el Número 4. (SPA & ENG.). 24p. (J). pap. 10.95 *(978-1-59381-135-8(7))*; lib. bdg. 20.95 *(978-1-59381-134-1(9))* Ozark Publishing.
—Colors & the Number 5, 11 vols. Sargent, Daina. 2004. (Learn to Read Ser.: 11). 24p. (J). pap. 10.95 *(978-1-59381-039-9(3))*; per. 10.95 *(978-1-59381-532-5(8))* Ozark Publishing.
—Colors & the Number 5/Los colores y el Número 5, 11 vols. Sargent, Daina. 2004. (Learn to Read Ser.: 11).Tr. of Los colores y el Número 5. (SPA & ENG.). 24p. (J). pap. 10.95 *(978-1-59381-137-2(3))*; lib. bdg. 20.95 *(978-1-59381-136-5(5))* Ozark Publishing.
—Colors & the Number 6, 11 vols. Sargent, Daina. 2004. (Learn to Read Ser.: 11). 24p. (J). pap. 10.95 *(978-1-59381-041-2(5))*; per. 10.95 *(978-1-59381-533-2(6))*; lib. bdg. 20.95 *(978-1-59381-040-5(7))* Ozark Publishing.
—Colors & the Number 6/Los Colores y el Número 6, 11 vols. Sargent, Daina. 2005. (Learn to Read Ser.: 11). (ENG & SPA.). 24p. (J). pap. 10.95 *(978-1-59381-139-6(X))* Ozark Publishing.
—Colors & the Number 7, 11 vols. Sargent, Daina. 2004. (Learn to Read Ser.: 11). 24p. (J). pap. 10.95 *(978-1-59381-043-6(1))*; per. 10.95 *(978-1-59381-534-9(4))*; lib. bdg. 20.95 *(978-1-59381-042-9(3))* Ozark Publishing.
—Colors & the Number 7/Los Colores y el Número 7, 11 vols. Sargent, Daina. 2004. (Learn to Read Ser.: 11).Tr. of Los colores y el Número 7. (SPA & ENG.). 24p. (J). pap. 10.95 *(978-1-59381-141-9(1))*; lib. bdg. 20.95 *(978-1-59381-140-2(3))* Ozark Publishing.
—Colors & the Number 8, 11 vols. Sargent, Daina. 2004. (Learn to Read Ser.: 11). 24p. (J). pap. 10.95 *(978-1-59381-045-0(8))*; lib. bdg. 20.95 *(978-1-59381-044-3(X))* Ozark Publishing.
—Colors & the Number 8/Los Colores y el Número 8, 11 vols. Sargent, Daina. 2004. (Learn to Read Ser.: 11).Tr. of Los colores y el Número 8. (SPA & ENG.). 24p. (J). pap. 10.95 *(978-1-59381-143-3(8))*; lib. bdg. 20.95 *(978-1-59381-142-6(X))* Ozark Publishing.
—Colors & the Number 9, 11 vols. Sargent, Daina. 2004. (Learn to Read Ser.: 11). 24p. (J). pap. 10.95 *(978-1-59381-047-4(4))*; lib. bdg. 20.95 *(978-1-59381-046-7(6))* Ozark Publishing.
—Colors & the Number 9/Los Colores y el Número 9, 11 vols. Sargent, Daina. 2004. (Learn to Read Ser.: 11).Tr. of Los colores y el Número 9. (SPA & ENG.). 24p. (J). pap. 10.95 *(978-1-59381-145-7(4))*; lib. bdg. 20.95 *(978-1-59381-144-0(6))* Ozark Publishing.
—Counting Coup Vol. 4: (Cheyenee) Be Proud, 20 vols. Sargent, Dave et al. l.t. ed. 2003. (Story Keeper Ser.). 42p. (J). lib. bdg. 23.60 *(978-1-56763-909-4(7))* Ozark Publishing.
—Cricket: (Seal Brown) Do Your Best, 30. Sargent, Dave & Sargent, Pat. 2003. (Saddle up Ser.: Vol. 20). 42p. (J). 20. lib. bdg. 22.60 *(978-1-56763-649-9(7))*; Vol. 20. pap. 10.95 *(978-1-56763-650-5(0))* Ozark Publishing.
—Dinky Duck: Be Prompt, 19 vols., Vol. 7. Sargent, Dave & Sargent, David M., Jr. 2003. (Feather Tales Ser.: 7). 42p. (J). pap. 10.95 *(978-1-56763-732-8(9))*; 2nd ed. lib. bdg. 20.95 *(978-1-56763-731-1(0))* Ozark Publishing.
—The Drought: Have Faith, 10 vols., Vol. 9. Sargent, Dave & Sargent, Pat. 2005. (Colorado Cowboys Ser.: 10). 32p. (J). pap. 10.95 *(978-1-59381-103-7(9))*; lib. bdg. 23.60 *(978-1-59381-102-0(0))* Ozark Publishing.
—Duke: (Dappled Palomino) Good Behavior, 30 vols., Vol. 23. Sargent, Dave & Sargent, Pat. 2003. (Saddle up Ser.: Vol. 23). 42p. (J). pap. 10.95 *(978-1-56763-682-6(9))*; lib. bdg. 23.60 *(978-1-56763-681-9(0))* Ozark Publishing.
—Dusty: (Grey Sabino) Be Helpful, 30 vols., Vol. 24. Sargent, Dave & Sargent, Pat. 2003. (Saddle up Ser.: Vol. 24). 42p. (J). pap. 10.95 *(978-1-56763-808-0(2))*; lib. bdg. 23.60 *(978-1-56763-807-3(4))* Ozark Publishing.
—Fields of Golden Corn Vol. 6: (Navajo) Be Energetic, 20 vols. Sargent, Dave et al. l.t. ed. 2003. (Story Keeper Ser.: 6). 42p. (J). pap. 10.95 *(978-1-56763-914-8(3))*; lib. bdg. 23.60 *(978-1-56763-913-1(5))* Ozark Publishing.
—Fierce Warriors Vol. 7: (Comanche) Learn Skills, 20 vols. Sargent, Dave et al. l.t. ed. 2004. (Story Keeper Ser.: 7). 48p. (J). pap. 10.95 *(978-1-56763-916-2(X))* Ozark Publishing.
—The Fire: A Second Chance, 10 vols., Vol. 10. Sargent, Dave & Sargent, Pat. 2005. (Colorado Cowboys Ser.: 10). 32p. (J). pap. 10.95 *(978-1-59381-105-1(5))* Ozark Publishing.
—Freckles: (Flea-bitten Grey) Be Proud of Old Glory, 30 vols., Vol. 26. Sargent, Dave & Sargent, Pat. 2003. (Saddle up Ser.: Vol. 26). 42p. (J). pap. 10.95 *(978-1-56763-810-3(4))*; lib. bdg. 23.60 *(978-1-56763-809-7(0))* Ozark Publishing.
—Ginger: (Lilac Roan) Be Likeable, 30 vols., Vol. 27. Sargent, Dave & Sargent, Pat. 2003. (Saddle up Ser.: Vol. 27). 42p. (J). pap. 10.95 *(978-1-56763-812-7(0))*; lib. bdg. 23.60 *(978-1-56763-811-0(2))* Ozark Publishing.
—Glenda Goose: Sharing, 19 vols., Vol. 8. Sargent, Dave & Sargent, David M., Jr. 2003. (Feather Tales Ser.: 8). 42p. (J). pap. 10.95 *(978-1-56763-734-2(5))*; 2nd ed. lib. bdg. 20.95 *(978-1-56763-733-5(7))* Ozark Publishing.
—Goober: (Silver Dapple) Appreciate Others, 30 vols., Vol. 29. Sargent, Dave & Sargent, Pat. 2003. (Saddle up Ser.: Vol. 29). 42p. (J). lib. bdg. 23.60 *(978-1-56763-689-5(6))* Ozark Publishing.
—Goober: (Sliver Dapple) Appreciate Others, 30 vols., Vol. 29. Sargent, Dave & Sargent, Pat. 2004. (Saddle up Ser.: Vol. 29). 42p. (J). pap. 10.95 *(978-1-56763-690-1(X))* Ozark Publishing.
—Grady: (Dappled Grey) Proud to Be an American, 30 vols., Vol. 30. Sargent, Dave & Sargent, Pat. 2003. (Saddle up Ser.: Vol. 30). 42p. (J). lib. bdg. 23.60 *(978-1-56763-813-4(9))* Ozark Publishing.
—Grady: Proud to Be an American, 30 vols. Sargent, Dave & Sargent, Pat. 2003. (Saddle up Ser.: Vol. 30). 42p. (J). pap. 10.95 *(978-1-56763-814-1(7))* Ozark Publishing.
—The Grizzly, 6 vols., Vol. 1. Sargent, Pat L. 2004. (Barney the Bear Killer Ser.: No. 1). 129p. (YA). pap. 10.95 *(978-1-56763-964-3(X))* Ozark Publishing.
—Gus: (Slate Grullo) Be Thankful, 30 vols., Vol. 32. Sargent, Dave & Sargent, Pat. 2003. (Saddle up Ser.: Vol. 32). 42p. (J). lib. bdg. 23.60 *(978-1-56763-693-2(4))*; pap. 10.95 *(978-1-56763-694-9(2))* Ozark Publishing.
—A Hole in the Sun: (Choctaw) Be Independent, 20, Vol. 1. Sargent, Dave et al. l.t. ed. 2003. (Story Keeper Ser.: 1). 42p. (J). pap. 6.95 *(978-1-56763-904-9(6))*; lib. bdg. 23.60 *(978-1-56763-903-2(8))* Ozark Publishing.
—Hondo: (Silver Dun) Look for Good in Others, 30 vols., Vol. 34. Sargent, Dave & Sargent, Pat. 2003. (Saddle up Ser.: Vol. 34). 42p. (J). pap. 10.95 *(978-1-56763-802-8(3))*; lib. bdg. 23.60 *(978-1-56763-801-1(5))* Ozark Publishing.
—Hoot: (Grullo) Be Creative, 30. Sargent, Dave & Sargent, Pat. 2003. (Saddle up Ser.: Vol. 35). 42p. (J). 35. pap. 6.95 *(978-1-56763-696-3(9))*; Vol. 35. lib. bdg. 23.60 *(978-1-56763-695-6(0))* Ozark Publishing.
—Hoot Owl: Mind Your Mamma, 19 vols., Vol. 9. Sargent, Dave & Sargent, David, Jr. 2003. (Feather Tales Ser.: 9). 42p. (J). pap. 10.95 *(978-1-56763-736-6(1))* Ozark Publishing.
—Hoot Owl: Mind Your Mamma, 20 vols., Vol. 9. Sargent, Dave & Sargent, David M., Jr. 2nd ed. 2003. (Feather Tales Ser.: 9). 42p. (J). lib. bdg. *(978-1-56763-735-9(3))* Ozark Publishing.
—Hummer Hummingbird: Being Small Is Okay, 19. Sargent, Dave & Sargent, David, Jr. 2003. (Feather Tales Ser.: 10). (J). 10. 42p. pap. 6.95 *(978-1-56763-738-0(8))*; Vol. 10. 2nd ed. 24p. lib. bdg. 20.95 *(978-1-56763-737-3(X))* Ozark Publishing.
—Introduction to Colors & Niumbers, 11 vols. Sargent, Daina. 2005. (Learn to Read Ser.: 11). 24p. (J). pap. 10.95 *(978-1-59381-051-1(2))* Ozark Publishing.
—Introduction to Colors & Numbers, 11 vols. Sargent, Daina. (Learn to Read Ser.: 11). 24p. (J). 2005. per. 10.95 *(978-1-59381-528-8(X))*; 2004. lib. bdg. 20.95 *(978-1-59381-050-4(4))* Ozark Publishing.
—Introduction to Colors & Numbers (BL) Introduccion a los colores y a los Numeros, 11 vols. Sargent, Daina. 2004. (Learn to Read Ser.: 11). (SPA & ENG.). 24p. (J). lib. bdg. 20.95 *(978-1-59381-148-8(9))* Ozark Publishing.
—Introduction to Colors & Numbers/Introduccion a los Colores Numeros, 11 vols. Sargent, Daina. l.t. ed. 2005. (Learn to Read Ser.: 11). (SPA & ENG.). 24p. (J). pap. 10.95 *(978-1-59381-149-5(7))* Ozark Publishing.
—The Jaguar, 8 vols. Sargent, Pat L. 2007. (Barney the Bear Killer Ser.: 8). 164p. (YA). lib. bdg. 26.25 *(978-1-59381-424-3(0))* Ozark Publishing.
—Kansas: Conquer Fear. Sargent, Daina. l.t. ed. 2004. (Double Trouble Ser.). 48p. (J). pap. 10.95 *(978-1-59381-125-9(X))*; lib. bdg. 23.60 *(978-1-59381-124-2(1))* Ozark Publishing.
—Keeping Ghosts Away Vol. 8: (Creek) Be Respectful, 20 vols. Sargent, Dave et al. l.t. ed. 2003. (Story Keeper Ser.: Vol. 8). 42p. (J). pap. 10.95 *(978-1-56763-918-6(6)*, 1228135) Ozark Publishing.
—Kitty Hawk: Stealing, 20. Sargent, Dave & Sargent, David, Jr. 2003. (Feather Tales Ser.: 11). 42p. (J). 11. pap. 6.95 *(978-1-56763-740-3(X))*; Vol. 11. 2nd ed. lib. bdg. 20.95 *(978-1-56763-739-7(6))* Ozark Publishing.
—Knocking the Rice Vol. 9: (Chippewa) Be Powerful, 20 vols. Sargent, Dave et al. l.t. ed. 2003. (Story Keeper Ser.: 9). 42p. (J). pap. 10.95 *(978-1-56763-920-9(8))*; lib. bdg. 23.60 *(978-1-56763-919-3(4))* Ozark Publishing.
—Ladder at the Door Vol. 10: (Hopi) Be Curious, 20 vols. Sargent, Dave et al. l.t. ed. 2004. (Story Keeper Ser.: 10). 48p. (J). pap. 10.95 *(978-1-56763-922-3(4))*; lib. bdg. 23.60 *(978-1-56763-921-6(6))* Ozark Publishing.
—Land of the Sun Vol. 11: (Ute) Respect Elders, 20 vols., Vol. 11. Sargent, Dave et al. l.t. ed. 2004. (Story Keeper Ser.: 11). 48p. (J). lib. bdg. 23.60 *(978-1-56763-923-0(2))*; pap. 10.95 *(978-1-56763-924-7(0))* Ozark Publishing.
—Lily: (Lilac Dun) A Second Chance, 30 vols., Vol. 38. Sargent, Dave & Sargent, Pat. 2003. (Saddle up Ser.: Vol. 38). 42p. (J). pap. 10.95 *(978-1-56763-698-7(5))*; lib. bdg. 23.60 *(978-1-56763-697-0(7))* Ozark Publishing.
—Little One Vol. 12: (Cherokee) Be Inventive, 20 vols. Sargent, Dave et al. l.t. ed. 2003. (Story Keeper Ser.: Vol. 12). 42p. (J). pap. 10.95 *(978-1-56763-926-1(7))*; Vol. 12. lib. bdg. 23.60 *(978-1-56763-925-4(9))* Ozark Publishing.
—Mack: (Medicine Hat Paint) Be a Leader, 30 vols., Vol. 39. Sargent, Dave & Sargent, Pat. 2003. (Saddle up Ser.: Vol. 39). 42p. (J). pap. 10.95 *(978-1-56763-700-7(0))* Ozark Publishing.
—Missouri: Teamwork. Sargent, Daina. l.t. ed. 2004. (Double Trouble Ser.). 48p. (J). pap. 10.95 *(978-1-59381-127-3(6))*; lib. bdg. 23.60 *(978-1-59381-126-6(8))* Ozark Publishing.
—Nick: (Linebacked Claybank Dun) Crime Does Not Pay, 30 vols., Vol. 42. Sargent, Dave & Sargent, Pat. 2003. (Saddle up Ser.: Vol. 42). 42p. (J). pap. 10.95

L

(978-1-56763-702-1(7)); lib. bdg. 23.60 *(978-1-56763-701-4(9))* Ozark Publishing.

—Nubbin: (Linebacked Apricot Dun) Freedom, 30 vols., Vol. 43. Sargent, Dave & Sargent, Pat. 2003. (Saddle up Ser.: Vol. 43). 42p. (J). pap. 10.95 *(978-1-56763-704-5(3))*; lib. bdg. 23.60 *(978-1-56763-703-8(5))* Ozark Publishing.

—On the Banks of the Wallowa River: (Nez Perce) Use Your Talent, 20 vols., Vol. 13. Sargent, Dave et al. l.t. ed. 2004. (Story Keeper Ser.: 13). 48p. (J). pap. 10.95 *(978-1-56763-928-5(3))*; lib. bdg. 23.60 *(978-1-56763-927-8(5))* Ozark Publishing.

—Once upon a Totem Pole Vol. 14: (Haida) Be Creative, 20 vols. Sargent, Dave et al. l.t. ed. 2003. (Story Keeper Ser.: 14). 42p. (J). pap. 10.95 *(978-1-56763-930-8(5))*; Vol. 14. lib. bdg. 23.60 *(978-1-56763-929-2(1))* Ozark Publishing.

—Pammie Pigeon: Keep Your Cool, 19 vols., Vol. 12. Sargent, Dave & Sargent, David M., Jr. 2003. (Feather Tales Ser.: 12). 42p. (J). pap. 10.95 *(978-1-56763-742-7(6))*; 2nd ed. lib. bdg. 20.95 *(978-1-56763-741-0(8))* Ozark Publishing.

—Penny Penguin: Be Kind to Others, 20 vols., Vol. 13. Sargent, Dave & Sargent, David M., Jr. 2nd ed. 2003. (Feather Tales Ser.: 13). 42p. (J). lib. bdg. 20.95 *(978-1-56763-743-4(4))* Ozark Publishing.

—Pete: (Pink-skinned Palomino) Be a Hero, 30 vols., Vol. 46. Sargent, Dave & Sargent, Pat. 2003. (Saddle up Ser.: Vol. 46). 42p. (J). lib. bdg. 23.60 *(978-1-56763-707-6(8))* Ozark Publishing.

—Pete: Pink-skinned Palomino) Be a Hero, 30 vols., Vol. 46. Sargent, Dave & Sargent, Pat. 2003. (Saddle up Ser.: Vol. 46). 42p. (J). pap. 10.95 *(978-1-56763-708-3(6))* Ozark Publishing.

—Petie Pelican: Be Proud of Yourself, 19 vols., Vol. 14. Sargent, Dave & Sargent, David M., Jr. 2003. (Feather Tales Ser.: 14). 42p. (J). pap. 10.95 *(978-1-56763-746-5(9))* Ozark Publishing.

—Petie Pelican: Be Proud of Yourself, 20 vols., Vol. 14. Sargent, Dave & Sargent, David, Jr. 2nd ed. 2003. (Feather Tales Ser.: 14). 42p. (J). lib. bdg. 20.95 *(978-1-56763-745-8(0))* Ozark Publishing.

—Pinkie Flamingo: Leaving Home, 19 vols., Vol. 15. Sargent, Dave & Sargent, David, Jr. 2003. (Feather Tales Ser.: 15). 42p. (J). pap. 10.95 *(978-1-56763-748-9(5))*; 2nd ed. lib. bdg. 20.95 *(978-1-56763-747-2(7))* Ozark Publishing.

—Ranger: (Olive Grullo) Be Honest, 30 vols., Vol. 48. Sargent, Dave & Sargent, Pat. 2003. (Saddle up Ser.: Vol. 48). 42p. (J). pap. 10.95 *(978-1-56763-710-6(8))*; lib. bdg. 23.60 *(978-1-56763-709-0(4))* Ozark Publishing.

—Rascal: (Red Dun) Responsible Leadership, 30 vols., Vol. 49. Sargent, Dave & Sargent, Pat. 2003. (Saddle up Ser.: Vol. 49). 42p. (J). pap. 10.95 *(978-1-56763-712-0(4))* Ozark Publishing.

—Rays of the Sun Vol. 15: (shoshone) Learn Lessons, 20 vols. Sargent, Dave et al. l.t. ed. 2004. (Story Keeper Ser.: 15). 48p. (J). pap. 10.95 *(978-1-56763-932-2(1))* Ozark Publishing.

—Rays of the Sun Vol. 15: (Shoshone) Learn Lessons, 20 vols. Sargent, Dave et al. l.t. ed. 2004. (Story Keeper Ser.: 15). 48p. (J). lib. bdg. 23.60 *(978-1-56763-931-5(3))* Ozark Publishing.

—Rocky: (Blue-eyed Palomino) Be Free, 30 vols., Vol. 51. Sargent, Dave & Sargent, Pat. 2003. (Saddle up Ser.: Vol. 51). 42p. (J). lib. bdg. 23.60 *(978-1-56763-713-7(2))* Ozark Publishing.

—Rusty: (Red Roan) Be Strong & Brave, 30 vols., Vol. 52. Sargent, Dave & Sargent, Pat. 2003. (Saddle up Ser.: Vol. 52). 42p. (J). pap. 10.95 *(978-1-56763-804-2(X))*; lib. bdg. 23.60 *(978-1-56763-803-5(1))* Ozark Publishing.

—Sandy Sea Gull: Making Friends, 20 vols., Vol. 16. Sargent, Dave & Sargent, David, Jr. 2nd ed. 2003. (Feather Tales Ser.: 16). 42p. (J). lib. bdg. 20.95 *(978-1-56763-749-6(3))* Ozark Publishing.

—Sonny: (Linebacked Yellow Dun) Have Orderly Manners, 30 vols., Vol. 54. Sargent, Dave & Sargent, Pat. 2003. (Saddle up Ser.: Vol. 54). 42p. (J). lib. bdg. 23.60 *(978-1-56763-715-1(9))* Ozark Publishing.

—Sonny: (Linebacked Yllow Dun) Have Orderly Manners, 30 vols., Vol. 54. Sargent, Dave & Sargent, Pat. 2003. (Saddle up Ser.: Vol. 54). 42p. (J). pap. 10.95 *(978-1-56763-716-8(7))* Ozark Publishing.

—Speedy Roadrunner: Helping Others, 19 vols., Vol. 17. Sargent, Dave & Sargent, David M., Jr. 2003. (Feather Tales Ser.: 17). 42p. (J). pap. 10.95 *(978-1-56763-752-6(3))*; 2nd ed. lib. bdg. 20.95 *(978-1-56763-751-9(5))* Ozark Publishing.

—Storky Stork: Be Trustworthy, 19 vols., Vol. 18. Sargent, Dave. 2003. (Feather Tales Ser.: 18). 42p. (J). pap. 10.95 *(978-1-56763-754-0(X))* Ozark Publishing.

—Storky Stork: Be Trustworthy, 20 vols., Vol. 18. Sargent, Dave & Sargent, David, Jr. 2nd ed. 2003. (Feather Tales Ser.: 18). 42p. (J). lib. bdg. 20.95 *(978-1-56763-753-3(1))* Ozark Publishing.

—A Strand of Wampum Vol. 2: Be Honest, 20 vols. Sargent, Dave et al. l.t. ed. 2003. (Story Keeper Ser.: 2). 42p. (J). lib. bdg. 23.60 *(978-1-56763-905-6(4))* Ozark Publishing.

—Summer Milky Way: (Blackfeet) Be Compassionate, 20 vols., Vol. 16. Sargent, Dave et al. l.t. ed. 2004. (Story Keeper Ser.: 16). 48p. (J). lib. bdg. 23.60 *(978-1-56763-933-9(X))*; pap. 10.95 *(978-1-56763-934-6(8))* Ozark Publishing.

—Sweetpea: (Purple Corn Welsh) Be Happy, 30 vols., Vol. 58. Sargent, Dave & Sargent, Pat. 2003. (Saddle up Ser.: Vol. 58). 42p. (J). pap. 10.95 *(978-1-56763-816-5(3))*; lib. bdg. 23.60 *(978-1-56763-815-8(5))* Ozark Publishing.

—Tattoos of Honor Vol. 17: (Osage) Be Gentle & Giving, 20 vols. Sargent, Dave et al. l.t. ed. 2004. (Story Keeper Ser.: Vol. 17). 42p. (J). pap. 10.95 *(978-1-56763-936-0(4))*; lib. bdg. 23.60 *(978-1-56763-935-3(6))* Ozark Publishing.

—The Timber Wolf, 6 vols., Vol. 3. Sargent, Pat. 2003. (Barney the Bear Killer Ser.: Vol. 3). 123p. (J). pap. 10.95 *(978-1-56763-968-1(2))*; lib. bdg. 26.25 *(978-1-56763-967-4(4))* Ozark Publishing.

—Tin Wren: Be Nice, 19 vols., Vol. 19. Sargent, Dave & Sargent, David, Jr. 2003. (Feather Tales Ser.: No. 19). 42p. (J). pap. 10.95 *(978-1-56763-756-4(6))*; 2nd ed. lib. bdg. 20.95 *(978-1-56763-755-7(8))* Ozark Publishing.

—Tom Turkey: Don't Bully, 19. Sargent, Dave & Sargent, David, Jr. 2003. (Feather Tales Ser.: 20). 42p. (J). 20. pap. 6.95 *(978-1-56763-758-8(2))*; Vol. 20. 2nd ed. lib. bdg. 20.95 *(978-1-56763-757-1(4))* Ozark Publishing.

—Topper: Son of Barney, 8. Sargent, Pat L. 2007. (Barney the Bear Killer Ser.: 7). 147p. (YA). lib. bdg. 25.25 *(978-1-56763-425-9(7))* Ozark Publishing.

—Tornado & Sweep, Bk. II. Sargent, Dave. Bowen, Debbie, ed. Zapata, Miguel, tr. from ENG. (SPA.). (Orig.). (J). (gr. k-6). pap. 6.95 *(978-1-56763-123-4(1))*; pap. 6.95 *(978-1-56763-126-5(6))* Ozark Publishing.

—Truth, Power & Freedom Vol. 19: (Sioux) Show Respect, 20 vols., Vol. 19. Sargent, Dave et al. l.t. ed. 2004. (Story Keeper Ser.: 19). 42p. (J). pap. 10.95 *(978-1-56763-940-7(2))* Ozark Publishing.

—Valley Oak Acorns: (Maidu) Be Helpful, 20 vols., Vol. 20. Sargent, Dave & Sargent, Pat. l.t. ed. 2005. (Story Keeper Ser.: 20). 42p. (J). (gr. -1 — 1). lib. bdg. 23.60 *(978-1-56763-941-4(0))* Ozark Publishing.

—Valley Oaks Acorns Vol. 20: (Maidu) Be Helpful, 20 vols. Sargent, Dave et al. l.t. ed. 2004. (Story Keeper Ser.: 20). 48p. (J). pap. 10.95 *(978-1-56763-942-1(9))* Ozark Publishing.

—Whiskers: (Roan) Pride & Peace, 30 vols., Vol. 59. Sargent, Dave & Sargent, Pat. 2003. (Saddle up Ser.: Vol. 59). 42p. (J). pap. 10.95 *(978-1-56763-806-6(6))* Ozark Publishing.

—Zeb: (Zebra Dun) Be Prepared, 30 vols., Vol. 60. Sargent, Dave & Sargent, Pat. 2003. (Saddle up Ser.: Vol. 60). 42p. (J). pap. 10.95 *(978-1-56763-718-2(3))*; lib. bdg. 23.60 *(978-1-56763-717-5(5))* Ozark Publishing.

Lenoir, Sue. The Bundle Keeper: (Pawnee) Be Responsible, 20 vols., Vol. 18. Sargent, Dave et al. 2004. (Story Keeper Ser.: No. 18). 42p. (J). lib. bdg. 23.60 *(978-1-56763-937-7(2))* Ozark Publishing.

—A Strand of Wampum Vol. 2: Be Honest, 20 vols. Sargent, Dave et al. l.t. ed. 2003. (Story Keeper Ser.: 2). 42p. (J). pap. 10.95 *(978-1-56763-906-3(2))* Ozark Publishing.

Lenox, August. Roy Rogers' Bullet & Trigger: Wild Horse Roundup. Beecher, Elizabeth. 2011. 28p. pap. 35.95 *(978-1-258-03850-2(1))* Literary Licensing, LLC.

Lensch, Chris. Comportamiento Con Libros de la Biblioteca. Tourville, Amanda Doering. 2011. (¡Así Debemos Ser!: Buenos Modales, Buen Comportamiento/Way to Be!: Manners Ser.).Tr. of Manners with a Library Book. (ENG & MUL.). 24p. (gr. -1-2). lib. bdg. 25.99 *(978-1-4048-6694-2(9))* Picture Window Bks.

—Comportamiento y Modales en el Patio de Juegos. Finn, Carrie. 2011. (¡Así Debemos Ser!: Buenos Modales, Buen Comportamiento/Way to Be!: Manners Ser.).Tr. of Manners on the Playground. (ENG, SPA & MUL.). 24p. (gr. -1-2). lib. bdg. 25.99 *(978-1-4048-6699-7(X))* Picture Window Bks.

—Comportamiento y Modales en la Biblioteca. Finn, Carrie. 2011. (¡Así Debemos Ser!: Buenos Modales, Buen Comportamiento/Way to Be!: Manners Ser.).Tr. of Manners in the Library. (ENG, SPA & MUL.). 24p. (gr. -1-2). lib. bdg. 25.99 *(978-1-4048-6697-3(3))* Picture Window Bks.

—Comportamiento y Modales en la Cafetería. Tourville, Amanda Doering. 2011. (¡Así Debemos Ser!: Buenos Modales, Buen Comportamiento/Way to Be!: Manners Ser.).Tr. of Manners in the Lunchroom. (ENG, SPA & MUL.). 24p. (gr. -1-2). lib. bdg. 25.99 *(978-1-4048-6695-9(7))* Picture Window Bks.

—Coral Reef: Hide & Seek. 2005. (ENG.). 10p. (J). bds. 7.95 *(978-1-58117-362-8(8))*, Intervisual/Piggy Toes) Bendon, Inc.

—Good Manners: At Play, Home, & School, 1 vol. Finn, Carrie & Picture Window Books Staff. 2008. (Way to Be!: Manners Ser.). (ENG.). 96p. (gr. -1-2). pap. 12.95 *(978-1-4048-5093-4(7))*, Nonfiction Picture Bks.) Picture Window Bks.

—Manners at a Friend's House, 1 vol. Tourville, Amanda Doering. 2009. (Way to Be!: Manners Ser.). (ENG.). 24p. (gr. -1-2). pap. 7.95 *(978-1-4048-5306-5(5))*; lib. bdg. 25.99 *(978-1-4048-5305-8(7))* Picture Window Bks. (Nonfiction Picture Bks.).

—Manners at School, 1 vol. Finn, Carrie. (Way to Be!: Manners Ser.). 2010. (ENG.). 32p. 8.99 *(978-1-4048-6511-2(X))*; 2009. 24p. (gr. -1-2). pap. 0.63 *(978-1-4048-5991-3(8))*; 2009. 24p. (gr. -1-2). pap. 2.76 *(978-1-4048-6050-6(9))* Picture Window Bks. (Nonfiction Picture Bks.).

—Manners at School [Scholastic]. Finn, Carrie. 2010. (Way to Be!: Manners Ser.). 24p. pap. 0.55 *(978-1-4048-6584-6(5))*, Nonfiction Picture Bks.) Picture Window Bks.

—Manners at the Table. Finn, Carrie. (Way to Be!: Manners Ser.). 24p. (gr. -1-2). 2009. pap. 0.63 *(978-1-4048-5992-0(6))*; 2007. (ENG.). lib. bdg. 25.99 *(978-1-4048-3155-1(X))*; 2007. (ENG.). per. 7.95 *(978-1-4048-3553-5(9))* Picture Window Bks. (Nonfiction Picture Bks.).

—Manners in Public. Finn, Carrie. (Way to Be!: Manners Ser.). 24p. (gr. -1-2). 2009. pap. 0.63 *(978-1-4048-5993-7(4))*; 2007. (ENG.). per. 7.95 *(978-1-4048-3555-9(5))* Picture Window Bks. (Nonfiction Picture Bks.).

—Manners in the Library. Finn, Carrie. (Way to Be!: Manners Ser.). 24p. (gr. -1-2). 2009. pap. 0.63 *(978-1-4048-5994-4(2))*; 2007. (ENG.). lib. bdg. 25.99 *(978-1-4048-3152-0(5)*, 1265722); 2007. (ENG.). per. 7.95 *(978-1-4048-3557-3(1)*, 1265722) Picture Window Bks. (Nonfiction Picture Bks.).

—Manners in the Lunchroom. Doering Tourville, Amanda. 2009. (Way to Be!: Manners Ser.). 24p. (gr. -1-2). pap. 2.76 *(978-1-4048-6051-3(7))*; (ENG.). 25.99 *(978-1-4048-5308-9(1))* Picture Window Bks. (Nonfiction Picture Bks.).

—Manners on the Playground. Finn, Carrie. 2009. (Way to Be!: Manners Ser.). 24p. (gr. -1-2). pap. 0.63 *(978-1-4048-5995-1(0))*; pap. 2.76 *(978-1-4048-6053-7(3))* Picture Window Bks. (Nonfiction Picture Bks.).

—Manners on the Playground, 1 vol. Finn, Carrie & Picture Window Books Staff. 2007. (Way to Be!: Manners Ser.). (ENG.). 24p. (gr. -1-2). 25.99 *(978-1-4048-3154-4(1))*, Nonfiction Picture Bks.) Picture Window Bks.

—Manners on the Playground, 1 vol. Finn, Carrie. 2007. (Way to Be!: Manners Ser.). (ENG.). 24p. (gr. -1-2). per. 7.95 *(978-1-4048-3559-7(8))*, Nonfiction Picture Bks.) Picture Window Bks.

—Manners on the School Bus, 1 vol. Tourville, Amanda Doering. 2009. (Way to Be!: Manners Ser.). (ENG.). 24p. (gr. -1-2). lib. bdg. 25.99 *(978-1-4048-5311-9(1))*, Nonfiction Picture Bks.) Picture Window Bks.

—Manners on the School Bus, 1 vol. Doering Tourville, Amanda. 2009. (Way to Be!: Manners Ser.). 24p. (gr. -1-2). (ENG.). pap. 7.95 *(978-1-4048-5312-6(X))*; pap. 2.76 *(978-1-4048-6052-0(5))* Picture Window Bks. (Nonfiction Picture Bks.).

—Manners on the School Bus (Comportamiento y Modales en el Autobús Escolar) Tourville, Amanda Doering. 2011. (¡Así Debemos Ser!: Buenos Modales, Buen Comportamiento/Way to Be!: Manners Ser.). (ENG, SPA & MUL.). 24p. (gr. -1-2). lib. bdg. 25.99 *(978-1-4048-6696-6(5))* Picture Window Bks.

—Manners on the Telephone. Finn, Carrie. (Way to Be!: Manners Ser.). 24p. (gr. -1-2). 2009. pap. 0.63 *(978-1-4048-5996-8(9))*; 2007. (ENG.). per. 7.95 *(978-1-4048-3561-0(X))* Picture Window Bks. (Nonfiction Picture Bks.).

—Manners on the Telephone, 1 vol. Finn, Carrie et al. 2007. (Way to Be!: Manners Ser.). (ENG.). 24p. (gr. -1-2). 25.99 *(978-1-4048-3156-8(8))*, Nonfiction Picture Bks.) Picture Window Bks.

—Manners with a Library Book, 1 vol. Tourville, Amanda Doering. 2009. (Way to Be!: Manners Ser.). (ENG.). 24p. (gr. -1-2). lib. bdg. 25.99 *(978-1-4048-5314-0(6))*, Nonfiction Picture Bks.) Picture Window Bks.

—Manners with a Library Book, 1 vol. Doering Tourville, Amanda. 2009. (Way to Be!: Manners Ser.). (ENG.). 24p. (gr. -1-2). pap. 7.95 *(978-1-4048-5315-7(4))*, Nonfiction Picture Bks.) Picture Window Bks.

—Who's Hiding Inside? Dinosaurs. Perez, Jessica. 2005. (Who's Hiding Inside Ser.). 12p. (J). bds. 7.95 *(978-1-58117-246-1(X))*, Intervisual/Piggy Toes) Bendon, Inc.

Lenski, Lois. Betsy-Tacy. Lovelace, Maud Hart. 60th anniv. ed. 2007. (Betsy-Tacy Ser.: 1). (ENG.). 144p. (J). (gr. 2-5). pap. 5.99 *(978-0-06-440096-1(4))* HarperCollins Pubs.

—A Letter to Popsey: A Story Parade Picture Book. La Rue, Mabel Guinnip. 2011. 28p. pap. 35.95 *(978-1-258-06342-9(5))* Literary Licensing, LLC.

Lenski, Lois. Cowboy Small. Lenski, Lois. 2006. (Lois Lenski Bks.). (ENG.). 32p. (J). (gr. k — 1). bds. 6.99 *(978-0-375-83570-4(9))*, Random Hse. Bks. for Young Readers) Random Hse. Children's Bks.

—The Little Airplane. Lenski, Lois. 2003. (Lois Lenski Bks.). (ENG.). 56p. (J). (gr. -1-k). reprint ed. 11.95 *(978-0-375-81079-4(X))*, Random Hse. Bks. for Young Readers) Random Hse. Children's Bks.

—Policeman Small. Lenski, Lois. 2006. (Lois Lenski Bks.). (ENG.). 32p. (J). (— 1). bds. 6.99 *(978-0-375-83569-8(5))*, Random Hse. Bks. for Young Readers) Random Hse. Children's Bks.

—Strawberry Girl. Lenski, Lois. Lenski. 60th anniv. ed. 2005. (ENG.). 208p. (J). (gr. 5-18). pap. 6.99 *(978-0-06-440585-0(0))* HarperCollins Pubs.

Lent, Blair. Tikki Tikki Tembo. Mosel, Arlene. 2008. (gr. k-2). 16.95 *(978-0-7569-8457-1(2))* Perfection Learning Corp.

—Tikki Tikki Tembo. Mosel, Arlene. 2007. (ENG.). 48p. (J). (gr. -1-3). 6.95 *(978-0-312-36748-0(1))* Square Fish.

—Tikki Tikki Tembo Book & CD Storytime Set. Mosel, Arlene. unabr. ed. 2012. (ENG.). (J). 12.99 *(978-1-4272-3211-3(3))* Macmillan Audio.

Lenton, Steven. Cosmic. Boyce, Frank Cottrell. unabr. ed. 2008. (ENG.). 320p. (J). (gr. 10-13). 23.95 *(978-1-4050-5464-5(6))*, Macmillan) Pan Macmillan GBR. Dist: Trans-Atlantic Pubns., Inc.

—Framed. Boyce, Frank Cottrell. unabr. ed. 2006. (ENG.). 320p. pap. 15.95 *(978-0-330-43425-6(X))* Macmillan Pubs., Ltd. GBR. Dist: Trans-Atlantic Pubns., Inc.

—Framed, 1. Boyce, Frank Cottrell. 2nd ed. 2008. (ENG.). 336p. 17.95 *(978-0-330-45292-2(4))*, Macmillan) Pan Macmillan GBR. Dist: Trans-Atlantic Pubns., Inc.

—Millions, 6. Boyce, Frank Cottrell & Boyce, Frank Cottrell. 2nd unabr. ed. 2008. (ENG.). 272p. 15.95 *(978-0-330-45084-3(0))*, Macmillan) Pan Macmillan GBR. Dist: Trans-Atlantic Pubns., Inc.

—Shifty Mcgifty & Slippery Sam. Corderoy, Tracey. 2013. (ENG.). 32p. (J). (gr. -1-3). 14.99 *(978-0-7636-6838-9(9))*, Nosy Crow) Candlewick Pr.

—Teddy Bear, Teddy Bear: And Other Favorite Nursery Rhymes. 2013. (ENG.). 22p. (gr. -1). bds. 8.95 *(978-1-58925-601-9(8))* Tiger Tales.

Lentz, Bob. The Attack on Pearl Harbor, 1 vol. Sutcliffe, Jane. 2006. (Disasters in History Ser.). (ENG.). 32p. (gr. 3-4). 29.99 *(978-0-7368-5477-1(0))*, Graphic Library) Capstone Pr., Inc.

—Book-O-Beards. Lemke, Donald. 2015. (Wearable Bks.). (ENG.). 12p. (gr. -1-1). bds. 7.99 *(978-1-62370-183-3(X))*, Wear-A-Book) Capstone Young Readers.

—Book-O-Hats. Lemke, Donald. 2015. (Wearable Bks.). (ENG.). 12p. (gr. -1-1). bds. 7.99 *(978-1-62370-184-0(8))*, Wear-A-Book) Capstone Young Readers.

—Book-O-Masks. Lemke, Donald. 2015. (Wearable Bks.). (ENG.). 12p. (gr. -1-1). bds. 7.99 *(978-1-62370-185-7(6))*, Wear-A-Book) Capstone Young Readers.

—Book-O-Teeth. Lemke, Donald B. 2015. (Wearable Bks.). (ENG.). 12p. (gr. -1-1). bds. 7.99 *(978-1-62370-186-4(4))*, Wear-A-Book) Capstone Young Readers.

—Gorillas, 1 vol. Welvaert, Scott R. 2005. (World of Mammals Ser.). (ENG.). 24p. (gr. 2-3). 23.32 *(978-0-7368-3718-7(3))*, Bridgestone Bks.) Capstone Pr., Inc.

—How to Draw Disgusting Aliens, 1 vol. Sautter, Aaron. 2007. (Drawing Cool Stuff Ser.). (ENG.). 32p. (gr. 3-4). 27.32 *(978-1-4296-0075-0(6))*, Edge Bks.) Capstone Pr., Inc.

Lentz, Bob, et al. Jackie Robinson: Baseball's Great Pioneer, 1 vol. Glaser, Jason. 2005. (Graphic Biographies Ser.). (ENG.). 32p. (gr. 3-4). 29.99 *(978-0-7368-4633-2(6))*, Graphic Library) Capstone Pr., Inc.

Lentz, Bob. Jackie Robinson: Gran Pionero del Béisbol. Glaser, Jason. 2006. (Biografías Gráficas Ser.). (ENG & SPA.). 32p. (gr. 3-4). 29.99 *(978-0-7368-6602-6(7))* Capstone Pr., Inc.

—Lions, 1 vol. Welvaert, Scott R. 2005. (World of Mammals Ser.). (ENG.). 24p. (gr. 2-3). 23.32 *(978-0-7368-3720-0(5))*, Bridgestone Bks.) Capstone Pr., Inc.

Lenz, Mary. Remember the Love. Jue, Thea. 2013. 36p. pap. 13.95 *(978-0-9827753-3-2(4))* Interdimensional Pr.

LEO, Inc Staff. Aldebaran Vol. 1, 3 vols., Vol. 1. LEO, Inc Staff. Leo. 2008. (ENG.). 104p. pap. 19.95 *(978-1-905460-57-1(0))* CineBook GBR. Dist: National Bk. Network.

Leo, Veronica. The Three Silver Coins: A Story from Tibet. Leo, Veronica, retold by. 2nd ed. 2011. (ENG.). 32p. (J). (gr. -1-3). pap. 14.95 *(978-1-55939-372-0(6))*, Snow Lion Publications, Inc.) Shambhala Pubns., Inc.

Leon, Gabriela. El Juego de Pelota Mixteca. Del Angel, Varinia. rev. ed. 2006. (Otra Escalera Ser.). (SPA & ENG.). 24p. (J). (gr. 2-4). pap. 9.95 *(978-968-5920-66-7(4))* Castillo, Ediciones, S. A. de C. V. MEX. Dist: Macmillan.

Leon, John Paul, jt. illus. see Jeanty, Georges.

Leon, Karen. As the Crow Flies. Higgins, Kitty. ed. 2004. (Reader's Theater Ser.). (J). pap. *(978-1-4108-2304-5(0)*, A23040) Benchmark Education Co.

—Battle for the Ballot. Howard, Annabelle. ed. 2004. (Reader's Theater Ser.). (J). pap. *(978-1-4108-2305-2(9)*, A23059) Benchmark Education Co.

—The Big Cheese. Howard, Annabelle. ed. 2004. (Reader's Theater Ser.). (J). pap. *(978-1-4108-2294-9(X)*, A2294X) Benchmark Education Co.

—The Corps of Discovery. Flounders, Anne. ed. 2004. (Reader's Theater Ser.). (J). pap. *(978-1-4108-2310-6(5)*, A23105) Benchmark Education Co.

—The Fifth Grade Votes. Kramer, Alan & Kramer, Candice. ed. 2004. (Reader's Theater Ser.). (J). pap. *(978-1-4108-2307-6(5)*, A23075) Benchmark Education Co.

—Jackie Robinson: Breaking Baseball's Barriers. Kramer, Alan. ed. 2004. (Reader's Theater Ser.). (J). pap. *(978-1-4108-2301-4(6)*, A23016) Benchmark Education Co.

—Lost City of the Inca. Meissner, David. ed. 2004. (Reader's Theater Ser.). (J). pap. *(978-1-4108-2308-3(3)*, A23083) Benchmark Education Co.

—Our New Home. Wall, Suzy. ed. 2004. (Reader's Theater Ser.). (J). pap. *(978-1-4108-2299-4(0)*, A22990) Benchmark Education Co.

—Why Coyote Stopped Imitating His Friends. Kramer, Candice. ed. 2004. (Reader's Theater Ser.). (J). pap. *(978-1-4108-2302-1(4)*, A23024) Benchmark Education Co.

Leon, Loni & Huston, Kyle. Can you Imagine..., 1. Leon, Loni. 2006. 49p. (J). 21.95 *(978-0-9728556-0-0(2))* Sullivan, Kelley Enterprises.

Leonard, Barbara & Holm, Sharon. All New Crafts for Halloween. Ross, Kathy. 2003. (All New Holiday Crafts for Kids Ser.). (ENG.). 48p. (gr. k-3). pap. 7.95 *(978-0-7613-1577-3(2))*, Millbrook Pr.) Lerner Publishing Group.

Leonard, Barry. Alphabet Connections: English-Spanish: 26 Picture Cards. Leonard, Barry, ed. 2004. 26p. (J). (gr. k-4). reprint ed. *(978-0-7567-7825-5(5))* DIANE Publishing Co.

Leonard, David. Daddy's Home! Parry, Rosanne. 2009. (ENG.). 20p. (J). bds. 6.99 *(978-0-8249-1823-1(1))*, Candy Cane Pr.) Ideals Pubns.

—The Extreme Team: Skateboard Moves. Christopher, Matt. 2013. (Passport to Reading Level 3 Ser.: 1). (ENG.). 32p. (J). (gr. 1-4). 3.99 *(978-0-316-25230-0(1))* Little, Brown Bks. for Young Readers.

—How to Clean Your Room. Spinelli, Eileen. 2009. (ENG.). 20p. (J). (gr. k-3). 18.99 *(978-0-8249-5551-9(X))*, Ideals Children's Bks.) Ideals Pubns.

—Today on Election Day. Stier, Catherine. 2012. (ENG.). 32p. (J). (gr. 1-4). 16.99 *(978-0-8075-8008-0(2))* Whitman, Albert & Co.

Leonard, Erskine. Prison to Palace. Pozdol, MaryBeth. 2004. 189p. (J). ring bd. 29.95 *(978-1-889723-43-3(6))* Family Harvest Church.

Leonard, Herb, jt. illus. see Leonhard, Herb.

Leonard, Kaycee. Chee Choo's Adventures, 1 vol. Bassler, Joni. 2007. (ENG.). 33p. 24.95 *(978-1-4241-8773-7(7))* America Star Bks.

Leonard, Michael. Bluegrass Breeze. Rhema, Dan. 2004. (J). per. 19.95 *(978-0-9729835-1-8(1))* Mesquite Tress Pr., LLC.

—One Tiny Twig, 1. Rhema, Dan. 2003. 32p. (J). per. 19.95 *(978-0-9729835-0-1(3))* Mesquite Tress Pr., LLC.

Leonard, Terry. Let's Get Going! The Step-by-Step Guide to Successful Outings with Children, 1 vol. Weisner, Candace. 2003. (ENG.). 172p. (J). pap. 9.95 *(978-0-88995-193-8(4))* Red Deer Pr. CAN. Dist: Ingram Pub. Services.

Leonard, Tom, et al. Extraordinary Migrations. Cooper, Sharon Katz. 2015. (Extraordinary Migrations Ser.). (ENG.). 24p. (gr. 2-3). lib. bdg. 103.96 *(978-1-4795-6247-3(5))* Picture Window Bks.

Leonard, Tom. Here Is Antarctica. Dunphy, Madeleine. 2008. (Web of Life Ser.). (ENG.). 32p. (J). (gr. -1-3). 16.95 *(978-0-9777539-4-9(8))* Web of Life Children's Bks.

—Here Is the African Savanna. Dunphy, Madeleine. 2006. (Web of Life Ser.). (ENG.). 32p. (J). (gr. -1-3). 16.95 *(978-0-9773795-3-8(1))*; pap. 9.95 *(978-0-9773795-2-1(3))* Web of Life Children's Bks.

—Here Is the Coral Reef. Dunphy, Madeleine. 2006. (Web of Life Ser.). (ENG.). 32p. (J). (gr. -1-3). 16.95 *(978-0-9773795-5-2(8))*; pap. 9.95 *(978-0-9773795-4-5(X))* Web of Life Children's Bks.

—One Small Place by the Sea. Brenner, Barbara. 2004. (One Small Place Ser.). (ENG.). 32p. (J). (gr. k-3). 16.99 *(978-0-688-17182-7(6))* HarperCollins Pubs.
—One Small Place in a Tree. Brenner, Barbara. 2004. (ENG.). 32p. (J). (gr. k-3). 17.99 *(978-0-688-17180-3(X))* HarperCollins Pubs.
Leonard, Tom. When Penguins Cross the Ice: The Emperor Penguin Migration. Cooper, Sharon Katz. 2015. (Extraordinary Migrations Ser.). (ENG.). 24p. (gr. 2-3). pap. 8.95 ***(978-1-4795-6102-5(9))*** Picture Window Bks.
Leonard, Tom. When Penguins Cross the Ice: The Emperor Penguin Migration. Cooper, Sharon Katz. 2015. (Extraordinary Migrations Ser.). (ENG.). 24p. (gr. 2-3). lib. bdg. 25.99 *(978-1-4795-6078-3(2))* Picture Window Bks.
—When Whales Cross the Sea: The Gray Whale Migration. Cooper, Sharon Katz. 2015. (Extraordinary Migrations Ser.). (ENG.). 24p. (gr. 2-3). lib. bdg. 25.99 *(978-1-4795-6079-0(0))* Picture Window Bks.
—Who Will Plant a Tree? Pallotta, Jerry. 2010. (ENG.). 32p. (J). (gr. -1-2). 15.95 *(978-1-58536-502-9(5))* Sleeping Bear Pr.
Leonard, Tom, jt. illus. see Daly, Catherine.
Leonardi, Rick. Darth Vader & the Lost Command: Vol 2. Blackman, Haden. 2012. (Star Wars: Darth Vader & the Lost Command Ser.). 24p. (J). 24.21 *(978-1-59961-981-1(4)*, Graphic Novels) Spotlight.
—Darth Vader & the Lost Command: Vol 3. Blackman, Haden. 2012. (Star Wars: Darth Vader & the Lost Command Ser.). 24p. (J). 24.21 *(978-1-59961-982-8(2)*, Graphic Novels) Spotlight.
—Darth Vader & the Lost Command: Vol 4. Blackman, Haden. 2012. (Star Wars: Darth Vader & the Lost Command Ser.). 24p. (J). 24.21 *(978-1-59961-983-5(0)*, Graphic Novels) Spotlight.
—Darth Vader & the Lost Command: Vol 5. Blackman, Haden. 2012. (Star Wars: Darth Vader & the Lost Command Ser.). 24p. (J). 24.21 *(978-1-59961-984-2(9)*, Graphic Novels) Spotlight.
Leonardi, Rick, et al. Spider-Man Bk. 1: The Complete Alien Costume Saga. Defalco, Tom. 2014. (ENG.). 488p. (J). (gr. 4-17). pap. 44.99 *(978-0-7851-8867-4(3))* Marvel Worldwide, Inc.
Leone, Jason. the Enchantress of Caratunk. Manna, Elizabeth, photos by. 2003. 30p. (J). (gr. 1-5). pap. 9.95 *(978-0-9729807-0-8(9))* Murray, David M.
Leone, Sergio. Peggy Finds the Theater. Hughes, Virginia. 2011. 186p. 42.95 *(978-1-258-10513-6(6))* Literary Licensing, LLC.
Leong, Sonia. Romeo & Juliet. Shakespeare, William & Appignanesi, Richard. 2007. (ENG.). 208p. (J). (gr. 2-8). pap. 12.95 *(978-0-8109-9325-9(2)*, Abrams Bks. for Young Readers) Abrams.
Leonhard, Herb. Billy's Mountain. Richardson, Steve. 2007. 52p. 14.95 *(978-0-9786422-0-4(1))* Impossible Dreams Publishing Co.
—The Faerie Garden Coloring Book. 2004. 24p. (J). 3.50 *(978-0-9763555-0-2(7))* Prancing Pony, The.
—I Know a Librarian Who Chewed on a Word, 1 vol. Knowlton, Laurie. 2012. (ENG.). 32p. (J). (gr. k-3). 16.99 *(978-1-58980-892-8(4))* Pelican Publishing Co., Inc.
—Kendall & Kyleah. Hill, Janet Muirhead. 2012. (J). pap. 13.00 *(978-1-937849-05-4(8))* Raven Publishing Inc. of Montana.
—Kendall's Storm. Hill, Janet Muirhead. 2011. (J). pap. 12.00 *(978-0-9820893-0-9(9))* Raven Publishing Inc. of Montana.
—Kyleah's Tree. Hill, Janet Muirhead. 2011. (J). pap. 12.00 *(978-0-9827377-9-8(3))* Raven Publishing Inc. of Montana.
—Matthew's Box. Reish, Kathleen. 2005. 48p. (J). 21.95 *(978-0-9762664-0-2(7)*, 3000) KBR Mutt's Pubns.
—The Quest Begins: Magic Bag Trilogy Book One. Watts, James. 2011. 410p. (YA). 24.95 *(978-1-936824-04-5(3))* Etcetera Pr. LLC.
—The Runaway Beignet. Morgan, Connie & Morgan, Connie Collins. 2014. (J). *(978-1-4556-1912-2(4))* Pelican Publishing Co., Inc.
—A Southern Child's Garden of Verses, 1 vol. Davis, David. 2010. (ENG.). 40p. (J). (gr. k-k). 17.99 *(978-1-58980-764-8(2))* Pelican Publishing Co., Inc.
—Southern Mother Goose, 1 vol. Davis, David. 2013. (ENG.). 40p. (J). (gr. k-4). 17.99 *(978-1-4556-1760-9(1))* Pelican Publishing Co., Inc.
—St. Patrick & the Three Brave Mice, 1 vol. Stengel, Joyce A. 2009. (ENG.). 32p. (J). (gr. k-3). 16.99 *(978-1-58980-663-4(8))* Pelican Publishing Co., Inc.
—Way Out West on My Little Pony, 1 vol. Peck, Jan. 2010. (ENG.). 32p. (J). (gr. k-3). 16.99 *(978-1-58980-697-9(2))* Pelican Publishing Co., Inc.
Leonhard, Herb. Sir Norman & the Dreaming Dragon. Leonhard, Herb. 2008. (ENG.). 32p. (J). 17.95 *(978-0-9763555-1-9(5))* Prancing Pony, The.
Leonhard, Herb & Leonard, Herb. Leonardo's Monster, 1 vol. Sutcliffe, Jane. 2010. (ENG.). 32p. (J). (gr. k-3). 16.99 *(978-1-58980-838-6(X))* Pelican Publishing Co., Inc.
Leoni, Nancy. Toby Goes to Camp, 1 vol. Leoni, Nancy. 2009. 21p. pap. 24.95 *(978-1-61546-417-3(4))* America Star Bks.
Leonidou, Niki. The Boat to Lullaby Bay. Poulter, J. R. 2014. 38p. (J). pap. 20.99 *(978-1-62994-921-5(3))* Tate Publishing & Enterprises, LLC.
—Dang, It's the Dragons. Poulter, J. R. 2014. 34p. (J). pap. 19.99 *(978-1-62994-920-8(5))* Tate Publishing & Enterprises, LLC.
Lepage, Catherine. Respect: A Girl's Guide to Getting Respect & Dealing When Your Line Is Crossed. Macavinta, Courtney & Pluym, Andrea Vander. 2005. (ENG.). 240p. (YA). (gr. 8-12). pap. 16.99 *(978-1-57542-177-3(1))* Free Spirit Publishing, Inc.
Leplar, Anna. All the Gold in the World. Leeson, Robert. 2004. (ENG.). 96p. 8.95 *(978-0-7136-4059-5(6)*, A & C Black) Bloomsbury Publishing Plc GBR. Dist: Consortium Bk. Sales & Distribution.
—The Wind in the Willows. Grahame, Kenneth. 256p. (J). *(978-1-4054-3774-5(X))* Parragon, Inc.
Leplar, Anna C. Noah's Ark. Adams, Georgie. 2014. (Early Reader Ser.). (ENG.). 64p. (J). (gr. k-2). pap. 7.99 *(978-1-4440-0789-3(0)*, Orion Children's Bks.) Hachette Children's Group GBR. Dist: Independent Pubs. Group.
LePlatt, Betsy. Mosquito, 1 vol. Kroll, Virginia. 2011. (ENG.). 32p. (J). (gr. k-3). 16.99 *(978-1-58980-883-6(5))* Pelican Publishing Co., Inc.
L'Eplattenier, Michelle. It's Okay to Talk to God. Neuls, Lillian. 2008. 12p. pap. 24.95 *(978-1-60703-855-9(2))* America Star Bks.
Lepley, Kathy. Frozen in Motion: Alaska's Glaciers. Hocker, Katherine M. Brubaker, Jill, ed. 2006. 54p. (J). spiral bd. 8.95 *(978-0-930931-76-6(9))* Alaska Geographic Assn.
Lepp, Kevin. Saving the Liberty Bell. Figley, Marty Rhodes. 2005. (On My Own History Ser.). (ENG.). 48p. (gr. 2-4). pap. 6.95 *(978-1-57505-696-8(8))* Lerner Publishing Group.
Lepp, Kevin. Saving the Liberty Bell. Lepp, Kevin, tr. Figley, Marty Rhodes. 2004. (On My Own History Ser.). (ENG.). 48p. (gr. 2-4). 25.26 *(978-1-57505-589-3(9))* Lerner Publishing Group.
Lepp, Royden. Barnabas Helps a Friend, 1 vol. Lepp, Royden. 2008. (I Can Read! / Barnabas Ser.). (ENG.). 32p. (J). (gr. -1-1). pap. 3.99 *(978-0-310-71585-6(7))* Zondervan.
—Happy Birthday Barnabas, 1 vol. Lepp, Royden. 2008. (I Can Read! / Barnabas Ser.). (ENG.). 32p. (J). (gr. -1-1). pap. 3.99 *(978-0-310-71586-3(5))* Zondervan.
Lepretre, Jean-Marc. Monster Machines! on the Farm. Vandewiele, Agnes. 2013. (Monster Machines! Ser.). (ENG.). 18p. (J). (gr. -1-1). bds. 12.99 *(978-1-4022-9247-7(3)*, Sourcebooks Jabberwocky) Sourcebooks, Inc.
Lepri, Nancy. A Lesson My Cat Taught Me. Weber, Saul. 2010. (ENG.). 38p. pap. 6.95 *(978-1-4528-1088-1(5))* CreateSpace Independent Publishing Platform.
Lerangis, Peter. The Colossus Rises, No. 1. Lerangis, Peter. 2012. (Seven Wonders Ser.). (ENG.). 112p. (J). (gr. 3-7). 2.99 *(978-0-06-223889-4(2))* HarperCollins Pubs.
Leray, Marjolaine. Little Red Hood. Leray, Marjolaine. Ardizzone, Sarah. Ardizzone, Sarah, tr. from FRE. 2013. (ENG.). 40p. (J). (gr. -1). 12.99 *(978-1-907912-00-9(2))* Phoenix Yard Bks. GBR. Dist: Independent Pubs. Group.
Lerch, Steffie. The Surprise Doll. Gipson, Morrell. 2005. 46p. (J). (gr. -1-2). reprint ed. 15.00 *(978-1-930900-18-9(X))* Purple Hse. Pr.
Lerot-Calvo, Florence. I'm Learning Japanese! A Language Adventure for Young People. Galan, Christian. 2010. (ENG & JPN.). 128p. (J). 19.95 *(978-4-8053-1074-8(X))* Tuttle Publishing.
Lervold, Erik. The Dung Beetle Bandits, 1 vol. Reynolds, Aaron. 2007. (Tiger Moth Ser.). (ENG.). 40p. (gr. 1-3). lib. bdg. 22.65 *(978-1-59889-317-5(3)*, Graphic Sparks) Stone Arch Bks.
—The Dung Beetle Bandits: Tiger Moth. Reynolds, Aaron. 2007. (Graphic Sparks Ser.). (ENG.). 40p. (gr. 1-3). pap. 5.95 *(978-1-59889-412-7(9)*, Graphic Sparks) Stone Arch Bks.
—The Fortune Cookies of Weevil, 1 vol. Reynolds, Aaron. 2007. (Tiger Moth Ser.). (ENG.). 40p. (gr. 1-3). lib. bdg. 22.65 *(978-1-59889-318-2(1)*, Graphic Sparks) Stone Arch Bks.
—The Fortune Cookies of Weevil: Tiger Moth. Reynolds, Aaron. 2007. (Graphic Sparks Ser.). (ENG.). 40p. (gr. 1-3). pap. 5.95 *(978-1-59889-413-4(7)*, Graphic Sparks) Stone Arch Bks.
—Insect Ninja: Tiger Moth. Reynolds, Aaron. 2006. (Graphic Sparks Ser.). (ENG.). 40p. (gr. 1-3). per. 5.95 *(978-1-59889-228-4(2)*, Graphic Sparks) Stone Arch Bks.
—Kung Pow Chicken: Tiger Moth. Reynolds, Aaron. 2008. (Graphic Sparks Ser.). (ENG.). 40p. (gr. 1-3). pap. 5.95 *(978-1-4342-0505-6(3)*, Graphic Sparks) Stone Arch Bks.
—The Pest Show on Earth, 1 vol. Reynolds, Aaron. 2008. (Tiger Moth Ser.). (ENG.). 40p. (gr. 1-3). lib. bdg. 22.65 *(978-1-4342-0454-7(5)*, Graphic Sparks) Stone Arch Bks.
—The Pest Show on Earth: Tiger Moth, 1 vol. Reynolds, Aaron. 2008. (Graphic Sparks Ser.). (ENG.). 40p. (gr. 1-3). per. 5.95 *(978-1-4342-0504-9(5)*, Graphic Sparks) Stone Arch Bks.
—Tiger Moth: Adventures of an Insect Ninja, 1 vol. Reynolds, Aaron. 2011. (Tiger Moth Ser.). (ENG.). 128p. (gr. 2-5). pap. 7.95 *(978-1-4342-3032-4(5)*, Graphic Sparks) Stone Arch Bks.
—Tiger Moth & the Dragon Kite Contest, 1 vol. Reynolds, Aaron. 2006. (Tiger Moth Ser.). (ENG.). 40p. (gr. 1-3). lib. bdg. 22.65 *(978-1-59889-056-3(5))*; per. 5.95 *(978-1-59889-229-1(0))* Stone Arch Bks. (Graphic Sparks).
Leschnikoff, Nancy. What's Happening to Me? (Girls Edition) Meredith, Susan. 2006. 48p. (J). pap. 6.99 *(978-0-7945-1267-5(4)*, Usborne) EDC Publishing.
Leslie, M. A. Tristen & the Magic Shop. Leslie, M. A. 2011. (ENG.). 184p. pap. 8.99 *(978-1-4610-0779-1(8))* CreateSpace Independent Publishing Platform.
Leslie, Melissa. Joey Discovers Astronomy. Ferraro, Lynn. 2005. (ENG.). 23p. per. 12.99 *(978-1-4134-9624-6(5))* Xlibris Corp.
—Joey's Day of Discovery. Ferraro, Lynn. 2005. (ENG.). 21p. per. 12.99 *(978-1-4134-9622-2(9))* Xlibris Corp.
Lesnick, Tina. Dragonfly Flight. Nettrour, Nelani. l.t. ed. 2003. 62p. (J). pap. 11.94 *(978-1-932657-02-9(9))* Third Millennium Pubns.
Lesnie, Phil. Once a Shepherd. Millard, Glenda. 2014. (ENG.). 32p. (J). (gr. -1-3). 16.99 *(978-0-7636-7458-8(3))* Candlewick Pr.
Less, Sally. Isaac the Frog. Irvin, Christine. 2004. 14p. (J). 7.95 *(978-0-9706654-9-2(0))* Sprite Pr.
Lessac, Frané. The Book Boat's In. Cotten, Cynthia. 2013. (ENG.). 32p. (J). 16.95 *(978-0-8234-2521-1(5))* Holiday Hse., Inc.
—Capital! Washington D. C. from A to Z. Melmed, Laura Krauss. 2006. (ENG.). 48p. (J). (gr. 1-6). 6.99 *(978-0-06-113614-6(X)*, Collins) HarperCollins Pubs.
—Clouds. Rockwell, Anne F. 2008. (Let's-Read-And-Find-Out Science 1 Ser.). (ENG.). 40p. (J). (gr. -1-1). pap. 5.99 *(978-0-06-445220-5(4)*, Collins) HarperCollins Pubs.
—The Day of the Elephant. Wilson, Barbara K. 32p. 2007. pap. *(978-0-207-20059-5(9))*; 2005. *(978-0-207-20055-7(6))* HarperCollins Pubs. Australia.
—The Donkey of Gallipoli: A True Story of Courage in World War I. Greenwood, Mark. 2008. (ENG.). 32p. (J). (gr. 1-4). 16.99 *(978-0-7636-3913-6(3))* Candlewick Pr.
—The Greatest Liar on Earth. Greenwood, Mark. 2012. (ENG.). 32p. (J). (gr. 2-5). 16.99 *(978-0-7636-6155-7(4))* Candlewick Pr.
—The Mayflower. Greenwood, Mark. 2014. (ENG.). 32p. (J). (gr. -1-3). 16.95 *(978-0-8234-2943-1(1))* Holiday Hse., Inc.
—Midnight. Greenwood, Mark. 2015. (ENG.). 32p. (J). (gr. k-4). 16.99 *(978-0-7636-7466-3(4))* Candlewick Pr.
—New York, New York! The Big Apple from A to Z. Melmed, Laura Krauss. 2008. (ENG.). 48p. (J). (gr. 1-6). pap. 6.99 *(978-0-06-054877-3(0)*, Collins) HarperCollins Pubs.
—New York, New York City: The Big Apple from A to Z. Melmed, Laura Krauss. 2005. (ENG.). 48p. (J). (gr. 1-6). 16.99 *(978-0-06-054874-2(6))* HarperCollins Pubs.
—The Turtle & the Island: A Folk Tale from Papua New Guinea. Quarto Generic Staff. 2012. (ENG.). 32p. (J). (gr. -1-2). pap. 8.99 *(978-1-84780-386-3(5)*, Frances Lincoln) Quarto Publishing Group UK GBR. Dist: Hachette Bk. Group.
—Wonderful Towers of Watts. Zelver, Patricia. 2005. (ENG.). 32p. (J). (gr. k-5). pap. 10.95 *(978-1-59078-255-2(0))* Boyds Mills Pr.
Lessac, Frané. Island Counting 1 2 3. Lessac, Frané. 2007. (ENG.). 24p. (J). (— 1). bds. 6.99 *(978-0-7636-3518-3(9))* Candlewick Pr.
Lester, Alison. Bibs & Boots. Lester, Alison. 2009. (ENG.). 16p. (J). (gr. k — 1). bds. 7.99 *(978-1-74175-508-4(5))* Allen & Unwin AUS. Dist: Independent Pubs. Group.
—Happy & Sad. Lester, Alison. 2009. (ENG.). 16p. (J). (gr. k — 1). bds. 7.99 *(978-1-74175-509-1(3))* Allen & Unwin AUS. Dist: Independent Pubs. Group.
—Magic Beach. Lester, Alison. 2006. (ENG.). 32p. (J). (gr. -1-k). pap. 11.99 *(978-1-74114-488-8(4))* Allen & Unwin AUS. Dist: Independent Pubs. Group.
—Noni the Pony. Lester, Alison. 2012. (ENG.). 32p. (J). (gr. -1-k). 15.99 *(978-1-4424-5959-5(X)*, Beach Lane Bks.) Beach Lane Bks.
Lester, Alison. Noni the Pony Goes to the Beach. Lester, Alison. 2015. (ENG.). 32p. (J). (gr. -1-3). 17.99 ***(978-1-4814-4625-9(8)***, Beach Lane Bks.) Beach Lane Bks.
Lester, Helen & Munsinger, Lynn. Happy Birdday, Tacky! Lester, Helen & Munsinger, Lynn. 2013. (Tacky the Penguin Ser.). (ENG.). 32p. (J). (gr. -1-3). 16.99 *(978-0-547-91228-8(5))* Houghton Mifflin Harcourt Publishing Co.
Lester, Mike. The Butt Book. Bennett, Artie. 2009. (ENG.). 32p. (J). (gr. k-2). 17.99 *(978-1-59990-311-8(3)*, Bloomsbury USA Childrens) Bloomsbury USA.
—Funny Bugs. Rothman, Cynthia Anne. l.t. ed. 2005. (Little Books & Big Bks.: Vol. 4). 8p. (gr. k-2). 23.00 net. *(978-0-8215-7513-0(9))* Sadlier, William H. Inc.
—Las Sombras. Calvert, Deanna. 2005. (Rookie Reader Español Ser.). (SPA & ESP.). 23p. (J). (gr. k-2). per. 4.95 *(978-0-516-24697-0(6)*, Children's Pr.) Scholastic Library Publishing.
—The Really Rotten Princess. Snodgrass, Lady Cecily. 2012. (Ready-To-Reads Ser.). (ENG.). 32p. (J). (gr. k-2). 15.99 *(978-1-4424-3326-7(4))*; pap. 3.99 *(978-1-4424-3325-0(6))* Simon Spotlight. (Simon Spotlight).
—The Really Rotten Princess & the Cupcake Catastrophe. Snodgrass, Lady Cecily. 2013. (Ready-To-Reads Ser.). (ENG.). 32p. (J). (gr. k-2). 16.99 *(978-1-4424-8974-5(X))*; pap. 3.99 *(978-1-4424-8973-8(1))* Simon Spotlight. (Simon Spotlight).
—Shadows. Calvert, Deanna. 2004. (Rookie Readers Ser.). 23p. (J). 12.60 *(978-0-7569-4333-2(7))* Perfection Learning Corp.
—Las Sombras: Shadows. Calvert, Deanna. 2005. (Rookie Reader Español Ser.). (SPA.). 24p. (gr. k-2). 19.50 *(978-0-516-24448-8(5)*, Children's Pr.) Scholastic Library Publishing.
—When Charlie McButton Lost Power. Collins, Suzanne. (ENG.). 32p. (J). (gr. -1-3). 2007. pap. 5.99 *(978-0-14-240857-5(3)*, Puffin); 2005. 16.99 *(978-0-399-24000-3(4)*, Putnam Juvenile) Penguin Publishing Group.
—When Charlie McButton Lost Power. Collins, Suzanne. 2009. 32p. 16.00 *(978-1-60686-529-3(3))* Perfection Learning Corp.
Lester, Roseanna. Sheldon Zab the Crab. Kucej, Kristine. 2009. 24p. pap. 11.49 *(978-1-4389-6204-7(5))* AuthorHouse.
—The Story of Rocco on Satterwhite Ridge: Spring Surprises. Thomas, Amy T. 2009. 16p. pap. 8.49 *(978-1-4389-3142-5(5))* AuthorHouse.
Lesynski, Loris. Cabbagehead. Lesynski, Loris. 2003. (ENG.). 32p. (J). (gr. k-3). 18.95 *(978-1-55037-805-4(8)*, 9781550378054); pap. 6.95 *(978-1-55037-804-7(X)*, 9781550378047) Annick Pr., Ltd. CAN. Dist: Firefly Bks., Ltd.
—Gatomagico. Lesynski, Loris. Canetti, Yanitzia, tr. from ENG. 2004. (SPA.). 32p. (J). (gr. -1-2). pap. 5.95 *(978-1-55037-874-0(0)*, 9781550378740) Annick Pr., Ltd. CAN. Dist: Firefly Bks., Ltd.
—Zigzag: Zoems for Zindergarten. Lesynski, Loris. 2004. (ENG.). 32p. (J). (gr. -1-1). pap. 10.95 *(978-1-55037-882-5(1)*, 9781550378825) Annick Pr., Ltd. CAN. Dist: Firefly Bks., Ltd.
Leszek, Cedryll. Harold the Owl Who Couldn't Sleep. Leadbetter, Lesley. 2012. 30p. (J). pap. *(978-1-921869-89-1(5)*, Digital Publishing Centre) Interactive Pubns. Pty, Ltd.
Lethcoe, Jason. You Wish. 2007. 215p. (J). *(978-1-4287-1806-7(0)*, Grosset & Dunlap) Penguin Publishing Group.
Lethcoe, Jason. Amazing Adventures from Zoom's Academy. Lethcoe, Jason. 2005. (ENG.). 160p. (J). (gr. 4-7). pap. 12.95 *(978-0-345-48355-3(3)*, Ballantine Bks.) Random House Publishing Group.
—The Capture of the Crimson Cape. Lethcoe, Jason. 2006. (Amazing Adventures from Zoom's Academy Ser.). (ENG.). 144p. (J). (gr. 4-7). pap. 12.95 *(978-0-345-48356-0(1)*, Ballantine Bks.) Random House Publishing Group.
LeTourneau, Anthony & Carlson, Josh. A Child's ABCs of Praise. Wiens, Patti. Spieler, Leah, ed. 2004. 60p. (J). pap. 14.99 *(978-0-9761408-0-1(2))* Creative Marketing Concepts, Inc.
LeTourneau, Anthony Alex. The Good Fun! Book: 12 Months of Parties That Celebrate Service. Duncan, Karen & Issa, Kate Hannigan. 2010. 64p. (J). (gr. 2-6). 15.95 *(978-0-9792918-5-2(2))* Blue Marlin Pubns.
—Hanni & Beth: Safe & Sound. 2007. (J). (gr. k-3). 17.95 *(978-0-9792918-0-7(1))* Blue Marlin Pubns.
—In the Shadow of the Mammoth. Clark, Patricia Nikolina. (J). 2005. 14.99 *(978-0-9674602-8-4(X))*; 2003. 190p. pap. 6.99 *(978-0-9674602-4-6(7))* Blue Marlin Pubns.
—Johnny Joins the Army. Beyers, Andrea. 2008. (Flower Kingdom Ser.: Vol. 2). 40p. (J). 16.95 *(978-0-9800754-1-0(6))* RockTuff.
LeTourneau, Anthony Alex, jt. illus. see Bone, Thomas H.
LeTourneau, Marie. Is a Worry Worrying You? Wolff, Ferida & Savitz, Harriet May. 2005. (ENG.). 32p. (J). (gr. -1-3). 15.95 *(978-0-9749303-2-9(6))*; per. 7.95 *(978-1-933718-05-7(6))* Tanglewood Pr.
—The Tiptoe Guide to Tracking Mermaids. Paquette, Ammi-Joan. 2012. (ENG.). 32p. (J). (gr. -1-3). 16.95 *(978-1-933718-59-0(5))* Tanglewood Pr.
LeTourneau, Marie. The Mice of Bistrot des Sept Frères. LeTourneau, Marie. Baty, Danielle Reed. 2006. (ENG.). 32p. (J). (gr. -1-3). 15.95 *(978-0-9749303-6-7(9))* Tanglewood Pr.
Letria, André. A Donkey Reads, 1 vol. 2011. (ENG.). 32p. (J). (gr. k-3). 16.95 *(978-1-59572-255-3(6))*; pap. 6.95 *(978-1-59572-256-0(4))* Star Bright Bks., Inc.
—If I Were a Book. Letria, José Jorge. 2014. (ENG.). 64p. 12.95 *(978-1-4521-2144-4(3))* Chronicle Bks. LLC.
Letria, André. Run Pumpkin, Run. Mejuto, Eva. 2007. (ENG.). 36p. (J). 17.95 *(978-84-96788-88-6(1))* OQO, Editora ESP. Dist: Baker & Taylor Bks.
Let's Draw Studio Staff. Four's a Crowd. Chanda, J-P. ed. 2005. (Teenage Mutant Ninja Turtles Ser.: No. 7). 24p. lib. bdg. 15.00 *(978-1-59054-834-5(9))* Fitzgerald Bks.
Leue, Mary. The Hermit's Handbook. Leue, Mary, photos by. Barry, Jack. Leue, Mary, ed. 2004. (Philaterra Ser.). 208p. pap. 12.95 *(978-1-878115-14-0(6))* Down-To-Earth-Bks.
Leung, Andrew. The Royal Waker-Upper. Masters, Elaine. 2003. (ENG.). 39p. (J). *(978-0-89610-992-6(5))* Island Heritage Publishing.
Leung, Hilary. The Legend of Ninja Cowboy Bear. Bruins, David. 2009. (Ninja Cowboy Bear Ser.). (ENG.). 32p. (J). (gr. -1-2). 16.95 *(978-1-55453-486-9(0))* Kids Can Pr., Ltd. CAN. Dist: Univ. of Toronto Pr.
—Ninja Cowboy Bear Presents the Way of the Ninja. Bruins, David. 2010. (Ninja Cowboy Bear Ser.). (ENG.). 32p. (J). (gr. -1-2). 16.95 *(978-1-55453-615-3(4))* Kids Can Pr., Ltd. CAN. Dist: Univ. of Toronto Pr.
—The Pirate Girl's Treasure. Leung, Peyton. 2012. (ENG.). 32p. (J). 16.95 *(978-1-55453-660-3(X))* Kids Can Pr., Ltd. CAN. Dist: Univ. of Toronto Pr.
Leung, Raymond. African Wildlife Nature Activity Book. Kavanagh, James. 2nd ed. 2011. (Nature Activity Book Ser.). (ENG.). 32p. (J). (gr. 4-7). 6.95 *(978-1-58355-574-3(9))* Waterford Pr., Inc.
—Arctic Wildlife Nature Activity Book. Kavanagh, James. 2nd ed. 2011. (Nature Activity Book Ser.). (ENG.). 32p. (J). (gr. 4-7). 6.95 *(978-1-58355-575-0(7))* Waterford Pr., Inc.
—Australian Wildlife. Kavanagh, James. 2nd ed. 2011. (Nature Activity Book Ser.). (ENG.). 32p. (J). (gr. 4-7). act. bk. ed. 6.95 *(978-1-58355-576-7(5))* Waterford Pr., Inc.
—Birds Nature Activity Book. Kavanagh, James. 2nd ed. 2011. (Nature Activity Book Ser.). (ENG.). 32p. (J). (gr. 4-7). 6.95 *(978-1-58355-577-4(3))* Waterford Pr., Inc.
—Dinosaurs Nature Activity Book. Kavanagh, James. 2nd ed. 2011. (Nature Activity Book Ser.). (ENG.). 32p. (J). (gr. 4-7). 6.95 *(978-1-58355-578-1(1))* Waterford Pr., Inc.
—Ducks Nature Activity Book. Kavanagh, James. 2nd ed. 2011. (Nature Activity Book Ser.). (ENG.). 32p. (J). (gr. 4-7). 6.95 *(978-1-58355-579-8(X))* Waterford Pr., Inc.
—Freshwater Fishing: A Waterproof Folding Guide to What a Novice Needs to Know. Kavanagh, James. 2010. (Duraguide Ser.). (ENG.). 1p. 6.95 *(978-1-58355-535-4(8))* Waterford Pr., Inc.
—Grasslands Wildlife: A Folding Pocket Guide to Familiar Species Found in Prairie Grasslands. Kavanagh, James. 2010. (Pocket Naturalist Guide Ser.). (ENG.). 1p. 6.95 *(978-1-58355-510-1(2))* Waterford Pr., Inc.
—Great Lakes Wildlife Nature Activity Book. Kavanagh, James. 2nd ed. 2011. (Nature Activity Book Ser.). (ENG.). 32p. (J). (gr. 4-7). 6.95 *(978-1-58355-580-4(3))* Waterford Pr., Inc.
—Hawaii Trees & Wildflowers: A Folding Pocket Guide to Familiar Species. Kavanagh, James. 2010. (Pocket Naturalist Guide Ser.). (ENG.). 1p. 6.95 *(978-1-58355-509-5(9))* Waterford Pr., Inc.
—Mammals Nature Activity Book. Kavanagh, James. 2nd ed. 2011. (Nature Activity Book Ser.). (ENG.). 32p. (J). (gr. 4-7). 6.95 *(978-1-58355-581-1(1))* Waterford Pr., Inc.
—My First Arctic Nature. Kavanagh, James. 2011. (Nature Activity Book Ser.). (ENG.). 32p. (J). (gr. 2-4). act. bk. ed. 6.95 *(978-1-58355-586-6(2))* Waterford Pr., Inc.
—My First Deserts Nature. Kavanagh, James. 2011. (Nature Activity Book Ser.). (ENG.). 32p. (J). (gr. 2-4). act. bk. ed. 6.95 *(978-1-58355-587-3(0))* Waterford Pr., Inc.
—My First Forests Nature. Kavanagh, James. 2011. (Nature Activity Book Ser.). (ENG.). 32p. (J). (gr. 2-4). act. bk. ed. 6.95 *(978-1-58355-588-0(9))* Waterford Pr., Inc.
—My First Grasslands Nature. Kavanagh, James. 2011. (Nature Activity Book Ser.). (ENG.). 32p. (J). (gr. 2-4). act. bk. ed. 6.95 *(978-1-58355-589-7(7))* Waterford Pr., Inc.

L

—My First Seashores Nature. Kavanagh, James. 2011. (Nature Activity Book Ser.). (ENG.). 32p. (J). (gr. 2-4). act. bk. ed. 6.95 *(978-1-58355-590-3(0))* Waterford Pr., Inc.

—My First Wetlands Nature. Kavanagh, James. 2011. (Nature Activity Book Ser.). (ENG.). 32p. (J). (gr. 2-4). act. bk. ed. 6.95 *(978-1-58355-591-0(9))* Waterford Pr., Inc.

—Pond Life Nature Activity Book. Kavanagh, James. 2nd ed. 2011. (Nature Activity Book Ser.). (ENG.). 32p. (J). (gr. 4-7). 6.95 *(978-1-58355-582-8(X))* Waterford Pr., Inc.

—Seashore Wildlife. Kavanagh, James. 2nd ed. 2011. (Nature Activity Book Ser.). (ENG.). 32p. (J). (gr. 4-7). act. bk. ed. 6.95 *(978-1-58355-584-2(6))* Waterford Pr., Inc.

—Southwest Desert Wildlife Nature. Kavanagh, James. 2nd ed. 2011. (Nature Activity Book Ser.). (ENG.). 32p. (J). (gr. 4-7). act. bk. ed. 6.95 *(978-1-58355-585-9(4))* Waterford Pr., Inc.

Leutwiler, Anita. Excuse Me, Is This India? Ravishankar, Anushka. 2003. 24p. (J). 14.95 *(978-81-86211-56-4(X))* Tara Publishing IND. Dist: Consortium Bk. Sales & Distribution.

LeVert, Mireille. Down at the Sea Hotel: A Greg Brown Song. Brown, Greg. 2007. (ENG.). 36p. (J). (gr. -1-2). 16.95 *(978-2-923163-34-5(6))* La Montagne Secrete CAN. Dist: Independent Pubs. Group.

Levert, Mireille. Tina & the Penguin. Dyer, Heather. 2004. (ENG.). 32p. (J). (gr. k-3). pap. 5.95 *(978-1-55337-767-2(2))* Kids Can Pr., Ltd. CAN. Dist: Univ. of Toronto Pr.

Levesque, Haude. If You Were Raised by a Dinosaur. Brooklyn, Isabella. 2013. (ENG.). 80p. (J). (gr. 2-5). pap. 9.95 *(978-1-62354-015-9(1),* Imagine Publishing) Charlesbridge Publishing, Inc.

LeVesque, Sherry, jt. photos by see Cavanaugh, Wendy.

Levin, Freddie. ABC Art Riddles. Murray, Carol. 2005. (ABC Riddles Ser.). 32p. (J). (gr. -1-3). 13.95 *(978-0-939217-58-8(9))* Peel Productions, Inc.

—ABC Math Riddles. Martin, Jannelle. 2003. (ABC Riddles Ser.). 32p. (J). 13.95 *(978-0-939217-57-1(0))* Peel Productions, Inc.

Levin, Freddie. 1-2-3 Draw Baby Animals. Levin, Freddie. Gordon, Freddie. 2006. (ENG.). 64p. (J). pap. 8.99 *(978-0-939217-45-8(7))* Peel Productions, Inc.

—1-2-3 Draw Horses. Levin, Freddie. 2004. (1-2-3 Draw Ser.). (ENG.). 64p. (J). pap. 8.99 *(978-0-939217-61-8(9))* Peel Productions, Inc.

Levin, Freddie. 1-2-3 Draw Mythical Creatures: A Step-by-Step Guide. Levin, Freddie. 2014. Orig. Title: 2003. 64p. (J). pap. ***(978-0-939217-06-9(6))*** Peel Productions, Inc.

Levin, Kate, jt. illus. see Glasser, Robin Preiss.

Levin, Lon. I'm Going to Read (Level 4) The Small Potatoes Club. 2007. (I'm Going to Read Ser.). 48p. (J). pap. 3.95 *(978-1-4027-3085-6(3))* Sterling Publishing Co., Inc.

—Monster Boy & the Classroom Pet. Emerson, Carl. 2008. (Monster Boy Ser.). 32p. (gr. -1-4). 28.50 *(978-1-60270-234-9(9),* Looking Glass Library) ABDO Publishing Co.

—Monster Boy & the Halloween Parade. Emerson, Carl. 2010. (Monster Boy Set 2 Ser.). 32p. (J). (gr. k-3). 28.50 *(978-1-60270-777-1(4))* ABDO Publishing Co.

—Monster Boy & the Scary Scouts. Emerson, Carl. 2010. (Monster Boy Set 2 Ser.). 32p. (J). (gr. k-3). 28.50 *(978-1-60270-778-8(2))* ABDO Publishing Co.

—Monster Boy at the Library. Emerson, Carl. 2008. (Monster Boy Ser.). 32p. (gr. -1-4). 28.50 *(978-1-60270-235-6(7),* Looking Glass Library) ABDO Publishing Co.

—Monster Boy's Art Project. Emerson, Carl. 2010. (Monster Boy Set 2 Ser.). 32p. (J). (gr. k-3). 28.50 *(978-1-60270-780-1(4))* ABDO Publishing Co.

—Monster Boy's Field Trip. Emerson, Carl. 2008. (Monster Boy Ser.). 32p. (gr. -1-4). 28.50 *(978-1-60270-236-3(5),* Looking Glass Library) ABDO Publishing Co.

—Monster Boy's First Day of School. Emerson, Carl. 2008. (Monster Boy Ser.). 32p. (gr. -1-4). 28.50 *(978-1-60270-237-0(3),* Looking Glass Library) ABDO Publishing Co.

—Monster Boy's Gym Class. Emerson, Carl. 2010. (Monster Boy Set 2 Ser.). 32p. (J). (gr. k-3). 28.50 *(978-1-60270-781-8(2))* ABDO Publishing Co.

—Monster Boy's School Lunch. Emerson, Carl. 2008. (Monster Boy Ser.). 32p. (gr. -1-4). 28.50 *(978-1-60270-238-7(1),* Looking Glass Library) ABDO Publishing Co.

—Monster Boy's Soccer Game. Emerson, Carl. 2008. (Monster Boy Ser.). 32p. (gr. -1-4). 28.50 *(978-1-60270-239-4(X),* Looking Glass Library) ABDO Publishing Co.

—Monster Boy's Valentine. Emerson, Carl. 2010. (Monster Boy Set 2 Ser.). 32p. (J). (gr. k-3). 28.50 *(978-1-60270-782-5(0))* ABDO Publishing Co.

Levin, Lon. Small Potatoes Club. Levin, Lon. 2007. (I'm Going to Read(r) Ser.). (ENG.). 40p. (J). (gr. 2-3). pap. 3.95 *(978-1-4027-3084-9(5))* Sterling Publishing Co., Inc.

Levine, Jennifer. When Kayla Was Kyle. Fabrikant, Amy. 2013. 32p. pap. 8.95 *(978-1-61286-154-8(7))* Avid Readers Publishing Group.

Levine, Lenora D. Special Words: A Story about Multicultural Families & Their Pets. Gomes, Linda Nunes. 2007. (YA). per. 12.99 *(978-1-934400-02-9(5))* Rock Village Publishing.

Levine, Robyn. I Can Do It! Io Puedo Hacer! Gabriel, Camila. 2011. (ENG.). 28p. pap. 12.95 *(978-1-4664-1557-7(6))* CreateSpace Independent Publishing Platform.

Levins Morales, Ricardo, jt. illus. see Barajas, Sal.

Levins, Tim. The Amazing Adventures of Superman!, 4 vols. Bird, Benjamin. 2015. (Amazing Adventures of Superman! Ser.). (ENG.). 32p. (gr. k-2). 95.96 ***(978-1-4795-8002-6(3))*** Picture Window Bks.

Levins, Tim. Batman Undercover. Weissburg, Paul. 2013. (Dark Knight Ser.). (ENG.). 88p. (gr. 2-3). pap. 5.95 *(978-1-4342-4213-6(7))* Stone Arch Bks.

—Batman vs. Catwoman, 1 vol. Bright, J. E. 2013. (DC Super Heroes Ser.). (ENG.). 56p. (gr. 2-3). lib. bdg. 25.32 *(978-1-4342-6013-0(5))* Stone Arch Bks.

Levins, Tim. Bubble Trouble! Bird, Benjamin. 2015. (Amazing Adventures of Superman! Ser.). (ENG.). 32p. (gr. k-2). pap. 3.95 ***(978-1-4795-6524-5(5))*** Picture Window Bks.

Levins, Tim. Cyborg Superman. Bright, J. E. 2013. (Man of Steel Ser.). (ENG.). 88p. (gr. 2-3). pap. 5.95 *(978-1-4342-4219-8(6))* Stone Arch Bks.

Levins, Tim. Day of the Bizarros! Bird, Benjamin & Siegel, Jerry. 2015. (Amazing Adventures of Superman! Ser.). (ENG.). 32p. (gr. k-2). pap. 3.95 ***(978-1-4795-6522-1(9))*** Picture Window Bks.

Levins, Tim. How to Draw the Joker, Lex Luthor, & Other DC Super-Villains. Sautter, Aaron. 2015. (Drawing DC Super Heroes Ser.). (ENG.). 32p. (gr. 3-6). lib. bdg. 27.32 *(978-1-4914-2155-0(X))* Capstone Pr., Inc.

—How to Draw Wonder Woman, Green Lantern, & Other DC Super Heroes. Sautter, Aaron. 2015. (Drawing DC Super Heroes Ser.). (ENG.). 32p. (gr. 3-6). lib. bdg. 27.32 *(978-1-4914-2154-3(1))* Capstone Pr., Inc.

Levins, Tim. Magic Monsters! Bird, Benjamin. 2015. (Amazing Adventures of Superman! Ser.). (ENG.). 32p. (gr. k-2). pap. 3.95 ***(978-1-4795-6525-2(3))*** Picture Window Bks.

Levins, Tim. Mxy's Magical Mayhem. Korte, Steve. 2013. (Man of Steel Ser.). (ENG.). 88p. (gr. 2-3). pap. 5.95 *(978-1-4342-4826-8(7));* 25.32 *(978-1-4342-4488-8(1))* Stone Arch Bks.

Levins, Tim. Supergirl's Pet Problem! Bird, Benjamin. 2015. (Amazing Adventures of Superman! Ser.). (ENG.). 32p. (gr. k-2). pap. 3.95 ***(978-1-4795-6523-8(7))*** Picture Window Bks.

Levins, Tim & DC Comics Staff. Batman Undercover, 1 vol. Weissburg, Paul. 2013. (Dark Knight Ser.). (ENG.). 88p. (gr. 2-3). 25.32 *(978-1-4342-4094-1(0))* Stone Arch Bks.

—Cyborg Superman, 1 vol. Bright, J. E. 2013. (Man of Steel Ser.). (ENG.). 88p. (gr. 2-3). 25.32 *(978-1-4342-4089-7(4))* Stone Arch Bks.

Levins, Tim, jt. illus. see Cavallaro, Mike.

Levins, Tim, jt. illus. see Doescher, Erik.

Leviskiy, Olga. Mr. Groundhog Wants the Day Off/El Senor Marmota Quiere el Dia Libre. Vojta, Pat Stemper. 2010. (ENG & SPA.). 32p. (J). (gr. 4-7). 16.95 *(978-1-934960-77-6(2),* Raven Tree Pr.,Csi) Continental Sales, Inc.

Levitas, Alex. Pick-A-Woowoo: Have You Ever Wondered about Angels? Alexandria, Chris. 2013. 34p. *(978-1-921883-50-7(2))* Pick-a-Woo Woo Pubs.

—Pick-A-Woowoo - Have You Ever Wondered about Angels? Alexandria, Chris. 2013. 34p. pap. *(978-1-921883-36-1(7))* Pick-a-Woo Woo Pubs.

Levitas, Alexander. Faiga Finds the Way. Brandeis, Batsheva. 2005. (Fun to Read Book Ser.). 120p. (J). pap. 9.95 *(978-1-929628-28-5(5))* Hachai Publishing.

—The Place That I Love. Cohen, R. G. 2006. 30p. (J). 10.95 *(978-1-929628-29-2(3))* Hachai Publishing.

—¡Tú También Puedes! La Vida de Barack Obama. Benatar, Raquel. 2009.Tr. of Yes, you can too! the Life of Barack Obama. (SPA & ENG.). 40p. (J). (gr. 4-9). 16.95 *(978-1-56492-365-3(7))* Laredo Publishing Co., Inc.

Levithan, David & Farmer, Jonathan, photos by. Every You, Every Me. Levithan, David. 2012. (ENG., 256p. (YA). (gr. 7). pap. 9.99 *(978-0-375-85451-4(7),* Ember) Random Hse. Children's Bks.

LeVitt, Mike. Ghsots of Whitner. LeVitt, J. A. 2004. 84p. (J). per. 10.95 *(978-1-932196-47-4(1))* WordWright.biz, Inc.

Levy, David B. Blue Va a la Escuela. Santomero, Angela C. 2003. (Pistas de Blue Ser.).Tr. of Blue Goes to School. (SPA.). (J). (gr. -1-2). lib. bdg. 11.25 *(978-0-613-90465-0(6),* Turtleback) Turtleback Bks.

—My Visit with Periwinkle. Inches, Alison. 2003. (Blue's Clues Ser.). (ENG.). 24p. (J). pap. 3.99 *(978-0-689-85230-5(4),* Simon Spotlight/Nickelodeon) Simon Spotlight/Nickelodeon.

Levy, Pamela R. Hector Afloat. Shreeve, Elizabeth. 2004. 71p. (J). lib. bdg. 15.00 *(978-1-4242-0902-6(1))* Fitzgerald Bks.

—Hector Afloat. Shreeve, Elizabeth. 2004. (Ready-For-Chapters Ser.: 3). (ENG.). 64p. (J). (gr. 1-4). pap. 6.99 *(978-0-689-86416-2(7),* Simon & Schuster/Paula Wiseman Bks.) Simon & Schuster/Paula Wiseman Bks.

—Hector Afloat. Shreeve, Elizabeth. 2004. (Adventures of Hector Fuller Ser.). 71p. (J). (gr. 1-4). lib. bdg. 8.62 *(978-1-4176-2863-6(4),* Turtleback) Turtleback Bks.

—Hector Finds a Fortune. Shreeve, Elizabeth. 2004. 68p. (J). lib. bdg. 15.00 *(978-1-4242-0903-3(X))* Fitzgerald Bks.

—Hector Finds a Fortune. Shreeve, Elizabeth. 2004. (Adventures of Hector Fuller Ser.). 68p. (J). (gr. 1-4). 11.65 *(978-0-7569-5527-4(0))* Perfection Learning Corp.

—Hector Finds a Fortune. Shreeve, Elizabeth. 2004. (Adventures of Hector Fuller Ser.). 68p. (J). (gr. 1-4). lib. bdg. 11.80 *(978-0-613-86966-9(4),* Turtleback) Turtleback Bks.

—Hector Springs Loose. Shreeve, Elizabeth. 2004. (Adventures of Hector Fuller Ser.). 67p. (J). (gr. 1-4). 11.65 *(978-0-7569-5528-1(9))* Perfection Learning Corp.

—Hector Springs Loose. Shreeve, Elizabeth. 2004. (Ready-For-Chapters Ser.). (ENG.). 64p. (J). (gr. 1-4). pap. 3.99 *(978-0-689-86414-8(0),* Simon & Schuster/Paula Wiseman Bks.) Simon & Schuster/Paula Wiseman Bks.

—Here Comes Peter Cottontail! Nelson, Steve & Rollins, Jack. 2015. (J). *(978-0-8249-1948-1(3),* Candy Cane Pr.); 2011. 16p. (J). bds. 10.99 *(978-0-8249-1843-9(6),* Candy Cane Pr.); 2007. (ENG.). 26p. (J). bds. 12.99 *(978-0-8249-6701-7(1));* 2007. (ENG.). 26p. (gr. -1-k). bds. 12.99 *(978-0-8249-6690-4(2),* Candy Cane Pr.); 2003. (ENG.). 26p. (J). (gr. -1-k). bds. 6.95 *(978-0-8249-4149-9(7),* Candy Cane Pr.) Ideals Pubns.

—Here Comes Peter Cottontail, Set. Nelson, Steve & Rollins, Jack. 2007. (ENG.). 26p. 16.99 *(978-0-8249-6689-8(9),* Candy Cane Pr.) Ideals Pubns.

—Walking Home Alone. Baker, Ginger. 2003. (Books for Young Learners). (ENG.). 16p. (J). 5.75 net. *(978-1-57274-604-6(1),* 2534, Bks. for Young Learners) Owen, Richard C. Pubs., Inc.

Levy, Ruth. Animals. Morris, Ting & Morris, Neil. 2006. (Sticky Fingers Ser.). 32p. (J). lib. bdg. 28.50 *(978-1-59771-025-1(3))* Sea-To-Sea Pubns.

Levy, Ruth & Cowne, Joanne. Dinosaurs. Morris, Ting & Morris, Neil. 2006. (Sticky Fingers Ser.). 32p. (J). lib. bdg. 28.50 *(978-1-59771-029-9(6))* Sea-To-Sea Pubns.

Levy, Shaun & Jamieson, Eden. The Fortieth Horse. Fiddick, Calay. 2006. 32p. (J). *(978-1-55306-876-1(9),* Epic Pr.) Essence Publishing.

Lew-McCabe, Minette. Make Your Own Hawaii Landmarks. 2007. *(978-1-59700-381-0(6))* Island Heritage Publishing.

Lew-Vriethoff, Joanne. Another Day As Emily. Spinelli, Eileen. (ENG.). 240p. (J). (gr. 3-7). 2015. 6.99 *(978-0-449-80989-1(7),* Yearling); 2014. 12.99 *(978-0-449-80987-7(0),* Knopf Bks. for Young Readers); 2014. lib. bdg. 15.99 *(978-0-449-80988-4(9),* Knopf Bks. for Young Readers) Random Hse. Children's Bks.

—The Dancing Pancake. Spinelli, Eileen. 2011. (ENG.). 256p. (J). (gr. 3-7). 6.99 *(978-0-375-85348-7(0),* Yearling) Random Hse. Children's Bks.

—Do You Know Dewey? Exploring the Dewey Decimal System. Cleary, Brian P. 2012. (Millbrook Picture Bks). (ENG.). 32p. (J). (gr. 2-5). lib. bdg. 22.60 *(978-0-7613-6676-8(8),* Millbrook Pr.) Lerner Publishing Group.

—I'm Big! Schafer, Milton. 2006. (J). *(978-1-4156-8150-3(3),* Dial) Penguin Publishing Group.

—Joey Daring, Caring, & Curious. Craver, Marcella Marino. 2014. (J). *(978-1-4338-1652-9(0));* pap. *(978-1-4338-1653-6(9))* American Psychological Assn. (Magination Pr.).

—Peace, Baby! Ashman, Linda. 2013. (ENG.). 32p. (J). (gr. -1-k). 15.99 *(978-1-4521-0613-7(4))* Chronicle Bks. LLC.

—The Punctuation Station. Cleary, Brian P. 2010. (ENG.). 32p. (J). (gr. k-3). lib. bdg. 16.95 *(978-0-8225-7852-9(2))* Lerner Publishing Group.

—Summerhouse Time. Spinelli, Eileen. 2007. (ENG.). 224p. (J). (gr. 3-7). 12.99 *(978-0-375-84061-6(3),* Knopf Bks. for Young Readers) Random Hse. Children's Bks.

—Summerhouse Time. Spinelli, Eileen. 2009. (ENG.). 240p. (J). (gr. 3-7). 5.99 *(978-0-440-42224-2(8),* Yearling) Random Hse. Children's Bks.

Lewellen, Emily. Piano & Laylee & the Cyberbully. Curatola Knowles, Carmela N. 2011. (J). pap. *(978-1-56484-279-4(7))* International Society for Technology in Education.

—Piano & Laylee Go Online. Curatola Knowles, Carmela N. 2011. (J). pap. *(978-1-56484-277-0(0))* International Society for Technology in Education.

—Piano & Laylee Learn about Acceptable Use Policies. Curatola Knowles, Carmela N. 2011. (J). 40p. *(978-1-56484-296-1(7));* 34p. pap. *(978-1-56484-281-7(9))* International Society for Technology in Education.

Lewin, Betsy. A Barnyard Collection: Click, Clack, Moo & More. Cronin, Doreen. 2010. (ENG.). 128p. (J). (gr. -1-3). 19.99 *(978-1-4424-1263-7(1),* Atheneum Bks. for Young Readers) Simon & Schuster Children's Publishing.

—A Busy Day at the Farm. Cronin, Doreen. 2009. (ENG.). 16p. (J). (gr. -1-k). pap. 6.99 *(978-1-4169-5518-4(6),* Little Simon) Little Simon.

—Clic, Clac, Plif, Plaf: Una Aventura de Contar. Cronin, Doreen. 2006. (gr. -1-k). per. 4.99 *(978-1-933032-03-0(0))* Lectorum Pubns., Inc.

—Clic, Clac, Plif, Plaf: Una Aventura de Contar. Cronin, Doreen. Rioja, Alberto Jimenez, tr. from ENG. 2006. (J). (gr. 5-6). 12.99 *(978-1-933032-11-5(1))* Lectorum Pubns., Inc.

—Click, Clack, 123. Cronin, Doreen. 2010. (ENG.). 24p. (J). (gr. -1 — 1). bds. 7.99 *(978-1-4169-9125-0(5),* Little Simon) Little Simon.

—Click, Clack, ABC. Cronin, Doreen. 2010. (ENG.). 24p. (J). (gr. -1 — 1). bds. 7.99 *(978-1-4169-9124-3(7),* Little Simon) Little Simon.

—Click, Clack, Boo! A Tricky Treat. Cronin, Doreen. 2013. (ENG.). 40p. (J). (gr. -1-2). 17.99 *(978-1-4424-6553-4(0))* Simon & Schuster Children's Publishing.

Lewin, Betsy. Click, Clack, Ho! Ho! Ho! Cronin, Doreen. 2015. (ENG.). 40p. (J). (gr. -1-2). 17.99 ***(978-1-4424-9673-6(8))*** Simon & Schuster Children's Publishing.

Lewin, Betsy. Click, Clack, Moo: Cows That Type. Cronin, Doreen & Simon and Schuster/LeapFrog Staff. 2008. (J). 13.99 *(978-1-59319-936-4(8))* LeapFrog Enterprises, Inc.

—Click, Clack, Moo: Cows That Type. Cronin, Doreen. (ENG.). (J). (gr. -1-3). 2011. 32p. 9.99 *(978-1-4424-3370-0(1));* 2010. 34p. 7.99 *(978-1-4424-0889-0(8));* Set. 2009. 16p. 14.99 *(978-1-4169-5516-0(X))* Little Simon. (Little Simon).

—Click, Clack, Peep! Cronin, Doreen. 2015. (ENG.). 40p. (J). (gr. -1-3). 17.99 *(978-1-4814-2411-0(4))* Simon & Schuster Children's Publishing.

—Click, Clack, Quackity-Quack: A Typing Adventure. Cronin, Doreen. 2008. (ENG.). 14p. (J). (gr. -1-k). 14.99 *(978-1-4169-5517-7(8),* Little Simon) Little Simon.

—Click, Clack, Quackity-Quack: An Alphabetical Adventure. Cronin, Doreen. 2005. (ENG.). 24p. (J). (gr. -1-3). 16.99 *(978-0-689-87715-5(3),* Atheneum Bks. for Young Readers) Simon & Schuster Children's Publishing.

—Click, Clack, Splish, Splash: A Counting Adventure. Cronin, Doreen. 2006. (ENG.). 24p. (J). (gr. -1-3). 16.99 *(978-0-689-87716-2(1),* Atheneum Bks. for Young Readers) Simon & Schuster Children's Publishing.

—Cowgirl Kate & Cocoa. Silverman, Erica. (Cowgirl Kate & Cocoa Ser.). (ENG.). 44p. (J). (gr. 1-4). 2006. pap. 5.95 *(978-0-15-205660-5(2));* 2005. 15.00 *(978-0-15-202124-5(8))* Houghton Mifflin Harcourt Publishing Co.

—Cowgirl Kate & Cocoa. Silverman, Erica. 2007. (Cowgirl Kate & Cocoa Ser.). (gr. 1-4). 15.95 *(978-0-7569-8043-6(7))* Perfection Learning Corp.

—Cowgirl Kate & Cocoa: Horse in the House. Silverman, Erica. 2010. (Cowgirl Kate & Cocoa Ser.). (ENG.). 44p. (J). (gr. 1-4). pap. 5.99 *(978-0-547-31672-7(0))* Houghton Mifflin Harcourt Publishing Co.

—Cowgirl Kate & Cocoa: Partners. Silverman, Erica. 2007. (Cowgirl Kate & Cocoa Ser.). (ENG.). 44p. (J). (gr. 1-4). pap. 5.95 *(978-0-15-206010-7(3))* Houghton Mifflin Harcourt Publishing Co.

—Cowgirl Kate & Cocoa: Rain or Shine. Silverman, Erica. 2009. (Cowgirl Kate & Cocoa Ser.). (ENG.). 44p. (J). (gr. 1-4). pap. 5.99 *(978-0-15-206602-4(0))* Houghton Mifflin Harcourt Publishing Co.

—Cowgirl Kate & Cocoa: Spring Babies. Silverman, Erica. 2011. (Cowgirl Kate & Cocoa Ser.: 6). (ENG.). 40p. (J). (gr. 1-4). pap. 5.99 *(978-0-547-56685-6(9))* Houghton Mifflin Harcourt Publishing Co.

—Dooby Dooby Moo. Cronin, Doreen. 2010. (Classic Board Bks.). (ENG.). 40p. (J). (gr. -1-k). 7.99 *(978-1-4424-0890-6(1),* Little Simon) Little Simon.

—Dooby Dooby Moo. Cronin, Doreen. 2006. (ENG.). 32p. (J). (gr. -1-3). 16.95 *(978-0-689-84507-9(3),* Atheneum Bks. for Young Readers) Simon & Schuster Children's Publishing.

—Dooby Dooby Moo. Cronin, Doreen. 2008. (Doreen Cronin: Click-Clack & More Ser.). (ENG.). 40p. (gr. -1-3). lib. bdg. 24.21 *(978-1-59961-423-6(5))* Spotlight.

—Dooby Dooby Moo. Cronin, Doreen. 2011. (J). (gr. -1-3). 29.95 *(978-0-545-04281-9(X))* Weston Woods Studios, Inc.

—Duck for President. Cronin, Doreen. 2004. (ENG.). 32p. (J). (gr. -1-3). 17.99 *(978-0-689-86377-6(2),* Atheneum Bks. for Young Readers) Simon & Schuster Children's Publishing.

—Duck for President. Cronin, Doreen. 2006. (Doreen Cronin: Click-Clack & More Ser.). (ENG.). 32p. (gr. -1-3). lib. bdg. 24.21 *(978-1-59961-091-7(4))* Spotlight.

—Dumpy la Rue. Winthrop, Elizabeth. rev. ed. 2004. (ENG.). 40p. (J). (gr. -1-3). reprint ed. pap. 8.99 *(978-0-8050-7535-9(6),* Holt, Henry & Co. Bks. For Young Readers) Holt, Henry & Co.

—Favorite Stories from Cowgirl Kate & Cocoa. Silverman, Erica. 2013. (Green Light Readers Level 2 Ser.). (ENG.). 32p. (J). (gr. 1-4). 12.99 *(978-0-544-02268-3(8))* Houghton Mifflin Harcourt Publishing Co.

—Favorite Stories from Cowgirl Kate & Cocoa: Partners. Silverman, Erica. ed. 2013. (Cowgirl Kate & Cocoa, Green Light Readers Ser.). (ENG.). 22p. (J). (gr. -1-3). lib. bdg. 13.55 *(978-0-606-33983-4(3),* Turtleback) Turtleback Bks.

—Favorite Stories from Cowgirl Kate & Cocoa: Rain or Shine. Silverman, Erica. 2013. (Green Light Readers Level 2 Ser.). (ENG.). 24p. (J). (gr. 1-4). pap. 3.99 *(978-0-544-10502-7(8))* Houghton Mifflin Harcourt Publishing Co.

—Favorite Stories from Cowgirl Kate & Cocoa: School Days. Silverman, Erica. 2014. (Green Light Readers Level 2 Ser.). (ENG.). 32p. (J). (gr. 1-4). 12.99 *(978-0-544-23017-0(5),* HMH Books For Young Readers) Houghton Mifflin Harcourt Publishing Co.

—Favorite Stories from Cowgirl Kate & Cocoa Partners. Silverman, Erica. 2013. (Green Light Readers Level 2 Ser.). (ENG.). 24p. (J). (gr. 1-4). 12.99 *(978-0-544-02266-9(1))* Houghton Mifflin Harcourt Publishing Co.

—Giggle, Giggle, Quack. Cronin, Doreen. 2011. (Classic Board Bks.). (ENG.). 34p. (J). (gr. -1-k). bds. 7.99 *(978-1-4424-0891-3(X),* Little Simon) Little Simon.

—Giggle, Giggle, Quack. Cronin, Doreen. 2006. (Doreen Cronin: Click-Clack & More Ser.). (ENG.). 32p. (gr. -1-3). lib. bdg. 24.21 *(978-1-59961-092-4(2))* Spotlight.

—Horse in the House. Silverman, Erica. 2009. (Cowgirl Kate & Cocoa Ser.). (ENG.). 44p. (J). (gr. 1-4). 15.00 *(978-0-15-205390-1(5))* Houghton Mifflin Harcourt Publishing Co.

—Jaja Jiji, Cuac. Cronin, Doreen. Jimenez, Alberto, tr. from ENG. 2003.Tr. of Giggle, Giggle, Quack. (SPA.). (J). 15.00 *(978-1-930332-46-1(7))* Lectorum Pubns., Inc.

—No Such Thing. Koller, Jackie French. 2012. (ENG.). 32p. (J). (gr. k-2). pap. 7.95 *(978-1-59078-911-7(3))* Boyds Mills Pr.

—Partners. Silverman, Erica. 2007. (Cowgirl Kate & Cocoa Ser.). pap. 7.93 *(978-1-4189-5237-2(0))* Houghton Mifflin Harcourt Trade & Reference Pubs.

—Partners. Silverman, Erica. 2007. (Cowgirl Kate & Cocoa Ser.). (gr. 1-4). 15.95 *(978-0-7569-8042-9(9))* Perfection Learning Corp.

—Pato para Presidente. Cronin, Doreen. 2008.Tr. of Duck for President. (SPA.). (J). (gr. k-2). pap. 7.99 *(978-1-930332-74-4(2),* LC32509) Lectorum Pubns., Inc.

—Pum, Cuac, Muu: Una Loca Aventura. Cronin, Doreen & Jiménez Rioja, Alberto. 2008. (SPA.). (J). pap. 5.99 *(978-1-933032-54-2(5));* 36p. 16.99 *(978-1-933032-53-5(7))* Lectorum Pubns., Inc.

—The Red-Hot Rattoons. Winthrop, Elizabeth. 2006. (ENG.). 224p. (J). (gr. 3-6). pap. 16.99 *(978-0-8050-7986-9(6),* Holt, Henry & Co. Bks. For Young Readers) Holt, Henry & Co.

—School Days. Silverman, Erica. 2008. (Cowgirl Kate & Cocoa Ser.). (ENG.). 48p. (J). (gr. 1-4). pap. 5.95 *(978-0-15-206130-2(4))* Houghton Mifflin Harcourt Publishing Co.

—So, What's It Like to Be a Cat? Kuskin, Karla. (ENG.). (J). (gr. -1-3). 2008. 40p. 7.99 *(978-0-689-85930-4(9));* 2005. 32p. 17.99 *(978-0-689-84733-2(5))* Simon & Schuster Children's Publishing. (Atheneum Bks. for Young Readers).

—Thump, Quack, Moo: A Whacky Adventure. Cronin, Doreen. 2008. (ENG.). 42p. (J). (gr. -1-2). 16.99 *(978-1-4169-1630-7(X),* Atheneum Bks. for Young Readers) Simon & Schuster Children's Publishing.

—Two Eggs, Please. Weeks, Sarah. 2007. (ENG.). 32p. (J). (gr. -1-1). reprint ed. 7.99 *(978-1-4169-2714-3(X),* Atheneum Bks. for Young Readers) Simon & Schuster Children's Publishing.

Lewin, Betsy. Good Night, Knight. Lewin, Betsy. 2015. (I Like to Read(r) Ser.). (ENG.). 24p. (J). (gr. -1-3). 6.99 *(978-0-8234-3315-5(3));* 14.95 *(978-0-8234-3206-6(8))* Holiday Hse., Inc.

—Thumpy Feet. Lewin, Betsy. 2014. (ENG.). 32p. (J). (gr. -1-1). 6.99 *(978-0-8234-3174-8(6))* Holiday Hse., Inc.

—Where Is Tippy Toes? Lewin, Betsy. 2010. (ENG.). 32p. (J). (gr. -1-2). 16.99 *(978-1-4169-3808-8(7)*, Atheneum Bks. for Young Readers) Simon & Schuster Children's Publishing.

—You Can Do It! Lewin, Betsy. 2014. (I Like to Read Ser.). (ENG.). 32p. (J). (gr. -1-3). 6.99 *(978-0-8234-3055-0(3))* Holiday Hse., Inc.

Lewin, Betsy, jt. illus. see Lewin, Ted.

Lewin, Ted. The Always Prayer Shawl. Oberman, Sheldon. 2005. (ENG.). 40p. (J). (gr. 2-7). pap. 10.95 *(978-1-59078-332-0(8))* Boyds Mills Pr.

—Babe Didrikson: Athlete of the Century. Knudson, R. R. 2015. (Women of Our Time Ser.). (ENG.). 80p. (J). (gr. 3-7). 7.99 *(978-0-14-751465-3(7)*, Puffin) Penguin Publishing Group.

Lewin, Ted. I See & See. 2016. (J). ***(978-0-8234-3544-9(X))*** Holiday Hse., Inc.

Lewin, Ted. Island of the Blue Dolphins. O'Dell, Scott. gif. ed. 2010. (ENG.). 192p. (J). (gr. 2-5). 22.00 *(978-0-547-42483-5(3))* Houghton Mifflin Harcourt Publishing Co.

—The Longest Night. Bauer, Marion Dane. 2009. (ENG.). 40p. (J). (gr. -1-3). 17.95 *(978-0-8234-2054-4(X))* Holiday Hse., Inc.

—One Green Apple. Bunting, Eve. 2006. (ENG.). 32p. (J). (gr. -1-3). 17.99 *(978-0-618-43477-0(1))* Houghton Mifflin Harcourt Publishing Co.

—Pennies in a Jar, 1 vol. Chaconas, Dori. 2007. (ENG.). 32p. (J). (gr. 1-5). 16.95 *(978-1-56145-422-8(2))* Peachtree Pubs.

Lewin, Ted. Peppe the Lamplighter. Bartone, Elisa. 2015. 32p. pap. 7.00 ***(978-1-61003-612-2(3))*** Center for the Collaborative Classroom.

Lewin, Ted. The World's Greatest Elephant. Helfer, Ralph. 2006. (ENG.). 48p. (J). (gr. 4-7). 17.99 *(978-0-399-24190-1(6)*, Philomel) Penguin Publishing Group.

Lewin, Ted. Animals Work. Lewin, Ted. 2014. (ENG.). 24p. (J). (gr. -1-3). 14.95 *(978-0-8234-3040-6(5))* Holiday Hse., Inc.

—At Gleason's Gym. Lewin, Ted. 2007. (ENG.). 40p. (J). (gr. k-4). 17.95 *(978-1-59643-231-4(4))* Roaring Brook Pr.

—Can You See Me? Lewin, Ted. 2014. (I Like to Read Ser.). (ENG.). 32p. (J). (gr. -1-3). 14.95 *(978-0-8234-2940-0(7))* Holiday Hse., Inc.

—How Much? Visiting Markets Around the World. Lewin, Ted. 2006. 40p. (J). (gr. k-4). 17.89 *(978-0-688-17553-5(8))* HarperCollins Pubs.

—Look! Lewin, Ted. (I Like to Read Ser.). (ENG.). 32p. (J). 2014. (gr. -1-3). 6.99 *(978-0-8234-3059-8(6))*; 2013. 14.95 *(978-0-8234-2607-2(6))* Holiday Hse., Inc.

—Lost City: The Discovery of Machu Picchu. Lewin, Ted. (ENG.). 48p. (J). (gr. 2-5). 2012. pap. 8.99 *(978-0-14-242580-0(X)*, Puffin); 2003. 17.99 *(978-0-399-23302-9(4)*, Philomel) Penguin Publishing Group.

—What Am I? Where Am I? Lewin, Ted. 2014. (ENG.). 32p. (J). (gr. -1-3). 6.99 *(978-0-8234-3180-9(0))* Holiday Hse., Inc.

Lewin, Ted & Lewin, Betsy. Balarama: A Royal Elephant. Lewin, Ted & Lewin, Betsy. 2009. (Adventures Around the World Ser.). (ENG.). 56p. (J). (gr. 1-6). 19.95 *(978-1-60060-265-8(7))* Lee & Low Bks., Inc.

Lewin, Ted, jt. illus. see Ichikawa, Satomi.

Lewis, Anthony. Amber Brown Horses Around. Danziger, Paula et al. (Amber Brown Ser.: 12). (ENG.). (J). 2015. 224p. (gr. 3-7). 5.99 *(978-0-14-751552-0(1)*, Puffin); 2014. 208p. (gr. 2-5). 14.99 *(978-0-399-16170-4(8)*, Putnam Juvenile) Penguin Publishing Group.

—Amber Brown Is on the Move. Danziger, Paula et al. 2014. (Amber Brown Ser.: 11). (ENG.). 192p. (J). (gr. 2-5). pap. 5.99 *(978-0-14-751223-9(9)*, Puffin) Penguin Publishing Group.

—Animal Sticker Atlas. Chancellor, Deborah. 2010. (ENG.). 32p. (J). (gr. k-2). pap. 6.99 *(978-0-7534-6444-1(6)*, Kingfisher) Roaring Brook Pr.

—¡Ataque de las Hormigas! James, Anne. Ramirez, Alma B., tr. from ENG. 2008. (Science Solves It! en Espanol Ser.). (SPA.). 32p. (J). (gr. -1-3). pap. 5.95 *(978-1-57565-278-8(1))* Kane Pr., Inc.

—¿Baño o Cama? Nilsen, Anna. Morell, Ivonne Bonsfill, tr. 2010. (SPA.). 12p. (J). 12.95 *(978-84-92691-23-4(9))* Roca Editorial De Libros ESP. Dist: Spanish Pubs., LLC.

—Bath or Bed? 2008. (Pick & Choose Ser.). (ENG.). 12p. (J). (gr. -1). bds. *(978-1-84643-239-2(1))* Child's Play International Ltd.

—Carrots or Peas? 2008. (Pick & Choose Ser.). (ENG.). 12p. (J). (gr. -1). bds. *(978-1-84643-242-2(1))* Child's Play International Ltd.

—Emergency, Call 911. Slater, Teddy. 2010. 16p. (J). *(978-0-545-24601-9(6))* Scholastic, Inc.

—Fire Prevention. Slater, Teddy. 2010. 16p. (J). *(978-0-545-24603-3(2))* Scholastic, Inc.

—Five Little Ducks. 2013. (Hands-On Songs Ser.). (ENG.). 12p. (gr. -1). bds. *(978-1-84643-630-7(3))* Child's Play International Ltd.

—Frank & Beans, 1 vol. Wargin, Kathy-jo. 2010. (I Can Read! / Frank & Beans Ser.). (ENG.). 32p. (J). pap. 3.99 *(978-0-310-71847-5(3))* Zonderkidz.

—Frank & Beans & the Grouchy Neighbor, 1 vol. Wargin, Kathy-jo. 2010. (I Can Read! / Frank & Beans Ser.). (ENG.). 32p. (J). pap. 3.99 *(978-0-310-71849-9(X))* Zonderkidz.

—Frank & Beans & the Scary Campout, 1 vol. Wargin, Kathy-jo. 2010. (I Can Read! / Frank & Beans Ser.). (ENG.). 32p. (J). pap. 3.99 *(978-0-310-71850-5(3))* Zonderkidz.

—Human Body Lift-The-Flap. Murrell, Deborah & Brooks, Susie. 2014. (Lift-The-Flap Tab Bks.). (ENG.). 16p. (J). (gr. k-1). bds. 9.99 *(978-0-7534-7060-2(8)*, Kingfisher) Roaring Brook Pr.

—Humpty Dumpty: Asl. 2013. (Hands-On Songs Ser.). (ENG.). 12p. (J). bds. *(978-1-84643-627-7(3))* Child's Play International Ltd.

—Jack & Jill. 2013. (Hands-On Songs Ser.). (ENG.). 12p. (gr. -1). bds. *(978-1-84643-629-1(X))* Child's Play International Ltd.

—The Lion Book of Prayers to Read & Know. Piper, Sophie. 2010. (ENG.). 96p. (J). (gr. k-2). 12.99 *(978-0-7459-6147-7(9))* Lion Hudson PLC GBR. Dist: Independent Pubs. Group.

—The Lion Read & Know Bible. Rock & Piper, Sophie. 2009. (ENG.). 384p. (J). (gr. k-2). 17.95 *(978-0-7459-4996-3(7))* Lion Hudson PLC GBR. Dist: Independent Pubs. Group.

—Little Jungle Explorers. 2007. (Little Explorers Ser.). (ENG.). 14p. (J). (gr. -1-k). bds. *(978-1-84643-036-7(4))* Child's Play International Ltd.

—Little Ocean Explorers. 2007. (Little Explorers Ser.). (ENG.). 14p. (J). (gr. -1-k). bds. *(978-1-84643-039-8(9))* Child's Play International Ltd.

—Little Snow Explorers. 2007. (Little Explorers Ser.). (ENG.). 14p. (J). (gr. -1-k). bds. *(978-1-84643-037-4(2))* Child's Play International Ltd.

—Little Space Explorers. 2007. (Little Explorers Ser.). (ENG.). 14p. (J). bds. *(978-1-84643-038-1(0))* Child's Play International Ltd.

—Meal Time. 2006. (Sign About Ser.). (ENG.). 12p. (J). (gr. -1). bds. *(978-1-84643-030-5(5))* Child's Play International Ltd.

—The Mess. Jensen, Patricia. 2003. (My First Reader Ser.). (ENG.). 32p. (J). 18.50 *(978-0-516-22932-4(X)*, Children's Pr.) Scholastic Library Publishing.

—My First Biography: Benjamin Franklin. Bauer, Marion Dane. 2011. (My First Biography Ser.). (ENG.). 32p. (J). (gr. -1-3). pap. 3.99 *(978-0-545-23256-2(2)*, Scholastic Nonfiction) Scholastic, Inc.

—Old MacDonald. 2013. (Hands-On Songs Ser.). (ENG.). 12p. (J). (gr. -1). bds. *(978-1-84643-628-4(1))* Child's Play International Ltd.

—¿Osito o Tren? Nilsen, Anna. Morell, Ivonne Bonsfill, tr. 2010. (SPA.). 12p. (J). 12.95 *(978-84-92691-25-8(5))* Roca Editorial De Libros ESP. Dist: Spanish Pubs., LLC.

—Play Time. 2006. (Sign About Ser.). (ENG.). 12p. (J). (gr. -1). bds. *(978-1-84643-031-2(3))* Child's Play International Ltd.

—Rescued by a Dog Called Flow. Goodhart, Pippa. 2006. 121p. (J). (gr. 4-7). pap. 6.95 *(978-1-903015-47-6(2))* Barn Owl Bks, London GBR. Dist: Independent Pubs. Group.

—Space Lift-The-Flap. Brooks, Susie. 2013. (Lift-The-Flap Tab Bks.). (ENG.). 16p. (J). (gr. -1-2). bds. 12.99 *(978-0-7534-6957-6(X)*, Kingfisher) Roaring Brook Pr.

—Stranger Danger. Slater, Teddy. 2010. 16p. (J). *(978-0-545-24605-7(9))* Scholastic, Inc.

Lewis, Anthony. Take a Pause, Paul: A Book about Commas. Powell, Marie. 2015. (Punctuation Station Ser.). (ENG.). 16p. (J). (gr. k-2). 17.95 ***(978-1-60753-731-1(1))*** Amicus Educational.

Lewis, Anthony. Teddy or Train? 2008. (Pick & Choose Ser.). (ENG.). 12p. (J). (gr. -1). bds. *(978-1-84643-241-5(3))* Child's Play International Ltd.

—Things That Go. Murrell, Deborah. 2012. (Lift-The-Flap Tab Bks.). (ENG.). 16p. (J). (gr. -1-1). bds. 9.99 *(978-0-7534-6787-9(9)*, Kingfisher) Roaring Brook Pr.

—¿Viento o Lluvia? Nilsen, Anna. Morell, Ivonne Bonsfill, tr. 2010. (SPA.). 12p. (J). 12.95 *(978-84-92691-29-6(8))* Roca Editorial De Libros ESP. Dist: Spanish Pubs., LLC.

—We Love You Baby. Davidson, Alice Joyce. 2004. (J). 9.99 *(978-1-890647-09-4(8))* TOMY International, Inc.

Lewis, Anthony. What Is That? A Book about Question Marks. Powell, Marie. 2015. (Punctuation Station Ser.). (ENG.). 16p. (J). (gr. k-2). 17.95 ***(978-1-60753-732-8(X))*** Amicus Educational.

Lewis, Anthony. The Wheels on the Bus: Asl. 2013. (Hands-On Songs Ser.). (ENG.). 12p. (J). bds. *(978-1-84643-626-0(5))* Child's Play International Ltd.

—Wind or Rain? 2008. (Pick & Choose Ser.). (ENG.). 12p. (J). (gr. -1). bds. *(978-1-84643-240-8(5))* Child's Play International Ltd.

—¿Zanahorias o Guisantes? Nilsen, Anna. Morell, Ivonne Bonsfill, tr. 2010. (SPA.). 12p. (J). 12.95 *(978-84-92691-27-2(1))* Roca Editorial De Libros ESP. Dist: Spanish Pubs., LLC.

Lewis, Benjamin E. Grandma Rocks! Scheve, Janice Rose. 2014. (ENG.). 24p. (J). pap. 8.99 *(978-1-63063-242-7(2))* Tate Publishing & Enterprises, LLC.

Lewis, Buddy. Bash & the Chocolate Milk Cows. Cole, Burton. 2015. (ENG.). 224p. (J). (gr. 3-7). pap. 8.99 *(978-1-4336-8530-9(2)*, B&H Kids) B&H Publishing Group.

Lewis, Cynthia. Perk up Your Ears: Discover Your Sense of Hearing. Cobb, Vicki. 2003. (Five Senses Ser.). (ENG.). 32p. (gr. 3-5). pap. 7.95 *(978-0-7613-1981-8(6)*, Millbrook Pr.) Lerner Publishing Group.

Lewis, E. B. Across the Alley. Michelson, Richard. 2006. (ENG.). 32p. (J). (gr. -1-3). 16.99 *(978-0-399-23970-0(7)*, Putnam Juvenile) Penguin Publishing Group.

Lewis, E. B. The Bat Boy & His Violin. Curtis, Gavin. 2015. 32p. pap. 8.00 ***(978-1-61003-618-4(2))*** Center for the Collaborative Classroom.

Lewis, E. B. Bippity Bop Barbershop. Tarpley, Natasha Anastasia. 2009. (ENG.). 32p. (gr. -1-1). pap. 7.00 *(978-0-316-03382-4(0))* Little, Brown Bks. for Young Readers.

—Circle Unbroken. Raven, Margot Theis. 2007. (ENG.). 48p. (J). (gr. -1-3). per. 8.99 *(978-0-312-37603-1(0))* Square Fish.

—D Is for Drinking Gourd: An African American Alphabet. Sanders, Nancy I. (ENG.). 40p. (J). (gr. k-6). 2009. pap. 7.95 *(978-1-58536-474-9(6))*; 2007. 17.95 *(978-1-58536-293-6(X))* Sleeping Bear Pr.

—Danitra Brown, Class Clown. Grimes, Nikki. 2005. 32p. (J). lib. bdg. 17.89 *(978-0-688-17291-6(1))*; (ENG.). (gr. 3). 16.99 *(978-0-688-17290-9(3)*, Amistad) HarperCollins Pubs.

—Each Kindness. Woodson, Jacqueline. 2012. (ENG.). 32p. (J). (gr. k-3). 16.99 *(978-0-399-24652-4(5)*, Nancy Paulsen Bks.) Penguin Publishing Group.

—The Everlasting Embrace. 2014. (ENG.). 40p. (J). (gr. -1-k). 17.99 *(978-0-670-78474-5(5)*, Viking Juvenile) Penguin Publishing Group.

—Homegrown House. Wong, Janet S. 2009. (ENG.). 40p. (J). (gr. -1-3). 16.99 *(978-0-689-84718-9(1)*, McElderry, Margaret K. Bks.) McElderry, Margaret K. Bks.

—I Love My Hair! Tarpley, Natasha Anastasia. 2014. 32p. pap. 7.00 *(978-1-61003-348-0(5))* Center for the Collaborative Classroom.

—I Love My Hair! Tarpley, Natasha Anastasia. 2003. (ENG.). 11p. (J). (gr. -1 — 1). bds. 6.99 *(978-0-316-52558-9(8))* Little, Brown Bks. for Young Readers.

—I Want to Be Free. Slate, Joseph. 2009. (ENG.). 32p. (J). (gr. 1-3). 16.99 *(978-0-399-24342-4(9)*, Putnam Juvenile) Penguin Publishing Group.

—Keeping the Night Watch. Smith, Hope Anita. 2014. (ENG.). 80p. (J). (gr. 5-8). pap. 9.99 *(978-0-312-65936-3(9))* Square Fish.

—The Legend of the Cape May Diamond. Noble, Trinka Hakes. rev. ed. 2007. (Legend (Sleeping Bear) Ser.). (ENG.). 40p. (J). (gr. 3-7). 17.95 *(978-1-58536-279-0(4))* Sleeping Bear Pr.

—My Best Friend. Rodman, Mary Ann. 2007. (ENG.). 32p. (J). (gr. -1-3). pap. 5.99 *(978-0-14-240806-3(9)*, Puffin) Penguin Publishing Group.

—My Best Friend. Rodman, Mary Ann. 2007. (gr. -1-3). 16.00 *(978-0-7569-8151-8(4))* Perfection Learning Corp.

—Night Boat to Freedom. Raven, Margot Theis. 2008. (ENG.). 40p. (J). (gr. 1-4). pap. 8.99 *(978-0-312-55018-9(9))* Square Fish.

—Pitching in for Eubie. Nolen, Jerdine. 2007. (ENG.). 32p. (J). (gr. k-3). 16.99 *(978-0-688-14917-8(0))* HarperCollins Pubs.

—The Secret World of Walter Anderson. Bass, Hester. 2014. (Candlewick Biographies Ser.). (ENG.). 48p. (J). (gr. 3-7). 14.99 *(978-0-7636-7116-7(9))* Candlewick Pr.

—The Secret World of Walter Anderson. Bass, Hester & Anderson, Walter Inglis. 2009. (ENG.). 48p. (J). (gr. 1-4). 17.99 *(978-0-7636-3583-1(9))* Candlewick Pr.

—Seeds of Freedom: The Peaceful Integration of Huntsville, Alabama. Bass, Hester. 2015. (ENG.). 32p. (J). (gr. k-3). 16.99 *(978-0-7636-6919-5(9))* Candlewick Pr.

—Stars above Us. Norman, Geoffrey. 2009. (ENG.). 32p. (J). (gr. k-3). 16.99 *(978-0-399-24724-8(6)*, Putnam Juvenile) Penguin Publishing Group.

—Tea Cakes for Tosh. Lyons, Kelly Starling. 2012. (ENG.). 32p. (J). (gr. k-3). 16.99 *(978-0-399-25213-6(4)*, Putnam Juvenile) Penguin Publishing Group.

—Trouper. Kearney, Meg. 2013. (ENG.). 32p. (J). (gr. -1-3). 16.99 *(978-0-545-10041-0(0)*, Scholastic Pr.) Scholastic, Inc.

—Under the Baobab Tree, 1 vol. Stiegemeyer, Julie. 2012. (ENG.). 32p. (J). 16.99 *(978-0-310-72561-9(5))* Zonderkidz.

—Virgie Goes to School with Us Boys. Howard, Elizabeth Fitzgerald. 2005. (gr. k-3). 18.00 *(978-0-7569-5088-0(0))* Perfection Learning Corp.

—Virgie Goes to School with Us Boys. Howard, Elizabeth Fitzgerald. 2005. (ENG.). 32p. (J). (gr. k-3). reprint ed. 7.99 *(978-0-689-87793-3(5)*, Simon & Schuster/Paula Wiseman Bks.) Simon & Schuster/Paula Wiseman Bks.

Lewis, E. B., jt. illus. see Lewis, Earl.

Lewis, Earl & Lewis, E. B. Coming on Home Soon. Woodson, Jacqueline. 2004. (ENG.). 32p. (J). (gr. k-3). 17.99 *(978-0-399-23748-5(8)*, Putnam Juvenile) Penguin Publishing Group.

—My Best Friend. Rodman, Mary Ann. 2005. (ENG.). 32p. (J). (gr. -1-3). 15.99 *(978-0-670-05989-8(7)*, Viking Juvenile) Penguin Publishing Group.

Lewis, Earl B. The First Step: How One Girl Put Segregation on Trial. Goodman, Susan E. 2016. (J). ***(978-0-8027-3741-0(2))*** Bloomsbury Pr.

Lewis, Earl B. Robin Hood & the Golden Arrow. San Souci, Robert D. 2010. (ENG.). 32p. (J). (gr. -1-3). 17.99 *(978-0-439-62538-8(6)*, Orchard Bks.) Scholastic, Inc.

Lewis, H. B. Mi Pinguino Oliver. Kimmel, Elizabeth Cody. 2004.Tr. of My Penguin Osbert. (SPA.). (J). 15.99 *(978-84-88342-68-3(3))* S.A. Kokinos ESP. Dist: Lectorum Pubns., Inc.

—My Penguin Osbert. Kimmel, Elizabeth Cody. (ENG.). 40p. (J). (gr. -1-3). 2011. pap. 6.99 *(978-0-7636-5730-7(1))*; 2008. 7.99 *(978-0-7636-3692-0(4))*; 2004. 16.99 *(978-0-7636-1699-1(0))* Candlewick Pr.

—My Penguin Osbert. Kimmel, Elizabeth Cody. 2005. 40p. pap. *(978-1-84428-565-5(0))* Walker Bks., Ltd.

—My Penguin Osbert Book & Toy Gift Set. Kimmel, Elizabeth Cody. 2007. (ENG.). 40p. (J). (gr. -1-3). 18.99 *(978-0-7636-3683-8(5))* Candlewick Pr.

—My Penguin Osbert in Love. Kimmel, Elizabeth Cody. 2010. (ENG.). 48p. (J). (gr. -1-3). 7.99 *(978-0-7636-5001-8(3))* Candlewick Pr.

—My Penguin Osbert in Love, Set. Kimmel, Elizabeth Cody & Buck, Lewis. 2008. (ENG.). 48p. (J). (gr. -1-3). 16.99 *(978-0-7636-3032-4(2))* Candlewick Pr.

Lewis, Jan. Baby's Bible Stories: The Birth of Jesus. Armadillo Publishing Staff. 2015. (ENG.). 24p. pap. 6.99 *(978-1-86147-484-1(9)*, Armadillo) Anness Publishing GBR. Dist: National Bk. Network.

Lewis, Jan. The Elves & the Shoemaker. Read, Lorna & Ladybird Books Staff. 2015. (First Favourite Tales Ser.). (ENG.). 32p. (J). (-k). 7.99 ***(978-1-4093-0628-3(3))*** Penguin Bks., Ltd. GBR. Dist: Independent Pubs. Group.

Lewis, Jan. The Emperor's New Clothes. 2015. (ENG.). 24p. (J). (gr. -1-2). bds. 6.99 *(978-1-86147-413-1(X)*, Armadillo) Anness Publishing GBR. Dist: National Bk. Network.

—First Fairy Tales: Cinderella. 2013. (ENG.). 24p. (J). (gr. -1-k). bds. 6.99 *(978-1-86147-334-9(6)*, Armadillo) Anness Publishing GBR. Dist: National Bk. Network.

—First Fairy Tales: Sleeping Beauty. 2013. (ENG.). 24p. (J). (gr. -1-k). bds. 6.99 *(978-1-86147-338-7(9)*, Armadillo) Anness Publishing GBR. Dist: National Bk. Network.

—First Fairy Tales: The Ugly Duckling. 2013. (ENG.). 24p. (J). (gr. -1-k). bds. 6.99 *(978-1-86147-333-2(8)*, Armadillo) Anness Publishing GBR. Dist: National Bk. Network.

—First Fairy Tales: Three Little Pigs. 2013. (ENG.). 24p. (J). (gr. -1-k). bds. 6.99 *(978-1-86147-331-8(1)*, Armadillo) Anness Publishing GBR. Dist: National Bk. Network.

—How to Be a Pirate in 7 Days or Less. Rees, Lesley. 2006. (How to be A Ser.). 32p. (J). (gr. k-3). 12.95 *(978-0-7534-6041-2(6)*, Kingfisher) Roaring Brook Pr.

—Look & Learn with Little Dino: Action Words. 2014. (ENG.). 24p. (J). (gr. k-2). bds. 6.99 *(978-1-86147-382-0(6)*, Armadillo) Anness Publishing GBR. Dist: National Bk. Network.

—Look & Learn with Little Dino: Busy Day. 2014. (ENG.). 24p. (J). (gr. k-2). bds. 6.99 *(978-1-86147-379-0(6)*, Armadillo) Anness Publishing GBR. Dist: National Bk. Network.

—Look & Learn with Little Dino: Count 123. 2014. (ENG.). 24p. (J). (gr. -1-1). bds. 6.99 *(978-1-86147-381-3(8)*, Armadillo) Anness Publishing GBR. Dist: National Bk. Network.

—Love from Santa, 6 vols. ed. 2013. (ENG.). 60p. (J). (gr. -1-2). bds. 7.99 *(978-1-86147-313-4(3)*, Armadillo) Anness Publishing GBR. Dist: National Bk. Network.

—Mother Goose Action Rhymes: Old MacDonald Had a Farm; One, Two, Buckle My Shoe; Round & Round the Garden; This Little Pig. 2004. 90p. (J). vinyl bd. *(978-1-902272-32-0(3))* Tucker Slingsby, Ltd.

—Mother Goose Rhymes: One, Two, Buckle My Shoe. 2015. (ENG.). 24p. bds. 6.99 *(978-1-86147-637-1(X)*, Armadillo) Anness Publishing GBR. Dist: National Bk. Network.

—Mother Goose Rhymes: Round & Round the Garden. 2015. (ENG.). 24p. bds. 6.99 *(978-1-86147-636-4(1)*, Armadillo) Anness Publishing GBR. Dist: National Bk. Network.

—My Big Book of Fairy Tales in Rhyme! Tucker Slingsby Ltd., Staff. 2004. 224p. (J). *(978-1-902272-31-3(5))* Tucker Slingsby, Ltd.

—My First 123. 2014. (ENG.). 24p. (J). (gr. -1-k). bds. 6.99 *(978-1-86147-371-4(0)*, Armadillo) Anness Publishing GBR. Dist: National Bk. Network.

—My First ABC. 2014. (ENG.). 24p. (J). (gr. -1-k). bds. 6.99 *(978-1-86147-372-1(9)*, Armadillo) Anness Publishing GBR. Dist: National Bk. Network.

—My First Animals. 2014. (ENG.). 24p. (J). (gr. -1-k). bds. 6.99 *(978-1-86147-373-8(7)*, Armadillo) Anness Publishing GBR. Dist: National Bk. Network.

—My First Colours. 2014. (ENG.). 24p. (J). (gr. -1-k). bds. 6.99 *(978-1-86147-374-5(5)*, Armadillo) Anness Publishing GBR. Dist: National Bk. Network.

—My Little Nursery Rhymes. 2015. (ENG.). 24p. bds. 6.99 *(978-1-86147-469-8(5)*, Armadillo) Anness Publishing GBR. Dist: National Bk. Network.

—My Mother Goose Collection: Action Rhymes. 2015. (ENG.). 24p. bds. 6.99 *(978-1-86147-646-3(9)*, Armadillo) Anness Publishing GBR. Dist: National Bk. Network.

—Old Macdonald Had a Farm - Mother Goose Rhymes. 2015. (ENG.). 24p. bds. 6.99 *(978-1-86147-468-1(7)*, Armadillo) Anness Publishing GBR. Dist: National Bk. Network.

—Performance. 2012. (First Time Ser.). (ENG.). 24p. (J). *(978-1-84643-487-4(7))* Child's Play International Ltd.

—The Pied Piper of Hamelin. 2006. (First Fairy Tales Ser.). 30p. (J). (gr. -1-3). lib. bdg. 28.50 *(978-1-59771-072-5(5))* Sea-To-Sea Pubns.

—School. 2012. (First Time Ser.). (ENG.). 24p. (J). *(978-1-84643-491-4(2))* Child's Play International Ltd.

—School Trip. 2012. (First Time Ser.). (ENG.). 24p. (J). *(978-1-84643-489-1(0))* Child's Play International Ltd.

—Small Bad Wolf. Taylor, Sean. 2004. (I Am Reading Ser.). 45p. (J). (gr. -1-3). 11.60 *(978-0-7569-5400-0(2))* Perfection Learning Corp.

—Sports Day. 2012. (First Time Ser.). (ENG.). 24p. (J). *(978-1-84643-488-4(2))* Child's Play International Ltd.

—The Princess & the Pea. 2015. (ENG.). 24p. bds. 6.99 *(978-1-86147-467-4(9)*, Armadillo) Anness Publishing GBR. Dist: National Bk. Network.

—This Little Pig - Mother Goose Rhymes. Armadillo Publishing Staff. 2015. (ENG.). 24p. bds. 6.99 *(978-1-86147-486-5(5)*, Armadillo) Anness Publishing GBR. Dist: National Bk. Network.

—Toby's Trousers. Cassidy, Anne. 2005. (Reading Corner Ser.). 24p. (J). (gr. k-3). lib. bdg. 22.80 *(978-1-59771-009-1(1))* Sea-To-Sea Pubns.

Lewis, Jan. Words: Turn the Wheels, Find the Pictures. 2015. (ENG.). 10p. bds. 14.99 ***(978-1-86147-660-9(4)***, Armadillo) Anness Publishing GBR. Dist: National Bk. Network.

—123: Turn the Wheels Learn to Count! 2015. (ENG.). 10p. (J). (gr. -1-12). bds. 14.99 ***(978-1-86147-661-6(2)***, Armadillo) Anness Publishing GBR. Dist: National Bk. Network.

Lewis, Jan. Look & Learn with Little Dino: Colour Fun. Lewis, Jan. 2014. (ENG.). 24p. (J). (gr. -1-2). bds. 6.99 *(978-1-86147-380-6(X)*, Armadillo) Anness Publishing GBR. Dist: National Bk. Network.

Lewis, Jenn. Valentine the Porcupine Dances Funny. Brown, Derrick. 2011. (ENG.). 44p. 20.00 *(978-1-935904-18-2(3))* Write Bloody Publishing.

Lewis, Jesse. The Stone Heart. Foster, D. S. 2012. (J). pap. 12.99 *(978-1-937331-14-6(8))* ShadeTree Publishing, LLC.

Lewis Jr, Daryl M. The 3Ds' Christmas. 2007. 30p. (J). 9.99 *(978-0-9776987-2-1(6))* Blackberry Pubns.

Lewis, K. E. Arturo & the Navidad Birds, 1 vol. Broyles, Anne. 2013. (ENG.). 32p. (J). (gr. k-3). 16.99 *(978-1-4556-1801-9(2))* Pelican Publishing Co., Inc.

—Will It Blow? Become a Volcano Detective at Mount St. Helens. Rusch, Elizabeth. 2007. (ENG.). 48p. (J). (gr. -1-3). per. 13.95 *(978-1-57061-509-2(8))* Sasquatch Bks.

Lewis, Kellie. Please Pass the Manners! Mealtime Tips for Everyone. Schaefer, Lola M. 2009. (ENG.). 12p. (J). (gr. -1-1). 7.99 *(978-1-4169-4826-1(0)*, Little Simon) Little Simon.

Lewis, Kim. I'll Always Be Your Friend. McBratney, Sam. 2004. (ENG.). 32p. (J). (gr. -1-3). pap. 6.99 *(978-0-06-055548-1(3)*, Harper Trophy) HarperCollins Pubs.

Lewis, Kim. Seymour & Henry. Lewis, Kim. 2009. (ENG.). 32p. (J). (gr. k-k). 15.99 *(978-0-7636-4243-3(6))* Candlewick Pr.

Lewis, Kim & Graef, Renee. Kirsten's Short Story Collection. Shaw, Janet. 2006. (American Girls Collection). 213p. (J). (gr. 3-8). 12.95 *(978-1-59369-323-7(0))* American Girl Publishing, Inc.

Lewis, Kimberly & Stead, Kevin. Ants, 1 vol. Whitecap Books Staff. 2010. (Investigate Ser.: 0). (ENG.). 64p. (J). (gr. 1-7). pap. 3.95 *(978-1-55285-129-6(X))* Whitecap Bks., Ltd. CAN. Dist: Midpoint Trade Bks., Inc.

Lewis-MacDougall, Patricia Ann & Fiegenschuh, Emily. How Things Came to Be: Inuit Stories of Creation, 1 vol. Qitsualik-Tinsley, Rachel & Qitsualik-Tinsley, Sean. 2015. (ENG.). 60p. (J). (gr. -1-k). 16.95 *(978-1-927095-78-2(6))* Inhabit Media Inc. CAN. Dist: Independent Pubs. Group.

Lewis-MacDougall, Patricia Ann & Owlkids Books Inc. Staff. Arctic Storm, No. 16. Wishinsky, Frieda. 2011. (Canadian Flyer Adventures Ser.: 16). (ENG.). 96p. (J). (gr. 1-4). pap. 7.95 *(978-1-926818-10-8(5)*, Maple Tree Pr.) Owlkids Bks. Inc. CAN. Dist: Perseus-PGW.

—Halifax Explodes! Wishinsky, Frieda. 2011. (Canadian Flyer Adventures Ser.: 17). (ENG.). 96p. (J). (gr. 1-4). pap. 7.95 *(978-1-926818-98-6(9)*, Maple Tree Pr.) Owlkids Bks. Inc. CAN. Dist: Perseus-PGW.

—Make It Fair!, No. 15. Wishinsky, Frieda. 2010. (Canadian Flyer Adventures Ser.: 15). (ENG.). 96p. (J). (gr. 1-4). pap. 7.95 *(978-1-897349-99-1(8)*, Maple Tree Pr.) Owlkids Bks. Inc. CAN. Dist: Perseus-PGW.

Lewis, Marisa. The Leopard Boy. Johnson, Julia. 2012. (ENG.). 96p. (J). (gr. 2-5). pap. 8.99 *(978-1-84780-213-2(3)*, Frances Lincoln Children's Bks.) Quarto Publishing Group UK GBR. Dist: Hachette Bk. Group.

Lewis, Naomi C. The New Neighbors. Ellis, Julie. 2009. (Rigby PM Stars Bridge Bks.). (ENG.). 16p. (gr. 2-3). pap. 8.70 *(978-1-4190-5507-2(0))* Rigby Education.

Lewis, Paul Owen. Storm Boy, 1 vol. Lewis, Paul Owen. 2008. (ENG.). 32p. (J). (gr. -1-3). pap. 8.95 *(978-1-55285-268-2(7))* Whitecap Bks., Ltd. CAN. Dist: Graphic Arts Ctr. Publishing Co.

Lewis, R. J. The Ballerina with Webbed Feet/la Bailarina Palmipeda. Van Scoyoc, Pam. Teichman, Diane E., tr. from ENG. l.t. ed. 2004. (ENG & SPA.). 40p. (J). (gr. k-2). lib. bdg. 16.98 *(978-0-9663629-2-3(6))* By Grace Enterprises.

—I Could Catch a Whale/ Yo Podria Pescar una Ballena. Van Scoyoc, Pam. Santillan-Cruz, Sylvia R., tr. l.t. ed. 2005. (ENG & SPA.). 32p. (J). (gr. k-2). lib. bdg. 16.98 *(978-0-9663629-5-4(0))* By Grace Enterprises.

Lewis, Rachel. Cook's Coloring Book: Simple Recipes for Beginners, 1 vol. Lewis, Rachel. 2015. (ENG.). 144p. pap. 12.99 ***(978-1-4236-3845-2(X))*** Gibbs Smith, Publisher.

Lewis, Rebecca. Tilli's Tale. Williams, Barbara A. 2004. 48p. (J). per. *(978-1-932077-52-0(9))* Athena Pr.

Lewis, Robert. Bloop Bloop. Feasel, PaPa. 2011. (ENG.). 24p. pap. 9.95 *(978-1-4505-3489-5(9))* CreateSpace Independent Publishing Platform.

Lewis, Robin Baird. Parfois Grand, Parfoit Petit. Stinson, Kathy. Homel, David, tr. from ENG. 2006. (FRE.). 23p. (J). (gr. -1-2). reprint ed. pap. 5.00 *(978-1-4223-5663-0(9))* DIANE Publishing Co.

—Red Is Best. Stinson, Kathy. (ENG.). (J). (gr. -1 — 1). 2011. 26p. bds., bds. 6.95 *(978-1-55451-364-2(2)*, 9781554513642); 25th ed. 2006. 32p. 19.95 *(978-1-55451-052-8(X)*, 9781554510528); 25th anniv. ed. 2006. 32p. pap. 6.95 *(978-1-55451-051-1(1)*, 9781554510511) Annick Pr., Ltd. CAN. Dist: Firefly Bks., Ltd.

Lewis, Simon. The Big Book of Baddies. Townsend, John. 2009. (ENG.). 32p. (J). (gr. 3-7). *(978-1-84732-301-9(4))* Carlton Bks., Ltd. GBR. Dist: Sterling Publishing Co., Inc.

Lewis, Stephen. Growing Money: A Complete Investing Guide for Kids. Karlitz, Gail & Honig, Debbie. ed. 2010. (ENG.). 144p. (J). (gr. 3-7). 8.99 *(978-0-8431-9905-5(9)*, Price Stern Sloan) Penguin Publishing Group.

—Nine Bright Pennies. Slater, Teddy & Scholastic, Inc. Staff. 2005. (Number Tales Ser.). (ENG.). 16p. (J). (gr. -1-1). pap. 2.99 *(978-0-439-69020-1(X))* Scholastic, Inc.

—Seven Magic Hats. Charlesworth, Liza. 2005. (Number Tales Ser.). (ENG.). 16p. (J). (gr. -1-1). pap. 2.99 *(978-0-439-69018-8(8))* Scholastic, Inc.

—Snow Friends. Jones, Milo. 2010. 16p. (J). pap. *(978-0-545-24823-5(X))* Scholastic, Inc.

Lewis, Stevie. A Cast Is the Perfect Accessory: And Other Lessons I've Learned. Gutknecht, Allison. 2014. (ENG.). 160p. (J). (gr. 2-5). 16.99 *(978-1-4424-8396-5(2))*; pap. 5.99 *(978-1-4424-8395-8(4))* Simon & Schuster/Paula Wiseman Bks. (Simon & Schuster/Paula Wiseman Bks.).

—Don't Wear Polka-Dot Underwear with White Pants: And Other Lessons I've Learned. Gutknecht, Allison. 2013. (ENG.). 160p. (J). (gr. 2-5). 15.99 *(978-1-4424-8393-4(8))*; pap. 5.99 *(978-1-4424-8392-7(X))* Simon & Schuster/Paula Wiseman Bks. (Simon & Schuster/Paula Wiseman Bks.).

—Finding Serendipity. Banks, Angelica. 2015. (ENG.). 288p. (J). (gr. 3-7). 16.99 *(978-1-62779-154-0(X)*, Holt, Henry & Co. Bks. For Young Readers) Holt, Henry & Co.

—Never Wear Red Lipstick on Picture Day: And Other Lessons I've Learned. Gutknecht, Allison. 2014. (ENG.). 176p. (J). (gr. 2-5). 16.99 *(978-1-4814-2959-7(0))*; pap. 6.99 *(978-1-4814-2958-0(2))* Simon & Schuster/Paula Wiseman Bks. (Simon & Schuster/Paula Wiseman Bks.).

—Pizza Is the Best Breakfast: And Other Lessons I've Learned. Gutknecht, Allison. 2015. (ENG.). 176p. (J). (gr. 2-5). pap. 6.99 *(978-1-4814-2961-0(2)*, Simon & Schuster/Paula Wiseman Bks.) Simon & Schuster/Paula Wiseman Bks.

Lewis, T. Tillena Lou's Day in the Sun. Tharp, Barbara et al. Denk, James, ed. 2nd ed. 2013. (My World & Me Ser.). (ENG.). 32p. (J). (gr. k-2). pap. *(978-1-888997-44-6(3)*, BioEd) Baylor College of Medicine.

Lewis, Wayne. Ted & the Combine Harvester. Lougher, Jenny. 2007. 23p. pap. *(978-1-905553-27-3(7))* BookPublishingWorld.

Ley, Mary. Tri-Son: The Little Triathlete. Ley, Mary. 2003. per. *(978-0-9707547-1-4(X))* Woodburn Graphics, Inc.

Leyhane, Vici & Baggott, Stella. Sticker Dolly Dressing Dolls. Watt, Fiona. 2006. (Usborne Activities Ser.). 23p. (J). pap. 8.99 *(978-0-7945-1389-4(1)*, Usborne) EDC Publishing.

—Sticker Dolly Dressing Princesses. Watt, Fiona. 2007. (Sticker Dolly Dressing Ser.). 32p. (J). pap. 8.99 *(978-0-7945-1390-0(5)*, Usborne) EDC Publishing.

Leyhane, Vici, jt. illus. see Baggott, Stella.

Leyssenne, Mathieu & Kraft, Jason. The Ultimate Pirate Handbook. Hamilton, Libby. 2015. (ENG.). 20p. (J). (gr. k-3). 19.99 ***(978-0-7636-7963-7(1)***, Templar) Candlewick Pr.

Leyva, Barbara. Henry & the Magic Window. Leyva, Barbara. l.t. ed. 2003. 50p. (J). 3.50 *(978-0-9729056-0-2(X)*, 0, Balticbard Publishing) Leyva, Barbara.

Leyva, Juan Camilo. Nettey Loves Shoeboxes. Delisle, Annette Gonzalez. 2011. 28p. pap. 9.99 *(978-1-61170-015-2(9))* Robertson Publishing.

Lhamo, Choki & Loday, Gyelsey, photos by. Bhutan: An Odyssey in Shangri-la with Choki & Gyelsey. Hawley, Michael. 2nd ed. 2003. 216p. lib. bdg. 10000.00 *(978-0-9742469-0-1(5)*, Big Bks. for Little People) Friendly Planet.

L'Hirondelle, Cheryl. Nieve. Griggs, Terry. 2010. (ENG.). 264p. (J). (gr. 4-10). pap. 14.95 *(978-1-897231-87-6(3))* Biblioasis CAN. Dist: Consortium Bk. Sales & Distribution.

Lhomme, Sandrine. The Earth Has Caught Cold. Galliez, Roxane Marie. 2009. 24p. (J). (gr. -1-3). 9.99 *(978-0-8416-7140-9(0))* Hammond World Atlas Corp.

—Farewell Sadness. Galliez, Roxane Marie. 2010. 24p. (J). 9.99 *(978-0-8416-7139-3(7))* Hammond World Atlas Corp.

Lhomme, Sandrine. Sammy the Snail's Amazing Day, 1 vol. Lhomme, Sandrine. Piu, Amandine. 2012. (My Baby Stories Ser.). (ENG.). 24p. (J). (gr. -1). bds. 9.95 *(978-2-7338-1981-4(X))* Auzou, Philippe Editions FRA. Dist: Consortium Bk. Sales & Distribution.

L'Hommedieu, Arthur John. Children of the Sun. L'Hommedieu, Arthur John. (GER.). (J). (gr. k-11). 10.99 *(978-0-85953-939-5(3))* Child's Play International Ltd. GBR. Dist: Child's Play-International.

Li, Deborah. Tricia & the Blue Cap. l.t. ed. 2003. 28p. (J). 7.95 net. *(978-0-9706654-5-4(8))* Sprite Pr.

Li, Xiaojun. Selvakumar Knew Better. Kroll, Virginia. 2009. (Selvakumar Knew Better Ser.). 32p. (J). (gr. -1-3). pap. 8.95 *(978-1-885008-36-7(8)*, Shen's Bks.) Lee & Low Bks., Inc.

Li, Yishan. Will Supervillains Be on the Final? Liberty Vocational. Novik, Naomi. 2011. (ENG.). 192p. pap. 10.99 *(978-0-345-51656-5(7)*, Del Rey) Random House Publishing Group.

Li, Yishan & Peng, Wang. The Murders in the Rue Morgue, & Other Tales. Poe, Edgar Allen & Morvan, Jean-David. 2013. (Classics Illustrated Deluxe Graphic Nove Ser.: 10). (ENG.). 144p. (J). (gr. 5-9). 17.99 *(978-1-59707-432-2(2))*; pap. 13.99 *(978-1-59707-431-5(4))* Papercutz.

Liang, Xiao Long. Battle of Red Cliffs. Dong Chen, Wei. 2013. (Three Kingdoms Ser.: 11). 176p. (gr. 5-12). pap. 9.99 *(978-89-98341-24-4(7))* JR Comics KOR. Dist: Lerner Publishing Group.

—Heroes & Chaos, Vol. 1. Chen, Wei Dong. 2013. (Three Kingdoms Ser.: 1). 176p. (gr. 5-12). pap. 9.99 *(978-89-94208-89-3(5))* JR Comics KOR. Dist: Lerner Publishing Group.

—Wagers & Vows. Dong Chen, Wei. 2013. (Three Kingdoms Ser.: 12). 176p. (gr. 5-12). pap. 9.99 *(978-89-98341-25-1(5))* JR Comics KOR. Dist: Lerner Publishing Group.

Liang, Xiao Long. The Brotherhood Restored, Vol. 7. Liang, Xiao Long. Chen, Wei Dong. 2013. (Three Kingdoms Ser.: 7). 176p. (gr. 5-12). pap. 9.99 *(978-89-94208-67-1(4))* JR Comics KOR. Dist: Lerner Publishing Group.

—Three Kingdoms, Vol. 9. Liang, Xiao Long. Chen, Wei Dong. 2013. (Three Kingdoms Ser.: 9). 176p. (gr. 5-12). pap. 9.99 *(978-89-98341-22-0(0))* JR Comics KOR. Dist: Lerner Publishing Group.

Liao, Jimmy. Filbert, the Good Little Fiend. Oram, Hiawyn. 2013. (ENG.). 32p. (J). (gr. -1-2). 15.99 *(978-0-7636-5870-0(7))* Candlewick Pr.

—The World Champion of Staying Awake. Taylor, Sean. 2011. (ENG.). 32p. (J). (gr. -1-2). 15.99 *(978-0-7636-4957-9(0))* Candlewick Pr.

Liao, Yivian. Activity Story Book: Sunshine & Her Big Blarney Smile. Hale, Linda. 2013. 26p. pap. *(978-1-927915-03-5(1))* Chase Enterprises.

—Sunshine & Her Big Blarney Smile. Hale, Linda. 2013. 26p. pap. *(978-1-927915-02-8(3))* Chase Enterprises.

Liautaud, Judy. Lulu Turns on the Night Light. Liautaud, Judy. 2013. 24p. pap. 12.95 *(978-1-883841-19-5(4))* City Creek Pr., Inc.

Libonn, Jula. One, Two, Buckle My Shoe: Math Activities for Young Children. Brown, Sam E. 2004. 112p. (Orig.). (gr. -1). pap. 8.95 *(978-0-87659-103-1(9)*, 10300) Gryphon Hse., Inc.

Lichtenheld, Tom. Camp Buccaneer. Smallcomb, Pam. ed. 2005. 58p. (J). lib. bdg. 15.00 *(978-1-59054-897-4(3))* Fitzgerald Bks.

—Duck! Rabbit! Rosenthal, Amy Krouse. (J). 2014. (ENG.). 40p. (gr. -1-k). bds. 7.99 *(978-1-4521-3733-9(1))*; 2009. (ENG.). 40p. (gr. -1-3). 16.99 *(978-0-8118-6865-5(6))*; 2009. 16.99 *(978-0-8118-8332-0(9))* Chronicle Bks. LLC.

—E-Mergency. Fields-Meyer, Ezra. 2014. (ENG.). 40p. (J). (gr. 3-7). 7.99 *(978-1-4521-3642-4(4))* Chronicle Bks. LLC.

—Exclamation Mark. Rosenthal, Amy Krouse. 2013. (ENG.). 56p. (J). 17.99 *(978-0-545-43679-3(6)*, Scholastic Pr.) Scholastic, Inc.

Lichtenheld, Tom. Goodnight, Goodnight, Construction Site. Rinker, Sherri Duskey. (ENG.). (J). (gr. -1 — 1). 2015. 66p. 15.99 ***(978-1-4521-4698-0(5))***; 2011. 32p. 16.99 *(978-0-8118-7782-4(5))* Chronicle Bks. LLC.

Lichtenheld, Tom. Goodnight, Goodnight Construction Site Sound Book. Rinker, Sherri Duskey. 2014. (ENG.). 12p. (J). (gr. -1 — 1). 12.99 *(978-1-4521-2824-5(3))* Chronicle Bks. LLC.

—I Wish You More. Rosenthal, Amy Krouse. 2015. (ENG.). 40p. (J). (gr. k-3). 14.99 *(978-1-4521-2699-9(2))* Chronicle Bks. LLC.

—It's Not Fair! Rosenthal, Amy Krouse. 2008. (ENG.). 40p. (J). (gr. -1-3). 16.99 *(978-0-06-115257-3(9))* HarperCollins Pubs.

—Shark vs. Train. Barton, Chris. (ENG.). (J). (gr. -1 — 1). 2015. 20p. bds. 6.99 *(978-0-316-37814-7(5))*; 2010. 40p. 18.00 *(978-0-316-00762-7(5))* Little, Brown Bks. for Young Readers.

—Sing. Raposo, Joe. 2013. (ENG.). 40p. (J). (gr. -1-3). 16.99 *(978-0-8050-9071-0(1)*, Holt, Henry & Co. Bks. For Young Readers) Holt, Henry & Co.

—Steam Train, Dream Train. Rinker, Sherri Duskey. 2013. (ENG.). 40p. (J). (gr. -1-1). 16.99 *(978-1-4521-0920-6(6))* Chronicle Bks. LLC.

Lichtenheld, Tom. Steam Train, Dream Train Sound Book. Rinker, Sherri Duskey. 2015. (ENG.). 12p. (J). (gr. -1-k). 12.99 ***(978-1-4521-2825-2(1))*** Chronicle Bks. LLC.

Lichtenheld, Tom. Stick & Stone. Ferry, Beth. 2015. (ENG.). 48p. (J). (gr. -1-3). 16.99 *(978-0-544-03256-9(X)*, HMH Books For Young Readers) Houghton Mifflin Harcourt Publishing Co.

—Wumbers. Rosenthal, Amy Krouse. 2012. (ENG.). 40p. (J). (gr. -1-1). 16.99 *(978-1-4521-1022-6(0))* Chronicle Bks. LLC.

—Wumbers. Rosenthal, Amy Krouse. 2015. (ENG.). 40p. (J). (gr. k-3). 7.99 *(978-1-4521-4122-0(3))* Chronicle Bks. LLC.

—Yes Day! Rosenthal, Amy Krouse. 2009. (ENG.). 40p. (J). (gr. -1-3). 14.99 *(978-0-06-115259-7(5))* HarperCollins Pubs.

—Zero the Hero. Holub, Joan. 2012. (ENG.). 40p. (J). (gr. 1-5). 17.99 *(978-0-8050-9384-1(2)*, Holt, Henry & Co. Bks. For Young Readers) Holt, Henry & Co.

Lichtenheld, Tom. Bridget's Beret. Lichtenheld, Tom. 2010. (ENG.). 40p. (J). (gr. -1-2). 16.99 *(978-0-8050-8775-8(3)*, Holt, Henry & Co. Bks. For Young Readers) Holt, Henry & Co.

—Cloudette. Lichtenheld, Tom. 2011. (ENG.). 40p. (J). (gr. -1-2). 17.99 *(978-0-8050-8776-5(1)*, Holt, Henry & Co. Bks. For Young Readers) Holt, Henry & Co.

—E-Mergency! Lichtenheld, Tom. 2011. (ENG.). 40p. (J). (gr. -1-17). 16.99 *(978-0-8118-7898-2(8))* Chronicle Bks. LLC.

—Everything I Know about Cars. Lichtenheld, Tom. 2005. (ENG.). 40p. (J). (gr. -1-3). 18.99 *(978-0-689-84382-2(8)*, Simon & Schuster Bks. For Young Readers) Simon & Schuster Bks. For Young Readers.

—Everything I Know about Pirates. Lichtenheld, Tom. 2003. (ENG.). 40p. (J). (gr. -1-3). pap. 7.99 *(978-0-689-86009-6(9)*, Simon & Schuster Bks. For Young Readers) Simon & Schuster Bks. For Young Readers.

—What Are You So Grumpy About? Lichtenheld, Tom. 2007. (ENG.). 40p. (J). (gr. -1-1). 7.00 *(978-0-316-06589-4(7))* Little, Brown Bks. for Young Readers.

Lichtenheld, Tom, jt. illus. see Rosenthal, Amy Krouse.

Lichtwardt, Rita. Barbie - A Perfect Christmas. 2011. (Book & Jewelry Ser.). (ENG.). 24p. (J). (gr. -1-1). 10.99 *(978-0-7944-2319-3(1))* Reader's Digest Assn., Inc., The.

Lida, Toshitsugu. Wolf's Rain. Bones. 2005. (Wolf's Rain Ser.). (ENG.). 184p. (YA). pap. 9.99 *(978-1-59116-718-1(3))* Viz Media.

—Wolf's Rain, 1. Bones & Nobumoto, Keiko. 2004. (Wolf's Rain Ser.). (ENG.). 184p. (YA). pap. 9.99 *(978-1-59116-591-0(1))* Viz Media.

Lida, Xing & Yi, Liu. Tracking Tyrannosaurs: Meet T. Rex's Fascinating Family, from Tiny Terrors to Feathered Giants. Sloan, Christopher. 2013. (ENG.). 48p. (J). (gr. 3-7). 18.95 *(978-1-4263-1374-5(8))*; lib. bdg. 27.90 *(978-1-4263-1375-2(6))* National Geographic Society. (National Geographic Children's Bks.).

Lidard, Kelly & Seeley, Douglas A. Chincoteague Daisy Chain. Seeley, Bonnie L. 2003. 32p. (J). bds. 12.95 *(978-0-9728380-0-9(7))* Seelcraft Publishing.

Lidberg, Micah. Rise & Fall. 2012. (ENG.). 20p. (gr. k). 16.00 *(978-1-907704-30-7(2))* Nobrow Ltd. GBR. Dist: Consortium Bk. Sales & Distribution.

Liddell, Daniel & Basta, Mary. California Native American Tribes: Mohave Tribe, 28 booklets. Boule, Mary Null. (California Native American Tribes). 52p. (J). (gr. 3-6). pap. 7.95 *(978-1-877599-73-6(5))* Merryant Pubs.

—Native Americans of North America, Set, 11. 2003. (Native Americans of North America). 48p. (J). (gr. 3-6). pap. 6.45 *(978-1-877599-61-3(1))* Merryant Pubs.

—Navajo People: SW Region, Set. Boule, Mary Null. (Native Americans of North America Ser.). 50-60p. (J). (gr. 3-6). pap. 7.95 *(978-1-877599-59-0(X))* Merryant Pubs.

Liddiment, Carol. How Many Donkeys? An Arabic Counting Tale. MacDonald, Margaret Read & Taibah, Nadia Jameel. 2012. (J). 34.28 *(978-1-61913-148-4(X))* Weigl Pubs., Inc.

—The Wooden Sword: A Jewish Folktale from Afghanistan. 2012. (ENG.). 32p. (J). (gr. k-3). 16.99 *(978-0-8075-9201-4(3))* Whitman, Albert & Co.

Lie, Vivian. Pink Feathers,Murky Pools & a Witch: A Lellaland Adventure. Masters, H. 2003. 52p. pap. *(978-1-84401-098-1(8))* Athena Pr.

Liebeck, Lisa. Count with Balloons. Rembisz, Linda. 2009. 28p. pap. 12.49 *(978-1-4490-1989-1(7))* AuthorHouse.

Lieber, Larry & Heck, Don. The Invincible Iron Man, Vol. 1. 2010. (ENG.). 208p. (J). (gr. 4-17). pap. 24.99 *(978-0-7851-4567-7(2))* Marvel Worldwide, Inc.

Lieber, Larry, jt. illus. see Romita, John.

Lieber, Steve, jt. illus. see Kano.

Lieberherr, Ruth. The Knottles. Mellon, Nancy. 2012. 32p. (J). pap. 11.95 *(978-1-62148-003-7(8))* SteinerBooks, Inc.

—Winter, Awake! Kroll, Linda. rev. ed. 2003. 32p. (J). pap. 11.95 *(978-0-88010-528-6(3))* SteinerBooks, Inc.

Liebert, Marjorie. The Kid from the Other Side. Liebert, Burt. l.t. ed. 2003. 192p. (YA). (gr. 5-7). pap. 7.95 *(978-0-9727499-0-9(X))* Creative Works.

Liebman, Simean. The Pigeon with the Sticky Stuck Neck. Arthur, Anne. 2004. (J). per. 7.99 *(978-0-9753320-0-9(7))* Riverbank Publishing.

Lieder, Rick. Sweep up the Sun. Frost, Helen. 2015. (ENG.). 32p. (J). (-k). 15.99 *(978-0-7636-6904-1(0))* Candlewick Pr.

Lieder, Rick, photos by. Step Gently Out. Frost, Helen. 2012. (ENG., 32p. (J). (gr. k-k). 15.99 *(978-0-7636-5601-0(1))* Candlewick Pr.

Liefeld, Rob. X-Force: Big Guns. Nicieza, Fabián. 2004. (X-Force Ser.). 136p. pap. 15.99 *(978-0-7851-1483-3(1))* Marvel Worldwide, Inc.

Liefeld, Rob, et al. X-Force: Under the Gun. 2011. (ENG.). 280p. (J). (gr. 4-17). 34.99 *(978-0-7851-4985-9(6))* Marvel Worldwide, Inc.

Liefeld, Rob & Hall, Bob. X-Force: Cable & the New Mutants. Simonson, Louise. 2011. (ENG.). 264p. (YA). (gr. 8-17). 24.99 *(978-0-7851-4970-5(8))* Marvel Worldwide, Inc.

Lieffering, Jan. Frank & Fiona Build a Fictional Story. Lynette, Rachel. 2013. (ENG.). 32p. (J). lib. bdg. 25.27 *(978-1-59953-587-6(4))*; (gr. 2-4). pap. 11.94 *(978-1-60357-561-4(8))* Norwood Hse. Pr.

Liegey, Daniel. I was Born to Be a Brother. Michels-Gualtieri, Zaydek G. 2005. (ENG.). 32p. (J). (gr. -1-3). 9.95 *(978-1-930775-10-7(5))* Platypus Media, L.L.C.

Liegey, Daniel, jt. illus. see Ramsey, Marcy Dunn.

Liepke, Peter, photos by. The Gypsies Never Came. Roos, Stephen. 2010. (ENG., 128p. (J). (gr. 3-7). pap. 7.99 *(978-1-4424-2940-6(2)*, Simon & Schuster Bks. For Young Readers) Simon & Schuster Bks. For Young Readers.

Lies, Brian. Deep in the Swamp. Bateman, Donna M. 2007. (ENG.). 32p. (J). (gr. -1-3). 16.95 *(978-1-57091-596-3(2))*; pap. 7.95 *(978-1-57091-597-0(0))* Charlesbridge Publishing, Inc.

—Finklehopper Frog. Livingston, Irene. 2008. (ENG.). 32p. (J). (gr. -1-2). pap. 7.95 *(978-1-58246-234-9(8)*, Tricycle Pr.) Ten Speed Pr.

—Lucky Duck. Weiss, Ellen. 2004. (Ready-to-Read Ser.). 31p. (J). (gr. -1-1). 11.65 *(978-0-7569-5618-9(8))* Perfection Learning Corp.

—Malcolm at Midnight. Beck, W. H. (ENG.). 272p. (gr. 2-5). 2015. (YA). pap. 7.99 *(978-0-544-33666-7(6)*, HMH Books For Young Readers); 2012. (J). 16.99 *(978-0-547-68100-9(3))* Houghton Mifflin Harcourt Publishing Co.

—Malcolm under the Stars. Beck, W. H. 2015. (ENG.). 272p. (J). (gr. 2-5). 16.99 *(978-0-544-39267-0(1)*, HMH Books For Young Readers) Houghton Mifflin Harcourt Publishing Co.

—More. Springman, I. C. 2012. (ENG.). 40p. (J). (gr. -1-3). 16.99 *(978-0-547-61083-2(1))* Houghton Mifflin Harcourt Publishing Co.

—Popcorn! Landau, Elaine. 2003. (ENG.). 32p. (J). (gr. 1-4). pap. 7.95 *(978-1-57091-443-0(5))* Charlesbridge Publishing, Inc.

Lies, Brian. Bats at the Library. Lies, Brian. 2008. (Bat Book Ser.). (ENG.). 32p. (J). (gr. -1-3). 16.00 *(978-0-618-99923-1(X))* Houghton Mifflin Harcourt Publishing Co.

—Bats in the Band. Lies, Brian. 2014. (Bat Book Ser.). (ENG.). 32p. (J). (gr. -1-3). 17.99 *(978-0-544-10569-0(9)*, HMH Books For Young Readers) Houghton Mifflin Harcourt Publishing Co.

Liese, Charles. Me & Caleb Again. Meyer, Franklyn E. 2006. (J). kivar 16.95 *(978-0-9789388-1-9(X))* Hester Publishing.

Liessner, Richard. The Foot Prince. Liessner, Richard. 2006. 24p. (J). 9.95 *(978-0-9766129-5-7(X))* Raindrop Bks.

Liest, Christina. The Graveyard Hounds, 1 vol. Hughes, Vi. 2009. (ENG.). 168p. (J). (gr. 3-5). pap. 12.95 *(978-1-896580-49-4(1))* Tradewind Bks. CAN. Dist: Orca Bk. Pubs. USA.

Lietha, Dan, et al. Dinosaur Pak & Stak. 2007. (J). 10.99 *(978-0-89051-486-3(0))* Master Bks.

Liew, Sonny, et al. Fairy Tales I Just Made Up: Snarky Bedtime Stories for Weirdo Children. Friesen, Ray. 2015. (ENG.). 80p. (J). (gr. 3-7). 18.95 *(978-0-9802314-4-1(2))* Don't Eat Any Bugs Prodns.

Liew, Sonny. The Shadow Hero. Yang, Gene Luen. 2014. (ENG.). 176p. (YA). (gr. 7-12). pap. 17.99 *(978-1-59643-697-8(2)*, First Second Bks.) Roaring Brook Pr.

—The Shadow Hero. Yang, Gene Luen. ed. 2014. lib. bdg. 30.60 *(978-0-606-35521-6(9))* Turtleback Bks.

Life, Kay. My Red Balloon. Bunting, Eve. 2005. (ENG.). 32p. (J). (gr. -1-2). 15.95 *(978-1-59078-263-7(1))* Boyds Mills Pr.

Life, Kay. Keys & Clues for Benny. Life, Kay, tr. 2004. (Adventures of Benny & Watch Ser.: No. 11). (ENG.). 32p. (J). (gr. 1-3). pap. 4.99 *(978-0-8075-4172-2(9))* Whitman, Albert & Co.

Ligasan, Darryl. Allie's Basketball Dream. Barber, Barbara E. 2013. (ENG.). 32p. (J). (gr. -1-5). pap. 9.95 *(978-1-880000-72-4(5))* Lee & Low Bks., Inc.

Light, Carol. Oops, a Curious Horse Big Book. Gansle, Sherry. 2003. 56p. (J). *(978-0-9745803-6-4(8))* Little Big Tomes.

—Oops, a Curious Horse Little Book. Gansle, Sherry. 2003. 52p. (J). *(978-0-9745803-7-1(6))* Little Big Tomes.

—Oops, a Curious Horse Story Book Reader. Gansle, Sherry. 2003. 58p. (J). *(978-0-9745803-5-7(X))* Little Big Tomes.

—Oops, a Curious Horse Story Telling Board. 2003. (J). *(978-0-9745803-4-0(1))* Little Big Tomes.

Light, Carol. Chickensing Big Book. Light, Carol. 2003. (J). *(978-0-9745803-2-6(5))* Little Big Tomes.

—Chickensing Little Book. Light, Carol. 2003. 108p. (J). *(978-0-9745803-3-3(3))* Little Big Tomes.

—Chickensing Story Book Reader. Light, Carol. 2003. 60p. (J). *(978-0-9745803-1-9(7))* Little Big Tomes.

Light, Kelly. Don't Blink! Rosenthal, Amy Krouse. 2015. (J). *(978-0-375-97364-2(8))* Random Hse., Inc.
—Elvis & the Underdogs. Lee, Jenny. 2013. (Elvis & the Underdogs Ser.: 1). (ENG.). 304p. (J). (gr. 3-7). 16.99 *(978-0-06-223554-1(0))* HarperCollins Pubs.
—Elvis & the Underdogs: Secrets, Secret Service, & Room Service. Lee, Jenny. (Elvis & the Underdogs Ser.: 2). (ENG.). 352p. (J). (gr. 3-7). 2015. pap. 6.99 *(978-0-06-223557-2(5))*; 2014. 16.99 *(978-0-06-223556-5(7))* HarperCollins Pubs.
—The Quirks & the Quirkalicious Birthday. Soderberg, Erin. 2015. (Quirks Ser.). (ENG.). 208p. (J). (gr. 3-6). 13.99 *(978-1-61963-370-4(1)*, Bloomsbury USA Childrens) Bloomsbury USA.
—We Read Phonics-Who Took the Cookbook? Orshoski, Paul. 2012. 32p. (J). 9.95 *(978-1-60115-347-0(3))*; pap. 4.99 *(978-1-60115-348-7(1))* Treasure Bay, Inc.
Light, Kelly. Louise Loves Art. Light, Kelly. 2014. (ENG.). 40p. (J). (gr. -1-3). 17.99 *(978-0-06-224817-6(0))* HarperCollins Pubs.
Light, Steve. Have You Seen My Monster? Light, Steven. 2015. (ENG.). 48p. (J). (-k). 16.99 *(978-0-7636-7513-4(X))* Candlewick Pr.
Light, Steve. The Christmas Giant. Light, Steve. 2010. (ENG.). 32p. (J). (gr. -1-2). 15.99 *(978-0-7636-4692-9(X))* Candlewick Pr.
—Have You Seen My Dragon? Light, Steve. 2014. (ENG.). 48p. (J). (-k). 16.99 *(978-0-7636-6648-4(3))* Candlewick Pr.
—I Am Happy: A Touch-and-Feel Book of Feelings. Light, Steve. 2005. 10p. (J). (gr. k-4). reprint ed. 13.00 *(978-0-7567-9630-3(X))* DIANE Publishing Co.
—Zephyr Takes Flight. Light, Steve. 2012. (ENG.). 40p. (J). (gr. -1-3). 16.99 *(978-0-7636-5695-9(X))* Candlewick Pr.
Lightburn, Ron. Frankenstink! A Cautionary Tale. 2015. (ENG.). 32p. (J). (gr. -1-3). 17.99 *(978-1-77049-694-1(7))* Tundra Bks. CAN. Dist: Random Hse., Inc.
—The Happily Ever Afternoon. Jennings, Sharon. 2006. (ENG.). 24p. (J). (gr. -1-k). pap. 7.95 *(978-1-55037-944-0(5)*, 9781550379440) Annick Pr., Ltd. CAN. Dist: Firefly Bks., Ltd.
—How Smudge Came, 1 vol. Gregory, Nan. (ENG.). 32p. (J). pap. 15.95 *(978-0-88995-161-7(6))* Red Deer Pr. CAN. Dist: Ingram Pub. Services.
—Juba This, Juba That. Becker, Helaine. 2011. (ENG.). 24p. (J). (gr. k-k). 17.95 *(978-0-88776-975-7(6)*, Tundra Bks.) Tundra Bks. CAN. Dist: Penguin Random Hse., LLC.
—Pumpkin People, 1 vol. Lightburn, Sandra. ed. 2009. (ENG.). 32p. (J). (gr. -1-5). 17.95 *(978-1-55109-681-0(1))* Nimbus Publishing, Ltd. CAN. Dist: Orca Bk. Pubs. USA.
—Roll On: Rick Hansen Wheels Around the World, 1 vol. Manson, Ainslie. 2013. (ENG.). 40p. (J). (gr. k-5). pap. 10.95 *(978-1-77100-268-4(9))* Greystone Books Ltd. CAN. Dist: Perseus-PGW.
Lightfoot, Martha. Digger to the Rescue. Archer, Mandy. 2012. (Busy Wheels Ser.). (ENG.). 24p. (J). (gr. -1-k). 15.99 *(978-1-60992-229-0(8))* QEB Publishing Inc.
—Fire Truck Is Flashing. Archer, Mandy. 2012. (Busy Wheels Ser.). (ENG.). 24p. (J). (gr. -1-k). 15.99 *(978-1-60992-228-3(X))* QEB Publishing Inc.
—The Lion's Share. 2009. (Finger Puppet Bks.). (ENG.). 24p. (J). (gr. -1-1). *(978-1-84643-248-4(0))* Child's Play International Ltd.
—Race Car Is Roaring. Archer, Mandy. 2012. (Busy Wheels Ser.). (ENG.). 24p. (J). (gr. -1-k). 15.99 *(978-1-60992-231-3(X))* QEB Publishing Inc.
—Tractor Saves the Day. Archer, Mandy. 2012. (Busy Wheels Ser.). (ENG.). 24p. (J). (gr. -1-k). 15.99 *(978-1-60992-230-6(1))* QEB Publishing Inc.
Ligi, Raffaella. See Inside Fairyland. Davidson, Susanna. 2007. (See Inside Board Bks). 14p. (J). (gr. -1-k). bds. 12.99 *(978-0-7945-1570-6(3)*, Usborne) EDC Publishing.
Lignell, Brent. Listen to the Raindrops: Featuring the Storm Song. Lignell, Kirk. 2007. 32p. (J). (gr. -1-3). 17.95 *(978-1-932399-15-8(1))* Huron River Pr.
Liguori, Kathy. The Ducks of Congress Park. Losey, Tori. 2004. 36p. (J). *(978-0-925168-97-9(1))* North Country Bks., Inc.
Liittschwager, David, photos by. Edible Schoolyard: A Universal Idea. Waters, Alice & Duane, Daniel. 2008. (ENG.). 80p. (gr. 13-17). 24.95 *(978-0-8118-6280-6(1))* Chronicle Bks. LLC.
Lilagan, Kenneth D. Ruby & Lucy Searching for Silly. Boodey, David M. 2010. (ENG.). 26p. pap. 9.99 *(978-1-4538-1881-7(2))* CreateSpace Independent Publishing Platform.
Lilje, Karen. The Little Red Hen. Orford, Margie. 2011. (Best Loved Tales for Africa Ser.). (ENG.). 32p. (J). (gr. k-2). pap. 10.95 *(978-1-77009-821-3(6))* Jacana Media ZAF. Dist: Independent Pubs. Group.
Liljeblad, Lynn. The Travels of Oso & Neo. Sherayko, Peter. 2011. (ENG.). 28p. pap. 9.95 *(978-1-4563-9961-0(6))* CreateSpace Independent Publishing Platform.
Lill, Debra. Music & Drum: Voices of War & Peace, Hope & Dreams. Robb, Laura. 2005. 32p. (J). reprint ed. 17.00 *(978-0-7567-9580-1(X))* DIANE Publishing Co.
Lilly, Kenneth. Atlas Visual de los Animales. Taylor, Barbara. 2nd ed. (Colección Atlas Visual). (SPA.). 64p. (YA). (gr. 5-8). *(978-84-216-1815-8(6)*, BU4894) Bruño, Editorial ESP. Dist: Lectorum Pubns., Inc.
—A Field Full of Horses. Hansard, Peter. 2008. (Read, Listen, & Wonder Ser.). (ENG.). 32p. (J). (gr. -1-3). pap. 8.99 *(978-0-7636-3828-3(5))* Candlewick Pr.
Lilly, Matthew. Charged Up: The Story of Electricity. Bailey, Jacqui. 2004. (Science Works). (ENG.). 32p. (gr. 3-6). 27.32 *(978-1-4048-0568-2(0))*; per. 7.95 *(978-1-4048-1129-4(X))* Picture Window Bks. (Nonfiction Picture Bks.).
—Cracking Up: A Story about Erosion, 1 vol. Bailey, Jacqui. 2006. (Science Works). (ENG.). 32p. (gr. 3-6). 27.32 *(978-1-4048-1594-0(5))*; per. 7.95 *(978-1-4048-1996-2(7))* Picture Window Bks. (Nonfiction Picture Bks.).
—A Drop in the Ocean: The Story of Water. Bailey, Jacqui. 2004. (Science Works). (ENG.). 32p. (gr. 3-6). 27.32 *(978-1-4048-0566-8(4))*; per. 7.95 *(978-1-4048-1127-0(3))* Picture Window Bks. (Nonfiction Picture Bks.).
—Monster Bones: The Story of a Dinosaur Fossil, 1 vol. Bailey, Jacqui. 2004. (Science Works). (ENG.). 32p. (gr. 3-6). 27.32 *(978-1-4048-0565-1(6)*, Nonfiction Picture Bks.) Picture Window Bks.
—The Rock Factory: The Story about the Rock Cycle. Bailey, Jacqui. 2006. (Science Works). (ENG.). 32p. (gr. 3-6). 27.32 *(978-1-4048-1596-4(1)*, Nonfiction Picture Bks.) Picture Window Bks.
—Sun up, Sun Down: The Story of Day & Night. Bailey, Jacqui. 2004. (Science Works). (ENG.). 32p. (gr. 3-6). 27.32 *(978-1-4048-0567-5(2))*; per. 7.95 *(978-1-4048-1128-7(1))* Picture Window Bks. (Nonfiction Picture Bks.).
Lim, Hwei. Our First Caribou Hunt, 1 vol. Noah, Jennifer & Giroux, Chris. 2015. (ENG.). 32p. (J). (gr. k-2). 10.95 ***(978-1-77227-022-8(9))*** Inhabit Media Inc. CAN. Dist: Independent Pubs. Group.
Lim, Kara. Demon Diary. Lee, Jee-Hyung. rev. ed. 192p. Vol. 2. 2003. (gr. 8-18). pap. 9.99 *(978-1-59182-155-7(X))*; Vol. 4. 2003. pap. 9.99 *(978-1-59182-157-1(6))*; Vol. 5. 2004. pap. 9.99 *(978-1-59182-430-5(3))*; Vol. 6. 2004. pap. 9.99 *(978-1-59182-431-2(1))* TOKYOPOP, Inc.
—Demon Diary, 7 vols., Vol. 7. Jee-Hyung, Lee. rev. ed. 2004. 192p. pap. 9.99 *(978-1-59182-432-9(X))* TOKYOPOP, Inc.
Lim, Ron. Meet the Marvel Super Heroes. Wyatt, Chris. 2nd ed. 2015. (ENG.). 160p. (J). (gr. 1-3). 12.99 *(978-1-4847-0670-1(6)*, Marvel Pr.) Disney Publishing Worldwide.
Lim, Ron & Millet, Jason. Reloaded Vol. I: In the Name of Patriotism. Rieber, John Ney. 2005. 144p. pap. 12.95 *(978-1-932796-23-0(1))* Devil's Due Publishing, Inc.
Lim, Ron & Rosenberg, Rachelle. Happy Holidays! From Avengers: Featuring the Voice of Stan Lee. Disney Book Group Staff & Thomas, Rich. 2014. (ENG.). 48p. (J). (gr. 1-3). 8.99 *(978-1-4847-1227-6(7)*, Marvel Pr.) Disney Publishing Worldwide.
Lim, Ron & Rosenberg, Rachelle. World of Reading: Ant-Man This Is Ant-Man: Level 1. Wyatt, Chris. 2015. (World of Reading Ser.). (ENG.). 32p. (J). (gr. -1-k). pap. 3.99 ***(978-1-4847-1455-3(5)****, Marvel Pr.) Disney Publishing Worldwide.
Lim, Ron & Rosenberg, Rachelle. World of Reading Falcon: This Is Falcon: Level 1. Marvel Book Group & Wong, Clarissa S. 2015. (World of Reading Ser.). (ENG.). 32p. (J). (gr. 1-3). pap. 3.99 *(978-1-4847-2259-6(0)*, Marvel Pr.) Disney Publishing Worldwide.
Lim, Ron & Troy, Andy. Star-Lord - Knowhere to Run. Wyatt, Chris. 2014. (ENG.). 128p. (J). (gr. 3-7). pap. 5.99 *(978-1-4847-1269-6(2)*, Marvel Pr.) Disney Publishing Worldwide.
Lim, Ron, jt. illus. see Bagley, Mark.
Lima, Graca. A Heart Alone in the Land of Darkness. Rozen, Beti. 2nd ed. 2004. Orig. Title: A Heart Alone in theLand of Darkness. 48p. 15.95 *(978-0-9642333-2-4(0))* Sem Fronteiras Pr., Ltd.
—Stolen Spirit. Rozen, Beti. 2nd ed. 2004. 32p. (gr. 3-7). pap. *(978-0-9642333-1-7(2))* Sem Fronteiras Pr., Ltd.
Lima, Sidney. Flights. McGregor, Don. 4th rev. ed. 2006. (Zorro Ser.). (ENG.). 96p. (J). pap. 7.95 *(978-1-59707-026-3(2))* Papercutz.
Limmer, Hannes. Lo Que los Ninos Quieren Saber. Leipe, Ulla. (SPA.). 180p. (YA). 11.95 *(978-84-241-5501-8(7)*, EV867) Everest Editora ESP. Dist: Continental Bk. Co., Inc.
Lin, Albert & Smith, Crystal. Questions for Kids: A Book to Discover a Child's Imagination & Knowledge. Smith, Michael. 2003. 208p. (J). (gr. k-4). pap. 9.95 *(978-0-9669437-1-9(6))* East West Discovery Pr.
Lin, Albert, jt. illus. see Smith, Crystal.
Lin, Grace. The Jade Necklace. Yee, Paul. 2006. 29p. (J). (gr. 4-8). reprint ed. 16.00 *(978-1-4223-5135-2(1))* DIANE Publishing Co.
—One Year in Beijing. Wang, Xiaohong. 2006. 32p. (J). (gr. -1-3). 16.95 *(978-0-9747302-5-7(4))* Chinasprout, Inc.
—Red Is a Dragon. Thong, Roseanne. 2014. 40p. pap. 7.00 *(978-1-61003-333-6(7))* Center for the Collaborative Classroom.
—Red Is a Dragon: A Book of Colors. Thong, Roseanne. 2008. (ENG.). 40p. (J). (gr. -1-17). pap. 7.99 *(978-0-8118-6481-7(2))* Chronicle Bks. LLC.
—Round Is a Mooncake: A Book of Shapes. Thong, Roseanne. 2014. (ENG.). 40p. (J). (gr. -1-k). 7.99 *(978-1-4521-3644-8(0))* Chronicle Bks. LLC.
—The Seven Chinese Sisters. Tucker, Kathy. 2003. (ENG.). 32p. (J). (gr. k-3). per. 6.99 *(978-0-8075-7310-5(8))* Whitman, Albert & Co.
—Where on Earth Is My Bagel? Park, Frances & Park, Ginger. 2013. (ENG.). 32p. (J). (gr. -1-4). 16.95 *(978-1-58430-033-5(7))* Lee & Low Bks., Inc.
Lin, Grace. Dim Sum for Everyone! Lin, Grace. (ENG.). (J). (gr. -1-2). 2014. 24p. bds. 6.99 *(978-0-385-75488-0(4)*, Knopf Bks. for Young Readers); 2003. 32p. 7.99 *(978-0-440-41770-5(8)*, Dragonfly Bks.) Random Hse. Children's Bks.
—Fortune Cookie Fortunes. Lin, Grace. 2006. (ENG.). 32p. (J). (gr. -1-2). 7.99 *(978-0-440-42192-4(6)*, Dragonfly Bks.) Random Hse. Children's Bks.
—Our Seasons. Lin, Grace. Mckneally, Ranida T. 2007. (ENG.). 32p. (J). (gr. k-3). pap. 7.95 *(978-1-57091-361-7(7))* Charlesbridge Publishing, Inc.
—The Red Thread: An Adoption Fairy Tale. Lin, Grace. 2007. (ENG.). 32p. (J). (gr. -1-3). 16.99 *(978-0-8075-6922-1(4))* Whitman, Albert & Co.
Lin, Grace, jt. illus. see Hong, Lily Toy.
Lin, Melanie, jt. illus. see Amber, Holly.
Lin, Yali. The Fishy Fountain. Thielbar, Melinda. 2010. (Manga Math Mysteries Ser.: 6). (ENG.). 48p. (gr. 3-5). 29.27 *(978-0-7613-4908-2(1))* Lerner Publishing Group.
—The Fishy Fountain: A Mystery with Multiplication & Division. Thielbar, Melinda. 2011. (Manga Math Mysteries Ser.: 6). (ENG.). 48p. (gr. 3-5). pap. 6.95 *(978-0-7613-8135-8(X)*, Graphic Universe) Lerner Publishing Group.
—#6 the Fishy Fountain: A Mystery with Multiplication & Division. Thielbar, Melinda. 2011. (Manga Math Mysteries Set II Ser.). pap. 39.62 *(978-0-7613-8363-5(8)*, Graphic Universe) Lerner Publishing Group.
Linares, Jairo. Cuentos de Fantasmas. Panamericana Staff, ed. 2003. (Coleccion el Pozo y el Pendulo Ser.). (SPA.). 138p. (YA). (gr. 4-7). pap. *(978-958-30-1066-8(9))* Panamericana Editorial.
—Pinocho. 2004. (Literatura Juvenil (Panamericana Editorial) Ser.).Tr. of Pinocchio. (SPA.). 283p. (J). (gr. 4-7). pap. *(978-958-30-0803-0(6)*, PV30464) Centro de Informacion y Desarrollo de la Comunicacion y la Literatura MEX. Dist: Lectorum Pubns., Inc.
Lincoln, Hazel. Little Snow Bear, 1 vol. Lincoln, Hazel. 2004. (ENG.). 32p. (J). pap. 17.95 *(978-0-86315-454-6(9))* Floris Bks. GBR. Dist: SteinerBooks, Inc.
Lind, Jenny. Navajo Coyote Tales, 1 vol. 2007. (ENG.). 50p. (gr. 2-18). reprint ed. pap. 9.99 *(978-0-941270-52-6(1))* Gibbs Smith, Publisher.
Lind, Kathleen & Simonis, Cheryl. Best Friends. Lind, Kathleen. 2005. (J). 4.95 *(978-1-58597-305-7(X))* Leathers Publishing.
Linda, Graves & Graves, Linda. Sister Bear: A Norse Tale, 0 vols. Yolen, Jane. 2011. (ENG.). 32p. (J). (gr. k-3). 17.99 *(978-0-7614-5958-3(8)*, 9780761459583, Amazon Children's Publishing) Amazon Publishing.
Lindahl, Larry, photos by. The Insider's Guide to Sedona. Andres, Dennis Michael. 2003. 222p. per. 16.95 *(978-0-9721202-1-0(1)*, 825-694) Meta Adventures Publishing & DIA Publishing.
Lindblad, Stefan. Strange Creatures. Orme, David. 2010. (Fact to Fiction Grafx Ser.). 36p. pap. 7.45 *(978-0-7891-7994-4(6))* Perfection Learning Corp.
Linde, Hermann. The Green Snake & the Beautiful Lily. Goethes Fairy Tale Staff. Allen, Joan deRis, ed. Heuscher, Julius E., tr. from GER. 2006. 53p. (J). (gr. 3-7). 25.00 *(978-0-88010-570-5(4))* SteinerBooks, Inc.
Linden, Martijn van der. The Prince Child. Rinck, Maranke. 2004. (ENG & GER.). 32p. (J). 16.95 *(978-1-932425-15-4(2)*, Lemniscaat) Boyds Mills Pr.
Lindenbaum, Pija. Mirabelle. Lindgren, Astrid. Dyssegaard, Elisabeth Kallick, tr. from SWE. 2003. 32p. (J). 15.00 *(978-91-29-65821-7(7))* R & S Bks. SWE. Dist: Macmillan.
Lindman. Flicka, Ricka, Dicka & the Little Dog. Lindman. 2013. (Flicka, Ricka, Dicka Ser.). (ENG.). 32p. (J). (gr. k-3). 9.99 *(978-0-8075-2509-8(X))* Whitman, Albert & Co.
—Flicka, Ricka, Dicka & the Strawberries. Lindman. 2013. (Flicka, Ricka, Dicka Ser.). (ENG.). 32p. (J). (gr. k-3). 9.99 *(978-0-8075-2512-8(X))* Whitman, Albert & Co.
—Flicka, Ricka, Dicka & the Three Kittens. Lindman. 2013. (Flicka, Ricka, Dicka Ser.). (ENG.). 32p. (J). (gr. k-3). 9.99 *(978-0-8075-2515-9(4))* Whitman, Albert & Co.
—Flicka, Ricka, Dicka & Their New Skates: Updated Edition with Paperdolls. Lindman. 2011. (ENG.). 32p. (J). (gr. k-2). 9.99 *(978-0-8075-2496-1(4))* Whitman, Albert & Co.
—Flicka, Ricka, Dicka Bake a Cake. Lindman. 2013. (Flicka, Ricka, Dicka Ser.). (ENG.). 32p. (J). (gr. k-3). 9.99 *(978-0-8075-2506-7(5))* Whitman, Albert & Co.
Lindman, Amy Sorvaag. Vegetable Soup - The Fruit Bowl. Jones, Susan Smith & Warren, Dianne. rev. ed. 2006. 64p. (J). (gr. -1-3). per. 14.95 *(978-0-9652736-0-2(1))* Oasis Pubns.
Lindman, Maj. Flicka, Ricka, Dicka & the New Dotted Dresses. Lindman, Maj. 2012. (Flicka, Ricka, Dicka Ser.). (ENG.). 32p. (J). (gr. k-3). 9.99 *(978-0-8075-2484-8(0))* Whitman, Albert & Co.
—Flicka, Ricka, Dicka & Their New Skates. Lindman, Maj. 2011. (ENG.). 32p. (J). (gr. k-2). 9.99 *(978-0-8075-2491-6(3))* Whitman, Albert & Co.
—Flicka, Ricka, Dicka Go to Market. Lindman, Maj. 2012. (ENG.). 32p. (J). (gr. k-3). 9.99 *(978-0-8075-2478-7(6))*; 9.99 *(978-0-8075-2479-4(4))* Whitman, Albert & Co.
Lindmark, Margaret. Braids - Trencitas. Contreras, Kathleen. 2009. (ENG & SPA.). 32p. (J). (gr. -1-3). 14.99 *(978-1-933032-27-6(8))* Lectorum Pubns., Inc.
—Fatima. Lipp, Frederick. 2006. 32p. (J). pap. *(978-1-59336-302-4(8))* Mondo Publishing.
Lindmark, Margaret. Sweet Memories/Dulces Recuerdos. Lindmark, Margaret. Contreras, Kathleen. 2014. (SPA & ENG.). 32p. (J). (gr. 2-4). pap. 14.99 *(978-1-933032-91-7(X))* Lectorum Pubns., Inc.
Lindner, Ellen & Purvis, Leland. A House Divided. Poe, Marshall. 2009. (Turning Points Ser.). (ENG.). 128p. (J). (gr. 3-7). pap. 8.99 *(978-1-4169-5057-8(5)*, Simon & Schuster/Paula Wiseman Bks.) Simon & Schuster/Paula Wiseman Bks.
Lindner, Ellen, jt. illus. see Purvis, Leland.
Lindro. To Live a Truer Life: A Story of the Hopedale Community. Hughes, Lynn Gordon. 2003. 32p. (J). 10.00 *(978-0-9725017-2-9(X))* Blackstone Editions.
Lindsay, Anne, photos by. Before It Wriggles Away. Wong, Janet S. 2006. (Meet the Author Ser.). (ENG.). 32p. (J). 14.95 *(978-1-57274-861-3(3)*, 735, Meet the Author) Owen, Richard C. Pubs., Inc.
Lindsay, Marion. The Case of the Feathered Mask. Webb, Holly. 2016. (ENG.). 192p. (J). ***(978-0-544-61993-7(5))*** Harcourt.
—The Case of the Phantom Cat. Webb, Holly. 2015. (Mysteries of Maisie Hitchins Ser.: 3). (ENG.). 176p. (J). (gr. 2-5). 15.99 ***(978-0-544-58243-9(8)****, HMH Books For Young Readers) Houghton Mifflin Harcourt Publishing Co.
Lindsay, Marion. Ready, Steady, Ghost! Baguley, Elizabeth. 2014. (ENG.). 32p. (J). (gr. -1-k). 16.99 *(978-1-4231-8039-5(9))* Hyperion Bks. for Children.
Lindsay, Marion. The Case of the Stolen Sixpence. Lindsay, Marion. Webb, Holly. 2014. (Mysteries of Maisie Hitchins Ser.: 1). (ENG.). 176p. (J). (gr. 2-5). 14.99 *(978-0-544-33928-6(2)*, HMH Books For Young Readers) Houghton Mifflin Harcourt Publishing Co.
Lindsay, Norman. The Magic Pudding. Lindsay, Norman. 2004. (New York Review Children's Collection). (ENG.). 184p. (J). (gr. 4-7). 19.95 *(978-1-59017-101-1(2)*, NYR Children's Collection) New York Review of Bks., Inc., The.
Lindsay, Sierra. Spindly the Spider. Lindsay, Sierra. 2012. 20p. pap. 10.99 *(978-0-9836641-9-2(6))* Kids At Heart Publishing & Bks.
Lindsey, Cath. Hairy Toe. Carthew, Mark. 2007. (Collins Big Cat Ser.). (ENG.). 24p. (J). pap. 8.99 *(978-0-00-722867-6(8))* HarperCollins Pubs. Ltd. GBR. Dist: Independent Pubs. Group.
Lindsey, Jessica. Eager Beavers. Burt, Vicky. 2012. 28p. pap. 13.99 *(978-1-937129-39-2(X))* Faithful Life Pubs.
—Hot Dog or Egg Sandwich? Burt, Vickie. 2013. 28p. pap. 13.99 *(978-1-937129-87-3(X))* Faithful Life Pubs.
Lindsey, Maurice. Dad Had Issues. Gadson, Cynthia. 2013. (ENG.). 24p. (J). pap. 19.99 *(978-1-62563-373-6(4))* Tate Publishing & Enterprises, LLC.
—Mom Had a Problem. Gadson, Cynthia. 2nd ed. 2013. (ENG.). 29p. (J). pap. 19.99 *(978-1-62563-366-8(1))* Tate Publishing & Enterprises, LLC.
—Show Me! Teach Me! Guide Me! Poetry Through a Child's Perspective. Gadson, Cynthia. 2nd ed. 2013. (ENG.). 24p. (J). pap. 19.99 *(978-1-62563-365-1(3))* Tate Publishing & Enterprises, LLC.
Lindsey, Michael. The Catarbie Conspiracy: Book 1 of the Houkura Series. deSouza, Sabrina. 2008. (Houkura Ser.: 1). 400p. pap. 14.95 *(978-0-9805090-0-7(9))* Houkura AUS. Dist: AtlasBooks Distribution.
Lindsey, Robin, photos by. Leopard & Silkie: One Boy's Quest to Save the Seal Pups. Peterson, Brenda. 2012. (ENG., 32p. (J). (gr. -1-3). 17.99 *(978-0-8050-9167-0(X)*, Holt, Henry & Co. Bks. For Young Readers) Holt, Henry & Co.
—Seal Pup Rescue. Peterson, Brenda. 2013. (My Readers Ser.). (ENG., 32p. (J). (gr. k-2). 15.99 *(978-1-250-02775-7(6))*; pap. 3.99 *(978-1-250-02776-4(4))* Square Fish.
Lindsley, Jennifer. The Fifolet, 1 vol. Downing, Johnette. 2015. (ENG.). 32p. (J). (gr. k-3). 16.99 *(978-1-4556-2036-4(X))* Pelican Publishing Co., Inc.
Lindstrom, Brita, jt. illus. see Peterson, Sara.
Lindstrom, Eva. Bertil & the Bathroom Elephants. Lindahl, Inger. Dyssegaard, Elisabeth Kallick, tr. 2003. 28p. (J). 15.00 *(978-91-29-65944-3(2))* R & S Bks. SWE. Dist: Macmillan.
Lindwall, Erika. The Moose & the Goose. Lindwall, Erika. 2013. 32p. pap. 11.95 *(978-1-940728-01-8(0)*, Simple Faith Bks.) Sunrise Mountain Bks.
Line Art Staff. Tennessee Jeopardy! Answers & Questions about Our State! Marsh, Carole. 2004. 32p. (J). (gr. 3-8). pap. 7.95 *(978-0-7933-9812-6(6))* Gallopade International.
Lineberger, Judy. Ick the Stick: Yes, I Can Read! Nature Series, Book 1. D'Agata, Tabatha Jean. 2006. (Yes, I Can Read! Ser.: 1). 24p. (J). pap. 6.95 *(978-1-934138-01-4(0))* Bouncing Ball Bks., Inc.
—Storm Tunes: Yes, I Can Read! Nature Series, Book 2. D'Agata, Tabatha Jean. 2006. (Yes, I Can Read! Ser.: Bk. 2). 30p. (J). pap. 6.95 *(978-1-934138-02-1(9))* Bouncing Ball Bks., Inc.
Linenthal, Peter. Look at Baby's House! 2008. (ENG.). 18p. (J). (gr. k — 1). bds. 6.99 *(978-0-525-42061-3(4)*, Dutton Juvenile) Penguin Publishing Group.
Linenthal, Peter. That's Our Custodian! Linenthal, Peter, photos by. Morris, Ann. 2003. (That's Our School Ser.). (ENG.). 32p. (gr. k-3). lib. bdg. 22.60 *(978-0-7613-2401-0(1)*, Millbrook Pr.) Lerner Publishing Group.
—That's Our Gym Teacher! Linenthal, Peter, photos by. Morris, Ann. 2003. (That's Our School Ser.). (ENG.). 32p. (gr. k-3). lib. bdg. 22.60 *(978-0-7613-2403-4(8)*, Millbrook Pr.) Lerner Publishing Group.
—That's Our Librarian! Linenthal, Peter, photos by. Morris, Ann. 2003. (That's Our School Ser.). (ENG.). 32p. (gr. k-3). lib. bdg. 22.60 *(978-0-7613-2400-3(3)*, Millbrook Pr.) Lerner Publishing Group.
—That's Our Nurse! Linenthal, Peter, photos by. Morris, Ann. 2003. (That's Our School Ser.). (ENG.). 32p. (gr. k-3). lib. bdg. 22.60 *(978-0-7613-2402-7(X)*, Millbrook Pr.) Lerner Publishing Group.
Linenthal, Peter, photos by. Grandma Hekmat Remembers: An Arab-American Family Story. Morris, Ann. 2003. (What Was It Like, Grandma? Ser.). (ENG., 32p. (gr. 2-5). lib. bdg. 22.60 *(978-0-7613-2864-3(5)*, Millbrook Pr.) Lerner Publishing Group.
Lingard, Darren. Getting Ahead: Drugs, Technology, & Competitive Advantage, 1 vol. Hile, Lori. 2012. (Ethics of Sports Ser.). (ENG.). 64p. (gr. 6-10). lib. bdg. 34.00 *(978-1-4329-5978-4(6))* Heinemann-Raintree.
Lingas, Leo. Escape from East Berlin. Downey, Glen. 2007. 48p. (J). lib. bdg. 23.08 *(978-1-4242-1635-2(4))* Fitzgerald Bks.
Lingenfelter, Jim. Fall Is Fun, 1 vol. Meister, Cari. 2010. (First Graphics: Seasons Ser.). (ENG.). 24p. (gr. 1-2). lib. bdg. 23.32 *(978-1-4296-4731-1(0))*; pap. 6.29 *(978-1-4296-5623-8(9))*; pap. 35.70 *(978-1-4296-5692-4(1))* Capstone Pr., Inc.
—Spring Is Special, 1 vol. Meister, Cari. 2010. (First Graphics: Seasons Ser.). (ENG.). 24p. (gr. 1-2). lib. bdg. 23.32 *(978-1-4296-4729-8(9))*; pap. 6.29 *(978-1-4296-5621-4(2))*; pap. 35.70 *(978-1-4296-5693-1(X))* Capstone Pr., Inc.
—Summer Is Super, 1 vol. Meister, Cari. 2010. (First Graphics: Seasons Ser.). (ENG.). 24p. (gr. 1-2). lib. bdg. 23.32 *(978-1-4296-4730-4(2))*; pap. 6.29 *(978-1-4296-5622-1(0))*; pap. 35.70 *(978-1-4296-5694-8(8))* Capstone Pr., Inc.
—Winter Is Wonderful, 1 vol. Meister, Cari. 2010. (First Graphics: Seasons Ser.). (ENG.). 24p. (gr. 1-2). lib. bdg. 23.32 *(978-1-4296-4732-8(9))*; pap. 6.29 *(978-1-4296-5624-5(7))*; pap. 35.70 *(978-1-4296-5695-5(6))* Capstone Pr., Inc.
Liniers. Escrito y Dibujado Por Enriqueta: TOON Level 3. 2015. (ENG & SPA.). 64p. (J). (gr. k). pap. 12.95 ***(978-1-935179-91-7(8))*** TOON Books / RAW Junior, LLC.
Liniers. The Big Wet Balloon (El Globo Grande y Mojado) Liniers. 2013. (ENG & SPA.). 32p. (J). (gr. -1-3). 12.95 *(978-1-935179-40-5(3))* TOON Books / RAW Junior, LLC.

L

—The Big Wet Balloon (El Globo Grande y Mojado) Liniers. 2013. (ENG & SPA.). 32p. (J). (gr. -1-3). pap. 4.99 (978-1-935179-39-9(X)) TOON Books / RAW Junior, LLC.

Liniers, Ricardo. The Big Wet Balloon. Liniers, Ricardo. 2013. (ENG.). 32p. (J). (gr. -1-3). 12.95 (978-1-935179-32-0(2)) TOON Books / RAW Junior, LLC.

Linke, Donald Q., Jr. IJustWantTo SLEEP for KIDS. Benett, Janet M. Kater, Mary, ed. 2005. (J). 56.97 net. (978-0-9744357-0-1(8)) IJustWantToSleep, Inc.

Linn, Laurent, jt. illus. see Nelson, Mary Beth.

Linsdell, Jo. Jasmine at Work. Rochelle, Maria. 2013. 34p. pap. 9.99 (978-0-9913342-1-6(3)) Draper Publishing.

Linsley, Paul. The Conifer Court Competition. Linsley, Sonja Paschal. 2006. 26p. (J). 18.95 (978-0-9766062-1-5(6), HGP 2005-2) Higher Ground Pr.

Linsley, Paul Adam. May I Have the First Dance? Linsley, Sonja Paschal. 2005. 24p. (J). 19.95 net. (978-0-9766062-0-8(8)) Higher Ground Pr.

Lintern, Tom. The Tooth Fairy Meets el Ratón Pérez. Laínez, René Colato. 2010. (ENG.). 32p. (J). (gr. -1-2). 15.99 (978-1-58246-296-7(8), Tricycle Pr.) Ten Speed Pr.

Linton, J. D., jt. illus. see Barnard, Frederick.

Linton, Jonathan. The Dance. Evans, Richard. 2014. (ENG.). 32p. (J). 16.99 (978-1-4814-3112-5(9), Simon & Schuster/Paula Wiseman Bks.) Simon & Schuster/Paula Wiseman Bks.

—The Spyglass: A Book about Faith. Evans, Richard. 2014. (ENG.). 32p. (J). (gr. -1-3). 16.99 (978-1-4814-3109-5(9), Simon & Schuster/Paula Wiseman Bks.) Simon & Schuster/Paula Wiseman Bks.

—The Tower: A Story of Humility. Evans, Richard. 2014. (ENG.). 32p. (J). (gr. -1-3). 16.99 (978-1-4814-3111-8(0), Simon & Schuster/Paula Wiseman Bks.) Simon & Schuster/Paula Wiseman Bks.

Linton, Vera. Skoob. Howell, Kathy. 2004. (J). per. 6.95 (978-1-59571-026-0(4)) Word Association Pubs.

Linville, S. Olga. Olga's Cats: An ABC Book. Anjou, Colette. 2005. 28p. (J). (gr. -1-3). per. 15.95 (978-0-9748933-5-8(8)) E & E Publishing.

Lionni, Leo. A Color of His Own. Lionni, Leo. 2006. (ENG.). 40p. (J). (gr. -1-k). reprint ed. 12.95 (978-0-375-83697-8(7), Knopf Bks. for Young Readers) Random Hse. Children's Bks.

—Frederick. Lionni, Leo. Mlawer, Teresa, tr. 2005. (SPA.). (J). pap. 6.99 (978-1-930332-81-2(5)) Lectorum Pubns., Inc.

—Inch by Inch. Lionni, Leo. unabr. ed. 2006. (J). (gr. -1-1). 18.95 (978-0-439-90585-5(0), WPCD699) Weston Woods Studios, Inc.

—Let's Make Rabbits. Lionni, Leo. 2010. (ENG.). 32p. (J). (gr. -1-2). pap. 6.99 (978-0-679-84019-0(2), Dragonfly Bks.) Random Hse. Children's Bks.

—Pezzettino. Lionni, Leo. 2006. 40p. (J). (gr. -1-3). lib. bdg. 17.99 (978-0-394-93156-2(4), Pantheon) Knopf Doubleday Publishing Group.

—Tillie & the Wall. Lionni, Leo. 2014. (ENG.). 32p. (J). (gr. -1-2). 17.99 (978-0-394-82155-9(6)); 20.99 (978-0-394-92155-6(0)) Random Hse. Children's Bks. (Knopf Bks. for Young Readers).

Liotta, Clayton. Dubs Goes to Washington: And Discovers the Greatness of America. Liotta, Clayton. Morris, Dick & McGann, Eileen. 2011. (ENG.). 42p. pap. 9.99 (978-1-4392-8026-3(6)) CreateSpace Independent Publishing Platform.

Lipchenko, Oleg. Alice's Adventures in Wonderland. Carroll, Lewis. 2009. (ENG.). 104p. (J). (gr. k-12). 22.95 (978-0-88776-932-0(2)) Tundra Bks. CAN. Dist: Random Hse., Inc.

—The Hunting of the Snark: An Agony in Eight Fits. Carroll, Lewis. 2012. (ENG.). 48p. (J). (gr. k-12). 17.95 (978-1-77049-407-7(3), Tundra Bks.) Tundra Bks. CAN. Dist: Penguin Random Hse., LLC.

Lipe, Barbara. Once upon A Monday. Roberts, Mary. 2004. 48p. (J). per. 19.95 (978-0-9744412-0-7(1)) DinRo.

Lipking, Ron. The Secret of the Silver Key. Perry, Phyllis J. 2003. (Fribble Mouse Library Mystery Ser.). 90p. (J). pap. 16.95 (978-1-932146-03-5(2)) Highsmith Inc.

—The Secrets of the Rock. Perry, Phyllis J. 2004. (Fribble Mouse Library Mystery Ser.). 96p. (J). 16.95 (978-1-932146-22-6(9), 1237661) Highsmith Inc.

Lipow, Dan, photos by. I Love Our Earth. Martin, Bill, Jr. & Sampson, Michael. 2009. (ENG., 32p. (J). (gr. -1-2). pap. 7.95 (978-1-58089-107-3(1)) Charlesbridge Publishing, Inc.

—I Love Our Earth / Amo Nuestra Tierra. Martin, Bill, Jr. & Sampson, Michael. ed. 2013. (ENG., 32p. (J). (gr. -1-2). pap. 7.95 (978-1-58089-557-6(3)) Charlesbridge Publishing, Inc.

Lipp, Tony. Rhyming Ricky Rutherford. Reid, Robin L. 2012. 24p. pap. 24.95 (978-1-4626-8896-8(9)) America Star Bks.

Lippincott, Gary. Come to the Fairies' Ball. Yolen, Jane. 2009. (ENG.). 32p. (J). (gr. 2-4). 17.95 (978-1-59078-464-8(2), Wordsong) Boyds Mills Pr.

Lippincott, Gary A. Hiding Glory. Chester, Laura. 2007. (ENG.). 160p. (J). (gr. 3-7). 18.95 (978-1-59543-616-0(2)) Willow Creek Pr., Inc.

—Jennifer Murdley's Toad: A Magic Shop Book. Coville, Bruce. 2007. (Magic Shop Book Ser.: 3). (ENG.). 176p. (J). (gr. 5-7). pap. 6.99 (978-0-15-206246-0(7)) Houghton Mifflin Harcourt Publishing Co.

—Jeremy Thatcher, Dragon Hatcher: A Magic Shop Book. Coville, Bruce. 20th ed. 2007. (Magic Shop Book Ser.: 2). (ENG.). 176p. (J). (gr. 5-7). pap. 6.99 (978-0-15-206252-1(1)) Houghton Mifflin Harcourt Publishing Co.

—Marvel the Marvelous. Chester, Laura. 2008. (ENG.). 176p. (J). 18.95 (978-1-59543-841-6(6)) Willow Creek Pr., Inc.

—The Skull of Truth: A Magic Shop Book. Coville, Bruce. 2007. (Magic Shop Book Ser.: 4). (ENG.). 208p. (J). (gr. 5-7). pap. 6.99 (978-0-15-206084-8(7)) Houghton Mifflin Harcourt Publishing Co.

Lipscombe, Nick, jt. illus. see Biggin, Gary.

Lisa Byers. Singled Out in Center Field: Diamonds Are A Girl's Best Friend - Book One. Robyn Washburn. 2009. 80p. pap. 12.00 (978-1-4389-6245-0(2)) AuthorHouse.

Lisansky, Sue. Cinderella. 2011. (First Fairy Tales Ser.). (ENG.). 20p. (J). (gr. -1-3). pap. 4.99 (978-1-934004-19-7(7)) Byeway Bks.

Lisette, Soleil. Cool Kids Cook: Fresh & Fit, 1 vol. De Las Casas, Dianne & Eliana, Kid. 2014. (ENG.). 64p. (J). (gr. 3-7). 14.95 (978-1-4556-1892-7(6)) Pelican Publishing Co., Inc.

Lishinski, Jamie. Let Your Light Shine. Lishinski, Ann King. Morello, Charles, ed. 2003. (J). pap. 9.95 (978-0-9709575-0-4(5)) Singing River Pubns.

Lisi, Margaret. Count on the Farm. Lisi, Branden. 2006. (J). lib. bdg. 15.95 (978-0-9771472-0-5(7)) Count On Learning.

Liska, Eliska. My Granny Loves Hockey. Weber, Lori. 2014. (ENG.). 32p. (J). (gr. -1-3). 16.95 (978-1-927018-43-9(9)) Simply Read Bks. CAN. Dist: Ingram Pub. Services.

—O'Shae the Octopus. Buble, Brandee. 2014. (ENG.). 32p. (J). (gr. -1-3). 15.95 (978-1-927018-56-9(0)) Simply Read Bks. CAN. Dist: Ingram Pub. Services.

Lisker, Sonia. Freckle Juice. Blume, Judy. 2014. (ENG.). 64p. (J). (gr. 1-5). pap. 5.99 (978-1-4814-1102-8(0), Atheneum Bks. for Young Readers) Simon & Schuster Children's Publishing.

Lisowski, Gabriel. Hardlucky: The Story of a Boy Who Learns How to Think Before He Acts. Chaikin, Miriam. 2012. (ENG.). 40p. (J). (gr. k-3). pap. 16.95 (978-1-61608-963-4(6), 608963, Sky Pony Pr.) Skyhorse Publishing Co., Inc.

Liss, Ira & Sorensen, Peter. Planetary Intelligence: 101 Easy Steps to Energy, Well-Being, & Natural Light. Hein, Simeon. 2006. 152p. per. 9.95 (978-0-9715863-5-2(7), 303 440-7393) Mount Baldy Pr., Inc.

Lissiat, Amy. The Short & Incredibly Happy Life of Riley. Thompson, Colin. 2006. 32p. (J). (978-0-7344-0806-8(4), Lothian Children's Bks.) Hachette Australia.

—The Short & Incredibly Happy Life of Riley. Thompson, Colin. 2007. (ENG.). 32p. (J). (gr. -1-3). 9.99 (978-1-933605-50-0(2)) Kane Miller.

Lister, Judy. Porcupines, Politicians & Plato. Kishkan, Dan. unabr. ed. (ENG.). 182p. pap. (978-0-920576-48-9(6)) Caitlin Pr., Inc.

Listokin, David & Connally, Perry L., Sr. Puffy the Watermelon. Switzer, Vern. 2004. 24p. (J). 15.95 (978-0-9753542-0-9(5)) Rural Farm Productions.

Litchfield, Jo. Baby Brother Look & Say. 2008. (Look & Say Board Bks). 12p. (J). bds. 7.99 (978-0-7945-2101-1(0), Usborne) EDC Publishing.

—Baby Sister Look & Say. 2008. (Look & Say Board Bks). 12p. (J). bds. 7.99 (978-0-7945-2102-8(9), Usborne) EDC Publishing.

—Backyard. Durber, Matt. 2007. (Look & Say Board Bks). 10p. (J). (gr. -1-k). bds. 7.99 (978-0-7945-1692-5(0), Usborne) EDC Publishing.

—Box of Trucks. 2004. (Boxed Jigsaws Ser.). 10p. (J). 11.99 (978-0-7945-0916-3(9), Usborne) EDC Publishing.

—Daisy Doctor. Brooks, Felicity. 2005. 24p. (J). pap. 6.95 (978-0-7945-0724-4(7), Usborne) EDC Publishing.

—Daisy the Doctor. Brooks, Felicity. 2008. (Jobs People Do Ser.). 23p. (J). (gr. 4-7). pap. 6.99 (978-0-7945-2214-8(9), Usborne) EDC Publishing.

—Dinosarios. Brooks, Felicity. 2004. (Titles in Spanish Ser.). (SPA.). 10p. (J). 4.95 (978-0-7460-6111-4(0), Usborne) EDC Publishing.

—Everyday Words in Spanish. Brooks, Felicity. rev. ed. 2004. (Everyday Words Ser.). 48p. (J). pap. 9.95 (978-0-7945-0881-4(2), Usborne) EDC Publishing.

—Farms lift & Look. Brooks, Felicity. 2005. 12p. (J). 9.95 (978-0-7945-0932-3(0), Usborne) EDC Publishing.

—First Book of Christmas Carols. 2004. (First Book of Christmas Carols Ser.). 24p. (J). 9.95 (978-0-7945-0596-7(1), Usborne) EDC Publishing.

—First Picture 123. 2005. (First Picture Board Books Ser.). 16p. (J). 11.95 (978-0-7945-0939-2(8), Usborne) EDC Publishing.

—First Picture Abc. 2005. (First Picture Board Books Ser.). 16p. (J). 11.95 (978-0-7945-0907-1(X), Usborne) EDC Publishing.

—First Picture Nursery Rhymes. 2005. (Usborne First Book Ser.). 16p. (J). (gr. -1-k). per. 11.99 (978-0-7945-1014-5(0), Usborne) EDC Publishing.

—First Picture Spanish. Brooks, Felicity & MacKinnon, Mairi. 2006. (First Picture Flap Bks.). 18p. (J). (gr. 1-4). bds. 14.99 (978-0-7945-1384-9(0), Usborne) EDC Publishing.

—First Shapes. MMStudios, photos by. Brooks, Felicity. 2007. (Usborne Look & Say Ser.). 12p. (J). (gr. -1-k). bds. 14.99 (978-0-7945-1450-1(2), Usborne) EDC Publishing.

—Frank the Farmer. Brooks, Felicity. (Jobs People Do Ser.). 23p. (J). 2005. (gr. -1-7). pap. 6.95 (978-0-7945-0723-7(9)); 2007. (gr. 4-7). pap. 6.99 (978-0-7945-1621-5(1)) EDC Publishing. (Usborne).

—Fred the Firefighter. Brooks, Felicity. (Jobs People Do Ser.). (J). 2004. (ENG.). 24p. pap. 6.95 (978-0-7945-0725-1(5)); 2006. 23p. (gr. -1). pap. 6.99 (978-0-7945-1496-9(0)) EDC Publishing. (Usborne).

—La Granja Minilibros Usborne. Brooks, Felicity. 2005. (SPA.). 10p. (J). 4.95 (978-0-7460-6110-7(2), Usborne) EDC Publishing.

—Jobs People Do. Brooks, Felicity. 2008. (Jobs People Do Ser.). 143p. (J). (gr. -1-3). 22.99 (978-0-7945-1998-8(9), Usborne) EDC Publishing.

—The Runaway Orange. Brooks, Felicity, ed. 2004. (Easy Reading Ser.). (ENG.). 1p. (J). (gr. -1-3). pap. 5.95 (978-0-7460-3029-5(0)) EDC Publishing.

—School Look & Say. Brooks, Felicity. 2005. 10p. (J). 7.95 (978-0-7945-1015-2(9), Usborne) EDC Publishing.

—Tessa the Teacher. Brooks, Felicity. 2006. 24p. (J). per. 6.99 (978-0-7945-0937-8(1), Usborne) EDC Publishing.

—Trains lift & Look. Brooks, Felicity. 2005. 12p. (J). 9.99 (978-0-7945-0935-4(5), Usborne) EDC Publishing.

—The Usborne Very First Dictionary. Young, Caroline & Brooks, Felicity. 2005. 64p. (J). (gr. -1-3). 11.95 (978-0-7945-1002-2(7), Usborne) EDC Publishing.

—Very First Words in Spanish. 2009. (Very First Words in Spanish Ser.). (SPA & ENG.). 18p. (J). (gr. -1). bds. 7.99 (978-0-7945-2446-3(X), Usborne) EDC Publishing.

—Vicky the Vet. Brooks, Felicity. 2004. (Jobs People Do Ser.). 24p. (J). pap. 6.95 (978-0-7945-0726-8(3)); (gr. -1). lib. bdg. 14.95 (978-1-58086-699-6(9)) EDC Publishing. (Usborne).

—Vicky the Vet Kid Kit. Brooks, Felicity. 2007. (Kid Kits Ser.). 23p. (J). pap. 15.99 (978-1-60130-008-9(5), Usborne) EDC Publishing.

Litchfield, Jo. Christmas. Litchfield, Jo. 2005. (Usborne Look & Say Ser.). 10p. (J). (gr. -1-k). bds. 9.95 (978-0-7945-1173-9(2), Usborne) EDC Publishing.

—First Words Look & Say. Litchfield, Jo. 2005. 18p. (J). 14.99 (978-0-7945-1024-4(8), Usborne) EDC Publishing.

Litchfield, Jo & Allen, Francesca. First Picture Fairytales. MMStudios, photos by. 2007. (First Picture Board Bks.). 16p. (J). (gr. -1-k). bds. 11.99 (978-0-7945-1460-0(X), Usborne) EDC Publishing.

—First Picture Nursery Rhymes With. 2006. 18p. (J). bds. 18.99 (978-0-7945-1489-1(8), Usborne) EDC Publishing.

—Home. Litchfield, Jo. 2006. (Usborne Look & Say Ser.). 12p. (J). (gr. -1-k). bds. 7.99 (978-0-7945-1425-9(1), Usborne) EDC Publishing.

—Jobs. Litchfield, Jo. 2006. (Usborne Look & Say Ser.). 10p. (J). (gr. -1-k). bds. 7.99 (978-0-7945-1353-5(0), Usborne) EDC Publishing.

Litchfield, Jo & Jones, Stephanie. First 1,2,3. Allman, Howard, photos by. 2006. (Usborne Look & Say Ser.). 20p. (J). (gr. -1-k). bds. 14.95 (978-0-7945-1219-4(4), Usborne) EDC Publishing.

Litten, Kristyna. Bike on, Bear! Liu, Cynthea. 2015. (ENG.). 32p. (J). (gr. -1-2). 17.99 **(978-1-4814-0506-5(3)**, Simon & Schuster/Paula Wiseman Bks.) Simon & Schuster/Paula Wiseman Bks.

Litten, Kristyna. Pins & Needles. Krensky, Stephen. 2014. (Penguin Core Concepts Ser.). (ENG.). 32p. (J). (gr. -1-k). 3.99 (978-0-448-46209-7(5), Grosset & Dunlap) Penguin Publishing Group.

—Pins & Needles Share a Dream. Krensky, Stephen. 2014. (Penguin Core Concepts Ser.). (ENG.). 32p. (J). (gr. -1-k). 3.99 (978-0-448-46210-3(9), Grosset & Dunlap) Penguin Publishing Group.

—Snoozefest. Berger, Samantha. 2015. (ENG.). 34p. (J). (gr. -1-k). 16.99 (978-0-8037-4046-4(8), Dial) Penguin Publishing Group.

—This Day in June. Pitman, Gayle E. 2013. (J). (978-1-4338-1658-1(X)); pap. (978-1-4338-1659-8(8)) American Psychological Assn. (Magination Pr.).

Litten, Kristyna. Hong Kong & Macau: a 3D Keepsake Cityscape. Litten, Kristyna. 2013. (Panorama Pops Ser.). (ENG.). 30p. (J). (gr. k-4). 8.99 (978-0-7636-6416-9(2)) Candlewick Pr.

—Rome: a 3D Keepsake Cityscape. Litten, Kristyna. 2013. (Panorama Pops Ser.). (ENG.). 15p. (J). (gr. k-12). 8.99 (978-0-7636-6415-2(4)) Candlewick Pr.

Litteral, Christopher. Sammy the Sea Turtle, 1 vol. Kruse, Robyn A. 2010. 18p. 24.95 (978-1-4489-4020-2(6)) PublishAmerica, Inc.

Little Airplane Productions. Go, Wonder Pets! Selig, Josh. 2008. (Wonder Pets! Ser.). (ENG.). 26p. (J). bds. 5.99 (978-1-4169-4723-3(X), Simon Spotlight/Nickelodeon) Simon Spotlight/Nickelodeon.

Little Airplane Productions & Fogarty, Alexandria. Baby Beaver Rescue. 2009. (Wonder Pets! Ser.). (ENG.). 24p. (J). (gr. -1-2). pap. 3.99 (978-1-4169-8499-3(2), Simon Spotlight/Nickelodeon) Simon Spotlight/Nickelodeon.

Little Airplane Productions & Scanlon, Michael. Off to School! 2009. (Wonder Pets! Ser.). (ENG.). 24p. (J). pap. 3.99 (978-1-4169-7197-9(1), Simon Spotlight/Nickelodeon) Simon Spotlight/Nickelodeon.

Little Airplane Productions Staff. How We Met! Scanlon, Michael. 2010. (Wonder Pets! Ser.). (ENG.). 24p. (J). pap. 3.99 (978-1-4424-0654-4(2), Simon Spotlight/Nickelodeon) Simon Spotlight/Nickelodeon.

Little, Elaine, photos by. My Family. Kinkade, Sheila. 2006. (ENG., 32p. (J). (gr. -1-3). 7.95 (978-1-57091-691-5(8)); 16.95 (978-1-57091-662-5(4)) Charlesbridge Publishing, Inc.

Little, Gary. My Story as Told by Sacagawea. Lohof, Arle & Jensen, Joyce. 2006. 32p. (J). (gr. 1-2). 3.95 (978-0-9711667-3-8(0)) Outlook Publishing, Inc.

Little, Jeanette. In Disguise! Undercover with Real Women Spies. Hunter, Ryan Ann. 2013. (ENG.). 176p. (J). (gr. 3-7). 17.99 (978-1-58270-383-1(3)); pap. 9.99 (978-1-58270-382-4(5)) Aladdin/Beyond Words.

Little, Kelli Ann. Rockabet: Classic Edition. Polark, Kelly. 2013. 32p. pap. 10.49 (978-0-9888462-0-3(9)) Big Smile Pr., LLC.

Littlechild, George. What's the Most Beautiful Thing You Know about Horses? Van Camp, Richard. 2013. (ENG.). 32p. (J). pap. 9.95 (978-0-89239-185-1(5)) Lee & Low Bks., Inc.

Littlechild, George. This Land Is My Land, 1 vol. Littlechild, George. 2013. (ENG.). 32p. (J). pap. 10.95 (978-0-89239-184-4(7), Children's Book Press) Lee & Low Bks., Inc.

Littlejohn, Anna. Divided Loyalties. Upham, Linda. 2007. 188p. per. (978-0-7552-0302-4(X)) Authors OnLine, Ltd.

Littlejohn, Brad. "A Is for All Aboard!", 1 vol. Kluth, Paula & Kluth, Victoria. 2009. (ENG.). 32p. (J). 16.95 (978-1-59857-071-7(4)) Brookes, Paul H. Publishing Co. Inc.

LittlePinkPebble. Queen Amina of Zari: Queens of Africa Book 1. Judybee. 2011. 28p. pap. (978-1-908218-43-8(6)) MX Publishing, Ltd.

—Queen Esther: Queens of Africa Book 4. Judybee. 2011. 28p. pap. (978-1-908218-52-0(5)) MX Publishing, Ltd.

—Queen Idi: Queens of Africa Book 5. Judybee. 2011. 24p. pap. (978-1-908218-55-1(X)) MX Publishing, Ltd.

—Queen Maked: Queens of Africa Book 2. Judybee. 2011. 28p. pap. (978-1-908218-46-9(0)) MX Publishing, Ltd.

—Queen Moremi: Queens of Africa Book 3. Judybee. 2011. 28p. pap. (978-1-908218-49-0(5)) MX Publishing, Ltd.

—The Zoo Crew Play Ball. Judybee. 2011. 40p. pap. (978-1-78092-000-9(8)) MX Publishing, Ltd.

Littler, Phil. The Three Frilly Goats Fluff. Guillain, Adam & Guillain, Charlotte. 2015. (ENG.). 32p. (J). **(978-0-7787-1935-9(9))** Crabtree Publishing Co.

Littlewood, Karin. Catherine's Story. Moore, Genevieve. 2010. (ENG.). 32p. (J). (gr. k-3). 17.95 (978-1-84507-655-9(9), Frances Lincoln) Quarto Publishing Group UK GBR. Dist: Perseus-PGW.

—Chanda & the Mirror of Moonlight. Bateson-Hill, Margaret. 2003. (Folk Tales Ser.). 32p. (J). (gr. 3-4). (978-1-84089-217-8(X)) Zero to Ten, Ltd.

—Christophe's Story. Cornwell, Nikki. 2012. (ENG.). 80p. (J). (gr. 3-6). pap. 8.99 (978-1-84780-250-7(8), Frances Lincoln) Quarto Publishing Group UK GBR. Dist: Hachette Bk. Group.

—Los Colores de Casa. Hoffman, Mary. 2003. (SPA.). 28p. (J). (gr. k-2). 20.99 (978-84-8452-223-2(7), MON32674) Fundacion Intermon ESP. Dist: Lectorum Pubns., Inc.

—The Day the Rains Fell. Faundez, Anne. 2010. (ENG.). 32p. (J). (gr. k-2). pap. 9.99 (978-1-84853-015-7(3)) Transworld Publishers Ltd. GBR. Dist: Independent Pubs. Group.

—Home for Christmas. Grindley, Sally. 2004. (ENG.). 32p. (J). (gr. k-17). 15.95 (978-1-84507-071-7(2), Frances Lincoln) Quarto Publishing Group UK GBR. Dist: Hachette Bk. Group.

—Home Now. Beake, Lesley. 2007. 32p. (J). (ENG.). (gr. -1-3). pap. 6.95 (978-1-58089-163-9(2)); (gr. k-3). 16.95 (978-1-58089-162-2(4)) Charlesbridge Publishing, Inc.

—Lucy & the Big Bad Wolf. Jungman, Ann. 2005. 120p. (J). (gr. -1-6). pap. 4.95 (978-1-903015-39-1(1)) Barn Owl Bks, London GBR. Dist: Independent Pubs. Group.

—Tara's Tree House. Dunmore, Helen. 2005. (Yellow Go Bananas Ser.). (ENG.). 48p. (J). (gr. 3-4). (978-0-7787-2743-9(2)); lib. bdg. (978-0-7787-2721-7(1)) Crabtree Publishing Co.

Littlewood, Karin. Immi's Gift, 1 vol. Littlewood, Karin. 2010. (ENG.). 32p. (J). (gr. -1-3). 15.95 (978-1-56145-545-4(8)) Peachtree Pubs.

Littlewort, Lizza. The Magic Fish. Orford, Margie. 2012. (Best Loved Tales for Africa Ser.). (ENG.). 32p. (J). (gr. k-2). pap. 9.95 (978-1-77009-822-0(4)) Jacana Media ZAF. Dist: Independent Pubs. Group.

Litwin, Mike. Isabella: Girl on the Go. Fosberry, Jennifer. 2012. (ENG.). 32p. (J). (gr. k-3). 16.99 (978-1-4022-6648-5(0), Sourcebooks Jabberwocky) Sourcebooks, Inc.

—Isabella: Star of the Story. Fosberry, Jennifer. 2013. (ENG.). 32p. (J). (-3). 16.99 (978-1-4022-7936-2(1), Sourcebooks Jabberwocky) Sourcebooks, Inc.

—My Name Is Not Alexander. Fosberry, Jennifer. 2011. (ENG.). 32p. (J). (gr. k-3). 16.99 (978-1-4022-5433-8(4), Sourcebooks Jabberwocky) Sourcebooks, Inc.

—My Name Is Not Isabella. Fosberry, Jennifer. 2008. 32p. (J). (gr. -1-3). lib. bdg. 19.99 (978-0-9802000-7-2(5)) Monkey Barrel Pr.

—My Name Is Not Isabella: Just How Big Can a Little Girl Dream? Fosberry, Jennifer. 2010. (ENG.). 32p. (J). (gr. k-3). 16.99 (978-1-4022-4395-0(2), Sourcebooks Jabberwocky) Sourcebooks, Inc.

Litwin, Mike. The Big Cowhuna. Litwin, Mike. 2015. (Welcome to Bermooda! Ser.: 3). (ENG.). 160p. (J). (gr. 2-5). 14.99 (978-0-8075-8720-1(6)) Whitman, Albert & Co.

—Crown of the Cowibbean. Litwin, Mike. 2014. (Welcome to Bermooda! Ser.: 2). (ENG.). 144p. (J). (gr. 2-5). 14.99 (978-0-8075-8719-5(2)) Whitman, Albert & Co.

—Lost in Bermooda. Litwin, Mike. 2014. (Welcome to Bermooda! Ser.: Book 1). (ENG.). 144p. (J). (gr. 2-5). 14.99 (978-0-8075-8718-8(4)) Whitman, Albert & Co.

Litz, Marnie Saebz. Saint Brendan & the Voyage Before Columbus. McGrew, Michael. 2005. 32p. 9.95 (978-0-8091-6705-0(0), 6705-0) Paulist Pr.

Litzinger, Rosanne. The Animals Watched: An Alphabet Book. Stewig, John Warren. 2007. (ENG.). 32p. (J). (gr. -1-3). 16.95 (978-0-8234-1906-7(1)) Holiday Hse., Inc.

—The Beckoning Cat: Based on a Japanese Folktale. Nishizuka, Koko. 2009. (ENG.). 32p. (J). (gr. -1-3). 16.95 (978-0-8234-2051-3(5)) Holiday Hse., Inc.

—Chicken Soup by Heart. Hershenhorn, Esther. 2010. (ENG.). 40p. (J). (gr. -1-3). 16.99 (978-1-4424-2197-4(5), Simon & Schuster Bks. For Young Readers) Simon & Schuster Bks. For Young Readers.

—The Frog Princess: A Tlingit Legend from Alaska. Kimmel, Eric A. 2005. (ENG.). 32p. (J). (gr. -1-3). 16.95 (978-0-8234-1618-9(6)) Holiday Hse., Inc.

—The Matzo Ball Boy. Shulman, Lisa. 2007. (ENG.). 32p. (J). (gr. -1-2). pap. 6.99 (978-0-14-240769-1(0), Puffin) Penguin Publishing Group.

—Snail's Good Night. Paul, Ann Whitford. 2008. (Holiday House Readers: Level 1 Ser.). (ENG.). 32p. (J). (gr. -1-3). 14.95 (978-0-8234-1912-8(6)) Holiday Hse., Inc.

Liu, Davy. The Giant Leaf: Take a Giant Leaf of Faith. Liu, Davy. 2009. (CHI.). (J). 1995.00 (978-0-9825050-0-7(0)) Kendu Films.

Liu, Kimi. Mira. Trujillo, Rafael E. 2009. (SPA.). 10p. (J). 5.99 (978-0-9765007-3-5(6)) Big-head fish.

—Mira: La Granja. Trujillo, Rafael E. 2009. (SPA.). 10p. (J). 5.99 (978-0-9765007-4-2(4)) Big-head fish.

—La ultima ola de Marianela. Trujillo, Rafael E. 2009. (SPA.). 16p. (J). 17.00 (978-0-9765007-6-6(0)) Big-head fish.

Liu, Siyu. A Thousand Peaks: Poems from China. Liu, Siyu, tr. Protopopescu, Orel O. 2003. (CHI & ENG.). 52p. (gr. 7-18). 19.95 (978-1-881896-24-1(2), THPE) Pacific View Pr.

LiveLearn, Robert. Hamster on the Run. Richter, Debra A. 2011. 24p. pap. 24.95 (978-1-4626-3897-0(X)) America Star Bks.

—Hamster on the Run, Let's Play in the Snow. Richter, Debra A. 2012. 28p. pap. 24.95 (978-1-4626-5064-4(3)) America Star Bks.

Liversidge, Cassie. Ice Cream! Grow Your Own Ingredients. 2015. (ENG.). 40p. (J). (gr. -1-3). 12.99 (978-1-63220-405-9(3), Sky Pony Pr.) Skyhorse Publishing Co., Inc.

Livesey, Robert. The Mounties, 1 vol. Smith, A. G. 2008. (Discovering Canada Ser.). (ENG.). 90p. (J). per. *(978-1-55005-135-3(0))* Fitzhenry & Whiteside, Ltd.

Livingston, Francis. Davy Crockett: Young Pioneer. Santrey, Laurence & Macken, JoAnn Early. 2008. 55p. (J). pap. *(978-0-439-02048-0(4))* Scholastic, Inc.

—Paul Revere, Son of Liberty. Brandt, Keith & Macken, JoAnn Early. 2007. 50p. (J). *(978-0-439-02017-6(4))* Scholastic, Inc.

Livingston, Jessica. My First Trip to the Bank. Kawa, Katie. 2012. (My First Adventures Ser.). (ENG.). 24p. (J). (gr. k-2). pap. 8.15 *(978-1-4339-6238-7(1))*; lib. bdg. 22.60 *(978-1-4339-6236-3(5))* Stevens, Gareth Publishing LLLP.

—My First Trip to the Bank: Mi Primera Visita Al Banco. Kawa, Katie. 2012. (My First Adventures / Mis primeras aventuras Ser.). (ENG & SPA.). 24p. (J). (gr. k-2). lib. bdg. 22.60 *(978-1-4339-6625-5(5))* Stevens, Gareth Publishing LLLP.

—My First Trip to the Dentist. Kawa, Katie. 2012. (My First Adventures Ser.). (ENG.). 24p. (J). (gr. k-2). pap. 8.15 *(978-1-4339-6243-1(8))*; lib. bdg. 22.60 *(978-1-4339-6241-7(1))* Stevens, Gareth Publishing LLLP.

—My First Trip to the Dentist: Mi Primera Visita Al Dentista. Kawa, Katie. 2012. (My First Adventures / Mis primeras aventuras Ser.). (ENG & SPA.). 24p. (J). (gr. k-2). lib. bdg. 22.60 *(978-1-4339-6627-9(1))* Stevens, Gareth Publishing LLLP.

—My First Trip to the Doctor. Kawa, Katie. 2012. (My First Adventures Ser.). (ENG.). 24p. (J). (gr. k-2). pap. 8.15 *(978-1-4339-6247-9(0))*; lib. bdg. 22.60 *(978-1-4339-6245-5(4))* Stevens, Gareth Publishing LLLP.

—My First Trip to the Library. Kawa, Katie. 2012. (My First Adventures Ser.). (ENG.). 24p. (J). (gr. k-2). pap. 8.15 *(978-1-4339-6251-6(9))*; lib. bdg. 22.60 *(978-1-4339-6249-3(7))* Stevens, Gareth Publishing LLLP.

—My First Trip to the Library: Mi Primera Visita a la Biblioteca. Kawa, Katie. 2012. (My First Adventures / Mis primeras aventuras Ser.). (ENG & SPA.). 24p. (J). (gr. k-2). lib. bdg. 22.60 *(978-1-4339-6631-6(X))* Stevens, Gareth Publishing LLLP.

—My First Trip to the Post Office. Kawa, Katie. 2012. (My First Adventures Ser.). (ENG.). 24p. (J). (gr. k-2). 22.60 *(978-1-4339-6253-0(5))*; pap. 8.15 *(978-1-4339-6255-4(1))* Stevens, Gareth Publishing LLLP.

—My First Trip to the Post Office: Mi Primera Visita Al Correo. Kawa, Katie. 2012. (My First Adventures / Mis primeras aventuras Ser.). (ENG & SPA.). 24p. (J). (gr. k-2). lib. bdg. 22.60 *(978-1-4339-6633-0(6))* Stevens, Gareth Publishing LLLP.

—My First Trip to the Zoo. Kawa, Katie. 2012. (My First Adventures Ser.). (ENG.). 24p. (J). (gr. k-2). pap. 8.15 *(978-1-4339-6259-2(4))*; lib. bdg. 22.60 *(978-1-4339-6257-8(8))* Stevens, Gareth Publishing LLLP.

—My First Trip to the Zoo: Mi Primera Visita Al Zoológico. Kawa, Katie. 2012. (My First Adventures / Mis primeras aventuras Ser.). (ENG & SPA.). 24p. (J). (gr. k-2). lib. bdg. 22.60 *(978-1-4339-6635-4(2))* Stevens, Gareth Publishing LLLP.

Livingston, Tim. Buddy & the Magic Chicken Tree, 2 bks. Livingston, Mary A. & Shufelberger, Amanda. 2014th ed. 2014. (ENG.). 34p. (J). 19.99 *(978-0-9635757-3-9(2))* Red Tail Publishing.

Livingston, Timothy J. FireStorm in the Forest: When a Forest Burns. Livingston, Timothy J. Livingston, Mary A. 2006. 32p. (J). 19.99 *(978-0-9635757-1-5(6))* Red Tail Publishing.

Liwksa, Renata. Once upon a Memory. Laden, Nina. 2013. (ENG.). 40p. (J). (gr. -1-1). 17.00 *(978-0-316-20816-1(7))* Little, Brown Bks. for Young Readers.

Liwska, Renata. Boom Snot Twitty This Way That Way. Cronin, Doreen. 2015. (ENG.). 32p. (J). (-k). 16.99 *(978-0-670-78577-3(6)*, Viking Juvenile) Penguin Publishing Group.

—The Christmas Quiet Book. Underwood, Deborah. 2012. (ENG.). 32p. (J). (gr. -1-3). 12.99 *(978-0-547-55863-9(5))* Houghton Mifflin Harcourt Publishing Co.

—The Loud Book! Underwood, Deborah. 2011. (ENG.). 32p. (J). (gr. -1-3). 12.99 *(978-0-547-39008-6(4))* Houghton Mifflin Harcourt Publishing Co.

—The Loud Book! Padded Board Book. Underwood, Deborah. 2015. (ENG.). 32p. (J). (— 1). bds. 8.99 *(978-0-544-43064-8(6)*, HMH Books For Young Readers) Houghton Mifflin Harcourt Publishing Co.

—A Puppy Is for Loving, 1 vol. Labatt, Mary. 2007. (Orca Echoes Ser.). (ENG.). 64p. (J). (gr. 2-3). per. 4.99 *(978-1-55143-477-3(6))* Orca Bk. Pubs. USA.

—The Quiet Book. Underwood, Deborah. (ENG.). 32p. (J). 2013. (— 1). bds. 8.99 *(978-0-544-05667-1(1))*; 2010. (gr. -1-3). 12.95 *(978-0-547-21567-9(3))* Houghton Mifflin Harcourt Publishing Co.

Liwska, Renata. The Red Wagon. Liwska, Renata. 2011. (ENG.). 32p. (J). (gr. -1-k). 16.99 *(978-0-399-25237-2(1)*, Philomel) Penguin Publishing Group.

—Red Wagon. Liwska, Renata. 2013. (ENG.). 32p. (J). (gr. -1-k). bds. 6.99 *(978-0-399-16239-8(9)*, Philomel) Penguin Publishing Group.

Liz, Pichon. Three Horrid Little Pigs. Liz, Pichon. 2010. 32p. pap. 7.95 *(978-1-58925-423-7(6))* Tiger Tales.

Liz Warren. Kimmy Finds Her Key. Harris-Wyrick, Wayne. 2013. 28p. pap. 11.99 *(978-0-9852661-8-9(X))* 4RV Publishing, LLC.

Liza, Behles, jt. illus. see Jocelyn, Sawyer.

Lizana, Lorenzo. The Adventures of Thumbs up Johnnie Banker Bill's Guide to Common Cents: Banker Bill's Guide to Common Cents. Bain, Michelle. 2007. (J). 14.95 *(978-0-9761421-9-5(8))* Pixie Stuff LLC.

—The Adventures of Thumbs up Johnnie Jimmy Jam Germ & the Happy Handshake: Jimmy Jam Germ & the Happy Handshake Version 2. Bain, Michelle. 2007. (J). 14.95 *(978-0-9761421-7-1(1))* Pixie Stuff LLC.

—The Adventures of Thumbs up Johnnie Johnnie Finds A Buddy: Johnnie Finds A Buddy Color Version 2. Bain, Michelle. 2007. (J). 14.95 *(978-0-9761421-6-4(3))* Pixie Stuff LLC.

—The Adventures of Thumbs up Johnnie Johnnie's Missing Boot! Johnnie's Missing Boot! Bain, Michelle. 2007. (J). 14.95 *(978-0-9761421-8-8(X))* Pixie Stuff LLC.

—The Adventures of Thumbs up Johnnie Rules of Thumb for Going Green: Rules of Thumb for Going Green. Bain, Michelle. 2008. 18p. (J). pap. 5.95 *(978-0-9795832-4-7(1))* Pixie Stuff LLC.

—The Adventures of Thumbs up Johnnie Thumbs up to Red, White & Blue! Thumbs up to Red, White & Blue! Bain, Michelle. 2007. 48p. (J). 14.95 *(978-0-9795832-2-3(5))* Pixie Stuff LLC.

—The Adventures of Thumbs up Johnnie Zipp, Little Digit & the Happy Signs: Zipp, Little Digit & the Happy Signs. Bain, Michelle. 2007. (J). 14.95 *(978-0-9795832-0-9(9))* Pixie Stuff LLC.

—Las aventuras de Juanito el Pulgarcito Juanito encuentra un Compañerito: Juanito encuentra un Compañerito. Bain, Michelle. 2006.Tr. of Johnnie Finds a Buddy. (SPA.). (J). 16.95 *(978-0-9761421-4-0(7))* Pixie Stuff LLC.

—Las aventuras de Juanito el Pulgarcito Liborio el Microbio y el apretón de Manos: Liborio el Microbio y el apretón de Manos. Bain, Michelle. 2007.Tr. of Jimmy Jam Germ & the Happy Handshake!. (SPA.). (J). pap. 16.95 *(978-0-9795832-1-6(7))* Pixie Stuff LLC.

—Las aventuras de Juanito el Pulgarcito Zipp, Pequeño Dígito, las señales y las Señas: Zipp, Pequeño Dígito, las señales y las Señas. Bain, Michelle. 2007.Tr. of Zipp, Digit & the Happy Signs!. (SPA.). 28p. (J). *(978-0-9795832-3-0(3))* Pixie Stuff LLC.

Lizano, Marc. Hidden. Dauvillier, Loïc & Salsedo, Greg. 2014. (ENG.). 80p. (J). (gr. 1-5). 16.99 *(978-1-59643-873-6(8)*, First Second Bks.) Roaring Brook Pr.

Lizatovic, Josip. Boom Chicka Boom. Weir, Liz. 2009. (ENG.). 80p. (J). pap. 11.95 *(978-0-86278-417-1(4))* O'Brien Pr., Ltd., The IRL. Dist: Dufour Editions, Inc.

Ljungberg, Jon. The Bully: A Discussion & Activity Story. Toews, Rita. 2011. 40p. (J). pap. 11.95 *(978-1-59850-102-5(X))* Youthlight, Inc.

—The Bully: A Discussion & Activity Story. Toews, Rita Y. l.t. ed. 2004. (ENG.). 40p. (J). *(978-0-9736224-0-9(7))* Birds Hill Publishing.

Ljungkvist, Laura. Yoo-Hoo, Ladybug! Fox, Mem. 2013. (ENG.). 32p. (J). (gr. -1-k). 16.99 *(978-1-4424-3400-4(7))* Simon & Schuster Children's Publishing.

Ljungkvist, Laura. Follow the Line. Ljungkvist, Laura. Ljungklist, Laura. 2006. (ENG.). 32p. (J). (gr. -1-k). 16.99 *(978-0-670-06049-8(6)*, Viking Juvenile) Penguin Publishing Group.

—Pepi Sings a New Song. Ljungkvist, Laura. 2010. (ENG.). 40p. (J). (gr. -1-3). 16.99 *(978-1-4169-9138-0(7)*, Beach Lane Bks.) Beach Lane Bks.

Llamas, Kristin. Sedrick the Snake. Jostand, Jeffrey Jay. 2008. 32p. pap. 24.95 *(978-1-4241-9944-0(1))* America Star Bks.

Llapashtica, Mentor. Dorothy & the Glasses. Brezinova, Ivona. 2007. 32p. (J). (ARA & ENG.). pap. 12.95 *(978-1-60195-088-8(8))*; (POL & ENG.). pap. 12.95 *(978-1-60195-099-4(3))* International Step by Step Assn.

Llewhellin, Gareth. Always There Bear. Granger, Trudi. 2015. (ENG.). 32p. (J). (-k). 16.99 *(978-1-63220-434-9(7)*, Sky Pony Pr.) Skyhorse Publishing Co., Inc.

Llewhellin, Gareth. Charles Reasoner's Little Cuddles. Reasoner, Charles. 2015. (Charles Reasoner's Little Cuddles Ser.). (ENG.). 10p. (gr. -1 — 1). bds. 23.96 ***(978-1-4795-8061-3(9)***, Charles Reasoners Little Cuddles) Picture Window Bks.

Lloyd, Anna. The Magical Labyrinth. Weaver, Ruth. 2013. (ENG.). 32p. (J). 16.95 *(978-1-922036-49-0(8))* Brolga Publishing AUS. Dist: Midpoint Trade Bks., Inc.

Lloyd-Diviny, Karen. Zoo Album. Morecroft, Richard & MacKay, Alison. 2008. (ENG.). 48p. (J). (gr. 3-7). pap. 9.95 *(978-1-59270-104-9(3))* Enchanted Lion Bks., LLC.

—Zoo Album. Morecroft, Richard et al. 2004. (ENG.). 48p. (J). (gr. 3). 17.95 *(978-1-59270-032-5(2))* Enchanted Lion Bks., LLC.

Lloyd, James. 77 Things You Absolutely Have to Do Before You Finish College. Bondy, Halley. 2014. (ENG.). 192p. (YA). (gr. 9). pap. 14.99 *(978-1-936976-00-3(5))* Zest Bks.

Lloyd, Megan. Betsy Ross. White, Becky. 2011. (ENG.). 32p. (J). 16.95 *(978-0-8234-1908-1(8))* Holiday Hse., Inc.

—A Big Boy Now. Spinelli, Eileen. 2012. (ENG.). 32p. (J). (gr. -1-3). 16.99 *(978-0-06-008673-2(4))* HarperCollins Pubs.

—Davy Crockett Gets Hitched. 2009. (ENG.). 32p. (J). (gr. -1-3). 16.95 *(978-0-8234-1837-4(5))* Holiday Hse., Inc.

—Earthquakes. Branley, Franklyn M. & Branley. 2005. (Let's-Read-And-Find-Out Science 2 Ser.). (ENG.). 40p. (J). (gr. k-4). pap. 5.99 *(978-0-06-445188-8(7))* HarperCollins Pubs.

Lloyd, Megan. Earthquakes. Branley, Franklyn M. 2015. (Let's-Read-And-Find-Out Science 2 Ser.). (ENG.). 40p. (J). (gr. -1-3). pap. 6.99 ***(978-0-06-238202-3(0))*** HarperCollins Pubs.

Lloyd, Megan. Earthquakes. Branley, Franklyn M. rev. ed. 2005. (Let's-Read-and-Find-Out Science Ser.). 40p. (J). (gr. k-4). (ENG.). 15.99 *(978-0-06-028008-6(5))*; lib. bdg. 16.89 *(978-0-06-028009-3(3))* HarperCollins Pubs.

—Fancy That. Hershenhorn, Esther. 2003. (ENG.). 32p. (J). (gr. k-3). tchr. ed. 16.95 *(978-0-8234-1605-9(4))* Holiday Hse., Inc.

—Miss Sally Ann & the Panther. Miller, Bobbi. 2012. (ENG.). 32p. (J). 16.95 *(978-0-8234-1833-6(2))* Holiday Hse., Inc.

—The Mixed-up Rooster. Edwards, Pamela Duncan. 2006. 32p. (J). (gr. -1-1). 15.99 *(978-0-06-028999-7(6)*, Tegen, Katherine Bks) HarperCollins Pubs.

—Thanksgiving at the Tappletons' Spinelli, Eileen. rev. ed. 2004. (ENG.). 32p. (J). (gr. -1-3). pap. 6.99 *(978-0-06-008672-5(6))* HarperCollins Pubs.

—Thanksgiving at the Tappletons' Spinelli, Eileen. 2005. (gr. -1-3). 17.00 *(978-0-7569-5762-9(1))* Perfection Learning Corp.

—This Is the Feast. Shore, Diane ZuHone. 2008. 32p. (J). (gr. -1-3). lib. bdg. 17.89 *(978-0-06-623795-4(5))* HarperCollins Pubs.

—This Is the Feast. Shore, Diane Z. (ENG.). 32p. (J). (gr. -1-3). 2011. pap. 6.99 *(978-0-06-443850-6(3))*; 2008. 16.99 *(978-0-06-623794-7(7))* HarperCollins Pubs.

—Too Many Turkeys. White, Linda Arms. 2010. (ENG.). 32p. (J). (gr. -1-3). 16.95 *(978-0-8234-2084-1(1))* Holiday Hse., Inc.

—Too Many Turkeys. White, Linda. 2011. (ENG.). 32p. (J). pap. 7.95 *(978-0-8234-2384-2(0))* Holiday Hse., Inc.

—Volcanoes. Branley, Franklyn M. & Branley. 2008. (Let's-Read-And-Find-Out Science 2 Ser.). (ENG.). 40p. (J). (gr. k-4). pap. 5.99 *(978-0-06-445189-5(5))* HarperCollins Pubs.

Lloyd, Sam. Dino-Baby. Sperring, Mark. 2013. (ENG.). 32p. (J). (gr. -1-1). 14.99 *(978-1-61963-151-9(2))*; lib. bdg. 15.89 *(978-1-61963-152-6(0))* Bloomsbury USA. (Bloomsbury USA Childrens).

Lloyd, Sam. Shape Sorters - Numbers, 2. Lloyd, Sam. ed. 2011. (Shape Sorters Ser.). (ENG.). 12p. (J). (gr. k-k). bds. 7.99 *(978-0-230-70962-1(1))* Macmillan Pubs., Ltd. GBR. Dist: Independent Pubs. Group.

—What's in Your Tummy Mummy? Lloyd, Sam. 2007. (ENG.). 24p. (J). (gr. -1-k). pap. 13.95 *(978-1-84365-091-1(6)*, Pavilion) Pavilion Bks. GBR. Dist: Independent Pubs. Group.

Lloyd, Sam, jt. illus. see Lloyd, Sam R.

Lloyd, Sam R. & Lloyd, Sam. Mr. Pusskins: A Love Story. Lloyd, Sam R. & Lloyd, Sam. 2006. (ENG.). 32p. (J). (gr. -1-3). 17.99 *(978-1-4169-2517-0(1)*, Atheneum Bks. for Young Readers) Simon & Schuster Children's Publishing.

—Mr. Pusskins & Little Whiskers: Another Love Story. Lloyd, Sam R. & Lloyd, Sam. 2008. (ENG.). 32p. (J). (gr. -1-3). 17.99 *(978-1-4169-5796-6(0)*, Atheneum Bks. for Young Readers) Simon & Schuster Children's Publishing.

Lo, Beth. Mahjong All Day Long. Lo, Ginnie. 2005. (ENG.). 32p. (J). (gr. -1-3). 16.95 *(978-0-8027-8941-9(2))* Walker & Co.

Lo Bianco, Nick. It's a Home Run, Charlie Brown! Shultz, Charles M. & Katschke, Judy. 2011. (Peanuts Ready-To-Reads Ser.). (ENG.). 32p. (gr. -1-2). lib. bdg. 24.21 *(978-1-59961-801-2(X))* Spotlight.

—It's Time for School, Charlie Brown. Shultz, Charles M. & Katschke, Judy. 2011. (Peanuts Ready-To-Reads Ser.). (ENG.). 32p. (gr. -1-2). lib. bdg. 24.21 *(978-1-59961-802-9(8))* Spotlight.

Lo Bianco, Peter. Lose the Blanket, Linus! Shultz, Charles M. & Bailer, Darice. 2011. (Peanuts Ready-To-Reads Ser.). (ENG.). 32p. (gr. -1-2). lib. bdg. 24.21 *(978-1-59961-804-3(4))* Spotlight.

—Lucy's Advice. Shultz, Charles M. & Katschke, Judy. 2011. (Peanuts Ready-To-Reads Ser.). (ENG.). 32p. (gr. -1-2). lib. bdg. 24.21 *(978-1-59961-805-0(2))* Spotlight.

—Make a Trade, Charlie Brown! Shultz, Charles M. & Bailer, Darice. 2011. (Peanuts Ready-To-Reads Ser.). (ENG.). 32p. (gr. -1-2). lib. bdg. 24.21 *(978-1-59961-806-7(0))* Spotlight.

—Snoopy: Flying Ace to the Rescue. Shultz, Charles M. & Bailer, Darice. 2011. (Peanuts Ready-To-Reads Ser.). (ENG.). 32p. (gr. -1-2). lib. bdg. 24.21 *(978-1-59961-807-4(9))* Spotlight.

Lo Cascio, Maria Cristina. Jesus Speaks to Me on My First Holy Communion. Burrin, Angela M. 2009. 39p. (J). (gr. 1-5). 12.95 *(978-1-59325-149-9(1))* Word Among Us Pr.

—Stories of Fairytale Castles. Lester, Anna. 2007. (Young Reading Series 1 Gift Bks). 48p. (J). (gr. 4-7). 8.99 *(978-0-7945-1679-6(3)*, Usborne) EDC Publishing.

Lo Famia, Jon. Charles Dickens/A Christmas Carol. Dickens, Charles. 2005. 48p. (gr. 5-8). 25.50 *(978-0-7910-9108-1(2))* Facts On File, Inc.

Lo Raso, Carlo, et al. My Little Pony Phonics Fun/[stories by Joanne Mattern]; [phonics Scope & Sequence by Cathy Toohey; Pictures by Carlo Lo Rosa ... [et Al.], 12 vols. Mattern, Joanne & Toohey, Cathy. 2008. (J). *(978-0-06-123171-1(1))*; *(978-0-06-123173-5(8))*; *(978-0-06-123174-2(6))*; *(978-0-06-123175-9(4))*; *(978-0-06-123176-6(2))*; *(978-0-06-123178-0(9))*; *(978-0-06-123179-7(7))*; *(978-0-06-123180-3(0))*; *(978-0-06-123181-0(9))*; *(978-0-06-123182-7(7))*; *(978-0-06-123183-4(5))*; *(978-0-06-123184-1(3))* HarperCollins Pubs. (Harper Trophy).

Lo Raso, Carlo. Watch Me Draw the Backyardigans' Incredible Adventures. 2012. (J). *(978-1-936309-42-9(4))* Quarto Publishing Group USA.

Lo Raso, Carlo, jt. illus. see Kurtz, John.

Lo, Rich. Father's Chinese Opera. Lo, Rich. 2014. (ENG.). 40p. (J). (gr. -1-k). 16.95 *(978-1-62873-610-6(0)*, Sky Pony Pr.) Skyhorse Publishing Co., Inc.

Lo, Talthau, photos by. The Disobedient Ducklings. Lo, Yer Jenny. 2008. 44p. pap. 24.95 *(978-1-60441-576-6(2))* America Star Bks.

Lobato, Arcadio. Volando por las Palabras. 2004.Tr. of Flying through Words. (SPA.). 48p. (J). 10.50 *(978-84-263-5018-3(6))* Vives, Luis Editorial (Edelvives) ESP. Dist: Lectorum Pubns., Inc.

Lobbecke, Eric. The Koala Bounces Back. Thomson, Jimmy. 2012. (ENG.). 32p. (J). (gr. k-2). 16.99 *(978-1-74275-007-1(9))* Random Hse. Australia AUS. Dist: Independent Pubs. Group.

Löbbecke, Eric. The Koala Bounces Back. Thomson, Jimmy. 2012. (ENG.). 32p. (J). (gr. k-2). pap. 9.99 *(978-1-74275-008-8(7))* Random Hse. Australia AUS. Dist: Independent Pubs. Group.

—The Koala Who Bounced. Thomson, Jimmy. 2011. (ENG.). 32p. (J). (gr. k-2). pap. 8.99 *(978-1-74275-224-2(1))* Random Hse. Australia AUS. Dist: Independent Pubs. Group.

Lobel, Adrianne, jt. illus. see Lobel, Arnold.

Lobel, Anita. All the World's a Stage. Davidson, Rebecca Piatt. 2003. 32p. (J). 16.89 *(978-0-06-029627-8(5))* HarperCollins Pubs.

—On Market Street. Lobel, Arnold. 25th anniv. ed. 2006. (ENG.). 40p. (J). (gr. -1-3). pap. 6.99 *(978-0-688-08745-6(0)*, Greenwillow Bks.) HarperCollins Pubs.

—So Happy! Henkes, Kevin. 2005. (ENG.). 32p. (J). (gr. -1-3). 16.99 *(978-0-06-056483-4(0)*, Greenwillow Bks.) HarperCollins Pubs.

Lobel, Anita. Animal Antics: A to Z. Lobel, Anita. 2005. 32p. (J). lib. bdg. 16.89 *(978-0-06-051815-8(4))* HarperCollins Pubs.

—Hello, Day! Lobel, Anita. 2008. (ENG.). 40p. (J). (gr. -1 — 1). 16.99 *(978-0-06-078765-3(1)*, Greenwillow Bks.) HarperCollins Pubs.

Lobel, Arnold. Miss Suzy. Young, Miriam. (J). 40th anniv. ed. 2004. 44p. 18.95 *(978-1-930900-28-8(7))*; 50th ed. 2014. (ENG.). 40p. (gr. -1-3). 18.95 *(978-1-930900-75-2(9))* Purple Hse. Pr.

Lobel, Arnold. Days with Frog & Toad. Lobel, Arnold. 2004. (I Can Read Book 2 Ser.). (ENG.). 64p. (J). (gr. -1-3). pap. 3.99 *(978-0-06-444058-5(3))*; 25th ed. 16.99 *(978-0-06-023963-3(8))* HarperCollins Pubs.

—Frog & Toad Are Friends. Lobel, Arnold. 2003. (I Can Read Book 2 Ser.). (ENG.). 64p. (J). (gr. -1-3). pap. 3.99 *(978-0-06-444020-2(6))* HarperCollins Pubs.

—The Frog & Toad Collection, Set. Lobel, Arnold. 2004. (I Can Read Book 2 Ser.). 13p. (J). (gr. k-3). pap. 11.99 *(978-0-06-058086-5(0))* HarperCollins Pubs.

—Frog & Toad Storybook Treasury. Lobel, Arnold. 2013. (I Can Read Book 2 Ser.). (ENG.). 256p. (J). (gr. -1-3). 11.99 *(978-0-06-229258-2(7))* HarperCollins Pubs.

—Sapo y Sepo, Inseparables. Lobel, Arnold. 2003. (SPA.). 68p. (J). (gr. -1-3). 12.95 *(978-84-204-3047-8(1))* Ediciones Alfaguara ESP. Dist: Lectorum Pubns., Inc., Santillana USA Publishing Co., Inc.

—Sapo y Sepo Son Amigos. Lobel, Arnold. 2003. (SPA.). 66p. (J). (gr. k-3). pap. 12.95 *(978-968-19-0714-3(0))* Aguilar, Altea, Taurus, Alfaguara, S.A. de C.V MEX. Dist: Santillana USA Publishing Co., Inc.

Lobel, Arnold & Lobel, Adrianne. The Frogs & Toads All Sang. Lobel, Arnold & Lobel, Adrianne. 2009. 32p. (J). (gr. -1-2). (ENG.). 16.99 *(978-0-06-180022-1(8))*; lib. bdg. 17.89 *(978-0-06-180023-8(6))* HarperCollins Pubs.

—Odd Owls & Stout Pigs: A Book of Nonsense. Lobel, Arnold & Lobel, Adrianne. 2009. (ENG.). 32p. (J). (gr. -1-2). 15.99 *(978-0-06-180054-2(6))* HarperCollins Pubs.

Locatelli, Ellen. Filastrocche Italiane- Italian Nursery Rhymes. 2013. 54p. *(978-1-938712-08-1(0))* Roxby Media Ltd.

Lochrie, Elizabeth. Big Jinny: The Story of a Grizzly Bear. Linderman, Frank B. et al. 2005. (ENG.). 130p. pap. 16.95 *(978-0-8032-8044-1(0)*, LINBIX, Bison Bks.) Univ. of Nebraska Pr.

Locke, Barbara K. Oliver's Ghost: A Spooky Tale from Nantucket. Bouton, Warren Hussey. 2003. (J). per. 5.95 *(978-0-9700555-3-8(6))* Hither Creek Pr.

Locke, Barbara Kauffmann. The Captain's Return: A Spooky Tale from Nantucket. Bouton, Warren Hussey. 2004. (J). per. 5.95 *(978-0-9700555-4-5(4))* Hither Creek Pr.

Locke, Gary. Bird, Bird, Bird! A Chirping Chant. Sayre, April Pulley. 2007. (American City Ser.). (ENG.). 32p. (J). (gr. k-3). 16.95 *(978-1-55971-978-0(8))* Cooper Square Publishing Llc.

—Raymie, Dickie, & the Bean: Why I Love & Hate My Brothers. Romano, Ray. 2007. 32p. (J). 18.00 *(978-1-4223-6806-0(8))* DIANE Publishing Co.

Locke, Margo. Lillie's Smile. Doolittle, Sara. 2011. 32p. (J). pap. 18.99 *(978-0-9827611-6-8(3)*, Catch the Spirit of Appalachia) Ammons Communications, Ltd.

Locke, Terry. Spencer Hurley & the Aliens: Book One: the Abduction, Vol. 1. Locke, Terry. Hucks, Robin, ed. 2008. (Spencer Hurley & the Aliens Ser.: 1). 256p. (J). per. 8.99 *(978-0-9786940-1-2(5))* Dream Workshop Publishing Co., LLC, The.

Locker, Thomas. Rembrandt & Titus: Artist & Son. Comora, Madeleine. 2005. (ENG.). 32p. (J). (gr. 2-5). 17.95 *(978-1-55591-490-5(X))* Fulcrum Publishing.

—Washington Irving's Rip Van Winkle. Foehner, Ashley & Irving, Washington. 2008. (ENG.). 32p. 12.95 *(978-1-55591-713-5(5))* Fulcrum Publishing.

Locker, Thomas. Hudson: The Story of a River. Locker, Thomas. Baron, Robert C. 2004. (ENG.). 32p. (J). 17.95 *(978-1-55591-512-4(4))* Fulcrum Publishing.

—Rip Van Winkle. Locker, Thomas. Foehner, Ashley P. 2008. (ENG.). 32p. (gr. -1-5). pap. 7.95 *(978-1-55591-675-6(9))* Fulcrum Publishing.

Lockhart, David. Hercules & Other Tales from Greek Myths. Coolidge, Olivia E. 2011. 120p. 39.95 *(978-1-258-02308-9(3))* Literary Licensing, LLC.

Lockheart, Susanna. If You Love a Christmas Tale. 2009. (ENG.). 24p. (J). (gr. -1-3). 18.99 *(978-0-7641-6267-1(5))* Barron's Educational Series, Inc.

Lockman, Darcy. Softball for Fun!, 1 vol. Lockman, Darcy. 2006. (For Fun!: Sports Ser.). (ENG.). 48p. (gr. 3-6). lib. bdg. 26.65 *(978-0-7565-1682-6(X)*, For Fun!) Compass Point Bks.

Lockman, Vic. Catechism for Young Children Coloring Book. Lockman, Vic. 2003. 24p. (J). (gr. -1-3). *(978-0-936175-41-6(9))* Lockman, Vic.

Lockspeiser, Nancy Flanders. Flexible You: 21 Stretches a Day for a 9-Lives Body: a Cat's Quick Guide to Stretching & Self-Massage. Lockspeiser, Nancy Flanders. 2004. 48p. spiral bd. 14.94 *(978-0-9752922-0-4(X))* Catamount Publishing LLC.

Lockwood, C. C., photos by. Tales of Mike the Tiger: Facts & Fun for Everyone. Baker, David G. & Stewart, Margaret Taylor. 2006. (ENG., 144p. (gr. 4-7). 19.95 *(978-0-8071-3118-3(0)*, 9780807131183) Louisiana State Univ. Pr.

Locsinto, Lucas. The Adventures of Seek & Save Volume 3: The Village. Swanepoel, Sharon. 2011. (J). *(978-0-9772647-6-6(9))* God's Glory Media.

Loday, Gyelsey, jt. photos by see Lhamo, Choki.

Lodge, Ali. Elephant Hide & Seek. Billam, Rosemary. 2006. (Reading Corner Ser.). (ENG.). 32p. (J). (gr. k-2). pap. 6.99 ***(978-0-7496-6556-2(4))*** Hodder & Stoughton GBR. Dist: Independent Pubs. Group.

Lodge, Ali. The Leopard & the Sky God. 2007. (Usborne First Reading: Level 3 Ser.). 48p. (J). (gr. -1-3). 8.99 *(978-0-7945-1838-7(9)*, Usborne) EDC Publishing.

L

—Moonlight Animals. Golding, Elizabeth. 2011. (ENG.). 12p. (J). 12.95 *(978-0-7624-4316-1(2))* Running Pr. Bk. Pubs.

—Moonlight Ocean. Golding, Elizabeth. 2012. (ENG.). 12p. (J). 12.95 *(978-0-7624-4486-1(X))* Running Pr. Bk. Pubs.

—My First Farmyard Tales: Eight Exciting Picture Stories for Little Ones. Baxter, Nicola. 2013. (ENG.). 16p. (J). (gr. -1-2). bds. 13.99 *(978-1-84322-990-2(0)*, Armadillo) Anness Publishing GBR. Dist: National Bk. Network.

—Noah's Ark: Baby's First Pop-up! Lodge, Yvette. gif. ed. 2006. 8p. (J). 19.95 *(978-1-57791-217-0(9))* Brighter Minds Children's Publishing.

Lodge, Alison. Clever Chameleon. Lodge, Alison. Lodge, Ali. 2005. 24p. (J). 15.99 *(978-1-84148-347-4(8))* Barefoot Bks., Inc.

Lodge, Bernard. Songs for Survival: Songs & Chants from Tribal Peoples Around the World. Siegen-Smith, Nikki, ed. 2005. 80p. (J). (gr. k-4). reprint ed. 19.00 *(978-0-7567-9404-0(8))* DIANE Publishing Co.

Lodge, Jo. Icky Sticky Monster Pop-Up. Lodge, Jo. Nosy Crow Staff. 2012. (ENG.). 12p. (J). (gr. -1-2). 12.99 *(978-0-7636-6173-1(2)*, Nosy Crow) Candlewick Pr.

—1, 2, 3, ¡Ya! Lodge, Jo. 2009. (SPA.). 12p. (J). bds. *(978-84-263-7278-9(3))* Vives, Luis Editorial (Edelvives).

Lodge, Katherine. Peach Tree Street, Vol. 2. Miranda, Anne. l.t. ed. 2005. (Little Books & Big Bks.: Vol. 10). 8p. (gr. k-2). 23.00 net. *(978-0-8215-7519-2(8))* Sadlier, William H. Inc.

Lodwick, Sarah. A Christmas Eve Victory. Spangenberg, Greg. l.t. ed. 2006. 32p. (J). 16.99 *(978-1-59879-140-2(0))* Lifevest Publishing, Inc.

—Churchy & the Light on Christmas Eve. Spangenberg, Greg. l.t. ed. 2006. 40p. (J). (gr. -1-7). 14.99 *(978-1-59879-017-7(X))* Lifevest Publishing, Inc.

Loebel, Bonnie. Duckling's First Adventure. Perry, Shelly. 2006. (ENG.). 56p. (J). per. 9.95 *(978-0-9787740-3-5(5))* Peppertree Pr., The.

Loebel-Fried, Caren. Naupaka: By Nona Beamer: Illustrations by Caren Loebel-Fried: Hawaiian Translation by Kaliko Beamer-Trapp: Music by Keola Beamer. Beamer, Winona Desha et al. 2008. (J). 14.95 *(978-1-58178-089-5(3))* Bishop Museum Pr.

Loebel-Fried, Caren Keala. Pua Polu: The Pretty Blue Hawaiian Flower. Beamer, Winona Desha & Beamer-Trapp, Kaliko. 2005. (HAW & ENG.). 36p. (J). audio compact disk 14.95 *(978-1-58178-041-3(9))* Bishop Museum Pr.

Loeffelholz, Sarah. Can You Just Imagine. 2007. 40p. (J). 14.95 *(978-0-9786850-1-0(6))* Overdue Bks.

—My Favorite Food. Robey, Stephanie. 2006. (J). 14.95 *(978-0-9786850-0-3(8))* Overdue Bks.

Loeffler, Trade. Zig & Wikki in Something Ate My Homework. Spiegelman, Nadja. Mouly, Francoise, ed. 2010. (ENG.). 40p. (J). (gr. -1-3). 12.95 *(978-1-935179-02-3(0))* TOON Books / RAW Junior, LLC.

Loeffler, Trade & Johnson, R. Kikuo. The Shark King. Johnson, R. Kikuo. 2012. (ENG.). 40p. (J). (gr. -1-3). 12.95 *(978-1-935179-16-0(0))* TOON Books / RAW Junior, LLC.

Loehle, Richard. Michael's Racing Machine. Lowery, Lawrence F. 2014. (ENG.). 36p. (J). pap. 11.95 *(978-1-941316-05-4(0))* National Science Teachers Assn.

Loehr, Jenny. Eek! I Hear a Squeak & the Scurrying of Little Feet. Carlson, Lavelle. 2006. (ENG.). 28p. (J). (gr. -1-3). 19.95 incl. audio compact disk *(978-0-9725803-8-0(7))* Children's Publishing.

—I Can Do That. Lederer, Susan. 2008. 28p. (J). per. 19.95 *(978-0-9789347-0-5(9))* Children's Publishing.

—I Can Say That. Lederer, Suzy. l.t. ed. 2006. 32p. (J). (gr. -1-3). 19.95 incl. audio compact disk *(978-0-9725803-7-3(9))* Children's Publishing.

Loehr, Patrick. Mucumber McGee & the Half-Eaten Hot Dog. Loehr, Patrick. 2007. 32p. (J). (gr. -1-3). lib. bdg. 16.89 *(978-0-06-082328-3(3)*, Tegen, Katherine Bks) HarperCollins Pubs.

Loewer, Jean. The Moonflower, 1 vol. Loewer, Peter. 2004. (ENG.). 32p. (J). (gr. 1-5). pap. 7.95 *(978-1-56145-314-6(5))* Peachtree Pubs.

LoFaro, Jerry. El Tesoro de Los Cuentos de Hadas. Publications International Ltd. Staff, ed. 2004. (SPA & ESP.). 384p. (J). 15.98 *(978-1-4127-0165-5(1)*, 3995001) Phoenix International Publications, Inc.

LoFaro, Jerry, et al. Treasury of Fairy Tales. Goldenburg, Dorothea & Killian, Bette. 2004. 320p. (J). 15.98 *(978-0-7853-7771-9(9)*, 3049205) Phoenix International Publications, Inc.

Lofting, Hugh. The Story of Doctor Dolittle, Original Version. Lofting, Hugh. 2010. (ENG.). 204p. (J). pap. 25.95 *(978-4-87187-305-5(6))* Ishi Pr. International.

Loftis, Cory. Of Giants & Ice. Bach, Shelby. 2013. (Ever Afters Ser.: 1). (ENG.). 368p. (J). (gr. 3-7). pap. 7.99 *(978-1-4424-3147-8(4)*, Simon & Schuster Bks. For Young Readers) Simon & Schuster Bks. For Young Readers.

Loftus, David & Terry, Chris, photos by. Jamie's Italy. Oliver, Jamie. 2006. (ENG., 320p. (gr. 8-17). 34.95 *(978-1-4013-0195-8(9))* Hyperion Pr.

Logan, Desiree. Princesses Do Not Wear Tattoos. Parker, Lisa L. Gray. 2011. 48p. pap. 24.95 *(978-1-4560-3281-4(X))* America Star Bks.

Logan, Laura. I Can Play It Safe. Feigh, Alison. 2008. (ENG.). 32p. (J). (gr. -1-3). 14.99 *(978-1-57542-285-5(9))* Free Spirit Publishing, Inc.

—Jesus Loves Me. 20p. (J). (gr. -1-k). 2009. 6.99 *(978-0-8249-1839-2(8))*; 2008. (ENG.). bds. 12.99 *(978-0-8249-6730-7(5))* Ideals Pubns. (Candy Cane Pr.).

—Lidia's Christmas Kitchen. Bastianich, Lidia Matticchio. 2010. (ENG.). 56p. (J). (gr. -1-3). 15.95 *(978-0-7624-3692-7(1))* Running Pr. Bk. Pubs.

—Storytime Stickers: Springtime with Bunny. Plourde, Lynn. 2012. (Storytime Stickers Ser.). (ENG.). 16p. (J). (gr. k). pap. 5.95 *(978-1-4027-8188-9(1))* Sterling Publishing Co., Inc.

—Ten Easter Eggs. Bodach, Vijaya. 2015. (ENG.). 22p. (J). (gr. -1-k). 8.99 *(978-0-545-74730-1(9)*, Cartwheel Bks.) Scholastic, Inc.

—That's My Mommy! Hodgman, Ann. 2013. *(978-1-58925-645-3(X))* Tiger Tales.

—Two to Cuddle. Spinelli, Eileen. 2009. (ENG.). 20p. (J). bds. 6.99 *(978-0-8249-1824-8(X)*, Candy Cane Pr.) Ideals Pubns.

Logan, Stephanie, jt. illus. see Noah, Ian.

Loh, Martin. Malaysian Children's Favourite Stories. Lyons, Kay. 2014. (ENG.). 64p. (J). pap. 12.95 *(978-0-8048-4401-7(1))* Tuttle Publishing.

Löhlein, Henning. Hamster Monster. Löhlein, Susanne. 2014. (ENG.). 32p. (J). 17.95 *(978-0-7358-4178-9(0))* North-South Bks., Inc.

Lohmann, Renate. The Bitty Twins on the Go. Hirsch, Jennifer. 2006. (J). *(978-1-59369-188-2(2))* American Girl Publishing, Inc.

—The Lucky Boots. 2006. (Famous Fables Ser.). (J). 6.99 *(978-1-59939-027-7(2))* Cornerstone Pr.

—The Queen & the Mouse: A Story about Friendship. Lang, Andrew. 2006. (J). *(978-1-59939-081-9(7)*, Reader's Digest Young Families, Inc.) Studio Fun International.

—The Wild Swans: A Tale of Persistence. Andersen, Hans Christian. 2006. (J). *(978-1-59939-093-2(0)*, Reader's Digest Young Families, Inc.) Studio Fun International.

Lohmann, Stephanie. Keeper at the Inn. McCurdy, Steve. 2007. 36p. 17.95 *(978-0-9761179-2-6(4))* StoryMaster Pr.

Lohr, Tyrel, jt. illus. see Watson, Travis.

Lohse, Otha Zackariah Edward. The Assassination of Abraham Lincoln, 1 vol. Olson, Kay Melchisedech & Melchisedech Olson, Kay. 2005. (Graphic History Ser.). (ENG.). 32p. (gr. 3-4). 29.99 *(978-0-7368-3831-3(7)*, Graphic Library) Capstone Pr., Inc.

—The Assassination of Abraham Lincoln, 1 vol. Olson, Kay Melchisedech. 2005. (Graphic History Ser.). (ENG.). 32p. (gr. 3-4). per. 8.10 *(978-0-7368-5241-8(7)*, Graphic Library) Capstone Pr., Inc.

Lohse, Otha Zackariah Edward & Schulz, Barbara. The Curse of King Tut's Tomb, 1 vol. Burgan, Michael & Hoena, Blake A. 2005. (Graphic History Ser.). (ENG.). 32p. (gr. 3-4). 29.99 *(978-0-7368-3833-7(3)*, Graphic Library) Capstone Pr., Inc.

Lohstoeter, Lori. Beatrice's Goat. McBrier, Page. 2004. (ENG.). 40p. (J). (gr. -1-3). reprint ed. 7.99 *(978-0-689-86990-7(8)*, Simon & Schuster/Paula Wiseman Bks.) Simon & Schuster/Paula Wiseman Bks.

—Cesar Chavez: A Hero for Everyone. Soto, Gary. 2003. (Milestone Ser.). (ENG.). 80p. (J). (gr. 2-5). pap. 5.99 *(978-0-689-85922-9(8)*, Simon & Schuster/Paula Wiseman Bks.) Simon & Schuster/Paula Wiseman Bks.

—How the Leopard Got His Spots. Kipling, Rudyard. 2005. (Rabbit Ears: A Classic Tale Ser.). 36p. (gr. 4-6). 25.65 *(978-1-59679-344-6(9))* Spotlight.

Loki & Splink. The Little Flower Bulb: Helping Children Bereaved by Suicide. Gormally, Eleanor. 2011. (ENG.). 32p. (J). (gr. -1-3). pap. 21.95 *(978-1-84730-260-1(2))* Veritas Pubns. IRL. Dist: Dufour Editions, Inc.

Lokus, Rex & Sánchez, Alvaro Iglesias. Milton Hershey's Sweet Idea: A Chocolate Kingdom. Cooper, Sharon Katz. 2015. (Story Behind the Name Ser.). (ENG.). 32p. (gr. 2-3). lib. bdg. 27.99 ***(978-1-4795-7137-6(7))*** Picture Window Bks.

Lola & Ivanke. Trucks. Krensky, Stephen. 2009. (Ready-To-Reads Ser.). (ENG.). 32p. (J). (gr. -1-1). pap. 3.99 *(978-1-4169-0236-2(8)*, Simon Spotlight) Simon Spotlight.

Lola & Ivanke & Lola. Easy to Be Green: Simple Activities You Can Do to Save the Earth. Bryant, Megan E. & O'Ryan, Ellie. 2009. (Little Green Bks.). (ENG.). 32p. (J). pap. 4.99 *(978-1-4169-7182-5(3)*, Simon Scribbles) Simon Scribbles.

Lollar, Cathy. I Can Do It! Quantrell, Angie. 2003. 9.99 *(978-1-56309-626-6(9))* Woman's Missionary Union.

Lombardo, Constance. Stunt Cat to the Stars. Lombardo, Constance. 2015. (Mr. Puffball Ser.: 1). (ENG.). 240p. (J). (gr. 3-7). 12.99 ***(978-0-06-232065-0(3))*** HarperCollins Pubs.

Lombardo, Irina. Let There Be Llamas! Kroll, Virginia. 2006. 31p. (J). pap. 11.95 *(978-0-8198-4519-1(1))* Pauline Bks. & Media.

Lombardo, Irina, jt. illus. see Curreli, Augusta.

Lomenech Gill, Olivia. Where My Wellies Take Me. Morpurgo, Michael & Morpurgo, Clare. 2013. (ENG.). 110p. (J). (gr. 1-4). 29.99 *(978-0-7636-6629-3(7)*, Templar) Candlewick Pr.

Lomofsky, Lynne & Laubscher, André. Taking the Cows Home. Schermbrucker, Reviva. 2011. (ENG.). 24p. (J). (gr. k-2). pap. 6.95 *(978-1-77009-862-6(3))* Jacana Media ZAF. Dist: Independent Pubs. Group.

Lonaytis, Olga. Grandpa Mouse & Little Mouse: A Tale about Respect for Elders. Grimm, Jacob & Grimm, Wilhelm K. 2006. (J). *(978-1-59939-088-8(4)*, Reader's Digest Young Families, Inc.) Studio Fun International.

London, Sean. Desolation Canyon. London, Jonathan. 2015. (ENG.). 168p. (YA). 23.99 ***(978-1-941821-60-2(X))***; pap. 12.99 *(978-1-941821-29-9(4))* Graphic Arts Ctr. Publishing Co. (West Winds Pr.).

Lonechild, Michael. Hidden Buffalo, 1 vol. Wiebe, Rudy. 2006. (ENG.). 32p. (J). (gr. -1-3). pap. 9.95 *(978-0-88995-334-5(1))* Red Deer Pr. CAN. Dist: Ingram Pub. Services.

Lonergan Iorio, John. Another Tree in the Yard. Sera, Lucia. 2004. 32p. (J). per. 16.95 *(978-1-932653-36-6(8))* Vocalis, Ltd.

Long, Carlos. Why Am I at the Red Table? Kamins, Julie Firstenberg. 2008. 32p. (J). 13.95 *(978-0-9771566-9-6(9))* Librujas.

Long, Chad Michael. The Lycan Journal. Long, Chad Michael, . 2nd ed. 2007. 141p. (YA). per. 12.95 *(978-0-615-18961-1(X))* Long Stories LLC.

Long, Corey. Use Your Imagination. Robinson, Vickie J. 2008. 24p. pap. 24.95 *(978-1-60703-825-2(0))* America Star Bks.

Long, Dave. The Marvelous Fountain: And other stories my grandma told Me. Filipi, Carmen. 2007.Tr. of Fuente Maravillosa y otros cuentos que me conto mi Abuela. (ENG & SPA.). 55p. (J). per. 14.95 *(978-0-9797814-0-7(X))* Hispanic Institute of Social Issues.

Long, DeWayne Lee. The Little Crooked Christmas Tree. Parker, Robert H. 2012. 32p. (J). pap. 15.00 *(978-0-9837382-9-9(7)*, Catch the Spirit of Appalachia) Ammons Communications, Ltd.

Long, Ethan. The Best Thanksgiving Ever! Slater, Teddy. 2007. (ENG.). 24p. (J). (gr. -1-3). pap. 5.99 *(978-0-439-87390-1(8)*, Cartwheel Bks.) Scholastic, Inc.

Long, Ethan. Big Cat. 2016. (J). ***(978-0-8234-3538-8(5))*** Holiday Hse., Inc.

Long, Ethan. The Book That Zack Wrote. 2011. (ENG.). 36p. (J). (gr. k-3). 11.99 *(978-1-60905-060-3(6))* Blue Apple Bks.

—Bunny Race! Maccarone, Grace. 2009. (J). *(978-0-545-11290-1(7))* Scholastic, Inc.

—Count on Culebra. Paul, Ann Whitford. 2010. (ENG.). 40p. (J). (gr. -1-3). pap. 6.95 *(978-0-8234-2310-1(7))* Holiday Hse., Inc.

—Count on Culebra: Go from 1 to 10 in Spanish. Paul, Ann Whitford. 2008. (ENG.). 40p. (J). (gr. -1-3). 16.95 *(978-0-8234-2124-4(4))* Holiday Hse., Inc.

—Draw with Scribbles & Ink: Draw & Paint Your Own Masterpieces! 2014. (ENG.). 48p. (J). (gr. 1-17). 14.95 *(978-1-60058-471-8(3))* Quarto Publishing Group USA.

—Drooling & Dangerous: The Riot Brothers Return! Amato, Mary. (ENG.). 176p. (J). 2008. (gr. 1-5). pap. 7.95 *(978-0-8234-2204-3(6))*; 2006. (gr. 4-7). 16.95 *(978-0-8234-1986-9(X))* Holiday Hse., Inc.

—Fiesta Fiasco. Paul, Ann Whitford. (ENG.). 32p. (J). (gr. -1-3). 2010. pap. 6.95 *(978-0-8234-2275-3(5))*; 2007. 16.95 *(978-0-8234-2037-7(X))* Holiday Hse., Inc.

—Fiesta Fiasco. Paul, Ann Whitford. 2012. pap. 18.95 *(978-1-4301-1099-6(6))* Live Oak Media.

Long, Ethan. Good Night! 2015. (ENG.). 20p. (J). (gr. -1 — 1). bds. 7.95 ***(978-1-4197-1366-8(3))*** Abrams.

Long, Ethan. Greedy Apostrophe: A Cautionary Tale. Carr, Jan. (ENG.). 32p. (J). (gr. 1-3). 2009. pap. 7.95 *(978-0-8234-2205-0(4))*; 2007. 17.95 *(978-0-8234-2006-3(X))* Holiday Hse., Inc.

—Halloween Sky Ride. Spurr, Elizabeth. (ENG.). 32p. (J). 2006. 6.95 *(978-0-8234-2041-4(8))*; 2005. (gr. -1-3). 16.95 *(978-0-8234-1870-1(7))* Holiday Hse., Inc.

—In, over & on the Farm. 2015. (J). Non-ISBN Publisher.

—It's Pooltime! 2012. (ENG.). 40p. (J). (gr. 1-4). 10.99 *(978-1-60905-201-0(3))* Blue Apple Bks.

—It's Raining Cats & Frogs! Ziefert, Harriet. 2015. (¡Hola, English! Ser.). (ENG & SPA.). 28p. (J). (gr. -1-3). 12.99 *(978-1-60905-508-0(X))* Blue Apple Bks.

—The Luckiest St. Patrick's Day Ever! Slater, Teddy. (J). 2008. (ENG.). 32p. (gr. -1-3). pap. 5.99 *(978-0-545-03943-7(6)*, Cartwheel Bks.); 2007. *(978-0-439-86648-4(0))* Scholastic, Inc.

—Manana, Iguana. Paul, Ann Whitford. 2005. (ENG.). 32p. (J). (gr. -1-3). 7.99 *(978-0-8234-1980-7(0))* Holiday Hse., Inc.

—Muddy As a Duck Puddle & Other American Similes. Lawlor, Laurie. 2010. (ENG.). 32p. (J). (gr. 1-5). 16.95 *(978-0-8234-2229-6(1))* Holiday Hse., Inc.

—Muddy as a Duck Puddle & Other American Similes. Lawlor, Laurie. 2011. (ENG.). 32p. (J). pap. 7.95 *(978-0-8234-2389-7(1))* Holiday Hse., Inc.

—One Little Chicken: A Counting Book. Elliott, David. 2007. (ENG.). 24p. (J). (gr. -1-3). 16.95 *(978-0-8234-1983-8(5))* Holiday Hse., Inc.

—Rick & Rack & the Great Outdoors. 2010. (ENG.). 40p. (J). (gr. 1-4). 10.99 *(978-1-60905-034-4(7))* Blue Apple Bks.

—Scribbles & Ink. 2012. (ENG.). 36p. (J). (gr. 2-5). 14.99 *(978-1-60905-205-8(6))* Blue Apple Bks.

—Scribbles & Ink Doodles for Two. 2012. (ENG.). 108p. (J). (gr. k-3). spiral bd. 14.99 *(978-1-60905-219-5(6))* Blue Apple Bks.

—Scribbles & Ink, the Contest. 2013. (ENG.). 72p. (J). (gr. k-3). 10.99 *(978-1-60905-351-2(6))* Blue Apple Bks.

—Snarf Attack, Underfoodle, & the Secret of Life: The Riot Brothers Tell All. Amato, Mary. 2006. (ENG.). 160p. (J). (gr. 4-7). pap. 7.95 *(978-0-8234-2062-9(0))* Holiday Hse., Inc.

—Stick Dog. Watson, Tom. 2013. (Stick Dog Ser.: 1). (ENG.). 192p. (J). (gr. 3-7). 12.99 *(978-0-06-211078-7(0))* HarperCollins Pubs.

—Stick Dog Wants a Hot Dog. Watson, Tom. 2013. 200p. (J). *(978-0-06-229593-4(4))* Harper & Row Ltd.

—Stick Dog Wants a Hot Dog. Watson, Tom. 2013. (Stick Dog Ser.: 2). (ENG.). 224p. (J). (gr. 3-7). 12.99 *(978-0-06-211080-0(2))* HarperCollins Pubs.

—Stinky & Successful: The Riot Brothers Never Stop! Amato, Mary. (ENG.). 160p. (J). 2008. (gr. 1-5). pap. 7.99 *(978-0-8234-2196-1(1))*; 2007. (gr. 2-5). 16.95 *(978-0-8234-2100-8(7))* Holiday Hse., Inc.

—Super Schnoz & the Gates of Smell. Urey, Gary. (Super Schnoz Ser.: 1). (ENG.). 160p. (J). (gr. 3-6). 2015. pap. 6.99 *(978-0-8075-7560-4(7))*; 2013. 14.99 *(978-0-8075-7555-0(0))* Whitman, Albert & Co.

—Take the Mummy & Run: The Riot Brothers Are on a Roll. Amato, Mary. (ENG.). 240p. (J). (gr. 1-5). 2010. pap. 7.95 *(978-0-8234-2273-9(9))*; 2009. 16.95 *(978-0-8234-2175-6(9))* Holiday Hse., Inc.

—Tortuga in Trouble. Paul, Ann Whitford. 2009. (ENG.). 32p. (J). (gr. -1-1). 16.95 *(978-0-8234-2180-0(5))* Holiday Hse., Inc.

—Trollerella. Stegman-Bourgeois, Karen M. 2006. (ENG.). 32p. (J). (gr. -1-3). 14.95 *(978-0-8234-1918-0(5))* Holiday Hse., Inc.

—The Ultimate Top Secret Guide to Taking over the World. Nesbitt, Kenn. 2011. (ENG.). 208p. (J). (gr. 4-8). pap. 10.99 *(978-1-4022-3834-5(7)*, Sourcebooks Jabberwocky) Sourcebooks, Inc.

—Wuv Bunnies from Outers Pace. Elliott, David. 2008. (ENG.). (J). 108p. (gr. 4-7). pap. 6.95 *(978-0-8234-2183-1(X))*; 112p. (gr. 2-4). 16.95 *(978-0-8234-1902-9(9))* Holiday Hse., Inc.

—The Zombie Nite Cafe. Kutner, Merrily. 2007. (ENG.). 32p. (J). (gr. -1-3). 16.95 *(978-0-8234-1963-0(0))* Holiday Hse., Inc.

Long, Ethan. Clara & Clem Take a Ride. Long, Ethan. 2012. (Penguin Young Readers, Level 1 Ser.). (ENG.). 32p. (J). (gr. k-1). mass mkt. 3.99 *(978-0-448-46264-6(8)*, Warne, Frederick Pubs.) Penguin Bks., Ltd. GBR. Dist: Penguin Random Hse., LLC.

—Clara & Clem Take a Ride (HC) Long, Ethan. 2012. (Penguin Young Readers, Level 1 Ser.). (ENG.). 32p. (J). (gr. k-1). 14.99 *(978-0-448-46271-4(0)*, Warne, Frederick Pubs.) Penguin Bks., Ltd. GBR. Dist: Penguin Random Hse., LLC.

—Clara & Clem under the Sea. Long, Ethan. 2014. (Penguin Young Readers, Level 1 Ser.). (ENG.). 32p. (J). (gr. k-1). pap. 3.99 *(978-0-448-47812-8(9)*, Warne, Frederick Pubs.) Penguin Bks., Ltd. GBR. Dist: Penguin Random Hse., LLC.

—The Croaky Pokey! Long, Ethan. (ENG.). 32p. (J). 2012. pap. 6.95 *(978-0-8234-2429-0(4))*; 2011. (gr. -1-1). 14.95 *(978-0-8234-2291-3(7))* Holiday Hse., Inc.

—In, over & on the Farm. Long, Ethan. 2015. (ENG.). 40p. (J). (gr. -1-k). 15.99 *(978-0-399-16907-6(5)*, Putnam Juvenile) Penguin Publishing Group.

—Max & Milo Go to Sleep! Long, Ethan. Long, Heather. 2013. (ENG.). 32p. (J). (gr. -1-3). 14.99 *(978-1-4424-5143-8(2)*, Simon & Schuster/Paula Wiseman Bks.) Simon & Schuster/Paula Wiseman Bks.

—Max & Milo the Mixed-Up Message. Long, Ethan. Long, Heather. 2013. (ENG.). 32p. (J). (gr. -1-3). 14.99 *(978-1-4424-5140-7(8)*, Simon & Schuster/Paula Wiseman Bks.) Simon & Schuster/Paula Wiseman Bks.

—My Dad, My Hero. Long, Ethan. 2011. (ENG.). 32p. (J). (gr. k-3). 12.99 *(978-1-4022-4239-7(5)*, Sourcebooks Jabberwocky) Sourcebooks, Inc.

—Pig Has a Plan. Long, Ethan. 2012. (I Like to Read Ser.). (ENG.). 32p. (J). 14.95 *(978-0-8234-2428-3(6))* Holiday Hse., Inc.

—Scribbles & Ink, Out of the Box. Long, Ethan. 2014. (Jump-Into-Chapters Ser.). (ENG.). 96p. (J). (gr. k-3). 12.99 *(978-1-60905-366-6(4))* Blue Apple Bks.

—Up, Tall & High! Long, Ethan. 2012. (ENG.). 40p. (J). (gr. -1-2). 15.99 *(978-0-399-25611-0(3)*, Putnam Juvenile) Penguin Publishing Group.

—The Wing Wing Brothers: Carnival de Math. Long, Ethan. 2013. (ENG.). 32p. (J). 15.95 *(978-0-8234-2604-1(1))* Holiday Hse., Inc.

—The Wing Wing Brothers Carnival de Math. Long, Ethan. 2014. (ENG.). 32p. (J). (gr. -1-1). 6.99 *(978-0-8234-3062-8(6))* Holiday Hse., Inc.

—The Wing Wing Brothers Geometry Palooza! Long, Ethan. 2014. (ENG.). 32p. (J). (gr. -1-1). 15.95 *(978-0-8234-2951-6(2))* Holiday Hse., Inc.

Long, Ethan. Manana, Iguana. Long, Ethan, tr. Paul, Ann Whitford. 2005. (ENG.). 32p. (J). (gr. -1-3). tchr. ed. 17.95 *(978-0-8234-1808-4(1))* Holiday Hse., Inc.

Long, Ethan, jt. illus. see Sun, Ru.

Long, John. Gogo Fish! The Story of the Western Australian State Fossil Emblem. Long, John. Ruse, Jill. 2004. 40p. (J). pap. *(978-1-920843-08-3(6))* Art Gallery of Western Australia, The.

Long, John & Ruse, Jill. Gogo Fish! The Story of the Western Australian State Fossil Emblem. Long, John. 2004. 40p. (J). *(978-1-920843-10-6(8))* Art Gallery of Western Australia, The.

Long, Laurel. The Legend of Holly Claus. Ryan, Brittney. 2004. (Julie Andrews Collection). 544p. (J). (gr. 4-18). 16.99 *(978-0-06-058511-2(0))*; lib. bdg. 17.89 *(978-0-06-058514-3(5))* HarperCollins Pubs. (Julie Andrews Collection).

Long, Laurel. The Twelve Days of Christmas. Long, Laurel. 2014. (ENG.). 32p. (J). (gr. -1-2). pap. 8.99 *(978-0-14-751286-4(7)*, Puffin) Penguin Publishing Group.

Long Liang, Xiao. Etched in Blood. Chen, Wei Dong. 2013. (Three Kingdoms Ser.: 5). 176p. (YA). (gr. 5-12). lib. bdg. 29.27 *(978-89-94208-98-5(4))* Lerner Publishing Group.

—The Family Plot. Chen, Wei Dong. 2013. (Three Kingdoms Ser.: 2). 176p. (YA). (gr. 5-12). lib. bdg. 29.27 *(978-89-94208-92-3(5))* Lerner Publishing Group.

—The Fortunate Sons. Dong Chen, Wei. 2013. (Three Kingdoms Ser.: 8). 176p. (gr. 5-12). pap. 9.99 *(978-89-98341-21-3(2))* JR Comics KOR. Dist: Lerner Publishing Group.

—Heroes & Chaos. Chen, Wei Dong. 2013. (Three Kingdoms Ser.: 1). 176p. (YA). (gr. 5-12). lib. bdg. 29.27 *(978-89-94208-90-9(9))* Lerner Publishing Group.

—Revenge & Betrayal. Chen, Wei Dong. 2013. (Three Kingdoms Ser.: 4). 176p. (YA). (gr. 5-12). lib. bdg. 29.27 *(978-89-94208-96-1(8))* Lerner Publishing Group.

—To Pledge Allegiance. Chen, Wei Dong. 2013. (Three Kingdoms Ser.: 3). 176p. (YA). (gr. 5-12). lib. bdg. 29.27 *(978-89-94208-94-7(1))* Lerner Publishing Group.

—War of Words. Dong Chen, Wei. 2013. (Three Kingdoms Ser.: 10). 176p. (gr. 5-12). pap. 9.99 *(978-89-98341-23-7(9))* JR Comics KOR. Dist: Lerner Publishing Group.

Long, Loren. The Day the Animals Came: A Story of Saint Francis Day. Weller, Frances Ward. 2006. 35p. (J). (gr. k-4). reprint ed. 17.00 *(978-1-4223-5396-7(6))* DIANE Publishing Co.

—I Dream of Trains. Johnson, Angela. 2003. (ENG.). 32p. (J). (gr. k-2). 17.99 *(978-0-689-82609-2(5)*, Simon & Schuster Bks. For Young Readers) Simon & Schuster Bks. For Young Readers.

Long, Loren, et al. Kat's Maps. Scieszka, Jon. 2011. (Jon Scieszka's Trucktown Ser.). (ENG.). 24p. (J). (gr. -1-1). 15.99 *(978-1-4169-4159-0(2)*, Simon Spotlight) Simon Spotlight.

Long, Loren. The Little Engine That Could. Piper, Watty & Penguin / LeapFrog. 2008. (J). 13.99 *(978-1-59319-938-8(4))* LeapFrog Enterprises, Inc.

—The Little Engine That Could. Piper, Watty. 2005. (Little Engine That Could Ser.). (ENG.). 48p. (J). (gr. -1-2). 17.99 *(978-0-399-24467-4(0)*, Philomel) Penguin Publishing Group.

—Nightsong. Berk, Ari. 2012. (ENG.). 48p. (J). (gr. -1-3). 17.99 *(978-1-4169-7886-2(0)*, Simon & Schuster Bks. For Young Readers) Simon & Schuster Bks. For Young Readers.

—Of Thee I Sing: A Letter to My Daughters. Obama, Barack. 2010. (ENG.). 40p. (J). (gr. k-12). 17.99 *(978-0-375-83527-8(X)*, Knopf Bks. for Young Readers) Random Hse. Children's Bks.

—Toy Boat. de Sève, Randall. 2007. (ENG.). 40p. (J). (gr. -1-2). 17.99 *(978-0-399-24374-5(7)*, Philomel) Penguin Publishing Group.

—Toy Boat. de Seve, Randall. 2014. (ENG.). 30p. (J). (gr. -1 — 1). bds. 7.99 *(978-0-399-16797-3(8)*, Philomel) Penguin Publishing Group.

—Wind Flyers. Johnson, Angela. 2007. (ENG.). 32p. (J). (gr. k-4). 17.99 *(978-0-689-84879-7(X)*, Simon & Schuster Bks. For Young Readers) Simon & Schuster Bks. For Young Readers.

Long, Loren. Blastin' the Blues. Long, Loren. Bildner, Phil. (Sluggers Ser.: 5). (ENG.). 448p. (J). (gr. 3-7). 2011. pap. 8.99 *(978-1-4169-1891-2(4))*; 2010. 15.99 *(978-1-4169-1867-7(1))* Simon & Schuster Bks. For Young Readers. (Simon & Schuster Bks. For Young Readers).

—The Drummer Boy. Long, Loren. 2008. (ENG.). 40p. (J). (gr. -1-k). 18.99 *(978-0-399-25174-0(X)*, Philomel) Penguin Publishing Group.

—Drummer Boy. Long, Loren. 2012. (ENG.). 40p. (J). (gr. -1-k). mass mkt. 7.99 *(978-0-14-242341-7(6)*, Puffin) Penguin Publishing Group.

—Game 3. Long, Loren. Bildner, Phil. 2008. (ENG.). 208p. (J). (gr. 2-5). 10.99 *(978-1-4169-1865-3(5)*, Simon & Schuster Bks. For Young Readers) Simon & Schuster Bks. For Young Readers.

—Great Balls of Fire. Long, Loren. Bildner, Phil. 2009. (Sluggers Ser.: 3). (ENG.). 224p. (J). (gr. 3-7). pap. 7.99 *(978-1-4169-1889-9(2)*, Simon & Schuster Bks. For Young Readers) Simon & Schuster Bks. For Young Readers.

—Home of the Brave. Long, Loren. Bildner, Phil. (Sluggers Ser.: 6). (ENG.). 336p. (J). (gr. 3-7). 2011. pap. 8.99 *(978-1-4169-1892-9(2))*; 2010. 15.99 *(978-1-4169-1868-4(X))* Simon & Schuster Bks. For Young Readers. (Simon & Schuster Bks. For Young Readers).

—Horsin' Around. Long, Loren. Bildner, Phil. 2009. (Sluggers Ser.: 2). (ENG.). 224p. (J). (gr. 3-7). pap. 8.99 *(978-1-4169-1888-2(4)*, Simon & Schuster Bks. For Young Readers) Simon & Schuster Bks. For Young Readers.

—Let's Doodle, Otis! Long, Loren. 2015. (Otis Ser.). (ENG.). 32p. (J). (gr. -1-k). 6.99 *(978-0-448-48405-1(6)*, Grosset & Dunlap) Penguin Publishing Group.

—Let's Go, Otis! Long, Loren. 2013. (Otis Ser.). (ENG.). 16p. (J). (gr. -1-2). pap. 6.99 *(978-0-448-47943-9(5)*, Grosset & Dunlap) Penguin Publishing Group.

—Magic in the Outfield. Long, Loren. Bildner, Phil. 2009. (Sluggers Ser.: 1). (ENG.). 160p. (J). (gr. 3-7). pap. 8.99 *(978-1-4169-1884-4(1)*, Simon & Schuster Bks. For Young Readers) Simon & Schuster Bks. For Young Readers.

—Mi Barco/Toy Boat. Long, Loren. de Sève, Randall & -Long, Sève. 2008. (SPA.). 40p. (J). (gr. -1-1). 18.99 *(978-84-261-3657-2(5))* Juventud, Editorial ESP. Dist: Lectorum Pubns., Inc.

—Otis. Long, Loren. (Otis Ser.). (J). (gr. -1-k). 2013. (SPA & ENG.). 40p. 7.99 *(978-0-14-751124-9(0)*, Puffin); 2011. (ENG.). 32p. bds. 8.99 *(978-0-399-25600-4(8)*, Philomel); 2009. (ENG.). 40p. 17.99 *(978-0-399-25248-8(7)*, Philomel) Penguin Publishing Group.

—Otis & the Puppy. Long, Loren. (Otis Ser.: 3). (ENG.). (J). (gr. -1-k). 2014. 38p. bds. 8.99 *(978-0-399-17196-3(7))*; 2013. 40p. 17.99 *(978-0-399-25469-7(2))* Penguin Publishing Group. (Philomel).

—Otis & the Scarecrow. Long, Loren. 2014. (Otis Ser.). (ENG.). 40p. (J). (gr. k-3). 17.99 *(978-0-399-16396-8(4)*, Philomel) Penguin Publishing Group.

—Otis & the Tornado. Long, Loren. 2011. (Otis Ser.: 2). (ENG.). 40p. (J). (gr. -1-2). 17.99 *(978-0-399-25477-2(3)*, Philomel) Penguin Publishing Group.

—An Otis Christmas. Long, Loren. 2013. (Otis Ser.: Bk. 4). (ENG.). 40p. (J). (gr. -1-2). 17.99 *(978-0-399-16395-1(6)*, Philomel) Penguin Publishing Group.

—Otis Loves to Play. Long, Loren. 2012. (Otis Ser.). (ENG.). 12p. (J). (gr. -1-k). bds. 5.99 *(978-0-448-46270-7(2)*, Grosset & Dunlap) Penguin Publishing Group.

—Otis's Busy Day. Long, Loren. 2014. (Otis Ser.). (ENG.). 32p. (J). (gr. k-1). pap. 3.99 *(978-0-448-48130-2(8)*, Warne, Frederick Pubs.) Penguin Bks., Ltd. GBR. Dist: Penguin Random Hse., LLC.

—Water, Water Everywhere. Long, Loren. Bildner, Phil. (Sluggers Ser.: 4). (ENG.). (J). (gr. 3-7). 2010. 288p. pap. 7.99 *(978-1-4169-1890-5(6))*; 2009. 304p. 14.99 *(978-1-4169-1866-0(3))* Simon & Schuster Bks. For Young Readers. (Simon & Schuster Bks. For Young Readers).

—When I Heard the Learn'd Astronomer. Long, Loren. Whitman, Walt. 2004. (ENG.). 32p. (J). (gr. k-4). 17.99 *(978-0-689-86397-4(7)*, Simon & Schuster Bks. For Young Readers) Simon & Schuster Bks. For Young Readers.

Long, Martha. A Keepsake Book of Love & Marriage: An enchanting way to say, I love You. Ramirez, Jeannette. 2007. 172p. (YA). 12.95 *(978-0-9794946-0-4(5))* Losantiville Pr., Inc.

Long, May, jt. illus. see Chu, Kate.

Long, Olivia. Billy Bumble Is Missing! Long, Olivia. Date not set. (Kaleidoscope Ser.). 32p. (J). (gr. -1-4). *(978-1-880042-02-1(9))* Shelf-Life Bks.

—The Boy & the Dog. Long, Olivia. Date not set. (Pets & Their People Ser.). 32p. (J). (gr. k-5). *(978-1-880042-07-6(X))* Shelf-Life Bks.

—The Dandelion Queen. Long, Olivia. Date not set. (Our Precious Planet Ser.). 32p. (J). (gr. -1-4). 9.95 *(978-1-880042-08-3(8)*, SL12461) Shelf-Life Bks.

—Diary of a Dog. Long, Olivia. Date not set. (Pets & Their People Ser.). 32p. (J). (gr. -1-4). 9.95 *(978-1-880042-06-9(1)*, SL12456) Shelf-Life Bks.

—The Elephant Who Forgot. Long, Olivia. Date not set. (Kaleidoscope Ser.). 32p. (J). (gr. -1-4). *(978-1-880042-05-2(3))* Shelf-Life Bks.

—A Horse of a Different Color. Long, Olivia. Date not set. (Kaleidoscope Ser.). 32p. (J). (gr. -1-4). 9.95 *(978-1-880042-01-4(0)*, SL12451) Shelf-Life Bks.

—Hortense, the Happy Hippo. Long, Olivia. Date not set. (Kaleidoscope Ser.). 32p. (J). (gr. -1-4). *(978-1-880042-03-8(7))* Shelf-Life Bks.

—The Impossible Peacock. Long, Olivia. Date not set. (Kaleidoscope Ser.). 32p. (J). (gr. -1-4). *(978-1-880042-04-5(5))* Shelf-Life Bks.

—There's a Dinosaur in My Bathtub! Long, Olivia. Date not set. (World of Dinosaurs Ser.). 32p. (J). (gr. -1-4). *(978-1-880042-11-3(8))* Shelf-Life Bks.

—Thunderbirds & Thunderbeings. Long, Olivia. Date not set. (Our Precious Planet Ser.). 32p. (J). (gr. -1-4). *(978-1-880042-10-6(X))* Shelf-Life Bks.

—Too Many Kittens. Long, Olivia. Date not set. (Pets & Their People Ser.). 32p. (J). (gr. -1-4). *(978-1-880042-09-0(6))* Shelf-Life Bks.

—Why Don't Cats Lay Eggs? Long, Olivia. Date not set. (Our Precious Planet Ser.). 32p. (J). (gr. -1-4). *(978-1-880042-12-0(6))* Shelf-Life Bks.

Long, Paulette Rich. Is There a Monster in My Closet? Paiva, Johannah Gilman. 2014. 32p. (J). (gr. -1-3). 7.99 ***(978-1-4867-0002-8(0))*** Flowerpot Children's Pr. Inc. CAN. Dist: Cardinal Pubs. Group.

Long, Paulette Rich. The Mouse & the Star. Condenzio, Mary. 2008. 13p. pap. 24.95 *(978-1-60441-449-3(9))* America Star Bks.

Long, Sylvia. Any Bear Can Wear Glasses: The Spectacled Bear & other Curious Creatures. Long, Matthew & Long, Thomas. 2005. 24p. (J). (gr. k-4). reprint ed. 17.00 *(978-0-7567-9763-8(2))* DIANE Publishing Co.

—Because You Are My Baby. Ward, Jennifer. 2007. (ENG.). 32p. (J). (gr. -1-1). 15.95 *(978-0-87358-911-6(4))* Cooper Square Publishing Llc.

—A Butterfly Is Patient. Aston, Dianna Hutts. 2011. (ENG.). 40p. (J). (gr. k-5). 16.99 *(978-0-8118-6479-4(0))* Chronicle Bks. LLC.

—A Butterfly Is Patient. Aston, Dianna. 2015. (ENG.). 40p. (J). (gr. k-3). 7.99 *(978-1-4521-4124-4(X))* Chronicle Bks. LLC.

—An Egg Is Quiet. Aston, Dianna Hutts. 2006. (J). 16.95 *(978-0-8118-5554-9(6))*; (ENG.). 36p. (gr. -1-7). 16.99 *(978-0-8118-4428-4(5))* Chronicle Bks. LLC.

—A Nest Is Noisy. Aston, Dianna Hutts. 2015. (ENG.). 40p. (J). (gr. k-3). 16.99 *(978-1-4521-2713-2(1))* Chronicle Bks. LLC.

Long, Sylvia. A Rock Is Lively. Aston, Dianna Hutts. (ENG.). 40p. (J). (gr. k-3). 2015. 7.99 ***(978-1-4521-4555-6(5))***; 2012. 16.99 *(978-1-4521-0645-8(2))* Chronicle Bks. LLC.

Long, Sylvia. A Seed Is Sleepy. Aston, Dianna Hutts & Hutts Aston, Dianna. 2007. (ENG.). 40p. (J). (gr. k-5). 16.99 *(978-0-8118-5520-4(1))* Chronicle Bks. LLC.

—Sylvia Long's Thumbelina. 2010. (ENG.). 58p. (J). (gr. k-5). 17.99 *(978-0-8118-5522-8(8))* Chronicle Bks. LLC.

Long, Sylvia. Twinkle, Twinkle, Little Star: A Traditional Lullaby. Long, Sylvia. 2006. (ENG.). 26p. (J). (gr. -1-7). bds. 6.99 *(978-0-8118-5230-2(X))* Chronicle Bks. LLC.

Long, Taillefer. Howard B. Wigglebottom on Yes or No: A Fable about Trust. Binkow, Howard. 2013. (Howard B. Wigglebottom Ser.). 32p. (J). (gr. -1-3). 15.00 *(978-0-9826165-8-1(9)*, We Do Listen) Thunderbolt Publishing.

Longabaugh, Kristen. The Bat Who Wore Glasses. Goss, Michael Anthony. 2005. (J). pap. *(978-1-933156-13-2(9))*; per. 16.99 *(978-1-933156-06-4(6))* GSVQ Publishing. (VisionQuest Kids).

Longfoot, Stephanie. All Things Bright & Beautiful. Taylor, Caroline. 2004. (My First Prayers Ser.). 10p. (J). bds. 3.99 *(978-1-85854-238-6(3))* Brimax Books Ltd. GBR. Dist: Byeway Bks.

—All Things Wise & Wonderful. Taylor, Caroline. 2004. (My First Prayers Ser.). 10p. (J). bds. 3.99 *(978-1-85854-239-3(1))* Brimax Books Ltd. GBR. Dist: Byeway Bks.

—Lord God Made Us All. Taylor, Caroline. 2004. (My First Prayers Ser.). 10p. (J). bds. 3.99 *(978-1-85854-243-0(X))* Brimax Books Ltd. GBR. Dist: Byeway Bks.

Longhi, Katya. Counting Change. Heos, Bridget. 2015. (Math World Ser.). 24p. (J). lib. bdg. 27.10 *(978-1-60753-462-4(2))* Amicus Educational.

—Do You Really Want a Bird? Heos, Bridget & Powell, Marie. 2013. (Do You Really Want a Pet? Ser.). (ENG.). 24p. (gr. 1-4). 27.10 *(978-1-60753-205-7(0))* Amicus Educational.

—Do You Really Want a Cat? Heos, Bridget. 2013. (Do You Really Want a Pet? Ser.). (ENG.). 24p. (gr. 1-4). 27.10 *(978-1-60753-203-3(4))* Amicus Educational.

—Do You Really Want a Dog? Heos, Bridget. 2013. (Do You Really Want a Pet? Ser.). (ENG.). 24p. (gr. 1-4). 27.10 *(978-1-60753-204-0(2))* Amicus Educational.

—Do You Really Want a Guinea Pig? Heos, Bridget. 2015. (Do You Really Want a Pet? Ser.). (ENG.). 24p. (gr. 1-3). 19.95 *(978-1-60753-749-6(4))* Amicus Educational.

—Do You Really Want a Hamster? Heos, Bridget. 2013. (Do You Really Want a Pet? Ser.). (ENG.). 24p. (gr. 1-4). 27.10 *(978-1-60753-206-4(9))* Amicus Educational.

—Do You Really Want a Horse? Heos, Bridget. 2013. (Do You Really Want a Pet? Ser.). (ENG.). 24p. (gr. 1-4). 27.10 *(978-1-60753-207-1(7))* Amicus Educational.

—Do You Really Want a Lizard? Heos, Bridget. 2015. (Do You Really Want a Pet? Ser.). (ENG.). 24p. (gr. 1-3). 19.95 *(978-1-60753-750-2(8))* Amicus Educational.

—Do You Really Want a Rabbit? Heos, Bridget. 2013. (Do You Really Want a Pet? Ser.). (ENG.). 24p. (gr. 1-4). 27.10 *(978-1-60753-208-8(5))* Amicus Educational.

—Do You Really Want a Snake? Heos, Bridget. 2015. (Do You Really Want a Pet? Ser.). (ENG.). 24p. (J). (gr. 1-3). 19.95 *(978-1-60753-751-9(6))* Amicus Educational.

—Do You Really Want a Turtle? Heos, Bridget. 2015. (Do You Really Want a Pet? Ser.). (ENG.). 24p. (J). (gr. 1-3). 19.95 *(978-1-60753-752-6(4))* Amicus Educational.

Longhi, Katya. Elephant. Perkins, Wendy. 2015. (J). pap. ***(978-1-68152-074-2(5))*** Amicus Educational.

Longhi, Katya. Making Graphs. Heos, Bridget. 2015. (Math World Ser.). 24p. (J). lib. bdg. 27.10 *(978-1-60753-463-1(0))* Amicus Educational.

—Manners at a Friend's House. Heos, Bridget. 2015. (Monstrous Manners Ser.). (ENG.). 24p. (gr. 1-3). 19.95 *(978-1-60753-743-4(5))* Amicus Educational.

—Manners at a Restaurant. Heos, Bridget. 2015. (Monstrous Manners Ser.). (ENG.). 24p. (gr. 1-3). 19.95 *(978-1-60753-744-1(3))* Amicus Educational.

Longhi, Katya. Manners at School. Heos, Bridget. 2015. (Monstrous Manners Ser.). (ENG.). 24p. (gr. 1-3). 19.95 ***(978-1-60753-745-8(1))*** Amicus Educational.

—Manners at the Store. Heos, Bridget. 2015. (Monstrous Manners Ser.). (ENG.). 24p. (gr. 1-3). 19.95 ***(978-1-60753-746-5(X))*** Amicus Educational.

—Manners on Vacation. Heos, Bridget. 2015. (Monstrous Manners Ser.). (ENG.). 24p. (gr. 1-3). 19.95 ***(978-1-60753-747-2(8))*** Amicus Educational.

—Manners with Technology. Heos, Bridget. 2015. (Monstrous Manners Ser.). (ENG.). 24p. (gr. 1-3). 19.95 ***(978-1-60753-748-9(6))*** Amicus Educational.

Longhi, Katya. Measure It. Heos, Bridget. 2015. (Math World Ser.). 24p. (J). lib. bdg. 27.10 *(978-1-60753-464-8(9))* Amicus Educational.

—Telling Time. Heos, Bridget. 2015. (Math World Ser.). 24p. (J). lib. bdg. 27.10 *(978-1-60753-461-7(4))* Amicus Educational.

Longino, Gina M. Livvie & Buggles. Longino, Gina M. 2010. (ENG.). 64p. pap. 9.15 *(978-1-4515-2572-4(9))* CreateSpace Independent Publishing Platform.

Longman, Mary. The Little Duck Sikihpsis. Cuthand, Beth. Cuthand, Stan, tr. ed. 2013. (ENG.). 34p. 18.00 *(978-1-894778-10-7(3))* Theytus Bks., Ltd. CAN. Dist: Univ. of Toronto Pr.

—Sikihpsis. Cuthand, Beth. Cuthand, Stan, tr. ed. 2007. (Little Duck Ser.). (CRE & ENG.). 28p. 17.00 *(978-1-894778-44-2(8))* Theytus Bks., Ltd. CAN. Dist: Univ. of Toronto Pr.

Longmore, Nickolai. The Little Princess. Snider, Lori L. 2005. 32p. (J). 3.99 *(978-0-9771700-0-5(4))* Mystic Arts, LLC.

—Nighttime Adventures Counting Sheep. Rock, Michelle L. 2006. 32p. (J). 3.99 net. *(978-0-9771700-1-2(2))* Mystic Arts, LLC.

Longo, Jason. Mommy Did You Know... An Adoption Story. Giroir, Constance H. 2005. 22p. per. 17.32 *(978-1-59926-397-7(1))* Xlibris Corp.

—Otto's Colorful Campus Tour - Syracuse University A-Z. 2004. (J). 9.99 *(978-1-933069-04-3(X))* Odd Duck Ink, Inc.

Longwood, Marc, photos by. Weekends for Two in Southern California 2003: 50 Romantic Getaways. Gleeson, Bill. 3rd rev. ed. 2003. (ENG.). 120p. (gr. 8-17). pap. 17.95 *(978-0-8118-4039-2(5))* Chronicle Bks. LLC.

Lonsdale, Mary. First Words Sticker Book. 2003. 12p. (J). bds. *(978-1-85854-658-2(3))* Autumn Publishing, Ltd.

—My Big Book of Numbers. Lebron, Karen. 2004. 48p. (J). 5.99 *(978-1-85854-317-8(7))* Brimax Books Ltd. GBR. Dist: Byeway Bks.

—My Prayers for Everyday. 2004. 10p. (J). bds. 7.99 *(978-1-85854-438-0(6))* Brimax Books Ltd. GBR. Dist: Byeway Bks.

—Whatever the Weather: When the Snow Comes. 2004. (Whatever the Weather Ser.). 10p. (J). bds. 4.99 *(978-1-85854-103-7(4))* Brimax Books Ltd. GBR. Dist: Byeway Bks.

—Whatever the Weather: When the Sun Shines. 2004. (Whatever the Weather Ser.). 10p. (J). bds. 4.99 *(978-1-85854-105-1(0))* Brimax Books Ltd. GBR. Dist: Byeway Bks.

—Whatever the Weather: When the Wind Blows. 2004. (Whatever the Weather Ser.). 10p. (J). bds. 4.99 *(978-1-85854-102-0(6))* Brimax Books Ltd. GBR. Dist: Byeway Bks.

Loomis, Jennifer A., photos by. Wildlife in the Rocky Mountains. Loomis, Jennifer A. unabr. ed. 2005. 100p. (J). 24.95 *(978-0-88045-159-8(9))* Stemmer Hse. Pubs.

Looney, Bill. The Flood of Noah: Legends & Lore of Survival. 2014. 24p. (J). 18.99 *(978-0-89051-801-4(7))* Master Bks.

—Noah, Didn't It Rain. Golden, William Lee. 2008. 29p. (J). (gr. -1-3). 13.99 incl. audio compact disk *(978-0-89221-683-3(2))* New Leaf Pr., Inc.

—Not Too Small at All: A Mouse Tale. Townsend, Stephanie Z. 2008. 30p. (J). (gr. -1). 12.99 *(978-0-89051-524-2(7))* Master Bks.

—The Vince Vance Rock & Roll Reader: Bedtime Stories, Poems, Songs, Jokes, Pictures & Other Real Cool Stuff for Kids of All Ages. Rice, Bob, photos by. Vance, Vince. Pennington, Carole, ed. 2003. 182p. (J). (gr. 3-8). per. *(978-0-9652918-0-4(4))* Fullerton Bks., Inc.

—What Ever Happened to the Wooly Mammoth: Life at the End of the Great Ice Age. Oard, Beverly & Oard, Michael. 2007. 72p. (J). 15.99 *(978-0-89051-508-2(5))* Master Bks.

Loopstra, Esther Dawn. Green Park, 1 vol. Shaskan, Trisha Speed. 2008. (Read-It! Readers: Character Education Ser.). (ENG.). 32p. (gr. k-2). 19.99 *(978-1-4048-4232-8(2)*, Easy Readers) Picture Window Bks.

LoParco, Chris. Z & the Cancer Meanie. St. Pierre-Ford, Hillary & Ford, Xander. 2011. (ENG.). 28p. pap. 12.95 *(978-1-4662-0833-9(3))* CreateSpace Independent Publishing Platform.

Loper, Carol J. The Miracle of Life. Loper, Ami M. 2007. (J). *(978-0-9678798-1-9(7))* Biblical Standards Pubns.

Lopes, Tom. In a Word: 750 Words & Their Fascinating Stories & Origins. Baker, Rosalie. 2003. (ENG.). 250p. (J). 17.95 *(978-0-8126-2710-7(5))* Cricket Bks.

Lopez, Alex. Goldilocks & the Three Bears: An Interactive Fairy Tale Adventure. Braun, Eric. 2015. (You Choose: Fractured Fairy Tales Ser.). (ENG.). 112p. (gr. 3-4). lib. bdg. 31.32 ***(978-1-4914-5855-6(0))*** Capstone Pr., Inc.

Lopez, Antonio Castro & Castro L., Antonio. El Día que Nevaron Tortillas. Hayes, Joe. Hayes, Joe, tr. 2003.Tr. of Day It Snowed Tortillas. (SPA & ENG.). 160p. (J). (gr. 4-6). pap. 12.95 *(978-0-938317-76-0(8))* Cinco Puntos Pr.

Lopez, Ayesha. Cinderella: An Interactive Fairy Tale Adventure. Braun, Eric & Gunderson, Jessica. 2015. (You Choose: Fractured Fairy Tales Ser.). (ENG.). 112p. (gr. 3-4). lib. bdg. 31.32 ***(978-1-4914-5854-9(2))*** Capstone Pr., Inc.

López, Casimiro de la Cruz, jt. illus. see Cruz, María Hernández de la.

Lopez, Cheyene. Jolly House: From the Lands of Jolly Happy Holidays. Lopez, Cheyene. l.t. ed. 2011. (ENG.). 52p. pap. 13.99 *(978-1-4610-4899-2(0))* CreateSpace Independent Publishing Platform.

Lopez, Cheyene & Lopez, Patricia. Captain Blue Wonder: The Adventures of Captain Blue Wonder. Lopez, Cheyene. l.t. ed. 2011. (ENG.). 32p. pap. 15.99 *(978-1-4611-4074-0(9))* CreateSpace Independent Publishing Platform.

Lopez, Claudia Navarro. La Nina Que Tenia el Mar Adentro. Chavez, Ricardo & Aguileta, Gabriela. rev. ed. 2005. (Castillo de la Lectura Verde Ser.). (SPA & ENG.). 136p. (J). (gr. -1-7). pap. 7.95 *(978-970-20-0176-8(5))* Castillo, Ediciones, S. A. de C. V. MEX. Dist: Macmillan.

Lopez, David. Blank Generation. 2013. (ENG.). 96p. (YA). (gr. 8-17). pap. 19.99 *(978-0-7851-6459-3(6))* Marvel Worldwide, Inc.

—Erik the Red Sees Green: A Story about Color Blindness. Anderson, Julie. 2013. (ENG.). 32p. (J). (gr. -1-2). 16.99 *(978-0-8075-2141-0(8))* Whitman, Albert & Co.

López Domínguez, Xan. Siete Casas, Siete Brujas y un Huevo. López Domínguez, Xan, tr. Sánchez, Gloria. 5th ed. 2005. (SPA.). 64p. (J). (gr. k-1). 6.95 *(978-84-348-6003-2(1))* SM Ediciones ESP. Dist: Iaconi, Mariuccia Bk. Imports.

Lopez, Jessica. Big Mouth's Bubble Gum. Lopez, Jessica. 2011. (ENG.). 38p. pap. 9.50 *(978-1-4664-1519-5(3))* CreateSpace Independent Publishing Platform.

—Big Mouth's Icecream. Lopez, Jessica. 2010. (ENG.). 42p. pap. 9.54 *(978-1-4499-7604-0(2))* CreateSpace Independent Publishing Platform.

Lopez, Loretta. I Remember Abuelito: A Day of the Dead Story. Levy, Janice & Arisa, Miguel. 2012.Tr. of Yo Recuerdo a Abuelito - Un Cuento del Dia de los Muertos. (SPA & ENG.). (J). *(978-1-61913-114-9(5))* Weigl Pubs., Inc.

—I Remember Abuelito/Yo Recuerdo a Abuelito: A Day of the Dead Story / un Cuento del Dia de los Muertos. Levy, Janice. Arisa, Miguel, tr. 2007. (SPA & ENG.). 32p. (J). (gr. -1-3). 6.99 *(978-0-8075-3517-2(6))* Whitman, Albert & Co.

—Say Hola to Spanish at the Circus. Elya, Susan Middleton. 2013. (ENG.). 32p. (J). (gr. -1-5). pap. 8.95 *(978-1-58430-042-7(6))* Lee & Low Bks., Inc.

—Say Hola to Spanish, Otra Vez (Again!) Elya, Susan Middleton. 2013. (SPA & ENG.). 32p. (J). (gr. -1-5). pap. 9.95 *(978-1-880000-64-9(4))*; pap. 8.95 *(978-1-880000-83-0(0))* Lee & Low Bks., Inc.

Lopez, Luz-Maria. How the Gods Created the Finger People, 1 vol. Moore, Elizabeth & Couvillon, Alice. 2011. (ENG & SPA.). 32p. (J). (gr. k-3). 18.99 *(978-1-58980-889-8(4))* Pelican Publishing Co., Inc.

Lopez, Lyle. Timmy & the Baseball Birthday Party. Dzidrums, Christine. 2012. 50p. pap. 6.99 *(978-0-9835393-8-4(3))* Creative Media Publishing.

Lopez, Lyle & Dzidrums, Joseph. Fair Youth: Emylee of Forest Springs. Dzidrums, Christine. 2012. 120p. pap. 9.99 *(978-1-938438-05-9(1))* Creative Media Publishing.

—Timmy Adopts a Girl Dog. Dzidrums, Christine. 2012. 48p. pap. 6.99 *(978-1-938438-03-5(5))* Creative Media Publishing.

López, Nivio. Companero de Suenos. López, Nivio, tr. Almena, Fernando & Artigot, Manuel. 6th ed. (SPA.). 217p. (J). (gr. 4-6). pap. *(978-84-216-1567-6(X)*, BU5118) Bruño, Editorial ESP. Dist: Lectorum Pubns., Inc.

López, Oscar J. Sing along with Abuelita Rosa: Hispanic Lullabies = Canciones de Cuna. 2006. (ENG & SPA.). 13p. (J). *(978-0-9788379-0-7(8))* Baby Abuelita Productions, Inc.

Lopez, Patricia. The Snow Feather: The Magic of Dreams. Lopez, Cheyene. l.t. ed. 2011. (ENG.). 32p. pap. 19.99 *(978-1-4610-4895-4(8))* CreateSpace Independent Publishing Platform.

Lopez, Patricia. A Dog Named Pom Pom & Friends. Lopez, Patricia. l.t. ed. 2011. (ENG.). 34p. pap. 15.99 *(978-1-4610-4886-2(9))* CreateSpace Independent Publishing Platform.

Lopez, Patricia, jt. illus. see Lopez, Cheyene.

Lopez, Paul. The Adventures of Melon & Turnip. Howell, Trisha Adelena. 2004. 32p. 15.95 *(978-1-931210-04-1(7))* Howell Canyon Pr.

—In the Jungle. Robinson, Fay. 2004. (Treasure Tree Ser.). 32p. (J). *(978-0-7166-1604-7(1))* World Bk., Inc.

Lopez, Paul, et al. Pinocchio's Nose Grows. Winkelman, Barbara Gaines. 2013. (Step into Reading Ser.). (ENG.). 32p. (J). (gr. -1-1). pap. 3.99 *(978-0-7364-1213-1(1)*, RH/Disney) Random Hse. Children's Bks.

Lopez, Paul & Hong, Denise. Why I Love My Mom: The Ultimate Gift of the Heart. Hong, Denise & Hong, Andrew. 2004. 32p. (J). lib. bdg. 17.99 *(978-0-9746503-4-0(X))* Platinum Bks.

Lopez, Paul, jt. illus. see Ewers, Joe.

López, Rafael. Book Fiesta! Celebrate Children's Day. Mora, Pat. 2009.Tr. of Celebremos el Día de los Niños, el Día de los Libros. (SPA & ENG.). 40p. (J). (gr. -1-1). 17.99 *(978-0-06-128877-7(2)*, Rayo) HarperCollins Pubs.

—The Cazuela That the Farm Maiden Stirred. Vamos, Samantha R. (ENG & SPA.). 32p. (J). (gr. k-3). 2013. pap.

L

8.95 *(978-1-58089-243-8(4))*; 2011. 17.95 *(978-1-58089-242-1(6))* Charlesbridge Publishing, Inc.

—Drum Dream Girl: How One Girl's Courage Changed Music. Engle, Margarita. 2015. (ENG.). 48p. (J). (gr. -1-3). 16.99 *(978-0-544-10229-3(0),* HMH Books For Young Readers) Houghton Mifflin Harcourt Publishing Co.

López, Rafael. Maybe Something Beautiful. Campoy, F. Isabel & Howell, Theresa. 2016. (ENG.). 40p. (J). ***(978-0-544-35769-3(8))*** Harcourt.

López, Rafael. My Name Is Celia: The Life of Celia Cruz. Brown, Monica. 2004.Tr. of Me Llamo Celia - La Vida de Celia Cruz. (ENG, SPA & MUL.). 32p. (J). (gr. k-3). 15.95 *(978-0-87358-872-0(X))* Cooper Square Publishing Llc.

—Nuestra California. Ryan, Pam Muñoz. 2008.Tr. of Our California. (SPA & ENG.). 48p. (J). (gr. 1-4). 17.95 *(978-1-58089-226-1(4))* Charlesbridge Publishing, Inc.

—Our California. Ryan, Pam Muñoz. 2008. (ENG.). 48p. (J). (gr. 1-4). 18.95 *(978-1-58089-116-5(0))*; per. 9.95 *(978-1-58089-117-2(9))* Charlesbridge Publishing, Inc.

—Tito Puente: Mambo King; Rey del Mambo. Brown, Monica. 2013. (ENG.). 32p. (J). (gr. -1-3). 17.99 *(978-0-06-122783-7(8),* Rayo) HarperCollins Pubs.

—Yum! Mmmm! Que Rico! America's Sproutings, 1 vol. Mora, Pat. 2007. 32p. (J). (gr. -1-3). lib. bdg. 16.95 *(978-1-58430-271-1(2))* Lee & Low Bks., Inc.

—Yum! ¡Mmmm! ¡Qué Rico! Americas' Sproutings. Mora, Pat. 2007. (ENG & SPA.). 32p. (J). pap. 9.95 *(978-1-60060-892-6(2))* Lee & Low Bks., Inc.

—Yum! ¡MmMm! ¡Qué Rico! Brotes de las Américas. Mora, Pat. 2009.Tr. of Yum! ¡MmMm! ¡Qué rico! America's Sproutings. (SPA.). 32p. (J). 17.95 *(978-1-60060-430-0(7))* Lee & Low Bks., Inc.

López, Rafael & Ada, Alma Flor. Yum! Mmmm! Qué Rico! Brotes de las Américas. Mora, Pat et al. 2009.Tr. of Yum! ¡MmMm! ¡Qué rico! America's Sproutings. (SPA & ENG.). 32p. (J). (gr. k-6). pap. 8.95 *(978-1-60060-268-9(1))* Lee & Low Bks., Inc.

López, Rafael, jt. illus. see Mora, Pat.

Lopez, Shana. Shakespeare's a Midsummer Night's Dream for Kids: 3 Short Melodramatic Plays for 3 Group Sizes. Kelso, Brendan. 2008. (ENG.). 54p. pap. 9.99 *(978-1-4196-8552-1(X))* CreateSpace Independent Publishing Platform.

—Shakespeare's Julius Caesar for Kids: 3 Short Melodramatic Plays for 3 Group Sizes. Kelso, Brendan P. Sidaris-Green, Hannah, ed. 2009. (Playing with Plays Ser.). (ENG.). 44p. pap. 9.99 *(978-1-4392-1355-1(0))* CreateSpace Independent Publishing Platform.

Lopez, Willie. Jack Crow Said Hello, 1 vol. Simmons, Lynn Sheffield. 2003. (ENG.). 128p. (J). (gr. 3-7). 10.95 *(978-1-58980-218-6(7))* Pelican Publishing Co., Inc.

Lopez, Xan. Barro de Medellín/ Mud of Medellin. Gómez Cerda, Alfredo. 2010. (SPA.). 146p. (YA). (gr. 5-8). *(978-84-263-6849-2(2))* Vives, Luis Editorial (Edelvives).

Lopiz, Violeta. Cuentos de la Abuela Amelia. Alcolea, Ana. 2009. (SPA.). 155p. (J). (gr. 3-5). pap. *(978-84-263-7271-0(6))* Vives, Luis Editorial (Edelvives).

Lopresti, Aaron, et al. Mystic: The Mathemagician, Vol. 6. Bedard, Tony. 2004. (Mystic Ser.). 160p. (YA). pap. 15.95 *(978-1-59314-039-7(8))* CrossGeneration Comics, Inc.

Lopresti, Sarah H., jt. illus. see Lucas, Stacey L.

Lopshire, Robert. I Want to Be Somebody New! Lopshire, Robert. 2009. (Beginner Books(R) Ser.). (ENG.). 48p. (J). (gr. -1-1). lib. bdg. 12.99 *(978-0-394-97616-7(9))*; 8.99 *(978-0-394-87616-0(4))* Random Hse. Children's Bks. (Random Hse. Bks. for Young Readers).

LoRaso, Carlo. My Little Pony: A Very Minty Christmas. Lange, Nikki Bataille. gif. ed. 2005. 22p. (J). (gr. -1-1). bds. 13.99 *(978-1-57791-191-3(1))* Brighter Minds Children's Publishing.

Lorbiecki, Marybeth & Heinzen, Kory S. Escaping Titanic: A Young Girl's True Story of Survival, 1 vol. Lorbiecki, Marybeth. 2012. (ENG.). 32p. (gr. 3-5). pap. 8.95 *(978-1-4048-7235-6(3))*; lib. bdg. 27.99 *(978-1-4048-7143-4(8))* Picture Window Bks. (Nonfiction Picture Bks.).

Lord, Jeremy. Meet Weary Dunlop. Saxby, Claire. 2015. (Meet... Ser.). (ENG.). 32p. (J). (gr. -1-k). 21.99 ***(978-0-85798-536-1(1))*** Random Hse. Australia AUS. Dist: Independent Pubs. Group.

Lord, John Vernon. The Giant Jam Sandwich. Lord, John Vernon. Burroway, Janet. 2009. (ENG.). 24p. (J). (gr. -1-3). bds. 7.99 *(978-0-547-15077-2(6))* Houghton Mifflin Harcourt Publishing Co.

Lord, Leonie. Ding Dong! Gorilla!, 1 vol. Robinson, Michelle. 2013. (ENG.). 32p. (J). (gr. -1-3). 15.95 *(978-1-56145-730-4(2))* Peachtree Pubs.

—The Super Hungry Dinosaur. Waddell, Martin. 2009. (ENG.). 32p. (J). (gr. -1-k). 16.99 *(978-0-8037-3446-3(8),* Dial) Penguin Publishing Group.

—The Super Swooper Dinosaur. Waddell, Martin. 2013. (J). *(978-1-4351-5000-3(7))* Barnes & Noble, Inc.

—Whiffy Wilson: The Wolf Who Wouldn't Wash. Hart, Caryl. 2012. (ENG.). 32p. (J). (gr. -1-k). pap. 10.99 *(978-1-4083-0919-3(X))* Hodder & Stoughton GBR. Dist: Independent Pubs. Group.

Lore, Erin. Timmy the Dragon. l.t. ed. 2007. 32p. (J). 8.95 *(978-0-9741562-7-9(2))* Yarrow Pr.

Lorencz, Bill, jt. illus. see Dias, Ron.

Lorenz, Albert. A Three-Minute Speech: Lincoln's Remarks at Gettysburg. Armstrong, Jennifer. 2003. (Milestone Ser.). (ENG.). 96p. (J). pap. 4.99 *(978-0-689-85622-8(9),* Simon & Schuster/Paula Wiseman Bks.) Simon & Schuster/Paula Wiseman Bks.

—The True Story Behind Lincoln's Gettysburg Address. Armstrong, Jennifer. 2013. (ENG.). 96p. (J). (gr. 2-5). 15.99 *(978-1-4424-9388-9(7))*; pap. 5.99 *(978-1-4424-9387-2(9))* Simon & Schuster/Paula Wiseman Bks. (Simon & Schuster/Paula Wiseman Bks.).

Lorenz, Jinye, Sr. Grandfather, the Tiger & Ryong. Lorenz, Jinye, Sr. Lorenz, Virginia O., Sr., ed. ltd. ed. 2005. 65p. (J). spiral bd. 14.95 *(978-1-888350-10-4(5))* Lighted Lamp Pr.

Lorenzetti, Doreen. Bridgetender's Boy. Barth, Linda J. 2004. *(978-0-930973-35-3(6))*; pap. *(978-0-930973-34-6(8))* Moore, Hugh Historical Park & Museums, Inc. (Canal History & Technology Pr.).

—Cathy Williams, Buffalo Soldier, 1 vol. Solomon, Sharon. 2010. (ENG.). 32p. (J). (gr. k-3). 16.99 *(978-1-58980-801-0(0))* Pelican Publishing Co., Inc.

Lorenzo, Gloria. Mountain Miracle: A Navtivity Story. Correa, Alvaro. 2008. 94p. (J). (gr. -1). pap. 14.95 *(978-1-933271-23-1(X))* Circle Pr.

Lorna, Balian & Lecla, Balian. The Aminal, 1 vol. Lorna, Balian. 2012. (ENG.). 48p. (J). pap. 7.95 *(978-1-59572-363-5(3))* Star Bright Bks., Inc.

Lorne, Patrick, photos by. Face-to-Face with the Ladybug: Little Garden Monster. Tracqui, Valérie. 2004. (Face-to-Face Ser.). 28p. (J). (gr. -1-2). 9.95 *(978-1-57091-453-9(2))* Charlesbridge Publishing, Inc.

Lornie, June. Alice's Adventures in Wonderland. Carroll, Lewis. 2013. 104p. pap. *(978-1-78201-037-1(8))* Evertype.

Losa, Ann. What Do You Say? Gillis, Jennifer Blizin. 2006. (Reader's Clubhouse Level 2 Reader Ser.). (ENG.). 24p. (J). (gr. 1-4). pap. 3.99 *(978-0-7641-3298-8(9))* Barron's Educational Series, Inc.

Losantos, Cristina. Beauty & the Beast: La Bella y la Bestia. 2007. (Bilingual Fairy Tales Ser.: BILI). (ENG & SPA.). 32p. (J). (gr. -1-3). pap. 6.95 *(978-0-8118-5970-7(3))* Chronicle Bks. LLC.

—Beauty & the Beast (La Bella y la Bestia) 2013. (Bilingual Fairy Tales Ser.). (SPA & ENG.). 32p. (J). (gr. 1-4). lib. bdg. 28.50 *(978-1-60753-355-9(3))* Amicus Educational.

—Bella y la Bestia. 2007. (Bilingual Fairy Tales Ser.: BILI).Tr. of Beauty & the Beast. (ENG & SPA.). 32p. (J). (gr. -1-3). 14.95 *(978-0-8118-5969-1(X))* Chronicle Bks. LLC.

—The Pied Piper: El Flautista de Hamelín. Cela, Jaume. 2008. (Bilingual Fairy Tales Ser.: BILI). (SPA & ENG.). 32p. (J). (gr. -1-3). 14.95 *(978-0-8118-6028-4(0))* Chronicle Bks. LLC.

Losh, Eric. Insectaside. Reffett, Frances. l.t. ed. 2006. 28p. (J). 8.00 net. *(978-0-9785886-0-1(6))* Chicory Pr.

Lostimolo, Stephanie. BeBa & the Curious Creature Catchers. Griffin, Lydia. l.t. ed. 2006. 32p. (J). 16.95 *(978-0-9770516-0-1(9))* Laffin Minor Pr.

Loter, Inc. The Big Ballet Show (Dora the Explorer) Golden Books. 2012. (Little Golden Book Ser.). (ENG & SPA.). 24p. (J). (gr. k-k). 3.99 *(978-0-307-93094-1(7),* Golden Bks.) Random Hse. Children's Bks.

Loter Inc. Staff. Clubhouse Christmas. Amerikaner, Susan & Disney Book Group Staff. 2008. (ENG.). 12p. (J). (gr. -1-k). bds. 6.99 *(978-1-4231-1253-2(9))* Disney Pr.

—Guess Who, Minnie! Reader's Digest Staff & Rhodes, Lilly. 2013. (Guess Who Ser.: 1). (ENG.). 10p. (J). (gr. -1-k). 10.99 *(978-0-7944-2555-5(0))* Reader's Digest Assn., Inc., The.

Loter, Inc. Staff. Huey, Dewey, & Louie's Rainy Day Adventure. Disney Book Group Staff & Ritchey, Kate. 2014. (World of Reading Ser.). (ENG.). 32p. (J). (gr. 1-3). pap. 3.99 *(978-1-4231-6965-9(4))* Disney Pr.

Loter Inc. Staff. Minnie: Case of the Missing Sparkle-Izer. Scollon, Bill. 2014. (World of Reading Pre-1 Ser.). (ENG.). 32p. (J). (gr. 3-5). lib. bdg. 24.21 *(978-1-61479-248-2(8))* Spotlight.

Loter Inc. Staff & Disney Storybook Art Team. Minnie's Rainbow. Higginson, Sheila Sweeny & Disney Book Group Staff. rev. ed. 2008. (ENG.). 24p. (J). (gr. -1-k). pap. 3.99 *(978-1-4231-0743-9(8))* Disney Pr.

—Minnie's Valentine. Higginson, Sheila Sweeny & Disney Book Group Staff. rev. ed. 2007. (ENG.). 24p. (J). (gr. -1-k). pap. 4.99 *(978-1-4231-0746-0(2))* Disney Pr.

Loter Inc. Staff, jt. illus. see Loter, John.

Loter, John & Loter Inc. Staff. Guess Who, Mickey! Reader's Digest Editors & Mitter, Matt. 2012. (Guess Who Ser.). (ENG.). 10p. (J). (gr. -1-k). 10.99 *(978-0-7944-2554-8(2))* Reader's Digest Assn., Inc., The.

Loter, John, jt. illus. see Horne, Philip.

Lott, Sheena. Island Santa, 1 vol. McFarlane, Sheryl. 2012. (ENG.). 32p. (J). (gr. k). 19.95 *(978-0-9880536-0-1(8))* Queen Alexandra Foundation for Children CAN. Dist: Orca Bk. Pubs. USA.

—Salmon Forest. Ellis, Sarah & Suzuki, David. 2006. (ENG.). 32p. (J). (gr. k-3). pap. 9.95 *(978-1-55365-163-5(4))* Greystone Books Ltd. CAN. Dist: Perseus-PGW.

—Singing the Dark, 1 vol. Sproule, Gail. 2006. (ENG.). 32p. (J). (gr. -1-3). per. 7.95 *(978-1-55041-348-9(1),* 1550413481) Fitzhenry & Whiteside, Ltd. CAN. Dist: Midpoint Trade Bks., Inc.

Lou, Cindy. The King of Ing Wants to Sing. Lou, Cindy, text. 2008. (J). 12.00 *(978-1-935332-00-8(7))* Kite Tales Publishing.

Lou Who, Carrie. Today Is My Birthday & I Have Nothing to Wear! Klitzner, Irene & Adams, Peggy. 2011. (ENG.). 48p. (J). 18.95 *(978-0-9846496-0-0(3))* Attitude Pie Publishing.

Loucks-Christenson, Lisa, photos by. Waiting Room to Heaven Presents: The Eagle Nest Coffee Bar & Cafe. Loucks-Christenson, Lisa. 2006. *(978-0-9771365-0-6(7),* Waiting Room to Heaven) Loucks-Christenson Publishing.

Loufane. Chick's Works of Art. Robberecht, Thierry. 2012. (ENG.). 30p. (J). (gr. -1-1). 15.95 *(978-1-60537-138-2(6))* Clavis Publishing.

—When Pigs Fly! Boonen, Stefan. 2004. 32p. (J). 6.95 *(978-1-58925-384-1(1))* Tiger Tales.

Loughran, P. J. Turning 15 on the Road to Freedom: My Story of the 1965 Selma to Montgomery March. 2015. (ENG.). 128p. (YA). (gr. 7). 19.99 *(978-0-8037-4123-2(5),* Dial) Penguin Publishing Group.

Loughridge, Stuart. Grandfather's Story Cloth. Gerdner, Linda & Langford, Sarah. 2008. (Grandfather's Story Cloth Ser.). 32p. (J). (gr. 2-4). 16.95 *(978-1-885008-34-3(1),* Shen's Bks.) Lee & Low Bks., Inc.

Louhi, Kristiina. Tundra Mouse Mountain. Jalonen, Riitta. Ledgard, J. M., tr. from FIN. 2006. (Picture books from around the World Seri Ser.). (ENG.). 56p. (J). (gr. k-2). 20.95 *(978-1-905341-05-4(9))* WingedChariot Pr. GBR. Dist: Independent Pubs. Group.

Louie, Ron. Animals Sing Aloha. Arita, Vera. 2009. 20p. pap. 7.95 *(978-1-933067-29-2(2))* Beachhouse Publishing, LLC.

Louie, Wes & Cannella, Marco. Island of Time. Montgomery, R. A. 2008. 144p. (J). (gr. 2-7). pap. 6.99 *(978-1-933390-28-4(X))* Chooseco LLC.

Louie, Wes, jt. illus. see Semionov, Vladimir.

Louis, Catherine. Liu & the Bird: A Journey in Chinese Calligraphy. Kazeroid, Sibylle, tr. from FRE. 2006. (FRE.). 40p. (J). (gr. -1-3). 16.95 *(978-0-7358-2050-0(3))* North-South Bks., Inc.

—What the Rat Told Me. Sellier, Marie. 2014. (ENG.). 32p. (J). (gr. k-3). 7.95 *(978-0-7358-4158-1(6))* North-South Bks., Inc.

Louis, Catherine & Fei, Wang. Legend of the Chinese Dragon. Sellier, Marie. Kazeroid, Sibylle, tr. from FRE. 2008. (ENG.). 40p. (J). (gr. -1-3). 15.95 *(978-0-7358-2152-1(6))* North-South Bks., Inc.

Louis, Dominique, jt. illus. see Luckey, Bud.

Louise, Cristina & McIlroy, Michelle. Where Is Paco Now? Louise, Cristina & McIlroy, Michelle. 2012. (SPA & ENG.). (J). *(978-1-934370-26-1(6),* Campanita Bks.) Editorial Campana.

Louise, Finnoula. Cookies Cookies: A Year of Holiday Treats. Louise, Finnoula. 2011. (ENG.). 20p. (J). bds. 11.95 *(978-0-9827951-1-8(4))* Woodglen Publishing LLC.

Louise, Karen. The Deep. Winton, Tim. 32p. (YA). pap. 13.95 *(978-1-86368-210-7(4))* Fremantle Pr. AUS. Dist: Independent Pubs. Group.

Louissaint, Louis. Makso. Heurtelou, Maude. (CRP.). 24p. (J). (gr. k-2). pap. 8.50 *(978-1-58432-005-0(2))* Educa Vision.

LouLou. Christopher Wren Avian Architect, 1 vol. Skinner, Tina. 2008. (ENG.). 32p. 15.99 *(978-0-7643-3169-5(8))* Schiffer Publishing, Ltd.

Lovass-Nagy, Nicole. I Wish I Had a Tail. Lepage, Michaele L. 2008. 20p. pap. 12.49 *(978-1-4343-4721-3(4))* AuthorHouse.

Love, Jeremy, et al. Frontline Vol. 4: Oneshots. McKeever, Sean et al. 2004. 160p. (YA). pap. 15.95 *(978-1-932796-16-2(9))* Devil's Due Publishing, Inc.

Love, Judy. The Baby Shower. Bunting, Eve. 2007. (ENG.). 28p. (J). (gr. -1-2). 15.95 *(978-1-58089-139-4(X))* Charlesbridge Publishing, Inc.

—The Big Test. Danneberg, Julie. 2011. (Mrs. Hartwells Classroom Adventures Ser.). (ENG.). 32p. (J). (gr. 1-4). 16.95 *(978-1-58089-360-2(0))*; pap. 6.95 *(978-1-58089-361-9(9))* Charlesbridge Publishing, Inc.

—Can I Bring My Pterodactyl to School, Ms. Johnson? Grambling, Lois G. 2006. (Prehistoric Pets Ser.). (ENG.). 32p. (J). (gr. k-3). 7.95 *(978-1-58089-141-7(1))* Charlesbridge Publishing, Inc.

—Can I Bring Saber to New York, Ms. Mayor? Grambling, Lois G. 2014. (Prehistoric Pets Ser.). (ENG.). 32p. (J). (gr. k-3). 17.95 *(978-1-58089-570-5(0))* Charlesbridge Publishing, Inc.

—Can I Bring Woolly to the Library, Ms. Reeder? Grambling, Lois G. 2012. 32p. (J). 16.95 *(978-1-60734-074-4(7))*; (ENG.). pap. 7.95 *(978-1-58089-282-7(5))*; (ENG.). lib. bdg. 16.95 *(978-1-58089-281-0(7))* Charlesbridge Publishing, Inc.

—Field-Trip Fiasco. Danneberg, Julie. 2015. (Mrs. Hartwells Classroom Adventures Ser.). (ENG.). 32p. (J). (gr. k-3). 16.95 *(978-1-58089-671-9(5))* Charlesbridge Publishing, Inc.

—First Year Letters. Danneberg, Julie. 2014. 32p. pap. 7.00 *(978-1-61003-320-6(5))* Center for the Collaborative Classroom.

—First Year Letters. Danneberg, Julie. 2003. (Mrs. Hartwells Classroom Adventures Ser.). (ENG.). 32p. (J). (gr. 1-4). 16.95 *(978-1-58089-084-7(9))*; pap. 6.95 *(978-1-58089-085-4(7))* Charlesbridge Publishing, Inc.

—¡Que Nervios! El Primer Día de Escuela. Danneberg, Julie. Mlawer, Teresa, tr. 2006. (Mrs. Hartwells Classroom Adventures Ser.). (SPA & ENG.). 32p. (J). (gr. k-3). pap. 7.95 *(978-1-58089-126-4(8))* Charlesbridge Publishing, Inc.

—Jake's 100th Day of School, 1 vol. Laminack, Lester L. (ENG.). 32p. (J). (gr. k-3). 2008. pap. 8.95 *(978-1-56145-463-1(X))*; 2006. 16.95 *(978-1-56145-355-9(2))* Peachtree Pubs.

—Last Day Blues. Danneberg, Julie. 2006. (Mrs. Hartwells Classroom Adventures Ser.). (ENG.). 32p. (J). (gr. k-3). 6.95 *(978-1-58089-104-2(7))* Charlesbridge Publishing, Inc.

Love, Judy, et al. Poetry Speaks to Children. Paschen, Elise. Collins, Billy et al, eds. 2005. (Poetry Speaks Experience Ser.). (ENG.). 112p. (gr. k-3). 19.95 *(978-1-4022-0329-9(2),* Sourcebooks MediaFusion) Sourcebooks, Inc.

Love, Judy. The Witch Who Wanted to Be a Princess. Grambling, Lois G. 2007. (ENG.). 32p. (J). (gr. k-3). 6.95 *(978-1-58089-063-2(6))* Charlesbridge Publishing, Inc.

Love, Judy, jt. illus. see Cartwright, Shannon.

Love, Terrence. Attention Without Tension: A Teacher's Handbook on Attention Deficit Disorders (ADHD & ADD) Copeland, Edna D. & Love, Valerie L. 2nd rev. ed. 2003. (ENG.). 175p. pap. 28.00 *(978-1-886941-01-4(7))* Specialty Pr., Inc.

Loveheart, Lucy & Clibbon, Lucy. The Fairyspotters Guide. Meg, Magic. 2007. (ENG.). 24p. (J). (gr. 2-4). *(978-1-84089-297-0(8))* Zero to Ten, Ltd.

Loveheart, Lucy, jt. illus. see Clibbon, Lucy.

Lovejoy, Brenda. The Kittens Thomas & Tut. Napthine, Margaret. 2006. (J). per. 16.00 *(978-0-9763993-2-2(6),* Ithaca Pr.) Authors & Artists Publishers of New York, Inc.

Lovell, Edith. Sheep of Many Colors: Coloring Book. Guzman, Maria Del C. 2013. 26p. pap. 5.99 *(978-0-9855639-4-3(X))* Guzman, Maria del C.

Lovell, Katie. Build a Picture Cars Sticker Book. Brooks, Felicity. 2013. (Build a Picture Sticker Bks.). (ENG.). (J). (gr. -1-3). 6.99 *(978-0-7945-3376-2(0),* Usborne) EDC Publishing.

—Build a Picture Tractors Sticker Book. Brooks, Felicity. ed. 2013. (Build a Picture Sticker Bks.). 24p. (J). pap. 6.99 *(978-0-7945-3319-9(1),* Usborne) EDC Publishing.

—Christmas Stencil Cards. 2007. (Christmas Stencil Cards Ser.). 16p. (J). 9.99 *(978-0-7945-1896-7(6),* Usborne) EDC Publishing.

—Dinosaur Fun. Watt, Fiona. 2009. (Preschool Activities Ser.). 24p. (J). (gr. -1). spiral bd. 12.99 *(978-0-7945-2133-2(9),* Usborne) EDC Publishing.

Lovell, Katie, jt. illus. see Harrison, Erica.

Lovell, Patty & Catrow, David. Have Fun, Molly Lou Melon. Lovell, Patty. 2012. (ENG.). 32p. (J). (gr. k-3). 16.99 *(978-0-399-25406-2(4),* Putnam Juvenile) Penguin Publishing Group.

Lovelock, Brian. Construction. Sutton, Sally. (ENG.). (J). 2015. 32p. (-k). bds. 6.99 ***(978-0-7636-7975-0(5))***; 2014. 34p. (gr. -1-2). 15.99 *(978-0-7636-7325-3(0))* Candlewick Pr.

Lovelock, Brian. Construir una Carretera (Roadwork) Sutton, Sally. 2013. (SPA.). 28p. (J). (-k). bds. 6.99 *(978-0-7636-6494-7(4))* Candlewick Pr. †

—Demolicion. Sutton, Sally. 2014. (SPA.). 22p. (J). (-k). bds. 6.99 *(978-0-7636-7031-3(6))* Candlewick Pr.

—Demolition. Sutton, Sally. (ENG.). (J). 2014. 22p. (-k). bds. 6.99 *(978-0-7636-6493-0(6))*; 2012. 32p. (gr. -1-2). 15.99 *(978-0-7636-5830-4(8))* Candlewick Pr.

—Did My Mother Do That? Holt, Sharon. 2010. (ENG.). 32p. (J). (gr. -1-2). 15.99 *(978-0-7636-4685-1(7))* Candlewick Pr.

—Flight of the Honey Bee. Huber, Raymond. (Read & Wonder Ser.). (ENG.). 32p. (J). (gr. -1-2). 2015. 6.99 *(978-0-7636-7648-3(9))*; 2013. 16.99 *(978-0-7636-6760-3(9))* Candlewick Pr.

—Roadwork. Sutton, Sally. (ENG.). (J). (gr. k-k). 2011. 28p. bds. 6.99 *(978-0-7636-4653-0(9))*; 2008. 32p. 15.99 *(978-0-7636-3912-9(5))* Candlewick Pr.

Loven, Beth Glick. The Great Monarch Butterfly Chase. Prior, R. W. 2013. (ENG.). 32p. (J). (gr. -1-3). 16.99 *(978-1-4814-2157-7(3),* Simon & Schuster Bks. For Young Readers) Simon & Schuster Bks. For Young Readers.

Loveridge, Matt. Dinosaur Disaster. Lubar, David. 2013. (Looniverse Ser.: 3). (ENG.). 96p. (J). (gr. 1-3). 15.99 *(978-0-545-49605-6(5))*; pap. 4.99 *(978-0-545-49606-3(3))* Scholastic, Inc.

—Meltdown Madness. Lubar, David. 2013. (Looniverse Ser.: 2). (ENG.). 96p. (J). (gr. 1-3). 15.99 *(978-0-545-49603-2(9))*; pap. 4.99 *(978-0-545-49604-9(7))* Scholastic, Inc.

Loveridge, Matt, et al. Pucks, Clubs, & Baseball Gloves: Reading & Writing Sports Poems, 1 vol. Ipcizade, Catherine et al. 2014. (Poet in You Ser.). (ENG.). 32p. (gr. 2-4). pap. 8.95 *(978-1-4795-2947-6(8))*; lib. bdg. 26.65 *(978-1-4795-2196-8(5))* Picture Window Bks.

Loveridge, Matt. Stage Fright. Lubar, David. 2014. (Looniverse Ser.: 4). (ENG.). 96p. (J). (gr. 1-3). 15.99 *(978-0-545-49607-0(1))* Scholastic, Inc.

—Stranger Things. Lubar, David. 2013. (Looniverse Ser.: 1). (ENG.). 96p. (J). (gr. 1-3). 15.99 *(978-0-545-49601-8(2))*; pap. 4.99 *(978-0-545-49602-5(0))* Scholastic, Inc.

—This Old Band. Wissinger, Tamera Will. 2014. (ENG.). 32p. (J). (gr. -1-k). 16.95 *(978-1-62873-595-6(3),* Sky Pony Pr.) Skyhorse Publishing Co., Inc.

Lovett, Louise Sheppa. A Happy Day. Lovett, Louise Sheppa, . 2008. 32p. (J). 18.50 *(978-0-9793419-0-8(6))* Tish & Co. LLC.

Lovett, Nate. Night of the Ghost Pirate (Paw Patrol) Golden Books. 2015. (Holographic Sticker Book Ser.). (ENG.). 64p. (J). (gr. -1-2). pap. 4.99 ***(978-0-553-52390-4(2),*** Golden Bks.) Random Hse. Children's Bks.

Lovett, Nate, jt. illus. see Golden Books Staff.

Lovett, Tracy M. Buck's Rodeo. Lovett, Tracy M. 2012. 470p. pap. 16.50 *(978-0-9819736-6-1(3))* Inclement Pr.

Lovsin, Polona. Boo-Hoo, Baby!, 1 vol. Llewellyn, Claire. 2013. (Start Reading Ser.). (ENG.). 24p. (gr. k-1). pap. 6.99 *(978-1-4765-3182-3(X))*; pap. 41.94 *(978-1-4765-3208-0(7))* Capstone Pr., Inc.

—Go Away, Baby!, 1 vol. Llewellyn, Claire. 2013. (Start Reading Ser.). (ENG.). 24p. (gr. k-1). pap. 6.99 *(978-1-4765-3183-0(8))*; pap. 41.94 *(978-1-4765-3214-1(1))* Capstone Pr., Inc.

—Good Night, Baby!, 1 vol. Llewellyn, Claire. 2013. (Start Reading Ser.). (ENG.). 24p. (gr. k-1). pap. 6.99 *(978-1-4765-3184-7(6))*; pap. 41.94 *(978-1-4765-3216-5(8))* Capstone Pr., Inc.

—Is It for Me?, 1 vol. Llewellyn, Claire. 2013. (Start Reading Ser.). (ENG.). 24p. (gr. k-1). pap. 6.99 *(978-1-4765-3185-4(4))*; pap. 41.94 *(978-1-4765-3221-9(4))* Capstone Pr., Inc.

Low, Alan M. Black Tortoise & the Dynasty Dragon. Wacker, Eileen. 2012. (Fujimini Adventure Ser.: Vol. 5). (ENG.). 40p. (J). (gr. -1-3). 10.99 *(978-1-4675-1741-6(0))* Oncekids.

Low, William. Ghost Hands. Barron, T. A. 2011. (ENG.). 40p. (J). (gr. k-3). 18.99 *(978-0-399-25083-5(2),* Philomel) Penguin Publishing Group.

—Me & Momma & Big John. Rockliff, Mara. 2012. (ENG.). 32p. (J). (gr. -1-2). 16.99 *(978-0-7636-4359-1(9))* Candlewick Pr.

Low, William. Henry & the Kite Dragon. Low, William, tr. Hall, Bruce Edward & Hall, Bruce. 2004. (ENG.). 32p. (J). (gr. 1-4). 17.99 *(978-0-399-23727-0(5),* Philomel) Penguin Publishing Group.

Low, William & Cobalt Illustrations Studio Staff. Daytime Nighttime. Low, William & Cobalt Illustrations Studio Staff. (ENG.). (J). (gr. -1-3). 2015. 28p. bds. 7.99 *(978-1-62779-172-4(8))*; 2014. 36p. 16.99 *(978-0-8050-9751-1(1))* Holt, Henry & Co. (Holt, Henry & Co. Bks. For Young Readers).

—The Last Days of Jesus: His Life & Times. O'Reilly, Bill. 2014. (ENG.). 320p. (YA). (gr. 5-12). 19.99

(978-0-8050-9877-8(1), Holt, Henry & Co. Bks. For Young Readers) Holt, Henry & Co.

—Machines Go to Work. Low, William & Cobalt Illustrations Studio Staff. 2009. (ENG.). 42p. (J). (gr. -1-1). 17.99 *(978-0-8050-8759-8(1)*, Holt, Henry & Co. Bks. For Young Readers) Holt, Henry & Co.

—Old Penn Station. Low, William & Cobalt Illustrations Studio Staff. 2007. (ENG.). 40p. (J). (gr. k-4). 18.99 *(978-0-8050-7925-8(4)*, Holt, Henry & Co. Bks. For Young Readers) Holt, Henry & Co.

—Los Últimos Días de Jesús. O'Reilly, Bill. Uxó, Carlos, tr. from ENG. 2015.Tr. of Last Days of Jesus. (SPA & ENG.). 320p. (J). (gr. 5). 25.99 *(978-1-62779-278-3(3)*, Holt, Henry & Co. Bks. For Young Readers) Holt, Henry & Co.

—Young Fu of the Upper Yangtze. Lewis, Elizabeth Foreman. 2008. (ENG.). 320p. (J). (gr. 5-9). pap. 8.99 *(978-0-312-38007-6(0))* Square Fish.

Lowe, David. Alphabet of Sports. Schwaeber, Barbie Heit. (Alphabet Bks.). (ENG.). 40p. 2011. (J). (gr. -1-3). 9.95 *(978-1-60727-446-9(9))*; 2009. 9.95 *(978-1-59249-994-6(5))*; 2008. (J). (gr. k-2). 15.95 *(978-1-59249-769-0(1))* Soundprints.

Lowe, Frank Allen. The King's Silverware. Riddle, Sharon Kay & Sanders, Nancy/Ida. 2007. 32p. (J). pap. 15.00 *(978-0-9761583-5-6(3))* Olive Leaf Pubns.

Lowe, Greg, photos by. Cook It in a Cup! Quick Meals & Treats Kids Can Cook in Silicone Cups. Myall, Julia. 2008. (ENG., 64p. (J). (gr. 1-9). 18.99 *(978-0-8118-5956-1(8))* Chronicle Bks. LLC.

Lowe, Isabel. The Truth at Last about the Little Red Hen. Price, Hugh. 2003. 16p. (J). pap. *(978-1-877228-19-3(2))* Steele Roberts Aotearoa Ltd.

Lowe, Jason, photos by. Fun Food. Rosenbaum, Stephanie. Williams, Chuck, ed. 2006. (ENG., 128p. 19.95 *(978-0-7432-7856-0(9)*, Free Pr.) Free Pr.

—The Silver Spoon. Phaidon Press Editors, ed. rev. ed. 2005. (ENG., 1264p. (gr. 8-17). 49.95 *(978-0-7148-4531-9(0))* Phaidon Pr. Ltd. GBR. Dist: Hachette Bk. Group.

Lowe, Tony. Troggle the Troll. Falk, Nicholas. 2013. (ENG.). 48p. (J). (-k). pap. 11.99 *(978-1-74275-601-1(8))* Random Hse. Australia AUS. Dist: Independent Pubs. Group.

Lowe, Vicky. Mary Margaret & the Perfect Pet Plan. MacLean, Christine Kole & Maclean, Christine. 2007. (ENG.). 192p. (J). (gr. 3-7). 6.99 *(978-0-14-240767-7(4)*, Puffin) Penguin Publishing Group.

Lowe, Wes. Augustine of Hippo. Carr, Simonetta. 2009. (ENG.). 62p. (J). 18.00 *(978-1-60178-073-7(7))* Reformation Heritage Bks.

—Sarky Puddleboat. Branson, Eve. 2011. 44p. (J). 14.99 *(978-1-4520-9754-1(2))* AuthorHouse.

Lowe, Wesley. Ajàyí Gb' Ìtum' Ìlù. ¿Ládo¿Ù, F¿Lák¿'. 2013. 34p. *(978-0-9866435-1-4(3))* Adubi Publishing.

—Alexander Trout's Amazing Adventure. Richardson, Steve. 2008. 75p. 16.95 *(978-0-9786422-2-8(8))* Impossible Dreams Publishing Co.

—Apollo 13. Zoehfeld, Kathleen Weidner. 2015. (Stepping Stone Book Ser.). (ENG.). 112p. (J). (gr. 2-5). pap. 4.99 *(978-0-385-39125-2(0))* Random Hse., Inc.

—Growing Trees. Stamper, Judith Bauer. 2010. (J). *(978-1-60617-127-1(5))* Teaching Strategies, Inc.

Lowe, Wesley. The Race Around the World (Totally True Adventures) Castaldo, Nancy. 2015. (Stepping Stone Book(TM) Ser.). (ENG.). 112p. (J). (gr. 2-5). 4.99 ***(978-0-553-52278-5(7)***, Random Hse. Bks. for Young Readers) Random Hse. Children's Bks.

Lowe, Wesley. The $25,000 Flight. Houran, Lori Haskins. 2014. (Stepping Stone Book Ser.). (ENG.). 112p. (J). (gr. 2-5). 4.99 *(978-0-385-38284-7(7)*, Random Hse. Bks. for Young Readers) Random Hse. Children's Bks.

Lowell, Shelley. This Is the Land of Two Suns: Paintings & Poetry, Lowell, Shelley. 2000th ltd. ed. 2005. 32p. per. 20.00 *(978-0-9765344-0-2(1))* Lowell, Shelley.

Lowenstein, Anna. Don't Call Me Cookie. Pasiadis, Vanessa. 2010. 178p. pap. 21.00 *(978-1-60911-470-1(1)*, Strategic Bk. Publishing) Strategic Book Publishing & Rights Agency (SBPRA).

Lowenstein, Sallie. Sir Kyle & Lady Madeline. Lowenstein, Sallie, . 2007. 32p. (J). 18.95 *(978-0-9658486-6-4(3))* Lion Stone Bks.

Lowenstein, Sallie. Waiting for Eugene. Lowenstein, Sallie. 2005. 208p. (J). 19.00 *(978-0-9658486-5-7(5))* Lion Stone Bks.

Lowery, Mike. All Aboard! Kai Dotlich, Rebecca. 2014. (ENG.). 32p. (J). (-k). 12.99 *(978-0-385-75420-0(5)*, Knopf Bks. for Young Readers) Random Hse. Children's Bks.

Lowery, Mike. Ancient Egypt. Jennings, Ken. 2015. (Ken Jennings' Junior Genius Guides). (ENG.). 160p. (J). (gr. 3-5). 19.99 ***(978-1-4814-2953-5(1)***, Little Simon) Little Simon.

Lowery, Mike. Bubble in the Bathtub. Nesbø, Jo. Chace, Tara F., tr. 2011. (Doctor Proctor's Fart Powder Ser.). (ENG.). 448p. (J). (gr. 3-7). pap. 7.99 *(978-1-4169-7975-3(1)*, Simon & Schuster/Paula Wiseman Bks.) Simon & Schuster/Paula Wiseman Bks.

—Bubble in the Bathtub. Nesbø, Jo. Chace, Tara, tr. from NOR. 2011. (Doctor Proctor's Fart Powder Ser.). (ENG.). 432p. (J). (gr. 3-7). 16.99 *(978-1-4169-7974-6(3)*, Simon & Schuster/Paula Wiseman Bks.) Simon & Schuster/Paula Wiseman Bks.

—Doctor Proctor's Fart Powder. Nesbø, Jo. Chace, Tara F., tr. 2010. (Doctor Proctor's Fart Powder Ser.). (ENG.). 288p. (J). (gr. 3-7). pap. 7.99 *(978-1-4169-7973-9(5)*, Simon & Schuster/Paula Wiseman Bks.) Simon & Schuster/Paula Wiseman Bks.

—Doctor Proctor's Fart Powder. Nesbø, Jo. Chace, Tara, tr. from GER. 2009. (Doctor Proctor's Fart Powder Ser.). (ENG.). 272p. (J). (gr. 3-7). 16.99 *(978-1-4169-7972-2(7)*, Simon & Schuster/Paula Wiseman Bks.) Simon & Schuster/Paula Wiseman Bks.

Lowery, Mike. The Gingerbread Man Loose at the Zoo. Murray, Laura. 2016. (J). ***(978-0-399-16867-3(2)***, Razorbill) Penguin Publishing Group.

Lowery, Mike. The Gingerbread Man Loose in the School. Murray, Laura. 2011. (ENG.). 32p. (J). (gr. k-3). 16.99 *(978-0-399-25052-1(2)*, Putnam Juvenile) Penguin Publishing Group.

—The Gingerbread Man Loose on the Fire Truck. Murray, Laura. 2013. (ENG.). 32p. (J). (gr. k-3). 16.99 *(978-0-399-25779-7(9)*, Putnam Juvenile) Penguin Publishing Group.

—Greek Mythology. Jennings, Ken. 2014. (Ken Jennings' Junior Genius Guides). (ENG.). 160p. (J). (gr. 3-5). 12.99 *(978-1-4814-2615-2(X))*; 18.99 *(978-1-4424-9849-5(8))*; pap. 7.99 *(978-1-4424-7330-0(4))* Little Simon. (Little Simon).

—The Human Body. Jennings, Ken. 2015. (Ken Jennings' Junior Genius Guides). (ENG.). 160p. (J). (gr. 3-5). pap. 7.99 *(978-1-4814-0173-9(4)*, Little Simon) Little Simon.

—The Magical Fruit. Nesbø, Jo. Chace, Tara F., tr. from NOR. 2013. (Doctor Proctor's Fart Powder Ser.). (ENG.). 320p. (J). (gr. 3-7). 16.99 *(978-1-4424-9342-1(9)*, Simon & Schuster/Paula Wiseman Bks.) Simon & Schuster/Paula Wiseman Bks.

—Maps & Geography. Jennings, Ken. 2014. (Ken Jennings' Junior Genius Guides). (ENG.). 160p. (J). (gr. 3-5). pap. 7.99 *(978-1-4424-7328-7(2)*, Little Simon) Little Simon.

—Moo Hoo. Ryan, Candace. 2012. (ENG.). 32p. (J). (gr. -1-k). 12.99 *(978-0-8027-2336-9(5))* Walker & Co.

—Random Body Parts, 1 vol. Bulion, Leslie. 2015. (ENG.). 48p. (gr. 3-6). 14.95 *(978-1-56145-737-3(X))* Peachtree Pubs.

—Ribbit Rabbit. Ryan, Candace. 2011. (ENG.). 32p. (J). (gr. -1-k). 12.99 *(978-0-8027-2180-8(X))* Walker & Co.

Lowery, Mike. Simple Machines. Ward, D. J. 2015. (Let's-Read-And-Find-Out Science 2 Ser.). (ENG.). 40p. (J). (gr. -1-3). pap. 6.99 ***(978-0-06-232147-3(1))*** HarperCollins Pubs.

Lowery, Mike. U. S. Presidents. Jennings, Ken. 2014. (Ken Jennings' Junior Genius Guides). (ENG.). 160p. (J). (gr. 3-5). pap. 7.99 *(978-1-4424-7332-4(0)*, Little Simon) Little Simon.

—Unscripted by Lainey McBride. Howie, Betsy. 2012. 183p. (J). *(978-0-545-39705-6(7))* Scholastic, Inc.

—What Can a Crane Pick Up? Kai Dotlich, Rebecca. 2012. (ENG.). 32p. (J). (gr. k-k). 16.99 *(978-0-375-86726-2(0))*; lib. bdg. 19.99 *(978-0-375-96726-9(5))* Random Hse. Children's Bks. (Knopf Bks. for Young Readers).

—What Can a Crane Pick Up? Kai Dotlich, Rebecca. 2014. (ENG.). 28p. (J). (-k). bds. 6.99 *(978-0-385-75383-8(7)*, Knopf Bks. for Young Readers) Random Hse. Children's Bks.

—Who Cut the Cheese? Nesbø, Jo. Chace, Tara F., tr. 2012. (Doctor Proctor's Fart Powder Ser.). (ENG.). 464p. (J). (gr. 3-7). pap. 7.99 *(978-1-4424-3308-3(6)*, Simon & Schuster/Paula Wiseman Bks.) Simon & Schuster/Paula Wiseman Bks.

—Who Cut the Cheese? Nesbø, Jo. Chace, Tara, tr. from NOR. 2012. (Doctor Proctor's Fart Powder Ser.). (ENG.). 464p. (J). (gr. 3-7). 16.99 *(978-1-4424-3307-6(8)*, Simon & Schuster/Paula Wiseman Bks.) Simon & Schuster/Paula Wiseman Bks.

Lowes, Tom. Casey's Four Holiday Celebrations. l.t. ed. 2003. 38p. (J). 16.95 *(978-0-9722099-9-1(9)*, C4HC) Caseys World Bks.

—Casey's Unexpected Friend. Stormer, Kate. l.t. ed. 2003. 38p. (J). 16.95 *(978-0-9722099-7-7(2)*, CUF) Caseys World Bks.

—The Rescue of Little Red. Stormer, Kate. 2005. 91p. (J). (gr. 3-5). per. 5.99 *(978-0-9765872-0-0(3))* Caseys World Bks.

—A Stranger in Casey's World. Stormer, Kate. l.t. ed. 2004. 32p. (J). 16.95 *(978-0-9647663-1-0(0))* Caseys World Bks.

—Teddy's TV Troubles. Cantor, Joanne. 2004. 36p. (J). mass mkt. 16.95 *(978-0-9647663-7-2(X))* HenschelHAUS Publishing.

Lowry, Judith. Home to Medicine Mountain. Santiago, Chiori. 2013. (ENG.). 32p. (J). (gr. 1-18). pap. 9.95 *(978-0-89239-176-9(6))* Lee & Low Bks., Inc.

Lowry, Lois. The Willoughbys. Lowry, Lois. 2008. (ENG.). 176p. (J). (gr. 1-4). 16.00 *(978-0-618-97974-5(3))* Houghton Mifflin Harcourt Publishing Co.

Lowry, Lois & Rohmann, Eric. Bless This Mouse. Lowry, Lois & Rohmann, Eric. 2011. (ENG.). 160p. (J). (gr. 2-5). 16.99 *(978-0-547-39009-3(2))* Houghton Mifflin Harcourt Publishing Co.

Loxton, Daniel. Evolution. Loxton, Daniel. 2010. (ENG.). 56p. (J). (gr. 3-8). 18.95 *(978-1-55453-430-2(5))* Kids Can Pr., Ltd. CAN. Dist: Univ. of Toronto Pr.

Loxton, Daniel & Smith, Jim W. W. Ankylosaur Attack. Loxton, Daniel. 2011. (Tales of Prehistoric Life Ser.). (ENG.). 32p. (J). (gr. -1-2). 16.95 *(978-1-55453-631-3(6))* Kids Can Pr., Ltd. CAN. Dist: Univ. of Toronto Pr.

—Plesiosaur Peril, 0 vols. Loxton, Daniel. 2014. (ENG.). 32p. (J). 16.95 *(978-1-55453-633-7(2))* Kids Can Pr., Ltd. CAN. Dist: Univ. of Toronto Pr.

—Pterosaur Trouble. Loxton, Daniel. 2013. (Tales of Prehistoric Life Ser.). (ENG.). 32p. (J). 16.95 *(978-1-55453-632-0(4))* Kids Can Pr., Ltd. CAN. Dist: Univ. of Toronto Pr.

Loy, Jessica. Weird & Wild Animal Facts. Loy, Jessica. 2015. (ENG.). 40p. (J). (gr. -1-3). 17.99 *(978-0-8050-7945-6(9)*, Holt, Henry & Co. Bks. For Young Readers) Holt, Henry & Co.

Loy, Nikki. David & Goliath. Page, Nick & Page, Claire. 2006. (Read with Me (Make Believe Ideas) Ser.). 31p. (J). (gr. k-2). *(978-1-84610-173-1(5))* Make Believe Ideas.

—The Good Samaritan. Page, Nick & Page, Claire. 2006. (Read with Me (Make Believe Ideas) Ser.). 31p. (J). (gr. k-2). *(978-1-84610-174-8(3))* Make Believe Ideas.

—Read with Me Jonah the Moaner: Sticker Activity Book. Page, Nick & Page, Claire. 2006. (Read with Me (Make Believe Ideas) Ser.). 12p. (J). (gr. k-2). pap. *(978-1-84610-183-0(2))* Make Believe Ideas.

Loyd, Mark. Big Ben: A Little Known Story. Loyd, Mark. ed. 2005. (J). *(978-0-9773317-1-0(7))* Too Fun Publshing.

Lozano, Hector. Dog Tacos. McChesney, Terry. McChesney, Ruth Lozano & Brannon, Brian, eds. 2010. (ENG.). 164p. pap. 9.95 *(978-1-4486-5663-9(X))* CreateSpace Independent Publishing Platform.

Lozano, Luciano. I (Don't) Like Snakes. Davies, Nicola. 2015. (ENG.). 32p. (J). (gr. k-4). 15.99 ***(978-0-7636-7831-9(7))*** Candlewick Pr.

Lozano, Luciano. Mister H. Nesquens, Daniel & Schimel, Lawrence. 2015. (J). 14.00 *(978-0-8028-5440-7(0)*, Eerdmans Bks For Young Readers) Eerdmans, William B. Publishing Co.

—Operation Alphabet. MacCuish, Al. 2011. (Ministry of Letters Ser.). (ENG.). 64p. (J). (gr. -1-k). 19.95 *(978-0-500-51584-6(0)*, 551584) Thames & Hudson.

Lozano, Omar. The Computer Meltdown. Sonneborn, Scott. 2015. (North Police Ser.). (ENG.). 32p. (gr. k-2). lib. bdg. 19.99 ***(978-1-4795-6485-9(0))*** Picture Window Bks.

—Meet the South Police. Sonneborn, Scott. 2015. (North Police Ser.). (ENG.). 32p. (gr. k-2). lib. bdg. 19.99 ***(978-1-4795-6486-6(9))*** Picture Window Bks.

—The Mystery of Santa's Sleigh. Sonneborn, Scott. 2015. (North Police Ser.). (ENG.). 32p. (gr. k-2). lib. bdg. 19.99 ***(978-1-4795-6484-2(2))*** Picture Window Bks.

Lozano, Omar. Ninja-Rella. Comeau, Joey. 2015. (Far Out Fairy Tales Ser.). (ENG.). 40p. (gr. 3-4). lib. bdg. 23.99 *(978-1-4342-9647-4(4))* Stone Arch Bks.

Lozano, Omar. The Reindeer Games. Sonneborn, Scott. 2015. (North Police Ser.). (ENG.). 32p. (gr. k-2). lib. bdg. 19.99 ***(978-1-4795-6487-3(7))*** Picture Window Bks.

Lubach, Peter. Mr. Mouse's Motel: Helping Others. Dinardo, Jeff. 2014. (Funny Bone Readers: Being a Friend Ser.). 24p. (gr. -1-1). pap. 4.99 *(978-1-939656-05-6(2))* Red Chair Pr.

—What Is the Moon Made Of? And Other Questions Kids Have about Space, 1 vol. Bowman, Donna H. (Kids' Questions Ser.). (ENG.). 24p. (gr. 1-2). 2011. pap. 7.49 *(978-1-4048-6726-0(0))*; 2009. lib. bdg. 25.99 *(978-1-4048-5529-8(7))* Picture Window Bks. (Nonfiction Picture Bks.).

Lubach, Vanessa. Dr Jekyll & Mr Hyde. Stevenson, Robert Louis. 2014. (Classics of Science Fiction Ser.). (ENG.). 64p. pap. 6.95 *(978-1-906230-15-9(3))* Real Reads Ltd. GBR. Dist: International Publishers Marketing.

—Jane Eyre. 2009. (Real Reads Ser.). 64p. (J). (gr. 4-8). 29.25 *(978-1-60754-667-2(1))* Windmill Bks.

—Wuthering Heights. Brontë, Emily. 2009. (Real Reads Ser.). 64p. (J). (gr. 4-8). 29.25 *(978-1-60754-670-2(1))* Windmill Bks.

Lubera, Logan. The Impending Storm: The Imperium Saga: Fall of the Imperium Trilogy, 3 vols., Vol. 1. Bowyer, Clifford B. 2003. (Imperium Saga: 1). (ENG.). 463p. (YA). 27.95 *(978-0-9744354-4-2(9)*, BK0001) Silver Leaf Bks., LLC.

Luberoff, William. My First Prayer Book. Cavanaugh, Karen. 2007. (Catholic Classics Ser.). 32p. (J). 3.95 *(978-0-88271-216-1(0))* Regina Pr., Malhame & Co.

Lubitsky, Maribeth Jenkins. Go-bez Nibe: Very Clever Firefly, 1 vol. Angelo, Tony. 2010. 48p. 24.95 *(978-1-4489-5184-0(4))* PublishAmerica, Inc.

Luca, Bogdan. They Shoot! They Score! Life's Lessons on Ice. Macdonald, Kelly. 2005. 32p. 9.99 *(978-0-9736893-0-3(7))* MacDonald, Kelly CAN. Dist: Hushion Hse. Publishing, Ltd.

Lucas, David. A Letter for Bear. 2013. (ENG.). 32p. (J). (gr. -1-2). 14.95 *(978-1-909263-13-0(3))* Flying Eye Bks. GBR. Dist: Consortium Bk. Sales & Distribution.

—Rubbaduck & Ruby Roo. Oram, Hiawyn. 2005. (ENG.). 28p. (J). (gr. -1-3). 15.95 *(978-1-59078-356-6(5))* Boyds Mills Pr.

LUCAS, David. Christmas at the Toy Museum. LUCAS, David. 2012. (ENG.). 32p. (J). (gr. -1-2). 15.99 *(978-0-7636-5868-7(5))* Candlewick Pr.

Lucas, David. The Lying Carpet. Lucas, David. (ENG.). (J). (gr. 4-7). 2013. 80p. pap. 10.99 *(978-1-84939-017-0(7))*; 2011. 78p. 15.99 *(978-1-84270-441-7(9))* Andersen Pr. GBR. Dist: Independent Pubs. Group.

—Peanut. Lucas, David. 2008. (ENG.). 32p. (J). (gr. k-k). 15.99 *(978-0-7636-3925-9(7))* Candlewick Pr.

—The Robot & the Bluebird. Lucas, David. 2008. (ENG.). 32p. (J). (gr. -1-3). 19.99 *(978-0-374-36330-7(7)*, Farrar, Straus & Giroux (BYR)) Farrar, Straus & Giroux.

Lucas, Diane. Adopting Jake. Black, Angie. 2010. 32p. pap. 12.95 *(978-1-935268-47-5(3))* Halo Publishing International.

—It's Time for Holi! Roy Shah, Amita. 2011. 24p. pap. 13.95 *(978-1-60844-943-9(2))* Dog Ear Publishing, LLC.

—Ka-Boom. Rininger, Alyce. 2012. 46p. pap. 13.95 *(978-1-61244-069-9(X))* Halo Publishing International.

—Keep Out!, 1 vol. Boudreau, Hélène. ed. 2010. (ENG.). 84p. (J). (gr. 1-4). pap. 8.95 *(978-1-55109-753-4(2))* Nimbus Publishing, Ltd. CAN. Dist: Orca Bk. Pubs. USA.

—Milton the Square Shell Turtle. Tatro, MaryAnn. 2013. 24p. pap. 11.95 *(978-1-61244-106-1(8))* Halo Publishing International.

—Sabrina the Girl with A Hole in Her Heart. Lewis, Wendy. 2011. (ENG.). 34p. pap. 10.95 *(978-1-4663-3473-1(8))* CreateSpace Independent Publishing Platform.

—The Seed Sower, Walter's Special Garden. Anderson, Debra. 2012. 24p. pap. 11.95 *(978-1-61244-097-2(5))* Halo Publishing International.

—Stella Saves the Game. E.A. Budd. 2012. 24p. pap. 12.95 *(978-1-61244-059-0(2))* Halo Publishing International.

Lucas, James. Gets a Shock. Simon, Francesca. 2004. (Little Yellow Dog Ser.: 1). (ENG.). 32p. (J). (gr. -1-k). pap. 7.99 *(978-1-84255-243-8(0)*, Orion Children's Bks.) Hachette Children's Group GBR. Dist: Independent Pubs. Group.

Lucas, James E. Little Yellow Dog Bites the Builder. Simon, Francesca. 2004. (Little Yellow Dog Ser.: 1). (ENG.). 32p. (J). (gr. -1-k). per. 7.99 *(978-1-84255-246-9(5)*, Orion Children's Bks.) Hachette Children's Group GBR. Dist: Independent Pubs. Group.

—Little Yellow Dog Says Look at Me. Simon, Francesca. 2004. (Little Yellow Dog Ser.: 1). (ENG.). 32p. (J). (gr. -1-k). pap. 7.99 *(978-1-84255-244-5(9)*, Orion Children's Bks.) Hachette Children's Group GBR. Dist: Independent Pubs. Group.

Lucas, Margeaux. Abby's Asthma & the Big Race. Golding, Theresa Martin. 2009. (ENG.). 32p. (J). (gr. 1-4). 16.99 *(978-0-8075-0465-9(3))* Whitman, Albert & Co.

—The Aliens Have Landed at Our School! Nesbitt, Kenn. 2006. (Giggle Poetry Ser.). (ENG.). 87p. (J). (gr. 1-6). per. 9.95 *(978-0-689-04864-7(5))* Meadowbrook Pr.

—Alpha Betti. Morton, Carlene. 2007. (ENG.). (J). (gr. -1-3). 17.95 *(978-1-932146-69-1(5)*, Upstart Bks.) Highsmith Inc.

—Cuando Sea Grande. Kittinger, Jo S. 2005. (Rookie Reader Español Ser.). (SPA & ESP.). 23p. (J). (gr. k-2). per. 4.95 *(978-0-516-24692-5(5)*, Children's Pr.) Scholastic Library Publishing.

—Cuando sea Grande: When I Grow Up. Kittinger, Jo S. 2005. (Rookie Reader Español Ser.). 24p. (gr. k-2). 19.50 *(978-0-516-24443-3(4)*, Children's Pr.) Scholastic Library Publishing.

—Dancing Dinos at the Beach. Lucas, Sally. 2010. (Step into Reading Ser.). (ENG.). 32p. (J). (gr. -1-1). pap. 3.99 *(978-0-375-85640-2(4))* Random Hse., Inc.

—Great Green Gator Graduation. Dadey, Debbie. 2006. (Swamp Monster in Third Grade Ser.). 58p. (J). pap. *(978-0-439-79401-5(3))* Scholastic, Inc.

—My Best Friend Is Moving. Parker, David. 2007. (J). *(978-0-545-00389-6(X))* Scholastic, Inc.

—Our Class Works Together. Parker, David. 2007. (J). *(978-0-545-00384-1(9))* Scholastic, Inc.

—P Is for Passover. Stone, Tanya Lee. 2003. (ENG.). 32p. (J). (gr. -1-k). mass mkt. 5.99 *(978-0-8431-0238-3(1)*, Price Stern Sloan) Penguin Publishing Group.

—Room 9 Writes a Report. Williams, Rozanne Lanczak. 2006. (Learn to Write Ser.). 16p. (J). (gr. k-2). pap. 3.49 *(978-1-59198-297-5(9)*, 6193) Creative Teaching Pr., Inc.

—Room 9 Writes a Report. Williams, Rozanne Lanczak. Maio, Barbara, ed. 2006. (J). per. 8.99 *(978-1-59198-357-6(6))* Creative Teaching Pr., Inc.

—Sharing My Room. Parker, David. 2007. (J). *(978-0-545-00386-5(5))* Scholastic, Inc.

—Signing at School: Sign Language for Kids, 1 vol. Clay, Kathryn. 2013. (Time to Sign Ser.). (ENG.). 32p. (gr. 1-2). 26.65 *(978-1-62065-052-3(5)*, Aplus Bks.) Capstone Pr., Inc.

—We Can All Play. Parker, David. 2007. (J). *(978-0-545-00390-2(3))* Scholastic, Inc.

Lucas, Stacey L., et al. Sara Safety, School Safety Pamphlet. LaBerge, Margaret M. 2004. (J). pap. *(978-0-9755561-0-8(X))* Reading Resc.

Lucas, Stacey L. & Lopresti, Sarah H. Sara Safety, Personal Safety: Kid's Activity Book. LaBerge, Margaret M. 2004. 21p. (J). pap. *(978-0-9755561-2-2(6))* Reading Resc.

Lucco, Kristine. Let's Visit Jerusalem! Adventures of Bella & Harry. Manzione, Lisa. ed. 2013. (Adventures of Bella & Harry Ser.: 1). (ENG.). 35p. (J). (gr. k-3). 16.95 *(978-1-937616-00-7(2))* Bella & Harry, LLC.

—Let's Visit London! Adventures of Bella & Harry. Manzione, Lisa. ed. 2011. (Adventures of Bella & Harry Ser.: 1). (ENG.). 35p. (J). (gr. k-3). 16.95 *(978-1-937616-03-8(7))* Bella & Harry, LLC.

Lucero, Jessica. Skulls. Marquitz, Tim. Milner, Isaac, ed. 2011. pap. 13.25 *(978-1-61572-354-6(4))* Damnation Bks.

Luchsinger, Linda. Waddling to the Pond. Poet, Jonny. 2011. 40p. pap. 24.95 *(978-1-4560-4033-8(2))* America Star Bks.

Lucini, Carmen. Tungaira: Miss Primeras Poesias. Plaza, José María & María, Plaza José. (SPA.). 96p. (J). 8.99 *(978-84-392-8115-3(3)*, EV4870) Gaviota Ediciones ESP. Dist: Lectorum Pubns., Inc.

Lucini, Chata. El Palacio de los Tres Ojos. Gisbert, Joan Manuel. 2006. (SPA.). 127p. (J). (gr. 4-7). pap. 10.99 *(978-84-263-4614-8(6))* Vives, Luis Editorial (Edelvives) ESP. Dist: Lectorum Pubns., Inc.

Lucke, Deb. Never Say Boo! Pulver, Robin. 2009. (ENG.). 32p. (J). (gr. -1-3). 16.95 *(978-0-8234-2110-7(4))* Holiday Hse., Inc.

—The Pilgrims' First Thanksgiving, 1 vol. Gunderson, Jessica. 2011. (Thanksgiving Ser.). (ENG.). 24p. (gr. 1-2). lib. bdg. 26.65 *(978-1-4048-6285-2(4))*; pap. 7.95 *(978-1-4048-6720-8(1))* Picture Window Bks. (Nonfiction Picture Bks.).

Lucke, Deb. The Book of Time Outs: A Mostly True History of the World's Biggest Troublemakers. Lucke, Deb. 2008. (ENG.). 32p. (J). (gr. 1-4). 15.99 *(978-1-4169-2829-4(4)*, Simon & Schuster Bks. For Young Readers) Simon & Schuster Bks. For Young Readers.

Luckemeyer, Norma. Johnny Coalboy. Witschen, Kay. 2003. (J). per. 5.95 *(978-0-9741352-0-5(8))* Dwitt Publishing.

Luckey, Bud & Louis, Dominique. Mater & the Ghost Light. RH Disney Staff. 2006. (Little Golden Book Ser.). (ENG.). 24p. (J). (gr. -1-2). 3.99 *(978-0-7364-2416-5(4)*, Golden/Disney) Random Hse. Children's Bks.

LuckySports. Adventures in SportsLand - the Golf Bully (with accompanying CD) The Golf Bully. LuckySports, . 2008. 32p. (J). pap. 19.95 *(978-0-935938-29-6(X))* LuckySports.

Lucot, Erica. I Sette Pesci: The Seven Fishes. Pursh, Eric. 2005. (J). per. *(978-0-9727319-3-5(8)*, Blacktypewriter Pr.) Pittsburgh Literary Arts Network LLC.

Lucy Cousins. Maisy's First Numbers: A Maisy Concept Book. Cousins, Lucy. 2013. (Maisy Ser.). (ENG.). 14p. (J). (-k). bds. 6.99 *(978-0-7636-6805-1(2))* Candlewick Pr.

Ludin, Marine. Snow Bears Never Lie. Said. 2013. (ENG.). 32p. (J). (gr. -1-3). 17.95 *(978-0-7358-4137-6(3))* North-South Bks., Inc.

Ludlam, Jamie. And Jake Makes Three. Whitaker, Sue. 2013. 108p. pap. *(978-1-907978-16-6(X))* ETA Publishing Hse.

—And Jake Makes Three & the Secret of Badlands. Whitaker, Sue. 2013. 92p. pap. *(978-1-907978-26-5(7))* ETA Publishing Hse.

—And Jake Makes Three in the Snow. Whitaker, Sue. 2013. 104p. pap. *(978-1-907978-21-0(6))* ETA Publishing Hse.

—And Jake Makes Three in the Vampires Den. Whitaker, Sue. Thomas-Brown, Cauline, ed. 2013. 86p. pap. *(978-1-907978-31-9(3))* ETA Publishing Hse.

Ludlow, Patricia. How the World Began: Creation in Myths & Legends. Cooper, Gilly Cameron. 2006. (ENG.). 48p. (J). (gr. 3-7). pap. 11.99 *(978-1-84476-246-0(7))* Anness Publishing GBR. Dist: National Bk. Network.

—O Come, All Ye Faithful. Augustine, Peg. 2007. 32p. (J). (gr. -1-3). 18.00 *(978-0-687-64304-2(X))* Abingdon Pr.

Ludlow, Patricia D. Casting the Gods Adrift: A Tale of Ancient Egypt. McCaughrean, Geraldine. 2003. (ENG.). 112p. (J). (gr. 4-7). 15.95 *(978-0-8126-2684-1(2))* Cricket Bks.

Ludvigsen, Henning. Project U. L. F. Clark, Stuart. 2007. (Project U.L.F. Ser.: 1). (ENG.). 418p. (YA). 27.95 *(978-0-9787782-0-0(0)*, BK0021) Silver Leaf Bks., LLC.

Ludy, Mark. When I Was a Boy... I Dreamed. Matott, Justin. 2004. (ENG.). 32p. (J). (gr. -1-4). *(978-0-9664276-2-2(9))* Green Pastures Publishing, Inc.

—When I Was a Girl ... I Dreamed. Matott, J. P. & Baker, Margaret. 2005. (ENG.). 32p. (J). (gr. -1-4). *(978-0-9664276-3-9(7))* Green Pastures Publishing, Inc.

Ludy, Mark. Jujo: The Youngest Tribesman. Ludy, Mark. 2007. (ENG.). 32p. (J). (gr. k-2). 16.95 *(978-0-9664276-5-3(3))* Green Pastures Publishing, Inc.

Lue Sue, Majella. Penina Levine Is a Hard-boiled Egg. O'Connell, Rebecca. 2009. (ENG.). 192p. (J). (gr. 3-7). pap. 14.99 *(978-0-312-55026-4(X))* Square Fish.

Luebs, Robin. How Do You Say Good Night? Moore, Raina. 2008. (ENG.). 32p. (J). (gr. -1-2). 16.99 *(978-0-06-083163-9(4))* HarperCollins Pubs.

—Who Said Coo? Ruddell, Deborah. 2010. (ENG.). 40p. (J). (gr. -1-2). 17.99 *(978-1-4169-8510-5(7)*, Beach Lane Bks.) Beach Lane Bks.

Luebs, Robin. Please Pick Me up, Mama! Luebs, Robin. 2009. (ENG.). 40p. (J). (gr. -1-k). 15.99 *(978-1-4169-7977-7(8)*, Beach Lane Bks.) Beach Lane Bks.

Luedecke, Bev. Birthday Beastie: All about Counting. Hall, Kirsten. 2003. (Beastieville Ser.). 32p. (J). 19.50 *(978-0-516-22891-4(9)*, Children's Pr.) Scholastic Library Publishing.

—Buried Treasure: All about Using a Map. Hall, Kirsten. 2003. (Beastieville Ser.). 32p. (J). 19.50 *(978-0-516-22894-5(3)*, Children's Pr.) Scholastic Library Publishing.

—Double Trouble: All about Colors. Hall, Kirsten. 2003. (Beastieville Ser.). 32p. (J). (gr. -1-1). 19.50 *(978-0-516-22892-1(7)*, Children's Pr.) Scholastic Library Publishing.

—First Day of School: All about Shapes & Sizes. Hall, Kirsten. 2004. (Beastieville Ser.). (ENG.). 32p. (J). (gr. k-1). pap. 3.95 *(978-0-516-24654-3(2)*, Children's Pr.) Scholastic Library Publishing.

—Good Times: All about the Seasons. Hall, Kirsten. 2004. (Beastieville Ser.). (J). 19.50 *(978-0-516-23648-3(2)*, Children's Pr.) Scholastic Library Publishing.

—Help! All about Telling Time. Hall, Kirsten. (Beastieville Ser.). 32p. (J). (gr. k-1). 2004. (ENG.). pap. 3.95 *(978-0-516-24655-0(0))*; 2003. 19.50 *(978-0-516-22890-7(0))* Scholastic Library Publishing. (Children's Pr.).

—Hide-And-Seek: All about Location. Hall, Kirsten. 2004. (Beastieville Ser.). (J). 19.50 *(978-0-516-23649-0(0)*, Children's Pr.) Scholastic Library Publishing.

—Hide-and-Seek: All about Location. Hall, Kirsten. 2005. (Beastieville Ser.). (ENG.). 32p. (J). (gr. k-1). pap. 3.95 *(978-0-516-25519-4(3)*, Children's Pr.) Scholastic Library Publishing.

—Let's Trade: All about Trading. Hall, Kirsten. (Beastieville Ser.). (J). (gr. k-1). 2005. (ENG.). 32p. pap. 3.95 *(978-0-516-25520-0(7))*; 2004. 19.50 *(978-0-516-22999-7(0))* Scholastic Library Publishing. (Children's Pr.).

—Little Lies: All about Math. Hall, Kirsten. (Beastieville Ser.). 32p. (J). (gr. k-1). 2004. (ENG.). pap. 3.95 *(978-0-516-24656-7(9))*; 2003. 19.50 *(978-0-516-22896-9(X))* Scholastic Library Publishing. (Children's Pr.).

—A Perfect Day: All about the Five Senses. Hall, Kirsten. (Beastieville Ser.). (J). (gr. k-1). 2005. (ENG.). 32p. pap. 3.95 *(978-0-516-25521-7(5))*; 2004. 19.50 *(978-0-516-24437-2(X))* Scholastic Library Publishing. (Children's Pr.).

—Slider's Pet: All about Nature. Hall, Kirsten. 2004. (Beastieville Ser.). (J). 19.50 *(978-0-516-22898-3(6)*, Children's Pr.) Scholastic Library Publishing.

—Tug-of-War: All about Balance. Hall, Kirsten. 2004. (Beastieville Ser.). 31p. (J). 19.50 *(978-0-516-22899-0(4)*, Children's Pr.) Scholastic Library Publishing.

—Vote for Me: All about Civics. Hall, Kirsten. 2003. (Beastieville Ser.). 32p. (J). 19.50 *(978-0-516-22897-6(8)*, Children's Pr.) Scholastic Library Publishing.

—What a Mess! All about Numbers. Hall, Kirsten. 2004. (Beastieville Ser.). (J). 19.50 *(978-0-516-23670-4(9)*, Children's Pr.) Scholastic Library Publishing.

Lueer, Carmen A. A Bunny Tail. Nees, Diane L. 2012. 44p. pap. 24.95 *(978-1-4626-9191-3(9))* America Star Bks.

Luenebrink, Judy. A Little Girl after God's Own Heart: Learning God's Ways in My Early Days. George, Elizabeth. 2006. 32p. (J). 14.99 *(978-0-7369-1545-8(1))* Harvest Hse. Pubs.

Lueth, Nathan. The Empty Room. Mikkelsen, Jon. 2008. (We Are Heroes Ser.). (ENG.). 40p. (gr. 2-3). lib. bdg. 22.65 *(978-1-4342-0791-3(9)*, Keystone Bks.) Stone Arch Bks.

—The Green Team. Mikkelsen, Jon. 2008. (We Are Heroes Ser.). (ENG.). 40p. (gr. 2-3). lib. bdg. 22.65 *(978-1-4342-0789-0(7)*, Keystone Bks.) Stone Arch Bks.

—Kids Against Hunger. Mikkelsen, Jon. 2008. (We Are Heroes Ser.). (ENG.). 40p. (gr. 2-3). lib. bdg. 22.65 *(978-1-4342-0790-6(0)*, Keystone Bks.) Stone Arch Bks.

—Race for Home. Mikkelsen, Jon. 2008. (We Are Heroes Ser.). (ENG.). 40p. (gr. 2-3). lib. bdg. 22.65 *(978-1-4342-0786-9(2)*, Keystone Bks.) Stone Arch Bks.

—Skateboard Buddy. Mikkelsen, Jon. 2008. (We Are Heroes Ser.). (ENG.). 40p. (gr. 2-3). lib. bdg. 22.65 *(978-1-4342-0788-3(9)*, Keystone Bks.) Stone Arch Bks.

—Storm Shelter. Mikkelsen, Jon. 2008. (We Are Heroes Ser.). (ENG.). 40p. (gr. 2-3). lib. bdg. 22.65 *(978-1-4342-0787-6(0)*, Keystone Bks.) Stone Arch Bks.

Lueth, Nathan, jt. illus. see Buckley, Harriet.

Luevano, Raul. Harriet the Ferret, 1 vol. Gifford, Dorinda. 2009. 20p. pap. 24.95 *(978-1-59129-405-4(3))* America Star Bks.

Lufkin, Raymond. We Were There with the California Forty-Niners. Holt, Stephen & Lewis, Oscar. 2011. 186p. 42.95 *(978-1-258-05988-0(6))* Literary Licensing, LLC.

Lugo, Patrick. Little Monk & the Mantis: A Bug, a Boy, & the Birth of a Kung Fu Legend. Fusco, John. 2012. (ENG.). 32p. (J). (gr. -1-2). 16.95 *(978-0-8048-4221-1(3))* Tuttle Publishing.

Luhrs, Henry. Dale Evans & Danger in Crooked Canyon. Hale, Helen. 2011. 280p. 47.95 *(978-1-258-02056-9(4))* Literary Licensing, LLC.

Luigart-Stayner, Becky & Luigart-Staynes, Becky, photos by. Southern Cakes: Sweet & Irresistible Recipes for Everyday Celebrations. McDermott, Nancie. 2007. (ENG.). 168p. (gr. 8-17). pap. 19.95 *(978-0-8118-5370-5(5))* Chronicle Bks. LLC.

Luigart-Staynes, Becky, jt. photos by see Luigart-Stayner, Becky.

Luisa, Gioffre-Suzuki. Worst Case of Pasketti-Itis. Asselin, Kristine Carlson. 2013. 24p. pap. 12.99 *(978-0-9889617-0-8(9))* 4RV Publishing, LLC.

Luiz, Fernando. Babies Love the Little Things. 2009. (ENG.). 10p. (J). (gr. -1). 7.95 *(978-1-58117-846-3(8)*, Intervisual/Piggy Toes) Bendon, Inc.

—Color Train, Color Train! Kelly, Martin. 2009. 20p. bds. 12.99 *(978-0-8249-1437-0(6)*, Candy Cane Pr.) Ideals Pubns.

—How to Be a Princess: A Girly Girl Book. 2009. 12p. (J). bds. 6.95 *(978-1-58117-850-0(6)*, Intervisual/Piggy Toes) Bendon, Inc.

Luizada, A. Legends of Queen Esther. Simhoni, S. Lask, I. M., tr. 2011. 62p. 36.95 *(978-1-258-09389-1(8))* Literary Licensing, LLC.

Lujan, Tonita. Little Boy with Three Names: Stories of Taos Pueblo. Clark, Ann Nolan. 2005. 75p. (J). (gr. 2-6). reprint ed. pap. 15.00 *(978-0-7567-9717-1(9))* DIANE Publishing Co.

Lukas, Mary. Five Blessings. Drogo, Susette. 2008. 24p. (J). pap. 15.00 *(978-0-9800611-8-5(0))* Orr Bks.

Lukatz, Casey. Coconut's Guide to Life: Life Lessons from a Girl's Best Friend. Chobanian, Elizabeth & American Girl Publishing Staff, eds. 2003. (Coconut Ser.). (ENG.). 32p. (J). 5.95 *(978-1-58485-771-6(4))* American Girl Publishing, Inc.

—Coconut's Guide to Life: Life Lessons from a Girl's Best Friend. Chobanian, Elizabeth, ed. 2003. (Coconut Ser.). 32p. (J). 21.95 *(978-1-58485-772-3(2))* American Girl Publishing, Inc.

—Top-Secret Code Book: Tricky, Fun Codes for You & Your Friends. Maring, Therese, ed. 2005. (American Girl Today Ser.). (ENG.). 32p. (J). (gr. 4-7). per. 5.95 *(978-1-59369-018-2(5)*, American Girl) American Girl Publishing, Inc.

Iukel, Onur. No Veggies for Me. Pierro, Rita. 2011. 32p. pap. 24.95 *(978-1-4626-4554-1(2))* America Star Bks.

Lukesh, Ronald E. My Favorite Dog & Cat Story: My Favorite Dog Story/My Favorite Cat Story. Lukesh, Jean A. 2013. 38p. (J). pap. 14.95 *(978-0-9888021-0-0(4))* Field Mouse Productions.

Lum, Bernice. Attack of the Alien Brain. Hartley, Steve. unabr. ed. 2015. (Oliver Fibbs Ser.: 1). (ENG.). 192p. (J). (gr. 2-5). pap. 8.99 *(978-1-4472-2023-7(4))* Pan Macmillan GBR. Dist: Independent Pubs. Group.

—The Attractive Truth about Magnetism, 1 vol. Swanson, Jennifer. 2012. (LOL Physical Science Ser.). (ENG.). 32p. (gr. 3-4). pap. 8.10 *(978-1-4296-9296-0(0))*; pap. 47.70 *(978-1-4296-9297-7(9)*, Fact Finders); lib. bdg. 26.65 *(978-1-4296-8603-7(0))* Capstone Pr., Inc.

—Everywear. Warwick, Ellen. 2008. (Planet Girl Ser.). (ENG.). 80p. (J). (gr. 5-18). 14.95 *(978-1-55337-799-3(0))* Kids Can Pr., Ltd. CAN. Dist: Univ. of Toronto Pr.

—Fully Woolly. Warwick, Ellen. 2007. (Planet Girl Ser.). (ENG.). 80p. (J). (gr. 5-9). 12.95 *(978-1-55337-798-6(2))* Kids Can Pr., Ltd. CAN. Dist: Univ. of Toronto Pr.

—The Gripping Truth about Forces & Motion, 1 vol. Biskup, Agnieszka. 2012. (LOL Physical Science Ser.). (ENG.). 32p. (gr. 3-4). pap. 8.10 *(978-1-4296-9298-4(7))*; pap. 47.70 *(978-1-4296-9299-1(5)*, Fact Finders); lib. bdg. 26.65 *(978-1-4296-8601-3(4))* Capstone Pr., Inc.

—Injeanuity. Warwick, Ellen. 2006. (Planet Girl Ser.). (ENG.). 80p. (J). (gr. 7-12). 12.95 *(978-1-55337-681-1(1))* Kids Can Pr., Ltd. CAN. Dist: Univ. of Toronto Pr.

—LOL Physical Science. Biskup, Agnieszka et al. 2012. (LOL Physical Science Ser.). (ENG.). 32p. (gr. 3-4). 106.60 *(978-1-4296-9153-6(0)*, Fact Finders) Capstone Pr., Inc.

—LOL Physical Science. Swanson, Jennifer et al. 2012. (LOL Physical Science Ser.). (ENG.). 32p. (gr. 3-4). pap. 190.80 *(978-1-4296-9305-9(3))*; pap. 31.80 *(978-1-4296-9304-2(5))* Capstone Pr., Inc. (Fact Finders).

—Mighty Maddie. Murphy, Stuart J. 2004. (MathStart Ser.). 40p. (J). 15.99 *(978-0-06-053159-1(2))*; (ENG.). (gr. -1-3). pap. 5.99 *(978-0-06-053161-4(4))* HarperCollins Pubs.

Lum, Bernice. Oliver Fibbs Vol. 4: The Clash of the Mega Robots. Hartley, Steve. unabr. ed. 2015. (Oliver Fibbs Ser.: 4). (ENG.). 208p. (J). (gr. 2-5). pap. 8.99 ***(978-1-4472-2032-9(3))*** Pan Macmillan GBR. Dist: Independent Pubs. Group.

—Oliver Fibbs & the Abominable Snow Penguin. Hartley, Steve. unabr. ed. 2015. (Oliver Fibbs Ser.: 3). (ENG.). 208p. (J). (gr. 2-5). pap. 8.99 ***(978-1-4472-2028-2(5))*** Pan Macmillan GBR. Dist: Independent Pubs. Group.

Lum, Bernice. Oliver Fibbs & the Giant Boy-Munching Bugs. Hartley, Steve. unabr. ed. 2015. (Oliver Fibbs Ser.: 2). (ENG.). 192p. (J). (gr. 2-5). pap. 8.99 *(978-1-4472-2024-4(2))* Pan Macmillan GBR. Dist: Independent Pubs. Group.

—The Shocking Truth about Electricity, 1 vol. Swanson, Jennifer Ann. 2012. (LOL Physical Science Ser.). (ENG.). 32p. (gr. 3-4). pap. 8.10 *(978-1-4296-9300-4(2)*, Fact Finders) Capstone Pr., Inc.

—The Shocking Truth about Electricity. Swanson, Jennifer. 2012. (LOL Physical Science Ser.). (ENG.). 32p. (gr. 3-4). pap. 47.70 *(978-1-4296-9301-1(0))*; lib. bdg. 26.65 *(978-1-4296-8602-0(2))* Capstone Pr., Inc. (Fact Finders).

—The Solid Truth about Matter, 1 vol. Weakland, Mark Andrew. 2012. (LOL Physical Science Ser.). (ENG.). 32p. (gr. 3-4). pap. 8.10 *(978-1-4296-9302-8(9)*, Fact Finders) Capstone Pr., Inc.

—The Solid Truth about Matter. Weakland, Mark. 2012. (LOL Physical Science Ser.). (ENG.). 32p. (gr. 3-4). pap. 47.70 *(978-1-4296-9303-5(7))*; lib. bdg. 26.65 *(978-1-4296-8427-9(5))* Capstone Pr., Inc. (Fact Finders).

—Stuff to Hold Your Stuff. Warwick, Ellen. 2006. (Planet Girl Ser.). (ENG.). 80p. (J). (gr. 6-18). 12.95 *(978-1-55337-745-0(1))* Kids Can Pr., Ltd. CAN. Dist: Univ. of Toronto Pr.

—3 Little Firefighters. Murphy, Stuart J. 2003. (MathStart 1 Ser.). (ENG.). 40p. (J). (gr. -1-3). pap. 5.99 *(978-0-06-000120-9(8))* HarperCollins Pubs.

Lum, Bernice. Stuff for Your Space. Lum, Bernice, tr. Warwick, Ellen. 2004. (Kids Can Do It Ser.). (ENG.). 40p. (J). (gr. 4-6). 6.95 *(978-1-55337-399-5(5))* Kids Can Pr., Ltd. CAN. Dist: Univ. of Toronto Pr.

Lum, J. Checkers & Dot at the Beach. Torres, J. 2013. (J). E-Book *(978-1-77049-448-0(0))* Tundra Bks.

—Checkers & Dot at the Beach. Torres, J. 2013. (Checkers & Dot Ser.). (ENG.). 16p. (J). (— 1). bds. 7.95 *(978-1-77049-444-2(8)*, Tundra Bks.) Tundra Bks. CAN. Dist: Penguin Random Hse., LLC.

—Checkers & Dot at the Zoo. Torres, J. 2012. (Checkers & Dot Ser.). (ENG.). 16p. (J). (gr. k — 1). bds. 7.95 *(978-1-77049-442-8(1)*, Tundra Bks.) Tundra Bks. CAN. Dist: Penguin Random Hse., LLC.

—Checkers & Dot on the Farm. Torres, J. 2013. (Checkers & Dot Ser.). (ENG.). 16p. (J). (— 1). bds. 7.95 *(978-1-77049-443-5(X)*, Tundra Bks.) Tundra Bks. CAN. Dist: Penguin Random Hse., LLC.

Lumb, Steve. Dance to the Beat. Afzal, Uz. 2005. (Collins Big Cat Ser.). (ENG.). 320p. (J). pap. 5.99 *(978-0-00-718576-4(6))* HarperCollins Pubs. Ltd. GBR. Dist: Independent Pubs. Group.

Lumb, Steve, photos by. My Party. Kelly, Maoliosa. 2005. (Collins Big Cat Ser.). (ENG.). 16p. (J). pap. 5.99 *(978-0-00-718533-7(2))* HarperCollins Pubs. Ltd. GBR. Dist: Independent Pubs. Group.

Lumer, Marc. Babel. Burston, Chaim & Naiditch, Dov. 2016. (J). ***(978-1-68115-514-2(1))*** Behrman Hse., Inc.

Lumer, Marc. Hashem Is Truly Everywhere. Altein, Chani. Rosenfeld, D. L. & Leverton, Yossi, eds. 2011. 28p. (J). 12.95 *(978-1-929628-57-5(9))* Hachai Publishing.

—The Search for the Stones. Blitz, Shmuel & Zakon, Miriam Stark. 2009. 96p. (J). *(978-1-4226-0934-7(0)*, Shaar Pr.) Mesorah Pubns., Ltd.

—The Torah Book of Opposites. Segal, Nechamy. 2012. 12p. (J). pap. 7.95 *(978-1-929628-67-4(6))* Hachai Publishing.

—When Miracles Happened- Wondrous Stories of Tzaddikim. 2009. 22p. (J). *(978-1-56871-484-4(X))* Targum Pr., Inc.

Lumley, Stef, photos by. London Sticker Book. Dickins, Rosie. Clarke, Phillip, ed. 2006. (Usborne Sticker Bks.). 15p. (J). (gr. 2-5). pap. 8.99 *(978-0-7945-1284-2(4)*, Usborne) EDC Publishing.

Lumsden, Colin. Apostles. 2003. (Bible Colour & Learn Ser.). 32p. pap. 2.50 *(978-1-903087-51-0(1))* DayOne Pubns. GBR. Dist: Send The Light Distribution LLC.

—Hebrews Men of Faith. 2003. (Bible Colour & Learn Ser.). 32p. pap. 2.50 *(978-1-903087-52-7(X))* DayOne Pubns. GBR. Dist: Send The Light Distribution LLC.

—John the Baptist. 2003. (Bible Colour & Learn Ser.). 32p. pap. 2.50 *(978-1-903087-44-2(9))* DayOne Pubns. GBR. Dist: Send The Light Distribution LLC.

—Miracles of Jesus. 2003. (Bible Colour & Learn Ser.). 32p. pap. 2.50 *(978-1-903087-48-0(1))* DayOne Pubns. GBR. Dist: Send The Light Distribution LLC.

—Parables of Jesus. 2003. (Bible Colour & Learn Ser.). 32p. pap. 2.50 *(978-1-903087-47-3(3))* DayOne Pubns. GBR. Dist: Send The Light Distribution LLC.

—People in the Life of Jesus. 2003. (Bible Colour & Learn Ser.). 32p. pap. 2.50 *(978-1-903087-49-7(X))* DayOne Pubns. GBR. Dist: Send The Light Distribution LLC.

—People in the Life of Paul. 2003. (Bible Colour & Learn Ser.). 32p. pap. 2.50 *(978-1-903087-50-3(3))* DayOne Pubns. GBR. Dist: Send The Light Distribution LLC.

—Story of Mary. 2003. (Bible Colour & Learn Ser.). 32p. pap. 2.50 *(978-1-903087-43-5(0))* DayOne Pubns. GBR. Dist: Send The Light Distribution LLC.

—Story of Paul. 2003. (Bible Colour & Learn Ser.). 32p. pap. 2.50 *(978-1-903087-46-6(5))* DayOne Pubns. GBR. Dist: Send The Light Distribution LLC.

—Story of Peter. 2003. (Bible Colour & Learn Ser.). 32p. pap. 2.50 *(978-1-903087-45-9(7))* DayOne Pubns. GBR. Dist: Send The Light Distribution LLC.

Lumsden, Matt. Crow No More. Burggraaf, Deborah. 2011. 28p. (J). pap. 10.95 *(978-0-9845161-8-6(2))* Protective Hands Communications.

Luna, Jose'. El Queso y la Rata: With English Subtitles. Luna, Jose'. 2006. (J). per. *(978-1-934379-00-4(X))* Printmedia Bks.

Luna, Lauren. The Stories True of Gabby Cockatoo. Houston, Alecia. 2010. 24p. pap. 11.25 *(978-1-60911-446-6(9)*, Strategic Bk. Publishing) Strategic Book Publishing & Rights Agency (SBPRA).

Luna, Margarita. Angela en el Cielo de Saturno. Baranda, Maria. rev. ed. 2006. (Castillo de la Lectura Naranja Ser.). (SPA & ENG.). 131p. (J). (gr. 4-7). pap. 7.95 *(978-968-5920-86-5(9))* Castillo, Ediciones, S. A. de C. V. MEX. Dist: Macmillan.

—La Isla de los Pollos. Estrada, Jorge Antonio. rev. ed. 2006. (Castillo de la Lectura Blanca Ser.). (SPA & ENG.). 48p. (J). (gr. k-2). pap. 6.95 *(978-968-5920-38-4(9))* Castillo, Ediciones, S. A. de C. V. MEX. Dist: Macmillan.

Luna, Tom & Alvarez, Laura. The Spots on the Jaguar: A Counting Book. Luna, Tom. 2005. (SPA & ENG.). 20p. (J). *(978-0-9716580-4-2(8))* Lectura Bks.

Lunch Lab LLC, Lunch Lab. Nelly Nitpick, Kid Food Critic. Candlewick Press, Candlewick. 2015. (Fizzy's Lunch Lab Ser.). (ENG.). 48p. (J). (gr. 1-4). pap. 5.99 *(978-0-7636-6885-3(0))* Candlewick Pr.

Lunch Lab Staff. Fizzy's Lunch Lab: Super Supper Throwdown. Candlewick Press Staff. 2014. (Fizzy's Lunch Lab Ser.). (ENG.). 64p. (J). (gr. 1-4). pap. 5.99 *(978-0-7636-6883-9(4))* Candlewick Pr.

Lund, Brian. G Is for Golden Boy: A Manitoba Alphabet. Verstraete, Larry. 2009. (Discover Canada Province by Province Ser.). (ENG.). 40p. (J). (gr. k-8). 17.95 *(978-1-58536-364-3(2))* Sleeping Bear Pr.

Lund, Nancy M. Chippy: The sea lion that lost its Way. Haller, Christine A. 2006. 20p. (J). 11.95 *(978-0-9771129-0-6(X))* Oxbow Bks.

Lundquist, David R., photos by. Clarabelle: Making Milk & So Much More. Peterson, Cris. 2013. (ENG.). 32p. (J). (gr. 4-6). pap. 7.95 *(978-1-62091-590-5(1))* Boyds Mills Pr.

—Fantastic Farm Machines. Peterson, Cris. 2006. (ENG.). 32p. (J). (gr. -1-3). 17.95 *(978-1-59078-271-2(2))* Boyds Mills Pr.

—Seed, Soil, Sun: Earth's Recipe for Food. Peterson, Cris. (ENG.). 32p. (J). (gr. k-4). 2012. pap. 7.95 *(978-1-59078-947-6(4))*; 2010. 17.95 *(978-1-59078-713-7(7))* Boyds Mills Pr.

Lundquist, Mary. Mission: Back to School: Top Secret Info for Rookie Students. Hood, Susan. 2016. (J). ***(978-0-375-97349-9(4))*** Random Hse., Inc.

Lundquist, Mary. Mission: New Baby. Hood, Susan. 2015. (ENG.). 32p. (J). (gr. -1-2). 16.99 *(978-0-385-37672-3(3))*; lib. bdg. 19.99 *(978-0-375-97324-6(9))* Random Hse. Children's Bks. (Random Hse. Bks. for Young Readers).

Lundquist, Mary. One Little, Two Little, Three Little Children. DiPucchio, Kelly. 2016. 32p. (J). (gr. -1-3). 17.99 ***(978-0-06-234866-1(3))*** HarperCollins Pubs.

Lundquist, Mary. Cat & Bunny. Lundquist, Mary. 2015. (ENG.). 32p. (J). (gr. -1-3). 17.99 *(978-0-06-228780-9(X))* HarperCollins Pubs.

Lundquist, Robert. Heather's Amazing Discovery: A True Story of Paleontology. Griffiths, Deborah. 2013. pap. *(978-0-9696612-0-7(7))* Courtenay & District Museum.

Lundy, Miranda, et al. Sacred Number: The Secret Quality of Quantities. Lundy, Miranda & Mcnaughton, Phoebe. 2005. (Wooden Bks.). (ENG.). 64p. 13.00 *(978-0-8027-1456-5(0))* Walker & Co.

Lunelli, Giuliano. Puss in Boots. Perrault, Charles. Bell, Anthea, tr. 2003. 24p. (J). (gr. 3-5). reprint ed. 18.00 *(978-0-7567-6600-9(1))* DIANE Publishing Co.

Lunn, Corey. Peekaboo Presents. Night & Day Studios. 2015. (Peekaboo Ser.). (ENG.). 20p. (J). (— 1). bds. 7.99 ***(978-0-7636-7567-7(9))*** Candlewick Pr.

Lunn, Naomi. The Fight Before Christmas. McCormack, Chris. 2013. 44p. (J). pap. *(978-0-9572875-4-9(2))* Batmack Ltd.

Lunzer, Lee. Betty Grable Paper Dolls. Lunzer, Lee. 2007. (ENG.). 16p. pap. 12.00 *(978-0-9790668-7-0(5))* Paper Studio Pr.

Lunzer, Lee, jt. illus. see Valliant, Regina.

Luo, Keyi. Colorful Childhood. 2004. (CHI.). (J). pap. 27.50 *(978-1-932002-47-8(2)*, Cozy Publishing Hse.) Cozy Graphics Corp.

Luo, Shiyin Sean. By the Light of the Moon. Goss, Leon. 2005. (J). pap. *(978-1-933156-12-5(0))*; per. 16.99 *(978-1-933156-05-7(8))* GSVQ Publishing. (VisionQuest Kids).

Lupton, David. Goodbye Brecken. 2012. 32p. (J). *(978-1-4338-1289-7(4))*; pap. *(978-1-4338-1290-3(8))* American Psychological Assn. (Magination Pr.).

Luque, Paco Diaz. Hawkeye: Blindspot. 2011. (ENG.). 136p. (YA). (gr. 8-17). pap. 15.99 *(978-0-7851-5601-7(1))* Marvel Worldwide, Inc.

Luraschi, Anna. Christmas Poems. Taplin, Sam. 2006. (Christmas Poems Ser.). 95p. (J). 12.99 *(978-0-7945-1471-6(5)*, Usborne) EDC Publishing.

—Illustrated Stories for Christmas. Chandler, Samuel. Spatz, Caroline, ed. 2010. (Illustrated Stories Ser.). 351p. (YA). (gr. 3-18). 14.99 *(978-0-7945-2687-0(X)*, Usborne) EDC Publishing.

—The Nutcracker. 2007. 24p. (J). 9.99 *(978-0-7945-1515-7(0)*, Usborne) EDC Publishing.

—The Usborne Book of Bedtime Rhymes. Taplin, Sam. 2008. (Usborne Book Of... Ser.). 12p. (J). (gr. -1-3). bds. 12.99 *(978-0-7945-1898-1(2)*, Usborne) EDC Publishing.

Lush, Debbie. Hot Like Fire. Bloom, Valerie. 2009. (ENG.). 192p. (J). (gr. 4-7). pap. 11.95 *(978-0-7475-9973-9(4))* Bloomsbury Publishing Plc GBR. Dist: Independent Pubs. Group.

Lustig, Loretta. The Little Red Hen: A Tale about Cooperation. 2006. (J). 6.99 *(978-1-59939-018-5(3))* Cornerstone Pr.

Luthardt, Kevin. The Vowel Family: A Tale of Lost Letters. Walker, Sally M. 2008. (ENG.). 32p. (J). (gr. k-3). lib. bdg. 16.95 *(978-0-8225-7982-3(0))* Lerner Publishing Group.

—Zoom!, 1 vol. Adams, Diane. (ENG.). 32p. (J). 2013. (gr. -1-1). 7.95 *(978-1-56145-683-3(7))*; 2005. (gr. k-1). 15.95 *(978-1-56145-332-0(3))* Peachtree Pubs.

Luthardt, Kevin. Flying!, 1 vol. Luthardt, Kevin. (ENG.). 32p. (J). (gr. -1-1). 2013. 7.95 *(978-1-56145-724-3(8))*; 2009. 15.95 *(978-1-56145-430-3(3))* Peachtree Pubs.

—Larabee, 1 vol. Luthardt, Kevin. (ENG.). 32p. (J). 2009. (gr. -1-1). pap. 7.95 *(978-1-56145-482-2(6))*; 2004. (gr. k-1). 15.95 *(978-1-56145-300-9(5))* Peachtree Pubs.

—Peep!, 1 vol. Luthardt, Kevin. (ENG.). 36p. (J). 2013. (gr. -1-1). 7.95 *(978-1-56145-682-6(9))*; 2003. (gr. k-1). 15.95 *(978-1-56145-046-6(4))* Peachtree Pubs.

—When Edgar Met Cecil, 1 vol. Luthardt, Kevin. 2013. (ENG.). 32p. (J). (gr. -1-3). 15.95 *(978-1-56145-706-9(X))* Peachtree Pubs.

Luthi, Morgan. Wall- E: Out There. Carlson, Bryce. 2010. (ENG.). 112p. (J). (gr. 3-6). pap. 9.99 *(978-1-60886-568-0(1))* Boom! Studios.

—Wall E Vol. 1: Recharge. Wheeler, Shannon & Torres, J. 2010. (ENG.). 112p. (J). 24.99 *(978-1-60886-554-3(1))* Boom! Studios.

Luthi, Morgan & Barks, Carl. Wall-E Vol. 1: Recharge. Wheeler, Shannon & Barks, Carl. Torres, J. 2010. (ENG.). 112p. (J). pap. 9.99 *(978-1-60886-512-3(6))* Boom! Studios.

Luthringer, Melisande. On the Farm: Interactive Fun with Fold-Out Play Scene, Reusable Stickers, & Punch-out, Stand-up Figures! Walter Foster Custom Creative Team. 2014. (Sticker, Punch-Out, & Play! Ser.). (ENG.). 12p. (J). (gr. -1-1). pap. 6.99 *(978-1-60058-718-4(6))* Quarto Publishing Group USA.

Lutz, Nancie Anne. Patsy & Freckles Make Christmas Cookies. Lutz, Nancie Anne. 2005. 25p. (J). *(978-0-9760064-1-1(3))* Dollworks.

—Patsy Ann Back Again. Lutz, Nancie Anne. 2005. 25p. (J). pap. 14.50 *(978-0-9760064-0-4(5))* Dollworks.

—Patsy Ann Paperdoll: Including Photographs of Patsy's Original Clothes. Lutz, Nancie Anne. 2005. 10p. (J). 14.50 *(978-0-9760064-2-8(1))* Dollworks.

Luu, Cindy. The Knot Guide for the Groom. Roney, Carley. 2005. (ENG.). 144p. (gr. 8-17). per. 14.95 *(978-0-8118-4614-1(8))* Chronicle Bks. LLC.

—The Knot Guide for the Mother of the Bride. Roney, Carley. 2005. (ENG.). 108p. (gr. 8-17). 16.95 *(978-0-8118-4636-3(9))* Chronicle Bks. LLC.

Lux, Eldon. Iris Wall, Cracker Cowgirl, 1 vol. Rey, Carol. 2012. (ENG.). 32p. (J). (gr. k-3). 16.99 *(978-1-4556-1525-4(0))* Pelican Publishing Co., Inc.

Luxbacher, Irene. The Imaginary Garden. Larsen, Andrew. 2009. (ENG.). 32p. (J). (gr. -1-2). 16.95 *(978-1-55453-279-7(5))* Kids Can Pr., Ltd. CAN. Dist: Univ. of Toronto Pr.

Luxbacher, Irene. The Jumbo Book of Art. Luxbacher, Irene. 2003. (Jumbo Bks.). (ENG.). 208p. (J). (gr. 3-8). 14.95 *(978-1-55074-762-1(2))* Kids Can Pr., Ltd. CAN. Dist: Univ. of Toronto Pr.

—The Jumbo Book of Outdoor Art. Luxbacher, Irene. 2006. (Jumbo Bks.). (ENG.). 144p. (J). (gr. 4-7). 16.95 *(978-1-55337-680-4(3))* Kids Can Pr., Ltd. CAN. Dist: Univ. of Toronto Pr.

—Mattoo, Let's Play! Luxbacher, Irene. 2010. (ENG.). 32p. (J). (gr. -1-2). 16.95 *(978-1-55453-424-1(0))* Kids Can Pr., Ltd. CAN. Dist: Univ. of Toronto Pr.

—123 I Can Build! Luxbacher, Irene. 2009. (Starting Art Ser.). (ENG.). 24p. (J). (gr. -1-2). 14.95 *(978-1-55453-315-2(5))*; pap. 6.95 *(978-1-55453-316-9(3))* Kids Can Pr., Ltd. CAN. Dist: Univ. of Toronto Pr.

—123 I Can Collage! Luxbacher, Irene. 2009. (Starting Art Ser.). (ENG.). 24p. (J). (gr. -1-2). 14.95 *(978-1-55453-313-8(9))*; pap. 6.95 *(978-1-55453-314-5(7))* Kids Can Pr., Ltd. CAN. Dist: Univ. of Toronto Pr.

—123 I Can Draw! Luxbacher, Irene. 2008. (Starting Art Ser.). (ENG.). 24p. (J). (gr. -1-3). 14.95 *(978-1-55453-039-7(3))*; pap. 5.95 *(978-1-55453-152-3(7))* Kids Can Pr., Ltd. CAN. Dist: Univ. of Toronto Pr.

—123 I Can Make Prints! Luxbacher, Irene. 2008. (Starting Art Ser.). (ENG.). 24p. (J). (gr. -1-3). 14.95 *(978-1-55453-040-3(7))*; pap. 5.95 *(978-1-55453-153-0(5))* Kids Can Pr., Ltd. CAN. Dist: Univ. of Toronto Pr.

—123 I Can Paint! Luxbacher, Irene. 2007. (Starting Art Ser.). (ENG.). 24p. (J). (gr. -1-2). 14.95 *(978-1-55453-037-3(7))*; pap. 5.95 *(978-1-55453-150-9(0))* Kids Can Pr., Ltd. CAN. Dist: Univ. of Toronto Pr.

—123 I Can Sculpt! Luxbacher, Irene. 2007. (Starting Art Ser.). (ENG.). 24p. (J). (gr. -1-3). pap. 5.95 *(978-1-55453-151-6(9))* Kids Can Pr., Ltd. CAN. Dist: Univ. of Toronto Pr.

Luxich, Matt. Invasion of the Gym Class Zombies. Nickel, Scott. 2008. (Graphic Sparks Ser.). (ENG.). 40p. (gr. 1-3). pap. 5.95 *(978-1-4342-0503-2(7))*; lib. bdg. 22.65 *(978-1-4342-0453-0(7))* Stone Arch Bks. (Graphic Sparks).

—Secret of the Summer School Zombies, 1 vol. Nickel, Scott. 2008. (School Zombies Ser.). (ENG.). 40p. (gr. 1-3). 22.65 *(978-1-4342-0760-9(9))*; pap. 5.95 *(978-1-4342-0856-9(7))* Stone Arch Bks. (Graphic Sparks).

—Ultimate Puzzle Challenge: Mind Mashers. Hovanec, Helene. 2010. (ENG.). 96p. (J). (gr. 2-5). pap. 5.95 *(978-1-4027-6204-8(6))* Sterling Publishing Co., Inc.

Luykx, Th. D. Oil Comes to Us. Wyler, Rose & McSpadden, Warren W. 2011. 32p. pap. 35.95 *(978-1-258-10512-9(8))* Literary Licensing, LLC.

LV Studio. Pat the Zoo (Pat the Bunny) Golden Books. 2012. (Touch-And-Feel Ser.). (ENG.). 16p. (J). (gr. k — 1). 14.99 *(978-0-307-97797-7(8),* Golden Bks.) Random Hse. Children's Bks.

LV Studio Staff, jt. illus. see Golden Books Staff.

Lý, Thu Hà. Indebted As Lord Chom/No Nhu Chua Chom: The Legend of the Forbidden Street. Song Hà. Smith, William, tr. from VIE. 2006. (ENG & VIE.). 32p. (J). (gr. 1-4). 16.95 *(978-0-9701654-6-6(3))* East West Discovery Pr.

Ly, Youme Nguy?n. Peace, Bugs, & Understanding: An Adventure in Sibling Harmony. Silver, Gail. 2014. (ENG.). 48p. (J). (gr. -1-3). 16.95 *(978-1-937006-63-1(8),* Plum Blossom Bks.) Parallax Pr.

Lyall, Dennis. The American Revolution. Rife, Douglas M. & Capaldi, Gina. 2009. (ENG.). 44p. (J). (gr. 3-17). 19.99 *(978-1-58476-612-4(3))* Innovative Kids.

—Letters for Freedom: the Civil War. Rife, Douglas M. & Capaldi, Gina. 2011. (ENG.). 44p. (J). (gr. 3-17). 19.99 *(978-1-60169-018-0(5))* Innovative Kids.

—Marshall: A Nantucket Sea Rescue. Stewart, Whitney. 2008. (ENG.). 32p. (J). (gr. -1-2). 2.95 *(978-1-59249-856-7(6))*; 6.95 *(978-1-59249-855-0(8))*; 10.95 *(978-1-59249-857-4(4))* Soundprints.

—The Upside-Down Voyage. Wuffson, Don L. 2005. (J). *(978-1-59336-334-5(6))*; pap. *(978-1-59336-335-2(4))* Mondo Publishing.

Lye, Michael. Choices: Stories for Assembly & P. S. H. E. Aspland, G. 2013. (ENG.). 64p. pap. 15.95 *(978-1-85741-077-8(7))* Southgate Pubs. GBR. Dist: Parkwest Pubns., Inc.

—Geography in the School Grounds. Hare, Ralph. 2013. (ENG.). 72p. pap. 15.95 *(978-1-85741-023-5(8))* Southgate Pubs. GBR. Dist: Parkwest Pubns., Inc.

—Home Stories: Talking about Personal, Social & Health Issues at Home. Aspland, Gordon. 2013. (ENG.). 30p. pap. 11.95 *(978-1-85741-130-0(7))* Southgate Pubs. GBR. Dist: Parkwest Pubns., Inc.

Lyford, Cabot. Arthur the Moose. Lyford, Cabot. l.t. ed. 2004. 32p. (J). lib. bdg. *(978-0-9748145-0-6(4))* Castlebay, Inc.

Lyle, Avis. The Bumpy Pumpkin. Inman, George, Jr. et al. 2004. 18p. (J). 8.95 *(978-0-9754696-0-6(6))* Bumpy Pumpkin.

Lyle, Kevin, jt. illus. see Chaisty, Chris.

Lyles, Christopher. Good-Bye, Jeepers: What to Expect When Your Pet Dies, 1 vol. Loewen, Nancy. 2011. (Life's Challenges Ser.). (ENG.). 24p. (J). (gr. 2-3). lib. bdg. 25.32 *(978-1-4048-6680-5(9),* Nonfiction Picture Bks.) Picture Window Bks.

—Once upon a Time: Writing Your Own Fairy Tale, 1 vol. Loewen, Nancy. 2009. (Writer's Toolbox Ser.). (ENG.). 32p. (gr. 2-4). lib. bdg. 26.65 *(978-1-4048-5335-5(9))*; pap. 8.95 *(978-1-4048-5336-2(7))* Picture Window Bks. (Nonfiction Picture Bks.).

—Saying Good-Bye to Uncle Joe: What to Expect When Someone You Love Dies, 1 vol. Loewen, Nancy. 2011. (Life's Challenges Ser.). (ENG.). 24p. (gr. 2-3). lib. bdg. 25.32 *(978-1-4048-6677-5(9),* Nonfiction Picture Bks.) Picture Window Bks.

—Share a Scare: Writing Your Own Scary Story, 1 vol. Loewen, Nancy. 2009. (Writer's Toolbox Ser.). (ENG.). 32p. (gr. 2-4). pap. 8.95 *(978-1-4048-5700-1(1),* Nonfiction Picture Bks.) Picture Window Bks.

—Show Me a Story: Writing Your Own Picture Book, 1 vol. Loewen, Nancy. 2009. (Writer's Toolbox Ser.). (ENG.). 32p. (gr. 2-4). pap. 8.95 *(978-1-4048-5342-3(1))*; lib. bdg. 26.65 *(978-1-4048-5341-6(3))* Picture Window Bks. (Nonfiction Picture Bks.).

—Sincerely Yours: Writing Your Own Letter, 1 vol. Loewen, Nancy. 2009. (Writer's Toolbox Ser.). (ENG.). 32p. (gr. 2-4). pap. 8.95 *(978-1-4048-5339-3(1))*; lib. bdg. 26.65 *(978-1-4048-5338-6(3))* Picture Window Bks. (Nonfiction Picture Bks.).

—Words, Wit, & Wonder: Writing Your Own Poem, 1 vol. Loewen, Nancy. 2010. (Writer's Toolbox Ser.). (ENG.). 32p. (gr. 2-4). pap. 8.95 *(978-1-4048-5345-4(6),* Nonfiction Picture Bks.) Picture Window Bks.

Lyles, Christopher, et al. Writer's Toolbox: Learn How to Write Letters, Fairy Tales, Scary Stories, Journals, Poems, & Reports, 1 vol. Loewen, Nancy. 2009. (Writer's Toolbox Ser.). (ENG.). 192p. (gr. 2-4). pap. 14.95 *(978-1-4048-5905-0(5),* Nonfiction Picture Bks.) Picture Window Bks.

Lyles, Christopher & Ouren, Todd. It's All about You: Writing Your Own Journal, 1 vol. Loewen, Nancy. 2009. (Writer's Toolbox Ser.). (ENG.). 32p. (gr. 2-4). pap. 8.95 *(978-1-4048-5698-1(6))*; lib. bdg. 26.65 *(978-1-4048-5520-5(3))* Picture Window Bks. (Nonfiction Picture Bks.).

Lyles, Christopher, jt. illus. see Beacon, Dawn.

Lyles, Christopher, jt. illus. see Doerrfeld, Cori.

Lyman, Mitzi. The Reading Rabbit. Yager, Jan. 32p. (J). 2014. (ENG.). 25.95 *(978-1-938998-00-3(6))*; 2013. pap. 17.95 *(978-1-938998-01-0(4))* Hannacroix Creek Bks., Inc.

Lyn, Jami. Cabo & Coral Go Surfing! Wahn, Udo. 2007. 48p. (J). pap. 17.95 *(978-0-615-17598-0(8))* Caboandcoral.com.

Lynch, Casey. Mighty Mike Builds a Nature Trail. Lynch, Kelly. 2011. (Mighty Mike Ser.). 32p. (gr. -1-2). 28.50 *(978-1-61641-130-5(9),* Looking Glass Library) ABDO Publishing Co.

—Mighty Mike Does What's Right! Lynch, Kelly. 2011. (Mighty Mike Ser.). 32p. (gr. -1-2). 28.50 *(978-1-61641-131-2(7),* Looking Glass Library) ABDO Publishing Co.

Lynch, Dan. Kid Scripts: Just What the Doctor Ordered. Kachmann, Rudy. 2005. (ENG.). 48p. (J). spiral bd. 12.95 *(978-1-893270-38-1(6))* Evangel Author Services.

Lynch, Emily S. Talking Is Hard for Me! Encouraging Communication in Children with Speech-Language Difficulties. Reinert, Linda M. 2013. 54p. pap. 18.95 *(978-1-60613-192-3(3))* Woodbine Hse.

Lynch, Jason. Worthwhile. Kirkpatrick, Taylor. 2003. 32p. (J). 15.95 *(978-0-9725420-0-5(0))* Chapman Pr., LLC.

Lynch, Josh, jt. illus. see Gray, Maureen.

Lynch, Kelly. Mighty Mike Builds a Ball Field. Lynch, Casey. 2011. (Mighty Mike Ser.). 32p. (gr. -1-2). 28.50 *(978-1-61641-128-2(7),* Looking Glass Library) ABDO Publishing Co.

—Mighty Mike Builds a Library. Lynch, Casey. 2011. (Mighty Mike Ser.). 32p. (gr. -1-2). 28.50 *(978-1-61641-129-9(5),* Looking Glass Library) ABDO Publishing Co.

—Mighty Mike Repairs a Playground. Lynch, Casey. 2011. (Mighty Mike Ser.). 32p. (gr. -1-2). 28.50 *(978-1-61641-132-9(5),* Looking Glass Library) ABDO Publishing Co.

—Mighty Mike Saves a School Bus. Lynch, Casey. 2011. (Mighty Mike Ser.). 32p. (gr. -1-2). 28.50 *(978-1-61641-133-6(3),* Looking Glass Library) ABDO Publishing Co.

Lynch, P. J. The Bee-Man of Orn. Stockton, Frank Richard. 2006. 44p. (J). (gr. k-4). reprint ed. 18.00 *(978-1-4223-5505-3(5))* DIANE Publishing Co.

—A Christmas Carol. Dickens, Charles. 2006. (ENG.). 160p. (Orig.). (J). (gr. 5-6). 19.99 *(978-0-7636-3120-8(5))* Candlewick Pr.

Lynch, P. J. The Christmas Miracle of Jonathan Toomey. Wojciechowski, Susan. 2015. (ENG.). 40p. (J). (gr. 1-4). 17.99 ***(978-0-7636-7822-7(8))*** Candlewick Pr.

Lynch, P. J. The Gift of the Magi. Henry, O. 2008. (ENG.). 40p. (J). (gr. 5-9). 15.99 *(978-0-7636-3530-5(8))* Candlewick Pr.

—Grandad's Prayers of the Earth. Wood, Douglas. 2009. 32p. pap. 6.99 *(978-0-7636-1865-0(9))*; (ENG.). (J). (gr. 1-4). pap. 7.99 *(978-0-7636-4675-2(X))* Candlewick Pr.

—Grandad's Prayers of the Earth. Wood, Douglas. 2004. 28p. (J). (gr. k-4). reprint ed. 17.00 *(978-0-7567-7101-0(3))* DIANE Publishing Co.

—Lincoln & His Boys. Wells, Rosemary. 2008. (ENG.). 96p. (J). (gr. 3-7). 16.99 *(978-0-7636-3723-1(8))* Candlewick Pr.

—Mysterious Traveler. Peet, Mal & Graham, Elspeth. 2013. (ENG.). 48p. (J). (gr. k-3). 15.99 *(978-0-7636-6232-5(1))* Candlewick Pr.

—No One but You. Wood, Douglas. 2011. (ENG.). 32p. (J). (gr. 1-4). 17.99 *(978-0-7636-3848-1(X))* Candlewick Pr.

—The Snow Queen. Andersen, Hans Christian. 2014. Orig. Title: Snedronningen. (ENG.). 48p. (J). (gr. k-2). pap. 10.99 *(978-1-84270-901-6(1))* Andersen Pr. GBR. Dist: Independent Pubs. Group.

—The Steadfast Tin Soldier. Andersen, Hans Christian & Lewis, Naomi. 2005.Tr. of Standhaftige Tinsoldat. (ENG.). 32p. (J). (gr. -1-4). pap. 11.99 *(978-1-84270-443-1(5))* Andersen Pr. GBR. Dist: Independent Pubs. Group.

—The Story of Britain from the Norman Conquest to the European Union. Dillon, Patrick. 2011. (ENG.). 352p. (J). (gr. 5-18). 21.99 *(978-0-7636-5122-0(2))* Candlewick Pr.

—When Jessie Came Across the Sea. Hest, Amy. 2003. (ENG.). 40p. (J). (gr. 1-4). pap. 6.99 *(978-0-7636-1274-0(X))* Candlewick Pr.

Lynch, P. J. The Boy Who Fell off the Mayflower, or John Howland's Good Fortune. Lynch, P. J. 2015. (ENG.). 64p. (J). (gr. 2-5). 17.99 ***(978-0-7636-6584-5(3))*** Candlewick Pr.

Lynch, Stephanie. The Tale of Squabbit. Young, Rachel & Young, Jackie. 2011. 42p. pap. 15.00 *(978-1-60911-360-5(8),* Eloquent Bks.) Strategic Book Publishing & Rights Agency (SBPRA).

Lynch, Tara. Mister Cool. Jones, Birdy. 2015. (ENG.). 34p. (J). (gr. 1-4). 16.95 *(978-1-57687-719-7(1),* powerHouse Bks.) powerHouse Cultural Entertainment, Inc.

Lynch, Todd, jt. illus. see Breckenridge, Trula.

Lynch, Tom. Around the World. Coy, John & Reonegro, Antonio. 2005. (ENG.). 32p. (J). (gr. 1-7). 17.95 *(978-1-58430-244-5(5))* Lee & Low Bks., Inc.

Lynch, Wayne. Baby Fox, 1 vol. Lang, Aubrey. 2003. (ENG.). 32p. (J). (gr. k-3). pap. *(978-1-55041-724-1(X))* Fitzhenry & Whiteside, Ltd.

—Baby Sea Turtle, 1 vol. Lang, Aubrey. 2007. (ENG.). 32p. (J). (gr. -1-3). *(978-1-55041-728-9(2))*; pap. *(978-1-55041-746-3(0))* Fitzhenry & Whiteside, Ltd.

Lynch, Wayne, photos by. Baby Black Bear, 1 vol. Lang, Aubrey. 2008. (ENG., 32p. (J). pap. *(978-1-55455-097-5(1))* Fitzhenry & Whiteside, Ltd.

—Baby Elephant, 1 vol. Lang, Aubrey. 2003. (ENG., 36p. (J). (gr. k-3). *(978-1-55041-715-9(0))* Fitzhenry & Whiteside, Ltd.

—Baby Fox. Lang, Aubrey. 2003. (Nature Babies Ser.). 36p. (J). (gr. -1-2). lib. bdg. 10.21 *(978-0-613-94173-0(X),* Turtleback) Turtleback Bks.

—Baby Grizzly, 1 vol. Lang, Aubrey. 2006. (Nature Babies Ser.). (ENG., (J). (gr. -1-3). 36p. 16.95 *(978-1-55041-577-3(8),* 1550415778); 32p. pap. 6.95 *(978-1-55041-579-7(4),* 1550415794) Fitzhenry & Whiteside, Ltd. CAN. Dist: Midpoint Trade Bks., Inc.

—Baby Ground Squirrel, 1 vol. Lang, Aubrey. 2004. (ENG., (J). (gr. k-3). 36p. pap. *(978-1-55041-799-9(1))*; 32p. *(978-1-55041-797-5(5))* Fitzhenry & Whiteside, Ltd.

—Baby Koala, 1 vol. Lang, Aubrey. 2004. (ENG., 36p. (J). pap. *(978-1-55041-876-7(9))* Fitzhenry & Whiteside, Ltd.

—Baby Koala, 1 vol. Lang, Aubrey. 2004. (Nature Babies Ser.). (ENG., 36p. (J). (gr. k-3). 13.95 *(978-1-55041-874-3(2),* 1550418742) Fitzhenry & Whiteside, Ltd. CAN. Dist: Midpoint Trade Bks., Inc.

—Baby Lion, 1 vol. Lang, Aubrey. (ENG., 36p. (J). (gr. k-3). 2004. pap. *(978-1-55041-713-5(4))*; 2003. *(978-1-55041-711-1(8))* Fitzhenry & Whiteside, Ltd.

—Baby Mountain Sheep, 1 vol. Lang, Aubrey. 2008. (ENG., 36p. (J). (gr. k-3). *(978-1-55455-043-2(2))* Fitzhenry & Whiteside, Ltd.

—Baby Mountain Sheep, 1 vol. Lang, Aubrey. 2007. (Nature Babies Ser.). (ENG., 36p. (J). (gr. -1-3). 15.95 *(978-1-55455-042-5(4),* 1554550424) Fitzhenry & Whiteside, Ltd. CAN. Dist: Midpoint Trade Bks., Inc.

—Baby Owl, 1 vol. Lang, Aubrey. 2004. (ENG., 36p. (J). (gr. k-3). pap. *(978-1-55041-798-2(3))* Fitzhenry & Whiteside, Ltd.

—Baby Owl, 1 vol. Lang, Aubrey. 2004. (Nature Babies Ser.). (ENG., 36p. (J). (gr. k-3). 13.95 *(978-1-55041-796-8(7),* 1550417967) Fitzhenry & Whiteside, Ltd. CAN. Dist: Midpoint Trade Bks., Inc.

—Baby Polar Bear, 1 vol. Lang, Aubrey. 2008. (ENG., 36p. *(978-1-55455-101-9(3))*; 32p. (J). pap. *(978-1-55455-102-6(1))* Fitzhenry & Whiteside, Ltd.

—Baby Porcupine, 1 vol. Lang, Aubrey. 2005. (ENG., 36p. (J). (gr. 4-7). pap. *(978-1-55041-562-9(X))* Fitzhenry & Whiteside, Ltd.

—Baby Porcupine, 1 vol. Lang, Aubrey. 2005. (Nature Babies Ser.). (ENG., 36p. (J). (gr. k-3). 15.95 *(978-1-55041-560-5(3),* 1550415603) Fitzhenry & Whiteside, Ltd. CAN. Dist: Midpoint Trade Bks., Inc.

—Baby Seal, 1 vol. Lang, Aubrey. 2004. (ENG., 36p. (J). (gr. k-3). pap. *(978-1-55041-726-5(6))* Fitzhenry & Whiteside, Ltd.

—Baby Sloth, 1 vol. Lang, Aubrey. 2004. (Nature Babies Ser.). (ENG., 36p. (J). pap. 5.95 *(978-1-55041-827-9(0),* 1550418270) Fitzhenry & Whiteside, Ltd. CAN. Dist: Midpoint Trade Bks., Inc.

—Sonoran Desert. 2008. (J). *(978-1-55971-984-1(2))*; pap. *(978-1-55971-985-8(0))* T&N Children's Publishing. (NorthWord Bks. for Young Readers).

Lynch, Wayne, photos by. The Arctic. Lynch, Wayne. 2007. (Our Wild World Ser.). (ENG., 64p. (J). (gr. 3-7). pap. 8.95 *(978-1-55971-961-2(3))* Cooper Square Publishing Llc.

—Arctic Alphabet: Exploring the North from A to Z. Lynch, Wayne. 2006. 32p. (J). (gr. k-4). reprint ed. 20.00 *(978-1-4223-5190-1(4))* DIANE Publishing Co.

—The Everglades. Lynch, Wayne. 2007. (Our Wild World Ser.). (ENG., 64p. (J). (gr. 3-7). 16.95 *(978-1-55971-970-4(2))*; pap. 9.95 *(978-1-55971-971-1(0))* Cooper Square Publishing Llc.

Lyndon, Janice. The Mark of the Wagarl. Little, Lorna. 2004. 28p. (J). *(978-1-875641-97-0(1))* Magabala Bks.

Lyndon, Tracy S. The Secret of Wattensaw Bayou. Hubbs, M. E. 2013. 170p. pap. 12.95 *(978-1-934610-76-3(3))* Bluewater Pubns.

Lyne, Alison. Bo & the Christmas Bandit, 1 vol. Simmons, Lynn. 2009. (Bo Ser.). (ENG.). 128p. (J). (gr. 3-6). pap. 8.95 *(978-1-58980-723-5(5))* Pelican Publishing Co., Inc.

—Petite Rouge: A Cajun Twist to an Old Tale, 1 vol. Hébert-Collins, Sheila. 2015. (ENG.). 32p. (J). (gr. k-3). 16.99 *(978-1-58980-602-3(6))* Pelican Publishing Co., Inc.

Lyne, Alison D. Thanksgiving Day Alphabet, 1 vol. Vidrine, Beverly Barras. 2006. (ENG.). 32p. (J). (gr. k-3). 8.95 *(978-1-58980-338-1(8))* Pelican Publishing Co., Inc.

Lyne, Alison Davis. Bo & the Roaring Pines, 1 vol. Simmons, Lynn Sheffield. 2008. (Bo Ser.). (ENG.). 120p. (J). (gr. 3-6). pap. 8.95 *(978-1-58980-522-4(4))* Pelican Publishing Co., Inc.

—Easter Day Alphabet, 1 vol. Vidrine, Beverly Barras. 2003. (ENG.). 32p. (J). (gr. k-k). pap. 8.95 *(978-1-58980-076-2(1))* Pelican Publishing Co., Inc.

—G Is for Grits: A Southern Alphabet, 1 vol. Bethea, Nikole. 2012. (ENG.). 32p. (J). (gr. k-3). 16.99 *(978-1-4556-1698-5(2))* Pelican Publishing Co., Inc.

—Halloween Alphabet, 1 vol. Vidrine, Beverly Barras. 2004. (ENG.). 32p. (J). (gr. k-1). pap. 8.95 *(978-1-58980-242-1(X))* Pelican Publishing Co., Inc.

—Jacques et la Canne à Sucre: A Cajun Jack & the Beanstalk, 1 vol. Hébert-Collins, Sheila. 2004. (FRE & ENG.). 32p. (J). (gr. k-3). pap. 16.99 *(978-1-58980-191-2(1))* Pelican Publishing Co., Inc.

—Kudzu Chaos, 1 vol. Lambe, Jennifer Holloway. 2003. (ENG.). 32p. (J). (gr. k-3). 16.99 *(978-1-58980-157-8(1))* Pelican Publishing Co., Inc.

Lyne, Alison Davis. Little Things Aren't Little ... When You're Little, 1 vol. Lyne, Alison Davis. Burrows, Mark. 2013. (ENG.). 32p. (J). (gr. -1-k). 16.99 *(978-1-4556-1791-3(1))* Pelican Publishing Co., Inc.

Lyne, William Rayford. Galisteo: Thothmes III's Colony in America, C. 1626 B. C.: the Tanoan-Egyptian Djed Festival Stone. Lyne, William Rayford, photos by. Lyne, William Rayford. 2011. (ENG.). 250p. pap. 25.00 *(978-0-9637467-3-3(1))* Creatopia Productions - Lamy, New Mexico.

Lynn, Bel. Gus, the Dinosaur Bus. Liu, Julia. 2013. (ENG.). 32p. (J). (gr. -1-3). 12.99 *(978-0-547-90573-0(4))* Houghton Mifflin Harcourt Publishing Co.

Lynn, Gaisterer. The Adventures Begin. Haller, Reese. 2005. (Fred the Mouse Ser.). 108p. (J). (gr. -1-3). per. 4.97 *(978-0-9616046-8-4(9))* Personal Power Pr.

Lynn, Rick. Lewis & Clark's Journey of Discovery: A Guide for Young Explorers. Conant, Susan Sens. 2004. 48p. (J). pap. *(978-0-9725584-1-9(1))* Little Blue Pr.

Lynn, Ronny. My Filipino Word Book: English - Tagalog - Ilokano. Fancy, Robin Lyn & Welch, Vala Jeanne. Gasmen, Imelda Fines, ed. 2007. 28p. (J). (gr. -1-3). 10.95 *(978-1-57306-276-3(6))* Bess Pr., Inc.

Lynn, Tammy. Happy Birthday Puppy: An I See Puppy Book. Lynn, Tammy. Stewart, Elaine, ed. 2006. 12p. (J). bds. 6.99 *(978-0-9774277-0-3(6),* 0-9774277-0-6) I See Puppy, LLP.

Lynne, Kimberlee. The Frog & the Mouse. 2011. (First Steps in Music Ser.). (ENG.). 32p. (J). (gr. k-2). 16.95 *(978-1-57999-802-8(X))* G I A Pubns., Inc.

Lyon, Belinda. My Book of Princess Stories. Baxter, Nicola. 2012. (ENG.). 80p. (J). (gr. k-4). pap. 9.99 *(978-1-84322-801-1(7))* Anness Publishing GBR. Dist: National Bk. Network.

Lyon, Carol. How & Why Stories: World Tales Kids Can Read & Tell. Hamilton, Martha & Weiss, Mitch. 2005. (World Storytelling from August House Ser.). (ENG.). 96p. (J). (gr. 1-7). pap. 15.95 *(978-0-87483-561-8(5))* August Hse. Pubs., Inc.

—Through the Grapevine: World Tales Kids Can Read & Tell. Hamilton, Martha & Weiss, Mitch. (ENG.). 128p. (J). (gr. 1-6). 2006. pap. 15.95 *(978-0-87483-624-0(7))*; 2005. 24.95 *(978-0-87483-625-7(5))* August Hse. Pubs., Inc.

Lyon, Chris. Calligraphy: From Beginner to Expert. Young, Caroline. 2006. (Usborne Guide Ser.). 48p. (J). (gr. 6). lib. bdg. 16.99 *(978-1-58086-934-8(3),* Usborne) EDC Publishing.

Lyon, Chris, et al. Diggers & Cranes. Young, Caroline. rev. ed. 2006. (Usborne Big Machines Ser.). 32p. (J). (gr. k-3). per. 6.95 *(978-0-7945-0840-1(5),* Usborne) EDC Publishing.

Lyon, Chris. Trucks. Castor, Harriet. 2006. (Big MacHines Ser.). 32p. (J). (gr. k). lib. bdg. 14.95 *(978-1-58086-847-1(9))* EDC Publishing.

Lyon, Chris, et al. Trucks. Castor, Harriet. rev. ed. 2004. (Usborne Big Machines Ser.). 31p. (J). (gr. -1). per. 6.95 *(978-0-7945-0839-5(1),* Usborne) EDC Publishing.

Lyon, Chris. The Usborne Book of Machines That Work. Young, Caroline & Castor, Harriet. 2004. (Young MacHines Ser.). 95p. (J). (gr. k). lib. bdg. 22.95 *(978-1-58086-031-4(1),* Usborne) EDC Publishing.

Lyon, Chris & Biggin, Gary. Bulldozers & Other Construction Machines. Butterfield, Moira. (J). mass mkt. 8.99 *(978-0-590-24556-2(2))* Scholastic, Inc.

Lyon, Chris & Gower, Teri. Tractors. Young, Caroline. 2004. (Young MacHines Ser.). 32p. (J). (gr. k). lib. bdg. 14.95 *(978-1-58086-616-3(6),* Usborne) EDC Publishing.

Lyon, David. Flight of the Buzby Bee. Lyon, David. 2005. 32p. (J). 16.95 *(978-0-9741328-0-8(2))* Lyon, Ernest Media Productions.

Lyon, Lea. Lailah's Lunchbox, 1 vol. Faruqi, Reem. 2015. (ENG.). 32p. (J). 16.95 ***(978-0-88448-431-8(9))*** Tilbury Hse. Pubs.

Lyon, Lea. The Miracle Jar: A Hanukkah Story. Penn, Audrey. (ENG.). 32p. (J). (gr. -1-3). 2009. pap. 8.95 *(978-1-933718-26-2(9))*; 2008. 16.95 *(978-1-933718-16-3(1))* Tanglewood Pr.

—Playing War, 1 vol. Beckwith, Kathy. 2005. (ENG.). 32p. (J). (gr. 3-6). 16.95 *(978-0-88448-267-3(7))* Tilbury Hse. Pubs.

—Say Something, 1 vol. Moss, Peggy. 2005. (ENG.). 32p. (J). (gr. 2-6). 16.95 *(978-0-88448-261-1(8))* Tilbury Hse. Pubs.

L

—Say Something: 10TH Anniversary Edition. Moss, Peggy. 2013. (ENG.). 32p. (J). pap. 7.95 (978-0-88448-360-1(6)) Tilbury Hse. Pubs.

Lyon, Lea. Keep Your Ear on the Ball, 1 vol. Lyon, Lea. Petrillo, Genevieve. 2007. (ENG.). 32p. (J). (gr. -1-3). 16.95 (978-0-88448-296-3(0)) Tilbury Hse. Pubs.

Lyon, Lea07/. Keep Your Ear on the Ball. Petrillo, Genevieve. 2010. 32p. (J). pap. 7.95 (978-0-88448-324-3(X)) Tilbury Hse. Pubs.

Lyon, Tammie. Best Season Ever, 1 vol. Manushkin, Fran. 2010. (Katie Woo Ser.). (ENG.). 32p. (gr. k-2). lib. bdg. 19.99 (978-1-4048-5730-8(3)) Picture Window Bks.

—The Big Lie, 1 vol. Manushkin, Fran. 2009. (Katie Woo Ser.). (ENG.). 32p. (gr. k-2). 19.99 (978-1-4048-5497-0(5)) Picture Window Bks.

—Boo, Katie Woo!, 1 vol. Manushkin, Fran. 2010. (Katie Woo Ser.). (ENG.). 32p. (gr. k-2). lib. bdg. 19.99 (978-1-4048-5987-6(X)); pap. 5.95 (978-1-4048-6366-8(4)) Picture Window Bks.

—Boss of the World, 1 vol. Manushkin, Fran. 2009. (Katie Woo Ser.). (ENG.). 32p. (gr. k-2). 19.99 (978-1-4048-5493-2(2)) Picture Window Bks.

—Bugs in My Hair?! Stier, Catherine. 2012. (J). 34.28 (978-1-61913-111-8(0)) Weigl Pubs., Inc.

—Bugs in My Hair?!, 1 vol. Stier, Catherine. 2010. (ENG.). 32p. (J). (gr. 1-4). pap. 6.99 (978-0-8075-0909-8(4)) Whitman, Albert & Co.

—Cartwheel Katie. Manushkin, Fran. 2015. (Katie Woo Ser.). (ENG.). 32p. (gr. k-2). 19.99 (978-1-4795-5894-0(X)) Picture Window Bks.

—Cowgirl Katie, 1 vol. Manushkin, Fran. 2014. (Katie Woo Ser.). (ENG.). 32p. (gr. k-2). lib. bdg. 19.99 (978-1-4795-2174-6(4)) Picture Window Bks.

—Eloise & the Big Parade. McClatchy, Lisa & Thompson, Kay. 2007. (Eloise Ser.). (ENG.). 32p. (J). (gr. -1-1). pap. 3.99 (978-1-4169-3523-0(1), Simon Spotlight) Simon Spotlight.

—Eloise Breaks Some Eggs. McNamara, Margaret & Thompson, Kay. 2005. (Eloise Ser.). (ENG.). 32p. (J). (gr. -1-1). pap. 3.99 (978-0-689-87368-3(9), Simon Spotlight) Simon Spotlight.

—Eloise Skates! McClatchy, Lisa. 2008. (Eloise Ser.). (ENG.). 32p. (J). (gr. -1-1). pap. 3.99 (978-1-4169-6406-3(1), Simon Spotlight) Simon Spotlight.

—Eloise Throws a Party! Knight, Hilary. 2008. (Eloise Ser.). (ENG.). 32p. (J). (gr. -1-1). pap. 3.99 (978-1-4169-6172-7(0), Simon Spotlight) Simon Spotlight.

—Eloise Visits the Zoo. Thompson, Kay & McClatchy, Lisa. 2009. (Eloise Ser.). (ENG.). 32p. (J). (gr. -1-1). pap. 3.99 (978-1-4169-8642-3(1), Simon Spotlight) Simon Spotlight.

—Eloise's Mother's Day Surprise. McClatchy, Lisa. 2009. (Eloise Ser.). (ENG.). 32p. (J). (gr. -1-1). pap. 3.99 (978-1-4169-7889-3(5), Simon Spotlight) Simon Spotlight.

—Fly High, Katie, 1 vol. Manushkin, Fran. 2014. (Katie Woo Ser.). (ENG.). 32p. (gr. k-2). lib. bdg. 19.99 (978-1-4795-2175-3(2)) Picture Window Bks.

—From Here to There. Skultety, Nancy. 2005. (ENG.). 32p. (J). (gr. -1-3). 15.95 (978-1-59078-092-3(2)) Boyds Mills Pr.

—The Gingerbread Bear. Dennis, Robert. (J). 2013. (ENG.). 32p. (gr. -1-k). 4.99 (978-0-545-48966-9(0)); 2012. (978-0-545-46767-4(5)) Scholastic, Inc. (Cartwheel Bks.).

—Good Morning, God! Bostrom, Kathleen Long. 2014. 20p. (J). bds. 6.99 (978-0-8249-1939-9(4), Candy Cane Pr.) Ideals Pubns.

—Good Night, God! Bostrom, Kathleen Long. 2014. 20p. (J). bds. 6.99 (978-0-8249-1940-5(8), Candy Cane Pr.) Ideals Pubns.

—Goodbye to Goldie, 1 vol. Manushkin, Fran. 2009. (Katie Woo Ser.). (ENG.). 32p. (gr. k-2). 19.99 (978-1-4048-5495-6(9)) Picture Window Bks.

—A Happy Day, 1 vol. Manushkin, Fran. 2009. (Katie Woo Ser.). (ENG.). 32p. (gr. k-2). 19.99 (978-1-4048-5496-3(7)) Picture Window Bks.

—Harriet Tubman. Bauer, Marion Dane. 2010. (My First Biography Ser.). (ENG.). 32p. (J). (gr. -1-3). pap. 3.99 (978-0-545-23257-9(0), Scholastic Nonfiction) Scholastic, Inc.

Lyon, Tammie. I Am Nibbles, Level 2. Froeb, Lori. 2015. (Rescue Readers Ser.: 3). (ENG.). 32p. (J). (gr. 1-3). pap. 3.99 **(978-0-7944-3455-7(X))** Studio Fun International.

Lyon, Tammie. It Doesn't Need to Rhyme, Katie: Writing a Poem with Katie Woo, 1 vol. Manushkin, Fran. 2013. (Katie Woo: Star Writer Ser.). (ENG.). 32p. (gr. k-2). pap. 5.95 (978-1-4795-1923-1(5)); lib. bdg. 19.99 (978-1-4048-8128-0(X)) Picture Window Bks.

—Just Like Always. Perry, Anne M. (Rookie Ready to Learn Ser.). (J). 2011. 40p. pap. 5.95 (978-0-531-26675-5(3)); 2011. 40p. (gr. -1-k). lib. bdg. 23.00 (978-0-531-26370-9(3)); 2005. (ENG.). 32p. (gr. 1-2). 19.50 (978-0-516-25154-7(6)) Scholastic Library Publishing. (Children's Pr.).

—Katie & the Class Pet, 1 vol. Manushkin, Fran. 2011. (Katie Woo Ser.). (ENG.). 32p. (gr. k-2). pap. 5.95 (978-1-4048-6856-4(9)); lib. bdg. 19.99 (978-1-4048-6520-4(9)) Picture Window Bks.

—Katie Finds a Job, 1 vol. Manushkin, Fran. 2011. (Katie Woo Ser.). (ENG.). 32p. (gr. k-2). pap. 5.95 (978-1-4048-6614-0(0)); lib. bdg. 19.99 (978-1-4048-6513-6(6)) Picture Window Bks.

—Katie Goes Camping, 1 vol. Manushkin, Fran. 2010. (Katie Woo Ser.). (ENG.). 32p. (gr. k-2). lib. bdg. 19.99 (978-1-4048-5731-5(1)) Picture Window Bks.

—Katie in the Kitchen, 1 vol. Manushkin, Fran. 2010. (Katie Woo Ser.). (ENG.). 32p. (gr. k-2). lib. bdg. 19.99 (978-1-4048-5724-7(9)) Picture Window Bks.

—Katie Saves Thanksgiving, 1 vol. Manushkin, Fran. 2010. (Katie Woo Ser.). (ENG.). 32p. (gr. k-2). lib. bdg. 19.99 (978-1-4048-5988-3(8)); pap. 5.95 (978-1-4048-6367-5(2)) Picture Window Bks.

—Katie Saves the Earth, 1 vol. Manushkin, Fran. 2013. (Katie Woo Ser.). (ENG.). 32p. (gr. k-2). pap. 5.95 (978-1-4048-8046-7(1)); lib. bdg. 19.99 (978-1-4048-7652-1(9)) Picture Window Bks.

—Katie Woo, 1 vol. Manushkin, Fran. (Katie Woo Ser.). (ENG.). 32p. (gr. k-2). 2014. lib. bdg. 599.64 (978-1-4795-4813-2(8)); 2013. pap. 130.90 (978-1-4048-8063-4(1)); 2013. pap. 23.80 (978-1-4048-8062-7(3)); 2013. lib. bdg. 79.96 (978-1-4048-8055-9(0)); 2013. lib. bdg. 599.66 (978-1-4048-8054-2(2)) Picture Window Bks.

—Katie Woo & Friends, 1 vol. Manushkin, Fran. 2012. (Katie Woo Ser.). (ENG.). 96p. (gr. k-2). pap. 4.95 (978-1-4048-7909-6(9)) Picture Window Bks.

—Katie Woo & Her Big Ideas, 1 vol. Manushkin, Fran. 2013. (Katie Woo Ser.). (ENG.). 96p. (gr. k-2). pap. 4.95 (978-1-4795-2026-8(8)) Picture Window Bks.

—Katie Woo Book Club Kit. Manushkin, Fran. 2013. (Katie Woo Ser.). (ENG.). 576p. (gr. k-2). pap. 29.70 (978-1-4795-5120-0(1)) Picture Window Bks.

—Katie Woo Celebrates, 1 vol. Manushkin, Fran. 2013. (Katie Woo Ser.). (ENG.). 96p. (gr. k-2). pap. 4.95 (978-1-4048-8100-6(X)) Picture Window Bks.

—Katie Woo, Don't Be Blue, 1 vol. Manushkin, Fran. 2013. (Katie Woo Ser.). (ENG.). 96p. (gr. k-2). pap. 4.95 (978-1-4048-8101-3(8)) Picture Window Bks.

—Katie Woo, Every Day's an Adventure, 1 vol. Manushkin, Fran. 2014. (Katie Woo Ser.). (ENG.). 96p. (gr. k-2). pap. 4.95 (978-1-4795-5211-5(9)) Picture Window Bks.

—Katie Woo Has the Flu, 1 vol. Manushkin, Fran. 2011. (Katie Woo Ser.). (ENG.). 32p. (gr. k-2). pap. 5.95 (978-1-4048-6504-0(2)); lib. bdg. 19.99 (978-1-4048-6518-1(7)) Picture Window Bks.

—Katie Woo Loves School, 1 vol. Manushkin, Fran. 2013. (Katie Woo Ser.). (ENG.). 96p. (gr. k-2). pap. 4.95 (978-1-4795-2027-5(6)) Picture Window Bks.

—Katie Woo Rules the School, 1 vol. Manushkin, Fran. 2011. (Katie Woo Ser.). (ENG.). 96p. (gr. k-2). pap. 4.95 (978-1-4048-7908-9(0)) Picture Window Bks.

—Katie Woo: Star Writer. Manushkin, Fran. 2013. (Katie Woo: Star Writer Ser.). (ENG.). 32p. (gr. k-2). pap. 35.70 (978-1-4795-1991-0(X)); lib. bdg. 119.94 (978-1-4048-8082-5(8)) Picture Window Bks.

Lyon, Tammie. Katie Woo, Super Scout. Manushkin, Fran. 2015. (Katie Woo Ser.). (ENG.). 32p. (gr. k-2). 19.99 **(978-1-4795-6178-0(9))** Picture Window Bks.

—Katie Woo Tries Something New. Manushkin, Fran. 2015. (Katie Woo Ser.). (ENG.). 96p. (gr. k-2). pap. 4.95 **(978-1-4795-6182-7(7))** Picture Window Bks.

Lyon, Tammie. Katie Woo, Where Are You?, 1 vol. Manushkin, Fran. 2011. (Katie Woo Ser.). (ENG.). 32p. (gr. k-2). pap. 5.95 (978-1-4048-6853-3(4)); lib. bdg. 19.99 (978-1-4048-6517-4(9)) Picture Window Bks.

—Katie Woo's Big Idea Journal: A Place for Your Best Stories, Drawings, Doodles, & Plans, 1 vol. Manushkin, Fran. 2014. (Katie Woo Ser.). (ENG.). 144p. (gr. k-2). 9.95 (978-1-62370-166-6(X)) Capstone Young Readers.

Lyon, Tammie. Katie's Happy Mother's Day. Manushkin, Fran. 2015. (Katie Woo Ser.). (ENG.). 32p. (gr. k-2). 19.99 **(978-1-4795-6179-7(7))** Picture Window Bks.

Lyon, Tammie. Katie's Lucky Birthday, 1 vol. Manushkin, Fran. 2011. (Katie Woo Ser.). (ENG.). 32p. (gr. k-2). pap. 5.95 (978-1-4048-6612-6(4)); lib. bdg. 19.99 (978-1-4048-6514-3(4)) Picture Window Bks.

—Katie's New Shoes, 1 vol. Manushkin, Fran. 2011. (Katie Woo Ser.). (ENG.). 32p. (gr. k-2). pap. 5.95 (978-1-4048-6855-7(0)); lib. bdg. 19.99 (978-1-4048-6519-8(5)) Picture Window Bks.

—Katie's Noisy Music. Manushkin, Fran. 2015. (Katie Woo Ser.). (ENG.). 32p. (gr. k-2). 19.99 (978-1-4795-5893-3(1)) Picture Window Bks.

—Let's Hear It for Almigal. Kupfer, Wendy. 2012. (ENG.). 32p. (J). (gr. k-2). 16.99 (978-0-9838294-0-9(3)) Handfinger Pr.

—Look at You, Katie Woo!, 1 vol. Manushkin, Fran. 2011. (Katie Woo Ser.). (ENG.). 112p. (gr. k-2). pap. 7.95 (978-1-4048-6596-9(9)) Picture Window Bks.

—Make-Believe Class, 1 vol. Manushkin, Fran. 2010. (Katie Woo Ser.). (ENG.). 32p. (gr. k-2). lib. bdg. 19.99 (978-1-4048-5732-2(X)) Picture Window Bks.

—Meet the Buddies! Hapka, Catherine. 2013. (World of Reading Ser.). (ENG.). 32p. (J). (gr. 1-3). pap. 3.99 (978-1-4231-6946-8(8)) Disney Pr.

—Moo, Katie Woo! Manushkin, Fran. 2013. (J). pap. 35.70 (978-1-4048-8093-1(3)); (ENG.). 32p. pap. 5.95 (978-1-4048-8047-4(X)); (ENG.). 32p. lib. bdg. 19.99 (978-1-4048-7653-8(7)) Picture Window Bks.

—Moving Day, 1 vol. Manushkin, Fran. 2010. (Katie Woo Ser.). (ENG.). 32p. (gr. k-2). pap. 5.95 (978-1-4048-6059-9(2)); lib. bdg. 19.99 (978-1-4048-5733-9(8)) Picture Window Bks.

—My Kitten, 0 vols. O'Hair, Margaret. 2011. (ENG.). 32p. (J). (gr. -1-2). 15.99 (978-0-7614-5811-1(5), 9780761458111, Amazon Children's Publishing) Amazon Publishing.

—My Pup, 0 vols. O'Hair, Margaret. 2010. (ENG.). 24p. (J). (gr. -1-2). bds. 7.99 (978-0-7614-5644-5(9), 9780761456445, Amazon Children's Publishing) Amazon Publishing.

—A Nervous Night, 1 vol. Manushkin, Fran. 2010. (Katie Woo Ser.). (ENG.). 32p. (gr. k-2). pap. 5.95 (978-1-4048-6060-5(6)); lib. bdg. 19.99 (978-1-4048-5725-4(7)) Picture Window Bks.

—No More Teasing, 1 vol. Manushkin, Fran. 2009. (Katie Woo Ser.). (ENG.). 32p. (gr. k-2). 19.99 (978-1-4048-5492-5(4)) Picture Window Bks.

—No Valentines for Katie, 1 vol. Manushkin, Fran. 2010. (Katie Woo Ser.). (ENG.). 32p. (gr. k-2). lib. bdg. 19.99 (978-1-4048-5986-9(1)); pap. 5.95 (978-1-4048-6365-1(6)) Picture Window Bks.

—Piggy Bank Problems, 1 vol. Manushkin, Fran. 2013. (Katie Woo Ser.). (ENG.). 32p. (gr. k-2). pap. 5.95 (978-1-4048-8048-1(8)); lib. bdg. 19.99 (978-1-4048-7654-5(5)) Picture Window Bks.

—The Princess & the Peanut Allergy. McClure, Wendy. 2012. (J). (978-1-61913-127-9(7)) Weigl Pubs., Inc.

—The Princess & the Peanut Allergy, 1 vol. McClure, Wendy. 2009. (ENG.). 32p. (J). (gr. 1-4). 16.99 (978-0-8075-6623-7(3)) Whitman, Albert & Co.

—Princess with a Purpose. Chapman, Kelly. 2010. 48p. (J). act. bk. ed. 6.99 (978-0-7369-2747-5(6)); 2010. 32p. (J). 14.99 (978-0-7369-2435-1(3)); 2009. pap. 12.99 (978-0-7369-2743-7(3)) Harvest Hse. Pubs.

—Psalms & Prayers for Little Ones. Nolan, Allia Zobel. 2014. 32p. (J). 12.99 (978-0-7369-5725-0(1)) Harvest Hse. Pubs.

—Red, White, & Blue & Katie Woo!, 1 vol. Manushkin, Fran. 2010. (Katie Woo Ser.). (ENG.). 32p. (gr. k-2). lib. bdg. 19.93 (978-1-4048-5985-2(3)); pap. 5.95 (978-1-4048-6364-4(8)) Picture Window Bks.

—Scholastic Reader Level 1: the Saturday Triplets #2: the Pumpkin Fair Problem. Kenah, Katharine. 2013. (Scholastic Reader Level 1 Ser.). (ENG.). 32p. (J). (gr. -1-2). pap. 3.99 (978-0-545-48144-1(9)) Scholastic, Inc.

—Scholastic Reader Level 1: the Saturday Triplets #3: Teacher Trouble! Kenah, Katharine. 2013. (Scholastic Reader Level 1 Ser.). (ENG.). 32p. (J). (gr. -1-2). pap. 3.99 (978-0-545-48145-8(7)) Scholastic, Inc.

—Sincerely, Katie: Writing a Letter with Katie Woo, 1 vol. Manushkin, Fran. 2013. (Katie Woo: Star Writer Ser.). (ENG.). 32p. (gr. k-2). pap. 5.95 (978-1-4795-1921-7(9)); lib. bdg. 19.99 (978-1-4048-8126-6(3)) Picture Window Bks.

—Star of the Show, 1 vol. Manushkin, Fran. 2011. (Katie Woo Ser.). (ENG.). 32p. (gr. k-2). pap. 5.95 (978-1-4048-6613-3(2)); lib. bdg. 19.99 (978-1-4048-6515-0(2)) Picture Window Bks.

—Stick to the Facts, Katie: Writing a Research Paper with Katie Woo, 1 vol. Manushkin, Fran. 2013. (Katie Woo: Star Writer Ser.). (ENG.). 32p. (gr. k-2). pap. 5.95 (978-1-4795-1925-5(1)); lib. bdg. 19.99 (978-1-4048-8130-3(1)) Picture Window Bks.

—Too Much Rain, 1 vol. Manushkin, Fran. 2009. (Katie Woo Ser.). (ENG.). 32p. (gr. k-2). 19.99 (978-1-4048-5494-9(0)) Picture Window Bks.

—The Tricky Tooth, 1 vol. Manushkin, Fran. 2011. (Katie Woo Ser.). (ENG.). 32p. (gr. k-2). pap. 5.95 (978-1-4048-6611-9(6)); lib. bdg. 19.99 (978-1-4048-6516-7(0)) Picture Window Bks.

—What Do You Think, Katie? Writing an Opinion Piece with Katie Woo, 1 vol. Manushkin, Fran. 2013. (Katie Woo: Star Writer Ser.). (ENG.). 32p. (gr. k-2). pap. 5.95 (978-1-4795-1926-2(X)); lib. bdg. 19.99 (978-1-4048-8131-0(X)) Picture Window Bks.

—What Happens Next, Katie? Writing a Narrative with Katie Woo, 1 vol. Manushkin, Fran. 2013. (Katie Woo: Star Writer Ser.). (ENG.). 32p. (gr. k-2). pap. 5.95 (978-1-4795-1924-8(3)); lib. bdg. 19.99 (978-1-4048-8129-7(8)) Picture Window Bks.

—What's in Your Heart, Katie? Writing in a Journal with Katie Woo, 1 vol. Manushkin, Fran. 2013. (Katie Woo: Star Writer Ser.). (ENG.). 32p. (gr. k-2). pap. 5.95 (978-1-4795-1922-4(7)); lib. bdg. 19.99 (978-1-4048-8127-3(1)) Picture Window Bks.

—Who Needs Glasses?, 1 vol. Manushkin, Fran. 2013. (Katie Woo Ser.). (ENG.). 32p. (gr. k-2). pap. 5.95 (978-1-4048-8049-8(6)); lib. bdg. 19.99 (978-1-4048-7655-2(3)) Picture Window Bks.

Lyon, Tammie. Adiós a Goldie. Lyon, Tammie. Manushkin, Fran. 2012. (Katie Woo en Español Ser.). (SPA.). 32p. (gr. k-2). pap. 5.95 (978-1-4048-7676-7(6)); lib. bdg. 19.99 (978-1-4048-7524-1(7)) Picture Window Bks.

—Basta de Burlas, 1 vol. Lyon, Tammie. Manushkin, Fran. 2012. (Katie Woo en Español Ser.). (SPA.). 32p. (gr. k-2). pap. 5.95 (978-1-4048-7677-4(4)); lib. bdg. 19.99 (978-1-4048-7525-8(5)) Picture Window Bks.

—La Gran Mentira, 1 vol. Lyon, Tammie. Manushkin, Fran. 2012. (Katie Woo en Español Ser.). (SPA.). 32p. (gr. k-2). pap. 5.95 (978-1-4048-7678-1(2)); lib. bdg. 19.99 (978-1-4048-7522-7(0)) Picture Window Bks.

—La Jefa Del Mundo, 1 vol. Lyon, Tammie. Manushkin, Fran. 2012. (Katie Woo en Español Ser.). (SPA.). 32p. (gr. k-2). pap. 5.95 (978-1-4048-7679-8(0)); lib. bdg. 19.99 (978-1-4048-7523-4(9)) Picture Window Bks.

—¡Soy Optimista! Lyon, Tammie. Parker, David. 2011. (SPA.). (J). (978-0-545-27356-5(0)) Scholastic, Inc.

Lyon, Tammie, jt. illus. see Cowdrey, Richard.

Lyon, Tammie, jt. illus. see Lyon, Tammie Speer.

Lyon, Tammie Speer. Eloise & the Snowman. McClatchy, Lisa & Thompson, Kay. 2006. (Eloise Ser.). (ENG.). 32p. (J). (gr. -1-1). pap. 3.99 (978-0-689-87451-2(0), Simon Spotlight) Simon Spotlight.

—Eloise at the Wedding. Thompson, Kay. 2006. (Eloise Ser.). (ENG.). 32p. (J). (gr. -1-1). pap. 3.99 (978-0-689-87449-9(9), Simon Spotlight) Simon Spotlight.

—Eloise's Summer Vacation. McClatchy, Lisa & Thompson, Kay. 2007. (Eloise Ser.). (ENG.). 32p. (J). (gr. -1-1). pap. 3.99 (978-0-689-87454-3(5), Simon Spotlight) Simon Spotlight.

—Grumbly Bunnies. Welch, Willy. 2004. 32p. (J). 15.95 (978-1-58089-086-1(5)) Charlesbridge Publishing, Inc.

—Hickory Dickory Dock! gif. ed. 2006. 10p. (J). (gr. -1-k). bds. 10.95 (978-1-57791-213-2(6)) Brighter Minds Children's Publishing.

—Mary Had a Little Lamb. 2006. 8p. (J). bds. 10.95 (978-1-57791-210-1(1)) Brighter Minds Children's Publishing.

—Now I Lay Me down to Sleep. 2006. 8p. (J). bds. 10.95 (978-1-57791-211-8(X)) Brighter Minds Children's Publishing.

—This Little Piggy. gif. ed. 2006. 10p. (J). bds. 10.95 (978-1-57791-212-5(8)) Brighter Minds Children's Publishing.

Lyon, Tammie Speer & Lyon, Tammie. Eloise & the Dinosaurs. McClatchy, Lisa & Thompson, Kay. 2007. (Eloise Ser.). (ENG.). 32p. (J). (gr. -1-1). pap. 3.99 (978-0-689-87453-6(7), Simon Spotlight) Simon Spotlight.

—Eloise & the Very Secret Room. Weiss, Ellen. 2006. (Eloise Ser.). (ENG.). 32p. (J). (gr. -1-1). pap. 3.99 (978-0-689-87450-5(2), Simon Spotlight) Simon Spotlight.

—Eloise Decorates for Christmas. McClatchy, Lisa & Knight, Hilary. 2007. (Eloise Ser.). (ENG.). 32p. (J). (gr. -1-1). pap. 3.99 (978-1-4169-4978-7(X), Simon Spotlight) Simon Spotlight.

—Eloise Goes to the Beach. Fry, Sonali & Knight, Hilary. 2007. (Eloise Ser.). (ENG.). 12p. (J). (gr. -1-2). 9.99 (978-1-4169-3344-1(1), Little Simon) Little Simon.

—Eloise's New Bonnet. McClatchy, Lisa & Thompson, Kay. 2007. (Eloise Ser.). (ENG.). 32p. (J). (gr. -1-1). pap. 3.99 (978-0-689-87452-9(9), Simon Spotlight) Simon Spotlight.

—Eloise's Pirate Adventure. McClatchy, Lisa. 2007. (Eloise Ser.). (ENG.). 32p. (J). (gr. -1-1). pap. 3.99 (978-1-4169-4979-4(8), Simon Spotlight) Simon Spotlight.

Lyona. I Will Fight Monsters for You. Balmes, Santi. 2015. (ENG.). 32p. (J). (gr. -1-2). 16.99 (978-0-8075-9056-0(8)) Whitman, Albert & Co.

Lyra, Rael & Albuquerque, Rafael. Jeremiah Harm. Giffen, Keith et al. 2007. (ENG.). 128p. per. 14.99 (978-1-934506-12-7(5)) Boom! Studios.

M

M. J. Studios Staff. The Incredible Dionsaur. Nichols, V. 128p. (J). (gr. k-6). pap., act. bk. ed. 2.95 (978-1-879424-64-7(9)) Nickel Pr.

M, Pierce, jt. illus. see Pierce, Mindy.

Ma, Wenhai. Tang Monk Disciples Monkey King. 2005. (Adventures of Monkey King Ser.: No. 3). 32p. (J). 16.95 (978-1-57227-084-8(5)) Pan Asia Pubns. (USA), Inc.

—Tang Monk Disciples Monkey King: English/Chinese. 2005. (Adventures of Monkey King Ser.: No. 3). (ENG & CHI.). 32p. (J). 16.95 (978-1-57227-086-2(1)) Pan Asia Pubns. (USA), Inc.

—Tang Monk Disciples Monkey King: English/Vietnamese. Do, Kim-Thu, tr. from ENG. 2005. (Adventures of Monkey King Ser.: No. 3). (ENG & VIE.). 32p. (J). 16.95 (978-1-57227-087-9(X)) Pan Asia Pubns. (USA), Inc.

Ma, Winnie. Circles of Round. Sturup, Signe. 2013. (ENG.). 40p. (J). (gr. k-3). 16.95 (978-1-927018-18-7(8)) Simply Read Bks. CAN. Dist: Ingram Pub. Services.

Maa'Dhoor, Lilian. Palabreríes: Retahílas, trabalenguas, Colmos y otros juegos de palabras. Hernandez, Eufemia. 2015. 48p. (J). (gr. k-3). pap. 10.99 **(978-970-58-0212-6(2))** Consejo Estatal Electoral MEX. Dist: Santillana USA Publishing Co., Inc.

Maas, Dorothy. Mr Dawson Had an Elephant. Work, Rhoda O. 2011. 128p. 40.95 (978-1-258-07973-4(9)) Literary Licensing, LLC.

Maas, Jason/A. Cows Can't Jump. Reisman, Dave. 2008. (ENG.). 44p. (J). (978-0-9801433-1-7(4)); pap. (978-0-9801433-0-0(6)) Jumping Cow Pr.

Maas, Rita, photos by. The Beach House Cookbook. Scott-Goodman, Barbara. 2005. (ENG., 156p. (gr. 8-17). 24.95 (978-0-8118-4308-9(4)) Chronicle Bks. LLC.

Maass, Mary Kurnick. Some Folks Like Cats: And Other Poems. Eastwick, Ivy O. 2003. (ENG.). 32p. (J). (gr. k-2). 15.95 (978-1-56397-450-2(9)) Boyds Mills Pr.

Maass, Robert, photos by. A Is for Autumn. Maass, Robert. 2011. (ENG., 32p. (J). (gr. -1-1). 16.99 (978-0-8050-9093-2(2), Holt, Henry & Co. Bks. For Young Readers) Holt, Henry & Co.

Mabee, Andrea, photos by. Dory Glory: Building A Boat from Stem to Stern. Mabee, Andrea. 2005. 67p. (YA). per. 15.95 (978-0-9630074-1-4(6)) Bass Cove Bks.

Maberry, Maranda. Stamps & Doodles for Girls. 2012. (Stamps & Doodles Ser.). (ENG.). 64p. (J). (gr. k). 14.95 (978-1-60710-456-8(3), Silver Dolphin Bks.) Baker & Taylor Publishing Group.

Maberry, Maranda, jt. illus. see Peterson, Stacy.

Mabey, Coline. A Christmas Kindness. Gevry, C. C. 2012. 24p. pap. 11.99 (978-0-9852661-4-1(7)) 4RV Publishing, LLC.

Mabire, Grégoire. Meggie Moon, 1 vol. Baguley, Elizabeth. 2005. (ENG.). 26p. (J). (gr. -1-3). pap. 16.00 (978-1-56148-474-4(1), Good Bks.) Skyhorse Publishing Co., Inc.

Mac, Sami. I Get a Baby Brother Instead. Vanorny-Barcus, LaVina. l.t. ed. 2011. (ENG.). 42p. pap. 14.95 (978-1-4610-8178-4(5)) CreateSpace Independent Publishing Platform.

—Perfect in Mother Nature's Eyes. Vanorny-Barcus, LaVina. 2010. (ENG.). 38p. pap. 15.95 (978-1-4505-9205-5(8)) CreateSpace Independent Publishing Platform.

—Perfecto en Los Ojos de la Madre Naturaleza: A Spanish/English Children's Book. Vanorny-Barcus, LaVina. l.t. ed. 2011. (ENG.). 42p. pap. 15.95 (978-1-4609-5739-4(3)) CreateSpace Independent Publishing Platform.

—Perfektni V Prirode Matky Oci: Perfect in Mother Nature's Eyes. Vanorny-Barcus, LaVina. 2010. (CZE & ENG.). 42p. pap. 15.95 (978-1-4515-3528-0(7)) CreateSpace Independent Publishing Platform.

MacAdam, Ian Paul. Donkey Oatie's Fashion Statement. Rath, Tom H. 2012. 32p. pap. (978-0-9866065-7-1(X)) Wood Islands Prints.

MacAdam, Reegory. Donkey Oatie's Impossible Dream. Rath, Tom H. 2012. 24p. pap. (978-0-9866065-5-7(3)) Wood Islands Prints.

Macadam, Winn. Will & the Magic Mirror. Macadam, Heather Dune. 2011. (ENG.). 102p. pap. 5.99 (978-1-4537-9863-8(3)) CreateSpace Independent Publishing Platform.

Macari, Mario Duilio. Funny Riddles for Kids: Squeaky Clean Easy Kid Riddles Drawn As Funny Kid's Cartoons in A Cool Comicbook Style. Macari, Mario Duilio, ed. 2007. 104p. (J). per. 10.00 (978-0-9766755-0-1(1)) Cartoonmario.com.

MacAulay, David. Building Big. MacAulay, David. 2006. 192p. reprint ed. 30.00 (978-1-4223-5328-8(1)) DIANE Publishing Co.

MacCarthy, Patricia. Forget-Me-Not Fairy Treasury. Musgrove, Marianne. 2013. (ENG.). 192p. (J). (gr. -1-3). (978-1-74308-536-3(2)) Hinkler Bks. Pty, Ltd.

MacCarthy, Patricia. Ocean Parade: A Counting Book. MacCarthy, Patricia. 2005. 24p. (J). (gr. -1-3). reprint ed. 12.00 (978-0-7567-8983-1(4)) DIANE Publishing Co.

MacCormick Secure Center, Residents. Another Sad Inning: Incarcerated Youth Reveal Their Trials, Tribulations & Loves. MacCormick SEcure Center, Residents. 2003. 90p. (YA). per. 17.00 *(978-0-9740184-1-6(4)*, MAC-2) Durland Alternatives Library.

MacDonald, Bruce. Two Fables of Aesop. Hamilton, Martha & Weiss, Mitch. 2005. (ENG.). 16p. (J). 5.75 *(978-1-57274-718-0(8)*, 2788, Bks. for Young Learners) Owen, Richard C. Pubs., Inc.

—Why Animals Never Got Fire: A Story of the Couer d'Alene Indians. Hamilton, Martha & Weiss, Mitch. 2005. (ENG.). 12p. (J). 5.75 *(978-1-57274-715-9(3)*, 2793, Bks. for Young Learners) Owen, Richard C. Pubs., Inc.

MacDonald, Clarke. Captain Lilly & the New Girl, 1 vol. Bellingham, Brenda. 2009. (Formac First Novels Ser.). (ENG.). 64p. (J). (gr. 1-5). 5.95 *(978-0-88780-855-5(7))* Formac Publishing Co., Ltd. CAN. Dist: Casemate Pubs. & Bk. Distributors, LLC.

—Lilly & the Hullabaloo, 1 vol. Bellingham, Brenda. 2008. (Formac First Novels Ser.). (ENG.). 64p. (gr. 2-5). (J). 5.95 *(978-0-88780-752-7(6))*; (YA). 14.95 *(978-0-88780-754-1(2))* Formac Publishing Co., Ltd. CAN. Dist: Casemate Pubs. & Bk. Distributors, LLC.

—Lilly & the Snakes. Bellingham, Brenda. 2007. (Formac First Novels Ser.: 37). (ENG & GER.). 64p. (J). (gr. 2-5). 14.95 *(978-0-88780-727-5(5))*; 4.95 *(978-0-88780-723-7(2))* Formac Publishing Co., Ltd. CAN. Dist: Casemate Pubs. & Bk. Distributors, LLC.

—Lilly Babysits Her Brother, 1 vol. Bellingham, Brenda. 2013. (Formac First Novels Ser.). (ENG.). 60p. (J). (gr. 2-3). 14.95 *(978-1-4595-0286-4(8))*; pap. 5.95 *(978-1-4595-0287-1(6))* Formac Publishing Co., Ltd. CAN. Dist: Casemate Pubs. & Bk. Distributors, LLC.

—Lilly Makes a Friend. Bellingham, Brenda. 2004. 62p. (J). lib. bdg. 12.00 *(978-1-4242-1221-7(9))* Fitzgerald Bks.

—Lilly Makes a Friend, 1 vol. Bellingham, Brenda. 2004. (Formac First Novels Ser.: 29). (ENG.). 64p. (J). (gr. 1-5). 4.95 *(978-0-88780-624-7(4))*; 14.95 *(978-0-88780-625-4(2))* Formac Publishing Co., Ltd. CAN. Dist: Casemate Pubs. & Bk. Distributors, LLC.

—Lilly Takes the Lead. Bellingham, Brenda. 2006. (Formac First Novels Ser.: 34). (ENG.). 64p. (gr. 2-5). 14.95 *(978-0-88780-703-9(8))*; (J). 4.95 *(978-0-88780-701-5(1))* Formac Publishing Co., Ltd. CAN. Dist: Casemate Pubs. & Bk. Distributors, LLC.

—Lilly Traps the Bullies. Bellingham, Brenda. 2011. (Formac First Novels Ser.). (ENG.). 64p. (J). (gr. 2-3). 14.95 *(978-0-88780-961-3(8))*; pap. 5.95 *(978-0-88780-959-0(6))* Formac Publishing Co., Ltd. CAN. Dist: Casemate Pubs. & Bk. Distributors, LLC.

—Lilly's Special Gift. Bellingham, Brenda. 2005. (Formac First Novels Ser.: 32). (ENG.). 64p. (gr. 2-5). 14.95 *(978-0-88780-665-0(1))* Formac Publishing Co., Ltd. CAN. Dist: Casemate Pubs. & Bk. Distributors, LLC.

MacDonald, Clarke & Kaulbach, Kathy. Lilly's Special Gift, 1 vol. Bellingham, Brenda. 2005. (Formac First Novels Ser.: 32). (ENG.). 64p. (gr. 2-5). 4.95 *(978-0-88780-664-3(3))* Formac Publishing Co., Ltd. CAN. Dist: Casemate Pubs. & Bk. Distributors, LLC.

MacDonald, John. Tsunami: The True Story of an April Fools' Day Disaster. Karwoski, Gail Langer. 2006. (ENG.). 64p. (gr. 5-12). lib. bdg. 17.95 *(978-1-58196-044-0(1)*, Darby Creek) Lerner Publishing Group.

MacDonald, Judy. Human Body A to Z. Galvin, Laura Gates. 2012. (ENG.). 40p. 9.95 *(978-1-60727-296-0(2))* Soundprints.

MacDonald, Ross. Boys of Steel: The Creators of Superman. Nobleman, Marc Tyler. (ENG.). 40p. (J). 2013. (gr. 5-6). 7.99 *(978-0-449-81063-7(1)*, Dragonfly Bks.); 2008. (gr. 1-4). 16.99 *(978-0-375-83802-6(3)*, Knopf Bks. for Young Readers) Random Hse. Children's Bks.

—Bye-Bye, Crib. McGhee, Alison. 2008. (ENG.). 32p. (J). (gr. -1-1). 16.99 *(978-1-4169-1621-5(0)*, Simon & Schuster/Paula Wiseman Bks.) Simon & Schuster/Paula Wiseman Bks.

—Grumpy Grandpa. Henson, Heather. 2009. (ENG.). 40p. (J). (gr. -1-3). 16.99 *(978-1-4169-0811-1(0)*, Atheneum Bks. for Young Readers) Simon & Schuster Children's Publishing.

—Hey Batta Batta Swing! The Wild Old Days of Baseball. Cook, Sally & Charlton, James. 2007. (ENG.). 56p. (J). (gr. 1-5). 18.99 *(978-1-4169-1207-1(X)*, McElderry, Margaret K. Bks.) McElderry, Margaret K. Bks.

—Hit the Road, Jack. Burleigh, Robert. 2012. (ENG.). 48p. (J). (gr. -1-3). 17.95 *(978-1-4197-0399-7(4)*, Abrams Bks. for Young Readers) Abrams.

Macdonald, Ross, pseud. The Adventure Collection: Treasure Island, the Jungle Book, Gulliver's Travels, White Fang, the Merry Adventures of Robin Hood, 0 vols. Swift, Jonathan et al. unabr. ed. 2012. (Heirloom Collection: 0). (ENG.). 1588p. 99.99 *(978-1-61218-416-6(2)*, 9781612184166) Amazon Publishing.

—The Enchanted Collection: Alice's Adventures in Wonderland; The Secret Garden; Black Beauty; The Wind in the Willows; Little Women, 0 vols. Sewell, Anna et al. unabr. ed. 2012. (Heirloom Collection: 0). (ENG.). 1634p. 99.99 *(978-1-61218-415-9(4)*, 9781612184159) Amazon Publishing.

MacDonald, Stella. Dead Hairy. Thomas, Debbie. 2011. (ENG.). 256p. (J). pap. 14.95 *(978-1-85635-678-7(7))* Mercier Pr., Ltd., The IRL. Dist: Dufour Editions, Inc.

—G. F. Woz Ere. Fitzmaurice, Gabriel. 2009. (ENG.). 96p. (J). pap. 12.95 *(978-1-85635-622-0(1))* Mercier Pr., Ltd., The IRL. Dist: Dufour Editions, Inc.

—Jungle Tangle. Thomas, Debbie. 2013. (ENG.). 320p. (J). pap. 14.95 *(978-1-78117-116-5(5))* Mercier Pr., Ltd., The IRL. Dist: Dufour Editions, Inc.

MacDonald, Suse. Alphabet Animals: A Slide-and-Peek Adventure. MacDonald, Suse. 2008. (ENG.). 28p. (J). (gr. -1-k). 12.99 *(978-1-4169-5045-5(1)*, Little Simon) Little Simon.

—Circus Opposites: An Interactive Extravaganza! MacDonald, Suse. 2010. (ENG.). 20p. (J). (gr. -1-2). bds. 11.99 *(978-1-4169-7154-2(8)*, Little Simon) Little Simon.

—Dino Shapes. MacDonald, Suse. 2014. (ENG.). 20p. (J). (gr. -1-2). bds. 7.99 *(978-1-4814-0093-0(2)*, Little Simon) Little Simon.

—Fish, Swish! Splash, Dash! Counting Round & Round. MacDonald, Suse. 2007. (ENG.). 30p. (J). (gr. -1-k). 9.99 *(978-1-4169-3605-3(X)*, Little Simon) Little Simon.

—Shape by Shape. MacDonald, Suse. 2009. (ENG.). 24p. (J). (gr. -1-3). 16.99 *(978-1-4169-7147-4(5)*, Little Simon) Little Simon.

MacDonall, Angus. Classic Myths. Judd, Mary Catherine. 2007. 172p. per. *(978-1-4065-4675-0(5))* Dodo Pr.

MacDougall, Larry. Hare & the Big Green Lawn. Robey, Katharine Crawford. 2006. (ENG.). 32p. (J). (gr. -1-3). 15.95 *(978-0-87358-889-8(4))* Cooper Square Publishing Llc.

MacDougall, Larry & Fiegenschuh, Emily. The Shadows That Rush Past: A Collection of Frightening Inuit Folktales. Qitsualik, Rachel A. 2011. (ENG.). 42p. (J). (gr. 3-6). 13.95 *(978-1-926569-46-8(6))* Inhabit Media Inc. CAN. Dist: Independent Pubs. Group.

MacEachern, Stephen. Earth-Friendly Buildings, Bridges & More: The Eco-Journal of Corry Lapont. Kaner, Etta. 2012. (ENG.). 64p. (J). 18.95 *(978-1-55453-570-5(0))* Kids Can Pr., Ltd. CAN. Dist: Univ. of Toronto Pr.

—Escapes! Scandiffio, Laura. 2003. (True Stories from the Edge Ser.). (ENG.). 176p. (J). (gr. 4-7). 18.95 *(978-1-55037-823-8(6)*, 9781550378238) Annick Pr., Ltd. CAN. Dist: Firefly Bks., Ltd.

—Gotcha! 18 Amazing Ways to Freak Out Your Friends. Acer, David. 2008. (ENG.). 48p. (J). (gr. 3-7). 16.95 *(978-1-55453-194-3(2))*; pap. 8.95 *(978-1-55453-195-0(0))* Kids Can Pr., Ltd. CAN. Dist: Univ. of Toronto Pr.

—How Football Works. Thomas, Keltie. 2010. (How Sports Work Ser.). (ENG.). 64p. (J). (gr. 3-6). pap. 10.95 *(978-1-897349-88-5(2)*, Maple Tree Pr.) Owlkids Bks. Inc. CAN. Dist: Perseus-PGW.

—38 Ways to Entertain Your Babysitter. Hunter, Dette. 2003. (ENG.). 48p. (J). (gr. -1-4). pap., act. bk. ed. 9.95 *(978-1-55037-794-1(9)*, 9781550377941) Annick Pr., Ltd. CAN. Dist: Firefly Bks., Ltd.

MacEachern, Stephen. The Kids Guide to Money Cent$ MacEachern, Stephen, tr. Thomas, Keltie. 2004. (ENG.). 56p. (J). 8.95 *(978-1-55337-391-9(X))*; (gr. 4-6). 8.95 *(978-1-55337-390-2(1))* Kids Can Pr., Ltd. CAN. Dist: Univ. of Toronto Pr.

MacEachern, Stephen & Owlkids Books Inc. Staff. How Soccer Works. Thomas, Keltie. 2007. (How Sports Work Ser.). (ENG.). 64p. (J). (gr. 3-6). pap. 10.95 *(978-1-897349-01-4(7)*, Maple Tree Pr.) Owlkids Bks. Inc. CAN. Dist: Perseus-PGW.

Macejko, Jeanne Anne. A Million Chameleons. 2004. (J). pap. 10.95 *(978-1-888836-13-4(X))* Shenango River Bks.

MacFarlane, John. Horace the Great Harmonica King. Mayerhofer, Felix. 2006. 31p. (J). (gr. -1-7). per. 16.95 *(978-1-60002-255-5(3)*, 4313) Mountain Valley Publishing, LLC.

MacGregor, Doug. The Incredible Tongue Twister That Swallowed My Sister: Another Santa Story by Doug MacGregor. MacGregor, Doug. ltd. ed. 2006. (J). per. *(978-0-9654843-5-0(1))* MacGregor, Doug.

Machas, Dimi. Tsaani: The Grizzly Bear Story. 2nd ed. 2005. 28p. (YA). 10.00 *(978-0-9767217-0-3(8))* Chickaloon Village Publishing.

Machen Pritchard, M. Ann. Phil the Pill & Friends: Making Positive Choices. Machen Pritchard, M. Ann. 2005. 75p. (J). per. 11.99 *(978-0-9772210-0-4(8)*, Phil the Pill & Friends) MAMP Creations.

Maciá, Raquel García. Jumping Jenny. Bari, Ellen. 2011. (Kar-Ben Favorites Ser.). (ENG.). 32p. (J). (gr. k-3). lib. bdg. 17.95 *(978-0-7613-5141-2(8)*, Kar-Ben Publishing) Lerner Publishing Group.

Macia, Raquel García. Jumping Jenny. Bari, Ellen. 2011. (ENG.). 32p. (J). (gr. k-3). pap. 7.95 *(978-0-7613-5143-6(4)*, Kar-Ben Publishing) Lerner Publishing Group.

Maciborski, Charmaine. Baby, Please Go to Sleep. Prendergast, R. L. 2013. (J). pap. *(978-0-9784548-4-5(7))* Dekko Publishing.

Macintosh, Tessa, photos by. Caribou Feed My Soul, 1 vol. Willett, Mindy & Enzoe, Pete. 2011. (Land Is Our Storyboo Ser.). (ENG., 32p. (J). (gr. 1-4). 16.95 *(978-1-897252-67-3(6))* Fifth Hse. Pubs. CAN. Dist: Ingram Pub. Services.

—Come & Learn with Me, 1 vol. Jumbo, Sheyenne & Willett, Mindy. 2009. (ENG., 32p. (J). (gr. 3-9). 16.95 *(978-1-897252-57-4(9))* Fifth Hse. Pubs. CAN. Dist: Ingram Pub. Services.

—The Delta Is My Home, 1 vol. McLeod, Tom & Willett, Mindy. 2008. (ENG., 32p. (J). (gr. 4-8). *(978-1-897252-32-1(3))* Fitzhenry & Whiteside, Ltd.

—Living Stories: Godi Weghàà Ets' Eèda, 1 vol. Highway, Tomson et al. ed. 2009. (ENG., 32p. *(978-1-897252-44-4(7))* Fitzhenry & Whiteside, Ltd.

—No Borders, 1 vol. Willett, Mindy & Enyagotailak, Darla. 2012. (ENG., 40p. (J). 16.95 *(978-1-927083-07-9(9))* Fifth Hse. Pubs. CAN. Dist: Ingram Pub. Services.

—We Feel Good Out Here, 1 vol. André, Julie-Ann et al. 2008. (ENG., 32p. (J). (gr. 4-7). 16.95 *(978-1-897252-33-8(1))* Fifth Hse. Pubs. CAN. Dist: Ingram Pub. Services.

Mack, David, et al. 411. Gandhi, Arun et al. 2004. (Marvel Heroes Ser.). 96p. (YA). pap. 11.99 *(978-0-7851-1255-6(3))* Marvel Worldwide, Inc.

Mack, Jeff. Boo, Bunny! Galbraith, Kathryn O. 2008. (ENG.). 40p. (J). (gr. -1-2). 16.00 *(978-0-15-216246-7(1))* Houghton Mifflin Harcourt Publishing Co.

—Boo, Bunny! Board Book. Galbraith, Kathryn O. 2012. (ENG.). 32p. (J). (gr. -1 — 1). bds. 5.99 *(978-0-547-81850-4(5))* Houghton Mifflin Harcourt Publishing Co.

—Cindy Moo. Mortensen, Lori. 2012. (ENG.). 32p. (J). (gr. -1-2). 16.99 *(978-0-06-204393-1(5))* HarperCollins Pubs.

—Creepy-Crawly Birthday. Howe, James. (Bunnicula & Friends Ser.: 6). (ENG.). 48p. (J). (gr. 1-3). 2008. pap. 3.99 *(978-0-689-85753-9(5))*; 2007. 16.99 *(978-0-689-85728-7(4))* Simon Spotlight. (Simon Spotlight).

—The Fright Before Christmas. Howe, James. (Bunnicula & Friends Ser.: 5). (ENG.). 48p. (J). (gr. 1-3). 2007. pap. 3.99 *(978-0-689-86941-9(X))*; 2006. 16.99 *(978-0-689-86939-6(8))* Simon Spotlight. (Simon Spotlight).

—Good News, Bad News. 2012. (ENG.). 40p. (J). (gr. -1-1). 16.99 *(978-1-4521-0110-1(8))* Chronicle Bks. LLC.

—Hot Fudge. Howe, James. 2006. (Bunnicula & Friends Ser.). 42p. (gr. k-4). 14.00 *(978-0-7569-7224-0(8))* Perfection Learning Corp.

—Hot Fudge. Howe, James. 2006. (Bunnicula & Friends Ser.: 2). (ENG.). 48p. (J). (gr. 1-3). pap. 3.99 *(978-0-689-85750-8(0)*, Simon Spotlight) Simon Spotlight.

—Hurry! Hurry! Bunting, Eve. (ENG.). (J). 2014. 40p. (gr. -1 — 1). pap. 6.99 *(978-0-544-22733-0(6)*, HMH Books For Young Readers); 2009. 32p. (gr. k — 1). bds. 6.99 *(978-0-15-206686-4(1))*; 2007. 40p. (gr. -1-3). 16.99 *(978-0-15-205410-6(3))* Houghton Mifflin Harcourt Publishing Co.

—Icky Sticky Chameleon. Bentley, Dawn. 2005. 18p. (J). 9.95 *(978-1-58117-086-3(6)*, Intervisual/Piggy Toes) Bendon, Inc.

—Mr. Duck Means Business. Sauer, Tammi. 2011. (ENG.). 32p. (J). (gr. -1-3). 15.99 *(978-1-4169-8522-8(0)*, Simon & Schuster/Paula Wiseman Bks.) Simon & Schuster/Paula Wiseman Bks.

—Rabbit-Cadabra! Howe, James. (Bunnicula & Friends Ser.: 4). (ENG.). 48p. (J). (gr. 1-3). 2007. pap. 3.99 *(978-0-689-85752-2(7))*; 2006. 16.99 *(978-0-689-85727-0(6))* Simon Spotlight. (Simon Spotlight).

—Scared Silly. Howe, James. 2006. (Bunnicula & Friends Ser.). 42p. (gr. 1-3). 14.00 *(978-0-7569-7225-7(6))* Perfection Learning Corp.

—Scared Silly. Howe, James. 2005. (Bunnicula & Friends Ser.: 3). (ENG.). 48p. (J). (gr. 1-3). 16.99 *(978-0-689-85726-3(8)*, Atheneum Bks. for Young Readers) Simon & Schuster Children's Publishing.

—Scared Silly. Howe, James. 2006. (Bunnicula & Friends Ser.: 3). (ENG.). 48p. (J). (gr. 1-3). pap. 3.99 *(978-0-689-85751-5(9)*, Simon Spotlight) Simon Spotlight.

—The Vampire Bunny. Howe, James. 2005. (Bunnicula & Friends Ser.). 41p. (J). (gr. 1-3). 11.65 *(978-0-7569-6832-8(1))* Perfection Learning Corp.

—The Vampire Bunny. Howe, James. 2005. (Bunnicula & Friends Ser.: 1). (ENG.). 48p. (J). (gr. 1-3). pap. 3.99 *(978-0-689-85749-2(7)*, Simon Spotlight) Simon Spotlight.

Mack, Jeff. Clueless Mcgee. Mack, Jeff. 2012. (Clueless Mcgee Ser.: 1). (ENG.). 240p. (J). (gr. 3-7). 12.99 *(978-0-399-25749-0(7)*, Philomel) Penguin Publishing Group.

—Clueless McGee & the Inflatable Pants, Bk. 2. Mack, Jeff. 2013. (Clueless Mcgee Ser.: 2). (ENG.). 256p. (J). (gr. 3-7). 12.99 *(978-0-399-25750-6(0)*, Philomel) Penguin Publishing Group.

—Clueless Mcgee Gets Famous. Mack, Jeff. 2014. (Clueless Mcgee Ser.: 3). (ENG.). 288p. (J). (gr. 3-7). 12.99 *(978-0-399-25751-3(9)*, Philomel) Penguin Publishing Group.

—Hippo & Rabbit. Mack, Jeff. 2011. (Scholastic Reader Level 1 Ser.). (ENG.). 32p. (J). (gr. -1-2). pap. 3.99 *(978-0-545-27445-6(1)*, Cartwheel Bks.) Scholastic, Inc.

—Hippo & Rabbit in Brave Like Me. Mack, Jeff. 2011. (Scholastic Reader Level 1 Ser.). (ENG.). 32p. (J). (gr. -1-2). pap. 3.99 *(978-0-545-28360-1(4)*, Cartwheel Bks.) Scholastic, Inc.

—Hush Little Polar Bear. Mack, Jeff. (ENG.). (J). (gr. -1-1). 2013. 36p. bds. 7.99 *(978-1-59643-945-0(9))*; 2008. 40p. 17.99 *(978-1-59643-368-7(X))* Roaring Brook Pr.

—Look! Mack, Jeff. 2015. (ENG.). 32p. (J). (gr. -1-k). 16.99 *(978-0-399-16205-3(4)*, Philomel) Penguin Publishing Group.

—The Things I Can Do. Mack, Jeff. 2013. (ENG.). 32p. (J). (gr. -1-1). 16.99 *(978-1-59643-675-6(1))* Roaring Brook Pr.

Mack, Jeff. Who Needs a Bath? Mack, Jeff. 2015. (ENG.). 40p. (J). (gr. -1-3). 17.99 ***(978-0-06-222028-8(4))*** HarperCollins Pubs.

Mack, Jeff. Who Wants a Hug? Mack, Jeff. 2015. (ENG.). 40p. (J). (gr. -1-3). 17.99 *(978-0-06-222026-4(8))* HarperCollins Pubs.

Mack, Jeff. Hot Fudge. Mack, Jeff, tr. Howe, James. 2004. (Bunnicula & Friends Ser.: 2). (ENG.). 48p. (J). (gr. 1-3). 16.99 *(978-0-689-85725-6(X)*, Atheneum Bks. for Young Readers) Simon & Schuster Children's Publishing.

—The Vampire Bunny. Mack, Jeff, tr. Henson, Heather et al. 2004. (Bunnicula & Friends Ser.: 1). (ENG.). 48p. (J). (gr. 1-3). 16.99 *(978-0-689-85724-9(1)*, Simon Spotlight) Simon Spotlight.

Mack, Kathryn. Super Cyclist. Carl, Dave. 2010. (ENG.). (J). pap. 12.00 *(978-0-9785160-8-6(7))* Etcetera Pr. LLC.

Mack, Stan. The Road to Revolution! Mack, Stan. Champlin, Susan. 2009. (Cartoon Chronicles of America Ser.). (ENG.). 128p. (J). (gr. 5-7). 16.99 *(978-1-59990-013-1(0)*, Bloomsbury USA Childrens) Bloomsbury USA.

Mack, Steve. AmazErasers: Sweet Shoppe. 2012. (AmazErasers Ser.). (ENG.). 48p. (J). (gr. k). 12.95 *(978-1-60710-431-5(8)*, Silver Dolphin Bks.) Baker & Taylor Publishing Group.

Mack, Steve. Foreman Frankie Is Handy. Goebel, Jenny. 2015. (ENG.). 32p. (J). (gr. -1-k). 3.99 ***(978-0-448-48099-2(9)**, Grosset & Dunlap) Penguin Publishing Group.

Mack, Steve. The Grouchies. Wagenbach, Debbie. 2009. 32p. (J). (gr. -1-3). 14.95 *(978-1-4338-0543-1(X))*; pap. 9.95 *(978-1-4338-0553-0(7))* American Psychological Assn. (Magination Pr.).

—Jurassic Poop: What Dinosaurs (and Others) Left Behind. Berkowitz, Jacob. 2006. (ENG.). 40p. (J). (gr. -1-3). 6.95 *(978-1-55337-867-9(9))*; 14.95 *(978-1-55337-860-0(1))* Kids Can Pr., Ltd. CAN. Dist: Univ. of Toronto Pr.

—Six Sheep Sip Thick Shakes: And Other Tricky Tongue Twisters. Cleary, Brian P. 2011. (Exceptional Reading & Language Arts Titles for Intermediate Grades Ser.). (ENG.). 32p. (J). (gr. k-4). lib. bdg. 16.95 *(978-1-58013-585-6(4))* Lerner Publishing Group.

—Stickley Sticks to It! A Frog's Guide to Getting Things Done. Miles, Brenda. 2014. (J). *(978-1-4338-1910-0(4)*, Magination Pr.) American Psychological Assn.

—Three Falafels in My Pita. Friedman, Maya. 2015. (ENG.). 12p. (J). (gr. -1 — 1). bds. 5.95 *(978-1-4677-3472-1(1)*, Kar-Ben Publishing) Lerner Publishing Group.

—Tikkun Olam Ted. Newman, Vivian. 2013. (Life Cycle Ser.). (ENG.). 12p. (J). (gr. -1 — 1). bds. 5.95 *(978-0-7613-9040-4(5)*, Kar-Ben Publishing) Lerner Publishing Group.

Mack, Travis. I'm Living My Dream: An inspirationsl Rhyme for all Ages in English & Spanish. Spencer, Mignon. 2008.Tr. of Hago mi sueno Realidad. (ENG & SPA.). 32p. (J). 12.99 *(978-0-9763871-2-1(3))* Solomon's Bks.

Mackall, Debbie. What Happens When I'm Asleep? Mackall, Deborah. 2008. (ENG.). 32p. (J). (gr. -1-k). 15.95 *(978-0-9762273-1-1(2))* Dimensions in Media, Inc.

Mackall, Deborah. Be Still! The Story of a Little Bird & How He Found His Purpose. Mackall, Deborah. 2nd ed. 2008. (ENG.). 32p. (J). (gr. -1-k). 15.95 *(978-0-9762273-3-5(9))* Dimensions in Media, Inc.

MacKay, Elly. Best Gifts, 1 vol. Skrypuch, Marsha Forchuk. 2nd ed. 2013. (ENG.). 32p. (J). 18.95 *(978-1-55455-283-2(4))* Fitzhenry & Whiteside, Ltd. CAN. Dist: Midpoint Trade Bks., Inc.

—Fall Leaves. Holland, Loretta. 2014. (ENG.). 32p. (J). (gr. -1-3). 16.99 *(978-0-544-10664-2(4)*, HMH Books For Young Readers) Houghton Mifflin Harcourt Publishing Co.

Mackay, Hugh. Brown Bear, 1 vol. Perry, Laurie. 2010. 22p. pap. 24.95 *(978-1-4489-5702-6(8))* PublishAmerica, Inc.

Mackay, John. Classic Children's Games from Scotland. Ross, Kendric. 128p. pap. 10.95 *(978-1-899827-12-1(9))* Scottish Children's Pr. GBR. Dist: Wilson & Assocs.

Mackay, Louis. What Makes a Tornado Twist? And Other Questions about Weather. Carson, Mary Kay. 2014. (Good Question! Ser.). (ENG.). 32p. (J). (gr. 1). 12.95 *(978-1-4549-0682-7(0))*; pap. 5.95 *(978-1-4549-0683-4(9))* Sterling Publishing Co., Inc.

MacKay, Mark. Missy Moo & Bailey Too Go down the Shore. Kilgannon, Amy. 2012. 22p. pap. 9.99 *(978-1-62050-745-2(5))* PlatyPr.

MacKenzie, Robert. Jack & the Beanstalk. 2008. (Classic Fairy Tale Collection). (ENG.). 32p. (J). (gr. -1-3). 14.95 *(978-1-4027-3064-1(0))* Sterling Publishing Co., Inc.

Mackenzie, Thomas. Aladdin & His Wonderful Lamp in Rhyme. Ransome, Arthur. 2011. (Calla Editions Ser.). (ENG.). 160p. (gr. 5). 30.00 *(978-1-60660-002-3(8))* Dover Pubns., Inc.

Mackey, James. Ava the Angelfish, 1 vol. Shaskan, Trisha Speed. 2008. (Read-It! Readers Ser.). (ENG.). 24p. (gr. -1-3). lib. bdg. 19.99 *(978-1-4048-4079-9(6)*, Easy Readers) Picture Window Bks.

Mackey, Kaitlin L. Little Bear & Honey Bee. MacKey, Esther L. 2012. 28p. 14.95 *(978-1-937260-10-1(0))* Sleepytown Pr.

Mackey, Stephen. Miki. Mackey, Stephen. 2012. (Miki Ser.). (ENG.). 48p. (J). (gr. -1-k). pap. 10.99 *(978-0-340-95065-4(X))* Hodder & Stoughton GBR. Dist: Independent Pubs. Group.

—Pushka. Mackey, Stephen. 2012. (ENG.). 48p. (J). (gr. k-2). 16.99 *(978-1-4449-0134-4(6))* Hodder & Stoughton GBR. Dist: Independent Pubs. Group.

Mackie, Clare. Crazy Creature Capers. Reidy, Hannah. 2003. (Crazy Creatures Ser.). 26p. (J). pap. *(978-1-84089-222-2(6))* Zero to Ten, Ltd.

—Crazy Creature Colors. Reidy, Hannah. 2003. (Crazy Creatures Ser.). 26p. (J). pap. *(978-1-84089-221-5(8))* Zero to Ten, Ltd.

—Crazy Creature Contrasts. Reidy, Hannah. 2003. (Crazy Creatures Ser.). 26p. (J). pap. *(978-1-84089-223-9(4))* Zero to Ten, Ltd.

—Crazy Creatures Counting. Reidy, Hannah. 2003. (Crazy Creatures Ser.). 26p. (J). pap. *(978-1-84089-220-8(X))* Zero to Ten, Ltd.

—Nonsense. Rosen, Michael. 2003. 48p. pap. *(978-0-7500-2671-0(5)*, Wayland) Hachette Children's Group.

Mackie, Marie-Anne. The Adventures of Hamish the Sea Eagle. MacKie, Ian. 2013. 24p. *(978-1-78148-614-6(X))* Grosvenor Hse. Publishing Ltd.

MacKinnon, Catherine-Anne. Babies Baby Flashcards. 2007. (Baby Flashcards Ser.). 16p. (J). (gr. -1-k). 9.99 *(978-0-7945-1571-3(1)*, Usborne) EDC Publishing.

—Cuddly Baby: Snuggletime. Watt, Fiona. 2006. 10p. (J). (gr. -1-k). bds. 8.99 *(978-0-7945-1070-1(1)*, Usborne) EDC Publishing.

—I Love You, Baby. Watt, Fiona. 2008. (Snuggletime Touchy-Feely Ser.). 10p. (J). (gr. -1-k). bds. 8.99 *(978-0-7945-2071-7(5)*, Usborne) EDC Publishing.

—Sleepy Baby. Watt, Fiona. 2006. (Snuggletime Board Bks.). 10p. (J). (gr. -1). bds., bds. 8.99 *(978-0-7945-1071-8(X)*, Usborne) EDC Publishing.

—Snuggletime Busy Baby. Watt, Fiona. 2005. 10p. (J). (gr. -1-k). per., bds. 8.99 *(978-0-7945-1054-1(X)*, Usborne) EDC Publishing.

MacKinnon, Catherine-Anne. Animals Baby Flashcards. MacKinnon, Catherine-Anne. 2007. (Baby Flashcards Ser.). 16p. (J). (gr. -1-k). 9.99 *(978-0-7945-1498-3(7)*, Usborne) EDC Publishing.

MacKinnon, Patsy. King of Keji, 1 vol. Coates, Jan. 2015. (ENG.). 32p. (J). (gr. k-3). pap. 12.95 ***(978-1-77108-281-5(X))*** Nimbus Publishing, Ltd. CAN. Dist: Orca Bk. Pubs. USA.

MacKinstry, Elizabeth. The Fairy Ring. Wiggin, Kate Douglas & Smith, Nora Archibald. 2008. 680p. pap. 20.95 *(978-1-59915-298-1(3))* Yesterday's Classics.

Mackintosh, Michelle. The Best Ever Birthday: Recipes Inspired by Margaret Fulton. Fulton-Keats, Louise. 2013. (ENG.). 80p. 19.95 *(978-1-74270-483-8(2))* Hardie Grant Bks. AUS. Dist: Random Hse., Inc.

—Genie in Charge. Badger, Meredith. 2013. (Tweenie Genie Ser.). (ENG.). 188p. (J). (gr. 2-4). pap. 9.99 (978-1-921848-83-4(9)) Hardie Grant Egmont Pty, Ltd. AUS. Dist: Independent Pubs. Group.
—Undercover. Badger, Meredith. 2007. (Fairy School Drop-Out Ser.). 144p. (J). (978-1-921098-71-0(6)) Hardie Grant Egmont Pty, Ltd.
MacLean, Amber. China's Daughters. Williams, Suzanne. 2011. (J). (978-1-881896-34-0(X)) Pacific View Pr.
Maclean, Andrew. Siff a Saff: A Straeon Eraill. Davies, Helen Emanuel. 2005. (WEL.). 64p. pap. (978-0-86381-364-1(X)) Gwasg Carreg Gwalch.
MacLean, Colin & MacLean, Moira. Baby's First Bible. Reader's Digest Staff. 2009. (ENG.). 20p. (J). (gr. -1 — 1). bds. 14.99 (978-0-7944-1942-4(9)) Reader's Digest Assn., Inc., The.
MacLean, Kerry Lee. Mindful Monkey, Happy Panda. Alderfer, Lauren. 2011. (ENG.). 32p. (J). (gr. -1-3). 16.95 (978-0-86171-683-8(3)) Wisdom Pubns.
MacLean, Kerry Lee. Peacefully Piggy Meditation. MacLean, Kerry Lee. 2004. (ENG.). 32p. (J). (gr. k-4). 6.99 (978-0-8075-6381-6(1)) Whitman, Albert & Co.
Maclean, Moira. Bible Adventures & Activities. Wright, Sally Ann. 2012. 144p. (J). pap. 11.95 (978-0-8198-1199-8(8)) Pauline Bks. & Media.
MacLean, Moira. First COLL of Bible Stories & Stickers: Daniel, Jonah, Jesus & Other Stories. Reynolds, Annette. 2004. 16p. pap. 8.95 (978-1-59325-045-4(2)) Word Among Us Pr.
—First COLL of Bible Stories & Stickers: Noahn, Samson, Jesus & Other Stories. Reynolds, Annette. 2004. 16p. pap. 8.95 (978-1-59325-044-7(4)) Word Among Us Pr.
—Knock, Knock! Who's There at Christmas? Howie, Vickie. 2004. 20p. (J). bds. 9.49 (978-0-7586-0649-5(4)) Concordia Publishing Hse.
—The Look & See Bible. Wright, Sally Ann. 2006. (Children's Bibles & Bible Story Collections). 94p. (J). (gr. -1-3). 12.95 (978-0-8091-6735-7(2), 6735-2) Paulist Pr.
—My First Christmas Sticker Book. Wright, Sally Ann. 2007. (J). (gr. -1-3). 6.95 (978-0-8198-4852-9(2)) Pauline Bks. & Media.
MacLean, Moira, jt. illus. see MacLean, Colin.
MacLeod, Gavin. Action Robots: A Pop-up Book Showing How They Work. Reeve, Tim. 2004. 14p. (YA). (gr. 4-10). reprint ed. 17.00 (978-0-7567-7284-0(2)) DIANE Publishing Co.
MacLure, Ashley. Beyond the Science Lab. Lindsey, Jason. 2012. 82p. pap. 16.95 (978-0-9854248-4-8(2)) Pinwheel Bks.
MacMenamin, John. Islands. Raine, Bonnie. 2003. 48p. (J). per. (978-1-931456-74-6(7)) Athena Pr.
—Two of Our Friends Are Doves. Coon, Thomas & Coon, Helene. 2003. 64p. (J). per. (978-1-932077-17-9(0)) Athena Pr.
MacMillan, Eric G. Khala Maninge - the Little Elephant That Cried a Lot: An African Fable. MacMillan, Ian C. 2nd ed. 2003. lib. bdg. 5.00 (978-0-9729698-0-2(2)) Maninge Mali.
Macnaughton, Tina. Are You Sad, Little Bear? A Book about Learning to Say Goodbye. Rivett, Rachel. (ENG.). (J). (-k). 2013. 32p. 9.99 (978-0-7459-6430-0(3)); 2010. 28p. 12.99 (978-0-7459-6137-8(1)) Lion Hudson PLC GBR. Dist: Independent Pubs. Group.
—An Arkful of Animal Prayers. Piper, Sophie. 2009. (ENG.). 64p. (J). (gr. -1-2). 9.95 (978-0-7459-6064-7(2)) Lion Hudson PLC GBR. Dist: Independent Pubs. Group.
—An Arkful of Animal Stories. Goodwin, John. 2008. 32p. (J). (gr. k-3). 13.95 (978-0-8198-0782-3(6)) Pauline Bks. & Media.
—One Magical Day, 1 vol. Freedman, Claire. 2007. (ENG.). 28p. (J). (gr. -1-1). pap. 16.95 (978-1-56148-567-3(5), Good Bks.) Skyhorse Publishing Co., Inc.
Macnaughton, Tina. One Special Christmas. Butler, M. Christina. 2013. (J). **(978-1-58925-145-8(8))** Tiger Tales.
Macnaughton, Tina. Where Snowflakes Fall. Freedman, Claire. 2012. 24p. (J). (978-1-4351-4321-0(3)) Barnes & Noble, Inc.
MacNeil, Chris. The Chipster's Sister. Wollman, Jessica. 2005. (Penelope Fritter: Super-Sitter Ser.: 1). (ENG.). 128p. (J). (gr. 3-7). pap. 7.99 (978-1-4169-0089-4(6), Simon & Schuster/Paula Wiseman Bks.) Simon & Schuster/Paula Wiseman Bks.
—Meet the Phonees. Wollman, Jessica. 2005. (Penelope Fritter: Super-Sitter Ser.: 2). (ENG.). 144p. (J). (gr. 3-7). pap. 4.99 (978-1-4169-0090-0(X), Simon & Schuster/Paula Wiseman Bks.) Simon & Schuster/Paula Wiseman Bks.
Maconachie, Roy, photos by. Cape Town. Bowden, Rob. 2006. (Global Cities Ser.). 64p. (gr. 5-8). 30.00 (978-0-7910-8856-2(1), Chelsea Hse.) Facts On File, Inc.
Macor, Jim. Frazier Fir, A Christmas Fable. Macor, Jim. 2007. 32p. (J). 17.95 (978-0-9785551-3-9(9)) Zuber Publishing.
MacPherson, Bruce. Josefina Javelina: A Hairy Tale. Lowell, Susan. 2005. (ENG.). 32p. (J). (gr. -1-3). 15.95 (978-0-87358-790-7(1)) Cooper Square Publishing Llc.
—Thank You, Aunt Tallulah! Coyle, Carmela Lavigna. 2006. (ENG.). 32p. (J). (gr. -1-3). 15.95 (978-0-87358-891-1(6)) Cooper Square Publishing Llc.
Macpherson, Carol. Littlestar, 1 vol. Grandmother Littlewolf. 2010. (ENG.). 19p. pap. 24.95 (978-1-4489-8619-4(2)) America Star Bks.
Macquignon, Stephen. Ferdinand Frog's Flight. Mayer, Marvin. 2011. 32p. pap. 15.55 (978-0-9832740-0-1(2)) 4RV Publishing, LLC.
—Why Am I Me? Harris-Wyrick, Wayne. 2011. 32p. pap. 17.99 (978-0-9828346-2-6(4)) 4RV Publishing, LLC.
MacRae, Jock. The Kids Book of Canada. Greenwood, Barbara. 2007. (Kids Book Of Ser.). (ENG.). 60p. (J). (gr. 4-7). 14.95 (978-1-55453-226-1(4)) Kids Can Pr., Ltd. CAN. Dist: Univ. of Toronto Pr.
Macy, Carolyn. Hawaiian Night Before Christmas, 1 vol. Macy, Carolyn. 2008. (Night Before Christmas Ser.). (ENG.). 32p. (gr. 1-3). 16.99 (978-1-58980-598-9(4)) Pelican Publishing Co., Inc.
Mada Design Inc. Kung Fu Panda. Chihak, Sheena & Loki. 2008. (I Can Find It Ser.). 22p. (J). 7.99 (978-0-696-23484-2(X)) Meredith Bks.
Mada Design, Inc Staff. Superman Versus Bizarro. Stratheam, Chris. 2010. (I Can Read Book 2 Ser.). (ENG.). 32p. (J). (gr. -1-3). pap. 3.99 (978-0-06-188516-7(9)) HarperCollins Pubs.
Mada Design Staff. Batman Classic: Gotham's Villains Unleashed! Sazaklis, John. 2009. (ENG.). 24p. (J). (gr. -1-3). pap. 3.99 (978-0-06-187856-5(1), HarperFestival) HarperCollins Pubs.
—Heads or Tails. Sudduth, Brent & Meredith Books Staff. 2008. 20p. (J). pap. 3.99 (978-0-696-23959-5(0)) Meredith Bks.
—Superman Classic: Superman & the Mayhem of Metallo. Stephens, Sarah Hines. 2010. (Superman Classics). (ENG.). 24p. (J). (gr. -1-3). pap. 3.99 (978-0-06-188529-7(0), HarperFestival) HarperCollins Pubs.
—Superman Versus Mongul. Teitelbaum, Michael. 2011. (I Can Read Book 2 Ser.). (ENG.). 32p. (J). (gr. -1-3). pap. 3.99 (978-0-06-188518-1(5)) HarperCollins Pubs.
Madan, Fredric C. & Ernst, Clara. Greer Garson Paper Dolls. Madan, Fredric C. 2007. (ENG.). 16p. pap. 12.00 (978-0-9790668-3-7(7)) Paper Studio Pr.
Madaras, Diana & Nielsen, Ric. Kitty Humbug's Christmas Tail. Madaras, Diana. 2009. 24p. 17.99 (978-1-892344-56-4(4)) Palomino Publishing.
Madden, Colleen. Green Fever. Brunstetter, Wanda E. 2013. (Double Trouble Ser.: 4). (ENG.). 160p. (J). pap. 5.99 (978-1-62416-286-2(X), Barbour Bks.) Barbour Publishing, Inc.
—Happy Sparkling Halloween. Spurr, Elizabeth. 2010. (Sparkling Stories Ser.). (ENG.). 14p. (J). (gr. k-k). bds. 5.95 (978-1-4027-7138-5(X)) Sterling Publishing Co., Inc.
—Happy Sparkling Hanukkah. Spurr, Elizabeth. 2011. (J). (978-1-4027-9660-9(9)) Sterling Publishing Co., Inc.
—Humble Pie. Brunstetter, Wanda E. 2014. (Double Trouble Ser.: 5). (ENG.). 160p. (J). pap. 5.99 (978-1-62836-389-0(4), Barbour Bks.) Barbour Publishing, Inc.
Madden, Colleen, et al. Little Red Riding Hood Stories Around the World: 3 Beloved Tales, 1 vol. Gunderson, Jessica. 2014. (Multicultural Fairy Tales Ser.). (ENG.). 32p. (gr. k-2). lib. bdg. 26.65 (978-1-4795-5435-5(9)) Picture Window Bks.
Madden, Colleen. Making New Friends. Blumenstock, Jacqueline & Pool, David. 2nd ed. 2005. 32p. (J). lib. bdg. 14.95 (978-0-9764647-1-6(3)) Big Brown Box, Inc., The.
Madden, Colleen, et al. Multicultural Fairy Tales, 1 vol. Gunderson, Jessica & Meister, Cari. 2014. (Multicultural Fairy Tales Ser.). (ENG.). 32p. (gr. k-2). 106.60 (978-1-4795-5547-5(9)) Picture Window Bks.
Madden, Colleen. Your Life As a Private on the Lewis & Clark Expedition, 1 vol. Gunderson, Jessica Sarah. 2012. (Way It Was Ser.). (ENG.). 32p. (gr. 2-3). pap. 7.95 (978-1-4048-7746-7(0), Nonfiction Picture Bks.) Picture Window Bks.
—Your Life As a Private on the Lewis & Clark Expedition, 1 vol. Gunderson, Jessica. 2012. (Way It Was Ser.). (ENG.). 32p. (gr. 2-3). lib. bdg. 25.99 (978-1-4048-7370-4(8), Nonfiction Picture Bks.) Picture Window Bks.
Madden, Colleen M. Diva Duck Dreams. Levy, Janice. 2012. (Diva Duck Ser.). 32p. (J). (gr. -1-4). 28.50 (978-1-61641-886-1(9)) Magic Wagon.
—Diva Duck Goes to Hollywood. Levy, Janice. 2012. (Diva Duck Ser.). 32p. (J). (gr. -1-4). 28.50 (978-1-61641-887-8(7)) Magic Wagon.
—Diva Duck Travels the World. Levy, Janice. 2012. (Diva Duck Ser.). 32p. (J). (gr. -1-4). 28.50 (978-1-61641-888-5(5)) Magic Wagon.
—Flip-Flop & the Absolutely Awful New Baby. Levy, Janice. 2011. (Flip-Flop Adventure Ser.). (ENG.). 32p. (J). (gr. k-3). 28.50 (978-1-61641-651-5(3)) Magic Wagon.
—Flip-Flop & the BFFs. Levy, Janice. 2011. (Flip-Flop Adventure Ser.). (ENG.). 32p. (J). (gr. k-3). 28.50 (978-1-61641-652-2(1)) Magic Wagon.
—Flip-Flop & the Bully Frogs Gruff. Levy, Janice. 2011. (Flip-Flop Adventure Ser.). (ENG.). 32p. (J). (gr. k-3). 28.50 (978-1-61641-653-9(X)) Magic Wagon.
Madden, Colleen M. Humble Pie. Brunstetter, Wanda E. 2014. 158p. (J). **(978-1-63058-967-7(5))** Barbour Publishing, Inc.
Madden, Colleen M. The Library Gingerbread Man. Enderle, Dotti. 2010. 32p. (J). (gr. -1). 17.95 (978-1-60213-048-7(5), Upstart Bks.) Highsmith Inc.
—School Rules for Diva Duck. Levy, Janice. 2012. (Diva Duck Ser.). 32p. (J). (gr. -1-4). 28.50 (978-1-61641-889-2(3)) Magic Wagon.
—Showtime for Flip-Flop. Levy, Janice. 2011. (Flip-Flop Adventure Ser.). (ENG.). 32p. (J). (gr. k-3). 28.50 (978-1-61641-654-6(8)) Magic Wagon.
—Water, Weed, & Wait. Fine, Edith Hope & Halpin, Angela Demos. 2010. (ENG.). 32p. (J). (gr. k-3). 15.99 (978-1-58246-320-9(4), Tricycle Pr.) Ten Speed Pr.
—What If a Stranger Approaches You?, 1 vol. Guard, Anara. 2011. (Danger Zone Ser.). (ENG.). 24p. (gr. 1-2). pap. 7.49 (978-1-4048-7031-4(8)); lib. bdg. 25.32 (978-1-4048-6683-6(3)) Picture Window Bks. (Nonfiction Picture Bks.).
—What If Everybody Did That?, 0 vols. Javernick, Ellen. 2010. (ENG.). 32p. (J). (gr. -1-2). 12.99 (978-0-7614-5686-5(4), 9780761456865, Amazon Children's Publishing) Amazon Publishing.
Madden-Lunsford, Lucy. Nothing Fancy about Kathryn & Charlie. Madden-Lunsford, Kerry. 2013. (ENG.). 36p. (J). pap. 14.95 (978-0-9828528-0-4(0)) Mockingbird Publishing.
Maddin, John. Letters of the West. Maddin, John. Walch, Michelle E. 2014. (Little Naturalist Ser.). (ENG.). 32p. (J). (gr. -1-k). 17.99 (978-1-940052-10-6(6)) Craigmore Creations.
Maddison, Kevin. Book of Greek Gods Pop-Up Board Games. Tango Books. 2007. (Pop-Up Board Games Ser.). (ENG.). 10p. (J). (gr. -1-2). 24.99 (978-1-85707-689-9(3)) Tango Bks. GBR. Dist: Independent Pubs. Group.
—Book of Roman Pop-Up Board Games. Fields, Sadie & Tango Books Staff. 2004. (Pop-Up Board Games Ser.). (ENG.). 10p. (J). (gr. -1-2). 24.99 (978-1-85707-597-7(8)) Tango Bks. GBR. Dist: Independent Pubs. Group.
Maddison, Lucy. I'm Telling on You! Poems about Brothers & Sisters. Moses, Brian. 2003. (ENG.). 60p. (J). pap. (978-0-330-36867-4(2), Pan) Pan Macmillan.
—The Practical Joker's Handbook 2. Dinneen, John. (ENG.). 80p. (J). pap. 4.95 (978-0-330-35524-7(4), Pan) Pan Macmillan GBR. Dist: Trafalgar Square Publishing.
Maddock, Monika. Horsing Around. Arena, Jacqueline. 2005. (Girlz Rock! Ser.). (J). pap. (978-1-59336-703-9(1)) Mondo Publishing.
—Pool Pals. Smith Dinbergs, Holly. 2005. (Girlz Rock! Ser.). (J). pap. (978-1-59336-705-3(8)) Mondo Publishing.
—School Play Stars. Mullins, Julie. 2005. (Girlz Rock! Ser.). (J). pap. (978-1-59336-706-0(6)) Mondo Publishing.
Maddocks, Maria. Animal Parade. Nolan, Allia Zobel. 2011. (ENG.). 10p. (J). (gr. -1 — 1). 12.99 (978-0-547-55867-7(8)) Houghton Mifflin Harcourt Publishing Co.
—Animal Parade. Zobel-Nolan, Allia. 2008. 10p. (J). (gr. -1). 12.95 (978-1-932915-63-1(X)) Sandvik Innovations, LLC.
—Baby's First Bible. Piper, Sophie. 2014. (ENG.). 40p. (J). (— 1). bds. 9.99 (978-0-7459-6411-9(7)) Lion Hudson PLC GBR. Dist: Independent Pubs. Group.
—The Christmas Story. Goodings, Christina. 2014. (ENG.). 6p. (J). (gr. -1-k). bds. 12.99 (978-0-7459-6380-8(3)) Lion Hudson PLC GBR. Dist: Independent Pubs. Group.
—Diggers & Dumpers. Wilding, Valerie. 2006. (Green Bananas Ser.). (ENG.). 48p. (J). (gr. -1-k). lib. bdg. (978-0-7787-1030-1(0)) Crabtree Publishing Co.
—Our Ballet Recital. Piggy Toes Press. 2005. (ENG.). 12p. (J). (gr. -1-3). 12.95 (978-1-58117-425-0(X), Intervisual/Piggy Toes) Bendon, Inc.
—Two Little Ballerinas: A Girly Girl Book. 2009. (ENG.). 10p. (J). 9.95 (978-1-58117-871-5(5), Intervisual/Piggy Toes) Bendon, Inc.
Mader, C. Roger. Lost Cat. Mader, C. Roger. 2013. (ENG.). 32p. (J). (gr. -1-3). 17.99 (978-0-547-97458-3(2)) Houghton Mifflin Harcourt Publishing Co.
—Tiptop Cat. Mader, C. Roger. 2014. (ENG.). 40p. (J). (gr. -1-3). 17.99 (978-0-544-14799-7(5), HMH Books For Young Readers) Houghton Mifflin Harcourt Publishing Co.
Madill, Douglas. Why Me, Lord? For victims of sexual & physical Abuse, 1 vol. Bissell, Sybil A. 2nd l.t. ed. 2004. Orig. Title: Why Me, Lord? for Victims of Sexual & Physical Abuse. (ENG.). 36p. pap. 7.95 (978-0-9747516-0-3(X), 1001) Heart Communications.
Madonna, Marissa. There's a Hole in the Bucket! 2013. (First Steps in Music Ser.). (ENG.). 32p. (J). (gr. k-2). 16.95 (978-1-57999-970-4(0)) G I A Pubns., Inc.
Madrid, Erwin. Amy Namey in Ace Reporter. McDonald, Megan. 2014. (Judy Moody Ser.: 3). (ENG.). 64p. (J). (gr. -1-1). 12.99 (978-0-7636-5715-4(8)) Candlewick Pr.
—Frank Pearl in the Awful Waffle Kerfuffle. McDonald, Megan. 2014. (Judy Moody Ser.: 4). (ENG.). 64p. (J). (gr. -1-1). 12.99 (978-0-7636-5717-8(4)) Candlewick Pr.
—Jessica Finch in Pig Trouble. McDonald, Megan. 2014. (Judy Moody Ser.: 1). (ENG.). 64p. (J). (gr. -1-1). 12.99 (978-0-7636-5718-5(2)); pap. 4.99 (978-0-7636-7027-6(8)) Candlewick Pr.
—Juniper Berry. Kozlowsky, M. P. (ENG.). 240p. (J). (gr. 3-7). 2012. pap. 5.99 (978-0-06-199870-6(2)); 2011. 15.99 (978-0-06-199869-0(9)) HarperCollins Pubs. (Waldon Pond Pr.).
—Little Rhino #1: My New Team. Howard, Ryan & Howard, Krystle. 2015. (Little Rhino Ser.: 1). (ENG.). 112p. (J). (gr. 2-5). pap. 4.99 (978-0-545-67490-4(5), Scholastic Paperbacks) Scholastic, Inc.
—Little Rhino #2: the Best Bat. Howard, Ryan & Howard, Krystle. 2015. (Little Rhino Ser.: 2). (ENG.). 112p. (J). (gr. 2-5). pap. 4.99 (978-0-545-67493-5(X), Scholastic Paperbacks) Scholastic, Inc.
—Little Rhino #2: the Best Bat - Library Edition. Howard, Ryan & Howard, Krystle. 2015. (Little Rhino Ser.: 2). (ENG.). 112p. (J). (gr. 2-5). 16.99 (978-0-545-67494-2(8), Scholastic Paperbacks) Scholastic, Inc.
Madrid, Erwin. Little Rhino #3: Dugout Hero. Howard, Ryan & Howard, Krystle. 2015. (Little Rhino Ser.: 3). (ENG.). 112p. (J). (gr. 2-5). pap. 4.99 **(978-0-545-67496-6(4),** Scholastic Paperbacks) Scholastic, Inc.
Madrid, Erwin. My New Team. Howard, Ryan & Howard, Krystle. 2015. (Little Rhino Ser.: 1). (ENG.). 112p. (J). (gr. 2-5). 16.99 (978-0-545-67491-1(3), Scholastic Paperbacks) Scholastic, Inc.
—The Prairie Thief. Wiley, Melissa. (ENG.). 224p. (J). (gr. 3-7). 2013. pap. 6.99 (978-1-4424-4057-9(0)); 2012. 15.99 (978-1-4424-4056-2(2)) McElderry, Margaret K. Bks. (McElderry, Margaret K. Bks.).
—Rudolph the Red-Nosed Reindeer - The Classic Story. Feldman, Thea. 2014. (Rudolph the Red-Nosed Reindeer Ser.). (ENG.). 40p. (J). (gr. -1-3). 12.99 (978-1-250-04760-1(9)) Square Fish.
—The Scary Places Map Book: Seven Terrifying Tours. Hennessy, B. G. 2012. (ENG.). 32p. (J). (gr. k-4). 15.99 (978-0-7636-4541-0(9)) Candlewick Pr.
—Stink Moody in Master of Disaster. McDonald, Megan. 2015. (Judy Moody Ser.: 5). (ENG.). 64p. (J). (gr. -1-1). 12.99 (978-0-7636-7218-8(1)) Candlewick Pr.
Madrid, Erwin. Triple Pet Trouble. McDonald, Megan. 2015. (Judy Moody Ser.: 6). (ENG.). 64p. (J). (gr. -1-1). 12.99 **(978-0-7636-7443-4(5))** Candlewick Pr.
Madrid, Erwin & Castelao, Patricia. Mermaids in the Backyard. Hapka, Catherine. 2013. (Stepping Stone Book Ser.). (ENG.). 112p. (J). (gr. 1-4). 4.99 (978-0-307-97637-6(8)) Random Hse., Inc.
—Mermaids in the Backyard. Hapka, Catherine. 2013. (Stepping Stone Book Ser.). (ENG.). 112p. (J). (gr. 1-4). lib. bdg. 12.99 (978-0-375-97120-4(3)) Random Hse., Inc.
Madsen, James. The Christmas House. Madsen, James. Bullman, Carol. 2009. 32p. (J). (gr. -1-3). 16.99 (978-0-8249-5598-4(6), Ideals Children's Bks.) Ideals Pubns.
Madsen, Jim. Adventure Bible Storybook, 1 vol. DeVries, Catherine. 2009. (Adventure Bible Ser.). (ENG.). 288p. (J). 16.99 (978-0-310-71637-2(3)) Zonderkidz.
—Adventures of Thor the Thunder God. Lunge-Larsen, Lise. 2007. (ENG.). 80p. (gr. 5-7). 19.95 (978-0-618-47301-4(7)) Houghton Mifflin Harcourt Publishing Co.
—The Crossing. Napoli, Donna Jo. 2011. (ENG.). 40p. (J). (gr. -1-3). 16.99 (978-1-4169-9474-9(2), Atheneum Bks. for Young Readers) Simon & Schuster Children's Publishing.
—Family Huddle. Manning, Peyton et al. 2009. (J). (ENG.). 32p. (gr. -1-3). 16.99 (978-0-545-15377-5(8)); (978-0-545-21351-6(7)) Scholastic, Inc. (Scholastic Pr.).
—How Does the Ear Hear? And Other Questions about the Five Senses. Stewart, Melissa. 2014. (Good Question! Ser.). (ENG.). 32p. (J). (gr. 1). 12.95 (978-1-4549-0672-8(3)) Sterling Publishing Co., Inc.
—The Jungle Book: Rikki-Tikki-Tavi Moves In. Kipling, Rudyard. 2008. (Easy Reader Classics Ser.). (ENG.). 32p. (gr. 4-7). lib. bdg. 24.21 (978-1-59961-336-9(0)) Spotlight.
—Legacy of the Claw. Grey, C. R. 2014. (Animas Ser.). (ENG.). 304p. (J). (gr. 3-7). 16.99 (978-1-4231-8038-8(0)) Disney Pr.
—The Little Shepherd Girl: A Christmas Story. Henry, Juliann. 2007. 32p. (J). (gr. -1-3). 14.99 (978-0-7814-4513-9(2)) Cook, David C.
—Marvin Makes Music. Hamlisch, Marvin. 2012. (ENG.). 32p. (J). (gr. -1-3). 17.99 (978-0-8037-3730-3(0), Dial) Penguin Publishing Group.
—A Spotlight for Harry. Kimmel, Eric A. 2010. (Stepping Stone Book Ser.). (ENG.). 112p. (J). (gr. 2-5). pap. 4.99 (978-0-375-85696-9(X)) Random Hse., Inc.
—Tuki & Moka: A Tale of Two Tamarins. Young, Judy. 2013. (ENG.). 32p. 16.99 (978-1-58536-795-5(8)) Sleeping Bear Pr.
—What Was Your Dream, Dr. King? And Other Questions About... Martin Luther King, Jr. Carson, Mary Kay. 2013. (Good Question! Ser.). (ENG.). 32p. (J). (gr. 2). 12.95 (978-1-4027-9622-7(6)); pap. 5.95 (978-1-4027-9045-4(7)) Sterling Publishing Co., Inc.
Madsen, Jim & Henderson, Meryl. Coretta Scott King: First Lady of Civil Rights. Stanley, George E. 2008. (Childhood of Famous Americans Ser.). (ENG.). 224p. (J). (gr. 3-7). pap. 5.99 (978-1-4169-6800-9(8), Simon & Schuster/Paula Wiseman Bks.) Simon & Schuster/Paula Wiseman Bks.
Madsen, Michelle, jt. illus. see Jeanty, Georges.
Madsen, Michelle, jt. illus. see Moline, Karl.
Madzel, D. E., jt. illus. see Robinson-Chavez, Kathryn A.
Maeda, Matsuo. The Turtle & the Warrior. Arai, Shizuko. 2014. (J). 8.95 (978-1-935523-69-7(4)) World Tribune Pr.
Maeda, Toshio. Adventure Kid - the Original Manga 1 Vol. 1: User Friendly. Maeda, Toshio. 2003. 208p. pap. 16.95 (978-1-58664-878-7(0), CMX 63501G, Manga 18) Central Park Media Corp.
Maeno, Itoko. Gift of Flowers. Paine, Penelope C. 2006. 24p. per. 5.95 (978-0-9707944-5-1(2)) Paper Posie.
—Gift of Love. Paine, Penelope C. 2006. 24p. per. 5.95 (978-0-7909-7443-9(6)) Paper Posie.
—Gift of Taste. Paine, Penelope C. 2006. 24p. per. 5.95 (978-0-9707944-6-8(0)) Paper Posie.
Maes, Ame. Tomorrow I Am a Big Sister, but Today I Am Me. Munoz, Ruby. 2008. 24p. pap. 24.95 (978-1-60672-862-8(8)) America Star Bks.
Maese, Fares. Soccer Longshot, 1 vol. Renner, C. J. et al. 2011. (Sports Illustrated Kids Graphic Novels Ser.). (ENG.). 56p. (gr. 2-3). lib. bdg. 25.32 (978-1-4342-2241-1(1)) Stone Arch Bks.
Maese, Fares & Aburto, Jesus. Soccer Longshot, 1 vol. Renner, C. J. et al. 2011. (Sports Illustrated Kids Graphic Novels Ser.). (ENG.). 56p. (gr. 2-3). pap. 7.19 (978-1-4342-3402-5(9)) Stone Arch Bks.
Maestro, Giulio. Eight Ate: A Feast of Homonym Riddles. Terban, Marvin. 2007. (ENG.). 64p. (J). (gr. -1-3). pap. 7.99 (978-0-618-76676-5(6)) Houghton Mifflin Harcourt Publishing Co.
—Guppies in Tuxedos: Funny Eponyms. Terban, Marvin. 2008. (ENG.). 64p. (J). (gr. 5-7). pap. 7.95 (978-0-547-03188-0(2)) Houghton Mifflin Harcourt Publishing Co.
—In a Pickle: And Other Funny Idioms. Terban, Marvin. 2007. (ENG.). 64p. (J). (gr. -1-3). pap. 7.99 (978-0-618-83001-5(4)) Houghton Mifflin Harcourt Publishing Co.
—Liberty or Death: The American Revolution: 1763-1783. Maestro, Betsy. 2005. 64p. (J). lib. bdg. 17.89 (978-0-688-08803-3(1)); (ENG.). (gr. 2-7). 18.99 (978-0-688-08802-6(3), Collins) HarperCollins Pubs.
—Mad As a Wet Hen! And Other Funny Idioms. Terban, Marvin. 2007. (ENG.). 64p. (J). (gr. -1-3). pap. 6.95 (978-0-618-83003-9(0)) Houghton Mifflin Harcourt Publishing Co.
—A More Perfect Union: The Story of Our Constitution. Maestro, Betsy. 2008. (American Story Ser.). (ENG.). 48p. (J). (gr. 2-7). pap. 7.99 (978-0-688-10192-3(5), Collins) HarperCollins Pubs.
—The New Americans: Colonial Times: 1620-1689. Maestro, Betsy. 2004. (American Story Ser.). (ENG.). 48p. (J). (gr. 2-7). pap. 7.99 (978-0-06-057572-4(7)) HarperCollins Pubs.
—The Story of Clocks & Calendars. Maestro, Betsy. 2004. (ENG.). 48p. (J). (gr. 2-7). pap. 9.99 (978-0-06-058945-5(0)) HarperCollins Pubs.
—Too Hot to Hoot: Funny Palindrome Riddles. Terban, Marvin. 2008. (ENG.). 64p. (J). (gr. 2-5). pap. 8.95 (978-0-618-19165-9(8)) Houghton Mifflin Harcourt Publishing Co.
—Your Foot's on My Feet! And Other Tricky Nouns. Terban, Marvin. 2008. (ENG.). 64p. (J). (gr. 2-5). pap. 7.99

(978-0-618-19166-6(6)) Houghton Mifflin Harcourt Publishing Co.

Maestro, Laura Hartman, jt. illus. see Muth, Jon J.

Magagna, Anna Marie. My Book about God's World. Mays, Blanche, ed. 2011. 28p. pap. 35.95 (978-1-258-10454-2(7)) Literary Licensing, LLC.

Magalinska, Ingrid. Charlie's Perfect Day. Likins, Kim. I.t. ed. 2003. 32p. (J). bds. (978-0-9729987-0-3(5)) Island Friends LLC.

Magallanes, Alejandro. Con Cuatro Alcanza. Hernandez, Claudia et al. rev. ed. 2006. (Otra Escalera Ser.). (ENG.). 36p. (J). pap. 8.95 (978-970-20-0811-8(5)) Castillo, Ediciones, S. A. de C. V. MEX. Dist: Macmillan.

—Quien Es Criminal? un Recorrido Por el Delito, la Ley, la Justicia y el Castigo en Mexico: Desde el Virreinato Hasta el Siglo XX. Guerra, Elisa Speckman. rev. ed. 2006. (Castillo de la Lectura Roja Ser.). 84p. (YA). (gr. 8-10). pap. 14.95 (978-970-20-0829-3(8)) Castillo, Ediciones, S. A. de C. V. MEX. Dist: Macmillan.

—Ruge! Baranda, Maria. 2009. (SPA.). (J). (gr. -1-k). bds. (978-968-5389-65-5(9)) El Naranjo, Ediciones.

Magaril, Mikhail. The Feather Merchants, & Other Tales of the Fools of Chelm. Sanfield, Steve. 2005. 102p. (J). (gr. 3-6). reprint ed. 16.00 (978-0-7567-8554-3(5)) DIANE Publishing Co.

Magdalena-Brown, Maria. My Little Book of Burrowing Owls. Irvin-Marston, Hope. 2nd ed. 2004. 32p. (J). pap. 7.95 (978-0-89317-054-7(2), WW-0542, Windward Publishing) Finney Co., Inc.

—My Little Book of Painted Turtles. Irvin-Marston, Hope. 2nd ed. 2004. 32p. (J). pap. 7.95 (978-0-89317-055-4(0), WW-0550, Windward Publishing) Finney Co., Inc.

—My Little Book of River Otters. Irvin-Marston, Hope. 2nd ed. 2004. 32p. (J). pap. 7.95 (978-0-89317-051-6(8), WW-0518, Windward Publishing) Finney Co., Inc.

—My Little Book of Timber Wolves. Irvin-Marston, Hope. 2nd ed. 2004. 32p. (J). pap. 7.95 (978-0-89317-052-3(6), WW-0526, Windward Publishing) Finney Co., Inc.

—My Little Book of Whitetails. Irvin-Marston, Hope. 2004. 32p. (J). pap. 7.95 (978-0-89317-050-9(X), WW-050X, Windward Publishing) Finney Co., Inc.

—My Little Book of Wood Ducks. Irvin-Marston, Hope. 2nd ed. 2004. 32p. (J). pap. 7.95 (978-0-89317-053-0(4), WW-0534, Windward Publishing) Finney Co., Inc.

Magee, Christopher. A Writer's Guide to Powerful Paragraphs. Pellegrino, Victor C. 2003. 187p. (YA). (gr. 7-18). pap. 18.95 (978-0-945045-05-2(0)) Maui Arthoughts Co.

Magee, Melanie. Mud Puddle Hunting Day. Grant, Callie. 2013. (ENG.). 20p. (J). bds. 8.99 (978-0-9854090-0-5(2)) Blanchard, Graham.

Magellan, Mauro. Max the Apartment Cat. Magellan, Mauro. 2013. 36p. pap. 12.95 (978-0-89334-887-8(2)) Green Dragon Bks.

Magenta, Emma. Orlando on a Thursday. Magenta, Emma. 2010. (ENG.). 32p. (J). (gr. -1-2). 15.99 (978-0-7636-4560-1(5)) Candlewick Pr.

Magerl, Caroline. Do-Wrong Ron. Herrick, Steven. 2005. (ENG.). 132p. (J). (gr. 1-5). pap. 11.99 (978-1-86508-661-3(4)) Allen & Unwin AUS. Dist: Independent Pubs. Group.

Magi, Jodi. Rich Man, Poor Man. Poulter, J. R. 2014. 30p. pap. 19.99 (978-1-63063-649-4(5)) Tate Publishing & Enterprises, LLC.

Magic Eye Studios. Rally Race. Porter, Alan J. 2010. (Cars Ser.). (ENG.). 112p. (J). (gr. 3-6). pap. 9.99 (978-1-60886-517-8(7)) Boom! Studios.

Magic Eye Studios, jt. illus. see Pastrovicchio, Lorenzo.

Magic Eye Studios Staff, et al. Prilla's Talent. Petrucha, Stefan. 2010. (Disney Fairies Ser.: 1). (ENG.). 80p. (J). (gr. 1-6). pap. 7.99 (978-1-59707-186-4(2));No. 1. 12.99 (978-1-59707-187-1(0)) Papercutz.

Maginn, Traci. Gilbert! Front & Center! McCord, Marianne. 2003. 24p. (J). per. 5.95 (978-0-9743352-0-9(7)) Jades Publishing.

Maglio-Macullar, Andrea. The Cat That Purred. Piantedosi, John J. 2014. (ENG.). (J). pap. 11.95 (978-1-56548-540-2(8)) New City Press of the Focolare.

Magnayon, Megan Coy. PuzzlePal Books: Cuddly Cow. Cohen, Melissa. 2013. (PuzzlePal Bks.). (ENG.). 10p. (J). (gr. -1). bds. 14.95 (978-1-60710-700-2(7), Silver Dolphin Bks.) Baker & Taylor Publishing Group.

—PuzzlePal Books: Dear Dinosaur. Cohen, Melissa. 2013. (PuzzlePal Bks.). (ENG.). 10p. (J). (gr. -1). bds. 14.95 (978-1-60710-699-9(X), Silver Dolphin Bks.) Baker & Taylor Publishing Group.

Magnette, Paul, jt. illus. see Newton, Vanessa.

Magniat, Jeffrey. Allosaurus. Mattern, Joanne. 2009. (Let's Read about Dinosaurs Ser.). 24p. (gr. -1-3). pap. 8.15 (978-0-8368-9418-9(9), Weekly Reader Leveled Readers) Stevens, Gareth Publishing LLLP.

—Ankylosaurus. Mattern, Joanne. 2009. (Let's Read about Dinosaurs Ser.). 24p. (gr. -1-3). pap. 8.15 (978-0-8368-9419-6(7), Weekly Reader Leveled Readers) Stevens, Gareth Publishing LLLP.

—Apatosaurus. Mattern, Joanne. 2007. (Let's Read about Dinosaurs Ser.). 24p. (gr. k-3). pap. 8.15 (978-0-8368-7702-1(0)); lib. bdg. 22.00 (978-0-8368-7695-6(4)) Stevens, Gareth Publishing LLLP. (Weekly Reader Leveled Readers).

—Apatosaurus/Apatosaurio. Mattern, Joanne. 2007. (Let's Read about Dinosaurs/ Conozcamos a los dinosaurios Ser.). (ENG & SPA.). 24p. (gr. k-3). lib. bdg. 22.00 (978-0-8368-8018-2(8), Weekly Reader Leveled Readers) Stevens, Gareth Publishing LLLP.

—Diplodocus. Mattern, Joanne. 2009. (Let's Read about Dinosaurs Ser.). 24p. (gr. -1-3). (J). lib. bdg. 22.00 (978-0-8368-9416-5(2)); pap. 8.15 (978-0-8368-9420-2(0)) Stevens, Gareth Publishing LLLP. (Weekly Reader Leveled Readers).

—Giganotosaurus. Mattern, Joanne. 2007. (Let's Read about Dinosaurs Ser.). 24p. (gr. k-3). pap. 8.15 (978-0-8368-7703-8(9), Weekly Reader Leveled Readers) Stevens, Gareth Publishing LLLP.

—Giganotosaurus/Gigantosaurio. Mattern, Joanne. 2007. (Let's Read about Dinosaurs/ Conozcamos a los dinosaurios Ser.). (ENG & SPA.). 24p. (gr. k-3). lib. bdg. 22.00 (978-0-8368-8019-9(6), Weekly Reader Leveled Readers) Stevens, Gareth Publishing LLLP.

—Oviraptor. Mattern, Joanne. 2009. (Let's Read about Dinosaurs Ser.). 24p. (gr. -1-3). (J). lib. bdg. 22.00 (978-0-8368-9417-2(0)); pap. 8.15 (978-0-8368-9421-9(9)) Stevens, Gareth Publishing LLLP. (Weekly Reader Leveled Readers).

—Stegosaurus. Mattern, Joanne. 2007. (Let's Read about Dinosaurs Ser.). 24p. (gr. k-3). lib. bdg. 22.00 (978-0-8368-7697-0(0), Weekly Reader Leveled Readers) Stevens, Gareth Publishing LLLP.

—Stegosaurus/Estegosaurio. Mattern, Joanne. 2007. (Let's Read about Dinosaurs/ Conozcamos a los dinosaurios Ser.). (ENG & SPA.). 24p. (gr. k-3). lib. bdg. 22.00 (978-0-8368-8020-5(X), Weekly Reader Leveled Readers) Stevens, Gareth Publishing LLLP.

—Triceratops. Mattern, Joanne. 2007. (Let's Read about Dinosaurs Ser.). 24p. (gr. k-3). pap. 8.15 (978-0-8368-7705-2(5)); lib. bdg. 22.00 (978-0-8368-7698-7(9)) Stevens, Gareth Publishing LLLP. (Weekly Reader Leveled Readers).

—Triceratops/Triceratops. Mattern, Joanne. 2007. (Let's Read about Dinosaurs/ Conozcamos a los dinosaurios Ser.). (ENG & SPA.). 24p. (gr. k-3). lib. bdg. 22.00 (978-0-8368-8021-2(8), Weekly Reader Leveled Readers) Stevens, Gareth Publishing LLLP.

—Tyrannosaurus Rex. Mattern, Joanne. 2007. (Let's Read about Dinosaurs Ser.). 24p. (gr. k-3). pap. 8.15 (978-0-8368-7706-9(3), Weekly Reader Leveled Readers) Stevens, Gareth Publishing LLLP.

—Tyrannosaurus Rex/Tiranosaurio Rex. Mattern, Joanne. 2007. (Let's Read about Dinosaurs/ Conozcamos a los dinosaurios Ser.). (ENG & SPA.). 24p. (gr. k-3). lib. bdg. 22.00 (978-0-8368-8022-9(6), Weekly Reader Leveled Readers) Stevens, Gareth Publishing LLLP.

—Velociraptor. Mattern, Joanne. 2007. (Let's Read about Dinosaurs Ser.). 24p. (gr. k-3). pap. 8.15 (978-0-8368-7707-6(1), Weekly Reader Leveled Readers) Stevens, Gareth Publishing LLLP.

—Velociraptor/Velociraptor. Mattern, Joanne. 2007. (Let's Read about Dinosaurs/ Conozcamos a los dinosaurios Ser.). (ENG & SPA.). 24p. (gr. k-3). lib. bdg. 22.00 (978-0-8368-8023-6(4), Weekly Reader Leveled Readers) Stevens, Gareth Publishing LLLP.

Magnisi, Angelica, jt. illus. see Magnisi, Sabrina.

Magnisi, Sabrina & Magnisi, Angelica. Miss Sabrina's Learn the Hail Mary As You Color the Rosary: A Guide for Children 6 - 9 & Up! Magnisi, Sabrina. 2005. 104p. (J). per. (978-1-933593-30-2(X)) Puarose Publishing.

Magno, Carlos. Transformers: Movie Prequel: Rising Storm: Vol 1. 2012. (Transformers: Dark of the Moon Movie Prequel Ser.). 24p. (J). 24.21 (978-1-59961-975-0(X), Graphic Novels) Spotlight.

—Transformers: Movie Prequel: Rising Storm: Vol 2. 2012. (Transformers: Dark of the Moon Movie Prequel Ser.). 24p. (J). 24.21 (978-1-59961-976-7(8), Graphic Novels) Spotlight.

—Transformers: Movie Prequel: Rising Storm: Vol 3. 2012. (Transformers: Dark of the Moon Movie Prequel Ser.). 24p. (J). 24.21 (978-1-59961-977-4(6), Graphic Novels) Spotlight.

—Transformers: Movie Prequel: Rising Storm: Vol 4. 2012. (Transformers: Dark of the Moon Movie Prequel Ser.). 24p. (J). 24.21 (978-1-59961-978-1(4), Graphic Novels) Spotlight.

Magno, Ryan. Sasquatch for Dinner. Robledo, Ronald J. Robledo, Victoria, ed. 2013. 32p. 18.99 (978-0-578-12711-8(3)) One Little Spark.

Magnum Photos Staff, photos by. Magnum Stories. Boot, Chris. rev. ed. 2004. (ENG., 512p. (gr. 8-17). 79.95 (978-0-7148-4245-5(1)) Phaidon Pr. Ltd. GBR. Dist: Hachette Bk. Group.

Magnus, Erica. Star Blanket. Brisson, Pat. 2003. (ENG.). 32p. (J). (gr. k-2). 15.95 (978-1-56397-889-0(X)) Boyds Mills Pr.

Magnuson, Diana. Home on the Range. Smithsonian Institution Staff. Schwaeber, Barbie H., ed. 2007. (ENG.). 32p. (J). (gr. -1-3). 9.85 (978-1-59249-686-0(5)) Soundprints.

—Hope Weavers. Ehrmantraut, Brenda. 2009. (J). (978-0-9729833-8-9(4)) Bubble Gum Pr.

—Jack & the Beanstalk: Classic Tales Edition. Adams, Alison. 2011. (Classic Tales Ser.). (J). (978-1-936258-68-0(4)) Benchmark Education Co.

—Not I, Not I. Hillert, Margaret. rev. exp. ed. 2006. (Beginning to Read Ser.). 32p. (J). (gr. -1-2). lib. bdg. 14.95 (978-1-59953-052-9(X)) Norwood Hse. Pr.

—Sacagawea. Krensky, Stephen. ed. 2005. 32p. (J). lib. bdg. 15.00 (978-1-59054-954-4(6)) Fitzgerald Bks.

—There's a Bear in My Chair. Magoun, James. 2004. (ENG.). 20p. (gr. k-2). pap. 5.95 (978-1-57874-080-2(0)) Kaeden Corp.

Magnuson, Natalie. La Gallinita Roja, 1 vol. Jones, Christianne C. Abello, Patricia, tr. from ENG. 2006. (Read-It! Readers en Español: Cuentos Folclóricos Ser.).Tr. of Little Red Hen. (SPA.). 32p. (gr. k-3). 19.99 (978-1-4048-1650-3(X), Easy Readers) Picture Window Bks.

—The Little Red Hen, 1 vol. Jones, Christianne C. (My First Classic Story Ser.). (ENG.). 32p. (gr. k-3). 2011. pap. 7.10 (978-1-4048-7356-8(2), My First Classic Story); 2010. lib. bdg. 21.32 (978-1-4048-6073-5(8), My First Classic Story); 2005. 19.99 (978-1-4048-0975-8(9), Easy Readers) Picture Window Bks.

Magoon, Scott. Big Mean Mike. Knudsen, Michelle. 2012. (ENG.). 40p. (J). (gr. -1-3). 15.99 (978-0-7636-4990-6(2)) Candlewick Pr.

—Chopsticks. Rosenthal, Amy Krouse. 2012. (Chopsticks Ser.). (ENG.). 40p. (J). (gr. -1-k). 16.99 (978-1-4231-0796-5(9)) Hyperion Pr.

—If Waffles Were Like Boys. Harper, Charise Mericle. 2011. (ENG.). 40p. (J). (gr. -1-1). 14.99 (978-0-06-177998-5(9)) HarperCollins Pubs.

Magoon, Scott. The Knights Before Christmas. Holub, Joan. 2015. (ENG.). 32p. (J). (gr. k-3). 16.99 **(978-0-8050-9932-4(8)**, Holt, Henry & Co. Bks. For Young Readers) Holt, Henry & Co.

Magoon, Scott. Mostly Monsterly. Sauer, Tammi. 2010. (ENG.). 40p. (J). (gr. -1-3). 15.99 (978-1-4169-6110-9(0), Simon & Schuster/Paula Wiseman Bks.) Simon & Schuster/Paula Wiseman Bks.

—The Nuts: Bedtime at the Nut House. Litwin, Eric. 2014. (ENG.). 32p. (J). (gr. -1-1). 18.00 (978-0-316-32244-7(X)) Little, Brown Bks. for Young Readers.

Magoon, Scott. The Nuts: Sing & Dance in Your Polka Dot Pants. Litwin, Eric. 2015. (ENG.). 32p. (J). (gr. -1-1). 18.00 **(978-0-316-32250-8(4))** Little Brown & Co.

Magoon, Scott. Otto: The Boy Who Loved Cars. LeReau, Kara. 2011. (ENG.). 32p. (J). (gr. -1-1). 15.99 (978-1-59643-484-4(8)) Roaring Brook Pr.

—Spoon. Rosenthal, Amy Krouse. 2009. (Spoon Ser.). (ENG.). 40p. (J). (gr. -1-k). 16.99 (978-1-4231-0685-2(7)) Hyperion Pr.

—Ugly Fish. LaReau, Kara. 2006. (ENG.). 40p. (J). (gr. -1-3). 16.99 (978-0-15-205082-5(5)) Houghton Mifflin Harcourt Publishing Co.

Magoon, Scott. The Boy Who Cried Bigfoot! Magoon, Scott. 2013. (ENG.). 48p. (J). (gr. -1-3). 17.99 (978-1-4424-1257-6(7), Simon & Schuster Bks. For Young Readers) Simon & Schuster/Paula Wiseman Bks.

—Breathe. Magoon, Scott. 2014. (ENG.). 40p. (J). (gr. -1-3). 17.99 (978-1-4424-1258-3(5), Simon & Schuster/Paula Wiseman Bks.) Simon & Schuster/Paula Wiseman Bks.

Magsamen, Sandra. Good Morning, Sunshine! Magsamen, Sandra. 2013. (ENG.). 12p. (J). (gr. -1 — 1). bds. 8.99 (978-0-545-43645-8(1), Cartwheel Bks.) Scholastic, Inc.

—Goodnight, Little One. Magsamen, Sandra. 2007. (Cloth Bks.). (ENG.). 6p. (J). (gr. -1 — 1). 13.00 (978-0-316-06594-8(3)) Little, Brown Bks. for Young Readers.

Maguire, Jake. The Turnarounders & the Arbuckle Rescue. Heneghan, Lou. 2013. 496p. pap. (978-0-9573523-1-5(X)) Natus Publishing.

Maguire, Kerry. Saber-Toothed Cats. Goodman, Susan E. 2006. (On My Own Science Ser.). (ENG.). 48p. (gr. 2-4). per. 6.95 (978-1-57505-851-1(0), First Avenue Editions) Lerner Publishing Group.

Maguire, Thomas Aquinas. The Wild Swans. Andersen, Hans Christian. 2012. (ENG.). 104p. (J). (gr. k). 24.95 (978-1-897476-36-9(1)) Simply Read Bks. CAN. Dist: Ingram Pub. Services.

Mah, Anna. It's Cool to Be Clever: The story of Edson C. Hendricks, the genius who invented the design for the Internet. Jones, Leanne. 2011. 40p. (978-1-897435-63-2(0)) Agio Publishing Hse.

Mah, Derek. Monsterology: Fabulous Lives of the Creepy, the Revolting, & the Undead. Slade, Arthur. 2005. (ENG.). 96p. (J). (gr. 4-7). pap. 8.95 (978-0-88776-714-2(1)) Tundra Bks. CAN. Dist: Random Hse., Inc.

—Villainology: Fabulous Lives of the Big, the Bad, & the Wicked. Slade, Arthur. 2007. (ENG.). 96p. (J). (gr. 4-7). per. 9.95 (978-0-88776-809-5(1)) Tundra Bks. CAN. Dist: Random Hse., Inc.

Mahal, Susan. Felicity's Cooking Studio. Athan, Polly et al. 2007. (American Girl Ser.). 56p. (J). (gr. 3-7). 15.95 (978-1-59369-266-7(8)) American Girl Publishing, Inc.

Mahan, Ben. All about Holidays. Kain, Kathleen. 2004. (Treasure Tree Ser.). 32p. (J). (978-0-7166-1644-3(0)) World Bk., Inc.

—All about Holidays: With Inspector McQ. Kain, Kathleen. 2004. (Early Literacy Library). 32p. (J). (gr. 2-5). 219.00 (978-0-7166-1647-4(5)) World Bk., Inc.

—Hi, I'm Blackbeary: The Fruit of the Spirit Is Peace. Carlson, Melody. 2004. (Beary Patch Bears Ser.). 96p. bds. 6.99 (978-1-58134-182-9(2)) Crossway.

—Molly the Great Misses the Bus: A Book about Being on Time. Marshall, Shelley. 2010. (Character Education with Super Ben & Molly the Great Ser.). 24p. (J). 22.60 (978-0-7660-3518-8(2)); pap. 7.95 (978-0-7660-3743-4(6)) Enslow Pubs., Inc. (Enslow Elementary).

—Molly the Great Respects the Flag: A Book about Being a Good Citizen. Marshall, Shelley. 2010. (Character Education with Super Ben & Molly the Great Ser.). 24p. (J). 22.60 (978-0-7660-3519-5(0)); pap. 7.95 (978-0-7660-3744-1(4)) Enslow Pubs., Inc. (Enslow Elementary).

—Molly the Great Tells the Truth: A Book about Honesty. Marshall, Shelley. 2010. (Character Education with Super Ben & Molly the Great Ser.). 24p. (J). 22.60 (978-0-7660-3520-1(4)); pap. 7.95 (978-0-7660-3745-8(2), Enslow Elementary) Enslow Pubs., Inc.

—Molly the Great's Messy Bed: A Book about Responsibility. Marshall, Shelley. 2010. (Character Education with Super Ben & Molly the Great Ser.). 24p. (J). 22.60 (978-0-7660-3517-1(4)); pap. 7.95 (978-0-7660-3742-7(8), Enslow Elementary) Enslow Pubs., Inc.

—The Story of Ronald Reagan. Pingry, Patricia A. 2006. (ENG.). 26p. (J). (gr. -1-k). bds. 7.69 (978-0-8249-6621-8(X), Candy Cane Pr.) Ideals Pubns.

—Super Ben Writes a Letter: A Book about Caring. Marshall, Shelley. 2010. (Character Education with Super Ben & Molly the Great Ser.). 24p. (J). 22.60 (978-0-7660-3516-4(6)); pap. 7.95 (978-0-7660-3741-0(X)) Enslow Pubs., Inc. (Enslow Elementary).

—Super Ben's Brave Bike Ride: A Book about Courage. Marshall, Shelley. 2010. (Character Education with Super Ben & Molly the Great Ser.). 24p. (J). 22.60 (978-0-7660-3515-7(8)); pap. 7.95 (978-0-7660-3740-3(1), Enslow Elementary) Enslow Pubs., Inc.

—Super Ben's Broken Cookie: A Book about Sharing. Marshall, Shelley. 2010. (Character Education with Super Ben & Molly the Great Ser.). 24p. (J). 22.60 (978-0-7660-3514-0(X)); pap. 7.95 (978-0-7660-3739-7(8)) Enslow Pubs., Inc. (Enslow Elementary).

—Super Ben's Dirty Hands: A Book about Healthy Habits. Marshall, Shelley. 2010. (Character Education with Super Ben & Molly the Great Ser.). 24p. (J). 22.60 (978-0-7660-3513-3(1)); pap. 7.95 (978-0-7660-3738-0(X), Enslow Elementary) Enslow Pubs., Inc.

Mahan, Benton. Friends Forever. Scelsa, Greg & Debney, John. Faulkner, Stacey, ed. 2006. (J). pap. 2.99 (978-1-59198-322-4(3)) Creative Teaching Pr., Inc.

—The Mouse Who Cried Cat, Vol. 4263. Williams, Rozanne Lanczak. 2005. (Reading for Fluency Ser.). 16p. (J). pap. 3.49 (978-1-59198-163-3(8), 4263) Creative Teaching Pr., Inc.

—My Picture Story. Williams, Rozanne Lanczak. 2006. (Learn to Write Ser.). 8p. (J). (gr. k-2). pap. 3.49 (978-1-59198-281-4(2), 6175) Creative Teaching Pr., Inc.

—My Picture Story. Williams, Rozanne Lanczak. Maio, Barbara & Faulkner, Stacey, eds. 2006. (J). per. 6.99 (978-1-59198-332-3(0)) Creative Teaching Pr., Inc.

—Today Is Somebody's Birthday. Williams, Rozanne Lanczak. 2005. (Reading for Fluency Ser.). 8p. (J). pap. 2.49 (978-1-59198-140-4(9), 4240) Creative Teaching Pr., Inc.

—Tuckerbean, 1 vol. Kalz, Jill. 2006. (Read-It! Readers: Adventures of Tuckerbean Ser.). (ENG.). 24p. (gr. -1-3). 19.99 (978-1-4048-1591-9(0), Easy Readers) Picture Window Bks.

—Tuckerbean at the Movies, 1 vol. Kalz, Jill. 2009. (Read-It! Readers: Adventures of Tuckerbean Ser.). (ENG.). 24p. (gr. -1-3). 19.99 (978-1-4048-5231-0(X), Easy Readers) Picture Window Bks.

—Tuckerbean in the Kitchen, 1 vol. Kalz, Jill. 2006. (Read-It! Readers: Adventures of Tuckerbean Ser.). (ENG.). 32p. (gr. -1-3). lib. bdg. 19.99 (978-1-4048-2402-7(2), Easy Readers) Picture Window Bks.

—Tuckerbean on the Moon, 1 vol. Kalz, Jill. 2009. (Read-It! Readers: Adventures of Tuckerbean Ser.). (ENG.). 24p. (gr. -1-3). 19.99 (978-1-4048-5234-1(4), Easy Readers) Picture Window Bks.

Mahbab, Mustashrik. Julius Caesar. Shakespeare, William. 2008. (ENG.). 208p. (YA). (gr. 7-11). pap. 12.95 (978-0-8109-7072-4(4), Amulet Bks.) Abrams.

Maher, Adele & Cline, Mike. Franky Fox's Fun with English Readers Level A1. Maher, Adele. 2007. 228p. (J). 26.99 (978-0-9777419-5-3(8)) Lingo Pr. LLC.

Maher, Alex. Diego in the Dark: Being Brave at Night. Stierle, Cynthia. 2008. (Go, Diego, Go! Ser.). (ENG.). 16p. (J). (gr. -1-2). pap. 6.99 (978-1-4169-5935-9(1), Simon Spotlight/Nickelodeon) Simon Spotlight/Nickelodeon.

—Diego's Sea Turtle Adventure. Ricci, Christine. 2006. 26p. (J). (978-0-7172-9870-9(1)) Scholastic, Inc.

—El Safari de Diego. 2007. (Go, Diego, Go! Ser.).Tr. of Diego's Safari Rescue. (SPA.). 24p. (J). (gr. -1-2). pap. 3.99 (978-1-4169-5998-4(X), Libros Para Ninos) Libros Para Ninos.

Maher, Bob. Emma & Topsy's Story: The Art of Loving & Letting Go. Edwards, Linda M. 2010. 20p. pap. 10.95 (978-1-60911-808-2(1), Eloquent Bks.) Strategic Book Publishing & Rights Agency (SBPRA).

Maher, Terre. A Maze Me: Poems for Girls. Nye, Naomi Shihab. (ENG.). 128p. (YA). (gr. 8). 2014. pap. 8.99 (978-0-06-058191-6(3)); 2005. 17.99 (978-0-06-058189-3(1)) HarperCollins Pubs. (Greenwillow Bks.).

Mahjouri. The Science of Sleep. Mahjouri. 2014. (ENG.). pap. 9.99 (978-1-941006-04-7(3)) SoGo Creation.

Mahomet, John. The Cunning Kwaku Anansi: Tales by the Fireside. Ansong, Anthony. I.t. ed. 2011. (ENG.). 36p. pap. 11.99 (978-1-4663-9733-0(0)) CreateSpace Independent Publishing Platform.

Mahoney, Daniel & Wood, Hannah. Ocean Wonders. Ranson, Erin. Top That! Staff, ed. 2007. (Sparkling Slide Book Ser.). (ENG.). 12p. (J). (gr. k). (978-1-84666-167-9(6), Tide Mill Pr.) Top That! Publishing PLC.

Mahoney, Daniel, jt. illus. see Mahoney, Daniel J.

Mahoney, Daniel J. The Happy Hippos. Charlesworth, Liza & Scholastic, Inc. Staff. 2005. (Number Tales Ser.). (ENG.). 16p. (J). (gr. -1-1). pap. 2.99 (978-0-439-69023-2(4)) Scholastic, Inc.

—I See a Monster! Young, Laurie. 2007. (Touch & Feel Ser.). 12p. (gr. -1-k). 15.95 (978-1-58117-574-5(4), Intervisual/Piggy Toes) Bendon, Inc.

—I See a Monster. 2008. (ENG.). 12p. (J). bds. 5.95 (978-1-58117-729-9(1), Intervisual/Piggy Toes) Bendon, Inc.

Mahoney, Daniel J. & Mahoney, Daniel. I See a Monster! Young, Laurie. 2006. (ENG.). 12p. (J). (gr. -1-k). bds. 10.95 (978-1-58117-483-0(7), Intervisual/Piggy Toes) Bendon, Inc.

Mahoney, Daniel J., jt. illus. see Wood, Hannah.

Mahoney, Paula J. Flying Jack. Petrie, Kathye Fetsko & Boyds Mills Press Staff. 2003. (ENG.). 32p. (J). (gr. k-2). 15.95 (978-1-56397-971-2(3)) Boyds Mills Pr.

Mahurin, Matt. Grumbles from the Forest: Fairy-Tale Voices with a Twist. Yolen, Jane & Dotlich, Rebecca Kai. 2013. (ENG.). 40p. (J). (gr. 2). 16.95 (978-1-59078-867-7(2), Wordsong) Boyds Mills Pr.

Mai Long. Tam & Cam/Tam Cam: The Ancient Vietnamese Cinderella Story. Minh Quoc. Smith, William, tr. from VIE. 2006. (ENG & VIE.). 32p. (J). (gr. 1-4). 16.95 (978-0-9701654-4-2(7)) East West Discovery Pr.

Mai, Vo-Dinh. The Coconut Monk. Hanh, Thich Nhat. 2009. (ENG.). 40p. (J). (gr. -1-3). pap. 10.95 (978-1-888375-97-8(3), Plum Blossom Bks.) Parallax Pr.

—The Hermit & the Well. Hanh, Thich Nhat & Parallax Press Staff. 2004. (ENG.). 36p. (J). 15.00 (978-1-888375-31-2(0)) Parallax Pr.

Mai-Wyss, Tatjana. Audrey (Cow) Bar-el, Dan. 2014.Tr. of Cow. (ENG.). 240p. (J). (gr. 2-5). 17.99 *(978-1-77049-602-6(5))* Tundra Bks. CAN. Dist: Penguin Random Hse., LLC.

—My Teacher Dances on the Desk. Gagliano, Eugene. 2009. (ENG.). 48p. (J). (gr. k-6). pap. 6.95 *(978-1-58536-446-6(0))* Sleeping Bear Pr.

Mai-Wyss, Tatjana. One Fine Shabbat. Barash, Chris. 2015. (J). ***(978-1-4677-5871-0(X)***, Kar-Ben Publishing) Lerner Publishing Group.

Mai-Wyss, Tatjana. The Passover Lamb. Marshall, Linda Elovitz. 2013. (ENG.). 32p. (J). (gr. 1-4). 17.99 *(978-0-307-93177-1(3))* Random Hse., Inc.

—That's Not How You Play Soccer, Daddy!, 1 vol. Shahan, Sherry. 2007. (ENG.). 32p. (J). (gr. -1-3). 15.95 *(978-1-56145-416-7(8)*, Peachtree Junior) Peachtree Pubs.

—A Tree for Emmy, 1 vol. Rodman, Mary Ann. 2009. (ENG.). 32p. (J). (gr. -1-3). 15.95 *(978-1-56145-475-4(3))* Peachtree Pubs.

—The Twelve Days of Christmas in South Carolina. Long, Melinda. 2010. (Twelve Days of Christmas in America Ser.). (ENG.). 32p. (J). (gr. k). 12.95 *(978-1-4027-6672-5(6))* Sterling Publishing Co., Inc.

—Whole-Y Cow! Fractions Are Fun. Souders, Taryn. 2010. (ENG & ACE.). 40p. (J). (gr. 1-4). 15.95 *(978-1-58536-460-2(6)*, 202182) Sleeping Bear Pr.

Maia, Chavez Larkin. My Mom's Not Cool. Rubi, Nicholas. 2008. 24p. (J). per. 12.95 *(978-0-9776906-4-0(4))* Blueline Publishing.

Maiborada, Tanya. The Hunting of the Great Bear: A Native American Folktale. Malaspina, Ann. 2013. (Folktales from Around the World Ser.). (ENG.). 24p. (J). (gr. k-3). 28.50 *(978-1-62323-616-8(9)*, 206383) Child's World, Inc., The.

Maiden, D. W. & Govoni, Dennis, photos by. Insects & Spiders. Walls, Suzanne L. 2012. 64p. (J). pap. 14.95 *(978-0-9841960-9-8(9))* Chantilly Books.

Maidment, Mikaila. Otter Lee Brave, 1 vol. Brown, Rena Cherry. 2012. (ENG.). 48p. (J). 16.99 *(978-0-7643-4155-7(3))* Schiffer Publishing, Ltd.

Maidment, Stella. The Star Child. Whelan, Olwyn. 2004. 40p. (J). 14.95 *(978-1-84458-039-2(3))* Avalon Publishing Group.

Maier, Ximena. La Casa de los Miedos. Alcantara, Ricardo. 2009. (SPA.). 141p. (J). (gr. 3-5). pap. *(978-84-263-7269-7(4))* Vives, Luis Editorial (Edelvives).

—Marcela. García Castellano, Ana. 2004. (SPA.). 80p. (J). pap. 9.99 *(978-84-667-2441-8(9))* Lectorum Pubns., Inc.

Maier, Ximena. Cuento para Susana. Maier, Ximena, tr. Aldecoa, Josefina. 2003. (AlfaGuay Ser.). (SPA.). 80p. *(978-84-204-6611-8(5))* Ediciones Alfaguara.

Maihack, Mike. Geeks, Girls, & Secret Identities. Jung, Mike. 2012. (J). (ENG.). 320p. (gr. 3-7). 16.99 *(978-0-545-33548-5(5))*; pap. *(978-0-545-33549-2(3))* Scholastic, Inc. (Levine, Arthur A. Bks.).

Mailer, Maggie. Lara's First Christmas. Howell, Alice O. 2004. 96p. (J). pap. 9.95 *(978-0-88010-553-8(4)*, Bell Pond Bks.) SteinerBooks, Inc.

Mailey, Maria C. & Neuburger, Jenny. I'm Good, I'm Beautiful, I'm Smart. Goss, Leon. 2005. (J). per. *(978-1-933156-02-6(3)*, VisionQuest Kids) GSVQ Publishing.

Malone, Heather. The Cats in the Doll Shop. McDonough, Yona Zeldis. 2012. (ENG.). 160p. (J). (gr. 3-7). pap. 5.99 *(978-0-14-242198-7(7)*, Puffin) Penguin Publishing Group.

—The Doll Shop Downstairs. McDonough, Yona Zeldis. 2011. (ENG.). 128p. (J). (gr. 2-5). 5.99 *(978-0-14-241691-4(6)*, Puffin) Penguin Publishing Group.

—How Oliver Olson Changed the World. Mills, Claudia. 2011. (ENG.). 128p. (J). (gr. 2-5). pap. 6.99 *(978-0-312-67282-9(9))* Square Fish.

—Remembering Mrs. Rossi. Hest, Amy. 2007. (ENG.). 192p. (J). (gr. 3-7). 14.99 *(978-0-7636-2163-6(3))* Candlewick Pr.

—Remembering Mrs. Rossi. Hest, Amy. 2010. (ENG.). 192p. (J). (gr. 3-7). 6.99 *(978-0-7636-4089-7(1))* Candlewick Pr.

Malone, Heather, jt. illus. see Malone, Heather Harms.

Malone, Heather Harms. How Oliver Olson Changed the World. Mills, Claudia. 2009. (ENG.). 112p. (J). (gr. 2-5). 15.95 *(978-0-374-33487-1(0)*, Farrar, Straus & Giroux (BYR)) Farrar, Straus & Giroux.

Malone, Heather Harms. Annie Glover Is Not a Tree Lover. Malone, Heather Harms. Beard, Darleen Bailey. 2009. (ENG.). 128p. (J). (gr. 2-5). 15.99 *(978-0-374-30351-8(7)*, Farrar, Straus & Giroux (BYR)) Farrar, Straus & Giroux.

Malone, Heather Harms & Malone, Heather. Princess Bess Gets Dressed. Cuyler, Margery. 2009. (ENG.). 32p. (J). (gr. -1-3). 15.99 *(978-1-4169-3833-0(8)*, Simon & Schuster Bks. For Young Readers) Simon & Schuster Bks. For Young Readers.

Malorano, Jamison. Snow Daze: The Storm, Adventure, Children, Educational, Exciting, Family Oriented. Cecca, John. Tick, David, ed. 2011. (ENG.). 78p. pap. 9.95 *(978-0-615-48741-0(6))* Todazebooks.com.

—Snow Daze (E3) The Storm. Cecca, John. Tick, David, ed. 2011. (ENG.). 78p. pap. 8.95 *(978-1-4679-3623-1(5))* CreateSpace Independent Publishing Platform.

Maison, Jerome, photos by. March of the Penguins: The Official Children's Book. Jacquet, Luc. 2005. (ENG.). 32p. (gr. -1). lib. bdg. 22.90 *(978-0-7922-6190-2(9))*; per. 5.95 *(978-0-7922-6183-4(6))* CENGAGE Learning.

Maiste, Piia. Anna's Teeth. Petrone, Epp. 2013. 94p. pap. *(978-9949-511-27-3(5))* Petrone Print.

Maizel, Karen. Big Brother Now: A Story about Me & Our New Baby. Sheldon, Annette. 2008. 32p. (J). (gr. -1-1). 14.95 *(978-1-4338-0381-9(X))*; pap. 9.95 *(978-1-4338-0382-6(8))* American Psychological Assn. (Magination Pr.).

—Big Sister Now: A Story about Me & Our New Baby. Sheldon, Annette. 2005. 32p. (J). (gr. -1-1). per. 9.95 *(978-1-59147-244-5(X))*; 14.95 *(978-1-59147-243-8(1))* American Psychological Assn. (Magination Pr.).

—Jake's Brave Night, 1 vol. Bowman, Crystal. 2007. (I Can Read! / the Jake Ser.). (ENG.). 32p. (J). (gr. -1-3). pap. 3.99 *(978-0-310-71456-9(7))* Zonderkidz.

—Package. Bauer, Roger. l.t. ed. 2005. (ENG.). 8p. (gr. k-2). pap. 4.95 *(978-1-879835-84-9(3))* Kaeden Corp.

—Time for a Bath! World of Discovery II. Mader, Jan. l.t. ed. 2005. (ENG.). 8p. (gr. k-1). pap. 4.95 *(978-1-879835-46-7(0))* Kaeden Corp.

Maizels, Jennie. Pop-Up New York. Maizels, Jennie. 2014. (ENG.). 12p. (J). (gr. k-4). 19.99 *(978-0-7636-7162-4(2))* Candlewick Pr.

Majado, Caio, et al. Drop In, 1 vol., Vol. 1. Lemke, Donald B. 2011. (Tony Hawk's 900 Revolution Ser.). (ENG.). 128p. (gr. 3-4). pap. 7.19 *(978-1-4342-3451-3(7))*; lib. bdg. 25.32 *(978-1-4342-3214-4(X))* Stone Arch Bks. (Tony Hawk's 900 Revolution).

Majado, Caio. Flipside, Vol. 11. Terrell, Brandon. 2013. (Tony Hawk's 900 Revolution Ser.). (ENG.). 128p. (gr. 3-4). lib. bdg. 25.32 *(978-1-4342-3842-9(3))* Stone Arch Bks.

—Flipside: Volume Eleven, 1 vol. Terrell, Brandon. 2013. (Tony Hawk's 900 Revolution Ser.). (ENG.). 128p. (gr. 3-4). pap. 7.19 *(978-1-4342-4895-4(X)*, Tony Hawk's 900 Revolution) Stone Arch Bks.

Majado, Caio, et al. Impulse, Vol. 2. Sherman, M. Zachary. 2011. (Tony Hawk's 900 Revolution Ser.). (ENG.). 128p. (gr. 3-4). pap. 7.19 *(978-1-4342-3452-0(5))*; lib. bdg. 25.32 *(978-1-4342-3203-8(4))* Stone Arch Bks. (Tony Hawk's 900 Revolution).

Majado, Caio. Zombified, Vol. 9. Hoena, Blake A. & Tortosa, Wilson. 2013. (Tony Hawk's 900 Revolution Ser.). (ENG.). 128p. (gr. 3-4). lib. bdg. 25.32 *(978-1-4342-3840-5(7))* Stone Arch Bks.

—Zombified: Volume Nine, 1 vol. Hoena, Blake A. 2013. (Tony Hawk's 900 Revolution Ser.). (ENG.). 128p. (gr. 3-4). pap. 7.19 *(978-1-4342-4898-5(4)*, Tony Hawk's 900 Revolution) Stone Arch Bks.

Majado, Caio & Emery, Thomas. Fall Line, Vol. 3. Sherman, M. Zachary. 2011. (Tony Hawk's 900 Revolution Ser.). (ENG.). 128p. (gr. 3-4). pap. 7.19 *(978-1-4342-3453-7(3))*; lib. bdg. 25.32 *(978-1-4342-3204-5(2))* Stone Arch Bks. (Tony Hawk's 900 Revolution).

Majado, Caio & Emery, Thomas J. Unchained, Vol. 4. Sherman, M. Zachary. 2011. (Tony Hawk's 900 Revolution Ser.). (ENG.). 128p. (gr. 3-4). pap. 7.19 *(978-1-4342-3454-4(1))*; lib. bdg. 25.32 *(978-1-4342-3215-1(8))* Stone Arch Bks. (Tony Hawk's 900 Revolution).

Majewski, Dawn. Borya & the Burps: An Eastern European Adoption Story. McNamara, Joan. 2005. 30p. (J). (gr. -1 — 1). 18.00 *(978-0-944934-31-9(5))* Perspectives Pr., Inc.

—Sam's Sister. Bond, Juliet C. 2004. (J). 18.00 *(978-0-944934-30-2(7))* Perspectives Pr., Inc.

Majewski, Julie. Color with Max! Activity & Coloring Book. Majewski, Anthony M. T. & Maximus. 2010. 16p. (J). pap., act. bk. ed. 4.99 *(978-0-615-38985-1(6))* Emarketing Of Michigan, LLC.

—Dog's Work Too! From Max's Point of View. Majewski, Anthony & "Max", Maximus. 2011. (ENG.). 28p. pap. 10.99 *(978-1-4392-3669-7(0))* CreateSpace Independent Publishing Platform.

Major, Rebekah. What Do You See in Me I am Who I am. Major, Gail Bacceli. 2013. (ENG.). 32p. (J). pap. 9.95 *(978-1-939289-22-3(X)*, Little Creek Bks.) Jan-Carol Publishing, INC.

Major, Rebekah. Mama Wrex. Major, Rebekah. 2014. (ENG.). (J). pap. 10.95 *(978-1-939289-46-9(7)*, Little Creek Bks.) Jan-Carol Publishing, INC.

Major, Sarah. Alphabet Tales. Major, Sarah. 2010. 112p. (J). pap. 39.95 *(978-0-9829873-3-9(1))* Child1st Pubns., LLC.

—Easy-for-Me Level C Books. Major, Sarah. 2012. pap. 64.95 *(978-1-936981-49-6(1))* Child1st Pubns., LLC.

—Easy-for-Me Reading Teaching Manual: A Snap for the teacher...a Cinch for the Child. Major, Sarah. 2nd ed. 2013. (ENG.). 324p. (J). pap. 59.95 *(978-1-936981-57-1(2))* Child1st Pubns., LLC.

—Right-Brained Addition & Subtraction: A Forget Memorization Book. Major, Sarah. 2013. (ENG.). 182p. (J). pap. 28.95 *(978-1-936981-54-0(8))* Child1st Pubns., LLC.

—Right-Brained Place Value: A Forget Memorization Book. Major, Sarah. 2013. 224p. (J). pap. 29.95 *(978-1-936981-55-7(6))* Child1st Pubns., LLC.

—SnapWords Mini-Lessons: How to Teach Each SnapWord Integrating Spelling, Writing, & Phonics Concepts. Major, Sarah. 2013. (ENG.). (J). pap. 14.95 *(978-1-936981-56-4(4))* Child1st Pubns., LLC.

—Writing the Visual, Kinesthetic, & Auditory Alphabet. Major, Sarah. 2007. 30p. (J). pap. 9.99 *(978-0-9829873-2-2(3))* Child1st Pubns., LLC.

Mak, Alice. This Is the Greatest Place! A Palace Inspired by the World of Small Animals. Tse, Brian. Steinhardt, Nancy S., ed. Wang, Ben, tr. from CHI. 2014. (ENG.). 44p. (J). (gr. -1-2). 12.95 *(978-0-9893776-2-1(8))* China Institute Gallery, China Institute in America.

Mak, Ding Sang. Everyday Life: Through Chinese Peasant Art. Morrissey, Tricia. 2009. (ENG.). 36p. (J). (gr. -1-5). pap. 9.95 *(978-1-934159-18-7(2))* ThingsAsian Pr.

Mak, Kam. Chinatown. Mak, Kam. 2016. 32p. (J). (gr. -1-3). pap. 6.99 *(978-0-06-443732-5(9))* HarperCollins Pubs.

Maka, Stephen, photos by. Life in a Wetland. Stewart, Melissa. 2003. (Ecosystems in Action Ser.). (ENG.). 72p. (gr. 5-9). lib. bdg. 26.60 *(978-0-8225-4687-0(6))* Lerner Publishing Group.

Maki, Jeffrey Stephen. The Adventures of Jason Roy Mouse: The Fun Adventures of a Little Mouse Who Uses His Diabetes to His Great Advantage. Maki, Jeffrey Stephen. 2010. (ENG.). 40p. pap. 12.95 *(978-1-4528-5330-7(4))* CreateSpace Independent Publishing Platform.

Maki, Tab. Timmy the Tiny Troubled Turtle, 1 vol. Syrstad, Suzi. 2009. 13p. pap. 24.95 *(978-1-61546-455-5(7))* PublishAmerica, Inc.

Maki, Yoko. Aishiteruze Baby, Vol. 3. Maki, Yoko. 2006. (Aishiteruze Baby Ser.). (ENG.). 208p. pap. 8.99 *(978-1-4215-0570-1(3))* Viz Media.

Makis, Sidney. Icy the Iceberg. Friend, Larry. 2008. 28p. pap. 13.95 *(978-1-4327-3777-1(5))* Outskirts Pr., Inc.

MAKOTO, Mizobuchi. Arceus & the Jewel of Life. MAKOTO, Mizobuchi. 2011. (Pokemon Ser.). (ENG.). 200p. (J). pap. 9.99 *(978-1-4215-3802-0(4))* Viz Media.

Makowski, Robin Lee. Dogs. 2004. (J). *(978-1-59203-088-0(2))* Learning Challenge, Inc.

—Sea Creatures. 2004. (J). *(978-1-59203-090-3(4))* Learning Challenge, Inc.

Makuc, Lucy. Christmas Drawing Wonderland! Besel, Jennifer M. 2013. (Holiday Sketchbook Ser.). (ENG.). (gr. 1-2). 40p. pap. 4.95 *(978-1-4765-3447-3(0))*; 24p. 24.65 *(978-1-4765-3092-5(0))* Capstone Pr., Inc. (First Facts).

—Drawing a Christmas Wonderland: A Step-By-Step Sketchpad, 1 vol. Besel, Jennifer M. 2014. (My First Sketchpads Ser.). (ENG.). 48p. pap. 5.95 *(978-1-4914-1748-5(X)*, First Facts) Capstone Pr., Inc.

—Drawing a Halloween Spooktacular: A Step-By-Step Sketchpad, 1 vol. Besel, Jennifer M. 2014. (My First Sketchpads Ser.). (ENG.). 48p. pap. 5.95 *(978-1-4914-1749-2(8)*, First Facts) Capstone Pr., Inc.

—Halloween Drawing Spooktacular! Besel, Jennifer M. 2013. (Holiday Sketchbook Ser.). (ENG.). (gr. 1-2). 40p. pap. 4.95 *(978-1-4765-3446-6(2))*; 24p. 24.65 *(978-1-4765-3091-8(2))* Capstone Pr., Inc. (First Facts).

—Holiday Sketchbook. Besel, Jennifer M. 2013. (Holiday Sketchbook Ser.). (ENG.). (gr. 1-2). 40p. pap. 19.80 *(978-1-4765-3653-8(8))*; 24p. lib. bdg. 98.60 *(978-1-4765-3652-1(X))* Capstone Pr., Inc. (First Facts).

—Thanksgiving Drawing Feast! Besel, Jennifer M. 2013. (Holiday Sketchbook Ser.). (ENG.). (gr. 1-2). 40p. pap. 4.95 *(978-1-4765-3448-0(9))*; 24p. 24.65 *(978-1-4765-3093-2(9))* Capstone Pr., Inc. (First Facts).

—Valentine's Day Drawing Treat! Besel, Jennifer M. 2013. (Holiday Sketchbook Ser.). (ENG.). (gr. 1-2). 40p. pap. 4.95 *(978-1-4765-3449-7(7))*; 24p. 24.65 *(978-1-4765-3094-9(7))* Capstone Pr., Inc. (First Facts).

Makuc, Lucy & Dynamo Limited Staff. Drawing Faces: A Step-By-Step Sketchbook, 1 vol. Bolte, Mari. 2014. (My First Sketchbook Ser.). (ENG.). 24p. (gr. 1-2). lib. bdg. 24.65 *(978-1-4914-0284-9(9))* Capstone Pr., Inc.

—Drawing Faces: A Step-By-Step Sketchpad, 1 vol. Bolte, Mari. 2014. (My First Sketchpads Ser.). (ENG.). 48p. (gr. 1-2). pap. 5.95 *(978-1-4914-0293-1(8)*, First Facts) Capstone Pr., Inc.

—Drawing Monsters: A Step-By-Step Sketchbook, 1 vol. Bolte, Mari. 2014. (My First Sketchbook Ser.). (ENG.). 24p. (gr. 1-2). lib. bdg. 24.65 *(978-1-4914-0282-5(2))* Capstone Pr., Inc.

—Drawing Monsters: A Step-By-Step Sketchpad, 1 vol. Bolte, Mari. 2014. (My First Sketchpads Ser.). (ENG.). 48p. (gr. 1-2). pap. 5.95 *(978-1-4914-0291-7(1)*, First Facts) Capstone Pr., Inc.

—Drawing Pets: A Step-By-Step Sketchbook, 1 vol. Bolte, Mari. 2014. (My First Sketchbook Ser.). (ENG.). 24p. (gr. 1-2). lib. bdg. 24.65 *(978-1-4914-0281-8(4))* Capstone Pr., Inc.

—Drawing Pets: A Step-By-Step Sketchpad, 1 vol. Bolte, Mari. 2014. (My First Sketchpads Ser.). (ENG.). 48p. (gr. 1-2). pap. 5.95 *(978-1-4914-0290-0(3)*, First Facts) Capstone Pr., Inc.

—Drawing Vehicles: A Step-By-Step Sketchbook, 1 vol. Bolte, Mari. 2014. (My First Sketchbook Ser.). (ENG.). 24p. (gr. 1-2). lib. bdg. 24.65 *(978-1-4914-0283-2(0))* Capstone Pr., Inc.

—Drawing Vehicles: A Step-By-Step Sketchpad, 1 vol. Bolte, Mari. 2014. (My First Sketchpads Ser.). (ENG.). 48p. (gr. 1-2). pap. 5.95 *(978-1-4914-0292-4(X)*, First Facts) Capstone Pr., Inc.

—My First Sketchbook, 1 vol. Bolte, Mari. 2014. (My First Sketchbook Ser.). (ENG.). 24p. (gr. 1-2). 98.60 *(978-1-4914-0285-6(7)*, First Facts) Capstone Pr., Inc.

Malak, Annabel. Cinderella. (Classic Stories Ser.). 48p. (J). (gr. -1-2). incl. audio *(978-2-921997-75-1(4))* Coffragants.

—Goldilocks & the Three Bears. (Classic Stories Ser.). 48p. (J). audio, audio compact disk *(978-2-921997-84-3(3))* Coffragants.

—The Three Little Pigs. Biddle, Charles, Jr. 2011. 16p. (J). pap. 12.95 *(978-2-89558-409-4(5))* Editions Alexandre Stanke CAN. Dist: AtlasBooks Distribution.

Malam, John. Ancient Egypt. Malam, John. 2004. (Picturing the Past Ser.). 32p. (J). 15.95 *(978-1-59270-021-9(7))* Enchanted Lion Bks., LLC.

—Library: From Ancient Scrolls to the Worldwide Web: A Building Works Book. Malam, John. 2006. 32p. (J). (gr. 4-18). reprint ed. 17.00 *(978-1-4223-5173-4(4))* DIANE Publishing Co.

—Theater: From First Rehearsal to Opening Night! a Building Works Book. Malam, John. 2006. 32p. (J). (gr. k-4). 17.00 *(978-1-4223-5179-6(3))* DIANE Publishing Co.

Maland, Nick. Big Blue Whale. Davies, Nicola. 2008. (Read, Listen, & Wonder Ser.). (ENG.). 32p. (J). (gr. -1-3). pap. 8.99 *(978-0-7636-3822-1(6))* Candlewick Pr.

Maland, Nick. Big Blue Whale. Davies, Nicola. 2015. 32p. pap. 7.00 ***(978-1-61003-542-2(9))*** Center for the Collaborative Classroom.

Maland, Nick. Oliver Who Travelled Far & Wide. Bergman, Mara. 2010. (Oliver Ser.). (ENG.). 32p. (J). (gr. -1-k). pap. 10.99 *(978-0-340-98164-1(4))* Hodder & Stoughton GBR. Dist: Independent Pubs. Group.

—Oliver Who Would Not Sleep! Bergman, Mara. 2007. (J). *(978-0-439-92827-4(3)*, Levine, Arthur A. Bks.) Scholastic, Inc.

—Snip Snap! What's That? Bergman, Mara. 2005. (ENG.). 32p. (J). (gr. -1-3). 16.99 *(978-0-06-077754-8(0)*, Greenwillow Bks.) HarperCollins Pubs.

—Wishing for Tomorrow: The Sequel to a Little Princess. McKay, Hilary. (ENG.). 288p. (J). (gr. 3-7). 2011. pap. 6.99 *(978-1-4424-0170-9(2))*; 2010. 16.99 *(978-1-4424-0169-3(9))* McElderry, Margaret K. Bks. (McElderry, Margaret K. Bks.).

—You've Got Dragons, 1 vol. Cave, Kathryn. 2003. (ENG.). 32p. (J). (gr. 1-5). 16.95 *(978-1-56145-284-2(X))* Peachtree Pubs.

—Yum Yum! What Fun! Bergman, Mara. 2009. (ENG.). 32p. (J). (gr. -1-2). 17.99 *(978-0-06-168860-7(6)*, Greenwillow Bks.) HarperCollins Pubs.

Malbrough, Michael & Fisher, G. W. Fire Proves Iron: Grounded Stars. Malbrough, Page. 2004. 80p. (YA). per. 9.95 *(978-0-9758883-0-8(7))* Malbrough, Michael.

Maldonado, Luis. Friends Having Fun. Maldonado, Luis, . 2007. 48p. (J). 3.95 *(978-0-9790699-1-8(2))* Empty Harbor Productions, LLC.

Male, Alan. Crocodile Crossing. Bull, Schuyler. 2005. (Amazing Animal Adventures Ser.). (ENG.). 36p. (J). (gr. -1-2). 15.95 *(978-1-59249-051-6(4)*, B7104); (gr. -1-2). pap. 6.95 *(978-1-59249-052-3(2)*, S7104); (gr. -1-2). 19.95 *(978-1-59249-390-6(4)*, BC7104); (gr. 2-2). 8.95 *(978-1-59249-391-3(2)*, SC7104) Soundprints.

—Crocodile Crossing. Bull, Schuyler M. 2003. (Soundprints' Amazing Animal Adventures! Ser.). (ENG.). 36p. (J). (gr. -1-3). 9.95 *(978-1-59249-060-8(3)*, PS7154); 2.95 *(978-1-59249-053-0(0)*, S7154) Soundprints.

Maleev, Alex. Daredevil: Out, 5. Bendis, Brian Michael. 2003. 208p. (YA). pap. 19.99 *(978-0-7851-1074-3(7))* Marvel Worldwide, Inc.

Maleev, Alex, et al. The Road to Civil War. 2007. (ENG.). 160p. (YA). (gr. 8-17). pap. 14.99 *(978-0-7851-1974-6(4))* Marvel Worldwide, Inc.

Maleev, Alexander, et al. Batman Vol. 1: No Man's Land. Gale, Bob & Grayson, Devin K. rev. ed. 2006. (Batman Ser.: Vol. 1). (ENG.). 200p. (YA). 17.99 *(978-1-56389-564-7(1))* DC Comics.

Malenfant, Isabelle. Once upon a Balloon, 1 vol. Galbraith, Bree. 2013. (ENG.). 32p. (J). (gr. -1-3). 19.95 *(978-1-4598-0324-4(8))* Orca Bk. Pubs. USA.

Malépart, Céline. Les Bisous. Stanké, Claudie. 2004. (Picture Bks.). (FRE.). 32p. (J). (gr. -1). *(978-2-89021-694-5(2))*; pap. *(978-2-89021-693-8(4))* Diffusion du livre Mirabel (DLM).

—Earth-Friendly Crafts: Clever Ways to Reuse Everyday Items. Ross, Kathy. (ENG.). 48p. (gr. 2-5). 2011. pap. 7.95 *(978-0-7613-7409-1(4))*; 2009. 26.60 *(978-0-8225-9099-6(9))* Lerner Publishing Group. (Millbrook Pr.).

—L' Héritage de Julien. Tremblay, Alain Ulysse. 2004. (Roman Jeunesse Ser.). (FRE.). 96p. (J). (gr. 4-7). pap. *(978-2-89021-682-2(9))* Diffusion du livre Mirabel (DLM).

Malepart, Celine. Sally Dog Little Undercover Agent. Richardson, Bill. 2003. (ENG.). 24p. (J). (gr. -1-2). pap. 6.95 *(978-1-55037-824-5(4)*, 9781550378245) Annick Pr., Ltd. CAN. Dist: Firefly Bks., Ltd.

—When Pigs Fly: A Piggy Pop-up Book! 2008. (ENG.). 12p. 16.95 *(978-1-58117-671-1(6)*, Intervisual/Piggy Toes) Bendon, Inc.

Malinow, Wendy. A Bit of Applause for Mrs. Claus. Schick-Jacobowitz, Jeannie et al. rev. ed. 2003. (ENG.). 64p. 9.95 *(978-1-4022-0140-0(0))* Sourcebooks, Inc.

Malkowski, Melissa. Larry the Turtle When Everyone Helps, Everyone Wins! Kleemann, Linda. 2005. (J). pap. 7.95 *(978-0-9776487-0-2(2))* Fencepost Communications Inc.

Mallam, Sally. The Man & the Fox. Shah, Idries. 2006. 32p. (J). (gr. -1). 18.00 *(978-1-883536-43-5(X))*; pap. 7.99 *(978-1-883536-60-2(X))* I S H K (Hoopoe Bks.).

Mallea, Cristian. Bigfoot & Adaptation, 1 vol. Collins, Terry. 2011. (Monster Science Ser.). (ENG.). 32p. (gr. 3-4). lib. bdg. 29.99 *(978-1-4296-6579-7(3)*, Graphic Library) Capstone Pr., Inc.

—Encountering Aliens: Eyewitness Accounts, 1 vol. Kincade, Chris. 2014. (Eyewitness to the Unexplained Ser.). (ENG.). 32p. (gr. 3-4). 29.99 *(978-1-4914-0244-3(X))* Capstone Pr., Inc.

—George Washington: The Rise of America's First President. Biskup, Agnieszka. 2012. (American Graphic Ser.). (ENG.). 32p. (gr. 3-4). pap. 47.70 *(978-1-4296-9335-6(5)*, Graphic Library); lib. bdg. 29.99 *(978-1-4296-8621-1(9))* Capstone Pr., Inc.

—George Washington: The Rise of America's First President, 1 vol. Biskup, Agnieszka Józefina. 2012. (American Graphic Ser.). (ENG.). 32p. (gr. 3-4). pap. 8.10 *(978-1-4296-9334-9(7)*, Graphic Library) Capstone Pr., Inc.

—Mummies & Sound, 1 vol. Wacholtz, Anthony. 2013. (Monster Science Ser.). (ENG.). 32p. (gr. 3-4). pap. 7.95 *(978-1-62065-818-5(6))*; 47.70 *(978-1-62065-819-2(4))*; 29.99 *(978-1-4296-9930-3(2))* Capstone Pr., Inc. (Graphic Library).

—Robert E. Lee: The Story of the Great Confederate General, 1 vol. Collins, Terry. 2011. (American Graphic Ser.). (ENG.). 32p. (gr. 3-4). lib. bdg. 29.99 *(978-1-4296-5475-3(9))*; pap. 8.10 *(978-1-4296-6269-7(7))*; pap. 47.70 *(978-1-4296-6436-3(3))* Capstone Pr., Inc. (Graphic Library).

Mallea, Cristian & Gervasio. Monster Science. Collins, Terry et al. 2013. (Monster Science Ser.). (ENG.). 32p. (gr. 3-4). lib. bdg. 299.90 *(978-1-4765-0427-8(X))*; lib. bdg. 59.98 *(978-1-4765-0426-1(1))* Capstone Pr., Inc. (Graphic Library).

Mallett, Keith. How Jelly Roll Morton Invented Jazz. Winter, Jonah. 2015. (ENG.). 32p. (J). (gr. k-3). 17.99 *(978-1-59643-963-4(7))* Roaring Brook Pr.

Mallett, Lisa. Forty-Eight Funny Faces: Use the Cling-On Stickers to Make Funny Faces! Golding, Elizabeth. 2015. (ENG.). 56p. (J). (gr. -1-2). pap. 8.99 *(978-1-4380-0599-7(7))* Barron's Educational Series, Inc.

Mallette, Dania. God Says I've Changed Your Dna: Walk As Children of the Light._Meli, Ayani & D., Jessie. 2013. 24p. pap. 12.00 *(978-0-9846315-7-5(7))* JWD Publishing.

—The Three Keys. Dimarco, Tony. 2010. 146p. pap. 9.95 *(978-0-9818391-2-7(6))* Panoply Pubns.

Mallory, Edgar. Hand Me down House. Norfleet, Mary Crockett. 2011. 98p. 38.95 *(978-1-258-07946-8(1))* Literary Licensing, LLC.

Mallory, Marilynn H. My Mother Talks to Trees, 1 vol. Gove, Doris. 2005. (ENG.). 32p. (J). (gr. k-3). pap. 7.95 *(978-1-56145-336-8(6)*, Q31285) Peachtree Pubs.

Malloy, Kalle. Jingle Bats. Jennings, Sharon. 72p. pap. *(978-1-897039-22-9(0))* High Interest Publishing (HIP).

Malone, Kyle. Miles Grand Adventures: The Denver Broncos Mascot's A-to-Z Journey Around Colorado. Merlatt, James & Frainier, Tamara. 2004. 32p. (J). 19.95 *(978-0-9759579-2-9(9))* Denver Broncos.

Malone, Nola Langner. Earrings! Viorst, Judith. 2010. (ENG.). 32p. (J). (gr. 1-5). 17.99 *(978-1-4424-1281-1(X),* Atheneum Bks. for Young Readers) Simon & Schuster Children's Publishing.

Malone, Peter. Agrippina: "Atrocious & Ferocious" Bridges, Shirin Yim. 2011. (Thinking Girl's Treasury of Dastardly Dames Ser.). (ENG.). 32p. (J). (gr. 3-8). 18.95 *(978-0-9834256-1-8(2))* Goosebottom Bks. LLC.

—The Boston Tea Party. Freedman, Russell. 2012. (ENG.). 40p. (J). 17.95 *(978-0-8234-2266-1(6))* Holiday Hse., Inc.

—The Boston Tea Party. Russell, Freedman. ed. 2013. (ENG.). 40p. (J). pap. 7.99 *(978-0-8234-2915-8(6))* Holiday Hse., Inc.

—Catherine de' Medici: "The Black Queen" Havemeyer, Janie. 2011. (Thinking Girl's Treasury of Dastardly Dames Ser.). (ENG.). 32p. (J). (gr. 3-8). 18.95 *(978-0-9834256-3-2(9))* Goosebottom Bks. LLC.

—Cleopatra: "Serpent of the Nile" Pack, Mary Fisk. 2011. (Thinking Girl's Treasury of Dastardly Dames Ser.). (ENG.). 32p. (J). (gr. 3-8). 18.95 *(978-0-9834256-0-1(4))* Goosebottom Bks. LLC.

—The Forest Child. Edwards, Richard. 2004. 28p. (J). reprint ed. *(978-0-7567-7850-7(6))* DIANE Publishing Co.

—Marie Antoinette "Madame Deficit" Hockinson, Liz. 2011. (Thinking Girl's Treasury of Dastardly Dames Ser.). (ENG.). 32p. (J). (gr. 3-8). 18.95 *(978-0-9834256-4-9(7))* Goosebottom Bks. LLC.

—Mary Tudor: "Bloody Mary" Maurer, Gretchen. 2011. (Thinking Girl's Treasury of Dastardly Dames Ser.). (ENG.). 32p. (J). (gr. 3-8). 18.95 *(978-0-9834256-2-5(0))* Goosebottom Bks. LLC.

—Njinga the Warrior Queen. Havemeyer, Janie. 2011. (Thinking Girl's Treasury of Dastardly Dames Ser.). (ENG.). 32p. (J). (gr. 3-8). 18.95 *(978-0-9834256-6-3(3))* Goosebottom Bks. LLC.

—The Nutcracker. Spinner, Stephanie. 2008. (ENG.). 40p. (J). (gr. -1-2). 17.99 *(978-0-375-84464-5(3))* Knopf, Alfred A. Inc.

Malone, Peter. Sergei Prokofiev's Peter & the Wolf: With a Fully-Orchestrated & Narrated CD. Malone, Peter. Prokofiev, Sergei. 2004. (ENG.). 40p. (J). (gr. -1-2). 19.95 *(978-0-375-82430-2(8),* Knopf Bks. for Young Readers) Random Hse. Children's Bks.

Maloney, Brenna. Ready Rabbit Gets Ready! Maloney, Brenna. 2015. (ENG.). 32p. (J). (gr. -1-k). 16.99 *(978-0-670-01549-8(0),* Viking Juvenile) Penguin Publishing Group.

Maloney, Cynthia, photos by. How Does God Listen? Lindahl, Kay. 2005. (ENG., 32p. (J). pap. 8.99 *(978-1-59473-084-9(9),* Skylight Paths Publishing) LongHill Partners, Inc.

Maloney, Jim. I Love Harry. Maloney, Jim. Buster Books Staff. 2013. (I Love One Direction Ser.). (ENG.). 96p. (J). (gr. 3-7). pap. 7.99 *(978-1-78055-213-2(0))* O'Mara, Michael Bks., Ltd. GBR. Dist: Independent Pubs. Group.

—I Love Liam. Maloney, Jim. 2013. (I Love One Direction Ser.). (ENG.). 96p. (J). (gr. 3-7). pap. 7.99 *(978-1-78055-217-0(3))* O'Mara, Michael Bks., Ltd. GBR. Dist: Independent Pubs. Group.

Maloney, Peter & Zekauskas, Felicia. One Foot, Two Feet. Maloney, Peter & Zekauskas, Felicia. 2011. (ENG.). 84p. (J). (gr. -1-k). 12.99 *(978-0-399-25446-8(3),* Putnam Juvenile) Penguin Publishing Group.

Maltaite, Will, jt. illus. see Peyo.

Maltman Dinwoodie, Heather. The Splendiddly Fazztabulous Grandmas. Sellen, Sandi. 2013. 32p. pap. *(978-1-77069-893-2(0))* Word Alive Pr.

Malvern, Corinne. The Night Before Christmas. Moore, Clement C. (Little Golden Board Book Ser.). (ENG.). (J). 2014. 26p. (-k). bds. 7.99 *(978-0-385-38474-2(2));* 2011. 24p. (gr. -1-k). 4.99 *(978-0-375-86359-2(1))* Random Hse. Children's Bks. (Golden Bks.).

—Nurse Nancy. Jackson, Kathryn. 2005. (Little Golden Book Ser.). (ENG.). 24p. (J). (gr. -1-2). 3.99 *(978-0-375-83262-8(9),* Golden Bks.) Random Hse. Children's Bks.

Malvezi, Irene. Draw Water & Other Things. Nissen Samuels, Linda. 2010. 48p. (J). pap. 15.98 *(978-1-905941-15-5(3))* Sigel Pr.

Mamada, Mineko. Which Is Round? Which Is Bigger? Mamada, Mineko. 2013. (ENG.). 24p. (J). 16.95 *(978-1-55453-973-4(0))* Kids Can Pr., Ltd. CAN. Dist: Univ. of Toronto Pr.

Mamata, Sue. Black, White & Beautiful. Harris, Amber. 2007. 25p. pap. 24.95 *(978-1-4241-8932-8(2))* PublishAmerica, Inc.

Mammano, Julie. Rhinos Who Play Baseball. Mammano, Julie. 2006. 24p. (J). (gr. k-4). reprint ed. 14.00 *(978-0-7567-9995-3(3))* DIANE Publishing Co.

Manak, Dave. Sabrina Animated. Gallagher, Mike. 2011. (Archie & Friends All-Stars Ser.: 13). (ENG.). 128p. (J). (gr. 4-7). pap. 9.95 *(978-1-879794-80-1(2),* Archie Comics) Archie Comic Pubns., Inc.

Manale, Steven Charles, et al. Eat It Up! Lip-Smacking Recipes for Kids. de Mariaffi, Elisabeth. 2nd ed. 2009. (ENG.). 96p. (J). (gr. 1-6). 19.95 *(978-1-897349-56-4(4))* Owlkids Bks. Inc. CAN. Dist: Perseus-PGW.

Manarino, Mark. Sourpuss Sue. McKenna, Jacqueline & Manarino-Leggett, Priscilla. 2011. 24p. pap. 24.95 *(978-1-4560-8939-9(0))* America Star Bks.

Manasau, Amos. The Curse of the Laulau Tree. Mesibere, Ellen. 2012. 34p. pap. *(978-9980-945-67-9(2))* University of Papua New Guinea Press.

—Wagabuibui, the Four Eyed Eagle. Charles, Novalyn. 2012. 38p. pap. *(978-9980-945-66-2(4))* University of Papua New Guinea Press.

Manasco, Katharine. An Exceptional Children's Guide to Touch: Teaching Social & Physical Boundaries to Kids. Manasco, Hunter. 2012. (ENG.). 72p. *(978-1-84905-871-1(7))* Kingsley, Jessica Ltd.

—The Way to A: Empowering Children with Autism Spectrum & Other Neurological Disorders to Monitor & Replace Aggression & Tantrum Behavior. Manasco, Hunter. 2006. 19p. spiral bd., wbk. ed. 18.95 *(978-1-931282-87-1(0))* Autism Asperger Publishing Co.

Manceau, Édouard. Tickle Monster. 2015. (ENG.). 32p. (J). (gr. -1-k). 14.95 *(978-1-4197-1731-4(6))* Abrams.

Mancek, Marjan. Let's Go to Work. Brunel, Aude. 2007. 32p. (J). (POL & ENG.). pap. 16.95 *(978-1-60195-101-4(9));* (ARA & ENG.). pap. 16.95 *(978-1-60195-089-5(6))* International Step by Step Assn.

Mancell, Doris. Tommy Tortoise Gets the Sugar Blues. Caraboolad, Arla. l.t. ed. 2011. (ENG.). 38p. pap. 8.99 *(978-1-4679-7980-1(5))* CreateSpace Independent Publishing Platform.

Manchess, Gregory. Cheyenne Medicine Hat. Heinz, Brian J. 2004. (ENG.). 32p. (J). (gr. 1-3). 19.95 *(978-1-56846-181-6(X))* Creative Co., The.

—Giving Thanks. London, Jonathan. 2011. (ENG.). 32p. (J). (gr. -1-2). pap. 6.99 *(978-0-7636-5594-5(5))* Candlewick Pr.

—The Last River: John Wesley Powell & the Colorado River Exploring Expedition. Waldman, Stuart. 2005. (Great Explorers Ser.). (ENG.). 48p. (J). (gr. 4-8). 19.95 *(978-1-931414-09-8(2),* 9781931414098) Mikaya Pr.

—Magellan's World. Waldman, Stuart. 2007. (Great Explorers Ser.). (ENG.). 48p. (J). (gr. 4-8). 22.95 *(978-1-931414-19-7(X),* 9781931414197) Mikaya Pr.

—Nanuk, Lord of the Ice. Heinz, Brian J. 2005. (J). *(978-0-936335-13-1(0));* pap. *(978-0-936335-14-8(9))* Ballyhoo BookWorks, Inc.

—Real Pirates: The Untold Story of the Whydah from Slave Ship to Pirate Ship. Garrett, Kenneth, photos by. Clifford, Barry. 2008. (ENG.). 32p. (J). (gr. 5). 16.95 *(978-1-4263-0279-4(7));* lib. bdg. 25.90 *(978-1-4263-0280-0(0))* National Geographic Society. (National Geographic Children's Bks.).

Mancini, Robert. The Billy-Goats Tough. O'Brien, Tim. 2007. (Collins Big Cat Ser.). (ENG.). 24p. (J). pap. 8.99 *(978-0-00-722863-8(5))* HarperCollins Pubs. Ltd. GBR. Dist: Independent Pubs. Group.

Mandarino, Gene. Losing Papou: One Child's Journey Towards Understanding & Accepting Death. Garrick, Lainie. l.t. ed. 2003. 32p. (J). *(978-0-9765725-0-3(8))* printONDEMANDpublisher.com.

Mander, Sanna. Design Line: History of Women's Fashion. Slee, Natasha. 2015. (ENG.). 16p. (J). (gr. 5). 17.99 ***(978-0-7636-7962-0(3),*** Big Picture Press) Candlewick Pr.

Manders, Jeff & Manders, John. Let's Have a Tree Party! Martin, David. 2012. (ENG.). 32p. (J). (gr. k-k). 15.99 *(978-0-7636-3704-0(1))* Candlewick Pr.

Manders, John. Case of the Psychic Hamster. McMahon, P. J. 2005. 153p. (J). lib. bdg. 15.38 *(978-1-4242-0404-5(6))* Fitzgerald Bks.

—The Case of the Psychic Hamster. McMahon, P. J. 4th ed. 2005. (Freaky Joe Club Ser.: 4). (ENG.). 128p. (J). (gr. 2-5). pap. 8.99 *(978-0-689-86263-2(6),* Simon & Schuster/Paula Wiseman Bks.) Simon & Schuster/Paula Wiseman Bks.

—Case of the Singing Sea Dragons. McMahon, P. J. 2005. 153p. (J). lib. bdg. 15.38 *(978-1-4242-0406-9(2))* Fitzgerald Bks.

—The Case of the Singing Sea Dragons. McMahon, P. J. 6th ed. 2005. (Freaky Joe Club Ser.: 6). (ENG.). 112p. (J). (gr. 2-5). pap. 8.99 *(978-1-4169-0050-4(0),* Simon & Schuster/Paula Wiseman Bks.) Simon & Schuster/Paula Wiseman Bks.

—The Case of the Smiling Shark. McMahon, P. J. 2004. (Freaky Joe Club Ser.: 2). (ENG.). 128p. (J). (gr. 2-5). pap. 7.99 *(978-0-689-86261-8(X),* Simon & Schuster/Paula Wiseman Bks.) Simon & Schuster/Paula Wiseman Bks.

—Case of the Smiling Shark. McMahon, P. J. 2004. 116p. (J). lib. bdg. 15.38 *(978-1-4242-0402-1(X))* Fitzgerald Bks.

—Cowboy Christmas. Sanders, Rob. 2012. (ENG.). 32p. (J). (gr. k-k). 10.99 *(978-0-375-86985-3(9),* Golden Bks.) Random Hse. Children's Bks.

—Dear Tyrannosaurus Rex. McClatchy, Lisa. 2010. (ENG.). 40p. (J). (gr. -1-2). 16.99 *(978-0-375-85608-2(0))* Random Hse., Inc.

—Finnegan & Fox: The Ten-Foot Cop. Wilbur, Helen L. 2013. (ENG.). 32p. (J). (gr. 1-4). 16.95 *(978-1-58536-784-9(2),* 202354) Sleeping Bear Pr.

—First-Base Hero: A Lift-the-Flap Pop-up Book. Hernandez, Keith. 2005. 12p. (J). (gr. k-4). reprint ed. 13.00 *(978-0-7567-8543-7(X))* DIANE Publishing Co.

—Goldie Socks & the Three Libearians. Hopkins, Jackie Mims. 2007. (J). *(978-1-932146-68-4(7));* (gr. -1-3). 17.95 *(978-1-932146-98-1(9))* Highsmith Inc. (Upstart Bks.).

—Henry & the Buccaneer Bunnies. Crimi, Carolyn. 2005. (ENG.). 40p. (J). (gr. -1-3). 15.99 *(978-0-7636-2449-1(7))* Candlewick Pr.

—Henry & the Buccaneer Bunnies. Crimi, Carolyn. 2009. (ENG.). 40p. (J). (gr. -1-3). pap. 6.99 *(978-0-7636-4540-3(0))* Candlewick Pr.

—Henry & the Crazed Chicken Pirates. Crimi, Carolyn. 2010. (ENG.). 40p. (J). (gr. -1-3). pap. 6.99 *(978-0-7636-4999-9(6))* Candlewick Pr.

—Jack & the Giant Barbecue. 0 vols. Kimmel, Eric A. 2012. (ENG.). 32p. (J). (gr. 1-3). 17.99 *(978-0-7614-6128-9(0),* 9780761461289, Amazon Children's Publishing) Amazon Publishing.

—Joe Bright & the Seven Genre Dudes. Hopkins, Jackie Mims. 2010. (J). 36p. (gr. 1-5). 17.95 *(978-1-60213-051-7(5));* *(978-1-60213-049-4(3))* Highsmith Inc. (Upstart Bks.).

—Lewis & Clark: A Prairie Dog for the President. Redmond, Shirley Raye. 2003. (Step into Reading Ser.). 48p. 14.00 *(978-0-7569-1697-8(6))* Perfection Learning Corp.

—Lewis & Clark: A Prairie Dog for the President. Redmond, Shirley Raye. 2003. (Step into Reading Ser.: No. 3). (ENG.). 48p. (J). (gr. k-3). pap. 3.99 *(978-0-375-81120-3(6),* Random Hse. Bks. for Young Readers) Random Hse. Children's Bks.

—Minnie's Diner: A Multiplying Menu. Dodds, Dayle Ann. 2007. (ENG.). 40p. (J). (gr. k-3). pap. 6.99 *(978-0-7636-3313-4(5))* Candlewick Pr.

—The Mystery of the Morphing Hockey Stick. McMahon, Patricia. 2004. 138p. (J). lib. bdg. 15.38 *(978-1-4242-0403-8(8))* Fitzgerald Bks.

—The Mystery of the Morphing Hockey Stick. McMahon, P. J. 3rd ed. 2004. (Freaky Joe Club Ser.: 3). (ENG.). 128p. (J). (gr. 2-5). pap. 8.99 *(978-0-689-86262-5(8),* Simon & Schuster/Paula Wiseman Bks.) Simon & Schuster/Paula Wiseman Bks.

—The Mystery of the Swimming Gorilla. McMahon, P. J. 2004. (Freaky Joe Club Ser.: 1). (ENG.). 128p. (J). (gr. 2-5). pap. 6.99 *(978-0-689-86260-1(1),* Simon & Schuster/Paula Wiseman Bks.) Simon & Schuster/Paula Wiseman Bks.

—Mystery of the Swimming Gorilla. McMahon, P. J. 2004. 106p. (J). lib. bdg. 15.38 *(978-1-4242-0401-4(1))* Fitzgerald Bks.

—The Perfect Nest. Friend, Catherine. 2007. (ENG.). 40p. (J). (gr. -1-2). 16.99 *(978-0-7636-2430-9(6))* Candlewick Pr.

—Pete & Fremont. Tripp, Jenny. 2008. (ENG.). 192p. (J). (gr. 3-7). pap. 12.95 *(978-0-15-206238-5(6))* Houghton Mifflin Harcourt Publishing Co.

—Pirates Go to School. Demas, Corinne. 2011. (ENG.). 32p. (J). (gr. -1-3). 16.99 *(978-0-545-20629-7(4),* Orchard Bks.) Scholastic, Inc.

—Santa's Reindeer Games. Berger, Samantha. 2011. (J). *(978-0-545-36866-7(9))* Scholastic, Inc.

—The Soldiers' Night Before Christmas. Holland, Trish & Ford, Christine. 2006. (Big Little Golden Book Ser.). (ENG.). 32p. (J). (gr. -1-2). 8.99 *(978-0-375-83795-1(7),* Golden Bks.) Random Hse. Children's Bks.

—Stinker & the Onion Princess. Griffin, Kitty & Combs, Kathy. 2005. (J). *(978-0-8037-2976-6(6),* Dial) Penguin Publishing Group.

—Turkey Day. Maccarone, Grace. 2010. (Scholastic Reader Level 1 Ser.). (ENG.). 32p. (J). (gr. -1-3). pap. 3.99 *(978-0-545-12001-2(2),* Cartwheel Bks.) Scholastic, Inc.

—What You Never Knew about Beds, Bedrooms, & Pajamas. Lauber, Patricia. 2008. (ENG.). 40p. (J). (gr. 1-4). 6.99 *(978-1-4169-6738-5(9),* Simon & Schuster Bks. For Young Readers) Simon & Schuster Bks. For Young Readers.

—What You Never Knew about Fingers, Forks, & Chopsticks. Lauber, Patricia. 2009. (ENG.). 36p. (J). (gr. 1-5). pap. 12.99 *(978-1-4424-0937-8(1),* Simon & Schuster Bks. For Young Readers) Simon & Schuster Bks. For Young Readers.

—Where's My Mummy? Crimi, Carolyn. (ENG.). 32p. (J). (gr. -1-3). 2009. 7.99 *(978-0-7636-4337-9(8));* 2008. 15.99 *(978-0-7636-3196-3(5))* Candlewick Pr.

—2030: A Day in the Life of Tomorrow's Kids. Daly, James & Zuckerman, Amy. 2009. (ENG.). 32p. (J). (gr. 1-3). 16.99 *(978-0-525-47860-7(4),* Dutton Juvenile) Penguin Publishing Group.

Manders, John, jt. illus. see Manders, Jeff.

Mandracchia, Charles, 8th. Showtoonz, Mandracchia, Charles, 8th, creator. 2nd l.t. ed. 2005. 38p. (J). per. 995.00 net. *(978-0-9721957-2-0(6),* Mandracchia Bks.) Mandracchia, Charles.

Mandrake, Tom & Zezelj, Danijel. The Call of Duty Vol. 2: The Precinct, 2 vols. Jones, Bruce & Austen, Chuck. 2003. (Call Ser.). 128p. (YA). pap. 9.99 *(978-0-7851-0974-7(9))* Marvel Worldwide, Inc.

Mandy, Stanley. Bella: The Birthday Party. Mandy, Stanley. 2010. 32p. (J). (gr. -1-k). 9.95 *(978-1-58925-850-1(9))* Tiger Tales.

—Bella: The Fairy Ball. Mandy, Stanley. 2010. 32p. (J). (gr. -1-k). 9.95 *(978-1-58925-851-8(7))* Tiger Tales.

Manetti, Francesco. What Could It Be? Nayar, Nandini. 2013. (ENG.). 28p. (J). (gr. -1). 11.95 *(978-81-8190-285-6(8))* Karadi Tales Co. Pvt. Ltd. IND. Dist: Consortium Bk. Sales & Distribution.

Manfre, Joey. Patch Land Adventures Book 2 Camping at Mimi's Ranch. Swick, Carmen D. Lambert, Page, ed. 2012. 40p. pap. 12.99 *(978-0-9831380-1-3(X))* Presbeau Publishing, Inc.

Manfredi, Federica. Kat & Mouse. de Campi, Alex. 2007. (Kat & Mouse; Teacher Torture Ser.: Vol. 2). 96p. pap. 5.99 *(978-1-59816-549-4(6))* TOKYOPOP, Inc.

—Kat & Mouse, Vol. 1. De, Campialex. 2006. (Kat & Mouse Ser.: Vol. 1). 96p. pap. 5.99 *(978-1-59816-548-7(8))* TOKYOPOP, Inc.

Manfredi, Frederica. Kat & Mouse, Vol. 4. De Campi, Alex. 2009. 112p. pap. 5.99 *(978-1-4278-1175-2(X))* TOKYOPOP, Inc.

Mangano, Tom. Dora. Beinstein, Phoebe. 2003. (Dora the Explorer Ser.). (ENG & SPA.). 12p. (J). bds. 7.99 *(978-0-689-85484-2(6),* Simon Spotlight/Nickelodeon) Simon Spotlight/Nickelodeon.

Mangano, Tom, et al. Dora's Rainbow Picnic. Ricci, Christine. 2007. (J). pap. *(978-1-4127-8927-1(3))* Publications International, Ltd.

Mangano, Tom. Dora's World Adventure! 2006. (Dora the Explorer Ser.). (ENG.). 24p. (J). (gr. -1-2). pap. 3.99 *(978-1-4169-2447-0(7),* Simon Spotlight/Nickelodeon) Simon Spotlight/Nickelodeon.

—Puppy Takes a Bath. Ricci, Christine. 2006. (Dora the Explorer Ser.: 10). (ENG.). 24p. (J). (gr. 3-7). pap. 3.99 *(978-1-4169-1483-9(8),* Simon Spotlight/Nickelodeon) Simon Spotlight/Nickelodeon.

Mangano, Tom & Miller, Victoria. Where Is Baby Jaguar? Driscoll, Laura. 2011. (Dora & Diego Ser.). (ENG.). 24p. (J). pap. 3.99 *(978-1-4424-1398-6(0),* Simon Spotlight/Nickelodeon) Simon Spotlight/Nickelodeon.

Mangelsen, Thomas, photos by. When Morning Comes. Hirschi, Ron. 2006. (ENG., 32p. (J). (gr. 1-3). pap. 9.95 *(978-1-59078-416-7(2))* Boyds Mills Pr.

—When Night Comes. Hirschi, Ron. 2006. (ENG., 32p. (J). (gr. 1-3). pap. 9.95 *(978-1-59078-417-4(0))* Boyds Mills Pr.

Mangelsen, Thomas D., photos by. The Animal in Me: Is Very Plain to See. Tye, Laurie. 2005. (ENG., 32p. (J). (gr. -1-k). per. 8.95 *(978-1-55868-898-8(6),* West Winds Pr.) Graphic Arts Ctr. Publishing Co.

Mangelsen, Thomas D. & Cooper, Deborah. Searching for Grizzlies. Mangelsen, Thomas D., photos by. Hirschi, Ron. 2005. (J). 17.95 *(978-1-4156-2797-6(5))* Boyds Mills Pr.

Mangiat, Jeff. Snakes. Scott, L. K. 2008. (ENG.). 24p. (J). (gr. 3-18). 19.95 *(978-1-58117-799-2(2),* Intervisual/Piggy Toes) Bendon, Inc.

Mangiat, Jeffrey. Allosaurus. Mattern, Joanne. 2009. (Let's Read about Dinosaurs Ser.). 24p. (J). (gr. -1-3). lib. bdg. 22.00 *(978-0-8368-9414-1(6),* Weekly Reader Leveled Readers) Stevens, Gareth Publishing LLLP.

—Ankylosaurus. Mattern, Joanne. 2009. (Let's Read about Dinosaurs Ser.). 24p. (J). (gr. -1-3). lib. bdg. 22.00 *(978-0-8368-9415-8(4),* Weekly Reader Leveled Readers) Stevens, Gareth Publishing LLLP.

Manglou, Gabrielle. Excuses Excuses. Ravishankar, Anushka. 2012. (ENG.). 48p. (J). (gr. k). 17.95 *(978-93-80340-12-8(5))* Tara Books Agency IND. Dist: Perseus-PGW.

Mangrum, Kaylea J. How to Draw Step-By-Step Using the Alphabet. Mangrum, Kaylea J. 2013. 38p. pap. 12.49 *(978-0-9883009-4-1(X))* Mangrum, Kaylea J.

—How to Draw Step-By-Step with Special Kids. Mangrum, Kaylea J. 2013. 38p. pap. 12.49 *(978-0-9883009-3-4(1))* Mangrum, Kaylea J.

—Tucker Goes to Kindergarten. Mangrum, Kaylea J. Bartch, Lea. 2013. 54p. pap. 14.99 *(978-0-9883009-5-8(8))* Mangrum, Kaylea J.

Mangum, James. The Silly Adventures of the Silly Name Gang: The Case of the Mixed-Up Families. Mangum, James. Spires, Sidney. ed. 2011. (ENG.). 48p. pap. 10.58 *(978-1-4610-5405-4(2))* CreateSpace Independent Publishing Platform.

Mangum, James A. The Fairy & the Chupacabra & Those Marfa Lights: A West Texas Fable. Mangum, James A. Spires, Sidney. 2008. 32p. (J). 17.95 *(978-0-9798391-5-3(7))* Hardy, John M. Publishing Co.

Manikandan, jt. illus. see Jones, K. L.

Manikoff, John. Shadow Moves: A Story for Families & Children Experiencing a Difficult or Traumatic Move. Sheppard, Caroline H. 2003. (J). pap. 10.00 *(978-1-931310-26-0(2))* National Institute for Trauma & Loss in Children (TLC), The.

Manion, Moira. The Vineyard Book. Johnston, Jack. 2005. 48p. (J). 25.00 *(978-0-9629880-0-4(6))* ACME Pr.

Manjula Padmanabhan. Unprincess! 2005. 98p. (J). *(978-0-14-333495-8(6),* Puffin) Penguin Publishing Group.

Mankamyer, Laura. The Adventures of the Stonycreek Gang. Mankamyer, Laura. l.t. ed. 2003. 84p. (J). 12.99 *(978-0-9728431-4-0(0))* Mankamyer, Laura.

Manley, Jeanette. In Search of Your Image: A Practical Guide to the Mental & Spiritual Aspects of Horsemanship. Hassler, Jill K. Jahiel, Jessica, ed. rev. ed. (ENG.). 384p. reprint ed. pap. 19.95 *(978-0-9632562-3-2(8),* 760) Goals Unlimited Pr.

Mann, Bethany. Show Off: How to Do Absolutely Everything. One Step at a Time. Stephens, Sarah Hines. 2009. (ENG.). 224p. (J). (gr. 5-9). pap. 18.99 *(978-0-7636-4599-1(0))* Candlewick Pr.

Mann, Clay. Collision. Carey, Mike. 2011. (ENG.). 112p. (J). (gr. 4-17). 19.99 *(978-0-7851-4668-1(7))* Marvel Worldwide, Inc.

—X-Men Legacy: Collison. Carey, Mike. 2011. (ENG.). 112p. (J). (gr. 4-17). pap. 14.99 *(978-0-7851-4669-8(5))* Marvel Worldwide, Inc.

Mann, Derek & Bouse, Biff. The Adventures of Robbie the Raindrop. Carroll, John. 2006. 32p. (J). pap. 21.99 *(978-1-59886-706-0(7))* Tate Publishing & Enterprises, LLC.

Mann, Jennifer K. Turkey Tot. Shannon, George. (ENG.). 32p. (J). 2014. (gr. -1-1). 6.99 *(978-0-8234-3175-5(4));* 2013. 16.95 *(978-0-8234-2379-8(4))* Holiday Hse., Inc.

Mann, Jennifer K. I Will Never Get a Star on Mrs. Benson's Blackboard. Mann, Jennifer K. 2015. (ENG.). 40p. (J). (gr. k-3). 16.99 *(978-0-7636-6514-2(2))* Candlewick Pr.

—Two Speckled Eggs. Mann, Jennifer K. 2014. (ENG.). 32p. (J). (gr. k-3). 14.99 *(978-0-7636-6168-7(6))* Candlewick Pr.

Mann, Lawrence. Stellarcadia. Grasso, Julie Anne. 2014. (Cardamom Ser.: Bk. 3). 128p. (J). pap. *(978-0-9873725-6-7(4))* Grasso, Julie Anne AUS. Dist: INT Bks.

Mann, William A. The Anhinga Tree. Maddock-Cowart, Donna. 2012. 74p. pap. 9.95 *(978-0-9836484-3-7(3))* Miglior Pr.

Manna, Giovanni. The Barefoot Book of Giants, Ghosts, & Goblins. Matthews, John. 2008. (ENG.). 80p. (J). 21.99 *(978-1-84686-235-9(3))* Barefoot Bks., Inc.

—The Barefoot Book of Knights. Matthews, John. (ENG.). 80p. (J). 2009. 19.99 *(978-1-84686-307-3(4));* 2005. (gr. 4-7). pap. 15.99 *(978-1-84148-205-7(6))* Barefoot Bks., Inc.

Manna, Giovanni. Knights. Matthews, John. 2014. (Barefoot Bks.). (ENG.). 79p. (J). (gr. 3-6). pap. 15.99 incl. audio compact disk ***(978-1-78285-165-3(8))*** Barefoot Bks., Inc.

Manna, Giovanni. Swing High, Swing Low. Coward, Fiona. 2005. (ENG.). 32p. (J). 16.99 *(978-1-84148-170-8(X))* Barefoot Bks., Inc.

—You & Me. Blackstone, Stella. 2009. (ENG.). 32p. (J). 14.99 *(978-1-84686-336-3(8))* Barefoot Bks., Inc.

Manni, Mia (Maio). Flora & the Silver Coins. Deluca, Laura. 2011. 40p. pap. 24.95 *(978-1-4560-7752-5(X))* America Star Bks.

Manning, Clarice. I Love My Baby Berimbau: an Introduction to the Berimbau in Capoeira. Bruno, Daphnie. 2011. (ENG.). 32p. pap. 9.95 *(978-1-4564-7994-7(6))* CreateSpace Independent Publishing Platform.

Manning, Eddie. Family Favourites. McKay-Lawton, Toni. 2007. (Just in Rhyme Ser.). 12p. (J). (gr. -1-3). *(978-1-84167-028-7(6))* Ransom Publishing Ltd.

—In Bloom. McKay-Lawton, Toni. 2007. (Just in Rhyme Ser.). 12p. (J). (gr. -1-3). pap. *(978-1-84167-030-0(8))* Ransom Publishing Ltd.

M

—Under the Sea. McKay-Lawton, Toni. 2007. (Just in Rhyme Ser.). 12p. (J). (gr. -1-3). *(978-1-84167-027-0(8))* Ransom Publishing Ltd.

Manning, Jane. Do Kangaroos Wear Seatbelts? Kurtz, Jane. Rossi, Ino, ed. 2005. (ENG.). 32p. (J). (gr. -1-k). 16.99 *(978-0-525-47358-9(0)*, Dutton Juvenile) Penguin Publishing Group.

—Little Elfie One. Jane, Pamela. 2015. (ENG.). 32p. (J). (gr. -1-3). 17.99 *(978-0-06-220673-2(7))* HarperCollins Pubs.

—Mac & Cheese & the Perfect Plan. Weeks, Sarah. 2012. 32p. (J). lib. bdg. 17.89 *(978-0-06-117083-6(6))*; (ENG.). 16.99 *(978-0-06-117082-9(8))*; (ENG.). pap. 3.99 *(978-0-06-117084-3(4))* HarperCollins Pubs.

—A Pet for Me. Hopkins, Lee Bennett. 2003. (I Can Read Bks.). (ENG.). 48p. (J). (gr. k-3). 15.99 *(978-0-06-029111-2(7))* HarperCollins Pubs.

—Snoring Beauty. Bardhan-Quallen, Sudipta. 2014. (J). *(978-0-06-087405-6(8))* Harper & Row Ltd.

—Snoring Beauty. Bardhan-Quallen, Sudipta. 2014. (ENG.). 32p. (J). (gr. -1-3). 17.99 *(978-0-06-087403-2(1))* HarperCollins Pubs.

—There's No Place Like School. Prelutsky, Jack. 2010. (ENG.). 32p. (J). (gr. k-5). 16.99 *(978-0-06-082338-2(0)*, Greenwillow Bks.) HarperCollins Pubs.

—There's No Place Like School: Classroom Poems. Prelutsky, Jack. 2010. 32p. (J). (gr. k-5). lib. bdg. 17.89 *(978-0-06-082339-9(9)*, Greenwillow Bks.) HarperCollins Pubs.

Manning, Jane. Cat Nights. Manning, Jane. 2008. 32p. (J). lib. bdg. 17.89 *(978-0-06-113889-8(4)*, Greenwillow Bks.) HarperCollins Pubs.

—Millie Fierce. Manning, Jane. 2012. (Millie Fierce Ser.). (ENG.). 32p. (J). (gr. -1-2). 16.99 *(978-0-399-25642-4(3)*, Philomel) Penguin Publishing Group.

—Millie Fierce Sleeps Out. Manning, Jane. 2014. (Millie Fierce Ser.). (ENG.). 32p. (J). (gr. -1-2). 16.99 *(978-0-399-16093-6(0)*, Philomel) Penguin Publishing Group.

Manning, Jane, jt. illus. see Jane, Pamela.

Manning, Jane K. Baa-Choo! Weeks, Sarah & Weeks. 2006. (I Can Read Book 1 Ser.). (ENG.). 32p. (J). (gr. k-3). pap. 3.99 *(978-0-06-443740-0(X))* HarperCollins Pubs.

—Beetle Mcgrady Eats Bugs! McDonald, Megan. 2005. (ENG.). 32p. (J). (gr. k-5). 17.99 *(978-0-06-001354-7(0)*, Greenwillow Bks.) HarperCollins Pubs.

—The Green Dog. Luke, Melinda. 2006. (Science Solves It Ser.). 32p. (J). pap. 7.99 *(978-0-15-356581-6(0))* Houghton Mifflin Harcourt School Pubs.

—The Just-So Woman. Blackwood, Gary L. 2006. (I Can Read Bks.). 48p. (J). (gr. -1-3). lib. bdg. 16.89 *(978-0-06-057728-5(2))* HarperCollins Pubs.

—Look Behind! Tales of Animal Ends. Schaefer, Lola M. & Miller, Heather Lynn. 2008. 32p. (J). (gr. -1-3). lib. bdg. 17.89 *(978-0-06-088394-2(4)*, Greenwillow Bks.) HarperCollins Pubs.

—Mac & Cheese. Weeks, Sarah. 2010. (I Can Read Book 1 Ser.). (ENG.). 32p. (J). (gr. -1-3). 16.99 *(978-0-06-117079-9(8))*; pap. 3.99 *(978-0-06-117081-2(X))* HarperCollins Pubs.

—Pip Squeak. Weeks, Sarah. (I Can Read Book 1 Ser.). 32p. (J). 2008. (ENG.). (gr. k-3). pap. 3.99 *(978-0-06-075638-3(1))*; 2007. (gr. -1-3). 15.99 *(978-0-06-075635-2(7)*, Geringer, Laura Book); 2007. (gr. -1-3). lib. bdg. 16.89 *(978-0-06-075637-6(3)*, Geringer, Laura Book) HarperCollins Pubs.

Manning, Lisa C. Falcons in the City. Manning, Lisa C. 2013. (ENG.). 40p. (J). pap. 14.95 *(978-1-59299-886-9(0))* Inkwater Pr.

Manning, Mary. Carolyn Quimby. Copp, Raymond. 2013. 110p. pap. 30.95 *(978-1-4575-2364-9(7))* Dog Ear Publishing, LLC.

—Hey Diddle Diddle. Everett, Melissa. 2013. (ENG.). 20p. (J). (gr. -1-3). 8.99 *(978-1-77093-536-5(3))* Flowerpot Children's Pr. Inc. CAN. Dist: Cardinal Pubs. Group.

Manning, Mary. I Wish I Was a Little. Everett, Melissa. Paiva, Johannah Gilman, ed. 2014. 20p. (J). 8.99 ***(978-1-77093-844-1(3))*** Flowerpot Children's Pr. Inc. CAN. Dist: Cardinal Pubs. Group.

Manning, Mary. Jack & the Beanstalk: An English Folktale. Malaspina, Ann. 2013. (Folktales from Around the World Ser.). (ENG.). 24p. (J). (gr. k-3). 28.50 *(978-1-62323-615-1(0)*, 206382) Child's World, Inc., The.

Manning, Maurie. The Hot Shots. Aboff, Marcie. 2004. 56p. (J). *(978-0-7652-3275-5(8))* Celebration Pr.

—Water Everywhere! Taylor-Butler, Christine. 2011. (Rookie Ready to Learn - First Science Ser.). 40p. (J). (gr. -1-k). lib. bdg. 23.00 *(978-0-531-26504-8(8)*, Children's Pr.) Scholastic Library Publishing.

Manning, Maurie J. Dear Child. Farrell, John. 2008. (ENG.). 32p. (J). (gr. -1-k). 16.95 *(978-1-59078-495-2(2))* Boyds Mills Pr.

—Getting to Know Ruben Plotnick. Rosenbluth, Roz. 2005. (ENG.). 32p. (J). (gr. k-2). 15.95 *(978-0-9729225-5-5(5))* Flashlight Pr.

—How Full Is Your Bucket? For Kids. Rath, Tom & Reckmeyer, Mary. 2009. (ENG.). 32p. (J). (gr. -1-3). 17.95 *(978-1-59562-027-9(3))* Gallup Pr.

—Looking for Home. Berry, Eileen M. 2006. 75p. (J). (gr. -1-3). per. *(978-1-59166-493-2(4))* BJU Pr.

—Sorry! Ludwig, Trudy. 2006. (ENG.). 32p. (J). (gr. 1-4). 15.99 *(978-1-58246-173-1(2)*, Tricycle Pr.) Ten Speed Pr.

—Tommy's Race. Hambrick, Sharon. 2004. (Fig Street Kids Ser.). 95p. (J). (gr. 1-2). 7.49 *(978-1-59166-286-0(9))* BJU Pr.

—Tommy's Rocket. Hambrick, Sharon. 2003. (Fig Street Kids Ser.). 83p. (J). (gr. 1-2). 7.49 *(978-1-59166-186-3(2))* BJU Pr.

—Water Everywhere! Taylor-Butler, Christine. 2005. (Rookie Reader Skill Set Ser.). (ENG.). 24p. (J). (gr. 1-2). per. 4.95 *(978-0-516-25285-8(2)*, Children's Pr.) Scholastic Library Publishing.

Manning, Maurie J. Kitchen Dance. Manning, Maurie J. 2008. (ENG.). 32p. (J). (gr. -1-3). 17.99 *(978-0-618-99110-5(7))* Houghton Mifflin Harcourt Publishing Co.

Manning, Maurie J. The Giant King. Manning, Maurie J., tr. Pelley, Kathleen. 2003. (New Child & Family Press Titles Ser.). 32p. (gr. -1-4). 14.95 *(978-0-87868-880-7(3)*, 8803, Child & Family Pr.) Child Welfare League of America, Inc.

—Tommy's Clubhouse. Manning, Maurie J., tr. Hambrick, Sharon. 2003. (Fig Street Kids Ser.). 78p. (J). (gr. 1-2). pap. 7.49 *(978-1-57924-993-9(0))* BJU Pr.

Manning, Mick & Granström, Brita. Charles Dickens: Scenes from an Extraordinary Life. 2014. (ENG.). 48p. (J). (gr. 3-7). pap. 12.99 *(978-1-84780-500-3(0)*, Frances Lincoln) Quarto Publishing Group UK GBR. Dist: Hachette Bk. Group.

—Charles Dickens: Scenes from an Extraordinary Life. Quarto Generic Staff. 2011. (ENG.). 48p. (J). (gr. 3-7). 18.95 *(978-1-84780-187-6(0)*, Frances Lincoln Children's Bks.) Quarto Publishing Group UK GBR. Dist: Hachette Bk. Group.

Manning, Mick & Granström, Brita. Dino-Dinners. Manning, Mick & Granström, Brita. 2015. (ENG.). 32p. (J). (gr. -1-1). pap. 9.99 ***(978-1-84780-665-9(1)***, Frances Lincoln) Quarto Publishing Group UK GBR. Dist: Hachette Bk. Group.

Manning, Mick & Granström, Brita. Drama School. 2009. (ENG.). 48p. (J). (gr. 2-5). 17.95 *(978-1-84507-845-4(4)*, Frances Lincoln) Quarto Publishing Group UK GBR. Dist: Hachette Bk. Group.

—Greek Hero. Manning, Mick & Granström, Brita. 2015. (Fly on the Wall Ser.). (ENG.). 40p. (J). (gr. k-3). pap. 9.99 *(978-1-84780-622-2(8)*, Frances Lincoln) Quarto Publishing Group UK GBR. Dist: Hachette Bk. Group.

—Nature School. 2009. (ENG.). 48p. (J). (gr. 1-5). 17.95 *(978-1-84507-843-0(8)*, Frances Lincoln) Quarto Publishing Group UK GBR. Dist: Perseus-PGW.

—Nature School. Quarto Generic Staff. 2009. (ENG.). 48p. (J). (gr. 2-5). pap. 9.95 *(978-1-84507-844-7(6)*, Frances Lincoln) Quarto Publishing Group UK GBR. Dist: Hachette Bk. Group.

—Pharaoh's Egypt. Manning, Mick & Granström, Brita. 2015. (Fly on the Wall Ser.). (ENG.). 40p. (J). (gr. k-3). pap. 9.99 *(978-1-84780-623-9(6)*, Frances Lincoln) Quarto Publishing Group UK GBR. Dist: Hachette Bk. Group.

—What Mr Darwin Saw. Manning, Mick. 2009. (ENG.). 48p. (J). (gr. 1-4). 17.95 *(978-1-84507-970-3(1)*, Frances Lincoln) Quarto Publishing Group UK GBR. Dist: Hachette Bk. Group.

—Woolly Mammoth. 2009. (ENG.). 32p. (J). (gr. -1-2). 16.95 *(978-1-84507-860-7(8)*, Frances Lincoln) Quarto Publishing Group UK GBR. Dist: Littlehampton Bk Services, Ltd.

Mannion, Steve, et al. Yabba Dabba Voodoo. Van Lente, Fred et al. 2009. (Tales from the Crypt Graphic Novels Ser.: 5). (ENG.). 96p. (J). (gr. 5-12). 12.95 *(978-1-59707-117-8(X))* Papercutz.

Manny. Willow, Too Soon, Too Late. storiesbypj.com. 2010. (ENG.). 26p. pap. 10.92 *(978-0-9841194-3-1(4))* Cowan, Pricilla J.

Manolis, Tim. Dragonflies of North America: A Color & learn Book for All Ages, with Activities. Biggs, Kathy. l.t. ed. 2007. (ENG.). 48p. (J). *(978-0-9677934-4-3(0))* Azalea Creek Publishing.

—Dragonflies of North America: A Color & Learn Book for All Ages, with Activities. Biggs, Kathy. l.t. ed. 2007. 48p. (J). cd-rom *(978-0-9677934-5-0(9))* Azalea Creek Publishing.

Manousos, Dave. Life Is Good & Other Reasons for Rhyme. Manousos, Dave. 2008. 36p. pap. 16.95 *(978-1-59858-590-2(8))* Dog Ear Publishing, LLC.

Mansfield, Andy. Follow the Star: A Pop-Up Christmas Journey. 2011. (ENG.). 12p. (J). (gr. -1-3). 19.99 *(978-1-4521-0358-7(5))* Chronicle Bks. LLC.

Mansfield, Phil. Eat Fresh Food: Awesome Recipes for Teen Chefs. Mansfield, Phil, photos by. Gold, Rozanne. 2009. (ENG.). 160p. (J). (gr. 7-18). 22.99 *(978-1-59990-282-1(6))*; (gr. 9-12). pap. 19.99 *(978-1-59990-445-0(4))* Bloomsbury USA. (Bloomsbury USA Childrens).

Mansmann, Leslie. When I'm with You. Elder, Elizabeth. ed. 2003. (ENG.). 32p. (J). 15.95 *(978-0-9671662-8-5(4))* Islandport Pr., Inc.

Manson, Beverlie. Beverlie Manson's Fairies: A Celebration of the Seasons. 2009. (ENG.). 48p. (J). (gr. -1). 16.95 *(978-1-905417-41-4(1))* Boxer Bks., Ltd. GBR. Dist: Sterling Publishing Co., Inc.

—Dreamland Fairies: Magical Bedtime Stories from Fairyland. Baxter, Nicola. 2012. (ENG.). 80p. (J). (gr. k-4). pap. 9.99 *(978-1-84322-806-6(8))* Anness Publishing GBR. Dist: National Bk. Network.

—The Mermaid's Secret Diaries. 2013. (ENG.). 96p. (J). (gr. -1-2). 9.95 *(978-1-907967-59-7(1))* Boxer Bks., Ltd. GBR. Dist: Sterling Publishing Co., Inc.

—My Treasury of Fairies & Elves: A Collection of 20 Magical Stories. Baxter, Nicola. 2012. (ENG.). 240p. (J). (gr. k-4). 18.99 *(978-1-84322-835-6(1))* Anness Publishing GBR. Dist: National Bk. Network.

—A Visit from the Tooth Fairy: Magical Stories & a Special Message from the Little Friend Who Collects Your Baby Teeth. Baxter, Nicola. 2013. (ENG.). 40p. (J). (gr. k-4). 14.99 *(978-1-84322-987-2(0)*, Armadillo) Anness Publishing GBR. Dist: National Bk. Network.

Manson, Christopher. Black Swan/White Crow. Lewis, J. Patrick. 2007. (ENG.). 32p. (J). (gr. 4-6). 9.99 *(978-1-4169-6158-1(5)*, Simon & Schuster/Paula Wiseman Bks.) Simon & Schuster/Paula Wiseman Bks.

—Good King Wenceslas. 2004. 25p. (J). (gr. k-4). reprint ed. 15.00 *(978-0-7567-8226-9(0))* DIANE Publishing Co.

—Over the River & Through the Wood. Child, Lydia Maria. 2014. (ENG.). 32p. (J). 14.95 *(978-0-7358-4191-8(8))* North-South Bks., Inc.

—Till Year's Good End. Nikola-lisa, W. 2009. (ENG.). 36p. (J). (gr. 1-4). 12.99 *(978-1-4424-0225-6(3)*, Atheneum Bks. for Young Readers) Simon & Schuster Children's Publishing.

Manson, Kayt. Molly Dolly - Dance with Me! Manson, Kayt. 2011. (ENG.). 12p. (J). (gr. k — 1). 8.99 *(978-1-84738-607-6(5))* Simon & Schuster, Ltd. GBR. Dist: Simon & Schuster, Inc.

Mansot, Fédérick. Diogenes' Lantern. Mansot, Fédérick, tr. Kerisel, Françoise. 2004. (ENG.). 22p. 6.95 *(978-0-89236-738-2(5))* Oxford Univ. Pr., Inc.

Mansur, Elisabeth Fahmi. Shuba & the Cyclone. Chandpai - Dhamrai Bangladeshi Students Staff. Kelly, Victoria, ed. 2011. (ENG.). 36p. (J). 17.95 *(978-0-9842146-6-2(6))* Concinnity Initiatives.

Mantell, Ahuva & Sperling, S. David. The Gift of Wisdom: The Books of Prophets & Writings. Steinbock, Steven E. 2004. (J). (gr. 4-6). pap. 13.95 *(978-0-8074-0752-3(6)*, 123944) URJ Pr.

Mantha, John. Canadian Exploration. Owens, Ann-Maureen & Yealland, Jane. 2008. (Kids Book Of Ser.). (ENG.). 56p. (J). (gr. 3-7). pap. 14.95 *(978-1-55453-257-5(4))* Kids Can Pr., Ltd. CAN. Dist: Univ. of Toronto Pr.

—Harry Houdini. MacLeod, Elizabeth. 2009. (Kids Can Read Ser.). (ENG.). 32p. (J). (gr. 1-3). 3.95 *(978-1-55453-299-5(X))*; 14.95 *(978-1-55453-298-8(1))* Kids Can Pr., Ltd. CAN. Dist: Univ. of Toronto Pr.

—The Kids Book of Aboriginal Peoples in Canada. Silvey, Diane. 2012. (Kids Book Of Ser.). (ENG.). 64p. (J). 14.95 *(978-1-55453-930-7(7))* Kids Can Pr., Ltd. CAN. Dist: Univ. of Toronto Pr.

—The Kids Book of Canada at War. MacLeod, Elizabeth. 2007. (Kids Book Of Ser.). (ENG.). 72p. (J). (gr. 4-7). 19.95 *(978-1-55453-003-8(2))* Kids Can Pr., Ltd. CAN. Dist: Univ. of Toronto Pr.

—The Kids Book of Canada's Railway: And How the CPR Was Built. Hodge, Deborah. 2008. (Kids Book Of Ser.). (ENG.). 48p. (J). (gr. 3-7). pap. 14.95 *(978-1-55453-256-8(6))* Kids Can Pr., Ltd. CAN. Dist: Univ. of Toronto Pr.

—The Kids Book of Canadian History. Hacker, Carlotta. 2009. (Kids Book Of Ser.). (ENG.). 72p. (J). (gr. 3-7). 14.95 *(978-1-55453-328-2(7))* Kids Can Pr., Ltd. CAN. Dist: Univ. of Toronto Pr.

—The Kids Book of Canadian Immigration. Hodge, Deborah. 2006. (Kids Book Of Ser.). (ENG.). 64p. (J). 19.95 *(978-1-55337-484-8(3))* Kids Can Pr., Ltd. CAN. Dist: Univ. of Toronto Pr.

—The Kids Book of Canadian Prime Ministers. Hancock, Pat. 2005. (Kids Book Of Ser.). (ENG.). 56p. (J). 19.95 *(978-1-55337-740-5(0))* Kids Can Pr., Ltd. CAN. Dist: Univ. of Toronto Pr.

—The Kids Book of Great Canadian Women. MacLeod, Elizabeth. 2006. (Kids Book Of Ser.). (ENG.). 64p. (J). 19.95 *(978-1-55337-820-4(2))* Kids Can Pr., Ltd. CAN. Dist: Univ. of Toronto Pr.

—The Kids Book of Great Canadians. MacLeod, Elizabeth. 2008. (Kids Book Of Ser.). (ENG.). 64p. (J). (gr. 3-7). pap. 14.95 *(978-1-55453-255-1(8))* Kids Can Pr., Ltd. CAN. Dist: Univ. of Toronto Pr.

—The Kids Book of World Religions. Glossop, Jennifer. 2013. (Kids Book Of Ser.). (ENG.). 64p. (J). pap. 14.95 *(978-1-55453-981-9(1))* Kids Can Pr., Ltd. CAN. Dist: Univ. of Toronto Pr.

—Lucy Maud Montgomery. MacLeod, Elizabeth. 2008. (ENG.). 32p. (J). (gr. -1-3). pap. 3.95 *(978-1-55453-056-4(3))*; (gr. 1-3). 14.95 *(978-1-55453-055-7(5))* Kids Can Pr., Ltd. CAN. Dist: Univ. of Toronto Pr.

—Marie Curie. MacLeod, Elizabeth. 2009. (Kids Can Read Ser.). (ENG.). 32p. (J). (gr. 1-3). 3.95 *(978-1-55453-297-1(3))*; 14.95 *(978-1-55453-296-4(5))* Kids Can Pr., Ltd. CAN. Dist: Univ. of Toronto Pr.

—The Old Ways. 1 vol. Chapman, Susan. 2014. (ENG.). 32p. (J). 17.95 *(978-1-927083-16-1(8))* Fifth Hse. Pubs. CAN. Dist: Ingram Pub. Services.

—Samuel de Champlain. MacLeod, Elizabeth. 2008. (Kids Can Read Ser.). (ENG.). 32p. (J). (gr. 1-3). 14.95 *(978-1-55453-049-6(0))*; pap. 3.95 *(978-1-55453-050-2(4))* Kids Can Pr., Ltd. CAN. Dist: Univ. of Toronto Pr.

—The Siege: Under Attack in Renaissance Europe. Shapiro, Stephen. 2007. (ENG.). 56p. (J). (gr. 5-12). 21.95 *(978-1-55451-108-2(9)*, 9781554511082); pap. 12.95 *(978-1-55451-107-5(0)*, 9781554511075) Annick Pr., Ltd. CAN. Dist: Firefly Bks., Ltd.

—Time of the Thunderbird. Silvey, Diane. 2008. (ENG.). 88p. (J). (gr. 6-5). pap. 11.99 *(978-1-55002-792-1(1)*, Sandcastle Bks.) Dundurn CAN. Dist: Ingram Pub. Services.

Mantha, John, et al. What Is the Statue of Liberty? Holub, Joan. 2014. (What Was... ? Ser.). (ENG.). 112p. (J). (gr. 3-7). 5.99 *(978-0-448-47917-0(6)*, Grosset & Dunlap) Penguin Publishing Group.

Mantha, John & Bennett, James. What Was the Battle of Gettysburg? O'Connor, Jim. 2013. (What Was... ? Ser.). (ENG.). (J). (gr. 3-7). 128p. 15.99 *(978-0-448-46575-3(2))*; 112p. pap. 5.99 *(978-0-448-46286-8(9))* Penguin Publishing Group. (Grosset & Dunlap).

Mantha, John & Holdcroft, Tina. Crusades. Scandiffio, Laura. 2009. (Kids at the Crossroads Ser.). (ENG.). 72p. (J). (gr. 4-6). 24.95 *(978-1-55451-147-1(X)*, 9781554511471); pap. 14.95 *(978-1-55451-146-4(1)*, 9781554511464) Annick Pr., Ltd. CAN. Dist: Firefly Bks., Ltd.

Mantha, John & Tomkinson, Tim. What Was Pearl Harbor? Demuth, Patricia Brennan. 2013. (What Was... ? Ser.). (ENG.). 112p. (J). (gr. 3-7). pap. 5.99 *(978-0-448-46462-6(4)*, Grosset & Dunlap) Penguin Publishing Group.

—What Was Pearl Harbor? Demuth, Patricia Brennan. 2013. (What Was... ? Ser.). (ENG.). 112p. (J). (gr. 3-7). 15.99 *(978-0-448-46580-7(9)*, Grosset & Dunlap) Penguin Publishing Group.

Mantilla, Maria Fernanda. Amores Eternos. Arciniega, Triunfo. 2003. (Primer Acto: Teatro Infantil y Juvenil Ser.). (SPA.). 55p. (J). (gr. -1-7). pap. *(978-958-30-0998-3(9))* Panamericana Editorial.

Mantle, Ben. Busy Bug Book. Watt, Fiona. ed. 2011. (Pull-Back Books Ser.). 10p. (J). ring bd. 24.99 *(978-0-7945-2941-3(0)*, Usborne) EDC Publishing.

—Five Little Pumpkins. Tiger Tales Staff. Tiger Tales Staff, ed. 2010. 24p. (J). (gr. -1-k). bds. 8.95 *(978-1-58925-856-3(8))* Tiger Tales.

—Hug! Tiger Tales Staff. 2013. (J). *(978-1-58925-637-8(9))* Tiger Tales.

—Land Shark. Ferry, Beth. 2015. (ENG.). 36p. (J). (gr. -1-k). 16.99 *(978-1-4521-2458-2(2))* Chronicle Bks. LLC.

—One Sheep, Blue Sheep. Wiley, Thom. 2012. (ENG.). 12p. (J). (— 1). bds. 6.99 *(978-0-545-40284-2(0)*, Cartwheel Bks.) Scholastic, Inc.

—Peek-A-Boo! Tiger Tales Staff. 2013. (J). *(978-1-58925-636-1(0))* Tiger Tales.

—Rocket Racers. Webb, Steve. 2014. (ENG.). 24p. (J). (-k). pap. 8.99 *(978-0-552-56673-5(X))* Transworld Publishers Ltd. GBR. Dist: Independent Pubs. Group.

—The Spooky Wheels on the Bus. Mills, J. Elizabeth. 2010. (ENG.). 24p. (J). (gr. -1-k). pap. 3.99 *(978-0-545-17480-0(5)*, Cartwheel Bks.) Scholastic, Inc.

—There Was an Old Dragon Who Swallowed a Knight. Klostermann, Penny Parker. 2015. (ENG.). 40p. (J). (gr. -1-2). 19.99 *(978-0-375-97355-0(9))* Random Hse., Inc.

—Trick or Treat: 12 Board Books, 12 vols. 2011. (J). *(978-1-4508-1914-5(1))* Phoenix International Publications, Inc.

—Trick or Treat: 12 Board Books, 12 vols. 2011. (J). *(978-1-4508-2461-3(7))*; *(978-1-4508-2465-1(X))*; *(978-1-4508-2458-3(7))*; *(978-1-4508-2459-0(5))*; *(978-1-4508-2460-6(9))*; *(978-1-4508-2457-6(9))*; *(978-1-4508-2462-0(5))*; *(978-1-4508-2468-2(4))*; *(978-1-4508-2464-4(1))*; *(978-1-4508-2463-7(3))*; *(978-1-4508-2467-5(6))*; *(978-1-4508-2466-8(8))* Publications International, Ltd.

Manton, Jimmy. Goddesses & Sirens. Demarco, Stacey. 2013. 165p. (J). pap. *(978-1-58270-381-7(7))* Beyond Words Publishing, Inc.

Manton, Jimmy. Gods & Titans. Demarco, Stacey. 2013. 160p. (J). ***(978-1-58270-380-0(9))*** Beyond Words Publishing, Inc.

Mantzke, Jurgen. The Adventures of the Rocky Mountain Tea Twerps. Hartman, Moreta. 2003. 56p. 18.95 *(978-0-9743937-0-4(3))* Hallelujah Acres Publishing.

Manu, jt. illus. see Chandu.

Manville, Ron, jt. photos by see Meppem, William.

Manwiller, S. A. The Adventures of Jack & Max: What Jack & Max Love. Manwiller, S. A. 2013. 30p. 19.99 *(978-0-9838427-4-3(4))* SevenHorns Publishing.

Manwiller, S. A. & Overly, Kristen V. The Adventures of Jack & Max the Truliest Meaning of Christmas. Manwiller, S. A. 2013. (ACH & ENG.). 38p. 24.99 *(978-0-9838427-7-4(9))* SevenHorns Publishing.

Manzel, Michael. Moby's Tale. 2004. 248p. (YA). pap. 19.95 *(978-0-9746345-0-0(6))* River of Life Publishing.

Mape, Michael. The Flying Fox & the Cockatoo. Baia, Edward. 2013. 22p. pap. *(978-9980-86-507-6(5))* University of Papua New Guinea Press.

Mape, Michael & Ella, Peter Leo. Isokau Akuaku: A Traditional Story from Central Province. Baia, Edward. 2013. 30p. pap. *(978-9980-86-494-9(X))* University of Papua New Guinea Press.

Maraja. Alice in Wonderland Picture Book. 2013. (Shape Bks.). (ENG.). 16p. (J). pap. 9.95 *(978-1-59583-701-1(9))* Laughing Elephant.

Marble, Abigail. Mi Enemiga Secreta. Ludwig, Trudy. Hernandez, Aurora, tr. 2007. (SPA.). 32p. (J). (gr. 1-4). 15.99 *(978-1-58246-203-5(8)*, Tricycle Pr.) Ten Speed Pr.

—My Secret Bully. Ludwig, Trudy. 2015. (ENG.). 32p. (J). (gr. 1-4). 7.99 *(978-0-553-50940-3(3)*, Dragonfly Bks.) Random Hse. Children's Bks.

—My Secret Bully. Ludwig, Trudy. rev. ed. 2005. (ENG.). 32p. (J). (gr. 1-4). 15.99 *(978-1-58246-159-5(7)*, Tricycle Pr.) Ten Speed Pr.

—Two for Joy. Amateau, Gigi. 2015. (ENG.). 96p. (J). (gr. 2-5). 14.99 *(978-0-7636-3010-2(1))* Candlewick Pr.

Marbury, Ja'Nitta. All Mixed Up. Marbury, Ja'Nitta. 2003. 22p. (J). pap. 22.50 *(978-0-9718307-3-8(8))* Shades of Me Publishing.

Marc, Sylvain. The Case of the Fatal Phantom, 3 vols. Kennedy, Emma. 2012. (Wilma Tenderfoot Ser.: 3). (ENG.). 368p. (J). (gr. 3-7). 16.99 *(978-0-8037-3542-2(1)*, Dial) Penguin Publishing Group.

Marc, Sylvain, et al. Wilma Tenderfoot - The Case of the Frozen Hearts. Kennedy, Emma. 2011. (Wilma Tenderfoot Ser.: 1). (ENG.). 352p. (J). (gr. 3-7). 16.99 *(978-0-8037-3540-8(5)*, Dial) Penguin Publishing Group.

Marc, Sylvain. Wilma Tenderfoot: the Case of the Fatal Phantom. Kennedy, Emma. 2013. (Wilma Tenderfoot Ser.: 3). (ENG.). 384p. (J). (gr. 3-7). pap. 7.99 *(978-0-14-242609-8(1)*, Puffin) Penguin Publishing Group.

Marc, Sylvain & Dorman, Brandon. The Case of the Putrid Poison, 2 vols. Kennedy, Emma. 2011. (Wilma Tenderfoot Ser.: 2). (ENG.). 336p. (J). (gr. 3-7). 16.99 *(978-0-8037-3541-5(3)*, Dial) Penguin Publishing Group.

Marcellino, Fred. Ouch! Babbitt, Natalie. pap. 18.95 incl. audio compact disk *(978-1-59112-350-7(X))*; pap. incl. audio compact disk *(978-1-59112-558-7(8))* Live Oak Media.

—Puss in Boots. Perrault, Charles. Arthur, Malcolm, tr. 2011. (ENG.). 32p. (J). (gr. -1-3). pap. 7.99 *(978-0-312-65945-5(8))* Square Fish.

—A Rat's Tale. Seidler, Tor. 2008. (ENG.). 192p. (J). (gr. 3-7). pap. 10.99 *(978-0-374-40031-6(8)*, Farrar, Straus & Giroux (BYR)) Farrar, Straus & Giroux.

Marcellus, Rhoald. Death Valley, Vol. 1. Cosby, Andrew & Stokes, Johanna. 2007. (ENG.). 128p. per. 14.99 *(978-1-934506-08-0(7))* Boom! Studios.

Marcero, Deborah. Sadie's Story. Heppermann, Christine & Koertge, Ronald. 2015. (Backyard Witch Ser.: 1). (ENG.). 176p. (J). (gr. 3-7). 16.99 *(978-0-06-233838-9(2)*, Collins Design) HarperCollins Pubs.

March, Chloe. My First 100 Words Book: A Lift-the-Flap, Pull-Tab Learning Book. Haney Perez, Jessica. 2005. (Learn to Read Ser.). 10p. (J). 10.95 *(978-1-58117-210-2(9)*, Intervisual/Piggy Toes) Bendon, Inc.

M

March, Guillermo, et al. Japones en Vinetas: Curso Basico de Japones a Traves del Manga. Bernabe, Marc. 5th ed. 2004. (SPA.). 293p. (YA). (gr. 8). per. 34.95 *(978-1-59497-074-0(2))* Public Square Bks.

Marchese, Stephen. The Flights of Marceau: Week Two. 2007. (ENG.). 60p. (J). 16.95 *(978-0-9797495-1-3(4))* Majestic Eagle Publishing.

Marchesi, Stephen. Box Turtle at Silver Pond Lane. Korman, Susan. 2005. (Smithsonian's Backyard Ser.). (ENG.). 32p. (J). (gr. -1-2). 15.95 *(978-1-56899-860-2(0),* B5020) Soundprints.

—Box Turtle at Silver Pond Lane: Smithsonians Backyard. Korman, Susan. 2005. (Smithsonian's Backyard Ser.). (ENG.). 32p. (J). (gr. -1-2). pap. 6.95 *(978-1-56899-935-7(6),* S5020) Soundprints.

—Deborah Saves the Day. Rottmann, Erik. 2008. (Arch Bks.). 16p. (J). (gr. k-4). pap. 1.99 *(978-0-7586-1457-5(8))* Concordia Publishing Hse.

—Dorothy Day: A Catholic Life of Action. Shaw, Maura D. 2004. (ENG.). 32p. (J). 12.99 *(978-1-59473-011-5(3),* Skylight Paths Publishing) LongHill Partners, Inc.

—The Flights of Marceau: Week One. 2007. (ENG.). 56p. (J). 16.95 *(978-0-9797495-0-6(6))* Majestic Eagle Publishing.

—Gandhi: India's Great Soul. Shaw, Maura D. 2003. (ENG.). 32p. (J). (gr. 1-3). 12.95 *(978-1-893361-91-1(8),* Skylight Paths Publishing) LongHill Partners, Inc.

—Glow-In-The-Dark Constellations. 2006. (J). *(978-1-59412-171-5(0))* Mud Puddle, Inc.

—Let's Read About — Pocahontas. Weinberger, Kimberly. 2003. (Scholastic First Biographies Ser.). (J). pap. *(978-0-439-56148-8(5))* Scholastic, Inc.

—Race to the Rescue. Brown, Joe. 2009. (J). *(978-0-545-13473-6(0))* Scholastic, Inc.

—Silver. Whelan, Gloria. 2004. (Stepping Stone Book(TM) Ser.). (ENG.). 64p. (J). (gr. 1-4). 3.99 *(978-0-394-89611-3(4),* Random Hse. Bks. for Young Readers) Random Hse. Children's Bks.

—Thich Nhat Hanh: Buddhism in Action. Shaw, Maura D. 2003. (ENG.). 32p. (J). (gr. 1-3). 12.95 *(978-1-893361-87-4(X),* Skylight Paths Publishing) LongHill Partners, Inc.

Marchesi, Stephen, et al. Who Is Jane Goodall? Edwards, Roberta. 2012. (Who Was... ? Ser.). (ENG.). 112p. (J). (gr. 3-7). 5.99 *(978-0-448-46192-2(7),* Grosset & Dunlap) Penguin Publishing Group.

Marchesi, Stephen. Who Was Nelson Mandela? Belviso, Meg & Pollack, Pamela D. 2014. (Who Was... ? Ser.). (ENG.). 112p. (J). (gr. 3-7). 5.99 *(978-0-448-47933-0(8),* Grosset & Dunlap) Penguin Publishing Group.

Marchesi, Stephen & Harrison, Nancy. Who Is J. K. Rowling? Pollack, Pam & Belviso, Meg. 2012. (Who Was... ? Ser.). (ENG.). 112p. (J). (gr. 3-7). pap. 5.99 *(978-0-448-45872-4(1),* Grosset & Dunlap) Penguin Publishing Group.

—Who Is Muhammad Ali? Buckley, James, Jr. 2014. (Who Was... ? Ser.). (ENG.). 112p. (J). (gr. 3-7). 5.99 *(978-0-448-47955-2(9),* Grosset & Dunlap) Penguin Publishing Group.

—Who Was Jesus? Morgan, Ellen. 2015. (Who Was... ? Ser.). (ENG.). 112p. (J). (gr. 3-7). 5.99 *(978-0-448-48320-7(3),* Grosset & Dunlap) Penguin Publishing Group.

—Who Was Maurice Sendak? Dubowski, Cathy East & Pascal, Janet. 2013. (Who Was... ? Ser.). (ENG.). 112p. (J). (gr. 3-7). pap. 4.99 *(978-0-448-46500-5(0),* Grosset & Dunlap) Penguin Publishing Group.

—Who Was Roald Dahl? Kelley, True. 2012. (Who Was... ? Ser.). (ENG.). 112p. (J). (gr. 3-7). pap. 5.99 *(978-0-448-46146-5(3),* Grosset & Dunlap) Penguin Publishing Group.

Marchesi, Stephen, jt. illus. see Harrison, Nancy.

Marchetti, Angela. A Donkey's Tale. Gorla, Stefano. 2013. 64p. (J). pap. 9.95 *(978-0-8198-1901-7(8))* Pauline Bks. & Media.

Marchus, Linda. The Gorilla Who Wanted to Dance. Marchus, Linda. 2003. 32p. (J). lib. bdg. 15.95 *(978-0-9723122-1-9(8))* Wee Read Publishing.

Marco, Harvey, jt. illus. see Niednagel, David.

Marconi, Gloria. Bela & the Gold Medallion. Preston, James, photos by. Smith, Loretta. 2012. 32p. pap. 13.00 *(978-1-930357-27-3(3))* Do The Write Thing, Inc.

Marcos, Pablo. Clara Barton & the American Red Cross. Marko, Eve. 2005. (Heroes of America Ser.). 237p. (gr. 3-8). 27.07 *(978-1-59679-255-5(8),* Abdo & Daughters) ABDO Publishing Co.

—Jackie Robinson. Hanft, Joshua E. 2005. (Heroes of America Ser.). 238p. (gr. 3-8). 27.07 *(978-1-59679-259-3(0),* Abdo & Daughters) ABDO Publishing Co.

—King Solomon's Mines. Haggard, H. Rider. 2005. (Great Illustrated Classics Ser.). 239p. (J). (gr. 3-8). 21.35 *(978-1-59679-244-9(2),* Abdo & Daughters) ABDO Publishing Co.

—A Little Princess: The Story of Sara Crewe. Burnett, Frances Hodgson. Warren, Eliza, ed. 2006. 239p. (YA). reprint ed. 10.00 *(978-0-7567-9835-2(3))* DIANE Publishing Co.

—Martin Luther King, Jr. Boyd, Herb. 2005. (Heroes of America Ser.). 239p. (gr. 3-8). 27.07 *(978-1-59679-258-6(2),* Abdo & Daughters) ABDO Publishing Co.

—Sherlock Holmes & the Case of the Hound of the Baskervilles. Doyle, Arthur. Vogel, Malvina G., ed. 2006. 237p. (YA). (gr. 4-8). 10.00 *(978-0-7567-9834-5(5))* DIANE Publishing Co.

Marder, Alan. Rocky & the Great Bird Race. Brutocao, W. J. 2010. (ENG.). 152p. pap. 7.99 *(978-1-4537-4951-7(9))* CreateSpace Independent Publishing Platform.

—Sancho at the Music Festival: With Rocky the Otter & Corky the Cormorant. Brutocao, W. J. 2011. (ENG.). 140p. pap. 7.99 *(978-1-4635-3585-8(6))* CreateSpace Independent Publishing Platform.

Marder, Larry. Beanworld: Tales of the Beanworld. Marder, Larry. Schutz, Diana, ed. 2012. (ENG.). 64p. 14.99 *(978-1-59582-897-2(4))* Dark Horse Comics.

Marderosian, Mark. Christmas Wishes. Herman, Gail. 2004. (J). *(978-0-439-66763-0(1))* Scholastic, Inc.

Mardinly, Berdan. Fresh Tarhana Soup - English. Mardinly, Berdan. 2008. (ENG.). 16p. (J). pap. 5.50 *(978-1-935125-05-1(2))* Robertson Publishing.

Mardon, John. Bats in the Garbage, 1 vol. Jennings, Sharon. 2003. (ENG.). 64p. (J). (gr. 2-5). pap. *(978-1-55041-723-4(1))* Fitzhenry & Whiteside, Ltd.

Marek, Jane. The Professor's Telescope. Moreau, Chris. 2006. (YA). 10.95 *(978-0-9785399-0-0(7));* cd-rom 7.95 *(978-0-9785399-2-4(3))* Windows of Discovery.

Maren, Julie. Celia Cruz, Queen of Salsa. Chambers, Veronica. 2008. (J). (gr. -1-3). 28.95 incl. audio compact disk *(978-1-4301-0284-7(5));* 25.95 incl. audio *(978-1-4301-0281-6(0));* pap. 16.95 incl. audio *(978-1-4301-0280-9(2))* Live Oak Media.

—Celia Cruz, Queen of Salsa. Chambers, Veronica. 2007. (ENG.). 40p. (J). (gr. k-3). pap. 6.99 *(978-0-14-240779-0(8),* Puffin) Penguin Publishing Group.

—Celia Cruz, Queen of Salsa. Chambers, Veronica. 2007. (gr. 2-5). 17.00 *(978-0-7569-8153-2(0))* Perfection Learning Corp.

—An Orange in January. Aston, Dianna Hutts. 2007. (ENG.). 32p. (J). (gr. -1-3). 16.99 *(978-0-8037-3146-2(9),* Dial) Penguin Publishing Group.

Maresca, Beth Anne. Megan Owlet. 2015. (ENG.). 32p. (J). (gr. -1-k). 16.99 *(978-1-63220-404-2(5),* Sky Pony Pr.) Skyhorse Publishing Co., Inc.

Margeson, John. Balls! Round 2. Rosen, Michael J. 2008. (Darby Creek Exceptional Titles Ser.). (ENG.). 80p. (gr. 4-8). 18.95 *(978-1-58196-066-2(2),* Darby Creek) Lerner Publishing Group.

—Scrubs Forever! McEwan, Jamie. 2008. (Darby Creek Exceptional Titles Ser.). (ENG.). 64p. (J). (gr. 2-5). lib. bdg. 14.95 *(978-1-58196-069-3(7),* Darby Creek) Lerner Publishing Group.

—Whitewater Scrubs. McEwan, Jamie. 2005. (ENG.). 80p. (J). (gr. 2-4). 14.99 *(978-1-58196-038-9(7),* Darby Creek) Lerner Publishing Group.

Margiotta, Kristen. Gustav Gloom & the Cryptic Carousel #4. Castro, Adam-Troy. (Gustav Gloom Ser.: 4). (ENG.). 248p. (J). (gr. 3-7). 2015. 7.99 ***(978-0-448-48719-9(5));*** 2014. 12.99 *(978-0-448-45836-6(5))* Penguin Publishing Group. (Grosset & Dunlap).

Margiotta, Kristen. Gustav Gloom & the Four Terrors, Vol. 3. Castro, Adam-Troy. 2013. (Gustav Gloom Ser.: 3). (ENG.). 232p. (J). (gr. 3-7). 12.99 *(978-0-448-45835-9(7),* Grosset & Dunlap) Penguin Publishing Group.

—Gustav Gloom & the Four Terrors #3. Castro, Adam-Troy. 2014. (Gustav Gloom Ser.: 3). (ENG.). 248p. (J). (gr. 3-7). 7.99 *(978-0-448-48330-6(0),* Grosset & Dunlap) Penguin Publishing Group.

Margiotta, Kristen. Gustav Gloom & the Inn of Shadows #5. Castro, Adam-Troy. 2015. (Gustav Gloom Ser.: 5). (ENG.). 248p. (J). (gr. 3-7). 12.99 ***(978-0-448-46458-9(6),*** Grosset & Dunlap) Penguin Publishing Group.

Margiotta, Kristen. Gustav Gloom & the Nightmare Vault, No. 2. Castro, Adam-Troy. 2013. (Gustav Gloom Ser.: 2). (ENG.). 232p. (J). (gr. 3-7). 12.99 *(978-0-448-45834-2(9),* Grosset & Dunlap) Penguin Publishing Group.

—Gustav Gloom & the Nightmare Vault #2. Castro, Adam-Troy. 2014. (Gustav Gloom Ser.: 2). (ENG.). 248p. (J). (gr. 3-7). 7.99 *(978-0-448-48329-0(7),* Grosset & Dunlap) Penguin Publishing Group.

—Gustav Gloom & the People Taker, No. 1. Castro, Adam-Troy. 2012. (Gustav Gloom Ser.: 1). (ENG.). 232p. (J). (gr. 3-7). 12.99 *(978-0-448-45833-5(0),* Grosset & Dunlap) Penguin Publishing Group.

—Gustav Gloom & the People Taker #1. Castro, Adam-Troy. 2014. (Gustav Gloom Ser.: 1). (ENG.). 248p. (J). (gr. 3-7). 7.99 *(978-0-448-48328-3(9),* Grosset & Dunlap) Penguin Publishing Group.

Margolis, Al. Boy in the Hoodie. Fontaine, Renee. 2012. 34p. (J). 19.95 *(978-1-61863-105-3(5))* Bookstand Publishing.

—Fucious: The True Story of the Ugly Duckling. Mastrud, Karen. 2012. 32p. (J). 24.95 *(978-1-61863-414-6(3))* Bookstand Publishing.

—Gabe's Nantucket Adventure: Daffodils, Dogs, & Cars. Thorpe, Rochelle O'Neal. Nakell, Euqenie, ed. l.t. ed. 2010. 28p. (YA). pap. 7.95 *(978-1-935706-02-1(0))* Wiggles Pr.

—The Playground Bully Blues. Ladin, Marc J. 2010. 26p. pap. 14.95 *(978-1-60844-377-2(9))* Dog Ear Publishing, LLC.

—Presents for Phoebe: Growing Independent. Rhode, Paul. 2011. 24p. (YA). pap. 9.95 *(978-1-935706-05-2(5))* Wiggles Pr.

—Seana's New Accessory. Faircloth, M. L. 2012. 26p. 19.95 *(978-1-61863-407-8(0))* Bookstand Publishing.

—Stories for Dreamers. Dultz, Dorothy. 2013. 68p. (J). pap. 9.95 *(978-1-61863-425-2(9))* Bookstand Publishing.

—Timothy Toot... . Finds A Hat. Tait, Barbara. 2011. 32p. (J). 24.95 *(978-1-58909-917-3(6))* Bookstand Publishing.

—Timothy Toot... Goes Fishing. Tait, Barbara. 2011. 28p. (J). 24.95 *(978-1-58909-879-4(X))* Bookstand Publishing.

—Virgil: The Bully from Cyberspace. Sanchez, Lorrie Christel & Blank, Carol. 2013. 54p. (J). 20.99 *(978-0-9891338-0-7(X))* Utterly Global.

—Virgil: The Bully from Cyberspace Teacher Edition. Sanchez, Lorrie Christel & Blank, Carol. 2013. 88p. 99.00 *(978-0-9891338-1-4(8))* Utterly Global.

Margolis, Al & Young, Bill. The Little Plum Tree. Rodhe, Paul & Wallas Reidy, Sarah. 2010. 24p. (J). pap. 9.95 *(978-1-935706-06-9(3))* Wiggles Pr.

Margolis, Lois. David's Tractor. Spinelli, Jami. l.t. ed. 2006. (J). 32p. 20.99 *(978-1-59879-242-3(3));* 27p. (gr. -1-3). per. 11.99 *(978-1-59879-241-6(5))* Lifevest Publishing, Inc.

Mari, Ian Robert, photos by. We Catch Them Falling. Ratto, Linda Lee. 2004. 225p. (YA). per. *(978-1-932496-08-6(4))* Penman Publishing, Inc.

Marichal, Poli. Julia: Cuando Los Grandes Eran Pequenos. Lazaro, Georgina. 2006. (SPA.). 30p. (YA). (gr. 8-10). 14.99 *(978-1-930332-58-4(0))* Lectorum Pubns., Inc.

Marie, Anne, jt. illus. see Ryan.

Marie, Berri. My Name Was Fear. Shadrick, Crystal Star. Stone, Karen, ed. 2013. 60p. pap. 12.95 *(978-1-935186-41-0(8))* Waldenhouse Pubs., Inc.

Marie, Paula Braxton. The Light in the Dark, 1. Keyes, Eric, 3rd et al. l.t. ed. 2004. (ENG.). 40p. (J). pap. 14.99 *(978-0-9722795-5-0(5),* Highest Good Pubns.) EbonyEnergy Publishing, Inc.

Marier, Chuck. Old MacDonald's Farm: Read Well Level K Unit 7 Storybook. Gunn, Barbara. 2004. (Read Well Level K Ser.). 20p. (J). *(978-1-57035-679-7(3))* Cambium Education, Inc.

Marimo, Ragawa, jt. illus. see Ragawa, Marimo.

Marin, Danny. You Wouldn't Like Me Without My Coffee. Millsaps, Grace & Murphy, Ryan. 2014. (ENG.). 40p. (J). (gr. k-2). 17.95 *(978-0-9904093-0-4(9))* Millfree Mursaps Media.

Marin, Liz. Rachel Beth & the Day the Towers Came Down, 1 vol. Marin, Dale Diane. 2009. 27p. pap. 24.95 *(978-1-60813-328-4(1))* America Star Bks.

Marín, Manuel. Palabras Manzana. Luján, Jorge et al. 2004. (Sopa de Libros Ser.). (SPA.). 96p. (J). pap. 12.99 *(978-84-667-2474-6(5))* Grupo Anaya, S.A. ESP. Dist: Lectorum Pubns., Inc.

Marin, Mary Rodriguez. Tulia y la Tecla Magica. Baranda, Maria. rev. ed. 2006. (Castillo de la Lectura, Serie Naranja). (SPA & ENG.). 160p. (J). (gr. 4-7). pap. 7.95 *(978-970-20-0177-5(3))* Castillo, Ediciones, S. A. de C. V. MEX. Dist: Macmillan.

Marini, Enrico. Rapaces. Dufaux, Jean. 2004. (SPA.). Vol. 1. 56p. pap. 17.95 *(978-1-59497-003-0(3));* Vol. 2. 56p. pap. 17.95 *(978-1-59497-004-7(1));* Vol. 3. 64p. pap. 17.95 *(978-1-59497-005-4(X))* Public Square Bks.

Mariniello, Cecco. Air Show. Suen, Anastasia. 2006. 30p. (J). (gr. k-4). reprint ed. 16.00 *(978-1-4223-5669-2(8))* DIANE Publishing Co.

Marino, Gianna. Night Animals. Marino, Gianna. 2015. (ENG.). 40p. (J). (gr. -1-k). 16.99 *(978-0-451-46954-0(2),* Viking Juvenile) Penguin Publishing Group.

Marino, Illustrator, Natalie, Natalie, jt. illus. see Marino, Natalie.

Marino, Michael F. Thanksgiving at Grandma's. Olson, Nancy. 2009. 24p. pap. 10.95 *(978-1-4251-8909-9(1))* Trafford Publishing.

Marino, Natalie. Guess What Happened to Me, Auntie Kate! Arden, Lynne. 2008. 52p. pap. 18.95 *(978-1-59858-733-3(1))* Dog Ear Publishing, LLC.

Marino, Natalie & Marino, Illustrator, Natalie, Natalie. A Place in the Sky. Singer, Maurene et al. 2005. 52p. (J). 16.00 *(978-0-9759382-0-1(7))* Carousel Pubns., Inc.

Marinov, Marin, jt. illus. see Beccia, Carlyn.

Marinsky, Jane. The Goat-Faced Girl: A Classic Italian Folktale. Sharpe, Leah Marinsky. 2009. 32p. (J). (gr. 1-4). 16.95 *(978-1-56792-393-3(3))* Godine, David R. Pub.

marion, designs & proctor, brian. Ellen G Goes Fishing. Crews, G. 2007. 28p. pap. 4.99 *(978-0-9795236-0-1(5))* Crews Pubns., LLC.

Mariscal, Javier. Senor Mundo & Me: A Happy Birthday Story. Summers, Kim. 2004. 31p. (J). (gr. k-4). 20.00 *(978-0-7567-7759-3(3))* DIANE Publishing Co.

Mariscal Vacas, Elisa. Tontos! Mariscal Vacas, Elisa. MARISCALACAS, ELISA, V. 2005. (SPA.). (J). 9.99 *(978-970-9705-06-5(7))* Serres, Ediciones, S. L. ESP. Dist: Lectorum Pubns., Inc.

Maritie. Bizz & Buzz Make Honey Buns. Leone, Dee. 2014. (Penguin Core Concepts Ser.). (ENG.). 32p. (J). (gr. -1-k). 3.99 *(978-0-448-47927-9(3),* Grosset & Dunlap) Penguin Publishing Group.

Marjoribanks, Karen & Edwards, William M. Chloe's New Baby Brother. Thiel, Annie. 2006. (Playdate Kids Ser.). 32p. (J). (gr. -1-3). 14.95 *(978-1-933721-01-9(4))* Playdate Kids Publishing.

Marjoribanks, Karen, jt. illus. see Edwards, William M.

Marjorie, Leggitt. Olympic National Park: Touch of the Tide Pool, Crack of the Glacier. Graf, Mike. 2012. (Adventures with the Parkers Ser.: 5). (ENG.). 96p. pap. 12.95 *(978-0-7627-7969-7(1),* Falcon Guides) Globe Pequot Pr., The.

—Rocky Mountain National Park: Peril on Long's Peak. Graf, Mike. 2012. (Adventures with the Parkers Ser.: 8). (ENG.). 96p. pap. 12.95 *(978-0-7627-7970-3(5),* Falcon Guides) Globe Pequot Pr., The.

Mark, Steve. Don't Behave Like You Live in a Cave. Verdick, Elizabeth. 2010. (Laugh & Learn Ser.). (ENG.). 128p. (J). (gr. 3-7). pap. 8.95 *(978-1-57542-353-1(7))* Free Spirit Publishing, Inc.

—Dude, That's Rude! (Get Some Manners) Espeland, Pamela & Verdick, Elizabeth. 2007. (Laugh & Learn Ser.). (ENG.). 128p. (J). (gr. 3-7). pap. 8.95 *(978-1-57542-233-6(6))* Free Spirit Publishing, Inc.

Markel, Marilyn, jt. illus. see Alarid, Carilyn.

Marklew, Gilly. Great Irish Heroes. Waters, Fiona. 2007. (ENG.). 66p. (J). 23.95 *(978-0-7171-3793-0(7))* Gill & MacMillan, Ltd. IRL. Dist: Dufour Editions, Inc.

Marko, Cyndi. Bok! Bok! Boom! Marko, Cyndi. 2014. (Kung Pow Chicken Ser.: 2). (ENG.). 80p. (J). (gr. k-2). 15.99 *(978-0-545-61064-3(8))* Scholastic, Inc.

—Heroes on the Side. Marko, Cyndi. 2014. (Kung Pow Chicken Ser.: 4). (ENG.). 80p. (J). (gr. k-2). 15.99 *(978-0-545-61077-3(X))* Scholastic, Inc.

—Kung Pow Chicken #1: Let's Get Cracking! (a Branches Book) Marko, Cyndi. 2014. (Kung Pow Chicken Ser.: 1). (ENG.). 80p. (J). (gr. k-2). pap. 4.99 *(978-0-545-61061-2(3))* Scholastic, Inc.

—Kung Pow Chicken #2: Bok! Bok! Boom! (a Branches Book) Marko, Cyndi. 2014. (Kung Pow Chicken Ser.: 2). (ENG.). 80p. (J). (gr. k-2). pap. 4.99 *(978-0-545-61063-6(X))* Scholastic, Inc.

—Kung Pow Chicken #3: the Birdy Snatchers (a Branches Book) Marko, Cyndi. 2014. (Kung Pow Chicken Ser.: 3). (ENG.). 80p. (J). (gr. k-2). pap. 4.99 *(978-0-545-61068-1(0))* Scholastic, Inc.

—Kung Pow Chicken #4: Heroes on the Side (a Branches Book) Marko, Cyndi. 2014. (Kung Pow Chicken Ser.: 4). (ENG.). 80p. (J). (gr. k-2). pap. 4.99 *(978-0-545-61074-2(5))* Scholastic, Inc.

—Let's Get Cracking! Marko, Cyndi. 2014. (Kung Pow Chicken Ser.: 1). (ENG.). 80p. (J). (gr. k-2). 15.99 *(978-0-545-61062-9(1))* Scholastic, Inc.

Markovitch, Evegeny, jt. illus. see Pollack, Gadi.

Marks, Alan. Black Beauty. Sewell, Anna. 2006. (Usborne Young Reading Ser.). 64p. (J). (gr. 2-5). 8.99 *(978-0-7945-1193-7(7),* Usborne) EDC Publishing.

—Black Beauty (Picture Book) Seabag-Montefiore, Mary. 2008. (Picture Book Classics Ser.). 24p. (J). 9.99 *(978-0-7945-2250-6(5),* Usborne) EDC Publishing.

—The Canterville Ghost. Wilde, Oscar. 2005. (Young Reading Ser.: Vol. 2). 64p. (J). (gr. 2-18). lib. bdg. 13.95 *(978-1-58086-781-8(2),* Usborne) EDC Publishing.

—A Christmas Carol. 2013. (ENG.). 24p. (J). 18.99 *(978-0-7945-2910-9(0),* Usborne) EDC Publishing.

—The Enchanted Castle. Sims, Lesley. 2007. (Young Reading Series 2 Gift Bks). 62p. (J). (gr. 4-7). 8.99 *(978-0-7945-1347-4(6),* Usborne) EDC Publishing.

—Family Pack. Markle, Sandra. 2011. (ENG.). 32p. (J). (gr. -1-3). 15.95 *(978-1-58089-217-9(5))* Charlesbridge Publishing, Inc.

—Finding Home. Markle, Sandra. 2010. (ENG.). 32p. (J). (gr. -1-3). pap. 7.95 *(978-1-58089-123-3(3))* Charlesbridge Publishing, Inc.

—Heidi. Spyri, Johanna. 2006. 63p. (J). (gr. 2). 8.99 *(978-0-7945-1237-8(2),* Usborne) EDC Publishing.

—Hip-Pocket Papa. Markle, Sandra. 2010. (ENG.). 32p. (J). (gr. -1-3). 15.95 *(978-1-57091-708-0(6))* Charlesbridge Publishing, Inc.

—The Little Mermaid. 2005. 48p. (J). (gr. 4-7). 8.95 *(978-0-7945-1122-7(8),* Usborne) EDC Publishing.

—Moonfleet: A Classic Tale of Smuggling. Falkner, John Meade. 2007. (Young Reading Series 3 Gift Bks). 63p. (J). (gr. 4-7). 8.99 *(978-0-7945-1906-3(7),* Usborne) EDC Publishing.

—A Mother's Journey. Markle, Sandra. (ENG.). 32p. (J). (gr. -1-3). 2006. pap. 7.95 *(978-1-57091-622-9(5));* 2005. 16.95 *(978-1-57091-621-2(7))* Charlesbridge Publishing, Inc.

—A Mother's Journey. Markle, Sandra. 2006. (gr. 4-7). 16.95 *(978-0-7569-6967-7(0))* Perfection Learning Corp.

—Pilot Mom. Duble, Kathleen Benner. 2004. 32p. (J). (gr. k-3). 15.95 *(978-1-57091-555-0(5))* Charlesbridge Publishing, Inc.

—The Railway Children. Sebag-Montefiore, Mary. 2007. (Young Reading Series 2 Gift Bks). 60p. (J). (gr. 4-7). 8.99 *(978-0-7945-1615-4(7),* Usborne) EDC Publishing.

—Snow School. Markle, Sandra. 2013. (ENG.). 32p. (J). (gr. -1-3). lib. bdg. 16.95 *(978-1-58089-410-4(0))* Charlesbridge Publishing, Inc.

—Spirit of the Forest: Tree Tales from Around the World. East, Helen & Maddern, Eric. 2003. 48p. (J). pap. 10.95 *(978-0-7112-1879-6(X),* Frances Lincoln) Quarto Publishing Group UK GBR. Dist: Perseus-PGW.

—Spooks' Surprise. Dolby, Karen. 2003. (Young Puzzle Adventures Ser.). 32p. (J). (gr. 1-18). lib. bdg. 12.95 *(978-1-58086-492-3(9))* EDC Publishing.

—The Stories of Knights. 2004. (Young Reading Series One Ser.). 48p. (J). (gr. 2-18). pap. 5.95 *(978-0-7945-0755-8(7),* Usborne) EDC Publishing.

—Stories of Knights & Castles. Milbourne, Anna. Doherty, Gillian, ed. 2007. (Stories for Young Children Ser.). 96p. (J). 16.99 *(978-0-7945-1466-2(9),* Usborne) EDC Publishing.

—The Story of Heidi. 2007. (Picture Book Classics Ser.). 24p. (J). (gr. -1-3). 9.99 *(978-0-7945-1716-8(1),* Usborne) EDC Publishing.

—The Story of Robin Hood. Jones, Rob Lloyd. 2010. (Picture Book Classics Ser.). 24p. (J). 9.99 *(978-0-7945-2859-1(7),* Usborne) EDC Publishing.

—Waiting for Ice. Markle, Sandra. 2012. (ENG.). 32p. (J). (gr. -1-3). 15.95 *(978-1-58089-255-1(8))* Charlesbridge Publishing, Inc.

Marlet, Nico & Frawley, Keith. Book of Dragons. 2014. (How to Train Your Dragon TV Ser.). (ENG.). 24p. (J). (gr. -1-5). 16.99 *(978-1-4814-2137-9(9),* Simon Spotlight) Simon Spotlight.

Marlette, Andy. Gator Alphabet ABC. Bianchi, Mike & Novak, Marisol. 2004. 32p. (J). (gr. -1-k). 6.95 *(978-1-58261-403-8(2))* Sports Publishing, LLC.

—Harry Loves Greens. Baldwin, Laura. 2012. 30p. (J). pap. 10.00 *(978-1-61153-013-1(X))* Light Messages Publishing.

—Harry Loves Turnips (Not!) Baldwin, Laura. 2012. 30p. (J). pap. 10.00 *(978-1-61153-023-0(7))* Light Messages Publishing.

—Swampmeet: A Gator Counting Book. Bianchi, Mike & Novak, Marisol. 2004. 32p. (J). (gr. -1-k). 6.95 *(978-1-58261-780-0(5))* Sports Publishing, LLC.

Marlin, Kathryn. God Made Kittens. Bennett, Marian. 2015. (Faith That Sticks Ser.). (ENG.). 30p. (J). pap. 3.99 ***(978-1-4964-0319-3(3))*** Tyndale Hse. Pubs.

Marlin, Kathryn. God Made Kittens. Bennett, Marian. 2014. (Happy Day Ser.). (ENG.). 16p. (J). pap. 2.49 *(978-1-4143-9479-4(9))* Tyndale Hse. Pubs.

—God Made Seasons. Shearer, Amelia. 2014. (Happy Day Ser.). (ENG.). 16p. (J). pap. 2.49 *(978-1-4143-9481-7(0))* Tyndale Hse. Pubs.

—God's Baby Animals. Redford, Margorie & Rice, Courtney. 2014. (Happy Day Ser.). (ENG.). 16p. (J). pap. 2.49 *(978-1-4143-9418-3(7))* Tyndale Hse. Pubs.

—I Love Church! Redford, Marjorie & Rice, Courtney. 2013. (Happy Day Ser.). (ENG.). 16p. (J). pap. 2.49 *(978-1-4143-9299-8(0))* Tyndale Hse. Pubs.

—My Bible Says. Redford, Marjorie. 2013. (Happy Day Ser.). (ENG.). 16p. (J). pap. 2.49 *(978-1-4143-9301-8(6))* Tyndale Hse. Pubs.

—My Bible Says. Redford, Marjorie. 2013. (Happy Day Ser.). (ENG.). 18p. (J). bds. 4.99 *(978-1-4143-9291-2(5))* Tyndale Hse. Pubs.

Marlin, Kathryn & Julien, Terry. God Always Cares. Beveridge, Amy. 2014. (Happy Day Ser.). (ENG.). 16p. (J). pap. 2.49 *(978-1-4143-9417-6(9))* Tyndale Hse. Pubs.

Marlow, Layn. Too Small for My Big Bed: Sleep Tight in Your Own Bed Tonight! Stewart, Amber. 2013. (ENG.). 32p. (J). (gr. -1 — 1). 14.99 *(978-0-7641-6587-0(9))* Barron's Educational Series, Inc.

Marlowe, Susan B. Goodnight, Boone. Greene, Melanie W. et al. 2012. (J). *(978-1-933251-80-6(8))* Parkway Pubs., Inc.

Marman, Richard. Mcalister's Spark. Marman, Richard. 2013. 364p. pap. *(978-1-909302-21-1(X))* Abela Publishing.

Marquez, David. Kestus. Hester, Phil. Morrissey, Paul, ed. 2011. (Day's Missing Ser.: 2). (ENG.). 144p. (YA). (gr. 7). 24.95 *(978-1-936393-10-7(7))*, Archaia Entertainment) Boom! Studios.

—Secret Warriors - Night, Vol. 5. Colak, Mirko & Hickman, Jonathan. 2011. (ENG.). 136p. (YA). (gr. 8-17). pap. 14.99 *(978-0-7851-4803-6(5))* Marvel Worldwide, Inc.

Marquez, Erick. The Binky Fairy. Shaw-Lott, Karen. 2009. 12p. pap. 11.00 *(978-1-60844-271-3(3))* Dog Ear Publishing, LLC.

Marquez, Francisca. Dig Those Dinosaurs. Houran, Lori Haskins. 2013. (ENG.). 24p. (J). (gr. -1-2). 15.99 *(978-0-8075-1579-2(5))* Whitman, Albert & Co.

—How to Spy on a Shark. Houran, Lori Haskins. 2015. (ENG.). 24p. (J). (gr. -1-2). 15.99 *(978-0-8075-3402-1(1))* Whitman, Albert & Co.

—A Trip into Space: An Adventure to the International Space Station. Houran, Lori Haskins. 2014. (ENG.). 24p. (J). (gr. -1-2). 15.99 *(978-0-8075-8091-2(0))* Whitman, Albert & Co.

Marquez, Sofia. Pepe Perez Mexican Mouse: Pepe Perez Comes to the United States: Book 1, 1 vol. Marquez, Sofia. 2009. 20p. pap. 24.95 *(978-1-61546-496-8(4))* America Star Bks.

Marquis, KariAnn. Seven Friends, 1 vol. Greeley, David. 2010. 38p. 24.95 *(978-1-4489-4101-8(6))* PublishAmerica, Inc.

Marrero, J. Julio & Maria Raise the Roof: English / Spanish Edition. Paul, Brian. 2011. (ENG.). 48p. pap. 15.00 *(978-1-4635-3515-5(5))* CreateSpace Independent Publishing Platform.

Marriot, Pat. El Dedo Magico. Dahl, Roald.Tr. of Magic Finger. (SPA.). 74p. (J). (gr. 3-5). 9.95 *(978-968-19-0621-4(7))* Aguilar Editorial MEX. Dist: Santillana USA Publishing Co., Inc.

Marriott, Pat. El Dedo Magico. Dahl, Roald. 2003.Tr. of Magic Finger. (SPA.). 74p. (gr. 3-5). pap. 11.95 *(978-958-24-0178-8(8))* Santillana COL. Dist: Santillana USA Publishing Co., Inc.

Marron, Jose, jt. illus. see Nugent, Suzanne.

Marron, Jose Luis, jt. illus. see Cannella, Marco.

Marroquin-Burr, Kristina. Learn to Draw Angry Birds Space. 2014. 64p. (J). (gr. 3-5). 33.27 *(978-1-939581-33-4(8))* Quarto Publishing Group USA.

Marrucchi, Elisa. Beautiful Brides. Lagonegro, Melissa. 2011. (Step into Reading Ser.). (ENG.). 32p. (J). (gr. k-3). pap. 3.99 *(978-0-7364-2685-5(X))* Random Hse., Inc.

—The Beauty of Nature. Random House Editors & Posner-Sanchez, Andrea. 2011. (Pictureback Ser.). (ENG.). 24p. (J). (gr. -1-2). pap. 3.99 *(978-0-7364-2771-5(6)*, RH/Disney) Random Hse. Children's Bks.

—Cinderella's Fairy Merry Christmas. Posner-Sanchez, Andrea. 2009. (Pictureback Ser.). (ENG.). 24p. (J). (gr. -1-2). pap. 3.99 *(978-0-7364-2622-0(1)*, RH/Disney) Random Hse. Children's Bks.

—Happy Birthday, Princess! (Disney Princess) Weinberg, Jennifer. 2012. (Step into Reading Ser.). (ENG.). 32p. (J). (gr. -1-1). pap. 3.99 *(978-0-7364-2859-0(3)*, RH/Disney) Random Hse. Children's Bks.

—The Little Mermaid - Songs from the Heart. Golden Books Staff. 2008. (Deluxe Coloring Book Ser.). (ENG.). 96p. (J). (gr. -1-2). pap. 3.99 *(978-0-7364-2497-4(0)*, Golden Bks.) Random Hse. Children's Bks.

—Sealed with a Kiss. Lagonegro, Melissa. 2005. (Step into Reading Ser.). (ENG.). 32p. (J). (gr. k-3). per. 3.99 *(978-0-7364-2363-2(X)*, RH/Disney) Random Hse. Children's Bks.

—Sweet & Spooky Halloween. Random House Disney Staff. 2007. (Pictureback(R) Ser.). (ENG.). 24p. (J). (gr. -1-2). pap. 3.99 *(978-0-7364-2453-0(9)*, RH/Disney) Random Hse. Children's Bks.

—Teachers' Pets (Disney Princess) Man-Kong, Mary. 2011. (Step into Reading Ser.). (ENG.). 32p. (J). (gr. k-3). pap. 3.99 *(978-0-7364-2778-4(3)*, RH/Disney) Random Hse. Children's Bks.

—Winter Wishes. Jordan, Apple J. 2006. (Step into Reading Ser.). (ENG.). 32p. (J). (gr. k-3). per. 3.99 *(978-0-7364-2409-7(1)*, RH/Disney) Random Hse. Children's Bks.

Marrucchi, Elisa, jt. illus. see Doescher, Erik.

Marrucchi, Elisa, jt. illus. see Emslie, Peter.

Mars, E., jt. illus. see Squire, M H.

Mars, W. T. The Friendly Frontier: The Story of the Canadian-American Border. Meyer, Edith Patterson. 2011. 304p. 48.95 *(978-1-258-09384-6(7))* Literary Licensing, LLC.

Marschall, Ken. On Board the Titanic: What It Was Like When the Great Liner Sank. Tanaka, Shelley. 2010. (I Was There Ser.). (ENG.). 48p. (J). (gr. k-2). pap. 9.95 *(978-1-897330-60-9(X))* Madison Pr. Bks. CAN. Dist: Independent Pubs. Group.

Marschell, Hannah. My Beautiful Bow: An Adoption Story. Goldman Marshall, Lauren. 2010. 36p. pap. 14.95 *(978-1-60844-395-6(7))* Dog Ear Publishing, LLC.

Marsden, Ken. Lucy's Grade School Adventure. Hansen, Jennifer. 2006. (J). *(978-0-9774822-7-6(8))* Crosam Pr.

Marsee, Kimberly. Daughter of the King: Daughter of the King: Book with Audio CD. Tucker, Terra. ed. 2007. 48p. (J). 19.95 *(978-0-9794578-0-7(7))* Tucker, Terra.

Marsh, Bobbi. Gaylord Goose. Christensen, Bob. 2011. 28p. pap. 12.95 *(978-1-61493-014-3(7))* Peppertree Pr., The.

Marsh, Bobbie. The Princess Mermaid & the Missing Sea Shells. Dipinto, Michael J. 2013. 36p. pap. 15.95 *(978-1-61493-151-5(8))* Peppertree Pr., The.

Marsh, Carole, photos by. The Mystery of Blackbeard the Pirate. Marsh, Carole. 2009. (Real Kids, Real Places Ser.). 150p. (J). 18.99 *(978-0-635-06992-4(X)*, Marsh, Carole Mysteries) Gallopade International.

Marsh, Dilleen. What Happens When People Die? Marsh, Dilleen, tr. 2003. (J). 12.95 *(978-1-57008-954-1(X))* Deseret Bk. Co.

Marsh, Jakob. EZ Times Table: An easy visual way to learn multiplication & division by playing with patterns & making friends with Numbers. Biesanz, Thomas. 2nd rev. ed. 2008. (ENG.). 80p. (J). per. 12.95 *(978-0-9799636-1-2(3))* Growth-Ink.

Marsh, Nancy. Path Winds Home. DeVos, Janie. l.t. ed. 2005. 32p. 16.95 *(978-0-9743758-0-9(2))* Red Engine Pr.

Marshall, Ann & Reeves, Jeni. Passover. Fishman, Cathy Goldberg. 2006. (On My Own Holidays Ser.). (ENG.). 48p. (gr. 2-4). 25.26 *(978-1-57505-656-2(9))* Lerner Publishing Group.

Marshall, Dan. Lydia Darragh: Quaker Patriot. Rand, Carol. (J). 15.95 *(978-0-945912-33-0(1))* Pippin Pr.

Marshall, Denise. Snow White & Rose Red: A Grimms' Fairy Tale. Brothers Grimm Staff. 2008. 28p. (J). 17.95 *(978-0-88010-591-0(7)*, Bell Pond Bks.) SteinerBooks, Inc.

Marshall, Felicia. Harriet Tubman & the Freedom Train. Gayle, Sharon. ed. 2005. (Ready-to-Read Ser.). 32p. (J). lib. bdg. 15.00 *(978-1-59054-960-5(0))* Fitzgerald Bks.

—Harriet Tubman & the Freedom Train. Gayle, Sharon. 2003. (Ready-To-read SOFA Ser.). (ENG.). 32p. (J). (gr. 1-3). pap. 3.99 *(978-0-689-85480-4(3)*, Simon Spotlight) Simon Spotlight.

—Keepers. Watts, Jeri Hanel. 2013. (ENG.). 32p. (J). (gr. -1-5). pap. 8.95 *(978-1-58430-013-7(2))* Lee & Low Bks., Inc.

—Loved Best. McKissack, Patricia C. 2005. (Ready-For-Chapters Ser.). (ENG.). 64p. (J). (gr. 2-5). pap. 4.99 *(978-0-689-86151-2(6)*, Simon & Schuster/Paula Wiseman Bks.) Simon & Schuster/Paula Wiseman Bks.

—The Night the Chimneys Fell. Figley, Marty Rhodes. 2009. (On My Own History Ser.). (ENG.). 48p. (gr. 2-4). 25.26 *(978-0-8225-7894-9(8))* Lerner Publishing Group.

—Robert Smalls Sails to Freedom. Brown, Susan Taylor. 2006. (On My Own History Ser.). (ENG.). 48p. (gr. 2-4). lib. bdg. 25.26 *(978-1-57505-872-6(3))* Lerner Publishing Group.

Marshall, H. Keene, jt. illus. see Miller, Bryan.

Marshall, Heidi Amenda. Petra's Adventure in Nievenheim. Marshall, Heidi Amenda. l.t. ed. 2003. 57p. (J). per. 7.99 *(978-0-9747445-0-6(6))* Landfall Co., The.

Marshall, Ian. Not Again, Frannie! A Frannie Flotnick Adventure. Turkovitz, Karen. Ryan, Linda et al, eds. unabr. ed. 2003. (YA). pap. 12.95 *(978-0-9679115-6-4(7))* Five Degrees of Frannie.

Marshall, James. Cinderella. Karlin, Barbara. unabr. ed. 2006. (J). (gr. -1-4). 29.95 *(978-0-439-84888-6(1)*, WHCD671); 18.95 *(978-0-439-84890-9(3)*, WPCD671) Weston Woods Studios, Inc.

—Miss Nelson Has a Field Day, 1 vol. Allard, Harry G., Jr. 2012. (ENG.). 32p. (J). (gr. -1-3). 10.99 *(978-0-547-75376-8(4))* Houghton Mifflin Harcourt Publishing Co.

—Miss Nelson Is Back, 1 vol. Allard, Harry G., Jr. 2011. (ENG.). 32p. (J). (gr. -1-3). 10.99 *(978-0-547-57718-0(4))* Houghton Mifflin Harcourt Publishing Co.

—Miss Nelson Is Missing!, 1 vol. Allard, Harry. 2007. (Read along Book & CD Ser.). (ENG.). 32p. (J). (gr. -1-3). 10.99 *(978-0-618-85281-9(6))* Houghton Mifflin Harcourt Publishing Co.

Marshall, Jamie. The Poopy Pekinese. Howell, Trisha Adelena. 2005. 32p. (J). 15.95 *(978-1-931210-09-6(8))* Howell Canyon Pr.

—The Stinky Shepherd. Howell, Trisha Adelena. 2005. 32p. (J). 15.95 *(978-1-931210-25-6(X))* Howell Canyon Pr.

Marshall, Janet. A Nantucket Nanny. Manley, Molly. 2005. (Little Limericks Ser.). (ENG.). 24p. (J). (gr. k-3). 12.95 *(978-1-889833-96-5(7)*, Commonwealth Editions) Applewood Bks.

—On a Vineyard Veranda. Manley, Molly. 2007. (Little Limericks Ser.). (ENG.). 24p. (J). (gr. k-3). 12.95 *(978-1-933212-46-3(2)*, Commonwealth Editions) Applewood Bks.

Marshall, Julia. The Daring Coast Guard Rescue of the Pendleton Crew. Barbo, Theresa Mitchell & Webster, W. Russell. 2013. Orig. Title: The Daring Coast Guard Rescue of the Pendleton Crew. (ENG.). 128p. (gr. 4-7). 14.99 *(978-1-62619-095-5(X)*, History Pr., The) Arcadia Publishing.

Marshall, Julia. Louisiana, the Jewel of the Deep South, 1 vol. Downing, Johnette. 2015. (ENG.). 32p. (J). (gr. k-3). 16.99 ***(978-1-4556-2096-8(3))*** Pelican Publishing Co., Inc.

Marshall, Julia. When Hurricane Katrina Hit Home. Karwoski, Gail Langer. 2013. Orig. Title: When Hurricane Katrina Hit Home. (ENG.). 192p. (gr. 4-7). 15.99 *(978-1-62619-083-2(6)*, History Pr., The) Arcadia Publishing.

Marshall, Laurie. Take Me with You When You Go. Venable, Alan. 2008. 112p. (J). 12.95 *(978-0-9777082-7-7(6))* One Monkey Bks.

Marshall, Natalie. Millie-Mae: In Autumn. 2014. (J). ***(978-1-4351-5612-8(9))*** Barnes & Noble, Inc.

Marshall, Natalie. Monster, Be Good! 2013. (ENG.). 28p. (J). (gr. -1-3). 12.99 *(978-1-60905-314-7(1))* Blue Apple Bks.

—Monster Needs One More. Ziefert, Harriet. 2013. (ENG.). 24p. (J). (-k). 12.99 *(978-1-60905-357-4(5))* Blue Apple Bks.

—Seaside Sandcastle! 2014. (J). *(978-1-4351-5505-3(X))* Barnes & Noble, Inc.

—Small Smaller Smallest. Fletcher, Corina. 2015. (ENG.). 12p. (J). (— 1). bds. 8.95 *(978-1-4549-1559-1(5))* Sterling Publishing Co., Inc.

Marshall, Natalie. Tiny Creatures: Touch & Feel Book. 2015. (J). ***(978-1-4351-5935-8(7))*** Barnes & Noble, Inc.

Marshall, Natalie. Up down Across. Fletcher, Corina. 2015. (ENG.). 12p. (J). (— 1). bds. 8.95 *(978-1-4549-1562-1(5))* Sterling Publishing Co., Inc.

—Zoo Fun: A Lift the Flap Guessing Book. 2013. (J). *(978-1-4351-4930-4(0))* Barnes & Noble, Inc.

Marshall, Natalie. This Little Piggy: A Fingers & Toes Nursery Rhyme Book. Marshall, Natalie. 2015. (ENG.). 12p. (J). (— 1). bds. 6.99 ***(978-0-545-76761-3(X)***, Cartwheel Bks.) Scholastic, Inc.

Marshall, Setsu. The Adventures of Tommy Toad. Rundstrom, Teressa. 2004. 40p. (J). per. *(978-1-932062-41-0(6))* Hability Solution Services, Inc.

Marshall, Todd, et al. Stegosaurus up Close: Plated Dinosaur. Dodson, Peter & Library Association Staff. 2010. (Zoom in on Dinosaurs! Ser.). 24p. (J). (gr. k-3). 22.60 *(978-0-7660-3334-4(1))* Enslow Pubs., Inc.

—Tyrannosaurus Rex up Close: Meat-Eating Dinosaur. Dodson, Peter & Library Association Staff. 2010. (Zoom in on Dinosaurs! Ser.). 24p. (J). (gr. k-3). 22.60 *(978-0-7660-3336-8(8))* Enslow Pubs., Inc.

Marshall, Todd & Bindon, John. Diplodocus up Close: Long-Necked Dinosaur. Dodson, Peter & Library Association Staff. 2010. (Zoom in on Dinosaurs! Ser.). 24p. (J). (gr. k-3). 22.60 *(978-0-7660-3333-7(3))* Enslow Pubs., Inc.

Marshall, Todd & Fields, Laura. Triceratops up Close: Horned Dinosaur. Dodson, Peter & Library Association Staff. 2010. (Zoom in on Dinosaurs! Ser.). 24p. (J). (gr. k-3). 22.60 *(978-0-7660-3335-1(X))* Enslow Pubs., Inc.

Marshall, Todd, jt. illus. see Csotonyi, Julius.

Marsico, Katie. A Baby Lobster Grows Up. Marsico, Katie. 2007. (Scholastic News Nonfiction Readers Ser.). (ENG.). 24p. (J). (gr. 1-2). 22.00 *(978-0-531-17475-3(1))* Scholastic Library Publishing.

—A Ladybug Larva Grows Up. Marsico, Katie. 2007. (Scholastic News Nonfiction Readers Ser.). (ENG.). 24p. (J). (gr. 1-2). 22.00 *(978-0-531-17478-4(6))* Scholastic Library Publishing.

—A Peachick Grows Up. Marsico, Katie. 2007. (Scholastic News Nonfiction Readers Ser.). (ENG.). 24p. (J). (gr. 1-2). 22.00 *(978-0-531-17480-7(8))* Scholastic Library Publishing.

Marstall, Bob. Butternut Hollow Pond. Heinz, Brian. 2006. (ENG.). 32p. (J). (gr. 2-6). pap. 6.95 *(978-0-8225-5993-1(5)*, First Avenue Editions) Lerner Publishing Group.

Marstall, Bob, et al. Mitch & Amy. Cleary, Beverly. 2008. (ENG.). 288p. (J). (gr. 3-7). 16.99 *(978-0-688-10806-9(7))* HarperCollins Pubs.

Marstall, Bob, jt. illus. see Robert, Marstall.

Marstall, Robert. B Is for Blue Planet: An Earth Science Alphabet. Strother, Ruth. 2011. (Sleeping Bear Alphabets Ser.). (ENG.). 40p. (J). (gr. k-6). lib. bdg. 16.95 *(978-1-58536-454-1(1))* Sleeping Bear Pr.

Marston, J. D., photos by. The Poems for Pequenines (Poemas Para Pequenines) 2004. (Baby Einstein Ser.). (SPA., 12p. (J). bds. *(978-970-718-159-5(1)*, Silver Dolphin en Español) Advanced Marketing, S. de R. L. de C. V.

Marta, Diana M. Firebug & the Mind Spark. Kisinger, E. Jean. 2012. 42p. pap. 12.50 *(978-0-615-58954-1(5))* Firebug Fairy Tales.

Martchenko, Michael. L' Anniversaire. Munsch, Robert. 2003. (Droles D'Histories Ser.).Tr. of Moira's Birthday. (FRE.). 24p. (J). (gr. k-18). pap. *(978-2-89021-114-8(2))* Diffusion du livre Mirabel (DLM).

—Le Dodo. Munsch, Robert. 2003. (Droles D'Histories Ser.).Tr. of Mortimer. (FRE.). 24p. (J). (gr. k-18). pap. *(978-2-89021-055-4(3))* Diffusion du livre Mirabel (DLM).

—Enough, 1 vol. Skrypuch, Marsha. 2003. (ENG.). 32p. (J). (gr. 2-4). pap. 9.95 *(978-1-55041-884-2(X)*, 155041884X) Fitzhenry & Whiteside, Ltd. CAN. Dist: Midpoint Trade Bks., Inc.

—Espera y Verás. Munsch, Robert. Aguirre, Rigo, tr. from ENG. 2004. (SPA.). 24p. (J). (gr. -1-2). pap. 5.95 *(978-1-55037-872-6(4)*, 9781550378726) Annick Pr., Ltd. CAN. Dist: Firefly Bks., Ltd.

—I Did It Because... How a Poem Happens. Lesynski, Loris. 2006. (ENG.). 64p. (J). (gr. 2-5). 19.95 *(978-1-55451-018-4(X)*, 9781554510184); pap. 9.95 *(978-1-55451-017-7(1)*, 9781554510177) Annick Pr., Ltd. CAN. Dist: Firefly Bks., Ltd.

—Kiss Me, I'm Perfect! Munsch, Robert. 2008. (J). (gr. -1-3). 11.65 *(978-0-7569-9007-7(6))* Perfection Learning Corp.

—Makeup Mess. Munsch, Robert. ed. 2004. (J). (gr. k-3). spiral bd. *(978-0-616-11124-6(X))* Canadian National Institute for the Blind/Institut National Canadien pour les Aveugles.

—Matthew & the Midnight Movie, 1 vol. Morgan, Allen. 2003. (ENG.). 32p. (YA). *(978-0-7737-6273-2(6))* Fitzhenry & Whiteside, Ltd.

—Matthew & the Midnight Pirates, 1 vol. Morgan, Allen. 2005. (First Flight Level 3 Ser.). (ENG.). 40p. (J). (gr. 1-3). lib. bdg. 11.95 *(978-1-55041-902-1(1)*, 1550419021) Fitzhenry & Whiteside, Ltd. CAN. Dist: Midpoint Trade Bks., Inc.

—Matthew & the Midnight Wrestlers, 1 vol. Morgan, Allen. 2005. (First Flight Level 3 Ser.). (ENG.). 40p. (J). (gr. 1-3). lib. bdg. 11.95 *(978-1-55041-915-3(3)*, 1550419153); per. 4.95 *(978-1-55041-916-0(1)*, 1550419161) Fitzhenry & Whiteside, Ltd. CAN. Dist: Midpoint Trade Bks., Inc.

—More Pies. Munsch, Robert. ed. 2004. (J). (gr. k-3). spiral bd. *(978-0-616-14590-6(X))* Canadian National Institute for the Blind/Institut National Canadien pour les Aveugles.

—Mortimer. Munsch, Robert. 2010. (ENG.). 26p. (J). (gr. -1). bds. 6.95 *(978-1-55451-228-7(X)*, 9781554512287) Annick Pr., Ltd. CAN. Dist: Firefly Bks., Ltd.

—Mortimer. Munsch, Robert. Canetti, Yanitzia, tr. from ENG. 2007. (SPA.). 24p. (J). (gr. -1-2). pap. 5.95 *(978-1-55451-109-9(7)*, 9781554511099) Annick Pr., Ltd. CAN. Dist: Firefly Bks., Ltd.

—The Paper Bag Princess. Munsch, Robert. 2009. (ENG.). 28p. (J). (gr. -1-2). bds. 6.95 *(978-1-55451-211-9(5)*, 9781554512119) Annick Pr., Ltd. CAN. Dist: Firefly Bks., Ltd.

—The Paper Bag Princess: The Story Behind the Story. Munsch, Robert. 25th anniv. ed. 2005. (ENG.). 64p. (J). (gr. -1-12). 19.95 *(978-1-55037-915-0(1)*, 9781550379150) Annick Pr., Ltd. CAN. Dist: Firefly Bks., Ltd.

—Pigs. 2014. (ENG.). 24p. (J). (gr. -1-k). bds. 6.95 *(978-1-55451-628-5(5)*, 9781554516285) Annick Pr., Ltd. CAN. Dist: Firefly Bks., Ltd.

—The Sandcastle Contest. Munsch, Robert. 2005. (ENG.). 32p. (J). (gr. -1-3). 4.99 *(978-0-439-74865-0(8)*, Cartwheel Bks.) Scholastic, Inc.

—Shoe Shakes. Lesynski, Loris. 2007. (ENG.). 32p. (J). (gr. -1-k). 19.95 *(978-1-55451-106-8(2)*, 9781554511068); pap. 9.95 *(978-1-55451-105-1(4)*, 9781554511051) Annick Pr., Ltd. CAN. Dist: Firefly Bks., Ltd.

—Smelly Socks. Munsch, Robert. 2005. (ENG.). 32p. (J). (gr. -1-3). pap. 4.99 *(978-0-439-64948-3(X)*, Cartwheel Bks.) Scholastic, Inc.

—Stephanie's Ponytail. Munsch, Robert. 2007. (Annikins Ser.). (ENG.). 24p. (J). (gr. -1-2). pap. 1.99 *(978-1-55451-114-3(3)*, 9781554511143) Annick Pr., Ltd. CAN. Dist: Firefly Bks., Ltd.

—Thomas' Snowsuit. Munsch, Robert. 2011. (ENG.). 24p. (J). (gr. -1 — 1). bds., bds. 6.95 *(978-1-55451-363-5(4)*, 9781554513635) Annick Pr., Ltd. CAN. Dist: Firefly Bks., Ltd.

—50 below Zero. Munsch, Robert. 2013. (ENG.). 22p. (J). (gr. -1-k). bds. 6.95 *(978-1-55451-532-5(7)*, 9781554515325) Annick Pr., Ltd. CAN. Dist: Firefly Bks., Ltd.

Martchenko, Michael. The Fire Station. Martchenko, Michael. Munsch, Robert. 2012. (ENG.). 24p. (J). (gr. -1-k). bds. 6.95 *(978-1-55451-423-6(1)*, 9781554514236) Annick Pr., Ltd. CAN. Dist: Firefly Bks., Ltd.

Martchenko, Michael. Matthew & the Midnight Firefighter, 1 vol. Martchenko, Michael, tr. Morgan, Allen. 2004. (First Flight Level 3 Ser.). (ENG.). 40p. (J). lib. bdg. 5.95 *(978-1-55041-875-0(0)*, 1550418750) Fitzhenry & Whiteside, Ltd. CAN. Dist: Midpoint Trade Bks., Inc.

Marten, Luanne. Measuring Length. Vogel, Julia. 2012. (Simple Measurement Ser.). (ENG.). 24p. (J). (gr. -1-2). 27.07 *(978-1-61473-279-2(5)*, 204984) Child's World, Inc., The.

—Measuring Temperature. Vogel, Julia. 2012. (Simple Measurement Ser.). (ENG.). 24p. (J). (gr. -1-2). 27.07 *(978-1-61473-280-8(9)*, 204985) Child's World, Inc., The.

—Measuring Time: the Calendar. Vogel, Julia. 2012. (Simple Measurement Ser.). (ENG.). 24p. (J). (gr. -1-2). 27.07 *(978-1-61473-281-5(7)*, 204986) Child's World, Inc., The.

—Measuring Time: the Clock. Vogel, Julia. 2012. (Simple Measurement Ser.). (ENG.). 24p. (J). (gr. -1-2). 27.07 *(978-1-61473-282-2(5)*, 204987) Child's World, Inc., The.

—Measuring Volume. Vogel, Julia. 2012. (Simple Measurement Ser.). (ENG.). 24p. (J). (gr. -1-2). 27.07 *(978-1-61473-283-9(3)*, 204988) Child's World, Inc., The.

—Measuring Weight. Vogel, Julia. 2012. (Simple Measurement Ser.). (ENG.). 24p. (J). (gr. -1-2). 27.07 *(978-1-61473-284-6(1)*, 204989) Child's World, Inc., The.

—Sophie & Sadie Build a Sonnet. StJohn, Amanda. 2011. (Poetry Builders Ser.). 32p. (J). (gr. 2-4). lib. bdg. 25.27 *(978-1-59953-440-4(1))* Norwood Hse. Pr.

Marten, Luanne. There Was an Old Woman Who Lived in a Shoe. Marten, Luanne. 2011. (Favorite Mother Goose Rhymes Ser.). (ENG.). 16p. (J). (gr. -1-2). lib. bdg. 25.64 *(978-1-60954-284-9(3)*, 200236) Child's World, Inc., The.

Marten, Luanne Voltmer. Can't-Wait Willow! Ziglar, Christy. 2013. 32p. (J). *(978-0-8249-5648-6(6))*, Ideals Children's Bks.) Ideals Pubns.

Martin, Alice, et al. When Two Saints Meet. Hunger, Bill. Ripley, Jill, ed. 100p. (Orig.). (YA). (gr. 6-12). pap. 9.95 *(978-0-9625782-0-5(7))* Two Saints Publishing.

Martin, Alison J. Charlie, the Brave Monkey. Martin, Alison J. 2013. 24p. pap. 13.97 *(978-1-62516-155-0(7)*, Strategic Bk. Publishing) Strategic Book Publishing & Rights Agency (SBPRA).

Martin, Alixandra. The Scariest Dream Ever. DiVencenzo, Maria T. 2010. (ENG.). 40p. (J). (gr. -1-k). 16.99 *(978-0-9816003-2-1(8))* Winterlake Pr.

Martin, Ana I. Pull & Play - Opposites. Larranaga, Ana M. ed. 2013. (Pull & Play Ser.). (ENG.). 10p. (J). (— 1). bds. 7.99 *(978-0-230-75040-1(0))* Pan Macmillan GBR. Dist: Independent Pubs. Group.

Martin, Anne E. A Tail & Two Kitties. Martin, Anne E. 2007. 40p. (J). (gr. -1-3). per. 13.99 *(978-1-59879-340-6(3))* Lifevest Publishing, Inc.

—There's A Ladybug in My House. Martin, Anne E. l.t. ed. 2006. 45p. (J). per. 12.99 *(978-1-59879-165-5(6))* Lifevest Publishing, Inc.

Martin, Brian. If Winning Isn't Everything, Why Do I Hate to Lose? Smith, Bryan. 2015. (ENG.). 32p. (J). pap. 10.95 ***(978-1-934490-85-3(7))*** Boys Town Pr.

Martin, Caroline & Davies, Nic. Girl 2 Girl: The Swap Book You Share with Your Friends. Reader, Jenny. 2003. 96p. (J). pap. *(978-0-439-56743-5(2))* Scholastic, Inc.

Martin, Cecile L. K. The Shark's Tooth. Rash, Ron. 2015. (Young Palmetto Bks.). (ENG.). 40p. (J). pap. 12.95 ***(978-1-61117-527-1(5))*** Univ. of South Carolina Pr.

Martin, Chris. Can I Tell You about ADHD? A Guide for Friends, Family & Professionals. Yarney, Susan. 2013. (Can I Tell You about... Ser.). (ENG.). 64p. pap. *(978-1-84905-359-4(6))* Kingsley, Jessica Ltd.

Martin, Courtney. Follow the Drinking Gourd: Come along the Underground Railroad. Coleman, Wim & Perrin, Pat. 2014. (Setting the Stage for Fluency Ser.). 40p. (gr. 3-5). pap. 8.95 *(978-1-939656-10-0(9))* Red Chair Pr.

Martin, Courtney A. Ballots for Belva: The True Story of a Woman's Race for the Presidency. Bardhan-Quallen, Sudipta. 2015. (ENG.). 32p. (J). (gr. k-5). 9.95 *(978-1-4197-1627-0(1)*, Abrams Bks. for Young Readers) Abrams.

Martin, Cynthia. Adventures in Sound with Max Axiom, Super Scientist, 1 vol. Sohn, Emily & Timmons, Anne. 2007. (Graphic Science Ser.). (ENG.). 32p. (gr. 3-4). per. 8.10 *(978-0-7368-7889-0(0)*, Graphic Library) Capstone Pr., Inc.

—Alley of Shadows, 1 vol. Brezenoff, Steve. (Vortex Bks.). (ENG.). 112p. (gr. 2-3). 2008. pap. 7.19 *(978-1-59889-922-1(8))*; 2007. 25.32 *(978-1-59889-856-9(6))* Stone Arch Bks. (Vortex Bks.).

—The American Presidency, 1 vol. Peterson, Christine. 2008. (Cartoon Nation Ser.). (ENG.). 32p. (gr. 3-4). lib. bdg. 29.99 *(978-1-4296-1330-9(0)*, Graphic Library) Capstone Pr., Inc.

—Aventuras con el Sonido con Max Axiom, Supercientífico. Sohn, Emily & Timmons, Anne. 2013. (Ciencia Gráfica Ser.). (SPA.). 32p. (gr. 3-4). lib. bdg. 29.99 *(978-1-62065-181-0(5))* Capstone Pr., Inc.

—Booker T. Washington: Gran Educador Norteamericano. Braun, Eric. 2006. (Biografías Graficas Ser.). (SPA.). 32p. (gr. 3-4). 29.99 *(978-0-7368-6599-9(3))* Capstone Pr., Inc.

—Booker T. Washington: Great American Educator, 1 vol. Braun, Eric. (Graphic Biographies Ser.). (ENG.). 32p. (gr. 3-4). 2006. per. 8.10 *(978-0-7368-6190-8(4))*; 2005. 29.99 *(978-0-7368-4630-1(1))* Capstone Pr., Inc. (Graphic Library).

—George Washington: Dirigiendo una Nueva Nación. Doeden, Matt. 2006. (Biografías Graficas Ser.). (SPA.). 32p. (gr. 3-4). 8.10 *(978-0-7368-9673-3(2))*; 29.99 *(978-0-7368-6605-7(1))* Capstone Pr., Inc.

—George Washington: Leading a New Nation. Doeden, Matt. 2005. (Graphic Biographies Ser.). (ENG.). 32p. (gr. 3-4). 29.99 *(978-0-7368-4963-0(7)*, Graphic Library) Capstone Pr., Inc.

—Green Berets, 1 vol. Glaser, Jason. 2006. (Warriors of History Ser.). (ENG.). 32p. (gr. 3-4). 27.32 *(978-0-7368-6430-5(X)*, Edge Bks.) Capstone Pr., Inc.

—Gulliver's Travels, 1 vol. Swift, Jonathan. 2008. (Classic Fiction Ser.). (ENG.). 72p. (gr. 2-3). lib. bdg. 26.65 *(978-1-4342-0449-3(9)*, Graphic Revolve) Stone Arch Bks.

—Hedy Lamarr & a Secret Communication System, 1 vol. Robbins, Trina. 2006. (Inventions & Discovery Ser.). (ENG.). 32p. (gr. 3-4). 8.10 *(978-0-7368-9641-2(4)*, Graphic Library) Capstone Pr., Inc.

—How to Draw Amazing Letters, 1 vol. Clay, Kathryn. 2009. (Drawing Fun Ser.). (ENG.). 32p. (gr. 3-4). 27.32 *(978-1-4296-2305-6(5)*, Snap Bks.) Capstone Pr., Inc.

—How to Draw Comic Heroes, 1 vol. Sautter, Aaron. 2007. (Drawing Cool Stuff Ser.). (ENG.). 32p. (gr. 3-4). 27.32 *(978-1-4296-0074-3(8)*, Edge Bks.) Capstone Pr., Inc.

—How to Draw Ferocious Dinosaurs, 1 vol. Sautter, Aaron. 2007. (Drawing Cool Stuff Ser.). (ENG.). 32p. (gr. 3-4). 27.32 *(978-1-4296-0076-7(4)*, Edge Bks.) Capstone Pr., Inc.

—How to Draw Manga Warriors, 1 vol. Sautter, Aaron. 2007. (Drawing Cool Stuff Ser.). (ENG.). 32p. (gr. 3-4). 27.32 *(978-1-4296-0078-1(0)*, Edge Bks.) Capstone Pr., Inc.

—A Journey into Adaptation with Max Axiom, Super Scientist, 1 vol. Biskup, Agnieszka & Schulz, Barbara. 2007. (Graphic Science Ser.). (ENG.). 32p. (gr. 3-4). per. 8.10 *(978-0-7368-7892-0(0)*, Graphic Library) Capstone Pr., Inc.

—Knights, 1 vol. Martin, Michael & Martin, Michael J. 2006. (Warriors of History Ser.). (ENG.). 32p. (gr. 3-4). 27.32 *(978-0-7368-6431-2(8)*, Edge Bks.) Capstone Pr., Inc.

—Knights, 1 vol. Lee, Adrienne. 2013. (Legendary Warriors Ser.). (ENG.). 32p. (gr. 1-2). 25.99 *(978-1-4765-3115-1(3)*, Blazers) Capstone Pr., Inc.

—Legendary Warriors. Lee, Adrienne. 2013. (Legendary Warriors Ser.). (ENG.). 32p. (gr. 1-2). 155.94 *(978-1-4765-3628-6(7)*, Blazers) Capstone Pr., Inc.

—Ninja, 1 vol. Glaser, Jason & Roley, Don. 2006. (Warriors of History Ser.). (ENG.). 32p. (gr. 3-4). 27.32 *(978-0-7368-6432-9(6)*, Edge Bks.) Capstone Pr., Inc.

—The Pony Express. Dunn, Joeming W. 2008. (Graphic History Ser.). 32p. 28.50 *(978-1-60270-184-7(9)*, Graphic Planet- Nonfiction) ABDO Publishing Co.

—The Salem Witch Trials. Dunn, Joeming W. 2008. (Graphic History Ser.). 32p. 28.50 *(978-1-60270-186-1(5)*, Graphic Planet- Nonfiction) ABDO Publishing Co.

—Samurai, 1 vol. Leavitt, Caroline. 2006. (Warriors of History Ser.). (ENG.). 32p. (gr. 3-4). 27.32 *(978-0-7368-6433-6(4)*, Edge Bks.) Capstone Pr., Inc.

—Samurai, 1 vol. Lee, Adrienne. 2013. (Legendary Warriors Ser.). (ENG.). 32p. (gr. 1-2). 25.99 *(978-1-4765-3113-7(7)*, Blazers) Capstone Pr., Inc.

—Shellshocked. Hammer, Cully et al. rev. ed. 2006. (ENG.). 144p. (YA). pap. 12.99 *(978-1-4012-0965-0(3))* DC Comics.

—Summer of Sabotage. Temple, Bob. 2008. (Vortex Bks.). (ENG.). 112p. (gr. 2-3). 25.32 *(978-1-4342-0799-9(4)*, Vortex Bks.) Stone Arch Bks.

—The Tempest. Conner, Daniel. 2008. (Graphic Shakespeare Ser.). 48p. (gr. 5-10). 29.93 *(978-1-60270-194-6(6)*, Graphic Planet- Fiction) ABDO Publishing Co.

Martin, Cynthia, et al. Theodore Roosevelt: Bear of a President, 1 vol. Olson, Nathan et al. 2007. (Graphic Biographies Ser.). (ENG.). 32p. (gr. 3-4). 29.99 *(978-0-7368-6849-5(6)*, 1264944, Graphic Library) Capstone Pr., Inc.

—Theodore Roosevelt: Bear of a President, 1 vol. Olson, Nathan et al. 2007. (Graphic Biographies Ser.). (ENG.). 32p. (gr. 3-4). per. 8.10 *(978-0-7368-7901-9(3)*, 1264944, Graphic Library) Capstone Pr., Inc.

Martin, Cynthia. Twelfth Night. Goodwin, Vincent & Shakespeare, William. 2008. (Graphic Shakespeare Ser.). 48p. (gr. 5-10). 29.93 *(978-1-60270-195-3(4)*, Graphic Planet- Fiction) ABDO Publishing Co.

—The U. S. Supreme Court. Fingeroth, Danny. 2008. (Cartoon Nation Ser.). (ENG.). 32p. (gr. 3-4). 29.99 *(978-1-4296-1985-1(6)*, Graphic Library) Capstone Pr., Inc.

—Vikings, 1 vol. Lee, Adrienne. 2013. (Legendary Warriors Ser.). (ENG.). 32p. (gr. 1-2). 25.99 *(978-1-4765-3116-8(1)*, Blazers) Capstone Pr., Inc.

—White Fang. London, Jack. 2007. (Graphic Classics). 32p. (gr. 4-7). 28.50 *(978-1-60270-055-0(9)*, Graphic Planet- Fiction) ABDO Publishing Co.

—The World of Food Chains with Max Axiom, Super Scientist, 1 vol. O'Donnell, Liam & Anderson, Bill. 2007. (Graphic Science Ser.). (ENG.). 32p. (gr. 3-4). 29.99 *(978-0-7368-6839-6(9)*, Graphic Library) Capstone Pr., Inc.

—The World of Food Chains with Max Axiom, Super Scientist, 1 vol. Anderson, Bill & O'Donnell, Liam. 2007. (Graphic Science Ser.). (ENG.). 32p. (gr. 3-4). per. 8.10 *(978-0-7368-7891-3(2)*, Graphic Library) Capstone Pr., Inc.

Martin, Cynthia & Anderson, Bill. Comprender el Calentamiento Global con Max Axiom, Supercientífico. Biskup, Agnieszka & Martin, Cynthia. Anderson, Bill. Strictly Spanish Translation Services Staff, tr. from ENG. 2012. (Ciencia Gráfica Ser.). (SPA.). 32p. (gr. 3-4). lib. bdg. 29.99 *(978-1-4296-9235-9(9))* Capstone Pr., Inc.

—Understanding Global Warming with Max Axiom, Super Scientist, 1 vol. Biskup, Agnieszka. (Graphic Science Ser.). (ENG.). 32p. (gr. 3-4). 2008. per. 8.10 *(978-1-4296-1767-3(5))*; 2007. 29.99 *(978-1-4296-0139-9(6))* Capstone Pr., Inc. (Graphic Library).

Martin, Cynthia & Beatty, Terry. The Story of the Star-Spangled Banner, 1 vol. Jacobson, Ryan. 2006. (Graphic History Ser.). (ENG.). 32p. (gr. 3-4). 29.99 *(978-0-7368-5493-1(2)*, Graphic Library) Capstone Pr., Inc.

Martin, Cynthia & Dominguez, Richard. Ciencia Gráfica. Biskup, Agnieszka & Sohn, Emily. 2013. (Ciencia Gráfica Ser.). (SPA.). 32p. (gr. 3-4). lib. bdg. 359.88 *(978-1-62065-186-5(6))* Capstone Pr., Inc.

Martin, Cynthia & Dominguez, Richard. Ciencia Gráfica. Biskup, Agnieszka & Sohn, Emily. 2013. (Ciencia Gráfica Ser.). (SPA.). 32p. (gr. 3-4). lib. bdg. 179.94 *(978-1-62065-185-8(8))* Capstone Pr., Inc.

Martin, Cynthia & Schoonover, Brent. Nathan Hale: Revolutionary Spy, 1 vol. Olson, Nathan & Glaser, Jason. 2006. (Graphic Biographies Ser.). (ENG.). 32p. (gr. 3-4). per. 8.10 *(978-0-7368-6199-1(8)*, Graphic Library) Capstone Pr., Inc.

—Nathan Hale: Revolutionary Spy. Olson, Nathan. 2005. (Graphic Biographies Ser.). (ENG.). 32p. (gr. 3-4). 29.99 *(978-0-7368-4968-5(8)*, Graphic Library) Capstone Pr., Inc.

—The Story of the Statue of Liberty, 1 vol. Niz, Xavier & Niz, Xavier W. 2006. (Graphic History Ser.). (ENG.). 32p. (gr. 3-4). 29.99 *(978-0-7368-5494-8(0)*, Graphic Library) Capstone Pr., Inc.

Martin, Cynthia & Schultz, Barbara. Sacagawea: Journey into the West, 1 vol. Gunderson, Jessica Sarah. 2006. (Graphic Biographies Ser.). (ENG.). 32p. (gr. 3-4). 29.99 *(978-0-7368-6499-2(7)*, Graphic Library) Capstone Pr., Inc.

Martin, Cynthia & Schulz, Barbara. The Attractive Story of Magnetism with Max Axiom, Super Scientist. Gianopoulos, Andrea. (Graphic Science Ser.). (ENG.). 32p. (gr. 3-4). 2008. pap. 8.10 *(978-1-4296-1769-7(1))*; 2007. lib. bdg. 29.99 *(978-1-4296-0141-2(8))* Capstone Pr., Inc. (Graphic Library).

—La Historia Atractiva del Magnetismo con Max Axiom, Supercientífico. Gianopoulos, Andrea. Strictly Spanish, LLC., tr. from ENG. 2012. (Ciencia Gráfica Ser.). (SPA.). 32p. (gr. 3-4). lib. bdg. 29.99 *(978-1-4296-9239-7(1))* Capstone Pr., Inc.

—A Journey into Adaptation with Max Axiom, Super Scientist, 1 vol. Biskup, Agnieszka & Schulz, Barbara. 2007. (Graphic Science Ser.). (ENG.). 32p. (gr. 3-4). 29.99 *(978-0-7368-6840-2(2)*, Graphic Library) Capstone Pr., Inc.

—A Journey Through the Digestive System with Max Axiom, Super Scientist, 1 vol. Sohn, Emily. 2009. (Graphic Science Ser.). (ENG.). 32p. (gr. 3-4). 29.99 *(978-1-4296-2336-0(5)*, Graphic Library) Capstone Pr., Inc.

—Sacagawea: Journey into the West, 1 vol. Gunderson, Jessica Sarah. 2006. (Graphic Biographies Ser.). (ENG.). 32p. (gr. 3-4). per. 8.10 *(978-0-7368-9663-4(5)*, Graphic Library) Capstone Pr., Inc.

—The Solid Truth about States of Matter with Max Axiom, Super Scientist, 1 vol. Biskup, Agnieszka. 2009. (Graphic Science Ser.). (ENG.). 32p. (gr. 3-4). pap. 8.10 *(978-1-4296-3451-9(0)*, Graphic Library) Capstone Pr., Inc.

—The Solid Truth about States of Matter with Max Axiom, Super Scientist. Biskup, Agnieszka. 2008. (Life Cycles Ser.). 24p. 289.10 *(978-1-4296-2451-0(5))* Capstone Pr., Inc.

—Un Viaje por la Adaptación con Max Axiom, Supercientífico. Biskup, Agnieszka & Martin, Cynthia. Schulz, Barbara. Strictly Spanish LLC. Staff, tr. 2013. (Ciencia Gráfica Ser.). (SPA & ENG.). 32p. (gr. 3-4). pap. 8.10 *(978-1-62065-977-9(8))*; lib. bdg. 29.99 *(978-1-62065-184-1(X))* Capstone Pr., Inc.

Martin, Cynthia & Timmons, Anne. Adventures in Sound with Max Axiom, Super Scientist. Sohn, Emily & Timmons, Anne. 2007. (Graphic Science Ser.). (ENG.). 32p. (gr. 3-4). 29.99 *(978-0-7368-6836-5(4)*, Graphic Library) Capstone Pr., Inc.

—Elizabeth Blackwell: America's First Woman Doctor. Robbins, Trina. 2006. (Graphic Biographies Ser.). (ENG.). 32p. (gr. 3-4). 29.99 *(978-0-7368-6497-8(0))*; per. 8.10 *(978-0-7368-9660-3(0))* Capstone Pr., Inc. (Graphic Library).

—Hedy Lamarr & a Secret Communication System, 1 vol. Robbins, Trina. 2006. (Inventions & Discovery Ser.). (ENG.). 32p. (gr. 3-4). 29.99 *(978-0-7368-6479-4(2)*, Graphic Library) Capstone Pr., Inc.

—Jane Goodall: Animal Scientist, 1 vol. Krohn, Katherine. 2006. (Graphic Biographies Ser.). (ENG.). 32p. (gr. 3-4). 29.99 *(978-0-7368-5485-6(1)*, Graphic Library) Capstone Pr., Inc.

—The Solid Truth about States of Matter with Max Axiom, Super Scientist, 1 vol. Biskup, Agnieszka. 2009. (Graphic Science Ser.). (ENG.). 32p. (gr. 3-4). lib. bdg. 29.99 *(978-1-4296-2339-1(X)*, Graphic Library) Capstone Pr., Inc.

—Wilma Rudolph: Olympic Track Star, 1 vol. Engfer, Lee. 2006. (Graphic Biographies Ser.). (ENG.). 32p. (gr. 3-4). 29.99 *(978-0-7368-5489-4(4)*, Graphic Library) Capstone Pr., Inc.

Martin, Dana. Johnstown Flood: An Up2U Historical Fiction Adventure. Mullarkey, John & Mullarkey, Lisa. 2013. (Up2U Adventures Ser.). 80p. (J). (gr. 2-5). lib. bdg. 27.07 *(978-1-61641-967-7(9)*, Calico Chapter Bks) Magic Wagon.

Martin, David Lozell. King Bartholomew & the Jesters Riddle. Mastromonaco, Pina. 2005. 32p. (J). (gr. -1-7). 15.95 *(978-0-9744307-1-3(4))* Merry Lane Pr.

Martin, David Lozell. Lucy & Bob: Brand New Readers. Martin, David Lozell. 2006. (Brand New Readers Ser.). (ENG.). 48p. (J). (gr. -1-3). pap. 5.99 *(978-0-7636-2722-5(4))* Candlewick Pr.

Martin, Dick. Play Ball. Hillert, Margaret. 2008. (Beginning-to-Read Bks.). 32p. (J). (gr. -1-3). lib. bdg. 19.93 *(978-1-59953-153-3(4))* Norwood Hse. Pr.

Martin, Don. My Day at the Zoo. Mademann Vaughan, Kathryn. 2004. (J). per. 19.95 *(978-0-9747447-1-1(9))* Chaser Media LLC.

Martin, Elizabeth B. I'm Not a Silly Goose. Martin, Elizabeth B., . ed. 2014. (ENG.). (J). 9.99 *(978-0-9910543-1-2(8))* Martin, Elizabeth B.

Martin, Fred. Condor Caper. Heimbuch, Carol Jo. 2008. 128p. pap. 11.50 *(978-1-59330-560-4(5))* Aventine Pr.

Martin, Iain C. Complete Theory Fun Factory. 2004. (ENG.). 96p. pap. 27.99 *(978-0-85162-181-4(3)*, 0851621813) Boosey & Hawkes, Inc.

—Fun Factory Violin Book. 2004. (ENG.). 32p. pap. 15.99 *(978-0-85162-183-8(X)*, 085162183X) Leonard, Hal Corp.

Martin, James R. Old King Stinky Toes. Graham, Baxter. 2005. 32p. (J). 15.95 *(978-0-9764791-0-9(9))* Drumstick Media.

Martin, Jan. Spies. Orme, David. 2010. (Fact to Fiction Grafx Ser.). 36p. pap. 7.45 *(978-0-7891-7998-2(9))* Perfection Learning Corp.

Martin, Jean-Francois. The Memory of an Elephant: An Unforgettable Journey. Strady, Sophie. 2014. (ENG.). 38p. (J). (gr. k-3). 18.99 *(978-1-4521-2903-7(7))* Chronicle Bks. LLC.

Martin, Jeannette. Kwame's Sound: An Acoustical Engineering Story. 2005. 39p. (J). per. 6.99 *(978-1-933758-02-2(3))* Engineering in Elementary.

Martin, John. Dorothea Creamer. Stiegemeyer, Julie. 2012. (Hero of Faith Ser.). (ENG.). 47p. (J). pap. 7.99 *(978-0-7586-3077-3(8))* Concordia Publishing Hse.

Martin, John F. In the Hands of the Enemy. Sheely, Robert. Killcoyne, Hope L., ed. 2003. (Adventures in America Ser.: Vol. 8). 75p. (gr. 4). 14.95 *(978-1-893110-31-1(1))* Silver Moon Pr.

—Seeking Safety. Weber, Judith Eichler. 2006. (Adventures in America Ser.). (J). *(978-1-893110-46-5(X))* Silver Moon Pr.

Martin Jourdenais, Norma Jean. The Kid's Book of Incredibly Fun Crafts. Gould, Roberta. 2004. (Williamson's Kids Can! Ser.). 128p. (J). pap. 14.95 *(978-1-885593-85-6(6)*, Williamson Bks.) Ideals Pubns.

Martin-Jourdenais, Norma Jean. 12 Easy Knitting Projects. Blanchette, Peg & Thibault, Terri. (ENG.). 64p. (J). (gr. 3-7). 2008. 12.95 *(978-0-8249-6784-0(4))*; 2006. pap. 8.95 *(978-0-8249-6785-7(2))* Ideals Pubns. (Williamson Bks.).

Martin, Joyce. The Amazing Animal ABC Book. Mock, Jean. 2005. (J). *(978-0-9767210-1-7(5))* JM2 Publishing Co.

—The Amazing Animal ABC Book the Study Guide. Mock, Jean. 2005. *(978-0-9767210-2-4(3))* JM2 Publishing Co.

Martin, Julie. Great Lakes Rhythm & Rhyme. Rodgers, Denise. 2004. 58p. (J). per. 14.95 incl. audio compact disk *(978-0-938682-81-3(4))* River Road Pubns., Inc.

—A Little Bit of Nonsense. Rodgers, Denise. (J). (gr. k-7). 16.95 *(978-0-9708382-0-9(4))* Creative Writing Pr., Inc.

Martin-Laranaga, Ana. Flap My Wings. Powell, Richard. 2003. 10p. (J). 5.95 *(978-1-58925-690-3(5))* Tiger Tales.

Martin-Larranaga, Ana. Butterfly at Home. 2007. (Butterfly Bks.). (J). bds. 5.95 *(978-1-58925-804-4(5))* Tiger Tales.

—Butterfly in the Garden. 2007. (Butterfly Bks.). (J). bds. 5.95 *(978-1-58925-803-7(7))* Tiger Tales.

—Butterfly in the Town. 2007. (Butterfly Bks.). (J). bds. 5.95 *(978-1-58925-805-1(3))* Tiger Tales.

—Butterfly on the Farm. 2007. (Butterfly Bks.). (J). bds. 5.95 *(978-1-58925-802-0(9))* Tiger Tales.

—Wag My Tail. Powell, Richard. 2003. 10p. (J). 5.95 *(978-1-58925-691-0(3))* Tiger Tales.

Martín Larrañaga, Ana. What's in the Box? Powell, Richard. 2004. (Ana's Mini Movers Ser.). 12p. (J). 5.95 *(978-1-58925-742-9(1))* Tiger Tales.

—What's in the Egg? Powell, Richard. 2004. (Ana's Mini Movers Ser.). 14p. (J). 5.95 *(978-1-58925-739-9(1))* Tiger Tales.

—Who Lives Here? Powell, Richard. 2004. (Ana's Mini Movers Ser.). 14p. (J). 5.95 *(978-1-58925-741-2(3))* Tiger Tales.

—Whose Hat Is That? Powell, Richard. 2004. (Ana's Mini Movers Ser.). 12p. (J). 5.95 *(978-1-58925-740-5(5))* Tiger Tales.

Martin, Laura & Kennedy, Seamus. The Hippity Dippity Witch. O' Byrne, Lorraine. 2012. 138p. pap. *(978-1-78176-391-9(7))* FeedARead.com.

Martin, Luanne. Must-Have Marvin! Ziglar, Christy. 2014. (Shine Bright Kids Ser.). 32p. (J). 14.99 *(978-0-8249-5657-8(5)*, Ideals Children's Bks.) Ideals Pubns.

Martin, Lyn. Busy Bees on Broadway. DeLand, M. Maitland. 2011. 32p. 15.95 *(978-1-60832-063-9(4))* Greenleaf Book Group.

Martin, M. J. Jazzmin's Jamboree. Danby, Aaron. 2005. 40p. 13.95 *(978-0-9730583-3-8(1))* Lion & Mouse Tales, Inc. CAN. Dist: Hushion Hse. Publishing, Ltd.

Martin, M. J. & Danby, Aaron. The Elusive Mr. Zee. 2004. 32p. 11.95 *(978-0-9730583-2-1(3))* Lion & Mouse Tales, Inc. CAN. Dist: Hushion Hse. Publishing, Ltd.

Martin, Marcos & Ramos, Humberto. Matters of Life & Death. 2011. (ENG.). 224p. (J). (gr. 4-17). pap., pap. 19.99 *(978-0-7851-5103-6(6))* Marvel Worldwide, Inc.

Martin, Marcos, jt. illus. see Azaceta, Paul.

Martin, McDonald. The Perfect Pet: Finding a pet that is dear to your Heart. Cantor, Don & Cantor, Michael. 2010. 30p. (J). pap. 9.95 *(978-0-9823906-6-5(1))* Wiggles Pr.

Martin, Miles J. Around the Clock: A Story about Telling Time. Jackson, Lora Z. 2011. 58p. 36.95 *(978-1-258-06483-9(9))* Literary Licensing, LLC.

Martin, Pedro. Don't Know Much about Dinosaurs. Davis, Kenneth C. 2004. (Picture Bks.: No. 7). 48p. (J). 15.99 *(978-0-06-028619-4(9))* HarperCollins Pubs.

—Don't Know Much about the Solar System. Davis, Kenneth C. 2004. (Don't Know Much About Ser.). (ENG.). 48p. (J). (gr. 1-4). pap. 6.99 *(978-0-06-446230-3(7))* HarperCollins Pubs.

—Hamster Champs. Murphy, Stuart J. 2005. (MathStart 3 Ser.). (ENG.). 40p. (J). (gr. 2). pap. 5.99 *(978-0-06-055773-7(7))* HarperCollins Pubs.

—The Presidents. Davis, Kenneth C. 2003. (Don't Know Much About Ser.). (ENG.). 64p. (J). (gr. 1-4). reprint ed. pap. 6.99 *(978-0-06-446231-0(5))* HarperCollins Pubs.

—Presidents. Davis, Kenneth C. rev. ed. 2009. (Don't Know Much About Ser.). (ENG.). 64p. (J). (gr. k-4). pap. 6.99 *(978-0-06-171823-6(8)*, Collins) HarperCollins Pubs.

Martin, Peter. The Short March to Wisdom. Yung Dong, Venerable & Jacobs, Marjorie. 2015. 64p. (J). pap. 0.00 ***(978-1-943211-00-5(0))*** Fo Guang Shan International Translation Ctr.

Martin, Richard. Black Beauty: And a Discussion of Kindness. Sewell, Anna. 2003. (Values in Action Illustrated Classics Ser.). 191p. (J). *(978-1-59203-028-6(9))* Learning Challenge, Inc.

Martin, Shawn. Peter's Christmas Eve Adventure, 1 vol. Organ, Betty. 2010. (ENG.). 32p. (J). (gr. k-3). 10.95 *(978-1-897174-68-5(3)*, Tuckamore Bks) Creative Bk. Publishing CAN. Dist: Orca Bk. Pubs. USA.

Martin, Sherry. Welcome Home, Indigeaux: A Louisiana Adventure. Woods, Wendy. 2013. (ENG.). (J). (gr. -1-3). 14.95 *(978-1-62086-246-9(8))* Mascot Bks., Inc.

Martin, Stephanie. The Red Caterpillar on College Street. Cooper, Afua. Date not set. 400p. (J). (gr. -1-3). pap. *(978-0-920813-87-4(9))* Sister Vision Pr.

Martin, Stuart. Changing Picture Bible Stories, 1 vol. Dowley, Tim. 2004. 14p. (J). 11.99 *(978-0-8254-7279-4(2)*, Candle Bks.) Lion Hudson PLC GBR. Dist: Kregel Pubns.

—Fly Away Home. Edgecombe, Jane. 2003. (J). 15.95 *(978-1-74047-152-7(0))* Book Co. Publishing Pty, Ltd., The AUS. Dist: Penton Overseas, Inc.

—Noah's Ark Pop-Up. Dowley, Tim. 2007. 6p. (J). bds. 14.99 *(978-0-8254-7330-2(6)*, Candle Bks.) Lion Hudson PLC GBR. Dist: Kregel Pubns.

—Puddle Pen Bible Stories, 1 vol. David, Juliet. 2010. (Candle Puddle Pen Ser.). 10p. (J). (gr. -1). bds. 12.99 *(978-0-8254-7394-4(2)*, Candle Bks.) Lion Hudson PLC GBR. Dist: Kregel Pubns.

Martin, Susan. Doug E Do. Tuey. 2006. 76p. pap. 16.95 *(978-1-4241-0295-2(2))* PublishAmerica, Inc.

Martin, W. Lyon. Rabbit's Song. Tucker, S. J. & Herring, Trudy. 2009. (ENG.). 32p. (J). lib. bdg. 16.95 *(978-0-9796834-7-3(5)*, Magical Child Bks.) Shades of White.

Martin, W. Lyon. Aidan's First Full Moon Circle: A Magical Child Story. Martin, W. Lyon. 2008. 32p. (J). (gr. -1-1). lib. bdg. 16.95 *(978-0-9796834-4-2(0))* Shades of White.

—An Ordinary Girl, A Magical Child. Martin, W. Lyon. 2008. (ENG.). 48p. (J). lib. bdg. 16.95 *(978-0-9796834-3-5(2)*, Magical Child Bks.) Shades of White.

Martin, Whitney. Cory's Stories: A Kid's Book about Living with ADHD. Kraus, Jeanne. 2004. 32p. (J). 14.95 *(978-1-59147-148-6(6))*; pap. 9.95 *(978-1-59147-154-7(0))* American Psychological Assn. (Magination Pr.).

—Finding the Right Spot: When Kids Can't Live with Their Parents. Levy, Janice. 2004. 48p. (J). 14.95 *(978-1-59147-073-1(0))*; pap. 9.95 *(978-1-59147-074-8(9))* American Psychological Assn. (Magination Pr.).

—Ginny Morris & Dads New Girlfriend. Gallagher, Mary Collins. 2006. (Ginny Morris Ser.). 63p. (J). (gr. 3-7). 14.95 *(978-1-59147-386-2(1))*; per. 9.95 *(978-1-59147-387-9(X))* American Psychological Assn. (Magination Pr.).

—Nine Is Not an Even Number. Gallagher, Mary Collins. 2005. 48p. (J). 14.95 *(978-1-59147-157-8(5))*; pap. 9.95 *(978-1-59147-158-5(3))* American Psychological Assn. (Magination Pr.).

—Pumpkin Hill. Spurr, Elizabeth. 2006. (ENG.). 32p. (J). (gr. -1-3). 16.95 *(978-0-8234-1869-5(3))* Holiday Hse., Inc.

—An Undone Fairy Tale. Lendler, Ian. 2005. (ENG.). 32p. (J). (gr. 1-5). 17.99 *(978-0-689-86677-7(1)*, Simon & Schuster Bks. For Young Readers) Simon & Schuster Bks. For Young Readers.

Martines, Donna. My ABCs: An ABC Book for Any Age. Spray, Michelle. Pasternack, Susan, ed. I.t. ed. 2006. 64p. (J). per. 8.95 *(978-0-9714160-4-8(4))* Bk. Shelf.

Martinez, Alitha, et al. Iron Man by Joe Quesada. Quesada, Joe & Tieri, Frank. 2013. (ENG.). 232p. (J). (gr. 4-17). pap. 24.99 *(978-0-7851-6736-5(6))* Marvel Worldwide, Inc.

Martinez, Alitha. The Quest for Dragon Mountain. Mayhall, Robin. 16th rev. ed. 2010. (Twisted Journeys (r) Ser.: 16). (ENG.). (J). (gr. 4-7). pap. 45.32 *(978-0-7613-6999-8(6))* Lerner Publishing Group.

Martinez, Alitha E. Kung Fu Masters. Tsang, Evonne. 2009. (Twisted Journeys (r) Ser.: 12). (ENG.). 112p. (J). (gr. 4-7). pap. 7.95 *(978-0-8225-8880-1(3))*; No. 12. 27.93 *(978-0-8225-8878-8(1)*, Graphic Universe) Lerner Publishing Group.

—My Boyfriend Bites, 3 vols., No. 3. Jolley, Dan. 2011. (My Boyfriend Is a Monster Ser.: 3). (ENG.). 128p. (YA). (gr. 7-12). 29.27 *(978-0-7613-5599-1(5))* Lerner Publishing Group.

—My Boyfriend Is a Monster - My Boyfriend Bites. Jolley, Dan. 2011. (My Boyfriend Is a Monster Ser.: 3). (ENG.). 128p. (YA). (gr. 7-12). pap. 9.95 *(978-0-7613-7078-9(1)*, Graphic Universe) Lerner Publishing Group.

—The Quest for Dragon Mountain. Mayhall, Robin. 2010. (Twisted Journeys (r) Ser.: 16). (ENG.). 112p. (J). (gr. 4-7). pap. 7.95 *(978-0-8225-9267-9(3)*, Graphic Universe); lib. bdg. 27.93 *(978-0-8225-9261-7(4))* Lerner Publishing Group.

Martínez, Andrés Vera. Babe Ruth. Delsante, Vito. 2009. (Before They Were Famous Ser.). (ENG.). 128p. (J). (gr. 3-7). pap. 8.99 *(978-1-4169-5071-4(0)*, Simon & Schuster/Paula Wiseman Bks.) Simon & Schuster/Paula Wiseman Bks.

Martinez, Andres Vera. Little White Duck: A Childhood in China. Martinez, Andres Vera. Liu, Na. 2012. (Single Titles Ser.). (ENG.). 108p. (gr. 4-7). pap. 9.95 *(978-0-7613-8115-0(5)*, Graphic Universe) Lerner Publishing Group.

Martínez, Andrés Vera. Little White Duck: A Childhood in China. Martínez, Andrés Vera. Liu, Na. 2012. (Single Titles Ser.). (ENG.). 108p. (gr. 4-7). lib. bdg. 29.27 *(978-0-7613-6587-7(7)*, Graphic Universe) Lerner Publishing Group.

Martinez, Andrew, photos by. The Pier at the End of the World, 1 vol. Erickson, Paul. 2014. (ENG., 32p. (J). 16.95 *(978-0-88448-382-3(7))* Tilbury Hse. Pubs.

Martinez, April. Toto's Tale. Hays, K. D. & Weidman, Meg. 2010. 248p. (J). pap. 14.99 *(978-1-936144-61-7(1)*, Zumaya Thresholds) Zumaya Pubns. LLC.

Martinez, Edward. Farmers Market. Parks, Carmen. ed. 2003. (Green Light Readers Level 2 Ser.). (ENG.). 24p. (J). (gr. -1-3). pap. 3.95 *(978-0-15-204841-9(3))* Houghton Mifflin Harcourt Publishing Co.

—Farmers Market/Dia de Mercado. Parks, Carmen. Flor Ada, Alma & Campoy, F. Isabel, trs. from ENG. 2010. (Green Light Readers Level 2 Ser.). (SPA & ENG.). 28p. (J). (gr. -1-3). pap. 3.99 *(978-0-547-36900-6(X))* Houghton Mifflin Harcourt Publishing Co.

—Tomás Rivera. Medina, Jane. 2004. (Green Light Readers Level 2 Ser.). (ENG.). 24p. (J). (gr. -1-3). pap. 3.95 *(978-0-15-205145-7(7))* Houghton Mifflin Harcourt Publishing Co.

Martinez, Enrique. Un Cambio de Piel. Remolina, Tere. (Barril Sin Fondo Ser.). (SPA.). (J). (gr. 3-5). pap. *(978-968-6465-20-4(0))* Casa de Estudios de Literatura y Talleres Artisticos Amaquemecan A.C. MEX. Dist: Lectorum Pubns., Inc.

—Danny Said Boobie. Pi Andreu, Andrés. 2011. (ENG.). 24p. pap. 15.00 *(978-1-4679-0668-5(9))* CreateSpace Independent Publishing Platform.

—El Deseo de Aurelio. Martínez, Rafael. 2006. (la Orilla del Viento Ser.). (SPA.). 48p. (J). (gr. 8-10). pap. *(978-968-16-7988-0(1))* Fondo de Cultura Economica.

—Lottery of Riddles. Lome, Emilio Angel. 2011. 46p. (gr. 2-5). pap. 6.95 *(978-968-19-0663-4(2))* Aguilar, Altea, Taurus, Alfaguara, S.A. de C.V MEX. Dist: Santillana USA Publishing Co., Inc.

—Los Pelusos, Cuentos Policiacos. Diaz, Enrique Perez. 2003. (SPA.). 95p. (J). (gr. 3-5). pap. 8.95 *(978-968-19-1018-1(4))* Santillana USA Publishing Co., Inc.

—Solo para Muchachos. Boullosa, Carmen. 2003. (SPA.). 60p. (J). (gr. 4-7). 11.95 *(978-968-19-0325-1(0))* Aguilar, Altea, Taurus, Alfaguara, S.A. de C.V MEX. Dist: Santillana USA Publishing Co., Inc.

Martinez, Enrique & Graullera, Fabiola. Del Otro Lado de los Suenos. Alberto, Eliseo. 2003. (SPA.). 32p. (J). (gr. k-3). 12.95 *(978-968-19-0473-9(7))* Aguilar, Altea, Taurus, Alfaguara, S.A. de C.V MEX. Dist: Santillana USA Publishing Co., Inc.

—Jose Marti: Cuatro cuentos Infantiles. Marti, Jose. (SPA.). 28p. (J). (gr. 3-5). 9.95 *(978-970-29-0522-6(2))* Santillana, Editorial, S.A. de C.V. MEX. Dist: Santillana USA Publishing Co., Inc.

—El Pais de las Sombras. Alvarez, Leticia Herrera. 2003. (SPA.). 48p. (J). (gr. 3-5). pap. 7.95 *(978-968-19-0535-4(0))* Santillana USA Publishing Co., Inc.

Martinez, Gayle Denise. Lean on Me, Lee. Valdez, Joseph G. 2012. 24p. pap. *(978-1-77067-670-1(8))* FriesenPress.

Martinez, Gil. La Princesa de Largos Cabellos. Van Haeringen, Annemarie. De Sterck, Goedele, tr. 2007. (Los Especiales de A la Orilla del Viento Ser.). (SPA.). 27p. (J). *(978-968-16-8471-6(0))* Fondo de Cultura Economica.

Martinez, Heather. The Big Halloween Scare. Banks, Steven. 2003. (SpongeBob SquarePants Ser.: Vol. 1). (ENG.). 32p. (J). (gr. k-2). pap. 3.99 *(978-0-689-84196-5(5)*, Simon Spotlight/Nickelodeon) Simon Spotlight/Nickelodeon.

—Camp Spongebob. Reisner, Molly & Ostrow, Kim. 2005. (Spongebob Squarepants Ser.). 32p. (gr. k-2). 14.00 *(978-0-7569-5424-6(X))* Perfection Learning Corp.

—Christmas with Krabby Klaws. David, Erica. 2010. (SpongeBob SquarePants Ser.). (ENG.). 16p. (J). pap. 5.99 *(978-1-4424-0805-0(7)*, Simon Spotlight/Nickelodeon) Simon Spotlight/Nickelodeon.

—Happy Birthday, SpongeBob! Chanda, J-P. 2005. (SpongeBob SquarePants Ser.). (ENG.). 24p. (J). pap. 3.99 *(978-0-689-87674-5(2)*, Simon Spotlight/Nickelodeon) Simon Spotlight/Nickelodeon.

—Ice-Cream Dreams. Krulik, Nancy. 2004. 22p. (J). lib. bdg. 15.00 *(978-1-4242-0975-0(7))* Fitzgerald Bks.

—Ice-Cream Dreams. 2004. (SpongeBob SquarePants Ser.). (ENG.). 24p. (J). pap. 3.99 *(978-0-689-86861-0(8)*, Simon Spotlight/Nickelodeon) Simon Spotlight/Nickelodeon.

—New Student Starfish. Miglis, Jenny. 2003. (SpongeBob SquarePants Ser.). (ENG.). 64p. (J). pap. 3.99 *(978-0-689-86164-2(8)*, Simon Spotlight/Nickelodeon) Simon Spotlight/Nickelodeon.

—Plankton's Christmas Surprise! (SpongeBob SquarePants) Random House. 2013. (Pictureback with Flaps Ser.). (ENG.). 16p. (J). (gr. -1-2). 4.99 *(978-0-449-81851-0(9)*, Random Hse. Bks. for Young Readers) Random Hse. Children's Bks.

—Shiver Me Timbers! Golden Books Staff. 2003. (Glow-In-the-Dark Sticker Book Ser.). (ENG.). 32p. (J). (gr. -1-2). pap. 3.99 *(978-0-307-10470-0(2)*, 14596695, Golden Bks.) Random Hse. Children's Bks.

—Sponge in Space! (SpongeBob SquarePants) Golden Books Staff. 2012. (Little Golden Book Ser.). (ENG.). 24p. (J). (gr. k-k). 3.99 *(978-0-307-92990-7(6)*, Golden Bks.) Random Hse., Inc.

—SpongeBob Airpants: The Lost Episode. Richards, Kitty. 2003. (SpongeBob SquarePants Ser.). (ENG.). 64p. (J). pap. 3.99 *(978-0-689-86163-5(X)*, Simon Spotlight/Nickelodeon) Simon Spotlight/Nickelodeon.

—SpongeBob Rocks! Chipponeri, Kelli. 2006. (SpongeBob SquarePants Ser.: 9). (ENG.). 32p. (J). (gr. -1-3). pap. 3.99 *(978-1-4169-1314-6(9)*, Simon Spotlight/Nickelodeon) Simon Spotlight/Nickelodeon.

Martinez, Heather. Star Wars: the Phantom Menace (Star Wars) Carbone, Courtney. 2015. (Little Golden Book Ser.). (ENG.). 24p. (J). (-k). 4.99 ***(978-0-7364-3542-0(5)***, Golden Bks.) Random Hse. Children's Bks.

Martinez, Heather. Top of the Class! Killeen, James. 2011. (Little Golden Book Ser.). (ENG.). 24p. (J). (gr. -1-2). 3.99 *(978-0-375-86568-8(3)*, Golden Bks.) Random Hse. Children's Bks.

—Where the Pirates Arrgh! (SpongeBob SquarePants) Wygand, Melissa. 2013. (Little Golden Book Ser.). (ENG.). 24p. (J). (-k). 3.99 *(978-0-307-98174-5(6)*, Golden Bks.) Random Hse. Children's Bks.

Martinez, Ivanova. Celebra el Halloween y el Dia de Muertos con Cristina y Su Conejito Azul. Flor Ada, Alma. 2006. (Cuentos para Celebrar / Stories to Celebrate Ser.). (SPA.). 30p. (gr. k-6). per. 11.95 *(978-1-59820-120-8(4)*, Alfaguara) Santillana USA Publishing Co., Inc.

—Celebrate Halloween & the Day of the Dead with Cristina & Her Blue Bunny. Flor Ada, Alma. 2006. (Cuentos para Celebrar / Stories to Celebrate Ser.). 30p. (gr. k-6). per. 11.95 *(978-1-59820-132-1(8))* Santillana USA Publishing Co., Inc.

Martinez, J-P Loppo. Dody the Dog Has a Rainbow. Derrick, Patricia. 2007. 32p. 18.95 incl. audio compact disk *(978-1-933818-10-8(7))* Animalations.

—Farley the Ferret of Farkleberry Farm. Derrick, Patricia. 2007. 32p. (J). (gr. -1-3). 18.95 incl. audio compact disk *(978-1-933818-12-2(3))* Animalations.

—Montgomery the Moose Can Shake His Caboose. Derrick, Patricia & Sibbett, Joyce. 2007. 32p. (J). (gr. -1). 18.95 incl. audio compact disk *(978-1-933818-18-4(2))* Animalations.

—Mr. Walrus & the Old School Bus. Derrick, Patricia. 2007. 32p. 18.95 incl. audio compact disk *(978-1-933818-13-9(1))* Animalations.

—Rathbone the Rat. Derrick, Patricia & O'Neil, Shirley. 2007. 32p. (J). (gr. -1-3). 18.95 incl. audio compact disk *(978-1-933818-17-7(4))* Animalations.

—Rickity & Snickity at the Balloon Fiesta. Derrick, Patricia. 2007. 32p. (J). (gr. -1-3). 18.95 incl. audio compact disk *(978-1-933818-11-5(5))* Animalations.

—Riley the Rhinoceros. Derrick, Patricia. 2007. 32p. (J). 18.95 incl. audio compact disk *(978-1-933818-15-3(8))* Animalations.

—Sly the Dragonfly. Derrick, Patricia. 2007. 32p. (J). (gr. -1-3). 18.95 incl. audio compact disk *(978-1-933818-16-0(6))* Animalations.

Martinez, Jorge. Androcles & the Lion. Sommer, Carl. 2014. (Sommer-Time Story Classics Ser.). (ENG.). 32p. (J). (gr. k-4). 16.95 *(978-1-57537-075-0(1))* Advance Publishing, Inc.

Martínez, Jorge, et al. Dare to Dream! Sommer, Carl. 2007. (Another Sommer-Time Story Ser.). (ENG.). 48p. (J). 23.95 incl. audio compact disk *(978-1-57537-723-0(3))*; (gr. -1-3). 9.95 *(978-1-57537-024-8(7))*; (gr. -1-3). 16.95 incl. audio compact disk *(978-1-57537-523-6(0))*; (gr. k-4). lib. bdg. 16.95 *(978-1-57537-073-6(5))* Advance Publishing, Inc.

Martinez, Jorge, et al. Dare to Dream! Sommer, Carl. 2014. (J). pap. ***(978-1-57537-951-7(1))*** Advance Publishing, Inc.

Martínez, Jorge, et al. Dare to Dream! ¡Atrévete a Soñar! Sommer, Carl. ed. 2009. 48p. (J). 26.95 incl. audio compact disk *(978-1-57537-176-4(6))* Advance Publishing, Inc.

—Dream. Sommer, Carl. 2009. (Quest for Success Ser.). (ENG.). 56p. (YA). pap. 4.95 *(978-1-57537-276-1(2))*; lib. bdg. 12.95 *(978-1-57537-251-8(7))* Advance Publishing, Inc.

—Dream (Sueña) Sommer, Carl. ed. 2009. (Quest for Success Bilingual Ser.). (SPA & ENG.). 104p. (YA). (gr. 6-18). lib. bdg. 14.95 *(978-1-57537-226-6(6))* Advance Publishing, Inc.

Martinez, Jorge. The Emperor & the Seed. Sommer, Carl. 2016. (J). ***(978-1-57537-946-3(5))*** Advance Publishing, Inc.

Martínez, Jorge. The Richest Poor Kid. Sommer, Carl. 2007. (Another Sommer-Time Story Ser.). (ENG.). 48p. (J). 23.95 incl. audio compact disk *(978-1-57537-724-7(1))*; (gr. -1-3). 9.95 *(978-1-57537-025-5(5))*; (gr. -1-3). 16.95 incl. audio compact disk *(978-1-57537-524-3(9))*; (gr. k-4). 16.95 *(978-1-57537-074-3(3))* Advance Publishing, Inc.

Martinez, Jorge. The Richest Poor Kid. Sommer, Carl. 2014. (J). pap. ***(978-1-57537-965-4(1))*** Advance Publishing, Inc.

—The Ugly Princess. Sommer, Carl. 2016. (J). ***(978-1-57537-948-7(1))*** Advance Publishing, Inc.

Martinez, Leovigildo. The Twenty-Five Mixtec Cats. Gollub, Matthew. 2004. (J). 32p. pap. 6.95 *(978-1-889910-29-1(5))*; *(978-1-889910-30-7(9))* Tortuga Pr.

—The Twenty-five Mixtec Cats. Gollub, Matthew W. rev. ed. 2004. 32p. (J). 15.95 *(978-1-889910-28-4(7))* Tortuga Pr.

—Uncle Snake. Gollub, Matthew. 2004. (J). *(978-1-889910-31-4(7))*; pap. *(978-1-889910-32-1(5))* Tortuga Pr.

Martinez, Michael. Nobody Likes Me: What Am I Doing Wrong? Williams, Justine. 2013. 20p. pap. 10.95 *(978-1-62212-778-8(1)*, Strategic Bk. Publishing) Strategic Book Publishing & Rights Agency (SBPRA).

Martinez, Miguel Fernandez. Uncle Scrooge, No. 365. Laban, Terry et al. Clark, John, ed. 2006. (Walt Disney's Uncle Scrooge Ser.). 64p. pap. 6.95 *(978-1-888472-25-7(1))* Gemstone Publishing, Inc.

Martinez, Natali. Nerdel's ABC Book. Kesselman, Robin & Kesselman, Marc. 2009. 38p. (J). 16.99 *(978-0-9823357-2-7(5))* Nerdel Co., The.

Martinez-Neal, Juana. Lellie the Different Elephant. Garza, Lois Ann. 2011. 36p. pap. 11.95 *(978-1-60047-592-4(2))* Wasteland Pr.

Martinez-Neal, Juana. La Madre Goose: Nursery Rhymes for Niños. Elya, Susan Middleton. 2016. (J). ***(978-0-399-25157-3(X)***, Putnam Adult) Penguin Publishing Group.

Martinez-Neal, Juana. The Messy One, 1 vol. Jones, Christianne C. (Little Boost Ser.). (ENG.). 32p. (gr. k-3). 2012. 7.95 *(978-1-4048-7417-6(8))*; 2011. lib. bdg. 22.65 *(978-1-4048-6651-5(5)*, Little Boost) Picture Window Bks.

Martinez Ricci, Andres. Electricity Is Everywhere CD+Book. Higgins, Nadia. 2010. (Science Rocks! Set 2 CD+Book Ser.). 32p. lib. bdg. 54.14 incl. cd-rom *(978-1-60270-991-1(2))* ABDO Publishing Co.

—Electricity Is Everywhere Site CD+Book. Higgins, Nadia. 2010. (Science Rocks! Set 2 Site CD+Book Ser.). 32p. lib. bdg. 84.14 incl. cd-rom *(978-1-61641-008-7(6))* ABDO Publishing Co.

—Excited about Energy CD+Book. Higgins, Nadia. 2010. (Science Rocks! Set 2 CD+Book Ser.). 32p. lib. bdg. 54.14 incl. cd-rom *(978-1-60270-992-8(0))* ABDO Publishing Co.

—Excited about Energy Site CD+Book. Higgins, Nadia. 2010. (Science Rocks! Set 2 Site CD+Book Ser.). 32p. lib. bdg. 84.14 incl. cd-rom *(978-1-61641-009-4(4))* ABDO Publishing Co.

—Marvelous Motion CD+Book. Higgins, Nadia. 2010. (Science Rocks! Set 2 CD+Book Ser.). 32p. lib. bdg. 54.14 incl. cd-rom *(978-1-60270-993-5(9))* ABDO Publishing Co.

—Marvelous Motion Site CD+Book. Higgins, Nadia. 2010. (Science Rocks! Set 2 Site CD+Book Ser.). 32p. lib. bdg. 84.14 incl. cd-rom *(978-1-61641-010-0(8))* ABDO Publishing Co.

—Mighty Magnet CD+Book. Higgins, Nadia. 2010. (Science Rocks! Set 2 CD+Book Ser.). 32p. lib. bdg. 54.14 incl. cd-rom *(978-1-60270-994-2(7))* ABDO Publishing Co.

—Mighty Magnet Site CD+Book. Higgins, Nadia. 2010. (Science Rocks! Set 2 Site CD+Book Ser.). 32p. lib. bdg. 84.14 incl. cd-rom *(978-1-61641-011-7(6))* ABDO Publishing Co.

—Stupendous Sound CD+Book. Higgins, Nadia. 2010. (Science Rocks! Set 2 CD+Book Ser.). 32p. lib. bdg. 54.14 incl. cd-rom *(978-1-60270-995-9(5))* ABDO Publishing Co.

—Stupendous Sound Site CD+Book. Higgins, Nadia. 2010. (Science Rocks! Set 2 Site CD+Book Ser.). 32p. lib. bdg. 84.14 incl. cd-rom *(978-1-61641-012-4(4))* ABDO Publishing Co.

—Super Shadows CD+Book. Higgins, Nadia. 2010. (Science Rocks! Set 2 CD+Book Ser.). 32p. lib. bdg. 54.14 incl. cd-rom *(978-1-60270-996-6(3))* ABDO Publishing Co.

—Super Shadows Site CD+Book. Higgins, Nadia. 2010. (Science Rocks! Set 2 Site CD+Book Ser.). 32p. lib. bdg. 84.14 incl. cd-rom *(978-1-61641-013-1(2))* ABDO Publishing Co.

Martinez, Rocio. The Fox & the Crow. 2007. (First Reading Level 1 Ser.). 32p. (J). (gr. -1-3). 8.99 *(978-0-7945-1813-4(3)*, Usborne) EDC Publishing.

—Las Adventuras de Pepe. Ballesteros, Jose Manuel & Manuel, Ballesteros Pastor José. (SPA.). 156p. (J). *(978-84-392-8118-4(8))* Gaviota Ediciones ESP. Dist: Lectorum Pubns., Inc.

—Por Qué? Munrriz, Mercedes & Munárriz Guezala, Mercedes. 2003. (SPA.). 16p. (J). *(978-84-667-2627-6(6))* Grupo Anaya, S.A. ESP. Dist: Lectorum Pubns., Inc.

—La Princesa Que No Sabia Estornudar. Canas, José & José, Cañas Torregrosa. (Leer Es Vivir Serie Teatro).Tr. of Princess Who Couldn't Sneeze. (SPA.). 48p. (J). 5.56 *(978-84-241-7716-4(9))* Everest Editora ESP. Dist: Lectorum Pubns., Inc.

—Qué Es? Munrriz, Mercedes & Munárriz Guezala, Mercedes. 2003. (SPA.). 16p. (J). *(978-84-667-2626-9(8))* Grupo Anaya, S.A. ESP. Dist: Lectorum Pubns., Inc.

Martinez, Rosemary. The Twin Kangaroo Treasure Hunt, a Gay Parenting Story. Martinez Jover, Carmen. 2013. 32p. pap. *(978-607-00-6545-3(X))* Martínez Jover, María del Carmen Dorotea.

Martinez, Sergio. Best of All. Lucado, Max. 2003. (Max Lucado's Wemmicks Ser.: 4). 32p. (J). 16.99 *(978-1-58134-501-8(1))* Crossway.

—Christmas Carols for a Kid's Heart, Vol. 3. Eareckson Tada, Joni & Wolgemuth, Bobbie. 2004. (Hymns for a Kid's Heart Ser.: 3). 96p. (J). 21.99 incl. audio compact disk *(978-1-58134-626-8(3))* Crossway.

—From Colonies to Country with George Washington. Hedstrom-Page, Deborah. 2007. (My American Journey Ser.). 82p. (J). (gr. 3-9). 9.99 *(978-0-8054-3265-7(5))* B&H Publishing Group.

—From Log Cabin to White House with Abraham Lincoln. Hedstrom-Page, Deborah. 2007. (My American Journey Ser.). 82p. (J). (gr. 3-9). 9.99 *(978-0-8054-3269-5(8))* B&H Publishing Group.

—From Settlement to City with Benjamin Franklin. Hedstrom-Page, Deborah. 2007. (My American Journey Ser.). 84p. (J). (gr. 3-9). 9.99 *(978-0-8054-3267-1(1))* B&H Publishing Group.

—From Slavery to Freedom with Harriet Tubman. Hedstrom-Page, Deborah. 2007. (My American Journey Ser.). 84p. (J). (gr. 3-9). 9.99 *(978-0-8054-3268-8(X))* B&H Publishing Group.

—The Prayer of Jabez for Young Hearts. Wilkinson, Bruce & Suggs, Robb. 2004. 32p. (J). (gr. -1-3). 15.99 *(978-0-8499-7932-3(3))* Nelson, Thomas Inc.

—Punchinello & the Most Marvelous Gift. Lucado, Max. 2004. (Max Lucado's Wemmicks Ser.: 5). 32p. (J). 15.99 *(978-1-58134-546-9(1))*; 2003. 28p. bds. 6.99 *(978-1-58134-562-9(3))* Crossway.

—Punchinello & the Most Marvelous Gift: And, Your Special Gift. Lucado, Max. 2007. (J). *(978-1-58134-877-4(0))* Crossway.

—You Are Mine. Lucado, Max. import ed. 2005. 28p. bds. *(978-1-85985-546-1(6)*, Candle Bks.) Lion Hudson PLC.

—You Are Special. Lucado, Max. rev. ed. 2007. 32p. (J). (gr. -1-3). 19.99 *(978-1-58134-894-1(0))* Crossway.

Martinez, Sonia. Meet Mary MacKillop. Murphy, Sally. (Meet... Ser.). (ENG.). (J). 2014. 36p. (gr. k). 13.99 *(978-1-74275-722-3(7))*; 2013. 32p. (gr. -1). 18.99 *(978-1-74275-721-6(9))* Random Hse. Australia AUS. Dist: Independent Pubs. Group.

Martinez, Tito. Mariana y el Albiqueno. Lantigua, Yanette. 2015. 24p. (J). (gr. -1-2). pap. 12.95 ***(978-9942-05-249-0(6)***, Alfaguara Infantil) Santillana Ecuador ECU. Dist: Santillana USA Publishing Co., Inc.

Martinez y Luis San Vicente, Enrique. Cuentos de Todo y de Nada. Sastrias, Marta. 2003. (SPA.). 82p. (J). (gr. 3-5). *(978-968-19-0551-4(2))* Aguilar, Altea, Taurus, Alfaguara, S.A. de C.V.

Martini, Angela. Ballerina Weather Girl. Stout, Shawn K. 2013. (Not-So-Ordinary Girl Ser.: 1). (ENG.). 192p. (J). (gr. 1-5). 15.99 *(978-1-4424-7402-4(5))*; pap. 5.99 *(978-1-4424-7401-7(7))* Simon & Schuster/Paula Wiseman Bks. (Simon & Schuster/Paula Wiseman Bks.).

—Best Friends Forever! Golosi, Rosanne. 2005. 64p. (J). *(978-0-439-80072-3(2))* Scholastic, Inc.

—Fiona Finkelstein, Big-Time Ballerina!! Stout, Shawn K. 2010. (ENG.). 192p. (J). pap. 4.99 *(978-1-4169-7109-2(2)*, Simon & Schuster/Paula Wiseman Bks.) Simon & Schuster/Paula Wiseman Bks.

—Fiona Finkelstein Meets Her Match!! Stout, Shawn K. 2010. (ENG.). 160p. (J). (gr. 1-5). 14.99 *(978-1-4169-7928-9(X)*, Simon & Schuster/Paula Wiseman Bks.) Simon & Schuster/Paula Wiseman Bks.

—I Heard a Rumor. Krulik, Nancy. 2007. (How I Survived Middle School Ser.: No. 3). 105p. (J). *(978-0-439-90091-1(3))* Scholastic, Inc.

—Miss Matched. Stout, Shawn K. 2013. (Not-So-Ordinary Girl Ser.: 2). (ENG.). (J). (gr. 1-5). 160p. 15.99 *(978-1-4424-7405-5(X))*; 176p. pap. 5.99 *(978-1-4424-7404-8(1))* Simon & Schuster/Paula Wiseman Bks. (Simon & Schuster/Paula Wiseman Bks.).

—Oops! I Did It (Again)! Wasserman, Robin. 2003. 96p. (J). *(978-0-439-55608-8(2))* Scholastic, Inc.

—Perfect World: I Was Soooo Embarrassed! Bligh, Deirdre. 2005. 62p. (J). *(978-0-439-80069-3(2))* Scholastic, Inc.

—A Smart Girl's Guide to Friendship Troubles: Dealing with Fights, Being Left Out & the Whole Popularity Thing. Criswell, Patti Kelley. 2003. (ENG.). 88p. pap. 9.95 *(978-1-58485-711-2(0))* American Girl Publishing, Inc.

—A Smart Girl's Guide to Parties: How to Be a Great Guest, Be a Happy Hostess, & Have Fun at Any Party. Lundsten, Apryl. Anton, Carrie, ed. 2010. (ENG.). 96p. (J). (gr. 4-7). pap. 9.95 *(978-1-59369-645-0(0))* American Girl Publishing, Inc.

—Stand up for Yourself & Your Friends: Dealing with Bullies & Bossiness, & Finding a Better Way. Criswell, Patti Kelley. 2009. (ENG.). 64p. (YA). (gr. 3-18). pap. 9.95 *(978-1-59369-482-1(2)*, American Girl) American Girl Publishing, Inc.

—Stand up for Yourself Journal: Quizzes & Questions to Help You Stand Strong Against Bullying. Falligant, Erin & American Girl Editors, eds. 2011. (ENG.). 64p. (J). spiral bd. 9.95 *(978-1-59369-910-9(7))* American Girl Publishing, Inc.

Martiniere, Stephan. Robonocchio. Lofficier, Randy & Lofficier, Jean-Marc. Pijuán Aragón, Miren, tr. 2004. (SPA.). 128p. (YA). per. 14.95 *(978-1-932983-25-8(2)*, Black Coat Pr.) HollywoodComics.com, LLC.

—Robonocchio. Lofficier, Randy & Lofficier, Jean-Marc. 2004. (FRE.). 128p. (YA). per. 14.95 *(978-1-932983-04-3(X)*, Black Coat Pr.) HollywoodComics.com, LLC.

Martino, Anita. Free to Be Gluten Free! Spergel, Heather. 2013. (ENG.). 48p. (J). 19.99 *(978-1-938501-18-0(7))* Turn the Page Publishing.

Martins, Ann-Kathrin & Fowler, Romana. I Don't Want to Be Grumpy Anymore! Fowler, Leona. 2011. 19p. (J). 12.95 *(978-1-58909-804-6(8))* Bookstand Publishing.

Martinsen, Sarah. Charlie & the Blanket Toss. Brown, Tricia. (ENG.). 32p. (J). 2015. pap. 10.99 ***(978-1-941821-66-4(9))***; 2014. 16.99 *(978-1-941821-07-7(3))* Graphic Arts Ctr. Publishing Co. (Alaska Northwest Bks.).

Martirosian, Patty Ann, et al. Early Modern Times Bk. 3: From Elizabeth the First to the Forty-Niners. Bauer, Susan Wise. 2004. (Story of the World Ser.: Vol. 3). (ENG.). 412p. pap., act. bk. ed. 36.95 *(978-0-9728603-2-1(0)*, 86032) Peace Hill Pr.

—Early Modern Times Vol. 3: From Elizabeth the First to the Forty-Niners. Bauer, Susan Wise. 2004. (Story of the World Ser.: 0). (ENG.). 432p. 21.95 *(978-0-9728603-0-7(4)*, 86030) Peace Hill Pr.

Marton, Jirina. Arctic Adventures: Tales from the Lives of Inuit Artists, 1 vol. Rivera, Raquel. 2007. (ENG.). 48p. (J). (gr. 2-18). 18.95 *(978-0-88899-714-2(0))* Groundwood Bks. CAN. Dist: Perseus-PGW.

—Fergie Tries to Fly. Cocks, Nancy. 2003. 16p. pap. *(978-2-89507-275-1(2))* Novalis Publishing.

—Marja's Skis, 1 vol. Pendziwol, Jean E. 2007. (ENG.). 32p. (J). (gr. -1-3). 17.95 *(978-0-88899-674-9(8))* Groundwood Bks. CAN. Dist: Perseus-PGW.

—Where, Oh Where, Is Fergie? Cocks, Nancy. 2003. 16p. pap. *(978-2-89507-273-7(6))* Novalis Publishing.

—You Can Count on Fergie. Cocks, Nancy. 2003. 16p. pap. *(978-2-89507-272-0(8))* Novalis Publishing.

Martorell, Antonio. Island Treasures: Growing up in Cuba: Includes Where the Flame Trees Bloom, under the Royal Palms, & Five Brand New Stories. Ada, Alma Flora. 2015. (ENG.). 240p. (J). (gr. 3-7). pap. 7.99 *(978-1-4814-2900-9(0))* Simon & Schuster Children's Publishing.

Martowiredjo, Salim. Indonesian Children's Favorite Stories. Suyenaga, Joan. 2015. (ENG.). 64p. (J). (gr. k-8). pap. 11.95 *(978-0-8048-4511-3(5))* Tuttle Publishing.

Marts, Doreen. Baxter the Tweeting Dog. 2012. (ENG.). 40p. (J). (gr. 1-4). 10.99 *(978-1-60905-199-0(8))* Blue Apple Bks.

—Look at Me! Look at Me! Williamson, Rose. 2014. (ENG.). 32p. (J). (gr. -1-k). 16.95 *(978-1-62914-617-1(X),* Sky Pony Pr.) Skyhorse Publishing Co., Inc.

Marts, Doreen Mulryan. Check, Please!, 3 vols. Stern, A. J. 2010. (Frankly, Frannie Ser.: 3). (ENG.). 128p. (J). (gr. 1-3). pap. 4.99 *(978-0-448-45352-1(5),* Grosset & Dunlap) Penguin Publishing Group.

—Doggy Day Care, 2 vols. Stern, A. J. 2010. (Frankly, Frannie Ser.: 2). (ENG.). 128p. (J). (gr. 1-3). pap. 4.99 *(978-0-448-45350-7(9),* Grosset & Dunlap) Penguin Publishing Group.

Marts, Doreen Mulryan. Even Monsters Say Good Night. 2015. (ENG.). 32p. (gr. -1-2). 14.95 *(978-1-62370-256-4(9))* Capstone Young Readers.

Marts, Doreen Mulryan. Fashion Frenzy. Stern, A. J. 2011. (Frankly, Frannie Ser.: 6). (ENG.). 128p. (J). (gr. 1-3). pap. 4.99 *(978-0-448-45544-0(7),* Grosset & Dunlap) Penguin Publishing Group.

—Frankly, Frannie, 1 vol. Stern, A. J. 2010. (Frankly, Frannie Ser.: 1). (ENG.). 128p. (J). (gr. 1-3). pap. 4.99 *(978-0-448-45348-4(7),* Grosset & Dunlap) Penguin Publishing Group.

—Frankly, Frannie: Books 1-3. Stern, A. J. 2014. (Frankly, Frannie Ser.). (ENG.). 384p. (J). (gr. 1-3). 8.99 *(978-0-448-48461-7(7),* Grosset & Dunlap) Penguin Publishing Group.

—Funny Business, 4 vols. Stern, A. J. 2011. (Frankly, Frannie Ser.: 4). (ENG.). 128p. (J). (gr. 1-3). pap. 4.99 *(978-0-448-45540-2(4),* Grosset & Dunlap) Penguin Publishing Group.

—Here Comes the... Trouble! Stern, A. J. 2012. (Frankly, Frannie Ser.: 9). (ENG.). 128p. (J). (gr. 1-3). pap. 4.99 *(978-0-448-45752-9(0),* Grosset & Dunlap) Penguin Publishing Group.

—Here Comes the... Trouble! Stern, A. J. ed. 2012. (Frankly, Frannie Ser.: 9). lib. bdg. 14.75 *(978-0-606-26653-6(4),* Turtleback) Turtleback Bks.

—Miss Fortune, 7 vols. Stern, A. J. 2012. (Frankly, Frannie Ser.: 7). (ENG.). 128p. (J). (gr. 1-3). pap. 4.99 *(978-0-448-45748-2(2),* Grosset & Dunlap) Penguin Publishing Group.

—My Pumpkin. Karr, Lily. 2014. (ENG.). 12p. (J). (gr. -1 — 1). bds. 4.99 *(978-0-545-49332-1(3),* Cartwheel Bks.) Scholastic, Inc.

—Principal for the Day. Stern, A. J. 2011. (Frankly, Frannie Ser.: 5). (ENG.). 128p. (J). (gr. 1-3). pap. 4.99 *(978-0-448-45542-6(0),* Grosset & Dunlap) Penguin Publishing Group.

—Rocking Out! Stern, A. J. 2012. (Frankly, Frannie Ser.: 8). (ENG.). 128p. (J). (gr. 1-3). 12.99 *(978-0-448-45751-2(2));* pap. 4.99 *(978-0-448-45750-5(4))* Penguin Publishing Group. (Grosset & Dunlap).

Martyr, Paula. New Tales from Alice's Wonderland: Dinah Plays Hide & Seek. Brown, Michele. 24p. (J). pap. 7.99 *(978-0-233-99535-9(8))* Andre Deutsch GBR. Dist: Trafalgar Square Publishing.

—New Tales from Alice's Wonderland: The Queen of Hearts & the Wibbly Wobbly Jelly. Brown, Michele. 24p. (J). pap. 7.95 *(978-0-233-99536-6(6))* Andre Deutsch GBR. Dist: Trans-Atlantic Pubns., Inc.

Martz, John, jt. illus. see Gauthier, Manon.

Maruda, Trotsky. Line & Circle. Maruda, Trotsky. 2004. 32p. (J). (ALB & ENG.). pap. *(978-1-84444-000-9(1));* (ARA & ENG.). pap. *(978-1-84444-002-3(8));* (BEN & ENG.). pap. *(978-1-84444-003-0(6));* (CZE & ENG.). pap. *(978-1-84444-005-4(2));* (ENG & PER.). pap. *(978-1-84444-006-1(0));* (PAN & ENG.). pap. *(978-1-84444-012-2(5));* (SER & ENG.). pap. *(978-1-84444-016-0(8));* (SOM & ENG.). pap. *(978-1-84444-017-7(6));* (ENG & TUR.). pap. *(978-1-84444-019-1(2));* (URD & ENG.). pap. *(978-1-84444-020-7(6));* (VIE & ENG.). pap. *(978-1-84444-021-4(4))* Mantra Lingua.

Marudu, Trotsky. Line & Circle. Menon, Radhika. 2004. (ENG & SPA.). 24p. (J). *(978-1-84444-018-4(4))* Mantra Lingua.

Maruyama, Ed, photos by. Games of Survival: Traditional Inuit Games for Elementary Students, 1 vol. Issaluk, Johnny. 2013. (ENG., 62p. (J). (gr. 3-6). 12.95 *(978-1-927095-21-8(2))* Inhabit Media Inc. CAN. Dist: Independent Pubs. Group.

Marvel Artists Staff & Olliffe, Pat. The Mighty Avengers. 2012. (Movie Theater Ser.). (ENG.). 32p. (J). (gr. k-2). 19.99 *(978-0-7944-2705-4(7))* Reader's Digest Assn., Inc., The.

Marvel Comics Staff. Art of Spider-Man Classic. 2011. (ENG.). 240p. (YA). (gr. 8-17). 49.99 *(978-0-7851-5750-2(6))* Marvel Worldwide, Inc.

—Captain America: First Vengeance. Lente, Fred Van. 2011. (ENG.). 96p. (YA). (gr. 8-17). 14.99 *(978-0-7851-5725-0(5))* Marvel Worldwide, Inc.

Marvel Comics Staff & Coipel, Olivier. The Mighty Thor: Fraction - Coipel. Fraction, Matt. 2011. (ENG.). 144p. (YA). (gr. 8-17). 24.99 *(978-0-7851-5691-8(7))* Marvel Worldwide, Inc.

Marvel Illustrators. Breakout! Siglain, Michael. 2012. (Avengers: Earth's Mightiest Heroes! Ser.). (ENG.). 24p. (J). (gr. -1-4). lib. bdg. 24.21 *(978-1-61479-001-3(9))* Spotlight.

—Hulk Versus the World. Rudnick, Elizabeth. 2012. (Avengers: Earth's Mightiest Heroes! Ser.). (ENG.). 24p. (J). (gr. -1-4). lib. bdg. 24.21 *(978-1-61479-002-0(7))* Spotlight.

—Iron Man Is Born. Rudnick, Elizabeth. 2012. (Avengers: Earth's Mightiest Heroes! Ser.). (ENG.). 24p. (J). (gr. -1-4). lib. bdg. 24.21 *(978-1-61479-003-7(5))* Spotlight.

—The Man in the Ant Hill. Castro, Nachie. 2012. (Avengers: Earth's Mightiest Heroes! Ser.). (ENG.). 24p. (J). (gr. -1-4). lib. bdg. 24.21 *(978-1-61479-004-4(3))* Spotlight.

—Thor the Mighty. Rudnick, Elizabeth. 2012. (Avengers: Earth's Mightiest Heroes! Ser.). (ENG.). 24p. (J). (gr. -1-4). lib. bdg. 24.21 *(978-1-61479-005-1(1))* Spotlight.

Marvin, Fred. Seven Animals Wag Their Tales. Bogot, Howard I. et al. 2005. 48p. (J). (gr. -1-1). pap. 9.95 *(978-1-930143-01-2(X));* (gr. k-3). 16.95 *(978-1-930143-00-5(1))* Simcha Media Group. (Devora Publishing).

Marxhausen, Ben & Koehler, Ed. Heaven is a Wonderful Place. Marxhausen, Joanne. 2nd ed. 2004. 48p. (J). (gr. -1-4). 9.49 *(978-0-7586-0681-5(8))* Concordia Publishing Hse.

Marxhausen, Benjamin & Koehler, Ed. El Cielo Es un Lugar Maravilloso. Marxhausen, Joanne. 2008. (SPA.). 48p. (J). (gr. -1). pap. 7.99 *(978-0-7586-1587-9(6))* Concordia Publishing Hse.

Mary Connors. Princess Bonnie & the Dragon. Claire Hamelin Bruyere. 2009. 16p. pap. 8.49 *(978-1-4389-8731-6(5))* AuthorHouse.

Mary Jean. Saint Hyacinth of Poland: The Story of the Apostle of the North. Windeatt, Mary F. 2009. (ENG.). 208p. (J). (gr. 1-8). reprint ed. pap. 13.95 *(978-0-89555-422-2(4))* TAN Bks.

Marzan, Jose, Jr. & Guerra, Pia. Y - The Last Man: Paper Dolls. Vaughan, Brian K. & Sudzuka, Goran. rev. ed. 2006. (Vertigo Ser.: Vol. 7). (ENG.). 144p. pap. 14.99 *(978-1-4012-1009-0(0),* Vertigo) DC Comics.

Marzan, Jose, Jr., jt. illus. see Guerra, Pia.

Marzel, Pépi. My First Hebrew Word Book. Groner, Judyth. 2005. (ENG.). 32p. (J). (gr. -1-2). lib. bdg. 17.95 *(978-1-58013-126-1(3),* Kar-Ben Publishing) Lerner Publishing Group.

Marzel, Pepi. My First Yiddish Word Book. Sussman, Joni. 2014. 32p. (J). (gr. -1-2). pap. 12.95 *(978-1-4677-5175-9(8),* Kar-Ben Publishing) Lerner Publishing Group.

Mas, Maribel. El Auto del Sr. Pulga. Barbot, Daniel. 2004. (SPA.). 28p. (J). pap. 6.99 *(978-980-257-260-1(8))* Ekare, Ediciones VEN. Dist: Lectorum Pubns., Inc.

Masciullo, Lucia. Family Forest. Kane, Kim. 2010. (ENG.). 32p. (J). (gr. -1-k). 22.99 *(978-1-921564-70-3(9))* Hardie Grant Bks. AUS. Dist: Independent Pubs. Group.

—When No-One's Looking: On the Farm. Fraillon, Zana. 2012. (ENG.). 24p. (J). (gr. -1-k). 16.99 *(978-1-921502-45-3(2))* Hardie Grant Bks. AUS. Dist: Independent Pubs. Group.

Mase, Naokata. The Rainy Trip Surprise. Mase, Naokata. Perry, Mia Lynn, tr. 2006. 24p. (J). (gr. -1-1). 19.95 incl. audio compact disk *(978-1-74126-436-4(7))* R.I.C. Pubns. AUS. Dist: SCB Distributors.

Masefield, Judith. The Box of Delights. Masefield, John. 2007. (ENG.). 312p. (J). (gr. 4-7). 17.95 *(978-1-59017-251-3(5),* NYR Children's Collection) New York Review of Bks., Inc., The.

Masel, Christy. Gorp's Dream: A Tale of Diversity, Tolerance, & Love in Pumpernickel Park. 2003. 36p. (J). 14.95 *(978-0-9724249-0-5(3))* Gorp Group Pr., The.

—Gorp's Dream: A Tale of Diversity, Tolerance, & Love in Pumpernickel Park. Chessen, Sherri. 2003. (ENG.). 36p. (J). pap. 7.95 *(978-0-9724249-1-2(1))* Gorp Group Pr., The.

Maser, Barry, jt. illus. see Moser, Barry.

Masheris, Bob. Cómo Contener el Fuego. Donahue, Jill Urban. 2011. (Cómo Mantenernos Seguros/How to Be Safe Ser.).Tr. of Contain the Flame. (SPA, ENG & MUL.). 24p. (gr. k-2). 25.99 *(978-1-4048-6887-8(9))* Picture Window Bks.

—Contain the Flame: Outdoor Fire Safety, 1 vol. Donahue, Jill Urban. 2008. (How to Be Safe! Ser.). (ENG.). 24p. (gr. k-2). 25.99 *(978-1-4048-4820-7(7),* Nonfiction Picture Bks.) Picture Window Bks.

—Juega Con Cuidado. Donahue, Jill Urban. 2011. (Cómo Mantenernos Seguros/How to Be Safe Ser.).Tr. of Play It Smart. (ENG, SPA & MUL.). 24p. (gr. k-2). 25.99 *(978-1-4048-6886-1(0))* Picture Window Bks.

—LAN's Plant. Riggs, Sandy. 2006. (Reader's Clubhouse Level 1 Reader Ser.). (ENG.). 24p. (J). (gr. 1-4). pap. 4.99 *(978-0-7641-3287-2(3))* Barron's Educational Series, Inc.

—Play It Smart: Playground Safety, 1 vol. Urban Donahue, Jill. 2008. (How to Be Safe! Ser.). (ENG.). 24p. (gr. k-2). 25.99 *(978-1-4048-4823-8(1),* Nonfiction Picture Bks.) Picture Window Bks.

—Say No & Go: Stranger Safety, 1 vol. Urban Donahue, Jill. 2008. (How to Be Safe! Ser.). (ENG.). 24p. (gr. k-2). 25.99 *(978-1-4048-4826-9(6),* Nonfiction Picture Bks.) Picture Window Bks.

Masheris, Robert. Away Go the Boats. Hillert, Margaret. 2008. (J). lib. bdg. 19.93 *(978-1-59953-146-5(1))* Norwood Hse. Pr.

—The Baby Bunny. Hillert, Margaret. 2008. 32p. (J). lib. bdg. 19.93 *(978-1-59953-188-5(7))* Norwood Hse. Pr.

—Up, up, & Away. Hillert, Margaret. 2008. 32p. (J). lib. bdg. 19.93 *(978-1-59953-151-9(8))* Norwood Hse. Pr.

Mashima, Hiro. Rave Master. Vol. 14. rev. ed. 2005. 200p. pap. 14.99 *(978-1-59532-019-3(9),* Tokyopop Kids) TOKYOPOP, Inc.

Mashima, Hiro. Rave Master, 21 vols. Mashima, Hiro. 2003. Vol. 3. rev. ed. 192p. (gr. 8-18). pap. 14.99 *(978-1-59182-210-3(6));* Vol. 5. 5th rev. ed. pap. 14.99 *(978-1-59182-212-7(2));* Vol. 6. rev. ed. 192p. pap. 14.99 *(978-1-59182-213-4(0))* TOKYOPOP, Inc. (Tokyopop Kids).

—Rave Master, 18 vols., Vol. 7. Mashima, Hiro. Dunn, Brian, tr. from JPN. rev. ed. 2004. 200p. pap. 14.99 *(978-1-59182-517-3(2),* Tokyopop Kids) TOKYOPOP, Inc.

—Rave Master, 21 vols., Vol. 11. Mashima, Hiro. Bourque, Jeremiah, tr. from JPN. rev. ed. 2004. 192p. (YA). pap. 14.99 *(978-1-59182-521-0(0),* Tokyopop Kids) TOKYOPOP, Inc.

—Rave Master. Mashima, Hiro. Vol. 13. rev. ed. 2005. 192p. pap. 14.99 *(978-1-59532-018-6(0));* Vol. 15. rev. ed. 2005. 192p. pap. 14.99 *(978-1-59532-020-9(2));* Vol. 17. 17th rev. ed. 2005. 192p. pap. 14.99 *(978-1-59532-022-3(9));* Vol. 18. 18th rev. ed. 2005. 200p. per. 14.99 *(978-1-59532-023-0(7));* Vol. 19. 19th rev. ed. 2006. 174p. (YA). pap. 14.99 *(978-1-59532-024-7(5));* Vol. 20. rev. ed. 2006. 191p. pap. 14.99 *(978-1-59532-025-4(3));* Vol. 22. 22nd rev. ed. 2006. 180p. per. 9.99 *(978-1-59532-626-3(X));* Vol. 24. 2007. 192p. pap. 9.99 *(978-1-59532-628-7(6));* Vol. 25. 2007. 192p. pap. 9.99 *(978-1-59532-629-4(4))* TOKYOPOP, Inc. (Tokyopop Kids).

Mashima, Hiro. Rave Master, Vol. 16. Mashima, Hiro, creator. rev. ed. 2005. (Rave Master Ser.). 192p. pap. 14.99 *(978-1-59532-021-6(0),* Tokyopop Kids) TOKYOPOP, Inc.

Masi, P. J. Alex Anklebone & Andy the Dog. Stevenson, Richard. 2005. (ENG.). 32p. (J). (gr. -1-17). *(978-1-896209-57-9(2))* Bayeux Arts, Inc.

Masiello, Ralph. The Flag We Love. Ryan, Pam Muñoz. 10th anniv. ed. 2006. (ENG.). 32p. (J). (gr. k-3). 17.95 *(978-1-57091-707-3(8))* Charlesbridge Publishing, Inc.

—The Icky Bug Counting Book. Pallotta, Jerry. 2004. (ENG.). 30p. (J). (-k). bds. 7.95 *(978-1-57091-624-3(1))* Charlesbridge Publishing, Inc.

—Mystic Phyles: Beasts. Brockway, Stephanie. 2011. (ENG.). 144p. (J). (gr. 4-7). pap. 15.95 *(978-1-57091-718-9(3))* Charlesbridge Publishing, Inc.

Masiello, Ralph. Bug Drawing Book: Simple Steps Make Anyone an Artist. Masiello, Ralph. 2004. (ENG.). 32p. (J). (gr. k-3). 16.95 *(978-1-57091-525-3(3))* Charlesbridge Publishing, Inc.

—Bug Drawing Book: Simple Steps to Make Anyone an Artist. Masiello, Ralph. 2004. (ENG.). 32p. (J). (gr. k-3). pap. 7.95 *(978-1-57091-526-0(1))* Charlesbridge Publishing, Inc.

—Ralph Masiello's Ancient Egypt Drawing Book. Masiello, Ralph. 2008. (Ralph Masiello's Drawing Bks.). (ENG.). 48p. (J). (gr. 3-7). pap. 7.95 *(978-1-57091-534-5(2))* Charlesbridge Publishing, Inc.

—Ralph Masiello's Christmas Drawing Book. Masiello, Ralph. 2013. (ENG.). 32p. (J). (gr. k-3). 17.95 *(978-1-57091-543-7(1));* pap. 7.95 *(978-1-57091-544-4(X))* Charlesbridge Publishing, Inc.

—Ralph Masiello's Dinosaur Drawing Book. Masiello, Ralph. 2005. (Ralph Masiello's Drawing Bks.). (ENG.). 48p. (J). (gr. k-3). 16.95 *(978-1-57091-527-7(X));* per. 7.95 *(978-1-57091-528-4(8))* Charlesbridge Publishing, Inc.

—Ralph Masiello's Dragon Drawing Book. Masiello, Ralph. 2007. (Fiery Good Time! Ser.). (ENG.). 64p. (J). (gr. 3-7). 17.95 *(978-1-57091-531-4(8));* pap. 9.95 *(978-1-57091-532-1(6))* Charlesbridge Publishing, Inc.

—Ralph Masiello's Fairy Drawing Book. Masiello, Ralph. 2013. (ENG.). 32p. (J). (gr. k-3). pap. 7.95 *(978-1-57091-540-6(7));* lib. bdg. 17.95 *(978-1-57091-539-0(3))* Charlesbridge Publishing, Inc.

—Ralph Masiello's Farm Drawing Book. Masiello, Ralph. 2012. (J). (ENG.). 32p. (gr. k-3). 16.95 *(978-1-57091-537-6(7));* (ENG.). 32p. (gr. k-3). pap. 7.95 *(978-1-57091-538-3(5));* (gr. 1-4). pap. 16.95 *(978-1-60734-082-9(8))* Charlesbridge Publishing, Inc.

—Ralph Masiello's Halloween Drawing Book. Masiello, Ralph. 2012. (ENG.). 32p. (J). (gr. k-3). pap. 7.95 *(978-1-57091-542-0(3))* Charlesbridge Publishing, Inc.

—Ralph Masiello's Ocean Drawing Book. Masiello, Ralph. 2006. (Ralph Masiello's Drawing Bks.). (ENG.). 32p. (J). (gr. k-3). pap. 7.95 *(978-1-57091-530-7(X),* 1258410) Charlesbridge Publishing, Inc.

—Ralph Masiello's Robot Drawing Book. Masiello, Ralph. 2011. (ENG.). 32p. (J). (gr. 1-4). 7.95 *(978-1-57091-536-9(9));* 16.95 *(978-1-57091-535-2(0))* Charlesbridge Publishing, Inc.

Masiello, Ralph, photos by. The Icky Bug Alphabet Book. Pallotta, Jerry. 32p. (J). (gr. -1-1). 10.95 *(978-0-933341-95-1(4))* Quinlan Pr.

Mask, Cynthia. Moon of the Wishing Night. Lamar, Gail Renfroe. 2004. 32p. (J). 17.95 *(978-1-57966-047-5(9),* River City Kids) River City Publishing.

Maslen, John & Hendra, Sue. Sight Words, First Grade, Set. Maslen, Bobby Lynn & Kertell, Lynn Maslen. 2010. (Bob Bks.). (ENG.). 120p. (J). (gr. -1-k). 16.99 *(978-0-545-01924-8(9),* Cartwheel Bks.) Scholastic, Inc.

—Sight Words Kindergarten, Set. Maslen, Bobby Lynn & Kertell, Lynn Maslen. 2010. (Bob Bks.). (ENG.). 120p. (J). (gr. -1-k). 16.99 *(978-0-545-01923-1(0),* Cartwheel Bks.) Scholastic, Inc.

Maslen, John R. Word Families, Set. Maslen, Bobby Lynn. 2006. (Bob Bks.). (ENG.). 16p. (J). (gr. -1-3). 16.99 *(978-0-439-84509-0(2),* Scholastic Paperbacks) Scholastic, Inc.

Maslen, John R. Compound Words, Set. Maslen, John R. Maslen, Bobby Lynn. 2006. (Bob Bks.). (ENG.). 16p. (J). (gr. -1-3). 16.99 *(978-0-439-84506-9(8),* Scholastic Paperbacks) Scholastic, Inc.

Maslen, John R. & Hendra, Sue. Alphabet. Kertell, Lynn Maslen. 2008. (Bob Bks.). (ENG.). 144p. (J). (gr. -1-3). 16.99 *(978-0-545-01921-7(4),* Cartwheel Bks.) Scholastic, Inc.

Maslen, John R., jt. illus. see Hendra, Sue.

Mason, Abi. The Soggy Saga of Samuel Sprat. Winbolt-Lewis, Martin. 2013. 24p. pap. *(978-1-78222-152-4(2))* Paragon Publishing, Rothersthorpe.

Mason, Alfonso & Mason, Ruth. English - French Counting Book, 1 vol. Baker, Mary E. 2010. 28p. pap. 24.95 *(978-1-4489-4347-0(7))* PublishAmerica, Inc.

—English - Spanish Counting Book. Baker, Mary. 2008. 24p. pap. 24.95 *(978-1-60672-035-6(X))* America Star Bks.

Mason, Bergetta. Turtle Games. Mason, Craig. 2003. 32p. (J). 4.99 *(978-0-9729153-0-4(3))* 1 Sleeve Publishing.

Mason, Charles, photos by. A Child's Alaska. Murphy, Claire Rudolf. 2012. (ENG., 48p. (J). (gr. 2-8). pap. 10.95 *(978-0-88240-859-0(3),* Alaska Northwest Bks.) Graphic Arts Ctr. Publishing Co.

Mason, Conrad. Illustrated Animal Stories. Sims, Lesley, ed. 2009. (Illustrated Stories Ser.). 352p. (YA). (gr. 3-18). 19.99 *(978-0-7945-2235-3(1),* Usborne) EDC Publishing.

—Illustrated Classics for Girls. Sims, Lesley. 2009. (Illustrated Stories Ser.). 384p. (YA). (gr. 3-18). 19.99 *(978-0-7945-2419-7(2),* Usborne) EDC Publishing.

Mason-Fry, Douglas L., photos by. I Like Being Me: Poems for Children about Feeling Special, Appreciating Others, & Getting Along. Lalli, Judy. 2007. (ENG., 64p. (J). (gr. -1-3). pap. 9.99 *(978-1-57542-025-7(2))* Free Spirit Publishing, Inc.

Mason, Janeen. Color, Color, Where Are You, Color? Koski, Mary B. 2004. (ENG.). (J). 28p. bds. 7.95 *(978-1-930650-34-3(5));* 32p. (gr. 1-3). 14.95 *(978-1-930650-35-0(3))* mTrellis Publishing, Inc.

—For Baby (For Bobbie) Denver, John. 2009. 36p. (J). (gr. -1-6). 19.95 incl. audio compact disk *(978-1-58469-120-4(4));* pap. 8.95 *(978-1-58469-121-1(2))* Dawn Pubns.

—Going Around the Sun: Some Planetary Fun. Berkes, Marianne Collins. 2008. 32p. (J). (gr. -1-4). 16.95 *(978-1-58469-099-3(2));* pap. 8.95 *(978-1-58469-100-6(X))* Dawn Pubns.

Mason, Janeen. The Gift of the Magpie, 1 vol. Mason, Janeen. 2011. (ENG.). 32p. (J). (gr. k-3). 16.99 *(978-1-58980-861-4(4))* Pelican Publishing Co., Inc.

—Ocean Commotion: Caught in the Currents, 1 vol. Mason, Janeen. 2012. (ENG.). 32p. (J). (gr. k-3). 16.99 *(978-1-58980-862-1(2))* Pelican Publishing Co., Inc.

—Ocean Commotion: Life on the Reef, 1 vol. Mason, Janeen. 2010. (ENG.). 32p. (J). (gr. k-3). 16.99 *(978-1-58980-783-9(9))* Pelican Publishing Co., Inc.

—Ocean Commotion: Sea Turtles, 1 vol. Mason, Janeen. 2006. (ENG.). 32p. (J). (gr. k-3). 16.99 *(978-1-58980-434-0(1))* Pelican Publishing Co., Inc.

Mason, Mark. Classroom Plays for Social Studies America in the 1800s, 4 vols. McCullough, L. E. 2003. 48p. (J). per. 7.99 *(978-1-56472-242-3(2))* Edupress, Inc.

—Classroom Plays for Social Studies American Biographies, 4. McCullough, L. E. 2003. 48p. (J). per. 7.99 *(978-1-56472-243-0(0))* Edupress, Inc.

—Classroom Plays for Social Studies Ancient Civilizations, 4 vols. McCullough, L. E. 2003. 48p. (J). per. 7.99 *(978-1-56472-240-9(6))* Edupress, Inc.

—Classroom Plays for Social Studies Early America, 4 vols. McCullough, L. E. 2003. 48p. (J). per. 7.99 *(978-1-56472-241-6(4))* Edupress, Inc.

—Following Directions 1-2. Schwartz, Linda. Scott, Kelly, ed. 2004. 64p. (J). pap. 10.99 *(978-1-59198-042-1(9),* 3397) Creative Teaching Pr., Inc.

—Following Directions 3-4. Schwartz, Linda. Martin, Kelly, ed. 2004. 64p. (J). pap. 10.99 *(978-1-59198-043-8(7),* 3398) Creative Teaching Pr., Inc.

—Primary Math Quiz Whiz, Vol. 428. Schwartz, Linda. VanBlaricum, Pam, ed. 2004. 128p. (J). (gr. 1-3). pap. 14.99 *(978-0-88160-371-2(6),* LW-428) Creative Teaching Pr., Inc.

—Primary Science Quiz Whiz, Vol. 429. Schwartz, Linda. VanBlaricum, Pam, ed. 2004. 128p. (J). (gr. 1-3). pap. 14.99 *(978-0-88160-372-9(4),* LW-429) Creative Teaching Pr., Inc.

—Traits of Good Writing, Grades 5-6. Heskett, Tracie. Fields, Kim et al, eds. ed. 2006. (Traits of Good Writing Ser.). (ENG.). 144p. (gr. 5-7). per. 16.99 *(978-1-4206-3593-5(X))* Teacher Created Resources, Inc.

Mason, Mark & Willardson, David. Leap into Literacy Fall. Geiser, Traci Ferguson & Boylan, Maureen McCourt. Cernek, Kim, ed. 2003. 160p. (J). (gr. k-2). pap. 17.99 *(978-1-57471-960-4(2),* 3376) Creative Teaching Pr., Inc.

Mason, Roberta Black. Tangle-Leina? I'll Tangle-Leina Them. Turner, Diane. 2008. 48p. pap. 24.95 *(978-1-60563-586-6(3))* America Star Bks.

Mason, Ruth, jt. illus. see Mason, Alfonso.

Mason, Sue. Fun Race. Goodhart, Pippa. 2013. (Start Reading Ser.). (ENG.). 24p. (gr. k-1). pap. 6.99 *(978-1-4765-4101-3(9))* Capstone Pr., Inc.

—Gamer, 1 vol. Durant, Alan. 2007. (Pathway Bks.). (ENG.). 72p. (gr. 2-3). lib. bdg. 23.99 *(978-1-59889-872-9(8),* Pathway Bks.) Stone Arch Bks.

—George & the Dragonfly. Blackford, Andy. 2014. (ReadZone Picture Bks.). (ENG.). 32p. (J). (gr. k-3). pap. 8.99 *(978-1-78322-423-4(1))* ReadZone Bks. GBR. Dist: Independent Pubs. Group.

—George & the Dragonfly. Blackford, Andy. 2011. (ENG.). 32p. (J). (gr. -1-k). pap. *(978-1-84089-624-4(8))* Zero to Ten, Ltd.

—Nature Detectives, 1 vol. Goodhart, Pippa. 2013. (Start Reading Ser.). (ENG.). 24p. (gr. k-1). pap. 6.99 *(978-1-4765-4121-1(3))* Capstone Pr., Inc.

—The Perfect Prince. Harrison, Paul. 2009. (ENG.). 32p. (J). (gr. -1-k). pap. *(978-1-84089-534-6(9))* Zero to Ten, Ltd.

Mason, Turning Bear. The Cost of Eggs: Hill House Farm Series. Smith, Sandra S. 2012. 24p. 24.95 *(978-1-4626-4928-0(9))* America Star Bks.

Massardier, Greg. Boo & Bear. Massardier, Greg, tr. Wyley, Enda. 2003. (Panda Cubs Ser.: 01). (ENG.). 48p. (J). pap. 9.95 *(978-0-86278-806-3(4))* O'Brien Pr., Ltd., The IRL. Dist: Dufour Editions, Inc.

Massari, Alida. Stories of the Saints. McAllister, Margaret. 2015. (ENG.). 48p. (J). (gr. 2-4). 17.99 *(978-0-7459-6445-4(1))* Lion Hudson PLC GBR. Dist: Independent Pubs. Group.

—The Story of Christmas. Joslin, Mary. 2014. (ENG.). 32p. (J). (gr. k-2). 14.99 *(978-0-7459-6937-4(2))* Lion Hudson PLC GBR. Dist: Independent Pubs. Group.

—Women of the Bible. McAllister, Margaret. 2013. (ENG.). 48p. (J). 16.99 *(978-1-61261-372-7(1))* Paraclete Pr., Inc.

Masse, José. Motherbridge of Love. Xinran, Xinran et al. 2007. (ENG.). 32p. (J). (gr. -1-5). 16.99 *(978-1-84686-047-8(4))* Barefoot Bks., Inc.

Masse, Josée. The Care & Keeping of You 2: The Body Book for Older Girls. Natterson, Cara. ed. 2013. lib. bdg. 24.50 *(978-0-606-31576-0(4),* Turtleback) Turtleback Bks.

—Follow Follow: A Book of Reverso Poems. Singer, Marilyn. 2013. (ENG.). 32p. (J). (gr. 1-4). 16.99 (978-0-8037-3769-3(6), Dial) Penguin Publishing Group.

—Frog & Friends. Bunting, Eve. 2011. (I Am A Reader! Ser.). (ENG.). 40p. (J). (gr. k-3). pap. 3.99 (978-1-58536-689-7(7)); lib. bdg. 9.95 (978-1-58536-548-7(3)) Sleeping Bear Pr.

—Frog & Friends: Outdoor Surprises. Bunting, Eve. 2013. (I AM a READER!: Frog & Friends Ser.). (ENG.). 48p. (J). (gr. 1-2). 9.95 (978-1-58536-807-5(5), 202361); pap. 3.99 (978-1-58536-808-2(3), 202370) Sleeping Bear Pr.

—Frog & Friends: Frog's Lucky Day 7. Bunting, Eve. 2014. (I Am a Reader!: Frog & Friends Ser.). (ENG.). 40p. (J). (gr. 1-2). 9.99 (978-1-58536-892-1(X), 203014) Sleeping Bear Pr.

—Mirror Mirror. Singer, Marilyn. 2010. (ENG.). 32p. (J). (gr. 1-4). 16.99 (978-0-525-47901-7(5), Dutton Juvenile) Penguin Publishing Group.

Masse, Josee. Motherbridge of Love. Xinran, Xinran & Mother's Bridge of Love Staff. 2013. (ENG.). 32p. (J). pap. 7.99 (978-1-78285-040-3(6)) Barefoot Bks., Inc.

Masse, Josée. The Princess Who Had Almost Everything. Levert, Mireille. 2008. (ENG.). 32p. (J). (gr. -1-3). 19.95 (978-0-88776-887-3(3), Tundra Bks.) Tundra Bks. CAN. Dist: Penguin Random Hse., LLC.

Masse, Josee. What Ship Is Not a Ship? Ziefert, Harriet. 2014. (ENG.). 40p. (J). (gr. k-4). 17.99 (978-1-60905-447-2(4)) Blue Apple Bks.

Masse, Josee. Goodnight, Sweet Pig. Masse, Josee. Bailey, Linda. 2007. (ENG.). 32p. (J). (gr. -1-k). 18.95 (978-1-55337-844-0(X)) Kids Can Pr., Ltd. CAN. Dist: Univ. of Toronto Pr.

Masse, Josée & Archer, Micha. Lola's Fandango. Witte, Anna. 2011. (ENG.). 48p. (J). 16.99 (978-1-84686-174-1(8)) Barefoot Bks., Inc.

Massey, Cal. My Name Is Oney Judge. Turner, Diane D. 2010. (J). pap. (978-0-88378-321-4(5)) Third World Press.

Massey, Call. My Name Is Oney Judge. Turner, Diane D. 2010. (ENG.). 40p. (J). 19.95 (978-0-88378-304-7(5)) Third World Press.

Massey, Ed, photos by. Casper, the Friendly Service Dog. Massey, Wayland. 2011. 28p. pap. 14.95 (978-1-936343-73-7(8)) Peppertree Pr., The.

Massey, Jane. Animales de la Granja. (Coloca y Siente). (SPA.). 10p. (J). (gr. k-2). bds. (978-968-5308-67-0(5), Silver Dolphin en Español) Advanced Marketing, S. de R. L. de C. V.

—Animales de la Selva. (Coloca y Siente). (SPA.). 10p. (J). (gr. k-2). bds. (978-968-5308-68-7(3), Silver Dolphin en Español) Advanced Marketing, S. de R. L. de C. V.

Massey, Jane. Do Dare Duck. Dunbar, Joyce. 2015. (ENG.). 32p. (J). (-k). pap. 9.99 **(978-1-78008-024-6(7))** Transworld Publishers Ltd. GBR. Dist: Independent Pubs. Group.

Massey, Jane. Fred & the Little Egg. Rawlinson, Julia. 2005. (ENG.). 25p. (J). pap. 16.00 (978-1-56148-468-3(7), Good Bks.) Skyhorse Publishing Co., Inc.

—I Love You, Blankie. Haft, Sheryl. 2015. (ENG.). 22p. (J). (gr. -1 — 1). bds. 8.99 (978-0-316-28356-4(8)) Little, Brown Bks. for Young Readers.

—Mascotas. (Coloca y Siente). (SPA.). 10p. (J). (gr. k-2). bds. (978-968-5308-66-3(7), Silver Dolphin en Español) Advanced Marketing, S. de R. L. de C. V.

—My Mommy Is Magic. Richards, Dawn. 2015. (ENG.). 32p. (J). (gr. -1-k). 8.99 (978-0-7641-6757-7(X)) Barron's Educational Series, Inc.

—Night-Night, Emily! Freedman, Claire. 2005. 32p. (J). 6.95 (978-1-58925-390-2(6)) Tiger Tales.

—Now We Have a Baby. Rock, Lois. 2014. (ENG.). 24p. (J). (gr. -1-k). bds. 7.99 (978-0-7459-6345-7(5)) Lion Hudson PLC GBR. Dist: Independent Pubs. Group.

Massey, Jane. Night-Night, Emily! Massey, Jane, tr. Freedman, Claire. 2003. 32p. (J). (gr. -1-1). tchr. ed. 15.95 (978-1-58925-032-1(X)) Tiger Tales.

Massey, Jane, jt. illus. see Pedler, Caroline.

Massey, Mitch & Kelleher, Michael. League of Super Groovy Crimefighters Trade Paperback. Campbell, Jan-Ives. 2003. (YA). per. 12.95 (978-0-9744216-0-5(X)) Ancient Studios.

Massini, Luca, jt. illus. see Calvetti, Leonello.

Massini, Sarah. Books Always Everywhere. Blatt, Jane. 2013. (J). (978-0-385-37535-1(2)) Random Hse., Inc.

—Love Always Everywhere. 2014. (ENG.). 32p. (J). (gr. -1-2). 16.99 (978-0-385-37552-8(2), Random Hse. Bks. for Young Readers) Random Hse. Children's Bks.

—Love Always Everywhere. 2014. (J). (978-0-385-37553-5(0)) Random Hse., Inc.

—Oodles of Noodles. Hendry, Diana. 2008. (Tiger Tales Ser.). 32p. (J). (gr. -1-2). 15.95 (978-1-58925-075-8(3)) Tiger Tales.

—Tulip & Rex Write a Story. Capucilli, Alyssa Satin. 2015. (ENG.). 32p. (J). (gr. -1-3). 17.99 (978-0-06-209416-2(5)) HarperCollins Pubs.

—Tulip Loves Rex. Capucilli, Alyssa Satin. 2013. (ENG.). 32p. (J). (gr. -1-3). 17.99 (978-0-06-209413-1(0), Tegen, Katherine Bks) HarperCollins Pubs.

Massironi, Daniela. Frankie the Frog. 2014. (J). **(978-1-4351-5573-2(4))** Barnes & Noble, Inc.

—Freddie the Fish. 2014. (J). **(978-1-4351-5574-9(2))** Barnes & Noble, Inc.

Massivebrain.com. The Tree & the Light. Strange, J. R. 2013. 48p. pap. 11.99 (978-0-9887214-0-1(6)) Firesidenook.

Masson, Annick. Bertha & the Frog Choir. Foccroulle, Luc. 2012. (ENG.). 32p. (J). (gr. -1-3). 17.95 (978-0-7358-4062-1(8)) North-South Bks., Inc.

—No, No, No! Callier, Marie-Isabelle. 2013. 32p. pap. 9.95 (978-1-4338-1312-2(2)); (J). (978-1-4338-1311-5(4)) American Psychological Assn. (Magination Pr.).

Mastin, Ian. The Lamb: PowerPoint Booklet. Cross, John R. 2007. (J). spiral bd. (978-1-890082-62-8(7)) GoodSeed International.

Mastnak, Rosemary. Cooking with Grandma. Mastnak, Rosemary. 2012. (ENG.). 28p. (J). (gr. -1-k). 16.99 (978-1-921564-19-2(9)) Hardie Grant Bks. AUS. Dist: Independent Pubs. Group.

—Dancing with Grandma. Mastnak, Rosemary. 2011. (ENG.). 28p. (J). (gr. -1-k). 16.99 (978-1-921288-90-6(6)) Hardie Grant Bks. AUS. Dist: Independent Pubs. Group.

Mastrangelo, Judy. What Do Bunnies Do All Day? 2003. (ENG.). 24p. (J). bds. 6.95 (978-0-8249-6520-4(5)) Ideals Pubns.

Mastrangelo, Judy. What Do Bunnies Do All Day? Mastrangelo, Judy. (J). 32p. pap. 4.95 (978-0-8249-5370-6(3), Ideals); 2006. (ENG.). 24p. (gr. -1-k). per. 3.95 (978-0-8249-5532-8(3), Ideals Children's Bks.) Ideals Pubns.

Mastroserio, Rocke. The Action Heroes Archives, Vol. 2. Kaler, David et al. rev. ed. 2007. (DC Archive Editions Ser.). (ENG.). 388p. (YA). 75.00 (978-1-4012-1346-6(4)) DC Comics.

Mata, Nina. Fettuccine & Four-Leaf Clovers: A Readers' Theater Script & Guide. Wallace, Nancy K. 2016. (J). **(978-1-62402-112-1(3))** Magic Wagon.

—Medals & Memorials: A Readers' Theater Script & Guide. Wallace, Nancy K. 2016. (J). **(978-1-62402-115-2(8))** Magic Wagon.

Mata, Nina. Princedom of Pea: A Readers' Theater Script & Guide. Wallace, Nancy K. 2013. (Readers' Theater: How to Put on a Production Ser.). 32p. (J). (gr. 2-6). lib. bdg. 28.50 (978-1-61641-988-2(1), Looking Glass Library-Nonfiction) Magic Wagon.

—Snow White & the Seven Dorks: A Readers' Theater Script & Guide. Wallace, Nancy K. 2013. (Readers' Theater: How to Put on a Production Ser.). 32p. (J). (gr. 2-6). lib. bdg. 28.50 (978-1-61641-990-5(3), Looking Glass Library- Nonfiction) Magic Wagon.

Mataya, David. Tales for Hard Times: A Story about Charles Dickens. Collins, David R. 2007. (Creative Minds Biographies Ser.). (ENG.). 64p. (gr. 4-8). pap. 8.95 (978-0-8225-6992-3(2)) Lerner Publishing Group.

Mate, Rae. Crocodiles Play! Heidbreder, Robert. 2009. (ENG.). 32p. (J). (gr. -1-3). 16.95 (978-1-894965-86-6(8)) Simply Read Bks. CAN. Dist: Ingram Pub. Services.

—Crocodiles Say... Heidbreder, Robert. 2005. (ENG.). 32p. (J). (gr. -1-3). 16.95 (978-1-894965-42-2(6)) Simply Read Bks. CAN. Dist: Ingram Pub. Services.

—Pussycat, Pussycat, Where Have You Been? Bar-el, Dan. 2011. (ENG.). 32p. (J). (gr. -1-3). 16.95 (978-1-897476-46-8(9)) Simply Read Bks. CAN. Dist: Ingram Pub. Services.

Mateer, Eric. Paint Me Terrified. Mateer, Eric. 2011. (ENG.). 72p. pap. 5.99 (978-1-4538-1131-3(1)) CreateSpace Independent Publishing Platform.

Matens, Margaret H. The Wisdom of Fishing. Matens, Margaret H. Armour, Christopher. 2010. (Wisdom Series Ser.: 0). (ENG.). 160p. pap. 6.95 (978-1-882959-53-2(1)) Foxglove Pr.

Mateo, Rosario. Un Agente Oportuno: Cuando la Penicilina Entra en Accion. Mariscal, Libia Barajas. rev. ed. 2006. (Otra Escalera Ser.). (SPA & ENG.). 24p. (J). (gr. 2-4). pap. 9.95 (978-968-5920-64-3(6)) Castillo, Ediciones, S. A. de C. V. MEX. Dist: Macmillan.

Mateo, Rosario & Sada, Margarita. Venir del Mar. Caban, Jose Alberto. rev. ed. 2006. (Otra Escalera Ser.). (SPA & ENG.). 24p. (J). (gr. 2-4). pap. 9.95 (978-968-5920-74-2(5)) Castillo, Ediciones, S. A. de C. V. MEX. Dist: Macmillan.

Maters, Ingrid. Samaya: The Deaf Baby Elephant. De Silva-Nijkamp, Tineke. 2005. 33p. (J). (978-955-599-438-5(2)) Sarvodaya Bk. Publishing Services.

Mateu, Francesca. The Little Mermaid. RH Disney Staff & Calmenson, Stephanie. 2003. (Pictureback(R) Ser.). (ENG.). 24p. (J). (gr. -1-2). pap. 3.99 (978-0-7364-2128-7(9), RH/Disney) Random Hse. Children's Bks.

Matheny, Jean Sherlock. I Want to Be a Christian: The Story of Blessed Kateri Tekakwitha. Paddock, Susan Star. Jaurequi, Leticia & Gomez, Elisa, trs. 2004. (J). (978-0-9747571-8-6(7)) Catholic World Mission.

Matheny, Melody. Rock, Stream, Tree. Zito, Ann R. 2010. 52p. pap. 11.00 (978-1-4520-7822-9(X)) AuthorHouse.

Mather, Daniel. Case File #3 the Accidental Accomplice. 2014. (Rabbids Invasion Ser.: 3). (ENG.). 96p. (J). (gr. 2-5). pap. 4.99 (978-1-4814-1720-4(7), Simon Spotlight) Simon Spotlight.

Mather, Daniel & Harrison, Nancy. Who Is Steven Spielberg? Spinner, Stephanie. 2013. (Who Was... ? Ser.). (ENG.). 112p. (J). (gr. 3-7). 5.99 (978-0-448-47935-4(4), Grosset & Dunlap) Penguin Publishing Group.

Mather-Smith, Charles. Inside Our Earth. Arnov Jr., Boris & Mindlin, Helen Mather-Smith. 2011. 160p. 41.95 (978-1-258-07682-5(9)) Literary Licensing, LLC.

Mathers, Petra. Button Up! Wrinkled Rhymes. Schertle, Alice. (ENG.). 40p. (J). (gr. -1-3). 2013. pap. 6.99 (978-0-544-02269-0(6)); 2009. 16.00 (978-0-15-205050-4(7)) Houghton Mifflin Harcourt Publishing Co.

—The Frogs Wore Red Suspenders. Prelutsky, Jack. 2005. (ENG.). 64p. (J). (gr. k-5). reprint ed. pap. 6.99 (978-0-06-073776-4(X), Greenwillow Bks.) HarperCollins Pubs.

—In Aunt Giraffe's Green Garden. Prelutsky, Jack. 2007. 64p. (J). (gr. -1-3). lib. bdg. 18.89 (978-0-06-623869-2(2)) HarperCollins Pubs.

Mathers, Petra. The McElderry Book of Mother Goose: Revered & Rare Rhymes. Mathers, Petra, compiled by. 2012. (ENG.). 96p. (J). (gr. k-5). 21.99 (978-0-689-85605-1(9), McElderry, Margaret K. Bks.) McElderry, Margaret K. Bks.

Matheson, Christie. Tap the Magic Tree. Matheson, Christie. 2013. (ENG.). 40p. (J). (gr. -1-3). 15.99 (978-0-06-227445-8(7), Greenwillow Bks.) HarperCollins Pubs.

—Touch the Brightest Star. Matheson, Christie. 2015. (ENG.). 40p. (J). (gr. -1-3). 15.99 (978-0-06-227447-2(3), Greenwillow Bks.) HarperCollins Pubs.

Mathew, Gillian. The Gift of Gold. Kowen, Dorothy. 2011. (ENG.). 24p. 13.95 (978-1-77009-796-4(1)) Jacana Media ZAF. Dist: Independent Pubs. Group.

Mathieu, Joe. Abby Cadabby Makes a Wish. Kleinberg, Naomi. 2010. (Sesame Street Ser.). (ENG.). 12p. (J). (gr. k — 1). bds. 4.99 (978-0-375-85935-9(7), Random Hse. Bks. for Young Readers) Random Hse. Children's Bks.

—The Cat in the Hat Knows a Lot about Christmas! (Dr. Seuss/Cat in the Hat) Rabe, Tish. 2013. (Big Golden Book Ser.). (ENG.). 48p. (J). (gr. -1-1). 9.99 (978-0-449-81495-6(5), Golden Bks.) Random Hse. Children's Bks.

—Dogs Don't Wear Sneakers. Numeroff, Laura Joffe. 2014. 40p. pap. 8.00 (978-1-61003-344-2(2)) Center for the Collaborative Classroom.

—Don't Be Silly, Mrs. Millie!, 0 vols. Cox, Judy. 2010. (ENG.). 32p. (J). (gr. k-3). pap. 6.99 (978-0-7614-5727-5(5), 9780761457275, Amazon Children's Publishing) Amazon Publishing.

—Get Moving with Elmo! (Sesame Street) Random House Staff. 2012. (ENG.). 12p. (J). (gr. k-k). bds. 5.99 (978-0-307-97666-6(1), Random Hse. Bks. for Young Readers) Random Hse. Children's Bks.

—Grouches Are Green. Kleinberg, Naomi. 2011. (ENG.). 12p. (J). (gr. k — 1). bds. 6.99 (978-0-375-86550-3(0), Random Hse. Bks. for Young Readers) Random Hse. Children's Bks.

—Happy Birthday, Mrs. Millie!, 0 vols. Cox, Judy. 2012. (ENG.). 32p. (J). (gr. k-3). 16.99 (978-0-7614-6126-5(4), 9780761461265, Amazon Children's Publishing) Amazon Publishing.

—Have You Seen My Dinosaur? Surgal, Jon. 2010. (Beginner Books Ser.). (ENG.). 48p. (J). (gr. -1-1). 8.99 (978-0-375-85639-6(0)) Random Hse. Children's Bks.

—Hello, Dragons! Hola, Dragones! Rodecker, Ron. 2005. (ENG & SPA.). 10p. (J). (gr. -1-2). reprint ed. 10.00 (978-0-7567-8937-4(0)) DIANE Publishing Co.

—Horses: Trotting! Prancing! Racing!, 0 vols. Hubbell, Patricia. 2011. (ENG.). 32p. (J). (gr. -1-3). 17.99 (978-0-7614-5949-1(9), 9780761459491, Amazon Children's Publishing) Amazon Publishing.

—Is My Face Red! A Book of Colorful Feelings. Kleinberg, Naomi. 2012. (ENG.). 12p. (J). (gr. k-k). bds. 5.99 (978-0-307-93055-2(6), Random Hse. Bks. for Young Readers) Random Hse. Children's Bks.

—Let's Visit Sesame Street. November, Deborah et al. 2010. (ENG.). 24p. (J). bds. 14.99 (978-0-7944-2101-4(6)) Reader's Digest Assn., Inc., The.

—Moose Crossing, 0 vols. Greene, Stephanie. 2010. (Moose & Hildy Ser.: 0). (ENG.). 64p. (J). (gr. 1-2). pap. 6.99 (978-0-7614-5699-5(6), 9780761456995, Amazon Children's Publishing) Amazon Publishing.

—Moose's Big Idea, 0 vols. Greene, Stephanie. 2010. (Moose & Hildy Ser.: 0). (ENG.). 64p. (J). (gr. 1-4). pap. 6.99 (978-0-7614-5698-8(8), 9780761456988, Amazon Children's Publishing) Amazon Publishing.

—Mrs. Millie Goes to Philly!, 0 vols. Cox, Judy. 2013. (ENG.). 27p. (J). (gr. -1-2). pap. 9.99 (978-1-4778-1680-6(1), 9781477816806, Amazon Children's Publishing) Amazon Publishing.

—The Nose Book. Dr. Seuss Enterprises Staff & Perkins, Al. 2003. (Bright & Early Board Books(TM) Ser.). (ENG.). 24p. (J). (gr. k — 1). bds. 4.99 (978-0-375-82493-7(6), Random Hse. Bks. for Young Readers) Random Hse. Children's Bks.

—Pick a Pumpkin, Mrs. Millie!, 0 vols. Cox, Judy. 2009. (ENG.). 32p. (J). (gr. -1-3). 15.99 (978-0-7614-5573-8(6), 9780761455738, Amazon Children's Publishing) Amazon Publishing.

—Pig Pickin', 0 vols. Greene, Stephanie. (Moose & Hildy Ser.). (ENG.). (J). (gr. -1-3). 2013. 68p. pap. 9.99 (978-1-4778-1684-4(4), 9781477816844); 2006. 32p. 14.99 (978-0-7614-5324-6(5), 9780761453246) Amazon Publishing. (Amazon Children's Publishing).

—Plant a Tree for Me! Kleinberg, Naomi. 2010. (ENG.). 12p. (J). (gr. k — 1). bds. 6.99 (978-0-375-85485-9(1), Random Hse. Bks. for Young Readers) Random Hse. Children's Bks.

—Read Around Sesame Street (Sesame Street) Albee, Sarah et al. 2014. (Step into Reading Ser.). (ENG.). 160p. (J). (gr. -1-1). pap. 7.99 (978-0-385-37411-8(9), Random Hse. Bks. for Young Readers) Random Hse. Children's Bks.

—The Sesame Street Dictionary. Hayward, Linda. 2004. (ENG.). 256p. (J). (gr. -1-2). 24.99 (978-0-375-82810-2(9), Random Hse. Bks. for Young Readers) Random Hse. Children's Bks.

—Sesame Street Guess Who, Easter Elmo! Guess Who Easter Elmo! Mitter, Matt. 2015. (Guess Who Ser.: 6). (ENG.). 10p. (J). (gr. -1-k). 10.99 (978-0-7944-3331-4(6)) Studio Fun International.

—The Show-Off, 0 vols. Greene, Stephanie. (Moose & Hildy Ser.). (ENG.). (J). (gr. 1-4). 2013. 50p. pap. 9.99 (978-1-4778-1686-8(0), 9781477816868); 2007. 64p. lib. bdg. 14.99 (978-0-7614-5374-1(1), 9780761453741) Amazon Publishing. (Amazon Children's Publishing).

—Too Many Cats. Houran, Lori Haskins. 2009. (Step into Reading Ser.). (ENG.). 32p. (J). (gr. -1-1). pap. 3.99 (978-0-375-85197-1(6)) Random Hse. Children's Bks.

—The Tooth Book. Seuss, Dr. 2003. (Bright & Early Board Books(TM) Ser.). (ENG.). 24p. (J). (— 1). bds. 4.99 (978-0-375-82492-0(8), Random Hse. Bks. for Young Readers) Random Hse. Children's Bks.

—Who Are the People in Your Neighborhood? Kleinberg, Naomi. 2009. (ENG.). 14p. (J). (gr. k — 1). bds. 7.99 (978-0-375-85138-4(0), Random Hse. Bks. for Young Readers) Random Hse. Children's Bks.

Mathieu, Joe. Big Bird's Big Book. Mathieu, Joe. Sesame Street Staff & Random House Editors. 2009. (Sesame Street Ser.). (ENG.). 14p. (J). (gr. k — 1). bds. 45.00 (978-0-394-89128-6(7), Random Hse. Bks. for Young Readers) Random Hse. Children's Bks.

Mathieu, Joe & Ruiz, Aristides. Hello, My Baby (Dr. Seuss/Cat in the Hat) Rabe, Tish. 2013. (Nifty Lift-And-Look Ser.). (ENG.). 12p. (J). (— 1). bds. 5.99 (978-0-449-81434-5(3), Random Hse. Bks. for Young Readers) Random Hse. Children's Bks.

—A Reindeer's First Christmas-New Friends for Christmas. Rabe, Tish. 2012. (Deluxe Pictureback Ser.). (ENG.). 32p. (J). (gr. -1-2). pap. 4.99 (978-0-307-97624-6(6), Random Hse. Bks. for Young Readers) Random Hse. Children's Bks.

—Spring into Summer! Rabe, Tish. 2012. (Deluxe Pictureback Ser.). (ENG.). 32p. (J). (gr. -1-2). pap. 4.99 (978-0-307-93057-6(2), Random Hse. Bks. for Young Readers) Random Hse. Children's Bks.

—Tree's Company. Golden Books Staff. 2011. (Reusable Sticker Book Ser.). (ENG.). 12p. (J). (gr. -1-2). 6.99 (978-0-375-86559-6(4), Golden Bks.) Random Hse. Children's Bks.

Mathieu, Joe, jt. illus. see Ruiz, Aristides.

Mathieu, Joe, jt. illus. see Urbanovic, Jackie.

Mathieu, Joseph, jt. illus. see Ruiz, Aristides.

Mathieu, Middy. I Love Ladybugs! Fisher, Meaghan. 2012. 16p. pap. 6.99 (978-1-938768-00-2(0)) Gypsy Pubns.

—What Would You Do If You Were Left at the Zoo? Hand, Renne. 2012. 24p. pap. 8.99 (978-1-938768-06-4(X)) Gypsy Pubns.

Mathis, Leslie. Be Satisfied with Who You Are. Fyne, Olga M. 2013. 24p. pap. 9.99 (978-1-61286-142-5(3)) Avid Readers Publishing Group.

—The Bedtime of the Sky & Other Sleepy-Bye Stories. Wolfe, Carolyn. 2010. 32p. pap. 11.25 (978-1-935105-57-2(4)) Avid Readers Publishing Group.

—Coyotebat. Hazelwood, K. D. 2010. 68p. pap. 14.99 (978-1-935105-52-7(3)) Avid Readers Publishing Group.

—Dollygal, Peacock, & the Serpent. Darlene, Cannon. 2011. 108p. pap. 19.95 (978-1-61286-001-5(X)) Avid Readers Publishing Group.

—Fluffy, a Puppy with a Purpose. Patterson, Eric. 2013. 146p. pap. 6.99 (978-1-61286-150-0(4)) Avid Readers Publishing Group.

—The Unhappy Little Dragon: Lessons Begin. Wolfe, Carolyn. 2009. 38p. pap. 12.99 (978-1-935105-42-8(6)) Avid Readers Publishing Group.

Mathis, Teresa, jt. illus. see Tom, Darcy.

Matijasevich, Astrid. Big Bill's Bed. Eggleton, Jill. 2003. (Rigby Sails Early Ser.). (ENG.). 16p. (gr. 1-2). pap. 6.95 (978-0-7578-8731-4(7)) Houghton Mifflin Harcourt Publishing Co.

—Flea & Big Bill. Eggleton, Jill. 2003. (Rigby Sails Early Ser.). (ENG.). 16p. (gr. 1-2). pap. 6.95 (978-0-7578-8722-2(8)) Houghton Mifflin Harcourt Publishing Co.

—Flea Goes Out! Eggleton, Jill. 2003. (Rigby Sails Early Ser.). (ENG.). 16p. (gr. 1-2). pap. 6.95 (978-0-7578-8737-6(6)) Houghton Mifflin Harcourt Publishing Co.

Matine, Laura. The Upside-Down Fish. Louise, Kate. 2015. (ENG.). 32p. (J). (gr. -1-k). 16.95 (978-1-62914-628-7(5), Sky Pony Pr.) Skyhorse Publishing Co., Inc.

Matiuzzo, Nick. Noise in the Night. Sullivan-Ringe, Laurie. 2008. 37p. pap. 24.95 (978-1-60672-476-7(2)) America Star Bks.

Matje, Martin. Harry & Lulu. Yorinks, Arthur. 32p. (J). pap. 4.99 (978-0-7868-1221-9(4)) Hyperion Paperbacks for Children.

—Stuart Goes to School. Pennypacker, Sara. 2005. (ENG.). 64p. (J). (gr. -1-3). reprint ed. per. 5.99 (978-0-439-30183-1(1), Scholastic Paperbacks) Scholastic, Inc.

—When It Starts to Snow. Gershator, Phillis. 2010. (ENG.). 32p. (J). (gr. -1-2). pap. 25.99 (978-0-8050-8871-7(7), Holt, Henry & Co. Bks. For Young Readers) Holt, Henry & Co.

Matkovich, Gregory. Red, 1 vol. Lloyd, Ashley. 2009. 19p. pap. 24.95 (978-1-61546-913-0(3)) PublishAmerica, Inc.

Mato. Best of Pokemon Adventures - Yellow. Kusaka, Hidenori. 2006. (Pokemon Ser.). (ENG.). 194p. (J). pap. 7.99 (978-1-4215-0929-7(6)) Viz Media.

—Pokémon Adventures. Kusaka, Hidenori. (Pokemon Ser.: 26). (ENG.). (J). 2015. 144p. pap. 9.99 (978-1-4215-3560-9(2)); 2014. 208p. pap. 9.99 (978-1-4215-3554-8(8)); 2013. 192p. pap. 9.99 (978-1-4215-3553-1(X)); 2013. 192p. pap. 9.99 (978-1-4215-3552-4(1)); 2013. 208p. pap. 9.99 (978-1-4215-3551-7(3)); 2013. 208p. pap. 9.99 (978-1-4215-3550-0(5)); 2013. 144p. pap. 9.99 (978-1-4215-3549-4(1)); 2011. 192p. pap. 9.99 (978-1-4215-3546-3(7)); Vol. 11. 2011. 192p. pap. 9.99 (978-1-4215-3545-6(9)) Viz Media.

—Pokémon Adventures, Vol. 27. Kusaka, Hidenori. 2015. (Pokemon Ser.: 27). (ENG.). 208p. (J). pap. 9.99 (978-1-4215-3561-6(0)) Viz Media.

Mato. Pokémon Adventures, Vol. 28. Kusaka, Hidenori. 2015. (Pokemon Ser.: 28). (ENG.). 208p. (J). pap. 9.99 **(978-1-4215-3562-3(9))** Viz Media.

Matoh, Sanami. Fake, 7 vols. Matoh, Sanami. rev. ed. 2003. 192p. Vol. 3. pap. 9.99 (978-1-59182-328-5(5)); Vol. 4. pap. 9.99 (978-1-59182-329-2(3)) TOKYOPOP, Inc.

—Fake, 7 vols., Vol. 5. Matoh, Sanami. Rymer, Nan, tr. from JPN. rev. ed. 2004. 192p. pap. 9.99 (978-1-59182-330-8(7)) TOKYOPOP, Inc.

Matoso, Madalena. At Our House. Minhós Martins, Isabel. 2013. (ENG.). 28p. 12.95 (978-1-84976-049-2(7)) Tate Publishing, Ltd. GBR. Dist: Abrams.

—My Neighbor Is a Dog. Martins, Isabel Minhós. Herring, John, tr. from POR. 2013. (ENG.). 32p. (J). (gr. -1-2). 16.95 (978-1-926973-68-5(2)) Owlkids Bks. Inc. CAN. Dist: Perseus-PGW.

—When I Was Born. Martins, Isabel Minhós. 2011. (ENG.). 32p. (gr. -1-3). 12.95 (978-1-85437-958-0(5)) Tate Publishing, Ltd. GBR. Dist: Abrams.

Matricardi, Luca. Frunk the Skunk. Mounts, Samia. 2008. (ENG.). 150p. (J). (gr. 4-6). pap. 9.95 (978-0-9798841-0-8(1)) 4N Publishing LLC.

M

Matsick, Anni. Eat It! Food Adventures with Marco Polo: Volume One: Leaving Home, 4 vols. Cavnar, Gracie. l.t. ed. 2012. (Eat It! Food Adventures with Marco Polo Ser.: 1). (ENG.). 160p. (J). (gr. 3). pap. 19.99 *(978-0-9846525-0-1(7),* S2P Pr.) Recipe for Success Foundation.

Matson, Don. Digging Tunnels, 1 vol. Macken, JoAnn Early. Saunders-Smith, Gail, ed. 2008. (Construction Zone Ser.). (ENG.). 24p. (gr. k-1). 24.65 *(978-1-4296-1234-0(7),* Pebble Plus) Capstone Pr., Inc.

Matson, Laurie. Jaz-O & 'G' in Key West. Matson, Laurie. l.t. ed. 2003. (J). 4.95 *(978-0-9673704-5-3(0))* Seastory Pr.

Matsoureff, Atanas. The Lost Island. Johnson, E. Pauline. 2004. (ENG.). 40p. (J). (gr. -1-3). 16.95 *(978-1-894965-07-1(8))* Simply Read Bks. CAN. Dist: Ingram Pub. Services.

Matsubuchi, Akemi, photos by. What Grows Here? Indoors: Favorite Houseplants for Every Situation. Hole, Jim. rev. ed. 2007. (ENG.). 288p. per. *(978-1-894728-06-5(8))* Hole's Greenhouses & Gardens, Ltd.

Matsuhashi, Toshimitsu, photos by. Life-Size Aquarium. Komiya, Teruyuki. Miyakoshi, Junko, tr. from JPN. 2010. (ENG., 48p. (gr. -1-2). 18.95 *(978-1-934734-59-9(4))* Seven Footer Pr.

—More Life-Size Zoo: An All-New Actual-Size Animal Encyclopedia. Komiya, Teruyuki. Miyakoshi, Junko, tr. 2010. (ENG., 48p. (gr. -1). 18.95 *(978-1-934734-19-3(5))* Seven Footer Pr.

Matsumoto, Natsumi. St. Dragon Girl. Matsumoto, Natsumi. (St. Dragon Girl Ser.: 6). (ENG.). (gr. 8-18). 2010. 208p. pap. 9.99 *(978-1-4215-2015-5(X));* 2008. 200p. pap. 8.99 *(978-1-4215-2010-0(9))* Viz Media.

Matsumoto, Tomo. Beauty Is the Beast. Matsumoto, Tomo. (Beauty Is the Beast Ser.). (ENG.). Vol. 1. 2005. 184p. pap. 8.99 *(978-1-4215-0289-2(5));* Vol. 2. 2006. 208p. pap. 8.99 *(978-1-4215-0352-3(2));* Vol. 3. 2006. 208p. pap. 8.99 *(978-1-4215-0353-0(0));* Vol. 4. 2006. 208p. pap. 8.99 *(978-1-4215-0354-7(9))* Viz Media.

Matsunaga, Judd. King's Kids Coloring Book. Fleming, Jesse, photos by. Date not set. (SPA.). 32p. (J). *(978-0-9703880-4-9(7))* King's Kids Trading Cards, Inc.

Matsunaga, Judd & Fleming, Jesse. King's Kids Coloring Book. Date not set. 32p. (J). *(978-0-9703880-3-2(9))* King's Kids Trading Cards, Inc.

Matsuoka, Mei. The Great Balloon Hullaballoo. Bently, Peter. 2014. (ENG.). 32p. (J). (gr. -1-3). 16.95 *(978-1-4677-3449-3(7))* Lerner Publishing Group.

—The Great Dog Bottom Swap. Bently, Peter. 2011. (ENG.). 32p. (J). (gr. -1-k). pap. 12.99 *(978-1-84270-988-7(7))* Andersen Pr. GBR. Dist: Independent Pubs. Group.

—The Great Sheep Shenanigans. Bently, Peter. 2012. (Andersen Press Picture Bks). (ENG.). 32p. (J). (gr. -1-3). 16.95 *(978-0-7613-8990-3(3))* Lerner Publishing Group.

Matsuoka, Mei. Footprints in the Snow. Matsuoka, Mei. 2008. (ENG.). 32p. (J). (gr. -1-1). 16.95 *(978-0-8050-8792-5(3),* Holt, Henry & Co. Bks. For Young Readers) Holt, Henry & Co.

Matsuoka, Yoko. If Chocolate Were Purple. Barton, Jen. gif. ed. 2013. (ENG.). 28p. (J). pap., instr.'s hndbk. ed. 10.89 *(978-0-615-78343-7(0),* Flickerfawn) Barton Bks.

Matsushita, Yoko. Descendants of Darkness. Matsushita, Yoko. 2006. (Descendants of Darkness Ser.: Vol. 10). (ENG.). 208p. pap. 9.99 *(978-1-4215-0321-9(2))* Viz Media.

—Descendants of Darkness. Matsushita, Yoko. DeConnick, Kelly Sue & Caselman, Lance. (Descendants of Darkness Ser.). (ENG.). Vol. 4. 2005. 184p. pap. 9.99 *(978-1-59116-702-0(7));* Vol. 11. 2006. 208p. (gr. 11). pap. 9.99 *(978-1-4215-0536-7(3))* Viz Media.

—Descendants of Darkness 8, Vol. 8. Matsushita, Yoko. 2005. (Descendants of Darkness Ser.). (ENG.). 184p. pap. 9.99 *(978-1-4215-0115-4(5))* Viz Media.

—Yami No Matsuei. Matsushita, Yoko. 2005. (Descendants of Darkness Ser.: Vol. 7). (ENG.). 192p. pap. 9.99 *(978-1-59116-983-3(6))* Viz Media.

—Yami No Matsuei. Matsushita, Yoko. Ury, David, tr. from JPN. 2005. (Descendants of Darkness Ser.: Vol. 6). (ENG.). 192p. pap. 9.99 *(978-1-59116-842-3(2))* Viz Media.

—Yami No Matsuei. Matsushita, Yoko. DeConnick, Kelly Sue & Caselman, Lance. 2004. (Descendants of Darkness Ser.). (ENG.). 200p. pap. 9.99 *(978-1-59116-507-1(5));* 2. 208p. pap. 9.99 *(978-1-59116-597-2(0))* Viz Media.

—Yami No Matsuei. Matsushita, Yoko. (Descendants of Darkness Ser.). (ENG.). Vol. 3. 2004. 200p. pap. 9.99 *(978-1-59116-460-9(5));* Vol. 5. 2005. 200p. pap. 9.99 *(978-1-59116-778-5(7));* Vol. 9. 2006. 192p. pap. 9.99 *(978-1-4215-0171-0(6))* Viz Media.

Matsuura, Tokihiko. Tuxedo Gin. Matsuura, Tokihiko. (Tuxedo Gin Ser.). (ENG.). 8. 2004. 200p. (YA). pap. 9.95 *(978-1-59116-489-0(3));* Vol. 1. 2003. 200p. pap. 9.95 *(978-1-59116-071-7(5));* Vol. 2. 2003. 192p. (YA). pap. 9.95 *(978-1-59116-072-4(3));* Vol. 3. 2003. 200p. (YA). pap. 9.95 *(978-1-59116-102-8(9));* Vol. 4. 2004. 200p. pap. 9.95 *(978-1-59116-131-8(2));* Vol. 5. 2004. 200p. pap. 9.95 *(978-1-59116-255-1(6));* Vol. 6. 2004. 200p. pap. 9.95 *(978-1-59116-322-0(6));* Vol. 7. 2004. 192p. pap. 9.95 *(978-1-59116-456-2(7));* Vol. 9. 2004. 200p. (YA). pap. 9.95 *(978-1-59116-585-9(7));* Vol. 10. 2005. 200p. (YA). pap. 9.95 *(978-1-59116-695-5(0));* Vol. 11. 2005. 192p. pap. 9.99 *(978-1-59116-744-0(2));* Vol. 12. 2005. 184p. pap. 9.99 *(978-1-59116-798-3(1));* Vol. 13. 2005. 200p. pap. 9.99 *(978-1-59116-861-4(9));* Vol. 14. 2005. 184p. pap. 9.99 *(978-1-4215-0033-1(7))* Viz Media.

Matsuzawa, Yoji, photos by. Gensundai Suizokukan. Sakanakun. 2010. (JPN., 48p. (J). *(978-4-09-217253-1(2))* Shogakukan.

Matt, Collins. A Picture Book of Harry Houdini. Adler, David A. & Adler, Michael S. 2010. (ENG.). 32p. (J). (gr. -1-3). pap. 7.99 *(978-0-8234-2302-6(6))* Holiday Hse., Inc.

Matt, Phelan & Phelan, Matt. Where I Live. Spinelli, Eileen. 2007. (ENG.). 112p. (J). (gr. 2-5). 16.99 *(978-0-8037-3122-6(1),* Dial) Penguin Publishing Group.

Matta, Gabriella & Legramandi, Francesco. I Am a Princess. Posner-Sanchez, Andrea. 2012. (Little Golden Book Ser.). (ENG.). 24p. (J). (gr. k-k). 3.99 *(978-0-7364-2906-1(9),* Golden/Disney) Random Hse. Children's Bks.

—The Sweetest Spring. Jordan, Apple. 2008. (Step into Reading Ser.). (ENG.). 32p. (J). (gr. k-3). pap. 3.99 *(978-0-375-84810-0(X))* Random Hse., Inc.

Matta, Gabriella, jt. illus. see Legramandi, Francesco.

Mattassi, Ezio. Pepito the Penguin, 1 vol. Mattassi, Ezio. 2009. 15p. pap. 24.95 *(978-1-61582-731-2(5))* PublishAmerica, Inc.

Mattel. Barbie What Shall I Be. Lombardi, Kristine. 2010. (Vinyl Shaped Purse Ser.). (ENG.). 72p. (J). (gr. -1-k). bds. 14.99 *(978-0-7944-2034-5(6))* Reader's Digest Assn., Inc., The.

Mattel & Ulkutay Design Group Staff. Barbie the Princess & the Popstar. Fontes, Justine. 2012. (Book & Jewelry Ser.: 1). (ENG.). 10p. (J). (gr. -1-3). bds. 9.99 *(978-0-7944-2580-7(1))* Reader's Digest Assn., Inc., The.

Mattel Barbie Staff. Barbie - A Fairy Secret. Fontes, Justine. 2011. (Panorama Sticker Storybook Ser.). (ENG.). 16p. (J). (gr. -1-2). pap. 7.99 *(978-0-7944-2171-7(7))* Reader's Digest Assn., Inc., The.

Mattel Barbie Staff & Ulkutay Design Group. Barbie the Princess & the Popstar. Fontes, Justine. 2012. (Panorama Sticker Storybook Ser.: 1). (ENG.). 24p. (J). (gr. -1-3). pap. 7.99 *(978-0-7944-2581-4(X))* Reader's Digest Assn., Inc., The.

Mattel Inc. Staff. Barbie Always in Style. 2011. (Storybook & Playset Ser.). (ENG.). 24p. (J). (gr. -1-1). 19.99 *(978-0-7944-2316-2(7))* Reader's Digest Assn., Inc., The.

—It's a Surprise Playhouse Storybook. Lombardi, Kristine. 2010. (Storybook & Playset Ser.). (ENG.). 16p. (J). (gr. -1-2). bds. 15.99 *(978-0-7944-2005-5(2))* Reader's Digest Assn., Inc., The.

Mattern, Scott. By Definition: Poems of Feelings. Holbrook, Sara. 2003. (ENG.). 48p. (J). (gr. 4-6). 15.95 *(978-1-59078-060-2(4));* pap. 8.95 *(978-1-59078-085-5(X))* Boyds Mills Pr.

Mattes-Ruggiero, Lynn. Where Did Grandma Go? Scanlon, Cara. 2008. (J). *(978-1-930596-85-6(5))* Amherst Pr.

—Where Did Grandpa Go? Scanlon, Cara. 2008. (J). *(978-1-930596-86-3(3))* Amherst Pr.

Matthes, Justice. The Red Sock Christmas. Frazier, Kelly. 2008. 25p. pap. 24.95 *(978-1-60610-704-1(6))* America Star Bks.

Mattheson, Jenny. The Great Tulip Trade. Brust, Beth Wagner. 2005. (Step into Reading Ser.). 48p. (J). (gr. 1-3). 11.65 *(978-0-7569-5160-3(7))* Perfection Learning Corp.

—Hanna & the Pajama Girls: The Case of the Sandy Keys. Wallach, Michelle. 2010. (ENG.). 108p. pap. 6.99 *(978-1-4537-6454-1(2))* CreateSpace Independent Publishing Platform.

—No Bows!, 1 vol. Duke, Shirley Smith. 2006. (ENG.). 32p. (J). (gr. k-1). 15.95 *(978-1-56145-356-6(0))* Peachtree Pubs.

Matthews, Ashley. Maya Visits a Hospital: Love Is the Best Medicine, 110 vols. Bucki, Jo Dee & O'Malley, John. Hicks, Mindy, ed. l.t. ed. 2007. 32p. (J). per. 4.95 *(978-0-9769069-0-2(2))* Strategic Visions, Inc.

Matthews, Bonnie. Blue Cheese Breath & Stinky Feet: How to Deal with Bullies. DePino, Catherine S. 2004. 48p. (J). 14.95 *(978-1-59147-111-0(7));* pap. 9.95 *(978-1-59147-112-7(5))* American Psychological Assn. (Magination Pr.).

—Coral Reefs. Earle, Sylvia A. 2003. (Jump into Science Ser.). (ENG.). 32p. (J). (gr. -1-3). 16.95 *(978-0-7922-6953-3(5))* National Geographic Society.

—What to Do When Bad Habits Take Hold: A Kid's Guide to Overcoming Nail Biting & More. Huebner, Dawn. 2008. 88p. (J). (gr. 6-12). pap. 15.95 *(978-1-4338-0383-3(6),* Magination Pr.) American Psychological Assn.

—What to Do When You Dread Your Bed: A Kid's Guide to Overcoming Problems with Sleep. Huebner, Dawn. 2008. (What to Do Guides for Kids Ser.). 93p. (J). (gr. 1-7). per. 15.95 *(978-1-4338-0318-5(6),* Magination Pr.) American Psychological Assn.

—What to Do When You Grumble Too Much: A Kid's Guide to Overcoming Negativity. Huebner, Dawn. 2006. ("What to Do" Guides for Kids Ser.). 88p. (J). (gr. 4-7). per. 15.95 *(978-1-59147-450-0(7),* Magination Pr.) American Psychological Assn.

—What to Do When Your Brain Gets Stuck: A Kid's Guide to Overcoming Ocd. Huebner, Dawn. 2007. 95p. (J). (gr. 3-7). per. 15.95 *(978-1-59147-805-8(7),* Magination Pr.) American Psychological Assn.

—What to Do When Your Temper Flares: A Kid's Guide to Overcoming Problems with Anger. Huebner, Dawn. 2007. (What-to-Do Guides for Kids Ser.). 95p. (J). (gr. 3-7). per. 15.95 *(978-1-4338-0134-1(5),* 4418005, Magination Pr.) American Psychological Assn.

Matthews, Brett. Tales of the Vampires. Edlund, Ben et al. 2004. (ENG.). 144p. pap. 15.95 *(978-1-56971-749-3(4))* Dark Horse Comics.

Matthews, Caitlin. StoryWorld: Quests & Adventures: Create-A-Story. Matthews, John. 2012. (Storyworld Ser.). (ENG.). (J). (gr. 4-7). 9.99 *(978-0-7636-5317-0(9),* Templar) Candlewick Pr.

Matthews, Derek. God Made Animals. Taylor, Jane & Macleod, Una. 2005. (Board Books God Made Ser.). (ENG.). 16p. (J). 3.99 *(978-1-85792-290-5(5))* Christian Focus Pubns. GBR. Dist: Send The Light Distribution LLC.

—God Made Me. Taylor, Jane & Macleod, Una. 2005. (Board Books God Made Ser.). (ENG.). 16p. (J). 3.99 *(978-1-85792-289-9(1))* Christian Focus Pubns. GBR. Dist: Send The Light Distribution LLC.

—Snappy Little Halloween. Steer, Dugald A. 2004. 20p. (J). (gr. k-4). reprint ed. 13.00 *(978-0-7567-7403-5(9))* DIANE Publishing Co.

Matthews, Elizabeth. Different Like Coco. Matthews, Elizabeth. 2007. (ENG.). 40p. (J). (gr. k-4). 16.99 *(978-0-7636-2548-1(5))* Candlewick Pr.

Matthews, Jacqueline M., jt. illus. see Matthews, Miriam.

Matthews, Jenny, photos by. Living in Bangladesh. Thomson, Ruth. 2006. (Living In- Ser.). 32p. (J). (gr. 4-7). lib. bdg. 27.10 *(978-1-59771-045-9(8))* Sea-To-Sea Pubns.

Matthews, Jenny, photos by. Children Growing up with War. Matthews, Jenny. 2014. (ENG., 48p. (J). (gr. 5). 17.99 *(978-0-7636-6942-3(3))* Candlewick Pr.

Matthews, John. The Everyday Easter Dress. Matthews, Elli. 2011. 24p. pap. 24.95 *(978-1-4560-9411-9(4))* America Star Bks.

Matthews, Melanie, jt. illus. see May, Kyla.

Matthews, Miriam & Matthews, Jacqueline M. A Whale Named Henry. Blanchet, M. Wylie. unabr. ed. (ENG.). 78p. (Orig.). (J). *(978-0-920080-33-7(2))* Harbour Publishing Co., Ltd.

Matthews, Rodney. Greek & Norse Legends. 2004. (Myths & Legends Ser.). 112p. (J). (gr. 6). lib. bdg. 20.95 *(978-1-58086-603-3(4))* EDC Publishing.

—Greek Myths & Legends. Evans, Cheryl & Millard, Anne. 2006. (Myths & Legends Ser.). 64p. (J). (gr. 6). lib. bdg. 18.95 *(978-1-58086-553-1(4))* EDC Publishing.

—Tales of King Arthur. rev. ed. 2007. (Usborne Classics Retold Ser.). 139p. (J). (gr. 4-7). per. 4.99 *(978-0-7945-1483-9(9),* Usborne) EDC Publishing.

Mattotti, Lorenzo. Hansel & Gretel. Gaiman, Neil. 2014. (ENG.). (J). (gr. 2-7). 56p. 16.95 *(978-1-935179-62-7(4));* 60p. 29.95 *(978-1-935179-65-8(9))* TOON Books / RAW Junior, LLC.

Mattozzi, Patricia. Santa's Prayer. Andes, Mary Lou. 2007. (J). (gr. -1-k). bds. 11.95 incl. cd-rom *(978-0-8198-7100-8(1))* Pauline Bks. & Media.

—Stations of the Cross for Children. Will, Julianne M. 2005. 32p. (J). (gr. -1-3). pap. 3.95 *(978-1-59276-153-1(4))* Our Sunday Visitor, Publishing Div.

Mattozzi, Patricia R. The Jesus Garden: An Easter Legend. Bosco, Antoinette. 2004. 44p. (J). 14.95 *(978-0-8198-3979-4(5),* 332-155) Pauline Bks. & Media.

—Little Book of Saints, 2 bks. Muldoon, Kathleen M. 2005. 24p. (J). Vol. 2. pap. 3.95 *(978-0-8198-4511-5(6),* 332-187); Vol. I. pap. 3.95 *(978-0-8198-4510-8(8),* 332-186) Pauline Bks. & Media.

Mattozzi, Patricia R. & Kinarney, Tom. My First Book of Saints. Muldoon, Kathleen M. & Wallace, Susan Helen. 2012. 128p. (J). 12.95 *(978-0-8198-4917-5(0))* Pauline Bks. & Media.

Mattucci, Sandra. Levi the Lightning Bug's Amazing Discovery. Mattucci, Sandra. 2012. 36p. 19.99 *(978-1-936453-08-5(8))* Bezalel Bks.

Matulay, Laszlo. We Were There at the First Airplane Flight. Sutton, Felix. 2013. (ENG.). 192p. (J). (gr. 3-8). pap. 6.99 *(978-0-486-49258-2(3))* Dover Pubns., Inc.

—We Were There at the First Airplane Flight. Sutton, Felix & Loening, Grover. 2011. 194p. 42.95 *(978-1-258-09600-7(5))* Literary Licensing, LLC.

Matuszak, Dagmara. Julio César. Rebscher, Susanne. Schleper, Frank, tr. from GER. 2009. (SPA.). 32p. (YA). (gr. 5-18). *(978-84-263-7255-0(4))* Vives, Luis Editorial (Edelvives).

Matyschenko, Tanya. Frogs by the Dozen. Bollen, Christine. l.t. ed. 2006. 24p. (J). per. 9.99 *(978-1-59879-115-0(X))* Lifevest Publishing, Inc.

Matysiak, Janek. System Shock, 1 vol. O'Donnell, Liam. 2006. (Graphic Quest Ser.). (ENG.). 88p. (gr. 3-3). pap. 5.95 *(978-1-59889-214-7(2),* Graphic Quest) Stone Arch Bks.

Matyuschenko, Tanya. An Angel in My Garden, 1 vol. Bollen, Christina. 2009. 47p. pap. 24.95 *(978-1-60813-661-2(2))* America Star Bks.

—Flying with the Geese, 1 vol. Bollen, Christine. 2010. 34p. 24.95 *(978-1-4489-4401-9(5))* PublishAmerica, Inc.

Matzen, Deon C. Chipper, the Heroic Chipmunk. Martin, Martha M. 2004. 32p. (J). (gr. -1-3). 16.95 *(978-0-9758580-0-4(9))* M & B Publishing.

Mauchline, Sarah. Posie Pixie & the Copper Kettle. Hill, Sarah. O'Gorman, Sarah, ed. 2013. 52p. pap. *(978-1-909302-20-4(1))* Abela Publishing.

—Posie Pixie & the Lost Matchbox. Hill, Sarah. O'Gorman, Sarah, ed. 2013. 60p. pap. *(978-1-909302-31-0(7))* Abela Publishing.

Mauerman, Nancy. Bearos. Mauerman, Nancy. Mauerman, John & Anderson, Amy, eds. l.t. ed. 2011. (ENG.). 30p. pap. 9.97 *(978-1-4664-3222-2(5))* CreateSpace Independent Publishing Platform.

Maughan, William. Horrible Hauntings: An Augmented Reality Collection of Ghosts & Ghouls. Bridges, Shirin Yim & Yim Bridges, Shirin. 2012. (ENG.). 24p. (gr. 6-7). 21.95 *(978-1-937463-99-1(0))* Goosebottom Bks. LLC.

Maughan, William L. Malian's Song. Bruchac, Marge. ed. 2006. (Vermont Folklife Center Children's Book Ser.). (ENG.). 32p. (J). (gr. -1-3). 16.95 *(978-0-916718-26-8(3))* Vermont Folklife Ctr.

Maunder, Brian. Polly's Little Kite. Maunder, Brian. 2014. (ENG.). 44p. (J). (gr. -1-3). pap. 11.95 *(978-1-56548-528-0(9))* New City Press of the Focolare.

Maureen, Roffey. A B C Animals Teach Me! 2014. (ENG.). 26p. (J). (gr. -1 — 1). bds. 5.99 *(978-0-7944-3017-7(1))* Reader's Digest Assn., Inc., The.

Maurice t, et al. Crossovers. Rodi, Rob. 2003. (Crossovers Ser.: Vol. 1). 160p. (YA). pap. 15.95 *(978-1-931484-85-5(6))* CrossGeneration Comics, Inc.

Mauricet. The Vampire from the Marshes. Vanholme, Virginie. 2008. (ENG.), 46p. pap. 11.95 *(978-1-905460-47-2(3))* CineBook GBR. Dist: National Bk. Network.

Mauro, Tony. Cold Case. Leonard, Julia Platt. 2011. (ENG.). 288p. (J). (gr. 3-7). 15.99 *(978-1-4424-2009-0(X),* Simon & Schuster/Paula Wiseman Bks.) Simon & Schuster/Paula Wiseman Bks.

Mauterer, Erin Marie. Los dos leemos-la Cama Colorada: Nivel 1. McKay, Sindy. 2006. (We Both Read Ser.). (SPA.). 48p. (J). (gr. -1-3). 7.99 *(978-1-891327-79-7(8));* pap. 3.99 *(978-1-891327-80-3(1))* Treasure Bay, Inc.

Mauzy, Barbara E. Don't Be a Schwoe: Manners, 1 vol. Mauzy, Barbara E. 2010. (ENG.). 64p. 14.99 *(978-0-7643-3428-3(X))* Schiffer Publishing, Ltd.

Maval Publishing Inc. Staff. Como el Viento Paso a Ser Tormenta. Hernandez, Mary L.Tr. of How the Tornado Got It's Wind. (SPA.). (J). (gr. -1-3). pap. 7.50 *(978-1-59134-015-7(2))* Maval Publishing, Inc.

Mavlian, Vatche. Spider-Man & Wolverine, 4 vols., Vol. 4. Matthews, Brett & Marvel Comics Staff. 2004. (Spider-Man Legends Ser.). 144p. (YA). pap. 13.99 *(978-0-7851-1297-6(9))* Marvel Worldwide, Inc.

Mavronis, Michelle. The Adventures of Rocky, Croaker & Spot. Gesser, Bernadette. 2008. 20p. pap. 24.95 *(978-1-60703-178-9(7))* America Star Bks.

Mawhinney, Art. Archie Babies. Kunkel, Mike. 2011. (Archie & Friends All-Stars Ser.: 11). (ENG.). 128p. (J). (gr. 2-5). pap. 9.95 *(978-1-879794-72-6(1),* Archie Comics) Archie Comic Pubns., Inc.

—Diego Saves the Sloth! Romay, Alexis. 2007. (Go, Diego, Go! Ser.: 4). (ENG.). 24p. (J). (gr. -1-2). pap. 3.99 *(978-1-4169-3470-7(7),* Simon Spotlight/Nickelodeon) Simon Spotlight/Nickelodeon.

—Diego's Arctic Rescue. 2009. (Go, Diego, Go! Ser.). (ENG.). 24p. (J). (gr. -1-2). pap. 3.99 *(978-1-4169-8504-4(2),* Simon Spotlight/Nickelodeon) Simon Spotlight/Nickelodeon.

—Diego's Birthday Surprise. Bergen, Lara. 2008. (Go, Diego, Go! Ser.: 8). (ENG.). 24p. (J). (gr. -1-1). pap. 3.99 *(978-1-4169-5431-6(7),* Simon Spotlight/Nickelodeon) Simon Spotlight/Nickelodeon.

—Diego's Halloween Party. Lindner, Brooke. 2008. (Go, Diego, Go! Ser.). (ENG.). 16p. (J). (gr. -1-k). bds. 5.99 *(978-1-4169-5497-2(X),* Simon Spotlight/Nickelodeon) Simon Spotlight/Nickelodeon.

—Diego's Ocean Adventure: A Book of Facts about Ocean Animals. Sollinger, Emily. 2008. (Go, Diego, Go! Ser.). (ENG.). 16p. (J). (gr. -1-2). pap. 6.99 *(978-1-4169-4781-3(7),* Simon Spotlight/Nickelodeon) Simon Spotlight/Nickelodeon.

—Diego's Wolf Pup Rescue. 2006. (Go, Diego, Go! Ser.: 1). (ENG.). 24p. (J). (gr. -1-2). pap. 3.99 *(978-1-4169-1559-1(1),* Simon Spotlight/Nickelodeon) Simon Spotlight/Nickelodeon.

—Dora & Diego Help the Dinosaur. ed. 2011. (Dora & Diego Ser.). (ENG.). 24p. (J). pap. 3.99 *(978-1-4424-1400-6(6),* Simon Spotlight/Nickelodeon) Simon Spotlight/Nickelodeon.

—Dora & Diego to the Rescue! 2010. (Go, Diego, Go! Ser.). (ENG.). 48p. (J). pap. 5.99 *(978-1-4424-0660-5(7),* Simon Spotlight/Nickelodeon) Simon Spotlight/Nickelodeon.

—Look & Find Disney Princess Worlds of Wonder. 2006. (Look & Find Books). (J). pap. 24.98 *(978-1-4127-6490-2(4))* Publications International, Ltd.

—Look & Find Open Season. 2007. 32p. (J). (gr. -1-3). lib. bdg. 7.98 *(978-1-4127-8889-2(7))* Publications International, Ltd.

—Olivia the Magnificent: A Lift-the-Flap Story. 2009. (Olivia TV Tie-In Ser.). (ENG.). 16p. (J). (gr. -1-2). pap. 6.99 *(978-1-4169-8297-5(3),* Simon Spotlight) Simon Spotlight.

—Roadwork! Lagonegro, Melissa & RH Disney Staff. 2008. (Step into Reading Ser.). (ENG.). 32p. (J). (gr. k-3). pap. 3.99 *(978-0-7364-2516-2(0),* RH/Disney) Random Hse. Children's Bks.

—Transformers. Burroughs, Caleb. 2007. (Look & Find (Publications International) Ser.). 16p. (J). (gr. -1-3). 7.98 *(978-1-4127-8673-7(8))* Publications International, Ltd.

Mawhinney, Art & Disney Storybook Artists Staff. Fairies. 2007. (Look & Find Ser.). 7.98 *(978-1-4127-7423-9(3))* Publications International, Ltd.

Mawhinney, Art & Johnson, Shane L. Olivia Meets Olivia. Bryant, Megan E. 2010. (Olivia TV Tie-In Ser.). (ENG.). 24p. (J). (gr. -1-2). 6.99 *(978-1-4169-9542-5(0),* Simon Spotlight) Simon Spotlight.

—OLIVIA Meets Olivia. 2011. (Olivia TV Tie-In Ser.). (ENG.). 24p. (J). (gr. -1-2). pap. 3.99 *(978-1-4424-4707-3(9),* Simon Spotlight) Simon Spotlight.

Mawhinney, Art, jt. illus. see DiCicco, Sue.

Mawhinney, Art, jt. illus. see Johnson, Shane L.

Mawson. The Tales of Henry Tuffin - Henry's Sore Foot & a New Arrival. Adams, Keith. Hewitt, Geoff, ed. 2013. 20p. pap. *(978-1-78222-105-0(0))* Paragon Publishing, Rothersthorpe.

Mawson, Alan. The Tales of Henry Tuffin - Henry Goes to School. Adams, Keith. Hewitt, Geoff, ed. 2013. 20p. pap. *(978-1-78222-103-6(4))* Paragon Publishing, Rothersthorpe.

—The Tales of Henry Tuffin - Henry's Christmas. Adams, Keith. Geoff Hewitt, ed. 2013. 32p. pap. *(978-1-78222-172-2(7))* Paragon Publishing, Rothersthorpe.

—The Tales of Henry Tuffin - the Day the Light Went Out. Adams, Keith. Hewitt, Geoff, ed. 2013. 20p. pap. *(978-1-78222-104-3(2))* Paragon Publishing, Rothersthorpe.

Max. El Ruiseñor. Bailer, Darice et al. 2007. (SPA & ENG.). 28p. (J). *(978-0-545-03029-8(3))* Scholastic, Inc.

—Thumbelina. Cosmic Debris Etc., Inc. Staff & Chronicle Books Staff. ed. 2004. (Bilingual Fairy Tales Ser.: BILI). (ENG & SPA.). 32p. (J). (gr. -1-7). 14.99 *(978-0-8118-3927-3(3))* Chronicle Bks. LLC.

Max and Sid Staff. Fun with Colors. Little Bee Books Staff & Brook-Piper, Holly. 2015. (Tiny Touch Ser.). (ENG.). 12p. (J). (gr. -1 — 1). bds. 4.99 *(978-1-4998-0001-2(0))* Little Bee Books Inc.

Max, Iman. DreamWorks' Dragons Vol.2: Dangers of the Deep. Titan Comics Staff & Furman, Simon. 2014. (Riders of Berk Ser.). (ENG.). 64p. (J). (gr. 3-7). pap. 6.99 *(978-1-78276-077-1(6),* Titan Comics) Titan Bks. Ltd. GBR. Dist: Random Hse., Inc.

Maxey, David. Cindy Big Hair: A Twisted (and Teased & Braided) Cinderella Story. Auerbach, Annie. 2005. 16p. (J). 12.95 *(978-1-58117-387-1(3),* Intervisual/Piggy Toes) Bendon, Inc.

Maxner, Pearl. The Hawaiian Bat: Ope'ape'a. Coste, Marion. 2005. (Latitude 20 Bks.). 30p. (J). (gr. 4-18). 14.99 *(978-0-8248-2797-7(X))* Univ. of Hawai'i Pr.

Maxwell, Cassandre. Fur, Fins, & Feathers: Abraham Dee Bartlett & the Invention of the Modern Zoo. 2015. 34p. (J). 17.00 ***(978-0-8028-5432-2(X)***, Eerdmans Bks For Young Readers) Eerdmans, William B. Publishing Co.

Maxwell, Cassandre. Silent Night: A Christmas Story. McCullough, L. E. 2006. 24p. (J). 7.95 *(978-0-88271-009-9(5))* Regina Pr., Malhame & Co.

—We Three Kings: A Christmas Story. McCullough, L. E. 2006. 24p. (J). 7.95 *(978-0-88271-010-5(9))* Regina Pr., Malhame & Co.

Maxwell, Jeremy. Ferdie the Fay Meets Flutterey the Butterfly: A Forest Fable. Robinson, Zan D. (Ferdie the Fay Adventure Ser.: No. 1). 52p. (Orig.). (J). (gr. -1-4). *(978-0-9635587-4-9(9))* Connors, E. W. Publishing Co.

Maxwell, Robert W. The Weeb Book. Maxwell, Robert W. 2009. 60p. pap. 20.00 *(978-1-59925-140-0(X))* Solid Ground Christian Bks.

May, Ashley. Jumpy the Turtle. Jeffords, Stephanie & Branum, Anita. 2012. 92p. pap. 20.00 *(978-1-936750-80-1(5))* Yorkshire Publishing Group.

May, Dan. Passage to Monterey. May, Dan, tr. Romeyn, Debra. 2003. (Adventures of Juan & Mariano Ser.: No. 1). 39p. (J). pap. 9.95 *(978-0-9729016-0-4(4))* Gossamer Bks.

May, Gillie. A contar con la sopa de Beto: Fiction-to-Fact Big Book. Schieber, Jennifer. enl. ed. 2004. (SPA.). (J). pap. 26.00 *(978-1-4108-2361-8(X)*, 2361X) Benchmark Education Co.

May, Gin. The Plumber & the Wishing Well. Maher, Liam. 2012. 24p. (gr. k-3). 19.95 *(978-1-61633-269-3(7))*; pap. 10.95 *(978-1-61633-268-6(9))* Guardian Angel Publishing, Inc.

May, Jason J. Save This Christmas! McCarthy, Rebecca. 2012. (Lego City Ser.). (ENG.). 24p. (J). (gr. -1-3). pap. 3.99 *(978-0-545-45727-9(0))* Scholastic, Inc.

May, Kate. Wish Fish. Hay, Sam. 2011. (My Phonics Readers: Level 2 Ser.). 24p. (J). (gr. -1-1). 24.25 *(978-1-84898-508-7(8))* Sea-To-Sea Pubns.

May, Kyla. The Dog Rules. La Rue, Coco. 2011. (ENG.). 128p. (J). (gr. 2-5). pap. 4.99 *(978-0-545-28261-1(6)*, Scholastic Paperbacks) Scholastic, Inc.

—A New Pig in Town. La Rue, Coco. 2013. 127p. (J). pap. *(978-0-545-46607-3(5))* Scholastic, Inc.

May, Kyla. Introducing Kyla May Miss. Behaves. May, Kyla. 2005. (Kyla May Miss. Behaves Ser.). (ENG.). 64p. (J). (gr. 2-5). pap. 5.99 *(978-0-8431-1370-9(7)*, Price Stern Sloan) Penguin Publishing Group.

—Kyla Miss. Behaves Around the World. May, Kyla. 2005. (Kyla May Miss. Behaves Ser.). (ENG.). 64p. (J). (gr. 2-5). pap. 5.99 *(978-0-8431-1371-6(5)*, Price Stern Sloan) Penguin Publishing Group.

May, Kyla & Matthews, Melanie. New Girl. Park, Louise. 2015. (Star Girl Ser.). (ENG.). 80p. (gr. 1-4). lib. bdg. 21.32 ***(978-1-4795-8275-4(1))*** Picture Window Bks.

—Odd One Out. Park, Louise. 2015. (Star Girl Ser.). (ENG.). 80p. (gr. 1-4). lib. bdg. 21.32 ***(978-1-4795-8276-1(X))*** Picture Window Bks.

—Three's a Crowd. Park, Louise. 2015. (Star Girl Ser.). (ENG.). 80p. (gr. 1-4). lib. bdg. 21.32 ***(978-1-4795-8278-5(6))*** Picture Window Bks.

—Winning Moves. Park, Louise. 2015. (Star Girl Ser.). (ENG.). 80p. (gr. 1-4). lib. bdg. 21.32 ***(978-1-4795-8277-8(8))*** Picture Window Bks.

May, Sandy. For the Love of Sapphire: The Promise. Mitchell, Gwendolyn. 2008. 27p. pap. 24.95 *(978-1-60813-029-0(0))* America Star Bks.

Mayberry, Maranda. My Day of Ballet. Feldman, Thea. 2007. (Magnix Imagination Activity Bks.). 6p. (J). (gr. -1-3). bds. 5.99 *(978-1-932915-41-9(9))* Sandvik Innovations, LLC.

Maydak, Michael. There's a Babirusa in My Bathtub: Fact & Fancy about Curious Creatures. Schur, Maxine Rose. 2009. 32p. (J). (gr. 2-7). pap. 8.95 *(978-1-58469-118-1(2))* Dawn Pubns.

Maydak, Michael S. Discovering Sharks & Rays. Field, Nancy H. 2003. (Discovering Nature Library). 40p. (J). (gr. 2-6). pap. 7.95 *(978-0-941042-33-8(2))* Dog-Eared Pubns.

Maydak, Michael S. Lifetimes. Rice, David L. 2015. 32p. pap. 9.00 ***(978-1-61003-549-1(6))*** Center for the Collaborative Classroom.

Maydak, Michael S. Millions of Monarchs. Roop, Connie & Roop, Peter. 2003. 30p. (J). *(978-0-439-43965-7(5))* Scholastic, Inc.

—Salmon Stream. Reed-jones, Carol. 2004. (Sharing Nature with Children Book Ser.). 32p. (YA). (gr. 4-7). 16.95 *(978-1-58469-014-6(3))*; pap. 7.95 *(978-1-58469-013-9(5))* Dawn Pubns.

—There's a Babirusa in My Bathtub: Fact & Fancy about Curious Creatures. Schur, Maxine Rose. 2009. 32p. (J). (gr. 2-7). 16.95 *(978-1-58469-117-4(4))* Dawn Pubns.

—The Web at Dragonfly Pond. Ellis, Brian. 2006. (Sharing Nature with Children Book Ser.). 32p. (J). (gr. 1-7). 16.95 *(978-1-58469-078-8(X))*; pap. 8.95 *(978-1-58469-079-5(8))* Dawn Pubns.

—Wild Stickers - Sharks & Rays. 2003. 4p. (J). 2.50 *(978-0-941042-34-5(0))* Dog-Eared Pubns.

Maydak, Mike. Gone Extinct! Parker, Katie. 2009. (ENG.). 24p. (J). (gr. k-17). 19.99 *(978-1-58476-941-5(6))* Innovative Kids.

Mayeaux, Alicia, jt. illus. see leger, Jarett.

Mayer, Bill. Brer Rabbit & Boss Lion. Kessler, Brad & Harris, Joel Chandler. 2004. (Rabbit Ears-A Classic Tale Ser.). 40p. (gr. k-5). 25.65 *(978-1-59197-760-5(6))* Spotlight.

—Hide & Sheep. Beaty, Andrea. 2011. (ENG.). 32p. (J). (gr. -1-3). 15.99 *(978-1-4169-2544-6(9)*, McElderry, Margaret K. Bks.) McElderry, Margaret K. Bks.

—The Monster Who Did My Math, 1 vol. Schnitzlein, Danny. (ENG.). 32p. (J). 2012. pap. 7.95 *(978-1-56145-668-0(3))*; 2007. 16.95 *(978-1-56145-420-4(6))* Peachtree Pubs.

—On My Very First School Day I Met... Stiles, Norman. 2005. (ENG.). 32p. (J). (gr. -1-3). 9.95 *(978-1-59687-182-3(2))* IBks., Inc.

—On My Very First School Day I Met... Stiles, Norman. 2005. 32p. (J). (gr. -1). 9.95 *(978-0-689-03924-9(7)*, Milk & Cookies) ibooks, Inc.

Mayer, Bill. Super Bugs. Meadows, Michelle. 2016. (J). ***(978-0-545-68756-0(X))*** Scholastic, Inc.

Mayer, Danuta. Tenzin's Deer. Soros, Barbara. (ENG.). 32p. (J). (gr. 2-4). 2007. pap. 7.99 *(978-1-84686-130-7(6))*; 2005. 16.99 *(978-1-905236-57-2(3))* Barefoot Bks., Inc.

—Tenzin's Deer: A Tibetan Tale. Soros, Barbara. 2003. 32p. (J). (gr. 2-5). 16.99 *(978-1-84148-811-0(9))* Barefoot Bks., Inc.

Mayer-Johnson. Full Schedule: A Picture Symbol Activity Book. McIlquham, Mary Caroline. 2005. 338p. spiral bd. 44.95 *(978-0-9768379-0-9(0))* Symtext Media.

Mayer, Jonathan. Anatomy of a Dragon. Doeden, Matt. 2013. (World of Dragons Ser.). (ENG.). 32p. (gr. 1-2). lib. bdg. 25.99 *(978-1-62065-145-2(9))* Capstone Pr., Inc.

—Dragon Behavior, 1 vol. Doeden, Matt. 2013. (World of Dragons Ser.). (ENG.). 32p. (gr. 1-2). lib. bdg. 25.99 *(978-1-62065-144-5(0))* Capstone Pr., Inc.

—Dragon Life, 1 vol. Doeden, Matt. 2008. (Dragons Ser.). (ENG.). 32p. (gr. 3-4). 27.32 *(978-1-4296-1297-5(5)*, Edge Bks.) Capstone Pr., Inc.

—Dragonatomy, 1 vol. Doeden, Matt. 2008. (Dragons Ser.). (ENG.). 32p. (gr. 3-4). 27.32 *(978-1-4296-1295-1(9)*, Edge Bks.) Capstone Pr., Inc.

Mayer, Jonathan & Pellegrino, Rich. The World of Dragons. Doeden, Matt. 2013. (World of Dragons Ser.). (ENG.). 32p. (gr. 1-2). lib. bdg. 103.96 *(978-1-62065-147-6(5)*, Blazers) Capstone Pr., Inc.

Mayer, Marianna, jt. illus. see Mayer, Mercer.

Mayer, Melody & Olson, Ed. The Crucifixion Part 1 ... the Road to the Cross Pt. I, Vol. 11: New Testament Volume 11 Life of Christ Part 11. Greiner, Ruth B. 2011. 36p. (J). pap. *(978-1-932381-41-2(4)*, 1011) Bible Visuals International, Inc.

—The Crucifixion Part 2 Christ Sacrifice Our Salvation Pt. 2, Vol. 12: New Testament Volume 12 Life of Christ Part 12. Greiner, Ruth B. 2011. 36p. (J). pap. *(978-1-932381-42-9(2)*, 1012) Bible Visuals International, Inc.

—Judgment the Wrath of God Vol. 44: New Testament Volume 44 Revelation Part 3. Greiner, Ruth B. 2010. 36p. (J). pap. *(978-1-932381-30-6(9)*, 1044) Bible Visuals International, Inc.

Mayer, Mercer, et al. Altogether, One at a Time. Konigsburg, E. L. & Haley, Gail E. 3rd ed. 2008. (ENG.). 96p. (J). (gr. 3-7). pap. 6.99 *(978-1-4169-5501-6(1)*, Atheneum Bks. for Young Readers) Simon & Schuster Children's Publishing.

Mayer, Mercer. The Great Brain. Fitzgerald, John D. 2004. (Great Brain Ser.). (ENG.). 192p. (J). (gr. 3-7). 5.99 *(978-0-14-240058-6(0)*, Puffin) Penguin Publishing Group.

—Me & My Little Brain. Fitzgerald, John D. 2004. (Great Brain Ser.). (ENG.). 144p. (J). (gr. 3-7). 5.99 *(978-0-14-240064-7(5)*, Puffin) Penguin Publishing Group.

—Me & My Little Brain. Fitzgerald, John D. 2004. (Great Brain Ser.). 137p. (gr. 3-7). 16.00 *(978-0-7569-2541-3(X))* Perfection Learning Corp.

—More Adventures of the Great Brain. Fitzgerald, John D. 2004. (Great Brain Ser.). (ENG.). 160p. (J). (gr. 3-7). pap. 5.99 *(978-0-14-240065-4(3)*, Puffin) Penguin Publishing Group.

—Outside My Window. Skorpen, Liesel Moak. 2004. 32p. (J). (gr. -1-3). 16.89 *(978-0-06-050775-6(6))* HarperCollins Pubs.

Mayer, Mercer. Bedtime Stories - Little Critter. Mayer, Mercer. 2013. (Little Critter Ser.). (ENG.). 144p. (J). (gr. -1-3). pap. 11.99 *(978-0-06-223640-1(7)*, HarperFestival) HarperCollins Pubs.

—The Best Teacher Ever No. 6. Mayer, Mercer. 2008. (Little Critter Ser.). (ENG.). 24p. (J). (gr. -1-2). pap. 3.99 *(978-0-06-053960-3(7)*, HarperFestival) HarperCollins Pubs.

—The Best Yard Sale. Mayer, Mercer. 2010. (Little Critter Ser.). (ENG.). 24p. (J). (gr. -1-2). pap. 3.99 *(978-0-06-147799-7(0)*, HarperFestival) HarperCollins Pubs.

—A Boy, a Dog, & a Frog. Mayer, Mercer. 2003. (Boy, a Dog, & a Frog Ser.). (ENG.). 32p. (J). (gr. -1-k). 6.99 *(978-0-8037-2880-6(8)*, Dial) Penguin Publishing Group.

—The Bravest Knight. Mayer, Mercer. 2007. (ENG.). 32p. (J). (gr. -1-3). 16.99 *(978-0-8037-3206-3(6)*, Dial) Penguin Publishing Group.

—Bye-Bye, Mom & Dad. Mayer, Mercer. 2004. (Little Critter Ser.). (ENG.). 24p. (J). (gr. -1-2). pap. 3.99 *(978-0-06-053945-0(3)*, HarperFestival) HarperCollins Pubs.

—The Fall Festival. Mayer, Mercer. 2009. (My First I Can Read Ser.). (ENG.). 32p. (J). (gr. -1-3). pap. 3.99 *(978-0-06-083551-4(6))* HarperCollins Pubs.

—The First Day of School No. 3. Mayer, Mercer. 2009. (Little Critter Ser.). (ENG.). 20p. (J). (gr. -1-2). pap. 6.99 *(978-0-06-053969-6(0)*, HarperFestival) HarperCollins Pubs.

—Frog Goes to Dinner. Mayer, Mercer. 2003. (Boy, a Dog, & a Frog Ser.). (ENG.). 32p. (J). (gr. -1-k). 6.99 *(978-0-8037-2884-4(0)*, Dial) Penguin Publishing Group.

—Frog on His Own. Mayer, Mercer. 2003. (Boy, a Dog, & a Frog Ser.). (ENG.). 32p. (J). (gr. -1-k). 6.99 *(978-0-8037-2883-7(2)*, Dial) Penguin Publishing Group.

—Frog, Where Are You? Mayer, Mercer. 2003. (Boy, a Dog, & a Frog Ser.). (ENG.). 32p. (J). (gr. -1-k). 6.99 *(978-0-8037-2881-3(6)*, Dial) Penguin Publishing Group.

—Going to the Firehouse. Mayer, Mercer. 2008. (My First I Can Read Ser.). (ENG.). 32p. (J). (gr. -1-3). 16.99 *(978-0-06-083546-0(X))*; pap. 3.99 *(978-0-06-083545-3(1))* HarperCollins Pubs.

—Going to the Sea Park. Mayer, Mercer. 2009. (My First I Can Read Ser.). (ENG.). 32p. (J). (gr. -1-3). pap. 3.99 *(978-0-06-083553-8(2))* HarperCollins Pubs.

—Good for Me & You. Mayer, Mercer. 2004. (Little Critter Ser.). (ENG.). 24p. (J). (gr. -1-2). pap. 3.99 *(978-0-06-053948-1(8)*, HarperFestival) HarperCollins Pubs.

—Grandma, Grandpa, & Me. Mayer, Mercer. 2007. (Little Critter Ser.). (ENG.). 24p. (J). (gr. -1-2). pap. 3.99 *(978-0-06-053951-1(8)*, HarperFestival) HarperCollins Pubs.

—A Green, Green Garden. Mayer, Mercer. 2011. (My First I Can Read Ser.). (ENG.). 32p. (J). (gr. -1-3). 16.99 *(978-0-06-083562-0(1))*; pap. 3.99 *(978-0-06-083561-3(3))* HarperCollins Pubs.

—Happy Halloween, Little Critter! Mayer, Mercer. 2004. (Little Critter Ser.). (ENG.). 16p. (J). (gr. -1-1). pap. 6.99 *(978-0-06-053971-9(2)*, HarperFestival) HarperCollins Pubs.

—Happy Mother's Day! Mayer, Mercer. 2009. (Little Critter Ser.). (ENG.). 20p. (J). (gr. -1-2). pap. 6.99 *(978-0-06-053970-2(4)*, HarperFestival) HarperCollins Pubs.

—Happy Valentine's Day, Little Critter! Mayer, Mercer. 2005. (Little Critter Ser.). (ENG.). 20p. (J). (gr. -1-3). pap. 6.99 *(978-0-06-053973-3(9)*, HarperFestival) HarperCollins Pubs.

—It's Earth Day!, No. 5. Mayer, Mercer. 2008. (Little Critter Ser.: No. 5). (ENG.). 24p. (J). (gr. -1-2). pap. 3.99 *(978-0-06-053959-7(3)*, HarperFestival) HarperCollins Pubs.

—It's Easter, Little Critter! Mayer, Mercer. 2007. (Little Critter Ser.). (ENG.). 20p. (J). (gr. -1-1). pap. 6.99 *(978-0-06-053974-0(7)*, HarperFestival) HarperCollins Pubs.

—Just a Big Storm. Mayer, Mercer. 2013. (Little Critter Ser.). (ENG.). 24p. (J). (gr. -1-2). pap. 3.99 *(978-0-06-147804-8(0)*, HarperFestival) HarperCollins Pubs.

—Just a Day at the Pond. Mayer, Mercer. 2008. (Little Critter Ser.). (ENG.). 24p. (J). (gr. -1-2). pap. 3.99 *(978-0-06-053961-0(5)*, HarperFestival) HarperCollins Pubs.

—Just a Kite. Mayer, Mercer. 2014. (My First I Can Read Ser.). (ENG.). 32p. (J). (gr. -1-3). 16.99 *(978-0-06-207197-2(1))* HarperCollins Pubs.

—Just a Little Critter Collection. Mayer, Mercer. 2005. (ENG.). 176p. (J). (gr. -1-2). 9.99 *(978-0-375-83255-0(6)*, Golden Bks.) Random Hse. Children's Bks.

—Just a Little Love. Mayer, Mercer. 2013. (My First I Can Read Ser.). (ENG.). 32p. (J). (gr. -1-3). 16.99 *(978-0-06-207196-5(3))* HarperCollins Pubs.

—Just a Little Luck. Mayer, Mercer. 2011. (Little Critter Ser.). (ENG.). 24p. (J). (gr. -1-2). pap. 3.99 *(978-0-06-147800-0(8)*, HarperFestival) HarperCollins Pubs.

—Just a Little Music. Mayer, Mercer. 2009. (Little Critter Ser.). (ENG.). 24p. (J). (gr. -1-3). pap. 3.99 *(978-0-06-053962-7(3)*, HarperFestival) HarperCollins Pubs.

—Just a Little Sick. Mayer, Mercer. 2009. (My First I Can Read Ser.). (ENG.). 32p. (J). (gr. -1-3). 16.99 *(978-0-06-083556-9(7))*; pap. 3.99 *(978-0-06-083555-2(9))* HarperCollins Pubs.

—Just a Little Too Little. Mayer, Mercer. 2012. (Little Critter Ser.). (ENG.). 24p. (J). (gr. -1-3). pap. 3.99 *(978-0-06-147802-4(4)*, HarperFestival) HarperCollins Pubs.

—Just a School Project. Mayer, Mercer. 2004. (Little Critter Ser.). (ENG.). 24p. (J). (gr. -1-2). pap. 3.99 *(978-0-06-053946-7(1)*, HarperFestival) HarperCollins Pubs.

—Just a Storybook Collection: Bye-Bye, Mom & Dad; Just a School Project; Just a Snowman; Good for Me & You; Just Big Enough; My Trip to the Hospital. Mayer, Mercer. 2012. (Little Critter Ser.). (ENG.). 176p. (J). (gr. -1-3). 11.99 *(978-0-06-213452-3(3))* HarperCollins Pubs.

—Just a Teacher's Pet. Mayer, Mercer. 2015. (My First I Can Read Ser.). (ENG.). 32p. (J). (gr. -1-3). pap. 3.99 *(978-0-06-147819-2(9))* HarperCollins Pubs.

—Just Big Enough. Mayer, Mercer. 2013. (Little Critter Ser.). (ENG.). 24p. (J). (gr. -1-2). pap. 3.99 *(978-0-06-147805-5(9)*, HarperFestival) HarperCollins Pubs.

—Just Critters Who Care. Mayer, Mercer. 2010. (My First I Can Read Ser.). (ENG.). 32p. (J). (gr. -1-3). 16.99 *(978-0-06-083560-6(5))*; pap. 3.99 *(978-0-06-083559-0(1))* HarperCollins Pubs.

—Just Fishing with Grandma. Mayer, Mercer. Mayer, Gina. 2015. (Little Critter Ser.). (ENG.). 24p. (J). (gr. -1-3). pap. 3.99 *(978-0-06-147808-6(3)*, HarperFestival) HarperCollins Pubs.

—Just Helping My Dad. Mayer, Mercer. 2011. (My First I Can Read Ser.). (ENG.). 32p. (J). (gr. -1-3). 16.99 *(978-0-06-083564-4(8))*; pap. 3.99 *(978-0-06-083563-7(X))* HarperCollins Pubs.

—Just Me & My Mom/Just Me & My Dad (Mercer Mayer's Little Critter) Mayer, Mercer. 2014. (Flip-It Pictureback Ser.). (ENG.). 48p. (J). (gr. -1-2). 4.99 *(978-0-385-37175-9(6)*, Random Hse. Bks. for Young Readers) Random Hse. Children's Bks.

—Just My Lost Treasure. Mayer, Mercer. 2014. (Little Critter Ser.). (ENG.). 24p. (J). (gr. -1-3). pap. 3.99 *(978-0-06-147806-2(7)*, HarperFestival) HarperCollins Pubs.

—Just One More Pet. Mayer, Mercer. 2013. (Little Critter Ser.). (ENG.). 24p. (J). (gr. -1-2). pap. 3.99 *(978-0-06-147807-9(5)*, HarperFestival) HarperCollins Pubs.

—Just Saving My Money. Mayer, Mercer. 2010. (My First I Can Read Ser.). (ENG.). 32p. (J). (gr. -1-3). pap. 3.99 *(978-0-06-083557-6(5))* HarperCollins Pubs.

—Little Critter: Just a Snowman. Mayer, Mercer. 2004. (Little Critter Ser.). (ENG.). 24p. (J). (gr. -1-2). pap. 3.99 *(978-0-06-053947-4(X)*, HarperFestival) HarperCollins Pubs.

—Little Critter: We Are Moving. Mayer, Mercer. 2012. (Little Critter Ser.). (ENG.). 24p. (J). (gr. -1-2). pap. 3.99 *(978-0-06-147803-1(2)*, HarperFestival) HarperCollins Pubs.

—Little Critter - Just a Little Love. Mayer, Mercer. 2013. (My First I Can Read Ser.). (ENG.). 20p. (J). (gr. -1-3). pap. 3.99 *(978-0-06-147815-4(6))* HarperCollins Pubs.

—Little Critter - Just a Special Day. Mayer, Mercer. 2014. (My First I Can Read Ser.). (ENG.). 32p. (J). (gr. -1-3). pap. 3.99 *(978-0-06-147817-8(2))* HarperCollins Pubs.

—Little Critter Collection. Mayer, Mercer. 2012. (My First I Can Read Ser.). (ENG.). 96p. (J). (gr. -1 — 1). pap. 11.99 *(978-0-06-207567-3(5))* HarperCollins Pubs.

Mayer, Mercer. Little Critter Fall Storybook Collection. Mayer, Mercer. 2015. (Little Critter Ser.). (ENG.). 192p. (J). (gr. -1-3). 11.99 ***(978-0-06-238032-6(X))*** HarperCollins Pubs.

Mayer, Mercer. Little Critter: Just a Kite. Mayer, Mercer. 2014. (My First I Can Read Ser.). (ENG.). 32p. (J). (gr. -1-3). pap. 3.99 *(978-0-06-147814-7(8))* HarperCollins Pubs.

—Little Critter Storybook Collection. Mayer, Mercer. 2005. (Little Critter Ser.). (ENG.). 176p. (J). (gr. -1-3). 11.99 *(978-0-06-082009-1(8)*, HarperFestival) HarperCollins Pubs.

—The Lost Dinosaur Bone. Mayer, Mercer. 2007. (Little Critter Ser.). (ENG.). 24p. (J). (gr. -1-3). pap. 3.99 *(978-0-06-053952-8(6)*, HarperFestival) HarperCollins Pubs.

—Merry Christmas, Little Critter! Mayer, Mercer. 2004. (Little Critter Ser.). (ENG.). 16p. (J). (gr. -1-1). pap. 6.99 *(978-0-06-053972-6(0)*, HarperFestival) HarperCollins Pubs.

—My Trip to the Hospital, No. 5. Mayer, Mercer. 2005. (Little Critter Ser.). (ENG.). 24p. (J). (gr. -1-2). pap. 3.99 *(978-0-06-053949-8(6)*, HarperFestival) HarperCollins Pubs.

—Octopus Soup, 0 vols. Mayer, Mercer. 2011. (ENG.). 24p. (J). (gr. k-3). 16.99 *(978-0-7614-5812-8(3)*, 9780761458128, Amazon Children's Publishing) Amazon Publishing.

—Phonics Fun. Mayer, Mercer. 2012. (My First I Can Read Ser.). (ENG.). 144p. (J). (gr. -1-k). pap. 12.99 *(978-0-06-147825-3(3))* HarperCollins Pubs.

—Sleeps Over. Mayer, Mercer. 2010. (Step into Reading Ser.). (ENG.). 32p. (J). (gr. -1-1). pap. 3.99 *(978-0-307-26203-5(0)*, Random Hse. Bks. for Young Readers) Random Hse. Children's Bks.

—Snowball Soup. Mayer, Mercer. 2007. (My First I Can Read Bks.). (ENG.). 32p. (J). (gr. -1-k). 16.99 *(978-0-06-083544-6(3))*; pap. 3.99 *(978-0-06-083543-9(5))* HarperCollins Pubs.

—This Is My Town. Mayer, Mercer. 2008. (My First I Can Read Ser.). (ENG.). 32p. (J). (gr. -1-3). pap. 3.99 *(978-0-06-083549-1(4))* HarperCollins Pubs.

—To the Rescue! Mayer, Mercer. 2008. (My First I Can Read Bks.). (ENG.). 32p. (J). (gr. -1-3). 16.99 *(978-0-06-083548-4(6))*; pap. 3.99 *(978-0-06-083547-7(8))* HarperCollins Pubs.

—Too Many Dinosaurs. Mayer, Mercer. (ENG.). 40p. (J). 2012. (gr. -1-2). pap. 6.99 *(978-0-8234-2543-3(6))*; 2011. 16.95 *(978-0-8234-2316-3(6))* Holiday Hse., Inc.

—What a Good Kitty. Mayer, Mercer. 2012. (My First I Can Read Ser.). (ENG.). 32p. (J). (gr. -1-3). 16.99 *(978-0-06-083566-8(4))*; pap. 3.99 *(978-0-06-083565-1(6))* HarperCollins Pubs.

—What Do You Do with a Kangaroo? Mayer, Mercer. 2008. (ENG.). (J). (gr. -1-3). 9.99 *(978-0-545-07457-5(6))*; 18.95 *(978-0-545-07460-5(6))* Scholastic, Inc.

Mayer, Mercer & Mayer, Marianna. A Boy, a Dog, a Frog & a Friend. Mayer, Mercer & Mayer, Marianna. 2003. (Boy, a Dog, & a Frog Ser.). (ENG.). 32p. (J). (gr. -1-k). 6.99 *(978-0-8037-2882-0(4)*, Dial) Penguin Publishing Group.

—One Frog Too Many. Mayer, Mercer & Mayer, Marianna. 2003. (Boy, a Dog, & a Frog Ser.). (ENG.). 32p. (J). (gr. -1-k). 6.99 *(978-0-8037-2885-1(9)*, Dial) Penguin Publishing Group.

Mayer, Uwe. The Stinking Story of Garbage. Daynes, Katie. (Usborne Young Reading: Series Two Ser.). (J). 2006. 64p. (gr. 4-7). per. 5.99 *(978-0-7945-1247-7(X))*; 2007. 62p. (gr. -1-3). 8.99 *(978-0-7945-1750-2(1))* EDC Publishing. (Usborne).

—Usborne the Children's Book of Art: Internet Linked. Dickins, Rosie. Armstrong, Carrie, ed. 2006. 64p. (J). (gr. 5-9). 14.99 *(978-0-7945-1223-1(2)*, Usborne) EDC Publishing.

Mayer, Uwe & McNee, Ian. The Story of Painting. Wheatley, Abigail. Riley, Janis, ed. 2007. (Story of Painting Ser.). 96p. (J). (gr. 4-7). pap. 10.99 *(978-0-7945-1678-9(5)*, Usborne) EDC Publishing.

Mayer, Uwe, jt. illus. see Chen, Kuo Kang.

Mayer, Uwe, jt. illus. see Donaera, Patrizia.

Mayer, Uwe, jt. illus. see Guille, Rosanne.

Mayer, Uwe, jt. illus. see Silver, Maggie.

Mayes, Steven. Introducing... Max, 1 vol. Mayes, Rosey. 2010. 16p. 24.95 *(978-1-4489-3895-7(3))* PublishAmerica, Inc.

Mayfield, Helen. The Enchanted Deer. 77p. (Orig.). (J). (gr. 6-18). pap. 4.00 *(978-1-884993-03-9(6))* Koldarana Pubns.

—The Island of the Three Sapphires. Robbins, Neal. 98p. (J). (gr. 6-18). pap. 4.00 *(978-1-884993-04-6(4))* Koldarana Pubns.

Mayhew, James. Classic Poems to Read Aloud. Berry, James. 2003. (Classic Collections). (ENG.). 256p. (J). (gr. 2-5). pap. 8.99 *(978-0-7534-5688-0(5)*, Kingfisher) Roaring Brook Pr.

—Shakespeare's Storybook: Folk Tales That Inspired the Bard. Ryan, Patrick. (ENG.). (J). 2009. 21.99 *(978-1-84686-271-7(X))*; 2006. 80p. (gr. 4-7). pap. 16.99 *(978-1-905236-86-2(7))* Barefoot Bks., Inc.

Mayhew, James. Boy. Mayhew, James. 2012. (ENG.). 32p. (J). (gr. -1-k). pap. 8.99 *(978-1-4083-1409-8(6))* Hodder & Stoughton GBR. Dist: Independent Pubs. Group.

—Katie & the Dinosaurs. Mayhew, James. 2015. (Katie Ser.). (ENG.). 32p. (J). (-k). 9.99 *(978-1-4083-3191-0(8))* Hodder & Stoughton GBR. Dist: Independent Pubs. Group.

—Katie & the Spanish Princess. Mayhew, James. 2009. (Katie Ser.). (ENG.). 32p. (J). (gr. -1-3). pap. 10.99 *(978-1-84616-248-0(3))* Hodder & Stoughton GBR. Dist: Independent Pubs. Group.

—Katie & the Starry Night. Mayhew, James. 2013. (Katie Ser.). (ENG.). 32p. (J). (-k). pap. 9.99 *(978-1-4083-0466-2(X))* Hodder & Stoughton GBR. Dist: Independent Pubs. Group.

—Katie's London Christmas. Mayhew, James. 2014. (Katie Ser.). (ENG.). 32p. (J). (-k). 16.99 *(978-1-4083-2641-1(8))* Hodder & Stoughton GBR. Dist: Independent Pubs. Group.

—Katie's Picture Show. Mayhew, James. 2014. (Katie Ser.). (ENG.). 32p. (J). (-k). 16.99 *(978-1-4083-3605-2(7))* Hodder & Stoughton GBR. Dist: Independent Pubs. Group.

Mayhew, Sara E. First Emperor. Low, Vicki. 2007. 48p. (J). lib. bdg. 23.08 *(978-1-4242-1626-0(5))* Fitzgerald Bks.

Maylin, Grace B., photos by. There Will Come Another: A Lesson from the Trees. Maylin, Grace B. 2007. per. *(978-0-9792384-0-6(4))* Maylin, Grace.

Maynard, Marc. Weather. Litchfield, Jo. 2008. (Usborne Look & Say Ser.). 12p. (J). (gr. -1-3). bds. 7.99 *(978-0-7945-1989-6(X)*, Usborne) EDC Publishing.

Mayne, Michael. A Wild Ride. Biggs, Pauline. 2004. 20p. (J). per. 12.95 *(978-0-9760129-0-0(1))* The Publishing Place LLC.

Mayo, Diana. The Children of Lir: A Celtic Legend. Casey, Dawn. 2004. 32p. (J). pap. *(978-1-85269-897-3(7))*; pap. *(978-1-85269-892-8(6))*; pap. *(978-1-85269-887-4(X))*; pap. *(978-1-85269-878-2(0))*; pap. *(978-1-85269-873-7(X))*; pap. *(978-1-85269-872-0(1))*; pap. *(978-1-85269-868-3(3))*; pap. *(978-1-85269-867-6(5))*; pap. *(978-1-85269-863-8(2))*; pap. *(978-1-85269-858-4(6))*; pap. *(978-1-85269-853-9(5))*; pap. *(978-1-85269-848-5(9))*; pap. *(978-1-85269-843-0(8))*; pap. *(978-1-85269-838-6(1))*; pap. *(978-1-85269-828-7(4))*; pap. *(978-1-85269-823-2(3))*; pap. *(978-1-85269-818-8(7))* Mantra Lingua.

—The Gingerbread Man. Lupton, Hugh. 2003. 24p. (J). (gr. k-3). 14.99 *(978-1-84148-056-5(8))* Barefoot Bks., Inc.

—Isis & Osiris. 2004. (J). *(978-1-84444-313-0(2))*; *(978-1-84444-314-7(0))*; *(978-1-84444-316-1(7))*; *(978-1-84444-318-5(3))*; 30p. *(978-1-84444-320-8(5))*; *(978-1-84444-321-5(3))*; *(978-1-84444-322-2(1))*; *(978-1-84444-324-6(8))*; *(978-1-84444-325-3(6))*; *(978-1-84444-326-0(4))*; 30p. *(978-1-84444-327-7(2))*; *(978-1-84444-328-4(0))*; *(978-1-84444-329-1(9))*; *(978-1-84444-331-4(0))*; (ENG & FRE.). 32p. pap. *(978-1-84444-319-2(1))* Mantra Lingua.

—My Little Picture Bible. Dorling Kindersley Publishing Staff. 2008. (ENG.). 80p. (J). (gr. -1 — 1). 7.99 *(978-0-7566-3997-6(2))* Dorling Kindersley Publishing, Inc.

—Pandora's Box. Barkow, Henriette. 2004. (ENG & ARA.). 32p. (J). pap. *(978-1-85269-898-0(5))*; pap. *(978-1-85269-894-2(2))*; pap. *(978-1-85269-893-5(4))*; pap. *(978-1-85269-889-8(6))*; pap. *(978-1-85269-884-3(5))*; pap. *(978-1-85269-879-9(9))*; pap. *(978-1-85269-874-4(8))*; pap. *(978-1-85269-869-0(1))*; pap. *(978-1-85269-864-5(0))*; pap. *(978-1-85269-859-1(4))*; pap. *(978-1-85269-854-6(3))*; pap. *(978-1-85269-849-2(7))*; pap. *(978-1-85269-844-7(6))*; pap. *(978-1-85269-839-3(X))*; pap. *(978-1-85269-834-8(9))*; pap. *(978-1-85269-829-4(2))*; pap. *(978-1-85269-824-9(1))*; pap. *(978-1-85269-819-5(5))* Mantra Lingua.

—Pandora's Box: English Only. Barkow, Henriette. 2004. (ENG.). 32p. (J). pap. *(978-1-84444-380-2(9))* Mantra Lingua.

—The Tiger & the Wise Man. Peters, Andrew Fusek. 2004. (Traditional Tales with a Twist Ser.). (ENG.). 32p. (J). *(978-1-904550-07-5(X))* Child's Play International Ltd.

—The Tiger & the Wise Man. Peters, Andrew. 2010. (Traditional Tales with a Twist Ser.). (ENG.). 32p. (J). (gr. -1-2). *(978-1-84643-346-7(0))* Child's Play International Ltd.

—Winter King, Summer Queen. Lister, Mary. 2007. (ENG.). 32p. (J). (gr. -1-3). pap. 9.99 *(978-1-84686-009-6(1))*; pap. 7.99 *(978-1-84686-080-5(6))* Barefoot Bks., Inc.

Mayo, Diana & Mistry, Nilesh. Isis & Osiris. Casey, Dawn. 2004. (ENG & BEN.). 32p. (J). pap. *(978-1-84444-315-4(9))*; pap. *(978-1-84444-323-9(X))*; pap. *(978-1-84444-330-7(2))*; pap. *(978-1-84444-433-5(3))*; pap. *(978-1-84444-434-2(1))*; pap. *(978-1-84444-435-9(X))* Mantra Lingua.

Mayo, Frank. An Alligator Adventure in Florida. Wilsdon, Christina. 2006. 26p. (J). 7.99 *(978-1-59939-010-9(8))* Cornerstone Pr.

—King Midas & the Golden Touch: A Tale about Greed. 2006. (J). 6.99 *(978-1-59939-022-2(1))* Cornerstone Pr.

Mays, Victor. Patrick Henry: Firebrand of the Revolution. Campion, Nardi Reeder. 2011. 272p. 47.95 *(978-1-258-04065-9(4))* Literary Licensing, LLC.

—Wells Fargo. Moody, Ralph. 2005. (ENG.). 186p. pap. 13.95 *(978-0-8032-8303-9(2)*, MOOWEX, Bison Bks.) Univ. of Nebraska Pr.

Mazali, Gustavo. Celebra el Cuatro de Julio con Campeon, el Gloton. Flor Ada, Alma. 2006. (Cuentos para Celebrar / Stories to Celebrate Ser.). (SPA.). 30p. (gr. k-6). per. 11.95 *(978-1-59820-119-2(0))* Santillana USA Publishing Co., Inc.

—Celebrate Fourth of July with Champ, the Scamp. Flor Ada, Alma. 2006. (Cuentos para Celebrar / Stories to Celebrate Ser.). 30p. (gr. k-6). per. 11.95 *(978-1-59820-131-4(X))* Santillana USA Publishing Co., Inc.

—Como Mamá. Munoz, Isabel. ed. 2006. (Eric & Julieta Ser.). (ENG & SPA.). 24p. (J). (gr. -1-3). pap. 3.99 *(978-0-439-78369-9(0))* Scholastic, Inc.

—Daddy Lost His Job. Moore-Mallinos, Jennifer. 2013. (Life Lessons Ser.). (ENG.). 32p. (J). (gr. -1-2). pap. 6.99 *(978-1-4380-0348-1(X))* Barron's Educational Series, Inc.

—A Day with Daddy. Gikow, Louise. 2004. (My First Reader Ser.). (ENG.). 32p. (J). (gr. k-1). pap. 3.95 *(978-0-516-25501-9(0)*, Children's Pr.) Scholastic Library Publishing.

—Desastre en la Cocina. Muñoz, Isabel. 2012. (Eric & Julieta Ser.). (SPA & ENG.). 24p. (J). (gr. -1-3). pap. 3.99 *(978-0-545-35581-0(8)*, Scholastic en Espanol) Scholastic, Inc.

—En el Museo. Munoz, Isabel. ed. 2011. (Eric & Julieta Ser.).Tr. of At the Museum. (SPA & ENG.). 24p. (J). (gr. -1-3). pap. 3.99 *(978-0-545-34512-5(X)*, Scholastic en Espanol) Scholastic, Inc.

—It's Mine (Es Mío) Munoz, Isabel. ed. 2006. (Eric & Julieta Ser.). (ENG & SPA.). 24p. (J). (gr. -1-3). pap. 3.99 *(978-0-439-78370-5(4))* Scholastic, Inc.

—Just Like Mom. Muñoz, Isabel. 2005. 22p. (J). pap. *(978-0-439-78844-1(7))* Scholastic, Inc.

—My First Handy Bible. Olesen, Cecilie. 2006. (ENG.). 64p. (gr. -1-k). bds. 12.99 *(978-1-59052-608-8(2)*, Multnomah) Doubleday Religious Publishing Group, The.

—Studying Is Hard. Moore-Mallinos, Jennifer. 2013. (Life Lessons Ser.). (ENG.). 32p. (J). (gr. -1-2). pap. 6.99 *(978-1-4380-0350-4(1))* Barron's Educational Series, Inc.

—Trucks & Diggers. Brooks, Felicity & Durber, Matt. 2008. (Magnet Bks.). 10p. (J). (gr. -1-3). bds. 19.99 *(978-0-7945-1907-0(5)*, Usborne) EDC Publishing.

—Where Is Eric? (¿Donde Está Eric?) Munoz, Isabel. 2006. (Eric & Julieta Ser.). (ENG & SPA.). 24p. (J). (gr. -1-3). pap. 3.99 *(978-0-439-78371-2(2))* Scholastic, Inc.

Maze, Deborah, jt. illus. see Williams, Garth.

Maze, Ellen. The Curse of Yama: The C. Walker Adventures. Ridley, K. F. 2011. (ENG.). 166p. pap. 7.50 *(978-1-4679-6891-1(9))* CreateSpace Independent Publishing Platform.

Mazellan, Ron. Finding Daddy: A Story of the Great Depression. Harper, Jo & Harper, Josephine. 2005. (ENG.). 48p. (J). (gr. k). 16.95 *(978-1-890515-31-7(0))* Turtle Bks.

—Irena's Jars of Secrets, 1 vol. Vaughan, Marcia. 2011. (ENG.). 40p. (J). 18.95 *(978-1-60060-439-3(0))* Lee & Low Bks., Inc.

—A Is for Abraham: A Jewish Family Alphabet. Michelson, Richard. 2008. (ENG.). 40p. (J). (gr. 1-4). 17.95 *(978-1-58536-322-3(7)*, 202126) Sleeping Bear Pr.

—Kids' Questions about Church & the Future. Fawcett, Cheryl & Newman, Robert C. 2003. 79p. pap. *(978-1-59402-084-1(1))* Regular Baptist Pr.

—Kids' Questions about God & Jesus. Fawcett, Cheryl & Newman, Robert C. 2003. 71p. pap. *(978-1-59402-081-0(7))* Regular Baptist Pr.

—We Will Walk. 2005. 16p. (J). pap. *(978-0-7367-2919-2(4))* Zaner-Bloser, Inc.

—You Can Be a Friend. Dungy, Tony & Dungy, Lauren. 2011. (ENG.). 32p. (J). (gr. -1-2). 16.99 *(978-1-4169-9771-9(7)*, Little Simon Inspirations) Little Simon Inspirations.

Mazellan, Ron. The Harmonica. Mazellan, Ron. Johnston, Tony. 2008. (ENG.). 32p. (J). (gr. 2-5). pap. 7.95 *(978-1-57091-489-8(3))* Charlesbridge Publishing, Inc.

Mazerac, Joseph. ANDY, Book 1: The Rise of David. Mazerac, Joseph. 2007. (ENG.). 96p. 9.99 *(978-0-9792770-0-9(0))* Old Time Stories.

Mazibuko, Luthando. How Riley Rescued the Hufffy Woofer. Garrott, Dawn E. 2015. (J). ***(978-1-61851-092-1(4))*** Baha'i Publishing.

Mazibuko, Luthando. Mema Says Good-Bye. Jaskwhich, Cynthia Sheperd. 2010. (J). *(978-0-87743-710-9(6))* Baha'i Publishing Trust, U.S.

Mazille, Capucine. My Take-Along Bible. Davidson, Alice Joyce. 2004. 20p. (J). bds. 9.99 *(978-0-89221-577-5(1))* New Leaf Pr., Inc.

—Red Riding Hood's Math Adventure. Harcourt, Lalie & Wortzman, Rickie. 2006. 19p. (J). (gr. k-4). reprint ed. 15.00 *(978-0-7567-9957-1(0))* DIANE Publishing Co.

Mazumdar, Sintu. Ben Brown & the Return of the Nephilim. Thorp, Michael C. 2010. 172p. (YA). pap. *(978-0-473-15580-3(X))* Free House Publishing.

Mazzara, Mauro. Dirty Rotten Rulers: History's Villains & Their Dastardly Deeds. Ticktock & Pipe, Jim. 2014. (ENG.). 64p. (J). (gr. 3-7). pap. 8.99 *(978-1-78325-163-6(8)*, TickTock Books) Octopus Publishing Group GBR. Dist: Hachette Bk. Group.

Mazzara, Mauro, jt. illus. see Finlayson, Luke.

Mazzei, Miriam. Does It Still Hurt. Pinto, Marie Parks. 2012. 30p. pap. 16.95 *(978-1-938812-02-6(6))* Full Court Pr.

—I Am Not Broken. Pinto, Marie Parks. 2012. (ENG.). 30p. pap. 16.95 *(978-1-938812-00-2(X))* Full Court Pr.

—Where Is Daddy? Pinto, Marie Parks. 2012. 30p. pap. 16.95 *(978-1-938812-06-4(9))* Full Court Pr.

Mazzola, Frank, Jr. The Ocean Alphabet Board Book. Pallotta, Jerry. 2003. (ENG.). 28p. (J). (-k). bds. 7.95 *(978-1-57091-524-6(5))* Charlesbridge Publishing, Inc.

Mazzon, Michelle, jt. illus. see Castellan, Andrea "Casty".

Mazzucchelli, David, jt. illus. see Hernandez, Gilbert.

Mazzucco, Jennifer. Little Johnny Buttermilk: After an Old English Folktale. Wahl, Jan. 2005. (ENG.). 32p. (J). (gr. -1-3). 15.95 *(978-0-87483-559-5(3))* August Hse. Pubs., Inc.

—The Pig Who Went Home on Sunday: An Appalachian Folktale. Davis, Donald. (ENG.). 40p. (J). (gr. -1-3). 2007. 7.95 *(978-0-87483-851-0(7))*; 2005. 16.95 *(978-0-87483-571-7(2))* August Hse. Pubs., Inc.

Mbairamadji, Koffi. African Savannah Stories, Volume 1. Mbairamadji, Koffi. 2006. 40p. (J). per. 17.49 *(978-1-59879-277-5(6))* Lifevest Publishing, Inc.

Mboya, Sharif. Heart Fealt Doses of Reality. Mboya, Sharif. 2004. 148p. (YA). per. 14.99 *(978-0-9754024-5-0(5))* Doses of Reality, Inc.

Mc Kelvey, Shawn. Timothy's Tic. Hurwitz, Kathleen A. 2008. 40p. (gr. -1 — 1). 16.99 *(978-1-4389-1924-9(7))* AuthorHouse.

McAdams, Caleb. Shubert. McAdams, Susan. 2008. 16p. per. 24.95 *(978-1-4241-9756-9(2))* America Star Bks.

McAdoo, Grami & McAdoo, O'Pa. In the Wake of Suicide: A Child's Journey. Kaulen, Diane Bouman. 2008. (J). (gr. 3-5). 14.95 *(978-0-9764026-5-7(3))* Longhorn Creek Pr.

McAdoo, O'Pa, jt. illus. see McAdoo, Grami.

McAliley, Susan, et al. Kit's Cooking Studio. Hirsch, Jennifer & Jones, Michelle. Witkowski, Teri, ed. 2007. (American Girl Ser.). 55p. (J). (gr. 3-7). 15.95 *(978-1-59369-267-4(6))* American Girl Publishing, Inc.

McAliley, Susan & Hunt, Robert. Happy New Year, Julie, Bk. 3. McDonald, Megan. 2007. (American Girl Ser.). (ENG.). 88p. (J). (gr. 3-7). 12.95 *(978-1-59369-292-6(7))* American Girl Publishing, Inc.

McAliley, Susan, jt. illus. see Rane, Walter.

McAlister, Bobbie. Prancing Deer: An Alegory, for Kids, for Parents, for Lovers... for Life. McAlister, Bobbie. 2011. (ENG.). 62p. pap. 13.99 *(978-1-4635-1512-6(X))* CreateSpace Independent Publishing Platform.

McAllan, Marina. Hey Diddle Diddle: The Story. Egan, Cecilia. 2015. (The Nursery Rhyme Story Ser.: 1). (ENG.). (J). pap. ***(978-1-925110-65-4(6)***, Leaves of Gold Pr.) Quillpen Pty. Ltd.

—Humpty Dumpty: The Story. Egan, Cecilia. 2015. (The Nursery Rhyme Story Ser.: 2). (ENG.). (J). pap. ***(978-1-925110-66-1(4)***, Leaves of Gold Pr.) Quillpen Pty. Ltd.

—Little Miss Muffet: The Story. Egan, Cecilia. 2015. (The Nursery Rhyme Story Ser.: 3). (ENG.). (J). pap. ***(978-1-925110-67-8(2)***, Leaves of Gold Pr.) Quillpen Pty. Ltd.

McAllister, Chris. Bullfrog Pops!, 1 vol. Walton, Rick. 2005. (ENG.). 32p. (J). (gr. 3-3). pap. 7.99 *(978-1-58685-840-7(8))* Gibbs Smith, Publisher.

—Bullfrog Pops! Adventures in Verbs & Objects, 1 vol. Walton, Rick. 2011. (ENG.). 36p. (J). (gr. 2-3). pap. 7.99 *(978-1-4236-2079-2(8))* Gibbs Smith, Publisher.

McArdle, Paula. The Adventures of Molly Whuppie & Other Appalachian Folktales. Shelby, Anne. 2007. (ENG.). 96p. (J). (gr. 3-7). 17.95 *(978-0-8078-3163-2(8))* Univ. of North Carolina Pr.

McAskin, Denice. Comprehension Crosswords Grade 4, 6 vols. Hemminger, Marcia. 2003. 32p. (J). 4.99 *(978-1-56472-188-4(4))* Edupress, Inc.

McAteer, Thomas. Basil's New Home: The Garden Rabbit Series - Part One. Vetter Squires, Diane. 2009. 28p. pap. 13.99 *(978-1-4490-0675-4(2))* AuthorHouse.

McAvinn, Douglas. Masterminds Riddlemath for Elementary: Whole Numbers, Addition, Subtraction, Multiplication, & Division. Opie, Brenda. 2004. (Masterminds Ser.). (ENG.). 91p. (gr. 1-4). per. 12.99 *(978-0-86530-604-2(4))* Incentive Pubns., Inc.

McBee, Scott. At the Seashore. Koeppel, Ruth. 2009. (ENG.). 10p. (J). (gr. -1-1). 12.99 *(978-1-58476-817-3(7))* Innovative Kids.

—In the Wild. Koeppel, Ruth. 2009. (ENG.). 10p. (J). (gr. -1-1). 15.99 *(978-1-58476-816-6(9))* Innovative Kids.

McBride, Earvin, Jr. The Adventurous Cyborg. McBride, Earvin, Jr. 2nd unabr. ed. 2003. (Amazing Sci-Fi & Adventure Heroes Ser.). 43p. (YA). (gr. 7-12). 4.95 *(978-1-892511-06-5(1))* MacBride, E. J. Pubn., Inc.

—The Bowdery Rodeo Cowboys of Texas. McBride, Earvin, Jr. 2nd unabr. ed. 2003. (Earvin MacBride's Amazing Sci-Fi & Adventure Heroes Ser.). 329p. (J). (gr. 7-12). pap. 4.95 *(978-1-892511-07-2(X))* MacBride, E. J. Pubn., Inc.

—Earvin MacBride's Amazing Sci-Fi & Adventure Heroes, 7 vols. McBride, Earvin, Jr. 2nd unabr. ed. 2003. (J). (gr. 7-12). pap. 25.95 *(978-1-892511-05-8(3))* MacBride, E. J. Pubn., Inc.

—The Eerie Adventures of Detective Omar Mendez. McBride, Earvin, Jr. 2nd unabr. ed. 2003. (Earvin MacBride's Amazing Sci-Fi & Adventure Heroes Ser.). 329p. (J). (gr. 7-12). pap. 5.95 *(978-1-892511-08-9(8))* MacBride, E. J. Pubn., Inc.

—Space - M. D. 3001. McBride, Earvin, Jr. 2nd unabr. ed. 2003. (Earvin MacBride's Amazing Sci-Fi & Adventure Heroes Ser.). 329p. (J). (gr. 7-12). pap. 4.95 *(978-1-892511-09-6(6))* MacBride, E. J. Pubn., Inc.

McBride, Marc. Deltora Shadowlands. Rodda, Emily. 2009. (Deltora Shadowlands Ser.). (ENG.). 384p. (J). (gr. 3-7). 14.99 *(978-0-545-05648-9(9))* Scholastic, Inc.

—Secrets of Deltora, 9 vols. Rodda, Emily. 2009. (Deltora Ser.: Bk. 9). (ENG.). 176p. (J). (gr. 3-7). 15.99 *(978-0-545-06933-5(5))* Scholastic, Inc.

McCabb, Jamie. Spike the Friendly Caterpillar. Martin, Anne E. I.t. ed. 2006. 53p. (J). per. 9.99 *(978-1-59879-127-3(3))* Lifevest Publishing, Inc.

McCabe, Dennis. Haunted Halloween: Color & Create with Spooky Stickers. 2004. 10p. (J). (gr. -1-18). bds. 4.99 *(978-1-57151-730-2(8))* Playhouse Publishing.

McCabe, Jane M. The Miracle of Sandy Duck: A True Story. Maxwell, Wayne F., Jr. 2003. 32p. (gr. k-4). lib. bdg. 15.00 *(978-0-9747023-0-8(7))* Pegasus Pubns.

McCabe, Steve. The Golden Key: Classic fairy Tales. MacDonald, George. 2008. 104p. (J). pap. *(978-0-88835-045-9(7))* Meany, P. D. Pubs.

McCafferty, Jan. The Best Friend Boom. Coe, Catherine. 2012. (Kid Cowboy Ser.: 2). (ENG.). 32p. (J). (gr. -1-2). pap. 7.99 *(978-1-4083-0692-5(1))* Hodder & Stoughton GBR. Dist: Independent Pubs. Group.

—Cake Test. Goodhart, Pippa. 2007. (Blue Bananas Ser.). (ENG.). 48p. (J). (gr. k-2). pap. 5.99 *(978-1-4052-2955-5(1))* Egmont Bks., Ltd. GBR. Dist: Independent Pubs. Group.

—Don't Be Greedy, Graham. Cox, Phil Roxbee. Tyler, Jenny, ed. 2006. (Cautionary Tales Ser.). 24p. (J). (gr. -1). lib. bdg. 15.99 *(978-1-58086-972-0(6))*; pap. 7.99 *(978-0-7945-1361-0(1))* EDC Publishing. (Usborne).

—Drawing Cartoons: Internet-Linked. Milbourne, Anna. 2006. (Art School Ser.). 64p. (J). (gr. 5). lib. bdg. 16.95 *(978-1-58086-507-4(0))* EDC Publishing.

—Fairy Things to Make & Do Kid Kit. Gilpin, Rebecca. 2004. (Kid Kits Ser.). 32p. (J). 15.99 *(978-1-58086-727-6(8))*; 15.99 *(978-1-58086-731-3(6))* EDC Publishing. (Usborne).

—The Games Player of Zob. Shipton, Paul. 2007. (Collins Big Cat Ser.). (ENG.). 48p. (J). pap. 8.99 *(978-0-00-723094-5(X))* HarperCollins Pubs. Ltd. GBR. Dist: Independent Pubs. Group.

—Horse Horror. Coe, Catherine. 2012. (Kid Cowboy Ser.: 4). (ENG.). 32p. (J). (gr. -1-2). pap. 7.99 *(978-1-4083-0693-2(X))* Hodder & Stoughton GBR. Dist: Independent Pubs. Group.

—Say Please, Louise! Roxbee Cox, Phil. Tyler, Jenny, ed. 2007. (Cautionary Tales Ser.). 23p. (J). (gr. -1-3). per. 7.99 *(978-0-7945-1726-7(9)*, Usborne) EDC Publishing.

—Sex, Puberty, & All That Stuff: A Guide to Growing Up. Bailey, Jacqui. 2004. (ENG.). 112p. (YA). pap. 12.99 *(978-0-7641-2992-6(9))* Barron's Educational Series, Inc.

—Showdown at Dawn. Coe, Catherine. 2012. (Kid Cowboy Ser.: 3). (ENG.). 32p. (J). (gr. -1-2). pap. 7.99 *(978-1-4083-0694-9(8))* Hodder & Stoughton GBR. Dist: Independent Pubs. Group.

—Wanda's Washing Machine. McQuinn, Anna. 2005. 20p. (J). (gr. -1-2). 12.95 *(978-1-58925-768-9(5))* Tiger Tales.

McCaffery, William. The Flea Circus. 2013. (J). *(978-0-307-97997-1(0))*; lib. bdg. *(978-0-375-97132-7(7))* Random Hse. Children's Bks.

McCaffrey, Brendan. Special Brothers & Sisters: Stories & Tips for Siblings of Children with a Disability or Serious Illness. Hames, Annette & McCaffrey, Monica, eds. 2005. (ENG.). 96p. (J). (gr. 4-7). per. *(978-1-84310-383-7(4))* Kingsley, Jessica Ltd.

McCaffrey, Susie. Ancient world - internet Linked. Chandler, Fiona. rev. ed. 2004. 96p. (J). pap. 14.95 *(978-0-7945-0816-6(2)*, Usborne) EDC Publishing.

McCaig, Dave & Brosseau, Pat. The Other Side. Aaron, Jason. rev. ed. 2007. (ENG.). 144p. pap. 12.99 *(978-1-4012-1350-3(2)*, Vertigo) DC Comics.

McCain, Kevin. Daddy Promises. Arquette, Kerry. 2005. 32p. (J). pap. 7.49 *(978-0-7586-0905-2(1))* Concordia Publishing Hse.

McCall, Anthony. And They Fell Fast Asleep. Cox, Roy. 2012. 48p. pap. 15.95 *(978-1-61493-045-7(7))* Peppertree Pr., The.

McCall, William L. My Very Special Brother. Hill, Genita. 2007. 40p. per. 24.95 *(978-1-4241-8852-9(0))* America Star Bks.

McCalla, Darrell. From the Lands of the Night, 1 vol. Mollel, Tololwa. 2014. (ENG.). 32p. (J). 19.95 *(978-0-88995-498-4(4))* Red Deer Pr. CAN. Dist: Ingram Pub. Services.

McCallum, Jodie. God's Christmas Gift. Navillus, Nell. 2006. (J). *(978-1-58173-595-6(2))* Sweetwater Pr.

—Happy Birthday, Jesus. Navillus, Nell. 2007. (J). *(978-1-60261-264-8(1))* Cliff Road Bks.

McCann, Emily. Animal Doodles. McCann, Emily. 2011. (Doodle On! Ser.). (ENG.). 160p. (J). (gr. k-4). 15.99 *(978-0-230-74485-1(0))* Macmillan Pubs., Ltd. GBR. Dist: Independent Pubs. Group.

McCann, Emma. Crocodile!, 1 vol. Norton, Liss. 2013. (Start Reading Ser.). (ENG.). 24p. (gr. k-1). pap. 6.99 *(978-1-4765-4093-1(4))* Capstone Pr., Inc.

McCann, Gerald. We Were There at the Opening of the Erie Canal. Meadowcroft, Enid Lamonte & Vigilante, Sylvester. 2011. 192p. 42.95 *(978-1-258-09742-4(7))* Literary Licensing, LLC.

McCann, Martin. Cooper's Pack — New York City: New York City, Vol. 1. Rudd, Brandon Kyle. 2007. 72p. (J). per. 14.95 *(978-0-9794882-0-7(6))* Cooper's Pack.

—Cooper's Pack Travel Guide to Alaska. Rudd, Brandon Kyle. 2011. (Cooper's Pack Ser.). (ENG.). 72p. (J). (gr. 1-6). pap. 12.95 *(978-0-9794882-3-8(0))* Cooper's Pack.

—Cooper's Pack Travel Guide to New York City. Rudd, Brandon Kyle. rev. ed. 2012. (ENG.). 72p. (J). (gr. 1-6). pap. 12.95 *(978-0-9794882-5-2(7))* Cooper's Pack.

McCann, Shawn. Catch the Wind. 2008. 38p. (J). pap. *(978-1-59298-244-8(1))* Beaver's Pond Pr., Inc.

—Why the Owl Has Big Ears. 2005. 32p. (J). (gr. -1-3). 8.75 *(978-0-9771466-0-4(X))* Goulasche Pr.

McCarter, Zack. Wellington's Windows. Randall, MarilynMae. 2003. 146p. (J). per. 15.00 *(978-0-9713589-6-6(6))* Ubavel's Gifts.

McCarthy, Dan. The Secret Twin. Orenstein, Denise Gosliner. 2007. 400p. (J). (gr. 7-12). 16.99 *(978-0-06-078564-2(0))* HarperCollins Pubs.

McCarthy, Kate. The Little Girl with a Loud Voice. McCarthy, Terry. 2013. 26p. pap. *(978-0-646-90439-9(6))* McCarthy, Kate.

McCarthy, Kevin. 20th Century Wars. Smith, Robert W. Hoffman, Nancy, ed. ed. 2006. (Spotlight on America Ser.). (ENG.). 96p. (gr. 5-9). pap. 13.99 *(978-1-4206-3219-4(1))* Teacher Created Resources, Inc.

McCarthy, Mary. A Closer Look. McCarthy, Mary. 2007. (ENG.). 40p. (J). (gr. -1-k). 17.99 *(978-0-06-124073-7(7)*, Greenwillow Bks.) HarperCollins Pubs.

McCarthy, Mary Tola. The Taming of the Halloween Monster: The Saga of the Gallant Platoon. Kaspee. 2003. 16p. 9.50 *(978-1-4120-0729-0(1))* Trafford Publishing.

McCarthy, Meghan. City Hawk: The Story of Pale Male. McCarthy, Meghan. 2007. (ENG.). 40p. (J). (gr. -1-3). 16.99 *(978-1-4169-3359-5(X)*, Simon & Schuster/Paula Wiseman Bks.) Simon & Schuster/Paula Wiseman Bks.

—Daredevil: The Daring Life of Betty Skelton. McCarthy, Meghan. 2013. (ENG.). 48p. (J). (gr. -1-3). 16.99 *(978-1-4424-2262-9(9)*, Simon & Schuster/Paula Wiseman Bks.) Simon & Schuster/Paula Wiseman Bks.

—Earmuffs for Everyone! How Chester Greenwood Became Known As the Inventor of Earmuffs. McCarthy, Meghan. 2015. (ENG.). 48p. (J). (gr. -1-3). 17.99 *(978-1-4814-0637-6(X)*, Simon & Schuster/Paula Wiseman Bks.) Simon & Schuster/Paula Wiseman Bks.

—Pop! The Invention of Bubble Gum. McCarthy, Meghan. 2010. (ENG.). 40p. (J). (gr. -1-3). 17.99 *(978-1-4169-7970-8(0)*, Simon & Schuster/Paula Wiseman Bks.) Simon & Schuster/Paula Wiseman Bks.

—Seabiscuit: The Wonder Horse. McCarthy, Meghan. 2008. (ENG.). 40p. (J). (gr. -1-3). 16.99 *(978-1-4169-3360-1(3)*, Simon & Schuster/Paula Wiseman Bks.) Simon & Schuster/Paula Wiseman Bks.

McCarthy, Pat, jt. illus. see Brodie, Neale.

McCarthy, Steve. Sally Go Round the Stars: Favourite Rhymes from an Irish Childhood. Webb, Sarah & Ranson, Claire. 2015. (ENG.). 64p. (J). pap. 17.00 (978-1-84717-675-2(5)) O'Brien Pr., Ltd., The IRL. Dist: Dufour Editions, Inc.

McCarthy, Steven. Sally Go Round the Stars: Favourite Rhymes for an Irish Childhood. Webb, Sarah & Ranson, Claire. 2012. (ENG.). 64p. (J). 26.00 (978-1-84717-211-2(3)) O'Brien Pr., Ltd., The IRL. Dist: Dufour Editions, Inc.

McCartney, Jen. Luke & His Amazing Space Bed. Sheridan, Luke. 2010. (ENG.). 32p. (J). (gr. -1-3). 17.95 (978-0-9814536-6-8(X), Cambridge House Pr.) Sterling & Ross Pubs.

McCartney, Michael David. A Real Name for Puppy. Alderton, Sylvia. 2006. (J). (978-1-930566-58-3(1), WestWind Pr.) Scott, D.& F. Publishing, Inc.

McCarty, Peter. Hermanos Bajo Cero. Seidler, Tor & Tor, Seidler. 2004. (Punto de Encuentro (Editorial Everest) Ser.).Tr. of Brothers Below Zero. (SPA.). 118p. (J). (gr. 5-12). pap., pap. 11.99 (978-84-241-8076-8(3)) Everest Editora ESP. Dist: Lectorum Pubns., Inc.

McCarty, Peter. Chloe. McCarty, Peter. 2012. 40p. (J). (gr. -1-1). (ENG.). 16.99 (978-0-06-114291-8(3)); lib. bdg. 17.89 (978-0-06-114292-5(1)) HarperCollins Pubs.

—Fabian Escapes. McCarty, Peter. rev. ed. 2007. (ENG.). 40p. (J). (gr. -1-1). 18.99 (978-0-8050-7713-1(8), Holt, Henry & Co. Bks. For Young Readers) Holt, Henry & Co.

—Fall Ball. McCarty, Peter. 2013. (ENG.). 32p. (J). (gr. -1-3). 16.99 (978-0-8050-9253-0(6), Holt, Henry & Co. Bks. For Young Readers) Holt, Henry & Co.

—First Snow. McCarty, Peter. 2015. (ENG.). 40p. (J). (gr. -1-3). 16.99 (978-0-06-218996-7(4)) HarperCollins Pubs.

—Henry in Love. McCarty, Peter. 2009. 48p. (J). (gr. -1-1). (ENG.). 16.99 (978-0-06-114288-8(3)); lib. bdg. 17.89 (978-0-06-114289-5(1)) HarperCollins Pubs.

—Hondo & Fabian. McCarty, Peter. 2007. (ENG.). 40p. (J). (gr. -1-1). per. 8.99 (978-0-312-36747-3(3)) Square Fish.

—Jeremy Draws a Monster. McCarty, Peter. 2009. (Jeremy & the Monster Ser.). (ENG.). 40p. (J). (gr. -1-1). 17.99 (978-0-8050-6934-1(8), Holt, Henry & Co. Bks. For Young Readers) Holt, Henry & Co.

—Little Bunny on the Move. McCarty, Peter. rev. ed. 2003. (ENG.). 32p. (J). (gr. -1-3). pap. 7.99 (978-0-8050-7259-4(4)) Square Fish.

—The Monster Returns. McCarty, Peter. 2012. (Jeremy & the Monster Ser.). (ENG.). 40p. (J). (gr. -1-1). 16.99 (978-0-8050-9030-7(4), Holt, Henry & Co. Bks. For Young Readers) Holt, Henry & Co.

—Moon Plane. McCarty, Peter. 2006. (ENG.). 40p. (J). (gr. -1-1). 18.99 (978-0-8050-7943-2(2), Holt, Henry & Co. Bks. For Young Readers) Holt, Henry & Co.

—T Is for Terrible. McCarty, Peter. 2008. (ENG.). 32p. (J). (gr. -1-1). pap. 7.99 (978-0-312-38423-4(8)) Square Fish.

McCaslin, Anna. The Owl Who Thinks He Is an Eagle. Ferer, Whitney H. 2003. 20p. (J). 14.95 (978-0-9729975-0-8(4), OWL1) Graphically Speaking, Inc.

McCauley, Adam. Ann & Nan Are Anagrams: A Mixed-Up Word Dilemma. Shulman, Mark. 2013. (ENG.). 36p. (J). (gr. k-3). 16.99 (978-1-4521-0914-5(1)) Chronicle Bks. LLC.

—Basketball Bats / Goof-Off Goalie. Hicks, Betty. 2009. (Gym Shorts Ser.). (ENG.). 128p. (J). (gr. 2-5). pap. 10.99 (978-0-312-58247-0(1)) Square Fish.

—Cheesie Mack Is Cool in a Duel. Cotler, Steve. 2013. (Cheesie Mack Ser.). (ENG.). 240p. (J). (gr. 3-7). 6.99 (978-0-375-86395-0(8), Yearling) Random Hse. Children's Bks.

—Cheesie Mack Is Cool in a Duel. Cotler, Steve. 2012. (Cheesie Mack Ser.). (ENG.). 240p. (J). (gr. 3-7). 15.99 (978-0-375-86438-4(5)) Random Hse., Inc.

—Cheesie Mack Is Not a Genius or Anything. Cotler, Steve. (Cheesie Mack Ser.). (ENG.). 240p. (J). (gr. 3-7). 2012. 6.99 (978-0-375-86394-3(X), Yearling); 2011. 15.99 (978-0-375-86437-7(7), Random Hse. Bks. for Young Readers); 2011. lib. bdg. 18.99 (978-0-375-96437-4(1), Random Hse. Bks. for Young Readers) Random Hse. Children's Bks.

—Da Wild, Da Crazy, Da Vinci. Scieszka, Jon. 2006. (Time Warp Trio Ser.: No. 14). 72p. (gr. 4-7). 15.00 (978-0-7569-6677-5(9)) Perfection Learning Corp.

—Hey Kid, Want to Buy a Bridge? Scieszka, Jon. 2004. (Time Warp Trio Ser.: 11). (ENG.). 96p. (J). (gr. 2-4). pap. 4.99 (978-0-14-240089-0(0), Puffin) Penguin Publishing Group.

—Hey Kid, Want to Buy a Bridge? Scieszka, Jon. 2005. (Time Warp Trio Ser.: No. 11). 74p. (gr. 4-7). 15.00 (978-0-7569-5988-3(8)) Perfection Learning Corp.

—June & August. Walsh, Vivian. 2009. (ENG.). 32p. (J). (gr. -1-3). 16.95 (978-0-8109-8410-3(5), Abrams Bks. for Young Readers) Abrams.

—Marco? Polo! Scieszka, Jon. 2008. (Time Warp Trio Ser.: 16). (ENG.). 96p. (J). (gr. 2-4). 4.99 (978-0-14-241177-3(9), Puffin) Penguin Publishing Group.

—Marco? Polo! Scieszka, Jon. 2008. (Time Warp Trio Ser.: No. 16). 90p. (J). (gr. 4-6). 12.65 (978-0-7569-8923-1(X)) Perfection Learning Corp.

—Me Oh Maya. Scieszka, Jon. 2005. (Time Warp Trio Ser.: 13). (ENG.). 96p. (J). (gr. 2-4). 4.99 (978-0-14-240300-6(8), Puffin) Penguin Publishing Group.

—Me Oh Maya. Scieszka, Jon. 2005. (Time Warp Trio Ser.: No. 13). 69p. (gr. 2-6). 15.00 (978-0-7569-5060-6(0)) Perfection Learning Corp.

—Oh Say, I Can't See, No. 15. Scieszka, Jon. 2007. (Time Warp Trio Ser.: 15). (ENG.). 80p. (J). (gr. 2-4). 4.99 (978-0-14-240808-7(5), Puffin) Penguin Publishing Group.

—Sam Samurai. Scieszka, Jon. 2004. (Time Warp Trio Ser.: 10). (ENG.). 96p. (J). (gr. 2-4). pap. 4.99 (978-0-14-240088-3(2), Puffin) Penguin Publishing Group.

—Sam Samurai. Scieszka, Jon. 2006. (Time Warp Trio Ser.: No. 10). 85p. (gr. 4-7). 15.00 (978-0-7569-6779-6(1)) Perfection Learning Corp.

—See You Later, Gladiator. Scieszka, Jon. 2004. (Time Warp Trio Ser.: 9). (ENG.). 96p. (J). (gr. 2-4). pap. 4.99 (978-0-14-240117-0(X), Puffin) Penguin Publishing Group.

—See You Later, Gladiator. Scieszka, Jon. 2004. (Time Warp Trio Ser.: No. 9). 87p. (J). (gr. 4-7). 12.65 (978-0-7569-5986-9(1)) Perfection Learning Corp.

—Sideways Stories from Wayside School. Sachar, Louis. (Wayside School Ser.). (ENG.). 128p. 2003. (J). (gr. 3-7). pap. 6.99 (978-0-380-69871-4(4)); 2004. (YA). (gr. 8-18). pap. 6.99 (978-0-380-73148-0(7)) HarperCollins Pubs.

—Swimming with Sharks / Track Attack. Hicks, Betty. 2010. (Gym Shorts Ser.). (ENG.). 128p. (J). (gr. 2-5). pap. 15.99 (978-0-312-60237-6(5)) Square Fish.

—Take Me to Your BBQ. Duval, Kathy. 2013. (ENG.). 40p. (J). (gr. -1-k). 16.99 (978-1-4231-2255-5(0)) Hyperion Pr.

—Viking It & Liking It. Scieszka, Jon. 2004. (Time Warp Trio Ser.: 12). (ENG.). 96p. (J). (gr. 2-4). pap. 4.99 (978-0-14-240002-9(5), Puffin) Penguin Publishing Group.

—Viking It & Liking It. Scieszka, Jon. 2004. (Time Warp Trio Ser.: No. 12). 73p. (gr. 2-6). 15.00 (978-0-7569-2589-5(4)) Perfection Learning Corp.

—Wayside School Gets a Little Stranger. Sachar, Louis. rev. ed. 2004. (Wayside School Ser.). (ENG.). 160p. (YA). (gr. 8-18). pap. 6.99 (978-0-380-73149-7(5)) HarperCollins Pubs.

—Wayside School Is Falling Down. Sachar, Louis. (Wayside School Ser.). 2003. 192p. (J). (gr. 3-7). pap. 6.99 (978-0-380-75484-7(3)); 2004. 160p. (YA). (gr. 8-18). pap. 6.99 (978-0-380-73150-3(9)) HarperCollins Pubs.

McCauley, Adam & Adam, Mccauley. Da Wild, Da Crazy, Da Vinci, No. 14. Scieszka, Jon. 2006. (Time Warp Trio Ser.: 14). (ENG.). 96p. (J). (gr. 2-4). 5.99 (978-0-14-240465-2(9), Puffin) Penguin Publishing Group.

McCauley, Adam, jt. illus. see Schick, Joel.

McCauley, Marlene & Children's Art-Friends of Kateri. Song of Kateri: Princess of the Eucharist. McCauley, Marlene. McCauley, R. Allan, ed. unabr. ed. 2005. 300p. (YA). (gr. 4-7). per. 14.95 (978-0-9633633-2-9(8)) Grace Hse. Publishing.

McCaw, Robert, photos by. Birds A to Z. McCaw, Robert. Earley, Chris G. 2009. (ENG.). 32p. (J). (gr. 1-5). 19.95 (978-1-55407-554-6(8), 9781554075546); pap. 7.95 (978-1-55407-500-3(9), 9781554075003) Firefly Bks., Ltd.

McClain, Tania. Big Jake Plants a Garden: Big Jake Adventures. McClain, Charles. Southern Lion Books, ed. 2013. 26p. (J). (978-1-935272-21-2(7)) Southern Lion Bks.

McClaine, Les. Bro-Jitsu: The Martial Art of Sibling Smackdown. Wilson, Daniel H. & Trippe, Dean. 2010. (ENG.). 160p. (YA). (gr. 7-18). pap. 12.99 (978-1-59990-279-1(6), Bloomsbury USA Childrens) Bloomsbury USA.

—The Middle Man: Volume 1. Grillo-Marxuach, Javier. 2006. 112p. per. 9.95 (978-0-9754193-7-3(4)) Viper Comics.

McCleary, Twila. Meesha, Guardian of Grand Mountain: Book One of the Guardian Series. Juckes, Deborah Sioux. 2005. (Guardian Ser.: Bk. 1). (YA). pap. 12.95 (978-0-9767748-0-8(1)) Red Earth Publishing.

—Meesha, Guardian of Grand Mountain: Book One of the Guardian Series. Juckes, Deborah Sioux. 2005. (YA). 18.95 (978-0-9767748-1-5(X)) Red Earth Publishing.

McClellan, David. The Eighth Day. Salerni, Dianne K. (Eighth Day Ser.: 1). (ENG.). (J). (gr. 3-7). 2015. 336p. pap. 6.99 (978-0-06-227216-4(0)); 2014. 320p. 16.99 (978-0-06-227215-7(2)) HarperCollins Pubs.

—The Guardian Herd - Stormbound. Alvarez, Jennifer Lynn. 2015. (Guardian Herd Ser.: 2). (ENG.). 320p. (J). (gr. 3-7). 16.99 (978-0-06-228609-3(9)) HarperCollins Pubs.

—Starbounders. Epstein, Adam Jay & Jacobson, Andrew. 2013. (Starbounders Ser.: 1). (ENG.). 320p. (J). (gr. 3-7). 16.99 (978-0-06-212022-9(0)) HarperCollins Pubs.

McClellan, Maddy. Friday the Scaredy Cat. McMahon, Kara. 2011. (Friday the Scaredy Cat Ser.). (ENG.). 24p. (J). (gr. -1-1). 15.99 (978-1-4424-3612-1(3)); pap. 3.99 (978-1-4424-2293-3(9)) Simon Spotlight. (Simon Spotlight).

—Pirate! Band 15. Gates, Susan. 2007. (Collins Big Cat Ser.). (ENG.). 48p. (J). pap. 8.99 (978-0-00-723095-2(8)) HarperCollins Pubs. Ltd. GBR. Dist: Independent Pubs. Group.

McClellan, Maddy. Playdates Are Not Scary! McMahon, Kara. 2015. (Friday the Scaredy Cat Ser.). (ENG.). 24p. (J). (gr. -1-1). pap. 3.99 (978-1-4814-3591-8(4), Simon Spotlight) Simon Spotlight.

McClellan, Maddy. The Scariest Day Ever ... So Far. McMahon, Kara. 2013. (Friday the Scaredy Cat Ser.). (ENG.). 24p. (J). (gr. -1-1). 16.99 (978-1-4424-6694-4(4), Simon Spotlight) Simon Spotlight.

—The Scariest Day Ever... So Far. McMahon, Kara. 2013. (Friday the Scaredy Cat Ser.). (ENG.). 24p. (J). (gr. -1-1). pap. 3.99 (978-1-4424-6693-7(6), Simon Spotlight) Simon Spotlight.

McClelland, Maddy. Mop Top. Graves, Sue. 2008. (Tadpoles Ser.). (ENG.). 24p. (J). (gr. -1-3). pap. (978-0-7787-3888-6(4)); lib. bdg. (978-0-7787-3857-2(4)) Crabtree Publishing Co.

—Mop Top. Graves, Sue. 2008. (Tadpoles Ser.). 23p. (J). (gr. -1-3). 17.15 (978-1-4178-0930-1(2), Turtleback) Turtleback Bks.

McClements, George. Dinosaur Woods: Can Seven Clever Critters Save Their Forest Home? McClements, George. 2009. (ENG.). 40p. (J). (gr. -1-2). 16.99 (978-1-4169-8626-3(X), Beach Lane Bks.) Beach Lane Bks.

—Night of the Veggie Monster. McClements, George. (ENG.). 32p. (J). (gr. -1-1). 2014. 7.99 (978-1-61963-180-9(6)); 2008. 16.99 (978-1-59990-061-2(0)) Bloomsbury USA. (Bloomsbury USA Childrens).

McCliggott, Timothy M. A Report on Quibnoida. McCliggott, Timothy M. 2007. 52p. (YA). pap. 17.00 (978-0-8059-7289-4(7)) Dorrance Publishing Co., Inc.

McClintic, Ben, jt. illus. see Woods, Christopher.

Mcclintock, Barbara. Animal Fables from Aesop. Aesop. 2012. (ENG.). 48p. (J). 17.95 (978-0-87923-913-8(1)) Godine, David R. Pub.

McClintock, Barbara. A Child's Garden of Verses. Stevenson, Robert Louis. 2011. (ENG.). 80p. (J). (gr. -1-3). 17.99 (978-0-06-028228-8(2)) HarperCollins Pubs.

—The Gingerbread Man. Aylesworth, Jim. 2010. (ENG.). 32p. (J). (gr. k — 1). bds. 6.99 (978-0-545-23514-3(6), Cartwheel Bks.) Scholastic, Inc.

—Goldilocks & the Three Bears. Aylesworth, Jim. 2003. (ENG.). 32p. (J). (gr. -1-3). 17.99 (978-0-439-39545-8(3), Scholastic Pr.) Scholastic, Inc.

—House of Dolls. Block, Francesca Lia. 2010. (ENG.). 80p. (J). (gr. 3-7). 15.99 (978-0-06-113094-6(X)) HarperCollins Pubs.

—Mary & the Mouse, the Mouse & Mary. Donofrio, Beverly. 2014. (Mary & the Mouse Ser.). (ENG.). 32p. (J). (gr. -1-2). 7.99 (978-0-385-38872-6(1), Dragonfly Bks.) Random Hse. Children's Bks.

—My Grandfather's Coat. Aylesworth, Jim. 2014. (ENG.). 32p. (J). (gr. -1-3). 17.99 (978-0-439-92545-7(2), Scholastic Pr.) Scholastic, Inc.

—Our Abe Lincoln. Aylesworth, Jim. 2009. (ENG.). 32p. (J). (gr. -1-3). 16.99 (978-0-439-92548-8(7), Scholastic Pr.) Scholastic, Inc.

Mcclintock, Barbara. A Tale of Two Bad Mice. Potter, Beatrix. 2007. (Rabbit Ears: A Classic Tale Ser.). 40p. (gr. -1-3). 25.65 (978-1-59961-314-7(X)) Spotlight.

McClintock, Barbara. Twelve Kinds of Ice. Obed, Ellen Bryan. 2012. (ENG.). 64p. (J). (gr. 1-4). 16.99 (978-0-618-89129-0(3)) Houghton Mifflin Harcourt Publishing Co.

—Where's Mommy? Donofrio, Beverly. 2014. (Mary & the Mouse Ser.). (ENG.). 32p. (J). (gr. -1-2). 17.99 (978-0-375-84423-2(6), Schwartz & Wade Bks.) Random Hse. Children's Bks.

McClintock, Barbara. Adèle & Simon. McClintock, Barbara. 2006. (ENG.). 36p. (J). (gr. -1-3). 17.99 (978-0-374-38044-1(9), Farrar, Straus & Giroux (BYR)) Farrar, Straus & Giroux.

—Adèle & Simon in America. McClintock, Barbara. 2008. (ENG.). 40p. (J). (gr. -1-3). 18.99 (978-0-374-39924-5(7), Farrar, Straus & Giroux (BYR)) Farrar, Straus & Giroux.

McCloskey, Kevin. A Dog Named Pavlov: Un Perro Llamado Pavlov. Campbell, Howard. 2010. 44p. (J). pap. 12.95 (978-0-9790350-4-3(X)) Stanley Publishing Co.

McCloskey, Robert. Henry Reed, Inc., Set. Robertson, Keith. abr. ed. (J). (gr. 4-7). 24.95 incl. audio (978-0-670-36800-6(8)) Live Oak Media.

—The Man Who Lost His Head. Bishop, Claire Huchet. 2009. (ENG.). 64p. (J). (gr. -1-3). 14.95 (978-1-59017-332-9(5), NYR Children's Collection) New York Review of Bks., Inc., The.

McCloskey, Robert. Homer Price. McCloskey, Robert. 2005. (Puffin Modern Classics Ser.). (ENG.). 160p. (J). (gr. 3-7). 6.99 (978-0-14-240415-7(2), Puffin) Penguin Publishing Group.

McClure, Jessica. Is Nothing Something? Kids' Questions & Zen Answers about Life, Death, Family, Friendship, & Everything in Between. Hanh, Thich Nhat. 2014. (ENG.). 40p. (J). (gr. -1-3). 16.95 (978-1-937006-65-5(4), Plum Blossom Bks.) Parallax Pr.

McClure, Nikki. All in a Day. Rylant, Cynthia. 2009. (ENG.). 32p. (J). (gr. -1-4). 18.95 (978-0-8109-8321-2(4), Abrams Bks. for Young Readers) Abrams.

—May the Stars Drip Down. Chatelain, Jeremy. 2014. (ENG.). 40p. (J). (gr. -1-2). 17.95 (978-1-4197-1024-7(9), Abrams Bks. for Young Readers) Abrams.

McClurkan, Rob. All Aboard! & Treasure. Cunningham, Anna. 2012. (Talk a Story Ser.). (ENG.). 16p. (J). (-k). pap. 7.99 (978-1-4451-0666-3(3)) Hodder & Stoughton GBR. Dist: Independent Pubs. Group.

—Pulling Back the Curtain on Magic! Higginson, Sheila Sweeny. 2015. (Science of Fun Stuff Ser.). (ENG.). 48p. (J). (gr. 1-3). 16.99 (978-1-4814-3702-8(X), Simon Spotlight) Simon Spotlight.

McClurkan, Rob. Aw, Nuts! McClurkan, Rob. 2014. (ENG.). 32p. (J). (gr. -1-3). 17.99 (978-0-06-231729-2(6)) HarperCollins Pubs.

McCluskey, Cindy. Chess for Children. Chandler, Murray & Milligan, Helen. 2004. (ENG.). 96p. 16.95 (978-1-904600-06-0(9)) Gambit Pubns., Ltd. GBR. Dist: Perseus Distribution.

McConkey, Barbara. Tulowly the Possum. Trowbridge, Terri. l.t. ed. 2005. 24p. (J). 9.95 (978-0-9766418-0-3(1)) Sidewalk Publishing.

McConnell, Clem. I Speak to Myself: Encouraging Words for Children. McConnell, Clem. 2007. 32p. (J). per. 5.00 (978-0-9673490-0-8(1)) Positive Strokes.

McConnell, James. Edgar Allan Poe. Poe, Edgar Allen. 2004. (Great American Short Stories Ser.). 80p. (gr. 4-7). lib. bdg. 24.00 (978-0-8368-4254-8(5), Gareth Stevens Learning Library) Stevens, Gareth Publishing LLLP.

—Edith Wharton. Wharton, Edith. 2004. (Great American Short Stories Ser.). 80p. (gr. 4-7). lib. bdg. 24.00 (978-0-8368-4256-2(1), Gareth Stevens Learning Library) Stevens, Gareth Publishing LLLP.

—Nathaniel Hawthorne. Hawthorne, Nathaniel. 2004. (Great American Short Stories Ser.). 80p. (gr. 4-7). lib. bdg. 24.00 (978-0-8368-4252-4(9), Gareth Stevens Learning Library) Stevens, Gareth Publishing LLLP.

McConnell, Sarah. Chewy Hughie. Clarke, Jane. 2006. (Collins Big Cat Ser.). (ENG.). 24p. (J). pap. 6.99 (978-0-00-718692-1(4)) HarperCollins Pubs. Ltd. GBR. Dist: Independent Pubs. Group.

—Dixie. Gilman, Grace. 2011. (I Can Read Book 1 Ser.). (ENG.). 32p. (J). (gr. -1-3). 16.99 (978-0-06-171914-1(5)); pap. 3.99 (978-0-06-171913-4(7)) HarperCollins Pubs.

—Dixie & the Big Bully. Gilman, Grace. 2013. (I Can Read Book 1 Ser.). (ENG.). 32p. (J). (gr. -1-3). 16.99 (978-0-06-208637-2(5)) HarperCollins Pubs.

—Dixie & the Good Deeds. Gilman, Grace. 2013. (I Can Read Book 1 Ser.). (ENG.). 32p. (J). (gr. -1-3). 16.99 (978-0-06-208657-0(X)); pap. 3.99 (978-0-06-208643-3(X)) HarperCollins Pubs.

—Dixie & the School Trip. Gilman, Grace. 2012. (I Can Read Book 1 Ser.). (ENG.). 32p. (J). (gr. -1-3). 16.99 (978-0-06-208609-9(X)); pap. 3.99 (978-0-06-208608-2(1)) HarperCollins Pubs.

—Dixie Loves School Pet Day. Gilman, Grace. 2011. (I Can Read Book 1 Ser.). (ENG.). 32p. (J). (gr. -1-3). 16.99 (978-0-06-171912-7(9)); pap. 3.99 (978-0-06-171911-0(0)) HarperCollins Pubs.

—Freda the Fearless. Courtenay, Lucy. 2012. (Scarlet Silver Ser.: 4). (ENG.). 96p. (J). (gr. 3-5). pap. 6.99 (978-0-340-95970-1(3)) Hodder & Stoughton GBR. Dist: Independent Pubs. Group.

—Impossible Island. Courtenay, Lucy. 2012. (Scarlet Silver Ser.: 2). (ENG.). 96p. (J). (gr. 3-5). pap. 6.99 (978-0-340-95968-8(1)) Hodder & Stoughton GBR. Dist: Independent Pubs. Group.

—I've Got Music! Molitoris, Cathy. 2006. (J). (978-0-439-88620-8(1)) Scholastic, Inc.

—Matey M'Lad. Courtenay, Lucy. 2012. (Scarlet Silver Ser.: 3). (ENG.). 96p. (J). (gr. 3-5). pap. 6.99 (978-0-340-95969-5(X)) Hodder & Stoughton GBR. Dist: Independent Pubs. Group.

—Vague Vagabond. Courtenay, Lucy. 2012. (Scarlet Silver Ser.: 6). (ENG.). 96p. (J). (gr. 3-5). pap. 6.99 (978-0-340-95972-5(X)) Hodder & Stoughton GBR. Dist: Independent Pubs. Group.

McConnell, Sarah. Loony Doubloon. McConnell, Sarah. Courtenay, Lucy. 2012. (Scarlet Silver Ser.: 5). (ENG.). 96p. (J). (gr. 3-5). pap. 6.99 (978-0-340-95971-8(1)) Hodder & Stoughton GBR. Dist: Independent Pubs. Group.

McCook, Eileen. Great Adventure Kids Coloring Book: Bible Story Coloring Book. Cavins, Emily. 2008. (Great Adventures: Kids Ser.). 48p. pap. 7.95 (978-1-934217-64-1(6)) Ascension Pr.

McCool, Arlene. The Proud Christmas Tree. Lawless, Mary Ann. 2006. (J). 12.95 (978-0-9772795-0-0(2)) Tuesday's Child.

McCord, David. The Great Raccoon Meets the Veterinarian. Reeder, Larry. 2011. (ENG.). 26p. pap. 9.95 (978-1-4636-9175-2(0)) CreateSpace Independent Publishing Platform.

McCord, Kathi. Prickle Says I'm Sorry. Wilkinson, Lisa. 2015. (Faith That Sticks Ser.). (ENG.). 26p. (J). pap. 3.99 (978-1-4964-0312-4(6)) Tyndale Hse. Pubs.

McCorkindale, Bruce & Youtsey, Scott. Sikulu & Harambe by the Zambezi River: An African Vversion of the Good Samaritan Story. Oguneye, Kunle. 2008. 32p. (J). (gr. -1-5). 14.99 (978-0-9777382-4-3(8)) Blue Brush Media.

McCorkle, Mark. Kim Possible Cine-Manga, 9 vols., Vol. 7. Schooley, Bob. 2004. 96p. pap. 14.99 (978-1-59182-570-8(9), Tokyopop Kids) TOKYOPOP, Inc.

—Kim Possible Cine-Manga: Animal Attraction & All the News, 9 vols., Vol. 5. Schooley, Bob. 2004. 96p. pap. 14.99 (978-1-59182-568-5(7), Tokyopop Kids) TOKYOPOP, Inc.

—Kim Possible Cine-Manga: Sink or Swim & Number One, 9 vols., Vol. 6. Schooley, Bob. 2004. 96p. pap. 14.99 (978-1-59182-569-2(5), Tokyopop Kids) TOKYOPOP, Inc.

McCoy, Dave. The Tooth That Mixed up Christmas. Polack, Peter J. 2010. (ENG.). 40p. pap. 17.95 (978-1-4528-4928-7(5)) CreateSpace Independent Publishing Platform.

McCoy, Derrick. Starchild's Adventures on Earth. McCoy, Angie. 2011. 24p. pap. 24.95 (978-1-4560-5053-5(2)) America Star Bks.

McCoy, Glenn. The Legend of Spud Murphy. Colfer, Eoin. 2005. (Eoin Colfer's Legend Of... Ser.). 95p. (gr. 2-6). 16.00 (978-0-7569-6514-3(4)) Perfection Learning Corp.

McCoy, Jody. The Genie & the Lamp: A Story of Creation. Beck, Timothy P. 2010. (ENG.). 82p. pap. 9.95 (978-1-4505-2002-7(2)) CreateSpace Independent Publishing Platform.

McCoy, John. Families Are Forever. Shemin, Craig. 2006. 34p. (J). (gr. -1-2). 16.95 (978-0-9728666-6-8(3)) As Simple As That Publishing.

—Families Are Forever. Shemin, Craig. l.t. ed. 2003. 34p. 9.95 (978-0-9728666-0-6(4), 1) As Simple As That Publishing.

—Families Are Forever. Shemin, Craig. l.t. ed. 2004. 34p. 9.95 (978-0-9728666-1-3(2), 1) As Simple As That Publishing.

McCoy, Virginia. The Rabbits' Race. Delaronde, Deborah L. ed. 2009. (Rabbit's Race Ser.). (ENG.). 50p. (gr. 4-6). 18.95 (978-1-894778-76-3(6)) Theytus Bks., Ltd. CAN. Dist: Univ. of Toronto Pr.

McCracken, Jaime, photos by. A Show & Tell Lesson. Pugh, Tracey D. l.t. ed. 2006. 32p. (J). 12.95 (978-1-59879-105-1(2)) Lifevest Publishing, Inc.

McCranie, Stephen. Belly Flop! Book 3. McCranie, Stephen. 3rd ed. 2012. (Mal & Chad Ser.: 3). (ENG.). 240p. (J). (gr. 3-7). pap. 9.99 (978-0-399-25658-5(X), Philomel) Penguin Publishing Group.

—Mal & Chad - Food Fight!, 2 vols. McCranie, Stephen. 2nd ed. 2012. (Mal & Chad Ser.: 2). (ENG.). 224p. (J). (gr. 3-7). 9.99 (978-0-399-25657-8(1), Philomel) Penguin Publishing Group.

—Mal & Chad - The Biggest, Bestest Time Ever! McCranie, Stephen. 2011. (Mal & Chad Ser.: 1). (ENG.). 224p. (J). (gr. 3-7). 9.99 (978-0-399-25221-1(5), Philomel) Penguin Publishing Group.

McCray, Ed. Jill Chill & the Baron of Glacier Mountain: Wonder Tales from the Book of Ed. McCray, Ed. Brewer, Tammy & Harms, Cathy, eds. 2003. 150p. (J). mass mkt. 14.95 (978-1-929515-26-4(X), Solovisions) Comic Library International.

McCrea, John. Theseus: Battling the Minotaur. Limke, Jeff. (Graphic Myths & Legends Ser.). (ENG.). 48p. (gr. 4-8). 2008. pap. 8.95 (978-0-8225-8517-6(0)); 2007. lib. bdg. 27.93 (978-0-8225-6756-1(3), Graphic Universe) Lerner Publishing Group.

McCreary, Jane. On the Trail of Bigfoot in Washington. Wilsdon, Christina. 2006. 26p. (J). 7.99 (978-1-59939-012-3(4)) Cornerstone Pr.

McCroskey, Christine. Lying Awake. Furbush, Helen. l.t. ed. 2004. 32p. (J). (gr. 1-6). 15.95 *(978-0-9741787-0-7(5)*, 1239134) Harbor Island Bks.

McCue, Lisa. The Babysitters. Chaconas, Dori. 2010. (Cork & Fuzz Ser.: 6). (ENG.). 32p. (J). (gr. 1-3). 13.99 *(978-0-670-01200-8(9)*, Viking Juvenile) Penguin Publishing Group.

—The Babysitters. Chaconas, Dori. 2014. (Cork & Fuzz Ser.: 6). (ENG.). 32p. (J). (gr. 1-3). pap. 3.99 *(978-0-448-48050-3(6)*, Warne, Frederick Pubs.) Penguin Bks., Ltd. GBR. Dist: Penguin Random Hse., LLC.

—Best Friends No. 1. Chaconas, Dori. 2010. (Cork & Fuzz Ser.: 1). (ENG.). 32p. (J). (gr. 1-3). mass mkt. 3.99 *(978-0-14-241593-1(6)*, Warne, Frederick Pubs.) Penguin Bks., Ltd. GBR. Dist: Penguin Publishing Group.

—Busy Bunnies. 2014. (ENG.). 14p. (J). (gr. -1 — 1). bds. 5.99 *(978-0-7944-3039-9(2))* Reader's Digest Assn., Inc., The.

—Busy Day Bunnies: A Carry along Treasury. Reader's Digest Staff. 2011. (Carry along Bks.). 20p. (J). (gr. -1-k). 14.99 *(978-0-7944-2168-7(7))* Reader's Digest Assn., Inc., The.

—The Collectors, 4 vols. Chaconas, Dori. 2010. (Cork & Fuzz Ser.: 4). (ENG.). 32p. (J). (gr. 1-3). mass mkt. 3.99 *(978-0-14-241714-0(9)*, Puffin) Penguin Publishing Group.

—Corduroy Goes to the Beach. Hennessy, B. G. 2006. (Corduroy Ser.). (ENG.). 20p. (J). (gr. 1-k). 11.99 *(978-0-670-06052-8(6)*, Viking Juvenile) Penguin Publishing Group.

—Corduroy Goes to the Doctor. Freeman, Don. 2005. (Corduroy Ser.). (ENG.). 14p. (J). (gr. -1 — 1). bds. 5.99 *(978-0-670-06031-3(3)*, Viking Juvenile) Penguin Publishing Group.

—Corduroy's Day. Freeman, Don. 2005. (Corduroy Ser.). (ENG.). 14p. (J). (gr. -1 — 1). bds. 5.99 *(978-0-670-06030-6(5)*, Viking Juvenile) Penguin Publishing Group.

—Corduroy's Fourth of July. Freeman, Don. 2007. (Corduroy Ser.). (ENG.). 16p. (J). (gr. -1 — 1). bds. 5.99 *(978-0-670-06159-4(X)*, Viking Juvenile) Penguin Publishing Group.

—Corduroy's Thanksgiving. 2006. (Corduroy Ser.). (ENG.). 16p. (J). (gr. -1 — 1). bds. 5.99 *(978-0-670-06108-2(5)*, Viking Juvenile) Penguin Publishing Group.

—Cork & Fuzz. Chaconas, Dori. 2005. (Cork & Fuzz Ser.: 1). (ENG.). 32p. (J). (gr. k-3). 13.99 *(978-0-670-03602-8(1)*, Viking Juvenile) Penguin Publishing Group.

—Cork & Fuzz - The Collectors. Chaconas, Dori. 2008. (Cork & Fuzz Ser.: 4). (ENG.). 32p. (J). (gr. k-3). 13.99 *(978-0-670-06286-7(3)*, Viking Juvenile) Penguin Publishing Group.

—Easter Parade. Berlin, Irving. 2003. 32p. (J). 16.89 *(978-0-06-029126-6(5))* HarperCollins Pubs.

—Finders Keepers, 5 vols. Chaconas, Dori. 2011. (Cork & Fuzz Ser.: 5). (ENG.). 32p. (J). (gr. 1-3). mass mkt. 3.99 *(978-0-14-241869-7(2)*, Puffin) Penguin Publishing Group.

—Good Sports. Chaconas, Dori. (Cork & Fuzz Ser.: 3). (ENG.). 32p. (J). 2010. (gr. 1-3). mass mkt. 3.99 *(978-0-14-241713-3(0)*, Puffin); 2007. (gr. k-3). 13.99 *(978-0-670-06145-7(X)*, Viking Juvenile) Penguin Publishing Group.

—Happy Hanukkah, Corduroy. Freeman, Don. 2009. (Corduroy Ser.). (ENG.). 16p. (J). (gr. -1 — 1). bds. 6.99 *(978-0-670-01127-8(4)*, Viking Juvenile) Penguin Publishing Group.

—How Do I Love You? Kimmelman, Leslie. 2005. 32p. (J). lib. bdg. 16.89 *(978-0-06-001201-4(3))* HarperCollins Pubs.

—Little Bear. Namm, Diane. (My First Reader Ser.). (ENG.). 32p. (J). (gr. k-1). 2004. pap. 3.95 *(978-0-516-24633-8(X))*; 2003. 18.50 *(978-0-516-22931-7(1))* Scholastic Library Publishing. (Children's Pr.).

—Little Raccoon Learns to Share. Packard, Mary. 2013. (Watch Me Grow Ser.). (ENG.). 24p. (J). (-k). 7.95 *(978-1-4027-7230-6(0))* Sterling Publishing Co., Inc.

—The Puppy Who Wanted a Boy. Thayer, Jane. 2005. (ENG.). 32p. (J). (gr. -1-3). pap. 6.99 *(978-0-06-052698-6(X))* HarperCollins Pubs.

—Short & Tall No. 2, 2 vols. Chaconas, Dori. 2010. (Cork & Fuzz Ser.: 2). (ENG.). 32p. (J). (gr. 1-3). mass mkt. 3.99 *(978-0-14-241594-8(4)*, Puffin) Penguin Publishing Group.

—Snot Stew. Wallace, Bill. 2nd ed. 2008. (ENG.). 96p. (J). (gr. 3-7). pap. 6.99 *(978-1-4169-5804-8(5)*, Simon & Schuster/Paula Wiseman Bks.) Simon & Schuster/Paula Wiseman Bks.

—Spring Cleaning. Chaconas, Dori. 2015. (Cork & Fuzz Ser.: 10). (ENG.). 32p. (J). (gr. 1-3). 14.99 *(978-0-670-01686-0(1)*, Warne, Frederick Pubs.) Penguin Bks., Ltd. GBR. Dist: Penguin Random Hse., LLC.

—Spring Is Here, Corduroy! Freeman, Don. 2007. (Corduroy Ser.). (ENG.). 16p. (J). (gr. -1-k). 4.99 *(978-0-448-44461-1(5))* Penguin Publishing Group.

—The Story of Peter Rabbit. Potter, Beatrix. 2005. (Easter Ornament Bks.). (ENG.). 20p. (J). (gr. -1-1). 10.99 *(978-0-7944-0527-4(4))* Studio Fun International.

—Swimming Lesson, 7 vols. Chaconas, Dori. 2011. (Cork & Fuzz Ser.: 7). (ENG.). 32p. (J). (gr. 1-3). 13.99 *(978-0-670-01281-7(5)*, Viking Juvenile) Penguin Publishing Group.

—The Swimming Lesson. Chaconas, Dori. 2014. (Cork & Fuzz Ser.: 7). (ENG.). 32p. (J). (gr. 1-3). pap. 3.99 *(978-0-448-48051-0(4)*, Warne, Frederick Pubs.) Penguin Bks., Ltd. GBR. Dist: Penguin Random Hse., LLC.

—Wait a Minute. Chaconas, Dori. (Cork & Fuzz Ser.: 9). (ENG.). 32p. (J). (gr. 1-3). 2015. pap. 3.99 *(978-0-14-750856-0(8))*; 2014. 14.99 *(978-0-670-01481-1(8))* Penguin Bks., Ltd. GBR. (Warne, Frederick Pubs.). Dist: Penguin Random Hse., LLC.

McCue, Lisa. Corduroy's Valentine's Day. McCue, Lisa. 2004. (Corduroy Ser.). (ENG.). 16p. (J). (gr. -1 — 1). bds. 5.99 *(978-0-670-03640-0(4)*, Viking Juvenile) Penguin Publishing Group.

—Snuggle Bunnies. McCue, Lisa. Falken, L. C. 2003. (Boardbooks - Board Book Ser.). (ENG.). 11p. (J). (gr. -1 — 1). bds. 6.99 *(978-0-7944-0040-8(X))* Reader's Digest Assn., Inc., The.

McCue, Lisa & Kong, Emilie. Halloween Is Here, Corduroy! Freeman, Don. 2007. (Corduroy Ser.). 16p. (J). (gr. -1-k). pap. 5.99 *(978-0-448-44563-2(8)*, Grosset & Dunlap) Penguin Publishing Group.

McCue, Lisa, jt. illus. see Barasch, Lynne.

McCue, Lisa, jt. illus. see Freeman, Don.

McCue, Patrick. Some Things Are Made to Smoke. Knapp-Grosz, Tamara & Loyd, Elizabeth. 2004. 20p. (J). pap. *(978-1-893974-23-4(5)*, Design Pr. Bks.) Savannah College of Art & Design Exhibitions.

McCullen, Sam. Ella the Superstar. Whybrow, Ian. 2007. (Collins Big Cat Ser.). (ENG.). 24p. (J). pap. 6.99 *(978-0-00-718681-5(9))* HarperCollins Pubs. Ltd. GBR. Dist: Independent Pubs. Group.

McCullough, Marilyn. Two by Two: Noah's Story in Rhyme. Kilpatrick, Leanne. 2013. 28p. pap. *(978-0-906672-67-9(8))* Oleander Pr., The.

McCullough, Sharon Pierce. Bunbun. (J). 12.99 *(978-1-84148-455-6(5))* Barefoot Bks., Inc.

McCully, Emily Arnold. Ballerina Swan. Kent, Allegra. 2012. (ENG.). 32p. (J). 16.95 *(978-0-8234-2373-6(5))* Holiday Hse., Inc.

—Ballerina Swan. Kent, Allegra. 2013. (ENG.). 32p. (J). pap. 6.99 *(978-0-8234-2906-6(7))* Holiday Hse., Inc.

—Ballywhinney Girl. Bunting, Eve. 2012. (ENG.). 32p. (J). (gr. -1-3). 16.99 *(978-0-547-55843-1(0))* Houghton Mifflin Harcourt Publishing Co.

—Black Is Brown Is Tan. Adoff, Arnold. 2004. (ENG.). 40p. (J). (gr. -1-3). reprint ed. pap. 6.99 *(978-0-06-443644-1(6)*, Amistad) HarperCollins Pubs.

—Dare the Wind: The Record-Breaking Voyage of Eleanor Prentiss & the Flying Cloud. Fern, Tracey E. 2014. (ENG.). 540p. (J). (gr. k-3). 17.99 *(978-0-374-31699-0(6)*, Farrar, Straus & Giroux (BYR)) Farrar, Straus & Giroux.

—The Helpful Puppy. Zarins, Kim. 2012. (ENG.). 32p. (J). 16.95 *(978-0-8234-2318-7(2))* Holiday Hse., Inc.

—The Helpful Puppy. Zarins, Kim. 2013. (ENG.). 32p. (J). pap. 6.99 *(978-0-8234-2919-6(9))* Holiday Hse., Inc.

—How to Eat Fried Worms. Rockwell, Thomas. ed. 2006. (ENG.). 128p. (J). (gr. 3-7). 6.99 *(978-0-440-42185-6(3)*, Yearling) Random Hse. Children's Bks.

—In Like a Lion, Out Like a Lamb. Bauer, Marion Dane. (ENG.). 32p. (J). 2012. pap. 6.95 *(978-0-8234-2432-0(4))*; 2011. (gr. -1-3). 16.95 *(978-0-8234-2238-8(0))* Holiday Hse., Inc.

—Nora's Ark. Kinsey-Warnock, Natalie. 2005. 32p. (J). 17.99 *(978-0-688-17244-2(X))* HarperCollins Pubs.

—The Taxing Case of the Cows: A True Story about Suffrage. Van Rynbach, Iris & Shea, Pegi Deitz. 2010. (ENG.). 32p. (J). (gr. 1-4). 16.99 *(978-0-547-23631-5(X))* Houghton Mifflin Harcourt Publishing Co.

—That's What Leprechauns Do. Bunting, Eve. 2006. (ENG.). 32p. (J). (gr. -1-3). 17.99 *(978-0-618-35410-8(7))* Houghton Mifflin Harcourt Publishing Co.

—That's What Leprechauns Do. Bunting, Eve. 2009. (ENG.). 32p. (J). (gr. -1-3). pap. 6.99 *(978-0-547-07673-7(8))* Houghton Mifflin Harcourt Publishing Co.

McCully, Emily Arnold. The Escape of Oney Judge: Martha Washington's Slave Finds Freedom. McCully, Emily Arnold. 2007. (ENG.). 32p. (J). (gr. 1-4). 17.99 *(978-0-374-32225-0(2)*, Farrar, Straus & Giroux (BYR)) Farrar, Straus & Giroux.

—First Snow. McCully, Emily Arnold. 2003. (ENG.). 32p. (J). (gr. -1-3). 17.99 *(978-0-06-623852-4(8))* HarperCollins Pubs.

—Late Nate in a Race. McCully, Emily Arnold. 2013. (I Like to Read Ser.). (ENG.). 24p. (J). pap. 6.99 *(978-0-8234-2755-0(2))* Holiday Hse., Inc.

—Little Ducks Go. McCully, Emily Arnold. (I Like to Read(r) Ser.). (ENG.). (J). (gr. -1-3). 2015. 24p. 6.99 *(978-0-8234-3300-1(5))*; 2014. 32p. 14.95 *(978-0-8234-2941-7(5))* Holiday Hse., Inc.

—My Heart Glow: Alice Cogswell, Thomas Gallaudet, & the Birth of American Sign Language. McCully, Emily Arnold. 2008. (ENG.). 40p. (gr. 1-4). 15.99 *(978-1-4231-0028-7(X))* Hyperion Pr.

—Pete Won't Eat. McCully, Emily Arnold. 2014. (ENG.). 32p. (J). (gr. -1-3). pap. 6.99 *(978-0-8234-3183-0(5))* Holiday Hse., Inc.

—Picnic. McCully, Emily Arnold. 2003. 32p. (J). (gr. -1-k). 16.89 *(978-0-06-623855-5(2))*; (ENG.). 17.99 *(978-0-06-623854-8(4))* HarperCollins Pubs.

—Sam & the Big Kids. McCully, Emily Arnold. (I Like to Read (r) Ser.). (ENG.). 32p. (J). 2014. (gr. 1-5). 6.99 *(978-0-8234-3060-4(X))*; 2013. 14.95 *(978-0-8234-2427-6(8))* Holiday Hse., Inc.

—School. McCully, Emily Arnold. 2005. 32p. (J). lib. bdg. 16.89 *(978-0-06-623857-9(9))* HarperCollins Pubs.

—The Secret Cave: Discovering Lascaux. McCully, Emily Arnold. 2010. (ENG.). 40p. (J). (gr. 1-4). 17.99 *(978-0-374-36694-0(2)*, Farrar, Straus & Giroux (BYR)) Farrar, Straus & Giroux.

—Strongheart: The World's First Movie Star Dog. McCully, Emily Arnold. 2014. (ENG.). 40p. (J). (gr. -1-3). 17.99 *(978-0-8050-9448-0(2)*, Holt, Henry & Co. Bks. For Young Readers) Holt, Henry & Co.

—Wonder Horse: The True Story of the World's Smartest Horse. McCully, Emily Arnold. 2010. (ENG.). 32p. (J). (gr. -1-3). 17.99 *(978-0-8050-8793-2(1)*, Holt, Henry & Co. Bks. For Young Readers) Holt, Henry & Co.

—3, 2, 1, Go! McCully, Emily Arnold. 2015. (I Like to Read(r) Ser.). (ENG.). 24p. (J). (gr. -1-3). 6.99 *(978-0-8234-3314-8(5))*; 14.95 *(978-0-8234-3288-2(2))* Holiday Hse., Inc.

McCune, Mark. Modern Fables. Gibbons, Ted & Wilcox, S. Michael. 2010. (J). 14.99 *(978-1-59955-307-8(4))* Cedar Fort, Inc./CFI Distribution.

McCurdy, Michael. The Founders: The 39 Stories Behind the U. S. Constitution. Fradin, Dennis Brindell. 2005. (ENG.). 144p. (J). (gr. 5-9). 22.95 *(978-0-8027-8972-3(2))* Walker & Co.

—Johnny Tremain. Forbes, Esther. l.t. ed. 2005. (ENG.). 440p. (YA). pap. 10.95 *(978-0-7862-7178-8(7))* Thorndike Pr.

—Knee-Deep in Blazing Snow: Growing up in Vermont. Hayford, James. 2005. (ENG.). 64p. (J). (gr. 5-17). 17.95 *(978-1-59078-338-2(7))* Boyds Mills Pr.

—Lucy's Christmas. Hall, Donald. 2007. (ENG.). 32p. (J). (gr. 1). pap. 10.95 *(978-1-56792-342-1(9))* Godine, David R. Pub.

—Lucy's Summer. Hall, Donald. 2008. (ENG.). 40p. (J). (gr. 1-18). pap. 10.95 *(978-1-56792-348-3(8))* Godine, David R. Pub.

—The Signers: The 56 Stories Behind the Declaration of Independence. Fradin, Dennis Brindell. 2003. (ENG.). 160p. (J). (gr. 5-18). 22.95 *(978-0-8027-8849-8(1))* Walker & Co.

—Tarzan. San Souci, Robert D. & Burroughs, Edgar Rice. 2004. 31p. (J). (gr. k-4). reprint ed. 16.00 *(978-0-7567-7576-6(0))* DIANE Publishing Co.

—The Train They Call New Orleans. Goodman, Steve. pap. 16.95 incl. audio *(978-1-59112-899-1(4))*; pap. incl. audio *(978-1-59112-901-1(X))*; pap. 18.95 incl. audio compact disk *(978-1-59112-903-5(6))*; pap. incl. audio compact disk *(978-1-59112-905-9(2))* Live Oak Media.

—The Train They Call the City of New Orleans. Goodman, Steve. 2003. 16.99 *(978-3-00-100280-8(8)*, Putnam Juvenile) Penguin Publishing Group.

McCurdy, Michael. Walden Then & Now: An Alphabetical Tour of Henry Thoreau's Pond. McCurdy, Michael. 2010. (ENG.). 32p. (J). (gr. k-12). 16.95 *(978-1-58089-253-7(1))* Charlesbridge Publishing, Inc.

McCuroy, Michael. American Fairy Tales: From Rip Van Winkle to the Rootabaga Stories. Philip, Neil, ed. 2004. 160p. (J). (gr. k-4). reprint ed. pap. 13.00 *(978-0-7567-8068-5(3))* DIANE Publishing Co.

McCurry, Steve, photos by. Looking East. McCurry, Steve. rev. ed. 2011. (ENG.). 128p. (gr. 8-17). 45.00 *(978-0-7148-4637-8(6))* Phaidon Pr., Inc.

McDaniel, Rick. Tuttle Stories. Murcray, Rod. 2012. 40p. pap. 14.95 *(978-1-61897-654-3(0)*, Strategic Bk. Publishing) Strategic Book Publishing & Rights Agency (SBPRA).

McDaniel, Scott, et al. Daredevil & Elektra: Fall from Grace. 2014. (ENG.). 464p. (J). (gr. 4-17). pap. 44.99 *(978-0-7851-8516-1(X))* Marvel Worldwide, Inc.

McDaniel, Thomas. Does This Belong Here? A Twiggyleaf Adventure. Goodwin, Carol. l.t. ed. 2003. 32p. (J). 14.95 *(978-0-9741072-1-9(2))* CornerWind Media, L.L.C.

—The Great Acorn: A Twiggyleaf Adventure. Goodwin, Carol. l.t. ed. 2004. 32p. (J). 14.95 *(978-0-9741072-2-6(0))* CornerWind Media, L.L.C.

—Tippy Needs A Home: A Twiggyleaf Adventure. Goodwin, Carol. l.t. ed. 32p. (J). 2004. 14.95 *(978-0-9741072-3-3(9))*; 2003. per. 14.95 *(978-0-09-741072-2(1))* CornerWind Media, L.L.C.

—What's the Hurry, Furry? A Twiggyleaf Adventure. Goodwin, Carol. l.t. ed. 2003. 32p. (J). 14.95 *(978-0-9741072-0-2(4))* CornerWind Media, L.L.C.

McDaniels, Preston. Blasts Off! Dowell, Frances O'Roark. 2011. (From the Highly Scientific Notebooks of Phineas L. MacGuire Ser.). (ENG.). 224p. (J). (gr. 3-7). pap. 5.99 *(978-1-4424-2204-9(1)*, Atheneum Bks. for Young Readers) Simon & Schuster Children's Publishing.

—The Eagle. Rylant, Cynthia. 2004. (Lighthouse Family Ser.: 3). (ENG.). 64p. (J). (gr. 1-5). 14.95 *(978-0-689-86243-4(1)*, Simon & Schuster Bks. For Young Readers) Simon & Schuster Bks. For Young Readers.

—The Eagle. Rylant, Cynthia. 2005. (Lighthouse Family Ser.: 3). (ENG.). 64p. (J). (gr. 1-5). pap. 4.99 *(978-0-689-86311-0(X)*, Simon & Schuster Bks. For Young Readers) Simon & Schuster Bks. For Young Readers.

—Erupts! Dowell, Frances O'Roark. 2006. (From the Highly Scientific Notebooks of Phineas L. MacGuire Ser.). (ENG.). 176p. (J). (gr. 3-7). 16.99 *(978-1-4169-0195-2(7)*, Atheneum Bks. for Young Readers) Simon & Schuster Children's Publishing.

—The Lord Is My Shepherd: Psalm 23 for Children. 2004. (Psalms for Children Ser.). (ENG.). 24p. (J). 10.00 *(978-0-8192-1986-2(X)*, Morehouse Publishing) Church Publishing, Inc.

—The Octopus. Rylant, Cynthia. 2005. (Lighthouse Family Ser.: 5). (ENG.). 64p. (J). (gr. 1-5). 17.99 *(978-0-689-86246-5(6)*, Simon & Schuster Bks. For Young Readers) Simon & Schuster Bks. For Young Readers.

—Phineas L. MacGuire ... Gets Cooking! 2014. (From the Highly Scientific Notebooks of Phineas L. MacGuire Ser.). (ENG.). 208p. (J). (gr. 3-7). 16.99 *(978-1-4814-0099-2(1)*, Atheneum Bks. for Young Readers) Simon & Schuster Children's Publishing.

—Phineas L. Macguire... Blasts Off! Dowell, Frances O'Roark. 2008. (From the Highly Scientific Notebooks of Phineas L. MacGuire Ser.). (ENG.). 208p. (J). (gr. 3-7). 16.99 *(978-1-4169-2689-4(5)*, Atheneum Bks. for Young Readers) Simon & Schuster Children's Publishing.

—Phineas L. Macguire... Erupts! Dowell, Frances O'Roark. 2007. (From the Highly Scientific Notebooks of Phineas L. MacGuire Ser.). (ENG.). 176p. (J). (gr. 3-7). pap. 6.99 *(978-1-4169-4734-9(5)*, Atheneum Bks. for Young Readers) Simon & Schuster Children's Publishing.

—Phineas L. MacGuire... Gets Slimed! Dowell, Frances O'Roark. (From the Highly Scientific Notebooks of Phineas L. MacGuire Ser.). (ENG.). (J). (gr. 3-7). 2010. 224p. pap. 5.99 *(978-1-4169-9775-7(X))*; 2007. 208p. 16.99 *(978-1-4169-0196-9(5))* Simon & Schuster Children's Publishing. (Atheneum Bks. for Young Readers).

—Phineas L. MacGuire... Gets Slimed! Dowell, Frances O'Roark. l.t. ed. 2008. (From the Highly Scientific Notebooks of Phineas L. MacGuire Ser.). 159p. (J). (gr. 3-7). 22.95 *(978-1-4104-0440-4(4))* Thorndike Pr.

—The Prince of Ireland & the Three Magic Stallions. 2003. (ENG.). 32p. (J). (gr. k-3). tchr. ed. 16.95 *(978-0-8234-1573-1(2))* Holiday Hse., Inc.

—Shout for Joy & Sing! Psalm 65 for Children. Webber, Christopher L. 2003. (Psalms for Children Ser.). (ENG.). 32p. 15.00 *(978-0-8192-1934-3(7)*, Morehouse Publishing) Church Publishing, Inc.

—The Squire & the Scroll: A Tale of the Rewards of a Pure Heart. Bishop, Jennie. 2009. (ENG.). 32p. (J). 15.99 *(978-1-59317-382-1(2))* Warner Pr. Pubs.

—The Squire & the Scroll: A Tale of the Rewards of a Pure Heart. 2004. (ENG.). 32p. (J). 12.99 *(978-1-59317-079-0(3))* Warner Pr. Pubs.

—The Storm. Rylant, Cynthia. 2003. (Lighthouse Family Ser.: 1). (ENG.). 80p. (J). (gr. 1-5). pap. 5.99 *(978-0-689-84882-7(X)*, Simon & Schuster Bks. For Young Readers) Simon & Schuster Bks. For Young Readers.

—The Three Gifts of Christmas. Bishop, Jennie. 2009. 32p. (J). (gr. 3-18). 15.99 incl. audio compact disk *(978-1-59317-378-4(4))* Warner Pr. Pubs.

—The Turtle. Rylant, Cynthia. 2006. (Lighthouse Family Ser.). 47p. (J). (gr. -1-3). 11.65 *(978-0-7569-6611-9(6))* Perfection Learning Corp.

—The Turtle. Rylant, Cynthia. (Lighthouse Family Ser.). (ENG.). 48p. (J). (gr. 1-5). 2006. pap. 4.99 *(978-0-689-86312-7(8))*; 2005. 14.95 *(978-0-689-86244-1(X))* Simon & Schuster Bks. For Young Readers. (Simon & Schuster Bks. For Young Readers).

—The Whale. Rylant, Cynthia. (Lighthouse Family Ser.: 2). (ENG.). (J). (gr. 1-5). 2004. 96p. pap. 5.99 *(978-0-689-84883-4(8))*; 2003. 64p. 15.99 *(978-0-689-84881-0(1))* Simon & Schuster Bks. For Young Readers. (Simon & Schuster Bks. For Young Readers).

McDaniels, Preston. A Perfect Snowman. McDaniels, Preston. 2007. (ENG.). 40p. (J). (gr. -1-3). 16.99 *(978-1-4169-1026-8(3)*, Simon & Schuster Bks. For Young Readers) Simon & Schuster Bks. For Young Readers.

McDee, Katie. Bridget & Bo Build a Blog. St. John, Amanda. 2012. 32p. (J). lib. bdg. 25.27 *(978-1-59953-507-4(6))* Norwood Hse. Pr.

—How Do We Know about Dinosaurs? A Fossil Mystery, 1 vol. Olien, Rebecca. 2011. (First Graphics: Science Mysteries Ser.). (ENG.). 24p. (gr. 1-2). pap. 6.29 *(978-1-4296-7173-6(4))*; pap. 35.70 *(978-1-4296-7177-4(7))*; lib. bdg. 23.32 *(978-1-4296-6095-2(3))* Capstone Pr., Inc.

—Where Do the Birds Go? A Migration Mystery, 1 vol. Olien, Rebecca. 2011. (First Graphics: Science Mysteries Ser.). (ENG.). 24p. (gr. 1-2). pap. 6.29 *(978-1-4296-7175-0(0))*; pap. 35.70 *(978-1-4296-7179-8(3))*; lib. bdg. 23.32 *(978-1-4296-6096-9(1))* Capstone Pr., Inc.

McDee, Katie, jt. illus. see Scott, Korey.

Mcdermot, Jessie. Clover. Coolidge, Susan. 2007. (ENG.). 168p. per. *(978-1-4065-1524-4(8))* Dodo Pr.

McDermott, Gerald. Gerald McDermott & You, 1 vol. Stott, Jon C. 2004. (Author & YOU Ser.). 128p. pap. 35.00 *(978-1-59158-175-8(3)*, LU1753, Greenwood Pr.) Greenwood Publishing Group, Inc.

McDermott, Gerald. Arrow to the Sun: A Pueblo Indian Tale. McDermott, Gerald. 2004. 37p. (J). (gr. k-3). reprint ed. pap. 14.00 *(978-0-7567-7103-4(X))* DIANE Publishing Co.

—The Light of the World. McDermott, Gerald. 2006. 32p. (J). 16.99 *(978-0-525-47488-3(9)*, Dutton Juvenile) Penguin Publishing Group.

McDermott, Robert. The Christmas Letter. Wood, Christine, photos by. Wood, Francis Eusene. Wood, Christine & Marken, Jon, eds. 2007. pap. 9.95 *(978-0-9746372-6-6(2))* Tip-Of-The-Moon Publishing Co.

McDermott, Robert W. Autumn's Reunion: A Story of Thanksgiving. Wood, Francis Eugene. Dean, Tina & Marken, Jon, eds. 2006. 47p. pap. 8.00 *(978-0-9746372-2-8(X))* Tip-Of-The-Moon Publishing Co.

McDonald, Amanda. Friday Night at the Zoo, 1 vol. McDonald, Regina. 2010. 16p. 24.95 *(978-1-4489-4090-5(7))* PublishAmerica, Inc.

McDonald, Candice Hartsough. Oliver at the Window. Shreeve, Elizabeth. 2009. (ENG.). 32p. (J). (gr. -1-1). 16.95 *(978-1-59078-548-5(7)*, Front Street) Boyds Mills Pr.

McDonald, Danielle. Fun Bums. 2014. (ENG.). 14p. (J). (gr. -1-k). bds. 5.99 *(978-1-74297-594-8(1))* Hardie Grant Egmont Pty. Ltd. AUS. Dist: Independent Pubs. Group.

McDonald, Eleanor. Beyond the Mirrors: The Study of the Mental & Spiritual Aspects of Horsemanship. Hassler, Jill K. Bartholomew, Jane, ed. rev. ed. (ENG.). 136p. pap. 15.95 *(978-0-9632562-1-8(1)*, 762) Goals Unlimited Pr.

McDonald, Jill. A Chanukah Present for Me! Scholastic, Inc. Staff & Karr, Lily. 2009. (ENG.). 7p. (J). (gr. k — 1). bds. 6.99 *(978-0-545-14874-0(X)*, Cartwheel Bks.) Scholastic, Inc.

—A Christmas Present for Me! Karr, Lily. 2009. (ENG.). 160p. (J). (gr. k — 1). bds. 6.99 *(978-0-545-13582-5(6)*, Cartwheel Bks.) Scholastic, Inc.

—A Farmer's Life for Me. Law, Jessica. 2013. (SPA.). 24p. (J). pap. 6.99 *(978-1-78285-025-0(2))* Barefoot Bks., Inc.

—Ghoulish Gang. 2008. (ENG.). 12p. (J). 9.95 *(978-1-58117-782-4(8)*, Intervisual/Piggy Toes) Bendon, Inc.

—A Hole in the Bottom of the Sea. Law, Jessica. 2013. (ENG.). 24p. (J). (gr. k-3). 16.99 *(978-1-84686-861-0(0))*; 9.99 *(978-1-84686-862-7(9))*; pap. 6.99 *(978-1-84686-948-8(X))* Barefoot Bks., Inc.

—Pocket Kisses. Perlman, Willa. 2011. (ENG.). 14p. (J). (gr. -1-17). 7.99 *(978-0-316-07787-3(9))* Little, Brown Bks. for Young Readers.

—Who's in the Farmyard? Gershator, Phillis. 2012. (ENG.). 24p. (J). bds. 14.99 *(978-1-84686-574-9(3))* Barefoot Bks., Inc.

—Who's in the Forest? Gershator, Phillis. 2010. (ENG.). 24p. (J). (gr. -1-k). 14.99 *(978-1-84686-476-6(3))* Barefoot Bks., Inc.

M

—Who's in the Garden? Gershator, Phillis. 2010. (ENG.). 13p. (J). (gr. -1). bds. 14.99 *(978-1-84686-403-2(8))* Barefoot Bks., Inc.

Mcdonald, Jill. Over in the Meadow Puzzle. Mcdonald, Jill. Fatus, Sophie. 2012. (ENG.). (J). 14.99 *(978-1-84686-746-0(0))* Barefoot Bks., Inc.

McDonald, Jill. Shapes: A Play-with-Me BK. McDonald, Jill. 2007. (ENG.). 10p. bds. 6.95 *(978-1-58117-604-9(X)*, Intervisual/Piggy Toes) Bendon, Inc.

McDonald, Jill & Reed, Susan. Over in the Meadow. McDonald, Jill. 2011. (ENG.). 24p. (J). (gr. 1-4). 16.99 *(978-1-84686-543-5(3))* Barefoot Bks., Inc.

McDonald, Joe, photos by. Snakes: Biggest! Littlest! Markle, Sandra. 2011. (Biggest! Littlest! Ser.). (ENG.). 32p. (J). pap. 10.95 *(978-1-59078-874-5(5))* Boyds Mills Pr.

McDonald, Kim. The Gold of Angel Island. Martin, Brian. 2007. 46p. (J). *(978-0-9798059-0-5(2))* Lunchbox Stories Inc.

—The Lost Ring. Martin, Brian. 2007. 42p. (J). *(978-0-9798059-1-2(0))* Lunchbox Stories Inc.

McDonald, Marion & Brown, Marion. The Missing Mom. McDonald, Marion. 2012. 30p. pap. 9.00 *(978-1-4349-8628-3(4)*, RoseDog Bks.) Dorrance Publishing Co., Inc.

McDonald, Mercedes. For a Girl Becoming. Harjo, Joy. 2009. (Sun Tracks Ser.: 66). (ENG.). 48p. (gr. -1). 17.95 *(978-0-8165-2797-7(0))* University of Arizona Pr.

—Hello Night/Hola Noche. Costales, Amy. 2007. (ENG, SPA & MUL.). 24p. (J). (gr. -1 — 1). 14.95 *(978-0-87358-927-7(0))* Cooper Square Publishing Llc.

McDonald, Patrick. Patrick & Hatrick, 1 vol. Borer, Christopher. 2010. 44p. pap. 24.95 *(978-1-4489-7978-3(1))* PublishAmerica, Inc.

McDonald, Steve. Fantastic Cities: A Coloring Book of Amazing Places Real & Imagined. 2015. (ENG.). 60p. pap. 14.95 ***(978-1-4521-4957-8(7))*** Chronicle Bks. LLC.

McDonald, Suzi. Henry & the Oranges: Henry's Wild Adventures. Hart, Janice. 2010. 32p. pap. 13.00 *(978-1-60860-911-6(1)*, Eloquent Bks.) Strategic Book Publishing & Rights Agency (SBPRA).

McDonald, Trevy. The Speech Family. McDonald, Charles. 2007. (J). 15.00 *(978-0-9670712-3-7(2))* zReyomi Publishing.

McDonnell, Janet. Adopted & Loved Forever. Dellinger, Annetta. 2009. 32p. 12.99 *(978-0-7586-1591-6(4))* Concordia Publishing Hse.

—God Makes Me His Child in Baptism. Wittenback, Janet. rev. ed. 2007. 32p. (J). (gr. -1-k). pap. 6.49 *(978-0-7586-1305-9(9))* Concordia Publishing Hse.

McDonnell, Janet. What to Do When Mistakes Make You Quake: A Kid's Guide to Accepting Imperfection. Freeland, Claire A.B. & Toner, Jacqueline B. 2015. (J). ***(978-1-4338-1930-8(9)***, Magination Pr.) American Psychological Assn.

McDonnell, Kevin. Turtle in the Tuba: Read Well Level K Unit 8 Storybook. Jones, Shelley V. & Sprick, Marilyn. 2004. (Read Well Level K Ser.). 20p. *(978-1-57035-672-8(6))* Cambium Education, Inc.

McDonnell, Patrick. The Skunk. Barnett, Mac. 2015. (ENG.). 40p. (J). (gr. -1-3). 17.99 *(978-1-59643-966-5(1))* Roaring Brook Pr.

McDonnell, Peter. Patrick Henry: Liberty or Death. Glaser, Jason. 2005. (Graphic Biographies Ser.). (ENG.). 32p. (gr. 3-4). 29.99 *(978-0-7368-4970-8(X)*, Graphic Library) Capstone Pr., Inc.

—The Pilgrims & the First Thanksgiving, 1 vol. Englar, Mary. 2006. (Graphic History Ser.). (ENG.). 32p. (gr. 3-4). 8.10 *(978-0-7368-9656-6(2))*; 29.99 *(978-0-7368-5492-4(4))* Capstone Pr., Inc. (Graphic Library).

—El Viaje del Mayflower. Lassieur, Allison. 2006. (Historia Gráficas Ser.). (SPA.). 32p. (gr. 3-4). 29.99 *(978-0-7368-6613-2(2))* Capstone Pr., Inc.

McElhinney, Glenn. The Demon Babysitter. Graves, Annie. 2015. (Nightmare Club Ser.: 7). (ENG.). 64p. (J). (gr. 2-5). lib. bdg. 25.32 *(978-1-4677-4355-6(0))*; pap. 6.99 ***(978-1-4677-6041-6(2)***, Darby Creek) Lerner Publishing Group.

—A Dog's Breakfast. Graves, Annie. 2015. (Nightmare Club Ser.: 1). (ENG.). 64p. (J). (gr. 2-5). pap. 6.99 *(978-1-4677-6042-3(0))*; lib. bdg. 25.32 *(978-1-4677-4350-1(X))* Lerner Publishing Group.

—Frankenkids. Graves, Annie. 2015. (Nightmare Club Ser.: 5). (ENG.). 64p. (J). (gr. 2-5). lib. bdg. 25.32 *(978-1-4677-4352-5(6))* Lerner Publishing Group.

—Guinea Pig Killer. Graves, Annie. 2015. (Nightmare Club Ser.: 4). (ENG.). 64p. (J). (gr. 2-5). pap. 6.99 *(978-1-4677-6044-7(7))*; lib. bdg. 25.32 *(978-1-4677-4351-8(8))* Lerner Publishing Group.

—The Hatching. Graves, Annie. 2015. (Nightmare Club Ser.: 8). (ENG.). 64p. (J). (gr. 2-5). lib. bdg. 25.32 *(978-1-4677-4354-9(2))*; pap. 6.99 ***(978-1-4677-6045-4(5)***, Darby Creek) Lerner Publishing Group.

—Help! My Brother's a Zombie. Graves, Annie. 2015. (J). (Nightmare Club Ser.: 2). (ENG.). 64p. (gr. 2-5). lib. bdg. 25.32 *(978-1-4677-4348-8(8))*; *(978-1-4677-7871-8(0))* Lerner Publishing Group.

—Mirrored. Graves, Annie. 2015. (Nightmare Club Ser.: 3). (ENG.). 64p. (J). (gr. 2-5). lib. bdg. 25.32 *(978-1-4677-4349-5(6))* Lerner Publishing Group.

—The Wolfling's Bite. Graves, Annie. 2015. (Nightmare Club Ser.: 6). (ENG.). 64p. (J). (gr. 2-5). lib. bdg. 25.32 *(978-1-4677-4353-2(4))*; pap. 6.99 ***(978-1-4677-6048-5(X)***, Darby Creek) Lerner Publishing Group.

McElligott, Matthew. The Spooky Book. Patschke, Steve. 2006. (ENG.). 32p. (J). (gr. -1-2). reprint ed. pap. 7.99 *(978-0-8027-8870-2(X))* Walker & Co.

McElligott, Matthew. Absolutely Not. McElligott, Matthew. 2006. (ENG.). 32p. (J). (gr. -1-3). 8.99 *(978-0-8027-8934-1(X))* Walker & Co.

—Backbeard: Pirate for Hire. McElligott, Matthew. 2007. (ENG.). 32p. (J). (gr. k-2). 16.95 *(978-0-8027-9632-5(X))* Walker & Co.

—Backbeard - Pirate for Hire. McElligott, Matthew. 2011. (ENG.). 32p. (J). (gr. k-4). pap. 7.99 *(978-0-8027-2265-2(2))* Walker & Co.

—Bean Thirteen. McElligott, Matthew. 2007. (ENG.). 32p. (J). (gr. k-3). 15.99 *(978-0-399-24535-0(9)*, Putnam Juvenile) Penguin Publishing Group.

—Benjamin Franklinstein Lives! McElligott, Matthew. Tuxbury, Larry David. (Benjamin Franklinstein Ser.: 1). (ENG.). (J). (gr. 3-7). 2011. 144p. 7.99 *(978-0-14-241935-9(4)*, Puffin); 2010. 128p. 12.99 *(978-0-399-25229-7(0)*, Putnam Juvenile) Penguin Publishing Group.

—Benjamin Franklinstein Meets Thomas Deadison. McElligott, Matthew. Tuxbury, Larry David. 2012. (Benjamin Franklinstein Ser.: 3). (ENG.). 160p. (J). (gr. 3-7). 12.99 *(978-0-399-25481-9(1)*, Putnam Juvenile) Penguin Publishing Group.

—Even Aliens Need Snacks. McElligott, Matthew. 2012. (ENG.). 40p. (J). (gr. k-8). 14.99 *(978-0-8027-2398-7(5)*, 226302) Walker & Co.

—Even Monsters Need Haircuts. McElligott, Matthew. 2015. (ENG.). 30p. (J). (gr. -1-2). bds. 6.99 *(978-0-8027-3839-4(7)*, Bloomsbury USA Childrens) Bloomsbury USA.

—Even Monsters Need Haircuts. McElligott, Matthew. (ENG.). (J). 2012. 40p. (gr. k-8). pap. 7.99 *(978-0-8027-2801-2(4))*; 2010. 32p. (gr. -1-2). 15.99 *(978-0-8027-8819-1(X))* Walker & Co.

—The Lion's Share. McElligott, Matthew. 2012. (ENG.). 32p. (J). (gr. k-8). pap. 8.99 *(978-0-8027-2360-4(8))* Walker & Co.

—The Lion's Share: A Tale of Halving Cake & Eating It, Too. McElligott, Matthew. 2009. (ENG.). 32p. (J). (gr. k-3). 16.99 *(978-0-8027-9768-1(7))* Walker & Co.

McElmurry, Jill. El Camioncito Azul. Schertle, Alice. 2013. (Little Blue Truck Ser.).Tr. of Little Blue Truck. (SPA.). 30p. (J). (— 1). bds. 7.99 *(978-0-547-98397-4(2))* Houghton Mifflin Harcourt Publishing Co.

—It's a Miracle! A Hanukkah Storybook. Spinner, Stephanie. 2007. (ENG.). 48p. (J). (gr. -1-3). 6.99 *(978-1-4169-5001-1(X)*, Simon & Schuster/Paula Wiseman Bks.) Simon & Schuster/Paula Wiseman Bks.

—Little Blue Truck. Schertle, Alice. (Little Blue Truck Ser.). (ENG.). (J). 2015. 30p. (— 1). bds. 12.99 *(978-0-544-05685-5(X)*, HMH Books For Young Readers); 2010. 32p. (gr. -1-3). 26.99 *(978-0-547-48248-4(5))*; 2008. 32p. (gr. -1-3). 17.99 *(978-0-15-205661-2(0))*; 2015. 30p. (— 1). bds. 7.99 ***(978-0-544-56803-7(6)***, HMH Books For Young Readers) Houghton Mifflin Harcourt Publishing Co.

—Little Blue Truck Farm Sticker Fun! Schertle, Alice. 2013. (Little Blue Truck Ser.). (ENG.). 24p. (J). (gr. -1-3). 5.99 *(978-0-544-06687-8(1))* Houghton Mifflin Harcourt Publishing Co.

—Little Blue Truck Leads the Way. Schertle, Alice. (Little Blue Truck Ser.). (ENG.). (J). 2012. 40p. (gr. -1-3). 26.99 *(978-0-547-85060-3(3))*; 2009. 40p. (gr. -1-3). 16.00 *(978-0-15-206389-4(7))*; 2015. 38p. (— 1). bds. 7.99 ***(978-0-544-56805-1(2)***, HMH Books For Young Readers) Houghton Mifflin Harcourt Publishing Co.

—Little Blue Truck's Christmas. Schertle, Alice. 2014. (Little Blue Truck Ser.). (ENG.). 24p. (J). (— 1). 14.99 *(978-0-544-32041-3(7)*, HMH Books For Young Readers) Houghton Mifflin Harcourt Publishing Co.

—The Pirate Princess. Bardhan-Quallen, Sudipta. 2012. (ENG.). 40p. (J). (gr. -1-3). 17.99 *(978-0-06-114242-0(5))* HarperCollins Pubs.

—Sharing the Bread: An Old-Fashioned Thanksgiving Story. Miller, Pat Zietlow. 2015. (ENG.). 32p. (J). (gr. -1-3). 17.99 *(978-0-307-98182-0(7)*, Schwartz & Wade Bks.) Random Hse. Children's Bks.

—The Tree Lady: The True Story of How One Tree-Loving Woman Changed a City Forever. Hopkins, H. Joseph. 2013. (ENG.). 32p. (J). (gr. k-5). 17.99 *(978-1-4424-1402-0(2)*, Beach Lane Bks.) Beach Lane Bks.

—Who Stole Mona Lisa? Knapp, Ruthie. 2010. (ENG.). 40p. (J). (gr. -1-3). 17.99 *(978-1-59990-058-2(0)*, Bloomsbury USA Childrens) Bloomsbury USA.

McElmurry, Jill. Little Blue Truck's Beep-Along Book. McElmurry, Jill. Schertle, Alice. 2015. (Little Blue Truck Ser.). (ENG.). 8p. (J). (— 1). bds. 12.99 ***(978-0-544-56812-9(5)***, HMH Books For Young Readers) Houghton Mifflin Harcourt Publishing Co.

McElmurry, Jill. Mario Makes a Move. McElmurry, Jill. 2012. (ENG.). 32p. (J). (gr. -1-2). 16.99 *(978-0-375-86854-2(2)*, Schwartz & Wade Bks.) Random Hse. Children's Bks.

McElmurry, Jill, jt. illus. see Szekeres, Cyndy.

McElrath-Eslick, Lori. Barefoot: Poems for Naked Feet. Weisburd, Stefi. 2008. (ENG.). 32p. (J). (gr. k-4). 16.95 *(978-1-59078-306-1(9)*, Wordsong) Boyds Mills Pr.

—Does God Know How to Tie Shoes? Carlstrom, Nancy White. 2009. 12p. (J). (gr. -1). 7.99 *(978-0-8028-5366-0(8))* Eerdmans, William B. Publishing Co.

—The Good Fire Helmet. Hoppey, Tim. 2010. (ENG.). 32p. (J). 16.95 *(978-1-934617-06-9(7)*, Alma Little) Elva Resa Publishing, LLC.

—If Jesus Came to My House. Thomas, Joan G. 2008. (HarperBlessings Ser.). (ENG.). 40p. (J). (gr. -1-3). 16.99 *(978-0-06-083942-0(2))* HarperCollins Pubs.

McElroy, Bonnie. Jagannath Coloring Book. McElroy, Bonnie. I.t. ed. 48p. (J). pap. 4.95 *(978-0-945475-29-3(2)*, 1203) Mandala Publishing.

McElroy, Kim. No More Night Mares: A Dream of Freedom. Van Zant, Dawn. 2005. (J). pap. 9.99 *(978-0-9761768-1-7(5))* Wild Heart Ranch, Inc.

McElvane, Catherine. Chipi Chipis, Small Shells of the Sea. Patterson, Irania. 2005.Tr. of Chipi Chipis, Caracolitos del Mar. (SPA.). 44p. (J). per. 12.99 *(978-1-59494-006-4(1))* CPCC Pr.

McEntee, Bill, jt. illus. see O'Kane, George.

McEvenue, Tim. Hats off to the President: A White House Mystery. Walsh, Brendan & Benchmark Education Co., LLC. 2014. (Text Connections Ser.). (J). (gr. 3). *(978-1-4509-9660-0(4))* Benchmark Education Co.

McEwan, Joseph. Who's Home? Faulkner, Keith. 12p. (J). (gr. -1). pap. 4.99 *(978-1-881445-33-3(X))* Sandvik Publishing.

McEwen, Katharine. Escape from Silver Street Farm. Davies, Nicola. 2013. (Silver Street Farm Ser.). (ENG.). 80p. (J). (gr. 2-5). 12.99 *(978-0-7636-6133-5(3))* Candlewick Pr.

—El Gato Que Desapareció Misteriosamente. Ahlberg, Allan. Abio, Carlos & Villegas, Mercedes, trs. 2009. (SPA.). 80p. (J). (gr. 2-4). pap. *(978-607-11-0111-2(5))* Aguilar, Altea, Taurus, Alfaguara, S.A. de C.V.

—I Love You, Little Monkey. Durant, Alan. 2007. (ENG.). 32p. (J). (gr. -1-1). 15.99 *(978-1-4169-2481-4(7)*, Simon & Schuster Bks. For Young Readers) Simon & Schuster Bks. For Young Readers.

—Send for a Superhero! Rosen, Michael. 2014. (ENG.). 40p. (J). (gr. -1-2). 16.99 *(978-0-7636-6438-1(3))* Candlewick Pr.

—That's Not Right! Durant, Alan. 2004. (Flying Foxes Ser.). 48p. (J). (gr. k-2). 13.10 *(978-0-7569-3057-8(X))* Perfection Learning Corp.

—That's Not Right. Durant, Alan. 2003. (Flying Foxes Ser.). (ENG.). 48p. (J). *(978-0-7787-1532-0(9))*; lib. bdg. *(978-0-7787-1486-6(1))* Crabtree Publishing Co.

—Tigerbear. Webb, Steve. 2012. (ENG.). 32p. (J). (gr. -1-k). pap. 10.99 *(978-1-84939-225-9(0))* Andersen Pr. GBR. Dist: Independent Pubs. Group.

—Welcome to Silver Street Farm. Davies, Nicola. 2012. (Silver Street Farm Ser.). (ENG.). 80p. (J). (gr. 2-5). 12.99 *(978-0-7636-5831-1(6))* Candlewick Pr.

—Welcome to Silver Street Farm. Davies, Nicola. 2013. (ENG.). 80p. (J). (gr. 2-5). pap. 4.99 *(978-0-7636-6443-5(X))* Candlewick Pr.

—Wheres My Darling Daughter. Kelly, Mij. 2006. (ENG.). 28p. (J). (gr. -1-k). pap. 16.00 *(978-1-56148-537-6(3)*, Good Bks.) Skyhorse Publishing Co., Inc.

McEwen, Katharine. Bear Hug. McEwen, Katharine. 2014. (ENG.). 32p. (J). (gr. -1-2). 15.99 *(978-0-7636-6630-9(0)*, Templar) Candlewick Pr.

McFadden, Brenda. Destanie's Journey. McFadden, Brenda. 2011. (ENG.). 174p. pap. 11.95 *(978-1-4611-0590-9(0))* CreateSpace Independent Publishing Platform.

McFadden, Joline. When the Bees Fly Home, 1 vol. Cheng, Andrea. 2005. (ENG.). 32p. (J). (gr. 3-6). 16.95 *(978-0-88448-238-3(3))* Tilbury Hse. Pubs.

McFall, Christie. America Underground. McFall, Christie. 2004. 80p. (J). (gr. 4-8). reprint ed. 14.00 *(978-0-7567-7712-8(7))* DIANE Publishing Co.

McFarland, Jim. Widget. McFarland, Lyn Rossiter. ed. 2004. (J). (gr. -1-k). spiral bd. *(978-0-616-11121-5(5))*; spiral bd. *(978-0-616-11122-2(3))* Canadian National Institute for the Blind/Institut National Canadien pour les Aveugles.

—Widget. McFarland, Lyn Rossiter. 2006. (ENG.). 32p. (J). (gr. -1-1). per. 7.99 *(978-0-374-48386-9(8))* Square Fish.

McFarland, Richard. Grandfather's Wrinkles. England, Kathryn. 2007. (ENG.). 32p. (J). (gr. k-3). 15.95 *(978-0-9729225-9-3(8))* Flashlight Pr.

McFarland, Shea. Ellie Finds a New Home. Carmichael, Heather. 2008. (ENG.). 36p. pap. 16.99 *(978-1-4389-2976-7(5))* AuthorHouse.

McFeeley, Dan. Westward, Ha-Ha!, 1800-1850. Levy, Elizabeth & Havlan, J. R. 2003. 160p. (J). pap. *(978-0-590-12257-3(6))* Scholastic, Inc.

McFeeley, Daniel. Dr. Laura Schlessinger's Where's God? Schlessinger, Laura. 2003. 40p. (J). (gr. -1-2). lib. bdg. 16.89 *(978-0-06-051910-0(X))* HarperCollins Pubs.

McG, Shane. 10 Little Hermit Crabs. Fox, Lee. (ENG.). 32p. (J). (-k). 2012. pap. 8.99 *(978-1-74237-952-4(4))*; 2010. 15.99 *(978-1-74175-739-2(8))* Allen & Unwin AUS. Dist: Independent Pubs. Group.

McG, Shane. Tennis, Anyone? McG, Shane. 2007. (ENG.). 40p. (J). (gr. k-3). 16.95 *(978-0-8225-6901-5(9)*, Carolrhoda Bks.) Lerner Publishing Group.

McGalry, James, jt. illus. see Aldous, Kate.

McGann, James. The Tailor & the Mouse. Feierabend, John M. 2012. (First Steps in Music Ser.). (ENG.). 32p. (J). (gr. -1-k). 16.95 *(978-1-57999-903-2(4))* G I A Pubns., Inc.

McGann, Oisín. Beyond the Cherry Tree. O'Brien, Joe. 2012. (ENG.). 224p. (J). pap. 12.95 *(978-1-84717-212-9(1))* O'Brien Pr., Ltd., The IRL. Dist: Dufour Editions, Inc.

McGann, Oisín. Mad Grandad's Flying Saucer. McGann, Oisín. 2003. (Flyers Ser.: 11). (ENG.). 64p. (J). pap. 9.95 *(978-0-86278-822-3(6))* O'Brien Pr., Ltd., The IRL. Dist: Dufour Editions, Inc.

McGary, Norman. The Adventures of Andy Ant: Lawn Mower on the Loose. O'Nan, Gerald D. 2014. (Morgan James Kids Ser.). (ENG.). 28p. (gr. -1-4). pap. 9.95 *(978-1-61448-673-2(5))* Morgan James Publishing.

—The Adventures of Andy Ant: The Swimming Hole Disaster. O'Nan, Lawrence W. & O'Nan, Gerald D. 2014. (Morgan James Kids Ser.). (ENG.). 34p. (gr. -1-4). pap. 9.95 *(978-1-61448-799-9(5))* Morgan James Publishing.

McGaw, Laurie. Avram's Gift. Blumberg, Margie. 48p. 2005. (YA). pap. 7.95 *(978-0-9624166-3-7(0))*; 2003. (J). (gr. 3-18). *(978-0-9624166-2-0(2))* MB Publishing, LLC.

—Journey to Ellis Island: How My Father Came to America. Bierman, Carol. 2010. (ENG.). 48p. (J). (gr. 4-7). pap. 10.95 *(978-1-897330-54-8(5))* Madison Pr. Bks. CAN. Dist: Independent Pubs. Group.

—A Little Something. Bosak, Susan V. 2008. 32p. (J). *(978-1-896232-06-5(X)*, TCP Pr.) Communication Project, The.

—Something to Remember Me By: A Story about Love & Legacies. Bosak, Susan V. 2003. 32p. pap. *(978-1-896232-02-7(7))*; (gr. 1-6). *(978-1-896232-01-0(9))* Communication Project, The. (TCP Pr.).

McGee, E. Alan, jt. photos by see Dawson, Sandy.

McGee, Holly. Hush Little Beachcomber. Moritz, Dianne. ed. 2011. (ENG.). 32p. (J). (gr. -1-1). 9.99 *(978-1-935279-81-5(5))* Kane Miller.

McGee, John F. Apes & Monkeys. Dennard, Deborah. 2003. (Our Wild World Ser.). (ENG.). 192p. (J). (gr. 2-5). 16.95 *(978-1-55971-863-9(3))* Cooper Square Publishing Llc.

—Chimpanzees. Dennard, Deborah. 2003. (Our Wild World Ser.). (ENG.). 48p. (J). (gr. 2-5). 10.95 *(978-1-55971-846-2(3))* Cooper Square Publishing Llc.

—Gorillas. Dennard, Deborah. 2003. (Our Wild World Ser.). (ENG.). 48p. (J). (gr. 2-5). 10.95 *(978-1-55971-844-8(7))*; pap. 7.95 *(978-1-55971-843-1(9))* Cooper Square Publishing Llc.

McGee, Mo. Alphabet Kingdom. Parent, Lauren A. 2009. (ENG.). 40p. (J). (gr. -1-1). pap. 8.95 *(978-1-55591-643-5(0))* Fulcrum Publishing.

McGee, Rick. Eleven Chickens in a Boat: A Story of Faith, Fear, & Feathers! 2013. (J). *(978-1-56722-974-5(3))* Word Aflame Pr.

McGee, Thomas. Multables, Inc. Osborne, Amy, ed. 3p. (J). (gr. 2-5). 13.99 *(978-0-9645004-0-2(X))* Multables, Inc.

Mcgee, Warner. ABC Animals (Dora the Explorer) Golden Books. 2013. (Color Plus Card Stock Ser.). (ENG.). 48p. (J). (gr. -1-2). pap. 3.99 *(978-0-307-98218-6(1)*, Golden Bks.) Random Hse. Children's Bks.

McGee, Warner. Ariel's Song. 2007. (Play a Tune Tale Ser.). 16p. (gr. -1-k). 12.98 *(978-1-4127-8829-8(3))* Publications International, Ltd.

Mcgee, Warner. Be a Ballerina! Golden Books Staff. 2010. (Glitter Sticker Book Ser.). (ENG.). 64p. (J). (gr. -1-2). pap. 4.99 *(978-0-375-85749-2(4)*, Golden Bks.) Random Hse. Children's Bks.

—Christmas Is Coming! (Dora the Explorer) Golden Books Staff. 2011. (Glitter Sticker Book Ser.). (ENG.). 64p. (J). (gr. -1-2). pap. 4.99 *(978-0-375-87393-5(7)*, Golden Bks.) Random Hse. Children's Bks.

McGee, Warner. Christmas Magic. Golden Books Staff. 2010. (Color Plus Gatefold Sticker Ser.). (ENG & SPA.). 16p. (J). (gr. -1-2). pap. 3.99 *(978-0-375-86525-1(X)*, Golden Bks.) Random Hse. Children's Bks.

Mcgee, Warner. Crystal Magic. Golden Books Staff. 2009. (Hologramatic Sticker Book Ser.). (ENG.). 48p. (J). (gr. -1-2). pap. 3.99 *(978-0-375-85555-9(6)*, Golden Bks.) Random Hse. Children's Bks.

McGee, Warner. Deep-Sea Countdown. Spelvin, Justin. 2006. (Backyardigans Ser.). (ENG.). 26p. (J). (gr. -1). bds. 5.99 *(978-1-4169-1484-6(6)*, Simon Spotlight/Nickelodeon) Simon Spotlight/Nickelodeon.

—Diego & the Baby Sea Turtles. Rao, Lisa. 2008. (Go, Diego, Go! Ser.: 8). (ENG.). 24p. (J). pap. 3.99 *(978-1-4169-5450-7(3)*, Simon Spotlight/Nickelodeon) Simon Spotlight/Nickelodeon.

—Diego rescata al bebé manatí (Diego's Manatee Rescue) Higginson, Sheila Sweeny. 2009. (Go, Diego, Go! Ser.). (SPA.). 24p. (J). pap. 3.99 *(978-1-4169-7983-8(2)*, Libros Para Ninos) Libros Para Ninos.

—Diego Saves a Butterfly. 2007. (Go, Diego, Go! Ser.: 3). (ENG.). 24p. (J). (gr. -1-1). pap. 3.99 *(978-1-4169-3364-9(6)*, Simon Spotlight/Nickelodeon) Simon Spotlight/Nickelodeon.

—Diego's Egyptian Expedition. 2009. (Go, Diego, Go! Ser.). (ENG.). 24p. (J). pap. 3.99 *(978-1-4169-6870-2(9)*, Simon Spotlight/Nickelodeon) Simon Spotlight/Nickelodeon.

—Diego's Family Christmas. Fernandez, Rafael. 2008. (Go, Diego, Go! Ser.). (ENG.). 16p. (J). (gr. -1-k). bds. 5.99 *(978-1-4169-5836-9(3)*, Simon Spotlight/Nickelodeon) Simon Spotlight/Nickelodeon.

—Extreme Rescue: Crocodile Mission. David, Erica. 2009. (Go, Diego, Go! Ser.). (ENG.). 24p. (J). pap. 3.99 *(978-1-4169-8515-0(8)*, Simon Spotlight/Nickelodeon) Simon Spotlight/Nickelodeon.

Mcgee, Warner. Go for the Gold! (Dora the Explorer) Golden Books. 2012. (Color Plus Stencil Ser.). (ENG.). 64p. (J). (gr. k-k). pap. 5.99 *(978-0-307-93134-4(X)*, Golden Bks.) Random Hse. Children's Bks.

McGee, Warner. Legend Hunters! Ricci, Christine. 2007. (Backyardigans Ser.: 9). (ENG.). 24p. (J). (gr. -1-2). pap. 3.99 *(978-1-4169-4058-6(8)*, Simon Spotlight/Nickelodeon) Simon Spotlight/Nickelodeon.

—Mission to Mars. 2006. (Backyardigans Ser.: 4). (ENG.). 24p. (J). (gr. -1-2). pap. 3.99 *(978-1-4169-1486-0(2)*, Simon Spotlight/Nickelodeon) Simon Spotlight/Nickelodeon.

—Monster Halloween Party. 2007. (Backyardigans Ser.). (ENG.). 14p. (J). (gr. -1-k). bds. 6.99 *(978-1-4169-3435-6(9)*, Simon Spotlight/Nickelodeon) Simon Spotlight/Nickelodeon.

Mcgee, Warner. Puzzle Party! (Dora the Explorer) Golden Books Staff. 2012. (Giant Coloring Book Ser.). (ENG.). 40p. (J). (gr. -1-2). pap. 9.99 *(978-0-307-97691-8(2)*, Golden Bks.) Random Hse. Children's Bks.

McGee, Warner. Run, Run, Koala! 2010. (Go, Diego, Go! Ser.). (ENG.). 24p. (J). (gr. -1-2). pap. 3.99 *(978-1-4169-9937-9(X)*, Simon Spotlight/Nickelodeon) Simon Spotlight/Nickelodeon.

Mcgee, Warner. Saddle Up! Golden Books Staff. 2011. (Big Coloring Book Ser.). (ENG.). 48p. (J). (gr. -1-2). pap. 6.99 *(978-0-375-86595-4(0)*, Golden Bks.) Random Hse. Children's Bks.

Mcgee, Warner & MJ Illustrations Staff. Dora's Chilly Day (Dora the Explorer) Rosebrough, Ellen. 2013. (Pictureback Series.). (ENG.). 16p. (J). (gr. -1-2). 3.99 *(978-0-449-81950-0(7)*, Random Hse. Bks. for Young Readers) Random Hse. Children's Bks.

McGee, Warner, jt. illus. see Moore, Saxton.

McGeehan, Dan. Bicycles Before the Store. Lynette, Rachel. 2012. (Before the Store Ser.). (ENG.). 32p. (J). (gr. 2-5). lib. bdg. 29.93 *(978-1-60973-676-7(1)*, 201248) Child's World, Inc., The.

—The Bizarre Origins of Kangaroo Court & Other Idioms. Ringstad, Arnold. 2012. (Idioms Ser.). (ENG.). 32p. (J). (gr. 3-6). 29.93 *(978-1-61473-231-0(0)*, 204938) Child's World, Inc., The.

—Bread Before the Store. Shaffer, Jody Jensen. 2012. (Before the Store Ser.). (ENG.). 32p. (J). (gr. 2-5). lib. bdg. 29.93 *(978-1-60973-629-3(X)*, 201250) Child's World, Inc., The.

—The Compelling Histories of Long Arm of the Law & Other Idioms. Ringstad, Arnold. 2012. (Idioms Ser.). (ENG.). 32p. (J). (gr. 3-6). 29.93 *(978-1-61473-232-7(9)*, 204939) Child's World, Inc., The.

—Earth. Owens, L. L. 2011. (Space Neighbors Ser.). (ENG.). 32p. (J). (gr. 1-4). lib. bdg. 27.07 *(978-1-60954-381-5(5)*, 200885) Child's World, Inc., The.

M

—Footballs Before the Store. Lynette, Rachel. 2012. (Before the Store Ser.). (ENG.). 32p. (J). (gr. 2-5). lib. bdg. 29.93 *(978-1-60973-675-0(3)*, 201251) Child's World, Inc., The.
—Ice Cream Before the Store. Bernard, Jan. 2012. (Before the Store Ser.). (ENG.). 32p. (J). (gr. 2-5). lib. bdg. 29.93 *(978-1-60973-677-4(X)*, 201252) Child's World, Inc., The.
—The Intriguing Sources of Hold Your Horses & Other Idioms. Ringstad, Arnold. 2012. (Idioms Ser.). (ENG.). 32p. (J). (gr. 3-6). 29.93 *(978-1-61473-233-4(7)*, 204940) Child's World, Inc., The.
—Jupiter. Owens, L. L. 2011. (Space Neighbors Ser.). (ENG.). 32p. (J). (gr. 1-4). lib. bdg. 27.07 *(978-1-60954-382-2(3)*, 200887) Child's World, Inc., The.
—Mars. Owens, L. L. 2011. (Space Neighbors Ser.). (ENG.). 32p. (J). (gr. 1-4). lib. bdg. 27.07 *(978-1-60954-383-9(1)*, 200886) Child's World, Inc., The.
—Mercury. Owens, L. L. 2011. (Space Neighbors Ser.). (ENG.). 32p. (J). (gr. 1-4). lib. bdg. 27.07 *(978-1-60954-384-6(X)*, 200883) Child's World, Inc., The.
—Neptune. Owens, L. L. 2011. (Space Neighbors Ser.). (ENG.). 32p. (J). (gr. 1-4). lib. bdg. 27.07 *(978-1-60954-385-3(8)*, 200890) Child's World, Inc., The.
—Opposites. Rosa-Mendoza, Gladys. Cifuentes, Carolina, ed. 2004. (English-Spanish Foundations Ser.: Vol. 5).Tr. of Opuestos. (ENG & SPA.). 20p. (J). (gr. -1-4). bds. 6.95 *(978-0-9679748-6-6(0))* Me+Mi Publishing.
—Opposites/Opuestos. Rosa-Mendoza, Gladys. Cifuentes, Carolina, ed. 2008. (English-Spanish Foundations Ser.). (gr. -1-k). bds. 6.95 *(978-1-931398-04-6(6))* Me+Mi Publishing.
—Orange Juice Before the Store. Jacobson, Ryan. 2012. (Before the Store Ser.). (ENG.). 32p. (J). (gr. 2-5). lib. bdg. 29.93 *(978-1-60973-678-1(8)*, 201253) Child's World, Inc., The.
—The over-The-Top Histories of Chew the Scenery & Other Idioms. Ringstad, Arnold. 2012. (Idioms Ser.). (ENG.). 32p. (J). (gr. 3-6). 29.93 *(978-1-61473-234-1(5)*, 204941) Child's World, Inc., The.
—Peanut Butter Before the Store. Bernard, Jan. 2012. (Before the Store Ser.). (ENG.). 32p. (J). (gr. 2-5). lib. bdg. 29.93 *(978-1-60973-679-8(6)*, 201254) Child's World, Inc., The.
—Pencils Before the Store. Lynette, Rachel. 2012. (Before the Store Ser.). (ENG.). 32p. (J). (gr. 2-5). lib. bdg. 29.93 *(978-1-60973-680-4(X)*, 201255) Child's World, Inc., The.
—Pluto & Other Dwarf Planets. Owens, L. L. 2011. (Space Neighbors Ser.). (ENG.). 32p. (J). (gr. 1-4). lib. bdg. 27.07 *(978-1-60954-386-0(6)*, 200891) Child's World, Inc., The.
—Saturn. Owens, L. L. 2011. (Space Neighbors Ser.). (ENG.). 32p. (J). (gr. 1-4). lib. bdg. 27.07 *(978-1-60954-387-7(4)*, 200888) Child's World, Inc., The.
—The Shocking Stories Behind Lightning in a Bottle & Other Idioms. Ringstad, Arnold. 2012. (Idioms Ser.). (ENG.). 32p. (J). (gr. 3-6). 29.93 *(978-1-61473-236-5(1)*, 204943) Child's World, Inc., The.
—Shoes Before the Store. Jacobson, Ryan. 2012. (Before the Store Ser.). (ENG.). 32p. (J). (gr. 2-5). lib. bdg. 29.93 *(978-1-60973-681-1(8)*, 201256) Child's World, Inc., The.
—Soda Pop Before the Store. Lynette, Rachel. 2012. (Before the Store Ser.). (ENG.). 32p. (J). (gr. 2-5). lib. bdg. 29.93 *(978-1-60973-682-8(6)*, 201257) Child's World, Inc., The.
—The Sun. Owens, L. L. 2011. (Space Neighbors Ser.). (ENG.). 32p. (J). (gr. 1-4). lib. bdg. 27.07 *(978-1-60954-388-4(2)*, 200882) Child's World, Inc., The.
—The Thrilling Sources of Push the Envelope & Other Idioms. Ringstad, Arnold. 2012. (Idioms Ser.). (ENG.). 32p. (J). (gr. 3-6). 29.93 *(978-1-61473-237-2(X)*, 204944) Child's World, Inc., The.
—Toilet Paper Before the Store. Lynette, Rachel. 2012. (Before the Store Ser.). (ENG.). 32p. (J). (gr. 2-5). lib. bdg. 29.93 *(978-1-60973-683-5(4)*, 201258) Child's World, Inc., The.
—Toothpaste Before the Store. Bernard, Jan. 2012. (Before the Store Ser.). (ENG.). 32p. (J). (gr. 2-5). lib. bdg. 29.93 *(978-1-60973-684-2(2)*, 201259) Child's World, Inc., The.
—The Unbelievable Origins of Snake Oil & Other Idioms. Ringstad, Arnold. 2012. (Idioms Ser.). (ENG.). 32p. (J). (gr. 3-6). 29.93 *(978-1-61473-238-9(8)*, 204945) Child's World, Inc., The.
—Uranus. Owens, L. L. 2011. (Space Neighbors Ser.). (ENG.). 32p. (J). (gr. 1-4). lib. bdg. 27.07 *(978-1-60954-389-1(0)*, 200889) Child's World, Inc., The.
—Venus. Owens, L. L. 2011. (Space Neighbors Ser.). (ENG.). 32p. (J). (gr. 1-4). lib. bdg. 27.07 *(978-1-60954-390-7(4)*, 200884) Child's World, Inc., The.
McGeehan, Dan & Moore, David, Jr. Being Safe around Water. Lindeen, Mary & Kesselring, Susan. 2011. (Be Safe Ser.). (ENG.). 24p. (J). (gr. k-3). lib. bdg. 27.07 *(978-1-60954-298-6(3)*, 200078) Child's World, Inc., The.
—Being Safe at Home. Lindeen, Mary & Kesselring, Susan. 2011. (Be Safe Ser.). (ENG.). 24p. (J). (gr. k-3). lib. bdg. 27.07 *(978-1-60954-299-3(1)*, 200079) Child's World, Inc., The.
McGeehan, Dan & Moore, David. Being Safe in Your Neighborhood. Lindeen, Mary & Kesselring, Susan. 2011. (Be Safe Ser.). (ENG.). 24p. (J). (gr. k-3). lib. bdg. 27.07 *(978-1-60954-370-9(X)*, 200081) Child's World, Inc., The.
—Being Safe on Wheels. Lindeen, Mary & Kesselring, Susan. 2011. (Be Safe Ser.). (ENG.). 24p. (J). (gr. k-3). lib. bdg. 27.07 *(978-1-60954-371-6(8)*, 200082) Child's World, Inc., The.
—Being Safe with Fire. Lindeen, Mary & Kesselring, Susan. 2011. (Be Safe Ser.). (ENG.). 24p. (J). (gr. k-3). lib. bdg. 27.07 *(978-1-60954-372-3(6)*, 200083) Child's World, Inc., The.
—Being Safe with Weather. Lindeen, Mary & Kesselring, Susan. 2011. (Be Safe Ser.). (ENG.). 24p. (J). (gr. k-3). lib. bdg. 27.07 *(978-1-60954-374-7(2)*, 200085) Child's World, Inc., The.
—Conjunctions. Heinrichs, Ann. 2010. (Language Rules! Ser.). (ENG.). 24p. (J). (gr. 1-4). lib. bdg. 27.07 *(978-1-60253-427-8(6)*, 200431) Child's World, Inc., The.
—Interjections. Heinrichs, Ann. 2010. (Language Rules! Ser.). (ENG.). 24p. (J). (gr. 1-4). lib. bdg. 27.07 *(978-1-60253-428-5(4)*, 200432) Child's World, Inc., The.
McGeehan, Dan & Moore, David, Jr. Nouns. Heinrichs, Ann. 2010. (Language Rules! Ser.). (ENG.). 24p. (J). (gr. 1-4). lib. bdg. 27.07 *(978-1-60253-429-2(2)*, 200433) Child's World, Inc., The.
—Prefixes & Suffixes. Heinrichs, Ann. 2010. (Language Rules! Ser.). (ENG.). 24p. (J). (gr. 1-4). lib. bdg. 27.07 *(978-1-60253-430-8(6)*, 200434) Child's World, Inc., The.
McGeehan, Dan & Moore, David. Pronouns. Heinrichs, Ann. 2010. (Language Rules! Ser.). (ENG.). 24p. (J). (gr. 1-4). lib. bdg. 27.07 *(978-1-60253-432-2(2)*, 200436) Child's World, Inc., The.
—Verbs. Heinrichs, Ann. 2010. (Language Rules! Ser.). (ENG.). 24p. (J). (gr. 1-4). lib. bdg. 27.07 *(978-1-60253-436-0(5)*, 200440) Child's World, Inc., The.
McGehee, Claudia. North Woods Girl. Bissonette, Aimee M. 2015. (ENG.). 32p. 16.95 ***(978-0-87351-966-3(3))*** Minnesota Historical Society Pr.
McGehee, Claudia. A Tallgrass Prairie Alphabet. McGehee, Claudia. 2004. (Bur Oak Book Ser.). 32p. (J). 17.95 *(978-0-87745-897-5(9))* Univ. of Iowa Pr.
McGhee, Chelsea. The Fox Behind the Chatterbox. Matalonis, Anne. 2008. 32p. pap. 17.95 *(978-1-59858-783-8(8))* Dog Ear Publishing, LLC.
McGhee, Katie Mariah & Herrera, Aaron Jeremiah. The Case of the Missing Chimpanzee from Classroom C2. McGhee, Katie Mariah. 2012. 28p. 24.95 *(978-1-4560-0039-4(X))* America Star Bks.
McGhee, Kerry. Princess Alice & the Dreadful Dragon. Bernhardt, William. 2007. 27p. (J). 19.99 *(978-1-930709-65-2(X))* HAWK Publishing Group.
McGhee, Stuart. The Great Reef Race. Perree, Leyland. 2nd ed. 2013. 36p. pap. 7.49 *(978-1-909587-26-7(5))* PlatyPr.
—The Unpleasant Tale of the Man-Eating Christmas Pudding. Perree, Leyland. 2013. 36p. pap. 5.99 *(978-1-909587-06-9(0))* PlatyPr.
McGill, Joshua. Proton Gator & Friends Coloring Book. Simone, Val Edward. 2011. 32p. (J). pap. 5.99 *(978-1-935296-27-0(2))* Morningside Publishing, LLC.
McGillivray, Kim & Zerbetz, Evon. Aleutian Sparrow. Hesse, Karen. 2005. (ENG.). 160p. (J). (gr. 4-9). reprint ed. pap. 7.99 *(978-1-4169-0327-7(5)*, McElderry, Margaret K. Bks.) McElderry, Margaret K. Bks.
McGinley-Nally, Sharon. Pigs in the Corner: Fun with Math & Dance. Axelrod, Amy. 2005. (ENG.). 40p. (J). (gr. -1-4). 11.99 *(978-1-4169-0335-2(6)*, Simon & Schuster/Paula Wiseman Bks.) Simon & Schuster/Paula Wiseman Bks.
McGinley-Nally, Sharon. Pigs at Odds: Fun with Math & Games. McGinley-Nally, Sharon. Axelrod, Amy. 2003. (ENG.). 40p. (J). (gr. -1-4). 7.99 *(978-0-689-86144-4(3)*, Simon & Schuster/Paula Wiseman Bks.) Simon & Schuster/Paula Wiseman Bks.
McGinness, Suzanne. My Bear Griz. Quarto Generic Staff. 2011. (ENG.). 32p. (J). (gr. -1-1). 17.95 *(978-1-84780-113-5(7)*, Frances Lincoln) Quarto Publishing Group UK GBR. Dist: Hachette Bk. Group.
McGinnis, Ben. Avoiding Injuries. Pinchbeck, Chris, photos by. Goodbody, Slim. 2007. (Slim Goodbody Good Health Guides). 32p. (gr. 2-6). lib. bdg. 26.00 *(978-0-8368-7739-7(X)*, Gareth Stevens Learning Library) Stevens, Gareth Publishing LLLP.
—Birds. Goodbody, Slim & Burstein, John. 2008. (Slim Goodbody's Inside Guide to Pets Ser.). 32p. (gr. 2-6). lib. bdg. 26.00 *(978-0-8368-8953-6(3)*, Gareth Stevens Learning Library) Stevens, Gareth Publishing LLLP.
—Cats. Goodbody, Slim & Burstein, John. 2008. (Slim Goodbody's Inside Guide to Pets Ser.). 32p. (gr. 2-6). lib. bdg. 26.00 *(978-0-8368-8954-3(1)*, Gareth Stevens Learning Library) Stevens, Gareth Publishing LLLP.
—Dogs. Goodbody, Slim & Burstein, John. 2008. (Slim Goodbody's Inside Guide to Pets Ser.). 32p. (gr. 2-6). lib. bdg. 26.00 *(978-0-8368-8955-0(X)*, Gareth Stevens Learning Library) Stevens, Gareth Publishing LLLP.
—Eating Right. Pinchbeck, Chris, photos by. Goodbody, Slim. 2007. (Slim Goodbody's Good Health Guides Ser.). 32p. (gr. 2-6). lib. bdg. 26.00 *(978-0-8368-7740-3(3)*, Gareth Stevens Learning Library) Stevens, Gareth Publishing LLLP.
—Exercising. Pinchbeck, Chris, photos by. Goodbody, Slim. 2007. (Slim Goodbody Good Health Guides). 32p. (gr. 2-6). lib. bdg. 26.00 *(978-0-8368-7741-0(1)*, Gareth Stevens Learning Library) Stevens, Gareth Publishing LLLP.
—Goldfish. Goodbody, Slim & Burstein, John. 2008. (Slim Goodbody's Inside Guide to Pets Ser.). 32p. (gr. 2-6). lib. bdg. 26.00 *(978-0-8368-8956-7(8)*, Gareth Stevens Learning Library) Stevens, Gareth Publishing LLLP.
—Guinea Pigs. Goodbody, Slim & Burstein, John. 2008. (Slim Goodbody's Inside Guide to Pets Ser.). 32p. (gr. 2-6). lib. bdg. 26.00 *(978-0-8368-8957-4(6)*, Gareth Stevens Learning Library) Stevens, Gareth Publishing LLLP.
—Keeping Clean. Pinchbeck, Chris, photos by. Goodbody, Slim. 2007. (Slim Goodbody Good Health Guides). 32p. (gr. 2-6). lib. bdg. 26.00 *(978-0-8368-7742-7(X)*, Gareth Stevens Learning Library) Stevens, Gareth Publishing LLLP.
—Keeping Safe. Pinchbeck, Chris, photos by. Goodbody, Slim. 2007. (Slim Goodbody Good Health Guides). 32p. (gr. 2-6). lib. bdg. 26.00 *(978-0-8368-7743-4(8)*, Gareth Stevens Learning Library) Stevens, Gareth Publishing LLLP.
—Rabbits. Goodbody, Slim & Burstein, John. 2008. (Slim Goodbody's Inside Guide to Pets Ser.). 32p. (gr. 2-6). lib. bdg. 26.00 *(978-0-8368-8958-1(4)*, Gareth Stevens Learning Library) Stevens, Gareth Publishing LLLP.
—Staying Well. Pinchbeck, Chris, photos by. Goodbody, Slim. 2007. (Slim Goodbody's Good Health Guides Ser.). 32p. (gr. 2-6). lib. bdg. 26.00 *(978-0-8368-7744-1(6)*, Gareth Stevens Learning Library) Stevens, Gareth Publishing LLLP.
McGinnis, Steve. Darling Saves Christmas: The Continuing Adventures of Darling the Curly Tailed Reindoe. Campbell, Cheryl. 2010. (ENG.). 30p. (J). 24.95 *(978-0-9828689-2-8(8)*, BQB Publishing) Boutique of Quality Books Publishing Co.
—Darling the Curly Tailed Reindoe. Campbell, Cheryl. 2010. (ENG.). 30p. (J). 24.95 *(978-0-9828689-3-5(6))* Boutique of Quality Books Publishing Co.
McGinty, Ian, et al. Hello Kitty: It's about Time. Chabot, Jacob. 2015. (Hello Kitty Ser.: 6). (ENG.). 64p. (J). pap. 7.99 *(978-1-4215-7769-2(0))* Viz Media.
—Hello Kitty: Work of Art. Chabot, Jacob. 2014. (Hello Kitty Ser.: 5). (ENG.). 64p. (J). pap. 7.99 *(978-1-4215-7542-1(6))* Viz Media.
McGinty, Ian. Uglydoll - Eat Dat!, Vol. 3. Nichols, Travis. 2014. (Uglydoll Ser.: 3). (ENG.). 80p. (J). pap. 7.99 *(978-1-4215-5724-3(X))* Viz Media.
—Which Way, Dude? No. 3: Lumpy Space Princess Saves the World. West, Tracey. 2015. (Adventure Time Ser.). (ENG.). 128p. (J). (gr. 3-7). 4.99 *(978-0-8431-8078-7(1)*, Price Stern Sloan) Penguin Publishing Group.
McGinty, Mick. Whales. Rosenthal, Sue. 2003. (Magic School Bus Fact Finder Ser.). (ENG.). 96p. (J). pap. 4.99 *(978-0-439-38174-1(6))* Scholastic, Inc.
McGoldrick, Bernita. Pretty Pretty Picky Penelope. McGoldrick, Bernita. 2010. 32p. pap. 12.95 *(978-1-935268-49-9(X))* Halo Publishing International.
McGowan, Jayme. One Bear Extraordinaire. 2015. (ENG.). 32p. (J). (gr. -1-3). 16.95 ***(978-1-4197-1654-6(9)***, Abrams Bks. for Young Readers) Abrams.
McGowan, Shane. Stella & the Movie Star. Costain, Meredith. 2015. (Legends in Their Own Lunchbox Ser.). (ENG.). 56p. (gr. 2-3). pap. 7.99 ***(978-1-4966-0261-9(7)***, Legends in Their Own Lunchbox) Capstone Classroom.
—Stella & the Pet Parade. Costain, Meredith. 2015. (Legends in Their Own Lunchbox Ser.). (ENG.). 48p. (gr. 1-2). pap. 7.99 ***(978-1-4966-0243-5(9)***, Legends in Their Own Lunchbox) Capstone Classroom.
—Stella, Circus Star. Costain, Meredith. 2015. (Legends in Their Own Lunchbox Ser.). (ENG.). 56p. (gr. 2-3). pap. 7.99 ***(978-1-4966-0255-8(2)***, Legends in Their Own Lunchbox) Capstone Classroom.
—Stella's Got Talent. Costain, Meredith. 2015. (Legends in Their Own Lunchbox Ser.). (ENG.). 48p. (gr. 1-2). pap. 7.99 ***(978-1-4966-0249-7(8)***, Legends in Their Own Lunchbox) Capstone Classroom.
McGrath, Liz. The Ghouls Come Haunting One by One, 1 vol. McDermott, Tom. 2010. (ENG.). 32p. (J). (gr. k-k). 16.99 *(978-1-58980-786-0(3))* Pelican Publishing Co., Inc.
McGrath, Liz. Even More/Todavía Más. McGrath, Liz. Quick, Barbara. de la Vega, Eida, tr. from ENG. 2004.Tr. of Todavía Más. (SPA & ENG.). 32p. (J). (gr. -1-3). 16.95 *(978-0-9720192-8-6(6)*, 626999, Raven Tree Pr.,Csi) Continental Sales, Inc.
McGrath, Michael, jt. illus. see Hyatt, Sean.
McGrath, Michael O'Neill. Patrons & Protectors: In Times of Need. 2003. (Patrons & Protectors Ser.: Vol. 3). 58p. (J). 18.95 *(978-1-56854-410-6(3))* Liturgy Training Pubns.
McGrath, Raymond. Dad & the Bike Race. Eggleton, Jill. 2003. (Rigby Sails Sailing Solo Ser.). (ENG.). 24p. (gr. 1-2). pap. 9.05 *(978-0-7578-3963-4(0))* Houghton Mifflin Harcourt Publishing Co.
—Fearless Phil: 3-in-1 Package. Eggleton, Jill. (Sails Literacy Ser.). 24p. (gr. 3-18). 57.00 *(978-0-7578-6996-9(3))* Rigby Education.
—Fearless Phil: 6 Small Books. Eggleton, Jill. (Sails Literacy Ser.). 24p. (gr. 3-18). 25.00 *(978-0-7578-6988-4(2))* Rigby Education.
—Fearless Phil: Big Book Only. Eggleton, Jill. (Sails Literacy Ser.). 24p. (gr. 3-18). 27.00 *(978-0-7578-6980-8(7))* Rigby Education.
—The Moon: Individual Title Six-Packs. (Sails Literacy Ser.). 16p. (gr. k-18). 27.00 *(978-0-7635-4426-3(4))* Rigby Education.
—My Alien: Individual Title Six-Packs. (Sails Literacy Ser.). 16p. (gr. k-18). 27.00 *(978-0-7635-4394-5(2))* Rigby Education.
—Where Are You, Mouse? Eggleton, Jill. 2003. (Rigby Sails Early Ser.). (ENG.). 16p. (gr. 1-2). pap. 6.95 *(978-0-7578-8741-3(4))* Houghton Mifflin Harcourt Publishing Co.
McGrath, Ryan. Swamp Band Lullaby. Joachimowski, Paula L. 2008. 32p. 17.99 *(978-1-59879-433-5(7))* Lifevest Publishing, Inc.
McGrath, Tom & Juta, Jason. Fantasy Field Guides, 1 vol. Sautter, A. J. 2014. (Fantasy Field Guides). (ENG.). 32p. (gr. 3-4). 109.28 *(978-1-4914-0705-9(0)*, Edge Bks.) Capstone Pr., Inc.
McGraw, Sheila. I Promise I'll Find You. Ward, Heather P. 2005. (ENG.). 32p. (J). (gr. -1-2). pap. 6.95 *(978-1-55209-094-7(9)*, 9781552090947) Firefly Bks., Ltd.
McGregor, Barbara. Mega Magna Forms Princess. Bryan, Sarah Jane & Beilenson, Suzanne. 2008. (Activity Book Ser.). 48p. (J). (gr. -1-3). spiral bd. 19.95 *(978-1-59359-808-2(4))* Peter Pauper Pr. Inc.
—The Wedding Planner's Daughter. Paratore, Coleen Murtagh. 2006. (Wedding Planner's Daughter Ser.). (ENG.). 208p. (J). (gr. 3-8). reprint ed. pap. 6.99 *(978-1-4169-1854-7(X)*, Simon & Schuster Bks. For Young Readers) Simon & Schuster Bks. For Young Readers.
McGregor, Malcolm. 100 Animals to Spot at the Zoo. Clarke, Phillip, ed. 2009. (Spotter's Cards Ser.). 52p. (J). 9.99 *(978-0-7945-2254-4(8)*, Usborne) EDC Publishing.
McGregor, Malcolm & Jackson, Ian. Animals Sticker Book. Clarke, Phillip & Khan, Sarah. Rogers, Kirsteen, ed. 2007. (Spotter's Guides Sticker Bks). 24p. (J). (gr. -1-3). pap. 8.99 *(978-0-7945-1744-1(7)*, Usborne) EDC Publishing.
McGregor, Tony L. The "I Love You" Story. Kelley, Walter P. 2004. (J). *(978-0-9729569-4-9(8))* BuTo, Ltd. Co.
McGrellis, Cynthia. The Longest Shortcut. Ayder, Earl. 2005. 40p. pap. 8.53 *(978-0-7578-9857-0(2))* Rigby Education.
McGrory, Anek. Mighty Monty. Hurwitz, Johanna. 2008. (Monty Ser.: 2). (ENG.). 112p. (J). (gr. 1-4). 15.99 *(978-0-7636-2977-9(4))* Candlewick Pr.
McGrory, Anik. Amazing Monty. Hurwitz, Johanna. 2013. (Monty Ser.). (ENG.). 112p. (J). (gr. k-4). pap. 5.99 *(978-0-7636-6561-6(4))* Candlewick Pr.
—Magical Monty. Hurwitz, Johanna. (Monty Ser.). (ENG.). 112p. (J). (gr. k-4). 2013. pap. 5.99 *(978-0-7636-6457-2(X))*; 2012. 15.99 *(978-0-7636-5008-7(0))* Candlewick Pr.
—Mighty Monty: More First-Grade Adventures. Hurwitz, Johanna. 2010. (Monty Ser.). (ENG.). 112p. (J). (gr. 1-4). pap. 5.99 *(978-0-7636-4786-5(1))* Candlewick Pr.
—Mostly Monty. Hurwitz, Johanna & McCrory, Anik. 2008. (Monty Ser.: 1). (ENG.). 96p. (J). (gr. 1-4). pap. 5.99 *(978-0-7636-4062-0(X))* Candlewick Pr.
—Mountain of Blintzes, 0 vols. Goldin, Barbara Diamond. 2010. (ENG.). 32p. (J). (gr. -1-2). pap. 6.99 *(978-0-7614-5790-9(9)*, 9780761457909, Amazon Children's Publishing) Amazon Publishing.
—You See a Circus, I See... Downs, Mike. 2006. (ENG.). 32p. (J). (gr. -1-3). pap. 7.95 *(978-1-58089-155-4(1))* Charlesbridge Publishing, Inc.
McGrory, Paul. Father Thames. Price, Robin. 2014. (London Deep Ser.). (ENG.). 144p. (J). (gr. 4-7). pap. 11.99 *(978-1-906132-04-0(6))* Mogzilla GBR. Dist: Independent Pubs. Group.
McGuckie, Cierra Jade. Mami, Que Es una Carcel? Stanglin, Jackie A. 2007. (J). (gr. -1-3). 40p. 13.99 *(978-1-59879-428-1(0))*; 36p. 19.99 *(978-1-59879-429-8(9))* Lifevest Publishing, Inc.
—What Is Jail, Mommy? Stanglin, Jackie A. l.t. ed. 2006. 40p. (J). 21.99 *(978-1-59879-252-2(0))*; (gr. -1-3). 13.99 *(978-1-59879-248-5(2))* Lifevest Publishing, Inc.
McGuinness, Áine. Marco: Master of Disguise. Boland, Gerry. 2012. (ENG.). 64p. (J). 12.95 *(978-1-84717-273-0(3))* O'Brien Pr., Ltd., The IRL. Dist: Dufour Editions, Inc.
—Marco Moves In. Boland, Gerry. 2012. (Rather Remarkable Grizzly Be Ser.). (ENG.). 64p. (J). 12.95 *(978-1-84717-229-7(6))* O'Brien Pr., Ltd., The IRL. Dist: Dufour Editions, Inc.
McGuinness, Ed. Amazing X-Men, Vol. 1. 2014. (ENG.). 136p. (YA). (gr. 8-17). pap. 17.99 *(978-0-7851-8821-6(5))* Marvel Worldwide, Inc.
McGuinness-Kelly, Tracy-Lee. Bad Cat. McGuinness-Kelly, Tracy-Lee. 2006. 29p. (J). (gr. k-4). reprint ed. 16.00 *(978-0-7567-9823-9(X))* DIANE Publishing Co.
McGuinness, Tracey, jt. illus. see McGuinness, Tracy.
McGuinness, Tracy. Brainiac's Bug Book: Creepy Crawly Activities. Tenah, Ann. 2005. (Activity Journals Ser.). 128p. 12.99 *(978-0-88088-362-7(6))* Peter Pauper Pr. Inc.
—Clutter Control: Tips & Crafts to Organize Your Bedroom, Backpack, Locker, Life. Falligant, Erin, ed. 2008. (ENG.). 64p. (J). (gr. 3-7). pap. 8.95 *(978-1-59369-341-1(9))* American Girl Publishing, Inc.
—Math Smarts: Tips, Tricks, & Secrets for Making Math More Fun! Long, Lynette. 2004. (AmericanGirl Library). (ENG.). 64p. (J). pap. 8.95 *(978-1-58485-875-1(3))* American Girl Publishing, Inc.
McGuinness, Tracy & McGuinness, Tracey. School Smarts Projects. Raymer, Dottie. 2007. (American Girl Library). (ENG.). 96p. (J). (gr. 3-7). pap. 8.95 *(978-1-59369-005-2(3)*, American Girl) American Girl Publishing, Inc.
McGuire, Bill. Buzz Beaker & the Cave Creatures. Meister, Cari. 2010. (Buzz Beaker Bks.). (ENG.). 32p. (gr. 2-3). pap. 6.25 *(978-1-4342-2797-3(9))*; 21.32 *(978-1-4342-2060-8(5))* Stone Arch Bks.
—Buzz Beaker & the Cool Caps, 1 vol. Meister, Cari. 2011. (Buzz Beaker Bks.). (ENG.). 32p. (gr. 2-3). pap. 6.25 *(978-1-4342-3055-3(4))*; lib. bdg. 21.32 *(978-1-4342-2526-9(7))* Stone Arch Bks.
—Buzz Beaker & the Growing Goo, 1 vol. Meister, Cari. 2011. (Buzz Beaker Bks.). (ENG.). 32p. (gr. 2-3). pap. 6.25 *(978-1-4342-3056-0(2))*; lib. bdg. 21.32 *(978-1-4342-2527-6(5))* Stone Arch Bks.
—Buzz Beaker & the Outer Space Trip. Meister, Cari. 2010. (Buzz Beaker Bks.). (ENG.). 32p. (gr. 2-3). pap. 6.25 *(978-1-4342-2800-0(2))*; 21.32 *(978-1-4342-2063-9(X))* Stone Arch Bks.
—Buzz Beaker & the Putt-Putt Contest. Meister, Cari. 2010. (Buzz Beaker Bks.). (ENG.). 32p. (gr. 2-3). pap. 6.25 *(978-1-4342-2799-7(5))*; 21.32 *(978-1-4342-2062-2(1))* Stone Arch Bks.
—Buzz Beaker & the Race to School, 1 vol. Meister, Cari. 2011. (Buzz Beaker Bks.). (ENG.). 32p. (gr. 2-3). pap. 6.25 *(978-1-4342-3057-7(0))*; lib. bdg. 21.32 *(978-1-4342-2528-3(3))* Stone Arch Bks.
—Buzz Beaker & the Speed Secret. Meister, Cari. 2010. (Buzz Beaker Bks.). (ENG.). 32p. (gr. 2-3). pap. 6.25 *(978-1-4342-2798-0(7))*; 21.32 *(978-1-4342-2061-5(3))* Stone Arch Bks.
—Buzz Beaker & the Super Fast Car, 1 vol. Meister, Cari. 2011. (Buzz Beaker Bks.). (ENG.). 32p. (gr. 2-3). pap. 6.25 *(978-1-4342-3058-4(9))* Stone Arch Bks.
McGuire, Bryan, jt. illus. see Menix, Cinda.
McGuire, Erin. Bite-Sized Magic: A Bliss Novel. Littlewood, Kathryn. (Bliss Bakery Trilogy Ser.: 3). (ENG.). 432p. (J). (gr. 3-7). 2015. pap. 6.99 *(978-0-06-208427-9(5))*; 2014. 16.99 *(978-0-06-208426-2(7))* HarperCollins Pubs. (Tegen, Katherine Bks).
—Breadcrumbs. Ursu, Anne. (ENG.). (J). (gr. 3-7). 2013. 336p. pap. 6.99 *(978-0-06-201506-8(0))*; 2011. 320p. 16.99 *(978-0-06-201505-1(2))* HarperCollins Pubs. (Waldon Pond Pr.).
—Breadcrumbs. Ursu, Anne. 2012. 320p. 55.00 *(978-0-449-01400-4(2))* Random Hse., Inc.
—A Dash of Magic: A Bliss Novel. Littlewood, Kathryn. 2013. (Bliss Bakery Trilogy Ser.: 2). (ENG.). 368p. (J). (gr. 3-7). 16.99 *(978-0-06-208429-3(1)*, Tegen, Katherine Bks) HarperCollins Pubs.
—French Ducks in Venice. Freymann-Weyr, Garret. 2011. (ENG.). 56p. (J). (gr. k-4). 16.99 *(978-0-7636-4173-3(1))* Candlewick Pr.
—Jelly Bean. Lord, Cynthia. 2014. (Shelter Pet Squad Ser.: 1). (ENG.). 128p. (J). (gr. 1-3). 16.99 *(978-0-545-63596-7(9))*; pap. 5.99 *(978-0-545-63597-4(7))* Scholastic, Inc. (Scholastic Pr.).
—Lucky for Good. Patron, Susan. 2012. (ENG.). 224p. (J). (gr. 3-7). pap. 6.99 *(978-1-4169-9059-8(3)*, Atheneum Bks.

for Young Readers) Simon & Schuster Children's Publishing.

—The Real Boy. Ursu, Anne. (ENG.). 352p. (J). (gr. 3-7). 2015. pap. 6.99 *(978-0-06-201508-2(7))*; 2013. 16.99 *(978-0-06-201507-5(9))* HarperCollins Pubs. (Walden Pond Pr.).

—Sleeping Beauty. Rylant, Cynthia. 2015. (J). *(978-1-4231-2108-4(2))* Disney Pr.

McGuire, Erin K. Lucky for Good. Patron, Susan. 2011. (ENG.). 224p. (J). (gr. 3-7). 16.99 *(978-1-4169-9058-1(5)*, Atheneum Bks. for Young Readers) Simon & Schuster Children's Publishing.

McGuire, Robert. Amelia Earhart: Female Pioneer in Flight. Mortensen, Lori. 2007. (Biographies Ser.). (ENG.). 24p. (gr. k-3). 25.99 *(978-1-4048-3728-7(0)*, Nonfiction Picture Bks.) Picture Window Bks.

—Frederick Douglass: Writer, Speaker, & Opponent of Slavery, 1 vol. Slade, Suzanne & Picture Window Books Staff. 2007. (Biographies Ser.). (ENG.). 24p. (gr. k-3). 25.99 *(978-1-4048-3102-5(9)*, Nonfiction Picture Bks.) Picture Window Bks.

—The Last Black King of the Kentucky Derby: The Story of Jimmy Winkfield. Hubbard, Crystal. 2008. (ENG.). 40p. (J). (gr. 1-6). 17.95 *(978-1-58430-274-2(7))* Lee & Low Bks., Inc.

—The White Elephant. Fleischman, Sid. 2006. 112p. (J). (gr. 3-6). lib. bdg. 16.89 *(978-0-06-113137-0(7))*; 15.99 *(978-0-06-113136-3(9))* HarperCollins Pubs. (Greenwillow Bks.).

McGuirk, Leslie. Gobble, Gobble, Tucker! McGuirk, Leslie. 2014. (ENG.). 32p. (J). (-k). bds. 7.99 *(978-0-7636-6887-7(7))* Candlewick Pr.

—Ho, Ho, Ho, Tucker! McGuirk, Leslie. (Candlewick Storybook Animation Ser.). (ENG.). (J). (-k). 2010. 32p. 8.99 *(978-0-7636-5043-8(9))*; 2005. 30p. bds. 7.99 *(978-0-7636-2582-5(5))* Candlewick Pr.

—Lucky Tucker. McGuirk, Leslie. 2008. (ENG.). 24p. (J). (gr. -1-k). pap. 4.99 *(978-0-7636-3389-9(5))* Candlewick Pr.

—The Moogees Move House. McGuirk, Leslie. 2012. (ENG.). 32p. (J). (gr. -1-2). 14.99 *(978-0-7636-5558-7(9))* Candlewick Pr.

—Tucker's Spooky Halloween. McGuirk, Leslie. (Candlewick Storybook Animation Ser.). (ENG.). (J). 2011. 32p. (gr. k-k). 8.99 *(978-0-7636-5113-8(0))*; 2009. 32p. (gr. k-k). 14.99 *(978-0-7636-4469-7(2))*; 2007. 28p. (gr. -1-k). bds. 7.99 *(978-0-7636-3181-9(7))* Candlewick Pr.

—Tucker's Valentine. McGuirk, Leslie. 2010. (ENG.). 28p. (J). (gr. -1-k). bds. 6.99 *(978-0-7636-4357-7(2))* Candlewick Pr.

—Wiggens Learns His Manners at the Four Seasons Restaurant. McGuirk, Leslie. Von Bidder, Alex. 2009. (ENG.). 32p. (J). (gr. -1-2). 16.99 *(978-0-7636-4014-9(X))* Candlewick Pr.

McHaffie, Natalie. C-Growl: The Daring Little Airplane. McHaffie, Natalie. 2004. 32p. 14.95 *(978-1-55125-015-1(2))* Vanwell Publishing, Ltd. CAN. Dist: Casemate Pubs. & Bk. Distributors, LLC.

McHale, Conor. Ancient Ireland Colouring Book: From Newgrange to the Vikings. McHale, Conor. 2014. (ENG.). 32p. (J). pap. 12.00 *(978-1-84717-629-5(1))* O'Brien Pr., Ltd., The IRL. Dist: Dufour Editions, Inc.

McHargue, D., et al. Ana Frank. Brown, Jonatha A. & Goff, Elizabeth Hudson. 2007. (Biografías Gráficas (Graphic Biographies) Ser.). (SPA.). 32p. (gr. 5-8). lib. bdg. 27.00 *(978-0-8368-7880-6(9))* Stevens, Gareth Publishing LLLP.

McHargue, D. The Battle of Gettysburg. Anderson, Dale & O'Hern, Kerri. 2006. (Graphic Histories Ser.). 32p. (gr. 5-8). lib. bdg. 27.00 *(978-0-8368-6204-1(X))* Stevens, Gareth Publishing LLLP.

—The Battle of the Alamo. Riehecky, Janet & O'Hern, Kerri. 2006. (Graphic Histories Ser.). 32p. (gr. 5-8). lib. bdg. 27.00 *(978-0-8368-6201-0(5))* Stevens, Gareth Publishing LLLP.

—César Chávez. Brown, Jonatha A. et al. 2007. (Biografías Gráficas (Graphic Biographies) Ser.). (SPA.). 32p. (gr. 5-8). lib. bdg. 27.00 *(978-0-8368-7879-0(5))* Stevens, Gareth Publishing LLLP.

—The Montgomery Bus Boycott. Walsh, Frank & O'Hern, Kerri. 2006. (Graphic Histories Ser.). 32p. (gr. 5-8). lib. bdg. 27.00 *(978-0-8368-6205-8(8))* Stevens, Gareth Publishing LLLP.

—Nelson Mandela. Holland, Gini & O'Hern, Kerri. 2006. (Graphic Biographies Ser.). 32p. (gr. 5-8). lib. bdg. 27.00 *(978-0-8368-6197-6(3))* Stevens, Gareth Publishing LLLP.

McHargue, Dove & Ellis, Rich. Will the Real Martian Please Stand Up? Kneece, Mark & Serling, Rod. 2009. (Twilight Zone Ser.). (ENG.). 72p. (YA). (gr. 7-10). pap. 9.99 *(978-0-8027-9727-8(X))* Walker & Co.

McHeffey, Adam. The Dyno-Mite Dog Show. 0 vols. Bonnett-Rampersaud, Louise. (Secret Knock Club Ser.: 0). (ENG.). 112p. (J). (gr. 1-4). 2015. pap. 9.99 *(978-0-7614-6325-2(9)*, 9780761463252); 2012. 12.99 *(978-0-7614-6213-2(9)*, 9780761462132) Amazon Publishing. (Amazon Children's Publishing).

McHeffey, Adam. Asiago, 0 vols. McHeffey, Adam. 2012. (ENG.). 32p. (J). (gr. k-3). 16.99 *(978-0-7614-6138-8(8)*, 9780761461388, Amazon Children's Publishing) Amazon Publishing.

McHenry, E. B. Poodlena. McHenry, E. B. 2004. (ENG.). 32p. (J). (gr. -1-3). 16.95 *(978-1-58234-824-7(3)*, Bloomsbury USA Childrens) Bloomsbury USA.

McHose, Jean. Tommy Wilson, Junior Veterinarian: The Case of the Wounded Jack Rabbit. Smith, Maggie Caldwell. 2005. 104p. (J). (gr. 3-6). pap. 7.95 *(978-1-889159-14-0(X))* Magpie Pr., Pine Mountain Club, CA.

McIlhany. A Toddler's Abc of Blessings. Prus, Jennifer. 2012. 20p. pap. 9.95 *(978-1-61633-256-3(5))* Guardian Angel Publishing, Inc.

McIlroy, Michelle, jt. illus. see Louise, Cristina.

McInerney, Kunyi June-Anne. Bush Games & Knucklebones. Kartinyeri, Doris. 2003. 32p. (J). pap. *(978-1-875641-81-9(5))* Magabala Bks.

McIntosh, Gabe. Parasaurolophus. Bailey, Gerry. 2011. (Smithsonian Prehistoric Zone Ser.). (ENG.). 32p. (J). (gr. k-3). *(978-0-7787-1799-7(2))*; pap. *(978-0-7787-1812-3(3))* Crabtree Publishing Co.

—Parasaurolophus Escapes. Bentley, Dawn. 2006. (Smithsonian's Prehistoric Pals Ser.). (ENG.). 36p. (J). 2.95 *(978-1-59249-645-7(8))*; (gr. -1-3). pap. 6.95 *(978-1-59249-643-3(1))* Soundprints.

McIntosh, Gabe, jt. illus. see Scalf, Christopher.

McIntosh, Gabe, jt. illus. see Scalf, Chris.

McIntosh, Iain. The Mystery of Meerkat Hill. McCall Smith, Alexander. 2013. (Precious Ramotswe Mysteries for Young Readers Ser.: 2). (ENG.). 112p. (J). (gr. 2-5). pap. 6.99 *(978-0-345-80446-4(5)*, Anchor) Knopf Doubleday Publishing Group.

—The Mystery of Meerkat Hill: A Precious Ramotswe Mystery for Young Readers. McCall Smith, Alexander. 2013. (Precious Ramotswe Mysteries for Young Readers Ser.: 2). (ENG.). 112p. (J). (gr. 2-5). 12.99 *(978-0-345-80458-7(9))*; lib. bdg. 13.99 *(978-0-345-80616-1(6))* Knopf Doubleday Publishing Group. (Anchor).

McInturff, Linda & Brownlie, Ian. One Day. Cunningham, Edie. 2004. 28p. (J). pap. *(978-1-932381-09-2(0)*, 6340) Bible Visuals International, Inc.

McInturff, Linda & Pope, Patricia. I Love to Tell the Story: A Visualized Gospel Song. 2010. 16p. (J). pap. *(978-1-932381-96-2(1)*, 6220) Bible Visuals International, Inc.

McInturff, Linda & Tweed, Sean. The Light of the World Is Jesus. 2004. 16p. (J). pap. *(978-1-932381-08-5(2))* Bible Visuals International, Inc.

McIntyre, Coleen. Baking with Friends: Recipes, Tips & Fun Facts for Teaching Kids to Bake. Davis, Sharon & Patton, Charlene. Beatty, Nicholas, ed. 2010. 78p. (J). *(978-0-9712368-2-0(8))* Goops Unlimited.

McIntyre, Connie, jt. illus. see Gage, Amy Glaser.

McIntyre, Georgina. Sammy Goes Flying. Elliott, Odette. 2011. (ENG.). 32p. (J). (gr. -1-k). pap. 9.99 *(978-1-84853-050-8(1))* Transworld Publishers Ltd. GBR. Dist: Independent Pubs. Group.

McIntyre, Louise. Flowers for Grandpa Dan: A Gentle Story to Help Children Understand Alzheimer's Disease. McIntyre, Connie. 2004. 20p. (J). 12.95 *(978-0-9677685-5-7(1))*; lib. bdg. 17.95 *(978-0-9677685-6-4(X))* Grannie Annie Family Story Celebration, The.

McIntyre, Sarah. Adventures of Riley: Dolphins in Danger. Lumry, Amanda & Hurwitz, Laura. 2005. 36p. 15.95 *(978-0-9748411-1-3(0))* Eaglemont Pr.

—Adventures of Riley: Mission to Madagascar. Lumry, Amanda & Hurwitz, Laura. 2005. 36p. (gr. 2-3). 15.95 *(978-0-9748411-2-0(9))* Eaglemont Pr.

—Amazon River Rescue. Lumry, Amanda & Hurwitz, Laura. 2004. (Adventures of Riley Ser.). 36p. 15.95 *(978-0-9662257-9-2(1))* Eaglemont Pr.

—Cakes in Space. Reeve, Philip. 2015. (Not-So-Impossible Tale Ser.). (ENG.). 224p. (J). (gr. 2-5). 12.99 *(978-0-385-38792-7(X))* Random Hse., Inc.

—Morris the Mankiest Monster. Andreae, Giles. 2011. (ENG.). 32p. (J). (gr. -1-k). pap. 12.99 *(978-0-552-55935-5(0))* Transworld Publishers Ltd. GBR. Dist: Independent Pubs. Group.

McIntyre, Sarah. Oliver & the Seawigs. Reeve, Philip. 2014. (Not-So-Impossible Tale Ser.). (ENG.). 208p. (J). (gr. 2-5). 12.99 *(978-0-385-38788-0(1)*, Random Hse. Bks. for Young Readers) Random Hse. Children's Bks.

McIntyre, Sarah. Tigers in Terai. Lumry, Amanda & Hurwitz, Laura. 2nd rev. ed. 2007. (Adventures of Riley (Unnumbered) Ser.). 36p. (J). (gr. -1-3). 15.95 *(978-1-60040-003-2(5))* Centro Bks., LLC.

—Tigers in Terai. Lumry, Amanda & Hurwitz, Laura. (Adventures of Riley Ser.). 36p. 2003. 15.95 *(978-0-9662257-7-8(5))*; 2nd ed. 2007. *(978-0-9748411-6-8(1))* Eaglemont Pr.

McIntyre, Sasha, et al. Franklin's Pond Phantom. Jennings, Sharon. 2005. 32p. (J). lib. bdg. 15.38 *(978-1-4242-1181-4(6))* Fitzgerald Bks.

McKay, Ann Marie. Hungry Mr. Gator. McLaughlin, Julie. 2005. (J). 15.99 *(978-0-933101-24-1(4))* Legacy Pubns.

—Mr. Gator Hits the Beach. McLaughlin, Julie. 2009. 32p. (J). 16.99 *(978-0-933101-56-2(2))* Legacy Pubns.

—Mr. Gator's up the Creek. McLaughlin, Julie. 2005. (J). 16.99 *(978-0-933101-23-4(6))* Legacy Pubns.

McKay, Donald. The Story of Mark Twain. Howard, Joan. Meadowcroft, Enid Lamonte, ed. 2011. 186p. 42.95 *(978-1-258-05565-3(1))* Literary Licensing, LLC.

McKay, Siobhan. Sharing Me: Helping Young Children Deal with Divorce. Alsop, Bonnie. 2013. 24p. pap. 11.50 *(978-1-62212-232-5(1)*, Strategic Bk. Publishing) Strategic Book Publishing & Rights Agency (SBPRA).

McKay, Traci. My Happy Gift. Langdown, Leanne Shea. 2011. 26p. pap. 6.99 *(978-1-61667-300-0(1))* Raider Publishing International.

McKean, Dave. Coraline. Gaiman, Neil. 3rd ed. 2003. (SPA.). 160p. *(978-84-7888-579-4(X)*, 1952) Emece Editores.

—Coraline. Gaiman, Neil. (P. S. Ser.). (ENG.). 2006. 192p. (gr. 6-8). pap. 12.99 *(978-0-06-113937-6(8)*, William Morrow Paperbacks); 2004. 224p. (YA). (gr. 8-18). pap. 8.99 *(978-0-06-057591-5(3))*; 2008. 176p. (J). (gr. 3). pap. 6.99 *(978-0-06-164969-1(4)*, HarperFestival) HarperCollins Pubs.

—Coraline. Gaiman, Neil. 2007. 151p. (J). (gr. 6-8). 60.00 *(978-1-59606-147-7(2))* Subterranean Pr.

—Coraline. Gaiman, Neil. 10th anniv. ed. 2012. (HarperClassics Ser.). (ENG.). 208p. (J). (gr. 3-18). pap. 6.99 *(978-0-380-80734-5(3))* HarperCollins Pubs.

—Coraline: Reading Group Guide. Gaiman, Neil. *(978-0-06-056878-8(X))* HarperCollins Pubs.

—Crazy Hair. Gaiman, Neil. (J). (gr. -1-3). 2015. (ENG.). 40p. pap. 6.99 *(978-0-06-057910-4(2))*; 2009. (ENG.). 40p. 18.99 *(978-0-06-057908-1(0))*; 2009. 32p. lib. bdg. 19.89 *(978-0-06-057909-8(9))* HarperCollins Pubs.

—The Day I Swapped My Dad for Two Goldfish. Gaiman, Neil. 64p. (J). (gr. k-3). 2006. (ENG.). pap. 7.99 *(978-0-06-058703-1(2))*; 2004. lib. bdg. 17.89 *(978-0-06-058702-4(4))*; 2004. (ENG.). 17.99 *(978-0-06-058701-7(6))* HarperCollins Pubs.

—Death: The Time of Your Life. Gaiman, Neil et al. Kahan, Bob, ed. rev. ed. 2006. (ENG.). 96p. (YA). pap. 12.99 *(978-1-56389-333-9(9))* DC Comics.

—The Graveyard Book. Gaiman, Neil. (J). 2010. (ENG.). 336p. (gr. 5). pap. 8.99 *(978-0-06-053094-5(4))*; 2008. 552p. pap. 17.99 *(978-0-06-170912-8(3))*; 2008. (ENG.). 320p. (gr. 5-7). 17.99 *(978-0-06-053092-1(8))*; 2008. 336p. (gr. 5-7). lib. bdg. 18.89 *(978-0-06-053093-8(6))* HarperCollins Pubs.

Mckean, Dave. The Graveyard Book. Gaiman, Neil. 2014. (ENG.). 352p. (J). (gr. 5-7). pap. 9.99 *(978-0-06-234918-7(X))* HarperCollins Pubs.

McKean, Dave. Los Lobos de la Pared. Gaiman, Neil. 2006.Tr. of Wolves in the Wall. (SPA.). 64p. 22.95 *(978-1-59497-222-5(2))* Public Square Bks.

—Mirrormask. Gaiman, Neil. ed. 2005. (ENG.). 80p. (J). (gr. 5). 16.99 *(978-0-06-082109-8(4))* HarperCollins Pubs.

Mckean, Dave. Mouse Bird Snake Wolf. Almond, David. 2013. (ENG.). 80p. (J). (gr. 2-5). 17.99 *(978-0-7636-5912-7(6))* Candlewick Pr.

McKean, Dave. The Savage. Almond, David. 2008. (ENG.). 80p. (J). (gr. 7). 17.99 *(978-0-7636-3932-7(X))* Candlewick Pr.

—Slog's Dad. Almond, David. 2011. (ENG.). 64p. (J). (gr. 5-18). 15.99 *(978-0-7636-4940-1(6))* Candlewick Pr.

—Varjak Paw. Said, S. F. 2005. (ENG.). 256p. (J). (gr. 3-7). reprint ed. pap. 6.99 *(978-0-440-42076-7(8)*, Yearling) Random Hse. Children's Bks.

—Wizard & Glass, 4 vols. King, Stephen. rev. ed. 2003. (Dark Tower Ser.: 4). (ENG.). (gr. 12-18). 752p. mass mkt. 8.99 *(978-0-451-21087-6(5)*, Signet); 720p. pap. 22.00 *(978-0-452-28472-2(4)*, Plume) Penguin Publishing Group.

—The Wolves in the Walls. Gaiman, Neil. (ENG.). 56p. (J). (gr. k). 2003. 17.99 *(978-0-380-97827-4(X))*; 2005. reprint ed. pap. 6.99 *(978-0-380-81095-6(6))* HarperCollins Pubs.

McKean, Dave. Mirrormask. McKean, Dave. ed. 2005. 80p. (J). lib. bdg. 17.89 *(978-0-06-082110-4(8))* HarperCollins Pubs.

McKee, Darren. Colors of Spring. Neusner, Dena Wallenstein. 2003. (Barney Ser.). (ENG.). 32p. (J). pap., act. bk. ed. 3.99 *(978-1-58668-305-4(5))* Scholastic, Inc.

—Musical Mystery Scooby Doo! Fertig, Michael P. 2007. (Scooby Doo Ser.). (J). (gr. -1-3). 12.98 *(978-1-4127-7429-1(2))* Publications International, Ltd.

—Zach Apologizes. Mulcahy, William. 2012. (Zach Rules Ser.). (ENG.). 32p. (J). (gr. -1-3). 12.99 *(978-1-57542-389-0(8))* Free Spirit Publishing, Inc.

McKee, David. Elmer & Butterfly. 2015. (J). *(978-1-4677-6327-1(6))* Lerner Publishing Group.

—Elmer & Super El. Mckee, David. 2012. (Andersen Press Picture Bks). (ENG.). 32p. (J). (gr. -1-3). 16.95 *(978-0-7613-8989-7(X))* Lerner Publishing Group.

—Elmer & the Birthday Quake. 2013. (ENG.). 32p. (J). (gr. -1-3). 16.95 *(978-1-4677-1117-3(9))* Lerner Publishing Group.

—Elmer & the Butterfly. 2015. (ENG.). 32p. (J). (gr. -1-3). 16.99 *(978-1-4677-6326-4(8))* Lerner Publishing Group.

—Elmer's Christmas. 2011. (Andersen Press Picture Books Ser.). (J). 16.95 *(978-0-7613-8088-7(4))* Andersen Pr. GBR. Dist: Lerner Publishing Group.

—The King of Quizzical Island. Snell, Gordon. 2009. (ENG.). 40p. (J). (gr. -1-3). 16.99 *(978-0-7636-3857-3(9))* Candlewick Pr.

—The Tickle Ghost. McKee, Brett. 2011. (ENG.). 32p. (J). (gr. k-2). 19.99 *(978-1-84939-246-4(3))* Andersen Pr. GBR. Dist: Independent Pubs. Group.

McKee, David. Charlotte's Piggy Bank. McKee, David. 2004. (ENG.). 32p. (J). pap. 12.95 *(978-1-84270-331-1(5))* Andersen Pr. GBR. Dist: Independent Pubs. Group.

—Denver. McKee, David. 2012. (ENG.). 32p. (J). (gr. -1-k). pap. 9.99 *(978-1-84939-389-8(3))* Andersen Pr. GBR. Dist: Independent Pubs. Group.

—Elmer, Level 4.9. McKee, David. 3rd ed. 2003. (Picture Books Collection). (SPA.). 32p. (J). (gr. k-3). 12.95 *(978-84-372-2186-1(2))* Altea, Ediciones, S.A. - Grupo Santillana ESP. Dist: Santillana USA Publishing Co., Inc.

—Elmer. McKee, David. (Historias Para Dormir Ser.). (SPA.). 32p. (J). (gr. k-3). pap. 9.95 *(978-968-19-1029-7(X))* Santillana USA Publishing Co., Inc.

—Elmer & Rose. McKee, David. 2010. (ENG.). 32p. (J). (gr. -1-3). 16.95 *(978-0-7613-5493-2(X))* Lerner Publishing Group.

—Elmer & Snake. McKee, David. 2013. (ENG.). 32p. (J). (gr. -1-3). 16.95 *(978-1-4677-2033-5(X))* Lerner Publishing Group.

—Elmer & the Big Bird. McKee, David. 2012. (Andersen Press Picture Bks). (ENG.). 32p. (J). (gr. -1-3). 16.95 *(978-1-4677-0319-2(2))* Lerner Publishing Group.

McKee, David. Elmer & the Flood. McKee, David. 2015. (ENG.). 32p. (J). (gr. -1-3). 17.99 ***(978-1-4677-9312-4(4))*** Lerner Publishing Group.

McKee, David. Elmer & the Hippos. McKee, David. 2010. (Andersen Press Picture Bks). (ENG.). 32p. (J). (gr. -1-3). 16.95 *(978-0-7613-6442-9(0))* Lerner Publishing Group.

—Elmer & the Lost Teddy. McKee, David. 2004. (Elmer Bks.). 32p. (J). 9.99 *(978-0-06-075243-9(2))* HarperCollins Pubs.

—Elmer & the Monster. McKee, David. 2014. 32p. (J). (gr. -1-3). 16.95 *(978-1-4677-4200-9(7))* Lerner Publishing Group.

—Elmer & the Rainbow. McKee, David. 2011. (Andersen Press Picture Bks). (ENG.). 32p. (J). (gr. -1-3). 16.95 *(978-0-7613-7410-7(8))* Lerner Publishing Group.

—Elmer & the Whales. McKee, David. 2014. (ENG.). 32p. (J). (gr. -1-3). 16.95 *(978-1-4677-3453-0(5))* Lerner Publishing Group.

—Elmer & Wilbur. McKee, David. 2004. (Elmer Bks.). 32p. (J). 9.99 *(978-0-06-075239-2(4))* HarperCollins Pubs.

—Elmer Board Book. McKee, David. 2014. 32p. (J). (gr. -1 — 1). bds. 7.99 *(978-0-06-232405-4(5)*, HarperFestival) HarperCollins Pubs.

—Elmer in the Snow. McKee, David. 2004. (Elmer Bks.). 32p. (J). 9.99 *(978-0-06-075240-8(8))* HarperCollins Pubs.

—Elmer's Baby Record Book. McKee, David. 2007. (ENG.). 32p. 15.99 *(978-1-84270-534-6(2))* Andersen Pr. GBR. Dist: Independent Pubs. Group.

—Elmer's Day. McKee, David. 2014. (Elmer Ser.). (ENG.). 16p. (J). (-k). 6.99 *(978-0-86264-496-3(8))* Andersen Pr. GBR. Dist: Independent Pubs. Group.

—Elmer's First Counting Book. McKee, David. Mckee, David. 2012. (Andersen Press Board Bks). (ENG.). 10p. (J). (gr. -1-2). bds. 7.95 *(978-0-7613-8999-6(7))* Lerner Publishing Group.

—Elmer's Opposites. McKee, David. Mckee, David. 2012. (Andersen Press Board Bks). (ENG.). 10p. (J). (gr. -1-2). bds. 7.95 *(978-0-7613-8998-9(9))* Lerner Publishing Group.

—Elmer's Special Day. McKee, David. 2009. (Andersen Press Picture Bks). (ENG.). 32p. (J). (gr. -1-3). 16.95 *(978-0-7613-5154-2(X)*, Carolrhoda Bks.) Lerner Publishing Group.

—Elmer's Weather. McKee, David. 2014. (Elmer Ser.). (ENG.). 16p. (J). (-k). 6.99 *(978-0-86264-494-9(1))* Andersen Pr. GBR. Dist: Independent Pubs. Group.

—George's Invisible Watch. McKee, David. McKee, Brett. 2013. (ENG.). 32p. (J). (gr. -1-k). pap. 8.99 *(978-1-84270-864-4(3))* Andersen Pr. GBR. Dist: Independent Pubs. Group.

—Gladiator. McKee, David. 2005. (ENG.). 32p. (J). (gr. k-2). pap. 12.99 *(978-1-84270-372-4(2))* Trafalgar Square Publishing.

—The Hill & the Rock. McKee, David. 2012. (ENG.). 32p. (J). (gr. -1-k). pap. 12.99 *(978-1-84939-305-8(2))* Andersen Pr. GBR. Dist: Independent Pubs. Group.

—Isabel's Noisy Tummy. McKee, David. 2013. (ENG.). 32p. (J). (gr. -1-k). pap. 9.99 *(978-1-84939-689-9(2))* Andersen Pr. GBR. Dist: Independent Pubs. Group.

—Melric: The Magician Who Lost His Magic. McKee, David. 2013. (Melric Ser.). (ENG.). 32p. (J). (gr. -1-k). 16.99 *(978-1-84939-439-0(3))* Andersen Pr. GBR. Dist: Independent Pubs. Group.

—Melric the Magician Who Lost His Magic. McKee, David. 2013. (Melric Ser.). (ENG.). 32p. (J). (gr. -1-k). pap. 12.99 *(978-1-84939-525-0(X))* Andersen Pr. GBR. Dist: Independent Pubs. Group.

—The Sad Story of Veronica: Who Played the Violin. McKee, David. 2014. (ENG.). 32p. (J). (gr. -1-k). pap. 9.99 *(978-1-84939-763-6(5))* Andersen Pr. GBR. Dist: Independent Pubs. Group.

—Tusk Tusk. McKee, David. 2007. (ENG.). 32p. (J). (gr. -1-2). pap. 13.99 *(978-1-84270-579-7(2))* Andersen Pr. GBR. Dist: Independent Pubs. Group.

—Zebra's Hiccups. McKee, David. 2009. (ENG.). 32p. (J). (gr. k-k). pap. 10.99 *(978-1-84270-923-8(2))* Andersen Pr. GBR. Dist: Independent Pubs. Group.

McKee, Karen & Griffin, Georgene. Hot Wings. 2004. (J). *(978-1-59203-091-0(2))* Learning Challenge, Inc.

McKendry, Joe. One Times Square: A Century of Change at the Crossroads of the World. McKendry, Joe. 2012. (ENG.). 64p. (J). 19.95 *(978-1-56792-364-3(X))* Godine, David R. Pub.

McKenna, Brenton. Living Alongside the Animals - Anangu Way. Wingfield, Eileen Wani & Austin, Emily Munyungka. 2009. (ENG.). 56p. (J). (gr. 3). pap. 11.95 *(978-1-86465-096-9(6))* IAD Pr. AUS. Dist: Independent Pubs. Group.

McKenna, Bridgett. Tumbleweed Christmas. McClure, Beverly Stowe. 2011. 24p. pap. 13.99 *(978-0-9832740-4-9(5))* 4RV Publishing, LLC.

McKenna, Lou. Math's Mate Orange: Student Pad. Wright, Joe. Tutos, Joanna, ed. 2013. 72p. pap. *(978-1-921535-55-0(5))* Educational Advantage Pty, Ltd.

—Math's Mate Rose: Student Pad. Wright, Joseph B. Tutos, Joanna, ed. 2013. 72p. pap. *(978-1-921535-56-7(3))* Educational Advantage Pty, Ltd.

McKenna, Mark, et al. Banana Tail. 2003. 32p. (J). 12.95 *(978-0-9727681-3-9(0))* Active Media Publishing, LLC.

McKenna, Mark. Timebreakers. Bedard, Tony. 2005. (Exiles Ser.). 168p. (YA). pap. 17.99 *(978-0-7851-1730-8(X))* Marvel Worldwide, Inc.

McKenna, Nancy Durrell, photos by. Nuevo Libro del Embarazo y Nacimiento: Guia Practica y Completa para Todos los Futuros Padres. Stoppard, Miriam. (SPA., 255p. pap. 20.99 *(978-958-04-5849-4(9))* Norma S.A. COL. Dist: Distribuidora Norma, Inc.

McKenna, Sharon Michelle. Good Morning, Sunshine: A Grandpa Story. 2006. 32p. (J). (gr. -1-3). 15.95 *(978-1-60108-003-5(4))* Red Cygnet Pr.

McKenna, Terry. Armor. Clarke, Catriona. 2007. (Usborne Beginners Ser.). 32p. (J). (gr. -1-3). 4.99 *(978-0-7945-1578-2(9)*, Usborne) EDC Publishing.

—Celts: Information for Young Readers - Level 2. Pratt, Leonie. 2007. (Usborne Beginners Ser.). 32p. (J). 4.99 *(978-0-7945-1580-5(0)*, Usborne) EDC Publishing.

—Pirates. Clarke, Catriona. 2006. (Beginners Social Studies: Level 2 Ser.). 32p. (J). (gr. 1-3). 4.99 *(978-0-7945-1332-0(8)*, Usborne) EDC Publishing.

McKenney, J. David. Careful What You Wish For. Petroff, Shani. 2010. (Bedeviled Ser.: 3). (ENG.). 240p. (J). (gr. 5-18). pap. 6.99 *(978-0-448-45113-8(1)*, Grosset & Dunlap) Penguin Publishing Group.

—Daddy's Little Angel, No. 1. Petroff, Shani. 2009. (Bedeviled Ser.: 1). (ENG.). 240p. (J). (gr. 5-7). pap. 7.99 *(978-0-448-45111-4(5)*, Grosset & Dunlap) Penguin Publishing Group.

—The Good, the Bad, & the Ugly Dress. Petroff, Shani. 2010. (Bedeviled Ser.: 2). (ENG.). 240p. (J). (gr. 5-7). pap. 6.99 *(978-0-448-45112-1(3)*, Grosset & Dunlap) Penguin Publishing Group.

—Love Struck. Petroff, Shani. 2010. (Bedeviled Ser.: 4). (ENG.). 240p. (J). (gr. 5-18). pap. 7.99 *(978-0-448-45114-5(X)*, Grosset & Dunlap) Penguin Publishing Group.

M

McKenny, Stewart & Moy, Phil. Monkey Business, 1 vol. Fisch, Sholly. 2013. (DC Super Friends Ser.). (ENG.). 32p. (gr. 1-2). 21.27 *(978-1-4342-4700-1(7))* Stone Arch Bks.
—Nothing to Fear, 1 vol. Fisch, Sholly. 2013. (DC Super Friends Ser.). (ENG.). 32p. (gr. 1-2). lib. bdg. 21.27 *(978-1-4342-4703-2(1))* Stone Arch Bks.
McKenny, Stewart & Moy, Philip. Wanted - The Super Friends. Fisch, Sholly. 2012. (DC Super Friends Ser.). (ENG.). 32p. (gr. 1-2). lib. bdg. 21.27 *(978-1-4342-4543-4(8))* Stone Arch Bks.
McKenzie, Heath. An A to Z of Fairies. Stills, Caroline. 2012. (ENG.). 24p. (J). (gr. k-k). 16.99 *(978-1-921714-50-4(6))* Little Hare Bks. AUS. Dist: Independent Pubs. Group.
—An ABC of Pirates. Stills, Caroline. 2010. (ENG.). 32p. (J). (gr. -1-1). 15.99 *(978-1-921272-77-6(5))* Little Hare Bks. AUS. Dist: Independent Pubs. Group.
—The Cocky Who Cried Dingo. Morrison, Yvonne. 2011. (ENG.). 24p. (J). (gr. -1). pap. 14.99 *(978-1-921714-94-8(8))* Hardie Grant Bks. AUS. Dist: Independent Pubs. Group.
—The Emu That Laid the Golden Egg. Morrison, Yvonne. 2013. (ENG.). 32p. (J). (gr. -1-k). 16.99 *(978-1-921894-00-8(8))* Little Hare Bks. AUS. Dist: Independent Pubs. Group.
—Eu Amo Você. Livro. Hathorn, Libby. Dalla, Juliana, tr. from ENG. 2012.Tr. of I love Your Book. (POR.). 36p. pap. *(978-1-921869-82-2(8)*, IP Kidz) Interactive Pubns. Pty, Ltd.
—Funny Little Dog. Mewburn, Kyle. 2010. (Pop Hooper's Perfect Pets Ser.: 2). (ENG.). 92p. (J). (gr. k-2). 9.99 *(978-1-921272-76-9(7))* Little Hare Bks. AUS. Dist: Independent Pubs. Group.
McKenzie, Heath. Kim's Fake Cake Bake. Clark, Sherryl. 2015. (J). pap. ***(978-1-4966-0256-5(0))*** Capstone Classroom.
—Kim's Pet Scoop. Clark, Sherryl. 2015. (J). pap. ***(978-1-4966-0238-1(2))*** Capstone Classroom.
—Kim's Super Science Day. Clark, Sherryl. 2015. (J). pap. ***(978-1-4966-0250-3(1))*** Capstone Classroom.
—Kim's Tug of War. Clark, Sherryl. 2015. (J). pap. ***(978-1-4966-0244-2(7))*** Capstone Classroom.
McKenzie, Heath. Mac O'Beasty, Bk. 2. Wallace, Adam. 2009. (ENG.). 40p. (J). pap. 15.97 *(978-0-9805564-5-2(7))* JoJo Publishing AUS. Dist: AtlasBooks Distribution.
McKenzie, Heath. Nerdy Ninjas vs the Really Really Bad Guys. Whamhower, Shogun. 2012. 137p. (J). ***(978-0-545-53736-0(3))*** Scholastic, Inc.
McKenzie, Heath. A New Friend for Marmalade. Reynolds, Alison. 2014. (ENG.). 40p. (J). (gr. -1-1). 15.99 *(978-1-4814-2046-4(1)*, Little Simon) Little Simon.
McKenzie, Heath. S. M. A. R. T. S. & the 3-D Danger. Metz, Melinda. 2015. (S. M. A. R. T. S. Ser.). (ENG.). 128p. (gr. 3-6). 21.32 ***(978-1-4965-0465-4(8))*** S.M.A.R.T.S. Learning System.
—S. M. A. R. T. S. & the Invisible Robot. Metz, Melinda. 2015. (S. M. A. R. T. S. Ser.). (ENG.). 128p. (gr. 3-6). 21.32 ***(978-1-4965-0463-0(1))*** S.M.A.R.T.S. Learning System.
—S. M. A. R. T. S. & the Missing UFO. Metz, Melinda. 2015. (S. M. A. R. T. S. Ser.). (ENG.). 128p. (gr. 3-6). lib. bdg. 21.32 ***(978-1-4965-0466-1(6))*** S.M.A.R.T.S. Learning System.
—S. M. A. R. T. S. & the Poison Plates. Metz, Melinda. 2015. (S. M. A. R. T. S. Ser.). (ENG.). 128p. (gr. 3-6). 21.32 ***(978-1-4965-0464-7(X))*** S.M.A.R.T.S. Learning System.
McKenzie, Heath. Sausage Curls. Cordina, Annette. 2012. (ENG.). 40p. (J). 23.49 *(978-0-9871448-8-1(X))* JoJo Publishing AUS. Dist: AtlasBooks Distribution.
—Scruffy Old Cat. Mewburn, Kyle. 2010. (Pop Hooper's Perfect Pets Ser.: 1). (ENG.). 186p. (J). (gr. k-2). 8.99 *(978-1-921272-75-2(9))* Little Hare Bks. AUS. Dist: Independent Pubs. Group.
—Slowcoach Turtle. Mewburn, Kyle. 2011. (Pop Hooper's Perfect Pets Ser.: 3). (ENG.). 92p. (J). (gr. k-2). 9.99 *(978-1-921541-23-0(7))* Little Hare Bks. AUS. Dist: Independent Pubs. Group.
—The Three Wallabies Gruff. Morrison, Yvonne. 2013. (ENG.). 32p. (J). (gr. -1-k). pap. 12.99 *(978-1-74297-715-7(4))* Little Hare Bks. AUS. Dist: Independent Pubs. Group.
—Town Possum, Outback Possum. Morrison, Yvonne. 2012. (ENG.). 22p. (J). (gr. -1-k). 16.99 *(978-1-921541-47-6(4))* Little Hare Bks. AUS. Dist: Independent Pubs. Group.
—A Year with Marmalade. Reynolds, Alison. 2013. (ENG.). 40p. (J). (gr. -1-1). 15.99 *(978-1-4424-8105-3(6)*, Little Simon) Little Simon.
McKenzie, Josie. Mrs. Potter's Cat. Abbott, D. K. 2007. 28p. per. 24.95 *(978-1-4241-8345-6(6))* America Star Bks.
McKeown, Christian. Nightmare in the Woods. Anglen, Becca. 2007. 36p. (J). pap. 9.00 *(978-0-8059-7655-7(8))* Dorrance Publishing Co., Inc.
McKeown, David. Scotty's Dream: Book & CD. Fant, Donna. Axford, Elizabeth C., ed. 2004. (ENG.). 16p. (J). audio compact disk 14.99 *(978-1-931844-17-8(8)*, PP1034) Piano Pr.
McKie, Roy. The Many Mice of Mr. Brice. Seuss, Dr. 2015. (Big Bright & Early Board Book Ser.). (ENG.). 24p. (J). (— 1). bds. 6.99 *(978-0-553-49733-5(2)*, Random Hse. Bks. for Young Readers) Random Hse. Children's Bks.
—Summer. Low, Alice. 2007. (Bright & Early Board Books Ser.). (ENG.). 24p. (J). (gr. k-1). bds. 4.99 *(978-0-375-83870-5(8)*, Random Hse. Bks. for Young Readers) Random Hse. Children's Bks.
McKie, Roy, jt. illus. see Seuss, Dr.
McKig, Susan. Let's Praise & Play: Children's Christian Mini-Piano Book. Advance Cal-Tech Inc. Staff. Kung, Edward, ed. 36p. (J). (gr. -1-6). *(978-0-943759-00-5(5))* Advance Cal Tech, Inc.
McKillip Thornburgh, Rebecca, jt. illus. see Molnar, Albert.
McKim, Brian & Yamauchi, Karl. Disneyland Detective: An Independent Guide to Discovering Disney's Legend, Lore, & Magic. Hawkins, Dave, photos by. Trahan, Kendra. 2004. (ENG.). 248p. (gr. 7-12). pap. 19.95 *(978-0-9717464-0-4(0))* PermaGrin Publishing.
McKimmie, Chris. Maisie Moo & Invisible Lucy. McKimmie, Chris. 2008. (ENG.). 32p. (J). (gr. k-2). 19.99 *(978-1-74175-134-5(9))* Allen & Unwin AUS. Dist: Independent Pubs. Group.
McKimmie, Chris. Scarlett & the Scratchy Moon. McKimmie, Chris. 2015. (ENG.). 32p. (J). (gr. -1-1). 19.99 ***(978-1-74331-515-6(5))*** Allen & Unwin AUS. Dist: Independent Pubs. Group.
McKimmie, Chris. Special Kev. McKimmie, Chris. 2009. (ENG.). 32p. (J). (gr. -1-3). 22.99 *(978-1-74175-550-3(6))* Allen & Unwin AUS. Dist: Independent Pubs. Group.
—Two Peas in a Pod. McKimmie, Chris. 2010. (ENG.). 32p. (J). (gr. -1-k). 23.99 *(978-1-74237-304-1(6))* Allen & Unwin AUS. Dist: Independent Pubs. Group.
McKinley, John. April Fool's Surprise. Klein, Abby. 2012. (Double Trouble Ser.: Vol. 2). (ENG.). 96p. (J). (gr. -1-3). pap. 5.99 *(978-0-545-29495-9(9)*, Scholastic Paperbacks) Scholastic, Inc.
—April Fool's Surprise. Klein, Abby. ed. 2012. lib. bdg. 16.00 *(978-0-606-23922-6(7)*, Turtleback) Turtleback Bks.
—Camping Catastrophe! Klein, Abby. 2008. (Ready, Freddy! Ser.: Bk. 14). 95p. (J). (gr. -1-3). 11.65 *(978-0-7569-8837-1(3))* Perfection Learning Corp.
—Camping Catastrophe! Klein, Abby. 2008. (Ready, Freddy! Ser.: 14). (ENG.). 96p. (J). (gr. -1-3). 5.99 *(978-0-439-89594-1(4)*, Blue Sky Pr., The) Scholastic, Inc.
—Halloween Fraidy-Cat. Klein, Abby. 2006. (Ready, Freddy! Ser.: 8). (ENG.). 96p. (J). (gr. -1-3). pap. 5.99 *(978-0-439-78457-3(3)*, Blue Sky Pr., The) Scholastic, Inc.
—Halloween Parade. Klein, Abby. 2009. (Ready, Freddy! Reader List: No. 3). 32p. (J). *(978-0-545-14174-1(5))* Scholastic, Inc.
—Homework Hassles. Klein, Abby. 2004. (Ready, Freddy! Ser.: 3). (ENG.). 96p. (J). (gr. -1-3). 5.99 *(978-0-439-55600-2(7)*, Blue Sky Pr., The) Scholastic, Inc.
—The King of Show-and-Tell. Klein, Abby. 2004. (Ready, Freddy! Ser.: 2). (ENG.). 96p. (J). (gr. -1-3). 5.99 *(978-0-439-55598-2(1)*, Blue Sky Pr., The) Scholastic, Inc.
—Looking for Leprechauns. Klein, Abby. 2009. (Ready, Freddy! Reader List: No. 2). (J). pap. *(978-0-545-09933-2(1)*, Scholastic) Scholastic, Inc.
—The One Hundredth Day of School! Klein, Abby. 2008. (Ready, Freddy! Ser.: Bk. 13). 94p. (J). (gr. -1-3). 11.65 *(978-0-7569-8836-4(5))* Perfection Learning Corp.
—The One Hundredth Day of School! Klein, Abby. 2008. (Ready, Freddy! Ser.: 13). (ENG.). 96p. (J). (gr. -1-3). 5.99 *(978-0-439-89593-4(6)*, Blue Sky Pr., The) Scholastic, Inc.
—The Pumpkin Elf Mystery. Klein, Abby. 2007. (Ready, Freddy! Ser.: Bk. 11). 95p. (J). (gr. -1-3). 11.65 *(978-0-7569-8301-7(0))* Perfection Learning Corp.
—The Reading Race. Klein, Abby. 2013. (Ready, Freddy! Ser.: 27). (ENG.). 96p. (J). (gr. 2-5). pap. 5.99 *(978-0-545-55044-4(0))* Scholastic, Inc.
—Ready, Freddy! #26: the Giant Swing. Klein, Abby. 2014. (Ready, Freddy! Ser.: 26). (ENG.). 96p. (J). (gr. 1-3). pap. 5.99 *(978-0-545-55043-7(2)*, Scholastic Paperbacks) Scholastic, Inc.
—Ready, Set, Snow! Klein, Abby. 2009. (Ready, Freddy! Ser.: 16). (ENG.). 96p. (J). (gr. -1-3). pap. 5.99 *(978-0-439-89596-5(0))* Scholastic, Inc.
—Save the Earth! Klein, Abby. 2012. (Ready, Freddy! Ser.: 25). (ENG.). 96p. (J). (gr. -1-3). pap. 5.99 *(978-0-545-29503-1(3)*, Scholastic Paperbacks) Scholastic, Inc.
McKinley, John. Second Grade Rules! Klein, Abby. 2014. 85p. (J). pap. ***(978-0-545-69031-7(5))*** Scholastic, Inc.
McKinley, John. Shark Attack! Klein, Abby. 2011. (Ready, Freddy! Ser.: 24). (ENG.). 96p. (J). (gr. -1-3). pap. 5.99 *(978-0-545-29500-0(9)*, Scholastic Paperbacks) Scholastic, Inc.
—Stop That Hamster! Klein, Abby. 2008. (Ready, Freddy! Ser.: Bk. 12). 95p. (gr. -1-3). 16.00 *(978-0-7569-8300-0(2))* Perfection Learning Corp.
—Thanks for Giving. Klein, Abby. 2009. (Ready, Freddy! Reader List: No. 4). 32p. (J). pap. *(978-0-545-14176-5(1))* Scholastic, Inc.
—Thanksgiving Turkey Trouble. Klein, Abby. 2008. (Ready, Freddy! Ser.: Bk. 15). 95p. (J). (gr. -1-3). 16.00 *(978-0-7569-8838-8(1))* Perfection Learning Corp.
—Thanksgiving Turkey Trouble. Klein, Abby. 2008. (Ready, Freddy! Ser.: 15). (ENG.). 96p. (J). (gr. -1-3). pap. 5.99 *(978-0-439-89595-8(2)*, Blue Sky Pr., The) Scholastic, Inc.
—Tooth Trouble. Klein, Abby. 2004. (Ready, Freddy! Ser.: 1). (ENG.). 96p. (J). (gr. -1-3). 5.99 *(978-0-439-55596-8(5)*, Blue Sky Pr., The) Scholastic, Inc.
Mckinley, John & McKinley, John. Don't Sit on My Lunch! Klein, Abby. 2005. (Ready, Freddy! Ser.: 4). (ENG.). 96p. (J). (gr. -1-3). 5.99 *(978-0-439-55602-6(3)*, Blue Sky Pr., The) Scholastic, Inc.
McKinley, John, jt. illus. see Mckinley, John.
McKinley, Kay, photos by. Un Desfile de Patrones. Freese, Joan. 2007. (Matemáticas en Nuestro Mundo (Math in Our World) Ser.). (SPA., 24p. (gr. 1-2). lib. bdg. 22.00 *(978-0-8368-8491-3(4)*, Weekly Reader Leveled Readers) Stevens, Gareth Publishing LLLP.
—Midiendo para una Búsqueda del Tesoro. Marrewa, Jennifer. 2008. (Matemáticas en Nuestro Mundo - Nivel 2 (Math in Our World - Level 2) Ser.). (SPA., 24p. (gr. 1-4). lib. bdg. 22.00 *(978-0-8368-9025-9(6)*, Weekly Reader Leveled Readers) Stevens, Gareth Publishing LLLP.
—Patterns on Parade. Freese, Joan. 2007. (Math in Our World Ser.). 24p. (gr. 1-2). lib. bdg. 22.00 *(978-0-8368-8473-9(6)*, Weekly Reader Leveled Readers) Stevens, Gareth Publishing LLLP.
—Usamos Matematicas en la Fiesta del Salon. Rauen, Amy & Ayers, Amy. 2007. (Matemáticas en Nuestro Mundo (Math in Our World) Ser.). (SPA., 24p. (gr. 1-2). lib. bdg. 22.00 *(978-0-8368-8493-7(0)*, Weekly Reader Leveled Readers) Stevens, Gareth Publishing LLLP.
—Using Math at the Class Party. Rauen, Amy. 2007. (Math in Our World Ser.). 24p. (gr. 1-2). lib. bdg. 22.00 *(978-0-8368-8475-3(2)*, Weekly Reader Leveled Readers) Stevens, Gareth Publishing LLLP.
—Using Money on a Shopping Trip. Marrewa, Jennifer. 2008. (Math in Our World: Level 2 Ser.). 24p. (gr. 1-4). lib. bdg. 22.00 *(978-0-8368-9004-4(3)*, Weekly Reader Leveled Readers) Stevens, Gareth Publishing LLLP.
—Vamos a Usar Dinero en un Viaje de Compras. Marrewa, Jennifer. 2008. (Matemáticas en Nuestro Mundo - Nivel 2 (Math in Our World - Level 2) Ser.). (SPA., 24p. (gr. 1-4). lib. bdg. 22.00 *(978-0-8368-9022-8(1)*, Weekly Reader Leveled Readers) Stevens, Gareth Publishing LLLP.
McKinney, Malachy. Pep, Polish & Paint. Harper, Helena. 2011. (ENG.). 40p. (J). pap. 8.86 *(978-0-9570530-0-7(2))* Harper Bks. GBR. Dist: Gardners Bks. Ltd.
McKinnon, Gay. The Smallest Carbon Footprint in the Land & Other Eco-Tales. Morgan, Anne. 2012. 80p. pap. *(978-1-922120-23-6(5)*, IP Kidz) Interactive Pubns. Pty, Ltd.
McKinnon, James. Koala Country: A Story of an Australian Eucalyptus Forest. Dennard, Deborah. 2005. (Wild Habitats Ser.: Vol. 17). (ENG.). 36p. (J). (gr. 1-4). 15.95 *(978-1-56899-887-9(2)*, B7018) Soundprints.
McKinnon, Joy. The Angel Explains Christmas Blessings. Mancil, Arlene. 2008. 16p. pap. 24.95 *(978-1-60813-297-3(8))* America Star Bks.
McKinnon, Margie & McKinnon, Tom W. Repair for Kids: A Children's Program for Recovery from Incest & Childhood Sexual Abuse. McKinnon, Margie & McKinnon, Tom W. 2008. 92p. (J). pap. 34.95 *(978-1-932690-57-6(3))* Loving Healing Pr., Inc.
McKinnon, Tom W., jt. illus. see McKinnon, Margie.
McKissock, Charmaine, jt. illus. see Peecock, Simon.
McKone, Mike. Avengers Academy Vol. 2: Will We Use This in the Real World? 2011. (ENG.). 168p. (J). (gr. 8-17). 24.99 *(978-0-7851-4496-0(X))* Marvel Worldwide, Inc.
—Avengers Academy - Permanent Record, Vol. 1. Gage, Christos. 2011. (ENG.). 120p. (J). (gr. 4-17). pap. 19.99 *(978-0-7851-4495-3(1))* Marvel Worldwide, Inc.
McKowen, Scott. The Adventures & the Memoirs of Sherlock Holmes. Doyle, Arthur. 2004. (Sterling Unabridged Classics Ser.). (ENG.). 576p. (J). 14.95 *(978-1-4027-1453-5(X))* Sterling Publishing Co., Inc.
—The Adventures of Huckleberry Finn. Twain, Mark. 2006. (Sterling Unabridged Classics Ser.). (ENG.). 320p. (YA). (gr. 4-7). 9.95 *(978-1-4027-2600-2(7))* Sterling Publishing Co., Inc.
—The Adventures of Tom Sawyer. Twain, Mark. 2004. (Sterling Unabridged Classics Ser.). (ENG.). 224p. (J). 9.95 *(978-1-4027-1460-3(2))* Sterling Publishing Co., Inc.
—Alice's Adventures in Wonderland. Carroll, Lewis. 2005. (Sterling Unabridged Classics Ser.). (ENG.). 136p. (J). (gr. 5-9). 9.95 *(978-1-4027-2502-9(7))* Sterling Publishing Co., Inc.
—Anne of Avonlea. Montgomery, L. M. 2008. (Sterling Unabridged Classics Ser.). (ENG.). 256p. (J). 9.95 *(978-1-4027-5428-9(0))* Sterling Publishing Co., Inc.
—Anne of Green Gables. Montgomery, L. M. 2004. (Sterling Unabridged Classics Ser.). (ENG.). 312p. (J). 9.95 *(978-1-4027-1451-1(3))* Sterling Publishing Co., Inc.
—Around the World in 80 Days. Verne, Jules. 2008. (Sterling Unabridged Classics Ser.). (ENG.). 224p. (J). 9.95 *(978-1-4027-5427-2(2))* Sterling Publishing Co., Inc.
—Black Beauty. Sewell, Anna. 2004. (Sterling Unabridged Classics Ser.). (ENG.). 208p. (J). 9.95 *(978-1-4027-1452-8(1))* Sterling Publishing Co., Inc.
—The Call of the Wild & White Fang. London, Jack. 2004. (Sterling Unabridged Classics Ser.). (ENG.). 312p. (J). 9.95 *(978-1-4027-1455-9(6))* Sterling Publishing Co., Inc.
—A Christmas Carol. Dickens, Charles. 2009. (Sterling Unabridged Classics Ser.). (ENG.). 96p. (Orig.). (J). (gr. 5). 9.95 *(978-1-4027-6690-9(4))* Sterling Publishing Co., Inc.
—Dracula. Stoker, Bram. 2010. (Sterling Unabridged Classics Ser.). (ENG.). 416p. (J). (gr. 5-18). 14.95 *(978-1-4027-7324-2(2))* Sterling Publishing Co., Inc.
—Grimm's Fairy Tales. Grimm, Jacob & Grimm, Wilhelm. 2009. (Sterling Unabridged Classics Ser.). (ENG.). 288p. (J). (gr. 5). 9.95 *(978-1-4027-6702-9(1))* Sterling Publishing Co., Inc.
—Journey to the Center of the Earth. Verne, Jules. 2007. (Sterling Unabridged Classics Ser.). (ENG.). 256p. (J). 9.95 *(978-1-4027-4337-5(8))* Sterling Publishing Co., Inc.
—The Jungle Book. Kipling, Rudyard. Rowe, John, ed. 2007. (Sterling Unabridged Classics Ser.). (ENG.). 352p. (J). 9.95 *(978-1-4027-4340-5(8))* Sterling Publishing Co., Inc.
—The Legend of Sleepy Hollow & Other Stories. Irving, Washington. 2013. (Sterling Unabridged Classics Ser.). (ENG.). 96p. (J). (gr. 5). 9.95 *(978-1-4549-0871-5(8))* Sterling Publishing Co., Inc.
—A Little Princess. Burnett, Frances Hodgson. 2004. (Sterling Unabridged Classics Ser.). (ENG.). 208p. (J). 9.95 *(978-1-4027-1454-2(8))* Sterling Publishing Co., Inc.
—Little Women. Alcott, Louisa May. 2004. (Sterling Unabridged Classics Ser.). (ENG.). 536p. (J). 14.95 *(978-1-4027-1458-0(0))* Sterling Publishing Co., Inc.
—The Merry Adventures of Robin Hood. Pyle, Howard. 2004. (Sterling Unabridged Classics Ser.). (ENG.). 344p. (J). 9.95 *(978-1-4027-1456-6(4))* Sterling Publishing Co., Inc.
—Oliver Twist. Dickens, Charles. 2008. (Sterling Unabridged Classics Ser.). (ENG.). 464p. (J). 14.95 *(978-1-4027-5425-8(6))* Sterling Publishing Co., Inc.
—Peter Pan. Barrie, J. M. 2008. (Sterling Unabridged Classics Ser.). (ENG.). 160p. (J). 9.95 *(978-1-4027-5426-5(4))* Sterling Publishing Co., Inc.
—Pinocchio. Collodi, Carlo. 2014. (Sterling Unabridged Classics Ser.). (ENG.). 184p. (J). (gr. 5). 9.95 *(978-1-4549-1220-0(0))* Sterling Publishing Co., Inc.
—Pollyanna. Porter, Eleanor H. 2013. (Sterling Unabridged Classics Ser.). (ENG.). 208p. (J). (gr. 5). 9.95 *(978-1-4027-9718-7(4))* Sterling Publishing Co., Inc.
—Robinson Crusoe. Defoe, Daniel. 2011. (Sterling Unabridged Classics Ser.). (ENG.). 288p. (J). 9.95 *(978-1-4027-8406-4(6))* Sterling Publishing Co., Inc.
—The Secret Garden. Burnett, Frances Hodgson. 2004. (Sterling Unabridged Classics Ser.). (ENG.). 248p. (J). 9.95 *(978-1-4027-1459-7(9))* Sterling Publishing Co., Inc.
—The Stories of Edgar Allan Poe. Poe, Edgar Allen. 2010. (Sterling Unabridged Classics Ser.). (ENG.). 344p. (J). (gr. 5-18). 14.95 *(978-1-4027-7325-9(0))* Sterling Publishing Co., Inc.
—The Story of King Arthur & His Knights. Pyle, Howard. 2005. (Sterling Unabridged Classics Ser.). (ENG.). 320p. (J). (gr. 5-9). 9.95 *(978-1-4027-2503-6(5)*, 1252056) Sterling Publishing Co., Inc.
—The Strange Case of Dr. Jekyll & Mr. Hyde. Stevenson, Robert Louis. 2011. (Sterling Unabridged Classics Ser.). (ENG.). 96p. (J). 9.95 *(978-1-4027-8402-6(3))* Sterling Publishing Co., Inc.
—The Swiss Family Robinson. Wyss, Johann David. 2006. (Sterling Unabridged Classics Ser.). (ENG.). 352p. (J). (gr. 4-7). 9.95 *(978-1-4027-2602-6(3))* Sterling Publishing Co., Inc.
—Treasure Island. Stevenson, Robert Louis. 2004. (Sterling Unabridged Classics Ser.). (ENG.). 232p. (J). 9.95 *(978-1-4027-1457-3(2))* Sterling Publishing Co., Inc.
—The Voyages of Doctor Dolittle. Lofting, Hugh. 2012. (Sterling Classics Ser.). (ENG.). 256p. (J). (gr. 5). 9.95 *(978-1-4027-9721-7(4))* Sterling Publishing Co., Inc.
McKowen, Scott, jt. illus. see Baum, L. Frank.
McKowen, Scott, jt. illus. see Grahame, Kenneth.
McLachlan, J. P. Twilla & the Fuzzy Finger. McLachlan, Joni. 2012. 20p. pap. *(978-0-9878035-2-8(2))* Insomniac Pr.
Mclanson, Matt. Dark Ryder. Brown, Liz. 2004. (New Series Canada). 91p. (J). pap. *(978-1-897039-02-1(6))* High Interest Publishing (HIP).
McLaren, Chesley. Princess Lessons. Cabot, Meg. 2003. (Princess Diaries Guidebook Ser.). (ENG.). 144p. (YA). (gr. 8-18). 15.99 *(978-0-06-052677-1(7)*, HarperTeen) HarperCollins Pubs.
McLaren, Duncan. Esther: The Brave Queen. Mackenzie, Carine. 2006. (Bible Time Ser.). (ENG.). 32p. (J). (gr. -1-2). pap. 3.99 *(978-1-84550-195-2(0))* Christian Focus Pubns. GBR. Dist: Send The Light Distribution LLC.
—Gideon: Soldier of God. MacKenzie, Carine. 2006. (Bible Time Ser.). (ENG.). 32p. (J). (gr. -1-2). pap. 3.99 *(978-1-84550-196-9(9))* Christian Focus Pubns. GBR. Dist: Send The Light Distribution LLC.
—Hannah: The Mother Who Prayer. MacKenzie, Carine. 2006. (Bible Time Ser.). (ENG.). 32p. (J). (gr. -1-2). pap. 3.99 *(978-1-84550-163-1(2))* Christian Focus Pubns. GBR. Dist: Send The Light Distribution LLC.
—John: The Baptist. MacKenzie, Carine. 2006. (Bible Time Ser.). (ENG.). 32p. (J). (gr. -1-2). pap. 3.99 *(978-1-84550-164-8(0))* Christian Focus Pubns. GBR. Dist: Send The Light Distribution LLC.
—Jonah: The Runaway Preacher. Mackenzie, Carine. 2006. (Bible Time Ser.). (ENG.). 32p. (J). (gr. -1-2). pap. 3.99 *(978-1-84550-165-5(9))* Christian Focus Pubns. GBR. Dist: Send The Light Distribution LLC.
—Joshua: The Brave Leader. Mackenzie, Carine. 2006. (Bible Time Ser.). (ENG.). 32p. (J). (gr. -1-2). pap. 3.99 *(978-1-84550-166-2(7))* Christian Focus Pubns. GBR. Dist: Send The Light Distribution LLC.
—Martha & Mary: Friends of Jesus. Mackenzie, Carine. 2006. (Bible Time Ser.). (ENG.). 32p. (J). (gr. -1-2). pap. 3.99 *(978-1-84550-167-9(5))* Christian Focus Pubns. GBR. Dist: Send The Light Distribution LLC.
—Mary: Mother of Jesus. MacKenzie, Carine. 2006. (Bible Time Ser.). (ENG.). 32p. (J). (gr. -1-2). pap. 3.99 *(978-1-84550-168-6(3))* Christian Focus Pubns. GBR. Dist: Send The Light Distribution LLC.
—Nehemiah: Builder for God. Mackenzie, Carine & Ross, Neil M. 2006. (Bible Time Ser.). (ENG.). 32p. (J). (gr. -1-2). pap. 3.99 *(978-1-84550-169-3(1))* Christian Focus Pubns. GBR. Dist: Send The Light Distribution LLC.
—Peter: The Apostle. MacKenzie, Carine. 2006. (Bible Time Ser.). (ENG.). 32p. (J). (gr. -1-2). pap. 3.99 *(978-1-84550-170-9(5))* Christian Focus Pubns. GBR. Dist: Send The Light Distribution LLC.
—Peter: The Fisherman. MacKenzie, Carine. 2006. (Bible Time Ser.). (ENG.). 32p. (J). (gr. -1-2). pap. 3.99 *(978-1-84550-171-6(3))* Christian Focus Pubns. GBR. Dist: Send The Light Distribution LLC.
—Rebekah: The Mother of Twins. Mackenzie, Carine. 2006. (Bible Time Ser.). (ENG.). 32p. (J). (gr. -1-2). pap. 3.99 *(978-1-84550-172-3(1))* Christian Focus Pubns. GBR. Dist: Send The Light Distribution LLC.
—Ruth: The Harvest Girl. MacKenzie, Carine. 2006. (Bible Time Ser.). (ENG.). 32p. (J). (gr. -1-2). pap. 3.99 *(978-1-84550-173-0(X))* Christian Focus Pubns. GBR. Dist: Send The Light Distribution LLC.
—Simon Peter: The Disciple. MacKenzie, Carine. 2006. (Bible Time Ser.). (ENG.). 32p. (J). (gr. -1-2). pap. 3.99 *(978-1-84550-174-7(8))* Christian Focus Pubns. GBR. Dist: Send The Light Distribution LLC.
McLaren, Keir. Henry Meets a Three-Legged Dog. McLaren, Keir. Demarie, Teresa, ed. 2011. (ENG.). 32p. pap. 9.95 *(978-1-4636-8233-0(6))* CreateSpace Independent Publishing Platform.
McLaughlin, David & Rocheleau, Paul, photos by. The Unfolding History of the Berkshires. McLaughlin, David. 2007. 92p. (J). pap. 18.95 *(978-0-9763500-5-7(X))* Pentacle Pr.
McLaughlin, Julie. The Art of the Possible: An Everyday Guide to Politics. Keenan, Edward. 2015. (ENG.). 64p. (J). (gr. 5-8). 16.95 ***(978-1-77147-068-1(2)***, Owlkids) Owlkids Bks. Inc. CAN. Dist: Perseus-PGW.
McLaughlin, Julie. Heroes of the Environment: True Stories of People Who Are Helping to Protect Our Planet. Rohmer, Harriet. 2009. (ENG.). 110p. (J). (gr. 4-9). 16.99 *(978-0-8118-6779-5(X))* Chronicle Bks. LLC.
—Why We Live Where We Live. Vermond, Kira. 2014. (ENG.). 48p. (J). (gr. 4-6). 17.95 *(978-1-77147-011-7(9)*, Owlkids) Owlkids Bks. Inc. CAN. Dist: Perseus-PGW.
McLaughlin, Tom. Catch That Rat. Hart, Caryl. 2013. (ENG.). 32p. (J). pap. 8.99 ***(978-1-84738-931-2(7))*** Simon & Schuster, Ltd. GBR. Dist: Simon & Schuster, Inc.
McLaughlin, Tom. Old MacDonald Had a Zoo. Jobling, Curtis. 2014. (ENG.). 32p. (J). (gr. -1-k). pap. 10.99 *(978-1-4052-6712-0(7))* Egmont Bks., Ltd. GBR. Dist: Independent Pubs. Group.

McLaughlin, Zack. What Eats What in a Forest Food Chain, 1 vol. Amstutz, Lisa J. 2012. (Food Chains Ser.). (ENG.). 24p. (gr. 2-3). 25.32 *(978-1-4048-7388-9(0))*; pap. 7.95 *(978-1-4048-7692-7(8))* Picture Window Bks.

—What Eats What in an Ocean Food Chain, 1 vol. Slade, Suzanne. 2012. (Food Chains Ser.). (ENG.). 24p. (gr. 2-3). 25.32 *(978-1-4048-7385-8(6))*; pap. 7.95 *(978-1-4048-7696-5(0))* Picture Window Bks.

McLean, Andrew. There's a Goat in My Coat. Milne, Rosemary. 2011. (ENG.). 32p. (J). (gr. -1-2). 19.99 *(978-1-74175-891-7(2))* Allen & Unwin AUS. Dist: Independent Pubs. Group.

McLean, Gill. I Wish... Harker, Jillian. 2010. (Picture Books Ser.). (J). (gr. -1-k). bds. *(978-1-4075-9462-0(1))* Parragon, Inc.

—Little Chick & the Secret of Sleep. Doyle, Malachy. 2012. (Storytime Ser.). (ENG.). 24p. (J). (gr. -1-1). 15.99 *(978-1-60992-232-0(8))* QEB Publishing Inc.

McLellen, Christoph Elizabeth, jt. illus. see Abbrederis, Christoph.

McLennan, Connie. Domitila: A Cinderella Tale from the Mexican Tradition. 2014. (ENG.). 32p. (J). pap. 9.95 *(978-1-885008-43-5(0)*, Shen's Bks.) Lee & Low Bks., Inc.

—Octavia & Her Purple Ink Cloud, 1 vol. Rathmell, Donna & Rathmell, Doreen. 2006. (ENG.). 32p. (J). (gr. -1-2). 15.95 *(978-0-9764943-5-5(3))*; pap. 9.95 *(978-1-60718-586-4(5))* Arbordale Publishing.

—The Rainforest Grew All Around, 1 vol. Mitchell, Susan K. 2007. (ENG.). 32p. (J). (gr. -1-2). 16.95 *(978-0-9768823-6-7(1))*; pap. 8.95 *(978-0-9777423-8-7(5))* Arbordale Publishing.

—Ready, Set ... Wait! What Animals Do Before a Hurricane, 1 vol. Zelch, Patti R. 2010. (ENG.). 32p. (J). (gr. -1-4). 16.95 *(978-1-60718-072-2(3))*; pap. 8.95 *(978-1-60718-083-8(9))* Arbordale Publishing.

—River Beds: Sleeping in the World's Rivers, 1 vol. Karwoski, Gail Langer. 2008. (ENG.). 32p. (J). (gr. -1-3). 16.95 *(978-0-9777423-4-9(2))*; pap. 8.95 *(978-1-934359-31-0(9))* Arbordale Publishing.

—Scottish Alphabet, 1 vol. Pittman, Rickey. 2008. (ENG.). 32p. (J). (gr. 1-3). 16.99 *(978-1-58980-596-5(8))* Pelican Publishing Co., Inc.

—Water Beds: Sleeping in the Ocean, 1 vol. Karwoski, Gail Langer. 2005. (ENG.). 32p. (J). (gr. -1-3). 15.95 *(978-0-9764943-1-7(0))*; pap. 8.95 *(978-1-934359-01-3(7))* Arbordale Publishing.

—Whose Nest Is This? Roemer, Heidi Bee. 2009. (ENG.). 32p. (J). (gr. -1-3). 16.95 *(978-1-58979-386-6(2))* Taylor Trade Publishing.

—The Wishing Tree. Thong, Roseanne. 2004. (Wishing Tree Ser.). 32p. (J). (gr. -1-3). 16.95 *(978-1-885008-26-8(0)*, Shen's Bks.) Lee & Low Bks., Inc.

McLeod, Bob. The New Mutants, Vol. 1. 2006. (ENG.). 240p. (J). (gr. 4-17). pap. 24.99 *(978-0-7851-2194-7(3))* Marvel Worldwide, Inc.

McLeod, Bob. SuperHero ABC. McLeod, Bob. 40p. (J). (gr. -1-3). 2008. (ENG.). pap. 7.99 *(978-0-06-074516-5(9))*; 2006. lib. bdg. 18.89 *(978-0-06-074515-8(0))* HarperCollins Pubs.

—Superhero ABC. McLeod, Bob. 2006. (ENG.). 40p. (J). (gr. -1-3). 17.99 *(978-0-06-074514-1(2))* HarperCollins Pubs.

McLeod, Chum. An Alien in My House, 1 vol. Nanji, Shenaaz. 2003. (ENG.). 24p. (J). (gr. -1-3). 15.95 *(978-1-896764-77-1(0))* Second Story Pr. CAN. Dist: Orca Bk. Pubs. USA.

—TLC Grow with Me! Rovetch, L. Bob. 2005. (J). *(978-1-58987-114-4(6))* Kindermusik International.

McLeod, David. Trixie - the Christmas Cow. Hastings, Leon. 2012. 18p. pap. *(978-1-84903-192-9(4))* Schiel & Denver Publishing Ltd.

McLeod, Herbert. Big Daddy Chinaberry: Love Given - Love Returned. McLeod, Rona. 2012. 24p. pap. 24.95 *(978-1-4626-7700-9(2))* America Star Bks.

McLeod, Kris Aro. Lizzie & the Last Day of School. Noble, Trinka Hakes. 2015. (ENG.). 32p. (J). (gr. k-2). 15.99 *(978-1-58536-895-2(4)*, 203811) Sleeping Bear Pr.

Mcleod, Rebecca. The Chronicles of Sir Hifford Wilkingford-Bisset: Part 1 ~ in the Beginning. Walford, Rod. l.t. ed. 2011. (ENG.). 32p. pap. 12.00 *(978-1-4663-3093-1(7))* CreateSpace Independent Publishing Platform.

McLimans, David. Gone Fishing: Ocean Life by the Numbers. McLimans, David. 2008. (ENG.). 40p. (J). (gr. -1-3). 16.99 *(978-0-8027-9770-4(9))* Walker & Co.

McLoughlin, Wayne. Bluestar's Prophecy. Hunter, Erin. (Warriors Super Edition Ser.: 2). (ENG.). (J). (gr. 3-7). 2010. 560p. pap. 7.99 *(978-0-06-158250-9(8))*; 2009. 544p. 17.99 *(978-0-06-158247-9(6))* HarperCollins Pubs.

—Cats of the Clans. Hunter, Erin. 2008. (Warriors Field Guide Ser.: No. 2). (ENG.). 112p. (J). (gr. 3-7). 16.99 *(978-0-06-145856-9(2))* HarperCollins Pubs.

—Code of the Clans. Hunter, Erin. 2009. (Warriors Field Guide Ser.: No. 3). 176p. (J). (gr. 3-7). (ENG.). 16.99 *(978-0-06-166009-2(4))*; lib. bdg. 17.89 *(978-0-06-166010-8(8))* HarperCollins Pubs.

—Here Is the Wetland. Dunphy, Madeleine. 2007. (Web of Life Ser.). (ENG.). 32p. (J). (gr. -1-3). 16.95 *(978-0-9773795-9-0(0))*; pap. 9.95 *(978-0-9773795-8-3(2))* Web of Life Children's Bks.

—Secrets of the Clans. Hunter, Erin. 2007. (Warriors Field Guide Ser.: No. 1). 176p. (J). (gr. 3-7). (ENG.). 15.99 *(978-0-06-123903-8(8))*; lib. bdg. 16.89 *(978-0-06-123904-5(6))* HarperCollins Pubs.

—Skyclan's Destiny. Hunter, Erin. (Warriors Super Edition Ser.: 3). 528p. (J). (gr. 3-7). 2011. (ENG.). pap. 7.99 *(978-0-06-169996-2(9))*; 2010. (ENG.). 17.99 *(978-0-06-169994-8(2))*; 2010. lib. bdg. 18.89 *(978-0-06-169995-5(0))* HarperCollins Pubs.

—The Untold Stories. Hunter, Erin. 2013. (Warriors Ser.). (ENG.). 320p. (J). (gr. 3-7). pap. 6.99 *(978-0-06-223292-2(4))* HarperCollins Pubs.

—Warriors: The Ultimate Guide. Hunter, Erin. 2013. (Warriors Ser.). (ENG.). 304p. (J). (gr. 3-7). 19.99 *(978-0-06-224533-5(3))* HarperCollins Pubs.

—Warriors - Tales from the Clans. 2014. (Warriors Novella Ser.). (ENG.). 320p. (J). (gr. 3-7). pap. 6.99 *(978-0-06-229085-4(1))* HarperCollins Pubs.

McLoughlin, Wayne. Warriors: Dawn of the Clans #6: Path of Stars. Hunter, Erin. 2015. (Warriors: Dawn of the Clans Ser.: 6). (ENG.). 352p. (J). (gr. 3-7). 16.99 ***(978-0-06-206366-3(9))*** HarperCollins Pubs.

McLoughlin, Wayne & Douglas, Allen. The First Battle. Hunter, Erin. 2015. (Warriors: Dawn of the Clans Ser.: 3). (ENG.). 352p. (J). (gr. 3-7). pap. 6.99 *(978-0-06-206356-4(1))* HarperCollins Pubs.

—A Forest Divided. Hunter, Erin. 2015. (Warriors Ser.: Bk. 5). (ENG.). 384p. (J). (gr. 3-7). 16.99 *(978-0-06-206362-5(6))* HarperCollins Pubs.

—The Sun Trail. Hunter, Erin. (Warriors: Dawn of the Clans Ser.: 1). (J). (gr. 3-7). 2014. (ENG.). 368p. pap. 6.99 *(978-0-06-206348-9(0))*; 2013. (ENG.). 352p. 16.99 *(978-0-06-206346-5(4))*; 2013. 352p. lib. bdg. 17.89 *(978-0-06-206347-2(2))* HarperCollins Pubs.

—Thunder Rising. Hunter, Erin. (Warriors: Dawn of the Clans Ser.: 2). (J). (gr. 3-7). 2014. (ENG.). 368p. pap. 6.99 *(978-0-06-206352-6(9))*; 2013. (ENG.). 352p. 16.99 *(978-0-06-206350-2(2))*; 2013. 352p. lib. bdg. 17.89 *(978-0-06-206351-9(0))* HarperCollins Pubs.

—Warriors: The First Battle. Hunter, Erin. 2014. (Warriors: Dawn of the Clans Ser.: 3). 352p. (J). (gr. 3-7). lib. bdg. 17.89 *(978-0-06-206355-7(3))* HarperCollins Pubs.

McMahon, Bob. Apple Days: A Rosh Hashanah Story. Soffer, Allison Sarnoff. 2014. (ENG.). 32p. (J). (gr. -1-2). 17.95 *(978-1-4677-1203-3(5))* Lerner Publishing Group.

—Apple Days: A Rosh Hashanah Story. Soffer, Allison. 2014. 32p. (J). (gr. -1-2). 7.95 *(978-1-4677-1204-0(3)*, Kar-Ben Publishing) Lerner Publishing Group.

McMahon, Bob. Something Rotten at Village Market. McMahon, Bob, tr. Fertig, Dennis. 2003. 60p. 11.60 net. *(978-0-7398-5170-8(5))* Steck-Vaughn.

McMahon, Bob & Mcmahon, Bob. Making Cents. Robinson, Elizabeth Keeler & Keeler Robinson, Elizabeth. 2008. (ENG.). 32p. (J). (gr. 1-4). 14.95 *(978-1-58246-214-1(3)*, Tricycle Pr.) Ten Speed Pr.

Mcmahon, Bob, jt. illus. see McMahon, Bob.

McMahon, Brad. Sinbad: Legend of the Seven Seas Pop-up. Auerbach, Annie. 2003. (Media Favorites!! Ser.). 10p. (J). 9.95 *(978-1-58117-171-6(4)*, Intervisual/Piggy Toes) Bendon, Inc.

McMahon, James P. Mister Pudge. McMahon, Kathleen A. 2009. 20p. pap. 8.50 *(978-1-4251-8704-0(8))* Trafford Publishing.

McMahon, Kelly. Comprehension Crosswords Grade 1, 6 vols. Shiotsu, Vicky. 2003. 32p. (J). 4.99 *(978-1-56472-185-3(X))* Edupress, Inc.

—Comprehension Crosswords Grade 2, 6 vols. Shiotsu, Vicky. 2003. 32p. (J). 4.99 *(978-1-56472-186-0(8))* Edupress, Inc.

—Phonics - The Gerbil Plays Guitar on the Girafee, Bk. 3. Crane, Kathy Dickerson. Klistoff, Lorin & Coan, Sharon, eds. ed. 2004. (Phonics (Teacher Created Resources) Ser.). (ENG.). 176p. pap. 17.99 *(978-0-7439-3017-8(7))* Teacher Created Resources, Inc.

McMahon, Wm. Franklin, photos by. We Came from Vietnam. Stanek, Muriel. 2004. 46p. (J). (gr. k-4). reprint ed. *(978-0-7567-7795-1(X))* DIANE Publishing Co.

McManus, Shawn. Captain Cold & the Blizzard Battle, 1 vol. Sonneborn, Scott. 2012. (DC Super-Villains Ser.). (ENG.). 56p. (gr. 2-3). pap. 5.95 *(978-1-4342-3897-9(0)*, DC Super-villains) Stone Arch Bks.

—Captain Cold & the Blizzard Battle, 1 vol. Sonneborn, Scott & Loughridge, Lee. 2012. (DC Super-Villains Ser.). (ENG.). 56p. (gr. 2-3). lib. bdg. 25.32 *(978-1-4342-3796-5(6)*, DC Super-villains) Stone Arch Bks.

—Joker on the High Seas, 1 vol. Bright, J. E. 2012. (DC Super-Villains Ser.). (ENG.). 56p. (gr. 2-3). pap. 5.95 *(978-1-4342-3895-5(4)*, DC Super-villains) Stone Arch Bks.

—Joker on the High Seas, 1 vol. Bright, J. E. & Loughridge, Lee. 2012. (DC Super-Villains Ser.). (ENG.). 56p. (gr. 2-3). lib. bdg. 25.32 *(978-1-4342-3794-1(X)*, DC Super-villains) Stone Arch Bks.

—Meteor of Doom, 1 vol. Kupperberg, Paul & Loughridge, Lee. (Superman Ser.). (ENG.). 56p. (gr. 2-3). 2013. pap. 4.95 *(978-1-4342-1734-9(5))*; 2009. lib. bdg. 25.32 *(978-1-4342-1568-0(7))* Stone Arch Bks. (DC Super Heroes).

—Sinestro & the Ring of Fear, 1 vol. Sutton, Laurie S. 2012. (DC Super-Villains Ser.). (ENG.). 56p. (gr. 2-3). pap. 5.95 *(978-1-4342-3899-3(7)*, DC Super-villains) Stone Arch Bks.

—Sinestro & the Ring of Fear, 1 vol. Sutton, Laurie S. & Loughridge, Lee. 2012. (DC Super-Villains Ser.). (ENG.). 56p. (gr. 2-3). lib. bdg. 25.32 *(978-1-4342-3798-9(2)*, DC Super-villains) Stone Arch Bks.

—Wolves. Buckingham, Mark & Willingham, Bill. rev. ed. 2006. (Fables Ser.: Vol. 8). (ENG.). 160p. pap. 17.99 *(978-1-4012-1001-4(5)*, Vertigo) DC Comics.

McManus, Shawn. Parasite's Power Drain, 1 vol. McManus, Shawn. Fein, Eric & Loughridge, Lee. (Superman Ser.). (ENG.). 56p. (gr. 2-3). 2013. pap. 4.95 *(978-1-4342-2261-9(6))*; 2010. lib. bdg. 25.32 *(978-1-4342-1862-7(1))* Stone Arch Bks. (DC Super Heroes).

—Two-Face's Double Take. McManus, Shawn. Manning, Matthew K. & Loughridge, Lee. (Batman Ser.). (ENG.). 56p. (gr. 2-3). 2013. pap. 4.95 *(978-1-4342-2264-0(0))*; 2010. lib. bdg. 25.32 *(978-1-4342-1878-0(3))* Stone Arch Bks. (DC Super Heroes).

McMaugh, Kimberly. Southpaw. Baird, Noah. 2013. 40p. pap. 13.95 *(978-1-938101-35-9(9))* Indigo Sea Pr., LLC.

McMenemy, Sarah. Berlin: a 3D Keepsake Cityscape. Candlewick Press, Candlewick Press. 2014. (Panorama Pops Ser.). (ENG.). 30p. (J). (gr. k-4). 8.99 *(978-0-7636-6472-5(3))* Candlewick Pr.

—Everybody Bonjours! Kimmelman, Leslie. 2008. (ENG.). 40p. (J). (gr. -1-2). 16.99 *(978-0-375-84443-0(0))* Knopf, Alfred A. Inc.

—Everybody Bonjours! Kimmelman, Leslie. 2015. (ENG.). 40p. (J). (gr. -1-2). pap. 7.99 *(978-0-553-50782-9(6)*, Dragonfly Bks.) Random Hse. Children's Bks.

—The First Rule of Little Brothers. Davis, Jill. 2008. (ENG.). 40p. (J). (gr. -1-2). 16.99 *(978-0-375-84046-3(X))* Knopf, Alfred A. Inc.

—The Louvre: A 3D Expanding Museum. Candlewick Press, Candlewick. 2014. (Panorama Pops Ser.). (ENG.). 64p. (J). (gr. k-4). 8.99 *(978-0-7636-7506-6(7))* Candlewick Pr.

—Tillie the Terrible Swede: How One Woman, a Sewing Needle, & a Bicycle Changed History. Stauffacher, Sue. 2011. (ENG.). 40p. (J). (gr. k-3). 17.99 *(978-0-375-84442-3(2)*, Knopf Bks. for Young Readers) Random Hse. Children's Bks.

—Venice: a 3D Keepsake Cityscape. Candlewick Press, Candlewick. 2014. (Panorama Pops Ser.). (ENG.). 20p. (J). (gr. k-4). 8.99 *(978-0-7636-7186-0(X))* Candlewick Pr.

McMenemy, Sarah. Paris: A 3D Keepsake Cityscape. McMenemy, Sarah. 2012. (Panorama Pops Ser.). (ENG.). 20p. (J). (gr. k-12). 8.99 *(978-0-7636-5894-6(4))* Candlewick Pr.

—Washington D. C. A 3D Keepsake Cityscape. McMenemy, Sarah. 2012. (Panorama Pops Ser.). (ENG.). 20p. (J). (gr. k-12). 8.99 *(978-0-7636-5935-6(5))* Candlewick Pr.

McMillan, Stephanie. Mischief in the Forest: A Yarn Yarn. Jensen, Derrick. 2010. (Flashpoint Press Ser.). (ENG.). 40p. (J). (gr. -1-k). pap. 14.95 *(978-1-60486-081-8(2))* PM Pr.

McMillion, Lindsey. Jacob Has Cancer: His Friends Want to Help. Cooper, Heather et al. 2012. (ENG.). 16p. (J). (gr. k-2). pap. 3.50 *(978-1-60443-012-7(5))* American Cancer Society, Inc.

McMorris, Kelley. Danger in Ancient Rome. Messner, Kate. 2015. (Ranger in Time Ser.: 2). (ENG.). 160p. (J). (gr. 2-5). pap. 5.99 *(978-0-545-63917-0(4)*, Scholastic Pr.) Scholastic, Inc.

—The Dead House. Johnson, Allen, Jr. 2014. (Blackwater Novels Ser.: Vol. 2). (ENG.). 212p. (J). (gr. 4-7). 14.99 *(978-1-933725-34-5(6))* Premium Pr. America.

—My Brother's Story. Johnson, Allen, Jr. 2014. (Blackwater Novels Ser.: Vol. 1). (ENG.). 191p. (J). (gr. 4-7). 14.99 *(978-1-933725-37-6(0))* Premium Pr. America.

—Rescue on the Oregon Trail. Messner, Kate. 2015. (Ranger in Time Ser.: 1). (ENG.). 144p. (J). (gr. 2-5). pap. 5.99 *(978-0-545-63914-9(X)*, Scholastic Pr.) Scholastic, Inc.

McMullan, Jim. Hogwash! Wilson, Karma. 2011. (ENG.). 40p. (J). (gr. -1-1). 16.99 *(978-0-316-98840-7(5))* Little, Brown Bks. for Young Readers.

—Horseplay! Wilson, Karma. 2012. (ENG.). 40p. (gr. -1-1). 16.99 *(978-0-316-93842-6(4))* Little Brown & Co.

—I Stink! McMullan, Kate. (ENG.). (J). (gr. -1-k). 2005. 34p. bds. 7.99 *(978-0-06-074592-9(4)*, HarperFestival); 2006. 40p. reprint ed. pap. 6.99 *(978-0-06-443836-0(8))* HarperCollins Pubs.

—I'm Bad! McMullan, Kate. 2008. (ENG.). 40p. (J). (gr. -1-3). 16.99 *(978-0-06-122971-8(7))* HarperCollins Pubs.

—I'm Big! McMullan, Kate. 2010. 40p. (J). (gr. -1-3). (ENG.). 16.99 *(978-0-06-122974-9(1))*; lib. bdg. 17.89 *(978-0-06-122975-6(X))* HarperCollins Pubs.

—I'm Brave! McMullan, Kate. 2014. (ENG.). 40p. (J). (gr. -1-3). 16.99 *(978-0-06-220318-2(5))* HarperCollins Pubs.

McMullan, Jim. I'm Cool! McMullan, Kate. 2015. 40p. (J). (gr. -1-3). 17.99 ***(978-0-06-230629-6(4))*** HarperCollins Pubs.

McMullan, Jim. I'm Dirty! McMullan, Kate. (ENG.). 40p. (J). (gr. -1-3). 2015. pap. 6.99 *(978-0-06-009295-5(5))*; 2006. 16.99 *(978-0-06-009293-1(9))* HarperCollins Pubs.

McMullan, Jim. I'm Dirty! Board Book. McMullan, Kate. 2015. (ENG.). 34p. (J). (gr. -1 — 1). bds. 7.99 ***(978-0-06-234318-5(1))*** HarperCollins Pubs.

McMullan, Jim. I'm Fast! McMullan, Kate. 2012. 40p. (J). (gr. -1-3). (ENG.). 16.99 *(978-0-06-192085-1(1))*; lib. bdg. 17.89 *(978-0-06-192086-8(X))* HarperCollins Pubs.

—I'm Mighty! McMullan, Kate. 2003. (ENG.). 40p. (J). (gr. -1-3). 17.99 *(978-0-06-009290-0(4))* HarperCollins Pubs.

—Julie Andrews' Collection of Poems, Songs, & Lullabies. Andrews, Julie & Hamilton, Emma Walton. 2009. (ENG.). 192p. (J). (gr. -1-17). 20.00 *(978-0-316-04049-5(5))* Little, Brown Bks. for Young Readers.

McMullen, Anne. Canyons, 1 vol. Webster, Christine. 2005. (Earthforms Ser.). (ENG.). 24p. (gr. 2-3). 23.32 *(978-0-7368-3711-8(6)*, Bridgestone Bks.) Capstone Pr., Inc.

—Everglades National Park. Graf, Mike & Snedden, Robert. 2003. (National Parks Ser.). (ENG.). 24p. (gr. 2-3). 23.32 *(978-0-7368-2219-0(4)*, Bridgestone Bks.) Capstone Pr., Inc.

—Oceans, 1 vol. Jackson, Kay. 2006. (Earthforms Ser.). (ENG.). 24p. (gr. 2-3). 23.32 *(978-0-7368-5406-1(1)*, 1252619, Bridgestone Bks.) Capstone Pr., Inc.

—Volcanoes. Niz, Xavier & Niz, Xavier W. 2005. (Earthforms Ser.). (ENG.). 24p. (gr. 2-3). 23.32 *(978-0-7368-4309-6(4)*, Bridgestone Bks.) Capstone Pr., Inc.

McMullen, Anne & Williams, Ted. States of Matter: A Question & Answer Book, 1 vol. Bayrock, Fiona. 2006. (Questions & Answers: Physical Science Ser.). (ENG.). 32p. (gr. 3-4). 26.65 *(978-0-7368-5448-1(7)*, Fact Finders) Capstone Pr., Inc.

McMullen, Brad. Secret at the Old Beaver Pond: El Secreto de la Lagunita de un Viejo Castor. Bruno, Susan. 2010. (ENG.). 50p. pap. 12.50 *(978-1-4537-7778-7(4))* CreateSpace Independent Publishing Platform.

McMullen, Nigel. Beauty & the Beast. Tyrrell, Melissa. 2005. (Fairytale Friends Ser.). 12p. (J). bds. 5.95 *(978-1-58117-153-2(6)*, Intervisual/Piggy Toes) Bendon, Inc.

—The Gingerbread Man. Tyrrell, Melissa. 2005. (Fairytale Friends Ser.: Vol. 8). 12p. (J). (gr. -1-k). bds. 5.95 *(978-1-58117-154-9(4)*, Intervisual/Piggy Toes) Bendon, Inc.

—Hansel & Gretel. Tyrrell, Melissa. 2005. (Fairytale Friends Ser.). 12p. (J). bds. 5.95 *(978-1-58117-152-5(8)*, Intervisual/Piggy Toes) Bendon, Inc.

—No Te Preocupes, Guille. Morton, Christine. (Buenas Noches Ser.). (SPA.). 26p. (J). (gr. k-3). 8.95 *(978-958-04-5088-7(9))* Norma S.A. COL. Dist: Distribuidora Norma, Inc.

—Pinocchio. Tyrrell, Melissa. 2005. (Fairytale Friends Ser.: Vol. 7). 12p. (J). (gr. -1-k). bds. 5.95 *(978-1-58117-151-8(X)*, Intervisual/Piggy Toes) Bendon, Inc.

McMullen, Nigel. Let's Dance, Grandma! McMullen, Nigel. 2014. (ENG.). 32p. (J). (gr. -1-3). 16.99 *(978-0-06-050747-3(0))* HarperCollins Pubs.

McMullen, T. C. Princess Annado Tandy's Versery Rhymes. Ruble, Kam. l.t. ed. 2007. 88p. (J). per. *(978-0-9779680-4-6(9))* Global Authors Pubns.

McMullin, Marcus. The Big Bend Guide. Parent, Laurence, photos by. Kimball, Allan. 2008. (ENG.). 104p. (YA). pap. 5.95 *(978-1-892588-20-3(X))* Great Texas Line Pr.

McMurry, Marena. Don't Even Think about It. Booth, Chrissie. 2011. 24p. pap. 24.95 *(978-1-4560-8289-5(2))* America Star Bks.

McNally, Bruce. Moose's Loose Tooth. Clarke, Jacqueline A. 2003. (J). *(978-0-439-41183-7(1))* Scholastic, Inc.

McNally, Tom. We Asked for Nothing. Waldman, Stuart. 2014. (ENG.). 208p. (J). (gr. 5-7). pap. 8.95 *(978-1-931414-50-0(5)*, 9781931414500) Mikaya Pr.

McNamara, Lisa. The Adventures of Betty Bunratty: This Is a Series of World Dream Travels of a Little Girl Named Betty Bunratty & Her Sidekick Michael. This Book Is Fun, Educational & Has Activity Pages. Soon the World Will Be Introduced to Her Cousin Eddy Moneypenny & His Side Kick Hamster Syd. Taylor, Eileen. 2011. (ENG.). 24p. pap. 11.99 *(978-1-4637-2828-1(X))* CreateSpace Independent Publishing Platform.

—The Adventures of Eddy Moneypenny. Taylor, Eileen. 2011. (ENG.). 24p. pap. 11.95 *(978-1-4662-3676-9(0))* CreateSpace Independent Publishing Platform.

McNaught, Harry. Howdy Doody's Lucky Trip. Kean, Edward. 2011. 30p. 35.95 *(978-1-258-02772-8(0))* Literary Licensing, LLC.

McNaughton, Colin. Dracula's Tomb. McNaughton, Colin. 2009. (ENG.). 24p. (J). (gr. k-4). 14.99 *(978-0-7636-4488-8(9))* Candlewick Pr.

—Gôl! McNaughton, Colin. Williams, Dylan, tr. from ENG. 2005.Tr. of Goal!. (WEL.). 30p. *(978-0-948930-79-9(9))* Cymdeithas Lyfrau Ceredigion.

McNaughton, Tina. What a Wonderful World! Chiew, Suzanne. 2013. (ENG.). 32p. (J). (gr. -1-1). 16.95 *(978-1-58925-129-8(6))* Tiger Tales.

McNaught, Jonathan & Offermann, Andrea. The Midnight Zoo. Hartnett, Sonya. 2011. (ENG.). 208p. (J). (gr. 5). 16.99 *(978-0-7636-5339-2(X))* Candlewick Pr.

McNeal, Drema & Teets, Ashley. Jake Learns All 8 Parts of Speech. 2010. (J). *(978-0-929915-55-5(0))* Headline Bks., Inc.

McNee, Ian. Illustrated Stories for Boys. Sims, Lesley & Stowell, Louie. 2007. (Usborne Illustrated Stories Ser.). 352p. (J). 19.99 *(978-0-7945-1420-4(0)*, Usborne) EDC Publishing.

—The Roman Soldier's Handbook: Everything a Beginner Soldier Needs to Know. Sims, Lesley. 2006. (English Heritage Ser.). 80p. (J). (gr. 4-7). 12.99 *(978-0-7945-0837-1(5)*, Usborne) EDC Publishing.

—The Story of Exploration. Claybourne, Anna. 2010. (Science Stories Ser.). 103p. (YA). (gr. 3-18). pap. 10.99 *(978-0-7945-2400-5(1)*, Usborne) EDC Publishing.

—Titanic. Claybourne, Anna & Daynes, Katie. 2006. (Usborne Young Reading Ser.). 64p. (J). (gr. 3-7). 8.99 *(978-0-7945-1269-9(0)*, Usborne) EDC Publishing.

—Treasure Island. 2006. 158p. (J). (gr. 5-9). per. 4.99 *(978-0-7945-1230-9(5)*, Usborne) EDC Publishing.

—True Stories of Gangsters. Brook, Henry. 2004. (True Adventure Stories Ser.). 144p. (J). pap. 4.95 *(978-0-7945-0722-0(0)*, Usborne) EDC Publishing.

—True Stories of the Blitz. Brook, Henry. 2006. (True Adventure Stories Ser.). 160p. (J). (gr. 4-7). per. 4.99 *(978-0-7945-1245-3(3)*, Usborne) EDC Publishing.

—Tutankhamun. Harvey, Gill. 2006. (Usborne Young Reading Ser.). 64p. (J). (gr. 3-7). 8.99 *(978-0-7945-1271-2(2)*, Usborne) EDC Publishing.

—The Usborne Official Pirate's Handbook. Taplin, Sam. 2007. (Usborne Official Handbooks Ser.). 80p. (J). (gr. -1-3). 12.99 *(978-0-7945-1463-1(4)*, Usborne) EDC Publishing.

McNee, Ian, jt. illus. see Mayer, Uwe.

McNeely, Tom. Isis & the Seven Scorpions, 1 vol. 2012. (Egyptian Myths Ser.). (ENG.). 32p. (gr. 3-4). pap. 7.95 *(978-1-4048-7241-7(8))*; lib. bdg. 27.99 *(978-1-4048-7150-2(0))* Picture Window Bks. (Nonfiction Picture Bks.).

McNeely, William. Jumpy the Frog Learns the Meaning of Love, 1 vol. Ross, Margaret Clark. 2010. 20p. pap. 24.95 *(978-1-4489-8370-4(3))* PublishAmerica, Inc.

McNeill, Jim. Dropping in on Andy Warhol. Stephens, Pamela Geiger. 2006. (J). 15.95 *(978-1-56290-433-3(7))* Crystal Productions.

—Dropping in on Grandma Moses. Stephens, Pamela. 2008. 32p. (J). 15.95 *(978-1-56290-598-9(8))* Crystal Productions.

—Dropping in on Grant Wood. Stephens, Pamela Greiger. 2005. (J). 15.95 *(978-1-56290-348-0(9))* Crystal Productions.

—Dropping in on Impressionists. Stephens, Pamela Geiger. 2009. (ENG.). 32p. (J). 15.95 *(978-1-56290-633-7(X))* Crystal Productions.

—Dropping in on Matisse. Stephens, Pamela Geiger. 2004. 32p. (J). 15.95 *(978-1-56290-322-0(5))* Crystal Productions.

—Dropping in on Picasso. Stephens, Pamela Geiger. 2004. 32p. (J). 15.95 *(978-1-56290-325-1(X))* Crystal Productions.

—Dropping in on Renaissance Artists. Geiger Stephens, Pamela. 2010. 32p. (J). 15.95 *(978-1-56290-658-0(5))* Crystal Productions.

—Dropping in on Romare Bearden. Stephens, Pamela Geiger. 2007. (ENG.). 32p. (J). 15.95 *(978-1-56290-539-2(2))* Crystal Productions.

McNevin, Dale. Crosby & Me, 1 vol. MacDonald, Hugh. ed. 2011. (ENG.). 32p. (J). (gr. 1-4). pap. 9.95 *(978-1-894838-50-4(5))* Acorn Pr., The CAN. Dist: Orca Bk. Pubs. USA.
—Everything That Shines. Weale, David. ed. (ENG.). 24p. pap. 6.95 *(978-0-9698606-8-6(4))* Acorn Pr., The CAN. Dist: Goose Lane Editions.
—Marty the Mailbox. Stretch, Ian. 2009. 24p. pap. 10.95 *(978-1-4251-8435-3(9))* Trafford Publishing.
—Three Tall Trees. Weale, David. ed. 2004. (ENG.). 24p. pap. 6.95 *(978-1-894838-13-9(0))* Acorn Pr., The CAN. Dist: Univ. of Toronto Pr.
McNicholas, Shelagh. Ballet Stars. Holub, Joan. 2012. (Step into Reading Ser.). (ENG.). 24p. (J). (gr. -1-1). pap. 3.99 *(978-0-375-86909-9(3))* Random Hse., Inc.
—Beautiful Ballerinas. Dombey, Elizabeth. 2014. (Penguin Core Concepts Ser.). (ENG.). 32p. (J). (gr. -1-k). 7.99 *(978-0-448-47791-6(2))*; 3.99 *(978-0-448-46714-6(3))* Penguin Publishing Group. (Grosset & Dunlap).
—Dear Daddy, I Love You. Allison, Catherine. 2014. (ENG.). (J). (gr. -1-3). *(978-1-74363-284-0(3))* Hinkler Bks. Pty, Ltd.
—Los Mejores Amigos. Anderson, Rachael. 2003. (SPA.). 120p. (J). (gr. 3-5). 9.95 *(978-84-204-4377-5(8))* Ediciones Alfaguara ESP. Dist: Santillana USA Publishing Co., Inc.
—My Ballet Dream. Geras, Adèle. 2012. (Tutu Tilly Ser.: 3). (ENG.). 32p. (J). (gr. k-2). pap. 10.99 *(978-1-4083-0980-3(7))* Hodder & Stoughton GBR. Dist: Independent Pubs. Group.
—Show Time with Sophia Grace & Rosie. Brownlee, Sophia Grace & McClelland, Rosie. 2014. (ENG.). 40p. (J). (gr. -1-k). 17.99 *(978-0-545-63135-8(1)*, Orchard Bks.) Scholastic, Inc.
—Soo's Boo-Boos: She's Got 10! Balsley, Tilda. 2013. (ENG.). 32p. (J). (gr. -1-2). 12.95 *(978-1-58925-118-2(0))* Tiger Tales.
—Tea Time with Sophia Grace & Rosie. Brownlee, Sophia Grace & McClelland, Rosie. 2013. (J). (ENG.). 40p. (gr. -1-k). 17.99 *(978-0-545-50214-6(4))*; pap. *(978-0-545-58534-7(1))* Scholastic, Inc. (Orchard Bks.).
—This Little Light of Mine. 2013. (ENG.). 12p. (J). (gr. -1-k). bds. 6.99 *(978-0-545-47768-0(9)*, Little Shepherd) Scholastic, Inc.
McNicholas, Shelagh. Tilly Tutu. McNicholas, Shelagh. Geras, Adèle. 2004. (ESP & SPA.). 28p. (J). 14.99 *(978-84-8488-091-2(5))* Serres, Ediciones, S. L. ESP. Dist: Lectorum Pubns., Inc.
McNicholas, Shelagh & Cascio, Maria Cristina Lo. Little Princess Treasury. Davidson, Susanna & Daynes, Katie. 2006. (English Heritage Ser.). 96p. (J). 7.99 *(978-0-7945-1442-6(1)*, Usborne) EDC Publishing.
McNicholas, Shelagh, jt. illus. see Cascio, Maria Cristina Lo.
McNicholas, Shelagh, jt. illus. see Colón, Raúl.
McNicholas, Shelagh, jt. illus. see Guicciardini, Desideria.
McNicolas, Shelagh. I Love Ponies. Aspley, Brenda. 2013. (ENG.). 20p. (J). (gr. -1-k). 7.99 *(978-1-84322-565-2(4)*, Armadillo) Anness Publishing GBR. Dist: National Bk. Network.
McNiven, Steve, et al. Coming Home, Vol. 4. Kesel, Barbara. 2003. (Meridian Traveler Ser.: Vol. 4). 160p. (YA). (gr. 6-18). pap. 9.95 *(978-1-59314-004-5(5))* CrossGeneration Comics, Inc.
—Going to Ground, Vol. 2. Kesel, Barbara. 2003. (Meridian Traveler Ser.: Vol. 2). 192p. (YA). (gr. 7-18). pap. 9.95 *(978-1-931484-69-5(4))* CrossGeneration Comics, Inc.
—Meridian, Vol. 6. Kesel, Barbara. 2003. (Meridian Ser.: Vol. 6). 160p. (YA). pap. 15.95 *(978-1-931484-95-4(3))* CrossGeneration Comics, Inc.
—Minister of Cadador, Vol. 5. Kesel, Barbara. (Meridian Traveler Ser.: Vol. 5). 160p. 2004. (YA). pap. 9.95 *(978-1-59314-050-2(9))*; 2003. (gr. 7-18). pap. 7.95 *(978-1-931484-70-1(8))* CrossGeneration Comics, Inc.
McNiven, Steve. The Sentry, Vol. 2. 2006. (ENG.). 152p. (J). (gr. 4-17). pap. 14.99 *(978-0-7851-1672-1(9))* Marvel Worldwide, Inc.
McNiven, Steve, et al. Taking the Skies, Vol. 3. Kesel, Barbara. 2003. (Meridian Traveler Ser.: Vol. 3). 160p. (YA). (gr. 6-18). pap. 9.95 *(978-1-931484-84-8(8))* CrossGeneration Comics, Inc.
McPartland, Dorothy. Wishing Stars. McPartland, Dorothy. 2004. 34p. (J). bds. 15.95 *(978-0-9755374-0-4(7))* Little Light Pr.
McPhail, David. All the Awake Animals Are Almost Asleep. Dragonwagon, Crescent. 2012. (ENG.). 40p. (J). (gr. -1-1). 16.99 *(978-0-316-07045-4(9))* Little Brown & Co.
—Animal Stackers. Belle, Jennifer. 2005. (ENG.). 40p. (gr. k-4). 15.99 *(978-0-7868-1834-1(4))* Hyperion Pr.
—Bunny's First Spring, 1 vol. Lloyd-Jones, Sally. 2015. (ENG.). 32p. (J). 15.99 *(978-0-310-73386-7(3))* Zonderkidz.
—La Colcha de Retazos, Level 3. Avery, Kristin. Flor Ada, Alma, tr. 2003. (Dejame Leer Ser.). (SPA.). 16p. (J). (gr. -1-3). 6.50 *(978-0-673-36303-9(1)*, Good Year Bks.) Celebration Pr.
—I Love You Because You're You. Baker, Liza. (ENG.). (J). (gr. -1-k). 2008. 24p. bds. 8.99 *(978-0-545-02931-5(7)*, Cartwheel Bks.); 2006. 9.99 *(978-0-439-69558-3(8))* Scholastic, Inc.
—Just Clowning Around: Two Stories. MacDonald, Steven. 2003. (Green Light Readers Level 1 Ser.). (ENG.). 24p. (J). (gr. -1-3). pap. 3.95 *(978-0-15-204856-3(1))* Houghton Mifflin Harcourt Publishing Co.
—Just Clowning Around: Two Stories. MacDonald, Steven. ed. 2003. (Green Light Readers — Level 1 Ser.). 20p. (gr. -1-3). lib. bdg. 13.50 *(978-0-613-66362-5(4)*, Turtleback) Turtleback Bks.
—The Orphan & the Mouse. Freeman, Martha. 2014. (ENG.). 176p. (J). (gr. 3-7). 16.95 *(978-0-8234-3167-0(3))* Holiday Hse., Inc.
—Peter Rabbit's Happy Easter. Maccarone, Grace. 2008. (ENG.). 11p. (J). (gr. -1-k). bds. 6.99 *(978-0-545-03784-6(0)*, Cartwheel Bks.) Scholastic, Inc.
—A Place for Nicholas. Floyd, Lucy. 2005. (Green Light Readers Level 2 Ser.). (ENG.). 24p. (J). (gr. -1-3). pap. 3.95 *(978-0-15-205149-5(X))* Houghton Mifflin Harcourt Publishing Co.
—A Place for Nicholas. Floyd, Lucy. 2005. (Green Light Readers Level 2 Ser.). 18p. (gr. k-2). 13.95 *(978-0-7569-5243-3(3))* Perfection Learning Corp.
—Tell Me the Day Backwards. Lamb, Albert. 2011. (ENG.). 40p. (J). (gr. -1-2). 15.99 *(978-0-7636-5055-1(2))* Candlewick Pr.
—When I Was King. Ashman, Linda. 2008. 32p. (J). (gr. -1-3). 17.89 *(978-0-06-029052-8(8))* HarperCollins Pubs.
—When Papa Comes Home Tonight. Spinelli, Eileen. 2009. (ENG.). 32p. (J). (gr. -1-k). 16.99 *(978-1-4169-1028-2(X)*, Simon & Schuster Bks. For Young Readers) Simon & Schuster Bks. For Young Readers.
McPhail, David. Andrew Draws. McPhail, David. 2014. (ENG.). 32p. (J). (gr. -1-3). 16.95 *(978-0-8234-3063-5(4))* Holiday Hse., Inc.
—Baby Pig Pig Talks. McPhail, David. 2014. (ENG.). 14p. (J). (— 1). bds. 6.95 *(978-1-58089-597-2(2))* Charlesbridge Publishing, Inc.
—Baby Pig Pig Walks. McPhail, David. 2014. (ENG.). 14p. (J). (— 1). bds. 6.95 *(978-1-58089-596-5(4))* Charlesbridge Publishing, Inc.
—Big Brown Bear's up & down Day. McPhail, David. 2005. 42p. (J). (gr. -1-3). reprint ed. 16.00 *(978-0-7567-8542-0(1))* DIANE Publishing Co.
—Boy, Bird, & Dog. McPhail, David. (I Like to Read Ser.). (ENG.). 24p. (J). 2012. (gr. -1-1). pap. 6.99 *(978-0-8234-2639-3(4))*; 2011. 14.95 *(978-0-8234-2346-0(8))* Holiday Hse., Inc.
—The Family Tree. McPhail, David. 2012. (ENG.). 40p. (J). (gr. -1-3). 16.99 *(978-0-8050-9057-4(6)*, Holt, Henry & Co. Bks. For Young Readers) Holt, Henry & Co.
—My Mother Goose: A Collection of Favorite Rhymes, Songs, & Concepts. McPhail, David. 2013. (ENG.). 96p. (J). (gr. -1-k). 19.99 *(978-1-59643-526-1(7))* Roaring Brook Pr.
—No! McPhail, David. 2009. (ENG.). 48p. (J). (gr. -1-3). 16.95 *(978-1-59643-288-8(8))* Roaring Brook Pr.
—Pig Pig Meets the Lion. McPhail, David. 2012. pap. 15.95 *(978-1-60734-080-5(1))*; (ENG.). 32p. (J). (gr. -1-3). 15.95 *(978-1-58089-358-9(9))* Charlesbridge Publishing, Inc.
—Pig Pig Returns. McPhail, David. 2011. (ENG.). 32p. (J). (gr. -1-3). 15.95 *(978-1-58089-356-5(2))* Charlesbridge Publishing, Inc.
—The Searcher & Old Tree. McPhail, David. (ENG.). 32p. (J). (gr. -1-2). 2011. pap. 7.95 *(978-1-58089-224-7(8))*; 2008. 15.95 *(978-1-58089-223-0(X))* Charlesbridge Publishing, Inc.
—Sisters. McPhail, David. 2003. (ENG.). 32p. (J). (gr. -1-3). 9.95 *(978-0-15-204659-0(3))* Houghton Mifflin Harcourt Publishing Co.
—The Teddy Bear. McPhail, David. 2005. (ENG.). 32p. (J). (gr. -1-1). reprint ed. pap. 8.99 *(978-0-8050-7882-4(7))* Square Fish.
—Weezer Changes the World. McPhail, David. 2009. (ENG.). 40p. (J). (gr. -1-2). 15.99 *(978-1-4169-9000-0(3)*, Beach Lane Bks.) Beach Lane Bks.
McPherson, Heath. The Big Picture Interactive Bible Stories for Toddlers, from the New Testament: Connecting Christ Throughout God's Story. B&H Editorial Staff, ed. 2014. (Gospel Project Ser.). (ENG.). 44p. (J). (— 1). bds. 9.99 *(978-1-4336-8429-6(2)*, B&H Kids) B&H Publishing Group.
—The Big Picture Interactive Bible Stories in 5 Minutes: Connecting Christ Throughout God's Story. B&H Editorial Staff, ed. 2014. (Gospel Project Ser.). (ENG.). 192p. (J). (gr. -1-3). 15.99 *(978-1-4336-8472-2(1)*, B&H Kids) B&H Publishing Group.
—Timmy & Tammy's Train of Thought. Chin, Oliver. 2007. (ENG.). 36p. (J). (gr. -1-3). 15.95 *(978-1-59702-008-4(7))* Immedium.
McPherson, Melinda. Taber Is Beautiful. DeGrasse, Samantha. 2011. 28p. pap. 12.56 *(978-1-4269-5825-0(0))* Trafford Publishing.
McPhillips, Robert. Let the Games Begin! Quinn, Jordan. 2015. (Kingdom of Wrenly Ser.: 7). (ENG.). 128p. (J). (gr. k-4). pap. 5.99 *(978-1-4814-2379-3(7)*, Little Simon) Little Simon.
—The Lost Stone. Quinn, Jordan. 2014. (Kingdom of Wrenly Ser.: 1). (ENG.). 128p. (J). (gr. k-4). pap. 5.99 *(978-1-4424-9690-3(8))*, Little Simon) Little Simon.
—The Scarlet Dragon. Quinn, Jordan. 2014. (Kingdom of Wrenly Ser.: 2). (ENG.). 128p. (J). (gr. k-4). pap. 5.99 *(978-1-4424-9693-4(2)*, Little Simon) Little Simon.
—Sea Monster! Quinn, Jordan. 2014. (Kingdom of Wrenly Ser.: 3). (ENG.). 128p. (J). (gr. k-4). pap. 5.99 *(978-1-4814-0072-5(X)*, Little Simon) Little Simon.
—The Secret World of Mermaids. Quinn, Jordan. 2015. (Kingdom of Wrenly Ser.: 8). (ENG.). 128p. (J). (gr. k-4). pap. 5.99 *(978-1-4814-3122-4(6)*, Little Simon) Little Simon.
—The Witch's Curse. Quinn, Jordan. 2014. (Kingdom of Wrenly Ser.: 4). (ENG.). 128p. (J). (gr. k-4). pap. 4.99 *(978-1-4814-0075-6(4)*, Little Simon) Little Simon.
McPhillips, Robert, jt. illus. see Bently, Peter.
McQuane, Antonia. Muinjij Becomes a Man. Joe, Saqamaw Mi'sel. 2012. (ENG.). 64p. pap. *(978-1-55081-167-4(3))* Breakwater Bks., Ltd.
McQuarrie, Ralph. The Adventures of Luke Skywalker, Jedi Knight. Disney Book Group Staff & DiTerlizzi, Tony. 2014. (ENG.). 64p. (J). (gr. 1-3). 19.99 *(978-1-4847-0668-8(4))* Disney Pr.
McQueen, Lucinda. The Little Red Hen. abr. ed. 2007. (ENG.). (J). (gr. -1-3). 9.99 *(978-0-545-00507-4(8))* Scholastic, Inc.
—Please Say Please, Grumpy Bunny! Fontes, Justine. 2007. (J). *(978-0-439-02012-1(3))* Scholastic, Inc.
—Spring Is Here, Grumpy Bunny! Korman, Justine. 2008. (Clifford's Bedtime Ser.). (ENG.). 64p. (J). (gr. -1-3). pap. 4.99 *(978-0-545-03402-9(7)*, Cartwheel Bks.) Scholastic, Inc.
—Turn the Key: Who Do You See? Katz, Julie & Merberg, Julie. 2011. (ENG.). 12p. (J). (gr. -1). bds. 11.99 *(978-1-935703-11-2(0))* Downtown Bookworks.
—Turn the Key: Around Town: Look & See! Merberg, Julie. 2012. (ENG.). 12p. (J). (gr. -1 — 1). bds. 11.99 *(978-1-935703-44-0(7))* Downtown Bookworks.
McQueen, Lucinda. The Little Red Hen. McQueen, Lucinda. abr. ed. 2007. (ENG.). (J). (gr. -1-3). 18.95 *(978-0-545-00511-1(6))* Scholastic, Inc.
McQueen, Stacey Dressen. How Dalia Put a Big Yellow Comforter Inside a Tiny Blue Box: And Other Wonders of Tzedakah. Heller, Linda. 2011. (ENG.). 32p. (J). (gr. -1-2). 16.99 *(978-1-58246-378-0(6)*, Tricycle Pr.) Ten Speed Pr.
McQueen, Todd. Bob & Rob & Corn on the Cob. McQueen, Todd. 2014. (ENG.). 32p. (J). (gr. -1-k). 16.95 *(978-1-62873-591-8(0)*, Sky Pony Pr.) Skyhorse Publishing Co., Inc.
McQuillan, David. The Legend of Lumpus & Ogols. Mcintyre, Mel. 2009. 28p. pap. 10.95 *(978-1-935137-96-2(4))* Guardian Angel Publishing, Inc.
McQuillan, Mary. Achoo! Good Manners Can Be Contagious! Kelly, Mij. 2009. (ENG.). 32p. (J). (gr. -1-2). 14.99 *(978-0-7641-6969-4(6))* Barron's Educational Series, Inc.
—Bare Bear. Moss, Miriam. 2005. (ENG.). 32p. (J). 16.95 *(978-0-8234-1934-0(7))* Holiday Hse., Inc.
—A Bed of Your Own. Kelly, Mij. 2011. 32p. (J). (gr. -1-1). pap. 8.99 *(978-0-7641-4768-5(4))* Barron's Educational Series, Inc.
—Have You Seen My Potty? Kelly, Mij. 2007. (ENG.). 32p. (J). (gr. -1-k). 12.99 *(978-0-7641-6030-1(3))* Barron's Educational Series, Inc.
—It's Not Fair. Harper, Anita. 2007. (ENG.). 32p. (J). (gr. -1-3). 16.95 *(978-0-8234-2094-0(9))* Holiday Hse., Inc.
—Preschool Time. Kelly, Mij. 2014. (ENG.). 32p. (J). (gr. -1 — 1). 14.99 *(978-0-7641-6655-6(7))* Barron's Educational Series, Inc.
McQuillan, Mary. Zoe Gets the Jitters! Gray, Kes. 2015. (Get Well Friends Ser.). (ENG.). 32p. (J). (-k). pap. 9.99 ***(978-1-4449-0026-2(9))*** Hodder & Stoughton GBR. Dist: Independent Pubs. Group.
McQuillan, Mary. Cluck O'Clock. McQuillan, Mary, tr. Gray, Kes. 2004. (ENG.). 32p. (J). (gr. k-3). tchr. ed. 17.95 *(978-0-8234-1809-1(X))* Holiday Hse., Inc.
McQuitty, LaVonia Corbin. Henrietta Hippo Learns to Dance. Ralls, Ken. 2nd ed. 2013. 24p. (J). 15.00 *(978-0-9884125-3-8(5))* Scribe's Closet Pubns., The.
—I'm Glad God Made Me... Me. Ware, Richard. 2013. 32p. (J). 17.00 *(978-0-9884125-4-5(3))* Scribe's Closet Pubns., The.
—Jesus Does Good Things. White, Susan K. 2013. 24p. (J). 15.00 *(978-0-9832570-6-6(X))* Scribe's Closet Pubns., The.
—Tinky Turtle Finds the Word. Oliver, Sheila. 2011. (ENG.). 16p. (J). 6.00 *(978-0-9801269-4-5(0))* Scribe's Closet Pubns., The.
McRae, Angel. J. A. M. S. & the Case of the Missing Tennessee Walking Horse. Speronis, Kathy. 2011. (ENG.). 94p. pap. 10.00 *(978-1-4609-6039-4(4))* CreateSpace Independent Publishing Platform.
McRae, Patrick. Leap into Space: Exploring the Universe & Your Place in It. Castaldo, Nancy F. 2008. (ENG.). 128p. (J). (gr. 3-7). 16.99 *(978-0-8249-6815-1(8))*; pap. 12.99 *(978-0-8249-6816-8(6))* Ideals Pubns. (Williamson Bks.).
McSwain, Ray. The Legend of Caribou Boy. Blondin, John & Blondin, George. Sundberg, Mary Rose, tr. ed. 2009. (Legend of Caribou Boy Ser.). (ENG & DGR.). 40p. pap. 19.95 *(978-1-894778-71-8(5))* Theytus Bks., Ltd. CAN. Dist: Univ. of Toronto Pr.
McSweeney, Ben. The Rithmatist. Sanderson, Brandon. 2014. (ENG.). 384p. (YA). (gr. 7). pap. 9.99 *(978-0-7653-3844-0(0)*, Tor Teen) Doherty, Tom Assocs., LLC.
McTeigue, Jane, jt. illus. see Miralles, Jose.
McVeigh, Kevin & Groff, David. What Was Ellis Island? Demuth, Patricia Brennan. 2014. (What Was... ? Ser.). (ENG.). 112p. (J). (gr. 3-7). 5.99 *(978-0-448-47915-6(X)*, Grosset & Dunlap) Penguin Publishing Group.
McVeigh, Kevin, jt. illus. see Groff, David.
McVeigh, Kevin, jt. illus. see Hammond, Ted.
McVeigh, Kevin, jt. illus. see Hinderliter, John.
McVeigh, Kevin, jt. illus. see Putra, Dede.
McWeeney, Tom. The Changing Tides: The Imperium Saga: Fall of the Imperium Trilogy, 3 vols., Vol. 2. Bowyer, Clifford B. 2005. (Imperium Saga: 2). (ENG.). 547p. (YA). 27.95 *(978-0-9744354-5-9(7)*, BK0005) Silver Leaf Bks., LLC.
—The Siege of Zoldex: The Imperium Saga: Fall of the Imperium Trilogy, 3 vols., Vol. 3. Bowyer, Clifford B. 2007. (Imperium Saga: 3). (ENG.). 556p. (YA). 29.95 *(978-0-9744354-6-6(5)*, BK0009) Silver Leaf Bks., LLC.
McWherter, Seth. I Should Have Been a Bear. Mcwherter, Barbara. 2011. 24p. pap. 24.95 *(978-1-4626-3532-0(6))* America Star Bks.
McWherter, Shelley. Oliver & His Mountain Climbing Adventures. Mcwherter, Barbara. 2012. 34p. 24.95 *(978-1-4626-7601-9(4))* America Star Bks.
McWilliam, Howard. Dinosaur Christmas. Pallotta, Jerry. (J). (gr. k-2). 2013. (ENG.). 32p. 12.99 *(978-0-545-43360-0(6))*; 2011. ***(978-0-545-24963-8(5))*** Scholastic, Inc.
—Ghost Detectors Volume 1: Let the Specter-Detecting Begin, Books 1-3. Enderle, Dotti. 2013. (Ghost Detectors Ser.: 1). (ENG.). 192p. (gr. 2-7). pap. 8.95 *(978-1-938063-28-2(7)*, Mighty Media Junior Readers) Mighty Media Pr.
McWilliam, Howard. Grow a Ghost! Enderle, Dotti. 2016. (J). ***(978-1-62402-100-8(X))*** Magic Wagon.
McWilliam, Howard. I Need My Monster. Noll, Amanda. 2009. (ENG.). 32p. (J). (gr. k-3). 16.95 *(978-0-9799746-2-5(3))* Flashlight Pr.
McWilliam, Howard. Spaced Out! Enderle, Dotti. 2016. (J). ***(978-1-62402-101-5(8))*** Magic Wagon.
—What I Saw in the Teachers' Lounge. Pallotta, Jerry. (J). (gr. k-2). 2015. (ENG.). 32p. 6.99 ***(978-0-545-38473-5(7)***, Cartwheel Bks.); 2012. ***(978-0-545-38472-8(9))*** Scholastic, Inc.
McWilliam, Howard. What If You Had Animal Feet? Markle, Sandra. 2015. (ENG.). 32p. (J). (gr. k-3). pap. 4.99 *(978-0-545-73312-0(X)*, Scholastic Paperbacks) Scholastic, Inc.
—What If You Had Animal Hair? Markle, Sandra. 2014. (ENG.). 32p. (J). (gr. 1-3). pap. 3.99 *(978-0-545-63085-6(1)*, Scholastic Paperbacks) Scholastic, Inc.
—What If You Had Animal Teeth? Markle, Sandra. 2013. (ENG.). 32p. (J). (gr. -1-3). pap. 3.99 *(978-0-545-48438-1(3)*, Scholastic Paperbacks) Scholastic, Inc.
—When a Dragon Moves In. Moore, Jodi. 2011. (When a Dragon Moves In Ser.). (ENG.). 32p. (J). (gr. k-2). 16.95 *(978-0-9799746-7-0(4))* Flashlight Pr.
Meachen Rau, Dana, et al. All about Me: My Book by Me - My Pinkie Finger - My Special Space. Meachen Rau, Dana & Franco-Feeney, Betsy. 2006. (ENG.). 93p. (J). (gr. k-2). 9.95 *(978-0-531-16924-7(3)*, Children's Pr.) Scholastic Library Publishing.
Mead, Tom. Fearsome Creatures of the Lumberwoods: 20 Chilling Tales from the Wilderness. Johnson, Hal. 2015. (ENG.). 176p. (J). (gr. 3-8). 14.95 ***(978-0-7611-8461-4(9))*** Workman Publishing Co., Inc.
Meade, Gregory S. I Just Might! E.C., Nanci. 2007. 20p. per. 9.95 *(978-1-59858-548-3(7))* Dog Ear Publishing, LLC.
Meade, Holly. And Then Comes Halloween. Brenner, Tom. (ENG.). 32p. (J). (gr. -1-3). 2011. pap. 6.99 *(978-0-7636-5299-9(7))*; 2009. 16.99 *(978-0-7636-3659-3(2))* Candlewick Pr.
—Hop! Root, Phyllis. 2010. (ENG.). 16p. (J). (gr. -1-2). bds. 5.99 *(978-0-7636-4879-4(5))* Candlewick Pr.
—Hush! A Thai Lullaby. Ho, Mingfong. ed. 2004. (J). (gr. -1-1). spiral bd. *(978-0-616-07255-4(4))* Canadian National Institute for the Blind/Institut National Canadien pour les Aveugles.
—In the Wild. Elliott, David. (ENG.). 32p. (J). (gr. -1-3). 2013. pap. 6.99 *(978-0-7636-6337-7(9))*; 2010. 16.99 *(978-0-7636-4497-0(8))* Candlewick Pr.
—Naamah & the Ark at Night. Bartoletti, Susan Campbell. 2011. (ENG.). 32p. (J). (gr. -1-3). 16.99 *(978-0-7636-4242-6(8))* Candlewick Pr.
—On the Farm. Elliott, David. (ENG.). 32p. (J). (gr. -1-2). 2012. pap. 6.99 *(978-0-7636-5591-4(0))*; 2008. 16.99 *(978-0-7636-3322-6(4))* Candlewick Pr.
—On the Farm. Elliott, David. ed. 2012. lib. bdg. 17.20 *(978-0-606-23810-6(7)*, Turtleback) Turtleback Bks.
—Rata-Pata-Scata-Fata: A Caribbean Story, 1 vol. Gershator, Phillis. 2005. (ENG.). 32p. (J). (gr. -1-3). 5.95 *(978-1-932065-95-4(4))*; 15.95 *(978-1-932065-94-7(6))* Star Bright Bks., Inc.
—That's What Friends Are For. Heide, Florence Parry. 2007. 40p. pap. 6.99 *(978-0-7636-3283-0(X))* Candlewick Pr.
—That's What Friends Are For. Heide, Florence Parry & Clief, Sylvia Van. 2007. (ENG.). 40p. (J). (gr. -1-3). 6.99 *(978-0-7636-2646-4(5))* Candlewick Pr.
—That's What Friends Are For. Heide, Florence Parry & Clief, Sylvia Van. 2007. 30p. (gr. -1-3). 17.00 *(978-0-7569-8126-6(3))* Perfection Learning Corp.
—Virginnie's Hat. Chaconas, Dori. 2007. (ENG.). 32p. (J). (gr. -1-1). 16.99 *(978-0-7636-2397-5(0))* Candlewick Pr.
Meade, Holly. If I Never Forever Endeavor. Meade, Holly. 2011. (ENG.). 32p. (J). (gr. -1-3). 15.99 *(978-0-7636-4071-2(9))* Candlewick Pr.
Meade, Sarah. ABCs for Little Yogis. Meade, Saci & Nonino, Lila. 2014. (ENG.). 26p. (gr. -1). 16.95 *(978-1-60887-340-1(4))* Mandala Publishing.
Meadow, Amy. Benny's Pets. Whimsy. 2005. 32p. (J). 15.95 *(978-0-9702675-0-4(9))* World of Whimsy Productions, LLC.
Meadows, Sarah. Hello Hokie Bird! Aryal, Aimee Sutter. 2003. (J). 18.95 *(978-0-9743442-0-1(6))* Mascot Bks., Inc.
Mebberson, Amy. Monsters, Inc: Laugh Factory. Benjamin, Paul. 2010. (ENG.). 112p. (J). pap. 9.99 *(978-1-60886-508-6(8))* Boom! Studios.
—Muppet Peter Pan. Randolph, Grace & Barks, Carl. 2010. (Muppet Show Ser.). (ENG.). 112p. (J). 24.99 *(978-1-60886-531-4(2))* Boom! Studios.
—Muppet Peter Pan. Randolph, Grace. 2010. (Muppet Show Ser.). (ENG.). 112p. (J). pap. 9.99 *(978-1-60886-507-9(X))* Boom! Studios.
—Muppet Sherlock Holmes. Storck, Patrick. 2011. (Muppet Show Ser.). 128p. pap. 9.99 *(978-1-60886-613-7(0))* Boom! Studios.
Mebberson, Amy & Rosa, Don. Monsters, Inc: Laugh Factory. Benjamin, Paul & Rosa, Don. 2010. (ENG.). 112p. (J). 24.99 *(978-1-60886-533-8(9))* Boom! Studios.
Mebberson, Amy, jt. illus. see Langridge, Roger.
Mecham, Janeal A. Christmas Gifts. Mecham, Janeal A. l.t. unabr. ed. 2003. 32p. (J). (gr. k-3). 12.95 *(978-1-932280-16-6(2)*, 80162) Granite Publishing & Distribution.
Meconis, Dylan. The Fifth Musketeer. Fontes, Justine & Fontes, Ron. 2012. (Twisted Journeys Ser.: 19). (ENG.). 112p. (J). (gr. 4-7). pap. 7.95 *(978-0-7613-8550-9(9))*; pap. 45.32 *(978-0-7613-9289-7(0))*; lib. bdg. 27.93 *(978-0-7613-4594-7(9))* Lerner Publishing Group. (Graphic Universe).
Meconni, Beppe. El Pulpo Campanero. Brignole, Giancarla, tr. (Fabulas De Familia Ser.). (SPA.). 32p. *(978-970-20-0262-8(1))* Castillo, Ediciones, S. A. de C. V.
Meddaugh, Susan. The Best Halloween of All. Wojciechowski, Susan. 2012. (ENG.). 24p. (J). (gr. -1-3). pap. 3.99 *(978-0-7636-6008-6(6))* Candlewick Pr.
—In the Haunted House. Bunting, Eve. 2013. (ENG.). 16p. (J). (gr. -1-3). 6.99 *(978-0-544-06670-0(7))* Houghton Mifflin Harcourt Publishing Co.
—No Nap. Bunting, Eve. 2014. (ENG.). 32p. (J). (— 1). 10.99 *(978-0-544-33917-0(7)*, HMH Books For Young Readers) Houghton Mifflin Harcourt Publishing Co.

Meddour, Wendy. A Hen in the Wardrobe. 2012. (Cinnamon Grove Ser.). (ENG.). 160p. (J). (gr. 3-7). pap. 7.99 *(978-1-84780-225-5(7)*, Frances Lincoln) Quarto Publishing Group UK GBR. Dist: Hachette Bk. Group.
Medeiros, Giovana. Fantastical Fairies Matching Game. Chronicle Books Staff. 2015. (ENG.). 36p. (J). (gr. -1-1). 14.99 ***(978-1-4521-3083-5(3))*** Chronicle Bks. LLC.
Medeiros, Jennifer. Curvey's Christmas Wish. Greber, Barbara. 2013. (ENG.). 24p. pap. 9.95 *(978-0-615-83310-1(1))* Grey Bear Publishing.
Medina, Hector. El Libro de Los Maravillosos Automatas de Juguete. Rendon, Gilberto. rev. ed. 2006. (SPA & ENG.). 96p. (YA). (gr. 7-10). pap. 12.95 *(978-968-5920-87-2(7))* Castillo, Ediciones, S. A. de C. V. MEX. Dist: Macmillan.
Medina, Juana. Smick! Cronin, Doreen. 2015. (ENG.). 34p. (J). (gr. -1-k). 16.99 *(978-0-670-78578-0(4)*, Viking Juvenile) Penguin Publishing Group.
Medina, Lan, et al. Minimum Carnage. 2013. (ENG.). 152p. (YA). (gr. 8-17). pap. 24.99 *(978-0-7851-6726-6(9))* Marvel Worldwide, Inc.
Medina, Paco. X-Men: First to Last. 2011. (ENG.). 128p. (YA). (gr. 8-17). 19.99 *(978-0-7851-5287-3(3))* Marvel Worldwide, Inc.
—X-Men - Curse of the Mutants. Gischler, Victor. 2011. (ENG.). 152p. (YA). (gr. 8-17). pap. 19.99 *(978-0-7851-4847-0(7))* Marvel Worldwide, Inc.
Medina, Paco & Barberi, Carlo. Nova - Rookie Season, No. 2. 2014. (ENG.). 136p. (J). (gr. 4-17). pap. 16.99 *(978-0-7851-6839-3(7))* Marvel Worldwide, Inc.
MEE (Minoru Tachikawa). Hyper Police, Vol. 3. MEE (Minoru Tachikawa). rev. ed. 2005. 192p. pap. 9.99 *(978-1-59532-296-8(5)*, Tokyopop Adult) TOKYOPOP, Inc.
Meehan, Patricia. Puedo Colorear Mi Mundo Musulman: Libro para Colorear. Emerick, Yahiya. 2010. (SPA.). 68p. pap. 5.95 *(978-1-4563-9975-7(6))* CreateSpace Independent Publishing Platform.
Meeks, Arone Raymond. Enora & the Black Crane. Meeks, Arone Raymond. 2nd ed. 2010. (ENG.). 36p. (J). (gr. k-2). pap. 16.95 *(978-1-921248-02-3(5))* Magabala Bks. AUS. Dist: Independent Pubs. Group.
Meens, Estelle. Boss No More. 2014. (J). *(978-1-4338-1641-3(5)*, Magination Pr.) American Psychological Assn.
Megahan, John & Rose, Melanie. W Is for Waves: An Ocean Alphabet. Smith, Marie & Smith, Roland. 2008. (ENG.). 32p. (J). (gr. k-6). 17.95 *(978-1-58536-254-7(9))* Sleeping Bear Pr.
Megale, Marina. Kids to the Rescue! First Aid Techniques for Kids. Boelts, Maribeth & Boelts, Darwin. rev. ed. 2003. (ENG.). 72p. (J). (gr. -1-7). pap. 9.95 *(978-1-884734-78-6(2))* Parenting Pr., Inc.
Meganck, Robert & Communication Design (Firm) Staff. Around the World with the Percussion Family!, 1 vol. Shaskan, Trisha Speed. 2010. (Musical Families Ser.). (ENG.). 24p. (gr. 2-3). lib. bdg. 24.65 *(978-1-4048-6044-5(4)*, Nonfiction Picture Bks.) Picture Window Bks.
—The Brass Family on Parade!, 1 vol. Shaskan, Trisha Speed. 2010. (Musical Families Ser.). (ENG.). 24p. (gr. 2-3). lib. bdg. 24.65 *(978-1-4048-6041-4(X)*, Nonfiction Picture Bks.) Picture Window Bks.
—The Keyboard Family Takes Center Stage!, 1 vol. Shaskan, Trisha Speed. 2010. (Musical Families Ser.). (ENG.). 24p. (gr. 2-3). lib. bdg. 24.65 *(978-1-4048-6045-2(2)*, Nonfiction Picture Bks.) Picture Window Bks.
—Opening Night with the Woodwind Family!, 1 vol. Shaskan, Trisha Speed. 2010. (Musical Families Ser.). (ENG.). 24p. (gr. 2-3). lib. bdg. 24.65 *(978-1-4048-6042-1(8)*, Nonfiction Picture Bks.) Picture Window Bks.
—The String Family in Harmony!, 1 vol. Shaskan, Trisha Speed. 2010. (Musical Families Ser.). (ENG.). 24p. (gr. 2-3). lib. bdg. 24.65 *(978-1-4048-6043-8(6)*, Nonfiction Picture Bks.) Picture Window Bks.
Megenhardt, Bill. Grandma Spoils Me. Wright, Mary H. l.t. ed. 2005. 32p. (J). lib. bdg. 16.95 *(978-0-9645493-4-0(4))* Bluebonnets, Boots & Bks. Pr.
—Who Is Santa? And How Did He Get to the North Pole? Bigalow, Stephen W. 2013. (ENG.). 144p. (J). (gr. 4-7). 19.95 *(978-0-9773757-3-8(0))* Profit Publishing.
Mehrlich, Cynthia. Splugworth Saves the Day, 1 vol. Mehrlich Iii, Ferdinand Paul. 2009. 43p. pap. 24.95 *(978-1-60836-765-8(7))* America Star Bks.
Meidell, Sherry. The Day the Picture Man Came. Gibbons, Faye. 2003. (ENG.). 32p. (YA). (gr. k-2). 16.95 *(978-1-56397-161-7(5))* Boyds Mills Pr.
—Full Steam Ahead. Gibbons, Faye. 2003. (ENG.). 32p. (J). (gr. k-2). 15.95 *(978-1-56397-858-6(X))* Boyds Mills Pr.
Meier, Kerry L. Adam's Grouchy Day. Muench-Williams, Heather. l.t. ed. 2005. (HRL Big Book Ser.). (J). (gr. -1-k). pap. 10.95 *(978-1-57332-320-8(9))*; pap. 10.95 *(978-1-57332-321-5(7))* Carson-Dellosa Publishing, LLC. (HighReach Learning, Incorporated).
—Caillou's Family & Friends. Jarrell, Pamela R. l.t. ed. 2005. (HRL Board Book Ser.). (J). (gr. k-18). pap. 10.95 *(978-1-57332-327-7(6)*, HighReach Learning, Incorporated) Carson-Dellosa Publishing, LLC.
—Caillov Visits the Farmer's Market. Vonthron, Satanta C. l.t. ed. 2005. (HRL Board Book Ser.). (J). (gr. -1-k). pap. 10.95 *(978-1-57332-310-9(1)*, HighReach Learning, Incorporated) Carson-Dellosa Publishing, LLC.
—If You Go into the Forest. Howard-Parlnam, Pam. l.t. ed. 2005. (HRL Board Book Ser.). (J). (gr. -1-k). pap. 10.95 *(978-1-57332-324-6(1)*, HighReach Learning, Incorporated) Carson-Dellosa Publishing, LLC.
Meier, Paul. Big Church. Pope, Amy. 2004. (J). bds. 9.99 *(978-1-4183-0008-1(X))* Christ Inspired, Inc.
—Crazy Old Lou. Parra, Jen. 2005. (J). bds. 9.99 *(978-1-4183-0063-0(2))* Christ Inspired, Inc.
—The Isle of Nam. Hansen, Eric. 2004. (J). bds. 9.99 *(978-1-4183-0016-6(0))* Christ Inspired, Inc.
—Princess Shannon & the Yellow Moon. Parra, Jen. 2004. (J). bds. 9.99 *(978-1-4183-0012-8(8))* Christ Inspired, Inc.
—The Ten Commandments. Alsbrooks, Stephanie. 2005. (J). bds. 9.99 *(978-1-4183-0064-7(0))* Christ Inspired, Inc.
Meier, Ty. Children of the Sea. Ruby, Anne. 2007. (YA). per. *(978-0-9787881-0-0(9))* Seachild.
Meierhofer, Brian. The Big Rescue: The Greenwood Forest Series, 1 vol. Knoch, Frank. 2010. 32p. pap. 24.95 *(978-1-4489-6158-0(0))* PublishAmerica, Inc.
Meijer, Marja. Anna's Tight Squeeze. De Smet, Marian. 2003. Orig. Title: Op Slot. 32p. (J). pap. 5.95 *(978-1-58925-378-0(7))* Tiger Tales.
Meilichson, Alex. Bubbie & Zadie Come to My House: A Story for Hanukkah. Bloom, Daniel Halevi. 2006. (ENG.). 32p. (J). (gr. -1-3). 16.95 *(978-0-7570-0298-4(6))* Square One Pubs.
Meirink, Tineke. Traveling by Airplane. Winters, Pierre. 2012. (Want to Know Ser.). (ENG.). 30p. (J). (gr. -1-k). 16.95 *(978-1-60537-137-5(8))* Clavis Publishing.
Meisel, Paul. After the Bell Rings: Poems about After-School Time. Shields, Carol Diggory. 2015. (ENG.). 32p. (J). (gr. 1-4). 16.99 *(978-0-8037-3805-8(6)*, Dial) Penguin Publishing Group.
—Barnyard Slam. Regan, Dian Curtis. (ENG.). 32p. (J). (gr. -1-3). 2010. pap. 6.95 *(978-0-8234-2306-4(9))*; 2009. 16.95 *(978-0-8234-1907-4(X))* Holiday Hse., Inc.
—Brendan & Belinda & the Slam Dunk! Rockwell, Anne F. & Rockwell. 2007. (Good Sports Ser.). 40p. (J). (gr. -1-1). 15.99 *(978-0-06-028443-5(9))* HarperCollins Pubs.
—The Cool Crazy Crickets Club. Elliott, David. 2010. (ENG.). 48p. (J). (gr. 1-4). 5.99 *(978-0-7636-4659-2(8))* Candlewick Pr.
—The Cool Crazy Crickets to the Rescue. Elliott, David. 2010. (ENG.). 48p. (J). (gr. 1-4). 4.99 *(978-0-7636-4658-5(X))* Candlewick Pr.
—Dear Baby: Letters from Your Big Brother. Sullivan, Sarah. 2005. (ENG.). 40p. (J). (gr. k-3). 14.99 *(978-0-7636-2126-1(9))* Candlewick Pr.
—Forces Make Things Move. Bradley, Kimberly Brubaker. 2005. (Let's-Read-And-Find-Out Science 2 Ser.). (ENG.). 40p. (J). (gr. k-4). pap. 5.99 *(978-0-06-445214-4(X)*, Collins) HarperCollins Pubs.
—Go Away, Dog. Nodset, Joan L. 2003. (My First I Can Read Ser.). (ENG.). 32p. (J). (gr. -1-3). pap. 3.99 *(978-0-06-444231-2(4))* HarperCollins Pubs.
—Go to Sleep, Groundhog. Cox, Judy. 2003. (ENG.). 32p. (gr. k-3). tchr. ed. 17.95 *(978-0-8234-1645-5(3))* Holiday Hse., Inc.
—Go to Sleep, Groundhog! Cox, Judy. 2004. (ENG.). 32p. (gr. k-3). reprint ed. pap. 7.99 *(978-0-8234-1874-9(X))* Holiday Hse., Inc.
—Harriet's Had Enough! Guest, Elissa Haden. 2009. (ENG.). 32p. (J). (gr. -1-2). 15.99 *(978-0-7636-3454-4(9))* Candlewick Pr.
—Katie Catz Makes a Splash. Rockwell, Anne F. 2003. (Good Sports Ser.). 40p. (J). (gr. -1-1). 15.99 *(978-0-06-028441-1(2))*; lib. bdg. 16.89 *(978-0-06-028445-9(5))* HarperCollins Pubs.
—Leprechaun under the Bed. Bateman, Teresa. 2012. (ENG.). 32p. (J). 17.95 *(978-0-8234-2221-0(6))* Holiday Hse., Inc.
—Light Is All Around Us. Pfeffer, Wendy. 2014. (Let's-Read-And-Find-Out Science 2 Ser.). (ENG.). 40p. (J). (gr. -1-3). 17.99 *(978-0-06-029121-1(4))* HarperCollins Pubs.
—The Little Red Hen & the Passover Matzah. Kimmelman, Leslie. (ENG.). 32p. (J). 2011. pap. 6.95 *(978-0-8234-2327-9(1))*; 2010. (gr. -1-3). 16.95 *(978-0-8234-1952-4(5))* Holiday Hse., Inc.
—Looking for Leprechauns. Keenan, Sheila. 2005. (J). *(978-0-439-68057-8(3))* Scholastic, Inc.
—Mr. Ouchy's First Day. Hennessy, B. G. 2007. (J). (gr. k-3). 27.95 incl. audio *(978-0-8045-6946-0(0))*; 29.95 incl. audio compact disk *(978-0-8045-4160-2(4))* Spoken Arts, Inc.
—Pop Bottle Science. Brunelle, Lynn. 2004. (ENG.). 128p. (gr. 2-6). pap. 17.95 *(978-0-7611-2980-6(4)*, 12980) Workman Publishing Co., Inc.
Meisel, Paul. Run for Your Life! A Day on the African Savanna. Schaefer, Lola M. 2016. (J). ***(978-0-8234-3555-5(5))*** Holiday Hse., Inc.
Meisel, Paul. Scat, Cat! Capucilli, Alyssa Satin. 2010. (My First I Can Read Ser.). (ENG.). 32p. (J). (gr. -1 — 1). 16.99 *(978-0-06-117754-5(7))*; pap. 3.99 *(978-0-06-117756-9(3))* HarperCollins Pubs.
—The Schmutzy Family. Rosenberg, Madelyn. 2012. (ENG.). 32p. (J). 16.95 *(978-0-8234-2371-2(9))* Holiday Hse., Inc.
—Swamp Chomp. Schaefer, Lola M. 2014. (ENG.). 32p. (J). (gr. -1-3). 16.95 *(978-0-8234-2407-8(3))* Holiday Hse., Inc.
—Take Care, Good Knight. Thomas, Shelley Moore. 2006. (ENG.). 32p. (J). (gr. -1-k). 16.99 *(978-0-525-47695-5(4)*, Dutton Juvenile) Penguin Publishing Group.
—The Three Bears' Christmas. Duval, Kathy. (ENG.). 32p. (J). (gr. -1-3). 2006. 6.95 *(978-0-8234-2039-1(6))*; 2005. 16.95 *(978-0-8234-1871-8(5))* Holiday Hse., Inc.
—The Three Bears' Christmas. Duval, Kathy. 2007. (J). *(978-0-545-05421-8(4))* Scholastic, Inc.
—The Three Bears' Halloween. Duval, Kathy. 2007. (ENG.). 32p. (J). (gr. -1-3). 16.95 *(978-0-8234-2032-2(9))* Holiday Hse., Inc.
—Trick or Treat? Martin, Bill, Jr. & Sampson, Michael. 2005. (ENG.). 32p. (J). (gr. -1-3). reprint ed. 7.99 *(978-1-4169-0262-1(7)*, Simon & Schuster/Paula Wiseman Bks.) Simon & Schuster/Paula Wiseman Bks.
—Vampire Baby. Bennett, Kelly. 2013. (ENG.). 32p. (J). (gr. -1-3). 15.99 *(978-0-7636-4691-2(1))* Candlewick Pr.
—We All Sing with the Same Voice. Miller, J. Philip & Greene, Sheppard M. 2005. (ENG.). 32p. (J). (gr. -1-2). reprint ed. pap. 6.99 *(978-0-06-073900-3(2))* HarperCollins Pubs.
—What Happens to Our Trash? Ward, D. J. 2012. (Let's-Read-And-Find-Out Science 2 Ser.). (ENG.). 40p. (J). (gr. k-4). 16.99 *(978-0-06-168756-3(1))*; pap. 5.99 *(978-0-06-168755-6(3))* HarperCollins Pubs. (Collins).
—What Happens to Our Trash? Ward, D. J. ed. 2012. (Let's-Read-And-Find-Out Science Stage 2 Ser.). 40p. lib. bdg. 16.00 *(978-0-606-23568-6(X)*, Turtleback) Turtleback Bks.
Meisel, Paul. What Is the World Made Of? Zoehfeld, Kathleen Weidner. 2015. (Let's-Read-And-Find-Out Science 2 Ser.). (ENG.). 32p. (J). (gr. -1-3). pap. 6.99 ***(978-0-06-238195-8(4))*** HarperCollins Pubs.
Meisel, Paul. What's So Bad about Gasoline? Fossil Fuels & What They Do. Rockwell, Anne F. 2009. (Let's-Read-And-Find-Out Science 2 Ser.). (ENG.). 40p. (J). (gr. k-4). 16.99 *(978-0-06-157528-0(3))*; pap. 5.99 *(978-0-06-157527-3(5))* HarperCollins Pubs. (Collins).
—What's the Matter in Mr. Whiskers' Room? Ross, Michael Elsohn. 2007. (ENG.). 48p. (J). (gr. 1-4). pap. 7.99 *(978-0-7636-3566-4(9))* Candlewick Pr.
—Why Are the Ice Caps Melting? The Dangers of Global Warming. Rockwell, Anne F. 2006. (Let's-Read-and-Find-Out Science Ser.). (ENG.). 40p. (J). (gr. k-4). 15.99 *(978-0-06-054669-4(7))*; pap. 5.99 *(978-0-06-054671-7(9)*, Collins) HarperCollins Pubs.
Meisel, Paul. See Me Dig. Meisel, Paul. (I Like to Read Ser.). (ENG.). 32p. (J). 2014. (gr. -1-3). 6.99 *(978-0-8234-3057-4(X))*; 2013. 14.95 *(978-0-8234-2743-7(9))* Holiday Hse., Inc.
—See Me Run. Meisel, Paul. (I Like to Read Ser.). (ENG.). 24p. (J). 2012. (gr. -1-1). pap. 6.99 *(978-0-8234-2638-6(6))*; 2011. 14.95 *(978-0-8234-2349-1(2))* Holiday Hse., Inc.
Meisel, Paul. Mooove Over! A Book about Counting by Twos. Meisel, Paul, tr. Bell, Karen Magnuson. 2004. (ENG.). 32p. (J). (gr. k-3). tchr. ed. 16.95 *(978-0-8234-1736-0(0))* Holiday Hse., Inc.
Meisel, Paul, jt. illus. see Truesdell, Sue.
Meisel, Paul, jt. illus. see Wilkin, Eloise.
Meissner, Amy. Grandpa's Clock, 1 vol. Gilmore, Rachna. 2006. (ENG.). 32p. (J). (gr. -1-3). 17.95 *(978-1-55143-333-2(8))* Orca Bk. Pubs. USA.
—Sam's Ride, 1 vol. Citra, Becky. 2009. (Orca Echoes Ser.). (ENG.). 64p. (J). (gr. 2-3). pap. 6.95 *(978-1-55469-160-9(5))* Orca Bk. Pubs. USA.
—Saving Sammy, 1 vol. Walters, Eric. 2014. (Orca Echoes Ser.). (ENG.). 64p. (J). (gr. 2-3). pap. 6.95 *(978-1-4598-0499-9(6))* Orca Bk. Pubs. USA.
—Sea Dog. Gaetz, Dayle Campbell. 2006. 62p. (J). lib. bdg. 20.00 *(978-1-4242-1249-1(9))* Fitzgerald Bks.
—Sea Dog, 1 vol. Gaetz, Dayle Campbell. 2006. (Orca Echoes Ser.). (ENG.). 64p. (J). (gr. 2-3). per. 6.95 *(978-1-55143-406-3(7))* Orca Bk. Pubs. USA.
—Seeing Orange, 1 vol. Cassidy, Sara. 2012. (Orca Echoes Ser.). (ENG.). 64p. (J). (gr. 2-3). pap. 6.95 *(978-1-55469-991-9(6))* Orca Bk. Pubs. USA.
—Seldovia Sam & the Blueberry Bear, Vol. 4. Springer, Susan Woodward. 2005. (Misadventures of Seldovia Sam Ser.). (ENG.). 64p. (J). (gr. -1-4). per. 6.95 *(978-0-88240-603-9(5)*, Alaska Northwest Bks.) Graphic Arts Ctr. Publishing Co.
—Seldovia Sam & the Sea Otter Rescue. Springer, Susan Woodward. 2003. (Misadventures of Seldovia Sam Ser.: Vol. 2). (ENG.). 64p. (J). (gr. -1-4). pap. 6.95 *(978-0-88240-571-1(3))* Graphic Arts Ctr. Publishing Co.
—Seldovia Sam & the Very Large Clam. Springer, Susan Woodward. 2003. (Misadventures of Seldovia Sam Ser.: 1). (ENG.). 64p. (J). (gr. -1-4). pap. 6.95 *(978-0-88240-570-4(5))* Graphic Arts Ctr. Publishing Co.
—Seldovia Sam & Wildfire Escape. Springer, Susan Woodward. 2005. (Misadventures of Seldovia Sam Ser.: Bk. 3). (ENG.). 64p. (J). (gr. -1-4). per. 6.95 *(978-0-88240-601-5(9))* Graphic Arts Ctr. Publishing Co.
—The Wrong Bus, 1 vol. Peterson, Lois. 2012. (Orca Echoes Ser.). (ENG.). 64p. (J). (gr. 2-3). pap. 6.95 *(978-1-55469-869-1(3))* Orca Bk. Pubs. USA.
Meister, Charles, jt. illus. see Landau, Helena Von.
Meister, Charles E. Our Little Crusader Cousin of Long Ago. Stein, Evaleen. 2007. 136p. per. 8.95 *(978-1-59915-243-1(6))* Yesterday's Classics.
Meister, Soizick. Dragon Tide, 1 vol. Lee, Ingrid. 2006. (ENG.). 32p. (J). (gr. -1-3). 17.95 *(978-1-55143-352-3(4))* Orca Bk. Pubs. USA.
Mejia, Estella. The Legend of the Colombian Mermaid. Balletta, Janet. 2013. 36p. (J). pap. 14.95 *(978-0-9856762-9-2(9))* WRB Pub.
Mejias, John & Mejias, John. The Hungry Brothers. 2009. (ENG.). 32p. (J). (gr. -1-2). 15.95 *(978-0-9798841-1-5(X))* 4N Publishing LLC.
Mejias, John, jt. illus. see Mejias, John.
Mejías, Mónica. Aprendiendo a Leer con Mili y Molo: Learn How to Read in Spanish. Mejías, Mónica. 2004.Tr. of: Lernen Sie Spanish Lesen, Impara a leggere in Spagnolo, Aprenda a ler Espanhol, Apprenez à lire L'espagnol. 40p. (J). audio compact disk 12.00 *(978-0-9753799-0-5(9))* Ediciones Alas, Inc.
Mekis, Pete. Tommy Books: Faith, 10 vols. Brown, Mark. l.t. ed. 2005. 24p. (J). 12.99 *(978-0-9762690-0-7(7))* Tommy Bks. Pubng.
—Tommy Books: Kings, 10 vols. Brown, Mark. l.t. ed. 2005. 24p. (J). 12.99 *(978-0-9762690-4-5(X))* Tommy Bks. Pubng.
—Tommy Books Vol. 2: Love, 10 vols. Brown, Mark. l.t. ed. 2005. 24p. (J). 12.99 *(978-0-9762690-1-4(5))* Tommy Bks. Pubng.
—Tommy Books Vol. 3: Too Busy, 10 vols. Brown, Mark. l.t. ed. 2005. 24p. (J). 12.99 *(978-0-9762690-2-1(3))* Tommy Bks. Pubng.
—Tommy Books Vol. 4: Praise, 10 vols. Brown, Mark. l.t. ed. 2005. 20p. (J). 12.99 *(978-0-9762690-3-8(1))* Tommy Bks. Pubng.
Melanson, Luc. Book of Big Brothers, 1 vol. Fagan, Cary. 2010. (ENG.). 32p. (J). (gr. -1-2). 17.95 *(978-0-88899-977-1(1))* Groundwood Bks. CAN. Dist: Perseus-PGW.
—How to Become a Perfect Princess in Five Days. Dube, Pierrette. 2009. (Rainy Day Readers Ser.). 32p. (J). (gr. -1-3). 22.60 *(978-1-60754-376-3(1))* Windmill Bks.
—Redheaded Robbie's Christmas Story. Luttrel, Bill. 2003. (ENG.). 32p. (J). (gr. k-6). 16.95 *(978-1-58536-136-6(4))* Sleeping Bear Pr.
—Rosario's Fig Tree, 1 vol. Wahl, Charis. 2015. (ENG.). 32p. (J). (gr. -1-2). 18.95 *(978-1-55498-341-4(X))* Groundwood Bks. CAN. Dist: Perseus-PGW.
Melanson, Matt. Against All Odds. Kropp, Paul. 2004. (New Series Canada). 87p. (J). pap. *(978-1-897039-06-9(9))* High Interest Publishing (HIP).
—The Kid Is Lost. Kropp, Paul. 2004. (New Series Canada). 88p. (J). pap. *(978-1-897039-04-5(2))* High Interest Publishing (HIP).
—Our Plane Is Down. Paton, Doug. 2004. (New Series Canada). 90p. (J). pap. *(978-1-897039-03-8(4))* High Interest Publishing (HIP).
—Student Narc. Kropp, Paul. 2004. (New Series Canada). 94p. (J). pap. *(978-1-897039-05-2(0))* High Interest Publishing (HIP).
Melaranci, Elisabetta, et al. Tinker Bell & the Day of the Dragon, No. 3. Machetto, Augusto et al. 2010. (Disney Fairies Ser.: 3). (ENG.). 80p. (J). (gr. 1-6). pap. 7.99 *(978-1-59707-128-4(5))* Papercutz.
Melaranci, Elisabetta & Urbano, Emilio. Tinker Bell & Her Magical Arrival. Gianatti, Silvia et al. 2012. (Disney Fairies Ser.: 9). (ENG.). 64p. (J). (gr. 1-6). 11.99 *(978-1-59707-324-0(5))*; pap. 7.99 *(978-1-59707-323-3(7))* Papercutz.
Melcher, Mary. Puppies Count. 2010. (J). *(978-1-58865-596-7(2))* Kidsbooks, LLC.
Melcher, Michele. Elvis: A Graphic Novel, 1 vol. Collins, Terry. 2011. (American Graphic Ser.). (ENG.). 32p. (gr. 3-4). lib. bdg. 29.99 *(978-1-4296-5476-0(7))*; pap. 8.10 *(978-1-4296-6266-6(2))*; pap. 47.70 *(978-1-4296-6434-9(7))* Capstone Pr., Inc. (Graphic Library).
Melchishua, Tewodross. Shango's Son. Winmilawe. 2012. 20p. pap. 9.95 *(978-0-9839318-0-5(1))* Gazing In Publishing.
Meldrum, Ned, photos by. Big Balloon, 1 vol. Dale, Jay. 2012. (Engage Literacy Yellow Ser.). (ENG., 32p. (gr. k-2). pap. 5.99 *(978-1-4296-8962-5(5)*, Engage Literacy) Capstone Pr., Inc.
—Circus Tricks, 1 vol. Giulieri, Anne. 2012. (Engage Literacy Green Ser.). (ENG., 32p. (gr. k-2). pap. 5.99 *(978-1-4296-9006-5(2)*, Engage Literacy) Capstone Pr., Inc.
—Cooking Pancakes, 1 vol. Giulieri, Anne. 2012. (Engage Literacy Red Ser.). (ENG., 32p. (gr. k-2). pap. 5.99 *(978-1-4296-8950-2(1)*, Engage Literacy) Capstone Pr., Inc.
—The Environment Park, 1 vol. Dale, Jay. 2012. (Engage Literacy Green Ser.). (ENG., 32p. (gr. k-2). pap. 5.99 *(978-1-4296-8997-7(8)*, Engage Literacy) Capstone Pr., Inc.
—Make a Secret Playhouse, 1 vol. Giulieri, Anne. 2012. (Engage Literacy Green Ser.). (ENG., 32p. (gr. k-2). pap. 5.99 *(978-1-4296-9001-0(1)*, Engage Literacy) Capstone Pr., Inc.
—My Big Sandwich, 1 vol. Dale, Jay. 2012. (Engage Literacy Red Ser.). (ENG., 32p. (gr. k-2). pap. 5.99 *(978-1-4296-8834-5(3)*, Engage Literacy) Capstone Pr., Inc.
—My Dinosaurs, 1 vol. Giulieri, Anne. 2012. (Engage Literacy Red Ser.). (ENG., 32p. (gr. k-2). pap. 5.99 *(978-1-4296-8938-0(2)*, Engage Literacy) Capstone Pr., Inc.
—My Rock Pool, 1 vol. Giulieri, Anne. 2012. (Engage Literacy Green Ser.). (ENG., 32p. (gr. k-2). pap. 5.99 *(978-1-4296-9013-3(5)*, Engage Literacy) Capstone Pr., Inc.
Meier, Kerry L. Caillou's Castle. Williams, Heather L. l.t. ed. 2005. (HRL Board Book Ser.). (J). (gr. -1-1). pap. 10.95 *(978-1-57332-291-1(1)*, HighReach Learning, Incorporated) Carson-Dellosa Publishing, LLC.
—Planting a Seed. Jarrell, Pamela R. l.t. ed. 2006. 12p. (J). (gr. -1-k). pap. 10.95 *(978-1-57332-350-5(0)*, HighReach Learning, Incorporated) Carson-Dellosa Publishing, LLC.
—Pretend. Mullican, Judy. l.t. ed. 2005. (HRL Board Book Ser.). 10p. (J). (gr. -1-1). pap. 10.95 *(978-1-57332-283-6(0)*, HighReach Learning, Incorporated) Carson-Dellosa Publishing, LLC.
Melhuish, Eva. Christmas Magic. Stainton, Sue. 2007. 32p. (J). (gr. -1-1). lib. bdg. 16.89 *(978-0-06-078572-7(1)*, Tegen, Katherine Bks) HarperCollins Pubs.
Melinda, Sheffler. Cuddles the Chocolate Cow & Friends. Edmond, Wally. 2006. 39p. (J). 14.95 *(978-1-59879-108-2(7))*; per. 9.99 *(978-1-59879-125-9(7))* Lifevest Publishing, Inc.
Melinda, Shoals. The Spritelees: A Christmas Tale about Kindness. 2006. 32p. (J). 16.00 *(978-0-9773460-0-4(5))* Spritelee Enterprises.
Melling, David. First Arabic Words. Morris, Neil. 2009. (First Words Ser.). (ARA & ENG.). 48p. (YA). (gr. 3-18). pap. 12.95 *(978-0-19-911135-0(9))* Oxford Univ. Pr., Inc.
—First Chinese Words. Morris, Neil. 2009. (First Words Ser.). (CHI & ENG.). 48p. (YA). (gr. 3-18). pap. 12.95 *(978-0-19-911205-0(3))* Oxford Univ. Pr., Inc.
—First Italian Words. 2009. (First Words Ser.). (ITA & ENG.). 48p. (J). (gr. 3-18). pap. 12.95 *(978-0-19-911100-8(6))* Oxford Univ. Pr., Inc.
—First Polish Words. 2009. (First Words Ser.). (POL & ENG.). 48p. (J). (gr. 3-18). pap. 12.95 *(978-0-19-911715-4(2))* Oxford Univ. Pr., Inc.
—First Russian Words. 2009. (First Words Ser.). (RUS & ENG.). 48p. (J). (gr. 3-18). pap. 12.95 *(978-0-19-911151-0(0))* Oxford Univ. Pr., Inc.
—Jerry's Trousers. Boswall, Nigel. 2003. (ENG.). 26p. (J). pap. 4.99 *(978-0-333-68359-0(5))* Macmillan Pubs., Ltd. GBR. Dist: Trafalgar Square Publishing.
Melling, David. Dont Worry Douglas. Melling, David. 2011. 32p. 12.95 *(978-1-58925-106-9(7))* Tiger Tales.
—Good Knight Sleep Tight. Melling, David. 2006. (ENG.). 32p. (J). (gr. k-2). pap. 9.99 *(978-0-340-86093-9(6))* Hodder & Stoughton GBR. Dist: Independent Pubs. Group.
—Hugless Dougless. Melling, David. 2010. (ENG.). 32p. (J). (gr. -1-2). 15.95 *(978-1-58925-098-7(2))* Tiger Tales.
—Splish, Splash, Splosh! Melling, David. 2013. (ENG.). 22p. (gr. -1). bds. 8.95 *(978-1-58925-643-9(3))* Tiger Tales.

—The Three Wishes. Melling, David. 2008. (ENG.). 32p. (J). (gr. -1-k). pap. 10.99 (978-0-340-93153-0(1)) Hodder & Stoughton GBR. Dist: Independent Pubs. Group.
—Two by Two & a Half. Melling, David. 2008. (ENG.). 32p. (J). (gr. -1-k). pap. 9.99 (978-0-340-90311-7(2)) Hodder & Stoughton GBR. Dist: Independent Pubs. Group.
Melling, David. Cold Enough for Snow. Melling, David, tr. McKay, Hilary. 2003. (Pudding Bag School Ser.: Bk. 2). 144p. (J). pap. (978-0-340-87750-0(2), Hodder Children's Books) Hachette Children's Group.
Melmon, Deborah. Adventures of Hound Hotel. Swanson Sateren, Shelley. 2015. (Adventures at Hound Hotel Ser.). (ENG.). 72p. (gr. 2-3). 95.96 **(978-1-4795-6291-6(2)**, Adventures at Hound Hotel) Picture Window Bks.
Melmon, Deborah. Albert Adds Up! May, Eleanor. 2014. (Mouse Math (r) Ser.). 32p. (gr. -1-1). 22.60 (978-1-57565-744-8(9)) Kane Pr., Inc.
—Albert Is Not Scared. May, Eleanor. 2013. (Mouse Math Ser.). (ENG.). 32p. (J). (gr. -1-1). pap. 7.95 (978-1-57565-629-8(9)); lib. bdg. 22.60 (978-1-57565-628-1(0)) Kane Pr., Inc.
—Albert Keeps Score. Skinner, Daphne. 2012. (Mouse Math Ser.). (ENG.). 32p. (J). (gr. -1-1). 7.95 (978-1-57565-444-7(X)); lib. bdg. 22.60 (978-1-57565-449-2(0)) Kane Pr., Inc.
Melmon, Deborah. Albert Starts School. May, Eleanor. 2015. (Mouse Math (r) Ser.). (ENG.). 32p. (J). (gr. -1-1). 22.60 **(978-1-57565-741-7(4))** Kane Pr., Inc.
Melmon, Deborah. Albert the Muffin-Maker. May, Eleanor. 2014. (Mouse Math Ser.). 32p. (gr. -1-1). lib. bdg. 22.60 (978-1-57565-631-1(0)) Kane Pr., Inc.
—Albert's Amazing Snail. May, Eleanor. 2012. (Mouse Math Ser.). (ENG.). 32p. (J). (gr. -1-1). 22.60 (978-1-57565-448-5(2)); pap. 7.95 (978-1-57565-442-3(3)) Kane Pr., Inc.
—Albert's Bigger Than Big Idea. May, Eleanor. 2013. (Mouse Math Ser.). 32p. (gr. -1-1). pap. 7.95 (978-1-57565-522-2(5)) Kane Pr., Inc.
—Baby Wants Mama, 0 vols. Loewen, Nancy. 2013. (ENG.). 24p. (J). (gr. -1-k). 14.99 (978-1-4778-1651-6(8), 9781477816516, Amazon Children's Publishing) Amazon Publishing.
—A Beach for Albert. May, Eleanor. 2013. (Mouse Math Ser.). 32p. (gr. -1-1). pap. 7.95 (978-1-57565-531-4(4)); lib. bdg. 22.60 (978-1-57565-530-7(6)) Kane Pr., Inc.
—Count off, Squeak Scouts! Driscoll, Laura. 2013. (Mouse Math Ser.). 32p. (J). (gr. -1-1). 22.60 (978-1-57565-524-6(1)); pap. 7.95 (978-1-57565-525-3(X)) Kane Pr., Inc.
—Fearless Freddie. Sateren, Shelley Swanson. 2015. (Adventures at Hound Hotel Ser.). (ENG.). 72p. (gr. 2-3). lib. bdg. 23.99 (978-1-4795-5898-8(2), Adventures at Hound Hotel) Picture Window Bks.
—Give up, Gecko!, 0 vols. MacDonald, Margaret Read. unabr. ed. 2013. (ENG.). 32p. (J). (gr. k-3). 16.99 (978-1-4778-1635-6(6), 9781477816356, Amazon Children's Publishing) Amazon Publishing.
—Growling Gracie. Sateren, Shelley Swanson. 2015. (Adventures at Hound Hotel Ser.). (ENG.). 72p. (gr. 2-3). lib. bdg. 23.99 (978-1-4795-5899-5(0), Adventures at Hound Hotel) Picture Window Bks.
—Holiday Helper. Abramson, Jill & O'Connor, Jane. 2014. (Penguin Young Readers, Level 2 Ser.). (ENG.). 32p. (J). (gr. 1-3). pap. 3.99 (978-0-448-45677-5(X), Warne, Frederick Pubs.) Penguin Bks., Ltd. GBR. Dist: Penguin Random Hse., LLC.
—Homesick Herbie. Sateren, Shelley Swanson. 2015. (Adventures at Hound Hotel Ser.). (ENG.). 72p. (gr. 2-3). lib. bdg. 23.99 (978-1-4795-5897-1(4), Adventures at Hound Hotel) Picture Window Bks.
—Hooray for Feet! Hunt, Connie. 2008. (J). (978-1-58728-699-5(8), Two-Can Publishing) T&N Children's Publishing.
—Hooray for Hands! Hunt, Connie. 2008. (J). (978-1-58728-700-8(5), Two-Can Publishing) T&N Children's Publishing.
Melmon, Deborah. Lost in the Mouseum. May, Eleanor. 2015. (Mouse Math (r) Ser.). (ENG.). 32p. (J). (gr. -1-1). 22.60 **(978-1-57565-643-4(4))** Kane Pr., Inc.
—Make a Wish, Albert: 3-D Shapes. Houran, Lori Haskins. 2015. (ENG.). 32p. (J). (gr. -1-1). lib. bdg. 22.60 **(978-1-57565-797-4(X))** Kane Pr., Inc.
Melmon, Deborah. Mice on Ice. May, Eleanor. 2013. (Mouse Math Ser.). 32p. (J). (gr. -1-1). 22.60 (978-1-57565-527-7(6)); pap. 7.95 (978-1-57565-528-4(4)) Kane Pr., Inc.
—The Mousier the Merrier. May, Eleanor. 2012. (Mouse Math Ser.). (ENG.). 32p. (J). (gr. -1-1). 22.60 (978-1-57565-447-8(4)); pap. 7.95 (978-1-57565-440-9(7)) Kane Pr., Inc.
—A Mousy Mess. Driscoll, Laura. 2014. (Mouse Math (r) Ser.). 32p. (J). (gr. -1-1). 22.60 (978-1-57565-646-5(9)) Kane Pr., Inc.
—Mudball Molly. Sateren, Shelley Swanson. 2015. (Adventures at Hound Hotel Ser.). (ENG.). 72p. (gr. 2-3). lib. bdg. 23.99 (978-1-4795-5900-8(8), Adventures at Hound Hotel) Picture Window Bks.
—On the Farm. Ring, Susan. 2008. (ENG.). 10p. (J). (gr. 3-17). 12.99 (978-1-58476-729-9(4)) Innovative Kids.
Melmon, Deborah. One Good Deed. Fields, Terri. 2015. (ENG.). 24p. (J). (gr. -1-3). pap. 7.99 **(978-1-4677-3479-0(9)**, Kar-Ben Publishing) Lerner Publishing Group.
—One Good Deed. Fields, Terri. 2015. (ENG.). 24p. (J). (gr. -1-3). 17.99 **(978-1-4677-3478-3(0))** Lerner Publishing Group.
Melmon, Deborah. Picnic at Camp Shalom. Jules, Jacqueline & Hechtkopf, Jacqueline. 2011. (Kar-Ben Favorites Ser.). (ENG.). 32p. (J). (gr. k-3). 17.95 (978-0-7613-6661-4(X), Kar-Ben Publishing) Lerner Publishing Group.
—Picnic at Camp Shalom. Jules, Jacqueline. 2011. (ENG.). 32p. (J). (gr. k-3). pap. 7.95 (978-0-7613-6662-1(8), Kar-Ben Publishing) Lerner Publishing Group.
—Puppy Parade. Abramson, Jill & O'Connor, Jane. 2013. (Penguin Young Readers, Level 2 Ser.). (ENG.). 32p. (J). (gr. 1-2). pap. 3.99 (978-0-448-45676-8(1)); 14.99 (978-0-448-46574-6(4)) Penguin Bks., Ltd. GBR. (Warne, Frederick Pubs.). Dist: Penguin Random Hse., LLC.
—Pups of the Spirit, 1 vol. Gorey, Jill & Haller, Nancy. 2015. (ENG.). 22p. (J). bds. 9.99 (978-0-310-74798-7(8)) Zonderkidz.
—The Right Place for Albert. Skinner, Daphne. 2012. (Mouse Math Ser.). (ENG.). 32p. (J). (gr. -1-1). 7.95 (978-1-57565-438-6(5)); lib. bdg. 22.60 (978-1-57565-446-1(6)) Kane Pr., Inc.
—Speak up, Tommy! Greene, Jacqueline Dembar. 2012. (Kar-Ben Favorites Ser.). (ENG.). 32p. (J). (gr. -1-3). lib. bdg. 17.95 (978-0-7613-7497-8(3), Kar-Ben Publishing) Lerner Publishing Group.
—Speak up, Tommy! Dembar Greene, Jacqueline. 2012. (Kar-Ben Favorites Ser.). (ENG.). 32p. (J). (gr. -1-3). 7.95 (978-0-7613-7498-5(1), Kar-Ben Publishing) Lerner Publishing Group.
Melmon, Deborah H. You Can Write a Story! A Story-Writing Recipe for Kids. Bullard, Lisa. 2007. (ENG.). 48p. (J). (gr. 1-4). 16.95 (978-1-58728-587-5(8)) Cooper Square Publishing Llc.
Melnychuk, Monika. Centsibility: The Planet Girl Guide to Money. Roderick, Stacey & Warwick, Ellen. 2008. (Planet Girl Ser.). (ENG.). 80p. (J). (gr. 4-7). 12.95 (978-1-55453-208-7(6)) Kids Can Pr., Ltd. CAN. Dist: Univ. of Toronto Pr.
—Girl in the Know: Your Inside-and-Out Guide to Growing Up. Katz, Anne. 2010. (ENG.). 112p. (J). (gr. 5-9). 18.95 (978-1-55453-303-9(1)) Kids Can Pr., Ltd. CAN. Dist: Univ. of Toronto Pr.
—Tastes Like Music: 17 Quirks of the Brain & Body. Birmingham, Maria. 2014. (ENG.). 40p. (J). (gr. 3-7). 17.95 (978-1-77147-010-0(0), Owlkids) Owlkids Bks. Inc. CAN. Dist: Perseus-PGW.
Melnyczuk, Peter. The Dragon Charmer. Hill, Douglas. 2005. 151p. (J). (gr. -1-k). pap. 4.95 (978-1-903015-36-0(7)) Barn Owl Bks, London GBR. Dist: Independent Pubs. Group.
Melo, Esperanca. Crocheting. Blakley Kinsler, Gwen & Young, Jackie. 2003. (Kids Can Do It Ser.). (ENG.). 40p. (J). (gr. 4-6). 6.95 (978-1-55337-177-9(1)) Kids Can Pr., Ltd. CAN. Dist: Univ. of Toronto Pr.
—JoJo the Giant. Barclay, Jane. 2012. (ENG.). 32p. (J). (gr. -1-1). 17.95 (978-0-88776-976-4(4), Tundra Bks.) Tundra Bks. CAN. Dist: Penguin Random Hse., LLC.
Melo, Esperança. Love You More, 1 vol. Musgrave, Susan. 2014. (ENG.). 24p. (J). (gr. -1-k). bds. 9.95 (978-1-4598-0240-7(3)) Orca Bk. Pubs. USA.
Melo, Esperanca. Merci Mister Dash! Kulling, Monica. 2011. (ENG.). 32p. (J). (gr. -1-2). 17.95 (978-0-88776-964-1(0), Tundra Bks.) Tundra Bks. CAN. Dist: Penguin Random Hse., LLC.
—Mister Dash & the Cupcake Calamity. Kulling, Monica. 2013. (ENG.). 32p. (J). (gr. -1-2). 17.95 (978-1-77049-396-4(4), Tundra Bks.) Tundra Bks. CAN. Dist: Penguin Random Hse., LLC.
Melo, Esperanca, jt. illus. see Slavin, Bill.
Melton, Eric. The House at the Bend of Contently Creek. Tuck, Helen. 2003. 107p. (J). pap. 11.95 (978-0-7414-1682-7(4)) Infinity Publishing.
Melton, Jo Lynn. Juanita Maria Sophia Bug Diva: Lived down South in the West. Blake-Brekke, Carri. 2004. (Mrs. B'S Story Time-.. with A Twist! Ser.). 20p. (J). pap. 11.95 incl. audio compact disk (978-0-9720549-3-5(6)) Mom's Pride Enterprises.
Melton, Jodi. Billy Bully Bug: Learns a Lesson in Hawaii. Blake-Brekke, Carri. 2003. (Mrs. B's Story Time... With a Twist! Ser.). 20p. (J). pap. 11.95 incl. audio compact disk (978-0-9720549-2-8(8)) Mom's Pride Enterprises.
Melville, Jacqui, photos by. Little Kitchen: 40 Delicious & Simple Things That Children Can Really Make. Pamni, Sabrina. 2010. 128p. pap. (978-1-74066-743-2(3)) Hardie Grant Bks. AUS. Dist: Independent Pubs. Group.
Melvin, Alice. An A to Z Treasure Hunt. Melvin, Alice. 2008. (ENG.). 32p. (J). (gr. -1-1). pap. 14.95 (978-1-85437-755-5(8)) Tate Publishing, Ltd. GBR. Dist: Abrams.
Melvin, Anita. Too Many Choices. Salyers, Rita. 2004. (J). per. 9.95 (978-0-9763423-0-4(8)) The Publishing Place LLC.
Melvin, Anita. What to do with Boogers. Melvin, Anita. 2004. 14p. (J). per. 9.95 (978-0-9760129-8-6(7)) The Publishing Place LLC.
Melvin, Anita Flannery. An Internet Adventure with Safari Sam. Fuzy, Jim. 2004. 24p. (J). per. 14.95 (978-0-9760129-7-9(9)) The Publishing Place LLC.
Melvin, James. Color with the Wright Brothers: See How They Made History. Tate, Suzanne. 2003. (Suzanne Tate's History Ser.). 32p. (J). pap. 2.95 (978-1-878405-41-8(1)) Nags Head Art, Inc.
—Danny & Daisy: A Tale of a Dolphin Duo. Tate, Suzanne. 2004. (Suzanne Tate's Nature Ser.: No. 13). 32p. (J). per. 10.95 (978-1-878405-44-9(6)) Nags Head Art, Inc.
—Flyer: A Tale of the Wright Dog. Tate, Suzanne. 2003. (Suzanne Tate's History Ser.). (J). pap. 4.95 (978-1-878405-42-5(X)) Nags Head Art, Inc.
—Great Sharky Shark: A Tale of a Big Hunter. Tate, Suzanne. 2004. (Suzanne Tate's Nature Ser.: No. 20). 32p. (J). per. 10.95 (978-1-878405-46-3(2)) Nags Head Art, Inc.
—Johnny Longlegs: A Tale of Big Birds. Tate, Suzanne. 2005. (Suzanne Tate's Nature Ser.: No. 28). 28p. (J). pap. 4.95 (978-1-878405-50-0(0)) Nags Head Art, Inc.
—Katie K. Whale: A Whale of a Tale. Tate, Suzanne. 2004. (Suzanne Tate's Nature Ser.: No. 17). 32p. (J). per. 10.95 (978-1-878405-47-0(0)) Nags Head Art, Inc.
—Rosie Ray: A Tale of Watery Wings. Tate, Suzanne. 2003. (Suzanne Tate's Nature Ser.: No. 25). 28p. (J). (gr. -1-3). pap. 4.95 (978-1-878405-40-1(3)) Nags Head Art, Inc.
—Sandy Seal: A Tale of Sea Dogs. Tate, Suzanne. l.t. ed. 2004. (Suzanne Tate's Nature Ser.: No. 27). 28p. (J). pap. 4.95 (978-1-878405-49-4(7)) Nags Head Art, Inc.
—Skippy Scallop: A Tale of Bright Blue Eyes. Tate, Suzanne. 2003. (Suzanne Tate's Nature Ser.: No. 26). 28p. (J). pap. 4.95 (978-1-878405-43-2(8)) Nags Head Art, Inc.
—Tammy Turtle: A Tale of Saving Sea Turtles. Tate, Suzanne. 2004. (Suzanne Tate's Nature Ser.: No. 11). 32p. (J). per. 10.95 (978-1-878405-45-6(4)) Nags Head Art, Inc.
—Teena Tortoise: A Tale of a Little Giant. Tate, Suzanne. 2012. 32p. (J). pap. 4.95 (978-1-878405-60-9(8)) Nags Head Art, Inc.
Memarzadeh, Sudabeh. Brush Barry Brush. Valderrama, Linda N. 2011. 32p. (J). pap. 11.95 (978-0-578-06605-9(X)) Shirley's Girl Pubns.
Menard, Adrienne. The Ghoul in Our School. Menard, Michele Rose. 2013. 36p. pap. 11.95 (978-0-9887969-9-7(6)) Four Menards, The.
Menard, John C. The Bees & the Bears. Menard, James. 2008. 36p. pap. 16.99 (978-1-4389-2150-1(0)) AuthorHouse.
Menchin, Scott. Bounce. Cronin, Doreen. 2007. (ENG.). 40p. (J). (gr. -1-3). 17.99 (978-1-4169-1627-7(X), Atheneum Bks. for Young Readers) Simon & Schuster Children's Publishing.
—My Yiddish Vacation. Skye, Ione. 2014. (ENG.). 32p. (J). (gr. k-3). 17.99 (978-0-8050-9512-8(8), Holt, Henry & Co. Bks. For Young Readers) Holt, Henry & Co.
—Rescue Bunnies. Cronin, Doreen. 2010. (ENG.). 32p. (J). (gr. -1-3). 16.99 (978-0-06-112871-4(6)) HarperCollins Pubs.
—Song of Middle C. McGhee, Alison. 2009. (ENG.). 32p. (J). (gr. k-3). 16.99 (978-0-7636-3013-3(6)) Candlewick Pr.
—Stretch. Cronin, Doreen. 2009. (ENG.). 40p. (J). (gr. -1-1). 15.99 (978-1-4169-5341-8(8), Atheneum Bks. for Young Readers) Simon & Schuster Children's Publishing.
—Wiggle. Cronin, Doreen. 2005. (ENG.). 40p. (J). (gr. -1-3). 15.99 (978-0-689-86375-2(6), Atheneum Bks. for Young Readers) Simon & Schuster Children's Publishing.
—Wiggle. Cronin, Doreen. 2006. (Doreen Cronin: Click-Clack & More Ser.). (ENG.). 36p. (gr. -1-3). lib. bdg. 24.21 (978-1-59961-093-1(0)) Spotlight.
Menchin, Scott. Harry Goes to Dog School. Menchin, Scott. 2012. (ENG.). 32p. (J). (gr. -1-3). 16.99 (978-0-06-195801-4(8)) HarperCollins Pubs.
—Taking a Bath with the Dog & Other Things That Make Me Happy. Menchin, Scott. 2013. (ENG.). 40p. (J). (gr. -1-3). 7.99 (978-0-7636-6335-3(2)) Candlewick Pr.
—What If Everything Had Legs? Menchin, Scott. 2011. (ENG.). 32p. (J). (gr. -1-3). 15.99 (978-0-7636-4220-4(7)) Candlewick Pr.
Menck, Kevin. Stories That End with a Prayer. Elkins, Stephen. 32p. (J). (gr. k-8). 12.98 (978-1-56919-003-6(8)) Wonder Workshop.
Mendelson, Harvey, photos by. Divine Kosher Cuisine: Catering to Family & Friends. Routenburg, Rise' & Wasser, Barbara. Keen, Annette, ed. 2006. 382p. 32.99 (978-0-9770172-0-1(6)) Congregation Agudat Achim.
Mendenhall, Cheryl. The Frog in the Pond. Mara, Wil. 2007. (Rookie Reader Skill Set Ser.). (ENG.). 32p. (J). (gr. -1-3). 19.50 (978-0-531-17541-5(3), Children's Pr.) Scholastic Library Publishing.
—God's Creation. Dalmatian Press Staff. 2004. (ENG.). 24p. (J). 2.99 (978-1-4037-0962-2(9), Spirit Pr.) Bendon, Inc.
—Joseph & His Coat of Many Colors. 2004. (ENG.). 24p. (J). 2.99 (978-1-4037-0966-0(1), Spirit Pr.) Bendon, Inc.
—Moses Baby in the Bulrushes. 2004. (ENG.). 24p. (J). 2.99 (978-1-4037-0963-9(7), Spirit Pr.) Bendon, Inc.
—Moses Parting the Red Sea. 2004. (ENG.). 24p. (J). 2.99 (978-1-4037-0964-6(5), Spirit Pr.) Bendon, Inc.
Mendes, Barbara. Max Said Yes! The Woodstock Story. Lipner, Joseph & Yasgur, Abigail. 2009. (ENG.). 32p. (J). (gr. k-2). 17.95 (978-0-615-21144-2(5)) Change the Universe Pr.
Mendes, Melissa. Jack Strong Takes a Stand. Greenwald, Tommy. 2013. (ENG.). 240p. (J). (gr. 4-7). 15.99 (978-1-59643-836-1(3)) Roaring Brook Pr.
Mendez, Simon. Animals All Day!, 1 vol. Diaz, Joanne Ruelos. 2014. (Animals All Day! Ser.). (ENG.). 32p. (gr. k-2). 106.60 (978-1-4795-5702-8(1)) Picture Window Bks.
—Animals by the Seashore, 1 vol. Diaz, Joanne Ruelos. 2014. (Animals All Day! Ser.). (ENG.). 32p. (gr. k-2). 26.65 (978-1-4795-5700-4(5)) Picture Window Bks.
—Animals in the Rain Forest, 1 vol. Diaz, Joanne Ruelos. 2014. (Animals All Day! Ser.). (ENG.). 32p. (gr. k-2). 26.65 (978-1-4795-5698-4(X)) Picture Window Bks.
—Animals on the African Savanna, 1 vol. Diaz, Joanne Ruelos. 2014. (Animals All Day! Ser.). (ENG.). 32p. (gr. k-2). 26.65 (978-1-4795-5701-1(3)) Picture Window Bks.
—Animals on the Farm, 1 vol. Diaz, Joanne Ruelos. 2014. (Animals All Day! Ser.). (ENG.). 32p. (gr. k-2). 26.65 (978-1-4795-5699-1(8)) Picture Window Bks.
—Asi Nace un Arbol. Llewellyn, Claire. 2004. (Colección Así Nace... / Starting Life Collection Ser.). (SPA.). 24p. (gr. k-6). pap. 10.95 (978-1-59437-449-4(X)) Santillana USA Publishing Co., Inc.
—Asi Nace un Pato. Llewellyn, Claire. 2004. (Colección Así Nace... / Starting Life Collection Ser.). (SPA.). 24p. (gr. k-6). pap. 10.95 (978-1-59437-448-7(1)) Santillana USA Publishing Co., Inc.
—Asi Nace una Mariposa. Llewellyn, Claire. Giraldo, Maria Cristina, tr. 2003. (Colección Así Nace... / Starting Life Collection Ser.). (SPA.). 24p. (gr. k-6). pap. 10.95 (978-1-59437-788-4(X)) Santillana USA Publishing Co., Inc.
—Asi Nace una Rana. Llewellyn, Claire. 2003. (Colección Así Nace... / Starting Life Collection Ser.). (SPA.). 24p. (gr. k-6). pap. 10.95 (978-1-59437-789-1(8)) Santillana USA Publishing Co., Inc.
—Bug Wars: Deadly Insects & Spiders Go Head to Head. Ticktock Media, Ltd. Staff & Parker, Steve. 2014. (Animal Wars Ser.). (ENG.). 80p. (J). (gr. 2-7). 12.99 (978-1-78325-146-9(8), TickTock Books) Octopus Publishing Group GBR. Dist: Hachette Bk. Group.
Mendez, Simon. Creatures of the Deep. Rake, Matthew. 2015. (Real-Life Monsters Ser.). (ENG.). 32p. (J). (gr. 3-6). 26.65 **(978-1-4677-6360-8(8))** Lerner Publishing Group.
Mendez, Simon. Ladybug. Llewellyn, Claire. 2004. (Starting Life Ser.). (ENG.). 24p. (J). (gr. k-3). 16.95 (978-1-55971-892-9(7)) Cooper Square Publishing Llc.
—Little Bear & the Wishing Tree, 1 vol. Landa, Norbert. 2007. (ENG.). 28p. (J). (gr. -1-2). pap. 16.95 (978-1-56148-566-6(7), Good Bks.) Skyhorse Publishing Co., Inc.
—Mama, Why? Wilson, Karma. 2011. (ENG.). 40p. (J). (gr. -1-2). 16.99 (978-1-4169-4205-4(X), McElderry, Margaret K. Bks.) McElderry, Margaret K. Bks.
—Muddypaws. Butterfield, Moira. (Picture Books Ser.). (J). 2010. (gr. -1-k). bds. (978-1-4075-8757-8(9)); 2008. 32p. (978-1-4075-1840-4(2)) Parragon, Inc.
—Myths & Monsters: Secrets Revealed. Edwards, Katie. 2004. 29p. (J). pap. 6.95 (978-1-57091-582-6(2)) Charlesbridge Publishing, Inc.
—One Winter's Night. Freedman, Claire. ed. 2009. (J). lib. bdg. (978-1-84895-013-9(6), Scholastic) Scholastic, Inc.
Mendez, Simon. Scaly, Slippery Creatures. Rake, Matthew. 2015. (Real-Life Monsters Ser.). (ENG.). 32p. (J). (gr. 3-6). pap. 7.99 **(978-1-4677-7645-5(9)**, Lerner Pubns.) Lerner Publishing Group.
Mendez, Simon. Duck. Mendez, Simon, tr. Llewellyn, Claire. 2004. (Starting Life Ser.). (ENG.). 24p. (J). (gr. k-3). 16.95 (978-1-55971-878-3(1)) Cooper Square Publishing Llc.
—Tree. Mendez, Simon, tr. Llewellyn, Claire. 2004. (Starting Life Ser.). (ENG.). 24p. (J). (gr. k-3). 16.95 (978-1-55971-879-0(X)) Cooper Square Publishing Llc.
Mendez, Simon & Warnes, Tim. My Little Box of Christmas Stories: One Winter's Night/Hurry, Santa!/a Magical Christmas/the Gift of Christmas/the Special Christmas Tree/the Christmas Bear. Freedman, Claire et al. 2013. (ENG.). (J). (gr. -1-1). pap. 8.95 (978-1-58925-443-5(0)) Tiger Tales.
Mendonca, Angela. Nursery Rhymes Island Style. Mendonca, Angela. 2013. 24p. pap. 9.99 (978-0-9843125-6-6(0)) Wealth of Wisdom LLC, A.
Mendoza, Carlos. Down under in Australia. Hulin, Pamela. 2007. 20p. per. 24.95 (978-1-4241-8929-8(2)) America Star Bks.
Mendoza, George. Colors of the Wind: The Story of Blind Artist & Champion Runner George Mendoza. Powers, J. L. 2014. (J). (978-1-930900-73-8(2)) Purple Hse. Pr.
Mendoza, Megan Elizabeth. Tony Loved to Learn. Riddle, Sharon Kay & Sanders, Nancy/Ida. 2007. 32p. (J). pap. 15.00 (978-0-9761583-6-3(1)) Olive Leaf Pubns.
Menéndez, Margarita. Acertijos, Chistes y Canciones: Chupachus. Menéndez, Margarita, tr. Fuertes, Gloria. 2003. (SPA.). 121p. (978-84-305-7803-0(X), SU5202) Susaeta Ediciones, S.A. ESP. Dist: Lectorum Pubns., Inc.
Mengert, Hollie E. Tumptin's Sneeze. Penrod, Kathy Webb. 2012. (ENG.). 36p. (J). (gr. -1-3). pap. 14.99 (978-1-62147-243-8(4)) Tate Publishing & Enterprises, LLC.
Menix, Cinda & McGuire, Bryan. Tenbrook Farms. Menix, Cinda. 2007. 67p. (J). (gr. 4-7). per. 23.99 (978-1-59879-338-3(1)) Lifevest Publishing, Inc.
Menking, Amanda & Fisher, Sean. The Happy Dragon, 1 vol. Bucher, Heatherly & Menking, Amanda. 2006. 32p. (J). (978-0-9790920-1-5(9)) MoonRattles.
Menten, Ted, jt. illus. see Denslow, W. W.
Mentis, Anastassios, photos by. Fiesta Latina: Fabulous Food for Sizzling Parties. Palomino, Rafael. 2006. (ENG., 144p. (gr. 8-17). 19.95 (978-0-8118-4410-9(2)) Chronicle Bks. LLC.
Menzel, Peter, photos by. What the World Eats. Menzel, Peter. D'Aluisio, Faith. 2008. (ENG., 160p. (YA). (gr. 1-4). 22.99 (978-1-58246-246-2(1), Tricycle Pr.) Ten Speed Pr.
Meppem, William, photos by. A Beautiful Bowl of Soup: The Best Vegetarian Recipes. Mitchell, Paulette. 2004. (ENG., 168p. (gr. 8-17). pap. 19.95 (978-0-8118-3528-2(6)) Chronicle Bks. LLC.
—The Glorious Soups & Stews of Italy. Marchetti, Domenica. 2006. (ENG., 168p. (gr. 8-17). pap. 19.95 (978-0-8118-4817-6(5)) Chronicle Bks. LLC.
Meppem, William & Manville, Ron, photos by. Luscious Chocolate Desserts. Longbotham, Lori. 2004. (ENG., 144p. (gr. 8-17). 19.95 (978-0-8118-3516-9(2)) Chronicle Bks. LLC.
Mercado, Jorge. Chicken Little. Sommer, Carl. 2014. (Sommer-Time Story Classics Ser.). (ENG.). 32p. (J). (gr. k-4). 16.95 (978-1-57537-076-7(X)) Advance Publishing, Inc.
—Divide to Conquer. Sommer, Carl & Aesop. 2009. (Quest for Success Ser.). (ENG.). 40p. (YA). pap. 4.95 (978-1-57537-275-4(4)); lib. bdg. 12.95 (978-1-57537-250-1(9)) Advance Publishing, Inc.
—Divide to Conquer(Divide y Venceras) Sommer, Carl & Aesop. ed. 2009. (Quest for Success Bilingual Ser.). (ENG & SPA.). 72p. (YA). lib. bdg. 14.95 (978-1-57537-225-9(8)) Advance Publishing, Inc.
—The Lion & the Mouse. Sommer, Carl. 2014. (Sommer-Time Story Classics Ser.). (ENG.). 32p. (J). (gr. k-4). 16.95 (978-1-57537-082-8(4)) Advance Publishing, Inc.
—The Lion & the Three Bulls. Sommer, Carl. 2014. (Sommer-Time Story Classics Ser.). (ENG.). 32p. (J). (gr. k-4). 16.95 (978-1-57537-083-5(2)) Advance Publishing, Inc.
—The Tiny Giant. Sommer, Carl & Aesop. 2009. (Quest for Success Ser.). (ENG.). 40p. (YA). pap. 4.95 (978-1-57537-286-0(X)); lib. bdg. 12.95 (978-1-57537-261-7(4)) Advance Publishing, Inc.
—Tiny Giant(La Gigante Pequeña) Sommer, Carl & Aesop. ed. 2009. (Quest for Success Bilingual Ser.). (ENG & SPA.). 72p. (YA). lib. bdg. 14.95 (978-1-57537-236-5(3)) Advance Publishing, Inc.
Mercado, Yehudi. Pantalones, TX: Don't Chicken Out. Mercado, Yehudi. 2013. (ENG.). 120p. (J). (gr. -1). 19.95 (978-1-936393-90-9(5)) Boom Entertainment, Inc.
Merced, Eric, jt. illus. see Wong, Scott.
Merced, Zuleika, photos by. Mujer de Medio Siglo... Atesorndo Vivencias. Merced, Zuleika. l.t. ed. 2003. 100p. (YA). pap. (978-1-931481-42-7(3)) LiArt-Literature & Art.
mercedes cecilia & mercedes cecilia. Kusikiy A Child from Taquile, Peru. mercedes cecilia. 2011. (J). pap. 24.99 (978-0-9844079-9-6(5)) Keepers of Wisdom and Peace Bks.
mercedes cecilia, jt. illus. see mercedes cecilia.

Mercer, Lynn. PC Polly to the Rescue. Allan, Jayne. 2003. (ENG.). 32p. (J). (gr. 1-18). pap. 10.95 *(978-0-9535413-8-6(X))* lynx publishing GBR. Dist: Dufour Editions, Inc.

Mercer, Matthew. The Monster Run. Butterworth, MyLinda. Day, Linda S., ed. l.t. ed. 2004. 32p. (J). (gr. -1-3). 14.95 *(978-1-890905-23-1(2)*, Writers Collective, The) Day to Day Enterprises.

Merchant, Donna. Goblins Will Be Seen: When It's Time for Halloween. Donnell, Frances. Hebert, Catherine, ed. 2005. 38p. (J). 16.95 *(978-0-9770893-0-7(4))* 2 Donn Bks.

Meredith, Samantha. 50 Things to Do on Vacation. Clarke, Catriona. 2007. (Activity Cards Ser.). 50p. (J). (gr. 4-7). 9.99 *(978-0-7945-1704-5(8)*, Usborne) EDC Publishing.

Meredith, Samantha & Wyk, Hanri van. Weddings Sticker Color Book. ed. 2011. (First Sticker Coloring Bks). 20p. (J). pap. 5.99 *(978-0-7945-3108-9(3)*, Usborne) EDC Publishing.

Merer, Laura. Fuzzy Ducky's Birthday: A Touch-and-Feel Pop-up Book. 2005. 10p. (J). 8.95 *(978-1-58117-324-6(5)*, Intervisual/Piggy Toes) Bendon, Inc.

—My Five Senses. 2010. (My World Ser.). (ENG.). 24p. (J). (gr. -1-1). pap. 8.15 *(978-1-61533-029-4(1))* Windmill Bks.

—My Senses/Mis Sentidos. Rosa-Mendoza, Gladys. 2007. (English Spanish Foundations Ser.). (ENG & SPA.). 20p. (J). (gr. -1-k). bds. 6.95 *(978-1-931398-21-3(6))* Me+Mi Publishing.

Merer, Laura Blanken. My Five Senses. 2010. (My World Ser.). (ENG.). 24p. (J). (gr. -1-1). lib. bdg. 22.60 *(978-1-60754-948-2(4))* Windmill Bks.

Meret, Sasha. Walking the Bible: An Illustrated Journey for Kids Through the Greatest Stories Ever Told. Meret, Sasha, tr. Feiler, Bruce. ed. 2004. 112p. (J). (gr. 2-7). 16.99 *(978-0-06-051117-3(6))* HarperCollins Pubs.

Merino, Jesus. Absolute Power. Loeb, Jeph. rev. ed. 2006. (Superman/Batman Ser.: Vol. 3). (ENG.). 128p. pap. 12.99 *(978-1-4012-0714-4(6))* DC Comics.

Merino, Jose Luis. Puss in Boots (El Gato Con Botas) Perrault, Charles. 2004. (Bilingual Fairy Tales Ser.: BILI). (ENG & SPA.). 32p. (gr. -1-7). pap. 6.99 *(978-0-8118-3924-2(9))* Chronicle Bks. LLC.

Merkel, Joe F. Evil Comes in Pairs. Egan, Kate. 2009. (Spider-Man Ser.). 64p. (J). (gr. 2-5). pap. 4.99 *(978-0-06-162625-8(2)*, HarperFestival) HarperCollins Pubs.

Merkel, Joe F. & Sazaklis, John. Surf's Up. Rao, Lisa. 2007. (Surf's Up Ser.). 32p. (J). (gr. -1-2). 4.99 *(978-0-06-115335-8(4)*, Harper Entertainment) HarperCollins Pubs.

Merker, Gerold, photos by. Zonata: The California Mountain Kingsnake. Mulks, Mitchell. 2004. 64p. pap. 15.95 *(978-0-9760770-0-8(0))* LM Digital.

Merkin, Richard. Leagues Apart: The Men & Times of the Negro Baseball Leagues. Ritter, Lawrence S. 2004. 35p. (J). (gr. k-4). reprint ed. pap. 12.00 *(978-0-7567-7714-2(3))* DIANE Publishing Co.

Merola, Caroline. Me in the Middle, 1 vol. Machado, Ana Maria. Unger, David, tr. from POR. 2003. (ENG.). 112p. (J). (gr. 3-6). pap. 4.95 *(978-0-88899-467-7(2))* Groundwood Bks. CAN. Dist: Perseus-PGW.

Merola, Caroline. Toni Biscotti's Magic Trick. Merola, Caroline. Cummins, Sarah, tr. from FRE. 2006. (Formac First Novels Ser.: 60). (ENG.). 64p. (J). (gr. 2-5). 14.95 *(978-0-88780-719-0(4))*; 4.95 *(978-0-88780-715-2(1))* Formac Publishing Co., Ltd. CAN. Dist: Casemate Pubs. & Bk. Distributors, LLC.

—La Trahison de Laurent Lareau. Merola, Caroline. 2003. (Premier Roman Ser.). (FRE.). 64p. (J). (gr. 1-4). pap. *(978-2-89021-645-7(4))* Diffusion du livre Mirabel (DLM).

Merola, Caroline. Jesus: A Story of Love. Merola, Caroline, tr. Dumont, C. & Lacoursiere, Suzanne. 2003. 32p. (J). mass mkt. 5.95 *(978-0-8198-3977-0(9)*, 332-153) Pauline Bks. & Media.

Merola, Marcelo & Nichx. The Chameleon Chronicles, Vol. 1. Leiter, Andrew S. 2005. (YA). per. 21.95 *(978-0-9767076-0-8(8))* Empowered Entertainment.

Merrell, David. Absolutely Lucy #6: Thanks to Lucy. Cooper, Ilene. 2013. (Stepping Stone Book(TM) Ser.). (ENG.). 112p. (J). (gr. 1-4). 4.99 *(978-0-375-86998-3(0))*; lib. bdg. 12.99 *(978-0-375-96998-0(5))* Random Hse. Children's Bks. (Random Hse. Bks. for Young Readers).

—The Fortress of the Treasure Queen. Abbott, Tony. 2004. (Secrets of Droon Ser.: No. 23). 115p. (J). lib. bdg. 15.38 *(978-1-4242-0312-3(0))* Fitzgerald Bks.

—Look at Lucy! Cooper, Ilene. 2009. (Stepping Stone Book(TM) Ser.: No. 3). (ENG.). 112p. (J). (gr. 1-4). 4.99 *(978-0-375-85558-0(0)*, Random Hse. Bks. for Young Readers) Random Hse. Children's Bks.

—Lucy on the Ball. Cooper, Ilene. 2011. (Stepping Stone Book(TM) Ser.). (ENG.). 112p. (J). (gr. 1-4). 4.99 *(978-0-375-85559-7(9)*, Random Hse. Bks. for Young Readers) Random Hse. Children's Bks.

—Lucy's Tricks & Treats. Cooper, Ilene. 2012. (Stepping Stone Book(TM) Ser.). (ENG.). 112p. (J). (gr. 1-4). 4.99 *(978-0-375-86997-6(2)*, Random Hse. Bks. for Young Readers) Random Hse. Children's Bks.

—The Riddle of Zorfendorf Castle. Abbott, Tony. 2005. (Secrets of Droon Ser.: No. 25). 124p. (J). lib. bdg. 15.38 *(978-1-4242-0310-9(4))* Fitzgerald Bks.

Merrell, Patrick & Schuna, Sam. Ogre Drool: 36 Tear-Off Placemats - Puzzles, Mazes, Brainteasers, Weird Facts, Jokes, & More! Bathroom Readers' Institute Staff. 2014. (ENG.). 72p. (gr. k-4). pap. 10.95 *(978-1-62686-070-4(X)*, Portable Pr.) Baker & Taylor Publishing Group.

—Scrambled Brains: 36 Tear-Off Placemats - Puzzles, Mazes, Brainteasers, Weird Facts, Jokes, & More! Bathroom Readers' Institute Staff. 2014. (ENG.). 72p. (gr. k-4). pap. 10.95 *(978-1-62686-039-1(4)*, Portable Pr.) Baker & Taylor Publishing Group.

Merrell, Vernon R. Wilbur's Great Adventure. Hilderbrandt, Sandra June. 2011. 32p. (J). 19.95 *(978-1-59649-587-6(1))* Whispering Pine Pr. International, Inc.

—Wilbur's Great Adventure. Hilderbrandt, Sandra June. Whispering Pine Press International, Inc. Staff, ed. 2011. (ENG.). 32p. (J). per. 12.95 *(978-1-59434-312-4(8))* Whispering Pine Pr. International, Inc.

Merrifield, Monarca. Inch Worm Inch Worm. Kayaalp, Suzan. 2013. 20p. pap. 12.95 *(978-1-62838-072-9(1))* Page Publishing Inc.

Merrill, Frank T. Boy Scouts in the White Mountains: the Story of a Long Hike. Eaton, Walter Prichard. 2006. (ENG.). 316p. per. 30.95 *(978-1-4286-4117-4(3))* Kessinger Publishing, LLC.

Merriman, Christi. The Wish: Johnny's Story. Bernal, Sandra Marie. 2011. 48p. pap. 24.95 *(978-1-4560-4934-8(8))* America Star Bks.

Merriman, Lisa P. Diabetes: The Ultimate Teen Guide. Moran, Katherine J. 2006. (It Happened to Me Ser.: 7). (ENG.). 192p. (gr. 8-12). per. 20.00 *(978-0-8108-5642-4(5))* Scarecrow Pr., Inc.

Merriman, Rachel. The Story of Me: A Girl's Journal. 2008. (ENG.). 144p. (J). (gr. 4-7). *(978-1-84597-624-8(X))* CICO Bks.

Merrison, Stacy. Paddle Tail. LeGrand, Hank, 3rd. l.t. ed. 2004. 63p. (J). per. 7.95 *(978-1-59466-020-7(4)*, Growing Years) Port Town Publishing.

Merritt, Kate. Indestructibles: Baby Babble. 2012. (Indestructibles Ser.). (ENG.). 12p. (J). (gr. k — 1). pap. 5.95 *(978-0-7611-6880-5(X)*, 16880) Workman Publishing Co., Inc.

—Indestructibles: Baby Faces. 2012. (Indestructibles Ser.). (ENG.). 12p. (J). (gr. k — 1). pap. 5.95 *(978-0-7611-6881-2(8)*, 16881) Workman Publishing Co., Inc.

—Indestructibles: Baby Night-Night. Pixton, Amy. 2014. (Indestructibles Ser.). (ENG.). 12p. (J). pap. 5.95 *(978-0-7611-8182-8(2)*, 18182) Workman Publishing Co., Inc.

—Indestructibles: Baby Peekaboo. Pixton, Amy. 2014. (Indestructibles Ser.). (ENG.). 12p. (J). pap. 5.95 *(978-0-7611-8181-1(4)*, 18181) Workman Publishing Co., Inc.

Merry, Alex. Jasper & the Magpie: Enjoying Special Interests Together. Mayfield, Dan. 2014. (ENG.). 36p. *(978-1-84905-579-6(3))* Kingsley, Jessica Ltd.

Merryweather, Jack. Kit Carson. Beals, Frank Lee. 2011. 194p. 42.95 *(978-1-258-08971-9(8))* Literary Licensing, LLC.

Mertins, Lisa. Jimmy Finds His Voice. Doti, James. 2013. (J). 14.95 *(978-1-935204-47-3(5)*, Jabberwocky Bks., Inc.) Hillcrest Publishing Group, Inc.

Merveille, David. Juke Box. Merveille, David. 2008. (ENG.). 48p. (J). (gr. 4-7). 9.99 *(978-1-933605-72-2(3))* Kane Miller.

Merwin, Decie. Happy Little Family. Caudill, Rebecca. 2004. 107p. (J). pap. 10.95 *(978-1-883937-72-0(8))* Bethlehem Bks.

—Schoolhouse in the Woods. Caudill, Rebecca. l.t. ed. 2004. (Fairchild Family Story Ser.: Bk. 2). 130p. (J). pap. 10.95 *(978-1-883937-80-5(9))* Bethlehem Bks.

—Schoolroom in the Parlor. Caudill, Rebecca. l.t. ed. 2005. (Fairchild Family Story Ser.). 145p. (J). (gr. 3-7). pap. 11.95 *(978-1-883937-82-9(5))* Bethlehem Bks.

—Up & down the River. Caudill, Rebecca. 2005. 143p. (J). (gr. -1-17). pap. 11.95 *(978-1-883937-81-2(7))* Bethlehem Bks.

Merz, Bruno. My Friend the Weather Monster. Smallman, Steve. 2012. (Storytime Ser.). (ENG.). 24p. (J). (gr. -1-1). 15.99 *(978-1-60992-234-4(4))* QEB Publishing Inc.

Meschenmoser, Sebastian. Learning to Fly. Meschenmoser, Sebastian. 2011. (ENG.). (J). pap. 5.99 *(978-1-935279-99-0(8))* Kane Miller.

Meschenmoser, Sebastian. Waiting for Winter. Meschenmoser, Sebastian. 2015. (ENG.). 58p. (J). (gr. k-3). 10.99 ***(978-1-61067-435-5(9))*** Kane Miller.

Meschenmoser, Sebastian. 3 Wishes for Pugman. Meschenmoser, Sebastian. 2012. (ENG.). 44p. (J). (gr. k-2). 22.99 *(978-0-9806070-9-3(4))* Wilkins Farago Pty. Ltd. AUS. Dist: Independent Pubs. Group.

Meschini, Leonardo. How to Draw Amazing Animals, 1 vol. McCurry, Kristen. 2013. (Smithsonian Drawing Bks.). (ENG.). 64p. (gr. 3-4). pap. 7.19 *(978-1-62065-726-3(0))*; pap. 41.70 *(978-1-62065-727-0(9))*; lib. bdg. 33.32 *(978-1-4296-9939-6(6))* Capstone Pr., Inc.

—The Prince & the Sphinx, 1 vol. 2012. (Egyptian Myths Ser.). (ENG.). 32p. (gr. 3-4). pap. 7.95 *(978-1-4048-7242-4(6))*; lib. bdg. 27.99 *(978-1-4048-7149-6(7))* Picture Window Bks. (Nonfiction Picture Bks.).

Meschini, Leonardo & Osterhold, Jared. Smithsonian Drawing Books. McCurry, Kristen. 2012. (Smithsonian Drawing Bks.). (ENG.). 64p. (gr. 3-4). pap. 13.90 *(978-1-62065-730-0(9))* Capstone Pr., Inc.

Meschini, Leonardo, jt. illus. see Osterhold, Jared.

Meserve, Jessica. Daisy Dawson & the Big Freeze. Voake, Steve. (Daisy Dawson Ser.). (ENG.). 96p. (J). (gr. 1-4). 2011. pap. 5.99 *(978-0-7636-5627-0(5))*; 2010. 14.99 *(978-0-7636-4729-2(2))* Candlewick Pr.

—Daisy Dawson & the Secret Pond. Voake, Steve. (Daisy Dawson Ser.: 2). (ENG.). 96p. (J). (gr. 1-4). 2010. pap. 5.99 *(978-0-7636-4730-8(6))*; 2009. 14.99 *(978-0-7636-4009-5(3))* Candlewick Pr.

—Daisy Dawson at the Beach. Voake, Steve. (Daisy Dawson Ser.: 4). (ENG.). (J). (gr. 1-4). 2012. 96p. pap. 5.99 *(978-0-7636-5946-2(0))*; 2011. 87p. 14.99 *(978-0-7636-5306-4(3))* Candlewick Pr.

—Daisy Dawson Is on Her Way! Voake, Steve. 2008. (Daisy Dawson Ser.: 1). (ENG.). 112p. (J). (gr. 1-4). 14.99 *(978-0-7636-3740-8(8))* Candlewick Pr.

—Daisy Dawson Is on Her Way! Voake, Steve. 2009. (Daisy Dawson Ser.: 1). (ENG.). 112p. (J). (gr. 1-4). pap. 5.99 *(978-0-7636-4294-5(0))* Candlewick Pr.

—Daisy Dawson on the Farm. Voake, Steve. 2012. (Daisy Dawson Ser.: 5). (ENG.). 96p. (J). (gr. 1-4). 14.99 *(978-0-7636-5882-3(0))* Candlewick Pr.

—Daisy Dawson on the Farm. Voake, Steve. 2013. (Daisy Dawson Ser.). (ENG.). 96p. (J). (gr. 1-4). pap. 5.99 *(978-0-7636-6340-7(9))* Candlewick Pr.

—Dibujemos Juntos. Thebo, Mimi. rev. ed. 2006. (Castillo de la Lectura Blanca Ser.). (ENG.). 64p. (J). (gr. k-2). pap. 6.95 *(978-970-20-0849-1(2))* Castillo, Ediciones, S. A. de C. V. MEX. Dist: Macmillan.

—Misty. Dencer, Christine. 2015. (Stanley & Me Ser.: 1). (ENG.). 34p. (J). 12.95 *(978-1-927018-59-0(5))* Simply Read Bks. CAN. Dist: Ingram Pub. Services.

—One Busy Day: A Story for Big Brothers & Sisters. Schaefer, Lola M. 2014. (ENG.). 40p. (J). (gr. -1-k). 16.99 *(978-1-4231-7112-6(8))* Hyperion Bks. for Children.

—One Special Day. Schaefer, Lola. 2012. (Story for Big Brothers & Sisters Ser.). (ENG.). 40p. (J). (gr. -1-k). 16.99 *(978-1-4231-3760-3(4))* Hyperion Pr.

Meserve, Jessica. Bedtime Without Arthur. Meserve, Jessica. 2010. (ENG.). 32p. (J). (gr. -1-3). 16.95 *(978-0-7613-5497-0(2))* Lerner Publishing Group.

Meserve, Jessica & Jones, Noah Z. Magic at the Bed & Biscuit. Carris, Joan Davenport. 2011. (Daisy Dawson Ser.). (ENG.). 128p. (J). (gr. 1-4). 15.99 *(978-0-7636-4306-5(8))* Candlewick Pr.

Meshon, Aaron. Take Me Out to the Yakyu. Meshon, Aaron. 2013. (ENG.). 40p. (J). (gr. -1-3). 16.99 *(978-1-4424-4177-4(1)*, Atheneum Bks. for Young Readers) Simon & Schuster Children's Publishing.

—Tools Rule! Meshon, Aaron. 2014. (ENG.). 40p. (J). (gr. -1-3). 17.99 *(978-1-4424-9601-9(0)*, Atheneum Bks. for Young Readers) Simon & Schuster Children's Publishing.

Mesquita, Camila. Elecciones Que Brillan. Camossa, Silvia. 2004. 64p. pap. 8.95 *(978-85-7416-193-8(4))* Callis Editora Ltda BRA. Dist: Independent Pubs. Group.

—Frida Kahlo. Lenero, Carmen. 2004. (Niñez de...Ser.). 24p. pap. 6.95 *(978-85-7416-216-4(7))* Callis Editora Ltda BRA. Dist: Independent Pubs. Group.

Messenger, Norman. Imagine. Messenger, Norman. 2005. (ENG.). 32p. (J). (gr. k-12). 17.99 *(978-0-7636-2757-7(7))* Candlewick Pr.

—The Land of Neverbelieve. Messenger, Norman. 2012. (ENG.). 32p. (J). (gr. 2-5). 17.99 *(978-0-7636-6021-5(3))* Candlewick Pr.

Messer, Celia. All Across Ohio: A Bird's Eye View with Worthington Cardinal, 7 bks. Gray, Susan. 2003. 24p. (J). 7.95 *(978-0-9742862-0-4(6))* Two's Company.

—Plain & Simple: A Bird's Eye View with Worthington Cardinal, 7 bks. Gray, Susan. 2003. 24p. (J). 7.95 *(978-0-9742862-4-2(9))* Two's Company.

—A River Ride: A Bird's Eye View with Worthington Cardinal, 7 bks. Gray, Susan. 2003. 24p. (J). 7.95 *(978-0-9742862-3-5(0))* Two's Company.

—Wagon-O! A Bird's Eye View with Worthington Cardinal, 7 bks. Gray, Susan. 2003. 24p. (J). 7.95 *(978-0-9742862-2-8(2))* Two's Company.

—We Can Fly! A Bird's Eye View with Worthington Cardinal, 7 bks. Gray, Susan. 2003. 24p. (J). 7.95 *(978-0-9742862-1-1(4))* Two's Company.

Messer, Celia, jt. illus. see Gray, Susan.

Messer, Corey. Cat, Cat, Feral Cat. Wolf, Clarissa. 2009. 28p. pap. 9.99 *(978-1-935105-26-8(4))* Avid Readers Publishing Group.

Messer, Jennifer K. Hoosier Heart. Messer, Luke. 2006. 32p. (J). 16.95 *(978-0-9786799-1-0(1))* Eva Publishing, LLC.

Messer, Jon. New York: The Empire State. Facklam, Margery & Thomas, Peggy. 2007. (ENG.). 40p. (J). (gr. 2-5). per. 7.95 *(978-1-57091-661-8(6))* Charlesbridge Publishing, Inc.

Messersmith, Patrick. Henrietta King: Rancher & Philanthropist. Alter, Judy. 2005. (Stars of Texas Ser.: 1). (ENG.). 72p. (gr. 4-7). 17.95 *(978-1-880510-98-8(7))* State Hse. Pr.

—Martín de León: Tejano Empresario. Alter, Judy. 2007. (Stars of Texas Ser.: 4). (ENG.). 72p. (gr. 4-7). 14.95 *(978-1-933337-08-1(7))* State Hse. Pr.

—Mirabeau B. Lamar: Second President of Texas. Alter, Judy. 2005. (Stars of Texas Ser.: 2). (ENG.). 72p. (gr. 4-7). 17.95 *(978-1-880510-97-1(9))* State Hse. Pr.

—Miriam Ma Ferguson: First Woman Governor of Texas. Alter, Judy. 2006. (Stars of Texas Ser.: 3). (ENG.). 72p. (gr. 4-7). 17.95 *(978-1-933337-01-2(X))* State Hse. Pr.

Messina, Lilli. Alice the Armadillo: A Tale of Self Discovery. Law, Felicia. 2010. (Animal Fair Values Ser.). 32p. (J). (gr. -1-3). pap. 10.55 *(978-1-60754-809-6(7))*; lib. bdg. 22.60 *(978-1-60754-805-8(4))* Windmill Bks.

—Florence the Flamingo: A Tale of Pride. Law, Felicia. 2010. (Animal Fair Values Ser.). (ENG.). 32p. (J). (gr. -1-3). pap. 10.55 *(978-1-60754-907-9(7))*; lib. bdg. 22.60 *(978-1-60754-901-7(8))* Windmill Bks.

—Limpopo the Lion: A Tale of Laziness & Lethargy. Law, Felicia. 2010. (Animal Fair Values Ser.). 32p. (J). (gr. -1-3). pap. 10.55 *(978-1-60754-808-9(9))*; lib. bdg. 22.60 *(978-1-60754-804-1(6))* Windmill Bks.

—Zanzibar the Zebra: A Tale of Individuality. Law, Felicia. 2010. (Animal Fair Values Ser.). 32p. (J). (gr. -1-3). pap. 10.55 *(978-1-60754-807-2(0))*; lib. bdg. 22.60 *(978-1-60754-803-4(8))* Windmill Bks.

Messina, Linda. FirstFires. Lightner, Laura. 2008. 27p. (J). 31.99 *(978-1-4363-4542-2(1))* Xlibris Corp.

Messing, Dave. How Different Is Good: Nick the Wise Old Cat. Sicks, Linda. 2010. (Importance of Friendship Ser.). 40p. (J). 18.95 *(978-1-936193-04-2(3))* Nick The Cat, LLC.

—Monty the Menace: Understanding Differences. Baum, Lonna. 2012. (ENG.). 32p. (J). 16.95 *(978-0-9839373-0-2(3))* Baum & Baum, LLC.

—Nick the Wise Old Cat: How I Found My Family. Sicks, Linda. 2010. (ENG.). 40p. (J). 18.95 *(978-1-936193-00-4(0))* Nick The Cat, LLC.

—Nick the Wise Old Cat How I Found My Family. Sicks, Linda. 2009. 32p. (J). 17.95 *(978-1-934878-63-7(4))* Mascot Bks., Inc.

—Nick's Holiday Celebration: Nick the Wise Old Cat. Sicks, Linda. 2010. (Importance of Family Ser.). 40p. (J). 18.95 *(978-1-936193-05-9(1))* Nick The Cat, LLC.

Messing, David. As-Tu Rempli un Seau Aujourd'hui? Un Guide du Bonheur Quotidien Pour Enfants. McCloud, Carol. 2012. (ENG & FRE.). 32p. (J). pap. 9.95 *(978-1-933916-92-7(3)*, Ferne Pr.) Nelson Publishing & Marketing.

—Fill a Bucket: A Guide to Daily Happiness for Young Children. McCloud, Carol et al. 2008. (ENG.). 24p. pap. 8.95 *(978-1-933916-28-6(1))* Nelson Publishing & Marketing.

—Has Llenado una Cubeta Hoy? Una Guia Diaria de Felicidades para Nios. McCloud, Carol. 2012. (ENG & SPA.). 32p. (J). pap. 9.95 *(978-1-933916-91-0(5)*, Ferne Pr.) Nelson Publishing & Marketing.

—Have You Filled a Bucket Today? A Guide to Daily Happiness for Kids. McCloud, Carol. (ENG.). 32p. 2007. 17.95 *(978-1-933916-16-3(8))*; 2006. (J). (gr. -1-3). pap. 9.95 *(978-0-9785075-1-0(7)*, Ferne Pr.) Nelson Publishing & Marketing.

—Myrtle the Hurdler: And Her Pink & Purple Polka-Dotted Girdle. Dillon-Butler, Marybeth. 2005. (ENG.). 32p. (J). (gr. -1-2). pap. 11.95 *(978-0-9785075-9-6(2)*, Ferne Pr.) Nelson Publishing & Marketing.

Messner, Dennis. Moopy el Monstruo Subterráneo/Moopy the Underground Monster. Meister, Cari. Heck, Claudia M., tr. from ENG. 2012. (Los Amigos Monstruos/Monster Friends Ser.). (SPA & MUL.). 32p. (gr. 2-3). lib. bdg. 21.32 *(978-1-4342-3785-9(0)*, Bilingual Stone Arch Readers) Stone Arch Bks.

—Moopy on the Beach, 1 vol. Meister, Cari. 2010. (Monster Friends Ser.). (ENG.). 32p. (gr. 2-3). pap. 6.25 *(978-1-4342-2304-3(3))*; lib. bdg. 21.32 *(978-1-4342-1874-2(0))* Stone Arch Bks.

—Moopy the Underground Monster, 1 vol. Meister, Cari. 2009. (Monster Friends Ser.). (ENG.). 32p. (gr. 2-3). 21.32 *(978-1-4342-1630-4(6))*; pap. 6.25 *(978-1-4342-1745-5(0))* Stone Arch Bks.

—Ora - El Monstruo Marino. Meister, Cari. Heck, Claudia M., tr. from ENG. 2012. (Los Amigos Monstruos/Monster Friends Ser.).Tr. of Ora - The Sea Monster. (MUL & SPA.). 32p. (gr. 2-3). lib. bdg. 21.32 *(978-1-4342-3784-2(2)*, Bilingual Stone Arch Readers) Stone Arch Bks.

—Ora - The Sea Monster. Meister, Cari. 2009. (Monster Friends Ser.). (ENG.). 32p. (gr. 2-3). pap. 6.25 *(978-1-4342-1746-2(9))* Stone Arch Bks.

—Ora at the Monster Contest, 1 vol. Meister, Cari. 2010. (Monster Friends Ser.). (ENG.). 32p. (gr. 2-3). pap. 6.25 *(978-1-4342-2305-0(1))*; lib. bdg. 21.32 *(978-1-4342-1875-9(9))* Stone Arch Bks.

—Ora the Sea Monster. Meister, Cari. 2009. (Monster Friends Ser.). (ENG.). 32p. (gr. 2-3). 21.32 *(978-1-4342-1631-1(4))* Stone Arch Bks.

—Snorp: The City Monster. Meister, Cari. 2009. (Monster Friends Ser.). (ENG.). 32p. (gr. 2-3). 21.32 *(978-1-4342-1632-8(2))*; pap. 6.25 *(978-1-4342-1747-9(7))* Stone Arch Bks.

—Snorp el Monstruo de la Ciudad/Snorp the City Monster, 1 vol. Meister, Cari. Heck, Claudia M., tr. from ENG. 2012. (Los Amigos Monstruos/Monster Friends Ser.). (MUL & SPA.). 32p. (gr. 2-3). lib. bdg. 21.32 *(978-1-4342-3783-5(4)*, Bilingual Stone Arch Readers) Stone Arch Bks.

—Snorp on the Slopes, 1 vol. Meister, Cari. 2010. (Monster Friends Ser.). (ENG.). 32p. (gr. 2-3). pap. 6.25 *(978-1-4342-2306-7(X))*; lib. bdg. 21.32 *(978-1-4342-1873-5(2))* Stone Arch Bks.

—Three Claws in the City, 1 vol. Meister, Cari. 2010. (Monster Friends Ser.). (ENG.). 32p. (gr. 2-3). pap. 6.25 *(978-1-4342-2307-4(8))*; lib. bdg. 21.32 *(978-1-4342-1872-8(4))* Stone Arch Bks.

—Three Claws the Mountain Monster. Meister, Cari. 2009. (Monster Friends Ser.). (ENG.). 32p. (gr. 2-3). 21.32 *(978-1-4342-1633-5(0))*; pap. 6.25 *(978-1-4342-1748-6(5))* Stone Arch Bks.

Mesturini, C. Astronaut. Caviezel, Giovanni. 2012. (Little People Shape Bks.). (ENG.). 10p. (J). (gr. k-2). bds. 8.99 *(978-0-7641-6573-3(9))* Barron's Educational Series, Inc.

—Ballerina. Caviezel, Giovanni. (Mini People Shape Bks.). (ENG.). 10p. (J). 2011. bds. 5.99 *(978-0-7641-6436-1(8))*; 2010. bds. 7.99 *(978-0-7641-6417-0(1))* Barron's Educational Series, Inc.

—Builder. Caviezel, Giovanni. (Mini People Shape Bks.). (ENG.). (J). 2011. 10p. bds. 5.99 *(978-0-7641-6437-8(6))*; 2009. 12p. (gr. -1-2). bds. 10.99 *(978-0-7641-6193-3(8))* Barron's Educational Series, Inc.

—Cowboy. Caviezel, Giovanni. (Mini People Shape Bks.). (ENG.). (J). 2011. 10p. bds. 5.99 *(978-0-7641-6438-5(4))*; 2009. 12p. (gr. -1-2). bds. 10.99 *(978-0-7641-6191-9(1))* Barron's Educational Series, Inc.

—Farmer. Caviezel, Giovanni. 2011. (Mini People Shape Bks.). (ENG.). 10p. (J). bds. 5.99 *(978-0-7641-6439-2(2))* Barron's Educational Series, Inc.

—Fireman's Safety Hints. Caviezel, Giovanni. 2012. (Little People Shape Bks.). (ENG.). 10p. (J). (gr. k-2). bds. 8.99 *(978-0-7641-6594-8(1))* Barron's Educational Series, Inc.

—Little Snowman. Caviezel, Giovanni. 2014. (Mini People Shape Bks.). (ENG.). 10p. (J). (gr. -1-2). bds. 4.99 *(978-0-7641-6737-9(5))* Barron's Educational Series, Inc.

—Nurse. Caviezel, Giovanni. (Mini People Shape Bks.). (ENG.). 10p. (J). 2011. bds. 5.99 *(978-0-7641-6440-8(6))*; 2008. (gr. -1-2). bds. 10.99 *(978-0-7641-6105-6(9))* Barron's Educational Series, Inc.

—Pirates! Caviezel, Giovanni. 2011. (Mini People Shape Bks.). (ENG.). 10p. (J). bds. 5.99 *(978-0-7641-6441-5(4))* Barron's Educational Series, Inc.

—Princess. Caviezel, Giovanni. 2008. (Little People Shape Bks.). (ENG.). 10p. (J). (gr. k-2). bds. 10.99 *(978-0-7641-6103-2(2))* Barron's Educational Series, Inc.

Mesturini, C., jt. illus. see Caviezel, Giovanni.

Mesturini, Cristina. Astronaut. Caviezel, Giovanni. 2009. (Mini People Shape Bks.). (ENG.). 12p. (J). (gr. -1-2). bds. 5.99 *(978-0-7641-6216-9(0))* Barron's Educational Series, Inc.

—Fairy. Caviezel, Giovanni. 2009. (Mini People Shape Bks.). (ENG.). 12p. (J). (gr. -1-2). bds. 5.99 *(978-0-7641-6218-3(7))* Barron's Educational Series, Inc.

—Little Elf. Caviezel, Giovanni. 2012. (Mini People Shape Bks.). (ENG.). 10p. (J). bds. 4.99 *(978-0-7641-6577-1(1))* Barron's Educational Series, Inc.
—My Own Human Body. Caviezel, Giovanni. 2012. (Little People Shape Bks.). (ENG.). 10p. (J). (gr. k-2). bds. 8.99 *(978-0-7641-6570-2(4))* Barron's Educational Series, Inc.
—Police Officer. Caviezel, Giovanni. 2009. (Mini People Shape Bks.). (ENG.). 12p. (J). (gr. -1-2). bds. 5.99 *(978-0-7641-6221-3(7))* Barron's Educational Series, Inc.
—Princess. Caviezel, Giovanni. 2009. (Mini People Shape Bks.). (ENG.). 12p. (J). (gr. -1-2). bds. 5.99 *(978-0-7641-6219-0(5))* Barron's Educational Series, Inc.
—Race Car Driver. Caviezel, Giovanni. 2009. (Mini People Shape Bks.). (ENG.). 12p. (J). (gr. -1-2). bds. 5.99 *(978-0-7641-6217-6(9))* Barron's Educational Series, Inc.
—Santa. Caviezel, Giovanni. 2012. (Mini People Shape Bks.). (ENG.). 10p. (J). bds. 4.99 *(978-0-7641-6578-8(X))* Barron's Educational Series, Inc.
Metcalf, Kristin. Emily Waits for Her Family. Zelaya, Carol. 2007. (Emily the Chickadee Ser.). 32p. (J). (gr. 2-3). 14.95 *(978-0-9796265-0-0(1))* Richlee Publishing.
Metcalf, Maggie. Franny & Mirus. Obray, C. J. 2011. (ENG.). 44p. pap. 11.99 *(978-1-4679-9330-2(1))* CreateSpace Independent Publishing Platform.
Metcalf, Paula. My Picture Encyclopedia. Phillips, Sarah. 2007. 64p. (J). (gr. k-2). *(978-1-84610-445-9(9))* Make Believe Ideas.
Metcalf, Tania. Gimme Five: Biblical Truths for Ages 9-12. Robinson, Ann. 2011. (ENG.). 54p. pap. 10.00 *(978-1-4538-6848-5(8))* CreateSpace Independent Publishing Platform.
Metola, Patricia. Hansel y Gretel (Colorin Colorado/That Is the End of the Story) Maestro, Pepe. 2009. (SPA.). 14p. (J). *(978-84-263-7179-9(5))* Vives, Luis Editorial (Edelvives).
Mets, Marilyn. Good-Bye Tonsils! Hatkoff, Craig & Hatkoff, Juliana Lee. 2004. (ENG.). 32p. (J). (gr. k-3). pap. 6.99 *(978-0-14-240133-0(1),* Puffin) Penguin Publishing Group.
Mets, Marilyn & Ledwon, Peter. Waiting for the Sun, 1 vol. Lohans, Alison. 2007. (ENG.). 32p. (YA). (gr. 8-12). per. 7.95 *(978-0-88995-358-1(9))* Red Deer Pr. CAN. Dist: Ingram Pub. Services.
Mets, Marilyn, jt. illus. see Ledwon, Peter.
Mettler, Joe. Don't eat your Broccoli! Morris, Lynn. 2007. 32p. (J). per. 6.95 *(978-0-9755548-2-1(4))* Log Cabin Bks.
Mettler, Rene. The Jungle. 2012. (ENG.). 36p. (J). (gr. -1-k). 12.99 *(978-1-85103-399-7(8))* Moonlight Publishing, Ltd. GBR. Dist: Independent Pubs. Group.
Mettler, René. Birds. Mettler, René. 2012. (ENG.). 38p. (J). (gr. -1-k). 12.99 *(978-1-85103-397-3(1))* Moonlight Publishing, Ltd. GBR. Dist: Independent Pubs. Group.
—Birds: Set of 6, 6, Set. Mettler, René. Harvey, Bev & Delafosse, Claude. 2006. (ENG.). 38p. (J). (gr. k-3). pap. 11.99 *(978-1-85103-107-8(3))* Moonlight Publishing, Ltd. GBR. Dist: Independent Pubs. Group.
—The Egg. Mettler, René. Mathews, Sarah. 2012. (ENG.). 34p. (J). (gr. -1-k). pap. 12.99 *(978-1-85103-380-5(7))* Moonlight Publishing, Ltd. GBR. Dist: Independent Pubs. Group.
—Jungle. Mettler, René. First Discovery Staff. 2006. (ENG.). 36p. (J). (gr. k-3). pap. 11.99 *(978-1-85103-183-2(9))* Moonlight Publishing, Ltd. GBR. Dist: Independent Pubs. Group.
Metu, jt. illus. see Lakes, Lofton.
Metzger, Jan. Slick 'n Slide. Lambert, Joyce. 2008. 36p. 9.95 *(978-0-9801146-0-7(8))* Lamweg Publishing.
Metzger, Steve & Antonini, Gabriele. Huggapotamus. 2011. (J). *(978-0-545-34352-7(6))* Scholastic, Inc.
Metzger, Wolfgang. Los Bomberos. Caballero, D., tr. 2006. (Junior (Silver Dolphin) Ser.). (SPA.). 16p. (J). (gr. 5). 9.95 *(978-970-718-344-5(6))* Baker & Taylor Publishing Group.
Meurer, Caleb. And the Winner Is... Miglis, Jenny. ed. 2005. (SpongeBob SquarePants Ser.: 4). 22p. (J). lib. bdg. 15.00 *(978-1-59054-824-0(8))* Fitzgerald Bks.
—And the Winner Is... Miglis, Jenny. 2004. (SpongeBob SquarePants Ser.). (ENG.). 24p. (J). pap. 3.99 *(978-0-689-86327-1(6),* Simon Spotlight/Nickelodeon) Simon Spotlight/Nickelodeon.
—Fly Like a Fish. Golden Books Staff. 2003. (Super Coloring Time Ser.). (ENG.). 64p. (J). (gr. -1-2). pap. 2.99 *(978-0-307-10124-2(X),* Golden Bks.) Random Hse. Children's Bks.
—Mr. FancyPants! Golden Books Staff & Smith, Geof. 2009. (Little Golden Book Ser.). (ENG.). 24p. (J). (gr. -1-2). 3.99 *(978-0-375-85121-6(6),* Golden Bks.) Random Hse. Children's Bks.
Meurer, Caleb. Star Wars: a New Hope (Star Wars) Smith, Geof. 2015. (Little Golden Book Ser.). (ENG.). 24p. (J). (-k). 4.99 ***(978-0-7364-3538-3(7),*** Golden Bks.) Random Hse. Children's Bks.
Meurer, Caleb. Stick Together! Golden Books Staff. 2007. (Stickerific Ser.). (ENG.). 32p. (J). (gr. -1-2). pap. 2.99 *(978-0-375-83485-1(0),* Golden Bks.) Random Hse. Children's Bks.
—Triceratops for Lunch. Golden Books Staff. 2010. (Little Golden Book Ser.). (ENG.). 24p. (J). (gr. -1-2). 3.99 *(978-0-375-86151-2(3),* Golden Bks.) Random Hse. Children's Bks.
—Winter Lights (Dinosaur Train) Posner-Sanchez, Andrea. 2013. (Little Golden Book Ser.). (ENG.). 24p. (J). (-k). 3.99 *(978-0-449-81658-5(3),* Golden Bks.) Random Hse. Children's Bks.
Meurer, Caleb, jt. illus. see Golden Books.
Meurer, Caleb, jt. illus. see Random House Staff.
Mey. Ana y la Maldicion de Las Pecas. Schuff, Nicolás & Fraticelli, Damin. 2013. (Coleccion Heroinas Ser.).Tr. of Ana & the Cursed Freckles. (SPA.). 96p. (J). (gr. 4-7). pap. *(978-987-1710-84-3(4))* Ediciones Urano S. A.
Meyer, Alison. Berc's Inner Voice. Ragan, Lyn. 2013. 24p. pap. 14.95 *(978-0-9860205-3-7(2))* HourGlass Publishing.
Meyer, Ashley M. Forget the Vet. Lynn, Elizabeth B. 2012. 32p. 24.95 *(978-1-936688-21-0(2))* AKA:yoLa.
Meyer, Chloe. The Butterfly & the Bee. Hurth, Barbi. 2008. 32p. pap. 24.95 *(978-1-60610-226-8(5))* America Star Bks.
Meyer-Hullmann, Kerstin. Das Grundschulwoerterbuch. (Duden Ser.). (GER.). 224p. (J). *(978-3-411-06061-0(1))* Bibliographisches Institut & F. A. Brockhaus AG DEU. Dist: International Bk. Import Service, Inc.
—Rechtschreibtraining fuer die 3. Klasse. (Duden-Lernminuten Ser.). (GER.). 44p. (J). wbk. ed. *(978-3-411-70801-7(8))* Bibliographisches Institut & F. A. Brockhaus AG DEU. Dist: International Bk. Import Service, Inc.
—Rechtschreibtraining fuer die 3. und 4. Klasse. (Duden-Lernminuten Ser.). (GER.). 44p. (J). wbk. ed. *(978-3-411-70811-6(5))* Bibliographisches Institut & F. A. Brockhaus AG DEU. Dist: International Bk. Import Service, Inc.
Meyer, Jane G. & Gannon, Ned. The Woman & the Wheat. Meyer, Jane G. & Gannon, Ned. 2009. 32p. (J). 18.00 *(978-0-88141-059-4(4))* St. Vladimir's Seminary Pr.
Meyer, Jean. Helen Keller, Girl of Courage. Sabin, Francene & Mattern, Joanne. 2006. 56p. (J). *(978-0-439-66043-3(2))* Scholastic, Inc.
Meyer, Jeff. You've Got a Friend. Eareckson Tada, Joni. 2004. 31p. (gr. -1-3). 14.99 *(978-1-58134-060-0(5))* Crossway.
Meyer, Karen. Halfback Attack. Christopher, Matt. ed. 2005. (Sports Classics II Ser.). 104p. (J). lib. bdg. 15.00 *(978-1-59054-752-6(7))* Fitzgerald Bks.
Meyer, Ken, Jr. Lucky Lionel. 2009. (J). *(978-1-60108-020-2(4))* Red Cygnet Pr.
Meyer, Kerry. Nursery Rhymes Touchy-Feely Board Book. Watt, Fiona. 2010. (Luxury Touchy-Feely Board Bks). 10p. (J). bds. 15.99 *(978-0-7945-2662-7(4),* Usborne) EDC Publishing.
Meyer, Kerstin. An Elk Dropped In. Steinhöfel, Andreas. Jaffa, Alisa, tr. from GER. 2006. (ENG.). 80p. (J). (gr. 1-5). 16.95 *(978-1-932425-80-2(2),* Lemniscaat) Boyds Mills Pr.
—Emma & the Blue Genie. Funke, Cornelia. Latsch, Oliver, tr. from GER. 2014. (ENG.). 96p. (J). (gr. 2-5). 9.99 *(978-0-385-37540-5(9),* Random Hse. Bks. for Young Readers) Random Hse. Children's Bks.
Meyer, Megan. The Great Adventures of Lamot the Liger. Meyer, Megan. 2010. (ENG.). 30p. 16.95 *(978-0-9830359-0-9(3))* Brosen Bks.
Meyer, Naama. Siddurchik: Prayer Book for Young Children. 2006. 32p. 12.95 *(978-965-229-328-2(8))* Gefen Publishing Hse., Ltd ISR. Dist: Gefen Bks.
Meyer, Nancy. Between Two Rivers: Stories from the Red Hills to the Gulf. Cerulean, Susan I. et al, eds. 2004. 352p. (YA). per. 21.95 *(978-0-9759339-0-9(6))* Red Hills Writers Project.
Meyer, Sarah. Detective Stephy Wephy Holmes in the Missing Cake. Rader, Josh. 2007. 36p. (J). (gr. -1-3). per. 14.99 *(978-1-59879-399-4(3))* Lifevest Publishing, Inc.
Meyer, Therese. La Petite Ballerine et Ses Amis les Cygnes (The Little Ballerina & Her Friends the Swans) Meyer, Therese. 2004. (FRE.). 52p. *(978-0-9750325-1-0(8))* Baby Swan.
Meyerhoff, Jill. How Many Are Here? Goldish, Meish. l.t. ed. 2005. (Sadlier Phonics Reading Program). 8p. (gr. -1-1). 23.00 net. *(978-0-8215-7344-0(6))* Sadlier, William H. Inc.
Meyerowitz, Rick. Paul Bunyan. Gleeson, Brian. 2004. (Rabbit Ears-A Classic Tale Ser.). 52p. (gr. k-5). 25.65 *(978-1-59197-767-4(3))* Spotlight.
Meyers, Haily. All Aboard California, 1 vol. Meyers, Haily. Meyers, Kevin. 2015. (ENG.). 22p. (J). bds. 9.99 ***(978-1-4236-4080-6(2))*** Gibbs Smith, Publisher.
—All Aboard NYC, 1 vol. Meyers, Haily. Meyers, Kevin. 2015. (ENG.). 22p. (J). bds. 9.99 ***(978-1-4236-4074-5(8))*** Gibbs Smith, Publisher.
—All Aboard Paris, 1 vol. Meyers, Haily. Meyers, Kevin. 2015. (ENG.). 22p. (J). bds. 9.99 ***(978-1-4236-4077-6(2))*** Gibbs Smith, Publisher.
Meyers, Jeff. Jason's First Day. Busic, Valerie. OI Foundation, ed. l.t. ed. 2004. 48p. per. 8.50 *(978-0-9642189-4-9(1))* Osteogenesis Imperfecta Foundation.
Meyers, Mark. The All-Star Joker. Kelly, David A. 2012. (Stepping Stone Book(TM) Ser.: Vol. 5). (ENG.). 112p. (J). (gr. 1-4). 4.99 *(978-0-375-86884-9(4));* lib. bdg. 12.99 *(978-0-375-96884-6(9))* Random Hse. Children's Bks. (Random Hse. Bks. for Young Readers).
—The All-Star Joker. Kelly, David A. ed. 2012. (Ballpark Mysteries Ser.: 5). lib. bdg. 14.75 *(978-0-606-26401-3(9),* Turtleback) Turtleback Bks.
—The Astro Outlaw. Kelly, David A. 2012. (Stepping Stone Book Ser.: No. 4). (ENG.). 112p. (J). (gr. 1-4). pap. 4.99 *(978-0-375-86883-2(6))* Random Hse., Inc.
—Ballpark Mysteries #10: the Rookie Blue Jay. Kelly, David A. 2015. (Stepping Stone Book(TM) Ser.). (ENG.). 112p. (J). (gr. 1-4). 4.99 *(978-0-385-37875-8(0),* Random Hse. Bks. for Young Readers) Random Hse. Children's Bks.
—Ballpark Mysteries #8: the Missing Marlin. Kelly, David A. 2014. (Stepping Stone Book(TM) Ser.). (ENG.). 112p. (J). (gr. 1-4). 4.99 *(978-0-307-97782-3(X),* Random Hse. Bks. for Young Readers) Random Hse. Children's Bks.
—Ballpark Mysteries #9: the Philly Fake. Kelly, David A. 2014. (Stepping Stone Book(TM) Ser.). (ENG.). 112p. (J). (gr. 1-4). 4.99 *(978-0-307-97785-4(4),* Random Hse. Bks. for Young Readers) Random Hse. Children's Bks.
—Counting Cows. Medlock-Adams, Michelle. 2010. 26p. (J). (gr. -1-k). 7.99 *(978-0-8249-1836-1(3),* Candy Cane Pr.) Ideals Pubns.
—The Fenway Foul-Up. Kelly, David A. 2011. (Stepping Stone Book(TM) Ser.: No. 1). (ENG.). 112p. (J). (gr. 1-4). pap. 4.99 *(978-0-375-86703-3(1))* Random Hse., Inc.
—Goldilocks Meets Desidero. Spetzler, Carl. 2011. 36p. pap. 16.86 *(978-1-4634-2684-2(4))* AuthorHouse.
—The L. A. Dodger. Kelly, David A. 2011. (Stepping Stone Book(TM) Ser.: No. 3). (ENG.). 112p. (J). (gr. 1-4). 4.99 *(978-0-375-86885-6(2),* Random Hse. Bks. for Young Readers) Random Hse. Children's Bks.
—The Pinstripe Ghost. Kelly, David A. 2011. (Stepping Stone Book Ser.: No. 2). (ENG.). 112p. (J). (gr. 1-4). 4.99 *(978-0-375-86704-0(X));* lib. bdg. 12.99 *(978-0-375-96704-7(4))* Random Hse. Children's Bks. (Random Hse. Bks. for Young Readers).
—The San Francisco Splash. Kelly, David A. 2013. (Stepping Stone Book Ser.). (ENG.). 112p. (J). (gr. 1-4). pap. 4.99 *(978-0-307-97779-3(X));* lib. bdg. 12.99 *(978-0-307-97780-9(3))* Random Hse., Inc.
—Stories to Make You Dream. Roozen, John. 2013. 120p. pap. 7.95 *(978-0-615-64557-5(7))* Windoggle.
—Take Me Out to the Ball Game. Norworth, Jack. 2011. 16p. (J). (gr. -1-k). bds. 10.99 *(978-0-8249-1852-1(5),* Candy Cane Pr.) Ideals Pubns.
—The Tiger Trouble. Kelly, David A. 2015. (Stepping Stone Book Ser.). (ENG.). 112p. (J). (gr. 1-4). pap. 4.99 *(978-0-385-37878-9(5))* Random Hse., Inc.
—Victricia Malicia: Book-Loving Buccaneer. Clickard, Carrie. 2012. (ENG.). 32p. (J). (gr. 2-4). 16.95 *(978-1-936261-12-3(X))* Flashlight Pr.
—The Wrigley Riddle. Kelly, David A. 2013. (Stepping Stone Book Ser.). (ENG.). 112p. (J). (gr. 1-4). pap. 4.99 *(978-0-307-97776-2(5))* Random Hse., Inc.
Meyers, Nancy. Operation: Oddball. Bankert, Lisa. 2007. 100p. per. 5.99 *(978-0-9795364-0-3(5))* Chowder Bay Bks.
—Planet Patrol: A Kids' Action Guide to Earth Care. Lorbiecki, Marybeth. 2005. (ENG.). 48p. (J). (gr. 4-7). 15.95 *(978-1-58728-514-1(2))* Cooper Square Publishing Llc.
Meyers, Nancy. Doodles 123. Meyers, Nancy. 2012. (Doodles Ser.). (ENG.). 64p. (J). (gr. k-5). pap. 7.95 *(978-1-61608-664-0(5),* 608664, Sky Pony Pr.) Skyhorse Publishing Co., Inc.
—Doodles ABC: Alphabet Fun with Dots to Join & Doodles to Do. Meyers, Nancy. 2012. (Doodles Ser.). (ENG.). 64p. (J). (gr. -1-1). pap. 7.95 *(978-1-61608-666-4(1),* 608666, Sky Pony Pr.) Skyhorse Publishing Co., Inc.
—Doodles Shapes. Meyers, Nancy. 2012. (Doodles Ser.). (ENG.). 64p. (J). (gr. k-5). pap. 7.95 *(978-1-61608-668-8(8),* 608668, Sky Pony Pr.) Skyhorse Publishing Co., Inc.
—Doodles Time. Meyers, Nancy. 2012. (Doodles Ser.). (ENG.). 64p. (J). (gr. k-5). pap. 7.95 *(978-1-61608-670-1(X),* 608670, Sky Pony Pr.) Skyhorse Publishing Co., Inc.
Meyers, Sarah. Sandy's Dream. Rader, Jared. 2007. 16p. (J). (gr. -1-3). 10.99 *(978-1-59879-398-7(5))* Lifevest Publishing, Inc.
Meynell, Louis. The Little Colonel's House Party. Johnston, Annie Fellows. 2007. 176p. per. *(978-1-4065-3514-3(1))* Dodo Pr.
Meyrand, Estelle. A Christmas Carol & the Remembrance of Mugby. Dickens, Charles. 2012. (Classics Illustrated Deluxe Graphic Novel Ser.: 9). (ENG.). 96p. (J). (gr. 2-8). pap. 11.99 *(978-1-59707-345-5(8))* Papercutz.
Meyrick, Kathryn. The Lost Music. 2010. (Child's Play Library). (ENG.). 32p. (J). *(978-1-84643-402-0(5))* Child's Play International Ltd.
Meza, Erika. Apple Picking Day! Ransom, Candice F. 2016. (J). pap. ***(978-0-553-53858-8(6))*** Random Hse. Children's Bks.
—Pumpkin Day! Ransom, Candice F. 2015. (Step into Reading Ser.). (ENG.). 32p. (J). (gr. -1-1). 12.99 ***(978-0-375-97466-3(0))*** Random Hse., Inc.
Mhasane, Ruchi. Bible Promises for a Little Boy. Joslin, Mary. 2014. (ENG.). 32p. (J). (gr. -1-2). 9.99 *(978-0-7459-6404-1(4))* Lion Hudson PLC GBR. Dist: Independent Pubs. Group.
—Bible Promises for a Little Girl. Joslin, Mary. 2014. (ENG.). 32p. (J). (gr. -1-2). 9.99 *(978-0-7459-6405-8(2))* Lion Hudson PLC GBR. Dist: Independent Pubs. Group.
Miao, Huai-Kuang, Sr. & Miao, Huai-Kuang. The Genesis of It All. Shaw, Luci. 2006. 32p. (J). (gr. -1-3). 17.95 *(978-1-55725-480-1(X))* Paraclete Pr., Inc.
Miao, Huai-Kuang, jt. illus. see Miao, Huai-Kuang, Sr.
Micale, Albert. The Long Trail: The Story of Buffalo Bill. Kolars, Frank. 2011. 190p. 42.95 *(978-1-258-05136-5(2))* Literary Licensing, LLC.
Miceli, Monica. Hielito, el Pinguino. Aldovini, Giulia. Brignole, Giancarla, tr. rev. ed. 2007. (Fabulas De Familia Ser.). (SPA & ENG.). 32p. (J). (gr. 4-7). pap. 6.95 *(978-970-20-0259-8(1))* Castillo, Ediciones, S. A. de C. V. MEX. Dist: Macmillan.
—El Rey Perezoso. Mostacchi, Massimo. Brignole, Giancarla, tr. rev. ed. 2006. (Fabulas De Familia Ser.). (SPA & ENG.). 32p. (J). (gr. k-4). pap. 6.95 *(978-970-20-0274-1(5))* Castillo, Ediciones, S. A. de C. V. MEX. Dist: Macmillan.
Michael A. Cicchetti. Healthy Fun with Benjamin & Jasmine: ABCs of the Human Body. Sherri L. Berner. 2009. 32p. pap. 12.99 *(978-1-4343-8297-9(4))* AuthorHouse.
Michael, Cavallaro, et al. The Wizard of Oz. Baum, L. Frank. 2005. (ENG.). 176p. (J). (gr. 3-7). 10.99 *(978-0-14-240471-3(3),* Puffin) Penguin Publishing Group.
Michael, Fitterling. The Elson Readers Teacher's Guide, Vol. 6. Newcomer, Mary Jane et al. 2005. (ENG.). 332p. (J). (gr. -1-12). tchr. ed., per. 20.95 *(978-1-890623-30-2(X))* Lost Classic Bks.
Michael, Joan. Let's Make Letters: ABC Kids. Behrens, Janice. 2007. (Let's Find Out Early Learning Bks.). (ENG.). 32p. (J). (gr. -1-3). 18.00 *(978-0-531-14867-9(X),* Children's Pr.) Scholastic Library Publishing.
—Let's Play a Five Senses Guessing Game. Miller, Amanda. 2007. (Let's Find Out Early Learning Bks.). (ENG.). 24p. (J). (gr. -1-3). 18.00 *(978-0-531-14871-6(8),* Children's Pr.) Scholastic Library Publishing.
Michael, Joan & Larsen, Eric. Let's Talk about Opposites, Morning to Night. Falk, Laine. 2007. (Let's Find Out Early Learning Bks.). (ENG.). 24p. (J). (gr. -1-3). 18.00 *(978-0-531-14872-3(6),* Children's Pr.) Scholastic Library Publishing.
Michaels, Lisa J. The Inner Light. Porada, Henry. 2013. 32p. pap. 12.99 *(978-1-937260-98-9(4))* Sleepytown Pr.
Michaud, Monique. Book of Dreams - the Ringtail Family. Michaud, Sylvie. 2012. 24p. pap. *(978-0-9782955-8-5(7))* Crafty Canuck, Inc.
—Book of Love - the Ringtail Family. Michaud, Sylvie. 2012. 24p. pap. *(978-1-927471-00-5(1))* Crafty Canuck, Inc.
—Book of Wishes - the Ringtail Family. Michaud, Sylvie. 2012. 24p. pap. *(978-0-9782955-9-2(5))* Crafty Canuck, Inc.
Michaud, Nancy. Heart of Stone. Monnar, Ana. 2007. 24p. (J). per. 11.99 *(978-0-9768035-5-3(0))* Readers Are Leaders U.S.A., Inc.
Michel, June. Going Places: True Tales from Young Travelers. 2003. 160p. (J). (gr. 4-12). pap. *(978-1-58270-070-0(2))* Beyond Words Publishing, Inc.
Michelle, Jean & D'Arrigo, Jay. Naba II: A Journey. Michelle, Jean. 2011. 20p. pap. 24.95 *(978-1-4626-4381-3(7))* America Star Bks.
Michelle, Nelson-Schmidt. Jonathan James & Whatif Monster. Michelle, Nelson-Schmidt. 2012. (ENG.). (J). 12.99 *(978-1-61067-131-6(7))* Kane Miller.
Michels-Boyce, Steven. When Jesus Was A Kid Like Me: A Counting Song about Jesus When He Was a Kid Like You & Me. 2005. (J). 15.95 *(978-0-9761477-0-1(X))* SoJam Pr.
Micich, Paul. The Littlest Angel. Tazewell, Charles. (ENG.). 32p. (J). (gr. -1-3). 2008. 8.99 *(978-0-8249-5575-5(7));* 2007. pap. 3.99 *(978-0-8249-5549-6(8))* Ideals Pubns. (Ideals Children's Bks.).
Mickle, Jed. The Forgotten Explorer? The Story of Amerigo Vespucci. Lambert, Lorene. 2005. (Who in the World Ser.). (ENG.). 56p. (gr. 2-4). per. 9.50 *(978-0-9728603-8-3(X),* 86038) Peace Hill Pr.
—Who in the World Was the Secretive Printer? The Story of Johannes Gutenberg. Beckham, Robert. 2005. (Who in the World Ser.). (ENG.). 40p. (gr. 2-18). pap. 9.50 *(978-0-9728603-6-9(3),* 86036) Peace Hill Pr.
—Who in the World Was the Unready King? The Story of Ethelred. Clark, Connie. 2005. (Who in the World Ser.). (ENG.). 54p. (gr. 2-18). pap. 9.50 *(978-0-9728603-7-6(1),* 86037) Peace Hill Pr.
Micucci, Charles. The Life & Times of Corn. Micucci, Charles. 2009. (ENG.). 32p. (J). (gr. -1-3). 16.99 *(978-0-618-50751-1(5))* Houghton Mifflin Harcourt Publishing Co.
Middlemiss, Laura B. The Great Hamstini. Middlemiss, David. 2010. 108p. *(978-1-907211-18-8(7))* Grosvenor Hse. Publishing Ltd.
Middleton, Charlotte. Summer Beat. Franco, Betsy. 2011. (ENG.). 36p. (J). (gr. -1-1). 14.99 *(978-1-4424-4339-6(1),* McElderry, Margaret K. Bks.) McElderry, Margaret K. Bks.
Middleton, Gayle. Color & Iron-Ons Book. Frantz, Jennifer. 2005. (My Little Pony Ser.). 32p. (J). (gr. -1-1). 3.99 *(978-0-06-074441-0(3),* HarperFestival) HarperCollins Pubs.
—My Little Pony: A Secret Gift. Benjamin, Ruth. 2006. 24p. (J). lib. bdg. 15.00 *(978-1-4242-1536-2(6))* Fitzgerald Bks.
—A Secret Gift/el Regalo Secreto. Benjamin, Ruth. Abboud, Adela, tr. from ENG. 2006. (I Can Read Bks.). (SPA & ENG.). 24p. (J). (gr. k-3). per. 3.99 *(978-0-06-112391-7(9),* Rayo) HarperCollins Pubs.
Middleton, Gayle & Edwards, Ken. Color & Poster Book. Bak, Jenny. 2006. (My Little Pony Ser.). 32p. (J). (gr. -1-1). 3.99 *(978-0-06-079470-5(4),* HarperFestival) HarperCollins Pubs.
Middleton, Joshua, et al. Flying Solo. Kesel, Barbara. 2003. (Meridian Traveler Ser.: Vol. 1). 192p. (YA). (gr. 7-18). pap. 9.95 *(978-1-931484-54-1(6))* CrossGeneration Comics, Inc.
Middleton, Mikell. Flitter, Flutter Butterfly. Jarrell, Pamela R. l.t. ed. 2005. (HRL Board Book Ser.). 12p. (J). (gr. -1-1). pap. 10.95 *(978-1-57332-286-7(5),* HighReach Learning, Incorporated) Carson-Dellosa Publishing, LLC.
—Helping in My Town. Hensley, Sarah M. l.t. ed. 2003. (HRL Big Book Ser.). 8p. (J). (gr. -1-1). pap. 10.95 *(978-1-57332-274-4(1));* pap. 10.95 *(978-1-57332-275-1(X))* Carson-Dellosa Publishing, LLC. (HighReach Learning, Incorporated).
Middleton, Taquon. Katy, the Cooking Kangaroo. Owens, Carmen. Otis, Michelle, ed. 2013. (J). pap. 12.95 *(978-0-9888644-5-0(2))* Knowledge Power Communications.
Middy Chilman, Thomas. Gooney Bird Greene. Lowry, Lois. 2004. (Gooney Bird Ser.: No. 1). 88p. (gr. 2-5). 16.00 *(978-0-7569-2583-3(5))* Perfection Learning Corp.
Midgorden, Barry. Scottosaurus the Little Dinosaur. Sage-Midgorden, Lucinda. 2010. (ENG.). 24p. pap. 9.95 *(978-1-4495-9762-7(9))* CreateSpace Independent Publishing Platform.
Midorikawa, Yuki. Natsume's Book of Friends. Midorikawa, Yuki. (Natsume's Book of Friends Ser.: 15). (ENG.). 2014. 192p. pap. 9.99 *(978-1-4215-5967-4(6));* 2011. 192p. pap. 9.99 *(978-1-4215-3274-5(3));* 2010. 200p. pap. 9.99 *(978-1-4215-3246-2(8));* 2010. 200p. pap. 9.99 *(978-1-4215-3245-5(X));* 2010. 208p. pap. 9.99 *(978-1-4215-3244-8(1));* 2010. 208p. pap. 9.99 *(978-1-4215-3243-1(3));* Vol. 5. 2011. 192p. pap. 9.99 *(978-1-4215-3247-9(6));* Vol. 6. 2011. 182p. pap. 9.99 *(978-1-4215-3248-6(4))* Viz Media.
Miele, Brianna. Eldy & Ohi. Sexton, Jessa Rose. 2012. 36p. pap. 8.00 *(978-0-9860150-9-0(1))* O'More Publishing.
Mier, Colin. Sam Sorts It Out. Cross, Gillian. 2005. (ENG.). 24p. (J). lib. bdg. 23.65 *(978-1-59646-702-6(9))* Dingles & Co.
Mier, Colin. Space Race. Blackman, Malorie. 2014. (ENG.). 80p. (J). (gr. k-2). pap. 7.99 ***(978-0-552-56893-7(7))*** Transworld Publishers Ltd. GBR. Dist: Independent Pubs. Group.
Mier, Vanessa. Animal Companions: In Our Hearts, Our Lives, & Our World. Pomerance, Diane. 2004. (YA). per. 9.95 *(978-0-9708500-3-4(4))* Polaire Pubns.
—Animal Companions: Your Friends, Teachers & Guides. Pomerance, Diane. 2003. 9.95 *(978-0-9708500-2-7(6))* Polaire Pubns.
Miesen, Christina. Baby Animals: With Flip the Flap Pages. Novick, Mary. 2008. (Mini Marvels Ser.). (ENG.). 12p. (J). (gr. k — 1). 6.95 *(978-1-921272-17-2(1))* Little Hare Bks. AUS. Dist: Independent Pubs. Group.
—Little Bugs: With Flip the Flap Pages. Novick, Mary. 2013. (Mini Marvels Ser.). (ENG.). 10p. (J). (gr. -1-k). 9.99

M

(978-1-921272-22-6(8)) Little Hare Bks. AUS. Dist: Independent Pubs. Group.

—Numbers. Novick, Mary & Peterson, Jenna. 2008. (Mini Marvels Ser.). (ENG.). 12p. (J). (gr. k — 1). 6.95 (978-1-921049-61-3(8)) Little Hare Bks. AUS. Dist: Independent Pubs. Group.

Migachyov, Larisa. Equations in Geometry: How to Make Your Child Successful in Math. Migachyov, Larisa. Migachyov, Dina. 2004. 267p. per. 29.99 (978-0-9672535-4-1(3)) Quaternion Pr.

Migdale, Lawrence. Cinco de Mayo: Celebrating the Traditions of Mexico. Hoyt-Goldsmith, Diane. 2008. (ENG.). 32p. (J). (gr. 3-7). 16.95 (978-0-8234-2107-7(4)) Holiday Hse., Inc.

—Cinco de Mayo: Celebrating the traditions of Mexico. Hoyt-Goldsmith, Diane. 2010. (ENG.). 32p. (J). (gr. 1-5). pap. 7.95 (978-0-8234-2279-1(8)) Holiday Hse., Inc.

—Three Kings Day: A Celebration at Christmastime. Hoyt-Goldsmith, Diane. 2004. (ENG.). 32p. (J). (gr. 4-6). tchr. ed. 16.95 (978-0-8234-1839-8(1)) Holiday Hse., Inc.

Migdale, Lawrence, photos by. Celebrating Chinese New Year. Hoyt-Goldsmith, Diane. (ENG.). 32p. (J). (gr. 4-6). pap. 6.95 (978-0-8234-1520-5(1)) Holiday Hse., Inc.

Migliari, Paola. I Am a Dump Truck. Page, Josephine. 2007. (ENG.). 4p. (J). (gr. k — 1). bds. 4.99 (978-0-439-91617-2(8), Cartwheel Bks.) Scholastic, Inc.

—I Am a Fire Truck. Page, Josephine. 2007. (ENG.). 4p. (J). (gr. k — 1). bds. 4.99 (978-0-439-91618-9(6)) Scholastic, Inc.

Miglio, Paige. Bunny Christmas: A Family Celebration. Walton, Rick. 2004. 32p. (J). (ENG.). 15.99 (978-0-06-008415-8(4)); lib. bdg. 16.89 (978-0-06-008416-5(2)) HarperCollins Pubs.

—What Do We Do with the Baby? Walton, Rick. 2008. 32p. (J). (gr. -1-k). lib. bdg. 17.89 (978-0-06-008420-2(0)) HarperCollins Pubs.

Miglio, Paige. Bear's Baby. Miglio, Paige. Date not set. 32p. (J). (gr. -1-18). 15.99 (978-0-06-029240-9(7)); pap. 5.99 (978-0-06-443741-7(8)); lib. bdg. 16.89 (978-0-06-029241-6(5)) HarperCollins Pubs.

Mignano, Daniel. Petey the One Lopped Eared Dog, 1 vol. Wingate, Barbara. 2009. 20p. pap. 24.95 (978-1-60836-931-7(5)) America Star Bks.

Mignola, Mike. Cosmic Odyssey. Starlin, Jim. Kahan, Bob, ed. rev. ed. 2009. (ENG.). 200p. pap. 19.99 (978-1-56389-051-2(8)) DC Comics.

—El Ejercito Perdido. Golden, Christopher. 2005. (Hellboy Ser.). (SPA.). 229p. per. 19.95 (978-1-59497-108-2(0)) Public Square Bks.

Migy. And Away We Go! Migy. 2014. (ENG.). 40p. (J). (gr. -1-1). 17.99 (978-0-8050-9901-0(8), Holt, Henry & Co. Bks. For Young Readers) Holt, Henry & Co.

Mihara, Mitsukazu. Mitsukazu Mihara - Haunted House. Mihara, Mitsukazu. 2006. 200p. (gr. 9-18). per. 9.99 (978-1-59816-321-6(3)) TOKYOPOP, Inc.

Mihara, Mitsukazu. Doll, 6 vols. Mihara, Mitsukazu, creator. rev. ed. 2005. Vol. 4. 192p. pap. 9.99 (978-1-59532-390-3(2)); Vol. 5. 176p. pap. 9.99 (978-1-59532-391-0(0)) TOKYOPOP, Inc.

Mihran, Turley Joyce. Totally Out There Gd Glacier Natl Park. Love, Donna. 2010. 0096p. (J). pap. 15.00 (978-0-87842-566-2(7)) Mountain Pr. Publishing Co., Inc.

Mike. Lemon Drop Rain: Poems & Drawings by Mr. Mike. Mike. l.t. ed. 2003. (ENG.). 180p. (J). pap. 14.95 (978-0-9658365-6-2(8)) Beetle Bug Bks.

—New Pet. Mike. l.t. ed. 2005. (ENG.). 32p. (J). lib. bdg. 14.95 (978-0-9658365-8-6(4)) Beetle Bug Bks.

Mikec, Larry. Firefly at Stony Brook Farm. Pfeffer, Wendy. 2005. (Smithsonian's Backyard Ser.). (ENG.). 32p. (J). (gr. -1-2). 15.95 (978-1-59249-282-4(7), BC5006) Soundprints.

—Firefly at Stonybrook Farm. Pfeffer, Wendy. 2004. (Smithsonian's Backyard Ser.). (ENG.). 32p. (J). (gr. -1-2). 8.95 (978-1-59249-306-7(8), SC5026); (gr. -1-3). 9.95 (978-1-59249-308-1(4), PB5076); (gr. -1-2). 19.95 (978-1-59249-307-4(6), BC5026); (gr. 2-2). 4.99 (978-1-59249-283-1(5), B5076) Soundprints.

MikeMotz.com. Yabut the Rabbit. Grimes, Craig & Washington, Aimee. 2011. (ENG.). 28p. pap. 9.95 (978-1-4662-1162-9(8)) CreateSpace Independent Publishing Platform.

Mikhail, Jess. Batter Splatter! Morgan, Ruth. 2005. (ENG.). 24p. (J). lib. bdg. 23.65 (978-1-59646-704-0(5)) Dingles & Co.

—Florentine & Pig. Katzler, Eva. 2012. (ENG.). 32p. (J). 17.89 (978-1-59990-949-3(9)); (gr. -1-6). 16.99 (978-1-59990-847-2(6)) Bloomsbury USA. (Bloomsbury USA Childrens).

—Mouse with No Name. Morgan, Michaela. 2004. (ENG.). 24p. (J). lib. bdg. 23.65 (978-1-59646-682-1(0)) Dingles & Co.

Mikhail, Jessica. Eleanore Won't Share, 1 vol. Gassman, Julie A. 2010. (Little Boost Ser.). (ENG.). 32p. (gr. k-3). lib. bdg. 22.65 (978-1-4048-6358-3(3), Little Boost) Picture Window Bks.

Mikimoto, Haruhiku. Ecole du Ciel, Vol. 2. Mikimoto, Haruhiku, creator. 2nd rev. ed. 2006. pap. 14.99 (978-1-59532-852-6(1), Tokyopop Adult) TOKYOPOP, Inc.

Mikki. The Calabash Tales. Abrams, Penny. 2011. 66p. 28.00 (978-1-4349-1169-8(1)) Dorrance Publishing Co., Inc.

Mikle, Toby. The Cookie That Saved My Family. Freund, William C. 2011. (J). (978-0-9846346-7-5(3)) Adibooks.com.

—My Family Forest. Voiles, Alison. 2010. 28p. pap. 13.99 (978-1-4389-1682-8(5)) AuthorHouse.

—Procrastimonsters! They're Everywhere. Hull, Claudia. 2012. 44p. pap. 15.95 (978-1-257-64007-2(0)) Shalako Pr.

—Sammy's Midnight Hunger. Chaudhary, Shahida. 2012. 38p. pap. 14.50 (978-1-61897-255-2(3), Strategic Bk. Publishing) Strategic Book Publishing & Rights Agency (SBPRA).

—Skippy the Dog in the Band. Palumbo, Mary Lou. 2009. 48p. pap. 19.49 (978-1-4389-9218-1(1)) AuthorHouse.

—Sleepytown Beagles Penny's 4th of July. Glass, Timothy. 2006. 24p. (J). per. 15.95 (978-1-888461-10-7(1)); 16.95 (978-1-888461-11-4(X)) Islewest Publishing.

Mikle, Toby, jt. illus. see Jones, Branson.

Mikler, Lisa M. Divine Providence: A Child's History of the United States. Smith, Ruth J. 2005. 224p. (J). per. 19.95 net. (978-0-9705618-5-5(7)) Bradford Pr., Inc.

—Liberty & Justice for All: A Child's History of the United States of America. Smith, Ruth J. 2003. 208p. (J). per. 19.95 (978-0-9705618-3-1(0)) Bradford Pr., Inc.

Miksch, Alison, photos by. Mastering the Grill: The Owner's Manual for Outdoor Cooking. Schloss, Andrew & Joachim, David. 2007. (ENG., 416p. (gr. 8-17). pap. 24.95 (978-0-8118-4964-7(3)) Chronicle Bks. LLC.

—Quick & Easy Thai: 70 Everyday Recipes. McDermott, Nancie. 2003. (ENG., 168p. (gr. 8-17). pap. 18.95 (978-0-8118-3731-6(9)) Chronicle Bks. LLC.

Miladovich, Dragana. Here I Am!, 1 vol. Brott, Ardyth. 2012. (ENG.). 32p. (J). (gr. 1-2). (978-0-88962-938-7(2)) Mosaic Pr.

Milagrito, El. La saga de los jugadores de Pelota. Rendon, Gilberto. rev. ed. 2003. (Castillo de la Lectura Roja Ser.). (SPA & ENG.). 240p. (J). pap. 8.95 (978-970-20-0335-9(0)) Castillo, Ediciones, S. A. de C. V. MEX. Dist: Macmillan.

Milam, C. J. Micah & the Magic Helmet: The Helmet & the Dragon. Parrish, Kat. 2011. (ENG.). 32p. (J). (gr. k-7). pap. 8.95 (978-0-938467-29-8(8), Headline Kids) Headline Bks., Inc.

Milano, Jacque. Stay-at-Home Hank: The Little Hummingbird That Couldn't Fly. Milano, Jacque. l.t. ed. 2003. 30p. (J). 9.95 (978-0-9728432-0-1(5)) Milano, Jacque & Assocs.

Milelli, Pascal. Seal Song, 1 vol. Spalding, Andrea. 2011. (ENG.). 32p. (J). (gr. -1-3). 19.95 (978-1-55469-242-2(3)) Orca Bk. Pubs. USA.

—Waiting for the Owl's Call. Whelan, Gloria. 2009. (Tales of the World Ser.). (ENG.). 32p. (J). (gr. 1-5). 17.95 (978-1-58536-418-3(5)) Sleeping Bear Pr.

Miles, David. Bernida: A Michigan Sailing Legend. Declercq, Al et al. 2014. (ENG.). 32p. (J). (gr. 1-4). 16.99 (978-1-58536-904-1(7), 203553) Sleeping Bear Pr.

—Brave Queen Esther, 1 vol. 2015. (I Can Read! / Adventure Bible Ser.). (ENG.). 32p. (J). pap. 3.99 (978-0-310-74666-9(3)) Zonderkidz.

—Cop's Night Before Christmas, 1 vol. Harrison, Michael. 2010. (Night Before Christmas Ser.). (ENG.). 32p. (J). (gr. k-3). 16.99 (978-1-58980-800-3(2)) Pelican Publishing Co., Inc.

—A Father's Love, 1 vol. Zondervan. 2014. (I Can Read! / Adventure Bible Ser.). (ENG.). 32p. (J). pap. 3.99 (978-0-310-73240-2(9)) Zonderkidz.

—God's Great Creation, 1 vol. Zondervan. 2014. (I Can Read! / Adventure Bible Ser.). (ENG.). 32p. (J). pap. 3.99 (978-0-310-73238-9(7)) Zondervan.

—Miracles of Jesus, 1 vol. Zondervan. 2014. (I Can Read! / Adventure Bible Ser.). (ENG.). 32p. (J). pap. 3.99 (978-0-310-73242-6(5)) Zonderkidz.

—Moses Leads the People, 1 vol. Zondervan. 2014. (I Can Read! / Adventure Bible Ser.). (ENG.). 32p. (J). pap. 3.99 (978-0-310-73236-5(0)) Zondervan.

—Noah's Voyage, 1 vol. Zondervan Bibles Staff. 2015. (I Can Read! / Adventure Bible Ser.). (ENG.). 32p. (J). pap. 3.99 (978-0-310-74683-6(3)) Zonderkidz.

Miles, Elizabeth. The Velveteen Rabbit. Williams, Margery. 2007. (ENG.). (J). (gr. -1-3). 18.95 (978-0-545-00512-8(4)); 9.99 (978-0-545-00510-4(8)) Scholastic, Inc.

Miles, Gail. Naughty Nicky & the Good Ship Oggy. Miles, Colin. 2013. 24p. pap. (978-1-909202-16-0(9)) Little Acorns Publishing.

Miles, Peregrine B. The Mucky Yucky Swamp. Smithrud, Norma. 2011. 28p. pap. 24.95 (978-1-4560-8790-6(8)) America Star Bks.

Milgram, Al, jt. illus. see Smith, Tod G.

Milgrim, David. Eddie Gets Ready for School. Milgrim, David. 2011. (ENG.). 32p. (J). (gr. -1-3). 8.99 (978-0-545-27329-9(3), Cartwheel Bks.) Scholastic, Inc.

—My Friend Lucky: A Love Story. Milgrim, David. 2010. (ENG.). 32p. (J). (gr. -1-2). 13.99 (978-1-4424-2937-6(2), Atheneum Bks. for Young Readers) Simon & Schuster Children's Publishing.

—Santa Duck. Milgrim, David. (ENG.). (J). (gr. -1 — 1). 2013. 30p. bds. 6.99 (978-0-399-16298-5(4), Nancy Paulsen Bks.); 2010. 32p. 12.99 (978-0-399-25541-0(9), Putnam Juvenile) Penguin Publishing Group.

—Some Monsters Are Different. Milgrim, David. 2013. (ENG.). 36p. (J). (gr. -1-k). 16.99 (978-0-8050-9519-7(5), Holt, Henry & Co. Bks. For Young Readers) Holt, Henry & Co.

—Swing Otto Swing! Milgrim, David. 2005. (Ready-to-Read Ser.). (J). (gr. -1-k). 11.65 (978-0-7569-6497-9(0)) Perfection Learning Corp.

Milgrom, Al. Avengers: West Coast Avengers: Sins of the Past. 2011. (ENG.). 248p. (J). (gr. 4-17). 34.99 (978-0-7851-5900-1(2)) Marvel Worldwide, Inc.

Milgrom, Al, et al. John Brown's Raid on Harpers Ferry. Glaser, Jason. 2005. (Graphic History Ser.). (ENG.). 32p. (gr. 3-4). 29.99 (978-0-7368-4369-0(8), Graphic Library) Capstone Pr., Inc.

Milgrom, Al. Jonas Salk & the Polio Vaccine, 1 vol. Krohn, Katherine E. 2006. (Inventions & Discovery Ser.). (ENG.). 32p. (gr. 3-4). 29.99 (978-0-7368-6483-1(0), Graphic Library) Capstone Pr., Inc.

—Secret Wars II. 2011. (ENG.). 264p. (J). (gr. 4-17). pap. 29.99 (978-0-7851-5830-1(8)) Marvel Worldwide, Inc.

Milgrom, Al, et al. Spider-Man: Deadly Foes of Spider-Man. 2011. (ENG.). 208p. (J). (gr. 4-17). pap. 24.99 (978-0-7851-5855-4(3)) Marvel Worldwide, Inc.

Milgrom, Al & Howell, Richard. Avengers - West Coast Avengers: Family Ties. 2011. (ENG.). 296p. (J). (gr. -1-17). 34.99 (978-0-7851-5500-3(7)) Marvel Worldwide, Inc.

Milgrom, Al & Smith, Tod G. Steve Jobs, Steve Wozniak, & the Personal Computer, 1 vol. Lemke, Donald B. 2006. (Inventions & Discovery Ser.). (ENG.). 32p. (gr. 3-4). pap. 8.10 (978-0-7368-9650-4(3)); pap. 47.70 (978-0-7368-9762-4(3)) Capstone Pr., Inc. (Graphic Library).

Milgrom, Al, jt. illus. see Purcell, Gordon.

Milgrom, Al, jt. illus. see Smith, Tod G.

Milian, Tomaso. Friends (Mostly) Joosse, Barbara M. 2010. 32p. (J). (gr. -1-3). (ENG.). 16.99 (978-0-06-088221-1(2)); lib. bdg. 17.89 (978-0-06-088222-8(0)) HarperCollins Pubs. (Greenwillow Bks.).

Milicevic, Adam. Hamster Cheeks. Delittle, Cathy. 2007. 32p. (J). 14.95 (978-1-892633-14-9(0)) Delittle Storyteller Co.

Miline, Bill, photos by. Big Bagel, Little Bagel. Shulman, Mark. 2006. 10p. (J). (gr. k-4). reprint ed. 6.00 (978-1-4223-5709-5(0)) DIANE Publishing Co.

—I'll Take a Dozen! Shulman, Mark. 2006. 12p. (J). (gr. k-4). reprint ed. 6.00 (978-1-4223-5725-5(2)) DIANE Publishing Co.

—My Square Breakfast. Shulman, Mark. 2006. 10p. (J). (gr. k-4). reprint ed. 6.00 (978-1-4223-5710-1(4)) DIANE Publishing Co.

—There's No Blue on a Bagel. Shulman, Mark. 2006. 12p. (J). (gr. k-4). reprint ed. 6.00 (978-1-4223-5711-8(2)) DIANE Publishing Co.

Militello, Joy. What Was My Mother Thinking? Hodkin, Faith. 2013. (J). 22.95 (978-1-933420-02-8(2)) Ravenwood Studios.

Milkau, Liz. Princess Backwards, 1 vol. Gray, Jane. 2003. (ENG.). 24p. (J). (gr. -1-3). 15.95 (978-1-896764-64-1(9)) Second Story Pr. CAN. Dist: Orca Bk. Pubs. USA.

Millar, H. The Phoenix & the Carpet. Nesbit, E. 2012. (Puffin Classics Ser.). (ENG.). 306p. (J). pap. 4.99 (978-0-14-134086-9(X), Puffin) Penguin Publishing Group.

Millar, H. R. Five Children & It. Nesbit, E. 2007. (ENG.). 178p. pap. 19.99 (978-1-4346-7586-6(6)); 198p. pap. 21.99 (978-1-4346-7587-3(4)) BiblioBazaar.

—Five Children & It. Nesbit, E. 2007. (ENG.). 204p. per. (978-1-4065-3077-3(8)) Dodo Pr.

Millar, H. R., jt. illus. see Fell, H. Granville.

Millar, H. R., jt. illus. see Nesbit, E.

Millard, Kerry. Nim's Island. Orr, Wendy. 2008. (ENG.). 128p. (gr. 3-7). 6.99 (978-0-385-73606-0(1), Yearling) Random Hse. Children's Bks.

—The Web. Hilton, Nette. 2013. (ENG.). 80p. (J). pap. 4.99 (978-1-61067-087-6(6)) Kane Miller.

Miller, Alexandra. The Beastie Book: An Alphabestiary. Harter, Penny. 2009. (ENG.). 56p. (J). 21.95 (978-1-934860-05-2(0)) Shenanigan Bks.

—Wisteria's Show & Tell Spectacular: Older Than the Dinosaurs. Grigsby, Susan. 2012. (J). (978-1-934860-12-0(3)) Shenanigan Bks.

Miller, Allan, jt. illus. see Miller, Christopher.

Miller, Antonia, et al. Art Projects. Allman, Howard, photos by. Watt, Fiona. 2005. 96p. (J). (gr. 5-9). 7.99 (978-0-7945-1111-1(2), Usborne) EDC Publishing.

Miller, Antonia. Art Skills. Watt, Fiona. 2004. (Art Ideas Ser.). (ENG.). 96p. (J). pap. 18.95 (978-0-7945-0351-2(9)) EDC Publishing.

—Drawing, Doodling & Coloring Fashion. Watt, Fiona. ed. 2013. (Activity Bks.). 128p. (J). pap. 13.99 (978-0-7945-3336-6(1), Usborne) EDC Publishing.

Miller, Antonia, et al. The Usborne Complete Book of Art Ideas. Watt, Fiona. 2006. (Art Ideas Ser.). 288p. (J). pap. 19.99 (978-0-7945-1439-6(1), Usborne) EDC Publishing.

Miller, Antonia & Figg, Non. Art Projects. Allman, Howard, photos by. Watt, Fiona. 2003. (Art Ideas Ser.). (ENG.). 96p. (J). (gr. 5-9). 18.95 (978-0-7945-0657-5(7), Usborne) EDC Publishing.

Miller, Antonia, jt. illus. see Baggott, Stella.

Miller, Bob. Finn the Foolish Fish: Trouble with Bubbles, Set. Paul, Sherry. (See How I Read Ser.). 32p. (Orig.). (J). (gr. -1-2). pap. 14.10 (978-0-675-01084-9(5)) CPI Publishing, Inc.

Miller, Bryan. I Love to Leap! Rundstrom, Teressa. 2004. 35p. (J). per. (978-1-932062-42-7(4)) Hability Solution Services, Inc.

Miller, Bryan & Marshall, H. Keene. Cherry the Sheep Finds Her Sheep Sound. Rundstrom, Teressa. 2004. 25p. (J). per. (978-1-932062-40-3(8)) Hability Solution Services, Inc.

Miller, Caroline. Beyond the River, 1 vol. Miller, Alex. 2011. (ENG.). 64p. (J). (978-0-7643-3741-3(6), Schiffer Publishing Ltd) Schiffer Publishing, Ltd.

Miller, Christopher & Miller, Allan. The Legend of Gid the Kid & the Black Bean Bandits, 2 bks., Bk.1. Miller, Christopher & Miller, Allan. 2007. (Heroes of Promise Ser.). (ENG.). 32p. (J). (gr. 1-5). 12.99 (978-1-59317-202-2(8)) Warner Pr. Pubs.

—The Legend of Ten-Gallon Sam & the Perilous Mine, 2 bks., Bk.2. Miller, Christopher & Miller, Allan. 2007. (Heroes of Promise Ser.). (ENG.). 32p. (J). (gr. -1-5). 12.99 (978-1-59317-225-1(7)) Warner Pr. Pubs.

Miller, Cliff. Rockwell: A Boy & His Dog. DiMare, Loren Spiotta et al. 2005. (ENG.). 32p. (J). 14.95 (978-0-7641-5790-5(6)) Barron's Educational Series, Inc.

Miller, Dave. Draw with the Cartoon Dude. 2011. (ENG.). 256p. (J). (gr. 2-4). pap. 16.99 (978-1-60905-068-9(1)) Blue Apple Bks.

Miller, David. Three Christmas Journeys. Willoughby, Robert. 2004. 24p. (gr. 3-7). pap. 5.00 (978-0-687-03482-6(5)) Abingdon Pr.

Miller, David Humphreys. Indian Friends & Foes: A Baker's Dozen Portraits from Pocahontas to Geronimo. Heiderstadt, Dorothy. 2011. 144p. 40.95 (978-1-258-08676-3(X)) Literary Licensing, LLC.

Miller, Dawn Ellen. Keri. McGee, Pamela M. 2012. 20p. pap. 24.95 (978-1-4626-8593-6(5)) America Star Bks.

—Keri: Dandelions. McGee, Pamela M. 2012. 24p. pap. 24.95 (978-1-4626-9977-3(4)) America Star Bks.

—Keri: The Wedding. McGee, Pamela M. 2013. 20p. pap. 24.95 (978-1-63004-171-7(8)) America Star Bks.

Miller, Dorcas S. Constellation Finder: A Guide to Patterns in the Night Sky with Star Stories from Around the World. Miller, Dorcas S. 2005. (ENG.). 64p. pap. 5.95 (978-0-912550-26-8(0)) Nature Study Guild.

Miller, Ed. Attack of the Evil Minions! Mayer, Kirsten. 2013. (ENG.). 32p. (J). (gr. -1-3). 12.99 (978-0-316-23444-3(3)) Little, Brown Bks. for Young Readers.

Miller, Ed. Minions: Dracula's Last Birthday. Rosen, Lucy. 2015. (ENG.). 32p. (J). (gr. -1-3). 7.99 (978-0-316-26693-2(0)) Little, Brown Bks. for Young Readers.

Miller, Edward. Alphabeep! A Zipping, Zooming ABC. Pearson, Debora. 2007. (ENG.). 36p. (J). (gr. -1-3). 6.95 (978-0-8234-2076-6(0)) Holiday Hse., Inc.

—Alphabeep: A Zipping, Zooming ABC. Pearson, Debora. 2007. (J). (gr. -1-3). 17.15 (978-1-4177-8559-9(4), Turtleback) Turtleback Bks.

—A Drop of Blood. Showers, Paul. 2004. (Let's-Read-and-Find-Out Science Ser.). 32p. (J). (gr. k-4). 15.99 (978-0-06-009108-8(8)); (ENG.). pap. 5.99 (978-0-06-009110-1(X), Collins); lib. bdg. 16.89 (978-0-06-009109-5(6)) HarperCollins Pubs.

—Fractions, Decimals, & Percents. Adler, David A. (ENG.). 32p. (J). 2011. pap. 7.99 (978-0-8234-2354-5(9)); 2010. (gr. 1-5). 17.95 (978-0-8234-2199-2(6)) Holiday Hse., Inc.

—Fractions, Decimals, & Percents. Adler, David A. 2010. (J). (978-0-545-25162-4(1)) Scholastic, Inc.

Miller, Edward, III. Fun with Roman Numerals. Adler, David A. 2008. (ENG.). 32p. (J). (gr. 1-5). 16.95 (978-0-8234-2060-5(4)) Holiday Hse., Inc.

Miller, Edward. Fun with Roman Numerals. Adler, David A. 2010. (ENG.). 32p. (J). (gr. 1-5). pap. 6.95 (978-0-8234-2255-5(0)) Holiday Hse., Inc.

—Gravity Is a Mystery. Branley, Franklyn M. 2007. (Let's-Read-and-Find-Out Science Ser.). 33p. (gr. k-4). 16.00 (978-0-7569-8103-7(4)) Perfection Learning Corp.

—Gravity Is a Mystery. Branley, Franklyn Mansfield. 2nd rev. ed. 2007. (Let's-Read-and-Find-Out Science Ser.). (ENG.). 40p. (J). (gr. k-4). 15.99 (978-0-06-028532-6(X)) HarperCollins Pubs.

—Gravity Is a Mystery. Branley, Franklyn M. 2nd rev. ed. 2007. (Let's-Read-And-Find-Out Science 2 Ser.). (ENG.). 40p. (J). (gr. k-4). pap. 5.99 (978-0-06-445201-4(8), Collins) HarperCollins Pubs.

—A House for Birdie. Murphy, Stuart J. 2004. (MathStart 1 Ser.). (ENG.). 40p. (J). (gr. -1). pap. 5.99 (978-0-06-052353-4(0)) HarperCollins Pubs.

—Millions, Billions, & Trillions. Adler, David A. 2013. (ENG.). 32p. (J). 16.95 (978-0-8234-2403-0(0)) Holiday Hse., Inc.

—Millions, Billions, & Trillions: Understanding Big Numbers. Adler, David A. 2014. (ENG.). 32p. (J). (gr. -1-3). 7.99 (978-0-8234-3049-9(9)) Holiday Hse., Inc.

—Money Madness. Adler, David A. (ENG.). 32p. (J). (gr. -1-3). 2010. pap. 6.95 (978-0-8234-2272-2(0)); 2009. 16.95 (978-0-8234-1474-1(4)) Holiday Hse., Inc.

—Mystery Math: A First Book of Algebra. Adler, David A. 2011. (ENG.). 32p. (J). 16.95 (978-0-8234-2289-0(5)) Holiday Hse., Inc.

—Mystery Math: A First Book of Algebra. Adler, David A. 2012. (ENG.). 32p. (J). (gr. 2-5). pap. 7.99 (978-0-8234-2548-8(7)) Holiday Hse., Inc.

—Nature Science Experiments: What's Hopping in a Dust Bunny? Bardhan-Quallen, Sudipta. 2010. (Mad Science Ser.). (ENG.). 64p. (J). (gr. 4-7). 12.95 (978-1-4027-2412-1(8)) Sterling Publishing Co., Inc.

—Perimeter, Area, & Volume. Adler, David A. 2013. (ENG.). 32p. (J). pap. 7.99 (978-0-8234-2763-5(3)) Holiday Hse., Inc.

—Perimeter, Area, & Volume: A Monster Book of Dimensions. Adler, David A. 2012. (ENG.). 32p. (J). 17.95 (978-0-8234-2290-6(9)) Holiday Hse., Inc.

Miller, Edward. Place Value. Adler, David A. 2016. (J). (978-0-8234-3550-0(4)) Holiday Hse., Inc.

Miller, Edward. Prices! Prices! Prices! Why They Go up & Down. Adler, David A. 2015. (ENG.). 32p. (J). (gr. 1-5). 17.95 (978-0-8234-3293-6(9)) Holiday Hse., Inc.

—Time Zones. Adler, David. 2011. (ENG.). 32p. (J). pap. 7.95 (978-0-8234-2385-9(9)) Holiday Hse., Inc.

—Time Zones. Adler, David A. 2010. (ENG.). 32p. (J). (gr. 1-5). 16.95 (978-0-8234-2201-2(1)) Holiday Hse., Inc.

—Triangles. Adler, David A. (ENG.). 32p. (J). (gr. 1-5). 2015. 7.99 (978-0-8234-3305-6(6)); 2014. 17.95 (978-0-8234-2378-1(6)) Holiday Hse., Inc.

—Working with Fractions. Adler, David A. (ENG.). 32p. (J). 2009. (gr. 1-5). pap. 7.99 (978-0-8234-2207-4(0)); 2007. (gr. 4-7). 16.95 (978-0-8234-2010-0(8)) Holiday Hse., Inc.

—You Can, Toucan, Math: Word Problem-Solving Fun. Adler, David A. (You Can, Toucan, Math Ser.). (ENG.). 32p. (J). (gr. -1-3). 2007. 6.95 (978-0-8234-2117-6(1)); 2006. 16.95 (978-0-8234-1919-7(3)) Holiday Hse., Inc.

Miller, Edward. Fireboy to the Rescue: A Fire Safety Book. Miller, Edward. (ENG.). 32p. (J). 2011. pap. 7.95 (978-0-8234-2344-6(1)); 2010. (gr. -1-3). 17.95 (978-0-8234-2222-7(4)) Holiday Hse., Inc.

—Recycling Day. Miller, Edward. 2014. (ENG.). 32p. (J). (gr. -1-3). 16.95 (978-0-8234-2419-1(7)) Holiday Hse., Inc.

—The Tooth Book: A Guide to Healthy Teeth & Gums. Miller, Edward. (ENG.). 32p. (J). 2009. (gr. -1-3). pap. 7.99 (978-0-8234-2206-7(2)); 2008. (gr. k-3). 17.95 (978-0-8234-2092-6(2)) Holiday Hse., Inc.

Miller, Erin L. The Sleepy Pelican Police. Handelsman, Valerie. 2005. (ENG.). 28p. (J). 7.95 (978-0-9748884-4-6(3)) Little Thoughts For Little Ones Publishing, Inc.

Miller, Frank. Autobiographix. Miller, Frank. Wagner, Matt et al. Schultz, Diana, ed. 2003. (ENG.). 104p. pap. 14.95 (978-1-59307-038-0(1)) Dark Horse Comics.

Miller, Fujiko. Bad Luck Boy. Brin, Susannah. 2003. (Romance Ser.). 60p. (J). pap. 4.95 (978-1-58659-458-9(3)) Artesian Pr.

—The Climb. Brin, Susannah. rev. ed. 2004. (Take Ten Ser.). 61p. (J). (gr. 4-12). pap. 4.95 (978-1-58659-042-0(1)) Artesian Pr.

—Connie's Secret. Epstein, Dwayne. 2003. (Romance Ser.). 58p. (J). pap. 4.95 (978-1-58659-460-2(5)) Artesian Pr.

—Crystal's Chance. Brin, Susannah. 2003. (Romance Ser.). 62p. (J). pap. 4.95 *(978-1-58659-459-6(1))* Artesian Pr.

—The Howling House. Schraff, Anne. rev. ed. 2004. (Standing Tall Mysteries Ser.). 51p. (J). (gr. 4-12). pap. 4.95 *(978-1-58659-083-3(9))* Artesian Pr.

—Search & Rescue. Brin, Susannah. rev. ed. 2004. (Take Ten Ser.). 62p. (J). (gr. 4-12). pap. 4.95 *(978-1-58659-043-7(X))* Artesian Pr.

—To Nicole with Love. West, Casey. 2003. (Romance Ser.). 60p. (J). pap. 4.95 *(978-1-58659-188-5(6))* Artesian Pr.

—Tough Guy. Brin, Susannah. rev. ed. 2004. (Take Ten Ser.). 62p. (J). (gr. 4-12). pap. 4.95 *(978-1-58659-045-1(6))* Artesian Pr.

Miller, Gina. Spooky Texas Tales. Tingle, Tim & Moore, James W. 2005. x, 85p. (J). pap. *(978-0-89672-566-9(9))* Texas Tech Univ. Pr.

Miller, Heidi. What the World Is Like to Bea Moore: The Treasure. Catanzarite, Lisa. 2009. 56p. pap. 17.26 *(978-1-4251-6321-1(1))* Trafford Publishing.

Miller, J. P. The House That Jack Built. Golden Books Staff. 2008. (Little Golden Book Ser.). (ENG.). 24p. (J). (gr. -1-2). 3.99 *(978-0-375-83530-8(X)*, Golden Bks.) Random Hse. Children's Bks.

—The Little Red Hen. Golden Books. 2015. (ENG.). 26p. (J). (-k). bds. 7.99 *(978-0-385-39094-1(7)*, Golden Bks.) Random Hse. Children's Bks.

—The Sweet Smell of Christmas. Scarry, Patricia M. 2003. (Scented Storybook Ser.). (ENG.). 36p. (J). (gr. -1-2). 9.99 *(978-0-375-82643-6(2)*, Golden Bks.) Random Hse. Children's Bks.

Miller, Jayna. Too Much Trick or Treat. Miller, Jayna. Thatch, Nancy, ed. 2005. 29p. (J). per. 19.95 *(978-0-933849-83-9(4))* landmark Hse., Ltd.

Miller, Jo. Day & Night, 1 vol. Hall, Margaret C. & Hall, Margaret. 2006. (Patterns in Nature Ser.). (ENG.). 24p. (gr. k-1). 24.65 *(978-0-7368-6338-4(9)*, Pebble Plus) Capstone Pr., Inc.

—Day & Night, 1 vol. Hall, Margaret C. Saunders-Smith, Gail, ed. 2006. (Patterns in Nature Ser.). (ENG.). 24p. (gr. k-1). per. 7.29 *(978-0-7368-9615-3(5)*, Pebble Plus) Capstone Pr., Inc.

—Phases of the Moon, 1 vol. Olson, Gillia M. 2006. (Patterns in Nature Ser.). (ENG.). 24p. (gr. k-1). 24.65 *(978-0-7368-6340-7(0)*, Pebble Plus) Capstone Pr., Inc.

—Phases of the Moon, 1 vol. Olson, Gillia M. Saunders-Smith, Gail, ed. 2006. (Patterns in Nature Ser.). (ENG.). 24p. (gr. k-1). per. 7.29 *(978-0-7368-9617-7(1)*, Pebble Plus) Capstone Pr., Inc.

—Seasons of the Year, 1 vol. Hall, Margaret C. & Hall, Margaret. 2006. (Patterns in Nature Ser.). (ENG.). 24p. (gr. k-1). 24.65 *(978-0-7368-6341-4(9)*, Pebble Plus) Capstone Pr., Inc.

—Seasons of the Year, 1 vol. Hall, Margaret C. Saunders-Smith, Gail, ed. 2006. (Patterns in Nature Ser.). (ENG.). 24p. (gr. k-1). per. 7.29 *(978-0-7368-9618-4(X)*, Pebble Plus) Capstone Pr., Inc.

Miller, Joanna. The Brass Serpent. Kimmel, Eric A. 2005. 32p. (J). 14.95 *(978-1-930143-41-8(9)*, 3419); pap. 9.95 *(978-1-930143-42-5(7)*, 3427) Simcha Media Group. (Devora Publishing).

Miller, Jonathan. When I Grow Up. 2011. 16p. (J). *(978-1-58865-637-7(3))* Kidsbooks, LLC.

—Winter, Spring, Summer, Fall. 2010. 16p. (J). *(978-1-58865-578-3(4))* Kidsbooks, LLC.

Miller, Josh, jt. illus. see Howard, Philip.

Miller, Joshua, jt. illus. see Howard, Philip.

Miller, Jules. When Night Became Day. 2015. (ENG.). 32p. (J). (gr. -1-k). 16.95 *(978-1-62914-632-4(3)*, Sky Pony Pr.) Skyhorse Publishing Co., Inc.

Miller, Jules. Ellie & the Truth about the Tooth Fairy. Miller, Jules. 2014. (ENG.). 36p. (J). (gr. -1-k). 16.95 *(978-1-62873-590-1(2)*, Sky Pony Pr.) Skyhorse Publishing Co., Inc.

Miller, Julia Love. The Other Day I Met a Bear. Feierabend, John M. 2014. (First Steps in Music Ser.). (ENG.). 32p. (J). (gr. -1-k). 16.95 *(978-1-62277-076-2(5))* G I A Pubns., Inc.

Miller, Justin. Devil's Canyon: Forensic Geography. McIntosh, Kenneth. 2007. (Crime Scene Club Ser.: Bk. 1). 144p. (YA). (gr. 9-12). 24.95 *(978-1-4222-0247-0(X))* Mason Crest.

—The Earth Cries Out: Forensic Chemistry & Environmental Science, 8 vols. McIntosh, Kenneth. 2007. (Crime Scene Club Ser.: Bk. 9). 144p. (YA). (gr. 9-12). lib. bdg. 24.95 *(978-1-4222-0254-8(2))* Mason Crest.

—If the Shoe Fits: Footwear Analysis, 7 vols. McIntosh, Kenneth. 2007. (Crime Scene Club Ser.). 144p. (YA). (gr. 9-12). lib. bdg. 24.95 *(978-1-4222-0253-1(4))* Mason Crest.

—Poison & Peril: Forensic Toxicology, 4 vols. McIntosh, Kenneth. 2007. (Crime Scene Club Ser.). 144p. (YA). (gr. 9-12). lib. bdg. 24.95 *(978-1-4222-0250-0(X))* Mason Crest.

—The Trickster's Image: Forensic Art, 3 vols. McIntosh, Kenneth. 2007. (Crime Scene Club Ser.). 144p. (YA). (gr. 9-12). lib. bdg. 24.95 *(978-1-4222-0249-4(6))* Mason Crest.

Miller, Kathy M., photos by. Chippy Chipmunk Parties in the Garden. Miller, Kathy M. 2009. (ENG., 40p. (gr. 2-3). 19.95 *(978-0-9840893-0-7(6))* Celtic Sunrise.

Miller, Kris Taft, jt. illus. see Wendland, Zachary.

Miller, Linzi. The Broken Law. Harris, Tumeka. Sea Breeze Productions & Phelps, Janice, eds. ed. 2006. 32p. (J). 14.95 *(978-0-9769366-0-2(7))* Dividion Group, LLC, The.

—The Goody Bag. Harris, Tumeka. Sea Breeze Productions, ed. 2006. 36p. (J). 14.95 *(978-0-9769366-2-6(3))* Dividion Group, LLC, The.

—Home Sweet Home. Harris, Tumeka. Sea Breeze Productions, ed. 2006. 36p. (J). 14.95 *(978-0-9769366-3-3(1))* Dividion Group, LLC, The.

—Trouble in Paradise. Harris, Tumeka. Sea Breeze Productions & Phelps, Janice, eds. 2006. 36p. (J). 14.95 *(978-0-9769366-1-9(5))* Dividion Group, LLC, The.

Miller, Margaret, photos by. POP! a Book about Bubbles. Bardley, Kimberly Brubaker. 2015. 40p. pap. 6.00 ***(978-1-61003-614-6(X))*** Center for the Collaborative Classroom.

Miller, Margaret, photos by. Baby Faces. Miller, Margaret. 2009. (Look Baby! Bks.). (ENG., 14p. (J). (gr. -1 — 1). 4.99 *(978-1-4169-7887-9(9)*, Little Simon) Little Simon.

—Baby Food. Miller, Margaret. 2009. (Look Baby! Bks.). (ENG., 14p. (J). (gr. -1 — 1). bds. 4.99 *(978-1-4169-8996-7(X)*, Little Simon) Little Simon.

—I Love Colors. Miller, Margaret. 2009. (Look Baby! Bks.). (ENG., 14p. (J). (gr. -1 — 1). 4.99 *(978-1-4169-7888-6(7)*, Little Simon) Little Simon.

—What's on My Head? Miller, Margaret. 2009. (Look Baby! Bks.). (ENG., 14p. (J). (gr. -1 — 1). 4.99 *(978-1-4169-8995-0(1)*, Little Simon) Little Simon.

Miller, Mark. Jake the Sadder Ladder. German, Lana. 2012. 20p. (-18). pap. 24.95 *(978-1-4626-9574-4(4))* America Star Bks.

Miller, Marlene. I Know Where the Freighters Go. Miller, Marlene. 2008. (ENG.). 32p. pap. 9.95 *(978-1-933916-29-3(X))* Nelson Publishing & Marketing.

Miller, Mike. Black Tide: Awakening of the Key. Bishop, Debbie. 2004. (ENG.). 208p. pap. 19.99 *(978-1-932431-00-1(4))* Left Field Angel Gate.

Miller, Mike, jt. illus. see Axworthy, Anni.

Miller, Nancy. Rockabye Baby Jesus. Tietz, Heather. 2011. 20p. 12.95 *(978-0-8091-6760-9(3))* Paulist Pr.

—Yes, Jesus Loves You. Tietz, Heather. 2009. 20p. (J). (gr. k-4). 14.95 *(978-0-8091-6743-2(3)*, Ambassador Bks.) Paulist Pr.

Miller, Nick. Native American Classics, Vol. 24. Smelcer, John E. et al. Pomplun, Tom et al, eds. 2013. Orig. Title: 2013. 144p. (YA). pap. 17.95 *(978-0-9825630-6-9(X))* Eureka Productions.

Miller, Paton. Sit! Stay! Sign! Margolis, Alysia. 2007. 32p. (J). *(978-1-4257-5919-3(X))* Margolis, Marion.

Miller, Peter, photos by. Vermont People. Miller, Peter. 5th ed. 2003. 144p. 34.95 *(978-0-9628064-6-9(3))*; pap. 22.95 *(978-0-9628064-9-0(8))* Silver Print Pr., Inc.

Miller, Phil, et al. The Great Chicago Fire Of 1871, 1 vol. Olson, Kay Melchisedech. 2006. (Disasters in History Ser.). (ENG.). 32p. (gr. 3-4). 29.99 *(978-0-7368-5480-1(0)*, Graphic Library) Capstone Pr., Inc.

—Henry Ford & the Model T, 1 vol. O'Hearn, Michael. 2006. (Inventions & Discovery Ser.). (ENG.). 32p. (gr. 3-4). 29.99 *(978-0-7368-6480-0(6)*, Graphic Library) Capstone Pr., Inc.

Miller, Phil. Isaac Newton & the Laws of Motion, 1 vol. Gianopoulos, Andrea & Barnett, Charles, III. 2007. (Inventions & Discovery Ser.). (ENG.). 32p. (gr. 3-4). pap. 8.10 *(978-0-7368-7899-9(8)*, 1264949, Graphic Library) Capstone Pr., Inc.

—Isaac Newton & the Laws of Motion [Scholastic]. Gianopoulos, Andrea & Barnett III, Charles. 2010. (Inventions & Discovery Ser.). 32p. pap. 0.45 *(978-1-4296-5969-7(6)*, Capstone Interactive Library) Capstone Digital.

Miller, Phil, et al. Matthew Henson: Arctic Adventurer, 1 vol. Hoena, Blake A. & Hoena, B. A. 2005. (Graphic Biographies Ser.). (ENG.). 32p. (gr. 3-4). 29.99 *(978-0-7368-4634-9(4)*, Graphic Library) Capstone Pr., Inc.

—Thomas Edison & the Lightbulb, 1 vol. Welvaert, Scott R. 2006. (Inventions & Discovery Ser.). (ENG.). 32p. (gr. 3-4). 29.99 *(978-0-7368-6489-3(X)*, Graphic Library) Capstone Pr., Inc.

—The Triangle Shirtwaist Factory Fire, 1 vol. Gunderson, Jessica Sarah & Gunderson, Jessica. 2006. (Disasters in History Ser.). (ENG.). 32p. (gr. 3-4). 29.99 *(978-0-7368-5483-2(5)*, Graphic Library) Capstone Pr., Inc.

Miller, Phil & Barnett, Charles, III. The Great San Francisco Earthquake & Fire, 1 vol. Burgan, Michael & Hoena, Blake A. 2007. (Disasters in History Ser.). (ENG.). 32p. (gr. 3-4). 29.99 *(978-1-4296-0155-9(8)*, Graphic Library) Capstone Pr., Inc.

—Isaac Newton & the Laws of Motion, 1 vol. Gianopoulos, Andrea & Capstone Press Editors. 2007. (Inventions & Discovery Ser.). (ENG.). 32p. (gr. 3-4). 29.99 *(978-0-7368-6847-1(X)*, Graphic Library) Capstone Pr., Inc.

Miller, Phil, jt. illus. see Barnett, Charles, III.

Miller, Rebecca. The Littlest Nephite in Nephi & the Brass Plates. Olsen, Bevan Lloyd. 2008. 14p. (J). (gr. 3-7). 15.99 *(978-1-59955-087-9(3))* Cedar Fort, Inc./CFI Distribution.

—Teeny Tiny Talks IV: My Eternal Family. Hammari, Kimiko. 2008. 116p. (J). pap. 12.99 *(978-1-59955-188-3(8))* Cedar Fort, Inc./CFI Distribution.

Miller, Richard. Along Little Dogie: Harley's Great Adventures. Pogo the Clown. 2005. (J). 12.95 *(978-0-9755253-3-3(6))* Chilinc Pubns.

—The Littlest Tiger: Harley's Great Adventures. Pogo the Clown. 2004. (J). 12.95 *(978-0-9755253-2-6(8))* Chilinc Pubns.

—Ricki Roars. Clown, Pogo the. 2006. 32p. (J). 12.95 *(978-0-9755253-8-8(7))* Chilinc Pubns.

Miller, Richard D. A Brave Little Lion: Harley's Great Adventures. Pogo the Clown. 2005. (J). 12.95 *(978-0-9755253-5-7(2))* Chilinc Pubns.

—The Great Blue Sky: Harley's Great Adventures. Pogo the Clown. 2005. (J). 12.95 *(978-0-9755253-6-4(0))* Chilinc Pubns.

—A Little Gray Mouse: Harley's Great Adventures. Pogo the Clown. 2005. (J). 12.95 *(978-0-9755253-7-1(9))* Chilinc Pubns.

—A Taste of Shrimp: Harley's Great Adventures. Pogo the Clown. 2005. (J). 12.95 *(978-0-9755253-4-0(4))* Chilinc Pubns.

Miller, Robert. A Dream Vacation. Haile, Carol J. 2003. 32p. (J). per. 19.95 *(978-0-9724699-0-6(7))* Panda Bear Pr.

Miller, Roger, photos by. United States Naval Academy: Annapolis. Foster, Linda. 2006. 168p. 39.95 *(978-0-911897-49-4(6))* Image Publishing, Ltd.

Miller, Ron. How Many Planets Circle the Sun? And Other Questions about Our Solar System. Carson, Mary Kay. 2014. (Good Question! Ser.). (ENG.). 32p. (J). (gr. 1). 12.95 *(978-1-4549-0668-1(5))* Sterling Publishing Co., Inc.

Miller, Ron. Special Effects: An Introduction to Movie Magic. Miller, Ron. 2006. (ENG.). 128p. (gr. 7-12). 26.60 *(978-0-7613-2918-3(8))* Lerner Publishing Group.

Miller, Russell. The Big Book of Gross Stuff. King, Bart. 2010. (ENG.). 304p. (YA). (gr. 5-6). pap. 19.99 *(978-1-4236-0746-5(5))* Gibbs Smith, Publisher.

Miller, Shane. Hawk of the Nile. Green, Robert James. 2012. 222p. 44.95 *(978-1-258-25119-2(1))*; pap. 29.95 *(978-1-258-25551-0(0))* Literary Licensing, LLC.

—Riddles, Riddles, Riddles: Enigmas & Anagrams, Puns & Puzzles, Quizzes & Conundrums! 2014. (ENG.). 256p. (J). (gr. 3-8). pap. 9.99 *(978-0-486-78186-0(0))* Dover Pubns., Inc.

Miller, Steve. Big Box, Little Box: The Forecast Calls for Potential Rain! Nash, Damien K. H. & Nash, Kathy. 2012. 80p. pap. 13.99 *(978-0-9846507-1-2(7))* Faith Bks. & MORE.

Miller, Susan. Step-by-Step. Taylor-Butler, Christine. 2005. (My First Reader Ser.). (ENG.). 32p. (J). (gr. k-1). lib. bdg. 18.50 *(978-0-516-24875-2(8)*, Children's Pr.) Scholastic Library Publishing.

Miller, Tom, jt. illus. see Fetherston, Catherine.

Miller, Victoria. Dora & the Unicorn King. 2011. (Dora the Explorer Ser.). (ENG.). 24p. (J). pap. 3.99 *(978-1-4424-1312-2(3)*, Simon Spotlight/Nickelodeon) Simon Spotlight/Nickelodeon.

—Dora in Wonderland (Dora the Explorer) Tillworth, Mary. 2014. (Pictureback Series.). (ENG.). 24p. (J). (gr. -1-2). 3.99 *(978-0-385-37119-3(5)*, Random Hse. Bks. for Young Readers) Random Hse. Children's Bks.

—Dora the Explorer to the Moon. Burroughs, Caleb. 2007. (Play a Tune Tale Ser.). 16p. (J). (gr. -1-3). 12.98 *(978-1-4127-8830-4(7))* Publications International, Ltd.

—Dora's Christmas Star (Dora the Explorer) Tillworth, Mary. 2013. (Glow-In-the-Dark Pictureback Ser.). (ENG.). 16p. (J). (gr. -1-2). 4.99 *(978-0-449-81780-3(6)*, Random Hse. Bks. for Young Readers) Random Hse. Children's Bks.

—Dora's Magic Watering Can. Rao, Lisa. 2008. (Dora the Explorer Ser.). (ENG.). 16p. (J). (gr. -1-1). pap. 4.99 *(978-1-4169-4772-1(8)*, Simon Spotlight/Nickelodeon) Simon Spotlight/Nickelodeon.

—Dora's Perfect Pumpkin. Larsen, Kirsten. 2007. (Dora the Explorer Ser.). (ENG.). 24p. (J). (gr. -1-3). pap. 3.99 *(978-1-4169-3438-7(3)*, Simon Spotlight/Nickelodeon) Simon Spotlight/Nickelodeon.

—Dora's Sleepover. Bergen, Lara Rice & Bergen, Lara. 2006. (Dora the Explorer Ser.: 12). (ENG.). 24p. (J). (gr. -1-1). pap. 3.99 *(978-1-4169-1508-9(7)*, Simon Spotlight/Nickelodeon) Simon Spotlight/Nickelodeon.

—Flowers for Mami Unicorn! 2010. (Dora the Explorer Ser.). (ENG.). 24p. (J). (gr. -1-2). pap. 3.99 *(978-1-4169-9064-2(X)*, Simon Spotlight/Nickelodeon) Simon Spotlight/Nickelodeon.

—I Love My Abuela! Ricci, Christine. 2009. (Dora the Explorer Ser.: 28). (ENG.). 24p. (J). pap. 3.99 *(978-1-4169-6866-5(0)*, Simon Spotlight/Nickelodeon) Simon Spotlight/Nickelodeon.

—Isa's Flower Garden (Dora the Explorer) Random House. 2014. (Glitter Board Book Ser.). (ENG.). 12p. (J). (— 1). bds. 6.99 *(978-0-385-37621-1(9)*, Random Hse. Bks. for Young Readers) Random Hse. Children's Bks.

—Lemonade with a Twist. Banks, Steven. 2004. (Fairly Oddparents Ser.). 32p. (J). (gr. k-2). 11.65 *(978-0-7569-1990-0(8))* Perfection Learning Corp.

—Rainbow Adventure. Golden Books Staff. 2010. (Super Color with Stickers Ser.). (ENG.). 96p. (J). (gr. -1-2). pap. 3.99 *(978-0-375-86350-9(8)*, Golden Bks.) Random Hse. Children's Bks.

—Rainbow Rescue! (Dora the Explorer) Golden Books. 2014. (Color Plus Chunky Crayons Ser.). (ENG.). 48p. (J). (gr. -1-2). pap. 3.99 *(978-0-385-37436-1(4)*, Golden Bks.) Random Hse. Children's Bks.

—A Royal Ball! (Dora & Friends) Golden Books. 2015. (Color Plus 1,000 Stickers Ser.). (ENG.). 64p. (J). (gr. -1-2). pap. 9.99 *(978-0-553-49766-3(9)*, Golden Bks.) Random Hse. Children's Bks.

—Save the Unicorn King! Golden Books Staff. 2011. (Paint Box Book Ser.). (ENG.). 48p. (J). (gr. -1-2). pap. 3.99 *(978-0-375-87391-1(0)*, Golden Bks.) Random Hse. Children's Bks.

—Super Babies! 2006. (Dora the Explorer Ser.: 18). (ENG.). 24p. (J). (gr. -1-3). pap. 3.99 *(978-1-4169-1485-3(4)*, Simon Spotlight/Nickelodeon) Simon Spotlight/Nickelodeon.

—Súper Bebés! Inches, Alison. 2006. (Dora la Exploradora Ser.). (SPA.). 24p. (J). (gr. -1-3). pap. 3.99 *(978-1-4169-2461-6(2)*, Libros Para Ninos) Libros Para Ninos.

—Tea Party in Wonderland (Dora the Explorer) Random House Staff. 2014. (Step into Reading Ser.). (ENG.). 32p. (J). (gr. -1-1). 3.99 *(978-0-449-81878-7(0))*; lib. bdg. 12.99 *(978-0-449-81879-4(9))* Random Hse. Children's Bks. (Random Hse. Bks. for Young Readers).

—Welcome to Wonderland! (Dora the Explorer) Golden Books. 2014. (Color Plus Chunky Crayons Ser.). (ENG.). 48p. (J). (gr. -1-2). pap. 3.99 *(978-0-449-81760-5(1)*, Golden Bks.) Random Hse. Children's Bks.

Miller, Victoria, jt. illus. see Aikins, Dave.

Miller, Victoria, jt. illus. see Mangano, Tom.

Miller, Victoria, jt. illus. see Perilli, Marilena.

Miller, Victoria, jt. illus. see Random House.

Miller, Woody. Meet the Howlers! Sayre, April Pulley. 2010. (ENG.). 32p. (J). (gr. -1-2). 16.95 *(978-1-57091-733-2(7))*; pap. 7.95 *(978-1-57091-734-9(5))* Charlesbridge Publishing, Inc.

—Tefilat Haderech: The Traveler's Prayer. 2012. (ENG.). 32p. (J). 17.95 *(978-0-939144-69-3(7))* EKS Publishing Co.

—Tefilat Haderech: The Traveler's Pryaer. 2012. (ENG.). 32p. (J). pap. 10.95 *(978-0-939144-68-6(9))* EKS Publishing Co.

—Zishe the Strongman. Rubinstein, Robert E. 2010. (Kar-Ben Favorites Ser.). (ENG.). 32p. (J). (gr. k-3). lib. bdg. 17.95 *(978-0-7613-3958-8(2)*, Kar-Ben Publishing) Lerner Publishing Group.

—Zishe the Strongman. Rubinstein, Robert. 2010. (Kar-Ben Favorites Ser.). (ENG.). 32p. (J). (gr. k-3). pap. 7.95 *(978-0-7613-3960-1(4)*, Kar-Ben Publishing) Lerner Publishing Group.

Millet, Claude & Millet, Denise. La Biblia: Los Grandes Relatos del Antiguo y del Nuevo Testamento. Marchon, Blandine. 4th ed.Tr. of Bible: Favorite Stories from the Old & New Testament. (SPA.). 158p. (J). (gr. 3-5). 25.56 *(978-84-263-3249-3(8))* Vives, Luis Editorial (Edelvives) ESP. Dist: Lectorum Pubns., Inc.

Millet, Denise, jt. illus. see Millet, Claude.

Millet, Esao & Millet, Jocelyn. The Boy's Book of Adventure: The Little Guidebook for Smart & Resourceful Boys. Lecreux, Michele & Gallais, Celia. 2013. (ENG.). 128p. (J). (gr. 3-7). 14.99 *(978-0-7641-6611-2(5))* Barron's Educational Series, Inc.

—The Girl's Book of Adventure: The Little Guidebook for Smart & Resourceful Girls. Lecreux, Michele & Gallais, Celia. 2013. (ENG.). 128p. (J). (gr. 3-7). 14.99 *(978-0-7641-6610-5(7))* Barron's Educational Series, Inc.

Millet, Jason, et al. Beyond Escape! 2007. (Choose Your Own Adventure Ser.: No. 15). 118p. (J). (gr. 4-7). per. 6.99 *(978-1-933390-15-4(8)*, CHCL15) Chooseco LLC.

—Escape. 2006. (Choose Your Own Adventure Ser.: No. 8). 124p. (J). (gr. 4-7). per. 6.99 *(978-1-933390-08-6(5)*, CHCL08) Chooseco LLC.

Millet, Jason. Freedom Songs: A Tale of the Underground Railroad, 1 vol. Robbins, Trina. 2008. (Historical Fiction Ser.). (ENG.). 56p. (gr. 2-3). pap. 6.25 *(978-1-4342-0495-0(2))*; lib. bdg. 25.32 *(978-1-4342-0445-5(6))* Stone Arch Bks. (Graphic Flash).

—Johnny Appleseed, 1 vol. Capstone Press Staff. 2003. (Tall Tales Ser.). (ENG.). 32p. (gr. 3-5). 27.32 *(978-0-7565-0458-8(9)*, CPB Grades 4-8) Compass Point Bks.

—War with the Evil Power Master. 2006. (Choose Your Own Adventure Ser.: No. 12). 123p. (J). (gr. 4-7). per. 6.99 *(978-1-933390-12-3(3)*, CHCL12) Chooseco LLC.

Millet, Jason, jt. illus. see Lim, Ron.

Millet, Jocelyn, jt. illus. see Millet, Esao.

Millett, Melanie. Teeny Tiny Talks: Junior Primary: I Will Follow God's Plan for Me, Vol. 1. Millett, Melanie. 2004. (J). per. 12.95 *(978-1-55517-778-2(6)*, Cedar Fort, Inc.) Cedar Fort, Inc./CFI Distribution.

Millican, JoAnn. Ballad of Koko-Ma. Millican, Jacob. 2003. (J). *(978-1-59404-014-6(1))* Peanut Butter Publishing.

Million, Liz. Elephant Rides Again. Harrison, Paul. 2009. (Get Ready (Windmill Books) Ser.). 32p. (J). (gr. k-2). lib. bdg. 22.60 *(978-1-60754-259-9(5))* Windmill Bks.

—Little Fred Riding Hood. Cox, Michael. 2006. (Red Bananas Ser.). (ENG.). 48p. (J). (gr. k-2). pap. 5.99 *(978-1-4052-1917-4(3))* Egmont Bks., Ltd. GBR. Dist: Independent Pubs. Group.

—Not so Silly Sausage. Gurney, Stella. 2011. 32p. pap. *(978-1-84089-707-4(4))* Zero to Ten, Ltd.

Mills, Lokken. Felipe the Flamingo. Conway, Jill Ker. 2006. (ENG.). 32p. (J). (gr. -1-3). 12.95 *(978-1-55591-547-6(7)*, 800.992.2908) Fulcrum Publishing.

Mills, Lokken. El Flamingo Felipe. Mills, Lokken. Conway, Jill Ker & Conway, Jill K. 2009. (SPA & ENG.). 32p. (J). (gr. k-3). pap. 9.95 *(978-1-55591-714-2(3))* Fulcrum Publishing.

Mills. Understanding Jason. Osborn. 2009. 24p. pap. 11.49 *(978-1-4389-4403-6(9))* AuthorHouse.

Mills, Christopher. Freddy Flamingo & the Kindertown Five. Gershenson, Harold P. 2005. 27p. (J). *(978-1-58987-070-3(0))* Kindermusik International.

—The Kindertown Fire Brigade. Gershenson, Harold P. 2006. (J). *(978-1-58987-019-2(0))* Kindermusik International.

—Noodles from Scratch. Gershenson, Harold P. 2006. (J). *(978-1-58987-007-9(7))* Kindermusik International.

Mills, Cindy. Cass Railroad Fun Book. 2007. 32p. (J). pap. 2.95 *(978-0-929915-74-6(7))* Headline Bks., Inc.

Mills, Dan, jt. photos by see Holmes, Robert.

Mills, Donald. The Night Before Christmas. Moore, Clement C. 2008. 30p. (J). (gr. -1-k). pap. 3.95 *(978-0-8249-5514-4(5))* Ideals Pubns.

Mills, Faythe. The Captain's Hat. Mercier, Deborah. 2007. 32p. (J). 17.99 *(978-0-9799410-0-9(8))* Minnewaska Pr.

Mills, Lori. Meet Toado & Friends. Mills, Linda Sue. I.t. ed. 2008. (ENG.). 30p. (J). 20.99 *(978-1-59879-246-1(6)*, Lifevest) Lifevest Publishing, Inc.

—Meet Toado & Friends. Brooks, Linda Sue. I.t. ed. 2008. (Toado & Friends Ser.). (ENG.). 30p. (J). (gr. -1-3). per. 11.99 *(978-1-59879-314-7(4)*, Lifevest) Lifevest Publishing, Inc.

Mills, Tom. What Am I? Easter. Lewis, Anne Margaret. 2012. (ENG.). 24p. (J). (gr. -1-k). 9.99 *(978-0-8075-8963-2(2))* Whitman, Albert & Co.

—What am I? Christmas. Lewis, Anne Margaret. 2011. (ENG.). 24p. (J). (gr. -1-k). 9.99 *(978-0-8075-8958-8(6))* Whitman, Albert & Co.

—What Am I? Florida. Lewis, Anne Margaret. 2012. (ENG.). 24p. (J). (gr. -1-k). 9.99 *(978-0-8075-8966-3(7))* Whitman, Albert & Co.

—What Am I? Halloween. Lewis, Anne Margaret. 2011. (ENG.). 24p. (J). (gr. -1-k). 9.99 *(978-0-8075-8959-5(4))* Whitman, Albert & Co.

—What am I? Illinois. Lewis, Anne Margaret. 2011. (ENG.). 24p. (J). (gr. -1-k). 9.99 *(978-0-8075-8960-1(8))* Whitman, Albert & Co.

—What Am I? Passover. Lewis, Anne Margaret. 2012. (ENG.). 24p. (J). (gr. -1-k). 9.99 *(978-0-8075-8971-7(3))* Whitman, Albert & Co.

—What Am I? Texas. Lewis, Anne Margaret. 2012. (ENG.). 24p. (J). (gr. -1-k). 9.99 *(978-0-8075-8982-3(9))* Whitman, Albert & Co.

Millsap, Lonnie. The Cow-Pie Chronicles. Butler, James L. 2013. (ENG.). 192p. (J). (gr. 2-4). pap. 9.95 (978-1-938778-32-2(4)) Publishing Syndicate.

Millward, Gwen. The Beasties. Nimmo, Jenny. 2012. (ENG.). 32p. (J). (gr. -1-k). pap. 8.99 (978-1-4052-4335-3(X)) Egmont Bks., Ltd. GBR. Dist: Independent Pubs. Group.

—The Bog Baby. Willis, Jeanne. 2009. (ENG.). 32p. (J). (gr. -1-2). 16.99 (978-0-375-86176-5(9), Schwartz & Wade Bks.) Random Hse. Children's Bks.

—Guess What I Found in Dragon Wood. Knapman, Timothy. 2007. (ENG.). 32p. (J). (gr. -1-3). 16.95 (978-1-59990-190-9(0), Bloomsbury USA Childrens) Bloomsbury USA.

—How Do You Hug a Porcupine? Isop, Laurie. 2011. (ENG.). 32p. (J). (gr. -1-1). 16.99 (978-1-4424-1291-0(7), Simon & Schuster Bks. For Young Readers) Simon & Schuster Bks. For Young Readers.

—The Snuggle Sandwich. Doyle, Malachy. 2013. (ENG.). 32p. (J). (gr. -1-k). pap. 9.99 (978-1-84939-420-8(2)) Andersen Pr. GBR. Dist: Independent Pubs. Group.

Millward, Hayley. Emerson Learns about Surgery. May, Erica. 2013. (ENG.). (J). (gr. -1-3). 14.95 (978-1-62086-279-7(4)) Mascot Bks., Inc.

Milne, Alex & Ruffolo, Rob. Mix & Match. Roe, David & Reader's Digest Editors. 2007. (ENG.). 12p. (J). (gr. -1-1). bds. 14.99 (978-0-7944-1286-9(6)) Reader's Digest Assn., Inc., The.

Milne, David. I Spy with My Little Eye: Baseball. Herzog, Brad. 2011. (I Spy Ser.). (ENG.). 32p. (J). (gr. 3-6). 13.95 (978-1-58536-496-1(7)) Sleeping Bear Pr.

Milne, David, photos by. I Spy with My Little Eye - Hockey. Napier, Matt. 2008. (ENG., 32p. (J). (gr. k-6). 13.95 (978-1-58536-365-0(0)) Sleeping Bear Pr.

Milne, Jessica. Jeremy & the Enchanted Theater. Citra, Becky. 2004. 64p. (J). lib. bdg. 20.00 (978-1-4242-1258-3(8)) Fitzgerald Bks.

—Jeremy & the Enchanted Theater, 1 vol. Citra, Becky. 2004. (Orca Echoes Ser.). (ENG.). 64p. (J). (gr. 2-3). pap. 6.95 (978-1-55143-322-6(2)) Orca Bk. Pubs. USA.

—Jeremy & the Fantastic Flying Machine, 1 vol. Citra, Becky. 2008. (Orca Echoes Ser.). (ENG.). 64p. (J). (gr. 2-3). pap. 6.95 (978-1-55143-950-1(6)) Orca Bk. Pubs. USA.

—Jeremy & the Golden Fleece, 1 vol. Citra, Becky. 2007. (Orca Echoes Ser.). (ENG.). 64p. (J). (gr. 2-3). per. 4.99 (978-1-55143-657-9(4)) Orca Bk. Pubs. USA.

Milne, Terry. Chocolate Porridge. Mahy, Margaret. 2014. (Early Reader Ser.). (ENG.). 80p. (J). 9.99 (978-1-4440-1130-2(8), Orion Children's Bks.) Hachette Children's Group GBR. Dist: Independent Pubs. Group.

Milner, Elizabeth B. Canoe Trip. Beasley, David R. 2006. 129p. (YA). per. 15.00 (978-0-915317-21-9(4)) Davus Publishing.

Milner, Fran & Brewer, Trish. Astrology for Regular People. Pluto Project Staff & Semkiw, Walter. 2007. (For Regular People Ser.). (ENG.). 198p. pap. 24.95 (978-0-9662982-7-7(6)) Pluto Project.

Milord, Susan. Pebble: A Story about Belonging. Milord, Susan. 2007. (ENG.). 32p. (J). (gr. -1-2). 15.99 (978-0-06-085807-0(9)) HarperCollins Pubs.

Milosevic, Tamara. The Wash Cloth & the Turtle. Knight, Deidre Denise. 2013. 36p. 17.95 (978-0-9893091-2-7(6)) Cube Marketing.

Milstrey, Dawn Bourdeau. I Can Sleep Alone. Mahr, Frank J. 2013. 34p. pap. 6.99 (978-1-4575-1895-9(3)) Dog Ear Publishing, LLC.

Miltenberger, Dave & Miltenberger, Jeri. Bessie's Little Mouse Day Care. Johnson, Gerald J. J. 2012. 32p. pap. 24.95 (978-1-62709-430-6(X)) America Star Bks.

Miltenberger, Dave, jt. illus. see Miltenberger, Jeri.

Miltenberger, Dave & Jeri. Officer Buck MacDuck. Johnson, Gerald J. J. 2013. 24p. pap. 24.95 (978-1-62709-429-0(6)) America Star Bks.

Miltenberger, Jeri & Miltenberger, Dave. Buffy Bunny. Johnson, Gerald J. J. 2011. 32p. pap. 24.95 (978-1-4512-5292-7(7)) America Star Bks.

—Miss Spinny, the Spider. Johnson, Gerald Jj. 2012. 24p. 24.95 (978-1-4626-6488-7(1)) America Star Bks.

—Misty's Christmas Present, 1 vol. Johnson, Gerald J. J. 2010. 32p. 24.95 (978-1-4512-1330-0(1)) PublishAmerica, Inc.

Miltenberger, Jeri, jt. illus. see Miltenberger, Dave.

Miltenberger, Jeri and Dave. Betty, the Chubby Butterfly. Johnson, Gerald J. J. 2011. 24p. pap. 24.95 (978-1-4489-3990-9(9)) America Star Bks.

Milton, Alexandra. Good Luck Baby Owls. Milton, Giles. 2012. (ENG.). 32p. (J). (gr. -1-k). 16.95 (978-1-907967-28-3(1)) Boxer Bks., Ltd. GBR. Dist: Sterling Publishing Co., Inc.

Milton, Freddy. Walt Disney's Comics, No. 687. Milton, Freddy. Erickson, Byron et al. Clark, John, ed. 2008. (Walt Disney's Comics & Stories Ser.). 64p. pap. 7.99 (978-1-888472-98-1(7)) Gemstone Publishing, Inc.

Milway, Alex. Alien Moon. Milway, Alex. 2014. (ENG.). 240p. (J). pap. 5.99 (978-1-61067-164-4(3)) Kane Miller.

—The Magma Conspiracy: Armed, Dangerous & Covered in Fur! Milway, Alex. 2013. (ENG.). 224p. (J). pap. 5.99 (978-1-61067-159-0(7)) Kane Miller.

—Operation Robot Storm: The Mythical 9th Division. Milway, Alex. 2013. (ENG.). 224p. (J). pap. 5.99 (978-1-61067-074-6(4)) Kane Miller.

Milway, Alex. Pigsticks & Harold & the Incredible Journey. Milway, Alex. (Candlewick Sparks Ser.). (ENG.). 84p. (J). (gr. k-4). 2015. pap. 3.99 (978-0-7636-8105-0(9)); 2014. 12.99 (978-0-7636-6615-6(7)) Candlewick Pr.

—Pigsticks & Harold & the Tuptown Thief. Milway, Alex. 2015. (ENG.). 80p. (J). (gr. k-4). 12.99 (978-0-7636-7809-8(0)) Candlewick Pr.

Milway, Alex. Terror of the Deep: Armed, Dangerous & Covered in Fur! Milway, Alex. 2013. (ENG.). 256p. (J). pap. 5.99 (978-1-61067-075-3(2)) Kane Miller.

Mims, Ashley. The Emperor's New Clothes. Namm, Diane. 2014. (Silver Penny Stories Ser.). (ENG.). 40p. (J). (gr. -1-1). 4.95 (978-1-4027-8428-6(7)) Sterling Publishing Co., Inc.

—The Little Mermaid. McFadden, Deanna & Andersen, Hans Christian. 2013. (Silver Penny Stories Ser.). (ENG.). 40p. (J). (gr. -1-1). 4.95 (978-1-4027-8336-4(1)) Sterling Publishing Co., Inc.

—Little Women. Alcott, Louisa May & Naxos of America Staff. 3rd ed. 2008. (Hear It Read It Classics Ser.: 0). (ENG.). 128p. (J). (gr. 2-4). 9.99 (978-1-4022-1169-0(4), Sourcebooks Jabberwocky) Sourcebooks, Inc.

—Rapunzel. McFadden, Deanna. 2012. (Silver Penny Stories Ser.). (ENG.). 40p. (J). (gr. -1-1). 4.95 (978-1-4027-8338-8(8)) Sterling Publishing Co., Inc.

Min, Ken. Hot, Hot Roti for Dada-Ji. Zia, F. 2011. (ENG.). 32p. (J). (gr. k-5). 17.95 (978-1-60060-443-0(9)) Lee & Low Bks., Inc.

Minagawa, Ryoji. Project Arms. Nanatsuki, Kyoichi. (Project Arms Ser.). (ENG.). Vol. 10. 2005. 216p. pap. 9.99 (978-1-4215-0073-7(6)); Vol. 12. 2006. 208p. pap. 9.99 (978-1-4215-0386-8(7)) Viz Media.

MinaLima. Bigfoot Is Missing! Lewis, J. Patrick & Nesbitt, Kenn. 2015. (ENG.). 40p. (J). (gr. 2-5). 17.99 (978-1-4521-1895-6(7)) Chronicle Bks. LLC.

Minami, Maki. S. A. Minami, Maki. 2008. (S. A. Ser.: 5). (ENG.). 192p. pap. 8.99 (978-1-4215-1748-3(5)) Viz Media.

Minch, Edwin & Minch, Jason. Caminos de Baja California: Geologia y Biologica Para Su Viaje. Minch, John & Minch, Edwin, photos by. Minch, Jason, photos by. Minch, John & Ledesma Vazquez, Jorge. Ledesma Vazquez, Jorge, tr. 2003. (SPA.). 192p. per. 23.95 (978-0-9631090-2-6(2)) Minch, John & Assocs., Inc.

Minch, Jason, jt. illus. see Minch, Edwin.

Minckler, Kathleen L. Bobo, Chen Odasye A / Bobo, the Sneaky Dog: Mancy's Haitian Folktale Collection. Lauture, Mireille B. 2010. 28p. pap. 12.49 (978-1-4520-6173-3(4)) AuthorHouse.

—Mancy's Haitian Folktale Collection: Father Misery. Lauture, Mireille B. 2011. 24p. pap. 12.50 (978-1-4634-3682-7(3)) AuthorHouse.

Mind Candy Ltd. Staff. Roary Eyes His Cards: Stories, Games, & 72 Collectible Playing Cards. Reader's Digest Editors & Bell, Megan. 2012. (Book & Collectible Cards Ser.). (ENG.). 64p. (J). (gr. 1-4). pap. 9.99 (978-0-7944-2601-9(8)) Reader's Digest Assn., Inc., The.

Mind Wave Inc. MoshiMoshiKawaii: Strawberry Princess Moshi's Activity Book. Mind Wave Inc. 2012. (MoshiMoshiKawaii Ser.). (ENG.). 28p. (J). (gr. -1-2). pap. 4.99 (978-0-7636-6237-0(2)) Candlewick Pr.

—Strawberry Moshi's Activity Book. Mind Wave Inc. 2012. (MoshiMoshiKawaii Ser.). (ENG.). 28p. (J). (gr. -1-2). pap. 4.99 (978-0-7636-6236-3(4)) Candlewick Pr.

Minekura, Kazuya. Saiyuki, 9 vols., Vol. 8. Minekura, Kazuya, creator. rev. ed. 2005. 192p. pap. 9.99 (978-1-59532-433-7(X)) TOKYOPOP, Inc.

Miner, Deb. I get Around. Miner, Deb. 2007. (ENG.). 32p. (J). bds. 11.00 (978-0-9794262-0-9(0)) do be you.

Miner, Julia. The Lighthouse Santa. Hunter, Sara Hoagland. 2011. 36p. (J). (gr. -1-3). 17.95 (978-1-61168-006-5(9)) Univ. Pr. of New England.

—The Unbreakable Code. Hunter, Sara Hoagland. 2007. (ENG.). 32p. (J). (gr. 1-3). per. 7.95 (978-0-87358-917-8(3)) Cooper Square Publishing Llc.

Ming, Choo Hill. Space Aliens in Our School. Cowley, Joy. 2011. (Dominie Joy Readers Ser.). (ENG.). 8p. (J). (gr. -1-3). pap. 4.67 (978-1-56270-755-2(8)) Dominie Pr., Inc.

Minger, Nancy. The Star Spangled Banner. Key, Francis Scott. 2010. 16p. (J). (gr. -1-1). 10.99 (978-0-8249-1838-5(X), Candy Cane Pr.) Ideals Pubns.

Mingming. Neon Genesis Evangelion Vol. 2: Campus Apocalypse, 4 vols. Mingming. 2011. (ENG.). 160p. pap. 10.99 (978-1-59582-661-9(0)) Dark Horse Comics.

Mingo, Norman & Ernst, Clara. Alice Faye Paper Dolls: Glamorous Movie Star Paper Dolls & Costumes. Mingo, Norman. 2007. 8p. pap. 12.00 (978-0-9795053-0-0(5)) Paper Studio Pr.

—Bette Davis Paper Dolls. Mingo, Norman. Taliadoros, Jenny, ed. 2007. (ENG.). 16p. pap. 12.00 (978-0-9790668-2-5(4)) Paper Studio Pr.

—Navy Scouts Paper Dolls. Mingo, Norman. Taliadoros, Jenny, ed. 2007. (ENG.). 16p. pap. 12.00 (978-0-9790668-3-2(2)) Paper Studio Pr.

—Rita Hayworth Paper Dolls. Mingo, Norman. Taliadoros, Jenny, ed. 2006. 16p. pap. 12.00 (978-0-9790668-0-1(8)) Paper Studio Pr.

Mingo, Norman & Ernt, Clara. Deanna Durbin Paper Dolls. Mingo, Norman. 2007. 16p. pap. 12.00 (978-0-9790668-5-6(9)) Paper Studio Pr.

Mingus, Cathi. Leading Ladies, 2 vols. Kimmel, Elizabeth Cody. 2012. (Forever Four Ser.: 2). (ENG.). 224p. (J). (gr. 3-7). pap. 6.99 (978-0-448-45549-5(8), Grosset & Dunlap) Penguin Publishing Group.

—A Smart Girl's Guide to Manners: The Secrets to Grace, Confidence, & Being Your Best. Holyoke, Nancy. Watkins, Michelle, ed. 2005. (ENG.). 120p. (J). (gr. 3). per. 9.95 (978-1-58485-983-3(0), American Girl) American Girl Publishing, Inc.

—Stories from New York, No. 3. Kimmel, Elizabeth Cody. 2012. (Forever Four Ser.: 3). (ENG.). 208p. (J). (gr. 3-7). pap. 6.99 (978-0-448-45550-1(1), Grosset & Dunlap) Penguin Publishing Group.

—#1 Forever Four. Kimmel, Elizabeth Cody. 2012. (Forever Four Ser.: 1). (ENG.). 224p. (J). (gr. 3-7). pap. 6.99 (978-0-448-45548-8(X), Grosset & Dunlap) Penguin Publishing Group.

Mini Pois Etc. Maks & Mila on a Special Journey. Bakker, Merel. 2013. 54p. (978-2-9700865-0-5(6)) Mila Publishing, Merel Bakker.

MiniKim, et al. Changing Moon. Mariolle, Mathieu. 2010. (Nola's Worlds Ser.: 1). (ENG.). 136p. (J). (gr. 6-9). 30.60 (978-0-7613-6502-0(8)); pap. 9.95 (978-0-7613-6538-9(9), Graphic Universe) Lerner Publishing Group.

—Even for a Dreamer Like Me. Mariolle, Mathieu. 2010. (Nola's Worlds Ser.: 3). (ENG.). 128p. (J). (gr. 6-9). 30.60 (978-0-7613-6505-1(2)); pap. 9.95 (978-0-7613-6541-9(9), Graphic Universe) Lerner Publishing Group.

—Ferrets & Ferreting Out. Mariolle, Mathieu. 2010. (Nola's Worlds Ser.: 2). (ENG.). 136p. (J). (gr. 6-9). 30.60 (978-0-7613-6504-4(4)) Lerner Publishing Group.

Minister, Peter. The Dawn of Planet Earth. Rake, Matthew. 2015. (Prehistoric Field Guides). (ENG.). 32p. (J). (gr. 3-6). 26.65 (978-1-4677-6348-6(9), Lerner Pubns.) Lerner Publishing Group.

—Dinosaurs Rule. Rake, Matthew. 2015. (Prehistoric Field Guides). (ENG.). 32p. (J). (gr. 3-6). 26.65 (978-1-4677-6349-3(7), Lerner Pubns.) Lerner Publishing Group.

Minnerly, Denise Bennett. Molly Meets Mona & Friends: A Magical Day in the Museum. 2004. (ENG.). 40p. (J). 17.95 (978-1-56290-324-4(1)) Crystal Productions.

Minnerly-Figueroa, Maria. Autism Spectrum Disorders Workbook: For Kids, Parents & Teachers Too. Basso, Michael. Scarfone, Dorothy, ed. 2011. (ENG.). 34p. pap. 14.95 (978-1-4564-0206-8(4)) CreateSpace Independent Publishing Platform.

Minnich, Matt. Sunburn: Bridging School to Home - C. Prokopchak, Ann. l.t. ed. 2003. (ENG.). 8p. (gr. k-1). pap. 4.95 (978-1-57874-014-7(2)) Kaeden Corp.

Minns, Karen M. C. Patterns in Arithmetic: Parent/Teacher Guide & Student Workbook: Book 1. Glenn, Suki & Carpenter, Susan. 2004. 305p. (YA). spiral bd. 45.00 (978-0-9729248-2-5(5)) Pattern Pr.

—Patterns in Arithmetic 2: Parent/Teacher Guide: Book 2. Glenn, Suki & Carpenter, Susan. 2005. 260p. (gr. 2-18). spiral bd. 22.00 (978-0-9729248-3-2(3)) Pattern Pr.

Minns, Karen Marie Christa. Patterns in Arithmetic 2: Student Workbook: Book 2. Glenn, Suki & Carpenter, Susan. 2005. (ENG.). 269p. (gr. 2-18). spiral bd. (978-0-9729248-5-6(X)) Pattern Pr.

Minor, Sarah. Pillow Talk: Loving affirmations to encourage & guide your Children. 2008. (ENG.). 96p. (YA). 16.95 (978-0-9816942-0-7(9)) Beck Global Publishing.

Minor, Wendell. Abe Lincoln Remembers. Turner, Ann Warren. 2003. (ENG.). 32p. (J). (gr. 1-4). pap. 6.99 (978-0-06-051107-4(9)) HarperCollins Pubs.

—Abraham Lincoln Comes Home. Burleigh, Robert. rev. ed. 2008. (ENG.). 40p. (J). (gr. 1-4). 16.95 (978-0-8050-7529-8(1), Holt, Henry & Co. Bks. For Young Readers) Holt, Henry & Co.

—Abraham Lincoln Comes Home. Burleigh, Robert. 2009. (J). (gr. 3-5). 27.95 incl. audio (978-0-8045-6977-4(0)) Spoken Arts, Inc.

—Abraham Lincoln Comes Home. Burleigh, Robert. 2014. (ENG.). 40p. (J). (gr. 1-4). 6.99 (978-1-250-03989-7(4)) Square Fish.

—America the Beautiful. Bates, Katherine Lee. 2006. (J). (gr. -1-3). pap. incl. audio (978-1-59112-953-0(2)); pap. 39.95 incl. audio compact disk (978-1-59112-957-8(5)) Live Oak Media.

—Bigger. Calvert, Patricia. 2003. (ENG.). 144p. (J). (gr. 3-7). pap. 8.95 (978-0-689-86003-4(X), Simon & Schuster/Paula Wiseman Bks.) Simon & Schuster/Paula Wiseman Bks.

—Cat, What Is That? Johnston, Tony. 2008. (ENG.). 32p. (J). pap. 10.95 (978-1-56792-351-3(8)) Godine, David R. Pub.

—The Eagles Are Back. George, Jean Craighead. 2013. (ENG.). 32p. (J). (gr. 1-3). 16.99 (978-0-8037-3771-6(8), Dial) Penguin Publishing Group.

—Edward Hopper Paints His World. Burleigh, Robert. 2014. (ENG.). 40p. (J). (gr. k-4). 17.99 (978-0-8050-8752-9(4), Holt, Henry & Co. Bks. For Young Readers) Holt, Henry & Co.

—Galápagos George. George, Jean Craighead. 2014. (ENG.). 40p. (J). (gr. k-3). 15.99 (978-0-06-028793-1(4)) HarperCollins Pubs.

—Galapagos Picture Book. George, Jean Craighead. Date not set. 32p. (J). (gr. k-3). 5.99 (978-0-06-443648-9(9)) HarperCollins Pubs.

—Ghost Ship. Clark, Mary Higgins. 2007. (ENG.). 40p. (J). (gr. 1-5). 17.99 (978-1-4169-3514-8(2), Simon & Schuster/Paula Wiseman Bks.) Simon & Schuster/Paula Wiseman Bks.

—Henry Knox: Bookseller, Soldier, Patriot. Silvey, Anita. 2010. (ENG.). 40p. (J). (gr. 1-4). 17.99 (978-0-618-27485-7(5)) Houghton Mifflin Harcourt Publishing Co.

—If You Spent a Day with Thoreau at Walden Pond. Burleigh, Robert. 2012. (ENG.). 36p. (J). (gr. k-4). 17.99 (978-0-8050-9137-3(8), Holt, Henry & Co. Bks. For Young Readers) Holt, Henry & Co.

—If You Were a Panda Bear. Minor, Florence F. 2013. (ENG.). 32p. (J). (gr. -1-3). 17.99 (978-0-06-195090-2(4), Tegen, Katherine Bks) HarperCollins Pubs.

—If You Were a Penguin. Minor, Florence F. 2009. 32p. (J). (gr. -1-2). lib. bdg. 18.89 (978-0-06-113098-4(2)) HarperCollins Pubs.

—Into the Woods: John James Audubon Lives His Dream. Burleigh, Robert. 2011. (ENG.). 40p. (J). (gr. 1-4). pap. 19.99 (978-1-4424-5337-1(0), Atheneum Bks. for Young Readers) Simon & Schuster Children's Publishing.

—The Last Polar Bear. George, Jean Craighead. (ENG.). 32p. (J). (gr. -1-2). 2014. pap. 6.99 (978-0-06-124069-0(9)); 2009. 16.99 (978-0-06-124067-6(2)) HarperCollins Pubs.

—The Last Train. Titcomb, Gordon. 2010. (ENG.). 32p. (J). (gr. -1-3). 17.99 (978-1-59643-164-5(4)) Roaring Brook Pr.

—Look to the Stars. Aldrin, Buzz. 2009. (ENG.). 40p. (J). (gr. 1-3). 17.99 (978-0-399-24721-7(1), Putnam Juvenile) Penguin Publishing Group.

—Luck: The Story of a Sandhill Crane. George, Jean Craighead. 2006. (Outdoor Adventures Ser.). 32p. (J). (gr. -1-3). (ENG.). 16.99 (978-0-06-008201-7(1), Geringer, Laura Book); 18.89 (978-0-06-008202-4(X)) HarperCollins Pubs.

—Luck: The Story of a Sandhill Crane. George, Jean Craighead. 2008. (J). (gr. k-4). 28.95 incl. audio compact disk (978-1-4301-0332-5(9)) Live Oak Media.

—A Lucky Thing: Poems & Paintings. Schertle, Alice. 2006. 28p. (J). (gr. 4-8). reprint ed. 17.00 (978-1-4223-5417-9(2)) DIANE Publishing Co.

—The Magical Christmas Horse. Clark, Mary Higgins. 2011. (ENG.). 40p. (J). (gr. -1-3). 17.99 (978-1-4169-9478-7(5), Simon & Schuster/Paula Wiseman Bks.) Simon & Schuster/Paula Wiseman Bks.

—Nibble Nibble. Brown, Margaret Wise. 2007. (ENG.). 32p. (J). (gr. -1-3). 17.99 (978-0-06-059208-0(7)) HarperCollins Pubs.

—Night Flight: Amelia Earhart Crosses the Atlantic. Burleigh, Robert. 2011. (ENG.). 40p. (J). (gr. -1-3). 17.99 (978-1-4169-6733-0(8), Simon & Schuster Bks. For Young Readers) Simon & Schuster Bks. For Young Readers.

—Rachel: The Story of Rachel Carson. Ehrlich, Amy. 2008. (ENG.). 32p. (J). (gr. -1-3). pap. 6.99 (978-0-15-206324-5(2)) Houghton Mifflin Harcourt Publishing Co.

—Reaching for the Moon. Aldrin, Buzz. (ENG.). 40p. (J). (gr. 1-4). 2008. 6.99 (978-0-06-055447-7(9), Collins); 2005. 17.99 (978-0-06-055445-3(2)) HarperCollins Pubs.

—Reaching for the Moon. Aldrin, Buzz. unabr. ed. 2005. (Picture Book Readalong Ser.). (gr. k-4). 28.95 incl. audio compact disk (978-1-59519-582-1(3)) Live Oak Media.

—The Seashore Book. Zolotow, Charlotte. 2004. (Reading Rainbow Bks.). (gr. -1-3). 17.00 (978-0-7569-4234-2(9)) Perfection Learning Corp.

—Sequoia. Johnston, Tony. 2014. (ENG.). 40p. (J). (gr. -1-3). 17.99 (978-1-59643-727-2(8)) Roaring Brook Pr.

—Shaker Hearts. Turner, Ann. 2006. 35p. (J). (gr. 4-8). pap. 11.00 (978-1-4223-5856-6(9)) DIANE Publishing Co.

—Sitting Bull Remembers. Turner, Ann Warren & Turner, Ann. 2007. (ENG.). 32p. (J). (gr. 1-4). 16.99 (978-0-06-051399-3(3)) HarperCollins Pubs.

—Snowboard Twist. George, Jean Craighead. 2004. (Outdoor Adventures Ser.). (ENG.). 32p. (J). 15.99 (978-0-06-050595-0(8)) HarperCollins Pubs.

—The Wolves Are Back. George, Jean Craighead. 2008. (J). (gr. 1-4). 25.95 incl. audio (978-1-4301-0591-6(7)) Live Oak Media.

—The Wolves Are Back. George, Jean Craighead. 2008. (ENG.). 32p. (J). (gr. -1-3). 16.99 (978-0-525-47947-5(3), Dutton Juvenile) Penguin Publishing Group.

Minor, Wendell. Christmas Tree! Minor, Wendell. Minor, Florence F. 2005. (ENG.). 40p. (J). (gr. -1-3). 16.99 (978-0-06-056034-8(7), Tegen, Katherine Bks) HarperCollins Pubs.

—Daylight Starlight Wildlife. Minor, Wendell. 2015. (ENG.). 32p. (J). (gr. -1-k). 17.99 (978-0-399-24662-3(2), Nancy Paulsen Bks.) Penguin Publishing Group.

—How Big Could Your Pumpkin Grow? Minor, Wendell. 2013. (ENG.). 32p. (J). (gr. -1-k). 16.99 (978-0-399-24684-5(3)) Penguin Publishing Group.

—If You Were a Penguin. Minor, Wendell. Minor, Florence F. 2008. (ENG.). 32p. (J). (gr. -1-2). 17.99 (978-0-06-113097-7(4), Tegen, Katherine Bks) HarperCollins Pubs.

—My Farm Friends. Minor, Wendell. (ENG.). (J). (gr. -1-k). 2013. 26p. bds. 6.99 (978-0-399-25799-5(3), Nancy Paulsen Bks.); 2011. 28p. 16.99 (978-0-399-24477-3(8), Putnam Juvenile) Penguin Publishing Group.

Minor, Wendell & Howell, Troy. America the Beautiful. Bates, Katharine Lee & Bates, Katharine. 2003. (ENG.). 32p. (J). (gr. -1-2). 18.99 (978-0-399-23885-7(9), Putnam Juvenile) Penguin Publishing Group.

Minor, Wendell, jt. illus. see Peterson, Stephanie.

Minter, Daniel. Ellen's Broom. Lyons, Kelly Starling. 2012. (ENG.). 32p. (J). (gr. k-3). 16.99 (978-0-399-25003-3(4), Putnam Juvenile) Penguin Publishing Group.

Mintzi, Vali. The Girl with a Brave Heart. Jahanforuz, Rita. 2013. (ENG.). 40p. (J). (gr. k-5). 16.99 (978-1-84686-929-7(3)) Barefoot Bks., Inc.

Mioroney, Tracy. A Child's Book of Parables. Froeb, Lori. 2003. 32p. (J). 15.99 (978-0-7847-1278-8(6), 04344) Standard Publishing.

Miracola, Jeff. Welcome to Monster Isle. Chin, Oliver. 2008. (ENG.). 36p. (J). (gr. -1-3). 15.95 (978-1-59702-016-9(8)) Immedium.

Miralles, Ana. Waluk. Ruiz, Emilio. Oliverio, Daniel, tr. 2013. (ENG.). 56p. (J). (gr. 2-5). pap. 7.95 (978-1-4677-1606-2(5)); lib. bdg. 26.60 (978-1-4677-1598-0(0)) Lerner Publishing Group. (Graphic Universe).

Miralles, Jose. The Golden Children's Bible. Golden Books Staff. 2006. (ENG.). 512p. (J). (gr. -1-2). 17.99 (978-0-307-16520-6(5), 16835, Golden Inspirational) Random Hse. Children's Bks.

Miralles, Jose & McTeigue, Jane. Christmas Star: A Light-up Shadow-Box Book. 2005. 10p. (J). (gr. k-4). reprint ed. 10.00 (978-0-7567-9559-7(1)) DIANE Publishing Co.

Miralles, Joseph. Pride & Prejudice. Austen, Jane. 2005. (Great Illustrated Classics Ser.). 236p. (gr. 3-8). 21.35 (978-1-59679-249-4(3)) Spotlight.

Miranda, Francisco. What Is My Song? Linn, Dennis et al. 2005. 32p. 16.95 (978-0-8091-6722-7(0), 6722-0) Paulist Pr.

Miranda, Inaki. Coffin Hill - Dark Endeavors, Vol. 2. Kittredge, Caitlin. 2015. (ENG.). 160p. pap. 14.99 (978-1-4012-5084-3(X), Vertigo) DC Comics.

Miranda, Pedro. A Collection of Street Games. Eckdahl, Judith & Eckdahl, Kathryn. O'Regan, Lucy, ed. 2005. 42p. pupil's gde. ed. 13.95 (978-0-9767200-0-3(0)) Lesen Pub.

Mirhady, Irandought. Thorn-Bush Boy: Pesare Tigh. Mirhady, Irandought. 2004. Orig. Title: Pesare Tigh. (PEO.). 63p. (YA). per. (978-0-9760323-0-4(9)) Mirhady, Farhad.

Mirocha, Paul. Amazing Armadillos. Mckerley, Jennifer. 2009. (Step into Reading Ser.). (ENG.). 48p. (J). (gr. k-3). pap. 3.99 (978-0-375-84352-5(3)) Random Hse., Inc.

—The Bee Tree. Cohn, Diana & Buchmann, Stephen. 2007. (ENG.). 40p. (J). (gr. 4-6). 17.95 (978-0-938317-98-2(9)) Cinco Puntos Pr.

—Hungry Plants. Batten, Mary. 2004. (Step into Reading Ser.). (ENG.). 48p. (J). (gr. 2-4). pap. 3.99 (978-0-375-82533-0(9), Random Hse. Bks. for Young Readers) Random Hse. Children's Bks.

—Mr Goethes Garden. Cohn, Diana. 2003. 32p. (J). 17.95 (978-0-88010-521-7(6)) SteinerBooks, Inc.

—Platypus! Clarke, Ginjer L. 2004. (Step into Reading Ser.). (ENG.). 32p. (J). (gr. -1-1). pap. 3.99 *(978-0-375-82417-3(0),* Random Hse. Bks. for Young Readers) Random Hse. Children's Bks.

Mirocha, Paul & Nicholson, Trudy. The Great North American Prairie: A Literary Field Guide. St. Antoine, Sara, ed. 2004. (Stories from Where We Live Ser.). (ENG.). 208p. (J). pap., instr.'s gde. ed. 10.95 *(978-1-57131-645-5(0))* Milkweed Editions.

—The North Atlantic Coast: A Literary Field Guide. St. Antoine, Sara, ed. 2004. (Stories from Where We Live Ser.). (ENG.). 288p. (J). pap., instr.'s gde. ed. 10.95 *(978-1-57131-643-1(4))* Milkweed Editions.

Mirocha, Paul, jt. illus. see Nicholson, Trudy.

Mirocha, Stephanie. My Little Book of Manatees. Marston, Hope Irvin. 2007. 32p. (J). (gr. k-5). pap. 7.95 *(978-0-89317-065-3(8),* Windward Publishing) Finney Co., Inc.

Miroglio, Brian. Mummy. Stoker, Bram. 2007. (Graphic Horror Ser.). 32p. (gr. 3-7). 28.50 *(978-1-60270-061-1(3),* Graphic Planet- Fiction) ABDO Publishing Co.

Mish. Softly Comes the Rain. Mish. 2005. 64p. (YA). per. 5.95 *(978-0-9766597-4-7(3))* Augusta Win Publishing.

Miskimins, Jason. The Bug in the Jug Wants a Hug. Cleary, Brian P. 2009. (Sounds Like Reading (r) Ser.: 1). (ENG.). (gr. -1-2). pap. 39.62 *(978-0-7613-4700-2(3))* Lerner Publishing Group.

—The Bug in the Jug Wants a Hug: A Short Vowel Sounds Book. Cleary, Brian P. & Maday, Alice M. 2009. (Sounds Like Reading (r) Ser.: 1). (ENG.). 32p. (gr. -1-2). lib. bdg. 23.93 *(978-0-7613-9503-4(2))* Lerner Publishing Group.

—The Clown in the Gown Drives the Car with the Star. Cleary, Brian P. 2009. (Sounds Like Reading (r) Ser.: 8). (ENG.). (gr. -1-2). pap. 39.62 *(978-0-7613-4707-1(0))* Lerner Publishing Group.

—The Clown in the Gown Drives the Car with the Star: A Book about Diphthongs & R-Controlled Vowel. Cleary, Brian P. & Maday, Alice M. 2009. (Sounds Like Reading (r) Ser.: 8). (ENG.). 32p. (gr. -1-2). lib. bdg. 23.93 *(978-0-8225-7637-2(6))* Lerner Publishing Group.

—The Frail Snail on the Trail. Cleary, Brian P. 2009. (Sounds Like Reading (r) Ser.: 4). (ENG.). (gr. -1-2). pap. 39.62 *(978-0-7613-4703-3(8))* Lerner Publishing Group.

—The Frail Snail on the Trail: Long Vowel Sounds with Consonant Blends. Cleary, Brian P. & Maday, Alice M. 2009. (Sounds Like Reading (r) Ser.: 4). (ENG.). 32p. (gr. -1-2). lib. bdg. 23.93 *(978-0-8225-7638-9(4))* Lerner Publishing Group.

—The Nice Mice in the Rice. Cleary, Brian P. 2009. (Sounds Like Reading (r) Ser.: 3). (ENG.). (gr. -1-2). pap. 39.62 *(978-0-7613-4702-6(X))* Lerner Publishing Group.

—The Nice Mice in the Rice: A Long Vowel Sound Book. Cleary, Brian P. & Maday, Alice M. 2009. (Sounds Like Reading (r) Ser.: 3). (ENG.). 32p. (gr. -1-2). lib. bdg. 23.93 *(978-0-8225-7628-0(7))* Lerner Publishing Group.

—The Peaches on the Beaches. Cleary, Brian P. 2009. (Sounds Like Reading (r) Ser.: 7). (ENG.). (gr. -1-2). pap. 39.62 *(978-0-7613-4706-4(2))* Lerner Publishing Group.

—The Peaches on the Beaches: A Book about Inflectional Endings. Cleary, Brian P. & Maday, Alice M. 2009. (Sounds Like Reading (r) Ser.: 7). (ENG.). 32p. (gr. -1-2). lib. bdg. 23.93 *(978-0-8225-7636-5(8))* Lerner Publishing Group.

—Stop, Drop, & Flop in the Slop. Cleary, Brian P. 2009. (Sounds Like Reading (r) Ser.: 2). (ENG.). (gr. -1-2). pap. 39.62 *(978-0-7613-4701-9(1))* Lerner Publishing Group.

—Stop, Drop, & Flop in the Slop: A Short Vowel Sounds Book with Consonant Blends. Cleary, Brian P. & Maday, Alice M. 2009. (Sounds Like Reading (r) Ser.: 2). (ENG.). 32p. (gr. -1-2). lib. bdg. 23.93 *(978-0-8225-7635-8(X))* Lerner Publishing Group.

—The Thing on the Wing Can Sing. Cleary, Brian P. 2009. (Sounds Like Reading (r) Ser.: 5). (ENG.). (gr. -1-2). pap. 39.62 *(978-0-7613-4704-0(6))* Lerner Publishing Group.

—The Thing on the Wing Can Sing: Short Vowel Sounds & Consonant Digraphs. Cleary, Brian P. & Maday, Alice M. 2009. (Sounds Like Reading (r) Ser.: 5). (ENG.). 32p. (gr. -1-2). lib. bdg. 23.93 *(978-0-8225-7639-6(2))* Lerner Publishing Group.

—Whose Shoes Would You Choose. Cleary, Brian P. 2009. (Sounds Like Reading (r) Ser.: 6). (ENG.). (gr. -1-2). pap. 39.62 *(978-0-7613-4705-7(4))* Lerner Publishing Group.

—Whose Shoes Would You Choose? A Long Vowel Sounds Book with Consonant Digraphs. Cleary, Brian P. & Maday, Alice M. 2009. (Sounds Like Reading (r) Ser.: 6). (ENG.). 32p. (gr. -1-2). lib. bdg. 23.93 *(978-0-8225-7640-2(6))* Lerner Publishing Group.

Misstigri. Princesses of World. Goyer, Katell. 2009. 3p. (J). (gr. -1-3). 17.99 *(978-0-8437-1445-6(X))* Hammond World Atlas Corp.

Mistry, Nilesh. A Calendar of Festivals: Celebrations from Around the World. Gilchrist, Cherry & Cann, Helen. 2005. (ENG.). 80p. (J). pap. 12.99 *(978-1-84148-970-4(0))* Barefoot Bks., Inc.

—Don't Bully Me. Robert, Na'ima bint. 2004. (POL & ENG.). 24p. (J). pap. *(978-1-84444-558-5(5))* Mantra Lingua.

—Fabulous Story of Fashion. Daynes, Katie. 2006. (Young Reading Series 2 Gift Bks.). 64p. (J). (gr. 2-5). 8.99 *(978-0-7945-1263-7(1),* Usborne) EDC Publishing.

—Marie Antoinette. Daynes, Katie. 2005. 64p. (J). 8.95 *(978-0-7945-1049-7(3),* Usborne) EDC Publishing.

—Nico's Octopus. Pitcher, Caroline. 2003. (ENG.). 32p. (J). (gr. k-3). 15.95 *(978-1-56656-483-0(2),* Crocodile Bks.) Interlink Publishing Group, Inc.

—The Revealing Story of Underwear. Daynes, Katie. 2006. (Young Reading Series 2 Gift Bks.). 64p. (J). (gr. 2-5). 8.99 *(978-0-7945-1352-8(2),* Usborne) EDC Publishing.

—Stories from the Silk Road. Gilchrist, Cherry. 2005. (ENG.). 80p. (J). pap. 12.99 *(978-1-84148-804-2(6))* Barefoot Bks., Inc.

—The Story of Divaali. Verma, Jatinder. 2007. (ENG.). 40p. (J). (gr. -1-3). pap. 7.99 *(978-1-84686-131-4(4))* Barefoot Bks., Inc.

—The Swirling Hijaab. Robert, Na'ima Bint. 2004. 24p. (J). *(978-1-85269-910-9(8));* (ARA & ENG.). pap. *(978-1-85269-119-6(0));* (URD & ENG.). pap. *(978-1-85269-143-1(3));* (BEN & ENG.). pap. *(978-1-85269-160-8(3));* (PER & ENG.). pap. *(978-1-85269-163-9(8));* (GER & ENG.). pap. *(978-1-85269-165-3(4));* (ITA & ENG.). pap. *(978-1-85269-167-7(0));* (PAN & ENG.). pap. *(978-1-85269-178-3(6));* (POR & ENG.). pap. *(978-1-85269-179-0(4));* (SER & ENG.). pap. *(978-1-85269-180-6(8));* (SOM & ENG.). pap. *(978-1-85269-181-3(6));* (SPA & ENG.). pap. *(978-1-85269-182-0(4));* (TAM & ENG.). pap. *(978-1-85269-188-2(3));* (TUR & ENG.). pap. *(978-1-85269-189-9(1));* (CZE & ENG.). pap. *(978-1-85269-629-0(X))* Mantra Lingua.

—The Swirling Hijaab: Le Foulard Qui Tourbillonne. Robert, Naima Bint, tr. 2004. (FRE & ENG.). 24p. (J). pap. *(978-1-85269-164-6(6))* Mantra Lingua.

—The Swirling Hijaab: Percja Valezuese. Robert, Na'ima Bint, tr. 2004. (ALB & ENG.). 24p. (J). pap. *(978-1-85269-105-9(0))* Mantra Lingua.

Mistry, Nilesh, jt. illus. see Mayo, Diana.

Mitchell, Anne. How to Grow a Hippo! Schantz, Becky. 2014. (ENG.). 32p. (J). (gr. -1-3). 14.95 *(978-1-62086-609-2(9))* Mascot Bks., Inc.

Mitchell, Anthony W. The Adventures of Sammy the Squirrel: Buying Shoes. Terrell, Andrea M. 2008. (ENG.). 28p. pap. 13.99 *(978-1-4343-5608-6(6))* AuthorHouse.

Mitchell, David. A Present for Paul. Ashley, Bernard. 2004. 28p. (J). *(978-1-85269-359-6(2)); (978-1-85269-360-2(6))* Mantra Lingua.

Mitchell, Derrick Lee. Miyah & Koala's First Day. Mitchell, Derrick Lee. Howard, Assuanta. 2012. 30p. 18.00 *(978-1-934947-69-2(5))* Asta Publications, LLC.

Mitchell, Gail A., photos by. Learning English the Cultural Way. Mitchell, Gail A. 2004. 40p. (J). per. 20.00 *(978-0-9653308-9-3(3))* Africana Homestead Legacy Pubs., Inc.

Mitchell, Ged. The Snowman's Coat & Other Science Questions, 4 vols. Naylor, Brenda & Naylor, Stuart. 32p. (J). pap. *(978-0-340-75755-0(8))* Hodder & Stoughton.

Mitchell, Hazel. Cassie & Mr. Ant. Powell, Glenda. 2008. 30p. (J). (gr. -1-3). per. 7.95 *(978-0-9779445-6-9(5))* Zoe Life Publishing.

—Double-Crossed at Cactus Flats: An Up2 U Western Adventure. Wallace, Rich. 2013. (Up2U Adventures Ser.). 80p. (J). (gr. 2-5). lib. bdg. 27.07 *(978-1-61641-966-0(0),* Calico Chapter Bks) Magic Wagon.

—F Is for Feelings. Millar, Goldie & Berger, Lisa. 2014. (ENG.). 40p. (J). (gr. -1-3). 15.99 *(978-1-57542-475-0(4))* Free Spirit Publishing, Inc.

—Fly, Emma, Fly. Suen, Anastasia. 2012. 66p. (J). *(978-1-61067-143-9(0))* Kane Miller.

—Hidden New Jersey. Barth, Linda J. 2012. (Search & Seek Bks.). (ENG.). 32p. (J). (gr. 1-4). 17.95 *(978-1-934133-23-1(X));* pap. 8.95 *(978-1-934133-40-8(X))* Charlesbridge Publishing, Inc. (Mackinac Island Press, Inc.).

—Luke's 1st Haircut. Marek, Catherine. ed. 2007. (ENG.). 32p. (J). (gr. -1-3). per. *(978-0-9748251-5-1(8))* Zoe Life Publishing.

—One Word Pearl. Groeneweg, Nicole. 2013. (ENG.). 32p. (J). (gr. k-3). 17.95 *(978-1-934133-53-8(1));* pap. 7.95 *(978-1-934133-54-5(X))* Charlesbridge Publishing, Inc. (Mackinac Island Press, Inc.).

—Sara's 1st Haircut. Marek, Catherine. l.t. ed. 2007. (ENG.). 32p. (J). (gr. -1-3). per. *(978-0-9748251-3-7(1))* Zoe Life Publishing.

—Save the Best for Last, Abby: All-Star Cheerleaders. Suen, Anastasia. 2013. (ENG.). 96p. (J). pap. 4.99 *(978-1-61067-001-2(9))* Kane Miller.

—Tick Tock, Taylor! All-Star Cheerleaders. Suen, Anastasia. 2013. (ENG.). 96p. (J). pap. 4.99 *(978-1-61067-000-5(0))* Kane Miller.

—Tickles the Bear Goes on a Cruise, 1 bk. Pighin, Marcel. 2006. 48p. (J). per. 10.49 *(978-0-9776679-7-0(9))* MP2ME Enterprise.

—Too Many Freckles! Gomez, Sally. 2008. (ENG.). 32p. pap. *(978-1-934363-32-4(4))* Zoe Life Publishing.

—Why Am I Here? A Story about Becoming The-Best-Version-of-Yourself! Kelly, Matthew. 2009. 60p. (J). 17.99 *(978-0-9841318-0-8(9))* Beacon Publishing.

Mitchell, Hazell. Imani's Moon. Brown-Wood, Janay. 2014. (ENG.). 32p. (J). (gr. 1-4). pap. 7.95 *(978-1-934133-58-3(2),* Mackinac Island Press, Inc.) Charlesbridge Publishing, Inc.

Mitchell, Hazle. The Naughty Grandmother. Bradley, Judy. 2012. (J). *(978-0-615-57032-7(1))* Bradley, Judy & Assocs., LLC.

Mitchell, Hetty. Martin Luther King Jr. Day. Lowery, Linda. rev. ed. 2003. (On My Own Holidays Ser.). (ENG.). 56p. (gr. 2-4). pap. 6.95 *(978-1-57505-709-5(3))* Lerner Publishing Group.

—Raggin' A Story about Scott Joplin. Mitchell, Barbara. 2003. (Creative Minds Biographies Ser.). (ENG.). 56p. (gr. 4-8). pap. 8.95 *(978-0-87614-589-0(6),* Carolrhoda Bks.) Lerner Publishing Group.

Mitchell, Jana Christy, jt. illus. see Christy, Jana.

Mitchell, Joanne & Hurst, Ceri. The Dragon Tattoo Book: With 24 Fabulous Temporary Tattoos! Virr, Paul. 2012. (ENG.). 32p. (J). (gr. 1-5). pap. 5.99 *(978-1-4380-0182-1(7))* Barron's Educational Series, Inc.

—The Fashion & Friendship Tattoo Book: With 24 Stylish Play Tattoos to Wear & Share! Virr, Paul. 2012. (ENG.). 32p. (J). (gr. 1-5). pap. 5.99 *(978-1-4380-0183-8(5))* Barron's Educational Series, Inc.

Mitchell Jr., Leonard. Stray's Great Adventure. Alexander, Troas James. 2010. 40p. pap. 15.95 *(978-1-60844-200-3(4))* Dog Ear Publishing, LLC.

Mitchell, Kathy. The Story of the Statue of Liberty. 2010. 26p. (J). (gr. -1-k). bds. 6.99 *(978-0-8249-1841-5(X),* Candy Cane Pr.) Ideals Pubns.

Mitchell, Lori. Holly Bloom's Garden. Ashman, Sarah & Parent, Nancy. (ENG.). 32p. (J). (gr. k-3). 2008. pap. 7.95 *(978-0-9799746-0-1(7));* 2004. 15.95 *(978-0-9729225-0-0(4))* Flashlight Pr.

Mitchell, Lori. Marfan Syndrome A-Z. Mitchell, Lori, compiled by. 2007. 36p. (J). pap. *(978-0-918335-14-2(0))* National Marfan Foundation, The.

Mitchell, Mark. A Bag of Lucky Rice. Reichart, George. 2004. (ENG.). 160p. pap. 10.95 *(978-1-56792-278-3(3))* Godine, David R. Pub.

Mitchell, Mark. Raising la Belle. Mitchell, Mark. (Professor Wigglestix & the Weather Ser.). 112p. 10.95 *(978-1-57168-703-6(3))* Eakin Pr.

Mitchell, Melanie. All Aboard Noah's Ark: A Touch & Feel Book. Price, Olivia. 2008. (ENG.). 12p. (J). (gr. -1). 12.95 *(978-1-58117-778-7(X),* Intervisual/Piggy Toes) Bendon, Inc.

—Are You Ticklish? McKendry, Sam. 2006. (ENG.). 12p. (J). (gr. -1-18). bds. 10.95 *(978-1-58117-376-5(8),* Intervisual/Piggy Toes) Bendon, Inc.

—Are You Ticklish? McKendry, Sam. ed. 2008. (ENG.). 12p. (J). bds. 5.95 *(978-1-58117-706-0(2),* Intervisual/Piggy Toes) Bendon, Inc.

—Are You Ticklish? A Touch & Tickle Book. McKendry, Sam. 2007. 15.95 *(978-1-58117-571-4(X),* Intervisual/Piggy Toes) Bendon, Inc.

—Are You Ticklish?/Tienes Cosquillas? McKendry, Sam. 2005. (ENG.). 12p. (J). (gr. -1-k). 10.95 *(978-1-58117-472-4(1),* Intervisual/Piggy Toes) Bendon, Inc.

—Bible Stories: A Touch & Feel Book. Price, Olivia. 2008. (ENG.). 12p. (J). (gr. -1). 12.95 *(978-1-58117-802-9(6),* Intervisual/Piggy Toes) Bendon, Inc.

—The Biggest Thing in the World. Steven, Kenneth C. 2013. (ENG.). 32p. (J). (gr. -1-k). 6.99 *(978-0-7459-6402-7(8))* Lion Hudson PLC GBR. Dist: Independent Pubs. Group.

—Christmas Story. Tebbs, Victoria. 2009. (See & Say! Ser.). (ENG.). 20p. (J). (gr. k — 1). 6.95 *(978-0-7459-4900-0(2))* Lion Hudson PLC GBR. Dist: Independent Pubs. Group.

—Curious Kitties: A Color Book. McKendry, Sam. 2007. (ENG.). 14p. (J). (gr. -1-3). bds. 5.95 *(978-1-58117-554-7(X),* Intervisual/Piggy Toes) Bendon, Inc.

—Curious Kitties: A Colors Book. McKendry, Sam. 2005. (ENG.). 16p. (J). bds. 9.95 *(978-1-58117-417-5(9),* Intervisual/Piggy Toes) Bendon, Inc.

—Deep in the Jungle. 2011. (ENG.). 6p. (J). (gr. -1-k). 14.95 *(978-1-61524-471-3(9),* Intervisual/Piggy Toes) Bendon, Inc.

—God's Winter Wonderland. Nolan, Allia Zobel. 2006. 10p. (J). bds. 8.99 *(978-0-8254-5526-1(X))* Kregel Pubns.

—Good Morning. 2008. (ENG.). 10p. (J). bds. 5.95 *(978-1-58117-708-4(9),* Intervisual/Piggy Toes) Bendon, Inc.

—Good Morning, Good Night! 2007. (Touch & Feel Ser.). 13p. 15.95 *(978-1-58117-572-1(8),* Intervisual/Piggy Toes) Bendon, Inc.

—Good Morning, Good Night! Imperato, Teresa. 2006. (ENG.). 12p. (J). (gr. -1-18). 9.95 *(978-1-58117-279-9(6),* Intervisual/Piggy Toes) Bendon, Inc.

—Good Morning, Good Night! A Touch & Feel Bedtime Book. 2006. 12p. (J). (gr. -1-k). 12.95 *(978-1-58117-461-8(6),* Intervisual/Piggy Toes) Bendon, Inc.

—Good Morning, Good Night Bilingual: Buenos Dias! Buenas Noches! 2005. (ENG & SPA.). 12p. (J). 9.95 *(978-1-58117-389-5(X),* Intervisual/Piggy Toes) Bendon, Inc.

—Good Night. 2008. (ENG.). 6p. (J). bds. 5.95 *(978-1-58117-709-1(7),* Intervisual/Piggy Toes) Bendon, Inc.

—Little Bunny's Bible, 1 vol. Zondervan & Lyons, P. J. 2015. (ENG.). 16p. (J). bds. 15.99 *(978-0-310-74444-3(X))* Zonderkidz.

—Little Chick's Bible, 1 vol. Zondervan & Lyons, P. J. 2015. (ENG.). 16p. (J). bds. 15.99 *(978-0-310-74780-2(5))* Zonderkidz.

—Molly Mouse Is Shy: A Story of Shyness. Gibbs, Lynne. 2009. (Let's Grow Together Ser.). 32p. (J). (gr. -1-2). pap. 10.55 *(978-1-60754-761-7(9));* lib. bdg. 22.60 *(978-1-60754-756-3(2))* Windmill Bks.

—My Little Bible Board Book, 1 vol. Goodings, Christina. 2008. (ENG.). 40p. 9.99 *(978-1-56148-609-0(4),* Good Bks.) Skyhorse Publishing Co., Inc.

—My Little Bible Board Book. Goodings, Christina. 2015. (ENG.). 40p. (J). (— 1). 9.99 *(978-0-7459-6046-3(4))* Lion Hudson PLC GBR. Dist: Independent Pubs. Group.

—Peepo Paw Printes. Prasadam, Smriti. 2008. (ENG.). 14p. (J). bds. 13.95 *(978-0-7475-9535-9(6))* Bloomsbury Publishing Plc GBR. Dist: Independent Pubs. Group.

—Teddy Bear Says Goodnight. Senior, Suzy. 2014. (Teddy Bear Says Ser.). (ENG.). 12p. (J). (— 1). bds. 7.99 *(978-0-7459-6436-2(2))* Lion Hudson PLC GBR. Dist: Independent Pubs. Group.

—Teddy Bear Says I Love You. Senior, Suzy. 2014. (Teddy Bear Says Ser.). (ENG.). 12p. (J). (— 1). bds. 7.99 *(978-0-7459-6437-9(0))* Lion Hudson PLC GBR. Dist: Independent Pubs. Group.

—Teddy Bear Says Let's Hug. Senior, Suzy. 2014. (Teddy Bear Says Ser.). (ENG.). 12p. (J). (— 1). bds. 7.99 *(978-0-7459-6439-3(7))* Lion Hudson PLC GBR. Dist: Independent Pubs. Group.

—Teddy Bear Says Wake Up! Senior, Suzy. 2014. (Teddy Bear Says Ser.). (ENG.). 12p. (J). (— 1). bds. 7.99 *(978-0-7459-6438-6(9))* Lion Hudson PLC GBR. Dist: Independent Pubs. Group.

—Time to Share: A Story of Sharing. Gibbs, Lynne. 2009. (Let's Grow Together Ser.). 32p. (J). (gr. -1-2). lib. bdg. 22.60 *(978-1-60754-757-0(0))* Windmill Bks.

—Wake up Little Ones. 2009. (ENG.). 12p. 10.95 *(978-1-58117-927-9(8),* Intervisual/Piggy Toes) Bendon, Inc.

—Who Do You Love? 2008. (ENG.). 6p. (J). bds. 5.95 *(978-1-58117-707-7(0),* Intervisual/Piggy Toes) Bendon, Inc.

—Who Do You Love? A Touch & Feel Book. Wang, Margaret. 2007. (gr. -1-k). 15.95 *(978-1-58117-570-7(1),* Intervisual/Piggy Toes) Bendon, Inc.

Mitchell, Nanci. Anna & Her Mommy. Champion, Gina. 2005. 36p. (J). (gr. k-6). pap. 10.00 *(978-1-884363-20-7(2))* Odenwald Pr.

Mitchell, Peter. Freaking Out: Real-Life Stories about Anxiety. Wells, Polly. 2013. (ENG.). 136p. (J). (gr. 7-12). 22.95 *(978-1-55451-545-5(9),* 9781554515455); pap. 12.95 *(978-1-55451-544-8(0),* 9781554515448) Annick Pr., Ltd. CAN. Dist: Firefly Bks., Ltd.

—I. D. Stuff That Happens to Define Us. Scowen, Kate, ed. 2010. (ENG.). 160p. (YA). (gr. 7-18). 24.95 *(978-1-55451-225-6(5),* 9781554512256); pap. 12.95 *(978-1-55451-224-9(7),* 9781554512249) Annick Pr., Ltd. CAN. Dist: Firefly Bks., Ltd.

Mitchell, Polly. Word Finding Vocabulary Test. Renfrew, Catherine. 4th ed. 16p. *(978-0-86388-335-4(4),* 003-1964) Speechmark Publishing Ltd.

Mitchell, Rhonda. Daddy Calls Me Man. Johnson, Angela. 2014. 32p. pap. 7.00 *(978-1-61003-309-1(4))* Center for the Collaborative Classroom.

Mitchell, Steven. Amazing Stories from Times Past: Devotions for Children & Families. Farenhorst, Christine. 2005. 142p. (J). (gr. 2-7). per. 8.99 *(978-0-87552-823-6(6))* P & R Publishing.

Mitchell, Susan. Christmas Lights. Bauer, Marion Dane. 2006. (ENG.). 10p. (J). (gr. -1-2). 12.99 *(978-0-689-86942-6(8),* Little Simon) Little Simon.

—Claire & the Unicorn Happy Ever After. Hennessy, B. G. 2006. (ENG.). 32p. (J). (gr. -1-3). 17.99 *(978-1-4169-0815-9(3),* Simon & Schuster Bks. For Young Readers) Simon & Schuster Bks. For Young Readers.

—Hugs for Baby! Zobel-Nolan, Allia. 2008. (Lift-the-Flap Hear-the-Sound Ser.). 10p. (J). (gr. -1). 12.95 *(978-1-932915-64-8(8))* Sandvik Innovations, LLC.

—The Little Christmas Elf. Smith, Nikki Shannon. 2011. (Little Golden Book Ser.). (ENG.). 24p. (J). (gr. -1-k). 4.99 *(978-0-375-87348-5(1),* Golden Bks.) Random Hse. Children's Bks.

—Mouse's Sock Tree. Metcalf, Paula. ed. 2014. (ENG.). 12p. (J). (— 1). bds. 7.99 *(978-0-230-76475-0(4))* Pan Macmillan GBR. Dist: Independent Pubs. Group.

—My Dad & Me. Capucilli, Alyssa Satin. 2009. (ENG.). 16p. (J). (gr. -1-1). 7.99 *(978-1-4169-5828-4(2),* Little Simon) Little Simon.

—My Mom & Me. Capucilli, Alyssa Satin. 2009. (ENG.). 16p. (J). (gr. -1-1). 7.99 *(978-1-4169-5829-1(0),* Little Simon) Little Simon.

—Nana's Bible Stories. Simpson, Roberta. 2007. (ENG.). 96p. (J). (gr. -1-3). 16.99 *(978-1-4003-1187-3(X))* Nelson, Thomas Inc.

—Paula Deen's Cookbook for the Lunch-Box Set. Deen, Paula. 2009. (ENG.). 192p. (J). (gr. 2-7). spiral bd. 21.99 *(978-1-4169-8268-5(X),* Simon & Schuster Bks. For Young Readers) Simon & Schuster Bks. For Young Readers.

—Paula Deen's My First Cookbook. Deen, Paula. 2008. (ENG.). 176p. (J). (gr. -1-3). spiral bd. 21.99 *(978-1-4169-5033-2(8),* Simon & Schuster Bks. For Young Readers) Simon & Schuster Bks. For Young Readers.

—Too Many Fairies: A Celtic Tale, 0 vols. MacDonald, Margaret Read. 2010. (ENG.). 32p. (J). (gr. -1-3). 17.99 *(978-0-7614-5604-9(X),* 9780761456049, Amazon Children's Publishing) Amazon Publishing.

Mitchell, Susan & Owlkids Books Inc. Staff. Whoosh! A Watery World of Wonderful Creatures, 0 vols. Baillie, Marilyn. 2014. (ENG.). 32p. (J). (gr. -1-2). 16.95 *(978-1-926973-98-2(4),* Owlkids) Owlkids Bks. Inc. CAN. Dist: Perseus-PGW.

Mitchell, Suzanne. Calvin's Giant Jumps. Mitchell, Marvin. 2003. 32p. 15.95 *(978-0-9727639-0-5(2))* Beachwalker Pr.

Mitchell, Tina. Crazy Colours. Lovell, Brandy. 2011. 42p. pap. *(978-0-9867761-0-6(6))* Bing Long Bks.

Mitchell, Tracy. The Great Divide: A Mathematical Marathon. Dodds, Dayle Ann. 2005. (ENG.). 32p. (J). (gr. k-4). reprint ed. pap. 6.99 *(978-0-7636-1592-5(7))* Candlewick Pr.

Mitchum, Lynn Tyner. Happy Being Me. Mitchum, Lynn Tyner. 2006. (J). bds. 21.95 *(978-0-9745191-0-4(3))* Lynn Tyner Mitchum & James Rogers.

Mithuna, R. Michael. Being Born: The Doula's Role. Hernandez, Jewel. 2008. (ENG.). 32p. (J). pap. 9.95 *(978-1-890772-83-3(6))* Hohm Pr.

Mithuna, R. Michael. El Nacimiento: El Papel de una Doula = Being Born: The Doula's Role. Mithuna, R. Michael. Hernandez, Jewel. 2009. (SPA & ENG.). (J). pap. *(978-1-890772-91-8(7))* Hohm Pr.

Mitsui Brown, Janet. Oshogatsu with Obaachan. 2005. (J). *(978-1-879965-24-9(0))* Polychrome Publishing Corp.

Mitsui, Eiichi, jt. illus. see Sakakura, Yoshinobu.

Mitsui-Kids, jt. illus. see Shogakukan.

Mittal, Shiekha. The Why & What of Epilepsy: A Book for Children & Teens. Karia, Roopal. 2008. 17p. pap. 24.95 *(978-1-60610-951-9(0))* America Star Bks.

Mittan, J. Barry, jt. photos by see Adeff, Jay.

Mitter, Kathryn. Cones. Hamilton, Laura. 2012. (Everyday 3-D Shapes Ser.). 24p. (J). (gr. -1-2). lib. bdg. 27.07 *(978-1-61641-872-4(9),* Looking Glass Library) Magic Wagon.

—Cubes. Hamilton, Laura. 2012. (Everyday 3-D Shapes Ser.). 24p. (J). (gr. -1-2). lib. bdg. 27.07 *(978-1-61641-873-1(7),* Looking Glass Library) Magic Wagon.

—Cylinders. Hamilton, Laura. 2012. (Everyday 3-D Shapes Ser.). 24p. (J). (gr. -1-2). lib. bdg. 27.07 *(978-1-61641-874-8(5),* Looking Glass Library) Magic Wagon.

—Duck for Turkey Day. Jules, Jacqueline. 2009. (ENG.). 32p. (J). (gr. 1-3). 16.99 *(978-0-8075-1734-5(8))* Whitman, Albert & Co.

—Eloise Has a Lesson. McNamara, Margaret & Thompson, Kay. 2005. (Eloise Ser.). (ENG.). 32p. (J). (gr. -1-1). pap. 3.99 *(978-0-689-87367-6(0),* Simon Spotlight) Simon Spotlight.

—Prisms. Hamilton, Laura. 2012. (Everyday 3-D Shapes Ser.). 24p. (J). (gr. -1-2). lib. bdg. 27.07 (978-1-61641-875-5(3), Looking Glass Library) Magic Wagon.

—Pyramids. Hamilton, Laura. 2012. (Everyday 3-D Shapes Ser.). 24p. (J). (gr. -1-2). lib. bdg. 27.07 (978-1-61641-876-2(1), Looking Glass Library) Magic Wagon.

—Raggedy Ann & the Birthday Surprise. Peters, Stephanie. 2003. (My First Raggedy Ann Ser.). (J). (gr. k-3). lib. bdg. 15.30 (978-0-613-67663-2(7), Turtleback) Turtleback Bks.

—Spheres. Hamilton, Laura. 2012. (Everyday 3-D Shapes Ser.). 24p. (J). (gr. -1-2). lib. bdg. 27.07 (978-1-61641-877-9(X), Looking Glass Library) Magic Wagon.

—Things I See at Baptism. Stiegemeyer, Julie. 2007. 20p. (J). (gr. -1-3). bds. 5.49 (978-0-7586-1246-5(X)) Concordia Publishing Hse.

—Things I See at Christmas. Stiegemeyer, Julie. 2005. 16p. (J). (gr. -1-17). bds. 5.49 (978-0-7586-0809-3(8)) Concordia Publishing Hse.

—What Does This Mean? Bergt, Carolyn. 16p. (gr. -1-k). 20.00 (978-0-570-05545-7(8), 54-0077) Concordia Publishing Hse.

Mitter, Kathy. Here Is the Church. Stohs, Anita. 2009. 32p. (J). (gr. -1). 8.99 (978-0-7586-1633-3(3)) Concordia Publishing Hse.

—Things I Hear in Church. Stiegemeyer, Julie. 2003. 20p. (J). bds. 5.49 (978-0-7586-0125-4(5)) Concordia Publishing Hse.

—Things I See at Easter. Stiegemeyer, Julie. 2005. 20p. (J). bds. 5.49 (978-0-7586-0797-3(0)) Concordia Publishing Hse.

—Things I See in Church. Stiegemeyer, Julie. 2003. 20p. (J). bds. 5.49 (978-0-7586-0357-9(6)) Concordia Publishing Hse.

—When Jesus Was Born. Hartman, Sara. 2007. 16p. (J). (gr. k-4). 1.99 (978-0-7586-1281-6(8)) Concordia Publishing Hse.

Miura, Taro. The Big Princess. Miura, Taro. 2015. (ENG.). 40p. (J). (-k). 14.99 (978-0-7636-7459-5(1)) Candlewick Pr.

—The Tiny King. Miura, Taro. 2013. (ENG.). 32p. (J). (-k). 14.99 (978-0-7636-6687-3(4)) Candlewick Pr.

Miyabe, Miyuki. The Book of Heroes. Miyabe, Miyuki. 2011. (ENG.). 350p. pap. 14.99 (978-1-4215-4083-2(5)) Viz Media.

Miyabi, Haruka. Lafcadio Hearn's Japanese Ghost Stories. Wilson, Sean Michael. 2007. 144p. (YA). per. (978-0-9788804-3-9(9)) Demented Dragon.

Miyake, Yoshi. Abigail Adams: Young Patriot. Sabin, Francene & Macken, JoAnn Early. 2007. 55p. (J). pap. (978-0-439-88003-9(3)) Scholastic, Inc.

—All about Pets. Kain, Kathleen. 2004. (Treasure Tree Ser.). 32p. (J). (978-0-7166-1626-9(2)) World Bk., Inc.

—Baby Jesus Visits the Temple. Maas, Alice E. 2004. (ENG.). 16p. (J). 1.99 (978-0-570-07575-2(0)) Concordia Publishing Hse.

—The Boy & the Goats. Hillert, Margaret. rev. exp. ed. 2006. (Beginning to Read Ser.). 32p. (J). (gr. -1-3). lib. bdg. 14.95 (978-1-59953-053-6(8)) Norwood Hse. Pr.

—Nicodemus & Jesus. Schkade, Jonathan. 2014. (Arch Bks.). (ENG.). 16p. (J). (gr. k-4). pap. 2.49 (978-0-7586-4606-4(2)) Concordia Publishing Hse.

—Take a Walk, Johnny. Hillert, Margaret. 2008. 32p. (J). lib. bdg. 19.93 (978-1-59953-152-6(6)) Norwood Hse. Pr.

—The Ten Commandments. Miller, Claire. 2004. (Arch Bks.). 16p. (J). 1.99 (978-0-7586-0672-3(9)) Concordia Publishing Hse.

Miyake, Yoski. Jesus, My Good Shepherd. Rottmann, Erik. 2005. (ENG.). 16p. (J). 1.99 (978-0-7586-0725-6(3)) Concordia Publishing Hse.

Miyakoshi, Wasoh. Seikai Trilogy Vol. 3: Banner of the Stars II, 3 vols. Morioka, Hiroyuki. rev. ed. 2004. 248p. pap. 9.99 (978-1-59182-859-4(7)) TOKYOPOP, Inc.

Miyares, Daniel. Bambino & Mr. Twain. Maltbie, P. I. 2012. (ENG.). 40p. (J). (gr. k-3). 15.95 (978-1-58089-272-8(8)) Charlesbridge Publishing, Inc.

—Papi's Bodega. Chambers, Veronica & Clampet, Jason. 2013. (J). (978-1-4231-0125-3(1)) Disney Pr.

—Waking up Is Hard to Do. Sedaka, Neil et al. 2010. (Book & CD Ser.). (ENG.). 26p. (J). (gr. k-12). 17.95 (978-1-936140-13-8(6), Imagine Publishing) Charlesbridge Publishing, Inc.

Miyares, Daniel. Float. Miyares, Daniel. 2015. (ENG.). 48p. (J). (gr. -1-3). 17.99 (978-1-4814-1524-8(7), Simon & Schuster Bks. For Young Readers) Simon & Schuster Bks. For Young Readers.

—Pardon Me! Miyares, Daniel. 2014. (ENG.). 40p. (J). (gr. -1-3). 16.99 (978-1-4424-8997-4(9), Simon & Schuster Bks. For Young Readers) Simon & Schuster Bks. For Young Readers.

Miyasaka, Kaho. Kare First Love, 10 vols. Miyasaka, Kaho. (Kare First Love Ser.). (ENG.). 2006. 208p. pap. 9.99 (978-1-4215-0547-3(9)); 2004. 200p. pap. 9.95 (978-1-59116-395-4(1)) Viz Media.

—Kare First Love, 10 vols. Miyasaka, Kaho. Watanabe, Akira, tr. from JPN. 2004. (Kare First Love Ser.: Vol. 1). (ENG.). 200p. pap. 9.95 (978-1-59116-394-7(3)) Viz Media.

—Kare First Love, 10 vols. Miyasaka, Kaho. (Kare First Love Ser.). (ENG.). Vol. 4. 2005. 192p. pap. 9.99 (978-1-59116-802-7(3)); Vol. 6. 2005. 200p. pap. 9.99 (978-1-4215-0139-0(2)); Vol. 7. 2006. 208p. pap. 9.99 (978-1-4215-0325-7(5)); Vol. 8. 2006. 208p. pap. 9.99 (978-1-4215-0546-6(0)) Viz Media.

Miyazaki, Hayao. The Art of Howl's Moving Castle. Miyazaki, Hayao. 2005. (Howl's Moving Castle Ser.). (ENG.). 256p. pap. 34.99 (978-1-4215-0049-2(3)) Viz Media.

—The Art of Porco Rosso. Miyazaki, Hayao. Searleman, Eric, ed. 2005. (Porco Rosso Ser.). (ENG.). 208p. pap. 34.99 (978-1-59116-704-4(3)) Viz Media.

—Castle in the Sky. Miyazaki, Hayao. 2003. (Castle in the Sky Ser.: 1). (ENG.). 164p. Vol. 1. pap. 9.95 (978-1-59116-170-7(3)); Vol. 2. pap. 9.95 (978-1-59116-171-4(1)); Vol. 3. pap. 9.95 (978-1-59116-172-1(X)); Vol. 4. pap. 9.95 (978-1-59116-173-8(8)) Viz Media.

—Howl's Moving Castle Film Comic, 4 vols., Vol. 2. Miyazaki, Hayao. 2005. (Howl's Moving Castle Ser.). (ENG.). 176p. pap. 9.99 (978-1-4215-0092-8(2)) Viz Media.

—Howl's Moving Castle Picture Book. Miyazaki, Hayao. 2005. (Howl's Moving Castle Ser.). (ENG.). 184p. pap. 19.99 (978-1-4215-0090-4(6)) Viz Media.

—My Neighbor Totoro. Miyazaki, Hayao. (My Neighbor Totoro Ser.: 4). (ENG.). 152p. 2005. pap. 9.99 (978-1-59116-700-6(0)); 2004. pap. 9.99 (978-1-59116-684-9(5)); 2004. pap. 9.99 (978-1-59116-699-3(3)); 2004. pap. 9.99 (978-1-59116-647-4(0)) Viz Media.

—Nausicaä of the Valley of the Wind. Miyazaki, Hayao. 2nd ed. 2004. (Nausicaa Ser.: 4). (ENG.). 138p. pap. 12.99 (978-1-59116-352-7(8)) Viz Media.

—Nausicaä of the Valley of the Wind, Vol. 1. Miyazaki, Hayao. Lewis, David & Smith, Toren, trs. from JPN. 2nd ed. 2004. (Nausicaa Ser.: 1). (ENG.). 136p. pap. 12.99 (978-1-59116-408-1(7)) Viz Media.

—Nausicaä of the Valley of the Wind. Miyazaki, Hayao. 2nd ed. 2004. (Nausicaa Ser.: 2). (ENG.). Vol. 2. 136p. pap. 12.99 (978-1-59116-350-3(1)); Vol. 3. 156p. pap. 12.99 (978-1-59116-410-4(9)); Vol. 5. 160p. pap. 12.99 (978-1-59116-412-8(5)); Vol. 6. 168p. pap. 12.99 (978-1-59116-354-1(4)); Vol. 7. 232p. pap. 12.99 (978-1-59116-355-8(2)) Viz Media.

—Ponyo. Miyazaki, Hayao. movie tie-in ed. 2009. (Ponyo on the Cliff Ser.: 1). (ENG.). 172p. (J). pap. 9.99 (978-1-4215-3077-2(5)) Viz Media.

—Ponyo Film Comic. Miyazaki, Hayao. movie tie-in ed. 2009. (Ponyo on the Cliff Ser.: 3). (ENG.). (J). 152p. pap. 9.99 (978-1-4215-3079-6(1)); 168p. pap. 9.99 (978-1-4215-3080-2(5)); 152p. pap. 9.99 (978-1-4215-3078-9(3)) Viz Media.

—Ponyo Picture Book. Miyazaki, Hayao. 2009. (Ponyo on the Cliff Ser.). (ENG.). 152p. (J). (gr. 2-7). pap. 19.99 (978-1-4215-3065-9(1)) Viz Media.

—Spirited Away. Miyazaki, Hayao. 2003. (Spirited Away Ser.: 5). (ENG & JPN.). 184p. pap. 9.95 (978-1-56931-795-2(X)); Vol. 4. 172p. pap. 9.95 (978-1-56931-794-5(1)) Viz Media.

Miyazaki, Hayao & Watsuki, Nobuhiro. The Art of My Neighbor Totoro. Miyazaki, Hayao & Watsuki, Nobuhiro. 2005. (My Neighbor Totoro Ser.). (ENG.). 176p. pap. 34.99 (978-1-59116-698-6(5)) Viz Media.

Miyazaki, Hayao, jt. illus. see Jones, Diana Wynne.

Miyazawa, Takeshi, jt. illus. see Alphona, Adrian.

Miyazoe, Ikuo. Biographical Comics: Christopher Columbus: The Merchant Adventurer. Saguchi, Kensaku. 2012. (Biographical Comic Ser.). (ENG.). 152p. (J). (gr. 3-6). 18.99 (978-1-4215-4973-6(5)); pap. 9.99 (978-1-4215-4974-3(3)) Shogakukan JPN. Dist: Simon & Schuster, Inc.

Mizobuchi, Makoto. Ranger & the Temple of the Sea. Mizobuchi, Makoto. Viz Media Staff. 2008. (Pokemon Ser.). (ENG.). 192p. (J). (gr. 1). pap. 9.99 (978-1-4215-2288-3(8)) Viz Media.

Mizsenko, Ingrid. La Abuela. Härtling, Peter. 2003. (SPA.). 103p. (J). (gr. 5-8). pap. 9.95 (978-968-19-0730-3(2)) Santillana USA Publishing Co., Inc.

Mizuno, Junko. Junko Mizuno's Hansel & Gretel. Mizuno, Junko. 2003. (Junko Mizuno Ser.). (ENG.). 144p. pap. 15.95 (978-1-56931-869-0(7)) Viz Media.

—Junko Mizuno's Princess Mermaid. Mizuno, Junko. 2003. (Junko Mizuno Ser.). (ENG.). 144p. pap. 15.95 (978-1-59116-117-2(7)) Viz Media.

Mizuno, Junko & Ishibash, Toshiharu. Yu's Cutie Dolls Vol. 3. Mizuno, Junko & Anzai, Yuko. 2003. (Collector File 003 Ser.). (ENG.). 48p. pap. 9.95 (978-1-56931-983-3(9)) Viz Media.

Mizuto, Aqua & Mizuto, Aqua. Yume Kira Dream Shoppe, Vol. 1. Mizuto, Aqua & Mizuto, Aqua. 2007. (Yume Kira Dream Shoppe Ser.). (ENG.). 200p. (gr. 8-18). pap. 8.99 (978-1-4215-1173-3(8)) Viz Media.

Mizuto, Aqua, jt. illus. see Mizuto, Aqua.

MJ Illustrations. Bubble Ball Game! (Bubble Guppies) Tillworth, Mary. 2015. (Pictureback Ser.). (ENG.). 16p. (J). (gr. -1-2). 4.99 (978-0-385-37439-2(9), Random Hse. Bks. for Young Readers) Random Hse. Children's Bks.

—Dora Goes to School/Dora Va a la Escuela (Dora the Explorer) Random House. 2014. (Pictureback(R) Ser.). (ENG.). 24p. (J). (gr. -1-2). 3.99 (978-0-385-37496-5(8), Random Hse. Bks. for Young Readers) Random Hse. Children's Bks.

MJ Illustrations. Haunted House Party! (Bubble Guppies) Random House. 2015. (Hologramatic Sticker Book Ser.). (ENG.). 64p. (J). (gr. -1-2). pap. 4.99 (978-0-385-38407-0(6), Golden Bks.) Random Hse. Children's Bks.

MJ Illustrations. Hide-And-Go-Swim! (Bubble Guppies) Random House. 2014. (Nifty Lift-And-Look Ser.). (ENG.). 12p. (J). (— 1). bds. 5.99 (978-0-385-38515-2(3), Random Hse. Bks. for Young Readers) Random Hse. Children's Bks.

MJ Illustrations. It's Time for Ballet! (Bubble Guppies) Tillworth, Mary. 2015. (Glitter Picturebook Ser.). (ENG.). 16p. (J). (gr. -1-2). 5.99 (978-0-553-52117-7(9), Random Hse. Bks. for Young Readers) Random Hse. Children's Bks.

MJ Illustrations. The Legend of Pinkfoot (Bubble Guppies) Tillworth, Mary. 2014. (Glow-In-the-Dark Pictureback Ser.). (ENG.). 16p. (J). (gr. -1-2). 4.99 (978-0-385-38411-7(4), Random Hse. Bks. for Young Readers) Random Hse. Children's Bks.

MJ Illustrations, et al. Super Sweet Treasury. Brooke, Samantha et al. 2012. (Strawberry Shortcake Ser.). (ENG.). 160p. (J). (gr. -1-k). 9.99 (978-0-448-46163-2(3), Grosset & Dunlap) Penguin Publishing Group.

MJ Illustrations Staff. Berry Bitty Bakers. Ackelsberg, Amy. 2011. (Strawberry Shortcake Ser.). (ENG.). 24p. (J). (gr. -1-k). pap. 4.99 (978-0-448-45695-9(8), Grosset & Dunlap) Penguin Publishing Group.

—A Fresh-n-Fruity Spring. Cecil, Lauren. 2010. (Strawberry Shortcake Ser.). (ENG.). 32p. (J). (gr. -1-k). 3.99 (978-0-448-45273-9(1), Grosset & Dunlap) Penguin Publishing Group.

—Have a Sweet Easter! 2010. (Strawberry Shortcake Ser.). (ENG.). 12p. (J). (gr. -1-k). bds. 5.99 (978-0-448-45272-2(3), Grosset & Dunlap) Penguin Publishing Group.

—Here Comes Bubble Bunny! (Bubble Guppies) Golden Books Staff. 2014. (Hologramatic Sticker Book Ser.). (ENG.). 48p. (J). (gr. -1-2). pap. 3.99 (978-0-385-37497-2(6), Golden Bks.) Random Hse. Children's Bks.

—Strawberry Shortcake's Spooky Night. Jacobs, Lana. 2011. (Strawberry Shortcake Ser.). (ENG.). 24p. (J). (gr. -1-k). mass mkt. 4.99 (978-0-448-45589-1(7), Grosset & Dunlap) Penguin Publishing Group.

—Valentine's Day Mix-Up. Ackelsberg, Amy. 2011. (Strawberry Shortcake Ser.). (ENG.). 24p. (J). (gr. -1-k). mass mkt. 4.99 (978-0-448-45696-6(6), Grosset & Dunlap) Penguin Publishing Group.

MJ Illustrations Staff, jt. illus. see Mcgee, Warner.

MJ Illustrations Staff, jt. illus. see Random House Beginners Books Staff.

MJ Illustrations Staff, jt. illus. see Random House Staff.

MJ Illustrations Staff, jt. illus. see Talkowski, Steve.

MMStudios & Allman, Howard, photos by. Big & Little: A Book about Opposites. 2007. (Usborne Look & Say Ser.). 18p. (J). (gr. -1-3). bds. 14.99 (978-0-7945-1884-4(2), Usborne) EDC Publishing.

Mo, Xiangyi. Access Asia: Primary Teaching & Learning Units. Glascodine, Carolyn, ed. 2003. 192p. pap. 35.95 (978-1-86366-345-8(2)) Education Services Australia Ltd. AUS. Dist: Cheng & Tsui Co.

Moates, Carol Meetze. A Light to Keep. Silcox, Diane. 2013. 30p. pap. 14.95 (978-1-938101-36-6(7)) Indigo Sea Pr., LLC.

Mochizuki, Chiemi. The Promise. Mochizuki, Chiemi. Randle, Walt R., ed. 2003. 38p. (J). (gr. 3-6). 16.99 (978-0-9720691-0-6(0)) Berkeley Major Publishing.

Mockford, Caroline. Cleo & Caspar. Blackstone, Stella. 2013. (ENG.). 24p. (J). pap. 6.99 (978-1-78285-053-3(8)) Barefoot Bks., Inc.

—Cleo in the Snow. Blackstone, Stella. 2013. (ENG.). 24p. (J). bds. 6.99 (978-1-78285-054-0(6)); lthr. 6.99 (978-1-78285-055-7(4)) Barefoot Bks., Inc.

—Cleo on the Move. Blackstone, Stella. 2013. (ENG.). 24p. (J). pap. 6.99 (978-1-78285-057-1(0)); bds. 6.99 (978-1-78285-056-4(2)) Barefoot Bks., Inc.

—Cleo the Cat. Blackstone, Stella. 2013. (ENG.). 24p. (J). pap. 6.99 (978-1-78285-051-9(1)) Barefoot Bks., Inc.

—Cleo the Cat. (J). 12.99 (978-1-84148-458-7(X)) Barefoot Bks., Inc.

—Cleo's Color Book. Blackstone, Stella. (J). 2010. (ENG.). 32p. pap. 6.99 (978-1-84686-440-7(2)); 2006. 0032p. 15.99 (978-1-905236-30-5(1)) Barefoot Bks., Inc.

—Cleo's Counting Book. Blackstone, Stella. 2003. (Cleo the Cat Ser.). (ENG.). 24p. (J). (gr. -1-3). 15.99 (978-1-84148-207-1(2)) Barefoot Bks., Inc.

—Come Here, Cleo! Blackstone, Stella. 2013. (ENG.). 24p. (J). pap. 6.99 (978-1-84148-330-6(3)) Barefoot Bks., Inc.

—The Elephants' Ears. Chamber, Catherine. 2004. 32p. (J). pap. 6.99 (978-1-84148-249-1(8)) Barefoot Bks., Inc.

—Talk with Me! Blackstone, Stella. 2009. (ENG.). 14p. (J). (gr. -1). bds. 7.99 (978-1-84686-180-2(2)) Barefoot Bks., Inc.

—Walk with Me! Blackstone, Stella. 2009. (ENG.). 14p. (J). (gr. -1). bds. 7.99 (978-1-84686-179-6(9)) Barefoot Bks., Inc.

Mockford, Caroline. Cleo's Color Book. Mockford, Caroline. Blackstone, Stella. 2007. (Cleo Ser.). (ENG.). 24p. (J). (gr. -1-k). bds. 6.99 (978-1-84686-060-7(1)) Barefoot Bks., Inc.

—What's This? A Seed's Story. Mockford, Caroline. 2007. (ENG.). 32p. (J). (gr. -1-1). pap. 7.99 (978-1-84686-071-3(7)) Barefoot Bks., Inc.

Mockler, Sean. Alex Has Had Enough! Johnson Mockler, Nicole. 2011. 64p. pap. (978-1-77067-334-2(2)) FriesenPress.

Modarressi, Mitra. Owlet's First Flight. Modarressi, Mitra. 2012. (ENG.). 32p. (J). (gr. -1-k). 16.99 (978-0-399-25526-7(5), Putnam Juvenile) Penguin Publishing Group.

—Taking Care of Mama. Modarressi, Mitra. 2010. (ENG.). 32p. (J). (gr. -1-k). 16.99 (978-0-399-25216-7(9), Putnam Juvenile) Penguin Publishing Group.

Modéré, Armelle. Solamente un Poco de Gripe. Modéré, Armelle. Dufresne, Didier & Modere, Armelle-dufresnedidier. Vinent, Julia, tr. 2003. (SPA.). 32p. (J). (gr. k-2). 15.99 (978-84-8470-123-1(9)) Corimbo, Editorial S.L. ESP. Dist: Lectorum Pubns., Inc.

Modica, Cathy, photos by. Niik & Bling: The Friendship Begins. Modica, Cathy. Van Eyck, Laura. l.t. ed. 2005. 40p. (J). 19.95 (978-0-9762466-0-2(0)) Wholesome Puppy Tales.

Modotti, Tina, photos by. Tina Modotti. Hooks, Margaret. rev. ed. 2005. (55s Ser.). (ENG., 128p. (gr. 8-17). 27.95 (978-0-7148-4566-1(3)) Phaidon Pr., Inc.

Modugno, Tina. Clarence the Clam. Lambert, Susan Dodd. 2013. 28p. pap. 6.95 (978-0-9883893-5-9(5)) Borgo Publishing.

Moeckel, Christine. Dick the Duck. Moeckel, Christine. l.t. ed. 2004. 31p. (J). spiral bd. 9.98 (978-0-9720350-2-6(8)) Duckpond Publishing, Inc.

Moeller, Bill, photos by. Crazy Horse: A Photographic Biography. Moeller, Bill. Moeller, Jan et al. rev. ed. 168p. (J). (gr. 4). pap. (978-0-87842-424-5(5), 648) Mountain Pr. Publishing Co., Inc.

Moeller mé illuminé, Jo. La Hormiguita ¿ A Folktale about the Perseverant Little Ant. 2005. (SPA.). (J). (978-0-9644678-4-2(4)) Bilingual Pubns.

Moeller, Richard. Grandpa Lolo's Navajo Saddle Blanket: La Tilma de Abuelito Lolo. Moeller, Richard, photos by. Garcia, Nasario. 2012. (J). (978-0-8263-5078-7(X)); pap. (978-0-8263-5080-0(1)); (SPA.). 72p. pap. (978-0-8263-5079-4(8)) Univ. of New Mexico Pr.

Moen Cabanting Ruth. All Around the Islands. Arita Vera. 2005. 24p. 12.95 (978-1-933067-09-4(8)) Mutual Publishing LLC.

Moen Cabanting, Ruth. 1-2-3 Waikiki Trolley. 2005. 20p. 7.95 (978-1-933067-06-3(3)) Beachhouse Publishing, LLC.

Moen, Ruth. Lio the Carousel Horse. Wing, Carol. 2010. 32p. 14.95 (978-1-933067-37-7(3)) Beachhouse Publishing, LLC.

—S Went Surfing in Hawai'i. Gillespie, Jane. 2013. (ENG.). 32p. (gr. -1). 12.95 (978-1-933067-50-6(0)) Beachhouse Publishing, LLC.

Moen, Tyler. Daddy Is That the Best You Got? Seelen, Christopher. 2005. 36p. (J). pap. 8.99 (978-0-9776385-0-5(2), Cotton Candy Pr.) Unveiled Media, LLC.

Moerbeck, Kees. Cinderella. Moerbeck, Kees, des. 2006. (Roly Poly Box Bks.). (ENG.). 24p. (J). (978-1-84643-019-0(4)) Child's Play International Ltd.

—Goldilocks. Moerbeck, Kees, des. 2006. (Roly Poly Box Bks.). (ENG.). 24p. (J). (978-1-84643-017-6(8)) Child's Play International Ltd.

—Three Little Pigs. Moerbeck, Kees, des. 2006. (Roly Poly Box Bks.). (ENG.). 24p. (J). (978-1-84643-018-3(6)) Child's Play International Ltd.

Moerbeek, Kees. Make 24 Paper Planes: Includes Awesome Launcher Kit! Golding, Elizabeth. 2015. (ENG.). 24p. (J). (gr. 2-6). pap. 10.99 (978-1-4380-0640-6(3)) Barron's Educational Series, Inc.

—Raggedy Ann & Andy & the Camel with the Wrinkled Knees. Gruelle, Johnny. collector's ed. 2003. (Raggedy Ann Ser.). (ENG.). 14p. (J). (gr. -1-2). 29.99 (978-0-689-85775-1(6), Little Simon) Little Simon.

Moerder, Lynne. Things That Go Burp! in the Night. Moerder, Lynne. 2015. (ENG.). 32p. (J). (gr. -1-k). 16.99 (978-1-4847-1669-4(8)) Hyperion Bks. for Children.

Moerner, John. Don't Play with Your Food!, Rock, Brian. 2005. 32p. (J). 14.99 (978-0-9754411-0-7(8)) First Light Publishing.

Mofett, Patricia. The Beast Beneath the Stairs, 1 vol. Dahl, Michael. 2007. (Library of Doom Ser.). (ENG.). 40p. (gr. 1-3). lib. bdg. 22.65 (978-1-59889-323-6(8)); per. 6.25 (978-1-59889-418-9(8)) Stone Arch Bks. (Zone Bks.).

Moffat, Ross. Cow Story. Arkangel, Brian. 2009. 24p. pap. 24.95 (978-1-60703-272-4(4)) America Star Bks.

Moffatt, Judith. Slide & Discover: It's Time! 2005. (Slide & Discover Ser.). 8p. (J). bds. 7.95 (978-1-58117-247-8(8), Intervisual/Piggy Toes) Bendon, Inc.

—Slide & Discover: What's My Job? 2005. (Slide & Discover Ser.). 8p. (J). bds. 7.95 (978-1-58117-248-5(6), Intervisual/Piggy Toes) Bendon, Inc.

Moffet, Patricia. Ghosts vs. Witches: Tussle of the Tricksters. O'Hearn, Michael. 2011. (Monster Wars Ser.). (ENG.). 32p. (gr. 3-4). pap. 47.70 (978-1-4296-7262-7(5)); lib. bdg. 27.32 (978-1-4296-6522-3(X)) Capstone Pr., Inc. (Edge Bks.).

Moffet, Patricia, et al. Monster Wars. O'Hearn, Michael. 2011. (Monster Wars Ser.). (ENG.). 32p. (gr. 3-4). pap. 31.80 (978-1-4296-7269-6(2)); pap. 190.80 (978-1-4296-7270-2(6)); lib. bdg. 109.28 (978-1-4296-6524-7(6)) Capstone Pr., Inc. (Edge Bks.).

Moffet, Patricia. Zombies vs. Mummies: Clash of the Living Dead. O'Hearn, Michael. 2011. (Monster Wars Ser.). (ENG.). 32p. (gr. 3-4). pap. 47.70 (978-1-4296-7268-9(4)); lib. bdg. 27.32 (978-1-4296-6520-9(3)) Capstone Pr., Inc. (Edge Bks.).

Mogensen, Jan. El Hijo del Elefante. Kipling, Rudyard. (Barril Sin Fondo Ser.).Tr. of Elephant's Child. (SPA.). (J). (gr. 3-5). pap. 8.76 (978-968-6465-06-8(5)) Casa de Estudios de Literatura y Talleres Artisticos Amaquemecan A.C. MEX. Dist: Lectorum Pubns., Inc.

Mogensen, Jan & Schroeder, Binnette. Crocodile, Crocodile. Kipling, Rudyard. 2003. Orig. Title: Krokodil, Krokodil. pap. 7.95 (978-1-56656-512-7(X)) Interlink Publishing Group, Inc.

Mogorrón, Guillermo. The Hunt for Hidden Treasure: A Mystery about Rocks. Beauregard, Lynda. 2012. (Summer Camp Science Mysteries Ser.: 3). (ENG.). 48p. (gr. 3-6). pap. 39.62 (978-0-7613-9270-5(X)); pap. 6.95 (978-0-7613-8545-5(2)); lib. bdg. 29.27 (978-0-7613-5690-5(8)) Lerner Publishing Group. (Graphic Universe).

Mogyorosi, Nicole. Three Dogs Go Walking. Post, Grace. 2009. 32p. pap. 24.95 (978-1-61546-147-9(7)) America Star Bks.

Mohamed, Sultan. The Story of Coffee. Mohamed, Sultan, tr. 2003. (ENG & AMH.). 24p. (J). (gr. 4-5). 15.99 (978-0-9605670-9-6(7)) Ananse Pr.

Mohrbacher, Peter. The Three Furies. Kingsley, Kaza. 2010. (Erec Rex Ser.: 4). (ENG.). 704p. (J). (gr. 5-9). 16.99 (978-1-4169-7990-6(5), Simon & Schuster Bks. For Young Readers) Simon & Schuster Bks. For Young Readers.

Mohrbacher, Peter, jt. illus. see Ng, James.

Moise, Nahomie. Big E, Meet Zeke, Your New Brother. Fichthorn, Ashley. 2011. 36p. pap. 24.95 (978-1-4560-6941-4(1)) America Star Bks.

Mojica, Victor Ramon. Little Miss History Travels to Mount Rushmore. Mojica, Barbara Ann. 2012. 36p. pap. 13.95 (978-0-9885030-0-7(X)) eugenus STUDIOS.

Mokona. Okimono Kimono. Mokona. Clamp Staff. 2010. (ENG.). 128p. pap. 12.99 (978-1-59582-456-1(1)) Dark Horse Comics.

Mola, Maria. Jeremy's Dreidel. Gellman, Ellie. 2012. (Hanukkah Ser.). 32p. (J). (gr. k-3). (ENG.). lib. bdg. 17.95 (978-0-7613-7507-4(4)); (SPA & ENG.). 7.95 (978-0-7613-7508-1(2)) Lerner Publishing Group. (Kar-Ben Publishing).

Molina, Adrian H., jt. illus. see RH Disney Staff.

Molina, Jorge, et al. Perfect World, Vol. 3. Parker, Jeff, ed. 2011. (ENG.). 144p. (J). (gr. 4-17). pap. 16.99 (978-0-7851-4666-7(0)) Marvel Worldwide, Inc.

Molina, Jorge & Kirby, Jack. Captain America: Man Out of Time. Waid, Mark. 2011. (ENG.). 144p. (J). (gr. 4-17). pap. 16.99 (978-0-7851-5129-6(X)) Marvel Worldwide, Inc.

M

Molinari, Carlo. Magic Tree House Fact Tracker #33: Vikings: A Nonfiction Companion to Magic Tree House #15: Viking Ships at Sunrise. Osborne, Mary Pope & Boyce, Natalie Pope. 2015. (Stepping Stone Book(TM) Ser.). (ENG.). 128p. (J). (gr. 2-5). 5.99 ***(978-0-385-38638-8(9))***, Random Hse. Bks. for Young Readers) Random Hse. Children's Bks.

Molinari, Carlo. Mary Walker Wears the Pants: The True Story of the Doctor, Reformer, & Civil War Hero. Harness, Cheryl. 2013. (ENG.). 32p. (J). (gr. 1-4). 16.99 *(978-0-8075-4990-2(8))* Whitman, Albert & Co.

—Sharks & Other Predators. Osborne, Mary Pope & Boyce, Natalie Pope. 2015. (Stepping Stone Book Ser.). (ENG.). 128p. (J). (gr. 2-5). 12.99 *(978-0-385-38642-5(7))*, Random Hse. Bks. for Young Readers) Random Hse. Children's Bks.

—Thank You, M'am. Hughes, Langston. 2014. (Classic Stories Ser.). (ENG.). 24p. (J). (gr. 3-6). 28.50 *(978-1-62323-621-2(5))*, 206389) Child's World, Inc., The.

—True Stories of the Civil War, 1 vol. Yomtov, Nelson. 2012. (Stories of War Ser.). (ENG.). 32p. (gr. 3-4). pap. 8.10 *(978-1-4296-9340-0(1))*; lib. bdg. 29.99 *(978-1-4296-8624-2(3))* Capstone Pr., Inc.

—True Stories of the Civil War. Yomtov, Nel. 2012. (Stories of War Ser.). (ENG.). 32p. (gr. 3-4). pap. 47.70 *(978-1-4296-9341-7(X))*, Graphic Library) Capstone Pr., Inc.

Molinari, Fernando. Bombón la Chihuahua Extraviada. Villacis, Alexandra. 2009. (SPA.). 252p. pap. 28.60 *(978-1-4251-5504-9(9))* Trafford Publishing.

—Bombón the Lost Chihuahua. Villacis, Alexandra. 2009. (SPA.). 258p. pap. 28.87 *(978-1-4251-5674-9(6))* Trafford Publishing.

—The Eye in the Graveyard. Dahl, Michael. 2007. (Library of Doom Ser.). (ENG.). 40p. (gr. 1-3). pap. 6.25 *(978-1-59889-423-3(4))*; lib. bdg. 22.65 *(978-1-59889-328-1(9))* Stone Arch Bks. (Zone Bks.).

—Isabel Allende: Memories for a Story: Isabel Allende: Recuerdos para un Cuento. Benatar, Raquel. Petersen, Patricia, tr. 2003. (SPA & ENG.). 32p. 16.95 *(978-1-55885-379-9(0))*, Piñata Books) Arte Publico Pr.

Moline, Karl, et al. Highway of Horror. Bedard, Tony. 2003. (Route 666 Ser.: Vol. 1). 160p. (YA). (gr. 7-18). pap. 15.95 *(978-1-931484-56-5(2))* CrossGeneration Comics, Inc.

—Most Haunted, Vol. 2. Bedard, Tony. 2004. (Route 666 Traveler Ser.: Vol. 2). 160p. (YA). pap. 9.95 *(978-1-59314-055-7(X))* CrossGeneration Comics, Inc.

—Route 666, Vol. 2. Bedard, Tony. 2003. (Route 666 Ser.: Vol. 2). 160p. (YA). pap. 15.95 *(978-1-931484-92-3(9))* CrossGeneration Comics, Inc.

—Route 666 Traveler: Highway of Horror. Bedard, Tony. 2004. (Route 666 Traveler Ser.). 160p. (YA). pap. 9.95 *(978-1-59314-041-0(X))* CrossGeneration Comics, Inc.

Moline, Karl & Madsen, Michelle. Buffy the Vampire Slayer, 4 vols. Allie, Scott et al. Allie, Scott & Hahn, Sierra, eds. 2013. (ENG.). 320p. 29.99 *(978-1-61655-127-8(5))* Dark Horse Comics.

Molinet, Michael. Before You Were Born. Molinet, Michael. Molinet, Kelly. 2003. 22p. (J). 12.99 *(978-0-9705996-7-4(6))* Practical Christianity Foundation.

—Just Like You. Molinet, Michael. Molinet, Kelly. 2004. 22p. (J). 15.99 *(978-1-932587-34-0(9))* Practical Christianity Foundation.

Molitor, Sherrie. The Lucky Nickel. DoNascimento, Nicole. 2014. (ENG.). 20p. (J). pap. 9.99 *(978-0-9835120-0-4(0))* DoNascimento.com/Bks.

Molk, Laurel. It's a ... It's a ... It's a Mitzvah. Suneby, Liz & Heiman, Diane. 2012. (ENG.). 32p. (J). 18.99 *(978-1-58023-509-9(3))*, Jewish Lights Publishing) LongHill Partners, Inc.

—That's a Mitzvah. Heiman, Diane & Suneby, Liz. 2014. (ENG.). 24p. (J). bds. 8.99 *(978-1-58023-804-5(1))*, Jewish Lights Publishing) LongHill Partners, Inc.

Molk, Laurel. Eeny, Meeny, Miney, Mo, & Flo. Molk, Laurel. 2015. (ENG.). 32p. (J). (gr. -1-k). 16.99 *(978-0-670-01538-2(5))*, Viking Juvenile) Penguin Publishing Group.

Mollett, Irene. Groundhog Breakfast, Soft Petals, & a Roof That Don't Leak Too Much, 1 vol. Williamson, Linda. 2009. 23p. pap. 24.95 *(978-1-60749-618-2(6))* America Star Bks.

Molloy, J. Christmas Terror Tales: Stories to Enjoy from October Through December. Folliard, Kevin. 2011. (ENG.). 92p. pap. 5.50 *(978-1-4637-8694-6(8))* CreateSpace Independent Publishing Platform.

Molloy, Michael. Jack - King of the Dogs. Molloy, Sheila. Steed, Tobias, ed. 2004. (Jack Ser.: 1). (ENG.). 100p. (J). (gr. 4-7). pap. 9.99 *(978-1-904872-30-6(1))*, Can of Worms Kids Pr.) Can of Worms Pr. GBR. Dist: Independent Pubs. Group.

Molloy, Sophie. The Cat Did Not Know. McCarthy, Margaret. 2006. (ENG.). 36p. (J). pap. 14.95 *(978-1-85390-923-8(8))* Veritas Pubns. IRL. Dist: Dufour Editions, Inc.

Molnar, Albert. Field Day. Jones, Melanie Davis. 2011. (Rookie Ready to Learn Ser.). 40p. (J). (ENG.). pap. 5.95 *(978-0-531-26826-1(8))*; (gr. -1-k). lib. bdg. 23.00 *(978-0-531-27176-6(5))* Scholastic Library Publishing. (Children's Pr.).

Molnar, Albert & McKillip Thornburgh, Rebecca. The School Box: Field Day - 100th Da of School - One Happy Classroom. Davis Jones, Melanie et al. 2004. (Rookie Reader Ser.). (ENG.). 96p. (J). (gr. k-2). 9.95 *(978-0-516-24554-6(6))*, Children's Pr.) Scholastic Library Publishing.

Momaday, N. Scott. Spirit Woman: The Teachings of the Shields. Andrews, Lynn V. 2007. (ENG.). 224p. (gr. 12-18). 14.95 *(978-1-58542-576-1(1))*, Tarcher) Penguin Publishing Group.

Momaday, N. Scott. Four Arrows & Magpie: A Kiowa Story. Momaday, N. Scott. 2006. 35p. (J). (gr. -1-3). pap. 9.95 *(978-1-930709-63-8(3))* HAWK Publishing Group.

Mombourquette, Paul. The Klondike Cat. Lawson, Julie. 2004. (ENG.). 32p. (J). (gr. k-3). 5.95 *(978-1-55337-766-5(4))* Kids Can Pr., Ltd. CAN. Dist: Univ. of Toronto Pr.

Mommaerts, Robb. Cinnamon & the April Shower. Johnson, Amy Crane. 2009. (ENG.). 32p. (J). (gr. -1-3). 16.95 *(978-1-934960-54-7(3))*, Raven Tree Pr.,Csi) Continental Sales, Inc.

—A Home for Pearl Squirrel. Johnson, Amy Crane. 2009. (ENG.). 32p. (J). (gr. -1-3). 16.95 *(978-1-934960-58-5(6))*, Raven Tree Pr.,Csi) Continental Sales, Inc.

—A Home for Pearl Squirrel: Una casa para la ardilla Perla, 4 vols. Crane Johnson, Amy. de la Vega, Eida, tr. rev. ed. 2004. (Solomon Raven Ser.: 1).Tr. of casa para la ardilla Perla. (SPA & ENG.). 32p. (J). (gr. 4-7). 16.95 *(978-0-9724973-4-3(X))*, 626999, Raven Tree Pr.,Csi) Continental Sales, Inc.

—Lewis Cardinal's First Winter. Johnson, Amy Crane. 2009. (ENG.). 32p. (J). (gr. 4-7). 16.95 *(978-1-934960-60-8(8))*, Raven Tree Pr.,Csi) Continental Sales, Inc.

—Mason Moves Away. Johnson, Amy Crane. 2009. (ENG.). 32p. (J). (gr. 4-7). 16.95 *(978-1-934960-56-1(X))*, Raven Tree Pr.,Csi) Continental Sales, Inc.

—Mason Moves Away/Mason se Muda: A Solomon Raven Story: un cuento del cuervo Salomon, 4 vols. Johnson, Amy Crane. de la Vega, Eida, tr. 2004. (Solomon Raven Ser.: 4).Tr. of Mason se Muda. (SPA & ENG.). 32p. (J). (gr. -1-3). 16.95 *(978-0-9720192-3-1(5))*, 626999, Raven Tree Pr.,Csi) Continental Sales, Inc.

Momokawa, Haruhiko. The Good Witch of the West, Vol. 6. Ogiwara, Noriko & Noriko, Ogiwara. 2008. (Good Witch of the West Ser.). 208p. (gr. 8-18). pap. 9.99 *(978-1-4278-0889-9(9))* TOKYOPOP, Inc.

Momose, Takeaki. Rahxephon. Izubuchi, Yutaka. 2004. (Rahxephon Ser.). (ENG.). (YA). 192p. pap. 9.95 *(978-1-59116-407-4(9))*; Vol. 2. 200p. pap. 9.95 *(978-1-59116-427-2(3))*; Vol. 3. 200p. pap. 9.95 *(978-1-59116-428-9(1))* Viz Media.

Mona, Larkins. Pablo's Art Adventures: Exploring the Studio. Mona, Larkins. 2004. 27p. (J). 14.99 *(978-0-9740841-3-8(1))* K&B Products.

Monaco, Octavia. Klimt & His Cat. Capatti, Bérénice. 2005. 40p. (J). 18.00 *(978-0-8028-5282-3(3))* Eerdmans, William B. Publishing Co.

—El Nacimiento de las Estaciones: El Mito de Demetery Persefone. Lossani, Chiara. 2009. (SPA.). (YA). (gr. 5-10). *(978-968-5389-62-4(4))* El Naranjo, Ediciones.

—Vincent Van Gogh & the Colors of the Wind. Lossani, Chiara & van Gogh, Vincent. 2011. 34p. (J). (gr. 2). 18.99 *(978-0-8028-5390-5(0))*, Eerdmans Bks For Young Readers) Eerdmans, William B. Publishing Co.

Monahan, Leo. The Twelve Days of Christmas. Monahan, Leo. 2007. (ENG.). 24p. (J). 19.95 *(978-1-58117-624-7(4))*, Intervisual/Piggy Toes) Bendon, Inc.

Monceaux, Morgan. My Heroes, My People: African Americans & Native Americans in Thewest. Monceaux, Morgan. Katcher, Ruth. 2004. 63p. (J). (gr. k-4). reprint ed. 18.00 *(978-0-7567-7868-2(9))* DIANE Publishing Co.

Mondragon, Manny. How Can I Be Special? Chinn, Jacqueline. 2003. (J). pap. 15.95 *(978-0-929526-55-3(4))* Double B Pubns.

Monelli, Marta. The Vanishing Gourds: A Sukkot Mystery. Axe-Bronk, Susan. 2012. (Sukkot & Simchat Torah Ser.). (ENG.). 24p. (J). (gr. -1-3). 7.95 *(978-0-7613-7504-3(X))*; lib. bdg. 17.95 *(978-0-7613-7503-6(1))* Lerner Publishing Group. (Kar-Ben Publishing).

Mones, Isidre. Bambi's Hide-and-Seek. Disney Staff & Posner-Sanchez, Andrea. 2013. (Step into Reading Ser.). (ENG.). 32p. (J). (gr. -1-1). lib. bdg. 12.99 *(978-0-7364-8009-3(9))*, Random Hse. Bks. for Young Readers) Random Hse. Children's Bks.

—Bambi's Hide-and-Seek. RH Disney Staff & Posner-Sanchez, Andrea. 2013. (Step into Reading Ser.). (ENG.). 32p. (J). (gr. -1-1). pap. 3.99 *(978-0-7364-1347-3(2))*, RH/Disney) Random Hse. Children's Bks.

—Cloudy with a Chance of Meatballs 3: Planet of the Pies. Barrett, Judi. 2013. (ENG.). 32p. (J). (gr. -1-3). 17.99 *(978-1-4424-9027-7(6))*, Atheneum Bks. for Young Readers) Simon & Schuster Children's Publishing.

—Puppy Mudge Has a Snack. Rylant, Cynthia. 2005. (Puppy Mudge Ser.). (gr. -1-k). 14.00 *(978-0-7569-5764-3(8))* Perfection Learning Corp.

—Puppy Mudge Has a Snack. Rylant, Cynthia. (Puppy Mudge Ser.). (ENG.). 32p. (J). (gr. -1-k). 2004. pap. 3.99 *(978-0-689-86995-2(9))*; 2003. 16.99 *(978-0-689-83981-8(2))* Simon Spotlight. (Simon Spotlight).

—Puppy Mudge Loves His Blanket. Rylant, Cynthia. (Puppy Mudge Ser.). (ENG.). 32p. (J). (gr. -1-k). 2005. pap. 3.99 *(978-1-4169-0336-9(4))*; 2004. 16.99 *(978-0-689-83983-2(9))* Simon Spotlight. (Simon Spotlight).

—Stingrays! Underwater Fliers. Gerber, Carole. 2015. (Step into Reading Ser.). (ENG.). 48p. (J). (gr. k-3). 12.99 *(978-0-375-97153-2(X))* Random Hse., Inc.

Mones, Isidre. Puppy Mudge Takes a Bath. Mones, Isidre. Rylant, Cynthia. 2004. (Puppy Mudge Ser.). (ENG.). 32p. (J). (gr. -1-k). pap. 3.99 *(978-0-689-86621-0(6))*, Simon Spotlight) Simon Spotlight.

Mones, Marc. Be Honest, Jess Lap Book. Garcia, Ellen. 2014. (MySELF Ser.). (J). (gr. -1-k). 27.00 *(978-1-4788-0508-3(0))* Newmark Learning LLC.

—Charlie Is Responsible Lap Book. Garcia, Ellen. 2014. (MySELF Ser.). (J). (gr. -1-k). 27.00 *(978-1-4788-0507-6(2))* Newmark Learning LLC.

—Disaster Day. Mckenzie, Precious. 2012. (ENG.). 24p. (gr. 2-3). pap. 7.95 *(978-1-61810-331-4(8))*; lib. bdg. 28.50 *(978-1-61810-198-3(6))* Rourke Educational Media.

—Fish Mission. Mckenzie, Precioius. 2013. (ENG.). 24p. (gr. -1-1). 25.64 *(978-1-62169-252-2(3))*; pap. 7.95 *(978-1-62169-210-2(8))* Rourke Educational Media.

—Go North! Greve, Meg. 2013. (ENG.). 24p. (gr. -1-1). 25.64 *(978-1-62169-248-5(5))*; pap. 7.95 *(978-1-62169-206-5(X))* Rourke Educational Media.

—I Can Be Kind Lap Book. Williams, Dinah. 2014. (MySELF Ser.). (J). (gr. -1-k). 27.00 *(978-1-4788-0504-5(8))* Newmark Learning LLC.

—I Show Respect. Linde, Barbara M. 2014. (J). (gr. -1). 3.99 *(978-1-4788-0468-0(8))* Newmark Learning LLC.

—I Show Respect Lap Book. Linde, Barbara M. 2014. (MySELF Ser.). (J). (gr. -1-k). 27.00 *(978-1-4788-0505-2(6))* Newmark Learning LLC.

—The Lake Mistake. Mckenzie, Precioius. 2013. (ENG.). 24p. (gr. -1-1). 25.64 *(978-1-62169-254-6(X))*; pap. 7.95 *(978-1-62169-212-6(4))* Rourke Educational Media.

—The Museum Mystery. Greve, Meg. 2013. (ENG.). 24p. (gr. -1-1). 25.64 *(978-1-62169-250-8(7))*; pap. 7.95 *(978-1-62169-208-9(6))* Rourke Educational Media.

—Surfing Safari. Mckenzie, Precioius. 2013. (ENG.). 24p. (gr. -1-1). 25.64 *(978-1-62169-253-9(1))*; pap. 7.95 *(978-1-62169-211-9(6))* Rourke Educational Media.

—Thanks for Sharing, Tommy. Giachetti, Julia. 2014. (J). (gr. -1). 3.99 *(978-1-4788-0466-6(1))* Newmark Learning LLC.

—Thanks for Sharing, Tommy Lap Book. Giachetti, Julia. 2014. (MySELF Ser.). (J). (gr. -1-k). 27.00 *(978-1-4788-0503-8(X))* Newmark Learning LLC.

—That's Not Fair! Lap Book. Daniel, Claire. 2014. (MySELF Ser.). (J). (gr. -1-k). 27.00 *(978-1-4788-0506-9(4))* Newmark Learning LLC.

—Time for a Trim. Reed, Jennifer. 2012. (ENG.). 24p. (gr. 1-2). pap. 7.95 *(978-1-61810-319-2(9))*; lib. bdg. 28.50 *(978-1-61810-186-0(2))* Rourke Educational Media.

—Vote for Me! Robertson, J. Jean. 2012. (ENG.). 24p. (gr. 1-2). pap. 7.95 *(978-1-61810-316-1(4))* Rourke Educational Media.

—Vote for Me! Robertson, Jean. 2012. (ENG.). 24p. (gr. 1-2). lib. bdg. 28.50 *(978-1-61810-183-9(8))* Rourke Educational Media.

—Wet & Wild Waterpark. Greve, Meg. 2013. (ENG.). 24p. (gr. -1-1). 25.64 *(978-1-62169-251-5(5))*; pap. 7.95 *(978-1-62169-209-6(4))* Rourke Educational Media.

Monescillo, Maria. Many Days, One Shabbat, 0 vols. Manushkin, Fran. 2011. (ENG.). 24p. (J). (gr. -1-3). 12.99 *(978-0-7614-5965-1(0))*, 9780761459651, Amazon Children's Publishing) Amazon Publishing.

—Mary Wrightly, So Politely. Bridges, Shirin Yim. 2013. (ENG.). 32p. (J). (gr. -1-3). 16.99 *(978-0-547-34248-1(9))* Houghton Mifflin Harcourt Publishing Co.

—The Tallest of Smalls, 1 vol. Lucado, Max. 2009. (ENG.). 32p. (gr. -1-2). 16.99 *(978-1-4003-1514-7(X))* Nelson, Thomas Inc.

Monescillo, Maria. Charlotte Jane Battles Bedtime. Monescillo, Maria. Wolfe, Myra. 2011. (ENG.). 32p. (J). (gr. -1-3). 16.99 *(978-0-15-206150-0(9))* Houghton Mifflin Harcourt Publishing Co.

Money, Greg. Princesses Don't Hit. Morrissey, Lynda I. 2012. 24p. pap. *(978-1-77097-976-5(X))* FriesenPress.

Moneymaker, Janet. Chemistry Pre-Level I. Keller, Rebecca W. 2005. (Real Science-4-Kids Ser.). 79p. (J). (gr. 1-3). 21095.00 *(978-0-9765097-0-7(9))* Gravitas Pubns., Inc.

Moneysmith, David. Mommy Breastfeeds My Baby Brother/ Mama Amamanta A Mi Hermanito. Repkin, Mark. 2011.Tr. of Mama Amamanta A Mi Hermanito. 24p. (J). pap. 9.99 *(978-0-9816538-1-5(2))* Istoria Hse.

Mongeau, Marc. The Bug House Family Restaurant, 1 vol. Brenna, Beverley. 2014. (ENG.). 64p. (J). (gr. 3-5). pap. 12.95 *(978-1-926890-01-2(9))* Tradewind Bks. CAN. Dist: Orca Bk. Pubs. USA.

—Mimi Power & the I-Don't-Know-What, 1 vol. Miles, Victoria. 2013. (ENG.). 224p. (J). (gr. 3-5). pap. 12.95 *(978-1-896580-65-4(3))* Tradewind Bks. CAN. Dist: Orca Bk. Pubs. USA.

—My Daddy's Footsteps. Barcelo, François. 2009. (My First Stories Ser.). 24p. (J). (gr. -1-3). 22.60 *(978-1-60754-359-6(1))*; pap. 8.15 *(978-1-60754-360-2(5))* Windmill Bks.

—My Mommy's Hands. Barcelo, François. 2009. (My First Stories Ser.). 24p. (J). (gr. -1-3). 22.60 *(978-1-60754-362-6(1))*; pap. 8.15 *(978-1-60754-365-7(6))* Windmill Bks.

—Shake Awakes, 1 vol. Heidbreder, Robert. 2012. (ENG.). 40p. (J). (gr. -1-3). 18.95 *(978-1-896580-71-5(8))* Tradewind Bks. CAN. Dist: Orca Bk. Pubs. USA.

—A World Full of Ghosts. Cotter, Charis. 2009. (ENG.). 48p. (J). (gr. 1-3). 19.95 *(978-1-55451-183-9(6))*, 9781554511839) Annick Pr., Ltd. CAN. Dist: Firefly Bks., Ltd.

Mongiovi, Jorge. Bugs & Spiders. Orme, David. 2010. (Fact to Fiction Ser.). 36p. pap. 7.45 *(978-0-7891-7990-6(3))* Perfection Learning Corp.

—Life in Space. Orme, Helen. 2008. (Trailblazers Ser.). 36p. pap. *(978-1-84167-690-6(X))* Ransom Publishing Ltd.

—Lost Animals. Orme, David. 2010. (Fact to Fiction Grafx Ser.). 36p. pap. 7.45 *(978-0-7891-7993-7(8))* Perfection Learning Corp.

Mongtomery Gibson, Jane. Don't Renege! It's Just an Egg! Mongtomery Gibson, Jane. 2005. (J). bds. 8.99 *(978-1-4183-0036-4(5))* Christ Inspired, Inc.

—In Olden Days. Mongtomery Gibson, Jane. 2005. (YA). bds. 8.99 *(978-1-4183-0042-5(X))* Christ Inspired, Inc.

—Jesus' Bread. Mongtomery Gibson, Jane. 2005. (J). bds. 8.99 *(978-1-4183-0028-9(4))* Christ Inspired, Inc.

—My Heart Goes with You. Mongtomery Gibson, Jane. 2005. (J). bds. 8.99 *(978-1-4183-0029-6(2))* Christ Inspired, Inc.

Mongtomgery Gibson, Jane. Angels Long. Mongtomgery Gibson, Jane. 2005. (YA). bds. 8.99 *(978-1-4183-0035-7(7))* Christ Inspired, Inc.

Monica, Brufton. Without Surprise. Maude, Tony. 2013. 60p. pap. *(978-2-917183-29-8(2))* Nigeria Baptist Convention, Pubns. Dept.

Monical, Olivia R. The Forest of Thinks. Monical, Olivia R. 2012. (ENG.). 28p. (J). pap. 10.95 *(978-1-57733-267-1(9))*, Papillon Publishing) Blue Dolphin Publishing, Inc.

Monick, Susie. A Boy & His God. Fite, Ramona. 2012. 36p. 22.50 *(978-1-937763-37-4(4))* Published by Westview, Inc.

Moniz, Michael. Wazzyjump. 2012. (ENG.). 44p. (J). (gr. -1-2). 16.95 *(978-1-897476-58-1(2))* Simply Read Bks. CAN. Dist: Ingram Pub. Services.

Moniz, Michael. The Cardinal & the Crow. Moniz, Michael. 2015. (ENG.). 40p. (J). 16.95 *(978-1-927018-58-3(7))* Simply Read Bks. CAN. Dist: Ingram Pub. Services.

Monkey, Micah, jt. illus. see Chambers-Goldberg, Micah.

Monkman, William Kent. A Coyote Columbus Story, 1 vol. King, Thomas. 2007. (ENG.). 32p. (J). (gr. -1-k). pap. 8.95 *(978-0-88899-830-9(9))* Groundwood Bks. CAN. Dist: Perseus-PGW.

Monks, Christian. The Wilkins Family Farm, 1 vol. May, Gary L. 2009. 75p. pap. 19.95 *(978-1-4489-2605-3(X))* America Star Bks.

Monks, Julie. Marcello Mouse & the Masked Ball, 6. Monks, Julie. 2012. (ENG.). 32p. (J). (gr. -1-k). pap. 8.99 *(978-0-230-70383-4(6))* Macmillan Pubs., Ltd. GBR. Dist: Independent Pubs. Group.

Monks, Lydia. Aaaarrgghh, Spider! 2004. (ENG.). 32p. (J). pap. *(978-1-4052-1044-7(3))* Egmont Bks., Ltd.

—Falling for Rapunzel. Wilcox, Leah. (ENG.). 32p. (J). 2005. (gr. k-3). pap. 5.99 *(978-0-14-240399-0(7))*, Puffin); 2003. (gr. -1-3). 15.99 *(978-0-399-23794-2(1))*, Putnam Juvenile) Penguin Publishing Group.

Monks, Lydia. Glitter Kitty. Bergman, Mara. (ENG.). 32p. (J). 2014. bds. 8.99 ***(978-1-4711-2216-3(6))***; 2005. (gr. -1-3). 16.99 *(978-0-689-87305-8(0))* Simon & Schuster, Ltd. GBR. Dist: Simon & Schuster, Inc.

Monks, Lydia. Mungo Monkey Has a Birthday Party. 2014. (ENG.). 14p. (J). (gr. -1). 12.99 *(978-1-4052-6866-0(2))* Egmont Bks., Ltd. GBR. Dist: Independent Pubs. Group.

—My Big (Strange) Happy Family. McCombie, Karen. 2009. (J). pap. *(978-0-385-73597-1(9))*, Yearling) Random Hse. Children's Bks.

—Princess Mirror-Belle & the Flying Horse, 3. Donaldson, Julia. 2013. (Princess Mirror-Belle Ser.: 3). (ENG.). 160p. (J). (gr. k-2). pap. 7.99 *(978-1-4472-2403-7(5))* Pan Macmillan GBR. Dist: Independent Pubs. Group.

—Princess Mirror-Belle & the Magic Shoes, 1. Donaldson, Julia. 2013. (Princess Mirror-Belle Ser.). (ENG.). 144p. (J). (gr. k-2). pap. 7.99 *(978-1-4472-2404-4(3))* Pan Macmillan GBR. Dist: Independent Pubs. Group.

—The Princess Mirror-Belle Collection, 3. Donaldson, Julia. unabr. ed. 2012. (Princess Mirror-Belle Ser.). (ENG.). 432p. (J). (gr. k-2). pap. 9.99 *(978-1-4472-0864-8(1))* Pan Macmillan GBR. Dist: Independent Pubs. Group.

—Queen Munch & Queen Nibble. Duffy, Carol Ann. 2008. (ENG.). 64p. (J). (gr. -1-3). *(978-1-59692-238-9(9))* MacAdam/Cage Publishing, Inc.

—Sharing a Shell Jigsaw Book. Donaldson, Julia. ed. 2008. (ENG.). 14p. (J). (gr. 3-6). 23.95 *(978-0-230-01640-8(5))*, Macmillan) Pan Macmillan GBR. Dist: Trans-Atlantic Pubns., Inc.

—Shout, Show & Tell! Agnew, Kate. 2005. (Green Bananas Ser.). (ENG.). 48p. (J). (gr. -1-1). *(978-0-7787-1040-0(8))* Crabtree Publishing Co.

—Shout, Show & Tell! Agnew, Kate. 2004. (Green Bananas Ser.). (ENG.). 48p. (J). (gr. k-2). pap. 5.99 *(978-1-4052-0875-8(9))* Egmont Bks., Ltd. GBR. Dist: Independent Pubs. Group.

—Shout, Show, & Tell. Agnew, Kate. 2005. (Green Bananas Ser.). (ENG.). 48p. (J). lib. bdg. *(978-0-7787-1024-0(6))* Crabtree Publishing Co.

—Waking Beauty. Wilcox, Leah. 2011. (ENG.). 32p. (J). (gr. -1-k). pap. 6.99 *(978-0-14-241538-2(3))*, Puffin) Penguin Publishing Group.

—What the Ladybug Heard. Donaldson, Julia. 2010. (ENG.). 32p. (J). (gr. -1-1). 17.99 *(978-0-8050-9028-4(2))*, Holt, Henry & Co. Bks. For Young Readers) Holt, Henry & Co.

Monks, Lydia & Okstad, Ella. My Super Sister, 1. Rees, Gwyneth. unabr. ed. 2013. (ENG.). 320p. (J). (gr. 4). pap. 6.99 *(978-0-330-46114-6(1))* Pan Macmillan GBR. Dist: Independent Pubs. Group.

Monlongo, Jorge. Enchanted, Vol. 3. Turner, James. 2013. (Mameshiba Ser.: 3). (ENG.). 80p. (J). pap. 6.99 *(978-1-4215-5524-9(7))* Viz Media.

—Mameshiba: We Could Be Heroes. Turner, James. 2012. (Mameshiba Ser.: 2). (ENG.). 80p. (J). pap. 6.99 *(978-1-4215-4128-0(9))* Viz Media.

Monlongo, Jorge. Trick Arrr Treat: A Pirate Halloween. Kimmelman, Leslie. 2015. (ENG.). 32p. (J). (gr. -1-2). 16.99 ***(978-0-8075-8061-5(9))*** Whitman, Albert & Co.

Monlongo, Jorge. Hello Kitty: Just Imagine. Monlongo, Jorge. Chabot, Jacob. 2014. (Hello Kitty Ser.: 4). (ENG.). 64p. (J). pap. 7.99 *(978-1-4215-7362-5(8))* Viz Media.

Monlongo, Jorge & Correll, Gemma. On the Loose!, Vol. 1. Turner, James. 2011. (Mameshiba Ser.: 1). (ENG.). 80p. (J). pap. 6.99 *(978-1-4215-3880-8(6))* Viz Media.

Monn, Margaret A. Cause I Live Here. Monn, Margaret A. 2011. 32p. pap. 24.95 *(978-1-4560-7311-4(7))* PublishAmerica, Inc.

Monnette, Kayla, jt. illus. see Monnette, Kimberly.

Monnette, Kimberly & Monnette, Kayla. I Wish, I Wish. Monnette, Kimberly. l.t. ed. 2011. (ENG.). 32p. pap. 9.99 *(978-1-4565-8498-6(7))* CreateSpace Independent Publishing Platform.

Monreal, Violeta. Manuela. Osorio, Marta. 6th ed. (SPA.). 32p. (J). (gr. 1-3). *(978-84-236-2674-8(1))* Edebé ESP. Dist: Lectorum Pubns., Inc.

—Manuela y el Mar. Osorio, Marta. 5th ed. (SPA.). (J). (gr. 1-3). pap. *(978-84-236-3390-6(X))* Edebé ESP. Dist: Lectorum Pubns., Inc.

Monroe, Chris. Big Little Brother. Kling, Kevin. 2011. (ENG.). 48p. (J). (gr. -1-2). 17.95 *(978-0-87351-844-4(6))*, Borealis Bk.) Minnesota Historical Society Pr.

—Big Little Mother. Kling, Kevin. 2013. (ENG.). 32p. (J). (gr. -1-3). 17.95 *(978-0-87351-911-3(6))*, Borealis Bk.) Minnesota Historical Society Pr.

—Cookie, the Walker. 2013. (ENG.). 32p. (J). (gr. -1-2). lib. bdg. 16.95 *(978-0-7613-5617-2(7))*, Carolrhoda Bks.) Lerner Publishing Group.

—Trash Mountain. Yolen, Jane. 2015. (J). *(978-1-4677-7170-2(8))*; (ENG.). 184p. (gr. 3-6). 16.99 *(978-1-4677-1234-7(5))* Lerner Publishing Group. (Carolrhoda Bks.).

Monroe, Chris. Bug on a Bike. Monroe, Chris. 2014. 32p. (J). (gr. -1-2). 16.95 *(978-1-4677-2154-7(9)*, Carolrhoda Bks.) Lerner Publishing Group.

—Monkey with a Tool Belt. Monroe, Chris. 2008. (Carolrhoda Picture Bks.). (ENG.). 32p. (J). (gr. -1-2). lib. bdg. 16.95 *(978-0-8225-7631-0(7)*, Carolrhoda Bks.) Lerner Publishing Group.

—Monkey with a Tool Belt & the Noisy Problem. Monroe, Chris. 2009. (Carolrhoda Picture Bks). (ENG.). 32p. (J). (gr. -1-2). 16.95 *(978-0-8225-9247-1(9)*, Carolrhoda Bks.) Lerner Publishing Group.

—Monkey with a Tool Belt & the Seaside Shenanigans. Monroe, Chris. 2011. (Carolrhoda Picture Books Ser.). (ENG.). 32p. (J). (gr. -1-2). lib. bdg. 16.95 *(978-0-7613-5616-5(9)*, Carolrhoda Bks.) Lerner Publishing Group.

—Sneaky Sheep. Monroe, Chris. 2010. (Carolrhoda Picture Bks.). (ENG.). 32p. (J). (gr. -1-3). lib. bdg. 16.95 *(978-0-7613-5615-8(0))* Lerner Publishing Group.

Monroe, Dan. Dad, I Wish I Was Your Age. Burwick, Josh. 2012. 40p. (J). pap. 14.99 *(978-0-9852146-3-0(5))* AuthorMike Ink.

Monroe, Daniel. What Do You Do, If You Lose Your Lalabaloo? Eleniak, Erika. 2013. 22p. pap. 9.99 *(978-0-9884468-7-8(1))* AuthorMike Ink.

Monroe Donovan, Jane. Winter's Gift. Monroe Donovan, Jane. 2004. (Holiday Ser.). (ENG.). 32p. (J). 16.95 *(978-1-58536-231-8(X))* Sleeping Bear Pr.

Monroe Donovan, Jane & Donovan, Jane Monroe. My Teacher Likes to Say. Brennan-Nelson, Denise. rev. ed. 2004. (ENG.). 32p. (J). (gr. k-6). 15.95 *(978-1-58536-212-7(3))* Sleeping Bear Pr.

Monroe Donovan, Jane, jt. illus. see Monroe, Michael Glenn.

Monroe, Joan Kiddell. The Great Barrier Reef. Patchett, Mary Elwyn. 2011. 210p. 44.95 *(978-1-258-08492-9(9))* Literary Licensing, LLC.

Monroe, Michael Glenn. Buzzy the Bumblebee. Brennan-Nelson, Denise. 2003. (ENG.). 32p. (J). (gr. k-6). pap. 6.95 *(978-1-58536-166-3(6))* Sleeping Bear Pr.

—Grady the Goose. Brennan-Nelson, Denise & Brennan-Nelson, Dense. rev. ed. 2006. (ENG.). 32p. (J). (gr. k-6). 16.95 *(978-1-58536-282-0(4))* Sleeping Bear Pr.

—I Saw It in the Garden. Brennan, Martin. 2006. 32p. (J). (gr. -1-3). 17.95 *(978-1-58726-296-8(7)*, Mitten Pr.) Ann Arbor Editions LLC.

—A Is for Ark: Noah's Journey. Monroe, Colleen. 2004. 38p. (gr. -1-1). pap. 17.95 *(978-0-9754942-0-2(1))* Storytime Pr., Inc.

—Little Florida. Crane, Carol. 2010. (My Little State Ser.). (ENG.). 22p. (J). 9.95 *(978-1-58536-487-9(8))* Sleeping Bear Pr.

—Little Illinois. Hershenhorn, Esther. 2011. (My Little State Ser.). (ENG.). 22p. (J). 9.95 *(978-1-58536-537-1(8))* Sleeping Bear Pr.

—Little Michigan. Brennan-Nelson, Denise. 2010. (My Little State Ser.). (ENG.). 22p. (J). 9.95 *(978-1-58536-479-4(7))* Sleeping Bear Pr.

—Little Ohio. Schonberg, Marcia. 2011. (My Little State Ser.). (ENG.). 20p. (J). 9.95 *(978-1-58536-527-2(0))* Sleeping Bear Pr.

—Little Texas. Crane, Carol. 2010. (My Little State Ser.). (ENG.). 22p. (J). 9.95 *(978-1-58536-488-6(6))* Sleeping Bear Pr.

—The Michigan Counting Book. Wargin, Kathy-jo. 2004. (Count Your Way Across the U. S. A. Ser.). (ENG.). 40p. (J). pap. 6.95 *(978-1-58536-245-5(X))* Sleeping Bear Pr.

—Penny: The Forgotten Coin. Brennan-Nelson, Denise. 2003. (ENG.). 32p. (J). (gr. k-6). 15.95 *(978-1-58536-128-1(3))* Sleeping Bear Pr.

—A Wish to Be a Christmas Tree. Monroe, Colleen. 2005. (Holiday Ser.). (ENG.). 20p. (J). (gr. -1-1). 8.99 *(978-1-58536-269-1(7)*, 202284) Sleeping Bear Pr.

—The Wonders of Nature Sketchbook: Learn about Nature & How to Draw It. Monroe, Colleen. 2006. 40p. (J). (gr. 4-7). lib. bdg. 15.00 *(978-0-9754942-1-9(X))* Storytime Pr., Inc.

Monroe, Michael Glenn & Monroe Donovan, Jane. Discover Florida, 2 bks. Crane, Carol. 2003. (ENG.). 40p. (J). 27.95 *(978-1-58536-226-4(3))* Sleeping Bear Pr.

Monroe, Michael Glenn & Tsairis, Jeannie Brett. Little South Carolina. Crane, Carol. 2011. (My Little State Ser.). (ENG.). 22p. (J). 9.95 *(978-1-58536-486-2(X))* Sleeping Bear Pr.

Monroy, Manuel. La Gitana de las Flores. Lujan, Jorge Elias. 2003. (SPA.). 32p. (J). (gr. k-3). pap. 8.95 *(978-968-19-0748-8(5))* Santillana USA Publishing Co., Inc.

—Una Mascota Inesperada. Chacek, Karen. rev. ed. 2007. (Castillo de la Lectura Blanca Ser.). (ENG.). 48p. (J). pap. 6.95 *(978-970-20-0850-7(6))* Castillo, Ediciones, S. A. de C. V. MEX. Dist: Macmillan.

—Rooster Gallo. Luján, Jorge. Amado, Elisa, tr. 2004. (ENG & SPA.). 24p. (J). 14.95 *(978-0-88899-558-2(X))* Groundwood Bks. CAN. Dist: Perseus-PGW.

—What Are You Doing?, 1 vol. Amado, Elisa. 2011. (ENG.). 32p. (J). (gr. -1-2). 16.95 *(978-1-55498-070-3(4))* Groundwood Bks. CAN. Dist: Perseus-PGW.

—When I Was a Boy Neruda Called Me Policarpo: A Memoir, 1 vol. Delano, Poli. Higgins, Sean, tr. from SPA. 2006. (ENG.). 96p. (J). (gr. 3-7). 15.95 *(978-0-88899-726-5(4))* Groundwood Bks. CAN. Dist: Perseus-PGW.

—Why Are You Doing That?, 1 vol. Amado, Elisa. 2014. (ENG.). 28p. (J). (gr. -1-2). 16.95 *(978-1-55498-453-4(X))* Groundwood Bks. CAN. Dist: Perseus-PGW.

Monson, Lois, photos by. God Is for Every Day(r) - Horse Dreams: Teach-a-Child Companion Book/DVD Set. Monson, Lois. 2008. 28p. (J). ring bd. 14.95 *(978-0-9727786-8-8(3))* JoySoul Corp.

Montagna, Frank. From Head to Toe: The Girls' Life Guide to Taking Care of You. Harrison, Emma. 2004. 124p. (J). *(978-0-439-44983-0(9))* Scholastic, Inc.

Montague, Christine. The Little Monkey & the Crocodile. Sithole, Thelma. 2007. 32p. per. 12.00 *(978-1-59858-204-8(6))* Dog Ear Publishing, LLC.

Montague, Ruth. The Gypsy Cholers Alphabet. Monroe, Judith W. 2006. (J). 7.00 *(978-0-9768370-2-2(1))* Seastory Pr.

Montaini-Klovdahl, Luisa. Why Do I Have To? A Book for Children Who Find Themselves Frustrated by Everyday Rules. Leventhal-Belfer, Laurie. 2008. (ENG.). 80p. pap. *(978-1-84310-891-7(7))* Kingsley, Jessica Ltd.

Montalto, Luisa. Big Dog Decisions, 1 vol. Jakubowski, Michele. 2014. (Sidney & Sydney Ser.). (ENG.). 128p. (gr. 1-3). 23.99 *(978-1-4795-5226-9(7))* Picture Window Bks.

—Dodgeball, Drama, & Other Dilemmas. Jakubowski, Michele. 2013. (Sidney & Sydney Ser.). (ENG.). 128p. (gr. 1-3). 8.95 *(978-1-4795-2116-6(7))*; lib. bdg. 23.99 *(978-1-4048-8061-0(5))* Picture Window Bks.

—Third Grade Mix-Up. Jakubowski, Michele. (Sidney & Sydney Ser.). (ENG.). 128p. (gr. 1-3). 2015. pap. 7.15 ***(978-1-4795-6754-6(X))***; 2013. 8.95 *(978-1-4048-8104-4(2))*; 2013. lib. bdg. 23.99 *(978-1-4048-8001-6(1))* Picture Window Bks.

Montalvo-Lagos, Tomas. Bakugan Battle Brawlers: The Battle Begins! Ballantine Books Staff & Cartoon Network Staff. 2008. (ENG.). 96p. (gr. 5). pap. 7.99 *(978-0-345-51368-7(1)*, Del Rey) Random House Publishing Group.

Montalvo, Rodolfo. The Contagious Colors of Mumpley Middle School. DeWitt, Fowler. 2013. (ENG.). 272p. (J). (gr. 2-5). 16.99 *(978-1-4424-7829-9(2)*, Atheneum Bks. for Young Readers) Simon & Schuster Children's Publishing.

Montañà, Marta. El Lobo y Los Siete Cabritos. Baller, Darice & Dominguez, Madelca. 2007. (SPA & ENG.). 28p. (J). *(978-0-545-02962-9(7))* Scholastic, Inc.

Montana, Scarlett. Lunch with a Blue Kitty. Montana, Scarlett. 2007. 41p. (J). pap. *(978-0-9796814-0-0(5))* Blue Kitty, The.

Montanari, Donata. Children Around the World. Montanari, Donata. 2004. (ENG.). 32p. (J). (gr. -1-2). pap. 7.95 *(978-1-55337-684-2(6))* Kids Can Pr., Ltd. CAN. Dist: Univ. of Toronto Pr.

Montanari, Eva. The Fabulous Flying Machines of Alberto Santos-Dumont. Griffith, Victoria. 2011. (ENG.). 32p. (J). (gr. k-4). 17.95 *(978-1-4197-0011-8(1)*, Abrams Bks. for Young Readers) Abrams.

—Princess Matilda. 2007. 24p. (J). (gr. -1-1). *(978-1-84539-276-5(0))* Meadowside Children's Bks.

—Show; Don't Tell! Secrets of Writing. Nobisso, Josephine. 2004. (ENG.). 40p. (J). (gr. 2-6). 28.95 *(978-0-940112-13-1(2))* Gingerbread Hse.

Montecalvo, Janet. A Day without Sugar / un día sin Azúcar. De Anda, Diane. Baeza Ventura, Gabriela, tr. 2012. (SPA & ENG.). (J). 17.95 *(978-1-55885-702-5(8)*, Piñata Books) Arte Publico Pr.

—Sofie & the City. Grant, Karima. 2006. (ENG.). 32p. (J). (gr. 1-3). 15.95 *(978-1-59078-273-6(9))* Boyds Mills Pr.

Montero Galan, Daniel. It's a Pain to Be a Princess! Gil, Carmen & Gil Martinez, Carmen. 2012. (ENG.). 28p. (J). (gr. k-2). 14.95 *(978-84-15241-78-2(X))* Cuento de Luz SL ESP. Dist: Perseus-PGW.

Montero, Jose Perez. The Best of Charles Dickens' Classics. Dickens, Charles & De Graaf, Anne. 2003. 240p. *(978-87-7247-184-6(0))* Scandinavia Publishing Hse.

—Gruff Ar Antur Yn y Beibl. Mortensen, Carl Anker. Davies, Aled, tr. from ENG. 2005. (WEL.). 66p. *(978-1-85994-503-2(1))* Cyhoeddiadau'r Gair.

—The Little Children's Bible Storybook. De Graaf, Anne. 2003. 448p. *(978-87-7247-132-7(6))* Scandinavia Publishing Hse.

—Seek & Find in the Bible. 2003. 64p. incl. cd-rom *(978-87-7247-305-5(3))* Scandinavia Publishing Hse.

Montero, Miguel. Mi Libro de Palabras, Oraciones y Cuentos. Ronnholm, Ursula O. Deliz, Osdila O., ed. (SPA.). 100p. (J). (gr. k-6). pap. 7.00 *(978-0-941911-02-3(0))* Two Way Bilingual, Inc.

Montes de Oca, Gonzalo. Cuba for Kids: Illustrated History Book/Libro de Historia Ilustrado. Roque-Velasco, Ismael. (SPA & ENG.). (J). (gr. 3-5). 16.00 net. *(978-0-9706319-0-9(1))* Roque-Velasco, Dr. Ismael.

Montes, Keoni. Kimo's Summer Vacation. Germain, Kerry. 2003. 52p. (J). 12.95 *(978-0-9705889-4-4(1))* Island Paradise Publishing.

Montez, Michele & Bodger, Lorraine. The New 50 Simple Things Kids Can Do to Save the Earth. Javna, John et al. 2009. (ENG.). 208p. pap. 14.99 *(978-0-7407-7746-2(7))* Andrews McMeel Publishing.

Montgomerie, Genevieve. Bullying, Change, Friendship & Trust. Vagner, Bohdanka. 2013. 106p. pap. *(978-1-921883-51-4(0)*, MBS Pr.) Pick-a-Woo Woo Pubs.

Montgomery Gibson, Jane. Claire, Claire! Wash Your Hair! Montgomery Gibson, Jane. 2005. (J). bds. 8.99 *(978-1-4183-0044-9(6))* Christ Inspired, Inc.

—Daddy's Valentine. Montgomery Gibson, Jane. 2005. (J). bds. 8.99 *(978-1-4183-0046-3(2))* Christ Inspired, Inc.

—Go Find Christmas. Montgomery Gibson, Jane. 2005. (YA). bds. 8.99 *(978-1-4183-0025-8(X))* Christ Inspired, Inc.

—God's Little Boy. Montgomery Gibson, Jane. 2005. (YA). bds. 8.99 *(978-1-4183-0034-0(9))* Christ Inspired, Inc.

—God's Little Girl. Montgomery Gibson, Jane. 2005. (YA). bds. 8.99 *(978-1-4183-0045-6(4))* Christ Inspired, Inc.

—Gracie Got Glasses. Montgomery Gibson, Jane. 2005. (J). bds. 8.99 *(978-1-4183-0039-5(X))* Christ Inspired, Inc.

—Hey, You Birds! Montgomery Gibson, Jane. 2004. (J). bds. 8.99 *(978-1-4183-0022-7(5))* Christ Inspired, Inc.

—How Do You Clean a Ballerina? Montgomery Gibson, Jane. 2005. (J). bds. 8.99 *(978-1-4183-0020-3(9))* Christ Inspired, Inc.

—I Touched Jesus Today. Montgomery Gibson, Jane. 2005. (YA). bds. 8.99 *(978-1-4183-0027-2(6))* Christ Inspired, Inc.

—I'll Tell You in Heaven. Montgomery Gibson, Jane. 2005. (YA). bds. 8.99 *(978-1-4183-0043-2(8))* Christ Inspired, Inc.

—The Inner Soul. Montgomery Gibson, Jane. 2005. (YA). bds. 8.99 *(978-1-4183-0049-4(7))* Christ Inspired, Inc.

—Jake the Fake Snake. Montgomery Gibson, Jane. 2005. (J). bds. 8.99 *(978-1-4183-0026-5(8))* Christ Inspired, Inc.

—Jesus Is! Montgomery Gibson, Jane. 2005. (J). bds. 8.99 *(978-1-4183-0033-3(0))* Christ Inspired, Inc.

—Jesus Loves Me. Montgomery Gibson, Jane. 2005. (J). bds. 8.99 *(978-1-4183-0048-7(9))* Christ Inspired, Inc.

—Jesus Smith or Jones. Montgomery Gibson, Jane. 2005. (YA). bds. 8.99 *(978-1-4183-0031-9(4))* Christ Inspired, Inc.

—The Keeper of Lost & Found. Montgomery Gibson, Jane. 2005. (YA). bds. 8.99 *(978-1-4183-0052-4(7))* Christ Inspired, Inc.

—A Little Bit Gone. Montgomery Gibson, Jane. 2005. (YA). bds. 8.99 *(978-1-4183-0037-1(3))* Christ Inspired, Inc.

—Mabel at the Table. Montgomery Gibson, Jane. 2005. (J). bds. 8.99 *(978-1-4183-0041-8(1))* Christ Inspired, Inc.

—Maggie Makeup. Montgomery Gibson, Jane. 2005. (J). bds. 9.99 *(978-1-4183-0030-2(6))* Christ Inspired, Inc.

—Maker of Prayer. Montgomery Gibson, Jane. 2005. (YA). bds. 8.99 *(978-1-4183-0047-0(0))* Christ Inspired, Inc.

—Mama's Wings. Montgomery Gibson, Jane. 2005. (YA). bds. 8.99 *(978-1-4183-0050-0(0))* Christ Inspired, Inc.

—Measure My Heart. Montgomery Gibson, Jane. 2005. (YA). bds. 8.99 *(978-1-4183-0023-4(3))* Christ Inspired, Inc.

—My Christmas Friend. Montgomery Gibson, Jane. 2005. (YA). bds. 8.99 *(978-1-4183-0066-1(7))* Christ Inspired, Inc.

—Oh Forsooth! I've Lost a Tooth! Montgomery Gibson, Jane. 2005. (J). bds. 8.99 *(978-1-4183-0021-0(7))* Christ Inspired, Inc.

—Pink Potatoes. Montgomery Gibson, Jane. 2005. (J). bds. 8.99 *(978-1-4183-0038-8(1))* Christ Inspired, Inc.

—Shiny Pants. Montgomery Gibson, Jane. 2005. (YA). bds. 8.99 *(978-1-4183-0032-6(2))* Christ Inspired, Inc.

—Sit down, Clown! Montgomery Gibson, Jane. 2005. (J). bds. 8.99 *(978-1-4183-0040-1(3))* Christ Inspired, Inc.

—Through Jesus Eyes. Montgomery Gibson, Jane. 2005. (J). bds. 8.99 *(978-1-4183-0024-1(1))* Christ Inspired, Inc.

Montgomery-Higham, Amanda. Monkey's Clever Tale. Montgomery-Higham, Amanda, tr. Peters, Andrew. 2003. (Traditional Tales with a Twist Ser.). (ENG.). 32p. (J). (gr. -1-2). *(978-0-85953-051-4(5))* Child's Play International Ltd.

Montgomery, Jason. Elvie Saves Christmas. Wilkes, Irene. 2010. 48p. (J). pap. 21.95 *(978-1-59299-537-0(3))* Inkwater Pr.

Montgomery, Lee. Ant. Hawcock, David. 2013. (Bouncing Bugs Ser.). (ENG.). 10p. (gr. -1). 10.99 *(978-1-60887-187-2(8))* Insight Editions LP.

—Bee. Hawcock, David. 2013. (Bouncing Bugs Ser.). (ENG.). 10p. (gr. -1). 10.99 *(978-1-60887-188-9(6))* Insight Editions LP.

Montgomery, Lee & Jackson, Ian. The Usborne World of Animals. Davidson, Susanna & Unwin, Mike. 2005. 128p. (J). pap. *(978-0-439-86321-6(X))* Scholastic, Inc.

Montgomery, Lee & Pastor, Terry. Fantastic Press-Out Flying Airplanes: Includes 18 Flying Models. Hawcock, David. 2015. (ENG.). 76p. (J). (gr. 2-5). 14.99 ***(978-0-486-80127-8(6))*** Dover Pubns., Inc.

Montgomery, Lee, jt. illus. see Gaudenzi, Giacinto.

Montgomery, Lewis B. The Case of the Poisoned Pig. Montgomery, Lewis B. 2009. (Milo & Jazz Mysteries Ser.). 96p. (J). (gr. 2-5). 22.60 *(978-1-57565-289-4(7))* Kane Pr., Inc.

Montgomery, Margaret. The Adventures of Anna Banana Shoeshine: Anna Banana Takes a Bath. 2006. 40p. (J). *(978-1-930401-49-5(3))* Central Coast Pr.

Montgomery, Michael. The Amazing Mr. Franklin: Or the Boy Who Read Everything, 1 vol. Ashby, Ruth. 2004. (ENG.). 144p. (J). (gr. 2-5). 12.95 *(978-1-56145-306-1(4))* Peachtree Pubs.

—Night Rabbits, 1 vol. Posey, Lee. 2007. (ENG.). 32p. (J). (gr. k-3). 7.95 *(978-1-56145-397-9(8))* Peachtree Pubs.

Montgomery, Michael G. Darling, Mercy Dog of World War I, 1 vol. Hart, Alison. 2013. (Dog Chronicles Ser.). (ENG.). 160p. (J). (gr. 2-5). 12.95 *(978-1-56145-705-2(1))* Peachtree Pubs.

—First Dog Fala, 1 vol. Van Steenwyk, Elizabeth. 2008. (ENG.). 32p. (J). (gr. k-3). 16.95 *(978-1-56145-411-2(7))* Peachtree Pubs.

—Santa's Eleven Months Off, 1 vol. Reiss, Mike. 2007. (ENG.). 32p. (J). (gr. k-3). 16.95 *(978-1-56145-421-1(4))* Peachtree Pubs.

Montgomery, R. A. & Thongmoon, Kriangsak. Journey under the Sea. Montgomery, R. A. 2006. (Choose Your Own Adventure Ser.: No. 2). 144p. (J). (gr. 4-7). per. 6.99 *(978-1-933390-02-4(6)*, CHCL02) Chooseco LLC.

Montgomery, Samantha. The Snoozies. Lujan Ed.D., Nan. 2012. 20p. pap. 24.95 *(978-1-4626-8831-9(4))* America Star Bks.

Montgomery, Violet. 3 Big Steps. Murphy, Eileen. 2008. 25p. pap. 24.95 *(978-1-60563-310-7(0))* America Star Bks.

Monti, Carmelo. Terry Trackhoe Goes Missing. Miller, M. 2011. (ENG.). 64p. pap. 7.99 *(978-1-4565-8091-9(4))* CreateSpace Independent Publishing Platform.

Montijo, Rhode. Attack of the Valley Girls. Trine, Greg. 6th ed. 2008. (Melvin Beederman, Superhero Ser.: 6). (ENG.). 144p. (J). (gr. 2-5). pap. 7.99 *(978-0-8050-8161-9(5))* Square Fish.

—The Brotherhood of the Traveling Underpants. Trine, Greg. 7th ed. 2009. (Melvin Beederman, Superhero Ser.: 7). (ENG.). 144p. (J). (gr. 2-5). pap. 8.99 *(978-0-8050-8163-3(1))* Square Fish.

—The Curse of the Bologna Sandwich. Trine, Greg. 2006. (Melvin Beederman, Superhero Ser.: 1). (ENG.). 144p. (J). (gr. 2-5). pap. 8.99 *(978-0-8050-7836-7(3))* Square Fish.

—The Fake Cape Caper. Trine, Greg. 5th rev. ed. 2007. (Melvin Beederman, Superhero Ser.: 5). (ENG.). 144p. (J). (gr. 2-5). pap. 8.99 *(978-0-8050-8159-6(3))* Square Fish.

—The Grateful Fred. Trine, Greg. 3rd rev. ed. 2006. (Melvin Beederman, Superhero Ser.: 3). (ENG.). 160p. (J). (gr. 2-5). pap. 8.99 *(978-0-8050-7922-7(X))* Square Fish.

—Invasion from Planet Dork. Trine, Greg. 2010. (Melvin Beederman, Superhero Ser.: 8). (ENG.). 144p. (J). (gr. 2-7). pap. 7.99 *(978-0-8050-8167-1(4))* Square Fish.

—The Revenge of the McNasty Brothers. Trine, Greg. 2nd rev. ed. 2006. (Melvin Beederman, Superhero Ser.: 2). (ENG.). 144p. (J). (gr. 2-5). pap. 7.99 *(978-0-8050-7837-4(1))* Square Fish.

—Super Grammar. Preciado, Tony. 2012. (ENG.). 176p. (J). (gr. 2-5). pap. 8.99 *(978-0-545-42515-5(8)*, Scholastic Reference) Scholastic, Inc.

—Terror in Tights. Trine, Greg. 4th rev. ed. 2007. (Melvin Beederman, Superhero Ser.: 4). (ENG.). 144p. (J). (gr. 2-5). pap. 8.99 *(978-0-8050-7924-1(6))* Square Fish.

Montijo, Rhode. Cloud Boy. Montijo, Rhode. 2011. (ENG.). 30p. (J). (gr. -1-1). pap. 13.99 *(978-1-4424-5227-5(7)*, Simon & Schuster Bks. For Young Readers) Simon & Schuster Bks. For Young Readers.

—The Halloween Kid. Montijo, Rhode. 2010. (ENG.). 32p. (J). (gr. -1-3). 14.99 *(978-1-4169-3575-9(4)*, Simon & Schuster Bks. For Young Readers) Simon & Schuster Bks. For Young Readers.

Montileaux, Donald F. The Enchanted Buffalo. Baum, L. Frank. 2010. 31p. (J). (gr. 2-5). 14.95 *(978-0-9822749-3-4(9)*, South Dakota State Historical Society Pr.) South Dakota State Historical Society Pr.

Montmeat, Jack. The Memory Tree. Neff, Fred. 2008. 36p. pap. 14.99 *(978-1-59858-854-5(0))* Dog Ear Publishing, LLC.

Montoya, Jeremy. Grandpa Lolo & Trampa: A Story of Surprise & Mystery = Abuelito Lolo y Trampa: Un Cuento de Sorpresa y Misterio. García, Nasario. 2014. (SPA & ENG.). (J). 9.99 *(978-1-936744-30-5(9))* LPD Pr.

—The Talking Lizard: New Mexico's Magic & Mystery. García, Nasario. 2014. (SPA & ENG.). (J). pap. *(978-1-936744-36-7(8)*, Rio Grande Bks.) LPD Pr.

Montoya, Jerry, jt. illus. see Randles, Slim.

Montoya, Robin Michelle. Tsa Ch'ayah/How the Turtle Got Its Squares: A Traditional Caddo Indian Children's Story. Weller, Sadie Bedoka. Chafe, Wallace, tr. 2005. (CAD & ENG.). 40p. (J). (gr. 3-7). per. 16.99 *(978-1-4134-8836-4(6))* Xlibris Corp.

Montpellier, Paul. Jason's New Dugout Canoe. Barber-Starkey, Joe. unabr. ed. (ENG.). 32p. (J). *(978-1-55017-229-4(8))* Harbour Publishing Co., Ltd.

Montross, Doug. The Blackbird's Nest: Saint Kevin of Ireland. Schroedel, Jenny. 2004. 32p. (J). 18.00 *(978-0-88141-258-1(9))* St. Vladimir's Seminary Pr.

Montserrat, Pep. Aladdin & the Magic Lamp (Aladino y la Lampara Maravillosa) Chronicle Books Staff. 2006. (Bilingual Fairy Tales Ser.: BILI). (ENG & SPA.). 32p. (J). (gr. -1-3). 14.95 *(978-0-8118-5061-2(7))* Chronicle Bks. LLC.

—Aladdin & the Magic Lamp/(Aladino y la Lampara Maravillosa) 2006. (Bilingual Fairy Tales Ser.: BILI). (ENG & SPA.). 32p. (J). (gr. -1-3). pap. 6.95 *(978-0-8118-5062-9(5))* Chronicle Bks. LLC.

—The Mcelderry Book of Greek Myths. Kimmel, Eric A. 2008. (ENG.). 112p. (J). (gr. 1-5). 21.99 *(978-1-4169-1534-8(6)*, McElderry, Margaret K. Bks.) McElderry, Margaret K. Bks.

—The Musicians of Bremen/Los Musicos de Bremen. Ros, Roser. 2005. (Bilingual Fairy Tales Ser.: BILI). (ENG & SPA.). 32p. (J). (gr. -1-3). 6.99 *(978-0-8118-4796-4(9))* Chronicle Bks. LLC.

Montserrat, Pep. Kafka y la Muneca Viajera. Sierra i Fabra, Jordi. 2006. (Tres Edades Ser.). (SPA.). 147p. (J). 28.95 *(978-84-7844-985-9(X))* Siruela, Ediciones S.A. ESP. Dist: Lectorum Pubns., Inc.

Moody, Jason. Wendell Has a Cracked Shell. Powers, Emily. 2008. 32p. (gr. -1-18). pap. 14.95 *(978-0-9801357-6-3(1))* Tree of Life Publishing Hse.

Moody, Julie. Fruit of the Spirit - Love. Sama, Kent. 2005. (J). bds. 9.99 *(978-1-4183-0060-9(8))* Christ Inspired, Inc.

—Great White Judgment. Hansen, Eric. 2005. (YA). bds. 9.99 *(978-1-4183-0059-3(4))* Christ Inspired, Inc.

—Shelby's 'Doption Story. Henson, Andora. 2004. (J). bds. 9.99 *(978-1-4183-0013-5(6))* Christ Inspired, Inc.

Moon, Jo. Buggy Buddies. ed. 2014. (Wipe-Clean Buggy Buddies Ser.). (ENG.). 10p. (J). (-k). 9.99 *(978-1-4472-6778-2(8))* Pan Macmillan GBR. Dist: Independent Pubs. Group.

—Counting. ed. 2014. (Wipe-Clean Buggy Buddies Ser.). (ENG.). 10p. (J). (— 1). 9.99 *(978-1-4472-6779-9(6))* Pan Macmillan GBR. Dist: Independent Pubs. Group.

—In the Pond. ed. 2014. (ENG.). 8p. (J). (— 1). 10.99 *(978-0-230-76660-0(9))* Pan Macmillan GBR. Dist: Independent Pubs. Group.

—Making Letters. 2006. (Making... Ser.). 14p. (J). (gr. -1-3). bds. 7.95 *(978-1-57791-248-4(9))* Brighter Minds Children's Publishing.

—Making Numbers. 2006. (Making... Ser.). 14p. (J). (gr. -1-3). bds. 7.95 *(978-1-57791-249-1(7))* Brighter Minds Children's Publishing.

—Making Shapes. Butler, Roberta. 2006. (Making... Ser.). 14p. (J). (gr. -1-3). bds. 7.95 *(978-1-57791-250-7(0))* Brighter Minds Children's Publishing.

—Noises. ed. 2014. (Wipe-Clean Buggy Buddies Ser.). (ENG.). 10p. (J). (— 1). 7.99 *(978-1-4472-6780-5(X))* Pan Macmillan GBR. Dist: Independent Pubs. Group.

—Under the Sea. ed. 2014. (ENG.). 8p. (J). (— 1). 10.99 *(978-0-230-76659-4(5))* Pan Macmillan GBR. Dist: Independent Pubs. Group.

—Whose Nose? Munro, Fiona & Phillipson, Fiona. 2011. (ENG.). 10p. (J). (gr. -1-k). bds. 6.99 *(978-0-8431-9811-9(7)*, Price Stern Sloan) Penguin Publishing Group.

Moon, Jung Who. Yongbi, the Invincible 1, Vol. 1. Ryu, Ki Woon. 2004. 200p. pap. 9.99 *(978-1-58664-967-8(1)*, CPM Manhwa) Central Park Media Corp.

Moon, Paul, jt. illus. see Boddy, James.

Moon, Poppy. How to be a Bully... NOT! Nass, Marcia. 2011. 56p. (J). pap. 16.95 *(978-1-59850-101-8(1))* Youthlight, Inc.

—Kicky's Friendship Card Game. 2011. (J). 17.95 (978-1-59850-097-4(X)) Youthlight, Inc.

Moonbot & Joyce, William. The Mischievians. Moonbot & Joyce, William. 2013. (ENG.). 56p. (J). (gr. k-3). 17.99 *(978-1-4424-7347-8(9),* Atheneum Bks. for Young Readers) Simon & Schuster Children's Publishing.

Mooney, Alyssa. Pet Parade. Velasquez, Maria. 2007. (J). pap. 21.00 *(978-0-15-379895-5(5))* Houghton Mifflin Harcourt School Pubs.

Mooney, Jim, et al. Essential Web of Spider-Man, Vol. 1. David, Peter. 2011. (ENG.). 528p. (J). (gr. 4-17). pap. 19.99 *(978-0-7851-5756-4(5))* Marvel Worldwide, Inc.

Mooney, Jim, jt. illus. see Buscema, John.

Moor, Becka, jt. illus. see Parker, Paul.

Moore, Clement C. & Gorsline, Douglas. The Night Before Christmas. Moore, Clement C., ed. 32p. (J). Random Hse. Children's Bks.

Moore, Clement C. & Porfirio, Guy. The Night Before Christmas. Moore, Clement C., ed. 2004. 20p. (J). 9.95 *(978-0-8249-6553-2(1))* Ideals Pubns.

Moore, Clement C. & Price, Margaret Evans. The Night Before Christmas. Moore, Clement C., ed. 2004. (Shape Bks.). (ENG.). 16p. (J). (gr. -1-3). pap. 9.95 *(978-1-59583-009-8(X),* 9781595830098, Green Tiger Pr.) Laughing Elephant.

Moore, Clement C. & Winget, Susan. The Night Before Christmas. Moore, Clement C., ed. 2004. 32p. 18.00 *(978-0-7412-1939-8(5))* Lang Graphics, Ltd.

Moore, Cyd. Arbor Day Square, 1 vol. Galbraith, Kathryn Osebold. 2010. (ENG.). 32p. (J). (gr. -1-3). 16.95 *(978-1-56145-517-1(2))* Peachtree Pubs.

—Diary of a Canadian Kid. Sleeping Bear Press. 2012. (Country Journal Ser.). (ENG.). 128p. (J). (gr. 4-8). pap. 11.95 *(978-1-58536-812-9(1),* 202346) Sleeping Bear Pr.

—Happy Halloween, Stinky Face. McCourt, Lisa. 2011. (ENG.). 32p. (J). (gr. k — 1). bds. 6.99 *(978-0-545-28542-1(9),* Cartwheel Bks.) Scholastic, Inc.

—He's Been a Monster All Day. Brennan-Nelson, Denise. 2013. (ENG.). 32p. (J). (gr. -1-1). 14.99 *(978-1-58536-827-3(X),* 202363) Sleeping Bear Pr.

—I Love You, Bunny Rabbit. Oppenheim, Shulamith. 2004. (ENG.). 32p. (J). (gr. -1-k). pap. 7.95 *(978-1-59078-337-5(9))* Boyds Mills Pr.

—I Love You, Stinky Face. McCourt, Lisa. (ENG.). (J). 2009. (gr. -1-3). 18.95 *(978-0-545-11944-3(8));* 2009. (gr. -1-3). 9.99 *(978-0-545-11757-9(7));* 2004. 16p. (gr. 3-7). bds. 6.99 *(978-0-439-63572-1(1));* 2003. 32p. (gr. -1-3). pap. 6.99 *(978-0-439-63469-4(5))* Scholastic, Inc.

—I Miss You, Stinky Face. McCourt, Lisa. 2009. (ENG.). (J). (gr. -1-3). 9.95 *(978-0-545-13849-9(3))* Scholastic, Inc.

—I Miss You, Stinky Face Board Book. McCourt, Lisa. 2014. (ENG.). 32p. (J). (gr. -1 — 1). bds. 6.99 *(978-0-545-74848-3(8),* Cartwheel Bks.) Scholastic, Inc.

—If You're Happy & You Know It. Raffi. 2007. (ENG.). 32p. (J). (gr. k — 1). bds. 6.99 *(978-0-375-82919-2(9),* Knopf Bks. for Young Readers) Random Hse. Children's Bks.

—Merry Christmas, Stinky Face. McCourt, Lisa. 2008. (ENG.). 32p. (J). (gr. k — 1). bds. 6.99 *(978-0-439-73123-2(2),* Cartwheel Bks.) Scholastic, Inc.

—Practical Plays: Grades 1-5. Marx, Pamela. 2nd rev. ed. 2007. 170p. (J). (gr. 1-6). per. 17.95 *(978-1-59647-196-2(4))* Good Year Bks.

—What Do Parents Do? (When You're Not Home), 1 vol. Ransom, Jeanie Franz. 2007. (ENG.). 32p. (J). (gr. k-3). 16.95 *(978-1-56145-409-9(5))* Peachtree Pubs.

—When It Snows. Nelson, Joanne. 2012. (Discovery Phonics Ser.). (ENG.). 16p. (J). (gr. -1-3). pap. 10.47 *(978-0-8136-1087-0(7))* Modern Curriculum Pr.

—Where Is the Night Train Going? Bedtime Poems. Spinelli, Eileen. 2005. (ENG.). 32p. (J). (gr. 2-3). pap. 9.95 *(978-1-59078-331-3(X))* Boyds Mills Pr.

—Willow. Brennan-Nelson, Denise & Brennan, Rosemarie. 2008. (ENG.). 32p. (J). (gr. k-6). 16.95 *(978-1-58536-342-1(1))* Sleeping Bear Pr.

—Willow & the Snow Day Dance. Brennan-Nelson, Denise. 2010. (ENG.). 32p. (J). (gr. k-6). lib. bdg. 16.95 *(978-1-58536-522-7(X))* Sleeping Bear Pr.

Moore, D., jt. illus. see De Angel, Miguel.

Moore, Danny. Hello Aubie! Aryal, Aimee. 2004. 22p. (J). 19.95 *(978-0-9743442-8-7(1))* Mascot Bks., Inc.

—Hello Big Al! Aryal, Aimee. 2004. 24p. (J). lib. bdg. 19.95 *(978-1-932888-03-4(9))* Mascot Bks., Inc.

—Hello Bully! Aryal, Aimee. 2004. 24p. (J). 19.95 *(978-0-9743442-6-3(5))* Mascot Bks., Inc.

—Hello Buzz! Aryal, Aimee. 2004. 24p. (J). 19.95 *(978-1-932888-27-0(6))* Mascot Bks., Inc.

—Hello, Mr. Met. Staub, Rusty. 2006. 24p. (J). lib. bdg. 17.95 *(978-1-932888-82-9(9))* Mascot Bks., Inc.

—Hello, Wally! Boston Red Sox. Remy, Jerry. 2006. 24p. (J). lib. bdg. 17.95 *(978-1-932888-80-5(2))* Mascot Bks., Inc.

—Let's Go, Yankees! Berra, Yogi. 2006. 24p. (J). 17.95 *(978-1-932888-81-2(0))* Mascot Bks., Inc.

—Wally the Green Monster & His Journey Through Red Sox Nation. Remy, Jerry. 2007. 24p. (J). 14.95 *(978-1-932888-89-8(6))* Mascot Bks., Inc.

Moore, Darryl. I Want It Now: Helping Children Deal with Frustration & Disappointment. Loftis, Chris & Lowenthal, Gary T. 2003. (Let's Talk Ser.). (ENG.). 48p. (J). pap. 12.95 *(978-0-88282-237-2(3),* Small Horizons) New Horizon Pr. Pubs., Inc.

Moore, David, Jr., jt. illus. see McGeehan, Dan.

Moore, Debra. Fluffy's Story Part 1 Fluffy's Journey. Joyce, Samantha & Joyce, Caroline. 2005. 48p. (J). 16.95 *(978-0-9770898-0-2(0))* Paw Print Publishing.

Moore, Dwain. The Adventures of Murphy the Mouse. Jones, Brenda. 2007. (J). per. 12.99 *(978-1-59712-069-2(3))* Catawba Publishing Co.

Moore, Eileen, photos by. Arizona Trails for Children: 135 Trails Across Arizona for Children & Adults. Moore, Eileen. 2005. 360p. (YA). (gr. 4-18). pap. 14.99 *(978-0-9672576-0-0(3))* Morten Moore Publishing.

Moore, Elyse. Miss Milli's Adventure: Garden Adventure Series. Cayce, Jw & Guy, K. T. 2011. 26p. pap. 13.95 *(978-1-4575-0002-2(7))* Dog Ear Publishing, LLC.

Moore, Emma V. The Littlest Giant: The Story of Vamana. Greene, Joshua M. 2014. (ENG.). 32p. (gr. -1). 16.99 *(978-1-60887-303-6(X))* Mandala Publishing.

Moore, Frances. Harriet Tubman: Hero of the Underground Railroad, 1 vol. Mortensen, Lori. 2007. (Biographies Ser.). (ENG.). 24p. (gr. k-3). lib. bdg. 25.99 *(978-1-4048-3103-2(7),* Nonfiction Picture Bks.) Picture Window Bks.

—India ABCs: A Book about the People & Places of India, 1 vol. Aboff, Marcie. 2006. (Country ABCs Ser.). (ENG.). 32p. (gr. k-5). 27.32 *(978-1-4048-1571-1(6),* Nonfiction Picture Bks.) Picture Window Bks.

Moore, Gareth. The Kids' Book of Mazes. Moore, Gareth. 2014. (ENG.). 192p. (J). (gr. 1-3). pap. 6.99 *(978-1-78055-248-4(3))* O'Mara, Michael Bks., Ltd. GBR. Dist: Independent Pubs. Group.

Moore, Gustav. Body Cycles. Ross, Michael Elsohn. 2003. (Cycles Ser.). 32p. (J). (gr. k-3). lib. bdg. 11.84 *(978-0-613-99000-4(5),* Turtleback) Turtleback Bks.

—Everybody's Somebody's Lunch, 1 vol. Mason, Cherie. 2005. (ENG.). 40p. (J). (gr. 3-6). 7.95 *(978-0-88448-200-0(6))* Tilbury Hse. Pubs.

—Re-Cycles. Ross, Michael Elsohn. 2003. (Cycles Ser.). (ENG.). 32p. (gr. 2-4). pap. 7.95 *(978-0-7613-1949-8(2),* First Avenue Editions) Lerner Publishing Group.

—Stone Wall Secrets. Thorson, Robert & Thorson, Kristine. 2010. 40p. (J). (gr. 3-7). 16.95 *(978-0-88448-195-9(6))* Tilbury Hse. Pubs.

Moore, Gustav. Stone Wall Secrets, 1 vol. Moore, Gustav. Thorson, Kristine & Thorson, Robert. 2014. (ENG.). 40p. (J). (gr. 2-7). 8.95 *(978-0-88448-229-1(4))* Tilbury Hse. Pubs.

Moore, Harry. Behold, No Cavities! A Visit to the Dentist. Willson, Sarah. 2007. (SpongeBob SquarePants Ser.: 15). (ENG.). 24p. (J). (gr. -1-3). pap. 3.99 *(978-1-4169-3566-7(5),* Simon Spotlight/Nickelodeon) Simon Spotlight/Nickelodeon.

—Bug Parade! (Bubble Guppies) Random House & Pohlmeyer, Krista. 2014. (Super Deluxe Pictureback Ser.). (ENG.). 24p. (J). (gr. -1-2). 5.99 *(978-0-385-38517-6(X),* Random Hse. Bks. for Young Readers) Random Hse. Children's Bks.

—The Case of the Vanished Squirrel. Lewman, David. 2008. (SpongeBob SquarePants Ser.). (ENG.). 16p. (J). (gr. -1-3). pap. 5.99 *(978-1-4169-4939-8(9),* Simon Spotlight/Nickelodeon) Simon Spotlight/Nickelodeon.

Moore, Harry, Jr. Double Trouble: The Case of the Missing Spatula - The Case of the Vanished Squirrel. Lewman, David. 2010. (SpongeBob SquarePants Ser.). (ENG.). 36p. (J). bds. 10.99 *(978-1-4424-1337-5(9),* Simon Spotlight/Nickelodeon) Simon Spotlight/Nickelodeon.

Moore, Harry. Just Say Please! Willson, Sarah. 2007. (SpongeBob SquarePants Ser.). (ENG.). 32p. (J). (gr. k-2). pap. 3.99 *(978-1-4169-4129-3(0),* Simon Spotlight/Nickelodeon) Simon Spotlight/Nickelodeon.

—Pick a Dad, Any Dad! Banks, Steven. ed. 2005. (Fairly Odd Parents Ser.: 7). 24p. (J). lib. bdg. 15.00 *(978-1-59054-804-2(3))* Fitzgerald Bks.

—Pup, Pup, & Away! (Paw Patrol) Random House. 2015. (Super Deluxe Pictureback Ser.). (ENG.). 24p. (J). (gr. -1-2). 5.99 *(978-0-553-50794-2(X),* Random Hse. Bks. for Young Readers) Random Hse. Children's Bks.

—SpongeBob's Slap Shot. Lewman, David. 2008. (SpongeBob SquarePants Ser.). (ENG.). 24p. (J). (gr. -1-3). pap. 3.99 *(978-1-4169-6153-6(4),* Simon Spotlight/Nickelodeon) Simon Spotlight/Nickelodeon.

Moore, Harry, jt. illus. see Random House Staff.

Moore, Inga. Horse Tales. 2005. (ENG.). 152p. (J). (gr. 4-7). 18.99 *(978-0-7636-2657-0(0))* Candlewick Pr.

—The Secret Garden. Burnett, Frances Hodgson. 2008. (ENG.). 272p. (J). (gr. 1-4). 22.99 *(978-0-7636-3161-1(2))* Candlewick Pr.

—The Secret Garden. Burnett, Frances Hodgson. 2010. (ENG.). 272p. (J). (gr. 1-4). pap. 14.99 *(978-0-7636-4732-2(2))* Candlewick Pr.

—The Wind in the Willows. Grahame, Kenneth. 184p. 2009. pap. 12.99 *(978-0-7606-4211-5(7));* 2003. (ENG.). (J). 21.99 *(978-0-7636-2242-8(7))* Candlewick Pr.

—The Wind in the Willows. Grahame, Kenneth. 2009. (Candlewick Illustrated Classic Ser.). (ENG.). 184p. (J). (gr. 5-12). pap. 14.99 *(978-0-7636-4211-2(8))* Candlewick Pr.

Moore, Inga. Captain Cat. Moore, Inga. 2013. (ENG.). 48p. (J). (gr. -1-2). 15.99 *(978-0-7636-6151-9(1))* Candlewick Pr.

—Six Dinner Sid. Moore, Inga. 2010. (ENG.). 32p. (J). (gr. -1-k). pap. 10.99 *(978-0-340-98895-4(9))* Hodder & Stoughton GBR. Dist: Independent Pubs. Group.

Moore, Jo. Sticker Dolly Dressing Parties. Watt, Fiona. ed. 2013. (Sticker Dolly Dressing Ser.). 34p. (J). pap. 8.99 *(978-0-7945-3370-0(1),* Usborne) EDC Publishing.

Moore, Jo, jt. illus. see Watton, Ross.

Moore, Jonathan & Harrison, Nancy. Who Was Alfred Hitchcock? Pollack, Pamela D. & Belviso, Meg. 2014. (Who Was... ? Ser.). (ENG.). 112p. (J). (gr. 3-7). pap. 4.99 *(978-0-448-48237-8(1),* Grosset & Dunlap) Penguin Publishing Group.

Moore, Jonathan & Harrison, Nancy. Who Was J. R. R. Tolkien? Pollack, Pamela D. & Belviso, Meg. 2015. (Who Was... ? Ser.). (ENG.). 112p. (J). (gr. 3-7). 5.99 ***(978-0-448-48302-3(5),*** Grosset & Dunlap) Penguin Publishing Group.

Moore, Kimberly. Arithmetic Village Presents King David Divide. Moore, Kimberly. 2nd ed. 2012. 24p. pap. *(978-0-9845731-9-6(4))* Roxby Media Ltd.

—Arithmetic Village Presents Linus Minus. Moore, Kimberly. 2nd ed. 2012. 24p. pap. *(978-0-9845731-7-2(8))* Roxby Media Ltd.

—Arithmetic Village Presents Tina Times. Moore, Kimberly. 2nd ed. 2012. 24p. pap. *(978-0-9845731-8-9(6))* Roxby Media Ltd.

Moore, Kimberly Ann. Arithmetic Village Presents Polly Plus. Moore, Kimberly Ann. 2nd ed. 2012. 24p. pap. *(978-0-9845731-6-5(X))* Roxby Media Ltd.

Moore, Kristen L. Is God Behind the Big Blue Sky? Moore, Katherine Roberts. 2010. 34p. pap. 13.95 *(978-1-60911-705-4(0),* Eloquent Bks.) Strategic Book Publishing & Rights Agency (SBPRA).

Moore, Lishia. Project Book: Ideas, Tips & Techniques for School Projects. Moore, Lishia, photos by. Wagner, Amy, photos by. Warner, Penny. Wagner, Amy, ed. 2007. 80p. pap. 9.98 *(978-1-887436-05-2(7))* Woodland Scenics.

Moore, Margie. Bartholomew's Blessing. Tolan, Stephanie S. 2004. 32p. (J). (gr. -1-3). lib. bdg. 16.89 *(978-0-06-001198-7(X))* HarperCollins Pubs.

—Bear of My Heart. Ryder, Joanne. 2009. (ENG.). 32p. (J). (gr. -1 — 1). bds. 8.99 *(978-1-4169-5472-9(4),* Little Simon) Little Simon.

—Blue-Ribbon Dad. Raisner Glass, Beth. 2011. (ENG.). 32p. (J). (gr. -1-2). 15.95 *(978-0-8109-9727-1(4),* Abrams Bks. for Young Readers) Abrams.

—A Horse's Tale: A Colonial Williamsburg Adventure. Lubner, Susan. 2008. (ENG.). 32p. (J). (gr. -1-1). 17.95 *(978-0-8109-9490-4(9),* Abrams Bks. for Young Readers) Abrams.

—It's Your First Day of School, Annie Claire. Carlstrom, Nancy White. 2009. (ENG.). 32p. (J). (gr. -1-2). 16.95 *(978-0-8109-4057-4(4),* Abrams Bks. for Young Readers) Abrams.

—Looking for Easter. Chaconas, Dori. 2012. (J). 34.28 *(978-1-61913-120-0(X))* Weigl Pubs., Inc.

—Looking for Easter, 1 vol. Chaconas, Dori. 2011. (ENG.). 32p. (J). (gr. -1-2). 6.99 *(978-0-8075-4750-2(6))* Whitman, Albert & Co.

—Mice Are Nice. Williams, Rozanne Lanczak. 2005. (Reading for Fluency Ser.). 16p. (J). pap. 3.49 *(978-1-59198-156-5(5),* 4256) Creative Teaching Pr., Inc.

—Ruby Bakes a Cake. Hill, Susan. 2004. (My First I Can Read Bks.). 32p. (J). (gr. k-3). lib. bdg. 16.89 *(978-0-06-008976-4(8))* HarperCollins Pubs.

—Ruby Bakes a Cake, 1 vol. Hill, Susan. 2010. (I Can Read! / Ruby Raccoon Ser.). (ENG.). 32p. (J). pap. 3.99 *(978-0-310-72022-5(2))* Zonderkidz.

—Ruby Paints a Picture, 1 vol. Hill, Susan. 2010. (I Can Read! / Ruby Raccoon Ser.). (ENG.). 32p. (J). pap. 3.99 *(978-0-310-72023-2(0))* Zonderkidz.

—Ruby's Perfect Day. Hill, Susan. 2006. (I Can Read Bks.). 32p. (J). (gr. -1-3). 15.99 *(978-0-06-008982-5(2))* HarperCollins Pubs.

—Ruby's Perfect Day, 1 vol. Hill, Susan. 2010. (I Can Read! / Ruby Raccoon Ser.). (ENG.). 32p. (J). pap. 3.99 *(978-0-310-72024-9(9))* Zonderkidz.

Moore, Michael. Ben Hurry: A Lesson in Patience, 1 vol. Peterson, Doug. 2006. (Big Idea Books / VeggieTown Values Ser.: Bk. 8). (ENG.). 32p. (J). (gr. -1-3). pap. 3.99 *(978-0-310-70743-1(9))* Zonderkidz.

—Cool Hand Cuke Vol. 5: A Lesson in Giving, 1 vol. Kenney, Cindy. 2006. (Big Idea Books / VeggieTown Values Ser.: Bk. 5). (ENG.). 32p. (J). (gr. -1-3). pap. 3.99 *(978-0-310-70738-7(2))* Zonderkidz.

—The Snooze Brothers: A Lesson in Responsibility, 1 vol. Kenney, Cindy & Peterson, Doug. 2006. (Big Idea Books / VeggieTown Values Ser.: Bk. 6). (ENG.). 32p. (J). (gr. -1-3). pap. 3.99 *(978-0-310-70739-4(0))* Zonderkidz.

—Veggietown Voyage, 1 vol. Kenney, Cindy et al. 2013. (Big Idea Bks.). (ENG.). 96p. (J). 7.99 *(978-0-310-72352-3(3))* Zonderkidz.

Moore, Michael & Big Idea Design Staff. How in the World?, 1 vol. Kenney, Cindy. 2005. (Big Idea Bks.). (ENG.). 24p. (J). (gr. -1-3). pap. 5.99 *(978-0-310-70937-4(7))* Zonderkidz.

Moore, Nicolette. Kimo's Surfing Lesson. Germain, Kerry. 2007. 48p. (gr. k-5). (J). 12.95 *(978-0-9705889-5-1(X));* pap. 12.95 *(978-0-9705889-3-7(3))* Island Paradise Publishing.

Moore, P. M. The Smallest Forest. Lewis, Regina N. 2013. 60p. pap. 12.95 *(978-1-935083-12-2(0))* CyPress Pubns.

—The Smallest Schoolhouse. Lewis, Regina N. 2007. 56p. (J). pap. 12.95 *(978-0-9776958-3-6(2))* CyPress Pubns.

Moore, Paul, photos by. Wine Lover Cooks with Wine: Great Recipes for the Essential Ingredient. Goldstein, Sidney. 2004. (ENG.). 224p. (gr. 8-17). pap. 24.95 *(978-0-8118-3022-5(5))* Chronicle Bks. LLC.

Moore, Phyllis M. The Smallest Toy Store, A Christmas Story. Lewis, Regina N. 2004. 44p. (J). per. 12.95 *(978-0-9672585-8-4(8))* CyPress Pubns.

Moore, Russell. Phonics Readers - Big Books: Grade 1, Bk. 10. Najimy, Norman. (Phonics Beginning Readers Ser.). (J). (gr. 1-18). 38.01 *(978-0-02-686023-9(6))* SRA/McGraw-Hill.

Moore, Sarah. The Amazing Adventures of Fizzlegrits Books 1 2 3 the Fizzlegrits Trilogy. Moore, David. 2011. (ENG.). 60p. pap. 13.50 *(978-1-4662-5873-0(X))* CreateSpace Independent Publishing Platform.

Moore, Sasha & Tilak, Brian. My Shaking Eyes. Elliott, Sherria L. 2013. 30p. pap. 12.99 *(978-0-9846963-2-1(6))* 4Elliott Publishing, Inc.

Moore, Saxton. Care Bears Lullaby: A Night Light Book. Flasterstein, Ran. 2007. 8p. (J). bds. 12.95 incl. audio compact disk *(978-1-57791-303-0(5),* Little Melody Pr.) Brighter Minds Children's Publishing.

Moore, Saxton & McGee, Warner. Plant a Garden. Sander, Sonia. 2008. (Care Bears Ser.). (ENG.). 24p. (J). (gr. -1-3). pap. 3.99 *(978-0-545-00908-9(1),* Scholastic) Scholastic, Inc.

Moore, Scott. The Battle of Antietam: The Bloodiest Day of Battle. Hama, Larry. 2007. (Graphic Battles of the Civil War Ser.). (ENG.). 48p. (YA). (gr. 4-7). lib. bdg. 31.95 *(978-1-4042-0775-2(9))* Rosen Publishing Group, Inc., The.

—The Battle of First Bull Run: The Civil War Begins. Hama, Larry. 2007. (Graphic Battles of the Civil War Ser.). (ENG.). 48p. (YA). (gr. 4-7). lib. bdg. 31.95 *(978-1-4042-0776-9(7))* Rosen Publishing Group, Inc., The.

—The Battle of Shiloh: Surprise Attack! Hama, Larry. 2007. (Graphic Battles of the Civil War Ser.). (ENG.). 48p. (YA). (gr. 4-7). lib. bdg. 31.95 *(978-1-4042-0779-0(1))* Rosen Publishing Group, Inc., The.

Moore, Sean L. What's up, Bear? A Book about Opposites. Wishinsky, Frieda. 2012. (ENG.). 32p. (J). (gr. -1-k). 16.95 *(978-1-926973-41-8(0),* Owlkids) Owlkids Bks. Inc. CAN. Dist: Perseus-PGW.

Moore, Sean L. & Owlkids Books Inc. Staff. Where Are You, Bear? A Canadian Alphabet Adventure. Wishinsky, Frieda. 2010. (ENG.). 32p. (J). (gr. -1-k). 17.95 *(978-1-897349-91-5(2))* Owlkids Bks. Inc. CAN. Dist: Perseus-PGW.

Moore, Trudy E. Kelly Kapers: Adventures of Kelly & Her Family. Moore, Trudy E. Kinderman, Robert W. 2011. 42p. pap. 23.00 *(978-1-4349-1035-6(0))* Dorrance Publishing Co., Inc.

Moore, Truman, photos by. Complete Charleston: A Guide to the Architecture, History & Gardens of Charleston & the Low Country. Moore, Margaret. 3rd ed. 2005. 304p. (YA). per. 19.95 *(978-0-9660144-2-6(1))* TM Photography, Inc.

Moore, Yvette. Heartland: A Prairie Sampler. Bannatyne-Cugnet, Jo. 2005. (ENG.). 40p. (J). (gr. k-12). pap. 9.95 *(978-0-88776-722-7(2),* Tundra Bks.) Tundra Bks. CAN. Dist: Penguin Random Hse., LLC.

—A Prairie Alphabet. Bannatyne-Cugnet, Jo. 2009. (ABC Our Country Ser.). (ENG.). 32p. (J). (gr. 1-4). pap. 7.95 *(978-0-88776-937-5(3))* Tundra Bks. CAN. Dist: Random Hse., Inc.

Moores, Ian & Thompson, Ian. Light & Sight. Richards, Jon. 2008. (Science Factory Ser.). 32p. (YA). (gr. 4-7). lib. bdg. 26.50 *(978-1-4042-3904-3(9))* Rosen Publishing Group, Inc., The.

Moores, Jeff. Good Luck Charlie. Kramer, Jennifer E. 2005. (Rookie Reader Skill Set Ser.). (ENG.). 32p. (J). (gr. k-2). pap. 4.95 *(978-0-516-25826-3(5),* Children's Pr.) Scholastic Library Publishing.

Moores, Susanna. It's Not Yours, It's Mine! Moores, Susanna. 2013. (Child's Play Library). (ENG.). 32p. (J). (gr. -1-2). *(978-1-84643-600-0(1))* Child's Play International Ltd.

Moose, David. A Soup Opera. Gill, Jim. 2009. (ENG.). 32p. (J). lib. bdg. *(978-0-9815721-0-9(3))* Gill, Jim Music.

Mora, Andy. Space Tourism. McMahon, Peter. 2011. (Machines of the Future Ser.). (ENG.). 40p. (J). 16.95 *(978-1-55453-368-8(6))* Kids Can Pr., Ltd. CAN. Dist: Univ. of Toronto Pr.

—Ultimate Trains. McMahon, Peter. 2010. (Machines of the Future Ser.). (ENG.). 40p. (J). (gr. 4-7). 16.95 *(978-1-55453-366-4(X))* Kids Can Pr., Ltd. CAN. Dist: Univ. of Toronto Pr.

Mora, Elsa. The Water & the Wild. Ormsbee, K. E. 2015. (ENG.). 448p. (J). (gr. 3-7). 16.99 *(978-1-4521-1386-9(6))* Chronicle Bks. LLC.

Mora, Francisco X. Delicious Hullabaloo (Pachanga Deliciosa) Mora, Pat. 2010. (J). (gr. -1-2). pap. 18.75 incl. audio compact disk *(978-1-4301-0837-5(1))* Live Oak Media.

Mora, Giovanni. Case of Pen Gone Missing/El Caso de la Pluma Perdida. Saldana, Rene. Villarroel, Carolina, tr. from ENG. 2009. (SPA & ENG.). 80p. (J). (gr. 3-7). pap. 9.95 *(978-1-55885-555-7(6),* Piñata Books) Arte Publico Pr.

—Rattling Chains & Other Stories for Children/Ruido de Cadenas y Otros Cuentos para Ninos. Garcia, Nasario. 2009. (SPA & ENG.). 160p. (J). (gr. 3-7). pap. 9.95 *(978-1-55885-544-1(0),* Piñata Books) Arte Publico Pr.

Mora, Julissa. Besties, Sleepovers, & Drama Queens: Questions & Answers about Friends. Loewen, Nancy & Skelley, Paula. 2015. (Girl Talk Ser.). (ENG.). 32p. (gr. 3-4). lib. bdg. 27.32 *(978-1-4914-1859-8(1))* Capstone Pr., Inc.

Mora, Julissa. Girl Talk. Loewen, Nancy & Skelley, Paula. 2015. (Girl Talk Ser.). (ENG.). 32p. (gr. 3-4). lib. bdg. 109.28 ***(978-1-4914-1862-8(1),*** Snap Bks.) Capstone Pr., Inc.

—Girl Talk: Questions & Answers about Daily Dramas, Disasters, & Delights. Loewen, Nancy. 2015. (ENG.). 112p. (gr. 3-4). pap. 12.95 ***(978-1-62370-218-2(6))*** Capstone Young Readers.

—Lunch Lines, Tryouts, & Making the Grade: Questions & Answers about School. Loewen, Nancy & Skelley, Paula. 2015. (Girl Talk Ser.). (ENG.). 32p. (gr. 3-4). lib. bdg. 27.32 ***(978-1-4914-1861-1(3),*** Snap Bks.) Capstone Pr., Inc.

Mora, Julissa. Siblings, Curfews, & How to Deal: Questions & Answers about Family Life. Loewen, Nancy & Skelley, Paula. 2015. (Girl Talk Ser.). (ENG.). 32p. (gr. 3-4). lib. bdg. 27.32 *(978-1-4914-1858-1(3))* Capstone Pr., Inc.

Mora, Julissa. Tangles, Growth Spurts, & Being You: Questions & Answers about Growing Up. Loewen, Nancy & Skelley, Paula. 2015. (Girl Talk Ser.). (ENG.). 32p. (gr. 3-4). lib. bdg. 27.32 ***(978-1-4914-1860-4(5),*** Snap Bks.) Capstone Pr., Inc.

Mora, Mauricio. Abra Cadabra, Patas de Cabra: A Spanish, English Story for Young Readers. Drew, Alejandrina. Satcher, David & Ford, Richard, trs. 41p. (J). pap. 15.95 *(978-1-57168-505-6(7))* Eakin Pr.

Mora, Pat & López, Rafael. Yum! Mmmm! Que Rico! America's Sproutings. Mora, Pat & López, Rafael. 2008. (SPA & ENG.). (J). (gr. k-6). 7.95 *(978-1-60060-267-2(3))* Lee & Low Bks., Inc.

Morais, Flavio. Voices in First Person: Reflections on Latino Identity. Rivera-Ortiz, Manuel, photos by. Carlson, Lori M., ed. 2008. (ENG.). 96p. (YA). (gr. 7-18). 17.99 *(978-1-4169-0635-3(5),* Atheneum Bks. for Young Readers) Simon & Schuster Children's Publishing.

Moraja, Melissa Perry. Jake's Adventures - the Secret of the Shark Tooth Crab Claw. Moraja, Melissa Perry. 2012. 118p. pap. *(978-0-9834751-8-7(0))* Roxby Media Ltd.

—Madison & G. A. - a Tale of the Slimy Spitball. Moraja, Melissa Perry. 2012. 94p. pap. *(978-0-9834751-7-0(2))* Roxby Media Ltd.

Morales, Andrew. Brady O'Brian Saves the Day. Mutrie, Matthew. 2007. 37p. pap. 24.95 *(978-1-4241-9009-6(6))* America Star Bks.

Morales, Carlos. Those Amazing Dogs: at the Pirate Bay: Book Four of the Those Amazing Dogs Series. Fenne, Edwin & Poehlmann, Jeffrey. 2011. (ENG.). 56p. pap. 5.99 *(978-1-4636-0164-5(6))* CreateSpace Independent Publishing Platform.

—Those Amazing Dogs: on the Coral Island: Book Five of the Those Amazing Dogs Series. Fenne, Edwin & Poehlmann, Jeffrey. 2011. (ENG.). 62p. pap. 5.99 *(978-1-4636-0193-5(X))* CreateSpace Independent Publishing Platform.
—Those Amazing Dogs Book Three: at the Arctic Circle: Book Three of the Those Amazing Dogs Series. Fenne, Edwin & Poehlmann, Jeffrey. 2011. (ENG.). 54p. pap. 5.99 *(978-1-4636-0142-3(5))* CreateSpace Independent Publishing Platform.
—Those Amazing Dogs Book Two: in the Viking Volcano: Book Two of the Those Amazing Dogs Series. Fenne, Edwin & Poehlmann, Jeffrey. 2011. (ENG.). 58p. pap. 5.99 *(978-1-4636-0133-1(6))* CreateSpace Independent Publishing Platform.
—Those Amazing Dogs: Trail of the Viking. Poehlmann, Jeffrey & Fenne, Edwin. 2011. (ENG.). 260p. pap. 10.49 *(978-1-4564-8705-8(1))* CreateSpace Independent Publishing Platform.
—Those Amazing Dogs:African River Adventure. Fenne, Edwin & Poehlmann, Jeffrey. 2011. (ENG.). 54p. pap. 5.99 *(978-1-4636-0130-0(1))* CreateSpace Independent Publishing Platform.
Morales, Fifi. Welcome to the USA. Bello, Ecrahim, photos by. Nohemi, Esther. Morris, Edwin, ed. l.t. ed. 2003. (YA). pap. *(978-1-931481-87-8(3))* LiArt-Literature & Art.
Morales, Jose. I-Can't & I-Can! Willow, Bim. 2012. 28p. pap. 8.99 *(978-0-9853574-3-6(6))* Mountan Creek Pubns.
Morales, Judith. Gracias a Johannes. Helguera, Luis Ignacio. 2003. (SPA.). *(978-968-494-086-4(6),* CI5287) Centro de Informacion y Desarrollo de la Comunicacion y la Literatura MEX. Dist: Lectorum Pubns., Inc.
Morales, Magaly. Chavela's Magic Chicle. Brown, Monica. 2008. (ENG & SPA.). (J). 15.95 *(978-0-87358-918-5(1),* Luna Rising) Northland Publishing.
—A Piñata in a Pine Tree: A Latino Twelve Days of Christmas. Mora, Pat. 2009. (ENG.). 32p. (J). (gr. -1-3). 16.00 *(978-0-618-84198-1(9))* Houghton Mifflin Harcourt Publishing Co.
—What Can You Do with a Paleta? Tafolla, Carmen. 2014. (ENG.). 32p. (J). (gr. -1-2). 7.99 *(978-0-385-75537-5(6),* Dragonfly Bks.) Random Hse. Children's Bks.
—What Can You Do with a Paleta? Tafolla, Carmen. 2009. (ENG.). 32p. (J). (gr. -1-2). 14.99 *(978-1-58246-221-9(6),* Tricycle Pr.) Ten Speed Pr.
—What Can You Do with a Paleta? (¿Que Puede Hacer con una Paleta?) Tafolla, Carmen. 2009. (SPA & ENG.). 32p. (J). (gr. -1-2). 14.99 *(978-1-58246-289-9(5),* Tricycle Pr.) Ten Speed Pr.
Morales, Yuyi. Cosechando Esperanza: La Historia de César Chávez. Krull, Kathleen. Campoy, F. Isabel & Flor Ada, Alma, trs. 2004. (SPA.). 48p. (J). (gr. -1-3). pap. 7.00 *(978-0-15-205169-3(4))* Houghton Mifflin Harcourt Publishing Co.
—Floating on Mama's Song: Flotando con la Canción de Mamá. Lacámara, Laura. 2010. (SPA & ENG.). 32p. (J). (gr. -1-2). 16.99 *(978-0-06-084368-7(3),* Tegen, Katherine Bks) HarperCollins Pubs.
—Los Gatos Black on Halloween. Montes, Marisa. rev. ed. 2006. (ENG.). 32p. (J). (gr. -1-3). 17.95 *(978-0-8050-7429-1(5),* Holt, Henry & Co. Bks. For Young Readers) Holt, Henry & Co.
—Harvesting Hope: The Story of Cesar Chavez. Krull, Kathleen. 2003. (ENG.). 48p. (J). (gr. -1-3). 17.00 *(978-0-15-201437-7(3))* Houghton Mifflin Harcourt Publishing Co.
—Ladder to the Moon. Soetoro-Ng, Maya. 2011. (ENG.). 48p. (J). (gr. -1-3). 16.99 *(978-0-7636-4570-0(2))* Candlewick Pr.
—Ladder to the Moon with CD. Soetoro-Ng, Maya. 2012. (ENG.). 48p. (J). (gr. -1-3). 19.99 *(978-0-7636-6006-2(X))* Candlewick Pr.
—My Abuelita. Johnston, Tony. 2009. (ENG.). 32p. (J). (gr. -1-3). 16.99 *(978-0-15-216330-3(1))* Houghton Mifflin Harcourt Publishing Co.
—Sand Sister. White, Amanda. 2004. 32p. (J). 16.99 *(978-1-84148-617-8(5))* Barefoot Bks., Inc.
Morales, Yuyi. Georgia in Hawaii: When Georgia O'Keeffe Painted What She Pleased. Morales, Yuyi. Novesky, Amy. 2012. (ENG.). 40p. (J). (gr. 1-4). 16.99 *(978-0-15-205420-5(0))* Houghton Mifflin Harcourt Publishing Co.
—Just in Case: A Trickster Tale & Spanish Alphabet Book. Morales, Yuyi. 2008. (ENG.). 40p. (J). (gr. -1-3). 18.99 *(978-1-59643-329-8(9))* Roaring Brook Pr.
—Niño: Wrestles the World. Morales, Yuyi. 2013. (ENG.). 36p. (J). (gr. -1-3). 16.99 *(978-1-59643-604-6(2))* Roaring Brook Pr.
Moran, Edna. Miracle Puzzlers. Schlegel, William. 2009. 64p. pap. 10.99 *(978-0-7586-1605-0(8))* Concordia Publishing Hse.
Moran, Edna Cabcabin. Can You Catch a Coqui Frog? Arita, Vera. 2009. (J). *(978-1-933067-27-8(6))* Beachhouse Publishing, LLC.
Moran, Edna Cabcabin. The Sleeping Giant: A Tale from Kauai. Moran, Edna Cabcabin, retold by. 2006. (J). *(978-1-933067-20-9(9))* Beachhouse Publishing, LLC.
Moran, Lyn. I Want That! Claus, Rimana. 2012. 36p. pap. 15.97 *(978-1-61897-838-7(1),* Strategic Bk. Publishing) Strategic Book Publishing & Rights Agency (SBPRA).
Moran, Michael. Ella Earns Her Own Money. Bullard, Lisa. 2013. (Cloverleaf Books — Money Basics Ser.). (ENG.). 24p. (gr. k-2). lib. bdg. 23.93 *(978-1-4677-0761-9(9),* Millbrook Pr.) Lerner Publishing Group.
—Iggy Loomis, a Hagfish Called Shirley. Allison, Jennifer. 2014. (ENG.). 208p. (J). (gr. 2-4). 16.99 *(978-0-8037-3781-5(5),* Dial) Penguin Publishing Group.
—Superkid in Training. Allison, Jennifer. 2014. (ENG.). 208p. (J). (gr. 2-4). pap. 6.99 *(978-0-14-242573-2(7),* Puffin) Penguin Publishing Group.
Moran, Michael & Moran, Mike. Do-4U the Robot Experiences Forces & Motion. Weakland, Mark. 2012. (In the Science Lab Ser.). (ENG.). 24p. (gr. 2-3). lib. bdg. 25.99 *(978-1-4048-7145-8(4),* Nonfiction Picture Bks.) Picture Window Bks.
Moran, Mike. Do-4U the Robot Experiences Forces & Motion. Weakland, Mark. 2012. (In the Science Lab Ser.). (ENG.). 24p. (gr. 2-3). pap. 8.95 *(978-1-4048-7239-4(6),* Nonfiction Picture Bks.) Picture Window Bks.
—Ella Earns Her Own Money. Bullard, Lisa. 2013. (Cloverleaf Books — Money Basics Ser.). (ENG.). 24p. (gr. k-2). pap. 6.95 *(978-1-4677-1511-9(5),* Millbrook Pr.) Lerner Publishing Group.
—Gabriel Gets a Great Deal. Bullard, Lisa. 2013. (Cloverleaf Books — Money Basics Ser.). (ENG.). 24p. (gr. k-2). pap. 6.95 *(978-1-4677-1512-6(3));* lib. bdg. 23.93 *(978-1-4677-0766-4(X))* Lerner Publishing Group. (Millbrook Pr.).
—I'm Fearsome & Furry! Meet a Werewolf. Bullard, Lisa. 2014. (Monster Buddies Ser.). (ENG.). 24p. (gr. k-2). lib. bdg. 23.93 *(978-0-7613-9189-0(4),* Millbrook Pr.) Lerner Publishing Group.
—I'm from Outer Space! Meet an Alien. Bullard, Lisa. 2014. (Monster Buddies Ser.). 24p. (gr. k-2). pap. 6.95 *(978-1-4677-4999-2(0));* (ENG.). lib. bdg. 23.93 *(978-0-7613-9193-7(2))* Lerner Publishing Group. (Millbrook Pr.).
—Let's Meet a Construction Worker. Heos, Bridget. 2013. (Cloverleaf Books — Community Helpers Ser.). (ENG.). 24p. (gr. k-2). pap. 6.95 *(978-1-4677-0799-2(6));* lib. bdg. 23.93 *(978-0-7613-9023-7(5))* Lerner Publishing Group. (Millbrook Pr.).
—Let's Meet a Doctor. Heos, Bridget. 2013. (Cloverleaf Books — Community Helpers Ser.). (ENG.). 24p. (gr. k-2). pap. 6.95 *(978-1-4677-0801-2(1));* lib. bdg. 23.93 *(978-0-7613-9028-2(6))* Lerner Publishing Group. (Millbrook Pr.).
—Poopendous! Bennett, Artie. 2012. (ENG.). 36p. (J). (gr. -1-3). 16.99 *(978-1-60905-190-7(4))* Blue Apple Bks.
—Stealing the Show. Finn, Perdita. 2006. (Time Flyers Ser.: Vol. 1). 109p. (J). pap. *(978-0-439-74433-1(4))* Scholastic, Inc.
Moran, Mike, jt. illus. see Moran, Michael.
Moran, Paul. The Boys' Summer Book. Campbell, Guy. 2011. (ENG.). 96p. (J). (gr. 1-3). 6.99 *(978-0-8431-9852-2(4),* Price Stern Sloan) Penguin Publishing Group.
—What If... Humans Were Like Animals? Taylor, Marianne. 2012. 128p. 7.99 *(978-1-78055-042-8(1),* Buster Bks.) O'Mara, Michael Bks., Ltd. GBR. Dist: Littlehampton Bk Services, Ltd.
—World's Greatest Who What Where When Quiz Book for Kids. 2003. 112p. (J). pap. 3.99 *(978-0-603-56100-9(4))* Egmont Bks., Ltd. GBR. Dist: Trafalgar Square Publishing.
Moran, Rosslyn. The Rainbow's End & Other Tales from the Ark. Rowlands, Avril. 128p. (J). pap. 6.95 *(978-0-7459-4073-1(0),* Lion Books) Lion Hudson PLC GBR. Dist: Trafalgar Square Publishing.
Morandi, Andrea. Bears. Parker, Steve. 2010. (I Love Animals Ser.). (ENG.). 24p. (J). (gr. 1-5). pap. 8.15 *(978-1-61533-232-8(4));* lib. bdg. 22.60 *(978-1-61533-226-7(X))* Windmill Bks.
—Owls. Parker, Steve. 2010. (I Love Animals Ser.). (ENG.). 24p. (J). (gr. 1-5). lib. bdg. 22.60 *(978-1-61533-229-8(4))* Windmill Bks.
Morandi, Andrea, jt. illus. see Cantucci, Alessandro.
Morandin, Mike. Do Chicks Ask for Snacks? Noticing Animal Behaviors. Rustad, Martha E. H. 2015. (ENG.). 24p. (J). (gr. k-2). 25.32 ***(978-1-4677-8558-7(X))*** Lerner Publishing Group.
Morchiladze, Manana. The Dark. Baghdasaryan, Rouzanna. 2007. 32p. (J). (ARA & ENG.). pap. 12.95 *(978-1-60195-086-4(1));* (POL & ENG.). pap. 12.95 *(978-1-60195-096-3(9))* International Step by Step Assn.
—The Littlest One. Kruk, Halya. 2007. 32p. (J). (POL & ENG.). pap. 14.95 *(978-1-60195-102-1(7));* (ARA & ENG.). pap. 14.95 *(978-1-60195-090-1(X))* International Step by Step Assn.
Mordan, C., jt. illus. see Mordan, C. B.
Mordan, C. B. Guinea Pig Scientists. Boring, Mel & Dendy, Leslie. 2014. (ENG.). 224p. (J). (gr. 5-12). pap. 12.99 *(978-1-250-05065-6(0))* Square Fish.
—Oh Rats! Marrin, Albert. 2014. (ENG.). 112p. (J). (gr. 5). pap. 8.99 *(978-0-14-751281-9(6),* Puffin) Penguin Publishing Group.
—Silent Movie. Avi. 2003. (ENG.). 48p. (J). (gr. -1-3). 19.99 *(978-0-689-84145-3(0),* Atheneum Bks. for Young Readers) Simon & Schuster Children's Publishing.
Mordan, C. B. & Mordan, C. Guinea Pig Scientists: Bold Self-Experimenters in Science & Medicine. Boring, Mel & Dendy, Leslie. rev. ed. 2005. (ENG.). 224p. (J). (gr. 5-12). 19.99 *(978-0-8050-7316-4(7),* Holt, Henry & Co. Bks. For Young Readers) Holt, Henry & Co.
Morden, Richard. Captain Cal & the Giant Straw, 1 vol. Dallimore, Jan. 2009. (Captain Cal Ser.). (ENG.). 56p. (gr. 2-3). lib. bdg. 19.99 *(978-1-4048-5510-6(6),* Chapter Readers) Picture Window Bks.
—Captain Cal & the Great Space Race, 1 vol. Dallimore, Jan. 2009. (Captain Cal Ser.). (ENG.). 56p. (gr. 2-3). lib. bdg. 19.99 *(978-1-4048-5508-3(4),* Chapter Readers) Picture Window Bks.
—Captain Cal & the Robot Army, 1 vol. Dallimore, Jan. 2009. (Captain Cal Ser.). (ENG.). 56p. (gr. 2-3). lib. bdg. 19.99 *(978-1-4048-5507-6(6),* Chapter Readers) Picture Window Bks.
More Gordon, Domenica. Archie. More Gordon, Domenica. 2012. (ENG.). 48p. (J). (gr. -1-1). 18.89 *(978-1-59990-947-9(2),* Bloomsbury USA Childrens) Bloomsbury USA.
Moreau, Hélène. What a Party!, 1 vol. Machado, Ana Maria. Amado, Elisa, tr. from POR. 2013. (ENG.). 32p. (J). (gr. -1-2). 18.95 *(978-1-55498-168-7(9))* Groundwood Bks. CAN. Dist: Perseus-PGW.
Moreiro, Enrique S. Pedrin y la Garza. Perera, Hilda & Hilda, Perera. 2005. (SPA.). 36p. (J). (gr. 3-5). 14.99 *(978-84-241-8637-1(0))* Everest Editora ESP. Dist: Lectorum Pubns., Inc.
—El Rey de las Octavas. Romeu, Emma. 2007. (SPA.). 40p. (J). (gr. 3-5). 17.99 *(978-1-933032-26-9(X))* Lectorum Pubns., Inc.
Moreiro, Enrique S. Federico García Lorca. Moreiro, Enrique S. Lázaro, Georgina. 2009. (Cuando los Grandes Eran Pequenos Ser.). (SPA.). 32p. (J). (gr. 4-6). 14.99 *(978-1-933032-39-9(1))* Lectorum Pubns., Inc.
Morejon, Tom. Puddles. Ladd, Debbie. 2006. 32p. (J). pap. 8.95 *(978-0-9727615-4-3(3))* Deb on Air Bks.
Moreland Krass, Melanie. Psalm 1 for Kidz: I'm So Happy I Want to Shout! Trudgian, Sherri. 2013. 32p. (J). *(978-0-9779194-6-8(3))* Little Sprout Publishing Hse.
Moreland, Melanie. Psalm 148: Let all Heaven & Earth Praise the Lord! 2006. 32p. (J). *(978-0-9779194-0-6(4),* Psalms for Kidz) Little Sprout Publishing Hse.
—Psalm 23: The Lord Is my Shepherd. I am His Lamb. 2007. 32p. (J). 10.00 *(978-0-9779194-1-3(2),* Psalms for Kidz) Little Sprout Publishing Hse.
Moreno, Chris. Toy Story: The Mysterious Stranger. Jolley, Dan. 2009. (ENG.). 112p. (J). 24.99 *(978-1-60886-523-9(1))* Boom! Studios.
Moreno, Chris & Fotos, Jay. Dracula vs. King Arthur #1. Beranek, Adam & Beranek, Christian. 2005. 40p. 2.95 *(978-0-9752582-2-4(2))* Silent Devil Productions.
Moreno, Rene King. Bravo! Guy, Ginger Foglesong. 2010. (SPA & ENG.). 32p. (J). (gr. -1-k). 16.99 *(978-0-06-173180-8(3),* Greenwillow Bks.) HarperCollins Pubs.
—Dias y Dias: Days & Days. Guy, Ginger Foglesong. 2011. (SPA & ENG.). (J). 16.99 *(978-0-06-173182-2(X),* Greenwillow Bks.) HarperCollins Pubs.
—Fiesta! Guy, Ginger Foglesong. 2007. (SPA.). 32p. (J). (gr. -1-3). 6.99 *(978-0-06-088226-6(3),* Greenwillow Bks.) HarperCollins Pubs.
—Fiesta! Board Book. Guy, Ginger Foglesong & Guy, Ginger F. 2003. (SPA & ENG.). 34p. (J). (gr. -1-3). bds. 7.99 *(978-0-06-009263-4(7),* Greenwillow Bks.) HarperCollins Pubs.
—Papi's Gift. Stanton, Karen. 2007. (ENG.). 32p. (J). (gr. 2-4). 16.95 *(978-1-59078-422-8(7))* Boyds Mills Pr.
—Siesta. Guy, Ginger Foglesong & Guy, Ginger F. 2005. (ENG & SPA.). 32p. (J). (gr. -1-k). 17.99 *(978-0-06-056061-4(4),* Greenwillow Bks.) HarperCollins Pubs.
—Siesta Board Book. Guy, Ginger Foglesong & Guy, Ginger F. 2009. (SPA & ENG.). 34p. (J). (gr. -1 — 1). bds. 7.99 *(978-0-06-168884-3(3),* Greenwillow Bks.) HarperCollins Pubs.
—Uncle Monarch & the Day of the Dead. Goldman, Judy. 2008. (ENG.). 32p. (J). (gr. 2-4). 16.95 *(978-1-59078-425-9(1))* Boyds Mills Pr.
—Under the Lemon Moon. Fine, Edith Hope. 2013.Tr. of Bajo la Luna de Limon. (ENG.). 32p. (J). pap. 8.95 *(978-1-58430-051-9(5))* Lee & Low Bks., Inc.
Moreno, Sergio. Cuenta Cuenta. Anaya, Hector. 2nd rev. ed. 2005. (Castillo de la Lectura Verde Ser.). (SPA & ENG.). 184p. (J). (gr. -1-7). pap. 7.95 *(978-970-20-0135-5(8))* Castillo, Ediciones, S. A. de C. V. MEX. Dist: Macmillan.
Morenton, Alice. Collins Big Cat - Royal Rap. Amholt, Laurence. 2015. (Collins Big Cat Ser.). (ENG.). 24p. pap. 7.95 ***(978-0-00-759113-8(6))*** HarperCollins Pubs. Ltd. GBR. Dist: Independent Pubs. Group.
Moreton, Daniel. I Knew Two Who Said Moo: A Counting & Rhyming Book. Barrett, Judi. 2003. (ENG.). 32p. (J). (gr. -1-3). 7.99 *(978-0-689-85935-9(X),* Atheneum Bks. for Young Readers) Simon & Schuster Children's Publishing.
—Lost! Trimble, Patti & Moran, Alex. 2003. (Green Light Readers Level 1 Ser.). (ENG.). 24p. (J). (gr. -1-3). pap. 3.95 *(978-0-15-204864-8(2))* Houghton Mifflin Harcourt Publishing Co.
—Lost! Trimble, Patti & Moran, Alex. ed. 2003. (Green Light Readers — Level 1 Ser.). (gr. -1-3). lib. bdg. 13.50 *(978-0-613-64539-3(1),* Turtleback) Turtleback Bks.
—What Day Is It? Moran, Alex & Trimble, Patti. 2003. (Green Light Readers Level 1 Ser.). (ENG.). 24p. (J). (gr. -1-3). pap. 3.95 *(978-0-15-204846-4(4))* Houghton Mifflin Harcourt Publishing Co.
—What Day Is It? Trimble, Patti. ed. 2003. (Green Light Readers — Level 1 Ser.). (gr. -1-3). lib. bdg. 13.50 *(978-0-613-66388-5(8),* Turtleback) Turtleback Bks.
—What Day Is It? (¿Qué Día es Hoy?) Moran, Alex. Campoy, F. Isabel & Flor Ada, Alma, trs. 2008. (Green Light Readers Level 1 Ser.). (ENG & SPA.). 28p. (J). (gr. -1-3). pap. 3.95 *(978-0-15-206281-1(5))* Houghton Mifflin Harcourt Publishing Co.
Moretti, Danilo. Dawning Star: Operation Quick Launch. Hammock, Lee & Jacobson, Justin. 2005. 208p. pap. 29.95 *(978-0-9763795-0-8(3),* BDV05001) Blue Devil Games.
Morgan, Christopher. One, Two, Buckle My Shoe. Everett, Melissa. 2013. (ENG.). 20p. (J). 8.99 *(978-1-77093-523-5(1))* Flowerpot Children's Pr. Inc. CAN. Dist: Cardinal Pubs. Group.
Morgan, Dennis W. Pumpkin Head Harvey. Morgan, Dennis W. 2013. 40p. pap. 14.99 *(978-0-9892295-1-7(3))* Dreamstreet Studios, Inc. (A Div. of DSMV Industries, Inc.).
Morgan-Jones, Tom. Boing-Boing the Bionic Cat & the Space Station. Hench, Larry. 2011. (Boing-Boing the Bionic Cat Ser.: 5). (ENG.). 96p. (J). (gr. 2-4). pap. 8.99 *(978-1-904872-07-8(7),* Can of Worms Kids Pr.) Can of Worms Pr. GBR. Dist: Independent Pubs. Group.
—The Boy Who Biked the World: On the Road to Africa. Humphreys, Alastair. 2012. (Boy Who Biked the World Ser.: 1). (ENG.). 192p. (J). (gr. 4-7). pap. 8.99 *(978-1-903070-75-8(9))* Eye Bks. GBR. Dist: Independent Pubs. Group.
—The Boy Who Biked the World: Riding the Americas. Humphreys, Alastair. 2015. (Boy Who Biked the World Ser.: 2). (ENG.). 192p. (J). (gr. 4-7). pap. 9.99 *(978-1-903070-87-1(2))* Eye Bks. GBR. Dist: Independent Pubs. Group.
—Mission: Explore Camping. Geography Collective Staff. 2011. (Mission Explore Ser.). (ENG.). 96p. (J). (gr. 4-7). pap. 7.99 *(978-1-904872-41-2(7),* Can of Worms Kids Pr.) Can of Worms Pr. GBR. Dist: Independent Pubs. Group.
—Mission: Explore on the Road. Geography Collective Staff. 2011. (Mission Explore Ser.). (ENG.). 96p. (J). (gr. 4-7). pap. 7.99 *(978-1-904872-38-2(7),* Can of Worms Kids Pr.) Can of Worms Pr. GBR. Dist: Independent Pubs. Group.
—Mission Explore Food. Geography Collective Staff. 2012. (Mission Explore Ser.). (ENG.). 272p. (J). (gr. 4-7). 32.95 *(978-1-904872-44-3(1),* Can of Worms Kids Pr.) Can of Worms Pr. GBR. Dist: Independent Pubs. Group.
Morgan, Mark & Gallenson, Ann. Town Website Project for Macromedia Dreamweaver MX 2004: Communicating Information & Ideas on the Web, 2 bks. Underwood, Dale & Aho, Kirsti. Dharkar, Anuja & McCain, Malinda, eds. 2003. 39p. spiral bd. 10.00 *(978-0-9742273-8-2(2),* Macromedia Education) Macromedia, Inc.
Morgan, Mary. When You Wander: A Search-and-Rescue Dog Story. Engle, Margarita. 2013. (ENG.). 32p. (J). (gr. -1-3). 16.99 *(978-0-8050-9312-4(5),* Holt, Henry & Co. Bks. For Young Readers) Holt, Henry & Co.
Morgan, Mary. Sleep Tight, Little Mouse. Morgan, Mary. 2015. (ENG.). 32p. (J). (gr. -1-2). bds. 6.99 *(978-0-553-49829-5(0),* Knopf Bks. for Young Readers) Random Hse. Children's Bks.
Morgan, Mary & Guevara, Susan. Wild Women of the Wild West. Winter, Jonah. 2011. (ENG.). 40p. (J). 16.95 *(978-0-8234-1601-1(1))* Holiday Hse., Inc.
Morgan, Nicolette. All about Me: Briana's Neighborhood. 2007. 24p. (J). 15.99 *(978-0-9793904-0-1(0))* It's Me Briana, LLC.
Morgan, Pau. Blast off! Doodle Book. Morgan, Pau. Young, Karen Romano. 2015. (Smithsonian Ser.). (ENG.). 128p. (J). (gr. 1-3). pap. 12.99 ***(978-0-448-48210-1(X),*** Grosset & Dunlap) Penguin Publishing Group.
Morgan, Pierr. Dragon Dancing. Morgan, Pierr. Schaefer, Carole Lexa & Schaefer, Carole. 2006. (ENG.). 40p. (J). (gr. -1-k). 16.99 *(978-0-670-06084-9(4),* Viking Juvenile) Penguin Publishing Group.
Morgan, Richard. The Fox & the Stork. 2005. (Reading Corner Ser.). 24p. (J). (gr. k-3). lib. bdg. 22.80 *(978-1-59771-011-4(3))* Sea-To-Sea Pubns.
—Leo's New Pet. Gowar, Mick. 2008. (Tadpoles Ser.). (ENG.). 24p. (J). (gr. -1-3). pap. *(978-0-7787-3886-2(8));* lib. bdg. *(978-0-7787-3855-8(8))* Crabtree Publishing Co.
—The Wheels on the Bus - The Boat on the Waves. 2013. (ENG.). 24p. (J). *(978-0-7787-1148-3(X))* Crabtree Publishing Co.
—The Wheels on the Bus; The Boat on the Waves. 2013. (ENG.). 24p. (J). pap. *(978-0-7787-1152-0(8))* Crabtree Publishing Co.
Morgan, Richard & Fennell, Tracy. Oliver Twist. Dickens, Charles. 2008. 48p. (J). (gr. 4-7). pap. 10.00 *(978-1-4190-5075-6(3))* Steck-Vaughn.
Morgan, Rick. An Illustrated Timeline of Inventions & Inventors, 1 vol. Spengler, Kremena T. 2011. (Visual Timelines in History Ser.). (ENG.). 32p. (gr. 3-4). pap. 7.49 *(978-1-4048-7017-8(2));* pap. 41.70 *(978-1-4048-7021-5(0))* Picture Window Bks. (Nonfiction Picture Bks.).
—An Illustrated Timeline of Inventions & Inventors, 1 vol. Spengler, Kremena T. 2011. (Visual Timelines in History Ser.). (ENG.). 32p. (gr. 3-4). lib. bdg. 27.99 *(978-1-4048-6662-1(0),* Nonfiction Picture Bks.) Picture Window Bks.
—An Illustrated Timeline of U. S. States, 1 vol. Wooster, Patricia. 2011. (Visual Timelines in History Ser.). (ENG.). 32p. (gr. 3-4). pap. 7.49 *(978-1-4048-7020-8(2));* lib. bdg. 27.99 *(978-1-4048-6663-8(9))* Picture Window Bks. (Nonfiction Picture Bks.).
—Rookie Racer. Pruett, Scott et al. 2005. (J). *(978-0-9670600-2-6(8))* Word Weaver Bks., Inc.
Morgan, Sally. The Last Dance. Morgan, Sally. 2013. (ENG.). 24p. (J). (gr. -1-k). 22.99 *(978-1-921714-84-9(0))* Little Hare Bks. AUS. Dist: Independent Pubs. Group.
Morgan, Tom & Mounts, Paul. Godzilla Saves America: A Monster Showdown in 3-D! Cerasini, Marc. 2006. 20p. (J). (gr. k-4). reprint ed. 12.00 *(978-1-4223-5409-4(1))* DIANE Publishing Co.
Morgan, Trish. A Lab's Tale. Malpass, Suzanne M. 2012. 38p. (J). 12.95 *(978-1-937406-68-4(7))* Mascot Bks., Inc.
Morgan, Vincent. Big Boy. Banks, Robin Washington. 2011. 20p. pap. 24.95 *(978-1-4560-7068-7(1))* PublishAmerica, Inc.
Morgin, W. J. & W., E. Sowing Beside All Waters: A Tale of the World in the Church. Leslie, Emma. 2007. 300p. 24.95 *(978-1-934671-06-1(1));* per. 14.95 *(978-1-934671-07-8(X))* Salem Ridge Press LLC.
Mori, Midori & Revels, Robert. Neem el Media Nino. Shah, Idries. Wirkala, Rita, tr. 2007. 32p. (J). 18.00 *(978-1-883536-96-1(0));* pap. 7.99 *(978-1-883536-97-8(9))* I S H K. (Hoopoe Bks.).
—Neem the Half-Boy. Shah, Idries. 2007. 32p. (J). (gr. -1). pap. 7.99 *(978-1-883536-95-4(2),* Hoopoe Bks.) I S H K.
Morice, Dave. A Visit from St. Alphabet. Morice, Dave. 2005. (ENG.). 24p. (Orig.). (J). (gr. -1-3). 9.95 *(978-1-56689-179-0(5))* Coffee Hse. Pr.
Moricuchi, Mique. Little Mouse Deer & the Crocodile. Hughes, Mónica. 2004. 24p. (J). lib. bdg. 23.65 *(978-1-59646-684-5(7))* Dingles & Co.
Morimoto, Sango. Taro & the Carnival of Doom. Morimoto, Sango. 2011. (Adventures of Taro Ser.: 3). (ENG.). 96p. (J). pap. 7.99 *(978-1-4215-3526-5(2))* Viz Media.
—Taro & the Magic Pencil. Morimoto, Sango. 2010. (Adventures of Taro Ser.). (ENG.). 104p. (J). pap. 7.99 *(978-1-4215-3524-1(6))* Viz Media.
—Taro & the Terror of Eats Street. Morimoto, Sango. 2011. (Adventures of Taro Ser.). (ENG.). 96p. (J). (gr. 1-4). pap. 7.99 *(978-1-4215-3525-8(4))* Viz Media.
Morin, Leane. The Carpet Boy's Gift, 1 vol. Shea, Pegi Deitz & Deitz Shea, Pegi. 2005. (ENG.). 40p. (J). (gr. 3-6). 16.95 *(978-0-88448-248-2(0))* Tilbury Hse. Pubs.
—Shy Mama's Halloween. Broyles, Anne. 2013. 32p. (J). pap. 12.00 *(978-1-62620-249-8(4))* Independent Pub.
Morin, Mauricio Gomez. Harvey Angel y la Nina Fantasma. Hendry, Diana. Alban, Rafael Segovia, tr. 2003. (la Orilla Del Viento Ser.). (SPA.). 166p. (J). reprint ed. pap., pap. 7.50 *(978-968-16-6723-8(9))* Fondo de Cultura Economica USA.

Morin, Paul. Mr. Hiroshi's Garden, 1 vol. Trottier, Maxine. 2006. (ENG.). 32p. (J). (gr. -1-3). 7.95 *(978-1-55005-152-0(0)*, 1550051520) Fitzhenry & Whiteside, Ltd. CAN. Dist: Midpoint Trade Bks., Inc.
—The Orphan Boy, 1 vol. Mollel, Tololwa M. 2nd rev. ed. 2008. (ENG.). 40p. (J). 21.95 *(978-1-55005-082-0(6)*, 1550050826) Fitzhenry & Whiteside, Ltd. CAN. Dist: Midpoint Trade Bks., Inc.
—The Vision Seeker, 1 vol. Freeman, Yusuf, photos by. Whetung, James. 2011. (ENG.). 32p. (J). pap. 9.95 *(978-1-55455-194-1(3))* Fitzhenry & Whiteside, Ltd. CAN. Dist: Midpoint Trade Bks., Inc.
—When God Made the Dakotas. Kessler, Tim. 2006. 32p. (J). (gr. k). 17.00 *(978-0-8028-5275-5(0)*, Eerdmans Bks For Young Readers) Eerdmans, William B. Publishing Co.
Morin, Paul, jt. illus. see Collier, John.
Morinaga, Ai. Duck Prince: Transformation, 6 bks, Bk. 1. Morinaga, Ai. Pannone, Frank, & Jackson, Laura & Kobayashi, Yoko, trs. from JPN. 2004. Orig. Title: Ahiruno Oujisama 1. 176p. pap. 9.99 *(978-1-58664-931-9(0)*, CMX 65201G, CPM Manga) Central Park Media Corp.
Morino, Brandon, et al. Skye the Troll: & Other Fairy Tales for Children. Skies, Apryl. 2010. (ENG.). 54p. pap. 16.99 *(978-1-4528-1719-4(7))* CreateSpace Independent Publishing Platform.
Morino, Sakana. Becoming a Dragon. Morino, Sakana. 2014. (J). 8.95 *(978-1-935523-67-3(8))* World Tribune Pr.
Moritsu, Wakako. O Holy Night: The First Christmas. Yamamoto, Makoto. 2005. 24p. (J). (gr. -1-3). per. 16.95 *(978-0-8198-5440-7(9))* Pauline Bks. & Media.
Moriuchi, Mique. Butterfly Girl. Puttock, Simon. 2007. (ENG.). 32p. (J). (gr. -1-k). 16.99 *(978-0-340-91145-7(X))* Hodder & Stoughton GBR. Dist: Independent Pubs. Group.
—Goodnight Prayers. Piper, Sophie. 2009. (ENG.). 64p. (J). (gr. -1-k). 9.99 *(978-0-7459-6065-4(0))* Lion Hudson PLC GBR. Dist: Independent Pubs. Group.
—I'll See You in the Morning. Jolley, Mike. 2008. (ENG.). (J). (gr. -1 — 1). bds. 6.99 *(978-0-8118-6543-2(6))* Chronicle Bks. LLC.
—Mix & Match Animals: Over 20 Different Animal Combinations! 2007. (ENG.). 10p. (gr. -1). 10.95 *(978-1-58117-603-2(1)*, Intervisual/Piggy Toes) Bendon, Inc.
Moriuchi, Mique. My Village: Rhymes from Around the World. 2015. (ENG & MUL.). 64p. (J). (gr. -1-1). 17.99 ***(978-1-84780-627-7(9)***, Frances Lincoln) Quarto Publishing Group UK GBR. Dist: Hachette Bk. Group.
Moriuchi, Mique. Talk Peace. Williams, Sam. 2005. 32p. (J). 16.95 *(978-0-8234-1936-4(3))* Holiday Hse., Inc.
—That's Love. Williams, Sam. 2006. 24p. (J). (gr. -1-3). 16.95 *(978-0-8234-2028-5(0))* Holiday Hse., Inc.
Moriuchi, Mique. The Very Best Teacher. Kim, YeShil. 2015. (ENG.). 24p. (J). (-3). 12.99 ***(978-1-4926-0998-8(6))*** Sourcebooks, Inc.
Morley, Amanda, et al. Fact & Fiction 1: Reece to the Rescue; Here Comes a Thunderstorm; Garden Giant; A Sunflower Life Cycle; Mugs Indoors & Outdoors; Cats Are Hunters; Beach Days; Oceans All Around Us, 8 bks., Set. McCarrier, Andrea et al. 2006. (ENG.). 16p. (J). pap. 120.00 *(978-1-893986-25-1(X))* Keep Bks.
Morley, Farah. The Spider & the Doves: The Story of the Hijra. 2012. (ENG.). 30p. (J). (gr. -1-2). 8.95 *(978-0-86037-449-7(1))* Kube Publishing Ltd. GBR. Dist: Consortium Bk. Sales & Distribution.
Morley, Taia. Anna's Table. Bunting, Eve. 2003. (ENG.). 32p. (J). (gr. 3-6). 16.95 *(978-1-55971-841-7(2))* Cooper Square Publishing Llc.
—Hurray for Spring. Hubbell, Patricia. 2005. (Picture Book Ser.). (ENG.). 32p. (J). (gr. -1-k). 15.95 *(978-1-55971-913-1(3))* Cooper Square Publishing Llc.
—Hurricane Watch. Stewart, Melissa. 2015. (Let's-Read-And-Find-Out Science 2 Ser.). (ENG.). 40p. (J). (gr. -1-3). pap. 6.99 *(978-0-06-232775-8(5))* HarperCollins Pubs.
—Looking Good! How to Get Stylin' with Your Friends. Hurley, Jo. 2007. 64p. (J). *(978-0-439-02013-8(1))* Scholastic, Inc.
—Slumber-ific! Great Sleepover Ideas for You & Your Friends. Hurley, Jo. 2007. 63p. (J). *(978-0-439-02015-2(8))* Scholastic, Inc.
Morley, Taia. The Sun & the Moon. DeCristofano, Carolyn Cinami. 2016. (J). pap. ***(978-0-06-233803-7(X))*** Harper & Row Ltd.
Morling, Donovan. The Disaster Caster. Carter, Grant Matthew. 2012. 38p. pap. 16.00 *(978-1-4349-8432-6(X)*, RoseDog Bks.) Dorrance Publishing Co., Inc.
Moro, Robin, et al. Read Aloud Spooky Stories. 2006. 320p. (J). (gr. 4-7). 15.98 *(978-0-7853-6338-5(6)*, 7159100) Publications International, Ltd.
Moroney, Christopher. Animal Alphabet: From Ape to Zebra. McMahon, Kara & Random House Disney Staff. 2005. (Sesame Street Start-to-Read Bks.). (ENG.). 20p. (J). (gr. k — 1). bds. 7.99 *(978-0-375-83228-4(9)*, Random Hse. Bks. for Young Readers) Random Hse. Children's Bks.
—Bamboozled. Rabe, Tish. 2011. (Little Golden Book Ser.). (ENG.). 24p. (J). (gr. -1-2). 3.99 *(978-0-375-87307-2(4)*, Golden Bks.) Random Hse. Children's Bks.
—Born to Run! Rabe, Tish. 2012. (Little Golden Book Ser.). (ENG.). 24p. (J). (gr. k-k). 3.99 *(978-0-307-93080-4(7)*, Golden Bks.) Random Hse. Children's Bks.
—Busy as a Bee! (Seuss/Cat in the Hat) Tillworth, Mary. 2012. (Write-On/Wipe-off Activity Book Ser.). (ENG.). 12p. (J). (gr. k — 1). bds. 9.99 *(978-0-307-93011-8(4)*, Golden Bks.) Random Hse., Inc.
—The Cat in the Hat - Cooking with the Cat. Worth, Bonnie. 2003. (Step into Reading Ser.). (ENG.). 32p. (J). (gr. -1-1). pap. 3.99 *(978-0-375-82494-4(4)*, 53560581, Random Hse. Bks. for Young Readers) Random Hse. Children's Bks.
—Elmo's Furry Friend (Sesame Street) Kleinberg, Naomi. 2013. (ENG.). 12p. (J). (— 1). bds. 4.99 *(978-0-385-37386-9(4)*, Random Hse. Bks. for Young Readers) Random Hse. Children's Bks.
—Elmo's Little Dreidel (Sesame Street) Kleinberg, Naomi. 2011. (ENG.). 12p. (J). (gr. k — 1). bds. 5.99 *(978-0-375-87396-6(1)*, Random Hse. Bks. for Young Readers) Random Hse. Children's Bks.
—Elmo's Monster Mash. Kleinberg, Naomi. 2010. (ENG.). 12p. (J). (gr. k — 1). 4.99 *(978-0-375-85804-8(0)*, Random Hse. Bks. for Young Readers) Random Hse. Children's Bks.
—Firsts! Kleinberg, Naomi. 2012. (Sesame Beginnings Ser.). (ENG.). 12p. (J). (gr. k-k). 6.99 *(978-0-307-93069-9(6)*, Random Hse. Bks. for Young Readers) Random Hse. Children's Bks.
—Happy Holi-Doodles! Golden Books. 2012. (Doodle Book Ser.). (ENG.). 128p. (J). (gr. -1-2). pap. 5.99 *(978-0-307-93198-6(6)*, Golden Bks.) Random Hse. Children's Bks.
—In Elmo's Easter Parade. Kleinberg, Naomi. 2009. (ENG.). 12p. (J). (gr. k — 1). bds. 4.99 *(978-0-375-84480-5(5)*, Random Hse. Bks. for Young Readers) Random Hse. Children's Bks.
—King Cecil the Sea Horse (Dr. Seuss/Cat in the Hat) Rabe, Tish. 2013. (Little Golden Book Ser.). (ENG.). 24p. (J). (-k). 3.99 *(978-0-449-81010-1(0)*, Golden Bks.) Random Hse. Children's Bks.
—Lovies. Kleinberg, Naomi. 2008. (Sesame Beginnings Ser.). (ENG.). 10p. (J). (gr. k — 1). bds. 6.99 *(978-0-375-84539-0(9)*, Random Hse. Bks. for Young Readers) Random Hse. Children's Bks.
—P Is for Potty! (Sesame Street) Random House. 2014. (Lift-The-Flap Ser.). (ENG.). 12p. (J). (— 1). bds. 5.99 *(978-0-385-38369-1(X)*, Random Hse. Bks. for Young Readers) Random Hse. Children's Bks.
—Potty Time! Sawyer, Parker K. 2006. (Sesame Beginnings Ser.). (ENG.). 12p. (J). (gr. k — 1). bds. 5.99 *(978-0-375-83695-4(0)*, Random Hse. Bks. for Young Readers) Random Hse. Children's Bks.
—Sesame Beginnings: It's Time! (Sesame Street) Kleinberg, Naomi. 2013. (Sesame Beginnings Ser.). (ENG.). 12p. (J). (— 1). bds. 6.99 *(978-0-307-98059-5(6)*, Random Hse. Bks. for Young Readers) Random Hse. Children's Bks.
—Sesame Beginnings: Oops! (Sesame Street) Kleinberg, Naomi. 2011. (Sesame Beginnings Ser.). (ENG.). 12p. (J). (gr. k — 1). bds. 6.99 *(978-0-375-87365-2(1)*, Random Hse. Bks. for Young Readers) Random Hse. Children's Bks.
—Sesame Street Elmo Goes to School. Shepherd, Jodie. 2012. (Lift-The-Flap Ser.: 1). (ENG.). 10p. (J). (gr. -1-k). bds. 10.99 *(978-0-7944-2585-2(2))* Reader's Digest Assn., Inc., The.
—So Big! Hays, Anna Jane. 2003. (Sesame Beginnings Ser.). (ENG.). 14p. (J). (gr. k — 1). bds. 7.99 *(978-0-375-81537-9(6)*, Random Hse. Bks. for Young Readers) Random Hse. Children's Bks.
—The Thinga-Ma-Jigger Is Coming Today! Rabe, Tish. 2010. (Little Golden Book Ser.). (ENG.). 24p. (J). (gr. -1-2). 3.99 *(978-0-375-85927-4(6)*, Golden Bks.) Random Hse. Children's Bks.
—Tummies! Albee, Sarah. 2010. (Sesame Beginnings Ser.). (ENG.). 12p. (J). (gr. k — 1). bds. 5.99 *(978-0-375-85484-2(3)*, Random Hse. Bks. for Young Readers) Random Hse. Children's Bks.
—Walkin' in a Sticker Wonderland! (Seuss/Cat in the Hat) Golden Books. 2012. (Holographic Sticker Book Ser.). (ENG.). 48p. (J). (gr. -1-2). pap. 3.99 *(978-0-307-93197-9(8)*, Golden Bks.) Random Hse. Children's Bks.
—What Shape Is a Grape? Webster, Christy. 2009. (ENG.). 20p. (J). (gr. k — 1). bds. 7.99 *(978-0-375-84536-9(4)*, Random Hse. Bks. for Young Readers) Random Hse. Children's Bks.
—1, 2, 3 Count with Me. Kleinberg, Naomi. 2005. (ENG.). 20p. (J). (gr. k — 1). bds. 7.99 *(978-0-375-83227-7(0)*, Random Hse. Bks. for Young Readers) Random Hse. Children's Bks.
Moroney, Trace. Bible Adventures. Nolan, Allia Zobel. 2007. 20p. (J). bds. 10.99 *(978-0-8254-5535-3(9))* Kregel Pubns.
—The Easter Story. Nolan, Allia Zobel. 2006. 24p. (J). pap. 3.99 *(978-0-8254-5534-6(0))* Kregel Pubns.
—My Bible Story Collection. Nolan, Allia Zobel. 2004. 96p. (J). 14.99 *(978-0-8254-5515-5(4))* Kregel Pubns.
—My First Book of Nursery Rhymes: Jigsaw Book. (My First Book Ser.). 12p. (J). *(978-1-74124-628-5(8))* Five Mile Pr. Pty Ltd. The.
—My First Book of Nursery Songs: Jigsaw Book. (My First Book Ser.). 12p. (J). *(978-1-74124-630-8(X))* Five Mile Pr. Pty Ltd. The.
—Stories Jesus Told. Littleton, Mark. 2004. 20p. (J). bds. 10.99 *(978-0-8254-5519-3(7))* Kregel Pubns.
—The Story of Noah's Ark. Nolan, Allia Zobel. 2006. 24p. (J). pap. 3.99 *(978-0-8254-5532-2(4))* Kregel Pubns.
Moroney, Trace. Bathtime: Baxter Bear Chubby. Moroney, Trace. 2008. (Baxter Bear Collection). 10p. (J). (gr. -1-1). bds. *(978-1-86463-175-3(9))* Brimax Books Ltd.
—Bedtime: The Baxter Bear Collection. Moroney, Trace. 2008. (Baxter Bear Collection). 10p. (gr. -1-1). bds. 5.99 *(978-1-86463-176-0(7))* Gardner Pubns.
—Dinnertime: Baxter Bear Chubby. Moroney, Trace. 2008. 10p. (J). (gr. -1-1). bds. 5.99 *(978-1-86463-174-6(0))* Gardner Pubns.
—Playtime. Moroney, Trace. 2008. (Baxter Bear Collection). 10p. (gr. -1-1). bds. 5.99 *(978-1-86463-177-7(5))* Gardner Pubns.
—Things I Love about Bedtime. Moroney, Trace. 2012. (ENG.). 16p. (J). (gr. -1-k). bds. 8.99 *(978-0-545-29016-6(3)*, Cartwheel Bks.) Scholastic, Inc.
Moroney, Tracey. A Child's Book of Miracles & Wonders. Tuck, Mildred. 2006. 28p. (J). (gr. -1-3). 15.99 *(978-0-7847-1437-9(1)*, 04076) Standard Publishing.
—Lift-the-Flap Bible. Jones, Sally Lloyd. 2011. (Lift-The-Flap Ser.). (ENG.). 20p. (J). (gr. -1-k). bds. 10.99 *(978-0-7944-2278-3(0))* Reader's Digest Assn., Inc., The.
Morozova, Anastasia. Rose-Pie. Sexton, Jessa Rose. 2011. 20p. pap. 6.00 *(978-0-9846244-0-9(6))* O'More Publishing.
Morrell, Cris. Basura No, Gracias! Pittar, Gill & Gill, Pittar. Rioja, Alberto Jiménez, tr. 2003. (Milly Molly Ser.). (SPA.). 24p. (J). pap. *(978-84-241-8695-1(8))* Everest Editora ESP. Dist: Lectorum Pubns., Inc.
—Las Ciruelas de Isa Bela. Pittar, Gill & Gill, Pittar. Rioja, Alberto Jiménez, tr. 2003. (Milly Molly Ser.). (SPA.). 24p. (J). pap. *(978-84-241-8687-6(7))* Everest Editora ESP. Dist: Lectorum Pubns., Inc.
—Milly & Molly's Monday. Pittar, Gill. 2nd rev. ed. 2003. 27p. *(978-1-877297-06-9(2))* Milly Molly Bks.
—Milly, Molly & Beaky. Pittar, Gill. 2005. 28p. (gr. -1). pap. *(978-1-86972-048-3(2))* Milly Molly Bks.
—Milly, Molly & the Ferryman. Pittar, Gill. 2004. 28p. pap. *(978-1-86972-004-9(0))* Milly Molly Bks.
—Milly, Molly & the Picnic. Pittar, Gill. 2005. 28p. (gr. -1). pap. *(978-1-86972-045-2(8))* Milly Molly Bks.
—Milly, Molly & the Runaway Bean. Pittar, Gill. 2005. 28p. (J). (gr. -1). pap. *(978-1-86972-049-0(0))* Milly Molly Bks.
—De Quien es Este Sombrero? Pittar, Gill & Gill, Pittar. Rioja, Alberto Jiménez, tr. 2003. (Milly Molly Ser.). (SPA.). 24p. (J). pap. *(978-84-241-8679-1(6))* Everest Editora ESP. Dist: Lectorum Pubns., Inc.
Morrill, Leslie. Nighty-Nightmare. Howe, James. 2007. (Bunnicula & Friends Ser.). (ENG.). 144p. (J). (gr. 3-7). pap. 5.99 *(978-1-4169-3966-5(0)*, Atheneum Bks. for Young Readers) Simon & Schuster Children's Publishing.
—Totally Disgusting! Wallace, Bill. 2008. (ENG.). 144p. (J). (gr. 3-7). pap. 5.99 *(978-1-4169-5805-5(3)*, Simon & Schuster/Paula Wiseman Bks.) Simon & Schuster/Paula Wiseman Bks.
Morrill, Leslie H. The Celery Stalks at Midnight. Howe, James. 2006. (Bunnicula & Friends Ser.). (ENG.). 144p. (J). (gr. 3-7). pap. 6.99 *(978-1-4169-2814-0(6)*, Atheneum Bks. for Young Readers) Simon & Schuster Children's Publishing.
Morris. The Daily Star. Léturgie, Jean & Fauche, Xavier. 2013. (ENG.). 48p. pap. 11.95 *(978-1-84918-160-0(8))* CineBook GBR. Dist: National Bk. Network.
—The Daltons Always on the Run. Goscinny, René. 2012. (Lucky Luke Adventure Ser.: Bk. 34). (ENG.). 48p. (J). (gr. 3-12). pap. 11.95 *(978-1-84918-119-8(5))* CineBook GBR. Dist: National Bk. Network.
—The Dashing White Cowboy. Goscinny, René. 2009. (ENG.). 46p. (J). (gr. -1-17). pap. 11.95 *(978-1-905460-66-3(X))* CineBook GBR. Dist: National Bk. Network.
—Doc Doxey's Elixir. 2013. (ENG.). 48p. pap. 11.95 *(978-1-84918-141-9(1))* CineBook GBR. Dist: National Bk. Network.
—Lucky Luke Versus Joss Jamon. Goscinny, Rene. 27th ed. 2011. (ENG.). 48p. (gr. 3-17). pap. 11.95 *(978-1-84918-071-9(7))* CineBook GBR. Dist: National Bk. Network.
—Lucky Luke Vol. 40: Phil Wire. 2013. (ENG.). 48p. pap. 11.95 *(978-1-84918-155-6(1))* CineBook GBR. Dist: National Bk. Network.
—Lucky Luke Vol. 43 the Bluefeet Are Coming! 2014. (ENG.). 48p. pap. 11.95 *(978-1-84918-173-0(X))* CineBook GBR. Dist: National Bk. Network.
—Lucky Luke Vol. 44: Lucky Luke Versus Pat Poker. 2014. (ENG.). 48p. pap. 11.95 *(978-1-84918-179-2(9))* CineBook GBR. Dist: National Bk. Network.
Morris, Alexander. Abc's of Health & Safety. Abramovitz, Melissa. 2012. 16p. pap. 9.95 *(978-1-61633-276-1(X))* Guardian Angel Publishing, Inc.
—Bearly Learning about Water. Esparza-Vela, Mary. 2012. 16p. pap. 9.95 *(978-1-61633-288-4(3))* Guardian Angel Publishing, Inc.
—Frankie's Perfect Home. McClure, Beverly Stowe. 2011. 16p. pap. 9.95 *(978-1-61633-162-7(3))* Guardian Angel Publishing, Inc.
—Juggerum. Kennedy, J. Aday. 2012. 16p. pap. 9.95 *(978-1-61633-348-5(0))* Guardian Angel Publishing, Inc.
—My Brother the Frog. McNamee, Kevin. 2011. 24p. 19.95 *(978-1-61633-167-2(4))*; pap. 10.95 *(978-1-61633-159-7(3))* Guardian Angel Publishing, Inc.
—The Water Cycle: Water Play Series Book 1. Calvani, Mayra. 2012. 20p. pap. 10.95 *(978-1-61633-237-2(9))* Guardian Angel Publishing, Inc.
Morris, Alfred. A Cure for the Daltons, Vol. 23. Goscinny, René. 2010. (ENG.). 48p. (J). (gr. 3-17). pap. 11.95 *(978-1-84918-034-4(2))* CineBook GBR. Dist: National Bk. Network.
—Jesse James. Goscinny, Rene. 2007. (Lucky Luke Ser.). (ENG.). 48p. (J). (gr. 4-7). per. 11.95 *(978-1-905460-14-4(7))* CineBook GBR. Dist: National Bk. Network.
—The Judge. 2010. (ENG.). 46p. (J). (gr. 3-17). pap. 11.95 *(978-1-84918-045-0(8))* CineBook GBR. Dist: National Bk. Network.
—The Tenderfoot. Goscinny, René. 2008. (ENG.). 48p. (J). (gr. -1-17). pap. 11.95 *(978-1-905460-65-6(1))* CineBook GBR. Dist: National Bk. Network.
—Western Circus. Goscinny, René. 2008. (ENG.). 48p. pap. 11.95 *(978-1-905460-55-7(4))* CineBook GBR. Dist: National Bk. Network.
Morris, Don. Luna & the Big Blur: A Story for Children Who Wear Glasses. Day, Shirley. 2008. 32p. (J). (gr. -1-3). 14.95 *(978-1-4338-0398-7(4))*; pap. 9.95 *(978-1-4338-0399-4(2))* American Psychological Assn. (Magination Pr.).
Morris, Douglas. Here I Am Look at Me! Morris, Deborah K. 2010. 36p. pap. 13.95 *(978-1-60911-739-9(5)*, Eloquent Bks.) Strategic Book Publishing & Rights Agency (SBPRA).
Morris, Garvin. Dump Dog. Morris, Garvin. (J). 2008. 32p. pap. 6.95 *(978-1-60108-022-6(0))*; 2007. 40p. (gr. -1-2). 15.95 *(978-1-60108-012-7(3))* Red Cygnet Pr.
Morris, Hannah. The Hyena & the Seven Little Kids. Bloch, Carole. 2012. (Best Loved Tales for Africa Ser.). (ENG.). 32p. (J). (gr. k-2). pap. 9.95 *(978-1-77009-820-6(8))* Jacana Media ZAF. Dist: Independent Pubs. Group.
Morris, Jackie. Can You See a Little Bear? Mayhew, James. 2006. (ENG.). 32p. (J). (gr. -1-1). pap. 8.99 *(978-1-84507-364-0(9)*, Frances Lincoln) Quarto Publishing Group UK GBR. Dist: Hachette Bk. Group.
—East of the Sun, West of the Moon. 2013. (ENG.). 176p. (J). (gr. 6-9). 15.99 *(978-1-84780-294-1(X)*, Frances Lincoln) Quarto Publishing Group UK GBR. Dist: Hachette Bk. Group.
—The Greatest Gift: The Story of the Other Wise Man. Summers, Susan. 2011. (ENG.). 30p. (J). 16.99 *(978-1-84686-578-7(6))* Barefoot Bks., Inc.
—How the Whale Became: And Other Stories. Hughes, Ted & Quarto Generic Staff. 2012. (ENG.). 96p. (J). (gr. k-3). pap. 14.99 *(978-1-84507-928-4(0)*, Frances Lincoln) Quarto Publishing Group UK GBR. Dist: Hachette Bk. Group.
—I Am Cat. Quarto Generic Staff. 2013. (ENG.). 32p. (J). (gr. k-3). 17.99 *(978-1-84780-135-7(8)*, Frances Lincoln) Quarto Publishing Group UK GBR. Dist: Hachette Bk. Group.
—The Ice Bear. 2014. (ENG.). 40p. (J). (gr. -1-2). pap. 9.99 *(978-1-84780-457-0(8)*, Frances Lincoln) Quarto Publishing Group UK GBR. Dist: Hachette Bk. Group.
—Jackie Morris Notebooks, Set. 2014. (ENG.). 48p. (J). (gr. k-17). pap. 15.99 *(978-0-7112-3572-4(4)*, Frances Lincoln) Quarto Publishing Group UK GBR. Dist: Hachette Bk. Group.
—Lord of the Forest. Pitcher, Caroline. (ENG.). 32p. (J). (gr. -1-2). 2009. pap. 8.95 *(978-1-84507-276-6(6))*; 2014. 6.99 *(978-1-84780-546-1(9))* Quarto Publishing Group UK GBR. (Frances Lincoln). Dist: Hachette Bk. Group.
—Mariana & the Merchild. Pitcher, Caroline. 2004. 32p. (J). (gr. -1-7). 17.00 *(978-0-8028-5204-5(1))* Eerdmans, William B. Publishing Co.
—Mariana & the Merchild: A Folk Tale from Chile. Pitcher, Caroline. 2006. 24p. (J). (gr. k-4). reprint ed. 17.00 *(978-1-4223-5136-9(X))* DIANE Publishing Co.
—Singing to the Sun. French, Vivian. 2008. 32p. (J). (gr. 2-3). 11.99 *(978-1-933605-94-4(4))* Kane Miller.
—The Snow Whale. Pitcher, Caroline. rev. ed. 2014. (ENG.). 32p. (J). (gr. -1-2). pap. 8.99 *(978-1-84507-717-4(2)*, Frances Lincoln) Quarto Publishing Group UK GBR. Dist: Hachette Bk. Group.
—Something about a Bear. Quarto Generic Staff. 2014. (ENG.). 32p. (J). (gr. -1-1). 17.99 *(978-1-84780-516-4(7)*, Frances Lincoln) Quarto Publishing Group UK GBR. Dist: Hachette Bk. Group.
—Starlight Sailor. Mayhew, James. (ENG.). 24p. (J). 2013. bds. 14.99 *(978-1-84686-936-5(6))*; 2012. pap. 6.99 *(978-1-84686-750-7(9))*; 2009. (gr. -1-3). 16.99 *(978-1-84686-185-7(3))* Barefoot Bks., Inc.
—Tell Me a Dragon. 2009. (ENG.). 32p. (J). (gr. -1-1). 17.99 *(978-1-84507-534-7(X)*, Frances Lincoln) Quarto Publishing Group UK GBR. Dist: Hachette Bk. Group.
Morris, Jackie. Y Tu Dragón, ¿Cómo Es? Morris, Jackie. 2010. (SPA.). 28p. (J). (gr. k-2). 14.95 *(978-84-92595-21-1(3))* Thule Ediciones, S. L. ESP. Dist: Independent Pubs. Group.
Morris, James R. Ranger Trails: Jobs of Adventure in America's Parks. Yanuchi, Lori & Yanuchi, Jeff. 2005. 64p. (J). per. 12.95 *(978-0-9670177-2-3(6))* Ridge Rock Pr.
Morris, Jean. The Wagon Train. Goscinny, René. 2008. (ENG.). 48p. pap. 11.95 *(978-1-905460-40-3(6))* CineBook GBR. Dist: National Bk. Network.
Morris, Jeanne L. Jody's Travelbooks for Kids Vol. I: Frankenmuth, Michigan. Arrathoon, Leigh A. & Davio, John. 48p. (J). (gr. 2-6). pap. 4.95 *(978-0-9648564-7-9(6))* Archus Pr., LLC.
—Jody's Travelbooks for Kids Vol. II: Holland, Michigan. Arrathoon, Leigh A. & Davio, John. 48p. (J). (gr. 2-6). pap. 4.95 *(978-0-9648564-8-6(4))* Archus Pr., LLC.
—Jody's Travelbooks for Kids Vol. III: Mackinaw, Michigan. Arrathoon, Leigh A. & Davio, John. 48p. (J). (gr. 2-6). pap. 4.95 *(978-0-9648564-9-3(2))* Archus Pr., LLC.
Morris, Jennifer. A Gluten-Free Birthday for Me! Fliess, Sue. 2013. (ENG.). 32p. (J). (gr. -1-2). 16.99 *(978-0-8075-2955-3(9))* Whitman, Albert & Co.
Morris, Jennifer & Morris, Jennifer E. If a Monkey Jumps onto Your School Bus. Cochran, Jean M. 2008. (ENG.). 32p. (J). (gr. -1-k). 16.95 *(978-0-9792035-2-7(X))* Pleasant St. Pr.
Morris, Jennifer E. It's Halloween Night! O'Connell, Jennifer Barrett. 2012. (ENG.). 32p. (J). (gr. -1-k). pap. 6.99 *(978-0-545-40283-5(2)*, Cartwheel Bks.) Scholastic, Inc.
—On a Dark, Dark Night. Cochran, Jean M. 2009. (ENG.). 32p. (J). (gr. k-2). 16.95 *(978-1-935025-00-9(7))* Pleasant St. Pr.
Morris, Jennifer E. Ice Cream Shop. Morris, Jennifer E. 2014. (Scholastic Reader Level 1 Ser.). (ENG.). 32p. (J). (gr. -1-1). pap. 3.99 *(978-0-545-61481-8(3))* Scholastic, Inc.
—May I Please Have a Cookie? Morris, Jennifer E. 2005. (Scholastic Reader Level 1 Ser.). (ENG.). 32p. (J). (gr. -1-3). per. 4.99 *(978-0-439-73819-4(9)*, Cartwheel Bks.) Scholastic, Inc.
—Please Write Back! Morris, Jennifer E. 2010. (Scholastic Reader Level 1 Ser.). (ENG.). 32p. (J). (gr. -1-3). pap. 3.99 *(978-0-545-11506-3(X)*, Cartwheel Bks.) Scholastic, Inc.
Morris, Jennifer E., jt. illus. see Morris, Jennifer.
Morris, Jessica. Treasure Delight: A Sweet Story about the Joy in Sharing. Lynn, Deidre. 2013. 36p. pap. 12.95 *(978-0-9893181-0-5(9))* LoveLight Media.
Morris, Julie, jt. illus. see Nieto-Phillips, John M.
Morris, Kiran. Lies Your Parents Tell You. O'Neil, Dave. 2005. 160p. pap. *(978-0-7344-0292-9(9)*, Lothian Children's Bks.) Hachette Australia.
Morris, Lillie. Wally the Whale Learns How to Be a Winner. Riner, Sherry. 2004. 43p. pap. 24.95 *(978-1-4137-3129-3(5))* PublishAmerica, Inc.
Morris, Michael. Puzzle Cards Letters. gif. ed. 2005. 16p. (J). 9.99 *(978-1-57791-188-3(1))* Brighter Minds Children's Publishing.

—Puzzle Cards Numbers. gif. ed. 2005. 16p. (J). 9.99 *(978-1-57791-187-6(3))* Brighter Minds Children's Publishing.

—Sad Sam & the Magic Cookies. Quest, Stacy. Wertheimer, Beverly & Ronsley, Jill, eds. 2006. (ENG.). (J). 16.95 *(978-1-932367-01-0(2))* BookBound Publishing.

Morris Publishing Company Staff. The Bounty Hunter, Vol. 26. Goscinny, René. 2011. (ENG.). 48p. pap. 11.95 *(978-1-84918-059-7(8))* CineBook GBR. Dist: National Bk. Network.

—The Escort, Vol. 18. Goscinny, René. 2009. (ENG.). 46p. (J). (gr. 4-7). pap. 11.95 *(978-1-905460-98-4(8))* CineBook GBR. Dist: National Bk. Network.

—Fingers. Banda, Lo Hartog Van. 2013. (ENG.). 48p. (J). (gr. 3-12). pap. 11.95 *(978-1-84918-138-9(1))* CineBook GBR. Dist: National Bk. Network.

—The Rivals of Painful Gulch. Goscinny, René. 2009. (ENG.). 48p. pap. 11.95 *(978-1-905460-60-1(0))* CineBook GBR. Dist: National Bk. Network.

Morris Publishing Company Staff. Seven Stories, Vol. 50. Goscinny, R. 2015. (ENG.). 48p. pap. 11.95 ***(978-1-84918-226-3(4))*** CineBook GBR. Dist: National Bk. Network.

Morris Publishing Company Staff. The Stagecoach. Goscinny, René. 2011. (ENG.). 48p. (J). (gr. 3-17). pap. 11.95 *(978-1-84918-052-8(0))* CineBook GBR. Dist: National Bk. Network.

Morris, Robin C. Sometimes I Worry Too Much: A Book to Help Children Who Worry When They Don't Need To. Huebner, Dawn. Schader, Karen, ed. 2003. (J). per. 17.95 *(978-1-58815-060-8(7)*, 63814) Childswork/Childsplay.

Morris, Samuel L. Gwynepe Slew the Dragon Almost. Diggs, Linda. Hanna, Ellen & Steier, John, eds. 2004. 49p. (J). (gr. k-6). 17.99 *(978-0-9754126-0-2(4))* Willie & Willie.

Morris, Sandra. Hoppity Hop, 6 pack. Holden, Pam. 2009. (Red Rocket Readers Ser.). 16p. (gr. -1-2). pap. *(978-1-877363-19-1(7)*, Red Rocket Readers) Flying Start Bks.

Morris, Susan. Elijah Helps the Widow. Thoreson-Snipes, Nanette. 2004. (ENG.). 16p. (J). 1.99 *(978-0-570-07574-5(2))* Concordia Publishing Hse.

—Elizabeth's Christmas Story. Dede, Vivian Hughes. 2004. 16p. (J). 1.99 *(978-0-7586-0478-1(5))* Concordia Publishing Hse.

—The Parable of the Talents. Dreyer, Nicole E. 2007. 16p. (J). (gr. k-4). 1.99 *(978-0-7586-1282-3(6))* Concordia Publishing Hse.

Morris, Ting. Barbed Wire on the Prairie. Goscinny, Rene & Spear, Luke. Spear, Luke, tr. from FRE. 2007. (ENG.). 48p. (J). (gr. 4-7). pap. 11.95 *(978-1-905460-24-3(4))* CineBook GBR. Dist: National Bk. Network.

—Tortillas for the Daltons. Goscinny, René. Spear, Luke, tr. from FRE. 2008. (ENG.). 48p. pap. 11.95 *(978-1-905460-49-6(X))* CineBook GBR. Dist: National Bk. Network.

Morris, Tony. Bear in the Barnyard. Robinson, Sue. 2004. (ENG.). 28p. (J). pap. 16.00 *(978-1-56148-430-0(X)*, Good Bks.) Skyhorse Publishing Co., Inc.

—Children's Guide to the Bible. Willoughby, Robert. 2003. 128p. 9.99 *(978-1-85999-072-8(X))* Scripture Union GBR. Dist: Gabriel Resources.

—When Zacchaeus Met Jesus. Frank, Penny. 2004. (Lion Story Bible Ser.). (ENG.). 24p. (J). (gr. k-2). pap. 30.00 *(978-0-7459-4925-3(8)*, Lion Books) Lion Hudson PLC GBR. Dist: Independent Pubs. Group.

Morrison, Cameron & Morrison, Connor. Why Bears Don't Live in Humble, 1 vol. Morrison, Maria. 2010. 26p. pap. 24.95 *(978-1-4489-9748-0(8))* PublishAmerica, Inc.

Morrison, Cathy. Abner Doubleday: Boy Baseball Pioneer, 11 vols. Dunham, Montrew. Underdown, Harold D., ed. 2nd ed. 2005. (Young Patriots Ser.: 11). (ENG.). 118p. (J). (gr. 4-7). 15.95 *(978-1-882859-49-8(9))*; pap. 9.95 *(978-1-882859-50-4(2))* Patria Pr., Inc. (Young Patriots Series).

—Alexander Hamilton: Young Statesman. Higgins, Helen Boyd. Underdown, Harold D., ed. 2nd rev. ed. 2008. (Young Patriots Ser.: 14). (ENG.). 120p. (J). (gr. 4-7). 15.95 *(978-1-882859-61-0(8))*; per. 9.95 *(978-1-882859-62-7(6))* Patria Pr., Inc. (Young Patriots Series).

—Animalogy: Animal Analogies, 1 vol. Berkes, Marianne Collins. 2011. (ENG.). 32p. (J). (gr. -1-3). 16.95 *(978-1-60718-127-9(4))*; pap. 8.95 *(978-1-60718-137-8(1))* Arbordale Publishing.

—Daisylocks, 1 vol. Berkes, Marianne. 2014. (ENG.). 32p. (J). (gr. -1-3). pap. 9.95 *(978-1-62855-215-7(8))* Arbordale Publishing.

—Dino Tracks, 1 vol. Rhonda Lucas Donald, Rhonda Lucas. 2013. (ENG.). 32p. (J). (gr. -1-3). 17.95 *(978-1-60718-619-9(5))* Arbordale Publishing.

—Dino Tracks, 1 vol. Donald, Rhonda Lucas. 2013. (ENG.). 32p. (J). (gr. -1-3). pap. 9.95 *(978-1-60718-631-1(4))* Arbordale Publishing.

—Dino Treasures, 1 vol. Donald, Rhonda Lucas. 2015. (ENG.). 32p. (J). (gr. k-3). 17.95 *(978-1-62855-450-2(9))* Arbordale Publishing.

—Eddie Rickenbacker: Boy Pilot & Racer, 6 vols. Sisson, Kathryn Cleven. rev. ed. 2003. (Young Patriots Ser.: 6). (ENG.). 120p. (J). (gr. 4-7). pap. 9.95 *(978-1-882859-13-9(8))* Patria Pr., Inc.

—Eddie Rickenbacker: Boy Pilot & Racer, 6 vols. Sisson, Kathryn Cleven. Underdown, Harold D., ed. rev. ed. 2003. (Young Patriots Ser.: 6). (ENG.). 120p. (J). (gr. 4-7). 15.95 *(978-1-882859-12-2(X))* Patria Pr., Inc.

—Evening Song. Zimelman, Nathan. 2003. (Books for Young Learners). (ENG.). 12p. (J). 5.75 net. *(978-1-57274-536-0(3)*, 2741, Bks. for Young Learners) Owen, Richard C. Pubs., Inc.

—Frederick Douglass: Young Defender of Human Rights. Myers, Elisabeth P. 2nd rev. ed. 2007. (Young Patriots Ser.: 13). Orig. Title: Frederick Douglass Boy Champion of Human Rights. (ENG.). 120p. (J). (gr. 4-7). per. 9.95 *(978-1-882859-58-0(8)*, Young Patriots Series) Patria Pr., Inc.

—Frederick Douglass: Young Defender of Human Rights. Myers, Elisabeth P. 2nd rev. ed. 2007. (Young Patriots Ser.: 13). (ENG.). 120p. (J). (gr. 4-7). 15.95 *(978-1-882859-57-3(X)*, Young Patriots Series) Patria Pr., Inc.

—George Rogers Clark: Boy of the Northwest Frontier, 8 vols. Wilkie, Katharine E. rev. ed. 2004. (Young Patriots Ser.: 8). (ENG.). 112p. (J). (gr. 4-7). 15.95 *(978-1-882859-43-6(X))*; pap. 9.95 *(978-1-882859-44-3(8))* Patria Pr., Inc.

Morrison, Cathy. If You Love Honey. Sullivan, Martha. 2015. (ENG.). 32p. (J). (gr. k-4). 16.95 ***(978-1-58469-533-2(1))*** Dawn Pubns.

Morrison, Cathy. John Audubon: Young Naturalist. Mason, Miriam E. 2nd rev. ed. 2006. (Young Patriots Ser.: 12). (ENG.). 120p. (J). (gr. 4-7). 15.95 *(978-1-882859-51-1(0))*; pap. 9.95 *(978-1-882859-52-8(9))* Patria Pr., Inc. (Young Patriots Series).

—John Hancock: Independent Boy. Sisson, Kathryn Cleven. Underdown, Harold D., ed. 2005. (Young Patriots Ser.: 9). (ENG.). 120p. (J). (gr. 4-7). 15.95 *(978-1-882859-45-0(6))*; pap. 9.95 *(978-1-882859-46-7(4))* Patria Pr., Inc.

—Mahalia Jackson: Gospel Singer & Civil Rights Champion, 7 vols. Dunham, Montrew. Underdown, Harold D., ed. 3rd rev. ed. 2003. (Young Patriots Ser.: 7). (ENG.). 120p. (J). (gr. 4-7). pap. 9.95 *(978-1-882859-39-9(1))*; 15.95 *(978-1-882859-38-2(3))* Patria Pr., Inc.

—La Naturaleza Recicla¿lo Haces Tú?, 1 vol. Lord, Michelle. 2013. (ENG & SPA.). 32p. (J). (gr. -1-4). 17.95 *(978-1-60718-711-0(6))* Arbordale Publishing.

—Nature Recycles: How about You?, 1 vol. Lord, Michelle. 2013. (ENG.). 32p. (J). (gr. -1-4). 17.95 *(978-1-60718-615-1(2))*; pap. 9.95 *(978-1-60718-627-4(6))* Arbordale Publishing.

Morrison, Cathy. Over on the Farm. Berkes, Marianne Collins. 2016. 32p. (J). (gr. -1-2). 16.95 ***(978-1-58469-548-6(X))*** Dawn Pubns.

Morrison, Cathy. Phillis Wheatley: Young Revolutionary Poet. Speicher, Helen Ross & Borland, Kathryn Kilby. 2nd rev. ed. 2005. (Young Patriots Ser.: 10). (ENG.). 120p. (J). (gr. 4-7). 15.95 *(978-1-882859-47-4(2)*, Young Patriots Series) Patria Pr., Inc.

—Phillis Wheatley: Young Revolutionary Poet, 10 vols. Borland, Kathryn Kilby & Speicher, Helen Ross. 2nd rev. ed. 2005. (Young Patriots Ser.: 10). (ENG.). 120p. (J). (gr. 4-7). pap. 9.95 *(978-1-882859-48-1(0)*, Young Patriots Series) Patria Pr., Inc.

—Pitter & Patter. Sullivan, Martha. 2015. (ENG.). 32p. (J). (gr. k-4). pap. 8.95 *(978-1-58469-509-7(9))* Dawn Pubns.

Morrison, Cathy. Saint Thomas Aquinas: Missionary of Truth. Trouvé, Marianne Lorraine. 2015. (J). pap. 8.95 ***(978-0-8198-9026-9(X))*** Pauline Bks. & Media.

—This Land Is Your Land, 1 vol. Ciocchi, Catherine. 2015. (ENG.). 32p. (J). (gr. k-3). 17.95 ***(978-1-62855-557-8(2))*** Arbordale Publishing.

Morrison, Cathy. Three Little Beavers, 1 vol. Diehl, Jean Heilprin. 2012. (ENG.). 32p. (J). (gr. -1-3). 17.95 *(978-1-60718-524-6(5))*; pap. 9.95 *(978-1-60718-533-8(4))* Arbordale Publishing.

Morrison, Cathy. The Tortoise & Hare's Amazing Race, 1 vol. Berkes, Marianne. 2015. (ENG & SPA.). 32p. (J). (gr. k-3). 17.95 ***(978-1-62855-635-3(8))*** Arbordale Publishing.

Morrison, Cathy. Esta Tierra, Es Tu País. Morrison, Cathy. Ciocchi, Catherine. 2015. (ENG.). 32p. (J). (gr. k-3). pap. 9.95 ***(978-1-62855-575-2(0))*** Arbordale Publishing.

Morrison, Cathy. La Plantita Margarita, 1 vol. Morrison, Cathy. Berkes, Marianne Collins & Toth, Rosalyna. 2014. (SPA.). 32p. (J). (gr. -1-3). pap. 9.95 *(978-1-62855-224-9(7))* Arbordale Publishing.

Morrison, Connor, jt. illus. see Morrison, Cameron.

Morrison, Frank. Ballerina Dreams: From Orphan to Dancer. DePrince, Michaela & DePrince, Elaine. 2014. (Step into Reading Ser.). (ENG.). 48p. (J). (gr. 2-4). 3.99 *(978-0-385-75515-3(5)*, Random Hse. Bks. for Young Readers) Random Hse. Children's Bks.

—George Crum & the Saratoga Chip, 1 vol. Taylor, Gaylia. 2006. (ENG.). 32p. (J). (gr. 1-5). 16.95 *(978-1-58430-255-1(0))* Lee & Low Bks., Inc.

—I Got the Rhythm. Schofield-Morrison, Connie. 2014. (ENG.). 32p. (J). (gr. -1-1). 17.89 *(978-1-61963-179-3(2)*, Bloomsbury USA Childrens) Bloomsbury USA.

—I Got the Rhythm. Schofield-Morrison, Connie. 2014. (ENG.). 32p. (J). (gr. -1-1). 16.99 *(978-1-61963-178-6(4)*, Bloomsbury USA Childrens) Bloomsbury USA.

—Jonron! Rodriguez, Alex. 2007. (SPA.). 32p. (J). (gr. -1-3). 16.99 *(978-0-06-115197-2(1)*, Rayo) HarperCollins Pubs.

—Keena Ford & the Second-Grade Mix-Up. Thomson, Melissa. (Keena Ford Ser.). (ENG.). 112p. (J). (gr. 1-3). 2009. 5.99 *(978-0-14-241396-8(8)*, Puffin); 2008. 15.99 *(978-0-8037-3263-6(5)*, Dial) Penguin Publishing Group.

—Keena Ford & the Secret Journal Mix-Up. Thomson, Melissa. 2011. (Keena Ford Ser.). (ENG.). 128p. (J). (gr. 1-3). 5.99 *(978-0-14-241937-3(0)*, Puffin) Penguin Publishing Group.

—Little Melba & Her Big Trombone. Russell-Brown, Katheryn. 2014. (ENG.). 40p. (J). 18.95 *(978-1-60060-898-8(1))* Lee & Low Bks., Inc.

—Long Shot: Never Too Small to Dream Big. Paul, Chris. 2009. (ENG.). 32p. (J). (gr. -1-3). 16.99 *(978-1-4169-5079-0(6)*, Simon & Schuster Bks. For Young Readers) Simon & Schuster Bks. For Young Readers.

—Out of the Ballpark. Rodriguez, Alex. 32p. (J). (gr. -1-3). 2012. (ENG.). pap. 6.99 *(978-0-06-115196-5(3))*; 2007. 17.89 *(978-0-06-115195-8(5))*; 2007. (ENG.). 16.99 *(978-0-06-115194-1(7))* HarperCollins Pubs.

—Play, Louis, Play! The True Story of a Boy & His Horn. Weinstein, Muriel Harris. (ENG.). 112p. (J). (gr. 2-4). 2013. pap. 5.99 *(978-1-59990-994-3(4))*; 2010. 15.99 *(978-1-59990-375-0(X))* Bloomsbury USA. (Bloomsbury USA Childrens).

—Quacky Baseball. Abrahams, Peter. 2011. (ENG.). 32p. (J). (gr. -1-3). 16.99 *(978-0-06-122978-7(4))* HarperCollins Pubs.

—Queen of the Scene. Queen Latifah. 2006. 32p. (J). (gr. -1-3). 17.89 incl. audio compact disk *(978-0-06-077857-6(1)*, Geringer, Laura Book) HarperCollins Pubs.

—Shoebox Sam, 1 vol. Barrett, Mary Brigid. 2011. (ENG.). 32p. (J). 15.99 *(978-0-310-71549-8(0))* Zonderkidz.

—Stars in the Shadows: The Negro League All-Star Game of 1934. Smith, Charles R., Jr. 2012. (ENG.). 112p. (J). (gr. 3-7). 14.99 *(978-0-689-86638-8(0)*, Atheneum Bks. for Young Readers) Simon & Schuster Children's Publishing.

—Sweet Music in Harlem. Taylor, Debbie A. 2014. 32p. pap. 9.00 *(978-1-61003-220-9(9))* Center for the Collaborative Classroom.

Morrison, Gordon. Dinosaurs. Kricher, John C. 2nd ed. 2013. (Peterson Field Guide Color-In Bks.). (ENG.). 64p. (J). 8.95 *(978-0-544-03255-2(1))* Houghton Mifflin Harcourt Publishing Co.

Morrison, Gordon, jt. illus. see Peterson, Roger Tory.

Morrison, Jeff. Tony Stewart. Carney, Larry. PC Treasures Staff, ed. 2009. (Nascar Drivers Coloring/Sticker Book Ser.). (ENG.). 96p. (J). pap. 6.95 *(978-1-60072-166-3(4))* PC Treasures, Inc.

Morrison, Jeff, jt. illus. see Houghton, Chris.

Morrison, Nancy. Land of the Angels, 1 vol. Sylvester, Sr. 2009. 32p. pap. 24.95 *(978-1-60836-888-4(2))* America Star Bks.

—Talking Memories. Sylvester, Sr. 2011. 36p. pap. 24.95 *(978-1-4489-4967-0(X))* America Star Bks.

Morrison, Taylor. The Buffalo Nickel. Morrison, Taylor. 2006. 32p. (J). (gr. 4-8). reprint ed. 16.00 *(978-1-4223-5858-0(5))* DIANE Publishing Co.

Morrison, Tyler. Goofus & Other Silly Poems, 1 vol. Wilson, Murray. 2010. 28p. pap. 24.95 *(978-1-4489-6288-4(9))* PublishAmerica, Inc.

Morriss, Deborah & Morstad, Julie. The Swing. Andersen, Hans Christian & Stevenson, Robert Louis. 2012.Tr. of Nattergalen. (ENG.). 16p. (J). 8.95 *(978-1-897476-48-2(5))* Simply Read Bks. CAN. Dist: Ingram Pub. Services.

Morrissey, Bridgette. Cross Katie Kross. Morrissey, Donna. 2012. (ENG.). 32p. (J). (gr. 3-7). 17.00 *(978-0-670-06479-3(3)*, Penguin Global) Penguin Publishing Group.

Morrissey, Dean. The Crimson Comet. Morrissey, Dean. Krensky, Stephen. 2006. 32p. (J). (gr. k-4). 17.89 *(978-0-06-008070-9(1))* HarperCollins Pubs.

—The Monster Trap. Morrissey, Dean. Krensky, Stephen. 2004. 40p. (J). lib. bdg. 17.89 *(978-0-06-052499-9(5))* HarperCollins Pubs.

—The Wizard Mouse. Morrissey, Dean. Krensky, Stephen. 2011. (ENG.). 32p. (J). (gr. k-4). 16.99 *(978-0-06-008066-2(3))* HarperCollins Pubs.

Morrissey, Kay, jt. photos by see Carrillo, Azalea.

Morrissey, Kay, jt. photos by see Ramirez, Antonio.

Morrow, E. Moose Shoes. Petersen, Jean. 2007. 52p. per. 24.95 *(978-1-4241-8399-9(5))* America Star Bks.

Morrow, George. The Marvellous Land of Snergs. Wyke-Smith, E. A. 2006. (Dover Children's Classics Ser.). (ENG.). 224p. (gr. 3-12). per. 10.95 *(978-0-486-45255-5(7))* Dover Pubns., Inc.

Morrow, Glenn, jt. illus. see Frankfeldt, Gwen.

Morrow, Gray. Carl Ben Eielson: Young Alaskan Pilot. Myers, Hortense & Burnett, Ruth. 2011. 200p. 44.95 *(978-1-258-01949-5(3))* Literary Licensing, LLC.

Morrow, Gray, et al. Marvel Masterworks Vol. 6: Captain America. Lee, Stan. 2012. (ENG.). 280p. (J). (gr. -1-17). 59.99 *(978-0-7851-5875-2(8))* Marvel Worldwide, Inc.

Morrow, J. T. Claude Monet. Krieg, Katherine. 2014. (World's Greatest Artists Ser.). (ENG.). 24p. (J). (gr. 2-5). 28.50 *(978-1-62687-348-3(8)*, 207188) Child's World, Inc., The.

—The Constellation Cassiopeia: The Story of the Queen. Owings, Lisa. 2013. (Constellations Ser.). (ENG.). 32p. (J). (gr. 2-5). 29.93 *(978-1-62323-484-3(0)*, 206252) Child's World, Inc., The.

—The Constellation Draco: The Story of the Dragon. Zee, Amy Van. 2013. (Constellations Ser.). (ENG.). 32p. (J). (gr. 2-5). 29.93 *(978-1-62323-485-0(9)*, 206253) Child's World, Inc., The.

—The Constellation Hercules: The Story of the Hero. York, J. 2013. (Constellations Ser.). (ENG.). 32p. (J). (gr. 2-5). 29.93 *(978-1-62323-486-7(7)*, 206254) Child's World, Inc., The.

—The Constellation Orion: The Story of the Hunter. Ringstad, Arnold. 2013. (Constellations Ser.). (ENG.). 32p. (J). (gr. 2-5). 29.93 *(978-1-62323-487-4(5)*, 206255) Child's World, Inc., The.

—The Constellation Scorpius: The Story of the Scorpion. Ringstad, Arnold. 2013. (Constellations Ser.). (ENG.). 32p. (J). (gr. 2-5). 29.93 *(978-1-62323-488-1(3)*, 206251) Child's World, Inc., The.

—The Constellation Taurus: The Story of the Bull. Ringstad, Arnold. 2013. (Constellations Ser.). (ENG.). 32p. (J). (gr. 2-5). 29.93 *(978-1-62323-483-6(2)*, 206256) Child's World, Inc., The.

—The Constellation Ursa Major: The Story of the Big Bear. Owings, Lisa. 2013. (Constellations Ser.). (ENG.). 32p. (J). (gr. 2-5). 29.93 *(978-1-62323-489-8(1)*, 206257) Child's World, Inc., The.

—The Constellation Ursa Minor: The Story of the Little Bear. Owings, Lisa. 2013. (Constellations Ser.). (ENG.). 32p. (J). (gr. 2-5). 29.93 *(978-1-62323-490-4(5)*, 206258) Child's World, Inc., The.

—Edgar Degas. Cernak, Linda. 2014. (World's Greatest Artists Ser.). (ENG.). 24p. (J). (gr. 2-5). 28.50 *(978-1-62687-349-0(6)*, 207189) Child's World, Inc., The.

—Issun Boshi (One-Inch Boy) A Japanese Folktale. Higgins, Nadia. 2011. (Folktales from Around the World Ser.). (ENG.). 24p. (J). (gr. k-3). 28.50 *(978-1-60973-139-7(5)*, 201143) Child's World, Inc., The.

—Leonardo Da Vinci. Cernak, Linda. 2014. (World's Greatest Artists Ser.). (ENG.). 24p. (J). (gr. 2-5). 28.50 *(978-1-62687-351-3(8)*, 207191) Child's World, Inc., The.

—Mary Cassatt. Cernak, Linda. 2014. (World's Greatest Artists Ser.). (ENG.). 24p. (J). (gr. 2-5). 28.50 *(978-1-62687-350-6(X)*, 207190) Child's World, Inc., The.

—Michelangelo. Bailer, Darice. 2014. (World's Greatest Artists Ser.). (ENG.). 24p. (J). (gr. 2-5). 28.50 *(978-1-62687-352-0(6)*, 207192) Child's World, Inc., The.

—Pablo Picasso. Bailer, Darice. 2014. (World's Greatest Artists Ser.). (ENG.). 24p. (J). (gr. 2-5). 28.50 *(978-1-62687-353-7(4)*, 207193) Child's World, Inc., The.

—Rembrandt. Bailer, Darice. 2014. (World's Greatest Artists Ser.). (ENG.). 24p. (J). (gr. 2-5). 28.50 *(978-1-62687-354-4(2)*, 207194) Child's World, Inc., The.

—Vincent Van Gogh. Cernak, Linda. 2014. (World's Greatest Artists Ser.). (ENG.). 24p. (J). (gr. 2-5). 28.50 *(978-1-62687-355-1(0)*, 207195) Child's World, Inc., The.

Morrow, J. T., jt. illus. see Rohrbach, Sophie.

Morrow, Jason. One Can Never Have Too Many Cats!! Lashley, Beverly. 2006. (J). *(978-0-9786835-0-4(1))* Two Tired Teachers Connection, Inc., The.

Morrow, Jt, jt. illus. see Rohrbach, Sophie.

Morse, Dorothy Bayley. Boy of the Pyramids: A Mystery of Ancient Egypt. Jones, Ruth Fosdick. 2011. 150p. 40.95 *(978-1-258-06798-4(6))* Literary Licensing, LLC.

Morse, Joe. Casey at the Bat. Thayer, Ernest L. 2010. (Visions in Poetry Ser.). (ENG.). 48p. (YA). pap. 9.95 *(978-1-55453-458-6(5))* Kids Can Pr., Ltd. CAN. Dist: Univ. of Toronto Pr.

—Hoop Genius: How a Desperate Teacher & a Rowdy Gym Class Invented Basketball. Coy, John. 2013. (ENG.). 32p. (J). (gr. 2-5). lib. bdg. 16.95 *(978-0-7613-6617-1(2)*, Carolrhoda Bks.) Lerner Publishing Group.

—Play Ball, Jackie! Krensky, Stephen. 2011. (Single Titles Ser.). (ENG.). 32p. (J). (gr. 2-5). lib. bdg. 16.95 *(978-0-8225-9030-9(1)*, Millbrook Pr.) Lerner Publishing Group.

Morse, Michelle. Captain Courage & the Fear-Squishing Shoes. Marshall, Stacey A. 2012. 16p. pap. 9.95 *(978-1-61633-319-5(7))* Guardian Angel Publishing, Inc.

—Captain Courage & the World's Most Shocking Secret Book 2. Marshall, Stacey A. 2013. 24p. 19.95 *(978-1-61633-431-4(2))* Guardian Angel Publishing, Inc.

—Emily, the Brave. McDuke, Doc. 2010. 20p. pap. 10.95 *(978-1-61633-065-1(1))* Guardian Angel Publishing, Inc.

Morse, Nessa Neilson. Lights of Imani. St. James, Leah. 2013. 28p. pap. 9.99 *(978-0-9853123-6-7(X))* Allen, Edward Publishing, LLC.

Morse, Patti. Tales of Zoftic. MacVicar, Andrea. 2007. 58p. (J). per. 16.95 *(978-0-9798395-0-4(5))* Inspiration Pr. Inc.

Morse, Scott. Magic Pickle. Morse, Scott. 2008. (Magic Pickle Ser.). (ENG.). 112p. (J). (gr. 2-5). pap. 9.99 *(978-0-439-87995-8(7)*, Graphix) Scholastic, Inc.

Morse, Tony. Armful of Memories. Honigsberg, Peter Jan. 2004. 32p. 17.95 *(978-1-57143-089-2(X))* RDR Bks.

—Pillow of Dreams. Honigsberg, Peter Jan. 2004. 32p. (gr. k-4). 17.95 *(978-1-57143-076-2(8))* RDR Bks.

Morstad, Julie. Beyond the Laughing Sky. Cuevas, Michelle. 2014. (ENG.). 160p. (J). (gr. 3-7). 16.99 *(978-0-8037-3867-6(6)*, Dial) Penguin Publishing Group.

—Julia, Child. 2014. (ENG.). 32p. (J). (gr. k-12). 17.99 *(978-1-77049-449-7(9))* Tundra Bks. CAN. Dist: Random Hse., Inc.

—Singing Away the Dark. Woodward, Caroline. 2011. (ENG.). 36p. (J). (gr. -1-3). 16.95 *(978-1-897476-41-3(8))* Simply Read Bks. CAN. Dist: Ingram Pub. Services.

—Swan: The Life & Dance of Anna Pavlova. Snyder, Laurel. 2015. (ENG.). 52p. (J). (gr. 1-4). 17.99 *(978-1-4521-1890-1(6))* Chronicle Bks. LLC.

—Think Again. Lawson, JonArno. 2010. (ENG.). 64p. (J). (gr. 5-18). 16.95 *(978-1-55453-423-4(2))* Kids Can Pr., Ltd. CAN. Dist: Univ. of Toronto Pr.

—This Is Sadie. O'Leary, Sara. 2015. (Sadie Mac Ser.). (ENG.). 32p. (J). (gr. -1-2). 17.99 *(978-1-77049-532-6(0))* Tundra Bks. CAN. Dist: Penguin Random Hse., LLC.

—When I Was Small. O'Leary, Sara. 2012. (ENG.). 32p. (J). (gr. -1-3). 16.95 *(978-1-897476-38-3(8))* Simply Read Bks. CAN. Dist: Ingram Pub. Services.

—When You Were Small. O'Leary, Sara. 2006. (ENG.). 32p. (J). (gr. -1-3). 16.95 *(978-1-894965-36-1(1))* Simply Read Bks. CAN. Dist: Ingram Pub. Services.

—Where You Came From. O'Leary, Sara. 2008. (ENG.). 32p. (J). (gr. -1-3). 16.95 *(978-1-894965-46-0(9))* Simply Read Bks. CAN. Dist: Ingram Pub. Services.

—Zingy. O'Leary, Sara & Opal, Paola. 2013. (Simply Small Ser.: 10). (ENG.). 24p. (J). (gr. k — 1). bds. 7.95 *(978-1-897476-75-8(2))* Simply Read Bks. CAN. Dist: Ingram Pub. Services.

Morstad, Julie. How To. Morstad, Julie. 2013. (ENG.). 36p. (J). (gr. -1-3). 16.95 *(978-1-897476-57-4(4))* Simply Read Bks. CAN. Dist: Ingram Pub. Services.

Morstad, Julie, jt. illus. see Morriss, Deborah.

Mortensen, Carl. Flea & Gang & the Tube Dogs. Mortensen, Carl. 2009. 16p. pap. 11.95 *(978-1-4251-8657-9(2))* Trafford Publishing.

Mortensen, Lyn. Effie May & Her Outrageous Hats. Mortensen, Lyn. 2006. (J). per. *(978-0-9767570-1-6(X))* Whitegate Bks.

—My Favorite Flower Is the Daisy... & other Silly Poems. Mortensen, Lyn. 2005. 48p. (J). per. *(978-0-9767570-0-9(1))* Whitegate Bks.

Mortimer, Alexander. Pick-a-WooWoo - KC the Conscious Camel: A furry jaunt to peace & Contentment. McRae, Suzanne. 12th ed. 2010. 32p. pap. *(978-0-9806520-3-1(0))* Pick-a-Woo Woo Pubs.

Mortimer, Anne. The Chocolate Cat. Stainton, Sue. 2007. 32p. (J). (gr. -1-3). 17.89 *(978-0-06-057246-4(9))* HarperCollins Pubs.

—The Lighthouse Cat. Stainton, Sue. 2004. (ENG.). 32p. (J). (gr. -1-2). 16.99 *(978-0-06-009604-5(7)*, Tegen, Katherine Bks) HarperCollins Pubs.

—The Owl & the Pussycat. Lear, Edward & Mortimer. 2006. (ENG.). 32p. (J). (gr. -1-4). 16.99 *(978-0-06-027228-9(7)*, Tegen, Katherine Bks) HarperCollins Pubs.

—A Pussycat's Christmas. Brown, Margaret Wise. 2009. (ENG.). 32p. (J). (gr. k-4). 9.99 *(978-0-06-186978-5(3)*, Tegen, Katherine Bks) HarperCollins Pubs.

—Sneakers, the Seaside Cat. Brown, Margaret Wise. 2005. (ENG.). 32p. (J). (gr. -1-3). pap. 6.99 *(978-0-06-443622-9(5))* HarperCollins Pubs.

Mortimer, Anne. Bunny's Easter Egg. Mortimer, Anne. 2010. (ENG.). 32p. (J). (gr. -1-2). 12.99 *(978-0-06-136664-2(1),* Tegen, Katherine Bks) HarperCollins Pubs.
—Christmas Mouse. Mortimer, Anne. 2013. (ENG.). 24p. (J). (gr. -1-3). 12.99 *(978-0-06-208928-1(5),* Tegen, Katherine Bks) HarperCollins Pubs.
—Pumpkin Cat. Mortimer, Anne. 2011. (ENG.). 24p. (J). (gr. -1-2). 14.99 *(978-0-06-187485-7(X),* Tegen, Katherine Bks) HarperCollins Pubs.
Mortimer, Lauren & Bennett, James. What Was the Boston Tea Party? Krull, Kathleen. 2013. (What Was... ? Ser.). (ENG.). (J). (gr. 3-7). 128p. 15.99 *(978-0-448-46576-0(0));* 112p. pap. 5.99 *(978-0-448-46288-2(5))* Penguin Publishing Group. (Grosset & Dunlap).
—What Was the Underground Railroad? McDonough, Yona Zeldis. 2013. (What Was... ? Ser.). (ENG.). 112p. (J). (gr. 3-7). 5.99 *(978-0-448-46712-2(7),* Grosset & Dunlap) Penguin Publishing Group.
Mortimer, Mitch. Ideas. Spiegel, Al. 2003. 32p. (J). lib. bdg. 13.99 *(978-0-9743553-0-6(5))* Crazy Man Press, LLC.
Morton, Ken. Cinderella. 2012. (ENG.). 24p. (J). (gr. -1-12). 5.99 *(978-1-84322-803-5(3))* Anness Publishing GBR. Dist: National Bk. Network.
—The Gingerbread Man (Floor Book) My First Reading Book. Brown, Janet. 2013. (ENG.). 24p. (J). (gr. -1-2). pap. 6.99 *(978-1-84322-900-1(5),* Armadillo) Anness Publishing GBR. Dist: National Bk. Network.
—Goldilocks & the Three Bears. 2012. (ENG.). 24p. (J). (gr. -1-12). 5.99 *(978-1-84322-838-7(6))* Anness Publishing GBR. Dist: National Bk. Network.
—Goldilocks & the Three Bears (Floor Book) My First Reading Book. Brown, Janet. 2013. (ENG.). 24p. (J). (gr. -1-2). pap. 6.99 *(978-1-84322-901-8(3),* Armadillo) Anness Publishing GBR. Dist: National Bk. Network.
—Hansel & Gretel: My First Reading Book. Brown, Janet. 2013. (ENG.). 24p. (J). (gr. -1-4). 5.99 *(978-1-84322-737-3(1),* Armadillo) Anness Publishing GBR. Dist: National Bk. Network.
—Jack & the Beanstalk: My First Reading Book. Brown, Janet. (ENG.). 24p. 2015. pap. 6.99 *(978-1-86147-474-2(1));* 2013. (J). (gr. -1-4). 5.99 *(978-1-84322-738-0(X))* Anness Publishing GBR. (Armadillo). Dist: National Bk. Network.
—Pinocchio: My First Reading Book. Brown, Janet. 2015. (ENG.). 24p. pap. 6.99 *(978-1-86147-475-9(X),* Armadillo) Anness Publishing GBR. Dist: National Bk. Network.
—Puss in Boots. Brown, Janet. 2012. (ENG.). 24p. (J). (gr. -1-12). 5.99 *(978-1-84322-848-6(3))* Anness Publishing GBR. Dist: National Bk. Network.
—Puss in Boots (Floor Book) My First Reading Book. Brown, Janet. 2013. (ENG.). 24p. (J). (gr. -1-2). pap. 6.99 *(978-1-84322-902-5(1),* Armadillo) Anness Publishing GBR. Dist: National Bk. Network.
—Red Riding Hood (Floor Book) My First Reading Book. Brown, Janet. 2015. (ENG.). 24p. (J). (gr. -1-1). pap. 6.99 *(978-1-86147-399-8(0),* Armadillo) Anness Publishing GBR. Dist: National Bk. Network.
—Snow White & the Seven Dwarves. Brown, Janet. 2012. (ENG.). 24p. (J). (gr. -1-12). 5.99 *(978-1-84322-850-9(5))* Anness Publishing GBR. Dist: National Bk. Network.
—Snow White & the Seven Dwarves (Floor Book) My First Reading Book. Brown, Janet. 2013. (ENG.). 30p. (J). (gr. -1-2). pap. 6.99 *(978-1-84322-903-2(X),* Armadillo) Anness Publishing GBR. Dist: National Bk. Network.
—The Three Billy Goats Gruff: My First Reading Book. 2013. (ENG.). 24p. 5.99 *(978-1-84322-832-5(7),* Armadillo) Anness Publishing GBR. Dist: National Bk. Network.
—The Three Billy Goats Gruff (Floor Book) Brown, Janet. 2015. (ENG.). 24p. (J). (gr. -1-1). pap. 6.99 *(978-1-86147-397-4(4),* Armadillo) Anness Publishing GBR. Dist: National Bk. Network.
—Three Little Pigs. Brown, Janet. 2012. (ENG.). 24p. (J). (gr. -1-12). 5.99 *(978-1-84322-813-4(0))* Anness Publishing GBR. Dist: National Bk. Network.
—Three Little Pigs (Floor Book) My First Reading Book. Brown, Janet. 2015. (ENG.). 24p. (J). (gr. -1-1). pap. 6.99 *(978-1-86147-396-7(6),* Armadillo) Anness Publishing GBR. Dist: National Bk. Network.
—The Ugly Duckling. Brown, Janet. 2012. (ENG.). 24p. (J). (gr. -1-12). 5.99 *(978-1-84322-851-6(3))* Anness Publishing GBR. Dist: National Bk. Network.
—The Ugly Duckling (Floor Book) My First Reading Book. Brown, Janet. 2015. (ENG.). 24p. (J). (gr. -1-1). pap. 6.99 *(978-1-86147-398-1(2),* Armadillo) Anness Publishing GBR. Dist: National Bk. Network.
—Witches, Wizards & Magicians. Baxter, Nicola. 2012. (ENG.). 80p. (J). (gr. k-4). pap. 9.99 *(978-1-84322-807-3(6))* Anness Publishing GBR. Dist: National Bk. Network.
Morton, Ken, jt. illus. see Brown, Janet.
Morton, Lisa. The Girl & the Mirror. Monnar, Alberto. Weiner, Linda, ed. 2008. per. 14.99 *(978-0-9768035-8-4(5))* Readers Are Leaders U.S.A., Inc.
Morton, Robert, et al. Why Do Tigers Have Stripes? Unwin, Mike. 2006. (Usborne Starting Point Science Ser.). 22p. (J). (gr. 1-4). pap. 4.99 *(978-0-7945-1408-2(1),* Usborne) EDC Publishing.
Morton, Robert. Why Do Tigers Have Stripes? Unwin, Mike. 2006. (Usborne Starting Point Science Ser.). 22p. (J). (gr. 1). lib. bdg. 12.99 *(978-1-58086-939-3(4),* Usborne) EDC Publishing.
Morton, Vivian. Power Reading: Nail-Biters! 2. Cole, Bob. 2005. 94p. (J). (gr. 6-18). vinyl bd. 89.95 *(978-1-883186-25-8(0),* PPNB2) National Reading Styles Institute, Inc.
Moscal, Manuela. The Unseen Paths of the Forest: 13 Tales about Love & Friendship. Panaitescu, Simona. 2012. (ENG.). 263p. pap. 14.95 *(978-1-4327-7908-5(7))* Outskirts Pr., Inc.
Mosedale, Julian. Bungleman. Strong, Jeremy. 2007. (Collins Big Cat Ser.). (ENG.). 32p. (J). pap. 8.99 *(978-0-00-723083-9(4))* HarperCollins Pubs. Ltd. GBR. Dist: Independent Pubs. Group.
—Mojo & Weeza & the New Hat: Band 04/Blue. Taylor, Sean. 2007. (Collins Big Cat Ser.). (ENG.). 16p. (J). pap. 5.99 *(978-0-00-718662-4(2))* HarperCollins Pubs. Ltd. GBR. Dist: Independent Pubs. Group.
Mosedale, Julian. Our Head Teacher Is a Super-Villain. Donbavand, Tommy & Harpercollins Staff. 2015. (Collins Big Cat Ser.). (ENG.). 32p. pap. 7.95 ***(978-0-00-759122-0(5))*** HarperCollins Pubs. Ltd. GBR. Dist: Independent Pubs. Group.
Moseley, Dudley. Pop-Up Bible Adventures. Dowley, Tim. 12p. (J). (gr. k-2). 2005. bds. 11.99 *(978-0-8254-7298-5(9));* 2. 2007. 11.99 *(978-0-8254-7328-9(4))* Lion Hudson PLC GBR. (Candle Bks.). Dist: Kregel Pubns.
Moseley, Keith. Where's the Knight? 2013. (Where's The ... ? Ser.). (ENG.). 24p. (J). 14.95 *(978-1-4027-8897-0(5))* Sterling Publishing Co., Inc.
Moseley, Rachel. Jordan & the Dreadful Golem. Goldman, Karen. 2013. (ENG.). 224p. (J). (gr. 4-7). 15.95 *(978-0-9838685-2-1(2))* Penlight Pubns.
Moseng, Elisabeth. Soccer Beat. Brug, Sandra Gilbert. 2012. (ENG.). 32p. (J). (gr. -1-1). 16.99 *(978-1-4424-8610-2(4),* McElderry, Margaret K. Bks.) McElderry, Margaret K. Bks.
Moser, Barry. The Blessing of the Beasts. Pochocki, Ethel. 2014. (ENG.). 40p. (J). pap. 15.99 *(978-1-61261-582-0(1))* Paraclete Pr., Inc.
—The Blessing of the Beasts. Pochocki, Ethel & Helms, Hal M. 2007. (ENG.). 40p. (J). (gr. -1-3). 18.95 *(978-1-55725-502-0(4))* Paraclete Pr., Inc.
—The Call of the Wild. London, Jack. 2011. (ENG.). 144p. (J). (gr. 4-9). pap. 8.99 *(978-1-4424-3411-0(2),* Simon & Schuster Bks. For Young Readers) Simon & Schuster Bks. For Young Readers.
—Cat Talk. MacLachlan, Patricia & Charest, Emily MacLachlan. 2013. 32p. (J). (gr. -1-3). (ENG.). 17.99 *(978-0-06-027978-3(8));* lib. bdg. 18.89 *(978-0-06-027979-0(6))* HarperCollins Pubs. (Tegen, Katherine Bks).
—The Cheshire Cheese Cat: A Dickens of a Tale, 1 vol. Deedy, Carmen Agra & Wright, Randall. 2011. (ENG.). 256p. (J). 16.95 *(978-1-56145-595-9(4))* Peachtree Pubs.
—Earthquack! Palatini, Margie. 2005. (ENG.). 32p. (J). (gr. -1-3). 7.99 *(978-1-4169-0260-7(0),* Simon & Schuster Bks. For Young Readers) Simon & Schuster Bks. For Young Readers.
—Franklin & Winston: A Christmas That Changed the World. Wood, Douglas. 2011. (ENG.). 40p. (J). (gr. 1-4). 16.99 *(978-0-7636-3383-7(6))* Candlewick Pr.
—I Can Make a Difference: A Treasury to Inspire Our Children. Edelman, Marian Wright & Edelman, Marian W. 2005. (ENG.). 112p. (J). (gr. 3-7). 21.99 *(978-0-06-028051-2(4),* Amistad) HarperCollins Pubs.
—Jack London's Dog. Wales, Dirk. 2008. 64p. (YA). (gr. 5-9). 17.95 *(978-0-9632459-3-9(7))* Great Plains Pr.
—Lousy Rotten Stinkin' Grapes. Palatini, Margie. 2009. (ENG.). 32p. (J). (gr. -1-3). 17.99 *(978-0-689-80246-1(3),* Simon & Schuster Bks. For Young Readers) Simon & Schuster Bks. For Young Readers.
—Oh, Harry! Kumin, Maxine. 2011. (ENG.). 32p. (J). (gr. -1-3). 16.99 *(978-1-59643-439-4(2))* Roaring Brook Pr.
—Once upon a Twice. Doyen, Denise. 2013. (Picture Book Ser.). (ENG.). 32p. (J). (gr. -1-2). pap. 7.99 *(978-0-449-81794-0(6),* Dragonfly Bks.) Random Hse. Children's Bks.
—One Small Garden. Nichol, Barbara. 2004. (ENG.). 56p. (J). (gr. 3-7). pap. 9.95 *(978-0-88776-687-9(0),* Tundra Bks.) Tundra Bks. CAN. Dist: Penguin Random Hse., LLC.
—Pilgrim's Progress. Schmidt, Gary D. 2008. 189p. (YA). (gr. 4-18). 16.50 *(978-0-8028-5346-2(3))* Eerdmans, William B. Publishing Co.
—The Pomegranate Witch. Doyen, Denise. 2013. (J). *(978-0-375-87057-6(1));* lib. bdg. *(978-0-375-97057-3(6))* Random Hse., Inc.
—Prairie Days. MacLachlan, Patricia. 2014. (J). *(978-1-4424-4191-0(7),* McElderry, Margaret K. Bks.) McElderry, Margaret K. Bks.
—The Three Silly Billies. Palatini, Margie. 2005. (ENG.). 32p. (J). (gr. -1-3). 17.99 *(978-0-689-85862-8(0),* Simon & Schuster Bks. For Young Readers) Simon & Schuster Bks. For Young Readers.
—Voices of Ancient Egypt. Winters, Kay. 2003. (ENG.). 32p. (J). (gr. 3-7). 16.95 *(978-0-7922-7560-2(8))* National Geographic Society.
Moser, Barry & Maser, Barry. Scary Stories. 2006. (ENG.). 184p. (J). (gr. 7-17). 16.95 *(978-0-8118-5414-6(0),* SeaStar Bks.) Chronicle Bks. LLC.
Moser, Barry & Moser, Cara. Sit, Truman! Harper, Dan. 2004. (ENG.). 32p. (J). (gr. -1-3). reprint ed. pap. 6.99 *(978-0-15-205068-9(X))* Houghton Mifflin Harcourt Publishing Co.
Moser, Cara, jt. illus. see Moser, Barry.
Moser, Chris & Moser, Liz. The Discoveries of Shuggs, A Curious Cat. Moser, Chris & Moser, Liz. 2011. (J). pap. 10.95 *(978-0-9842881-9-9(8))* Capital City Bks. LLC.
Moser, Liz, jt. illus. see Moser, Chris.
Moses, Grandma. The Night Before Christmas. 2007. (ENG.). 32p. (J). (gr. k-4). 17.95 *(978-0-7893-1568-7(8))* Universe Publishing.
—A Prayer in Spring. Frost, Robert. 2013. (ENG.). 32p. (J). (gr. 2-5). 7.98 *(978-0-7893-2481-8(4),* Rizzoli Universe Promotional Bks.) Rizzoli International Pubns., Inc.
Moses, Will. Hansel & Gretel. Moses, Will. 2006. (ENG.). 40p. (J). (gr. -1-3). 17.99 *(978-0-399-24234-2(1),* Philomel) Penguin Publishing Group.
—Mary & Her Little Lamb: The True Story of Famous Nursery Rhyme. Moses, Will. 2011. (ENG.). 40p. (J). (gr. k-3). 17.99 *(978-0-399-25154-2(5),* Philomel) Penguin Publishing Group.
—Raining Cats & Dogs: A Collection of Irresistible Idioms & Illustrations to Tickle the Funny Bones. Moses, Will. 2008. (ENG.). 40p. (J). (gr. k-3). 17.99 *(978-0-399-24233-5(3),* Philomel) Penguin Publishing Group.
—Will Moses' Mother Goose. Moses, Will. (ENG.). (J). (gr. -1-k). 2012. 28p. bds. 6.99 *(978-0-399-16109-4(0));* 2003. 64p. 18.99 *(978-0-399-23744-7(5))* Penguin Publishing Group. (Philomel).
Mosher, Barry. The Mushroom Man. Pochocki, Ethel. 2006. 26p. (J). (gr. 3-7). reprint ed. *(978-0-88448-278-9(2))* Tilbury Hse. Pubs.
Mosher, Scott, jt. illus. see Tucker, Lewis R.
Mosier, Scott & Son, Eugene. Marvel Universe Ultimate Spider-Man Volume 6. 2014. (ENG.). 88p. (J). (gr. -1-17). pap. 9.99 *(978-0-7851-8815-5(0))* Marvel Worldwide, Inc.
Mosqueda, Olga, jt. illus. see Disney Storybook Art Team.
Mosqueda, Olga, jt. illus. see Disney Storybook Artists Staff.
Mosqueda, Olga T. & Tucker, Marianne. Learn to Draw Plus Disney Winnie the Pooh. 2012. (J). *(978-1-936309-68-9(8))* Quarto Publishing Group USA.
Mosquito, Angel. Werewolves & States of Matter, 1 vol. Slingerland, Janet. 2011. (Monster Science Ser.). (ENG.). 32p. (gr. 3-4). pap. 8.10 *(978-1-4296-7333-4(8));* pap. 47.70 *(978-1-4296-7334-1(6));* lib. bdg. 29.99 *(978-1-4296-6578-0(5))* Capstone Pr., Inc. (Graphic Library).
Moss, Marissa. Mira's Diary: Bombs over London. 2014. (ENG.). 190p. (J). (gr. 2-8). 12.99 *(978-1-939547-12-5(1))* Creston Bks.
Moss, Marissa. Alien Eraser Reveals the Secret of Evolution. Moss, Marissa. 2009. (ENG.). 56p. (J). (gr. 3-7). pap. 6.99 *(978-0-7636-4419-2(6));* (Max Disaster Ser.: Bk. 3). 15.99 *(978-0-7636-3579-4(0))* Candlewick Pr.
—Alien Eraser to the Rescue. Moss, Marissa. 2009. (Max Disaster Ser.: No. 1). (ENG.). 56p. (J). (gr. 3-7). pap. 6.99 *(978-0-7636-4407-9(2))* Candlewick Pr.
—The All-New Amelia. Moss, Marissa. (ENG.). (J). 2013. 5.99 *(978-1-4169-1289-7(4));* 2007. 40p. (gr. 2-5). 12.99 *(978-1-4169-0908-8(7))* Simon & Schuster/Paula Wiseman Bks. (Simon & Schuster/Paula Wiseman Bks.).
—Amelia Tells All. Moss, Marissa. 2007. (Amelia Ser.). (ENG.). 64p. (J). (gr. 2-5). 9.99 *(978-1-4169-0918-7(4),* Simon & Schuster/Paula Wiseman Bks.) Simon & Schuster/Paula Wiseman Bks.
—Amelia Writes Again. Moss, Marissa. (Amelia Ser.). (ENG.). (J). (gr. 2-5). 2012. 32p. pap. 6.99 *(978-1-4169-1285-9(1));* 2006. 40p. 12.99 *(978-1-4169-0904-0(4))* Simon & Schuster/Paula Wiseman Bks. (Simon & Schuster/Paula Wiseman Bks.).
—Amelia's 5th-Grade Notebook. Moss, Marissa. 2006. (Amelia Ser.). (ENG.). (J). 5.99 *(978-1-4169-1292-7(4));* 40p. (gr. 2-5). 12.99 *(978-1-4169-0912-5(5))* Simon & Schuster/Paula Wiseman Bks. (Simon & Schuster/Paula Wiseman Bks.).
—Amelia's 6th-Grade Notebook. Moss, Marissa. 2005. (Amelia Ser.). (ENG.). 80p. (J). (gr. 4-7). 12.99 *(978-0-689-87040-8(X),* Simon & Schuster/Paula Wiseman Bks.) Simon & Schuster/Paula Wiseman Bks.
—Amelia's 7th-Grade Notebook. Moss, Marissa. 2007. (Amelia Ser.). (ENG.). 80p. (J). (gr. 5-8). 12.99 *(978-1-4169-3661-9(0),* Simon & Schuster/Paula Wiseman Bks.) Simon & Schuster/Paula Wiseman Bks.
—Amelia's Are-We-There-Yet Longest Ever Car Trip. Moss, Marissa. (Amelia Ser.). (ENG.). 40p. (J). (gr. 2-5). 2012. pap. 6.99 *(978-1-4169-1287-3(8));* 2006. 10.99 *(978-1-4169-0906-4(0))* Simon & Schuster/Paula Wiseman Bks. (Simon & Schuster/Paula Wiseman Bks.).
—Amelia's Back-to-School Survival Guide: Vote 4 Amelia - Amelia's Guide to Babysitting. Moss, Marissa. 2012. (Amelia Ser.). (ENG.). 160p. (J). (gr. 5-8). 12.99 *(978-1-4424-4349-5(9),* Simon & Schuster/Paula Wiseman Bks.) Simon & Schuster/Paula Wiseman Bks.
—Amelia's BFF. Moss, Marissa. 2011. (Amelia Ser.). (ENG.). 64p. (J). (gr. 5-8). 9.99 *(978-1-4424-0376-5(4),* Simon & Schuster/Paula Wiseman Bks.) Simon & Schuster/Paula Wiseman Bks.
—Amelia's Book of Notes & Note Passing. Moss, Marissa. 2006. (Amelia Ser.). (ENG.). 80p. (J). (gr. 4-7). 9.95 *(978-0-689-87446-8(4),* Simon & Schuster/Paula Wiseman Bks.) Simon & Schuster/Paula Wiseman Bks.
—Amelia's Boredom Survival Guide. Moss, Marissa. (Amelia Ser.). (ENG.). 64p. (J). (gr. 2-5). 2013. pap. 6.99 *(978-1-4424-8369-9(5));* 2006. 12.99 *(978-1-4169-0916-3(8))* Simon & Schuster/Paula Wiseman Bks. (Simon & Schuster/Paula Wiseman Bks.).
—Amelia's Boy Survival Guide. Moss, Marissa. 2012. (Amelia Ser.). (ENG.). 80p. (J). (gr. 4-8). 9.99 *(978-1-4424-4084-5(8),* Simon & Schuster/Paula Wiseman Bks.) Simon & Schuster/Paula Wiseman Bks.
—Amelia's Bully Survival Guide. Moss, Marissa. (Amelia Ser.). (ENG.). 40p. (J). (gr. 2-5). 2012. pap. 6.99 *(978-1-4169-1288-0(6));* 2006. 9.95 *(978-1-4169-0907-1(9))* Simon & Schuster/Paula Wiseman Bks. (Simon & Schuster/Paula Wiseman Bks.).
—Amelia's Cross-My-Heart, Hope-to-Die Guide to the Real, True You! Moss, Marissa. 2010. (Amelia Ser.). (ENG.). 64p. (J). (gr. 5-8). bds. 9.99 *(978-1-4169-8710-9(X),* Simon & Schuster/Paula Wiseman Bks.) Simon & Schuster/Paula Wiseman Bks.
—Amelia's Family Ties. Moss, Marissa. 2013. (Amelia Ser.). (ENG.). (J). 5.99 *(978-1-4169-1293-4(2),* Simon & Schuster/Paula Wiseman Bks.) Simon & Schuster/Paula Wiseman Bks.
—Amelia's Guide to Babysitting. Moss, Marissa. 2008. (Amelia Ser.). (ENG.). 80p. (J). (gr. 5-8). 9.99 *(978-1-4169-5051-6(6),* Simon & Schuster/Paula Wiseman Bks.) Simon & Schuster/Paula Wiseman Bks.
—Amelia's Guide to Gossip: The Good, the Bad, & the Ugly. Moss, Marissa. 2006. (Amelia Ser.). (ENG.). 80p. (J). (gr. 5-8). 9.95 *(978-1-4169-1475-4(7),* Simon & Schuster/Paula Wiseman Bks.) Simon & Schuster/Paula Wiseman Bks.
—Amelia's Itchy-Twitchy, Lovey-Dovey Summer at Camp Mosquito. Moss, Marissa. 2008. (Amelia Ser.). (ENG.). 80p. (J). (gr. 5-8). 12.99 *(978-1-4169-4722-6(1),* Simon & Schuster/Paula Wiseman Bks.) Simon & Schuster/Paula Wiseman Bks.
—Amelia's Longest, Biggest, Most-Fights-Ever Family Reunion. Moss, Marissa. 2006. (Amelia Ser.). (ENG.). 80p. (J). (gr. 4-7). 12.99 *(978-0-689-87447-5(2),* Simon & Schuster/Paula Wiseman Bks.) Simon & Schuster/Paula Wiseman Bks.
—Amelia's Middle School Survival Guide: Amelia's Most Unforgettable Embarrassing Moments, Amelia's Guide to Gossip. Moss, Marissa. 2009. (Amelia Ser.). (ENG.). 160p. (J). (gr. 5-8). 14.99 *(978-1-4169-7987-6(5),* Simon & Schuster/Paula Wiseman Bks.) Simon & Schuster/Paula Wiseman Bks.
—Amelia's Most Unforgettable Embarrassing Moments. Moss, Marissa. 2005. (Amelia Ser.). (ENG.). 80p. (J). (gr. 4-7). 12.99 *(978-0-689-87041-5(8),* Simon & Schuster/Paula Wiseman Bks.) Simon & Schuster/Paula Wiseman Bks.
—Amelia's Must-Keep Resolutions for the Best Year Ever! Moss, Marissa. 2006. (Amelia Ser.). (ENG.). 40p. (J). (gr. 4-7). 12.99 *(978-1-4169-3361-8(1),* Simon & Schuster/Paula Wiseman Bks.) Simon & Schuster/Paula Wiseman Bks.
—Amelia's Notebook. Moss, Marissa. 2006. (Amelia Ser.). (ENG.). (J). 5.99 *(978-1-4169-1286-6(X));* 40p. (gr. 2-5). 12.99 *(978-1-4169-0905-7(2))* Simon & Schuster/Paula Wiseman Bks. (Simon & Schuster/Paula Wiseman Bks.).
—Amelia's School Survival Guide. Moss, Marissa. 2006. (Amelia Ser.). (ENG.). 64p. (J). (gr. 2-5). 12.99 *(978-1-4169-0915-6(X),* Simon & Schuster/Paula Wiseman Bks.) Simon & Schuster/Paula Wiseman Bks.
—Amelia's Science Fair Disaster. Moss, Marissa. 2008. (Amelia Ser.). (ENG.). 80p. (J). (gr. 5-8). 9.99 *(978-1-4169-6494-0(0),* Simon & Schuster/Paula Wiseman Bks.) Simon & Schuster/Paula Wiseman Bks.
—Amelia's Summer Survival Guide: Amelia's Longest, Biggest, Most-Fights-Ever Family Reunion; Amelia's Itchy-Twitchy, Lovey-Dovey Summer at Camp Mosquito. Moss, Marissa. 2011. (Amelia Ser.). (ENG.). 160p. (J). (gr. 5-8). 12.99 *(978-1-4424-2331-2(5),* Simon & Schuster/Paula Wiseman Bks.) Simon & Schuster/Paula Wiseman Bks.
—Blood Diaries: Tales of a 6th-Grade Vampire. Moss, Marissa. 2014. (ENG.). 136p. (J). (gr. 2-7). 13.00 *(978-1-939547-05-7(9))* Creston Bks.
—The Fake Friend! Moss, Marissa. 2012. (Daphne's Diary of Daily Disasters Ser.). (ENG.). 96p. (J). (gr. 2-5). 9.99 *(978-1-4424-4014-2(7));* pap. 5.99 *(978-1-4424-4015-9(5))* Simon & Schuster/Paula Wiseman Bks. (Simon & Schuster/Paula Wiseman Bks.).
—Friendship Survival Guide: And Trying to Be the Best BFF Amelia. Moss, Marissa. 2013. (Amelia Ser.). (ENG.). 144p. (J). (gr. 5-8). 12.99 *(978-1-4424-8304-0(0),* Simon & Schuster/Paula Wiseman Bks.) Simon & Schuster/Paula Wiseman Bks.
—Max Disaster Bk. 2: Alien Eraser Unravels the Mystery of the Pyramids. Moss, Marissa. 2009. (Max Disaster Ser.: No. 2). (ENG.). 56p. (J). (gr. 3-7). pap. 6.99 *(978-0-7636-4408-6(0))* Candlewick Pr.
—The Name Game! Moss, Marissa. 2011. (Daphne's Diary of Daily Disasters Ser.). (ENG.). 80p. (J). (gr. 2-5). pap. 5.99 *(978-1-4424-1738-0(2));* lib. bdg. 9.99 *(978-1-4424-2676-4(4))* Simon & Schuster/Paula Wiseman Bks. (Simon & Schuster/Paula Wiseman Bks.).
—The Vampire Dare! Moss, Marissa. 2011. (Daphne's Diary of Daily Disasters Ser.). (ENG.). 80p. (J). (gr. 2-5). pap. 5.99 *(978-1-4424-1737-3(4));* lib. bdg. 9.99 *(978-1-4424-2677-1(2))* Simon & Schuster/Paula Wiseman Bks. (Simon & Schuster/Paula Wiseman Bks.).
—Vote 4 Amelia. Moss, Marissa. 2007. (Amelia Ser.). (ENG.). 80p. (J). (gr. 4-7). 9.99 *(978-1-4169-2789-1(1),* Simon & Schuster/Paula Wiseman Bks.) Simon & Schuster/Paula Wiseman Bks.
Mossiano, Sage. My New Mommy. Mossiano, Lilly. 2012. 28p. pap. 24.95 *(978-1-4626-8898-2(5))* PublishAmerica, Inc.
Most, Andee. I Am Special: Jesus Is Our Friend. Plum, Joan Ensor & Plum, Paul S. 5th ed. 2007. 112p. (J). (gr. k-1). per. 11.95 *(978-1-59276-296-5(4))* Our Sunday Visitor, Publishing Div.
Mostow, Sarah. Alpacas All the Way (A Slightly True Story) Talmadge, Joyce. 2011. (ENG.). 32p. pap. 12.95 *(978-0-615-48761-8(0))* Overlook Farm.
Mostyn, David. Amazing Magic Tricks. 2014. (ENG.). 128p. (J). (gr. 2). 9.99 *(978-0-486-78034-4(1))* Dover Pubns., Inc.
—Close-Up Magic. Lane, Mike. 2012. (Miraculous Magic Tricks Ser.). (ENG.). 32p. (J). (gr. 3-6). pap. 11.75 *(978-1-4488-6737-0(1));* lib. bdg. 26.50 *(978-1-61533-515-2(3))* Windmill Bks.
—Hairy Mole's Adventures on the High Seas. Owen, Christopher. 2007. (Hairy Mole the Pirate Ser.). 80p. (J). per. *(978-1-84167-563-3(6))* Ransom Publishing Ltd.
—I'm Not Wearing That! Clarke, Jane. 2005. (ENG.). 24p. (J). lib. bdg. 23.65 *(978-1-59646-716-3(9))* Dingles & Co.
—Mind Magic. Lane, Mike. 2012. (Miraculous Magic Tricks Ser.). 32p. (J). (gr. 3-6). pap. 11.75 *(978-1-4488-6735-6(5));* lib. bdg. 26.50 *(978-1-61533-514-5(5))* Windmill Bks.
—Spring-Heeled Jack. Pullman, Philip. 2004. (ENG.). 112p. (gr. 3-7). per. 5.99 *(978-0-440-41881-8(X),* Yearling) Random Hse. Children's Bks.
—Toad Swims for his Life! Atkins, Jill. 2004. (ENG.). 24p. (J). lib. bdg. 23.65 *(978-1-59646-712-5(6))* Dingles & Co.
Mostyn, David, jt. illus. see Charbonnel, Olivier.
Mostyn, David, jt. illus. see Spoor, Mike.
Mosz, Gosia. Hanukkah Moon. Da Costa, Deborah. 2007. (Hanukkah Ser.). (ENG.). 32p. (J). (gr. 1-4). 10.95 *(978-1-58013-245-9(6),* Kar-Ben Publishing) Lerner Publishing Group.
Motley, Chris and Jim Young. Pollywogs & Other Friends. Hardy, Ed & Young, Jim. 2007. 28p. per. 24.95 *(978-1-4137-2834-7(0))* America Star Bks.
Motley, T. The Golden Ass of Lucius Apuleius. Usher, M. D. 2011. (ENG.). 112p. (J). 17.95 *(978-1-56792-418-3(2))* Godine, David R. Pub.
Moton, Veronica. Beauty & the Firefly: A Book about Self Esteem. Moton, Veronica. 2010. (ENG.). 30p. pap. 9.99 *(978-1-4505-9351-9(8))* CreateSpace Independent Publishing Platform.

M

Motoyama, Keiko. Bears, Bears, Everywhere. Milios, Rita. rev. ed. 2003. (Rookie Reader Español Ser.). (ENG.). 32p. (J). (gr. k-2). pap. 4.95 *(978-0-516-27830-8(4),* Children's Pr.) Scholastic Library Publishing.

—I Can Tell the Truth. Burch, Regina G. & Donovan Guntly, Jenette. 2004. (Doing the Right Thing Ser.). 16p. (gr. -1-2). lib. bdg. 20.00 *(978-0-8368-4249-4(9),* Gareth Stevens Learning Library) Stevens, Gareth Publishing LLLP.

—Lost Puppy, Found Puppy. Williams, Rozanne Lanczak. 2006. (Learn to Write Ser.). 16p. (J). (gr. k-2). pap. 3.49 *(978-1-59198-296-8(0),* 6190) Creative Teaching Pr., Inc.

—Lost Puppy, Found Puppy. Williams, Rozanne Lanczak. Maio, Barbara, ed. 2006. (J). per. 8.99 *(978-1-59198-347-7(9))* Creative Teaching Pr., Inc.

—Peter's Easter Story. Dreyer, Nicole E. 2004. (Arch Bks.). (ENG.). 16p. (J). 1.99 *(978-0-7586-0477-4(7))* Concordia Publishing Hse.

—The Prince & the Potty. Lewison, Wendy Cheyette. 2006. (ENG.). 40p. (J). (gr. -1 — 1). 14.99 *(978-0-689-87808-4(7),* Simon & Schuster Bks. For Young Readers) Simon & Schuster Bks. For Young Readers.

Mottashed, Susie. Who Lives in Your Backyard? Creating a journal that opens your eyes & heart to nature's nearby Wonders. Mottashed, Susie. 2005. 96p. 24.95 *(978-0-9759300-0-7(1))* Sketches From The Heart Publishing.

Motz, Mike. At the Park with Tommy & Scales. Little, Celeste. 2012. 26p. (J). (-18). 12.95 *(978-1-60131-139-9(7),* Castlebridge Bks.) Big Tent Bks.

—The House on the Hill in Stinkyville. Haitz, Rochelle. 2010. (ENG.). 30p. pap. 9.99 *(978-1-4505-7794-6(6))* CreateSpace Independent Publishing Platform.

—Mommy's Coming Home from Treatment. Crosson, Denise D. 2009. (ENG.). 44p. (J). (gr. -1-3). pap. 14.95 *(978-0-9799869-4-9(X))* Central Recovery Pr.

—Mommy's Gone to Treatment. Crosson, Denise D. 2008. (ENG.). 44p. (J). (gr. k-3). pap. 14.95 *(978-0-9799869-1-8(5))* Central Recovery Pr.

—The Old Cookie Jar. Snow, Susie. 2012. 34p. pap. 19.99 *(978-1-61996-595-9(X))* Salem Publishing Solutions, Inc.

—Scales. Little, Celeste. 2012. 24p. (J). 12.95 *(978-1-60131-116-0(8))* Big Tent Bks.

—The Smiling Burro. Esparza-Vela, Mary. 2012. 16p. pap. 9.95 *(978-1-61633-323-2(5))* Guardian Angel Publishing, Inc.

—Thank You God for Onions. Tennisiwood, Mark. 2006. (J). 14.95 *(978-1-60131-003-3(X))* Big Tent Bks.

—The Treasure of Trust: The Hidden Treasures of My Kingdom Pals. Page, Julie & Adams, Sabrina. McTeer, Rhonda, ed. 2005. 72p. (J). (gr. 4-7). 14.95 *(978-0-9748251-0-6(7),* 825106) Zoe Life Publishing.

—You Can't Take the Dinosaur Home. Esparza- Vela, Mary. 2013. 16p. pap. 9.95 *(978-1-61633-364-5(2))* Guardian Angel Publishing, Inc.

Mouchet, Klutt, jt. illus. see Schmitz, Cecile.

Mould, Chris. Captain Beastlie's Pirate Party. Coats, Lucy. 2014. (ENG.). 32p. (J). (gr. -1-2). 15.99 *(978-0-7636-7399-4(4),* Nosy Crow) Candlewick Pr.

—Sandwich that Jack Made. Graham, Elspeth. 2004. (ENG.). 24p. (J). lib. bdg. 23.65 *(978-1-59646-698-2(7))* Dingles & Co.

—School Trip. Hawes, Alison. 2004. (ENG.). 24p. (J). lib. bdg. 23.65 *(978-1-59646-694-4(4))* Dingles & Co.

Mould, Chris. The Icy Hand. Mould, Chris. 2008. (Something Wickedly Weird Ser.: 2). (ENG.). 176p. (J). (gr. 5-9). 9.95 *(978-1-59643-385-4(X))* Roaring Brook Pr.

—The Treasure Keepers. Mould, Chris. 2010. (Something Wickedly Weird Ser.: 6). (ENG.). 192p. (J). (gr. 5-9). 13.99 *(978-1-59643-389-2(2))* Roaring Brook Pr.

Moulder, Bob. Armour. Tango Books Staff. 2011. (3-Dimensional Exploration Bks.). (ENG.). 20p. (J). (gr. -1-2). 22.95 *(978-1-85707-664-6(8))* Tango Bks. GBR. Dist: Independent Pubs. Group.

—Hit It!, 1 vol. Hardcastle, Michael. 2006. (Graphic Quest Ser.). (ENG.). 88p. (gr. 3-3). per. 5.95 *(978-1-59889-164-5(2),* Graphic Quest) Stone Arch Bks.

—The Loch Ness Monster & Other Lake Mysteries. Jeffrey, Gary. 2006. (Graphic Mysteries Ser.). (ENG.). 48p. (gr. 5-8). pap. 14.05 *(978-1-4042-0807-0(0))* Rosen Publishing Group, Inc., The.

—My Brother's a Keeper, 1 vol. Hardcastle, Michael. 2006. (Graphic Quest Ser.). (ENG.). 88p. (gr. 3-3). lib. bdg. 23.99 *(978-1-59889-081-5(6),* 1256168, Graphic Quest) Stone Arch Bks.

Moulder, Bob, jt. illus. see Spender, Nik.

Moulding, Lynne. Colin Car: Bath Books That Float. Rivers-Moore, Debbie. 2012. (Water Wheels Ser.). (ENG.). 8p. (J). 5.99 *(978-1-4380-7221-0(X))* Barron's Educational Series, Inc.

—Danny Digger: Bath Books That Float. Rivers-Moore, Debbie. 2012. (Water Wheels Ser.). (ENG.). 8p. (J). 5.99 *(978-1-4380-7222-7(8))* Barron's Educational Series, Inc.

—Firetruck Fred: Bath Books That Float. Rivers-Moore, Debbie. 2012. (Water Wheels Ser.). (ENG.). 8p. (J). 5.99 *(978-1-4380-7223-4(6))* Barron's Educational Series, Inc.

—Tractor Tim: Bath Books That Float. Rivers-Moore, Debbie. 2012. (Water Wheels Ser.). (ENG.). 8p. (J). 5.99 *(978-1-4380-7224-1(4))* Barron's Educational Series, Inc.

Moulton, Kathy. Six Small Rabbits. Moulton, Kathy. 2011. (ENG.). 28p. pap. 12.95 *(978-0-615-43516-9(5))* CreateSpace Independent Publishing Platform.

—A View from You. Moulton, Kathy. 2011. (ENG.). 48p. pap. 14.95 *(978-0-615-44147-4(5))* Moulton, Kathy Verner.

Mouly, Françoise, jt. illus. see Spiegelman, Art.

Mount, Arthur. Picnic on a Cloud. Icanberry, Mark. 2010. (Look, Learn & Do Ser.). 48p. (J). (gr. -1-3). pap. 7.95 *(978-1-893327-02-3(7))* Look, Learn & Do Pubns.

—The Ultimate Bar Book: The Comprehensive Guide to over 1,000 Cocktails. Hellmich, Mittie. 2006. (ENG.). 476p. (gr. 8-17). 19.95 *(978-0-8118-4351-5(3))* Chronicle Bks. LLC.

Mount, Arthur, jt. illus. see Eckel, Jessie.

Mounter, Paddy. Agent Arthur's Island Adventures. Sims, Lesley. 2003. (Puzzle Adventures Ser.). 48p. (J). (gr. 3). lib. bdg. 12.95 *(978-1-58086-463-3(5))* EDC Publishing.

—Aladdin & His Magical Lamp. 2004. (1001 Things to Spot Ser.). 48p. (J). (gr. 1). lib. bdg. 14.95 *(978-1-58086-558-6(5),* Usborne) EDC Publishing.

—Ali Baba & the Forty Thieves. 2004. (Young Reading Ser.: Vol. 1). 48p. (J). (gr. 2-18). lib. bdg. 13.95 *(978-1-58086-642-2(5),* Usborne) EDC Publishing.

—Jack & the Beanstalk. Daynes, Katie. 2006. 48p. (J). 8.99 *(978-0-7945-1238-5(0),* Usborne) EDC Publishing.

Mountford, Katie. The Notre Dame Spirit. Lenhart, Kristin & Passamani, Julia. 2012. 30p. (J). 19.95 *(978-0-9859377-0-6(X))* Corby Books.

Mounts, Paul, jt. illus. see Morgan, Tom.

Mouravlova, Yulia. Tales of the Little Hedgehogs: Fairy Plays. Haupt, Wolfgang & Bland, Janice. 2009. (J). *(978-0-88734-978-2(1))* Players Pr., Inc.

Mourning, Tuesday. Back on the Beam, 1 vol. Maddox, Jake. 2009. (Jake Maddox Girl Sports Stories Ser.). (ENG.). 72p. (gr. 2-3). 23.99 *(978-1-4342-1211-5(4))* Stone Arch Bks.

—Ballet Bullies, 1 vol. Maddox, Jake & Berne, Emma Carlson. 2009. (Jake Maddox Girl Sports Stories Ser.). (ENG.). 72p. (gr. 2-3). 23.99 *(978-1-4342-1604-5(7))* Stone Arch Bks.

—Billy & Milly, Short & Silly. Feldman, Eve B. 2009. (ENG.). 32p. (J). (gr. -1-k). 16.99 *(978-0-399-24651-7(7),* Putnam Juvenile) Penguin Publishing Group.

—Blueberry Queen, 1 vol. Peschke, Marci. 2011. (Kylie Jean Ser.). (ENG.). 112p. (gr. 2-3). pap. 5.95 *(978-1-4048-6615-7(9));* lib. bdg. 21.32 *(978-1-4048-6756-7(2))* Picture Window Bks. (Kylie Jean).

—Cheer Challenge. Maddox, Jake. 2008. (Jake Maddox Girl Sports Stories Ser.). (ENG.). 72p. (gr. 2-3). lib. bdg. 23.99 *(978-1-4342-0468-4(5));* per. 5.95 *(978-1-4342-0518-6(5))* Stone Arch Bks.

Mourning, Tuesday. Cupcake Queen. Peschke, Marci. (Kylie Jean Ser.). (ENG.). 112p. (gr. 2-3). 2015. pap. 5.95 ***(978-1-4795-6753-9(1),*** Kylie Jean); 2013. 8.95 *(978-1-4048-8102-0(6));* 2013. lib. bdg. 21.32 *(978-1-4048-7580-7(8))* Picture Window Bks.

Mourning, Tuesday. Dancing Queen, 1 vol. Peschke, Marci. 2012. (Kylie Jean Ser.). (ENG.). 112p. (gr. 2-3). pap. 5.95 *(978-1-4048-7209-7(4));* lib. bdg. 21.32 *(978-1-4048-6798-7(8))* Picture Window Bks. (Kylie Jean).

—Drama Queen, 1 vol. Peschke, Marci. 2011. (Kylie Jean Ser.). (ENG.). 112p. (gr. 2-3). lib. bdg. 21.32 *(978-1-4048-6757-4(0),* Kylie Jean) Picture Window Bks.

—Drama Queen, 1 vol. Peschke, Marci. 2011. (Kylie Jean Ser.). (ENG.). 112p. (gr. 2-3). pap. 5.95 *(978-1-4048-6616-4(7),* Kylie Jean) Picture Window Bks.

—Fashion Queen. Peschke, Marci. 2015. (Kylie Jean Ser.). (ENG.). 112p. (gr. 2-3). 8.95 *(978-1-4795-5881-0(8))* Picture Window Bks.

—Field Hockey Firsts, 1 vol. Maddox, Jake. 2009. (Jake Maddox Girl Sports Stories Ser.). (ENG.). 72p. (gr. 2-3). 23.99 *(978-1-4342-1606-9(3))* Stone Arch Bks.

—Football Queen, 1 vol. Peschke, Marci. 2012. (Kylie Jean Ser.). (ENG.). 112p. (gr. 2-3). pap. 5.95 *(978-1-4048-7210-3(8));* lib. bdg. 21.32 *(978-1-4048-6799-4(6))* Picture Window Bks. (Kylie Jean).

—Full Court Dreams. Maddox, Jake. 2008. (Jake Maddox Girl Sports Stories Ser.). (ENG.). 72p. (gr. 2-3). lib. bdg. 23.99 *(978-1-4342-0469-1(3));* per. 5.95 *(978-1-4342-0519-3(3))* Stone Arch Bks.

—Green Queen, 1 vol. Peschke, Marci. 2014. (Kylie Jean Ser.). (ENG.). 112p. (gr. 2-3). 21.32 *(978-1-4795-2351-1(8),* Kylie Jean) Picture Window Bks.

—Half-Pipe Prize, 1 vol. Maddox, Jake. 2009. (Jake Maddox Girl Sports Stories Ser.). (ENG.). 72p. (gr. 2-3). 23.99 *(978-1-4342-1607-6(1))* Stone Arch Bks.

—Hoop Doctor, 1 vol. Maddox, Jake & Berne, Emma Carlson. 2009. (Jake Maddox Girl Sports Stories Ser.). (ENG.). 72p. (gr. 2-3). 23.99 *(978-1-4342-1605-2(5))* Stone Arch Bks.

—Hoop Queen, 1 vol. Peschke, Marci. 2011. (Kylie Jean Ser.). (ENG.). 112p. (gr. 2-3). lib. bdg. 21.32 *(978-1-4048-5962-3(4),* Kylie Jean) Picture Window Bks.

—Hoop Queen, 1 vol. Peschke, Marci. 2011. (Kylie Jean Ser.). (ENG.). 112p. (gr. 2-3). pap. 5.95 *(978-1-4048-6617-1(5),* Kylie Jean) Picture Window Bks.

—Horseback Hopes, 1 vol. Maddox, Jake. 2009. (Jake Maddox Girl Sports Stories Ser.). (ENG.). 72p. (gr. 2-3). 23.99 *(978-1-4342-1214-6(9))* Stone Arch Bks.

—Icky, Sticky, Hairy Scary Bible Stories: 60 Poems for Kids. Schkade, Jonathan. 2010. 125p. (J). pap. 14.99 *(978-0-7586-2671-4(1))* Concordia Publishing Hse.

—Jump Serve. Maddox, Jake. 2008. (Jake Maddox Girl Sports Stories Ser.). (ENG.). 72p. (gr. 2-3). lib. bdg. 23.99 *(978-1-4342-0470-7(7));* per. 5.95 *(978-1-4342-0520-9(7))* Stone Arch Bks.

—Kylie Jean, 1 vol. Peschke, Marci. (Kylie Jean Ser.). (ENG.). 112p. (gr. 2-3). 2014. 298.48 *(978-1-4795-4545-2(7));* 2013. 85.28 *(978-1-4048-8050-4(X));* 2013. 255.84 *(978-1-4048-8051-1(8))* Picture Window Bks. (Kylie Jean).

—Kylie Jean Craft Queen, 1 vol. Ventura, Marne et al. 2014. (Kylie Jean Craft Queen Ser.). (ENG.). 112p. (gr. 2-3). pap. 9.95 *(978-1-4795-2971-1(0))* Picture Window Bks.

—Kylie Jean Party Craft Queen, 1 vol. Ventura, Marne & Peschke, Marci. 2014. (Kylie Jean Craft Queen Ser.). (ENG.). 32p. (gr. 2-3). lib. bdg. 25.99 *(978-1-4795-2191-3(4))* Picture Window Bks.

—Kylie Jean Pirate Craft Queen, 1 vol. Meinking, Mary & Peschke, Marci. 2014. (Kylie Jean Craft Queen Ser.). (ENG.). 32p. (gr. 2-3). lib. bdg. 25.99 *(978-1-4795-2192-0(2))* Picture Window Bks.

—Kylie Jean Rodeo Craft Queen, 1 vol. Meinking, Mary & Peschke, Marci. 2014. (Kylie Jean Craft Queen Ser.). (ENG.). 32p. (gr. 2-3). lib. bdg. 25.99 *(978-1-4795-2190-6(6))* Picture Window Bks.

—Kylie Jean Summer Camp Craft Queen, 1 vol. Ventura, Marne & Peschke, Marci. 2014. (Kylie Jean Craft Queen Ser.). (ENG.). 32p. (gr. 2-3). lib. bdg. 25.99 *(978-1-4795-2193-7(0))* Picture Window Bks.

—Over the Net, 1 vol. Maddox, Jake. 2009. (Jake Maddox Girl Sports Stories Ser.). (ENG.). 72p. (gr. 2-3). 23.99 *(978-1-4342-1213-9(0))* Stone Arch Bks.

—Party Queen, 1 vol. Peschke, Marci. 2013. (Kylie Jean Ser.). (ENG.). 112p. (gr. 2-3). lib. bdg. 21.32 *(978-1-4048-7582-1(4))* Picture Window Bks.

Mourning, Tuesday. Pirate Queen. Peschke, Marci. (Kylie Jean Ser.). (ENG.). 112p. (gr. 2-3). 2015. pap. 5.95 ***(978-1-4795-8020-0(1),*** Kylie Jean); 2013. 8.95 *(978-1-4048-8103-7(4));* 2013. lib. bdg. 21.32 *(978-1-4048-7581-4(6))* Picture Window Bks.

Mourning, Tuesday. Rodeo Queen, 1 vol. Peschke, Marci. 2011. (Kylie Jean Ser.). (ENG.). 112p. (gr. 2-3). pap. 5.95 *(978-1-4048-6618-8(3));* lib. bdg. 21.32 *(978-1-4048-5961-6(6))* Picture Window Bks. (Kylie Jean).

—Running Rivals. Maddox, Jake. 2008. (Jake Maddox Girl Sports Stories Ser.). (ENG.). 72p. (gr. 2-3). 23.99 *(978-1-4342-0778-4(1))* Stone Arch Bks.

—Singing Queen, 1 vol. Peschke, Marci. 2012. (Kylie Jean Ser.). (ENG.). 112p. (gr. 2-3). pap. 5.95 *(978-1-4048-7211-0(6));* lib. bdg. 21.32 *(978-1-4048-6800-7(3))* Picture Window Bks. (Kylie Jean).

—Skater's Secret, 1 vol. Maddox, Jake. 2009. (Jake Maddox Girl Sports Stories Ser.). (ENG.). 72p. (gr. 2-3). 23.99 *(978-1-4342-1212-2(2))* Stone Arch Bks.

—Soccer Queen. Peschke, Marci. 2015. (Kylie Jean Ser.). (ENG.). 112p. (gr. 2-3). 21.32 *(978-1-4795-5882-7(6))* Picture Window Bks.

—Soccer Spirit. Maddox, Jake. 2008. (Jake Maddox Girl Sports Stories Ser.). (ENG.). 72p. (gr. 2-3). 23.99 *(978-1-4342-0780-7(3))* Stone Arch Bks.

—Spelling Queen, 1 vol. Peschke, Marci. 2012. (Kylie Jean Ser.). (ENG.). 112p. (gr. 2-3). pap. 5.95 *(978-1-4048-7212-7(4));* lib. bdg. 21.32 *(978-1-4048-6801-4(1))* Picture Window Bks. (Kylie Jean).

—Stolen Bases. Maddox, Jake. 2008. (Jake Maddox Girl Sports Stories Ser.). (ENG.). 72p. (gr. 2-3). 23.99 *(978-1-4342-0779-1(X))* Stone Arch Bks.

—Storm Surfer, 1 vol. Maddox, Jake. 2008. (Jake Maddox Girl Sports Stories Ser.). (ENG.). 72p. (gr. 2-3). lib. bdg. 23.99 *(978-1-4342-0471-4(5));* per. 5.95 *(978-1-4342-0521-6(5))* Stone Arch Bks.

—Summer Camp Queen, 1 vol. Peschke, Marci. 2013. (Kylie Jean Ser.). (ENG.). 112p. (gr. 2-3). lib. bdg. 21.32 *(978-1-4048-7583-8(2))* Picture Window Bks.

—Tennis Trouble. Maddox, Jake. 2008. (Jake Maddox Girl Sports Stories Ser.). (ENG.). 72p. (gr. 2-3). 23.99 *(978-1-4342-0781-4(1))* Stone Arch Bks.

—The Two & Only Kelly Twins. Hurwitz, Johanna. 2013. (ENG.). 96p. (J). (gr. 1-4). 14.99 *(978-0-7636-5602-7(X))* Candlewick Pr.

—Valentine Queen, 1 vol. Peschke, Marci. 2014. (Kylie Jean Ser.). (ENG.). 112p. (gr. 2-3). 21.32 *(978-1-4795-2352-8(6),* Kylie Jean) Picture Window Bks.

Moursund, Gry. Snake in the Grass. Sande, Hans. Vetleseter, Tonje, tr. from NOR. 2008. 40p. (J). (gr. -1-1). 16.95 *(978-0-9815761-0-7(9))* Mackenzie Smiles, LLC.

Moussa, Karen M. The Secret of the Sand. Valeska, John & Fripp, Jean. Fripp, Jean, ed. 2003. (Dolphin Watch Ser.). 32p. (J). (gr. k-5). pap. 5.99 *(978-0-9701008-2-5(5))* Bicast, Inc.

Moutafis, Greg. Hero Corps: The Rookie. Becker, Jason Earl. 2005. (YA). per. 7.95 *(978-0-9765125-0-9(5))* Baby Shark Productions.

Moutarde & Blanchin, Matthieu. Half & Half-Voyage into Space. Kemoun, Hubert Ben & Grenier, Christian. 2008. 48p. (J). 9.95 *(978-1-60115-209-1(4));* pap. 4.99 *(978-1-60115-210-7(8))* Treasure Bay, Inc.

Movshina, Marina. Angels Do That. Cox, Tracey M. 2012. 16p. pap. 9.95 *(978-1-61633-299-0(9))* Guardian Angel Publishing, Inc.

—Buster Bear & Uncle B. Kennedy, J. Aday. 2012. 20p. pap. 10.95 *(978-1-61633-235-8(2))* Guardian Angel Publishing, Inc.

—Golden Daffodils. Maher, Liam. 2010. 20p. pap. 10.95 *(978-1-61633-073-6(2))* Guardian Angel Publishing, Inc.

—If I Could Be Anything. McNamee, Kevin. 2009. 16p. pap. 9.95 *(978-1-61633-011-8(2))* Guardian Angel Publishing, Inc.

—Just for Today. McNamee, Kevin. 2012. 16p. pap. 9.95 *(978-1-61633-314-0(6))* Guardian Angel Publishing, Inc.

—Kitty Kerplunking: Preposition Fun. Reeg, Cynthia. 2006. 24p. (J). E-Book 9.95 incl. cd-rom *(978-1-933090-27-6(8))* Guardian Angel Publishing, Inc.

—My Grandma's Kitchen Rules. Kirk, Bill. 2009. 24p. pap. 10.95 *(978-1-935137-88-7(3))* Guardian Angel Publishing, Inc.

—Romeo's Rescue. Reed, Emma & Reed, Jennifer. 2012. 24p. pap. 10.95 *(978-1-61633-247-1(6))* Guardian Angel Publishing, Inc.

—Too Many Kitties. Clineff, Jeff. 2007. 22p. (J). E-Book 9.95 incl. cd-rom *(978-1-933090-45-0(6))* Guardian Angel Publishing, Inc.

—Too Many Kitties. Clineff, Jeff. 2007. (ESK.). 24p. (J). 9.95 *(978-1-933090-10-8(3))* Guardian Angel Publishing, Inc.

Mowatt, Ken N. The First Fry Bread: A Gibxsan Story. Smith, M. Jane. Wheeler, Jordan, ed. 2012. 32p. pap. *(978-1-4602-0226-5(0))* FriesenPress.

Mowery, Linda Williams & Murphy, Emmy Lou. The Bible Is the Best Book. Why? Gunderson, Vivian D. 36p. (J). (gr. 4-8). pap., wbk. ed. 2.00 *(978-0-915374-00-7(5))* Rapids Christian Pr., Inc.

Mowll, Joshua, et al. Operation Typhoon Shore. Mowll, Joshua. 2008. (ENG.). 288p. (J). (gr. 5). pap. 8.99 *(978-0-7636-3808-5(0))* Candlewick Pr.

Moxley, Sheila. El Baile del Elefante: Recuerdos de la India. Heine, Theresa. 2005. (SPA.). 44p. (gr. 2-3). 22.99 *(978-84-8452-356-7(X))* Fundacion Intermon ESP. Dist: Lectorum Pubns., Inc.

—Diary of a Princess: A Tale from Marco Polo's Travels. Maisner, Heather. 2006. 26p. (gr. k-4). reprint ed. pap. 8.00 *(978-1-4223-5302-8(8))* DIANE Publishing Co.

—Elephant Dance: A Journey to India. Heine, Theresa. 2006. (ENG.). 40p. (J). 7.99 *(978-1-905236-79-4(4))* Barefoot Bks., Inc.

—Elephant Dance: Memories of India. Heine, Teresa & Heine, Theresa. 2004. (ENG.). 40p. (J). 16.99 *(978-1-84148-917-9(4))* Barefoot Bks., Inc.

—Stone Girl Bone Girl: The Story of Mary Anning. Anholt, Laurence. 2006. (ENG.). 32p. (J). (gr. k-3). pap. 8.99 *(978-1-84507-700-6(8),* Frances Lincoln Children's Bks.) Quarto Publishing Group UK GBR. Dist: Hachette Bk. Group.

Moxley, Sheila. Grandpa's Garden. Moxley, Sheila. Fry, Stella. 2012. (ENG.). 40p. (J). pap. 7.99 *(978-1-84686-809-2(2))* Barefoot Bks., Inc.

Moxley, Sheila. Come to the Great World: Poems from Around the Globe. Moxley, Sheila, tr. Cooling, Wendy, ed. 2004. (ENG.). 48p. (J). (gr. k-3). tchr. ed. 17.95 *(978-0-8234-1822-0(7))* Holiday Hse., Inc.

Moxley, Sheila, jt. illus. see Jago.

Moy, Phil, jt. illus. see McKenny, Stewart.

Moy, Philip. Attack of the Virtual Villains. Wayne, Matt. 2012. (Batman: the Brave & the Bold Ser.). (ENG.). 32p. (gr. 2-3). lib. bdg. 21.27 *(978-1-4342-4546-5(2))* Stone Arch Bks.

Moy, Philip, jt. illus. see McKenny, Stewart.

Moya, Patricia. Parade of Lights. Sharpe, Gerald. 2007. (What Lies Beneath the Bed Ser.). 487p. (J). per. 11.00 *(978-1-933894-01-0(6))* IJN Publishing, Inc.

—Tommy's Tales. Sharpe, Gerald. 2006. (Tommy's Tales Ser.). 300p. (J). per. 7.00 *(978-1-933894-00-3(8))* IJN Publishing, Inc.

Moyer, Brett, jt. illus. see Stauffer, Lori.

Moyer, J. Ben & Elvis: The Miracle of a Stormy Christmas. Page, J. & Rainier, S. T. 2012. 28p. pap. 8.99 *(978-0-9829669-4-5(6))* Elv Enterprises.

Moyer, Tom. The Adventures of Drew & Ellie: The Daring Rescue. Noland, Charles. 2nd ed. 2006. 92p. (J). per. 7.95 *(978-0-9789297-2-5(1))* TMD Enterprises.

Moyers, William. Three Together: Story of the Wright Brothers & Their Sister. Mills, Lois. 2011. 160p. 41.95 *(978-1-258-05968-2(1))* Literary Licensing, LLC.

—Wild Stallion. Murphy, Bud. 2011. 176p. 42.95 *(978-1-258-05633-9(X))* Literary Licensing, LLC.

Moyler, Alan. The Curies & Radium. Rubin, Elizabeth. 2011. 122p. 40.95 *(978-1-258-09479-9(7))* Literary Licensing, LLC.

Mozi, Jennifer. The Adventures of Mr. Chicken Butt. Bidelman, Jeff. 2013. (ENG.). (J). 14.95 *(978-1-62086-354-1(5))* Mascot Bks., Inc.

Mozlak, Rose Mary Casciano, jt. illus. see Casciano, Christie.

Mozley, Peggy. Alphascripts: The ABC's of the Bible. Wimbrey, Crystal M. 2006. 56p. 14.95 *(978-1-933285-63-4(X))* Brown Bks. Publishing Group.

Mozz. In Search of the Holey Whale: The Top Secret Riddles & Left-Handed Scribbles of Mozz. Mozz. 2008. 176p. (J). (gr. 3-6). lib. bdg. 17.95 *(978-0-9726130-3-3(X))* Goofy Guru Publishing.

MpMann. Inanna's Tears. Vollmar, Rob. 2011. (ENG.). 136p. (YA). (gr. 7). 19.95 *(978-1-932386-79-0(3),* Archaia Entertainment) Boom! Studios.

mpMann. Some New Kind of Slaughter: Or, Lost in the Flood (And How We Found Home Again) Lewis, A. David. 2009. (ENG.). 144p. (YA). (gr. 7-18). 19.95 *(978-1-932386-53-0(X))* Boom Entertainment, Inc.

Mrozek, Elizabeth. The Fifth Chair. Mrozek, Elizabeth. 2013. 38p. 19.95 *(978-1-935766-80-3(5))* Windy City Pubs.

Mshindu. Fun with Letters. Taylor, Maxwell. Date not set. (Fun with Ser.: Vol. 3). (J). (gr. -1-1). pap. 3.95 *(978-1-881316-42-8(4))* A & B Distributors & Pubs. Group.

Mucha-Sullivan, Emily V., jt. illus. see Mucha-Sullivan, Kalie A.

Mucha-Sullivan, Kalie A. & Mucha-Sullivan, Emily V. My Favorite Time of Year. Mucha Aydlott, Julie A. I.t. ed. 2004. 22p. (J). 5.95 *(978-0-9746093-2-4(3))* San Diego Business Accounting Solutions a Non CPA Firm.

Muckle, Christine. The Adventures of Annika. Saunders, Vivien. 2013. 42p. pap. *(978-1-909730-02-1(5))* Abbotsley Publishing.

Mudd, Barbra. Poseidon's Adventures: My Life as a Raindrop. Benhardt, Will. 2011. (ENG.). 46p. pap. 10.50 *(978-1-4663-1991-2(7))* CreateSpace Independent Publishing Platform.

Mudgal, Nishant, et al. How to Draw the Darkest, Baddest Graphic Novels, 1 vol. Singh, Asavari. 2011. (Drawing Ser.). (ENG.). 48p. (gr. 3-4). lib. bdg. 31.32 *(978-1-4296-6594-0(7))* Capstone Pr., Inc.

Muehlenhardt, Amy Bailey. Beauty & the Beast, 1 vol. Jones, Christianne C. (My First Classic Story Ser.). (ENG.). 32p. (gr. k-3). 2013. pap. 7.10 *(978-1-4795-1851-7(4));* 2010. lib. bdg. 21.32 *(978-1-4048-6081-0(9))* Picture Window Bks. (My First Classic Story).

—Classroom Cookout, 1 vol. Blackaby, Susan. 2004. (Read-It! Readers Ser.). (ENG.). 32p. (gr. -1-3). 19.99 *(978-1-4048-0583-5(4),* Easy Readers) Picture Window Bks.

—A Fire Drill with Mr. Dill, 1 vol. Blackaby, Susan. 2004. (Read-It! Readers Ser.). (ENG.). 32p. (gr. -1-3). 19.99 *(978-1-4048-0584-2(2),* Easy Readers) Picture Window Bks.

—Hatching Chicks, 1 vol. Blackaby, Susan. 2004. (Read-It! Readers Ser.). (ENG.). 32p. (gr. -1-3). 19.99 *(978-1-4048-0585-9(0),* Easy Readers) Picture Window Bks.

—I Drive a Backhoe, 1 vol. Bridges, Sarah. 2006. (Working Wheels Ser.). (ENG.). 24p. (gr. -1-2). 25.99

(978-1-4048-1604-6(6), Nonfiction Picture Bks.) Picture Window Bks.
—I Drive a Fire Engine, 1 vol. Bridges, Sarah. 2006. (Working Wheels Ser.). (ENG.). 24p. (gr. -1-2). 25.99 (978-1-4048-1606-0(2), Nonfiction Picture Bks.) Picture Window Bks.
—I Drive a Freight Train, 1 vol. Bridges, Sarah. 2006. (Working Wheels Ser.). (ENG.). 24p. (gr. -1-2). 25.99 (978-1-4048-1607-7(0), Nonfiction Picture Bks.) Picture Window Bks.
—I Drive a Street Sweeper, 1 vol. Bridges, Sarah. 2006. (Working Wheels Ser.). (ENG.). 24p. (gr. -1-2). 25.99 (978-1-4048-1608-4(9), Nonfiction Picture Bks.) Picture Window Bks.
—Johnny Appleseed, 1 vol. Blair, Eric. 2011. (My First Classic Story Ser.).Tr. of Johnny Appleseed. (ENG.). 32p. (gr. k-3). pap. 7.10 (978-1-4048-7367-4(8), My First Classic Story) Picture Window Bks.
—Johnny Appleseed, 1 vol. Blair, Eric. Robledo, Sol, tr. 2006. (Read-It! Readers en Español: Cuentos Exagerados Ser.).Tr. of Johnny Appleseed. (SPA.). 32p. (gr. k-3). 19.99 (978-1-4048-1655-8(0), Easy Readers) Picture Window Bks.
—Kids Talk about Bullying, 1 vol. Finn, Carrie. 2006. (Kids Talk Jr Ser.). (ENG.). 32p. (gr. -1-2). lib. bdg. 25.99 (978-1-4048-2315-0(8), Nonfiction Picture Bks.) Picture Window Bks.
—Kids Talk about Fairness, 1 vol. Finn, Carrie. 2006. (Kids Talk Jr Ser.). (ENG.). 32p. (gr. -1-2). lib. bdg. 25.99 (978-1-4048-2316-7(6), Nonfiction Picture Bks.) Picture Window Bks.
—Pitch In! Kids Talk about Cooperation. Nettleton, Pamela Hill. 2004. (Kids Talk Ser.). (ENG.). 32p. (gr. 2-5). 27.32 (978-1-4048-0621-4(0), Nonfiction Picture Bks.) Picture Window Bks.
—Rapunzel: A Retelling of the Grimms' Fairy Tale, 1 vol. Jones, Christianne C. 2013. (My First Classic Story Ser.). (ENG.). 32p. (gr. k-3). pap. 7.10 (978-1-4795-1852-4(2), My First Classic Story) Picture Window Bks.
—Whose Gloves Are These? A Look at Gloves Workers Wear - Leather, Cloth, & Rubber, 1 vol. Salas, Laura Purdie. 2006. (Whose Is It?: Community Workers Ser.). (ENG.). 24p. (gr. -1-2). lib. bdg. 25.99 (978-1-4048-1599-5(6), Nonfiction Picture Bks.) Picture Window Bks.
—Whose Hat Is This? A Look at Hats Workers Wear - Hard, Tall, & Shiny, 1 vol. Cooper, Sharon Katz. 2006. (Whose Is It?: Community Workers Ser.). (ENG.). 24p. (gr. -1-2). lib. bdg. 25.99 (978-1-4048-1600-8(3), Nonfiction Picture Bks.) Picture Window Bks.
—Whose Shoes Are These? A Look at Workers' Footwear - Slippers, Sneakers, & Boots, 1 vol. Salas, Laura Purdie. 2006. (Whose Is It?: Community Workers Ser.). (ENG.). 24p. (gr. -1-2). 25.99 (978-1-4048-1601-5(1), 1253204, Nonfiction Picture Bks.) Picture Window Bks.
—Whose Tools Are These? A Look at Tools Workers Use - Big, Sharp, & Smooth, 1 vol. Cooper, Sharon Katz. 2006. (Whose Is It?: Community Workers Ser.). (ENG.). 24p. (gr. -1-2). lib. bdg. 25.99 (978-1-4048-1602-2(X), Nonfiction Picture Bks.) Picture Window Bks.
—The Word of the Day, 1 vol. Blackaby, Susan. 2004. (Read-It! Readers Ser.). (ENG.). 32p. (gr. -1-3). 19.99 (978-1-4048-0588-0(5), Easy Readers) Picture Window Bks.
Muehlenhardt, Amy Bailey. Beginner's Guide to Drawing: Animals, Bugs, Dinosaurs, & Other Cool Stuff! Muehlenhardt, Amy Bailey. 2010. (Sketch It! Ser.). (ENG.). 144p. (gr. k-4). pap. 14.95 (978-1-4048-6166-4(1), Nonfiction Picture Bks.) Picture Window Bks.
—Drawing & Learning about Bugs: Using Shapes & Lines, 1 vol. Muehlenhardt, Amy Bailey. 2004. (Sketch It! Ser.). (ENG.). 24p. (gr. k-4). 25.99 (978-1-4048-0270-4(3), Nonfiction Picture Bks.) Picture Window Bks.
—Drawing & Learning about Cars: Using Shapes & Lines, 1 vol. Muehlenhardt, Amy Bailey. 2004. (Sketch It! Ser.). (ENG.). 24p. (gr. k-4). 25.99 (978-1-4048-0269-8(X), Nonfiction Picture Bks.) Picture Window Bks.
—Drawing & Learning about Faces: Using Shapes & Lines. Muehlenhardt, Amy Bailey. 2004. (Sketch It! Ser.). (ENG.). 24p. (gr. k-4). 25.99 (978-1-4048-0271-1(1), 1229557, Nonfiction Picture Bks.) Picture Window Bks.
—Drawing & Learning about Fashion: Using Shapes & Lines, 1 vol. Muehlenhardt, Amy Bailey. 2005. (Sketch It! Ser.). (ENG.). 24p. (gr. k-4). lib. bdg. 25.99 (978-1-4048-1191-1(5), 1243855, Nonfiction Picture Bks.) Picture Window Bks.
Mueller, Janet. A Star from Grandma. Mueller, Janet. 2004. (J). pap. 8.96 (978-0-9746932-3-1(5)) Stella Bks, Inc.
Müeller, Jörg. The Bear Who Wanted to Be a Bear. Steiner, Jörg. 2nd ed. 2007. (ENG.). 44p. (J). (gr. 2-4). 16.95 (978-0-9762056-0-9(2)) Heryin Publishing Corp.
Mueller, Mike, photos by. Pickup Trucks. Zuehlke, Jeffrey. 2007. (Motor Mania Ser.). (ENG.). 48p. (gr. 4-7). lib. bdg. 26.60 (978-0-8225-6564-2(1)) Lerner Publishing Group.
Mueller, Miranda. Gardening with Grandma. Brunsvold, Eric. 2010. 24p. pap. 9.95 (978-0-615-38944-8(9)) Specialized Printing, LLC.
—Mishka: An Adoption Tale. 2007. 32p. (J). 16.95 (978-1-933084-01-5(4)) DRT Pr.
Mueller, Pete. Black Out! Animals That Live in the Dark. Clarke, Ginjer L. 2008. (Penguin Young Readers, Level 3 Ser.). (ENG.). 48p. (J). (gr. 1-3). mass mkt. 3.99 (978-0-448-44824-4(6), Warne, Frederick Pubs.) Penguin Bks., Ltd. GBR. Dist: Penguin Random Hse., LLC.
—Bug Out! The World's Creepiest, Crawliest Critters. Clarke, Ginjer L. 2007. (Penguin Young Readers, Level 3 Ser.). (ENG.). 48p. (J). (gr. 1-3). pap. 3.99 (978-0-448-44543-4(3), Warne, Frederick Pubs.) Penguin Bks., Ltd. GBR. Dist: Penguin Random Hse., LLC.
—Bug Out! The World's Creepiest, Crawliest Critters. Clarke, Ginjer L. 2007. (All Aboard Science Reader Ser.). (gr. -1-3). 14.00 (978-0-7569-8168-6(9)) Perfection Learning Corp.
—Fake Out! Animals That Play Tricks. Clarke, Ginjer L. 2007. (Penguin Young Readers, Level 3 Ser.). (ENG.). 48p. (J). (gr. 1-3). mass mkt. 3.99 (978-0-448-44656-1(1), Grosset & Dunlap) Penguin Publishing Group.
—Fake Out! Animals That Play Tricks. Clarke, Ginjer L. 2007. (All Aboard Science Reader Ser.). 48p. (gr. 1-3). 14.00 (978-0-7569-8170-9(0)) Perfection Learning Corp.
—Far Out! Animals That Do Amazing Things. Clarke, Ginjer L. 2009. (Penguin Young Readers, Level 3 Ser.). (ENG.). 48p. (J). (gr. 1-3). mass mkt. 3.99 (978-0-448-44826-8(2), Grosset & Dunlap) Penguin Publishing Group.
—Freak Out! Animals Beyond Your Wildest Imagination. Clarke, Ginjer L. 2006. (Penguin Young Readers, Level 4 Ser.). (ENG.). 48p. (J). (gr. 3-4). mass mkt. 3.99 (978-0-448-44308-9(2), Warne, Frederick Pubs.) Penguin Bks., Ltd. GBR. Dist: Penguin Random Hse., LLC.
—Freak Out! Animals Beyond Your Wildest Imagination. Clarke, Ginjer L. 2007. (All Aboard Science Reader Ser.). 48p. (gr. 1-3). 14.00 (978-0-7569-8173-0(5)) Perfection Learning Corp.
—Gross Out! Animals That Do Disgusting Things. Clarke, Ginjer L. 2006. (Penguin Young Readers, Level 4 Ser.). (ENG.). 48p. (J). (gr. 3-4). mass mkt. 3.99 (978-0-448-44390-4(2), Grosset & Dunlap) Penguin Publishing Group.
—Gross Out! Animals That Do Disgusting Things. Clarke, Ginjer L. 2007. (All Aboard Science Reader Ser.). 46p. (gr. 1-3). 14.00 (978-0-7569-8172-3(7)) Perfection Learning Corp.
—Maxed Out! Gigantic Creatures from the Past. Clarke, Ginjer L. 2010. (Penguin Young Readers, Level 3 Ser.). (ENG.). 48p. (J). (gr. 1-3). mass mkt. 3.99 (978-0-448-44827-5(0), Grosset & Dunlap) Penguin Publishing Group.
—Watch Out! The World's Most Dangerous Creatures. Clarke, Ginjer L. 2012. (Penguin Young Readers, Level 3 Ser.). (ENG.). 48p. (J). (gr. 1-3). pap. 3.99 (978-0-448-45108-4(5), Warne, Frederick Pubs.) Penguin Bks., Ltd. GBR. Dist: Penguin Random Hse., LLC.
Mueller, Pete, jt. illus. see Mueller, Peter R.
Mueller, Peter. Pets: Step-by-Step Insructions for 23 Favorite Animals. Walter Foster Creative Team. 2011. (Learn to Draw Ser.). 32p. (J). (gr. 1-4). 28.50 (978-1-936309-17-7(3)) Quarto Publishing Group USA.
Mueller, Peter R. & Mueller, Pete. Honeybees. Milton, Joyce. 2003. (Penguin Young Readers, Level 3 Ser.). (ENG.). 48p. (J). (gr. 1-3). pap. 3.99 (978-0-448-42846-8(6), Warne, Frederick Pubs.) Penguin Bks., Ltd. GBR. Dist: Penguin Random Hse., LLC.
Muellner, Nancy. The Hustle & Bustle of Poor Mrs. Tustle. Berggren, Joyce D. 2010. 32p. pap. 12.95 (978-0-9819860-5-0(6)) Amber Skye Publishing LLC.
Mugambi, Christina Nkirote. Maybe the Truth about Santa. Powell Zalewski, Amy. 2005. 32p. (J). (gr. -1-3). 15.00 (978-0-9773608-1-9(4)) Shiny Red Ball Publishing.
Mugnaini, Joe, jt. illus. see Bradbury, Ray.
Mugnaini, Joseph. The Halloween Tree. Bradbury, Ray. ed. 2007. (ENG.). 160p. (J). (gr. 3-7). reprint ed. 15.99 (978-0-394-82409-3(1), Knopf Bks. for Young Readers) Random Hse. Children's Bks.
Muhammad, Raychelle. Fit Boys Like You. Muhammad, Raychelle. l.t. ed. 2012. (ENG.). 30p. pap. 9.95 (978-1-4663-9279-3(7)) CreateSpace Independent Publishing Platform.
—Fit Girls Like You. Muhammad, Raychelle. l.t. ed. 2012. (ENG.). 30p. pap. 9.95 (978-1-4663-9252-6(5)) CreateSpace Independent Publishing Platform.
Mühle, Jörg. Be at the Ark by Eight. Hub, Ulrich. 2012. (J). 12.00 (978-0-8028-5410-0(9), Eerdmans Bks For Young Readers) Eerdmans, William B. Publishing Co.
—Becoming the Wolf. Hub, Ulrich & Ragg-Kirkby, Helena. 2012. (J). 12.00 (978-0-8028-5409-4(5), Eerdmans Bks For Young Readers) Eerdmans, William B. Publishing Co.
Muhle, Jorg. See Inside Pirate Ships. Jones, Rob Lloyd. 2007. (See Inside Board Bks). 15p. (J). (gr. -1-3). bds. 12.99 (978-0-7945-1601-7(7), Usborne) EDC Publishing.
Muhn, Gu-seon. Mango Trees: Philippines. Kim, Tae-yeon. Cowley, Joy, ed. 2015. (Global Kids Storybooks Ser.). (ENG.). 32p. (gr. 1-4). 26.65 **(978-1-925246-07-0(8))**; 26.65 **(978-1-925246-33-9(7))**; 7.99 **(978-1-925246-59-9(0))** ChoiceMaker Pty. Ltd., The AUS. (Big and SMALL). Dist: Lerner Publishing Group.
Muirhead, Deborah, jt. illus. see Dancy, Deborah.
Mukherjee, Aiswarya & S., Bijan. My Family! ABCs with Keesha. 2011. (J). pap. 2.99 (978-0-9767273-9-2(0)) Dodi Pr.
Mukherjee, Aniruddha. Siddhartha Gautama: The Life of the Buddha - Based on Original Sources. Seth, Shantum. adapted ed. 2014. (Life of the Buddha Ser.). (ENG.). 64p. pap. 6.95 (978-1-906230-61-6(7)) Real Reads Ltd. GBR. Dist: International Publishers Marketing.
Mukhida, Zul & Card, Vanessa. Buddhist Vihara. Ganeri, Anita. 2004. (ENG.). 32p. pap. (978-0-7136-5498-1(8), A & C Black) Bloomsbury Publishing Plc.
Mukthavaram, Vasantha. Aesop's Fables: Eternal Leaf Art. Mukthavaram, Vasantha. 2011. (ENG.). (J). 19.99 (978-0-615-46456-5(4)) Vikasam.
Mulabdic, Sonja. The Gift of Odin. Quednau, Marion. 2007. (ENG.). 192p. (J). (gr. 4-6). pap. 9.95 (978-1-55451-075-7(9), 9781554510757) Annick Pr., Ltd. CAN. Dist: Firefly Bks., Ltd.
Mulazzani, Simona. Animal Supermarket. Zoboli, Giovanna & Watkinson, Laura. 2015. 26p. (J). 16.00 (978-0-8028-5448-3(6), Eerdmans Bks For Young Readers) Eerdmans, William B. Publishing Co.
—The Big Book of Slumber. Zoboli, Giovanna. 2014. 28p. (J). pap. 16.00 (978-0-8028-5439-1(7)) Eerdmans, William B. Publishing Co.
—I Wish I Had... Zoboli, Giovanna & Mathews, Leslie. 2013. (J). 16.00 (978-0-8028-5415-5(X), Eerdmans Bks For Young Readers) Eerdmans, William B. Publishing Co.
Mulazzani, Simona. Tree of Wonder. Messner, Kate. 2015. (ENG.). 36p. (J). (gr. k-3). 16.99 **(978-1-4521-1248-0(7))** Chronicle Bks. LLC.
Mulholland, Bailey. Grandpa Isn't Grandpa Anymore. Durben, Toni. 2006. (J). lib. bdg. (978-1-933556-33-8(1)) Publishers' Graphics, L.L.C.
Mulkey Young, Kim. Under Three Flags: Exploring Early St. Louis History. Hoessle, Maureen. 2004. (J). pap. 14.95 (978-1-891442-28-5(7)) Virginia Publishing Corp.
Mullaly, Glen. How Electricity Works. Swanson, Jennifer. 2011. (How Things Work Ser.). (ENG.). 32p. (J). (gr. 2-5). 28.50 (978-1-60973-216-5(2), 201158) Child's World, Inc., The.
—How MP3 Players Work. Jacobson, Ryan. 2011. (How Things Work Ser.). (ENG.). 32p. (J). (gr. 2-5). 28.50 (978-1-60973-220-2(0), 201161) Child's World, Inc., The.
—How Submarines Work. Swanson, Jennifer. 2011. (How Things Work Ser.). (ENG.). 32p. (J). (gr. 2-5). 28.50 (978-1-60973-222-6(7), 201163) Child's World, Inc., The.
—How Telescopes, Binoculars, & Microscopes Work. Jacobson, Ryan. 2011. (How Things Work Ser.). (ENG.). 32p. (J). (gr. 2-5). 28.50 (978-1-60973-214-1(6), 201164) Child's World, Inc., The.
—How Toilets Work. Jacobson, Ryan. 2011. (How Things Work Ser.). (ENG.). 32p. (J). (gr. 2-5). 28.50 (978-1-60973-223-3(5), 201166) Child's World, Inc., The.
—How Wind Turbines Work. Jacobson, Ryan. 2011. (How Things Work Ser.). (ENG.). 32p. (J). (gr. 2-5). 28.50 (978-1-60973-224-0(3), 201167) Child's World, Inc., The.
Mullan, G. E. Canticle: Biblical Songs Illuminated. Shea, John. 2009. (J). 29.95 (978-1-58459-427-7(6)) World Library Pubns.
Mullan, Michael. Karl & Carolina Uncover the Parts of a Book, 1 vol. Donovan, Sandy. 2010. (In the Library). (ENG.). 24p. (gr. k-4). lib. bdg. 25.99 (978-1-4048-5760-5(5)); pap. 7.29 (978-1-4048-6107-7(6)) Picture Window Bks. (Nonfiction Picture Bks.).
Mullen, Lana. Cats! Train Your Owner! Ewing, Susan. Cider Mill Press Staff, ed. 2008. (My-T-Smart(tm) Flash Cards Ser.). (ENG.). 32p. 14.95 (978-1-933662-77-0(8)) Cider Mill Pr. Bk. Pubs., LLC.
Müller, Chris. The Griffin & the Dinosaur: How Adrienne Mayor Discovered a Fascinating Link Between Myth & Science. Aronson, Marc & Mayor, Adrienne. 2014. (ENG.). 48p. (J). (gr. 5). 18.99 (978-1-4263-1108-6(7), National Geographic Children's Bks.) National Geographic Society.
Muller, Cristina. Claudia y Daniel. Strepponi, Blanca. 2004. (SPA.). 28p. (J). pap. 7.99 (978-980-257-268-7(3)) Ekare, Ediciones VEN. Dist: Lectorum Pubns., Inc.
Muller, Daniel. Knights of the Castle. Linke, Uwe. 2008. (ENG.). 20p. (J). (gr. -1-3). 11.95 (978-0-7358-2201-6(8)) North-South Bks., Inc.
—Two Birthdays. Thorup, Bryce. 2005. (J). 18.95 (978-0-9765964-0-0(7)) Round Tower Pr.
Müller, Hildegard. The Cowboy. Maccarone, Grace. 2015. (I Like to Read(r) Ser.). (ENG.). 24p. (J). (gr. -1-3). 14.95 (978-0-8234-3202-8(5)) Holiday Hse., Inc.
Müller, Hildegard. The Cowboy. Müller, Hildegard. 2015. (I Like to Read(r) Ser.). (ENG.). 24p. (J). (gr. -1-3). 6.99 (978-0-8234-3316-2(1)) Holiday Hse., Inc.
Muller, Ruth. Doctor Matthews' Family Christmas. Thorup, Bryce. 2005. (J). 18.95 (978-0-9765964-1-7(5)) Round Tower Pr.
Mullerova, Lucie. Un Loro en Mi Granja. Bruno, Pep. 2009. (SPA.). 32p. (J). (gr. 1-3). (978-84-263-7341-0(0)) Vives, Luis Editorial (Edelvives).
Mullett, Viv. The Case of the Cat with the Missing Ear: From the Notebooks of Edward R. Smithfield, D. V. M. Emerson, Scott. 2011. (Adventures of Samuel Blackthorne Ser.: 1). (ENG.). 240p. (J). (gr. 3-7). pap. 11.99 (978-0-689-87615-8(7), Simon & Schuster Bks. For Young Readers) Simon & Schuster Bks. For Young Readers.
Mulligan, Todd. The Story Behind Santa Sacks. Moore, Brian L. 2004. 32p. (978-0-9732651-0-1(8)) Hills-n-Hollows Publishing.
Mullin, Michael, jt. illus. see Skewes, John.
Mulock, Julian. Bees. Hodge, Deborah. 2004. (Denver Museum of Nature & Science Bks.). (ENG.). 32p. (J). (gr. k-3). 5.95 (978-1-55337-656-9(0)) Kids Can Pr., Ltd. CAN. Dist: Univ. of Toronto Pr.
—What's That Bug? Everyday Insects & Their Really Cool Cousins. Froman, Nan. 2010. (ENG.). 32p. (J). (gr. 4-7). pap. 8.95 (978-1-897330-56-2(1)) Madison Pr. Bks. CAN. Dist: Independent Pubs. Group.
Mumper-Drumm, Heidrun. A Web of Good Manners - Grown-up Manners for Young People. Hillings, Phyllis & Hillings, Pamela. (J). 19.95 (978-0-9725364-1-7(8)) Perrin & Kabel Publishing.
Muncaster, Harriet. Happy Halloween, Witch's Cat! Muncaster, Harriet. 2015. (ENG.). 32p. (J). (gr. -1-3). 15.99 (978-0-06-222916-8(8)) HarperCollins Pubs.
Mundie, Ken. Two Fires in the Night: The Third Part of the Crazy Horse Chronicles. Jepperson, Richard. 2003. viii, 56p. (YA). (gr. 7-12). 16.95 (978-0-9672012-2-1(5)) String of Beads Pubns.
Mundy, Jen. Lily's Little Life Lessons: Lily's Laces. Coniglio, Rebecca Perlman. 2013. (ENG.). 24p. (J). (gr. -1-3). 14.95 (978-1-62086-408-1(8)) Mascot Bks., Inc.
—Mommy, Mommy! Is This for Me? Connolly, Megan B. 2013. (ENG.). (J). 14.95 (978-1-62086-356-5(1)) Mascot Bks., Inc.
—N Is for Nepal. Adhikary, Anita. 2011. (J). 14.95 (978-1-936319-52-7(7)) Mascot Bks., Inc.
Munger, Nancy, et al. Best-Loved Christmas Stories. Olive, Teresa et al. 2014. (ENG.). 102p. (J). 9.99 (978-0-7586-4661-3(5)) Concordia Publishing Hse.
Munger, Nancy. Bethlehem Town: Where Jesus Was Born. Hoffman, Patricia. 2003. 32p. (J). 9.49 (978-0-7586-0412-5(2)) Concordia Publishing Hse.
—David & Goliath: A Story about Trusting in God: Based on 1 Samuel 17:1/50. Pingry, Patricia A. 2005. (Children of the Bible Ser.). (ENG.). 23p. (J). bds. 6.95 (978-0-8249-6570-9(1)) Ideals Pubns.
—Jesus in the Temple: Based on Luke 2:40/52. Pingry, Patricia A. 2008. (ENG.). 26p. (J). bds. 6.95 (978-0-8249-6569-3(8)) Ideals Pubns.
—Little Visits for Toddlers. Simon, Mary Manz. 3rd ed. 2006. (Little Visits Ser.). Orig. Title: Little Visits 1-2-3. 275p. (J). (gr. -1-3). per. 13.49 (978-0-7586-0845-1(4)) Concordia Publishing Hse.
—My Story of Jesus. Holder, Jennifer. 2014. (Happy Day Ser.). (ENG.). 16p. (J). pap. 2.49 (978-1-4143-9325-4(3)) Tyndale Hse. Pubs.
—The Parable of the Lily, 1 vol. Higgs, Liz Curtis. 10th anniv. ed. 2007. (Parable Ser.). (ENG.). 32p. (gr. -1-2). 7.99 (978-1-4003-0844-6(5)) Nelson, Thomas Inc.
—La Parabola del Lirio. Higgs, Liz Curtis. 2005.Tr. of Parable of the Lily. 32p. (J). (gr. -1-3). pap. 5.99 (978-0-8254-1327-8(3)) Kregel Pubns.
—The Story of the Star-Spangled Banner. Pingry, Patricia A. 2014. (Story of Ser.). 24p. (J). bds. 6.99 (978-0-8249-1930-6(0), Candy Cane Pr.) Ideals Pubns.
—The Sunflower Parable, 1 vol. Higgs, Liz Curtis. 10th anniv. ed. 2007. (Parable Ser.). (ENG.). 32p. (gr. -1-2). 7.99 (978-1-4003-0845-3(3)) Nelson, Thomas Inc.
—Why I Trust You, God. Adams, Michelle Medlock. 2006. 20p. (J). (gr. -1). bds. 5.49 (978-0-7586-0913-7(2)) Concordia Publishing Hse.
Muniz, Jim. Divine Time, Vol. 3. Aguirre-Sacasa, Roberto. 2005. (Marvel Knights 4 Ser.). 144p. (YA). pap. 14.99 (978-0-7851-1678-3(8)) Marvel Worldwide, Inc.
Muñoz, Claudio. !Bravo, Rosina! Thomas, Maria Jose & Thomas, María José. 2005. (SPA.). 48p. (J). (gr. -1-5). 10.40 (978-980-257-242-7(X), EK33833) Ekare, Ediciones VEN. Dist: Lectorum Pubns., Inc.
—Captain & Matey Set Sail. Laurence, Daniel. 2003. (I Can Read Bks.). 64p. (gr. 1-3). 15.00 (978-0-7569-1402-8(7)) Perfection Learning Corp.
—Just Another Morning. Ashman, Linda. 2004. (ENG.). 32p. (J). (gr. -1-3). 15.99 (978-0-06-029053-5(6)) HarperCollins Pubs.
Munoz, Claudio. Tia Isa Quiere un Carro. Medina, Meg. 2012.Tr. of Tia Isa Wants a Car. (SPA.). 32p. (J). (gr. -1-2). pap. 6.99 (978-0-7636-5751-2(4)) Candlewick Pr.
Muñoz, Claudio. Tia Isa Wants a Car. Medina, Meg. 2011. (ENG.). 32p. (J). (gr. -1-2). 15.99 (978-0-7636-4156-6(1)) Candlewick Pr.
Munoz, Olga M. Opposites Are Fun. Milne, Barbara L. W. l.t. ed. 2005. 40p. (J). 19.95 (978-0-9708796-0-8(1), TLConcepts, Inc.) Tender Learning Concepts.
Munoz, Rie. Goodbye, My Island. Rogers, Jean. 2015. (ENG.). 96p. (J). (gr. 7-9). 21.99 **(978-1-943328-15-4(3)**, Alaska Northwest Bks.) Graphic Arts Ctr. Publishing Co.
Muñoz, William. The Call of the Osprey. Muñoz, William, photos by. Patent, Dorothy Hinshaw. 2015. (Scientists in the Field Ser.). (ENG.). 80p. (J). (gr. 5-7). 18.99 (978-0-544-23268-6(2), HMH Books For Young Readers) Houghton Mifflin Harcourt Publishing Co.
—Life in a Desert. Muñoz, William, photos by. Patent, Dorothy Hinshaw. 2003. (Ecosystems in Action Ser.). (ENG.). 72p. (gr. 5-9). 26.60 (978-0-8225-2140-2(7)) Lerner Publishing Group.
Muñoz, William, photos by. The Buffalo & the Indians: A Shared Destiny. Patent, Dorothy Hinshaw. 2006. (ENG.). 96p. (J). (gr. 5-7). 19.00 (978-0-618-48570-3(8)) Houghton Mifflin Harcourt Publishing Co.
Munoz, William, photos by. Homesteading: Settling America's Heartland. Patent, Dorothy Hinshaw. 2013. 48p. (J). pap. 12.00 (978-0-87842-605-8(1)) Mountain Pr. Publishing Co., Inc.
—The Horse & the Plains Indians: A Powerful Partnership. Patent, Dorothy Hinshaw. 2012. (ENG.). 112p. (J). (gr. 5-7). 17.99 (978-0-547-12551-0(8)) Houghton Mifflin Harcourt Publishing Co.
Muñoz, William, photos by. The Lewis & Clark Trail: Then & Now. Patent, Dorothy Hinshaw. 2006. 60p. (J). (gr. 4-8). reprint ed. 20.00 (978-1-4223-5732-3(5)) DIANE Publishing Co.
—Saving Audie: A Pit Bull Puppy Gets a Second Chance. Patent, Dorothy Hinshaw. 2011. (ENG.). 48p. (J). (gr. 2-4). 17.99 (978-0-8027-2272-0(5)) Walker & Co.
Munro, Roxie. Crocodiles, Camels & Dugout Canoes: Eight Adventurous Episodes. Zaunders, Bo. 2006. 48p. (J). (gr. 4-8). reprint ed. 17.00 (978-1-4223-5397-4(4)) DIANE Publishing Co.
—The Great Bridge-Building Contest. Zaunders, Bo. 2006. 30p. (J). (gr. 4-8). reprint ed. 17.00 (978-1-4223-5239-7(0)) DIANE Publishing Co.
—Texas Rangers: Legendary Lawmen. Spradlin, Michael P. 2008. (ENG.). 32p. (J). (gr. 3-6). 16.95 (978-0-8027-8096-6(2)) Walker & Co.
Munro, Roxie. Hatch!, 0 vols. Munro, Roxie. 2011. (ENG.). 40p. (J). (gr. k-6). 17.99 (978-0-7614-5882-1(4), 9780761458821, Amazon Children's Publishing) Amazon Publishing.
—The Inside-Outside Book of New York City. Munro, Roxie. 2005. 44p. (J). (gr. 4-8). reprint ed. 16.00 (978-0-7567-9455-2(2)) DIANE Publishing Co.
—Market Maze. Munro, Roxie. 2015. (ENG.). 32p. (J). (gr. -1-3). 16.95 (978-0-8234-3092-5(8)) Holiday Hse., Inc.
Munsinger, Lynn. ABC School's for Me! Katz, Susan B. 2015. (ENG.). 32p. (J). (gr. -1-k). 16.99 (978-0-545-53092-7(X), Scholastic Pr.) Scholastic, Inc.
—All for Me & None for All. Lester, Helen. 2012. (ENG.). 32p. (J). (gr. -1-3). 16.99 (978-0-547-68834-3(2)) Houghton Mifflin Harcourt Publishing Co.
—Batter up Wombat. Lester, Helen. ed. 2006. (ENG.). 32p. (J). (gr. k-3). 24.80 (978-1-4287-0160-1(5), Follettbound) Follett School Solutions.
—Beatrice Doesn't Want To. Numeroff, Laura Joffe. 2008. (ENG.). 32p. (J). (gr. -1-2). pap. 7.99 (978-0-7636-3843-6(9)) Candlewick Pr.
—Best Friends Pretend. Strauss, Linda Leopold. 2014. (ENG.). 14p. (J). (gr. -1 — 1). bds. 6.99 (978-0-545-45171-0(X), Cartwheel Bks.) Scholastic, Inc.
—Bunny Tails. Brenner, Barbara et al. 2005. 32p. 15.95 (978-0-689-03925-6(5), Milk & Cookies) ibooks, Inc.
Munsinger, Lynn. Ginny Louise & the School Field Day. Sauer, Tammi. 2016. (J). **(978-1-4847-3044-7(5))** Disney Pr.
Munsinger, Lynn. Ginny Louise & the School Showdown. Sauer, Tammi. 2015. (ENG.). 32p. (J). (gr. -1-k). 16.99 (978-1-4231-6853-9(4)) Disney Pr.

M

—Hooway for Wodney Wat, 1 vol. Lester, Helen. 2011. (ENG.). 32p. (J). (gr. -1-3). 10.99 *(978-0-547-55217-0(3))* Houghton Mifflin Harcourt Publishing Co.

—Howliday Inn. Howe, James. 2006. 195p. (gr. 3-7). 16.00 *(978-0-7569-6807-6(0))* Perfection Learning Corp.

—Howliday Inn. Howe, James. 2nd ed. 2006. (Bunnicula & Friends Ser.). (ENG.). 224p. (J). (gr. 3-7). pap. 6.99 *(978-1-4169-2815-7(4))*, Atheneum Bks. for Young Readers) Simon & Schuster Children's Publishing.

—Hunter's Best Friend at School. Elliott, Laura Malone. 2005. (gr. -1-2). 17.00 *(978-0-7569-5786-5(9))* Perfection Learning Corp.

—Hunter's Best Friend at School. Elliott, Laura Malone. 2005. (ENG.). 32p. (J). (gr. -1-2). reprint ed. pap. 6.99 *(978-0-06-075319-1(6))*, Tegen, Katherine Bks) HarperCollins Pubs.

—Hurty Feelings. Lester, Helen. 2007. (ENG.). 32p. (J). (gr. -1-3). 6.95 *(978-0-618-84062-5(1))* Houghton Mifflin Harcourt Publishing Co.

—Hurty Feelings. Lester, Helen. 2014. (Laugh-Along Lessons Ser.). (ENG.). 32p. (J). (gr. -1-3). 8.99 *(978-0-544-10622-2(9))* Houghton Mifflin Harcourt Publishing Co.

—It Wasn't My Fault. Lester, Helen. alt. ed. 2013. (Laugh-Along Lessons Ser.). (ENG.). 32p. (J). (gr. -1-3). 8.99 *(978-0-544-00323-1(3))* Houghton Mifflin Harcourt Publishing Co.

—The Jellybeans & the Big Art Adventure. Numeroff, Laura Joffe & Evans, Nate. 2012. (ENG.). 32p. (J). (gr. -1-2). 17.95 *(978-1-4197-0171-9(1))*, Abrams Bks. for Young Readers) Abrams.

—The Jellybeans & the Big Book Bonanza. Numeroff, Laura Joffe & Evans, Nate. 2010. (ENG.). 32p. (J). (gr. -1-3). 17.95 *(978-0-8109-8412-7(1))*, Abrams Bks. for Young Readers) Abrams.

—The Jellybeans & the Big Dance. Numeroff, Laura Joffe & Evans, Nate. 2008. (ENG.). 32p. (J). (gr. -1-1). 17.95 *(978-0-8109-9352-5(X))*, Abrams Bks. for Young Readers) Abrams.

—The Jellybeans Love to Dance. Numeroff, Laura Joffe & Evans, Nate. 2013. (ENG.). 24p. (J). (gr. -1 — 1). bds. 7.95 *(978-1-4197-0622-6(5))*, Abrams Appleseed) Abrams.

—The Jellybeans Love to Read. Numeroff, Laura Joffe & Evans, Nate. 2014. (ENG.). 24p. (J). (gr. -1 — 1). bds. 7.95 *(978-1-4197-1162-6(8))*, Abrams Appleseed) Abrams.

—Listen, Buddy. Lester, Helen. 2013. (Laugh-Along Lessons Ser.). (ENG.). 32p. (J). (gr. -1-3). 8.99 *(978-0-544-00322-4(5))* Houghton Mifflin Harcourt Publishing Co.

—The Loch Mess Monster. Lester, Helen. 2014. (ENG.). 32p. (J). (gr. -1-3). 16.99 *(978-0-544-09990-6(7))*, HMH Books For Young Readers) Houghton Mifflin Harcourt Publishing Co.

—Lots of Lambs. Numeroff, Laura Joffe. 2012. (ENG.). 20p. (J). (gr. k — 1). 9.99 *(978-0-547-40206-2(6))* Houghton Mifflin Harcourt Publishing Co.

—Me First. Lester, Helen. 2013. (Laugh-Along Lessons Ser.). (ENG.). 32p. (J). (gr. -1-3). 8.99 *(978-0-544-00321-7(7))* Houghton Mifflin Harcourt Publishing Co.

Munsinger, Lynn. Miss Nelson Is Missing! Lester, Helen. 2015. 32p. pap. 7.00 ***(978-1-61003-507-1(0))*** Center for the Collaborative Classroom.

Munsinger, Lynn. La Mochila de Lin, Level 2. Lester, Helen. Flor Ada, Alma, tr. from ENG. 3rd ed. 2003. (Dejame Leer Ser.).Tr. of Lin's Backpack. (SPA.). 8p. (J). (gr. -1-1). 6.50 *(978-0-673-36291-9(4))*, Good Year Bks.) Celebration Pr.

—One Monkey Too Many. Koller, Jackie French. 2003. (ENG.). 32p. (J). (gr. -1-3). pap. 7.00 *(978-0-15-204764-1(6))* Houghton Mifflin Harcourt Publishing Co.

—Ponyella. Numeroff, Laura Joffe & Evans, Nate. 2011. (ENG.). 32p. (J). (gr. -1-k). 16.99 *(978-1-4231-0259-5(2))* Hyperion Pr.

—A Porcupine Named Fluffy. Lester, Helen. 2013. (Laugh-Along Lessons Ser.). (ENG.). 32p. (J). (gr. -1-3). 8.99 *(978-0-544-00319-4(5))* Houghton Mifflin Harcourt Publishing Co.

—Rock 'N' Roll Mole. Crimi, Carolyn. 2011. (ENG.). 32p. (J). (gr. -1-k). 16.99 *(978-0-8037-3166-0(3))*, Dial) Penguin Publishing Group.

—The Sheep in Wolf's Clothing. Lester, Helen. 2014. (Laugh-Along Lessons Ser.). (ENG.). 32p. (J). (gr. -1-3). 8.99 *(978-0-544-23300-3(X))*, HMH Books For Young Readers) Houghton Mifflin Harcourt Publishing Co.

—Spot the Plot: A Riddle Book of Book Riddles. Lewis, J. Patrick. 2009. (ENG.). 36p. (J). (gr. -1-3). 15.99 *(978-0-8118-4668-4(7))* Chronicle Bks. LLC.

—String of Hearts. Elliott, Laura Malone. 2010. (ENG.). 32p. (J). (gr. -1-2). 16.99 *(978-0-06-000085-1(6))*, Tegen, Katherine Bks) HarperCollins Pubs.

—Tacky & the Haunted Igloo. Lester, Helen. 2015. (Tacky the Penguin Ser.). (ENG.). 32p. (J). 16.99 *(978-0-544-33994-1(0))*, HMH Books For Young Readers) Houghton Mifflin Harcourt Publishing Co.

—Tacky & the Winter Games. Lester, Helen. 2007. (Tacky the Penguin Ser.). (ENG.). 32p. (J). (gr. -1-3). 6.95 *(978-0-618-95674-6(3))* Houghton Mifflin Harcourt Publishing Co.

—Tacky Goes to Camp. Lester, Helen. 2009. (Tacky the Penguin Ser.). (ENG.). 32p. (J). (gr. -1-3). 16.00 *(978-0-618-98812-9(2))* Houghton Mifflin Harcourt Publishing Co.

—Tacky in Trouble. Lester, Helen. 2005. (Tacky the Penguin Ser.). (ENG.). 32p. (J). (gr. -1-3). 6.95 *(978-0-618-38008-4(6))* Houghton Mifflin Harcourt Publishing Co.

—Tacky the Penguin. Lester, Helen. (Tacky the Penguin Ser.). (ENG.). 32p. (J). (gr. -1-3). 2008. bds. 7.99 *(978-0-547-13344-7(8))*; 2006. 10.99 *(978-0-618-73754-3(5))* Houghton Mifflin Harcourt Publishing Co.

—Tackylocks & the Three Bears. Lester, Helen. 2004. (Tacky the Penguin Ser.). (ENG.). 32p. (J). (gr. -1-3). 6.99 *(978-0-618-43953-9(6))* Houghton Mifflin Harcourt Publishing Co.

—Tacky's Christmas. Lester, Helen. 2010. (Tacky the Penguin Ser.). (ENG.). 32p. (J). (gr. -1-3). 16.99 *(978-0-547-17208-8(7))* Houghton Mifflin Harcourt Publishing Co.

—The Teeny Tiny Ghost & the Monster, Vol. 3. Winters, Kay. 2004. (ENG.). 32p. (J). (gr. -1-3). 14.99 *(978-0-06-028884-6(1))* HarperCollins Pubs.

—Thanksgiving Day Thanks. Elliott, Laura Malone. 2013. (ENG.). 32p. (J). (gr. -1-3). 17.99 *(978-0-06-000236-7(0))* HarperCollins Pubs.

—Underwear! Monsell, Mary Elise. 2010. (ENG.). 16p. (J). (gr. -1-k). bds. 7.99 *(978-0-8075-8310-4(3))* Whitman, Albert & Co.

—What Aunts Do Best / What Uncles Do Best. Numeroff, Laura Joffe. 2004. (ENG.). 32p. (J). (gr. -1-3). 17.99 *(978-0-689-84825-4(0))*, Simon & Schuster Bks. For Young Readers) Simon & Schuster Bks. For Young Readers.

—What Brothers Do Best. Numeroff, Laura Joffe. 2012. (ENG.). 20p. (J). (gr. -1 — 1). bds. 6.99 *(978-1-4521-1073-8(5))* Chronicle Bks. LLC.

—What Puppies Do Best. Numeroff, Laura Joffe. 2011. (ENG.). 32p. (J). (gr. -1-2). 14.99 *(978-0-8118-6601-9(7))* Chronicle Bks. LLC.

—What Sisters Do Best. Numeroff, Laura Joffe. (ENG.). (J). (gr. -1 — 1). 2012. 20p. bds. 6.99 *(978-1-4521-1074-5(3))*; 2009. 44p. 15.99 *(978-0-8118-6545-6(2))* Chronicle Bks. LLC.

—The Wizard, the Fairy, & the Magic Chicken: A Story about Teamwork. Lester, Helen. 2014. (Laugh-Along Lessons Ser.). (ENG.). 32p. (J). (gr. -1-3). 8.99 *(978-0-544-22064-5(1))*, HMH Books For Young Readers) Houghton Mifflin Harcourt Publishing Co.

—Wodney Wat's Wobot. Lester, Helen. 2011. (ENG.). 32p. (J). (gr. -1-3). 16.99 *(978-0-547-36756-9(2))* Houghton Mifflin Harcourt Publishing Co.

—Zany Zoo. Wise, William. 11th ed. 2007. (ENG.). 32p. (J). (gr. k-3). 6.95 *(978-0-618-95686-9(7))* Houghton Mifflin Harcourt Publishing Co.

Munsinger, Lynn. Nighty-Night, Cooper. Munsinger, Lynn. Numeroff, Laura Joffe. 2013. (ENG.). 32p. (J). (gr. -1-3). 16.99 *(978-0-547-40205-5(8))* Houghton Mifflin Harcourt Publishing Co.

Munsinger, Lynn, jt. illus. see Lester, Helen.

Munz, Casey "Naanaage Binesik". Sshtaa taa Haa! Oh No! 2004. (OJI & ENG.). 16p. (J). per. *(978-0-9758801-0-4(1))* Bay Mills Indian Community.

Munzo, Claudio. Tia Isa Quiere un Carro. Medina, Meg. 2012.Tr. of Tia Isa Wants a Car. (SPA.). 32p. (J). (gr. -1-2). 15.99 *(978-0-7636-6129-8(5))* Candlewick Pr.

Muradov, Roman. Goldfish on Vacation. Lloyd-Jones, Sally. 2016. (J). ***(978-0-385-38611-1(7))*** Bantam Doubleday Dell Large Print Group, Inc.

Muraida, Thelma. Cecilia & Miguel Are Best Friends. Bertrand, Diane Gonzales. Ventura, Gabriela Baeza, tr. 2014.Tr. of Cecilia y Miguel Son Mejores Amigos. (SPA & ENG.). 32p. 17.95 *(978-1-55885-794-0(X))* Arte Publico Pr.

—Clara & the Curandera / Clara y la Curandera. Brown, Monica & Ventura, Gabriela Baeza. 2011. (J). 16.95 *(978-1-55885-700-1(1))*, Piñata Books) Arte Publico Pr.

—My Big Sister / Mi Hermana Mayor. Caraballo, Samuel. 2012. (ENG & SPA.). (J). (gr. 3-8). 16.95 *(978-1-55885-750-6(6))*, Piñata Books) Arte Publico Pr.

Muraida, Thelma. The Place Where You Live / El Lugar donde Vives. Muraida, Thelma. Luna, James & Ventura, Gabriela Baeza. 2015. (SPA & ENG.). 32p. (J). (gr. k-3). 17.95 ***(978-1-55885-813-8(X))*** Arte Publico Pr.

Murakami, Jon. Geckos Go to Bed. 2008. 24p. 8.95 *(978-1-933067-26-1(8))* Beachhouse Publishing, LLC.

—Geckos Make a Rainbow. 2010. 28p. pap. 8.95 *(978-1-933067-38-4(1))* Beachhouse Publishing, LLC.

Murakami, Maki. Gravitation, Vol. 12. Yoshimoto, Ray, tr. from JPN. rev. ed. 2005. 192p. pap. 9.99 *(978-1-59532-415-3(1))* TOKYOPOP, Inc.

Murakami, Maki. Gravitation, 12 vols. Murakami, Maki. rev. ed. Vol. 3. 2003. 192p. (gr. 8-18). pap. 9.99 *(978-1-59182-335-3(8))*; Vol. 4. 2004. 208p. (gr. 8-18). pap. 9.99 *(978-1-59182-336-0(6))*; Vol. 5. 2004. 208p. (gr. 8-18). pap. 9.99 *(978-1-59182-337-7(4))*; Vol. 10. 2005. 216p. pap. 9.99 *(978-1-59182-342-1(0))*; Vol. 11. 2005. 176p. pap. 9.99 *(978-1-59532-414-6(3))* TOKYOPOP, Inc.

Murakami, Yasanuri & Kimura, ken. 999 Frogs & a Little Brother. 2015. (ENG.). 40p. (J). 17.95 *(978-0-7358-4202-1(7))* North-South Bks., Inc.

Murakami, Yoshiko, jt. illus. see Karakida, Toshihiko.

Murariu, Lorraine. Peter Rabbit & My Tulips. Gulino, ViTina Corso. 2012. 26p. (J). pap. 9.95 *(978-1-61863-275-3(2))* Bookstand Publishing.

Murase, Sho. City under the Basement. Petrucha, Stefan & Kinney, Sarah. 2009. (Nancy Drew Graphic Novels: Girl Detectiv Ser.: 18). (ENG.). 96p. (J). (gr. 3-7). pap. 7.95 *(978-1-59707-154-3(4))*; 18th ed. 12.95 *(978-1-59707-155-0(2))* Papercutz.

—Cliffhanger. Petrucha, Stefan & Kinney, Sarah. 2009. (Nancy Drew Graphic Novels: Girl Detectiv Ser.: 19). (ENG.). 96p. (J). (gr. 3-7). 12.95 *(978-1-59707-166-6(8))*; pap. 7.95 *(978-1-59707-165-9(X))* Papercutz.

—The Demon of River Heights. Petrucha, Stefan. 2005. (Nancy Drew: Girl Detective Ser.). 88p. (gr. 3-8). 24.21 *(978-1-59961-057-3(4))* Spotlight.

—Doggone Town. Petrucha, Stefan & Kinney, Sarah. 2008. (Nancy Drew Graphic Novels: Girl Detectiv Ser.: 13). (ENG.). 112p. (J). (gr. 3-7). pap. 7.95 *(978-1-59707-098-0(X))* Papercutz.

—Global Warning. Petrucha, Stefan. 8th rev. ed. 2007. (Nancy Drew Graphic Novels: Girl Detectiv Ser.: 8). (ENG.). 112p. (J). (gr. 3-7). pap. 7.95 *(978-1-59707-051-5(3))* Papercutz.

—The Haunted Dollhouse. Petrucha, Stefan. 2005. (Nancy Drew: Girl Detective Ser.). 88p. (gr. 3-7). 24.21 *(978-1-59961-059-7(0))* Spotlight.

—High School Musical Mystery. Petrucha, Stefan & Kinney, Sarah. 2010. (Nancy Drew Graphic Novels: Girl Detectiv Ser.: 20). (ENG.). 96p. (J). (gr. 3-7). pap. 8.99 *(978-1-59707-178-9(1))* Papercutz.

—The Lost Verse, No. 21. Petrucha, Stefan & Kinney, Sarah. 2010. (Nancy Drew Graphic Novels: Girl Detectiv Ser.: 21). (ENG.). 96p. (J). (gr. 3-7). pap. 8.99 *(978-1-59707-195-6(1))* Papercutz.

—Monkey Wrench Blues, No. 11. Petrucha, Stefan & Kinney, Sarah. 11th rev. ed. 2007. (Nancy Drew Graphic Novels: Girl Detectiv Ser.: 11). (ENG.). 112p. (J). (gr. 3-7). pap. 7.95 *(978-1-59707-076-8(9))* Papercutz.

—Nancy Drew: Together with the Hardy Boys. Conway, Gerry. 2011. (Nancy Drew the New Case Files Ser.: 3). (ENG.). 64p. (J). (gr. 3-7). pap. 7.99 *(978-1-59707-262-5(1))* Papercutz.

—The Nancy Drew Diaries. Petrucha, Stefan. 2014. (Nancy Drew Diaries: 1). (ENG.). 176p. (J). (gr. 3-7). pap. 9.99 *(978-1-59707-501-5(9))* Papercutz.

—Night of the Living Chatchke. Petrucha, Stefan & Kinney, Sarah. 2009. (Nancy Drew Graphic Novels: Girl Detectiv Ser.: 17). (ENG.). 96p. (J). (gr. 3-7). pap. 7.95 *(978-1-59707-143-7(9))*; 17th ed. 12.95 *(978-1-59707-144-4(7))* Papercutz.

—Sleight of Dan. Petrucha, Stefan & Kinney, Sarah. 2008. (Nancy Drew Graphic Novels: Girl Detectiv Ser.: 14). (ENG.). 112p. (J). (gr. 3-7). 12.95 *(978-1-59707-108-6(0))*; 14th ed. pap. 7.95 *(978-1-59707-107-9(2))* Papercutz.

—Tiger Counter. Petrucha, Stefan & Kinney, Sarah. 2008. (Nancy Drew Graphic Novels: Girl Detectiv Ser.: 15). (ENG.). 96p. (J). (gr. 3-7). 12.95 *(978-1-59707-119-2(6))*; pap. 7.95 *(978-1-59707-118-5(8))* Papercutz.

—Vampire Slayer. Petrucha, Stefan & Kinney, Sarah. 2010. (Nancy Drew the New Case Files Ser.: 1). (ENG.). 64p. (J). (gr. 3-7). pap. 6.99 *(978-1-59707-213-7(3))* Papercutz.

—A Vampire's Kiss. Petrucha, Stefan & Kinney, Sarah. 2010. (Nancy Drew the New Case Files Ser.: 2). (ENG.). 64p. (J). (gr. 3-7). 10.99 *(978-1-59707-234-2(6))*;No. 2. pap. 6.99 *(978-1-59707-233-5(8))* Papercutz.

—What Goes Up... Petrucha, Stefan & Kinney, Sarah. 2009. (Nancy Drew Graphic Novels: Girl Detectiv Ser.: 16). (ENG.). 96p. (J). (gr. 3-7). 12.95 *(978-1-59707-135-2(8))*;No. 16. pap. 7.95 *(978-1-59707-134-5(X))* Papercutz.

—Writ in Stone. Petrucha, Stefan. 2005. (Nancy Drew: Girl Detective Ser.). 88p. (gr. 3-9). 24.21 *(978-1-59961-058-0(2))* Spotlight.

Murase, Sho & Guzman, Carlos Jose. The Disoriented Express. Petrucha, Stefan & Kinney, Sarah. 10th rev. ed. 2007. (Nancy Drew Graphic Novels: Girl Detectiv Ser.: 10). (ENG.). 112p. (J). (gr. 3-7). pap. 7.95 *(978-1-59707-066-9(1))* Papercutz.

Murata, Yusuke. Eyeshield 21. Inagaki, Riichiro. 2007. (Eyeshield 21 Ser.: Vol. 12). (ENG.). 208p. pap. 7.99 *(978-1-4215-1061-3(8))* Viz Media.

—Eyeshield 21, Vol. 1. Inagaki, Riichird & Inagaki, Riichiro. 2005. (Eyeshield 21 Ser.). (ENG.). 208p. (YA). (gr. 11-17). pap. 9.99 *(978-1-59116-752-5(3))* Viz Media.

—Eyeshield 21. Inagaki, Riichiro. (Eyeshield 21 Ser.). (ENG.). Vol. 2. 2005. 208p. pap. 9.99 *(978-1-59116-809-6(0))*; Vol. 3. 2005. 200p. pap. 9.99 *(978-1-59116-874-4(0))*; Vol. 4. 2005. 200p. pap. 9.99 *(978-1-4215-0074-4(4))*; Vol. 6. 2006. 208p. pap. 9.99 *(978-1-4215-0274-8(7))*; Vol. 7. 2006. 208p. pap. 9.99 *(978-1-4215-0405-6(7))*; Vol. 8. 2006. 208p. pap. 9.99 *(978-1-4215-0637-1(8))*; Vol. 9. 2006. 208p. (gr. 11). pap. 9.99 *(978-1-4215-0638-8(6))*; Vol. 13. 2007. 216p. pap. 7.99 *(978-1-4215-1062-0(6))* Viz Media.

Murawski, Darlyne A. Face to Face with Caterpillars. Murawski, Darlyne A. 2007. (Face to Face with Animals Ser.). (ENG.). 32p. (J). (gr. 2-5). 16.95 *(978-1-4263-0052-3(2))*; lib. bdg. 25.90 *(978-1-4263-0053-0(0))* National Geographic Society. (National Geographic Children's Bks.).

Murawski, Darlyne A., photos by. Spiders & Their Webs. Murawski, Darlyne A. 2007. 31p. (J). reprint ed. 17.00 *(978-1-4223-6813-8(0))* DIANE Publishing Co.

Murawski, Kevin. Harold's Birthday Surprise: Harold & the Purple Crayon. Marsoli, Lisa Ann. 2005. 10p. (J). 6.95 *(978-1-58117-261-4(3))*, Intervisual/Piggy Toes) Bendon, Inc.

Murch, Frank. Jed Smith: Trail Blazer of the West. Latham, Frank. McHugh, Michael J., ed. 2003. 121p. pap. 6.95 *(978-1-930367-86-9(4))* Christian Liberty Pr.

Murchison, Leon, et al. Struggle for Freedom & Henry Box Brown: A Read along Book. Johnston, Brenda A. & Pruitt, Pamela. McCluskey, John A., ed. (Read-Along Bk.). 22p. (J). (gr. 2-4). reprint ed. pap. 4.00 incl. audio *(978-0-913678-16-9(3))* New Day Pr.

Murdocca, Sal. Abe Lincoln at Last! Osborne, Mary Pope. 2011. (Stepping Stone Book(TM) Ser.: No. 47). (ENG.). 128p. (J). (gr. 2-5). 12.99 *(978-0-375-86825-2(9))*; lib. bdg. 15.99 *(978-0-375-96825-9(3))* Random Hse. Children's Bks. (Random Hse. Bks. for Young Readers).

—Abraham Lincoln: Abe Lincoln at Last! Osborne, Mary Pope & Boyce, Natalie Pope. 2011. (Stepping Stone Book Ser.: No. 25). (ENG.). 128p. (J). (gr. 2-5). lib. bdg. 12.99 *(978-0-375-97024-5(X))*, Random Hse. Bks. for Young Readers) Random Hse. Children's Bks.

—Abraham Lincoln No. 47: A Nonfiction Companion to Magic Tree House - Abe Lincoln at Last! Boyce, Natalie Pope & Osborne, Mary Pope. 2011. (Stepping Stone Book(TM) Ser.: No. 25). (ENG.). 128p. (J). (gr. 2-5). 5.99 *(978-0-375-87024-8(5))*, Random Hse. Bks. for Young Readers) Random Hse. Children's Bks.

—American Revolution: A Nonfiction Companion to Revolutionary War on Wednesday. Osborne, Mary Pope & Boyce, Natalie Pope. 2004. (Stepping Stone Book(TM) Ser.: No. 11). (ENG.). 128p. (J). (gr. 2-5). pap. 5.99 *(978-0-375-82379-4(4))*, Random Hse. Bks. for Young Readers) Random Hse. Children's Bks.

—Ancient Rome & Pompeii: A Nonfiction Companion to Vacation under the Volcano. Osborne, Mary Pope & Boyce, Natalie Pope. 2006. (Stepping Stone Book(TM) Ser.: No. 14). (ENG.). 128p. (J). (gr. 1-4). 5.99 *(978-0-375-83220-8(3))*; (gr. 2-5). lib. bdg. 12.99 *(978-0-375-93220-5(8))* Random Hse. Children's Bks. (Random Hse. Bks. for Young Readers).

—Barcos Vikingos al Amanecer. Osborne, Mary Pope. Brovelli, Marcela, tr. from ENG. 2007. (Casa del Arbol Ser.: No. 15).Tr. of Viking Ships at Sunrise. (SPA.). 73p. (J). per. 4.95 *(978-1-933032-21-4(9))* Lectorum Pubns., Inc.

—Blizzard of the Blue Moon. Osborne, Mary Pope. 2007. (Stepping Stone Book(TM) Ser.: No. 36). (ENG.). 144p. (J). (gr. 2-5). 4.99 *(978-0-375-83038-9(3))*, Random Hse. Bks. for Young Readers) Random Hse. Children's Bks.

—Carnival at Candlelight. Osborne, Mary Pope & PLC Editors Staff. 2006. (Magic Tree House Ser.: No. 33). 105p. (gr. 2-6). 15.00 *(978-0-7569-6690-4(6))* Perfection Learning Corp.

—Carnival at Candlelight. Osborne, Mary Pope. 2006. (Stepping Stone Book(TM) Ser.: No. 33). (ENG.). 144p. (J). (gr. 2-5). 4.99 *(978-0-375-83034-1(0))*, Random Hse. Bks. for Young Readers) Random Hse. Children's Bks.

—The Case of the Dirty Clue. Stanley, George Edward. 2005. (Ready-for-Chapters Ser.). (J). lib. bdg. 15.00 *(978-1-59054-898-1(1))* Fitzgerald Bks.

—The Case of the Dirty Clue. Stanley, George E. 2003. (Third-Grade Detectives Ser.: 7). (ENG.). 80p. (J). (gr. 1-4). pap. 4.99 *(978-0-689-86357-8(8))*, Simon & Schuster/Paula Wiseman Bks.) Simon & Schuster/Paula Wiseman Bks.

—China: Land of the Emperor's Great Wall. Osborne, Mary Pope & Boyce, Natalie Pope. 2014. (Stepping Stone Book Ser.). (ENG.). 128p. (J). (gr. 2-5). pap. 5.99 *(978-0-385-38635-7(4))*, Random Hse. Bks. for Young Readers) Random Hse. Children's Bks.

—Christmas in Camelot, Bk. 29. Osborne, Mary Pope. 2009. (Stepping Stone Book(TM) Ser.: No. 29). (ENG.). 144p. (J). (gr. 2-5). 4.99 *(978-0-375-85812-3(1))*, Random Hse. Bks. for Young Readers) Random Hse. Children's Bks.

—The Clue of the Left-Handed Envelope. Stanley, George E. 2004. (Third-Grade Detectives Ser.: Bk. 1). (ENG.). 144p. (J). (gr. 1-4). pap. 5.99 *(978-0-689-87106-1(6))*, Simon & Schuster/Paula Wiseman Bks.) Simon & Schuster/Paula Wiseman Bks.

—A Crazy Day with Cobras. Osborne, Mary Pope. (Stepping Stone Book Ser.: No. 45). (ENG.). (J). 2012. 144p. (gr. 1-4). 4.99 *(978-0-375-86795-8(3))*; 2011. 128p. (gr. 2-5). 12.99 *(978-0-375-86823-8(2))* Random Hse. Children's Bks. (Random Hse. Bks. for Young Readers).

—Dancing Granny, 1 vol. Winthrop, Elizabeth & Winthrop. 2003. (ENG.). 32p. (J). 16.95 *(978-0-7614-5141-9(2))* Marshall Cavendish Corp.

—Danger in the Darkest Hour. Osborne, Mary Pope. 2015. (Stepping Stone Book Ser.: No. 1). (ENG.). 192p. (J). (gr. 2-5). 14.99 *(978-0-553-49772-4(3))*, Random Hse. Bks. for Young Readers) Random Hse. Children's Bks.

—Dark Day in the Deep Sea. Osborne, Mary Pope. 2008. (Stepping Stone Book(TM) Ser.: No. 39). (ENG.). 128p. (J). (gr. 2-5). lib. bdg. 14.99 *(978-0-375-93731-6(5))*, Random Hse. Bks. for Young Readers) Random Hse. Children's Bks.

—Dark Day in the Deep Sea. Osborne, Mary Pope & Osborne, Magic Tree. 2009. (Stepping Stone Book(TM) Ser.: No. 39). (ENG.). 144p. (J). (gr. 2-5). 4.99 *(978-0-375-83732-6(9))* Random Hse., Inc.

—Dinosaurs: A Nonfiction Companion to Dinosaurs Before Dark. Osborne, Will & Osborne, Mary Pope. 2004. (Magic Tree House Research Guides: No. 1). 119p. 16.00 *(978-0-7569-2209-2(7))* Perfection Learning Corp.

—Dinosaurs Before Dark, 1 vol., Set. Osborne, Mary Pope. 2008. (Stepping Stone Book(TM) Ser.: No. 1). (ENG.). (J). (gr. 1-4). 9.99 *(978-0-375-84405-8(8))*, Random Hse. Bks. for Young Readers) Random Hse. Children's Bks.

—Dinosaurs Before Dark. Osborne, Mary Pope. 20th anniv. ed. 2012. (Stepping Stone Book Ser.). (ENG.). 96p. (J). (gr. k-3). 14.99 *(978-0-375-86988-4(3))*; lib. bdg. 17.99 *(978-0-375-96988-1(8))* Random Hse., Inc.

—Dog Heroes: A Nonfiction Companion to Magic Tree House No. 46 Dogs in the Dead of Night. Osborne, Mary Pope & Boyce, Natalie Pope. 2011. (Stepping Stone Book(TM) Ser.: No. 24). (ENG.). 128p. (J). (gr. 1-4). 5.99 *(978-0-375-86012-6(6))*, Random Hse. Bks. for Young Readers) Random Hse. Children's Bks.

—Dogs in the Dead of Night. Osborne, Mary Pope. (Stepping Stone Book(TM) Ser.: No. 46). (ENG.). (J). (gr. 2-5). 2013. 144p. 4.99 *(978-0-375-86796-5(1))*; 2011. 128p. 12.99 *(978-0-375-86824-5(0))*; 2011. 128p. lib. bdg. 15.99 *(978-0-375-96824-2(5))* Random Hse. Children's Bks. (Random Hse. Bks. for Young Readers).

—Dolphins & Sharks: Dolphins at Daybreak. Osborne, Mary Pope & Boyce, Natalie Pope. 2003. (Stepping Stone Book(TM) Ser.: No. 9). (ENG.). 128p. (J). (gr. 2-5). 5.99 *(978-0-375-82377-0(8))*, Random Hse. Bks. for Young Readers) Random Hse. Children's Bks.

—Dolphins at Daybreak; Ghost Town at Sundown; Lions at Lunchtime; Polar Bears Past Bedtime, 4 vols. Osborne, Mary Pope. 2003. (Magic Tree House Ser.: Nos. 9-12). (ENG.). (J). (gr. 3-7). 19.96 *(978-0-375-82553-8(3))*, Random Hse. Bks. for Young Readers) Random Hse. Children's Bks.

—Dragon of the Red Dawn. Osborne, Mary Pope. 2008. (Stepping Stone Book(TM) Ser.: No. 37). (ENG.). 144p. (J). (gr. 2-5). 4.99 *(978-0-375-83728-9(0))* Random Hse., Inc.

—Eve of the Emperor Penguin. Osborne, Mary Pope. 2008. (Stepping Stone Book(TM) Ser.: No. 40). (ENG.). 128p. (J). (gr. 2-5). 11.99 *(978-0-375-83733-3(7))*, Random Hse. Bks. for Young Readers) Random Hse. Children's Bks.

—Eve of the Emperor Penguin. Osborne, Mary Pope. 2009. (Stepping Stone Book(TM) Ser.: No. 40). (ENG.). 144p. (J). (gr. 2-5). 4.99 *(978-0-375-83734-0(5))* Random Hse., Inc.

—Games & Puzzles from the Tree House. Osborne, Mary Pope & Boyce, Natalie Pope. 2010. (Stepping Stone Book(TM) Ser.). (ENG.). 256p. (J). (gr. 1-4). act. bk. ed. 5.99 *(978-0-375-86216-8(1))*, Random Hse. Bks. for Young Readers) Random Hse. Children's Bks.

—A Ghost Tale for Christmas Time. Osborne, Mary Pope. (Stepping Stone Book(TM) Ser.: No. 44). (ENG.). 128p. (J). (gr. 2-5). 2012. pap. 4.99 (978-0-375-85653-2(6)); 2010. 12.99 (978-0-375-85652-5(8)); 2010. lib. bdg. 15.99 (978-0-375-95652-2(2)) Random Hse. Children's Bks. (Random Hse. Bks. for Young Readers).

—Ghosts: A Nonfiction Companion to a Good Night for Ghosts. Osborne, Mary Pope & Boyce, Natalie Pope. 2009. (Stepping Stone Book(TM) Ser.: No. 20). (ENG.). 128p. (J). (gr. 1-4). 5.99 (978-0-375-84666-3(2)); (gr. 2-5). lib. bdg. 12.99 (978-0-375-94666-0(7)) Random Hse., Inc.

—A Good Night for Ghosts. Osborne, Mary Pope. 2009. (Magic Tree House Ser.: No. 42). 112p. (J). Non-ISBN Publisher.

—A Good Night for Ghosts. Osborne, Mary Pope. (Stepping Stone Book(TM) Ser.: No. 42). (ENG.). (J). (gr. 2-5). 2011. 144p. 4.99 (978-0-375-85649-5(8)); 2009. 128p. 11.99 (978-0-375-85648-8(X)); 2009. 128p. lib. bdg. 14.99 (978-0-375-95648-5(4)) Random Hse. Children's Bks. (Random Hse. Bks. for Young Readers).

—Haunted Castle on Hallows Eve. Osborne, Mary Pope. (Stepping Stone Book(TM) Ser.: No. 30). (ENG.). (J). (gr. 2-5). 2010. 144p. pap. 4.99 (978-0-375-86090-4(8)); 2003. 128p. lib. bdg. 13.99 (978-0-375-92521-4(X)) Random Hse. Children's Bks. (Random Hse. Bks. for Young Readers).

—Heroes for All Times: A Nonfiction Companion High Time for Heroes. Osborne, Mary Pope & Boyce, Natalie Pope. 2014. (Stepping Stone Book(TM) Ser.). (ENG.). 128p. (J). (gr. 2-5). 5.99 (978-0-375-87027-9(X), Random Hse. Bks. for Young Readers) Random Hse. Children's Bks.

—High Tide in Hawaii. Osborne, Mary Pope. 2003. (Stepping Stone Book(TM) Ser.: No. 28). (ENG.). 96p. (J). (gr. 1-4). pap. 4.99 (978-0-375-80616-2(4), Random Hse. Bks. for Young Readers) Random Hse. Children's Bks.

—High Time for Heroes. Osborne, Mary Pope. 2014. (ENG.). 128p. (J). (gr. 2-5). (Stepping Stone Book(TM) Ser.). lib. bdg. 15.99 (978-0-307-98050-2(2)); (Stepping Stone Book Series: Bk. 51). 12.99 (978-0-307-98049-6(9)) Random Hse. Children's Bks. (Random Hse. Bks. for Young Readers).

—La Hora de los Juegos Olimpicos. Osborne, Mary Pope. Brovelli, Marcela, tr. 2007. (Casa del Arbol Ser.: No. 16).Tr. of Hour of the Olympics Games. (ENG & SPA.). 68p. (J). per. 4.95 (978-1-933032-22-1(7)) Lectorum Pubns., Inc.

—Horse Heroes: Stallion by Starlight. Osborne, Mary Pope & Boyce, Natalie Pope. 2013. (Stepping Stone Book(TM) Ser.). (ENG.). 128p. (J). (gr. 1-4). 5.99 (978-0-375-87026-2(1)); lib. bdg. 12.99 (978-0-375-97026-9(6)) Random Hse. Children's Bks. (Random Hse. Bks. for Young Readers).

—Hurry Up, Houdini! Osborne, Mary Pope. 2013. (Stepping Stone Book Ser.: No. 50). (ENG.). 128p. (J). (gr. 2-5). 12.99 (978-0-307-98045-8(6)); lib. bdg. 15.99 (978-0-307-98046-5(4)) Random Hse. Children's Bks. (Random Hse. Bks. for Young Readers).

—The Knight at Dawn, 1 vol., Set. Osborne, Mary Pope. 2008. (Stepping Stone Book Ser.: No. 2). (ENG.). (J). (gr. 1-4). 9.99 (978-0-375-84406-5(6), Random Hse. Bks. for Young Readers) Random Hse. Children's Bks.

—The Knight at Dawn. Osborne, Mary Pope. 20th anniv. ed. 2013. (Stepping Stone Book Ser.). (ENG.). 96p. (J). (gr. 1-4). 14.99 (978-0-449-81822-0(5)); 17.99 (978-0-449-81823-7(3)) Random Hse., Inc.

—Leonardo Da Vinci: A Nonfiction Companion to Monday with a Mad Genius. Osborne, Mary Pope & Boyce, Natalie Pope. 2009. (Stepping Stone Book(TM) Ser.: No. 19). (ENG.). 128p. (J). (gr. 2-5). 5.99 (978-0-375-84665-6(4)); lib. bdg. 12.99 (978-0-375-94665-3(9)) Random Hse. Children's Bks. (Random Hse. Bks. for Young Readers).

—Leprechaun in Late Winter. Osborne, Mary Pope. (Stepping Stone Book(TM) Ser.: No. 43). (ENG.). (J). (gr. 2-5). 2012. 144p. 4.99 (978-0-375-85651-8(X)); 2010. 128p. 12.99 (978-0-375-85650-1(1)); 2010. 128p. lib. bdg. 15.99 (978-0-375-95650-8(6)) Random Hse. Children's Bks. (Random Hse. Bks. for Young Readers).

—Leprechauns & Irish Folklore: A Nonfiction Companion to Leprechaun in Late Winter. Osborne, Mary Pope & Boyce, Natalie Pope. 2010. (Stepping Stone Book Ser.: No. 21). (ENG.). 128p. (J). (gr. 1-4). 5.99 (978-0-375-86009-6(6)); (gr. 2-5). lib. bdg. 12.99 (978-0-375-96009-3(0)) Random Hse. Children's Bks. (Random Hse. Bks. for Young Readers).

—Magic Tree House: Vacation under the Volcano; Day of the Dragon King; Viking Ships at Sunrise; Hour of the Olympics, 4 vols. Osborne, Mary Pope. 2008. (Magic Tree House Ser.: Nos. 13-16). (ENG.). (J). (gr. k-3). 19.96 (978-0-375-84661-8(1), Random Hse. Bks. for Young Readers) Random Hse. Children's Bks.

—Magic Tree House #3: Mummies in the Morning. Osborne, Mary Pope. 2014. (Stepping Stone Book Ser.). (ENG.). 96p. (J). (gr. 1-4). 14.99 (978-0-385-38758-3(X), Random Hse. Bks. for Young Readers) Random Hse. Children's Bks.

—Magic Tree House #47: Abe Lincoln at Last! Osborne, Mary Pope. 2013. (Stepping Stone Book(TM) Ser.). (ENG.). 144p. (J). (gr. 2-5). 4.99 (978-0-375-86797-2(X), Random Hse. Bks. for Young Readers) Random Hse. Children's Bks.

Murdocca, Sal. Magic Tree House #50: Hurry up, Houdini! Osborne, Mary Pope. 2015. (Stepping Stone Book(TM) Ser.). (ENG.). 144p. (J). (gr. 2-5). 4.99 **(978-0-307-98048-9(0)**, Random Hse. Bks. for Young Readers) Random Hse. Children's Bks.

—Magic Tree House #53: Shadow of the Shark. Osborne, Mary Pope. 2015. (Stepping Stone Book(TM) Ser.). (ENG.). 144p. (J). (gr. 2-5). lib. bdg. 15.99 **(978-0-553-51082-9(7)**, Random Hse. Bks. for Young Readers) Random Hse. Children's Bks.

Murdocca, Sal. Magic Tree House: Animal Games & Puzzles. Osborne, Mary Pope & Boyce, Natalie Pope. 2015. (Stepping Stone Book(TM) Ser.). (ENG.). 256p. (J). (gr. 2-5). 5.99 (978-0-553-50840-6(7), Random Hse. Bks. for Young Readers) Random Hse. Children's Bks.

—Magic Tree House Fact Tracker #30: Ninjas & Samurai: A Nonfiction Companion to Magic Tree House #5: Night of the Ninjas. Osborne, Mary Pope & Boyce, Natalie Pope. 2014. (Stepping Stone Book(TM) Ser.). (ENG.). 128p. (J). (gr. 2-5). 5.99 (978-0-385-38632-6(X), Random Hse. Bks. for Young Readers) Random Hse. Children's Bks.

—Magic Tree House Survival Guide. Osborne, Mary Pope & Boyce, Natalie Pope. 2014. (Stepping Stone Book(TM) Ser.). (ENG.). 144p. (J). (gr. 2-5). 12.99 (978-0-553-49737-3(5), Random Hse. Bks. for Young Readers) Random Hse. Children's Bks.

—Magic Tree House Volumes 21-24 Boxed Set: American History Quartet, 4 vols. Osborne, Mary Pope. 2014. (ENG.). 96p. (J). (gr. 1-4). 19.96 (978-0-385-38957-0(4), Random Hse. Bks. for Young Readers) Random Hse. Children's Bks.

—Monday with a Mad Genius. Osborne, Mary Pope. 2007. (Stepping Stone Book(TM) Ser.: No. 38). (ENG.). 128p. (J). (gr. 2-5). 11.99 (978-0-375-83729-6(9)); lib. bdg. 14.99 (978-0-375-93729-3(3)) Random Hse. Children's Bks. (Random Hse. Bks. for Young Readers).

—Monday with a Mad Genius. Osborne, Mary Pope. 2009. (Stepping Stone Book(TM) Ser.: No. 38). (ENG.). 144p. (J). (gr. 2-5). 4.99 (978-0-375-83730-2(2)) Random Hse., Inc.

—Moonlight on the Magic Flute. Osborne, Mary Pope. 2009. (Stepping Stone Book(TM) Ser.: No. 41). (ENG.). 128p. (J). (gr. 2-5). 11.99 (978-0-375-85646-4(3)); lib. bdg. 14.99 (978-0-375-95646-1(8)) Random Hse. Children's Bks. (Random Hse. Bks. for Young Readers).

—Moonlight on the Magic Flute. Osborne, Mary Pope. 2010. (Stepping Stone Book(TM) Ser.: No. 41). (ENG.). 144p. (J). (gr. 2-5). pap. 4.99 (978-0-375-85647-1(1)) Random Hse., Inc.

—The Mystery of the Enchanted Dog, 4 vols., Set. Osborne, Mary Pope. 2009. (ENG.). 96p. (J). (gr. 1-4). 19.96 (978-0-375-85811-6(3), Random Hse. Bks. for Young Readers) Random Hse. Children's Bks.

—Night of the New Magicians. Osborne, Mary Pope. 2007. (Stepping Stone Book(TM) Ser.: No. 35). (ENG.). 144p. (J). (gr. 2-5). 4.99 (978-0-375-83036-5(7), Random Hse. Bks. for Young Readers) Random Hse. Children's Bks.

—Pandas & Other Endangered Species: A Perfect Time for Pandas. Osborne, Mary Pope & Boyce, Natalie Pope. 2012. (Stepping Stone Book(TM) Ser.: No. 26). (ENG.). 128p. (J). (gr. 1-4). 5.99 (978-0-375-87025-5(3), Random Hse. Bks. for Young Readers) Random Hse. Children's Bks.

—Penguins & Antarctica: A Nonfiction Companion to Eve of the Emperor Penguin. Osborne, Mary Pope & Boyce, Natalie Pope. 2008. (Stepping Stone Book(TM) Ser.: No. 18). (ENG.). 128p. (J). (gr. 2-5). 5.99 (978-0-375-84664-9(6), Random Hse. Bks. for Young Readers) Random Hse. Children's Bks.

—A Perfect Time for Pandas. Osborne, Mary Pope. 2012. (Stepping Stone Book(TM) Ser.: No. 48). (ENG.). 128p. (J). (gr. 2-5). 12.99 (978-0-375-86826-9(7)); lib. bdg. 15.99 (978-0-375-96826-6(1)) Random Hse. Children's Bks. (Random Hse. Bks. for Young Readers).

—A Perfect Time for Pandas. Osborne, Mary Pope. 2014. (Stepping Stone Book(TM) Ser.). (ENG.). 144p. (J). (gr. 2-5). pap. 4.99 (978-0-375-86798-9(8)) Random Hse., Inc.

—Pilgrims: A Nonfiction Companion to Thanksgiving on Thursday. Osborne, Mary Pope & Boyce, Natalie Pope. 2005. (Stepping Stone Book(TM) Ser.: No. 13). (ENG.). 128p. (J). (gr. 1-4). 5.99 (978-0-375-83219-2(X)); (gr. 2-5). lib. bdg. 12.99 (978-0-375-93219-9(4)) Random Hse. Children's Bks. (Random Hse. Bks. for Young Readers).

—Polar Bears & the Arctic: A Nonfiction Companion to Polar Bears Past Bedtime. Osborne, Mary Pope & Boyce, Natalie Pope. 2007. (Stepping Stone Book Ser.: No. 16). (ENG.). 128p. (J). (gr. 1-4). 5.99 (978-0-375-83222-2(X)); (gr. 2-5). lib. bdg. 12.99 (978-0-375-93222-9(4)) Random Hse. Children's Bks. (Random Hse. Bks. for Young Readers).

—Sabertooths & the Ice Age: A Nonfiction Companion to Sunset of the Sabertooth. Osborne, Mary Pope & Boyce, Natalie Pope. 2005. (Stepping Stone Book(TM) Ser.: No. 12). (ENG.). 128p. (J). (gr. 2-5). 5.99 (978-0-375-82380-0(8)); lib. bdg. 12.99 (978-0-375-92380-7(2)) Random Hse. Children's Bks. (Random Hse. Bks. for Young Readers).

—Sea Monsters: A Nonfiction Companion to Dark Day in the Deep Sea. Osborne, Mary Pope & Boyce, Natalie Pope. 2008. (Magic Tree House Research Guides: No. 17). 121p. (J). (gr. 1-5). 12.65 (978-0-7569-8809-8(8)) Perfection Learning Corp.

—Sea Monsters: A Nonfiction Companion to Dark Day in the Deep Sea. Osborne, Mary Pope & Boyce, Natalie Pope. 2008. (Stepping Stone Book Ser.: No. 17). (ENG.). 128p. (J). (gr. 1-4). 5.99 (978-0-375-84663-2(8)); (gr. 2-5). lib. bdg. 12.99 (978-0-375-94663-9(2)) Random Hse., Inc.

—Season of the Sandstorms. Osborne, Mary Pope. 2006. (Stepping Stone Book(TM) Ser.: No. 34). (ENG.). 144p. (J). (gr. 2-5). 4.99 (978-0-375-83032-7(4), Random Hse. Bks. for Young Readers) Random Hse. Children's Bks.

—The Secret of the Green Skin. Stanley, George E. 2003. (Third-Grade Detectives Ser.: 6). (ENG.). 64p. (J). (gr. 1-4). pap. 4.99 (978-0-689-85378-4(5), Simon & Schuster/Paula Wiseman Bks.) Simon & Schuster/Paula Wiseman Bks.

—The Secret of the Green Skin. Stanley, George Edward. ed. 2005. (Third-Grade Detectives Ser.: Bk. 6). 62p. (J). lib. bdg. 15.00 (978-1-59054-916-2(3)) Fitzgerald Bks.

—Snakes & Other Reptiles: A Nonfiction Companion to a Crazy Day with Cobras. Osborne, Mary Pope & Boyce, Natalie Pope. 2011. (Stepping Stone Book(TM) Ser.: No. 23). (ENG.). 128p. (J). (gr. 1-4). 5.99 (978-0-375-86011-9(8)); (gr. 2-5). lib. bdg. 12.99 (978-0-375-96011-6(2)) Random Hse., Inc.

—Soccer: A Nonfiction Companion to Magic Tree House #52: Soccer on Sunday. Osborne, Mary Pope & Boyce, Natalie Pope. 2014. (Stepping Stone Book(TM) Ser.: No. 29). (ENG.). 128p. (J). (gr. 2-5). lib. bdg. 12.99 (978-0-385-38630-2(3), Random Hse. Bks. for Young Readers) Random Hse. Children's Bks.

—Soccer: Soccer on Sunday. Osborne, Mary Pope & Boyce, Natalie Pope. 2014. (Stepping Stone Book(TM) Ser.: No. 29). (ENG.). 128p. (J). (gr. 2-5). 5.99 (978-0-385-38629-6(X), Random Hse. Bks. for Young Readers) Random Hse. Children's Bks.

—Soccer on Sunday. Osborne, Mary Pope. 2014. (Magic Tree House Ser.: No. 52). (ENG.). 128p. (J). (gr. 2-5). 12.99 (978-0-307-98053-3(7), Random Hse. Bks. for Young Readers) Random Hse. Children's Bks.

—Stallion by Starlight. Osborne, Mary Pope. (Stepping Stone Book(TM) Ser.). (ENG.). (J). (gr. 2-5). 2014. 144p. pap. 4.99 (978-0-307-98044-1(8)); 2013. 128p. 12.99 (978-0-307-98040-3(5)); 2013. 128p. lib. bdg. 15.99 (978-0-307-98042-7(1)) Random Hse. Children's Bks. (Random Hse. Bks. for Young Readers).

—Summer of the Sea Serpent. Osborne, Mary Pope. 2011. (Stepping Stone Book(TM) Ser.: No. 31). (ENG.). 144p. (J). (gr. 2-5). 4.99 (978-0-375-86491-9(1), Random Hse. Bks. for Young Readers) Random Hse. Children's Bks.

—Tsunamis & Other Natural Disasters: A Nonfiction Companion to High Tide in Hawaii. Osborne, Mary Pope & Boyce, Natalie Pope. 2007. (Stepping Stone Book(TM) Ser.: No. 15). (ENG.). 128p. (J). (gr. 1-4). 5.99 (978-0-375-83221-5(1), Random Hse. Bks. for Young Readers) Random Hse. Children's Bks.

—Vacaciones Al Pie de un Volcan. Osborne, Mary Pope. Brovelli, Marcela, tr. from ENG. 2007. (Casa del Arbol Ser.: No. 13).Tr. of Vacation under the Colcano. (SPA.). 74p. (J). per. 4.95 (978-1-933032-19-1(7)) Lectorum Pubns., Inc.

—Winter of the Ice Wizard. Osborne, Mary Pope. 2004. (Stepping Stone Book(TM) Ser.: No. 32). (ENG.). 128p. (gr. 2-5). 11.95 (978-0-375-82736-5(6)); lib. bdg. 13.99 (978-0-375-92736-2(0)) Random Hse. Children's Bks. (Random Hse. Bks. for Young Readers).

—Winter of the Ice Wizard. Osborne, Mary Pope. 2011. (Stepping Stone Book(TM) Ser.: No. 32). (ENG.). 144p. (J). (gr. 2-5). 4.99 (978-0-375-87395-9(3), Random Hse. Bks. for Young Readers) Random Hse. Children's Bks.

Murdocca, Sal. Buenos Días, Gorilas. Murdocca, Sal. Osborne, Mary Pope & Brovelli, Marcela. 2014. (SPA.). 88p. (J). (gr. 2-4). pap. 4.95 (978-1-933032-93-1(6)) Lectorum Pubns., Inc.

—Búfalos Antes del Desayuno. Murdocca, Sal. Osborne, Mary Pope & Brovelli, Marcela. 2008. (Casa del Arbol Ser.: No. 18).Tr. of Buffalo Before Breakfast. (SPA.). (J). (gr. 2-4). pap. 4.95 (978-1-933032-48-1(0)) Lectorum Pubns., Inc.

—Esta Noche en el Titanic. Murdocca, Sal. Osborne, Mary Pope. 2008. (Casa del Arbol Ser.: No. 17).Tr. of Tonight on the Titanic. (SPA.). (J). (gr. 2-4). pap. 4.95 (978-1-933032-47-4(2)) Lectorum Pubns., Inc.

—Jueves de Acción de Gracias. Murdocca, Sal. Osborne, Mary Pope & Brovelli, Marcela. 2014. (SPA.). 88p. (J). (gr. 2-4). pap. 4.95 (978-1-933032-94-8(4)) Lectorum Pubns., Inc.

—Maremoto en Hawái. Murdocca, Sal. Osborne, Mary Pope & Brovelli, Marcela. 2014. (SPA.). 88p. (J). (gr. 2-4). pap. 4.95 (978-1-933032-95-5(2)) Lectorum Pubns., Inc.

—Miedo Escénico en una Noche de Verano. Murdocca, Sal. Osborne, Mary Pope & Brovelli, Marcela. 2014. (SPA.). 86p. (J). (gr. 2-4). pap. 4.95 (978-1-933032-92-4(8)) Lectorum Pubns., Inc.

—Perros Salvajes a la Hora de la Cena. Murdocca, Sal. Osborne, Mary Pope & Brovelli, Marcela. 2008. (Casa del Arbol Ser.: No. 20).Tr. of Dingoes at Dinnertime. (SPA.). (J). (gr. 2-4). pap. 4.95 (978-1-933032-50-4(2)) Lectorum Pubns., Inc.

—Tigres Al Anochecer. Murdocca, Sal. Osborne, Mary Pope & Brovelli, Marcela. 2008. (Casa del Arbol Ser.: No. 19).Tr. of Tigers at Twilight. (SPA.). (J). (gr. 2-4). pap. 4.95 (978-1-933032-49-8(9)) Lectorum Pubns., Inc.

Murdocca, Sal. Ancient Greece & the Olympics: A Nonfiction Companion to Hour of the Olympics. Murdocca, Sal, tr. Osborne, Mary Pope & Boyce, Natalie Pope. 2004. (Stepping Stone Book(TM) Ser.: No. 10). (ENG.). 128p. (J). (gr. 2-5). pap. 5.99 (978-0-375-82378-7(6)); lib. bdg. 12.99 (978-0-375-92378-4(0)) Random Hse. Children's Bks. (Random Hse. Bks. for Young Readers).

—Summer of the Sea Serpent. Murdocca, Sal, tr. Osborne, Mary Pope. 2004. (Stepping Stone Book(TM) Ser.: No. 31). (ENG.). 128p. (J). (gr. 2-5). 11.95 (978-0-375-82735-8(8), Random Hse. Bks. for Young Readers) Random Hse. Children's Bks.

Murdocca, Sal & Vilela, Luiz. Magic Tricks from the Tree House. Osborne, Mary Pope & Boyce, Natalie Pope. 2013. (Stepping Stone Book(TM) Ser.). (ENG.). 128p. (J). (gr. 2-5). 4.99 (978-0-449-81790-2(3), Random Hse. Bks. for Young Readers) Random Hse. Children's Bks.

Murdocca, Sal, jt. illus. see Osborne, Will.

Murdocca, Salvatore. The Case of the Bank-Robbing Bandit. Stanley, George E. 2004. (Third-Grade Detectives Ser.: 9). (ENG.). 80p. (J). (gr. 1-4). pap. 4.99 (978-0-689-86489-6(2), Simon & Schuster/Paula Wiseman Bks.) Simon & Schuster/Paula Wiseman Bks.

—The Mystery of the Stolen Statue. Stanley, George E. 2004. (Third-Grade Detectives Ser.: 10). (ENG.). 80p. (J). (gr. 1-4). pap. 5.99 (978-0-689-86491-9(4), Simon & Schuster/Paula Wiseman Bks.) Simon & Schuster/Paula Wiseman Bks.

—The Riddle of the Stolen Sand. Stanley, George E. 2003. (Third-Grade Detectives Ser.: 5). (ENG.). 64p. (J). (gr. 1-4). pap. 4.99 (978-0-689-85376-0(9), Simon & Schuster/Paula Wiseman Bks.) Simon & Schuster/Paula Wiseman Bks.

—The Secret of the Wooden Witness. Stanley, George E. 2004. (Third-Grade Detectives Ser.: 8). (ENG.). 80p. (J). (gr. 1-4). pap. 4.99 (978-0-689-86487-2(6), Simon & Schuster/Paula Wiseman Bks.) Simon & Schuster/Paula Wiseman Bks.

Murfield, Anna. Adventures in the Weeping Willow Tree. Goebel, Kelly. 2013. 26p. pap. 9.99 (978-1-937165-49-9(3)) Orange Hat Publishing.

—Growing up Cranberry. Gray, Shannon. 2012. 24p. pap. 9.50 (978-1-937165-27-7(2)) Orange Hat Publishing.

—The Perfect Puppy. Marquardt, Michelle. 2013. 24p. pap. 9.99 (978-1-937165-65-9(5)) Orange Hat Publishing.

—Sharlene & Her Animal Friends. Merline, Sharlene, Rongner, Bridget, ed. 2012. 106p. pap. 8.99 (978-1-937165-09-3(4)) Orange Hat Publishing.

Murfin, Teresa. Back-to-School Rules. Friedman, Laurie. 2011. (Carolrhoda Picture Books Ser.). (ENG.). 32p. (J). (gr. k-3). lib. bdg. 16.95 (978-0-7613-6070-4(0)) Lerner Publishing Group.

—Birthday Rules. Friedman, Laurie B. 2015. (J). (gr. k-3). (ENG.). 32p. lib. bdg. 16.99 (978-0-7613-6071-1(9)); (978-1-4677-6177-2(X)) Lerner Publishing Group. (Carolrhoda Bks.).

—I'm Not Afraid of This Haunted House. Friedman, Laurie. 2005. (ENG.). 32p. (J). (gr. k-3). 16.95 (978-1-57505-751-4(4), Carolrhoda Bks.) Lerner Publishing Group.

—Magic Mess! Ryan, Margaret. 2010. (Airy Fairy Ser.). (ENG.). 80p. (gr. 2-4). lib. bdg. 24.21 (978-1-59961-497-7(9)) Spotlight.

—Magic Mistakes! Ryan, Margaret. 2010. (Airy Fairy Ser.). (ENG.). 80p. (gr. 2-4). lib. bdg. 24.21 (978-1-59961-499-1(5)) Spotlight.

—Naughty Toes. Bonwill, Ann. 2011. 32p. 15.95 (978-1-58925-103-8(2)); pap. 7.95 (978-1-58925-430-5(9)) Tiger Tales.

—Thanksgiving Rules. Friedman, Laurie. 2009. (Carolrhoda Picture Bks). (ENG.). 32p. (J). (gr. k-3). 16.95 (978-0-8225-7983-0(9), Carolrhoda Bks.) Lerner Publishing Group.

Murguia, Bethanie. Buglette, the Messy Sleeper. Murguia, Bethanie. 2011. (ENG.). 32p. (J). (gr. -1-2). 15.99 (978-1-58246-375-9(1), Tricycle Pr.) Ten Speed Pr.

—Snippet the Early Riser. Murguia, Bethanie. 2013. (ENG.). 40p. (J). (gr. -1-2). 15.99 (978-1-58246-460-2(X), Knopf Bks. for Young Readers) Random Hse. Children's Bks.

Murguia, Bethanie Deeney. The Best-Ever Bookworm Book. Kuipers, Alice. 2014. (ENG.). 40p. (J). (gr. -1-1). 17.00 (978-0-316-21200-7(8)) Little, Brown Bks. for Young Readers.

Murguia, Bethanie Deeney. Princess Fairy Ballerina. 2016. (J). **(978-0-545-73240-6(9))** Scholastic, Inc.

Murguia, Bethanie Deeney. The Best Parts of Christmas. Murguia, Bethanie Deeney. 2015. (ENG.). 32p. (J). (gr. -1-2). 14.99 **(978-0-7636-7556-1(3))** Candlewick Pr.

Murguia, Bethanie Deeney. I Feel Five! Murguia, Bethanie Deeney. 2014. (ENG.). 32p. (J). (gr. -1-3). 14.99 (978-0-7636-6291-2(7)) Candlewick Pr.

—Zoe's Room (No Sisters Allowed) Murguia, Bethanie Deeney. 2013. (ENG.). 40p. (J). (gr. -1-k). 16.99 (978-0-545-45781-1(5), Levine, Arthur A. Bks.) Scholastic, Inc.

Murguia, Jose J. Uarhiri sapirhatiecheri Jukambekua: La velacion de los Angelitos. Andrade, Mary J., photos by. Andrade, Mary J. 2005. Orig. Title: The Vigil of the Little Angels. 40p. (J). (gr. 3-6). pap. 9.95 (978-0-9665876-8-5(5)) La Oferta Publishing Co.

Murley, Karen O. Every Monday Morning. Hutton, Linda. 2005. 32p. (J). (gr. 4-7). 10.99 (978-0-8254-2895-1(5)) Kregel Pubns.

Muro, Jenny. The Little Pig. Waterbury, Matthew. 2013. 16p. pap. 24.95 (978-1-4512-2919-6(4)) America Star Bks.

Muronaka, Michael & Kaylor, Emiko. Adventures in Japanese. Peterson, Hiromi & Omizo, Naomi. 2004. (JPN & ENG.). Vol. 2. (gr. 7-10). pap., tchr. ed., ldr.'s hndbk. ed. 59.95 (978-0-88727-322-3(X)); Vol. 2. 210p. (gr. 7-10). pap., wbk. ed. 19.95 (978-0-88727-321-6(1)); Vol. 3. (gr. 9-11). pap., tchr. ed., ldr.'s hndbk. ed. 59.95 (978-0-88727-398-8(X)) Cheng & Tsui Co.

—Adventures in Japanese Level 1, 4 vols. Peterson, Hiromi & Omizo, Naomi. 2nd ed. 2005. pap., stu. ed., wbk. ed. 24.95 (978-0-88727-450-3(1)) Cheng & Tsui Co.

Murphy, Aileen. The Bravest Girl in School. Gaynor, Kate. 2013. 20p. pap. (978-0-9555787-4-8(4)) Special Stories Publishing.

Murphy, Andrea. Wilkinson Tales: A Collection of Adventure Short Stories for Young People. Wilkinson, Richard Fergus. 2010. 88p. pap. 27.49 (978-1-4490-5489-2(7)) AuthorHouse.

Murphy, Betsy. A Christmas Problem for Samuel James. Yaun, Ellen R. 59p. (J). (gr. 2-5). pap. 5.95 (978-0-9673970-1-6(4)) Blue Chip Publishing.

Murphy, Bob. Two-B & the Rock 'n' Roll Band, Set. Paul, Sherry. (See How I Read Ser.). 32p. (Orig.). (J). (gr. -1-2). pap. 14.10 (978-0-675-01082-5(9)) CPI Publishing, Inc.

Murphy, Brendán. Ready for School, Murphy? Murphy, Brendán. 2015. (ENG.). 40p. (J). (gr. -1-k). 16.99 (978-1-4847-0740-1(0)) Disney Publishing Worldwide.

Murphy, Charles R. Chickadees At Night. Smith, Bill O. 2012. 32p. (978-0-615-56972-7(2)) Smith, Bill O.

Murphy, Chris. Mango's Revenge. Logue, Stephanie. 2006. (J). pap. (978-1-59336-769-5(4)) Mondo Publishing.

Murphy, David. Sir Mike. Black, Robyn Hood. 2006. (Rookie Reader Skill Set Ser.). (ENG.). 32p. (J). (gr. k-2). per. 4.95 (978-0-516-25020-5(5), Children's Pr.) Scholastic Library Publishing.

Murphy, Dennis. From the Farm to You Coloring Book. Triplett, Annette. Vale, Joe, ed. 2012. 28p. (J). (978-0-933842-34-2(1)) Univ. of Missouri, Extension.

Murphy, Emmy Lou, jt. illus. see Mowery, Linda Williams.

Murphy, Fredrick. Batboy's Crazy Day. Poole, Catherine Cheyenne. 2008. 24p. pap. 8.95 (978-1-935105-18-3(3)) Avid Readers Publishing Group.

Murphy, Ivan. Gadzooks: The Christmas Goose, 1 vol. Kent, Jennifer McGrath. ed. 2011. (ENG.). 32p. (J). (gr. -1-2). 19.95 (978-1-55109-794-7(X)) Nimbus Publishing, Ltd. CAN. Dist: Orca Bk. Pubs. USA.

Murphy, Jill. A Bad Spell for the Worst Witch. Murphy, Jill. 2014. (Worst Witch Ser.). (ENG.). 128p. (J). (gr. 3-7). pap. 5.99 (978-0-7636-7252-2(1)) Candlewick Pr.

—Five Minutes' Peace. Murphy, Jill. 2012. (ENG.). 24p. (J). (gr. -1 — 1). bds. 6.99 (978-0-399-25707-0(1), Putnam Juvenile) Penguin Publishing Group.

M

—Mr. Large in Charge. Murphy, Jill. 2007. (ENG.). 40p. (J). (gr. -1-3). 16.99 *(978-0-7636-3504-6(9))* Candlewick Pr.

Murphy, Jill. On the Way Home. Murphy, Jill. 2nd rev. ed. 2007. (ENG.). 36p. (J). (gr. k-2). pap. 11.95 ***(978-0-230-01584-5(0))*** Pan Macmillan GBR. Dist: Independent Pubs. Group.

—The Worst Witch & the Wishing Star. Murphy, Jill. 2015. (Worst Witch Ser.). (ENG.). 208p. (J). (gr. 3-7). 14.99 ***(978-0-7636-7000-9(6))*** Candlewick Pr.

Murphy, Jill. The Worst Witch Saves the Day. Murphy, Jill. 2014. (Worst Witch Ser.). (ENG.). 160p. (J). (gr. 3-7). pap. 5.99 *(978-0-7636-7255-3(6))* Candlewick Pr.

—The Worst Witch to the Rescue. Murphy, Jill. (Worst Witch Ser.). (ENG.). 176p. (J). (gr. 3-7). 2015. pap. 5.99 ***(978-0-7636-7862-3(7))***; 2014. 14.99 *(978-0-7636-6999-7(7))* Candlewick Pr.

Murphy, Jobi. In Search of the Time & Space Machine. Abela, Deborah. 2005. (Spy Force Ser.). 256p. (Orig.). (J). 14.95 *(978-1-74051-765-2(2)*, Simon & Schuster Bks. For Young Readers) Simon & Schuster Bks. For Young Readers.

—Muddled-Up Farm, 1 vol. Dumbleton, Mike. 2013. (ENG.). 32p. (J). 16.99 *(978-1-59572-630-8(6))*; pap. 6.99 *(978-1-59572-631-5(4))* Star Bright Bks., Inc.

Murphy, Kelly. Alex & the Amazing Time Machine. Cohen, Rich. 2013. (ENG.). 176p. (J). (gr. 3-7). pap. 6.99 *(978-1-250-02729-0(2))* Square Fish.

Murphy, Kelly. Anton & Cecil, Book 2: Cats on Track. Martin, Lisa & Martin, Valerie. 2015. (Anton & Cecil Ser.: 2). (ENG.). 272p. (J). (gr. 3-7). 16.95 ***(978-1-61620-419-8(2))*** Algonquin Bks. of Chapel Hill.

Murphy, Kelly. The Basilisk's Lair. LaFevers, R. L. (Nathaniel Fludd, Beastologist Ser.: 2). (ENG.). 160p. (J). (gr. 1-4). 2011. pap. 5.99 *(978-0-547-54957-6(1))*; 2nd ed. 2010. 15.00 *(978-0-547-23867-8(3))* Houghton Mifflin Harcourt Publishing Co.

—Behind the Bookcase. Steensland, Mark. 2013. (ENG.). 288p. (J). (gr. 3-7). 6.99 *(978-0-385-74072-2(7)*, Yearling) Random Hse. Children's Bks.

—Brand-New Baby Blues. Appelt, Kathi. 2009. (ENG.). 32p. (J). (gr. -1-1). 16.99 *(978-0-06-053233-8(5))* HarperCollins Pubs.

—The Case of the Missing Moonstone (the Wollstonecraft Detective Agency, Book 1) Stratford, Jordan. 2015. (Wollstonecraft Detective Agency Ser.). (ENG.). 240p. (J). (gr. 3-7). 16.99 *(978-0-385-75440-8(X)*, Knopf Bks. for Young Readers) Random Hse. Children's Bks.

—Creepy Monsters, Sleepy Monsters. Yolen, Jane. (ENG.). 32p. (J). (gr. -1-2). 2013. 5.99 *(978-0-7636-6283-7(6))*; 2011. 14.99 *(978-0-7636-4201-3(0))* Candlewick Pr.

—Face Bug. Siskind, Fred, photos by. Lewis, J. Patrick. 2013. (ENG.). 36p. (J). (gr. 1-5). 16.95 *(978-1-59078-925-4(3)*, Wordsong) Boyds Mills Pr.

—Fiona's Luck. Bateman, Teresa. 2009. (ENG.). 32p. (J). (gr. -1-3). pap. 7.95 *(978-1-57091-643-4(8))* Charlesbridge Publishing, Inc.

—Flight of the Phoenix Bk. 1. LaFevers, R. L. 2010. (Nathanial Fludd, Beastologist Ser.: 1). (ENG.). 144p. (J). (gr. 1-4). pap. 5.99 *(978-0-547-40845-3(5))* Houghton Mifflin Harcourt Publishing Co.

—Loony Little: An Environmental Tale. Aston, Dianna Hutts. 2007. (ENG.). 40p. (J). (gr. -1-3). 6.99 *(978-0-7636-3562-6(6))* Candlewick Pr.

—Masterpiece. Broach, Elise. 2010. (ENG.). 320p. (J). (gr. 4-7). pap. 7.99 *(978-0-312-60870-5(5))* Square Fish.

—The Miniature World of Marvin & James. Broach, Elise. 2014. (Masterpiece Adventures Ser.: 1). (ENG.). 112p. (J). (gr. 1-4). 15.99 *(978-0-8050-9190-8(4)*, Holt, Henry & Co. Bks. For Young Readers) Holt, Henry & Co.

—The Mouse with the Question Mark Tail. Peck, Richard. 2013. (ENG.). 240p. (J). (gr. 3-7). 16.99 *(978-0-8037-3838-6(2)*, Dial) Penguin Publishing Group.

—Over at the Castle. Ashburn, Boni. 2010. (ENG.). 32p. (J). (gr. -1-1). 15.95 *(978-0-8109-8414-1(8)*, Abrams Bks. for Young Readers) Abrams.

—Romping Monsters, Stomping Monsters. Yolen, Jane. 2013. (ENG.). 32p. (J). (gr. -1-2). 14.99 *(978-0-7636-5727-7(1))* Candlewick Pr.

—The Scorpions of Zahir. Brodien-Jones, Christine. 2012. (ENG.). 384p. (J). (gr. 5). 17.99 *(978-0-385-73933-7(8)*, Delacorte Bks. for Young Readers) Random Hse. Children's Bks.

—Secrets at Sea. Peck, Richard. 2011. (ENG.). 256p. (J). (gr. 3-7). 16.99 *(978-0-8037-3455-5(7)*, Dial) Penguin Publishing Group.

—The Unicorn's Tale. LaFevers, R. L. 2012. (Nathanial Fludd, Beastologist Ser.: 4). (ENG.). 160p. (J). (gr. 1-4). pap. 5.99 *(978-0-547-85079-5(4))* Houghton Mifflin Harcourt Publishing Co.

—The Wyverns' Treasure. LaFevers, R. L. 2012. (Nathanial Fludd, Beastologist Ser.: 3). (ENG.). 160p. (J). (gr. 1-4). pap. 5.99 *(978-0-547-85823-4(X))* Houghton Mifflin Harcourt Publishing Co.

Murphy, Kelly & Brewster, Patience. Masterpiece. Broach, Elise. 2008. (ENG.). 304p. (J). (gr. 4-7). 16.99 *(978-0-8050-8270-8(0)*, Holt, Henry & Co. Bks. For Young Readers) Holt, Henry & Co.

Murphy, Kelly & Revoy, Antoine. Haunted Houses. San Souci, Robert D. 2012. (Are You Scared Yet? Ser.). (ENG.). 304p. (J). (gr. 4-7). pap. 7.99 *(978-0-312-55136-0(3))* Square Fish.

Murphy, Liz. ABC Dentist: Healthy Teeth from A to Z. Ziefert, Harriet. 2012. (ENG.). 36p. (J). (gr. -1-3). pap. 6.99 *(978-1-60905-274-4(9))* Blue Apple Bks.

—ABC Dentist: Healthy Teeth from A to Z. Ziefert, Harriet. 2012. (ENG.). 36p. (J). (gr. -1-3). 16.99 *(978-1-60905-320-8(6))* Blue Apple Bks.

—ABC Doctor: Staying Healthy from A to Z. Ziefert, Harriet. 2012. (ENG.). 36p. (J). (gr. -1-3). 16.99 *(978-1-60905-319-2(2))* Blue Apple Bks.

—ABC Doctor: Staying Healthy from A to Z. Ziefert, Harriet. 2012. (ENG.). 36p. (J). (gr. -1-3). pap. 6.99 *(978-1-60905-273-7(0))* Blue Apple Bks.

—Broadway Barks. Peters, Bernadette. 2008. (ENG.). 40p. (J). (gr. -1-3). 17.95 *(978-1-934706-00-8(0))* Blue Apple Bks.

—Poodles Don't Play Tennis. Rizzuto, Katherine. 2013. (ENG.). 32p. (J). 19.99 *(978-1-938501-06-7(3))* Turn the Page Publishing.

—Stella & Charlie, Friends Forever. Peters, Bernadette. 2015. (ENG.). 40p. (J). (gr. -1-2). 17.99 *(978-1-60905-535-6(7))* Blue Apple Bks.

—Stella Is a Star! Peters, Bernadette & Blue Apple Staff. 2010. (ENG.). 40p. (J). (gr. k-4). 17.99 *(978-1-60905-008-5(8))* Blue Apple Bks.

Murphy, Liz. A Dictionary of Dance. Murphy, Liz. Ziefert, Harriet. 2012. (ENG.). 36p. (J). (gr. -1-3). pap. 6.99 *(978-1-60905-045-0(2))* Blue Apple Bks.

Murphy, Mary. Are You My Mommy? Murphy, Mary. 2015. (ENG.). 16p. (J). (gr. -1 — 1). bds. 6.99 *(978-0-7636-7372-7(2))* Candlewick Pr.

—How Kind! Murphy, Mary. 2004. (ENG.). 24p. (J). (gr. k-k). bds. 6.99 *(978-0-7636-2307-4(5))* Candlewick Pr.

—A Kiss Like This. Murphy, Mary. 2012. (ENG.). 32p. (J). (gr. k-k). 12.99 *(978-0-7636-6182-3(1))* Candlewick Pr.

—Panda Foo & the New Friend. Murphy, Mary. 2007. (ENG.). 32p. (J). (gr. k-k). 15.99 *(978-0-7636-3405-6(0))* Candlewick Pr.

—Quick Duck! Murphy, Mary. 2013. (ENG.). 16p. (J). (— 1). bds. 6.99 *(978-0-7636-6022-2(1))* Candlewick Pr.

—Say Hello Like This. Murphy, Mary. 2014. (ENG.). 32p. (J). (-k). 12.99 *(978-0-7636-6951-5(2))* Candlewick Pr.

Murphy, Mary Elizabeth. I Kissed the Baby! Murphy, Mary Elizabeth. 2004. (ENG.). 24p. (J). (— 1). bds. 6.99 *(978-0-7636-2443-9(8))* Candlewick Pr.

Murphy, Matt. Man of the Atom, Vol. 2. Newman, Paul S. 2005. (Doctor Solar Ser.: Vol. 2). (ENG.). 200p. 49.95 *(978-1-59307-327-5(5))* Dark Horse Comics.

Murphy, Patrick J. Las Armas de Fuego. Reiter, David P. Rosales-Martinez, Guadalupe, tr. from ENG. 2010.Tr. of Real Guns. (SPA.). 32p. (YA). *(978-1-921479-44-1(2))* Interactive Pubns. Pty, Ltd.

—Real Guns. Reiter, David P. 2007. 32p. (J). *(978-1-876819-83-5(9)*, IP Kidz) Interactive Pubns. Pty, Ltd.

Murphy, Scott. Overboard, 1 vol. Brezenoff, Steve. 2012. (Return to Titanic Ser.). (ENG.). 112p. (gr. 2-3). pap. 6.95 *(978-1-4342-3912-9(8))*; lib. bdg. 23.99 *(978-1-4342-3302-8(2))* Stone Arch Bks. (Return to Titanic).

—Stowaways, 1 vol. Brezenoff, Steve. 2012. (Return to Titanic Ser.). (ENG.). 112p. (gr. 2-3). pap. 6.95 *(978-1-4342-3910-5(1))*; lib. bdg. 23.99 *(978-1-4342-3300-4(6))* Stone Arch Bks. (Return to Titanic).

—Time Voyage, 1 vol. Brezenoff, Steve. 2012. (Return to Titanic Ser.). (ENG.). 112p. (gr. 2-3). pap. 6.95 *(978-1-4342-3909-9(8))*; lib. bdg. 23.99 *(978-1-4342-3299-1(9))* Stone Arch Bks. (Return to Titanic).

—An Unsinkable Ship, 1 vol. Brezenoff, Steve. 2012. (Return to Titanic Ser.). (ENG.). 112p. (gr. 2-3). pap. 6.95 *(978-1-4342-3911-2(X))*; lib. bdg. 23.99 *(978-1-4342-3301-1(4))* Stone Arch Bks. (Return to Titanic).

Murphy, Stuart J. ¡Bien Hecho, Ajay! 2011. (Isil Ser.).Tr. of Good Job, Ajay!. (SPA.). 32p. (J). (-k). 14.95 *(978-1-58089-486-9(0))*; pap. 6.95 *(978-1-58089-487-6(9))* Charlesbridge Publishing, Inc.

—Camille's Team. 2011. (Isil Ser.). (ENG.). 32p. (J). (gr. -1-k). 14.95 *(978-1-58089-458-6(5))*; pap. 6.95 *(978-1-58089-459-3(3))* Charlesbridge Publishing, Inc.

—Emma Hace Amigos. 2011. (Isil Ser.). (SPA & ENG.). 32p. (J). (-k). 14.95 *(978-1-58089-482-1(8))*; pap. 6.95 *(978-1-58089-483-8(6))* Charlesbridge Publishing, Inc.

—Emma's Friendwich. 2010. (Isil Ser.). (ENG.). 32p. (J). (gr. -1-k). 14.95 *(978-1-58089-450-0(X))* Charlesbridge Publishing, Inc.

—Freda Organiza una Merienda. 2011. (Isil Ser.). (SPA & ENG.). 32p. (J). (-k). 14.95 *(978-1-58089-488-3(7))*; pap. 6.95 *(978-1-58089-489-0(5))* Charlesbridge Publishing, Inc.

—Left, Right, Emma! 2012. (Isil Ser.). (ENG.). 32p. (J). (-k). 14.95 *(978-1-58089-472-2(0))*; pap. 6.95 *(978-1-58089-473-9(9))* Charlesbridge Publishing, Inc.

—Percy Se Enoja. 2012. (Isil Ser.). (SPA & ENG.). 32p. (J). (-k). 14.95 *(978-1-58089-492-0(5))*; pap. 6.95 *(978-1-58089-493-7(3))* Charlesbridge Publishing, Inc.

Murphy, Terri. Arch Books: The Centurion at the Cross. Bohnet, Eric C. 2007. (Arch Bks.). (J). 1.99 *(978-0-7586-1260-1(5))* Concordia Publishing Hse.

—Dance Y'all, Dance. Bennett, Kelly. 2010. (ENG.). 32p. (J). (gr. k-2). 16.95 *(978-1-933979-65-6(8))* Bright Sky Pr.

—My School. 2010. (My World Ser.). (ENG.). 24p. (J). (gr. -1-1). pap. 8.15 *(978-1-61533-039-3(9))*; lib. bdg. 22.60 *(978-1-60754-953-6(0))* Windmill Bks.

—My School/Mi Escuela. Rosa-Mendoza, Gladys. 2007. (English Spanish Foundations Ser.). (ENG & SPA.). (J). (gr. -1-k). bds. 6.95 *(978-1-931398-23-7(2))* Me+Mi Publishing.

—One Day I Went Rambling. Bennett, Kelly. 2012. (ENG.). 24p. (J). (gr. k-3). 17.95 *(978-1-936474-06-6(9))* Bright Sky Pr.

—The Ten Plagues. Hartman, Sara. 2006. 16p. (J). 1.99 *(978-0-7586-0875-8(6))* Concordia Publishing Hse.

Murphy, Tom. A Bear & His Boy. Bryan, Sean & Thomas, Evan. 2011. (ENG.). 32p. (J). (gr. -1-k). 14.95 *(978-1-61145-027-9(6)*, 611027, Arcade Publishing) Skyhorse Publishing Co., Inc.

—A Boy & His Bunny. Bryan, Sean. 2011. (ENG.). 32p. (J). (gr. -1-k). 14.95 *(978-1-61145-023-1(3)*, 611023, Arcade Publishing) Skyhorse Publishing Co., Inc.

—A Girl & Her Gator. Bryan, Sean. 2011. (ENG.). 32p. (J). (gr. -1-k). 14.95 *(978-1-61145-032-3(2)*, 611032, Arcade Publishing) Skyhorse Publishing Co., Inc.

—The Juggling Pug. Bryan, Sean. (ENG.). 32p. (J). 2014. (-k). 12.95 *(978-1-62873-596-3(1))*; 2011. (gr. -1-k). 12.95 *(978-1-61608-329-8(8)*, 608329) Skyhorse Publishing Co., Inc. (Sky Pony Pr.).

Murr, Bob. How to Beat Granddad at Checkers. Cardie, John P. 2007. 62p. per. 15.95 *(978-1-59879-390-1(X))* Lifevest Publishing, Inc.

Murray, Alison. Princess Penelope & the Runaway Kitten. Nosy Crow Staff. 2013. (ENG.). 32p. (J). (gr. -1-2). 15.99 *(978-0-7636-6952-2(0)*, Nosy Crow) Candlewick Pr.

Murray, Alison. Hickory Dickory Dog. Murray, Alison. 2014. (ENG.). 32p. (J). (-k). 16.99 *(978-0-7636-6826-6(5))* Candlewick Pr.

—One Two That's My Shoe! Murray, Alison. 2012. (ENG.). 32p. (J). (gr. -1-1). 16.99 *(978-1-4231-4329-1(9))* Hyperion Pr.

Murray, Bill. Under African Skies. Barksdale-Hall, Roland. 2010. (Stories by Brother Barksdale Ser.). (J). 24.95 *(978-0-9825842-7-9(X))*; pap. 18.95 *(978-0-9825842-8-6(8))* Africana Homestead Legacy Pubs., Inc. (Nefu Bks.).

Murray, Carol. Cooking with Ginger: Ginger Gets Lost Book I. Keenan, Penny. 2005. (J). per. 19.95 *(978-1-932604-23-8(5))* Tennessee Valley Publishing.

Murray, D. Leaf & the Rushing Waters: Twig Stories. Marshall, Jo. 2011. (ENG.). 370p. pap. 13.95 *(978-1-4611-3578-4(8))* CreateSpace Independent Publishing Platform.

Murray, D. W. Leaf & the Sky of Fire: Twig Stories. Marshall, Jo. 2011. (ENG.). 320p. pap. 12.95 *(978-1-4563-0092-0(X))* CreateSpace Independent Publishing Platform.

Murray, James. Tilda Pinkerton's Magical Hats. Shelton, Angela. 2013. 196p. pap. 11.99 *(978-0-9859443-7-7(4))* Quiet Owl Bks.

Murray, Martine. Henrietta the Great Go-Getter. Murray, Martine. 2010. (Henrietta Ser.). (ENG.). 96p. (J). (gr. k-2). 10.99 *(978-1-74175-450-6(X))* Allen & Unwin AUS. Dist: Independent Pubs. Group.

Murray, Patricia. Make It & Pray It. Murray, Patricia. gif. ed. 2005. 110p. (J). (gr. 3-7). 22.00 *(978-0-88489-895-5(4))* St. Mary's Pr. of MN.

—Make It & Pray It: The Rosary Kit for Young People, 10 pack. Murray, Patricia. 2005. 63p. (J). (gr. -1-7). 58.75 *(978-0-88489-870-2(9))* St. Mary's Pr. of MN.

Murray, Paula. Pupazzo's Colorful World. Keylock, Joanna Murray. Pelayo, Ruben, tr. 2006.Tr. of colorido mundo de Pupazzo. (J). 10.00 *(978-1-889289-62-5(0))* Ye Olde Font Shoppe.

Murray, Rhett E. The Aaronic Priesthood: Seven Principles That Will Make This Power a Part of Your Daily Life. Daybell, Chad. 2003. 100p. (YA). pap. 8.95 *(978-1-55517-717-1(4)*, 77174) Cedar Fort, Inc./CFI Distribution.

Murray, Sean. Trollhunters. del Toro, Guillermo & Kraus, Daniel. 2015. (Trollhunters Ser.). (ENG.). 320p. (YA). (gr. 7-12). 18.99 *(978-1-4231-2598-3(3))* Hyperion Bks. for Children.

Murray, Steven. Arguing: Word by Word, 1 vol. Slavens, Elaine. (Lorimer Deal with It Ser.). (ENG.). 32p. (J). (gr. 4-6). 2010. 24.95 *(978-1-55277-498-4(8))*; 2004. 12.95 *(978-1-55028-820-9(2))* Lorimer, James & Co., Ltd., Pubs. CAN. Dist: Casemate Pubs. & Bk. Distributors, LLC.

—Authority: Deal with It Before It Deals with You, 1 vol. Aikins, Anne Marie. 2005. (Lorimer Deal with It Ser.). (ENG.). 32p. (J). (gr. 4-6). 12.95 *(978-1-55028-869-8(5))* Lorimer, James & Co., Ltd., Pubs. CAN. Dist: Casemate Pubs. & Bk. Distributors, LLC.

—Competition: From Start to Finish, 1 vol. Messier, Mireille. 2004. (Lorimer Deal with It Ser.). (ENG.). 32p. (J). (gr. 4-6). 12.95 *(978-1-55028-832-2(6))* Lorimer, James & Co., Ltd., Pubs. CAN. Dist: Casemate Pubs. & Bk. Distributors, LLC.

—Fighting: Without Coming to Blows, 1 vol. Slavens, Elaine. 2nd ed. 2010. (Lorimer Deal with It Ser.). (ENG.). 32p. (J). (gr. 4-6). 24.95 *(978-1-55277-501-1(1))* Lorimer, James & Co., Ltd., Pubs. CAN. Dist: Casemate Pubs. & Bk. Distributors, LLC.

—Fighting: Without Coming to Blows, 1 vol. Slavens, Elaine & James Lorimer and Company Ltd. Staff. 2nd ed. 2010. (Lorimer Deal with It Ser.). (ENG.). 32p. (J). (gr. 4-6). pap. 12.95 *(978-1-55277-517-2(8))* Lorimer, James & Co., Ltd., Pubs. CAN. Dist: Casemate Pubs. & Bk. Distributors, LLC.

—Girlness: Body & Soul, 1 vol. Peters, Diane. 2005. (Lorimer Deal with It Ser.). (ENG.). 32p. (J). (gr. 4-6). pap. 12.95 *(978-1-55028-891-9(1))* Lorimer, James & Co., Ltd., Pubs. CAN. Dist: Casemate Pubs. & Bk. Distributors, LLC.

—Guyness: Body & Soul, 1 vol. Pitt, Steve. 2005. (Lorimer Deal with It Ser.). (ENG.). 32p. (J). (gr. 4-6). pap. 12.95 *(978-1-55028-892-6(X))* Lorimer, James & Co., Ltd., Pubs. CAN. Dist: Casemate Pubs. & Bk. Distributors, LLC.

—Misconduct: Deal with It Without Bending the Rules, 1 vol. Aikins, Anne Marie. 2005. (Lorimer Deal with It Ser.). (ENG.). 32p. (J). (gr. 4-6). 12.95 *(978-1-55028-871-1(7))* Lorimer, James & Co., Ltd., Pubs. CAN. Dist: Casemate Pubs. & Bk. Distributors, LLC.

—Racism: Deal with It Before It Gets under Your Skin, 1 vol. Aikins, Anne Marie. (Lorimer Deal with It Ser.). (ENG.). 32p. (J). (gr. 4-6). 2010. 24.95 *(978-1-55277-495-3(3))*; 2004. 12.95 *(978-1-55028-844-5(X))* Lorimer, James & Co., Ltd., Pubs. CAN. Dist: Casemate Pubs. & Bk. Distributors, LLC.

Murrell, Diane. Friends Learn about Tobin. Murrell, Diane. 2007. (ENG.). 29p. (J). (gr. -1-3). 16.95 *(978-1-932565-41-6(8))* Future Horizons, Inc.

—Oliver Onion: The Onion Who Learns to Accept & Be Himself. Murrell, Diane. 2004. 40p. (J). (gr. -1-4). 16.95 *(978-1-931282-64-2(1))* Autism Asperger Publishing Co.

Murrish, Layne Keeton. Bubbles & Billy Sandwalker. Mogavera, Cyndie Lepori & Richards, Courtland William. 2nd ed. 2012. 106p. pap. 19.95 *(978-0-9856754-0-0(3))* IAMPress.

Musacchia, Vince. Scooby-Doo! The Case of the Disappearing Scooby Snacks. 2005. (Media Favorites!! Ser.). 22p. (J). 9.95 *(978-1-58117-214-0(1)*, Intervisual/Piggy Toes) Bendon, Inc.

Muscarello, James. Bad Rats. Drachman, Eric. 2008. (ENG.). 32p. (J). (gr. -1-3). 18.95 *(978-0-9703809-4-4(1))* Kidwick Bks.

—Ellison the Elephant. Drachman, Eric. 2005. (ENG.). 32p. (J). (gr. -1-2). 18.95 *(978-0-9703809-1-3(7))* Kidwick Bks.

—A Frog Thing. Drachman, Eric. 2006. (ENG.). 32p. (J). (gr. -1-2). 18.95 *(978-0-9703809-3-7(3))* Kidwick Bks.

—Leo the Lightning Bug. Drachman, Eric. l.t. ed. 2005. (ENG.). 32p. (J). (gr. -1-2). 18.95 *(978-0-9703809-0-6(9))* Kidwick Bks.

Muschinske, Emily. Fingerprint Critters: Turning Your Prints into Fun Art. 2006. 48p. (J). pap. *(978-0-439-81338-9(7))* Scholastic, Inc.

—Let's Draw a Bear with Squares. Campbell, Kathy Kuhtz. 2004. (Let's Draw with Shapes Ser.). 24p. (J). (gr. k-1). lib. bdg. 22.60 *(978-1-4042-2501-5(3)*, PowerKids Pr.) Rosen Publishing Group, Inc., The.

—Let's Draw a Bird with Shapes. Randolph, Joanne. 2005. (Let's Draw with Shapes Ser.). 24p. (J). (gr. k-1). lib. bdg. 22.60 *(978-1-4042-2792-7(X)*, PowerKids Pr.) Rosen Publishing Group, Inc., The.

—Let's Draw a Bird with Shapes: Vamos a Dibujar un Ave Usando Figuras. Randolph, Joanne. 2005. (Let's Draw with Shapes / Vamos a Dibujar con Figuras Ser.). (J). 22.60 *(978-1-4042-7555-3(X)*, PowerKids Pr.) Rosen Publishing Group, Inc., The.

—Let's Draw a Butterfly with Circles. Randolph, Joanne. 2005. (Let's Draw with Shapes Ser.). 24p. (J). (gr. k-1). lib. bdg. 22.60 *(978-1-4042-2500-8(5)*, PowerKids Pr.) Rosen Publishing Group, Inc., The.

—Let's Draw a Butterfly with Circles: Vamos a Dibujar una Mariposa Usando Circulos. Randolph, Joanne. 2004. (Let's Draw with Shapes / Vamos a Dibujar con Figuras Ser.). (ENG & SPA.). 24p. (J). (gr. -1-1). lib. bdg. 22.60 *(978-1-4042-7500-3(2)*, PowerKids Pr.) Rosen Publishing Group, Inc., The.

—Let's Draw a Dinosaur with Shapes. Randolph, Joanne. 2005. (Let's Draw with Shapes Ser.). 24p. (J). (gr. k-1). lib. bdg. 22.60 *(978-1-4042-2793-4(8)*, PowerKids Pr.) Rosen Publishing Group, Inc., The.

—Let's Draw a Fire Truck with Shapes. Randolph, Joanne. 2005. (Let's Draw with Shapes Ser.). 24p. (J). (gr. k-1). lib. bdg. 22.60 *(978-1-4042-2794-1(6)*, PowerKids Pr.) Rosen Publishing Group, Inc., The.

—Let's Draw a Fire Truck with Shapes: Vamos a Dibujar un Camion de Bomberos Usando Figuras. Randolph, Joanne. 2005. (Let's Draw with Shapes / Vamos a Dibujar con Figuras Ser.). (ENG & SPA.). (J). 22.60 *(978-1-4042-7556-0(8)*, PowerKids Pr.) Rosen Publishing Group, Inc., The.

—Let's Draw a House with Shapes. Randolph, Joanne. 2005. (Let's Draw with Shapes Ser.). 24p. (J). (gr. k-1). lib. bdg. 22.60 *(978-1-4042-2795-8(4)*, PowerKids Pr.) Rosen Publishing Group, Inc., The.

—Let's Draw a House with Shapes: Vamos a Dibujar una Casa Usando Figuras. Randolph, Joanne. 2005. (Let's Draw with Shapes / Vamos a Dibujar con Figuras Ser.). (ENG & SPA.). (J). 22.60 *(978-1-4042-7558-4(4)*, PowerKids Pr.) Rosen Publishing Group, Inc., The.

—Let's Draw a School Bus with Shapes. Randolph, Joanne. 2005. (Let's Draw with Shapes Ser.). 24p. (J). (gr. k-1). lib. bdg. 22.60 *(978-1-4042-2791-0(1)*, PowerKids Pr.) Rosen Publishing Group, Inc., The.

—Let's Draw a School Bus with Shapes: Vamos a Dibujar un Autobus Escolar Usando Figuras. Randolph, Joanne. 2005. (Let's Draw with Shapes / Vamos a Dibujar con Figuras Ser.). (ENG & SPA.). (J). 22.60 *(978-1-4042-7557-7(6)*, PowerKids Pr.) Rosen Publishing Group, Inc., The.

—Let's Draw a Truck with Shapes. Randolph, Joanne. 2005. (Let's Draw with Shapes Ser.). 24p. (J). (gr. k-1). lib. bdg. 22.60 *(978-1-4042-2796-5(2)*, PowerKids Pr.) Rosen Publishing Group, Inc., The.

—Let's Draw a Truck with Shapes: Vamos a Dibujar un Camion Usando Figuras. Randolph, Joanne. 2005. (Let's Draw with Shapes / Vamos a Dibujar con Figuras Ser.). (ENG & SPA.). (J). 22.60 *(978-1-4042-7554-6(1)*, PowerKids Pr.) Rosen Publishing Group, Inc., The.

Muschinske, Emily. Let's Draw a Fish with Triangles: Vamos a Dibujar un Pez Usando Triangulos. Muschinske, Emily, tr. Campbell, Kathy Kuhtz. 2004. (Let's Draw with Shapes / Vamos a Dibujar con Figuras Ser.). (ENG & SPA.). 24p. (J). (gr. -1-1). lib. bdg. 22.60 *(978-1-4042-7505-8(3)*, PowerKids Pr.) Rosen Publishing Group, Inc., The.

—Let's Draw a Frog with Ovals: Vamos a Dibujar una Rana Usando Ovalos. Muschinske, Emily, tr. Campbell, Kathy Kuhtz. 2004. (Let's Draw with Shapes / Vamos a Dibujar con Figuras Ser.). (ENG & SPA.). 24p. (J). (gr. -1-1). lib. bdg. 22.60 *(978-1-4042-7503-4(7)*, PowerKids Pr.) Rosen Publishing Group, Inc., The.

—Let's Draw a Horse with Rectangles. Muschinske, Emily, tr. Randolph, Joanne. 2004. (Let's Draw with Shapes Ser.). 24p. (gr. -1-1). 22.60 *(978-1-4042-2502-2(1)*, PowerKids Pr.) Rosen Publishing Group, Inc., The.

Musheno, Erica. Krumbuckets. Mohr, L. C. 2007. (ENG.). 144p. (J). (gr. 2-7). 13.95 *(978-0-9769417-6-7(7))* Blooming Tree Pr.

Muss, Angela. Frog & Me. 2012. (Puppet Pals Ser.). (ENG.). 10p. (J). bds. *(978-1-84643-476-1(9))* Child's Play International Ltd.

—Guess Who? Noah's Ark: A Flip-The-Flap Book. Goodings, Christina. 2014. (ENG.). 6p. (J). (— 1). bds. 9.99 *(978-0-7459-6496-6(6))* Lion Hudson PLC GBR. Dist: Independent Pubs. Group.

—Little Bear's Sparkly Christmas. Stone, Julia. 2014. (ENG.). 6p. (J). (gr. -1-k). bds. 8.99 *(978-0-7459-6262-7(9))* Lion Hudson PLC GBR. Dist: Independent Pubs. Group.

—Monkey & Me. 2012. (Puppet Pals Ser.). (ENG.). 10p. (J). bds. *(978-1-84643-475-4(0))* Child's Play International Ltd.

—Panda & Me. 2012. (Puppet Pals Ser.). (ENG.). 10p. (J). bds. *(978-1-84643-473-0(4))* Child's Play International Ltd.

—Penguin & Me. 2012. (Puppet Pals Ser.). (ENG.). 10p. (J). bds. *(978-1-84643-474-7(2))* Child's Play International Ltd.

Musselman, Christian, jt. illus. see Duarte, Pamela.

Mussenbrock, Anne. The Christmas Surprise. Meyer, Brigit. 2004. 10p. (J). bds. 5.99 *(978-1-59384-061-7(6))* Parklane Publishing.

—Merry Christmas, Little Bear. Meyer, Brigit. 2004. 10p. (J). bds. 5.99 *(978-1-59384-062-4(4))* Parklane Publishing.

Muszynski, Eva. Brer Rabbit down the Well. Stowell, Louie. 2010. (First Reading Level 2 Ser.). 32p. (J). 6.99 *(978-0-7945-2674-0(8)*, Usborne) EDC Publishing.

Muth, Jon J. Blowin' in the Wind. Dylan, Bob. 2011. (ENG.). 28p. (J). (gr. k-3). 17.95 *(978-1-4027-8002-8(8))* Sterling Publishing Co., Inc.

—The Christmas Magic. Thompson, Lauren. 2009. (ENG.). 40p. (J). (gr. -1-3). 16.99 *(978-0-439-77497-0(7)*, Scholastic Pr.) Scholastic, Inc.

—City Dog, Country Frog. Willems, Mo. 2010. (ENG.). 64p. (J). (gr. -1-k). 17.99 *(978-1-4231-0300-4(9))* Hyperion Pr.

—A Family of Poems: My Favorite Poetry for Children. Kennedy, Caroline. 2005. (ENG.). 144p. (J). (gr. -1-17). 19.95 *(978-0-7868-5111-9(2))* Hyperion Pr.

—I Will Hold You 'Til You Sleep. Zuckerman, Linda. 2006. (J). *(978-0-439-43421-8(1)*, Levine, Arthur A. Bks.) Scholastic, Inc.

—Mr. George Baker. Hest, Amy. 2007. (Reading Rainbow Bks.). (ENG.). 32p. (J). (gr. k-3). 6.99 *(978-0-7636-3308-0(9))* Candlewick Pr.

—No Dogs Allowed! Manzano, Sonia. 2005. (J). 27.95 incl. audio *(978-0-8045-6927-9(4)*, SAC6927); 29.95 incl. audio compact disk *(978-0-8045-4101-5(9)*, SACD4101) Spoken Arts, Inc.

—Old Turtle & the Broken Truth. Wood, Douglas. 2003. (ENG.). 64p. (J). (gr. -1-3). 17.99 *(978-0-439-32109-9(3))* Scholastic, Inc.

—Poems to Learn by Heart. Kennedy, Caroline. 2013. (ENG.). 194p. (J). (gr. -1-17). 19.99 *(978-1-4231-0805-4(1))* Hyperion Pr.

—Poems to Learn by Heart. Kennedy, Caroline & Sampson, Ana. 2014. (ENG.). 224p. 19.95 *(978-1-78243-145-9(4))* O'Mara, Michael Bks., Ltd. GBR. Dist: Independent Pubs. Group.

—Poems to Share. Kennedy, Caroline. 2008. 32p. 17.99 *(978-1-4231-1658-5(5))* Hyperion Pr.

Muth, Jon J. No Dogs Allowed! Muth, Jon J. Manzano, Sonia. 2004. (ENG.). 32p. (J). (gr. -1-2). 16.99 *(978-0-689-83088-4(2)*, Atheneum Bks. for Young Readers) Simon & Schuster Children's Publishing.

—Stone Soup. Muth, Jon J. (ENG.). (J). (gr. -1-3). 2011. 9.99 *(978-0-545-35394-6(7))*; 2003. 32p. 17.99 *(978-0-439-33909-4(X)*, Scholastic Pr.) Scholastic, Inc.

—Zen Ghosts. Muth, Jon J. 2012. (ENG.). (J). (gr. -1-3). 9.99 *(978-0-545-43428-7(9))* Scholastic, Inc.

—Zen Shorts. Muth, Jon J. 2005. (ENG.). 40p. (J). (gr. -1-3). 17.99 *(978-0-439-33911-7(1))* Scholastic, Inc.

—Zen Ties. Muth, Jon J. 2008. (ENG.). 40p. (J). (gr. -1-3). 17.99 *(978-0-439-63425-0(3)*, Scholastic Pr.) Scholastic, Inc.

Muth, Jon J. & Buscema, John. Galactus the Devourer. 2014. (ENG.). 184p. (J). (gr. 4-17). pap. 24.99 *(978-0-7851-8562-8(3))* Marvel Worldwide, Inc.

Muth, Jon J. & Maestro, Laura Hartman. A Family Christmas. Kennedy, Caroline. rev. ed. 2007. (ENG.). 333p. (gr. 7-17). 26.95 *(978-1-4013-2227-4(1))* Hyperion Pr.

Muths, Tohn. Princess Dessabelle Makes a Friend. Dzidrums, Christine. 2011. 32p. (J). pap. 9.99 *(978-0-9826435-6-3(X))*; 17.99 *(978-0-9826435-7-0(8))* Creative Media Publishing.

Muths, Tohn Fayette. Princess Dessabelle: Tennis Star. Dzidrums, Christine. 2013. 50p. pap. 10.99 *(978-1-938438-34-9(5))* Creative Media Publishing.

Muzak, Warren. Dixie & Taco Vol. 2: Dixie & Taco go to the Zoo: Enfield CT Version. Monkeys, J. 2011. (ENG.). 34p. pap. 10.00 *(978-1-4663-4521-8(7))* CreateSpace Independent Publishing Platform.

—Dixie & Taco Go to Grandmother's House. Monkeys, J. 2011. (ENG.). 28p. pap. 10.00 *(978-1-4611-1328-7(8))* CreateSpace Independent Publishing Platform.

—Dixie & Taco Go to the Zoo. Monkeys, J. 2011. (ENG.). 34p. pap. 10.00 *(978-1-4636-9251-3(X))* CreateSpace Independent Publishing Platform.

My Wolf Dog. A Peek into the Secret Little Ones of Turtle Back Island. Avignone, June. 2004. 40p. (J). pap. *(978-0-9654628-2-2(X))* Mill Street Forward, The.

Myagmardorj, Enkhtungalag. The Doll That Flew Away. Batkhuu, Kh. 2007. 32p. (J). (POL & ENG.). pap. 12.95 *(978-1-60195-098-7(5))*; (ARA & ENG.). pap. 12.95 *(978-1-60195-092-5(6))* International Step by Step Assn.

Mycek-Wodecki, Anna. How Would It Feel? Goddard, Mary Beth. 2005. (ENG.). 32p. (J). (gr. -1-6). 15.95 *(978-1-59143-050-6(X)*, Bear Cub Bks.) Bear & Co.

Mycek-Wodecki, Anna. The Bilingual Dog. Mycek-Wodecki, Anna. Abt, Diana, tr. 2008. (Minutka Ser.). (SPA & ENG.). 48p. (J). (gr. -1-k). 9.95 *(978-1-84059-509-3(4))* Milet Publishing.

—The Bilingual Dog/Iki Dilli Kopek. Mycek-Wodecki, Anna. Erdogan, Fatih, tr. 2008. (Minutka Ser.). (TUR & ENG.). 48p. (J). (gr. -1-k). 9.95 *(978-1-84059-510-9(8))* Milet Publishing.

—La Cagnetta Bilingue (The Bilingual Dog) Mycek-Wodecki, Anna. Umicini, Roberta, tr. 2008. (Minutka Ser.). (ITA & ENG.). 48p. (J). (gr. -1-k). 9.95 *(978-1-84059-513-0(2))* Milet Publishing.

—Minutka: The Bilingual Dog & Friends. Mycek-Wodecki, Anna. ed. 2009. (Minutka Ser.). 48p. (J). (gr. k — 1). (POL & ENG.). 9.95 *(978-1-84059-523-9(X))*; (SPA & ENG.). 9.95 *(978-1-84059-527-7(2))* Milet Publishing.

Myer, Ed. A Blimp in the Blue. Robertson, J. Jean. 2013. (ENG.). 24p. (gr. -1-1). 25.64 *(978-1-62169-270-6(1))*; pap. 7.95 *(978-1-62169-228-7(0))* Rourke Educational Media.

—The Chili Challenge. Greve, Meg. 2013. (ENG.). 24p. (gr. -1-1). 25.64 *(978-1-62169-268-3(X))*; pap. 7.95 *(978-1-62169-226-3(4))* Rourke Educational Media.

—Clam Beach. Robertson, J. Jean. 2013. (ENG.). 24p. (gr. -1-1). 25.64 *(978-1-62169-271-3(X))*; pap. 7.95 *(978-1-62169-229-4(9))* Rourke Educational Media.

—Flipper Island. Robertson, J. Jean. 2013. (ENG.). 24p. (gr. -1-1). 25.64 *(978-1-62169-272-0(8))*; pap. 7.95 *(978-1-62169-230-0(2))* Rourke Educational Media.

—Glaciers! Robertson, J. Jean. 2013. (ENG.). 24p. (gr. -1-1). 25.64 *(978-1-62169-273-7(6))*; pap. 7.95 *(978-1-62169-231-7(0))* Rourke Educational Media.

—In the Big City. Suen, Anastasia. 2012. (ENG.). 24p. (gr. k-1). pap. 7.95 *(978-1-61810-302-4(4))*; lib. bdg. 28.50 *(978-1-61810-169-3(2))* Rourke Educational Media.

—In the Doghouse. Steinkraus, Kyla. 2012. (ENG.). 24p. (gr. 2-3). pap. 7.95 *(978-1-61810-332-1(6))*; lib. bdg. 28.50 *(978-1-61810-199-0(4))* Rourke Educational Media.

—Johnny Appleseed. Suen, Anastasia. 2012. (ENG.). 24p. (gr. k-1). pap. 7.95 *(978-1-61810-301-7(6))*; lib. bdg. 28.50 *(978-1-61810-168-6(4))* Rourke Educational Media.

—Jungle Journey. Robertson, J. Jean. 2013. (ENG.). 24p. (gr. -1-1). 25.64 *(978-1-62169-241-6(8))*; pap. 7.95 *(978-1-62169-199-0(3))* Rourke Educational Media.

—Kangaroo Country. Robertson, J. Jean. 2013. (ENG.). 24p. (gr. -1-1). 25.64 *(978-1-62169-240-9(X))*; pap. 7.95 *(978-1-62169-198-3(5))* Rourke Educational Media.

—Let's Meet a Firefighter. Bellisario, Gina. 2013. (Cloverleaf Books — Community Helpers Ser.). (ENG.). 24p. (gr. k-2). pap. 6.95 *(978-1-4677-0802-9(X))*; lib. bdg. 23.93 *(978-0-7613-9025-1(1))* Lerner Publishing Group. (Millbrook Pr.).

—Let's Meet a Librarian. Bellisario, Gina. 2013. (Cloverleaf Books — Community Helpers Ser.). (ENG.). 24p. (gr. k-2). pap. 6.95 *(978-1-4677-0803-6(8))*; lib. bdg. 23.93 *(978-0-7613-9027-5(8))* Lerner Publishing Group. (Millbrook Pr.).

—Little Red Riding Hood. Selleck, Richelle. 2012. (ENG.). 24p. (gr. 2-3). pap. 7.95 *(978-1-61810-324-6(5))*; lib. bdg. 28.50 *(978-1-61810-191-4(9))* Rourke Educational Media.

—Money down the Drain. Steinkraus, Kyla. 2012. (ENG.). 24p. (gr. 2-3). pap. 7.95 *(978-1-61810-329-1(6))*; lib. bdg. 28.50 *(978-1-61810-196-9(X))* Rourke Educational Media.

—The Mountain Thrill. Greve, Meg. 2013. (ENG.). 24p. (gr. -1-1). 25.64 *(978-1-62169-266-9(3))*; pap. 7.95 *(978-1-62169-224-9(8))* Rourke Educational Media.

—Off to Pluto! Robertson, Jean J. 2013. (ENG.). 24p. (gr. -1-1). 25.64 *(978-1-62169-274-4(4))* Rourke Educational Media.

—Off to Pluto! Robertson, J. Jean. 2013. (ENG.). 24p. (gr. -1-1). pap. 7.95 *(978-1-62169-232-4(9))* Rourke Educational Media.

—A Ship & Shells. Greve, Meg. 2013. (ENG.). 24p. (gr. -1-1). 25.64 *(978-1-62169-267-6(1))*; pap. 7.95 *(978-1-62169-225-6(6))* Rourke Educational Media.

—Sledding in Summer? Robertson, J. Jean. 2013. (ENG.). 24p. (gr. -1-1). 25.64 *(978-1-62169-275-1(2))*; pap. 7.95 *(978-1-62169-233-1(7))* Rourke Educational Media.

—The Tooth Fairy. Suen, Anastasia. 2012. (ENG.). 24p. (gr. k-1). pap. 7.95 *(978-1-61810-307-9(5))*; lib. bdg. 28.50 *(978-1-61810-174-7(9))* Rourke Educational Media.

—Watch for Whales! Greve, Meg. 2013. (ENG.). 24p. (gr. -1-1). 25.64 *(978-1-62169-269-0(8))*; pap. 7.95 *(978-1-62169-227-0(2))* Rourke Educational Media.

—We're Going on a Dinosaur Dig. Suen, Anastasia. 2012. (ENG.). 24p. (gr. k-1). pap. 7.95 *(978-1-61810-299-7(0))*; lib. bdg. 28.50 *(978-1-61810-166-2(8))* Rourke Educational Media.

Myers, Alishea. The Adventures of Brady Bean: Operation: Canine Caper. Wafer, C. K. 2008. (J). pap. 5.95 *(978-0-9797580-1-0(7))* CK Bks.

—The Adventures of Brady Bean: Operation: Georgie Porgie. Wafer, C. K. & Wafer, C. K. 2007. (J). pap. 5.95 *(978-0-9797580-0-3(9))* CK Bks.

Myers, Bernice & Myers, Lou. Sailing on a Very Fine Day. Ives, Burl. 2011. 32p. pap. 35.95 *(978-1-258-04002-4(6))* Literary Licensing, LLC.

Myers, Christopher. Autobiography of My Dead Brother. Myers, Walter Dean. 2006. (ENG.). 224p. (YA). (gr. 9). pap. 9.99 *(978-0-06-058293-7(6)*, Amistad) HarperCollins Pubs.

—Firebird. Copeland, Misty. 2014. (ENG.). 40p. (J). (gr. k-3). 17.99 *(978-0-399-16615-0(7)*, Putnam Juvenile) Penguin Publishing Group.

—Jazz. Myers, Walter Dean. (ENG.). 48p. (J). 2008. pap. 12.95 *(978-0-8234-2173-2(2))*; 2006. (gr. -1-3). 18.95 *(978-0-8234-1545-8(7))* Holiday Hse., Inc.

—Lies & Other Tall Tales. Hurston, Zora Neale & Thomas, Joyce Carol. (ENG.). 40p. (J). 2015. (gr. -1-3). pap. 6.99 *(978-0-06-000657-0(9))*; 2005. (gr. 1-5). 17.99 *(978-0-06-000655-6(2))* HarperCollins Pubs.

—Monster. Myers, Walter Dean. 2004. (Monster Ser.). (ENG.). 304p. (YA). (gr. 8). reprint ed. pap. 9.99 *(978-0-06-440731-1(4)*, Amistad) HarperCollins Pubs.

—We Are America: A Tribute from the Heart. Myers, Walter Dean. (ENG.). 40p. (J). (gr. 1-5). 2015. pap. 6.99 *(978-0-06-052310-7(7))*; 2011. 16.99 *(978-0-06-052308-4(5))* HarperCollins Pubs. (Collins).

Myers, Christopher. My Pen. Myers, Christopher. 2015. (ENG.). 32p. (J). (gr. -1-k). 16.99 *(978-1-4231-0371-4(8))* Hyperion Bks. for Children.

—Nighttime Symphony. Myers, Christopher. Timbaland. 2014. (ENG.). 32p. (J). 16.99 *(978-1-4424-1208-8(9)*, Atheneum Bks. for Young Readers) Simon & Schuster Children's Publishing.

Myers, Christopher, jt. illus. see Myers, Christopher A.

Myers, Christopher A. & Myers, Christopher. Blues Journey. Myers, Walter Dean. 2007. (ENG.). 48p. (J). (gr. -1-3). pap. 8.95 *(978-0-8234-2079-7(5))* Holiday Hse., Inc.

Myers, Doug. Seeing the Sky: 100 Projects, Activities & Explorations in Astronomy. Schaaf, Fred. 2012. (Dover Children's Science Bks.). (ENG.). 224p. (C). (gr. 8). pap. 14.95 *(978-0-486-48888-2(8))* Dover Pubns., Inc.

Myers, Glenn. Solomon Builds the Temple: 1 Kings 5:1-8:66. 2005. (Little Learner Bible Story Books). 16p. (J). pap. 2.29 *(978-0-7586-0944-1(2))* Concordia Publishing Hse.

—Stephen Stands Strong. Stiegemeyer, Julie. 2004. (ENG.). 16p. (J). 1.99 *(978-0-570-07576-9(9))* Concordia Publishing Hse.

Myers, Kristen. Piper's Great Adventures. Lowry, Mark & Bolton, Martha. 2005. (ENG.). 124p. (J). 15.99 *(978-1-58229-474-2(7)*, Howard Bks.) Howard Books.

Myers, Lawrence E. Glow-In-The-Dark Zombie Science. Hall, Kirsten. 2009. 32p. (J). pap. *(978-0-545-22626-4(0))* Scholastic, Inc.

—Night Sky. Salzano, Tammi J. 2009. 48p. (J). pap. *(978-0-545-13832-1(9))* Scholastic, Inc.

—Space. Dakota, Heather. 2008. 64p. (J). pap. *(978-0-545-08503-8(9))* Scholastic, Inc.

Myers, Lou, jt. illus. see Myers, Bernice.

Myers, Marie Honre. Little Duck. Barrows, Marjorie. 2011. 50p. 35.95 *(978-1-258-08897-2(5))* Literary Licensing, LLC.

Myers, Matt. Scarecrow Magic. Masessa, Ed. 2015. (ENG.). 32p. (J). (gr. -1-k). 16.99 *(978-0-545-69109-3(5))* Scholastic, Inc.

Myers, Matt, jt. illus. see Myers, Matthew.

Myers, Matthew. A Is for Musk Ox. Cabatingan, Erin. 2012. (Musk Ox Ser.: 1). (ENG.). 36p. (J). (gr. k-2). 16.99 *(978-1-59643-676-3(X))* Roaring Brook Pr.

—Bartholomew Biddle & the Very Big Wind. Ross, Gary. 2012. (ENG.). 96p. (J). (gr. 1-4). 17.99 *(978-0-7636-4920-3(1))* Candlewick Pr.

—Battle Bunny. Scieszka, Jon & Barnett, Mac. 2013. (ENG.). 32p. (J). (gr. k-4). 14.99 *(978-1-4424-4673-1(0)*, Simon & Schuster Bks. For Young Readers) Simon & Schuster Bks. For Young Readers.

—Clink. DiPucchio, Kelly. 2011. (ENG.). 32p. (J). (gr. -1-2). 16.99 *(978-0-06-192928-1(X))* HarperCollins Pubs.

—Danger Goes Berserk. Barnett, Mac. 2012. (Brixton Brothers Ser.: 4). (ENG.). 256p. (J). (gr. 3-7). 15.99 *(978-1-4424-3977-1(7)*, Simon & Schuster Bks. For Young Readers) Simon & Schuster Bks. For Young Readers.

—Musk Ox Counts. Cabatingan, Erin. 2013. (Musk Ox Ser.: 2). (ENG.). 36p. (J). (gr. k-2). 16.99 *(978-1-59643-798-2(7))* Roaring Brook Pr.

—What James Said. Rosenberg, Liz. 2015. (ENG.). 32p. (J). (gr. k-3). 16.99 *(978-1-59643-908-5(4))* Roaring Brook Pr.

—The World According to Musk Ox. Cabatingan, Erin. 2014. (Musk Ox Ser.: 3). (ENG.). 40p. (J). (gr. k-2). 17.99 *(978-1-59643-799-9(5))* Roaring Brook Pr.

Myers, Matthew & Myers, Matt. Tyrannosaurus Dad. Rosenberg, Liz. 2011. (ENG.). 32p. (J). (gr. -1-1). 16.99 *(978-1-59643-531-5(3))* Roaring Brook Pr.

Myers, Matthew, jt. illus. see Rex, Adam.

Myers, Shari. Rising above Global Warming. DeFrancesco, B. J. 2007. 46p. (J). per. 19.95 *(978-0-9801555-0-1(9))* Argus Enterprises International, Inc.

—The Wild Adventures of a Curious Princess. McGhee, Heather. 2008. (J). per. 9.99 *(978-0-9788985-9-5(1))* Better Be Write Pub., A.

Myers, V. G. Mind-Boggling Word Puzzles. Gardner, Martin. 2010. (Dover Children's Activity Bks.). (ENG.). 96p. (J). (gr. 3-5). pap. 4.99 *(978-0-486-47496-0(8))* Dover Pubns., Inc.

Myler, Terry. Back up the Beanstalk. Keilty, Derek. 2003. (Chimps Ser.: 5). (ENG.). 64p. (J). pap. 10.95 *(978-1-901737-45-5(4))* Anvil Bks., Ltd. IRL. Dist: Dufour Editions, Inc.

—Cookie & Curley. Mulligan, Frank. 2003. (Chimps Ser.: 2). (ENG.). 64p. (J). (gr. k-18). pap. 9.95 *(978-1-901737-38-7(1))* Anvil Bks., Ltd. IRL. Dist: Dufour Editions, Inc.

—A Fresh Start. Regan, Peter. 2004. (Shannon Harps Ser.: 03). (ENG.). 112p. (J). per. 10.95 *(978-1-901737-49-3(7))* Anvil Bks., Ltd. IRL. Dist: Dufour Editions, Inc.

—The Return of the Big Bad Wolf. Farrell, Liam. 2004. (ENG.). 64p. (J). pap. 10.95 *(978-1-901737-48-6(9))* Anvil Bks., Ltd. IRL. Dist: Dufour Editions, Inc.

—Riverside: The Curse. Regan, Peter. 2004. (Riverside Ser.). (ENG.). 127p. (J). pap. 11.95 *(978-1-901737-46-2(2))* Anvil Bks., Ltd. IRL. Dist: Dufour Editions, Inc.

—Shannon Harps. Regan, Peter. 2003. (Shannon Harps Ser.: 01). (ENG.). 128p. (J). (gr. 3-18). pap. 10.95 *(978-1-901737-41-7(1))* Anvil Bks., Ltd. IRL. Dist: Dufour Editions, Inc.

—Something New, Vol. 2. Regan, Peter. 2004. (Shannon Harps Ser.: 02). (ENG.). 112p. (J). pap. 10.95 *(978-1-901737-52-3(7))* Anvil Bks., Ltd. IRL. Dist: Dufour Editions, Inc.

—True Story of the Three Little Pigs & the Big Bad Wolf. Farrell, Liam. 2nd rev. ed. 2012. (ENG.). 192p. (J). pap. 13.95 *(978-1-85635-682-4(5))* Mercier Pr., Ltd., The IRL. Dist: Dufour Editions, Inc.

—Two Mad Dogs. Harrison, Cora. 2003. (Chimps Ser.: 4). (ENG.). 64p. (J). pap. 10.95 *(978-1-901737-44-8(6))* Anvil Bks., Ltd. IRL. Dist: Dufour Editions, Inc.

—Where's Jacko? Hickey, Tony. 2006. (ENG.). 64p. (J). pap. 10.95 *(978-1-901737-47-9(0))* Anvil Bks., Ltd. IRL. Dist: Dufour Editions, Inc.

N

N Gallerie Studios. The Island Hunters - Book III: The Legend of Brown Eyed James. Walford, N. E. 2012. 180p. (J). 26.99 *(978-0-9818347-6-4(0))* N Gallerie Pr. LLC.

N Gallerie Studios. The Island Hunters Book II: Trail of the Tomb Robbers, 12 vols., Vol. 2. N Gallerie Studios, . 2nd ed. 2012.Tr. of Los Cazadores de la Isla. (ENG.). 130p. (J). 14.99 *(978-0-9818347-7-1(9))* N Gallerie Pr. LLC.

—The Island Hunters Book III: The Legend of Brown Eyed James, 12 vols., Vol. 3. N Gallerie Studios, . 3rd ed. 2012.Tr. of Los Cazadores de la Isla. (ENG.). 196p. (J). 16.99 *(978-0-9818347-8-8(7))* N Gallerie Pr. LLC.

Naba, Dajana. Crowder Pea, Don't Bite! Jones, Angela & Jones, Sourou. 2010. 16p. pap. 9.99 *(978-1-60911-735-1(2)*, Eloquent Bks.) Strategic Book Publishing & Rights Agency (SBPRA).

Nadaskay, Lori. Baseball Billy. Johnson, Sandi. Johnson, Britt, ed. l.t. ed. 2003. 12p. (J). (gr. k-5). spiral bd. 5.99 *(978-1-929063-30-7(X)*, 320) Moons & Stars Publishing For Children.

Nadeau, Janice. All about Grandmas. Schotter, Roni. 2012. (ENG.). 32p. (J). (gr. -1-k). 16.99 *(978-0-8037-3714-3(9)*, Dial) Penguin Publishing Group.

—Cinnamon Baby. Winstanley, Nicola. 2011. (ENG.). 32p. (J). (gr. -1-2). 16.95 *(978-1-55337-821-1(0))* Kids Can Pr., Ltd. CAN. Dist: Univ. of Toronto Pr.

—Harvey, 1 vol. Bouchard, Hervé. Mixter, Helen, tr. from FRE. 2010. (ENG.). 168p. (gr. 4-18). 19.95 *(978-1-55498-075-8(5))* Groundwood Bks. CAN. Dist: Perseus-PGW.

—The Tooth Mouse. Hood, Susan. 2012. (ENG.). 32p. (J). 16.95 *(978-1-55453-565-1(4))* Kids Can Pr., Ltd. CAN. Dist: Univ. of Toronto Pr.

Nadel, Carolina. Daddy's Home. Nadel, Carolina. 2012. 32p. 19.95 *(978-0-9792761-4-9(4))* Mookind Pr.

Nadler, Ellis. Neville the Devil. Lawrence, Michael. 2012. (Jiggy Mccue Ser.: 7). (ENG.). 352p. (J). (gr. 3-7). pap. 8.99 *(978-1-84362-879-8(1))* Hodder & Stoughton GBR. Dist: Independent Pubs. Group.

Naenix, Robin. Jessie's Walk. Brewer, Dottie A. 2004. 20p. (J). 4.95 *(978-0-9707945-7-4(6))* Billion $ Baby Pubns.

—Saul the Pelican. Brewer, Dottie A. 2004. 30p. (J). 4.95 *(978-0-9707945-9-8(2))* Billion $ Baby Pubns.

Nagai, Tomohiro. Full Metal Panic - Overload!, Vol. 5. Gatou, Shouji. 2006. (Full Metal Panic: Overload! Ser.). 200p. (YA). pap. 9.99 *(978-1-4139-0342-3(8))* ADV Manga.

Nagar, Sachin. Photo Booth. Helfand, Lewis. 2011. (Campfire Graphic Novels Ser.). (ENG.). 80p. (gr. 3-7). pap. 9.99 *(978-93-80028-65-1(2)*, Campfire) Kalyani Navyug Media Pty. Ltd. IND. Dist: Random Hse., Inc.

—Sundarkaand: Triumph of Hanuman. Tulsidas. 2013. (Campfire Graphic Novels Ser.). (ENG.). 72p. (J). (gr. 5). pap. 9.99 *(978-93-80741-70-3(7)*, Campfire) Kalyani Navyug Media Pty. Ltd. IND. Dist: Random Hse., Inc.

—The Treasured Thief. Foley, Ryan. 2012. (Campfire Graphic Novels Ser.). (ENG.). 64p. (J). (gr. 3-7). pap. 9.99 *(978-93-80741-11-6(1)*, Campfire) Kalyani Navyug Media Pty. Ltd. IND. Dist: Random Hse., Inc.

Nagar, Sachin, jt. illus. see Banerjee, Sankha.

Nagara, Innosanto. A Is for Activist. Nagara, Innosanto. 2012. (ENG.). 28p. bds. 15.00 *(978-0-9883448-9-1(0))* Kupu Kupu Pr.

Nagaraju, Harsha. Deep Sea Creatures. Yelagalawadi, Jyoti. 2004. 32p. (J). 14.99 *(978-0-9725901-2-9(9))* Lekha Pubs., LLC.

—Laugh with Dinosaurs. Yelagalawadi, Jyoti. 2004. 32p. (J). 14.99 *(978-0-9725901-1-2(0))* Lekha Pubs., LLC.

Nagle, Paul. Fred Threads: Book One: the Interview. Oswalt, Kay. 2012. (ENG.). 36p. 18.99 *(978-1-4624-0070-6(1)*, Inspiring Voices) Author Solutions, Inc.

Nagle, Shane. Are You for Wheel? The Most Amazing Cars Ever. Davis, Tony. 2008. (ENG.). 150p. (J). (gr. 3-6). pap. 13.95 *(978-1-74166-280-1(X))* Random Hse. Australia AUS. Dist: Independent Pubs. Group.

Nagulakonda, Rajesh. Krishna - Defender of Dharma. Taneja, Sweta. 2013. (Campfire Graphic Novels Ser.). (ENG.). 152p. (gr. 5). pap. 14.99 *(978-93-80741-12-3(X)*, Campfire) Kalyani Navyug Media Pty. Ltd. IND. Dist: Random Hse., Inc.

Nagy, Ian. How to Write Your Life Story. Fletcher, Ralph. 2007. 112p. (J). (gr. 3-7). 15.99 *(978-0-06-050770-1(5))* HarperCollins Pubs.

Nagy, Krisztina. Fuzzy Bear Goes to School. Bentley, Dawn. 2005. (Fuzzy Bear Ser.). 10p. (J). 10.95 *(978-1-58117-124-2(2)*, Intervisual/Piggy Toes) Bendon, Inc.

—Fuzzy Bear's Bedtime. Bentley, Dawn. 2005. (Fuzzy Bear Ser.). 10p. (J). (gr. -1-k). act. bk. ed. 10.95 *(978-1-58117-055-9(6)*, Intervisual/Piggy Toes) Bendon, Inc.

Nagy, Krisztina. Animal Lullabies. Nagy, Krisztina, tr. Ross, Mandy. 2003. (Poems for the Young Ser.). (ENG.). 32p. (J). *(978-0-85953-116-0(3))* Child's Play International Ltd.

Nagy, Krisztina Kállai. The Lion Storyteller Bedtime Book. Hartman, Bob. 2015. (ENG.). 128p. (J). (gr. k-2). pap. 16.99 ***(978-0-7459-6494-2(X))*** Lion Hudson PLC GBR. Dist: Independent Pubs. Group.

Nagy, Krisztina Kallai. The Lion Storyteller Christmas Book. Hartman, Bob. 2013. (Storyteller Tales Ser.). (ENG.). 128p. (J). (gr. k-2). pap. 14.99 *(978-0-7459-6379-2(X))* Lion Hudson PLC GBR. Dist: Independent Pubs. Group.

Nagy, Robert. Talisman of Zandria, 1. Norris, Christine. 2005. 187p. (YA). pap. 14.95 *(978-1-885093-44-8(6)*, LBF/Hadrosaur) Hadrosaur Pr.

Nahabedian, Dallas. The Boy Who Wouldn't Hug. Gemstone, Rose. 2010. (ENG.). 26p. pap. 9.13 *(978-1-4515-9543-7(3))* CreateSpace Independent Publishing Platform.

Naifeh, Ted. Kin. Black, Holly. (Good Neighbors Ser.: 1). (ENG.). (J). (gr. 7). 2009. 128p. pap. 9.99 *(978-0-439-85565-5(9))*; 2008. 144p. 16.99 *(978-0-439-85562-4(4))* Scholastic, Inc. (Graphix).

—Kind. Black, Holly. (Good Neighbors Ser.: 3). (ENG.). 128p. (J). 2011. (gr. 7-7). pap. 12.99 *(978-0-439-85567-9(5))*; 2010. (gr. 3-7). 16.99 *(978-0-439-85564-8(0))* Scholastic, Inc. (Graphix).

—Kith. Black, Holly. (Good Neighbors Ser.: 2). (ENG.). 128p. (J). 2010. (gr. 3-7). pap. 12.99 *(978-0-439-85566-2(7))*;

2009. (gr. 7-18). 16.99 *(978-0-439-85563-1(2))* Scholastic, Inc. (Graphix).

Nakahara, Aya. Love. Com, Volume 1. Nakahara, Aya. 2007. (Love. com Ser.). 18.70 *(978-1-4178-1299-8(0),* Turtleback) Turtleback Bks.

—Love.com, Vol. 11. Nakahara, Aya. Rolf, Pookie, tr. from JPN. 2009. (Love Com Ser.: 11). (ENG.). 184p. pap. 9.99 *(978-1-4215-2369-9(8))* Viz Media.

Nakai, Ryan. The Adventures of Young Starbury: Practice Makes Perfect. Marbury, Stephon & Dean, Marshall. 2007. 36p. (J). 12.99 *(978-0-9798250-0-2(8))* Godspeed Pr.

Nakajo, Hisaya. For You in Full Blossom Vol. 2. Nakajo, Hisaya. 2004. (Hana-Kimi Ser.: Vol. 2). (ENG.). 200p. pap. 9.95 *(978-1-59116-398-5(6))* Viz Media.

—Hana-Kimi. Nakajo, Hisaya. (Hana-Kimi Ser.). (ENG.). Vol. 9. 2005. 192p. pap. 9.99 *(978-1-4215-0138-3(4));* Vol. 16. 2007. 184p. pap. 9.99 *(978-1-4215-0991-4(1));* Vol. 17. 2007. 184p. pap. 9.99 *(978-1-4215-0992-1(X))* Viz Media.

—Sugar Princess: Skating to Win. Nakajo, Hisaya. 2008. (Sugar Princess: Skating to Win Ser.: 1). (ENG.). 184p. (gr. 2). pap. 8.99 *(978-1-4215-1930-2(5))* Viz Media.

—Sugar Princess - Skating to Win. Nakajo, Hisaya. 2008. (Sugar Princess - Skating to Win Ser.: 2). (ENG.). 216p. (gr. 2). pap. 8.99 *(978-1-4215-1931-9(3))* Viz Media.

Nakasone, Shaun. Ethan the Ending Eater. Ladd, Debbie. 2008. 64p. (J). 17.95 *(978-0-9727615-2-9(7))* Deb on Air Bks.

—Nurse Robin's Hats. Ladd, Debbie. 2006. 52p. (J). 16.95 *(978-0-9727615-3-6(5))* Deb on Air Bks.

Nakata, Hiroe. All of Baby, Nose to Toes. Adler, Victoria. 2009. (ENG.). 32p. (J). (gr. k — 1). 14.99 *(978-0-8037-3217-9(1),* Dial) Penguin Publishing Group.

—All of Baby Nose to Toes. Adler, Victoria. 2011. (ENG.). 30p. (J). (gr. k — 1). bds. 6.99 *(978-0-8037-3531-6(6),* Dial) Penguin Publishing Group.

—Baby Shoes. Slater, Dashka. 2008. (ENG.). 24p. (J). (gr. -1-1). bds. 7.95 *(978-1-59990-273-9(7),* Bloomsbury USA Childrens) Bloomsbury USA.

—Duck Tents. Berry, Lynne. 2009. (ENG.). 32p. (J). (gr. -1-k). 16.95 *(978-0-8050-8696-6(X),* Holt, Henry & Co. Bks. For Young Readers) Holt, Henry & Co.

—Grandma Calls Me Gigglepie. Lester, J. D. 2011. (ENG.). 26p. (J). (— 1). bds. 7.99 *(978-0-375-85904-5(7),* Robin Corey Bks.) Random Hse. Children's Bks.

—I Love Fall! Simon, Mary Manz et al. 2009. (ENG.). 12p. (J). (gr. -1-1). bds. 6.99 *(978-1-4169-3609-1(2),* Little Simon) Little Simon.

—Mommy Calls Me Monkeypants. Lester, J. D. 2009. (ENG.). 26p. (J). (— 1). bds. 7.99 *(978-0-375-84502-4(X),* Robin Corey Bks.) Random Hse. Children's Bks.

—Not That Tutu! Colman, Michelle Sinclair. 2013. (ENG.). 20p. (J). (— 1). bds. 7.99 *(978-0-307-97698-7(X),* Robin Corey Bks.) Random Hse. Children's Bks.

—Ocean Babies. Rose, Deborah Lee. 2005. (ENG.). 32p. (J). (gr. -1-3). 16.95 *(978-0-7922-6669-3(2));* 25.90 *(978-0-7922-8312-6(0))* National Geographic Society. (National Geographic Children's Bks.).

—Snow Happy! Hubbell, Patricia. 2010. (ENG.). 32p. (J). (gr. -1-2). 15.99 *(978-1-58246-329-2(8),* Tricycle Pr.) Ten Speed Pr.

—Tell Me My Story, Mama. Lund, Deborah S. 2004. 40p. (J). lib. bdg. 16.89 *(978-0-06-028877-8(9))* HarperCollins Pubs.

—This Is the Way a Baby Rides. Meyers, Susan. 2005. (ENG.). 32p. (J). (gr. -1-1). 15.95 *(978-0-8109-5763-3(9),* Abrams Bks. for Young Readers) Abrams.

—Two Is for Twins. Lewison, Wendy Cheyette. 2011. (ENG.). 28p. (J). (gr. -1 — 1). bds. 6.99 *(978-0-670-01310-4(2),* Viking Juvenile) Penguin Publishing Group.

Nam, Doan. Gordon & Li Li Count in Mandarin. McSween, Michele. 2010. 32p. 9.99 *(978-0-9820881-3-5(2))* McWong Ink.

—Gordon & Li Li Learn Animals in Mandarin. McSween, Michele. 2010. 32p. 9.99 *(978-0-9820881-2-8(4))* McWong Ink.

Nanatsuki, Kyoichi. The Gallows Bell. Nanatsuki, Kyoichi. Minagawa, Ryoji. 2005. (Project Arms Ser.: Vol. 8). (ENG.). 216p. pap. 9.99 *(978-1-59116-732-7(9))* Viz Media.

—Project Arms, Vol. 13. Nanatsuki, Kyoichi. 2006. (Project Arms Ser.). (ENG.). 208p. pap. 9.99 *(978-1-4215-0502-2(9))* Viz Media.

Nance, Dan. The Story of the H. L. Hunley & Queenie's Coin. Hawk, Frank. 2004. (ENG.). 40p. (J). (gr. k-6). 16.95 *(978-1-58536-218-9(2))* Sleeping Bear Pr.

Nancy Raj. Malli. Jeeva Raghunath & Nayar, Deeya. 2005. (HIN & ENG.). 16p. (J). *(978-81-8146-089-9(8))* Tulika Pubs.

Nancy, Scheibe. Karner's Quest for Blue Lupine. Dickens, Sara Jo. 2014. (J). 18.95 *(978-1-59298-923-2(3))* Beaver's Pond Pr., Inc.

Nanny Fanny. Touch the Stars: A Children's Book. Fanny, Nanny. 2013. 32p. pap. 12.99 *(978-1-61204-275-6(9),* Strategic Bk. Publishing) Strategic Book Publishing & Rights Agency (SBPRA).

Nanten, Yutaka. Cowboy Bebop Vl. ed. 2005. 192p. pap. 9.99 *(978-1-59816-038-3(9))* TOKYOPOP, Inc.

Nap, Dug & Sweet, Melissa. Weather! A Book about Pink Snow, Fighting Kites, Lightning Rods, Rains of Frogs, Typhoons, Tornadoes, & Ice Balls from Space. Rupp, Rebecca. 2003. (ENG.). 144p. (J). (gr. 3-7). pap. 14.95 *(978-1-58017-420-6(5),* 67420) Storey Publishing, LLC.

Napier, Louise S. Kate's Fan. Ballard, Elizabeth Silance. 2008. 48p. (J). pap. 18.95 *(978-0-9706823-3-8(6))* Righter Publishing Co., Inc.

Nardandrea, Swannee. Funny, Dust & Honey & the Giant Carrot. Stroud, David Wayne. l.t. ed. 2005. 32p. (J). 17.95 *(978-0-9762835-2-2(2))* Shooting Star Publishing.

Nardi, Tisa. Princess the Pygmy Goat. Carmen, Indigo. 2009. 24p. pap. 24.95 *(978-1-60703-824-5(2))* America Star Bks.

Nascimbene, Yan. The Creative Collection of American Short Stories. Chronicle Staff. 2010. (ENG.). 272p. (J). (gr. 4-7). 28.95 *(978-1-56846-202-8(6),* Creative Editions) Creative Co., The.

—Crouching Tiger. Compestine, Ying Chang. 2011. (ENG.). 40p. (J). (gr. 1-4). 16.99 *(978-0-7636-4642-4(3))* Candlewick Pr.

—E Is for Eiffel Tower: A France Alphabet. Wilbur, Helen L. 2010. (Discover the World Ser.). (ENG.). 40p. (J). (gr. 1-3). 17.95 *(978-1-58536-505-0(X),* 202199) Sleeping Bear Pr.

—Eight Dolphins of Katrina: A True Tale of Survival. Coleman, Janet Wyman. 2013. (ENG.). 40p. (J). (gr. 1-4). lib. bdg. 17.99 *(978-0-547-71923-8(X))* Houghton Mifflin Harcourt Publishing Co.

—First Grade Jitters. Quackenbush, Robert. 2010. (ENG.). 32p. (J). (gr. k-2). 16.99 *(978-0-06-077632-9(3))* HarperCollins Pubs.

—Into the Air: An Illustrated Timeline of Flight. Hunter, Ryan Ann et al. 2003. (ENG.). 48p. (J). (gr. -1-3). 16.95 *(978-0-7922-5120-0(2))* National Geographic Society.

—Yuki & the One Thousand Carriers. Whelan, Gloria. 2008. (Tales of the World Ser.). (ENG.). 32p. (J). (gr. -1-3). 17.95 *(978-1-58536-352-0(9))* Sleeping Bear Pr.

Nascimbeni, Barbara. Images of God. Delval, Marie-Hélène. 2011. 90p. (J). (gr. -1-3). 16.50 *(978-0-8028-5391-2(9),* Eerdmans Bks For Young Readers) Eerdmans, William B. Publishing Co.

Nascimbeni, Barbara. Little Miss Muffet. (Classic Books with Holes Ser.). (ENG.). (J). 2015. 16p. ***(978-1-84643-678-9(8));*** 2012. 14p. bds. *(978-1-84643-511-9(0));* 2012. 16p. pap. *(978-1-84643-500-3(5))* Child's Play International Ltd.

Nascimbeni, Barbara. The Tortoise & the Hare, 1 vol. Piumini, Roberto & Aesop. 2011. (Storybook Classics Ser.). (ENG.). 32p. (gr. 3-4). lib. bdg. 25.32 *(978-1-4048-6503-7(9),* Fiction Picture Bks.) Picture Window Bks.

—Undersea Adventure. Harrison, Paul. 2011. 32p. pap. *(978-1-84089-638-1(8))* Zero to Ten, Ltd.

Nascimbeni, Barbara. Animals & Their Families. Nascimbeni, Barbara. Zimic, Lesley, tr. from FRE. 2012. (ENG.). 72p. (J). (gr. -1 — 1). 17.95 *(978-1-926973-32-6(1))* Owlkids Bks. Inc. CAN. Dist: Perseus-PGW.

Nascimbeni, Barbara, jt. illus. see Kubler, Annie.

Nash, Gisele. The Wise Man's Last Wish: A Christmas Tale. Alexander, Marilee. 2012. (ENG.). 23p. (J). 23.95 *(978-1-4327-8307-5(6));* pap. 14.95 *(978-1-4327-8040-1(9))* Outskirts Pr., Inc.

Nash, Joshua. Moose N' Me. Loggins, Kenny. 2013. (ENG.). 32p. (J). (gr. -1-3). 14.95 *(978-0-578-07552-5(0),* Imagine Publishing) Charlesbridge Publishing, Inc.

Nash, Kelli. Jemma's Got the Travel Bug, 1 vol. Glick, Susan. 2010. (ENG.). 32p. (J). 14.99 *(978-0-7643-3632-4(0))* Schiffer Publishing, Ltd.

—Mallory the Forgetful Duck, 1 vol. Allen, Elaine. 2012. (ENG.). 40p. (J). 16.99 *(978-0-7643-4069-7(7))* Schiffer Publishing, Ltd.

Nash, Kelli. Olly Explores 7 Wonders of the Chesapeake Bay, 1 vol. Allen, Elaine Ann. 2015. (ENG.). 32p. (J). 16.99 ***(978-0-7643-4938-6(4),*** 9780764349386) Schiffer Publishing, Ltd.

Nash, Kelli. Olly the Oyster Cleans the Bay, 1 vol. Allen, Elaine Ann. 2008. (ENG.). 30p. (J). 13.95 *(978-0-87033-603-4(7),* Cornell Maritime Pr./Tidewater Pubs.) Schiffer Publishing, Ltd.

—Olly's Treasure, 1 vol. Allen, Elaine Ann. 2011. (ENG.). 40p. (J). *(978-0-7643-3772-7(6),* Schiffer Publishing Ltd) Schiffer Publishing, Ltd.

Nash, Mike, et al. Drawing. 2012. (Drawing Ser.). (ENG.). 48p. (gr. 3-4). lib. bdg. 62.64 *(978-1-4296-8228-2(0));* lib. bdg. 187.92 *(978-1-4296-8229-9(9))* Capstone Pr., Inc.

—How to Draw the Coolest, Most Creative Tattoo Art, 1 vol. 2012. (Drawing Ser.). (ENG.). 48p. (gr. 3-4). lib. bdg. 31.32 *(978-1-4296-7539-0(X))* Capstone Pr., Inc.

—How to Draw the Meanest, Most Terrifying Monsters, 1 vol. 2012. (Drawing Ser.). (ENG.). 48p. (gr. 3-4). lib. bdg. 31.32 *(978-1-4296-7538-3(1))* Capstone Pr., Inc.

Nash, Scott. Betsy Red Hoodie. Levine, Gail Carson. 2010. (ENG.). 40p. (J). (gr. -1-3). 16.99 *(978-0-06-146870-4(3))* HarperCollins Pubs.

—Betsy Who Cried Wolf. Levine, Gail Carson. 2005. (ENG.). 40p. (J). (gr. -1-3). reprint ed. pap. 6.99 *(978-0-06-443640-3(3))* HarperCollins Pubs.

—The Bugliest Bug. Shields, Carol Diggory. 2005. (ENG.). 32p. (J). (gr. -1-3). pap. 7.99 *(978-0-7636-2293-0(1))* Candlewick Pr.

—The Cat in the Rhinestone Suit. Cash, John Carter. 2012. (ENG.). 32p. (J). (gr. -1-3). 17.99 *(978-1-4169-7483-3(0),* Little Simon Inspirations) Little Simon Inspirations.

—Catch That Baby! Coffelt, Nancy. 2011. (ENG.). 40p. (J). (gr. -1-3). 16.99 *(978-1-4169-9148-9(4),* Simon & Schuster/Paula Wiseman Bks.) Simon & Schuster/Paula Wiseman Bks.

—Flat Stanley. Brown, Jeff. 2006. (Flat Stanley Ser.). (ENG.). 40p. (J). (gr. -1-3). 17.99 *(978-0-06-112904-9(6))* HarperCollins Pubs.

—Hooper Humperdink...? Not Him! Seuss, Dr. 2006. (Bright & Early Books(R) Ser.). (ENG.). 48p. (J). (gr. -1-k). 8.99 *(978-0-679-88129-2(8),* Random Hse. Bks. for Young Readers) Random Hse. Children's Bks.

—My Beastly Brother. Leuck, Laura. 2003. 32p. (J). (gr. -1-1). 16.89 *(978-0-06-029548-6(1))* HarperCollins Pubs.

—My Creature Teacher. Leuck, Laura. 2004. (ENG.). 32p. (J). (gr. -1-1). 15.99 *(978-0-06-029694-0(1))* HarperCollins Pubs.

—Saturday Night at the Dinosaur Stomp. Shields, Carol Diggory. 2008. (ENG.). 32p. (J). (gr. -1-3). pap. 6.99 *(978-0-7636-3887-0(0))* Candlewick Pr.

—Solomon Snow & the Silver Spoon. Umansky, Kaye. 2007. (ENG.). 304p. (J). (gr. 2-5). 12.99 *(978-0-7636-3218-2(X))* Candlewick Pr.

—Solomon Snow & the Stolen Jewel. Umansky, Kaye. 2007. (ENG.). 256p. (J). (gr. 2-5). 12.99 *(978-0-7636-2793-5(3))* Candlewick Pr.

—Stanley in Space. Brown, Jeff. ed. 2003. (Flat Stanley Ser.: 3). (gr. k-3). lib. bdg. 14.75 *(978-0-613-66735-7(2),* Turtleback) Turtleback Bks.

—Uh-Oh, Baby! Coffelt, Nancy. 2013. (ENG.). 40p. (J). (gr. -1-3). 16.99 *(978-1-4169-9149-6(2),* Simon & Schuster/Paula Wiseman Bks.) Simon & Schuster/Paula Wiseman Bks.

Nash, Scott. The High-Skies Adventures of Blue Jay the Pirate. Nash, Scott. 2012. (ENG.). 368p. (J). (gr. 4-7). 17.99 *(978-0-7636-3264-9(3))* Candlewick Pr.

—Tuff Fluff: The Case of Duckie's Missing Brain. Nash, Scott. 2004. (J). 101.94 *(978-0-7636-2503-0(5));* (ENG.). 40p. (gr. 1-4). 16.99 *(978-0-7636-1882-7(9))* Candlewick Pr.

Nash, Scott & Pamintuan, Macky. Flat Stanley - His Original Adventure! Brown, Jeff. 40th anniv. ed. 2013. (Flat Stanley Ser.). (ENG.). 96p. (J). (gr. 1-5). pap. 4.99 *(978-0-06-009791-2(4))* HarperCollins Pubs.

—Invisible Stanley. Brown, Jeff. 2009. (Flat Stanley Ser.). (ENG.). 112p. (J). (gr. 2-5). pap. 4.99 *(978-0-06-009792-9(2))* HarperCollins Pubs.

—Stanley & the Magic Lamp. Brown, Jeff. 2009. (Flat Stanley Ser.). (ENG.). 128p. (J). (gr. 2-5). pap. 4.99 *(978-0-06-009793-6(0))* HarperCollins Pubs.

—Stanley, Flat Again! Brown, Jeff. (Flat Stanley Ser.). 96p. (J). (gr. 2-5). 2009. (ENG.). pap. 4.99 *(978-0-06-442173-7(2));* 2003. (ENG.). 15.99 *(978-0-06-009551-2(2));* 2003. lib. bdg. 16.89 *(978-0-06-029826-5(X))* HarperCollins Pubs.

—Stanley's Christmas Adventure. Brown, Jeff. 2010. (Flat Stanley Ser.). (ENG.). 96p. (J). (gr. 2-5). pap. 4.99 *(978-0-06-442175-1(9))* HarperCollins Pubs.

Nashton, Nashon. Marshall Island Legends & Stories. Kelin, Daniel. 2003. 160p. 22.95 *(978-1-57306-141-4(7));* 272p. pap. 9.95 *(978-1-57306-140-7(9))* Bess Pr., Inc.

Nasmith, Ted. Auld Lang Syne: The Story of Scotland's Most Famous Poet, Robert Burns, 1 vol. Findon, Joanne. 2004. (ENG.). 32p. (J). pap. 8.95 *(978-1-55005-121-6(0),* 1550051210) Fitzhenry & Whiteside, Ltd. CAN. Dist: Midpoint Trade Bks., Inc.

Nassief, Adel. First Christmas. Macdonald, Alastair. 2008. (ENG.). 56p. 22.50 *(978-1-59962-055-8(3),* Welcome Bks) Rizzoli International Pubns., Inc.

—Primera Navidad. Macdonald, Alastair. Canetti, Yanitzia, tr. from ENG. 2008. (SPA.). 22.50 *(978-1-59962-058-9(8),* Welcome Bks) Rizzoli International Pubns., Inc.

Nassner, Alyssa. Halloween Scratchers. Golden, Erin Lee. 2012. (ENG.). 40p. (J). (gr. 2-17). 9.95 *(978-1-4521-0985-5(0))* Chronicle Bks. LLC.

—Lullaby & Kisses Sweet: Poems to Love with Your Baby. 2015. (ENG.). 44p. (J). (gr. -1-1). bds. 15.95 *(978-1-4197-1037-7(0))* Abrams.

—Montessori - Shape Work. George, Bobby & George, June. 2013. (Montessori Ser.). (ENG.). 18p. (J). (gr. -1-k). bds. 9.95 *(978-1-4197-0935-7(6),* Abrams Appleseed) Abrams.

—Montessori: Letter Work. George, Bobby & George, June. 2012. (ENG.). 24p. (J). (gr. -1-k). bds., bds. 9.95 *(978-1-4197-0411-6(7),* Abrams Appleseed) Abrams.

—Montessori: Number Work. George, Bobby & George, June. 2012. (Montessori Ser.). (ENG.). 24p. (J). (gr. -1-k). bds., bds. 9.95 *(978-1-4197-0412-3(5),* Abrams Appleseed) Abrams.

—Secrets of the Apple Tree. Brown, Carron. 2014. (ENG.). 36p. (J). 12.99 *(978-1-61067-243-6(7))* Kane Miller.

—Secrets of the Rain Forest. Brown, Carron. 2015. (ENG.). 36p. (J). 12.99 *(978-1-61067-325-9(5))* Kane Miller.

—Secrets of the Seashore. Brown, Carron. 2014. (ENG.). 36p. (J). 12.99 *(978-1-61067-309-9(3))* Kane Miller.

Nast, Thomas. The Fat Boy. 2011. (American Antiquarian Society Ser.). (ENG.). 24p. (gr. 1). 24.95 *(978-1-4290-9736-9(1))* Applewood Bks.

—A Visit from St. Nicholas. Moore, Clement C. 2006. (ENG.). 24p. (gr. -1-1). pap. 24.95 *(978-1-55709-592-3(2))* Applewood Bks.

Nastanlieva, Vanya. The New Arrival. Nastanlieva, Vanya. 2013. (ENG.). 36p. (J). (gr. -1-3). 16.95 *(978-1-927018-13-2(7))* Simply Read Bks. CAN. Dist: Ingram Pub. Services.

Nastari, Nadine. Mr. TLC (Three-Legged Cat) 2007. 36p. (J). spiral bd. 14.95 *(978-0-9798387-5-0(4))* Nastari, Nadine.

Nasu, Yukie. Here Is Greenwood, 1. Nasu, Yukie. Smith, Joe. 2004. (Here Is Greenwood Ser.). (ENG.). 208p. (YA). pap. 9.99 *(978-1-59116-604-7(7))* Viz Media.

—Here Is Greenwood. Nasu, Yukie. 2005. (Here Is Greenwood Ser.). (ENG.). (YA). Vol. 2. 216p. pap. 9.99 *(978-1-59116-605-4(5));* Vol. 3. 200p. pap. 9.99 *(978-1-59116-606-1(3))* Viz Media.

Natale, Vince. Passion & Poison: Tales of Shape-Shifters, Ghosts, & Spirited Women, 0 vols. Del Negro, Janice M. 2013. (ENG.). 64p. (J). (gr. 5-7). pap. 9.99 *(978-1-4778-1685-1(2),* 9781477816851, Amazon Children's Publishing) Amazon Publishing.

Natalini, Sandro & Baruzzi, Agnese. The True Story of Goldilocks. Natalini, Sandro & Baruzzi, Agnese. 2009. (ENG.). 18p. (J). (gr. -1-3). 14.99 *(978-0-7636-4475-8(7))* Candlewick Pr.

Natalini, Sandro, jt. illus. see Baruzzi, Agnese.

Natarajan, Srividya. Kali & the Rat Snake. Whitaker, Zai. 2006. (ENG.). 32p. (J). (gr. 1-4). 10.99 *(978-1-933605-10-4(3))* Kane Miller.

Natchev, Alexi. The Elijah Door. Strauss, Linda Leopold. 2012. (ENG.). 32p. (J). 16.95 *(978-0-8234-1911-1(8))* Holiday Hse., Inc.

—Rock-a-Bye Farm. Hamm, Diane Johnston. 2008. (ENG.). 32p. (J). (gr. -1 — 1). 7.99 *(978-1-4169-3621-3(1),* Little Simon) Little Simon.

Natelli, Kenny. Jimmy the Gnome Won't Leave His Home, 1 vol. Welch, Enc. 2009. 17p. pap. 24.95 *(978-1-60836-679-8(0))* America Star Bks.

Nath, Vann & Pourlseth, Phal. Sinat & the Instrument of the Heart: A Story of Cambodia. pierSath, Chath. 2010. (Make Friends Around the World Ser.). (ENG.). 32p. (J). (gr. k-3). 9.95 *(978-1-60727-117-8(6));* 9.95 *(978-1-60727-098-0(6));* 9.95 *(978-1-60727-116-1(8));* 19.95 *(978-1-60727-097-3(8));* 16.95 *(978-1-60727-087-4(0));* pap. 6.95 *(978-1-60727-088-1(9))* Soundprints.

Nathan, Cheryl. Earthquakes: Earth's Mightiest Moments. Harrison, David L. 2004. (Earth Works). (ENG.). 32p. (J). (gr. 1-2). 15.95 *(978-1-59078-243-9(7))* Boyds Mills Pr.

—Glaciers: Nature's Icy Caps. Harrison, David L. 2006. (Earth Works). (ENG.). 32p. (J). (gr. 1-3). 15.95 *(978-1-59078-372-6(7))* Boyds Mills Pr.

—The Kissing Skunks. Deak, Gloria. 2006. 40p. (J). (gr. -1). 16.95 *(978-1-932065-46-6(6))* Star Bright Bks., Inc.

—Let's Visit Israel. Groner, Judye & Wikler, Madeline. 2004. (ENG.). 12p. (J). (gr. -1 — 1). bds. 5.95 *(978-1-58013-087-5(9),* Kar-Ben Publishing) Lerner Publishing Group.

—Mountains: The Tops of the World. Harrison, David L. 2005. (Earth Works). (ENG.). 32p. (J). (gr. 1-4). 15.95 *(978-1-59078-326-9(3))* Boyds Mills Pr.

—My Brother Needs a Boa, 1 vol. Weston, Anne. 2005. (ENG.). 32p. (J). (gr. -1-3). 15.95 *(978-1-932065-96-1(2))* Star Bright Bks., Inc.

—Oceans: The Vast, Mysterious Deep. Harrison, David L. 2003. (Earth Works). (ENG.). 32p. (J). (gr. k-2). 15.95 *(978-1-59078-018-3(3))* Boyds Mills Pr.

—Rivers: Nature's Wondrous Waterways. Harrison, David L. 2003. (Earthworks Ser.). (ENG.). 32p. (J). (gr. k-2). 15.95 *(978-1-56397-968-2(3))* Boyds Mills Pr.

Nathan, Cheryl & Gutierrez, Akemia. Ella's Trip to Israel. Newman, Vivian. 2011. (Israel Ser.). (ENG.). 24p. (J). (gr. -1 — 1). pap. 8.95 *(978-0-7613-6029-2(8),* Kar-Ben Publishing) Lerner Publishing Group.

Nathan, James. Can You Survive a Global Blackout? An Interactive Doomsday Adventure. Doeden, Matt. 2015. (You Choose: Doomsday Ser.). (ENG.). 112p. (gr. 3-4). lib. bdg. 31.32 ***(978-1-4914-5850-1(X),*** You Choose Bks.) Capstone Pr., Inc.

—Can You Survive a Zombie Apocalypse? Wacholtz, Anthony. 2015. (You Choose: Doomsday Ser.). (ENG.). 112p. (gr. 3-4). pap. 6.95 ***(978-1-4914-5925-6(5))*** Capstone Pr., Inc.

—You Choose: Doomsday. Hoena, Blake & Doeden, Matt. 2015. (You Choose: Doomsday Ser.). (ENG.). 112p. (gr. 3-4). 125.28 ***(978-1-4914-6968-2(4),*** You Choose Bks.) Capstone Pr., Inc.

Nathan, Jared. All the Beautiful Butterflies: Wendell's Adventures Are Just Beginning. Nathan, Jared. 2010. (ENG.). 56p. pap. 11.99 *(978-1-4536-7384-3(9))* CreateSpace Independent Publishing Platform.

Nation, Tate. My Purple Kisses. Hahn, Blair. 2011. (My Purple Toes Ser.). 26p. (J). bds. 10.99 *(978-0-9844556-7-6(1))* My Purple Toes, LLC.

—My Purple Toes. Hahn, Blair. 2010. 24p. (J). 10.99 *(978-0-9844556-4-5(7))* My Purple Toes, LLC.

—Yo, Millard Fillmore! And All Those Other Presidents You Don't Know. Cleveland, Will & Alvarez, Mark. rev. ed. 2011. (ENG.). 128p. (J). (gr. 2-9). pap. 7.95 *(978-1-935212-41-6(9),* Prospecta Pr.) Easton Studio Pr., LLC.

—Yo, Sacramento! (And All Those Other State Capitals You Don't Know) - Memorize Them All (Forever) in 20 Minutes-Without Trying! Cleveland, Will & Alvarez, Mark. 2011. (ENG.). 128p. (J). (gr. 3-7). pap. 7.95 *(978-1-935212-38-6(9),* Prospecta Pr.) Easton Studio Pr., LLC.

National Gallery Staff. First Christmas. 2010. (ENG.). 32p. (J). (gr. -1-2). pap. 8.95 *(978-1-84780-001-5(7),* Frances Lincoln) Quarto Publishing Group UK GBR. Dist: Hachette Bk. Group.

Natsumoto, Masato. Lost War Chronicles, Vol. 2. rev. ed. 2006. (Mobile Suit Gundam Ser.). 160p. pap. 9.99 *(978-1-59816-214-1(4),* Tokyopop Kids) TOKYOPOP, Inc.

—Mobile Suit Gundam Lost War Chronicles, 2 vols., Vol. 1. Chiba, Tomohiro & Games, Incbandai. 2006. (Mobile Suit Gundam Ser.). 144p. (gr. 8-12). pap. 9.99 *(978-1-59816-213-4(6),* Tokyopop Kids) TOKYOPOP, Inc.

Natti, S., jt. illus. see Natti, Susanna.

Natti, Susanna. The Barking Treasure Mystery. Adler, David A. 2005. (Cam Jansen Ser.: 19). (ENG.). 64p. (J). (gr. 2-5). 3.99 *(978-0-14-240319-8(9),* Puffin) Penguin Publishing Group.

—Beany & the Dreaded Wedding. Wojciechowski, Susan. 2005. (Beany Adventures Ser.). 121p. (J). 13.65 *(978-0-7569-6498-6(9))* Perfection Learning Corp.

—Beany & the Magic Crystal. Wojciechowski, Susan. 2005. (Beany Adventures Ser.). 87p. (J). lib. bdg. 13.65 *(978-0-7569-5836-7(9))* Perfection Learning Corp.

—Beany Goes to Camp. Wojciechowski, Susan. 2005. (Beany Adventures Ser.). 104p. (J). (gr. 4-7). 13.65 *(978-0-7569-6499-3(7))* Perfection Learning Corp.

—Beany (Not Beanhead) Wojciechowski, Susan. 2005. (Beany Adventures Ser.). 68p. (J). lib. bdg. 12.65 *(978-0-7569-5835-0(0))* Perfection Learning Corp.

—Birthday Mystery. Adler, David A. 2005. (Cam Jansen Ser.: 20). (ENG.). 64p. (J). (gr. 2-5). 3.99 *(978-0-14-240354-9(7),* Puffin) Penguin Publishing Group.

—Cam Jansen: The Mystery of the Stolen Diamonds. Adler, David A. 2004. (Cam Jansen Ser.: 1). (ENG.). 64p. (J). (gr. 2-5). pap. 3.99 *(978-0-14-240010-4(6),* Puffin) Penguin Publishing Group.

—Cam Jansen - The First Day of School Mystery, 22 vols. Adler, David A. 2005. (Cam Jansen Ser.: 22). (ENG.). 64p. (J). (gr. 2-5). 3.99 *(978-0-14-240326-6(1),* Puffin) Penguin Publishing Group.

—Cam Jansen - The Tennis Trophy Mystery. Adler, David A. 2005. (Cam Jansen Ser.: 23). (ENG.). 64p. (J). (gr. 2-5). 3.99 *(978-0-14-240290-0(7),* Puffin) Penguin Publishing Group.

—Cam Jansen & the Catnapping Mystery. Adler, David A. 2005. (Cam Jansen Ser.). 58p. (gr. 2-5). 14.00 *(978-0-7569-5045-3(7))* Perfection Learning Corp.

—The Catnapping Mystery, 18 vols. Adler, David A. 2005. (Cam Jansen Ser.: 18). (ENG.). 64p. (J). (gr. 2-5). 3.99 *(978-0-14-240289-4(3)*, Puffin) Penguin Publishing Group.

—The Chocolate Fudge Mystery, 14 vols. Adler, David A. 2004. (Cam Jansen Ser.: 14). (ENG.). 64p. (J). (gr. 2-5). 3.99 *(978-0-14-240211-5(7)*, Puffin) Penguin Publishing Group.

—The Ghostly Mystery, Vol. 16. Adler, David A. 2005. (Cam Jansen Ser.: 16). (ENG.). 64p. (J). (gr. 2-5). 3.99 *(978-0-14-240287-0(7)*, Puffin) Penguin Publishing Group.

—Midnight Moon. Watson, Clyde. 2006. (ENG.). 24p. (J). (gr. -1-k). *(978-1-59692-162-7(5))* MacAdam/Cage Publishing, Inc.

—The Molly Shoe Mystery, No. 14. Adler, David A. 2008. (Young Cam Jansen Ser.: 14). (ENG.). 32p. (J). (gr. k-3). 14.99 *(978-0-670-06142-6(5)*, Viking Juvenile) Penguin Publishing Group.

—Mystery at the Haunted House, 13 vols. Adler, David A. 2004. (Cam Jansen Ser.: 13). (ENG.). 64p. (J). (gr. 2-5). 3.99 *(978-0-14-240210-8(9)*, Puffin) Penguin Publishing Group.

—The Mystery of Flight 427: Inside a Crash Investigation. Adler, David A. 2004. (Cam Jansen Ser.: No. 12). 56p. (J). pap. *(978-0-439-13384-5(X)*, Puffin) Penguin Publishing Group.

—The Mystery of Flight 54, 12 vols. Adler, David A. 2004. (Cam Jansen Ser.: 12). (ENG.). 64p. (J). (gr. 2-5). 3.99 *(978-0-14-240179-8(X)*, Puffin) Penguin Publishing Group.

—The Mystery of the Carnival Prize, 9 vols. Adler, David A. 2004. (Cam Jansen Ser.: 9). (ENG.). 64p. (J). (gr. 2-5). 3.99 *(978-0-14-240018-0(1)*, Puffin) Penguin Publishing Group.

—The Mystery of the Circus Clown, 7 vols. Adler, David A. 2004. (Cam Jansen Ser.: 7). (ENG.). 64p. (J). (gr. 2-5). 3.99 *(978-0-14-240016-6(5)*, Puffin) Penguin Publishing Group.

—The Mystery of the Gold Coins, 5 vols. Adler, David A. 2004. (Cam Jansen Ser.: 5). (ENG.). 64p. (J). (gr. 2-5). 3.99 *(978-0-14-240014-2(9)*, Puffin) Penguin Publishing Group.

—The Mystery of the Monkey House. Adler, David A. 2004. (Cam Jansen Ser.: 10). (ENG.). 64p. (J). (gr. 2-5). 3.99 *(978-0-14-240019-7(X)*, Puffin) Penguin Publishing Group.

—The Mystery of the Monster Movie, 8 vols. Adler, David A. 2004. (Cam Jansen Ser.: 8). (ENG.). 64p. (J). (gr. 2-5). 3.99 *(978-0-14-240017-3(3)*, Puffin) Penguin Publishing Group.

—The Mystery of the Stolen Corn Popper, 11 vols. Adler, David A. 2004. (Cam Jansen Ser.: 11). (ENG.). 64p. (J). (gr. 2-5). 3.99 *(978-0-14-240178-1(1)*, Puffin) Penguin Publishing Group.

—The Mystery of the Television Dog, 4 vols. Adler, David A. 2004. (Cam Jansen Ser.: 4). (ENG.). 64p. (J). (gr. 2-5). 3.99 *(978-0-14-240013-5(0)*, Puffin) Penguin Publishing Group.

—The Mystery of the U. F. O., 2 vols. Adler, David A. 2004. (Cam Jansen Ser.: 2). (ENG.). 64p. (J). (gr. 2-5). 3.99 *(978-0-14-240011-1(4)*, Puffin) Penguin Publishing Group.

—The Scary Snake Mystery. Adler, David A. 2005. (Cam Jansen Ser.: 17). (ENG.). 64p. (J). (gr. 2-5). 3.99 *(978-0-14-240288-7(5)*, Puffin) Penguin Publishing Group.

—The School Play Mystery. Adler, David A. 2005. (Cam Jansen Ser.: 21). (ENG.). 64p. (J). (gr. 2-5). 3.99 *(978-0-14-240355-6(5)*, Puffin) Penguin Publishing Group.

—The Secret Service Mystery. Adler, David A. 2008. (Cam Jansen Ser.: 26). (ENG.). 64p. (J). (gr. 2-5). 3.99 *(978-0-14-241074-5(8)*, Puffin) Penguin Publishing Group.

—The Secret Service Mystery. Adler, David A. 2008. (Cam Jansen Ser.: Bk. 26). 57p. (J). (gr. 2-5). 11.65 *(978-0-7569-8917-0(5))* Perfection Learning Corp.

—The Snowy Day Mystery, 24 vols. Adler, David A. 2005. (Cam Jansen Ser.: 24). (ENG.). 64p. (J). (gr. 2-5). 3.99 *(978-0-14-240417-1(9)*, Puffin) Penguin Publishing Group.

—The Speedy Car Mystery, 16 vols. Adler, David A. 2010. (Young Cam Jansen Ser.: 16). (ENG.). 32p. (J). (gr. 1-3). 14.99 *(978-0-670-06143-3(3)*, Viking Juvenile) Penguin Publishing Group.

—The Triceratops Pops Mystery, 15 vols. Adler, David A. 2004. (Cam Jansen Ser.: 15). (ENG.). 64p. (J). (gr. 2-5). 3.99 *(978-0-14-240206-1(0)*, Puffin) Penguin Publishing Group.

—The Valentine Baby Mystery. Adler, David A. 25th ed. 2006. (Cam Jansen Ser.: 25). (ENG.). 80p. (J). (gr. 2-5). 3.99 *(978-0-14-240694-6(5)*, Puffin) Penguin Publishing Group.

—Young Cam Jansen & the 100th Day of School, 15 vols. Adler, David A. 2010. (Young Cam Jansen Ser.: 15). (ENG.). 32p. (J). (gr. 1-3). mass mkt. 3.99 *(978-0-14-241685-3(1)*, Puffin) Penguin Publishing Group.

—Young Cam Jansen & the 100th Day of School Mystery, 15 vols. Adler, David A. 2009. (Young Cam Jansen Ser.: 15). (ENG.). 32p. (J). (gr. 1-3). 13.99 *(978-0-670-06172-3(7)*, Viking Juvenile) Penguin Publishing Group.

—Young Cam Jansen & the Circus Mystery. Adler, David A. 2013. (Young Cam Jansen Ser.: 17). (ENG.). 32p. (J). (gr. 1-3). pap. 3.99 *(978-0-448-46614-9(7)*, Warne, Frederick Pubs.) Penguin Bks., Ltd. GBR. Dist: Penguin Random Hse., LLC.

—Young Cam Jansen & the Circus Mystery. Adler, David A. 2011. (Young Cam Jansen Ser.: 17). (ENG.). 32p. (J). (gr. k-3). 14.99 *(978-0-670-01242-8(4)*, Viking Juvenile) Penguin Publishing Group.

—Young Cam Jansen & the Double Beach Mystery. Adler, David A. 2003. (Young Cam Jansen Ser.: 8). (ENG.). 32p. (J). (gr. 1-3). mass mkt. 3.99 *(978-0-14-250079-8(8)*, Puffin) Penguin Publishing Group.

—Young Cam Jansen & the Double Beach Mystery. Adler, David A. ed. 2003. (Young Cam Jansen — Penguin Young Readers Level 3 Ser.: 8). 30p. (gr. -1-3). lib. bdg. 13.55 *(978-0-613-67477-5(4)*, Turtleback) Turtleback Bks.

—Young Cam Jansen & the Goldfish Mystery. Adler, David A. 2014. (Young Cam Jansen Ser.: 19). (ENG.). 32p. (J). (gr. 1-3). pap. 3.99 *(978-0-14-242224-3(X)*, Warne, Frederick Pubs.) Penguin Bks., Ltd. GBR. Dist: Penguin Random Hse., LLC.

—Young Cam Jansen & the Goldfish Mystery. Adler, David A. 2013. (Young Cam Jansen Ser.: 19). (ENG.). 32p. (J). (gr. 1-3). 14.99 *(978-0-670-01259-6(9)*, Viking Adult) Penguin Publishing Group.

Natti, Susanna. Young Cam Jansen & the Knock, Knock Mystery. Adler, David A. (Young Cam Jansen Ser.: 20). (ENG.). 32p. (J). (gr. 1-3). 2015. pap. 3.99 ***(978-0-14-242225-0(8))***; 2014. 14.99 *(978-0-670-01261-9(0))* Penguin Bks., Ltd. GBR. (Warne, Frederick Pubs.). Dist: Penguin Random Hse., LLC.

Natti, Susanna. Young Cam Jansen & the Lions' Lunch Mystery. Adler, David A. 2007. (Young Cam Jansen Ser.: 13). (ENG.). 32p. (J). (gr. k-3). 13.99 *(978-0-670-06171-6(9)*, Viking Juvenile) Penguin Publishing Group.

—Young Cam Jansen & the Lions' Lunch Mystery, No. 13. Adler, David A. 2008. (Young Cam Jansen Ser.: 13). (ENG.). 32p. (J). (gr. 1-3). mass mkt. 3.99 *(978-0-14-241176-6(0)*, Puffin) Penguin Publishing Group.

—Young Cam Jansen & the Magic Bird Mystery. Adler, David A. 2013. (Young Cam Jansen Ser.: 18). (ENG.). 32p. (J). (gr. 1-3). pap. 3.99 *(978-0-448-46613-2(9)*, Warne, Frederick Pubs.) Penguin Bks., Ltd. GBR. Dist: Penguin Random Hse., LLC.

—Young Cam Jansen & the Magic Bird Mystery, 18 vols. Adler, David A. 2012. (Young Cam Jansen Ser.: 18). (ENG.). 32p. (J). (gr. 1-3). 14.99 *(978-0-670-01257-2(2)*, Viking Juvenile) Penguin Publishing Group.

—Young Cam Jansen & the Molly Shoe Mystery, No. 14. Adler, David A. 2009. (Young Cam Jansen Ser.: 14). (ENG.). 32p. (J). (gr. 1-3). mass mkt. 3.99 *(978-0-14-241402-6(6)*, Puffin) Penguin Publishing Group.

—Young Cam Jansen & the New Girl Mystery. Adler, David A. (Young Cam Jansen Ser.: 10). (ENG.). 32p. (J). 2005. (gr. 1-3). mass mkt. 3.99 *(978-0-14-240353-2(9)*, Puffin); Vol. 10. 2004. (gr. k-3). 13.99 *(978-0-670-05915-7(3)*, Viking Juvenile) Penguin Publishing Group.

—Young Cam Jansen & the New Girl Mystery. Adler, David A. 2005. (Young Cam Jansen Ser.: Bk. 10). 32p. (gr. k-2). 14.00 *(978-0-7569-5522-9(X))* Perfection Learning Corp.

—Young Cam Jansen & the Speedy Car Mystery, 16 vols. Adler, David A. 2011. (Young Cam Jansen Ser.: 16). (ENG.). 32p. (J). (gr. 1-3). mass mkt. 3.99 *(978-0-14-241868-0(4)*, Puffin) Penguin Publishing Group.

—Young Cam Jansen & the Spotted Cat Mystery. Adler, David A. 2007. (Young Cam Jansen (prebound) Ser.). 31p. (gr. -1-3). 14.00 *(978-0-7569-8155-6(7))* Perfection Learning Corp.

—Young Cam Jansen & the Substitute Mystery, No. 11. Adler, David A. 2006. (Young Cam Jansen Ser.: 11). (ENG.). 32p. (J). (gr. 1-3). mass mkt. 3.99 *(978-0-14-240660-1(0)*, Puffin) Penguin Publishing Group.

—Young Cam Jansen & the Zoo Note Mystery. Adler, David A. (ENG.). (J). 2013. (Puffin Young Readers, L3 Ser.). 31p. (gr. -1-3). pap. 3.99 *(978-0-448-46633-0(3))*; 2004. (Young Cam Jansen Ser.: 9). 32p. (gr. 1-3). mass mkt. 3.99 *(978-0-14-240204-7(4))* Penguin Publishing Group. (Puffin).

Natti, Susanna & Natti, S. Young Cam Jansen & the Spotted Cat Mystery, No. 12. Adler, David A. 2007. (Young Cam Jansen Ser.: 12). (ENG.). 32p. (J). (gr. 1-3). pap. 3.99 *(978-0-14-241012-7(8)*, Puffin) Penguin Publishing Group.

Nauck, Todd, et al. Deadpool/Amazing Spider-Man/Hulk: Identity Wars. 2011. (ENG.). 112p. (J). (gr. 4-17). 19.99 *(978-0-7851-5568-3(6))* Marvel Worldwide, Inc.

Nauck, Todd, jt. illus. see Frenz, Ron.

Naughton, Terry. My Personal Panther. Cesak, Jerry. 2012. (J). *(978-0-578-10507-9(1))* U. S. ISBN Agency.

Naujokaitis, Pranas T. Belches, Burps, & Farts - Oh My! Bennett, Artie. 2014. (ENG.). 40p. (J). (gr. -1-3). 17.99 *(978-1-60905-392-5(3))* Blue Apple Bks.

—Dinosaurs in Space. 2012. (ENG.). 40p. (J). (gr. 1-4). 11.99 *(978-1-60905-253-9(6))* Blue Apple Bks.

—The Radically Awesome Adventures of the Animal Princess. 2013. (ENG.). 40p. (J). (gr. 1-4). 11.99 *(978-1-60905-296-6(X))* Blue Apple Bks.

—The Totally Awesome Epic Quest of the Brave Boy Knight. 2011. (ENG.). 40p. (J). (gr. 1-4). 11.99 *(978-1-60905-099-3(1))* Blue Apple Bks.

Nault, S. &R. Mr Scruffpot's Pony. Nault, Susan. 2013. 30p. pap. *(978-0-9870744-1-6(5))* Kingdom Pr.

Nausley, Kathy. The Gift. Sheets, Judy. 2005. 40p. (J). lib. bdg. 24.00 *(978-0-9726451-2-6(8))* Sheets, Judy.

Nautilus Studio Staff. The Planet of the Snake. Bruneau, Clotilde et al. 2015. (ENG.). 48p. (J). (gr. 4-8). pap. 7.95 ***(978-1-4677-6027-0(7)***, Graphic Universe) Lerner Publishing Group.

Nava, Francisco. La Vaca Roja. Lujan, Jorge Elias. 2003. (SPA.). 27p. (J). (gr. k-3). pap. 7.95 *(978-968-19-0629-0(2))* Santillana USA Publishing Co., Inc.

Navarra, Nino. How to Draw Nickelodeon Teenage Mutant Ninja Turtles: /step-By-Step Illustrations by Niño Navarra. 2014. 64p. (J). *(978-1-939581-17-4(6))* Quarto Publishing Group USA.

—Ooze Control. Random House Staff. 2013. (Glow-In-the-Dark Pictureback Ser.). (ENG.). 16p. (J). (gr. -1-2). pap. 4.99 *(978-0-307-98229-2(7)*, Random Hse. Bks. for Young Readers) Random Hse. Children's Bks.

Navarro, Larry. The Story of Jack Frost. ed. 2012. lib. bdg. 13.55 *(978-0-606-26920-9(7)*, Turtleback) Turtleback Bks.

Navía, Miguel. Mari Pepa y el Club de los Pirados. Cerdá, Alfredo Gómez. 2010. (Librosaurio Ser.). (SPA.). 116p. (J). (gr. 4-7). 13.95 *(978-84-7942-398-8(6))* Heinemann Iberia, S.A. ESP. Dist: Independent Pubs. Group.

Nayberg, Yevgenia. The Wren & the Sparrow. Lewis, J. Patrick. 2014. (J). *(978-1-4677-6210-6(5)*, Kar-Ben Publishing) Lerner Publishing Group.

Nayler, Sarah. Flash Harriet & the Loch Ness Monster. Wallace, Karen. 2007. (Collins Big Cat Ser.). (ENG.). 160p. (J). pap. 8.99 *(978-0-00-723082-2(6))* HarperCollins Pubs. Ltd. GBR. Dist: Independent Pubs. Group.

Nayler, Sarah. Shredder. Kebbe, Jonathan. 2014. (ENG.). 80p. (J). (gr. k-2). pap. 7.99 ***(978-0-552-56898-2(8))*** Transworld Publishers Ltd. GBR. Dist: Independent Pubs. Group.

Nayler, Sarah. Bebé a Bordo. Nayler, Sarah. Gray, Kes & GRAY, KES. 2004. (ESP & SPA.). 28p. (J). 16.99 *(978-84-8488-087-5(7))* Serres, Ediciones, S. L. ESP. Dist: Lectorum Pubns., Inc.

Nazar, Alexandria. Little Blue Planet. Riggs, Jon & Evanoff, Corrine R. 2014. (ENG.). 24p. (J). (-5). 16.95 *(978-1-939621-07-8(0))* ORO Editions.

Nazareth, Carla. Nuestros Derechos. Carvalho et al. 2003. (SPA.). 48p. (J). (gr. k-2). pap. 8.50 *(978-84-241-8335-6(5))* Everest Editora ESP. Dist: Lectorum Pubns., Inc.

Nazario, Rafael. Mr. Blue Butterfly. Kennedy, Kirk. 2013. (ENG.). (J). (gr. -1-3). 14.95 *(978-1-62086-256-8(5))* Mascot Bks., Inc.

Nazif, Iwan. DreamWorks' Dragons Vol. 1: Dragon Down (How to Train Your Dragon TV) Titan Comics Staff & Furman, Simon. 2014. (Riders of Berk Ser.). (ENG.). 64p. (J). (gr. 3-7). pap. 6.99 *(978-1-78276-076-4(8)*, Titan Comics) Titan Bks. Ltd. GBR. Dist: Random Hse., Inc.

Nazran, Govinder. Aladdin. 2014. (Storyteller Book Ser.). (ENG.). 48p. (J). (gr. 2-5). pap. 7.99 *(978-1-84322-790-8(8)*, Armadillo) Anness Publishing GBR. Dist: National Bk. Network.

Neal, Bill. A Little Piece of Ground. Laird, Elizabeth. 2006. (ENG.). 240p. (J). (gr. 4-6). pap. 9.95 *(978-1-931859-38-7(8))* Haymarket Bks.

Neal, Christopher Silas. Go to Sleep, Little Farm. Ray, Mary Lyn. (ENG.). (J). 2015. 38p. (— 1). bds. 8.99 ***(978-0-544-57916-3(X))***; 2014. 40p. (gr. -1-3). 16.99 *(978-0-544-15014-0(7))* Houghton Mifflin Harcourt Publishing Co. (HMH Books For Young Readers).

Neal, Christopher Silas. Lifetime: The Amazing Numbers in Animal Lives. Schaefer, Lola M. 2013. (ENG.). 40p. (J). (gr. -1-3). 17.99 *(978-1-4521-0714-1(9))* Chronicle Bks. LLC.

—Over & under the Snow. Messner, Kate. (ENG.). 44p. (J). 2014. (gr. k-3). 7.99 *(978-1-4521-3646-2(7))*; 2011. (gr. -1-3). 16.99 *(978-0-8118-6784-9(6))* Chronicle Bks. LLC.

Neal, Jill Faith. Aunt Linda's Shape Book. Dudley, Linda S. 2007. (ENG.). 32p. per. 24.95 *(978-1-4241-8618-1(8))* America Star Bks.

Neal, Penelope. Moose with Loose Poops. Cowan, Charlotte. 2008. (Dr. Hippo Ser.). (ENG.). 32p. (J). (gr. -1-2). 17.95 *(978-0-9753516-5-9(6))* Hippocratic Pr., The.

Nealon, Eve, jt. illus. see Espinola, Nicole.

Neary, Paul. Nick Fury vs. S. H. I. E. L. D. 2011. (ENG.). 304p. (J). (gr. 4-17). 39.99 *(978-0-7851-5901-8(0))* Marvel Worldwide, Inc.

—S. H. I. E. L. D. Nick Fury vs. S. H. I. E. L. D. 2013. (ENG.). 304p. (J). (gr. 4-17). pap. 29.99 *(978-0-7851-8500-0(3))* Marvel Worldwide, Inc.

Neate, Andy. Hewitch. Deveze, Winky. 2006. (J). *(978-0-9787174-0-7(6))* Love Bug Bks.

Needham, James M. Many Biomes, One Earth. Collard, Sneed B., III. 2009. (ENG.). 32p. (J). (gr. k-3). pap. 7.95 *(978-1-57091-632-8(2))* Charlesbridge Publishing, Inc.

Neel, Julien. Secret Diary. Burrell, Carol Klio. 2012. (Lou! Ser.: 1). (ENG.). 48p. (J). (gr. 6-9). lib. bdg. 27.93 *(978-0-7613-8776-3(5)*, Graphic Universe) Lerner Publishing Group.

—Summertime Blues. Burrell, Carol Klio. 2012. (Lou! Ser.: 2). (ENG.). 48p. (J). (gr. 6-9). lib. bdg. 27.93 *(978-0-7613-8777-0(3)*, Graphic Universe) Lerner Publishing Group.

Neel, Julien. Down in the Dumps. Neel, Julien. 2012. (Lou! Ser.: 3). (ENG.). 48p. (J). (gr. 6-9). pap. 8.95 *(978-0-8225-9165-8(0)*, Graphic Universe) Lerner Publishing Group.

—Down in the Dumps. Neel, Julien. Burrell, Carol Klio. 2012. (Lou! Ser.: 3). (ENG.). 48p. (J). (gr. 6-9). lib. bdg. 27.93 *(978-0-7613-8779-4(X)*, Graphic Universe) Lerner Publishing Group.

—Lou! Neel, Julien. 2012. (Lou! Ser.). 48p. (J). (gr. 4-8). lib. bdg. 55.86 *(978-0-7613-8903-3(2)*, Graphic Universe) Lerner Publishing Group.

—Lou! 6Pack Set. Neel, Julien. 2012. (Lou! Ser.). 48p. (J). (gr. 4-8). pap. 102.03 *(978-0-7613-9288-0(2)*, Graphic Universe) Lerner Publishing Group.

—Lou! Single Copy Set. Neel, Julien. 2012. (Lou! Ser.). 48p. (J). (gr. 4-8). pap. 17.01 *(978-0-7613-9287-3(4)*, Graphic Universe) Lerner Publishing Group.

—The Perfect Summer. Neel, Julien. 2012. (Lou! Ser.: 4). (ENG.). 48p. (J). (gr. 6-9). pap. 8.95 *(978-0-8225-9169-6(3)*, Graphic Universe) Lerner Publishing Group.

—The Perfect Summer. Neel, Julien. Burrell, Carol Klio. 2012. (Lou! Ser.: 4). (ENG.). 48p. (J). (gr. 6-9). lib. bdg. 27.93 *(978-0-7613-8780-0(3)*, Graphic Universe) Lerner Publishing Group.

—Secret Diary. Neel, Julien. 2012. (Lou! Ser.). 48p. (J). (gr. 4-8). pap. 51.02 *(978-0-7613-9285-9(8))*; (ENG.). (gr. 6-9). pap. 8.95 *(978-0-7613-8868-5(0))* Lerner Publishing Group. (Graphic Universe).

—Summertime Blues. Neel, Julien. 2012. (Lou! Ser.). 48p. (J). (gr. 4-8). pap. 51.02 *(978-0-7613-9286-6(6))*; (ENG.). (gr. 6-9). pap. 8.95 *(978-0-7613-8869-2(9))* Lerner Publishing Group. (Graphic Universe).

Neel, Preston. Oh My, It Must Be the Sky! Appleton-Smith, Laura. 2004. (Book to Remember Ser.). (ENG.). 52p. pap. 8.95 *(978-1-929262-21-2(3)*, Books To Remember) Flyleaf Publishing.

—Queen Bee Needs to Be Free. Appleton-Smith, Laura. 2005. (Book to Remember Ser.). (ENG.). 35p. pap. 8.95 *(978-1-929262-43-4(4)*, Books To Remember) Flyleaf Publishing.

Neely, Keith. Play Ball Like the Hall of Famers: Tips for Kids from 19 Baseball Greats, 1 vol. Krasner, Steven. 2005. (ENG.). 208p. (J). (gr. 5-9). pap. 14.95 *(978-1-56145-339-9(0))* Peachtree Pubs.

—St. Jude: A Friend in Hard Times. Aquilina, Michael, III. 2004. 76p. (J). 14.95 *(978-0-8198-7075-9(7)*, 332-371) Pauline Bks. & Media.

Neely, Keith R. Something Is Wrong at My House: A Book about Parents' Fighting. Davis, Diane. 2010.Tr. of Algo anda mal en mi Casa. (SPA & ENG.). 32p. (J). (gr. -1-3). pap. 9.95 *(978-1-884734-65-6(0))*; lib. bdg. 16.95 *(978-1-884734-66-3(9))* Parenting Pr., Inc.

Neely, Scott. The Case of the Cheese Thief, 1 vol. Bright, J. E. 2014. (You Choose Stories: Scooby-Doo Ser.). (ENG.). 112p. (gr. 2-3). pap. 6.95 *(978-1-4342-7927-9(8)*, You Choose Bks.) Capstone Pr., Inc.

Neely, Scott. The Curse of Atlantis. Sutton, Laurie S. 2015. (You Choose Stories: Scooby-Doo Ser.). (ENG.). 112p. (gr. 2-3). lib. bdg. 31.32 ***(978-1-4965-0477-7(1))*** Stone Arch Bks.

Neely, Scott. The Fright at Zombie Farm. Sutton, Laurie S. 2015. (You Choose Stories: Scooby-Doo Ser.). (ENG.). 112p. (gr. 2-3). lib. bdg. 31.32 *(978-1-4342-9713-6(6)*, You Choose Bks.) Capstone Pr., Inc.

—The Ghost of the Bermuda Triangle, 1 vol. Sutton, Laurie S. 2014. (You Choose Stories: Scooby-Doo Ser.). (ENG.). 112p. (gr. 2-3). 31.32 *(978-1-4342-9126-4(X)*, You Choose Bks.) Capstone Pr., Inc.

—The House on Spooky Street. Sutton, Laurie S. 2015. (You Choose Stories: Scooby-Doo Ser.). (ENG.). 112p. (gr. 2-3). lib. bdg. 31.32 *(978-1-4342-9714-3(4)*, You Choose Bks.) Capstone Pr., Inc.

—The Mystery of the Aztec Tomb, 1 vol. Sutton, Laurie S. 2014. (You Choose Stories: Scooby-Doo Ser.). (ENG.). 112p. (gr. 2-3). 31.32 *(978-1-4342-9127-1(8)*, You Choose Bks.) Capstone Pr., Inc.

—The Mystery of the Maze Monster, 1 vol. Sazaklis, John. 2014. (You Choose Stories: Scooby-Doo Ser.). (ENG.). 112p. (gr. 2-3). pap. 6.95 *(978-1-4342-7928-6(6)*, You Choose Bks.) Capstone Pr., Inc.

Neely, Scott. The Secret of the Flying Saucer. Sutton, Laurie S. 2015. (You Choose Stories: Scooby-Doo Ser.). (ENG.). 112p. (gr. 2-3). lib. bdg. 31.32 ***(978-1-4965-0478-4(X))*** Stone Arch Bks.

Neely, Scott. The Secret of the Sea Creature, 1 vol. Sutton, Laurie S. 2014. (You Choose Stories: Scooby-Doo Ser.). (ENG.). 112p. (gr. 2-3). pap. 6.95 *(978-1-4342-7925-5(1)*, You Choose Bks.) Capstone Pr., Inc.

—The Terror of the Bigfoot Beast, 1 vol. Sutton, Laurie S. 2014. (You Choose Stories: Scooby-Doo Ser.). (ENG.). 112p. (gr. 2-3). pap. 6.95 *(978-1-4342-7926-2(X)*, You Choose Bks.) Capstone Pr., Inc.

Neff, Henry H. The Fiend & the Forge. Neff, Henry H. 2010. (Tapestry Ser.: Bk. 3). (ENG.). 560p. (J). (gr. 3-7). lib. bdg. 20.99 *(978-0-375-93898-6(2)*, Random Hse. Bks. for Young Readers) Random Hse. Children's Bks.

—The Maelstrom: Book Four of the Tapestry. Neff, Henry H. (Tapestry Ser.). (ENG.). 480p. (J). (gr. 3-7). 2013. 7.99 *(978-0-375-87148-1(9))*; 2012. lib. bdg. 19.99 *(978-0-375-95707-9(3)*, Random Hse. Bks. for Young Readers) Random Hse. Children's Bks.

Negrin, Fabian. El Milagro de la Primera Flora de Nochebuena; Un Cuento Mexicano Sobre la Navidad. Oppenheim, Joanne F. 2003. (SPA & ENG.). 32p. (J). 16.99 *(978-1-84148-308-5(7))* Barefoot Bks., Inc.

—The Miracle of the First Poinsettia. Oppenheim, Joanne F. 2003. (ENG.). 32p. (J). 16.99 *(978-1-84148-245-3(5))* Barefoot Bks., Inc.

—Miracle of the First Poinsettia. Oppenheim, Joanne F. 32p. 8.99 *(978-1-84148-364-1(8))* Barefoot Bks., Inc.

—The Riverbank. Darwin, Charles. 2010. (ENG.). 32p. (J). (gr. 1-3). 17.95 *(978-1-56846-207-3(7)*, Creative Editions) Creative Co., The.

—Wizard Tales. 2003. 96p. 19.95 *(978-1-55285-558-4(9))* Whitecap Bks., Ltd. CAN. Dist: Graphic Arts Ctr. Publishing Co.

Negrin, Fabian. The Perfect Knight. Negrin, Fabian, tr. Gousseff, Catherine. 2004. (ENG.). 22p. 6.95 *(978-0-89236-739-3(3))* Oxford Univ. Pr., Inc.

—Prince Orpheus. Negrin, Fabian, tr. Du Bouchet, Paule. 2004. (ENG.). 22p. 6.95 *(978-0-89236-737-5(7))* Oxford Univ. Pr., Inc.

Nel, Molly. Color, 1 vol. Niz, Ellen. 2006. (Our Physical World Ser.). (ENG.). 24p. (gr. 1-2). 24.65 *(978-0-7368-5400-9(2)*, First Facts) Capstone Pr., Inc.

—Hearing, 1 vol. Olien, Rebecca. 2005. (Senses Ser.). (ENG.). 24p. (gr. 1-2). 24.65 *(978-0-7368-4301-0(9)*, First Facts) Capstone Pr., Inc.

—Tasting, 1 vol. Olien, Rebecca. 2005. (Senses Ser.). (ENG.). 24p. (gr. 1-2). 24.65 *(978-0-7368-4304-1(3)*, First Facts) Capstone Pr., Inc.

Nel, Molly, jt. illus. see Collins, Tami.

Neibert, Alissa. Count Your Way Through South Africa. Haskins, Jim & Benson, Kathleen. 2006. (Count Your Way Ser.). (ENG.). 24p. (gr. 2-5). lib. bdg. 19.93 *(978-1-57505-883-2(9)*, Millbrook Pr.) Lerner Publishing Group.

Neidigh, Sherry. Bailey & the Beagle Brigade. Heit Schwaeber, Barbie. 2011. (ENG.). 32p. (J). 6.95 *(978-1-60727-218-2(0))* Soundprints.

—Count down to Fall, 1 vol. Hawk, Fran. 2009. (ENG.). 32p. (J). (gr. -1-3). 16.95 *(978-1-934359-94-5(7))* Arbordale Publishing.

—Deep in the Desert, 1 vol. Donald, Rhonda Lucas. 2011. (ENG.). 32p. (J). (gr. -1-3). 16.95 *(978-1-60718-125-5(8))*; pap. 8.95 *(978-1-60718-135-4(5))* Arbordale Publishing.

N

—Falcons. Lynch, Wayne. 2005. (Our Wild World Ser.). (ENG.). 48p. (J). (gr. 2-5). 10.95 *(978-1-55971-911-7(7))* Cooper Square Publishing Llc.

—Falcons. Lynch, Wayne, photos by. Lynch, Wayne. 2005. (Our Wild World Ser.). (ENG.). 48p. (J). (gr. 2-5). pap. 7.95 *(978-1-55971-912-4(5))* Cooper Square Publishing Llc.

—Vultures. Lynch, Wayne, photos by. Lynch, Wayne. 2005. (Our Wild World Ser.). (ENG.). 48p. (J). (gr. 2-5). pap. 7.95 *(978-1-55971-918-6(4))* Cooper Square Publishing Llc.

Neidigh, Sherry. Who Needs That Nose? Neidigh, Sherry, tr. Warrick, Karen Clemens. 2004. (ENG.). 32p. (J). (gr. -1-k). 15.95 *(978-1-55971-887-5(0))* Cooper Square Publishing Llc.

Neighbor, Douglas. My Grandpa Tom & Me, 1 vol. Godell, Rick. 2009. 29p. pap. 24.95 *(978-1-61546-026-7(8))* America Star Bks.

Neilan, Eujin Kim. The Best Winds. Williams, Laura E. 2006. (ENG.). 32p. (J). (gr. -1-2). 16.95 *(978-1-59078-274-3(7))* Boyds Mills Pr.

—Fly Free! Thong, Roseanne. 2010. (ENG.). 32p. (J). (gr. 2-4). 17.95 *(978-1-59078-550-8(9))* Boyds Mills Pr.

—Imagine a Dragon. Pringle, Laurence. 2008. (ENG.). 32p. (J). (gr. 2-4). 16.95 *(978-1-56397-328-4(6))* Boyds Mills Pr.

—Rabbit & the Dragon King: Based on a Korean Folk Tale. San Souci, Daniel. 2006. (ENG.). 32p. (J). (gr. 1-4). pap. 9.95 *(978-1-59078-418-1(9))* Boyds Mills Pr.

Neild, Robyn. My One-of-a-Kind Fashion Design. Ward, Wendy. 2014. (ENG.). 128p. (J). (gr. 4-8). pap. 14.99 *(978-1-4022-9541-6(3)*, Sourcebooks Jabberwocky) Sourcebooks, Inc.

Neill, John R. Little Wizard Stories of Oz. Baum, L. Frank. 2011. (Dover Children's Classics Ser.). (ENG.). 160p. (J). (gr. 3-5). pap. 14.99 *(978-0-486-47644-5(8))* Dover Pubns., Inc.

—The Silver Princess in Oz. Thompson, Ruth Plumly & Baum, L. Frank. 2011. 248p. 46.95 *(978-1-258-01166-6(2))* Literary Licensing, LLC.

—A Wonderful Welcome to Oz: The Marvelous Land of Oz, Ozma of Oz, & the Emerald City of Oz. Baum, L. Frank. Maguire, Gregory, ed. 2006. (Modern Library Classics Ser.). (ENG.). 624p. per. 15.95 *(978-0-8129-7494-2(8)*, Modern Library) Random House Publishing Group.

Neilson, Ginger. Gunter the Underwater Elephant. Neilson, Ginger. 2011. 32p. pap. 15.99 *(978-0-9832740-2-5(9))* 4RV Publishing, LLC.

Neilson, Heidi. Play, Said the Earth to Air. Lewis, Richard. 2013. (ENG.). 44p. (J). (gr. -1). pap. 12.00 *(978-1-929299-12-6(5))* Touchstone Ctr. Pubns.

Neira, Muyi. Los Siete Mejores Cuentos Rabes. Escobar, Melba. 2004. (SPA.). (J). (gr. 3-5). *(978-958-04-7212-4(2))* Norma S.A.

Neitz, Erica. Shapesville. Mills, Andy & Osborn, Becky. 2003. (ENG.). 32p. (J). 15.95 *(978-0-936077-47-5(6))* Shelter Pubns., Inc.

Neitz, Erica. Shapesville. Neitz, Erica, tr. Mills, Andy & Osborn, Becky. 2003. (ENG.). 32p. (J). pap. 12.95 *(978-0-936077-44-4(1))* Shelter Pubns., Inc.

Nelligan, Kevin, jt. illus. see Ocello, Salvatore.

Nellis, Philip. Themes to Remember, 3, Vol. 1. Persons, Marjorie Kiel. 2007. 124p. (J). lib. bdg. 31.95 incl. audio compact disk *(978-0-9794947-0-3(2))* Classical Magic, Inc.

—Themes to Remember Teacher's Guide Vol. 2: A Theme Recognition Based Method for Teaching Music Appreciation, 2 vols. Persons, Marjorie Kiel. 2003. 128p. tchr. ed. 24.95 *(978-0-9675997-4-8(1))* Classical Magic, Inc.

Nellis, Philip & Johnson, George Ann. Antonin Dvorak from the New World with Lyrics. Persons, Marjorie Kiel. 2004. 80p. (J). lib. bdg. 31.95 *(978-0-9675997-6-2(8))* Classical Magic, Inc.

—Classical Karaoke for Kids. Persons, Marjorie Kiel. 2003. 128p. (J). lib. bdg. 31.95 *(978-0-9675997-2-4(5))* Classical Magic, Inc.

—Themes to Remember, Volume 2, Vol. 2. Persons, Marjorie Kiel. rev. ed. 2004. 128p. (J). lib. bdg. 31.95 *(978-0-9675997-5-5(X))* Classical Magic, Inc.

Nelms, Kate. See What a Seal Can Do. Butterworth, Chris. 2013. (ENG.). 32p. (J). (gr. k-4). 14.99 *(978-0-7636-6574-6(6))* Candlewick Pr.

—See What a Seal Can Do. Butterworth, Christine. 2015. (Read & Wonder Ser.). (ENG.). 32p. (J). (gr. -1-3). 6.99 *(978-0-7636-7649-0(7))* Candlewick Pr.

Nelson, Andy. The Impressionists Coloring Book. Nelson, Andy. 2nd ed. 2004. 96p. (Orig.). (J). (gr. 1-6). pap. 8.95 *(978-0-929636-26-9(0))* Syren Bk. Co.

Nelson, Anndria. School Rules! Williams, Shannon. 2010. 36p. pap. 16.99 *(978-1-4520-3924-4(0))* AuthorHouse.

Nelson, Annika. Dominga's Wonderful Year/El Año Maravilloso del Domingo. Yonikus, Sandi. 2005. (SPA & ENG.). 32p. (J). 16.95 *(978-0-8146-2876-8(1))* Liturgical Pr.

Nelson, Annika & Diaz, David. Canto Familiar. Soto, Gary. 2007. (ENG.). 96p. (J). (gr. 2-5). pap. 7.95 *(978-0-15-205885-2(0))* Houghton Mifflin Harcourt Publishing Co.

Nelson, Annika M. Colors of Me. Barnes, Brynne. 2011. (ENG.). 28p. 15.95 *(978-1-58536-541-8(6))* Sleeping Bear Pr.

Nelson, Casey. The Boy Who Ate America. Jones, Nathan Smith. 2007. 32p. (J). (gr. -1-3). 16.95 *(978-1-59038-814-3(3)*, Shadow Mountain) Shadow Mountain Publishing.

—My First Book of Temples. Buck, Deanna Draper. 2012. (J). bds. 15.99 *(978-1-60907-158-5(1))* Deseret Bk. Co.

Nelson, Christine. Heavenites Angels to Zebras Board Book with Audio CD. Collison, Shauna. 2007. 26p. (J). 15.95 *(978-0-9792510-0-9(1))* Revelation Products LLC.

—Heavenites Learning to Count on God Board Book with audio CD. Collisin, Shauna. 2007. 22p. (J). 15.95 *(978-0-9792510-1-6(X))* Revelation Products LLC.

Nelson, Craig. I'll Be with You Always. Eareckson Tada, Joni. 2004. 32p. (gr. 8-12). 14.99 *(978-1-58134-000-6(1))* Crossway.

Nelson, Don. How the World Began. Heal, Edith. 2012. 112p. 39.95 *(978-1-258-23527-7(1))*; pap. 24.95 *(978-1-258-24549-8(3))* Literary Licensing, LLC.

Nelson, Douglas, jt. illus. see Nelson, Ray.

Nelson, Ernist. Atlantis Motherland. Collins, Robert, photos by. Flying Eagle & Whispering Wind. 2004. 168p. (YA). 39.00 *(978-0-9719580-0-5(9))* COSMIC VORTEX.

Nelson, Gail M. Go Eat, Pete. Nelson, Gail M. Nelson, Katie M. 2013. 32p. pap. 9.99 *(978-1-936499-05-2(3))* Jewel Publishing.

Nelson, Holly. Believe & You're There at the Miracles of Jesus. Johnson, Alice W. & Warner, Allison H. 2009. 96p. (J). pap. 8.95 *(978-1-59038-722-1(8))* Deseret Bk. Co.

—Believe & You're There When the Stone Was Rolled Away. Johnson, Alice W. & Warner, Allison H. 2009. 96p. (J). pap. 8.95 *(978-1-59038-723-8(6))* Deseret Bk. Co.

—Believe & You're There When the White Dove Descended. Johnson, Alice W. & Warner, Allison H. 2009. 96p. (J). pap. 8.95 *(978-1-59038-721-4(X))* Deseret Bk. Co.

Nelson, Jane E. God Makes It Right: Three Stories for Children Based on Favorite Bible Verses. Murphy, Elspeth Campbell. 72p. (J). *(978-1-55513-109-8(3))* Cook, David C.

Nelson, Jim. The Curse of King Tut's Mummy. Zoehfeld, Kathleen Weidner. 2007. (Stepping Stone Book(TM) Ser.). (ENG.). 112p. (J). (gr. 2-5). per. 4.99 *(978-0-375-83862-0(7)*, Random Hse. Bks. for Young Readers) Random Hse. Children's Bks.

—Finding the First T. Rex. Zoehfeld, Kathleen Weidner. 2014. (Stepping Stone Book Ser.). (ENG.). 112p. (J). (gr. 2-5). 4.99 *(978-0-375-84662-5(X)*, Random Hse. Bks. for Young Readers) Random Hse. Children's Bks.

—Looking for Bigfoot. Worth, Bonnie. 2010. (Step into Reading Ser.). (ENG.). 48p. (J). (gr. 2-4). pap. 3.99 *(978-0-375-86331-8(1))* Random Hse., Inc.

Nelson, Judy. Desert Tails. Reasoner, Charles. 2011. (Tail Spin Bks.). (ENG.). 14p. (J). (gr. -1). 9.99 *(978-1-934650-93-6(5))* Just For Kids Pr., LLC.

—Ocean Tails. Reasoner, Charles. 2011. (Tail Spin Bks.). (ENG.). 14p. (J). (gr. -1-3). bds. 9.99 *(978-1-934650-92-9(7))* Just For Kids Pr., LLC.

—Whose Ears? Kenna, Kara. 2011. (Whose Whose Bks.). (ENG.). 10p. (gr. -1-k). bds. 9.99 *(978-1-935498-52-0(5))* Just For Kids Pr., LLC.

—Whose Eyes? Kenna, Kara. 2011. (Whose Whose Bks.). (ENG.). 10p. (gr. -1-k). bds. 9.99 *(978-1-935498-51-3(7))* Just For Kids Pr., LLC.

—Whose Feet? Kenna, Kara. 2011. (Whose Whose Bks.). (ENG.). 12p. (J). (gr. -1). bds. 9.99 *(978-1-935498-53-7(3))* Just For Kids Pr., LLC.

Nelson, Judy A. Whose Nose? Kenna, Kara. 2011. (Whose Whose Bks.). (ENG.). 10p. (gr. -1-k). bds. 9.99 *(978-1-935498-54-4(1))* Just For Kids Pr., LLC.

Nelson, Kadir. Abe's Honest Words. Rappaport, Doreen. 2009. (J). (gr. 2-4). 27.95 incl. audio *(978-0-8045-6984-2(3))* Spoken Arts, Inc.

—All God's Critters. Staines, Bill. 2009. (ENG.). 36p. (J). (gr. k-3). 16.99 *(978-0-689-86959-4(2)*, Simon & Schuster Bks. For Young Readers) Simon & Schuster Bks. For Young Readers.

—Big Jabe. Nolen, Jerdine. 2003. (ENG.). 32p. (J). (gr. k-5). pap. 7.99 *(978-0-06-054061-6(3)*, Amistad) HarperCollins Pubs.

—Big Jabe. Nolen, Jerdine. 2004. (gr. 1). 17.00 *(978-0-7569-3184-1(3))* Perfection Learning Corp.

—Coretta Scott. Shange, Ntozake. 32p. (J). (gr. -1-4). 2011. (ENG.). pap. 6.99 *(978-0-06-125366-9(9))*; 2009. (ENG.). 17.99 *(978-0-06-125364-5(2))*; 2009. lib. bdg. 18.89 *(978-0-06-125365-2(0))* HarperCollins Pubs. (Tegen, Katherine Bks).

—Dancing in the Wings. Allen, Debbie. 2003. (ENG.). 32p. (J). (gr. -1-3). 6.99 *(978-0-14-250141-2(7)*, Puffin) Penguin Publishing Group.

—Dancing in the Wings. Allen, Debbie. 2003. (J). (gr. -1-3). 14.65 *(978-0-7569-7022-2(9))* Perfection Learning Corp.

—Ellington Was Not a Street. Shange, Ntozake. 2004. (ENG.). 40p. (J). (gr. k-6). 17.99 *(978-0-689-82884-3(5)*, Simon & Schuster Bks. For Young Readers) Simon & Schuster Bks. For Young Readers.

—Ellington Was Not a Street. Shange, Ntozake. 2005. (J). 29.95 *(978-0-439-77582-3(5)*, WHCD672) Weston Woods Studios, Inc.

—Henry's Freedom Box: A True Story from the Underground Railroad. Levine, Ellen. 2007. (ENG.). 40p. (J). (gr. -1-3). 17.99 *(978-0-439-77733-9(X)*, Scholastic Pr.) Scholastic, Inc.

—Henry's Freedom Box: A True Story from the Underground Railroad. Levine, Ellen. 2011. (J). (gr. 2-5). 29.95 *(978-0-545-13455-2(2))* Weston Woods Studios, Inc.

—Hewitt Anderson's Great Big Life. Nolen, Jerdine. (ENG.). 40p. (J). (gr. k-3). 2013. 7.99 *(978-1-4424-6035-5(0))*; 2005. 17.99 *(978-0-689-86866-5(9))* Simon & Schuster/Paula Wiseman Bks. (Simon & Schuster/Paula Wiseman Bks.).

—I Have a Dream, 1 vol. King, Martin Luther, Jr. 2012. (ENG.). 40p. (J). (gr. k-12). 18.99 *(978-0-375-85887-1(3)*, Schwartz & Wade Bks.) Random Hse. Children's Bks.

—Mama Miti: Wangari Maathai & the Trees of Kenya. Napoli, Donna Jo. 2010. (ENG.). 40p. (J). (gr. -1-3). 18.99 *(978-1-4169-3505-6(3)*, Simon & Schuster/Paula Wiseman Bks.) Simon & Schuster/Paula Wiseman Bks.

—Michael's Golden Rules. Jordan, Deloris. 2007. (ENG.). 32p. (J). (gr. 1-5). 16.99 *(978-0-689-87016-3(7)*, Simon & Schuster/Paula Wiseman Bks.) Simon & Schuster/Paula Wiseman Bks.

—Moses: When Harriet Tubman Led Her People to Freedom. Weatherford, Carole Boston. 2006. (ENG.). 44p. (J). (gr. k-3). 15.99 *(978-0-7868-5175-1(9)*, Jump at the Sun) Hyperion Bks. for Children.

—A Nation's Hope: The Story of Boxing Legend Joe Louis. De la Peña, Matt. (ENG.). 40p. (J). (gr. 1-3). 2013. 8.99 *(978-0-14-751061-7(9)*, Puffin); 2011. 17.99 *(978-0-8037-3167-7(1)*, Dial) Penguin Publishing Group.

—Please, Baby, Please. Lee, Spike & Lee, Tonya Lewis. 2007. (Classic Board Bks.). (ENG.). 32p. (J). (gr. -1-k). bds. 7.99 *(978-1-4169-4911-4(9)*, Little Simon) Little Simon.

—Please, Baby, Please. Lee, Spike & Lee, Tonya Lewis. 2006. (ENG.). 38p. (J). (gr. -1-3). reprint ed. 7.99 *(978-0-689-83457-8(8)*, Simon & Schuster Bks. For Young Readers) Simon & Schuster Bks. For Young Readers.

—Please, Puppy, Please. Lee, Tonya Lewis & Lee, Spike. 2005. (ENG.). 32p. (J). (gr. -1-3). 17.99 *(978-0-689-86804-7(9)*, Simon & Schuster Bks. For Young Readers) Simon & Schuster Bks. For Young Readers.

—The Real Slam Dunk. Richardson, Charisse K. 2005. (ENG.). 80p. (J). (gr. k-3). 4.99 *(978-0-14-240212-2(5)*, Puffin) Penguin Publishing Group.

—Salt in His Shoes: Michael Jordan in Pursuit of a Dream. Jordan, Deloris & Jordan, Roslyn M. 2003. (ENG.). 32p. (J). (gr. -1-3). pap. 7.99 *(978-0-689-83419-6(5)*, Simon & Schuster Bks. For Young Readers) Simon & Schuster Bks. For Young Readers.

—Salt in His Shoes: Michael Jordan in Pursuit of a Dream. Jordan, Deloris & Jordan, Roslyn M. ed. 2003. lib. bdg. 18.40 *(978-0-613-89001-4(9)*, Turtleback) Turtleback Bks.

—A Strong Right Arm: The Story of Mamie Peanut Johnson. Green, Michelle Y. 2004. (ENG.). 128p. (J). (gr. 3-7). 5.99 *(978-0-14-240072-2(6)*, Puffin) Penguin Publishing Group.

—Testing the Ice: A True Story about Jackie Robinson. Robinson, Sharon. 2009. (ENG.). 40p. (J). (gr. 2-5). 18.99 *(978-0-545-05251-1(3)*, Scholastic Pr.) Scholastic, Inc.

—Thunder Rose. Nolen, Jerdine. 2007. (ENG.). 32p. (J). (gr. k-3). pap. 7.00 *(978-0-15-206006-0(5))* Houghton Mifflin Harcourt Publishing Co.

—Thunder Rose. Nolen, Jerdine. 2007. (gr. k-3). 17.00 *(978-0-7569-8199-0(9))* Perfection Learning Corp.

—The Village That Vanished. Grifalconi, Ann. 2004. (ENG.). 40p. (J). (gr. k-3). reprint ed. pap. 7.99 *(978-0-14-240190-3(0)*, Puffin) Penguin Publishing Group.

Nelson, Kadir. Baby Bear. Nelson, Kadir. 2014. (ENG.). 40p. (J). (gr. -1-3). 17.99 *(978-0-06-224172-6(9))* HarperCollins Pubs.

—Change Has Come: An Artist Celebrates Our American Spirit. Nelson, Kadir. Obama, Barack. 2009. (ENG.). 64p. (J). (gr. 1). 12.99 *(978-1-4169-8955-4(2)*, Simon & Schuster Bks. For Young Readers) Simon & Schuster Bks. For Young Readers.

—Heart & Soul: The Story of America & African Americans. Nelson, Kadir. (J). (gr. 1-5). 2013. (ENG.). 112p. pap. 8.99 *(978-0-06-173079-5(3))*; 2011. (ENG.). 108p. 19.99 *(978-0-06-173074-0(2))*; 2011. 108p. lib. bdg. 20.89 *(978-0-06-173076-4(9))* HarperCollins Pubs.

—He's Got the Whole World in His Hands. Nelson, Kadir. 2005. (ENG.). 32p. (J). (gr. -1-3). 17.99 *(978-0-8037-2850-9(6)*, Dial) Penguin Publishing Group.

—He's Got the Whole World in His Hands. Nelson, Kadir. unabr. ed. 2006. (J). (gr. -1-2). 29.95 *(978-0-439-90581-7(8))* Weston Woods Studios, Inc.

—If You Plant a Seed. Nelson, Kadir. 2015. (ENG.). 32p. (J). (gr. -1-3). 18.99 *(978-0-06-229889-8(5))* HarperCollins Pubs.

—Nelson Mandela. Nelson, Kadir. 2013. 40p. (J). (gr. -1-4). (ENG.). 17.99 *(978-0-06-178374-6(9))*; lib. bdg. 18.89 *(978-0-06-178376-0(5))* HarperCollins Pubs. (Tegen, Katherine Bks).

—We Are the Ship: The Story of Negro League Baseball. Nelson, Kadir. 2008. (ENG.). 96p. (J). (gr. 3-7). 18.99 *(978-0-7868-0832-8(2)*, Jump at the Sun) Hyperion Bks. for Children.

Nelson, Kadir, jt. illus. see Kelley, Gary.

Nelson, Mary Beth. Elmo's World: Love! McMahon, Kara. 2004. (Sesame Street Elmo's World Ser.). (ENG.). 12p. (J). (gr. k-1). bds. 4.99 *(978-0-375-82843-0(5)*, Random Hse. Bks. for Young Readers) Random Hse. Children's Bks.

—First Flap-Book Library. RH Disney Staff et al. 2008. (Sesame Street Elmo's World Ser.). (ENG.). 12p. (J). (gr. k-1). bds. 9.99 *(978-0-375-84512-3(7)*, Random Hse. Bks. for Young Readers) Random Hse. Children's Bks.

Nelson, Mary Beth & Linn, Laurent. Elmo's Big Word Book/el Libro Grande de Palabras de Elmo. Barrett, John E., photos by. 2006. (Elmo's Big Word Book/el Libro Grande de Palabras de Elmo Ser.). (SPA, ENG, MUL & ANG.). 12p. (J). (gr. -1 — 1). 8.95 *(978-0-87358-906-2(8))* Cooper Square Publishing Llc.

Nelson, Marybeth, jt. illus. see Weiss, Ellen.

Nelson, Megan. Hey Guys: A Story about Going to Day Camp. Freedman, Sharon. 2004. (ENG.). 39p. 24.95 *(978-1-4137-2422-6(1))* PublishAmerica, Inc.

Nelson, Michiyo. My First 100 Words. Scholastic, Inc. Staff. 2008. (Sign Language Ser.). (ENG.). 32p. (J). (gr. -1-3). pap. 6.99 *(978-0-545-05657-1(8)*, Cartwheel Bks.) Scholastic, Inc.

—Sign Language: My First 100 Words. Scholastic Book Editors. 2008. 32p. (gr. -1-3). 17.00 *(978-0-7569-8911-8(6))* Perfection Learning Corp.

Nelson, Ray & Nelson, Douglas. Greetings from America: Postcards from Donovan Willoughby. Nelson, Ray & Nelson, Douglas. Tronslin, Andrea, ed. 2nd ed. 48p. (J). (gr. k-5). 14.95 *(978-1-56977-409-0(9))* Flying Rhinoceros, Inc.

Nelson, S. D. Crazy Horse's Vision. Bruchac, Joseph. 2006. (gr. 1-4). 20.45 *(978-0-7569-6691-1(4))* Perfection Learning Corp.

—Dance in a Buffalo Skull. Zitkala-Sa. 2007. (Prairie Tales Ser.). 40p. (J). (gr. -1-2). 14.95 *(978-0-9777955-2-9(7)*, South Dakota State Historical Society Pr.) South Dakota State Historical Society Pr.

—Greet the Dawn: The Lakota Way. 2012. (J). 18.95 *(978-0-9845041-6-9(8)*, South Dakota State Historical Society Pr.) South Dakota State Historical Society Pr.

Nelson, S. D. Jim Thorpe's Bright Path, 1 vol. Nelson, S. D., tr. Bruchac, Joseph. 2004. (ENG.). 40p. (J). (gr. 1-4). 17.95 *(978-1-58430-166-0(X))* Lee & Low Bks., Inc.

Nelson, Sarah. Alphabeasties. Werner, Sharon et al. 2010. (ENG.). 26p. (J). (gr. k-12). 15.99 *(978-1-60905-003-0(7))* Blue Apple Bks.

Nelson-Schmidt, Michelle. Bob Is a Unicorn. Nelson-Schmidt, Michelle. 2014. (ENG.). 28p. (J). 14.99 *(978-1-61067-155-2(4))* Kane Miller.

—Cats, Cats! Nelson-Schmidt, Michelle. ed. 2011. (ENG.). 32p. (J). pap. 5.99 *(978-1-61067-042-5(6))* Kane Miller.

—Dogs, Dogs! Nelson-Schmidt, Michelle. ed. 2011. (ENG.). 32p. (J). pap. 5.99 *(978-1-61067-041-8(8))* Kane Miller.

—Jonathan James & the Whatif Monster. Nelson-Schmidt, Michelle. 2013. (ENG.). 32p. (J). pap. 6.99 *(978-1-61067-118-7(X))* Kane Miller.

Nelson, Scott. Patch the Porcupine & the Bike Shop Job. Nelson, Scott. 2004. 28p. (J). 14.95 *(978-0-9745715-3-9(9))* KRBY Creations, LLC.

Nelson, Scott, photos by. Humvees: High Mobility in the Field. Teitelbaum, Michael. 2006. (Mighty Military Machines Ser.). 48p. (J). (gr. 4-7). lib. bdg. 25.27 *(978-0-7660-2661-2(2))* Enslow Pubs., Inc.

Nelson, Shannon. Ryan's Vitiligo. May, Cynthia. 2003. (J). pap. 8.95 *(978-0-615-12578-7(6))* May, Cynthia D.

Nelson, Thea, jt. illus. see Smith, Nina.

Nelson, Will, et al. Alphabet of Bears. Schwaeber, Barbie Heit. 2011. (Alphabet Bks.). (ENG.). 40p. (J). (gr. -1-3). 17.95 *(978-1-60727-668-5(2))* Soundprints.

—Alphabet of Bears. Schwaeber, Barbie Heit. 2007. (Alphabet Of... Ser.). (ENG.). 40p. (J). 15.95 *(978-1-59249-689-1(X))* Soundprints.

Nelson, Will. Black Bear Cub at Sweet Berry Trail. Galvin, Laura Gates. 2008. (ENG.). 32p. (J). (gr. k-2). 6.95 *(978-1-59249-775-1(6))*; pap. 8.95 *(978-1-59249-777-5(2))*; 19.95 *(978-1-59249-776-8(4))*; 16.95 *(978-1-59249-773-7(X))*; pap. 6.95 *(978-1-59249-774-4(8))* Soundprints.

—Panda Bear Cub. Moody-Luther, Jacqueline. 2006. (ENG.). 32p. (J). pap. 3.95 *(978-1-59249-585-6(0))* Soundprints.

Nelson, William. Then & Now Stories. Stonesifer, Gertrude. 2003. (ENG.). 112p. (J). 21.95 *(978-1-878044-86-0(9))* Mayhaven Publishing, Inc.

Nemet, Andrea. Are You Sleeping Little One. Schmidt, Hans-Christian. Lindgren, Laura, tr. from GER. 2012. (ENG.). 18p. (J). (gr. k-k). bds. 6.95 *(978-0-7892-1120-0(3)*, Abbeville Kids) Abbeville Pr., Inc.

Nemet, Andreas. When a Coconut Falls on Your Head. Schmidt, Hans-Christian & Schmid, A, HC;Nemet. 2009. (ENG.). 12p. (J). (gr. -1). bds. 9.95 *(978-0-7358-2242-9(5))* North-South Bks., Inc.

Nemett, Barry & Nemett, Laini. Adam's Crayons. Leopold, Nikia Speliakos Clark. 2011. (J). *(978-0-9817519-1-7(1))* Galileo Pr.

Nemett, Laini, jt. illus. see Nemett, Barry.

Neogi, Joyeeta. Mummy's Gorgeous Hair. Williams, Vivienne. 2013. 26p. pap. *(978-0-9576680-9-6(0))* Williams, Vivienne.

NeonSeon. Life of Shouty: Food & Fitness, bk. 2. NeonSeon. 2011. (Life of Shouty Ser.: 2). (ENG.). 32p. (J). 14.95 *(978-0-9842069-1-9(4))* RIXKIN.

—Life of Shouty: Good Habits, bk. 1. NeonSeon. 2010. (Life of Shouty Ser.: No. 1). (ENG.). 32p. (J). (gr. 3-18). 14.95 *(978-0-9842069-0-2(6))* RIXKIN.

Nepomniachi, Leonid. El Monstruo Graciopeo. Dayan, Linda Marcos. (Barril Sin Fondo Ser.). (SPA.). (J). (gr. 3-5). pap. *(978-968-6465-60-0(X))* Casa de Estudios de Literatura y Talleres Artisticos Amaquemecan A.C. MEX. Dist: Lectorum Pubns., Inc.

Nepomniatchi, Leonid. Los Artistas de Las Plumas: The Feather Artists. Barrera, Norma Anabel. rev. ed. 2006. (Otra Escalera Ser.). (SPA & ENG.). 36p. (J). (gr. 2-4). pap. 9.95 *(978-968-5920-53-7(2))* Castillo, Ediciones, S. A. de C. V. MEX. Dist: Macmillan.

Neradova, Maria. Princess Tales. Ruzicka, Oldrich & Kolcavova, Klara. 2015. (Children's Theatre Ser.). (ENG.). 20p. (J). (gr. -1-3). bds. 14.95 ***(978-1-63322-008-9(7))*** Quarto Publishing Group USA.

Nerlove, Miriam. Greenhorn. Olswanger, Anna. 2012. (ENG.). (J). 48p. 17.95 *(978-1-58838-235-1(4)*, Junebug Bks.); E-Book 9.99 *(978-1-60306-159-9(2)*, NewSouth Bks.) NewSouth, Inc.

Nesbit, E. & Millar, H. R. Five Children & It. Nesbit, E. 2004. (ENG.). 240p. (gr. 12-18). 14.00 *(978-0-14-303915-0(6)*, Penguin Classics) Penguin Publishing Group.

Nesterova, Natalia. Ein Schmetterling Ohne Flügel. Powers, David M. F. Vail, Sue, tr. 2013. 42p. pap. 9.99 *(978-0-9860373-3-7(8))* Pants On Fire Pr.

Nestler, David. The Art of Dave Nestler. 2003. 48p. (YA). (gr. 12-18). pap. *(978-0-86562-065-0(2))* Anabas Marketing, Ltd.

Nethery, Susan. Horsing Around. Shulman, Mark. 2005. (Storytime Stickers Ser.). (ENG.). 16p. (J). (gr. k-2). pap. 5.95 *(978-1-4027-1808-3(X))* Sterling Publishing Co., Inc.

Nettis, Donna. Jabari Makes a Splash. Grier, Kerry. 2010. (ENG.). 26p. pap. 9.99 *(978-1-4515-3836-6(7))* CreateSpace Independent Publishing Platform.

Nettrour, Autumn. Imagynairs of Jemmidar. Nettrour, Nelani. 2003. 78p. pap. 11.95 *(978-1-929381-99-9(9)*, Third Millennium Publishing) Sci Fi-Arizona, Inc.

—Nunkey's Adventures, Bk. 1. Nettrour, Nelani. 2003. 70p. (J). pap. 11.95 *(978-1-929381-17-3(4)*, Third Millennium Publishing) Sci Fi-Arizona, Inc.

Nettrour, Heather. All about Krammer: Dogtails 2. Nettrour, Nelani A. 2005. 100p. pap. 11.95 *(978-1-932657-30-2(4))* Third Millennium Pubns.

—Banshees Bk. 2: Dragon Lands. Nettrour, Nelani. l.t. ed. 2003. 114p. (J). pap. 11.95 *(978-1-932657-03-6(7))* Third Millennium Pubns.

—The Dragon Lands Bk. 1: The Ripple. Nettrour, Nelani. 2003. 100p. pap. 11.95 *(978-1-929381-46-3(8)*, Third Millennium Publishing) Sci Fi-Arizona, Inc.

—Jodi & the Seasons. Nettrour, Nelani. l.t. ed. 2004. 88p. pap. 11.95 *(978-1-932657-16-6(9))* Third Millennium Pubns.

—Jodi's Bugs. Nettrour, Nelani. l.t. ed. 2003. 66p. (J). pap. 11.95 *(978-1-932657-04-3(5))* Third Millennium Pubns.
—Meeshu's Keep Bk. 1: Dragon Guardians. Nettrour, Nelani. 2005. 113p. pap. 14.95 *(978-1-932657-37-1(1))* Third Millennium Pubns.
Neu, Debra. ABC Literacy Storytimes: Storytimes to Promote Literacy & Learning. Lohnes, Marilyn. 2008. 251p. pap. 19.95 *(978-1-60213-023-4(X)*, Upstart Bks.) Highsmith Inc.
Neubecker, Robert. The Great Dog Wash. Braeuner, Shellie. 2009. (ENG.). 32p. (J). (gr. -1-1). 15.99 *(978-1-4169-7116-0(5)*, Simon & Schuster Bks. For Young Readers) Simon & Schuster Bks. For Young Readers.
—I Got Two Dogs. Lithgow, John. 2008. (ENG.). 40p. (J). (gr. -1-1). 17.99 *(978-1-4169-5881-9(9)*, Simon & Schuster Bks. For Young Readers) Simon & Schuster Bks. For Young Readers.
—The President's Stuck in the Bathtub: Poems about the Presidents. Katz, Susan. 2012. (ENG.). 64p. (J). (gr. 1-4). 18.99 *(978-0-547-18221-6(X))* Houghton Mifflin Harcourt Publishing Co.
—The Problem with Not Being Scared of Monsters. Richards, Dan. 2014. (ENG.). 32p. (J). (gr. -1-3). 15.95 *(978-1-62091-024-5(1))* Boyds Mills Pr.
—School Fever. Bagert, Brod. 2015. (ENG.). 40p. (J). (gr. 1-3). 8.99 *(978-0-14-751450-9(9)*, Puffin) Penguin Publishing Group.
—Shiver Me Timbers! Pirate Poems & Paintings. Florian, Douglas. 2012. (ENG.). 32p. (J). (gr. 1-5). 16.99 *(978-1-4424-1321-4(2)*, Beach Lane Bks.) Beach Lane Bks.
—Sophie Peterman Tells the Truth! Weeks, Sarah. 2009. (ENG.). 32p. (J). (gr. -1-3). 16.99 *(978-1-4169-8686-7(3)*, Beach Lane Bks.) Beach Lane Bks.
—Space Boy & His Dog. Regan, Dian Curtis. 2015. (ENG.). 32p. (J). (gr. -1-2). 16.95 *(978-1-59078-955-1(5))* Boyds Mills Pr.
—Tick Tock Clock. Cuyler, Margery. 2012. (My First I Can Read Ser.). (ENG.). 32p. (J). (gr. -1 — 1). 16.99 *(978-0-06-136309-2(X))*; pap. 3.99 *(978-0-06-136311-5(1))* HarperCollins Pubs.
Neubecker, Robert. Linus the Vegetarian T. Rex. Neubecker, Robert. 2013. (ENG.). 40p. (J). (gr. -1-3). 16.99 *(978-1-4169-8512-9(3)*, Beach Lane Bks.) Beach Lane Bks.
—Too Many Monsters! A Halloween Counting Book. Neubecker, Robert. 2010. (ENG.). 26p. (J). (gr. -1-k). bds. 7.99 *(978-1-4424-0172-3(9)*, Little Simon) Little Simon.
—What Little Boys Are Made Of. Neubecker, Robert. 2012. (ENG.). 32p. (J). (gr. -1-3). 14.99 *(978-0-06-202355-1(1))* HarperCollins Pubs.
—Winter Is for Snow. Neubecker, Robert. 2013. (ENG.). 32p. (J). (gr. -1-k). 16.99 *(978-1-4231-7831-6(9))* Hyperion Pr.
Neuburger, Jenny. Andre' Angel in a Poodle Suit. Danner, Pamela. 2003. 32p. (J). per. *(978-0-9728429-0-7(X)*, 4290X) Poodle Suit Publishing.
Neuburger, Jenny, jt. illus. see Mailey, Maria C.
Neuendorf, Silvio. No Quiero Verte Mas! Abedí, Isabel & Neuendorf, Abedi -. 2003. (SPA.). 196p. (J). (gr. -1-3). 17.99 *(978-84-261-3303-8(7))* Juventud, Editorial ESP. Dist: Lectorum Pubns., Inc.
Neufeld, Josh. A Few Perfect Hours & Other Stories from Southeast Asia & Central Europe. 2004. (ENG.). 128p. (gr. 8). pap. 12.95 *(978-1-891867-79-8(2))* Alternative Comics.
Neufeld, Juliana. God Loves Hair. Shraya, Vivek. 2014. (ENG.). 112p. (gr. 6). pap. 18.95 *(978-1-55152-543-3(7)*, 399) Arsenal Pulp Pr. CAN. Dist: Consortium Bk. Sales & Distribution.
—House of Robots. Patterson, James & Grabenstein, Chris. 2014. (House of Robots Ser.). (ENG.). 352p. (J). (gr. 3-7). 13.99 *(978-0-316-40591-1(4))* Little Brown & Co.
Neufeld, Juliana. Treasure Hunters. Patterson, James & Grabenstein, Chris. (Treasure Hunters Ser.: 1). (ENG.). 480p. (J). (gr. 3-7). 2015. pap. 8.00 ***(978-0-316-20757-7(8))***; 2013. 14.99 *(978-0-316-20756-0(X))* Little Brown & Co.
Neufeld, Juliana. Treasure Hunters. Patterson, James et al. 2013. 451p. (J). *(978-0-316-24262-2(4))* Little Brown & Co.
—Treasure Hunters: Danger down the Nile. Patterson, James & Grabenstein, Chris. 2014. (Treasure Hunters Ser.). (ENG.). 480p. (J). (gr. 3-7). 14.99 *(978-0-316-37086-8(X))* Little Brown & Co.
Neufeld, Juliana. Treasure Hunters: Secret of the Forbidden City. Patterson, James & Grabenstein, Chris. 2015. (Treasure Hunters Ser.: 3). (ENG.). 448p. (J). (gr. 3-7). 14.99 ***(978-0-316-28480-6(7))*** Little Brown & Co.
Neuhaus, Julia. I Am Ivan Crocodile! Gouichoux, René. 2015. (ENG.). 36p. (J). (gr. k-3). 16.99 ***(978-0-9806711-3-1(2))*** Berbay Publishing AUS. Dist: Independent Pubs. Group.
Neuman, Richard. It's Time to Combine. Gabel, Stacey. 2009. 24p. pap. 13.95 *(978-1-60844-121-1(0))* Dog Ear Publishing, LLC.
—The New Blue Tractor. Gabel, Stacey. 2007. 24p. per. 13.95 *(978-1-59858-424-0(3))* Dog Ear Publishing, LLC.
Neusca, Guy, Jr. & Porter, Lynda C. Tofu Ling & the Angel: Seeds of Corruptions. Beasley, Jonathan & Porter, Rosanna I. 2009. (ENG.). (YA). pap. 16.00 *(978-0-615-31157-9(1))* Hero Builder Comics.
Neuville, Loyal de. The Surprise Party. Cohen, Lee. 2010. (ENG.). 32p. (J). (gr. -1-12). lib. bdg. 16.95 *(978-1-934960-85-1(3)*, Raven Tree Pr.,Csi) Continental Sales, Inc.
Nevarez, Lisa. Dodger the Dragon, 1 vol. McMilin, Jack. 2009. pap. 24.95 *(978-1-60703-930-3(3))* PublishAmerica, Inc.
Nevarez, Lisa D. The Water Dog. McMilin, Jack D. 2011. 24p. pap. 24.95 *(978-1-4626-0544-6(3))* America Star Bks.
Neves, Diogenes & Walker, Cory. Masters of the Universe: He-Man's Icons of Evil. Kirkman, Robert. 2004. (Masters of the Universe Ser.). 160p. (YA). pap. 9.95 *(978-1-59314-040-3(1))* CrossGeneration Comics, Inc.
Neveu, Fred. Caillou's Dinosaur Day. Vonthron, Satanta C. l.t. ed. 2004. (HRL Board Book Ser.). (J). (gr. -1-1). pap. 10.95 *(978-1-57332-288-1(1)*, HighReach Learning, Incorporated) Carson-Dellosa Publishing, LLC.
—The Dinosaur Surprise. Howard-Parham, Pam. l.t. ed. 2004. (HRL Little Book Ser.). (J). (gr. -1-1). pap. 10.95 *(978-1-57332-294-2(6))*; pap. 10.95 *(978-1-57332-293-5(8))* Carson-Dellosa Publishing, LLC. (HighReach Learning, Incorporated).
Neville, Bill. Colorful File Folder Games: Skill-Building Center Activities for Language Arts & Math. Pyne, Lynette & Pressnall, Debra Olson. 2005. (Colorful File Folder Games Ser.). (ENG.). 160p. (gr. 1-1). per. 22.99 *(978-1-59441-089-5(5)*, CD-104049) Carson-Dellosa Publishing, LLC.
Nevins, Daniel. With a Mighty Hand: The Story in the Torah. Ehrlich, Amy. 2013. (ENG.). 224p. (J). (gr. k-12). 29.99 *(978-0-7636-4395-9(5))* Candlewick Pr.
Newberry, Clare Turlay. Marshmallow. Newberry, Clare Turlay. 2008. 32p. (J). (gr. -1-1). (ENG.). 16.99 *(978-0-06-072486-3(2))*; lib. bdg. 17.89 *(978-0-06-072487-0(0))* HarperCollins Pubs.
Newberry, Loretta. Sundancer. Marlow, Herb. 2004. 56p. (J). lib. bdg. 21.95 *(978-1-893595-39-2(0))*; per. 14.95 *(978-1-893595-41-5(2))* Four Seasons Bks., Inc.
Newbigging, Martha. Archers, Alchemists, & 98 Other Medieval Jobs You Might Have Loved or Loathed. Galloway, Priscilla. 2003. (Jobs in History Ser.). (ENG.). 96p. (J). (gr. 4-7). pap. 16.95 *(978-1-55037-810-8(4)*, 9781550378108) Annick Pr., Ltd. CAN. Dist: Firefly Bks., Ltd.
—Attack of the Killer Video Book: Tips & Tricks for Young Directors. Shulman, Mark & Krog, Hazlitt. 2nd enl. ed. 2012. (ENG.). 76p. (J). (gr. 5-12). 24.95 *(978-1-55451-367-3(7)*, 9781554513673); pap. 14.95 *(978-1-55451-366-6(9)*, 9781554513666) Annick Pr., Ltd. CAN. Dist: Firefly Bks., Ltd.
—Ballplayers & Bonesetters: One Hundred Ancient Aztec & Maya Jobs You Might Have Adored or Abhorred. Coulter, Laurie. 2008. (ENG.). 96p. (J). (gr. 4-7). 25.95 *(978-1-55451-141-9(0)*, 9781554511419); pap. 16.95 *(978-1-55451-140-2(2)*, 9781554511402) Annick Pr., Ltd. CAN. Dist: Firefly Bks., Ltd.
—Cowboys & Coffin Makers: One Hundred 19th-Century Jobs You Might Have Feared or Fancied. Coulter, Laurie. 2007. (Jobs in History Ser.). (ENG.). 96p. (J). (gr. 4-7). 25.95 *(978-1-55451-068-9(6)*, 9781554510689); pap. 16.95 *(978-1-55451-067-2(8)*, 9781554510672) Annick Pr., Ltd. CAN. Dist: Firefly Bks., Ltd.
—The Dirt on Dirt. Bourgeois, Paulette. 2008. (ENG.). 48p. (J). (gr. 3-7). pap. 7.95 *(978-1-55453-102-8(0))* Kids Can Pr., Ltd. CAN. Dist: Univ. of Toronto Pr.
—Jared Lester, Fifth Grade Jester. Kyi, Tanya Lloyd. 2006. (ENG.). 74p. (J). (gr. 3-5). pap. 7.95 *(978-1-55451-025-2(2)*, 9781554510252) Annick Pr., Ltd. CAN. Dist: Firefly Bks., Ltd.
—Pharaohs & Foot Soldiers: One Hundred Ancient Egyptian Jobs You Might Have Desired or Dreaded. Butcher, Kristin. 2009. (Jobs in History Ser.). (ENG.). 96p. (J). (gr. 4-6). 25.95 *(978-1-55451-171-6(2)*, 9781554511716); pap. 16.95 *(978-1-55451-170-9(4)*, 9781554511709) Annick Pr., Ltd. CAN. Dist: Firefly Bks., Ltd.
—Research Ate My Brain: The Panic-Proof Guide to Surviving Homework. Toronto Public Library & Toronto Public Library. 2005. (ENG.). 96p. (J). (gr. 5-12). 19.95 *(978-1-55037-939-6(9)*, 9781550379396) Annick Pr., Ltd. CAN. Dist: Firefly Bks., Ltd.
—Research Ate My Brain: The Panic-Proof Guide to Surviving Homework. Toronto Public Library. 2005. (ENG.). 96p. (J). (gr. 5-12). pap. 8.95 *(978-1-55037-938-9(0)*, 9781550379389) Annick Pr., Ltd. CAN. Dist: Firefly Bks., Ltd.
—Warriors & Wailers: One Hundred Ancient Chinese Jobs You Might Have Relished or Reviled. Tsiang, Sarah. 2012. (Jobs in History Ser.). (ENG.). 96p. (J). (gr. 3-7). 25.95 *(978-1-55451-391-8(X)*, 9781554513918); pap. 16.95 *(978-1-55451-390-1(1)*, 9781554513901) Annick Pr., Ltd. CAN. Dist: Firefly Bks., Ltd.
Newbigging, Mary. Kings & Carpenters: One Hundred Bible Land Jobs You Might Have Praised or Panned. Coulter, Laurie. 2010. (Jobs in History Ser.). (ENG.). 96p. (J). (gr. 3-6). 25.95 *(978-1-55451-227-0(1)*, 9781554512270); pap. 16.95 *(978-1-55451-226-3(3)*, 9781554512263) Annick Pr., Ltd. CAN. Dist: Firefly Bks., Ltd.
Newborne, David / F. The Lion That Finally Roared: Inspirational Story of Purpose & Destiny. Chidebelu-Eze / Dove Publishing, Chibueze Obi. 2008. 80p. (J). 17.99 *(978-0-9766578-5-9(6))*; pap. 11.99 *(978-0-9766578-6-6(4))* Dove Publishing, Inc.
—The Tales of Tortoise: Inspirational Stories of Wisdom. Chidebelu-Eze/Dove Publishing, Chibueze / Obi. 2005. (ENG.). 76p. (J). 16.00 *(978-0-9766578-0-4(5))* Dove Publishing, Inc.
Newcomb, Kristene. Festus & His New Job. Balmer, Fred. 2004. 26p. (J). per. 7.00 *(978-0-9760790-1-9(1))* Folsom Fallies Pr.
—Festus & the Hole in the Fence Gang. Balmer, Fred. 2005. 33p. (J). per. 7.00 *(978-0-9760790-3-3(8))* Folsom Fallies Pr.
—Festus & the Missing Bag of Feed. Balmer, Fred. 2004. 26p. (J). per. 7.00 *(978-0-9760790-0-2(3))* Folsom Fallies Pr.
—Festus & the Monster. Balmer, Fred. 2004. 27p. (J). per. 6.95 *(978-0-9760790-2-6(X))* Folsom Fallies Pr.
—Festus & the Stranger. Balmer, Fred. Miller, Callie, ed. 2007. 30p. (J). per. 7.00 *(978-0-9760790-4-0(6))* Folsom Fallies Pr.
Newcomb, Kristene. Molly Q's Trash Travels Through the Water Cycle. Newcomb, Kristene. Paschall, Patricia, ed. 2007. 32p. (J). per. 8.00 *(978-0-9760790-9-5(7))* Folsom Fallies Pr.
Newcome, Zita. This Royal Baby. Newcome, Zita. ed. 2013. (ENG.). 12p. (J). (— 1). bds. 14.99 *(978-0-230-77284-7(6))* Pan Macmillan GBR. Dist: Independent Pubs. Group.
Newell, Brian. The Bird Lady. Jones, Angela. 2009. 16p. pap. 7.31 *(978-1-4251-8612-8(2))* Trafford Publishing.
Newell, Claudia. Design It! The Ordinary Things You Use Every Day & the Not-So-Ordinary Ways They Came to Be. Arato, Rona. 2010. (ENG.). 72p. (J). (gr. 4-7). pap. 20.95 *(978-0-88776-846-0(6))* Tundra Bks. CAN. Dist: Random Hse., Inc.
Newell, Keith. Cars. Brooks, Felicity. 2008. (Usborne Lift & Look Ser.). 12p. (J). (gr. -1-3). bds. 9.99 *(978-0-7945-1958-2(X)*, Usborne) EDC Publishing.
—Construction Sites. Brooks, Felicity. 2010. (Lift & Look Board Bks.). 12p. (J). bds. 9.99 *(978-0-7945-2728-0(0)*, Usborne) EDC Publishing.
Newell, Keith, jt. illus. see Van Wyk, Hanri.
Newell, Lennette. Welcome to the World. Wyatt, Valerie. 2011. (ENG.). 24p. (J). 14.95 *(978-1-55453-593-4(X))* Kids Can Pr., Ltd. CAN. Dist: Univ. of Toronto Pr.
Newey, Gail. The Barefoot Book of Faeries. Batt, Tanya Robyn. (ENG.). 64p. (J). 2009. 19.99 *(978-1-84686-317-2(1))*; 2008. (gr. -1-3). 15.99 *(978-1-84686-163-5(2))* Barefoot Bks., Inc.
—Faerie Stickers. 15.00 *(978-1-84148-177-7(7))* Barefoot Bks., Inc.
—My Mama Hung the World for Me. Katz, Susan B. 2009. (J). *(978-1-84686-269-4(8))* Barefoot Bks., Inc.
Newgarden, Mark. Bow-Wow's Nightmare Neighbors. Cash, Megan Montague. 2014. (ENG.). 64p. (J). (gr. k-3). 17.99 *(978-1-59643-640-4(9))* Roaring Brook Pr.
Newhouse, Judy. Hey Ranger! Kids Ask Questions about Rocky Mountain National Park. Justesen, Kim Williams. 2005. (Hey Ranger! Ser.). (ENG.). 48p. (J). (gr. -1-12). pap. 9.95 *(978-0-7627-3848-9(0)*, Falcon Guides) Globe Pequot Pr., The.
Newhouse, Maxwell. Emily Carr: At the Edge of the World. Bogart, Jo Ellen. 2003. (ENG.). 40p. (J). (gr. 5-18). 22.95 *(978-0-88776-640-4(4)*, Tundra Bks.) Tundra Bks. CAN. Dist: Penguin Random Hse., LLC.
—Laura Secord: A Story of Courage. Lunn, Janet. 2012. (ENG.). 32p. (J). (gr. 2-4). pap. 9.95 *(978-1-77049-384-1(0)*, Tundra Bks.) Tundra Bks. CAN. Dist: Penguin Random Hse., LLC.
Newkirk, Errol Q. Arrione's Daddies!, 1 vol. Edison-Clark, Gina. 2010. 24p. pap. 24.95 *(978-1-4489-6511-3(X))* PublishAmerica, Inc.
—I Just Want My Daddy! Edison-Clark, Gina. 2008. 13p. pap. 24.95 *(978-1-60672-026-4(0))* America Star Bks.
Newland, g. f. Sticks 'N Stones 'N Dinosaur Bones. Enik, Ted. 2013. 42p. pap. 12.99 *(978-1-939322-10-4(3))* Pixel Mouse Hse.
Newland, Gillian. Big & Small, Room for All. Bogart, Jo Ellen. 2009. (ENG.). 32p. (J). (gr. k-k). 18.95 *(978-0-88776-891-0(1)*, Tundra Bks.) Tundra Bks. CAN. Dist: Penguin Random Hse., LLC.
—The Magician of Auschwitz, 1 vol. Kacer, Kathy. 2014. (ENG.). 32p. (J). (gr. 3-5). 18.95 *(978-1-927583-46-3(2))* Second Story Pr. CAN. Dist: Orca Bk. Pubs. USA.
Newland, Gillian & Second Story Press Staff. A Chanukah Noel: A True Story, 1 vol. Jennings, Sharon. 2010. (ENG.). 24p. (J). (gr. k-3). 15.95 *(978-1-897187-74-6(2))* Second Story Pr. CAN. Dist: Orca Bk. Pubs. USA.
Newlun, Shawn. The Sleep Fairy. Peterson, Janie & Peterson, Macy. 2003. (ENG.). 32p. (J). (gr. -1-5). 16.95 *(978-0-9714405-0-0(6))* Behave'n Kids Pr.
Newman, Barbara. Bones & the Apple Pie Mystery. Adler, David A. (Bones Ser.: 10). (ENG.). 32p. (J). (gr. 1-3). 2014. pap. 3.99 *(978-0-448-48231-6(2))*; 2013. 14.99 *(978-0-670-01300-5(5))* Penguin Bks., Ltd. GBR. (Warne, Frederick Pubs.). Dist: Penguin Publishing Group.
—Bones & the Birthday Mystery, No. 5. Adler, David A. 2009. (Bones Ser.: 5). (ENG.). 32p. (J). (gr. 1-3). mass mkt. 3.99 *(978-0-14-241432-3(8)*, Puffin) Penguin Publishing Group.
—Bones & the Cupcake Mystery, No. 3. Adler, David A. 2008. (Bones Ser.: 3). (ENG.). 32p. (J). (gr. 1-3). mass mkt. 3.99 *(978-0-14-241147-6(7)*, Puffin) Penguin Publishing Group.
—Bones & the Dinosaur Mystery, No. 4. Adler, David A. 2009. (Bones Ser.: 4). (ENG.). 32p. (J). (gr. 1-3). mass mkt. 3.99 *(978-0-14-241341-8(0)*, Puffin) Penguin Publishing Group.
—Bones & the Math Test Mystery. Adler, David A. 2010. (Bones Ser.: 6). (ENG.). 32p. (J). (gr. 1-3). mass mkt. 3.99 *(978-0-14-241519-1(7)*, Puffin) Penguin Publishing Group.
—Bones & the Roller Coaster Mystery, 7 vols. Adler, David A. (Bones Ser.: 7). (ENG.). 32p. (J). (gr. 1-3). 2010. mass mkt. 3.99 *(978-0-14-241687-7(8)*, Puffin); No. 7. 2009. 13.99 *(978-0-670-06340-6(1)*, Viking Juvenile) Penguin Publishing Group.
Newman, Barbara Johansen. Barnyard Purim. Terwilliger, Kelly. 2012. (Purim Ser.). (ENG.). 32p. (J). (gr. k-3). pap. 7.95 *(978-0-7613-4514-5(0))*; lib. bdg. 17.95 *(978-0-7613-4513-8(2))* Lerner Publishing Group. (Kar-Ben Publishing).
—Bones & the Big Yellow Mystery, No. 1. Adler, David A. 2008. (Bones Ser.: 1). (ENG.). 32p. (J). (gr. 1-3). mass mkt. 3.99 *(978-0-14-241042-4(X)*, Warne, Frederick Pubs.) Penguin Bks., Ltd. GBR. Dist: Penguin Random Hse., LLC.
—Bones & the Big Yellow Mystery. Adler, David A. 2008. (Puffin Easy-to-Read Ser.). 32p. (gr. k-3). 14.00 *(978-0-7569-8914-9(0))* Perfection Learning Corp.
—Bones & the Clown Mix-Up Mystery, No. 8. Adler, David A. 2011. (Bones Ser.: 8). (ENG.). 32p. (J). (gr. 1-3). 3.99 *(978-0-14-241825-3(0)*, Puffin) Penguin Publishing Group.
—Bones & the Dinosaur Mystery. Adler, David A. 2005. (Jeffrey Bones Mystery Ser.: No. 4). 32p. (J). *(978-0-670-05970-6(6)*, Viking Adult) Penguin Publishing Group.
—Bones & the Dog Gone Mystery, No. 2. Adler, David A. 2008. (Bones Ser.: 2). (ENG.). 32p. (J). (gr. 1-3). mass mkt. 3.99 *(978-0-14-241043-1(8)*, Warne, Frederick Pubs.) Penguin Bks., Ltd. GBR. Dist: Penguin Random Hse., LLC.
—Bones & the Dog Gone Mystery. Adler, David A. 2008. (Puffin Easy-to-Read Ser.: Bk. 2). 32p. (gr. k-3). 14.00 *(978-0-7569-8916-3(7))* Perfection Learning Corp.
—The Case of the Barfy Birthday. Torrey, Michele. 2009. (Doyle & Fossey, Science Detectives Ser.: 4). (ENG.). 96p. (J). pap. 6.95 *(978-1-4027-4964-3(3))* Sterling Publishing Co., Inc.
—The Case of the Crooked Carnival. Torrey, Michele. 2010. (Doyle & Fossey, Science Detectives Ser.). (ENG.). 96p. (J). (gr. 4-7). pap. 6.95 *(978-1-4027-4965-0(1))* Sterling Publishing Co., Inc.
—The Case of the Graveyard Ghost. Torrey, Michele. 2009. (Doyle & Fossey, Science Detectives Ser.: 3). (ENG.). 96p. (J). pap. 6.95 *(978-1-4027-4963-6(5))* Sterling Publishing Co., Inc.
—The Case of the Terrible T. Rex. Torrey, Michele. 2010. (Doyle & Fossey, Science Detectives Ser.). (ENG.). 96p. (J). (gr. 3-5). pap. 6.95 *(978-1-4027-4966-7(X))* Sterling Publishing Co., Inc.
—Glamorous Garbage. 2015. (ENG.). 40p. (J). (gr. k-3). 16.95 *(978-1-62091-626-1(6))* Boyds Mills Pr.
—The Night Before the Tooth Fairy. Wing, Natasha. 2003. (Night Before Ser.). (ENG.). 32p. (J). (gr. -1-3). pap. 4.99 *(978-0-448-43252-6(8)*, Grosset & Dunlap) Penguin Publishing Group.
—Shoo! Scat!, 1 vol. Grambling, Lois G. & Grambling. 2004. (ENG.). 32p. (J). 16.95 *(978-0-7614-5167-9(6))* Marshall Cavendish Corp.
Newman, Barbara Johansen, jt. illus. see Torrey, Michele.
Newman, Ben. Professor Astro Cat's Frontiers of Space. Walliman, Dominic. 2013. (ENG.). 64p. (J). (gr. 2-6). 24.00 *(978-1-909263-07-9(9))* Flying Eye Bks. GBR. Dist: Consortium Bk. Sales & Distribution.
Newman, Heather. And Sometimes Y. Schultz, Leslie & Braulick, J. J. M. 2013. 302p. pap. 12.99 *(978-1-937848-07-1(8))* Do Life Right, Inc.
Newman, Jeff. Can One Balloon Make an Elephant Fly? Richards, Dan. 2016. (J). *(978-1-4424-5215-2(3))* Simon & Schuster Bks. For Young Readers.
—Phoebe & Digger. Springstubb, Tricia. 2013. (ENG.). 32p. (J). (gr. -1-2). 16.99 *(978-0-7636-5281-4(4))* Candlewick Pr.
Newman, Jeff. The Boys. Newman, Jeff. 2010. (ENG.). 40p. (J). (gr. -1-2). 17.99 *(978-1-4169-5012-7(5)*, Simon & Schuster Bks. For Young Readers) Simon & Schuster Bks. For Young Readers.
—Hand Book. Newman, Jeff. 2011. (ENG.). 40p. (J). (gr. -1-3). 15.99 *(978-1-4169-5013-4(3)*, Simon & Schuster Bks. For Young Readers) Simon & Schuster Bks. For Young Readers.
Newman, Jeff & Santat, Dan. Carnivores. Reynolds, Aaron. 2013. (ENG.). 40p. (J). (gr. -1-3). 16.99 *(978-0-8118-6690-3(4))* Chronicle Bks. LLC.
Newman, Langley. Black History Playing Card Deck: With 52 Portraits of Distinguished Black Americans. Holt, Deloris L. (History Channel Ser.). 120p. pap. 12.00 *(978-1-57281-422-6(5)*, HCBH55) U.S. Games Systems, Inc.
Newman, Mark. Polar Bears. Newman, Mark. 2010. (ENG.). 32p. (J). (gr. -1-3). 16.99 *(978-0-8050-8999-8(3)*, Holt, Henry & Co. Bks. For Young Readers) Holt, Henry & Co.
Newman, Winifred Barnum & Barnum-Newman, Winifred. To Market, to Market. Barnum-Newman, Winifred. 2010. (Favorite Children's Songs Ser.). (ENG.). 16p. (J). (gr. -1-2). 25.64 *(978-1-60253-532-9(9)*, 200114) Child's World, Inc., The.
Newmann, Ed. Marvin Monster's Big Date. 2007. (ENG.). 32p. (J). (gr. -1-3). 6.95 *(978-0-9792371-4-0(9))* Keene Publishing.
—Marvin Monster's Teacher Jitters. 2006. (ENG.). 48p. (J). (gr. 4-7). per. 6.95 *(978-0-9766805-3-6(X))* Keene Publishing.
Newsom, Carol. The Emperor's New Clothes: A Country Storybook. Gill, Vince. 2006. 30p. (J). (gr. 4-8). reprint ed. 17.00 *(978-1-4223-5729-3(5))* DIANE Publishing Co.
—Give My Regards to Broadway. Cohan, George M. & Schwaeber, Barbie. 2008. (American Favorites Ser.). (ENG.). 32p. (J). (gr. -1-3). 8.95 *(978-1-59249-727-0(6))*; 14.95 *(978-1-59249-726-3(8))* Soundprints.
Newsom, Tom. The First Noel. 2006. 14p. (J). (gr. k-4). reprint ed. 8.00 *(978-1-4223-5413-1(X))* DIANE Publishing Co.
—My First Night Before Christmas. Moore, Clement C. 2008. (ENG.). 12p. (J). 9.95 *(978-1-58117-808-1(5)*, Intervisual/Piggy Toes) Bendon, Inc.
—The Mystery of the Cupboard. Banks, Lynne Reid. 2004. (Indian in the Cupboard Ser.: No. 4). (ENG.). 256p. (J). (gr. 4-18). pap. 6.99 *(978-0-380-72013-2(2))* HarperCollins Pubs.
—The Night Before Christmas. Moore, Clement C. 2007. (ENG.). 18p. (J). (gr. -1-3). 19.95 *(978-1-4037-2947-7(6)*, Intervisual/Piggy Toes) Bendon, Inc.
Newsom, Tom. The Night Before Christmas. Moore, Clement C. 2012. (J). ***(978-1-4508-5375-0(7))*** Publications International, Ltd.
Newsom, Tom. Our Family Christmas Album: A Book about Us! 2008. (ENG.). 24p. (J). 12.95 *(978-1-58117-795-4(X)*, Intervisual/Piggy Toes) Bendon, Inc.
—Our Night Before Christmas: Memory Book - A Book about Us! 2008. (ENG.). 24p. (YA). (gr. 2-18). 12.95 *(978-1-58117-796-1(8)*, Intervisual/Piggy Toes) Bendon, Inc.
Newsome, Andy. The Gift of the Gold Coin. Bauld, Jane S. Carpenter, Christina D., ed. Date not set. 32p. (J). (gr. -1-5). 15.95 *(978-1-886440-03-6(4))* Portunus Publishing Co.
Newton, Jill. Crash Bang Donkey! 2015. (J). ***(978-1-4896-3858-8(X))*** Weigl Pubs., Inc.
Newton, Jill. Daniel & the Beast of Babylon. McGough, Roger. 2004. (ENG.). 32p. (J). (gr. k-2). pap. 11.00 *(978-0-7459-4753-2(0))* Lion Hudson PLC GBR. Dist: Independent Pubs. Group.
—The Fox & the Stork. Kuenzler, Lou & Powell, Jillian. 2012. (Aesop's Awesome Rhymes Ser.: 4). (ENG.). 48p. (J). (gr. k-2). pap. 7.99 *(978-1-4083-0971-1(8))* Hodder & Stoughton GBR. Dist: Independent Pubs. Group.

N

—Keeping up with Cheetah. Camp, Lindsay. 2004. 28p. (J). (gr. -1-2). (978-1-85269-150-9(6)) Mantra Lingua.

—Larry & Rita. Michalak, Jamie. 2007. (Brand New Readers Ser.). (ENG.). 48p. (J). (gr. -1-3). 14.99 (978-0-7636-2963-2(4)) Candlewick Pr.

—Monkey's Noisy Jungle. Ziefert, Harriet. 2007. bds. 7.95 (978-1-59354-598-7(3)) Blue Apple Bks.

—Old MacNoah Had an Ark. Lloyd-Jones, Sally. 2008. (HarperBlessings Ser.). 32p. (J). (gr. -1-2). 17.89 (978-0-06-055718-8(4)) HarperCollins Pubs.

—The Town Mouse & the Country Mouse. Kuenzler, Lou & Powell, Jillian. 2012. (Aesop's Awesome Rhymes Ser.: 3). (ENG.). 48p. (J). (gr. k-2). pap. 7.99 (978-1-4083-0970-4(X)) Hodder & Stoughton GBR. Dist: Independent Pubs. Group.

Newton, Jill. Don't Wake Mr Bear! Newton, Jill. 2011. (ENG.). 32p. (J). (gr. -1). 17.99 (978-1-4052-4965-2(X)); pap. 9.99 (978-1-4052-4966-9(8)) Egmont Bks., Ltd. GBR. Dist: Independent Pubs. Group.

Newton, Keith. Ghost Island. Gilligan, Shannon. 2008. (Dragonlarks Ser.). 80p. (J). (gr. k-3). pap. 7.99 (978-1-933390-57-4(3)) Chooseco LLC.

—The Lake Monster Mystery. Gilligan, Shannon. 2009. (Dragonlarks Ser.). 80p. (J). (gr. k-3). pap. 7.99 (978-1-933390-60-4(3)) Chooseco LLC.

—Sand Castle. Montgomery, R. A. 2008. 80p. (J). (gr. k-3). pap. 7.99 (978-1-933390-59-8(X)) Chooseco LLC.

Newton, Kimberly. Earl's Big Adventure in Costa Rica. Haidar, Hanna. Hutcheson, Meredith, ed. 2007. 22p. (J). per. 7.99 (978-0-9800975-0-4(9)) Old Silver Pr.

—Earl's Big Adventure in Costa Rica. Haidar, Hanna. 2nd ed. 2012. 22p. (J). (978-0-9800975-2-8(5)) Old Silver Pr.

—Earl's Big Adventure in Japan. Haidar, Hanna. 2012. 26p. (J). (978-0-9800975-1-1(7)) Old Silver Pr.

Newton, Pilar. No Descanso Para Sparky. Arruzza, Rick. 2004. (SPA.). 24p. (J). mass mkt. 7.95 (978-0-9744509-3-3(6)) Three Spots Productions.

—No Rest for Sparky. Arruzza, Rick. 2004. 24p. (J). mass mkt. 7.95 (978-0-9744509-2-6(8)) Three Spots Productions.

—El Paseo de Sparky. Arruzza, Rick. 2003. (SPA.). 24p. mass mkt. 7.95 (978-0-9744509-1-9(X)) Three Spots Productions.

—Sparky's Walk. Arruzza, Rick. 2003. 24p. (J). mass mkt. 7.95 (978-0-9744509-0-2(1)) Three Spots Productions.

Newton, Vanessa. One Love: Based on the Song by Bob Marley. Marley, Cedella & Marley, Bob. 2011. (ENG.). 32p. (J). (gr. -1-1). 16.99 (978-1-4521-0224-5(4)) Chronicle Bks. LLC.

Newton, Vanessa. Let Freedom Sing. Newton, Vanessa. 2009. (ENG.). 40p. (J). (gr. k-12). 16.99 (978-1-934706-90-9(6)) Blue Apple Bks.

Newton, Vanessa & Magnette, Paul. Think Big. Scanlon, Liz Garton. 2012. (ENG.). 32p. (J). (gr. -1-6). 16.99 (978-1-59990-611-9(2), 226295, Bloomsbury USA Childrens) Bloomsbury USA.

Newton, Vanessa Brantley. Baby Faces. Loehr, Mallory. 2012. (ENG.). 12p. (J). (gr. k — 1). 7.99 (978-0-375-87031-6(8), Random Hse. Bks. for Young Readers) Random Hse. Children's Bks.

—Brand New School, Brave New Ruby. Barnes, Derrick. 2008. (Ruby & the Booker Boys Ser.: 1). (ENG.). 144p. (J). (gr. 2-5). pap. 5.99 (978-0-545-01760-2(2), Scholastic Paperbacks) Scholastic, Inc.

—The Girl Who Heard Colors. Harris, Marie. 2013. (ENG.). 32p. (J). (gr. -1-k). 16.99 (978-0-399-25643-1(1), Nancy Paulsen Bks.) Penguin Publishing Group.

—Go, Jade, Go! Dungy, Tony & Dungy, Lauren. 2013. (Ready-To-Reads Ser.). (ENG.). 32p. (J). (gr. k-2). 16.99 (978-1-4424-5467-5(9)); pap. 3.99 (978-1-4424-5466-8(0)) Simon Spotlight. (Simon Spotlight).

—Here Comes the Parade! Dungy, Tony & Dungy, Lauren. 2014. (Ready-To-Reads Ser.). (ENG.). 32p. (J). (gr. k-2). pap. 3.99 (978-1-4424-5469-9(5), Simon Spotlight) Simon Spotlight.

—I Can Do It! Holland, Trish. 2014. (Little Golden Book Ser.). (ENG.). 24p. (J). (-k). 3.99 (978-0-449-81310-2(X), Golden Bks.) Random Hse. Children's Bks.

—Justin & the Bully. Dungy, Tony & Dungy, Lauren. 2012. (Ready-To-Reads Ser.). (ENG.). 32p. (J). (gr. k-2). 15.99 (978-1-4424-5719-5(8)); pap. 3.99 (978-1-4424-5718-8(X)) Simon Spotlight. (Simon Spotlight).

—The Missing Cupcake Mystery. Dungy, Tony & Dungy, Lauren. 2013. (Ready-To-Reads Ser.). (ENG.). 32p. (J). (gr. k-2). 16.99 (978-1-4424-5464-4(4)); pap. 3.99 (978-1-4424-5463-7(6)) Simon Spotlight. (Simon Spotlight).

—Mister & Lady Day: Billie Holiday & the Dog Who Loved Her. Novesky, Amy. 2013. (ENG.). 32p. (J). (gr. -1-3). 16.99 (978-0-15-205806-7(0)) Houghton Mifflin Harcourt Publishing Co.

—Ruby Goldberg's Bright Idea. Humphrey, Anna. 2013. (ENG.). 144p. (J). (gr. 3-7). 15.99 (978-1-4424-8027-8(0), Simon & Schuster Bks. For Young Readers) Simon & Schuster Bks. For Young Readers.

—Ruby's New Home. Dungy, Tony & Dungy, Lauren. 2011. (Ready-To-Reads Ser.). (ENG.). 32p. (J). (gr. k-2). pap. 3.99 (978-1-4169-9784-9(9)); lib. bdg. 15.99 (978-1-4424-2948-2(8)) Simon Spotlight. (Simon Spotlight).

—A Team Stays Together! Dungy, Tony & Dungy, Lauren. 2011. (Ready-To-Reads Ser.). (ENG.). 32p. (J). (gr. k-2). 15.99 (978-1-4424-3540-7(2)); pap. 3.99 (978-1-4424-3539-1(9)) Simon Spotlight. (Simon Spotlight).

—Thanksgiving for Emily Ann. Johnston, Teresa. 2014. (ENG.). 32p. (J). (gr. -1-k). 6.99 (978-0-545-43413-3(0), Cartwheel Bks.) Scholastic, Inc.

—Trivia Queen/Supreme. Barnes, Derrick D. 2008. (Ruby & the Booker Boys Ser.: 2). (ENG.). 144p. (J). (gr. 2-5). pap. 5.99 (978-0-545-01761-9(0)) Scholastic, Inc.

Nex, Anthony, photos by. Little Feet Love. 2009. 12p. 7.95 (978-1-58117-881-4(6), Intervisual/Piggy Toes) Bendon, Inc.

—Little Hands Love. 2009. (ENG., 12p. (J). 8.95 (978-1-58117-851-7(4), Intervisual/Piggy Toes) Bendon, Inc.

Neyret, Aurélie. Bedtime Is Canceled. Meng, Cece. 2012. (ENG.). 32p. (J). (gr. -1-3). 16.99 (978-0-547-63668-9(7)) Houghton Mifflin Harcourt Publishing Co.

Nez, John. Bubble Trouble. Gabriel, Nat. 2004. 32p. (J). lib. bdg. 20.00 (978-1-4242-1085-5(2)) Fitzgerald Bks.

—Bubble Trouble. Gabriel, Nat. 2004. (Science Solves It Ser.). 32p. (gr. -1-3). 15.00 (978-0-7569-4286-1(1)) Perfection Learning Corp.

—The Creeping Tide. Herman, Gail. 2003. (Science Solves It! Ser.). 32p. (J). pap. 5.95 (978-1-57565-128-6(9)) Kane Pr., Inc.

—The Dragon Painter. 2006. (First Reading Level 4 Ser.). 48p. (J). (gr. 1-4). 8.99 (978-0-7945-1275-0(5), Usborne) EDC Publishing.

—Gotcha! Dussling, Jennifer. 2003. (Science Solves It! Ser.). 32p. (J). pap. 5.95 (978-1-57565-124-8(6)) Kane Pr., Inc.

—My Vacation Diary. 2008. (ENG.). 24p. (J). (gr. -1-3). pap. 14.99 (978-0-8249-5581-6(1), Ideals Children's Bks.) Ideals Pubns.

—New Dog in Town. Herman, Gail. 2006. (Social Studies Connects). 32p. (J). (gr. -1-3). pap. 5.95 (978-1-57565-165-1(3)) Kane Pr., Inc.

—Tod el Apretado: Math Matters en Espanol. Skinner, Daphne. 2005. (SPA.). 32p. (J). pap. 5.95 (978-1-57565-155-2(6)) Kane Pr., Inc.

Nez, John. One Smart Cookie. Nez, John. 2006. (ENG.). 32p. (J). (gr. k-3). lib. bdg. 16.99 (978-0-8075-6099-0(5)) Whitman, Albert & Co.

Nez, John. Bubble Trouble. Nez, John, tr. Gabriel, Nat. 2004. (Science Solves It! Ser.). 32p. (J). pap. 5.95 (978-1-57565-133-0(5)) Kane Pr., Inc.

Nez, John, jt. illus. see Bliss, Harry.

Nez, John A. Daisy Diaz Shakes up Camp. Harkrader, Lisa. 2009. (Social Studies Connects Complete Set Ser.). 32p. (J). (gr. k-7). pap. 5.95 (978-1-57565-292-4(7)) Kane Pr., Inc.

—No Money? No Problem! Haskins, Lori. 2004. (Social Studies Connects). 32p. (J). (gr. k-2). pap. 5.95 (978-1-57565-141-5(6)) Kane Pr., Inc.

—Pet Peeves! Willson, Sarah. 2005. (Social Studies Connects). 32p. (J). pap. 5.95 (978-1-57565-149-1(1)) Kane Pr., Inc.

Nez, John Abbott. Dancing Clock. Metzger, Steve. 2011. 32p. 12.95 (978-1-58925-100-7(8)); (J). pap. 7.95 (978-1-58925-429-9(5)) Tiger Tales.

Nez, John Abbott. The Twelve Days of Christmas in Washington. Nez, John Abbott. 2011. (Twelve Days of Christmas in America Ser.). (ENG.). 32p. (J). (gr. k-3). 12.95 (978-1-4027-7068-5(5)) Sterling Publishing Co., Inc.

Nez, Jon. Mouse's Christmas Cookie, 0 vols. Thomas, Patricia. 2013. (ENG.). 22p. (J). (gr. -1-2). 14.99 (978-1-4778-4704-6(9), 9781477847046, Amazon Children's Publishing) Amazon Publishing.

—Peter Panda Melts Down! Bennett, Artie. 2014. (ENG.). 40p. (J). (gr. -1-k). 16.99 (978-1-60905-411-3(3)) Blue Apple Bks.

Ng-Benitez, Shirley. Danny & the Blue Cloud: Coping with Childhood Depression. Foley, James. 2016. (J). (978-1-4338-2103-5(6), Magination Pr.) American Psychological Assn.

Ng, Drew. Falling Star. Cutting, Robert. 2007. 48p. (J). lib. bdg. 23.08 (978-1-4242-1625-3(7)) Fitzgerald Bks.

—Marco Polo & the Roc. Boyd, David. 2007. 48p. (J). lib. bdg. 23.08 (978-1-4242-1621-5(4)) Fitzgerald Bks.

—Pearl Harbor. Boyd, David. 2007. 48p. (J). lib. bdg. 23.08 (978-1-4242-1640-6(0)) Fitzgerald Bks.

Ng, James. The Secret of Ashona. Kingsley, Kaza. (Erec Rex Ser.: 5). (ENG.). 528p. (J). (gr. 5-9). 2013. pap. 8.99 (978-1-4169-7993-7(X)); 2012. 16.99 (978-1-4169-7992-0(1)) Simon & Schuster Bks. For Young Readers. (Simon & Schuster Bks. For Young Readers).

Ng, James & Mohrbacher, Peter. The Three Furies. Kingsley, Kaza. 2011. (Erec Rex Ser.: 4). (ENG.). 576p. (J). (gr. 5-9). pap. 8.99 (978-1-4169-7991-3(3), Simon & Schuster Bks. For Young Readers) Simon & Schuster Bks. For Young Readers.

Ng, Leandro. Passage 2: HIV/AIDS — First Love. Roman, Annette. 2005. (1 World Manga Ser.: Vol. 2). (ENG.). 40p. (J). pap. 3.99 (978-0-8213-6406-2(5)) World Bank Pubns.

—1 World Manga. Roman, Annette. (1 World Manga Ser.: Vol. 3). (ENG.). 2006. 40p. pap. 3.99 (978-1-4215-0366-0(2)); Vol. 1. 2005. 40p. pap. 3.99 (978-1-4215-0364-6(6)); Vol. 2. 2005. 40p. pap. 3.99 (978-1-4215-0365-3(4)); Vol. 5. 2007. 240p. pap. 3.99 (978-1-4215-1169-6(X)) Viz Media.

Ng, Leandro & Wong, Walden. One World Manga, Vols. 1-6. Roman, Annette. 2007. (1 World Manga Ser.). (ENG.). 240p. (gr. 1). pap. 9.99 (978-1-4215-1584-7(9)) Viz Media.

Ng, Neiko. Hop, Hop Bunny. Seresin, Lynn & Schwartz, Betty Ann. 2015. (Follow-Along Book Ser.). (ENG.). 10p. (J). (gr. -1 — 1). bds. 9.99 (978-1-4521-2464-3(7)) Chronicle Bks. LLC.

—Run, Run Piglet. Schwartz, Betty Ann & Seresin, Lynn. 2015. (Follow-Along Book Ser.). (ENG.). 10p. (J). (gr. -1 — 1). bds. 9.99 (978-1-4521-2467-4(1)) Chronicle Bks. LLC.

—Woodland Christmas: A Festive Wintertime Pop-Up Book. Yeretskaya, Yevgeniya. 2013. (ENG.). 6p. 19.95 (978-1-60580-954-0(3)) Jumping Jack Pr.

Ng, Robyn. I Had a Favorite Hat. Ashburn, Boni. 2015. (ENG.). 32p. (J). (gr. -1-3). 16.95 (978-1-4197-1462-7(7), Abrams Bks. for Young Readers) Abrams.

Ng, Simon. Tales from Gold Mountain, 1 vol. Yee, Paul. 2011. (ENG.). 64p. (J). (gr. 1-5). pap. 14.95 (978-1-55498-125-0(5)) Groundwood Bks. CAN. Dist: Perseus-PGW.

Ngo. The Teaser Monster. Ngo, Lap. 2012. 24p. (J). 11.99 (978-0-9838321-9-5(6)) Higher Ground Pr.

Ngui, Marc. The Big Book of Pop Culture: A How-To Guide for Young Artists. Niedzviecki, Hal. 2007. (ENG.). 183p. (YA). (gr. 7-12). pap. 14.95 (978-1-55451-055-9(4), 9781554510559) Annick Pr., Ltd. CAN. Dist: Firefly Bks., Ltd.

—Watch This Space: Designing, Defending & Sharing Public Spaces. Dyer, Hadley. 2010. (ENG.). 80p. (J). (gr. 5-9). 18.95 (978-1-55453-293-3(0)) Kids Can Pr., Ltd. CAN. Dist: Univ. of Toronto Pr.

Nguyen, Albert. Artemisia of Caria. Bridges, Shirin Yim & Yim Bridges, Shirin. 2010. (Thinking Girl's Treasury of Real Princesses Ser.). (ENG.). 24p. (J). (gr. 3-8). 18.95 (978-0-9845098-1-2(X)) Goosebottom Bks. LLC.

—Hatshepsut of Egypt. Bridges, Shirin Yim. 2010. (Thinking Girl's Treasury of Real Princesses Ser.). (ENG.). 24p. (J). (gr. 3-8). 18.95 (978-0-9845098-0-5(1)) Goosebottom Bks. LLC.

—Isabella of Castile. Bridges, Shirin Yim. 2010. (Thinking Girl's Treasury of Real Princesses Ser.). (ENG.). 24p. (J). (gr. 3-8). 18.95 (978-0-9845098-4-3(4)) Goosebottom Bks. LLC.

—Nur Jahan of India. Bridges, Shirin Yim & Yim Bridges, Shirin. 2010. (Thinking Girl's Treasury of Real Princesses Ser.). (ENG.). 24p. (J). (gr. 3-8). 18.95 (978-0-9845098-5-0(2)) Goosebottom Bks. LLC.

—Qutlugh Terkan Khatun of Kirman. Bridges, Shirin Yim & Yim Bridges, Shirin. 2010. (Thinking Girl's Treasury of Real Princesses Ser.). (ENG.). 24p. (J). (gr. 3-8). 18.95 (978-0-9845098-3-6(6)) Goosebottom Bks. LLC.

—Sacajawea of the Shoshone. Yim, Natasha. 2012. (Thinking Girl's Treasury of Real Princesses Ser.). (ENG.). 32p. (J). (gr. 3-8). 18.95 (978-0-9845098-6-7(0)) Goosebottom Bks. LLC.

Nguyen, Bich. The Tet Pole/Su Tich Cay Neu Ngay Tet: The Story of Tet Festival. Tran, Quoc. Smith, William, tr. from VIE. 2006. (ENG & VIE.). 32p. (J). (gr. 1-4). 16.95 (978-0-9701654-5-9(5)) East West Discovery Pr.

Nguyen, Cindy. Angel from Heaven. Capozzola, Christine. 2014. (Morgan James Kids Ser.). (ENG.). 28p. pap. 9.95 (978-1-63047-189-7(5)) Morgan James Publishing.

Nguyen, Duke, jt. illus. see Kuon, Vuthy.

Nguyen, Dustin. April Showers & Cinco de Mayo, 1 vol. Stone Arch Books. 2014. (Batman: Li'l Gotham Ser.). (ENG.). 32p. (gr. 2-3). 21.27 (978-1-4342-9220-9(7)) Stone Arch Bks.

—Christmas & New Year's Eve, 1 vol. Stone Arch Books. 2014. (Batman: Li'l Gotham Ser.). (ENG.). 32p. (gr. 2-3). 21.27 (978-1-4342-9217-9(7)) Stone Arch Bks.

—Comic con & Labor Day. Kane, Bob. 2015. (Batman: Li'l Gotham Ser.). (ENG.). 32p. (gr. 2-3). lib. bdg. 21.27 (978-1-4342-9736-5(5)) Stone Arch Bks.

—Halloween & Thanksgiving, 1 vol. Stone Arch Books. 2014. (Batman: Li'l Gotham Ser.). (ENG.). 32p. (gr. 2-3). 21.27 (978-1-4342-9208-7(8)) Stone Arch Bks.

—Month of Waters & Independence Day. Kane, Bob. 2015. (Batman: Li'l Gotham Ser.). (ENG.). 32p. (gr. 2-3). lib. bdg. 21.27 (978-1-4342-9666-5(0)) Stone Arch Bks.

—Mother's Day & Father's Day, 1 vol. Stone Arch Books. 2014. (Batman: Li'l Gotham Ser.). (ENG.). 32p. (gr. 2-3). 21.27 (978-1-4342-9221-6(5)) Stone Arch Bks.

—Sandwich Day & Our Family Album. Kane, Bob. 2015. (Batman: Li'l Gotham Ser.). (ENG.). 32p. (gr. 2-3). lib. bdg. 21.27 (978-1-4342-9737-2(3)) Stone Arch Bks.

—St. Patrick's Day & Easter, 1 vol. Stone Arch Books. 2014. (Batman: Li'l Gotham Ser.). (ENG.). 32p. (gr. 2-3). 21.27 (978-1-4342-9219-3(3)) Stone Arch Bks.

—Tropical Getaway & Bird Watching. Kane, Bob. 2015. (Batman: Li'l Gotham Ser.). (ENG.). 32p. (gr. 2-3). lib. bdg. 21.27 (978-1-4342-9735-8(7)) Stone Arch Bks.

—Valentine's Day & the Lunar New Year, 1 vol. Stone Arch Books. 2014. (Batman: Li'l Gotham Ser.). (ENG.). 32p. (gr. 2-3). 21.27 (978-1-4342-9218-6(5)) Stone Arch Bks.

Nguyen, Dustin Tri. Batman: Li'l Gotham, 1 vol. Stone Arch Books. 2014. (Batman: Li'l Gotham Ser.). (ENG.). 32p. (gr. 2-3). 127.62 (978-1-4342-9529-3(X)) Stone Arch Bks.

Nguyen, Tao. Mighty Mite: A New Beginning. Nguyen, Tao. 2006. (J). 14.95 (978-0-9776282-1-6(3)) Amazing Factory, The.

Nguyen, Taohuu. Mighty Mite 2: Zoo Gone Wild. Nguyen, Taohuu. 2007. (J). 14.95 (978-0-9788469-2-3(3)) Amazing Factory, The.

—Mighty Mite 3: Good Mites, Bad Mites. Nguyen, Taohuu. 2007. (J). 14.95 (978-0-9790302-3-9(4)) Amazing Factory, The.

Nguyen, Vincent. Bandit, 0 vols. Rostoker-Gruber, Karen. 2008. (ENG.). 40p. (J). (gr. -1-3). 15.99 (978-0-7614-5382-6(2), 9780761453826, Amazon Children's Publishing) Amazon Publishing.

—Bandit's Surprise, 0 vols. Rostoker-Gruber, Karen. 2010. (ENG.). 32p. (J). (gr. -1-3). 15.99 (978-0-7614-5623-0(6), 9780761456230, Amazon Children's Publishing) Amazon Publishing.

—Buzz. Spinelli, Eileen. 2010. (ENG.). 32p. (J). (gr. -1-3). 15.99 (978-1-4169-4925-1(9), Simon & Schuster Bks. For Young Readers) Simon & Schuster Bks. For Young Readers.

—The Crabfish. 2010. (First Steps in Music Ser.). (ENG.). 24p. (J). (gr. -1-k). 16.95 (978-1-57999-772-4(4)) G I A Pubns., Inc.

—The Dragon & the Turtle. Paul, Donita K. & Denmark, Evangeline. 2010. (ENG.). 40p. (J). (gr. k-12). 11.99 (978-0-307-44644-2(1), WaterBrook Pr.) Doubleday Religious Publishing Group, The.

—The Dragon & the Turtle Go on Safari. Paul, Donita K. & Denmark, Evangeline. 2011. (ENG.). 40p. (J). (gr. k-12). 11.99 (978-0-307-44645-9(X), WaterBrook Pr.) Doubleday Religious Publishing Group, The.

—Gorilla Garage, 0 vols. Shulman, Mark. (ENG.). (J). (gr. -1-3). 2013. 42p. pap. 9.99 (978-1-4778-1663-9(1), 9781477816639); 2009. 40p. 17.99 (978-0-7614-5461-8(6), 9780761454618) Amazon Publishing. (Amazon Children's Publishing).

—Jungle Bullies, 0 vols. Kroll, Steven. (ENG.). 32p. (J). (gr. -1-2). 2010. 16.99 (978-0-7614-5297-3(4), 9780761452973); 2006. pap. 7.99 (978-0-7614-5620-9(1), 9780761456209) Amazon Publishing. (Amazon Children's Publishing).

—Polar Bears' Home: A Story about Global Warming. Bergen, Lara. 2008. (Little Green Bks.). (ENG.). 24p. (J). (gr. -1-1). pap. 3.99 (978-1-4169-6787-3(7), Little Simon) Little Simon.

—The Truly Terribly Horrible Sweater... That Grandma Knit. Macomber, Debbie & Carney, Mary Lou. 2009. (ENG.). 32p. (J). (gr. -1-2). 16.99 (978-0-06-165093-2(5)) HarperCollins Pubs.

Nhem, Sopaul. Half Spoon of Rice: A Survival Story of the Cambodian Holocaust. Smith, Icy. 2009. (J). (gr. 2-7). 19.95 (978-0-9821675-8-8(X)) East West Discovery Pr.

Nicely, Darthy. Where Is Grandmother? Lampkin, Laveta M. 2011. 36p. pap. 24.95 (978-1-4626-1579-7(1)) America Star Bks.

Nicholai, Rachel, et al. Bird Adventures. Nicholai, Rachel et al. 2006. (Adventure Story Collection Ser.). 28p. (J). (gr. 2-6). pap. 10.00 (978-1-58084-246-4(1)) Lower Kuskokwim Schl. District.

Nicholas, Corasue. The Tag-a-long Trio: Zak, Lizze & Ben Too! Malokas, Ann. 2007. (J). 15.95 (978-0-9708415-8-2(2)) Guilty Mom Pr.

Nicholas, Frank. Wildcat, the Seminole: The Florida War. Clark, Electa. 2011. 194p. 42.95 (978-1-258-06128-9(7)) Literary Licensing, LLC.

Nicholas, Jacob. When My Nose Runs, Where Does It Go? Rogala, Jennifer. 2006. 36p. per. 11.95 (978-1-58939-866-5(1)) Virtualbookworm.com Publishing, Inc.

Nicholas, Kristin. Kids Knitting. Hartlove, Chris, photos by. Falick, Melanie. 2003. (ENG.). 128p. (J). pap. 15.95 (978-1-57965-241-8(7), 85241) Artisan.

Nicholls, Calvin. The World Before This One: A Novel Told in Legend. Martin, Rafe. 2005. (ENG.). 208p. (J). (gr. 3-7). per. 5.99 (978-0-590-37980-9(1), Levine, Arthur A. Bks.) Scholastic, Inc.

Nicholls, Emma, jt. illus. see Wallis, Diz.

Nicholls, Paul. Candle Pop-Up Bible Atlas, 1 vol. Dowley, Tim & David, Juliet. 2014. (ENG.). 16p. (J). 16.99 (978-1-78128-100-0(9), Candle Bks.) Lion Hudson PLC GBR. Dist: Kregel Pubns.

—I Want to Be A... Pirate. 2014. (J). (978-1-4351-5500-8(9)) Barnes & Noble, Inc.

—My World: My Busy Day. Wang, Adria. 2005. 10p. (J). 4.95 (978-1-58117-251-5(6), Intervisual/Piggy Toes) Bendon, Inc.

—My World: My Family. Wang, Adria. 2005. (My World Bks.). 10p. (J). 4.95 (978-1-58117-252-2(4), Intervisual/Piggy Toes) Bendon, Inc.

—My World: My Outdoors. Wang, Adria. 2005. (My World Bks.). 10p. (J). 4.95 (978-1-58117-249-2(4), Intervisual/Piggy Toes) Bendon, Inc.

—My World: My Playtimes Toys. Wang, Adria. 2005. 10p. (J). 4.95 (978-1-58117-250-8(8), Intervisual/Piggy Toes) Bendon, Inc.

—Twinkle, Star of the Week. Holub, Joan. 2012. (J). (978-1-61913-137-8(4)) Weigl Pubs., Inc.

—Twinkle, Star of the Week. Holub, Joan. 2010. (ENG.). 32p. (J). (gr. 1-3). 16.99 (978-0-8075-8131-5(3)) Whitman, Albert & Co.

Nichols, Chris. King for a Day. Goss, Leon. 2005. (J). pap. (978-1-933156-09-5(0)); per. 16.99 (978-1-933156-01-9(5)) GSVQ Publishing. (VisionQuest Kids).

Nichols, Clayton. Faith Found New, 1. Showell, Isaiah, Sr. 2004. 82p. (YA). per. 15.00 incl. audio compact disk (978-0-9754489-0-8(0)) Divine Intertwine Publishing.

Nichols, Dave. Help Your Buddy Learn English, Bk. 1. Claire, Elizabeth. l.t. ed. 2003. 64p. 15.00 (978-0-937630-04-4(7)) Eardley Pubns.

Nichols, Garry, jt. illus. see Reibeling, Brandon.

Nichols, Garry, jt. illus. see Yesh, Jeff.

Nichols, Jon, jt. illus. see Nichols, Tucker.

Nichols, Lori. No, No, Kitten! Thomas, Shelley Moore. 2015. (ENG.). 40p. (J). (gr. -1-2). 16.95 (978-1-62091-631-5(2)) Boyds Mills Pr.

—This Orq. (He Cave Boy.) Elliott, David. 2014. (ENG.). 40p. (J). (gr. -1). 15.95 (978-1-62091-521-9(9)) Boyds Mills Pr.

Nichols, Lori. Maple. Nichols, Lori. 2014. (ENG.). 32p. (J). (gr. -1-k). 16.99 (978-0-399-16085-1(X), Nancy Paulsen Bks.) Penguin Publishing Group.

—Maple & Willow Together. Nichols, Lori. 2014. (ENG.). 32p. (J). (gr. -1-k). 16.99 (978-0-399-16283-1(6), Nancy Paulsen Bks.) Penguin Publishing Group.

Nichols, Paul. Pirate Sticker Book. Watt, Fiona. ed. 2011. (Sticker Activity Books Ser.). 24p. (J). pap. 8.99 (978-0-7945-2915-4(1), Usborne) EDC Publishing.

Nichols, Travis. Monstrous Fun: A Doodle & Activity Book. Nichols, Travis. 2015. (ENG.). 64p. (J). (gr. 3-7). 7.99 (978-0-8431-7882-1(5), Price Stern Sloan) Penguin Publishing Group.

Nichols, Tucker & Nichols, Jon. Crabtree. 2013. (ENG.). 32p. (J). (gr. -1-3). 17.95 (978-1-936365-82-1(0)) McSweeney's Publishing.

Nicholson, Kat & Cardy, Jason. A Midsummer Night's Dream. Shakespeare, William. Bryant, Clive, ed. 2012. (ENG.). 144p. (gr. 6). lib. bdg. 24.95 (978-1-907127-44-1(5)) Classical Comics GBR. Dist: Perseus-PGW.

Nicholson, Kat, jt. illus. see Cardy, Jason.

Nicholson, Trudy. Alligator Crossing. Douglas, Marjory Stoneman & Milkweed Editions Staff. 2003. (ENG.). 192p. (J). (gr. 3-8). pap. 7.95 (978-1-57131-644-8(2)) Milkweed Editions.

Nicholson, Trudy & Mirocha, Paul. The South Atlantic Coast & Piedmont: A Literary Field Guide. Milkweed Editions Staff. St. Antoine, Sara, ed. 2006. (Stories from Where We Live Ser.). (ENG.). 256p. (J). (gr. 4-7). per. 10.95 (978-1-57131-664-6(7)) Milkweed Editions.

Nicholson, Trudy, jt. illus. see Mirocha, Paul.

Nicholson, William. The Velveteen Collection Set: The Velveteen Principles & the Velveteen Rabbit, 2 vols. Williams, Margery & Raiten-D'Antonio, Toni. 2005. (ENG.). 296p. (gr. -1-3). 19.95 *(978-0-7573-0347-0(1))* Health Communications, Inc.

—The Velveteen Rabbit. Williams, Margery. 2011. (Dover Children's Classics Ser.). (ENG.). 48p. (J). (gr. k-5). pap. 8.99 *(978-0-486-48606-2(0))* Dover Pubns., Inc.

—The Velveteen Rabbit. Williams, Margery. ed. 2014. (ENG.). 48p. (J). (gr. -1-k). pap. 9.99 *(978-1-4052-1054-6(0))* Egmont Bks., Ltd. GBR. Dist: Independent Pubs. Group.

—The Velveteen Rabbit. Williams, Margery. 2005. (ENG.). 96p. (J). (gr. -1-1). 9.95 *(978-0-7573-0333-3(1))* Health Communications, Inc.

—The Velveteen Rabbit. Williams, Margery. 44p. (J). (gr. 2-3). pap. 3.50 *(978-0-8072-1346-9(2)*, Listening Library) Random Hse. Audio Publishing Group.

—The Velveteen Rabbit. Williams, Margery. 2014. (ENG.). 48p. (J). (gr. -1-2). 19.99 *(978-0-385-37566-5(2)*, Doubleday Bks. for Young Readers) Random Hse. Children's Bks.

—The Velveteen Rabbit Book & Charm. Williams, Margery. 2006. 40p. (J). (gr. -1-3). pap. 4.99 *(978-0-06-076067-0(2)*, HarperFestival) HarperCollins Pubs.

Nicholson, William. The Velveteen Rabbit, or, How Toys Become Real. Bianco, Margery Williams. 2015. (J). pap. ***(978-1-4677-9307-0(8)***, First Avenue Editions) Lerner Publishing Group.

Nichx, jt. illus. see Merola, Marcelo.

Nickelodeon Staff. Discover with Dora: Books & Magnetic Playset, Set. Reader's Digest Staff. 2010. (Magnetic Playset Ser.). (ENG.). 16p. (J). (gr. -1-2). bds. 15.99 *(978-0-7944-2003-1(6))* Reader's Digest Assn., Inc., The.

—Dora Music Player. Reader's Digest Staff. 10th anniv. ed. 2010. (Music Player Storybook Ser.). (ENG.). 40p. (J). (gr. -1). bds. 19.99 *(978-0-7944-2033-8(8))* Reader's Digest Assn., Inc., The.

Nicklaus, Carol. ¿Adonde Vamos? Dentro y Fuera de tu mente. Carlson, Dale. Guix, Joan Carles, tr. from ENG. 2004.Tr. of In & Out of your Mind. Where are we Going?. (SPA.). 64p. *(978-84-9754-117-6(0)*, 88303) Ediciones Oniro S.A.

—Are You Human, or What? Carlson, Dale Bick & Carlson, Hannah. 2008. (ENG.). 143p. (gr. 7-18). pap. 14.95 *(978-1-884158-33-9(1))* Bick Publishing Hse.

—Elmo's ABC Book. November, Deborah. 2007. (Big Bird's Favorites Board Bks.). (ENG.). 24p. (J). (gr. k — 1). bds. 4.99 *(978-0-375-84037-1(0)*, Random Hse. Bks. for Young Readers) Random Hse. Children's Bks.

—The Mountain of Truth. Carlson, Dale Bick. 2nd ed. 2005. (ENG.). 169p. (gr. 8-12). reprint ed. pap. 14.95 *(978-1-884158-30-8(7))* Bick Publishing Hse.

—Sometimes I Share. Linn, Margot. 2005. (I'm Going to Read(r) Ser.). (ENG.). 28p. (J). (gr. -1-k). pap. 3.95 *(978-1-4027-2090-1(4))* Sterling Publishing Co., Inc.

—Talk: Teen Art of Communication. Carlson, Dale Bick. Khaimar, Kishore, ed. 2006. (ENG.). 154p. (gr. 7-18). pap. 14.95 *(978-1-884158-32-2(3))* Bick Publishing Hse.

—The Teen Brain Book: Who & What Are You? Carlson, Dale. Teasdale, Nancy, ed. 2004. (ENG.). 230p. (gr. 7-12). pap. 14.95 *(978-1-884158-29-2(3))* Bick Publishing Hse.

—Who Said What? Philosophy Quotes for Teens. Carlson, Dale. 2003. (ENG.). 224p. (gr. 7-12). pap. 14.95 *(978-1-884158-28-5(5))* Bick Publishing Hse.

Nicklaus, Carol, jt. illus. see Carlson, Al.

Nickle, John. The Brixen Witch. DeKeyser, Stacy. (ENG.). 208p. (J). (gr. 3-7). 2013. pap. 6.99 *(978-1-4424-3329-8(9))*; 2012. 15.99 *(978-1-4424-3328-1(0))* McElderry, Margaret K. Bks. (McElderry, Margaret K. Bks.).

—Hans My Hedgehog: A Tale from the Brothers Grimm. Grimm, Jacob & Grimm, Wilhelm K. 2012. (ENG.). 40p. (J). (gr. k-3). 16.99 *(978-1-4169-1533-1(8)*, Atheneum Bks. for Young Readers) Simon & Schuster Children's Publishing.

—Never Take a Shark to the Dentist: And Other Things Not to Do. Barrett, Judi. 2008. (ENG.). 34p. (J). (gr. -1-3). 17.99 *(978-1-4169-0724-4(6)*, Atheneum Bks. for Young Readers) Simon & Schuster Children's Publishing.

—Who Pushed Humpty Dumpty? And Other Notorious Nursery Tale Mysteries. Levinthal, David. 2012. (ENG.). 40p. (J). (gr. -1-3). 17.99 *(978-0-375-84195-8(4))*; 20.99 *(978-0-375-94595-3(4))* Random Hse. Children's Bks. (Schwartz & Wade Bks.).

Nicol, Brock. Little Sam's Secret Place. Walters Iii, Harry C. 2012. 44p. 24.95 *(978-1-937763-41-1(2))*; pap. 14.95 *(978-1-937763-40-4(4))* Published by Westview, Inc.

Nicolas, Otero. How Chile Came to New Mexico. Anaya, Rudolfo A. Nasario, Garcia, tr. 2014. 48p. (gr. -1-3). 24.95 *(978-1-936744-20-6(1)*, Rio Grande Bks.) LPD Pr.

Nicolson, Cynthia Pratt & Slavin, Bill. The Jumbo Book of Space. Nicolson, Cynthia Pratt et al. 2007. (Jumbo Bks.). (ENG.). 208p. (J). 17.95 *(978-1-55453-020-5(2))* Kids Can Pr., Ltd. CAN. Dist: Univ. of Toronto Pr.

Nidenoff, Michele. Sleeping Dragons All Around, 1 vol. Fitch, Sheree. ed. 2014. (ENG.). 32p. (J). (gr. -1-3). pap. 12.95 *(978-1-55109-772-5(9))* Nimbus Publishing, Ltd. CAN. Dist: Orca Bk. Pubs. USA.

Niednagel, David & Marco, Harvey. Your Key to Sports Success: Using Your Unique Brain Type to Maximize Athletic Performance. Niednagel, Jonathan P. 8th rev. ed. 2005. 408p. (Orig.). pap. 24.95 *(978-0-916309-01-5(0))* Cerebral Press International.

Nielander, Amy. The Ladybug Race. Nielander, Amy. 2015. (ENG.). 40p. (J). 19.95 ***(978-0-7649-7187-7(5)***, POMEGRANATE KIDS) Pomegranate Communications, Inc.

Nieländer, Peter. La Bicicleta Robada. Preller, James. 5th ed. 2007. (Nino Puzle Ser.). (SPA.). 78p. (J). (gr. -1-3). 13.95 *(978-84-263-5272-9(3))* Vives, Luis Editorial (Edelvives) ESP. Dist: Ediciones Urano S. A.

—El Hamster Desaparecido. Preller, James. 5th ed. 2007. (Nino Puzle Ser.). (SPA.). 78p. (J). (gr. -1-3). 13.95 *(978-84-263-5269-9(3))* Vives, Luis Editorial (Edelvives) ESP. Dist: Ediciones Urano S. A.

Nielsen, Gwyn English & Colby, Devon English. Serendipity & the Dream Catcher. Nielsen, Gwyn English. 2003. 176p. (gr. 3-7). pap. 5.95 *(978-0-9660726-2-4(6))* C.G.S. Pr.

Nielsen, Janet Marie. A Song for Me: A Muslim Holiday Story. Abdelsalam, Lisa. 2006. 34p. (J). *(978-0-9755975-1-4(5))* Abdelsalam Corp.

Nielsen, Julia L. How to Draw Cool Fashions, 1 vol. Clay, Kathryn. 2009. (Drawing Fun Ser.). (ENG.). 32p. (gr. 3-4). lib. bdg. 27.32 *(978-1-4296-3406-9(5)*, Snap Bks.) Capstone Pr., Inc.

Nielsen, Kay. The Twelve Dancing Princesses & Other Fairy Tales. Quiller-Couch, Sir Arthur. 2012. (Calla Editions Ser.). (ENG.). 224p. (gr. 4). 40.00 *(978-1-60660-025-2(7))* Dover Pubns., Inc.

Nielsen, Ric, jt. illus. see Madaras, Diana.

Nielsen, Shaw. How Do You Feed a Hungry Giant? A Munch-and-Sip Pop-Up Book. Friedman, Caitlin. 2011. (ENG.). 30p. (J). (gr. -1-2). 18.95 *(978-0-7611-5752-6(2)*, 15752) Workman Publishing Co., Inc.

Nielson, Cliff. The Challenge. Pearson, Ridley. 2009. (Steel Trapp Ser.: Bk. 1). (ENG.). 336p. (J). (gr. 3-7). pap. 7.99 *(978-1-4231-0803-0(5))* Hyperion Pr.

Nielson, Doug, jt. illus. see Storey, Linda.

Nielson, Ginger. The Adventures of Cali. Lallouz, Michele. 2007. 32p. (J). pap. 9.95 *(978-0-9793004-0-0(1))* Cali Publishing.

—Carla's Cloud Catastrophe. Reinke, Beth Bence. 2011. 28p. pap. 14.99 *(978-0-9828346-0-2(8))* 4RV Publishing, LLC.

—Count 1, 2, 3 with Me. Arnold, Connie. 2013. 24p. pap. 12.99 *(978-1-940310-12-1(1))* 4RV Publishing, LLC.

—Daniel & the Harmonica. Dubreuil, Robert. Eisenstadter, Dave, ed. 2010. 48p. (J). (gr. 1-7). 16.95 *(978-0-88045-088-1(6))* Stemmer Hse. Pubs.

—A Dinner Date for Dilly. Jones, Rena. 2012. 28p. pap. 14.99 *(978-0-9852661-2-7(0))* 4RV Publishing, LLC.

—I Like Pink. Zabel, Vivian. 2013. 28p. pap. 12.99 *(978-0-9889617-1-5(7))* 4RV Publishing, LLC.

—A New Friend for Dilly. Jones, Rene'. 2011. 32p. pap. 14.99 *(978-0-9826423-0-6(X))* 4RV Publishing, LLC.

—Pony Strings & Critter Things. Jones, Rena. 2012. 28p. pap. 14.99 *(978-0-9838018-0-1(0))* 4RV Publishing, LLC.

Nielson, Ginger. Willow, an Elephant's Tale. Nielson, Ginger. 2012. 32p. pap. 11.65 *(978-0-9852661-1-0(2))* 4RV Publishing, LLC.

Nielson, Sam. Neversink. Wolverton, Barry. (ENG.). (J). (gr. 3-7). 2013. 320p. pap. 6.99 *(978-0-06-202793-1(X))*; 2012. 304p. 16.99 *(978-0-06-202791-7(3))* HarperCollins Pubs. (Waldon Pond Pr.).

—Neversink. Wolverton, Barry. 2012. xiii, 287p. (J). *(978-0-06-202792-4(1))* Longman Publishing.

—The Zoo at the Edge of the World. Gale, Eric Kahn. (ENG.). 240p. (J). (gr. 3-7). 2015. pap. 6.99 ***(978-0-06-212517-0(6))***; 2014. 16.99 *(978-0-06-212516-3(8))* HarperCollins Pubs.

Niemann, Christoph. The Boy with Two Belly Buttons. Dubner, Stephen J. 2007. 32p. (J). (gr. -1-1). 17.89 *(978-0-06-113403-6(1))* HarperCollins Pubs.

Niemann, Christoph. The Pet Dragon: A Story about Adventure, Friendship, & Chinese Characters. Niemann, Christoph. 2008. 40p. (J). (gr. -1-3). (ENG.). 16.99 *(978-0-06-157776-5(6))*; lib. bdg. 17.89 *(978-0-06-157777-2(4))* HarperCollins Pubs. (Greenwillow Bks.).

—Subway. Niemann, Christoph. 2010. 40p. (J). (gr. -1-k). (ENG.). 16.99 *(978-0-06-157779-6(0))*; lib. bdg. 17.89 *(978-0-06-157780-2(4))* HarperCollins Pubs. (Greenwillow Bks.).

—That's How! Niemann, Christoph. 2011. (ENG.). 32p. (J). (gr. -1-k). 16.99 *(978-0-06-201963-9(5)*, Greenwillow Bks.) HarperCollins Pubs.

Nieminen, Lotta. Walk This World. Broom, Jenny. 2013. (ENG.). 24p. (J). (gr. k-3). 17.99 *(978-0-7636-6895-2(8)*, Big Picture Press) Candlewick Pr.

Niepold, Mil & Verdu, Jeanyves. Oooh! Picasso. Niepold, Mil & Verdu, Jeanyves. 2009. (ENG.). 48p. (J). (gr. k-3). 14.99 *(978-1-58246-265-3(8)*, Tricycle Pr.) Ten Speed Pr.

Nieto, Gina L. My Angel & Me. Nieto, Nancy. 2003. 19p. (J). *(978-1-932046-04-5(6))* Pastime Pr.

Nieto, Laura. La Patrulla Del Castillo Volador/ the Flying Castle Patrol. Nieto, Laura. 2009. (ENG & SPA.). 206p. (YA). 24.95 *(978-9962-629-70-2(5))* Piggy Pr. Bks.

Nieto-Phillips, John M. & Morris, Julie. Telma, la Hormiguita. Nieto-Phillips, John M. & Morris, Julie. 2006. (ENG & SPA.). 29p. (J). *(978-0-9772852-3-5(5))*; pap. *(978-0-9772852-2-8(7))* Lectura Bks.

Nievelstein, Ralf. The Secret of the Twelfth Continent. Michaelis, Antonia. Hosmer-Dillard, Mollie, tr. from GER. 2013. (ENG.). 288p. (J). (gr. 3-6). 14.95 *(978-1-62087-539-1(X)*, 620539, Sky Pony Pr.) Skyhorse Publishing Co., Inc.

Nighthawk, Tori. Don't Judge a Bird by Its Feathers. Nighthawk, Tori. 2013. (ENG.). 60p. (J). (gr. -1-3). 17.99 *(978-0-9858811-9-1(4))* Stone, Anne Publishing.

Nightingale, Jenny. Think Green! Getz, Jeanine Behr. 2008. (ENG.). 32p. (J). 15.50 *(978-0-9797362-0-9(X))* Kids Think Big LLC.

Nightow, Yasuhiro. Break Out, 13 vols., Vol. 5. Nightow, Yasuhiro. 2005. (Trigun Maximum Ser.). (ENG.). 208p. pap. 9.95 *(978-1-59307-344-2(5))* Dark Horse Comics.

Nihei, Tsutomu. Biomega, 6 vols. Nihei, Tsutomu. 2010. (Biomega Ser.: 2). (ENG.). 216p. pap. 12.99 *(978-1-4215-3185-4(2))*; 220p. pap. 12.99 *(978-1-4215-3184-7(4))* Viz Media.

—Wolverine Legends Vol. 5: Snikt! Nihei, Tsutomu. 2003. (Wolverine Legends Ser.). 120p. (YA). (gr. 7-18). pap. 13.99 *(978-0-7851-1239-6(1))* Marvel Worldwide, Inc.

Nihoff, Tim. I Fooled You: Ten Stories of Tricks, Jokes & Switcheroos. Hurwitz, Johanna, ed. 2010. (ENG.). 192p. (J). (gr. 4-7). 16.99 *(978-0-7636-3789-7(0))*; pap. 6.99 *(978-0-7636-4877-0(9))* Candlewick Pr.

—Otter Everywhere: Brand New Readers. Webster, Christine. 2007. (Brand New Readers Ser.). (ENG.). 48p. (J). (gr. -1-3). pap. 5.99 *(978-0-7636-2922-9(7))* Candlewick Pr.

—Teddy Bear Addition. McGrath, Barbara Barbieri. 2014. (McGrath Math Ser.). (ENG.). 32p. (J). (gr. -1-3). pap. 7.95 *(978-1-58089-425-8(9))* Charlesbridge Publishing, Inc.

—Teddy Bear Counting. McGrath, Barbara Barbieri. 2010. (McGrath Math Ser.). (ENG.). 32p. (J). (gr. -1-2). 16.95 *(978-1-58089-215-5(9))*; pap. 7.95 *(978-1-58089-216-2(7))* Charlesbridge Publishing, Inc.

—Teddy Bear Math. McGrath, Barbara Barbieri. 2011. (McGrath Math Ser.). (ENG.). 32p. (J). (gr. k-3). 16.95 *(978-1-58089-283-4(3))*; pap. 7.95 *(978-1-58089-284-1(1))* Charlesbridge Publishing, Inc.

—Teddy Bear Patterns. McGrath, Barbara Barbieri. 2013. (McGrath Math Ser.). (ENG.). 32p. (J). (gr. -1-2). pap. 7.95 *(978-1-58089-423-4(2))*; lib. bdg. 16.95 *(978-1-58089-422-7(4))* Charlesbridge Publishing, Inc.

—Teddy Bear Subtraction. McGrath, Barbara Barbieri. 2014. (J). *(978-1-60734-652-4(4))* Charlesbridge Publishing, Inc.

—Teddy Bear, Teddy Bear, School Day Math. McGrath, Barbara Barbieri. 2012. (McGrath Math Ser.). (ENG.). 32p. (J). (gr. -1-3). 16.95 *(978-1-58089-420-3(8))*; pap. 7.95 *(978-1-58089-421-0(6))* Charlesbridge Publishing, Inc.

Nijland, Stern, jt. illus. see Haan, Linda de.

Nikiel, Laura Gibbons. Egermeier's ABC Bible Storybook: Favorite Stories Adapted for Young Children. Egermeier, Elsie E. Rhodes, Karen, ed. 2006. (ENG.). 56p. (gr. -1-k). 12.99 *(978-1-59317-156-8(0))* Warner Pr. Pubs.

—Egermeier's ABC Bible Storybook: Favorite Stories Adapted for Young Children. Egermeier, Elsie. Rhodes, Karen, ed. 2007. (ENG.). 56p. (J). (gr. -1-5). 14.99 incl. audio compact disk *(978-1-59317-198-8(6))* Warner Pr. Pubs.

—In Jesse's Shoes: Appreciating Kids with Special Needs. Lewis, Beverly. 2007. (ENG.). 32p. (J). (gr. -1-4). 11.99 *(978-0-7642-0313-8(4))* Bethany Hse. Pubs.

Niland, Deborah. This Little Piggy Went Dancing. Wild, Margaret. 2014. (ENG.). 24p. (J). (-k). 15.99 *(978-1-74331-511-8(2))* Allen & Unwin AUS. Dist: Independent Pubs. Group.

Niland, Deborah. Annie's Chair. Niland, Deborah. 2005. 32p. (J). *(978-0-670-04249-4(8))* Penguin Books Australia.

—When Coco Was a Kitten. Niland, Deborah. 2009. (Toddler Tales Ser.). (ENG.). 24p. (J). (gr. -1). 7.99 *(978-1-935279-10-5(6))* Kane Miller.

Niland, Kilmeny. Two Bad Teddies. Niland, Kilmeny. 2010. (ENG.). 24p. (J). (gr. -1-k). 14.99 *(978-1-921541-05-6(9))* Little Hare Bks. AUS. Dist: Independent Pubs. Group.

—Two Tough Teddies. Niland, Kilmeny. (ENG.). 24p. (J). (gr. -1-k). 2010. pap. 8.99 *(978-1-921272-38-7(4))*; 2008. 14.95 *(978-1-921272-05-9(8))* Little Hare Bks. AUS. Dist: Independent Pubs. Group.

Niles, Kim. Westie the Dog. Anjou, Colette. 2005. 28p. (J). (gr. -1-3). per. 15.95 *(978-0-9748933-6-5(6))* E & E Publishing.

Nilesh, Misty. The Seven Wise Princesses: A Medieval Persian Epic. Tarnowska, Wafa'. 2008. (ENG.). 96p. (J). (gr. 5-9). 19.99 *(978-1-84686-250-2(7))* Barefoot Bks., Inc.

Nille, Peggy. The Drummer Boy. Min, SooHyeon. 2015. (MySELF Bookshelf Ser.). (ENG.). 32p. (J). (gr. k-2). pap. 11.94 *(978-1-60357-696-3(7))*; lib. bdg. 22.60 *(978-1-59953-661-3(7))* Norwood Hse. Pr.

Nilsen, Anna. The Amazeing Voyage of Charles Darwin. Nilsen, Anna. 2003. 32p. (Orig.). pap., act. bk. ed. *(978-1-877003-28-8(X))* Little Hare Bks. AUS. Dist: HarperCollins Pubs. Australia.

—Robotics: Maths, Games & Puzzles. Nilsen, Anna. 2004. 32p. pap., act. bk. ed. *(978-1-877003-61-5(1))* Little Hare Bks. AUS. Dist: HarperCollins Pubs. Australia.

Nilsen, Mary Ylvisaker, photos by. The Blessing of Feelings. Nilsen, Erika. 2007. 32p. (J). 10.95 *(978-0-9627147-4-0(7))* Zion Publishing.

Nilsson, Al. The Tennessee Tater. Nilsson, Al. 2003. (YA). per. *(978-0-9741294-9-5(6)*, MSP) Main St Publishing, Inc.

Nilsson, Troy, 2nd. Hiroshima Stones: The Shadow Stones of Hiroshima. Nilsson, Troy, 2nd. 2003. 248p. (YA). pap. 9.95 *(978-0-9724771-0-9(1)*, Nilsson, Troy) Nilsson Media.

—Hiroshima Stones: The Shadow Stones of Hiroshima - a Story of Love & War. Nilsson, Troy, 2nd. collector's aut. ed. 2003. Orig. Title: Hiroshima Stones. 248p. (YA). 24.95 *(978-0-9724771-1-6(X)*, Nilsson, Troy) Nilsson Media.

Ninaltowski, Eric. Confession, 1 vol. Miller, Mike S. 2008. (Z Graphic Novels / Hand of the Morning Star Ser.). (ENG.). 160p. (YA). (gr. 8-11). pap. 6.99 *(978-0-310-71371-5(4))* Zondervan.

Niño, Alex. Herman Melville/Moby Dick. Melville, Herman. 2005. 48p. (gr. 5-8). 25.50 *(978-0-7910-9106-7(6))* Facts On File, Inc.

Nippert, Brenda & Nippert, George. An Alphabet of Catholic Saints, bks. 13000. Nippert, Brenda & Nippert, George. 3rd ed. 2006. (ENG.). 64p. (J). pap. 11.95 *(978-0-9787035-1-6(0))* Joseph's Heartprint.

—An Alphabet of Mary, bks. 3000. Nippert, Brenda & Nippert, George. 2012. (ENG.). 64p. (J). pap. 12.95 *(978-0-9787035-0-9(2))* Joseph's Heartprint.

Nippert, George, jt. illus. see Nippert, Brenda.

Nirattisai, Preston. Welcome Aboard the Disneyland Railroad! The Complete Disneyland Railroad Reference Guide. DeGaetano, Steve. 2004. 318p. 64.95 *(978-0-9758584-0-0(8))* Steam Passages Pubns.

Nishi, Yoshiyuki. Muhyo & Roji's Bureau of Supernatural Investigation. Nishi, Yoshiyuki. 2007. (Muhyo & Roji's Bureau of Supernatural Investigation Ser.: 1). (ENG.). 208p. (gr. 8-18). pap. 7.99 *(978-1-4215-1376-8(5))* Viz Media.

—Muhyo & Roji's Bureau of Supernatural Investigation, Vol. 18. Nishi, Yoshiyuki. 2010. (Muhyo & Roji's Bureau of Supernatural Investigation Ser.: 18). (ENG.). 192p. pap. 9.99 *(978-1-4215-2840-3(1))* Viz Media.

Nishii. The Adventures of the Big Dog & the Little Dog: They First Meet! Johnsen, Erin L. 2013. 32p. pap. 24.95 *(978-1-4626-2346-4(8))* America Star Bks.

Nishimori, Hiroyuki. Cheeky Angel. Nishimori, Hiroyuki. Yamazaki, Joe, tr. from JPN. (Cheeky Angel Ser.: Vol. 7). (ENG.). (YA). 2005. 184p. pap. 9.95 *(978-1-59116-839-3(2))*; 2004. 200p. pap. 9.95 *(978-1-59116-620-7(9))* Viz Media.

—Cheeky Angel. Nishimori, Hiroyuki. (Cheeky Angel Ser.). (ENG.). 3. 2004. 200p. (YA). pap. 9.95 *(978-1-59116-503-3(2))*; Vol. 2. 2004. 200p. (YA). pap. 9.95 *(978-1-59116-467-8(2))*; Vol. 5. 2005. 200p. (YA). pap. 9.95 *(978-1-59116-631-3(4))*; Vol. 6. 2005. 192p. (YA). pap. 9.95 *(978-1-59116-774-7(4))*; Vol. 8. 2005. 192p. pap. 9.99 *(978-1-59116-979-6(8))*; Vol. 9. 2005. 192p. pap. 9.99 *(978-1-4215-0069-0(8))*; Vol. 11. 2006. 194p. pap. 9.99 *(978-1-4215-0317-2(4))*; Vol. 12. 2006. 208p. pap. 9.99 *(978-1-4215-0446-9(4))*; Vol. 13. 2006. 208p. pap. 9.99 *(978-1-4215-0447-6(2))* Viz Media.

Nishiyama, Akira & Komatsu, Eiko. Wonderful Houses Around the World. Komatsu, Yoshio, photos by. 2004. (ENG.). 43p. (J). pap. 9.95 *(978-0-936070-34-6(X))* Shelter Pubns., Inc.

Nister, Ernest. Merry Magic-Go-Round: An Antique Book of Changing Pictures. 2005. 14p. (J). (gr. k-4). reprint ed. 19.00 *(978-0-7567-9156-8(1))* DIANE Publishing Co.

Nitzberg, Chuck. Travels with Charlie: Across the Midwest. Bhagat-Clark, Duryan & Backer, Miles. 2014. (ENG.). 36p. (J). (gr. 1-4). 14.99 *(978-1-60905-462-5(8))* Blue Apple Bks.

—Travels with Charlie: Travelin' the Northeast. Backer, Miles. 2013. (ENG.). 36p. (J). (gr. 1-4). 14.99 *(978-1-60905-355-0(9))* Blue Apple Bks.

—Travels with Charlie - Down South. Backer, Miles. 2013. (ENG.). 36p. (J). (gr. 1-4). 14.99 *(978-1-60905-353-6(2))* Blue Apple Bks.

—Travels with Charlie - Way Out West. Backer, Miles. 2013. (ENG.). 36p. (J). (gr. 1-4). 14.99 *(978-1-60905-354-3(0))* Blue Apple Bks.

Nitzsche, Shane. Arizona Activity Book, 1 vol. Ellis, Paula. 2012. 64p. (J). (gr. 2-3). pap. 5.95 *(978-1-59193-288-8(2))* Adventure Pubns., Inc.

—Constellations Activity Book, 1 vol. Jacobson, Ryan. 2012. 64p. (J). (gr. 2-3). pap. 5.95 *(978-1-59193-325-0(0))* Adventure Pubns., Inc.

—The Ghost of J. Stokely. Temple, Bob. 2008. (Shade Bks.). (ENG.). 80p. (gr. 2-3). 23.99 *(978-1-4342-0796-8(X)*, Shade Bks.) Stone Arch Bks.

—Texas Activity Book, 1 vol. Ellis, Paula. 2012. 64p. (J). (gr. 2-3). pap. 5.95 *(978-1-59193-376-2(5))* Adventure Pubns., Inc.

—Yellowstone & Grand Teton Activity Book. Ellis, Paula. 2011. 64p. (J). (gr. 2-3). pap. 5.95 *(978-1-59193-356-4(0))* Adventure Pubns., Inc.

—Yosemite Activity Book, 1 vol. Ellis, Paula. 2013. 64p. (J). (gr. 2-3). pap. 5.95 *(978-1-59193-299-4(8))* Adventure Pubns., Inc.

Nivola, Claire A. Emma's Poem: The Voice of the Statue of Liberty. Glaser, Linda. (ENG.). 32p. (J). (gr. -1-3). 2013. pap. 7.99 *(978-0-544-10508-9(7))*; 2010. 17.99 *(978-0-547-17184-5(6))* Houghton Mifflin Harcourt Publishing Co.

—The Flag Maker: A Story of the Star-Spangled Banner. Bartoletti, Susan Campbell. 2007. (ENG.). 32p. (J). (gr. 2-5). 6.95 *(978-0-618-80911-0(2))* Houghton Mifflin Harcourt Publishing Co.

—The Silent Witness: A True Story of the Civil War. Friedman, Robin. 2008. (ENG.). 32p. (J). (gr. -1-3). pap. 6.99 *(978-0-547-01436-4(8))* Houghton Mifflin Harcourt Publishing Co.

Nivola, Claire A. Life in the Ocean: The Story of Oceanographer Sylvia Earle, 1 vol. Nivola, Claire A. 2012. (ENG.). 32p. (J). (gr. -1-3). 17.99 *(978-0-374-38068-7(6)*, Farrar, Straus & Giroux (BYR)) Farrar, Straus & Giroux.

—Orani: My Father's Village. Nivola, Claire A. 2011. (ENG.). 36p. (J). (gr. -1-3). 16.99 *(978-0-374-35657-6(2)*, Frances Foster Bks.) Farrar, Straus & Giroux.

—Planting the Trees of Kenya: The Story of Wangari Maathai. Nivola, Claire A. 2008. (ENG.). 32p. (J). (gr. k-3). 18.99 *(978-0-374-39918-4(2)*, Farrar, Straus & Giroux (BYR)) Farrar, Straus & Giroux.

—Star Child. Nivola, Claire A. 2014. (ENG.). 40p. (J). (gr. k-3). 16.99 *(978-0-374-37182-1(2)*, Farrar, Straus & Giroux (BYR)) Farrar, Straus & Giroux.

Niwano, Makoto. Deltora Quest 1. Rodda, Emily. 2011. (Deltora Quest Ser.). (ENG.). 202p. (gr. 8-12). pap. 10.99 *(978-1-935429-28-9(0))* Kodansha America, Inc.

—Deltora Quest 2. Rodda, Emily. 2011. (Deltora Quest Ser.). (ENG.). 206p. (gr. 8-12). pap. 10.99 *(978-1-935429-29-6(9))* Kodansha America, Inc.

Nix, Pamela, jt. illus. see Paulson, Arlie.

Nixon, Chris. Crocodile Cake. Morgan, Palo. 2010. (ENG.). 40p. (J). (gr. -1-k). 17.95 *(978-1-921361-55-5(7))* Fremantle Pr. AUS. Dist: Independent Pubs. Group.

Nixon, John. Stitches. Morrison, Kevin. 2003. 32p. (J). 12.95 *(978-1-929039-15-9(8))* Ambassador Bks., Inc.

Nixon, Tom. Sled Dog Wisdom: Humorous & Heartwarming Tales from Alaska's Mushers. 2006. (ENG.). 64p. 4.95 *(978-0-9745014-5-1(X))* Epicenter Pr., Inc.

No New Art Needed, jt. illus. see Disney Storybook Artists Staff.

No, Yi-Jung. Visitor. No, Yi-Jung, creator. 2005. 192p. (YA). pap. 9.99 *(978-1-59532-342-2(2))* TOKYOPOP, Inc.

Noad, Jordan. Isabella & the Merry Mouse House: A Christmas Story Coloring Book. Pachek, Mary C. 2009. 34p. pap. 14.49 *(978-1-4389-8467-4(7))* AuthorHouse.

Noah, Ian & Logan, Stephanie. Mike's Math Club Presents the Monstrously Fun Fraction Book. Noah, Ian & Logan, Stephanie. Milken-Noah, Joni et al, eds. 2003. 382p. pap. 24.95 *(978-0-9646425-1-5(4))* Milken Family Foundation.

Nobati, Eugenia. ¡A la Busqueda del Tesoro! White, Amy. Kratky, Lada J., tr. 2009. (Colección Fácil de Leer Ser.). (SPA.). 16p. (gr. k-2). pap. 5.99 *(978-1-60396-418-0(5))* Ediciones Alfaguara ESP. Dist: Santillana USA Publishing Co., Inc.

—Bat's Big Game. Aesop. 2012. (J). 34.28 *(978-1-61913-131-6(5))* Weigl Pubs., Inc.

N

—Bat's Big Game. MacDonald, Margaret Read. 2008. (ENG.). 32p. (J). (gr. k-3). 16.99 *(978-0-8075-0587-8(0))* Whitman, Albert & Co.

—Celebrate Mardi Gras with Joaquin. Flor Ada, Alma. 2006. (Cuentos para Celebrar / Stories to Celebrate Ser.). 30p. (gr. k-6). per. 11.95 *(978-1-59820-128-4(X))* Santillana USA Publishing Co., Inc.

Nobens, C. A. Bashful Ball Pythons. Doudna, Kelly. 2013. (Unusual Pets Ser.). (ENG.). 24p. (J). (gr. -1-3). 24.21 *(978-1-61783-397-7(5))* ABDO Publishing Co.

—The Best Thing about Christmas. Tangvald, Christine Harder. 2014. (Faith That Sticks Ser.). (ENG.). 27p. (J). pap. 3.99 *(978-1-4964-0087-1(9))* Tyndale Hse. Pubs.

—El Bolígrafo del Cerdo. Scheunemann, Pam. 2007. (Cuentos de Animales Ser.). (SPA & ENG.). 24p. (J). (gr. k-3). lib. bdg. 24.21 *(978-1-59928-659-4(9)*, SandCastle) ABDO Publishing Co.

—El Caracol de la Tortuga. Salzmann, Mary Elizabeth. 2007. (Cuentos de Animales Ser.). (SPA & ENG.). 24p. (J). (gr. k-3). lib. bdg. 24.21 *(978-1-59928-657-0(2)*, SandCastle) ABDO Publishing Co.

—Cheeky Chinchillas. Doudna, Kelly. 2013. (Unusual Pets Ser.). (ENG.). 24p. (J). (gr. -1-3). 24.21 *(978-1-61783-398-4(3))* ABDO Publishing Co.

—Elephant Trunks. Kompelien, Tracy. 2006. (Fact & Fiction Ser.). 24p. (J). pap. 48.42 *(978-1-59679-936-3(6))* ABDO Publishing Co.

Nobens, C. A. God Made You Special. Holder, Jennifer. (Happy Day Ser.). (ENG.). (J). 2015. 16p. pap. 2.49 ***(978-1-4964-1110-5(2)**, Happy Day)*; 2014. 28p. pap. 3.99 *(978-1-4964-0086-4(0))* Tyndale Hse. Pubs.

Nobens, C. A. Hilarious Hedgehogs. Doudna, Kelly. 2013. (Unusual Pets Ser.). (ENG.). 24p. (J). (gr. -1-3). 24.21 *(978-1-61783-399-1(1))* ABDO Publishing Co.

—Horse Shoes. Tuminelly, Nancy. 2006. (Fact & Fiction Ser.). 24p. (J). pap. 48.42 *(978-1-59679-944-8(7))* ABDO Publishing Co.

—I Can Pray! Stortz, Diane & Holder, Jennifer. 2014. (Faith That Sticks Ser.). (ENG.). 28p. (J). pap. 3.99 *(978-1-4964-0085-7(2))* Tyndale Hse. Pubs.

—Kangaroo Boxers. Hanson, Anders. 2006. (Fact & Fiction Ser.). 24p. (J). pap. 48.42 *(978-1-59679-946-2(3))* ABDO Publishing Co.

—Lion Manes. Kompelien, Tracy. 2006. (Fact & Fiction Ser.). 24p. (J). pap. 48.42 *(978-1-59679-950-9(1))* ABDO Publishing Co.

—Magnificent Macaws. Kuskowski, Alex. 2013. (Unusual Pets Ser.). (ENG.). 24p. (J). (gr. -1-3). 24.21 *(978-1-61783-400-4(9))* ABDO Publishing Co.

—Las Orejas del Conejo. Doudna, Kelly. 2007. (Cuentos de Animales Ser.).Tr. of Rabbit Ears. (SPA & ENG.). 24p. (J). (gr. k-3). lib. bdg. 24.21 *(978-1-59928-669-3(6)*, SandCastle) ABDO Publishing Co.

—Los Pantaloncillos del Canguro. Hanson, Anders. 2007. (Cuentos de Animales Ser.). (SPA & ENG.). 24p. (J). (gr. k-3). lib. bdg. 24.21 *(978-1-59928-655-6(6)*, SandCastle) ABDO Publishing Co.

—Pig Pens. Scheunemann, Pam. 2006. (Fact & Fiction Ser.). 24p. (J). pap. 48.42 *(978-1-59679-960-8(9))* ABDO Publishing Co.

—Portly Potbellied Pigs. Kuskowski, Alex. 2013. (Unusual Pets Ser.). (ENG.). 24p. (J). (gr. -1-3). 24.21 *(978-1-61783-401-1(7))* ABDO Publishing Co.

—Rabbit Ears. Doudna, Kelly. 2006. (Fact & Fiction Ser.). 24p. (J). pap. 48.42 *(978-1-59679-962-2(5))* ABDO Publishing Co.

—Rhino Horns. Hanson, Anders. 2006. (Fact & Fiction Ser.). 24p. (J). pap. 48.42 *(978-1-59679-964-6(1))* ABDO Publishing Co.

—Special Memories. Williams, Rozanne Lanczak. Maio, Barbara, ed. 2006. (J). per. 8.99 *(978-1-59198-360-6(6))* Creative Teaching Pr., Inc.

—Tricky Tarantulas. Kuskowski, Alex. 2013. (Unusual Pets Ser.). (ENG.). 24p. (J). (gr. -1-3). 24.21 *(978-1-61783-402-8(5))* ABDO Publishing Co.

—La Tuba Del Rinoceronte. Hanson, Anders. 2006. (Realidad y Ficción Ser.). (SPA.). 24p. (J). 48.42 *(978-1-59928-666-2(1))* ABDO Publishing Co.

—La Tuba del Rinoceronte. Hanson, Anders. 2007. (Cuentos de Animales Ser.). (SPA & ENG.). 24p. (J). (gr. k-3). lib. bdg. 24.21 *(978-1-59928-665-5(3)*, SandCastle) ABDO Publishing Co.

—Turtle Shells. Salzmann, Mary Elizabeth. 2006. (Fact & Fiction Ser.). 24p. (J). pap. 48.42 *(978-1-59679-970-7(6))* ABDO Publishing Co.

—Los Zapatos de la Potranca. Tuminelly, Nancy. 2007. (Cuentos de Animales Ser.). (SPA & ENG.). 24p. (J). (gr. k-3). lib. bdg. 24.21 *(978-1-59928-677-8(7)*, SandCastle) ABDO Publishing Co.

—Zebra Stripes. Kompelien, Tracy. 2006. (Fact & Fiction Ser.). 24p. (J). pap. 48.42 *(978-1-59679-972-1(2))* ABDO Publishing Co.

Nobens, Cheryl. Colores - Colors. 2006. (ENG & SPA.). (J). bds. 5.99 *(978-1-934113-03-5(4))* Little Cubans, LLC.

—How to Make a Friend. Williams, Rozanne Lanczak. 2005. (Reading for Fluency Ser.). 16p. (J). pap. 3.49 *(978-1-59198-155-8(7)*, 4255) Creative Teaching Pr., Inc.

Nobens, Cheryl A. Elephant Trunks. Kompelien, Tracy. 2006. (Animal Tales Ser.). (ENG.). 24p. (J). (gr. k-3). lib. bdg. 24.21 *(978-1-59679-935-6(8)*, SandCastle) ABDO Publishing Co.

—Horse Shoes. Tuminelly, Nancy. 2006. (Animal Tales Ser.). (ENG.). 24p. (J). (gr. k-3). lib. bdg. 24.21 *(978-1-59679-943-1(9)*, SandCastle) ABDO Publishing Co.

—Kangaroo Boxers. Hanson, Anders. 2006. (Animal Tales Ser.). (ENG.). 24p. (J). (gr. k-3). lib. bdg. 24.21 *(978-1-59679-945-5(5)*, SandCastle) ABDO Publishing Co.

—Pig Pens. Scheunemann, Pam. 2006. (Animal Tales Ser.). (ENG.). 24p. (J). (gr. k-3). lib. bdg. 24.21 *(978-1-59679-959-2(5)*, SandCastle) ABDO Publishing Co.

—Rabbit Ears. Doudna, Kelly. 2006. (Animal Tales Ser.). (ENG.). 24p. (J). (gr. k-3). lib. bdg. 24.21 *(978-1-59679-961-5(7)*, SandCastle) ABDO Publishing Co.

—Rhino Horns. Hanson, Anders. 2006. (Animal Tales Ser.). (ENG.). 24p. (J). (gr. k-3). lib. bdg. 24.21 *(978-1-59679-963-9(3)*, SandCastle) ABDO Publishing Co.

—Turtle Shells. Salzmann, Mary Elizabeth. 2006. (Animal Tales Ser.). (ENG.). 24p. (J). (gr. k-3). lib. bdg. 24.21 *(978-1-59679-969-1(2)*, SandCastle) ABDO Publishing Co.

—Zebra Stripes. Kompelien, Tracy. 2006. (Animal Tales Ser.). (ENG.). 24p. (J). (gr. k-3). lib. bdg. 24.21 *(978-1-59679-971-4(4)*, SandCastle) ABDO Publishing Co.

Noble, Amy. Creepy Chicago: A Ghosthunter's Tales of the City's Scariest Sites. Bielski, Ursula. 2010. (ENG.). 135p. (J). pap. 7.95 *(978-1-933272-28-3(7))* Thunder Bay Pr.

Noble, Edwin & Grieve, Walter G. The Natural History Story Book. Talbot, Ethel. 2008. 336p. pap. 13.95 *(978-1-59915-295-0(9))* Yesterday's Classics.

Noble, Penny. Jerboth Weaves a Song. Brown, Linda Kayse. 2007. (ENG.). 20p. (J). pap. 9.95 *(978-0-9769742-0-8(7))* Bay Villager, The.

Noble, Roger. Bedtime Baby. 1 vol. Baker, Jaime. 2010. 16p. pap. 24.95 *(978-1-4489-6234-1(X))* PublishAmerica, Inc.

Noble, Sheilagh. Let's Look at Eyes. Sideri, Simona. 2003. (Let's Look at Ser.). 24p. (J). *(978-1-84089-146-1(7))* Zero to Ten, Ltd.

—Let's Look at Mouths. Sideri, Simona. 2003. (Let's Look at Ser.). 24p. (J). *(978-1-84089-147-8(5))* Zero to Ten, Ltd.

Noble, Stuart, jt. illus. see Grant, Sophia.

Noble, Trinka Hakes. Apple Tree Christmas. Noble, Trinka Hakes. 2005. (Holiday Ser.). (ENG.). 32p. (J). (gr. -1-3). 16.95 *(978-1-58536-270-7(0))* Sleeping Bear Pr.

Nobles, Scott, photos by. Button Girl: 25 Pretty Projects from Belts to Barrettes. Bruder, Mikyla. 2005. (ENG., 64p. (J). (gr. 4-17). 12.95 *(978-0-8118-4553-3(2))* Chronicle Bks. LLC.

Nodel, Norman. Yossi & Laibel Learn to Help. Rosenfeld, Dina. 2012. 14p. (J). 6.95 *(978-1-929628-62-9(5))* Hachai Publishing.

Noé. The Ant & the Grasshopper. Sommer, Carl. 2016. (J). lib. bdg. ***(978-1-57537-925-8(2))*** Advance Publishing, Inc.

—The Donkey, Fox, & the Lion. Sommer, Carl. 2016. (J). lib. bdg. ***(978-1-57537-926-5(0))*** Advance Publishing, Inc.

—The Eagle & the Chickens. Sommer, Carl. 2016. (J). ***(978-1-57537-945-6(7))*** Advance Publishing, Inc.

Noé. The Great Deception. Sommer, Carl. 2009. (Quest for Success Ser.). (ENG.). 40p. (YA). pap. 4.95 *(978-1-57537-279-2(7))*; lib. bdg. 12.95 *(978-1-57537-254-9(1))* Advance Publishing, Inc.

—The Great Deception(El Gran Engaño) Sommer, Carl. ed. 2009. (Quest for Success Bilingual Ser.). (ENG & SPA.). 72p. (YA). lib. bdg. 14.95 *(978-1-57537-228-0(2))* Advance Publishing, Inc.

—The Sonics on Tour: The Respiratory System. Reif, Cheryl. 2012. (J). lib. bdg. *(978-1-57537-900-5(7))* Advance Publishing, Inc.

Noe, Ignacio. The Country Mouse & the City Mouse. Sommer, Carl. 2014. (Sommer-Time Story Classics Ser.). (ENG.). 32p. (J). (gr. k-4). 16.95 *(978-1-57537-080-4(8))* Advance Publishing, Inc.

—The Emperor's New Clothes. Sommer, Carl. 2014. (Sommer-Time Story Classics Ser.). (ENG.). 32p. (J). (gr. k-4). 16.95 *(978-1-57537-081-1(6))* Advance Publishing, Inc.

—The Little Red Hen. Sommer, Carl. 2014. (Sommer-Time Story Classics Ser.). (ENG.). 32p. (J). (gr. k-4). 16.95 *(978-1-57537-084-2(0))* Advance Publishing, Inc.

—Little Red Riding Hood. Sommer, Carl. 2014. (Sommer-Time Story Classics Ser.). (ENG.). 32p. (J). (gr. k-4). 16.95 *(978-1-57537-077-4(8))* Advance Publishing, Inc.

Noel, Green. God Made Me: The Safe Touch Coloring Book. Beth, Robinson. 2007. 20p. (J). pap. 3.99 *(978-0-9799092-0-7(1))* Robinson, Beth.

Noel III, jt. illus. see Rio, Adam del.

Noeth, Chris, et al. Zombielicious! Bilgrey, Marc et al. 3rd ed. 2008. (Tales from the Crypt Graphic Novels Ser.: 3). (ENG.). 112p. (J). (gr. 5-12). 12.95 *(978-1-59707-091-1(2))* Papercutz.

Noh, Mi Young. Threads of Time, 11 vols., Vol. 6. Noh, Mi Young. 6th rev. ed. 2006. (Threads of Time Ser.). 192p. per. 9.99 *(978-1-59532-037-7(7))* TOKYOPOP, Inc.

Noh, Seong-bin. Where Are You, Sun Bear? Malaysia. Choi, Eun-Mi. Cowley, Joy, ed. 2015. (Global Kids Storybooks Ser.). (ENG.). 32p. (gr. 1-4). 26.65 ***(978-1-925246-02-5(7))***; 26.65 ***(978-1-925246-28-5(0))***; 7.99 ***(978-1-925246-54-4(X))*** ChoiceMaker Pty. Ltd., The AUS. (Big and SMALL). Dist: Lerner Publishing Group.

Noiset, Michele. The Alphabet. Rosa-Mendoza, Gladys. Cifuentes, Carolina, ed. 2004. (English-Spanish Foundations Ser.).Tr. of El Alfabeto. (ENG & SPA.). 32p. (J). bds. 6.95 *(978-0-9679748-0-4(1))* Me+Mi Publishing.

—Colors & Shapes. Rosa-Mendoza, Gladys. Cifuentes, Carolina, ed. 2004. (English-Spanish Foundations Ser.).Tr. of Los Colores y las Figuras. (ENG & SPA.). 20p. (J). bds. 6.95 *(978-0-9679748-3-5(6))* Me+Mi Publishing.

—English-Spanish Foundations Series: The Alphabet; Numbers; Colors & Shapes. Rosa-Mendoza, Gladys. Cifuentes, Carolina, ed. 2004. (Spanish Foundations Ser.). (ENG & SPA.). (J). bds. 19.95 *(978-0-9679748-1-1(X))* Me+Mi Publishing.

—Numbers. Rosa-Mendoza, Gladys. Cifuentes, Carolina, ed. 2004. (English-Spanish Foundations Ser.).Tr. of Los Numeros. (ENG & SPA.). 20p. (J). bds. 6.95 *(978-0-9679748-2-8(8))* Me+Mi Publishing.

—We Read Phonics-Bugs on the Bus. Orshoski, Paul. 2010. 32p. (J). 9.95 *(978-1-60115-325-8(2))*; pap. 4.99 *(978-1-60115-326-5(0))* Treasure Bay, Inc.

Nój, Nahta. Color Create: Animals. Broom, Jenny. 2012. (ENG.). 32p. (J). (gr. k). 16.95 *(978-1-60710-493-3(8)*, Silver Dolphin Bks.) Baker & Taylor Publishing Group.

Noj, Nahta. The Lion & the Mouse: Turn-And-Tell Tales. Broom, Jenny. 2014. (ENG.). 32p. (J). (gr. -1-2). 14.99 *(978-0-7636-6619-4(X)*, Templar) Candlewick Pr.

—The Tortoise & the Hare. Ritchie, Alison. 2015. (ENG.). 32p. (J). (-k). 15.99 *(978-0-7636-7601-8(2)*, Templar) Candlewick Pr.

Nojiri, Housuke. Rocket Girls - The Last Planet. Nojiri, Housuke. 2011. (Rocket Girls Ser.). (ENG.). 250p. pap. 13.99 *(978-1-4215-3765-8(6))* Viz Media.

Nolan, Amanda M. Emily: Dream Believe Achieve. Symington, Martha M. 2008. 36p. pap. *(978-1-897435-21-2(5))* Agio Publishing Hse.

Nolan, Dennis. An Ellis Island Christmas. Leighton, Maxinne Rhea. 2005. (ENG.). 32p. (J). (gr. k-3). pap. 6.99 *(978-0-14-240506-2(X)*, Puffin) Penguin Publishing Group.

—Saint Francis of Assisi: A Life of Joy. Kennedy, Robert F., Jr. 2005. (ENG.). 32p. (J). (gr. k-4). 18.99 *(978-0-7868-1875-4(1))* Hyperion Pr.

—William Shakespeare's a Midsummer Night's Dream. Coville, Bruce. 2003. (ENG.). 48p. (J). (gr. k-3). pap. 7.99 *(978-0-14-250168-9(9)*, Puffin) Penguin Publishing Group.

—William Shakespeare's a Midsummer Night's Dream. 2003. (J). (gr. 2-5). lib. bdg. 16.65 *(978-0-613-92494-8(0)*, Turtleback) Turtleback Bks.

Nolan, Dennis. Hunters of the Great Forest. Nolan, Dennis. 2014. (ENG.). 40p. (J). (gr. -1-2). 17.99 *(978-1-59643-896-5(7))* Roaring Brook Pr.

—Sea of Dreams. Nolan, Dennis. 2011. (ENG.). 40p. (J). (gr. -1-2). 16.99 *(978-1-59643-470-7(8))* Roaring Brook Pr.

Noll, Cheryl. Bokuden & the Bully: [A Japanese Folktale]. Krensky, Stephen. 2009. (On My Own Folklore Ser.). (ENG.). 48p. (gr. 2-4). pap. 6.95 *(978-1-58013-847-5(0)*, First Avenue Editions) Lerner Publishing Group.

Noll, Cheryl Kirk. The Black Regiment of the American Revolution. Brennan, Linda. 2005. 32p. (J). (gr. 4-7). per. 8.95 *(978-1-931659-18-5(4))* Moon Mountain Publishing, Inc.

—Bokuden & the Bully. Krensky, Stephen. 2008. (On My Own Folklore Ser.). (ENG.). 48p. (gr. 2-4). lib. bdg. 25.26 *(978-0-8225-7547-4(7)*, Millbrook Pr.) Lerner Publishing Group.

Nolte, Larry. Flowers: Read Well Level K Unit 9 Storybook. Gunn, Barbara & Dunn, Richard. 2004. (Read Well Level K Ser.). 20p. (J). *(978-1-57035-680-3(7))* Cambium Education, Inc.

—Mi Perrito, Level 1. Greene, Inez. Flor Ada, Alma, tr. 3rd ed. 2003. (Dejame Leer Ser.). (SPA.). 8p. (J). (gr. -1-k). 6.50 *(978-0-673-36289-6(2)*, Good Year Bks.) Celebration Pr.

—Monkey Business: Read Well Level K Unit 3 Storybook. Sprick, Marilyn. 2003. (Read Well Level K Ser.). 20p. (J). *(978-1-57035-675-9(0))* Cambium Education, Inc.

Noon, Connie & Zraick, Robert. Dinosaurs & Donuts. Moor-Doucette, Saba. 2013. 28p. pap. 10.95 *(978-0-578-13447-5(0))* Gratitude Works.

Noon, Steve. A City Through Time. Steele, Philip & Dorling Kindersley Publishing Staff. 2013. (ENG.). 48p. (J). (gr. 2-5). 17.99 *(978-1-4654-0249-3(7))* Dorling Kindersley Publishing, Inc.

—The Story of the Titanic. Dorling Kindersley Publishing Staff. 2012. (ENG.). 48p. (J). (gr. 3-7). 17.99 *(978-0-7566-9171-4(0))* Dorling Kindersley Publishing, Inc.

—A Street Through Time. Millard, Anne. 2012. (ENG.). 48p. (J). (gr. 5-12). 17.99 *(978-0-7566-9792-1(1))* Dorling Kindersley Publishing, Inc.

Noonan, Julia. Baby Bat's Lullaby. Mitchard, Jacquelyn. 2004. 32p. (J). (gr. -1-1). lib. bdg. 16.89 *(978-0-06-050761-9(6))* HarperCollins Pubs.

—Over the Rainbow. Harburg, E. Y. & Arlen, Harold. 2004. 24p. (J). (gr. 4-8). reprint ed. 16.00 *(978-0-7567-7340-3(7))* DIANE Publishing Co.

—Over the Rainbow. Harburg, E. Y. Date not set. 32p. (J). 5.99 *(978-0-06-443677-9(2))* HarperCollins Pubs.

—Sweetwater. Yep, Laurence. 2004. 191p. (J). pap. 5.99 *(978-0-06-056029-4(0))* HarperCollins Pubs.

Noone, Cathleen L. Among the Buildings That Touch the Sky: Philadelphia. Kelly, Elaine A. & Carl, Jean R. 2009. *(978-0-578-06873-2(7))* U. S. ISBN Agency.

Noordeman, Jelmer, et al. Unusual Creatures: A Mostly Accurate Account of Some of the Earth's Strangest Animals. Hearst, Michael. 2012. (ENG.). 112p. (J). (gr. 3-7). 17.99 *(978-1-4521-0467-6(0))* Chronicle Bks. LLC.

Norberg, Ken. Angel George Series James Needs a Miracle. Lynn, Debbie. 2006. (J). 15.95 *(978-0-9771318-9-1(0))* Hope Harvest Publishing.

Norbu, Tenzing. Shantideva: How to Wake up a Hero. Townshend, Dominique. 2015. (ENG.). 64p. (J). 22.95 ***(978-1-61429-058-2(X))*** Wisdom Pubns.

Norcross, David. Dylan Discovers His Brain ! Almarode, John. 2010. 28p. pap. 12.99 *(978-1-4490-5491-5(9))* AuthorHouse.

Norcross, Harry. The Nature of Study Skills: Hardworking Helen K Honeybee Study Skills 3. Cali, Charlene C. 56p. (J). (gr. 8-9). 14.95 *(978-1-57543-101-7(7))* MAR*CO Products, Inc.

Nord, Mary. ABC Talking Book Adventures. McTaggart, Stephen & McTaggart, Debra. (Talking Book Adventures Ser.). 12p. (J). (gr. -1-18). 16.95 *(978-0-9627001-2-5(6))* Futech Educational Products, Inc.

—Bookee Presents 1, 2, 3 Count with Me. McTaggart, Stephen & McTaggart, Debra. (Talking Book Adventures Ser.). 14p. (J). (gr. -1-18). 16.95 *(978-0-9627001-3-2(4))* Futech Educational Products, Inc.

—Bookee Presents Colors, Shapes & Sounds. Kidd, Ron. (Talking Book Adventures Ser.). 12p. (J). (gr. -1-18). 16.95 *(978-0-9627001-1-8(8))* Futech Educational Products, Inc.

—Bookee's Sounds Around. McTaggart, Stephen & McTaggart, Debra. (Talking Book Adventures Ser.). 12p. (J). (gr. -1-18). 16.95 *(978-0-9627001-0-1(X))* Futech Educational Products, Inc.

Nordenstrom, Michael. Hina & the Sea of Stars. Nordenstrom, Michael, adapted by. 2003. 32p. 10.95 *(978-1-57306-167-4(0))* Bess Pr., Inc.

Nordhagen, Ted, jt. illus. see Ross, Gary.

Nordll, Ernest. Roy Rogers on the Double-R Ranch. Beecher, Elizabeth. 2011. 78p. 37.95 *(978-1-258-03590-7(1))* Literary Licensing, LLC.

Nordqvist, Sven. Findus Plants Meatballs. Nordqvist, Sven. Large, Nathan, tr. from SWE. 2013. (ENG.). 28p. (J). (gr. -1-3). *(978-1-907359-29-3(X))* Hawthorn Pr.

—Pancakes for Findus. Nordqvist, Sven. 2008. (Findus & Pettson Ser.). (ENG.). 28p. (J). *(978-1-903458-79-2(X))* Hawthorn Pr.

Noreika, Robert. Marsh Morning. Berkes, Marianne. 2011. (ENG.). 32p. (J). (gr. k-3). pap. 6.95 *(978-0-7613-7462-6(0)*, Millbrook Pr.) Lerner Publishing Group.

—Marsh Music. Berkes, Marianne. 2011. (ENG.). 32p. (J). (gr. k-3). pap. 6.95 *(978-0-7613-7461-9(2)*, Millbrook Pr.) Lerner Publishing Group.

—Seashells by the Seashore. Berkes, Marianne Collins. 2004. (Sharing Nature with Children Book Ser.). 32p. (J). (gr. -1-5). 16.95 *(978-1-58469-035-1(6))*; pap. 8.95 *(978-1-58469-034-4(8))* Dawn Pubns.

Norell, Aaron. Guardian Angels Vol. 1: True Stories of Guidance & Protection. Smitten, Susan. rev. ed. 2004. (Ghost Stories Ser.). (ENG.). 224p. (J). (gr. 4). pap. *(978-1-894877-59-6(4))* Lone Pine Publishing.

—Urban Legends: Strange Stories Behind Modern Myths, Vol. 1. Mott, A. S. rev. ed. 2004. (Ghost Stories Ser.). (ENG.). 232p. (J). (gr. 4). pap. *(978-1-894877-41-1(1))* Ghost Hse. Bks CAN. Dist: Lone Pine Publishing.

—Werewolves & Shapeshifters, Vol. 1. Zenko, Darren. rev. ed. 2004. (Ghost Stories Ser.). (ENG.). 216p. (J). (gr. 4). pap. *(978-1-894877-53-4(5))* Lone Pine Publishing.

Norheim, Karen. Clarabelle the Cat Loses Her Hair. Theis, Patricia & Theis, Matthew. 2008. 24p. pap. 12.95 *(978-1-59858-865-1(6))* Dog Ear Publishing, LLC.

Norie, Rooney. Gracie's Hill. Knights, Nancy. 2007. 28p. per. 7.95 *(978-1-58275-192-4(7))* Black Forest Pr.

Noriega, Fernando. Poemas para la Paz. Torices, José Gonzalez et al. 2004.Tr. of Poems for Peace. (SPA.). 68p. (J). (gr. 2-3). 14.99 *(978-84-241-8726-2(1))* Everest Editora ESP. Dist: Lectorum Pubns., Inc.

Norling, Beth. Ghost Hunter. Hunt, Julie. 2011. (Little Else Ser.: 3). (ENG.). 80p. (J). (gr. 2-4). 10.99 *(978-1-74175-878-8(5))* Allen & Unwin AUS. Dist: Independent Pubs. Group.

—Naked Bunyip Dancing. Herrick, Steven. 2008. (ENG.). 208p. (J). (gr. 3-7). 16.95 *(978-1-59078-499-0(5)*, Front Street) Boyds Mills Pr.

—On the Run. Hunt, Julie. 2011. (Little Else Ser.: 2). (ENG.). 64p. (J). (gr. 2-4). 10.99 *(978-1-74175-876-4(9))* Allen & Unwin AUS. Dist: Independent Pubs. Group.

—The Simple Things. Condon, Bill. 2015. 168p. (J). (gr. 3-5). 9.99 *(978-1-74331-724-2(7))* Allen & Unwin AUS. Dist: Independent Pubs. Group.

—Trick Rider. Hunt, Julie. 2011. (Little Else Ser.: 1). (ENG.). 64p. (J). (gr. 2-4). 10.99 *(978-1-74175-877-1(7))* Allen & Unwin AUS. Dist: Independent Pubs. Group.

Norling, Beth. Las Hermanitas Son... Norling, Beth. 2008. (SPA & ENG.). 24p. (J). (gr. -1-1). 4.99 *(978-1-933605-93-7(6)*, Libros del Mundo) Kane Miller.

—Los Hermanitos Son... Norling, Beth. 2008. (SPA & ENG.). 24p. (J). (gr. -1-1). bds. 4.99 *(978-1-933605-92-0(8)*, Libros del Mundo) Kane Miller.

—The Stone Baby. Norling, Beth. 2004. 32p. (J). (gr. k-2). *(978-0-7344-0353-7(4)*, Lothian Children's Bks.) Hachette Australia.

Norman, Dean. In the Dark Cave, 1 vol. Watson, Richard A. 2005. (ENG.). 32p. (J). (gr. -1-2). 5.95 *(978-1-59572-038-2(3))* Star Bright Bks., Inc.

Norman, Justin & Starkings, Richard. Solstice. Seagle, Steven T. 2005. per. 12.95 *(978-0-9766761-1-9(7))* Active Images.

Norman, Vera Stone. Guide Book for Language, Grade Three: Shepherd-Parkman Language Series. Parkman, Mary Rosetta. 2011. 236p. 46.95 *(978-1-258-08037-2(0))* Literary Licensing, LLC.

Normand, Hal. Souvenirs from Space: The Oscar E. Monnig Meteorite Gallery. Alter, Judy. 2007. (ENG.). 24p. (J). (gr. 4-7). pap. 4.95 *(978-0-87565-346-4(4))* Texas Christian Univ. Pr.

Normand, Jean-Pierre. Polaris: A Celebration of Polar Science, 1 vol. Czerneda, Julie E., ed. 2007. (ENG.). 173p. (J). (gr. -1). per. 6.95 *(978-0-88995-372-7(4))* Red Deer Pr. CAN. Dist: Ingram Pub. Services.

Norona, Bill, jt. illus. see Alley, Ashleigh.

Norridge, Terry. Assalamu Alaykum. Kayani, M. S. Hewitt, Ibrahim, ed. 2nd ed. 2009. (ENG.). 22p. (J). (gr. -1-1). 8.95 *(978-0-86037-347-6(9))* Kube Publishing Ltd. GBR. Dist: Consortium Bk. Sales & Distribution.

—Muslim Nursery Rhymes. McDermott, Mustafa Yusuf. 2nd ed. 2009. (ENG.). 29p. (J). (gr. -1-k). 8.95 *(978-0-86037-342-1(8))* Kube Publishing Ltd. GBR. Dist: Consortium Bk. Sales & Distribution.

Norrington, Leonie. Dino-School - Counting. Bedford, David & Worthington, Leonie. 2012. (Dino-School Ser.). (ENG.). 22p. (J). (— 1). bds. 8.99 *(978-1-921894-30-5(X))* Hardie Grant Egmont Pty. Ltd. AUS. Dist: Independent Pubs. Group.

Norris, Aaron, jt. illus. see Jones, Penny.

Norris, Judy-Jo Harris. The CBARCs of Cannon Bay: Storm Clouds over Cannon Bay, 5 bks, Bk.3. Norris, David A. 2012. 128p. (YA). pap. 16.95 *(978-1-937493-30-1(X))* Dancing Moon Pr.

Norstrand, Torstein. The Curse of the King. Lerangis, Peter. 2015. (Seven Wonders Ser.: Bk. 4). (ENG.). 320p. (J). (gr. 3-7). 17.99 *(978-0-06-207049-4(5))* HarperCollins Pubs.

—Lost in Babylon. Lerangis, Peter. 2014. (Seven Wonders Ser.: 2). (ENG.). 400p. (J). (gr. 3-7). pap. 6.99 *(978-0-06-207044-9(4))* HarperCollins Pubs.

—The Tomb of Shadows. Lerangis, Peter. (Seven Wonders Ser.: 3). (ENG.). (J). (gr. 3-7). 2015. 368p. pap. 6.99

(978-0-06-207047-0(9)); 2014. 304p. 17.99 *(978-0-06-207046-3(0))* HarperCollins Pubs.

Norstrand, Torstein & Reagan, Mike. The Colossus Rises. Lerangis, Peter. 2013. (Seven Wonders Ser.: 1). (ENG.). 384p. (J). (gr. 3-7). pap. 6.99 *(978-0-06-207041-8(X))* HarperCollins Pubs.

Norstrand, Torstein, jt. illus. see Reagan, Mike.

North, Ryan. Dinosaur Comics. North, Ryan. 2005. 112p. 14.99 *(978-0-7560-0518-4(3))* Teacher's Discovery.

Northcott, Ed. Degrassi the Next Generation Extra Credit Suddenly, Last Summer. Torres, J. 2nd ed. 2006. (Degrassi the Next Generation Ser.). (ENG.). 128p. (J). pap. *(978-1-55168-320-1(2))* Fenn, H. B. & Co., Ltd.

Northcutt, Leslie L., jt. illus. see Taylor, David W., Jr.

Northfield, Gary. Derek the Sheep. Northfield, Gary. 2009. (ENG.). 64p. (J). (gr. k-2). 16.95 *(978-0-7475-9424-6(4))* Bloomsbury Publishing Plc GBR. Dist: Independent Pubs. Group.

Northway, Jennifer. That's Mine! 2011. (ENG.). 32p. (J). (gr. -1-k). 16.95 *(978-1-84780-215-6(X)*, Frances Lincoln) Quarto Publishing Group UK GBR. Dist: Hachette Bk. Group.

Norton, Carolyn. A Kid's Multicultural Math Adventure: Amazing Activities to Explore Math's Global Roots! McCallum, Ann. 2004. (Williamson Multicultural Kids Can! Book Ser.). 128p. (J). pap. 14.95 *(978-1-885593-92-4(9)*, Williamson Bks.) Ideals Pubns.

Norton, Carolyn McIntyre. The Secret Life of Math: Discover How (and Why) Numbers Have Survived from the Cave Dwellers to Us! McCallum, Ann. 2005. (Kids Can Ser.). (ENG.). 128p. (J). (gr. 3-7). per. 14.25 *(978-0-8249-6755-0(0))*; (gr. 4-7). 14.95 *(978-0-8249-6779-6(8))* Ideals Pubns. (Williamson Bks.).

Norton, Dorothy S. Ice Age Mammals of North America: A Guide to the Big, the Hairy, & the Bizarre, Vol. 1. Lange, Ian. rev. ed. 224p. (J). (gr. 4). pap. *(978-0-87842-403-0(2)*, 329) Mountain Pr. Publishing Co., Inc.

—Rocks from Space: Meteorites & Meteorite Hunters. Norton, O. Richard. Ort, Kathleen & Carey, Jennifer, eds. 2nd rev. ed. 467p. (J). (gr. 4-12). pap. 32.00 *(978-0-87842-373-6(7)*, 325) Mountain Pr. Publishing Co., Inc.

Norton, Mike. By Hook or by Web, 1 vol. Baltazar, Art & Aureliani, Franco. 2012. (Young Justice Ser.). (ENG.). 32p. (gr. 2-3). 21.27 *(978-1-4342-4556-4(X))* Stone Arch Bks.

—Hack & You Shall Find, 1 vol. Baltazar, Art & Aureliani, Franco. 2012. (Young Justice Ser.). (ENG.). 32p. (gr. 2-3). 21.27 *(978-1-4342-4555-7(1))* Stone Arch Bks.

—Haunted, 1 vol. Baltazar, Art & Aureliani, Franco. 2012. (Young Justice Ser.). (ENG.). 32p. (gr. 2-3). lib. bdg. 21.27 *(978-1-4342-4553-3(5))* Stone Arch Bks.

—Mega Man 5: Rock of Ages. Flynn, Ian. 2013. (Mega Man Ser.: 5). (ENG.). 104p. (gr. 4-7). pap. 11.99 *(978-1-936975-48-8(3)*, Archie Comics) Archie Comic Pubns., Inc.

—Monkey Business, 1 vol. Baltazar, Art & Aureliani, Franco. 2012. (Young Justice Ser.). (ENG.). 32p. (gr. 2-3). 21.27 *(978-1-4342-4554-0(3))* Stone Arch Bks.

Norton, Mike, jt. illus. see Alphona, Adrian.

Noruzi, Charlotte. Necessary Noise: Stories about Our Families as They Really Are. Cart, Michael. 2003. 256p. (J). (gr. 12-18). lib. bdg. 16.89 *(978-0-06-027500-6(6))* HarperCollins Pubs.

—Necessary Noise: Stories about Our Families as They Really Are. Cart, Michael. 2006. (ENG.). 256p. (YA). (gr. 8-12). reprint ed. pap. 8.99 *(978-0-06-051437-2(X)*, HarperTeen) HarperCollins Pubs.

Noto, Phil. Wolverine & Jubilee: Curse of the Mutants. Immonen, Kathryn. 2011. (ENG.). 96p. (YA). (gr. 8-17). pap., pap. 14.99 *(978-0-7851-5546-1(5))* Marvel Worldwide, Inc.

—Wolverine & Jubilee: Curse of the Mutants. 2011. (ENG.). 120p. (YA). (gr. 8-17). 19.99 *(978-0-7851-5775-5(1))* Marvel Worldwide, Inc.

Nouf, Feras. My Bonus Mom! Taking the Step Out of Stepmom. Butcher, Tami. 2011. (ENG.). 56p. (J). 16.95 *(978-1-58985-081-1(5))* Five Star Pubns., Inc.

Nourigat, Natalie. Debt Dangers: A Book in the Series Marvels of Money ... for Kids. Nourigat, Paul. 2012. (Marvels of Money for Kids Ser.: 4). (ENG.). 38p. (J). lib. bdg. 12.29 *(978-1-936872-03-9(X))* FarBeyond Publishing LLC.

—Earning Excitement: a book in the series Marvels of Money ... for Kids. Nourigat, Paul. 2014. (Marvels of Money for Kids Ser.: 1). 38p. (J). pap. 9.29 *(978-1-936872-21-3(8))* FarBeyond Publishing LLC.

—Earning Excitement: A Book in the Series Marvels of Money ... for Kids. Nourigat, Paul. l.t. ed. 2012. (Marvels of Money for Kids Ser.: 1). (ENG.). 38p. (J). 12.29 *(978-1-936872-01-5(3))* FarBeyond Publishing LLC.

—Giving Greatness: A Book in the Series Marvels of Money ... for Kids. Nourigat, Paul. 2012. (Marvels of Money for Kids Ser.: 3). (ENG.). 38p. (J). lib. bdg. 12.29 *(978-1-936872-04-6(8))* FarBeyond Publishing LLC.

—Spending Success: A Book in the Series Marvels of Money ... for Kids. Nourigat, Paul. 2014. (Marvels of Money for Kids Ser.: 2). 38p. (J). pap. *(978-1-936872-22-0(6))* FarBeyond Publishing LLC.

—Terrific Tools for Money: A Book in the Series Marvels of Money ... for Kids. Nourigat, Paul. 2012. (Marvels of Money for Kids Ser.: 5). (ENG.). 38p. (J). lib. bdg. 12.89 *(978-1-936872-05-3(6))* FarBeyond Publishing LLC.

—Wrapped up in You. Jolley, Dan. 2012. (My Boyfriend Is a Monster Ser.: 6). (ENG.). 128p. (YA). (gr. 7-12). pap. 9.95 *(978-0-8225-9425-3(0))*; lib. bdg. 29.27 *(978-0-7613-6856-4(6))* Lerner Publishing Group. (Graphic Universe).

Novak, Matt. No Zombies Allowed. Novak, Matt. 2014. (ENG.). 32p. (J). (gr. -1-1). 16.99 *(978-1-4814-2540-7(4)*, Atheneum Bks. for Young Readers) Simon & Schuster Children's Publishing.

—A Wish for You. Novak, Matt. 2010. 32p. (J). 16.99 *(978-0-06-155202-1(X)*, Greenwillow Bks.) HarperCollins Pubs.

Novak, Steven. A Caring Deed for Becky. Widgen, Susan. 2012. 36p. pap. 8.99 *(978-1-60820-579-0(7))* MLR Pr., LLC.

Novak, Steven. Snow Man Is My Friend. Novak, Steven. l.t. ed. 2011. (ENG.). 38p. pap. 8.99 *(978-0-615-55460-0(1))* Quiet Corner Pr.

Novoa, Teresa. Azul. (Cocorolos Ser.). (SPA.). 12p. (J). (gr. -1-k). bds. 7.95 *(978-84-294-6923-3(0))* Santillana USA Publishing Co., Inc.

—Una Buena Costumbre. Paloma, David & Paloma Sanllehi, David. 2003. (Caballo Alado Series-Al Galope Ser.). (SPA & ENG.). 24p. (J). (gr. k-2). pap. 5.95 *(978-84-7864-671-5(X))* Combel Editorial, S.A. ESP. Dist: Independent Pubs. Group.

—Rojo. (Cocorolos Ser.). (SPA.). 12p. (J). (gr. -1-k). bds. 7.95 *(978-84-294-6921-9(4))* Santillana USA Publishing Co., Inc.

Novoa, Teresa. Si Ves un Monte de Espuma y Otros Poemas. Novoa, Teresa, tr. Garralón, Ana et al. (SPA.). 127p. (J). *(978-84-207-0019-9(3)*, GS31219) Grupo Anaya, S.A. ESP. Dist: Lectorum Pubns., Inc.

Nowak, Cheri. The Horseshoe. Nelson, Suzanne. 2012. (J). 14.95 *(978-1-937406-49-3(0))* Mascot Bks., Inc.

Nowakowski, Voytek. Flight of the Outcasts, 1 vol. McGrath, Alister. 2011. (Aedyn Chronicles Ser.). (ENG.). 176p. (J). (gr. 4-7). 14.99 *(978-0-310-71813-0(9))* Zondervan.

Noyes, Deborah. African Acrostics: A Word in Edgeways. Noyes, Deborah, photos by. Harley, Avis. ed. 2012. lib. bdg. 18.40 *(978-0-606-23808-3(5)*, Turtleback) Turtleback Bks.

Noyes, Deborah, photos by. African Acrostics: A Word in Edgeways. Harley, Avis. 2012. (ENG., 40p. (J). (gr. 3-7). pap. 7.99 *(978-0-7636-5818-2(9))* Candlewick Pr.

Noyes, Diana. The Tickle Bug. Noyes, Diana. l.t. ed. 2005. 20p. (J). per. 9.99 *(978-1-59879-080-1(3))* Lifevest Publishing, Inc.

Noyes, Eli. From Wibbleton to Wobbleton: Adventures with the Elements of Music & Movement. Harding, James. 2014. (Pentatonic Press Integrated Learning Ser.: 3). (ENG.). 201p. pap. 32.00 *(978-0-9773712-5-9(5))* Pentatonic Pr.

Noyes, Leighton. Bubbles in the Bathroom. Martineau, Susan. 2011. (Everyday Science Experiments Ser.). (ENG.). 24p. (J). (gr. 3-6). pap. 10.60 *(978-1-61533-409-4(2))*; lib. bdg. 25.25 *(978-1-61533-371-4(1))* Windmill Bks.

—Bugs in the Garden. Martineau, Susan. 2011. (Everyday Science Experiments Ser.). (ENG.). 24p. (J). (gr. 3-6). pap. 10.60 *(978-1-61533-408-7(4))*; lib. bdg. 25.25 *(978-1-61533-370-7(3))* Windmill Bks.

—Fizz in the Kitchen. Martineau, Susan. 2011. (Everyday Science Experiments Ser.). (ENG.). 24p. (J). (gr. 3-6). pap. 10.60 *(978-1-61533-411-7(4)*, 1328714); lib. bdg. 25.25 *(978-1-61533-373-8(8)*, 1328714) Windmill Bks.

—Julius Caesar's Sandals. Bailey, Gerry & Foster, Karen. 2008. (Stories of Great People Ser.). (ENG.). 40p. (J). (gr. 3-6). pap. *(978-0-7787-3717-9(9))*; lib. bdg. *(978-0-7787-3695-0(4))* Crabtree Publishing Co.

—Shadows in the Bedroom. Martineau, Susan. 2011. (Everyday Science Experiments Ser.). (ENG.). 24p. (J). (gr. 3-6). pap. 10.60 *(978-1-61533-410-0(6))*; lib. bdg. 25.25 *(978-1-61533-372-1(X))* Windmill Bks.

—50 French Phrases: Games & Activities to Teach Language Essentials. Martineau, Susan. 2009. (ENG.). 32p. (J). (gr. 2-7). pap. 7.99 *(978-0-7641-4340-3(9))* Barron's Educational Series, Inc.

Noyes, Leighton & Radford, Karen. Columbus's Chart. Bailey, Gerry & Foster, Karen. 2008. (Stories of Great People Ser.). 37p. (J). (gr. 3-7). 20.80 *(978-1-4178-0889-2(6)*, Turtleback) Turtleback Bks.

—Galileo's Telescope. Bailey, Gerry & Foster, Karen. 2008. (Stories of Great People Ser.). (ENG.). 40p. (J). (gr. 3-6). lib. bdg. *(978-0-7787-3694-3(6))*; pap. *(978-0-7787-3716-2(0))* Crabtree Publishing Co.

—Marco Polo's Silk Purse. Bailey, Gerry & Foster, Karen. 2008. (Stories of Great People Ser.). 37p. (J). (gr. 3-7). 20.80 *(978-1-4178-0891-5(8)*, Turtleback) Turtleback Bks.

—Mother Teresa's Alms Bowl. Ganeri, Anita. 2008. (Stories of Great People Ser.). 37p. (J). (gr. 3-7). 19.85 *(978-1-4178-0893-9(4)*, Turtleback) Turtleback Bks.

—Mozart's Wig. Bailey, Gerry & Foster, Karen. 2008. (Stories of Great People Ser.). (ENG.). 40p. (J). (gr. 3-6). lib. bdg. *(978-0-7787-3696-7(2))* Crabtree Publishing Co.

—Queen Victoria's Diamond. Bailey, Gerry & Foster, Karen. 2008. (Stories of Great People Ser.). (ENG.). 40p. (J). (gr. 3-6). lib. bdg. *(978-0-7787-3697-4(0))*; pap. *(978-0-7787-3719-3(5))* Crabtree Publishing Co.

Noyes, Leighton, jt. illus. see Radford, Karen.

Nugent, Cynthia. The Aunts Come Marching. Richardson, Bill. 2007. (ENG.). 32p. (J). (gr. -1-3). 15.95 *(978-1-55192-990-3(2))* Raincoast Bk. Distribution CAN. Dist: Perseus-PGW.

—The Emerald Curse, 1 vol. Rose, Simon. 2006. (ENG.). 115p. (J). (gr. 3-6). per. 7.95 *(978-1-896580-90-6(4))* Tradewind Bks. CAN. Dist: Orca Bk. Pubs. USA.

—I Want to Go to the Moon. Saunders, Tom. 2012. (ENG.). 32p. (J). (gr. -1-2). 16.95 *(978-1-897476-56-7(6))* Simply Read Bks. CAN. Dist: Ingram Pub. Services.

—Mister Got to Go: The Cat that Wouldn't Leave, 1 vol. Simmie, Lois. 2003. (ENG.). 32p. (J). (gr. -1-3). pap. 9.95 *(978-0-88995-157-0(8))* Red Deer Pr. CAN. Dist: Ingram Pub. Services.

—Mr Got to Go Where Are You, 1 vol. Simmie, Lois. 2014. (ENG.). 32p. (J). 19.95 *(978-0-88995-490-8(9))* Red Deer Pr. CAN. Dist: Ingram Pub. Services.

—A Time to Be Brave. Stuchner, Joan Betty. 2014. (Stepping Stone Book(TM) Ser.). (ENG.). 112p. (J). (gr. 2-5). 4.99 *(978-0-385-39205-1(2)*, Random Hse. Bks. for Young Readers) Random Hse. Children's Bks.

Nugent, Suzanne. Cup of Death. Gilligan, Shannon. 2006. (Choose Your Own Adventure Ser.). 120p. (J). (gr. 2-7). per. 6.99 *(978-1-933390-70-3(0))* Chooseco LLC.

Nugent, Suzanne & Donploypetch, Jintanan. Search for the Mountain Gorillas. Wallace, Jim. 2008. (Choose Your Own Adventure Ser.: No. 25). 125p. (J). (gr. 4-7). pap. 6.99 *(978-1-933390-25-3(5))* Chooseco LLC.

Nugent, Suzanne & Marron, Jose. Secret of the Ninja. Leibold, Jay. 2007. (Choose Your Own Adventure Ser.: Vol. 16). 124p. (J). (gr. 4-7). per. 6.99 *(978-1-933390-16-1(6))* Chooseco LLC.

Numberman, Neil. Flip & Fin: Super Sharks to the Rescue! Gill, Timothy. 2016. 32p. (J). (gr. -1-3). 15.99 ***(978-0-06-224301-0(2)**, Collins Design)* HarperCollins Pubs.

Numberman, Neil. Flip & Fin: We Rule the School! Gill, Timothy. 2014. (ENG.). 32p. (J). (gr. -1-3). 14.99 *(978-0-06-224300-3(4)*, Greenwillow Bks.) HarperCollins Pubs.

—In Big Hairy Drama. Reynolds, Aaron. 2010. (Joey Fly, Private Eye Ser.: 2). (ENG.). 128p. (J). (gr. 2-4). pap. 14.99 *(978-0-8050-9110-6(6))* Square Fish.

Numberman, Neil, jt. illus. see Weaver, Brian M.

Nuñez, Ruddy. El mejor regalo del mundo: La leyenda de la vieja Belén. Alvarez, Julia. 2013. (ENG & SPA.). (J). pap. 12.95 *(978-1-62263-149-0(8)*, Alfaguara) Santillana USA Publishing Co., Inc.

Nunez, Jose Luis. Cuando Mi Mama Me Lee/When My Mama Reads to Me. Elkus, Julie. Fagin, Cristina, tr. from ENG. 2005. (SPA & ENG.). 24p. (J). (gr. -1-3). 8.95 *(978-1-933197-06-7(4))* Orange Frazer Pr.

Núñez, Pablo. El Guardián de la Luna. Núñez, Pablo, tr. Sierra i Fabra, Jordi. (SPA.). 80p. 15.95 *(978-84-207-6282-1(2))* Grupo Anaya, S.A. ESP. Dist: Distribooks, Inc.

Nuñez, Ruddy. El Mejor Regalo del Mundo; The Best Gift of All: La Leyenda de la Vieja Belen; The Legend of La Vieja Belen. Alvarez, Julia. Espaillat, Rhina P., tr. 2009. (Bilingual Bks). (SPA & ENG.). 32p. (gr. 3-5). 14.99 *(978-1-60396-325-1(1))* Santillana USA Publishing Co., Inc.

Nuñez, Veronica. Saving Sleepy Walter: Fitztown Fairies Tale. Fitzsimons, Morgan. 2010. (ENG.). 32p. pap. 9.99 *(978-1-4528-5756-5(3))* CreateSpace Independent Publishing Platform.

Nunn, Paul. Firefighter Gil! (Bubble Guppies) Tillworth, Mary. 2013. (Pictureback(R) Ser.). (ENG.). 24p. (J). (gr. -1-2). 3.99 *(978-0-449-81770-4(9)*, Random Hse. Bks. for Young Readers) Random Hse. Children's Bks.

Nunn, Paul, jt. illus. see Random House Staff.

Nunn, Paul E. Uncle Arthur's Art Studio. Forrester, Emma. 2008. (Spiderwick Chronicles). (ENG.). 48p. (J). (gr. 2-7). 10.99 *(978-1-4169-4955-8(0)*, Simon Scribbles) Simon Scribbles.

Nunnally, Carson. How Sparkles Came About: The Adventures of Sparkles. Wellings, Chris R. 2011. 32p. pap. 24.95 *(978-1-4560-4119-9(3))* America Star Bks.

Nurullah, Seitu. Froggie Sang Tenor. Fogerty, Ramona. 2005. (FRE.). (J). per. 15.00 *(978-0-9759889-0-9(5))* Potential Psychotherapy Counseling & Remedial Service.

Nutt, Don. Eagles of Lincoln. Hammer, Larry. l.t. ed. 2011. (ENG.). 36p. pap. 6.95 *(978-1-4637-2716-1(X))* CreateSpace Independent Publishing Platform.

Nutt, Robert. Amy's Light. Nutt, Robert. 2010. 44p. (J). (gr. -1-3). 16.95 *(978-1-58469-128-0(X))*; pap. 8.95 *(978-1-58469-129-7(8))* Dawn Pubns.

Nyamor, Eric. The Adventures of Princess Zari. Pope, Cheryl Lynn. 2009. 34p. pap. 12.99 *(978-0-9840660-1-8(2))* Second Time Media & Communications.

—Choices: Upper Elementary. Jackson, Sharinese. 2010. 112p. pap. 12.95 *(978-0-9840660-3-2(9))* Second Time Media & Communications.

Nye, Penny. My Kindergarten Year. 2003. 41p. (J). spiral bd. 7.00 net. *(978-1-890703-33-2(8)*, Bookmates) Penny Laine Papers, Inc.

Nyeu, Tao. Bunny Days. Nyeu, Tao. 2010. (ENG.). 48p. (J). (gr. -1-k). 16.99 *(978-0-8037-3330-5(5)*, Dial) Penguin Publishing Group.

Nyhus, Svein. What Does the Fox Say? Ylvis & Løchstøer, Christian. 2013. (ENG.). 32p. (J). (gr. -1-3). 17.99 *(978-1-4814-2223-9(5)*, Simon & Schuster Bks. For Young Readers) Simon & Schuster Bks. For Young Readers.

—Why Kings & Queens Don't Wear Crowns. Louise, Märtha. Sevig-Fajardo, Mari Elise, tr. from NOR. 2005. Orig. Title: Hvorfor de kongelige ikke har krone på Hodet. 32p. (J). 17.95 *(978-1-57534-037-1(2)*, CSC 100) Skandisk, Inc.

—Why Kings & Queens Don't Wear Crowns (with CD) Märtha Louise, Princess. Sevig-Fajardo, Mari Elise, tr. from NOR. 2006. Orig. Title: Fvorfor de kongelige ikke har krone på Hodet. 32p. (J). 19.95 incl. audio compact disk *(978-1-57534-038-8(0)*, CSC 100C) Skandisk, Inc.

Nyman, Ingrid. Do You Know Pippi Longstocking? Lindgren, Astrid. Dyssegaard, Elisabeth Kallick, tr. 2005. 32p. (J). pap. 4.95 *(978-91-29-66203-0(6))* R & S Bks. SWE. Dist: Macmillan.

O

O Donovan, Christina. Are You My Brown Bear? Ziefert, Harriet. 2015. (¡Hola, English! Ser.). (ENG & SPA.). 28p. (J). (gr. -1-3). 12.99 *(978-1-60905-512-7(8))* Blue Apple Bks.

Oakes, Terry. Classic Tales of Horror: A Pop-Up Book. Oakes, Terry. Delalandre, Benoit. 2011. (ENG.). 22p. (J). (gr. -1-2). 19.99 *(978-1-85707-729-2(6))* Tango Bks. GBR. Dist: Independent Pubs. Group.

Oakley, Graham. The Church Mouse. Oakley, Graham. 2010. (ENG.). 36p. (J). (gr. k-4). 9.99 *(978-1-935279-69-3(6))* Kane Miller.

Oakley, Jacqui. The Complete Novels of Jane Austen: Emma, Pride & Prejudice, Sense & Sensibility, Northanger Abbey, Mansfield Park, Persuasion, & Lady Susan, 0 vols. Austen, Jane. unabr. ed. 2012. (Heirloom Collection: 0). (ENG.). 1120p. 99.99 *(978-1-61218-414-2(6)*, 9781612184142) Amazon Publishing.

—Lighting Our World: A Year of Celebrations. Rondina, Catherine. 2012. (ENG.). 32p. (J). 17.95 *(978-1-55453-594-1(8))* Kids Can Pr., Ltd. CAN. Dist: Univ. of Toronto Pr.

Oapos, Jem, jt. illus. see Bronte, Jules.

Oatman, M. Scott. He Said Yes: The Story of Father Mychal Judge. Lynch, Kelly Ann. 2007. 32p. (J). (gr. -1-3). 12.95 *(978-0-8091-6740-1(9)*, 6740-1) Paulist Pr.

Obata, Claudia. The Lion's Drum: A Retelling of an African Folk Tale. Gregory, Steven. 2007. 32p. (J). 13.95 *(978-0-615-15540-1(5))* Words & Music.

Obata, Takeshi. Death Note, 13 vols. Ohba, Tsugumi. (Death Note Ser.). (ENG.). 200p. Vol. 1. 2005. pap. 9.99 *(978-1-4215-0168-0(6))*; Vol. 2. 2005. pap. 9.99 *(978-1-4215-0169-7(4))*; Vol. 3. 2006. pap. 9.99 *(978-1-4215-0170-3(8))* Viz Media.

—Hikaru No Go. Hotta, Yumi. (Hikaru No Go Ser.: 15). (ENG.). 2009. 216p. pap. 9.99 *(978-1-4215-2192-3(X))*; 2009. 216p. pap. 9.99 *(978-1-4215-1510-6(5))*; 2008. 200p. pap. 7.95 *(978-1-4215-1508-3(3))*; 2007. 208p. pap. 9.99 *(978-1-4215-1067-5(7))*; 2007. 208p. pap. 9.99 *(978-1-4215-1066-8(9))*; Vol. 1. 2004. 192p. pap. 9.99 *(978-1-59116-222-3(X))*; Vol. 2. 2004. 192p. pap. 9.99 *(978-1-59116-496-8(0))*; Vol. 5. 2005. 208p. pap. 9.99 *(978-1-59116-689-4(6))*; Vol. 6. 2006. 208p. pap. 7.95 *(978-1-4215-0275-5(5))*; Vol. 7. 2006. 208p. pap. 7.95 *(978-1-4215-0641-8(6))*; Vol. 8. 2006. 208p. pap. 7.95 *(978-1-4215-0642-5(4))*; Vol. 11. 2008. 208p. (gr. 4). pap. 7.95 *(978-1-4215-1068-2(5))* Viz Media.

—Hikaru No Go Vol. 4. Hotta, Yumi. 2005. (Hikaru No Go Ser.). (ENG.). 200p. pap. 9.99 *(978-1-59116-688-7(8))* Viz Media.

Obata, Takeshi, jt. illus. see Hotta, Yumi.

Obata, Takeshi, jt. illus. see Shindo, Hikaru.

Ober, Jonathan & Willoughby, Yuko. John & Betty Stam: Missionary Martyrs to China. Weitzel, Karen E. 2008. (ENG.). 52p. (J). pap. *(978-1-932381-12-2(0)*, 5190) Bible Visuals International, Inc.

Ober, Jonathan, jt. illus. see Hertzler, Frances B.

Oberdieck, Bernhard. The Princess & the Pea. 2007. (Classic Fairy Tale Collection). (ENG.). 24p. (J). (gr. -1-2). 14.95 *(978-1-4027-3065-8(9))* Sterling Publishing Co., Inc.

Oberdieck, Bernhard & Gordeev, Denis. A Princess Primer: A Fairy Godmother's Guide to Being a Princess. Peters, Stephanie True. 2006. (ENG.). 32p. (J). (gr. k-3). 19.99 *(978-0-525-47765-5(9)*, Dutton Juvenile) Penguin Publishing Group.

Oberlin, Linda. Eco in the Garden. Oberlin, Linda. 2013. 26p. pap. 10.00 *(978-0-9911382-0-3(1))* Little Worm Publishing.

Oberman, Sheldon & Cohen, Sheldon. The Flying Canoe. Fischman, Sheila, tr. from FRE. 2004. (ENG.). 24p. (J). (gr. 3-7). 15.95 *(978-0-88776-636-7(6)*, Tundra Bks.) Tundra Bks. CAN. Dist: Penguin Random Hse., LLC.

Obregón, José María. Cambio Climático: Los Gases de Efecto Invernadero y la Capa de Ozono. Faust, Daniel R. 2009. (Historietas Juveniles: Peligros Del Medioambiente (Jr. Graphic Environmental Dangers) Ser.). (SPA.). 24p. (gr. 3-6). (YA). lib. bdg. 25.25 *(978-1-4358-8462-5(0))*; pap. 10.60 *(978-1-4358-8463-2(9))* Rosen Publishing Group, Inc., The.

Obregon, Jose Maria. Mitologia Egipcia: Isis y Osiris. Daning, Tom. 2009. (Historietas Juveniles: Mitologías (Jr. Graphic Mythologies) Ser.). (SPA.). 24p. (J). (gr. 3-6). lib. bdg. 25.25 *(978-1-4358-8567-7(8))* Rosen Publishing Group, Inc., The.

—Mitología Africana: Anansi. Herdling, Glenn. 2009. (Historietas Juveniles: Mitologías (Jr. Graphic Mythologies) Ser.). (SPA.). 24p. (J). (gr. 3-6). 25.25 *(978-1-4358-8565-3(1))* Rosen Publishing Group, Inc., The.

Obregón, José María. Mitologia Mesoamericana: Quetzalcóatl. Daning, Tom. 2009. (Historietas Juveniles: Mitologías (Jr. Graphic Mythologies) Ser.). (SPA.). 24p. (J). (gr. 3-6). lib. bdg. 25.25 *(978-1-4358-8569-1(4))* Rosen Publishing Group, Inc., The.

—Mitologia Romana: Rómulo y Remo. Daning, Tom. 2009. (Historietas Juveniles: Mitologías (Jr. Graphic Mythologies) Ser.). (SPA.). 24p. (J). (gr. 3-6). lib. bdg. 25.25 *(978-1-4358-8570-7(8))* Rosen Publishing Group, Inc., The.

Obrero, Rudy. Sweet Dreams, Curious George. Anderson, R. P. 2005. (J). (gr. -1-k). pap. *(978-0-618-69493-8(5))* Houghton Mifflin Harcourt Trade & Reference Pubs.

O'Brien, Anne. Goodnight Kuu~Kuu: My Cozy All Day Village Safari. Njenga, Wamoro P. 2010. (ENG.). 40p. pap. 13.70 *(978-1-4528-9552-9(X))* CreateSpace Independent Publishing Platform.

O'Brien, Anne Sibley. Flower Garden. Havill, Juanita. 2015. 32p. pap. 7.00 ***(978-1-61003-503-3(8))*** Center for the Collaborative Classroom.

O'Brien, Anne Sibley. Jamaica Tag-Along, 1 vol. Havill, Juanita. 2011. (ENG.). 32p. (J). (gr. -1-3). 10.99 *(978-0-547-48105-0(5))* Houghton Mifflin Harcourt Publishing Co.

—Jamaica's Blue Marker. Havill, Juanita. 2003. (ENG.). 32p. (J). (gr. -1-3). pap. 6.95 *(978-0-618-36917-1(1))* Houghton Mifflin Harcourt Publishing Co.

—Jamaica's Find, 1 vol. Havill, Juanita. 2009. (Read along Book & CD Ser.). (ENG.). 32p. (J). (gr. -1-3). 10.99 *(978-0-547-11961-8(5))* Houghton Mifflin Harcourt Publishing Co.

—Jouanah: A Hmong Cinderella. Coburn, Jewell Reinhart & Lee, Tzexa Cherta. 2014. (ENG.). 32p. (J). pap. 8.95 *(978-1-885008-41-1(4)*, Shen's Bks.) Lee & Low Bks., Inc.

O

—Moon Watchers: Shirin's Ramadan Miracle, 1 vol. Jalali, Reza. 2010. (ENG.). 32p. (J). (gr. 2-7). 16.95 *(978-0-88448-321-2(5),* Harpswell Pr.) Tilbury Hse. Pubs.

—Talking Walls. Knight, Margy Burns. 2004. 34p. (gr. 3-8). 19.45 *(978-0-7569-4256-4(X))* Perfection Learning Corp.

—Talking Walls: Discover Your World. Knight, Margy Burns. 2014. 64p. (J). 18.95 *(978-0-88448-356-4(8))* Tilbury Hse. Pubs.

—Welcoming Babies, 1 vol. Burns Knight, Margy. 2005. (ENG.). 40p. (J). (gr. k-4). 7.95 *(978-0-88448-124-9(7))* Tilbury Hse. Pubs.

—What Will You Be, Sara Mee? Avraham, Kate Aver. 2010. (ENG.). 32p. (J). (gr. -1-3). 16.95 *(978-1-58089-210-0(8));* pap. 7.95 *(978-1-58089-211-7(6))* Charlesbridge Publishing, Inc.

—Who Belongs Here? Burns Knight, Margy et al. 2nd ed. 2005. 40p. (gr. 3-8). pap., tchr. ed., tchr.'s training gde. ed. 9.95 *(978-0-88448-111-9(5))* Tilbury Hse. Pubs.

—Who Belongs Here? An American Story. Knight, Margy Burns. 2004. 32p. 19.45 *(978-0-7569-2426-3(X))* Perfection Learning Corp.

O'Brien, Anne Sibley. I'm New Here. O'Brien, Anne Sibley. 2015. (ENG.). 32p. (J). (gr. k-3). lib. bdg. 16.95 *(978-1-58089-612-2(X))* Charlesbridge Publishing, Inc.

—The Legend of Hong Kil Dong: The Robin Hood of Korea. O'Brien, Anne Sibley. 2008. (ENG.). 48p. (J). (gr. 4-7). per. 8.95 *(978-1-58089-303-9(1))* Charlesbridge Publishing, Inc.

—A Path of Stars. O'Brien, Anne Sibley. 2012. (ENG.). 40p. (J). (gr. k-3). 15.95 *(978-1-57091-735-6(3))* Charlesbridge Publishing, Inc.

O'Brien, Anne Sibley & O'Brien, Perry Edmond. After Gandhi: One Hundred Years of Nonviolent Resistance. O'Brien, Anne Sibley & O'Brien, Perry Edmond. 2009. (ENG.). 192p. (J). (gr. 4-7). 24.95 *(978-1-58089-129-5(2))* Charlesbridge Publishing, Inc.

O'Brien, John. Abe Lincoln: His Wit & Wisdom from A to Z. Schroeder, Alan. 2015. (ENG.). 32p. (J). (gr. 1-5). 17.95 *(978-0-8234-2420-7(0))* Holiday Hse., Inc.

—Ben Franklin: His Wit & Wisdom from A to Z. Schroeder, Alan. 2011. (ENG.). 32p. (J). (gr. 1-5). 16.95 *(978-0-8234-1950-0(9))* Holiday Hse., Inc.

—Ben Franklin: His Wit & Wisdom from A-Z. Schroeder, Alan. 2012. (ENG.). 32p. (J). pap. 7.95 *(978-0-8234-2435-1(9))* Holiday Hse., Inc.

—Blockhead: The Life of Fibonacci. D'Agnese, Joseph. 2010. (ENG.). 40p. (J). (gr. 1-4). 17.99 *(978-0-8050-6305-9(6),* Holt, Henry & Co. Bks. For Young Readers) Holt, Henry & Co.

—The Cat in Numberland. Ekeland, Ivar. 2006. (ENG.). 56p. (J). (gr. 3-9). 19.95 *(978-0-8126-2744-2(X))* Cricket Bks.

—I Know a Shy Fellow Who Swallowed a Cello. Garriel, Barbara S. 2004. (ENG.). 32p. (J). (gr. k-3). 17.95 *(978-1-59078-043-5(4))* Boyds Mills Pr.

—I Know a Shy Fellow Who Swallowed a Cello. Garriel, Barbara. 2012. (ENG.). 32p. (J). (gr. k-2). pap. 6.95 *(978-1-59078-946-9(6))* Boyds Mills Pr.

—Our Liberty Bell. Magaziner, Henry Jonas. 2007. (ENG.). 32p. (J). (gr. 1-5). 5.95 *(978-0-8234-2081-0(7))* Holiday Hse., Inc.

—¿Quién Fue Mark Twain? (Who Was Mark Twain?) Prince, April Jones. 2009. (¿Quién Fue... ? / Who Was... ? Ser.). (SPA.). 112p. (gr. 3-5). pap. 9.99 *(978-1-60396-424-1(X))* Santillana USA Publishing Co., Inc.

—¿Quién Fue Tomás Jefferson? (Who Was Thomas Jefferson?) Fradin, Dennis Brindell. 2009. (¿Quién Fue... ? / Who Was... ? Ser.). (SPA.). 112p. (gr. 3-5). pap. 9.99 *(978-1-60396-425-8(8))* Santillana USA Publishing Co., Inc.

—Thomas Jefferson Builds a Library. Rosenstock, Barb. 2013. (ENG.). 32p. (J). (gr. 3-6). 16.95 *(978-1-59078-932-2(6),* Calkins Creek) Boyds Mills Pr.

—Who Was Abigail Adams? Kelley, True. 2014. (Who Was... ? Ser.). (ENG.). 112p. (J). (gr. 3-7). 5.99 *(978-0-448-47890-6(0),* Grosset & Dunlap) Penguin Publishing Group.

—Who Was Ben Franklin? Fradin, Dennis Brindell. 2003. (Who Was... ? Ser.). 105p. (gr. 4-7). 15.00 *(978-0-7569-1589-6(9))* Perfection Learning Corp.

—Who Was Elvis Presley? Edgers, Geoff. 2007. (Who Was... ? Ser.). 105p. (gr. 2-5). 15.00 *(978-0-7569-8164-8(6))* Perfection Learning Corp.

O'Brien, John, et al. Who Was Marco Polo? Holub, Joan. 2007. (Who Was... ? Ser.). (ENG.). 112p. (J). (gr. 3-7). pap. 5.99 *(978-0-448-44540-3(9),* Grosset & Dunlap) Penguin Publishing Group.

O'Brien, John. Who Was Marco Polo? Holub, Joan. 2007. (Who Was... ? Ser.). 105p. (gr. 4-7). 15.00 *(978-0-7569-8165-5(4))* Perfection Learning Corp.

—Who Was Mark Twain? Prince, April Jones. 2004. (Who Was... ? Ser.). 105p. (gr. 3-7). 16.00 *(978-0-7569-4590-9(9))* Perfection Learning Corp.

—Who Was Thomas Alva Edison? Frith, Margaret. 2005. (Who Was... ? Ser.). 106p. (gr. 3-7). 15.00 *(978-0-7569-5830-5(X))* Perfection Learning Corp.

—Who Was William Shakespeare? Mannis, Celeste Davidson & Davidson, Mannis. 2006. (Who Was... ? Ser.). (ENG.). 112p. (J). (gr. 3-7). pap. 5.99 *(978-0-448-43904-4(2),* Grosset & Dunlap) Penguin Publishing Group.

—Who Was William Shakespeare? Mannis, Celeste Davidson & Kramer, Sydelle. 2006. (Who Was... ? Ser.). 105p. (gr. 2-6). 15.00 *(978-0-7569-6952-3(2))* Perfection Learning Corp.

O'Brien, John. Who Were the Brothers Grimm? Reed, Avery. 2015. (Who Was... ? Ser.). (ENG.). 112p. (J). (gr. 3-7). 5.99 ***(978-0-448-48314-6(9),*** Grosset & Dunlap) Penguin Publishing Group.

O'Brien, John & Harrison, Nancy. Quién Fue Marco Polo? Holub, Joan. 2012. (Who Was... ? Ser.). (ENG & SPA.). 112p. (J). (gr. 3-7). pap. 7.99 *(978-0-448-46174-8(9),* Grosset & Dunlap) Penguin Publishing Group.

—Who Is Michelle Obama? Stine, Megan. 2013. (Who Was... ? Ser.). (ENG.). 112p. (J). (gr. 3-7). 4.99 *(978-0-448-47863-0(3),* Grosset & Dunlap) Penguin Publishing Group.

—Who Was Betsy Ross? Buckley, James, Jr. 2014. (Who Was... ? Ser.). (ENG.). 112p. (J). (gr. 3-7). 4.99 *(978-0-448-48243-9(6),* Grosset & Dunlap) Penguin Publishing Group.

—Who Was Elvis Presley? Edgers, Geoff. 2007. (Who Was... ? Ser.). (ENG.). 112p. (J). (gr. 3-7). pap. 5.99 *(978-0-448-44642-4(1),* Grosset & Dunlap) Penguin Publishing Group.

—Who Was Galileo? Demuth, Patricia Brennan. 2015. (Who Was... ? Ser.). (ENG.). 112p. (J). (gr. 3-7). 5.99 *(978-0-448-47985-9(0),* Grosset & Dunlap) Penguin Publishing Group.

O'Brien, John, jt. illus. see Harrison, Nancy.

O'Brien, John A. Air Is All Around You. Branley, Franklyn M. 2006. (Let's-Read-And-Find-Out Science 1 Ser.). (ENG.). 40p. (J). (gr. -1-3). pap. 5.99 *(978-0-06-059415-2(2),* Collins) HarperCollins Pubs.

—The Curious Adventures of Jimmy McGee. Estes, Eleanor. 2005. (ENG.). 224p. (J). (gr. 2-5). pap. 10.95 *(978-0-15-205517-2(7))* Houghton Mifflin Harcourt Publishing Co.

—The Fastest Game on Two Feet: And Other Poems about How Sports Began. Low, Alice. 2009. (ENG.). 40p. (J). (gr. 1-5). 17.95 *(978-0-8234-1905-0(3))* Holiday Hse., Inc.

—Our Liberty Bell. Magaziner, Henry Jonas. 2007. (ENG.). 32p. (J). (gr. 1-5). 15.95 *(978-0-8234-1892-3(8))* Holiday Hse., Inc.

—The Twelve Days of Christmas. 2003. (ENG.). 32p. (J). (gr. k-2). pap. 8.95 *(978-1-59078-086-2(8))* Boyds Mills Pr.

—Underwear: What We Wear under There. Swain, Ruth Freeman. 2008. (ENG.). 32p. (J). (gr. 1-5). 16.95 *(978-0-8234-1920-3(7))* Holiday Hse., Inc.

O'Brien, John A., et al. Who Was Thomas Alva Edison? Frith, Margaret. 2005. (Who Was... ? Ser.). (ENG.). 112p. (J). (gr. 3-7). pap. 5.99 *(978-0-448-43765-1(1),* Grosset & Dunlap) Penguin Publishing Group.

O'Brien, John A. & Harrison, Nancy. Who Was Helen Keller? Thompson, Gare. 2003. (Who Was... ? Ser.). (ENG.). 112p. (J). (gr. 3-7). pap. 5.99 *(978-0-448-43144-4(0),* Grosset & Dunlap) Penguin Publishing Group.

—Who Was Louis Armstrong? McDonough, Yona Zeldis. 2004. (Who Was... ? Ser.). (ENG.). 112p. (J). (gr. 3-7). pap. 5.99 *(978-0-448-43368-4(0),* Grosset & Dunlap) Penguin Publishing Group.

—Who Was Mark Twain? Prince, April Jones. 2004. (Who Was... ? Ser.). (ENG.). 112p. (J). (gr. 3-7). pap. 5.99 *(978-0-448-43319-6(2),* Grosset & Dunlap) Penguin Publishing Group.

O'Brien, Laurel. Chester's Field. Riley, Christine. 2004. 296p. (J). per. 17.50 *(978-0-9740683-6-7(5))* Authors & Artists Publishers of New York, Inc.

O'Brien, Patrick. Captain Raptor & the Moon Mystery. O'Malley, Kevin. 2005. (Captain Raptor Ser.). (ENG.). 32p. (J). (gr. k-5). 17.99 *(978-0-8027-8935-8(8))* Walker & Co.

—Captain Raptor & the Space Pirates. O'Malley, Kevin. 2007. (Captain Raptor Ser.). (ENG.). 32p. (J). (gr. k-3). 16.95 *(978-0-8027-9571-7(4))* Walker & Co.

O'Brien, Patrick. The Mutiny on the Bounty. O'Brien, Patrick. 2007. (ENG.). 40p. (J). (gr. 3-6). 17.95 *(978-0-8027-9587-8(0))* Walker & Co.

—You Are the First Kid on Mars. O'Brien, Patrick. 2009. (ENG.). 32p. (J). (gr. k-3). 16.99 *(978-0-399-24634-0(7),* Putnam Juvenile) Penguin Publishing Group.

O'Brien, Perry Edmond, jt. illus. see O'Brien, Anne Sibley.

O'Brien, Renee McMullen. The Amazing Mocha & His Courageous Journey. O'Brien, Renee McMullen. 2009. 28p. pap. 12.95 *(978-1-936051-60-1(5))* Peppertree Pr., The.

O'Brien, Tim. The Hunger Games. Collins, Suzanne. 2009. 384p. pap. *(978-1-4071-0908-4(1),* Scholastic) Scholastic, Inc.

—Moonshiner's Son. Reeder, Carolyn. 2003. (ENG.). 208p. (J). (gr. 3-7). pap. 6.99 *(978-0-689-85550-4(8),* Simon & Schuster/Paula Wiseman Bks.) Simon & Schuster/Paula Wiseman Bks.

Obrist, Jürg. Complex Cases: Three Major Mysteries for You to Solve. Obrist, Jürg. 2006. (Mini-Mysteries for You to Solve Ser.). (ENG.). 96p. (gr. 4-6). 23.93 *(978-0-7613-3419-4(X),* Millbrook Pr.) Lerner Publishing Group.

Oburkova, Eva. Toby's Travels Through Time: Puzzle Adventures in Dinosaur Days. Oburkova, Eva. 2007. (Toby's Travels Through Time: Puzzle Adventures in Dinosaur Days Ser.). 32p. (gr. k-3). lib. bdg. 28.00 *(978-0-8368-7497-6(8),* Gareth Stevens Learning Library) Stevens, Gareth Publishing LLLP.

O'Byrne, Nicola. Open Very Carefully: A Book with Bite. Bromley, Nick. 2013. (ENG.). 32p. (J). (gr. -1-2). 15.99 *(978-0-7636-6163-2(5),* Nosy Crow) Candlewick Pr.

O'Byrne, Nicola. Count & Color - Swim. O'Byrne, Nicola. 2013. (ENG.). 56p. (J). (gr. -1-k). pap. 9.99 *(978-1-60905-299-7(4))* Blue Apple Bks.

—Fly. O'Byrne, Nicola. 2013. (ENG.). 56p. (J). (gr. -1-k). pap. 9.99 *(978-1-60905-342-0(7))* Blue Apple Bks.

O'Byrne, Nicola. Use Your Imagination. O'Byrne, Nicola. 2015. (ENG.). 36p. (J). (gr. -1-2). 15.99 ***(978-0-7636-8001-5(X),*** Nosy Crow) Candlewick Pr.

O'Byrne, Nicola & Hudson, Katy. Animal Teachers. Halfmann, Janet. 2014. (ENG.). 36p. (J). (gr. -1-3). 17.99 *(978-1-60905-391-8(5))* Blue Apple Bks.

O'Callaghan, Gemma. Half a Man. Morpurgo, Michael. 2015. (ENG.). 64p. (J). (gr. 5). 16.99 *(978-0-7636-7747-3(7))* Candlewick Pr.

O'Callahan, Laura. Herman & Marguerite: An Earth Story, 1 vol. O'Callahan, Jay. 2003. (ENG.). 36p. (J). (gr. k-3). pap. 7.95 *(978-1-56145-283-5(1))* Peachtree Pubs.

Ocampo Ruiz, Jose Alfonso & Smith, Tod. Dracula, 1 vol. Fuentes, Benny & Stoker, Bram. 2008. (Classic Fiction Ser.). (ENG.). 72p. (gr. 2-3). pap. 6.95 *(978-1-4342-0498-1(7),* 1278680, Graphic Revolve) Stone Arch Bks.

Ocello, Salvatore & Nelligan, Kevin. Peppy Up: Eat Your Best, Be Your Best! Nelligan, Patty. 2013. 32p. pap. 12.95 *(978-1-939418-41-8(0))* Writer of the Round Table Pr.

Ochoa, Ana. Lupe Lupita, Where Are You?/Lupe Lupita, Donde Estas? Rosa-Mendoza, Gladys. 2005. (English-Spanish Foundations Ser.). (SPA & ENG.). 20p. (J). (gr. -1). bds. 6.95 *(978-1-931398-16-9(X))* Me+Mi Publishing.

—Lupe Lupita, Where Are You?/Lupe Lupita Donde Estas? Rosa-Mendoza, Gladys. 2007. (English Spanish Foundations Ser.). 20p. (gr. -1-k). pap. 19.95 *(978-1-931398-62-4(8))* Me+Mi Publishing.

—So Many Me's. Neasi, Barbara J. (Rookie Ready to Learn Ser.). (J). 2011. 40p. pap. 5.95 *(978-0-531-26677-9(X));* 2011. 40p. (gr. -1-k). lib. bdg. 23.00 *(978-0-531-26372-3(X));* 2003. 32p. 19.50 *(978-0-516-22883-9(8))* Scholastic Library Publishing. (Children's Pr.).

—Una Vaca Querida. Antillano, Laura. (Literary Encounters Ser.). (SPA.). (J). (gr. 3-5). pap. *(978-968-494-077-2(7),* CI7709) Centro de Informacion y Desarrollo de la Comunicacion y la Literatura MEX. Dist: Lectorum Pubns., Inc.

Ochoa, Ana. Muchas Veces Yo. Ochoa, Ana. Neasi, Barbara J. 2011. (Rookie Ready to Learn Español Ser.). (SPA.). 40p. (J). pap. 5.95 *(978-0-531-26789-9(X));* lib. bdg. 23.00 *(978-0-531-26121-7(2))* Scholastic Library Publishing. (Children's Pr.).

Ochoa, Francisco. La Plaza. Deltoro, Antonio. 2004.Tr. of Plaza. (SPA.). (J). (gr. k-2). pap. 11.99 *(978-968-494-045-1(9))* Centro de Informacion y Desarrollo de la Comunicacion y la Literatura MEX. Dist: Lectorum Pubns., Inc.

O'Connell, Caitlin & Rodwell, Timothy. A Baby Elephant in the Wild. O'Connell, Caitlin. 2014. (ENG.). 40p. (J). (gr. -1-3). 16.99 *(978-0-544-14944-1(0),* HMH Books For Young Readers) Houghton Mifflin Harcourt Publishing Co.

O'Connell, Dave. Always Late Nate. Krivitzky, Nathan & Nathan, Krivitzky. 2009. (ENG.). 32p. (J). pap. 10.95 *(978-1-933916-41-5(9))* Nelson Publishing & Marketing.

O'Connell, Jennifer. The Eye of the Whale: A Rescue Story, 1 vol. O'Connell, Jennifer. 2013. (ENG.). 32p. (J). 16.95 *(978-0-88448-335-9(5))* Tilbury Hse. Pubs.

O'Connell, Jennifer Barrett. A Garden of Whales. Davis, Maggie Steincrohn. 2008. (ENG.). 32p. (J). (gr. -1-2). reprint ed. pap. 6.95 *(978-0-944475-35-5(3),* 9780944475355) Firefly Bks., Ltd.

O'Connell, Lorraine. Super Soap (Team Umizoomi) Random House Staff. 2013. (Step into Reading Ser.). (ENG.). 24p. (J). (gr. -1-2). pap. 3.99 *(978-0-449-81387-4(8),* Random Hse. Bks. for Young Readers) Random Hse. Children's Bks.

O'Connell, Lorraine, jt. illus. see Random House Staff.

OConner, Kim. Nika Goes to Camp. Melkonian, Sheyda Mia. 2011. 28p. pap. 14.95 *(978-1-4575-0524-9(X))* Dog Ear Publishing, LLC.

O'Connor, Bailey, jt. illus. see O'Connor, Marcy.

O'Connor, George. Alien Feast. Simmons, Michael. 2009. (Chronicles of the First Invasion Ser.: 1). (ENG.). 240p. (J). (gr. 3-7). 16.95 *(978-1-59643-281-9(0))* Roaring Brook Pr.

—Captain Awesome & the Easter Egg Bandit. Kirby, Stan. 2015. (Captain Awesome Ser.: 13). (ENG.). 128p. (J). (gr. k-4). pap. 5.99 *(978-1-4814-2558-2(7),* Little Simon) Little Simon.

—Captain Awesome & the Missing Elephants. Kirby, Stan. 2014. (Captain Awesome Ser.: 10). (ENG.). 128p. (J). (gr. k-4). 15.99 *(978-1-4424-8995-0(2));* pap. 5.99 *(978-1-4424-8994-3(4))* Little Simon. (Little Simon).

—Captain Awesome & the New Kid. Kirby, Stan. 2012. (Captain Awesome Ser.: 3). (ENG.). 128p. (J). (gr. k-4). 16.99 *(978-1-4424-4200-9(X));* pap. 5.99 *(978-1-4424-4199-6(2))* Little Simon. (Little Simon).

—Captain Awesome & the Ultimate Spelling Bee. Kirby, Stan. 2013. (Captain Awesome Ser.: 7). (ENG.). 128p. (J). (gr. k-2). 15.99 *(978-1-4424-5156-8(4));* pap. 4.99 *(978-1-4424-5158-2(0))* Little Simon. (Little Simon).

—The Captain Awesome Collection: A MI-TEE Boxed Set: Captain Awesome to the Rescue!; Captain Awesome vs. Nacho Cheese Man; Captain Awesome & the New Kid; Captain Awesome Takes a Dive. Kirby, Stan. ed. 2013. (Captain Awesome Ser.). (ENG.). 512p. (J). (gr. k-2). pap. 23.99 *(978-1-4424-8977-6(4),* Little Simon) Little Simon.

—Captain Awesome Gets Crushed. Kirby, Stan. 2013. (Captain Awesome Ser.: 9). (ENG.). 128p. (J). (gr. k-2). pap. 4.99 *(978-1-4424-8212-8(5));* 16.99 *(978-1-4424-8213-5(3))* Little Simon. (Little Simon).

—Captain Awesome Goes to Superhero Camp. Kirby, Stan. 2015. (Captain Awesome Ser.: 14). (ENG.). 128p. (J). (gr. k-4). pap. 5.99 *(978-1-4814-3153-8(6),* Little Simon) Little Simon.

—Captain Awesome Saves the Winter Wonderland. Kirby, Stan. 2012. (Captain Awesome Ser.: 6). (ENG.). 128p. (J). (gr. k-4). 16.99 *(978-1-4424-4335-8(9));* pap. 5.99 *(978-1-4424-4334-1(0))* Little Simon. (Little Simon).

—Captain Awesome, Soccer Star. Kirby, Stan. 2012. (Captain Awesome Ser.: 5). (ENG.). 128p. (J). (gr. k-4). 16.99 *(978-1-4424-4332-7(4));* pap. 5.99 *(978-1-4424-4331-0(6))* Little Simon. (Little Simon).

—Captain Awesome Takes a Dive. Kirby, Stan. 2012. (Captain Awesome Ser.: 4). (ENG.). 128p. (J). (gr. k-2). pap. 4.99 *(978-1-4424-4202-3(6));* 16.99 *(978-1-4424-4203-0(4))* Little Simon. (Little Simon).

—Captain Awesome to the Rescue! Kirby, Stan. 2012. (Captain Awesome Ser.: 1). (ENG.). 128p. (J). (gr. k-2). 16.99 *(978-1-4424-4090-6(2));* pap. 5.99 *(978-1-4424-3561-2(5))* Little Simon. (Little Simon).

—Captain Awesome vs. Nacho Cheese Man. Kirby, Stan. 2012. (Captain Awesome Ser.: 2). (ENG.). 128p. (J). (gr. -1-2). 15.99 *(978-1-4424-4091-3(0));* (gr. k-4). pap. 5.99 *(978-1-4424-3563-6(1))* Little Simon. (Little Simon).

—Captain Awesome vs. the Evil Babysitter. Kirby, Stan. 2014. (Captain Awesome Ser.: 11). (ENG.). 128p. (J). (gr. k-4). pap. 5.99 *(978-1-4814-0446-4(6),* Little Simon) Little Simon.

—Captain Awesome vs. the Spooky, Scary House. Kirby, Stan. 2013. (Captain Awesome Ser.: 8). (ENG.). 128p. (J). (gr. k-2). 15.99 *(978-1-4424-7255-6(3));* pap. 5.99 *(978-1-4424-7254-9(5))* Little Simon. (Little Simon).

—Hollywood. Abela, Deborah. 2007. (Spy Force Ser.: 4). (ENG.). 240p. (J). (gr. 3-7). pap. 10.99 *(978-1-4169-3969-6(5),* Simon & Schuster/Paula Wiseman Bks.) Simon & Schuster/Paula Wiseman Bks.

—Mission: The Nightmare Vortex. Abela, Deborah. 2005. (Spy Force Ser.: 3). (ENG.). 256p. (J). (gr. 3-7). 9.95 *(978-0-689-87359-1(X),* Simon & Schuster/Paula Wiseman Bks.) Simon & Schuster/Paula Wiseman Bks.

O'Connor, George. Aphrodite: Goddess of Love. O'Connor, George. 2013. (Olympians Ser.: 6). (ENG.). 80p. (J). (gr. 4-9). 17.99 *(978-1-59643-947-4(5));* pap. 9.99 *(978-1-59643-739-5(1))* Roaring Brook Pr. (First Second Bks.).

—Ares. O'Connor, George. 2015. (Olympians Ser.: 7). (ENG.). 80p. (J). (gr. 4-9). pap. 9.99 *(978-1-62672-013-8(4),* First Second Bks.) Roaring Brook Pr.

—Athena Bk. 2: Grey-Eyed Goddess. O'Connor, George. 2010. (Olympians Ser.: 2). (ENG.). 80p. (J). (gr. 4-9). 16.99 *(978-1-59643-649-7(2));* pap. 9.99 *(978-1-59643-432-5(5))* Roaring Brook Pr. (First Second Bks.).

—Hades: Lord of the Dead. O'Connor, George. 2012. (Olympians Ser.: 4). (ENG.). 80p. (J). (gr. 4-9). 17.99 *(978-1-59643-761-6(8));* pap. 9.99 *(978-1-59643-434-9(1))* Roaring Brook Pr. (First Second Bks.).

—Hera: The Goddess & Her Glory. O'Connor, George. 2011. (Olympians Ser.: 3). (ENG.). 80p. (J). (gr. 4-9). 17.99 *(978-1-59643-724-1(3));* pap. 9.99 *(978-1-59643-433-2(3))* Roaring Brook Pr. (First Second Bks.).

—If I Had a Raptor. O'Connor, George. 2014. (ENG.). 32p. (J). (gr. -1-2). 15.99 *(978-0-7636-6012-3(4))* Candlewick Pr.

—If I Had a Triceratops. O'Connor, George. 2015. (ENG.). 32p. (J). (gr. -1-2). 15.99 *(978-0-7636-6013-0(2))* Candlewick Pr.

—Kapow! O'Connor, George. 2007. (ENG.). 48p. (J). (gr. -1-3). 12.99 *(978-1-4169-6847-4(4),* Simon & Schuster/Paula Wiseman Bks.) Simon & Schuster/Paula Wiseman Bks.

—Ker-Splash! O'Connor, George. 2010. (ENG.). 40p. (J). (gr. -1-3). 19.99 *(978-1-4424-2196-7(7),* Simon & Schuster Bks. For Young Readers) Simon & Schuster Bks. For Young Readers.

—Poseidon: Earth Shaker. O'Connor, George. 2013. (Olympians Ser.: 5). (ENG.). 80p. (J). (gr. 4-9). 16.99 *(978-1-59643-828-6(2));* pap. 9.99 *(978-1-59643-738-8(3))* Roaring Brook Pr. (First Second Bks.).

—Zeus: King of the Gods. O'Connor, George. 2010. (Olympians Ser.: 1). (ENG.). 80p. (J). (gr. 4-9). 17.99 *(978-1-59643-625-1(5));* pap. 9.99 *(978-1-59643-431-8(7))* Roaring Brook Pr. (First Second Bks.).

O'Connor, George, jt. illus. see Sycamore, Hilary.

O'Connor, Jeff. You & Your Horse: How to Whisper Your Way into Your Horse's Life. Mackall, Dandi Daley. 2009. (ENG.). 128p. (J). (gr. 4-8). pap. 5.99 *(978-1-4169-6449-0(5),* Simon & Schuster/Paula Wiseman Bks.) Simon & Schuster/Paula Wiseman Bks.

O'Connor, John. Ben Over Night. McPhail, David. Ellis, Sarah, ed. 2003. (ENG.). 32p. pap. *(978-1-55041-802-6(5))* Fitzhenry & Whiteside, Ltd.

—The Blue Door, 1 vol. McPhail, David & McPhail. 2005. (First Flight Level 1 Ser.). (ENG.). 32p. (J). pap. 4.95 *(978-1-55041-917-7(X),* 155041917X) Fitzhenry & Whiteside, Ltd. CAN. Dist: Midpoint Trade Bks., Inc.

O'Connor, Marcy & O'Connor, Bailey. Little Bee the Size of a Pe. Ceballos, Jacalyn Martin. 2011. 28p. pap. 24.95 *(978-1-4626-3005-9(7))* America Star Bks.

O'Connor, Niamh. George Washington Carver: Teacher, Scientist, & Inventor. Mortensen, Lori. 2007. (Biographies Ser.). (ENG.). 24p. (gr. k-3). lib. bdg. 25.99 *(978-1-4048-3725-6(6),* Nonfiction Picture Bks.) Picture Window Bks.

O'Connor, Niamh, jt. illus. see Garvey, Brann.

O'Connor, Shannon. Rags the Recycled Doll. Jackson, Ann. 2004. 49p. 12.95 *(978-1-57197-405-1(9))* Pentland Pr., Inc.

O'Connor, Tim. The Journeys of Wobblefoot the Beginning. Cogar, Tubal U. et al. Cogar, Karen S., ed. 2003. (J). pap. 17.50 *(978-0-9747149-0-5(9))* Wobblefoot Ltd.

—Mi Biblia Pijama. Holmes, Andy. ed. 2008. (SPA.). 64p. (J). (gr. -1). bds. 13.99 *(978-1-4143-1979-7(7),* Tyndale Espanol) Tyndale Hse. Pubs.

—Mighty Acts of God: A Family Bible Story Book. Meade, Starr. 2010. 288p. (J). 24.99 *(978-1-4335-0604-8(1))* Crossway.

—Read 'n' See DVD Bible, 1 vol. Elkins, Stephen. 2006. (ENG.). 176p. (gr. -1-3). 19.99 *(978-1-59145-486-1(7))* Nelson, Thomas Inc.

—The Word & Song Bible. Elkins, Stephen. 2004. (J). 34.99 incl. audio *(978-0-8054-3012-7(1));* 34.99 incl. audio compact disk *(978-0-8054-3018-9(0));* 448p. (gr. -1-5). 19.99 *(978-0-8054-1689-3(7))* B&H Publishing Group.

Oda, Eiichiro. Buggy the Clown, Vol. 2. Oda, Eiichiro. 2003. (One Piece Ser.). (ENG.). 200p. pap. 9.99 *(978-1-59116-057-1(X))* Viz Media.

—For Whom the Bell Tolls. Oda, Eiichiro. 2004. (One Piece Ser.: Vol. 5). (ENG.). 200p. pap. 9.99 *(978-1-59116-615-3(2))* Viz Media.

—The Oath, Vol. 6. Oda, Eiichiro. 2005. (One Piece Ser.). (ENG.). 200p. pap. 9.99 *(978-1-59116-723-5(X))* Viz Media.

—One Piece. Oda, Eiichiro. (One Piece Ser.: 57). (ENG.). 2011. 208p. pap. 9.99 *(978-1-4215-3851-8(2));* 2011. 192p. pap. 9.99 *(978-1-4215-3850-1(4));* 2010. 208p. pap. 9.99 *(978-1-4215-3471-8(1));* 2010. 208p. pap. 9.99 *(978-1-4215-3470-1(3));* 2010. 232p. pap. 9.99 *(978-1-4215-3465-7(7));* 2010. 208p. pap. 9.99 *(978-1-4215-3466-4(5));* 2010. 232p. pap. 9.99

(978-1-4215-3467-1(3)); 2010. 216p. pap. 9.99 (978-1-4215-3468-8(1)); 2010. 216p. pap. 9.99 (978-1-4215-3469-5(X)); 2005. 200p. pap. 9.99 (978-1-59116-852-2(X)); 2004. 208p. pap. 9.99 (978-1-59116-337-4(4)); 2003. 216p. pap. 9.99 (978-1-56931-901-7(4)); Vol. 3. 2004. 200p. pap. 9.99 (978-1-59116-184-4(3)); Vol. 8. 2005. 192p. pap. 9.99 (978-1-4215-0075-1(2)); Vol. 9. 2006. 208p. pap. 9.99 (978-1-4215-0191-8(0)); Vol. 11. 2006. 208p. pap. 9.99 (978-1-4215-0663-0(7)) Viz Media.

—One Piece, Vol. 18. Oda, Eiichiro. Caselman, Lance. 2008. (One Piece Ser.: 18). (ENG.). 232p. pap. 9.99 (978-1-4215-1512-0(1)) Viz Media.

—One Piece: East Blue 10-11-12. Oda, Eiichiro. 2010. (One Piece 3-In-1 Ser.). (ENG.). 600p. 14.99 (978-1-4215-3628-6(5)) Viz Media.

—One Piece: East Blue 4-5-6. Oda, Eiichiro. 2010. (One Piece 3-In-1 Ser.). (ENG.). 600p. pap. 14.99 (978-1-4215-3626-2(9)) Viz Media.

—One Piece: East Blue 7-8-9. Oda, Eiichiro. 2010. (One Piece 3-In-1 Ser.). (ENG.). 592p. pap. 14.99 (978-1-4215-3627-9(7)) Viz Media.

Oda, Kancho. The Moon Princess, 1 vol. McCarthy, Ralph F. 2013. (Kodansha Children's Bilingual Classics Ser.). (ENG.). 48p. 9.95 (978-1-56836-527-5(6)) Kodansha America, Inc.

Oda, Takashi. We Are Dolphins. Grooms, Molly. 2004. (ENG.). 32p. (J). (gr. -1-2). pap. 7.95 (978-1-55971-904-9(4)) Cooper Square Publishing Llc.

Odermatt, Brian. The Wonders of Waldorf Chemistry: Notes from a Teacher's Notebook. Mitchell, David. 2004. 250p. (gr. 7-9). per. 22.00 (978-1-888365-16-0(1)) Waldorf Pubns.

Odom, Kelly. It's Not Easy Being a Purple Goose. Parrish, Edith E. 2011. 44p. pap. 24.95 (978-1-4626-4207-6(1)) America Star Bks.

—Sarah the Purple Goose Gets Lost. Parrish, Edith. 2011. 34p. 23.95 (978-1-60844-930-9(0)) Dog Ear Publishing, LLC.

Odone, Jamison. The Bedtime Train. Cowley, Joy. 2008. (ENG.). 32p. (J). (gr. k-2). 16.95 (978-1-59078-493-8(6), Front Street) Boyds Mills Pr.

—Mole Had Everything. 2012. (ENG.). 40p. (J). (gr. -1-3). 14.99 (978-1-60905-224-9(2)) Blue Apple Bks.

Odone, Jamison. Alice's Adventures in Wonderland. Odone, Jamison. 2010. (Stickfiguratively Speaking Ser.). (ENG.). 192p. (gr. 2-3). 14.95 (978-1-935557-61-6(0)) PublishingWorks.

Odriozola, Elena. Marte y Las Princesas Voladores. Baranda, María. 2007. (la Orilla del Viento Ser.). (SPA.). 35p. (J). pap. (978-968-16-8141-8(X)) Fondo de Cultura Economica.

—The Opposite, 1 vol. MacRae, Tom. 2006. (ENG.). 32p. (J). (gr. k-3). 15.95 (978-1-56145-371-9(4)) Peachtree Pubs.

—The Story Blanket, 1 vol. Wolff, Ferida & Savitz, Harriet May. 2008. (ENG.). 32p. (J). (gr. -1-3). 16.95 (978-1-56145-466-2(4), Peachtree Junior) Peachtree Pubs.

—What I Do with Vegetable Glue. Chandler, Susan. 2012. (ENG.). 24p. (J). (gr. k-3). 16.95 (978-1-61608-661-9(0), 608661, Sky Pony Pr.) Skyhorse Publishing Co., Inc.

Oe, Patricia Daly. Blue Mouse, Yellow Mouse. Oe, Patricia Daly. 2007. (R. I. C. Story Chest Ser.). 20p. (J). (gr. -1-k). 11.95 incl. audio compact disk (978-1-74126-439-5(1)) R.I.C. Pubns. AUS. Dist: SCB Distributors.

—Where Are My Stripes? Oe, Patricia Daly. 2007. (R. I. C. Story Chest Ser.). 20p. (J). (gr. -1-k). 11.95 incl. audio compact disk (978-1-74126-438-8(3)) R.I.C. Pubns. AUS. Dist: SCB Distributors.

Oechsli, Kelly. The Birthday Car. Hillert, Margaret. rev. exp. ed. 2006. (Beginning to Read Ser.). 30p. (J). (gr. -1-3). lib. bdg. 14.95 (978-1-59953-043-7(0)) Norwood Hse. Pr.

—The Haunted House. Rose, Dorothy. 2014. (ENG.). 24p. (J). (gr. -1-k). pap. 13.99 (978-1-4814-2646-6(X), Little Simon) Little Simon.

—A House for Little Red. Hillert, Margaret. rev. ed. 2006. (Beginning to Read Ser.). 32p. (J). (gr. -1-3). lib. bdg. 19.93 (978-1-59953-029-1(5)) Norwood Hse. Pr.

Oehlers, Adam. Celeste, Nick & the Magical Tea Party. Atkinson, Joelie & Dinkles. 2013. (ENG.). 32p. (J). 16.95 (978-1-921596-80-3(5)) Brolga Publishing AUS. Dist: Midpoint Trade Bks., Inc.

—Lulu & the Purple Pebble. Badaoui, Chad. 2013. (ENG.). 32p. (J). 16.95 (978-1-921596-53-7(8)) Brolga Publishing AUS. Dist: Midpoint Trade Bks., Inc.

Oehm, Kent. Appalachian Christmas ABCs. Hall, Francie. 2010. (ENG.). 53p. (J). 16.95 (978-1-57072-328-5(1)) Overmountain Pr.

Oelofsen, Vian. That Dog! Hay, Sam. 2011. (My Phonics Readers: Level 2 Ser.). 24p. (J). (gr. -1-1). 24.25 (978-1-84898-510-0(X)) Sea-To-Sea Pubns.

Oelofsen, Vian. Mom & Dad Don't Live Together Anymore. Stinson, Kathy. rev. ed. 2007. (ENG.). 24p. (J). (gr. -1-2). 19.95 (978-1-55451-094-8(5), 9781554510948); pap. 6.95 (978-1-55451-093-1(7), 9781554510931) Annick Pr., Ltd. CAN. Dist: Firefly Bks., Ltd.

Oelrich, Deborah, photos by. Amazing Creatures. 2009. 48p. pap. 19.00 (978-1-4343-6713-6(4)) AuthorHouse.

Oeltjenbruns, Joni. Basil & Parsley, 1 vol. Clairmont, Patsy. 2007. (Tails from the Pantry Ser.: 5). (ENG.). 32p. (gr. -1-2). 9.99 (978-1-4003-1039-5(3)) Nelson, Thomas Inc.

—Christmas Around the World. Kelley, Emily. rev. ed. 2003. (On My Own Holidays Ser.). (ENG.). 48p. (gr. 2-4). pap. 6.95 (978-1-57505-580-0(5)) Lerner Publishing Group.

—La Navidad Alrededor del Mundo. Kelley, Emily. Translations.com Staff, tr. 2005. (Yo Solo: Festividades (on My Own Holidays) Ser.). (SPA & ENG.). 48p. (gr. 2-4). lib. bdg. 25.26 (978-0-8225-3116-6(X), Ediciones Lerner) Lerner Publishing Group.

—The Numbers of My Jewish Year. Gold-Vukson, Marji E. 2006. (ENG.). 12p. (J). (gr. -1 — 1). bds. 5.95 (978-1-58013-148-3(4), Kar-Ben Publishing) Lerner Publishing Group.

—Trick-or-Treat on Milton Street. Bullard, Lisa. 2004. (Carolrhoda Picture Books Ser.). (ENG.). 32p. (J). (gr. k-4). pap. 6.95 (978-1-57505-793-4(X)) Lerner Publishing Group.

—5 Cheesy Stories: About Friendship, Bravery, Bullying, & More, 1 vol. Clairmont, Patsy. 2007. (Tails from the Pantry Ser.). (ENG.). 144p. (gr. -1-2). 15.99 (978-1-4003-1042-5(3)) Nelson, Thomas Inc.

Oeming, Michael, et al. Fear Itself: The Home Front. 2012. (ENG.). 240p. (YA). (gr. 8-17). pap. 24.99 (978-0-7851-5667-3(4)) Marvel Worldwide, Inc.

Oeming, Michael. Who Killed Retro Girl?, Vol. 1. 2011. (ENG.). 100p. (gr. 13-17). 24.99 (978-0-7851-5671-0(2)) Marvel Worldwide, Inc.

Oeming, Michael Avon. Powers: The Definitive Collection. 2011. (ENG.). 600p. (gr. 13-17). 34.99 (978-0-7851-5316-0(0)) Marvel Worldwide, Inc.

—Powers Vol. 4: Supergroup. Bendis, Brian Michael. 2003. 176p. (YA). (gr. 8-18). 29.95 (978-1-58240-290-1(6)) Image Comics.

—Takio. Bendis, Brian Michael. 2011. (ENG.). 96p. (J). (gr. -1-17). 9.95 (978-0-7851-5326-9(8)) Marvel Worldwide, Inc.

—Takio 2. 2013. (ENG.). 120p. (J). (gr. -1-17). 16.99 (978-0-7851-6553-8(3)) Marvel Worldwide, Inc.

Oesch, Brian. Our Presidents Rock!, 1 vol. Turner, Juliette. 2014. (ENG.). 320p. (J). pap. 15.99 (978-0-310-73095-8(3)) Zonderkidz.

Offen, Hilda. Mrs Pepperpot & the Treasure: A Classic Story with a Touch of Magic. Proysen, Alf. 2013. (ENG.). 32p. (J). (gr. k-2). pap. 10.99 (978-1-84941-866-9(7), Red Fox) Random House Children's Books GBR. Dist: Independent Pubs. Group.

—Mrs Pepperpot Minds the Baby: A Classic Story with a Touch of Magic. Proysen, Alf. 2013. (ENG.). 32p. (J). (gr. k-2). pap. 10.99 (978-1-84941-864-5(0), Red Fox) Random House Children's Books GBR. Dist: Independent Pubs. Group.

Offermann, Andrea. The Boneshaker. Milford, Kate. 2011. (ENG.). 384p. (J). (gr. 5-7). pap. 7.99 (978-0-547-55004-6(9)) Houghton Mifflin Harcourt Publishing Co.

—The Broken Lands. Milford, Kate. (ENG.). 464p. 2015. (J). (gr. 5-7). pap. 8.99 (978-0-544-43942-9(2), HMH Books For Young Readers); 2012. (YA). (gr. 7). 16.99 (978-0-547-73966-3(4)) Houghton Mifflin Harcourt Publishing Co.

—A Path Begins. White, J. A. 2014. (Thickety Ser.: 1). (ENG.). 496p. (J). (gr. 5-7). 16.99 (978-0-06-225724-6(2), Tegen, Katherine Bks) HarperCollins Pubs.

—The Shepherd of Weeds, Bk. 3. Appelbaum, Susannah. 2012. (Poisons of Caux Ser.: Bk. 3). (ENG.). 464p. (J). (gr. 4-7). 7.99 (978-0-440-42249-5(3)) Random Hse. Children's Bks.

—The Whispering Trees. White, J. A. 2015. (Thickety Ser.: 2). (ENG.). 528p. (J). (gr. 5). 16.99 (978-0-06-225729-1(3), Tegen, Katherine Bks) HarperCollins Pubs.

Offermann, Andrea, jt. illus. see McNaughtt, Jonathan.

Officer, Robyn. Sariah McDuff: Primary Program Diva. Setzer, Lee Ann. 2004. 61p. (J). pap. 4.95 (978-1-55517-786-7(7)) Cedar Fort, Inc./CFI Distribution.

Offner, Naomi. Purple Puppy. Faith, Susan. 2005. 32p. (J). 19.95 (978-0-9707793-0-4(5)) Purple People, Inc.

Offredi, James, jt. illus. see Collins, Mike.

Offredi, James, jt. illus. see Roach, David.

Ogasawara, Tomofumi. Mobile Suit Gundam Seed, Vol. 1. Goto, Liu & Yatate, Hajime. 2005. (Mobile Suit Gundam Seed (Novels) Ser.). 272p. pap. 7.99 (978-1-59532-881-6(5), Tokyopop Kids) TOKYOPOP, Inc.

Ogata, Michael. New Friend for Nai'a. 2009. (J). (978-1-56647-912-7(6)) Mutual Publishing LLC.

Ogawa, Grace. Angeldevil V: Tales, Tools, Pawns & Fools. Ogawa, Grace. 2010. 228p. (YA). pap. 12.00 (978-0-9769275-8-7(6)) Eltsar Pr.

Ogawa, Yayoi. Tramps Like Us. Ogawa, Yayoi. 2005. 192p. Vol. 4. rev. ed. pap. 14.99 (978-1-59532-142-8(X)); Vol. 6. 6th rev. ed. pap. 14.99 (978-1-59532-144-2(6)) TOKYOPOP, Inc. (Tokyopop Adult).

Ogden, Betina. Archie the Big Good Wolf Vol. 9: Band 15/Emerald. Baillie, Allan. 2007. (Collins Big Cat Ser.). (ENG.). 32p. (J). pap. 8.99 (978-0-00-723421-9(X)) HarperCollins Pubs. Ltd. GBR. Dist: Independent Pubs. Group.

—Littlest Pumpkin. Herman, R. A. 2006. (ENG.). (J). (gr. -1-3). 18.95 (978-0-439-89837-9(4)) Scholastic, Inc.

—The Littlest Pumpkin. Herman, R. A. 2006. (ENG.). (J). (gr. -1-3). 9.99 (978-0-439-89555-2(3)) Scholastic, Inc.

—Pal Saves the Day. Herman, R. A. 2004. (Pal the Pony Ser.). 32p. (J). pap. (978-0-439-64985-8(4)); pap. (978-0-439-57746-5(2)) Scholastic, Inc.

—A Stocking for Jesus. Arruda, Suzanne M. 2005. (J). pap. 7.95 (978-0-8198-7076-6(5), 332-372) Pauline Bks. & Media.

Ogene, Chuma C. I Wish for Snow. Perkins, Nicole D. 2005. (J). per. 19.95 (978-0-9755566-0-3(6)) Azreal Publishing Co.

Ogilvie, Sara. Dogs Don't Do Ballet. Kemp, Anna. 2010. (ENG.). 32p. (J). (gr. -1-3). 17.99 (978-1-4169-9839-6(X), Simon & Schuster Bks. For Young Readers) Simon & Schuster Bks. For Young Readers.

—Dogs Don't Do Ballet. Kemp, Anna. 2010. (ENG.). 32p. pap. (978-1-84738-474-4(9)) Simon & Schuster, Ltd.

—Meet the Parents. Bently, Peter. 2014. (ENG.). 32p. (J). (gr. -1-3). 17.99 (978-1-4814-1483-8(6), Simon & Schuster/Paula Wiseman Bks.) Simon & Schuster/Paula Wiseman Bks.

—Rhinos Don't Eat Pancakes. Kemp, Anna. 2015. (J). (978-1-4814-3844-5(1), Simon & Schuster Bks. For Young Readers) Simon & Schuster Bks. For Young Readers.

Ogilvie, Sara. Rhinos Don't Eat Pancakes. Kemp, Anna. 2015. (ENG.). 32p. (J). (gr. -1-3). 16.99 (978-1-4814-3845-2(X), Simon & Schuster/Paula Wiseman Bks.) Simon & Schuster/Paula Wiseman Bks.

Ogilvie, Sara. The Worst Princess. Kemp, Anna. 2014. (ENG.). 32p. (J). (gr. -1-2). 16.99 (978-0-385-37125-4(X)) Random Hse., Inc.

Ogilvy, Shelli. Alphabet Bird Collection. 2009. (ENG.). 56p. (J). (gr. -1-2). 16.95 (978-1-57061-618-1(3)) Sasquatch Bks.

Ogiwara, Noriko. Mirror Sword & Shadow Prince. Ogiwara, Noriko. 2011. (ENG.). 450p. 21.99 (978-1-4215-3725-2(7)) Viz Media.

Ogle, Nancy, jt. illus. see Ogle, Nancy Gray.

Ogle, Nancy Gray. Looking at Wild Cats. Hodge, Deborah. 2008. (Kids Can Read Ser.). (ENG.). 32p. (J). (gr. k-1). pap. 3.95 (978-1-55453-285-8(X)) Kids Can Pr., Ltd. CAN. Dist: Univ. of Toronto Pr.

Ogle, Nancy Gray & Ogle, Nancy. Bats. Mason, Adrienne. 2003. (Kids Can Press Wildlife Ser.). (ENG.). 32p. (J). (gr. k-3). 5.95 (978-1-55337-525-8(4)) Kids Can Pr., Ltd. CAN. Dist: Univ. of Toronto Pr.

—Otters. Mason, Adrienne. 2003. (Kids Can Press Wildlife Ser.). (ENG.). 32p. (J). (gr. k-3). 5.95 (978-1-55337-407-7(X)) Kids Can Pr., Ltd. CAN. Dist: Univ. of Toronto Pr.

—Owls. Mason, Adrienne. 2004. (Kids Can Press Wildlife Ser.). (ENG.). 32p. (J). (gr. k-5). 7.95 (978-1-55337-624-8(2)) Kids Can Pr., Ltd. CAN. Dist: Univ. of Toronto Pr.

—Skunks. Mason, Adrienne. 2006. (Kids Can Press Wildlife Ser.). (ENG.). 32p. (J). (gr. k-5). 6.95 (978-1-55337-734-4(6)) Kids Can Pr., Ltd. CAN. Dist: Univ. of Toronto Pr.

—Snakes. Mason, Adrienne. 2005. (Kids Can Press Wildlife Ser.). (ENG.). 32p. (J). (gr. k-5). 6.95 (978-1-55337-628-6(5)) Kids Can Pr., Ltd. CAN. Dist: Univ. of Toronto Pr.

Ogo, Luis S. Illuminating the Legacy: A Coloring & Activity Book of the CNMI's History. Sanchez, John Joseph P. 2006. 106p. (J). (gr. 4-5). pap. (978-1-878453-89-1(0)) Univ. of Guam, Micronesian Area Research Ctr.

Oh, Charlotte. First Look at Insects. Gates Galvin, Laura. 2011. (ENG.). 16p. (J). (978-1-60727-223-6(7)) Soundprints.

Oh, Daniella. The 3 Trees. 2008. Orig. Title: Les 3 Arbres. 32p. (J). (gr. -1-1). 8.95 (978-0-8198-7426-9(4)) Pauline Bks. & Media.

Oh, Jiwon. Mr. Monkey's Classroom. Oh, Jiwon. 2005. 32p. (J). (gr. -1-2). lib. bdg. 15.89 (978-0-06-055722-5(2)) HarperCollins Pubs.

Oh, Lee. Where the Winds Meet: Mongolia. Joo, Mi-hwa. Cowley, Joy, ed. 2015. (Global Kids Storybooks Ser.). (ENG.). 32p. (gr. 1-4). 26.65 **(978-1-925246-03-2(5))**; 26.65 **(978-1-925246-29-2(9))**; 7.99 **(978-1-925246-55-1(8))** ChoiceMaker Pty. Ltd., The AUS. (Big and SMALL). Dist: Lerner Publishing Group.

Oh, Mo, jt. illus. see Timmons, Anne.

Oh Rhe Bar Ghun. Peigenz, 8 vols., Vol. 1. Oh Rhe Bar Ghun. 2004. (Peigenz Ser.: Vol. 1). 192p. (YA). per. 9.95 (978-1-59697-021-2(9)) Infinity Studios LLC.

Oh, Seung-min. Good Friends: Symbiotic Relationships. Jang, Ki-hwa & Kim, In-sook. Cowley, Joy, ed. 2015. (Science Storybooks Ser.). (ENG.). 32p. (gr. k-3). 26.65 **(978-1-925246-20-9(5))**; 7.99 **(978-1-925246-72-8(8))** ChoiceMaker Pty. Ltd., The AUS. (Big and SMALL). Dist: Lerner Publishing Group.

—Good Friends: Symbiotic Relationships. Jang, Ki-hwa & Kim, In-sook. Cowley, Joy, ed. 2015. (Science Storybooks Ser.). (ENG.). 32p. (gr. k-3). 26.65 **(978-1-925246-46-9(9)**, Big and SMALL) ChoiceMaker Pty. Ltd., The AUS. Dist: Lerner Publishing Group.

O'Hara, Cynthia, jt. illus. see Amory, Deanna.

O'hehir, Trisha. The Toothpaste Secret. O'hehir, Trisha. 2003. 56p. (J). (gr. 2-6). 9.95 (978-0-9659236-1-3(4)) Perio Reports.

O'Herron, Mary. A Letter from Marty: Grandma & Grandpa's Cat. O'Herron, Mary. 2004. 32p. (J). (gr. -1-1). pap. 8.95 (978-0-9664732-4-7(8)) Countinghouse Pr., Inc.

Ohi, Debbie Ridpath. I'm Bored. Black, Michael Ian. 2012. (ENG.). 40p. (J). (gr. -1-3). 17.99 (978-1-4424-1403-7(0), Simon & Schuster Bks. For Young Readers) Simon & Schuster Bks. For Young Readers.

Ohi, Debbie Ridpath. Mitzi Tulane, Preschool Detective, in What's That Smell? McLaughlin, Lauren. 2016. (J). **(978-0-375-97176-1(9))** Random Hse., Inc.

Ohi, Debbie Ridpath. Naked! Black, Michael Ian. 2014. (ENG.). 40p. (J). (gr. -1-3). 17.99 (978-1-4424-6738-5(X), Simon & Schuster Bks. For Young Readers) Simon & Schuster Bks. For Young Readers.

—The One in the Middle Is the Green Kangaroo. Blume, Judy. 2014. (ENG.). 48p. (J). (gr. 1-5). pap. 5.99 (978-1-4814-1131-8(4), Atheneum Bks. for Young Readers) Simon & Schuster Children's Publishing.

—The Pain & the Great One. Blume, Judy. 2014. (ENG.). 48p. (J). (gr. 1-5). pap. 5.99 (978-1-4814-1145-5(4), Atheneum Bks. for Young Readers) Simon & Schuster Children's Publishing.

Ohi, Debbie Ridpath. Ruby Rose on Her Toes. Sanders, Rob. 2016. 32p. (J). (gr. -1-3). 15.99 **(978-0-06-223569-5(9))** HarperCollins Pubs.

Ohi, Debbie Ridpath. Where Are My Books? Ohi, Debbie Ridpath. 2015. (ENG.). 40p. (J). (gr. -1-3). 17.99 (978-1-4424-6741-5(X), Simon & Schuster Bks. For Young Readers) Simon & Schuster Bks. For Young Readers.

Ohi, Ruth. Beneath the Bridge. Hutchins, Hazel J. & Hutchins, Hazel. 2004. (ENG.). 24p. (J). (gr. -1-k). 19.95 (978-1-55037-859-7(7), 9781550378597) Annick Pr., Ltd. CAN. Dist: Firefly Bks., Ltd.

—Chicken, Pig, Cow Horse Around. 2011. (Chicken, Pig, Cow Ser.). (ENG.). 32p. (J). (gr. -1-k). pap. 6.95 (978-1-55451-244-7(1), 9781554512447) Annick Pr., Ltd. CAN. Dist: Firefly Bks., Ltd.

—Naomi's Road, 1 vol. Kogawa, Joy. 2005. (ENG.). 120p. (Orig.). (J). pap. 9.95 (978-1-55005-115-5(6)) Fitzhenry & Whiteside, Ltd. CAN. Dist: Ingram Pub. Services.

—Naomi's Tree, 1 vol. Kogawa, Joy. 2011. (ENG.). 32p. (J). (gr. 1-4). pap. 9.95 (978-1-55455-184-2(6)) Fitzhenry & Whiteside, Ltd. CAN. Dist: Midpoint Trade Bks., Inc.

—No Monsters Here, 1 vol. Jennings, Sharon. 2006. (ENG.). 24p. (J). (gr. -1-1). pap. 7.95 (978-1-55041-789-0(4), 1550417894) Fitzhenry & Whiteside, Ltd. CAN. Dist: Midpoint Trade Bks., Inc.

—The Sidewalk Rescue. Hutchins, Hazel J. & Hutchins, Hazel. 2004. (ENG.). 32p. (J). (gr. -1-1). pap. 7.95 (978-1-55037-830-6(9), 9781550378306) Annick Pr., Ltd. CAN. Dist: Firefly Bks., Ltd.

Ohi, Ruth. Chicken, Pig, Cow. Ohi, Ruth. 2008. (Chicken, Pig, Cow Ser.). (ENG.). 32p. (J). (gr. -1-k). 19.95 (978-1-55451-157-0(7), 9781554511570); pap. 6.95 (978-1-55451-156-3(9), 9781554511563) Annick Pr., Ltd. CAN. Dist: Firefly Bks., Ltd.

—Chicken, Pig, Cow, & the Purple Problem. Ohi, Ruth. 2010. (Chicken, Pig, Cow Ser.). (ENG.). 32p. (J). (gr. -1-k). 19.95 (978-1-55451-219-5(0), 9781554512195); pap. 6.95 (978-1-55451-218-8(2), 9781554512188) Annick Pr., Ltd. CAN. Dist: Firefly Bks., Ltd.

—Chicken, Pig, Cow Horse Around. Ohi, Ruth. 2011. (Chicken, Pig, Cow Ser.). (ENG.). 32p. (J). (gr. -1-k). 19.95 (978-1-55451-245-4(X), 9781554512454) Annick Pr., Ltd. CAN. Dist: Firefly Bks., Ltd.

—Chicken, Pig, Cow on the Move. Ohi, Ruth. 2009. (Chicken, Pig, Cow Ser.). (ENG.). 32p. (J). (gr. -1-k). 19.95 (978-1-55451-194-5(1), 9781554511945); pap. 6.95 (978-1-55451-193-8(3), 9781554511938) Annick Pr., Ltd. CAN. Dist: Firefly Bks., Ltd.

—Clara & the Bossy. Ohi, Ruth. 2006. (Ruth Ohi Picture Book Ser.). (ENG.). 32p. (J). (gr. -1-1). 19.95 (978-1-55037-943-3(7), 9781550379433); pap. 5.95 (978-1-55037-942-6(9), 9781550379426) Annick Pr., Ltd. CAN. Dist: Firefly Bks., Ltd.

—The Couch Was a Castle. Ohi, Ruth. 2006. (Ruth Ohi Picture Book Ser.). (ENG.). 24p. (J). (gr. -1-1). 19.95 (978-1-55451-014-6(7), 9781554510146) Annick Pr., Ltd. CAN. Dist: Firefly Bks., Ltd.

—Fox & Squirrel. Ohi, Ruth. 2013. (ENG.). 32p. (J). (gr. -1-2). (978-1-4431-1914-6(8)) Scholastic Canada, Ltd.

—Me & My Brother. Ohi, Ruth. 2007. (Ruth Ohi Picture Book Ser.). (ENG.). 24p. (J). (gr. -1-k). 19.95 (978-1-55451-092-4(9), 9781554510924); pap. 5.95 (978-1-55451-091-7(0), 9781554510917) Annick Pr., Ltd. CAN. Dist: Firefly Bks., Ltd.

—Me & My Sister. Ohi, Ruth. 2005. (ENG.). 24p. (J). (gr. -1 — 1). 19.95 (978-1-55037-893-1(7), 9781550378931) Annick Pr., Ltd. CAN. Dist: Firefly Bks., Ltd.

—A Trip with Grandma. Ohi, Ruth. 2007. (Ruth Ohi Picture Book Ser.). (ENG.). 32p. (J). (gr. -1-2). pap. 5.95 (978-1-55451-071-9(6), 9781554510719) Annick Pr., Ltd. CAN. Dist: Firefly Bks., Ltd.

Ohi, Ruth, jt. illus. see Krykorka, Vladyana.

Ohkami, Mineko. Dragon Knights, 17 vols., Vol. 7. Ohkami, Mineko. Yoshida, Agnes, tr. from JPN. rev. ed. 2003. (Graphic Novel-Manga Ser.). 208p. (gr. 8-18). pap. 9.99 (978-1-59182-111-3(8)) TOKYOPOP, Inc.

—Dragon Knights, 17 vols. Ohkami, Mineko. rev. ed. 2003. (Graphic Novel-Manga Ser.). 192p. Vol. 10. pap. 9.99 (978-1-59182-114-4(2)); Vol. 11. pap. 9.99 (978-1-59182-115-1(0)) TOKYOPOP, Inc.

—Dragon Knights, 17 vols., Vol. 12. Ohkami, Mineko. Nakamura, Yuki, tr. from JPN. rev. ed. 2004. (Graphic Novel-Manga Ser.). 200p. pap. 9.99 (978-1-59182-440-4(0)) TOKYOPOP, Inc.

—Dragon Knights. Ohkami, Mineko. Vol. 18. rev. ed. 2005. 208p. pap. 9.99 (978-1-59182-961-4(5)); Vol. 21. 21st rev. ed. 2005. 192p. pap. 9.99 (978-1-59532-634-8(0)); Vol. 22. 22nd rev. ed. 2006. 200p. per. 9.99 (978-1-59532-635-5(9)); Vol. 24. 24th rev. ed. 2007. 208p. per. 9.99 (978-1-59816-797-9(9)) TOKYOPOP, Inc.

—Dragon Knights: Volume 12, Vol. 12. Ohkami, Mineko. 2004. (Dragon Knights Ser.). 210p. lib. bdg. 20.90 (978-1-4176-5944-9(0), Turtleback) Turtleback Bks.

—Dragon Knights: Volume 14, Vol. 14. Ohkami, Mineko. 2004. (Dragon Knights Ser.). 210p. lib. bdg. 20.90 (978-1-4176-5945-6(9), Turtleback) Turtleback Bks.

—Dragon Knights: Volume 16, Vol. 16. Ohkami, Mineko. 2004. (Dragon Knights Ser.). 210p. lib. bdg. 20.90 (978-1-4176-5946-3(7), Turtleback) Turtleback Bks.

—Dragon Knights: Volume 18, Vol. 18. Ohkami, Mineko. 2005. (Dragon Knights Ser.). 210p. lib. bdg. 20.90 (978-1-4176-5947-0(5), Turtleback) Turtleback Bks.

Ohkami, Mineko. Dragon Knights, Vol. 19. Ohkami, Mineko, creator. 19th rev. ed. 2005. 192p. pap. 9.99 (978-1-59182-962-1(3)) TOKYOPOP, Inc.

OHora, Zachariah. The Pet Project: Cute & Cuddly Vicious Verses. Wheeler, Lisa. 2013. (ENG.). 40p. (J). (gr. -1-3). 16.99 (978-1-4169-7595-3(0), Atheneum Bks. for Young Readers) Simon & Schuster Children's Publishing.

—Tyrannosaurus Wrecks! Bardhan-Quallen, Sudipta. 2014. (ENG.). 32p. (J). (gr. -1-3). 14.95 (978-1-4197-1035-3(4), Abrams Bks. for Young Readers) Abrams.

—Wolfie the Bunny. Dyckman, Ame. 2015. (ENG.). 40p. (J). (gr. -1-1). 17.00 (978-0-316-22614-1(9)) Little, Brown Bks. for Young Readers.

OHora, Zachariah. No Fits, Nilson! OHora, Zachariah. 2013. (ENG.). 32p. (J). (gr. -1-k). 16.99 (978-0-8037-3852-2(8), Dial) Penguin Publishing Group.

—Stop Snoring, Bernard! OHora, Zachariah. 2011. (ENG.). 32p. (J). (gr. -1-2). 17.99 (978-0-8050-9002-4(9), Holt, Henry & Co. Bks. For Young Readers) Holt, Henry & Co.

—Stop Snoring, Bernard! OHora, Zachariah. 2012. (ENG.). 32p. (J). (gr. -1-2). pap. 6.99 (978-1-250-00717-9(8)) Square Fish.

Ohtsuka, Tommy, et al. Flesh for the Beast. Komada, Yoshihiro et al. Pannone, Frank, ed. 2004. 132p. pap. 9.99 (978-1-58655-556-6(1), SSNOV-0419) Media Blasters, Inc.

Ohtsuka, Tommy. 15-Love. 2011. (ENG.). 144p. (J). (gr. 4-17). pap. 14.99 (978-0-7851-1334-8(7)) Marvel Worldwide, Inc.

Oien, Jennifer. Tessie the Toad. Grandma Poo Poo. 2008. 28p. pap. 24.95 (978-1-60610-325-8(3)) America Star Bks.

Ok, SeoJeong. Oh That Snow! Kim, JeongHo. 2015. (MySELF Bookshelf Ser.). (ENG.). 32p. (J). (gr. k-2). pap. 11.94 (978-1-60357-697-0(5)); lib. bdg. 22.60 (978-1-59953-662-0(5)) Norwood Hse. Pr.

O

Okamoto, Alan. Kingdom of Nu - TJ's Tale: TJ's Tale. Okamoto, Rod. 2006. (J). per. 19.95 *(978-0-9764116-0-4(1))* Nutrishare Publishing.

—Max Goes to the Moon: A Science Adventure with Max the Dog. Bennett, Jeffrey. 2nd ed. 2012. (Science Adventures with Max the Dog Ser.). (ENG.). 32p. (J). (gr. 2-4). 15.00 *(978-1-937548-20-9(1))* Big Kid Science.

O'Kane, George & McEntee, Bill. Hook Em's Colorful Campus Tour - University of Texas A-Z: Forty Acres (A-Z) 2004. (J). 9.99 *(978-1-933069-01-2(5))* Odd Duck Ink, Inc.

O'Kane, George & Weikert, Dana. Baldwin's Colorful Campus Tour - Boston College A-Z. 2004. (J). 9.99 *(978-1-933069-00-5(7))* Odd Duck Ink, Inc.

Oke, Rachel, jt. illus. see Haynes, Jason.

O'Keefe, Laurie. Gopher to the Rescue! A Volcano Recovery Story, 1 vol. Jennings, Terry Catasús. 2012. (ENG.). 32p. (J). (gr. -1-4). 17.95 *(978-1-60718-131-6(2))*; pap. 9.95 *(978-1-60718-141-5(X))* Arbordale Publishing.

OKeefe, Raven. If Your Possum Go Daylight. Lofficier, Randy. 2009. (ENG.). 60p. (J). pap. 12.95 *(978-1-934543-78-8(0))* HollywoodComics.com, LLC.

O'Keeffe, Neil. American Horses. Moody, Ralph. 2004. (ENG.). 185p. pap. 14.95 *(978-0-8032-8301-5(6)*, MOOAMX, Bison Bks.) Univ. of Nebraska Pr.

Oketch, Alphonce Omondi. Rfaud Tastes Wisdom. Carlson, Martin D. 2013. 36p. pap. 11.00 *(978-0-9848791-2-0(9))* BoCook Publishing.

O'Kif. I'm Taller Than You! Benjamin, A. H. 2008. (Tadpoles Ser.). (ENG.). 24p. (J). (gr. -1-3). lib. bdg. *(978-0-7787-3854-1(X))* Crabtree Publishing Co.

—I'm Taller Than You! Benjamin, A. H. 2008. (Tadpoles Ser.). 23p. (J). (gr. -1-3). 17.15 *(978-1-4178-0927-1(2)*, Turtleback) Turtleback Bks.

—Muncle Trogg. Foxley, Janet. 2012. (ENG.). 224p. (J). (gr. 2-5). 14.99 *(978-0-545-37800-0(1)*, Chicken Hse., The) Scholastic, Inc.

—No Somos Irrompibles (12 Cuentos de Chicos Enamorados) 2003. (SPA.). 143p. (J). (gr. 8-12). pap. 9.95 *(978-950-511-243-2(2))* Santillana USA Publishing Co., Inc.

—La Tarea Segun Natacha. Pescetti, Luis María. 2003. (Coleccion Derechos Del Nino Ser.). (SPA.). 32p. (J). (gr. 3-5). pap. 7.95 *(978-84-204-5836-6(8))* Santillana USA Publishing Co., Inc.

O'Kif. Two Hungry Birds. Adeney, Anne. 2008. (Reading Corner Ser.). (ENG.). 24p. (J). (gr. k-2). pap. 6.99 ***(978-0-7496-7693-3(0))*** Hodder & Stoughton GBR. Dist: Independent Pubs. Group.

Okonji, Azuka. Malaik: A Poetry Collection for Children & Those Who Love Them. Chukwumerije, Dikeogu. 2012. 60p. pap. *(978-0-9557940-9-4(9))* Afriscope Publishing.

Oksner, Judith. Snowball: The Dancing Cockatoo. Montgomery, Sy. 2013. (ENG.). 64p. (J). pap. 15.00 *(978-0-87233-156-3(3))* Bauhan Publishing LLC.

Okstad, Ella, jt. illus. see Monks, Lydia.

Okstad, Ella K. Princess Kitty. Metzger, Steve. 2016. (J). ***(978-0-06-230662-3(6))*** Harper & Row Ltd.

Okum, David. Napoleon's Last Stand. Boyd, David. 2007. 48p. (J). lib. bdg. 23.08 *(978-1-4242-1639-0(7))* Fitzgerald Bks.

—Rebel Prince. Downey, Glen. 2007. 48p. (J). lib. bdg. 23.08 *(978-1-4242-1642-0(7))* Fitzgerald Bks.

Oladimeji, Solomon. Alexia Goes to School! Edwards-Tomdio, Stacy. l.t. ed. 2011. (ENG.). 34p. pap. 12.95 *(978-1-4611-1184-9(6))* CreateSpace Independent Publishing Platform.

Olafsdottir, Linda. The Enormous Turnip. Olmstead, Kathleen. 2013. (J). *(978-1-4027-8344-9(2))* Sterling Publishing Co., Inc.

Olafsdottir, Linda, jt. illus. see Zilber, Denis.

Olan, Agnieszka. The Forgotten Birthday. Lenington, Paula. 2011. 28p. pap. 24.95 *(978-1-4560-2711-7(5))* America Star Bks.

Olberg, Henry. The Magical Tooth Fairies: A Surprise in Mexico. 2012. (J). ***(978-0-86715-568-6(X))*** Edition Q, Inc.

Oldfield, Rachel. Outdoor Opposites. Williams, Brenda. 2015. 32ppp. (J). (gr. -1-2). 9.99 ***(978-1-78285-095-3(3))*** Barefoot Bks., Inc.

Oldfield, Rachel. Up, up, Up! Reed, Susan. 2010. (ENG.). 24p. (J). (gr. -1-2). 16.99 *(978-1-84686-369-1(4))* Barefoot Bks., Inc.

Oldham, Cindi. Marianne's Secret Cousins. Williams, Annie Morris. 2005. (Family History Adventures for Young Readers Ser.: 2). 240p. (J). per. 10.00 *(978-0-9645272-8-7(6))* Field Stone Pubs.

Oldham, Marion. Carrots, Just a Little Boy. Molesworth, Mary Louisa. 2004. reprint ed. pap. 22.95 *(978-1-4179-3800-1(5))* Kessinger Publishing, LLC.

Oldland, Nicholas. Big Bear Hug. Oldland, Nicholas. 2009. (ENG.). 32p. (J). (gr. -1-2). 16.95 *(978-1-55453-464-7(X))* Kids Can Pr., Ltd. CAN. Dist: Univ. of Toronto Pr.

—The Busy Beaver. Oldland, Nicholas. 2011. (ENG.). 32p. (J). 16.95 *(978-1-55453-749-5(5))* Kids Can Pr., Ltd. CAN. Dist: Univ. of Toronto Pr.

—Dinosaur Countdown. Oldland, Nicholas. 2012. (ENG.). 24p. (J). 15.95 *(978-1-55453-834-8(3))* Kids Can Pr., Ltd. CAN. Dist: Univ. of Toronto Pr.

—Making the Moose Out of Life. Oldland, Nicholas. 2010. (ENG.). 32p. (J). (gr. -1-2). 16.95 *(978-1-55453-580-4(8))* Kids Can Pr., Ltd. CAN. Dist: Univ. of Toronto Pr.

Oldroyd, Mark. John Henry. Krensky, Stephen. 2007. (On My Own Folklore Ser.). (ENG.). 48p. (gr. 2-4). per. 6.95 *(978-0-8225-6477-5(7)*, First Avenue Editions) Lerner Publishing Group.

—John Henry. Krensky, Stephen. 2006. (On My Own Folklore Ser.). (ENG.). 48p. (gr. 2-4). lib. bdg. 25.26 *(978-1-57505-887-0(1)*, Millbrook Pr.) Lerner Publishing Group.

—Leif Eriksson. Knudsen, Shannon. 2005. (On My Own Biography Ser.). (ENG.). 48p. (gr. 2-4). pap. 6.95 *(978-1-57505-828-3(6))*; lib. bdg. 25.26 *(978-1-57505-649-4(6)*, Carolrhoda Bks.) Lerner Publishing Group.

—Sarah Emma Edmonds Was a Great Pretender: The True Story of a Civil War Spy. Jones, Carrie. 2011. (Carolrhoda Picture Bks). (ENG.). 32p. (J). (gr. 2-5). 17.95 *(978-0-7613-5399-7(2)*, Carolrhoda Bks.) Lerner Publishing Group.

—Stowaway? Jarman, Julia. 2007. (Collins Big Cat Ser.). (ENG.). 48p. (J). pap. 8.99 *(978-0-00-723088-4(5))* HarperCollins Pubs. Ltd. GBR. Dist: Independent Pubs. Group.

Olds, Irene. How Do the Children Pray? Denis, Toni. 2010. 16p. 10.99 *(978-1-4490-5164-8(2))* AuthorHouse.

O'Leary Brown, Erin. El Cuento Dorado, un Libro de Aventura, la Historia de Goldentail. Hoffmann, Dana Marie. 2004. (SPA.). 42p. (J). 9.95 *(978-0-9753106-1-8(5))* Hoffmann Partnership, The.

—The Golden Tale, A Goldentail Adventure Story Book. Hoffmann, Dana. 2004. (ENG.). 44p. (J). 19.95 *(978-0-9753106-0-1(7))* Hoffmann Partnership, The.

—The Golden Tale, A Goldentail Adventure Story Book. Hoffmann, Dana Marie. 2004. 42p. (J). 9.95 *(978-0-9753106-3-2(1))* Hoffmann Partnership, The.

—Here Little Teacup! up! Up! Hoffmann, Catherine E. & Hoffmann, Dana Marie. 2005. 16p. (J). 6.95 *(978-0-9753106-2-5(3))* Hoffmann Partnership, The.

—In My Backyard. Curry, Don L. 2011. (Rookie Ready to Learn Ser.). 32p. (J). pap. 5.95 *(978-0-531-26697-7(4))*; (gr. -1-k). lib. bdg. 23.00 *(978-0-531-26416-4(5))* Scholastic Library Publishing. (Children's Pr.).

O'Leary Brown, Erin. En Mi Patio. O'Leary Brown, Erin. Curry, Don L. 2011. (Rookie Ready to Learn Español Ser.). (SPA.). 32p. (J). lib. bdg. 23.00 *(978-0-531-26116-3(6)*, Children's Pr.) Scholastic Library Publishing.

O'Leary, John. ¡En Busca del Tesoro del Pirata! O'Leary, John. 2005. (SPA & ENG.). 14p. (J). (gr. -1-k). 15.95 *(978-84-7864-794-1(5))* Combel Editorial, S.A. ESP. Dist: Independent Pubs. Group.

—Goldilocks: A Pop-Up Book. O'Leary, John. 2015. (ENG.). 16p. (J). (gr. -1-k). 19.99 *(978-1-85707-888-6(8))* Tango Bks. GBR. Dist: Independent Pubs. Group.

Oleynikov, Igor. The King with Horse's Ears & Other Irish Folktales. 2009. (Folktales of the World Ser.). (ENG.). 96p. (J). (gr. 3-7). 14.95 *(978-1-4027-3772-5(6))* Sterling Publishing Co., Inc.

—Mahalia Mouse Goes to College. Lithgow, John. 2007. (ENG.). 40p. (J). (gr. -1-3). 17.99 *(978-1-4169-2715-0(8)*, Simon & Schuster Bks. For Young Readers) Simon & Schuster Bks. For Young Readers.

—The Nightingale. Andersen, Hans Christian. 2007.Tr. of Nattergalen. (ENG.). 40p. (J). (gr. k). lib. bdg. 16.50 *(978-1-933327-31-0(6))*; (gr. 1). 15.95 *(978-1-933327-30-3(8))* Purple Bear Bks., Inc.

—Tiny Bear's Bible, 1 vol. Lloyd-Jones, Sally. 2015. (ENG.). 22p. (J). bds. 15.99 *(978-0-310-74787-1(2))* Zonderkidz.

—Tiny Bear's Bible, 1 vol. Lloyd-Jones, Sally. (Furry Bible Stories Ser.). (ENG.). 22p. (J). (gr. -1-k). 2009. pap. 14.99 *(978-0-310-71818-5(X))*; 2007. 14.99 *(978-0-310-71082-0(0))* Zonderkidz.

—Who Came First. Dargaw, Kate. 2008. 32p. 15.95 *(978-1-933327-45-7(6))* Purple Bear Bks., Inc.

Olien, Jessica. Shark Detective! Olien, Jessica. 2015. (ENG.). 32p. (J). (gr. -1-3). 17.99 ***(978-0-06-235714-4(X))*** HarperCollins Pubs.

Oliffe, Pat, et al. The X-Men. Marvel Press Group Staff et al. 2nd ed. 2014. (Origin Story Ser.). (ENG.). 48p. (J). (gr. 1-3). 8.99 *(978-1-4231-7226-0(4))* Marvel Worldwide, Inc.

Oliphant, Manelle. At the Beach, 1 vol. Spurr, Elizabeth. 2013. (ENG.). 22p. (J). (gr. -1 — 1). bds. 6.95 *(978-1-56145-583-6(0))* Peachtree Pubs.

—In the Garden, 1 vol. Spurr, Elizabeth. 2012. (ENG.). 22p. (J). bds. 6.95 *(978-1-56145-581-2(4))* Peachtree Pubs.

—In the Woods, 1 vol. Spurr, Elizabeth. 2012. (ENG.). 22p. (J). bds. 6.95 *(978-1-56145-582-9(2))* Peachtree Pubs.

—The Rescue Begins in Delaware. Earl, Cheri Pray & Williams, Carol Lynch. ed. 2013. (Just in Time Ser.: 1). (ENG.). 144p. (J). (gr. 3-7). pap. 9.95 *(978-1-938301-74-2(9))* Familius LLC.

—Sweet Secrets in Pennsylvania. Williams, Carol Lynch & Earl, Cheri Pray. ed. 2013. (Just in Time Ser.: 2). (ENG.). 152p. (J). (gr. 3-7). pap. 9.95 *(978-1-938301-76-6(5))* Familius LLC.

Oliva, Octavio. My Ducky Buddy. Smith, Michael & Wang, Emily. 2011. (CHI & ENG.). 23p. (J). *(978-0-9821675-7-1(1))* East West Discovery Pr.

—My Ducky Buddy. Smith, Michael. 2011. 23p. (J). *(978-0-9821675-4-0(7))* East West Discovery Pr.

—My Ducky Buddy/Mi Amigo el Pato. Smith, Michael. 2011. (ENG & SPA.). 24p. (J). (gr. -1-3). 12.95 *(978-0-9821675-5-7(5))* East West Discovery Pr.

—Relativity. Smith, Michael. 2011. 30p. (J). *(978-0-9799339-8-1(6))* East West Discovery Pr.

Oliva, Octavio. Grasshopper Buddy. Oliva, Octavio. Smith, Michael. 2012. (SPA & ENG.). (J). *(978-0-9856237-0-8(5))* East West Discovery Pr.

—Relativity: Relatividad. Oliva, Octavio. Smith, Michael. 2011. (SPA & ENG.). (J). *(978-0-9832278-3-0(7))* East West Discovery Pr.

Olive, Phyllis Carol. The Gift of the Holy Ghost. Olive, Phyllis Carol. unabr. ed. 2003. 25p. (J). (gr. k-4). 12.95 *(978-1-932280-08-1(1)*, 80081) Granite Publishing & Distribution.

Oliver, Alison. The Adventures of Huckleberry Finn: A Camping Primer. Adams, Jennifer. ed. 2014. (ENG.). 22p. (J). bds. 9.99 ***(978-1-4236-3622-9(8))*** Gibbs Smith, Publisher.

Oliver, Alison. Alice in Wonderland: A Colors Primer, 1 vol. Adams, Jennifer. 2012. (ENG.). 22p. (gr. k-1). bds. 9.99 *(978-1-4236-2477-6(7))* Gibbs Smith, Publisher.

—Alice in Wonderland Playset: A Babylit(r) Color Primer Board Book & Playset, 1 vol. Adams, Jennifer. ed. 2014. (ENG.). (J). bds. 19.99 *(978-1-4236-3644-1(9))* Gibbs Smith, Publisher.

—Anna Karenina: A BabyLit Fashion Primer, 1 vol. Adams, Jennifer. 2013. (ENG.). 22p. (gr. k-1). bds. 9.99 *(978-1-4236-3483-6(7))* Gibbs Smith, Publisher.

—Button-Lit Wearable Classic Literature Button Box, 1 vol. Gibbs Smith & Adams, Jennifer. 2012. (ENG.). 200p. 220.00 *(978-1-4236-3138-5(2))* Gibbs Smith, Publisher.

—A Christmas Carol: A BabyLit Colors Primer, 1 vol. Adams, Jennifer. 2012. (ENG.). 22p. (J). (gr. k-1). bds. 9.99 *(978-1-4236-2575-9(7))* Gibbs Smith, Publisher.

Oliver, Alison. Don Quixote: A Spanish Language Primer, 1 vol. Adams, Jennifer. 2015. (ENG.). 22p. (J). (gr. k-1). bds. 9.99 ***(978-1-4236-3875-9(1))*** Gibbs Smith, Publisher.

Oliver, Alison. Dracula: A BabyLit Counting Primer, 1 vol. Adams, Jennifer. 2012. (ENG.). 22p. (J). (gr. k-1). bds. 9.99 *(978-1-4236-2480-6(7))* Gibbs Smith, Publisher.

—Frankenstein: An Anatomy Primer. Adams, Jennifer. 2014. (ENG.). 22p. (gr. k-1). bds. 9.99 *(978-1-4236-3741-7(0))* Gibbs Smith, Publisher.

—Jabberwocky: A Nonsense Primer, 1 vol. Adams, Jennifer. 2013. (ENG.). 22p. (gr. k-1). bds. 9.99 *(978-1-4236-3408-9(X))* Gibbs Smith, Publisher.

—Jane Eyre: A Counting Primer, 1 vol. Adams, Jennifer. 2012. (ENG.). 22p. (J). (gr. k-1). bds. 9.99 *(978-1-4236-2474-5(2))* Gibbs Smith, Publisher.

Oliver, Alison. The Jungle Book: An Animal Primer. Adams, Jennifer. 2014. (ENG.). 22p. (J). bds. 9.99 ***(978-1-4236-3548-2(5))*** Gibbs Smith, Publisher.

Oliver, Alison. Moby-Dick. Adams, Jennifer. 2013. (ENG.). 22p. (gr. k-1). bds. 9.99 *(978-1-4236-3204-7(4))* Gibbs Smith, Publisher.

Oliver, Alison. Moby-Dick: Board Book & Playset, 1 vol. Adams, Jennifer. 2015. (ENG.). 22p. (J). 19.99 ***(978-1-4236-3871-1(9))*** Gibbs Smith, Publisher.

Oliver, Alison. Pride & Prejudice: A Counting Primer, 1 vol. Adams, Jennifer. 2011. (ENG.). 22p. (J). (gr. k-1). bds. 9.99 *(978-1-4236-2202-4(2))* Gibbs Smith, Publisher.

—Pride & Prejudice: Counting Primer Book & Playset. Adams, Jennifer. 2013. (ENG.). 22p. (J). bds. 19.99 *(978-1-4236-3515-4(9))* Gibbs Smith, Publisher.

—Romeo & Juliet: A BabyLit Counting Primer, 1 vol. Adams, Jennifer. 2011. (ENG.). 22p. (J). (gr. k-1). bds. 9.99 *(978-1-4236-2205-5(7))* Gibbs Smith, Publisher.

Oliver, Alison. The Secret Garden: A Flowers Primer, 1 vol. Adams, Jennifer. 2015. (ENG.). 22p. (J). (gr. k-1). bds. 9.99 ***(978-1-4236-3872-8(7))*** Gibbs Smith, Publisher.

Oliver, Alison. Sense & Sensibility: An Opposites Primer, 1 vol. Adams, Jennifer. 2013. (ENG.). 22p. (gr. k-1). bds. 9.99 *(978-1-4236-3170-5(6))* Gibbs Smith, Publisher.

Oliver, Alison. The Wonderful Wizard of Oz. Adams, Jennifer. 2014. (ENG.). 22p. (J). bds. 9.99 ***(978-1-4236-3718-9(6))*** Gibbs Smith, Publisher.

Oliver, Alison. Wuthering Heights: A Weather Primer. Adams, Jennifer. 2013. (ENG.). 22p. (gr. k-1). bds. 9.99 *(978-1-4236-3173-6(0))* Gibbs Smith, Publisher.

Oliver, Angel. The Adventures of Little Sprout. Rowland, Dawn. 2010. 32p. 12.99 *(978-1-4490-7725-9(0))* AuthorHouse.

Oliver, Jenni. A Summer to Die. Lowry, Lois. 2007. (ENG.). 160p. (YA). (gr. 7-12). per. 7.99 *(978-0-385-73420-2(4)*, Delacorte Bks. for Young Readers) Random Hse. Children's Bks.

Oliver, Julia. My Bedtime Angel. Darens, Cat. 2010. 18p. (J). (gr. -1-k). 7.95 *(978-0-8091-6745-6(X)*, Ambassador Bks.) Paulist Pr.

—My Morning Angel. Darens, Cat. 2010. 18p. (J). (gr. -1-k). 7.95 *(978-0-8091-6753-1(0)*, Ambassador Bks.) Paulist Pr.

Oliver, Liana. Buntley's Wing Kit. Adams, Paul Robert. 2012. 34p. pap. *(978-0-9871712-6-9(7))* Fastnet Bks.

Oliver, Maria Fernanda. Retablillo de Navidad. Nazoa, Aquiles.Tr. of Christmas Nativity. (SPA.). (J). (gr. 3-5). 10.95 *(978-980-257-067-6(2))* Ekare, Ediciones VEN. Dist: Lectorum Pubns., Inc.

Oliver, Mark. Aquanauts. Harvey, Damian. 2009. (Robo-Runners Ser.: 6). (ENG.). 112p. (J). (gr. k-2). pap. 8.99 *(978-0-340-94494-3(3)*, Hodder Children's Books) Hachette Children's Group GBR. Dist: Independent Pubs. Group.

—Are You Sleeping? Harris, Brooke. 2010. (Rising Readers Ser.). (J). 3.49 *(978-1-60719-685-3(9))* Newmark Learning LLC.

—Bear Went over the Mountain. Fuerst, Jeffrey B. 2010. (Rising Readers Ser.). (J). 3.49 *(978-1-60719-686-0(7))* Newmark Learning LLC.

—Let's Read! Monsters: An Owner's Guide. Emmett, Jonathan. ed. 2014. (Let's Read! Ser.). (ENG.). 400p. (J). (gr. k-2). pap. 7.99 *(978-1-4472-3697-9(1))* Pan Macmillan GBR. Dist: Independent Pubs. Group.

—Speak up, Spike. Ewart, Franzeska G. 2005. (Yellow Go Bananas Ser.). (ENG.). 48p. (J). (gr. 3-4). *(978-0-7787-2744-6(0))*; lib. bdg. *(978-0-7787-2722-4(X))* Crabtree Publishing Co.

—Tunnel Racers. Harvey, Damian. 2009. (Robo-Runners Ser.: 2). (ENG.). 112p. (J). (gr. k-2). pap. 8.99 *(978-0-340-94486-8(2)*, Hodder Children's Books) Hachette Children's Group GBR. Dist: Independent Pubs. Group.

Oliver, Mark. Robot Dog, 1 vol. Oliver, Mark. 2005. (ENG.). 28p. (J). pap. 16.00 *(978-1-56148-489-8(X)*, Good Bks.) Skyhorse Publishing Co., Inc.

Oliver, Narelle. The Best Beak in Boonaroo Bay. Oliver, Narelle. 48p. (YA). pap. *(978-0-85091-671-3(2)*, Lothian Children's Bks.) Hachette Australia.

—Sand Swimmers: The Secret Life of Australia's Desert Wilderness. Oliver, Narelle. 2015. (ENG.). 40p. (J). (gr. 2-5). 16.99 *(978-0-7636-6761-0(7))* Candlewick Pr.

—Twilight Hunt, 1 vol. Oliver, Narelle. 2007. (Seek-and-Find Bks.). (ENG.). 32p. (J). (gr. k-3). 16.95 *(978-1-59572-107-5(X))* Star Bright Bks., Inc.

Oliver, Stephen, photos by. Tamanos. 2005. (Coleccion Primeras Imagenes).Tr. of My First Look at Sizes. (SPA.). (J). (gr. -1-18). pap. 7.95 *(978-950-11-0907-8(0)*, SGM9070) Sigmar ARG. Dist: Continental Bk. Co., Inc.

Oliver, Tony. Frogs Sing Songs. Winer, Yvonne. 2003. 32p. (J). pap. 6.95 *(978-1-57091-549-9(0))*; (gr. -1-4). 16.95 *(978-1-57091-548-2(2))* Charlesbridge Publishing, Inc.

Olivera, Ramon. ABCs on Wings. Olivera, Ramon. 2015. (ENG.). 40p. (J). (gr. -1-2). 17.99 *(978-1-4814-3242-9(7)*, Little Simon) Little Simon.

Olivetti, Ariel. Phazer: A Man Lost in Alternative Universes. Nicieza, Mariano. 2008. 48p. (YA). per. 14.95 *(978-0-9740212-7-0(X))* Cedar Grove Bks.

Olivetti, Ariel, et al. Thor: Heaven & Earth. 2012. (ENG.). 112p. (YA). (gr. 8-17). pap. 14.99 *(978-0-7851-4833-3(7))* Marvel Worldwide, Inc.

Olivetti, Ariel, jt. illus. see Kano.

Oller, Erika. Cats, Cats, Cats! Newman, Lesléa. 2004. (ENG.). 32p. (J). (gr. -1-3). reprint ed. 7.99 *(978-0-689-86697-5(6)*, Simon & Schuster Bks. For Young Readers) Simon & Schuster Bks. For Young Readers.

—Dogs, Dogs, Dogs! Newman, Lesléa. 2011. (ENG.). 30p. (J). (gr. -1-3). pap. 16.99 *(978-1-4424-5228-2(5)*, Simon & Schuster Bks. For Young Readers) Simon & Schuster Bks. For Young Readers.

Ollerenshaw, Sue. Practical Guide to Teaching Reading Skills at All Levels: With Examples in French, German & Spanish. Ollerenshaw, Jenny. 2003. (FRE, GER, SPA & ENG.). 36p. pap. 10.00 *(978-0-9532440-6-5(7))* Advance Materials Ltd. GBR. Dist: Cambridge Univ. Pr.

Olliffe, Pat. The Avengers: An Origin Story. Thomas, Rich, Jr. 2nd ed. 2013. (Origin Story Ser.). (ENG.). 48p. (J). (gr. 1-3). 8.99 *(978-1-4231-8308-2(8))* Marvel Worldwide, Inc.

—The Mighty Avengers: An Origin Story. Thomas, Rich. 2012. (Origin Story Ser.). (ENG.). 48p. (J). (gr. 1-3). 8.99 *(978-1-4231-4841-8(X)*, Marvel Pr.) Disney Publishing Worldwide.

Olliffe, Pat, et al. Spider-Man: An Origin Story. Thomas, Rich, Jr. 2nd ed. 2013. (ENG.). 48p. (J). (gr. 1-3). 8.99 *(978-1-4231-8306-8(1))* Marvel Worldwide, Inc.

Olliffe, Pat. The Story of the X-Men Level 2 Reader. Macri, Thomas. 2013. (World of Reading Ser.). (ENG.). 32p. (J). (gr. 1-3). pap. 3.99 *(978-1-4231-7224-6(8))* Marvel Worldwide, Inc.

—Thor: An Origin Story. Thomas, Rich. 2013. (Origin Story Ser.). (ENG.). 48p. (J). (gr. 1-3). 8.99 *(978-1-4231-7215-4(9))* Marvel Worldwide, Inc.

Olliffe, Pat, jt. illus. see Marvel Artists Staff.

Olliffe, Patrick. Frankenstein: the Graphic Novel. Powell, Martin. 2012. (ENG.). 110p. pap. 9.99 *(978-1-4792-7227-3(2))* CreateSpace Independent Publishing Platform.

Ollweiler, D. R. The Strange Wish. Ollweiler, Angela Messina. 2010. 112p. pap. 10.95 *(978-1-60844-274-4(8))* Dog Ear Publishing, LLC.

Olmos, Roger. The Silly Nanny Goat. Bruno, Pepe & Bruno, Pep. 2007. (ENG.). 36p. (J). 17.95 *(978-84-96788-86-2(5))* OQO, Editora ESP. Dist: Baker & Taylor Bks.

—The Thing That Hurts Most in the World. Liván, Paco. 2007. (ENG.). 36p. (J). 17.95 *(978-84-96788-89-3(X))* OQO, Editora ESP. Dist: Baker & Taylor Bks.

—Las Trenzas del Abuelo. Figueras, Nuria. 2003. (Libros para Soñar Ser.). (SPA.). 32p. *(978-84-8464-180-3(5))* Kalandraka Editora, S.L. ESP. Dist: Lectorum Pubns., Inc.

Olofsdotter, Marie, jt. illus. see Adler, Michael S.

Olrun, Prudy, jt. illus. see Amos, Muriel.

Olsen, Christian. Make the World a Better Place! My Sharing Time, Talent & Treasure Activity Book. Flikkema, Elizabeth. 2006. 47p. 19.95 *(978-0-9774155-0-2(3))* Learning to Give.

Olsen, Greg. I Am a Child of God. 2004. (J). 17.95 *(978-1-57734-933-4(4))* Covenant Communications, Inc.

Olson, Cindy. A ferret in a Garret. Hoffman, Peter. 2008. 36p. (J). 24.99 *(978-0-9790247-6-4(5))* Artpacks.

Olson, Ed. Christ & the Church Vol. 42: New Testament Volume 42 Revelation Part 1. Greiner, Ruth B. 2010. 36p. (J). pap. *(978-1-932381-29-0(5)*, 1042) Bible Visuals International, Inc.

—Clopper & the Lost Boy, 1 vol. King, Emily. 2009. 32p. (J). 12.99 *(978-0-8254-2946-0(3))* Kregel Pubns.

—Clopper & the Night Travelers. King, Emily. 2007. 32p. (J). (gr. -1-3). 10.99 *(978-0-8254-3066-4(6))* Kregel Pubns.

—Clopper the Christmas Donkey, 1 vol. King, Emily. 2003. 32p. (J). 12.99 *(978-0-8254-3069-5(0))* Kregel Pubns.

—The Little Man in the Map: With Clues to Remember All 50 States. Martonyi, E. Andrew. 2007. (ENG.). 64p. (J). (gr. -1-3). pap. 19.95 *(978-0-9785100-4-6(6))* Schoolside Pr.

Olson, Ed & Willoughby, Yuko. Ly Huy's Escape: A Story of Vietnam. Carvin, Rose-Mae. Neal, Sharon & Mayer, Kristin, eds. 2010. (ENG.). 40p. (J). spiral bd. *(978-1-932381-13-9(9)*, 5275) Bible Visuals International, Inc.

Olson, Ed, jt. illus. see Hertzler, Frances H..

Olson, Ed, jt. illus. see Hertzler, Frances.

Olson, Ed, jt. illus. see Mayer, Melody.

Olson, Jennifer Gray. Ninja Bunny. 2015. (ENG.). 32p. (J). (gr. -1-2). 16.99 *(978-0-385-75493-4(0)*, Knopf Bks. for Young Readers) Random Hse. Children's Bks.

Olson, Johan, jt. illus. see Olson, John.

Olson, John & Olson, Johan. Los Cuentos de la Casa del Arbol. Munoz, Norma. rev. ed. 2005. (Castillo de la Lectura Blanca Ser.). (SPA & ENG.). 72p. (J). (gr. -1-3). pap. 6.95 *(978-970-20-0124-9(2))* Castillo, Ediciones, S. A. de C. V. MEX. Dist: Macmillan.

Olson, Julie. Already Asleep. 2006. (ENG.). 32p. (J). (gr. -1-3). 12.95 *(978-0-9766805-6-7(4))* Keene Publishing.

—Dear Cinderella. Moore, Marian & Kensington, Mary Jane. 2012. (ENG.). 32p. (J). (gr. -1-k). 12.99 *(978-0-545-34220-9(1)*, Orchard Bks.) Scholastic, Inc.

—Herd of Cows! Flock of Sheep! Walton, Rick. 2011. (ENG.). 36p. (gr. 2-3). pap. 7.99 *(978-1-4236-2090-7(9))* Gibbs Smith, Publisher.

—The Kickball Kids, 1 vol. Meister, Cari. 2009. (My First Graphic Novel Ser.). (ENG.). 32p. (gr. k-2). pap. 6.25 *(978-1-4342-1410-2(9))*; lib. bdg. 23.32 *(978-1-4342-1294-8(7))* Stone Arch Bks. (My First Graphic Novel).

—Little Penguin: The Emperor of Antarctica, 0 vols. London, Jonathan. 2011. (ENG.). 36p. (J). (gr. -1-3). 17.99

(978-0-7614-5954-5(5), 9780761459545, Amazon Children's Publishing) Amazon Publishing.
—The Opposites of My Jewish Year. Dion, L. M. 2005. (Very First Board Bks.). (ENG.). 12p. (J). (gr. -1 — 1). bds. 5.95 (978-1-58013-113-1(1), Kar-Ben Publishing) Lerner Publishing Group.
—Purple. Hickman, Kirt. 2012. 32p. pap. 15.99 (978-0-9796330-8-9(7)) Quillrunner Publishing LLC.
Olson, Julie. Discover America: From Sea to Shining Sea. Olson, Julie. 2014. (J). 17.99 (978-1-60907-855-3(1), Shadow Mountain) Shadow Mountain Publishing.
Olson, Meagan, jt. illus. see Gandy, Meg.
Olson, Robert, photos by. Alaska - Hints of Paradise: Photographs & Essays by Robert Olson. Olson, Robert. 2004. 160p. 39.95 (978-0-9749570-0-5(3)) Visions Of Nature.
Olson, Ryan. I Lost My Sock. Jakary, Lin. 2008. 40p. (J). (gr. -1-3). 16.99 (978-1-934867-01-3(2)) Wocto Publishing.
Olson, Stan. Johnny Appleseed. Kunstler, James Howard. 2005. (Rabbit Ears-A Classic Tale Ser.). 36p. (J). (gr. k-5). 25.65 (978-1-59197-765-0(7)) Spotlight.
Olson, Tom. The Tale of the Not-So-Perfect Christmas Tree. Cruikshank, Fran. 2005. 17p. (J). 9.95 (978-1-59971-055-6(2)) Aardvark Global Publishing.
Olten, Manuela. I Know Something You Don't Know. Raab, Brigitte. 2010. (ENG.). 32p. (J). (gr. -1-3). 16.95 (978-0-7358-2303-7(0)) North-South Bks., Inc.
—Mama, I Can't Sleep. Raab, Brigitte. 2012. (ENG.). 32p. (J). (gr. -1-k). 16.95 (978-1-61608-965-8(2), 608965, Sky Pony Pr.) Skyhorse Publishing Co., Inc.
—Where Does Pepper Come From. Raab, Brigitte, photos by. James, J. Alison, tr. from GER. 2008. 28p. (J). (gr. -1-3). pap. 6.95 (978-0-7358-2218-4(2)) North-South Bks., Inc.
—Where Does Pepper Come From? And Other Fun Facts. Raab, Brigitte. 2006. (ENG.). 32p. (J). (gr. -1-3). 15.95 (978-0-7358-2070-8(8)) North-South Bks., Inc.
O'Malley, Jason. Kirby's Derby: Pop-Up Animals on Wheels. White, George. 2013. (ENG.). 7p. 16.95 (978-1-60580-285-5(9)) Jumping Jack Pr.
O'Malley, Kathleen. A Fishy Story. Zimelman, Nathan. 2003. (Books for Young Learners). (ENG.). 16p. (J). pap. 5.75 (978-1-57274-538-4(X), 2453, Bks. for Young Learners) Owen, Richard C. Pubs., Inc.
—Five-Minute Mini-Mysteries. Smith, Stan. 2003. (ENG.). 96p. pap. 6.95 (978-1-4027-0031-6(8)) Sterling Publishing Co., Inc.
O'Malley, Kathy. How Fox Became Red. Hamilton, Martha & Weiss, Mitch. 2005. (ENG.). 12p. (J). 5.75 (978-1-57274-717-3(X), 2749, Bks. for Young Learners) Owen, Richard C. Pubs., Inc.
—Lazy Days of Summer. Young, Judy. rev. ed. 2007. (ENG.). 32p. (J). (gr. k-6). 15.95 (978-1-58536-241-7(7)) Sleeping Bear Pr.
—Murphy's Three Homes: A Story for Children in Foster Care. Gilman, Jan Levinson. 2008. 32p. (J). (gr. -1-2). 14.95 (978-1-4338-0384-0(4)); pap. 9.95 (978-1-4338-0385-7(2)) American Psychological Assn. (Magination Pr.).
—Prairie Numbers: An Illinois Number Book. Wargin, Kathy-jo. 2006. (Count Your Way Across the U. S. A. Ser.). (ENG.). 40p. (J). (gr. -1-3). 17.95 (978-1-58536-180-9(1)) Sleeping Bear Pr.
O'Malley, Kevin. The Birthday Pet, 0 vols. Javernick, Ellen. 2012. (ENG.). 32p. (J). (gr. k-3). pap. 7.99 (978-0-7614-6238-5(4), 9780761462385, Amazon Children's Publishing) Amazon Publishing.
—How They Croaked: The Awful Ends of the Awfully Famous. Bragg, Georgia. 2012. (ENG.). 192p. (J). (gr. 5-14). pap. 9.99 (978-0-8027-2794-7(8), Bloomsbury USA Childrens) Bloomsbury USA.
—How They Croaked: The Awful Ends of the Awfully Famous. Bragg, Georgia. 2011. (ENG.). (J). (gr. 5-8). 144p. 17.99 (978-0-8027-9817-6(9)); 192p. lib. bdg. 18.89 (978-0-8027-9818-3(7)) Walker & Co.
—If Beaver Had a Fever, 0 vols. Ketteman, Helen. 2011. (ENG.). 32p. (J). (gr. -1-3). 16.99 (978-0-7614-5951-4(0), 9780761459514, Amazon Children's Publishing) Amazon Publishing.
—Miss Malarkey Leaves No Reader Behind. Finchler, Judy. 2010. (Miss Malarkey Ser.). (ENG.). 32p. (J). (gr. k-3). pap. 7.99 (978-0-8027-2098-6(6)) Walker & Co.
—Miss Malarkey's Field Trip. Finchler, Judy. 2006. (Miss Malarkey Ser.). (ENG.). 32p. (J). (gr. k-4). 6.95 (978-0-8027-8917-4(X)) Walker & Co.
O'Malley, Kevin, et al. Once upon a Cool Motorcycle Dude. O'Malley, Kevin. 2005. (ENG.). 32p. (J). (gr. 1-5). 16.99 (978-0-8027-8947-1(1)) Walker & Co.
—Once upon a Royal Superbaby. O'Malley, Kevin. 2010. (ENG.). 40p. (J). (gr. k-3). 16.99 (978-0-8027-2164-8(8)) Walker & Co.
O'Malley, Kevin. The Planets in Our Solar System. Branley, Franklyn M. 2015. (Let's-Read-And-Find-Out Science 2 Ser.). (ENG.). 32p. (J). (gr. -1-3). pap. 6.99 **(978-0-06-238194-1(6))** HarperCollins Pubs.
O'Malley, Kevin. Slugs in Love, 0 vols. Pearson, Susan. 2012. (ENG.). 32p. (J). (gr. -1-3). pap. 7.99 (978-0-7614-6248-4(1), 9780761462484, Amazon Children's Publishing) Amazon Publishing.
—Someday Is Not a Day of the Week. Brennan-Nelson, Denise. 2005. (ENG.). 32p. (J). (gr. k-6). 15.95 (978-1-58536-243-1(3)) Sleeping Bear Pr.
—Testing Miss Malarkey. Finchler, Judy. 2003. (Miss Malarkey Ser.). (ENG.). 32p. (J). (gr. k-4). pap. 7.99 (978-0-8027-7624-2(8)) Walker & Co.
—Twelve Days: A Christmas Countdown. Snell, Gordon. 2005. 30p. (J). (gr. -1-2). reprint ed. 16.00 (978-0-7567-9403-3(X)) DIANE Publishing Co.
O'Malley, Kevin. Animal Crackers Fly the Coop. O'Malley, Kevin. 2010. (ENG.). 40p. (J). (gr. k-3). 16.99 (978-0-8027-9837-4(3)) Walker & Co.
—Backpack Stories. O'Malley, Kevin. 2009. (ENG.). 32p. (J). (gr. 2-4). 16.99 (978-0-8075-0504-5(8)) Whitman, Albert & Co.
—Congratulations, Miss Malarkey! O'Malley, Kevin. Finchler, Judy. 2009. (Miss Malarkey Ser.). (ENG.). 32p. (J). (gr. k-3). 16.99 (978-0-8027-9835-0(7)) Walker & Co.
—Gimme Cracked Corn & I Will Share. O'Malley, Kevin. 2007. (ENG.). 32p. (J). (gr. k-3). 16.95 (978-0-8027-9684-4(2)) Walker & Co.
—Lucky Leaf. O'Malley, Kevin. 2007. (ENG.). 32p. (J). (gr. -1-2). 7.99 (978-0-8027-9647-9(8)) Walker & Co.
—Mount Olympus Basketball. O'Malley, Kevin. 2005. (ENG.). 32p. (J). (gr. 1-4). pap. 7.99 (978-0-8027-7728-7(7)) Walker & Co.
Omary, Rachel. Animals in Dari. l.t. ed. 2003. 4p. (J). spiral bd. 10.95 (978-0-9740535-3-0(8)) Knight Publishing.
—Animals in Farsi. l.t. ed. 2003. 4p. (J). spiral bd. 10.95 (978-0-9740535-4-7(6)) Knight Publishing.
—Animals in Pashto. l.t. ed. 2003. 4p. (J). spiral bd. 10.95 (978-0-9740535-5-4(4)) Knight Publishing.
—Shapes & Colors in Dari. 2004. 5p. (J). spiral bd. 14.95 (978-0-9740535-7-8(0)) Knight Publishing.
—Shapes & Colors in Farsi. l.t. ed. 2004. 5p. (J). spiral bd. 14.95 (978-0-9740535-6-1(2)) Knight Publishing.
—Shapes & Colors in Pashto. l.t. ed. 2004. 5p. (J). spiral bd. 14.95 (978-0-9740535-8-5(9)) Knight Publishing.
O'Meara, Stephen, photos by. Into the Volcano: A Volcano Researcher at Work. O'Meara, Donna. 2007. (ENG.). 56p. (J). (gr. 3-7). 9.95 (978-1-55337-693-4(5)) Kids Can Pr., Ltd. CAN. Dist: Univ. of Toronto Pr.
O'Meara, Tim, photos by. Viva Frida. Morales, Yuyi. 2014. (ENG.). 40p. (J). (gr. -1-3). 17.99 (978-1-59643-603-9(4)) Roaring Brook Pr.
Omishi, Ray. Sorcerer Hunters Vol. 2: Authentic Relaunch. rev. ed. 2005. 192p. pap. 9.99 (978-1-59532-495-5(X)) TOKYOPOP, Inc.
—Sorcerer Hunters Authentic Relaunch. 2005. Vol. 1. 208p. pap. 9.99 (978-1-59532-494-8(1)); Vol. 3. 192p. pap. 9.99 (978-1-59532-496-2(8)) TOKYOPOP, Inc.
Omoto, Garrett. Kai the 'Opihi Gets the Point. Omoto, Gail. 2006. 32p. (J). 16.95 (978-1-933835-05-1(2)) Partners in Development Foundation.
—Ke Kino - The Body. 2006. Orig. Title: Ke Kino. (HAW.). 16p. (J). 8.95 (978-1-933835-02-0(8)) Partners in Development Foundation.
—Na Waihooluu. 2006.Tr. of Colors. (HAW & ENG.). 16p. (J). 8.95 (978-1-933835-00-6(1)) Partners in Development Foundation.
—Pili the 'Iwa Bird Shares the Letter B: Book #1 in the Gift of Reading Series. Hu, Lorna. 2013. (J). pap. 9.95 (978-1-933835-28-0(1)) Partners in Development Foundation.
—Pili the 'Iwa Bird Shares the Letter P: Book #2 in the Gift of Reading Series. 2013. (Gift of Reading Ser.: Bk. 2). (J). (978-1-933835-27-3(3)) Partners in Development Foundation.
—Tutu Books Preschool Library, 3 bks. 2006. (ENG & HAW.). 48p. (YA). 29.95 (978-1-933835-04-4(4)) Partners in Development Foundation.
—'Umi Keiki Li'i Li'i - Ten Little Children. 2006. Orig. Title: 'Umi Keiki Li'i Li'i. (HAW.). 16p. (J). 8.95 (978-1-933835-01-3(X)) Partners in Development Foundation.
ón, Daniel & Groff, David. Where Is the Empire State Building? Pascal, Janet. 2015. (Where Is... ? Ser.). (ENG.). 112p. (J). (gr. 3-7). 5.99 (978-0-448-48426-6(9), Grosset & Dunlap) Penguin Publishing Group.
O'Neal, Kerry. I Wish I Could Fly/I Can Fly! The Lonely Caterpillar BOOK I & the Lonely Butterfly BOOK II. O'Neal, Kerry. l.t. ed. 2006. 60p. (J). 29.99 (978-1-59879-197-6(4)) Lifevest Publishing, Inc.
O'Neal-Thorpe, Rochelle. Gabe & the Bike: Riding the Minuteman Trail. O'Neal-Thorpe, Rochelle. 2010. 30p. (J). pap. 12.95 (978-0-9823906-8-9(8)) Wiggles Pr.
—Gabe & the Park & his Big Toy Box: The Adventures of Gabe Series. O'Neal-Thorpe, Rochelle. 2010. 38p. (J). pap. 10.95 (978-0-9823906-9-6(6)) Wiggles Pr.
O'Neil, Sharron. Who Lives in the Sea?/Qui'n Vive en el Mar? Rosa-Mendoza, Gladys. 2007. (English Spanish Foundations Ser.). (ENG & SPA.). 20p. (J). (gr. -1-k). bds. 6.95 (978-1-931398-24-4(0)) Me+Mi Publishing.
O'Neill, Catharine. Benjy: A Ferocious Fairy Tale. O'Connor, Edwin. 2006. 96p. (J). reprint ed. pap. 12.00 (978-1-4223-5421-6(0)) DIANE Publishing Co.
—J. B. Wigglebottom & the Parade of Pets: True Ringside Tales, BBQ, & down-Home Recipes. Sathre, Vivian. 2013. (ENG.). 96p. (J). (gr. 2-5). pap. 13.99 (978-1-4814-2159-1(X), Atheneum Bks. for Young Readers) Simon & Schuster Children's Publishing.
O'Neill, Catharine. Annie & Simon. O'Neill, Catharine. 2008. (ENG.). 64p. (J). (gr. k-4). 15.99 (978-0-7636-2688-4(0)) Candlewick Pr.
—Annie & Simon: The Sneeze & Other Stories. O'Neill, Catharine. (Candlewick Sparks Ser.). (ENG.). 64p. (J). (gr. k-4). 2015. pap. 3.99 (978-0-7636-7788-6(4)); 2013. 15.99 (978-0-7636-4921-0(X)) Candlewick Pr.
O'Neill, Dave. The Boston Balloonies. Shankman, Ed. (Shankman & O'Neill Ser.). (J). (gr. -1-3). 2012. (ENG.). 40p. pap. 12.95 (978-1-933212-66-1(7)); 2008. 36p. 14.95 (978-1-933212-76-0(4)) Applewood Bks. (Commonwealth Editions).
—The Bourbon Street Band Is Back. Shankman, Ed. 2011. (Shankman & O'Neill Ser.). (ENG.). 32p. (gr. -1-3). 14.95 (978-1-933212-79-1(9), Commonwealth Editions) Applewood Bks.
—Champ & Me by the Maple Tree. Shankman, Ed. 2010. (Shankman & O'Neill Ser.). (ENG.). 32p. (gr. -1-3). 14.95 (978-0-9819430-5-3(5), Commonwealth Editions) Applewood Bks.
—The Cods of Cape Cod. Shankman, Ed. 2009. (Shankman & O'Neill Ser.). (ENG.). 32p. (gr. -1-3). 14.95 (978-1-933212-78-4(0), Commonwealth Editions) Applewood Bks.
—I Met a Moose in Maine One Day. Shankman, Ed. 2008. (Shankman & O'Neill Ser.). (ENG.). 32p. (J). (gr. -1-3). 14.95 (978-1-933212-77-7(2), Commonwealth Editions) Applewood Bks.
—My Grandma Lives in Florida. Shankman, Ed. 2013. (Shankman & O'Neill Ser.). (ENG.). 32p. (J). (gr. -1-3). 14.95 (978-1-933212-35-7(7), Commonwealth Editions) Applewood Bks.
O'Neill, Gemma. Monty's Magnificent Mane. O'Neill, Gemma. 2015. (ENG.). 40p. (J). (gr. -1-2). 15.99 (978-0-7636-7593-6(8), Templar) Candlewick Pr.
—Oh Dear, Geoffrey! O'Neill, Gemma. 2014. (ENG.). 32p. (J). (gr. -1-2). 15.99 (978-0-7636-6659-0(9), Templar) Candlewick Pr.
O'Neill, Jacquie. Figure Skating. 2010. (Sticker Stories Ser.). (ENG.). 16p. (J). (gr. -1-k). pap. 5.99 (978-0-448-45343-9(6), Grosset & Dunlap) Penguin Publishing Group.
O'Neill-McGrath, Michael. Jesus A to Z. O'Neill-McGrath, Michael. 2007. 32p. 16.99 (978-1-58459-332-4(6)) World Library Pubns.
O'Neill, Michael Patrick, photos by. Ocean Magic. O'Neill, Michael Patrick, . 2008. 48p. (J). (gr. 1-4). 19.95 (978-0-9728653-5-7(7)) Batfish Bks.
—Shark Encounters. O'Neill, Michael Patrick, . 2008. 48p. (J). (gr. 1-4). 19.95 (978-0-9728653-4-0(9)) Batfish Bks.
O'Neill, Michael Patrick, photos by. Fishy Friends: A Journey Through the Coral Kingdom. O'Neill, Michael Patrick. 2003. 64p. (J). 19.95 (978-0-9728653-0-2(6)) Batfish Bks.
—Let's Explore Coral Reefs. O'Neill, Michael Patrick. 2006. 32p. (J). 15.95 (978-0-9728653-3-3(0)) Batfish Bks.
—Let's Explore Sea Turtles. O'Neill, Michael Patrick. 2006. 32p. (J). 15.95 (978-0-9728653-2-6(2)) Batfish Bks.
—Let's Explore Sharks. O'Neill, Michael Patrick. 2006. 32p. (J). 15.95 (978-0-9728653-1-9(4)) Batfish Bks.
O'Neill, Philomena. Dance Me, Daddy, 1 vol. Morgan, Cindy. (ENG.). (J). 2014. 24p. bds. 6.99 (978-0-310-72584-8(4)); 2009. 32p. (gr. -1-2). 16.99 (978-0-310-71762-1(0)) Zonderkidz.
—Equal Shmequal. Kroll, Virginia. 2005. (Math Adventures Ser.). (ENG.). 32p. (J). (gr. k-3). per. 7.95 (978-1-57091-892-6(9)) Charlesbridge Publishing, Inc.
—Little Shrew Caboose. Stolberg, Tina. 2009. (ENG.). 32p. (J). (gr. k-2). 16.95 (978-0-9792035-7-2(0)) Pleasant St. Pr.
—The Thanksgiving Bowl, 1 vol. Kroll, Virginia. 2007. (ENG.). 32p. (J). (gr. k-3). 16.99 (978-1-58980-365-7(5)) Pelican Publishing Co., Inc.
—Toads & Tessellations. Morrisette, Sharon. 2012. (ENG.). 32p. (J). (gr. 2-5). 16.95 (978-1-58089-354-1(6)); pap. 7.95 (978-1-58089-355-8(4)) Charlesbridge Publishing, Inc.
O'Neill, Rachael. Baby! 2014. (ENG.). 8p. (J). (gr. -1 — 1). 9.99 (978-0-7641-6738-6(3)) Barron's Educational Series, Inc.
—Bad Rat. Wallacel, Karen. 2011. (My Phonics Readers: Level 1 Ser.). 24p. (J). (gr. -1-1). 24.25 (978-1-84898-504-9(5)) Sea-To-Sea Pubns.
—Fairy Colors. Repchuk, Caroline. 2007. (ENG.). 5p. (J). (gr. k — 1). bds. 5.99 (978-0-439-88704-5(6), Cartwheel Bks.) Scholastic, Inc.
—I Won't Do That Today: A Story of Stubbornness. Davies, Gill. 2009. (Let's Grow Together Ser.). 32p. (J). (gr. -1-2). pap. 10.55 (978-1-60754-765-5(1)); lib. bdg. 22.60 (978-1-60754-758-7(9)) Windmill Bks.
—My First Library: With Nine Colorful Books. (J). (978-1-85479-804-6(9)) O'Mara, Michael Bks., Ltd.
—A Special Wish: A Story of Confidence. Davies, Gill. 2009. (Let's Grow Together Ser.). 32p. (J). (gr. -1-2). pap. 10.55 (978-1-60754-769-3(4)); lib. bdg. 22.60 (978-1-60754-760-0(0)) Windmill Bks.
O'Neill, Rachael. Do You Want a Hug, Honey Bunny? O'Neill, Rachael. 2008. (Tiger Tales Ser.). 12p. (J). (gr. -1-k). 8.95 (978-1-58925-829-7(0)) Tiger Tales.
O'Neill, Sean, et al. Adventures in Science. Yomtov, Nel. 2012. (Adventures in Science Ser.). (ENG.). 32p. (gr. 3-4). pap. 190.80 (978-1-4296-8470-5(4)); pap. 31.80 (978-1-4296-8469-9(0)) Capstone Pr., Inc. (Graphic Library).
—Adventures in Science. Yomtov, Nel et al. 2012. (Adventures in Science Ser.). (ENG.). 32p. (gr. 3-4). lib. bdg. 119.96 (978-1-4296-8172-8(1), Graphic Library) Capstone Pr., Inc.
O'Neill, Sean. When Volcanoes Erupt!, 1 vol. Yomtov, Nelson. 2012. (Adventures in Science Ser.). (ENG.). 32p. (gr. 3-4). pap. 8.10 (978-1-4296-7990-9(5)); lib. bdg. 29.99 (978-1-4296-7547-5(0)) Capstone Pr., Inc. (Graphic Library).
—When Volcanoes Erupt! Yomtov, Nel. 2012. (Adventures in Science Ser.). (ENG.). 32p. (gr. 3-4). pap. 47.70 (978-1-4296-8468-2(2), Graphic Library) Capstone Pr., Inc.
—Will & Wendy Build a Website with Digital Tools. Bailer, Darice. 2013. (ENG.). 32p. (J). lib. bdg. 25.27 (978-1-59953-584-5(X)); (gr. 2-4). pap. 11.94 (978-1-60357-558-4(8)) Norwood Hse. Pr.
O'Neill, Todd. Mary Cohen's Tuneful Introduction to 2nd Finger Spacing: Easy Well-Known Pieces for Violin. Cohen, Mary. 2003. (Faber Edition Ser.). (ENG.). 24p. pap. 10.25 (978-0-571-51806-7(0)) Faber & Faber, Ltd. GBR. Dist: Alfred Publishing Co., Inc.
Oneones. Happy Birthday Coco. Oneones. 2006. (ENG.). 56p. (J). 9.99 (978-1-933605-13-5(8)) Kane Miller.
Ong, Cheri. Being Different Is a Good Thing. Ong, Cheri. Ong, Alvin. 2011. (ENG.). 34p. pap. 9.99 (978-1-4663-6718-0(0)) CreateSpace Independent Publishing Platform.
Ong, Cristina. I Knew You Could! A Book for All the Stops in Your Life. Dorfman, Craig. 2003. (Little Engine That Could Ser.). (ENG.). 32p. (J). (gr. -1-2). 11.99 (978-0-448-43148-2(3), Grosset & Dunlap) Penguin Publishing Group.
—I'm a Good Friend! Parker, David. 2004. (J). pap. (978-0-439-62807-5(5)) Scholastic, Inc.
Ong, Wilson. Mommy Promises. Steigemeyer, Julie. 2008. 32p. pap. 7.49 (978-0-7586-1479-7(9)) Concordia Publishing Hse.
—Paper Son: Lee's Journey to America. James, Helen Foster & Loh, Virginia Shin-Mui. 2013. (Tales of Young Americans Ser.). (ENG.). 32p. (J). (gr. 1-4). 16.99 (978-1-58536-833-4(4), 202366) Sleeping Bear Pr.
—T Is for Tutu: A Ballet Alphabet. Rodriguez, Sonia & Browning, Kurt. 2011. (ENG.). 32p. (gr. k-5). 16.95 (978-1-58536-312-4(X)) Sleeping Bear Pr.
Onishi, Satoru. Quien Se Esconde? Onishi, Satoru. 2007. 31p. (gr. -1-k). 17.50 (978-1-4177-9749-3(5), Turtleback) Turtleback Bks.
Ono, Toshihiro. Seikai Trilogy: Banner of the Stars: The Shape of Bonds, 3 vols., Vol. 2. Morioka, Hiroyuki. rev. ed. 2004. (Seikai Trilogy). 200p. pap. 9.99 (978-1-59182-858-7(9)) TOKYOPOP, Inc.
Onoda, Yuta. Wild Wings. Lewis, Gill. (ENG.). 304p. (J). (gr. 3-7). 2012. pap. 7.99 (978-1-4424-1446-4(4)); 2011. 18.99 (978-1-4424-1445-7(6)) Simon & Schuster Children's Publishing. (Atheneum Bks. for Young Readers).
Onque, Sulaiman. It's in the Book: Good Ol' Friends, 9. 3rd ed. 2005. (ENG.). 60p. (J). per. (978-0-9763841-2-0(4)) Anointed Pubs.
Onyefulu, Ifeoma, photos by. Deron Goes to Nursery School. Onyefulu, Ifeoma. (First Experiences Ser.). (ENG.). 32p. (J). (gr. -1-1). 2015. pap. 9.99 (978-1-84780-252-1(4)); 2010. 17.99 (978-1-84507-864-5(0)) Quarto Publishing Group UK GBR. (Frances Lincoln). Dist: Hachette Bk. Group.
—Grandma Comes to Stay. Onyefulu, Ifeoma. 2015. (First Experiences Ser.). (ENG.). 32p. (J). (gr. -1-1). pap. 9.99 (978-1-84780-251-4(6), Frances Lincoln) Quarto Publishing Group UK GBR. Dist: Hachette Bk. Group.
Oobayashi, Kaoru. Biographical Comics: the Wright Brothers: Challengers of the AIR. Imamura, Keiko & Imamura, Keiko. 2012. (Biographical Comic Ser.). (ENG.). 152p. (J). (gr. 3-6). 18.99 (978-1-4215-4320-8(6)) Shogakukan JPN. Dist: Simon & Schuster, Inc.
—Biographical Comics: the Wright Brothers: Challengers of the AIR. Imamura, Keiko. 2012. (Biographical Comic Ser.). (ENG.). 152p. (J). (gr. 3-6). pap. 9.99 (978-1-4215-4321-5(4)) Shogakukan JPN. Dist: Simon & Schuster, Inc.
Opal, Paola. Saffy & Ollie. 2012. (Simply Small Ser.). (ENG.). 24p. (J). (gr. -1 — 1). bds. 7.95 (978-1-897476-69-7(8)) Simply Read Bks. CAN. Dist: Ingram Pub. Services.
—Stinky Skunk Mel. Winters, Kari-Lynn & Van Turennout, Paola. George, Kallie, ed. 2014. (ENG.). 32p. (J). (gr. -1-3). 15.95 (978-1-897476-83-3(3)) Simply Read Bks. CAN. Dist: Ingram Pub. Services.
Opatz, Shane. Behind the Zoo: Find Out What the Animals Eat & Do at Irvine Park Zoo, Chippewa Falls, Wisconsin. Opatz, Shane, photos by. Holtz, Monica Stauber. 2011. (J). (978-0-9837617-1-6(X)) Holtz Creative Enterprises.
Opie, David. Border Breakdown: The Fall of the Berlin Wall. Smith, Molly. 32p. (J). (gr. 1-6). 2010. (ENG.). 9.95 (978-1-60727-126-0(5)); 2010. (ENG.). 19.95 (978-1-60727-125-3(7)); 2010. (ENG.). 16.95 (978-1-60727-123-9(0)); 2010. (ENG.). pap. 6.95 (978-1-60727-124-6(9)); 2009. (ENG.). 17.95 (978-1-60727-121-3(5)); 2009. 17.95 incl. audio (978-1-60727-102-4(8)); 2009. pap. 9.95 incl. audio (978-1-60727-103-1(6)) Soundprints.
—Dozer's Run: A True Story of a Dog & His Race. Levy, Debbie & Panza, Rosana. 2014. (ENG.). 32p. (J). (gr. 1-4). 16.99 (978-1-58536-896-9(2), 203665) Sleeping Bear Pr.
—Monkey & the Engineer. 2007. 24p. (J). 14.95 (978-0-9793972-6-4(X)) JD Publishing.
Oppenheimer, Nancy. Tali's Jerusalem Scrapbook. Rouss, Sylvia A. 2003. 32p. (J). (gr. 1-4). 14.95 (978-1-930143-68-5(0)); pap. 9.95 (978-1-930143-69-2(9)) Simcha Media Group. (Pitspopany Pr.).
Opsahl, Gail Kohler. Talking with My Treehouse Friends about Cancer: An Activity Book for Children of Parents with Cancer. Van Dernoot, Peter R. & van Dernoot, Peter R. 2007. (ENG.). 24p. (J). pap. 9.95 (978-1-55591-630-5(9)) Fulcrum Publishing.
Opseth, Katie. Beginning Knitting: Stitches with Style, 1 vol. Olson, Kay Melchisedech & Boonyadhistam, Thiranut. 2006. (Crafts Ser.). (ENG.). 32p. (gr. 3-4). 27.32 (978-0-7368-6473-2(3), Snap Bks.) Capstone Pr., Inc.
Oquendo, Lisa. Abecedario. 2006. (SPA.). bds. 5.99 (978-1-934113-04-2(2)) Little Cubans, LLC.
—Números - Numbers. 2006. (ENG & SPA.). (J). bds. 5.99 (978-1-934113-01-1(8)) Little Cubans, LLC.
Orbaan, Albert. Thunder Rolling: The Story of Chief Joseph. Miller, Helen Markley. 2011. 190p. 42.95 (978-1-258-06189-0(9)) Literary Licensing, LLC.
Orbach, Ruth. Acorns & Stew, Too. Orbach, Ruth. ed. 2011. (ENG.). 32p. (J). 10.99 (978-1-61067-017-3(5)) Kane Miller.
Orback, Craig. Benjamin Banneker: Pioneering Scientist. Wadsworth, Ginger. 2003. (On My Own Biography Ser.). (ENG.). 48p. (gr. 2-4). 25.26 (978-0-87614-916-4(6)); per. 6.95 (978-0-87614-104-5(1), Carolrhoda Bks.) Lerner Publishing Group.
—Benjamin Banneker: Pioneering Scientist. Wadsworth, Ginger. 2006. (On My Own Biographies Ser.). 47p. (gr. 2-5). 17.00 (978-0-7569-6705-5(8)) Perfection Learning Corp.
—Boys Camp: Zee's Story. Jazynka, Kitson & Tripp, Valerie. 2015. (ENG.). 144p. (J). (gr. 1-5). 14.99 (978-1-62914-754-3(0), Sky Pony Pr.) Skyhorse Publishing Co., Inc.
—Bronco Charlie & the Pony Express. Brill, Marlene Targ. 2004. (On My Own History Ser.). (ENG.). 48p. (gr. 2-4). pap. 6.95 (978-1-57505-618-0(6)); lib. bdg. 25.26 (978-1-57505-587-9(2)) Lerner Publishing Group.
—Bronco Charlie y el Pony Express. Brill, Marlene Targ. Translations.com Staff, tr. 2005. (Yo Solo: Historia (on My Own History) Ser.). (SPA.). 48p. (gr. 2-4). lib. bdg. 25.26 (978-0-8225-2991-0(2), Ediciones Lerner) Lerner Publishing Group.

—Clara Morgan & the Oregon Trail Journey. Figley, Marthy Rhodes. 2011. (History Speaks: Picture Books Plus Reader's Theater Ser.). 48p. pap. 56.72 *(978-0-7613-7631-6(3))*; (ENG.). (gr. 2-4). 27.93 *(978-0-7613-5878-7(1)*, Millbrook Pr.) Lerner Publishing Group.

—Gifts from the Enemy. Ludwig, Trudy. 2014. (HumanKIND Project Ser.). (ENG.). 32p. (gr. 2-7). 16.95 *(978-1-935952-97-8(8))* White Cloud Pr.

—Hot Pursuit: Murder in Mississippi. Deutsch, Stacia & Cohon, Rhody. 2010. (ENG.). 40p. (J). (gr. 3-5). pap. 7.95 *(978-0-7613-3956-4(6))*; lib. bdg. 17.95 *(978-0-7613-3955-7(8))* Lerner Publishing Group. (Kar-Ben Publishing).

—John Adams Speaks for Freedom. Hopkinson, Deborah. ed. 2005. 32p. (J). lib. bdg. 15.00 *(978-1-59054-992-6(9))* Fitzgerald Bks.

—John Adams Speaks for Freedom. Hopkinson, Deborah. 2005. (Ready-To-read SOFA Ser.). (ENG.). 32p. (J). (gr. 1-3). pap. 3.99 *(978-0-689-86907-5(X)*, Simon Spotlight) Simon Spotlight.

—John Greenwood's Journey to Bunker Hill. Figley, Marty Rhodes. 2010. (History Speaks: Picture Books Plus Reader's Theater Ser.). (ENG.). 48p. (gr. 2-4). pap. 9.95 *(978-0-7613-6134-3(0))*; lib. bdg. 27.93 *(978-1-58013-673-0(7)*, Millbrook Pr.) Lerner Publishing Group.

—Keeping the Promise: A Torah's Journey. Lehman-Wilzig, Tami. 2004. (ENG.). 32p. (J). (gr. k-3). pap. 9.95 *(978-1-58013-118-6(2)*, Kar-Ben Publishing) Lerner Publishing Group.

—Nate's Story, Bk. 2. Jazynka, Kitson. 2013. (ENG.). 144p. (J). (gr. 2-5). 14.95 *(978-1-62087-981-8(6)*, 620981, Sky Pony Pr.) Skyhorse Publishing Co., Inc.

—Nature's Paintbox: A Seasonal Gallery of Art & Verse. Thomas, Patricia. 2007. (Millbrook Picture Books Ser.). (ENG.). 32p. (J). (gr. 2-4). lib. bdg. 16.95 *(978-0-8225-6807-0(1)*, Millbrook Pr.) Lerner Publishing Group.

—Paul Bunyan. 2007. (On My Own Folklore Ser.). (ENG.). 48p. (gr. 2-4). per. 6.95 *(978-0-8225-6479-9(3)*, First Avenue Editions) Lerner Publishing Group.

—Paul Revere's Ride, 1 vol. Mortensen, Lori. 2009. (Our American Story Ser.). (ENG.). 32p. (gr. 1-3). lib. bdg. 26.65 *(978-1-4048-5537-3(8)*, Nonfiction Picture Bks.) Picture Window Bks.

—Prisoner for Liberty. Figley, Marty Rhodes. (On My Own History Ser.). (ENG.). 48p. (gr. 2-4). 2009. pap. 6.95 *(978-0-8225-9022-4(0)*, First Avenue Editions); 2008. lib. bdg. 25.26 *(978-0-8225-7280-0(X)*, Millbrook Pr.) Lerner Publishing Group.

—Survival in the Snow. Wadsworth, Ginger. 2009. (On My Own History Ser.). (ENG.). 48p. (gr. 2-4). 25.26 *(978-0-8225-7892-5(1))* Lerner Publishing Group.

—Susan B. Anthony: Fighter for Freedom & Equality. Slade, Suzanne & Picture Window Books Staff. 2007. (Biographies Ser.). (ENG.). 24p. (gr. k-3). 25.99 *(978-1-4048-3104-9(5)*, Nonfiction Picture Bks.) Picture Window Bks.

—An Uncommon Revolutionary: A Story about Thomas Paine. Waxman, Laura Hamilton. 2003. (Creative Minds Biographies Ser.). (ENG.). 64p. (gr. 4-8). 22.60 *(978-1-57505-180-2(X)*, Carolrhoda Bks.) Lerner Publishing Group.

—Washington Is Burning. Figley, Marty Rhodes. 2007. (On My Own History Ser.). (ENG.). 48p. (gr. 2-4). per. 6.95 *(978-0-8225-6050-0(X)*, First Avenue Editions) Lerner Publishing Group.

—Zack's Story, Bk. 1. Dokey, Cameron. 2013. (ENG.). 128p. (J). (gr. 2-5). 14.95 *(978-1-62087-528-5(4)*, 620528, Sky Pony Pr.) Skyhorse Publishing Co., Inc.

Orban, Paul. Father of the American Navy: John Barry. Anderson, Floyd. 2011. 188p. 42.95 *(978-1-258-07454-8(0))* Literary Licensing, LLC.

Orchard, Eric. Anything but Hank! Wells, Zachariah et al. 2008. (ENG.). 50p. (J). (gr. k-3). 19.95 *(978-1-897231-36-4(9))* Biblioasis CAN. Dist: Consortium Bk. Sales & Distribution.

—Bluenose Adventure. Halsey, Jacqueline. 2013. (ENG.). 32p. (J). (gr. -1-3). 16.95 *(978-1-4595-0280-2(9))* Formac Publishing Co., Ltd. CAN. Dist: Casemate Pubs. & Bk. Distributors, LLC.

—The Terrible, Horrible, Smelly Pirate, 1 vol. Muller, Carrie & Halsey, Jacqueline. ed. 2008. (ENG.). 32p. (J). (gr. k-3). pap. 10.95 *(978-1-55109-655-1(2))* Nimbus Publishing, Ltd. CAN. Dist: Orca Bk. Pubs. USA.

Ord, G. W. Tommy Smith's Animals. Selous, Edmund. 2009. 166p. pap. 9.95 *(978-1-59915-376-6(9))* Yesterday's Classics.

Ord, Mandy. Sensitive Creatures. Ord, Mandy. 2012. (ENG.). 304p. (YA). (gr. 9). pap. 19.95 *(978-1-74237-216-7(3))* Allen & Unwin AUS. Dist: Independent Pubs. Group.

Ordas, Emi. Sticker Dressing Extreme Sports. Gillespie, Lisa Jane. 2014. (Usborne Activities Ser.). (ENG.). 24p. (J). (gr. -1-3). 8.99 *(978-0-7945-3164-5(4)*, Usborne) EDC Publishing.

—Sticker Dressing Warriors. Gillespie, L. ed. 2013. (Sticker Dressing Ser.). 34p. (J). pap. 8.99 *(978-0-7945-3353-3(1)*, Usborne) EDC Publishing.

Ordaz, Francisco. The Very First Christmas. Maier, Paul L. (J). 2004. 20p. (gr. -1-k). bds. 7.49 *(978-0-7586-0689-1(3))*; 2003. 32p. (gr. 1-5). 7.49 *(978-0-7586-0616-7(8))* Concordia Publishing Hse.

—The Very First Easter. Maier, Paul L. (J). 2005. 20p. bds. 7.49 *(978-0-7586-0717-1(2))*; 2004. 32p. pap. 7.49 *(978-0-7586-0627-3(3))*; 2004. 32p. 13.49 *(978-0-570-07053-5(8))* Concordia Publishing Hse.

Ordaz, Frank. Be Careful, Kangaroo! Langeland, Deirdre. 2005. (Soundprints' Read-and-Discover Ser.). (ENG.). 48p. (J). (gr. -1-1). 12.95 *(978-1-59249-146-9(4)*, PS2010) Soundprints.

—The Titanic Game. Warner, Michael N. 2007. (ENG.). 201p. (J). pap. 9.95 *(978-0-9744446-2-8(6))* All About Kids Publishing.

—Waves of Grace. Doherty, Patrick. 2007. 160p. (J). (gr. 9-12). pap. 9.95 *(978-0-9744446-6-6(9))* All About Kids Publishing.

Ordóñez, María Antonia. Beba y la Isla Nena: Beba & the Little Island. Landrón, Rafael & Landrón, José Rafael. 2010. (SPA & ENG.). 32p. (J). *(978-1-934370-05-6(3)*, Campanita Bks.) Editorial Campana.

Ordóñez, Miguel. Your Baby's First Word Will Be DADA. Fallon, Jimmy. 2015. (ENG.). (J). (gr. -1 — -1). 40p. 16.99 ***(978-1-250-00934-0(0))***; 16p. bds. 7.99 ***(978-1-250-07181-1(X))*** Feiwel & Friends.

O'Reilly, John, jt. illus. see Teo, Ali.

Orellana, Nery. Before She Gets Her Period: Talking with Your Daughter about Menstruation. Gillooly, Jessica B. 2003. 163p. (J). pap. 13.95 *(978-0-9622036-9-5(6))* Perspective Publishing, Inc.

Oren, Rony. The Animated Menorah: Travels on a Space Dreidel. Sidon, Ephraim. 2007. (Animated Holydays Ser.). 48p. 17.95 *(978-965-7108-80-2(2)*, Lambda) Urim Pubns. ISR. Dist: Coronet Bks.

Origin Communications. Princess Amara & the Magic Fruit. 2007. 23p. (J). 15.99 *(978-0-9800538-0-7(3))* Ufodike, Ekwutosi.

Origlio, Peter. Charlie & Albert. 2007. 22p. (J). pap. 12.95 *(978-0-9801329-0-8(8))* Charlie & Albert.

Oriol, Elsa. The Patchwork Torah. Ofanansky, Allison. 2014. (Sukkot & Simchat Torah Ser.). (ENG.). 32p. (J). (gr. -1-5). 17.95 *(978-1-4677-0426-7(1))*; 7.95 *(978-1-4677-0427-4(X))* Lerner Publishing Group. (Kar-Ben Publishing).

Orkrania, Alexia. I'm Just a Little Cow. Reasoner, Charles. 2014. (ENG.). 12p. (gr. -1). *(978-1-78244-588-3(9))* Top That! Publishing PLC.

—I'm Just a Little Horse. Ross, Eilidh. 2014. (ENG.). 12p. (gr. -1). *(978-1-78244-589-0(7))* Top That! Publishing PLC.

—123 Dreams. Graham, Oakley. 2014. (Turn & Learn Ser.). (ENG.). 12p. (J). (gr. -1-3). *(978-1-78244-534-0(X))* Top That! Publishing PLC.

Orlandi, Lorenzo. Look Inside the Time of Jesus. Rock, Lois. 2014. (ENG.). 8p. (J). (gr. k-2). bds. 14.99 *(978-0-7459-6398-3(6))* Lion Hudson PLC GBR. Dist: Independent Pubs. Group.

Orlando, jt. illus. see Gribel, Christiane.

Orman, Roscoe. Ricky & Mobo. 2007. (J). 14.95 *(978-1-59299-255-3(2))* Inkwater Pr.

Orme, Harinani. Kili & the Singing Snails. Crowl, Janice. 2011. (J). 16.95 *(978-1-58178-104-5(0))* Bishop Museum Pr.

—Pulelehua & Mamaki. Crowl, Janice. 2009. (J). 14.95 *(978-1-58178-090-1(7)*, Kamahoi Pr.) Bishop Museum Pr.

Ormerod, Jan. Adios, Ratoncito. Harris, Robie H. Rioja, Alberto Jiménez, tr. (SPA.). (J). (gr. k-2). 16.00 *(978-1-930332-34-8(3)*, LC8567) Lectorum Pubns., Inc.

—The Buffalo Storm. Applegate, Katherine. 2014. (ENG.). 32p. (J). (gr. -1-3). pap. 6.99 *(978-0-544-33921-7(5)*, HMH Books For Young Readers) Houghton Mifflin Harcourt Publishing Co.

—Goodbye Mousie. Harris, Robie H. 2004. (ENG.). 32p. (J). (gr. -1-3). reprint ed. 16.99 *(978-0-689-87134-4(1)*, Simon & Schuster/Paula Wiseman Bks.) Simon & Schuster/Paula Wiseman Bks.

—I Am Not Going to School Today! Harris, Robie H. 2003. (ENG.). 32p. (J). (gr. -1-3). 17.99 *(978-0-689-83913-9(8)*, McElderry, Margaret K. Bks.) McElderry, Margaret K. Bks.

—Itsy-Bitsy Animals. Wild, Margaret. 2012. (ENG.). 24p. (J). (gr. k-k). 16.99 *(978-1-921714-42-9(5))* Little Hare Bks. AUS. Dist: Independent Pubs. Group.

—Itsy-Bitsy Animals. Wild, Margaret. 2013. (ENG.). 24p. (J). (-k). pap. 9.99 *(978-1-74297-468-2(6))* Little Hare Bks. AUS. Dist: Independent Pubs. Group.

—Itsy-Bitsy Babies. Wild, Margaret. 2011. (ENG.). 24p. (J). (gr. -1 — 1). pap. 8.99 *(978-1-921541-89-6(X))* Little Hare Bks. AUS. Dist: Independent Pubs. Group.

—Mama's Day. Ashman, Linda. 2011. (ENG.). 32p. (J). (gr. -1-1). pap. 16.99 *(978-1-4424-5233-6(1)*, Simon & Schuster Bks. For Young Readers) Simon & Schuster Bks. For Young Readers.

—May I Pet Your Dog? The How-to Guide for Kids Meeting Dogs (and Dogs Meeting Kids) Calmenson, Stephanie. 2007. (ENG.). 32p. (J). (gr. -1-3). 9.95 *(978-0-618-51034-4(6))* Houghton Mifflin Harcourt Publishing Co.

—Ponko & the South Pole. Hooper, Meredith & Quarto Generic Staff. 2012. (ENG.). 32p. (J). (gr. -1-1). pap. 8.99 *(978-1-84780-403-7(9)*, Frances Lincoln) Quarto Publishing Group UK GBR. Dist: Hachette Bk. Group.

Ormerod, Jan. Lizzie Nonsense. Ormerod, Jan. 2004. 40p. (J). *(978-1-877003-59-2(X))* Little Hare Bks. AUS. Dist: HarperCollins Pubs. Australia.

—Water Witcher. Ormerod, Jan. 2008. (ENG.). 32p. (J). (gr. -1). pap. 13.99 *(978-1-921272-16-5(3))* Little Hare Bks. AUS. Dist: Independent Pubs. Group.

Ornia-Blanco, Miguel. Cold Feet, 1 vol. Dahl, Michael. 2010. (Monster Street Ser.). (ENG.). 32p. (gr. 1-3). lib. bdg. 22.65 *(978-1-4048-6070-4(3)*, Monster Street) Picture Window Bks.

—In One Ear, Out the Other, 1 vol. Dahl, Michael. 2010. (Monster Street Ser.). (ENG.). 32p. (gr. 1-2). lib. bdg. 22.65 *(978-1-4048-6068-1(1)*, Monster Street) Picture Window Bks.

—Two Heads Are Better Than One, 1 vol. Dahl, Michael. 2010. (Monster Street Ser.). (ENG.). 32p. (gr. 1-2). lib. bdg. 22.65 *(978-1-4048-6067-4(3)*, Monster Street) Picture Window Bks.

Ornoff, Theresa. Logan's Journey. Heath, Kathy & Martin, Karla. 2007. 32p. (J). (gr. -1-3). lib. bdg. 17.95 *(978-1-933982-02-1(0))* Bumble Bee Publishing.

O'Rourke, Page Eastburn. Henry Lleva la Cuenta. Skinner, Daphne. 2007. (Math Matters Ser.). 32p. (J). (gr. -1-3). pap. 5.95 *(978-1-57565-250-4(1))* Kane Pr., Inc.

—Que Sigue, Nina? Math Matters en Espanol. Kassirer, Sue. 2005. 32p. (J). pap. 5.95 *(978-1-57565-152-1(1))* Kane Pr., Inc.

—Slow down, Sara! Driscoll, Laura. 2003. (Science Solves It! Ser.). 32p. (J). pap. 5.95 *(978-1-57565-125-5(4))* Kane Pr., Inc.

—Where's Harley? Felton, Carol & Felton, Amanda. 2003. (Math Matters Ser.). 32p. (J). pap. 5.95 *(978-1-57565-132-3(7))* Kane Pr., Inc.

O'Rourke, Ryan. Alphabet Trains. Vamos, Samantha R. 2015. (ENG.). 32p. (J). (gr. -1-2). lib. bdg. 14.95 *(978-1-58089-592-7(1))* Charlesbridge Publishing, Inc.

—Eight Days Gone. McReynolds, Linda. 2012. (ENG.). 40p. (J). (gr. k-3). 16.95 *(978-1-58089-364-0(3))* Charlesbridge Publishing, Inc.

—Lisa Loeb's Silly Sing-Along: The Disappointing Pancake & Other Zany Songs. Loeb, Lisa. 2011. (ENG.). 24p. (J). (gr. -1-2). 14.95 *(978-1-4027-6915-3(6))* Sterling Publishing Co., Inc.

—One Big Rain: Poems for Every Season. ed. 2014. (ENG.). 32p. (J). (gr. 2-5). pap. 7.95 *(978-1-57091-717-2(5))* Charlesbridge Publishing, Inc.

O'Rourke, Ryan. Bella Lost & Found. O'Rourke, Ryan. 2014. (ENG.). 40p. (J). (gr. -1-3). 17.99 *(978-0-06-221861-2(1))* HarperCollins Pubs.

—Bella, Up, Up & Away. O'Rourke, Ryan. 2016. (J). 17.99 *(978-0-06-221863-6(8))* HarperCollins Pubs.

Orpinas, Jean-Paul. Jack Sparrow: The Siren Song. Kidd, Rob. 2006. 122p. (J). lib. bdg. 16.00 *(978-1-4242-1571-3(4))* Fitzgerald Bks.

Orpinas, Jean-Paul, et al. Wall-E. Vick-E & RH Disney Staff. 2008. (Little Golden Book Ser.). (ENG.). 24p. (J). (gr. -1-2). 3.99 *(978-0-7364-2422-6(9)*, RH/Disney) Random Hse. Children's Bks.

Orpinas, Jean-Paul & Tilley, Scott. Cars. 2006. (Little Golden Book Ser.). (ENG.). 24p. (J). (gr. -1-2). 3.99 *(978-0-7364-2347-2(8)*, Golden/Disney) Random Hse. Children's Bks.

Orpinas, Jean-Paul, jt. illus. see Disney Storybook Artists Staff.

Orpinas, Jean-Paul, jt. illus. see Tilley, Scott.

Orr, Forrest W. Swift Rivers. Meigs, Cornelia & Holm, Jennifer L. 2004. (ENG.). 288p. (J). (gr. 5). pap. 8.99 *(978-0-8027-7703-4(1))* Walker & Co.

Orr, Katherine. Discover Hawaii's Volcanoes: Birth by Fire. Cook, Mauliola. rev. ed. 2010. (ENG.). 44p. pap. *(978-1-59700-849-5(4))* Island Heritage Publishing.

Orsolini, Laura. Lulu the Shy Piglet. Jeong, SoYun. rev. ed. 2014. (MySELF Bookshelf: Social & Emotional Learning/Self-Worth Ser.). (ENG.). 32p. (J). (gr. k-2). pap. 11.94 *(978-1-60357-654-3(1))*; lib. bdg. 22.60 *(978-1-59953-645-3(5))* Norwood Hse. Pr.

Ortac, Feride. Sharp Kids Activity. Ortac, Arda. 2009. 80p. Bk. 1. pap. 9.00 *(978-1-60743-151-0(3))*; Bk. 02. pap. 9.00 *(978-1-60743-152-7(1))* Independent Pub.

Ortakales, Denise. Good Morning, Garden. Brenner, Barbara. 2004. (ENG.). 32p. (J). (gr. -1-k). 15.95 *(978-1-55971-888-2(9))* Cooper Square Publishing Llc.

Ortega, Damian. Alegre Roger y el Tesoro Submarino. French, Vivian. Solana, María T., tr. 2006. (la Orilla Del Viento Ser.). (SPA.). 125p. (J). pap. 7.50 *(978-968-16-6837-2(5)*, 163) Fondo de Cultura Economica USA.

Ortega, David. I Am Special. Lisl, Charlotte. 2006. 16p. (J). 9.99 *(978-1-4120-8911-1(5))* Trafford Publishing.

Ortega, James. Snowflakes in June. Ortiz, Andrea. 2013. 36p. 14.00 *(978-0-9884237-9-4(0))* CLF Publishing.

Ortega, Jose. Agua Agua Agua, Level 2. Mora, Pat. Flor Ada, Alma, tr. 3rd ed. 2003. (Dejame Leer Ser.). (SPA.). 16p. (J). (gr. -1-1). 6.50 *(978-0-673-36292-6(2)*, Good Year Bks.) Celebration Pr.

—Fiesta. McConnie Zapater, Beatriz. 2005. (Multicultural Celebrations Ser.). 32p. (J). 4.95 *(978-1-59373-009-3(8))* Bunker Hill Publishing, Inc.

Ortega, Macarena. The Turtle's Shell. Campos, Paula. 2008.Tr. of tortuga Golosa. (J). pap. 14.95 *(978-0-9801147-5-1(6))* Jorge Pinto Bks.

Ortelli, Barbara. Thankyouplease. Winters, Pierre. 2011. (ENG.). 32p. (J). (gr. -1-k). 15.95 *(978-1-60537-099-6(1))* Clavis Publishing.

Ortiz, Ada. Does It Really Rain Cats & Dogs? Whaley, Michelle Marie. 2008. 36p. pap. 24.95 *(978-1-60563-233-9(3))* America Star Bks.

Ortiz Montanez, Nivea. The Gang & the Biggest Book in the World. Quinones, Juan Carlos. 2004. (Purple Ser.). 48p. (J). *(978-1-57581-438-4(2))* Ediciones Santillana, Inc.

—The Lost Sock. Iturrondo, Angeles Molina & Iguina, Adriana. 2004. (Green Ser.). 24p. (J). *(978-1-57581-434-6(X))* Ediciones Santillana, Inc.

—La Pandilla Bajo el Arbol. Quinones, Juan Carlos. 2004. (Purple Ser.). (SPA.). 44p. (J). (gr. 3-5). pap. 5.95 *(978-1-57581-439-1(0))* Santillana USA Publishing Co., Inc.

Ortiz, Nivea. Sopa de Hortalizas. Molina, Angeles. 2004. (SPA & ENG.). (J). *(978-0-8477-0131-5(X))* Univ. of Puerto Rico Pr.

Ortiz, Oscar. The Poet Upstairs. Cofer, Judith Ortiz. 2012. (J). (gr. 5-9). 16.95 *(978-1-55885-704-9(4)*, Piñata Books) Arte Publico Pr.

—La Poeta Del Piso de Arriba. Ortiz Cofer, Judith. Baeza Ventura, Gabriela, tr. from ENG. 2014. (SPA.). (J). 17.95 *(978-1-55885-788-9(5)*, Piñata Books) Arte Publico Pr.

Osada, Ryuta. Othello. Shakespeare, William. 2009. (Manga Shakespeare Ser.). (ENG.). 208p. (YA). (gr. 7-11). pap. 12.95 *(978-0-8109-8350-2(8)*, Amulet Bks.) Abrams.

Osadchuk, Keit. When I Was Big. Kaplan, Debbie. 2010. (J). pap. *(978-1-57043-318-4(6))* Eckankar.

Osban, Rodger. Maria & the Stars of Nazca (Maria y las Estrellas de Nazca) Jepson-Gilbert, Anita. Casis, Carmen A., tr. 2004.Tr. of Maria y las Estrellas de Nazca. (SPA & ENG.). 32p. (J). pap. incl. audio compact disk *(978-0-9749745-0-7(1))* TAE Nazca Resources.

—Maria & the Stars of Nazca (Maria y las Estrellas de Nazca), without audio CD. Jepson-Gilbert, Anita. 2004.Tr. of Maria y las Estrellas de Nazca. (ENG & SPA.). pap. 14.95 *(978-0-9749745-1-4(X))* TAE Nazca Resources.

Osborn, Jim. Manners Made Easy. Moore, June Hines. 2004. 96p. pap., tchr. ed., stu. ed. 9.99 *(978-0-8054-3770-6(3))* B&H Publishing Group.

Osborn, Kathy. A Horse in the House & Other Strange but True Animal Stories. Ablow, Gail. 2007. (ENG.). 40p. (J). (gr. 1-4). 17.99 *(978-0-7636-2838-3(7))* Candlewick Pr.

Osborn, Tonia Bennington. Rupert's Tales: A Book of Bedtime Stories. Kyrja. 2014. (ENG.). 64p. (J). (gr. 5-8). 19.99 *(978-0-7643-4694-1(6))* Schiffer Publishing, Ltd.

—Rupert's Tales: The Wheel of the Year - Samhain, Yule, Imbolc, & Ostara. Kyrja. 2012. 64p. (J). 19.99 *(978-0-7643-3987-5(7))* Schiffer Publishing, Ltd.

—Rupert's Tales: The Wheel of the Year Activity Book. Kyrja. 2012. 40p. (J). pap. 9.99 *(978-0-7643-4020-8(4))* Schiffer Publishing, Ltd.

Osborne, Amber. Puffy Buffy Jones Jones Osborne Dadoot Da Do. Osborne, Amber. Osborne, Dwight. ed. 2006. (J). pap. 11.99 *(978-0-9786431-0-2(0))* AAO Publishing.

Osborne, Graham. Build Your Own Steam Locomotive: A Complete, Easy-to-Assemble Model. Farrington, Karen & Constable, Nick. 2004. 34p. (J). (gr. 4-8). reprint ed. pap. 17.00 *(978-0-7567-8261-0(9))* DIANE Publishing Co.

Osborne, Richard. Animal Stories: Young Readers. Thomas, David, ed. 2011. 190p. 42.95 *(978-1-258-10206-7(4))* Literary Licensing, LLC.

—Teenage Animal Stories. Carter, Russell Gordon. 2011. 252p. 46.95 *(978-1-258-09864-3(4))* Literary Licensing, LLC.

—Teenage Horse Stories. Thomas, David, ed. 2011. 252p. 46.95 *(978-1-258-09866-7(0))* Literary Licensing, LLC.

Osborne, Will & Murdocca, Sal. Rain Forests: A Nonfiction Companion to Afternoon on the Amazon. Osborne, Mary Pope. 2012. (Stepping Stone Book Ser.: No. 5). (ENG.). 128p. (J). (gr. 2-5). lib. bdg. 12.99 *(978-0-375-91355-6(6)*, Random Hse. Bks. for Young Readers) Random Hse. Children's Bks.

—Twisters & Other Terrible Storms: A Nonfiction Companion to Twister on Tuesday. Osborne, Mary Pope. 2003. (Stepping Stone Book(TM) Ser.: No. 8). (ENG.). 128p. (J). (gr. 2-5). 5.99 *(978-0-375-81358-0(6))*; lib. bdg. 12.99 *(978-0-375-91358-7(0))* Random Hse. Children's Bks. (Random Hse. Bks. for Young Readers).

Oseid, Kelsey. How to Face Paint. Atwood, Megan. 2013. (Make Your Own Fun Ser.). (ENG.). 24p. (J). (gr. 1-4). 28.50 *(978-1-62323-560-4(X)*, 206326) Child's World, Inc., The.

—How to Make Paper Airplanes. Adams, B. 2013. (Make Your Own Fun Ser.). (ENG.). 24p. (J). (gr. 1-4). 28.50 *(978-1-62323-562-8(6)*, 206328) Child's World, Inc., The.

—Iris & Ian Learn about Interjections. Bailer, Darice. 2015. (Language Builders Ser.). (ENG.). 32p. (J). (gr. 2-4). pap. 11.94 *(978-1-60357-707-6(6))*; lib. bdg. 25.27 *(978-1-59953-672-9(2))* Norwood Hse. Pr.

—Magic Tricks with String. Adams, B. 2013. (Make Your Own Fun Ser.). (ENG.). 24p. (J). (gr. 1-4). 28.50 *(978-1-62323-561-1(8)*, 206333) Child's World, Inc., The.

Osenchakov, Yuri. Snyder: The Pig's Tale. Nilsen, Morten. 2007. 116p. 24.95 *(978-0-9774906-0-8(2))* Counterbalance Bks.

O'Shaughnessy, Nancy. Where Do the Bubbles Go? Macaluso, Jennifer. 2006. (ENG.). 40p. (J). (gr. -1-3). pap. 21.99 *(978-1-4259-3929-8(5))* AuthorHouse.

O'Shea, Bonnie. Henrietta the Farmer & the Long, Long, Long, Long Vacation! Winter, Christopher. 2012. 32p. pap. 13.95 *(978-1-60594-856-0(X))* Aeon Publishing Inc.

O'Shea, Miranda. The Tale of the Little Duckling: Who Am I & Where Do I Belong? Weinstein, Grit. 2010. (ENG.). 44p. pap. 14.95 *(978-1-4536-4437-9(7))* CreateSpace Independent Publishing Platform.

Oshida, Tim. The Society's Traitor. (The Discoveries of Arthur Grey ser.: 1). (ENG.). (J). (gr. 4-8). 2012. 298p. 27.99 *(978-0-9852202-0-4(1))*; 2nd ed. 2015. 304p. 27.99 ***(978-1-943317-00-4(3))*** Panama Hat Publishing, Ltd.

Oshii, Mamoru, jt. illus. see Katsura, Masakazu.

Osker, Denise. All White Dogs Love Mud. Davis, Dayna. 14p. (J). (gr. 1-5). pap. *(978-0-9660350-1-8(1))* Suzalooz Pr.

Osmond, Jack. A Fishy Adventure. Osmond, Joanne H. 2013. 152p. pap. 12.99 *(978-1-933334-26-4(6))* Vision Tree, Ltd., The.

Osnaya, Ricardo. Ali Baba & the Forty Thieves, 1 vol. Manning, Matthew K. 2010. (Classic Fiction Ser.). (ENG.). 72p. (gr. 2-3). 26.65 *(978-1-4342-1988-6(7))*; pap. 7.15 *(978-1-4342-2776-8(6))* Stone Arch Bks. (Graphic Revolve).

Osorio, Sergio. Ajedrez Infantil: Diviertete Con el Juego Mas Inteligente! Kidder, Harvey. 2005.Tr. of Chess for Children. (SPA.). 128p. (YA). (gr. 2). pap. *(978-968-403-315-3(X))* Selector, S.A. de C.V.

—El Arca de Noé. Fernandez, Francisco. 2005. (Historia de la Biblia Ser.). (SPA.). 64p. (J). pap. 4.70 *(978-970-643-872-0(6))* Selector, S.A. de C.V. MEX. Dist: Lectorum Pubns., Inc.

—La Creacion. Fernandez, Francisco. 2005. (Historia de la Biblia Ser.). (SPA.). 64p. (J). pap. 4.70 *(978-970-643-871-3(8))* Selector, S.A. de C.V. MEX. Dist: Lectorum Pubns., Inc.

—Jonas. Fernandez, Francisco. 2005. (Historia de la Biblia Ser.). (SPA.). 64p. (J). pap. 4.70 *(978-970-643-876-8(9))* Selector, S.A. de C.V. MEX. Dist: Lectorum Pubns., Inc.

—Los Milagros de Jesus. Fernandez, Francisco. 2005. (Historia de la Biblia Ser.). (SPA.). 64p. (J). pap. 4.70 *(978-970-643-882-9(3))* Selector, S.A. de C.V. MEX. Dist: Lectorum Pubns., Inc.

—Moises. Fernandez, Francisco. 2005. (Historia de la Biblia Ser.). (SPA.). 64p. (J). pap. 4.70 *(978-970-643-875-1(0))* Selector, S.A. de C.V. MEX. Dist: Lectorum Pubns., Inc.

Osorno, Laura. Invitacion a la Fiesta del Gran Gorila. Baena, Gloria. 2003. (SPA.). 32p. (J). 8.95 *(978-958-04-7072-4(3))* Norma S.A. COL. Dist: Distribuidora Norma, Inc.

Ospital, Genevelve. The Story of the Infinipede. Kamke, Bridget. 2003. (J). 19.95 *(978-0-9744306-0-7(9))* You Can Do It! Productions.

Osterhold, Jared. Cooks up a Surprise. 2011. (Olivia TV Tie-In Ser.). (ENG.). 24p. (J). (gr. -1-2). pap. 3.99 *(978-1-4424-1384-9(0),* Simon Spotlight) Simon Spotlight.

—For the Love of Bubbles. Banks, Steven et al. 2006. (SpongeBob SquarePants Ser.: 12). (ENG.). 64p. (J). pap. 4.99 *(978-1-4169-1633-8(4),* Simon Spotlight/Nickelodeon) Simon Spotlight/Nickelodeon.

—How to Draw Incredible Ocean Animals, 1 vol. McCurry, Kristen. 2013. (Smithsonian Drawing Bks.). (ENG.). 64p. (gr. 3-4). pap. 7.19 *(978-1-62065-728-7(7));* pap. 41.70 *(978-1-62065-729-4(5));* lib. bdg. 33.32 *(978-1-4296-9940-2(X))* Capstone Pr., Inc.

—Olivia & the Babies. 2010. (Olivia TV Tie-In Ser.). (ENG.). 24p. (J). (gr. -1-2). pap. 3.99 *(978-1-4169-9529-6(3),* Simon Spotlight) Simon Spotlight.

—OLIVIA & the Pet Project. 2015. (Olivia TV Tie-In Ser.). (ENG.). 24p. (J). (gr. -1-1). pap. 3.99 *(978-1-4814-2895-8(0),* Simon Spotlight) Simon Spotlight.

—OLIVIA Becomes a Vet. 2011. (Olivia TV Tie-In Ser.). (ENG.). 24p. (J). (gr. -1-1). 16.99 *(978-1-4424-2860-7(0));* pap. 3.99 *(978-1-4424-2859-1(7))* Simon Spotlight. (Simon Spotlight).

—Olivia Claus. 2010. (Olivia TV Tie-In Ser.). (ENG.). 24p. (J). (gr. -1-1). 16.99 *(978-1-4424-0662-9(3),* Simon Spotlight) Simon Spotlight.

—OLIVIA Goes Camping. 2011. (Olivia TV Tie-In Ser.). (ENG.). 24p. (J). (gr. -1-1). 15.99 *(978-1-4424-2253-7(X));* pap. 3.99 *(978-1-4424-2135-6(5))* Simon Spotlight. (Simon Spotlight).

—OLIVIA Goes to the Library. 2013. (Olivia TV Tie-In Ser.). (ENG.). 24p. (J). (gr. -1-1). 16.99 *(978-1-4424-8479-5(9));* pap. 3.99 *(978-1-4424-8478-8(0))* Simon Spotlight. (Simon Spotlight).

—OLIVIA Helps Mother Nature. 2014. (Olivia TV Tie-In Ser.). (ENG.). 24p. (J). (gr. -1-1). pap. 3.99 *(978-1-4424-9664-4(9),* Simon Spotlight) Simon Spotlight.

—Olivia Leaps! Barton, Elizabeth & Shaw, Natalie. 2009. (Olivia TV Tie-In Ser.). (ENG.). 12p. (J). (gr. -1-1). bds. 6.99 *(978-1-4169-8572-3(7),* Simon Spotlight) Simon Spotlight.

—Olivia Leaps! Shaw, Natalie. 2010. (Olivia TV Ser.). (ENG.). 12p. (J). bds. 8.99 *(978-1-84738-612-0(1))* Simon & Schuster Children's Publishing.

—OLIVIA Loves Halloween. Testa, Maggie. 2014. (Olivia TV Tie-In Ser.). (ENG.). 24p. (J). (gr. -1-1). pap. 3.99 *(978-1-4814-0462-4(8),* Simon Spotlight) Simon Spotlight.

—OLIVIA Makes a Charm Bracelet. McDoogle, Farrah. 2012. (Olivia TV Tie-In Ser.). (ENG.). 16p. (J). (gr. -1-2). pap. 6.99 *(978-1-4424-4163-7(1),* Simon Spotlight) Simon Spotlight.

—OLIVIA Measures Up. 2013. (Olivia TV Tie-In Ser.). (ENG.). 24p. (J). (gr. -1-1). 15.99 *(978-1-4424-5974-8(3));* pap. 3.99 *(978-1-4424-5973-1(5))* Simon Spotlight. (Simon Spotlight).

—Olivia Opens a Lemonade Stand. 2010. (Olivia TV Tie-In Ser.). (ENG.). 24p. (J). (gr. -1-2). pap. 3.99 *(978-1-4169-9932-4(9),* Simon Spotlight) Simon Spotlight.

—OLIVIA Plants a Garden. 2011. (Olivia TV Tie-In Ser.). (ENG.). 24p. (J). (gr. -1-1). pap. 3.99 *(978-1-4424-1675-8(0),* Simon Spotlight) Simon Spotlight.

—OLIVIA Plants a Garden. Sollinger, Emily. 2011. (Olivia TV Tie-In Ser.). (ENG.). 24p. (J). (gr. -1-1). 16.99 *(978-1-4424-2011-3(1),* Simon Spotlight) Simon Spotlight.

—OLIVIA Plays Soccer. 2013. (Olivia TV Tie-In Ser.). (ENG.). 24p. (J). (gr. -1-1). 16.99 *(978-1-4424-7249-5(9),* Simon Spotlight) Simon Spotlight.

—OLIVIA Plays Soccer. Gallo, Tina. 2013. (Olivia TV Tie-In Ser.). (ENG.). 24p. (J). (gr. -1-1). pap. 3.99 *(978-1-4424-7248-8(0),* Simon Spotlight) Simon Spotlight.

—OLIVIA Takes a Trip. 2010. (Olivia TV Tie-In Ser.). (ENG.). 24p. (J). (gr. -1-1). 16.99 *(978-1-4424-1381-8(6),* Simon Spotlight) Simon Spotlight.

—OLIVIA Takes a Trip. 2010. (Olivia TV Tie-In Ser.). (ENG.). 24p. (J). (gr. -1-1). pap. 3.99 *(978-1-4169-9933-1(7),* Simon Spotlight) Simon Spotlight.

—OLIVIA Talks Turkey. McDoogle, Farrah. 2011. (Olivia TV Tie-In Ser.). (ENG.). 16p. (J). (gr. -1-1). pap. 5.99 *(978-1-4424-3061-7(3),* Simon Spotlight) Simon Spotlight.

—OLIVIA Wishes on a Star. 2014. (Olivia TV Tie-In Ser.). (ENG.). 24p. (J). (gr. -1-2). pap. 3.99 *(978-1-4814-1769-3(X),* Simon Spotlight) Simon Spotlight.

—The Search for the Book of Thoth, 1 vol. 2012. (Egyptian Myths Ser.). (ENG.). 32p. (gr. 3-4). pap. 7.95 *(978-1-4048-7243-1(4));* lib. bdg. 27.99 *(978-1-4048-7151-9(9))* Picture Window Bks. (Nonfiction Picture Bks.).

Osterhold, Jared & Johnson, Shane L. Olivia & Her Great Adventures. Falconer, Ian et al. 2012. (J). *(978-1-4351-4316-6(7),* Simon Spotlight) Simon Spotlight.

Osterhold, Jared & Meschini, Leonardo. Smithsonian Drawing Books. McCurry, Kristen. 2013. (Smithsonian Drawing Bks.). (ENG.). 64p. (gr. 3-4). lib. bdg. 66.64 *(978-1-4296-9941-9(8))* Capstone Pr., Inc.

Osterhold, Jared, jt. illus. see Meschini, Leonardo.

Ostermeyer, Tim, photos by. Titus & Tiana: Lesson for Baby Tigers. 2011. 18.95 *(978-0-9794228-6-7(8))* Ostermeyer Photography.

Ostin, Joyce, photos by. Hollywood Moms: Photographs by Joyce Ostin. 2005. 112p. (YA). reprint ed. 30.00 *(978-0-7567-9363-0(7))* DIANE Publishing Co.

Ostrom, Bob. An Airplane Daydream. Meier, Joanne. 2008. (Herbster Readers: the First Day of School: Level 4 Readers: Machines Ser.). (ENG.). 32p. (J). (gr. -1-2). 25.64 *(978-1-60253-025-6(4),* 200338) Child's World, Inc., The.

—Alex & the Box Shop: The Sound of X. Minden, Cecilia. 2010. (Sounds of Phonics Ser.). (ENG.). 24p. (J). (gr. -1-2). 25.64 *(978-1-60253-422-3(5),* 200878) Child's World, Inc., The.

—April. Kelley, C. 2014. (Twelve Magic Months Ser.). (ENG.). 24p. (J). (gr. k-3). 27.07 *(978-1-62687-362-9(3),* 207202) Child's World, Inc., The.

—The Aquarium Adventure. Meier, Joanne D. & Minden, Cecilia. 2009. (Herbster Readers: Teamwork at Lotsaluck Camp: Level 3 Readers: Careers Ser.). (ENG.). 32p. (J). (gr. -1-2). 25.64 *(978-1-60253-209-0(5),* 200304) Child's World, Inc., The.

—August. Kelley, C. 2014. (Twelve Magic Months Ser.). (ENG.). 24p. (J). (gr. k-3). 27.07 *(978-1-62687-363-6(1),* 207203) Child's World, Inc., The.

—Baseball Jokes. Rosenberg, Pam. 2014. (Laughing Matters Ser.). (ENG.). 24p. (J). (gr. 1-4). 27.07 *(978-1-62323-993-0(1),* 206782) Child's World, Inc., The.

—The Best Cookies of All. Minden, Cecilia & Meier, Joanne D. 2009. (Herbster Readers: Teamwork at Lotsaluck Camp: Level 3 Readers: Careers Ser.). (ENG.). 32p. (J). (gr. -1-2). 25.64 *(978-1-60253-210-6(9),* 200305) Child's World, Inc., The.

—Best Mates on the Boat. Meier, Joanne. 2008. (Herbster Readers: the First Day of School: Level 4 Readers: Machines Ser.). (ENG.). 32p. (J). (gr. -1-2). 25.64 *(978-1-60253-028-7(9),* 200339) Child's World, Inc., The.

—Big Dude-L Book. Mayer, Kirsten. 2013. (Adventure Time Ser.). (ENG.). 128p. (J). (gr. 3-7). 12.99 *(978-0-8431-7465-6(X),* Price Stern Sloan) Penguin Publishing Group.

—The Big Race. Minden, Cecilia. 2008. (Herbster Readers: the First Day of School: Level 3 Readers: Sports Ser.). (ENG.). 32p. (J). (gr. -1-2). 25.64 *(978-1-60253-022-5(X),* 200332) Child's World, Inc., The.

—Bug Jokes. Rosenberg, Pam. 2014. (Laughing Matters Ser.). (ENG.). 24p. (J). (gr. 1-4). 27.07 *(978-1-62323-994-7(X),* 206783) Child's World, Inc., The.

—A Bully-Free Bus. Hall, Pamela. 2012. (Bully-Free World Ser.). 24p. (J). (gr. -1-4). 27.07 *(978-1-61641-844-1(3))* Magic Wagon.

—A Bully-Free Party. Hall, Pamela. 2012. (Bully-Free World Ser.). 24p. (J). (gr. -1-4). 27.07 *(978-1-61641-845-8(1))* Magic Wagon.

—A Bully-Free Playground. Hall, Pamela. 2012. (Bully-Free World Ser.). 24p. (J). (gr. -1-4). 27.07 *(978-1-61641-846-5(X))* Magic Wagon.

—A Bully-Free School. Hall, Pamela. 2012. (Bully-Free World Ser.). 24p. (J). (gr. -1-4). 27.07 *(978-1-61641-847-2(8))* Magic Wagon.

—Carrie's Surprise: The Sound of Hard C. Meier, Joanne. 2010. (Sounds of Phonics Ser.). (ENG.). 24p. (J). (gr. -1-2). 25.64 *(978-1-60253-395-0(4),* 200852) Child's World, Inc., The.

—Cindy, Cedric, & the Circus: The Sound of Soft C. Minden, Cecilia. 2010. (Sounds of Phonics Ser.). (ENG.). 24p. (J). (gr. -1-2). 25.64 *(978-1-60253-396-7(2),* 200851) Child's World, Inc., The.

—Dan's Darn Dog: The Sound of D. Meier, Joanne. 2010. (Sounds of Phonics Ser.). (ENG.). 24p. (J). (gr. -1-2). 25.64 *(978-1-60253-397-4(0),* 200853) Child's World, Inc., The.

—December. Kelley, C. 2014. (Twelve Magic Months Ser.). (ENG.). 24p. (J). (gr. k-3). 27.07 *(978-1-62687-364-3(X),* 207204) Child's World, Inc., The.

—Dinosaur Jokes. Rosenberg, Pam. 2014. (Laughing Matters Ser.). (ENG.). 24p. (J). (gr. 1-4). 27.07 *(978-1-62323-995-4(8),* 206784) Child's World, Inc., The.

—Dinosaurs Then & Wow! Shulman, Mark. 2005. (Storytime Stickers Ser.). (ENG.). 16p. (J). (gr. k-2). pap. 5.95 *(978-1-4027-1805-2(5))* Sterling Publishing Co., Inc.

—The Drawing Lesson. Minden, Cecilia & Meier, Joanne D. 2009. (Herbster Readers: Teamwork at Lotsaluck Camp: Level 1 Readers: Shapes Ser.). (ENG.). 32p. (J). (gr. -1-2). 25.64 *(978-1-60253-212-0(5),* 200289) Child's World, Inc., The.

—An Energy Expert at Home. Meier, Joanne D. & Minden, Cecilia. 2009. (Herbster Readers: Teamwork at Lotsaluck Camp: Level 4 Readers: the Environment Ser.). (ENG.). 32p. (J). (gr. -1-2). 25.64 *(978-1-60253-226-7(5),* 200309) Child's World, Inc., The.

—Every Drop Helps! Meier, Joanne D. & Minden, Cecilia. 2009. (Herbster Readers: Teamwork at Lotsaluck Camp: Level 4 Readers: the Environment Ser.). (ENG.). 32p. (J). (gr. -1-2). 25.64 *(978-1-60253-227-4(3),* 200310) Child's World, Inc., The.

—February. Kelley, C. 2014. (Twelve Magic Months Ser.). (ENG.). 24p. (J). (gr. k-3). 27.07 *(978-1-62687-365-0(8),* 207205) Child's World, Inc., The.

—The Fire Truck Adventure. Meier, Joanne. 2008. (Herbster Readers: the First Day of School: Level 4 Readers: Machines Ser.). (ENG.). 32p. (J). (gr. -1-2). 25.64 *(978-1-60253-027-0(0),* 200340) Child's World, Inc., The.

—Fran & Fay Find a Bird: The Sound of F. Meier, Joanne. 2010. (Sounds of Phonics Ser.). (ENG.). 24p. (J). (gr. -1-2). 25.64 *(978-1-60253-400-1(4),* 200856) Child's World, Inc., The.

—Friends till the End! ed. 2005. (Teenage Mutant Ninja Turtles Ser.: No. 3). 24p. (J). lib. bdg. 15.00 *(978-1-59054-833-2(7))* Fitzgerald Bks.

—Gary Gets a Gift: The Sound of Hard G. Meier, Joanne. 2010. (Sounds of Phonics Ser.). (ENG.). 24p. (J). (gr. -1-2). 25.64 *(978-1-60253-401-8(2),* 200858) Child's World, Inc., The.

—Gina & the Magic Bear: The Sound of Soft G. Meier, Joanne. 2010. (Sounds of Phonics Ser.). (ENG.). 24p. (J). (gr. -1-2). 25.64 *(978-1-60253-402-5(0),* 200857) Child's World, Inc., The.

—Gross-Out Jokes. Rosenberg, Pam. 2014. (Laughing Matters Ser.). (ENG.). 24p. (J). (gr. 1-4). 27.07 *(978-1-62323-996-1(6),* 206785) Child's World, Inc., The.

—The Halloween Costume Contest. Minden, Cecilia & Meier, Joanne D. 2009. (Herbster Readers: Teamwork at Lotsaluck Camp: Level 2 Readers: Holidays Ser.). (ENG.). 32p. (J). (gr. -1-2). 25.64 *(978-1-60253-217-5(6),* 200296) Child's World, Inc., The.

—Holly & Hank's Snow Holiday: The Sound of H. Meier, Joanne. 2010. (Sounds of Phonics Ser.). (ENG.). 24p. (J). (gr. -1-2). 25.64 *(978-1-60253-403-2(9),* 200859) Child's World, Inc., The.

—The Home Run. Meier, Joanne. 2008. (Herbster Readers: the First Day of School: Level 3 Readers: Sports Ser.). (ENG.). 32p. (J). (gr. -1-2). 25.64 *(978-1-60253-018-8(1),* 200333) Child's World, Inc., The.

—Hospital Helper. Meier, Joanne D. & Minden, Cecilia. 2009. (Herbster Readers: Teamwork at Lotsaluck Camp: Level 3 Readers: Careers Ser.). (ENG.). 32p. (J). (gr. -1-2). 25.64 *(978-1-60253-218-2(4),* 200300) Child's World, Inc., The.

—How a Library Works. StJohn, Amanda. 2012. (Library Skills Ser.). (ENG.). 24p. (J). (gr. -1-2). 28.50 *(978-1-61473-247-1(7),* 204949) Child's World, Inc., The.

—How an e-Book Works. StJohn, Amanda. 2012. (Library Skills Ser.). (ENG.). 24p. (J). (gr. -1-2). 28.50 *(978-1-61473-248-8(5),* 204950) Child's World, Inc., The.

—How to Check Out a Book. StJohn, Amanda. 2012. (Library Skills Ser.). (ENG.). 24p. (J). (gr. -1-2). 28.50 *(978-1-61473-249-5(3),* 204951) Child's World, Inc., The.

—How to Find a Book. StJohn, Amanda. 2012. (Library Skills Ser.). (ENG.). 24p. (J). (gr. -1-2). 28.50 *(978-1-61473-250-1(7),* 204952) Child's World, Inc., The.

—How to Find Information Online. StJohn, Amanda. 2012. (Library Skills Ser.). (ENG.). 24p. (J). (gr. -1-2). 28.50 *(978-1-61473-251-8(5),* 204953) Child's World, Inc., The.

—How to Treat a Book. StJohn, Amanda. 2012. (Library Skills Ser.). (ENG.). 24p. (J). (gr. -1-2). 28.50 *(978-1-61473-252-5(3),* 204954) Child's World, Inc., The.

—I Like Potatoes. Scelsa, Greg. Faulkner, Stacey, ed. 2006. (J). pap. 2.99 *(978-1-59198-316-3(9))* Creative Teaching Pr., Inc.

—It's Time to Listen. Meier, Joanne. 2008. (Herbster Readers: the First Day of School: Level 2 Readers: Manners Ser.). (ENG.). 32p. (J). (gr. -1-2). 25.64 *(978-1-60253-013-3(0),* 200325) Child's World, Inc., The.

—January. Kelley, C. 2014. (Twelve Magic Months Ser.). (ENG.). 24p. (J). (gr. k-3). 27.07 *(978-1-62687-366-7(6),* 207206) Child's World, Inc., The.

—Jeff's Job: The Sound of J. Minden, Cecilia. 2010. (Sounds of Phonics Ser.). (ENG.). 24p. (J). (gr. -1-2). 25.64 *(978-1-60253-406-3(3),* 200862) Child's World, Inc., The.

—July. Kelley, C. 2014. (Twelve Magic Months Ser.). (ENG.). 24p. (J). (gr. k-3). 27.07 *(978-1-62687-367-4(4),* 207207) Child's World, Inc., The.

—June. Kelley, C. 2014. (Twelve Magic Months Ser.). (ENG.). 24p. (J). (gr. k-3). 27.07 *(978-1-62687-368-1(2),* 207208) Child's World, Inc., The.

—Knock-Knock Jokes. Rosenberg, Pam. 2014. (Laughing Matters Ser.). (ENG.). 24p. (J). (gr. 1-4). 27.07 *(978-1-62323-997-8(4),* 206786) Child's World, Inc., The.

—Lilly's Lost Lunch: The Sound of L. Meier, Joanne. 2010. (Sounds of Phonics Ser.). (ENG.). 24p. (J). (gr. -1-2). 25.64 *(978-1-60253-408-7(X),* 200864) Child's World, Inc., The.

—The Make-Believe Store. Meier, Joanne D. & Minden, Cecilia. 2009. (Herbster Readers: Teamwork at Lotsaluck Camp: Level 1 Readers: Shapes Ser.). (ENG.). 32p. (J). (gr. -1-2). 25.64 *(978-1-60253-214-4(1),* 200291) Child's World, Inc., The.

—Making a Bully-Free World. Hall, Pamela. 2012. (Bully-Free World Ser.). 24p. (J). (gr. -1-4). 27.07 *(978-1-61641-848-9(6))* Magic Wagon.

—March. Kelley, C. 2014. (Twelve Magic Months Ser.). (ENG.). 24p. (J). (gr. k-3). 27.07 *(978-1-62687-369-8(0),* 207209) Child's World, Inc., The.

—Max & the Mail: The Sound of M. Meier, Joanne. 2010. (Sounds of Phonics Ser.). (ENG.). 24p. (J). (gr. -1-2). 25.64 *(978-1-60253-409-4(8),* 200865) Child's World, Inc., The.

—May. Kelley, C. 2014. (Twelve Magic Months Ser.). (ENG.). 24p. (J). (gr. k-3). 27.07 *(978-1-62687-370-4(4),* 207210) Child's World, Inc., The.

—Mom's Birthday Surprise. Minden, Cecilia & Meier, Joanne D. 2009. (Herbster Readers: Teamwork at Lotsaluck Camp: Level 1 Readers: Shapes Ser.). (ENG.). 32p. (J). (gr. -1-2). 25.64 *(978-1-60253-221-2(4),* 200288) Child's World, Inc., The.

—Monster Jokes. Rosenberg, Pam. 2014. (Laughing Matters Ser.). (ENG.). 24p. (J). (gr. 1-4). 27.07 *(978-1-62323-998-5(2),* 206787) Child's World, Inc., The.

—The Most Unbelievable First Day of School: A Storytime Book. Minden, Cecilia. 2008. (Herbster Readers: the First Day of School Ser.). (ENG.). 32p. (J). (gr. -1-2). 25.64 *(978-1-60253-029-4(7),* 200343) Child's World, Inc., The.

—The Nice Clean Park. Meier, Joanne D. & Minden, Cecilia. 2009. (Herbster Readers: Teamwork at Lotsaluck Camp: Level 4 Readers: the Environment Ser.). (ENG.). 32p. (J). (gr. -1-2). 25.64 *(978-1-60253-213-7(3),* 200312) Child's World, Inc., The.

—Nick & Ned: The Sound of N. Minden, Cecilia. 2010. (Sounds of Phonics Ser.). (ENG.). 24p. (J). (gr. -1-2). 25.64 *(978-1-60253-410-0(1),* 200866) Child's World, Inc., The.

—November. Kelley, C. 2014. (Twelve Magic Months Ser.). (ENG.). 24p. (J). (gr. k-3). 27.07 *(978-1-62687-371-1(2),* 207211) Child's World, Inc., The.

—October. Kelley, C. 2014. (Twelve Magic Months Ser.). (ENG.). 24p. (J). (gr. k-3). 27.07 *(978-1-62687-372-8(0),* 207212) Child's World, Inc., The.

—Pam's Trip to the Park: The Sound of P. Meier, Joanne. 2010. (Sounds of Phonics Ser.). (ENG.). 24p. (J). (gr. -1-2). 25.64 *(978-1-60253-413-1(6),* 200869) Child's World, Inc., The.

—Postcards from All Over. Minden, Cecilia & Meier, Joanne D. 2009. (Herbster Readers: Teamwork at Lotsaluck Camp: Level 3 Readers: Careers Ser.). (ENG.). 32p. (J). (gr. -1-2). 25.64 *(978-1-60253-223-6(0),* 200301) Child's World, Inc., The.

—Prepare for Blastoff! Meier, Joanne D. & Minden, Cecilia. 2009. (Herbster Readers: Teamwork at Lotsaluck Camp: Level 3 Readers: Careers Ser.). (ENG.). 32p. (J). (gr. -1-2). 25.64 *(978-1-60253-219-9(2),* 200302) Child's World, Inc., The.

—Purple Paint Everywhere! Meier, Joanne. 2008. (Herbster Readers: the First Day of School: Level 1 Readers: Colors Ser.). (ENG.). 32p. (J). (gr. -1-2). 25.64 *(978-1-60253-008-9(4),* 200317) Child's World, Inc., The.

—Raising Your Hand. Minden, Cecilia. 2008. (Herbster Readers: the First Day of School: Level 2 Readers: Manners Ser.). (ENG.). 32p. (J). (gr. -1-2). 25.64 *(978-1-60253-015-7(7),* 200326) Child's World, Inc., The.

—Roy on the Ranch: The Sound of R. Minden, Cecilia. 2010. (Sounds of Phonics Ser.). (ENG.). 24p. (J). (gr. -1-2). 25.64 *(978-1-60253-415-5(2),* 200871) Child's World, Inc., The.

—The Runaway Train. Minden, Cecilia. 2008. (Herbster Readers: the First Day of School: Level 4 Readers: Machines Ser.). (ENG.). 32p. (J). (gr. -1-2). 25.64 *(978-1-60253-024-9(6),* 200341) Child's World, Inc., The.

—Santa's Little Helpers (Team Umizoomi) Random House. 2013. (Glow-In-the-Dark Pictureback Ser.). (ENG.). 16p. (J). (gr. -1-1). 4.99 *(978-0-449-81881-7(0),* Random Hse. Bks. for Young Readers) Random Hse. Children's Bks.

—Sara at the Store: The Sound of S. Minden, Cecilia. 2010. (Sounds of Phonics Ser.). (ENG.). 24p. (J). (gr. -1-2). 25.64 *(978-1-60253-416-2(0),* 200872) Child's World, Inc., The.

—Save the Kitten!/Buster's Big Day (Team Umizoomi) Random House. 2014. (Deluxe Pictureback Ser.). (ENG.). 32p. (J). (gr. -1-2). 4.99 *(978-0-385-37520-7(4),* Random Hse. Bks. for Young Readers) Random Hse. Children's Bks.

—Saying "Thank You" Minden, Cecilia. 2008. (Herbster Readers: the First Day of School: Level 2 Readers: Manners Ser.). (ENG.). 32p. (J). (gr. -1-2). 25.64 *(978-1-60253-016-4(5),* 200327) Child's World, Inc., The.

—School Jokes. Rosenberg, Pam. 2014. (Laughing Matters Ser.). (ENG.). 24p. (J). (gr. 1-4). 27.07 *(978-1-62323-999-2(0),* 206788) Child's World, Inc., The.

—The Secret. Murphy, Steve & Murphy, Sonia. 2004. (Teenage Mutant Ninja Turtles Ser.). 32p. (J). (gr. k-2). 11.65 *(978-0-7569-5401-7(0))* Perfection Learning Corp.

—September. Kelley, C. 2014. (Twelve Magic Months Ser.). (ENG.). 24p. (J). (gr. k-3). 27.07 *(978-1-62687-373-5(9),* 207213) Child's World, Inc., The.

—Sharing the Green Ball. Minden, Cecilia. 2008. (Herbster Readers: the First Day of School: Level 1 Readers: Colors Ser.). (ENG.). 32p. (J). (gr. -1-2). 25.64 *(978-1-60253-006-5(8),* 200318) Child's World, Inc., The.

—Skateboarding Friends. Minden, Cecilia. 2008. (Herbster Readers: the First Day of School: Level 3 Readers: Sports Ser.). (ENG.). 32p. (J). (gr. -1-2). 25.64 *(978-1-60253-021-8(1),* 200331) Child's World, Inc., The.

—Smile for the Dentist. Minden, Cecilia & Meier, Joanne D. 2009. (Herbster Readers: Teamwork at Lotsaluck Camp: Level 3 Readers: Careers Ser.). (ENG.). 32p. (J). (gr. -1-2). 25.64 *(978-1-60253-215-1(X),* 200303) Child's World, Inc., The.

—The Soccer Game. Meier, Joanne. 2008. (Herbster Readers: the First Day of School: Level 3 Readers: Sports Ser.). (ENG.). 32p. (J). (gr. -1-2). 25.64 *(978-1-60253-020-1(3),* 200334) Child's World, Inc., The.

—Staying Bully-Free Online. Hall, Pamela. 2012. (Bully-Free World Ser.). 24p. (J). (gr. -1-4). 27.07 *(978-1-61641-849-6(4))* Magic Wagon.

—Step-by-Step Experiments with Electricity. Hagler, Gina. 2012. (Step-By-Step Experiments Ser.). (ENG.). 32p. (J). (gr. 1-4). lib. bdg. 29.93 *(978-1-60973-338-4(X),* 201230) Child's World, Inc., The.

—Step-by-Step Experiments with Insects. Marsico, Katie. 2012. (Step-By-Step Experiments Ser.). (ENG.). 32p. (J). (gr. 1-4). lib. bdg. 29.93 *(978-1-60973-339-1(8),* 201231) Child's World, Inc., The.

—Step-by-Step Experiments with Life Cycles. Marsico, Katie. 2012. (Step-By-Step Experiments Ser.). (ENG.). 32p. (J). (gr. 1-4). lib. bdg. 29.93 *(978-1-60973-587-6(0),* 201232) Child's World, Inc., The.

—Step-by-Step Experiments with Light & Vision. Jacobson, Ryan. 2012. (Step-By-Step Experiments Ser.). (ENG.). 32p. (J). (gr. 1-4). lib. bdg. 29.93 *(978-1-60973-588-3(9),* 201233) Child's World, Inc., The.

—Step-by-Step Experiments with Magnets. Hagler, Gina. 2012. (Step-By-Step Experiments Ser.). (ENG.). 32p. (J). (gr. 1-4). lib. bdg. 29.93 *(978-1-60973-589-0(7),* 201234) Child's World, Inc., The.

—Step-by-Step Experiments with Soils. Hagler, Gina. 2012. (Step-By-Step Experiments Ser.). (ENG.). 32p. (J). (gr. 1-4). lib. bdg. 29.93 *(978-1-60973-592-0(7),* 201238) Child's World, Inc., The.

—Step-by-Step Experiments with Sound. Hagler, Gina. 2012. (Step-By-Step Experiments Ser.). (ENG.). 32p. (J). (gr. 1-4). lib. bdg. 29.93 *(978-1-60973-593-7(5),* 201239) Child's World, Inc., The.

—Step-by-Step Experiments with Taste & Digestion. Marsico, Katie. 2012. (Step-By-Step Experiments Ser.). (ENG.). 32p. (J). (gr. 1-4). lib. bdg. 29.93 *(978-1-60973-614-9(1),* 201240) Child's World, Inc., The.

—Step-by-Step Experiments with the Water Cycle. Duke, Shirley. 2012. (Step-By-Step Experiments Ser.). (ENG.). 32p. (J). (gr. 1-4). lib. bdg. 29.93 *(978-1-60973-615-6(X),* 201241) Child's World, Inc., The.

—Taking Turns. Meier, Joanne. 2008. (Herbster Readers: the First Day of School: Level 2 Readers: Manners Ser.). (ENG.). 32p. (J). (gr. -1-2). 25.64 *(978-1-60253-014-0(9),* 200328) Child's World, Inc., The.

—Teamwork at Lotsaluck Camp: A Storytime Book. Meier, Joanne D. & Minden, Cecilia. 2009. (Herbster Readers: Teamwork at Lotsaluck Camp Ser.). (ENG.). 32p. (J). (gr. -1-2). 25.64 *(978-1-60253-229-8(X),* 200313) Child's World, Inc., The.

—Ted & Tim: The Sound of T. Minden, Cecilia. 2010. (Sounds of Phonics Ser.). (ENG.). 24p. (J). (gr. -1-2). 25.64 *(978-1-60253-417-9(9),* 200873) Child's World, Inc., The.

—The Thanksgiving Play. Minden, Cecilia & Meier, Joanne D. 2009. (Herbster Readers: Teamwork at Lotsaluck Camp: Level 2 Readers: Holidays Ser.). (ENG.). 32p. (J). (gr. -1-2). 25.64 *(978-1-60253-230-4(3),* 200297) Child's World, Inc., The.

—Tongue Twisters. Rosenberg, Pam. 2014. (Laughing Matters Ser.). (ENG.). 24p. (J). (gr. 1-4). 27.07 *(978-1-62687-000-0(4),* 206789) Child's World, Inc., The.

—The Tractor Saves the Day. Minden, Cecilia. 2008. (Herbster Readers: the First Day of School: Level 4 Readers: Machines Ser.). (ENG.). 32p. (J). (gr. -1-2).

O

25.64 *(978-1-60253-023-2(8)*, 200342) Child's World, Inc., The.

—A Tree for the City. Minden, Cecilia & Meier, Joanne D. 2009. (Herbster Readers: Teamwork at Lotsaluck Camp: Level 4 Readers: the Environment Ser.). (ENG.). 32p. (J). (gr. -1-2). 25.64 *(978-1-60253-222-9(2)*, 200307) Child's World, Inc., The.

—Valentines for Everyone. Minden, Cecilia & Meier, Joanne D. 2009. (Herbster Readers: Teamwork at Lotsaluck Camp: Level 2 Readers: Holidays Ser.). (ENG.). 32p. (J). (gr. -1-2). 25.64 *(978-1-60253-232-8(X)*, 200298) Child's World, Inc., The.

—A Walk Across Town. Minden, Cecilia & Meier, Joanne D. 2009. (Herbster Readers: Teamwork at Lotsaluck Camp: Level 4 Readers: the Environment Ser.). (ENG.). 32p. (J). (gr. -1-2). 25.64 *(978-1-60253-233-5(8)*, 200308) Child's World, Inc., The.

—Wendy & the Dog Wash: The Sound of W. Meier, Joanne. 2010. (Sounds of Phonics Ser.). (ENG.). 24p. (J). (gr. -1-2). 25.64 *(978-1-60253-421-6(7)*, 200877) Child's World, Inc., The.

—The Winning Basket. Minden, Cecilia. 2008. (Herbster Readers: the First Day of School: Level 3 Readers: Sports Ser.). (ENG.). 32p. (J). (gr. -1-2). 25.64 *(978-1-60253-019-5(X)*, 200335) Child's World, Inc., The.

—Wishing for a Red Balloon. Minden, Cecilia. 2008. (Herbster Readers: the First Day of School: Level 1 Readers: Colors Ser.). (ENG.). 32p. (J). (gr. -1-2). 25.64 *(978-1-60253-009-6(2)*, 200321) Child's World, Inc., The.

—Wrinkles. Miller, Pam. 2005. (Rookie Readers Ser.). (ENG.). 32p. (J). (gr. k-2). lib. bdg. 19.50 *(978-0-516-24860-8(X)*, Children's Pr.) Scholastic Library Publishing.

—Wrinkles. Miller, Pam. 2006. (Rookie Reader Skill Set Ser.). (ENG.). 32p. (J). (gr. k-2). per. 4.95 *(978-0-516-25021-2(3)*, Children's Pr.) Scholastic Library Publishing.

Ostrovsky, Alexsandr. Birthday: Companies-Products-Services. Ostrovsky, Alexsandr. (Childrens Ser.). (Orig.). (J). pap. 14.95 *(978-0-934393-17-1(6))* Rector Pr., Ltd.

—Clouds: Companies-Products-Services. Ostrovsky, Alexsandr. (Childrens Ser.). (Orig.). (J). pap. 14.95 *(978-0-934393-20-1(6))* Rector Pr., Ltd.

—Paper Kite. Ostrovsky, Alexsandr. (Childrens Ser.). (Orig.). (J). pap. 14.95 *(978-0-934393-18-8(4))* Rector Pr., Ltd.

Ostrowski, Justin. Sky, the Blue Bunny. Vezeau, Sheila. 2012. 16p. pap. 24.95 *(978-1-4626-7533-3(6))* America Star Bks.

O'Such, Holly. Aunt Ruby, Do I Look Like God? 2004. (J). lib. bdg. 9.95 *(978-0-9745122-0-4(6))* Urban Advocacy.

O'Sullivan, Tom & Bacon, Paul. Shirley Temple's Fairyland: The Wild Swans; Beauty & the Beast; Rumpelstiltskin; the Sleeping Beauty. 2011. 62p. 36.95 *(978-1-258-04207-3(X))* Literary Licensing, LLC.

Osuna, Rosa. No es Facil, Pequena Ardilla. 2004.Tr. of It's Not Easy, Little Squirrel. (SPA.). (J). 15.99 *(978-84-8464-202-2(X))* Kalandraka Editora, S.L. ESP. Dist: Lectorum Pubns., Inc.

Oswald, Ash. Camp Chaos. Badger, Meredith. 2008. (Go Girl! Ser.: 11). (ENG.). 96p. (Orig.). (J). (gr. 2-4). pap. 4.99 *(978-0-312-34645-4(X))* Square Fish.

—Catch Me If You Can. Kalkipsakis, Thalia. 2008. (Go Girl! Ser.: 8). (ENG.). 96p. (J). (gr. 2-4). pap. 4.99 *(978-0-312-34654-6(9))* Feiwel & Friends.

—Dancing Queen. Kalkipsakis, Thalia. 2008. (Go Girl! Ser.: 7). (ENG.). 96p. (Orig.). (J). (gr. 2-4). pap. 4.99 *(978-0-312-34651-5(4))* Square Fish.

—Deep Waters. Larry, H. I. 2008. (Zac Power Ser.: 2). (ENG.). 96p. (J). (gr. 3-6). pap. 5.99 *(978-0-312-34655-3(7))* Square Fish.

—Frozen Fear. Larry, H. I. 2008. (Zac Power Ser.: 4). (ENG.). 96p. (J). (gr. 3-6). pap. 4.99 *(978-0-312-34656-0(5))* Square Fish.

—Go Girl! #10: Basketball Blues. Kalkipsakis, Thalia. 2008. (Go Girl! Ser.: 10). (ENG.). 96p. (Orig.). (J). (gr. 2-4). pap. 4.99 *(978-0-312-34646-1(8))* Feiwel & Friends.

—Go Girl! #12: Back to School. Badger, Meredith. 2008. (Go Girl! Ser.: 12). (ENG.). 96p. (Orig.). (J). (gr. 2-4). pap. 4.99 *(978-0-312-34648-5(4))* Square Fish.

—Lunchtime Rules. Steggall, Vicki. 2007. (Go Girl! Ser.: 4). (ENG.). 96p. (Orig.). (J). (gr. 2-4). per. 4.99 *(978-0-312-34644-7(1))* Square Fish.

—Mind Games. Larry, H. I. 2008. (Zac Power Ser.: 3). (ENG.). 96p. (J). (gr. 3-6). pap. 4.99 *(978-0-312-34657-7(3))* Square Fish.

—The New Girl. McAuley, Rowan. 2008. (Go Girl! Ser.: 9). (ENG.). 96p. (Orig.). (J). (gr. 2-4). pap. 4.99 *(978-0-312-34649-2(2))* Feiwel & Friends.

—Poison Island. Larry, H. I. 2008. (Zac Power Ser.: 1). (ENG.). 96p. (J). (gr. 3-6). pap. 5.99 *(978-0-312-34659-1(X))* Square Fish.

—The Secret Club. Perry, Chrissie. 2007. (Go Girl! Ser.: 1). (ENG.). 96p. (Orig.). (J). (gr. 2-4). per. 4.99 *(978-0-312-34652-2(2))* Square Fish.

—Sister Spirit. Kalkipsakis, Thalia. 2007. (Go Girl! Ser.: 3). (ENG.). 96p. (Orig.). (J). (gr. 2-4). per. 4.99 *(978-0-312-34643-0(3))* Square Fish.

—Sleepover! McAuley, Rowan. 2008. (Go Girl! Ser.: 5). (ENG.). 96p. (J). (gr. 2-4). pap. 4.99 *(978-0-312-34641-6(7))* Square Fish.

—Surf's Up! Perry, Chrissie. 2008. (Go Girl! Ser.: 6). (ENG.). 96p. (Orig.). (J). (gr. 2-4). pap. 4.99 *(978-0-312-34647-8(6))* Feiwel & Friends.

—The Worst Gymnast. Kalkipsakis, Thalia. 2007. (Go Girl! Ser.: 2). (ENG.). 96p. (Orig.). (J). (gr. 2-4). per. 4.99 *(978-0-312-34642-3(5))* Square Fish.

Oswald, Bonnie. The Creation. Brady, Janeen. 2008. (J). 16.99 *(978-1-59955-139-5(X))* Cedar Fort, Inc./CFI Distribution.

Oswald, Pete. Chickens Don't Fly: And Other Fun Facts. DiSiena, Laura Lyn & Eliot, Hannah. 2014. (Did You Know? Ser.). (ENG.). 32p. (J). (gr. -1-3). 17.99 *(978-1-4424-9353-7(4))*; pap. 5.99 *(978-1-4424-9326-1(7))* Little Simon. (Little Simon).

—Hippos Can't Swim: And Other Fun Facts. DiSiena, Laura Lyn & Eliot, Hannah. 2014. (Did You Know? Ser.). (ENG.). 32p. (J). (gr. -1-3). 17.99 *(978-1-4424-9352-0(6))*; pap. 5.99 *(978-1-4424-9324-7(0))* Little Simon. (Little Simon).

—Rainbows Never End: And Other Fun Facts. DiSiena, Laura Lyn & Eliot, Hannah. 2014. (Did You Know? Ser.). (ENG.). 32p. (J). (gr. -1-3). 17.99 *(978-1-4814-0277-4(3))*; pap. 5.99 *(978-1-4814-0275-0(7))* Little Simon. (Little Simon).

Oswald, Pete & Spurgeon, Aaron. Did You Know? Hippos Can't Swim; Chickens Don't Fly; Rainbows Never End; Trains Can Float. DiSiena, Laura Lyn & Eliot, Hannah. ed. 2014. (Did You Know? Ser.). (ENG.). 128p. (J). (gr. -1-3). pap. 23.99 *(978-1-4814-3032-6(7)*, Little Simon) Little Simon.

—Saturn Could Sail: And Other Fun Facts. DiSiena, Laura Lyn & Eliot, Hannah. 2014. (Did You Know? Ser.). (ENG.). 32p. (J). (gr. -1-3). 17.99 *(978-1-4814-1429-6(1))*; pap. 6.99 *(978-1-4814-1428-9(3))* Little Simon. (Little Simon).

—Trains Can Float: And Other Fun Facts. DiSiena, Laura Lyn & Eliot, Hannah. 2014. (Did You Know? Ser.). (ENG.). 32p. (J). (gr. -1-3). 17.99 *(978-1-4814-0281-1(1)*, Little Simon) Little Simon.

Ot, Elli. Iris y el Gato Negro. Ot, Elli. Brignole, Giancarla, tr. rev. ed. 2007. (Fabulas De Familia Ser.). 32p. (J). (gr. k-4). pap. 6.95 *(978-970-20-0275-8(3))* Castillo, Ediciones, S. A. de C. V. MEX. Dist: Macmillan.

Ota, Yuko. Detective Frankenstein. Johnson, Alaya Dawn. 2011. (Twisted Journeys (r) Ser.: 17). (ENG.). 112p. (J). (gr. 4-7). pap. 7.95 *(978-0-8225-8943-3(5))*; pap. 45.32 *(978-0-7613-7613-2(5))*; lib. bdg. 27.93 *(978-0-8225-8942-6(7))* Lerner Publishing Group. (Graphic Universe).

—The Secret Ghost: A Mystery with Distance & Measurement. Thielbar, Melinda. 2010. (Manga Math Mysteries Ser.: 3). (ENG.). 48p. (gr. 3-5). pap. 6.95 *(978-0-7613-5245-7(7)*, Graphic Universe) Lerner Publishing Group.

Ota, Yuko & Studio, Xian Nu. A Match Made in Heaven. Robbins, Trina. 2013. (My Boyfriend Is a Monster Ser.: 8). (ENG.). 128p. (YA). (gr. 7-12). pap. 9.95 *(978-1-4677-0732-9(5)*, Graphic Universe) Lerner Publishing Group.

Otero, Nicolas. How Hollyhocks Came to New Mexico. Anaya, Rudolfo. Garcia, Nasario, tr. 2012. 48p. 24.95 *(978-1-936744-12-1(0)*, Rio Grande Bks.) LPD Pr.

Otero, Sole. All-American Girl Style: Fun Fashions You Can Sketch, 1 vol. Bolte, Mari. 2013. (Drawing Fun Fashions Ser.). (ENG.). 32p. (J). (gr. 3-4). lib. bdg. 27.32 *(978-1-62065-039-4(8)*, Snap Bks.) Capstone Pr., Inc.

—Patrick & Paula Learn about Prepositions. Atwood, Megan. 2015. (Language Builders Ser.). (ENG.). 32p. (J). (gr. 2-4). pap. 11.94 *(978-1-60357-708-3(4))*; lib. bdg. 25.27 *(978-1-59953-673-6(0))* Norwood Hse. Pr.

—The People Could Fly: An African-American Folktale. Malaspina, Ann. 2013. (Folktales from Around the World Ser.). (ENG.). 24p. (J). (gr. k-3). 28.50 *(978-1-62323-617-5(7)*, 206385) Child's World, Inc., The.

—Quinn & Penny Investigate How to Research, 1 vol. Troupe, Thomas Kingsley. 2011. (In the Library). (ENG.). 24p. (gr. k-4). lib. bdg. 25.99 *(978-1-4048-6290-6(0)*, Nonfiction Picture Bks.) Picture Window Bks.

Otey Little, Mimi. Yoshiko & the Foreigner. Otey Little, Mimi. 2004. 31p. (J). (gr. 4-8). reprint ed. 16.00 *(978-0-7567-7510-0(8))* DIANE Publishing Co.

O'Toole, Jeanette. Animals. Filipek, Nina. 2009. (Bright Basics Ser.). 12p. (J). (gr. -1-k). bds. 11.40 *(978-1-60754-688-7(4))* Windmill Bks.

—Cinderella. Filipek, Nina. 2009. (Fairy Tale Firsts Ser.). 12p. (J). (gr. -1-k). bds. 11.40 *(978-1-60754-691-7(4))* Windmill Bks.

—Colors. Filipek, Nina. 2009. (Bright Basics Ser.). 12p. (J). (gr. -1-k). bds. 11.40 *(978-1-60754-687-0(6))* Windmill Bks.

—Counting. Filipek, Nina. 2009. (Bright Basics Ser.). 12p. (J). (gr. -1-k). bds. 11.40 *(978-1-60754-686-3(8))* Windmill Bks.

—The Gingerbread Man. Filipek, Nina. 2009. (Fairy Tale Firsts Ser.). 12p. (J). (gr. -1-k). bds. 11.40 *(978-1-60754-694-8(9))* Windmill Bks.

—Goldilocks & the Three Bears. Filipek, Nina. 2009. (Fairy Tale Firsts Ser.). 12p. (J). (gr. -1-k). bds. 11.40 *(978-1-60754-689-4(2))* Windmill Bks.

—The Three Little Pigs. Filipek, Nina. 2009. (Fairy Tale Firsts Ser.). 12p. (J). (gr. -1-k). bds. 11.40 *(978-1-60754-693-1(0))* Windmill Bks.

—The Ugly Duckling. Filipek, Nina & Andersen, Hans Christian. 2009. (Fairy Tale Firsts Ser.). 12p. (J). (gr. -1-k). bds. 11.40 *(978-1-60754-692-4(2))* Windmill Bks.

—Words. Filipek, Nina. 2009. (Bright Basics Ser.). 12p. (J). (gr. -1-k). bds. 11.40 *(978-1-60754-685-6(X))* Windmill Bks.

O'Toole, Jeanette, jt. illus. see Canals, Sonia.

O'Toole, Julianne. The Smelly Shoe. Giangregorio, Kimberly A. 2012. 24p. pap. 24.95 *(978-1-4626-9387-0(3))* America Star Bks.

Otoshi, Kathryn. Maneki Neko: The Tale of the Beckoning Cat. Lendroth, Susan. 2010. (J). *(978-1-885008-39-8(2)*, Shen's Bks.) Lee & Low Bks., Inc.

—Marcello: The Movie Mouse. Hockinson, Liz. 2005. (ENG.). 40p. (J). (gr.-k). 16.95 *(978-0-9723946-2-8(1))* KO Kids Bks.

Otoshi, Kathryn. What Emily Saw. Otoshi, Kathryn. 2004. (ENG.). 36p. (J). (gr. -1-12). 16.95 *(978-0-9723946-0-4(5))* KO Kids Bks.

Otoshi, Kathryn. The Saddest Little Robot. Otoshi, Kathryn, tr. Gage, Brian. 2004. (ENG.). 90p. (J). 16.95 *(978-1-932360-05-9(0)*, Soft Skull Pr.) Counterpoint LLC.

Otoshi, Kathryn & Ciccarelli, Gary. Bedtime Safari. Friden, Chris. 2007. (J). *(978-0-9758785-3-8(0))* Haydenburri Lane.

Ott, Margot Janet. Invincible. Romansky, Sally Rosenberg. 2006. (J). pap. 8.95 *(978-0-9723729-4-7(6))* Imagination Stage, Inc.

Ott, Thomas. We Have Always Lived in the Castle. Jackson, Shirley. deluxe ed. 2006. (Penguin Classics Deluxe Edition Ser.). (ENG.). 160p. (gr. 12-18). 17.00 *(978-0-14-303997-6(0)*, Penguin Classics) Penguin Publishing Group.

Otterstätter, Sara. Avati: Discovering Arctic Ecology, 1 vol. Pelletier, Mia. 2013. (ENG.). 46p. (J). (gr. 2-5). 14.95 *(978-1-927095-13-3(1))* Inhabit Media Inc. CAN. Dist: Independent Pubs. Group.

Ottinger, Jon. My Little Red Lunchbox Book. Pugliano-Martin, Carol. 2004. (Sparkle Shape Bks.). 10p. (J). (gr. -1-18). bds. 6.99 *(978-1-57151-716-6(2))* Playhouse Publishing.

Ottley, Matt. Tree: A Little Story about Big Things. Parker, Danny. 2015. (ENG.). 32p. (J). (gr. -1-k). 13.99 ***(978-1-74297-860-4(6))*** Little Hare Bks. AUS. Dist: Independent Pubs. Group.

Ottley, Matt & Sheehan, Peter. Charlie Burr & the Three Stolen Dollars. Morgan, Sally et al. 2011. (ENG.). 128p. (J). (gr. 3-7). pap. 13.99 *(978-1-921714-04-7(2))* Little Hare Bks. AUS. Dist: Independent Pubs. Group.

Oud, Pauline. Big Sister Sarah. Oud, Pauline. 2013. (ENG.). 32p. (J). (gr. -1-k). 15.95 *(978-1-60537-151-1(3))* Clavis Publishing.

—Eating with Lily & Milo. Oud, Pauline. 2010. (Lily & Milo Ser.). (ENG.). 30p. (J). (gr. k — 1). 12.95 *(978-1-60537-055-2(X))* Clavis Publishing.

—Getting Dressed with Lily & Milo. Oud, Pauline. 2010. (Lily & Milo Ser.). (ENG.). 30p. (J). (gr. k — 1). 12.95 *(978-1-60537-060-6(6))* Clavis Publishing.

—Going to the Beach with Lily & Milo. Oud, Pauline. 2011. (Lily & Milo Ser.). (ENG.). 28p. (J). (gr. k — 1). 12.95 *(978-1-60537-094-1(0))* Clavis Publishing.

—Going to the Zoo with Lily & Milo. Oud, Pauline. 2011. (Lily & Milo Ser.). (ENG.). 28p. (J). (gr. k — 1). 12.95 *(978-1-60537-093-4(2))* Clavis Publishing.

—Having a Party with Lily & Milo. Oud, Pauline. 2012. (Clavis Toddler: Skills Ser.). (ENG.). 24p. (J). (— 1). 12.95 *(978-1-60537-129-0(7))* Clavis Publishing.

Oudinot, Wanda & Baum, Kipley, photos by. Colors of a City: Philadelphia. Sedlacek, Jan Gill. 2012. 46p. (J). pap. 14.00 *(978-0-9836878-7-0(0))* Aperture Pr., LLC.

Ouellet, Joanne. The Memory Stone, 1 vol. MacDonald, Anne Louise. 2003. (ENG.). 24p. (J). (gr. -1-2). 7.95 *(978-1-55109-442-7(8))* Nimbus Publishing, Ltd. CAN. Dist: Orca Bk. Pubs. USA.

Oughton, Taylor. I Love My Brother. Galvin, Laura Gates. 2008. (ENG.). 16p. (J). (gr. -1-k). bds. 6.95 *(978-1-59249-866-6(3))* Soundprints.

Oughton, Taylor, et al. I Love My Sister. Galvin, Laura Gates. 2011. (I Love My... Ser.). (ENG.). 16p. (J). (gr. -1-k). 6.95 *(978-1-60727-311-0(X))* Soundprints.

Oughton, Taylor. Loon at Northwood Lake. Ring, Elizabeth. 2005. (Smith Sonian's Backyard Ser.). 32p. (J). (gr. -1-3). (ENG.). 6.95 *(978-1-59249-482-8(X)*, S5017); pap. 8.95 incl. audio *(978-1-59249-491-0(9)*, SC5013) Soundprints.

—Mallard Duck at Meadow View Pond. Pfeffer, Wendy. (Smithsonian's Backyard Ser.). (ENG.). 32p. (J). (gr. -1-2). 2005. 19.95 *(978-1-56899-958-6(5)*, BC5021); 2005. pap. 4.95 *(978-1-56899-957-9(7)*, B5071); 2003. 9.95 *(978-1-56899-961-6(5)*, PB5071); 2003. 8.95 *(978-1-59249-063-9(8)*, SC5021) Soundprints.

—Mallard Duck at Mountain View Pond. Pfeffer, Wendy. 2005. (Smithsonian's Backyard Ser.). (ENG.). 32p. (J). (gr. -1-2). 15.95 *(978-1-56899-956-2(9)*, B5021) Soundprints.

Oulmet, David. Dare to Be Scared: Thirteen Stories to Chill & Thrill. San Souci, Robert D. 2003. (Dare to Be Scared Ser.). (ENG.). 144p. (J). (gr. 3-7). 17.95 *(978-0-8126-2688-9(5))* Cricket Bks.

—Dare to Be Scared 4: Thirteen More Tales of Terror. San Souci, Robert D. 2009. (Dare to Be Scared Ser.: 4). (ENG.). 229p. (J). (gr. 2-9). 17.95 *(978-0-8126-2754-1(7))* Cricket Bks.

—Double-Dare to Be Scared: Another Thirteen Chilling Tales. San Souci, Robert D. 2004. (Dare to Be Scared Ser.). (ENG.). 144p. (J). 17.95 *(978-0-8126-2716-9(4))* Cricket Bks.

—Triple-Dare to Be Scared: Thirteen Further Freaky Tales. San Souci, Robert D. 2007. (Dare to Be Scared Ser.). (ENG.). 240p. (J). (gr. 2-9). 16.95 *(978-0-8126-2749-7(0))* Cricket Bks.

Ouren, Todd. La Bella Durmiente. Blair, Eric. Abello, Patricia, tr. from ENG. 2006. (Read-It! Readers en Español: Cuentos de Hadas Ser.). (SPA.). 32p. (gr. k-3). 19.99 *(978-1-4048-1639-8(9)*, Easy Readers) Picture Window Bks.

—Birthdays. Haugen, Brenda. 2003. (Holidays & Celebrations Ser.). (ENG.). 24p. (gr. k-3). 25.99 *(978-1-4048-0198-1(7)*, Nonfiction Picture Bks.) Picture Window Bks.

—Camping in Green, 1 vol. Jones, Christianne C. 2007. (Know Your Colors Ser.). (ENG.). 24p. (gr. -1-1). lib. bdg. 25.99 *(978-1-4048-3107-0(X)*, 1265677, Nonfiction Picture Bks.) Picture Window Bks.

—The Capitol Building. Stille, Darlene R. 2008. (Our Nation's Pride Ser.). 32p. (gr. -1-3). 28.50 *(978-1-60270-112-0(1)*, Looking Glass Library- Nonfiction) Magic Wagon.

—Christmas. Haugen, Brenda. 2003. (Holidays & Celebrations Ser.). (ENG.). 24p. (gr. k-3). 25.99 *(978-1-4048-0192-9(8)*, Nonfiction Picture Bks.) Picture Window Bks.

—Do Polar Bears Snooze in Hollow Trees? A Book about Animal Hibernation. Salas, Laura Purdie. 2006. (Animals All Around Ser.). (ENG.). 24p. (gr. -1-2). lib. bdg. 25.99 *(978-1-4048-2231-3(3)*, Nonfiction Picture Bks.) Picture Window Bks.

—Downhill Fun: A Counting Book about Winter, 1 vol. Dahl, Michael. 2004. (Know Your Numbers Ser.). (ENG.). 24p. (gr. -1-2). per. 7.95 *(978-1-4048-1092-1(7)*, Nonfiction Picture Bks.) Picture Window Bks.

—Eggs & Legs: Counting by Twos, 1 vol. Dahl, Michael. 2005. (Know Your Numbers Ser.). (ENG.). 24p. (gr. -1-2). 25.99 *(978-1-4048-0945-1(7)*, Nonfiction Picture Bks.) Picture Window Bks.

—The Frog Prince: A Retelling of the Grimm's Fairy Tale, 1 vol. Blair, Eric. 2013. (My First Classic Story Ser.). (ENG.). 32p. (gr. k-3). pap. 7.10 *(978-1-4795-1853-1(0)*, My First Classic Story) Picture Window Bks.

—The Frog Prince: A Retelling of the Grimm's Fairy Tale, 1 vol. Blair, Eric et al. 2010. (My First Classic Story Ser.). (ENG.). 32p. (gr. k-3). lib. bdg. 21.32 *(978-1-4048-6083-4(5)*, My First Classic Story) Picture Window Bks.

—From the Garden: A Counting Book about Growing Food. Dahl, Michael. 2004. (Know Your Numbers Ser.). (ENG.). 24p. (gr. -1-2). 25.99 *(978-1-4048-0578-1(8)*, 1229520); per. 7.95 *(978-1-4048-1116-4(8))* Picture Window Bks. (Nonfiction Picture Bks.).

—El Gato Con Botas: Versión del Cuento de los Hermanos Grimm. Blair, Eric. Abello, Patricia, tr. from ENG. 2006. (Read-It! Readers en Español: Cuentos de Hadas Ser.). (SPA.). 32p. (gr. k-3). 19.99 *(978-1-4048-1635-0(6)*, Easy Readers) Picture Window Bks.

—Un Gran Edificio: Un Libro para Contar Sobre Construcción. Dahl, Michael. 2010. (Apréndete Tus Números/Know Your Numbers Ser.).Tr. of One Big Building - A Counting Book about Construction. (ENG, SPA & MUL.). 24p. (gr. -1-2). lib. bdg. 25.99 *(978-1-4048-6294-4(3))* Picture Window Bks.

—Huevos y Patas: Cuenta de Dos en Dos. Dahl, Michael. 2010. (Apréndete Tus Números/Know Your Numbers Ser.).Tr. of Eggs & Legs/Counting by Twos. (MUL & SPA.). 24p. (gr. -1-2). lib. bdg. 25.99 *(978-1-4048-6296-8(X))* Picture Window Bks.

—I Am a Sea Horse: The Life of a Dwarf Sea Horse, 1 vol. Shaskan, Trisha Speed. 2008. (I Live in the Ocean Ser.). (ENG.). 24p. (gr. -1-2). lib. bdg. 25.99 *(978-1-4048-4728-6(6)*, Nonfiction Picture Bks.) Picture Window Bks.

—I Am a Sea Turtle: The Life of a Green Sea Turtle, 1 vol. Stille, Darlene R. 2004. (I Live in the Ocean Ser.). (ENG.). 24p. (gr. -1-2). 25.99 *(978-1-4048-0597-2(4)*, Nonfiction Picture Bks.) Picture Window Bks.

—I Am an Octopus: The Life of a Common Octopus, 1 vol. Shaskan, Trisha Speed. 2008. (I Live in the Ocean Ser.). (ENG.). 24p. (gr. -1-2). lib. bdg. 25.99 *(978-1-4048-4729-3(4)*, Nonfiction Picture Bks.) Picture Window Bks.

—In the Buffalo Pasture. Stockland, Patricia M. 2009. (Barnyard Buddies Set 2 Ser.). 24p. (gr. -1-2). 27.07 *(978-1-60270-641-5(7)*, Looking Glass Library-Nonfiction) Magic Wagon.

—In the Cattle Yard. Stockland, Patricia M. 2007. (Barnyard Buddies Ser.). 24p. (gr. -1-2). 27.07 *(978-1-60270-022-2(2)*, Looking Glass Library-Nonfiction) Magic Wagon.

—In the Chicken Coop. Stockland, Patricia M. 2007. (Barnyard Buddies Ser.). 24p. (gr. -1-2). 27.07 *(978-1-60270-023-9(0)*, Looking Glass Library-Nonfiction) Magic Wagon.

—In the Goat Yard. Stockland, Patricia M. 2009. (Barnyard Buddies Set 2 Ser.). 24p. (gr. -1-2). 27.07 *(978-1-60270-642-2(5)*, Looking Glass Library-Nonfiction) Magic Wagon.

—In the Goose Pen. Stockland, Patricia M. 2009. (Barnyard Buddies Set 2 Ser.). 24p. (gr. -1-2). 27.07 *(978-1-60270-643-9(3)*, Looking Glass Library-Nonfiction) Magic Wagon.

—In the Horse Stall. Stockland, Patricia M. 2007. (Barnyard Buddies Ser.). 24p. (gr. -1-2). 27.07 *(978-1-60270-024-6(9)*, Looking Glass Library-Nonfiction) Magic Wagon.

—In the Llama Yard. Stockland, Patricia M. 2009. (Barnyard Buddies Set 2 Ser.). 24p. (gr. -1-2). 27.07 *(978-1-60270-644-6(1)*, Looking Glass Library-Nonfiction) Magic Wagon.

—In the Pig Pen. Stockland, Patricia M. 2007. (Barnyard Buddies Ser.). 24p. (gr. -1-2). 27.07 *(978-1-60270-025-3(7)*, Looking Glass Library-Nonfiction) Magic Wagon.

—In the Rabbit Hutch. Stockland, Patricia M. 2009. (Barnyard Buddies Set 2 Ser.). 24p. (gr. -1-2). 27.07 *(978-1-60270-645-3(X)*, Looking Glass Library-Nonfiction) Magic Wagon.

—In the Sheep Pasture. Stockland, Patricia M. 2007. (Barnyard Buddies Ser.). 24p. (gr. -1-2). 27.07 *(978-1-60270-026-0(5)*, Looking Glass Library-Nonfiction) Magic Wagon.

—In the Turkey Pen. Stockland, Patricia M. 2009. (Barnyard Buddies Set 2 Ser.). 24p. (gr. -1-2). 27.07 *(978-1-60270-646-0(8)*, Looking Glass Library-Nonfiction) Magic Wagon.

—Lots of Ladybugs! Counting by Fives, 1 vol. Dahl, Michael. 2005. (Know Your Numbers Ser.). (ENG.). 24p. (gr. -1-2). 25.99 *(978-1-4048-0944-4(9)*, Nonfiction Picture Bks.) Picture Window Bks.

—¡Montones de Mariquitas! Cuenta de Cinco en Cinco. Dahl, Michael. 2010. (Apréndete Tus Números/Know Your Numbers Ser.).Tr. of Lots of Ladybugs! - Counting by Fives. (SPA & MUL.). 24p. (gr. -1-2). lib. bdg. 25.99 *(978-1-4048-6297-5(8))* Picture Window Bks.

—The National Anthem. Hall, M. C. 2008. (Our Nation's Pride Ser.). 32p. (gr. -1-3). 28.50 *(978-1-60270-113-7(X)*, Looking Glass Library- Nonfiction) Magic Wagon.

—On the Duck Pond. Stockland, Patricia M. 2007. (Barnyard Buddies Ser.). 24p. (gr. -1-2). 27.07 *(978-1-60270-027-7(3)*, Looking Glass Library-Nonfiction) Magic Wagon.

—One Big Building: A Counting Book about Construction, 1 vol. Dahl, Michael. 2004. (Know Your Numbers Ser.). (ENG.). 24p. (gr. -1-2). per. 7.95 *(978-1-4048-1120-1(6)*, Nonfiction Picture Bks.) Picture Window Bks.

—El Pescador y Su Mujer: Versión del Cuento de los Hermanos Grimm. Blair, Eric. Abello, Patricia, tr. 2006. (Read-It! Readers en Español: Cuentos de Hadas Ser.). (SPA.). 32p. (gr. k-3). 19.99 *(978-1-4048-1630-5(5)*, Easy Readers) Picture Window Bks.

—The Pledge of Allegiance. Doering Tourville, Amanda. 2008. (Our Nation's Pride Ser.). 32p. (gr. -1-3). 28.50 *(978-1-60270-114-4(8)*, Looking Glass Library- Nonfiction) Magic Wagon.

—El Principe Encantado. Blair, Eric. Abello, Patricia, tr. from ENG. 2006. (Read-It! Readers en Español: Cuentos de Hadas Ser.).Tr. of Frog Prince. (SPA.). 32p. (gr. k-3). 19.99 *(978-1-4048-1631-2(3)*, Easy Readers) Picture Window Bks.

—Puss in Boots: A Retelling of the Grimm's Fairy Tale, 1 vol. Blair, Eric. 2011. (My First Classic Story Ser.). (ENG.). 32p. (gr. k-3). pap. 7.10 *(978-1-4048-7359-9(7)*, My First Classic Story) Picture Window Bks.

—Puss in Boots: A Retelling of the Grimm's Fairy Tale, 1 vol. Blair, Eric et al. 2010. (My First Classic Story Ser.). (ENG.). 32p. (gr. k-3). lib. bdg. 21.32 *(978-1-4048-6078-0(9)*, My First Classic Story) Picture Window Bks.

—Red Eyes or Blue Feathers: A Book about Animal Colors, 1 vol. Stockland, Patricia M. 2005. (Animal Wise Ser.). (ENG.). 24p. (gr. k-2). 25.99 *(978-1-4048-0931-4(7)*, Nonfiction Picture Bks.) Picture Window Bks.

—Sand, Leaf, or Coral Reef: A Book about Animal Habitats. Stockland, Patricia M. 2005. (Animal Wise Ser.). (ENG.). 24p. (gr. k-2). 25.99 *(978-1-4048-0932-1(5)*, Nonfiction Picture Bks.) Picture Window Bks.

—Sleeping Beauty: A Retelling of the Grimm's Fairy Tale, 1 vol. Blair, Eric. 2011. (My First Classic Story Ser.). (ENG.). 32p. (gr. k-3). pap. 7.10 *(978-1-4048-7360-5(0)*, My First Classic Story) Picture Window Bks.

—Sleeping Beauty: A Retelling of the Grimm's Fairy Tale, 1 vol. Blair, Eric et al. 2010. (My First Classic Story Ser.). (ENG.). 32p. (gr. k-3). lib. bdg. 21.32 *(978-1-4048-6080-3(0)*, My First Classic Story) Picture Window Bks.

—The Star-Spangled Banner: America's National Anthem & Its History, 1 vol. 2003. (Patriotic Songs Ser.). (ENG.). 24p. (gr. -1-4). 25.99 *(978-1-4048-0175-2(8)*, Nonfiction Picture Bks.) Picture Window Bks.

—The Statue of Liberty. Stille, Darlene R. 2008. (Our Nation's Pride Ser.). 32p. (gr. -1-3). 28.50 *(978-1-60270-115-1(6)*, Looking Glass Library- Nonfiction) Magic Wagon.

—Strange Dances & Long Flights: A Book about Animal Behavior. Stockland, Patricia M. 2005. (Animal Wise Ser.). (ENG.). 24p. (gr. k-2). 25.99 *(978-1-4048-0936-9(8)*, Nonfiction Picture Bks.) Picture Window Bks.

—Stripes, Spots, or Diamonds: A Book about Animal Patterns. Stockland, Patricia M. 2005. (Animal Wise Ser.). (ENG.). 24p. (gr. k-2). 25.99 *(978-1-4048-0934-5(1)*, Nonfiction Picture Bks.) Picture Window Bks.

—Thanksgiving. Haugen, Brenda. 2003. (Holidays & Celebrations Ser.). (ENG.). 24p. (gr. k-3). 25.99 *(978-1-4048-0191-2(X)*, Nonfiction Picture Bks.) Picture Window Bks.

—Tom Thumb: A Retelling of the Grimm's Fairy Tale, 1 vol. Blair, Eric. 2013. (My First Classic Story Ser.). (ENG.). 32p. (gr. k-3). pap. 7.10 *(978-1-4795-1847-0(6)*, My First Classic Story) Picture Window Bks.

—Tom Thumb: A Retelling of the Grimm's Fairy Tale, 1 vol. Blair, Eric et al. 2010. (My First Classic Story Ser.). (ENG.). 32p. (gr. k-3). lib. bdg. 21.32 *(978-1-4048-6071-1(1)*, My First Classic Story) Picture Window Bks.

—The United States Flag. Doering Tourville, Amanda. 2008. (Our Nation's Pride Ser.). 32p. (gr. -1-3). 28.50 *(978-1-60270-116-8(4)*, Looking Glass Library- Nonfiction) Magic Wagon.

—Valentine's Day. Haugen, Brenda. 2003. (Holidays & Celebrations Ser.). (ENG.). 24p. (gr. k-3). 25.99 *(978-1-4048-0193-6(6)*, Nonfiction Picture Bks.) Picture Window Bks.

—Veteran's Day. Tourville, Amanda Doering. 2008. (Our Nation's Pride Ser.). 32p. (gr. -1-3). 28.50 *(978-1-60270-117-5(2)*, Looking Glass Library- Nonfiction) Magic Wagon.

—You're a Grand Old Flag: A Jubilant Song about Old Glory, 1 vol. 2003. (Patriotic Songs Ser.). (ENG.). 24p. (gr. -1-4). 25.99 *(978-1-4048-0173-8(1)*, Nonfiction Picture Bks.) Picture Window Bks.

Ouren, Todd, jt. illus. see Lyles, Christopher.

Ousley, Clayton Gerard, photos by. Charley Finds A Family. Duchene-Marshall, Michele A. Marshall, Alan David, ed. l.t. ed. 2004. Orig. Title: Charley finds a Home. 20p. (J). spiral bd. 10.00 *(978-0-9761675-2-5(2))* Storybook Acres.

—Shirley's Red Satin Shoes. Duchene-Marshall, Michele A. Marshall, Alan David, ed. l.t. ed. 2003. 17p. (J). spiral bd. 10.00 *(978-0-9761675-1-8(4))* Storybook Acres.

Outohak, Diana. Lulu Learns about Reporting: Ending the Tattle Battle. Golden, Pam. 2007. 28p. (J). pap. 18.95 *(978-0-9659650-8-8(2))* Roedway Pr.

Ovakimyan, Liza. Johnathan & Geneva the Adventures of Zeallionaire Kid's. Perry, Melanie Denise. Neal, Albert, ed. 2013. 34p. pap. 11.99 *(978-0-9911077-1-1(3))* Sankofa Pr.

—Jonathan y Geneva Las Aventuras de Los Zeallionaire Kids. Perry, Melanie Denise. Neal, Albert, ed. 2013. 34p. pap. 11.99 *(978-0-9911077-0-4(5))* Sankofa Pr.

Ovani, Germano. The Monkey King. 2007. (Young Reading Series 1 Gift Bks). 47p. (J). (gr. -1-3). 8.99 *(978-0-7945-1593-5(2)*, Usborne) EDC Publishing.

Overly, Kristen V., jt. illus. see Manwiller, S. A.

Overwater, Georgien. Enormous Turnip. Daynes, Katie. 2006. (First Reading Level 3 Ser.). 48p. (J). (gr. 1-4). 8.99 *(978-0-7945-1376-4(X)*, Usborne) EDC Publishing.

—The Three Little Pigs. 2007. (Usborne First Reading: Level 3 Ser.). 48p. (J). 8.99 *(978-0-7945-1598-0(3)*, Usborne) EDC Publishing.

Ovresat, Laura. Bath Time. Gerver, Jane E. 2004. (My First Reader Ser.). 31p. (J). 18.50 *(978-0-516-24677-2(1)*, Children's Pr.) Scholastic Library Publishing.

—Did You See Chip? Yee, Wong Herbert. 2004. (Green Light Readers Level 2 Ser.). (ENG.). 24p. (J). (gr. -1-3). pap. 3.95 *(978-0-15-205096-2(5))* Houghton Mifflin Harcourt Publishing Co.

—Guess Who Baby Animals. Reader's Digest Staff & Shepherd, Jodie. 2011. (Guess Who Ser.). (ENG.). 10p. (J). (gr. -1-k). bds. 7.99 *(978-0-7944-2196-0(2))* Reader's Digest Assn., Inc., The.

—Ocean Friends. Shepherd, Jodie. 2007. (Guess Who Ser.). (ENG.). 12p. (J). (gr. -1-k). bds. 8.99 *(978-0-7944-1122-0(3))* Reader's Digest Assn., Inc., The.

—The Picnic. Williams, David K. & Williams, David. 2006. (Green Light Readers Level 1 Ser.). (ENG.). 24p. (J). (gr. -1-3). pap. 3.95 *(978-0-15-205782-4(X))* Houghton Mifflin Harcourt Publishing Co.

—The Picnic. Williams, David K. 2006. (Green Light Readers Level 1 Ser.). (gr. -1-1). 13.95 *(978-0-7569-7209-7(4))* Perfection Learning Corp.

—Tick Tock. Williams, David K. & Williams, David. 2006. (Green Light Readers Level 1 Ser.). (ENG.). 24p. (J). (gr. -1-3). pap. 3.95 *(978-0-15-205605-6(X))* Houghton Mifflin Harcourt Publishing Co.

Owen, Elizabeth. Lilly in the Middle, 1 vol. Bellingham, Brenda. 2003. (Formac First Novels Ser.: 25). (ENG.). 64p. (J). (gr. 1-5). 4.95 *(978-0-88780-589-9(2))*; 14.95 *(978-0-88780-590-5(6))* Formac Publishing Co., Ltd. CAN. Dist: Casemate Pubs. & Bk. Distributors, LLC.

Owen, Erich. Beast Academy Guide 3B. Batterson, Jason. 2012. 104p. (J). pap. 15.00 *(978-1-934124-42-0(7))* AoPS Inc.

—Beast Academy Guide 3C. Batterson, Jason. 2012. 112p. pap. 15.00 *(978-1-934124-44-4(3))* AoPS Inc.

—Kung Fu Klutz & Karate Cool, Vol. 1. Seidenberg, Mark & Milky, D. J. 2007. (Manga Chapters Ser.). 96p. (gr. 2-4). pap. 4.99 *(978-1-59816-052-9(4))* TOKYOPOP, Inc.

Owen, James A. The Dragon's Apprentice. Owen, James A. (Chronicles of the Imaginarium Geographica Ser.: 5). (ENG.). (YA). (gr. 7). 2012. 400p. pap. 9.99 *(978-1-4169-5898-7(3))*; 2010. 384p. 17.99 *(978-1-4169-5897-0(5))* Simon & Schuster Bks. For Young Readers. (Simon & Schuster Bks. For Young Readers).

—The Dragons of Winter. Owen, James A. (Chronicles of the Imaginarium Geographica Ser.: 6). (ENG.). (YA). (gr. 7). 2013. 416p. pap. 9.99 *(978-1-4424-1224-8(0))*; 2012. 400p. 17.99 *(978-1-4424-1223-1(2))* Simon & Schuster Bks. For Young Readers. (Simon & Schuster Bks. For Young Readers).

—The First Dragon. Owen, James A. (Chronicles of the Imaginarium Geographica Ser.: 7). (ENG.). 304p. (YA). (gr. 7). 2014. pap. 12.99 *(978-1-4424-1227-9(5))*; 2013. 17.99 *(978-1-4424-1226-2(7))* Simon & Schuster Bks. For Young Readers. (Simon & Schuster Bks. For Young Readers).

—Here, There Be Dragons. Owen, James A. (Chronicles of the Imaginarium Geographica Ser.: 1). (ENG.). (YA). (gr. 7-12). 2007. 352p. pap. 11.99 *(978-1-4169-1228-6(2))*; 2006. 336p. 19.99 *(978-1-4169-1227-9(4))* Simon & Schuster Bks. For Young Readers. (Simon & Schuster Bks. For Young Readers).

—The Indigo King. Owen, James A. (Chronicles of the Imaginarium Geographica Ser.: 3). (ENG.). (YA). (gr. 7). 2010. 400p. pap. 9.99 *(978-1-4169-5108-7(3))*; 2008. 352p. 17.99 *(978-1-4169-5107-0(5))* Simon & Schuster Bks. For Young Readers. (Simon & Schuster Bks. For Young Readers).

—Lost Treasures of the Pirates of the Caribbean. Owen, James A. Owen, Jeremy. 2011. (ENG.). 32p. (J). (gr. 3-7). pap. 16.99 *(978-1-4424-3093-8(1))*, Simon & Schuster Bks. For Young Readers) Simon & Schuster Bks. For Young Readers.

—The Search for the Red Dragon. Owen, James A. 2008. (Chronicles of the Imaginarium Geographica Ser.: 2). (ENG.). (YA). (gr. 7). 400p. pap. 9.99 *(978-1-4169-4851-3(1))*; 384p. 17.99 *(978-1-4169-4850-6(3))* Simon & Schuster Bks. For Young Readers. (Simon & Schuster Bks. For Young Readers).

—The Shadow Dragons. Owen, James A. 2009. (Chronicles of the Imaginarium Geographica Ser.: 4). (ENG.). 352p. (YA). (gr. 7-18). 18.99 *(978-1-4169-5879-6(7)*, Simon & Schuster Bks. For Young Readers) Simon & Schuster Bks. For Young Readers.

Owen, Ken & Owen, Siân. Golwg Gyntaf Ar Bethau Byw. Wadsworth, Pamela. 2005. (WEL.). 24p. pap. *(978-1-85596-250-7(0))* Dref Wen.

—Gwahanol Blanhigion Ac Anifeiliaid. Wadsworth, Pamela. 2005. (WEL.). 24p. pap. *(978-1-85596-223-1(3))* Dref Wen.

Owen, R. Emmett. The Go Ahead Boys & Simon's Mine. Kay, Ross. 2007. 184p. per. *(978-1-4065-1857-3(3))* Dodo Pr.

Owen, Ramon. Shadi, the Shadow Who Wanted to Be Free. Cyr, Joe. 2010. 40p. pap. 14.95 *(978-1-936343-08-9(8))* Peppertree Pr., The.

—Two Happy Stories. Cyr, Joe. 2007. 36p. per. 12.95 *(978-1-934246-73-3(5))* Peppertree Pr., The.

Owen, Rob. Spy Boy, Cheyenne, & Ninety-Six Crayons: A "Mardi Gras" Indian's Story, 1 vol. Owen, Rob. 2013. (ENG.). 32p. (J). (gr. k-3). 16.99 *(978-1-4556-1799-9(7))* Pelican Publishing Co., Inc.

Owen, Ruth. Xtreme! Woods, Mark. 2010. (Top Score Maths Ser.). 32p. pap. *(978-0-237-54282-5(X))* Evans Brothers, Ltd.

Owen, Siân, jt. illus. see Owen, Ken.

Owens, Emily. Whatever the Weather. Peysin, Shainy. Rosenfeld, Dina & Leverton, Yossi, eds. 2011. 32p. (J). 12.95 *(978-1-929628-56-8(0))* Hachai Publishing.

Owens, Mary Beth. The Dump Man's Treasures. Plourde, Lynn. ed. 2008. (ENG.). 32p. (J). (gr. -1-3). 15.95 *(978-0-89272-725-4(X))* Down East Bks.

—A Penny for a Hundred. Pochocki, Ethel. 2005. 31p. (J). (gr. 2-5). pap. 9.95 *(978-1-883937-52-2(3))* Bethlehem Bks.

—Saints & Heroes. Pochocki, Ethel. 2012. 258p. (YA). pap. 15.95 *(978-1-932350-51-7(9))* Bethlehem Bks.

—The Story of the Sea Glass. Dodd, Anne Westcott. ed. 2006. (ENG.). 32p. (J). (gr. -1-17). 15.95 *(978-0-89272-416-1(1))* Down East Bks.

Owenson, Meg. Jars of Hope: How One Woman Helped Save 2,500 Children During the Holocaust. Roy, Jennifer. 2015. (Encounter: Narrative Nonfiction Picture Bks.). (ENG.). 32p. (gr. 3-5). lib. bdg. 26.65 *(978-1-4914-6072-6(5))* Encounter Bks.

Owings, Rae. Max & Friends. Surman, Susan. 150p. (J). (gr. k-3). 9.99 *(978-0-88092-452-8(7))* Royal Fireworks Publishing Co.

Owl, William. Sam & Charlie (and Sam Too) at Camp! Kimmelman, Leslie. 2015. (ENG.). 48p. (J). (gr. k-3). 13.99 *(978-0-8075-7217-7(9))* Whitman, Albert & Co.

Owl, William, jt. illus. see Tambellini, Stefano.

Owlkids Books Inc. Staff, jt. illus. see Attoe, Steve.

Owlkids Books Inc. Staff, jt. illus. see Barron, Ashley.

Owlkids Books Inc. Staff, jt. illus. see Bennett, Jamie.

Owlkids Books Inc. Staff, jt. illus. see Caron, Romi.

Owlkids Books Inc. Staff, jt. illus. see Chin, Carl.

Owlkids Books Inc. Staff, jt. illus. see Cho, Michael.

Owlkids Books Inc. Staff, jt. illus. see Dávila, Claudia.

Owlkids Books Inc. Staff, jt. illus. see Delisle, Anne-Claire.

Owlkids Books Inc. Staff, jt. illus. see Eastman, Dianne.

Owlkids Books Inc. Staff, jt. illus. see Eid, Jean-Paul.

Owlkids Books Inc. Staff, jt. illus. see Franson, Leanne.

Owlkids Books Inc. Staff, jt. illus. see Geoffroi, Remie.

Owlkids Books Inc. Staff, jt. illus. see Griffiths, Dean.

Owlkids Books Inc. Staff, jt. illus. see Hall, Greg.

Owlkids Books Inc. Staff, jt. illus. see Hammill, Matt.

Owlkids Books Inc. Staff, jt. illus. see Hanmer, Clayton.

Owlkids Books Inc. Staff, jt. illus. see Herrbach, Stéphanie.

Owlkids Books Inc. Staff, jt. illus. see Kain, Bob.

Owlkids Books Inc. Staff, jt. illus. see Kicksee, John.

Owlkids Books Inc. Staff, jt. illus. see Kim, Soyeon.

Owlkids Books Inc. Staff, jt. illus. see Kulak, Jeff.

Owlkids Books Inc. Staff, jt. illus. see Lewis-MacDougall, Patricia Ann.

Owlkids Books Inc. Staff, jt. illus. see MacEachern, Stephen.

Owlkids Books Inc. Staff, jt. illus. see Mitchell, Susan.

Owlkids Books Inc. Staff, jt. illus. see Moore, Sean L.

Owlkids Books Inc. Staff, jt. illus. see Pérez, Ramón.

Owlkids Books Inc. Staff, jt. illus. see Richard, Laurent.

Owlkids Books Inc. Staff, jt. illus. see Ritchie, Scot.

Owlkids Books Inc. Staff, jt. illus. see Schwartz, Roslyn.

Owlkids Books Inc. Staff, jt. illus. see Storms, Patricia.

Owlkids Books Inc. Staff, jt. illus. see Wallace, Mary.

Owlkids Books Inc. Staff, jt. illus. see Whamond, Dave.

Owsley, Anthony. Crazy Concoctions: A Mad Scientist's Guide to Messy Mixtures. Brown, Jordan D. 2012. (ENG.). 80p. (J). (gr. 3-7). 14.95 *(978-1-936140-51-0(9)*, Imagine Publishing) Charlesbridge Publishing, Inc.

—Ouch! The Weird & Wild Ways Your Body Deals with Agonizing Aches, Ferocious Fevers, Lousy Lumps, Crummy Colds, Bothersome Bites, Breaks, Bruises, & Burns & Makes Them Feel Better! Rhatigan, Joe. 2013. (ENG.). 80p. (J). (gr. 3-7). 14.95 *(978-1-62354-005-0(4)*, Imagine Publishing) Charlesbridge Publishing, Inc.

—Ouch! The Weird & Wild Ways Your Body Deals with Agonizing Aches, Ferocious Fevers, Lousy Lumps, Crummy Colds, Bothersome Bites, Breaks, Bruises & Burns & Makes Them Feel Better! Rhatigan, Joe. 2015. (ENG.). 80p. (J). (gr. 4-7). pap. 9.95 *(978-1-62354-053-1(4)*, Imagine Publishing) Charlesbridge Publishing, Inc.

—The Super Concentrated Brain De-Clogger Book: Hundreds of Games, Puzzles & Other Fun Activites That Are Positively Guaranteed to Remove Brain Sludge, Liquidate Blocked Brain Cells, & Stomp Out Boredom! Press, Applesauce & Rhatigan, Joe. 2012. (ENG.). 528p. (J). (gr. 3). pap. 14.95 *(978-1-60433-228-5(X)*, Applesauce Pr.) Cider Mill Pr. Bk. Pubs., LLC.

Oxenbury, Helen. Alice Through the Looking-Glass. Carroll, Lewis. 2009. (ENG.). 208p. (J). (gr. 3-7). pap. 14.99 *(978-0-7636-4262-4(2))* Candlewick Pr.

—Alice's Adventures in Wonderland. Carroll, Lewis. 2003. (ENG.). 208p. (J). (gr. 3-7). pap. 14.99 *(978-0-7636-2049-3(1))* Candlewick Pr.

—Big Momma Makes the World. Root, Phyllis. 2007. (ENG.). 48p. (J). (gr. -1-3). pap. 7.99 *(978-0-7636-2600-6(7))* Candlewick Pr.

—Charley's First Night. Hest, Amy. 2012. (ENG.). 32p. (J). (gr. -1-2). 15.99 *(978-0-7636-4055-2(7))* Candlewick Pr.

—El Desayuno de Tomas. Cutler, Ivor. (SPA.). 30p. (J). (gr. k-3). pap. 6.95 *(978-1-56014-629-2(X))* Santillana USA Publishing Co., Inc.

—Diez Deditos de Las Manos y Diez Deditos de Los Pies / Ten Little Fingers & Ten Little Toes Bilingual Board Book. Fox, Mem. 2012. (ENG & SPA.). 38p. (J). (gr. k — 1). bds. 6.99 *(978-0-547-87006-9(X))* Houghton Mifflin Harcourt Publishing Co.

—Farmer Duck. Waddell, Martin. (Candlewick Storybook Audio Ser.). (ENG.). 40p. (J). 2011. (-k). 8.99 *(978-0-7636-5112-1(5))*; 2008. (gr. -1-k). 14.99 *(978-0-7636-3512-1(X))* Candlewick Pr.

—La Gran Mamá Hace el Mundo. Root, Phyllis. 2004. (SPA.). (J). 23.99 *(978-84-88342-48-5(9))* S.A. Kokinos ESP. Dist: Lectorum Pubns., Inc.

—The Growing Story. Krauss, Ruth. 2007. (ENG.). 40p. (J). (gr. -1-3). 16.99 *(978-0-06-024716-4(9))* HarperCollins Pubs.

—King Jack & the Dragon. Bently, Peter. 2011. (ENG.). 32p. (J). (gr. -1-k). 17.99 *(978-0-8037-3698-6(3)*, Dial) Penguin Publishing Group.

—King Jack & the Dragon Board Book. Bently, Peter. 2013. (ENG.). 14p. (J). (gr. -1 — 1). bds. 7.99 *(978-0-8037-3987-1(7)*, Dial) Penguin Publishing Group.

—So Much! Cooke, Trish. 2008. (ENG.). 48p. (J). (gr. -1-2). pap. 6.99 *(978-0-7636-4091-0(3))* Candlewick Pr.

—Ten Little Fingers & Ten Little Toes. Fox, Mem. (ENG.). 2010. 38p. (gr. k — 1). bds. 8.99 *(978-0-547-36620-3(5))*; 2008. 40p. (J). (gr. -1 — 1). 16.99 *(978-0-15-206057-2(X))* Houghton Mifflin Harcourt Publishing Co.

—Ten Little Fingers & Ten Little Toes Lap Board Book. Fox, Mem. 2011. (ENG.). 38p. (J). (gr. k — 1). bds. 11.99 *(978-0-547-58103-3(3))* Houghton Mifflin Harcourt Publishing Co.

—There's Going to Be a Baby. Burningham, John. 48p. (J). 2014. (ENG.). (-k). 7.99 *(978-0-7636-7265-2(3))*; 2010. *(978-0-7445-4996-6(5))*; 2010. (ENG.). (gr. -1-k). 16.99 *(978-0-7636-4907-4(4))* Candlewick Pr.

Oxenbury, Helen. The Three Little Wolves & the Big Bad Pig. Trivizas, Eugene. 2015. 32p. pap. 8.00 ***(978-1-61003-621-4(2))*** Center for the Collaborative Classroom.

Oxenbury, Helen. The Three Little Wolves & the Big Bad Pig. Trivizas, Eugene. 2004. (ENG.). 16p. (J). 24.95 *(978-1-4052-0669-3(1))* Egmont Bks., Ltd. GBR. Dist: Trafalgar Square Publishing.

—The Three Little Wolves & the Big Bad Pig: A Pop-up Storybook. Trivizas, Eugene. 2006. 16p. (J). (gr. k-4). reprint ed. 27.00 *(978-0-7567-9913-7(9))* DIANE Publishing Co.

—Los Tres Lobitos y el Cochino Feroz. Trivizas, Eugene. 2003. (SPA.). 32p. (J). (gr. k-3). pap. 12.99 *(978-980-257-246-5(2)*, EK1366) Ekare, Ediciones VEN. Dist: Kane Miller, Lectorum Pubns., Inc.

—Vamos a Caca de Um Urso. Rosen, Michael. 2004. Orig. Title: We're Going on a Bear Hunt. (ENG & POR.). 33p. (J). pap. *(978-1-85269-715-0(6))* Mantra Lingua.

—We're Going on a Bear Hunt. 2004. 33p. (J). *(978-1-85269-713-6(X))*; *(978-1-85269-719-8(9))*; (ENG & ARA.). pap. *(978-1-85269-707-5(5))* Mantra Lingua.

—We're Going on a Bear Hunt. Rosen, Michael. 2004. (J). 32p. *(978-1-85269-706-8(7))*; 32p. *(978-1-85269-710-5(5))*; 32p. *(978-1-85269-711-2(3))*; 32p. *(978-1-85269-716-7(4))*; 32p. *(978-1-85269-718-1(0))*; 32p. *(978-1-85269-720-4(2))*; (ENG & BEN.). 33p. pap. *(978-1-85269-708-2(3))*; (ENG & PAN.). 33p. pap. *(978-1-85269-714-3(8))*; (ENG & URD.). 33p. pap. *(978-1-85269-721-1(0))*; (ENG & FRE.). 33p. pap. *(978-1-85269-712-9(1))* Mantra Lingua.

—We're Going on a Bear Hunt. Rosen, Michael. 2003. (ENG.). 36p. (J). (gr. -1-3). pap. 7.99 *(978-0-689-85349-4(1)*, McElderry, Margaret K. Bks.) McElderry, Margaret K. Bks.

—We're Going on a Bear Hunt. Rosen, Michael. ed. 2003. (gr. k-3). 18.40 *(978-0-613-61665-2(0)*, Turtleback) Turtleback Bks.

—We're Going on a Bear Hunt: Anniversary Edition of a Modern Classic. Rosen, Michael. ed. 2009. (Classic Board Bks.). (ENG.). 36p. (J). (gr. -1-k). bds. 8.99 *(978-1-4169-8712-3(6)*, Little Simon) Little Simon.

—We're Going on a Bear Hunt: Anniversary Edition of a Modern Classic. Rosen, Michael. ed. 2009. (ENG.). 40p. (J). (gr. -1-3). 18.99 *(978-1-4169-8711-6(8)*, McElderry, Margaret K. Bks.) McElderry, Margaret K. Bks.

—We're Going on a Bear Hunt: Sound Book. Rosen, Michael. 2014. (ENG.). 40p. (J). (gr. -1-2). 19.99 *(978-0-7636-7702-2(7))* Candlewick Pr.

—When Charley Met Grampa. Hest, Amy. 2013. (ENG.). 40p. (J). (gr. -1-2). 15.99 *(978-0-7636-5314-9(4))* Candlewick Pr.

Oxenbury, Helen. Baby Love Set: All Fall down - Clap Hands - Say Goodnight - Tickle, Tickle. Oxenbury, Helen. gif. ed. 2009. (ENG.). 40p. (J). (gr. -1 — 1). bds. 7.99 *(978-1-4169-9546-3(3)*, Little Simon) Little Simon.

—The Helen Oxenbury Nursery Collection. Oxenbury, Helen. 2014. (ENG.). 96p. (J). (gr. -1-1). 22.99 *(978-1-4052-6742-7(9))* Egmont Bks., Ltd. GBR. Dist: Independent Pubs. Group.

—It's My Birthday. Oxenbury, Helen. 2010. (ENG.). 24p. (J). (gr. -1-k). bds. 8.99 *(978-0-7636-4970-8(8))* Candlewick Pr.

—Pig Tale. Oxenbury, Helen. 2010. (ENG.). 32p. (J). (gr. -1-1). 16.99 *(978-1-4424-2153-0(3))*, McElderry, Margaret K. Bks.) McElderry, Margaret K. Bks.

Oxenbury, Helen, jt. illus. see Rosen, Michael.

Oxfam (Afghanistan) Staff, photos by. Around the World - Playtime. Petty, Kate. 2013. (Around the World Ser.). (ENG.). 32p. (J). (gr. -1-1). pap. 8.99 *(978-1-84507-555-2(2)*, Frances Lincoln) Quarto Publishing Group UK GBR. Dist: Hachette Bk. Group.

Oxfam Staff. W Is for World Big Book: A Round-the-World ABC. Cave, Kathryn. 2004. 32p. (J). pap. *(978-1-84507-026-7(7)*, Frances Lincoln) Quarto Publishing Group UK.

Oxford Bible Staff. Abraham Lincoln, 1 vol. Raum, Elizabeth. 2012. (American Biographies Ser.). (ENG.). 48p. (gr. 4-6). lib. bdg. 32.00 *(978-1-4329-6453-5(4)*, NA-h) Heinemann-Raintree.

—George Washington, 1 vol. Rand, Casey. 2012. (American Biographies Ser.). (ENG.). 48p. (gr. 4-6). lib. bdg. 32.00 *(978-1-4329-6452-8(6)*, NA-h) Heinemann-Raintree.

—Langston Hughes, 1 vol. Gallagher, Brigid. 2012. (American Biographies Ser.). (ENG.). 48p. (gr. 4-6). lib. bdg. 32.00 *(978-1-4329-6455-9(0)*, NA-h) Heinemann-Raintree.

—Malcolm X, 1 vol. Fay, Gail. 2012. (American Biographies Ser.). (ENG.). 48p. (gr. 4-6). lib. bdg. 32.00 *(978-1-4329-6456-6(9)*, NA-h) Heinemann-Raintree.

—Medgar Evers, 1 vol. Weil, Ann. 2012. (American Biographies Ser.). (ENG.). 48p. (gr. 4-6). lib. bdg. 32.00 *(978-1-4329-6454-2(2)*, NA-h) Heinemann-Raintree.

Oyama, Misuzu. Rue de la Nuit: Labyrinth. 2010. (ENG.). 40p. (gr. 1). 25.95 *(978-1-935557-02-9(5))* PublishingWorks.

Ozaki, Kaori. Immortal Rain. Ozaki, Kaori, creator. rev. ed. 2005. Vol. 5. 216p. pap. 9.99 *(978-1-59182-991-1(7))*; Vol. 6. 192p. pap. 9.99 *(978-1-59532-799-4(1))* TOKYOPOP, Inc.

Ozama, Marcel & Dzama, Marcel. Bed, Bed, Bed. Might Be Giants Staff et al. 2003. (ENG.). 48p. (gr. -1-5). 16.95 *(978-0-7432-5024-5(9))* Simon & Schuster.

Ozzy. The Leprechaun. Smyth, Jimmy. 2013. 32p. pap. *(978-0-9569314-1-2(3))* Smith, Jimmy.

O

P

P, N. Alphabet Country: A Read-Together ABC Game. P, N. 2012. (ENG.). 26p. (J). spiral bd. 9.00 *(978-0-615-59362-3(3))* Easy Reach Corp.

P, N. Down on the Ranch: A Counting Book, 1. P, N., text. 2011. 24p. (J). spiral bd. 9.00 *(978-0-615-50973-0(8))* Easy Reach Corp.

PA Illustrator. Annabelle Discovers the Missing Lunch Money. Hauf, Kyle. 2011. 36p. pap. 24.95 *(978-1-4560-3656-0(4))* America Star Bks.

—Hooray! We're Making Memories Today! Gittens, Sandra L. 2011. 48p. pap. 24.95 *(978-1-4560-0914-4(1))* America Star Bks.

Paarmann, Lesley, photos by. Please Let Me Help: I Need Validation. Paarmann, Al. unabr. ed. 2003. 150p. (YA). pap. 12.95 *(978-0-9715963-1-3(X))* Paarmann, Al International.

Paccia, Abbey. Alex the Ant Goes to the Beach. Dickey, Eric Wayne. 2014. (ENG.). 32p. (J). (gr. k-2). 17.99 *(978-1-940052-08-3(4))* Craigmore Creations.

Pace, Brittany Lee Ann. Walter S. (Spy) Pigeon, 1 vol. Collier, Kathy Lynn. 2009. 20p. pap. 24.95 *(978-1-60813-543-1(8))* America Star Bks.

Pace, Christine. Kipper Finds a Home: A White Squirrel Parable Volume 1. Guess, Catherine Ritch. 2005. (ENG.). 32p. (J). (gr. -1-7). pap. 13.95 *(978-1-933341-00-2(9))* CRM.

Pacheco, Alma Rosa & Pacheco, Guadalupe. Felicia y Odicia. Palacios, Maria Eugenia Blanco & Blanco, Maria. rev. ed. 2005. (Castillo de la Lectura Blanca Ser.). (SPA & ENG.). 56p. (J). (gr. -1-3). pap. 6.95 *(978-970-20-0125-6(0))* Castillo, Ediciones, S. A. de C. V. MEX. Dist: Macmillan.

—Que Te Pasa, Calabaza! Ortiz, Orlando & Ortiz, Orlando. rev. ed. 2007. (Castillo de la Lectura Blanca Ser.). (SPA & ENG.). 72p. (J). (gr. k-2). pap. 6.95 *(978-970-20-0172-0(2))* Castillo, Ediciones, S. A. de C. V. MEX. Dist: Macmillan.

Pacheco, Alma Rosa, jt. illus. see Pacheco, Luis Gabriel.

Pacheco, Carlos. Fantastic Four: Extended Family. Buscema, John. 2011. (ENG.). 232p. (YA). (gr. 8-17). pap. 24.99 *(978-0-7851-5303-0(9))* Marvel Worldwide, Inc.

Pacheco, Carlos, et al. Fantastic Four - Resurrection of Galactus. 2011. (ENG.). 200p. (J). (gr. 4-17). 24.99 *(978-0-7851-4476-2(5))* Marvel Worldwide, Inc.

Pacheco, Carlos & Klein, Nic. Captain America, Vol. 3. 2014. (ENG.). 136p. (J). (gr. 4-17). 24.99 *(978-0-7851-8951-0(3))* Marvel Worldwide, Inc.

Pacheco, Gabriel. I Dreamt... A Book about Hope, 1 vol. Olmos, Gabriela. Amado, Elisa, tr. from SPA. 2013. (ENG.). 40p. (J). (gr. k-3). 18.95 *(978-1-55498-330-8(4))* Groundwood Bks. CAN. Dist: Perseus-PGW.

—El Papalote y el Nopal. Petterson, Aline. 2003. (SPA.). 34p. (J). (gr. 3-5). 15.95 *(978-968-19-0750-1(7))* Santillana USA Publishing Co., Inc.

—El Pollito de la Avellaneda. Rubio, Antonio. 2006. 32p. (J). (gr. 5-7). 15.99 *(978-84-96388-12-3(3))* Lectorum Pubns., Inc.

Pacheco, Guadalupe, jt. illus. see Pacheco, Alma Rosa.

Pacheco, Jorge M. Harry & Hannah: The American Adventure. Herrington, Chris. 2003. (Adventures of Harry & Hannah Ser.). (ENG.). 72p. (J). (gr. 1-5). 15.00 *(978-0-9722343-0-6(6))* Herrington Teddy Bears.

Pacheco, Luis Gabriel & Pacheco, Alma Rosa. Juegos Recreativos para Ninos. 2003. (SPA.). 182p. (J). pap. *(978-970-651-625-1(5))* Editorial Oceano De Mexico, S.A. DE C.V.

Pacheco, Luis Gabriel, jt. illus. see Alvarado, Dalia.

Pacheco, Robert. Trade on the Taos Mountain Trail. 2010. (ENG.). 48p. (J). pap. 16.99 *(978-0-9823445-0-7(3))* Vanishing Horizons.

Packer, Emily. Dramatizando la Gallinita Roja: Un Cuento para Contar y Actuar. Thistle, Louise. l.t. ed. 2003.Tr. of Dramatizing the Little Red Hen. (SPA.). 32p. (J). (gr. k-2). pap. 10.00 *(978-0-9644186-4-6(9))* Literature Dramatization Pr.

—Dramatizing the Little Red Hen. Thistle, Louise. Landes, William-Alan, ed. l.t. ed. 2003. 32p. (J). (gr. k-2). pap. 10.00 *(978-0-9644186-5-3(7))* Literature Dramatization Pr.

Packer, Neil. The Iliad. Cross, Gillian. 2015. (ENG.). 160p. (J). (gr. 3-7). 19.99 *(978-0-7636-7832-6(5))* Candlewick Pr.

Packer, Neil. The Odyssey. Cross, Gillian. 2012. (ENG.). 178p. (J). (gr. 3-7). 19.99 *(978-0-7636-4791-9(8))* Candlewick Pr.

Pacovskà, Kveta. Flying. Pacovskà, Kveta. 2005.Tr. of Turme. 39p. (J). reprint ed. 20.00 *(978-0-7567-8532-1(4))* DIANE Publishing Co.

Padavick, Nate. Know Your State Activity Book Utah, 1 vol. Hansen Moench, Megan. 2015. (ENG.). 272p. pap. 14.99 *(978-1-4236-4056-1(X))* Gibbs Smith, Publisher.

—Know Your State Activity Book Washington, 1 vol. Hansen Moench, Megan. 2015. (ENG.). 272p. pap. 14.99 *(978-1-4236-4059-2(4))* Gibbs Smith, Publisher.

Padgett, Dave. Ellie Bean the Drama Queen: A Children's Book about Sensory Processing Disorder. Harding, Jennie. 2011. (ENG.). 48p. (J). (gr. -1-4). pap. 9.95 *(978-1-935567-27-1(6))* Sensory Resources.

Padilla, Ariel. The Argon Deception, 1 vol. Krueger, Jim & Rogers, Bud. 2008. (Z Graphic Novels / Tomo Ser.). (ENG.). 160p. (J). (gr. 4-7). pap. 6.99 *(978-0-310-71303-6(X))* Zondervan.

—The Battle for Argon Falls, 1 vol. Rogers, Bud & Krueger, Jim. 2012. (Z Graphic Novels / Tomo Ser.). (ENG.). 160p. (J). pap. 6.99 *(978-0-310-71307-4(2))* Zondervan.

—Betrayal of Trust, 1 vol. Krueger, Jim & Zondervan Publishing Staff. Rogers, Bud, ed. 2009. (Z Graphic Novels / Tomo Ser.). (ENG.). 160p. (J). pap. 6.99 *(978-0-310-71306-7(4))* Zondervan.

—Child of Destiny, 1 vol. Krueger, Jim & Rogers, Bud. 2008. (Z Graphic Novels / Tomo Ser.). (ENG.). 160p. (J). (gr. 4-7). pap. 6.99 *(978-0-310-71302-9(1))* Zondervan.

—I Was an Eighth-Grade Ninja, 1 vol. Simmons, Andrew & Averdonz, N. R. 2007. (Z Graphic Novels / Tomo Ser.). (ENG.). 160p. (J). (gr. 3-7). pap. 6.99 *(978-0-310-71300-5(5))* Zonderkidz.

—My Double-Edged Life, 1 vol. Kreuger, Jim & Averdonz, N. R. 2007. (Z Graphic Novels / Tomo Ser.). (ENG.). 160p. (J). (gr. 3-7). pap. 6.99 *(978-0-310-71301-2(3))* Zonderkidz.

—Secret Alliance, 1 vol. Rogers, Bud & Krueger, Jim. 2008. (Z Graphic Novels / Tomo Ser.). (ENG.). 160p. (J). pap. 6.99 *(978-0-310-71304-3(8))* Zondervan.

—Truth Revealed, 1 vol. Rogers, Bud et al. 2009. (Z Graphic Novels / Tomo Ser.). (ENG.). 160p. (J). pap. 6.99 *(978-0-310-71305-0(6))* Zonderkidz.

Padilla, Eren Star. Smiling at the Rain. Padilla, Felix M. 32p. (J). (gr. 3-18). 16.00 *(978-0-9710860-4-3(4))* Libros, Encouraging Cultural Literacy.

Padmanabhan, Manjula. I Am Different. 2011. (MUL & ENG.). 32p. (J). (gr. 1-4). pap. 7.95 *(978-1-57091-640-3(3))* Charlesbridge Publishing, Inc.

Padovano, Chris. The Butterfly Princess. Newton, Chelle. 2012. 44p. pap. 11.99 *(978-1-61286-129-6(6))* Avid Readers Publishing Group.

—Gold Old Gets a Little Help from His Friends. Carothers, Nina. Nilsen, Richard J., ed. 2013. 32p. pap. 12.97 *(978-1-937376-29-1(X))* All Star Pr.

—Pink Ink's Purpose. Carothers, Nina. Nilsen, Richard J., ed. 2013. 36p. pap. 12.97 *(978-1-937376-26-0(5))* All Star Pr.

—Red Ed & the True Meaning of Christmas. Carothers, Nina. Nilsen, Richard J., ed. 2013. 32p. pap. 12.97 *(978-1-937376-27-7(3))* All Star Pr.

—The Wonderful World of Color Olors. Carothers, Nina. Nilsen, Richard J., ed. 2013. 36p. pap. 12.97 *(978-1-937376-28-4(1))* All Star Pr.

Padron, Alicia. ABC, Baby Me! Katz, Susan B. 2010. (ENG.). 28p. (J). (— 1). bds. 7.99 *(978-0-375-86679-1(5)*, Robin Corey Bks.) Random Hse. Children's Bks.

—The Birthday Bears. Huven, Kim. 2010. 10p. bds. 10.95 *(978-1-60747-774-7(2)*, Pickwick Pr.) Phoenix Bks., Inc.

—I Love You All Year Round. Shubuck, Sheila. 2008. (ENG.). 16p. (J). (gr. -1). 10.95 *(978-1-58117-786-2(0)*, Intervisual/Piggy Toes) Bendon, Inc.

Padrón, Angela. My Body Belongs to Me: A Book about Body Safety. Starishevsky, Jill. 2014. (ENG.). 32p. (J). (gr. -1-3). 12.99 *(978-1-57542-461-3(4))* Free Spirit Publishing, Inc.

Padron, Aya. My First Book of Chinese Words: An ABC Rhyming Book. Wu, Faye-Lynn. 2013. (ENG & CHI.). 32p. (J). (gr. -1 — 1). 12.95 *(978-0-8048-4367-6(8))* Tuttle Publishing.

—My First Book of Japanese Words: An ABC Rhyming Book. Brown, Michelle Haney. 2013. (ENG & JPN.). 32p. (J). 12.95 *(978-4-8053-1201-8(7))* Tuttle Publishing.

—My First Book of Korean Words: An ABC Rhyming Book. Park, Kyubyong & Amen, Henry J. 2012. (ENG.). 26p. (J). (gr. -1 — 1). 12.95 *(978-0-8048-4273-0(6))* Tuttle Publishing.

Padur, Simone. 3 on a Moonbeam. Sandilands, Joyce. 2004. 64p. *(978-0-9734383-1-4(2))* Whitlands Publishing, Ltd.

Paes, Rob. Mighty Machines. 2003. 12p. (J). (gr. k-3). 20.00 *(978-0-7567-6652-8(4))* DIANE Publishing Co.

Pagano, Mark. Today's Okay. Cheha, Jacob. 2010. (ENG.). 32p. pap. 9.97 *(978-1-4563-1652-5(4))* CreateSpace Independent Publishing Platform.

Pagay, Jeff. Mele da Mynah's Noisy 'Ohana. Geshell, Carmen. 2004. 24p. 10.95 *(978-1-57306-225-1(1))* Bess Pr., Inc.

—The Surf Rats of Waikiki Beach. Geshell, Carmen. 2004. 24p. 10.95 *(978-1-57306-226-8(X))* Bess Pr., Inc.

—Waltah Melon: Local-Kine Hero. Geshell, Carmen. 2004. 24p. (J). 10.95 *(978-1-57306-205-3(7))* Bess Pr., Inc.

Page. Don't Be Afraid of the Storm. Caban, Connie. 2011. 32p. pap. 12.95 *(978-1-936343-97-3(5))* Peppertree Pr., The.

Page, Debbie. Chickadee - the Traveler, 11 vols. Keaster, Diane W. l.t. ed. 2004. (ZC Horses: Vol. 8). (ENG.). 80p. (J). per. 7.95 *(978-0-9721496-7-9(8))* ZC Horses Series of Children's Bks.

Page, Debbie, et al. Darby - the Cow Dog, 9 vols. Keaster, Diane W. l.t. ed. 2005. (ZC Horses: 9). (ENG.). 68p. (J). per. 7.95 *(978-0-9721496-8-6(6))* ZC Horses Series of Children's Bks.

Page, Debbie. Goldie - the Wise, 25 vols. Keaster, Diane W. l.t. ed. 2004. (ZC Horses: 7). (ENG.). 87p. (J). per. 7.95 *(978-0-9721496-6-2(X))* ZC Horses Series of Children's Bks.

—Leroy - the Stallion, 25 vols. Keaster, Diane W. l.t. ed. 2003. (ZC Horses: 6). (ENG.). 79p. (J). per. 7.95 *(978-0-9721496-5-5(1))* ZC Horses Series of Children's Bks.

—Tawny-The Beauty. Keaster, Diane. 2013. 70p. pap. 7.95 *(978-0-9791719-2-5(X))* ZC Horses Series of Children's Bks.

Page, Gail. How to Be a Good Cat. 2011. (ENG.). 32p. (J). (gr. -1-1). 17.89 *(978-1-59990-475-7(6)*, Bloomsbury USA Childrens) Bloomsbury USA.

Page, Gail. How to Be a Good Dog. Page, Gail. (ENG.). 32p. (J). (gr. -1-3). 2007. pap. 7.99 *(978-1-59990-151-0(X))*; 2006. 15.95 *(978-1-58234-683-0(6))* Bloomsbury USA. (Bloomsbury USA Childrens).

Page, Mark. No Boys Allowed! Scholastic, Inc. Staff & Taylor-Butler, Christine. 2004. (Just for You Ser.). (ENG.). 32p. pap. 3.99 *(978-0-439-56856-2(0)*, Teaching Resources) Scholastic, Inc.

—The Two Tyrones. Hudson, Wade. 2004. 32p. (J). lib. bdg. 15.00 *(978-1-4242-0239-3(6))* Fitzgerald Bks.

—The Two Tyrones. Hudson, Wade. 2004. (Just for You Ser.). (ENG.). 32p. (gr. 2-3). pap. 3.99 *(978-0-439-56866-1(8)*, Teaching Resources) Scholastic, Inc.

Page, Philip. Macbeth: Livewire Shakespeare. Page, Philip, ed. Petit, Marilyn, ed. 2005. (Picture This! Shakespeare Ser.). (ENG.). 64p. per. 8.99 *(978-0-7641-3140-0(0))* Barron's Educational Series, Inc.

—Romeo & Juliet. Page, Philip, ed. Petit, Marilyn, ed. 2005. (Picture This! Shakespeare Ser.). (ENG.). 64p. per. 8.99 *(978-0-7641-3144-8(3))* Barron's Educational Series, Inc.

Page, Robin. A Chicken Followed Me Home! Questions & Answers about a Familiar Fowl. Page, Robin. 2015. (ENG.). 40p. (J). (gr. k-5). 17.99 *(978-1-4814-1028-1(8)*, Beach Lane Bks.) Beach Lane Bks.

Page, Terry. The Fathers of the Friendly Forest. Page, Terry. 24p. (J). (gr. 2-6). pap. 4.00 *(978-1-887864-69-5(5))*; lib. bdg. 7.00 *(978-1-887864-38-1(5))* Boo Bks., Inc.

—The Fathers of the Friendly Forest Coloring Book. Page, Terry. 32p. (J). (gr. -1-5). pap. 3.00 *(978-1-887864-39-8(3))* Boo Bks., Inc.

—The Saddest Centaur. Page, Terry. 24p. (J). (gr. 2-6). pap. 4.00 *(978-1-887864-68-8(7))*; lib. bdg. 7.00 *(978-1-887864-36-7(9))* Boo Bks., Inc.

—The Saddest Centaur Coloring Book. Page, Terry. 32p. (J). (gr. -1-5). pap. 3.00 *(978-1-887864-37-4(7))* Boo Bks., Inc.

Page, Tyler. The Bark in Space. Robbins, Trina. 2013. (Chicagoland Detective Agency Ser.: 5). (ENG.). 64p. (gr. 4-8). pap. 6.95 *(978-1-4677-0725-1(2))*; lib. bdg. 29.27 *(978-0-7613-8166-2(X))* Lerner Publishing Group. (Graphic Universe).

—The Big Flush. Robbins, Trina. 2012. (Chicagoland Detective Agency Ser.: 4). (ENG.). 64p. (gr. 4-8). pap. 6.95 *(978-0-8225-9161-0(8))*; lib. bdg. 29.27 *(978-0-7613-8165-5(1))* Lerner Publishing Group. (Graphic Universe).

—The Drained Brains Caper. Robbins, Trina. 2010. (Chicagoland Detective Agency Ser.: 1). (ENG.). 64p. (gr. 4-8). pap. 6.95 *(978-0-7613-5635-6(5)*, Graphic Universe); lib. bdg. 29.27 *(978-0-7613-4601-2(5))* Lerner Publishing Group.

—The Maltese Mummy. Robbins, Trina. 2011. (Chicagoland Detective Agency Ser.: 2). (ENG.). 64p. (gr. 4-8). 29.27 *(978-0-7613-4615-9(5))*; pap. 6.95 *(978-0-7613-5636-3(3)*, Graphic Universe) Lerner Publishing Group.

—A Midterm Night's Scheme. Robbins, Trina. 2014. (Chicagoland Detective Agency Ser.: 6). (ENG.). 64p. (gr. 4-8). lib. bdg. 29.27 *(978-0-7613-8167-9(8)*, Graphic Universe) Lerner Publishing Group.

—Night of the Living Dogs. Robbins, Trina. 2012. (Chicagoland Detective Agency Ser.). 64p. (gr. 4-8). (J). pap. 39.62 *(978-0-7613-9313-9(7)*, Graphic Universe); (ENG.). lib. bdg. 29.27 *(978-0-7613-4616-6(3))* Lerner Publishing Group.

—The Night of the Living Dogs. Robbins, Trina. 2012. (Chicagoland Detective Agency Ser.: 3). (ENG.). 64p. (gr. 4-8). pap. 6.95 *(978-0-7613-5637-0(1)*, Graphic Universe) Lerner Publishing Group.

Paglia, Rhonda & Galaska, Taylor. The Little Lambs & the Very Special Mission. Paglia, Rhonda. 2013. 44p. pap. 12.95 *(978-0-9899141-1-6(9))* Angels Landing.

Pagnoni, Roberta. The Christmas Star. Caviezel, Giovanni. 2013. (ENG.). 10p. (J). (gr. -1 — 1). bds. 6.99 *(978-0-7641-6624-2(7))* Barron's Educational Series, Inc.

—Humpty Dumpty's Nursery Rhymes. 2010. (ENG.). 10p. (J). (gr. -1-k). bds. 7.99 *(978-0-7641-6278-7(0))* Barron's Educational Series, Inc.

—It's Easter Time. 2010. (ENG.). 10p. (J). (gr. -1-k). bds. 6.99 *(978-0-7641-6334-0(5))* Barron's Educational Series, Inc.

Pagnoni, Roberta, et al. My Ballet Bag. Ravera, Giuseppe. 2015. (ENG.). 8p. (J). (gr. -1-k). bds. 6.99 *(978-0-7641-6786-7(3))* Barron's Educational Series, Inc.

Pagnoni, Roberta. Spring. Caviezel, Giovanni. 2013. (My First Seasons Ser.). (ENG.). 10p. (J). (gr. -1 — 1). bds. 6.99 *(978-0-7641-6585-6(2))* Barron's Educational Series, Inc.

—Summer. Caviezel, Giovanni. 2013. (My First Seasons Ser.). (ENG.). 10p. (J). (gr. -1 — 1). bds. 6.99 *(978-0-7641-6586-3(0))* Barron's Educational Series, Inc.

Pagnoni, Roberta & Rigo, Laura. Gingerbread Man House. Ravera, Giuseppe. 2015. (ENG.). 8p. (J). (gr. -1-k). bds. 6.99 *(978-0-7641-6784-3(7))* Barron's Educational Series, Inc.

—The Nutcracker. Barron's Editorial Staff. 2015. (Little People Shape Bks.). (ENG.). 10p. (J). (gr. -1 — 1). bds. 7.99 *(978-0-7641-6796-6(0))* Barron's Educational Series, Inc.

Pagnoni, Roberta & Rigo, Laura. The Twelve Days of Christmas. 2013. (ENG.). 24p. (J). (gr. -1 — 1). bds. 10.99 *(978-0-7641-6622-8(0))* Barron's Educational Series, Inc.

Pagnoni, Roberta, jt. illus. see Rigo, L.

Pagona, Aurora. The Magical Purple-Blue Frog, 1 vol. De Jesus, Opal. 2010. 16p. pap. 24.95 *(978-1-4489-5925-9(X))* PublishAmerica, Inc.

Paillot, Jim. Back to School, Weird Kids Rule! Gutman, Dan. 2014. (My Weird School Special Ser.). (ENG.). 144p. (J). (gr. 1-5). pap. 5.99 *(978-0-06-220685-5(0))* HarperCollins Pubs.

—Bunny Double, We're in Trouble! Gutman, Dan. 2014. (My Weird School Special Ser.). (ENG.). 144p. (J). (gr. 1-5). pap. 4.99 *(978-0-06-228400-6(2))* HarperCollins Pubs.

—Coach Hyatt Is a Riot! Gutman, Dan. 2008. (My Weird School Daze Ser.: 4). 112p. (J). (gr. 1-5). lib. bdg. 15.89 *(978-0-06-155408-7(1))*; 4th ed. (ENG.). pap. 4.99 *(978-0-06-155406-3(5))* HarperCollins Pubs.

—Coach Hyatt Is a Riot! Gutman, Dan. 2009. (My Weird School Daze Ser.: No. 4). 106p. (J). (gr. 2-5). 12.90 *(978-1-4178-3168-5(5)*, Turtleback) Turtleback Bks.

—Deck the Halls, We're off the Walls! Gutman, Dan. 2013. (My Weird School Special Ser.). (ENG.). 144p. (J). (gr. 1-5). pap. 5.99 *(978-0-06-220682-4(6))* HarperCollins Pubs.

—Dr. Brad Has Gone Mad! Gutman, Dan. 2009. (My Weird School Daze Ser.: 7). 112p. (J). (gr. 1-5). (ENG.). pap. 4.99 *(978-0-06-155412-4(X))*; lib. bdg. 15.89 *(978-0-06-155414-8(6))* HarperCollins Pubs.

—Dr. Carbles Is Losing His Marbles! Gutman, Dan. 2007. (My Weird School Ser.: 19). 112p. (J). (ENG.). (gr. 1-5). pap. 4.99 *(978-0-06-123477-4(X))*; (gr. 2-5). lib. bdg. 15.89 *(978-0-06-123478-1(8))* HarperCollins Pubs.

—Dr. Carbles Is Losing His Marbles! Gutman, Dan. 2007. (My Weird School Ser.: No. 19). 99p. (J). (gr. 2-5). 11.65 *(978-0-7569-8810-4(1))* Perfection Learning Corp.

—Dr. Nicholas Is Ridiculous! Gutman, Dan. 2013. (My Weirder School Ser.: 8). 112p. (J). (gr. 1-5). 15.89 *(978-0-06-204219-4(X))*; (ENG.). pap. 4.99 *(978-0-06-204218-7(1))* HarperCollins Pubs.

—Fun Excuse to Stay up Late. Overdeck, Laura. 2013. (Bedtime Math Ser.). (ENG.). 96p. (J). (gr. -1-2). 15.99 *(978-1-250-03585-1(6))* Feiwel & Friends.

—The Great Turkey Race. Metzger, Steve. 2006. (J). *(978-0-439-85930-1(1))* Scholastic, Inc.

—It's Halloween, I'm Turning Green! Gutman, Dan. 2013. (My Weird School Special Ser.). 144p. (J). (gr. 1-5). (ENG.). pap. 5.99 *(978-0-06-220679-4(6))*; lib. bdg. 16.89 *(978-0-06-220680-0(X))* HarperCollins Pubs.

—Klink & Klank: Accepting Differences. Dinardo, Jeff. 2014. (Funny Bone Readers: Being a Friend Ser.). 24p. (gr. -1-1). pap. 4.99 *(978-1-939656-04-9(4))* Red Chair Pr.

—Mayor Hubble Is in Trouble! Gutman, Dan. 2012. (My Weirder School Ser.: 6). 112p. (J). (gr. 1-5). (ENG.). pap. 4.99 *(978-0-06-204212-5(2))*; lib. bdg. 15.89 *(978-0-06-204213-2(0))* HarperCollins Pubs.

Paillot, Jim. Miss Brown Is Upside Down! Gutman, Dan. 2015. (My Weirdest School Ser.: 3). (ENG.). 112p. (J). (gr. 1-5). pap. 4.99 *(978-0-06-228427-3(4))* HarperCollins Pubs.

Paillot, Jim. Miss Child Has Gone Wild! Gutman, Dan. 2011. (My Weirder School Ser.: 1). 112p. (J). (gr. 1-5). (ENG.). pap. 4.99 *(978-0-06-196916-4(8))*; lib. bdg. 15.89 *(978-0-06-196917-1(6))* HarperCollins Pubs.

—Miss Daisy Is Crazy! Gutman, Dan. 2004. (My Weird School Ser.: 1). (ENG.). 96p. (J). (gr. 1-5). pap. 4.99 *(978-0-06-050700-8(4))* HarperCollins Pubs.

—Miss Holly Is Too Jolly! Gutman, Dan. 2006. (My Weird School Ser.: 14). (ENG.). 112p. (J). (gr. 1-5). pap. 4.99 *(978-0-06-085382-2(4))* HarperCollins Pubs.

—Miss Klute Is a Hoot! Gutman, Dan. 2014. (My Weirder School Ser.: 11). 112p. (J). (gr. 1-5). 15.89 *(978-0-06-219845-7(9))*; (ENG.). pap. 4.99 *(978-0-06-219844-0(0))* HarperCollins Pubs.

—Miss Kraft Is Daft! Gutman, Dan. 2012. (My Weirder School Ser.: 7). 112p. (J). (gr. 1-5). (ENG.). pap. 4.99 *(978-0-06-204215-6(7))*; lib. bdg. 15.89 *(978-0-06-204216-3(5))* HarperCollins Pubs.

—Miss Kraft Is Daft! Gutman, Dan. ed. 2012. (My Weirder School Ser.: 7). lib. bdg. 14.75 *(978-0-606-27125-7(2)*, Turtleback) Turtleback Bks.

—Miss Laney Is Zany! Gutman, Dan. 2010. (My Weird School Daze Ser.: 8). 112p. (J). (gr. 1-5). (ENG.). pap. 4.99 *(978-0-06-155415-5(4))*; lib. bdg. 15.89 *(978-0-06-155417-9(0))* HarperCollins Pubs.

—Miss Lazar Is Bizarre! Gutman, Dan. 2005. (My Weird School Ser.: 9). (ENG.). 96p. (J). (gr. 1-5). pap. 4.99 *(978-0-06-082225-5(2))* HarperCollins Pubs.

—Miss Mary Is Scary! Gutman, Dan. 2010. (My Weird School Daze Ser.: 10). 112p. (J). (gr. 1-5). (ENG.). pap. 4.99 *(978-0-06-170397-3(4))*; lib. bdg. 15.89 *(978-0-06-170398-0(2))* HarperCollins Pubs.

—Miss Small Is off the Wall! Gutman, Dan. 2005. (My Weird School Ser.: 5). (ENG.). 112p. (J). (gr. 1-5). pap. 4.99 *(978-0-06-074518-9(5))* HarperCollins Pubs.

—Miss Suki Is Kooky! Gutman, Dan. 2007. (My Weird School Ser.: 17). (ENG.). 112p. (J). (gr. 1-5). pap. 4.99 *(978-0-06-123473-6(7))* HarperCollins Pubs.

—Miss Suki Is Kooky! Gutman, Dan. ed. 2007. (My Weird School Ser.: 17). 13.55 *(978-1-4177-7430-2(4)*, Turtleback) Turtleback Bks.

—Mom, There's a Dinosaur in Beeson's Lake. Trueit, Trudi Strain. 2010. (Secrets of a Lab Rat Ser.). (ENG.). 160p. (J). (gr. 3-7). 14.99 *(978-1-4169-7593-9(4)*, Simon & Schuster/Paula Wiseman Bks.) Simon & Schuster/Paula Wiseman Bks.

—Mom, There's a Dinosaur in Beeson's Lake. Trueit, Trudi. 2011. (Secrets of a Lab Rat Ser.). (ENG.). 160p. (J). (gr. 3-7). pap. 5.99 *(978-1-4169-6112-3(7)*, Simon & Schuster/Paula Wiseman Bks.) Simon & Schuster/Paula Wiseman Bks.

—Mr. Burke Is Berserk! Gutman, Dan. 2012. (My Weirder School Ser.: 4). 112p. (J). (gr. 1-5). (ENG.). pap. 4.99 *(978-0-06-196922-5(2))*; lib. bdg. 15.89 *(978-0-06-196923-2(0))* HarperCollins Pubs.

—Mr. Cooper Is Super! Gutman, Dan. 2015. (My Weirdest School Ser.: 1). (ENG.). 112p. (J). (gr. 1-5). pap. 4.99 *(978-0-06-228421-1(5))* HarperCollins Pubs.

Paillot, Jim. Mr. Cooper Is Super! Gutman, Dan. 2015. (My Weirdest School Ser.: 1). lib. bdg. 14.75 *(978-0-606-36482-9(X))* Turtleback Bks.

Paillot, Jim. Mr. Docker Is off His Rocker! Gutman, Dan. 2006. (My Weird School Ser.: 10). (ENG.). 112p. (J). (gr. 1-5). pap. 4.99 *(978-0-06-082227-9(9))* HarperCollins Pubs.

—Mr. Granite Is from Another Planet!, No. 3. Gutman, Dan. 2008. (My Weird School Daze Ser.: 3). (ENG.). 112p. (J). (gr. 1-5). pap. 4.99 *(978-0-06-134611-8(X))* HarperCollins Pubs.

—Mr. Harrison Is Embarrassin'! Gutman, Dan. 2011. (My Weirder School Ser.: 2). 112p. (J). (gr. 1-5). (ENG.). pap. 4.99 *(978-0-06-196918-8(4))*; lib. bdg. 15.89 *(978-0-06-196919-5(2))* HarperCollins Pubs.

—Mr. Hynde Is Out of His Mind! Gutman, Dan. 2005. (My Weird School Ser.: 6). 112p. (J). (ENG.). (gr. 1-5). pap. 4.99 *(978-0-06-074520-2(7))*; (gr. 2-5). lib. bdg. 15.89 *(978-0-06-074521-9(5))* HarperCollins Pubs.

—Mr. Jack Is a Maniac! Gutman, Dan. 2014. (My Weirder School Ser.: 10). (ENG.). 112p. (J). (gr. 1-5). pap. 3.99 *(978-0-06-219841-9(6))* HarperCollins Pubs.

—Mr. Klutz Is Nuts!, No. 2. Gutman, Dan. 2004. (My Weird School Ser.: 2). (ENG.). 112p. (J). (gr. 1-5). pap. 4.99 *(978-0-06-050702-2(0))* HarperCollins Pubs.

—Mr. Louie Is Screwy! Gutman, Dan. 2007. (My Weird School Ser.: 20). (ENG.). 112p. (J). (gr. 1-5). pap. 4.99 *(978-0-06-123479-8(6))* HarperCollins Pubs.

—Mr. Macky Is Wacky! Gutman, Dan. 2006. (My Weird School Ser.: 15). (ENG.). 112p. (J). (gr. 1-5). pap. 4.99 *(978-0-06-114151-5(8))* HarperCollins Pubs.

—Mr. Macky Is Wacky! Gutman, Dan. ed. 2007. (My Weird School Ser.: 15). lib. bdg. 14.75 *(978-1-4177-7429-6(0)*, Turtleback) Turtleback Bks.

—Mr. Sunny Is Funny! Gutman, Dan. 2008. (My Weird School Daze Ser.: 2). 112p. (J). (gr. 1-5). (ENG.). pap. 4.99 *(978-0-06-134609-5(8))*;No. 2. lib. bdg. 15.89 *(978-0-06-134610-1(1))* HarperCollins Pubs.
—Mr. Tony Is Full of Baloney! Gutman, Dan. 2010. (My Weird School Daze Ser.: 11). 112p. (J). (gr. 1-5). (ENG.). pap. 4.99 *(978-0-06-170399-7(0))*; lib. bdg. 15.89 *(978-0-06-170400-0(8))* HarperCollins Pubs.
—Mrs. Cooney Is Loony! Gutman, Dan. 2005. (My Weird School Ser.: 7). (ENG.). 112p. (J). (gr. 1-5). pap. 4.99 *(978-0-06-074522-6(3))* HarperCollins Pubs.
—Mrs. Dole Is Out of Control! Gutman, Dan. 2008. (My Weird School Daze Ser.: 1). (ENG.). 112p. (J). (gr. 1-5). pap. 4.99 *(978-0-06-134607-1(1))* HarperCollins Pubs.
—Mrs. Jafee Is Daffy! Gutman, Dan. 2009. (My Weird School Daze Ser.: 6). 128p. (J). (gr. 1-5). (ENG.). pap. 4.99 *(978-0-06-155411-7(1))*; lib. bdg. 15.89 *(978-0-06-155413-1(8))* HarperCollins Pubs.
—Mrs. Kormel Is Not Normal! Gutman, Dan. 2006. (My Weird School Ser.: 11). (ENG.). 96p. (J). (gr. 1-5). pap. 4.99 *(978-0-06-082229-3(5))* HarperCollins Pubs.
—Mrs. Lilly Is Silly! Gutman, Dan. 2011. (My Weirder School Ser.: 3). 112p. (J). (gr. 1-5). (ENG.). pap. 4.99 *(978-0-06-196920-1(6))*; lib. bdg. 15.89 *(978-0-06-196921-8(4))* HarperCollins Pubs.
—Mrs. Lizzy Is Dizzy! Gutman, Dan. 2010. (My Weird School Daze Ser.: 9). 112p. (J). (gr. 1-5). (ENG.). pap. 4.99 *(978-0-06-155416-2(2))*; lib. bdg. 15.89 *(978-0-06-155418-6(9))* HarperCollins Pubs.
—Mrs. Patty Is Batty! Gutman, Dan. 2006. (My Weird School Ser.: 13). (ENG.). 112p. (J). (gr. 1-5). pap. 4.99 *(978-0-06-085380-8(8))* HarperCollins Pubs.
—Mrs. Roopy Is Loopy! Gutman, Dan. 2004. (My Weird School Ser.: 3). (ENG.). 96p. (J). (gr. 1-5). pap. 4.99 *(978-0-06-050704-6(7))* HarperCollins Pubs.
—Mrs. Yonkers Is Bonkers! Gutman, Dan. 2007. (My Weird School Ser.: 18). (ENG.). 112p. (J). (gr. 1-5). pap. 4.99 *(978-0-06-123475-0(3))* HarperCollins Pubs.
—Mrs. Yonkers Is Bonkers! Gutman, Dan. ed. 2007. (My Weird School Ser.: 18). 14.75 *(978-1-4177-8222-2(6)*, Turtleback) Turtleback Bks.
—Ms. Beard Is Weird! Gutman, Dan. 2012. (My Weirder School Ser.: 5). 112p. (J). (gr. 1-5). (ENG.). pap. 4.99 *(978-0-06-204209-5(2))*; lib. bdg. 15.89 *(978-0-06-204210-1(6))* HarperCollins Pubs.
—Ms. Coco Is Loco! Gutman, Dan. 2007. (My Weird School Ser.: 16). (ENG.). 112p. (J). (gr. 1-5). pap. 4.99 *(978-0-06-114153-9(4))* HarperCollins Pubs.
—Ms. Coco Is Loco! Gutman, Dan. ed. 2007. (My Weird School Ser.: 16). 14.75 *(978-1-4177-7428-9(2)*, Turtleback) Turtleback Bks.
—Ms. Cuddy Is Nutty! Gutman, Dan. 2015. (My Weirdest School Ser.: 2). (ENG.). 112p. (J). (gr. 1-5). pap. 4.99 *(978-0-06-228424-2(X))* HarperCollins Pubs.
—Ms. Hannah Is Bananas! Gutman, Dan. 2004. (My Weird School Ser.: 4). (ENG.). 96p. (J). (gr. 1-5). pap. 4.99 *(978-0-06-050706-0(3))* HarperCollins Pubs.
—Ms. Krup Cracks Me Up! Gutman, Dan. 2008. (My Weird School Ser.: 21). (ENG.). 112p. (J). (gr. 1-5). pap. 4.99 *(978-0-06-134605-7(5))* HarperCollins Pubs.
—Ms. Lagrange Is Strange! Gutman, Dan. 2005. (My Weird School Ser.: 8). (ENG.). 112p. (J). (gr. 1-5). pap. 4.99 *(978-0-06-082223-1(6))* HarperCollins Pubs.
—Ms. Leakey Is Freaky! Gutman, Dan. 2011. (My Weird School Daze Ser.: 12). 112p. (J). (gr. 1-5). lib. bdg. 15.89 *(978-0-06-170403-1(2))* HarperCollins Pubs.
—Ms. Leakey Is Freaky! No. 12. Gutman, Dan. 2011. (My Weird School Daze Ser.: 12). (ENG.). 112p. (J). (gr. 1-5). pap. 4.99 *(978-0-06-170402-4(4))* HarperCollins Pubs.
—Ms. Sue Has No Clue! Gutman, Dan. 2013. (My Weirder School Ser.: 9). (ENG.). 112p. (J). (gr. 1-5). pap. 4.99 *(978-0-06-219838-9(6))* HarperCollins Pubs.
—Ms. Todd Is Odd! Gutman, Dan. 2006. (My Weird School Ser.: 12). (ENG.). 112p. (J). (gr. 1-5). pap. 4.99 *(978-0-06-082231-6(7))* HarperCollins Pubs.
—The My Weird School Collection, Bks. 1-4. Gutman, Dan. 2010. (My Weird School Ser.). (J). (gr. 1-5). pap. 15.99 *(978-0-06-189489-3(3))* HarperCollins Pubs.
—My Weird School Daze! Gutman, Dan. 2007. (J). *(978-1-4287-4814-9(8))* HarperCollins Pubs.
—My Weird School Daze 12-Book Box Set, 12 vols. Gutman, Dan. 2013. (My Weird School Daze Ser.). (ENG.). 500p. (J). (gr. 1-5). pap. 45.00 *(978-0-06-228891-2(1))* HarperCollins Pubs.
—My Weird School Special - Oh, Valentine, We've Lost Our Minds! Gutman, Dan. 2014. (My Weird School Special Ser.). (ENG.). 144p. (J). (gr. 1-5). pap. 5.99 *(978-0-06-228403-7(7))* HarperCollins Pubs.
—My Weird School Special: Back to School, Weird Kids Rule! Gutman, Dan. 2014. (My Weird School Special Ser.). 144p. (J). (gr. 1-5). lib. bdg. 16.89 *(978-0-06-220686-2(9))* HarperCollins Pubs.
—My Weird School Special: Bunny Double, We're in Trouble! Gutman, Dan. 2014. (My Weird School Special Ser.). 144p. (J). (gr. 1-5). lib. bdg. 16.89 *(978-0-06-228401-3(0))* HarperCollins Pubs.
—My Weird School Special: Deck the Halls, We're off the Walls! Gutman, Dan. 2013. (My Weird School Special Ser.). 144p. (J). (gr. 1-5). lib. bdg. 16.89 *(978-0-06-220683-1(4))* HarperCollins Pubs.
—My Weird Writing Tips. Gutman, Dan. 2013. (My Weird School Ser.). (ENG.). 160p. (J). (gr. 3-7). 16.99 *(978-0-06-209107-9(7))*; pap. 5.99 *(978-0-06-209106-2(9))* HarperCollins Pubs.
—My Weirder School #10: Mr. Jack Is a Maniac! Gutman, Dan. 2014. (My Weirder School Ser.: 10). 112p. (J). (gr. 1-5). lib. bdg. 15.89 *(978-0-06-219842-6(4))* HarperCollins Pubs.
—My Weirder School #12 - Mrs. Lane Is a Pain! Gutman, Dan. 2014. (My Weirder School Ser.: 12). (ENG.). 112p. (J). (gr. 1-5). pap. 4.99 *(978-0-06-219847-1(5))* HarperCollins Pubs.
—My Weirder School #12: Mrs. Lane Is a Pain! 2014. (My Weirder School Ser.: 12). 112p. (J). (gr. 1-5). lib. bdg. 15.89 *(978-0-06-219848-8(3))* HarperCollins Pubs.
—My Weirder School #9: Ms. Sue Has No Clue! Gutman, Dan. 2013. (My Weirder School Ser.: 9). 112p. (J). (gr. 1-5). lib. bdg. 15.89 *(978-0-06-219839-6(4))* HarperCollins Pubs.
—My Weirdest School #2: Ms. Cuddy Is Nutty! Gutman, Dan. 2015. (My Weirdest School Ser.: 2). 112p. (J). (gr. 1-5). lib. bdg. 15.89 *(978-0-06-228425-9(8))* HarperCollins Pubs.
—No Girls Allowed (Dogs Okay) Trueit, Trudi. (Secrets of a Lab Rat Ser.). (ENG.). 128p. (J). (gr. 3-7). 2010. pap. 5.99 *(978-1-4169-6111-6(9))*; 2009. 14.99 *(978-1-4169-7592-2(6))* Simon & Schuster/Paula Wiseman Bks. (Simon & Schuster/Paula Wiseman Bks.).
—Officer Spence Makes No Sense! Gutman, Dan. 2009. (My Weird School Daze Ser.: 5). 112p. (J). (gr. 1-5). (ENG.). pap. 4.99 *(978-0-06-155409-4(X))*; lib. bdg. 15.89 *(978-0-06-155410-0(3))* HarperCollins Pubs.
—Scab for Treasurer? Trueit, Trudi. 2011. (Secrets of a Lab Rat Ser.). (ENG.). 160p. (J). (gr. 3-7). 15.99 *(978-1-4169-7594-6(2))*; pap. 5.99 *(978-1-4169-6113-0(5))* Simon & Schuster/Paula Wiseman Bks. (Simon & Schuster/Paula Wiseman Bks.).
Paillot, Jim. They're There on Their Vacation. Cleary, Brian P. 2015. (ENG.). 32p. (J). (gr. 2-5). 26.65 ***(978-0-7613-9033-6(2)***, Millbrook Pr.) Lerner Publishing Group.
Paillot, Jim. This Time It's Personal. Overdeck, Laura. 2014. (Bedtime Math Ser.). (ENG.). 96p. (J). (gr. -1-2). 15.99 *(978-1-250-04096-1(5))* Feiwel & Friends.
—The Truth Comes Out. Overdeck, Laura. 2015. (Bedtime Math Ser.). (ENG.). 96p. (J). (gr. -1-2). 15.99 *(978-1-250-04775-5(7))* Feiwel & Friends.
—The Turkey Train. Metzger, Steve. 2013. (ENG.). 32p. (J). (gr. -1-k). 6.99 *(978-0-545-49229-4(7)*, Cartwheel Bks.) Scholastic, Inc.
Paine, Colin. Big George & the Winter King. Pringle, Eric. 2004. (ENG.). 208p. (J). pap. 12.99 *(978-0-7475-6341-9(1))* Bloomsbury Publishing Plc GBR. Dist: Independent Pubs. Group.
Painted Daisies Inc. Staff. Shermit's Adventure to Sprinkle Island. Painted Daisies Inc. Staff. Borgatti, Katherine. 2010. (ENG.). 32p. (J). 15.95 *(978-0-615-34491-1(7))* Painted Daisies Inc.
Paj, Eduardo. What If an Alligator Ate an Avalanche. Macalino, Damien. 2013. 32p. pap. 10.00 *(978-0-9836303-8-8(0))* Crystal Mosaic Bks.
Pajot, Lauren. Machine Gun Inventors: A Military History Coloring Book. Segel, Robert G. 2012. 16p. 4.95 *(978-0-9823918-2-2(X))* Chipotle Publishing, LLC.
Pak, Amy. History Through the Ages - America's History: Historical Timeline Figures (Explorers to 21st Century) Pak, Amy. 2003. (J). pap. 29.95 *(978-0-9720265-2-9(5))* Home Schl. in the Woods.
—History Through the Ages - Napoleon to Now: Historical Timeline Figures (1750 AD - Present) Pak, Amy. 2003. (J). pap. 19.95 *(978-0-9720265-3-6(3))* Home Schl. in the Woods.
Pak, Kenard. Flowers Are Calling. Gray, Rita. 2015. (ENG.). 32p. (J). (gr. -1-3). 16.99 *(978-0-544-34012-1(4)*, HMH Books For Young Readers) Houghton Mifflin Harcourt Publishing Co.
—Have You Heard the Nesting Bird? Gray, Rita. 2014. (ENG.). 32p. (J). (gr. -1-3). 16.99 *(978-0-544-10580-5(X)*, HMH Books For Young Readers) Houghton Mifflin Harcourt Publishing Co.
Pak, Mi-Son. The Seven Brothers & the Big Dipper/Heungbu, Nolbu & the Magic Gourds. 2008. (Korean Folk Tales for Children Ser.: Vol. 4). (ENG & KOR.). 43p. (J). (gr. 2-5). lib. bdg. 14.50 *(978-0-930878-74-0(4))* Hollym International Corp.
Pak, Mi-Son & Kim, Yon-Kyong. The Greedy Princess/the Rabbit & the Tiger. 2008. (Korean Folk Tales for Children Ser.: Vol. 7). (ENG & KOR.). 45p. (J). (gr. 2-5). lib. bdg. 14.50 *(978-0-930878-90-0(6))* Hollym International Corp.
Pal, Erika. Armel's Revenge. Cornwell, Nicki. 2012. (ENG.). 96p. (J). (gr. 3-6). pap. 8.99 *(978-1-84780-224-8(9)*, Frances Lincoln) Quarto Publishing Group UK GBR. Dist: Hachette Bk. Group.
—I See the Moon. Mitton, Jacqueline & Quarto Generic Staff. 2011. (ENG.). 32p. (J). (gr. -1-2). 17.95 *(978-1-84507-633-7(8)*, Frances Lincoln) Quarto Publishing Group UK GBR. Dist: Hachette Bk. Group.
—Off to Market. Dale, Elizabeth. 2013. (ENG.). 32p. (J). (gr. -1-3). 17.99 *(978-1-84780-338-2(5)*, Frances Lincoln) Quarto Publishing Group UK GBR. Dist: Hachette Bk. Group.
Palacios G., Sara Helena. De Aqui para Alla. Segovia, Silvia. rev. ed. 2007. (Castillo de la Lectura Blanca Ser.). (SPA & ENG.). 56p. (J). (gr. k-2). pap. 6.95 *(978-970-20-0197-3(8))* Castillo, Ediciones, S. A. de C. V. MEX. Dist: Macmillan.
Palacios, John. Readers' Theater: Scripts for Young Readers. Stewart, Kelly, ed. 2009. 16p. (J). pap. 16.95 *(978-1-60184-146-9(9))*; pap. 16.95 *(978-1-60184-148-3(5))*; pap. 16.95 *(978-1-60184-150-6(7))*; pap. 16.95 *(978-1-60184-152-0(3))*; pap. 16.95 *(978-1-60184-154-4(X))*; pap. 16.95 *(978-1-60184-160-5(4))*; pap. 16.95 *(978-1-60184-166-7(3))* Primary Concepts/Concepts to Go.
—Readers' Theater: Scripts for Young Readers: How the Tiger Got Its Stripes. 2009. 16p. (J). pap. 16.95 *(978-1-60184-162-9(0))* Primary Concepts/Concepts to Go.
—Readers' Theater: Scripts for Young Readers: the Monkey & the Crocodile. Stewart, Kelly, ed. 2009. 16p. (J). pap. 16.95 *(978-1-60184-164-3(7))* Primary Concepts/Concepts to Go.
—Readers' Theater: Scripts for Young Readers: the Peach Boy. Stewart, Kelly, ed. 2009. 16p. (J). pap. 16.95 *(978-1-60184-156-8(6))* Primary Concepts/Concepts to Go.
—Readers' Theater: Scripts for Young Readers: the Spear Throwing Contest. Stewart, Kelly, ed. 2009. 16p. (J). pap. 16.95 *(978-1-60184-158-2(2))* Primary Concepts/Concepts to Go.
Palacios, Sara. Henry Holton Takes the Ice. Bradley, Sandra. 2015. (ENG.). 40p. (J). (gr. k-3). 16.99 *(978-0-8037-3856-0(0)*, Dial) Penguin Publishing Group.
Palacios, Sara. Lola Knows a Lot. McCarthy, Jenna. 2016. 32p. (J). (gr. -1-3). 17.99 ***(978-0-06-225017-9(5))*** HarperCollins Pubs.
Palacios, Sara. Marisol McDonald & the Clash Bash/Marisol Mcdonald y la Fiesta Sin Igual. Brown, Monica. 2013. (ENG & SPA.). 40p. (J). 18.95 *(978-0-89239-273-5(8))* Lee & Low Bks., Inc.
—Marisol Mcdonald Doesn't Match / Marisol Mcdonald no Combina. Brown, Monica. 2013. (SPA & ENG.). 32p. (J). (gr. -1-3). 17.95 *(978-0-89239-235-3(5))* Lee & Low Bks., Inc.
Palacios, Sara Helena. Conoce a Gabriela Mistral: Get to Know Gabriela Mistral. Leon, Georgina Lazaro. 2014. (Personajes Del Mundo Hispnico Ser.). (ENG & SPA.). 32p. (J). (gr. -1-3). 15.95 *(978-1-61435-351-5(4)*, Alfaguara) Santillana USA Publishing Co., Inc.
Palacious, John. Readers' Theater Paul Bunyan: Scripts for Young Readers. 2009. 16p. (J). pap. *(978-1-60184-144-5(2))* Primary Concepts/Concepts to Go.
Palagonia, Peter. Matzah & Miracles: A Passover Musical & Chapter Book. Akselrad, January & Young, Jennifer. 2012. (ENG.). 88p. (J). 15.00 *(978-0-9822134-8-3(4))* See The Wish.
Palatini, Margie. Hogg, Hogg, & Hog. Palatini, Margie. 2011. (ENG.). 32p. (J). (gr. -1-3). 15.99 *(978-1-4424-0322-2(5)*, Simon & Schuster Bks. For Young Readers) Simon & Schuster Bks. For Young Readers.
—The Zoey Zone. Palatini, Margie. (ENG.). 192p. (J). (gr. 3-6). 2010. pap. 6.99 *(978-0-06-113900-0(9))*; 2008. 10.99 *(978-0-06-113898-0(3))* HarperCollins Pubs. (Tegen, Katherine Bks).
Palen, Debbie. How Not to Babysit Your Brother. Hapka, Cathy & Titlebaum, Ellen. 2005. (Step into Reading Ser.). (ENG.). 48p. (J). (gr. 2-4). pap. 3.99 *(978-0-375-82856-0(7)*, Random Hse. Bks. for Young Readers) Random Hse. Children's Bks.
—How Not to Start Third Grade. Hapka, Cathy & Titlebaum, Ellen. 2007. (Step into Reading Ser.). (ENG.). 48p. (J). (gr. 2-4). pap. 3.99 *(978-0-375-83904-7(6)*, Random Hse. Bks. for Young Readers) Random Hse. Children's Bks.
—In the Garden. Greenburg, J. C. 2003. (Stepping Stone Book(TM) Ser.: Bk. 4). (ENG.). 96p. (J). (gr. 1-4). 3.99 *(978-0-375-81280-4(6)*, Random Hse. Bks. for Young Readers) Random Hse. Children's Bks.
—The Period Book: Everything You Don't Want to Ask (But Need to Know) Gravelle, Karen & Gravelle, Jennifer. 2nd rev. ed. 2006. (ENG.). 160p. (J). (gr. 3-7). per. 10.99 *(978-0-8027-7736-2(8))* Walker & Co.
—The Sunrise Band: Cooperating. Dinardo, Jeff. 2014. (Funny Bone Readers: Being a Friend Ser.). 24p. (gr. -1-1). pap. 4.99 *(978-1-939656-06-3(0))* Red Chair Pr.
—The Ultimate Girls' Guide to Science: From Backyard Experiments to Winning the Nobel Prize. Hoyt, Beth Caldwell & Ritter, Erica. 2004. 128p. (J). (gr. 4-12). pap. *(978-1-58270-092-2(3))* Beyond Words Publishing, Inc.
Paley, Joan. The Emperor Lays an Egg. Guiberson, Brenda Z. Schonhorst, Elizabeth, ed. rev. ed. 2004. (ENG.). 32p. (J). (gr. -1-3). pap. 8.99 *(978-0-8050-7636-3(0))* Square Fish.
—The Secret Life of the Woolly Bear Caterpillar. Pringle, Laurence. 2014. (ENG.). 32p. (J). (gr. k-2). 16.95 *(978-1-62091-000-9(4))* Boyds Mills Pr.
—Star of the Sea: A Day in the Life of a Starfish. Halfmann, Janet. 2011. (ENG.). 32p. (J). (gr. k-2). 17.99 *(978-0-8050-9073-4(8)*, Holt, Henry & Co. Bks. For Young Readers) Holt, Henry & Co.
Palin, Nicki. Flip the Flaps: Baby Animals. Wilson, Hannah. 2012. (Flip the Flaps Ser.). (ENG.). 32p. (J). (gr. -1-1). 6.99 *(978-0-7534-6849-4(2)*, Kingfisher) Roaring Brook Pr.
—Flip the Flaps: Farm Animals. Wallace, Karen. 2012. (Flip the Flaps Ser.). (ENG.). 32p. (J). (gr. -1-1). pap. 6.99 *(978-0-7534-6738-1(0)*, Kingfisher) Roaring Brook Pr.
—Flip the Flaps: Jungle Animals. Wilson, Hannah. 2012. (Flip the Flaps Ser.). (ENG.). 32p. (J). (gr. -1-1). pap. 6.99 *(978-0-7534-6859-3(X)*, Kingfisher) Roaring Brook Pr.
—Flip the Flaps: Planet Earth. Goldsmith, Mike. 2012. (Flip the Flaps Ser.). (ENG.). 32p. (J). (gr. -1-1). pap. 6.99 *(978-0-7534-6860-9(3)*, Kingfisher) Roaring Brook Pr.
Pallace, Chris. Skallywaggs Card Game: The Mix-n-match Pirate Game. 2005. (YA). *(978-0-9768848-0-4(1))* Bent Castle Workshops.
Pallace, Chris, jt. illus. see Serwacki, Kevin.
Palmer, Barbara A. A Clue Book for Boo-Boo. 2012. 32p. (J). *(978-0-9728228-3-1(6))* Palmer, Barbara A.
—The Journey of Cattail. 2012. 26p. (J). *(978-0-9728228-4-8(4))* Palmer, Barbara A.
Palmer, Barbara A. Finding Fido the Feline: Flip Book with American Sign Language. Palmer, Barbara A. 2004. (J). bds. 11.99 *(978-0-9728228-1-7(X))* Palmer, Barbara A.
—The Journey of Cattail. Palmer, Barbara A. 2004. 26p. (J). 16.95 *(978-0-9728228-0-0(1))* Palmer, Barbara A.
Palmer, Evan. Jurassic Farts: A Spotter's Guide. Grossblatt, Ben & Rippley, P. U. 2015. (ENG.). 22p. (J). (gr. -1-5). 15.99 *(978-1-4521-4421-4(4))* Chronicle Bks. LLC.
Palmer, Gary. H Is for Hook: A Fishing Alphabet. Young, Judy. 2008. (Sports Ser.). (ENG.). 40p. (J). (gr. 3-7). 17.95 *(978-1-58536-347-6(2))* Sleeping Bear Pr.
—Handkerchief Quilt. Crane, Carol. 2010. (ENG.). 32p. (J). (gr. k-3). 15.95 *(978-1-58536-344-5(8))* Sleeping Bear Pr.
—Net Numbers: A South Carolina Numbers Book. Crane, Carol. 2006. (Count Your Way Across the U. S. A. Ser.). (ENG.). 40p. (J). (gr. -1-3). 17.95 *(978-1-58536-202-8(6))* Sleeping Bear Pr.
—T Is for Tar Heel: A North Carolina Alphabet. Crane, Carol. 2003. (Discover America State by State Ser.). (ENG.). 40p. (J). 17.95 *(978-1-58536-082-6(1))* Sleeping Bear Pr.
—Wright Numbers: A North Carolina Number Book. Crane, Carol. 2005. (Count Your Way Across the USA Ser.). (ENG.). 40p. (J). (gr. k-5). 16.95 *(978-1-58536-196-0(8))* Sleeping Bear Pr.
Palmer, James. The Little Red Hen: Classic Tales Series. Smith, Carrie. 2011. (Classic Tales Ser.). (J). *(978-1-936258-66-6(8))* Benchmark Education Co.
—Pinocchio & Peter Pan: Selections from Two Classic Children's Novels. Collodi, Carlo et al. 2014. (Text Connections Ser.). (J). (gr. 3). *(978-1-4509-9648-8(5))* Benchmark Education Co.
Palmer, Jan. Raggedy Ann & Rags. Gruelle, Johnny. 2010. (Raggedy Ann Ser.). (ENG.). 40p. (J). (gr. -1-2). 19.99 *(978-1-4424-2198-1(3)*, Simon & Schuster Bks. For Young Readers) Simon & Schuster Bks. For Young Readers.
Palmer, Judd. Driftwood Ellesmere. Davidge, James. 2010. (Driftwood Saga Ser.). (ENG.). 206p. (J). (gr. 8-12). 7.95 *(978-1-896209-81-4(5))* Bayeux Arts, Inc. CAN. Dist: Chicago Distribution Ctr.
Palmer, Kate S. Baseball Fun. Geddes, Diana E. Kaeden Corp. Staff, ed. 2003. (ENG.). 12p. (gr. k-2). pap. 5.95 *(978-1-879835-72-6(X))* Kaeden Corp.
—Day at the Races: World of Discovery II. Bauer, Roger. l.t. ed. 2006. (ENG.). 8p. (gr. k-2). pap. 4.95 *(978-1-879835-48-1(7))* Kaeden Corp.
—Hockey Practice. Geddes, Diana E. 2005. (ENG.). 12p. (gr. k-2). pap. 5.95 *(978-1-57874-001-7(0)*, Kaeden Bks.) Kaeden Corp.
—Let's Play Basketball. Geddes, Diana E. Kaeden Corp. Staff, ed. 2005. (ENG.). 16p. (gr. k-1). pap. 5.95 *(978-1-879835-55-9(X))* Kaeden Corp.
—My Brother Wants to Be Like Me. Mader, Jan. l.t. ed. 2005. (ENG.). 16p. (gr. k-2). pap. 5.95 *(978-1-879835-27-6(4)*, Kaeden Bks.) Kaeden Corp.
—Nick Goes Fishing: World of Discovery II. Yukish, Joseph. l.t. ed. 2003. (ENG.). 12p. (gr. k-2). pap. 5.95 *(978-1-879835-47-4(9))* Kaeden Corp.
Palmer, Kate S., jt. illus. see Palmer, Kate Salley.
Palmer, Kate Salley. Almost Invisible Blk Patriots. Palmer, Kate Salley. 2008. (ENG.). 56p. (J). pap. 11.95 *(978-0-9667114-6-2(7))* Warbranch Pr., Inc.
Palmer, Kate Salley & Palmer, Kate S. Bird Feeder, 6-pack: 6 Copies, 6 vols. Coulton, Mia. 2006. (ENG.). 16p. (gr. k-2). pap. 5.95 *(978-1-879835-71-9(1))* Kaeden Corp.
Palmer, Kimmy. Olivia's Tree, 1 vol. Flatley, Paula Chorman. 2010. 16p. pap. 24.95 *(978-1-4489-5870-2(9))* America Star Bks.
Palmer, Ruth. Alice Ray & the Salem Witch Trials. Knudsen, Shannon. 2011. (History Speaks: Picture Books Plus Reader's Theater Ser.). 48p. pap. 56.72 *(978-0-7613-7629-3(1))*; (ENG.). (gr. 2-4). 27.93 *(978-0-7613-5879-4(X)*, Millbrook Pr.); (ENG.). (gr. 2-4). pap. 9.95 *(978-0-7613-7114-4(1))* Lerner Publishing Group.
—Good Night Central Park. Gamble, Adam & Jasper, Mark. 2013. (Good Night Our World Ser.). (ENG.). 20p. (J). (— 1). bds. 9.95 *(978-1-60219-082-5(8))* Our World of Books.
—Good Night New Mexico. Gamble, Adam & Jasper, Mark. 2014. (Good Night Our World Ser.). (ENG.). 20p. (J). (— 1). bds. 9.95 *(978-1-60219-088-7(7))* Our World of Books.
—Good Night Pittsburgh. Gamble, Adam & Jasper, Mark. 2012. (Good Night Our World Ser.). (ENG.). 20p. (J). (gr. k — 1). bds. 9.95 *(978-1-60219-073-3(9))* Our World of Books.
Palmer, Ruth. Good Night Twin Cities. Gamble, Adam & Jasper, Mark. 2015. (ENG.). 20p. (J). (— 1). bds. 9.95 ***(978-1-60219-232-4(4))*** Our World of Books.
Palmer, Ruth. I Hate Everyone. Kelly, Mij. 2003. 32p. (YA). *(978-1-85602-362-7(1)*, Pavilion Children's Books) Pavilion Bks.
—Peter Rabbit & the Pumpkin Patch. Potter, Beatrix. 2013. (Peter Rabbit Ser.). (ENG.). 32p. (J). pap. 3.99 *(978-0-7232-7124-6(0)*, Warne) Penguin Publishing Group.
Palmer, Scott. The Lord's Supper... Let's Get Ready! Donahue, Laurie & Phillips, Paul. 2005. 96p. per. 10.99 *(978-0-9718306-6-0(5))* LifeSong Pubs.
Palmiotti, Jimmy. John Constantine, Hellblazer: Red Sepulchre. Carey, Mike. rev. ed. 2005. (Hellblazer Ser.). (ENG.). 208p. pap. 12.99 *(978-1-4012-0485-3(6)*, Vertigo) DC Comics.
—Street Justice. Andreyko, Marc. 2005. (Manhunter Ser.). (ENG.). 128p. (YA). pap. 12.99 *(978-1-4012-0728-1(6))* DC Comics.
Palmisciano, Diane. The Big Something. Giff, Patricia Reilly. 2012. (Fiercely & Friends Ser.). (ENG.). 40p. (J). (gr. -1-3). 6.99 *(978-0-545-24459-6(5)*, Orchard Bks.); 16.99 *(978-0-545-43369-3(X))* Scholastic, Inc.
—Fair Is Fair! Dussling, Jennifer. 2003. (Math Matters Ser.). 32p. (J). (gr. 1-3). pap. 5.95 *(978-1-57565-131-6(9))* Kane Pr., Inc.
—Fiercely & Friends: the Big Something. Giff, Patricia Reilly. 2013. (Fiercely & Friends Ser.). (ENG.). 40p. (J). (gr. k-2). pap. 3.99 *(978-0-545-24463-3(3)*, Scholastic Paperbacks) Scholastic, Inc.
—Fiercely & Friends: the Sneaky Snow Fox. Giff, Patricia Reilly. (Fiercely & Friends Ser.). (ENG.). 40p. (J). (gr. k-2). 2013. pap. 3.99 *(978-0-545-24461-9(7)*, Scholastic Paperbacks); 2012. 16.99 *(978-0-545-43378-5(9)*, Orchard Bks.) Scholastic, Inc.
—Follow That Clue! Walker, Nan. 2008. (Social Studies Connects Ser.). 32p. (J). (gr. -1-3). pap. 5.95 *(978-1-57565-274-0(9))* Kane Pr., Inc.
—Follow That Clue! Walker, Nan. 2009. (Social Studies Connects (r) Ser.). (ENG.). (J). (gr. k-2). pap. 33.92 *(978-0-7613-4805-4(0))* Lerner Publishing Group.
—The Garden Monster. Giff, Patricia Reilly. (Fiercely & Friends Ser.). (J). (gr. k-2). 2014. (ENG.). 40p. 16.99 *(978-0-545-43379-2(7))*; 2013. *(978-0-545-24460-2(9))* Scholastic, Inc. (Orchard Bks.).
—Gifts from the Heart. Osteen, Victoria. 2010. (ENG.). 32p. (J). (gr. -1-2). 17.99 *(978-1-4169-5551-1(8)*, Little Simon Inspirations) Little Simon Inspirations.
—Lo Justo Es Justo! Dussling, Jennifer A. 2008. (Math Matters en Espanol Ser.). (SPA.). 32p. (J). (gr. -1-3). pap. 5.95 *(978-1-57565-269-6(2))* Kane Pr., Inc.

P

—Mac & Cheese, Pleeeeze! May, Eleanor. 2008. (Math Matters Ser.). 32p. (J). (gr. -1-3). pap. 5.95 (978-1-57565-260-3(9)) Kane Pr., Inc.

—Monster Bug. Hayward, Linda. 2004. 32p. (J). lib. bdg. 20.00 (978-1-4242-1097-8(6)) Fitzgerald Bks.

—Monster Bug. Hayward, Linda. 2004. (Science Solves It Ser.). 32p. (gr. -1-3). 15.00 (978-0-7569-4313-4(2)) Perfection Learning Corp.

—The Sneaky Snow Fox. Giff, Patricia Reilly. 2012. (Fiercely & Friends Ser.). (ENG.). 40p. (J). (gr. k-2). 6.99 (978-0-545-24458-9(7), Orchard Bks.) Scholastic, Inc.

—Unexpected Treasures. Osteen, Victoria. 2009. (ENG.). 32p. (J). (gr. -1-3). 16.99 (978-1-4169-5550-4(X), Little Simon Inspirations) Little Simon Inspirations.

Palmisciano, Diane. Monster Bug. Palmisciano, Diane, tr. Lunney, Linda Hayward. 2004. (Science Solves It! Ser.). 32p. (J). pap. 5.95 (978-1-57565-135-4(1)) Kane Pr., Inc.

Palmisciano, Diane & Brooks, Erik. A Case for Jenny Archer. Conford, Ellen. 2nd ed. 2006. (ENG.). 64p. (J). (gr. 1-4). per. 10.99 (978-0-316-01486-1(9)) Little, Brown Bks. for Young Readers.

—Jenny Archer, Author. Conford, Ellen. 2006. (ENG.). 64p. (J). (gr. 1-4). per. 12.99 (978-0-316-01487-8(7)) Little, Brown Bks. for Young Readers.

—A Job for Jenny Archer. Conford, Ellen. 2006. (ENG.). 80p. (J). (gr. 1-4). per. 14.99 (978-0-316-01484-7(2)) Little, Brown Bks. for Young Readers.

—What's Cooking, Jenny Archer? Conford, Ellen. 2006. (ENG.). 80p. (J). (gr. 1-4). per. 10.99 (978-0-316-01488-5(5)) Little, Brown Bks. for Young Readers.

Palmore, lyende, jt. illus. see Breckenridge, Trula.

Palmquist, Eric. Rasmus & the Vagabond. Lindgren, Astrid. Bothmer, Gerry, tr. from SWE. 2014. (ENG.). 180p. pap. 9.95 (978-0-87486-597-4(2)) Plough Publishing Hse.

Palomares, Franz. Angelica's Hope: A Story for Young People & Their Parents about the Need to Talk about Things That No One Talks About. Nelson, Annabelle. 2003. (SPA.). (978-0-9656732-9-7(4)) WHEEL Council, Inc., The.

—Ricardo's Pain: A Story for Young People & Their Parents about Staying Strong, Finding Courage & Overcoming Adversity. Nelson, Annabelle. 2003. (SPA.). (978-0-9656732-8-0(6)) WHEEL Council, Inc., The.

Palone, Terry & Permane, Terry, photos by. Thomas & the Treasure. Hooke, R. Schuyler. 2008. (Thomas & Friends Ser.). (ENG.). 24p. (J). (gr. -1-2). pap. 3.99 (978-0-375-84287-0(X), Random Hse. Bks. for Young Readers) Random Hse. Children's Bks.

Palumbo, Debi. Santa, NASA y el Hombre en la Luna. Kaplan, Richard et al.Tr. of Santa, NASA & the Man in the Moon. (SPA.). (Orig.). (J). (gr. -1-5). pap. 14.95 (978-0-9649608-1-7(8)) Batyah Productions, Inc.

Paluseka, Julia. Sparkles Visits the Farm. Wellings, Chris. 2011. 36p. pap. 24.95 (978-1-4560-4102-1(9)) America Star Bks.

Pamintuan, Macky. The African Safari Discovery. Brown, Jeff. 2010. (Flat Stanley's Worldwide Adventures Ser.: 6). (ENG.). 112p. (J). (gr. 2-5). pap. 4.99 (978-0-06-143000-8(5));No. 6. 15.99 (978-0-06-143001-5(3)) HarperCollins Pubs.

—Alfred Zector, Book Collector. DiPucchio, Kelly. 2010. (ENG.). 32p. (J). (gr. -1-1). 16.99 (978-0-06-000581-8(5)) HarperCollins Pubs.

—Alien in My Pocket: Radio Active. Ball, Nate. 2014. (Alien in My Pocket Ser.: 3). (ENG.). 144p. (J). (gr. 1-5). 15.99 (978-0-06-231493-2(9)); pap. 4.99 (978-0-06-221627-4(9)) HarperCollins Pubs.

—Alien in My Pocket - Blast Off! Ball, Nate. 2014. (Alien in My Pocket Ser.: 1). (ENG.). 160p. (J). (gr. 1-5). pap. 4.99 (978-0-06-221623-6(6)) HarperCollins Pubs.

—Alien in My Pocket - The Science Unfair. Ball, Nate. 2014. (Alien in My Pocket Ser.: 2). (ENG.). 144p. (J). (gr. 1-5). pap. 4.99 (978-0-06-221625-0(2)) HarperCollins Pubs.

—Alien in My Pocket #5: Ohm vs. Amp. Ball, Nate. 2015. (Alien in My Pocket Ser.: 5). (ENG.). 144p. (J). (gr. 1-5). 15.99 (978-0-06-231489-5(0)) HarperCollins Pubs.

—The Amazing Mexican Secret. Brown, Jeff. 2010. (Flat Stanley's Worldwide Adventures Ser.: 5). (ENG.). 112p. (J). (gr. 2-5). pap. 4.99 (978-0-06-142998-9(8));No. 5. 15.99 (978-0-06-142999-6(6)) HarperCollins Pubs.

—April Fool's Day. Keene, Carolyn. 2009. (Nancy Drew & the Clue Crew Ser.: 19). (ENG.). 96p. (J). (gr. 1-4). pap. 4.99 (978-1-4169-7518-2(7), Simon & Schuster/Paula Wiseman Bks.) Simon & Schuster/Paula Wiseman Bks.

—The Australian Boomerang Bonanza. Brown, Jeff. 2011. (Flat Stanley's Worldwide Adventures Ser.: 8). (ENG.). 112p. (J). (gr. 2-5). 15.99 (978-0-06-157435-1(X)) HarperCollins Pubs.

—The Australian Boomerang Bonanza No. 8. Brown, Jeff. 2011. (Flat Stanley's Worldwide Adventures Ser.: 8). (ENG.). 112p. (J). (gr. 2-5). pap. 4.99 (978-0-06-143018-3(8)) HarperCollins Pubs.

—Babysitting Bandit. Keene, Carolyn. 2009. (Nancy Drew & the Clue Crew Ser.: 23). (ENG.). 96p. (J). (gr. 1-4). pap. 4.99 (978-1-4169-7813-8(5), Simon & Schuster/Paula Wiseman Bks.) Simon & Schuster/Paula Wiseman Bks.

—Baseball from A to Z. Spradlin, Michael P. 2010. (ENG.). 32p. (J). (gr. -1-3). 16.99 (978-0-06-124081-2(8)) HarperCollins Pubs.

—Bedtime at the Swamp. Crow, Kristyn. 2008. (ENG.). 32p. (J). (gr. -1-1). 16.99 (978-0-06-083951-2(1)) HarperCollins Pubs.

Pamintuan, Macky. Believe - Coloring Book: Think, Act, & Be Like Jesus, 1 vol. Zondervan. 2015. (ENG.). 64p. (J). pap. 4.99 (978-0-310-75222-6(1)) Zonderkidz.

Pamintuan, Macky. Buggy Breakout. Keene, Carolyn. 2010. (Nancy Drew & the Clue Crew Ser.: 25). (ENG.). 96p. (J). (gr. 1-4). pap. 4.99 (978-1-4169-7814-5(3), Simon & Schuster/Paula Wiseman Bks.) Simon & Schuster/Paula Wiseman Bks.

—Camp Creepy. Keene, Carolyn. 2010. (Nancy Drew & the Clue Crew Ser.: 26). (ENG.). 96p. (J). (gr. 1-4). pap. 4.99 (978-1-4169-9438-1(6), Simon & Schuster/Paula Wiseman Bks.) Simon & Schuster/Paula Wiseman Bks.

—Cape Mermaid Mystery. Keene, Carolyn. 2012. (Nancy Drew & the Clue Crew Ser.: 32). (ENG.). 96p. (J). (gr. 1-4). pap. 4.99 (978-1-4424-4625-0(0), Simon & Schuster/Paula Wiseman Bks.) Simon & Schuster/Paula Wiseman Bks.

—The Case of the Sneaky Snowman. Keene, Carolyn. 2009. (Nancy Drew & the Clue Crew Set II Ser.). 96p. (gr. 2-4). 24.21 (978-1-59961-640-7(8)) Spotlight.

—Case of the Sneaky Snowman. Keene, Carolyn. 5th ed. 2006. (Nancy Drew & the Clue Crew Ser.: 5). (ENG.). 96p. (J). (gr. 1-4). pap. 4.99 (978-1-4169-1254-5(1), Simon & Schuster/Paula Wiseman Bks.) Simon & Schuster/Paula Wiseman Bks.

—Cat Burglar Caper. Keene, Carolyn. 2010. (Nancy Drew & the Clue Crew Ser.: 27). (ENG.). 96p. (J). (gr. 1-4). pap. 4.99 (978-1-4169-9436-7(X), Simon & Schuster/Paula Wiseman Bks.) Simon & Schuster/Paula Wiseman Bks.

—Chick-Napped! Keene, Carolyn. 13th ed. 2008. (Nancy Drew & the Clue Crew Ser.: 13). (ENG.). 96p. (J). (gr. 1-4). pap. 5.99 (978-1-4169-5522-1(4), Simon & Schuster/Paula Wiseman Bks.) Simon & Schuster/Paula Wiseman Bks.

—Chick-Napped! Keene, Carolyn. 2009. (Nancy Drew & the Clue Crew Set II Ser.). 96p. (gr. 2-4). 24.21 (978-1-59961-641-4(6)) Spotlight.

—The Cinderella Ballet Mystery. Keene, Carolyn. 4th ed. 2006. (Nancy Drew & the Clue Crew Ser.: 4). (ENG.). 96p. (J). (gr. 1-4). pap. 4.99 (978-1-4169-1256-9(8), Simon & Schuster/Paula Wiseman Bks.) Simon & Schuster/Paula Wiseman Bks.

—The Cinderella Ballet Mystery. Keene, Carolyn. 2007. (Nancy Drew & the Clue Crew Ser.). 83p. (gr. 1-4). 24.21 (978-1-59961-345-1(X)) Spotlight.

—The Circus Scare. Keene, Carolyn. 2009. (Nancy Drew & the Clue Crew Set II Ser.). 96p. (gr. 2-4). 24.21 (978-1-59961-642-1(4)) Spotlight.

—Cooking Camp Disaster. Keene, Carolyn. 2013. (Nancy Drew & the Clue Crew Ser.: 35). (ENG.). 96p. (J). (gr. 1-4). pap. 4.99 (978-1-4169-9466-4(1), Simon & Schuster/Paula Wiseman Bks.) Simon & Schuster/Paula Wiseman Bks.

—Cupcake Chaos. Keene, Carolyn. 2013. (Nancy Drew & the Clue Crew Ser.: 34). (ENG.). 96p. (J). (gr. 1-4). pap. 5.99 (978-1-4424-5351-7(6), Simon & Schuster/Paula Wiseman Bks.) Simon & Schuster/Paula Wiseman Bks.

—Dance Off. Keene, Carolyn. 2011. (Nancy Drew & the Clue Crew Ser.: 30). (ENG.). 96p. (J). (gr. 1-4). pap. 4.99 (978-1-4169-9459-6(9), Simon & Schuster/Paula Wiseman Bks.) Simon & Schuster/Paula Wiseman Bks.

—Designed for Disaster. Keene, Carolyn. 2011. (Nancy Drew & the Clue Crew Ser.: 29). (ENG.). 96p. (J). (gr. 1-4). pap. 4.99 (978-1-4169-9439-8(4), Simon & Schuster/Paula Wiseman Bks.) Simon & Schuster/Paula Wiseman Bks.

—Double Take. Keene, Carolyn. 2009. (Nancy Drew & the Clue Crew Ser.: 21). (ENG.). 96p. (J). (gr. 1-4). pap. 4.99 (978-1-4169-7812-1(7), Simon & Schuster/Paula Wiseman Bks.) Simon & Schuster/Paula Wiseman Bks.

—Dude, Where's My Spaceship? Greenburg, Dan. 2006. (Stepping Stone Book(TM) Ser.: No. 1). (ENG.). 96p. (J). (gr. 1-4). 3.99 (978-0-375-83344-1(7), Random Hse. Bks. for Young Readers) Random Hse. Children's Bks.

—Earth Day Escapade. Keene, Carolyn. 2009. (Nancy Drew & the Clue Crew Ser.: 18). (ENG.). 96p. (J). (gr. 1-4). pap. 4.99 (978-1-4169-7218-1(8), Simon & Schuster/Paula Wiseman Bks.) Simon & Schuster/Paula Wiseman Bks.

—The Fashion Disaster. Keene, Carolyn. 6th ed. 2007. (Nancy Drew & the Clue Crew Ser.: 6). (ENG.). 96p. (J). (gr. 1-4). pap. 4.99 (978-1-4169-3485-1(5), Simon & Schuster/Paula Wiseman Bks.) Simon & Schuster/Paula Wiseman Bks.

—The Fashion Disaster. Keene, Carolyn. 2009. (Nancy Drew & the Clue Crew Set II Ser.). 96p. (gr. 2-4). 24.21 (978-1-59961-643-8(2)) Spotlight.

—Flat Stanley: Show & Tell, Flat Stanley! Brown, Jeff. 2014. (I Can Read Book 2 Ser.). (ENG.). 32p. (J). (gr. -1-3). 16.99 (978-0-06-218976-9(X)); pap. 3.99 (978-0-06-218975-2(1)) HarperCollins Pubs.

Pamintuan, Macky. Flat Stanley - On Ice. Brown, Jeff. 2015. (I Can Read Book 2 Ser.). (ENG.). 32p. (J). (gr. -1-3). pap. 3.99 (978-0-06-218981-3(6)) HarperCollins Pubs.

Pamintuan, Macky. Flat Stanley & the Firehouse. Brown, Jeff. 2011. (I Can Read Book 2 Ser.). (ENG.). 32p. (J). (gr. -1-3). 16.99 (978-0-06-143006-0(4)); pap. 3.99 (978-0-06-143009-1(9)) HarperCollins Pubs.

Pamintuan, Macky. Flat Stanley & the Firehouse. Houran, Lori Haskins. 2013. 32p. (J). (978-1-4351-5055-3(4)) Barnes & Noble, Inc.

Pamintuan, Macky. Flat Stanley & the Haunted House. Brown, Jeff. 2010. (I Can Read Book 2 Ser.). (ENG.). 32p. (J). (gr. -1-3). 16.99 (978-0-06-143004-6(8)); pap. 3.99 (978-0-06-143005-3(6)) HarperCollins Pubs.

—Flat Stanley & the Very Big Cookie. Brown, Jeff. 2015. (I Can Read Book 2 Ser.). (ENG.). 32p. (J). (gr. -1-3). 16.99 (978-0-06-218979-0(4)); pap. 3.99 (978-0-06-218978-3(6)) HarperCollins Pubs.

—Flat Stanley at Bat. Brown, Jeff. 2012. (I Can Read Book 2 Ser.). (ENG.). 32p. (J). (gr. k-3). 16.99 (978-0-06-143010-7(2)); pap. 3.99 (978-0-06-143012-1(9)) HarperCollins Pubs.

—The Flat Stanley Collection, Set. Brown, Jeff. 2013. (Flat Stanley Ser.). 400p. (J). (gr. 1-5). pap. 14.99 (978-0-06-180247-8(6)) HarperCollins Pubs.

—Flat Stanley Goes Camping. Brown, Jeff. 2013. (I Can Read Book 2 Ser.). (ENG.). 32p. (J). (gr. -1-3). 16.99 (978-0-06-143013-8(7)); pap. 3.99 (978-0-06-143015-2(3)) HarperCollins Pubs.

—Flat Stanley's Worldwide Adventures #10: Showdown at the Alamo. Brown, Jeff. 2013. (Flat Stanley's Worldwide Adventures Ser.: 10). (ENG.). 112p. (J). (gr. 1-5). 15.99 (978-0-06-218988-2(3)) HarperCollins Pubs.

—Flat Stanley's Worldwide Adventures #12: Escape to California. Brown, Jeff. 2014. (Flat Stanley's Worldwide Adventures Ser.: 12). (ENG.). 128p. (J). (gr. 1-5). pap. 4.99 (978-0-06-218990-5(5)) HarperCollins Pubs.

—The Flower Show Fiasco. Keene, Carolyn. 2014. (Nancy Drew & the Clue Crew Ser.: 37). (ENG.). 96p. (J). (gr. 1-4). pap. 4.99 (978-1-4424-8668-3(6), Simon & Schuster/Paula Wiseman Bks.) Simon & Schuster/Paula Wiseman Bks.

—The Flying Chinese Wonders. Greenhut, Josh & Brown, Jeff. 2011. (Flat Stanley's Worldwide Adventures Ser.: 7). (ENG.). 96p. (J). (gr. 1-5). 15.99 (978-0-06-143003-9(X)); pap. 4.99 (978-0-06-143002-2(1)) HarperCollins Pubs.

—Framed in France. Brown, Jeff. 2014. (Flat Stanley's Worldwide Adventures Ser.: 11). (ENG.). 128p. (J). (gr. 1-5). 15.99 (978-0-06-218985-1(9)); pap. 4.99 (978-0-06-218984-4(0)) HarperCollins Pubs.

—Grand Old Flag. Nussbaum, Ben. 2006. (American Favorites Ser.). (ENG.). 32p. (J). (gr. -1-3). 14.95 (978-1-59249-572-6(9)); 9.95 (978-1-59249-593-1(1)) Soundprints.

—The Great Egyptian Grave Robbery. Pennypacker, Sara & Brown, Jeff. 2009. (Flat Stanley's Worldwide Adventures Ser.: 2). (ENG.). 96p. (J). (gr. 2-5). pap. 4.99 (978-0-06-142992-7(9)) HarperCollins Pubs.

—The Great Egyptian Grave Robbery No. 2. Pennypacker, Sara & Brown, Jeff. 2009. (Flat Stanley's Worldwide Adventures Ser.: 2). (ENG.). 96p. (J). (gr. 2-5). 15.99 (978-0-06-142993-4(7)) HarperCollins Pubs.

—The Halloween Hoax. Keene, Carolyn. 9th ed. 2007. (Nancy Drew & the Clue Crew Ser.: 9). (ENG.). 96p. (J). (gr. 1-4). pap. 4.99 (978-1-4169-3664-0(5), Simon & Schuster/Paula Wiseman Bks.) Simon & Schuster/Paula Wiseman Bks.

—The Halloween Hoax. Keene, Carolyn. 2009. (Nancy Drew & the Clue Crew Set II Ser.). 96p. (gr. 2-4). 24.21 (978-1-59961-644-5(0)) Spotlight.

—I Saw an Ant on the Railroad Track. Prince, Joshua. 2006. (ENG.). 24p. (J). (gr. -1-k). 14.95 (978-1-4027-2183-0(8), 1252268) Sterling Publishing Co., Inc.

—The Intrepid Canadian Expedition. Brown, Jeff. 2009. (Flat Stanley's Worldwide Adventures Ser.: 4). (ENG.). 112p. (J). (gr. 2-5). 15.99 (978-0-06-142997-2(X)) HarperCollins Pubs.

—The Intrepid Canadian Expedition Vol. 4. Brown, Jeff. 2009. (Flat Stanley's Worldwide Adventures Ser.: 4). (ENG.). 112p. (J). (gr. 2-5). pap. 4.99 (978-0-06-142996-5(1)) HarperCollins Pubs.

—Lights, Camera ... Cats! Keene, Carolyn. 8th ed. 2007. (Nancy Drew & the Clue Crew Ser.: 8). (ENG.). 96p. (J). (gr. 1-4). pap. 4.99 (978-1-4169-3957-3(1), Simon & Schuster/Paula Wiseman Bks.) Simon & Schuster/Paula Wiseman Bks.

—Lights, Camera... Cats! Keene, Carolyn. 2009. (Nancy Drew & the Clue Crew Set II Ser.). 96p. (gr. 2-4). 24.21 (978-1-59961-645-2(9)) Spotlight.

—The Make-a-Pet Mystery. Keene, Carolyn. 2012. (Nancy Drew & the Clue Crew Ser.: 31). (ENG.). 96p. (J). (gr. 1-4). pap. 5.99 (978-1-4169-9464-0(5), Simon & Schuster/Paula Wiseman Bks.) Simon & Schuster/Paula Wiseman Bks.

—Mall Madness. Keene, Carolyn. 15th ed. 2008. (Nancy Drew & the Clue Crew Ser.: 15). (ENG.). 96p. (J). (gr. 1-4). pap. 4.99 (978-1-4169-5900-7(9), Simon & Schuster/Paula Wiseman Bks.) Simon & Schuster/Paula Wiseman Bks.

—Mall Madness. Keene, Carolyn. 2009. (Nancy Drew & the Clue Crew Set II Ser.). 96p. (gr. 2-4). 24.21 (978-1-59961-646-9(7)) Spotlight.

—Max & Maddy & the Bursting Balloons Mystery. McCall Smith, Alexander. 2008. (ENG.). 80p. (J). (gr. 2-4). pap. 4.95 (978-1-59990-217-3(6), Bloomsbury USA Childrens) Bloomsbury USA.

—The Mount Rushmore Calamity. Brown, Jeff. 2009. (Flat Stanley's Worldwide Adventures Ser.: 1). (ENG.). 96p. (J). (gr. 2-5). 15.99 (978-0-06-142991-0(0)); pap. 4.99 (978-0-06-142990-3(2)) HarperCollins Pubs.

—A Musical Mess. Keene, Carolyn. 2014. (Nancy Drew & the Clue Crew Ser.: 38). (ENG.). 96p. (J). (gr. 1-4). pap. 4.99 (978-1-4424-9512-8(X), Simon & Schuster/Paula Wiseman Bks.) Simon & Schuster/Paula Wiseman Bks.

—The Nancy Drew & the Clue Crew Collection: Sleepover Sleuths; Scream for Ice Cream; Pony Problems; the Cinderella Ballet Mystery; Case of the Sneaky Snowman. Keene, Carolyn. ed. 2014. (Nancy Drew & the Clue Crew Ser.). (ENG.). 480p. (J). (gr. 1-4). 24.99 (978-1-4814-1472-2(0), Simon & Schuster/Paula Wiseman Bks.) Simon & Schuster/Paula Wiseman Bks.

—The Night Before Baseball at the Park by the Bay. Schnell, David. 2013. (ENG.). 32p. 0.00 (978-0-9891043-0-2(3)) Prospect Palo Alto Publishing.

—Pirates Coming Through, 24 vols., Vol. 4257. Williams, Rozanne Lanczak. 2005. (Reading for Fluency Ser.). 16p. (J). pap. 3.49 (978-1-59198-157-2(3), 4257) Creative Teaching Pr., Inc.

—Pony Problems. Keene, Carolyn. 3rd ed. 2006. (Nancy Drew & the Clue Crew Ser.: 3). (ENG.). 80p. (J). (gr. 1-4). pap. 4.99 (978-1-4169-1815-8(9), Simon & Schuster/Paula Wiseman Bks.) Simon & Schuster/Paula Wiseman Bks.

—Pony Problems. Keene, Carolyn. 2007. (Nancy Drew & the Clue Crew Ser.). (ENG.). 80p. (gr. 1-4). 24.21 (978-1-59961-346-8(8)) Spotlight.

—Princess Mix-Up Mystery, No. 24. Keene, Carolyn. 2009. (Nancy Drew & the Clue Crew Ser.: 24). (ENG.). 96p. (J). (gr. 1-4). pap. 5.99 (978-1-4169-7811-4(9), Simon & Schuster/Paula Wiseman Bks.) Simon & Schuster/Paula Wiseman Bks.

—The Pumpkin Patch Puzzle. Keene, Carolyn. 2012. (Nancy Drew & the Clue Crew Ser.: 33). (ENG.). 112p. (J). (gr. 1-4). pap. 4.99 (978-1-4169-9465-7(3), Simon & Schuster/Paula Wiseman Bks.) Simon & Schuster/Paula Wiseman Bks.

—The Science Unfair. Ball, Nate. 2014. (Alien in My Pocket Ser.: 2). (ENG.). 144p. (J). (gr. 1-5). 15.99 (978-0-06-231494-9(7)) HarperCollins Pubs.

—Scream for Ice Cream. Keene, Carolyn. 2nd ed. 2006. (Nancy Drew & the Clue Crew Ser.: 2). (ENG.). 96p. (J). (gr. 1-4). pap. 4.99 (978-1-4169-1253-8(3), Simon & Schuster/Paula Wiseman Bks.) Simon & Schuster/Paula Wiseman Bks.

—Scream for Ice Cream. Keene, Carolyn. 2007. (Nancy Drew & the Clue Crew Ser.). (ENG.). 89p. (gr. 1-4). 24.21 (978-1-59961-347-5(6)) Spotlight.

—The Secret of the Scarecrow. Keene, Carolyn. 2013. (Nancy Drew & the Clue Crew Ser.: 36). (ENG.). 96p. (J). (gr. 1-4). pap. 4.99 (978-1-4424-5353-1(2), Simon & Schuster/Paula Wiseman Bks.) Simon & Schuster/Paula Wiseman Bks.

—Showdown at the Alamo. Brown, Jeff. 2013. (Flat Stanley's Worldwide Adventures Ser.: 10). (ENG.). 112p. (J). (gr. 1-5). pap. 4.99 (978-0-06-218987-5(5)) HarperCollins Pubs.

—Ski School Sneak. Keene, Carolyn. 11th ed. 2007. (Nancy Drew & the Clue Crew Ser.: 11). (ENG.). 96p. (J). (gr. 1-4). pap. 5.99 (978-1-4169-4936-7(4), Simon & Schuster/Paula Wiseman Bks.) Simon & Schuster/Paula Wiseman Bks.

—Ski School Sneak. Keene, Carolyn. 2009. (Nancy Drew & the Clue Crew Set II Ser.). 96p. (gr. 2-4). 24.21 (978-1-59961-647-6(5)) Spotlight.

—Sleepover Sleuths. Keene, Carolyn. 2006. (Nancy Drew & the Clue Crew Ser.: 1). (ENG.). 96p. (J). (gr. 1-4). pap. 5.99 (978-1-4169-1255-2(X), Simon & Schuster/Paula Wiseman Bks.) Simon & Schuster/Paula Wiseman Bks.

—Sleepover Sleuths. Keene, Carolyn. 2007. (Nancy Drew & the Clue Crew Ser.). (ENG.). 81p. (gr. 1-4). 24.21 (978-1-59961-348-2(4)) Spotlight.

—Stanley in Space. Brown, Jeff. 2009. (Flat Stanley Ser.). (ENG.). 128p. (J). (gr. 2-5). pap. 4.99 (978-0-06-442174-4(0)) HarperCollins Pubs.

Pamintuan, Macky. Telescope Troubles. Ball, Nate. 2016. (Alien in My Pocket Ser.: 7). 144p. (J). (gr. 1-5). pap. 4.99 (978-0-06-237088-4(X)) HarperCollins Pubs.

Pamintuan, Macky. Thanksgiving Thief. Keene, Carolyn. 2008. (Nancy Drew & the Clue Crew Ser.: 16). (ENG.). 96p. (J). (gr. 1-4). pap. 4.99 (978-1-4169-6777-4(X), Simon & Schuster/Paula Wiseman Bks.) Simon & Schuster/Paula Wiseman Bks.

—Thanksgiving Thief. Keene, Carolyn. 2009. (Nancy Drew & the Clue Crew Set II Ser.). 96p. (gr. 2-4). 24.21 (978-1-59961-648-3(3)) Spotlight.

—Ticket Trouble. Keene, Carolyn. 10th ed. 2007. (Nancy Drew & the Clue Crew Ser.: 10). (ENG.). 96p. (J). (gr. 1-4). pap. 4.99 (978-1-4169-4733-2(7), Simon & Schuster/Paula Wiseman Bks.) Simon & Schuster/Paula Wiseman Bks.

—Ticket Trouble. Keene, Carolyn. 2009. (Nancy Drew & the Clue Crew Set II Ser.). 96p. (gr. 2-4). 24.21 (978-1-59961-649-0(1)) Spotlight.

—Time Thief. Keene, Carolyn. 2011. (Nancy Drew & the Clue Crew Ser.: 28). (ENG.). 96p. (J). (gr. 1-4). pap. 4.99 (978-1-4169-9458-9(0), Simon & Schuster/Paula Wiseman Bks.) Simon & Schuster/Paula Wiseman Bks.

—Treasure Trouble. Keene, Carolyn. 2009. (Nancy Drew & the Clue Crew Ser.: 20). (ENG.). 96p. (J). (gr. 1-4). pap. 4.99 (978-1-4169-7809-1(7), Simon & Schuster/Paula Wiseman Bks.) Simon & Schuster/Paula Wiseman Bks.

—The U. S. Capital Commotion. Brown, Jeff. 2011. (Flat Stanley's Worldwide Adventures Ser.: 9). (ENG.). 112p. (J). (gr. 2-5). pap. 4.99 (978-0-06-143019-0(6)) HarperCollins Pubs.

—Unicorn Uproar. Keene, Carolyn. 2009. (Nancy Drew & the Clue Crew Ser.: 22). (ENG.). 96p. (J). (gr. 1-4). pap. 4.99 (978-1-4169-7810-7(0), Simon & Schuster/Paula Wiseman Bks.) Simon & Schuster/Paula Wiseman Bks.

—The US Capital Commotion. Brown, Jeff. 2011. (Flat Stanley's Worldwide Adventures Ser.: 9). (ENG.). 112p. (J). (gr. 2-5). 15.99 (978-0-06-157436-8(8)) HarperCollins Pubs.

—Valentine's Day Secret. Keene, Carolyn. 12th ed. 2007. (Nancy Drew & the Clue Crew Ser.: 12). (ENG.). 80p. (J). (gr. 1-4). pap. 5.99 (978-1-4169-4944-2(5), Simon & Schuster/Paula Wiseman Bks.) Simon & Schuster/Paula Wiseman Bks.

—Valentine's Day Secret. Keene, Carolyn. 2009. (Nancy Drew & the Clue Crew Set II Ser.). 96p. (gr. 2-4). 24.21 (978-1-59961-650-6(5)) Spotlight.

—Valentine's Day Secret. Keene, Carolyn. 2008. (Nancy Drew & the Clue Crew Ser.). 85p. (J). (gr. 1-4). 14.75 (978-1-4178-1133-5(1)) Turtleback Bks.

—Wedding Day Disaster. Keene, Carolyn. 2008. (Nancy Drew & the Clue Crew Ser.: 17). (ENG.). 96p. (J). (gr. 1-4). pap. 5.99 (978-1-4169-6778-1(8), Simon & Schuster/Paula Wiseman Bks.) Simon & Schuster/Paula Wiseman Bks.

—The Zoo Crew. Keene, Carolyn. 14th ed. 2008. (Nancy Drew & the Clue Crew Ser.: 14). (ENG.). 96p. (J). (gr. 1-4). pap. 4.99 (978-1-4169-5899-4(1), Simon & Schuster/Paula Wiseman Bks.) Simon & Schuster/Paula Wiseman Bks.

—The Zoo Crew. Keene, Carolyn. 2009. (Nancy Drew & the Clue Crew Set II Ser.). 96p. (gr. 2-4). 24.21 (978-1-59961-651-3(3)) Spotlight.

Pamintuan, Macky & Wang, Qi. Grand Old Flag. Schwaeber, Barbie. Nussbaum, Ben, ed. 2006. (Smithsonian American Favorites Ser.). (ENG.). 32p. (J). (gr. -1-3). 9.85 (978-1-59249-650-1(4)) Soundprints.

Pamintuan, Macky, jt. illus. see Nash, Scott.

Pamment, Katie. The Prince & the Pauper. Twain, Mark. 2008. (Young Reading Series 2 Gift Books Ser.). 63p. (J). 8.99 (978-0-7945-1818-9(4), Usborne) EDC Publishing.

Pan, Hui-Mei. El Cochinito en mi Bolsillo, 1 vol. Pan, Hui-Mei. Vernescu, Maritza, tr. from ENG. 2004.Tr. of Piggy in My Pocket. (SPA.). 32p. (J). bds. 5.95 (978-1-932065-04-6(0), 1-718-794-9112) Star Bright Bks., Inc.

—Piggy in My Pocket (Spanish/English), 1 vol. Pan, Hui-Mei. del Risco, Eida, tr. 2004. (ENG & SPA.). 32p. (J). bds. 5.95 (978-1-932065-11-4(3)) Star Bright Bks., Inc.

—¿Qué hay en la bolsa de Abuelita? Pan, Hui-Mei. 2004.Tr. of What's in Grandma's Grocery Bag?. (SPA.). 16p. (J). bds. 6.25 (978-1-932065-05-3(9)) Star Bright Bks., Inc.

Panaccione, Nancy. Emma's Very Busy Week. Dakota, Heather. 2009. 31p. (J). *(978-0-545-17227-1(6))* Scholastic, Inc.

Pancheshnaya, Dasha. Silent As a Stone: Mother Maria of Paris & the Trash Can Rescue. Forest, Jim. 2007. (ENG.). 32p. (J). 18.00 *(978-0-88141-314-4(3))* St. Vladimir's Seminary Pr.

Pandya, Yamini. Nyagrodha. Kalpish Ratna. 2006. 287p. (J). *(978-0-670-04969-1(7)*, Puffin) Penguin Publishing Group.

Paneva, Valya. The Adventures of Martha & Sully. Wright, Karen. 2011. (ENG.). 40p. pap. 9.95 *(978-1-4637-2069-8(6))* CreateSpace Independent Publishing Platform.

Pang, Alex. The A-10 Thunderbolt. Hansen, Ole Steen. 2005. (Cross-Sections Ser.). (ENG.). 32p. (gr. 3-4). 27.32 *(978-0-7368-5251-7(4)*, 1244013, Edge Bks.) Capstone Pr., Inc.

—The AH-64 Apache Helicopter, 1 vol. Hansen, Ole Steen. 2005. (Cross-Sections Ser.). (ENG.). 32p. (gr. 3-4). 27.32 *(978-0-7368-5250-0(6)*, 1244012, Edge Bks.) Capstone Pr., Inc.

—The B-2 Spirit Stealth Bomber, 1 vol. Hansen, Ole Steen. 2005. (Cross-Sections Ser.). (ENG.). 32p. (gr. 3-4). 27.32 *(978-0-7368-5255-5(7)*, 1244017, Edge Bks.) Capstone Pr., Inc.

—The F/A-22 Raptor. Hansen, Ole Steen. 2005. (Cross-Sections Ser.). (ENG.). 32p. (gr. 3-4). 27.32 *(978-0-7368-5253-1(0)*, 1244015, Edge Bks.) Capstone Pr., Inc.

—The HMMWV Humvee, 1 vol. Parker, Steve. 2007. (Cross-Sections Ser.). (ENG.). 32p. (gr. 3-4). 27.32 *(978-1-4296-0093-4(4)*, Edge Bks.) Capstone Pr., Inc.

—The LCAC Military Hovercraft, 1 vol. Parker, Steve. 2007. (Cross-Sections Ser.). (ENG.). 32p. (gr. 3-4). 27.32 *(978-1-4296-0095-8(0)*, Edge Bks.) Capstone Pr., Inc.

—The M2 Bradley Infantry Fighting Vehicle, 1 vol. Parker, Steve. 2007. (Cross-Sections Ser.). (ENG.). 32p. (gr. 3-4). 27.32 *(978-1-4296-0092-7(6)*, Edge Bks.) Capstone Pr., Inc.

—The M270 Multiple Launch Rocket, 1 vol. Parker, Steve. 2007. (Cross-Sections Ser.). (ENG.). 32p. (gr. 3-4). 27.32 *(978-1-4296-0096-5(9)*, Edge Bks.) Capstone Pr., Inc.

—Speed Machines. Parker, Steve. 2010. (How It Works Ser.). 40p. (J). (gr. 3-18). lib. bdg. 19.95 *(978-1-4222-1800-6(7)*, 1317938) Mason Crest.

Pang, Alex, jt. illus. see Fox, Christyan.

Pang, YaWen Ariel. P Is for Pumpkin: God's Harvest Alphabet, 1 vol. Wargin, Kathy-jo. 2008. (ENG.). 40p. (J). (gr. -1-3). 15.99 *(978-0-310-71180-3(0))* Zonderkidz.

Pangbourne, Daniel. Learn with Me 123. Pangbourne, Daniel, photos by. Bulloch, Ivan & James, Diane. 2007. (ENG.). 46p. (J). (gr. -1 — 1). pap. 6.95 *(978-1-58728-622-3(X))* Cooper Square Publishing Llc.

Pangbourne, Daniel, photos by. Learn with Me ABC. Bulloch, Ivan & James, Diane. 2007. (ENG., 45p. (J). (gr. -1-3). pap. 6.95 *(978-1-58728-599-8(1))* Cooper Square Publishing Llc.

Pankhurst, Kate. Big Red Balloon. Fine, Anne. 2013. (Blue Bananas Ser.). (ENG.). 48p. (J). (gr. k-2). pap. 5.99 *(978-1-4052-5433-5(5))* Egmont Bks., Ltd. GBR. Dist: Independent Pubs. Group.

Pankhurst, Kate. A Friend in Need! Jarman, Julia. 2015. (Friends Ser.: 2). (ENG.). 96p. (J). (gr. 2-4). 6.99 ***(978-1-84939-576-2(4))*** Andersen Pr. GBR. Dist: Independent Pubs. Group.

Pankhurst, Kate. Make Friends - Break Friends. Jarman, Julia. 2015. (Friends Ser.: 1). (ENG.). 96p. (J). (gr. 2-4). pap. 6.99 *(978-1-84939-509-0(8))* Andersen Pr. GBR. Dist: Independent Pubs. Group.

—Midnight Feast Magic: Sleepover Fun & Food. Boursnell, Clive, photos by. Peters, Rosalind. 2009. (ENG.). 64p. (J). (gr. 3-6). pap. 15.95 *(978-1-84507-783-9(0)*, Frances Lincoln) Quarto Publishing Group UK GBR. Dist: Hachette Bk. Group.

Pankhurst, Kate. New Friend Old Friends. Jarman, Julia. 2015. (Friends Ser.: 3). (ENG.). 112p. (J). (gr. 2-4). 6.99 ***(978-1-78344-004-7(X))*** Andersen Pr. GBR. Dist: Independent Pubs. Group.

—The Three Billy Goats Gruff. adapted ed. 2015. (My First Fairy Tales Ser.). (ENG.). 32p. (J). 7.99 ***(978-1-58925-459-6(7))*** Tiger Tales.

Pankratz, Justin. Blue Monkey. 2003. (J). 5.95 *(978-0-9742637-0-0(2))* Pankratz Creations.

—Humpty Dumpty, Back Together Again? Summers, Sherri Pankratz. 2003. 32p. (J). 8.95 *(978-0-9742637-1-7(0))* Pankratz Creations.

Pannell, Nick. Daddy Keeps Us Free. Mann, Scott. 2011. 36p. pap. 24.95 *(978-1-4560-6075-6(9))* America Star Bks.

Panosian, Dan. Doom in a Box. Sudduth, Brent & Meredith Books Staff. 2008. 22p. (J). pap. 3.99 *(978-0-696-23956-4(6))* Meredith Bks.

—Grodd's Army. West, Tracey. 2010. (Batman: the Brave & the Bold Ser.). (ENG.). 64p. (J). (gr. 1-3). pap. 4.99 *(978-0-448-45384-2(3)*, Grosset & Dunlap) Penguin Publishing Group.

—Night of the Mummy. West, Tracey. 2010. (Batman: the Brave & the Bold Ser.). (ENG.). 64p. (J). (gr. 3-7). pap. 4.99 *(978-0-448-45339-2(8)*, Grosset & Dunlap) Penguin Publishing Group.

Panse, Sonal. Just Too Little. Miller, Judith J. 2013. 16p. pap. 9.95 *(978-1-61633-413-0(4))* Guardian Angel Publishing, Inc.

—Rescue Dog. Duncan, Al. 2005. (J). per. 10.00 *(978-0-9754298-6-0(8)*, Ithaca Pr.) Authors & Artists Publishers of New York, Inc.

Pantaleon, Tamara, photos by. The Magic Tree: Home of the Fairies. Pantaleon, Tamara. 2011. (ENG., 24p. pap. 12.99 *(978-1-4565-0911-8(X))* CreateSpace Independent Publishing Platform.

Pantic, Dunja. Mom, Mac & Cheese, Please! Olin, Marilyn. 2013. (ENG.). 28p. (J). (gr. -1-1). 16.95 *(978-1-62087-995-5(6)*, 620995, Sky Pony Pr.) Skyhorse Publishing Co., Inc.

Pantoja, Maria Kristina. The Hundred-Dollar Robber: A Mystery with Money. Thielbar, Melinda. 2009. (Manga Math Mysteries Ser.: 2). (ENG.). 48p. (gr. 3-5). 29.27 *(978-0-7613-3854-3(3))* Lerner Publishing Group.

—The Lost Key: A Mystery with Whole Numbers. Thielbar, Melinda. 2009. (Manga Math Mysteries Ser.: 1). (ENG.). 48p. (gr. 3-5). 29.27 *(978-0-7613-3853-6(5))* Lerner Publishing Group.

Pantoja, Tintin. The Ancient Formula: A Mystery with Fractions. Thielbar, Melinda. 2011. (Manga Math Mysteries Ser.: 5). (ENG.). 48p. (gr. 3-5). pap. 6.95 *(978-0-7613-8134-1(1)*, Graphic Universe) Lerner Publishing Group.

—The Ancient Formula No. 5: A Mystery with Fractions. Thielbar, Melinda. 2010. (Manga Math Mysteries Ser.: 5). (ENG.). 48p. (gr. 3-5). 29.27 *(978-0-7613-4907-5(3))* Lerner Publishing Group.

—The Hundred-Dollar Robber: A Mystery with Money. Thielbar, Melinda. 2010. (Manga Math Mysteries Ser.: 2). (ENG.). 48p. (gr. 3-5). pap. 6.95 *(978-0-7613-5243-3(0)*, Graphic Universe) Lerner Publishing Group.

—The Lost Key: A Mystery with Whole Numbers. Thielbar, Melinda. 2010. (Manga Math Mysteries Ser.: 1). (ENG.). 48p. (gr. 3-5). pap. 6.95 *(978-0-7613-5244-0(9)*, Graphic Universe) Lerner Publishing Group.

—#5 the Ancient Formula: A Mystery with Fractions. Thielbar, Melinda. 2011. (Manga Math Mysteries Set II Ser.). pap. 39.62 *(978-0-7613-8362-8(X)*, Graphic Universe) Lerner Publishing Group.

Paolini, Alison. Carina & Her Care Partner Gramma. Hall, Kirk. 2013. 26p. 19.95 *(978-1-61314-158-8(0))*; pap. 15.95 *(978-1-61314-171-7(8))* Innovo Publishing, LLC.

—Carson & His Shaky Paws Grampa. Hall, Kirk. 2011. 24p. (J). pap. 15.95 *(978-1-61314-009-3(6))*; lib. bdg. 19.95 *(978-1-936076-91-8(8))* Innovo Publishing, LLC.

Papaleo, Antonio. The Kite Who Was Scared of Heights. Williams, Simon. 2013. 38p. pap. *(978-1-910053-36-2(8))* Legend Pr.

Paparone, Pam. Flip, Float, Fly: Seeds on the Move. Macken, JoAnn Early. 2008. (ENG.). 32p. (J). (gr. 1-5). 16.95 *(978-0-8234-2043-8(4))* Holiday Hse., Inc.

—Where Do Chicks Come From? Sklansky, Amy E. 2005. (Let's-Read-and-Find-Out-Science Ser.). 40p. (J). (gr. -1-1). (ENG.). 15.99 *(978-0-06-028892-1(2))*; lib. bdg. 16.89 *(978-0-06-028893-8(0))* HarperCollins Pubs.

Paparone, Pam, jt. illus. see Paparone, Pamela.

Paparone, Pamela. A Big Surprise. Butler, Kristi T. 2005. (Green Light Readers Level 1 Ser.). (ENG.). 24p. (J). (gr. -1-3). pap. 3.95 *(978-0-15-205141-9(4))* Houghton Mifflin Harcourt Publishing Co.

—The Greatest Invention: The Story of Walter Hunt. Polette, Nancy. 2008. (ENG.). 32p. (J). *(978-0-15-205824-1(9))* Harcourt Trade Pubs.

—The Little School Bus. Roth, Carol. 2004. (ENG.). 32p. (J). (gr. k-1). pap. 7.95 *(978-0-7358-1905-4(X))* North-South Bks., Inc.

—Nobody Owns the Sky. Lindbergh, Reeve. 2004. 32p. (J). *(978-1-85269-342-8(8))*; *(978-1-85269-343-5(6))*; *(978-1-85269-344-2(4))*; *(978-1-85269-345-9(2))*; *(978-1-85269-347-3(9))* Mantra Lingua.

—Ten Dirty Pigs: An Upside-Down Turn Around. Roth, Carol. 2008. (ENG.). 22p. (J). (gr. -1-k). bds. 7.95 *(978-0-7358-2213-9(1))* North-South Bks., Inc.

—Where Do Chicks Come From? Sklansky, Amy E. 2005. (Let's-Read-and-Find-Out Science 1 Ser.). (ENG.). 40p. (J). (gr. -1-3). pap. 5.99 *(978-0-06-445212-0(3)*, Collins) HarperCollins Pubs.

Paparone, Pamela. Five Little Ducks. Paparone, Pamela. 2005. (Cheshire Studio Book Ser.). (ENG.). 24p. (J). bds. 6.95 *(978-0-7358-1857-6(6))* North-South Bks., Inc.

Paparone, Pamela & Paparone, Pam. Of Numbers & Stars: The Story of Hypatia. Love, D. Anne. 2006. (ENG.). 32p. (J). (gr. 4-8). 16.95 *(978-0-8234-1621-9(6))* Holiday Hse., Inc.

—Raindrop, Plop! Lewison, Wendy Cheyette. Paparone, Pamela, tr. 2004. (ENG.). 32p. (J). (gr. -1-k). 15.99 *(978-0-670-03620-2(X)*, Viking Juvenile) Penguin Publishing Group.

Pape, Jane. Adventures of the Six Cousins. Blyton, Enid. 2013. (ENG.). 330p. (J). 16.50 *(978-1-84135-589-4(5))* Award Pubns. Ltd. GBR. Dist: Parkwest Pubns., Inc.

Pape, Wendy Fehrle. Tea & Cookie. LeBlanc, Ellen Lieb. 2005. (J). bds. *(978-0-9773010-0-3(1))* Talmage Publishing.

Papeo, Maria Eugenia & Saumell, Marina. Why Is My Name Sam? Canady, Mary Monica. 2008. 24p. pap. 24.95 *(978-1-60474-028-8(0))* America Star Bks.

Papi, Liza. Carnavalia! African-Brazilian Folklore & Crafts. Papi, Liza. 2004. 48p. (J). (gr. k-4). reprint ed. 20.00 *(978-0-7567-7760-9(7))* DIANE Publishing Co.

Papile, Christopher, et al. Adopted: The Ultimate Teen Guide. Washburn, Chris, photos by. Slade, Suzanne Buckingham. 2007. (It Happened to Me Ser.: 20). (ENG.). 272p. (gr. 8-12). 61.00 *(978-0-8108-5774-2(X))* Scarecrow Pr., Inc.

Papish, Adam. Sissy's Christmas Program. Seglie, Susan & Schiefelbein, Janis. Zagorski, Astrid, tr. 2003. (ENG & SPA.). (J). 4.95 *(978-0-9747243-1-7(9))* Seglie, Susan M.

Papish, Ram & Papish, Ram. The Little Fox: An Alaska Adventure. Papish, Ram. 2008. (ENG.). 38p. (gr. 3-7). 15.95 *(978-1-889963-87-7(9))* Univ. of Alaska Pr.

Papish, Ram, jt. illus. see Papish, Ram.

Paplinksie, Cecilia. Color Me Happy. Harris, Sally M. 2009. 24p. pap. 10.95 *(978-1-935137-75-7(1))* Guardian Angel Publishing, Inc.

Papp, Kathy, jt. illus. see Papp, Robert.

Papp, Lisa. My Mom's Wedding. Bunting, Eve. 2006. (ENG.). 32p. (J). (gr. k-6). 16.95 *(978-1-58536-288-2(3))* Sleeping Bear Pr.

—One for All: A Pennsylvania Number Book. Noble, Trinka Hakes. 2005. (Count Your Way Across the USA Ser.). (ENG.). 40p. (J). (gr. k-5). 16.95 *(978-1-58536-200-4(X))* Sleeping Bear Pr.

Papp, Lisa & Papp, Robert. The Town That Fooled the British: A War of 1812 Story. Papp, Lisa & Papp, Robert. 2011. (Tales of Young Americans Ser.). (ENG.). 32p. (J). (gr. 1-5). 16.95 *(978-1-58536-484-8(3))* Sleeping Bear Pr.

Papp, Lisa, jt. illus. see Papp, Robert.

Papp, Robert. The Amazing Mystery Show. 2010. (Boxcar Children Mysteries Ser.). (ENG.). 128p. (J). (gr. 2-5). pap. 4.99 *(978-0-8075-0315-7(0))*;No. 123. 14.99 *(978-0-8075-0314-0(2))* Whitman, Albert & Co.

—Anna Maria's Gift. Shefelman, Janice Jordan. 2011. (Stepping Stone Book Ser.). (ENG.). 112p. (J). (gr. 2-5). pap. 4.99 *(978-0-375-85882-6(2))* Random Hse. Children's Bks.

—The Battles. Papp, Lisa & Noble, Trinka Hakes. 2013. (American Adventures Ser.). (ENG.). 88p. (J). (gr. 3-6). pap. 9.99 *(978-1-58536-861-7(X)*, 202368) Sleeping Bear Pr.

—Best Friends Forever? Medearis, Angela Shelf. 2004. 124p. (J). *(978-0-439-52330-1(3))* Scholastic, Inc.

—The Box That Watch Found. 2007. (Boxcar Children Ser.: No. 113). (ENG.). 128p. (J). (gr. 2-5). lib. bdg. 14.99 *(978-0-8075-5568-2(1))*; per. 4.99 *(978-0-8075-5569-9(X))* Whitman, Albert & Co.

—Bravo, Mia! Yep, Laurence. England, Tamara, ed. 2008. (ENG.). 136p. (J). (gr. 3). pap. 6.95 *(978-1-59369-410-4(5))* American Girl Publishing, Inc.

—The Clue in the Recycling Bin. 2011. (Boxcar Children Mysteries Ser.). (ENG.). 128p. (J). (gr. 2-5). pap. 4.99 *(978-0-8075-1209-8(5))* Whitman, Albert & Co.

—The Clue in the Recycling Bin. 2011. (Boxcar Children Mysteries Ser.). (ENG.). 128p. (J). (gr. 2-5). lib. bdg. 14.99 *(978-0-8075-1208-1(7))* Whitman, Albert & Co.

—The Creature in Ogopogo Lake. 2006. (Boxcar Children Mysteries Ser.: 108). (ENG.). 128p. (J). (gr. 2-5). per. 5.99 *(978-0-8075-1337-8(7))* Whitman, Albert & Co.

—The Cupcake Caper. 2010. (Boxcar Children Mysteries Ser.). (ENG.). 128p. (J). (gr. 2-5). 14.99 *(978-0-8075-1373-6(3))*;No. 125. pap. 4.99 *(978-0-8075-1374-3(1))* Whitman, Albert & Co.

—Encyclopedia Brown & the Case of the Jumping Frogs. Sobol, Donald J. 2005. (Encyclopedia Brown Ser.). 69p. (J). (gr. 3-7). 13.15 *(978-0-7569-5100-9(3))* Perfection Learning Corp.

—From Sea to Shining Sea, 1 vol. 2011. (Boxcar Children Mysteries Ser.). (ENG.). 384p. (J). (gr. 2-5). pap. 8.99 *(978-0-8075-0891-6(8))* Whitman, Albert & Co.

—The Game Store Mystery. 2005. (Boxcar Children Ser.: No. 104). (ENG.). 128p. (J). (gr. 2-5). 14.99 *(978-0-8075-2738-2(6))*; per. 4.50 *(978-0-8075-2739-9(4))* Whitman, Albert & Co.

—The Ghost in the First Row, Vol. 112. 2007. (Boxcar Children Ser.). (ENG.). 128p. (J). (gr. 2-5). per. 4.50 *(978-0-8075-5567-5(3))* Whitman, Albert & Co.

—The Ghost of the Chattering Bones. 2007. (Boxcar Children Ser.). 120p. 15.00 *(978-0-7569-7611-8(1))* Perfection Learning Corp.

—The Ghost of the Chattering Bones. 2005. (Boxcar Children Ser.: No. 102). (ENG.). 128p. (J). (gr. 2-5). pap. 4.50 *(978-0-8075-0874-9(8))* Whitman, Albert & Co.

—The Giant Yo-Yo Mystery. 2006. (Boxcar Children Ser.: No. 107). (ENG.). 128p. (J). (gr. 2-5). per. 4.50 *(978-0-8075-0879-4(9))* Whitman, Albert & Co.

—The Great Detective Race. 2008. (Boxcar Children Ser.: No. 115). (ENG.). 128p. (J). (gr. 2-5). 14.99 *(978-0-8075-5573-6(8))* Whitman, Albert & Co.

—The Great Detective Race. 2008. (Boxcar Children Ser.: No. 115). (ENG.). 128p. (J). (gr. 2-5). pap. 4.99 *(978-0-8075-5574-3(6))* Whitman, Albert & Co.

—The Great Turkey Heist. 2011. (Boxcar Children Mysteries Ser.: No. 129). (ENG.). 128p. (J). (gr. 2-5). 4.99 *(978-0-8075-3051-1(4))*; lib. bdg. 14.99 *(978-0-8075-3050-4(6))* Whitman, Albert & Co.

—A Horse Named Dragon. 2008. (ENG.). 128p. (J). (gr. 2-5). (Boxcar Children Mysteries Ser.: 114). per. 5.99 *(978-0-8075-5572-9(X))*; (Boxcar Children Ser.: No. 114). lib. bdg. 14.99 *(978-0-8075-5571-2(1))* Whitman, Albert & Co.

—Lanie, Bk. 1. Kurtz, Jane. Hirsch, Jennifer, ed. 2010. (ENG.). 112p. (J). (gr. 5). pap. 6.95 *(978-1-59369-682-5(5)*, American Girl) American Girl Publishing, Inc.

—Lanie's Real Adventures. Kurtz, Jane. 2010. (American Girl Today Ser.). (ENG.). 112p. (YA). (gr. 3-18). 12.95 *(978-1-59369-685-6(X))* American Girl Publishing, Inc.

—Lanie's Real Adventures, Bk. 2. Kurtz, Jane. England, Tamara, ed. 2010. (ENG.). 112p. (YA). (gr. 3-18). pap. 6.95 *(978-1-59369-683-2(3)*, American Girl) American Girl Publishing, Inc.

—The Last Brother: A Civil War Tale. Noble, Trinka Hakes. 2006. (Tales of Young Americans Ser.). (ENG.). 32p. (J). (gr. 3-7). 17.95 *(978-1-58536-253-0(0))* Sleeping Bear Pr.

—M Is for Meow: A Cat Alphabet. Wilbur, Helen L. rev. ed. 2006. (ENG.). 40p. (J). (gr. k-6). 17.95 *(978-1-58536-304-9(9))* Sleeping Bear Pr.

—Mia, Bk. 1. Yep, Laurence. England, Tamara, ed. 2008. (ENG.). 136p. (gr. 3-18). pap. 6.95 *(978-1-59369-409-8(1))* American Girl Publishing, Inc.

—Monkey Trouble. 2011. (Boxcar Children Mysteries Ser.). (ENG.). 128p. (J). (gr. 2-5). pap. 4.99 *(978-0-8075-5240-7(2))* Whitman, Albert & Co.

—Monkey Trouble. 2011. (Boxcar Children Mysteries Ser.). (ENG.). 128p. (J). (gr. 2-5). lib. bdg. 14.99 *(978-0-8075-5239-1(9))* Whitman, Albert & Co.

—The Mystery of the Orphan Train. 2005. (Boxcar Children Ser.: No. 105). (ENG.). 128p. (J). (gr. 2-5). lib. bdg. 14.99 *(978-0-8075-5558-3(4))*; per. 4.50 *(978-0-8075-5559-0(2))* Whitman, Albert & Co.

—The Pumpkin Head Mystery, No. 124. 2010. (Boxcar Children Mysteries Ser.). (ENG.). 128p. (J). (gr. 2-5). pap. 4.99 *(978-0-8075-6669-5(1))* Whitman, Albert & Co.

—Quake! Disaster in San Francisco 1906, 1 vol. Karwoski, Gail Langer. 2004. (ENG.). 192p. (J). (gr. 3-7). 15.95 *(978-1-56145-310-8(2))* Peachtree Pubs.

—The Rock 'n' Roll Mystery. 2006. (Boxcar Children Ser.: No. 109). (ENG.). 128p. (J). (gr. 2-5). lib. bdg. 14.99 *(978-0-8075-7089-0(3))*; per. 4.50 *(978-0-8075-7090-6(7))* Whitman, Albert & Co.

—The Scarlet Stockings Spy. Noble, Trinka Hakes. 2004. (Tales of Young Americans Ser.). (ENG.). 48p. (J). (gr. 1-7). 16.95 *(978-1-58536-230-1(1))* Sleeping Bear Pr.

—The Seattle Puzzle. 2007. (Boxcar Children Ser.: No. 111). (ENG.). 128p. (J). (gr. 2-5). lib. bdg. 14.99 *(978-0-8075-5560-6(6))*; per. 4.99 *(978-0-8075-5561-3(4))* Whitman, Albert & Co.

—The Secret of the Mask. 2007. (Boxcar Children Ser.: No. 110). (ENG.). 128p. (J). (gr. 2-5). lib. bdg. 14.99 *(978-0-8075-5564-4(9))*; per. 4.99 *(978-0-8075-5565-1(7))* Whitman, Albert & Co.

—Spooktacular Special. 2013. (Boxcar Children Mysteries Ser.). (ENG.). 368p. (J). (gr. 2-5). 9.99 *(978-0-8075-7605-2(0))* Whitman, Albert & Co.

—The Spy Game. 2009. (Boxcar Children Mysteries Ser.). (ENG.). 128p. (J). (gr. 2-5). pap. 4.99 *(978-0-8075-7604-5(2))* Whitman, Albert & Co.

—The Spy in the Bleachers. 2010. (Boxcar Children Mysteries Ser.). (ENG.). 128p. (J). (gr. 2-5). 14.99 *(978-0-8075-7606-9(9))*;No. 122. pap. 4.99 *(978-0-8075-7607-6(7))* Whitman, Albert & Co.

—The Sword of the Silver Knight. 2005. (Boxcar Children Ser.: No. 103). (ENG.). 128p. (J). (gr. 2-5). per. 4.99 *(978-0-8075-0876-3(4))* Whitman, Albert & Co.

—Titanicat. Crisp, Marty. 2008. (ENG.). 40p. (J). (gr. k-6). 17.95 *(978-1-58536-355-1(3))* Sleeping Bear Pr.

—The Vanishing Passenger. 2006. (Boxcar Children Ser.: No. 106). (ENG.). 128p. (J). (gr. 2-5). 14.99 *(978-0-8075-1066-7(1))* Whitman, Albert & Co.

—The Zombie Project. 2011. (Boxcar Children Mysteries Ser.: No. 128). (ENG.). 128p. (J). (gr. 2-5). 4.99 *(978-0-8075-9493-3(8))*; lib. bdg. 14.99 *(978-0-8075-9492-6(X))* Whitman, Albert & Co.

Papp, Robert & Papp, Kathy. The Pumpkin Head Mystery. 2010. (Boxcar Children Mysteries Ser.). (ENG.). 128p. (J). (gr. 2-5). 14.99 *(978-0-8075-6668-8(3))* Whitman, Albert & Co.

Papp, Robert & Papp, Lisa. P Is for Princess: A Royal Alphabet. Layne, Deborah & Layne, Steven. rev. ed. 2007. (ENG.). 40p. (J). (gr. k-6). 17.95 *(978-1-58536-306-3(5))* Sleeping Bear Pr.

Papp, Robert, jt. illus. see Papp, Lisa.

Papp, Robert L. The Dog-Gone Mystery. 2009. (Boxcar Children Mysteries Ser.). (ENG.). 128p. (J). (gr. 2-5). lib. bdg. 14.99 *(978-0-8075-1658-4(9))*; pap. 5.99 *(978-0-8075-1657-7(0))* Whitman, Albert & Co.

—The Spy Game. 2009. (Boxcar Children Mysteries Ser.). (ENG.). 128p. (J). (gr. 2-5). 14.99 *(978-0-8075-7603-8(4))* Whitman, Albert & Co.

—Superstar Watch. 2009. (Boxcar Children Mysteries Ser.). (ENG.). 128p. (J). (gr. 2-5). pap. 4.99 *(978-0-8075-7668-7(9))*; lib. bdg. 14.99 *(978-0-8075-7667-0(0))* Whitman, Albert & Co.

—The Vampire Mystery. 2009. (Boxcar Children Mysteries Ser.). (ENG.). 128p. (J). (gr. 2-5). pap. 4.99 *(978-0-8075-8461-3(4))*; lib. bdg. 14.99 *(978-0-8075-8460-6(6))* Whitman, Albert & Co.

Paprocki, Greg. Curious George's Big Book of Curiosity. Rey, H. A. & Rey, Margret. 2005. (Curious George Ser.). (ENG.). 48p. (J). (gr. -1-3). 11.99 *(978-0-618-58338-6(6))* Houghton Mifflin Harcourt Publishing Co.

—Math-Terpieces: The Art of Problem-Solving. Tang, Greg. 2003. (ENG.). 32p. (J). (gr. 2-5). 18.99 *(978-0-439-44388-3(1))* Scholastic, Inc.

Paprocki, Greg. Storyland: the Marvelous Mccrittersons — Road Trip to Grandma's: A Story Coloring Book. Paprocki, Beth. 2015. (ENG.). 32p. (J). (gr. k-5). pap. 3.99 ***(978-0-486-79383-2(4))*** Dover Pubns., Inc.

Paprocki, Greg & Hines, Anna Grossnickle. Curious George & Me! Perez, Monica & Houghton Mifflin Company Editors. 2007. (Curious George Ser.). (ENG.). 56p. (J). (gr. -1-3). 9.95 *(978-0-618-73762-8(6))* Houghton Mifflin Harcourt Publishing Co.

Paprocki, Greg, jt. illus. see Anderson, Derek.

Paquette Jr., Edward D. Kammy the Chameleon Goes to School. Paquette, Heather. 2012. 24p. pap. 24.95 *(978-1-62709-765-9(1))* America Star Bks.

Paquin, Pauline. Carry Me Mama, 1 vol. Devine, Monica. 2005. (ENG.). 32p. (J). pap. 9.95 *(978-1-55005-150-6(4)*, 1550051504) Fitzhenry & Whiteside, Ltd. CAN. Dist: Midpoint Trade Bks., Inc.

Paramonova, Lea. Princess Charming. Wildsmith, Sarah. 2013. 32p. pap. 14.99 *(978-1-62380-970-6(3)*, Harmony Ink Pr.) Dreamspinner Pr.

Paraschiv, Doina. Christopher's Adventures: A Prayer on Angel Wings. Parr, Susan Sherwood. 2004. (ENG.). 16p. 10.95 *(978-0-9728590-3-5(9)*, KID-E Bks.) Word Prodns.

—Christopher's Adventures: Chris Visits the Hospital, Vol. 2. Parr, Susan Sherwood. 2nd alt. ed. 2013. (ENG.). 24p. (J). pap. 8.95 *(978-0-9827998-8-8(8)*, KID-E Bks.) Word Prodns.

Paraskevas, Michael. On My Way to Bed. Maizes, Sarah. 2013. (ENG.). 40p. (J). (gr. -1-1). 16.99 *(978-0-8027-2366-6(7))*; lib. bdg. 17.89 *(978-0-8027-2367-3(5))* Walker & Co.

—On My Way to School. Maizes, Sarah. 2014. (ENG.). 40p. (J). (gr. -1-1). 16.99 *(978-0-8027-3700-7(5))* Walker & Co.

—On My Way to the Bath. Maizes, Sarah. (ENG.). (J). (gr. -1-1). 2014. 32p. bds. 7.99 *(978-0-8027-3734-2(X))*; 2012. 40p. lib. bdg. 16.89 *(978-0-8027-2365-9(9))*; 2012. 40p. 15.99 *(978-0-8027-2364-2(0))* Walker & Co.

—Peter Pepper's Pet Spectacular. Paraskevas, Betty. 2007. 32p. (J). (gr. 2-6). pap. 14.95 *(978-1-60095-257-9(7))* Carson-Dellosa Publishing, LLC.

Parathian, Hannah. Peppy - a Long Way from Home. Hevesi, Rachel. 2008. 48p. pap. *(978-1-906210-76-2(4))* Grosvenor Hse. Publishing Ltd.

Pardo DeLange, Alex. Pepita & the Bully: Pepita y la Peleonera. Lachtman, Ofelia Dumas. Baeza Ventura, Gabriela, tr. 2011. (SPA & ENG.). 32p. (J). (gr. -1-3). 16.95 *(978-1-55885-689-9(7)*, Piñata Books) Arte Publico Pr.

P

Parekh, Rikin. The Beekeeper. Morgan, Bernard. Emecz, Steve, ed. 2007. 28p. per. (978-1-904312-26-0(8)) MX Publishing, Ltd.

—Pszczelarz. Morgan, Bernard P. Juraszek, Barbara, tr. 2008. 28p. pap. (978-1-904312-44-4(6)) MX Publishing, Ltd.

Parent, Dan. Archie Meets Glee. Aguirre-Sacasa, Roberto. 2013. (Archie & Friends All-Stars Ser.: 20). (ENG.). 112p. (gr. 5). pap. 12.99 (978-1-936975-45-7(9), Archie Comics) Archie Comic Pubns., Inc.

Parent, Lauren. I'm Different but I'm Special. Parent, Lauren. l.t. ed. 2006. 21p. (J). (gr. -1-3). per. 10.99 (978-1-59879-259-1(8)) Lifevest Publishing, Inc.

Parett, Lisa. The Girls' Life Guide to Being a Style Superstar! Lundsten, Apryl. 2004. 124p. (J). (978-0-439-44984-7(7)) Scholastic, Inc.

—The Girls' Life Guide to Being the Best You! White, Kelly. 2003. 124p. (J). (978-0-439-44978-6(2)) Scholastic, Inc.

Paris, Pat. Jesus Walks Away. Carolyn, Berg. 2003. (Arch Bks.). 16p. (J). 2.49 (978-0-7586-0504-7(8)) Concordia Publishing Hse.

—A Meal for Many: My Gift for Jesus. Rottmann, Erik. 2003. (Arch Bks.). (ENG.). 16p. (J). (gr. k-4). 1.99 (978-0-7586-0377-7(0)) Concordia Publishing Hse.

Parish, Herman & Sweat, Lynn. Amelia Bedelia Talks Turkey. Parish, Herman. 2008. (Amelia Bedelia Ser.). 64p. (J). (gr. k-4). lib. bdg. 17.89 (978-0-06-084353-3(5), Greenwillow Bks.) HarperCollins Pubs.

Parish, Shannon. The Best Belcher. Medlyn, Lynda Lee & Staudenmier, Kelley Anne. 2008. (ENG.). 32p. (J). (gr. k-2). lib. bdg. (978-0-9793738-0-0(8)) Window Box Pr. LLC.

—The Monster Solution. Zimet, Sara Goodman. 2005. 32p. (J). 16.95 (978-0-9645159-1-8(1), 1245168) Discovery Pr. Pubns., Inc.

Parish, Steve. Clown Fish Finds a Friend. Johnson, Rebecca. 2005. (Animal Storybooks Ser.). 24p. (gr. k-3). lib. bdg. 22.00 (978-0-8368-5969-0(3), Gareth Stevens Learning Library) Stevens, Gareth Publishing LLLP.

—The Cranky Crocodile. Johnson, Rebecca. 2005. (Animal Storybooks Ser.). 24p. (gr. k-3). lib. bdg. 22.00 (978-0-8368-5970-6(7), Gareth Stevens Learning Library) Stevens, Gareth Publishing LLLP.

—The Kangaroos' Great Escape. 2005. (Animal Storybooks Ser.). 24p. (gr. k-3). lib. bdg. 22.00 (978-0-8368-5971-3(5), Gareth Stevens Learning Library) Stevens, Gareth Publishing LLLP.

—Little Dolphin's Big Leap. Johnson, Rebecca. 2005. (Animal Storybooks Ser.). 24p. (gr. k-3). lib. bdg. 22.00 (978-0-8368-5973-7(1), Gareth Stevens Learning Library) Stevens, Gareth Publishing LLLP.

—The Proud Pelican's Secret. Johnson, Rebecca. 2005. (Animal Storybooks Ser.). 24p. (gr. k-3). lib. bdg. 22.00 (978-0-8368-5974-4(X), Gareth Stevens Learning Library) Stevens, Gareth Publishing LLLP.

—Sea Turtle's Clever Plan. Johnson, Rebecca. 2005. (Animal Storybooks Ser.). 24p. (gr. k-3). lib. bdg. 22.00 (978-0-8368-5975-1(8), Gareth Stevens Learning Library) Stevens, Gareth Publishing LLLP.

—Tree Frog Hears a Sound. Johnson, Rebecca. 2005. (Animal Storybooks Ser.). 24p. (gr. k-3). lib. bdg. 22.00 (978-0-8368-5976-8(6), Gareth Stevens Learning Library) Stevens, Gareth Publishing LLLP.

Parisi, Anthony. Monster for President. Pollock, Hal. 2008. 28p. 14.95 (978-0-9816554-1-3(6)) Esquire Publishing, Inc.

Park, Andy. The Fairies of Bladderwhack Pond. Bishop, Debbie. 2003. (Fairies of Bladderwhack Pond Ser.: Vol. 1). (ENG.). 152p. (J). (gr. 4-9). 19.99 (978-1-932431-01-8(2)) Left Field,Angel Gate.

Park, Clare, photos by. Yoga for Kids. Lark, Liz. 2005. 127p. (J). reprint ed. pap. 20.00 (978-0-7567-9410-1(2)) DIANE Publishing Co.

Park, Darcie. S Is for Silver: A Nevada Alphabet. Coerr, Eleanor. 2004. (State Ser.). (ENG.). 40p. (J). 17.95 (978-1-58536-117-5(8)) Sleeping Bear Pr.

Park, Hye-Jin. Chronicles of the Cursed Sword, 10 vols. Yuy, Beub-Ryong. 2003.Tr. of Pa Keum Gee. 176p. (gr. 8-18). Vol. 1. pap. 9.99 (978-1-59182-254-7(8)); Vol. 2. pap. 9.99 (978-1-59182-255-4(6)); Vol. 3. pap. 9.99 (978-1-59182-256-1(4)) TOKYOPOP, Inc.

Park, Hyeondo. My Boyfriend Is a Monster - Under His Spell. Croall, Marie P. 2011. (My Boyfriend Is a Monster Ser.: 4). (ENG.). 128p. (YA). (gr. 7-12). pap. 9.95 (978-0-7613-7076-5(5), Graphic Universe) Lerner Publishing Group.

—Under His Spell, 4 vols., No. 4. Croall, Marie P. 2011. (My Boyfriend Is a Monster Ser.: 4). (ENG.). 128p. (YA). (gr. 7-12). 29.27 (978-0-7613-5602-8(9)) Lerner Publishing Group.

—Veda: Assembly Required. Teer, Samuel. 2015. (ENG.). 144p. pap. 14.99 (978-1-61655-497-2(5)) Dark Horse Comics.

Park, Janie Jaehyun. Count Your Way Through Zimbabwe. Haskins, Jim & Benson, Kathleen. 2006. (Count Your Way Ser.). (ENG.). 24p. (gr. 2-5). lib. bdg. 19.93 (978-1-57505-885-6(5), Millbrook Pr.) Lerner Publishing Group.

Park, Julie. Deedee's Easter Surprise. Kinnear, Kay. 2003. 25p. (J). pap. 9.99 (978-0-7459-4443-2(4), Lion Books) Lion Hudson PLC GBR. Dist: Trafalgar Square Publishing.

Park, Jung-a, jt. illus. see Gwangjo.

Park, Kathy. Clara's Red Balloon. Lee, Jc. 2011. 40p. pap. 24.95 (978-1-4560-2491-8(4)) America Star Bks.

Park, Keun. The Three Pig Sisters. Kim, Cecil. 2015. (MySELF Bookshelf Ser.). (ENG.). 32p. (J). (gr. k-2). pap. 11.94 (978-1-60357-689-5(4)); lib. bdg. 22.60 (978-1-59953-654-5(4)) Norwood Hse. Pr.

Park, Laura. Get Me Out of Here! Patterson, James & Tebbetts, Chris. 2012. (Middle School Ser.: 2). (ENG.). 288p. (J). (gr. 3-7). 15.99 (978-0-316-20671-6(7)) Little Brown & Co.

—How I Survived Bullies, Broccoli, & Snake Hill. Patterson, James & Tebbetts, Chris. 2013. (Middle School Ser.: 4). (ENG.). 336p. (J). (gr. 3-7). 14.00 (978-0-316-23175-6(4)) Little Brown & Co.

—I Even Funnier: A Middle School Story. Patterson, James & Grabenstein, Chris. 2013. (I Funny Ser.: 2). (ENG.). 368p. (J). (gr. 3-7). 13.99 (978-0-316-20697-6(0)) Little Brown & Co.

—I Funny: A Middle School Story. Patterson, James & Grabenstein, Chris. (I Funny Ser.: 1). (ENG.). 320p. (J). (gr. 3-7). 2015. pap. 8.00 (978-0-316-20692-1(X)); 2013. 13.99 (978-0-316-32200-3(8)) Little Brown & Co.

—I Funny: A Middle School Story. Grabenstein, Chris. Patterson, James, ed. 2012. 303p. (J). 11.99 (978-0-316-22638-7(6), 1351607) Little Brown & Co.

—I Funny: A Middle School Story. Grabenstein, Chris & Patterson, James. 2012. (I Funny Ser.: 1). (ENG.). 320p. (J). (gr. 3-7). 15.99 (978-0-316-20693-8(8)) Little Brown & Co.

—I Totally Funniest: A Middle School Story. Patterson, James & Grabenstein, Chris. 2015. (I Funny Ser.). (ENG.). 336p. (J). (gr. 3-7). 13.99 (978-0-316-40593-5(0)) Little Brown & Co.

Park, Laura. Just My Rotten Luck. Patterson, James & Tebbetts, Chris. 2015. (Middle School Ser.: 7). (ENG.). 320p. (J). (gr. 3-7). 13.99 **(978-0-316-28477-6(7))** Little Brown & Co.

Park, Laura. Save Rafe! Patterson, James & Tebbetts, Chris. 2014. (Middle School Ser.: 6). (ENG.). 288p. (J). (gr. 3-7). 13.99 (978-0-316-32212-6(1)) Little Brown & Co.

—Save Rafe! Patterson, James & Tebbetts, Christopher. 2014. 269p. (J). (978-0-316-28629-9(X)) Little Brown & Co.

—The Worst Years of My Life. Patterson, James & Tebbetts, Chris. (Middle School Ser.: Bk. 1). (ENG.). (J). (gr. 3-7). 2014. 320p. 13.99 (978-0-316-32202-7(4)); 2013. pap. 0.01 (978-0-316-25251-5(4)); 2012. 336p. pap. 8.00 (978-0-316-10169-1(9)) Little Brown & Co.

—The Worst Years of My Life. Patterson, James & Tebbetts, Chris. 2011. (Middle School Ser.: 1). (ENG.). 288p. (J). (gr. 3-7). 15.99 (978-0-316-10187-5(7)) Little, Brown Bks. for Young Readers.

—The Worst Years of My Life. Patterson, James & Tebbetts, Chris. ed. 2012. (Middle School Ser.: 1). lib. bdg. 18.45 (978-0-606-26164-7(8), Turtleback) Turtleback Bks.

Park, Laura & Swaab, Neil. The Middle School Set: The Worst Years of My Life; Get Me Out of Here!; My Brother Is a Big, Fat Liar; How I Survived Bullies, Broccoli & Snake Hill. Patterson, James et al. 2013. (ENG.). 1184p. (J). (gr. 3-7). 60.00 (978-0-316-25091-7(0)) Little Brown & Co.

Park, Meg. Anna, Banana, & the Big-Mouth Bet. Rissi, Anica Mrose. 2015. (J). pap. (978-1-4814-1612-2(X), Simon & Schuster Bks. For Young Readers) Simon & Schuster Bks. For Young Readers.

—Anna, Banana, & the Friendship Split. Rissi, Anica Mrose. 2015. (Anna, Banana Ser.: 1). (ENG.). 128p. (J). (gr. 1-5). 15.99 (978-1-4814-1605-4(7), Simon & Schuster Bks. For Young Readers) Simon & Schuster Bks. For Young Readers.

—Anna, Banana, & the Monkey in the Middle. Rissi, Anica Mrose. 2015. (Anna, Banana Ser.: 2). (ENG.). 128p. (J). (gr. 1-5). 15.99 (978-1-4814-1608-5(1), Simon & Schuster Bks. For Young Readers) Simon & Schuster Bks. For Young Readers.

Park, Meg. Anna, Banana, & the Puppy Parade. Rissi, Anica Mrose. 2016. (J). pap. **(978-1-4814-1615-3(4)**, Simon & Schuster Bks. For Young Readers) Simon & Schuster Bks. For Young Readers.

Park, Mi-Ok. Booyoung & Sea Turtle's Adventure: God's Creatures' Adventures Series 1. Roh, Grace S. 2013. 52p. pap. 17.50 (978-1-62212-718-4(8), Strategic Bk. Publishing) Strategic Book Publishing & Rights Agency (SBPRA).

Park, Min-Seo. Blazin' Barrels. Park, Min-Seo. 192p. rev. ed. 2005. (Blazin' Barrels Ser.: Vol. 3). per. 9.99 (978-1-59532-560-0(3)); Vol. 2. 2nd rev. ed. 2005. pap. 9.99 (978-1-59532-559-4(X)); Vol. 4. 4th rev. ed. 2006. (Blazin' Barrels Ser.). per. 9.99 (978-1-59532-561-7(1)) TOKYOPOP, Inc.

Park, Sang-Sun. Les Bijoux, 6 vols. Jo, Eun-Ha. 2004. 200p. Vol. 4. 4th rev. ed. pap. 14.99 (978-1-59182-693-4(4)); Vol. 5. 5th rev. ed. pap. 14.99 (978-1-59182-694-1(2)) TOKYOPOP, Inc. (Tokyopop Adult).

Park, Sarah. The Modern Age Vol. 4: From Victoria's Empire to the End of the USSR. Bauer, Susan Wise. 2005. (Story of the World Ser.: Vol. 4). (ENG.). 503p. (gr. 4-8). per. 16.95 (978-0-9728603-3-8(9), 86033) Peace Hill Pr.

Park, Seung-bum. Mother to the Poor: The Life of Blessed Teresa of Calcutta. Ko, Jung-wook. 2008. Orig. Title: Mongdangyeonpili Doen Mother Teresa. (KOR.). (J). (gr. 3-5). pap. 14.95 (978-0-8198-4863-5(8)) Pauline Bks. & Media.

Park, Soyoo H. Look What We've Brought You from Korea: Crafts, Games, Recipes, Stories & Other Cultural Activities from Korean-Americans. Shalant, Phyllis. (J). (gr. 2-18). pap. 7.95 (978-0-382-24994-5(1)) Silver, Burdett & Ginn, Inc.

Park, Sung-Woo. Peigenz, 8 vols. Oh Rhe Bar Ghun. (Peigenz Ser.: Vol. 2). (YA). Vol. 2. 2004. 192p. per. 9.95 (978-1-59697-022-9(7)); Vol. 3. 2004. 176p. per. 9.95 (978-1-59697-023-6(5)); Vol. 4. 2005. 176p. per. 9.95 (978-1-59697-024-3(3)); Vol. 5. 2005. 176p. per. 9.95 (978-1-59697-025-0(1)); Vol. 6. 2006. 176p. per. 9.95 (978-1-59697-026-7(X)); Vol. 7. 2006. 176p. per. 9.95 (978-1-59697-027-4(8)); Vol. 8. 2006. 192p. per. 9.95 (978-1-59697-028-1(6)) Infinity Studios LLC.

—Zero, 10 vols. Ihm, Dar-Young. (Zero Ser.: Vol. 5). (YA). Vol. 5. 2007. 204p. per. 9.95 (978-1-59697-035-9(9)); Vol. 6. 2007. 204p. per. 9.95 (978-1-59697-036-6(7)); Vol. 7. 2007. 204p. per. 9.95 (978-1-59697-037-3(5)); Vol. 8. 2008. 204p. per. 9.95 (978-1-59697-038-0(3)); Vol. 9. 2008. 204p. per. 9.95 (978-1-59697-039-7(1)); Vol. 10. 2008. 230p. per. 9.95 (978-1-59697-040-3(5)) Infinity Studios LLC.

Park, Sung-Woo. Now. Park, Sung-Woo. 2006. (NOW Ser.: Vol. 5). 217p. Vol. 5. (YA). per. 9.95 (978-1-59697-185-1(1)); Vol. 7. (YA). per. 9.95 (978-1-59697-187-5(8)); Vol. 8. (YA). per. 9.95 (978-1-59697-188-2(6)); Vol. 9. per. 9.95 (978-1-59697-189-9(4)) Infinity Studios LLC.

Park, Trip. Ant, Ant, Ant! An Insect Chant. Sayre, April Pulley. 2005. (American City Ser.). (ENG.). 32p. (J). (gr. k-3). 15.95 (978-1-55971-922-3(2)) Cooper Square Publishing Llc.

—Battle of the Dum Diddys. Stine, R. L. 2007. (Rotten School Ser.: 12). (ENG.). 128p. (J). (gr. 3-7). 12.99 (978-0-06-078833-9(X)) HarperCollins Pubs.

—Battle of the Dum Diddys. Stine, R. L. 2011. (Rotten School Ser.: No. 12). 128p. (gr. 2-5). 24.21 (978-1-59961-836-4(2)) Spotlight.

—The Big Blueberry Barf-Off! Stine, R. L. 2005. (Rotten School Ser.: No. 1). 128p. (J). (ENG.). 6.99 (978-0-06-078586-4(1)); lib. bdg. 14.89 (978-0-06-078587-1(X)) HarperCollins Pubs.

—The Big Blueberry Barf-Off! Stine, R. L. 2011. (Rotten School Ser.: No. 1). 128p. (gr. 2-5). 24.21 (978-1-59961-825-8(7)) Spotlight.

—The Big Blueberry Barf-Off! Stine, R. L. 2008. (Rotten School Ser.: 1). (ENG.). 128p. (J). (gr. 3-7). pap. 5.99 (978-0-06-078588-8(8)) HarperCollins Pubs.

—Calling All Birdbrains. Stine, R. L. 2007. (Rotten School Ser.: No. 15). (ENG.). 128p. (J). (gr. 3-7). 6.99 (978-0-06-123275-6(0)) HarperCollins Pubs.

—Dudes, the School Is Haunted! Stine, R. L. 2011. (Rotten School Ser.: No. 7). 128p. (gr. 2-5). 24.21 (978-1-59961-831-9(1)) Spotlight.

—Dumb Clucks. Stine, R. L. 2008. (Rotten School Ser.: 16). (ENG.). 128p. (J). (gr. 3-7). 6.99 (978-0-06-123278-7(5)) HarperCollins Pubs.

—The Good, the Bad & the Very Slimy. Stine, R. L. 2008. (Rotten School Ser.: 3). (ENG.). 128p. (J). (gr. 3-7). pap. 5.99 (978-0-06-078594-9(2)) HarperCollins Pubs.

—The Good, the Bad & the Very Slimy. Stine, R. L. 2011. (Rotten School Ser.: No. 3). 128p. (gr. 2-5). 24.21 (978-1-59961-827-2(3)) Spotlight.

—Got Cake? Stine, R. L. 2007. (Rotten School Ser.: 13). (ENG.). 128p. (J). (gr. 3-7). 12.99 (978-0-06-123269-5(6)) HarperCollins Pubs.

—The Great Smelling Bee. Stine, R. L. 2008. (Rotten School Ser.: 2). (ENG.). 128p. (J). (gr. 3-7). pap. 5.99 (978-0-06-078591-8(8)) HarperCollins Pubs.

—The Great Smelling Bee. Stine, R. L. 2011. (Rotten School Ser.: No. 2). 128p. (gr. 2-5). 24.21 (978-1-59961-826-5(5)) Spotlight.

—The Heinie Prize. Stine, R. L. 2006. (Rotten School Ser.: No. 6). 128p. (J). pap. 4.99 (978-0-06-078816-2(X), Harper Trophy) HarperCollins Pubs.

—The Heinie Prize. Stine, R. L. 2011. (Rotten School Ser.: No. 6). 128p. (gr. 2-5). 24.21 (978-1-59961-830-2(3)) Spotlight.

—Lose, Team, Lose! Stine, R. L. 2008. (Rotten School Ser.: 4). (ENG.). 128p. (J). (gr. 3-7). pap. 5.99 (978-0-06-078810-0(0)) HarperCollins Pubs.

—Lose, Team, Lose! Stine, R. L. 2011. (Rotten School Ser.: No. 4). 128p. (gr. 2-5). 24.21 (978-1-59961-828-9(1)) Spotlight.

—Night of the Creepy Things. Stine, R. L. (Rotten School Ser.: Bk. 14). 4.99 (978-0-06-123274-9(2)) HarperCollins Pubs.

—Party Poopers. Stine, R. L. (Rotten School Ser.: Bk. 9). 4.99 (978-0-06-078826-1(7)) HarperCollins Pubs.

—Party Poopers. Stine, R. L. 2011. (Rotten School Ser.: No. 9). 128p. (gr. 2-5). 24.21 (978-1-59961-833-3(8)) Spotlight.

—Punk'd & Skunked. Stine, R. L. 2011. (Rotten School Ser.: No. 11). 128p. (gr. 2-5). 24.21 (978-1-59961-835-7(4)) Spotlight.

—Punk'd & Skunked. Stine, R. L. 2007. (Rotten School Ser.: 11). (ENG.). 128p. (J). (gr. 3-7). 6.99 (978-0-06-078830-8(5)) HarperCollins Pubs.

—Rotten School - Dudes, the School Is Haunted! Stine, R. L. 2009. (Rotten School Ser.: No. 7). 128p. (J). pap. 4.99 (978-0-06-078820-9(8), Harper Trophy) HarperCollins Pubs.

—Rotten School #12: Battle of the Dum Diddys. Stine, R. L. 4.99 (978-0-06-078835-3(6)) HarperCollins Pubs.

—Rotten School #15: Calling All Birdbrains. Stine, R. L. 4.99 (978-0-06-123277-0(7)) HarperCollins Pubs.

—Rotten School #16: Dumb Clucks. Stine, R. L. 4.99 (978-0-06-123280-0(7)) HarperCollins Pubs.

—The Rottenest Angel. Stine, R. L. (Rotten School Ser.: Bk. 10). 4.99 (978-0-06-078829-2(1)) HarperCollins Pubs.

—The Rottenest Angel. Stine, R. L. 2011. (Rotten School Ser.: No. 10). 128p. (gr. 2-5). 24.21 (978-1-59961-834-0(6)) Spotlight.

—The Rottenest Angel. Stine, R. L. 2006. (Rotten School Ser.: 10). (ENG.). 128p. (J). (gr. 3-7). 6.99 (978-0-06-078827-8(5)) HarperCollins Pubs.

—Shake, Rattle, & Hurl! Stine, R. L. 2006. (Rotten School Ser.: No. 5). (ENG.). 128p. (J). (gr. 3-7). 6.99 (978-0-06-078811-7(9)) HarperCollins Pubs.

—Shake, Rattle, & Hurl! Stine, R. L. 2008. (Rotten School Ser.: 5). (ENG.). 128p. (J). (gr. 3-7). pap. 5.99 (978-0-06-078813-1(5)) HarperCollins Pubs.

—Shake, Rattle, & Hurl! Stine, R. L. 2011. (Rotten School Ser.: No. 5). 128p. (gr. 2-5). 24.21 (978-1-59961-829-6(X)) Spotlight.

—The Teacher from Heck. Stine, R. L. 2009. (Rotten School Ser.: No. 8). 128p. (J). pap. 4.99 (978-0-06-078823-0(2), Harper Trophy) HarperCollins Pubs.

—The Teacher from Heck. Stine, R. L. 2011. (Rotten School Ser.: No. 8). 128p. (gr. 2-5). 24.21 (978-1-59961-832-6(X)) Spotlight.

—Trout, Trout, Trout: (A Fish Chant) Sayre, April Pulley. 2007. (American City Ser.). (ENG.). 32p. (J). (gr. k-3). pap. 8.95 (978-1-55971-979-7(6)) Cooper Square Publishing Llc.

Park, Yeong-jin. What Lives in the Sea? Marine Life. Gam Do, Rin Bo. Cowley, Joy, ed. 2015. (Science Storybooks Ser.). (ENG.). 32p. (gr. k-3). 7.99 **(978-1-925246-77-3(9)**, Big and SMALL) ChoiceMaker Pty. Ltd., The AUS. Dist: Lerner Publishing Group.

—What Lives in the Sea? Marine Life. Gam Do, Rin Bo. Cowley, Joy, ed. 2015. (Science Storybooks Ser.). (ENG.). 32p. (gr. k-3). 26.65 **(978-1-925246-51-3(5)**, Big and SMALL) ChoiceMaker Pty. Ltd., The AUS. Dist: Lerner Publishing Group.

—What Lives in the Sea? Marine Life. Gam Do, Rin Bo. Cowley, Joy, ed. 2015. (Science Storybooks Ser.). (ENG.). 32p. (gr. k-3). 26.65 **(978-1-925246-25-4(6)**, Big and SMALL) ChoiceMaker Pty. Ltd., The AUS. Dist: Lerner Publishing Group.

Parke, Steven. Medusa's Daughter. Fuqua, Jonathon Scott. 2012. (YA). (978-0-9745645-8-6(3)) Active Media Publishing, LLC.

Parker, Andy. House that Jack Built. Goodhart, Pippa. 2004. (ENG.). 24p. (J). lib. bdg. 23.65 (978-1-59646-700-2(2)) Dingles & Co.

—Mekanimals Clockwork Safari. 2004. 8p. (J). bds. 12.95 (978-1-59223-145-4(4), Silver Dolphin Bks.) Baker & Taylor Publishing Group.

—Mekanimals Cyber Bugs. 2004. 8p. (J). bds. 12.95 (978-1-59223-146-1(2), Silver Dolphin Bks.) Baker & Taylor Publishing Group.

Parker, Ant. The Amazing Machines - Truckload of Fun, 10 bks., Set. Mitton, Tony. 2007. (Amazing Machines Ser.). (ENG.). 24p. (J). (gr. -1-k). 24.99 (978-0-7534-6154-9(4), Kingfisher) Roaring Brook Pr.

—Charlie Chick, 1. Denchfield, Nick. ed. 2014. (Charlie Chick Ser.). (ENG.). 400p. (J). 12.99 (978-1-4472-5764-6(2)) Pan Macmillan GBR. Dist: Independent Pubs. Group.

—Forest Adventure. Mitton, Tony. 2015. (Amazing Animals Ser.). (ENG.). 24p. (J). (gr. -1-1). pap. 4.99 (978-0-7534-7229-3(5), Kingfisher) Roaring Brook Pr.

—Muddle Builders: A Magnetic Play Book. 2011. (Muddle Bks.). (ENG.). 8p. (J). (gr. -1-2). 10.99 (978-0-7641-6423-1(6)) Barron's Educational Series, Inc.

—Penelope the Piglet. Denchfield, Nick. ed. 2008. (ENG.). 16p. (J). (gr. 2-5). bds. 13.95 (978-0-230-01615-6(4), Macmillan) Pan Macmillan GBR. Dist: Trans-Atlantic Pubns., Inc.

—Sherman Swaps Shells. Clarke, Jane. 2003. (Flying Foxes Ser.). (ENG.). 48p. (J). lib. bdg. (978-0-7787-1485-9(3)) Crabtree Publishing Co.

—Who Eats? Lewis, Edwina. 2003. (Who... Ser.). 16p. (YA). (978-1-85602-470-9(9), Pavilion Children's Books) Pavilion Bks.

—Who Jumps? Lewis, Edwina. 2003. (Who... Ser.). 16p. (YA). (978-1-85602-447-1(4), Pavilion Children's Books) Pavilion Bks.

—Who Plays? Lewis, Edwina. 2003. (Who... Ser.). 16p. (J). (978-1-85602-469-3(5), Pavilion Children's Books) Pavilion Bks.

—Who Swims? Lewis, Edwina. 2003. (Who... Ser.). 16p. (YA). (978-1-85602-448-8(2), Pavilion Children's Books) Pavilion Bks.

Parker, Buzz, jt. illus. see Ivie, Emily.

Parker, Buzz, jt. illus. see Reger, Rob.

Parker, Curtis. DreddieLocks & the Three Slugs. Hyde, Margaret E. 2003. 36p. (J). lib. bdg. 16.95 (978-1-888108-07-1(X)) Budding Artists, Inc.

—Dreddielocks & the Three Slugs, 1 vol. Hyde, Margaret, ed. 2003. (ENG.). 36p. (J). (gr. k-3). 17.99 (978-1-58980-231-5(4)) Pelican Publishing Co., Inc.

Parker, David. Csi Expert! Forensic Science for Kids. Schulz, Karen K. 2008. (ENG.). 160p. (gr. 5-8). pap. 19.95 (978-1-59363-312-7(2)) Prufrock Pr.

Parker, Edward, photos by. Istanbul. Bowden, Rob. 2007. (Global Cities Ser.). 64p. (gr. 5-8). lib. bdg. 30.00 (978-0-7910-8850-0(2), Chelsea Hse.) Facts On File, Inc.

—Rio de Janeiro. Scoones, Simon. 2006. (Global Cities Ser.). 61p. (gr. 5-8). 30.00 (978-0-7910-8857-9(X), Chelsea Hse.) Facts On File, Inc.

Parker, Edward, photos by. Mexico City. Parker, Edward. 2006. (Global Cities Ser.). 64p. (gr. 5-8). 30.00 (978-0-7910-8854-8(5), Chelsea Hse.) Facts On File, Inc.

Parker, Gretel. Pinwheel Days, 1 vol. Tarlow, Ellen. 2007. (ENG.). 32p. (J). (gr. -1-3). pap. 6.95 (978-1-59572-059-7(6)) Star Bright Bks., Inc.

Parker, Jack. Ernie the Ermine. Patterson, Horace. 2007. 28p. per. 7.99 (978-1-58942-374-9(7)) R.H. Boyd Publishing Corp.

Parker, Jake. Apple ABC. McNamara, Margaret. 2012. (J). (978-0-439-72809-6(6)) Scholastic, Inc.

—Apples A to Z. McNamara, Margaret. 2012. (ENG.). 40p. (J). (gr. -1-k). 17.99 (978-0-439-72808-9(8)) Scholastic, Inc.

—The Astonishing Secret of Awesome Man. Chabon, Michael. 2011. (ENG.). 40p. (J). (gr. -1-3). 17.99 (978-0-06-191462-1(2)) HarperCollins Pubs.

—The Girl Who Wouldn't Brush Her Hair. Bernheimer, Kate. 2013. (ENG.). 40p. (J). (gr. -1-3). 17.99 (978-0-375-86878-8(X), Schwartz & Wade Bks.) Random Hse. Children's Bks.

—The Tooth Fairy Wars. Coombs, Kate. 2014. (ENG.). 40p. (J). (gr. -1-3). 17.99 (978-1-4169-7915-9(8)) Simon & Schuster Children's Publishing.

Parker, Jeff. Wonderland, Vol. 1. Gage, Christos, Allie, Scott & Hahn, Sierra, eds. 2013. (ENG.). 144p. pap. 17.99 (978-1-61655-145-2(3)) Dark Horse Comics.

Parker, Laurie. It Really Said Christmas. 2003. (J). (978-0-9729615-0-9(X)) Parker, Laurie.

Parker, Laurie. It Really Said Christmas. Parker, Laurie. 2005. (J). pap. 17.95 (978-0-9772096-0-6(1)) Wild Hare Publishing.

Parker, Nancy Winslow. Who Will I Be? A Halloween Rebus Story. Neitzel, Shirley. 2005. 32p. (J). lib. bdg. 13.89 (978-0-06-056068-3(1)) HarperCollins Pubs.

Parker, Paul & Moor, Becka. Snakes. MacLaine, James. 2014. (Usborne Beginners Ser.). (ENG.). 32p. (J). (gr. 1-4). 4.99 (978-0-7945-2686-3(1), Usborne) EDC Publishing.

Parker-Rees, Guy. Ants in Your Pants! Jarman, Julia. 2011. (ENG.). 32p. (J). (gr. -1-k). pap. 10.99 *(978-1-4083-0525-6(9))* Hodder & Stoughton GBR. Dist: Independent Pubs. Group.

Parker-Rees, Guy. Are You My Daddy? Oliver, Ilanit. 2015. (ENG.). 12p. (J). (gr. -1-k). 8.99 ***(978-0-545-77558-8(2)***, Cartwheel Bks.) Scholastic, Inc.

Parker-Rees, Guy. Diggory Digger & the Dinosaurs. Bently, Peter. 2013. (ENG.). 32p. (J). (gr. -1-k). pap. 10.99 *(978-1-4052-6118-0(8))* Egmont Bks., Ltd. GBR. Dist: Independent Pubs. Group.

—Dinosaurumpus! Mitton, Tony. (ENG.). (J). (gr. -1-k). 2014. 30p. bds. 6.99 *(978-0-545-69480-3(9)*, Cartwheel Bks.); 2003. 32p. 16.99 *(978-0-439-39514-4(3)*, Orchard Bks.) Scholastic, Inc.

—Giraffes Can't Dance. Andreae, Giles. (J). (gr. -1-3). 2012. (ENG.). 32p. bds. 6.99 *(978-0-545-39255-6(1)*, Cartwheel Bks.); 2008. (ENG.). 9.99 *(978-0-545-09738-3(X))*; 2007. 24.95 incl. audio *(978-0-439-02733-5(0))* Scholastic, Inc.

—Giraffes Can't Dance. Andreae, Giles. unabr. ed. 2011. (J). (gr. -1-1). 29.95 *(978-0-439-02734-2(9))* Weston Woods Studios, Inc.

—Giraffes Can't Dance: Number Rumba. Andreae, Giles. 2014. (ENG.). 12p. (J). (gr. -1 — 1). bds. 7.99 *(978-0-545-63996-5(4)*, Cartwheel Bks.) Scholastic, Inc.

—K Is for Kissing a Cool Kangaroo. Andreae, Giles. 2009. (ENG.). 32p. (J). (gr. -1-3). pap. 6.99 *(978-0-439-53128-3(4)*, Scholastic Paperbacks) Scholastic, Inc.

—Never Ask a Dinosaur to Dinner. Edwards, Gareth. 2015. (ENG.). 32p. (J). (gr. -1-k). 17.99 *(978-0-545-81296-2(8)*, Scholastic Pr.) Scholastic, Inc.

—Playful Little Penguins. Mitton, Tony. 2007. (ENG.). 32p. (J). (gr. -1-1). 15.95 *(978-0-8027-9710-0(5))* Walker & Co.

—Thunderbelle's Song. Wallace, Karen. 2010. (Monster Mountain Ser.: 6). (ENG.). 32p. (J). (gr. k-2). pap. 6.99 *(978-1-84362-628-2(4))* Hodder & Stoughton GBR. Dist: Independent Pubs. Group.

Parker-Rees, Guy. Party Time with Littlebob & Plum. Parker-Rees, Guy. 2012. (Littlebob & Plum Ser.). (ENG.). 20p. (J). (gr. -1-k). 16.99 *(978-1-4083-0443-3(0))* Hodder & Stoughton GBR. Dist: Independent Pubs. Group.

Parker, Rick. Breaking Down, No. 2. Petrucha, Stefan. 2011. (Papercutz Slices Ser.: 2). (ENG.). 64p. (J). (gr. 5-12). 10.99 *(978-1-59707-245-8(1))* Papercutz.

—The Farting Dead. Petrucha, Stefan. 2013. (Papercutz Slices Ser.: 5). (ENG.). 64p. (J). (gr. 5-12). pap. 7.99 *(978-1-59707-453-7(5))* Papercutz.

—Harry Potty & the Deathly Boring. Petrucha, Stefan. 2010. (Papercutz Slices Ser.: 1). (ENG.). 64p. (J). (gr. 5-12). 10.99 *(978-1-59707-218-2(4))*; pap. 7.99 *(978-1-59707-217-5(6))* Papercutz.

—My Name Is Orange - Secret Agent Orange! Salicrup, Jim et al. 2012. (Annoying Orange Graphic Novels Ser.: 1). (ENG.). 64p. (J). (gr. 2-7). 10.99 *(978-1-59707-362-2(8))* Papercutz.

—Orange You Glad You're Not Me? Salicrup, Jim et al. 2013. (Annoying Orange Graphic Novels Ser.: 2). (ENG.). 64p. (J). (gr. 2-7). 10.99 *(978-1-59707-391-2(1))* Papercutz.

—Orange You Glad You're Not Me? No. 2. Salicrup, Jim et al. 2013. (Annoying Orange Graphic Novels Ser.: 2). (ENG.). 64p. (J). (gr. 2-7). pap. 6.99 *(978-1-59707-390-5(3))* Papercutz.

—Papercutz Slices #4: the Hunger Pains. Petrucha, Stefan. 2012. (Papercutz Slices Ser.: 4). (ENG.). 64p. (J). (gr. 5-12). 10.99 *(978-1-59707-313-4(X))* Papercutz.

—Papercutz Slices #5: the Farting Dead. Petrucha, Stefan. 2013. (Papercutz Slices Ser.: 5). (ENG.). 64p. (J). (gr. 5-12). 11.99 *(978-1-59707-454-4(3))* Papercutz.

—Percy Jackson & the Ovolactovegetarians, No. 3. Petrucha, Stefan & Kinney-Petrucha, Margo. 2011. (Papercutz Slices Ser.: 3). (ENG.). 64p. (J). (gr. 5-12). pap. 6.99 *(978-1-59707-264-9(8))* Papercutz.

—Secret Agent Orange. Salicrup, Jim et al. 2012. (Annoying Orange Graphic Novels Ser.: 1). (ENG.). 64p. (J). (gr. 2-7). pap. 6.99 *(978-1-59707-361-5(X))* Papercutz.

Parker, Rick, et al. Wickeder. Gerrold, David et al. 2010. (Tales from the Crypt Graphic Novels Ser.: 9). (ENG.). 64p. (J). (gr. 5-12). 10.99 *(978-1-59707-216-8(8))*; pap. 6.99 *(978-1-59707-215-1(X))* Papercutz.

Parker, Rick. Breaking Down. Parker, Rick. Petrucha, Stefan. 2011. (Papercutz Slices Ser.: 2). (ENG.). 64p. (J). (gr. 5-12). pap. 6.99 *(978-1-59707-244-1(3))* Papercutz.

Parker, Robert A. Grandfather Tang's Story. Tompert, Ann. 2015. (ENG.). 32p. (J). (gr. -1-2). 16.99 *(978-0-517-57487-4(X))*; lib. bdg. 19.99 *(978-0-517-57272-6(9))* Random Hse. Children's Bks. (Knopf Bks. for Young Readers).

Parker, Robert Andrew. Across the Blue Pacific: A World War II Story. Borden, Louise & Borden, Louise W. 2006. (ENG.). 48p. (J). (gr. -1-3). 17.00 *(978-0-618-33922-8(1))* Houghton Mifflin Harcourt Publishing Co.

—Action Jackson. Greenberg, Jan & Jordan, Sandra. 2007. (ENG.). 32p. (J). (gr. 1-5). per. 7.99 *(978-0-312-36751-0(1))* Square Fish.

—Action Jackson. Jordan, Sandra & Greenberg, Jan. pap. incl. audio *(978-1-59112-961-5(3))*; pap. incl. audio compact disk *(978-1-59112-965-3(6))* Live Oak Media.

—The Impossible Major Rogers. Gauch, Patricia Lee. 2008. (J). *(978-1-59078-334-4(4))* Boyds Mills Pr.

—The Magician's Visit: A Passover Tale. Peretz, I. L. & Goldin, Barbara Diamond. 2006. 28p. (J). (gr. 4-8). reprint ed. 15.00 *(978-1-4223-5408-7(3))*; pap. 5.00 *(978-1-4223-5400-1(8))* DIANE Publishing Co.

—Who Was Albert Einstein? Brallier, Jess M. 2003. (Who Was... ? Ser.). 105p. (gr. 4-7). 15.00 *(978-0-7569-1586-5(4))* Perfection Learning Corp.

Parker, Ron. Voices from the Wild: An Animal Sensagoria, 1 vol. Bouchard, David. 2014. (ENG.). 72p. (J). 24.95 *(978-1-55455-295-5(8))* Fitzhenry & Whiteside, Ltd. CAN. Dist: Midpoint Trade Bks., Inc.

Parker, Zac. We Like to Nurse Too. Young, Mary. 2009. 32p. (J). (gr. -1). pap. 9.95 *(978-1-890772-98-7(4))* Hohm Pr.

Parker, Zachary. Nos Gusta Vivir Verde= We Like to Live Green. Young, Mary. 2010. (SPA.). 32p. (J). pap. 9.95 *(978-1-935387-01-5(4))* Hohm Pr.

—We Like to Live Green. Young, Mary. 2010. 32p. (J). pap. 9.95 *(978-1-935387-00-8(6))* Hohm Pr.

Parkins, David. The Adventures of Old Bo Bear. Schertle, Alice. 2005. (J). 16.95 *(978-978-081-183-9(4))* Chronicle Bks. LLC.

—Aunt Nancy & the Bothersome Visitors. Root, Phyllis. 2007. (ENG.). 64p. (J). (gr. 2-5). 16.99 *(978-0-7636-3074-4(8))* Candlewick Pr.

—Ben the Inventor, 1 vol. Stevenson, Robin. 2011. (Orca Echoes Ser.). (ENG.). 64p. (J). (gr. 2-3). pap. 6.95 *(978-1-55469-802-8(2))* Orca Bk. Pubs. USA.

—Ben's Robot, 1 vol. Stevenson, Robin. 2010. (Orca Echoes Ser.). (ENG.). 64p. (J). (gr. 2-3). pap. 6.95 *(978-1-55469-153-1(2))* Orca Bk. Pubs. USA.

—Brigadier: Gentle Hero. Andrekson, Judy. 2009. (True Horse Stories Ser.). (ENG.). 96p. (J). (gr. 4-7). pap. 7.95 *(978-0-88776-904-7(7))* Tundra Bks. CAN. Dist: Random Hse., Inc.

—Captain Pepper's Pets. Grindley, Sally. 2004. 48p. (J). pap. *(978-0-7534-1042-4(7)*, Kingfisher) Roaring Brook Pr.

—Don't Eat That! Charles, Veronika Martenova. 2008. (Easy-To-Read Spooky Tales Ser.). (ENG.). 56p. (J). (gr. k-3). pap. 5.95 *(978-0-88776-857-6(1))* Tundra Bks. CAN. Dist: Random Hse., Inc.

—Don't Enter the House! Charles, Veronika Martenova. 2008. (Easy-To-Read Spooky Tales Ser.). (ENG.). 56p. (J). (gr. k-3). pap. 5.95 *(978-0-88776-856-9(3))* Tundra Bks. CAN. Dist: Random Hse., Inc.

—Don't Forget! Charles, Veronika Martenova. 2008. (Easy-To-Read Spooky Tales Ser.). (ENG.). 56p. (J). (gr. k-3). pap. 5.95 *(978-0-88776-859-0(8))* Tundra Bks. CAN. Dist: Random Hse., Inc.

—Don't Go in There! Charles, Veronika Martenova. 2007. (Easy-To-Read Spooky Tales Ser.). (ENG.). 56p. (J). (gr. k-3). pap. 5.95 *(978-0-88776-781-4(8)*, Delacorte Bks. for Young Readers) Random Hse. Children's Bks.

—Don't Go into the Forest! Charles, Veronika Martenova. 2007. (Easy-To-Read Spooky Tales Ser.). (ENG.). 56p. (J). (gr. k-3). pap. 5.95 *(978-0-88776-778-4(8)*, Delacorte Bks. for Young Readers) Random Hse. Children's Bks.

—Don't Go near the Water! Charles, Veronika Martenova. 2007. (Easy-To-Read Spooky Tales Ser.). (ENG.). 56p. (J). (gr. k-3). pap. 5.95 *(978-0-88776-780-7(X)*, Delacorte Bks. for Young Readers) Random Hse. Children's Bks.

—Don't Open the Door! Charles, Veronika Martenova. 2007. (Easy-To-Read Spooky Tales Ser.). (ENG.). 56p. (J). (gr. k-3). pap. 5.95 *(978-0-88776-779-1(6)*, Delacorte Bks. for Young Readers) Random Hse. Children's Bks.

—Don't Talk to Strangers! Charles, Veronika Martenova. 2008. (Easy-To-Read Spooky Tales Ser.). (ENG.). 56p. (J). (gr. k-3). pap. 5.95 *(978-0-88776-847-7(4))* Tundra Bks. CAN. Dist: Penguin Random Hse., LLC.

—Don't Touch That! Charles, Veronika Martenova. 2008. (Easy-To-Read Spooky Tales Ser.). (ENG.). 56p. (J). (gr. k-3). pap. 5.95 *(978-0-88776-858-3(X))* Tundra Bks. CAN. Dist: Random Hse., Inc.

—Don't Walk Alone at Night! Charles, Veronika Martenova. 2007. (Easy-To-Read Spooky Tales Ser.). (ENG.). 56p. (J). (gr. k-3). pap. 5.95 *(978-0-88776-782-1(6)*, Delacorte Bks. for Young Readers) Random Hse. Children's Bks.

—Egyptian Diary: The Journal of Nakht. Platt, Richard. 2014. (ENG.). 128p. (J). (gr. 4-7). pap. 6.99 *(978-0-7636-7054-2(5))* Candlewick Pr.

—Fosta: Marathon Master. Andrekson, Judy. 2008. (True Horse Stories Ser.). (ENG.). 104p. (J). (gr. 4-7). pap. 7.95 *(978-0-88776-838-5(5))* Tundra Bks. CAN. Dist: Random Hse., Inc.

—Gilgamesh the Hero. McCaughrean, Geraldine. 2004. 96p. (J). (gr. 6-9). 20.00 *(978-0-8028-5262-5(9))* Eerdmans, William B. Publishing Co.

—Going Up! Elisha Otis's Trip to the Top. Kulling, Monica. (Great Idea Ser.). (ENG.). 32p. (J). (gr. k-3). 2014. pap. 7.99 *(978-1-77049-516-6(9))*; 2012. 17.95 *(978-1-77049-240-0(2))* Tundra Bks. CAN. (Tundra Bks.). Dist: Penguin Random Hse., LLC.

—Gunner: Hurricane Horse. Andrekson, Judy. 2010. (True Horse Stories Ser.). (ENG.). 104p. (J). (gr. 4-7). pap. 7.95 *(978-0-88776-905-4(5))* Tundra Bks. CAN. Dist: Random Hse., Inc.

—I Always, Always Get My Way. Krasnesky, Thad. 2009. (ENG.). 32p. (J). (gr. k-2). 16.95 *(978-0-9799746-4-9(X))* Flashlight Pr.

—I'm a Truck Driver. London, Jonathan. 2010. (ENG.). 32p. (J). (gr. -1-2). 14.99 *(978-0-8050-7989-0(0)*, Holt, Henry & Co. Bks. For Young Readers) Holt, Henry & Co.

—In the Bag! Margaret Knight Wraps It Up. Kulling, Monica. (Great Idea Ser.). (ENG.). 32p. (J). (gr. k-3). 2013. pap. 7.95 *(978-1-77049-515-9(0))*; 2011. 17.95 *(978-1-77049-239-4(9))* Tundra Bks. CAN. (Tundra Bks.). Dist: Penguin Random Hse., LLC.

—The Inside Tree. Smith, Linda. 2010. (ENG.). 32p. (J). (gr. -1-3). 16.99 *(978-0-06-028241-7(X))* HarperCollins Pubs.

—It's Not about the Apple! Charles, Veronika Martenova. 2010. (Easy-To-Read Wonder Tales Ser.). (ENG.). 64p. (J). (gr. k-3). pap. 5.95 *(978-0-88776-955-9(1))* Tundra Bks. CAN. Dist: Random Hse., Inc.

—It's Not about the Crumbs! Charles, Veronika Martenova. 2010. (Easy-To-Read Wonder Tales Ser.). (ENG.). 64p. (J). (gr. k-3). pap. 5.95 *(978-0-88776-953-5(5))* Tundra Bks. CAN. Dist: Random Hse., Inc.

—It's Not about the Diamonds! Charles, Veronika Martenova. 2013. (Easy-To-Read Wonder Tales Ser.). (ENG.). 64p. (J). (gr. k-3). pap. 5.95 *(978-1-77049-328-5(X))* Tundra Bks. CAN. Dist: Random Hse., Inc.

—It's Not about the Hunter! Charles, Veronika Martenova. 2010. (Easy-To-Read Wonder Tales Ser.). (ENG.). 56p. (J). (gr. k-3). pap. 5.95 *(978-0-88776-948-1(9))* Tundra Bks. CAN. Dist: Random Hse., Inc.

—It's Not about the Pumpkin! Charles, Veronika Martenova. 2010. (Easy-To-Read Wonder Tales Ser.). (ENG.). 64p. (J). (gr. k-3). pap. 5.95 *(978-0-88776-949-8(7))* Tundra Bks. CAN. Dist: Penguin Random Hse., LLC.

—It's Not about the Rose! Charles, Veronika Martenova. 2010. (Easy-To-Read Wonder Tales Ser.). (ENG.). 64p. (J). (gr. k-3). pap. 5.95 *(978-0-88776-954-2(3))* Tundra Bks. CAN. Dist: Random Hse., Inc.

—JB Andrew: Mustang Magic. Andrekson, Judy. 2008. (True Horse Stories Ser.). (ENG.). 88p. (J). (gr. 4-7). pap. 7.95 *(978-0-88776-837-8(7))* Tundra Bks. CAN. Dist: Random Hse., Inc.

—Jeepers Creepers: A Monstrous ABC. Leuck, Laura. 2003. (ENG.). 32p. (J). (gr. -1-7). 15.95 *(978-0-8118-3509-1(X)*, 53408263) Chronicle Bks. LLC.

—Little Squire: The Jumping Pony. Andrekson, Judy. 2007. (True Horse Stories Ser.). (ENG.). 80p. (J). (gr. 4-7). pap. 7.95 *(978-0-88776-770-8(2))* Tundra Bks. CAN. Dist: Random Hse., Inc.

—Miskeen: The Dancing Horse. Andrekson, Judy. 2007. (True Horse Stories Ser.). (ENG.). 96p. (J). (gr. 4-7). pap. 7.95 *(978-0-88776-771-5(0))* Tundra Bks. CAN. Dist: Random Hse., Inc.

—Pirate Island Treasure, 1 vol. Helmer, Marilyn. 2013. (Orca Echoes Ser.). (ENG.). 64p. (J). (gr. 2-3). pap. 6.95 *(978-1-4598-0165-3(2))* Orca Bk. Pubs. USA.

—Prince for a Princess, 1 vol. Walters, Eric. 2012. (Orca Echoes Ser.). (ENG.). 64p. (J). (gr. 2-3). pap. 6.95 *(978-1-4598-0200-1(4))* Orca Bk. Pubs. USA.

—Roman Diary: The Journal of Iliona, a Young Slave. Platt, Richard. 2014. (ENG.). 128p. (J). (gr. 4-7). pap. 6.99 *(978-0-7636-7053-5(7))* Candlewick Pr.

—Roman Diary: The Journal of Iliona of Mytilini, Who Was Captured & Sold As a Slave in Rome, AD 107. Platt, Richard. 2009. (ENG.). 64p. (J). (gr. 3-7). 18.99 *(978-0-7636-3480-3(8))* Candlewick Pr.

—Shhhhh! Everybody's Sleeping. Markes, Julie. 32p. (J). (gr. -1-1). 2005. lib. bdg. 16.89 *(978-0-06-053791-3(4))*; 2004. (ENG.). 16.99 *(978-0-06-053790-6(6))* HarperCollins Pubs.

—Skye Above, 1 vol. Walters, Eric. 2014. (Orca Echoes Ser.). (ENG.). 64p. (J). (gr. 2-3). pap. 6.95 *(978-1-4598-0701-3(4))* Orca Bk. Pubs. USA.

—Spic-And-Span! Lillian Gilbreth's Wonder Kitchen. 2014. (Great Idea Ser.). (ENG.). 32p. (J). (gr. k-3). 17.99 *(978-1-77049-380-3(8))* Tundra Bks. CAN. Dist: Random Hse., Inc.

—That Cat Can't Stay. Krasnesky, Thad. 2010. (ENG.). 32p. (J). (gr. k-2). 16.95 *(978-0-9799746-5-6(8))* Flashlight Pr.

—The Water Horse. King-Smith, Dick. 2007. (ENG.). 128p. (J). (gr. 1-4). 5.99 *(978-0-375-84231-3(4)*, Yearling) Random Hse. Children's Bks.

—When the Worst Happens: Extraordinary Stories of Survival. Kyi, Tanya Lloyd. 2014. (ENG.). 128p. (J). (gr. 5-8). pap. 14.95 *(978-1-55451-682-7(X)*, 9781554516827) Annick Pr., Ltd. CAN. Dist: Firefly Bks., Ltd.

Parkins, David & Firth, Barbara. Webster J. Duck. Waddell, Martin. 2004. (ENG.). 32p. (J). (-k). pap. 6.99 *(978-0-7636-2431-6(4))* Candlewick Pr.

Parkinson, Cheryl. Santa's Stormy Christmas Eve. Parkinson, Cheryl, tr. MacLennan, David. 2004. 32p. 7.95 *(978-0-9731960-0-9(9))* Full Satchel Pr. CAN. Dist: Wilson & Assocs.

Parkinson, Kate. Grace. Parkinson, Kate. 2015. (I Like to Read(r) Ser.). (ENG.). 24p. (J). (gr. -1-3). 6.99 *(978-0-8234-3317-9(X))*; 14.95 *(978-0-8234-3207-3(6))* Holiday Hse., Inc.

Parkinson, Kathy. When I Feel Good about Myself. Spelman, Cornelia Maude. 2003. (Way I Feel Ser.). (ENG.). 24p. (J). (gr. -1-1). 15.99 *(978-0-8075-8887-1(3))*; pap. 6.99 *(978-0-8075-8901-4(2))* Whitman, Albert & Co.

—When I Feel Jealous. Spelman, Cornelia Maude. 2003. (Way I Feel Bks.). (ENG.). 24p. (J). (gr. -1-1). 6.99 *(978-0-8075-8902-1(0))*; 15.99 *(978-0-8075-8886-4(5))* Whitman, Albert & Co.

—When I Feel Scared. Spelman, Cornelia Maude. 2010. (ENG.). 16p. (J). (gr. -1-k). bds. 7.99 *(978-0-8075-8905-2(5))* Whitman, Albert & Co.

—When I Feel Scared. Spelman, Cornelia. 2012. (J). *(978-1-61913-141-5(2))* Weigl Pubs., Inc.

—When I Feel Worried. Spelman, Cornelia Maude. 2013. (Way I Feel Bks.). (ENG.). 24p. (J). (gr. -1-1). 15.99 *(978-0-8075-8893-2(8))* Whitman, Albert & Co.

—When I Feel Worried. Maude Spelman, Cornelia & Spelman, Cornelia Maude. 2014. (Way I Feel Bks.). (ENG.). 24p. (J). (gr. -1-1). pap. 6.99 *(978-0-8075-8895-6(4))* Whitman, Albert & Co.

—When I Miss You. Spelman, Cornelia Maude. (ENG.). (J). (gr. -1-k). 2010. 16p. bds. 7.99 *(978-0-8075-8904-5(7))*; 2004. 24p. pap. 6.99 *(978-0-8075-8903-8(9))* Whitman, Albert & Co.

Parks, Paul, jt. illus. see Damerum, Kanako.

Parks, Phil. Basement of the Undead, 1 vol. Strange, Jason. 2011. (Jason Strange Ser.). (ENG.). 72p. (gr. 2-3). pap. 6.25 *(978-1-4342-3433-9(9))*; lib. bdg. 23.99 *(978-1-4342-3234-2(4))* Stone Arch Bks.

Parks, Phil. Blazing Courage. Halls, Kelly Milner. 2015. (ENG.). 96p. (J). (gr. 4-8). lib. bdg. 25.32 ***(978-1-4677-7219-8(4)***, Darby Creek) Lerner Publishing Group.

Parks, Phil. Every Day's a Holiday: Amusing Rhymes for Happy Times. Koontz, Dean. 2003. 144p. (J). 18.89 *(978-0-06-008585-8(1))* HarperCollins Pubs.

—Faceless Friend, 1 vol. Strange, Jason. 2011. (Jason Strange Ser.). (ENG.). 72p. (gr. 2-3). pap. 6.25 *(978-1-4342-3431-5(2))*; lib. bdg. 23.99 *(978-1-4342-3232-8(8))* Stone Arch Bks.

—The Mothman's Shadow, 1 vol. Strange, Jason. 2011. (Jason Strange Ser.). (ENG.). 72p. (gr. 2-3). pap. 6.25 *(978-1-4342-3093-5(7))* Stone Arch Bks.

—Realm of Ghosts, 1 vol. Strange, Jason. 2011. (Jason Strange Ser.). (ENG.). 72p. (gr. 2-3). pap. 6.25 *(978-1-4342-3096-6(1))*; 23.99 *(978-1-4342-2962-5(9))* Stone Arch Bks.

—Robot Santa: The Further Adventures of Santa's Twin. Koontz, Dean. 2004. (Santa's Twin Ser.: Bk. 2). 72p. (J). 20.89 *(978-0-06-050944-6(9))* HarperCollins Pubs.

—Santa's Twin. Koontz, Dean. 2004. (Santa's Twin Ser.: Bk. 1). (ENG.). 64p. pap. 12.95 *(978-0-06-057223-5(X)*, William Morrow Paperbacks) HarperCollins Pubs.

—To Wake the Dead, 1 vol. Strange, Jason. 2011. (Jason Strange Ser.). (ENG.). 72p. (gr. 2-3). pap. 6.25 *(978-1-4342-3094-2(5))*; 23.99 *(978-1-4342-2963-2(7))* Stone Arch Bks.

—Zombie Winter, 1 vol. Strange, Jason. 2011. (Jason Strange Ser.). (ENG.). 72p. (gr. 2-3). pap. 6.25 *(978-1-4342-3095-9(3))* Stone Arch Bks.

Parks, Phil & Dal Lago, Alberto. Full Moon Horror, 1 vol. Strange, Jason. 2011. (Jason Strange Ser.). (ENG.). 72p. (gr. 2-3). pap. 6.25 *(978-1-4342-3434-6(7))*; lib. bdg. 23.99 *(978-1-4342-3235-9(2))* Stone Arch Bks.

—Text 4 Revenge, 1 vol. Strange, Jason. 2011. (Jason Strange Ser.). (ENG.). 72p. (gr. 2-3). pap. 6.25 *(978-1-4342-3432-2(0))*; lib. bdg. 23.99 *(978-1-4342-3233-5(6))* Stone Arch Bks.

Parks, Phil, jt. illus. see Soleiman, Serg.

Parlagreco, Aurora M., jt. illus. see Rogers, Jacqueline.

Parlett, George & Bleach, James. Young Marvelman Classic - Volume 1. Anglo, Mick. 2011. (ENG.). 168p. (J). (gr. -1-17). 34.99 *(978-0-7851-5504-1(X))* Marvel Worldwide, Inc.

Parlin, Tim. Milton Hershey. Sutcliffe, Jane. 2003. (History Maker Biographies Ser.). (ENG.). 48p. (gr. 3-6). 27.93 *(978-0-8225-0247-0(X)*, Lerner Pubns.) Lerner Publishing Group.

Parmar, Tavisha. The Class Photograph. 2005. (J). *(978-81-902492-1-8(5))* Vivera Bks.

Parme, Fabrice. Caesar, Who's He? Surget, Alain & Yeardley, Glynne. 2014. 95p. (J). ***(978-1-4351-5328-8(6))*** Barnes & Noble, Inc.

—Cleopatra Must Be Saved! Surget, Alain & Yeardley, Glynne. 2014. 95p. (J). ***(978-1-4351-5329-5(4))*** Barnes & Noble, Inc.

—Danger at the Circus! Surget, Alain & Yeardley, Glynne. 2014. 95p. (J). ***(978-1-4351-5334-9(0))*** Barnes & Noble, Inc.

—Prisoners in the Pyramid. Surget, Alain & Yeardley, Glynne. 2014. 94p. (J). ***(978-1-4351-5326-4(X))*** Barnes & Noble, Inc.

Parmelee, George. Gerald Giraffe's Garage. Beresford, J. R. 2013. (ENG.). 32p. (J). (gr. -1-3). 11.95 *(978-0-9860321-0-3(7))* Tuscarora Publishing Company.

Parmenter, Wayne. Little Colt's Palm Sunday. Adams, Michelle Medlock. 2005. (ENG.). 28p. (J). 14.95 *(978-0-8249-5503-8(X))* Ideals Pubns.

—When Christmas Came. Spinelli, Eileen. 2006. (ENG.). 32p. (J). (gr. k-3). bds. 16.95 *(978-0-8249-5507-6(2)*, Ideals Pr.) Ideals Pubns.

Paroline, Michelle, jt. illus. see Paroline, Shelli.

Paroline, Shelli. Adventure Time. Lamb, Braden. 2014. (Adventure Time Ser.: 3). (ENG.). 128p. (J). (gr. 4). 34.99 *(978-1-60886-347-1(6))* Boom! Studios.

—Adventure Time, Vol. 1. North, Ryan & Lamb, Branden. 2012. (Adventure Time Ser.). (ENG.). 128p. (J). (gr. 4). pap. 14.99 *(978-1-60886-280-1(1))* Boom! Studios.

—Ice Age: Past, Presents, & Future! Monroe, Caleb & Lamb, Branden. 2012. (ENG.). 24p. (J). (gr. -1-3). pap. 3.99 *(978-1-60886-269-6(0))* Boom! Studios.

—Ice Age: Where There's Thunder. Lamb, Branden & Boom Studios Staff. 2012. (Ice Age Ser.). (ENG.). 24p. (J). (gr. -1). pap. 3.99 *(978-1-60886-262-7(3))* Boom! Studios.

—Muppet Snow White. Snider, Jesse Blaze. 2010. (Muppet Show Ser.). 112p. (J). (gr. 3-6). pap. 9.99 *(978-1-60886-574-1(6))* Boom! Studios.

—Tricky Fox Tales. Schweizer, Chris. 2011. (Tricky Journeys Ser.: 3). (ENG.). 64p. (J). (gr. 2-4). pap. 6.95 *(978-0-7613-7861-7(8)*, Graphic Universe) Lerner Publishing Group.

Paroline, Shelli & Lamb, Braden. Adventure Time. North, Ryan. 2013. (Adventure Time Ser.: 1). (ENG.). 128p. (J). (gr. 4). Vol. 1. 34.99 *(978-1-60886-324-2(7))*; Vol. 2. 34.99 *(978-1-60886-321-1(2))* Boom! Studios.

—Adventure Time Vol. 2. North, Ryan. 2013. (Adventure Time Ser.). (ENG.). 112p. (J). (gr. 4). pap. 14.99 *(978-1-60886-323-5(9))* Boom! Studios.

—Adventure Time Vol. 3. North, Ryan. 2013. (Adventure Time Ser.). (ENG.). 112p. (J). (gr. 4). pap. 14.99 *(978-1-60886-317-4(4))* Boom! Studios.

Paroline, Shelli & Lamb, Branden. Hidden Treasure, Vol. 5. Monroe, Caleb & Paroline, Shelli. 2013. (Ice Age Ser.: 5). (ENG.). 24p. (J). (gr. -1-4). pap. 3.99 *(978-1-60886-301-3(8))* Boom! Studios.

—Ice Age, Vol. 2. Monroe, Caleb. 2012. (Ice Age Ser.). (ENG.). 24p. (J). (gr. k). pap. 3.99 *(978-1-60886-253-5(4))* Boom! Studios.

Paroline, Shelli & Paroline, Michelle. Tricky Fox Tales. Schweizer, Chris. 2011. (Tricky Journeys Ser.: 3). (ENG.). (J). (gr. 2-4). pap. 39.62 *(978-0-7613-8627-8(0))*; No. 3. 64p. lib. bdg. 27.93 *(978-0-7613-6605-8(9))* Lerner Publishing Group. (Graphic Universe).

Parot, Annelore. Kokeshi Style: Design Your Own Kokeshi Fashions. 2012. (ENG.). 120p. 14.99 *(978-1-4521-1372-2(6))* Chronicle Bks. LLC.

Parpan, Justin. Gwango's Lonesome Trail. 2006. 32p. (J). (gr. -1-3). 15.95 *(978-1-60108-004-2(2))* Red Cygnet Pr.

Parr, Martin, photos by. Martin Parr. Williams, Val. rev. ed. 2004. (ENG., 352p. (gr. 8-17). pap. 49.95 *(978-0-7148-4389-6(X))* Phaidon Pr. Ltd. GBR. Dist: Hachette Bk. Group.

—Think of England. rev. ed. 2004. (ENG., 144p. (gr. 8-17). pap. 35.00 *(978-0-7148-4454-1(3))* Phaidon Pr. Ltd. GBR. Dist: Hachette Bk. Group.

Parr, Todd. The Family Book. Parr, Todd. 2003. (ENG.). 32p. (J). (gr. -1-1). 17.00 *(978-0-316-73896-5(4))* Little, Brown Bks. for Young Readers.

—El Gran Libro de la Amistad. Parr, Todd. Morell, Ivonne Bonsfill, tr. 2010. (Mundo de Todd Ser.). (SPA.). 10p. (J). 17.95 *(978-84-92691-19-7(0))* Roca Editorial De Libros ESP. Dist: Spanish Pubs., LLC.

—The I Love You Book. Parr, Todd. 2009. (ENG.). 32p. (J). (gr. -1-1). 9.99 *(978-0-316-01985-9(2))* Little, Brown Bks. for Young Readers.

P

Parra, John. Green Is a Chile Pepper: A Book of Colors. Thong, Roseanne Greenfield. 2014. (ENG & SPA.). 40p. (J). (gr. -1-k). 16.99 *(978-1-4521-0203-0(1))* Chronicle Bks. LLC.

—Marvelous Cornelius: Hurricane Katrina & the Spirit of New Orleans. Bildner, Phil. 2015. (ENG.). 44p. (J). (gr. k-3). 16.99 *(978-1-4521-2578-7(3))* Chronicle Bks. LLC.

—My Name Is Gabriela/Me Llamo Gabriela: The Life of Gabriela Mistral/la Vida de Gabriela Mistral. Brown, Monica. 2005. (SPA, MUL & ENG.). 32p. (J). (gr. -1-3). 15.95 *(978-0-87358-859-1(2))* Rowman & Littlefield Publishers, Inc.

—P Is for Pinata. Johnston, Tony. 2008. (Discover the World Ser.). (ENG.). 40p. (J). (gr. 1-5). 17.95 *(978-1-58536-144-1(5))* Sleeping Bear Pr.

Parra, John. Round Is a Tortilla. Thong, Roseanne. 2015. (ENG.). 40p. (J). (gr. -1-k). 7.99 ***(978-1-4521-4568-6(7))*** Chronicle Bks. LLC.

Parra, John. Round Is a Tortilla: A Book of Shapes. Thong, Roseanne Greenfield. 2013. (ENG.). 40p. (J). (gr. -1-k). 16.99 *(978-1-4521-0616-8(9))* Chronicle Bks. LLC.

—Waiting for the Biblioburro. Brown, Monica. 2011. (ENG.). 32p. (J). (gr. k-3). 16.99 *(978-1-58246-353-7(0),* Tricycle Pr.) Ten Speed Pr.

Parra, Rocio. Globito Manual. Reyes, Carlos Jose. 2004. (Primer Acto: Teatro Infantil y Juvenil Ser.). (SPA.). 30p. (J). (gr. -1-7). pap. *(978-958-30-0317-2(4))* Panamericana Editorial.

—Lucy Es Pecosa. Arciniegas, Triunfo. 2004. (Primer Acto: Teatro Infantil y Juvenil Ser.). (SPA.). 43p. (J). (gr. -1-7). pap. *(978-958-30-0316-5(6))* Panamericana Editorial.

—Sirilko y la Flauta. Rodriguez, Julia. 2004. (Primer Acto: Teatro Infantil y Juvenil Ser.). (SPA.). 28p. (J). (gr. 4-7). pap. *(978-958-30-0315-8(8))* Panamericana Editorial.

Parramon's Editorial Team Staff, photos by. Metal. Parramon's Editorial Team Staff. Parramon's Editorial Team. 2004. (Let's Create! Ser.). 32p. (gr. 1-4). lib. bdg. 26.00 *(978-0-8368-4016-2(X),* Gareth Stevens Learning Library) Stevens, Gareth Publishing LLLP.

—Papier-Mâché. Parramon's Editorial Team Staff. 2004. (Let's Create! Ser.). 32p. (gr. 1-4). lib. bdg. 26.00 *(978-0-8368-4017-9(8),* Gareth Stevens Learning Library) Stevens, Gareth Publishing LLLP.

—Recyclables. Parramon's Editorial Team Staff. 2004. (Let's Create! Ser.). 32p. (gr. 1-4). lib. bdg. 26.00 *(978-0-8368-4018-6(6),* Gareth Stevens Learning Library) Stevens, Gareth Publishing LLLP.

—Stones & "Stuff" Parramon's Editorial Team Staff. 2004. (Let's Create! Ser.). 32p. (gr. 1-4). lib. bdg. 26.00 *(978-0-8368-4019-3(4),* Gareth Stevens Learning Library) Stevens, Gareth Publishing LLLP.

Parris, Kitty. If I Were a Monkey. Batchler, Darla. 2005. 24p. (J). bds. 12.95 *(978-0-9746959-2-1(0))* Falcon Publishing LTD.

Parrish, Emma. Doodle Farm: Oodles of Mooing, Oinking, & Quacking Doodles to Complete & Create. 2010. (ENG.). 64p. (J). pap. 7.95 *(978-0-7624-3970-6(X))* Running Pr. Bk. Pubs.

—Halloween Doodles: Spooky Designs to Complete & Create. 2009. (ENG.). 64p. (J). pap. 7.95 *(978-0-7624-3760-3(X))* Running Pr. Bk. Pubs.

Parrish, Fayrene. Pancho Saves the Day: Shipmates Learning Adventures Venture. Parrish, Fayrene. 2010. 42p. (J). 15.95 *(978-0-9826717-8-8(4))* Rondo Bks.

Parrish, Maxfield. The Knave of Hearts. Saunders, Louise. 2008. (Calla Editions Ser.). (ENG.). 40p. (gr. 3). 30.00 *(978-1-60660-001-6(X))* Dover Pubns., Inc.

—The STORY of ALADDIN & the MAGICAL LAMP. Anonymous. Craft, Richard et al, eds. 2011. (ENG.). 66p. pap. 14.95 *(978-1-4681-5299-9(8))* CreateSpace Independent Publishing Platform.

—The STORY of GULNARE of the SEA. Anonymous. Craft, Richard et al, eds. 2011. (ENG.). 24p. pap. 12.75 *(978-1-4681-5350-7(1))* CreateSpace Independent Publishing Platform.

—The STORY of PRINCE AGIB. Anonymous. Craft, Richard et al, eds. 2011. (ENG.). 26p. pap. 12.75 *(978-1-4681-5355-2(2))* CreateSpace Independent Publishing Platform.

—The Story of the Fisherman & the Genie. Anonymous. Craft, Richard et al, eds. 2011. (ENG.). 24p. pap. 12.75 *(978-1-4681-5340-8(4))* CreateSpace Independent Publishing Platform.

Parrott, Heather. Dale the Uniclyde: An adventure in Friendship. von Rosenberg, Byron. 2007. 22p. (J). 11.95 *(978-0-9759858-6-1(8))* Red Mountain Creations.

Parry, Alan. The Kregel Pictorial Guide to the Tabernacle, 1 vol. Dowley, Tim. 2003. (Kregel Pictorial Guide Ser.). 32p. pap. 11.99 *(978-0-8254-2468-7(2))* Kregel Pubns.

Parry, Jo. Albert & Sarah Jane. Doyle, Malachy. 2007. (Storytime Ser.). (ENG.). 24p. (J). (gr. -1-17). lib. bdg. 15.99 *(978-1-59566-336-8(3))* QEB Publishing Inc.

—Alphabet Farm. Top That Publishing Staff, ed. 2007. (Magnetic - Alphabet Ser.). 10p. (J). (gr. -1). bds. *(978-1-84666-272-0(9),* Tide Mill Pr.) Top That! Publishing PLC.

—Alphabet Farm (large Version) Top That!. 2007. 10p. (J). (gr. -1). *(978-1-84666-553-0(1),* Tide Mill Pr.) Top That! Publishing PLC.

—Beetle Bugs Party: A Counting Book. Depisco, Dorothea. 2005. 10p. (J). (gr. -1-3). 10.95 *(978-1-58117-415-1(2),* Intervisual/Piggy Toes) Bendon, Inc.

—Bluebird's Nest. DePrisco, Dorothea. 2006. (ENG.). 16p. (J). 9.95 *(978-1-58117-390-1(3),* Intervisual/Piggy Toes) Bendon, Inc.

—Bluebird's Nest. DePrisco, Dorothea. 2006. (ENG.). 14p. (gr. -1-k). 5.95 *(978-1-58117-504-2(3),* Intervisual/Piggy Toes) Bendon, Inc.

—Candle Bible for Kids, 1 vol. David, Juliet. 2011. (ENG.). 400p. (J). (gr. k). 16.99 *(978-1-85985-827-1(9),* Candle Bks.) Lion Hudson PLC GBR. Dist: Kregel Pubns.

—Candle Bible for Kids Board Book, 1 vol. David, Juliet. 2014. (ENG.). 42p. (J). bds. 9.99 *(978-1-78128-101-7(7),* Candle Bks.) Lion Hudson PLC GBR. Dist: Kregel Pubns.

—Candle Prayers for Kids, 1 vol. Freedman, Claire. 2014. (ENG.). 128p. (J). 12.99 *(978-1-78128-102-4(5),* Candle Bks.) Lion Hudson PLC GBR. Dist: Kregel Pubns.

—The Christmas Story, 1 vol. David, Juliet. 2009. (Candle Read & Play Ser.). 12p. (J). bds. 11.99 *(978-0-8254-7400-2(0),* Candle Bks.) Lion Hudson PLC GBR. Dist: Kregel Pubns.

—Color Safari (large Version) Top That!. 2007. 10p. (J). (gr. -1). *(978-1-84666-554-7(X),* Tide Mill Pr.) Top That! Publishing PLC.

—Daddy Loves You So Much, 1 vol. Thomas Nelson Publishing Staff. 2015. (ENG.). 20p. (J). bds. 9.99 *(978-0-529-12335-0(5))* Nelson, Thomas Inc.

—The Easter Story, 1 vol. David, Juliet. 2015. (ENG.). 12p. (J). bds. 3.99 *(978-1-85985-992-6(5),* Candle Bks.) Lion Hudson PLC GBR. Dist: Kregel Pubns.

—The Great Flood, 1 vol. David, Juliet. 2014. (ENG.). 12p. (J). bds. 3.99 *(978-1-85985-991-9(7),* Candle Bks.) Lion Hudson PLC GBR. Dist: Kregel Pubns.

—Jungle Numbers. Top That Publishing Staff, ed. 2007. (Magnetic - Numbers Ser.). 10p. (J). (gr. -1). bds. *(978-1-84666-163-1(3),* Tide Mill Pr.) Top That! Publishing PLC.

—Jungle Numbers (large Version) Top That!. 2007. 10p. (J). (gr. -1). *(978-1-84666-552-3(3),* Tide Mill Pr.) Top That! Publishing PLC.

—Magnetic Color Safari. Ranson, Erin. 2007. 10p. (J). (gr. -1-3). *(978-1-84666-361-1(X),* Tide Mill Pr.) Top That! Publishing PLC.

—Magnetic Playtime Shapes. Ranson, Erin. 2007. (Magnetic Playtime Shapes Ser.). 10p. (J). (gr. -1-3). *(978-1-84666-363-5(6),* Tide Mill Pr.) Top That! Publishing PLC.

—Mommy Loves You So Much, 1 vol. Thomas Nelson Publishing Staff. 2015. (ENG.). 20p. (J). bds. 9.99 *(978-0-529-12338-1(X))* Nelson, Thomas Inc.

—My First Fairy Tales: Eight Exciting Picture Stories for Little Ones. Baxter, Nicola. 2013. (ENG.). 16p. (J). (gr. -1-2). bds. 13.99 *(978-1-84322-991-9(9),* Armadillo) Anness Publishing GBR. Dist: National Bk. Network.

—Playtime Shapes (large Version) Top That!. 2007. 10p. (J). (gr. -1). *(978-1-84666-555-4(8),* Tide Mill Pr.) Top That! Publishing PLC.

—Ten Christmas Lights: Count the Lights from One to Ten! Imperato, Teresa. 2005. (ENG.). 20p. (J). 10.95 *(978-1-58117-321-5(0),* Intervisual/Piggy Toes) Bendon, Inc.

—Traditional Fairy Tales: Eight Exciting Picture Stories for Little Ones. Baxter, Nicola & Francis, Jan. 2013. (ENG.). 16p. (J). (gr. -1-2). 13.99 *(978-1-84322-992-6(7),* Armadillo) Anness Publishing GBR. Dist: National Bk. Network.

Parry, Linda. Badger's Christmas Day. Parry, Alan. 2004. (gr. -1-3). 15.00 *(978-0-687-09703-6(7))* Abingdon Pr.

—Badger's Easter Surprise. Parry, Alan. 2004. (Oaktree Wood Ser.). 16p. (gr. -1-3). 15.00 *(978-0-687-04813-7(3))* Abingdon Pr.

—Badger's Lovely Day. Parry, Alan. 2004. (Oaktree Wood Ser.). (gr. -1-3). 5.00 *(978-0-687-09712-8(6))* Abingdon Pr.

—The Bible Made Easy: A Pop-Up, Pull-Out, Interactive Bible Adventure. Parry, Alan. (J). 14.99 *(978-1-85608-399-7(3))* Hunt, John Publishing Ltd. GBR. Dist: O. M. Literature.

—Discover Oaktree Woods: A Touch & Feel Book. Parry, Alan. 2004. 9.00 *(978-0-687-02741-5(1))* Abingdon Pr.

—The First Seven Days. Parry, Alan. 2004. (gr. -1-3). 9.00 *(978-0-687-04910-3(5))* Abingdon Pr.

—Goodnight Prayers. Parry, Alan. 2004. (Oaktree Wood Ser.). 32p. (gr. -1-3). 10.00 *(978-0-687-09705-0(3))* Abingdon Pr.

—Mouse Can't Sleep. Parry, Alan. 2004. (Oaktree Wood Ser.). (gr. -1-3). 5.00 *(978-0-687-09711-1(8))* Abingdon Pr.

—Never Mind Squirrel. Parry, Alan. 2004. (Oaktree Wood Ser.). (gr. -1-3). 5.00 *(978-0-687-09710-4(X))* Abingdon Pr.

—Rabbit Helps Out. Parry, Alan. 2004. (gr. -1-3). 5.00 *(978-0-687-09713-5(4))* Abingdon Pr.

—Woodland Bible Stories. Parry, Alan. 2004. bds. 16.00 *(978-0-687-02664-7(4))* Abingdon Pr.

Parsloe, Alismarie. Wesley's World. Brown, Kathy. 2011. 36p. pap. 24.95 *(978-1-4489-8461-9(0))* America Star Bks.

Parsons, Arielle, jt. illus. see Stanley, Christopher Heath.

Parsons, Garry. Digging for Dinosaurs. Waite, Judy. 2003. (Flying Foxes Ser.). (ENG.). 48p. (J). lib. bdg. *(978-0-7787-1483-5(7))* Crabtree Publishing Co.

—The Dinosaurs Are Having a Party! Jones, Gareth P. 2015. (J). *(978-1-4677-6317-2(5))* Lerner Publishing Group.

—The Four Franks. Mayfield, Sue. 2005. (Blue Go Bananas Ser.). (ENG.). 48p. (J). (gr. 1-2). *(978-0-7787-2651-7(7))* Crabtree Publishing Co.

—G. E. M. Clarke, Jane. 2008. (ENG.). 32p. (J). (gr. -1-k). pap. 9.95 *(978-0-09-948012-9(3))* Transworld Publishers Ltd. GBR. Dist: Independent Pubs. Group.

—George & the Big Bang. Hawking, Lucy & Hawking, Stephen W. 2012. (George's Secret Key Ser.). (ENG.). 336p. (J). (gr. 3-7). 18.99 *(978-1-4424-4005-0(8),* Simon & Schuster Bks. For Young Readers) Simon & Schuster Bks. For Young Readers.

—George & the Big Bang. Hawking, Stephen W. & Hawking, Lucy. 2013. (George's Secret Key Ser.). (ENG.). 304p. (J). (gr. 3-7). pap. 11.99 *(978-1-4424-4006-7(6),* Simon & Schuster Bks. For Young Readers) Simon & Schuster Bks. For Young Readers.

—George's Cosmic Treasure Hunt. Hawking, Stephen W. & Hawking, Lucy. 2009. (George's Secret Key Ser.). (ENG.). 320p. (J). (gr. 3-7). 19.99 *(978-1-4169-8671-3(5),* Simon & Schuster Bks. For Young Readers) Simon & Schuster Bks. For Young Readers.

—George's Cosmic Treasure Hunt. Hawking, Lucy & Hawking, Stephen W. 2011. (George's Secret Key Ser.). (ENG.). 352p. (J). (gr. 3-7). pap. 11.99 *(978-1-4424-2175-2(4),* Simon & Schuster Bks. For Young Readers) Simon & Schuster Bks. For Young Readers.

—George's Secret Key to the Universe. Hawking, Stephen W. & Hawking, Lucy. (George's Secret Key Ser.). (ENG.). (J). (gr. 3-7). 2009. 336p. pap. 10.99 *(978-1-4169-8584-6(0));* 2007. 304p. 21.99 *(978-1-4169-5462-0(7))* Simon & Schuster Bks. For Young Readers. (Simon & Schuster Bks. For Young Readers).

—George's Secret Key to the Universe. Hawking, Stephen W. & Hawking, Lucy. l.t. ed. 2008. (Literacy Bridge Middle Reader Ser.). 359p. (J). (gr. 3-7). 24.95 *(978-1-4104-0638-5(5))* Thorndike Pr.

—Movie Maker: The Ultimate Guide to Making Films. Grabham, Tim et al. 2010. (ENG.). 48p. (J). (gr. 3-7). 19.99 *(978-0-7636-4949-4(X))* Candlewick Pr.

—Nuddy Ned. Gray, Kes. 2014. (ENG.). 32p. (J). (gr. -1-k). 13.99 *(978-1-4088-3659-0(9),* 161263, Bloomsbury USA Childrens) Bloomsbury USA.

Parsons, Garry. The Tooth Fairy's Christmas. Bently, Peter. 2014. (J). ***(978-1-4351-5739-2(7))*** Barnes & Noble, Inc.

Parsons, Garry. Wrong Kind of Bark. Donaldson, Julia. 2004. (Red Bananas Ser.). (ENG.). 48p. (J). (gr. k-2). pap. 5.99 *(978-1-4052-1062-1(1))* Egmont Bks., Ltd. GBR. Dist: Independent Pubs. Group.

—The Wrong Kind of Bark. Donaldson, Julia. 2005. (Red Bananas Ser.). (ENG.). 48p. (J). lib. bdg. *(978-0-7787-1073-8(4));* (gr. 1-3). *(978-0-7787-1089-9(0))* Crabtree Publishing Co.

Parsons, Garry. Krong! Parsons, Garry. 2006. 32p. (J). (gr. -1-3). 15.95 *(978-1-58925-061-1(3))* Tiger Tales.

Parsons, Garry, jt. illus. see Sharratt, Nick.

Parsons, Gary. Spooky Soccer. Doyle, Malachy. 2010. (Red Bananas Ser.). (ENG.). 48p. (J). (gr. k-2). pap. 5.99 *(978-1-4052-4924-9(2))* Egmont Bks., Ltd. GBR. Dist: Independent Pubs. Group.

—Would You Believe It? Agnew, Kate. (ENG.). 128p. (J). pap. 7.50 *(978-1-4052-0520-7(2))* Egmont Bks., Ltd. GBR. Dist: Trafalgar Square Publishing.

Parsons, Gary & Richards, Lucy. Animals in School. Donaldson, Julia. 2013. (ENG.). 90p. (J). (gr. k-2). pap. 6.99 *(978-1-4052-6210-1(9))* Egmont Bks., Ltd. GBR. Dist: Independent Pubs. Group.

Parsons, Jackie & Larranaga, Ana Martin. Three Little Duckies. Jugran, Jan. 2006. (ENG.). 6p. (J). (gr. -1 — 1). 14.99 *(978-1-58476-352-9(3),* IKIDS) Innovative Kids.

Parsons, Sally. Madeline Island ABC Coloring Book. Henry, Marcia. 2008. (ENG.). 32p. (J). (gr. k-6). pap. 6.95 *(978-0-9817723-0-1(7))* Univ. of Wisconsin Pr.

Partis, Joanne. Bella's Butterfly Ball. Nilsen, Anna. 2012. (ENG.). 20p. (J). (gr. -1-1). pap. 9.99 *(978-1-84365-194-9(7),* Pavilion Children's Books) Pavilion Bks. GBR. Dist: Independent Pubs. Group.

—Bella's Midsummer Secret. Nilsen, Anna. 2005. (ENG.). 18p. (J). (gr. -1-1). pap. 9.99 *(978-1-84458-338-6(4),* Pavilion Children's Books) Pavilion Bks. GBR. Dist: Independent Pubs. Group.

Partis, Joanne. Look at Me! Partis, Joanne. 2007. (Baby Bks.). (ENG.). 10p. (J). (gr. k — 1). 4.99 *(978-1-84458-365-2(1))* Pavilion Bks. GBR. Dist: Independent Pubs. Group.

Parton, Paua. Room 17 Where History Comes Alive! Book I-Indians. Parton, Paula. 2007. 128p. 19.95 *(978-0-9794815-2-9(X))* Bellissima Publishing, LLC.

Parton, Paula. I Always Wondered. Parton, Paula. 2009. 44p. pap. 11.95 *(978-1-935118-48-0(X))* Bellissima Publishing, LLC.

—Room 17 - Where History Comes Alive - Missions. Parton, Paula. 2010. 126p. pap. 8.95 *(978-1-935630-19-7(9))* Bellissima Publishing, LLC.

—Room 17 Where History Comes Alive Book I — Indians. Parton, Paula. 2007. 128p. per. 8.95 *(978-0-9794815-0-5(3))* Bellissima Publishing, LLC.

—We Love Christmas! Parton, Paula. 2009. 30p. pap. 11.95 *(978-1-935118-84-8(6))* Bellissima Publishing, LLC.

Parts, Art, jt. illus. see Grabas, Peter.

Parvensky Barwell, Catherine A. Tommi Goes Camping, 4 vols. Parvensky Barwell, Catherine A. Barwell, Matthew W. et al, eds. 2006. 40p. (J). 14.95 *(978-0-9774409-3-1(1),* TL004) ILT Publishing.

Paschkis, Julie. Albert the Fix-It Man, 1 vol. Lord, Janet. (ENG.). 32p. (J). 2015. (gr. 1-3). pap. 7.95 *(978-1-56145-830-1(9));* 2008. (gr. k-3). 15.95 *(978-1-56145-433-4(8))* Peachtree Pubs.

—Building on Nature: The Life of Antoni Gaudí. Rodriguez, Rachel Victoria. 2009. (ENG.). 32p. (J). (gr. k-3). 18.99 *(978-0-8050-8745-1(1),* Holt, Henry & Co. Bks. For Young Readers) Holt, Henry & Co.

—Fat Cat: A Danish Folktale. MacDonald, Margaret Read. 2005. (ENG.). 32p. (J). (gr. -1-2). pap. 8.95 *(978-0-87483-765-0(0))* August Hse. Pubs., Inc.

—Glass Slipper, Gold Sandal: A Worldwide Cinderella. Fleischman, Paul. 2007. (ENG.). 32p. (J). (gr. k-5). 17.99 *(978-0-8050-7953-1(X),* Holt, Henry & Co. Bks. For Young Readers) Holt, Henry & Co.

—The Great Smelly, Slobbery, Small-Tooth Dog: A Folktale from Great Britain. 2007. (ENG.). 32p. (J). (gr. -1-3). 16.95 *(978-0-87483-808-4(8))* August Hse. Pubs., Inc.

—Head, Body, Legs: A Story from Liberia. Paye, Won-Ldy & Lippert, Margaret H. 2006. (gr. -1-3). lib. bdg. 18.00 *(978-0-7569-6925-7(5))* Perfection Learning Corp.

—Head, Body, Legs: A Story from Liberia. Paye, Won-Ldy & Lippert, Margaret H. 2005. (ENG.). 32p. (J). (gr. -1-3). pap. 7.99 *(978-0-8050-7890-9(8))* Square Fish.

—Here Comes Grandma! Lord, Janet. rev. ed. 2005. (ENG.). 32p. (J). (gr. -1-k). 14.99 *(978-0-8050-7666-0(2),* Holt, Henry & Co. Bks. For Young Readers) Holt, Henry & Co.

—Mrs. Chicken & the Hungry Crocodile. Paye, Won-Ldy & Lippert, Margaret H. 2014. (ENG.). 32p. (J). (gr. -1-2). pap. 6.99 *(978-1-250-04673-4(4))* Square Fish.

—The Night of the Moon: A Muslim Holiday Story. Khan, Hena. 2008. (ENG.). 32p. (J). (gr. -1-3). 16.99 *(978-0-8118-6062-8(0))* Chronicle Bks. LLC.

—Pablo Neruda: Poet of the People. Brown, Monica. 2011. (ENG.). 300p. (J). (gr. 1-4). 17.99 *(978-0-8050-9198-4(X),* Holt, Henry & Co. Bks. For Young Readers) Holt, Henry & Co.

—Summer Birds: The Butterflies of Maria Merian. Engle, Margarita. 2010. (ENG.). 32p. (J). (gr. k-3). 17.99 *(978-0-8050-8937-0(3),* Holt, Henry & Co. Bks. For Young Readers) Holt, Henry & Co.

—Through Georgia's Eyes. Rodriguez, Rachel Victoria. rev. ed. 2006. (ENG.). 32p. (J). (gr. k-3). 18.99 *(978-0-8050-7740-7(5),* Holt, Henry & Co. Bks. For Young Readers) Holt, Henry & Co.

—Twist: Yoga Poems. Wong, Janet S. 2007. (ENG.). 40p. (J). (gr. 2-5). 18.99 *(978-0-689-87394-2(8),* McElderry, Margaret K. Bks.) McElderry, Margaret K. Bks.

—Where Is Catkin?, 1 vol. Lord, Janet. (ENG.). 32p. (J). (gr. -1-1). 2013. 7.95 *(978-1-56145-684-0(5));* 2010. 16.95 *(978-1-56145-523-2(7))* Peachtree Pubs.

—Who Put the Cookies in the Cookie Jar? Shannon, George. 2013. (ENG.). 32p. (J). (gr. -1-1). 16.99 *(978-0-8050-9197-7(1),* Holt, Henry & Co. Bks. For Young Readers) Holt, Henry & Co.

Paschkis, Julie. Flutter & Hum / Aleteo y Zumbido: Animal Poems / Poemas de Animales. Paschkis, Julie. 2015. (ENG & SPA.). 32p. (J). (gr. -1-3). 17.99 *(978-1-62779-103-8(5),* Holt, Henry & Co. Bks. For Young Readers) Holt, Henry & Co.

—Knock on Wood: Poems about Superstitions. Paschkis, Julie. Wong, Janet S. 2003. (ENG.). 40p. (J). (gr. 2-5). 19.99 *(978-0-689-85512-2(5),* McElderry, Margaret K. Bks.) McElderry, Margaret K. Bks.

—Mooshka, a Quilt Story, 1 vol. Paschkis, Julie. 2012. (ENG.). 32p. (J). 16.95 *(978-1-56145-620-8(9))* Peachtree Pubs.

—P. Zonka Lays an Egg, 1 vol. Paschkis, Julie. 2015. (ENG.). 32p. (J). (gr. 1-3). 16.95 *(978-1-56145-819-6(8))* Peachtree Pubs.

Pascoe, Jed. Performance Poems. Moses, Brian, ed. 2013. (ENG.). 80p. pap. 16.50 *(978-1-85741-087-7(4))* Southgate Pubs. GBR. Dist: Parkwest Pubns., Inc.

—Rip-Roaring Round Book. Kempton, Clive & Atkin, Alan. 2013. (ENG.). 112p. pap. 21.50 *(978-1-85741-062-4(9))* Southgate Pubs. GBR. Dist: Parkwest Pubns., Inc.

Pascoe, Pete. A Pig Called Pete. Bowater, Alan. 2009. (Pig Called Pete Ser.). 32p. (J). (gr. -1-2). 22.60 *(978-1-60754-558-3(6));* pap. 10.55 *(978-1-60754-559-0(4))* Windmill Bks.

—A Pig Called Pete Meets a Cat Called Kitty. Bowater, Alan. 2009. (Pig Called Pete Ser.). 32p. (J). (gr. -1-2). 22.60 *(978-1-60754-561-3(6));* pap. 10.55 *(978-1-60754-562-0(4))* Windmill Bks.

—A Pig Called Pete Meets a Cow Called Carlotta. Bowater, Alan. 2009. (Pig Called Pete Ser.). 32p. (J). (gr. -1-2). 22.60 *(978-1-60754-567-5(5));* pap. 10.55 *(978-1-60754-568-2(3))* Windmill Bks.

—A Pig Called Pete Meets a Dog Called Doug. Bowater, Alan. 2009. (Pig Called Pete Ser.). 32p. (J). (gr. -1-2). 22.60 *(978-1-60754-564-4(0));* pap. 10.55 *(978-1-60754-565-1(9))* Windmill Bks.

—A Pig Called Pete Meets a Sheep Called Sean. Bowater, Alan. 2009. (Pig Called Pete Ser.). 32p. (J). (gr. -1-2). 22.60 *(978-1-60754-570-5(5));* pap. 10.55 *(978-1-60754-571-2(3))* Windmill Bks.

Pascuzzo, Philip. No Ordinary Apple: A Story about Eating Mindfully. Marlowe, Sara. 2013. (ENG.). 36p. (J). (gr. -1-3). 16.95 *(978-1-61429-076-6(8))* Wisdom Pubns.

Pasishnychenko, Oksana. Twinkle, Twinkle, Little Star. Everett, Melissa. 2013. (ENG.). 20p. (J). (gr. -1-3). 8.99 *(978-1-77093-534-1(7))* Flowerpot Children's Pr. Inc. CAN. Dist: Cardinal Pubs. Group.

Passarella, Jennie. U.S. Presidents & Their Animal Friends. Autrey, Jacquelyn & Yeager, Alice. 2004. 32p. (J). *(978-1-59421-005-1(5))* Seacoast Publishing, Inc.

Passicot, Monique. The Day the Rabbi Disappeared: Jewish Holiday Tales of Magic. Schwartz, Howard. 2003. (JPS Young Adult Story Collections). (ENG.). 80p. pap. 13.00 *(978-0-8276-0757-6(1))* Jewish Pubn. Society.

Passman, Emily. Dancing With My Mother. Bissex, Rachel. 2003. 14p. (J). spiral bd. 10.00 *(978-0-9742516-0-8(7))* Minimal Pr., The.

Pastars, Chris. Washington Farm-Toons Coloring & Activity Book. O'Neil, Patrick. 2nd ed. 2003. (J). *(978-0-9742610-0-3(9))* Applied Database Technology, Inc.

Pastel, Elyse & Pastel, Elyse. Tutu Twins. Bergen, Lara. 2008. (ENG.). 24p. (J). (gr. k-17). per. 3.99 *(978-1-58476-615-5(8))* Innovative Kids.

Pastel, Elyse, jt. illus. see Pastel, Elyse.

Pastis, Stephan. Mistakes Were Made. Pastis, Stephan. 2013. (Timmy Failure Ser.: No. 1). (ENG.). 304p. (J). (gr. 3-7). 14.99 *(978-0-7636-6050-7(7));* 100.00 *(978-0-7636-6689-7(0))* Candlewick Pr.

—Now Look What You've Done. Pastis, Stephan. 2014. (Timmy Failure Ser.: No. 2). (ENG.). 288p. (J). (gr. 3-7). 14.99 *(978-0-7636-6051-2(5))* Candlewick Pr.

—Timmy Failure: Mistakes Were Made. Pastis, Stephan. 2015. (Timmy Failure Ser.). (ENG.). 320p. (J). (gr. 3-7). pap. 7.99 *(978-0-7636-6927-0(X))* Candlewick Pr.

Pastor, Terry & Haggerty, Tim. The Solar System (Al Majmoo'a Al Shamsiya) Bone, Emily. Ibrahim, Nouran, tr. 2012. (ENG & ARA.). 32p. (J). 6.99 *(978-99921-94-35-5(9),* 149893) Bloomsbury USA.

—The Solar System Internet Referenced. Bone, Emily. 2010. (Beginner's Science Ser.). 32p. (J). (gr. 1). 4.99 *(978-0-7945-2812-6(0),* Usborne) EDC Publishing.

Pastor, Terry, jt. illus. see Montgomery, Lee.

Pastore, Vicki. The Apostles' Creed. 2007. 32p. (J). (gr. -1-3). per. 7.95 *(978-0-8091-6738-8(7),* 6738-8) Paulist Pr.

Pastrovicchio, Lorenzo. Mouse Magic. Ambrosio, Stefano. 2010. (ENG.). 112p. (J). 24.99 *(978-1-60886-550-5(9));* Vol. 1. pap. 9.99 *(978-1-60886-541-3(X))* Boom! Studios.

—Why, Mommy!!, 1 vol. Alvarez, Miguel et al. 2009. 17p. pap. 24.95 *(978-1-60749-429-4(9))* America Star Bks.

Pastrovicchio, Lorenzo & Magic Eye Studios. Wizards of Mickey - Grand Tournament, Vol. 2. Ambrosio, Stefano. 2010. (Wizards of Mickey Ser.). (ENG.). 128p. (J). (gr. 3-6). pap. 9.99 *(978-1-60886-564-2(9))* Boom! Studios.

Pastuchiv, Olga. Riparia's River, 1 vol. Caduto, Michael J. 2010. (ENG.). 32p. (J). (gr. k-7). 16.95 *(978-0-88448-327-4(4))* Tilbury Hse. Pubs.

Patacchiola, Amy. Unplugged Play: No Batteries. No Plugs. Pure Fun. Conner, Bobbi. 2007. (ENG.). 516p. (J). (gr. -1-5). 27.95 *(978-0-7611-4114-3(6),* 14114); pap. 16.95 *(978-0-7611-4390-1(4),* 14390) Workman Publishing Co., Inc.

Patagonia School. Lillie's Treasures/Los tesoros de Lili. Chesne, Sabrina. Capasso, Diana, tr. 2004. (ENG & SPA.). 32p. per. 15.00 *(978-0-9630310-9-9(0))* Will Hall Bks.

Patch, Michael. Santa's Sugar. Gerencher, Jane. 2012. 51p. 15.50 *(978-0-9852501-3-3(5))* Inkwell Productions, LLC.

—Tales of the Lush Green Woods. Patch, Lisa. 2012. 42p. 16.50 *(978-0-9852501-5-7(1))* Inkwell Productions, LLC.

—Who Is in That Shell? Amdahl Elco, Anita & Weikert Stelmach, Katherine. 2012. 130p. (J). pap. 13.50 *(978-0-9883568-0-1(5))* Inkwell Productions, LLC.

Patch, Sebastion. Thimble the Fairy's Acorns & Tea. The Fairy, Thimble. 2011. (ENG.). 48p. (J). 8.99 *(978-0-9827304-0-9(3))* Eleve Publishing.

Pate, Rodney. Joe Louis, My Champion, 1 vol. Pate, Rodney, tr. Miller, William. 2004. (ENG.). 32p. (J). 16.95 *(978-1-58430-161-5(9))* Lee & Low Bks., Inc.

Pate, Rodney S. Jackie Robinson. Walker, Sally M. Translations.com Staff, tr. 2005. (Yo Solo: Biografías (on My Own Biographies) Ser.). (SPA & ENG.). 48p. (gr. 2-4). lib. bdg. 25.26 *(978-0-8225-3126-5(7),* Ediciones Lerner) Lerner Publishing Group.

—Joe Louis, My Champion. Miller, William. 2004. (ENG.). 32p. (J). pap. 10.95 *(978-1-60060-426-3(9))* Lee & Low Bks., Inc.

—A Lesson for Martin Luther King, Jr. Patrick, Denise Lewis. 2003. (Ready-To-read COFA Ser.). (ENG.). 32p. (J). (gr. k-2). pap. 3.99 *(978-0-689-85397-5(1),* Simon Spotlight) Simon Spotlight.

Patenaude, Brian. Firefly Fred. Porter, Todd. 2004. (ENG.). 36p. (J). (gr. -1-3). 19.95 *(978-1-932278-00-2(1))* Mayhaven Publishing, Inc.

Patent, Dorothy Hinshaw. Dogs on Duty: Soldiers' Best Friends on the Battlefield & Beyond. Patent, Dorothy Hinshaw. 2012. (ENG.). 48p. (J). (gr. 2-10). 16.99 *(978-0-8027-2845-6(6));* 17.89 *(978-0-8027-2846-3(4))* Walker & Co.

Paterson, Alys. The Shape of My Heart. Sperring, Mark. 2012. (ENG.). 32p. (J). lib. bdg. 15.89 *(978-1-59990-963-9(4));* (gr. -1-k). 16.99 *(978-1-59990-962-2(6))* Bloomsbury USA. (Bloomsbury USA Childrens).

Paterson, Diane. Love, Lizzie: Letters to a Military Mom. McElroy, Lisa Tucker. (ENG.). 32p. (J). (gr. 1-5). 2009. pap. 6.99 *(978-0-8075-4778-6(6));* 2005. lib. bdg. 16.99 *(978-0-8075-4777-9(8))* Whitman, Albert & Co.

—You Go Away, 1 vol. Corey, Dorothy. 2008. (ENG.). 32p. (J). (gr. -1-k). pap. 6.99 *(978-0-8075-9443-8(1))* Whitman, Albert & Co.

Paterson, Diane. Hurricane Wolf. Paterson, Diane. 2006. (ENG.). 32p. (J). (gr. k-3). lib. bdg. 16.99 *(978-0-8075-3438-0(2))* Whitman, Albert & Co.

Patete, Christine. Super Phil & the Missing Mom. Tucker, Mark. 2003. 24p. (J). 4.50 *(978-1-882440-01-6(3))* God's World Pubns. Inc.

—Super Phil & the Sphiddle of the Rinks. Tucker, Mark. 2003. (J). 4.50 *(978-1-882440-02-3(1))* God's World Pubns. Inc.

Pathak, Ashutosh. Arnie & the Chawl of Colour. Rao, Chatura. 2004. 100p. pap. *(978-0-14-333592-4(8),* Puffin) Penguin Publishing Group.

Patience, John. I Can Read. Gikow, Louise. 2004. (My First Reader Ser.). 31p. (J). 18.50 *(978-0-516-24678-9(X),* Children's Pr.) Scholastic Library Publishing.

—I Can Read. Gikow, Louise A. 2005. (My First Reader Ser.). (ENG.). 32p. (J). (gr. k-1). pap. 3.95 *(978-0-516-25114-1(7),* Children's Pr.) Scholastic Library Publishing.

Patients from East Tennessee Children's Hospital. East Tennessee from a to Z. McMillan, Jenna. 2013. (ENG.). 26p. 20.00 *(978-0-9830954-2-2(6))* Books by Kids LLC.

Patkau, Karen. One Hungry Heron, 1 vol. Beck, Carolyn. 2014. (ENG.). 32p. (J). 17.95 *(978-1-55455-361-7(X))* Fitzhenry & Whiteside, Ltd. CAN. Dist: Midpoint Trade Bks., Inc.

—One Watermelon Seed, 1 vol. Lottridge, Celia. 2012. (ENG.). 32p. (J). pap. 9.95 *(978-1-55455-222-1(2))* Fitzhenry & Whiteside, Ltd. CAN. Dist: Midpoint Trade Bks., Inc.

Patkau, Karen. Creatures Yesterday & Today. Patkau, Karen. 2012. (ENG.). 32p. (J). (gr. 1-4). pap. 8.95 *(978-1-77049-310-0(7),* Tundra Bks.) Tundra Bks. CAN. Dist: Penguin Random Hse., LLC.

Patlan, Alyssa A. The Magical City of Northopolis; a Christmas Story. Banda, Rey A. 2012. 50p. (-18). pap. 16.95 *(978-0-615-69125-1(0))* Northopolis.

Patradol Kitcharoen. Pandi's Adventures in Afric. Alfred Sole. 2012. 86p. pap. 23.97 *(978-1-61897-493-8(9),* Strategic Bk. Publishing) Strategic Book Publishing & Rights Agency (SBPRA).

Patricelli, Leslie. Be Careful, Icarus! Holub, Joan. 2015. (ENG.). 22p. (J). (gr. -1 — 1). bds. 6.95 ***(978-1-4197-1677-5(8))*** Abrams.

Patricelli, Leslie. Be Patient, Pandora! Holub, Joan. 2014. (Mini Myths Ser.). (ENG.). 24p. (J). (gr. -1 — 1). bds. 6.95 *(978-1-4197-0951-7(8),* Abrams Appleseed) Abrams.

—Brush Your Hair, Medusa! Holub, Joan. 2015. (Mini Myths Ser.). (ENG.). 24p. (J). (gr. -1 — 1). bds. 6.95 *(978-1-4197-0953-1(4))* Abrams.

—Make a Wish, Midas! Holub, Joan. 2015. (Mini Myths Ser.). (ENG.). 24p. (J). (gr. -1 — 1). bds. 6.95 *(978-1-4197-0952-4(6))* Abrams.

—Play Nice, Hercules! Holub, Joan. 2014. (Mini Myths Ser.). (ENG.). 24p. (J). (gr. -1 — 1). bds. 6.95 *(978-1-4197-0954-8(2),* Abrams Appleseed) Abrams.

Patricelli, Leslie. Please Share, Aphrodite! Holub, Joan. 2015. (ENG.). 22p. (J). (gr. -1 — 1). bds. 6.95 ***(978-1-4197-1678-2(6))*** Abrams.

Patricelli, Leslie. Baby Happy Baby Sad. Patricelli, Leslie. 2008. (Leslie Patricelli Board Bks.). (ENG.). 24p. (J). (— 1). bds. 6.99 *(978-0-7636-3245-8(7))* Candlewick Pr.

—Big Little. Patricelli, Leslie. 2003. (Leslie Patricelli Board Bks.). (ENG.). 24p. (J). (— 1). bds. 6.99 *(978-0-7636-1951-0(5))* Candlewick Pr.

—Binky. Patricelli, Leslie. 2005. (Leslie Patricelli Board Bks.). (ENG.). 24p. (J). (— 1). bds. 6.99 *(978-0-7636-2364-7(4))* Candlewick Pr.

—The Birthday Box. Patricelli, Leslie. (Leslie Patricelli Board Bks.). (ENG.). (J). 2009. 26p. (gr. k — 1). bds. 6.99 *(978-0-7636-4449-9(8));* 2007. 32p. (gr. -1-k). 15.99 *(978-0-7636-2825-3(5))* Candlewick Pr.

—Blankie. Patricelli, Leslie. 2005. (Leslie Patricelli Board Bks.). (ENG.). 24p. (J). (— 1). bds. 6.99 *(978-0-7636-2363-0(6))* Candlewick Pr.

Patricelli, Leslie. Boo! Patricelli, Leslie. 2015. (Leslie Patricelli Board Bks.). (ENG.). 26p. (J). (— 1). bds. 6.99 ***(978-0-7636-6320-9(4))*** Candlewick Pr.

Patricelli, Leslie. Fa la La. Patricelli, Leslie. 2012. (Leslie Patricelli Board Bks.). (ENG.). 26p. (J). (gr. k — 1). bds. 6.99 *(978-0-7636-3247-2(3))* Candlewick Pr.

—Faster! Faster! Patricelli, Leslie. (Leslie Patricelli Board Bks.). (ENG.). (J). (-k). 2013. 30p. bds. 6.99 *(978-0-7636-6222-6(4));* 2012. 32p. 15.99 *(978-0-7636-5473-3(6))* Candlewick Pr.

—Faster! Faster!/Mas Rapido! Mas Rapido! Patricelli, Leslie. 2013. (Leslie Patricelli Board Bks.). (ENG.). 30p. (J). (-k). bds. 6.99 *(978-0-7636-6611-8(4))* Candlewick Pr.

—Grande Pequeño. Patricelli, Leslie. Rozarena, P., tr. 2003. (SPA.). 25p. (J). (gr. -1-k). bds. 7.95 *(978-970-29-0988-0(0))* Santillana USA Publishing Co., Inc.

—Higher! Higher! Patricelli, Leslie. 2010. (Leslie Patricelli Board Bks.). (ENG.). 30p. (J). (-k). bds. 6.99 *(978-0-7636-4433-8(1))* Candlewick Pr.

—Hop! Hop! Patricelli, Leslie. 2015. (Leslie Patricelli Board Bks.). (ENG.). 26p. (J). (— 1). bds. 6.99 *(978-0-7636-6319-3(0))* Candlewick Pr.

—Huggy Kissy. Patricelli, Leslie. 2012. (Leslie Patricelli Board Bks.). (ENG.). 26p. (J). (gr. k — 1). bds. 6.99 *(978-0-7636-3246-5(5))* Candlewick Pr.

—No No Yes Yes. Patricelli, Leslie. 2008. (Leslie Patricelli Board Bks.). (ENG.). 24p. (J). (— 1). bds. 6.99 *(978-0-7636-3244-1(9))* Candlewick Pr.

—The Patterson Puppies & the Midnight Monster Party. Patricelli, Leslie. 2010. (ENG.). 32p. (J). (gr. -1-k). 14.99 *(978-0-7636-3243-4(0))* Candlewick Pr.

—The Patterson Puppies & the Rainy Day. Patricelli, Leslie. 2009. (ENG.). 40p. (J). (gr. -1-k). 14.99 *(978-0-7636-3242-7(2))* Candlewick Pr.

—Potty. Patricelli, Leslie. 2010. (Leslie Patricelli Board Bks.). (ENG.). 28p. (J). (gr. k — 1). bds. 6.99 *(978-0-7636-4476-5(5))* Candlewick Pr.

—Quiet Loud. Patricelli, Leslie. 2003. (Leslie Patricelli Board Bks.). (ENG.). 24p. (J). (gr. k — 1). bds. 6.99 *(978-0-7636-1952-7(3))* Candlewick Pr.

—Silencio Ruido. Patricelli, Leslie. Rozarena, P., tr. 2003. (SPA.). 25p. (J). (gr. -1-k). bds. 7.95 *(978-970-29-0987-3(2))* Santillana USA Publishing Co., Inc.

—Tickle. Patricelli, Leslie. 2014. (Leslie Patricelli Board Bks.). (ENG.). 26p. (J). (— 1). bds. 6.99 *(978-0-7636-6322-3(0))* Candlewick Pr.

—Toot. Patricelli, Leslie. 2014. (Leslie Patricelli Board Bks.). (ENG.). 24p. (J). (— 1). bds. 6.99 *(978-0-7636-6321-6(2))* Candlewick Pr.

—Tubby. Patricelli, Leslie. 2010. (Leslie Patricelli Board Bks.). (ENG.). 28p. (J). (— 1). bds. 6.99 *(978-0-7636-4567-0(2))* Candlewick Pr.

—Yummy Yucky. Patricelli, Leslie. 2003. (Leslie Patricelli Board Bks.). (ENG.). 24p. (J). (gr. k — 1). bds. 6.99 *(978-0-7636-1950-3(7))* Candlewick Pr.

Patrick, Jean L. S. & Faricy, Patrick. Face to Face with Mount Rushmore. Patrick, Jean L. S. 2008. (J). *(978-0-9798823-1-9(1))* Mount Rushmore Bookstores.

Patrick, Scot. Pink Milk Sea Coloring Book. Frances, Dee. Date not set. 32p. (J). pap. 3.00 *(978-1-885519-26-9(5))* DDDD Pubns.

Patrick, Tom. Hurray for Snow! Tyrell, Melissa. enl. ed. 2005. (ENG.). 10p. (J). (gr. -1-3). 4.95 *(978-1-58117-118-1(8),* Intervisual/Piggy Toes) Bendon, Inc.

PatrickGeorge. A Drove of Bullocks: A Compilation of Animal Group Names. PatrickGeorge. 2011. (ENG.). 48p. (J). (gr. 2). pap. 12.99 *(978-0-9562558-0-8(9))* PatrickGeorge GBR. Dist: Independent Pubs. Group.

—A Filth of Starlings: A Compilation of Bird & Aquatic Animal Group Names. PatrickGeorge. 2011. (ENG.). 48p. (J). (gr. 2). pap. 12.99 *(978-0-9562558-1-5(7))* PatrickGeorge GBR. Dist: Independent Pubs. Group.

Patrizzi, Barbara. O Is for Oystercatcher: A Book of Seaside ABCs. Patrizzi, Barbara. 2003. 55p. 15.95 *(978-1-59322-008-2(1))* Down The Shore Publishing Corp.

Patterson, Annie. How Does a Caterpillar Become a Butterfly? And Other Questions about Butterflies. Stewart, Melissa. 2014. (Good Question! Ser.). (ENG.). 32p. (J). (gr. 1). 12.95 *(978-1-4549-0666-7(9))* Sterling Publishing Co., Inc.

—Too Hot? Too Cold? Keeping Body Temperature Just Right. Arnold, Caroline. 2013. (ENG.). 32p. (J). (gr. 1-4). pap. 7.95 *(978-1-58089-277-3(9))* Charlesbridge Publishing, Inc.

—Turtle, Turtle, Watch Out! Sayre, April Pulley. 2010. (ENG.). 32p. (J). (gr. k-3). pap. 7.95 *(978-1-58089-149-3(7))* Charlesbridge Publishing, Inc.

—Whale Snow. Edwardson, Debby Dahl. 2004. (ENG.). 32p. (J). (gr. -1-3). pap. 7.95 *(978-1-57091-394-5(3))* Charlesbridge Publishing, Inc.

Patterson, Bill. Rudolph's Night Off. Black, Baxter A. 2011. (ENG.). 32p. (J). (gr. -1-3). 19.95 *(978-0-939343-54-6(1))* Coyote Cowboy Co.

Patterson, Geoffrey. The Elephant's Child. Kipling, Rudyard. 2010. (ENG.). 36p. (J). (gr. -1-2). pap. 8.95 *(978-1-84507-492-0(0),* Frances Lincoln) Quarto Publishing Group UK GBR. Dist: Hachette Bk. Group.

Patterson, Nancy. May the Magnificent Lighthouse. Patterson, Nancy. 2012. 24p. 18.95 *(978-0-615-61021-4(8))* Bayberry Cottage Gallery.

Patterson, Robin. 101 Cool Pool Games for Children: Fun & Fitness for Swimmers of All Levels. Rodomista, Kim. 2006. (SmartFun Activity Bks.). (ENG.). 160p. (gr. -1). per. 14.95 *(978-0-89793-483-1(0),* Hunter Hse.) Turner Publishing Co.

Patteson, Neida. Adina de Zavala: "Angel of the Alamo" Her Life Story Presented Through the Clothes She Wore. Patteson, Neida. 2003. (Women of Texas Ser.: Vol. 3). Orig. Title: Angel of the Alamo. 32p. (J). (gr. 4-8). pap. 14.95 *(978-0-9629001-2-9(5))* Smiley Co.

Patti, Sheila. Ollie Ollie Ox in Free. Ferguson, Linda. 2004. 189p. (YA). per. *(978-0-9755288-0-8(7))* Ferguson, Linda.

Patton, Julia. Are You Listening, Jack? Garcia, Ellen. 2014. (J). (gr. -1). 3.99 *(978-1-4788-0472-7(6))* Newmark Learning LLC.

—Are You Listening, Jack? Lap Book. Garcia, Ellen. 2014. (MySELF Ser.). (J). (gr. -1-k). 27.00 *(978-1-4788-0509-0(9))* Newmark Learning LLC.

—Be Patient, Maddie Lap Book. Garcia, Ellen. 2014. (MySELF Ser.). (J). (gr. -1-k). 27.00 *(978-1-4788-0512-0(9))* Newmark Learning LLC.

—Clean up, Everybody Lap Book. Sparks, Stacey. 2014. (MySELF Ser.). (J). (gr. -1-k). 27.00 *(978-1-4788-0514-4(5))* Newmark Learning LLC.

—I Can Follow the Rules. Williams, Dinah. 2014. (J). (gr. -1). 3.99 *(978-1-4788-0473-4(4))* Newmark Learning LLC.

—I Can Follow the Rules Lap Book. Williams, Dinah. 2014. (MySELF Ser.). (J). (gr. -1-k). 27.00 *(978-1-4788-0510-6(2))* Newmark Learning LLC.

—I Can Stay Calm. Daniel, Claire. 2014. (J). (gr. -1). 3.99 *(978-1-4788-0474-1(2))* Newmark Learning LLC.

—I Can Stay Calm Lap Book. Daniel, Claire. 2014. (MySELF Ser.). (J). (gr. -1-k). 27.00 *(978-1-4788-0511-3(0))* Newmark Learning LLC.

—I Take Turns. Linde, Barbara M. 2014. (J). (gr. -1). 3.99 *(978-1-4788-0476-5(9))* Newmark Learning LLC.

—I Take Turns Lap Book. Linde, Barbara M. 2014. (MySELF Ser.). (J). (gr. -1-k). 27.00 *(978-1-4788-0513-7(7))* Newmark Learning LLC.

—PB&J Hooray! Your Sandwich's Amazing Journey from Farm to Table. Nolan, Janet. 2014. (ENG.). 32p. (J). (gr. -1-2). 16.99 *(978-0-8075-6397-7(8))* Whitman, Albert & Co.

Patton, Lucia. Surprise on Wheels. Friskey, Margaret. 2004. reprint ed. pap. 15.95 *(978-1-4191-1496-0(4))* Kessinger Publishing, LLC.

Patton, Scott. Stories Told under the Sycamore Tree: Bible Plant Object Lessons. Patton, Scott, tr. Hahn, Samuel J. 2003. 191p. (J). pap. 19.95 *(978-0-7880-1972-2(4))* CSS Publishing Co.

Patzelt, Kasie. Land of Pink. Sanders, Roy E. 2007. (Not So Far Ago Ser.). 37p. (J). (gr. -1-3). 19.99 *(978-1-59879-327-7(6))* Lifevest Publishing, Inc.

—Twiggle. Staton, Debbie. 2007. (J). (gr. -1-3). 17.99 *(978-1-59879-362-8(4));* 26p. per. 12.99 *(978-1-59879-199-0(0))* Lifevest Publishing, Inc.

Paul, Kate. The Adventures of Jake & George: Jake Gets a New Brother. Swift, K. Marie. 2010. 26p. pap. 11.75 *(978-1-60693-863-8(0),* Eloquent Bks.) Strategic Book Publishing & Rights Agency (SBPRA).

Paul, Korky. Dinosaur Poems. Foster, John. 2nd rev. ed. 2004. (ENG.). 32p. (YA). 10.95 *(978-0-19-276305-1(9))* Oxford Univ. Pr., Inc.

—Dragon Poems. Foster, John L. 2nd rev. ed. 2004. (ENG.). 32p. (YA). pap. 10.95 *(978-0-19-276307-5(5))* Oxford Univ. Pr., Inc.

—Fantastic Football Poems. Foster, John. 2008. (ENG.). 32p. (YA). (gr. 4-7). pap. 10.95 *(978-0-19-276349-5(0))* Oxford Univ. Pr., Inc.

—First Day. Gray, Kes. 2007. (Collins Big Cat Ser.). (ENG.). 24p. (J). pap. 6.99 *(978-0-00-718666-2(5))* HarperCollins Pubs. Ltd. GBR. Dist: Independent Pubs. Group.

—Mr. Crookodile. Bush, John. 2006. (Blue Bananas Ser.). (ENG.). 48p. (J). (gr. k-2). pap. 5.99 *(978-1-4052-2229-7(8))* Egmont Bks., Ltd. GBR. Dist: Independent Pubs. Group.

—Pa Jinglebob - The Fastest Knitter in the West. Arrigan, Mary. 2005. (Red Bananas Ser.). (ENG.). 48p. (J). lib. bdg. *(978-0-7787-1072-1(6))* Crabtree Publishing Co.

—The Rascally Cake. Paul, Jeanne Wi & Willis, Jeanne. 2011. (ENG.). 32p. (J). (gr. k-k). pap. 8.99 *(978-1-84270-717-3(5))* Andersen Pr. GBR. Dist: Independent Pubs. Group.

—Snail's Legs. Harvey, Damian. 2006. (ENG.). 32p. (J). (gr. -1-4). 15.95 *(978-1-84507-112-7(3),* Frances Lincoln) Quarto Publishing Group UK GBR. Dist: Perseus-PGW.

—The Very Noisy House. Rhodes, Julie & Quarto Generic Staff. 2014. (ENG.). 32p. (J). (gr. -1-k). 17.99 *(978-1-84507-983-3(3),* Frances Lincoln) Quarto Publishing Group UK GBR. Dist: Hachette Bk. Group.

Paul, Korky. You Tell Me! McGough, Roger et al. 2015. (ENG.). 96p. (J). (gr. 2-6). pap. 7.99 ***(978-1-84780-444-0(6),*** Frances Lincoln) Quarto Publishing Group UK GBR. Dist: Hachette Bk. Group.

Paul, Leonard. Long Powwow Nights, 1 vol. Bouchard, David & Aleekuk, Pam. 2009. (ENG.). 32p. (J). (gr. 1-4). 23.95 *(978-0-88995-427-4(5))* Red Deer Pr. CAN. Dist: Ingram Pub. Services.

—Pisim Finds Her Miskinow. Dumas, William. 2013. (ENG & CRE.). 48p. (YA). *(978-1-55379-394-6(3),* 9781553793946, HighWater Pr.) Portage & Main Pr.

Paul Reising. Beyond All Imagination: The First Souvenir. Leigh-Anna Tehan. 2009. 44p. pap. 18.49 *(978-1-4389-6452-2(8))* AuthorHouse.

Paul, Ruth. Hedgehog's Magic Tricks. Paul, Ruth. 2013. (ENG.). 32p. (J). (gr. -1-2). 12.99 *(978-0-7636-6385-8(9))* Candlewick Pr.

—Red Panda's Candy Apples. Paul, Ruth. 2014. (ENG.). 32p. (J). (gr. -1-2). 14.99 *(978-0-7636-6758-0(7))* Candlewick Pr.

Pauling, Galen T. Q. T. Pie Meets Smart E. Sanders, Stephanie. I.t. ed. 2003. (Q.T. Pie Ser.). 36p. (J). mass mkt. 4.99 *(978-0-9670875-4-2(6),* 313-533-7383) SanPaul Group, LLC, The.

Paull, Grace. Forgotten Island. Coatsworth, Elizabeth Jane. 2011. 74p. 36.95 *(978-1-258-07461-6(3))* Literary Licensing, LLC.

Paulsen, Ruth Wright. La Tortilleria. Paulsen, Gary. Andujar, Gloria Dearagon, tr. from ENG. 2006.Tr. of Tortilla Factory. 27p. (J). (gr. k-4). reprint ed. 16.00 *(978-1-4223-5319-6(2))* DIANE Publishing Co.

Paulson, Arlie & Nix, Pamela. Tummel the Tumbleweed. Nix, Pamela. Barnes, Trisha, ed. 2011. 26p. (J). pap. 7.99 *(978-0-9815914-9-0(3))* River Canyon Pr.

Paulson, Judy. Baby Tawnies. Paulson, Judy. 2013. (ENG.). 32p. (J). (gr. -1-k). pap. 11.99 *(978-1-74275-577-9(1))* Random Hse. Australia AUS. Dist: Independent Pubs. Group.

Paun, Alexandra. Old Man Nate's Halloween Tale. Paun, Alexandra. 2011. (ENG.). 34p. pap. 7.00 *(978-1-4663-3017-7(1))* CreateSpace Independent Publishing Platform.

Pavey, Peter. One Dragon's Dream. Pavey, Peter. 2009. (ENG.). 40p. (J). (gr. -1-2). 17.99 *(978-0-7636-4470-3(6))* Candlewick Pr.

Pavlova, Vera. A Child's Bedtime Companion. Henry, Sandy. 2005. 26p. (J). (gr. -1-2). per. 12.95 *(978-1-929039-31-9(X))* Ambassador Bks., Inc.

—Daddy's Good Cookin' Johnson, Vincent L. 2006. 32p. (J). 16.95 *(978-0-9657033-3-8(9))* Marzetta Bks.

Pavlovic, Milan. Hey Canada! Bowers, Vivien. 2012. (ENG.). 72p. (J). (gr. 2-5). 19.95 *(978-1-77049-255-4(0))* Tundra Bks. CAN. Dist: Random Hse., Inc.

Pawelak, Lydia, photos by. The Ballet Book: The Young Performer's Guide to Classical Dance. Bowes, Deborah. 2007. (Young Performer's Guide Ser.). (ENG., 144p. (J). (gr. 3-9). pap. 14.95 *(978-1-55209-353-5(0),* 9781552093535) Firefly Bks., Ltd.

Pawlak, Pawel. Excuse Me... Are You a Witch? Horn, Emily. 2004. (ENG.). 32p. (J). (gr. -1-2). pap. 7.95 *(978-1-58089-103-5(9))* Charlesbridge Publishing, Inc.

Pax, H. H. -. Metta's Bedtime Stories. World Peace, Metta & McBride, Heddrick. 2013. 36p. pap. 12.95 *(978-0-615-70075-5(6))* McBride, Heddrick.

Paxton, Cameron L. Arthur, the Talking Goat. Cromwell, Daisy. 2007. 52p. (J). pap. 18.99 *(978-0-9800675-1-4(0))* Mirror Publishing.

Payne, C. F. Brave Harriet. Moss, Marissa. 2015. 32p. pap. 8.00 ***(978-1-61003-492-0(9))*** Center for the Collaborative Classroom.

Payne, C. F. Bunnicula in a Box: Bunnicula; Howliday Inn; the Celery Stalks at Midnight; Nighty-Nightmare; Return to Howliday Inn; Bunnicula Strikes Again; Bunnicula Meets Edgar Allan Crow. Howe, James. ed. 2013. (Bunnicula & Friends Ser.). (ENG.). 1136p. (J). (gr. 3-7). pap. 41.99 *(978-1-4424-8521-1(3),* Atheneum Bks. for Young Readers) Simon & Schuster Children's Publishing.

—Casey at the Bat: A Ballad of the Republic Sung in the Year 1888. Thayer, Ernest L. 2003. (ENG.). 40p. (J). (gr. -1-3). 17.99 *(978-0-689-85494-1(3),* Simon & Schuster Bks. For Young Readers) Simon & Schuster Bks. For Young Readers.

—Hide-and-Squeak. Frederick, Heather Vogel. 2011. (ENG.). 32p. (J). (gr. -1-1). 16.99 *(978-0-689-85570-2(2),* Simon & Schuster Bks. For Young Readers) Simon & Schuster Bks. For Young Readers.

—Late for School. Martin, Steve. 2010. (ENG.). 32p. (gr. -1-1). 17.99 *(978-0-446-55702-3(1))* Grand Central Publishing.

—The Legend of the Curse of the Bambino. Shaughnessy, Dan. 2005. (ENG.). 32p. (J). (gr. k-3). 16.95 *(978-0-689-87235-8(6),* Simon & Schuster/Paula Wiseman Bks.) Simon & Schuster/Paula Wiseman Bks.

—Lineup for Yesterday. Nash, Ogden. 2011. (ENG.). 56p. (J). (gr. 1-3). 19.99 *(978-1-56846-212-7(3),* Creative Editions) Creative Co., The.

—Lineup for Yesterday ABC Baseball Cards. Nash, Ogden. 2013. (ENG.). (J). (gr. 1-3). 12.99 *(978-1-56846-249-3(2),* Creative Editions) Creative Co., The.

—Micawber. Lithgow, John. 2005. (ENG.). 40p. (J). (gr. -1-3). reprint ed. 7.99 *(978-0-689-83542-1(6),* Simon & Schuster Bks. For Young Readers) Simon & Schuster Bks. For Young Readers.

—Mousetronaut: Based on a (Partially) True Story. Kelly, Mark. 2012. (ENG.). 40p. (J). (gr. -1-3). 17.99 *(978-1-4424-5824-6(0),* Simon & Schuster/Paula Wiseman Bks.) Simon & Schuster/Paula Wiseman Bks.

—Mousetronaut Goes to Mars. Kelly, Mark. 2013. (ENG.). 40p. (J). (gr. -1-3). 16.99 *(978-1-4424-8426-9(8),* Simon & Schuster/Paula Wiseman Bks.) Simon & Schuster/Paula Wiseman Bks.

—Pop's Bridge. Bunting, Eve. 2006. (ENG.). 32p. (J). (gr. -1-3). 17.99 *(978-0-15-204773-3(5))* Houghton Mifflin Harcourt Publishing Co.

—Shoeless Joe & Black Betsy. Bildner, Phil. 2006. (ENG.). 40p. (J). (gr. k-3). reprint ed. 7.99 *(978-0-689-87437-6(5),* Simon & Schuster Bks. For Young Readers) Simon & Schuster Bks. For Young Readers.

—The Shot Heard 'Round the World. Bildner, Phil. 2010. (ENG.). 32p. (J). (gr. k-3). 16.99 *(978-1-4424-2195-0(9),* Simon & Schuster Bks. For Young Readers) Simon & Schuster Bks. For Young Readers.

—To Dare Mighty Things: The Life of Theodore Roosevelt. Rappaport, Doreen. 2013. (ENG.). 48p. (J). (gr. 1-3). 17.99 *(978-1-4231-2488-7(X))* Hyperion Pr.

—Turkey Bowl. Bildner, Phil. 2008. (ENG.). 32p. (J). (gr. k-3). 15.99 *(978-0-689-87896-1(6),* Simon & Schuster Bks. For Young Readers) Simon & Schuster Bks. For Young Readers.

Payne, C. F. Mighty Jackie: The Strike-Out Queen. Payne, C. F., tr. Moss, Marissa. 2004. (ENG.). 32p. (J). (gr. k-3). 17.99 *(978-0-689-86329-5(2),* Simon & Schuster/Paula Wiseman Bks.) Simon & Schuster/Paula Wiseman Bks.

P

Payne, Emerald M. Brown Eyes: Ojos Marrones. Payne, Yadira V. Payne, Yadira V., ed. 2004. (MUL.). (J). pap. 12.50 *(978-0-9747350-1-6(9))* Payne, Yadira V. Publishing.

Payne, Henry. The Ear Book. Perkins, Al. (Bright & Early Board Books(TM) Ser.). (ENG.). (J). (— 1). 2008. 24p. bds. 4.99 *(978-0-375-84279-5(9))*; 2007. 36p. 8.99 *(978-0-375-84251-1(9))* Random Hse. Children's Bks. (Random Hse. Bks. for Young Readers).

Payne, Kay. Beth's Fella. Strong, Frances Dinkins. 2006. 112p. (J). pap. 9.95 *(978-0-9720267-6-5(2))* Learning Abilities Bks.

Payne, Mark. Hilhairyass Poems: By a Six Year Old Adult. Lebachen, Medyhne. 2012. 76p. (YA). *(978-0-9872816-4-7(X))* Heart Space Pubns Pty Ltd (Australia).

Payne, Rachel & Song, Danielle. Miss Spellin' Helen. Payne, Jody. 2012. 148p. pap. 6.99 *(978-0-9846687-0-0(5))* Absalon Pr.

Payne, Stephanie. Cappy's Playground Adventure. O'Hanlon, Toni. 2012. (ENG.). 32p. pap. 9.95 *(978-1-4664-3105-8(9))* CreateSpace Independent Publishing Platform.

—KiddiCards. O'Hanlon, Toni. 2011. (ENG.). 32p. pap. 9.95 *(978-1-4610-0807-1(7))* CreateSpace Independent Publishing Platform.

—KiddiVersity KiddiCards Rhyming Edition - Modules Three & Four. O'Hanlon, Toni. 2011. (ENG.). 32p. pap. 9.95 *(978-1-4610-2761-4(6))* CreateSpace Independent Publishing Platform.

—KiddiVersity KiddiCards Rhyming Edition- Modules Seven & Eight. O'Hanlon, Toni. 2011. (ENG.). 36p. pap. 9.95 *(978-1-4610-3094-2(3))* CreateSpace Independent Publishing Platform.

—KiddiVersity KiddiCards Rhyming Edition Modules Five & Six. O'Hanlon, Toni. 2011. (ENG.). 32p. pap. 9.95 *(978-1-4610-3079-9(X))* CreateSpace Independent Publishing Platform.

—KiddiVersity KiddiCards Rhyming Edition Modules Nine & Ten. O'Hanlon, Toni. 2011. (ENG.). 34p. pap. 9.95 *(978-1-4610-3101-7(X))* CreateSpace Independent Publishing Platform.

—KiddiVersity's KiddiCards Rhyming Edition Modules Eleven & Twelve. O'Hanlon, Toni. 2011. (ENG.). 32p. pap. 9.95 *(978-1-4610-3103-1(6))* CreateSpace Independent Publishing Platform.

Payne, Tony. Things to Make & Doodle: Exciting Projects to Color, Cut, & Create. 2012. (ENG.). 64p. (J). pap. 12.95 *(978-0-7624-4289-8(1))* Running Pr. Bk. Pubs.

Payne, Yadira V. ¡Viva los Colores! Payne, Yadira V. 2004. (MUL.). (J). pap. 12.50 *(978-0-9747350-9-0(0))* Payne, Yadira V. Publishing.

Peabody, Rob. Achy Ali. Hersey, Jodi. 2011. pap. 5.00 *(978-1-4276-5272-0(4))* Aardvark Global Publishing.

Peach-Pit Press Staff. DearS, Vol. 2. Peach-pit. rev. ed. 2005. 208p. pap. 9.99 *(978-1-59532-309-5(0)*, Tokyopop Adult) TOKYOPOP, Inc.

—DearS, Vol. 3. rev. ed. 2005. (DearS Ser.). 208p. pap. 9.99 *(978-1-59532-310-1(4)*, Tokyopop Adult) TOKYOPOP, Inc.

Peach-Pit Press Staff. DearS, Vol. 5. Peach-Pit Press Staff. rev. ed. 2006. (DearS Ser.). 192p. pap. 9.99 *(978-1-59532-797-0(5)*, Tokyopop Adult) TOKYOPOP, Inc.

Peacock, Ausa M. As My Heart Awakes: A Waldorf Reader for Early Third Grade. Pittis, Arthur M. Mitchell, David S., ed. 2005. (J). bds. 10.00 *(978-1-888365-62-7(5))* Waldorf Pubns.

—Fee Fi Fo Fum: A Waldorf Reader for Late Second Grade. Pittis, Arthur M. Mitchell, David S., ed. 2005. (J). bds. 10.00 *(978-1-888365-63-4(3))* Waldorf Pubns.

—Sun So Hot I Froze to Death: A Waldorf Reader for Advanced Fourth Grade. Pittis, Arthur M. Mitchell, David S., ed. 2005. (J). bds. 12.00 *(978-1-888365-65-8(X))* Waldorf Pubns.

—When I Hear My Heart Wonder: A Waldorf Reader for Late Third Grade. Pittis, Arthur M. Mitchell, David S., ed. 2005. (J). bds. 10.00 *(978-1-888365-66-5(8))* Waldorf Pubns.

Peacock, Bessie Merle. Benny the Beetle, 1 vol. Peacock-Williams, Carol A. & Williams, Christy Jo. 2010. 28p. 24.95 *(978-1-4489-8373-5(8))* PublishAmerica, Inc.

Peacock, Phyllis Hornung. Pythagoras & the Ratios: A Math Adventure. Ellis, Julie. 2010. (ENG.). 32p. (J). (gr. 2-5). pap. 7.95 *(978-1-57091-776-9(0))* Charlesbridge Publishing, Inc.

—Pythagoras & the Ratios: A Math Adventure. Ellis, Julie. 2010. (ENG.). 32p. (J). (gr. 2-5). 16.95 *(978-1-57091-775-2(2))* Charlesbridge Publishing, Inc.

Peacock, Ralph. Wulf the Saxon: A Story of the Norman Conquest. Henty, G. A. 2010. (Dover Children's Classics Ser.). (ENG.). 352p. (YA). (gr. 3-8). pap. 8.95 *(978-0-486-47595-0(6))* Dover Pubns., Inc.

Peacock, Robert M., photos by. Southern Cocktails: Dixie Drinks, Party Potions, & Classic Libations. Gee, Denise. 2007. (ENG., 120p. (gr. 8-17). 14.95 *(978-0-8118-5243-2(1))* Chronicle Bks. LLC.

Peacock, Sarah. Ladybird's Remarkable Relaxation: How Children (And Frogs, Dogs, Flamingos & Dragons) Can Use Yoga Relaxation to Help Deal with Stress, Grief, Bullying & Lack of Confidence. Chissick, Michael. 2013. (ENG.). 48p. *(978-1-84819-146-4(4))* Kingsley, Jessica Ltd.

Peake, Mervyn. Grimm's Household Tales. Grimm, Jacob & Grimm, Wilhelm. 2012. 303p. 22.50 *(978-0-7123-5858-3(7))* British Library, The GBR. Dist: Chicago Distribution Ctr.

—The Hunting of the Snark. Carroll, Lewis. 2004. 64p. *(978-0-413-74380-0(2))* Methuen Publishing Ltd.

Pearce, Carl. Attention, Girls! A Guide to Learn all about Your AD/HD. Quinn, Patricia O. 2009. 112p. (J). (gr. 4-7). 16.95 *(978-1-4338-0447-2(6))*; pap. 12.95 *(978-1-4338-0448-9(4))* American Psychological Assn. (Magination Pr.).

Pearce, Carl. John Deere's Powerful Idea: The Perfect Plow. Collins, Terry. 2015. (Story Behind the Name Ser.). (ENG.). 32p. (gr. 2-3). lib. bdg. 27.99 ***(978-1-4795-7138-3(5))*** Picture Window Bks.

Pearce, Carl. The No-Dogs-Allowed Rule. Sheth, Kashmira. 2012. (ENG.). 128p. (J). (gr. 1-3). 14.99 *(978-0-8075-5694-8(7))* Whitman, Albert & Co.

—The Silence Seeker. Morley, Ben. 2009. (ENG.). 32p. (J). (gr. k-2). pap. 14.99 *(978-1-84853-003-4(X))* Transworld Publishers Ltd. GBR. Dist: Independent Pubs. Group.

Pearce, Gillian M. Growing up Pagan: A Workbook for Wiccan Families, 1 vol. Hill, Raine. 2009. (ENG.). 64p. pap., wbk. ed. 19.99 *(978-0-7643-3143-5(4))* Schiffer Publishing, Ltd.

Pearcey, Dawn. Escape Plans. Posesorski, Sherie. 2005. 272p. (J). (gr. 5). 8.95 *(978-1-55050-177-3(1))* Coteau Bks. CAN. Dist: Fitzhenry & Whiteside, Ltd.

Pearl, Debi & Pearl, Michael. Listen to My Dream. Pearl, Debi. 2009. (ENG.). 40p. pap. 6.95 *(978-0-9819737-1-5(X))* No Greater Joy Ministries, Inc.

Pearl, Michael, jt. illus. see Pearl, Debi.

Pearlman, Esther, jt. illus. see Pearlman, Larry.

Pearlman, Larry & Pearlman, Esther. Cute Li'l Donkeys: (Raisin' & Grazin') 2014. (J). *(978-0-935047-81-3(6))* Americas Group, The.

Pearn, Kayley. Even Cows Wear Moo Moos. Hackett, J. J. 2013. 24p. pap. 14.95 *(978-0-9897242-1-0(2)*, Over the Rainbow) Pearn & Assocs. Inc.

Pearse, Alfred. A Tale of the Western Plains. Henty, G. A. 2006. (Dover Children's Classics Ser.). (ENG.). 352p. (YA). (gr. 3-8). per. 8.95 *(978-0-486-45261-6(1))* Dover Pubns., Inc.

Pearse, Asha. Wizard of Oz. 2014. (ENG.). 16p. (J). (gr. -1-4). 7.99 ***(978-1-4867-0009-7(8))*** Flowerpot Children's Pr. Inc. CAN. Dist: Cardinal Pubs. Group.

Pearse, Stephen. Native Trees of British Columbia. Pearse, Stephen, tr. Halter, Reese & Turner, Nancy J. rev. ed. 2003. 96p. pap. *(978-0-9684143-3-0(8))* Global Forest Pr. CAN. Dist: Lone Pine Publishing.

Pearson, David, jt. illus. see Custard, P. T.

Pearson, Jason. Astonishing X-Men: Monstrous. 2011. (ENG.). 120p. (YA). (gr. 8-17). 19.99 *(978-0-7851-5114-2(1))* Marvel Worldwide, Inc.

Pearson, Jason, jt. illus. see Huat, Tan Eng.

Pearson, Larry Leroy. The Three Little Jayhawks. Sanner, Jennifer Jackson, ed. 2006. 40p. (J). per. 20.00 *(978-0-9742918-1-9(1))* Kansas Alumni Assoc.

Pearson, Luke. Hilda & the Bird Parade. 2013. (Hildafolk Ser.). (ENG.). 44p. (J). (gr. k). 24.00 *(978-1-909263-06-2(0))* Flying Eye Bks. GBR. Dist: Consortium Bk. Sales & Distribution.

—Hilda & the Black Hound. 2014. (Hildafolk Ser.). (ENG.). 64p. (J). (gr. k). 24.00 *(978-1-909263-18-5(4))* Flying Eye Bks. GBR. Dist: Consortium Bk. Sales & Distribution.

—Hilda & the Troll. 2013. (Hildafolk Ser.). (ENG.). 40p. (J). (gr. k). 18.95 *(978-1-909263-14-7(1))* Flying Eye Bks. GBR. Dist: Consortium Bk. Sales & Distribution.

Pearson, Maria. Animal Stencil Cards. 2008. (Stencil Cards Ser.). 16p. (J). 9.99 *(978-0-7945-1961-2(X)*, Usborne) EDC Publishing.

—Spooky Stencil Cards. 2008. (Stencil Cards Ser.). 16p. (J). 9.99 *(978-0-7945-2415-9(X)*, Usborne) EDC Publishing.

Pearson, Maria, jt. illus. see Field, Mandy.

Pearson, Tracey Campbell. Tuck-in Time. Gerber, Carole. 2014. (ENG.). 40p. (J). (gr. -1 — 1). 16.99 *(978-0-374-37860-6(6)*, Farrar, Straus & Giroux (BYR)) Farrar, Straus & Giroux.

Pearson, Tracey Campbell. Bob. Pearson, Tracey Campbell. 2006. (ENG.). 32p. (J). (gr. -1-1). reprint ed. 8.99 *(978-0-374-40871-8(8))* Square Fish.

—Elephant's Story. Pearson, Tracey Campbell. 2013. (ENG.). 40p. (J). (gr. -1-3). 17.99 *(978-0-374-39913-9(1)*, Farrar, Straus & Giroux (BYR)) Farrar, Straus & Giroux.

Pearson, Victoria, photos by. Dinner Parties: Simple Recipes for Easy Entertaining. Strand, Jessica. 2004. (ENG., 132p. (gr. 8-17). 16.95 *(978-0-8118-4298-3(3))* Chronicle Bks. LLC.

—Four Seasons Pasta. Fletcher, Janet. 2004. (ENG., 132p. (gr. 8-17). pap. 19.95 *(978-0-8118-3908-2(7))* Chronicle Bks. LLC.

—Sangria: Fun & Festive Recipes. Hellmich, Mittie. 2004. (ENG., 80p. (gr. 8-17). 16.95 *(978-0-8118-4290-7(8))* Chronicle Bks. LLC.

Pease, Tristyn. Noah's Little Lamb, 1 vol. Jelsma, Amber. 2010. 32p. pap. 24.95 *(978-1-4489-6068-2(1))* PublishAmerica, Inc.

Peat, Fern Bisel. A Child's Garden of Verses Shape Book. Stevenson, Robert Louis. 2011. (ENG.). 16p. (J). pap. 9.95 *(978-1-59583-429-4(X)*, Darling & Co.) Laughing Elephant.

—The Sugar-Plum Tree & Other Verses: Includes a Read-and-Listen. Field, Eugene. 2010. (Dover Read & Listen Ser.). (ENG.). 80p. (J). (gr. 1-5). pap. 14.99 *(978-0-486-47675-9(8))* Dover Pubns., Inc.

Peattie, Gary. Christmas Time in the Mountains. Luton, Mildred. 2003. 44p. (Orig.). (gr. 1-6). pap. 6.95 *(978-0-87516-434-2(X))* DeVorss & Co.

Peavler, Amy & Peavler, Jan. The King the Queen & the Princess. Peavler, Amy & Peavler, Jan. 2006. 40p. (J). per. *(978-0-9787672-2-8(5))* Lotus Petal Publishing.

Peavler, Jan, jt. illus. see Peavler, Amy.

Peck, Beth. Just Like Josh Gibson. Johnson, Angela. 2007. (J). 14.65 *(978-0-7569-8088-7(7))* Perfection Learning Corp.

—Just Like Josh Gibson. Johnson, Angela. (ENG.). 32p. (J). 2004. (gr. -1-2). 17.99 *(978-0-689-82628-3(1))*; 2007. (gr. k-2). reprint ed. 7.99 *(978-1-4169-2728-0(X))* Simon & Schuster Bks. For Young Readers. (Simon & Schuster Bks. For Young Readers).

Peck, Beth. Matthew & Tilly. Jones, Rebecca C. 2015. 32p. pap. 7.00 ***(978-1-61003-532-3(1))*** Center for the Collaborative Classroom.

Peck, Beth. Megan's Year: An Irish Traveler's Story. Whelan, Gloria. 2011. (Tales of the World Ser.). (ENG.). 32p. (gr. k-5). lib. bdg. 16.95 *(978-1-58536-449-7(5))* Sleeping Bear Pr.

—Music for the End of Time. Bryant, Jen. 2005. 32p. (J). (gr. 4-5). 17.00 *(978-0-8028-5229-8(7))* Eerdmans, William B. Publishing Co.

Peck, Bill. Kiernan's Jam. Moore, Nancy Delano. 2006. (J). 10.00 *(978-0-9785775-0-6(7))* Moore, Hullihen.

Peck, Everett. Mose the Fireman. Metaxas, Eric. 2004. (Rabbit Ears-A Classic Tale Ser.). 40p. (gr. k-5). 25.65 *(978-1-59197-766-7(5))* Spotlight.

Peck, Jamie. Oscar Potter & His Late-Night Visitor. Mastin, Marcus. l.t. ed. 2011. (ENG.). 32p. pap. 9.95 *(978-1-4679-2362-0(1))* CreateSpace Independent Publishing Platform.

Peck, Karna. Abrea Ansus. Hauser, Sheri. aut. ed. 2005. 26p. (YA). per. *(978-0-9766718-7-9(5))* Glorybound Publishing.

—Tomasena: Moving from Doubt to Faith. Hauser, Sheri. aut. ed. 2005. 304p. (YA). 39.50 *(978-0-9766718-3-1(2))* Glorybound Publishing.

Peck, Lillian Hoban. The Little Brute Family. Hoban, Russell. 2004. (Sunburst Bks.). 17.00 *(978-0-7569-3301-2(3))* Perfection Learning Corp.

Pecos NM After School Program Staff. Another Voice Sings in the Forest. Luna, Abuela. 2010. (ENG.). 40p. pap. 14.95 *(978-1-4505-7166-1(2))* CreateSpace Independent Publishing Platform.

Pecos,, 4th & 5th grade Art Students, & 5th grade Art Students. How the Earth Heard Music. Luna, Abuela. 2010. (ENG.). 66p. pap. 17.95 *(978-1-4515-5629-2(2))* CreateSpace Independent Publishing Platform.

Pedersen, Janet. Bath Time, 1 vol. Spinelli, Eileen & Spinelli. 2003. (ENG.). 32p. (J). 14.95 *(978-0-7614-5117-4(X))* Marshall Cavendish Corp.

—In Memory of Gorfman T. Frog. Donovan, Gail. 2009. (ENG.). 192p. (J). (gr. 4-7). 16.99 *(978-0-525-42085-9(1)*, Dutton Juvenile) Penguin Publishing Group.

—Jake Drake, Class Clown. Clements, Andrew. 2007. (Jake Drake Ser.: Bk. 4). (ENG.). 80p. (J). (gr. 2-5). pap. 5.99 *(978-1-4169-4912-1(7)*, Atheneum Bks. for Young Readers) Simon & Schuster Children's Publishing.

—Jake Drake, Teacher's Pet. Clements, Andrew. 2007. (Jake Drake Ser.: 3). (ENG.). 96p. (J). (gr. 2-5). pap. 5.99 *(978-1-4169-3932-0(6)*, Atheneum Bks. for Young Readers) Simon & Schuster Children's Publishing.

—Sneezy Louise. Breznak, Irene. 2009. (Picture Book Ser.). (ENG.). 40p. (J). (gr. -1-2). 15.99 *(978-0-375-85169-8(0))* Random Hse. Children's Bks.

—Thea's Tree. Jackson, Alison. 2008. (ENG.). 32p. (J). (gr. 1-18). 16.99 *(978-0-525-47443-2(9)*, Dutton Juvenile) Penguin Publishing Group.

Pedersen, Janet & Frazee, Marla. Bully Buster. Clements, Andrew. 2007. (Jake Drake Ser.: Bk. 1). (ENG.). 96p. (J). (gr. 2-5). pap. 5.99 *(978-1-4169-3933-7(4)*, Atheneum Bks. for Young Readers) Simon & Schuster Children's Publishing.

—Jake Drake, Know-It-All. Clements, Andrew. 2007. (Jake Drake Ser.: Bk. 2). (ENG.). 96p. (J). (gr. 2-5). pap. 5.99 *(978-1-4169-3931-3(8)*, Atheneum Bks. for Young Readers) Simon & Schuster Children's Publishing.

Pedersen, Janet, jt. illus. see Frazee, Marla.

Pedersen, Judy. Seedfolks. Fleischman, Paul. 2004. (Joanna Cotler Bks.). (ENG.). 112p. (YA). (gr. 8-18). pap. 8.99 *(978-0-06-447207-4(8))* HarperCollins Pubs.

Pedersen, Robert H. Seeds of Awareness: A Journey Towards Self Realization. Pedersen, Robert H., photos by. 2003. 96p. pap. 24.95 *(978-0-9744163-0-4(4))* Awareness Pubns.

Pedersen, Vilhelm. The Stories of Hans Christian Andersen: A New Translation from the Danish. Andersen, Hans Christian et al. Frank, Diana Crone & Frank, Jeffrey Crone, eds. 2005. (ENG.). 304p. per. 23.95 *(978-0-8223-3693-8(6))* Duke Univ. Pr.

Pedersen, Vilhelm, jt. illus. see Fröhlich, Lorenz.

Pederson, Gunda. Susie Sunflower. Harris, Mary Beth. 2010. 24p. 16.49 *(978-1-4520-5171-0(2))* AuthorHouse.

Pederson, Judy. Gifts from the Sea. Kinsey-Warnock, Natalie. 2005. (ENG.). 128p. (J). (gr. 3-7). 5.99 *(978-0-440-41970-9(0)*, Yearling) Random Hse. Children's Bks.

Pedigo, Kim Tran. Having Fun with Kandai the Elephant. Pedigo, Kim Tran. 2012. 36p. pap. 12.95 *(978-1-61244-105-4(X))* Halo Publishing International.

Pedlar, Caroline. Have You Seen Christmas? Howie, Vicki. 2006. 29p. (J). (gr. -1-3). 18.00 *(978-0-687-49678-5(0))* Abingdon Pr.

Pedlar, Elaine. A Shelter in Our Car. Gunning, Monica. 2013. (ENG.). 32p. (J). pap. 8.95 *(978-0-89239-308-4(4)*, Children's Book Press) Lee & Low Bks., Inc.

Pedlar, Elaine & Tonel. Birthday in the Barrio. Dole, Mayra L. 2004.Tr. of Cumpleaños en el Barrio. (ENG & SPA.). 32p. (J). 16.95 *(978-0-89239-194-3(4))* Lee & Low Bks., Inc.

Pedler, Caroline. A Cuddle for Little Duck. Freedman, Claire. 2009. (ENG.). 20p. (J). (gr. -1-k). bds. 8.99 *(978-0-545-07797-2(4)*, Cartwheel Bks.) Scholastic, Inc.

—Don't Wake the Bear! Smallman, Steve. 2012. (ENG.). 32p. (J). (gr. -1-3). 9.99 *(978-0-545-33299-6(0)*, Cartwheel Bks.) Scholastic, Inc.

—It's Potty Time! Corderoy, Tracey. 2014. (ENG.). 18p. (gr. -1-k). bds. 8.99 *(978-1-58925-574-6(7))* Tiger Tales.

—A Night Night Prayer, 1 vol. Parker, Amy. (ENG.). (J). 2015. 24p. pap. 3.99 *(978-0-7180-3652-2(2))*; 2014. 20p. bds. 9.99 *(978-1-4003-2431-6(9))* Nelson, Thomas Inc.

—A Sparkly Ballet Story. Baxter, Nicola. 2014. (ENG.). 14p. (J). (gr. -1-1). bds. 7.99 *(978-1-84322-546-1(8)*, Armadillo) Anness Publishing GBR. Dist: National Bk. Network.

—A Sparkly Pony Story. Baxter, Nicola. 2014. (ENG.). 14p. (J). (gr. -1-1). bds. 7.99 *(978-1-84322-545-4(X)*, Armadillo) Anness Publishing GBR. Dist: National Bk. Network.

—Touch & Feel Petting Zoo. Grieser, Jeanne K. 2010. (ENG.). 20p. (J). (gr. k — 1). bds. 9.95 *(978-1-4027-6524-7(X))* Sterling Publishing Co., Inc.

—When Grandma Saved Christmas. Hubery, Julia. 2014. 32p. (J). (gr. -1-3). 16.99 *(978-1-58925-164-9(4))* Tiger Tales.

Pedler, Caroline & Massey, Jane. My Little Box of Bedtime Stories: Can't You Sleep, Puppy?/Time to Sleep, Little Bear!/What Are You Doing in My Bed?/Sleep Tight, Giner Kitten/Good Night, Emily!/Don't Be Afraid, Little Ones. Warnes, Tim et al. 2013. (ENG.). (J). (gr. -1-1). pap. 8.95 *(978-1-58925-442-8(2))* Tiger Tales.

Pedro, Javier Martínez. Migrant. Mateo, José Manuel. 2014. (ENG & SPA.). 22p. (J). (gr. 3-17). 17.95 *(978-1-4197-0957-9(7)*, Abrams Bks. for Young Readers) Abrams.

Peecock, Simon & McKissock, Charmaine. An Amazing Storytelling Cat. Williams, Jan. 2013. 120p. pap. *(978-0-9568148-6-9(7))* Swift Publishing.

Peek, Jeannette. My Daddy Is A Fire Fighter: My Daddy Is A Fireman. Beckler, Bruce. l.t. ed. 2004. 16p. (J). 5.59 *(978-0-9745210-8-4(6))* Myers Publishing Co.

—My Mommy Is A Nurse. Beckler, Bruce. l.t. ed. 2004. 20p. (J). 5.59 *(978-0-9745210-9-1(4))* Myers Publishing Co.

Peel, Stephanie. Little Rabbit Waits for the Moon. Shoshan, Beth. 2013. (J). *(978-1-4351-4802-4(9))* Barnes & Noble, Inc.

Peer, Kate. Let's Take a Walk in the Rain. Johnson, Kathy. 2012. 28p. pap. 13.54 *(978-1-4669-3252-4(X))* Trafford Publishing.

Peer, Nancy. Mermaid Tears: A Magical Sea Tale. Lasaracina, Barbara. 2010. 28p. pap. 11.99 *(978-1-60844-451-9(1))* Dog Ear Publishing, LLC.

Peet, Bill. The Caboose Who Got Loose, 1 vol. Peet, Bill. 2008. (Read along Book & CD Ser.). (ENG.). 48p. (J). (gr. -1-3). 10.99 *(978-0-618-95979-2(3))* Houghton Mifflin Harcourt Publishing Co.

Peggykauffman.com Staff & Kauffman, Margaret. Raja: Story of a Racehorse. Hambleton, Anne. 2011. (ENG.). 272p. (J). (gr. 4-7). pap. 12.95 *(978-0-615-54029-0(5))* Old Bow Publishing.

Peguero, Phillip. Neecie & the Sparkling Spring. Barrett, Anna Pearl. Weston, Eunice Guy, ed. 2004. (Neecie Bks.: Vol. 5). 70p. (J). (gr. 1-6). 7.95 *(978-0-9661330-5-9(6))* Over the Rainbow Productions.

Peguy, Laurence. The Abominable Snowman, Montgomery, R. A. 2007. (Choose Your Own Adventure Ser.). 144p. (J). (gr. 4-7). per. 6.99 *(978-1-933390-01-7(8)*, CHCL01) Chooseco LLC.

—Smoke Jumpers. Montgomery, R. A. 2009. (Choose Your Own Adventure Ser.: No. 29). 144p. (J). (gr. 2-7). pap. 6.99 *(978-1-933390-29-1(8))* Chooseco LLC.

Peinador, Angeles. Ay, Luna, Luna, Lunita... Canetti, Yanitzia James et al. 2006. (Coleccion Rascacielos Ser.). (SPA.). 32p. (J). (gr. 2-3). 14.99 *(978-84-241-8774-3(1))* Everest Editora ESP. Dist: Lectorum Pubns., Inc.

Peirce, Lincoln. Big Nate Flips Out. 2013. 216p. (J). *(978-0-06-224637-0(2))* Harper & Row Ltd.

Peirce, Lincoln. Big Nate: Fun Blaster: Cheezy Doodles, Crazy Comix, & Loads of Laughs! Peirce, Lincoln. 2012. (Big Nate Activity Book Ser.: 2). (ENG.). 224p. (J). (gr. 3-7). 10.99 *(978-0-06-209045-4(3))* HarperCollins Pubs.

—Big Nate: Game On! Peirce, Lincoln. 2013. (ENG.). 224p. (J). pap. 9.99 *(978-1-4494-2777-1(4))* Andrews McMeel Publishing.

—Big Nate: Mr. Popularity. Peirce, Lincoln. 2014. (Big Nate Ser.). (ENG.). 224p. (J). (gr. 3-7). pap. 9.99 *(978-0-06-208700-3(2))* HarperCollins Pubs.

—Big Nate: The Crowd Goes Wild! Peirce, Lincoln. 2014. (Big Nate Ser.). (ENG.). 224p. (J). 9.99 *(978-1-4494-3634-6(X))* Andrews McMeel Publishing.

—Big Nate — Genius Mode. Peirce, Lincoln. 2013. (Big Nate Ser.). (ENG.). 224p. (J). (gr. 3-7). pap. 9.99 *(978-0-06-208698-3(7))* HarperCollins Pubs.

—Big Nate — Here Goes Nothing. Peirce, Lincoln. 2012. (Big Nate Comix Ser.: 2). (ENG.). 224p. (J). (gr. 3-7). pap. 9.99 *(978-0-06-208696-9(0))* HarperCollins Pubs.

—Big Nate — In a Class by Himself. Peirce, Lincoln. (Big Nate Ser.: 1). (ENG.). (J). (gr. 3-7). 2015. 224p. pap. 6.99 *(978-0-06-226359-7(6))*; 2012. 240p. 12.99 *(978-0-06-220773-9(3))* HarperCollins Pubs.

—Big Nate — In the Zone. Peirce, Lincoln. 2014. (Big Nate Ser.: 6). 224p. (J). (gr. 3-7). (ENG.). 13.99 *(978-0-06-199665-8(3))*; lib. bdg. 14.89 *(978-0-06-199666-5(1))* HarperCollins Pubs.

—Big Nate — What Could Possibly Go Wrong? Peirce, Lincoln. 2012. (Big Nate Comix Ser.: 1). (ENG.). 224p. (J). (gr. 3-7). pap. 9.99 *(978-0-06-208694-5(4))* HarperCollins Pubs.

—Big Nate - Fun Blaster. Peirce, Lincoln. 2015. (Big Nate Activity Book Ser.: 2). (ENG.). 224p. (J). (gr. 3-7). pap. 6.99 *(978-0-06-234951-4(1))* HarperCollins Pubs.

—Big Nate - In a Class by Himself. Peirce, Lincoln. 2010. (Big Nate Ser.: 1). 224p. (J). (gr. 3-7). (ENG.). 12.99 *(978-0-06-194434-5(3))*; lib. bdg. 14.89 *(978-0-06-194435-2(1))* HarperCollins Pubs.

—Big Nate Boredom Buster. Peirce, Lincoln. 2014. (Big Nate Activity Book Ser.: 1). (ENG.). 224p. (J). (gr. 3-7). pap. 6.99 *(978-0-06-233800-6(5))* HarperCollins Pubs.

—Big Nate Boredom Buster: Super Scribbles, Cool Comix, & Lots of Laughs. Peirce, Lincoln. 2011. (Big Nate Activity Book Ser.: 1). (ENG.). 224p. (J). (gr. 3-7). 10.99 *(978-0-06-206094-5(5))* HarperCollins Pubs.

—Big Nate Doodlepalooza. Peirce, Lincoln. 2013. (Big Nate Ser.). (ENG.). 224p. (J). (gr. 3-7). 10.99 *(978-0-06-211114-2(0))* HarperCollins Pubs.

—Big Nate Flips Out. Peirce, Lincoln. 2013. (Big Nate Ser.). 224p. (J). (gr. 3-7). (ENG.). 13.99 *(978-0-06-199663-4(7))*; lib. bdg. 14.89 *(978-0-06-199664-1(5))* HarperCollins Pubs.

—Big Nate Goes for Broke. Peirce, Lincoln. 2012. (Big Nate Ser.: 4). 224p. (J). (gr. 3-7). (ENG.). 12.99 *(978-0-06-199661-0(0))*; lib. bdg. 14.89 *(978-0-06-199662-7(9))* HarperCollins Pubs.

—Big Nate Laugh-O-Rama. Peirce, Lincoln. 2014. (Big Nate Activity Book Ser.: 4). (ENG.). 224p. (J). (gr. 3-7). pap. 6.99 *(978-0-06-211116-6(7))* HarperCollins Pubs.

—Big Nate Lives It Up. Peirce, Lincoln. 2015. (Big Nate Ser.: 7). 224p. (J). (gr. 3-7). lib. bdg. 13.89 *(978-0-06-211109-8(4))* HarperCollins Pubs.

—Big Nate Makes the Grade. Peirce, Lincoln. Harper, Chuck et al. 2012. (ENG.). 224p. (J). 9.99 *(978-1-4494-2566-1(6))* Andrews McMeel Publishing.

—Big Nate on a Roll. Peirce, Lincoln. (Big Nate Ser.: 3). 224p. (J). (gr. 3-7). 2015. (ENG.). pap. 6.99 *(978-0-06-228357-3(X))*; 2011. (ENG.). 12.99 *(978-0-06-194438-3(6))*; 2011. lib. bdg. 14.89 *(978-0-06-194439-0(4))* HarperCollins Pubs.

—Big Nate Strikes Again. Peirce, Lincoln. (Big Nate Ser.: 2). 224p. (J). (gr. 3-7). 2015. (ENG.). pap. 6.99 *(978-0-06-228358-0(8))*; 2010. (ENG.). 12.99 *(978-0-06-194436-9(X))*; 2010. lib. bdg. 14.89 *(978-0-06-194437-6(8))* HarperCollins Pubs.

Peirce, Lincoln. Big Nate Super Scribbler. Peirce, Lincoln. 2015. (Big Nate Activity Book Ser.: 5). (ENG.). 224p. (J). (gr. 3-7). pap. 6.99 ***(978-0-06-234922-4(8))*** HarperCollins Pubs.

Peirce, Lincoln. Big Nate Triple Play Box Set. Peirce, Lincoln. 2013. (Big Nate Ser.). (ENG.). (J). (gr. 3-7). pap. 16.99 *(978-0-06-228360-3(X))* HarperCollins Pubs.

Pekarsky, Mel. The Magic Beans. Hillert, Margaret. rev. ed. 2006. (Beginning to Read Ser.). 32p. (J). (gr. -1-3). lib. bdg. 19.93 *(978-1-59953-025-3(2))* Norwood Hse. Pr.

—The Three Goats. Hillert, Margaret. rev. ed. 2006. (Beginning to Read Ser.). 30p. (J). (gr. -1-3). lib. bdg. 19.93 *(978-1-59953-027-7(9))* Norwood Hse. Pr.

Pelaez, Ricardo. Corre con Caballos. Burks, Brian. Vinos, Maria, tr. 2003. (la Orilla Del Viento Ser.). (SPA.). 96p. (J). per. 7.50 *(978-968-16-7057-3(4)*, 168) Fondo de Cultura Economica USA.

—En un Martes Trece... Otero, Armando Leiero. 2006. (SPA & ENG.). 36p. (J). (gr. -1-3). pap. 9.95 *(978-968-5920-55-1(9))* Castillo, Ediciones, S. A. de C. V. MEX. Dist: Macmillan.

—Sonidos, Olores y Colores - la Comunicacion en el Mundo Animal. Ruiz, Maria Emilia Beyer. rev. ed. 2006. (Otra Escalera Ser.). (SPA & ENG.). 36p. (J). (gr. 4). pap. 9.95 *(978-968-5920-79-7(6))* Castillo, Ediciones, S. A. de C. V. MEX. Dist: Macmillan.

Pelham, David. Here Comes Santa: A Mini Holiday Pop-Up. Pelham, David. ed. 2008. (ENG.). 18p. (J). 11.99 *(978-1-4169-5440-8(6)*, Little Simon) Little Simon.

Pelham, David. Sam's Sandwich. Pelham, David. 2015. (ENG.). 24p. (J). (gr. -1-2). 9.99 ***(978-0-7636-7808-1(2))*** Candlewick Pr.

Pelham, David. Stuff & Nonsense: A Touch-and-Feel Book with a Pop-Up Surprise! Pelham, David. 2009. (ENG.). 16p. (J). (gr. -1-2). 14.99 *(978-1-4169-5907-6(6)*, Little Simon) Little Simon.

—Trail: Paper Poetry. Pelham, David. 2007. (ENG.). 12p. (J). (gr. -1-2). 26.99 *(978-1-4169-4894-0(5)*, Little Simon) Little Simon.

Pelham, Sophie. Colors. Pelham, Sophie. 2014. (ENG.). 18p. (J). (gr. -1-k). 6.99 *(978-0-8431-7242-3(8)*, Price Stern Sloan) Penguin Publishing Group.

Peli, Peli. Candida. Silvera, Elvia. 2005. (SPA.). (J). (gr. 2-3). pap. 7.95 *(978-980-257-281-6(0))* Ekare, Ediciones VEN. Dist: Iaconi, Mariuccia Bk. Imports.

Pelicano, Christopher J. Credo: I Believe. Ellis, Colette. Avakoff, Caroline, ed. 2009. (Faith & Life Ser.). 121p. (J). pap. 7.95 *(978-0-89870-898-1(2))* Ignatius Pr.

Pellaton, Karen E. The Official M&M's(r) Brand History of Chocolate. 2004. 32p. (YA). (gr. 1-9). 16.95 *(978-1-57091-448-5(6))*; pap. 6.95 *(978-1-57091-449-2(4))* Charlesbridge Publishing, Inc.

—The Official M&M's(r) Brand History of the Calendar. Brimner, Larry Dane. 2004. 32p. (YA). 16.95 *(978-1-57091-431-7(1))*; pap. 6.95 *(978-1-57091-432-4(X))* Charlesbridge Publishing, Inc.

Pellé, Serge. Nomads, Vol. 3. Runberg, Sylvain. 2011. (ENG.). 56p. pap. 13.95 *(978-1-84918-080-1(6))* CineBook GBR. Dist: National Bk. Network.

—Orbital Vol. 1: Scars. Runberg, Sylvain. Saincatin, Jerome, tr. from FRE. 2009. (ENG.). 47p. pap. 11.95 *(978-1-905460-89-2(9))* CineBook GBR. Dist: National Bk. Network.

—Orbital Vol. 2: Ruptures. Runberg, Sylvain. Saincatin, Jerome, tr. from FRE. 2009. (ENG.). 55p. pap. 13.95 *(978-1-905460-95-3(3))* CineBook GBR. Dist: National Bk. Network.

Pelle, Serge. Orbital Vol. 5: Justice. Runberg, Sylvain. 2014. (ENG.). 56p. pap. 13.95 *(978-1-84918-172-3(1))* CineBook GBR. Dist: National Bk. Network.

Pelleg, Tirtsa. I Wish I Were a King. Krohn, Genendel. 50p. 13.95 *(978-1-58330-590-4(4))* Feldheim Pubs.

—The Miracle of the Other Stories: Timeless Tales from the Lives of Our Sages. Krohn, Genendel. 2003. 56p. (J). 14.99 *(978-1-58330-650-5(1))* Feldheim Pubs.

—Who Is the Builder? Krohn, Genendel. 32p. 13.99 *(978-1-58330-515-7(7))* Feldheim Pubs.

Pellegata, Donna. The Harp Mouse Chooses Her Home: The Adventure Begins. 2008. 24p. (J). pap. 6.95 *(978-0-9742174-1-3(7))* Heart & Harp LLC.

Pellegrini, Will. Peppy's Shadow. Trimble, Marcia. 2003. 32p. (J). (gr. -1-3). 15.95 *(978-1-891577-70-3(0))*; pap. 7.95 *(978-1-891577-71-0(9))* Images Pr.

Pellegrino, Rich. Real-World Dragons, 1 vol. Doeden, Matt. 2013. (World of Dragons Ser.). (ENG.). 32p. (gr. 1-2). lib. bdg. 25.99 *(978-1-62065-146-9(7)*, Blazers) Capstone Pr., Inc.

Pellegrino, Rich, jt. illus. see Mayer, Jonathan.

Pellegrino, Richard. The Battle of the Olympians & the Titans, 1 vol. 2011. (Greek Myths Ser.). (ENG.). 32p. (gr. 4-5). lib. bdg. 27.99 *(978-1-4048-6667-6(1)*, Nonfiction Picture Bks.) Picture Window Bks.

—Stowaway Monster, 1 vol. Dahl, Michael. (Dragonblood Ser.). (ENG.). 40p. (gr. 1-3). 2010. pap. 6.25 *(978-1-4342-2312-8(4))*; 2009. 22.65 *(978-1-4342-1259-7(9))* Stone Arch Bks. (Zone Bks.).

—Terror Beach, 1 vol. Dahl, Michael. (Dragonblood Ser.). (ENG.). 40p. (gr. 1-3). 2010. pap. 6.25 *(978-1-4342-2313-5(2))*; 2009. 22.65 *(978-1-4342-1263-4(7))* Stone Arch Bks. (Zone Bks.).

—The Thing in the Woods. Brezenoff, Steve. 2008. (Shade Bks.). (ENG.). 80p. (gr. 2-3). 23.99 *(978-1-4342-0795-1(1)*, Shade Bks.) Stone Arch Bks.

Pelletier, Ninon. Night Boy, 1 vol. Carter, Anne Laurel. 2012. (ENG.). 32p. (J). (gr. -1-3). 19.95 *(978-1-55469-402-0(7))* Orca Bk. Pubs. USA.

Pelletier, Paul, et al. Baptism of Fire, Vol. 2. Bedard, Tony. 2003. (Negation Ser.: Vol. 2). 160p. (YA). pap. 12.95 *(978-1-931484-59-6(7))* CrossGeneration Comics, Inc.

—Negation, Vol. 3. Bedard, Tony. 2003. (Negation Ser.: Vol. 3). 160p. (YA). pap. 15.95 *(978-1-931484-90-9(2))* CrossGeneration Comics, Inc.

—Shock & Awe, Vol. 3. Bedard, Tony. 2004. (Negation Ser.: Vol. 4). 160p. (YA). pap. 15.95 *(978-1-59314-046-5(0))* CrossGeneration Comics, Inc.

Pelling, Lenny. Summer Days. Pelling, Lenny. 2010. (Pen Pals Forever Ser.: 1). (ENG.). 64p. (J). (gr. k-2). 6.99 *(978-1-86471-900-0(1))* Random Hse. Australia AUS. Dist: Independent Pubs. Group.

Pels, Winslow. Cricket at the Manger. Fine, Edith Hope. 2005. (ENG.). 32p. (J). (gr. k-2). 15.95 *(978-1-56397-993-4(4))* Boyds Mills Pr.

Pels, Winslow Pinney. Hansel y Cretel. Cross, Ruth Belov. 2003. (SPA.). pap. *(978-0-439-19894-3(1)*, SO30113) Scholastic GBR. Dist: Lectorum Pubns., Inc.

Peltier, Sylvia M. Nanny & I. Peltier, Sylvia M. 2003. 32p. (YA). (gr. -1-18). 16.95 *(978-0-9724394-0-4(4))* Sylables.

Pelton, Bonnie L. Bryanna Global Warrior: Attack of the Alaska Aerial Wolf Hunters, 1 vol. Ball Sr., Frank J. 2009. 23p. pap. 24.95 *(978-1-61582-587-5(8))* America Star Bks.

—Planet Earth Past, Present, Future: Bryanna Global Warrior Book 3, 1 vol. Ball Sr., Frank J. 2010. 34p. pap. 24.95 *(978-1-4489-8321-6(5))* PublishAmerica, Inc.

Peluso, Beth A. The Charcoal Forest: How Fire Helps Animals & Plants. Peluso, Beth A. 2007. 56p. (J). (gr. -1-3). pap. 12.00 *(978-0-87842-532-7(2))* Mountain Pr. Publishing Co., Inc.

Peluso, Martina. Dara's Clever Trap: A Story from Cambodia. Flanagan, Liz et al. 2014. 48p. (J). pap. 7.99 *(978-1-78285-103-5(8))* Barefoot Bks., Inc.

—Feraj & the Magic Lute: An Arabian Folktale. Malaspina, Ann. 2013. (Folktales from Around the World Ser.). (ENG.). 24p. (J). (gr. k-3). 28.50 *(978-1-62323-613-7(4)*, 206380) Child's World, Inc., The.

—Joseph & the Sabbath Fish. Kimmel, Eric A. 2011. (Shabbat Ser.). (ENG.). 32p. (J). (gr. k-3). pap. 7.95 *(978-0-7613-5909-8(5))*; lib. bdg. 17.95 *(978-0-7613-5908-1(7))* Lerner Publishing Group. (Kar-Ben Publishing).

Peluso, Martina. Og's Ark. Marks, Allison & Marks, Wayne. 2015. (J). ***(978-1-4677-6149-9(4)***, Kar-Ben Publishing) Lerner Publishing Group.

Peluso, Martina. The Princess of the Springs. Finch, Mary & Barefoot Books. 2014. 48p. (J). pap. 7.99 *(978-1-78285-101-1(1))* Barefoot Bks., Inc.

—Romeo & Juliet. Marion, Dominique & Shakespeare, William. 2013. (Big Picture Book Ser.). (ENG.). 40p. (J). (gr. 1). 14.95 *(978-2-7338-2119-0(9))* Auzou, Philippe Editions FRA. Dist: Consortium Bk. Sales & Distribution.

Pena, Amado M., Jr. Amadito & Spider Woman. Goldman, Lisa Bear. 2003. 32p. (J). 15.95 *(978-1-885772-30-5(0))* Kiva Publishing, Inc.

Pena, Willie R. Sweet & Shorts! Short Stories Made of 100 Important Sight Words a First Grader Should Know. Pena, Diana R. 2010. (ENG.). 40p. pap. 10.99 *(978-1-4505-5669-9(8))* CreateSpace Independent Publishing Platform.

—What I Like: A Fun, Basic Reading Book for Kindergarteners & First Graders. Pena, Diana R. 2010. (ENG.). 40p. pap. 10.99 *(978-1-4515-6443-3(0))* CreateSpace Independent Publishing Platform.

Pender, Rachel. Well... What's All That Drilling About? Stone, Andrew & Bryan, Jessica. 2007. 40p. (J). 7.95 *(978-0-9641186-3-8(7))* American Ground Water Trust.

Pendergrass, Mark D. May I See the King? Daubenspeck, Julie & Daubenspeck, Vince. 2009. (ENG.). 32p. (gr. k). 14.95 *(978-1-59700-797-9(8))* Island Heritage Publishing.

Penfield, James. Dinosaurs & Other Prehistoric Animals. Baltzer, Rochelle. 2015. (J). *(978-1-62402-081-0(X))* Magic Wagon.

—Dogs & Cats. Baltzer, Rochelle. 2015. (J). *(978-1-62402-080-3(1))* Magic Wagon.

Penfield, James. Monsters & Other Mythical Creatures. Baltzer, Rochelle. 2015. (J). ***(978-1-62402-083-4(6))*** Magic Wagon.

—Pirates on the High Seas. Baltzer, Rochelle. 2015. (J). ***(978-1-62402-084-1(4))*** Magic Wagon.

—A Royal Court in Its Kingdom. Baltzer, Rochelle. 2015. (J). ***(978-1-62402-085-8(2))*** Magic Wagon.

Peng, Cathy. Yo-Yo & Yeou-Cheng Ma, Finding Their Way: Amazing Asian Americans. Louie, Ai-Ling. 2012. (Biographies of Amazing Asian Americans Ser.: 2). (ENG.). 48p. (J). pap. 16.99 *(978-0-9787465-0-6(3))* Dragoneagle Pr.

Peng, Chao. Band of Brothers. Dong Chen, Wei. 2013. (Monkey King Ser.: 18). 176p. (gr. 6-12). pap. 9.99 *(978-89-94208-63-3(1))* JR Comics KOR. Dist: Lerner Publishing Group.

—The Dual. Dong Chen, Wei. 2013. (Monkey King Ser.: 14). 176p. (gr. 6-12). pap. 9.99 *(978-89-94208-59-6(3))* JR Comics KOR. Dist: Lerner Publishing Group.

—Expulsion of Sun Wu. Dong Chen, Wei. 2013. (Monkey King Ser.: 7). 176p. (YA). (gr. 6-12). pap. 9.99 *(978-89-94208-51-0(8))* Lerner Publishing Group.

—The Expulsion of Sun Wu Kong. Chen, Wei Dong. 2013. (Monkey King Ser.: 7). 176p. (YA). (gr. 6-12). lib. bdg. 29.27 *(978-89-94208-75-6(5))* Lerner Publishing Group.

—Fanning the Flames. Dong Chen, Wei. 2013. (Monkey King Ser.: 15). 176p. (gr. 6-12). pap. 9.99 *(978-89-94208-60-2(7))* JR Comics KOR. Dist: Lerner Publishing Group.

—Fight to the Death. Chen, Wei Dong. 2013. (Monkey King Ser.: 11). 176p. (YA). (gr. 6-12). lib. bdg. 29.27 *(978-89-94208-79-4(8))* Lerner Publishing Group.

—Fight to the Death. Dong Chen, Wei. 2013. (Monkey King Ser.: 11). 176p. (YA). (gr. 6-12). pap. 9.99 *(978-89-94208-56-5(9))* Lerner Publishing Group.

—Golden Temple. Dong Chen, Wei. 2013. (Monkey King Ser.: 16). 176p. (gr. 6-12). pap. 9.99 *(978-89-94208-61-9(5))* JR Comics KOR. Dist: Lerner Publishing Group.

—The Journey Ends. Dong Chen, Wei. 2013. (Monkey King Ser.: 20). 176p. (gr. 6-12). pap. 9.99 *(978-89-94208-65-7(8))* JR Comics KOR. Dist: Lerner Publishing Group.

—The Lost Children. Chen, Wei Dong. 2013. (Monkey King Ser.: 12). 176p. (YA). (gr. 6-12). lib. bdg. 29.27 *(978-89-94208-80-0(1))* Lerner Publishing Group.

—Lost Children. Dong Chen, Wei. 2013. (Monkey King Ser.: 12). 176p. (YA). (gr. 6-12). pap. 9.99 *(978-89-94208-57-2(7))* Lerner Publishing Group.

—Masters & Disciples. Dong Chen, Wei. 2013. (Monkey King Ser.: 19). 176p. (gr. 6-12). pap. 9.99 *(978-89-94208-64-0(X))* JR Comics KOR. Dist: Lerner Publishing Group.

—Monkey King: Birth of the Stone Monkey. Chen, Wei Dong. 2012. (Monkey King Ser.: 1). (ENG.). 176p. (gr. 5-8). lib. bdg. 29.27 *(978-89-94208-69-5(0))* JR Comics KOR. Dist: Lerner Publishing Group.

—Monkey King: Enemies & a New Friend. Chen, Wei Dong. 2012. (Monkey King Ser.: 4). (ENG.). 176p. (gr. 5-8). lib. bdg. 29.27 *(978-89-94208-72-5(0))* JR Comics KOR. Dist: Lerner Publishing Group.

—Monkey King: Journey to the West. Chen, Wei Dong. 2012. (Monkey King Ser.: 3). (ENG.). 176p. (gr. 5-8). lib. bdg. 29.27 *(978-89-94208-71-8(2))* JR Comics KOR. Dist: Lerner Publishing Group.

—Monkey King: The Bane of Heaven. Chen, Wei Dong. 2012. (Monkey King Ser.: 2). (ENG.). 176p. (gr. 5-8). lib. bdg. 29.27 *(978-89-94208-70-1(4))* JR Comics KOR. Dist: Lerner Publishing Group.

—Monkey King: The Sacred Tree. Chen, Wei Dong. 2012. (Monkey King Ser.: 6). (ENG.). 176p. (gr. 5-8). lib. bdg. 29.27 *(978-89-94208-74-9(7))* JR Comics KOR. Dist: Lerner Publishing Group.

—Monkey King: Three Trials. Chen, Wei Dong. 2012. (Monkey King Ser.: 5). (ENG.). 176p. (gr. 5-8). lib. bdg. 29.27 *(978-89-94208-73-2(9))* JR Comics KOR. Dist: Lerner Publishing Group.

—Realm of Infant King. Dong Chen, Wei. 2013. (Monkey King Ser.: 10). 176p. (YA). (gr. 6-12). pap. 9.99 *(978-89-94208-54-1(2))* Lerner Publishing Group.

—The Realm of the Infant King. Chen, Wei Dong. 2013. (Monkey King Ser.: 10). 176p. (YA). (gr. 6-12). lib. bdg. 29.27 *(978-89-94208-78-7(X))* Lerner Publishing Group.

—The Seven Sisters. Dong Chen, Wei. 2013. (Monkey King Ser.: 17). 176p. (gr. 6-12). pap. 9.99 *(978-89-94208-62-6(3))* JR Comics KOR. Dist: Lerner Publishing Group.

—The Stolen Kingdom. Chen, Wei Dong. 2013. (Monkey King Ser.: 9). 176p. (YA). (gr. 6-12). lib. bdg. 29.27 *(978-89-94208-77-0(1))* Lerner Publishing Group.

—Stolen Kingdom. Dong Chen, Wei. 2013. (Monkey King Ser.: 9). 176p. (YA). (gr. 6-12). pap. 9.99 *(978-89-94208-53-4(4))* Lerner Publishing Group.

—Treasures of Mt Kings. Dong Chen, Wei. 2013. (Monkey King Ser.: 8). 176p. (YA). (gr. 6-12). pap. 9.99 *(978-89-94208-52-7(6))* Lerner Publishing Group.

—Treasures of the Mountain Kings. Chen, Wei Dong. 2013. (Monkey King Ser.: 8). 176p. (YA). (gr. 6-12). lib. bdg. 29.27 *(978-89-94208-76-3(3))* Lerner Publishing Group.

—Trust & Temptation. Dong Chen, Wei. 2013. (Monkey King Ser.: 13). 176p. (gr. 6-12). pap. 9.99 *(978-89-94208-58-9(5))* JR Comics KOR. Dist: Lerner Publishing Group.

Peng, Wang, jt. illus. see Li, Yishan.

Penhale, Douglas. Why Seals Blow Their Noses: Canadian Wildlife in Fact & Fiction, 1 vol. Swanson, Diane. (ENG.). 80p. (J). pap. 12.95 *(978-1-55110-038-8(X))* Whitecap Bks., Ltd. CAN. Dist: Graphic Arts Ctr. Publishing Co.

Penk, Kathryn. Little Tree's Mightiest Deed. Edgren, Elizabeth. 2009. 36p. pap. 12.95 *(978-1-59858-825-5(7))* Dog Ear Publishing, LLC.

Penn, Audrey, et al. The Kissing Hand. 2010. 23.05 *(978-0-7569-9299-6(0))* Natl Bk. Network.

Penn, Briony. The Kids Book of Canadian Geography. Penn, Briony. 2008. (ENG.). 56p. (J). (gr. 3-7). 19.95 *(978-1-55074-890-1(4))* Kids Can Pr., Ltd. CAN. Dist: Univ. of Toronto Pr.

Penn, Karen V. The Doll at the Christmas Bazaar: Christmas Miracles. O'Neal-Thorpe, Rochelle. 2010. 32p. (J). pap. 9.95 *(978-0-9823906-2-7(9))* Wiggles Pr.

Pennell, Lauren. The Phantom Stallion. Pennell, Kathleen. 2003. (Pony Investigators Ser.: Vol. 4). 118p. (J). (gr. 3-7). pap. 5.95 *(978-1-930353-73-2(1))* Masthof Pr.

Pennell, Rhett / R. Look Left, Look Right, Look Left Again. Pate, Ginger. 2013. 28p. (J). 8.50 *(978-1-880851-30-2(X))* Greene Bark Pr., Inc.

Penner, Fred. Animal Boogie. Harter, Debbie. 2011. (ENG.). 62p. (J). pap. 9.99 *(978-1-84686-620-3(0))* Barefoot Bks., Inc.

Penner, Stephen. Professor Barrister's Dinosaur Mysteries #1: The Case of the Truncated Troodon. Penner, Stephen. 2010. 44p. pap. 19.25 *(978-1-60888-005-8(2))* Nimble Bks. LLC.

—Professor Barrister's Dinosaur Mysteries #4: The Case of the Colorful Caudipteryx. Penner, Stephen. 2011. 62p. pap. 14.99 *(978-1-60888-111-6(3))* Nimble Bks. LLC.

Penney, Ian. A Noteworthy Tale. Mutchnick, Brenda & Casden, Ron. 2004. 30p. (J). (gr. k-4). reprint ed. 19.00 *(978-0-7567-7654-1(6))* DIANE Publishing Co.

Pennington, Beverly A. Jonathan's Discovery. Pennington, Beverly A. 2006. 29p. (J). (gr. -1-3). pap. 12.95 *(978-1-56167-920-1(8))* American Literary Pr.

Pennington, Craig. Grandma's Christmas Tree. Sinke, Grandma Janet Mary. l.t. ed. 2004. (Grandma Janet Mary Ser.). 50p. (J). *(978-0-9742732-1-1(X))* My Grandma & Me Pubs.

—Grandma's Treasure Chest. Grandma Janet Mary. l.t. ed. 2005. (Grandma Janet Mary Ser.). 50p. (J). 16.95 *(978-0-9742732-3-5(6))* My Grandma & Me Pubs.

—Grandpa's Fishin' Friend. Grandma Janet Mary. 2nd ed. 2007. (Grandma Janet Mary Ser.). 28p. (J). 16.95 *(978-0-9742732-7-3(9))* My Grandma & Me Pubs.

—I Wanna Go to Grandma's House. Sinke, Grandma Janet Mary. 2003. (Grandma Janet Mary Ser.). 50p. (J). *(978-0-9742732-0-4(1))* My Grandma & Me Pubs.

—I Wanna Go to Grandma's House & Grandma's Treasure Chest, 2, Set. Sinke, Janet Mary. 2006. 80p. (J). *(978-0-9742732-6-6(0))* My Grandma & Me Pubs.

—Priscilla Mcdoodlenut Doodle Mcmae Asks, Why? Sinke, Janet Mary. 2007. 40p. (J). 17.95 *(978-0-9742732-8-0(7))* My Grandma & Me Pubs.

Pennington, Jack & Tank, Daniel. Joseph. Brand, Ruth. 2004. 87p. (J). 19.99 *(978-0-8280-1854-8(5)*, 104-522) Review & Herald Publishing Assn.

—Joseph. 2004. 87p. (J). pap. *(978-0-8280-1855-5(3))* Review & Herald Publishing Assn.

Pennington, Kelly. With My Little Box of Crayons. Wooten, Laura. 2008. 50p. pap. 18.95 *(978-1-4251-7103-2(6))* Trafford Publishing.

Pennington, Mark. How the World Was Made: A Cherokee Creation Myth. Yasuda, Anita. 2012. (Short Tales Native American Myths Ser.). 32p. (J). (gr. 3-6). lib. bdg. 24.21 *(978-1-61641-881-6(8))* Magic Wagon.

—Shade Changing: The American Scream. Milligan, Peter. rev. ed. 2009. (ENG.). 168p. pap. 17.99 *(978-1-4012-0046-6(X))* DC Comics.

—Sky Woman & the Big Turtle: An Iroquois Creation Myth. Yasuda, Anita. 2012. (Short Tales Native American Myths Ser.). 32p. (J). (gr. 3-6). lib. bdg. 24.21 *(978-1-61641-882-3(6))* Magic Wagon.

—The Warrior Twins: A Navajo Hero Myth. Yasuda, Anita. 2012. (Short Tales Native American Myths Ser.). 32p. (J). (gr. 3-6). lib. bdg. 24.21 *(978-1-61641-884-7(2))* Magic Wagon.

Pennington, Mark & Villarrubia, Jose. Cut Here, 3 vols. Carey, Mike & Fern, Jim. rev. ed. 2007. (Crossing Midnight Ser.). (ENG.). 128p. pap. 9.99 *(978-1-4012-1341-1(3)*, Vertigo) DC Comics.

Pennington, Mark, jt. illus. see Sears, Bart.

Penny, Agnes M. The Story of Our Lady of Victory. Penny, Agnes M. 2008. 24p. (J). 4.50 *(978-0-9788687-2-7(2))* Requiem Pr.

Pennypacker, Mona. Ghost Fever (Mal de Fantasma) Hayes, Joe. 2004. (ENG & SPA.). 80p. (J). (gr. 4-6). 14.95 *(978-0-938317-83-8(0))* Cinco Puntos Pr.

Pennypacker, Mona, jt. illus. see Hill, Vicki Trego.

Pentangelo, Manuela. A Day with My Dad. Waite, Lance. 2008. 24p. (J). (gr. -1-3). 17.99 *(978-1-60131-015-6(3)*, Parents Publishing Group) Big Tent Bks.

Pentangelo, Manuela. To the Rescue: Chicco Adventures. Pentangelo, Manuela. 2010. (ENG.). 24p. pap. 10.10 *(978-1-4536-1960-5(7))* CreateSpace Independent Publishing Platform.

Pentney, Ryan. Cyclops Tells All: The Way Eye See It. Loewen, Nancy. 2014. (Other Side of the Myth Ser.). (ENG.). 32p. (gr. 2-3). pap. 6.95 *(978-1-4795-2937-7(0))* Picture Window Bks.

—Cyclops Tells All: The Way EYE See It, 1 vol. Loewen, Nancy. 2014. (Other Side of the Myth Ser.). (ENG.). 32p. (gr. 2-3). lib. bdg. 26.65 *(978-1-4795-2180-7(9))* Picture Window Bks.

—Pandora Tells All: Not the Curious Kind, 1 vol. Loewen, Nancy. 2014. (Other Side of the Myth Ser.). (ENG.). 32p. (gr. 2-3). pap. 6.95 *(978-1-4795-2938-4(9))* Picture Window Bks.

Pentney, Ryan, jt. illus. see Gilpin, Stephen.

Peoples, Alan. James the Circus Boy. 2013. 80p. pap. 11.99 *(978-1-62839-474-0(9))* Salem Publishing Solutions, Inc.

Peot, Margaret. Inkblot: Drip, Splat, & Squish Your Way to Creativity. Peot, Margaret. 2011. (ENG.). 56p. (J). (gr. 6-18). 19.95 *(978-1-59078-720-5(X))* Boyds Mills Pr.

Pep, Joe. Sonic the Hedgehog Archives. Gallagher, Mike et al. Pellerito, Mike, ed. 2007. (Sonic the Hedgehog Archives Ser.: 2). (ENG.). 112p. (J). (gr. 4-7). pap. 7.95 *(978-1-879794-21-4(7)*, Archie Comics) Archie Comic Pubns., Inc.

Pepin, Jacques. Kids Cook French: Les Enfants Cuisinent en Francais. Pepin, Claudine. 2015. (ENG & FRE.). 96p. 21.99 *(978-1-59253-953-6(X)*, Quarry Books) Quarto Publishing Group USA.

Pepis, Aaron, photos by. What You Will See Inside a Mosque. Khan, Aisha Karen. 32p. (J). 2008. (ENG., pap. 8.99 *(978-1-59473-257-7(4))*; 2003. (gr. 1-5). 16.95 *(978-1-893361-60-7(8))* LongHill Partners, Inc. (Skylight Paths Publishing).

—What You Will See Inside a Mosque. Khan, Aisha Karen. 2003. 32p. *(978-2-89507-398-7(8))* Novalis Publishing.

Perard, Victor. Pete Cow Puncher a Story of the Texas Plains. Ames, Joseph B. 2005. reprint ed. pap. 31.95 *(978-0-7661-9421-2(3))* Kessinger Publishing, LLC.

Perciopelo. Susana Worrywart & the Magical Teddy Bear Balloon. Burke, Ellinor Rozecki. 2003. 32p. (J). 17.99 *(978-0-9741586-3-1(1))* Comfort Tales, LLC.

—Susana Worrywart & the Magical Teddy Bear Balloon: With CD for Relaxation. Burke, Ellinor Rozecki. 2003. 32p. (J). 27.00 incl. audio compact disk *(978-0-9741586-0-0(7))* Comfort Tales, LLC.

Percival, Tom. And He's the Good Guy. Landy, Derek. 2007. (Skulduggery Pleasant Ser.: 1). (ENG.). 400p. (J). (gr. 5-7). 17.99 *(978-0-06-123115-5(0))* HarperCollins Pubs.

—Curses for Sale, 1 vol. Brezenoff, Steve. 2012. (Ravens Pass Ser.). (ENG.). 96p. (gr. 2-3). pap. 6.15 *(978-1-4342-4209-9(9))*; lib. bdg. 23.99 *(978-1-4342-3763-7(X))* Stone Arch Bks.

—Monster & Me, 1 vol. Marsh, Robert. 2009. (Monster & Me Ser.). (ENG.). 40p. (gr. 1-3). lib. bdg. 22.65 *(978-1-4342-1589-5(X)*, Graphic Sparks) Stone Arch Bks.

—Monster in the Outfield, 1 vol. Marsh, Robert. 2009. (Monster & Me Ser.). (ENG.). 40p. (gr. 1-3). lib. bdg. 22.65 *(978-1-4342-1590-1(3)*, Graphic Sparks) Stone Arch Bks.

—Monster Moneymaker, 1 vol. Marsh, Robert. 2010. (Monster & Me Ser.). (ENG.). 40p. (gr. 1-3). lib. bdg. 22.65 *(978-1-4342-1891-9(0),* Graphic Sparks) Stone Arch Bks.

—New in Town, 1 vol. Brezenoff, Steve. 2012. (Ravens Pass Ser.). (ENG.). 96p. (gr. 2-3). pap. 6.15 *(978-1-4342-4210-5(2));* lib. bdg. 23.99 *(978-1-4342-3793-4(1))* Stone Arch Bks.

—Scepter of the Ancients. Landy, Derek. (Skulduggery Pleasant Ser.: Bk. 1). (ENG.). 416p. (J). 2009. pap. 3.99 *(978-0-06-173155-6(2),* Harper Trophy); 2008. (gr. 5). pap. 7.99 *(978-0-06-123117-9(7))* HarperCollins Pubs.

—The Sleeper, 1 vol. Brezenoff, Steve. 2012. (Ravens Pass Ser.). (ENG.). 96p. (gr. 2-3). pap. 6.15 *(978-1-4342-4211-2(0));* lib. bdg. 23.99 *(978-1-4342-3792-7(3))* Stone Arch Bks.

—Witch Mayor, 1 vol. Brezenoff, Steve. 2012. (Ravens Pass Ser.). (ENG.). 96p. (gr. 2-3). pap. 6.15 *(978-1-4342-4212-9(9));* lib. bdg. 23.99 *(978-1-4342-3791-0(5))* Stone Arch Bks.

Percival, Tom. Jack's Amazing Shadow. Percival, Tom. 2013. (ENG.). 32p. (J). (gr. -1-k). pap. 9.99 *(978-1-84365-220-5(X),* Pavilion) Pavilion Bks. GBR. Dist: Independent Pubs. Group.

Percy, Graham. Tales from the Arabian Nights. 2011. (10-Minute Bedtime Stories Ser.). (ENG.). 64p. (J). (gr. k-4). 14.99 *(978-1-84365-144-4(0),* Pavilion Children's Books) Pavilion Bks. GBR. Dist: Independent Pubs. Group.

Percy, Graham. The Ant & the Grasshopper. Percy, Graham. 2009. (Aesop's Fables Ser.). (ENG.). 32p. (J). (gr. k-3). 28.50 *(978-1-60253-201-4(X),* 200033) Child's World, Inc., The.

—The Heron & the Fish. Percy, Graham. 2009. (Aesop's Fables Ser.). (ENG.). 32p. (J). (gr. k-3). 28.50 *(978-1-60253-202-1(8),* 200037) Child's World, Inc., The.

—The Tortoise & the Hare. Percy, Graham. 2009. (Aesop's Fables Ser.). (ENG.). 32p. (J). (gr. k-3). 28.50 *(978-1-60253-204-5(4),* 200040) Child's World, Inc., The.

Percy, Sally. Donde Dormiras Pequena Liebre? Cain, Sheridan. (SPA.). (J). (gr. k-2). pap. 16.95 *(978-84-488-0869-3(X),* BS3556) Beascoa, Ediciones S.A. ESP. Dist: Lectorum Pubns., Inc.

Pérez, Carmen. A Cat Is Chasing Me Through This Book!, 1 vol. Bird, Benjamin. 2014. (Tom & Jerry Ser.). (ENG.). 32p. (gr. -1-2). 21.32 *(978-1-4795-5229-0(1))* Picture Window Bks.

—Don't Give This Book a Bowl of Milk!, 1 vol. Bird, Benjamin. 2014. (Tom & Jerry Ser.). (ENG.). 32p. (gr. -1-2). 21.32 *(978-1-4795-5230-6(5))* Picture Window Bks.

—There's a Mouse Hiding in This Book!, 1 vol. Bird, Benjamin. 2014. (Tom & Jerry Ser.). (ENG.). 32p. (gr. -1-2). 21.32 *(978-1-4795-5228-3(3))* Picture Window Bks.

—This Book Is Not a Piece of Cheese!, 1 vol. Bird, Benjamin. 2014. (Tom & Jerry Ser.). (ENG.). 32p. (gr. -1-2). 21.32 *(978-1-4795-5231-3(3))* Picture Window Bks.

Pérez, Daniel, et al. Alice in Wonderland, 1 vol. Carroll, Lewis. 2009. (Classic Fiction Ser.). (ENG.). 72p. (gr. 2-3). lib. bdg. 26.65 *(978-1-4342-1585-7(7),* Graphic Revolve) Stone Arch Bks.

—The Hound of the Baskervilles. Doyle, Arthur. 2008. (Classic Fiction Ser.). (ENG.). 72p. (gr. 2-3). 26.65 *(978-1-4342-0755-5(2),* Graphic Revolve) Stone Arch Bks.

—The Seven Voyages of Sinbad, 1 vol. Powell, Martin. 2010. (Classic Fiction Ser.). (ENG.). 72p. (gr. 2-3). 26.65 *(978-1-4342-1987-9(9));* pap. 7.15 *(978-1-4342-2775-1(8))* Stone Arch Bks. (Graphic Revolve).

Pérez, Daniel & Ferran, Daniel. Macbeth, 1 vol. Shakespeare, William. 2011. (Shakespeare Graphics Ser.). (ENG.). 88p. (gr. 2-3). pap. 7.15 *(978-1-4342-3447-6(9),* Shakespeare Graphics) Stone Arch Bks.

Perez, Debi. It's Blue Like You! A Story about Loyalty. Pantelides, Sherry. 2007. 32p. (J). 12.99 *(978-0-9771076-1-2(2))* Lacey Productions.

—It's Red Like Me! A Story about the Blood of Jesus. Pantelides, Sherry. 2007. (J). lib. bdg. 12.99 *(978-0-9771076-0-5(4))* Lacey Productions.

—Make A Choice to Rejoice! A Story about Being Cheerful. Pantelides, Sherry. 2007. 32p. (J). 12.99 *(978-0-9771076-2-9(0))* Lacey Productions.

Perez, Dorothy Thompson. Cómo Participar en la Liturgia: Un Libro de Para los Ninos Anglicanos-Episcopales. Kitch, Anne E. Martell, Oswald Perez, tr. 2008. 48p. pap. 10.00 *(978-0-8192-2331-9(X),* Morehouse Publishing) Church Publishing, Inc.

—What We Do in Advent: An Anglican Kids' Activity Book. Kitch, Anne E. 2006. (ENG.). 48p. (gr. -1-2). pap. 10.00 *(978-0-8192-2195-7(3),* Morehouse Publishing) Church Publishing, Inc.

—What We Do in Church: An Anglican Child's Activity Book. Kitch, Anne E. 2004. (ENG.). 48p. pap. 10.00 *(978-0-8192-2105-6(8),* Morehouse Publishing) Church Publishing, Inc.

—What We Do in Lent: A Child's Activity Book. Kitch, Anne E. 2007. 48p. pap. 10.00 *(978-0-8192-2278-7(X),* Morehouse Publishing) Church Publishing, Inc.

Perez, Esther Ido. Let's Go Camping & Discover Our Nature. Yerushalmi, Miriam. 2007. 28p. (J). (gr. 2-4). 16.50 *(978-0-911643-38-1(9))* Aura Printing, Inc.

Perez-Fessenden, Lourdes. Daddy & I. Perez-Fessenden, Lourdes. 2012. 34p. pap. *(978-0-9840862-3-8(4))* Roxby Media Ltd.

Perez, George, et al. Essential Avengers, Vol. 8. Shooter, Jim & Wolfman, Marv. 2012. (ENG.). 488p. (J). (gr. 4-17). pap. 19.99 *(978-0-7851-6322-0(0))* Marvel Worldwide, Inc.

—Essential Fantastic Four - Volume 9. 2013. (ENG.). 512p. (J). (gr. 4-17). pap. 19.99 *(978-0-7851-8410-2(4))* Marvel Worldwide, Inc.

—Radiant, Vol. 2. Kesel, Barbara. 2004. (Solus Ser.: Vol. 2). 160p. (YA). pap. 15.95 *(978-1-59314-057-1(6))* CrossGeneration Comics, Inc.

Perez, George. The Serpent Crown. 2005. (ENG.). 136p. (J). (gr. 4-17). pap. 15.99 *(978-0-7851-1700-1(8))* Marvel Worldwide, Inc.

Perez, George, et al. Solus. Kesel, Barbara. 2003. (Solus Ser.: Vol. 1). 160p. (YA). pap. 15.95 *(978-1-931484-97-8(X))* CrossGeneration Comics, Inc.

Perez, George & Pollard, Keith. Fantastic Four: The Overthrow of Doom. Wein, Len & Wolfman, Marv. 2011. (ENG.). 192p. (J). (gr. 4-17). 29.99 *(978-0-7851-5605-5(4))* Marvel Worldwide, Inc.

Perez, Gerry. Hello CavMan! Aryal, Aimee. 2004. 24p. (J). 19.95 *(978-0-9743442-3-2(0))* Mascot Bks., Inc.

—Hello Joe Bruin! Aryal, Aimee. 2004. 24p. (J). 19.95 *(978-1-932888-15-7(2))* Mascot Bks., Inc.

—Hello, Ralphie! Aryal, Aimee. 2007. 24p. (J). lib. bdg. 14.95 *(978-1-932888-34-8(9))* Mascot Bks., Inc.

—Hello Tommy Trojan! Aryal, Aimee. 2004. 24p. (J). 19.95 *(978-1-932888-08-9(X))* Mascot Bks., Inc.

Pérez, Javier Serrano. The Shadow Mother. Virgo, Seán. 2014. (ENG.). 64p. (J). (gr. 6). 21.95 *(978-0-88899-971-9(2))* Groundwood Bks. CAN. Dist: Perseus-PGW.

Perez, Jose S. The Banjoman/El Hombre del Banjo. Perez, Jose S. Norman, Tyler. 2004. (ENG & SPA.). 32p. (J). 12.95 *(978-1-57072-292-9(7))* Overmountain Pr.

Perez, Lucia Angela. Hablando Con Madre Tierra. Argueta, Jorge. 2006.Tr. of Talking with Mother Earth. (ENG & SPA.). 32p. (J). (gr. k-3). 17.95 *(978-0-88899-626-8(8))* Groundwood Bks. CAN. Dist: Perseus-PGW.

Perez, Maureen T. Caring - Companion Book. Cesena, Denise. I.t. ed. 2003. 12p. (J). 2.00 *(978-0-9740418-7-2(4))* Night Light Pubns., LLC.

Perez, Maureen T. Caring. Perez, Maureen T. Cesena, Denise. I.t. ed. 2003. 28p. (J). 10.00 *(978-0-9740418-6-5(6))* Night Light Pubns., LLC.

Perez, Maureen T. & Cesena, Denise. Friendliness. Perez, Maureen T. I.t. ed. 2003. 28p. (J). 10.00 *(978-0-9740418-0-3(7))* Night Light Pubns., LLC.

—Friendliness - Companion Book. Perez, Maureen T. I.t. ed. 2003. 12p. (J). 2.00 *(978-0-9740418-1-0(5))* Night Light Pubns., LLC.

Perez, Maureen T., jt. illus. see Cesena, Denise.

Perez-Moliere, Mamie. Los Tres Naufragos. Barsy, Kalman. 2004. (Orange Ser.). (SPA.). 40p. (J). (gr. 3-5). pap. 5.95 *(978-1-57581-469-8(2))* Santillana USA Publishing Co., Inc.

—La Niña y la Estrella. Leon, Georgina Lazaro. 2003. (Yellow Ser.). (SPA.). 31p. (gr. k-3). pap. 7.95 *(978-1-57581-436-0(6))* Santillana USA Publishing Co., Inc.

Perez, Pere. The Guardian, Vol. 1. Miller, Bryan Q. 2013. (ENG.). 144p. pap. 14.99 *(978-1-4012-3824-7(6))* DC Comics.

Perez, Peter L. Presiona Aqui. Perez, Peter L. Tullet, Hervé. 2012. (SPA & ENG.). 56p. (J). (gr. -1-3). 15.99 *(978-1-4521-1287-9(8))* Chronicle Bks. LLC.

Perez, Ramon, et al. Captain America: Allies & Enemies. 2011. (ENG.). 136p. (YA). (gr. 8-17). pap., pap. 16.99 *(978-0-7851-5502-7(3))* Marvel Worldwide, Inc.

Perez, Ramon. The Country of Wolves, 1 vol. Flaherty, Louise & Christopher, Neil. 2013. (ENG.). 108p. (J). (gr. 7). 24.95 *(978-1-927095-04-1(2))* Inhabit Media Inc. CAN. Dist: Independent Pubs. Group.

Pérez, Ramón. The Country of Wolves, 1 vol. Christopher, Neil. 2015. (ENG.). 108p. (YA). (gr. 7). pap. 19.95 ***(978-1-927095-35-5(2))*** Inhabit Media Inc. CAN. Dist: Independent Pubs. Group.

Pérez, Ramón. Max Finder Mystery Collected Casebook, Vol. 6. Battle, Craig. 2012. (Max Finder Mystery Collected Casebook Ser.: 6). (ENG.). 96p. (J). (gr. 3). pap. 9.95 *(978-1-926973-21-0(6))* Owlkids Bks. Inc. CAN. Dist: Perseus-PGW.

Perez, Ramon. Tale of Sand. Henson, Jim & Juhl, Jerry. Christy, Stephen & Robinson, Chris, eds. 2011. (ENG.). 120p. (YA). (gr. 2). 29.95 *(978-1-936393-09-1(3))* Boom Entertainment, Inc.

Pérez, Ramón & Owlkids Books Inc. Staff. Fear This Book: Your Guide to Fright, Horror, & Things That Go Bump in the Night. Szpirglas, Jeff. 2006. (ENG.). 64p. (J). (gr. 3-6). pap. 9.95 *(978-1-897066-67-6(8),* Maple Tree Pr.) Owlkids Bks. Inc. CAN. Dist: Perseus-PGW.

—Max Finder Mystery Collected Casebook, Vol. 4. O'Donnell, Liam & Battle, Craig. 2010. (Max Finder Mystery Collected Casebook Ser.: 4). (ENG.). 96p. (J). (gr. 3-6). pap. 9.95 *(978-1-897349-80-9(7))* Owlkids Bks. Inc. CAN. Dist: Perseus-PGW.

—Max Finder Mystery Collected Casebook, Vol. 5. Battle, Craig. 2011. (Max Finder Mystery Collected Casebook Ser.: 5). (ENG.). 96p. (J). (gr. 3-6). pap. 9.95 *(978-1-926818-12-2(1))* Owlkids Bks. Inc. CAN. Dist: Perseus-PGW.

Pérez, Ramón K. Cyclist BikeList: The Book for Every Rider. Robinson, Laura. 2010. (ENG.). 64p. (J). (gr. 4-7). pap. 17.95 *(978-0-88776-784-5(2))* Tundra Bks. CAN. Dist: Random Hse., Inc.

Perez, Sara. Is a Spider an Insect? Ikids Staff & Schimel, Lawrence. 2009. (ENG.). 22p. (J). (gr. -1-1). 9.99 *(978-1-58476-820-3(7),* IKIDS) Innovative Kids.

—What's in the Egg? Ikids Staff & Schimel, Lawrence. 2009. (ENG.). 22p. (J). (gr. -1-1). 9.99 *(978-1-58476-821-0(5),* IKIDS) Innovative Kids.

Pérez, Sara Rojo. The Ant & the Grasshopper: A Retelling of Aesop's Fable, 1 vol. White, Mark & Aesop Enterprise Inc. Staff. 2011. (My First Classic Story Ser.). (ENG.). 24p. (gr. k-3). lib. bdg. 21.32 *(978-1-4048-6505-1(5),* My First Classic Story) Picture Window Bks.

—The Ant & the Grasshopper: A Retelling of Aesop's Fable, 1 vol. White, Mark. 2011. (My First Classic Story Ser.). (ENG.). 24p. (gr. k-3). pap. 7.10 *(978-1-4048-7363-6(5),* My First Classic Story) Picture Window Bks.

—The Fox & the Grapes: A Retelling of Aesop's Fable, 1 vol. White, Mark. 2013. (My First Classic Story Ser.). (ENG.). 24p. (gr. k-3). pap. 7.10 *(978-1-4795-1856-2(5),* My First Classic Story) Picture Window Bks.

—The Fox & the Grapes: A Retelling of Aesop's Fable, 1 vol. White, Mark & Aesop Enterprise Inc. Staff. 2011. (My First Classic Story Ser.). (ENG.). 24p. (gr. k-3). lib. bdg. 21.32 *(978-1-4048-6508-2(X),* My First Classic Story) Picture Window Bks.

—The Fox & the Grapes: A Retelling of Aesop's Fable. White, Mark. 2008. (Read-It! Readers: Fables Ser.). (ENG.). 24p. (gr. k-3). per. 3.95 *(978-1-4048-0467-8(6),* Easy Readers) Picture Window Bks.

—El Leon y el Raton: Versión de la Fábula de Esopo. White, Mark. Abello, Patricia, tr. from ENG. 2006. (Read-It! Readers en Español: Fábulas Ser.).Tr. of Lion & the Mouse - A Retelling of Aesop's Fable. (SPA.). 24p. (gr. k-3). 19.99 *(978-1-4048-1623-7(2),* Easy Readers) Picture Window Bks.

—The Lion & the Mouse: A Retelling of Aesop's Fable, 1 vol. White, Mark. 2010. (My First Classic Story Ser.). (ENG.). 24p. (gr. k-3). pap. 7.10 *(978-1-4048-7365-0(1),* My First Classic Story) Picture Window Bks.

—The Lion & the Mouse: A Retelling of Aesop's Fable, 1 vol. White, Mark & Aesop Enterprise Inc. Staff. 2010. (My First Classic Story Ser.). (ENG.). 24p. (gr. k-3). lib. bdg. 21.32 *(978-1-4048-6525-9(X),* My First Classic Story) Picture Window Bks.

—Why Do We Recycle? Science Made Simple! Ikids Staff. 2009. (ENG.). 22p. (J). (gr. -1-1). 9.99 *(978-1-58476-935-4(1))* Innovative Kids.

—Why Does the Wind Blow? Science Made Simple! Ikids Staff. 2009. (ENG.). 20p. (J). (gr. -1-1). 9.99 *(978-1-58476-934-7(3))* Innovative Kids.

—The Wolf in Sheep's Clothing: A Retelling of Aesop's Fable, 1 vol. White, Mark. 2013. (My First Classic Story Ser.). (ENG.). 24p. (gr. k-3). pap. 7.10 *(978-1-4795-1857-9(3),* My First Classic Story) Picture Window Bks.

—The Wolf in Sheep's Clothing: A Retelling of Aesop's Fable, 1 vol. White, Mark & Aesop Enterprise Inc. Staff. 2011. (My First Classic Story Ser.). (ENG.). 24p. (gr. k-3). lib. bdg. 21.32 *(978-1-4048-6509-9(8),* My First Classic Story) Picture Window Bks.

—La Zorra y Las Uvas. White, Mark. Abello, Patricia, tr. 2008. (Read-It! Readers en Español: Cuentos Folclóricos Ser.). (SPA.). 24p. (gr. k-3). per. 3.95 *(978-1-4048-2141-5(4),* Easy Readers) Picture Window Bks.

Perez-Stable, Deborah. That Blessed Christmas Night. Chaconas, Dori. 2004. 32p. (J). 18.00 *(978-0-687-00626-7(0))* Abingdon Pr.

Perez, Thierry. Carla & Leo's World of Dance. Relota, Agatha. 2011. (ENG.). 112p. (J). (gr. 1-3). 19.95 *(978-0-500-51560-0(3),* 551560) Thames & Hudson.

Perez-Torres, Juliana. George, Candy, & the Raccoon. Gilbert, George. 2008. 40p. pap. 16.99 *(978-1-4389-2848-7(3))* AuthorHouse.

Perilli, Marilena & Miller, Victoria. The Princess & the Ring (Dora & Friends) Tillworth, Mary. 2015. (Little Golden Book Ser.). (ENG.). 24p. (J). (-k). 3.99 *(978-0-553-49768-7(5),* Golden Bks.) Random Hse. Children's Bks.

Perilli, Marilena & Tomita, Kuni. Doggy Day. Buckley, MacKenzie. 2014. (Big Golden Book Ser.). (ENG.). 48p. (J). (gr. -1-2). 9.99 *(978-0-385-37501-6(8),* Golden Bks.) Random Hse. Children's Bks.

Perin, Pauline. The Bully of Glendale Pond. Smith, Clyde R. 2012. 24p. (-18). pap. 24.95 *(978-1-4626-7795-5(9))* America Star Bks.

Peringer, Stephen Mercer. Jordan's Hair. Spruill, Edward L. & Spruill, Sonya. 2005. 16p. (J). (gr. -1-3). 8.00 *(978-0-8170-1484-1(5))* Judson Pr.

Peris, Carme. ¡No Quiero Bañarme! Produccions Editorials, Trèvol & Trèvol, S. A. 2005. (Cucú Ser.). (SPA & ENG.). 16p. (J). (gr. -1-k). pap. 6.95 *(978-84-7864-841-2(0))* Combel Editorial, S.A. ESP. Dist: Independent Pubs. Group.

Peris, Nuria, jt. illus. see Sandoval, Sergio.

Perkins, Chelsea. Have You Ever Seen a Wild Bird Dance? Yost, B. L. 2008. 16p. pap. 24.95 *(978-1-60703-127-7(2))* America Star Bks.

Perkins, Ken. Does God Love Michael's Two Daddies. Butt, Sheila K. 2007. (ENG.). 16p. (J). pap. 7.95 *(978-0-932859-94-5(1))* Apologetics Pr., Inc.

Perkins, Lori L., jt. illus. see Perkins, William C.

Perkins, Lucy. The American Twins of the Revolution. Perkins, Lucy. 2007. 232p. per. 12.95 *(978-0-9776786-7-9(9))* Salem Ridge Press LLC.

Perkins, Lucy Fitch. The American Twins of the Revolution. Perkins, Lucy Fitch. 2008. 240p. 22.95 *(978-1-934671-19-1(3))* Salem Ridge Press LLC.

Perkins, Lynne Rae. Seed by Seed: The Legend & Legacy of John Appleseed Anniversary. Codell, Esmé Raji. 2012. 32p. (J). (gr. -1-3). 17.89 *(978-0-06-145516-2(4),* Greenwillow Bks.) HarperCollins Pubs.

—Seed by Seed: The Legend & Legacy of John Appleseed Chapman. Codell, Esmé Raji. 2012. (ENG.). 32p. (J). (gr. -1-3). 16.99 *(978-0-06-145515-5(6),* Greenwillow Bks.) HarperCollins Pubs.

Perkins, Lynne Rae. The Cardboard Piano. Perkins, Lynne Rae. 2008. 32p. (J). (gr. -1-3). lib. bdg. 18.89 *(978-0-06-154266-4(0));* (ENG.). 17.99 *(978-0-06-154265-7(2))* HarperCollins Pubs. (Greenwillow Bks.).

—Nuts to You. Perkins, Lynne Rae. 2014. (ENG.). 272p. (J). (gr. 3-7). 16.99 *(978-0-06-009275-7(0),* Greenwillow Bks.) HarperCollins Pubs.

—Pictures from Our Vacation. Perkins, Lynne Rae. 2007. 32p. (J). (gr. k-3). 17.89 *(978-0-06-085098-2(1),* Greenwillow Bks.) HarperCollins Pubs.

—Pictures from Our Vacation. Perkins, Lynne Rae. Perkins, Lynne R. 2007. (ENG.). 32p. (J). (gr. k-3). 17.99 *(978-0-06-085097-5(3),* Greenwillow Bks.) HarperCollins Pubs.

—Snow Music. Perkins, Lynne Rae. 2003. 40p. (J). lib. bdg. 16.89 *(978-0-06-623958-3(3))* HarperCollins Pubs.

—Snow Music. Perkins, Lynne Rae. Perkins, Lynne R. 2003. (ENG.). 40p. (J). (gr. -1-3). 16.99 *(978-0-06-623956-9(7),* Greenwillow Bks.) HarperCollins Pubs.

Perkins, Mair. Boris the Lost Badger. Hainsworth, B. R. 2012. 42p. pap. *(978-1-78148-585-9(2))* Grosvenor Hse. Publishing Ltd.

Perkins, Mike, jt. illus. see Guice, Butch.

Perkins, Nancy. Mother Goose Coloring Book. Greenaway, Kate. 2013. (Dover Coloring Bks.). (ENG.). 48p. (J). (gr. -1-8). pap. 3.99 *(978-0-486-22883-9(5))* Dover Pubns., Inc.

Perkins, Nicole & Frisk, Maria. I Believe God Will: Book of Devotion & Prayer for Children. Perkins, Nicole. 2008. 32p. (J). 7.00 *(978-0-9755566-1-0(4))* Azreal Publishing Co.

Perkins, R. Earth Whispers. 32p. (J). (gr. 3-18). 16.00 *(978-0-9710860-2-9(8))* Libros, Encouraging Cultural Literacy.

Perkins, Rodney R., jt. illus. see VanDerTuuk-Perkins, Jennifer E.

Perkins, Ruth. Dozens & Dozens of Cousins & Cousins. Young, Elizabeth L. 2012. 30p. 20.95 *(978-1-61633-353-9(7));* pap. 12.95 *(978-1-61633-352-2(9))* Guardian Angel Publishing, Inc.

Perkins, Stephanie. The Mystery of the Silver Statue. Perkins, Raymond. 2011. (ENG.). 96p. pap. 12.95 *(978-1-4637-7933-7(X))* CreateSpace Independent Publishing Platform.

Perkins, Terrell D. I Know When the Rainbow Comes. Perkins, Miss Quinn. 2013. 28p. pap. 9.95 *(978-0-9851628-0-1(5))* Soulful Storytellers, Inc.

Perkins, William C. & Perkins, Lori L. What Makes Honey? Perkins, Myrna. 32p. (Orig.). (J). (gr. -1-3). pap. 3.95 *(978-0-937729-03-8(5))* Markins Enterprises.

Perks, Brad, photos by. Inspirational Harvest & Hope: Brad Perks California Vineyards. Perks, Brad. 2008. 128p. (YA). 24.95 *(978-0-9788442-1-9(1))* Perks, Brad Lightscapes Photo Gallery.

Perla, Brian. NiNi Spergelini: Guitar-Ific! Spergel, Heather. 2013. (NiNi Spergelini Ser.: 1). (ENG.). 32p. (J). 18.99 *(978-0-9832148-5-4(9))* Turn the Page Publishing.

Perlin, Don, et al. Essential Defenders, Vol. 6. Gruenwald, Mark & Grant, Stephen. 2011. (ENG.). 498p. (J). (gr. 4-17). pap. 19.99 *(978-0-7851-5754-0(9))* Marvel Worldwide, Inc.

Perlman, Janet. The Delicious Bug. Perlman, Janet. (ENG.). 32p. (J). 2013. 7.95 *(978-1-77138-034-8(9));* 2009. (gr. -1-2). 16.95 *(978-1-55337-996-6(9))* Kids Can Pr., Ltd. CAN. Dist: Univ. of Toronto Pr.

—The Penguin & the Pea. Perlman, Janet. 2006. (ENG.). 32p. (J). (gr. -1-3). 7.95 *(978-1-55337-983-6(7))* Kids Can Pr., Ltd. CAN. Dist: Univ. of Toronto Pr.

Perlow, Janet. Show Dog. 2007. 40p. (J). pap. 14.95 incl. audio compact disk *(978-0-9795049-0-7(2))* Kidz Entertainment, Inc.

—Show Dog Coloring Book. 2007. 40p. (J). pap. 4.95 *(978-0-9795049-1-4(0))* Kidz Entertainment, Inc.

Perlyn, Amanda. The Biggest & Brightest Light: The Magic of Helping Others. Perlyn, Marilyn. 2nd rev. ed. 2013. (ENG.). 48p. (J). (gr. 1-5). 17.95 *(978-1-934759-75-2(9))* Reed, Robert D. Pubs.

Permane, Terry, jt. photos by see Palone, Terry.

Pernisco, Atilio. Grandma's Pear Tree. Santillan, Suzanne. 2010. (ENG.). 32p. (J). (gr. 4-7). 16.95 *(978-1-934960-82-0(9),* Raven Tree Pr.,Csi) Continental Sales, Inc.

—Grandma's Pear Tree/El Peral de Abuela. Santillan, Suzanne. 2010. (ENG & SPA.). 32p. (J). (gr. 4-7). 16.95 *(978-1-934960-80-6(2),* Raven Tree Pr.,Csi) Continental Sales, Inc.

Pérols, Sylvaine. El Raton y Otros Roedores. Pérols, Sylvaine. Millet, Claude et al. Jeunesse, Gallimard & Delafosse, Claude, trs. (Coleccion Mundo Maravilloso). (SPA.). 40p. (J). (gr. 2-4). *(978-84-348-3727-0(7),* SM5471) SM Ediciones ESP. Dist: Lectorum Pubns., Inc.

Perols, Sylvaine. The Body. Perols, Sylvaine, creator. 2007. (ENG.). 36p. (J). (gr. k-3). pap. 11.99 *(978-1-85103-225-9(8))* Moonlight Publishing, Ltd. GBR. Dist: Independent Pubs. Group.

Perras, Marielle. Bravery Is like Love. Chalifoux, Lisa M. 2009. 24p. pap. 10.99 *(978-1-4269-0942-9(X))* Trafford Publishing.

Perrault, Charles, jt. illus. see Clarke, Harry.

Perret, Delphine. The Pointless Leopard: What Good Are Kids Anyway? Gutman, Colas & Seegmuller, Stephanie. 2014. (ENG.). 48p. (YA). (gr. 2-4). pap. 9.99 *(978-1-78269-040-5(9),* Pushkin Children's Bks.) Pushkin Pr., Ltd. GBR. Dist: Random Hse., Inc.

Perret, Delphine. Pedro & George. Perret, Delphine. 2015. (ENG.). 32p. (J). (gr. -1-3). 17.99 *(978-1-4814-2925-2(6))* Simon & Schuster Children's Publishing.

Perrett, Lisa. Keeker & the Crazy, Upside-Down Birthday. Higginson, Hadley. 2008. (ENG.). 56p. (J). (gr. k-3). pap. 4.99 *(978-0-8118-6256-1(9))* Chronicle Bks. LLC.

—Keeker & the Pony Camp Catastrophe, Bk. 5. Higginson, Hadley. 2007. (Keeker & the Sneaky Pony Ser.: KEEK). (ENG.). (J). (gr. k-3). 52p. lib. bdg. 15.50 *(978-0-8118-5596-9(1));* 56p. per. 4.99 *(978-0-8118-5597-6(X))* Chronicle Bks. LLC.

—Keeker & the Springtime Surprise. Higginson, Hadley. 2007. (Keeker & the Sneaky Pony Ser.: KEEK). (ENG.). 58p. (J). (gr. k-3). per. 4.99 *(978-0-8118-5599-0(6))* Chronicle Bks. LLC.

—Sparkling Princess ABC. 2013. (Sparkling Stories Ser.). (ENG.). 14p. (J). bds. 5.95 *(978-1-4027-8886-4(X))* Sterling Publishing Co., Inc.

—Sparkling Princess Colors. 2014. (Sparkling Stories Ser.). (ENG.). 14p. (J). (gr. -1-k). bds. 5.95 *(978-1-4549-1249-1(9))* Sterling Publishing Co., Inc.

—Sparkling Princess Opposites. 2014. (Sparkling Stories Ser.). (ENG.). 14p. (J). (gr. -1-k). bds. 5.95 *(978-1-4549-1250-7(2))* Sterling Publishing Co., Inc.

—Sugar & Spice. Wax, Wendy. 2007. (ENG.). 24p. (J). (gr. 1-4). per. 3.99 *(978-1-58476-614-8(X),* IKIDS) Innovative Kids.

—Sugar & Spice - Fashion Girls. Innovative Kids Staff. 2006. (ENG.). 10p. (J). (gr. -1-1). 19.99 *(978-1-58476-487-8(2),* IKIDS) Innovative Kids.

—You've Got Spirit! Cheers, Chants, Tips, & Tricks Every Cheerleader Needs to Know. Hunt, Sara R. 2013. (ENG.). 48p. (gr. 3-6). lib. bdg. 30.60 (978-0-7613-8634-6(3), Millbrook Pr.) Lerner Publishing Group.

Perri, Anthony F. Repo Elf. Sims, Tom. 2008. (ENG.). 104p. (J). 12.95 (978-0-9787213-4-3(9), Cambridge House Pr.) Sterling & Ross Pubs.

Perrin, Martine. Look Who's There! Perrin, Martine. Martens, Marianne, tr. from FRE. 2011. (ENG.). 16p. (J). (gr. -1-k). bds. 8.99 (978-0-8075-7676-2(X)) Whitman, Albert & Co.

—What Do You See? Perrin, Martine. 2011. (ENG.). 16p. (J). (gr. -1-k). bds. 8.99 (978-0-8075-6712-8(4)) Whitman, Albert & Co.

Perrine, Doug. Sharks: Biggest! Littlest! Perrine, Doug, photos by. Markle, Sandra. 2008. (Biggest! Littlest! Ser.). (ENG.). 32p. (J). (gr. -1-2). 16.95 (978-1-59078-513-3(4)) Boyds Mills Pr.

Perrine, Doug, photos by. Sharks: Biggest! Littlest! Markle, Sandra. 2011. (Biggest! Littlest! Ser.). (ENG., 32p. (J). pap. 10.95 (978-1-59078-873-8(7)) Boyds Mills Pr.

Perrins, Karen. The Frog King: An African Folktale. StJohn, Amanda. 2011. (Folktales from Around the World Ser.). (ENG.). 24p. (J). (gr. k-3). 28.50 (978-1-60973-137-3(9), 201145) Child's World, Inc., The.

Perritt, Jordona. Cowgirls Dream. Johnson, Sandi. Date not set. (Kooky Kountry Ser.). (J). (gr. -1-6). 8.99 (978-1-929063-56-7(3)) Moons & Stars Publishing For Children.

Perron, Debra. Imagination Goodnight. Burlinson, J. 2005. 24p. (J). 14.95 (978-1-59879-068-9(4)) Lifevest Publishing, Inc.

Perroud, Benoît. Caco the Little Orphan Cat: O Gatinho Órfão. Heymelaux, Jasmin. Canuto, Louise, tr. from ENG. 2010. (ENG & POR.). 28p. (J). pap. 14.00 (978-1-58432-689-2(1)) Educa Vision.

—Coco: The Little Orphan Cat. Heymelaux, Jasmin & Biggs, Harry. 2006. (J). 16.00 (978-1-58432-234-4(9)) Educa Vision.

Perry, Aumi Kauffman. Brutus the Bull. Bean, Margo Cronbaugh. 2013. 24p. 19.95 (978-1-61633-373-7(1)); pap. 11.95 (978-1-61633-374-4(X)) Guardian Angel Publishing, Inc.

—Buffaloed Badger. Bean, Margo Cronbaugh. 2012. 24p. 19.95 (978-1-61633-239-6(5)); pap. 11.95 (978-1-61633-240-2(9)) Guardian Angel Publishing, Inc.

Perry, Charles, photos by. The Legend of Scarface. Perry, Charles. 2005. (ENG., 12p. (J). 5.75 (978-1-57274-752-4(8), 2764, Bks. for Young Learners) Owen, Richard C. Pubs., Inc.

Perry, Craig Rex & Preston, Felicia. Ricky & Friends Go to Africa. Van Dyke, Tony & Van Dyke, Tracey. ed. 2003. (Encouraging African-Americans in Their Walk Ser.). (ENG.). 64p. (J). pap. 5.99 (978-0-8024-0902-7(4), Lift Every Voice) Moody Pubs.

Perry, Curtis. Always Remember You Are Loved: When a Child Seeks Guidance on Cyber & Peer Bullying. Washington, Angel D. 2012. 40p. pap. 9.95 (978-0-9860041-1-7(1)) Angel's Diary.

Perry, Diana Torri. Clumsy Claudia & the Gentle Forest Friends, 1 vol. Perry, Brad Lee. 2010. 56p. pap. 16.95 (978-1-4489-4633-4(6)) America Star Bks.

Perry, Fred. Cymbeline: Graphic Novel. Shakespeare, William. 2010. (Graphic Shakespeare Set 2 Ser.). 48p. (J). (gr. 5-9). 29.93 (978-1-60270-763-4(4)) ABDO Publishing Co.

—Julius Caesar: Graphic Novel. Shakespeare, William. 2010. (Graphic Shakespeare Set 2 Ser.). 48p. (J). (gr. 5-9). 29.93 (978-1-60270-765-8(0)) ABDO Publishing Co.

Perry, Gala. A Girl's Guide to Growing up - Booklet, 10 per packet. Smith, Liz. 2005. (J). 63.95 (978-1-55942-207-9(6)) Witcher Productions.

Perry, Georgia. The Bouncing Ball. Kelly, Deborah. 2014. (ENG.). 32p. (J). (gr. -1-k). 15.99 (978-0-85798-004-5(1)) Random Hse. Australia AUS. Dist: Independent Pubs. Group.

Perry, Gina Marie. Dirty Gertie, 1 vol. Mortensen, Lori. 2009. (Read-It! Readers: Character Education Ser.). (ENG.). 32p. (gr. k-2). 19.99 (978-1-4048-4234-2(9), Easy Readers) Picture Window Bks.

Perry, Jennifer A. TJ & the Good Luck Cricket. Szish, Jill Henry. 2007. 32p. per. 24.95 (978-1-4241-8502-3(5)) America Star Bks.

Perry, Lee Ann. Why, Daddy, Why Are There Stars in the Sky? Freeman, Chip. 2012. 20p. (-18). pap. 11.95 (978-1-937770-23-5(0), SPC Bks.) RPJ & Co., Inc.

Perry, Margie. Birdie School Days: The First Day of School. Perrine, David L. 2005. (J). pap. 15.00 (978-0-8059-6699-2(4)) Dorrance Publishing Co., Inc.

Perry, Marie. A Gift for Sadia. Perry, Marie. l.t. ed. 2005. 32p. (J). lib. bdg. 15.95 (978-0-9755675-1-7(9)) Buttonweed Pr., L.L.C.

Perry, Marie/Fritz. Cecil's New Year's Eve Tail. Perry, Marie/Fritz. 2007. 32p. (J). lib. bdg. (978-0-9755675-2-4(7)) Buttonweed Pr., L.L.C.

Perry, Matt, jt. illus. see Unalp, Janet.

Perry, Rex. All Things Bright & Beautiful. 2004. 24p. (J). lib. bdg. 8.00 (978-1-4242-0638-4(3)) Fitzgerald Bks.

—Over the River & Through the Woods. 2004. 24p. (J). lib. bdg. 8.00 (978-1-4242-0640-7(5)) Fitzgerald Bks.

—'Twas the Night Before Christmas. 2004. 24p. (J). lib. bdg. 8.00 (978-1-4242-0641-4(3)) Fitzgerald Bks.

Perry, Rex. Coco's Girls. Perry, Rex. 2008. (ENG.). 36p. (YA). per. 12.95 (978-0-9740212-1-8(0), Sapling Bks.) Cedar Grove Bks.

Persiani, Tony. The Day-Glo Brothers: The True Story of Bob & Joe Switzer's Bright Ideas & Brand-New Colors. Barton, Chris. 2009. (ENG.). 44p. (J). (gr. 2-5). 19.95 (978-1-57091-673-1(X)) Charlesbridge Publishing, Inc.

Persico, Zoe. My Grandparents. Harrington, Claudia. 2016. (J). **(978-1-62402-105-3(0))** Magic Wagon.

—My Military Mom. Harrington, Claudia. 2016. (J). **(978-1-62402-106-0(9))** Magic Wagon.

—My Mom & Dad. Harrington, Claudia. 2016. (J). **(978-1-62402-107-7(7))** Magic Wagon.

—My Two Dads. Harrington, Claudia. 2016. (J). **(978-1-62402-108-4(5))** Magic Wagon.

—My Two Homes. Harrington, Claudia. 2016. (J). **(978-1-62402-109-1(3))** Magic Wagon.

—My Two Moms. Harrington, Claudia. 2016. (J). **(978-1-62402-110-7(7))** Magic Wagon.

Pertile, Paula. The Gingerbread Man. 2010. (J). (978-1-60617-141-7(0)) Teaching Strategies, Inc.

—Number One Puppy. Wilson, Zachary. 2011. (Rookie Ready to Learn Ser.). 40p. (J). pap. 5.95 (978-0-531-26748-6(2)); (gr. -1-k). lib. bdg. 23.00 (978-0-531-26448-5(3)) Scholastic Library Publishing. (Children's Pr.).

Perucca, Nancy Call. Multiplication Camp. Perucca, Nancy Call. Evans, Renee Call. 2004. (J). pap. 29.95 (978-0-9748074-0-9(0)) Nancy's Artworks.

—Sea Notes on the Keyboard: The Fast & Fun Way to Learn the Notes on the Keyboard! Perucca, Nancy Call. Evans, Renee Call. 2004. 32p. (J). pap. 9.95 (978-0-9748074-1-6(9)) Nancy's Artworks.

Perunko, Linda. My Grandma Is an Angel Now. Havens, Sarita. 2008. 12p. pap. 24.95 (978-1-60672-350-0(2)) America Star Bks.

Peruzzo, Nicolas. Safari Dreams. Peruzzo, Nicolas. 2012. 26p. pap. 9.99 (978-1-61225-162-2(5)) Mirror Publishing.

Pervan, Ivo & Bemporad, Alex, photos by. Fate Did Not Let Me Go: A Mother's Farewell Letter, 1 vol. Ollendorff, Valli. 2003. (ENG., 48p. 5.95 (978-1-58980-153-0(9)) Pelican Publishing Co., Inc.

Pesce, Carol. The Look Book: 50 Iconic Beauties & How to Achieve Their Signature Styles. Stalder, Erika. 2011. (ENG.). 128p. (YA). (gr. 7-18). pap. 18.99 (978-0-9819733-8-8(8)) Zest Bks.

Peschel, Georgia. A Real Meal Table Fable. Chen, Sam. 2007. 60p. (J). (978-0-9800764-0-0(4)) Uncle Jim's Publishing.

Pesenti, Antonia. Alphabetical Sydney. Bell, Hilary. 2013. (ENG.). 56p. (J). (gr. -1). 19.99 (978-1-74223-370-3(8), UNSW Press) NewSouth Publishing AUS. Dist: Independent Pubs. Group.

Peskimo. Alphablock. Franceschelli, Christopher. 2013. (Alphablock Ser.). (ENG.). 104p. (J). (gr. -1 — 1). bds. 16.95 (978-1-4197-0936-4(4), Abrams Appleseed) Abrams.

Peskimo. Dinoblock. Franceschelli, Christopher. 2015. (Alphablock Ser.). (ENG.). 96p. (J). (gr. -1 — 1). bds. 16.95 **(978-1-4197-1674-4(3)**, Abrams Appleseed) Abrams.

Petelinsek, Kathleen. Acrostic Poems. Simons, Lisa M. Bolt. 2015. (Poetry Party Ser.). (ENG.). 24p. (J). (gr. 2-5). 27.07 (978-1-63143-692-5(9), 208527) Child's World, Inc., The.

—Actions/Las Acciones. Berendes, Mary. 2008. (WordBooks/Libros de Palabras Ser.). (SPA & ENG.). 24p. (J). (gr. k-3). 25.64 (978-1-59296-987-6(9), 201085) Child's World, Inc., The.

—Adjectives. Gregory, Josh. 2013. (Explorer Junior Library: the Parts of Speech Ser.). (ENG.). 24p. (J). (gr. 1-4). 25.64 (978-1-62431-180-2(6), 203040); pap. 12.79 (978-1-62431-312-7(4), 203042) Cherry Lake Publishing.

—Adverbs. Gregory, Josh. 2013. (Explorer Junior Library: the Parts of Speech Ser.). (ENG.). 24p. (J). (gr. 1-4). 25.64 (978-1-62431-183-3(0), 203052); pap. 12.79 (978-1-62431-315-8(9), 203054) Cherry Lake Publishing.

—Animals. Thornborough, Kathy. 2014. (Talking Hands Ser.). (ENG.). 24p. (J). (gr. k-3). 25.64 (978-1-62687-314-8(3), 207154) Child's World, Inc., The.

—Animals/Los Animales. Berendes, Mary. 2007. (WordBooks/Libros de Palabras Ser.). (SPA & ENG.). 24p. (J). (gr. k-3). 25.64 (978-1-59296-795-7(7), 201086) Child's World, Inc., The.

—Beauty & the Beast. Higgins, Nadia. 2013. (Fairy Tale Collection). (ENG.). 24p. (J). (gr. k-3). 28.50 (978-1-62323-607-6(X), 206374) Child's World, Inc., The.

—Being Respectful Online. Truesdell, Ann. 2013. (Explorer Junior Library: Information Explorer Junior Ser.). (ENG.). 24p. (J). (gr. 1-4). 28.50 (978-1-62431-131-4(8), 202844); pap. 12.79 (978-1-62431-263-2(2), 202846) Cherry Lake Publishing.

—Birthday Crafts. Berendes, Mary & Eick, Jean. 2011. (CraftBooks Ser.). (ENG.). 24p. (J). (gr. 1-4). 27.07 (978-1-60954-231-3(2), 200125) Child's World, Inc., The.

—Careers/Las Carreras. Berendes, Mary. 2008. (WordBooks/Libros de Palabras Ser.). (SPA & ENG.). 24p. (J). (gr. k-3). 25.64 (978-1-59296-988-3(7), 201088) Child's World, Inc., The.

—Cinco de Mayo. Heinrichs, Ann. 2013. (Holidays & Celebrations Ser.). (ENG.). 32p. (J). (gr. k-3). 27.07 (978-1-62323-505-5(7), 206277) Child's World, Inc., The.

—Cinderella. Higgins, Nadia. 2013. (Fairy Tale Collection). (ENG.). 24p. (J). (gr. k-3). 28.50 (978-1-62323-608-3(8), 206375) Child's World, Inc., The.

—Cinquain Poems. Simons, Lisa M. Bolt. 2015. (Poetry Party Ser.). (ENG.). 24p. (J). (gr. 2-5). 27.07 (978-1-63143-693-2(7), 208528) Child's World, Inc., The.

—Clothes/la Ropa. Berendes, Mary. 2008. (WordBooks/Libros de Palabras Ser.). (SPA & ENG.). 24p. (J). (gr. k-3). 25.64 (978-1-59296-989-0(5), 201089) Child's World, Inc., The.

—Colors & Shapes. Thornborough, Kathy. 2014. (Talking Hands Ser.). (ENG.). 24p. (J). (gr. k-3). 25.64 (978-1-62687-315-5(1), 207155) Child's World, Inc., The.

—Concrete Poems. Pearson, Yvonne. 2015. (Poetry Party Ser.). (ENG.). 24p. (J). (gr. 2-5). 27.07 (978-1-63143-694-9(5), 208529) Child's World, Inc., The.

—Conjunctions. Marsico, Katie. 2013. (Explorer Junior Library: the Parts of Speech Ser.). (ENG.). 24p. (J). (gr. 1-4). 25.64 (978-1-62431-181-9(4), 203044); pap. 12.79 (978-1-62431-313-4(2), 203046) Cherry Lake Publishing.

—Crafting with Duct Tape. Rau, Dana Meachen. 2013. (How-To Library). (ENG.). 32p. (J). (gr. 3-6). 28.50 (978-1-62431-147-5(4), 202908); pap. 14.21 (978-1-62431-279-3(9), 202910) Cherry Lake Publishing.

—Crafting with Recyclables. Rau, Dana Meachen. 2013. (How-To Library). (ENG.). 32p. (J). (gr. 3-6). 28.50 (978-1-62431-146-8(6), 202904); pap. 14.21 (978-1-62431-278-6(0), 202906) Cherry Lake Publishing.

—Creating Digital Brochures. Newman, Heather. 2013. (Explorer Library: Information Explorer Ser.). (ENG.). 32p. (J). (gr. 4-8). 28.50 (978-1-62431-128-4(8), 202832); pap. 14.21 (978-1-62431-260-1(8), 202834) Cherry Lake Publishing.

—Creating Halloween Crafts. Rau, Dana Meachen. 2013. (How-To Library). (ENG.). 32p. (J). (gr. 3-6). 28.50 (978-1-62431-149-9(0), 202916); pap. 14.21 (978-1-62431-281-6(0), 202918) Cherry Lake Publishing.

—Creating Thanksgiving Crafts. Rau, Dana Meachen. 2013. (How-To Library). (ENG.). 32p. (J). (gr. 3-6). 28.50 (978-1-62431-148-2(2), 202912); pap. 14.21 (978-1-62431-280-9(2), 202914) Cherry Lake Publishing.

—Creating Winter Crafts. Rau, Dana Meachen. 2013. (How-To Library). (ENG.). 32p. (J). (gr. 3-6). 28.50 (978-1-62431-150-5(4), 202920); pap. 14.21 (978-1-62431-282-3(9), 202922) Cherry Lake Publishing.

—Days & Times. Thornborough, Kathy. 2014. (Talking Hands Ser.). (ENG.). 24p. (J). (gr. k-3). 25.64 (978-1-62687-316-2(X), 207156) Child's World, Inc., The.

—Days & Times (Los Días y Las Horas) Berendes, Mary. 2008. (WordBooks/Libros de Palabras Ser.). (ENG.). 24p. (J). (gr. k-3). 25.64 (978-1-59296-990-6(9), 201090) Child's World, Inc., The.

—Easter Crafts. Eick, Jean. 2011. (CraftBooks Ser.). (ENG.). 24p. (J). (gr. 1-4). 27.07 (978-1-60954-233-7(9), 200127) Child's World, Inc., The.

—Family & Friends. Thornborough, Kathy. 2014. (Talking Hands Ser.). (ENG.). 24p. (J). (gr. k-3). 25.64 (978-1-62687-317-9(8), 207157) Child's World, Inc., The.

—Feelings & Emotions. Thornborough, Kathy. 2014. (Talking Hands Ser.). (ENG.). 24p. (J). (gr. k-3). 25.64 (978-1-62687-318-6(6), 207158) Child's World, Inc., The.

—Feelings/Las Emociones. Berendes, Mary. 2007. (WordBooks/Libros de Palabras Ser.). (SPA & ENG.). 24p. (J). (gr. k-3). 25.64 (978-1-59296-797-1(3), 201091) Child's World, Inc., The.

—The Fisherman & His Wife. Felix, Rebecca. 2013. (Fairy Tale Collection). (ENG.). 24p. (J). (gr. k-3). 28.50 (978-1-62323-611-3(8), 206378) Child's World, Inc., The.

—Folding Origami. Rau, Dana Meachen. 2013. (How-To Library). (ENG.). 32p. (J). (gr. 3-6). 28.50 (978-1-62431-145-1(8), 202900); pap. 14.21 (978-1-62431-277-9(2), 202902) Cherry Lake Publishing.

—Food. Thornborough, Kathy. 2014. (Talking Hands Ser.). (ENG.). 24p. (J). (gr. k-3). 25.64 (978-1-62687-319-3(4), 207159) Child's World, Inc., The.

—Food/la Comida. Berendes, Mary. 2007. (WordBooks/Libros de Palabras Ser.). (SPA & ENG.). 24p. (J). (gr. k-3). 25.64 (978-1-59296-798-8(1), 201092) Child's World, Inc., The.

—Greetings & Phrases. Thornborough, Kathy. 2014. (Talking Hands Ser.). (ENG.). 24p. (J). (gr. k-3). 25.64 (978-1-62687-320-9(8), 207160) Child's World, Inc., The.

—Haikus. Simons, Lisa M. Bolt. 2015. (Poetry Party Ser.). (ENG.). 24p. (J). (gr. 2-5). 27.07 (978-1-63143-695-6(3), 208531) Child's World, Inc., The.

—Hansel & Gretel. Higgins, Nadia. 2013. (Fairy Tale Collection). (ENG.). 24p. (J). (gr. k-3). 28.50 (978-1-62323-609-0(6), 206376) Child's World, Inc., The.

—Holidays & Celebrations (Los Días de Fiestas y Las Celebraciones) Berendes, Mary. 2008. (WordBooks/Libros de Palabras Ser.). (SPA & ENG.). 24p. (J). (gr. k-3). 25.64 (978-1-59296-991-3(7), 201093) Child's World, Inc., The.

—House/la Casa. Berendes, Mary. 2008. (WordBooks/Libros de Palabras Ser.). (SPA & ENG.). 24p. (J). (gr. k-3). 25.64 (978-1-59296-992-0(5), 201094) Child's World, Inc., The.

—How to Handle Cyberbullies. Truesdell, Ann. 2013. (Explorer Library: Information Explorer Ser.). (ENG.). 32p. (J). (gr. 4-8). 28.50 (978-1-62431-127-7(X), 202828); pap. 14.21 (978-1-62431-259-5(4), 202830) Cherry Lake Publishing.

—How to Write a Comic Book. Yomtov, Nelson. 2013. (Explorer Junior Library: How to Write Ser.). (ENG.). 24p. (J). (gr. 1-4). lib. bdg. 25.64 (978-1-62431-187-1(3), 203072) Cherry Lake Publishing.

—How to Write a Comic Book. Yomtov, Nel. 2013. (Explorer Junior Library: How to Write Ser.). (ENG.). 24p. (J). (gr. 1-4). pap. 12.79 (978-1-62431-319-6(1), 203074) Cherry Lake Publishing.

—How to Write a Fractured Fairy Tale. Yomtov, Nel. 2013. (Explorer Junior Library: How to Write Ser.). (ENG.). 24p. (J). (gr. 1-4). 25.64 (978-1-62431-186-4(5), 203068); pap. 12.79 (978-1-62431-318-9(3), 203070) Cherry Lake Publishing.

—How to Write a Lab Report. Yomtov, Nel. 2013. (Explorer Junior Library: How to Write Ser.). (ENG.). 24p. (J). (gr. 1-4). 25.64 (978-1-62431-185-7(7), 203064); pap. 12.79 (978-1-62431-317-2(5), 203066) Cherry Lake Publishing.

—How to Write a Memoir. Yomtov, Nel. 2013. (Explorer Junior Library: How to Write Ser.). (ENG.). 24p. (J). (gr. 1-4). 25.64 (978-1-62431-188-8(1), 203076); pap. 12.79 (978-1-62431-320-2(5), 203078) Cherry Lake Publishing.

—Independence Day Crafts. Berendes, Mary. 2011. (CraftBooks Ser.). (ENG.). 24p. (J). (gr. 1-4). lib. bdg. 27.07 (978-1-60954-235-1(5), 200129) Child's World, Inc., The.

—Interjections. Marsico, Katie. 2013. (Explorer Junior Library: the Parts of Speech Ser.). (ENG.). 24p. (J). (gr. 1-4). 25.64 (978-1-62431-184-0(9), 203056); pap. 12.79 (978-1-62431-316-5(7), 203058) Cherry Lake Publishing.

—Learn French Words. York, J. 2014. (Foreign Language Basics Ser.). (ENG.). 24p. (J). (gr. 2-5). 27.07 (978-1-62687-374-2(7), 207121) Child's World, Inc., The.

—Learn German Words. York, J. 2014. (Foreign Language Basics Ser.). (ENG.). 24p. (J). (gr. 2-5). 27.07 (978-1-62687-375-9(5), 207122) Child's World, Inc., The.

—Learn Japanese Words. York, J. 2014. (Foreign Language Basics Ser.). (ENG.). 24p. (J). (gr. 2-5). 27.07 (978-1-62687-376-6(3), 207123) Child's World, Inc., The.

—Learn Mandarin Chinese Words. York, J. 2014. (Foreign Language Basics Ser.). (ENG.). 24p. (J). (gr. 2-5). 27.07 (978-1-62687-377-3(1), 207124) Child's World, Inc., The.

—Learn Russian Words. York, J. 2014. (Foreign Language Basics Ser.). (ENG.). 24p. (J). (gr. 2-5). 27.07 (978-1-62687-378-0(X), 207125) Child's World, Inc., The.

—Learn Spanish Words. York, J. 2014. (Foreign Language Basics Ser.). (ENG.). 24p. (J). (gr. 2-5). 27.07 (978-1-62687-379-7(8), 207126) Child's World, Inc., The.

—Learning & Sharing with a Wiki. Fontichiaro, Kristin & Truesdell, Ann. 2013. (Explorer Junior Library: Information Explorer Junior Ser.). (ENG.). 24p. (J). (gr. 1-4). 28.50 (978-1-62431-132-1(6), 202848); pap. 12.79 (978-1-62431-264-9(0), 202850) Cherry Lake Publishing.

—Limericks. Pearson, Yvonne. 2015. (Poetry Party Ser.). (ENG.). 24p. (J). (gr. 2-5). 27.07 (978-1-63143-696-3(1), 208532) Child's World, Inc., The.

—The Little Mermaid. Felix, Rebecca. 2013. (Fairy Tale Collection). (ENG.). 24p. (J). (gr. k-3). 28.50 (978-1-62323-612-0(6), 206379) Child's World, Inc., The.

—Little Red Riding Hood. Higgins, Nadia. 2013. (Fairy Tale Collection). (ENG.). 24p. (J). (gr. k-3). 28.50 (978-1-62323-610-6(X), 206377) Child's World, Inc., The.

—Las Máquinas. Berendes, Mary. 2007. (WordBooks/Libros de Palabras Ser.).Tr. of Machines. (ENG.). 24p. (J). (gr. k-3). 25.64 (978-1-59296-799-5(X), 201095) Child's World, Inc., The.

—Measuring Length. Bailer, Darice. 2014. (Explorer Junior Library: Math Explorer Junior Ser.). (ENG.). 24p. (J). (gr. 1-4). 28.50 (978-1-62431-647-0(6), 203100) Cherry Lake Publishing.

—Measuring Temperature. Bailer, Darice. 2014. (Explorer Junior Library: Math Explorer Junior Ser.). (ENG.). 24p. (J). (gr. 1-4). 28.50 (978-1-62431-648-7(4), 203104) Cherry Lake Publishing.

—Measuring Time with a Calendar. Bailer, Darice. 2014. (Explorer Junior Library: Math Explorer Junior Ser.). (ENG.). 24p. (J). (gr. 1-4). 28.50 (978-1-62431-649-4(2), 203108) Cherry Lake Publishing.

—Measuring Time with a Clock. Reinke, Beth Bence. 2014. (Explorer Junior Library: Math Explorer Junior Ser.). (ENG.). 24p. (J). (gr. 1-4). 28.50 (978-1-62431-650-0(6), 203112) Cherry Lake Publishing.

—Measuring Volume. Reinke, Beth Bence. 2014. (Explorer Junior Library: Math Explorer Junior Ser.). (ENG.). 24p. (J). (gr. 1-4). 28.50 (978-1-62431-651-7(4), 203116) Cherry Lake Publishing.

—Measuring Weight. Reinke, Beth Bence. 2014. (Explorer Junior Library: Math Explorer Junior Ser.). (ENG.). 24p. (J). (gr. 1-4). 28.50 (978-1-62431-652-4(2), 203120) Cherry Lake Publishing.

—Narrative Poems. Pearson, Yvonne. 2015. (Poetry Party Ser.). (ENG.). 24p. (J). (gr. 2-5). 27.07 (978-1-63143-699-4(6), 208534) Child's World, Inc., The.

—Neighborhood/el Barrio. Berendes, Mary. 2008. (WordBooks/Libros de Palabras Ser.). (SPA & ENG.). 24p. (J). (gr. k-3). 25.64 (978-1-59296-993-7(3), 201096) Child's World, Inc., The.

—Nouns. Gregory, Josh. 2013. (Explorer Junior Library: the Parts of Speech Ser.). (ENG.). 24p. (J). (gr. 1-4). 25.64 (978-1-62431-177-2(6), 203028); pap. 12.79 (978-1-62431-309-7(4), 203030) Cherry Lake Publishing.

—People/Las Personas. Berendes, Mary. 2007. (WordBooks/Libros de Palabras Ser.). (SPA & ENG.). 24p. (J). (gr. k-3). 25.64 (978-1-59296-800-8(7), 201097) Child's World, Inc., The.

—Prepositions. Marsico, Katie. 2013. (Explorer Junior Library: the Parts of Speech Ser.). (ENG.). 24p. (J). (gr. 1-4). 25.64 (978-1-62431-182-6(2), 203048); pap. 12.79 (978-1-62431-314-1(0), 203050) Cherry Lake Publishing.

—Pronouns. Marsico, Katie. 2013. (Explorer Junior Library: the Parts of Speech Ser.). (ENG.). 24p. (J). (gr. 1-4). 25.64 (978-1-62431-178-9(4), 203032); pap. 12.79 (978-1-62431-310-3(8), 203034) Cherry Lake Publishing.

—Prose Poems. Pearson, Yvonne. 2015. (Poetry Party Ser.). (ENG.). 24p. (J). (gr. 2-5). 27.07 (978-1-63143-697-0(X), 208530) Child's World, Inc., The.

—Questions & Answers. Thornborough, Kathy. 2014. (Talking Hands Ser.). (ENG.). 24p. (J). (gr. k-3). 25.64 (978-1-62687-321-6(6), 207161) Child's World, Inc., The.

—Reading & Learning from Informational Text. Hamer, Jennifer L. 2013. (Explorer Junior Library: Information Explorer Junior Ser.). (ENG.). 24p. (J). (gr. 1-4). 28.50 (978-1-62431-134-5(2), 202856); pap. 12.79 (978-1-62431-266-3(7), 202858) Cherry Lake Publishing.

—Rhyming Poems. Simons, Lisa M. Bolt. 2015. (Poetry Party Ser.). (ENG.). 24p. (J). (gr. 2-5). 27.07 (978-1-63143-698-7(8), 208533) Child's World, Inc., The.

—School. Thornborough, Kathy. 2014. (Talking Hands Ser.). (ENG.). 24p. (J). (gr. k-3). 25.64 (978-1-62687-322-3(4), 207162) Child's World, Inc., The.

—School/la Escuela. Berendes, Mary. 2008. (WordBooks/Libros de Palabras Ser.). (SPA & ENG.). 24p. (J). (gr. k-3). 25.64 (978-1-59296-994-4(1), 201098) Child's World, Inc., The.

—Seasons. Thornborough, Kathy. 2014. (Talking Hands Ser.). (ENG.). 24p. (J). (gr. k-3). 25.64 (978-1-62687-323-0(2), 207163) Child's World, Inc., The.

—Sports & Games/Los Deportes y Los Juegos. Berendes, Mary. 2007. (WordBooks/Libros de Palabras Ser.). (SPA & ENG.). 24p. (J). (gr. k-3). 25.64 (978-1-59296-802-2(3), 201099) Child's World, Inc., The.

—Starting Your Own Blog. Truesdell, Ann & Fontichiaro, Kristin. 2013. (Explorer Junior Library: Information Explorer Junior Ser.). (ENG.). 24p. (J). (gr. 1-4). 28.50 (978-1-62431-133-8(4), 202852); pap. 12.79 (978-1-62431-265-6(9), 202854) Cherry Lake Publishing.

—Understanding & Creating Infographics. Fontichiaro, Kristin. 2013. (Explorer Library: Information Explorer Ser.). (ENG.). 32p. (J). (gr. 4-8). 28.50 (978-1-62431-126-0(1), 202824); pap. 14.21 (978-1-62431-258-8(6), 202826) Cherry Lake Publishing.

—Using Digital Maps. Matteson, Adrienne. 2013. (Explorer Library: Information Explorer Ser.). (ENG.). 32p. (J). (gr. 4-8). 28.50 (978-1-62431-129-1(6), 202836); pap. 14.21 (978-1-62431-261-8(6), 202838) Cherry Lake Publishing.

—Verbs. Gregory, Josh. 2013. (Explorer Junior Library: the Parts of Speech Ser.). (ENG.). 24p. (J). (gr. 1-4). 25.64 (978-1-62431-179-6(2), 203036); pap. 12.79 (978-1-62431-311-0(6), 203038) Cherry Lake Publishing.

—Weather. Thornborough, Kathy. 2014. (Talking Hands Ser.). (ENG.). 24p. (J). (gr. k-3). 25.64 *(978-1-62687-324-7(0),* 207164) Child's World, Inc., The.

—Weird-But-True Facts about Crafts. Coss, Lauren. 2013. (Weird-But-True Facts Ser.). (ENG.). 32p. (J). (gr. 2-5). 28.50 *(978-1-61473-413-0(5),* 205117) Child's World, Inc., The.

—Weird-But-True Facts about Inventions. Ringstad, Arnold. 2013. (Weird-But-True Facts Ser.). (ENG.). 32p. (J). (gr. 2-5). 28.50 *(978-1-61473-415-4(1),* 205119) Child's World, Inc., The.

—Weird-But-True Facts about Science. Ringstad, Arnold. 2013. (Weird-But-True Facts Ser.). (ENG.). 32p. (J). (gr. 2-5). 28.50 *(978-1-61473-417-8(8),* 205121) Child's World, Inc., The.

—Weird-But-True Facts about the U. S. Military. Ringstad, Arnold. 2013. (Weird-But-True Facts Ser.). (ENG.). 32p. (J). (gr. 2-5). 28.50 *(978-1-61473-420-8(8),* 205124) Child's World, Inc., The.

—Work. Thornborough, Kathy. 2014. (Talking Hands Ser.). (ENG.). 24p. (J). (gr. k-3). 25.64 *(978-1-62687-325-4(9),* 207165) Child's World, Inc., The.

Petelinsek, Kathleen. Crafting with Tissue Paper. Petelinsek, Kathleen. 2014. (How-To Library). (ENG.). 32p. (J). (gr. 3-6). 28.50 *(978-1-63137-779-2(5),* 205359) Cherry Lake Publishing.

—Learning to Sew. Petelinsek, Kathleen. 2014. (How-To Library). (ENG.). 32p. (J). (gr. 3-6). 28.50 *(978-1-63137-780-8(9),* 205363) Cherry Lake Publishing.

—Little Jack Horner. Petelinsek, Kathleen. 2011. (Favorite Mother Goose Rhymes Ser.). (ENG.). 16p. (J). (gr. -1-2). lib. bdg. 25.64 *(978-1-60954-280-1(0),* 200232) Child's World, Inc., The.

—Making Clay Bead Crafts. Petelinsek, Kathleen. 2014. (How-To Library). (ENG.). 32p. (J). (gr. 3-6). 28.50 *(978-1-63137-777-8(9),* 205351) Cherry Lake Publishing.

—Making Jewelry with Rubber Bands. Petelinsek, Kathleen. 2014. (How-To Library). (ENG.). 32p. (J). (gr. 3-6). 28.50 *(978-1-63137-781-5(7),* 205367) Cherry Lake Publishing.

—Making Sock Puppets. Petelinsek, Kathleen. 2014. (How-To Library). (ENG.). 32p. (J). (gr. 3-6). 28.50 *(978-1-63137-782-2(5),* 205371) Cherry Lake Publishing.

—Modeling Clay Creations. Petelinsek, Kathleen. 2014. (How-To Library). (ENG.). 32p. (J). (gr. 3-6). 28.50 *(978-1-63137-783-9(3),* 205375) Cherry Lake Publishing.

—Pipe Cleaner Crafts. Petelinsek, Kathleen. 2014. (How-To Library). (ENG.). 32p. (J). (gr. 3-6). lib. bdg. 28.50 *(978-1-63137-784-6(1),* 205379) Cherry Lake Publishing.

Peten, Chantal. A Day at the Museum. Ducatteau, Florence. 2013. (Want to Know Ser.). (ENG.). 32p. (J). (gr. k-2). 16.95 *(978-1-60537-142-9(4))* Clavis Publishing.

Peter, Joshua. Where Is Beau? Grinnell, Suzanne. 2008. 24p. pap. 12.99 *(978-1-59858-612-1(2))* Dog Ear Publishing, LLC.

Peters, Andy & Hewett, Angela. My First 1000 Words. Giles, Sophie & Davis, Kate. 2014. (ENG.). 125p. 17.50 *(978-1-84135-642-6(5))* Award Pubns. Ltd. GBR. Dist: Parkwest Pubns., Inc.

Peters, Darcy. Little Rumely Man. Silcox, Beth Douglass. 2012. 36p. pap. 12.99 *(978-0-9832514-2-2(6))* Gypsy Heart Pr.

Peters, Kathryn. A Pet for Elizabeth Rose. Peters, Kathryn. l.t. ed. 2005. 42p. (J). 8.99 *(978-0-9752647-9-9(6))* Proton Arts.

Peters, Liam. Bewitched in Oz, 1 vol. Burns, Laura J. 2014. (Bewitched in Oz Ser.). (ENG.). 256p. (gr. 4-8). 12.95 *(978-1-62370-129-1(5));* lib. bdg. 27.48 *(978-1-4342-9207-0(X))* Stone Arch Bks.

Peters, Ramona. Strawberry Thanksgiving. Jennings, Paulla. 2005. (Multicultural Celebrations Ser.). 32p. (J). 4.95 *(978-1-59373-010-9(1))* Bunker Hill Publishing, Inc.

Peters, Rob. Bye, Bye Boogeyman. Davies, Donna M. Bailin-Rembar, Jill, ed. 2013. 32p. pap. 9.95 *(978-0-9853082-5-4(7))* All Hallows Eve Pr.

—Eartha Gets Well. Falk, Kristi & Falk, Daniel. 2012. (ENG.). 30p. (J). 24.95 *(978-1-937084-27-1(2),* BQB Publishing) Boutique of Quality Books Publishing Co.

—Jessica & Madison: Being Beautiful. Taylor, Derrick & Garnett, Kaila. 2012. 38p. pap. 8.00 *(978-1-62050-492-5(8));* 14.95 *(978-1-61364-734-9(4))* DTaylor Bks.

—Night of the Candy Creepers. Davies, Donna. 2013. 32p. pap. 9.95 *(978-0-9853082-1-6(4))* All Hallows Eve Pr.

—Pete's Big Paws - Hardcover. Richter, Cindy. 2012. 32p. 15.99 *(978-0-9849732-0-0(6))* Coast View Publishing.

Peters, Robert. Da Goodie Monsta: Chase Dem Nightmares Away. Peters, Robert. 2009. 28p. (YA). lib. bdg. *(978-0-9823906-7-2(X))* Wiggles Pr.

Peterschmidt, Betsy. Blackbird Fly. Kelly, Erin Entrada. 2015. (ENG.). 304p. (J). (gr. 3-7). 16.99 *(978-0-06-223861-0(2),* Greenwillow Bks.) HarperCollins Pubs.

Petersen, Alexander. Tracks Count: A Guide to Counting Animal Prints. Engel, Steve. 2014. (Little Naturalist Ser.). (ENG.). 32p. (J). (gr. -1-k). 17.99 *(978-1-940052-07-6(6))* Craigmore Creations.

Petersen, Darla & Shields, Erik P. There's a Monster under the Captain's Bed!!! Erik's Monster. Aunt Darla. Date not set. 32p. 16.00 *(978-0-9658926-1-2(1))* Poet Tree Pubns.

Petersen, David. Mouse Guard - Winter 1152, Vol. 2. Petersen, David. Illidge, Joseph Phillip, ed. 2009. (Mouse Guard Ser.: 2). (ENG.). 192p. (J). (gr. 2-18). 24.95 *(978-1-932386-74-5(2))* Boom Entertainment, Inc.

—Snowy Valentine. Petersen, David. 2011. (ENG.). 32p. (J). (gr. -1-3). 14.99 *(978-0-06-146378-5(7))* HarperCollins Pubs.

Petersen, David, jt. illus. see Villavert, Armand, Jr.

Petersen, Jeff. Bum, Christmas! Bum!! Gage, Brian. 2004. (ENG.). 40p. 17.95 *(978-1-932360-55-4(7))* Counterpoint LLC.

Petersen, Sheli. Gigi & the Birthday Ring. Fernandez, Giselle. 2005. (J). *(978-1-56492-358-5(4))* Laredo Publishing Co., Inc.

Petersen, William. Amigos de Jesús 2009: A Bilingual Catechetical Program. un Programa Catequético BilingüE. Advent 2008 - November 2009. Aguinaco, Carmen F. 2008.Tr. of Friends of Jesus 2009. (ENG & SPA.). 408p. (J). pap. 99.00 *(978-0-89570-503-7(6))* Claretian Pubns.

Petersham, Maud & Petersham, Miska. A Child's Own Book of Verse, Book One (Yesterday's Classics) Skinner, Ada & Wickes, Frances. 2006. (J). pap. 8.95 *(978-1-59915-051-2(4))* Yesterday's Classics.

—A Child's Own Book of Verse, Book Three (Yesterday's Classics) Skinner, Ada & Wickes, Frances. 2006. (J). pap. 8.95 *(978-1-59915-053-6(0))* Yesterday's Classics.

—A Child's Own Book of Verse, Book Two (Yesterday's Classics) Skinner, Ada & Wickes, Frances. 2006. (J). pap. 8.95 *(978-1-59915-052-9(2))* Yesterday's Classics.

—Rootabaga Stories. Sandburg, Carl. 2003. (ENG.). 192p. (J). (gr. 2-5). pap. 6.95 *(978-0-15-204714-6(X))* Houghton Mifflin Harcourt Publishing Co.

Petersham, Miska, jt. illus. see Petersham, Maud.

Peterson, Barbara. Greek & Latin Roots: Teaching Vocabulary to Improve Reading Comprehension. Callella, Trisha. Rous, Sheri, ed. 2004. 144p. pap. 16.99 *(978-0-88160-381-1(3),* LW-438) Creative Teaching Pr., Inc.

—I Have, Who Has? Language Arts Grades 1-2. Callella, Trisha. Taylor, Jennifer, ed. 2007. (J). per. 19.99 *(978-1-59198-429-0(7))* Creative Teaching Pr., Inc.

—Prefixes & Suffixes: Teaching Vocabulary to Improve Reading Comprehension. Callella, Trisha. Williams, Carolea & Rous, Sheri, eds. 2004. 144p. pap. 16.99 *(978-0-88160-380-4(5),* LW-437) Creative Teaching Pr., Inc.

Peterson, Ben. John Henry, 1 vol. Jones, Christianne C. 2013. (My First Classic Story Ser.).Tr. of John Henry. (ENG.). 32p. (gr. k-3). pap. 7.10 *(978-1-4795-1861-6(1),* My First Classic Story) Picture Window Bks.

—John Henry, 1 vol. Jones, Christianne C. Robledo, Sol, tr. (Read-It! Readers en Español: Cuentos Exagerados Ser.).Tr. of John Henry. (SPA.). 32p. (gr. k-3). 2008. per. 3.95 *(978-1-4048-2174-3(0));* 2006. 19.99 *(978-1-4048-1654-1(2))* Picture Window Bks. (Easy Readers).

—El Ninito de Jengibre, 1 vol. Blair, Eric. Abello, Patricia, tr. from ENG. 2006. (Read-It! Readers en Español: Cuentos Folclóricos Ser.).Tr. of Gingerbread Man. (SPA.). 32p. (gr. k-3). 19.99 *(978-1-4048-1647-3(X),* Easy Readers) Picture Window Bks.

Peterson, Brandon. Chimera. Marz, Ron. 2003. 160p. (YA). pap. 15.95 *(978-1-931484-96-1(1))* CrossGeneration Comics, Inc.

Peterson, Brandon, et al. Mystic Traveler: The Demon Queen, Vol. 2. Marz, Ron. 2004. (Mystic Traveler Ser.). 160p. (YA). pap. 9.95 *(978-1-59314-037-3(1))* CrossGeneration Comics, Inc.

Peterson, Brandon. Ultimate X-Men - The Tempest, Vol. 9. 2006. (ENG.). 112p. (J). (gr. -1-17). pap. 10.99 *(978-0-7851-1404-8(1))* Marvel Worldwide, Inc.

Peterson, Brandon, et al. X-Men: X-Cutioner's Song. Lobdell, Scott et al. 2011. (ENG.). 368p. (J). (gr. 4-17). 49.99 *(978-0-7851-5610-9(0))* Marvel Worldwide, Inc.

Peterson, Brandon, jt. illus. see Ribic, Esad.

Peterson, Carol. Jump into Science: Themed Science Fairs, 1 vol. Peterson, Carol. 2007. 152p. (gr. 3-7). per. 35.00 *(978-1-59158-413-1(2),* TIP4132, Teacher Ideas Pr.) Libraries Unlimited, Inc.

Peterson, Carol A. Pony Pointers: How to Safely Care for Your Horse or Pony. Bennett, Kathy. 2004. 48p. (J). per. 7.99 *(978-0-9763209-0-6(8))* Trail Trotters Bk. Ranch.

Peterson, Dawn. Amasa Walker's Spendid Garment. Chetkowski, Emily. 2003. 48p. (gr. 5-8). reprint ed. pap. 9.95 *(978-0-911469-21-9(4))* Hood, Alan C. & Co., Inc.

—Children's Tea & Etiquette: Brewing Good Manners in Young Minds. Johnson, Dorothea et al. 2006. 39p. (J). (gr. 4-7). 19.95 *(978-0-9663478-9-0(7))* Benjamin Pr.

—Mabel Takes the Ferry, 1 vol. Chetkowski, Emily. 2nd ed. 2012. (ENG.). 32p. (J). pap. 12.95 *(978-1-934031-99-5(2),* 0da48001-1b7b-4d70-849d-d13163dabbc6) Islandport Pr., Inc.

Peterson, Gary. Gray Wolf's Search, 1 vol. Swanson, Bruce & Swanson, Bill. 2007. (ENG.). 24p. (J). (gr. -1-2). 14.95 *(978-0-9779183-1-7(9),* 7th Generation) Book Publishing Co.

—Native Athletes in Action: Sports Stars Past & Present. Schilling, Vincent. 2007. (Native Trailblazers Ser.). (ENG.). 128p. (YA). (gr. 3-11). pap. 9.95 *(978-0-9779183-0-0(0),* 7th Generation) Book Publishing Co.

Peterson, Ingela. Ellie & Pinky's Pop-Up Shapes. 2003. (First Concepts Ser.). 10p. (J). 7.95 *(978-1-58117-184-6(6),* Intervisual/Piggy Toes) Bendon, Inc.

Peterson, Joel & Rogers, Jacqueline. The Littles & the Surprise Thanksgiving Guests. 2004. (Littles First Readers Ser.). 105p. (J). *(978-0-439-68704-1(7))* Scholastic, Inc.

Peterson, Kathleen. Girls Who Choose God. Krishna, McArthur & Spalding, Bethany Brady. 2014. (J). 17.99 *(978-1-60907-882-9(9),* Ensign Peak) Shadow Mountain Publishing.

Peterson, Kathleen. Girls Who Choose God: Stories of Strong Women from the Book of Mormon. Krishna, McArthur & Spalding, Bethany Brady. 2015. (J). 18.99 *(978-1-62972-101-9(8))* Deseret Bk. Co.

Peterson, Kathleen. Koa's Seed. Han, Carolyn. 2004. 32p. (J). 14.95 *(978-1-933067-02-5(0))* Beachhouse Publishing, LLC.

—Moon Mangoes. Shapiro, Lindy. 2011. 36p. 14.95 *(978-1-933067-42-1(X))* Beachhouse Publishing, LLC.

Peterson Kathleen. Pele & Poliahu. Collins Malia. 2005. 24p. 14.95 *(978-1-933067-13-1(6))* Mutual Publishing LLC.

Peterson, Lennie. When You Have to Say Goodbye: Loving & Letting Go of Your Pet. Mansfield, Monica. 2011. (ENG.). 32p. (J). (gr. k). 8.95 *(978-0-9831032-1-9(6),* BeanPole Bks.) Harren Communications, LLC.

Peterson, Lynn Ihsen. Twice a Hero: Polish American Heroes of the American Revolutuion. Wales, Dirk. 2007. 31p. (J). (gr. 4-9). 18.95 incl. audio compact disk *(978-0-9632459-4-6(5))* Great Plains Pr.

Peterson, Mary. No Time to Nap. Madison, Mike. 2007. (J). (gr. -1-3). *(978-1-59714-046-1(5))* Heyday.

—Ocean Soup. Swinburne, Stephen R. alt. ed. 2010. (ENG.). 32p. (J). (gr. k-3). pap. 7.95 *(978-1-58089-201-8(9))* Charlesbridge Publishing, Inc.

—Ocean Soup: Tide-Pool Poems. Swinburne, Stephen R. 2010. (ENG.). 32p. (J). (gr. k-3). 16.95 *(978-1-58089-200-1(0))* Charlesbridge Publishing, Inc.

—Wiggle & Waggle. Arnold, Caroline. 2009. (ENG.). 48p. (J). (gr. k-3). pap. 5.95 *(978-1-58089-307-7(4))* Charlesbridge Publishing, Inc.

—Wooby & Peep: A Story of Unlikely Friendship. Liu, Cynthea. 2013. (ENG.). 40p. (J). (gr. -1-2). 14.95 *(978-1-4027-9644-9(7))* Sterling Publishing Co., Inc.

Peterson, Mary. Piggies in the Pumpkin Patch. Peterson, Mary. Rofé, Jennifer. 2010. (ENG.). 28p. (J). (gr. -1-2). 16.95 *(978-1-57091-460-7(5));* pap. 7.95 *(978-1-57091-461-4(3))* Charlesbridge Publishing, Inc.

Peterson, Mary Joseph. Basic Prayers in My Pocket. 2009. 32p. (J). pap. 1.95 *(978-0-8198-1173-8(4))* Pauline Bks. & Media.

—My First Book about Jesus. Tebo, Mary Elizabeth. 2008. 64p. (J). (gr. 1-3). pap. 7.95 *(978-0-8198-4865-9(4))* Pauline Bks. & Media.

—Saint Clare of Assisi: A Light for the World. Trouve, Marianne Lorraine. 2009. (J). pap. 7.95 *(978-0-8198-7122-0(2))* Pauline Bks. & Media.

Peterson, Melanie. Explorers of the Word: Episode 1: the Creation. Burshek, Edward & Burshek, Tonja. 2007. (ENG.). 76p. per. 19.95 *(978-1-4241-6691-6(8))* America Star Bks.

Peterson, Nancy. Tenkita, Jumping on One Patita. Peterson, Mitzi & Peay Peterson, Mitzi. 2011. (ENG.). 32p. pap. 9.99 *(978-1-4564-5797-6(7))* CreateSpace Independent Publishing Platform.

Peterson, Rick. ¿A Qué Huele? Un Libro Sobre el Olfato. Meachen Rau, Dana. Abello, Patricia, tr. from ENG. 2008. (Nuestro Asombroso Cuerpo: Los Cinco Sentidos Ser.). (SPA.). 24p. (gr. k-3). 25.99 *(978-1-4048-3831-4(7))* Picture Window Bks.

—Beaky's Guide to Caring for Your Bird, 1 vol. Thomas, Isabel. 2014. (Pets' Guides). (ENG.). 32p. (gr. 1-3). pap. 8.29 *(978-1-4846-0266-9(8));* 26.65 *(978-1-4846-0259-1(5))* Heinemann-Raintree. (Heinemann First Library).

—Bunny's Guide to Caring for Your Rabbit, 1 vol. Ganeri, Anita. 2013. (Pets' Guides). (ENG.). 32p. (gr. 1-3). pap. 8.29 *(978-1-4329-7142-7(5));* lib. bdg. 26.65 *(978-1-4329-7135-9(2))* Heinemann-Raintree. (Heinemann First Library).

—The Chicken & the Worm. McBrier, Page. 2008. 36p. (J). *(978-0-9798439-2-1(8))* Heifer Project International.

—Chirp, Chirp! Crickets in Your Backyard. Loewen, Nancy. 2005. (Backyard Bugs Ser.). (ENG.). 24p. (gr. -1-3). lib. bdg. 25.99 *(978-1-4048-1141-6(9),* Nonfiction Picture Bks.) Picture Window Bks.

—Florida. Bruun, Erik. 2006. (ENG.). 48p. (J). (gr. -1-17). 9.95 *(978-1-57912-231-7(0),* 81231, Black Dog & Leventhal Pubs. Inc.) Hachette Bks.

—Garden Wigglers: Earthworms in Your Backyard. Loewen, Nancy. 2005. (Backyard Bugs Ser.). (ENG.). 24p. (gr. -1-3). lib. bdg. 25.99 *(978-1-4048-1144-7(3),* Nonfiction Picture Bks.) Picture Window Bks.

—Giggle's Guide to Caring for Your Gerbils, 1 vol. Thomas, Isabel. 2014. (Pets' Guides). (ENG.). 32p. (gr. 1-3). pap. 8.29 *(978-1-4846-0267-6(6));* 26.65 *(978-1-4846-0260-7(9))* Heinemann-Raintree. (Heinemann First Library).

—Goldie's Guide to Caring for Your Goldfish, 1 vol. Ganeri, Anita. 2013. (Pets' Guides). (ENG.). 32p. (gr. 1-3). pap. 8.29 *(978-1-4329-7139-7(5));* lib. bdg. 26.65 *(978-1-4329-7132-8(8))* Heinemann-Raintree. (Heinemann First Library).

—Gordon's Guide to Caring for Your Guinea Pigs, 1 vol. Thomas, Isabel. 2014. (Pets' Guides). (ENG.). 32p. (gr. 1-3). pap. 8.29 *(978-1-4846-0268-3(4));* 26.65 *(978-1-4846-0261-4(7))* Heinemann-Raintree. (Heinemann First Library).

—Henrietta's Guide to Caring for Your Chickens, 1 vol. Thomas, Isabel. 2014. (Pets' Guides). (ENG.). 32p. (gr. 1-3). pap. 8.29 *(978-1-4846-0269-0(2));* 26.65 *(978-1-4846-0262-1(5))* Heinemann-Raintree. (Heinemann First Library).

—Holy Guacamole! And Other Scrumptious Snacks. Fauchald, Nick. 2008. (Kids Dish Ser.). (ENG.). 32p. (gr. 1-3). lib. bdg. 26.65 *(978-1-4048-3995-3(X),* Nonfiction Picture Bks.) Picture Window Bks.

—Keep on Rollin' Meatballs: And Other Delicious Dinners. Fauchald, Nick. 2008. (Kids Dish Ser.). (ENG.). 32p. (gr. 1-3). lib. bdg. 26.65 *(978-1-4048-3998-4(4),* Nonfiction Picture Bks.) Picture Window Bks.

—Kitty's Guide to Caring for Your Cat, 1 vol. Ganeri, Anita. 2013. (Pets' Guides). (ENG.). 32p. (gr. 1-3). pap. 8.29 *(978-1-4329-7137-3(9));* lib. bdg. 26.65 *(978-1-4329-7130-4(1))* Heinemann-Raintree. (Heinemann First Library).

—Look! A Book about Sight, 1 vol. Meachen Rau, Dana. 2005. (Amazing Body: the Five Senses Ser.). (ENG.). 24p. (gr. k-3). 25.99 *(978-1-4048-1019-8(6),* Nonfiction Picture Bks.) Picture Window Bks.

—Look! [Scholastic]: A Book about Sight. Meachen Rau, Dana. 2010. (Amazing Body: the Five Senses Ser.). 24p. pap. 0.56 *(978-1-4048-4390-5(6),* Nonfiction Picture Bks.) Picture Window Bks.

—Nibble's Guide to Caring for Your Hamster, 1 vol. Ganeri, Anita. 2013. (Pets' Guides). (ENG.). 32p. (gr. 1-3). pap. 8.29 *(978-1-4329-7140-3(9));* lib. bdg. 26.65 *(978-1-4329-7133-5(6))* Heinemann-Raintree. (Heinemann First Library).

—¡Oye! Un Libro Sobre el Oído. Meachen Rau, Dana. Abello, Patricia, tr. from ENG. 2008. (Nuestro Asombroso Cuerpo: Los Cinco Sentidos Ser.). (SPA.). 24p. (gr. k-3). lib. bdg. 25.99 *(978-1-4048-3830-7(9))* Picture Window Bks.

—Puffy Popovers: And Other Get-Out-of-Bed Breakfasts. Fauchald, Nick. 2008. (Kids Dish Ser.). (ENG.). 32p. (gr. 1-3). lib. bdg. 26.65 *(978-1-4048-3996-0(8),* Nonfiction Picture Bks.) Picture Window Bks.

—Ruff's Guide to Caring for Your Dog, 1 vol. Ganeri, Anita. 2013. (Pets' Guides). (ENG.). 32p. (gr. 1-3). pap. 8.29 *(978-1-4329-7138-0(7));* lib. bdg. 26.65 *(978-1-4329-7131-1(X))* Heinemann-Raintree. (Heinemann First Library).

—Shhhh... A Book about Hearing. Meachen Rau, Dana. 2005. (Amazing Body: the Five Senses Ser.). (ENG.). 24p. (gr. k-3). 25.99 *(978-1-4048-1018-1(8),* Nonfiction Picture Bks.) Picture Window Bks.

—Shhhh... [Scholastic]: A Book about Hearing. Meachen Rau, Dana. 2010. (Amazing Body: the Five Senses Ser.). 24p. pap. 0.56 *(978-1-4048-6541-9(1),* Nonfiction Picture Bks.) Picture Window Bks.

—Slinky's Guide to Caring for Your Snake, 1 vol. Thomas, Isabel. 2014. (Pets' Guides). (ENG.). 32p. (gr. 1-3). pap. 8.29 *(978-1-4846-0270-6(6));* 26.65 *(978-1-4846-0263-8(3))* Heinemann-Raintree. (Heinemann First Library).

—Sniff, Sniff [Scholastic]: A Book about Smell. Meachen Rau, Dana. 2010. (Amazing Body: the Five Senses Ser.). 24p. pap. 0.56 *(978-1-4048-6542-6(X),* Nonfiction Picture Bks.) Picture Window Bks.

—Soft & Smooth, Rough & Bumpy: A Book about Touch. Meachen Rau, Dana. 2005. (Amazing Body: the Five Senses Ser.). (ENG.). 24p. (gr. k-3). 25.99 *(978-1-4048-1022-8(6),* Nonfiction Picture Bks.) Picture Window Bks.

—Soft & Smooth, Rough & Bumpy [Scholastic]: A Book about Touch. Meachen Rau, Dana. 2010. (Amazing Body: the Five Senses Ser.). 24p. pap. 0.56 *(978-1-4048-6544-0(6),* Nonfiction Picture Bks.) Picture Window Bks.

—Squeak's Guide to Caring for Your Pet Rats or Mice, 1 vol. Thomas, Isabel. 2014. (Pets' Guides). (ENG.). 32p. (gr. 1-3). pap. 8.29 *(978-1-4846-0271-3(4));* 26.65 *(978-1-4846-0264-5(1))* Heinemann-Raintree. (Heinemann First Library).

—Winnie's Guide to Caring for Your Horse or Pony, 1 vol. Ganeri, Anita. 2013. (Pets' Guides). (ENG.). 32p. (gr. 1-3). pap. 8.29 *(978-1-4329-7141-0(7));* lib. bdg. 26.65 *(978-1-4329-7134-2(4))* Heinemann-Raintree. (Heinemann First Library).

—Yum! A Book about Taste. Meachen Rau, Dana. 2005. (Amazing Body: the Five Senses Ser.). (ENG.). 24p. (gr. k-3). 25.99 *(978-1-4048-1021-1(8),* Nonfiction Picture Bks.) Picture Window Bks.

—Yum! [Scholastic]: A Book about Taste. Meachen Rau, Dana. 2010. (Amazing Body: the Five Senses Ser.). 24p. pap. 0.56 *(978-1-4048-6543-3(8),* Nonfiction Picture Bks.) Picture Window Bks.

Peterson, Rick & Yesh, Jeff. ¡Mira! Un Libro Sobre la Vista. Meachen Rau, Dana. Abello, Patricia, tr. from ENG. 2008. (Nuestro Asombroso Cuerpo: Los Cinco Sentidos Ser.). (SPA.). 24p. (gr. k-3). lib. bdg. 25.99 *(978-1-4048-3829-1(5))* Picture Window Bks.

Peterson, Roger Tory & Morrison, Gordon. Seashores. Kricher, John C. Peterson, Roger Tory, ed. 2nd ed. 2013. (Peterson Field Guide Color-In Bks.). (ENG.). 64p. (J). 8.95 *(978-0-544-03399-3(X))* Houghton Mifflin Harcourt Publishing Co.

Peterson, Roger Tory & Savage, Virginia. Wildflowers. Tenenbaum, Frances & Peterson, Roger Tory. 2013. (Peterson Field Guide Color-In Bks.). (ENG.). 64p. (J). 8.95 *(978-0-544-02697-1(7))* Houghton Mifflin Harcourt Publishing Co.

Peterson, Sara & Lindstrom, Brita. The Clock & the Mouse: A Teaching Rhyme about Time. Turley, Sandy. 2006. 32p. (J). lib. bdg. 26.95 *(978-0-9778548-0-6(9))* Helps4Teachers.

Peterson, Scott, photos by. Pizza: More Than 60 Recipes for Delicious Homemade Pizza. Morgan, Diane & Gemignani, Tony. 2005. (ENG., 168p. (gr. 8-17). per. 18.95 *(978-0-8118-4554-0(0))* Chronicle Bks. LLC.

Peterson, Shauna, jt. illus. see Rooney, Ronnie.

Peterson-Shea, Julie. Echoes of Kansas Past. Boeve, Eunice. 2012. 176p. pap. 10.99 *(978-0-9851196-9-0(1))* Rowe Publishing and Design.

Peterson, Stacy. Just Grandma & Me: The Fill-In, Tear-Out, Fold-Up Book of Fun for Girls & Their Grandmas. Magruder, Trula & American Girl Editors, eds. 2011. (ENG.). 96p. (J). spiral bd. 10.95 *(978-1-59369-870-6(4))* American Girl Publishing, Inc.

—Just Mom & Me: The Tear-Out, Punch-Out, Fill-Out Book of Fun for Girls & Their Moms. Falligant, Erin, ed. 2008. (ENG.). 96p. (J). (gr. 4-7). spiral bd. 10.95 *(978-1-59369-340-4(0))* American Girl Publishing, Inc.

—My Family Vacation: A Book about Me! Sund, Mike. 2008. (ENG.). 24p. (YA). (gr. 2-18). 12.95 *(978-1-58117-792-3(5),* Intervisual/Piggy Toes) Bendon, Inc.

—Oodles of Horses: A Collection of Posters, Doodles, Cards, Stencils, Crafts, Stickers, Frames & Lots More for Girls Who Love Horses! Magruder, Trula, ed. 2010. (ENG.). 80p. (J). spiral bd. 12.95 *(978-1-59369-672-6(8))* American Girl Publishing, Inc.

Peterson, Stacy & Maberry, Maranda. My Pod: Libro de Cuentos y Reproductor Personal de Musica. Miller, Sara. 2007. (SPA.). 38p. (J). (gr. -1-3). *(978-970-718-495-4(7),* Silver Dolphin en Español) Advanced Marketing, S. de R. L. de C. V.

Peterson, Stacy & Watkins, Michelle. Friends: Making Them & Keeping Them. Criswell, Patti Kelley. 2006. (ENG.). 80p. (J). pap. 9.95 *(978-1-59369-154-7(8))* American Girl Publishing, Inc.

Peterson, Stephanie & Minor, Wendell. The Buffalo Are Back. Cimarusti, Marie Torres & George, Jean Craighead. 2010. (ENG.). 32p. (J). (gr. k-3). 16.99 *(978-0-525-42215-0(3),* Dutton Juvenile) Penguin Publishing Group.

Petete, Christine. Super Phil. Tucker, Mark. 2003. (J). 4.50 *(978-1-882440-00-9(5))* God's World Pubns. Inc.

Petosa-Sigel, Kristi. HOKU the Stargazer: The Exciting Pirate Adventure! Crowe, Ellie & Fry, Juliet. 2009. (ENG.). 28p. (J). *(978-1-59700-601-9(7))* Island Heritage Publishing.

Petricić, Dušan. In the Tree House. Larsen, Andrew. 2013. (ENG.). 32p. (J). 16.95 *(978-1-55453-635-1(9))* Kids Can Pr., Ltd. CAN. Dist: Univ. of Toronto Pr.

Petricic, Dusan. Bagels from Benny. Davis, Aubrey. 2005. (ENG.). 32p. (J). (gr. 3). 7.95 *(978-1-55337-749-8(4))* Kids Can Pr., Ltd. CAN. Dist: Univ. of Toronto Pr.

—Better Together. Shapiro, Sheryl & Shapiro, Simon. 2011. (ENG.). 32p. (J). (gr. -1-1). 19.95 *(978-1-55451-279-9(4),* 9781554512799); pap. 8.95 *(978-1-55451-278-2(6),* 9781554512782) Annick Pr., Ltd. CAN. Dist: Firefly Bks., Ltd.

Petricic, Dusan. InvisiBill. Fergus, Maureen. 2015. (ENG.). 40p. (J). (gr. k-4). 17.99 ***(978-1-77049-613-2(0))*** Tundra Bks. CAN. Dist: Penguin Random Hse., LLC.

Petricic, Dusan. Jacob Two-Two & the Dinosaur. Richler, Mordecai. 2009. (Jacob Two-Two Ser.). (ENG.). 104p. (J). (gr. 4-7). 10.95 *(978-0-88776-926-9(8))* Tundra Bks. CAN. Dist: Random Hse., Inc.

—Jacob Two-Two Meets the Hooded Fang. Richler, Mordecai. 2009. (Jacob Two-Two Ser.). (ENG.). 96p. (J). (gr. 4-7). 10.95 *(978-0-88776-925-2(X))* Tundra Bks. CAN. Dist: Random Hse., Inc.

—Jacob Two-Two on the High Seas. Fagan, Cary. 2009. (Jacob Two-Two Ser.). (ENG.). 112p. (J). (gr. 4-7). 10.95 *(978-0-88776-895-8(4))* Tundra Bks. CAN. Dist: Random Hse., Inc.

—Jacob Two-Two's First Spy Case. Richler, Mordecai. 2009. (Jacob Two-Two Ser.). (ENG.). 168p. (J). (gr. 4-7). 10.95 *(978-0-88776-927-6(6))* Tundra Bks. CAN. Dist: Random Hse., Inc.

—Lickety-Split. Heidbreder, Robert. 2007. (ENG.). 32p. (J). (gr. -1-2). 15.95 *(978-1-55337-710-8(9))* Kids Can Pr., Ltd. CAN. Dist: Univ. of Toronto Pr.

—The Man with the Violin. Stinson, Kathy. 2013. (ENG.). 32p. (J). (gr. k-3). 19.95 *(978-1-55451-565-3(3),* 9781554515653) Annick Pr., Ltd. CAN. Dist: Firefly Bks., Ltd.

—Mattland. Hutchins, Hazel & Herbert, Gail. 2008. (ENG.). 32p. (J). (gr. -1-2). 19.95 *(978-1-55451-121-1(6),* 9781554511211); pap. 8.95 *(978-1-55451-120-4(8),* 9781554511204) Annick Pr., Ltd. CAN. Dist: Firefly Bks., Ltd.

—Mr. Zinger's Hat. Fagan, Cary. 2012. (ENG.). 32p. (J). (gr. -1-1). 17.95 *(978-1-77049-253-0(4))* Tundra Bks. CAN. Dist: Random Hse., Inc.

Petricic, Dusan. Mud Puddle. 2015. (ENG.). 26p. (J). (gr. -1 — 1). bds. 6.95 ***(978-1-55451-754-1(0),*** 9781554517541) Annick Pr., Ltd. CAN. Dist: Firefly Bks., Ltd.

Petricic, Dusan. Mud Puddle. Munsch, Robert. 2012. (ENG.). 32p. (J). (gr. -1-2). 19.95 *(978-1-55451-427-4(4),* 9781554514274); pap. 9.95 *(978-1-55451-426-7(6),* 9781554514267) Annick Pr., Ltd. CAN. Dist: Firefly Bks., Ltd.

—My New Shirt. Fagan, Cary. 2007. (ENG.). 32p. (J). (gr. -1-1). 18.95 *(978-0-88776-715-9(X),* Tundra Bks.) Tundra Bks. CAN. Dist: Penguin Random Hse., LLC.

—Ned Mouse Breaks Away, 1 vol. Wynne-Jones, Tim. 2003. (ENG.). 68p. (J). (gr. 3-18). 14.95 *(978-0-88899-474-5(5))* Groundwood Bks. CAN. Dist: Perseus-PGW.

—On Tumbledown Hill, 1 vol. Wynne-Jones, Tim. 2008. (ENG.). 32p. (J). (gr. -1-3). pap. 8.95 *(978-0-88995-409-0(7))* Red Deer Pr. CAN. Dist: Ingram Pub. Services.

—The Queen's Feet, 1 vol. Ellis, Sarah. 2008. (ENG.). 32p. (J). (gr. -1-3). 6.95 *(978-0-88995-414-4(3))* Red Deer Pr. CAN. Dist: Ingram Pub. Services.

—When Apples Grew Noses & White Horses Flew: Tales of Ti-Jean, 1 vol. Andrews, Jan. 2011. (ENG.). 72p. (J). (gr. 1-5). 16.95 *(978-0-88899-952-8(6))* Groundwood Bks. CAN. Dist: Perseus-PGW.

Petrie, H. D., photos by. All God's Creatures; Jesus Loves Me. ed. 2005. 32p. (J). spiral bd. *(978-0-9774115-0-4(8))* AGC Outreach Ministry.

Petrlik, Andrea. All Aboard the Yellow School Bus: Follow the Bus Through the Pages on a Counting Adventure! Cabral, Jeane. Top That Publishing Staff, ed. 2008. (Story Book Ser.). 20p. (J). (gr. -1). *(978-1-84666-543-1(4),* Tide Mill Pr.) Top That! Publishing PLC.

—Chatterbox Turtle. Rider, Cynthia. 2004. (ENG.). 24p. (J). lib. bdg. 23.65 *(978-1-59646-696-8(0))* Dingles & Co.

—Hansel & Gretel. 2007. (Flip-Up Fairy Tales Ser.). (ENG.). 24p. (J). (gr. -1-2). *(978-1-84643-090-9(9))* Child's Play International Ltd.

—Shoo, Fly! 2008. (J). *(978-0-545-03046-5(3))* Scholastic, Inc.

—The Story of Noah's Ark. Ranson, Erin. 2007. (Interactive Magnetic Book Ser.). 10p. (J). (gr. -1). *(978-1-84666-359-8(8),* Tide Mill Pr.) Top That! Publishing PLC.

Petroff, Kathryn. A Daddy's Love Through a Girl's Eye. Williams, Joyce. 2012. 58p. pap. 9.99 *(978-0-9852729-3-7(7))* Faith Bks. & MORE.

Petrone, Valeria. Big Girl Panties. Manushkin, Fran. 2012. (ENG.). 24p. (J). (gr. k — 1). bds. 7.99 *(978-0-307-93152-8(8),* Robin Corey Bks.) Random Hse. Children's Bks.

—The Boy & the Tigers. Bannerman, Helen. 2004. (Little Golden Book Ser.). (ENG.). 24p. (J). (gr. -1-2). 3.99 *(978-0-375-82719-8(6),* Golden Bks.) Random Hse. Children's Bks.

—Colors All Around: A Turn & Pop Book. Imperato, Teresa. 2005. (Turn & Pop Book Ser.). 10p. (J). bds. 5.95 *(978-1-58117-277-5(X),* Intervisual/Piggy Toes) Bendon, Inc.

—Dos en el Zoológico: Un Libro para Contar. Smith, Danna. 2011.Tr. of Two at the Zoo - A Counting Book. (ENG & SPA.). 30p. (J). (gr. k — 1). bds. 4.99 *(978-0-547-58137-8(8))* Houghton Mifflin Harcourt Publishing Co.

—Double the Ducks. Murphy, Stuart J. 2003. (MathStart Ser.). 40p. (J). 15.99 *(978-0-06-028922-5(8))* HarperCollins Pubs.

—Fish & Frog: Brand New Readers. Knudsen, Michelle. 2005. (Brand New Readers Ser.). (ENG.). 8p. (J). (gr. -1-3). pap. 5.99 *(978-0-7636-2457-6(8))* Candlewick Pr.

—Fish & Frog Big Book: Brand New Readers. Knudsen, Michelle. 2010. (Brand New Readers Ser.). (ENG.). 48p. (J). (gr. -1-3). pap. 24.99 *(978-0-7636-4810-7(8))* Candlewick Pr.

—How Many Ducks in a Row? A Turn & Pop Book. Imperato, Teresa. 2005. 10p. (J). bds. 5.95 *(978-1-58117-278-2(8),* Intervisual/Piggy Toes) Bendon, Inc.

—Lasso the Moon. Holland, Trish. 2005. (Little Golden Book Ser.). (ENG.). 24p. (J). (gr. -1-2). 3.99 *(978-0-375-83289-5(0),* Golden Bks.) Random Hse. Children's Bks.

—Pirate Nap: A Book of Colors. Smith, Danna. 2011. (ENG.). 40p. (J). lib. bdg. 14.99 *(978-0-547-57531-5(9))* Houghton Mifflin Harcourt Publishing Co.

—Plumply, Dumply Pumpkin. Serfozo, Mary. 2006. (Classic Board Bks.). (ENG.). 28p. (J). (gr. -1-1). 6.99 *(978-0-689-86277-9(6),* Little Simon) Little Simon.

—Potty Animals: What to Know When You've Gotta Go! Vestergaard, Hope. 2010. (ENG.). 32p. (J). (gr. -1-1). 14.95 *(978-1-4027-5996-3(7))* Sterling Publishing Co., Inc.

—The Pup Speaks Up. Hays, Anna Jane. 2003. (Step into Reading Ser.). (gr. -1-1). 14.00 *(978-0-7569-1696-1(8))* Perfection Learning Corp.

—The Pup Speaks Up. Hays, Anna Jane. 2003. (Step into Reading Ser.). (ENG.). 32p. (J). (gr. -1-1). pap. 3.99 *(978-0-375-81232-3(6),* Random Hse. Bks. for Young Readers) Random Hse. Children's Bks.

—Red Truck. Hamilton, Kersten. 2012. (ENG.). 24p. (J). (gr. -1-k). bds. 6.99 *(978-0-670-01467-5(2),* Viking Juvenile) Penguin Publishing Group.

—Two at the Zoo. Smith, Danna. 2009. (ENG.). 32p. (J). (gr. k — 1). 16.00 *(978-0-547-04982-3(X))* Houghton Mifflin Harcourt Publishing Co.

—Way down Deep in the Deep Blue Sea. Peck, Jan. 2004. (ENG.). 32p. (J). (gr. -1-3). 17.99 *(978-0-689-85110-0(3),* Simon & Schuster Bks. For Young Readers) Simon & Schuster Bks. For Young Readers.

—Way Far Away on a Wild Safari. Peck, Jan. 2006. (ENG.). 32p. (J). (gr. -1-3). 17.99 *(978-1-4169-0072-6(1),* Simon & Schuster Bks. For Young Readers) Simon & Schuster Bks. For Young Readers.

—Way up High in a Tall Green Tree. Peck, Jan. 2005. (ENG.). 32p. (J). (gr. -1-3). 17.99 *(978-1-4169-0071-9(3),* Simon & Schuster Bks. For Young Readers) Simon & Schuster Bks. For Young Readers.

—Yellow Copter. Hamilton, Kersten. 2015. (ENG.). 32p. (J). (-k). 16.99 *(978-0-451-46991-5(7))* Penguin Bks., Ltd. GBR. Dist: Penguin Random Hse., LLC.

Petropouleas, Niko. From a Street Kid: Stephen Lungu's Incredible Life Journey. Cope Bowley, Tonia. 2012. 192p. pap. *(978-1-78003-380-8(X))* Pen Pr. Pubs., Ltd.

Petropoulos, John. Plato the Platypus Plumber (Part-Time) Edwards, Hazel. 2010. 36p. (J). 14.95 *(978-1-921479-37-3(X))* Interactive Pubns. Pty, Ltd. AUS. Dist: SPD-Small Pr. Distribution.

Petrosino, Tamara. Cat Show. Harvey, Jayne. 2003. (Penguin Young Readers, Level 2 Ser.). (ENG.). 32p. (J). (gr. 1-2). mass mkt. 3.99 *(978-0-448-43112-3(2),* Warne, Frederick Pubs.) Penguin Bks., Ltd. GBR. Dist: Penguin Random Hse., LLC.

—Dog Poems. Crawley, Dave. 2007. (ENG.). 32p. (J). (gr. 4-6). 16.95 *(978-1-59078-454-9(5),* Wordsong) Boyds Mills Pr.

—No Plain Hair. 2006. (I'm Going to Read(r) Ser.). (ENG.). 32p. (J). (gr. 1-2). pap. 3.95 *(978-1-4027-3083-2(7))* Sterling Publishing Co., Inc.

Petrossi, Fabrizio. Fry Cook Freak-Out! (SpongeBob SquarePants) Golden Books. 2014. (Color Plus Chunky Crayons Ser.). (ENG.). 48p. (J). (gr. -1-2). pap. 3.99 *(978-0-385-37430-9(5),* Golden Bks.) Random Hse. Children's Bks.

Petrossi, Fabrizio. Puppy Birthday to You! (Paw Patrol) Golden Books. 2015. (Little Golden Book Ser.). (ENG.). 24p. (J). (-k). 4.99 ***(978-0-553-52277-8(9),*** Golden Bks.) Random Hse. Children's Bks.

Petrossi, Fabrizio. The Sponge Who Saved Christmas (SpongeBob SquarePants) Wygand, Melissa. 2012. (Big Golden Book Ser.). (ENG.). 48p. (J). (gr. k-k). 9.99 *(978-0-307-97596-6(7),* Golden Bks.) Random Hse. Children's Bks.

Petrossi, Fabrizio, jt. illus. see Golden Books Staff.

Petrossi, Fabrizio, jt. illus. see Random House Staff.

Petrov, Anton. Jesus lo Hizo por Mi. Mackall, Dandi Daley. 2008. (SPA.). 28p. (J). (gr. -1). pap. 7.99 *(978-0-7586-1585-5(X))* Concordia Publishing Hse.

—The Lighthouse Boy: A Story about Courage. Schneider, Richard H. 2007. (ENG.). 32p. (J). (gr. -1-3). pap. 8.99 *(978-0-8249-5557-1(9),* Guideposts) Ideals Pubns.

—Moving Day for Sam: A Story about Change. Kennedy, Pamela. 2007. 32p. (J). (gr. -1-3). 8.99 *(978-0-8249-5558-8(7),* GPKids) Ideals Pubns.

Petrova, Valeria. God Thought of It First. Keener, Joan N. 2006. 28p. (J). 14.99 *(978-0-7847-1432-4(0),* 04016) Standard Publishing.

Petru, Suzin. Autumn's Indigo. Costanza, Francine. 2012. 30p. 24.95 *(978-1-4626-6523-5(3))* America Star Bks.

Petruccelli, Jessica, jt. illus. see Fennell, Kristen.

Petruccio, Stephen & Petruccio, Stephen. Dolphin's Rescue. Halfmann, Janet. (Smithsonian Oceanic Colection Ser.). (ENG.). 32p. (J). (gr. -1-2). 8.95 *(978-1-59249-429-3(3),* SC4028) Soundprints.

Petruccio, Stephen, jt. illus. see Petruccio, Stephen.

Petruccio, Steven James, et al. Alphabet of Ocean Animals. Galvin, Laura Gates. 2009. (ENG.). 40p. 9.95 *(978-1-60727-024-9(2))* Soundprints.

—Alphabet of Ocean Animals. Galvin, Laura Gates. 2007. (ENG.). 40p. (J). (gr. k-2). 15.95 *(978-1-59249-690-7(3))* Soundprints.

Petruccio, Steven James. Dolphin's First Day: The Story of a Bottlenose Dolphin. Zoehfeld, Kathleen Weidner. (Smithsonian Oceanic Collection). (J). 2009. 24.95 incl. audio compact disk *(978-1-59249-666-2(0));* 2003. (ENG.). 32p. (gr. -1-3). pap. 6.95 *(978-1-59249-056-1(5),* S4001) Soundprints.

—Dolphin's Rescue: The Story of a Pacific White-Sided Dolphin. Halfmann, Janet. (Smithsonian Oceanic Collection Ser.). (ENG.). 32p. (J). 2011. (gr. -1-3). 19.95 *(978-1-60727-646-3(1));* 2011. (gr. -1-3). 8.95 *(978-1-60727-647-0(X));* 2005. (gr. -1-3). 19.95 *(978-1-59249-430-9(7),* BC4028); 2005. (gr. -1-3). 4.95 *(978-1-59249-427-9(7),* B4078); 2005. (gr. -1-3). pap. 6.95 *(978-1-59249-428-6(5),* S4028); 2005. (gr. 1-3). 15.95 *(978-1-59249-426-2(9),* B4028) Soundprints.

—Great White Shark: Ruler of the Sea. Zoehfeld, Kathleen Weidner. (Smithsonian Oceanic Collection). (J). 2009. 24.95 incl. audio compact disk *(978-1-59249-664-8(4));* 2005. (ENG.). 32p. (gr. -1-2). per. 6.95 *(978-1-59249-196-4(0),* S4006) Soundprints.

—Manatee Winter. Zoehfeld, Kathleen Weidner. 2005. (ENG.). 32p. (J). (gr. -1-2). 8.95 *(978-1-59249-072-1(7),* SC4003) Soundprints.

—Narwhal: The Unicorn of the Sea. Halfmann, Janet. 2008. (ENG.). 32p. (J). (gr. -1-2). 19.95 *(978-1-59249-872-7(8))* Soundprints.

—Narwhal: Unicorn of the Sea. Halfmann, Janet. 2008. (ENG.). 32p. (J). (gr. -1-2). 16.95 *(978-1-59249-868-0(X));* 4.95 *(978-1-59249-869-7(8));* pap. 6.95 *(978-1-59249-870-3(1));* pap. 9.95 *(978-1-59249-871-0(X))* Soundprints.

—Puffer's Surprise. Winkelman, Barbara Gaines. (Smithsonian Oceanic Collection Ser.). (ENG.). 32p. (J). (gr. -1-3). 2011. 19.95 *(978-1-60727-658-6(5));* 2011. 8.95 *(978-1-60727-659-3(3));* 2005. 15.95 *(978-1-59249-032-5(8),* B4024); 2003. 19.95 *(978-1-59249-035-6(2),* BC4024); 2003. 4.95 *(978-1-59249-033-2(6),* B4074); 2003. 8.95 *(978-1-59249-062-2(X),* SC4024); 2003. 9.95 *(978-1-59249-038-7(7),* PB4074); 2003. 6.95 *(978-1-59249-034-9(4),* S4024) Soundprints.

—Seahorse Reef: A Story of the South Pacific. Walker, Sally M. 2005. (ENG.). 32p. (J). (gr. -1-2). pap. 6.95 *(978-1-56899-938-8(0),* S4020); (Smithsonian Oceanic Collection: No. 20). 15.95 *(978-1-56899-869-5(4),* B4020) Soundprints.

Petrulis, Sarah. AIDS in the Endzone. Albright, Kendra S. & Gavigan, Karen W., eds. 2014. (Young Palmetto Bks.). (ENG.). 40p. pap. 12.95 *(978-1-61117-424-3(4))* Univ. of South Carolina Pr.

Petrusek, Brett. El Lobo y los Siete Cabritos. Blair, Eric. Abello, Patricia, tr. from ENG. 2006. (Read-It! Readers en Español: Cuentos de Hadas Ser.). (SPA.). 32p. (gr. k-3). 19.99 *(978-1-4048-1645-9(3),* Easy Readers) Picture Window Bks.

Petsch, Maggie, photos by. Dora the A-Dora-ble Duck. Petsch, Maggie, text. 2004. (J). per. 9.95 *(978-0-9715860-4-8(7))* From the Asylum Bks. & Pr.

Pett, Mark. The Boy & the Airplane. Pett, Mark. 2013. (ENG.). 40p. (J). 15.99 *(978-1-4424-5123-0(8),* Simon & Schuster Bks. For Young Readers) Simon & Schuster Bks. For Young Readers.

—The Girl & the Bicycle. Pett, Mark. 2014. (ENG.). 40p. (J). 16.99 *(978-1-4424-8319-4(9),* Simon & Schuster Bks. For Young Readers) Simon & Schuster Bks. For Young Readers.

—The Girl Who Never Made Mistakes. Pett, Mark. Rubinstein, Gary. 2011. (ENG.). 32p. (J). (gr. k-3). 14.99 *(978-1-4022-5544-1(6),* Sourcebooks Jabberwocky) Sourcebooks, Inc.

Pett, Mark. Lizard from the Park. Pett, Mark. 2015. (ENG.). 40p. (J). (gr. -1-3). 17.99 ***(978-1-4424-8321-7(0),*** Simon & Schuster Bks. For Young Readers) Simon & Schuster Bks. For Young Readers.

Pettingill, Charla. One to Ten NYC. Puck. 2013. (ENG.). 22p. (J). (— 1). bds. 9.95 *(978-1-938093-19-7(4))* Duo Pr. LLC.

Petty, Colin. The Three Little Pigs: A Tale about Working Hard. 2006. (J). 6.99 *(978-1-59939-016-1(7))* Cornerstone Pr.

Petty, William Kevin. Steamduck Learns to Fly! Bush, Emilie P. 2012. 36p. pap. 11.95 *(978-0-9849028-1-1(3))* Coal City Stories.

Peyo. The Purple Smurf, No. 1. Delporte, Yvan. 2010. (Smurfs Graphic Novels Ser.: 1). (ENG.). 56p. (J). (gr. 2-5). 10.99 *(978-1-59707-207-6(9))* Papercutz.

—The Purple Smurfs. Delporte, Yvan. 2010. (Smurfs Graphic Novels Ser.: 1). (ENG.). 56p. (J). (gr. 2-5). pap. 5.99 *(978-1-59707-206-9(0))* Papercutz.

—The Smurfs & the Magic Flute. Delporte, Yvan. 2010. (Smurfs Graphic Novels Ser.: 2). (ENG.). 64p. (J). (gr. 2-5). pap. 5.99 *(978-1-59707-208-3(7));* 10.99 *(978-1-59707-209-0(5))* Papercutz.

Peyo. Astro Smurf Blasts Off! Peyo. 2013. (Smurfs Classic Ser.). (ENG.). 24p. (J). (gr. -1-2). pap. 3.99 *(978-1-4424-8514-3(0),* Simon Spotlight) Simon Spotlight.

—The Astrosmurf. Peyo. Gos. 2011. (Smurfs Graphic Novels Ser.: 7). (ENG.). 56p. (J). (gr. 2-5). 10.99 *(978-1-59707-251-9(6))* Papercutz.

—The Astrosmurf. Peyo. Gos. 2011. (Smurfs Graphic Novels Ser.: 7). (ENG.). 56p. (J). (gr. 2-5). pap. 5.99 *(978-1-59707-250-2(8))* Papercutz.

—Find the 100 Smurfs! Peyo. 2012. (Smurfs Classic Ser.). (ENG.). 12p. (J). (gr. -1-2). bds. 9.99 *(978-1-4424-5350-0(8),* Simon Spotlight) Simon Spotlight.

—The Giant Smurf. Peyo. 2013. (Smurfs Classic Ser.). (ENG.). 24p. (J). (gr. -1-2). pap. 3.99 *(978-1-4424-6178-9(0),* Simon Spotlight) Simon Spotlight.

—I Smurf You! Peyo. Mitter, Matt. 2011. (Smurfs Classic Ser.). (ENG.). 14p. (J). (gr. -1-k). bds. 10.99 *(978-1-4424-3606-0(9),* Simon Spotlight) Simon Spotlight.

—It's a Smurfy World! Peyo. 2013. (Smurfs Classic Ser.). (ENG.). 16p. (J). (gr. -1-k). bds. 7.99 *(978-1-4424-6709-5(6),* Simon Spotlight) Simon Spotlight.

—Meet Smurfette. Peyo. 2011. (Smurfs Classic Ser.). (ENG.). 24p. (J). pap. 3.99 *(978-1-4424-2290-2(4),* Simon Spotlight) Simon Spotlight.

—Off to School! Peyo. 2011. (Smurfs Classic Ser.). (ENG.). 32p. (J). (gr. k-2). pap. 3.99 *(978-1-4424-2138-7(X));* lib. bdg. 15.99 *(978-1-4424-3062-4(1))* Simon Spotlight. (Simon Spotlight).

—Papa Smurf's Favorite Things. Peyo. 2013. (Smurfs Classic Ser.). (ENG.). 12p. (J). (gr. -1-k). bds. 5.99 *(978-1-4424-6167-3(5),* Simon Spotlight) Simon Spotlight.

—Rain, Rain, Smurf Away. Peyo. 2012. (Smurfs Classic Ser.). (ENG.). 24p. (J). (gr. -1-3). pap. 3.99 *(978-1-4424-3600-8(X),* Simon Spotlight) Simon Spotlight.

—Sky-High Smurf. Peyo. 2014. (Smurfs Classic Ser.). (ENG.). 16p. (J). (gr. -1-3). 5.99 *(978-1-4424-9740-5(8),* Simon Spotlight) Simon Spotlight.

—Smurf Cake. Peyo. 2013. (Smurfs Classic Ser.). (ENG.). 32p. (J). (gr. k-2). 16.99 *(978-1-4424-8493-1(4));* pap. 3.99 *(978-1-4424-8492-4(6))* Simon Spotlight. (Simon Spotlight).

—The Smurf Championship Games. Peyo. 2012. (Smurfs Classic Ser.). (ENG.). 32p. (J). (gr. k-2). pap. 3.99 *(978-1-4424-4993-0(4),* Simon Spotlight) Simon Spotlight.

—Smurf vs. Smurf. Peyo. 2012. (Smurfs Graphic Novels Ser.: 12). (ENG.). 56p. (J). (gr. 2-5). 10.99 *(978-1-59707-321-9(0));* pap. 5.99 *(978-1-59707-320-2(2))* Papercutz.

—The Smurfette, No. 4. Peyo. Delporte, Yvan. 2011. (Smurfs Graphic Novels Ser.: 4). (ENG.). 64p. (J). (gr. 2-5). 10.99 *(978-1-59707-237-3(0));* pap. 5.99 *(978-1-59707-236-6(2))* Papercutz.

—Smurfette & the Beast: A Smurftastic Pop-Up Book. Peyo. 2013. (Smurfs Classic Ser.). (ENG.). 12p. (J). (gr. -1-3). 17.99 *(978-1-4424-8317-0(2),* Simon Spotlight) Simon Spotlight.

—Smurfiness to Go! A Smurfin' Big Adventure, Meet Smurfette!, Lazy Smurf Takes a Nap, the Thankful Smurf, Rain, Rain Smurf Away, the 100th Smurf. Peyo. ed. 2012. (Smurfs Classic Ser.). (ENG.). 144p. (J). (gr. -1-2). pap. 15.99 *(978-1-4424-6520-6(4),* Simon Spotlight) Simon Spotlight.

—The Smurfs #8: the Smurf Apprentice. Peyo. Gos et al. 2011. (Smurfs Graphic Novels Ser.: 8). (ENG.). 56p. (J). (gr. 2-5). 10.99 *(978-1-59707-280-9(X));* pap. 5.99 *(978-1-59707-279-3(6))* Papercutz.

—The Smurfs #9: Gargamel & the Smurfs. Peyo. Gos & Delporte, Yvan. 2011. (Smurfs Graphic Novels Ser.: 9). (ENG.). 56p. (J). (gr. 2-5). 10.99 *(978-1-59707-290-8(7));* pap. 5.99 *(978-1-59707-289-2(3))* Papercutz.

—The Smurfs & the Howlibird. Peyo. Delporte, Yvan & Gos. 2011. (Smurfs Graphic Novels Ser.: 6). (ENG.). 56p. (J). (gr. 2-5). pap. 5.99 *(978-1-59707-260-1(5))* Papercutz.

—The Smurfs & the Howlibird. Peyo. Delporte, Peyo et al. 2011. (Smurfs Graphic Novels Ser.: 6). (ENG.). 56p. (J). (gr. 2-5). 10.99 *(978-1-59707-261-8(3))* Papercutz.

—The Smurfs & the Magic Egg. Peyo. 2014. (Smurfs Classic Ser.). (ENG.). 32p. (J). (gr. k-2). pap. 3.99 *(978-1-4424-9570-8(7),* Simon Spotlight) Simon Spotlight.

—Smurfs Mini Library: Rise & Shine; Happy Smurfdays; Fun & Games; Making Music; Whatever the Weather. Peyo. ed. 2014. (Smurfs Classic Ser.). (ENG.). 70p. (J). (gr. -1-2). bds. 6.99 *(978-1-4424-9543-2(X),* Simon Spotlight) Simon Spotlight.

—The Snow Giant. Peyo. 2011. (Smurfs Classic Ser.). (ENG.). 32p. (J). pap. 3.99 *(978-1-4424-2892-8(9),* Simon Spotlight) Simon Spotlight.

—The Snow Giant. Peyo. 2011. (Smurfs Classic Ser.). (ENG.). 32p. (J). 15.99 *(978-1-4424-3610-7(7),* Simon Spotlight) Simon Spotlight.

—Welcome, Baby Smurf! Peyo. 2014. (Smurfs Classic Ser.). (ENG.). 24p. (J). (gr. -1-2). pap. 3.99 *(978-1-4424-9542-5(1),* Simon Spotlight) Simon Spotlight.

—Who's That Smurf? Peyo. 2013. (Smurfs Classic Ser.). (ENG.). 18p. (J). (gr. -1-1). bds. 5.99 *(978-1-4424-7235-8(9),* Simon Spotlight) Simon Spotlight.

—Why Do You Cry, Baby Smurf? Peyo. 2013. (Smurfs Classic Ser.). (ENG.). 32p. (J). (gr. k-2). 15.99 *(978-1-4424-6193-2(4));* pap. 3.99 *(978-1-4424-6191-8(8))* Simon Spotlight. (Simon Spotlight).

Peyo & Maltaite, Will. Benny Breakiron #2: Madame Adolphine. Peyo. 2013. (Benny Breakiron Ser.: 2). (ENG.). 64p. (J). (gr. 2-12). 11.99 *(978-1-59707-436-0(5))* Papercutz.

—The Red Taxis. Peyo. 2013. (Benny Breakiron Ser.: 1). (ENG.). 64p. (J). (gr. 2-12). 11.99 *(978-1-59707-409-4(8))* Papercutz.

Peyo, Peyo. The Smurf King. Delporte, Yvan. 2010. (Smurfs Graphic Novels Ser.: 3). (ENG.). 64p. (J). (gr. 2-5). 10.99 *(978-1-59707-225-0(7));* pap. 5.99 *(978-1-59707-224-3(9))* Papercutz.

Peyo, Peyo. The Smurfs & the Egg. Peyo, Peyo. Delporte, Yvan. 2011. (Smurfs Graphic Novels Ser.: 5). (ENG.). 64p. (J). (gr. 2-5). 10.99 *(978-1-59707-247-2(8));* pap. 5.99 *(978-1-59707-246-5(X))* Papercutz.

Peyrols, Sylvaine, et al. Volcanoes. Peyrols, Sylvaine et al. 2013. (ENG.). 36p. (J). (-k). 12.99 *(978-1-85103-420-8(X))* Moonlight Publishing, Ltd. GBR. Dist: Independent Pubs. Group.

Peyrols, Sylvaine. The Body. Peyrols, Sylvaine. 2012. (ENG.). 36p. (J). (gr. -1-k). 12.99 *(978-1-85103-396-6(3))* Moonlight Publishing, Ltd. GBR. Dist: Independent Pubs. Group.

—Crocodile. Peyrols, Sylvaine. 2012. (ENG.). (J). (gr. k-3). pap. 11.99 *(978-1-85103-317-1(3))* Moonlight Publishing, Ltd. GBR. Dist: Independent Pubs. Group.

—Dolphins. Peyrols, Sylvaine. Biard, Philippe & Krawczyk, Sabine. 2012. (ENG.). 32p. (J). (gr. k-3). pap. 11.99 *(978-1-85103-364-5(5))* Moonlight Publishing, Ltd. GBR. Dist: Independent Pubs. Group.

—The Human Body. Peyrols, Sylvaine. Jeunesse, Gallimard. 2007. (First Discovery Book Ser.). (ENG.). 24p. (J). (gr. -1-k). pap. 5.99 *(978-0-439-91088-0(9))* Scholastic, Inc.

—Ladybugs & Other Insects. Peyrols, Sylvaine. Jeunesse, Gallimard. 2007. (First Discovery Book Ser.). (ENG.). 24p. (J). (gr. -1-k). pap. 5.99 *(978-0-439-91086-6(2))* Scholastic, Inc.

Pez. Los Grendelines. Bornemann, Elsa. 2003.Tr. of Grendelines. (SPA.). 70p. (J). (gr. 3-5). pap. 11.95 *(978-950-511-244-9(0))* Alfaguara S.A. de Ediciones ARG. Dist: Santillana USA Publishing Co., Inc.

—Silencio, Ninos! Y Otros Cuentos. Wolf, Ema. (Torre de Papel Ser.).Tr. of Quiet, Children! & Other Stories. (SPA.). 116p. (J). (gr. 4-6). 8.95 *(978-958-04-3927-1(3))* Norma S.A. COL. Dist: Distribuidora Norma, Inc.

Pezzali, Walter & Sfar, Joann. Sardine in Outer Space 5. Guibert, Emmanuel. 5th ed. 2008. (Sardine in Outer Space Ser.: 5). (ENG.). 112p. (J). (gr. 1-5). pap. 15.99 *(978-1-59643-380-9(9)*, First Second Bks.) Roaring Brook Pr.

Pezzali, Walter, jt. illus. see Sfar, Joann.

Pfeiffer, Judith. We Didn't Know. 2012. 8p. (J). *(978-0-7367-2742-6(6))* Zaner-Bloser, Inc.

—Zippers. Boland, Janice. 2003. (Books for Young Learners). (ENG.). 8p. (J). pap. 15.00 *(978-1-57274-700-5(5)*, BB2220, Bks. for Young Learners) Owen, Richard C. Pubs., Inc.

Pfister, Marcus. Hopper's Easter Surprise. Siegenthaler, Kathrin & Sieegenthaler, Pfist. 2010. (ENG.). 26p. (J). (gr. -1 — 1). bds. 7.95 *(978-0-7358-2266-5(2))* North-South Bks., Inc.

Pfister, Marcus. Copycat Charlie. Pfister, Marcus. 2009. (ENG.). 12p. (J). (gr. -1). bds. 6.95 *(978-0-7358-2222-1(0))* North-South Bks., Inc.

—La Estrella de Navidad. Pfister, Marcus. 2005. (SPA.). 14p. (J). (gr. -1-3). 6.95 *(978-0-7358-2012-8(0))* North-South Bks., Inc.

—The Friendly Monsters. Pfister, Marcus. 2008. (ENG.). 32p. (J). (gr. -1-3). 18.95 *(978-0-7358-2206-1(9))* North-South Bks., Inc.

—Just Like Daddy. Pfister, Marcus. 2009. (ENG.). 32p. (J). (gr. -1-k). 16.95 *(978-0-7358-2224-5(7))* North-South Bks., Inc.

—Milo & the Magical Stones. Pfister, Marcus. 2010. (ENG.). 32p. (J). (gr. k-3). 17.95 *(978-0-7358-2253-5(0))* North-South Bks., Inc.

—Rainbow Fish Colors/Colores. Pfister, Marcus. 2005. (ENG & SPA.). 24p. (J). 4.99 *(978-0-7358-1978-8(5))* North-South Bks., Inc.

—Rainbow Fish Discovers the Deep Sea. Pfister, Marcus. 2009. (ENG.). 32p. (J). (gr. k-3). 18.95 *(978-0-7358-2248-1(4))* North-South Bks., Inc.

—Rainbow Fish Finds His Way. Pfister, Marcus. James, J. Alison, tr. from GER. 2006. (Rainbow Fish (North-South Books) Ser.). (ENG.). 32p. (J). (gr. k-3). 18.95 *(978-0-7358-2084-5(8))* North-South Bks., Inc.

Pfisterer Clark, Pem. An Elephant Story for Alex. McKown, Martha. 2009. 24p. pap. 11.99 *(978-1-4389-4435-7(7))* AuthorHouse.

Pfleegor, Gina. I Like Gum. Tango-Hampton, Doreen. 2007. (ENG.). 32p. (J). (gr. -1-3). 15.95 *(978-0-9726614-2-3(5))* Shenanigan Bks.

—What If There Is a Fire?, 1 vol. Guard, Anara. 2011. (Danger Zone Ser.). (ENG.). 24p. (gr. 1-2). pap. 7.49 *(978-1-4048-7033-8(4))*; lib. bdg. 25.32 *(978-1-4048-6685-0(X))* Picture Window Bks. (Nonfiction Picture Bks.).

Pfloog, Jan. What Can an Animal Do? Lowery, Lawrence F. 2012. (ENG.). 40p. (J). pap. 12.95 *(978-1-936959-45-7(3))* National Science Teachers Assn.

Pflueger, Maura McArdle. Hello Albert! F. Aryal, Aimee. 2004. 24p. (J). 19.95 *(978-1-932888-12-6(8))* Mascot Bks., Inc.

Pham, Khoi. Chaos War. Pak, Greg. 2011. (ENG.). 168p. (YA). (gr. 8-17). pap. 19.99 *(978-0-7851-5131-9(1))* Marvel Worldwide, Inc.

Pham, LeUyen. Akimbo & the Snakes. McCall Smith, Alexander. 2006. (Akimbo Ser.: 3). (ENG.). 80p. (J). (gr. 2-4). 9.95 *(978-1-58234-705-9(0)*, Bloomsbury USA Childrens) Bloomsbury USA.

—All Fall Down. Barrett, Mary Brigid. 2014. (ENG.). 16p. (J). (-k). bds. 6.99 *(978-0-7636-4430-7(7))* Candlewick Pr.

—Alvin Ho: Allergic to Babies, Burglars, & Other Bumps in the Night. Look, Lenore. 2013. (Alvin Ho Ser.). (ENG.). 192p. (J). (gr. 1-4). 15.99 *(978-0-375-87033-0(4)*, Schwartz & Wade Bks.) Random Hse. Children's Bks.

—Alvin Ho: Allergic to Birthday Parties, Science Projects, & Other Man-Made Catastrophes. Look, Lenore. (Alvin Ho Ser.). (ENG.). 192p. (J). (gr. 1-4). 2011. 6.99 *(978-0-375-87369-0(4)*, Yearling); 2010. 15.99 *(978-0-375-86335-6(4)*, Schwartz & Wade Bks.) Random Hse. Children's Bks.

—Alvin Ho: Allergic to Camping, Hiking, & Other Natural Disasters. Look, Lenore. 2010. (Alvin Ho Ser.). (ENG.). 192p. (J). (gr. 1-4). 6.99 *(978-0-375-85750-8(8)*, Yearling) Random Hse. Children's Bks.

—Alvin Ho: Allergic to Girls, School, & Other Scary Things. Look, Lenore. (Alvin Ho Ser.). (ENG.). (J). (gr. 1-4). 2009. 192p. 6.99 *(978-0-375-84930-5(0)*, Yearling); 2008. 176p. 15.99 *(978-0-375-83914-6(3)*, Schwartz & Wade Bks.) Random Hse. Children's Bks.

—Alvin Ho: Allergic to the Great Wall, the Forbidden Palace, & Other Tourist Attractions. Look, Lenore. 2014. (Alvin Ho Ser.). (ENG.). 176p. (J). (gr. 1-4). 15.99 *(978-0-385-36972-5(7)*, Schwartz & Wade Bks.) Random Hse. Children's Bks.

—Alvin Ho: Allergic to Babies, Burglars, & Other Bumps in the Night. Look, Lenore. 2014. (Alvin Ho Ser.). (ENG.). 192p. (J). (gr. 1-4). 6.99 *(978-0-385-38600-5(1)*, Yearling) Random Hse. Children's Bks.

—Alvin Ho: Allergic to Dead Bodies, Funerals, & Other Fatal Circumstances. Look, Lenore. 2012. (Alvin Ho Ser.). (ENG.). 208p. (J). (gr. 1-4). 6.99 *(978-0-307-97695-6(5)*, Yearling) Random Hse. Children's Bks.

Pham, LeUyen. Alvin Ho: Allergic to the Great Wall, the Forbidden Palace, & Other Tourist Attractions. Look, Lenore. 2015. (Alvin Ho Ser.). (ENG.). 176p. (J). (gr. 1-4). 6.99 ***(978-0-553-52055-2(5)***, Yearling) Random Hse. Children's Bks.

Pham, LeUyen. Any Which Wall. Snyder, Laurel. 2010. (ENG.). 256p. (J). (gr. 3-7). pap. 7.99 *(978-0-375-85561-0(0))* Random Hse., Inc.

—Bedtime for Mommy. Rosenthal, Amy Krouse. 2010. (ENG.). 32p. (J). (gr. -1-k). 16.99 *(978-1-59990-341-5(5)*, Bloomsbury USA Childrens) Bloomsbury USA.

—Before I Was Your Mother. Lasky, Kathryn. 2007. (ENG.). 40p. (J). (gr. -1-3). pap. 6.99 *(978-0-15-205842-5(7))* Houghton Mifflin Harcourt Publishing Co.

—Best Friends Forever. Moore, Julianne. 2011. (Freckleface Strawberry Ser.). (ENG.). 40p. (J). (gr. -1-3). 17.89 *(978-1-59990-552-5(3)*, Bloomsbury USA Childrens) Bloomsbury USA.

—Bo at Ballard Creek. Hill, Kirkpatrick. 2013. (ENG.). 288p. (J). (gr. 3-7). 16.99 *(978-0-8050-9351-3(6)*, Holt, Henry & Co. Bks. For Young Readers) Holt, Henry & Co.

—Bo at Ballard Creek. Hill, Kirkpatrick. 2014. (ENG.). 304p. (J). (gr. 3-7). pap. 7.99 *(978-1-250-04425-9(1))* Square Fish.

—Bo at Iditarod Creek. Hill, Kirkpatrick. 2014. (ENG.). 288p. (J). (gr. 3-7). 15.99 *(978-0-8050-9352-0(4)*, Holt, Henry & Co. Bks. For Young Readers) Holt, Henry & Co.

—Boy of Mine. Asim, Jabari. 2010. (ENG.). 20p. (J). (gr. -1 — 1). bds. 6.99 *(978-0-316-73577-3(9))* Little, Brown Bks. for Young Readers.

—The Boy Who Loved Math: The Improbable Life of Paul Erdös. Heiligman, Deborah. 2013. (ENG.). 48p. (J). (gr. -1-2). 17.99 *(978-1-59643-307-6(8))* Roaring Brook Pr.

—Freckleface Strawberry. Moore, Julianne. 2007. (Freckleface Strawberry Ser.). (ENG.). 32p. (J). (gr. -1-3). 17.99 *(978-1-59990-107-7(2)*, Bloomsbury USA Childrens) Bloomsbury USA.

—Freckleface Strawberry: Best Friends Forever. Moore, Julianne. 2011. (Freckleface Strawberry Ser.). (ENG.). 40p. (J). (gr. -1-8). 16.99 *(978-1-59990-551-8(5)*, Bloomsbury USA Childrens) Bloomsbury USA.

—Freckleface Strawberry & the Dodgeball Bully. Moore, Julianne. 2009. (Freckleface Strawberry Ser.). (ENG.). 40p. (J). (gr. k-2). 17.89 *(978-1-59990-317-0(2)*, Bloomsbury USA Childrens) Bloomsbury USA.

Pham, LeUyen. Freckleface Strawberry: Backpacks! Moore, Julianne. 2015. (Step into Reading Ser.). (ENG.). 32p. (J). (gr. -1-1). lib. bdg. 15.99 ***(978-0-375-97367-3(2)***, Random Hse. Bks. for Young Readers) Random Hse. Children's Bks.

—Freckleface Strawberry: Lunch, or What's That? Moore, Julianne. 2015. (Step into Reading Ser.). (ENG.). 32p. (J). (gr. -1-1). lib. bdg. 15.99 ***(978-0-375-97366-6(4)***, Random Hse. Bks. for Young Readers) Random Hse. Children's Bks.

Pham, LeUyen. Girl of Mine. Asim, Jabari. 2010. (ENG.). 20p. (J). (gr. -1 — 1). bds. 6.99 *(978-0-316-73578-0(7))* Little, Brown Bks. for Young Readers.

—God's Dream. Tutu, Desmond & Abrams, Douglas Carlton. 2008. (ENG.). 40p. (J). (gr. k-12). 16.99 *(978-0-7636-3388-2(7))* Candlewick Pr.

—God's Dream. Abrams, Douglas Carlton & Tutu, Desmond. 2010. (ENG.). 32p. (J). (— 1). bds. 7.99 *(978-0-7636-4742-1(X))* Candlewick Pr.

—Grace for President. DiPucchio, Kelly. 2012. (ENG.). 40p. (J). (gr. 1-3). 16.99 *(978-1-4231-3999-7(2))* Hyperion Pr.

Pham, LeUyen. Hillary Clinton. Markel, Michelle. 2016. 40p. (J). (gr. -1-3). 17.99 ***(978-0-06-238122-4(9))*** HarperCollins Pubs.

—Isabella for Real. Palatini, Margie. 2016. (J). ***(978-0-544-14846-8(0))*** Harcourt.

Pham, LeUyen. Monster Makeovers. DiPucchio, Kelly. 2006. (J). *(978-0-7868-5181-2(3))* Hyperion Bks. for Children.

—My Chocolate Year: A Novel with 12 Recipes. Herman, Charlotte. 2008. (ENG.). 192p. (J). (gr. 3-7). 15.99 *(978-1-4169-3341-0(7)*, Simon & Schuster Bks. For Young Readers) Simon & Schuster Bks. For Young Readers.

—Pat-a-Cake. Barrett, Mary Brigid. 2014. (ENG.). 16p. (J). (-k). bds. 6.99 *(978-0-7636-4358-4(0))* Candlewick Pr.

—The Princess in Black. Hale, Shannon & Hale, Dean. (Princess in Black Ser.). (ENG.). 96p. (J). (gr. k-3). 2015. pap. 6.99 *(978-0-7636-7888-3(0))*; 2014. 14.99 *(978-0-7636-6510-4(X))* Candlewick Pr.

—Samantha Hansen Has Rocks in Her Head. Viau, Nancy. 2008. (ENG.). 192p. (YA). (gr. 3-7). 15.95 *(978-0-8109-7299-5(9)*, Amulet Bks.) Abrams.

—Shoe-la-La! Beaumont, Karen. 2011. (ENG.). 40p. (J). (gr. -1-3). 16.99 *(978-0-545-06705-8(7)*, Scholastic Pr.) Scholastic, Inc.

—Shoe-La-la! Beaumont, Karen. 2013. (ENG.). 32p. (J). (gr. -1 — 1). bds. 6.99 *(978-0-545-59478-3(2)*, Cartwheel Bks.) Scholastic, Inc.

—A Stick Is an Excellent Thing: Poems Celebrating Outdoor Play. Singer, Marilyn. 2012. (ENG.). 40p. (J). (gr. -1-3). 17.99 *(978-0-547-12493-3(7))* Houghton Mifflin Harcourt Publishing Co.

—Twenty-One Elephants. Bildner, Phil. 2004. (ENG.). 40p. (J). (gr. -1-3). 17.99 *(978-0-689-87011-8(6)*, Simon & Schuster Bks. For Young Readers) Simon & Schuster Bks. For Young Readers.

—Vampirina Ballerina. Pace, Anne Marie. 2012. (Vampirina Ser.). (ENG.). 40p. (J). (gr. -1-k). 14.99 *(978-1-4231-5753-3(2))* Hyperion Pr.

—Vampirina Ballerina Hosts a Sleepover. Pace, Anne Marie. 2013. (Vampirina Ser.). (ENG.). 40p. (J). (gr. -1-k). 16.99 *(978-1-4231-7570-4(0))* Hyperion Pr.

—Whose Knees Are These? Asim, Jabari. 2006. (ENG.). 20p. (J). (gr. -1 — 1). bds. 6.99 *(978-0-316-73576-6(0))* Little, Brown Bks. for Young Readers.

—Whose Toes Are Those? Asim, Jabari. 2006. (ENG.). 11p. (J). (gr. -1 — 1). bds. 6.99 *(978-0-316-73609-1(0))* Little, Brown Bks. for Young Readers.

Pham, LeUyen. All the Things I Love about You. Pham, LeUyen. 2010. (ENG.). 40p. (J). (gr. -1-3). 14.99 *(978-0-06-199029-8(9))* HarperCollins Pubs.

—Big Sister, Little Sister. Pham, LeUyen. 2005. (ENG.). 40p. (J). (gr. -1-3). 15.99 *(978-0-7868-5182-9(1))* Hyperion Pr.

—A Piece of Cake. Pham, LeUyen. 2014. (ENG.). 40p. (J). (gr. -1-3). 16.99 *(978-0-06-199264-3(X))* HarperCollins Pubs.

Pham, LeUyen, jt. illus. see Scribner, Joanne.

Pham, LeUyen, jt. illus. see Shed, Greg.

Pham, Thien. Level Up. Yang, Gene Luen. 2011. (ENG.). 160p. (YA). (gr. 7). 19.99 *(978-1-59643-714-2(6))*; pap. 16.99 *(978-1-59643-235-2(7))* Roaring Brook Pr. (First Second Bks.).

Pham, Thien. Sumo. Pham, Thien. 2012. (ENG.). 112p. (YA). (gr. 9-12). pap. 14.99 *(978-1-59643-581-0(X)*, First Second Bks.) Roaring Brook Pr.

Pham, Xuan. The Turtle Who Couldn't Swim. Petersen, Pat. 2012. 28p. 24.95 *(978-1-4626-8615-5(X))*; pap. 24.95 *(978-1-4626-4847-4(9))* America Star Bks.

Phan, Henry, et al. When Watute Wants Some Water. Sarja, Jennifer. 2005. 36p. (J). (gr. -1-3). 20.00 *(978-0-9773451-0-6(6))* Youth Inkwell Publishing.

Phatak, Bhakti. Basava & the Dots of Fire. Chadha, Radhika. 2005. 24p. (J). *(978-81-8146-165-0(7))* Tulika Pubs.

Phelan, Matt. Always. Stott, Ann. 2008. (ENG.). 32p. (J). (gr. k-k). 15.99 *(978-0-7636-3232-8(5))* Candlewick Pr.

—A Box Full of Kittens. Manzano, Sonia. 2007. (ENG.). 40p. (J). (gr. -1-3). 17.99 *(978-0-689-83089-1(0)*, Atheneum Bks. for Young Readers) Simon & Schuster Children's Publishing.

—Flora's Very Windy Day. Birdsall, Jeanne. (ENG.). 32p. (J). (gr. -1-3). 2013. pap. 6.99 *(978-0-547-99485-7(0))*; 2010. 16.99 *(978-0-618-98676-7(6))* Houghton Mifflin Harcourt Publishing Co.

—The Higher Power of Lucky. Patron, Susan. (ENG.). (J). (gr. 4-6). 2008. 160p. pap. 7.99 *(978-1-4169-7557-1(8)*, Atheneum Bks. for Young Readers); 2006. 144p. 17.99 *(978-1-4169-0194-5(9)*, Atheneum/Richard Jackson Bks.) Simon & Schuster Children's Publishing.

—I'll Be There. Stott, Ann. 2011. (ENG.). 32p. (J). (gr. -1-2). 14.99 *(978-0-7636-4711-7(X))* Candlewick Pr.

—Lucky Breaks. Patron, Susan. (ENG.). (J). (gr. 3-7). 2010. 208p. pap. 7.99 *(978-1-4169-9772-6(5))*; 2009. 192p. 16.99 *(978-1-4169-3998-6(9))* Simon & Schuster Children's Publishing. (Atheneum Bks. for Young Readers).

—Marilyn's Monster. Knudsen, Michelle. 2015. (ENG.). 40p. (J). (gr. -1-3). 15.99 *(978-0-7636-6011-6(6))* Candlewick Pr.

—Miss Emily. Muten, Burleigh. 2014. (ENG.). 144p. (J). (gr. 2-5). 15.99 *(978-0-7636-5734-5(4))* Candlewick Pr.

—The New Girl... & Me. Robbins, Jacqui. 2006. (ENG.). 32p. (J). (gr. -1-2). 17.99 *(978-0-689-86468-1(X)*, Atheneum/Richard Jackson Bks.) Simon & Schuster Children's Publishing.

—The Seven Wonders of Sassafras Springs. Birney, Betty G. 2007. 210p. 17.00 *(978-0-7569-8075-7(5))* Perfection Learning Corp.

—The Seven Wonders of Sassafras Springs. Birney, Betty G. (ENG.). 224p. (J). (gr. 3-7). 2007. pap. 7.99 *(978-1-4169-3489-9(8))*; 2005. 16.95 *(978-0-689-87136-8(8))* Simon & Schuster Children's Publishing. (Atheneum Bks. for Young Readers).

—Spilling Ink: A Young Writer's Handbook. Potter, Ellen & Mazer, Anne. 2010. (ENG.). 288p. (J). (gr. 4-9). pap., instr.'s hndbk. ed. 9.99 *(978-1-59643-628-2(X))* Square Fish.

—Two of a Kind. Robbins, Jacqui. 2009. (ENG.). 32p. (J). (gr. -1-2). 16.99 *(978-1-4169-2437-1(X)*, Atheneum Bks. for Young Readers) Simon & Schuster Children's Publishing.

—Very Hairy Bear. Schertle, Alice. ed. 2012. lib. bdg. 17.20 *(978-0-606-26605-5(4)*, Turtleback) Turtleback Bks.

—Xander's Panda Party. Park, Linda Sue. 2013. (ENG.). 40p. (J). (gr. -1-3). 16.99 *(978-0-547-55865-3(1))* Houghton Mifflin Harcourt Publishing Co.

Phelan, Matt. Around the World. Phelan, Matt. (ENG.). 240p. (J). (gr. 4-7). 2014. pap. 12.99 *(978-0-7636-6925-6(3))*; 2011. 24.99 *(978-0-7636-3619-7(3))* Candlewick Pr.

—Bluffton. Phelan, Matt. 2013. (ENG.). 240p. (J). (gr. 4-7). 22.99 *(978-0-7636-5079-7(X))* Candlewick Pr.

—Druthers. Phelan, Matt. 2014. (ENG.). 32p. (J). (-k). 15.99 *(978-0-7636-5955-4(X))* Candlewick Pr.

—The Storm in the Barn. Phelan, Matt. 2009. (ENG.). 208p. (J). (gr. 5). 24.99 *(978-0-7636-3618-0(5))* Candlewick Pr.

Phelan, Matt, jt. illus. see Matt, Phelan.

Phelan, Matt, jt. illus. see Trueman, Matthew.

Phelan, Michele-lee. Mythic Oracle: Wisdom of the Ancient Greek Pantheon. Mellado, Carisa. 2012. (ENG.). 160p. (YA). (gr. 7). pap. 17.99 *(978-1-58270-325-1(6))* Simon Pulse/Beyond Words.

Phelan, Nicky. I'm Proud to Be Me: Poems for Children & Their Parents. Fitzmaurice, Gabriel. 2005. (ENG.). 96p. (J). pap. 12.95 *(978-1-85635-474-5(1))* Mercier Pr., Ltd., The IRL. Dist: Dufour Editions, Inc.

—Penny in Space. O'Hely, Eileen. 2009. (ENG.). 225p. (J). pap. 14.95 *(978-1-85635-571-1(3))* Mercier Pr., Ltd., The IRL. Dist: Dufour Editions, Inc.

—Penny on Safari. O'Hely, Eileen. 2010. (ENG.). 192p. (J). pap. 15.95 *(978-1-85635-572-8(1))* Mercier Pr., Ltd., The IRL. Dist: Dufour Editions, Inc.

—Penny the Pencil. O'Hely, Eileen. 2005. (ENG.). 200p. (J). pap. 13.95 *(978-1-85635-475-2(X))* Mercier Pr., Ltd., The IRL. Dist: Dufour Editions, Inc.

—Splat: And Other Great Poems. Fitzmaurice, Gabriel & Macdonald, Stella. 2012. (ENG.). 96p. (J). pap. 13.95 *(978-1-85635-953-5(0))* Mercier Pr., Ltd., The IRL. Dist: Dufour Editions, Inc.

Phelps Williams, Janice. Still Her Spirit Sings: One Dog's Love, Lessons, Life & Legacy. 2010. 32p. (J). (gr. k-2). 16.95 *(978-0-9760220-1-5(X))* Kidzpoetz Publishing.

Phil Brannan & Sunni Brannan. Juanita's Flowers. Sally Spencer. 2009. 32p. pap. 14.49 *(978-1-4389-4841-6(7))* AuthorHouse.

Philbrick, Katie, jt. illus. see Stockton, Greta.

Philip Dadd. William Tell Told Again - Illustrated in Color. Wodehouse, P. G. 2009. 76p. pap. 14.95 *(978-1-60386-208-0(0)*, Watchmaker Publishing) Wexford College Pr.

Philipp, Cathy, et al, photos by. On the Trail Again: Malibu to Santa Barbara, 1. Philipp, Cathy. 2004. 252p. per. *(978-0-9655848-1-4(X))* Philipp, Cathy Publishing.

Philippe, Dupasquier. A Country Far Away. Gray, Nigel. 2012. 32p. pap. *(978-0-9808760-2-4(8))* Vivid Publishing.

Philips, Chad, photos by. Help Me Learn Addition. Marzollo, Jean. 2013. (ENG., 32p. (J). pap. 6.99 *(978-0-8234-2759-8(5))* Holiday Hse., Inc.

—Help Me Learn Subtraction. Marzollo, Jean. 2013. (ENG., 32p. (J). pap. 6.99 *(978-0-8234-2822-9(2))* Holiday Hse., Inc.

Philips, Mike. Collins Big Cat - Own Goal. MacPhail, Catherine. 2015. (Collins Big Cat Ser.). (ENG.). 24p. pap. 7.95 ***(978-0-00-759114-5(4))*** HarperCollins Pubs. Ltd. GBR. Dist: Independent Pubs. Group.

Phillippi, Faith, jt. illus. see Beatty, Connie.

Phillips. Bubbie's Baby. Phillips, . 2006. 28p. (J). 14.99 *(978-0-9774552-0-1(3))* Danza Pubns.

Phillips, Alan, pseud. The Sleepover Surprise. Cushing, Mims. 2010. 24p. pap. 12.95 *(978-1-936343-01-0(0))* Peppertree Pr., The.

Phillips, Andrea, jt. illus. see Phillips, Elizabeth.

Phillips, Chad. Help Me Learn Numbers 0-20. Phillips, Chad, photos by. Marzollo, Jean. 2011. (ENG.). 32p. (J). 15.95 *(978-0-8234-2334-7(4))* Holiday Hse., Inc.

—Help Me Learn Subtraction. Phillips, Chad, photos by. Marzollo, Jean. 2012. (ENG.). 32p. (J). 15.95 *(978-0-8234-2401-6(4))* Holiday Hse., Inc.

Phillips, Chad, photos by. Help Me Learn Addition. Marzollo, Jean. 2012. (ENG., 32p. (J). 15.95 *(978-0-8234-2398-9(0))* Holiday Hse., Inc.

—Help Me Learn Numbers 0-20. Marzollo, Jean. 2012. (ENG., 32p. (J). (gr. -1-1). pap. 6.99 *(978-0-8234-2542-6(8))* Holiday Hse., Inc.

Phillips, Craig. The Alchemist War, 1 vol. Seven, John. 2013. (Time-Tripping Faradays Ser.). (ENG.). 160p. (gr. 4-5). 9.95 *(978-1-62370-011-9(6))*; (YA). pap. 5.95 *(978-1-4342-6438-1(6))*; (gr. 4-5). lib. bdg. 25.32 *(978-1-4342-6028-4(3))* Stone Arch Bks.

—Apollo & the Battle of the Birds. Holub, Joan & Williams, Suzanne. 2014. (Heroes in Training Ser.: 6). (ENG.). 128p. (J). (gr. 1-4). 16.99 *(978-1-4424-8846-5(8))*; pap. 5.99 *(978-1-4424-8845-8(X))* Simon & Schuster/Paula Wiseman Bks. (Simon & Schuster/Paula Wiseman Bks.).

—Ares & the Spear of Fear. Holub, Joan & Williams, Suzanne. 2014. (Heroes in Training Ser.: 7). (ENG.). 112p. (J). (gr. 1-4). pap. 5.99 *(978-1-4424-8848-9(4)*, Simon & Schuster/Paula Wiseman Bks.) Simon & Schuster/Paula Wiseman Bks.

—Bogus to Bubbly: An Insider's Guide to the World of Uglies. Westerfeld, Scott. 2008. (Uglies Ser.). (ENG.). 208p. (YA). (gr. 7). pap. 8.99 *(978-1-4169-7436-9(9)*, Simon Pulse) Simon Pulse.

—Chasing Shadows. Avasthi, Swati. 2013. (ENG.). 320p. (gr. 9). (J). 17.99 *(978-0-375-86342-4(7))*; (YA). lib. bdg. 20.99 *(978-0-375-96341-4(3))* Random Hse. Children's Bks. (Knopf Bks. for Young Readers).

—Chasing Shadows. Avasthi, Swati. 2015. (ENG.). 336p. (YA). (gr. 9). pap. 10.99 *(978-0-375-86343-1(5))* Random Hse., Inc.

—Crius & the Fright of Night. Holub, Joan & Williams, Suzanne. 2015. (Heroes in Training Ser.: 9). (ENG.). 96p. (J). (gr. 1-4). pap. 5.99 *(978-1-4814-3506-2(X)*, Simon & Schuster/Paula Wiseman Bks.) Simon & Schuster/Paula Wiseman Bks.

—Disguised & Dangerous. Mason, Jane B. & Hines-Stephens, Sarah. 2011. 92p. (J). *(978-0-545-37469-9(3))* Scholastic, Inc.

—The Dragon of Rome, 1 vol. Seven, John. 2013. (Time-Tripping Faradays Ser.). (ENG.). 160p. (gr. 4-5). 9.95 *(978-1-62370-012-6(4))*; lib. bdg. 25.32 *(978-1-4342-6029-1(1))* Stone Arch Bks.

—Dragon's Lair. West, Tracey. 2010. (Hiro's Quest Ser.: 4). (ENG.). 96p. (J). (gr. 2-5). 4.99 *(978-0-545-21477-3(7)*, Scholastic Paperbacks) Scholastic, Inc.

—Enemy Rising. West, Tracey. 2010. (Hiro's Quest Ser.: 1). (ENG.). 96p. (J). (gr. 2-5). 4.99 *(978-0-545-16288-3(2)*, Scholastic Paperbacks) Scholastic, Inc.

—Hades & the Helm of Darkness. Holub, Joan & Williams, Suzanne. 2013. (Heroes in Training Ser.: 3). (ENG.). 128p. (J). (gr. 1-4). 15.99 *(978-1-4424-5725-6(2))*; pap. 5.99 *(978-1-4424-5267-1(6))* Simon & Schuster/Paula Wiseman Bks. (Simon & Schuster/Paula Wiseman Bks.).

—Hyperion & the Great Balls of Fire. Holub, Joan & Williams, Suzanne. 2013. (Heroes in Training Ser.: 4). (ENG.). 144p. (J). (gr. 1-4). 16.99 *(978-1-4424-5803-1(8))*; pap. 5.99 *(978-1-4424-5269-5(2))* Simon & Schuster/Paula Wiseman Bks. (Simon & Schuster/Paula Wiseman Bks.).

—Let Sleeping Dogs Spy. Mason, Jane B. & Hines-Stephens, Sarah. 2012. 91p. (J). pap. *(978-0-545-37470-5(7))* Scholastic, Inc.

—Poseidon & the Sea of Fury. Holub, Joan & Williams, Suzanne. 2012. (Heroes in Training Ser.: 2). (ENG.). 128p. (J). (gr. 1-4). 15.99 *(978-1-4424-5798-0(8))*; pap. 5.99 *(978-1-4424-5265-7(X))* Simon & Schuster/Paula Wiseman Bks. (Simon & Schuster/Paula Wiseman Bks.).

—Sidewayz Glory. Strasser, Todd. 2006. (DriftX Ser.: 3). (ENG.). 208p. (YA). (gr. 9-12). pap. 10.99 *(978-1-4169-0583-7(9)*, Simon Pulse) Simon Pulse.

—Slide or Die. Strasser, Todd. 2006. (DriftX Ser.: 1). (ENG.). 224p. (YA). (gr. 9-18). pap. 10.99 *(978-1-4169-0581-3(2)*, Simon & Schuster/Paula Wiseman Bks.) Simon & Schuster/Paula Wiseman Bks.

—The Time-Tripping Faradays, 1 vol. Seven, John. (Time-Tripping Faradays Ser.). (ENG.). 160p. (gr. 4-5). 2014. 50.65 *(978-1-4342-9473-9(0))*; 2013. 50.65 *(978-1-4342-8994-0(X))* Stone Arch Bks.

—Typhon & the Winds of Destruction. Holub, Joan & Williams, Suzanne. 2013. (Heroes in Training Ser.: 5). (ENG.). 112p. (J). (gr. 1-4). 15.99 *(978-1-4424-8844-1(1))*; pap.

5.99 *(978-1-4424-8842-7(5))* Simon & Schuster/Paula Wiseman Bks. (Simon & Schuster/Paula Wiseman Bks.).
—Zeus & the Thunderbolt of Doom. Holub, Joan & Williams, Suzanne. 2012. (Heroes in Training Ser.: 1). (ENG.). 112p. (J). (gr. 1-4). 16.99 *(978-1-4424-5787-4(2))*; pap. 5.99 *(978-1-4424-5263-3(3))* Simon & Schuster/Paula Wiseman Bks. (Simon & Schuster/Paula Wiseman Bks.).
Phillips, Craig, jt. illus. see Impey, Allison.
Phillips, Dave. Magic Marks the Spot. Carlson, Caroline. 2013. (ENG.). 368p. (J). pap. *(978-0-06-231467-3(X))* Harper & Row Ltd.
—Magic Marks the Spot. Carlson, Caroline. (Very Nearly Honorable League of Pirates Ser.: 1). (ENG.). (J). (gr. 3-7). 2014. 384p. pap. 6.99 *(978-0-06-219435-0(6))*; 2013. 368p. 16.99 *(978-0-06-219434-3(8))* HarperCollins Pubs.
—Palace of Dreams. Epstein, Adam Jay & Jacobson, Andrew. (Familiars Ser.: 4). (ENG.). 336p. (J). (gr. 3-7). 2015. pap. 6.99 *(978-0-06-212031-1(X))*; No. 4. 2013. 16.99 *(978-0-06-212029-8(8))* HarperCollins Pubs.
Phillips, Dave. The Terror of the Southlands. Carlson, Caroline. 2014. (ENG.). 336p. (J). pap. ***(978-0-06-236178-3(3))*** Harper & Row Ltd.
—The Terror of the Southlands. Carlson, Caroline. 2015. (Very Nearly Honorable League of Pirates Ser.: 2). (ENG.). 352p. (J). (gr. 3-7). pap. 6.99 ***(978-0-06-219437-4(2))*** HarperCollins Pubs.
Phillips, Dave. The Very Nearly Honorable League of Pirates - The Terror of the Southlands. Carlson, Caroline. 2014. (Very Nearly Honorable League of Pirates Ser.: 2). (ENG.). 336p. (J). (gr. 3-7). 16.99 *(978-0-06-219436-7(4))* HarperCollins Pubs.
Phillips, Dawn. Alexis & Ralph the Dragon. Kowalski, Bernard. 2009. 32p. pap. 24.95 *(978-1-60749-167-5(2))* America Star Bks.
Phillips, Deborah. The Adventures of Pelican Mcfeet: The Big Lumpy Green Monster. Brady, Carolyn. 2008. 32p. pap. 16.95 *(978-1-4389-3539-3(0))* AuthorHouse.
Phillips-Duke, Barbara Jean & Duke, Barbara. Stop, Drop, & Chill. Scholastic, Inc. Staff & Barnes, Derrick D. 2004. (Just for You Ser.). (ENG.). 32p. pap. 3.99 *(978-0-439-56870-8(6)*, Teaching Resources) Scholastic, Inc.
Phillips, Elizabeth & Phillips, Andrea. The Blueberry Princess. Phillips, Elizabeth. 2008. 25p. pap. 24.95 *(978-1-60672-097-4(X))* America Star Bks.
Phillips, Gary. My Body Is Mine! Osilaja, Peter Deji. 2007. (J). (gr. k-2). pap. 8.95 *(978-1-884413-84-1(6))*; lib. bdg. 14.95 *(978-1-884413-83-4(8))* Kidsafety of America.
Phillips, Gary R. New Old Shoes. Blessing, Charlotte. 2009. (ENG.). 32p. (J). (gr. k-3). 16.95 *(978-0-9792035-6-5(2))* Pleasant St. Pr.
—Ocean Hide & Seek, 1 vol. Kramer, Jennifer Evans. 2009. (ENG.). 32p. (J). (gr. -1-3). 16.95 *(978-1-934359-91-4(2))*; pap. 8.95 *(978-1-60718-036-4(7))* Arbordale Publishing.
Phillips, Hope Ann. Show & Tell. Taylor, Myonna. 2012. 32p. 24.95 *(978-1-4626-7798-6(3))* America Star Bks.
Phillips, Ian. The Kids' Money Book. McGillian, Jamie Kyle. 2006. 96p. (J). (gr. 4-8). reprint ed. 18.00 *(978-0-7567-9900-7(7))* DIANE Publishing Co.
Phillips, Jane B. Big Book of Fun: Creative Learning Activities for Home & School. Haas, Carolyn B. 2nd ed. 2003. 288p. (J). (gr. -1-7). reprint ed. pap. 14.95 *(978-1-55652-020-4(4))* Chicago Review Pr., Inc.
Phillips, Jillian. Animals Everywhere. Ikids Staff. 2010. (ENG.). 20p. (J). (gr. -1-17). 6.99 *(978-1-60169-006-7(1))* Innovative Kids.
—Green Start - Little Helpers. Ikids Staff. 2010. (ENG.). 20p. (J). (gr. -1-17). 6.99 *(978-1-60169-007-4(X))* Innovative Kids.
—One Tree. Bockol, Leslie & Ikids Staff. 2009. (ENG.). 20p. (J). (gr. -1-1). 6.99 *(978-1-58476-811-1(8))* Innovative Kids.
Phillips, Laverne. Grandma, Will You Clap! Mandelkom, Carole. 2013. 16p. pap. 10.95 *(978-1-61493-196-6(8))* Peppertree Pr., The.
Phillips, Linda T. Red Book Pets Vets & Snakes. Bjornsen, Holly. 2011. 51p. (YA). pap. 16.95 *(978-0-9828950-1-6(1))* Entry Way Publishing.
Phillips, Louise. I Heard a Little Baa. MacLeod, Elizabeth. 2007. (ENG.). 30p. (J). bds. 7.95 *(978-1-55453-179-0(9))* Kids Can Pr., Ltd. CAN. Dist: Univ. of Toronto Pr.
Phillips, Matt. Doc Block. Marx, David F. 2006. (Reader's Clubhouse Level 1 Reader Ser.). (ENG.). 24p. (J). (gr. 1-4). pap. 3.99 *(978-0-7641-3288-9(1))* Barron's Educational Series, Inc.
—The Mega-Deluxe Capitalization Machine. Martin, Justin McCory. 2004. (Grammar Tales Ser.). (ENG.). 16p. (J). (gr. 3-7). pap. 3.25 *(978-0-439-45821-4(8))* Scholastic, Inc.
—What Can I Be? Meister, Cari. 2003. (Rookie Readers Ser.). 24p. (J). 19.50 *(978-0-516-22876-1(5)*, Children's Pr.) Scholastic Library Publishing.
Phillips, Mike. Bad Kids Vol. 1: The Worst Behaved Children in History, 1. Robinson, Tony. unabr. ed. 2009. (ENG.). 144p. 28.50 *(978-0-230-73787-7(0)*, Macmillan) Pan Macmillan GBR. Dist: Trans-Atlantic Pubns., Inc.
—Circles. Bailey, Gerry & Law, Felicia. 2014. (ENG.). 32p. (J). *(978-0-7787-0507-9(2))* Crabtree Publishing Co.
—The Gargling Gorilla. Mahy, Margaret. 2007. (Collins Big Cat Ser.). (ENG.). 40p. (J). pap. 8.99 *(978-0-00-723089-1(3))* HarperCollins Pubs. Ltd. GBR. Dist: Independent Pubs. Group.
—Goat in a Boat. Grindley, Sally. 2011. (My Phonics Readers: Level 3 Ser.). 24p. (J). (gr. -1-1). 24.25 *(978-1-84898-515-5(0))* Sea-To-Sea Pubns.
—Lintball Leo's Not-So-Stupid Questions about Your Body, 1 vol. Larimore, Walt et al. 2003. (ENG.). 128p. (J). pap. 7.99 *(978-0-310-70545-1(2))* Zonderkidz.
—Poppy the Pirate Dog. Kessler, Liz. (Candlewick Sparks Ser.). (ENG.). 64p. (J). (gr. k-4). 2015. pap. 3.99 *(978-0-7636-7661-2(6))*; 2013. 14.99 *(978-0-7636-6569-2(X))* Candlewick Pr.
—Poppy the Pirate Dog & the Missing Treasure. Kessler, Liz. 2015. (ENG.). 64p. (J). (gr. k-4). 14.99 *(978-0-7636-7497-7(4))* Candlewick Pr.
Phillips, Mike. Poppy the Pirate Dog's New Shipmate. Kessler, Liz. (Candlewick Sparks Ser.). (ENG.). 64p. (J). (gr. k-4). 2015. pap. 3.99 ***(978-0-7636-8031-2(1))***; 2014. 14.99 *(978-0-7636-6751-1(X))* Candlewick Pr.
Phillips, Mike. Snail Trail. Grindley, Sally. 2011. (My Phonics Readers: Level 3 Ser.). 24p. (J). (gr. -1-1). 24.25 *(978-1-84898-512-4(6))* Sea-To-Sea Pubns.
—Spheres. Bailey, Gerry & Law, Felicia. 2014. (ENG.). 32p. (J). lib. bdg. *(978-0-7787-0510-9(2))* Crabtree Publishing Co.
—Stone Age Geometry - Circles. Bailey, Gerry & Law, Felicia. 2014. (Stone Age Geometry Ser.). (ENG.). 32p. (J). pap. *(978-0-7787-0513-0(7))* Crabtree Publishing Co.
—Stone Age Geometry - Cubes. Bailey, Gerry & Law, Felicia. 2014. (Stone Age Geometry Ser.). (ENG.). 32p. (J). *(978-0-7787-0508-6(0))*; pap. *(978-0-7787-0514-7(5))* Crabtree Publishing Co.
—Stone Age Geometry - Lines. Bailey, Gerry & Law, Felicia. 2014. (Stone Age Geometry Ser.). (ENG.). 32p. (J). *(978-0-7787-0509-3(9))*; pap. *(978-0-7787-0515-4(3))* Crabtree Publishing Co.
—Stone Age Geometry - Squares. Bailey, Gerry & Law, Felicia. 2014. (Stone Age Geometry Ser.). (ENG.). 32p. (J). *(978-0-7787-0511-6(0))*; pap. *(978-0-7787-0517-8(X))* Crabtree Publishing Co.
—Stone Age Geometry -Triangles. Bailey, Gerry & Law, Felicia. 2014. (Stone Age Geometry Ser.). (ENG.). 32p. (J). lib. bdg. *(978-0-7787-0512-3(9))* Crabtree Publishing Co.
—Stuff That Scares Your Pants Off! The Science Scoop on More Than 30 Terrifying Phenomena! Murphy, Glenn. 2011. (ENG.). 192p. (J). (gr. 3-7). pap. 16.99 *(978-1-59643-633-6(6))* Roaring Brook Pr.
—Why Is Snot Green? And Other Extremely Important Questions (And Answers) Murphy, Glenn. 2009. (ENG.). 240p. (J). (gr. 3-7). pap. 11.99 *(978-1-59643-500-1(3))* Square Fish.
—The World's Best Book: The Spookiest, Smelliest, Wildest, Oldest, Weirdest, Brainiest, & Funniest Facts. Payne, Jan. 2009. (ENG.). 256p. (J). (gr. 3-18). 12.95 *(978-0-7624-3755-9(3)*, Running Pr. Kids) Running Pr. Bk. Pubs.
—Worst Children's Jobs in History. Robinson, Tony. 3rd unabr. ed. 2005. (ENG.). 112p. pap. 12.99 *(978-0-330-44286-2(4))* Macmillan Pubs., Ltd. GBR. Dist: Independent Pubs. Group.
Phillips, Mike. Esos Estupidos Ordenadores. Phillips, Mike. Coleman, Michael. (Coleccion Esa Gran Cultura).Tr. of Crashing Computers. (SPA.). 160p. (YA). (gr. 5-8). 7.96 *(978-84-272-2136-9(3))* Molino, Editorial ESP. Dist: Lectorum Pubns., Inc.
Phillips, Mike & Brooks, Rosie. Cowries, Coins, Credit: The History of Money, 1 vol. Bailey, Gerry & Law, Felicia. 2006. (My Money Ser.). (ENG.). 24p. (gr. 4-6). 30.65 *(978-0-7565-1676-5(5)*, CPB Grades 4-8) Compass Point Bks.
—Get Rich Quick? Earning Money, 1 vol. Bailey, Gerry & Law, Felicia. 2006. (My Money Ser.). (ENG.). 24p. (gr. 4-6). 30.65 *(978-0-7565-1674-1(9)*, CPB Grades 4-8) Compass Point Bks.
—Money, It's Our Job: Money Careers, 1 vol. Bailey, Gerry & Law, Felicia. 2006. (My Money Ser.). (ENG.). 24p. (gr. 4-6). 30.65 *(978-0-7565-1675-8(7)*, CPB Grades 4-8) Compass Point Bks.
—What's It All Worth? The Value of Money, 1 vol. Bailey, Gerry & Law, Felicia. 2006. (My Money Ser.). (ENG.). 24p. (gr. 4-6). 30.65 *(978-0-7565-1673-4(0)*, CPB Grades 4-8) Compass Point Bks.
Phillips, Rachael. Christian Stories. Ganeri, Anita. 2014. (Storyteller Ser.). (ENG.). 32p. (J). (gr. 2-4). pap. 10.99 *(978-1-78388-007-2(4))* Tulip Books GBR. Dist: Independent Pubs. Group.
—The Easter Story. Ganeri, Anita. 2003. (Festival Stories Ser.). 24p. (J). pap. *(978-0-237-52475-3(9))* Evans Brothers, Ltd.
—The Easter Story. Ganeri, Anita. 2003. (Festival Stories Ser.). (ENG.). 24p. (J). pap. 10.99 *(978-0-237-52531-6(3))* Evans Brothers, Ltd. GBR. Dist: Independent Pubs. Group.
—Hindu Stories. Ganeri, Anita. 2014. (Storyteller Ser.). (ENG.). 32p. (J). (gr. 2-4). pap. 10.99 *(978-1-78388-008-9(2))* Tulip Books GBR. Dist: Independent Pubs. Group.
—Islamic Stories. Ganeri, Anita. 2014. (Storyteller Ser.). (ENG.). 32p. (J). (gr. 2-4). pap. 10.99 *(978-1-78388-009-6(0))* Tulip Books GBR. Dist: Independent Pubs. Group.
—The Passover Story. Ganeri, Anita. 2004. (Holiday Stories Ser.). (J). lib. bdg. 22.80 *(978-1-58340-491-1(0))* Black Rabbit Bks.
—Sikh Stories. Ganeri, Anita. 2003. (Storyteller Ser.). 30p. (J). *(978-0-237-52037-3(0))* Evans Brothers, Ltd.
—Sikh Stories. Ganeri, Anita. 2014. (Storyteller Ser.). (ENG.). 32p. (J). (gr. 2-4). pap. 10.99 *(978-1-78388-011-9(2))* Tulip Books GBR. Dist: Independent Pubs. Group.
Phillips, Sean. Kingpin: Thug. Jones, Bruce. Youngquist, Jeff, ed. 2004. (Spider-Man Ser.). 160p. pap. 14.99 *(978-0-7851-1225-9(1))* Marvel Worldwide, Inc.
Phillips, Zelmer. Live Performance, Vol. 1. Burroughs, William S. Hoffman, Kathelin, ed. (C). 12.95 incl. audio *(978-0-929856-00-1(7))* Caravan of Dreams Productions.
Phillipson, Andy, jt. illus. see Tucker, Marianne.
Philpot, Graham. The Emperor & the Nightingale. 2007. (First Reading Level 4 Ser.). 48p. (J). (gr. -1-3). 8.99 *(978-0-7945-1614-7(9)*, Usborne) EDC Publishing.
—The Fish That Talked. 2008. (Usborne First Reading: Level 3 Ser.). 48p. (J). 8.99 *(978-0-7945-1945-2(8)*, Usborne) EDC Publishing.
—Hansel & Gretel. 2007. (First Fairy Tales Ser.). 32p. (J). (gr. -1-3). lib. bdg. 28.50 *(978-1-59771-075-6(X))* Sea-To-Sea Pubns.
—Tales from Pinocchio. Rossendale, Helen. 2011. (10-Minute Bedtime Stories Ser.). (ENG.). 88p. (J). (gr. k-4). 14.99 *(978-1-84365-147-5(5)*, Pavilion Children's Books) Pavilion Bks. GBR. Dist: Independent Pubs. Group.
Philpot, Heather. Caperucita Roja. Boase, Wendy. Puncel, Maria, tr. (Primeros Cuentos Ser.). (SPA.). 28p. (J). (gr. k-3). pap. 7.95 *(978-1-56014-458-8(0))* Santillana USA Publishing Co., Inc.
Philpott, Keith. Tiger Pups. Harvey, Tom et al. 2009. 32p. (J). (gr. k-2). lib. bdg. 18.89 *(978-0-06-177314-3(X))*; (ENG.). 17.99 *(978-0-06-177309-9(3)*, Collins) HarperCollins Pubs.
Phinn, Gervase. Who Am I? Phinn, Gervase. 2012. (Andersen Press Picture Bks). (ENG.). 32p. (J). (gr. -1-3). 16.95 *(978-0-7613-8996-5(2))* Lerner Publishing Group.
Phipps, Bebe. An Old Salem Christmas, 1840. Smith, Karen Cecil. 2008. (J). 14.95 *(978-1-933251-46-2(8))* Parkway Pubs., Inc.
Phipps, Catherine Wood. Erika Flowers. Seeds of Grace. Desch, Sandra Lee. 2013. 80p. pap. 10.00 *(978-1-61170-144-9(9))* Robertson Publishing.
Phipps, Michael. War of the Black Curtain. Dashner, James. 2005. (Jimmy Fincher Saga: Bk. 4). per. 14.99 *(978-1-55517-879-6(0))* Cedar Fort, Inc./CFI Distribution.
Phoenix Books Staff. Baby's First Stories & Songs: Read, Sing, & Play. 2014. 22p. (J). bds. ***(978-1-4508-8585-0(3)***, 1450885853) Publications International, Ltd.
—Disney(r) PIXAR Cars! Can Drive! 2015. 11p. (J). bds. ***(978-1-4508-8633-8(7)***, 1450886337) Publications International, Ltd.
—Sofia the First - Sofia's Royal Day: Includes 6 Punch-Out Play Pieces. Publications International Ltd. Staff, ed. 2015. 14p. (J). bds. ***(978-1-4508-8884-4(4)***, 1450888844) Publications International, Ltd.
Phoenix Books Staff. Sofia the First Royal Picnic - Little Sound Book. 2014. 12p. (J). bds. 9.98 *(978-1-4508-7487-8(8)*, 0b73a7ef-ea68-4afb-b340-9a4f6fc740c0) Phoenix International Publications, Inc.
—Thomas' Piano Book. 2014. 14p. (J). bds. 12.98 *(978-1-4508-6584-5(4)*, 1450865844) Phoenix International Publications, Inc.
Phoenix International Staff. Baby Einstein: Little Piano Book. 2014. 12p. (J). bds. 12.98 *(978-1-4508-7546-2(7)*, 1450875467) Publications International, Ltd.
—Princess Sofia. 2012. 10p. (J). bds. 14.98 *(978-1-4508-6822-8(3)*, e41cac27-3be3-41b8-8dc5-7fb934c0ea6b) Phoenix International Publications, Inc.
—Sesame at the Zoo Look & Find. 2014. 24p. (J). 7.98 *(978-1-4508-8417-4(2)*, 1450884172) Phoenix International Publications, Inc.
—Sesame Street(r) Big Fire Truck. 2014. 10p. (J). bds. *(978-1-4508-7442-7(8)*, 88c653bc-7055-470d-ae38-8642c9dd9e9d) Phoenix International Publications, Inc.
—Thomas & Friends(r) - Thomas' Piano Book. deluxe ed. 2014. 12p. (J). bds. 17.98 *(978-1-4127-4552-9(7)*, 1412745527) Phoenix International Publications, Inc.
Phong, Ann. Going Home, Coming Home. Tran, Truong. 2003.Tr. of Ve Nha Tham Que Hu'o'Ng. (ENG & VIE.). 32p. (J). 16.95 *(978-0-89239-179-0(0))* Lee & Low Bks., Inc.
Photodisc-Getty Staff, Images, photos by. We Both Read-Being Safe. McKay, Sindy. 2003. (We Both Read Ser.). 44p. (J). (gr. 1-2). 7.99 *(978-1-891327-51-3(8))*; pap. 5.99 *(978-1-891327-52-0(6))* Treasure Bay, Inc.
PhotoDisc Staff, photos by. National Honor Roll, 13 vols. NHR Staff, ed. (YA). Vol. 5. 2005. 485p. *(978-1-932654-17-2(8))*; Vol. 5. 2004. 491p. *(978-1-932654-06-6(2))*; Vol. 6. 2005. *(978-1-932654-18-9(6))* National Honor Roll, LLC.
Platt, Robert. My Sugar Bear. Comley, Kathlyn. 2004. (J). bds. 9.99 *(978-1-4183-0001-2(2))* Christ Inspired, Inc.
Piatti, Federico. Dead Wings, 1 vol. Dahl, Michael. 2010. (Dragonblood Ser.). (ENG.). 40p. (gr. 1-3). lib. bdg. 22.65 *(978-1-4342-1926-8(7)*, Zone Bks.) Stone Arch Bks.
—Dragon Cowboy, 1 vol. Dahl, Michael. 2010. (Dragonblood Ser.). (ENG.). 40p. (gr. 1-3). lib. bdg. 22.65 *(978-1-4342-1927-5(5)*, Zone Bks.) Stone Arch Bks.
—Eye of the Monster, 1 vol. Dahl, Michael. 2010. (Dragonblood Ser.). (ENG.). 40p. (gr. 1-3). lib. bdg. 22.65 *(978-1-4342-1928-2(3)*, Zone Bks.) Stone Arch Bks.
—The Girl Who Breathed Fire. Dahl, Michael. 2010. (Dragonblood Ser.). (ENG.). 40p. (gr. 1-3). lib. bdg. 22.65 *(978-1-4342-1925-1(9)*, Zone Bks.) Stone Arch Bks.
—The Missing Fang, 1 vol. Dahl, Michael. 2010. (Dragonblood Ser.). (ENG.). 40p. (gr. 1-3). lib. bdg. 22.65 *(978-1-4342-1923-7(2)*, Zone Bks.) Stone Arch Bks.
—Wings above the Waves, 1 vol. Dahl, Michael. 2010. (Dragonblood Ser.). (ENG.). 40p. (gr. 1-3). lib. bdg. 22.65 *(978-1-4342-1924-4(0)*, Zone Bks.) Stone Arch Bks.
Piazza, Gail. The Alphabet War: A Story about Dyslexia. Robb, Diane Burton. 2004. (ENG.). 32p. (J). (gr. 2-5). 16.99 *(978-0-8075-0302-7(9))* Whitman, Albert & Co.
Pica, Steve. Beach Riddles. Doering, Jennie Spray. 2006. (Silly Millies Level 3 Ser.). (ENG.). 32p. (gr. 1-3). lib. bdg. 21.27 *(978-0-7613-2885-8(8)*, Millbrook Pr.) Lerner Publishing Group.
Picanyol. The Comic Book Bible. Matas, Toni. 2013. (ENG.). 162p. (J). (gr. k). 12.95 *(978-1-60710-788-0(0)*, Silver Dolphin Bks.) Baker & Taylor Publishing Group.
—Discovering Jesus, the Light: Children's Bible. Matas, Toni. 2010. (ENG.). 50p. pap. 14.99 *(978-1-4515-5718-3(3))* CreateSpace Independent Publishing Platform.
—Discovering Jesus, the Word: Children's Bible. Matas, Toni. 2010. (ENG.). 44p. pap. 14.99 *(978-1-4515-5396-3(X))* CreateSpace Independent Publishing Platform.
—Saint Francis of Assisi, Messenger of Peace. Matas, Toni. 2013. 64p. (J). 8.95 *(978-0-8198-7297-5(0))* Pauline Bks. & Media.
—St. Ignatius of Loyola, Leading the Way. Matas, Toni. 2013. (J). 8.95 *(978-0-8198-7298-2(9))* Pauline Bks. & Media.
Picard, Charline. Eva from Stockholm. Pellegrini, Isabelle. 2014. (AV2 Fiction Readalong Ser.: Vol. 125). (ENG.). 32p. (J). (gr. -1-3). lib. bdg. 34.28 *(978-1-4896-2265-5(9)*, AV2 by Weigl) Weigl Pubs., Inc.
Picayo, Mario & Picayo, Pablo. Four Wishes for Robbie. 2012. (J). *(978-1-934370-19-3(3))*, Campanita Bks.) Editorial Campana.
Picayo, Pablo, jt. illus. see Picayo, Mario.
Piccione, Dana. The Funny, Naughty Bunny: A Bilingual Book in English & German. Wreggelsworth, Irene. 2010. (ENG.). 102p. pap. 26.99 *(978-1-4537-2122-3(3))* CreateSpace Independent Publishing Platform.
—Help, Children! - The Monsters Kidnapped Santa Claus: Bilingual Book in English & Spanish. Wreggelsworth, Irene. ed. 2010. (ENG.). 120p. pap. 26.99 *(978-1-4537-1272-6(0))* CreateSpace Independent Publishing Platform.
Pichelli, Sara. Death of Spider-Man Fallout. Dragotta, Nick & Hickman, Jonathan. 2011. (ENG.). 136p. (YA). (gr. 8-17). 24.99 *(978-0-7851-5912-4(6))* Marvel Worldwide, Inc.
Pichelli, Sara, jt. illus. see Lashley, Ken.
Pichon, Liz. Beautiful Bananas, 1 vol. Laird, Elizabeth. 2013. (ENG.). 32p. pap. 7.95 *(978-1-56145-691-8(8))* Peachtree Pubs.
—Dave. Hendra, Sue. 2013. (ENG.). 32p. (J). (gr. -1-k). pap. 10.99 *(978-1-4449-1295-1(X))* Hodder & Stoughton GBR. Dist: Independent Pubs. Group.
—The First Christmas, 1 vol. Ellis, Gwen. 2007. 10p. (J). bds. 15.99 *(978-0-8254-5538-4(3))* Kregel Pubns.
—Red Riding Hood & the Sweet Little Wolf. Mortimer, Rachael. 2013. 32p. 12.95 *(978-1-58925-117-5(2))* Tiger Tales.
—Spinderella. Donaldson, Julia. 2005. (Blue Go Bananas Ser.). (ENG.). 48p. (J). (gr. 1-2). lib. bdg. *(978-0-7787-2628-9(2))* Crabtree Publishing Co.
—The Three Billy Goats Fluff. Mortimer, Rachael. 2013. (ENG.). 32p. (J). (gr. -1-2). pap. 7.95 *(978-1-58925-439-8(2))* Tiger Tales.
—Three Billy Goats Fluff. Mortimer, Rachael. 2011. 36p. 15.95 *(978-1-58925-101-4(6))* Tiger Tales.
Pichon, Liz. Bored Bill. Pichon, Liz. 2006. 32p. (J). (gr. -1-3). 15.95 *(978-1-58925-053-6(2))* Tiger Tales.
—The Brilliant World of Tom Gates: Read It & Go Ha! Ha! Ha! Pichon, Liz. 2014. (Tom Gates Ser.: 1). (ENG.). 256p. (J). (gr. 3-7). 12.99 *(978-0-7636-7472-4(9))* Candlewick Pr.
—Everything's Amazing (Sort Of) Pichon, Liz. 2015. (Tom Gates Ser.: 3). (ENG.). 416p. (J). (gr. 3-7). 12.99 *(978-0-7636-7473-1(7))* Candlewick Pr.
—The Three Horrid Little Pigs. Pichon, Liz. 2008. 32p. (J). (gr. -1-2). 15.95 *(978-1-58925-077-2(X))* Tiger Tales.
—Tom Gates: Excellent Excuses (And Other Good Stuff) Pichon, Liz. 2015. (Tom Gates Ser.: 2). (ENG.). 352p. (J). (gr. 3-7). 12.99 *(978-0-7636-7474-8(5))* Candlewick Pr.
Pichon, Liz. Beautiful Bananas. Pichon, Liz, tr. Laird, Elizabeth. 2004. (ENG.). 32p. (J). 15.95 *(978-1-56145-305-4(6))* Peachtree Pubs.
Pichon, Liz, jt. illus. see Ursell, Martin.
Picini, Frank. Robots. Gifford, Clive. 2008. (ENG.). 32p. (J). (gr. 3-9). 21.99 *(978-1-4169-6414-8(2)*, Atheneum Bks. for Young Readers) Simon & Schuster Children's Publishing.
Pickering, Jimmy. Araminta Spookie: The Sword in the Grotto. Sage, Angie. 2006. (Araminta Spookie Ser.: Bk. 2). 160p. (J). (gr. 2-5). 8.99 *(978-0-06-077484-4(3)*, Tegen, Katherine Bks) HarperCollins Pubs.
—Bubble Trouble. Krensky, Stephen. 2004. (Ready-to-Read Ser.). 32p. (J). (gr. -1-1). lib. bdg. 11.80 *(978-0-613-88999-5(1)*, Turtleback) Turtleback Bks.
—Frognapped. Sage, Angie. (Araminta Spookie Ser.: 3). (J). (gr. 2-5). 2008. (ENG.). 224p. pap. 6.99 *(978-0-06-077489-9(4))*; 2007. 128p. 8.99 *(978-0-06-077487-5(8))*; 2007. 208p. lib. bdg. 14.89 *(978-0-06-077488-2(6))* HarperCollins Pubs. (Tegen, Katherine Bks).
—Ghostsitters. Sage, Angie. (Araminta Spookie Ser.: 5). (ENG.). 224p. (J). (gr. 1-5). 2009. pap. 4.99 *(978-0-06-144925-3(3))*; 2008. 8.99 *(978-0-06-144922-2(9))* HarperCollins Pubs. (Tegen, Katherine Bks).
—My Haunted House. Sage, Angie. (Araminta Spookie Ser.: 1). (ENG.). (J). (gr. 2-5). 2008. 160p. pap. 5.99 *(978-0-06-077483-7(5))*; 2006. 144p. 8.99 *(978-0-06-077481-3(9))* HarperCollins Pubs. (Tegen, Katherine Bks).
—Shivery Shades of Halloween. Siddals, Mary McKenna. 2014. (ENG.). 32p. (J). (-k). lib. bdg. 15.99 *(978-0-375-97181-5(5)*, Random Hse. Bks. for Young Readers) Random Hse. Children's Bks.
—Sloop John B: A Pirate's Tale. Jardine, Alan. 2005. (ENG.). 32p. (J). (gr. 4-7). 17.95 *(978-1-59687-181-6(4))* IBks., Inc.
—Sloop John B: A Pirate's Tale. Jardine, Alan. 2005. 32p. 17.95 *(978-0-689-03596-8(9)*, Milk & Cookies) ibooks, Inc.
—The Swamps of Sleethe: Poems from Beyond the Solar System. Prelutsky, Jack. 2009. (ENG.). 40p. (J). (gr. 1-4). 16.99 *(978-0-375-84674-8(3))* Knopf, Alfred A. Inc.
—The Sword in the Grotto. Sage, Angie. 2008. (Araminta Spookie Ser.: 2). (ENG.). 176p. (J). (gr. 2-5). pap. 5.99 *(978-0-06-077486-8(X)*, Tegen, Katherine Bks) HarperCollins Pubs.
—Vampire Brat. Sage, Angie. (Araminta Spookie Ser.: 4). (J). (gr. 2-5). 2009. (ENG.). 224p. pap. 6.99 *(978-0-06-077492-9(4)*, Tegen, Katherine Bks); 2007. 128p. 8.99 *(978-0-06-077490-5(8))* HarperCollins Pubs.
Pickering, Jimmy. Skelly & Femur. Pickering, Jimmy. 2009. (ENG.). 32p. (J). (gr. -1-2). 12.99 *(978-1-4169-7143-6(2)*, Simon & Schuster Bks. For Young Readers) Simon & Schuster Bks. For Young Readers.
—Skelly the Skeleton Girl. Pickering, Jimmy. 2007. (ENG.). 32p. (J). (gr. -1-2). 14.99 *(978-1-4169-1192-0(8)*, Simon & Schuster Bks. For Young Readers) Simon & Schuster Bks. For Young Readers.

P

Pickering, Jimmy. My Imagination Kit. Pickering, Jimmy, tr. Fulmer, Jeffrey. 2003. (J). 24p. 15.95 *(978-1-59336-008-5(8))*; 23p. pap. *(978-1-59336-009-2(6))* Mondo Publishing.

Pickering, Lynne. James & the Naughty Seagull. Pickering, Lynne. 2013. 32p. pap. 13.50 *(978-1-62857-333-6(3)*, Strategic Bk. Publishing) Strategic Book Publishing & Rights Agency (SBPRA).

Pickering, Russell, photos by. Counting at the Market. Rauen, Amy. 2008. (Getting Started with Math Ser.). 16p. (gr. -1-2). lib. bdg. 19.00 *(978-0-8368-8981-9(9)*, Weekly Reader Leveled Readers) Stevens, Gareth Publishing LLLP.

—Usamos Dinero en el Puesto de Limonada. Rauen, Amy & Ayers, Amy. 2007. (Matemáticas en Nuestro Mundo (Math in Our World) Ser.). (SPA., 24p. (gr. 1-2). lib. bdg. 22.00 *(978-0-8368-8490-6(6)*, Weekly Reader Leveled Readers) Stevens, Gareth Publishing LLLP.

—Using Money at the Lemonade Stand. Rauen, Amy & Ayers, Amy. 2007. (Math in Our World Ser.). 24p. (gr. 1-2). lib. bdg. 22.00 *(978-0-8368-8472-2(8)*, Weekly Reader Leveled Readers) Stevens, Gareth Publishing LLLP.

—Vamos a Contar en el Mercado. Rauen, Amy. 2008. (Matemáticas para Empezar (Getting Started with Math) Ser.).Tr. of Counting at the Market. (SPA., 16p. (gr. -1-2). lib. bdg. 19.00 *(978-0-8368-8991-8(6)*, Weekly Reader Leveled Readers) Stevens, Gareth Publishing LLLP.

Pickering, Todd, photos by. Lagunitas Creek: Hope in Restoration. Pickering, Todd. 2005. 60p. (YA). pap. 15.00 *(978-0-615-12910-5(2))* Pickering, Todd.

Pickersgill, Peter. A Distinguished Old Bentley Drove down to the Sea, 1 vol. Rae, Lisa. 2007. (ENG.). 28p. (J). (gr. -1-2). pap. 8.95 *(978-1-897174-05-0(5)*, Tuckamore Bks) Creative Bk. Publishing CAN. Dist: Orca Bk. Pubs. USA.

Pickett, Danny. Colorful Spring. Moran, Erin. 2005. 32p. (J). mass mkt. 15.95 *(978-0-9763778-0-1(2))* Seal Rock Publishing, LLC.

Pickett, Justine, jt. illus. see Pickett, Robert.

Pickett, Robert & Pickett, Justine. Cat. Pickett, Robert & Pickett, Justine, photos by. 2004. 32p. (J). lib. bdg. 27.10 *(978-1-58340-431-7(7))* Black Rabbit Bks.

—Dog. Pickett, Robert & Pickett, Justine, photos by. 2004. 32p. (J). lib. bdg. 27.10 *(978-1-58340-430-0(9))* Black Rabbit Bks.

Pickman, Marian. Clarence Blooms in Winter. Anbinder, Adrienne. 2009. 40p. pap. 16.99 *(978-1-4389-7028-8(5))* AuthorHouse.

Pidgeon, Jean. Brush Your Teeth, Please: A Pop-Up Book. 2013. (Pop-Up Book Ser.: 2). (ENG.). 12p. (J). (gr. -1-k). 14.99 *(978-0-7944-3040-5(6))* Reader's Digest Assn., Inc., The.

Pidlubny, Donna. PeaceMaker. Ronco, Dan. 2004. (YA). per. 15.49 *(978-0-9752711-4-8(8))* Winterwolf Publishing.

Piemme, P. I. Shasta Indian Tales. Holsinger, Rosemary. 2003. 48p. (YA). (gr. -1-18). pap. 5.95 *(978-0-87961-129-3(4))* Naturegraph Pubs., Inc.

Pien, Lark. Long Tail Kitty. Pien, Lark. 2009. (ENG.). 64p. (J). (gr. -1-3). 17.99 *(978-1-934706-44-2(2))* Blue Apple Bks.

—Mr. Elephanter. Pien, Lark. 2010. (ENG.). 32p. (J). (gr. k-4). 14.99 *(978-0-7636-4409-3(9))* Candlewick Pr.

Pien, Lark, jt. illus. see Yang, Gene Luen.

Pienkowski, Jan, et al. The First Noel: A Christmas Carousel. Pienkowski, Jan. 2004. (ENG.). 1p. (J). (gr. k-12). 14.99 *(978-0-7636-2190-2(0))* Candlewick Pr.

Pienkowski, Jan. The Thousand Nights & One Night. Walser, David. 2011. (Calla Editions Ser.). (ENG.). 160p. (J). (gr. 5). 25.00 *(978-1-60660-020-7(6))* Dover Pubns., Inc.

Pienkowski, Jan. The Glass Mountain: Tales from Poland. Pienkowski, Jan. Walser, David. 2014. (ENG.). 104p. (J). (gr. 2-4). 17.99 *(978-0-7636-7320-8(X))* Candlewick Pr.

Pierard, John. My Teacher Flunked the Planet. Coville, Bruce. 2005. (My Teacher Bks.: 4). (ENG.). 176p. (J). (gr. 3-7). pap. 6.99 *(978-1-4169-0331-4(3)*, Simon & Schuster/Paula Wiseman Bks.) Simon & Schuster/Paula Wiseman Bks.

—My Teacher Fried My Brains. Coville, Bruce. (My Teacher Bks.: 2). (ENG.). 176p. (J). (gr. 3-7). 2014. 17.99 *(978-1-4814-0431-0(8))*; 2005. pap. 6.99 *(978-1-4169-0332-1(1))* Simon & Schuster/Paula Wiseman Bks. (Simon & Schuster/Paula Wiseman Bks.).

—My Teacher Glows in the Dark. Coville, Bruce. 2005. (My Teacher Bks.: 3). (ENG.). 144p. (J). (gr. 3-7). pap. 6.99 *(978-1-4169-0333-8(X)*, Simon & Schuster/Paula Wiseman Bks.) Simon & Schuster/Paula Wiseman Bks.

Pierard, John W. Arthur Conan Doyle. Doyle, Arthur et al. Pomplun, Tom, ed. 2nd ed. 2005. (Graphic Classics Ser.: Vol. 2). 144p. pap. 11.95 *(978-0-9746648-5-9(5))* Eureka Productions.

Pierce Clark, Donna. The Lost Treasure of Hawkins Cave. Snowden, Gary. 2013. 112p. pap. 7.99 *(978-1-938768-10-1(8))* Gypsy Pubns.

Pierce, Dave G. R Is for Reading Books. Hill, Cheryl E. 2012. 56p. pap. 17.99 *(978-0-9859770-0-9(0))* N.O.A.H Bks.

Pierce, Joanne Y. Mint's Christmas Message. Spitz, Mary Y. 2003. 32p. 14.95 *(978-0-9724570-0-2(3))* Mother Moose Pr.

Pierce, Julie A. An Army ABC Book. Pirog, Kristen T. 2007. 32p. (J). per. 14.99 *(978-1-59879-324-6(1))* Lifevest Publishing, Inc.

—A Marine ABC Book. Pirog, Kristen T. l.t. ed. 2006. 32p. (J). per. 16.99 *(978-1-59879-221-8(0))* Lifevest Publishing, Inc.

Pierce, Kim. Lepi's Golden America. Comman, Sabrina. 2003. 108p. 20.00 *(978-0-9719167-6-0(4))*; per. 12.00 *(978-0-9719167-5-3(6))* Open Bk. Publishing.

Pierce, Linda. Dr. Bessie Rehwinkel. Sutton, A. Trevor. 2012. (Hero of Faith Ser.). (ENG.). 47p. (J). pap. 7.99 *(978-0-7586-3078-0(6))* Concordia Publishing Hse.

Pierce, M. Deborah. Dandylion: The Most Misunderstood Flower. Bremer, Terry. 2003. 32p. (J). lib. bdg. 15.00 *(978-1-931646-90-1(2))* Beaver's Pond Pr., Inc.

Pierce, Matthew. Swirly. Saunders, Sara. 2012. 32p. (J). 7.99 *(978-0-8280-2681-9(5))* Review & Herald Publishing Assn.

Pierce, Mindy. The Night Before the 100th Day of School. Wing, Natasha. 2005. (Night Before Ser.). (ENG.). 32p. (J). (gr. -1-3). pap. 4.99 *(978-0-448-43923-5(9)*, Grosset & Dunlap) Penguin Publishing Group.

Pierce, Mindy & M, Pierce. The Night Before Summer Camp. Wing, Natasha. 2007. (Night Before Ser.). (ENG.). 32p. (J). (gr. -1-3). pap. 4.99 *(978-0-448-44639-4(1)*, Grosset & Dunlap) Penguin Publishing Group.

Pierfederici, Franco. Tron: Movie Adaptation. 2011. (ENG.). 112p. (J). (gr. 4-17). pap., pap. 9.99 *(978-0-7851-5320-7(9))* Marvel Worldwide, Inc.

Pierfederici, Mirco, jt. illus. see Dodson, Terry.

Pierfederici, Mirco, jt. illus. see Edwards, Neil.

Pierola, Mabel. La Lechera. Sarfatti, Esther, tr. from ENG. 2006. (Bilingual Tales Ser.). (SPA.). 24p. (J). (gr. -1-3). pap. 3.99 *(978-0-439-77377-5(6)*, Scholastic en Espanol) Scholastic, Inc.

Pierotti, Yvonne. The Tortoise & the Birds. Nnodim, Paul. 32p. (J). 2012. 24.95 *(978-1-937622-09-1(6))*; 2010. 14.95 *(978-0-9825842-9-3(6))* Africana Homestead Legacy Pubs., Inc. (Nefu Bks.).

Pierre, Chevelin. Babou & the Dream Maker. Papillon, Margaret. Devillers, Edith, tr. 2011. (ENG.). 36p. pap. 10.00 *(978-1-4637-3745-0(9))* CreateSpace Independent Publishing Platform.

Pierre-Louis, Phillip. The Reason for the Season. Ellen, Chantal. 2007. 32p. (J). (gr. k-2). 15.95 *(978-0-9786786-1-6(3))* Lions Den Publishing, LLC.

Pietila, David. Send Me the Soap #1: The Emerald Isle Adventure. Schlesinger, Gretchen. 2006. (J). 11.95 *(978-0-9778536-0-1(8))* Eco-thumb Publishing Co.

—Send Me the Soap #1: The Emerald Isle Adventure (lib. Bdg.) Schlesinger, Gretchen. 2006. (J). lib. bdg. *(978-0-9778536-1-8(6))* Eco-thumb Publishing Co.

—Send Me the Soap #2: The Amazon Adventure. Schlesinger, Gretchen. 2007. (J). 11.95 *(978-0-9778536-2-5(4))* Eco-thumb Publishing Co.

Pigford, Grady A., jt. illus. see Ward, Patricia R.

Pighin, Marcel & Daggett, Irma. Tickles the Bear, 1 bk. Pighin, Marcel. 2005. 92p. (J). per. 7.99 *(978-0-9717947-5-7(8))* MP2ME Enterprise.

Pignataro, Anna. Genesis-the Book with Seventy Faces: A Guide for the Family. Takac, Esther. 2008. 241p. (J). (gr. 3-9). 24.95 *(978-1-932687-92-7(0)*, Pitspopany Pr.) Simcha Media Group.

—Once upon a Time in the Kitchen. Odell, Carol. 2010. (Myths, Legends, Fairy & Folktales Ser.). (ENG.). 48p. (J). (gr. 1-4). 12.95 *(978-1-58536-518-0(1)*, 202208) Sleeping Bear Pr.

—Star. Prior, Natalie Jane. 2009. (ENG.). 28p. (J). (gr. -1). 5.99 *(978-1-935279-07-5(6))* Kane Miller.

—Sun. Prior, Natalie Jane. 2009. (ENG.). 28p. (J). (gr. -1). 5.99 *(978-1-935279-06-8(8))* Kane Miller.

—The Wonderful Whisper. Kwaymullina, Ezekiel. 2014. (ENG.). 32p. (J). (gr. -1-1). 16.99 *(978-1-921894-16-9(4))* Little Hare Bks. AUS. Dist: Independent Pubs. Group.

Pignataro, Anna. Mama, Will I Be Yours Forever? Pignataro, Anna. 2013. (ENG.). 32p. (J). (gr. -1-k). pap. 4.99 *(978-0-545-46074-3(3)*, Cartwheel Bks.) Scholastic, Inc.

—Mama, Will You Hold My Hand? Pignataro, Anna. 2010. (ENG.). 32p. (J). (gr. -1-k). pap. 4.99 *(978-0-545-16986-8(0)*, Cartwheel Bks.) Scholastic, Inc.

Pigni, Guido. The Story of Giraffe. Hermsen, Ronald. 2007. (ENG.). 32p. (J). (gr. k-2). 16.95 *(978-1-932425-87-1(X)*, Front Street) Boyds Mills Pr.

Pike, Jay Scott, et al. Marvel Masterworks: Atlas Era Jungle Adventures - Volume 3. 2013. (ENG.). 280p. (J). (gr. -1-17). 74.99 *(978-0-7851-5927-8(4)*, Marvel Pr.) Disney Publishing Worldwide.

Pilar, Bella. How to Raise Your Parents: A Teen Girl's Survival Guide. Burningham, Sarah O'Leary. 2008. (ENG.). 144p. (YA). (gr. 8-17). pap. 12.99 *(978-0-8118-5696-6(8))* Chronicle Bks. LLC.

Pilatowski, Boris. Diego Rana-Pintor. Cortes, Eunice & Cortes, Laura. 2003. (SPA.). 56p. (J). (gr. 3-5). pap. 13.95 *(978-968-19-0604-7(7))* Santillana USA Publishing Co., Inc.

Pilcher, Steve. Pixar Animation Studio Artist Showcase over There. Pilcher, Steve. 2014. (Pixar Animation Studios Artist Showcase Ser.). (ENG.). 40p. (J). (gr. -1-k). 17.99 *(978-1-4231-4793-0(6))* Hyperion Bks. for Children.

Pileggi, Steve. Four Pals on a Field Trip: An Adventure with Friends Who Are Different. Tucker, Angel. 2013. (Four Pals Ser.). (ENG.). 34p. (J). (gr. -1-3). pap. 8.95 *(978-1-62086-487-6(8))* Mascot Bks., Inc.

—Heather & Avery & the Magic Kite. Deubreau, Sharon. l.t. ed. 2006. 23p. (J). per. 11.99 *(978-1-59879-143-3(5))* Lifevest Publishing, Inc.

—Who Moved My Cheese? An A-Mazing Way to Change & Win! For Kids. Johnson, Spencer. 2003. (ENG.). 64p. (J). (gr. -1-3). 20.99 *(978-0-399-24016-4(0)*, Putnam Juvenile) Penguin Publishing Group.

Pileggi, Steven. Annoying Alex. Monnar, Alexander. 2008. (J). per. 14.99 *(978-0-9768035-9-1(3))* Readers Are Leaders U.S.A., Inc.

Pilgrim, Cheryl. Hound Dawg. Vermillion, Patricia. 2015. (ENG.). 40p. 21.95 *(978-0-87565-615-1(3))* Texas Christian Univ. Pr.

Pilkey, Dav. Julius. Johnson, Angela. 2015. 32p. pap. 7.00 ***(978-1-61003-548-4(8))*** Center for the Collaborative Classroom.

Pilkey, Dav. The Adventures of Captain Underpants. Pilkey, Dav. (Captain Underpants Ser.: 1). (ENG.). (J). (gr. 2-5). 2013. 144p. 9.99 *(978-0-545-49908-8(9))*; 2005. 128p. 12.99 *(978-0-439-75668-6(5))* Scholastic, Inc.

—The Adventures of Ook & Gluk, Kung-Fu Cavemen from the Future. Pilkey, Dav. (Captain Underpants Ser.). (ENG.). 176p. (J). (gr. 2-5). 2011. 5.99 *(978-0-545-38577-0(6))*; 2010. 9.99 *(978-0-545-17530-2(5))* Scholastic, Inc.

—The Adventures of Super Diaper Baby. Pilkey, Dav. 2014. (ENG.). 144p. (J). (gr. 3-7). 9.99 *(978-0-545-66544-5(2))* Scholastic, Inc.

—Las Aventuras de Uuk y Gluk, Cavernícolas del Futuro y Maestros de Kung Fu. Pilkey, Dav. 2011. (Captain Underpants Ser.). (SPA.). 176p. (J). (gr. 2-5). pap. 5.99 *(978-0-545-27916-1(X)*, Scholastic en Espanol) Scholastic, Inc.

—El Capitán Calzoncillos y la Feroz Batalla Contra el Niño Mocobiónico: La Noche de los Mocos Vivientes. Pilkey, Dav. 2005. (Captain Underpants Ser.: 6). Orig. Title: Captain Underpants & the Big, Bad Battle of the Bionic Booger Boy: the Night of the Nasty Nostril Nuggets. (SPA & ENG.). 176p. (J). (gr. 2-5). mass mkt. 5.99 *(978-0-439-66204-8(4)*, Scholastic en Espanol) Scholastic, Inc.

—El Capitan Calzoncillos y la Feroz Batalla Contra el Nino Mocobionico Pt. 2: La Venganza de los Ridiculos Mocorobots. Pilkey, Dav. Azaola, Miguel, tr. 2005. (Captain Underpants Ser.: Bk. 7). Orig. Title: Captain Underpants & the Big, Bad Battle of the Bionic Booger Boy, Part 2: The Revenge of the Ridiculous Robo-Boogers. (SPA & ENG.). 176p. (J). (gr. 2-5). pap. 5.99 *(978-0-439-66205-5(2)*, Scholastic en Espanol) Scholastic, Inc.

—Captain Underpants & the Attack of the Talking Toilets. Pilkey, Dav. 2014. (Captain Underpants Ser.: Bk. 2). (ENG.). 160p. (J). (gr. 2-5). 9.99 *(978-0-545-59932-0(6))* Scholastic, Inc.

—Captain Underpants & the Big, Bad Battle of the Bionic Booger Boy Part 1: The Night of the Nasty Nostril Nuggets. Pilkey, Dav. 2003. (Captain Underpants Ser.: 6). (ENG.). 176p. (J). (gr. 2-5). pap. 5.99 *(978-0-439-37610-5(6))* Scholastic, Inc.

—Captain Underpants & the Big, Bad Battle of the Bionic Booger Boy Part 2: The Revenge of the Ridiculous Robo-Boogers. Pilkey, Dav. 2003. (Captain Underpants Ser.: 7). (ENG.). 176p. (J). (gr. 2-5). 16.99 *(978-0-439-37611-2(4))*; pap. 5.99 *(978-0-439-37612-9(2))* Scholastic, Inc.

—Captain Underpants & the Invasion of the Incredibly Naughty Cafeteria Ladies from Outer Space: (And the Subsequent Assault of the Equally Evil Lunchroom Zombie Nerds) Pilkey, Dav. collector's ed. 2008. (Captain Underpants Ser.: 3). (ENG.). 144p. (J). (gr. 2-5). 12.99 *(978-0-545-07302-8(2))* Scholastic, Inc.

—Captain Underpants & the Preposterous Plight of the Purple Potty People. Pilkey, Dav. 2006. (Captain Underpants Ser.: 8). (ENG.). 176p. (J). (gr. 2-5). 5.99 *(978-0-439-37614-3(9))* Scholastic, Inc.

—Captain Underpants & the Revolting Revenge of the Radioactive Robo-Boxers. Pilkey, Dav. 2013. (Captain Underpants Ser.: 10). (ENG.). 192p. (J). (gr. 2-5). 9.99 *(978-0-545-17536-4(4))* Scholastic, Inc.

—Captain Underpants & the Terrifying Return of Tippy Tinkletrousers. Pilkey, Dav. 2012. (Captain Underpants Ser.: 9). (ENG.). 304p. (J). (gr. 2-5). 9.99 *(978-0-545-17534-0(8))* Scholastic, Inc.

—Dog Breath! The Horrible Trouble with Hally Tosis. Pilkey, Dav. 3rd ed. 2004. (Scholastic Bookshelf Ser.). (ENG.). 32p. (J). (gr. -1-3). pap. 6.99 *(978-0-439-59839-2(7)*, Scholastic Paperbacks) Scholastic, Inc.

—Dogzilla. Pilkey, Dav. 2014. 32p. pap. 7.00 *(978-1-61003-187-5(3))* Center for the Collaborative Classroom.

—Dragon's Halloween. Pilkey, Dav. 2003. (Dragon's Tales Ser.: Bk. 5). (ENG.). 48p. (J). (gr. -1-3). pap. 5.99 *(978-0-439-54847-2(0)*, Orchard Bks.) Scholastic, Inc.

—Dumb Bunnies' Easter. Pilkey, Dav. 2009. (Dumb Bunnies Ser.). (ENG.). 32p. (J). (gr. -1-3). 16.99 *(978-0-545-03946-8(0))* Scholastic, Inc.

—The Hallo-Wiener. Pilkey, Dav. 2014. (ENG.). 32p. (J). (gr. -1-k). bds. 6.99 *(978-0-545-66136-2(6))* Scholastic, Inc.

—The Invasion of the Potty Snatchers. Pilkey, Dav. Scholastic Canada Ltd. Staff. 2011. (Captain Underpants Ser.: 2). (ENG.). 128p. (J). (gr. 2-5). 9.99 *(978-0-545-17532-6(1))* Scholastic, Inc.

—The Tra-la-Laa-Rific, Bks. 1-4, Set. Pilkey, Dav. 2007. (Captain Underpants Ser.). (ENG.). (J). (gr. 2-5). 23.96 *(978-0-545-02287-3(8))* Scholastic, Inc.

Pillion, Dean. Those Amazing Engineers. Forbes, Charlotte. 2nd rev. ed. 2005. (Those Amazing... Ser.). (ENG.). 30p. (J). pap. 10.95 *(978-0-9772799-0-6(1))* Trilogy Pubns. LLC.

—Those Amazing Scientists. Forbes, Charlotte & Forbes, Charlotte. 2007. 26p. (J). *(978-0-9772799-1-3(X))* Trilogy Pubns. LLC.

Pillo, Cary. Do All Bugs Have Wings? And Other Questions Kids Have about Bugs, 1 vol. Slade, Suzanne. 2010. (Kids' Questions Ser.). (ENG.). 24p. (gr. 1-2). lib. bdg. 25.99 *(978-1-4048-5761-2(3)*, Nonfiction Picture Bks.) Picture Window Bks.

—Gentle Willow: A Story for Children about Dying. Mills, Joyce C. 2nd ed. 2003. 32p. (J). 14.95 *(978-1-59147-071-7(4))*; pap. 9.95 *(978-1-59147-072-4(2))* American Psychological Assn. (Magination Pr.).

—God Gave Me: Wade Hudson. Hudson, Wade. 2004. 16p. (J). bds. 8.00 *(978-0-687-02590-9(7))* Abingdon Pr.

—How Do Tornadoes Form? And Other Questions Kids Have about Weather, 1 vol. Slade, Suzanne. (Kids' Questions Ser.). (ENG.). 24p. (gr. 1-2). 2010. lib. bdg. 25.99 *(978-1-4048-6048-3(7))*; 2011. pap. 7.49 *(978-1-4048-6731-4(7))* Picture Window Bks. (Nonfiction Picture Bks.).

—Party Princess. Braver, Vanita. 2005. (Teach Your Children Well Ser.). 24p. (J). (gr. -1). per. 8.95 *(978-1-58760-038-8(2)*, Child & Family Pr.) Child Welfare League of America, Inc.

—Sally Sore Loser: A Story about Winning & Losing. Sileo, Frank J. 2012. (J). 14.95 *(978-1-4338-1189-0(8))*; pap. 9.95 *(978-1-4338-1190-6(1))* American Psychological Assn. (Magination Pr.).

—Sammy the Elephant & Mr. Camel: A Story to Help Children Overcome Bedwetting. Mills, Joyce C. & Crowley, Richard J. 2nd ed. 2005. 32p. (J). 14.95 *(978-1-59147-247-6(4))*; pap. 9.95 *(978-1-59147-248-3(2))* American Psychological Assn. (Magination Pr.).

—Striped Shirts & Flowered Pants: A Story about Alzheimer's Disease for Young Children. Schnurbush, Barbara. 2006. 32p. (J). (gr. -1-3). 14.95 *(978-1-59147-475-3(2))*; per. 9.95 *(978-1-59147-476-0(0))* American Psychological Assn. (Magination Pr.).

—Werewolf Moon. Hanford, Juliana. 2009. (Science Solves It! Complete Set Ser.). 32p. (J). (gr. k-7). pap. 5.95 *(978-1-57565-291-7(9))* Kane Pr., Inc.

—Where Is My Mommy? Coping When a Parent Leaves (and Doesn't Come Back) Kilgore, Mary & Kilgore, Mitchell. 2010. (ENG.). 32p. (J). (gr. -1-4). pap. 12.95 *(978-1-884734-46-5(4))* Parenting Pr., Inc.

—Who Invented Basketball? And Other Questions Kids Have about Sports, 1 vol. Slade, Suzanne. (Kids' Questions Ser.). (ENG.). 24p. (gr. 1-2). 2010. lib. bdg. 25.99 *(978-1-4048-6049-0(5))*; 2011. pap. 7.49 *(978-1-4048-6730-7(9))* Picture Window Bks. (Nonfiction Picture Bks.).

—Why Do Dogs Drool? And Other Questions Kids Have about Dogs, 1 vol. Slade, Suzanne. 2010. (Kids' Questions Ser.). (ENG.). 24p. (gr. 1-2). lib. bdg. 25.99 *(978-1-4048-5762-9(1)*, Nonfiction Picture Bks.) Picture Window Bks.

Pillo, Cary. Jenny Is Scared! When Sad Things Happen in the World. Pillo, Cary, tr. Shuman, Carol. 2003. 32p. (J). (gr. k-3). pap. 9.95 *(978-1-59147-003-8(X))*; 14.95 *(978-1-59147-002-1(1))* American Psychological Assn. (Magination Pr.).

Pillot, édéric. The Most Beautiful Images from the Bible: Sharing the Stories with Children. Mrowiec, Katia. 2012. 48p. 19.95 *(978-0-8091-6766-1(2))* Paulist Pr.

Pilo, Cary. Rena & Rio Build a Rhyme. Hall, Pamela. 2011. (Poetry Builders Ser.). 32p. (J). (gr. 2-4). lib. bdg. 25.27 *(978-1-59953-439-8(8))* Norwood Hse. Pr.

Pilorget, Bruno. The Great Wave: A Children's Book Inspired by Hokusai. Massenot, Véronique. 2011. (ENG.). 32p. (J). (gr. -1). 14.95 *(978-3-7913-7058-3(8))* Prestel Publishing.

—Journey on the Clouds: A Children's Book Inspired by Marc Chagall. Massenot, Véronique. 2011. (ENG.). 32p. (J). (gr. -1). 14.95 *(978-3-7913-7057-6(X))* Prestel Publishing.

Pilston, Jim. Total Feng Shui: Bring Health, Wealth, & Happiness into Your Life. Too, Lillian. 2004. (ENG.). 288p. (gr. 8-17). pap. 19.95 *(978-0-8118-4530-4(3))* Chronicle Bks. LLC.

Pilsworth, Graham. Confederation. Staunton, Ted. 2004. (Dreadful Truth Ser.). (ENG.). 80p. (J). (gr. 3-8). *(978-0-88780-630-8(9))* Formac Publishing Co., Ltd.

—The Halifax Citadel. Grant, Vicki. 2003. (Dreadful Truth Ser.). (ENG.). 80p. (J). (gr. 3-8). *(978-0-88780-599-8(X))* Formac Publishing Co., Ltd.

Pilutti, Deb. The Twelve Days of Christmas in Michigan. Thoms, Susan Collins. 2010. (Twelve Days of Christmas in America Ser.). (ENG.). 32p. (J). (gr. k). 12.95 *(978-1-4027-6351-9(4))* Sterling Publishing Co., Inc.

Pilutti, Deb. Bear & Squirrel Are Friends ... Yes, Really! Pilutti, Deb. 2015. (ENG.). 40p. (J). (gr. -1-3). 17.99 *(978-1-4814-2913-9(2)*, Simon & Schuster Bks. For Young Readers) Simon & Schuster Bks. For Young Readers.

—Ten Rules of Being a Superhero. Pilutti, Deb. 2014. (ENG.). 32p. (J). (gr. -1-2). 16.99 *(978-0-8050-9759-7(7)*, Holt, Henry & Co. Bks. For Young Readers) Holt, Henry & Co.

Pilz, M. H. The Best Mother's Day Ever. May, Eleanor. 2010. (Social Studies Connects Ser.). 32p. (J). (gr. 1-3). pap. 5.95 *(978-1-57565-299-3(4))* Kane Pr., Inc.

Pilz, M. H. A Thousand Theos: Doubling. Houran, Lori Haskins. 2015. (ENG.). 32p. (J). (gr. 1-3). pap. 5.95 ***(978-1-57565-803-2(8))*** Kane Pr., Inc.

Pilz, M. H. The Yum-Yum House. Walker, Nan. 2009. (Math Matters Complete Set Ser.). 32p. (J). (gr. 3-5). pap. 5.95 *(978-1-57565-290-0(0))* Kane Pr., Inc.

Pinchbeck, Neil. Crash, Bang, Yell! 16p. (J). *(978-1-85792-366-7(9))* Christian Focus Pubns. GBR. Dist: Riverside.

—The Praying Man. 16p. (J). *(978-1-85792-363-6(4))* Christian Focus Pubns. GBR. Dist: Riverside.

—Rescue on the Road. 16p. (J). *(978-1-85792-365-0(0))* Christian Focus Pubns. GBR. Dist: Riverside.

—There's a Hole in My Roof! 16p. (J). *(978-1-85792-361-2(8))* Christian Focus Pubns. GBR. Dist: Riverside.

Pinckney, Jerry. God Bless the Child. Holiday, Billie & Herzog, Arthur, Jr. 2005. 30p. (J). (gr. 4-8). reprint ed. 17.00 *(978-0-7567-9650-1(4))* DIANE Publishing Co.

Pinder, Andrew. The Boys' Doodle Book: Amazing Pictures to Complete & Create. 2008. (ENG.). 128p. (J). (gr. k-7). pap. 12.95 *(978-0-7624-3506-7(2))* Running Pr. Bk. Pubs.

—Diary of Dorkius Maximus. Collins, Tim. 2014. (Diary of Dorkius Maximus Ser.: 1). (ENG.). 192p. (J). (gr. 4-6). 8.99 *(978-1-78055-027-5(8))* O'Mara, Michael Bks., Ltd. GBR. Dist: Independent Pubs. Group.

—Diary of Dorkius Maximus in Egypt. Collins, Tim. 2014. (Diary of Dorkius Maximus Ser.: 2). (ENG.). 192p. (J). (gr. 4-6). pap. 8.99 *(978-1-78055-028-2(6))* O'Mara, Michael Bks., Ltd. GBR. Dist: Independent Pubs. Group.

—Diary of Dorkius Maximus in Pompeii. Collins, Tim. 2015. (Diary of Dorkius Maximus Ser.: 3). (ENG.). 192p. (J). (gr. 4-6). pap. 8.99 *(978-1-78055-268-2(8))* O'Mara, Michael Bks., Ltd. GBR. Dist: Independent Pubs. Group.

—Dinosaur Doodles: Amazing Pictures to Complete & Create. 2011. (ENG.). 128p. (J). pap. 12.95 *(978-0-7624-3894-5(0))* Running Pr. Bk. Pubs.

—Fangs a Lot: Final Notes from a Totally Lame Vampire. Collins, Tim. 2014. (ENG.). 320p. (J). (gr. 5-9). 13.99 *(978-1-4814-2134-8(4)*, Simon & Schuster/Paula Wiseman Bks.) Simon & Schuster/Paula Wiseman Bks.

—The Girls' Doodle Book: Amazing Pictures to Complete & Create. 2008. (ENG.). 128p. (J). (gr. k-7). pap. 12.95 *(978-0-7624-3505-0(4))* Running Pr. Bk. Pubs.

—The London Activity Book: With Palaces, Puzzles & Pictures to Colour. Bailey, Ellen & Mosedale, Julian. 2013. (ENG.). 64p. (J). (gr. 2-4). pap. 7.99 *(978-1-78055-095-4(2))* O'Mara, Michael Bks., Ltd. GBR. Dist: Independent Pubs. Group.

—Notes from a Hairy-Not-Scary Werewolf. Collins, Tim. 2013. (ENG.). 288p. (J). (gr. 5-9). 12.99 *(978-1-4424-8207-4(9)*, Simon & Schuster/Paula Wiseman Bks.) Simon & Schuster/Paula Wiseman Bks.

—Notes from a Totally Lame Vampire: Because the Undead Have Feelings Too! Collins, Tim. 2010. (ENG.). 336p. (J). (gr. 5-9). 12.99 *(978-1-4424-1183-8(X)*, Simon & Schuster/Paula Wiseman Bks.) Simon & Schuster/Paula Wiseman Bks.

—Off with Their Heads! All the Cool Bits in British History. Oliver, Martin. 2014. (ENG.). 128p. (J). (gr. 4-7). 8.99 *(978-1-78055-134-0(7))* O'Mara, Michael Bks., Ltd. GBR. Dist: Independent Pubs. Group.

—Out of This World: All the Cool Stuff about Space You Want to Know. Gifford, Clive. 2012. (J). *(978-1-60652-571-5(9))* Reader's Digest Assn., Inc., The.

—Prince of Dorkness: More Notes from a Totally Lame Vampire. Collins, Tim. 2011. (ENG.). 336p. (J). (gr. 5-9). 12.99 *(978-1-4424-3388-5(4)*, Simon & Schuster/Paula Wiseman Bks.) Simon & Schuster/Paula Wiseman Bks.

Pindroh, Paula. First Look at Dinosaurs. Galvin, Laura Gates. 2011. (First Look At... (Soundprints) Ser.). (ENG.). 16p. 6.95 *(978-1-60727-285-4(7))* Soundprints.

Pine, Hank. Polly Perfect & the Tragic Fart. Richmond, Jacob. 2012. (ENG.). 64p. (J). pap. 9.95 *(978-1-897411-36-0(7))* Bayeux Arts, Inc. CAN. Dist: Chicago Distribution Ctr.

Pineda, Jesus. Sentimientos. Jauregui, Patricia. Jauregui, Reginald, ed. l.t. ed. 2004. (SPA.). 39p. (YA). pap. 19.95 *(978-1-931481-41-0(5))* LiArt-Literature & Art.

Pinelli, Amerigo. Bites, 1 vol. Brezenoff, Steve. 2013. (Ravens Pass Ser.). (ENG.). 96p. (gr. 2-3). pap. 5.95 *(978-1-4342-6217-2(0))*; lib. bdg. 23.99 *(978-1-4342-4617-2(5))* Stone Arch Bks.

—Cheaters, 1 vol. Brezenoff, Steve. 2013. (Ravens Pass Ser.). (ENG.). 96p. (gr. 2-3). lib. bdg. 23.99 *(978-1-4342-4616-5(7))* Stone Arch Bks.

—Chillax! How Ernie Learns to Chill Out, Relax, & Take Charge of His Anger. Craver, Marcella Marino. 2011. 64p. (J). pap. 9.95 *(978-1-4338-1037-4(9)*, Magination Pr.) American Psychological Assn.

—Lost Island, 1 vol. Brezenoff, Steve. 2013. (Ravens Pass Ser.). (ENG.). 96p. (gr. 2-3). pap. 5.95 *(978-1-4342-6214-1(6))*; lib. bdg. 23.99 *(978-1-4342-4614-1(0))* Stone Arch Bks.

—No Place Like Home, 1 vol. Brezenoff, Steve. 2013. (Ravens Pass Ser.). (ENG.). 96p. (gr. 2-3). pap. 5.95 *(978-1-4342-6215-8(4))*; lib. bdg. 23.99 *(978-1-4342-4615-8(9))* Stone Arch Bks.

—Shield Up! Craver, Marcella Marino. 2014. 64p. (J). pap. *(978-1-4338-1651-2(2)*, Magination Pr.) American Psychological Assn.

—Tracking an Assassin! Nickolas Flux & the Assassination of Abraham Lincoln, 1 vol. Yomtov, Nelson. 2014. (Nickolas Flux History Chronicles Ser.). (ENG.). 32p. (gr. 3-4). lib. bdg. 29.99 *(978-1-4914-0252-8(0))* Capstone Pr., Inc.

Pinero, Eimi. Four Little Witches, 1 vol. Perkins, T. J. 2015. (ENG.). 40p. (J). 12.99 ***(978-0-7643-4943-0(0)***, 9780764349430) Schiffer Publishing, Ltd.

Pinfold, Levi. Black Dog. Pinfold, Levi. 2012. (ENG.). 32p. (J). (gr. -1-3). 15.99 *(978-0-7636-6097-0(3)*, Templar) Candlewick Pr.

—The Django. Pinfold, Levi. 2010. (ENG.). 40p. (J). (gr. k-4). 16.99 *(978-0-7636-4788-9(8)*, Templar) Candlewick Pr.

Pinfold, Levi, jt. illus. see Wyatt, David.

Pingk, Rubin. Samurai Santa: A Very Ninja Christmas. Pingk, Rubin. 2015. (ENG.). 40p. (J). (gr. -1-3). 17.99 *(978-1-4814-3057-9(2)*, Simon & Schuster Bks. For Young Readers) Simon & Schuster Bks. For Young Readers.

Pinkham, Pamela, jt. illus. see Verhoef, Sharon.

Pinkney, Brian. Boycott Blues: How Rosa Parks Inspired a Nation. Pinkney, Andrea Davis. 2008. (ENG.). 40p. (J). (gr. k-3). 16.99 *(978-0-06-082118-0(3)*, Greenwillow Bks.) HarperCollins Pubs.

—Busy-Busy Little Chick. Harrington, Janice N. 2013. (ENG.). 32p. (J). (gr. -1-1). 15.99 *(978-0-374-34746-8(8)*, Farrar, Straus & Giroux (BYR)) Farrar, Straus & Giroux.

—Cut from the Same Cloth: American Women of Myth, Legend, & Tall Tale. San Souci, Robert D. 2005. 140p. 17.00 *(978-0-7569-6284-5(6))* Perfection Learning Corp.

—The Dark-Thirty: Southern Tales of the Supernatural. McKissack, Patricia C. 2004. 122p. (J). (gr. 5-8). reprint ed. pap. 17.00 *(978-0-7567-7601-5(5))* DIANE Publishing Co.

—The Dark-Thirty: Southern Tales of the Supernatural. McKissack, Patricia C. 2006. (ENG.). 128p. (J). (gr. 3-7). 18.95 *(978-0-679-81863-2(4)*, Knopf Bks. for Young Readers) Random Hse. Children's Bks.

—Duke Ellington. Pinkney, Andrea Davis. 2006. (ENG.). 32p. (J). (gr. k-4). pap. 6.99 *(978-0-7868-1420-6(9)*, Jump at the Sun) Hyperion Bks. for Children.

—Ella Fitzgerald: The Tale of a Vocal Virtuosa. Pinkney, Andrea Davis. 2007. (ENG.). 32p. (J). (gr. k-4). pap. 6.99 *(978-0-7868-1416-9(0)*, Jump at the Sun) Hyperion Bks. for Children.

—Hand in Hand: Ten Black Men Who Changed America. Pinkney, Andrea Davis. 2012. (ENG.). 243p. (YA). (gr. 4-7). 19.99 *(978-1-4231-4257-7(8))* Hyperion Pr.

—Jackie's Bat. Lorbiecki, Marybeth. 2006. (ENG.). 40p. (J). (gr. k-3). 17.99 *(978-0-689-84102-6(7)*, Simon & Schuster Bks. For Young Readers) Simon & Schuster Bks. For Young Readers.

—Little Diva. LaChanze. 2010. (ENG.). 32p. (J). (gr. -1-3). 16.99 *(978-0-312-37010-7(5))* Feiwel & Friends.

—Sit-in: How Four Friends Stood Up by Sitting Down. Pinkney, Andrea Davis. 2011. (J). 37.75 *(978-1-4498-6817-8(7))* Recorded Bks., LLC.

—Sojourner Truth's Step-Stomp Stride. Pinkney, Andrea Davis. 2009. (ENG.). 32p. (J). (gr. k-4). 16.99 *(978-0-7868-0767-3(9)*, Jump at the Sun) Hyperion Bks. for Children.

—Thumbelina. Andersen, Hans Christian. 2003. 40p. (J). 17.89 *(978-0-688-17477-4(9))* HarperCollins Pubs.

—Where Does the Trail Lead? Albert, Burton. 2008. (ENG.). 40p. (J). (gr. -1-3). 13.99 *(978-1-4169-7138-2(6)*, Simon & Schuster/Paula Wiseman Bks.) Simon & Schuster/Paula Wiseman Bks.

Pinkney, Brian. The Dream Keeper & Other Poems. Pinkney, Brian. Hughes, Langston. 2007. (ENG.). 96p. (J). (gr. 3-7). 16.99 *(978-0-679-84421-1(X)*, Knopf Bks. for Young Readers) Random Hse. Children's Bks.

—Max Found Two Sticks. Pinkney, Brian. 2nd ed. 2005. (Stories to Go! Ser.). (ENG.). 40p. (J). 4.99 *(978-1-4169-0310-9(0)*, Simon & Schuster/Paula Wiseman Bks.) Simon & Schuster/Paula Wiseman Bks.

Pinkney, Brian. On the Ball. Pinkney, Brian. 2015. (ENG.). 40p. (J). (gr. -1-k). 17.99 ***(978-1-4847-2329-6(5))*** Disney Pr.

Pinkney, J. Brian. Happy Birthday, Martin Luther King. Marzollo, Jean. 2006. (Scholastic Bookshelf Ser.). (ENG.). 32p. (J). (gr. -1-3). per. 6.99 *(978-0-439-78224-1(4)*, Scholastic Paperbacks) Scholastic, Inc.

Pinkney, Jane. The Mice of Nibbling Village. Greaves, Margaret. 2011. (ENG.). 32p. (J). (gr. -1-k). 14.99 *(978-1-84365-189-5(0)*, Pavilion Children's Books) Pavilion Bks. GBR. Dist: Independent Pubs. Group.

—Mouse Mischief. Greaves, Margaret. 2013. (ENG.). 32p. (J). (gr. -1-k). 14.99 *(978-1-84365-223-6(4)*, Pavilion) Pavilion Bks. GBR. Dist: Independent Pubs. Group.

Pinkney, Jerry. The All-I'll-Ever-Want Christmas Doll. McKissack, Patricia C. 2007. (J). *(978-0-375-83615-2(2)*, Schwartz & Wade Bks.) Random Hse. Children's Bks.

—The All-I'll-Ever-Want Christmas Doll. McKissack, Patricia C. 2007. (ENG.). 40p. (J). (gr. -1-3). 17.99 *(978-0-375-83759-3(0)*, Schwartz & Wade Bks.) Random Hse. Children's Bks.

—Las Fabulas de Esopo. 2004.Tr. of Aesop's Fables. (SPA.). (J). pap. 10.99 *(978-84-316-7164-8(5))* Vicens-Vives, Editorial, S.A. ESP. Dist: Lectorum Pubns., Inc.

—The Further Adventures of Spider: West African Folktales. Arkhurst, Joyce Cooper. 2012. (Passport to Reading Level 4 Ser.). (ENG.). 32p. (J). (gr. -1-3). pap. 4.99 *(978-0-316-20345-6(9))* Little, Brown Bks. for Young Readers.

—God Bless the Child. Holiday, Billie & Herzog, Arthur, Jr. 2008. (ENG.). 40p. (J). (gr. -1-3). per. 7.99 *(978-0-06-443646-5(2))* HarperCollins Pubs.

—God Bless the Child. Holiday, Billie. 2004. 32p. (J). lib. bdg. 17.89 *(978-0-06-029487-8(6)*, Amistad) HarperCollins Pubs.

—Goin' Someplace Special. McKissack, Patricia C. 2008. (ENG.). 40p. (J). (gr. -1-3). 7.99 *(978-1-4169-2735-8(2)*, Simon & Schuster/Paula Wiseman Bks.) Simon & Schuster/Paula Wiseman Bks.

—The Moon over Star. Aston, Dianna Hutts. 2008. (ENG.). 32p. (J). (gr. 1-3). 17.99 *(978-0-8037-3107-3(8)*, Dial) Penguin Publishing Group.

Pinkney, Jerry, et al. Music from Our Lord's Holy Heaven. Pinkney, Gloria Jean. 2005. 48p. (J). (gr. -1-18). lib. bdg. 18.89 incl. audio compact disk *(978-0-06-000769-0(9))* HarperCollins Pubs.

Pinkney, Jerry. The Old African. Lester, Julius. 2005. (ENG.). 80p. (J). (gr. k-3). 21.99 *(978-0-8037-2564-5(7)*, Dial) Penguin Publishing Group.

—Song of the Trees. Taylor, Mildred D. 2003. (ENG.). 64p. (J). (gr. 3-7). 5.99 *(978-0-14-250075-0(5)*, Puffin) Penguin Publishing Group.

—A Starlit Snowfall. Willard, Nancy. 2011. (ENG.). 32p. (J). (gr. -1-1). 6.99 *(978-0-316-18366-6(0))* Little Brown & Co.

—The Tales of Uncle Remus: The Adventures of Brer Rabbit. Lester, Julius. 2006. (Puffin Modern Classics Ser.). (ENG.). 160p. (J). (gr. 3-7). 5.99 *(978-0-14-240720-2(8)*, Puffin) Penguin Publishing Group.

—Undersea Animals: A Dramatic Dimensional Visit to Strange Underwater Realms. Buxton, Jane H. 2008. (ENG.). 12p. (J). (gr. -1-3). 14.95 *(978-1-4263-0334-0(3)*, National Geographic Children's Bks.) National Geographic Society.

Pinkney, Jerry. The Little Red Hen. Pinkney, Jerry. 2006. (ENG.). 32p. (J). (gr. -1-3). 17.99 *(978-0-8037-2935-3(9)*, Dial) Penguin Publishing Group.

—Rikki-Tikki-Tavi. Pinkney, Jerry. Kipling, Rudyard. 2004. (ENG.). 48p. (J). (gr. -1-3). reprint ed. pap. 6.99 *(978-0-06-058785-7(7))* HarperCollins Pubs.

—Three Little Kittens. Pinkney, Jerry. 2010. (ENG.). 40p. (J). (gr. -1-k). 16.99 *(978-0-8037-3533-0(2)*, Dial) Penguin Publishing Group.

Pinkney, Myles C. Shades of Black: A Celebration of Our Children. Pinkney, Sandra L. 2006. (ENG.). 24p. (J). (gr. k — 1). bds. 6.99 *(978-0-439-80251-2(2)*, Cartwheel Bks.) Scholastic, Inc.

Pinkney, Myles C., photos by. I Am Latino: the Beauty in Me. Pinkney, Sandra L. 2013. (ENG., 28p. (J). (gr. -1-1). bds. 6.99 *(978-0-316-23385-9(4))* Little, Brown Bks. for Young Readers.

—It's Raining Laughter. Grimes, Nikki. 2005. (ENG., 32p. (J). (gr. -1-3). pap. 10.95 *(978-1-59078-077-0(9))* Boyds Mills Pr.

Pinkwater, Jill. Beautiful Yetta: The Yiddish Chicken. Pinkwater, Daniel M. 2010. (ENG.). 32p. (J). (gr. -1-2). 16.99 *(978-0-312-55824-6(4))* Feiwel & Friends.

—Beautiful Yetta's Hanukkah Kitten. Pinkwater, Daniel M. 2014. (ENG.). 32p. (J). (gr. -1-2). 17.99 *(978-0-312-62134-6(5))* Feiwel & Friends.

—Dancing Larry, 1 vol. Pinkwater, Daniel M. 2006. (ENG.). 32p. (J). (gr. -1-3). 16.95 *(978-0-7614-5220-1(6))* Marshall Cavendish Corp.

—Young Larry, 1 vol. Pinkwater, Daniel M. 2005. (ENG.). 32p. (J). pap. 5.95 *(978-0-7614-5177-8(3))* Marshall Cavendish Corp.

Pinnock, Nathan. The Sacrament. Bytheway, John. 2013. 18.99 *(978-1-60907-790-7(3))* Deseret Bk. Co.

Pino, Pablo. Dreamboy. Damiron, Anya. 2010. (SPA.). 26p. (J). *(978-9945-421-42-2(5))* Lucia Stories.

—Inventor Boy. Damiron, Anya. 2010. (SPA.). 26p. (J). *(978-9945-00-157-0(4))* Lucia Stories.

—Nino Inventor. Damiron, Anya. 2010. 26p. (J). *(978-9945-00-153-2(1))* Lucia Stories.

Pinto, Dan. Hedgehug's Halloween. Sutton, Benn. 2013. (ENG.). 40p. (J). (gr. -1-3). 9.99 *(978-0-06-196104-5(3))* HarperCollins Pubs.

Pinto, Dan. Hedgehug: A Sharp Lesson in Love. Pinto, Dan. Sutton, Benn. 2011. (ENG.). 40p. (J). (gr. -1-2). 9.99 *(978-0-06-196101-4(9))* HarperCollins Pubs.

Pinto, Sara. Kids Cook 1-2-3: Recipes for Young Chefs Using Only 3 Ingredients. Gold, Rozanne. 2006. (ENG.). 144p. (J). (gr. 4-6). 17.95 *(978-1-58234-735-6(2)*, Bloomsbury USA Childrens) Bloomsbury USA.

Pinto, Sara. The Alphabet Room. Pinto, Sara. 2003. (ENG.). 56p. (J). (gr. k-k). bds. 17.99 *(978-1-58234-841-4(3)*, Bloomsbury USA Childrens) Bloomsbury USA.

—Apples & Oranges: Going Bananas with Pairs. Pinto, Sara. 2007. (ENG.). 32p. (J). (gr. -1-2). 16.95 *(978-1-59990-103-9(X)*, Bloomsbury USA Childrens) Bloomsbury USA.

Pintor, Ruben. Growing up Yanomamö: Missionary Adventures in the Amazon Rainforest. Dawson, Mike. 2009. (ENG.). 336p. pap. 19.95 *(978-1-60265-009-1(8))* Grace Acres Pr.

Pintozzi, Connie, jt. illus. see Pintozzi, Nick.

Pintozzi, Nick, et al. Bentley & the Great Fire. Pintozzi, Nick. 2004. 16.95 *(978-0-9749465-2-8(4))*; 120p. per. 17.95 *(978-0-9749465-1-1(6))* BentDaiSha, LLC.

—Bentley Finds a Home. Pintozzi, Nick. l.t. ed. 2004. 102p. per. 17.95 *(978-0-9749465-0-4(8))* BentDaiSha, LLC.

Pintozzi, Nick & Pintozzi, Connie. Bentley & the Cactus Rustlers. Pintozzi, Nick. 2006. per. 11.00 *(978-0-9749465-4-2(0))* BentDaiSha, LLC.

Piotti, Dania. Outside with Lil Boo. Bookins, Daddy. 2012. 38p. pap. 13.50 *(978-0-9848019-3-0(6))* Inkwell Productions, LLC.

Pipe, Jasper. The Adventures of Miss Turtle. Hong, Catherine Thao. 2012. 24p. (J). pap. *(978-0-9873790-0-9(3))* Icky Grass Books.

Piper, Molly. Rosey & Amanda. Piper, Molly. Date not set. (J). (gr. k-6). pap. 7.95 *(978-1-891360-01-5(9))* Little Deer Pr.

Piper, Tom. Animal Rain. Nevis, Lance. Laible MBA, Steve William, ed. 2012. 36p. pap. 10.99 *(978-0-9850142-7-8(X))* Kodel Group, LLC, The.

—The Pollywog Prince. Nevis, Lance. Laible MBA, Steve William, ed. 2012. 46p. pap. 10.99 *(978-0-9850142-8-5(8))* Kodel Group, LLC, The.

—Silly Stew. Nevis, Lance. Laible MBA, Steve William, ed. 2012. 50p. pap. 10.99 *(978-0-9850142-9-2(6))* Kodel Group, LLC, The.

Pippin, Barbara. Gramma's Glasses. Guiffre, William. 2008. 32p. (J). (gr. -1-3). pap. 9.95 *(978-1-931650-35-9(7))* Bks. for Children Publishing.

—Gramma's Glasses. Guiffre, William A. 2008. 32p. (J). (gr. -1-7). lib. bdg. 17.95 *(978-1-931650-19-9(5))* Bks. for Children Publishing.

Pippin, Kristin A. & Pippin, Sheila C. Katrina: Through Mango's Eyes. Pippin, Sheila C. 2007. (J). (gr. -1-5). pap. 12.95 *(978-1-56167-956-0(9))* American Literary Pr.

Pippin-Mathur, Courtney. Maya Was Grumpy. 2013. (J). *(978-0-545-62077-2(5))* Flashlight Pr.

Pippin-Mathur, Courtney. Maya Was Grumpy. Pippin-Mathur, Courtney. 2013. (ENG.). 32p. (J). (gr. k-2). 16.95 *(978-1-936261-13-0(8))* Flashlight Pr.

Pippin, Sheila C., jt. illus. see Pippin, Kristin A.

Pirnot, Karen Hutchins. Just Hanging Out, a Collection of Poems for Kids. Klanot, Khaya Dawn. 2008. 48p. pap. 16.95 *(978-0-9814894-5-2(1))* Peppertree Pr., The.

Pirnot, Karen Hutchins. Keeper of the Lullabies, a Book for Grandmothers Who Cherish the World of Children. Pirnot, Karen Hutchins. 2007. 36p. per. 12.95 *(978-1-934246-90-0(5))* Peppertree Pr., The.

—Night Traveler. Pirnot, Karen Hutchins. 2007. 24p. per. 12.95 *(978-1-934246-97-9(2))* Peppertree Pr., The.

Pisapia, Biasco & Brughera, Pamela. The Chilly Mammoth, 1 vol. Pavanello, Roberto. Zeni, Marco, tr. from ITA. 2013. (Echo & the Bat Pack Ser.). (ENG.). 128p. (gr. 2-3). 9.95 *(978-1-4342-4889-3(5))* Stone Arch Bks.

—The Dancing Vampire. Pavanello, Roberto. Zeni, Marco, tr. from ITA. 2012. (Echo & the Bat Pack Ser.). (ENG.). 128p. (gr. 2-3). 23.99 *(978-1-4342-3837-5(7)*, Echo & the Bat Pack) Stone Arch Bks.

—The Ghost of Dr. Mold. Pavanello, Roberto. Zeni, Marco, tr. from ITA. 2012. (Echo & the Bat Pack Ser.). (ENG.). 128p. (gr. 2-3). 23.99 *(978-1-4342-3834-4(2)*, Echo & the Bat Pack) Stone Arch Bks.

—King Tut's Grandmother, 1 vol. Pavanello, Roberto. Zeni, Marco, tr. from ITA. 2012. (Echo & the Bat Pack Ser.). (ENG.). 128p. (gr. 2-3). 9.95 *(978-1-4342-4245-7(5))*; lib. bdg. 23.99 *(978-1-4342-3823-8(7)*, Echo & the Bat Pack) Stone Arch Bks.

—The Midnight Witches, 1 vol. Pavanello, Roberto. Zeni, Marco, tr. from ITA. 2012. (Echo & the Bat Pack Ser.). (ENG.). 128p. (gr. 2-3). 9.95 *(978-1-4342-4246-4(3))*; lib. bdg. 23.99 *(978-1-4342-3822-1(9)*, Echo & the Bat Pack) Stone Arch Bks.

—The Pirate with the Golden Tooth, 1 vol. Pavanello, Roberto. Zeni, Marco, tr. from ITA. (Echo & the Bat Pack Ser.). (ENG.). 128p. (gr. 2-3). 2013. 9.95 *(978-1-4342-4888-6(7))*; 2012. 23.99 *(978-1-4342-3836-8(9)*, Echo & the Bat Pack) Stone Arch Bks.

—The Thing in the Sewers, 1 vol. Pavanello, Roberto. Zeni, Marco, tr. from ITA. 2012. (Echo & the Bat Pack Ser.). (ENG.). 128p. (gr. 2-3). 9.95 *(978-1-4342-4247-1(1))*; 23.99 *(978-1-4342-3824-5(5)*, Echo & the Bat Pack) Stone Arch Bks.

—Treasure in the Graveyard, 1 vol. Pavanello, Roberto. Zeni, Marco, tr. from ITA. 2012. (Echo & the Bat Pack Ser.). (ENG.). 128p. (gr. 2-3). 9.95 *(978-1-4342-4248-8(X))*; lib. bdg. 23.99 *(978-1-4342-2249-7(7)*, Echo & the Bat Pack) Stone Arch Bks.

Piscopo, Samantha. The Missing Vowel. Cox-Sands, Angela. 2008. 20p. pap. 24.95 *(978-1-60813-028-3(2))* America Star Bks.

Pistacchio. The Three Little Pigs Count To 100. Maccarone, Grace. 2015. (ENG.). 32p. (J). (gr. -1-2). 16.99 ***(978-0-8075-7901-5(7))*** Whitman, Albert & Co.

Pistorius, Anna. The True Book of Birds We Know. Friskey, Margaret. 2011. 48p. pap. 35.95 *(978-1-258-09819-3(9))* Literary Licensing, LLC.

Pita, Lorena. Crisol & His Star. Ibarrola, Begonia. 2013. (ENG.). 32p. (J). *(978-84-95923-50-9(5))* Primera Persona.

Pitcairn, Ansel. Portraits of African-American Heroes. Bolden, Tonya. 2005. (ENG.). 96p. (J). (gr. 3-7). pap. 12.99 *(978-0-14-240473-7(X)*, Puffin) Penguin Publishing Group.

Pitcher, Jeff. Hop, Skip & Jump into Reading. Howlett, Bruce et al. 2003. (J). Bk. 1. 9.00 *(978-0-9704183-4-0(5))*; Bk. 2. 9.00 *(978-0-9704183-3-3(7)*, Sound Reading); Bk. 3. 9.00 *(978-0-9704183-8-8(8)*, Sound Reading) Sound Reading Solutions.

Pitre, Dawn. Beauty's Secret. Gano, Debra. 2008. (Heartlight Girls Ser.). 54p. (J). 17.95 *(978-0-9787689-0-4(6))* Heartlight Girls.

Pitt, Sarah. Animal Friends on the Farm. Reasoner, Charles. 2009. (3D Board Bks.). 12p. (J). (gr. -1-k). bds. 9.99 *(978-1-934650-35-6(8))* Just For Kids Pr., LLC.

—Animals in the Jungle. Reasoner, Charles. 2009. (3D Board Bks.). 12p. (J). (gr. -1-k). bds. 9.99 *(978-1-934650-38-7(2))* Just For Kids Pr., LLC.

—The Busy Christmas Stable, 1 vol. David, Juliet. 2010. (Candle Peek-A-boo Ser.). (ENG.). 8p. (J). (gr. -1-2). 11.99 *(978-1-85985-803-5(1)*, Candle Bks.) Lion Hudson PLC GBR. Dist: Kregel Pubns.

—Colors in the Garden. Reasoner, Charles. 2009. (3D Board Bks.). 12p. (J). (gr. -1-k). bds. 9.99 *(978-1-934650-40-0(4))* Just For Kids Pr., LLC.

—First Words at the Park. Reasoner, Charles. 2009. (3D Board Bks.). 12p. (J). (gr. -1-k). bds. 9.99 *(978-1-934650-39-4(0))* Just For Ks Pr., LLC.

—Noah's Busy Boat, 1 vol. David, Juliet. 2010. (Candle Peek-A-boo Ser.). (ENG.). 8p. (J). bds. 11.99 *(978-0-8254-7393-7(4)*, Candle Bks.) Lion Hudson PLC GBR. Dist: Kregel Pubns.

—Numbers under the Sea. Reasoner, Charles. 2009. (3D Board Bks.). 12p. (J). (gr. -1-k). bds. 9.99 *(978-1-934650-37-0(4))* Just For Kids Pr., LLC.

—Shapes at the Beach. Reasoner, Charles. 2009. (3D Board Bks.). 12p. (J). (gr. -1-k). bds. 9.99 *(978-1-934650-36-3(6))* Just For Kids Pr., LLC.

—Time for Bed Bible Stories, 1 vol. David, Juliet & Dowley, Tim. 2010. (ENG.). 96p. (J). (gr. -1-k). 12.99 *(978-1-85985-778-6(7)*, Candle Bks.) Lion Hudson PLC GBR. Dist: Kregel Pubns.

—Tractor Trouble Drive Through Storybook. Reader's Digest Staff. 2011. (Drive-Through Storybooks Ser.). (ENG.). 10p. (J). (gr. -1-1). bds. 12.99 *(978-0-7944-2169-4(5))* Reader's Digest Assn., Inc., The.

Pittman, Gail. Anna's Choice. Carter, Catherine. 2005. 24p. (J). (gr. 3-7). 12.95 *(978-1-893062-79-5(1))* Quail Ridge Pr., Inc.

Pitz, Henry. Amigo, Circus Horse. Cooper, Page. 2011. 240p. 46.95 *(978-1-258-06394-8(8))* Literary Licensing, LLC.

Pitzer, Marjorie W., photos by. I Like Berries, Do You? Pitzer, Marjorie W. 2013. (ENG., 14p. (J). bds. 11.95 *(978-1-60613-183-1(4))* Woodbine Hse.

—My up & down & All Around Book. Pitzer, Marjorie W. 2008. 16p. (J). (gr. -1-1). pap. 10.95 *(978-1-890627-90-4(9))* Woodbine Hse.

Pitzer, Suzanne. Talking about Divorce & Separation: A Dialogue Between Parent & Child. Grollman, Earl A. 2005. (J). *(978-1-56123-155-3(X))* Centering Corp.

Piu, Amandine. Shelby the Flying Snail, 1 vol. Hanna, Virginie. 2012. (My Little Picture Book Ser.). (ENG.). 32p. (J). (gr. -1). pap. 6.95 *(978-2-7338-1946-3(1))* Auzou, Philippe Editions FRA. Dist: Consortium Bk. Sales & Distribution.

Piven, Hanoch. What Presidents Are Made Of. 2012. (ENG.). 40p. (J). (gr. 1-5). 7.99 *(978-1-4424-4433-1(9)*, Atheneum Bks. for Young Readers) Simon & Schuster Children's Publishing.

Piven, Hanoch. Let's Make Faces. Piven, Hanoch. 2013. (ENG.). 40p. (J). (gr. -1-3). 16.99 *(978-1-4169-1532-4(X))* Simon & Schuster Children's Publishing.

—My Dog Is As Smelly As Dirty Socks: And Other Funny Family Portraits. Piven, Hanoch. 2012. (ENG.). 40p. (J). (gr. -1-3). pap. 7.99 *(978-0-307-93089-7(0)*, Dragonfly Bks.) Random Hse. Children's Bks.

—What Cats Are Made Of. Piven, Hanoch. 2009. (ENG.). 40p. (J). (gr. -1-3). 16.99 *(978-1-4169-1531-7(1)*, Atheneum Bks. for Young Readers) Simon & Schuster Children's Publishing.

Piwowarski, Marcin. La Biblia en un Año para Niños. Davies, Rhona. 2007.Tr. of One Year Children's Bible. (SPA.). 352p. (J). (gr. 1-5). 19.99 *(978-1-4143-1500-3(7)*, Tyndale Espanol) Tyndale Hse. Pubs.

—The One Year Children's Bible. Davies, Rhona. 2007. (ENG.). 352p. (J). (gr. 1-5). 19.99 *(978-1-4143-1499-0(X))* Tyndale Hse. Pubs.

—The Road to Christmas Day. Godfrey, Jan. 2008. 32p. (J). (gr. -1-1). 14.95 *(978-0-8198-6487-1(0))* Pauline Bks. & Media.

—The Road to Easter Day. Godfrey, Jan. 2009. 32p. (J). (gr. -1-1). 14.95 *(978-0-8198-6486-4(2))* Pauline Bks. & Media.

Pixley, Pippa. The Princess & the Pea. Andersen, Hans Christian. 2012. (Fairytale Pop-Ups Ser.). (ENG.). 16p. (J). (gr. k-2). 18.99 *(978-1-85707-816-9(0))* Tango Bks. GBR. Dist: Independent Pubs. Group.

Pixton, Kaaren. Hickory Dickory Dock: Hey Baby! Look at the Mouse that Went up the Clock — Big Ben in London! Sickler, Jonas & Pixton, Amy. 2011. (Indestructibles Ser.). (ENG.). 12p. (J). (gr. k — 1). pap. 5.95 *(978-0-7611-5921-6(5)*, 15921) Workman Publishing Co., Inc.

—Old Macdonald Had a Farm: Hey Baby! Look at These Animals on the Farm — in Bolivia! Sickler, Jonas & Pixton, Amy. 2011. (Indestructibles Ser.). (ENG.). 12p. (J). (gr. k — 1). pap. 5.95 *(978-0-7611-5922-3(3)*, 15922) Workman Publishing Co., Inc.

Pixton, Kaaren, jt. illus. see Sickler, Jonas.

Pizzoli, Greg. Just Itzy. Krumwiede, Lana. 2015. (ENG.). 40p. (J). (-k). 15.99 *(978-0-7636-5811-3(1))* Candlewick Pr.

P

—Not Very Scary. Brendler, Carol. 2014. (ENG.). 40p. (J). (gr. -1-1). 12.99 (978-0-374-35547-0(9), Farrar, Straus & Giroux (BYR)) Farrar, Straus & Giroux.

Pizzoli, Greg. Number One Sam. Pizzoli, Greg. 2014. (ENG.). 40p. (J). (gr. -1-k). 16.99 (978-1-4231-7111-9(X)) Hyperion Bks. for Children.

—Templeton Gets His Wish. Pizzoli, Greg. 2015. (ENG.). 48p. (J). (gr. -1-k). 16.99 (978-1-4847-1274-0(9)) Disney Pr.

—The Watermelon Seed. Pizzoli, Greg. 2013. (ENG.). 40p. (J). (gr. -1-k). 16.99 (978-1-4231-7101-0(2)) Disney Pr.

Place, Francois. Meeting Cezanne. Morpurgo, Michael. 2013. (ENG.). 80p. (J). (gr. 2-5). 15.99 (978-0-7636-4896-1(5)) Candlewick Pr.

Place, François. Tales of a Lost Kingdom: A Journey into Northwest Pakistan. L'Homme, Erik. 2007. (ENG.). 48p. (J). (gr. 3-18). 17.95 (978-1-59270-072-1(1)) Enchanted Lion Bks., LLC.

Place, Francois. Toby Alone. De Fombelle, Timothée. Ardizzone, Sarah, tr. from FRE. 2009. (ENG.). 400p. (J). (gr. 4-7). 17.99 (978-0-7636-4181-8(2)) Candlewick Pr.

—Toby & the Secrets of the Tree. De Fombelle, Timothée. Ardizzone, Sarah, tr. from FRE. 2010. (ENG.). 432p. (J). (gr. 4-7). 16.99 (978-0-7636-4655-4(5)) Candlewick Pr.

Placides, Del S. The Safe Place. Vogel-Placides, Joan Katherine. 2013. 58p. 13.99 (978-0-9888718-3-0(1)) DOMINIONHOUSE Publishing & Design.

Plafkin-Hurwitz, Marsha. Up 2 Snuff: Illustrated Book for Children. Plafkin-Hurwitz, Marsha. 2nd ed. 2010. 32p. (J). pap. (978-0-578-05270-0(9)) Art as Responsa LLC.

Plagens, Frances. Imagine This! Froh, Joanne. 2006. 32p. (J). 19.95 (978-0-9777640-0-6(1)) Joanne Frances Pr.

Planer, Geoffrey. And Then There Were Three. Seymour, Jane & Keach, James. 2003. (This One & That One Ser.: Vol. 5). (ENG.). 32p. (J). (gr. -1-3). 12.99 (978-1-932431-09-4(8)) Left Field,Angel Gate.

—Boing! No Bouncing on the Bed. Seymour, Jane & Keach, James. 2003. (This One & That One Ser.: Vol. 1). (ENG.). 32p. (J). (gr. -1-3). 12.99 (978-1-932431-06-3(3)) Left Field,Angel Gate.

—Fried Pies & Roast Cake. Seymour, Jane & Keach, James. 2003. (This One & That One Ser.: Vol. 5). (ENG.). 32p. (J). (gr. -1-3). 12.99 (978-1-932431-10-0(1)) Left Field,Angel Gate.

—The Other One: You Make Me Happy. Seymour, Jane & Keach, James. gif. ed. 2003. (This One & That One Ser.). (ENG.). 16p. (J). (gr. -1-3). 5.99 (978-1-932431-57-5(8)) Left Field,Angel Gate.

—Splat! The Tale of a Colorful Cat. Seymour, Jane & Keach, James. 2003. (This One & That One Ser.: Vol. 2.). (ENG.). 32p. (J). (gr. -1-3). 12.99 (978-1-932431-07-0(1)) Left Field,Angel Gate.

—Yum! A Tale of Two Cookies. Seymour, Jane & Keach, James. 2nd ed. 2003. (This One & That One Ser.: Vol. 3). (ENG.). 32p. (J). (gr. -1-3). 12.99 (978-1-932431-08-7(X)) Left Field,Angel Gate.

Plant, Andrew. Ancient Animals: Saber-Toothed Cat. Thomson, Sarah L. 2014. (ENG.). 32p. (J). (gr. 1-4). pap. 5.95 (978-1-58089-407-4(0)); lib. bdg. 12.95 (978-1-58089-400-5(3)) Charlesbridge Publishing, Inc.

—It's True! We Came from Slime. McNamara, Ken. 2006. (It's True! Ser.). (ENG.). 96p. (J). (gr. 5-8). 19.95 (978-1-55037-953-2(4), 9781550379532); pap. 5.95 (978-1-55037-952-5(6), 9781550379525) Annick Pr., Ltd. CAN. Dist: Firefly Bks., Ltd.

—A Platypus, Probably. Collard, Sneed B., III. 2005. (ENG.). 32p. (J). (gr. k-3). per. 7.95 (978-1-57091-584-0(9)) Charlesbridge Publishing, Inc.

Plant, Beth. Brandy & the Mascot: Brandy the Golden Retriever; Author's Version. Finch, Donna. l.t. ed. 2010. (ENG.). 34p. pap. 9.25 (978-1-4563-2318-9(0)) CreateSpace Independent Publishing Platform.

Plante, Beth. Brandy & the Big Dig: Brandy the Golden Retriever: Author's Version. Finch, Donna. l.t. ed. 2010. (ENG.). 36p. pap. 9.25 (978-1-4538-8414-0(9)) CreateSpace Independent Publishing Platform.

—Brandy & the Rapids, 1 vol. Finch, Donna. 2009. 36p. pap. 24.95 (978-1-60749-150-7(8)) America Star Bks.

—Brandy & the Rapids: Brandy, the Golden Retriever. Finch, Donna. l.t. ed. 2010. (ENG.). 32p. pap. 9.25 (978-1-4564-9107-9(5)) CreateSpace Independent Publishing Platform.

Platt, Brian. Triplet Tales. Cushion, Hazel. 2006. 32p. pap. (978-0-9547092-1-1(7)) Accent Pr. Ltd.

Platt, Greg. Alphie & the Alphabets: A Fun Way to Learn to Read. Sayles, Alayne. 2005. 44p. (J). spiral bd. 79.95 incl. audio compact disk (978-0-9767506-0-4(0)) Reading Studio Pr.

Platt, Jason. Early Social Skills Stories: Going Potty. Hodson, Sarah E. 2013. (J). (978-0-7606-1408-2(3)) LinguiSystems, Inc.

Platt, Pierre. Bye-Bye, Katy, Vol. 3. Michaels, David. l.t. ed. 2005. (Sadlier Phonics Reading Program). 8p. (gr. -1-1). 23.00 net. (978-0-8215-7354-9(3)) Sadlier, William H. Inc.

Platt, Sharal. Goliaths's Secret. Feuer, Bonnie. 2013. (ENG.). 38p. (J). 18.50 (978-0-9825468-8-8(2)) Connecticut Pr., The.

Playcrib. Six Fingers & the Blue Warrior. Laar-Yond C.T. 2013. 36p. pap. 14.00 (978-1-62212-177-9(5), Strategic Bk. Publishing) Strategic Book Publishing & Rights Agency (SBPRA).

Player, Micah. Around the World Matching Game. Chronicle Books Staff. 2013. (ENG.). 72p. (J). (gr. -1-1). bds. 14.99 (978-1-4521-1699-0(7)) Chronicle Bks. LLC.

—Binny for Short. McKay, Hilary. (ENG.). (J). (gr. 3-7). 2014. 320p. pap. 7.99 (978-1-4424-8276-0(1)); 2013. 304p. 16.99 (978-1-4424-8275-3(3)) McElderry, Margaret K. Bks. (McElderry, Margaret K. Bks.).

—Chloe, Instead. 2012. (ENG.). 32p. (J). (gr. -1-1). 15.99 (978-0-8118-7865-4(1)) Chronicle Bks. LLC.

—Lately Lily ABC Travel Flash Cards. Chronicle Books Editors. 2014. (ENG.). 26p. (J). (gr. -1-17). 14.99 (978-1-4521-1524-5(9)) Chronicle Bks. LLC.

Plecas, Jennifer. Agapanthus Hum & the Eyeglasses. Cowley, Joy. 2013. (Penguin Young Readers, Level 3 Ser.). (ENG.). 32p. (J). (gr. 1-3). pap. 3.99 (978-0-448-46477-0(2), Warne, Frederick Pubs.) Penguin Bks., Ltd. GBR. Dist: Penguin Random Hse., LLC.

—The Basket Ball. Codell, Esmé Raji. 2011. (ENG.). 32p. (J). (gr. -1-3). 17.95 (978-1-4197-0007-1(3), Abrams Bks. for Young Readers) Abrams.

—Emma's Strange Pet. Little, Jean. (I Can Read Book 3 Ser.). 64p. (J). (gr. k-3). 2004. (ENG.). pap. 3.99 (978-0-06-444259-6(4)); 2003. 15.99 (978-0-06-028350-6(5)) HarperCollins Pubs.

—Get Well, Good Knight. Thomas, Shelley Moore. 2004. (Penguin Young Readers, Level 3 Ser.). (ENG.). 48p. (J). (gr. 1-3). 3.99 (978-0-14-240050-0(5), Warne, Frederick Pubs.) Penguin Bks., Ltd. GBR. Dist: Penguin Random Hse., LLC.

—Get Well, Good Knight. Thomas, Shelley Moore. 2004. (Easy-to-Read Ser.). 44p. (gr. k-3). 14.00 (978-0-7569-2923-7(7)) Perfection Learning Corp.

—Happy Birthday, Good Knight. Thomas, Shelley Moore. 2014. (Penguin Young Readers, Level 3 Ser.). (ENG.). 48p. (J). (gr. 1-3). pap. 3.99 (978-0-448-46374-2(1), Warne, Frederick Pubs.) Penguin Bks., Ltd. GBR. Dist: Penguin Random Hse., LLC.

—I, Fly. Heos, Bridget. 2015. (ENG.). 48p. (J). (gr. -1-3). 17.99 (978-0-8050-9469-5(5), Holt, Henry & Co. Bks. For Young Readers) Holt, Henry & Co.

—Please Is a Good Word to Say. Joosse, Barbara M. 2007. (J). (978-1-4287-4649-7(8), Philomel) Penguin Publishing Group.

Plecas, Jennifer. Bah! Said the Baby. Plecas, Jennifer. 2015. (ENG.). 32p. (J). (gr. -1-k). 16.99 (978-0-399-16606-8(8), Philomel) Penguin Publishing Group.

Pledger, Maurice. Animal World. 2011. (Pledger Sticker Book Ser.). (ENG.). 80p. (J). (gr. -1). 10.95 (978-1-60710-167-3(X), Silver Dolphin Bks.) Baker & Taylor Publishing Group.

—Daisy Duckling's Adventure. 2014. (ENG.). 16p. (J). (gr. -1). bds. 10.95 (978-1-62686-015-5(7), Silver Dolphin Bks.) Baker & Taylor Publishing Group.

—Dinosaurs & Bugs. 2014. (ENG.). 120p. (J). (gr. -1). act. bk. ed. 12.95 (978-1-62686-106-0(4), Silver Dolphin Bks.) Baker & Taylor Publishing Group.

—Dottie Dolphin Plays Hide-And-Seek. 2015. (Friendship Tales Ser.). (ENG.). 16p. (gr. -1). bds. 10.95 (978-1-62686-344-6(X), Silver Dolphin Bks.) Baker & Taylor Publishing Group.

—Into the Wild. 2014. (ENG.). 120p. (J). (gr. -1). act. bk. ed. 12.95 (978-1-62686-107-7(2), Silver Dolphin Bks.) Baker & Taylor Publishing Group.

—Jungle. 2008. (Pledger Sounds Ser.). (ENG.). 16p. (J). (gr. k). 18.95 (978-1-59223-472-1(0), Silver Dolphin Bks.) Baker & Taylor Publishing Group.

—Jungles & Oceans. 2015. (Animal Kingdom Ser.). (ENG.). 120p. (gr. -1). act. bk. ed. 12.95 (978-1-62686-108-4(0), Silver Dolphin Bks.) Baker & Taylor Publishing Group.

—Nature Trails: Baby Animals. 2014. (Maurice Pledger Nature Trails Ser.). (ENG.). 16p. (J). (gr. -1). 12.95 (978-1-62686-038-4(6), Silver Dolphin Bks.) Baker & Taylor Publishing Group.

—Nature Trails: Beetles & Bugs. 2013. (Maurice Pledger Nature Trails Ser.). (ENG.). 16p. (J). (gr. -1). 12.95 (978-1-60710-590-9(X), Silver Dolphin Bks.) Baker & Taylor Publishing Group.

—Nature Trails: Dinosaurs. 2013. (Maurice Pledger Nature Trails Ser.). (ENG.). 16p. (J). (gr. -1). 12.95 (978-1-60710-589-3(6), Silver Dolphin Bks.) Baker & Taylor Publishing Group.

—Nighttime. 2007. (Pledger Sounds Ser.). (ENG.). 16p. (J). (gr. k). 18.95 (978-1-59223-471-4(2), Silver Dolphin Bks.) Baker & Taylor Publishing Group.

—Noisy Nature: in the Jungle. Martin, Ruth. 2015. (ENG.). 12p. (J). (gr. -1). 16.95 (978-1-62686-104-6(8), Silver Dolphin Bks.) Baker & Taylor Publishing Group.

—Noisy Nature: in the Ocean. 2015. (Noisy Nature Ser.). (ENG.). 12p. (J). (gr. -1). 16.95 (978-1-62686-105-3(6), Silver Dolphin Bks.) Baker & Taylor Publishing Group.

—Noisy Nature: on the Farm. Martin, Ruth. 2015. (ENG.). 12p. (J). (gr. -1). 16.95 (978-1-62686-103-9(X), Silver Dolphin Bks.) Baker & Taylor Publishing Group.

—Olivia Owl Finds a Friend. 2013. (Maurice Pledger Surprises Ser.). (ENG.). 16p. (J). (gr. -1). bds. 10.95 (978-1-60710-884-9(4), Silver Dolphin Bks.) Baker & Taylor Publishing Group.

—Oscar Otter & the Goldfish. 2013. (Maurice Pledger Surprises Ser.). (ENG.). 16p. (J). (gr. -1). bds. 10.95 (978-1-60710-883-2(6), Silver Dolphin Bks.) Baker & Taylor Publishing Group.

—Ping-Ping Panda's Bamboo Journey. 2015. (Friendship Tales Ser.). (ENG.). 16p. (J). (gr. -1). bds. 10.95 (978-1-62686-345-3(8), Silver Dolphin Bks.) Baker & Taylor Publishing Group.

—Sounds of the Wild: Animals. Davies, Valerie. 2015. (Pledger Sounds Ser.). (ENG.). 16p. (J). (gr. k). 18.95 (978-1-62686-049-0(1), Silver Dolphin Bks.) Baker & Taylor Publishing Group.

—Sounds of the Wild: Birds. 2015. (Pledger Sounds Ser.). (ENG.). 16p. (J). (gr. k). 18.95 (978-1-62686-417-7(9), Silver Dolphin Bks.) Baker & Taylor Publishing Group.

—Sounds of the Wild: Bugs. 2015. (Pledger Sounds Ser.). (ENG.). 16p. (J). (gr. k). 18.95 (978-1-62686-418-4(7), Silver Dolphin Bks.) Baker & Taylor Publishing Group.

—Sounds of the Wild: Desert. 2015. (Pledger Sounds Ser.). (ENG.). 16p. (J). (gr. k). 18.95 (978-1-62686-419-1(5), Silver Dolphin Bks.) Baker & Taylor Publishing Group.

—Sounds of the Wild: Forest. 2012. (Pledger Sounds Ser.). (ENG.). 16p. (J). (gr. k). 18.95 (978-1-60710-371-4(0), Silver Dolphin Bks.) Baker & Taylor Publishing Group.

—Sounds of the Wild: Safari. 2015. (Pledger Sounds Ser.). (ENG.). 16p. (J). (gr. k). 18.95 (978-1-62686-420-7(9), Silver Dolphin Bks.) Baker & Taylor Publishing Group.

Pledger, Maurice. Bobby Bear & the Honeybees. Pledger, Maurice. 2014. (Friendship Tales Ser.). (ENG.). 16p. (J). (gr. -1). bds. 10.95 (978-1-62686-189-3(7), Silver Dolphin Bks.) Baker & Taylor Publishing Group.

Plessix, Michel. The Gates of Dawn. Grahame, Kenneth. Johnson, Joe, tr. 2003. (Wind in the Willows Ser.: Vol. 3). (ENG.). 32p. (gr. 4-7). pap. 15.95 (978-1-56163-245-9(7)) NBM Publishing Co.

Ploog, Michael G. L. Frank Baum's the Life & Adventures of Santa Claus. Ploog, Michael G. 2003. 80p. (YA). (gr. 7-12). reprint ed. 25.00 (978-0-7567-6682-5(6)) DIANE Publishing Co.

Ploog, Mike. The Puppet, the Professor, & the Prophet. Dematteis, J. M. 3rd rev. ed. 2007. 144p. (J). (gr. 4-7). 9.99 (978-1-4231-0063-8(8)) Hyperion Pr.

—Stardust Kid. DeMatteis, J. M. 2008. (ENG.). 128p. pap. 14.99 (978-1-934506-04-2(4)) Boom! Studios.

Ploss, Skip. If Picasso Were a Fish. Ploss, Skip. 2006. 40p. (J). (gr. k-2). 15.99 (978-1-4116-9220-6(9)) Lulu Enterprises Inc.

Plumbe, Scott. Bodyguards! From Gladiators to the Secret Service. Butts, Ed. 2012. (ENG.). 124p. (J). (gr. 4-7). 24.95 (978-1-55451-437-3(1), 9781554514373); pap. 14.95 (978-1-55451-436-6(3), 9781554514366) Annick Pr., Ltd. CAN. Dist: Firefly Bks., Ltd.

Plume, Ilse. Saint Francis & the Wolf. Langton, Jane P. 2007. (ENG.). 32p. (J). (gr. -1-3). 16.95 (978-1-56792-320-9(8)) Godine, David R. Pub.

—The Year Comes Round: Haiku Through the Seasons. Farrar, Sid. 2012. (ENG.). 32p. (J). (gr. -1-2). 16.99 (978-0-8075-8129-2(1)) Whitman, Albert & Co.

Plume, Ilse. The Farmer in the Dell. Plume, Ilse, adapted by. 2010. (ENG.). 32p. pap. 8.95 (978-1-56792-390-2(9)) Godine, David R. Pub.

Plumlee, Buddy. The Ants. McClure, Brian D. 2009. (Brian D. Mcclure Childrens Book Collection). 57p. (J). (gr. -1-3). 16.95 (978-1-933426-10-5(1)) Universal Flag Publishing.

—The Birds & the Frogs. McClure, Brian D. 2009. (Brian D. Mcclure Childrens Book Collection). 37p. (J). (gr. -1-3). 16.95 (978-1-933426-13-6(6)) Universal Flag Publishing.

—The Meal. McClure, Brian D. 2009. (Brian D. Mcclure Childrens Book Collection). 59p. (J). (gr. -1-3). 16.95 (978-1-933426-04-4(7)) Universal Flag Publishing.

—The Up down Day. McClure, Brian D. 2009. (Brian D. Mcclure Childrens Book Collection). 47p. (J). (gr. -1-3). 14.95 (978-1-933426-07-5(1)) Universal Flag Publishing.

Plumley, Alea. Animals, Vegetables & Minerals from A to Z. O'Donnell, Sallie. l.t. ed. 2005. 60p. pap. 9.95 (978-0-9764982-5-4(1)) Legacy Publishing Services, Inc.

Pluum, Ave. Katrina's New Room. Weinstein, Natalie. 2004. (J). pap. 19.95 (978-0-9749531-0-6(5)) Images For Presentation.

Pocock, Aaron. Bailey Beats the Blah. Tyrrell, Karen. 2013. 34p. pap. (978-0-9872740-4-5(X)) Digital Future Press.

—The Orange Ray. Blake-Wilson, Pamela. 2010. (Colour Code Ser.: Bk. 2). 266p. pap. (978-0-9806520-6-2(5)) Pick-a-Woo Woo Pubs.

—Pick-a-WooWoo - Robbie the Butterfly: An enlightening story of Transformation, 16 vols., Vol. 13. Larson, Robert. 2010. 28p. pap. (978-0-9806520-2-4(2)) Pick-a-Woo Woo Pubs.

—The Red Ray. Blake-Wilson, Pamela. 2009. (Colour Code Ser.: Bk. 1). 246p. (J). pap. (978-0-9806520-0-0(6)) Pick-a-Woo Woo Pubs.

Podgurski, Sharon. I'm Adopted, I'm Special. Rice, Beth. 2008. 32p. pap. 12.95 (978-0-9817572-0-9(0)) Peppertree Pr., The.

Poe, Edgar Allen. Edgar Allan Poe Collection. Poe, Edgar Allen. 2005. (Adventure Classics Ser.). 176p. (J). pap. 6.99 (978-0-06-075881-3(3), HarperFestival) HarperCollins Pubs.

Poer, Nancy Jewel. Mia's Apple Tree. Poer, Nancy Jewel. 2004. 34p. (J). 21.95 (978-0-9740413-1-5(9)) White Feather Publishing.

Poes, Nancy. Loco Dog & the Dust Devil in the Railyard. Heller, Marcy. 2007. 30p. (J). (gr. -1-7). 19.95 (978-1-929115-17-4(2)) Azro Pr., Inc.

Pogany, Willy. The Adventures of Odysseus & the Tale of Troy. Colum, Padraic. 2004. (Dover Children's Classics Ser.). (ENG.). 176p. (J). (gr. 3-8). pap. 6.95 (978-0-486-43455-1(9)) Dover Pubns., Inc.

—The Adventures of Odysseus & the Tale of Troy. Colum, Padraic. 2008. 164p. pap. (978-1-4068-2730-9(4)) Echo Library.

—The Children of Odin: The Book of Northern Myths. Colum, Padraic. 2008. 216p. (gr. 5-9). pap. (978-1-4065-9868-1(2)) Dodo Pr.

—The Children of Odin: The Book of Northern Myths. Colum, Padraic. 2004. (ENG.). 288p. (J). (gr. 5-9). pap. 9.99 (978-0-689-86885-6(5), Simon & Schuster/Paula Wiseman Bks.) Simon & Schuster/Paula Wiseman Bks.

—The Children's Homer: The Adventures of Odysseus & the Tale of Troy. Colum, Padraic. 2004. (ENG.). 256p. (J). (gr. 5-9). pap. 9.99 (978-0-689-86883-2(9), Simon & Schuster/Paula Wiseman Bks.) Simon & Schuster/Paula Wiseman Bks.

—The Golden Cockerel: From the Original Russian Fairy Tale of Alexander Pushkin. Pogany, Elaine. 2013. (Dover Children's Classics Ser.). (ENG.). 48p. (J). (gr. 5-8). pap. 14.95 (978-0-486-49115-8(3)) Dover Pubns., Inc.

—The Golden Fleece: And the Heroes Who Lived Before Achilles. Colum, Padraic. 2004. 316p. (J). (gr. 5). 17.60 (978-0-7569-4048-5(6)) Perfection Learning Corp.

—The Golden Fleece: And the Heroes Who Lived Before Achilles. Colum, Padraic. 2004. (ENG.). 320p. (J). (gr. 5-9). pap. 10.99 (978-0-689-86884-9(7), Simon & Schuster/Paula Wiseman Bks.) Simon & Schuster/Paula Wiseman Bks.

—The Golden Fleece & the Heroes Who Lived Before Achilles. Colum, Padraic. 2007. 144p. pap. 8.99 (978-1-4209-3040-5(0)) Digireads.com.

—The Golden Fleece & the Heroes Who Lived Before Achilles. Colum, Padraic. 2010. (Looking Glass Library). (ENG.). 368p. (J). (gr. 3-7). 10.99 (978-0-375-86709-5(0)) Random Hse., Inc.

—The King of Ireland's Son. Colum, Padraic. ed. 2009. 308p. pap. 12.95 (978-1-59915-083-3(2)) Yesterday's Classics.

—The Story of the Golden Fleece. Colum, Padraic. unabr. ed. 2005. (Dover Children's Classics Ser.). (ENG.). 256p. (J). (gr. 3-5). per. 5.95 (978-0-486-44366-9(3)) Dover Pubns., Inc.

—Tanglewood Tales. Hawthorne, Nathaniel. 2009. 272p. pap. 11.95 (978-1-59915-091-8(3)) Yesterday's Classics.

—A Treasury of Poems for Children. Edgar, M. G. 2010. (Dover Children's Classics Ser.). (ENG.). 272p. (J). (gr. -1-3). pap. 9.99 (978-0-486-47376-5(7)) Dover Pubns., Inc.

Poh, Jennie. I Love You to the Moon. Harrod-Eagles, Cynthia. 2014. (ENG.). 20p. (gr. -1). bds. 8.95 (978-1-58925-642-2(5)) Tiger Tales.

Pohl, David. Pawns. Roberts, Willo Davis. 2012. (ENG.). 160p. (J). (gr. 5-9). pap. 8.99 (978-0-689-83320-5(2), Simon & Schuster/Paula Wiseman Bks.) Simon & Schuster/Paula Wiseman Bks.

Pohle, Peter. Solomon's Temple Model, 1 vol. Dowley, Tim. 2011. (Candle Discovery Ser.). 20p. (J). (gr. 2-4). 14.99 (978-0-8254-7425-5(6), Candle Bks.) Lion Hudson PLC GBR. Dist: Kregel Pubns.

poho. Late October. Cowart, Logan. 2011. (ENG.). 42p. pap. 9.99 (978-1-4610-5645-4(4)) CreateSpace Independent Publishing Platform.

Pohrt, Tom. Finding Susie. O'Connor, Sandra Day. 2009. (ENG.). 40p. (J). (gr. k-3). 16.99 (978-0-375-84103-3(2), Knopf Bks. for Young Readers) Random Hse. Children's Bks.

—The Little Gentleman. Pearce, Philippa. 2004. 208p. (J). (gr. 3-18). lib. bdg. 16.89 (978-0-06-073161-8(3)) HarperCollins Pubs.

—The Walls of Cartagena. Durango, Julia. 2008. (ENG.). 160p. (J). (gr. 3-7). 15.99 (978-1-4169-4102-6(9), Simon & Schuster Bks. For Young Readers) Simon & Schuster Bks. For Young Readers.

—The Wishing Bone, & Other Poems. Mitchell, Stephen. 2003. (ENG.). 56p. (J). (gr. k-12). 16.99 (978-0-7636-1118-7(2)) Candlewick Pr.

Pohrte, Juliann, jt. illus. see Pohrte, Olivia.

Pohrte, Olivia & Pohrte, Juliann. In the Land of Liviaann. Pohrte, Kathysue & Pohrte, Olivia. Pohrte, Juliann. Pohrte, Kathysue, ed. l.t. ed. 2003. 36p. (J). pap. 17.95 (978-0-9722296-0-9(4), 872493); (gr. -1-6). 12.95 (978-0-9722296-1-6(2), 872493) Pohrte, Dorey Publishing, Inc.

Point, Susan, jt. illus. see Fernandes, Roger.

Poirier, Nadine. Busy Kids' Colors, Shapes & Sizes. Jaramillo, Gloria. 2008. (Busy Kids Ser.). 36p. (J). (gr. -1-k). bds. 12.99 (978-2-7641-1677-7(2)) Gardner Pubns.

Poitier, Anton. Colors: Match the Words & Colors. 2014. (Twisters Ser.). (ENG.). 10p. (J). (gr. -1 — 1). bds. 7.99 (978-0-7641-6687-7(5)) Barron's Educational Series, Inc.

Poitier, Anton. Numbers. 2015. (Twisters Ser.). (ENG.). 10p. (J). (gr. -1 — 1). bds. 7.99 (978-0-7641-6809-3(6)) Barron's Educational Series, Inc.

Poitier, Anton. Opposites: Twist & Find the Opposite. 2014. (Twisters Ser.). (ENG.). 10p. (J). (gr. -1 — 1). bds. 7.99 (978-0-7641-6688-4(3)) Barron's Educational Series, Inc.

Poitier, Anton. Shapes. 2015. (Twisters Ser.). (ENG.). 10p. (J). (gr. -1 — 1). bds. 7.99 (978-0-7641-6810-9(X)) Barron's Educational Series, Inc.

Poitras, Jim. The Drum Calls Softly. Bouchard, David & Willier, Shelley. 2008. 120p. (ENG.). (J). (gr. 4-7). 24.95 (978-0-88995-421-2(6), 0889954216); 4th ed. (FRE & ENG.). 24.95 (978-0-88995-424-3(0)) Red Deer Pr. CAN. Dist: Midpoint Trade Bks., Inc., Ingram Pub. Services.

Pokrovskaya, Liya, photos by. Saving Yasha: The Incredible True Story of an Adopted Moon Bear. Kvatum, Lia. 2012. (ENG., 32p. (J). (gr. -1-3). 16.95 (978-1-4263-1051-5(X)); lib. bdg. 25.90 (978-1-4263-1076-8(5)) National Geographic Society. (National Geographic Children's Bks.).

Polacco, Patricia. Because of Thursday. 2016. (J). (978-1-4814-2140-9(9), Simon & Schuster Bks. For Young Readers) Simon & Schuster Bks. For Young Readers.

—When Lightning Comes in a Jar. Polacco, Ernest L. 2007. (ENG.). 40p. (J). (gr. k-3). 6.99 (978-0-14-240350-1(4), Puffin) Penguin Publishing Group.

Polacco, Patricia. The Art of Miss Chew. Polacco, Patricia. 2012. (ENG.). 32p. (J). (gr. k-3). 17.99 (978-0-399-25703-2(9), Putnam Juvenile) Penguin Publishing Group.

—Betty Doll. Polacco, Patricia. 2004. (ENG.). 40p. (J). (gr. -1-3). reprint ed. pap. 7.99 (978-0-14-240196-5(X), Puffin) Penguin Publishing Group.

—The Blessing Cup. Polacco, Patricia. 2013. (ENG.). 48p. (J). (gr. -1-3). 17.99 (978-1-4424-5047-9(9), Simon & Schuster Bks. For Young Readers) Simon & Schuster Bks. For Young Readers.

—Bully. Polacco, Patricia. 2012. (ENG.). 48p. (J). (gr. 2-5). 17.99 (978-0-399-25704-9(7), Putnam Juvenile) Penguin Publishing Group.

—Bun Bun Button. Polacco, Patricia. 2011. (ENG.). 36p. (J). (gr. -1-k). 17.99 (978-0-399-25472-7(2), Putnam Juvenile) Penguin Publishing Group.

—Emma Kate. Polacco, Patricia. (ENG.). (J). (gr. -1-k). 2008. 32p. pap. 6.99 (978-0-14-241196-4(5), Puffin); 2005. 40p. 17.99 (978-0-399-24452-0(2), Philomel) Penguin Publishing Group.

—Fiona's Lace. Polacco, Patricia. 2014. (ENG.). 48p. (J). (gr. -1-3). 17.99 (978-1-4424-8724-6(0), Simon & Schuster/Paula Wiseman Bks.) Simon & Schuster/Paula Wiseman Bks.

—For the Love of Autumn. Polacco, Patricia. 2008. (ENG.). 40p. (J). (gr. 1-4). 17.99 (978-0-399-24541-1(3), Philomel) Penguin Publishing Group.

—G Is for Goat. Polacco, Patricia. 2006. (ENG.). 32p. (J). (gr. -1-k). reprint ed. pap. 6.99 (978-0-14-240550-5(7), Puffin) Penguin Publishing Group.

—Gifts of the Heart. Polacco, Patricia. 2013. (ENG.). 40p. (J). (gr. k-3). 17.99 (978-0-399-16094-3(9), Putnam Juvenile) Penguin Publishing Group.

—Ginger & Petunia. Polacco, Patricia. 2007. (ENG.). 40p. (J). (gr. -1-3). 17.99 *(978-0-399-24539-8(1)*, Philomel) Penguin Publishing Group.
—The Graves Family. Polacco, Patricia. 2006. (ENG.). 48p. (J). (gr. k-3). reprint ed. pap. 6.99 *(978-0-14-240635-9(X)*, Puffin) Penguin Publishing Group.
—The Graves Family. Polacco, Patricia. 2006. (gr. k-3). 17.00 *(978-0-7569-6715-4(5))* Perfection Learning Corp.
—In Our Mothers' House. Polacco, Patricia. 2009. (ENG.). 48p. (J). (gr. 1-3). 17.99 *(978-0-399-25076-7(X)*, Philomel) Penguin Publishing Group.
—January's Sparrow. Polacco, Patricia. 2009. (ENG.). 96p. (J). (gr. 3-7). 22.99 *(978-0-399-25077-4(8)*, Philomel) Penguin Publishing Group.
—John Philip Duck. Polacco, Patricia. 2004. (ENG.). 48p. (J). (gr. k-4). 17.99 *(978-0-399-24262-5(7)*, Philomel) Penguin Publishing Group.
—The Junkyard Wonders. Polacco, Patricia. 2010. (ENG.). 48p. (J). (gr. 1-4). 17.99 *(978-0-399-25078-1(6)*, Philomel) Penguin Publishing Group.
—Just in Time, Abraham Lincoln. Polacco, Patricia. 2011. (ENG.). 48p. (J). (gr. 2-4). 17.99 *(978-0-399-25471-0(4)*, Putnam Juvenile) Penguin Publishing Group.
—The Keeping Quilt: 25th Anniversary Edition. Polacco, Patricia. ed. 2013. (ENG.). 64p. (J). (gr. -1-3). 17.99 *(978-1-4424-8237-1(0)*, Simon & Schuster/Paula Wiseman Bks.) Simon & Schuster/Paula Wiseman Bks.
—The Lemonade Club. Polacco, Patricia. 2007. (ENG.). 48p. (J). (gr. 1-4). 17.99 *(978-0-399-24540-4(5)*, Philomel) Penguin Publishing Group.
—Mommies Say Shhh! Polacco, Patricia. (ENG.). (J). (gr. -1 — 1). 2007. 32p. bds. 6.99 *(978-0-399-24720-0(3))*; 2005. 40p. 16.99 *(978-0-399-24341-7(0))* Penguin Publishing Group. (Philomel).
—Mr. Wayne's Masterpiece. Polacco, Patricia. 2014. (ENG.). 40p. (J). (gr. k-3). 17.99 *(978-0-399-16095-0(7)*, Putnam Adult) Penguin Publishing Group.
—Oh, Look! Polacco, Patricia. 2004. (ENG.). 32p. (J). (gr. -1-3). 16.99 *(978-0-399-24223-6(6)*, Philomel) Penguin Publishing Group.
—An Orange for Frankie. Polacco, Patricia. 2004. (ENG.). 48p. (J). (gr. 1-4). 17.99 *(978-0-399-24302-8(X)*, Philomel) Penguin Publishing Group.
—Rotten Richie & the Ultimate Dare. Polacco, Patricia. 2006. (ENG.). 48p. (J). (gr. k-3). 17.99 *(978-0-399-24531-2(6)*, Philomel) Penguin Publishing Group.
—Someone for Mr. Sussman. Polacco, Patricia. 2008. (ENG.). 40p. (J). (gr. 1-3). 17.99 *(978-0-399-25075-0(1)*, Philomel) Penguin Publishing Group.
—Something about Hensley's. Polacco, Patricia. 2006. (ENG.). 48p. (J). (gr. -1-3). 17.99 *(978-0-399-24538-1(3)*, Philomel) Penguin Publishing Group.
—Thank You, Mr. Falker. Polacco, Patricia. 2012. (ENG.). 40p. (J). (gr. k-3). 12.99 *(978-0-399-25762-9(4)*, Philomel) Penguin Publishing Group.
—Tucky Jo & Little Heart. Polacco, Patricia. 2015. (ENG.). 48p. (J). (gr. -1-3). 17.99 *(978-1-4814-1584-2(0)*, Simon & Schuster Bks. For Young Readers) Simon & Schuster Bks. For Young Readers.
Polan, Jason. Mermaid in Chelsea Creek. Tea, Michelle. 2013. (ENG.). 240p. (gr. 5-11). 19.95 *(978-1-938073-36-6(3))* McSweeney's Publishing.
Polastri, Rosa Elena. El Misterio del Condor. Brignole, Giancarla, tr. (Fabulas De Familia Ser.). (SPA.). 32p. *(978-970-20-0270-3(2))* Castillo, Ediciones, S. A. de C. V.
Polat, Ercan. Makkah & Madinah Activity Book. Gunes, Aysenur. 2015. (Discover Islam Sticker Activity Bks.). (ENG.). 32p. (J). 5.95 *(978-0-86037-544-9(7))* Kube Publishing Ltd. GBR. Dist: Consortium Bk. Sales & Distribution.
—Mosques of the World Activity Book. Gunes, Aysenur. 2015. (Discover Islam Sticker Activity Bks.). (ENG.). 32p. (J). 5.95 *(978-0-86037-539-5(0))* Kube Publishing Ltd. GBR. Dist: Consortium Bk. Sales & Distribution.
Polchlopek, Mary Ann. Little Orly & the Cricket. Lutterbach, Johanna. 2008. 24p. pap. 11.49 *(978-1-4389-0656-0(0))* AuthorHouse.
Polhamus, Bruce, jt. illus. see Speer, Julie.
Polhemus, Coleman. Return to Daemon Hall: Evil Roots. Nance, Andrew. 2011. (ENG.). 256p. (YA). (gr. 7-12). 18.99 *(978-0-8050-8748-2(6)*, Holt, Henry & Co. Bks. For Young Readers) Holt, Henry & Co.
Polhemus, Coleman. The Crocodile Blues. Polhemus, Coleman. 2007. (ENG.). 48p. (J). (gr. -1-2). 16.99 *(978-0-7636-3543-5(X))* Candlewick Pr.
Police, Lou. My Very Own Bible. Fletcher, Betty & Harvest House Publishers Staff. 2008. 96p. (J). (gr. -1-3). 6.99 *(978-0-7369-2153-4(2))* Harvest Hse. Pubs.
Poling, Kyle. Can We Ring the Liberty Bell? Rustad, Martha. 2014. (Cloverleaf Books (tm) — Our American Symbols Ser.). 24p. (gr. k-2). (J). lib. bdg. 23.93 *(978-1-4677-2137-0(9))*; pap. 6.95 *(978-1-4677-4467-6(0))* Lerner Publishing Group. (Millbrook Pr.).
—Can You Sing the Star-Spangled Banner? Rustad, Martha. 2014. (Cloverleaf Books (tm) — Our American Symbols Ser.). 24p. (gr. k-2). (J). lib. bdg. 23.93 *(978-1-4677-2136-3(0))*; pap. 6.95 *(978-1-4677-4469-0(7))* Lerner Publishing Group. (Millbrook Pr.).
—The Delicious Dairy Group, 1 vol. Lee, Sally. 2011. (First Graphics: Myplate & Healthy Eating Ser.). (ENG.). 24p. (gr. 1-2). pap. 6.29 *(978-1-4296-7159-0(9))*; lib. bdg. 23.32 *(978-1-4296-6092-1(9))*; pap. 35.70 *(978-1-4296-7165-1(3))* Capstone Pr., Inc.
—Easter Bunny's Basket. Karr, Lily. 2011. (ENG.). 10p. (J). (gr. k — 1). bds. 6.99 *(978-0-545-27940-6(2)*, Cartwheel Bks.) Scholastic, Inc.
—The Eco-Family's Guide to Living Green, 1 vol. Johnson, J. Angelique. 2010. (Point It Out! Tips for Green Living Ser.). (ENG.). 24p. (gr. 2-3). lib. bdg. 25.99 *(978-1-4048-6026-1(6)*, Nonfiction Picture Bks.) Picture Window Bks.
—The Eco-Neighbor's Guide to a Green Community, 1 vol. Johnson, J. Angelique. 2010. (Point It Out! Tips for Green Living Ser.). (ENG.). 24p. (gr. 2-3). lib. bdg. 25.99 *(978-1-4048-6028-5(2)*, Nonfiction Picture Bks.) Picture Window Bks.
—The Eco-Shopper's Guide to Buying Green, 1 vol. Johnson, J. Angelique. 2010. (Point It Out! Tips for Green Living Ser.). (ENG.). 24p. (gr. 2-3). lib. bdg. 25.99 *(978-1-4048-6029-2(0)*, Nonfiction Picture Bks.) Picture Window Bks.
—The Eco-Student's Guide to Being Green at School, 1 vol. Johnson, J. Angelique. 2010. (Point It Out! Tips for Green Living Ser.). (ENG.). 24p. (gr. 2-3). lib. bdg. 25.99 *(978-1-4048-6027-8(4)*, Nonfiction Picture Bks.) Picture Window Bks.
—Five Hungry Pandas! A Count & Crunch Book. Barad-Cutler, Alexis. 2014. (ENG.). 10p. (J). (gr. -1 — 1). bds. 6.99 *(978-0-545-53183-2(7)*, Cartwheel Bks.) Scholastic, Inc.
—The Great Grains Group, 1 vol. Aboff, Marcie. 2011. (First Graphics: Myplate & Healthy Eating Ser.). (ENG.). 24p. (gr. 1-2). pap. 6.29 *(978-1-4296-7161-3(0))*; lib. bdg. 23.32 *(978-1-4296-6088-4(0))*; pap. 35.70 *(978-1-4296-7167-5(X))* Capstone Pr., Inc.
—The Incredible Vegetable Group, 1 vol. Aboff, Marcie. 2011. (First Graphics: Myplate & Healthy Eating Ser.). (ENG.). 24p. (gr. 1-2). pap. 6.29 *(978-1-4296-7163-7(7))*; lib. bdg. 23.32 *(978-1-4296-6089-1(9))*; pap. 35.70 *(978-1-4296-7169-9(6))* Capstone Pr., Inc.
—Let's Meet a Dentist. Heos, Bridget. 2013. (Cloverleaf Books — Community Helpers Ser.). (ENG.). 24p. (gr. k-2). pap. 6.95 *(978-1-4677-0800-5(3))*; lib. bdg. 23.93 *(978-0-7613-9029-9(4))* Lerner Publishing Group. (Millbrook Pr.).
—Let's Meet a Teacher. Heos, Bridget. 2013. (Cloverleaf Books — Community Helpers Ser.). (ENG.). 24p. (gr. k-2). pap. 6.95 *(978-1-4677-0805-0(4))*; lib. bdg. 23.93 *(978-0-7613-9026-8(X))* Lerner Publishing Group. (Millbrook Pr.).
—Rocks & Minerals. Tomecek, Steve. 2010. (Jump into Science Ser.). (ENG.). 32p. (J). (gr. -1-3). 16.95 *(978-1-4263-0538-2(9))*; lib. bdg. 25.90 *(978-1-4263-0539-9(7))* National Geographic Society. (National Geographic Children's Bks.).
—Spooky Boo: A Halloween Adventure. Karr, Lily. 2011. (ENG.). 12p. (J). (gr. -1 — 1). bds. 6.99 *(978-0-545-29867-4(9)*, Cartwheel Bks.) Scholastic, Inc.
Poling, Kyle. Ten Flying Brooms. Oliver, Ilanit. 2015. (ENG.). 24p. (J). (gr. -1-k). 3.99 ***(978-0-545-81336-5(0)***, Cartwheel Bks.) Scholastic, Inc.
Poling, Kyle. There's a Dinosaur in My Soup! Boniface, William. 2012. (ENG.). 12p. (J). (gr. -1-1). bds. 9.99 *(978-1-4424-4610-6(2)*, Little Simon) Little Simon.
—What Is Inside the Lincoln Memorial? Rustad, Martha. 2014. (Cloverleaf Books (tm) — Our American Symbols Ser.). 24p. (gr. k-2). (J). lib. bdg. 23.93 *(978-1-4677-2135-6(2))*; pap. 6.95 *(978-1-4677-4468-3(9))* Lerner Publishing Group. (Millbrook Pr.).
—Why Are There Stripes on the American Flag? Rustad, Martha. 2014. (Cloverleaf Books (tm) — Our American Symbols Ser.). 24p. (gr. k-2). (J). lib. bdg. 23.93 *(978-1-4677-2140-0(9))*; pap. 6.95 *(978-1-4677-4465-2(4))* Lerner Publishing Group. (Millbrook Pr.).
—Yummy Bunny Easter Treats! Boniface, William. 2013. (ENG.). 12p. (J). (gr. -1-1). 9.99 *(978-1-4424-5724-9(4)*, Little Simon) Little Simon.
Poling, Kyle & Swift, Gary. First Graphics: Myplate & Healthy Eating. Aboff, Marcie & Lee, Sally. 2011. (First Graphics: Myplate & Healthy Eating Ser.). (ENG.). 24p. (gr. 1-2). pap. 37.74 *(978-1-4296-7171-2(8))*; lib. bdg. 116.60 *(978-1-4296-6094-5(5))*; pap. 214.20 *(978-1-4296-7172-9(6))* Capstone Pr., Inc.
Polinko, Les. KenKarta: Battle of the Onoxmon. Karevold, Alison. Malone, Susan Mary, ed. 2011. 300p. (J). 25.98 *(978-0-9843166-3-2(9))* Artists' Orchard, LLC, The.
Polinko, Les. The Ganorch under the Porch. Polinko, Les. Donaldson, Connie. 2013. 36p. pap. 9.95 *(978-0-9836682-3-7(X))* Hearthstone Rose.
Polis, Gary A. Scorpion Man: Exploring the World of Scorpions. Pringle, Laurence. 2008. (ENG.). 48p. (J). (gr. 1-3). 11.99 *(978-1-4169-7574-8(8)*, Simon & Schuster/Paula Wiseman Bks.) Simon & Schuster/Paula Wiseman Bks.
Polito, Mike. My Special Angel: A Bedtime Story. Donald, Diana. 2005. 33p. (J). (gr. -1-3). incl. audio compact disk *(978-1-894290-01-2(1))* Heart of the Matter Publishing.
Pollack, Barbara. Deep Freeze. Muldrow, Diane. 2007. (Dish Ser.: 12). (ENG.). 160p. (J). (gr. 4-7). pap. 6.99 *(978-0-448-44693-6(6)*, Grosset & Dunlap) Penguin Publishing Group.
—Sweet-and-Sour Summer. Muldrow, Diane. 2007. (Dish Ser.: 9). (ENG.). 160p. (J). (gr. 4-7). pap. 6.99 *(978-0-448-44661-5(8)*, Grosset & Dunlap) Penguin Publishing Group.
Pollack, Barbara, jt. illus. see Pollak, Barbara.
Pollack, Gadi. The Lost Treasure of Tikkun Hamiddos Island. Chait, Baruch. (Good Middos Ser.: Vol. 2). 62p. 25.99 *(978-1-58330-478-5(9))* Feldheim Pubs.
—The Terrifying Trap of the Bad Middos Pirates, 2 vols. Chait, Baruch. (Good Middos Ser.). 96p. 25.99 *(978-1-58330-664-2(1))* Feldheim Pubs.
Pollack, Gadi. Purimshpiel. Pollack, Gadi, contrib. by. 19.99 *(978-1-58330-596-6(3))*; (ENG & FRE.). 21.95 *(978-1-58330-601-7(3))*; (ENG & HEB.). *(978-1-58330-611-6(0))* Feldheim Pubs.
Pollack, Gadi & Markovitch, Evegeny. The Miniature Puppet Theater Book. Schreiber, Elisheva. (J). 14.95 *(978-1-58330-617-8(X))* Feldheim Pubs.
Pollak, Barbara. Boiling Point. Muldrow, Diane. 2007. (Dish Ser.: 3). (ENG.). 160p. (J). (gr. 4-7). pap. 6.99 *(978-0-448-44528-1(X)*, Grosset & Dunlap) Penguin Publishing Group.
—Girl Stuff: A Survival Guide to Growing Up. Guest, Elissa Haden & Blackstone, Margaret. 2006. (ENG.). 192p. (J). (gr. 5-7). pap. 8.95 *(978-0-15-205679-7(3))* Houghton Mifflin Harcourt Publishing Co.
—Heart to Heart with Mallory. Friedman, Laurie. (Mallory Ser.: 6). (ENG.). 160p. (J). (gr. 2-5). 2007. per. 5.95 *(978-0-8225-7133-9(1)*, First Avenue Editions); 2006. lib. bdg. 15.95 *(978-1-57505-932-7(0)*, Twenty-First Century Bks.) Lerner Publishing Group.
—Honestly, Mallory! Friedman, Laurie. (Mallory Ser.: 8). (ENG.). 160p. (J). (gr. 2-5). 2008. pap. 5.95 *(978-1-58013-840-6(3)*, First Avenue Editions); 2007. 15.95 *(978-0-8225-6193-4(X)*, Carolrhoda Bks.) Lerner Publishing Group.
—In Business with Mallory. Friedman, Laurie. (Mallory Ser.: 5). (ENG.). 160p. (J). (gr. 2-5). 2007. per. 5.95 *(978-0-8225-6561-1(7)*, First Avenue Editions); 2006. 15.95 *(978-1-57505-925-9(8)*, Carolrhoda Bks.) Lerner Publishing Group.
—Into the Mix. Muldrow, Diane. 4th ed. 2007. (Dish Ser.: 4). (ENG.). 160p. (J). (gr. 4-7). pap. 6.99 *(978-0-448-44529-8(8)*, Grosset & Dunlap) Penguin Publishing Group.
—Mallory on Board. Friedman, Laurie. (Mallory Ser.: 7). (ENG.). 176p. (J). (gr. 2-5). 2008. per. 5.95 *(978-0-8225-9023-1(9)*, First Avenue Editions); 2007. 15.95 *(978-0-8225-6194-1(8)*, Carolrhoda Bks.) Lerner Publishing Group.
—On the Back Burner. Muldrow, Diane. 2007. (Dish Ser.: 6). (ENG.). 160p. (J). (gr. 4-7). pap. 6.99 *(978-0-448-44531-1(X)*, Grosset & Dunlap) Penguin Publishing Group.
—Stirring It Up. Muldrow, Diane. 2007. (Dish Ser.: 1). (ENG.). 160p. (J). (gr. 4-7). pap. 4.99 *(978-0-448-44526-7(3)*, Grosset & Dunlap) Penguin Publishing Group.
—Turning up the Heat, No. 2. Muldrow, Diane. 2nd ed. 2007. (Dish Ser.: 2). (ENG.). 160p. (J). (gr. 4-7). pap. 4.99 *(978-0-448-44527-4(1)*, Grosset & Dunlap) Penguin Publishing Group.
Pollak, Barbara & Pollack, Barbara. A Measure of Thanks. Muldrow, Diane. 2007. (Dish Ser.: 10). (ENG.). 160p. (J). (gr. 4-7). pap. 6.99 *(978-0-448-44662-2(6)*, Grosset & Dunlap) Penguin Publishing Group.
Pollak, Monika. Russell's World: A Story for Kids about Autism. Amenta, Charles A. 2011. 40p. (J). (gr. -1-3). 14.95 *(978-1-4338-0975-0(3)*, Magination Pr.) American Psychological Assn.
Pollard, Brian. Heroes of History for Young Readers - George Washington: America's Patriot. Meloche, Renee Taft. 2006. (Heroes of History Ser.). (ENG.). 32p. 8.99 *(978-1-932096-28-6(0))* Emerald Bks.
—Heroes of History for Young Readers - Meriwether Lewis: Journey Aross America. Meloche, Renee Taft. 2006. (Heroes of History Ser.). (ENG.). 32p. (gr. -1-3). 8.99 *(978-1-932096-27-9(2))* Emerald Bks.
Pollard, Bryan. Daniel Boone: Bravery on the Frontier. Meloche, Renee Taft. 2009. (Heroes of History for Young Readers Ser.). 32p. (J). (gr. 1). 8.99 *(978-1-932096-61-3(2))* Emerald Bks.
—Heroes for Young Readers - Cameron Townsend: Planting God's Word. Meloche, Renee. 2004. (Heroes for Young Readers Ser.). (ENG.). 32p. (J). 8.99 *(978-1-57658-241-1(8))* YWAM Publishing.
—Heroes for Young Readers - Hudson Taylor: Friend of China. Meloche, Renee. 2004. 32p. 8.99 *(978-1-57658-234-3(5))* YWAM Publishing.
—Heroes for Young Readers - Jim Elliot: A Light for God. Meloche, Renee. 2004. (Heroes for Young Readers Ser.). (ENG.). 32p. 8.99 *(978-1-57658-235-0(3))* YWAM Publishing.
—Heroes for Young Readers - Jonathan Goforth: Never Give Up. Meloche, Renee. 2004. (Heroes for Young Readers Ser.). (ENG.). 32p. (J). 8.99 *(978-1-57658-242-8(6))* YWAM Publishing.
—Heroes for Young Readers - Lottie Moon: A Generous Offering. Meloche, Renee. 2004. (Heroes for Young Readers Ser.). (ENG.). 32p. 8.99 *(978-1-57658-243-5(4))* YWAM Publishing.
—Heroes for Young Readers Activity Guide Package Books 1-4: Includes: Activity Guide, Audio CD, & Books 1-4. Meloch, Renee. 2005. (Heroes for Young Readers Ser.). (ENG.). 55.94 incl. audio compact disk *(978-1-57658-375-3(9))* YWAM Publishing.
—Heroes for Young Readers Activity Guide Package Books 13-16: Includes: Activity Guide, Audio CD, & Books 13-16. Meloche, Renee Taft. 2006. (ENG.). 55.94 incl. audio compact disk *(978-1-57658-378-4(3))* YWAM Publishing.
—Heroes for Young Readers Activity Guide Package Books 5-8: Includes: Activity Guide, Audio CD, & Books 5-8. Meloche, Renee Taft. 2005. (Heroes for Young Readers Ser.). (ENG.). 57.94 incl. audio compact disk *(978-1-57658-376-0(7))* YWAM Publishing.
—Heroes for Young Readers Activity Guide Package Books 9-12: Includes: Activity Guide, Audio CD, & Books 9-12. Meloche, Renee Taft. 2005. (Heroes for Young Readers Ser.). (ENG.). 55.94 incl. audio compact disk *(978-1-57658-377-7(5))* YWAM Publishing.
—Heroes of History for Young Readers - Clara Barton: Courage to Serve. Meloche, Renee Taft. 2006. (Heroes of History for Young Readers Ser.). (ENG.). 32p. (gr. -1). 8.99 *(978-1-932096-33-0(7))* Emerald Bks.
—Heroes of History for Young Readers - George Washington Carver: America's Scientist. Meloche, Renee Taft. 2006. (Heroes for Young Readers Ser.). (ENG.). 32p. (gr. 1-4). 8.99 *(978-1-932096-17-0(5))* Emerald Bks.
Pollard, Deborah Hanna. The Legend of Scary Mary: The Journey to Leadership Collection Adventure 2. Smith, I. J. 2004. 96p. (J). 16.95 *(978-0-9727273-1-0(0))* Green Owl, Inc.
—The Musical Fort. Smith, I. J. 2003. 53p. (J). 14.95 *(978-0-9727273-0-3(2))* Green Owl, Inc.
Pollard, Keith, et al. Avengers Epic Collection: Judgement Day. Stern, Roger & Defalco, Tom. 2014. (ENG.). 464p. (J). (gr. 4-17). pap. 34.99 *(978-0-7851-8894-0(0))* Marvel Worldwide, Inc.
—Fantastic Four: Reunited They Stand. Wolfman, Marv & Mantlo, Bill. 2013. (ENG.). 168p. (J). (gr. 4-17). pap. 24.99 *(978-0-7851-6286-5(0))* Marvel Worldwide, Inc.
Pollard, Keith, jt. illus. see Perez, George.
Pollard, Keith, jt. illus. see Tuska, George.
Pollard, Simon, photos by. Insects: Biggest! Littlest! Markle, Sandra. 2011. (Biggest! Littlest! Ser.). (ENG., 32p. (J). pap. 10.95 *(978-1-59078-872-1(9))* Boyds Mills Pr.
—Spiders: Biggest! Littlest! Markle, Sandra. 2011. (Biggest! Littlest! Ser.). (ENG., 32p. (J). pap. 10.95 *(978-1-59078-875-2(3))* Boyds Mills Pr.
Pollard, Susie. The Scrawny Little Tree. Mehler, Ed. 2011. (ENG.). 48p. (J). (gr. -1-k). 6.99 *(978-0-8431-9860-7(5)*, Price Stern Sloan) Penguin Publishing Group.
Pollema-Cahill, Phyllis. Always My Brother, 1 vol. Reagan, Jean. 2010. (ENG.). 32p. (J). (gr. 1-5). 16.95 *(978-0-88448-313-7(4))* Tilbury Hse. Pubs.
Pollock, Mary Ellen. A Whole Different Animal. Pollock, Jim. 2007. 89p. (J). 17.00 net. *(978-0-9763675-2-9(1))* First Flight Bks.
Polly Jr., Jimmy Wayne. The Mop Heads, 1 vol. Hayes, Angela. 2009. 14p. pap. 24.95 *(978-1-61546-006-9(3))* America Star Bks.
Polseno, Jo. Charles Carroll & the American Revolution. Lomask, Milton. 2011. 188p. 42.95 *(978-1-258-07263-6(7))* Literary Licensing, LLC.
Polsky, Beanie. Tapuchim & Dvash. Cohen, Penny L. 2012. 36p. 24.95 *(978-1-4626-7769-6(X))*; pap. 24.95 *(978-1-4626-6667-6(1))* PublishAmerica, Inc.
Poluzzi, Alessandro. Centaurs. Jeffrey, Gary. 2012. (Graphic Mythical Creatures Ser.). (ENG.). 24p. (J). (gr. 3-5). pap. 8.15 *(978-1-4339-6753-5(7))*; lib. bdg. 23.95 *(978-1-4339-6751-1(0))* Stevens, Gareth Publishing LLLP. (Gareth Stevens Learning Library).
Poluzzi, Allesandro. The Oregon Trail. Jeffrey, Gary. 2012. (Graphic History of the American West Ser.). (ENG.). 24p. (J). (gr. 3-8). pap. 8.15 *(978-1-4339-6745-0(6)*, Gareth Stevens Learning Library); (gr. 4-7). lib. bdg. 23.95 *(978-1-4339-6743-6(X))* Stevens, Gareth Publishing LLLP.
Polyansky, Nikita. Botero: Paintings & Works on Paper. Bloncourt, Nelson & Botero, Fernando. 2013. (ENG.). 252p. 125.00 *(978-0-9881745-1-1(0))* Glitterati, Inc.
—Fanny the Flying French Bulldog. Bloncourt, Nelson. 2014. (ENG.). 40p. 20.00 *(978-0-9851696-3-3(X))* Glitterati, Inc.
Polyansky, Nikita. The Sleeping Beauty: A Journey to the Ballet of the Marinsky Theatre. Polyansky, Nikita. Ebong, Ima. 2006. (ENG.). 48p. (J). (gr. 3-17). 20.00 *(978-0-9721152-0-9(X))* Glitterati, Inc.
Pombo, Luis, jt. illus. see Pombo, Luis G.
Pombo, Luis G. & Pombo, Luis. Redondo: O Cuando los Circulos Se Convierten en Esferas. Hernandez, Claudia. 2007. (Otra Escalera Ser.). (ENG.). 36p. (J). (gr. 1-3). pap. 8.95 *(978-970-20-0840-8(9))* Castillo, Ediciones, S. A. de C. V. MEX. Dist: Macmillan.
Pomerantz, Norman. Billy Brahman: The Story of A Calf. Roop, James Q. 2011. 28p. 35.95 *(978-1-258-01757-6(1))* Literary Licensing, LLC.
Pomeroy, John. Un Ninito Los Guiara. Perkins, Greg. 2005. 16p. (J). (gr. 4-7). 8.99 *(978-1-59185-826-3(7)*, Charisma Kids) Charisma Media.
Pomeroy, John. A Little Child Shall Lead Them. Pomeroy, John. 2005. 24p. (J). 9.99 *(978-1-59185-632-0(9)*, Charisma Kids) Charisma Media.
Pommier, Maurice. Jesús. Le Guillou, Philippe. Pérez, Berta Herreros, tr. 2008. (Tras Los Pasos de ... Ser.). (SPA.). 128p. (J). (gr. 4-7). pap. 14.95 *(978-84-9801-197-5(3))* Blume ESP. Dist: Independent Pubs. Group.
Pon, Cynthia. Music Everywhere! Ajmera, Maya & Derstine, Elise Hofer. 2014. (ENG.). 32p. (J). (gr. -1-3). pap. 7.95 *(978-1-57091-937-4(2))* Charlesbridge Publishing, Inc.
Ponce, José María. San Manuel Bueno, Mártir. Unamuno, Miguel de & Unamuno, Miguel de. Cabrales Arteaga, José Manuel, ed. 2010. (SPA.). 128p. ***(978-84-667-2636-8(5))*** Grupo Anaya, S.A.
Pond, Brenda, photos by. The Princess Who Lost Her Scroll of the Dead: Ancient Egypt - an Underworld Adventure. Pond, Roy. 2010. (ENG., 108p. pap. 7.95 *(978-1-4538-1527-4(9))* CreateSpace Independent Publishing Platform.
Pongetti, Freda. Why the Chimes Rang. Pongetti, Freda, adapted by. 2007. 18p. (J). 21.00 net. *(978-0-9796625-0-8(8))* GDG Publishing.
Ponnay, Brenda. Secret Agent Josephine in Paris. Ponnay, Brenda. 2013. 32p. 19.99 *(978-1-62395-524-3(6))* Xist Publishing.
Pons, Bernadette. I Love You, Good Night. Buller, Jon & Schade, Susan. 2006. (ENG.). 28p. (J). (gr. -1 — 1). 7.99 *(978-0-689-86212-0(1)*, Little Simon) Little Simon.
—I Love You, Good Night: Lap Edition. Buller, Jon & Schade, Susan. 2013. (ENG.). 28p. (J). (gr. -1 — 1). bds. 12.99 *(978-1-4424-8539-6(6)*, Little Simon) Little Simon.
—Muriel's Red Sweater. Dokas, Dara Sanders & Dokas, Dara. 2009. (ENG.). 32p. (J). (gr. -1-k). 16.99 *(978-0-525-47962-8(7)*, Dutton Juvenile) Penguin Publishing Group.
—Scrubba Dub. Van Laan, Nancy. 2008. (ENG.). 32p. (J). (gr. -1-1). 8.99 *(978-1-4169-7859-6(3))*, Simon & Schuster/Paula Wiseman Bks.) Simon & Schuster/Paula Wiseman Bks.
Pont, Charles E. Fun with String: A Collection of String Games, Useful Braiding & Weaving, Knot Work & Magic with String & Rope. Leeming, Joseph. 2011. (Dover Children's Activity Bks.). (ENG.). 192p. (J). (gr. 3-8). reprint ed. pap. 10.95 *(978-0-486-23063-4(5))* Dover Pubns., Inc.
Ponte, June. Middle Eastern Crafts Kids Can Do! Hartman, Sarah. 2006. (Multicultural Crafts Kids Can Do! Ser.). 32p. (J). (gr. 3-4). lib. bdg. 23.94 *(978-0-7660-2456-4(3)*, Enslow Elementary) Enslow Pubs., Inc.
—Nifty Thrifty Animal Crafts. Gabriel, Faith K. 2007. (Nifty Thrifty Crafts for Kids Ser.). 32p. (J). (gr. 3-4). lib. bdg. 23.94 *(978-0-7660-2779-4(1)*, Enslow Elementary) Enslow Pubs., Inc.
—Nifty Thrifty Art Crafts. Miller, Heather. 2007. (Nifty Thrifty Crafts for Kids Ser.). 32p. (J). (gr. 3-7). lib. bdg. 23.94 *(978-0-7660-2780-0(5)*, Enslow Elementary) Enslow Pubs., Inc.

P

—Nifty Thrifty Math Crafts. Hollow, Michele C. 2007. (Nifty Thrifty Crafts for Kids Ser.). 32p. (J). (gr. 3-4). lib. bdg. 23.94 *(978-0-7660-2781-7(3)*, 1264782, Enslow Elementary) Enslow Pubs., Inc.

—Nifty Thrifty Music Crafts. Niven, Felicia Lowenstein. 2007. (Nifty Thrifty Crafts for Kids Ser.). 32p. (J). (gr. 3-4). lib. bdg. 23.94 *(978-0-7660-2784-8(8)*, 1264783, Enslow Elementary) Enslow Pubs., Inc.

—Nifty Thrifty Space Crafts. Boekhoff, P. M. 2007. (Nifty Thrifty Crafts for Kids Ser.). 32p. (J). (gr. 3-4). lib. bdg. 23.94 *(978-0-7660-2783-1(X)*, Enslow Elementary) Enslow Pubs., Inc.

—Nifty Thrifty Sports Crafts. Hollow, Michele C. 2007. (Nifty Thrifty Crafts for Kids Ser.). 32p. (J). (gr. 3-4). lib. bdg. 23.94 *(978-0-7660-2782-4(1)*, Enslow Elementary) Enslow Pubs., Inc.

—Thanksgiving Day Crafts. Erlbach, Arlene & Erlbach, Herbert. 2005. (Fun Holiday Crafts Kids Can Do! Ser.). 32p. (J). lib. bdg. 23.94 *(978-0-7660-2345-1(1)*, Enslow Elementary) Enslow Pubs., Inc.

Ponti, Claude. Pockety: The Tortoise Who Lived As She Pleased. Seyvos, Florence. Provata-Carlone, Mika, tr. from FRE. 2014. (ENG.). 64p. (YA). (gr. 2-4). pap. 9.99 *(978-1-78269-025-2(5)*, Pushkin Children's Bks.) Pushkin Pr., Ltd. GBR. Dist: Random Hse., Inc.

Ponti, Claude. El Arbol Sin Fin. Ponti, Claude. 2006. (SPA.). 44p. (J). *(978-84-8470-231-3(6))* Corimbo, Editorial S.L.

—DeZert Isle. Ponti, Claude. Holliday, Mary Martin, tr. from FRE. 2003. (ENG.). 64p. (J). 16.95 *(978-1-56792-237-0(6))* Godine, David R. Pub.

Ponzio, Jean-Michel. Civilisation, 2 vols. Marazano, Richard. 2010. (ENG.). 55p. pap. 13.95 *(978-1-84918-043-6(1))* CineBook GBR. Dist: National Bk. Network.

—The Sons of Ares, 2 vols. Marazano, Richard. (ENG.). 2010. 55p. pap. 13.95 *(978-1-84918-015-3(6))*; 2009. 56p. pap. 13.95 *(978-1-84918-002-3(4))* CineBook GBR. Dist: National Bk. Network.

Pool, Cathy. Second Chance: A Tale of Two Puppies, 1 vol. Masrud, Judy. 2006. 81p. (J). (gr. 1-7). per. 9.95 *(978-0-9774142-0-8(5)*, Birdseed Books for Kids) Birdseed Bks.

Pool, Joyce Oudkerk, photos by. Delicious Dips. Morgan, Diane. 2004. (ENG., 124p. (gr. 8-17). 16.95 *(978-0-8118-4220-4(7))* Chronicle Bks. LLC.

Pool, Steve, photos by. Welcome to Michael's: Great Food, Great People, Great Party! McCarty, Michael. 2007. (ENG., 240p. 40.00 *(978-0-316-11815-6(X))* Little Brown & Co.

Poole, Amy Lowry. The Pea Blossom. Poole, Amy Lowry, retold by. 2006. (ENG.). 32p. (J). reprint ed. 6.95 *(978-0-8234-2018-6(3))* Holiday Hse., Inc.

Poole, Helen. ABC Hanukkah Hunt. Balsley, Tilda. 2013. 32p. 17.95 *(978-1-4677-1637-6(5))*; (ENG.). (J). (gr. -1-2). 7.95 *(978-1-4677-0421-2(0)*, Kar-Ben Publishing); (ENG.). (J). (gr. -1-2). lib. bdg. 17.95 *(978-1-4677-0420-5(2)*, Kar-Ben Publishing) Lerner Publishing Group.

—Are You Scared, Jacob? Lap Book. Daniel, Claire. 2014. (MySELF Ser.). (J). (gr. -1-k). 27.00 *(978-1-4788-0501-4(3))* Newmark Learning LLC.

—The Birdhouse That Jack Built. Greve, Meg. 2012. (ENG.). 24p. (gr. k-1). pap. 7.95 *(978-1-61810-300-0(8))*; lib. bdg. 28.50 *(978-1-61810-167-9(6))* Rourke Educational Media.

—The Day I Felt Sad. Garcia, Ellen. 2014. (J). (gr. -1). 3.99 *(978-1-4788-0461-1(0))* Newmark Learning LLC.

—The Day I Felt Sad Lap Book. Garcia, Ellen. 2014. (MySELF Ser.). (J). (gr. -1-k). 27.00 *(978-1-4788-0498-7(X))* Newmark Learning LLC.

—Don't Worry, Mason. Smith, Molly. 2014. (J). (gr. -1). 3.99 *(978-1-4788-0463-5(7))* Newmark Learning LLC.

—Don't Worry, Mason Lap Book. Smith, Molly. 2014. (MySELF Ser.). (J). (gr. -1-k). 27.00 *(978-1-4788-0500-7(5))* Newmark Learning LLC.

—Humpty Dumpty. Greve, Meg. 2012. (ENG.). 24p. (gr. 1-2). pap. 7.95 *(978-1-61810-313-0(X))*; lib. bdg. 28.50 *(978-1-61810-180-8(3))* Rourke Educational Media.

—I Was So Mad. Giachetti, Julia. 2014. (J). (gr. -1). 3.99 *(978-1-4788-0462-8(9))* Newmark Learning LLC.

—I Was So Mad Lap Book. Giachetti, Julia. 2014. (MySELF Ser.). (J). (gr. -1-k). 27.00 *(978-1-4788-0499-4(8))* Newmark Learning LLC.

—Itsy Bitsy Spider. Hord, Colleen. 2012. (ENG.). 24p. (gr. 1-2). pap. 7.95 *(978-1-61810-310-9(5))*; lib. bdg. 28.50 *(978-1-61810-177-8(3))* Rourke Educational Media.

—Jealous of Josie. Linde, Barbara M. 2014. (J). (gr. -1). 3.99 *(978-1-4788-0465-9(3))* Newmark Learning LLC.

—Jealous of Josie Lap Book. Linde, Barbara M. 2014. (MySELF Ser.). (J). (gr. -1-k). 27.00 *(978-1-4788-0502-1(1))* Newmark Learning LLC.

—Let's Get Pizza. Greve, Meg. 2012. (ENG.). 24p. (gr. k-1). pap. 7.95 *(978-1-61810-306-2(7))*; lib. bdg. 28.50 *(978-1-61810-173-0(0))* Rourke Educational Media.

—Little Miss Midge. Hord, Colleen. 2012. (ENG.). 24p. (gr. 1-2). pap. 7.95 *(978-1-61810-311-6(3))*; lib. bdg. 28.50 *(978-1-61810-178-5(1))* Rourke Educational Media.

—Mud Pie Queen. Greve, Meg. 2012. (ENG.). 24p. (gr. k-1). pap. 7.95 *(978-1-61810-303-1(2))*; lib. bdg. 28.50 *(978-1-61810-170-9(6))* Rourke Educational Media.

—My Happy Day. Giachetti, Julia. 2014. (J). (gr. -1). 3.99 *(978-1-4788-0460-4(2))* Newmark Learning LLC.

—My Happy Day Lap Book. Giachetti, Julia. 2014. (MySELF Ser.). (J). (gr. -1-k). 27.00 *(978-1-4788-0497-0(1))* Newmark Learning LLC.

—Puddle Pen Christmas, 1 vol. David, Juliet. 2010. (Candle Puddle Pen Ser.). (ENG.). 10p. (J). (gr. -1-k). bds. 12.99 *(978-1-85985-868-4(6)*, Candle Bks.) Lion Hudson PLC GBR. Dist: Kregel Pubns.

—Who's Mr. Goldfluss? Hord, Colleen. 2012. (ENG.). 24p. (gr. 1-2). pap. 7.95 *(978-1-61810-318-5(0))*; lib. bdg. 28.50 *(978-1-61810-185-3(4))* Rourke Educational Media.

Poole, Helen. Clara's Crazy Curls, 1 vol. Poole, Helen. 2014. (ENG.). 40p. (gr. -1-3). 14.95 *(978-1-62370-043-0(4))* Capstone Young Readers.

Poole, Steven R. Simon the Guide Dog. Reid, Christy. 2012. 38p. 24.95 *(978-1-4626-6052-0(5))* America Star Bks.

Poole, Susie. Baby Parade. O'Connell, Rebecca. 2013. (ENG.). 24p. (J). (gr. -1 — 1). 15.99 *(978-0-8075-0509-0(9))* Whitman, Albert & Co.

—Baby Party. O'Connell, Rebecca. 2015. (ENG.). 24p. (J). (gr. -1 — 1). 15.99 *(978-0-8075-0512-0(9))* Whitman, Albert & Co.

—The First Rainbow. Box, Su. 2009. (ENG.). 24p. (J). (gr. -1-k). bds. 6.95 *(978-0-7459-6904-6(6)*, Lion Children's) Lion Hudson PLC GBR. Dist: Independent Pubs. Group.

—You Are Very Special. Box, Su. 2003. 32p. (J). pap. 6.95 *(978-0-8198-8807-5(9)*, 332-417) Pauline Bks. & Media.

—You Are Very Special: With a Special Surprise for You Inside! Box, Su. 2011. (ENG.). 12p. (J). (gr. -1-k). bds. 7.99 *(978-0-7459-6300-6(5))* Lion Hudson PLC GBR. Dist: Independent Pubs. Group.

Poole, Susie. A Christmas Journey. Poole, Susie. 2014. (ENG.). 48p. (gr. -1-3). 12.99 *(978-1-4336-8343-5(1)*, B&H Kids) B&H Publishing Group.

Poole, Tracy. Pinta & Polly Go to the Moon, 1 vol. Franklin, Cathy. 2009. 27p. pap. 24.95 *(978-1-60813-861-6(5))* America Star Bks.

Pooler, Paige. Autumn's Secret Gift. Allen, Elise & Stanford, Halle. 2014. (Enchanted Sisters Ser.). (ENG.). 128p. (J). (gr. 2-4). 15.99 *(978-1-61963-256-1(X))*; pap. 5.99 *(978-1-61963-254-7(3))* Bloomsbury USA. (Bloomsbury USA Childrens).

—Autumn's Secret Gift. Allen, Elise & Stanford, Halle. ed. 2014. lib. bdg. 16.00 *(978-0-606-35519-3(7))* Turtleback Bks.

—Cleared for Takeoff. DeVillers, Julia. 2012. (Liberty Porter, First Daughter Ser.: 3). (ENG.). 224p. (J). (gr. 3-7). pap. 7.99 *(978-1-4169-9131-1(X)*, Simon & Schuster/Paula Wiseman Bks.) Simon & Schuster/Paula Wiseman Bks.

—Liberty Porter, First Daughter. DeVillers, Julia. (Liberty Porter, First Daughter Ser.: 1). (ENG.). (J). (gr. 3-7). 2010. 192p. pap. 6.99 *(978-1-4169-9127-4(1))*; 2009. 176p. 15.99 *(978-1-4169-9126-7(3))* Simon & Schuster/Paula Wiseman Bks. (Simon & Schuster/Paula Wiseman Bks.).

—New Girl in Town. DeVillers, Julia. (Liberty Porter, First Daughter Ser.: 2). (ENG.). (J). (gr. 3-7). 2011. 224p. pap. 6.99 *(978-1-4169-9129-8(8))*; 2010. 208p. 15.99 *(978-1-4169-9128-1(X))* Simon & Schuster/Paula Wiseman Bks. (Simon & Schuster/Paula Wiseman Bks.).

—Spring's Sparkle Sleepover. Allen, Elise & Stanford, Halle. 2015. (Enchanted Sisters Ser.). (ENG.). 128p. (J). (gr. 2-4). 15.99 *(978-1-61963-296-7(9))*; pap. 5.99 *(978-1-61963-269-1(1))* Bloomsbury USA. (Bloomsbury USA Childrens).

—Spring's Sparkle Sleepover. Allen, Elise & Stanford, Halle. ed. 2015. lib. bdg. 16.00 *(978-0-606-36218-4(5))* Turtleback Bks.

—Summer's Friendship Games. Allen, Elise & Stanford, Halle. 2015. (Enchanted Sisters Ser.). (ENG.). 128p. (J). (gr. 2-4). 15.99 *(978-1-61963-271-4(3)*, Bloomsbury USA Childrens) Bloomsbury USA.

—Winter's Flurry Adventure. Allen, Elise & Stanford, Halle. 2014. (Enchanted Sisters Ser.). (ENG.). 128p. (J). (gr. 2-4). 15.99 *(978-1-61963-297-4(7))*; pap. 5.99 *(978-1-61963-267-7(5))* Bloomsbury USA. (Bloomsbury USA Childrens).

—Winter's Flurry Adventure. Allen, Elise & Stanford, Halle. ed. 2014. lib. bdg. 16.00 *(978-0-606-36217-7(7))* Turtleback Bks.

Poon, Janice. Claire & the Bakery Thief. Poon, Janice. 2008. (ENG.). 104p. (J). (gr. 2-5). 15.95 *(978-1-55453-286-5(8))*; pap. 7.95 *(978-1-55453-245-2(0))* Kids Can Pr., Ltd. CAN. Dist: Univ. of Toronto Pr.

—Claire & the Water Wish. Poon, Janice. 2009. (ENG.). 120p. (J). (gr. 2-5). 7.95 *(978-1-55453-382-4(1))*; 15.95 *(978-1-55453-381-7(3))* Kids Can Pr., Ltd. CAN. Dist: Univ. of Toronto Pr.

Poortvliet, Rien. Boris. Haar, Jaap Ter & Mearns, Martha. 2009. (J). pap. *(978-0-921100-72-0(8))* Inheritance Pubns.

Pop Art Properties Staff. Amazing Story of Cell Phone Technology. Enz, Tammy. 2013. (STEM Adventures Ser.). (ENG.). 32p. (gr. 3-4). 29.99 *(978-1-4765-0137-6(8)*, Graphic Library) Capstone Pr., Inc.

—Amazing Story of Space Travel. Biskup, Agnieszka. 2013. (STEM Adventures Ser.). (ENG.). 32p. (gr. 3-4). 29.99 *(978-1-4765-0124-6(6)*, Graphic Library) Capstone Pr., Inc.

—Amazing Story of the Combustion Engine. Bolte, Mari. 2013. (STEM Adventures Ser.). (ENG.). 32p. (gr. 3-4). 29.99 *(978-1-4765-3103-8(X)*, Graphic Library) Capstone Pr., Inc.

—STEM Adventures. Enz, Tammy & Biskup, Agnieszka. 2013. (STEM Adventures Ser.). (ENG.). 32p. (gr. 3-4). lib. bdg. 119.96 *(978-1-4765-0464-3(4)*, Graphic Library) Capstone Pr., Inc.

—Terrific Tale of Television Technology. Enz, Tammy. 2013. (STEM Adventures Ser.). (ENG.). 32p. (gr. 3-4). 29.99 *(978-1-4765-0138-3(6)*, Graphic Library) Capstone Pr., Inc.

Pop Art Studios. Engineering a Totally Rad Skateboard with Max Axiom, Super Scientist, 1 vol. Enz, Tammy. 2013. (Graphic Science & Engineering in Action Ser.). (ENG.). 32p. (gr. 3-4). pap. 7.95 *(978-1-62065-703-4(1)*, Graphic Library) Capstone Pr., Inc.

—Engineering an Awesome Recycling Center with Max Axiom, Super Scientist, 1 vol. Bethea, Nikole Brooks. 2013. (Graphic Science & Engineering in Action Ser.). (ENG.). 32p. (gr. 3-4). pap. 7.95 *(978-1-62065-699-0(X)*, Graphic Library) Capstone Pr., Inc.

Pop Art Studios Staff. Engineering a Totally Rad Skateboard with Max Axiom, Super Scientist, 1 vol. Enz, Tammy. 2013. (Graphic Science & Engineering in Action Ser.). (ENG.). 32p. (gr. 3-4). lib. bdg. 29.99 *(978-1-4296-9935-8(3)*, Graphic Library) Capstone Pr., Inc.

—Engineering an Awesome Recycling Center with Max Axiom, Super Scientist, 1 vol. Bethea, Nikole Brooks. 2013. (Graphic Science & Engineering in Action Ser.). (ENG.). 32p. (gr. 3-4). lib. bdg. 29.99 *(978-1-4296-9934-1(5)*, Graphic Library) Capstone Pr., Inc.

Pope, Kate, jt. illus. see Pope, Liz.

Pope, Kevin. The Exploding Toilet: Modern Urban Legends. 2005. (ENG.). 112p. (J). (gr. -1-9). pap. 7.95 *(978-0-87483-715-5(4)*, 1231866) August Hse. Pubs., Inc.

—Scared Witless: Thirteen Eerie Tales to Tell. Hamilton, Martha & Weise, Mutch. 2015. (ENG.). 64p. (J). (gr. 3-6). pap. 8.95 ***(978-1-939160-95-9(2))*** August Hse. Pubs., Inc.

Pope, Kevin. Scared Witless: Thirteen Eerie Tales to Tell. Hamilton, Martha & Weiss, Mitch. 2006. (ENG.). 64p. (J). (gr. 3-7). 15.95 *(978-0-87483-796-4(0))* August Hse. Pubs., Inc.

Pope, Lauren, jt. illus. see Huber, Becca.

Pope, Liz & Pope, Kate. If I Were a... Ballerina. Hegarty, Pat. 2008. (If I Were A Ser.). 10p. (J). (gr. -1-k). bds. 6.95 *(978-1-58925-834-1(7))* Tiger Tales.

—If I Were a... Firefighter. Hegarty, Pat. 2008. 12p. (J). (gr. -1). bds. 6.95 *(978-1-58925-839-6(8))* Tiger Tales.

—If I Were a... Princess. Hegarty, Pat. 2008. 12p. (J). (gr. -1). bds. 6.95 *(978-1-58925-838-9(X))* Tiger Tales.

—If I Were a... Soccer Star. Hegarty, Pat. 2008. (If I Were A Ser.). 10p. (J). (gr. -1-k). bds. 6.95 *(978-1-58925-835-8(5))* Tiger Tales.

Pope, Patricia, jt. illus. see McInturff, Linda.

Pope, Paul. Battling Boy. Pope, Paul. 2013. (Battling Boy Ser.: 1). (ENG.). 208p. (J). (gr. 5-12). 24.99 *(978-1-59643-805-7(3))*; pap. 15.99 *(978-1-59643-145-4(8))* Roaring Brook Pr. (First Second Bks.).

Pope, Richie. American Graphic. Biskup, Agnieszka & Collins, Terry. 2012. (American Graphic Ser.). (ENG.). 32p. (gr. 3-4). pap. 15.90 *(978-1-4296-9494-0(7))*; pap. 95.40 *(978-1-4296-9338-7(X))*; pap. 572.40 *(978-1-4296-9339-4(8))* Capstone Pr., Inc. (Graphic Library).

—Louis Armstrong: Jazz Legend, 1 vol. Collins, Terry. 2012. (American Graphic Ser.). (ENG.). 32p. (gr. 3-4). pap. 8.10 *(978-1-4296-9336-3(3))*; pap. 47.70 *(978-1-4296-9337-0(1)*, Graphic Library); lib. bdg. 29.99 *(978-1-4296-8622-8(7))* Capstone Pr., Inc.

Pope, T. The Dog & the Frog: The Change. Letcher, MaKayla. l.t. ed. 2011. (ENG.). 50p. pap. 11.99 *(978-1-4664-8225-8(7))* CreateSpace Independent Publishing Platform.

Popeo, Joanie. Dancing on the Sand: A Story of an Atlantic Blue Crab. Hollenbeck, Kathleen M. (Smithsonian Oceanic Collection). (ENG.). 32p. (J). (gr. -1-2). 2005. per. 6.95 *(978-1-59249-194-0(4)*, S4017); 2004. 15.95 *(978-1-56899-730-8(2)*, B4017) Soundprints.

—Sockeye's Journey Home: The Story of a Pacific Salmon. Winkelman, Barbara Gaines. 2005. (Smithsonian Oceanic Collection: Vol. 19). (ENG.). 32p. (J). (gr. -1-2). 15.95 *(978-1-56899-829-9(5)*, B4019) Soundprints.

—Sockeye's Journey Home: The Story of a Pacific Salmon. Winkelman, Barbara Gaines & Thomas, Peter. 2003. (ENG.). 32p. (J). (gr. -1-3). 9.95 *(978-1-56899-834-3(1)*, PB4069) Soundprints.

Popescu, Anna Ildiko. Stamps & Doodles for Boys. 2012. (Stamps & Doodles Ser.). (ENG.). 64p. (J). (gr. k). 14.95 *(978-1-60710-457-5(1)*, Silver Dolphin Bks.) Baker & Taylor Publishing Group.

Popeson, Pamela. The African Elephant: American Museum of Natural History Book & Diorama. Weiss, Ellen. 2005. 64p. (J). (gr. 4-8). reprint ed. pap. 11.00 *(978-0-7567-8823-0(4))* DIANE Publishing Co.

Popko, Wendy. Hidden Michigan. Lewis, Anne Margaret & Campbell, Janis. 2006. (ENG.). 40p. (J). (gr. 1-4). 12.95 *(978-1-934133-01-9(9)*, Mackinac Island Press, Inc.) Charlesbridge Publishing, Inc.

—How Do I Cure This Cold? Williamson, Greg. 2005. (J). 7.99 *(978-0-9666076-4-2(3))* Peerless Publishing, L.L.C.

—Why Do I Have to Wear Glasses? Williamson, Greg. 2005. (J). 12.99 *(978-0-9666076-5-9(1))* Peerless Publishing, L.L.C.

Popkp, Wendy. Why Do I Have to Wear Glasses? Williamson, Greg. 2005. (J). pap. 7.99 *(978-0-9666076-3-5(5))* Peerless Publishing, L.L.C.

Poplawska, Yolanda. Halifax Harbour 123 (BB) A Counting Book about Halifax Harbour, 1 vol. 2014. (ENG.). 10p. (J). (gr. -1-k). bds., bds. 9.95 *(978-1-77108-002-6(7))* Nimbus Publishing, Ltd. CAN. Dist: Orca Bk. Pubs. USA.

Popov, Nikolai. Amazonia: Indigenous Tales from Brazil, 1 vol. Springer, Jane, tr. from POR. 2013. (ENG.). 96p. (J). (gr. 4). 24.95 *(978-1-55498-185-4(9))* Groundwood Bks. CAN. Dist: Perseus-PGW.

Popp, K. Wendy. One Candle. Bunting, Eve. 2004. (ENG.). 40p. (J). (gr. -1-3). pap. 6.99 *(978-0-06-008560-5(6))* HarperCollins Pubs.

—Where the Sunrise Begins. Wood, Douglas. 2010. (ENG.). 40p. (J). (gr. -1-3). 17.99 *(978-0-689-86172-7(9)*, Simon & Schuster Bks. For Young Readers) Simon & Schuster Bks. For Young Readers.

Poppen, Alex. A Brother-Sister Team. Bitner, Pamela. 2008. 16p. pap. 24.95 *(978-1-60474-583-2(5))* America Star Bks.

Populoh, Valeska M. Dinosaur Name Poems/Poemas de Nombres de Dinosaurios. Cunningham, Steven C. Gorospe, Myriam, tr. 2009. (SPA.). 70p. (J). pap. 12.95 *(978-0-9721241-6-4(0))* Three Conditions Pr.

Porcellino, John. The Next Day. Gilmore, Jason & Peterson, Paul. Jansen, Alex & Poplak, Richard, eds. 2011. (ENG.). 104p. (YA). pap. 16.95 *(978-0-9864884-1-2(0))* Pop Sandbox, Inc. CAN. Dist: Diamond Bk. Distributors.

Porcellino, John. Thoreau at Walden. Porcellino, John. 2009. (ENG.). 112p. (J). (gr. 5-18). pap. 9.99 *(978-1-4231-0039-3(5))* Hyperion Pr.

Porcheron, Tammy. Hairy Beary Book Two Bk. 2,Vol. 2: The Great Waterfall, 3 bks. Lewis, Carolyn. DeVince, James, ed. 2003. (Hairy Beary Ser.: 2). 42p. (J). pap. 9.95 *(978-0-9712641-1-3(2))* J M D's Business Services.

Porcheron, Tammy & DeVince, James. The Hairy Beary Adventure Series, 3 bks. Lewis, Carolyn & DeVince, James. 2005. 122p. (J). pap. 24.95 *(978-0-9712641-3-7(9))* J M D's Business Services.

—Hairy Beary Book Three: The Blue Ribbon Hero, 3 bks., Vol. 3. Lewis, Carolyn & DeVince, James. 2003. (Hairy Beary Ser.: 3). 46p. (J). pap. 9.95 *(978-0-9712641-2-0(0))* J M D's Business Services.

Porfirio, Guy. The Day I Could Fly. Loux, Lynn Crosbie. 2003. (ENG.). 32p. (J). (gr. k-3). 15.95 *(978-1-55971-866-0(8))* Cooper Square Publishing Llc.

—Esperanza Means Hope. Harvey, Gwen. 2010. (J). *(978-0-910037-51-8(5))*; pap. *(978-0-910037-52-5(3))* Arizona Historical Society.

—Grandpa's Little One. Crystal, Billy. 2006. 40p. (J). (gr. -1-k). lib. bdg. 17.89 *(978-0-06-078174-3(2))* HarperCollins Pubs.

—Juan y los Frijoles Magicos (Jack & the Beanstalk), Grades PK-3. Ottolenghi, Carol. 2005. (Keepsake Stories Ser.). (SPA & ENG.). 32p. (J). (gr. -1-3). pap. 3.99 *(978-0-7696-3816-4(3))* Carson-Dellosa Publishing, LLC.

—Junk Man's Daughter. Levitin, Sonia. rev. ed. 2007. (Tales of Young Americans Ser.). (ENG.). 32p. (J). (gr. 3-7). 17.95 *(978-1-58536-315-5(4))* Sleeping Bear Pr.

—The Littlest Angel. Tazewell, Charles. 2004. 32p. (J). 16.95 *(978-0-8249-5473-4(4))* Ideals Pubns.

—Sheldon's Adventures in Heaven. Wallace-Lang, Maxine Lois. 2003. 48p. (J). 12.99 *(978-0-8280-1508-0(2))* Review & Herald Publishing Assn.

Porfirio, Guy, jt. illus. see Moore, Clement C.

Pornkerd, Vorrarit, et al. The Case of the Silk King. Gilligan, Shannon. 2006. (Choose Your Own Adventure Ser.). 116p. (J). (gr. 4-7). per. 6.99 *(978-1-933390-14-7(X)*, CHCL14) Chooseco LLC.

—The Lost Jewels of Nabooti. 2006. (Choose Your Own Adventure Ser.: No. 4). 131p. (J). (gr. 4-7). per. 6.99 *(978-1-933390-04-8(2)*, CHCL04) Chooseco LLC.

—Space & Beyond. 2006. (Choose Your Own Adventure Ser.: No. 3). 131p. (J). (gr. 4-8). per. 6.99 *(978-1-933390-03-1(4)*, CHCL03) Chooseco LLC.

Pornkerd, Vorrarit & Yaweera, Sasiprapa. Mystery of the Maya. Donploypetch, Jintanan. 2006. (Choose Your Own Adventure Ser.: No. 5). 131p. (J). (gr. 4-7). per. 6.99 *(978-1-933390-05-5(0)*, CHCL05) Chooseco LLC.

Porras, Javier Fernando. Cenicienta. Perrault, Charles. 2003. (Coleccion Letras Pegadas Ser.). (SPA.). 70p. (J). (gr. -1-7). pap. *(978-958-30-0547-3(9))* Panamericana Editorial.

—Historias de Amores y Desvarios en America. 2004. (Literatura Juvenil (Panamericana Editorial) Ser.). (SPA.). 179p. (J). (gr. -1-7). pap. *(978-958-30-0569-5(X)*, PV4378) Centro de Informacion y Desarrollo de la Comunicacion y la Literatura MEX. Dist: Lectorum Pubns., Inc.

—The Lazy Bee. Quiroga, Horacio. Leal, Mireya Fonseca, ed. 2003. (Library of Tale Ser.). (SPA.). 12p. (J). (gr. -1-7). pap. *(978-958-30-0988-4(1))* Panamericana Editorial.

Port, Cynthia. Kibble Talk. Port, Cynthia. 2013. 214p. pap. 9.99 *(978-0-9912278-0-8(8))* Port, Cynthia L.

Porter, Jane. Duck Sock Hop. Kohuth, Jane. 2012. (ENG.). 32p. (J). (gr. -1-k). 16.99 *(978-0-8037-3712-9(2)*, Dial) Penguin Publishing Group.

Porter, Janice. The Chocolate Tree: [A Mayan Folktale]. Lowery, Linda & Keep, Richard. 2009. (On My Own Folklore Ser.). (ENG.). 48p. (gr. 2-4). pap. 6.95 *(978-1-58013-851-2(9)*, First Avenue Editions) Lerner Publishing Group.

Porter, Janice Lee. Allen Jay & the Undergound Railroad, 4 bks., Set. Brill, Marlene Targ. 2007. (Readalongs for Beginning Readers Ser.). (J). (gr. 1-3). pap. 37.95 incl. audio *(978-1-59519-947-8(0))* Live Oak Media.

—Allen Jay & the Underground Railroad, 4 bks., Set. 2006. (Readalongs for Beginning Readers Ser.). (J). (gr. 2-5). pap. 39.95 incl. audio compact disk *(978-1-59519-951-5(9))* Live Oak Media.

—Allen Jay y el Ferrocarril Subterraneo. Brill, Marlene Targ. Translations.com Staff, tr. from ENG. 2007. (Yo Solo: Historia (on My Own History) Ser.). (SPA.). 48p. (gr. 2-4). lib. bdg. 25.26 *(978-0-8225-7784-3(4)*, Ediciones Lerner) Lerner Publishing Group.

—Aunt Clara Brown: Official Pioneer. Lowery, Linda. 2006. (On My Own Biographies Ser.). 48p. 16.95 *(978-0-7569-6699-7(X))* Perfection Learning Corp.

—Bessie Coleman: Daring to Fly. Walker, Sally M. 2003. (On My Own Biography Ser.). (ENG.). 48p. (gr. 2-4). pap. 6.95 *(978-0-87614-103-8(3)*, Carolrhoda Bks.) Lerner Publishing Group.

—Family. Monk, Isabell. 2005. (Carolrhoda Picture Bks.). (ENG.). 32p. (J). (gr. k-4). per. 10.95 *(978-1-57505-917-4(7))* Lerner Publishing Group.

—Jesse Owens. Sutcliffe, Jane. 2006. (On My Own Biographies Ser.). 48p. 17.00 *(978-0-7569-6702-4(3))* Perfection Learning Corp.

—The Tale of la Llorona: A Mexican Folktale. Lowery, Linda & Keep, Richard. 2007. (On My Own Folklore Ser.). (ENG.). 48p. (gr. 2-4). lib. bdg. 25.26 *(978-0-8225-6378-5(9)*, Millbrook Pr.) Lerner Publishing Group.

—Yuvi's Candy Tree. Simpson, Lesley. 2011. (ENG.). 32p. (J). (gr. k-3). pap. 7.95 *(978-0-7613-5652-3(5))*; lib. bdg. 17.95 *(978-0-7613-5651-6(7))* Lerner Publishing Group. (Kar-Ben Publishing).

Porter, Lynda C., jt. illus. see Neusca, Guy, Jr.

Porter, Matthew. Fox on the Loose! Porter, Matthew. 2014. (ENG.). 20p. (J). (— 1). bds. 9.99 *(978-1-57061-928-1(X))* Sasquatch Bks.

—The Rise & Fall of Oscar the Magician: A Monkey World Adventure. Porter, Matthew. 2015. (ENG.). 32p. (J). (gr. -1-3). 17.99 *(978-1-57061-929-8(8))* Sasquatch Bks.

Porter, Sue. McGillycuddy Could! Edwards, Pamela Duncan. 2005. 32p. (J). (gr. -1-1). 14.99 *(978-0-06-029001-6(3))* HarperCollins Pubs.

Porter, Tammy. A Wondrous World of Home. Feather, Tami Flaming. 2012. 24p. pap. 24.95 *(978-1-4626-4544-2(5))* America Star Bks.

Porterfield, Scott. Zangadoo Kangaroo & the Mysterious Boomerang. Lee, Karin. 2012. 94p. pap. 6.99 (978-0-9847428-2-0(4)) Zangadoo Entertainment.

Portis, Antoinette. Froodle. Portis, Antoinette. 2014. (ENG.). 32p. (J). (gr. -1-3). 16.99 (978-1-59643-922-1(X)) Roaring Brook Pr.

—Kindergarten Diary. Portis, Antoinette. 2010. 32p. (J). (gr. -1-3). (ENG.). 12.99 (978-0-06-145691-6(8)); lib. bdg. 14.89 (978-0-06-145692-3(6)) HarperCollins Pubs.

—Not a Box. Portis, Antoinette. 2006. 32p. (J). (gr. -1 — 1). (ENG.). 14.99 (978-0-06-112322-1(6)); lib. bdg. 14.89 (978-0-06-112323-8(4)) HarperCollins Pubs.

—Not a Box Board Book. Portis, Antoinette. 2011. (ENG.). 28p. (J). (gr. -1 — 1). bds. 7.99 (978-0-06-199442-5(1), HarperFestival) HarperCollins Pubs.

—Not a Stick. Portis, Antoinette. 2007. (ENG.). 32p. (J). (gr. -1-1). 14.99 (978-0-06-112325-2(0)) HarperCollins Pubs.

—A Penguin Story. Portis, Antoinette. 2008. (ENG.). 40p. (J). (gr. -1-3). 17.99 (978-0-06-145688-6(8)) HarperCollins Pubs.

—Princess Super Kitty. Portis, Antoinette. 2011. (ENG.). 40p. (J). (gr. -1-3). 14.99 (978-0-06-182725-9(8)) HarperCollins Pubs.

Portman, Michelle Eva. Compost, by Gosh! An Adventure with Vermicomposting. Portman, Michelle Eva. l.t. ed. 2003. (ENG.). 42p. (J). 16.95 (978-0-942256-16-1(6), Falcon Guides) Globe Pequot Pr., The.

Portnoi, Jeremy. The Animated Jewish Year. Wool, Danny & Yudin, Yefim (Chaim). 2006. 88p. 19.95 (978-965-7108-79-6(9), Lambda) Urim Pubns. ISR. Dist: Lambda Pubs., Inc.

Portnoy, Amy. The Magical Ms. Plum. Becker, Bonny. 2011. (ENG.). 112p. (J). (gr. 1-4). 5.99 (978-0-375-84760-8(X), Yearling) Random Hse. Children's Bks.

Portwood, Andrew. Escamas de Dragon y Hojas de Sauce. Givens, Terryl L. (SPA.). (J). pap. 7.95 (978-958-04-4168-7(5)) Norma S.A. COL. Dist: Distribuidora Norma, Inc., Lectorum Pubns., Inc.

Poryes, Michael. The Trouble with Boys, 2 vols., Vol. 2. 2004. (That's So Raven Ser.). 96p. pap. 14.99 (978-1-59182-807-5(4), Tokyopop Kids) TOKYOPOP, Inc.

Posada, Mia. Dazzling Dragonflies: A Life Cycle Story. Glaser, Linda. 2008. (Linda Glaser's Classic Creatures Ser.). (ENG.). 32p. (gr. k-3). lib. bdg. 22.60 (978-0-8225-6753-0(9), Millbrook Pr.) Lerner Publishing Group.

—The Long, Long Journey: The Godwit's Amazing Migration. Markle, Sandra. 2013. (ENG.). 32p. (J). (gr. k-3). lib. bdg. 26.60 (978-0-7613-5623-3(1), Millbrook Pr.) Lerner Publishing Group.

Posada, Mia. Guess What Is Growing Inside This Egg. Posada, Mia. 2007. (ENG.). 32p. (J). (gr. k-3). 15.95 (978-0-8225-6192-7(1), Millbrook Pr.) Lerner Publishing Group.

—Who Was Here? Discovering Wild Animal Tracks. Posada, Mia. 2014. 32p. (J). (gr. k-3). 16.95 (978-1-4677-1871-4(8), Millbrook Pr.) Lerner Publishing Group.

Posen, Mick. Titanic: The Search for the Lost Fugitives. Croy, Anita. 2012. (ENG.). 48p. (J). (gr. 3-7). 16.99 (978-0-7534-6672-8(4), Kingfisher) Roaring Brook Pr.

POST, L. E. E. Texas Animals Big & Small. Post, Lee. 2008. 32p. pap. 9.95 (978-1-934443-33-0(6)) ExpandingBooks.com.

Post, Lee. Alaska! Big & Small: A big book of Alaskan Animals from itsy-bitsy to Gigantic. Post, Lee. 2007. 32p. per. 9.95 (978-1-934443-94-1(8)) ExpandingBooks.com.

Postgate, Daniel. The Little Red Hen. 2006. (First Reading Level 3 Ser.). 48p. (J). (gr. 1-4). 8.99 (978-0-7945-1375-7(1), Usborne) EDC Publishing.

—My Auntie Susan. Bird, Shelia May. 2008. (Tadpoles Ser.). 23p. (J). (gr. -1-3). 17.15 (978-1-4178-0931-8(0), Turtleback) Turtleback Bks.

—My Auntie Susan. Bird, Shelia May. 2008. (Tadpoles Ser.). (ENG.). 24p. (J). (gr. -1-3). pap. (978-0-7787-3889-3(2)); lib. bdg. (978-0-7787-3858-9(2)) Crabtree Publishing Co.

Postgate, Daniel. Rumpled Stilton Skin. 2015. (ENG.). 32p. (J). (978-0-7787-1930-4(8)) Crabtree Publishing Co.

Postgate, Daniel. The Ugly Duckling. 2006. (First Reading Level 4 Ser.). 48p. (J). (gr. 1-4). 8.99 (978-0-7945-1274-3(7), Usborne) EDC Publishing.

Postgate, Daniel. Esa Inmensa Galaxia. Postgate, Daniel. Poskitt, Kjartan. (SPA.). 158p. (YA). (gr. 5-8). (978-84-272-2055-3(3)) Molino, Editorial ESP. Dist: Lectorum Pubns., Inc.

—Esas Endiabladas Mates. Postgate, Daniel. Poskitt, Kjartan. (SPA.). 176p. (YA). (gr. 5-8). (978-84-272-2064-5(2)) Molino, Editorial ESP. Dist: Lectorum Pubns., Inc.

—Esas Insignificantes Fracciones. Postgate, Daniel. Poskitt, Kjartan. (SPA.). 160p. (YA). (gr. 5-8). (978-84-272-2068-3(5)) Molino, Editorial ESP. Dist: Lectorum Pubns., Inc.

—Smelly Bill, 1 vol. Postgate, Daniel. 2010. (ENG.). 32p. (J). (gr. -1-2). pap. 6.99 (978-0-8075-7463-8(5)) Whitman, Albert & Co.

Postgate, Daniel. Esos Extintos Dinosaurios. Postgate, Daniel, tr. Oliver, Martin. 2003. (Coleccion Esa Gran Cultura).Tr. of Dead Dinosaurs. (SPA.). 134p. (YA). 7.96 (978-84-272-2137-6(1)) Molino, Editorial ESP. Dist: Lectorum Pubns., Inc.

Postier, Jim. Best Little Wingman. Allen, Janet. 2005. (ENG.). 32p. (J). (gr. k-2). 15.95 (978-1-59078-197-5(X)) Boyds Mills Pr.

—Goose Moon. Arden, Carolyn. 2004. (ENG.). 32p. (J). (gr. k-7). 15.95 (978-1-59078-040-4(X)) Boyds Mills Pr.

Poston, Valerie Williams. ArbeZ ZebrA Teaches A to Z, 3 vols., Vol. 1. 2007. 33p. (J). spiral bd. 39.99 (978-0-9779063-0-7(2)) Gain Literacy Skills / Lynette Gain Williams.

Pottenkulam, Pooja. Sunshine for Amma. Husain, Zakir & Mishra, Samina. 2004. 16p. (J). (978-81-89013-41-7(6)) Zubaan.

Potter, Beatrix. The Tale of Peter Rabbit. 2014. (J). pap. (978-1-4677-5772-0(1), First Avenue Editions) Lerner Publishing Group.

Potter, Beatrix. The Peter Rabbit & Friends Treasury. Potter, Beatrix. 2006. 240p. (J). (gr. k-4). reprint ed. 20.00 (978-1-4223-5452-0(0)) DIANE Publishing Co.

—Peter Rabbit Rainbow Shapes & Colors. Potter, Beatrix. 2006. (Peter Rabbit Seedlings Ser.). (ENG.). 10p. (J). (gr. k-18). bds. 5.99 (978-0-7232-5722-6(1), Puffin) Penguin Publishing Group.

—Sgeulachd Bheniamin Coineanach. Potter, Beatrix. MacDonald, James, 1st, tr. from ENG. 2008.Tr. of Tale of Benjamin Bunny. (GAE.). 64p. (J). (978-0-9552326-4-0(3)) Grace Note Pubns.

—Sgeulachd Pheadair Rabaid. Potter, Beatrix. MacDonald, James, 1st, tr. from ENG. 2008.Tr. of Tale of Peter Rabbit. (GAE.). 84p. (978-0-9552326-3-3(5)) Grace Note Pubns.

Potter, Debra. I am the Music Man. 2005. (Classic Books with Holes Board Book Ser.). (ENG.). 14p. (J). bds. (978-1-904550-60-0(6)) Child's Play International Ltd.

—I Am the Music Man. (Classic Books with Holes Big Book Ser.). (ENG.). 16p. (J). 2006. (gr. -1-3). (978-1-84643-010-7(0)); 2005. pap. (978-1-904550-34-1(7)) Child's Play International Ltd.

Potter, Diane. Ups & Downs. Potter, Diane, ed. Potter, Michael. 2010. (ENG.). 62p. pap. 12.98 (978-1-4537-8966-7(9)) CreateSpace Independent Publishing Platform.

Potter, Giselle. Beatrice Spells Some Lulus & Learns to Write a Letter. Best, Cari. 2013. (ENG.). 32p. (J). (gr. k-3). 16.99 (978-0-374-39904-7(2), Farrar, Straus & Giroux (BYR)) Farrar, Straus & Giroux.

—The Boy Who Loved Words. Schotter, Roni. 2006. (ENG.). 40p. (J). (gr. -1-3). 17.99 (978-0-375-83601-5(2), Schwartz & Wade Bks.) Random Hse. Children's Bks.

—The Brave Little Seamstress. Osborne, Mary Pope. 2006. 32p. (gr. -1-3). 17.00 (978-0-7569-6613-3(2)) Perfection Learning Corp.

—Cecil the Pet Glacier. Harvey, Matthea. 2012. (ENG.). 40p. (J). (gr. -1-3). 17.99 (978-0-375-86773-6(2)); 20.99 (978-0-375-96773-3(7)) Random Hse. Children's Bks. (Schwartz & Wade Bks.).

—C'mon an' Swing in My Tree! 2005. 14p. (J). bds. 16.95 incl. audio compact disk (978-0-9763012-0-2(2)) Cow Heard Records.

—The Hare & the Tortoise. Bolt, Ranjit. 2006. (ENG.). 64p. (J). (gr. -1-3). 19.99 (978-1-905236-54-1(9)) Barefoot Bks., Inc.

—Kate & the Beanstalk. Osborne, Mary Pope. 2005. (ENG.). 40p. (J). (gr. -1-3). reprint ed. 7.99 (978-1-4169-0818-0(8), Simon & Schuster/Paula Wiseman Bks.) Simon & Schuster/Paula Wiseman Bks.

—The Little Piano Girl: The Story of Mary Lou Williams, Jazz Legend. MacDonald, Maryann & Ingalls, Ann. 13th ed. 2010. (ENG.). 32p. (J). (gr. 1-4). 17.00 (978-0-618-95974-7(2)) Houghton Mifflin Harcourt Publishing Co.

—Moo, Moo, Brown Cow! Have You Any Milk? Gershator, Phillis. 2011. (ENG.). 40p. (J). (gr. -1-2). 16.99 (978-0-375-86744-6(9)) Random Hse. Children's Bks.

—Mr. Semolina-Semolinus. Manna, Anthony L. & Mitakidou, Christodoula. 2004. (ENG.). 40p. (J). (gr. -1-3). 19.99 (978-0-689-86698-2(4), Simon & Schuster/Paula Wiseman Bks.) Simon & Schuster/Paula Wiseman Bks.

—The Orphan: A Cinderella Story from Greece. Manna, Anthony & Mitakidou, Christodoula. 2011. (ENG.). 40p. (J). (gr. -1-3). 16.99 (978-0-375-86691-3(4), Schwartz & Wade Bks.) Random Hse. Children's Bks.

—Sleeping Bobby. Osborne, Mary Pope & Osborne, Will. 2005. (ENG.). 40p. (J). (gr. -1-3). 18.99 (978-0-689-87668-4(8), Atheneum Bks. for Young Readers) Simon & Schuster Children's Publishing.

—Three Cheers for Catherine the Great! Best, Cari. 2003. (Catherine the Great Ser.). (ENG.). 32p. (J). (gr. -1-3). pap. 7.99 (978-0-374-47551-2(2)) Square Fish.

Potter, Giselle. The Honest-to-Goodness Truth. Potter, Giselle. McKissack, Patricia C. 2003. (ENG.). 40p. (J). (gr. -1-3). 7.99 (978-0-689-85395-1(5), Simon & Schuster/Paula Wiseman Bks.) Simon & Schuster/Paula Wiseman Bks.

Potter, Heather. Pearl Verses the World. Murphy, Sally. 2011. (ENG.). 80p. (J). (gr. 3-7). 14.99 (978-0-7636-4821-3(3)) Candlewick Pr.

Potter, Katherine. Always Be Safe. Schulz, Kathy. 2003. (Rookie Reader Skill Set Ser.). (ENG.). (J). (gr. k-2). pap. 4.95 (978-0-516-26965-8(8), Children's Pr.) Scholastic Library Publishing.

—Old House, New House, 0 vols. Gershator, Phillis. 2009. (ENG.). 32p. (J). (gr. -1-3). 17.99 (978-0-7614-5386-4(5), 9780761453864, Amazon Children's Publishing) Amazon Publishing.

Potter, Lori. The Little Cat, the Wonderful Witch, & the Clever Mouse. Stuart, Lisa Marie. 2008. 60p. pap. 21.95 (978-1-59858-691-6(2)) Dog Ear Publishing, LLC.

Potter, Melisande. Dick Whittington & His Cat. 2006. (ENG.). 32p. (J). (gr. -1-3). 16.95 (978-0-8234-1987-6(8)) Holiday Hse., Inc.

—Pizza for the Queen. Castaldo, Nancy F. 2005. (ENG.). 32p. (J). (gr. -1-3). 16.95 (978-0-8234-1865-7(0)) Holiday Hse., Inc.

—Traveling Tom & the Leprechaun. Bateman, Teresa. 2007. (ENG.). 32p. (J). (gr. -1-3). 16.95 (978-0-8234-1976-0(2)) Holiday Hse., Inc.

Pottie, Marjolein. The Best Bottom. Minne, Brigitte. 2006. (ENG.). 32p. (J). (gr. -1-3). pap. 5.95 (978-1-59687-387-2(6)) IBks., Inc.

—The Best Bottom. Minne, Brigitte. 2004. 32p. (J). 15.95 (978-0-689-03595-1(0), Milk & Cookies) ibooks, Inc.

—Qui?! Nielandt, Dirk. Sarfati, Sonia, tr. from DUT. 2004. (Picture Bks.). (FRE.). 32p. (J). (gr. -1). (978-2-89021-679-2(9)); pap. (978-2-89021-678-5(0)) Diffusion du livre Mirabel (DLM).

—Qui Est-Ce Qui... Nielandt, Dirk. Sarfati, Sonia, tr. from DUT. 2004. (Picture Bks.). (FRE.). 32p. (J). (gr. -1). (978-2-89021-681-5(0)); pap. (978-2-89021-680-8(2)) Diffusion du livre Mirabel (DLM).

Potts Dawson, Eileen. H Is for Hawkeye. Wagner, Jay. 2003. (J). 16.95 (978-1-931599-11-5(4), Trails Bks.) Big Earth Publishing.

Potts, Sam, jt. illus. see Seeley, Scott.

Poulin, Stephane. Earth to Audrey. Hughes, Susan. 2007. (ENG.). 32p. (J). (gr. k-3). 6.95 (978-1-55453-165-3(9)) Kids Can Pr., Ltd. CAN. Dist: Univ. of Toronto Pr.

—La Forêt aux Mille et un Périls, Tome 2. Côté, Denis. 2004. (Roman Jeunesse Ser.). (FRE.). 96p. (J). (gr. 4-7). pap. (978-2-89021-696-9(9)) Diffusion du livre Mirabel (DLM).

Poulin, Stéphane. Little Zizi. Lenain, Thierry. Zolinsky, Daniel, tr. from FRE. 2008. (ENG.). 32p. (J). (gr. k-1). 16.95 (978-1-933693-05-7(3)) Cinco Puntos Pr.

Poupard, et al. Why Are We Here Again? Beka. 2007. (Rugger Boys Ser.). (ENG.). 48p. (J). (gr. 4-7). per. 9.99 (978-1-905460-33-5(3)) CineBook GBR. Dist: National Bk. Network.

Poupart, Jean-Sébastien. Caillou Leads the Parade. Sulgit, Nicole. 2004. (J). (978-0-7853-9949-0(6)) Publications International, Ltd.

Pouriseth, Phal, jt. illus. see Nath, Vann.

Póveda Piérola, Mabel. La Lechera. Combel Editorial Staff & Samaniego, Félix María. 2005. (Caballo Alado Clásico Series-Al Paso Ser.). (SPA & ENG.). 24p. (J). (gr. -1-k). 7.95 (978-84-7864-852-8(6)) Combel Editorial, S.A. ESP. Dist: Independent Pubs. Group.

Povenmire, Dan, jt. illus. see Jeff, Marsh.

Povey, Andrea. The Witch Who Liked to Wear Pink. Kane, Gillian. 2013. 24p. pap. 11.50 (978-1-62516-315-8(0), Strategic Bk. Publishing) Strategic Book Publishing & Rights Agency (SBPRA).

Powell, Consie. Baby Bear Isn't Hungry. Ross, Michael Elsohn. 2006. (ENG.). 26p. (J). (gr. -1-4). 10.95 (978-1-930238-24-4(X)) Yosemite Assn.

—Bird on My Hand (hardcover) Making Friends with Chickadees, 1 vol. Bevis, Mary. 2014. (ENG.). 32p. (J). (gr. 1-2). 17.95 (978-0-9883508-9-2(0)) Raven Productions, Inc.

—Bird on My Hand (softcover) Making Friends with Chickadees. Bevis, Mary. 2014. (ENG.). 32p. (J). (gr. 1-2). pap. 9.95 (978-0-9883508-8-5(2)) Raven Productions, Inc.

—A Day in the Salt Marsh, 1 vol. Kurtz, Kevin. 2007. (ENG.). 32p. (J). (gr. -1-3). 15.95 (978-0-9768823-5-0(3)); pap. 9.95 (978-1-934359-19-8(X)) Arbordale Publishing.

—Nature's Patchwork Quilt: Understanding Habitats. Miché, Mary. 2012. 32p. (J). (gr. k-6). 16.95 (978-1-58469-169-3(7)); (ENG.). pap. 8.95 (978-1-58469-170-9(0)) Dawn Pubns.

—Old Woman Winter. Bevis, Mary. 2010. 32p. (J). (gr. 1-2). pap. 9.95 (978-0-9819307-6-3(X)) Raven Productions, Inc.

—Who Lives in the Snow? Jones, Jennifer Berry. 2012. (ENG.). 32p. (gr. -1-3). pap. 8.95 (978-1-57098-444-0(1)) Rinehart, Roberts Pubs.

—Wolf Song. Bevis, Mary. 2007. 32p. (gr. 1-2). 18.95 (978-0-9794202-0-7(2)); pap. 12.95 (978-0-9794202-1-4(0)) Raven Productions, Inc.

Powell, Consie. Old Dog Cora & the Christmas Tree. Powell, Consie. 2003. 32p. (J). (gr. 1-2). lib. bdg. 14.95 (978-0-9677057-6-7(2)) Raven Productions, Inc.

Powell, Consie, jt. illus. see Bevis, Mary.

Powell, Debbie. Trucks. Powell, Debbie. 2012. (ENG.). 16p. (J). (gr. -1 — 1). bds. 5.99 (978-0-7636-5934-9(7)) Candlewick Pr.

Powell, James. The Adventures of Rady Red Comb. Tingwald, Jady Ann. 2005. 33p. (J). (gr. 1-6). 9.00 (978-0-9706728-1-0(0)) New Millenium Pr., The.

—Orrie's Christmas. Tingwald, July Ann. 2007. 42p. 9.00 (978-0-9706728-5-8(3)) New Millenium Pr., The.

Powell, Jonathan. Making Sense of Sex: A Forthright Guide to Puberty, Sex & Relationships for People with Asperger's Syndrome. Attwood, Sarah. 2008. (ENG.). 320p. (gr. 4-12). pap. (978-1-84310-374-5(5)) Kingsley, Jessica Ltd.

Powell, Luciana Navarro. Alphasaurus. Bryant, Megan E. 2012. (ENG.). 20p. (J). (gr. -1 — 1). bds. 9.99 (978-1-4521-0748-6(3)) Chronicle Bks. LLC.

—Busy Little Dinosaurs: A Touch-And-Feel Alphabet Book. Schwartz, Betty & Seresin, Lynn. 2015. (Back-And-Forth Bks.). (ENG.). 22p. (gr. -1 — 1). bds. 9.99 (978-1-62370-234-2(8)) Capstone Young Readers.

—Colorasaurus. Bryant, Megan E. 2012. (ENG.). 20p. (J). (gr. -1 — 1). bds. 9.99 (978-1-4521-0814-8(5)) Chronicle Bks. LLC.

—Countasaurus. Bryant, Megan E. 2012. (ENG.). 20p. (J). (gr. -1 — 1). bds. 9.99 (978-1-4521-0747-9(5)) Chronicle Bks. LLC.

—I Take Care of Myself!/Me Se Cuidar! Rosa-Mendoza, Gladys. 2007. (English Spanish Foundations Ser.). (ENG & SPA.). 20p. (J). (gr. -1-k). bds. 6.95 (978-1-931398-22-0(4)) Me+Mi Publishing.

Powell, Luciana Navarro. Puppies, Puppies, Everywhere! A Back-And-Forth Opposites Book. Schwartz, Betty & Seresin, Lynn. 2015. (J). (978-1-62370-236-6(4)) Capstone Young Readers.

Powell, Luciana Navarro. Shapeasaurus. Bryant, Megan E. 2012. (ENG.). 18p. (J). (gr. -1 — 1). bds. 9.99 (978-1-4521-0815-5(3)) Chronicle Bks. LLC.

—Ten Playful Tigers: A Touch-And-Feel Counting Book. Schwartz, Betty & Seresin, Lynn. 2015. (Back-And-Forth Bks.). (ENG.). 22p. (gr. -1 — 1). bds. 9.99 (978-1-62370-233-5(X)) Capstone Young Readers.

Powell, Luciana Navarro. You're It, Little Red Fish! A Back-And-Forth Color Book. Schwartz, Betty & Seresin, Lynn. 2015. (J). (978-1-62370-235-9(6)) Capstone Young Readers.

Powell, Nate. The Year of the Beasts. Castellucci, Cecil. 2012. (ENG.). 192p. (YA). (gr. 7-12). 16.99 (978-1-59643-686-2(7)) Roaring Brook Pr.

—The Year of the Beasts. Castellucci, Cecil. 2014. (ENG.). 208p. (YA). (gr. 7-12). pap. 9.99 (978-1-250-05076-2(6)) Square Fish.

Powell, Nathan. Heroes of Olympus, Book One the Lost Hero: the Graphic Novel. Riordan, Rick & Venditti, Robert. 2014. (Heroes of Olympus Ser.). (ENG.). 192p. (J). (gr. 5-9). pap. 12.99 (978-1-4231-6325-1(7)) Hyperion Bks. for Children.

Powell, Polly. I Howl, I Growl: Southwest Animal Antics. Vaughn, Marcia. 2003. (ENG.). 26p. (J). (gr. -1-k). 7.95 (978-0-87358-835-5(5)) Cooper Square Publishing Llc.

Powell, Rick. Who's Haunting the White House? The President's Mansion & the Ghosts Who Live There. Belanger, Jeff. 2012. (ENG.). 64p. (J). (gr. 5). pap. 9.95 (978-1-4549-0026-9(1)) Sterling Publishing Co., Inc.

Power, Margaret. The Sea's Secret. Bursztynski, Susan. 2004. iv, 36p. (J). pap. (978-0-7608-6737-2(2)) Sundance/Newbridge Educational Publishing.

—The Silver Brumby: Including Elyne Mitchell's Ast Brumby Story, 'Wild Echoes Ringing' Mitchell, Elyne. 2003. 232p. (978-0-207-19862-5(4)) HarperCollins Pubs. Australia.

Powers, Don. The Silver Donkey. Hartnett, Sonya. 2014. (ENG.). 272p. (J). (gr. 5). 16.99 (978-0-7636-7211-9(4)) Candlewick Pr.

Powers, Leon R., photos by. The Forgotten Expedition: The 1907 Baker University Expedition into Idaho & Oregon. Powers, Leon R. 2011. 200p. (YA). pap. 16.95 (978-0-9800208-1-6(6)) Look-About Bks.

Powers, Mark, et al. Tara's Tiara: Paperback. Powers, Mark & Powers, Megan. 2012. 130p. (J). pap. 14.95 (978-0-9853817-0-7(1)) Pendentive Pubns.

Powers, Mireille Xioulan, jt. illus. see Colby, J. Z.

Powers, Richard M. Land of the Pharaohs. Cottrell, Leonard. 2012. 130p. 40.95 (978-1-258-23853-7(5)); pap. 25.95 (978-1-258-24652-5(X)) Literary Licensing, LLC.

Poydar, Nancy. The Bad-News Report Card. Poydar, Nancy. 2006. (ENG.). 32p. (J). (gr. -1-3). 16.95 (978-0-8234-1992-0(4)) Holiday Hse., Inc.

—The Biggest Test in the Universe. Poydar, Nancy. 2005. (ENG.). 32p. (J). (gr. -1-3). 16.95 (978-0-8234-1944-9(4)) Holiday Hse., Inc.

—Bus Driver. Poydar, Nancy. 2012. (ENG.). 32p. (J). 15.95 (978-0-8234-2411-5(1)) Holiday Hse., Inc.

—Busy Bea. Poydar, Nancy. 2013. (ENG.). 32p. (J). (gr. -1-2). 16.99 (978-1-4814-2161-4(1), McElderry, Margaret K. Bks.) McElderry, Margaret K. Bks.

—Cool Ali. Poydar, Nancy. 2014. (ENG.). 32p. (J). (gr. -1-2). 16.99 (978-1-4814-2531-5(5), McElderry, Margaret K. Bks.) McElderry, Margaret K. Bks.

—No Fair Science Fair. Poydar, Nancy. 2011. (ENG.). 32p. (J). (gr. -1-3). 14.95 (978-0-8234-2269-2(0)) Holiday Hse., Inc.

—The Perfectly Horrible Halloween. Poydar, Nancy. 2005. (ENG.). 32p. (J). (gr. k-3). pap. 6.95 (978-0-8234-1769-8(7)) Holiday Hse., Inc.

—Zip, Zip... Homework. Poydar, Nancy. 2008. (ENG.). 32p. (J). (gr. -1-3). 16.95 (978-0-8234-2090-2(6)) Holiday Hse., Inc.

Poynter, Linda. My Invisible Friends. Whitedove, Michelle. l.t. ed. 2005. 30p. (gr. -1-3). spiral bd. 18.95 (978-0-9714908-4-0(8)) Whitedove Pr.

Pozzo, Adam Dal. The Wiggles Christmas Song & Activity Book. 2006. (ENG.). 44p. per. 10.95 (978-1-876871-88-8(1), 1876871881) Music Sales Corp.

Prahin, Andrew. Brimsby's Hats. Prahin, Andrew. 2013. (ENG.). 40p. (J). (gr. -1-3). 15.99 (978-1-4424-8147-3(1), Simon & Schuster Bks. For Young Readers) Simon & Schuster Bks. For Young Readers.

Praker, Jon. 5 - Dorp the Scottish Dragon: In the Bermuda Triangle, bk. 5. Johnson, Sandi. Brundige, Britt & Durant, Sybrina, eds. 2014. 5. (ENG.). 30p. (J). (gr. -1-6). pap. 12.99 (978-1-929063-62-8(8), 161) Moons & Stars Publishing For Children.

Prange, Beckie. Song of the Water Boatman & Other Pond Poems. Sidman, Joyce. 2005. (ENG.). 32p. (J). (gr. -1-3). 17.99 (978-0-618-13547-9(2)) Houghton Mifflin Harcourt Publishing Co.

—Ubiquitous: Celebrating Nature's Survivors. Sidman, Joyce. 2010. (ENG.). 40p. (J). (gr. 1-4). 17.00 (978-0-618-71719-4(6)) Houghton Mifflin Harcourt Publishing Co.

Prap, Lila. I Like Black & White. Hicks, Barbara Jean. 2006. 24p. (J). (gr. -1-3). 9.95 (978-1-58925-056-7(7)) Tiger Tales.

—I Like Colors. Hicks, Barbara Jean. 2006. 24p. (J). (gr. -1-3). 9.95 (978-1-58925-057-4(5)) Tiger Tales.

Prap, Lila. Animals Speak. Prap, Lila. 2006. (ENG & MUL.). 40p. (J). 15.95 (978-0-7358-2058-6(9)) North-South Bks., Inc.

—Daddies. Prap, Lila. 2009. (ENG.). 32p. (J). (gr. -1-3). pap. 6.95 (978-0-7358-2240-5(9)) North-South Bks., Inc.

—Papas. Prap, Lila. Campy, F. Isabel & Flor Ada, Alma, trs. 2009. (SPA.). 32p. (J). (gr. -1-3). 6.95 (978-0-7358-2245-0(X)) North-South Bks., Inc.

Prasetya, Erwin & Campidelli, Maurizio. Revenge/Sacrifice, Vol. 2. Smith, Brian & Levine, Cory. 2013. (Monsuno Ser.: 2). (ENG.). 64p. (J). pap. 7.99 (978-1-4215-5689-5(8)) Viz Media.

Prater, John. I Love My Bed. Prater, John. 2007. (ENG.). 32p. (J). (gr. k-k). pap. 9.99 (978-0-340-85536-2(3)) Hodder & Stoughton GBR. Dist: Independent Pubs. Group.

Prater, Linda. Afikomen Mambo. Black, Joe. 2011. (ENG.). 24p. (J). (gr. -1 — 1). pap. 8.95 (978-0-7613-5639-4(8), Kar-Ben Publishing) Lerner Publishing Group.

—Vivian & Victor Learn about Verbs. Malaspina, Ann. 2015. (Language Builders Ser.). (ENG.). 32p. (J). (gr. 2-4). pap. 11.94 (978-1-60357-702-1(5)); lib. bdg. 25.27 (978-1-59953-667-5(6)) Norwood Hse. Pr.

Prater, Linda, jt. illus. see Brown, Richard E.

Prato, Rodica. Journeys in Time: A New Atlas of American History. Buckley, Susan & Leacock, Elspeth. 2003. (ENG.). 48p. (J). (gr. 5-7). pap. 7.99 (978-0-618-31114-9(9)) Houghton Mifflin Harcourt Publishing Co.

—King Midas & the Golden Touch. Metaxas, Eric. 2007. (Rabbit Ears: A Classic Tale Ser.). 36p. (gr. -1-3). 25.65 (978-1-59961-309-3(3)) Spotlight.

Pratt, Christine Joy. Sea Queens: Women Pirates Around the World. Yolen, Jane. (ENG.). 112p. (J). (gr. 2-5). 2010. pap. 9.95 *(978-1-58089-132-5(2))*; 2008. 18.95 *(978-1-58089-131-8(4))* Charlesbridge Publishing, Inc.

—This Is America: The American Spirit in Places & People. Robb, Don. 2005. (ENG.). 32p. (J). (gr. 1-4). pap. 7.95 *(978-1-57091-605-2(5))* Charlesbridge Publishing, Inc.

Pratt, Liz. Jelly Bean Row, 1 vol. Pynn, Susan. 2011. (ENG.). 32p. (J). (gr. k-5). pap. 9.95 *(978-1-897174-80-7(2),* Tuckamore Bks) Creative Bk. Publishing CAN. Dist: Orca Bk. Pubs. USA.

Pratt, Lizz. If It's No Trouble... a Big Polar Bear, 1 vol. Dalrymple, Lisa. 2012. (ENG.). 32p. (J). (gr. k-3). 12.95 *(978-1-897174-95-1(0),* Tuckamore Bks) Creative Bk. Publishing CAN. Dist: Orca Bk. Pubs. USA.

Pratt, Ned, photos by. The House of Wooden Santas, 1 vol. Major, Kevin. gif. ed. 2004. (ENG.). 96p. (J). 34.95 *(978-0-88995-249-2(3))* Red Deer Pr. CAN. Dist: Fitzhenry & Whiteside, Ltd.

Pratt, Pierre. Albert, the Dog Who Liked to Ride in Taxis. Zarin, Cynthia. 2004. (ENG.). 32p. (J). (gr. -1-3). 18.99 *(978-0-689-84762-2(9),* Atheneum/Richard Jackson Bks.) Simon & Schuster Children's Publishing.

—Doors in the Air, 1 vol. Weale, David. 2012. (ENG.). 32p. (J). (gr. -1-3). 19.95 *(978-1-55469-250-7(4))* Orca Bk. Pubs. USA.

—Le Géant de la Forêt: Un Voyage Musical. Ziskind, Hélio & Duchesne, Christiane. 2014. (FRE.). 48p. (J). (gr. k-2). 16.95 *(978-2-923163-36-9(2))* La Montagne Secrete CAN. Dist: Independent Pubs. Group.

—The Ladder. Rasmussen, Halfdan. Nelson, Marilyn, tr. from DAN. 2006. (ENG.). 62p. (J). (gr. -1-3). 17.99 *(978-0-7636-2282-4(6))* Candlewick Pr.

—No-Matter-What Friend, 1 vol. Winters, Kari-Lynn. 2014. (ENG.). 32p. (J). (gr. k-2). 16.95 *(978-1-896580-83-8(1))* Tradewind Bks. CAN. Dist: Orca Bk. Pubs. USA.

—Skunkdog. Jenkins, Emily. 2008. (ENG.). 32p. (J). (gr. -1-3). 16.95 *(978-0-374-37009-1(5),* Farrar, Straus & Giroux (BYR)) Farrar, Straus & Giroux.

—That New Animal. Jenkins, Emily & Jenkins, Emily P. 2005. (ENG.). 32p. (J). (gr. -1-1). 17.99 *(978-0-374-37443-3(0),* Farrar, Straus & Giroux (BYR)) Farrar, Straus & Giroux.

Pratt-Serafini, Kristin Joy. Saguaro Moon: A Desert Journal. 2004. (Sharing Nature with Children Book Ser.). 32p. (YA). 16.95 *(978-1-58469-037-5(2))* Dawn Pubns.

Pratt Serafini, Kristin Joy. A Swim Through the Sea. 2006. (Simply Nature Bks.). 26p. (J). (gr. -1). bds. 7.95 *(978-1-58469-080-1(1))* Dawn Pubns.

Pratt-Serafini, Kristin Joy. The Forever Forest: Kids Save a Tropical Treasure. Pratt-Serafini, Kristin Joy. Crandell, Rachel. 2008. 32p. (J). (gr. k-5). 16.95 *(978-1-58469-101-3(8))* Dawn Pubns.

—A Walk in the Rainforest. Pratt-Serafini, Kristin Joy. 2007. (Simply Nature Book Ser.). 26p. (J). (gr. -1 — 1). bds. 7.95 *(978-1-58469-088-7(7))* Dawn Pubns.

Pratt, Susan. Look at Little Lucy, 1 vol. Welty, Carolyn. 2009. 16p. pap. 24.95 *(978-1-60813-444-1(X))* America Star Bks.

Pratt-Thomas, Leslie. Shackles. Wentworth, Marjory. 2009. (ENG.). 36p. (J). 16.99 *(978-0-933101-06-7(6))* Legacy Pubns.

Prebeg, Rick, photos by. Into the Jungle. Prebeg, Rick. 2005. (J). *(978-1-933248-05-9(X))* World Quest Learning.

—Looking for Lions. Prebeg, Rick. 2005. (J). *(978-1-933248-12-7(2))* World Quest Learning.

—Night Cat. Prebeg, Rick. 2005. (J). *(978-1-933248-15-8(7))* World Quest Learning.

—You've Got Cheetah Mail. Prebeg, Rick. 2005. (J). *(978-1-933248-11-0(4))* World Quest Learning.

Prebenna, David. Peekaboo, Elmo! (Sesame Street) Allen, Constance. 2014. (Big Bird's Favorites Board Bks.). (ENG.). 24p. (J). (— 1). bds. 4.99 *(978-0-449-81483-3(1),* Random Hse. Bks. for Young Readers) Random Hse. Children's Bks.

—Zip! Pop! Hop! And Other Fun Words to Say. Muntean, Michaela. 2008. (Big Bird's Favorites Board Bks.). (ENG.). 24p. (J). (gr. k — 1). bds. 4.99 *(978-0-375-84209-2(8),* Random Hse. Bks. for Young Readers) Random Hse. Children's Bks.

Premise Entertainment. The Spirit of Lindy. Weeks, Kermit. 2011. (J). 19.95 *(978-0-9790267-1-3(7))* KWIP, Inc.

Prentice, Priscilla. When You Just Have to Roar! Robertson, Rachel. 2015. (ENG.). 32p. (J). (gr. -1-k). 15.95 *(978-1-60554-362-8(4))* Redleaf Pr.

Press, Jenny. Bedtime Tales. Baxter, Nicola. 2013. (ENG.). 80p. (J). (gr. -1-k). pap. 9.99 *(978-1-84322-952-0(8))* Anness Publishing GBR. Dist: National Bk. Network.

—Book of Five-Minute Farmyard Tales. Baxter, Nicola. 2013. (ENG.). 80p. (J). (gr. -1-k). pap. 9.99 *(978-1-84322-953-7(6))* Anness Publishing GBR. Dist: National Bk. Network.

—A Book of Five-Minute Kitten Tales: A Treasury of over 35 Bedtime Stories. Baxter, Nicola. 2013. (ENG.). 80p. (J). (gr. -1-12). pap. 9.99 *(978-1-84322-888-2(2))* Anness Publishing GBR. Dist: National Bk. Network.

—A Book of Five-Minute Teddy Bear Tales: A Treasury of over 35 Bedtime Stories. Baxter, Nicola. 2013. (ENG.). 80p. pap. 9.99 *(978-1-84322-889-9(0))* Anness Publishing GBR. Dist: National Bk. Network.

—My Little Treasury of Bedtime Stories. Baxter, Nicola. 2013. (ENG.). 320p. (J). (gr. -1-k). 12.99 *(978-1-84322-729-8(0))* Anness Publishing GBR. Dist: National Bk. Network.

—My Little Treasury of Stories & Rhymes. Baxter, Nicola. 2013. (ENG.). 320p. (J). (gr. -1-k). 12.99 *(978-1-84322-904-9(8))* Anness Publishing GBR. Dist: National Bk. Network.

—My Wonderful Treasury of Five-Minute Stories. Baxter, Nicola. 2012. (ENG.). 256p. (J). (gr. k-4). 18.99 *(978-1-84322-805-9(X))* Anness Publishing GBR. Dist: National Bk. Network.

—Peter Pan. Barrie, J. M. 2013. (Storyteller Book Ser.). (ENG.). 48p. (J). (gr. k-5). pap. 7.99 *(978-1-84322-884-4(X),* Armadillo) Anness Publishing GBR. Dist: National Bk. Network.

—A Storyteller Book Sleeping Beauty. Young, Lesley. 2013. (ENG.). 48p. (J). (gr. -1-12). pap. 7.99 *(978-1-84322-910-0(2),* Armadillo) Anness Publishing GBR. Dist: National Bk. Network.

—Tales from the Toy Box. Baxter, Nicola. 2012. (ENG.). 80p. (J). (gr. k-4). pap. 9.99 *(978-1-84322-951-3(X))* Anness Publishing GBR. Dist: National Bk. Network.

Pressey, Deborah. On My Way to the Market. Pair, Karma A. 2009. 24p. pap. 15.00 *(978-1-4389-6299-3(1))* AuthorHouse.

Preston, Carole. Restless Owl & Other Stories. Littlewood, Graham. 2010. (ENG.). 56p. pap. *(978-1-84748-778-0(5))* Athena Pr.

Preston, Felicia, jt. illus. see Perry, Craig Rex.

Preston-Gannon, Frann. Acorn. Schaefer, Lola M. 2016. (J). *(978-1-4521-1242-8(8))* Chronicle Bks. LLC.

Preston, Graham. The Good Wagon. Clark, Paul. 2012. (J). lthr. *(978-1-921633-88-1(3),* Even Before Publishing) Wombat Bks.

Preston, Halsey. Never Play Checkers with a Leapfrog. Day, Todd. 2012. 122p. (-18). pap. 12.95 *(978-1-937004-88-0(0))* Old Line Publishing, LLC.

Preuss, Sarah Louise. Annie: A Small Ant with Some Big Questions. Diggle, David Mark. 2011. 24p. (J). pap. *(978-0-9871658-2-4(8))* Diggle de Doo Productions Pty, Ltd.

—Bella: Shares Her Sticky Plan. Diggle, David Mark. 2011. 24p. (J). pap. *(978-0-9871658-9-3(5))* Diggle de Doo Productions Pty, Ltd.

—Douglas: Pays the Price for Not Paying Attention. Diggle, David Mark. 2011. 24p. (J). pap. *(978-0-9871658-5-5(2))* Diggle de Doo Productions Pty, Ltd.

—Lilly: The Crazy Little Van. Diggle, David Mark. 2011. 26p. (J). pap. *(978-0-9871658-4-8(4))* Diggle de Doo Productions Pty, Ltd.

—Malana: Learns When Enough Is Enough. Diggle, David Mark. 2011. 24p. (J). pap. *(978-0-9871658-7-9(9))* Diggle de Doo Productions Pty, Ltd.

—Paco: The High-Performance Penguin. Diggle, David Mark. 2011. 24p. (J). pap. *(978-0-9871658-1-7(X))* Diggle de Doo Productions Pty, Ltd.

—Reggie: Learns to Roll with It. Diggle, David Mark. 2011. 24p. (J). pap. *(978-0-9871658-3-1(6))* Diggle de Doo Productions Pty, Ltd.

—Sally: And Her Singing Stage Debut. Diggle, David Mark. 2011. 24p. (J). pap. *(978-0-9871658-6-2(0))* Diggle de Doo Productions Pty, Ltd.

—Samantha: One Finger, One Nose, A Whole Lot of Bugs. Diggle, David Mark. 2011. 24p. (J). pap. *(978-0-9871658-0-0(1))* Diggle de Doo Productions Pty, Ltd.

Prevac, Rose Anne. Toby, the Pet Therapy Dog, & His Hospital Friends. Hammond, Charmaine. 2011. (ENG.). 36p. (J). pap. 12.99 *(978-0-9836045-0-1(9),* Kendahl Hse. Pr.) Youngs, Bettie Bks.

Prevec, Rose Anne. Toby, the Pet Therapy Dog, Says Be a Buddy Not a Bully. Hammond, Charmaine. 2013. (ENG.). (J). pap. 12.95 *(978-0-9836045-5-6(X),* Kendahl Hse. Pr.) Youngs, Bettie Bks.

Previn, Alicia L. The Strange Disappearance of Walter Tortoise. Previn, Alicia L. 2013. 36p. pap. 12.99 *(978-0-9847107-1-3(X))* Previn, Lovely Pubns.

Previn, Stacey. Being a Good Citizen: A Book about Citizenship, 1 vol. Small, Mary. 2005. (Way to Be! Ser.). (ENG.). 24p. (gr. k-2). lib. bdg. 25.99 *(978-1-4048-1050-1(1),* Nonfiction Picture Bks.) Picture Window Bks.

—Being Considerate. Donahue, Jill Lynn. 2007. (Way to Be! Ser.). (ENG.). 24p. (gr. -1-2). lib. bdg. 25.99 *(978-1-4048-3777-5(9),* Nonfiction Picture Bks.) Picture Window Bks.

—Being Fair: A Book about Fairness, 1 vol. Small, Mary. 2005. (Way to Be! Ser.). (ENG.). 24p. (gr. k-2). lib. bdg. 25.99 *(978-1-4048-1051-8(X),* Nonfiction Picture Bks.) Picture Window Bks.

—Being Respectful: A Book about Respectfulness, 1 vol. Small, Mary. 2005. (Way to Be! Ser.). (ENG.). 24p. (gr. k-2). lib. bdg. 25.99 *(978-1-4048-1053-2(6),* Nonfiction Picture Bks.) Picture Window Bks.

—Being Responsible: A Book about Responsibility, 1 vol. Small, Mary. 2005. (Way to Be! Ser.). (ENG.). 24p. (gr. k-2). lib. bdg. 25.99 *(978-1-4048-1052-5(8),* Nonfiction Picture Bks.) Picture Window Bks.

—Being Trustworthy: A Book about Trustworthiness, 1 vol. Small, Mary. 2005. (Way to Be! Ser.). (ENG.). 24p. (gr. k-2). lib. bdg. 25.99 *(978-1-4048-1054-9(4),* Nonfiction Picture Bks.) Picture Window Bks.

—Caring: A Book about Caring, 1 vol. Small, Mary. 2005. (Way to Be! Ser.). (ENG.). 24p. (gr. k-2). lib. bdg. 25.99 *(978-1-4048-1049-5(8),* Nonfiction Picture Bks.) Picture Window Bks.

—Ser Digno de Confianza. Small, Mary. 2011. (¡Así Debemos Ser!/Way to Be! Ser.).Tr. of Being Trustworthy. (ENG, SPA & MUL.). 24p. (gr. -1-2). lib. bdg. 25.99 *(978-1-4048-6691-1(4))* Picture Window Bks.

—Ser Honesto. Donahue, Jill Lynn. 2011. (¡Así Debemos Ser!/Way to Be! Ser.).Tr. of Being Honest. (ENG, SPA & MUL.). 24p. (gr. -1-2). lib. bdg. 25.99 *(978-1-4048-6689-8(2))* Picture Window Bks.

—Venezuela ABCs: A Book about the People & Places of Venezuela, 1 vol. Cooper, Sharon Katz. 2007. (Country ABCs Ser.). (ENG.). 32p. (gr. k-5). lib. bdg. 27.32 *(978-1-4048-2250-4(X),* Nonfiction Picture Bks.) Picture Window Bks.

—Way to Be! How to Be Brave, Responsible, Honest, & an All-Around Great Kid, 1 vol. Donahue, Jill Lynn & Small, Mary. 2010. (Way to Be! Ser.). (ENG.). 128p. (gr. -1-2). pap. 12.95 *(978-1-4048-6400-9(8),* Nonfiction Picture Bks.) Picture Window Bks.

Prevost, Mikela. Elan, Son of Two Peoples. Hyde, Heidi Smith. 2014. (Life Cycle Ser.). (ENG.). 32p. (J). (gr. k-3). 17.95 *(978-0-7613-9051-0(0),* Kar-Ben Publishing) Lerner Publishing Group.

—Trouble Talk. Ludwig, Trudy. 2008. (ENG.). 32p. (J). (gr. 1-4). 15.99 *(978-1-58246-240-0(2),* Tricycle Pr.) Ten Speed Pr.

Prewett, Maggie. The Old Frangipani Tree at Flying Fish Point. Saffioti, Trina. 2010. (ENG.). 28p. (J). (gr. 1-7). 18.95 *(978-1-921248-60-3(2))* Magabala Bks. AUS. Dist: Independent Pubs. Group.

Preza, Bruno Gonzalez. Juana Ines. Lazaro, Georgina. 2007. (SPA.). 32p. (J). (gr. 3-5). 14.99 *(978-1-930332-57-7(2))* Lectorum Pubns., Inc.

Prezio, Victor. Teenage Frontier Stories. Furman, A. L., ed. 2011. 256p. 47.95 *(978-1-258-09865-0(2))* Literary Licensing, LLC.

Price, Andy. Rarity. Cook, Katie. 2015. (J). ***(978-1-61479-335-9(2))*** Spotlight.

Price, Caroline. The New Jumbo Book of Easy Crafts. Sadler, Judy Ann. 2009. (Jumbo Bks.). (ENG.). 176p. (J). (gr. -1-2). pap. 18.95 *(978-1-55453-239-1(6))* Kids Can Pr., Ltd. CAN. Dist: Univ. of Toronto Pr.

Price, Carolyn. Vine & Branches, ol. 3. Hakowski, Maryann. 2003. (Resources for Youth Retreats Ser.: Vol. 3). 176p. (J). (gr. 6-7). pap. 24.95 *(978-0-88489-323-3(5))* St. Mary's Pr. of MN.

Price, Christine. Frederic Chopin, Son of Poland, Early Years. Wheeler, Opal. 2007. 160p. (J). per. 12.95 *(978-1-933573-11-3(2),* 4716) Zeezok Publishing, LLC.

—Frederic Chopin, Son of Poland Later Years. Wheeler, Opal. 2007. 160p. (J). per. 12.95 *(978-1-933573-09-0(0),* 4717) Zeezok Publishing, LLC.

—The Molliwumps. Maiden, Cecil. 2004. 160p. 12.95 *(978-0-9714612-9-1(5))* Green Mansion Pr. LLC.

Price, Christine, jt. illus. see Van Loon, Hendrik.

Price, Dana. What Does Your Daddy Do? Pierce, Heather Vowell. 2010. 32p. pap. 16.49 *(978-1-4520-1723-5(9))* AuthorHouse.

Price, David & Ursell, Martin. Birds & Beasts: Animal songs, games & Activities. Roberts, Sheena. 2006. (Classroom Music Ser.). (ENG.). 80p. (J). (gr. 1-6). *(978-0-7136-5653-4(0),* A & C Black) Bloomsbury Publishing Plc.

Price, Hattie Longstreet. A Little Maid of Newport. Curtis, Alice. 2006. (Little Maid Ser.). (ENG.). 212p. (J). (gr. 4-7). pap. 12.95 *(978-1-55709-339-4(3))* Applewood Bks.

Price, Margaret Evans. The Betty Fairy Book. 2006. (Shape Bks.). (ENG.). 16p. (J). pap. 9.95 *(978-1-59583-092-0(8),* Green Tiger Pr.) Laughing Elephant.

—A Child's Book of Myths. 2011. (Dover Read & Listen Ser.). (ENG.). 144p. (J). (gr. 3-8). pap. 14.99 *(978-0-486-48370-2(3))* Dover Pubns., Inc.

Price, Margaret Evans, et al. A Christmas Treasury. Dover et al. 2014. (ENG.). 96p. (J). (gr. 1-5). pap. 12.99 *(978-0-486-78184-6(4))* Dover Pubns., Inc.

Price, Margaret Evans. Hansel & Gretel. Grimm, Jacob & Grimm, Wilhelm K. 2005. (Shape Bks.). (ENG.). 16p. (J). (gr. -1-3). 9.95 *(978-1-59583-012-8(X),* 9781595830128, Green Tiger Pr.) Laughing Elephant.

—The Night Before Christmas. Moore, Clement C. 2009. (Dover Children's Classics Ser.). (ENG.). 16p. (J). (gr. k-5). pap. 6.99 *(978-0-486-47369-7(4))* Dover Pubns., Inc.

Price, Margaret Evans. Mother Goose: Book of Rhymes. Price, Margaret Evans, as told by. 2007. (Shape Bks.). (ENG.). 16p. (J). (gr. 4-7). pap. 9.95 *(978-1-59583-134-7(7),* 9781595831347, Green Tiger Pr.) Laughing Elephant.

Price, Margaret Evans, jt. illus. see Moore, Clement C.

Price, Michael, jt. illus. see Adams, Kevin.

Price, Nick. Aesop's Fables. 2004. (Young Reading Series Two Ser.). 64p. (J). (gr. 2-18). pap. 5.95 *(978-0-7945-0409-0(4),* Usborne) EDC Publishing.

—Animal Legends. 2004. 48p. (J). (gr. 2-18). (Young Reading Series One Ser.). pap. 5.95 *(978-0-7945-0408-3(6))*; (Young Reading Ser.: Vol. 1). lib. bdg. 13.95 *(978-1-58086-660-6(3))* EDC Publishing. (Usborne).

—Band of Friends. Morgan, Michaela. 2005. (ENG.). 24p. (J). lib. bdg. 23.65 *(978-1-59646-734-7(7))* Dingles & Co.

—The Invisible Womble. Beresford, Elisabeth. 2012. (Wombles Ser.). (ENG.). 112p. (J). (gr. 3-5). pap. 12.99 *(978-1-4088-0834-4(X),* 30799) Bloomsbury USA.

—Little Jack Horner. Blane, Francisco. 2010. (Rising Readers Ser.). (J). 3.49 *(978-1-60719-701-0(4))* Newmark Learning LLC.

—Little Jack Horner Eats Pie. Blane, Francisco. 2009. (Reader's Theater Nursery Rhymes & Songs Set B Ser.). 48p. (J). pap. *(978-1-60859-158-9(1))* Benchmark Education Co.

—Magical Animals. 2004. (Young Reading Series One Ser.). 48p. (J). (gr. 2-18). pap. 5.95 *(978-0-7945-0454-0(X),* Usborne) EDC Publishing.

—The Snow Womble. Beresford, Elisabeth. 2013. (Wombles Ser.). (ENG.). 32p. (J). pap. 12.99 *(978-1-4088-3424-4(3),* 160309, Bloomsbury USA Childrens) Bloomsbury USA.

—Tim's Head, Shoulders, Knees, & Toes. Jeffries, Katherine. 2009. (Reader's Theater Nursery Rhymes & Songs Set B Ser.). 48p. (J). pap. *(978-1-60859-169-5(7))* Benchmark Education Co.

—Tumtum & Nutmeg: the Rose Cottage Adventures. Bearn, Emily. 2013. (Tumtum & Nutmeg Ser.: 2). (ENG.). 416p. (J). (gr. 3-7). pap. 7.99 *(978-0-316-08598-4(7))* Little, Brown Bks. for Young Readers.

—The Wandering Wombles. Beresford, Elisabeth. 2012. (Wombles Ser.). (ENG.). 224p. (J). (gr. 3-5). pap. 12.99 *(978-1-4088-0833-7(1))* Bloomsbury USA.

—The Wombles. Beresford, Elisabeth. 2012. (Wombles Ser.). (ENG.). 240p. (J). (gr. 3-5). pap. 12.99 *(978-1-4088-0837-5(4))*; 31.99 *(978-1-4088-2180-0(X),* 71107, Bloomsbury USA Childrens) Bloomsbury USA.

—The Wonderful Wizard of Oz. 2009. (ENG.). 12p. (J). 8.95 *(978-1-58117-856-2(5),* Intervisual/Piggy Toes) Bendon, Inc.

Price, Rebecca. A Lump of Clay. Holliday, Bobby. 2010. 28p. (J). 18.99 *(978-0-9829082-1-0(0))* Lady Hawk Pr.

Price, Ryan. The Raven. Poe, Edgar Allen. 2006. (Visions in Poetry Ser.). (ENG.). 48p. (YA). (gr. 7-18). 17.95 *(978-1-55337-473-2(8))* Kids Can Pr., Ltd. CAN. Dist: Univ. of Toronto Pr.

Price, Susan D. Sing Christmas. Bosley, Judith A. l.t. ed. Date not set. (J). (gr. -1-k). pap. 10.95 *(978-0-930809-26-3(2))* Grand Bks., Inc.

Price, Tom. Champion Sleeper. 2008. 32p. (J). pap. 9.95 *(978-0-9748226-1-7(2))* Murphy's Bone Publishing.

Price, Traer. The Mouse & the Buddha. Price, Kathryn. 2006. (ENG.). 36p. (J). (gr. -1-k). 14.95 *(978-0-9773812-0-3(X))* Little Hse. Pr.

Priceman, Marjorie. The Bake Shop Ghost. Ogburn, Jacqueline K. 2008. (ENG.). 32p. (J). (gr. -1-3). pap. 6.99 *(978-0-547-07677-5(0))* Houghton Mifflin Harcourt Publishing Co.

—The Blue Ribbon Day. Couric, Katie. 2004. (ENG.). 32p. (gr. k-2). 15.95 *(978-0-385-50142-2(0),* Doubleday) Doubleday Religious Publishing Group, The.

—The Blue Ribbon Day. Couric, Katie & Couric, Katherine. 2004. (ENG.). 32p. (gr. 3-6). lib. bdg. 17.95 *(978-0-385-51292-3(9),* Doubleday) Doubleday Religious Publishing Group, The.

—Cold Snap. Spinelli, Eileen. 2012. (ENG.). 40p. (J). (gr. k-3). 17.99 *(978-0-375-85700-3(1),* Knopf Bks. for Young Readers) Random Hse. Children's Bks.

—Jazz Age Josephine: Dancer, Singer- Who's That, Who? Why That's Miss Josephine Baker, to You! Winter, Jonah. 2012. (ENG.). 40p. (J). (gr. -1-3). 16.99 *(978-1-4169-6123-9(2),* Atheneum Bks. for Young Readers) Simon & Schuster Children's Publishing.

—Julie Andrews' Treasury for All Seasons: Poems & Songs to Celebrate the Year. Andrews, Julie & Hamilton, Emma Walton. 2012. (ENG.). 192p. (J). (gr. -1-17). 19.99 *(978-0-316-04051-8(7))* Little, Brown Bks. for Young Readers.

Priceman, Marjorie. Miracle on 133rd Street. Manzano, Sonia. 2015. (ENG.). 48p. (J). (gr. -1-3). 17.99 ***(978-0-689-87887-9(7))*** Simon & Schuster Children's Publishing.

Priceman, Marjorie. Paris in the Spring with Picasso. Yolleck, Joan. 2010. (ENG.). 40p. (J). (gr. -1-3). 17.99 *(978-0-375-83756-2(6),* Schwartz & Wade Bks.) Random Hse. Children's Bks.

—The Ride: The Legend of Betsy Dowdy. Griffin, Kitty. 2010. (ENG.). 40p. (J). (gr. -1-3). 16.99 *(978-1-4169-2816-4(2),* Atheneum Bks. for Young Readers) Simon & Schuster Children's Publishing.

—Serefina under the Circumstances. Theroux, Phyllis. 2004. 30p. (J). (gr. k-4). reprint ed. *(978-0-7567-7756-2(9))* DIANE Publishing Co.

—Zin! Zin! Zin! A Violin. Moss, Lloyd. 2004. (gr. -1-3). 18.00 *(978-0-7569-1919-1(3))* Perfection Learning Corp.

—Zin! Zin! Zin! A Violin. Moss, Lloyd. 2005. (Stories to Go! Ser.). (ENG.). 32p. (J). (gr. -1-3). 4.99 *(978-1-4169-0838-8(2),* Simon & Schuster/Paula Wiseman Bks.) Simon & Schuster/Paula Wiseman Bks.

Priceman, Marjorie. Hot Air: The (Mostly) True Story of the First Hot-Air Balloon Ride. Priceman, Marjorie. 2005. (ENG.). 40p. (J). (gr. -1-3). 17.99 *(978-0-689-82642-9(7),* Atheneum Bks. for Young Readers) Simon & Schuster Children's Publishing.

—How to Make a Cherry Pie & See the U. S. A. Priceman, Marjorie. 2013. (ENG.). 40p. (J). (gr. k-3). 7.99 *(978-0-385-75293-0(8),* Dragonfly Bks.) Random Hse. Children's Bks.

Priddis, C. Michael. A Prophet in Palmyra. Daybell, Chad G. 2004. (Dare to Be True Adventure Ser.: 1). 110p. (YA). pap. 9.95 *(978-1-932898-00-2(X),* 9800X) Spring Creek Bk. Co.

Priddy, Roger. Fluffy Chick & Friends. Priddy, Roger. 2005. (Touch & Feel Cloth Bks.). (ENG.). 10p. (J). (gr. -1 — 1). 11.99 *(978-0-312-49430-8(0),* Priddy Bks.) St. Martin's Pr.

Pride, Matthew. A Star Named Little One (Boy) Dukovich, Amanda J. l.t. ed. 2006. 32p. (J). (gr. -1). 15.99 *(978-1-59879-189-1(3))* Lifevest Publishing, Inc.

—A Star Named Little One (Girl) Dukovich, Amanda J. l.t. ed. 2006. 32p. (J). (gr. -1-k). 15.99 *(978-1-59879-090-0(0))* Lifevest Publishing, Inc.

Priest, Dick. White Ruff: Famous Dog Stories. Balch, Glenn. 2011. 240p. 46.95 *(978-1-258-09962-6(4))* Literary Licensing, LLC.

Priest, Saira, photos by. If We Were... Priest, Saira, des. l.t. ed. 2003. 20p. 12.95 *(978-0-9726628-7-1(1))* Niche Publishing & Marketing.

Priestley, Alice. A Gift for Gita. Gilmore, Rachna. 2004. 24p. (J). *(978-1-85269-403-6(3))*; *(978-1-85269-407-4(6))*; *(978-1-85269-408-1(4))*; *(978-1-85269-409-8(2))* Mantra Lingua.

—Mom & Mum Are Getting Married!, 1 vol. Setterington, Ken. 2004. (ENG.). 24p. (J). (gr. -1-3). 15.95 *(978-1-896764-84-9(3))* Second Story Pr. CAN. Dist: Orca Bk. Pubs. USA.

—Out on the Ice in the Middle of the Bay. Cumming, Peter. 10th rev. anniv. ed. 2004. (ENG.). 32p. (J). (gr. k-3). 19.95 *(978-1-55037-871-9(6),* 9781550378719); pap. 9.95 *(978-1-55037-870-2(8),* 9781550378702) Annick Pr., Ltd. CAN. Dist: Firefly Bks., Ltd.

—Roses for Gita. Gilmore, Rachna. 2004. 24p. (J). *(978-1-85269-367-1(3))*; *(978-1-85269-369-5(X))* Mantra Lingua.

—Roses for Gita. Gilmore, Rachna. 2005. 24p. (J). (gr. 3-6). pap. 7.95 *(978-0-88448-224-6(3))* Tilbury Hse. Pubs.

Priestley, Chris. Billy Wizard. Priestley, Chris. 2005. (Young Corgi Ser.). (ENG.). 90p. (J). per. 6.99 *(978-0-552-54689-8(5))* Transworld Publishers Ltd. GBR. Dist: Independent Pubs. Group.

Prieto, Antonio. Rooly & Flora's Reunion: A Story of Cuba. Martinez, Raul. 2006. (ENG.). 32p. (J). pap. 6.95 *(978-1-59249-658-7(X))* Soundprints.

Prieto, Iván. What a Snout! Liván, Paco. 2007. (ENG.). 48p. (J). 18.95 *(978-84-96788-87-9(3))* OQO, Editora ESP. Dist: Baker & Taylor Bks.

Prigmore, Shane. Planet Kindergarten. Ganz-Schmitt, Sue. 2014. (ENG.). 40p. (J). (gr. -1-k). 16.99 *(978-1-4521-1893-2(0))* Chronicle Bks. LLC.

Prigmore, Shane. Planet Kindergarten: 100 Days in Orbit. Ganz-Schmitt, Sue. 2016. (J). ***(978-1-4521-3776-6(5))*** Chronicle Bks. LLC.

Prigmore, Shane. Spaceheadz. Scieszka, Jon. (Spaceheadz Ser.: 3). (ENG.). (J). (gr. 2-5). 2012. 224p. pap. 5.99 *(978-1-4169-7956-2(5))*; 2011. 224p. 15.99 *(978-1-4169-7955-5(7))*; 2010. 144p. 14.99 *(978-1-4169-7951-7(4))*; Set. 2013. 864p. 23.99 *(978-1-4424-9858-7(7))* Simon & Schuster Bks. For Young Readers. (Simon & Schuster Bks. For Young Readers).

—SPHDZ 4 Life! Scieszka, Jon. 2013. (Spaceheadz Ser.: 4). (ENG.). 192p. (J). (gr. 2-5). pap. 5.99 *(978-1-4169-7958-6(1))*;Bk. 4. 16.99 *(978-1-4169-7957-9(3))* Simon & Schuster Bks. For Young Readers. (Simon & Schuster Bks. For Young Readers).

—SPHDZ Book #1! Scieszka, Jon. 2011. (Spaceheadz Ser.: 1). (ENG.). 192p. (J). (gr. 2-5). pap. 7.99 *(978-1-4424-1986-5(5))*, Simon & Schuster Bks. For Young Readers) Simon & Schuster Bks. For Young Readers.

—SPHDZ Book #2! Scieszka, Jon. (Spaceheadz Ser.: 2). (ENG.). (J). (gr. 2-5). 2011. 256p. pap. 6.99 *(978-1-4169-7954-8(9))*; 2010. 240p. 14.99 *(978-1-4169-7953-1(0))* Simon & Schuster Bks. For Young Readers. (Simon & Schuster Bks. For Young Readers).

Primavera, Elise. Fred & Anthony Meet the Heinie Goblins from the Black Lagoon. Fred, Anthony. rev. ed. 2008. 128p. 14.99 *(978-0-7868-3681-9(4))* Hyperion Bks. for Children.

Primavera, Elise. Auntie Claus: Home for the Holidays. Primavera, Elise. 2009. (ENG.). 40p. (J). (gr. -1-3). 17.99 *(978-1-4169-5485-9(6)*, Simon & Schuster/Paula Wiseman Bks.) Simon & Schuster/Paula Wiseman Bks.

—Fred & Anthony Escape from the Netherworld. Primavera, Elise. Arevamirp, Esile. 2007. (ENG.). 128p. (J). (gr. 2-6). pap. 4.99 *(978-0-7868-3678-9(4))* Hyperion Pr.

—Fred & Anthony Meet the Demented Super-Degerm-O Zombie. Primavera, Elise. Arevamirp, Esile. 2007. (ENG.). 128p. (J). (gr. 2-6). pap. 4.99 *(978-0-7868-3680-2(6))* Hyperion Pr.

—Fred & Anthony Meet the Heinie Goblins from the Black Lagoon. Primavera, Elise. rev. ed. 2008. (ENG.). 128p. (J). (gr. 2-4). pap. 4.99 *(978-0-7868-3682-6(2))* Hyperion Bks. for Children.

—Libby of High Hopes. Primavera, Elise. 2012. (Libby of High Hopes Ser.). (ENG.). 192p. (J). (gr. 2-5). 14.99 *(978-1-4169-5542-9(9)*, Simon & Schuster/Paula Wiseman Bks.) Simon & Schuster/Paula Wiseman Bks.

Primavera, Elise. Project Blue Ribbon. Primavera, Elise. 2015. (Libby of High Hopes Ser.). (ENG.). 288p. (J). (gr. 2-5). 16.99 ***(978-1-4169-5543-6(7)***, Simon & Schuster Bks. For Young Readers) Simon & Schuster Bks. For Young Readers.

Primavera, Elise. The Secret Order of the Gumm Street Girls. Primavera, Elise. 2008. (ENG.). 464p. (J). (gr. 3-7). pap. 8.99 *(978-0-06-056948-8(4))* HarperCollins Pubs.

Primeau, Chuck. Detective Chase McCain- Save That Cargo! King, Trey. 2013. (Lego City Ser.). (ENG.). 24p. (J). (gr. -1-3). 3.99 *(978-0-545-51573-3(4))* Scholastic, Inc.

—Rise of the Guardians: Worlds of Wonder. Reader's Digest Staff. deluxe ed. 2012. (ENG.). 24p. (J). (gr. k-2). 19.99 *(978-0-7944-2803-7(7))* Reader's Digest Assn., Inc., The.

Primm, Patricia. Tennessee Ocean Frogs. Dudley, Marie Luther. 2008. 24p. pap. 24.95 *(978-1-60474-261-9(5))* America Star Bks.

Primm, Thomas. Tinkum's Dog. Newth, Rebecca. 2005. 32p. (J). 15.00 *(978-0-9630310-7-5(4))* Will Hall Bks.

Primmasone, Bruce. Rufus' Big Scare. Hasan, K. A. 2011. 48p. pap. 24.95 *(978-1-4626-0660-3(1))* America Star Bks.

Prince, Andrea. Lucy & the Halloween Miracle. Morgan, Emily. 2013. 24p. 16.99 *(978-0-9910324-8-8(9))* Mindstir Media.

Prince, Brian. Katie the Cricket. Jonell, Bob. 2009. 12p. pap. 24.95 *(978-1-61546-280-3(5))* America Star Bks.

—Penny the Chinstrap Penguin, 1 vol. Jonell, Bob. 2010. 22p. 24.95 *(978-1-4489-5334-9(0))* PublishAmerica, Inc.

Princess Marie. Katoufs in Nursery Rhymes: Mother Goose. Kole, Ted & Genet, John, eds. 24p. (J). 50.00 *(978-0-9641381-1-7(5))* Kreative Character Kreations, Inc.

Pringle, Victoria. Coyote & the Sky: How the Sun, Moon, & Stars Began. Garcia, Emmett Shkeme & Garcia, Emmett. 2006. (ENG.). 32p. (J). (gr. 6-18). 18.95 *(978-0-8263-3730-6(9))* Univ. of New Mexico Pr.

—Sister Rabbit's Tricks. Garcia, Emmett Shkeme. 2013. (ENG.). 40p. (J). pap. 18.95 *(978-0-8263-5268-2(5))* Univ. of New Mexico Pr.

Priscilla, Louis. Ranch Mystery: Young Readers. Coombs, Charles. 2011. 188p. 42.95 *(978-1-258-09854-4(7))* Literary Licensing, LLC.

Pritchard, Louise. Charlie & Chippo Meet a Ghost. Tossell, David H. 2012. 24p. pap. *(978-1-908773-25-8(1))* Iponymous Publishing, Ltd.

Pritchett and Hull Associates. Cooper Has Diabetes. Olson, Karen. 2003. (ENG.). 34p. (J). 9.95 *(978-0-939838-82-0(6))* Pritchett & Hull Assocs., Inc.

Pritchett and Hull Associates, Inc. Cooper Gets a Cast. Olson, Karen. 2003. (J). 4.50 *(978-0-939838-86-8(9))* Pritchett & Hull Assocs., Inc.

Pritelli, Maria Cristina. Everything Is a Poem: the Best of J. Patrick Lewis. Lewis, J. Patrick. 2014. (ENG.). 88p. (J). (gr. 1-3). 24.99 *(978-1-56846-240-0(9)*, Creative Editions) Creative Co., The.

—Sailing the Unknown. Rosen, Michael J. 2014. (ENG.). 40p. (J). (gr. 1-3). pap. 12.00 *(978-0-89812-976-2(1)*, Creative Paperbacks) Creative Co., The.

—Sailing the Unknown: Around the World with Captain Cook. Rosen, Michael J. 2012. (ENG.). 40p. (J). (gr. 1-3). 19.99 *(978-1-56846-216-5(6)*, Creative Editions) Creative Co., The.

—See Inside the Second World War. Jones, Rob Lloyd. ed. 2012. (See Inside Board Bks). 16p. (J). ring bd. 13.99 *(978-0-7945-3085-3(0)*, Usborne) EDC Publishing.

Probert, Tim. Pickle: The (Formerly) Anonymous Prank Club of Fountain Point Middle School. Baker, Kimberly. 2012. (ENG.). 240p. (J). (gr. 3-7). 15.99 *(978-1-59643-765-4(0))* Roaring Brook Pr.

—Pickle: The (Formerly) Anonymous Prank Club of Fountain Point Middle School. Baker, Kim. 2014. (ENG.). 256p. (J). (gr. 3-7). pap. 6.99 *(978-1-250-04427-3(8))* Square Fish.

—A Whole New Ballgame. Bildner, Phil. 2015. (Rip & Red Ser.). (ENG.). 256p. (J). (gr. 3-7). 15.99 *(978-0-374-30130-9(1)*, Farrar, Straus & Giroux (BYR)) Farrar, Straus & Giroux.

Proch, Gregory & Allred, Scott. How to Get Rich on the Oregon Trail. Olson, Tod. 2009. (How to Get Rich Ser.). (ENG.). 48p. (J). (gr. 5-9). lib. bdg. 27.90 *(978-1-4263-0413-2(7)*, National Geographic Children's Bks.) National Geographic Society.

Proch, Gregory, jt. illus. see Allred, Scott.

Procter, Bill. It Happened in the Goldfish Bowl. Procter, Diann. 2007. 28p. pap. 24.95 *(978-1-4241-8357-9(X))* America Star Bks.

proctor, brian, jt. illus. see marion, designs.

Proctor, Jon. The First & Final Voyage: The Sinking of the Titanic, 1 vol. Peters, Stephanie True. 2008. (Historical Fiction Ser.). (ENG.). 56p. (gr. 2-3). pap. 6.25 *(978-1-4342-0494-3(4)*, Graphic Flash) Stone Arch Bks.

—True Stories of World War I, 1 vol. Yomtov, Nelson. 2012. (Stories of War Ser.). (ENG.). 32p. (gr. 3-4). pap. 8.10 *(978-1-4296-9344-8(4))*; lib. bdg. 29.99 *(978-1-4296-8625-9(1))* Capstone Pr., Inc.

—True Stories of World War I. Yomtov, Nel. 2012. (Stories of War Ser.). (ENG.). 32p. (gr. 3-4). pap. 47.70 *(978-1-4296-9345-5(2)*, Graphic Library) Capstone Pr., Inc.

Proctor, Peter. Wallie Exercises. Active Spud Press & Ettinger, Steve. 2011. 32p. (J). (gr. -1-3). 15.95 *(978-0-9845388-0-5(1))* Active Spud Pr.

Prodor, Bob. The Duchess Ranch of Old John Ware. Davidge, James. 2010. (ENG.). 104p. pap. 10.95 *(978-1-897411-18-6(9))* Bayeux Arts, Inc. CAN. Dist: Chicago Distribution Ctr.

Producciones, Sunset, jt. illus. see Sunset Producciones.

Proferes, Jo. Be Brave, Tah-Hy! The Journey of Chief Joseph's Daughter. Williams, Jack R. 2012. (ENG.). 134p. (J). (gr. 3-7). pap. 29.95 *(978-0-87422-313-2(X))* Washington State Univ. Pr.

Proimos, James. Year of the Jungle. Collins, Suzanne. 2013. (ENG.). 40p. (J). (gr. -1-7). 17.99 *(978-0-545-42516-2(6)*, Scholastic Pr.) Scholastic, Inc.

Proimos, James, Jr. Apocalypse Bow Wow. Proimos, James, Jr. Proimos, James, III. 2015. (ENG.). 224p. (J). (gr. 3-6). 13.99 *(978-1-61963-442-8(2)*, Bloomsbury USA Childrens) Bloomsbury USA.

Proimos, James. Knuckle & Potty Destroy Happy World. Proimos, James. 2012. (ENG.). 80p. (J). (gr. 2-5). 12.99 *(978-0-8050-9155-7(6)*, Holt, Henry & Co. Bks. For Young Readers) Holt, Henry & Co.

—Todd's TV. Proimos, James. 2010. (ENG.). 40p. (J). (gr. -1-3). 15.99 *(978-0-06-170985-2(9)*, Tegen, Katherine Bks) HarperCollins Pubs.

Project Firefly. All of Life Is a School. Weeks, Kermit. 2007. 64p. (J). 19.95 *(978-0-9790267-0-6(9))* KWIP, Inc.

Project Firefly Animation Studios. The Adventures of Lady: The Big Storm. Pearson, Iris & Merrill, Mike. Pearson, Iris, ed. rev. ed. 2007. 34p. (J). 11.99 *(978-0-9789984-2-4(1))* Adventures of Lady LLC, The.

—The Adventures of Lady: The Big Storm Coloring Book. Pearson, Iris & Merrill, Mike. Pearson, Iris, ed. 2007. 34p. (J). pap. 5.49 *(978-0-9789984-3-1(X))* Adventures of Lady LLC, The.

Prole, Helen. Baby Jesus Is Born, 1 vol. David, Juliet. 2007. (Candle Bible for Toddlers Ser.). 24p. (J). (gr. -1-k). bds. 8.99 *(978-0-8254-7202-2(4)*, Candle Bks.) Lion Hudson PLC GBR. Dist: Kregel Pubns.

—Candle Bible for Toddlers, 1 vol. David, Juliet. 2006. (Candle Bible for Toddlers Ser.). 400p. (J). (gr. -1-k). 14.99 *(978-0-8254-7311-1(X)*, Candle Bks.) Lion Hudson PLC GBR. Dist: Kregel Pubns.

—Candle Bible for Toddlers, 1 vol. David, Juliet. 2015. (ENG.). 400p. (J). 19.99 *(978-1-78128-201-4(3)*, Candle Bks.) Lion Hudson PLC GBR. Dist: Kregel Pubns.

—Candle Bible for Toddlers Carry along Bible Fun. David, Juliet. 2007. (Candle Bible for Toddlers Ser.). (J). pap. 12.99 *(978-0-8254-7336-4(5)*, Candle Bks.) Lion Hudson PLC GBR. Dist: Kregel Pubns.

—Candle Prayers for Toddlers, 1 vol. David, Juliet. 2010. (Candle Bible for Toddlers Ser.). (ENG.). 128p. (J). 11.99 *(978-1-85985-679-6(9)*, Candle Bks.) Lion Hudson PLC GBR. Dist: Kregel Pubns.

—Candle Prayers for Toddlers & Candle Bible for Toddlers, 2 vols. David, Juliet. 2009. (Candle Bible for Toddlers Ser.). 528p. (J). 24.99 *(978-0-8254-7380-7(2)*, Candle Bks.) Lion Hudson PLC GBR. Dist: Kregel Pubns.

—Follow the Star, 1 vol. David, Juliet. 2005. (Poster Sticker Bks.). 8p. (J). (gr. k-2). pap. 6.99 *(978-0-8254-7304-3(7)*, Candle Bks.) Lion Hudson PLC GBR. Dist: Kregel Pubns.

—Learn & Play: Chalkboard Activities. David, Juliet. 2007. (Candle Bible for Toddlers Ser.). 12p. (J). (gr. -1-k). bds. 11.99 *(978-0-8254-7331-9(4)*, Candle Bks.) Lion Hudson PLC GBR. Dist: Kregel Pubns.

—My Very First Bible & Prayers, 1 vol. David, Juliet & Ayliffe, Alex. 2014. (Candle Bible for Toddlers Ser.). (ENG.). 64p. (J). 9.99 *(978-1-78128-152-9(1)*, Candle Bks.) Lion Hudson PLC GBR. Dist: Kregel Pubns.

—Noah & His Great Ark, 1 vol. David, Juliet. 2007. (Candle Bible for Toddlers Ser.). 24p. (J). (gr. -1-k). act. bk. ed. 6.99 *(978-0-8254-7345-6(4)*, Candle Bks.) Lion Hudson PLC GBR. Dist: Kregel Pubns.

—The Very First Christmas, 1 vol. David, Juliet. 2007. (Candle Bible for Toddlers Ser.). 24p. (J). (gr. -1-k). act. bk. ed. 6.99 *(978-0-8254-7353-1(5)*, Candle Bks.) Lion Hudson PLC GBR. Dist: Kregel Pubns.

Prosek, James. Bird, Butterfly, Eel. Prosek, James. Keats, John. 2009. (ENG.). 40p. (J). (gr. 1-5). 17.99 *(978-0-689-86829-0(4)*, Simon & Schuster Bks. For Young Readers) Simon & Schuster Bks. For Young Readers.

—The Day My Mother Left. Prosek, James. 2009. (ENG.). 304p. (J). (gr. 4-7). pap. 7.99 *(978-1-4169-0771-8(8)*, Simon & Schuster Bks. For Young Readers) Simon & Schuster Bks. For Young Readers.

—A Good Day's Fishing. Prosek, James. 2004. (ENG.). 40p. (J). (gr. 1-5). 17.99 *(978-0-689-85327-2(0)*, Simon & Schuster Bks. For Young Readers) Simon & Schuster Bks. For Young Readers.

Prosmitsky, Jenya. Hairy, Scary, Ordinary: What Is an Adjective? Cleary, Brian P. 2006. (Words Are Categorical Ser.). (gr. 2-4). 17.00 *(978-0-7569-6882-3(8))* Perfection Learning Corp.

—To Root, to Toot, to Parachute: What Is a Verb? Cleary, Brian P. 2006. (Words Are Categorical Ser.). (gr. 2-4). 17.00 *(978-0-7569-6884-7(4))* Perfection Learning Corp.

—The Wedding That Saved a Town. Strom, Yale. 2008. (ENG.). 32p. (J). (gr. 2-4). pap. 7.95 *(978-0-8225-7380-7(6)*, Kar-Ben Publishing) Lerner Publishing Group.

Prosofsky, Merle, photos by. The Essential Canadian Christmas Cookbook. Walker, Lovoni. rev. ed. 2005. (ENG., 160p. pap. *(978-1-55105-552-7(X))* Lone Pine Publishing.

—The Essential Christmas Cookbook, Vol. 1. Walker, Lovoni. rev. ed. 2004. (ENG., 160p. pap. *(978-1-55105-446-9(9))* Lone Pine Publishing.

Prosofsky, Merle, jt. photos by see Samol, Nanette.

Prothero, Tiffany. Curtains! A High School Musical Mystery. Dahl, Michael. 2008. (Vortex Bks.). (ENG.). 112p. (gr. 2-3). 25.32 *(978-1-4342-0801-9(X)*, Vortex Bks.) Stone Arch Bks.

—The Mummy at Midnight. Brezenoff, Steve. 2008. (Shade Bks.). (ENG.). 80p. (gr. 2-3). 23.99 *(978-1-4342-0797-5(8)*, Shade Bks.) Stone Arch Bks.

Proudfoot, Peter R., et al. Creepy Critters: A Pop-Up Book of Creatures That Jump, Crawl, & Fly. 2012. (ENG.). 14p. (J). (gr. k-3). 15.95 *(978-0-8109-8942-9(5)*, Abrams Bks. for Young Readers) Abrams.

Proulx, Denis. Little Rina Meets Baby Brother. Loccisano, Rina Fuda. 2011. 48p. pap. 24.95 *(978-1-4512-6299-5(X))* America Star Bks.

—Lucky's Lick. Esparza-Vela, Mary. 2013. 16p. pap. 9.95 *(978-1-61633-406-2(1))* Guardian Angel Publishing, Inc.

—Scotty's Feeder & the Secret Tower. Stein, Clem. 2011. 40p. 16.99 *(978-1-4567-3191-5(2))* AuthorHouse.

Proulx, Denis. The Adventures of Sir Sniffsalot & His Friends. Gould, Terry. 2007. 48p. (gr. -1-3). pap. 15.99 *(978-0-9789057-3-6(3))* Huntington Ludlow Media Group.

—Aunt Ruby's Kisses, 1 vol. Averette, Sonya M. 2009. 35p. pap. 24.95 *(978-1-60749-045-6(5))* America Star Bks.

—Austin & the Bully. Milot, Carryanne. 2012. 40p. pap. *(978-1-77097-970-3(0))* FriesenPress.

—Stuck. M a. 2011. (ENG.). 38p. (J). (gr. 1-5). 15.77 *(978-1-935204-33-6(5)*, Jabberwocky Bks., Inc.) Hillcrest Publishing Group, Inc.

Prout, Louise. Crime Time: Australians Behaving Badly. Bursztynski, Sue. 2009. (ENG.). 186p. (YA). pap. 10.95 *(978-1-876462-76-5(0)*, Ford Street Publishing) Hybrid Pubs. AUS. Dist: International Publishers Marketing.

Provantini, Silvia. The Runaway Pancake. 2006. (First Reading Level 4 Ser.). 48p. (J). (gr. 1-4). 8.99 *(978-0-7945-1276-7(3)*, Usborne) EDC Publishing.

Provencher, Annemarie. Susu of the Frufru. Finneron, Karyn A. 2012. 32p. (-18). pap. 9.99 *(978-0-9857362-0-0(8))* Nana's Stories.

Provensen, Alice. A Day in the Life of Murphy. Provensen, Alice. unabr. rev. ed. 2005. (J). (gr. -1-2). 28.95 incl. audio compact disk *(978-1-59519-538-8(6))* Live Oak Media.

—A Day in the Life of Murphy. Provensen, Alice. 2003. (ENG.). 40p. (J). (gr. -1-3). 17.99 *(978-0-689-84884-1(6)*, Simon & Schuster Bks. For Young Readers) Simon & Schuster Bks. For Young Readers.

—A Day in the Life of Murphy. Provensen, Alice. 2006. (ENG.). 40p. (J). (gr. -1-3). reprint ed. 7.99 *(978-1-4169-1800-4(0)*, Simon & Schuster/Paula Wiseman Bks.) Simon & Schuster/Paula Wiseman Bks.

—The Master Swordsman & the Magic Doorway: Two Legends from Ancient China. Provensen, Alice. 2014. (ENG.). 40p. (J). (gr. k-3). 19.99 *(978-1-4814-2874-3(8)*, Simon & Schuster Bks. For Young Readers) Simon & Schuster Bks. For Young Readers.

Provensen, Alice & Provensen, Martin. The Color Kittens. Brown, Margaret Wise. 2003. (Little Golden Book Ser.). (ENG.). 24p. (J). (gr. -1-2). 3.99 *(978-0-307-02141-0(6)*, Golden Bks.) Random Hse. Children's Bks.

—The Fuzzy Duckling. Werner Watson, Jane. 2012. (Golden Baby Ser.). (ENG.). 24p. (J). (gr. k — 1). bds. 6.99 *(978-0-307-92966-2(3)*, Golden Bks.) Random Hse., Inc.

—The Glorious Flight: Across the Channel with Louis Bleriot. Provensen, Alice & Provensen, Martin. 2010. (ENG.). 40p. (J). (gr. 5-8). 17.99 *(978-0-670-34259-4(9)*, Viking Juvenile) Penguin Publishing Group.

Provensen, Alice, jt. illus. see Provensen, Martin.

Provensen, Martin & Provensen, Alice. The Color Kittens. Brown, Margaret Wise. 2009. (Little Golden Treasures Ser.). (ENG.). 26p. (J). (gr. k — 1). bds. 4.99 *(978-0-375-85335-7(9)*, Golden Bks.) Random Hse., Inc.

—The Fuzzy Duckling. Watson, Jane Werner. 2015. (Little Golden Book Ser.). (ENG.). 24p. (J). (-k). 3.99 *(978-0-553-52213-6(2)*, Golden Bks.) Random Hse. Children's Bks.

Provensen, Martin, jt. illus. see Provensen, Alice.

Provenzano, Jeannine. Stashi the Rainbow Star: Her Journey Home. Venditti, Stacey Marie. 2008. 52p. pap. 24.95 *(978-1-60474-786-7(2))* America Star Bks.

Prud'homme, Jules. Leo's Midnight Rescue. Leblanc, Louise. 2004. 62p. (J). lib. bdg. 12.00 *(978-1-4242-1217-0(0))* Fitzgerald Bks.

—Leo's Skiing Surprise. Leblanc, Louise. 2007. (Formac First Novels Ser.). (ENG.). 64p. (gr. 2-5). 14.95 *(978-0-88780-738-1(0))* Formac Publishing Co., Ltd. CAN. Dist: Casemate Pubs. & Bk. Distributors, LLC.

—Leo's Skiing Surprise, 1 vol. Leblanc, Louise. Cummins, Sarah, tr. from FRE. 2007. (Formac First Novels Ser.). (ENG.). 64p. (gr. 2-5). 4.95 *(978-0-88780-736-7(4))* Formac Publishing Co., Ltd. CAN. Dist: Casemate Pubs. & Bk. Distributors, LLC.

Prud'homme, Jules & Jules, Prud'homme. Leo's Midnight Rescue, 1 vol. Leblanc, Louise. Cummins, Sarah, tr. from FRE. 2004. (Formac First Novels Ser.: 53). (ENG.). 64p. (J). (gr. 2-5). 4.95 *(978-0-88780-640-7(6))*; 14.95 *(978-0-88780-641-4(4))* Formac Publishing Co., Ltd. CAN. Dist: Casemate Pubs. & Bk. Distributors, LLC.

—Leo's Poster Challenge, 1 vol. Leblanc, Louise. Prud'homme, Jules & Cummins, Sarah, trs. from FRE. 2003. (Formac First Novels Ser.). (ENG.). 64p. (J). (gr. 2-5). 4.95 *(978-0-88780-608-7(2))*; 14.95 *(978-0-88780-609-4(0))* Formac Publishing Co., Ltd. CAN. Dist: Casemate Pubs. & Bk. Distributors, LLC.

Pruett, Mary. Color the Western Birds. 2010. (Pruett Ser.). (ENG.). 32p. (J). pap. 4.99 *(978-0-87108-957-1(2))* Pruett Publishing Co.

Pruitt, Ginny. All the Muchos in the World: A Special Story about Love. Carson, Diana Pastora. 2006. 32p. (J). pap. 8.95 *(978-0-8198-0779-3(6))* Pauline Bks. & Media.

—One Hundred First Communions. Kelly, Veronica & Goody, Wendy. 2003. (J). (gr. k-5). 14.95 *(978-0-9657218-2-0(5))* WhipperSnapper Bks.

Pruitt, Gwendolyn. The Blake Family Vacation. Ross, Jill. 2010. (ENG.). 130p. (J). (gr. 3-7). pap. 9.95 *(978-1-59825-950-6(4))* Shenanigans Series.

—The Real Nitty-Gritty. Ross, Jill. 2010. (ENG.). 60p. (J). (gr. 3-7). pap. 9.95 *(978-1-59825-949-0(0))* Shenanigans Series.

—What's the Matter, Mr. Ticklebritches? Ross, Jill. 2010. (ENG.). 70p. (J). (gr. 3-7). pap. 9.95 *(978-1-59825-948-3(2))* Shenanigans Series.

Pruitt, Jason. Saving Nidia. Thigpen, Meredith. 2007. 32p. (J). (gr. -1-3). 17.99 *(978-1-59886-814-2(4))* Tate Publishing & Enterprises, LLC.

Prunier, James & Galeron, Henri. Dinosaurs. Jeunesse, Gallimard et al. 2007. (First Discovery Book Ser.). (ENG.). 24p. (J). (gr. -1-k). pap. 5.99 *(978-0-439-91089-7(7))* Scholastic, Inc.

Prunier, James, jt. illus. see Grant, Donald.

Pryor, Jim. Joey Gonzalez, Great American. Robles, Tony. 2008. (ENG.). (J). (gr. -1-3). 15.95 *(978-0-9767269-3-7(9))* WND Bks, Inc.

Pryor, John-Thomas. Midrak Earthshaker. Nanavati, Daniel. 2013. 132p. pap. *(978-1-908867-06-3(X))* FootSteps Pr.

Pryor, Sean. The Catechist's Magic Kit: 80 Simple Tricks for Teaching Catholicism to Kids. Stagnaro, Angelo. 2009. (ENG.). 256p. pap. 29.95 *(978-0-8245-2518-7(3))* Crossroad Publishing Co., The.

Przybylek, Leslie. Big Bear's Arkansas ABCs. Sandage, Charley. 2004. 56p. (J). (gr. k-2). pap. 14.95 *(978-0-9638956-9-1(9))* Archeological Assessments, Inc.

Psacharopulo, Alessandra. The Firefighter. Goebel, Jenny. 2015. (ENG.). 32p. (J). (gr. -1-k). pap. 3.99 ***(978-0-448-48101-2(4)***, Grosset & Dunlap) Penguin Publishing Group.

—Is It Hanukkah Yet? Barash, Chris. 2015. (ENG.). 32p. (J). (gr. -1-2). 16.99 ***(978-0-8075-3384-0(X))*** Whitman, Albert & Co.

Psacharopulo, Alessandra. Is It Passover Yet? Barash, Chris. 2015. (ENG.). 32p. (J). (gr. -1-2). 16.99 *(978-0-8075-6330-4(7))* Whitman, Albert & Co.

Puddle, Patricia. Rascals Sing at the Opera House: Adventures of Rascals, Polly & Gertie. Puddle, Patricia. 2011. (ENG.). 108p. pap. 7.99 *(978-1-4664-7185-6(9))* CreateSpace Independent Publishing Platform.

Puebla, Teo. Antonio Machado para Ninos. Machado, Antonio. 2003. (SPA.). 248p. *(978-84-305-9532-7(5)*, SU30132) Susaeta Ediciones, S.A. ESP. Dist: Lectorum Pubns., Inc.

—Dos Plumas de Aguila. Gómez Cerdá, Alfredo et al. 2003. (SPA.). 32p. (gr. 3-5). 14.99 *(978-84-241-8028-7(3))* Everest Editora ESP. Dist: Lectorum Pubns., Inc.

Puerta, Carlos. El Libro de la Selva. Puerta, Carlos, tr. Kipling, Rudyard & Solari, Maria J.Tr. of Jungle Book. (SPA.). 92p. (J). (gr. 5-8). pap. 12.95 *(978-84-204-5766-6(3))* Santillana USA Publishing Co., Inc.

Pugh, Jonathan. www.Here-I-Am. Stannard, Russell. 2011. (ENG.). 160p. (YA). (gr. 5-8). pap. 9.95 *(978-1-890151-85-0(8))* Templeton Pr.

Puglisi, Adriana. The Pet Store Pet Show, 1 vol. Gallagher, Diana G. 2014. (Pet Friends Forever Ser.). (ENG.). 88p. (gr. 1-3). 23.99 *(978-1-4795-2177-7(9))* Picture Window Bks.

—Problem Pup, 1 vol. Gallagher, Diana G. 2014. (Pet Friends Forever Ser.). (ENG.). 88p. (gr. 1-3). 23.99 *(978-1-4795-2176-0(0))* Picture Window Bks.

Puglisi, Adriana, jt. illus. see Juarez, Adriana.

Puig Rosado, Fernando. The Good Little Devil & Other Tales. Gripari, Pierre. Lewis, Sophie, tr. 2014. (ENG.). 300p. (YA). (gr. 4-7). 20.00 *(978-1-78269-008-5(5)*, Pushkin Children's Bks.) Pushkin Pr., Ltd. GBR. Dist: Random Hse., Inc.

Pukac, Michael & Stephen, Marchesi. The Flights of Marceau: Week Three. 2008. (ENG.). 64p. (J). 16.95 *(978-0-9797495-2-0(2))* Majestic Eagle Publishing.

Pulido, Rene. Costumes of Asia: A Connoisseur's Coloring Book. Heiter, Celeste. 2010. (ENG.). 48p. (J). (gr. k-5). pap. 4.95 *(978-1-934159-20-0(4))* ThingsAsian Pr.

—Fashion Asia: Patterns & Designs of Traditional Cultures. Heiter, Celeste. 2010. (ENG.). 224p. (J). (gr. -1-3). pap. 9.95 *(978-1-934159-19-4(0))* ThingsAsian Pr.

Pullan, Jack. Dear Dragon Flies a Kite. Hillert, Margaret. 2015. (Beginning-To-Read Ser.). (ENG.). 32p. (J). (gr. k-2). pap. 10.60 *(978-1-60357-709-0(2))*; lib. bdg. 21.27 *(978-1-59953-674-3(9))* Norwood Hse. Pr.

Pullan, Jack. Dear Dragon Gets a Hole-In-One. Hillert, Margaret. 2015. (Beginning-To-Read Ser.). (ENG.). 32p. (J). (gr. k-2). pap. 10.60 ***(978-1-60357-790-8(4))***; lib. bdg. 22.60 ***(978-1-59953-705-4(2))*** Norwood Hse. Pr.

P

—Dear Dragon Gets a Pet. Hillert, Margaret. 2015. (Beginning-To-Read Ser.). (ENG.). 32p. (J). (gr. k-2). pap. 10.60 ***(978-1-60357-791-5(2))***; lib. bdg. 22.60 ***(978-1-59953-706-1(0))*** Norwood Hse. Pr.

Pullan, Jack. Dear Dragon Goes to Grandpa's Farm. Hillert, Margaret. 2015. (Beginning-To-Read Ser.). (ENG.). 32p. (J). (gr. k-2). pap. 10.60 *(978-1-60357-710-6(6))*; lib. bdg. 21.27 *(978-1-59953-675-0(7))* Norwood Hse. Pr.

—Dear Dragon Goes to the Aquarium. Hillert, Margaret. 2015. (Beginning-To-Read Ser.). (ENG.). 32p. (J). (gr. k-2). pap. 10.60 *(978-1-60357-712-0(2))*; lib. bdg. 21.27 *(978-1-59953-677-4(3))* Norwood Hse. Pr.

Pullan, Jack. Dear Dragon Goes to the Beach. Hillert, Margaret. 2015. (Beginning-To-Read Ser.). (ENG.). 32p. (J). (gr. k-2). pap. 10.60 ***(978-1-60357-789-2(0))***; lib. bdg. 22.60 ***(978-1-59953-704-7(4))*** Norwood Hse. Pr.

Pullan, Jack. Dear Dragon Goes to the Police Station. Hillert, Margaret. 2015. (Beginning-To-Read Ser.). 32p. (J). (gr. k-2). pap. 10.60 *(978-1-60357-711-3(4))*; lib. bdg. 21.27 *(978-1-59953-676-7(5))* Norwood Hse. Pr.

Pullan, Jack. Dear Dragon Learns to Read. Hillert, Margaret. 2015. (Beginning-To-Read Ser.). (ENG.). 32p. (J). (gr. k-2). pap. 10.60 ***(978-1-60357-792-2(0))***; lib. bdg. 22.60 ***(978-1-59953-707-8(9))*** Norwood Hse. Pr.

Pullan, Jack, jt. illus. see Epstein, Len.

Pullen, Zachary. Alfred Nobel: The Man Behind the Peace Prize. Wargin, Kathy-jo. 2009. (ENG.). 32p. (J). (gr. k-6). 17.95 *(978-1-58536-281-3(6))* Sleeping Bear Pr.

—The Bambino & Me. Hyman, Zachary. 2014. (ENG.). 48p. (J). (gr. 1-4). 17.99 *(978-1-77049-627-9(0))* Tundra Bks. CAN. Dist: Random Hse., Inc.

Pullen, Zachary. The Bambino & Me. Hyman, Zachary. 2015. (ENG.). 48p. (J). (gr. 1-4). pap. 7.99 ***(978-1-77049-628-6(9))*** Tundra Bks. CAN. Dist: Penguin Random Hse., LLC.

Pullen, Zachary. Finn McCool & the Great Fish. Bunting, Eve. 2010. (ENG.). 38p. (J). (gr. k-6). 16.95 *(978-1-58536-366-7(9))* Sleeping Bear Pr.

—Francis & Eddie: The True Story of America's Underdogs. Herzog, Brad. 2013. (ENG.). 32p. (J). 17.95 *(978-0-9849919-2-1(1))* Why Not Bks.

—The Greatest Game Ever Played. Bildner, Phil. 2006. (ENG.). 40p. (J). (gr. k-3). 17.99 *(978-0-399-24171-0(X)*, Putnam Juvenile) Penguin Publishing Group.

—John Appleseed: A Trail of Trees. Winters, Kay. 2007. (J). *(978-1-4263-0101-8(4))* National Geographic Society.

—Lipman Pike: America's First Home Run King. Michelson, Richard. 2011. (ENG.). 32p. (J). (gr. 1-4). 16.95 *(978-1-58536-465-7(7)*, 202186) Sleeping Bear Pr.

—S Is for Story: A Writer's Alphabet. Hershenhorn, Esther. 2009. (ENG.). 40p. (J). (gr. 1-4). 17.95 *(978-1-58536-439-8(8)*, 202167) Sleeping Bear Pr.

—The Toughest Cowboy: Or How the Wild West Was Tamed. Frank, John. 2004. (ENG.). 48p. (J). (gr. 1-3). 17.95 *(978-0-689-83461-5(6)*, Simon & Schuster Bks. For Young Readers) Simon & Schuster Bks. For Young Readers.

Pullen, Zachary. Friday My Radio Flyer Flew. Pullen, Zachary. 2008. (ENG.). 32p. (J). (gr. -1-2). 17.99 *(978-1-4169-3983-2(0)*, Simon & Schuster Bks. For Young Readers) Simon & Schuster Bks. For Young Readers.

—The Toughest Cowboy: Or How the Wild West Was Tamed. Pullen, Zachary. Frank, John. 2008. (ENG.). 48p. (J). (gr. 1-3). 7.99 *(978-0-689-83462-2(4)*, Simon & Schuster/Paula Wiseman Bks.) Simon & Schuster/Paula Wiseman Bks.

Pulles, Elizabeth. Little Library Literacy: Lizo's Song Ndebele. Hodson, Christopher. 2007. pap. *(978-0-521-70282-9(8))* Cambridge Univ. Pr.

—Little Library Literacy: Lizo's Song Siswati. Hodson, Christopher. 2007. pap. *(978-0-521-70286-7(0))* Cambridge Univ. Pr.

—Little Library Literacy: Lizo's Song Xhosa. Hodson, Christopher. 2007. pap. *(978-0-521-70283-6(6))* Cambridge Univ. Pr.

Pulley, Kelly. Adam & Eve in the Garden, 1 vol. Zondervan Publishing Staff. 2008. (I Can Read! / the Beginner's Bible Ser.). (ENG.). 32p. (J). (gr. -1-1). pap. 3.99 *(978-0-310-71552-8(0))* Zonderkidz.

—All Aboard with Noah!, 1 vol. DeVries, Catherine & Zondervan Publishing Staff. 2009. (Beginner's Bible Ser.). (ENG.). 12p. (J). bds. 7.99 *(978-0-310-71726-3(4))* Zonderkidz.

—Baby Jesus Is Born, 1 vol. Zondervan Publishing Staff. 2009. (I Can Read! / the Beginner's Bible Ser.). (ENG.). 32p. (J). (gr. -1-2). pap. 3.99 *(978-0-310-71780-5(9))* Zonderkidz.

—Baby Moses & the Princess, 1 vol. Zondervan Publishing Staff. 2009. (I Can Read! / the Beginner's Bible Ser.). (ENG.). 32p. (J). pap. 3.99 *(978-0-310-71767-6(1))* Zonderkidz.

—The Beginner's Bible: Timeless Children's Stories. 2014. (Beginner's Bible (Zonderkidz) Ser.). (ENG.). (gr. -1-k). 16.97 *(978-0-310-72924-2(6))* Zondervan.

Pulley, Kelly. The Beginner's Bible All about Jesus Sticker & Activity Book, 1 vol. Zondervan Publishing Staff. 2015. (Beginner's Bible Ser.). (ENG.). 16p. (J). pap. 3.99 ***(978-0-310-74693-5(0))*** Zonderkidz.

Pulley, Kelly. Beginner's Bible Collector's Edition: Timeless Children's Stories, 1 vol. Zondervan Publishing Staff. 2014. (Beginner's Bible Ser.). (ENG.). 512p. (J). 39.99 *(978-0-310-74734-5(1))* Zonderkidz.

—The Beginner's Bible Come Celebrate Easter, 1 vol. Zondervan Bibles Staff. 2015. (Beginner's Bible Ser.). (ENG.). 16p. (J). pap., act. bk. ed. 3.99 *(978-0-310-74733-8(3))* Zonderkidz.

—The Beginner's Bible Stories about Jesus, 1 vol. Zondervan Publishing Staff. 2015. (Beginner's Bible Ser.). (ENG.). 22p. (J). bds. 9.99 *(978-0-310-74740-6(6))* Zonderkidz.

—Bridget's Blog. Witherow, Wendy. 2007. 95p. (J). pap. *(978-1-934306-09-3(6))* Mission City Pr., Inc.

—Daniel & the Lions, 1 vol. Zondervan Publishing Staff. 2008. (I Can Read! / the Beginner's Bible Ser.). (ENG.). 32p. (J). (gr. -1-1). pap. 3.99 *(978-0-310-71551-1(2))* Zonderkidz.

—David & the Giant, 1 vol. Zondervan Publishing Staff. 2008. (I Can Read! / the Beginner's Bible Ser.). (ENG.). 32p. (J). (gr. -1-1). pap. 3.99 *(978-0-310-71550-4(4))* Zonderkidz.

—Jesus & His Friends, 1 vol. Zondervan Publishing Staff. ed. 2009. (I Can Read! / the Beginner's Bible / ¡Yo Sé Leer! Ser.). (SPA & ENG.). 32p. (J). pap. 3.99 *(978-0-310-71889-5(9))* Zonderkidz.

—Jesus Feeds the People, 1 vol. Zondervan Publishing Staff. 2010. (I Can Read! / the Beginner's Bible Ser.). (ENG.). 32p. (J). pap. 3.99 *(978-0-310-71779-9(5))* Zonderkidz.

—Jesus Saves the World, 1 vol. Zondervan Publishing Staff. 2008. (I Can Read! / the Beginner's Bible Ser.). (ENG.). 32p. (J). (gr. -1-1). pap. 3.99 *(978-0-310-71553-5(9))* Zonderkidz.

—Joseph & His Brothers, 1 vol. Zondervan Publishing Staff. 2009. (I Can Read! / the Beginner's Bible Ser.). (ENG.). 32p. (J). pap. 3.99 *(978-0-310-71731-7(0))* Zonderkidz.

—The Lost Son: Based on Luke 15:11-32, 1 vol. Zondervan Publishing Staff. 2009. (I Can Read! / the Beginner's Bible Ser.). (ENG.). 32p. (J). pap. 3.99 *(978-0-310-71781-2(7))* Zonderkidz.

—Miranda's Makeover. Witherow, Wendy. 2007. 93p. (J). *(978-1-934306-11-6(8))* Mission City Pr., Inc.

—Moses & the King, 1 vol. Zondervan Bibles Staff. 2009. (I Can Read! / the Beginner's Bible Ser.). (ENG.). 32p. (J). pap. 3.99 *(978-0-310-71800-0(7))* Zonderkidz.

—Queen Esther Helps God's People, 1 vol. Zondervan Publishing Staff. 2008. (I Can Read! / the Beginner's Bible Ser.). (ENG.). 32p. (J). pap. 3.99 *(978-0-310-71815-4(5))* Zonderkidz.

—The Story of David. Pingry, Patricia A. 2012. (J). *(978-0-8249-1886-6(X)*, Candy Cane Pr.) Ideals Pubns.

—The Story of Jesus. Pingry, Patricia A. 2011. (Little Bible Bks). 22p. (J). (gr. -1-k). bds. 6.99 *(978-0-8249-1854-5(1)*, Candy Cane Pr.) Ideals Pubns.

—The Story of Joshua. Pingry, Patricia A. 2012. (Little Bible Bks). 22p. (J). bds. 6.99 *(978-0-8249-1871-2(1)*, Candy Cane Pr.) Ideals Pubns.

—Timeless Children's Stories, 1 vol. Zondervan Publishing Staff. rev. ed. 2005. (Beginner's Bible Ser.). (ENG.). 512p. (J). 16.99 *(978-0-310-70962-6(8))* Zonderkidz.

—The Very First Christmas, 1 vol. 2008. (Beginner's Bible Ser.). (ENG.). 32p. (J). pap. 47.76 *(978-0-310-71816-1(3))*; pap. 1.99 *(978-0-310-71826-0(0))* Zonderkidz.

—The Very First Easter, 1 vol. Zondervan Publishing Staff. 2009. (Beginner's Bible Ser.). (ENG.). 32p. (J). pap. 47.76 *(978-0-310-71817-8(1))*; pap. 1.99 *(978-0-310-71827-7(9))* Zonderkidz.

Pulley, Kelly. Adan y Eva en el Jardin, 1 vol. Pulley, Kelly. Zondervan Publishing Staff. ed. 2009. (I Can Read! / the Beginner's Bible / ¡Yo Sé Leer! Ser.).Tr. of Adam & Eve in the Garden. (SPA & ENG.). 32p. (J). pap. 3.99 *(978-0-310-71892-5(9))* Zonderkidz.

—The Cycling Wangdoos. Pulley, Kelly. 2011. 32p. (J). (gr. -1-3). 16.95 *(978-0-9820812-1-1(9)*, Frog Legs Ink) Gauthier Pubns. Inc.

—Daniel y los Leones, 1 vol. Pulley, Kelly. Zondervan Publishing Staff. ed. 2009. (I Can Read! / the Beginner's Bible / ¡Yo Sé Leer! Ser.).Tr. of Daniel & the Lions. (SPA & ENG.). 32p. (J). pap. 3.99 *(978-0-310-71891-8(0))* Zonderkidz.

—David & the Giant (David y el Gigante), 1 vol. Pulley, Kelly. Zondervan Publishing Staff. ed. 2009. (I Can Read! / the Beginner's Bible / ¡Yo Sé Leer! Ser.). (SPA & ENG.). 32p. (J). pap. 3.99 *(978-0-310-71890-1(2))* Zonderkidz.

—Jesus Saves the World, 1 vol. Pulley, Kelly. Zondervan Publishing Staff. ed. 2009. (I Can Read! / the Beginner's Bible / ¡Yo Sé Leer! Ser.). (SPA & ENG.). 32p. (J). pap. 3.99 *(978-0-310-71893-2(7))* Zonderkidz.

—Jonas y el Gran Pez, 1 vol. Pulley, Kelly. Zondervan Publishing Staff. ed. 2009. (I Can Read! / the Beginner's Bible / ¡Yo Sé Leer! Ser.).Tr. of Jonah & the Big Fish. (SPA & ENG.). 32p. (J). pap. 3.99 *(978-0-310-71887-1(2))* Zonderkidz.

—Noah & the Ark, 1 vol. Pulley, Kelly. Zondervan Publishing Staff. ed. 2009. (I Can Read! / the Beginner's Bible / ¡Yo Sé Leer! Ser.). (SPA & ENG.). 32p. (J). pap. 3.99 *(978-0-310-71886-4(4))* Zonderkidz.

—Ten Unusual Features of Lulu McDunn. Pulley, Kelly. 2010. 32p. (J). (gr. -1). 16.95 *(978-0-9820812-7-3(8)*, Frog Legs Ink) Gauthier Pubns. Inc.

Pulley, Kelly & Reed, Lisa. God Is Bigger Than the Boogie Man. Vischer, Phil. 2014. (VeggieTales Book Ser.). 16p. (J). bds. 12.99 *(978-0-8249-1943-6(2)*, Candy Cane Pr.) Ideals Pubns.

—Jolly Old Santa's Workshop Activity Book. Traditional. 2014. 16p. (J). 4.99 *(978-0-8249-5665-3(6)*, Ideals Children's Bks.) Ideals Pubns.

—Silent Night. Traditional. 2014. (VeggieTales Book Ser.). 16p. (J). bds. 12.99 *(978-0-8249-1934-4(3)*, Candy Cane Pr.) Ideals Pubns.

Pulsar Studios Staff. Cheer Captain, 1 vol. Maddox, Jake. 2011. (Jake Maddox Girl Sports Stories Ser.). (ENG.). 72p. (gr. 2-3). 23.99 *(978-1-4342-2551-1(8))* Stone Arch Bks.

—Drive to the Hoop, 1 vol. Maddox, Jake. 2011. (Jake Maddox Girl Sports Stories Ser.). (ENG.). 72p. (gr. 2-3). 23.99 *(978-1-4342-2500-9(3))* Stone Arch Bks.

—Victory Vault, 1 vol. Maddox, Jake. 2011. (Jake Maddox Girl Sports Stories Ser.). (ENG.). 72p. (gr. 2-3). 23.99 *(978-1-4342-2498-9(8))* Stone Arch Bks.

Punch, Melissa, photos by. Gadgetology: Kitchen Fun with Your Kids, Using 35 Cooking Gadgets for Simple Recipes, Crafts, Games, & Experiments. Abrams, Pam. 2007. (ENG., 96p. (gr. 4-7). spiral bd. 14.95 *(978-1-55832-346-9(5))* Harvard Common Pr.

Punniyamurthi, Kavitha. Lucy's Purple Pullover. Punniyamurthi, Kavitha. 2010. 16p. pap. 9.95 *(978-1-61633-075-0(9))* Guardian Angel Publishing, Inc.

Purcell, Gordon, et al. Benjamin Franklin: Un Genio Norteamericano. Olson, Kay Melchisedech. 2006. (Biografías Gráficas Ser.). (SPA.). 32p. (gr. 3-4). 29.99 *(978-0-7368-6598-2(5))* Capstone Pr., Inc.

Purcell, Gordon. George Eastman & the Kodak Camera, 1 vol. Fandel, Jennifer & Milgrom, Al. 2007. (Inventions & Discovery Ser.). (ENG.). 32p. (gr. 3-4). pap. 8.10 *(978-0-7368-7900-2(5)*, Graphic Library) Capstone Pr., Inc.

—The Trojan Horse: The Fall of Troy. Fontes, Ron et al. 2006. (Graphic Myths & Legends Ser.). (ENG.). 48p. (gr. 4-8). 27.93 *(978-0-8225-3065-5(6))* Lerner Publishing Group.

Purcell, Gordon & Beatty, Terry. The Creation of the U. S. Constitution, 1 vol. Burgan, Michael & Hoena, Blake A. 2006. (Graphic History Ser.). (ENG.). 32p. (gr. 3-4). 29.99 *(978-0-7368-6491-6(1)*, Graphic Library) Capstone Pr., Inc.

—The Creation of the U. S. Constitution. Burgan, Michael. 2006. (Graphic History Ser.). (ENG.). 32p. (gr. 3-4). pap. 8.10 *(978-0-7368-9653-5(8)*, Graphic Library) Capstone Pr., Inc.

—The First Moon Landing, 1 vol. Adamson, Thomas K. 2006. (Graphic History Ser.). (ENG.). 32p. (gr. 3-4). 29.99 *(978-0-7368-6492-3(X))*; per. 8.10 *(978-0-7368-9654-2(6))* Capstone Pr., Inc. (Graphic Library).

—Thomas Jefferson: Great American, 1 vol. Doeden, Matt. 2006. (Graphic Biographies Ser.). (ENG.). 32p. (gr. 3-4). 29.99 *(978-0-7368-5488-7(6)*, Graphic Library) Capstone Pr., Inc.

Purcell, Gordon & Milgrom, Al. Charles Darwin & the Theory of Evolution, 1 vol. Adamson, Heather. 2007. (Inventions & Discovery Ser.). (ENG.). 32p. (gr. 3-4). 29.99 *(978-1-4296-0145-0(0)*, Graphic Library) Capstone Pr., Inc.

—George Eastman & the Kodak Camera, 1 vol. Fandel, Jennifer & Milgrom, Al. 2007. (Inventions & Discovery Ser.). (ENG.). 32p. (gr. 3-4). 29.99 *(978-0-7368-6848-8(8)*, Graphic Library) Capstone Pr., Inc.

Purcell, Gordon & Schulz, Barbara. Benjamin Franklin: An American Genius, 1 vol. Olson, Kay Melchisedech. 2005. (Graphic Biographies Ser.). (ENG.). 32p. (gr. 3-4). 29.99 *(978-0-7368-4629-5(8)*, Graphic Library) Capstone Pr., Inc.

—Eleanor Roosevelt: First Lady of the World. Jacobson, Ryan. 2005. (Graphic Biographies Ser.). (ENG.). 32p. (gr. 3-4). 29.99 *(978-0-7368-4969-2(6)*, Graphic Library) Capstone Pr., Inc.

—The Trojan Horse: The Fall of Troy - A Greek Legend. Fontes, Ron & Fontes, Justine. 2007. (Graphic Myths & Legends Ser.). (ENG.). 48p. (gr. 4-8). per. 8.95 *(978-0-8225-6484-3(X))* Lerner Publishing Group.

Purcell, Rebecca. Super Chicken! Purcell, Rebecca. 2013. (ENG.). 14p. (J). (— 1). bds. 7.99 *(978-0-545-45170-3(1)*, Cartwheel Bks.) Scholastic, Inc.

Purchase, Brendan. Alfie Potts: Alfie & the Mind Virus. Hibbitts, Mark. 2011. (ENG.). 40p. (J). *(978-1-907498-60-2(5)*, Book Shaker) Lean Marketing Pr.

—Alfie Potts: Alfie & the Seminar. Hibbitts, Mark. 2011. (ENG.). 40p. pap. *(978-1-907498-75-6(3)*, Book Shaker) Lean Marketing Pr.

Purdy, Joanne. It Happened One Night in the Barn. Kormos, Lawrence. 2007. 24p. *(978-1-55452-192-0(0))* Essence Publishing.

Purnell, Gerald. Am I a Color Too? Cole, Heidi & Vogl, Nancy. 2005. 32p. (J). (gr. -1-3). 15.95 *(978-0-9740190-5-5(4))* Illumination Arts Publishing Co., Inc.

—God's Promise. Moss, Maureen. 2008. 30p. (J). (gr. -1-3). 15.95 *(978-0-9740190-7-9(0))* Illumination Arts Publishing Co., Inc.

—A Home Run for Bunny. Anderson, Richard. 2013. (ENG.). (J). (gr. -1-3). 16.95 *(978-0-9855417-2-9(5))* Inspire Every Child dba Illumination Arts.

Purnell, Teresa. The Rainforest Family & Those Terrible Toads. Lamond, Peter. 2011. 92p. pap. 27.25 *(978-1-60976-297-1(5)*, Eloquent Bks.) Strategic Book Publishing & Rights Agency (SBPRA).

Purves, Jeff, et al. Hulk Visionaries, Vol. 3. 2006. (ENG.). 192p. (J). (gr. 4-17). pap. 19.99 *(978-0-7851-2095-7(5))* Marvel Worldwide, Inc.

Purvis, Leland. Defiance, Bk. 2. Jablonski, Carla. 2011. (Resistance Ser.: 2). (ENG.). 128p. (YA). (gr. 7-12). pap. 17.99 *(978-1-59643-292-5(6)*, First Second Bks.) Roaring Brook Pr.

—Resistance, Bk. 1. Jablonski, Carla. 2010. (Resistance Ser.: 1). (ENG.). 128p. (YA). (gr. 7-12). pap. 17.99 *(978-1-59643-291-8(8)*, First Second Bks.) Roaring Brook Pr.

—Sons of Liberty. Poe, Marshall. 2008. (Turning Points Ser.). (ENG.). 128p. (J). (gr. 3-7). pap. 8.99 *(978-1-4169-5067-7(2)*, Simon & Schuster/Paula Wiseman Bks.) Simon & Schuster/Paula Wiseman Bks.

—Victory: Resistance Book 3. Jablonski, Carla. 2012. (Resistance Ser.: 3). (ENG.). 128p. (YA). (gr. 7-3). pap. 17.99 *(978-1-59643-293-2(4)*, First Second Bks.) Roaring Brook Pr.

Purvis, Leland & Lindner, Ellen. Little Rock Nine. Poe, Marshall. 2008. (Turning Points Ser.). (ENG.). 128p. (J). (gr. 3-7). pap. 7.99 *(978-1-4169-5066-0(4)*, Simon & Schuster/Paula Wiseman Bks.) Simon & Schuster/Paula Wiseman Bks.

Purvis, Leland, jt. illus. see Lindner, Ellen.

Pushee, Marisa. The Adventures of Miss Chief: Miss Chief Goes to School. Hyde, Noreen. 2007. 28p. per. 9.95 *(978-1-59858-368-7(9))* Dog Ear Publishing, LLC.

Put, Klaartje van der. Little Cat: Finger Puppet Book. Chronicle Books Staff & Image Books Staff. 2014. (Little Finger Puppet Board Bks.). (ENG.). 12p. (J). (gr. -1 — 1). bds. 6.99 *(978-1-4521-2916-7(9))* Chronicle Bks. LLC.

—Little Chick: Finger Puppet Book. Image Books Staff. 2015. (ENG.). 12p. (J). (gr. -1 — 1). bds. 6.99 *(978-1-4521-2917-4(7))* Chronicle Bks. LLC.

—Little Chicken. Image Books Staff. 2012. (Little Finger Puppet Board Bks.: FING). (ENG.). 12p. (J). (gr. -1 — 1). bds. 6.99 *(978-1-4521-0811-7(0))* Chronicle Bks. LLC.

—Little Dolphin. Image Books Staff. 2012. (Little Finger Puppet Board Bks.: FING). (ENG.). 12p. (J). (gr. -1 — 1). bds. 6.99 *(978-1-4521-0816-2(1))* Chronicle Bks. LLC.

Put, Klaartje van der. Little Fox: Finger Puppet Book. ImageBooks Staff & Chronicle Books Staff. 2015. (ENG.). 12p. (J). (gr. -1 — 1). 6.99 ***(978-1-4521-4230-2(0))*** Chronicle Bks. LLC.

Put, Klaartje van der. Little Horse: Finger Puppet Book. ImageBooks Staff. 2013. (Little Finger Puppet Board Bks.). (ENG.). 12p. (J). (gr. -1 — 1). bds. 6.99 *(978-1-4521-1249-7(5))* Chronicle Bks. LLC.

—Little Monkey. ImageBooks Staff. 2013. (Little Finger Puppet Board Bks.). (ENG.). 12p. (J). (gr. -1 — 1). bds. 6.99 *(978-1-4521-1250-3(9))* Chronicle Bks. LLC.

Put, Klaartje van der. Little Moose: Finger Puppet Book. Chronicle Books Staff & ImageBooks Staff. 2015. (ENG.). 12p. (J). (gr. -1 — 1). 6.99 ***(978-1-4521-4231-9(9))*** Chronicle Bks. LLC.

Put, Klaartje van der. Little Pig. Image Books Staff & Chronicle Books Staff. 2012. (Little Finger Puppet Board Bks.). (ENG.). 12p. (J). (gr. -1 — 1). bds. 6.99 *(978-1-4521-0817-9(X))* Chronicle Bks. LLC.

—Little Seal: Finger Puppet Book. Image Books Staff. 2012. (Little Finger Puppet Board Bks.: FING). (ENG.). 12p. (J). (gr. -1 — 1). 6.99 *(978-1-4521-0812-4(9))* Chronicle Bks. LLC.

—Little Shark: Finger Puppet Book. ImageBooks Staff. 2013. (Little Finger Puppet Board Bks.). (ENG.). 12p. (J). (gr. -1 — 1). bds. 6.99 *(978-1-4521-1251-0(7))* Chronicle Bks. LLC.

—Little Zebra. ImageBooks Staff. 2013. (Little Finger Puppet Board Bks.). (ENG.). 12p. (J). (gr. -1 — 1). bds. 6.99 *(978-1-4521-1252-7(5))* Chronicle Bks. LLC.

Puth, Klaus. 101 Pep-Up Games for Children: Refreshing, Recharging, Refocusing. Bartl, Allison. 2007. (SmartFun Activity Bks.). (ENG.). 160p. pap. 14.95 *(978-0-89793-495-4(4))*; spiral bd. 19.95 *(978-0-89793-496-1(2))* Turner Publishing Co. (Hunter Hse.).

—101 Relaxation Games for Children: Finding a Little Peace & Quiet in Between. Bartl, Allison. 2007. (SmartFun Activity Bks.). (ENG.). 160p. (J). (gr. 3). per. 14.95 *(978-0-89793-493-0(8)*, Hunter Hse.) Turner Publishing Co.

Putman, Stanley. Lion-Hearted Quakers. Haines, Marie. 2011. 152p. 41.95 *(978-1-258-03120-6(5))* Literary Licensing, LLC.

Putra, Dede & Harrison, Nancy. Who Was Rachel Carson? Fabiny, Sarah. 2014. (Who Was... ? Ser.). (ENG.). 112p. (J). (gr. 3-7). 4.99 *(978-0-448-47959-0(1)*, Grosset & Dunlap) Penguin Publishing Group.

Putra, Dede & McVeigh, Kevin. What Were the Salem Witch Trials? Holub, Joan. 2015. (What Was... ? Ser.). (ENG.). 112p. (J). (gr. 3-7). 5.99 ***(978-0-448-47905-7(2)***, Grosset & Dunlap) Penguin Publishing Group.

Puttapipat, Niroot. Jingle Bells: A Magical Cut-Paper Edition. Pierpont, James Lord. 2015. (ENG.). 12p. (J). (gr. -1-3). 19.99 ***(978-0-7636-7821-0(X))*** Candlewick Pr.

Puttapipat, Niroot. The Night Before Christmas: A Magical Cut-Paper Edition. Moore, Clement C. 2007. (ENG.). 24p. (J). (gr. -1-3). 19.99 *(978-0-7636-3469-8(7))* Candlewick Pr.

Puybaret, Eric. How Deep Is the Ocean? Zoehfeld, Kathleen Weidner. 2016. (J). pap. ***(978-0-06-232819-9(0))*** HarperCollins Pubs.

Puybaret, Eric. In Search of Happiness. Saumande, Juliette. Weller, Andrew, tr. from FRE. 2010. 32p. (J). (gr. -1-2). 14.99 *(978-0-8416-7141-6(9))* Hammond World Atlas Corp.

Puybaret, Éric. Manfish: A Story of Jacques Cousteau. Berne, Jennifer. 2008. (ENG.). 40p. (J). (gr. 1-4). 16.99 *(978-0-8118-6063-5(9))* Chronicle Bks. LLC.

—Manfish: The Story of Jacques Cousteau. Berne, Jennifer. 2015. (ENG.). 38p. (J). (gr. k-3). 9.99 *(978-1-4521-4123-7(1))* Chronicle Bks. LLC.

Puybaret, Eric. The Night Before Christmas. Moore, Clement C. 2010. (Book & CD Ser.). (ENG.). 26p. (J). (gr. k-12). 19.95 *(978-1-936140-06-0(3)*, Imagine Publishing) Charlesbridge Publishing, Inc.

—Over the Rainbow. 2010. (Book & CD Ser.). (ENG.). 26p. (J). (gr. k-12). 17.95 *(978-1-936140-00-8(4)*, Imagine Publishing) Charlesbridge Publishing, Inc.

—Over the Rainbow (Board) 2014. (ENG.). 22p. (J). (gr. k-12). bds. 7.95 *(978-1-62354-044-9(5)*, Imagine Publishing) Charlesbridge Publishing, Inc.

—Puff, the Magic Dragon. Yarrow, Peter & Lipton, Lenny. (ENG.). (J). 2012. 24p. (gr. k — 1). bds. 7.95 *(978-1-4549-0114-3(4))*; 2010. 32p. (gr. k-2). pap. 9.95 incl. audio compact disk *(978-1-4027-7216-0(5))*; 2007. 24p. 16.95 *(978-1-4027-5279-7(2))*; 2007. 24p. (gr. -1-2). 16.95 *(978-1-4027-5219-3(9))*; 2007. 24p. (gr. -1-2). 16.95 *(978-1-4027-4782-3(9))* Sterling Publishing Co., Inc.

—Puff, the Magic Dragon Pop-Up. Yarrow, Peter & Lipton, Lenny. 2011. (ENG.). 14p. (J). (gr. 1). 26.95 *(978-1-4027-8711-9(1))* Sterling Publishing Co., Inc.

—When You Wish upon a Star. Harline, Leigh & Wshington, Ned. 2011. (ENG.). 28p. (J). (gr. k-12). 17.95 *(978-1-936140-35-0(7)*, Yarrow, Peter Bks.) Charlesbridge Publishing, Inc.

Pye, Ali. Mouse's First Night at Moonlight School. Puttock, Simon. 2015. (ENG.). 32p. (J). (gr. -1-2). 16.99 *(978-0-7636-7607-0(1)*, Nosy Crow) Candlewick Pr.

—Something Delicious. Lewis, Jill. 2014. (Little Somethings Ser.: 1). (ENG.). 32p. (J). (gr. -1-k). pap. 9.99 *(978-1-4052-6238-5(9))* Egmont Bks., Ltd. GBR. Dist: Independent Pubs. Group.

Pye, Ali. Something Missing. Lewis, Jill. 2015. (Little Somethings Ser.). (ENG.). 32p. (J). (gr. -1-k). pap. 10.99 ***(978-1-4052-6819-6(0))*** Egmont Bks., Ltd. GBR. Dist: Independent Pubs. Group.

Pye, Ali. Where Is Fred? Hardy, Edward. 2013. (ENG.). 32p. (J). (gr. -1-k). pap. 9.99 *(978-1-4052-5403-8(3))* Egmont Bks., Ltd. GBR. Dist: Independent Pubs. Group.

Pye, Ali. Something Different. Pye, Ali. Lewis, Jill. 2014. (Little Somethings Ser.: 2). (ENG.). 32p. (J). (gr. -1-k). pap. 9.99 *(978-1-4052-6808-0(5))* Egmont Bks., Ltd. GBR. Dist: Independent Pubs. Group.

Pye, Trevor. Billy Mcbrown. Eggleton, Jill. (Sails Literacy Ser.). 24p. (gr. 1-18). 27.00 *(978-0-7578-6202-1(0))*;Pack. 57.00 *(978-0-7578-8620-1(5))* Rigby Education.
—The Fire. Eggleton, Jill. 2003. (Rigby Sails Early Ser.). (ENG.). 16p. (gr. 1-2). pap. 6.95 *(978-0-7578-8663-8(9))* Houghton Mifflin Harcourt Publishing Co.
—The Ice-Cream Machine. Eggleton, Jill. 2003. (Rigby Sails Early Ser.). (ENG.). 16p. (gr. 1-2). pap. 6.95 *(978-0-7578-8728-4(7))* Houghton Mifflin Harcourt Publishing Co.
—Mickey Maloney's Missing Bag. Eggleton, Jill. 2004. (Rigby Sails Early Ser.). (ENG.). 16p. (gr. 1-2). pap. 6.95 *(978-0-7578-9299-8(X))* Houghton Mifflin Harcourt Publishing Co.
—Stories of the Wild West Gang. Cowley, Joy. 2012. (Gecko Press Titles Ser.). (ENG.). 368p. (gr. -1-1). 16.95 *(978-1-877579-21-9(1))* Gecko Pr. NZL. Dist: Lerner Publishing Group.
Pyers, Kelsey. The Adventures of Granny: Granny Goes to the Zoo. Eberhart, Nancy. 2007. (J). 24p. per. 10.99 *(978-1-59879-372-7(1))*; (gr. -1-3). 13.99 *(978-1-59879-373-4(X))* Lifevest Publishing, Inc.
—Anabelle's Wish. Eberhart, Nancy. 2007. (J). 22p. per. 9.99 *(978-1-59879-370-3(5))*; (gr. -1-3). 13.99 *(978-1-59879-371-0(3))* Lifevest Publishing, Inc.
Pyle, Charles S. & Pyle, Chuck. No Easy Way: The Story of Ted Williams & the Last .400 Season. Bowen, Fred. 2010. (ENG.). 32p. (J). (gr. k-3). 16.99 *(978-0-525-47877-5(9))*, Dutton Juvenile) Penguin Publishing Group.
Pyle, Chuck. Freddie & Flossie. Hope, Laura Lee. ed. 2005. 32p. (J). lib. bdg. 15.00 *(978-1-59054-999-5(6))* Fitzgerald Bks.
—Freddie & Flossie. Hope, Laura Lee. 2005. (Bobbsey Twins Ser.). (ENG.). 32p. (J). (gr. -1-k). pap. 3.99 *(978-1-4169-0270-6(8))*, Simon Spotlight) Simon Spotlight.
—Freddie & Flossie & Snap. Hope, Laura Lee. 2005. (Bobbsey Twins Ser.). (ENG.). 32p. (J). (gr. -1-k). pap. 13.99 *(978-1-4169-0267-6(8))*, Simon Spotlight) Simon Spotlight.
—Freddie & Flossie & the Train Ride. Hope, Laura Lee. 2005. (Bobbsey Twins Ser.). (ENG.). 32p. (J). (gr. -1-k). pap. 13.99 *(978-1-4169-0269-0(4))*, Simon Spotlight) Simon Spotlight.
—Freddie & Flossie at the Beach. Hope, Laura Lee. 2005. (Bobbsey Twins Ser.). (ENG.). 32p. (J). (gr. -1-k). pap. 13.99 *(978-1-4169-0268-3(6))*, Simon Spotlight) Simon Spotlight.
Pyle, Chuck, jt. illus. see Pyle, Charles S.
Pyle, Howard. The Merry Adventures of Robin Hood. 2015. (J). *(978-1-4677-5841-3(8))*, First Avenue Editions) Lerner Publishing Group.
Pyle, Howard. Pepper & Salt & the Wonder Clock, Set. Pyle, Howard. 2006. (Foundations Ser.). 385p. (J). 45.00 *(978-1-933859-14-9(8))* ISI Bks.
—The Story of King Arthur & His Knights. Pyle, Howard. 2006. (ENG.). 416p. (gr. 12-18). 6.95 *(978-0-451-53024-0(1))*, Signet Classics) Penguin Publishing Group.
Pyle, Kevin C. Bad for You: Exposing the War on Fun! Pyle, Kevin C. Cunningham, Scott. 2014. (ENG.). 192p. (YA). (gr. 7). pap. 12.99 *(978-0-8050-9289-9(7))*, Holt, Henry & Co. Bks. For Young Readers) Holt, Henry & Co.
—Katman. Pyle, Kevin C. 2009. (ENG.). 144p. (YA). (gr. 7-12). pap. 12.99 *(978-0-8050-8285-2(9))*, Holt, Henry & Co. Bks. For Young Readers) Holt, Henry & Co.
—Take What You Can Carry. Pyle, Kevin C. 2012. (ENG.). 176p. (YA). (gr. 7-12). pap. 14.99 *(978-0-8050-8286-9(7))* Square Fish.
Pylypchuck, Anna. Chocalin! Calvani, Mayra. 2009. 24p. pap. 10.95 *(978-1-935137-69-6(7))* Guardian Angel Publishing, Inc.
Pym, T. Snezhnaya Koroleva - the Snow Queen. Andersen, Hans Christian. 2013. 56p. *(978-1-909115-60-6(6))* Planet, The.
Pynaert, Andrea. Clashmore Mike Comes Home. Guibert, Susan Mullen & O'Shaughnessy, Brendan. 2012. 24p. (J). 19.95 *(978-0-9859377-3-7(4))* Corby Books.
—Clashmore Mike_Dublin to Dome. Guibert, Susan Mullen & O'Shaughnessy, Brendan. 2012. 36p. (J). 19.95 *(978-0-9859377-1-3(8))* Corby Books.

Q

Q, Likit. B Is for Bangkok. Brown, Janet. 2011. (Alphabetical World Ser.). (ENG.). 47p. (J). (gr. k-4). 12.95 *(978-1-934159-26-2(3))* ThingsAsian Pr.
Qovaizi, Mo. Riley & the Sleeping Dragon: A Journey Around Beijing. McCartney, Tania Maree. 2008. 32p. (J). pap. *(978-0-9804750-0-5(7))* McCartney, Tania AUS. Dist: Jones, Dennis & Assocs. Pty, Ltd.
QTA Media Staff, et al. Atlas of Africa, 1 vol. Foster, Karen. 2008. (Picture Window Books World Atlases Ser.). (ENG.). 32p. (gr. 2-4). pap. 8.95 *(978-1-4048-3888-8(0))*, Nonfiction Picture Bks.) Picture Window Bks.
—Atlas of Australia, 1 vol. Foster, Karen. 2008. (Picture Window Books World Atlases Ser.). (ENG.). 32p. (gr. 2-4). pap. 8.95 *(978-1-4048-3889-5(9))*, Nonfiction Picture Bks.) Picture Window Bks.
—Atlas of Europe, 1 vol. Foster, Karen. 2008. (Picture Window Books World Atlases Ser.). (ENG.). 32p. (gr. 2-4). pap. 8.95 *(978-1-4048-3890-1(2))*, Nonfiction Picture Bks.) Picture Window Bks.
—Atlas of North America, 1 vol. Foster, Karen. 2008. (Picture Window Books World Atlases Ser.). (ENG.). 32p. (gr. 2-4). pap. 8.95 *(978-1-4048-3893-2(7))*, Nonfiction Picture Bks.) Picture Window Bks.
—Atlas of South America, 1 vol. Foster, Karen. 2008. (Picture Window Books World Atlases Ser.). (ENG.). 32p. (gr. 2-4). pap. 8.95 *(978-1-4048-3895-6(3))*, Nonfiction Picture Bks.) Picture Window Bks.
—Atlas of Southwest & Central Asia, 1 vol. Law, Felicia. 2008. (Picture Window Books World Atlases Ser.). (ENG.). 32p. (gr. 2-4). pap. 8.95 *(978-1-4048-3892-5(9))*, Nonfiction Picture Bks.) Picture Window Bks.
—Atlas of the Far East & Southeast Asia, 1 vol. Law, Felicia. 2008. (Picture Window Books World Atlases Ser.). (ENG.). 32p. (gr. 2-4). pap. 8.95 *(978-1-4048-3891-8(0))*, Nonfiction Picture Bks.) Picture Window Bks.
—Atlas of the Poles & Oceans, 1 vol. Foster, Karen. 2008. (Picture Window Books World Atlases Ser.). (ENG.). 32p. (gr. 2-4). pap. 8.95 *(978-1-4048-3894-9(5))*, Nonfiction Picture Bks.) Picture Window Bks.
Quach, Lam. Baby Chronicles: My Very Own Story: From Pre-Natal to Pre-School. Lebovics, Dania. 2007. (ENG.). 72p. spiral bd. 19.95 *(978-0-9699203-7-3(7))*, 9780969920373) Kiddy Chronicles Publishing CAN. Dist: Firefly Bks., Ltd.
Quackenbush, Marcia, jt. illus. see Dyrud, Chris Wold.
Quackenbush, Robert. Henry's Awful Mistake. Quackenbush, Robert, photos by. rev. deluxe ed. 2005. 40p. (J). (gr. k-2). reprint ed. 12.95 *(978-0-9712757-0-6(X))* Quackenbush, Robert Studios.
Quadflieg, Roswitha. La Historia Interminable. Quadflieg, Roswitha, tr. Ende, Michael. Sáenz, Miguel, tr.Tr. of Unendliche Geschichte. (SPA.). 424p. (J). 9.95 *(978-84-204-3226-7(1))* Ediciones Alfaguara ESP. Dist: Santillana USA Publishing Co., Inc.
Qualls, Sean. Before John Was a Jazz Giant: A Song of John Coltrane. Weatherford, Carole Boston. 2008. (ENG.). 32p. (J). (gr. k-4). 17.99 *(978-0-8050-7994-4(7))*, Holt, Henry & Co. Bks. For Young Readers) Holt, Henry & Co.
—Bird in a Box. Pinkney, Andrea Davis. 2012. (ENG.). 288p. (J). (gr. 3-7). pap. 8.00 *(978-0-316-07402-5(0))* Little, Brown Bks. for Young Readers.
—Bird in a Box. Pinkney, Andrea Davis. ed. 2012. lib. bdg. 18.45 *(978-0-606-26157-9(5))*, Turtleback) Turtleback Bks.
—Dizzy. Winter, Jonah. 2006. (J). 16.99 *(978-0-439-50736-3(7))*, Levine, Arthur A. Bks.) Scholastic, Inc.
—Emmanuel's Dream: The True Story of Emmanuel Ofosu Yeboah. Thompson, Laurie Ann. 2015. (ENG.). 40p. (J). (gr. -1-3). 17.99 *(978-0-449-81744-5(X))*, Schwartz & Wade Bks.) Random Hse. Children's Bks.
—Freedom Song: The Story of Henry "Box" Brown. Walker, Sally M. 2012. (ENG.). 40p. (J). (gr. -1-3). 17.99 *(978-0-06-058310-1(X))* HarperCollins Pubs.
—Giant Steps to Change the World. Lee, Spike & Lee, Tonya Lewis. 2011. (ENG.). 40p. (J). (gr. -1). 18.99 *(978-0-689-86815-3(4))*, Simon & Schuster Bks. For Young Readers) Simon & Schuster Bks. For Young Readers.
Qualls, Sean. Jump Back, Paul: The Life & Poems of Paul Laurence Dunbar. Derby, Sally. 2015. (ENG.). 128p. (J). (gr. 4-7). 16.99 ***(978-0-7636-6070-3(1))*** Candlewick Pr.
Qualls, Sean. Little Cloud & Lady Wind. Morrison, Toni & Morrison, Slade. 2010. (ENG.). 32p. (J). pap. 7.99 *(978-1-4169-8524-2(7))*, Simon & Schuster Bks. For Young Readers) Simon & Schuster Bks. For Young Readers.
—Little Cloud & Lady Wind. Morrison, Toni & Morrison, Slade. 2010. (ENG.). 32p. (J). (gr. -1-3). 16.99 *(978-1-4169-8523-5(9))*, Simon & Schuster/Paula Wiseman Bks.) Simon & Schuster/Paula Wiseman Bks.
—Lullaby (for a Black Mother) Hughes, Langston. 2013. (ENG.). 32p. (J). (gr. -1-3). 16.99 *(978-0-547-36265-6(X))* Houghton Mifflin Harcourt Publishing Co.
—The Poet Slave of Cuba: A Biography of Juan Francisco Manzano. Engle, Margarita. ed. 2011. (ENG & SPA.). 208p. (YA). (gr. 7-12). pap. 9.99 *(978-0-312-65928-8(8))* Square Fish.
—Skit-Scat Raggedy Cat: Ella Fitzgerald. Orgill, Roxane. 2010. (ENG.). 48p. (J). (gr. k-4). 17.99 *(978-0-7636-1733-2(4))* Candlewick Pr.
—Skit-Scat Raggedy Cat: Ella Fitzgerald. Orgill, Roxane. 2012. (Candlewick Biographies Ser.). (ENG.). 48p. (J). (gr. 3-7). 14.99 *(978-0-7636-6459-6(6))*; pap. 4.99 *(978-0-7636-6458-9(8))* Candlewick Pr.
Qualls, Sean, jt. illus. see Alko, Selina.
Quarello, Maurizio A. C. The Frog Prince. Namm, Diane. 2013. (Silver Penny Stories Ser.). (ENG.). 40p. (J). (gr. -1-1). 4.95 *(978-1-4027-8429-3(5))* Sterling Publishing Co., Inc.
—The Glutton. Albo, Pablo. 2007. (ENG.). 48p. (J). 18.95 *(978-84-96788-91-6(1))* OQO, Editora ESP. Dist: Baker & Taylor Bks.
—Jack & the Beanstalk. Namm, Diane. 2012. (Silver Penny Stories Ser.). (ENG.). 40p. (J). (gr. -1-1). 4.95 *(978-1-4027-8433-0(3))* Sterling Publishing Co., Inc.
—King Midas. Olmstead, Kathleen. 2014. (Silver Penny Stories Ser.). (ENG.). 40p. (J). (gr. -1-1). 4.95 *(978-1-4027-8346-3(9))* Sterling Publishing Co., Inc.
Quarello, Maurizio A. C. Mister Doctor: Janusz Korczak & the Orphans of the Warsaw Ghetto. Cohen-Janca, Irène. 2015. (ENG.). 68p. (J). (gr. 4-7). 24.95 ***(978-1-55451-715-2(X))***, 9781554517152) Annick Pr., Ltd. CAN. Dist: Firefly Bks., Ltd.
Quarello, Maurizio A. C. Rumpelstiltskin. McFadden, Deanna. 2014. (Silver Penny Stories Ser.). (ENG.). 40p. (J). (gr. -1-1). 4.95 *(978-1-4027-8340-1(X))* Sterling Publishing Co., Inc.
—The Tooth Gnashing Witch. Meroto, Tina. 2007. (ENG.). 48p. (J). 18.95 *(978-84-96788-82-4(2))* OQO, Editora ESP. Dist: Baker & Taylor Bks.
Quateman, India. Daddy Daughter Dinner Dance: A Father's Steps to a Blended Family That Really Works. Quateman, India. Quateman, Bill. 2003. 96p. 17.95 *(978-0-9729866-0-1(X))* Angel Mind.
Quay, Emma. Goodnight, Me. Daddo, Andrew. 2007. (ENG.). 32p. (J). (gr. -1-k). 12.99 *(978-1-59990-153-4(6))*, Bloomsbury USA Childrens) Bloomsbury USA.
Queen, Dana. Runty's Adventure: A Story of Love. Castleton, Chaffee. 2010. 97p. (J). pap. 17.95 *(978-0-578-06109-2(0))* Castleton, Julia J.
Querin, Pamela. What Is God Like? Lewis, Beverly. 2008. (ENG.). 32p. (J). (gr. -1-3). 14.99 *(978-0-7642-0466-1(1))* Bethany Hse. Pubs.
—What Is Heaven Like? Lewis, Beverly. 2006. (ENG.). 32p. (J). (gr. -1-3). 15.99 *(978-0-7642-0184-4(0))* Bethany Hse. Pubs.
Quesada, Joe & Kubert, Andy. Origin. 2006. (ENG.). 160p. (J). (gr. 4-17). pap. 14.99 *(978-0-7851-0965-5(X))* Marvel Worldwide, Inc.
Quesada, Maria Fe. Adivina, Adivinanza. Everest. (SPA.). (J). pap. 5.56 *(978-84-241-8037-9(2))* Everest Editora ESP. Dist: Lectorum Pubns., Inc.
Quick, Jen Lee. Off*Beat, Vol. 1. 2005. 184p. (YA). (gr. 8-18). pap. 14.99 *(978-1-59816-132-8(6))*, Tokyopop Kids) TOKYOPOP, Inc.
Quigley, Sebastian. The Dinosaur Museum: An Unforgettable, Interactive Virtual Tour Through Dinosaur History. U. S. National Geographic Society Staff. 2008. (ENG.). 24p. (J). (gr. 1-4). 19.95 *(978-1-4263-0335-7(1))*, National Geographic Children's Bks.) National Geographic Society.
—Legendary Journeys: Ships. Steele, Philip & Lavery, Brian. 2011. (Legendary Journeys Ser.). (ENG.). 32p. (J). (gr. 3-7). 19.99 *(978-0-7534-6681-0(3))*, Kingfisher) Roaring Brook Pr.
—Origami Adventures: Animals. Robinson, Nick. 2014. (Origami Adventures Ser.). (ENG.). 76p. (J). (gr. 1). spiral bd. 15.95 *(978-1-60710-763-7(5))*, Silver Dolphin Bks.) Baker & Taylor Publishing Group.
—Origami Adventures: Oceans. Terry, Nicolas. 2015. (Origami Adventures Ser.). (ENG.). 76p. (J). (gr. 1). spiral bd. 15.95 *(978-1-62686-251-7(6))*, Silver Dolphin Bks.) Baker & Taylor Publishing Group.
Quigley, Sebastion. Origami Adventures: Dinosaurs. Robinson, Nick. 2014. (Origami Adventures Ser.). (ENG.). 76p. (J). (gr. 1). spiral bd. 15.95 *(978-1-60710-762-0(7))*, Silver Dolphin Bks.) Baker & Taylor Publishing Group.
Quinn, Courtney. The Little Hospital Book. Dyan, Penelope. 2008. 108p. 19.95 *(978-1-935118-09-1(9))*; pap. 8.95 *(978-1-935118-08-4(0))* Bellissima Publishing, LLC.
—The Warrior Mouse of Forest Hollow. Dyan, Penelope. 2008. 108p. 17.95 *(978-1-935118-00-8(5))* Bellissima Publishing, LLC.
Quinn, Kitty. The Hummingbird Garden. Schwarz, Evelyn. 2012. (ENG.). 34p. (J). pap. 16.95 *(978-1-4327-9815-4(4))* Outskirts Pr., Inc.
Quinn, Paris. Shadow & Light, Vol. 4. Quinn, Paris. 2003. (ENG.). 48p. (YA). pap. 10.95 *(978-1-56163-327-2(5))*, Amerotica) NBM Publishing Co.
Quinn, Peter. Gramma I'm Bored. Quanstrom, Brenda. 2011. (ENG.). 30p. pap. 13.63 *(978-1-4662-5399-5(1))* CreateSpace Independent Publishing Platform.
Quinn, Savannah. Slowpoke the Sloth. Patterson, Drake. 2014. 34p. (J). pap. 9.99 *(978-1-62407-245-1(3))* PlatyPr.
Quinones, Joe, et al. The Amazing Spider-Man. Weisman, Greg. 2010. (ENG.). 136p. (J). (gr. 4-17). pap. 14.99 *(978-0-7851-4612-4(1))* Marvel Worldwide, Inc.
Quintero, José. Lo Que Sí y lo Que No. Murguía, Verónica. rev. ed. 2006. (Otra Escalera Ser.). (SPA & ENG.). 24p. (J). (gr. 2-4). pap. 9.95 *(978-968-5920-56-8(7))* Castillo, Ediciones, S. A. de C. V. MEX. Dist: Macmillan.
Quintero, michelle. Ollie Otter's Special Gift: A Story from Quiet Pond. Reminick, Gerald. 2013. 32p. (J). 10.00 *(978-1-889901-60-2(1))*, Palo Alto Bks.) Glencannon Pr.
Quitely, Frank. Neil Gaiman's Neverwhere. Carey, Mike & Fabry, Glenn. rev. ed. 2007. (ENG.). 224p. pap. 19.99 *(978-1-4012-1007-6(4))* DC Comics.
Quraishi, Ibrahim. The Story of Hurry. Williams, Emma. 2014. (ENG.). 38p. (J). (gr. -1-2). 16.95 *(978-1-60980-589-0(5))*, Triangle Square) Seven Stories Pr.
Q2A Staff. Christopher Columbus & the Voyage of 1492. Abnett, Dan. 2007. (Jr. Graphic Biographies Ser.). (ENG.). 24p. (gr. 3-8). pap. 10.60 *(978-1-4042-2143-7(3))*, PowerKids Pr.) Rosen Publishing Group, Inc., The.
Q2AMedia Services Private Ltd, Q2AMedia Services. Drawing Appaloosas & Other Handsome Horses, 1 vol. Young, Rae. 2014. (Drawing Horses Ser.). (ENG.). 32p. (gr. 3-4). lib. bdg. 27.32 *(978-1-4765-4001-6(2))*, Snap Bks.) Capstone Pr., Inc.
—Drawing Arabians & Other Amazing Horses, 1 vol. Young, Rae. 2014. (Drawing Horses Ser.). (ENG.). 32p. (gr. 3-4). lib. bdg. 27.32 *(978-1-4765-3995-9(2))*, Snap Bks.) Capstone Pr., Inc.
—Drawing Barrel Racers & Other Speedy Horses, 1 vol. Young, Rae. 2014. (Drawing Horses Ser.). (ENG.). 32p. (gr. 3-4). lib. bdg. 27.32 *(978-1-4765-3994-2(4))*, Snap Bks.) Capstone Pr., Inc.
—Drawing Friesians & Other Beautiful Horses, 1 vol. Young, Rae. 2014. (Drawing Horses Ser.). (ENG.). 32p. (gr. 3-4). lib. bdg. 27.32 *(978-1-4765-3996-6(0))*, Snap Bks.) Capstone Pr., Inc.
—Drawing Horses, 1 vol. Young, Rae. 2014. (Drawing Horses Ser.). (ENG.). 32p. (gr. 3-4). lib. bdg. 163.92 *(978-1-4765-4667-4(3))*, Snap Bks.) Capstone Pr., Inc.
—Drawing Mustangs & Other Wild Horses, 1 vol. Young, Rae. 2014. (Drawing Horses Ser.). (ENG.). 32p. (gr. 3-4). lib. bdg. 27.32 *(978-1-4765-4002-3(0))*, Snap Bks.) Capstone Pr., Inc.
—Drawing Thoroughbreds & Other Elegant Horses, 1 vol. Young, Rae. 2014. (Drawing Horses Ser.). (ENG.). 32p. (gr. 3-4). lib. bdg. 27.32 *(978-1-4765-3993-5(6))*, Snap Bks.) Capstone Pr., Inc.
Q2AMedia Services Private Ltd Staff. The Ultimate Guide to Drawing Horses, 1 vol. Young, Rae. 2013. (Drawing Horses Ser.). (ENG.). 144p. (gr. 3-4). pap. 14.95 *(978-1-4765-3992-8(8))*, Snap Bks.) Capstone Pr., Inc.

R

R. Z. Novit Graphic Design Staff. Alphabet Aa to Zz. Novit, Renee Z. (Kidz & Katz Educational Learning Book Ser.). 16p. (J). (gr. -1). pap. 7.95 *(978-1-883371-00-5(7))* Kidz & Katz Publishing Co.
Raasch, Peg. Reaching Your Goals: The Ultimate Teen Guide. Courtright, Anne. 2009. (It Happened to Me Ser.: 23). (ENG.). 298p. 50.00 *(978-0-8108-5572-4(0))* Scarecrow Pr., Inc.
Rabei, Carolina. Crunch! Rabei, Carolina. 2015. (Child's Play Library). (ENG.). 36p. (J). pap. ***(978-1-84643-732-8(6))*** Child's Play International Ltd.
Rabenau, Francesca von. Keka en el Museo de Arte de Ponce. Valldejuly, Frances Bragan. 2004. (SPA.). 60p. 21.95 *(978-1-56328-269-0(0))* Editorial Plaza Mayor, Inc.
Rabley, Stephen & Ursell, Martin. Red Rock/Roca Roja. Rabley, Stephen. 2009. (Let's Read! Bks.). (FRE & ENG.). 32p. (J). (gr. 3-7). pap. 4.99 *(978-0-7641-4360-1(3))* Barron's Educational Series, Inc.
Rabon, Elaine Hearn. Hattie & the Higgledy-Piggledy Hedge. Dolson, Carol Bland. 2012. (ENG.). 32p. (J). 18.95 *(978-0-9827614-4-1(9))* Miglior Pr.
—Tim & Sally's Beach Adventure. Thrasher, Grady. 2008. 48p. (J). (gr. -1-3). 18.95 *(978-1-58818-161-9(8))* Hill Street Pr., LLC.
—Tim & Sally's Vegetable Garden. Thrasher, Grady. 2007. 48p. (J). (gr. -1-3). lib. bdg. 18.95 *(978-1-58818-131-2(6))* Hill Street Pr., LLC.
—Tim & Sally's Year in Poems. Thrasher, Grady. 2010. 56p. (J). 18.95 *(978-0-9827614-0-3(6))* Miglior Pr.
Rabou, John. Look Inside the Bible - Life of Jesus, 1 vol. Dowley, Tim & Bewley, Robert. 2011. (Candle Discovery Ser.). (ENG.). 16p. (J). (gr. 2-4). 11.99 *(978-1-85985-823-3(6))*, Candle Bks.) Lion Hudson PLC GBR. Dist: Kregel Pubns.
Raboy, Mac. Adam Strange. Binder, Otto & Fox, Gardner. rev. ed. 2006. (Archives Ser.: Vol. 2). (ENG.). 228p. (YA). 49.99 *(978-1-4012-0780-9(4))* DC Comics.
Rachel, Drapkin. Puffs In: Christmas in Puffville. Joseph, Costa & Christopher, Romero. 2013. 46p. pap. 15.95 *(978-1-62882-016-4(0))* Keith Pubns., LLC.
Rachel Henson. The Angry Thunderstorm. Carol Henson Keesee. 2009. 40p. pap. 20.00 *(978-1-4389-4334-3(2))* AuthorHouse.
Racine, Victoria. The Absolute Truth about Lying. Lopez, Christopher P. 2011. 36p. pap. 24.95 *(978-1-4626-3245-9(9))* America Star Bks.
Rackham, Arthur. Aesop's Fables. Aesop. Jones, V. S. Vernon, tr. from GEC. 2003. (Barnes & Noble Classics Ser.). (ENG.). 304p. pap. 8.95 *(978-1-59308-062-4(X))* Barnes & Noble, Inc.
—Aesop's Fables. Jones, Vernon. 2007. 160p. (J). pap. 5.00 *(978-0-9788914-4-2(9))* Kahley, Glenn.
—The Cat & the Birds: And Other Fables by Aesop. Aesop. 2014. 72p. 12.00 *(978-0-7123-5722-7(X))* British Library, The GBR. Dist: Chicago Distribution Ctr.
—Cinderella. 2012. (Calla Editions Ser.). (ENG.). 112p. (gr. 4). 25.00 *(978-1-60660-029-0(X))* Dover Pubns., Inc.
—Cuentos de Andersen. Andersen, Hans Christian & Andersen. 2003. (SPA.). 240p. 24.95 *(978-84-261-0273-7(5))*, JV30115) Juventud, Editorial ESP. Dist: Lectorum Pubns., Inc., Distribooks, Inc.
—Cuentos de Grimm. Grimm, Jacob & Grimm. (Coleccion Cuentos Universales). (SPA.). 144p. (YA). (gr. 4-18). *(978-84-261-1098-5(3))*, JV30116) Juventud, Editorial ESP. Dist: Lectorum Pubns., Inc.
—Fairy Tales from Many Lands. Andersen, Hans Christian. 2014. (ENG.). 164p. (J). (gr. k-3). 22.99 *(978-1-4052-6741-0(0))* Egmont Bks., Ltd. GBR. Dist: Independent Pubs. Group.
—The Night Before Christmas. Moore, Clement C. 2012. 32p. pap. 5.99 *(978-1-61720-437-1(4))* Wilder Pubns., Corp.
—Poor Cecco. Bianco, Margery Williams. 2013. (ENG.). 168p. (J). (gr. 3-12). pap. 9.99 *(978-0-486-49226-1(5))* Dover Pubns., Inc.
—Sleeping Beauty. Evans, C. S. 2012. (ENG.). 104p. (J). 12.95 *(978-1-59583-457-7(5))*, Green Tiger Pr.) Laughing Elephant.
—The Wind in the Willows. Grahame, Kenneth. 2012. (ENG.). 264p. *(978-1-904919-51-3(0))*, Collector's Library, The) Pan Macmillan.
Rackham, Arthur & Bedford, F. D. The Complete Adventures of Peter Pan Includes: The Little White Bird, Peter Pan in Kensington Gardens(Illustrated) & Peter. Barrie, J. M. 2013. 326p. *(978-1-78139-361-1(3))* Benediction Classics.
Rackham, Arthur, jt. illus. see Bedford, Francis Donkin.
Racklin-Siegel, Alison. Jacob's Travels. 2005. (ENG & HEB.). 32p. (J). per. 10.95 *(978-0-939144-53-2(0))* EKS Publishing Co.
Racklin-Siegel, Carol. Lech Lecha: The Story of Abraham & Rebecca. 2004. (HEB & ENG.). 32p. (J). per. 10.95 *(978-0-939144-49-5(2))* EKS Publishing Co.
—Noah's Ark. 2003. 32p. (J). per. 10.95 *(978-0-939144-42-6(5))* EKS Publishing Co.
Racz, Michael. The Roman Colosseum: The Story of the World's Most Famous Stadium & Its Deadly Games. Mann, Elizabeth. 2006. (Wonders of the World Book Ser.). (ENG.). 48p. (J). (gr. 4-8). pap. 9.95 *(978-1-931414-17-3(3))*, 9781931414173) Mikaya Pr.
Radaviciute, Diana. Tambien Los Insectos Son Perfectos. Blanco, Alberto. 2005.Tr. of Insects Are Perfect, Too. (SPA.). (J). (gr. k-2). pap. 10.95 *(978-968-494-054-3(8))* Centro de Informacion y Desarrollo de la Comunicacion y la Literatura MEX. Dist: Iaconi, Mariuccia Bk. Imports.
Rader, Laura. The Best Smelling Christmas Book Ever: 9 Scents to Scratch & Sniff! Ziefert, Harriet. 2004. 18p. (J). (gr. k-4). reprint ed. 13.00 *(978-0-7567-7600-8(7))* DIANE Publishing Co.
—Run, Turkey, Run! Mayr, Diane. 2009. (ENG.). 32p. (J). (gr. -1-2). pap. 7.99 *(978-0-8027-8481-0(X))*, Bloomsbury USA Childrens) Bloomsbury USA.

Q

—Silly Pig. Linn, Margot. 2005. (I'm Going to Read(r) Ser.). (ENG.). 32p. (J). (gr. k-1). pap. 3.95 *(978-1-4027-2097-0(1))* Sterling Publishing Co., Inc.

—What to Expect at Preschool. Murkoff, Heidi. 2003. (What to Expect Kids Ser.). (ENG.). 24p. (J). (gr. -1-k). pap. 3.99 *(978-0-06-052920-8(2)*, HarperFestival) HarperCollins Pubs.

—What to Expect When Mommy's Having a Baby. Murkoff, Heidi. 2004. (What to Expect Kids Ser.). (ENG.). 24p. (J). (gr. -1-3). pap. 3.99 *(978-0-06-053802-6(3)*, HarperFestival) HarperCollins Pubs.

Rader, Laura. The Twelve Days of Christmas in California. Rader, Laura. 2009. (Twelve Days of Christmas in America Ser.). (ENG.). 32p. (J). (gr. k-3). 12.95 *(978-1-4027-6247-5(X))* Sterling Publishing Co., Inc.

—When Santa Lost His Ho! Ho! Ho! Rader, Laura. 2008. (ENG.). 40p. (J). (gr. -1-3). 14.99 *(978-0-06-114139-3(9))* HarperCollins Pubs.

Rader, Laura & Utt, Mary Ann. A Child's Story of Thanksgiving. 24p. (J). 7.95 *(978-0-8249-5327-0(4)*, Ideals Children's Bks.) Ideals Pubns.

Radford, Karen & Dreidemy, Joëlle. Storybook Homes. Bailey, Gerry. 2013. (ENG.). 32p. (J). *(978-0-7787-0288-7(X))*; pap. *(978-0-7787-0298-6(7))* Crabtree Publishing Co.

Radford, Karen & Noyes, Leighton. Armstrong's Moon Rock. Bailey, Gerry & Foster, Karen. 2008. (Stories of Great People Ser.). (ENG.). 40p. (J). (gr. 3-8). lib. bdg. *(978-0-7787-3684-4(9))*; (gr. 5-8). pap. *(978-0-7787-3706-3(3))* Crabtree Publishing Co.

—Cleopatra's Coin. Bailey, Gerry & Foster, Karen. 2008. (Stories of Great People Ser.). (ENG.). 40p. (J). (gr. 3-8). pap. *(978-0-7787-3707-0(1))*; lib. bdg. *(978-0-7787-3685-1(7))* Crabtree Publishing Co.

—Columbus's Chart. Bailey, Gerry & Foster, Karen. 2008. (Stories of Great People Ser.). (ENG.). 40p. (J). (gr. 3-8). pap. *(978-0-7787-3708-7(X))*; lib. bdg. *(978-0-7787-3686-8(5))* Crabtree Publishing Co.

—Leonardo's Pallete. Bailey, Gerry & Foster, Karen. 2008. (Stories of Great People Ser.). (ENG.). 40p. (J). (gr. 3-8). lib. bdg. *(978-0-7787-3687-5(3))* Crabtree Publishing Co.

—Marco Polo's Silk Purse. Bailey, Gerry & Foster, Karen. 2008. (Stories of Great People Ser.). (ENG.). 40p. (J). (gr. 3-8). pap. *(978-0-7787-3710-0(1))*; lib. bdg. *(978-0-7787-3688-2(1))* Crabtree Publishing Co.

—Martin Luther King Jr.'s Microphone. Bailey, Gerry & Foster, Karen. 2008. (Stories of Great People Ser.). (ENG.). 40p. (J). (gr. 3-8). pap. *(978-0-7787-3711-7(X))*; lib. bdg. *(978-0-7787-3689-9(X))* Crabtree Publishing Co.

—Mother Teresa's Alms Bowl. Ganeri, Anita. 2008. (Stories of Great People Ser.). (ENG.). 40p. (J). (gr. 3-8). pap. *(978-0-7787-3712-4(8))* Crabtree Publishing Co.

—Shakespeare's Quill. Bailey, Gerry & Foster, Karen. 2008. (Stories of Great People Ser.). (ENG.). 40p. (J). (gr. 3-7). lib. bdg. *(978-0-7787-3691-2(1))*; pap. *(978-0-7787-3713-1(6))* Crabtree Publishing Co.

—Sitting Bull's Tomahawk. Bailey, Gerry & Foster, Karen. 2008. (Stories of Great People Ser.). (ENG.). 40p. (J). (gr. 3-8). pap. *(978-0-7787-3714-8(4))*; lib. bdg. *(978-0-7787-3692-9(X))* Crabtree Publishing Co.

—The Wright Brothers' Glider. Bailey, Gerry & Foster, Karen. 2008. (Stories of Great People Ser.). (ENG.). 40p. (J). (gr. 3-8). pap. *(978-0-7787-3715-5(2))*; lib. bdg. *(978-0-7787-3693-6(8))* Crabtree Publishing Co.

Radford, Karen, jt. illus. see Noyes, Leighton.

Raditz, JoAnne. The Mud House Mystery: A Wild Bunch Adventure. Savageau, Tony. 2004. (J). pap. 9.95 *(978-0-9759737-0-7(3))* Blue Mustang Pr.

Radjev, Priya. Untangling the Ivy League. Zawel, Marc. Burns, Adam, ed. 2005. (College Prowler: Untangling the Ivy League Ser.). 567p. per. 24.95 *(978-1-59658-500-3(5))* College Prowler, Inc.

Radjou, Anna Nazaretz. A Book for Elie. Trooboff, Rhoda. 2008. (ENG.). 31p. pap. 15.00 *(978-0-9773536-1-3(3))* Tenley Circle Pr.

Radmanovic, Ljubica. Color Me Trendy. Radmanovic, Rada. 2010. 68p. pap. 14.99 *(978-1-4520-5795-8(8))* AuthorHouse.

Radtke, Becky. Catholic Corner: Puzzles & Activities: Year C, Ages 5-7. Lucey, Marcia T., ed. 2007. 67p. pap. 14.95 incl. cd-rom *(978-1-58459-362-1(8))* World Library Pubns.

—Four Square: The Personal Writing Coach, Grades 1-3. Burke, Mary F. 2005. 112p. (J). pap. 12.95 *(978-1-57310-446-3(9))* Teaching & Learning Co.

—Hey! There's Science in My Literature! Grades 1-2. Dunn, Justine. 2007. (Rigby Best Teachers Press Ser.). 96p. per. 13.99 *(978-1-4190-2848-9(0))* Houghton Mifflin Harcourt Supplemental Pubs.

—Hey! There's Social Studies in My Literature! Grades 1-2. Dunn, Justine. 2007. (Rigby Best Teachers Press Ser.). 96p. per. 13.99 *(978-1-4190-3400-8(6))* Houghton Mifflin Harcourt Supplemental Pubs.

Radtke, Becky J. Four Square: A Companion to the Four Square Writing Method: Writing in the Content Areas for Grades 1-4. Gould, Judith S. & Gould, Evan Jay. Mitchell, Judy, ed. 2004. 112p. (J). pap. 11.95 *(978-1-57310-421-0(3))* Teaching & Learning Co.

Radunsky, Vladimir. Advice to Little Girls. Twain, Mark. 2013. (ENG.). 24p. (gr. k). 14.95 *(978-1-59270-129-2(9))* Enchanted Lion Bks., LLC.

—Hip Hop Dog. Raschka, Chris. 2010. (ENG.). 32p. (J). (gr. -1-3). 16.99 *(978-0-06-123963-2(1))* HarperCollins Pubs.

—On a Beam of Light: A Story of Albert Einstein. Berne, Jennifer. 2013. (ENG.). 56p. (J). (gr. 1-4). 17.99 *(978-0-8118-7235-5(1))* Chronicle Bks. LLC.

Radunsky, Vladimir. What Does Peace Feel Like? Radunsky, Vladimir. 2004. (ENG.). 24p. (J). (gr. -1-3). 17.99 *(978-0-689-86676-0(3)*, Atheneum Bks. for Young Readers) Simon & Schuster Children's Publishing.

Radzinski, Kandy. I Is for Idea: An Inventions Alphabet. Schonberg, Marcia. (Science Ser.). (ENG.). (J). 2006. 40p. (gr. -1-3). pap. 7.95 *(978-1-58536-327-8(8))*; 2005. 48p. (gr. k-5). 16.95 *(978-1-58536-257-8(3))* Sleeping Bear Pr.

Radzinski, Kandy. What Cats Want for Christmas. Radzinski, Kandy. rev. ed. 2007. (ENG.). 32p. (J). (gr. k-6). 16.95 *(978-1-58536-340-7(5))* Sleeping Bear Pr.

—What Dogs Want for Christmas. Radzinski, Kandy. 2008. (ENG.). 32p. (J). (gr. k-6). 16.95 *(978-1-58536-363-6(4))* Sleeping Bear Pr.

—Where to Sleep. Radzinski, Kandy. 2009. (ENG.). 32p. (J). (gr. k-6). 15.95 *(978-1-58536-436-7(3))* Sleeping Bear Pr.

Rae, John. Reynard the Fox & Other Fables. Larned, W. T. & La Fontaine, Jean de. 2014. (ENG.). 96p. (J). (gr. 3-8). pap. 12.99 *(978-0-486-78197-6(6))* Dover Pubns., Inc.

Raff, Anna. Simple Machines: Wheels, Levers, & Pulleys. Adler, David A. 2015. (ENG.). 32p. (J). (gr. -1-3). 17.95 *(978-0-8234-3309-4(9))* Holiday Hse., Inc.

—Things That Float & Things That Don't. Adler, David A. (ENG.). 32p. (J). 2014. (gr. -1-2). 7.99 *(978-0-8234-3176-2(2))*; 2013. 16.95 *(978-0-8234-2862-5(1))* Holiday Hse., Inc.

—World Rat Day: Poems about Real Holidays You've Never Heard Of. Lewis, J. Patrick. 2013. (ENG.). 40p. (J). (gr. k-3). 15.99 *(978-0-7636-5402-3(7))* Candlewick Pr.

Raffaella, Ligi. My First Fairyland Book. Davidson, Susanna & Stowell, Louie. ed. 2012. (My First Book Ser.). 16p. (J). ring bd. 6.99 *(978-0-7945-3227-7(6)*, Usborne) EDC Publishing.

Raga, Silvia. Billy on the Ball. Harrison, Paul. 2010. 32p. pap. *(978-1-84089-634-3(5))* Zero to Ten, Ltd.

—The Birthday Surprise. Oliver, Jane. 2009. (Get Ready (Windmill Books) Ser.). 32p. (J). (gr. k-2). lib. bdg. 22.60 *(978-1-60754-257-5(9))* Windmill Bks.

—Molly Is New. Turpin, Nick. 2010. 32p. pap. *(978-1-84089-650-3(7))* Zero to Ten, Ltd.

—Mr. Bickle & the Ghost. Gurney, Stella. 2009. (Get Ready (Windmill Books) Ser.). 32p. (J). (gr. k-2). lib. bdg. 22.60 *(978-1-60754-260-5(9))* Windmill Bks.

Ragan, Jewel Coochie. Lost & Found. Ragan, Jewel Coochie. 2012. 46p. pap. 11.11 *(978-0-9853809-1-5(8))* Ragan, Jewel.

Ragawa, Marimo. Baby & Me. Ragawa, Marimo. (Baby & Me Ser.: 17). (ENG.). 2009. 184p. pap. 9.99 *(978-1-4215-2470-2(8))*; 2009. 192p. pap. 9.99 *(978-1-4215-2469-6(4))*; 2009. 200p. (gr. 8-18). pap. 8.99 *(978-1-4215-2468-9(6))*; Vol. 2. 2006. 208p. pap. 8.99 *(978-1-4215-0573-2(8))*; Vol. 14. 2009. 200p. pap. 8.99 *(978-1-4215-2467-2(8))* Viz Media.

Ragawa, Marimo & Marimo, Ragawa. Baby & Me, Vol. 5. Ragawa, Marimo & Marimo, Ragawa. Robertson, Ian, ed. 2007. (Baby & Me Ser.: 5). (ENG.). 192p. pap. 8.99 *(978-1-4215-1008-8(1))* Viz Media.

Ragel-Dial, Tasha, photos by. Say What?, a Photo Book of Inspirational Bible Verses for Kids - Featuring the Photography of Tasha Ragel-Dial. Ragel-Dial, Tasha. 2013. 24p. 22.95 *(978-1-61493-215-4(8))* Peppertree Pr., The.

Raghuraman, Savitri. Horace Leclaire & His Bottles of Air. Sundaram, Siddhartha & Raghuraman, Renuka S. 2008. 36p. pap. 9.99 *(978-1-935105-03-9(5))* Avid Readers Publishing Group.

Ragland, Teresa. God's Fig Tree. Kile, Joan. 2005. 32p. (J). pap. 7.95 *(978-1-57736-345-3(0))* Providence Hse Pubs.

—God's Fruit Tree. Kile, Joan. 2005. (Musty the Mustard Seed Ser.). 28p. (J). (gr. -1-4). per. 7.95 *(978-1-57736-344-6(2))* Providence Hse Pubs.

—God's Mustard Seed: Volume 1, Vol. 1. Kile, Joan. 2005. (Musty the Mustard Seed Ser.). 32p. (J). (gr. -1-3). per. 11.95 *(978-1-57736-342-2(6))* Providence Hse Pubs.

—God's Protecting Angels. Kile, Joan. 2005. (Musty the Mustard Seed Ser.). 28p. (J). (gr. -1-4). per. 7.95 *(978-1-57736-346-0(9))* Providence Hse Pubs.

—God's Rugged Cross. Kile, Joan. 2005. (Musty the Mustard Seed Ser.). 32p. (Orig.). (J). (gr. -1-3). per. 4.95 *(978-1-57736-343-9(4))* Providence Hse Pubs.

Raglin, Tim. The Elephant's Child: From the Just So Stories. Kipling, Rudyard. 2005. (Rabbit Ears: A Classic Tale Ser.). 42p. (gr. -1-3). 25.65 *(978-1-59679-343-9(0))* Spotlight.

—How the Camel Got His Hump. Kipling, Rudyard. 2005. (Rabbit Ears: A Classic Tale Ser.). 28p. (gr. 2-7). 25.65 *(978-1-59197-749-0(5))* Spotlight.

—How the Rhinoceros Got His Skin. Kipling, Rudyard. 2005. (Rabbit Ears: A Classic Tale Ser.). 28p. (gr. 2-7). 25.65 *(978-1-59197-750-6(9))* Spotlight.

—Pecos Bill. Gleeson, Brian. 2004. (Rabbit Ears-A Classic Tale Ser.). 36p. (gr. k-5). 25.65 *(978-1-59197-768-1(1))* Spotlight.

—The Sheep in Wolf's Clothing. Hartman, Bob. 2014. (ENG.). 28p. (J). (gr. k-2). 16.99 *(978-0-7459-6515-4(6))* Lion Hudson PLC GBR. Dist: Independent Pubs. Group.

—We Both Read Bilingual Edition-The Well-Mannered Monster/el Monstruo Debuenos Modales. Brown, Marcy & Haley, Dennis. ed. 2011. (ENG & SPA.). 44p. (J). pap. 5.99 *(978-1-60115-044-8(X))* Treasure Bay, Inc.

—We Both Read-the Well-Mannered Monster. Brown, Marcy & Haley, Dennis. 2006. (We Both Read Ser.). 40p. (J). (gr. -1-4). 7.99 *(978-1-891327-65-0(8))* Treasure Bay, Inc.

—We Both Read-The Well-Mannered Monster. Brown, Marcy & Haley, Dennis. 2006. (We Both Read Ser.). 44p. (J). (gr. -1-4). pap. 5.99 *(978-1-891327-66-7(6))* Treasure Bay, Inc.

—We Read Phonics-I Want to Be a Cowboy! McKay, Sindy. 2012. 32p. (J). 9.95 *(978-1-60115-351-7(1))*; pap. 4.99 *(978-1-60115-352-4(X))* Treasure Bay, Inc.

—The Well-Mannered Monster: Monstruo de Buenos Modales. Brown, Marcy et al. 2010. 41p. (J). *(978-1-60115-043-1(1))* Treasure Bay, Inc.

—The Wolf Who Cried Boy. Hartman, Bob. 2004. (ENG.). 32p. (J). (gr. k-3). pap. 6.99 *(978-0-14-240159-0(5)*, Puffin) Penguin Publishing Group.

—The Wolf Who Cried Boy. Hartman, Bob. 2004. (Picture Puffins Ser.). (gr. k-3). 17.00 *(978-0-7569-2950-3(4))* Perfection Learning Corp.

—The 13 Days of Halloween. Greene, Carol. 2009. (ENG.). 32p. (J). (gr. k-3). 14.99 *(978-1-4022-3096-7(6)*, Sourcebooks Jabberwocky) Sourcebooks, Inc.

Rahn, Jess. Meet Sneazle, 1. Hollis, Randy. 2004. 20p. (J). 6.95 *(978-0-9758815-0-7(7))* SNZ Publishing.

Raible, Alton. The Egypt Game. Snyder, Zilpha Keatley. (ENG.). (J). (gr. 3-7). 2009. 240p. pap. 7.99 *(978-1-4169-9051-2(8))*; 2007. 224p. 17.99 *(978-1-4169-6065-2(1))* Simon & Schuster Children's Publishing. (Atheneum Bks. for Young Readers).

—The Headless Cupid. Snyder, Zilpha Keatley. 2009. (Stanley Family Ser.). (ENG.). 224p. (J). (gr. 3-7). 16.99 *(978-1-4169-9532-6(3)*, Atheneum Bks. for Young Readers) Simon & Schuster Children's Publishing.

—The Witches of Worm. Snyder, Zilpha Keatley. 2009. (ENG.). (J). (gr. 3-7). 192p. 16.99 *(978-1-4169-9531-9(5))*; 208p. pap. 6.99 *(978-1-4169-9053-6(4))* Simon & Schuster Children's Publishing. (Atheneum Bks. for Young Readers).

Raichert, Lance. Treasury of Values for Children. 2012. 159p. (J). *(978-1-4508-3729-3(8))* Phoenix International Publications, Inc.

Raidt, Gerda. In the New World: A Family in Two Centuries. Holtei, Christa & Woofter, Susi. 2015. (ENG.). 40p. (J). (gr. k-3). lib. bdg. 17.95 *(978-1-58089-630-6(8))* Charlesbridge Publishing, Inc.

—Six Swans. Grimm, J. & W. & Brothers Grimm. 2014. (ENG.). 32p. (J). (gr. k-3). 17.95 *(978-0-7358-4172-7(1))* North-South Bks., Inc.

Railton, Fanny, jt. illus. see Sanborn, F. C.

Raimondi, Pablo. Full Throttle. Reilly, Matthew. 2006. (ENG.). 224p. (J). (gr. 5-9). pap. 10.99 *(978-1-4169-0228-7(7)*, Simon & Schuster/Paula Wiseman Bks.) Simon & Schuster/Paula Wiseman Bks.

RainboWindow. Leviticus, I Love You. RainboWindow. l.t. ed. 2009. (RainboWindow Ser.: Vol. 3). (ENG.). 32p. (J). 14.99 *(978-1-931552-03-5(7)*, 03-931552) Rocksand, LLC.

Raines, Morgan. Grizzer the Goofy Wolf. Raines, Kristy. 2007. (ENG.). 80p. per. 11.95 *(978-1-59594-132-9(0)*, Wingspan Pr.) WingSpan Publishing.

Rainey, Merrill. Frog. Frog? Frog! Understanding Sentence Types, 1 vol. Loewen, Nancy. 2013. (Language on the Loose Ser.). (ENG.). 24p. (gr. 2-4). 27.32 *(978-1-4048-8321-5(5))*; pap. 7.95 *(978-1-4795-1920-0(0))* Picture Window Bks.

Rainier, S. T. Curiosity Strikes: Ben & Elvis Adventures. Rainier, S. T. Page, J. 2011. 28p. (J). pap. 8.99 *(978-0-9829669-3-8(8))* Elv Enterprises.

Rainmaker Entertainment, jt. illus. see Rainmaker Entertainment Staff.

Rainmaker Entertainment Staff & Rainmaker Entertainment. Barbie & the Diamond Castle. Man-Kong, Mary. 2008. (Little Golden Book Ser.). (ENG.). 24p. (J). (gr. -1-2). 3.99 *(978-0-375-87508-3(5)*, Golden Bks.) Random Hse. Children's Bks.

Raiz, James, jt. illus. see Johnson, Drew.

Raizk, Leyla Marie. Happy Birthday, Ohio: Celebrating Ohio's Bicentennial 1803-2003, 1. Raizk, Mary Ann. 2003. 32p. (J). pap. 14.95 *(978-1-882203-97-0(6))* Orange Frazer Pr.

Rajagopalan, Ashok. The Runaway Peppercorn. Ramadurai, Suchitra. 2005. 28p. (J). *(978-81-8146-119-3(3))* Tulika Pubs.

Rajcak, Hélène. Small & Tall Tales of Extinct Animals. Laverdunt, Damien. 2012. (Gecko Press Titles Ser.). (ENG.). 80p. (gr. -1). 22.95 *(978-1-877579-06-6(8))* Gecko Pr. NZL. Dist: Lerner Publishing Group.

Rajic, Alex. The Alefbet Illuminated. Rajic, Alex. 2010. (ENG.). 56p. 0.00 *(978-0-615-38180-0(4))* Cenozoic Pr.

Rajvanshi, Ayush. Revenge of the Puppets. D'souza, Nadine. 2013. (ENG.). 32p. (J). (gr. -1). pap. 9.95 *(978-81-8190-197-2(5))* Karadi Tales Co. Pvt. Ltd. IND. Dist: Consortium Bk. Sales & Distribution.

Rakitin, Sarah. Little Hands Create! Art & Activities for Kids Ages 3 to 6. Dall, Mary Doerfler. (J). 2008. (ENG.). 20p. pap. 12.95 *(978-0-8249-8664-3(4))*; 2004. pap. 12.95 *(978-1-885593-65-8(1))* Ideals Pubns. (Williamson Bks.).

—Using Color in Your Art! Choosing Colors for Impact & Pizzazz. Henry, Sandi. 2005. (Kids Can Ser.). (ENG.). 128p. (J). (gr. 3-7). pap. 12.95 *(978-0-8249-6754-3(2)*, Williamson Bks.) Ideals Pubns.

—Using Color in Your Art! Chossing Colors for Impact & Pizzazz. Henry, Sandi. 2005. (Williamson Kids Can! Ser.). 128p. (J). (gr. 3-7). 14.95 *(978-0-8249-6772-7(0)*, Williamson Bks.) Ideals Pubns.

Rakola, Matthew, photos by. Try This! 50 Fun Experiments for the Mad Scientist in You. Young, Karen Romano. 2014. (ENG., 160p. (J). (gr. 5). pap. 16.99 *(978-1-4263-1711-8(5)*, National Geographic Children's Bks.) National Geographic Society.

Rakusin, Sudie. Savannah Blue's Activity Book/Libro de Actividades de Savannah Azul. Sforza, Daniella, ed. Spagnoli, Maria Eugenia, tr. 2005.Tr. of Libro de Actividades de Savannah Azul. (SPA & ENG.). 48p. (J). 10.95 *(978-0-9664805-4-2(6))* Winged Willow Pr.

Rakusin, Sudie. Dear Calla Roo... Love, Savannah Blue No. 2: A Letter about Getting Sick & Feeling Better. Rakusin, Sudie. 2003. 32p. (J). (gr. -1-4). 16.95 *(978-0-9664805-3-5(8))* Winged Willow Pr.

Rallis, Chris. Owls: Birds of the Night. Sollinger, Emily. 2014. (Penguin Young Readers, Level 3 Ser.). (ENG.). 48p. (J). (gr. 1-3). pap. 3.99 *(978-0-448-48135-7(9)*, Warne, Frederick Pubs.) Penguin Bks., Ltd. GBR. Dist: Penguin Random Hse., LLC.

Ralph, Karin. Mayda Saves the Day. Ryan, Mike. 2004. 60p. (J). (gr. 1-5). 14.95 *(978-0-9701319-3-5(3))* Temenos Pr.

Ralston, Peter, photos by. Island Journal: An Annual Publication of the Island Institute, 20. Platt, D. D. & Conkling, Philip, eds. 20th ed. 2003. (Island Journals: 20). 96p. pap. 9.95 *(978-0-942719-33-8(6))* Island Institute.

—Island Journal: An Annual Publication of the Island Institute, Vol. 21. annuals Platt, D. D., ed. 2005. (Island Journals: 21). 96p. pap. 16.95 *(978-0-942719-35-2(2))* Island Institute.

Ralte, Albert Lalmuanpuia. Adventures in Human Values - Series 4: Strength, Bravery, Gratitude, Acceptance, Discipline, Happiness, Cooperation, Hope, Self-Control. Nambiar, Vinesh. 2012. (J). pap. 9.99 *(978-0-9798986-3-1(3))* Human Values 4 Kids Foundation, The.

Raluca, Cristina Cirti. Good Girls Do. Hall, Tara. 2013. 36p. pap. 9.99 *(978-1-61286-192-0(X))* Avid Readers Publishing Group.

Ramá, Sue. It's Time for Preschool! Codell, Esmé Raji. 2012. 40p. (J). (gr. -1-k). (ENG.). 15.99 *(978-0-06-145518-6(0))*; lib. bdg. 16.89 *(978-0-06-145519-3(9))* HarperCollins Pubs. (Greenwillow Bks.).

Rama, Sue. Little Ones Talk with God: A Book of Prayers. Wangerin, Walter, Jr. et al. 2006. 56p. 7.49 *(978-0-7586-1132-1(3))* Concordia Publishing Hse.

—Subway Ride. Miller, Heather Lynn. 2011. (ENG.). 32p. (J). (gr. -1-3). pap. 7.95 *(978-1-58089-112-7(8))* Charlesbridge Publishing, Inc.

—Super Sam! Ries, Lori. 2007. (ENG.). 32p. (J). (gr. -1-k). pap. 6.95 *(978-1-58089-171-4(3))* Charlesbridge Publishing, Inc.

Ramá, Sue. Where Shabbat Lives. Fabiyi, Jan Goldin. 2008. (ENG.). 12p. (J). (gr. -1 — 1). bds. 5.95 *(978-0-8225-8946-4(X)*, Kar-Ben Publishing) Lerner Publishing Group.

Rama, Sue. Yum! Yuck! A Foldout Book of People Sounds. Park, Linda Sue & Durango, Julia. 2005. (ENG.). 36p. (J). (gr. -1-3). 9.95 *(978-1-57091-659-5(4))* Charlesbridge Publishing, Inc.

Ramaiah, Rajiv. I Don't Want to Be the Mom Today. Park, Laura. 2011. (ENG.). 30p. pap. 9.99 *(978-1-4609-5983-1(3))* CreateSpace Independent Publishing Platform.

Ramajo, Fernando, photos by. Postres 2. 2003. (Cocina para Todos Ser.). (SPA., 28p. *(978-958-30-1059-0(6))* Panamericana Editorial.

Ramaswamy, Maya. U Sier Lapalang: A Khasi Tale. 2005. (J). *(978-81-89020-31-6(5))* Katha.

—Walk the Rainforest with Niwupah. Datta, Aparajita & Manjrekar, Nima. 2004. (J). *(978-81-89020-15-6(3))* Katha.

Rambo, Angela. The Story of Rhu the Fairy. Plumier, Lea. 2012. 208p. pap. 11.95 *(978-1-61477-039-8(5))* Bellissima Publishing, LLC.

Ramel, Charlotte. There's a Pig in My Class! Thydell, Johanna & Martens, Helle. 2014. (ENG.). 32p. (J). (gr. -1-3). 16.95 *(978-0-8234-3168-7(1))* Holiday Hse., Inc.

Ramey, Cindy. Where Have All the Fairies Gone? Auxier, Bryan. l.t. ed. 2005. 24p. (J). pap. 7.95 *(978-0-9719144-3-8(5))* Where? Pr., Inc.

Ramirez, Alberto. Uno and the Raptor Pack: The Journey Begins! Blasing, George. 2007. (J). 4.95 *(978-0-9797304-1-2(4))* Raining Popcorn Media.

—Dinosaur George Prehistoric Safari: Raptor Island. Blasing, George. 2007. (J). 4.95 *(978-0-9797304-2-9(2))* Raining Popcorn Media.

Ramírez, Antonio & Morrissey, Kay, photos by. V antologia nuevo Milenio: Narración (Cuentos) y Poesía. Kassandra, ed. l.t. ed. 2004. (SPA., 100p. (YA). pap. 12.00 *(978-1-931481-86-1(5))* LiArt-Literature & Art.

Ramirez, Elizandro de los Angeles. Pin Pon. Batres, Ethel. 2010. (SPA.). 16p. (J). (gr. -1-1). pap. incl. audio compact disk *(978-99922-1-351-3(5))* Piedra Santa, Editorial.

Ramirez, Gamaliel. The Night We Almost Saw the Three Kings. 32p. (J). (gr. 1-18). 16.00 *(978-0-9710860-8-1(7))* Libros, Encouraging Cultural Literacy.

Ramirez, Herman. Stories of Mexico's Independence Days & Other Bilingual Children's Fables. Torres, Eliseo & Sawyer, Timothy L. 2005. (ENG & SPA.). 70p. (J). (gr. 3-7). pap. 15.95 *(978-0-8263-3886-0(0))* Univ. of New Mexico Pr.

Ramirez, Jose. Frog & His Friends Save Humanity/la Rana y Sus Amigos Salvan ALA Humanidad. Villaseñor, Victor. Ochoa, Edna, tr. 2005. (ENG & SPA.). 32p. (J). (gr. -1). 16.95 *(978-1-55885-429-1(0)*, Piñata Books) Arte Publico Pr.

—Goodnight, Papito Dios/Buenos Noches, Papito Dios. Villasenor, Victor. Villarroel, Carolina, tr. 2007. (SPA & ENG.). 32p. (J). (gr. -1-2). 16.95 *(978-1-55885-467-3(3)*, Piñata Books) Arte Publico Pr.

—Quinito's Neighborhood (El Vecindario de Quinito) Cumpiano, Ina. 2005. (ENG & SPA.). 24p. (J). (gr. -1-1). 16.95 *(978-0-89239-209-4(6))* Lee & Low Bks., Inc.

Ramirez, José. Quinito's Neighborhood (El Vecindario de Quinito) Cumpiano, Ina. 2013. (ENG & SPA.). 32p. (J). (gr. -1-3). pap. 9.95 *(978-0-89239-229-2(0))* Lee & Low Bks., Inc.

Ramirez, Orlando L. Captain Cheech. Marin, Cheech. 2008. 32p. (J). (gr. -1-3). lib. bdg. 17.89 *(978-0-06-113208-7(X))* HarperCollins Pubs.

—Cheech the School Bus Driver. Marin, Cheech. 2007. 32p. (J). (gr. -1-3). lib. bdg. 17.89 *(978-0-06-113202-5(0))* HarperCollins Pubs.

—Cheech y el Autobus Fantasma. Marin, Cheech. Fabiancic, Miriam, tr. 2009. (SPA.). 32p. (J). (gr. -1-3). 17.99 *(978-0-06-113214-8(4)*, Rayo) HarperCollins Pubs.

Ramirez, Samuel. Pancho the Green Parrot Lays an Egg, 1 vol. Sanchez, Juanita L. 2009. 24p. pap. 24.95 *(978-1-61546-150-9(7))* America Star Bks.

Ramos, Amy Jones. The Treasure Hunt Fish & Miss Bernadette's Wish. Martin, Brenda Darnley. 2009. 40p. pap. 14.95 *(978-0-9841074-1-4(X))* Jimsam Inc. Publishing.

Ramos, Beatriz Helena. Ack! Icky, Sticky, Gross Stuff Underground. Rosenberg, Pam. 2007. (Icky, Sticky, Gross-Out Bks.). (ENG.). 24p. (J). (gr. 3-6). 27.07 *(978-1-59296-900-5(3)*, 200353) Child's World, Inc., The.

—Eek! Icky, Sticky, Gross Stuff in Your Food. Rosenberg, Pam. 2007. (Icky, Sticky, Gross-Out Bks.). (ENG.). 24p. (J). (gr. 3-6). 27.07 *(978-1-59296-895-4(3)*, 200354) Child's World, Inc., The.

—Eew! Icky, Sticky, Gross Stuff in Your Body. Rosenberg, Pam. 2007. (Icky, Sticky, Gross-Out Bks.). (ENG.). 24p. (J). (gr. 3-6). 27.07 *(978-1-59296-894-7(5)*, 200355) Child's World, Inc., The.

—Ugh! Icky, Sticky, Gross Stuff in the Hospital. Rosenberg, Pam. 2007. (Icky, Sticky, Gross-Out Bks.). (ENG.). 24p. (J). (gr. 3-6). 27.07 *(978-1-59296-897-8(X)*, 200356) Child's World, Inc., The.

—Yecch! Icky, Sticky, Gross Stuff in Your House. Rosenberg, Pam. 2007. (Icky, Sticky, Gross-Out Bks.). (ENG.). 24p. (J). (gr. 3-6). 27.07 *(978-1-59296-898-5(8)*, 200357) Child's World, Inc., The.

—Yikes! Icky, Sticky, Gross Stuff Underwater. Rosenberg, Pam. 2007. (Icky, Sticky, Gross-Out Bks.). (ENG.). 24p. (J). (gr. 3-6). 27.07 *(978-1-59296-901-2(1)*, 200358) Child's World, Inc., The.

—Yuck! Icky, Sticky, Gross Stuff in Your Garden. Rosenberg, Pam. 2007. (Icky, Sticky, Gross-Out Bks.). (ENG.). 24p. (J). (gr. 3-6). 27.07 *(978-1-59296-896-1(1)*, 200359) Child's World, Inc., The.

Ramos, Humberto, et al. Captain America: To Serve & Protect. Waid, Mark. 2011. (ENG.). 192p. (J). (gr. 4-17). 24.99 *(978-0-7851-5082-4(X))* Marvel Worldwide, Inc.

Ramos, Humberto. Spider-Man: Big Time. Slott, Dan. 2011. (ENG.). 144p. (J). (gr. 4-17). pap. 14.99 *(978-0-7851-4624-7(5))* Marvel Worldwide, Inc.

Ramos, Humberto, et al. Spider-Man - Trouble on the Horizon. 2013. (ENG.). 112p. (J). (gr. 4-17). pap. 16.99 *(978-0-7851-6004-5(3))* Marvel Worldwide, Inc.

Ramos, Humberto, jt. illus. see Martin, Marcos.

Ramos, José. Echo & Narcissus. Sanderson, Jeannette & Benchmark Education Co., LLC. 2014. (Text Connections Ser.). (J). (gr. 3). *(978-1-4509-9668-6(X))* Benchmark Education Co.

—Opinions about Odysseus: A Greek Hero. Swain, Cynthia & Benchmark Education Co., LLC. 2014. (Text Connections Ser.). (J). (gr. 3). *(978-1-4509-9669-3(8))* Benchmark Education Co.

Ramos, Manuel Joao. The Boy Who Did Not Like Television. Zink, Rui. Dreher, Patrick, tr. from POR. 2004. (ENG.). 24p. (J). *(978-1-931561-96-9(6))* MacAdam/Cage Publishing, Inc.

Ramotar, Alexandra, jt. illus. see Ahmad, Maryam.

Rampley, Leigh, jt. illus. see Huffman, Jared.

Ramsey, Ann Louise. Me, the Tree. Ramsey, Ann Louise. 2006. (ENG.). 56p. (J). 19.95 *(978-0-9645663-4-7(6))* Crown Peak Publishing.

Ramsey, Jayne. Boomerang, the Farm Cat. Mustaine Hettinger, Cynthia. 2004. (Electra's Acres Ser.: 4). 32p. (J). per. 14.95 *(978-0-9746330-5-3(4))* Anton Berkshire Publishing.

—Casey the Confused Cow. Mustaine Hettinger, Cynthia. 2003. (Electra's Acres Ser.). 32p. (J). per. 14.95 *(978-0-9746330-1-5(1))* Anton Berkshire Publishing.

—Doc the Pygmy Goat. Mustaine Hettinger, Cynthia. 2003. (Electra's Acres Ser.). 32p. (J). per. 14.95 *(978-0-9746330-0-8(3))* Anton Berkshire Publishing.

—Penelope, the Busy Hen. Mustaine Hettinger, Cynthia. 2004. (Electra's Acres Ser.: Bk. 3). 32p. (J). per. 14.95 *(978-0-9746330-4-6(6))* Anton Berkshire Publishing.

—Travis, the Shetland Sheep. Mustaine Hettinger, Cynthia. 2004. (Electra's Acres Ser.: Bk. 5). 32p. (J). per. 14.95 *(978-0-9746330-6-0(2))* Anton Berkshire Publishing.

Ramsey, L. A. From Plowboy to Mormon Prophet Being a Short History of Joseph Smith for Children. Morton, William A. 2004. reprint ed. pap. 30.95 *(978-1-4179-6860-2(5))* Kessinger Publishing, LLC.

Ramsey, Marcy. Anyone Can Eat Squid!, 0 vols. Naylor, Phyllis Reynolds. 2009. (Simply Sarah Ser.: 0). (ENG.). 80p. (J). (gr. 2-5). pap. 9.99 *(978-0-7614-5540-0(X)*, 9780761455400, Amazon Children's Publishing) Amazon Publishing.

—Cuckoo Feathers, 0 vols. Naylor, Phyllis Reynolds. 2009. (Simply Sarah Ser.: 0). (ENG.). 96p. (J). (gr. 2-5). pap. 6.99 *(978-0-7614-5541-7(8)*, 9780761455417, Amazon Children's Publishing) Amazon Publishing.

—David & His Friend, Jonathan. Dietrich, Julie. 2005. (Arch Bks.). (ENG.). 16p. (J). 1.99 *(978-0-7586-0723-2(7))* Concordia Publishing Hse.

—Eating Enchiladas, 0 vols. Naylor, Phyllis Reynolds. 2011. (Simply Sarah Ser.: 0). (ENG.). 80p. (J). (gr. 1-4). pap. 6.99 *(978-0-7614-5885-2(9)*, 9780761458852, Amazon Children's Publishing) Amazon Publishing.

—Patches & Scratches, 0 vols. Naylor, Phyllis Reynolds. 2007. (Simply Sarah Ser.: 0). (ENG.). 80p. (J). (gr. 2-6). 14.99 *(978-0-7614-5347-5(4)*, 9780761453475, Amazon Children's Publishing) Amazon Publishing.

—Patches & Scratches, 0 vols. Naylor, Phyllis Reynolds. 2010. (Simply Sarah Ser.: 0). (ENG.). 80p. (J). (gr. 2-6). pap. 6.99 *(978-0-7614-5731-2(3)*, 9780761457312, Amazon Children's Publishing) Amazon Publishing.

Ramsey, Marcy Dunn. Beddy Bye in the Bay, 1 vol. Cummings, Priscilla. 2010. (ENG.). 32p. 14.99 *(978-0-7643-3450-4(6))* Schiffer Publishing, Ltd.

—Beetle Boddiker, 1 vol. Cummings, Priscilla. 2008. (ENG.). 30p. (J). (gr. k-7). 13.95 *(978-0-87033-602-7(9)*, Cornell Maritime Pr./Tidewater Pubs.) Schiffer Publishing, Ltd.

—Counties of Maryland's Lower Eastern Shore, 1 vol. Bunting, Elaine & D'Amario, Patricia. 2004. (Our Maryland Counties Ser.). (ENG.). 168p. (J). 19.95 *(978-0-87033-555-6(3)*, Cornell Maritime Pr./Tidewater Pubs.) Schiffer Publishing, Ltd.

—I Was Born to Be a Sister. Michels-Gualtieri, Akaela S. 2005. (ENG.). 32p. (J). (gr. 4-7). 9.95 *(978-1-930775-11-4(3))* Platypus Media, L.L.C.

—I Will Keep Trying! Parker, David. 2005. (J). pap. *(978-0-439-73588-9(2))* Scholastic, Inc.

—Mookey the Monkey Gets over Being Teased. Lonczak, Heather Suzanne. 2006. 32p. (J). (gr. -1-3). 14.95 *(978-1-59147-479-1(5))*; 9.95 *(978-1-59147-480-7(9))* American Psychological Assn. (Magination Pr.).

—Osprey Adventure. Curtis, Jennifer Keats. 2008. (ENG.). 32p. (J). (gr. 3-7). 13.95 *(978-0-87033-593-8(6)*, Cornell Maritime Pr./Tidewater Pubs.) Schiffer Publishing, Ltd.

—Santa Claws: The Christmas Crab. Cummings, Priscilla. 2006. 32p. (J). 10.50 *(978-0-87033-576-1(6)*, Cornell Maritime Pr./Tidewater Pubs.) Schiffer Publishing, Ltd.

—Saving Squeak: The Otter Tale, 1 vol. Curtis, Jennifer Keats. 2010. (ENG.). 32p. (J). 14.99 *(978-0-7643-3588-4(X))* Schiffer Publishing, Ltd.

—Secret of Belle Meadow, 1 vol. McVicker, Mary. 2004. (ENG.). 152p. (J). per. 9.95 *(978-0-87033-554-9(5)*, Cornell Maritime Pr./Tidewater Pubs.) Schiffer Publishing, Ltd.

Ramsey, Marcy Dunn & Liegey, Daniel. I Was Born to be a Brother/I Was Born to be a Sister. Michels-Gualtieri, Zaydek G. & Michels-Gualtieri, Akaela S. 2005. (ENG.). 32p. 34.95 *(978-1-930775-21-3(0))* Platypus Media, L.L.C.

Ramsey, Marshall. The Big Birthday Surprise: Junior Discovers Giving. Ramsey, Dave. 2003. 26p. (J). 7.95 *(978-0-9726323-2-4(8))* Lampo Licensing, LLC.

—Careless at the Carnival: Junior Discovers Spending. Ramsey, Dave. 2003. 26p. (J). 7.95 *(978-0-9726323-1-7(X))* Lampo Licensing, LLC.

—My Fantastic Fieldtrip: Junior Discovers Saving. Ramsey, Dave. 2003. 26p. (J). 7.95 *(978-0-9726323-3-1(6))* Lampo Licensing, LLC.

Ramstad, Ralph L. Science Fiction Pioneer: A Story about Jules Verne. Streissguth, Tom. 2003. (Creative Minds Biographies Ser.). (ENG.). 64p. (gr. 4-8). pap. 8.95 *(978-1-57505-623-4(2))* Lerner Publishing Group.

Ramstein, Anne-Margot, jt. illus. see Arégui, Matthias.

Ranchetti, Sebastiano. In the Arctic. Ottina, Laura. 2009. (Learn with Animals Ser.). (ENG.). 24p. (J). (gr. -1-2). pap. 8.15 *(978-1-4339-2088-2(3))*; lib. bdg. 22.00 *(978-1-4339-1911-4(7))* Stevens, Gareth Publishing LLLP. (Weekly Reader Leveled Readers).

—In the Forest. Ottina, Laura. 2009. (Learn with Animals Ser.). (ENG.). 24p. (J). (gr. -1-2). pap. 8.15 *(978-1-4339-2089-9(1))*; lib. bdg. 22.00 *(978-1-4339-1912-1(5))* Stevens, Gareth Publishing LLLP. (Weekly Reader Leveled Readers).

—In the Jungle. Ottina, Laura. 2009. (Learn with Animals Ser.). (ENG.). 24p. (J). (gr. -1-2). pap. 8.15 *(978-1-4339-2090-5(5))*; lib. bdg. 22.00 *(978-1-4339-1913-8(3))* Stevens, Gareth Publishing LLLP. (Weekly Reader Leveled Readers).

—In the Sea. Ottina, Laura. 2009. (Learn with Animals Ser.). (ENG.). 24p. (J). (gr. -1-2). pap. 8.15 *(978-1-4339-2091-2(3))*; lib. bdg. 22.00 *(978-1-4339-1914-5(1))* Stevens, Gareth Publishing LLLP. (Weekly Reader Leveled Readers).

—On the Farm. Ottina, Laura. 2009. (Learn with Animals Ser.). (ENG.). 24p. (J). (gr. -1-2). pap. 8.15 *(978-1-4339-2092-9(1))*; lib. bdg. 22.00 *(978-1-4339-1915-2(X))* Stevens, Gareth Publishing LLLP. (Weekly Reader Leveled Readers).

—On the Savanna. Ottina, Laura. 2009. (Learn with Animals Ser.). (ENG.). 24p. (J). (gr. -1-2). pap. 8.15 *(978-1-4339-2093-6(X))*; lib. bdg. 22.00 *(978-1-4339-1916-9(8))* Stevens, Gareth Publishing LLLP. (Weekly Reader Leveled Readers).

Rand, Colleen. Big Bunny. Rand, Colleen. Rand, Betseygail. 2011. (ENG.). 32p. (J). (gr. -1-2). 14.99 *(978-1-58246-376-6(X)*, Tricycle Pr.) Ten Speed Pr.

Rand, Paul. I Know a Lot of Things. Rand, Ann. 2009. (ENG.). 40p. (J). (gr. -1-1). 16.99 *(978-0-8118-6615-6(7))* Chronicle Bks. LLC.

Rand, Ted. Here Are My Hands. Archambault, John & Martin, Bill, Jr. 2007. (ENG.). 32p. (J). (gr. -1-k). pap. 25.95 *(978-0-8050-8119-0(4)*, Holt, Henry & Co. Bks. For Young Readers) Holt, Henry & Co.

—If Not for the Cat. Prelutsky, Jack. 2004. (ENG.). 40p. (J). (gr. -1-3). 17.99 *(978-0-06-059677-4(5)*, Greenwillow Bks.) HarperCollins Pubs.

Rand, Ted. Mailing May. Tunnell, Michael O. 2015. 32p. pap. 7.00 ***(978-1-61003-610-8(7))*** Center for the Collaborative Classroom.

Rand, Ted. Mountain Wedding. Gibbons, Faye. 2005. (ENG.). 32p. (J). (gr. k-2). pap. 8.95 *(978-1-59078-324-5(7))* Boyds Mills Pr.

—The Night Before Christmas. Moore, Clement C. 2014. (ENG.). 32p. (J). 17.95 *(978-0-7358-4106-2(3))* North-South Bks., Inc.

Rand, Tracy. The World According to August: One Good Friend. Westendorf, Sandra. 2011. *(978-0-9868424-0-5(0))* Purple Birch Publishing.

Randall, Emma. The Elf Boogie. Jones, Christianne C. 2015. (Holiday Jingles Ser.). (ENG.). 20p. (gr. -1 — 1). bds. 5.99 ***(978-1-4795-6493-4(1))*** Picture Window Bks.

—The Reindeer Dance. Jones, Christianne C. 2015. (Holiday Jingles Ser.). (ENG.). 20p. (gr. -1 — 1). bds. 5.99 ***(978-1-4795-6496-5(6))*** Picture Window Bks.

—The Santa Shimmy. Jones, Christianne C. 2015. (Holiday Jingles Ser.). (ENG.). 20p. (gr. -1 — 1). bds. 5.99 ***(978-1-4795-6494-1(X))*** Picture Window Bks.

—The Snowman Shuffle. Jones, Christianne C. 2015. (Holiday Jingles Ser.). (ENG.). 20p. (gr. -1 — 1). bds. 5.99 ***(978-1-4795-6495-8(8))*** Picture Window Bks.

Randall, Jack. The Old Lady of Wasilla Lake: A Story of the Red-necked Grebes of Wasilla Lake, Alaska. Randall, Jack. Mishler, Clark James, photos by. 2005. 48p. (YA). lib. bdg. 24.95 *(978-1-930580-81-7(9)*, Ulyssian Pubns.) Pine Orchard, Inc.

Randall, Lee Brandt. Texas State Bird Pageant. Michael, Todd. 2005. 32p. (J). (gr. -1-3). 16.95 *(978-1-893062-75-7(9))* Quail Ridge Pr., Inc.

Randall, Ron. Amaterasu: Return of the Sun. Storrie, Paul D. 2007. (Graphic Myths & Legends Ser.). (ENG.). 48p. (gr. 4-8). lib. bdg. 27.93 *(978-0-8225-5968-9(4))* Lerner Publishing Group.

—Amaterasu: Return of the Sun - A Japanese Myth. Storrie, Paul D. 2008. (Graphic Myths & Legends Ser.). (ENG.). 48p. (gr. 4-8). per. 8.95 *(978-0-8225-6573-4(0))* Lerner Publishing Group.

—The Amnesia Countdown. Oirich, Alan. 2003. (Jewish Hero Corps. Ser.: 1). 24p. (J). pap. 3.95 *(978-1-932443-06-6(1)*, JHC1, Shayach Comics) Judaica Pr., Inc., The.

—Beowulf: Monster Slayer. Storrie, Paul D. 2008. (Graphic Myths & Legends Ser.). (ENG.). 48p. (gr. 4-8). pap. 8.95 *(978-0-8225-8512-1(X))* Lerner Publishing Group.

—Guan Yu: Blood Brothers to the End [A Chinese Legend]. Jolley, Dan. 2009. (Graphic Myths & Legends Ser.). (ENG.). 48p. (gr. 4-8). pap. 8.95 *(978-1-58013-890-1(X))* Lerner Publishing Group.

—Psyche & Eros: The Lady & the Monster [A Greek Myth]. Croall, Marie P. 2009. (Graphic Myths & Legends Ser.). (ENG.). 48p. (gr. 4-8). pap. 8.95 *(978-1-58013-827-7(6))* Lerner Publishing Group.

—Thor & Loki: In the Land of Giants - A Norse Myth. Limke, Jeff. (Graphic Myths & Legends Ser.). (ENG.). 48p. (gr. 4-8). 2007. per. 8.95 *(978-0-8225-6481-2(5))*; 2006. 27.93 *(978-0-8225-3087-9(2))* Lerner Publishing Group.

—Tristan & Isolde: The Warrior & the Princess - A British Legend. Limke, Jeff. 2008. (Graphic Myths & Legends Ser.). (ENG.). 48p. (gr. 4-8). lib. bdg. 27.93 *(978-0-8225-7526-9(4)*, Graphic Universe) Lerner Publishing Group.

—Tristan & Isolde: The Warrior & the Princess [A British Legend]. Limke, Jeff. 2009. (Graphic Myths & Legends Ser.). (ENG.). 48p. (gr. 4-8). pap. 8.95 *(978-1-58013-889-5(6))* Lerner Publishing Group.

Randall, Ron, jt. illus. see Guinan, Paul.

Randazzo, Tony. Race Cars. Ikids Staff. 2009. (ENG.). 10p. (J). (gr. -1-1). 15.99 *(978-1-58476-939-2(4))* Innovative Kids.

Randles, Slim & Montoya, Jerry. Ol' Jimmy Dollar. 2015. (J). ***(978-1-936744-40-4(6))*** LPD Pr.

Randolph, Carolyn. Dinkey the Donkey. Phillips, Rachelle. Lt. ed. 2004. 24p. (J). 7.50 *(978-0-9748591-5-6(X)*, MSP) Main St Publishing, Inc.

Random House. All of My Friends! (Dora & Friends) Tillworth, Mary. 2015. (Friendship Box Ser.). (ENG.). 48p. (J). (-k). bds. 10.99 ***(978-0-553-52090-3(3)***, Random Hse. Bks. for Young Readers) Random Hse. Children's Bks.

Random House. Batter up!/¡a Batear!(SpongeBob SquarePants) Lewman, David & Gomez, Yuliana. 2014. (Pictureback Series.). (ENG.). 24p. (J). (gr. -1-2). 3.99 *(978-0-385-38436-0(X)*, Random Hse. Bks. for Young Readers) Random Hse. Children's Bks.

—Bear Hugs! (Julius Jr.) Posner-Sanchez, Andrea. 2014. (Bright & Early Board Books Ser.). (ENG.). 24p. (J). (-k). bds. 4.99 *(978-0-553-50863-5(6)*, Random Hse. Bks. for Young Readers) Random Hse. Children's Bks.

—Bedtime Explorers!/¡Exploradores a la Hora de Dormir! (Dora the Explorer) Gomez, Yuliana. 2014. (Pictureback Series.). (ENG.). 24p. (J). (gr. -1-2). 3.99 *(978-0-385-38410-0(6)*, Random Hse. Bks. for Young Readers) Random Hse. Children's Bks.

—Friend or Foe? (Teenage Mutant Ninja Turtles) Gilbert, Matthew. 2014. (Junior Novel Ser.). (ENG.). 128p. (J). (gr. 3-7). 5.99 *(978-0-385-38505-3(6)*, Random Hse. Bks. for Young Readers) Random Hse. Children's Bks.

—Frosty the Snowman Pictureback (Frosty the Snowman) Man-Kong, Mary. 2014. (Pictureback(R) Ser.). (ENG.). 24p. (J). (gr. -1-2). 3.99 *(978-0-385-38724-8(5)*, Random Hse. Bks. for Young Readers) Random Hse. Children's Bks.

—Here Comes Peter Cottontail Pictureback (Peter Cottontail) Man-Kong, Mary. 2015. (Pictureback Ser.). (ENG.). 16p. (J). (gr. -1-2). 4.99 *(978-0-553-50821-5(0)*, Random Hse. Bks. for Young Readers) Random Hse. Children's Bks.

—Merry Christmas, Pocoyo (Pocoyo) Depken, Kristen L. 2013. (Glitter Board Book Ser.). (ENG.). 12p. (J). (— 1). bds. 6.99 *(978-0-449-81903-6(5)*, Random Hse. Bks. for Young Readers) Random Hse. Children's Bks.

—Mr. Peabody & Sherman Junior Novelization (Mr. Peabody & Sherman) David, Erica. 2014. (Junior Novel Ser.). (ENG.). 128p. (J). (gr. 2-5). 5.99 *(978-0-385-37141-4(1)*, Random Hse. Bks. for Young Readers) Random Hse. Children's Bks.

—Mutant Mayhem! (Teenage Mutant Ninja Turtles) Gilbert, Matthew. 2014. (Junior Novel Ser.). (ENG.). 128p. (J). (gr. 3-7). 5.99 *(978-0-385-37433-0(X)*, Random Hse. Bks. for Young Readers) Random Hse. Children's Bks.

—Open the Door & Explore! (Julius Jr.) Depken, Kristen L. 2015. (Pictureback with Flaps Ser.). (ENG.). 16p. (J). (gr. -1-2). 4.99 *(978-0-553-51017-1(7)*, Random Hse. Bks. for Young Readers) Random Hse. Children's Bks.

—Show Me the Bunny! (SpongeBob SquarePants) Banks, Steven. 2014. (Step into Reading Ser.). (ENG.). 24p. (J). (gr. -1-1). 3.99 *(978-0-385-37608-2(1)*, Random Hse. Bks. for Young Readers) Random Hse. Children's Bks.

—Snow Day! (Frosty the Snowman) Carbone, Courtney. 2014. (Step into Reading Ser.). (ENG.). 32p. (J). (gr. -1-1). 3.99 *(978-0-385-38726-2(1)*, Random Hse. Bks. for Young Readers) Random Hse. Children's Bks.

—Soccer Start/Estrella de Futbol! (SpongeBob SquarePants) Lewman, David. Gomez, Yuliana, tr. 2014. (Pictureback Series.). (ENG.). 24p. (J). (gr. -1-2). 3.99 *(978-0-385-37929-6(3)*, Random Hse. Bks. for Young Readers) Random Hse. Children's Bks.

Random House. Sticker Hunt! (Julius Jr.) Homberg, Ruth. 2015. (Step into Reading Ser.). (ENG.). 24p. (J). (gr. -1-1). 4.99 ***(978-0-553-52475-8(5)***, Random Hse. Bks. for Young Readers) Random Hse. Children's Bks.

—Teenage Mutant Ninja Turtles Deluxe Step into Reading (Teenage Mutant Ninja Turtles) James, Hollis. 2015. (Step into Reading Ser.). (ENG.). 24p. (J). (gr. -1-1). 4.99 ***(978-0-553-52286-0(8)***, Random Hse. Bks. for Young Readers) Random Hse. Children's Bks.

Random House. UmiCar's Big Race/la Gran Carrera de UmiCar (Team Umizoomi) Gomez, Yuliana. 2014. (Pictureback Series.). (ENG.). 24p. (J). (gr. -1-2). 3.99 *(978-0-385-38437-7(8)*, Random Hse. Bks. for Young Readers) Random Hse. Children's Bks.

Random House. Wally's Best Friends. Depken, Kristen L. 2015. (Friendship Box Ser.). (ENG.). 48p. (J). (-k). bds. 10.99 ***(978-0-553-52311-9(2)***, Random Hse. Bks. for Young Readers) Random Hse. Children's Bks.

—Wild Predators (Wild Kratts) Kratt, Chris & Kratt, Martin. 2015. (Step into Reading Ser.). (ENG.). 32p. (J). (gr. -1-1). 3.99 ***(978-0-553-52472-7(0)***, Random Hse. Bks. for Young Readers) Random Hse. Children's Bks.

Random House. Wild Reptiles: Snakes, Crocodiles, Lizards, & Turtles (Wild Kratts) Kratt, Chris & Kratt, Martin. 2015. (Step into Reading Ser.). (ENG.). 32p. (J). (gr. k-4). 3.99 *(978-0-553-50775-1(3))*; lib. bdg. 12.99 *(978-0-553-50776-8(1))* Random Hse. Children's Bks. (Random Hse. Bks. for Young Readers).

Random House. Big Fish, Little Fish: a Book of Opposites (Bubble Guppies) Random House. 2015. (Bright & Early Board Books(TM) Ser.). (ENG.). 24p. (J). (-k). bds. 4.99 *(978-0-385-38442-1(4)*, Random Hse. Bks. for Young Readers) Random Hse. Children's Bks.

—Dora's Farm Rescue! (Dora the Explorer) Random House. 2014. (Super Deluxe Pictureback Ser.). (ENG.). 24p. (J). (gr. -1-2). 5.99 *(978-0-385-38516-9(1)*, Random Hse. Bks. for Young Readers) Random Hse. Children's Bks.

Random House. Epic Turtle Tales (Teenage Mutant Ninja Turtles) Random House. 2015. (Pictureback(R) Ser.). (ENG.). 96p. (J). (gr. -1-2). 9.99 ***(978-0-553-52471-0(2)***, Random Hse. Bks. for Young Readers) Random Hse. Children's Bks.

—Five Fin-Tastic Stories (Bubble Guppies) Random House. 2015. (Step into Reading Ser.). (ENG.). 144p. (J). (gr. -1-1). pap. 7.99 ***(978-0-553-52116-0(0)***, Random Hse. Bks. for Young Readers) Random Hse. Children's Bks.

Random House. Five Playtime Tales (Nick, Jr.) Random House. 2015. (Step into Reading Ser.). (ENG.). 160p. (J). (gr. -1-1). 7.99 *(978-0-553-50859-8(8)*, Random Hse. Bks. for Young Readers) Random Hse. Children's Bks.

—Five Undersea Stories (SpongeBob SquarePants) Random House. 2015. (Step into Reading Ser.). (ENG.). 160p. (J). (gr. -1-1). 7.99 *(978-0-553-50860-4(1)*, Random Hse. Bks. for Young Readers) Random Hse. Children's Bks.

—Funny-Side Up: A SpongeBob Joke Book. Random House. 2014. (Junior Novel Ser.). (ENG.). 128p. (J). (gr. 3-7). 5.99 *(978-0-385-37432-3(1)*, Random Hse. Bks. for Young Readers) Random Hse. Children's Bks.

—Here Comes Peter Cottontail. Random House. 2015. (Bright & Early Board Books Ser.). (ENG.). 24p. (J). (-k). bds. 4.99 *(978-0-553-50975-5(6)*, Random Hse. Bks. for Young Readers) Random Hse. Children's Bks.

—Hooray for Dads! (SpongeBob SquarePants) Random House. 2014. (Pictureback Series.). (ENG.). 24p. (J). (gr. -1-2). 4.99 *(978-0-385-37607-5(3)*, Random Hse. Bks. for Young Readers) Random Hse. Children's Bks.

—It's a SpongeBob Christmas! (SpongeBob SquarePants) Random House. 2013. (Pictureback Series.). (ENG.). 24p. (J). (gr. -1-2). 3.99 *(978-0-385-37856-7(4)*, Random Hse. Bks. for Young Readers) Random Hse. Children's Bks.

—Moms Are the Best! (SpongeBob SquarePants) Random House. Wilson, Sarah. 2014. (Step into Reading Ser.). (ENG.). 32p. (J). (gr. -1-1). 3.99 *(978-0-385-37499-6(2)*, Random Hse. Bks. for Young Readers) Random Hse. Children's Bks.

—The Mutant Files (Teenage Mutant Ninja Turtles) Random House. 2014. (Super Deluxe Pictureback Ser.). (ENG.). 24p. (J). (gr. -1-2). 5.99 *(978-0-385-38746-0(6)*, Random Hse. Bks. for Young Readers) Random Hse. Children's Bks.

Random House. The Park Is Open. Random House. Shealy, Dennis R. 2015. (Pictureback Ser.). (ENG.). 16p. (J). (gr. -1-2). 4.99 ***(978-0-553-53692-8(3)***, Random Hse. Bks. for Young Readers) Random Hse. Children's Bks.

—Patrol Pals (Paw Patrol) Random House. 2015. (Friendship Box Ser.). (ENG.). 48p. (J). (— 1). bds. 10.99 ***(978-0-553-50796-6(6)***, Random Hse. Bks. for Young Readers) Random Hse. Children's Bks.

Random House. Pups to the Rescue! (Paw Patrol) Random House. 2014. (Pictureback Ser.). (ENG.). 16p. (J). (gr. -1-1). 3.99 *(978-0-385-38444-5(0)*, Random Hse. Bks. for Young Readers) Random Hse. Children's Bks.

—SpongeBob's Slap Shot (SpongeBob SquarePants) Random House. 2014. (Pictureback Series.). (ENG.). 24p. (J). (gr. -1-2). 3.99 *(978-0-385-37852-9(1)*, Random Hse. Bks. for Young Readers) Random Hse. Children's Bks.

—Team Colors (Paw Patrol) Random House. 2015. (Big Bright & Early Board Book Ser.). (ENG.). 24p. (J). (— 1). bds. 6.99 *(978-0-553-49771-7(5)*, Random Hse. Bks. for Young Readers) Random Hse. Children's Bks.

—The Teenage Mutant Ninja Turtles Collection (Teenage Mutant Ninja Turtles) Random House. 2015. (Junior Novel Ser.). (ENG.). 384p. (J). (gr. 3-7). 9.99 *(978-0-553-50896-3(2)*, Random Hse. Bks. for Young Readers) Random Hse. Children's Bks.

—Teenage Mutant Ninja Turtles: Special Edition Movie Novelization (Teenage Mutant Ninja Turtles) Random House. David, Erica. 2014. (Junior Novel Ser.). (ENG.). 128p. (J). (gr. 3-7). 9.99 *(978-0-553-51110-9(6)*, Random Hse. Bks. for Young Readers) Random Hse. Children's Bks.

Random House & Golden Books Staff. To the Hall of Doors! Random House & Golden Books Staff. 2014. (Lift-The-Flap Ser.). (ENG.). 16p. (J). (-k). bds. 14.99 *(978-0-553-49855-4(X)*, Random Hse. Bks. for Young Readers) Random Hse. Children's Bks.

Random House & Miller, Victoria. Fairytale Magic (Dora the Explorer) Depken, Kristen L. 2014. (Step into Reading Ser.). (ENG.). 24p. (J). (gr. -1-1). 3.99 *(978-0-385-37503-0(4)*, Random Hse. Bks. for Young Readers) Random Hse. Children's Bks.

Random House & Song, Jennifer. Crayon Craze! (Julius Jr.) Tillworth, Mary. 2015. (Step into Reading Ser.). (ENG.). 24p. (J). (gr. -1-1). 4.99 *(978-0-553-50893-2(8)*, Random Hse. Bks. for Young Readers) Random Hse. Children's Bks.

—Howdy-Doodle-Doo! Tillworth, Mary. 2014. (Step into Reading Ser.). (ENG.). 24p. (J). (gr. -1-1). 4.99 *(978-0-553-49856-1(8)*, Random Hse. Bks. for Young Readers) Random Hse. Children's Bks.

Random House Audio Publishing Group Staff. Barbie: Thumbelina. Landolf, Diane Wright. 2009. (Step into Reading Ser.). (ENG.). 32p. (J). (gr. -1-1). pap. 3.99 *(978-0-375-85690-7(0)*, Random Hse. Bks. for Young Readers) Random Hse. Children's Bks.

Random House Beginners Books Staff & MJ Illustrations Staff. Dora Loves Boots (Dora the Explorer) Inches, Alison. 2013. (Pictureback Series.). (ENG.). 16p. (J). (gr. -1-2). 4.99 *(978-0-385-37345-6(7)*, Random Hse. Bks. for Young Readers) Random Hse. Children's Bks.

R

—Dump Truck Trouble/Let's Build a Doghouse! (Bubble Guppies) Tillworth, Mary. 2014. (Deluxe Pictureback Ser.). (ENG.). 32p. (J). (gr. -1-2). 4.99 *(978-0-385-37526-9(3),* Random Hse. Bks. for Young Readers) Random Hse. Children's Bks.

Random House Dictionary Staff & Aikins, Dave. You're Fired! (SpongeBob SquarePants) Random House Dictionary Staff. 2014. (Pictureback Series.). (ENG.). 24p. (J). (gr. -1-2). 3.99 *(978-0-385-37431-6(3),* Random Hse. Bks. for Young Readers) Random Hse. Children's Bks.

Random House Disney Staff. Beauty: Aurora's Sleepy Kitten. Redbank, Tennant. 2014. (Stepping Stone Book(TM) Ser.). (ENG.). 64p. (J). (gr. 2-5). 5.99 *(978-0-7364-3266-5(3),* RH/Disney) Random Hse. Children's Bks.

—The Christmas Party. Posner-Sanchez, Andrea. 2014. (Step into Reading Ser.). (ENG.). 24p. (J). (gr. -1-1). 4.99 *(978-0-7364-3279-5(5),* RH/Disney) Random Hse. Children's Bks.

—Firefighters! (Disney/Pixar Cars) Berrios, Frank. 2014. (Little Golden Book Ser.). (ENG.). 24p. (J). (-k). 3.99 *(978-0-7364-3169-9(1),* Golden/Disney) Random Hse. Children's Bks.

—Game On! Jordan, Apple & Amerikaner, Susan. 2012. (Step into Reading Ser.). (ENG.). 32p. (J). (gr. -1-1). pap. 3.99 *(978-0-7364-2889-7(5),* RH/Disney) Random Hse. Children's Bks.

—A Skipping Day (Disney Junior: Jake & the Neverland Pirates) Posner-Sanchez, Andrea. 2012. (Little Golden Book Ser.). (ENG.). 24p. (J). (gr. k-k). 3.99 *(978-0-7364-3029-6(6),* Golden/Disney) Random Hse. Children's Bks.

—A Tale of Two Sisters. Lagonegro, Melissa. 2013. (Step into Reading Ser.). (ENG.). 32p. (J). (gr. -1-1). 3.99 *(978-0-7364-3120-0(9),* RH/Disney) Random Hse. Children's Bks.

—To Protect & Serve. Berrios, Frank. 2015. (Step into Reading Ser.). (ENG.). 24p. (J). (gr. -1-1). 4.99 *(978-0-7364-3282-5(5),* RH/Disney) Random Hse. Children's Bks.

—Woody's White Christmas. Depken, Kristen L. 2010. (Pictureback(R) Ser.). (ENG.). 12p. (J). (gr. -1 — 1). bds. 6.99 *(978-0-7364-2682-4(5),* RH/Disney) Random Hse. Children's Bks.

Random House Disney Staff. Anna's Act of Love - Elsa's Icy Magic, 2 bks. in 1. Random House Disney Staff. 2013. (Pictureback(R) Ser.). (ENG.). 24p. (J). (gr. -1-2). 4.99 *(978-0-7364-3061-6(X),* RH/Disney) Random Hse. Children's Bks.

—Brave Firefighters (Disney Planes: Fire & Rescue) Random House Disney Staff. 2014. (Step into Reading Ser.). (ENG.). 32p. (J). (gr. -1-1). 3.99 *(978-0-7364-3240-5(X),* RH/Disney) Random Hse. Children's Bks.

—Frozen Little Golden Book (Disney Frozen) Random House Disney Staff. 2013. (Little Golden Book Ser.). (ENG.). 24p. (J). (-k). 3.99 *(978-0-7364-3051-7(2),* Golden/Disney) Random Hse. Children's Bks.

—Journey to the Ice Palace. Random House Disney Staff. 2013. (Jumbo Coloring Book Ser.). (ENG.). 224p. (J). (gr. -1-2). pap. 5.99 *(978-0-7364-3121-7(7),* Golden/Disney) Random Hse. Children's Bks.

—A New Reindeer Friend. Random House Disney Staff. 2014. (Big Golden Book Ser.). (ENG.). 32p. (J). (gr. -1-2). 9.99 *(978-0-7364-3295-5(7),* Golden/Disney) Random Hse. Children's Bks.

—Planes: Fire & Rescue Paper Airplane Book (Disney Planes Fire & Rescue) Random House Disney Staff. 2015. (Full-Color Activity Book with Stickers Ser.). (ENG.). 48p. (J). (gr. -1-2). pap. 4.99 *(978-0-7364-3124-8(1),* Golden/Disney) Random Hse. Children's Bks.

—The Power of a Princess, 6 bks. in 1. Random House Disney Staff. 2014. (Jumbo Coloring Book Ser.). (ENG.). 224p. (J). (gr. -1-2). pap. 5.99 *(978-0-7364-3162-0(4),* Golden/Disney) Random Hse. Children's Bks.

—Race Team. Random House Disney Staff. 2008. (Step into Reading Ser.). (ENG.). 32p. (J). (gr. k-3). pap. 3.99 *(978-0-7364-2571-1(3),* RH/Disney) Random Hse. Children's Bks.

—Snow Place Like Home. Random House Disney Staff. 2013. (Giant Coloring Book Ser.). (ENG.). 40p. (J). (gr. -1-2). pap. 9.99 *(978-0-7364-3117-0(9),* Golden/Disney) Random Hse. Children's Bks.

—Squiggles & Giggles (Disney/Pixar) Random House Disney Staff. 2011. (Deluxe Doodle Book Ser.). (ENG.). 256p. (J). (gr. -1-2). pap. 9.99 *(978-0-7364-2791-3(0),* Golden/Disney) Random Hse. Children's Bks.

—Sweet & Spunky. Random House Disney Staff. 2014. (Color Plus Chunky Crayons Ser.). (ENG.). 48p. (J). (gr. -1-2). pap. 3.99 *(978-0-7364-3154-5(3),* Golden/Disney) Random Hse. Children's Bks.

—Time to Shine! Random House Disney Staff. 2015. (Hologramatic Sticker Book Ser.). (ENG.). 64p. (J). (gr. -1-2). pap. 4.99 *(978-0-7364-3323-5(6),* Golden/Disney) Random Hse. Children's Bks.

—Wreck-It Ralph Little Golden Book (Disney Wreck-It Ralph) Random House Disney Staff. 2012. (Little Golden Book Ser.). (ENG.). 24p. (J). (gr. k-k). 3.99 *(978-0-7364-2972-6(7),* Golden/Disney) Random Hse. Children's Bks.

Random House Editors. Barbie in a Christmas Carol. Man-Kong, Mary. 2010. (Pictureback Ser.). (ENG.). 24p. (J). (gr. -1-2). pap. 3.99 *(978-0-375-86482-7(2),* Random Hse. Bks. for Young Readers) Random Hse. Children's Bks.

—Barbie in a Mermaid Tale. Webster, Christy. 2010. (Step into Reading Ser.). (ENG.). 32p. (J). (gr. -1-1). pap. 3.99 *(978-0-375-86450-6(4),* Random Hse. Bks. for Young Readers) Random Hse. Children's Bks.

Random House Editors, et al. Batman's Hero Files (DC Super Friends) Wrecks, Billy. 2015. (Step into Reading Ser.). (ENG.). 24p. (J). (gr. -1-1). 4.99 *(978-0-553-50808-6(3),* Random Hse. Bks. for Young Readers) Random Hse. Children's Bks.

Random House Editors. Fashion Fairytale. Man-Kong, Mary & Hashimoto, Meika. 2010. (Pictureback Ser.). (ENG.). 16p. (J). (gr. -1-2). pap. 3.99 *(978-0-375-86030-0(4),* Random Hse. Bks. for Young Readers) Random Hse. Children's Bks.

—A Friend at the Zoo/un Amigo en el Zoologico (Bubble Guppies) Tillworth, Mary. Gomez, Yuliana, tr. 2014. (Pictureback Series.). (ENG.). 24p. (J). (gr. -1-2). 3.99 *(978-0-385-37928-1(5),* Random Hse. Bks. for Young Readers) Random Hse. Children's Bks.

—Joker's Joyride - Built for Speed. Shealy, Dennis. 2010. (Deluxe Pictureback Ser.). (ENG.). 32p. (J). (gr. -1-2). pap. 4.99 *(978-0-375-85967-0(5),* Random Hse. Bks. for Young Readers) Random Hse. Children's Bks.

Random House Editors. Don't Be a Jerk, It's Christmas! Random House Editors. 2013. (Big Golden Book Ser.). (ENG.). 40p. (J). (gr. -1-2). 12.99 *(978-0-449-81766-7(0),* Golden Bks.) Random Hse. Children's Bks.

Random House Editors & Aikins, Dave. Food Fight! Carbone, Courtney. 2015. (Step into Reading Ser.). (ENG.). 24p. (J). (gr. -1-1). pap. 4.99 *(978-0-385-38773-6(3),* Random Hse. Bks. for Young Readers) Random Hse. Children's Bks.

—SpongeBob Movie Tie-In Deluxe Step into Reading (SpongeBob SquarePants) Carbone, Courtney. 2015. (Step into Reading Ser.). (ENG.). 24p. (J). (gr. -1-1). lib. bdg. 12.99 *(978-0-385-38774-3(1),* Random Hse. Bks. for Young Readers) Random Hse. Children's Bks.

Random House Editors & Disney Storybook Artists Staff. I Am Cinderella. Random House Editors & Posner-Sanchez, Andrea. 2011. (Shaped Board Book Ser.). (ENG.). 12p. (J). (— 1). bds. 4.99 *(978-0-7364-2769-2(4),* Golden/Disney) Random Hse. Children's Bks.

Random House Editors & Golden Books Staff. Nickelodeon Story Time Collection (Nickelodeon) Random House Editors. 2014. (ENG.). 320p. (J). (gr. -1-2). 15.99 *(978-0-385-38777-4(6),* Golden Bks.) Random Hse. Children's Bks.

Random House Editors & Random House Staff. I Can Be a Movie Star. Random House Editors & Random House Staff. 2010. (Pictureback Favorites Ser.). (ENG.). 80p. (J). (gr. -1-2). 7.99 *(978-0-375-86089-8(4),* Random Hse. Bks. for Young Readers) Random Hse. Children's Bks.

Random House Editors & Spaziante, Patrick. The Casey Chronicles (Teenage Mutant Ninja Turtles) Gilbert, Matthew. 2015. (Junior Novel Ser.). (ENG.). 128p. (J). (gr. 3-7). 5.99 *(978-0-553-50865-9(2),* Random Hse. Bks. for Young Readers) Random Hse. Children's Bks.

—Too Much Ooze! (Teenage Mutant Ninja Turtles) Random House Editors. 2015. (Step into Reading Ser.). (ENG.). 24p. (J). (gr. -1-1). 4.99 *(978-0-553-50866-6(0),* Random Hse. Bks. for Young Readers) Random Hse. Children's Bks.

Random House Editors & VanTuyle, David. Bath Party! Webster, Christy. 2015. (Step into Reading Ser.). (ENG.). 24p. (J). (gr. -1-1). pap. 4.99 *(978-0-385-38767-5(9),* Random Hse. Bks. for Young Readers) Random Hse. Children's Bks.

Random House Staff. Barbie: A Fairy Secret. Webster, Christy. 2011. (Step into Reading Ser.). (ENG.). 32p. (J). (gr. -1-1). pap. 3.99 *(978-0-375-86775-0(9),* Random Hse. Bks. for Young Readers) Random Hse. Children's Bks.

—Barbie - Princess & the Popstar. Trimble, Irene. 2012. (Junior Novel Ser.). (ENG.). 128p. (J). (gr. 3-7). 4.99 *(978-0-307-97626-0(2),* Random Hse. Bks. for Young Readers) Random Hse. Children's Bks.

—Barbie -Fairy Secret. Man-Kong, Mary. 2011. (Pictureback Ser.). (ENG.). 16p. (J). (gr. -1-2). pap. 3.99 *(978-0-375-86555-8(1),* Random Hse. Bks. for Young Readers) Random Hse. Children's Bks.

—Barbie & the Three Musketeers. Man-Kong, Mary. 2009. (Step into Reading Ser.). (ENG.). 32p. (J). (gr. -1-1). pap. 3.99 *(978-0-375-86007-2(X),* Random Hse. Bks. for Young Readers) Random Hse. Children's Bks.

—Barbie Fairytale Collection. 2011. (Step into Reading Ser.). (ENG.). 160p. (J). (gr. -1-1). pap. 7.99 *(978-0-375-87255-6(8),* Random Hse. Bks. for Young Readers) Random Hse. Children's Bks.

—Best Little Board Book Ever. Scarry, Richard. 2013. (ENG.). 24p. (J). (— 1). bds. 4.99 *(978-0-449-81901-2(9),* Random Hse. Bks. for Young Readers) Random Hse. Children's Bks.

—Beware the Shadow Phoenix (Winx Club) Bright, J. E. 2013. (Junior Novel Ser.). (ENG.). 128p. (J). (gr. 3-7). 4.99 *(978-0-449-81775-9(X),* Random Hse. Bks. for Young Readers) Random Hse. Children's Bks.

—Brain Freeze! Bright, J. E. 2010. (Step into Reading Ser.). (ENG.). 32p. (J). (gr. -1-1). pap. 3.99 *(978-0-375-86221-2(8))* Random Hse., Inc.

—Fairy Dreams. Man-Kong, Mary. 2013. (Step into Reading Ser.). (ENG.). 32p. (J). (gr. -1-1). 3.99 *(978-0-449-81628-8(1),* Random Hse. Bks. for Young Readers) Random Hse. Children's Bks.

—A Fairy-Tail Adventure. Man-Kong, Mary. 2012. (Pictureback Series.). (ENG.). 16p. (J). (gr. -1-2). pap. 3.99 *(978-0-307-92977-8(9),* Random Hse. Bks. for Young Readers) Random Hse. Children's Bks.

—Fairytale Favorites (Barbie) Man-Kong, Mary. 2012. (Pictureback Favorites Ser.). (ENG.). 80p. (J). (gr. -1-2). 7.99 *(978-0-307-93117-7(X),* Random Hse. Bks. for Young Readers) Random Hse. Children's Bks.

—Go, Go, Thomas! - Express Coming Through. Awdry, Wilbert V. 2013. (Deluxe Pictureback Ser.). (ENG.). 32p. (J). (gr. -1-2). pap. 4.99 *(978-0-307-98216-2(5),* Random Hse. Bks. for Young Readers) Random Hse. Children's Bks.

—Good Night, Pocoyo (Pocoyo) Depken, Kristen L. 2013. (Bright & Early Board Books Ser.). (ENG.). 24p. (J). (-k). bds. 4.99 *(978-0-307-98163-9(0),* Random Hse. Bks. for Young Readers) Random Hse. Children's Bks.

—Good Night, Thomas (Thomas & Friends) Awdry, Wilbert V. 2012. (Glow-In-the-Dark Board Book Ser.). (ENG.). 12p. (J). (gr. k-k). bds. 6.99 *(978-0-307-97697-0(1),* Random Hse. Bks. for Young Readers) Random Hse. Children's Bks.

—Green Lantern vs. the Meteor Monster! Wrecks, Billy. 2011. (Pictureback(R) Ser.). (ENG.). 24p. (J). (gr. -1-2). pap. 3.99 *(978-0-375-87297-6(3),* Random Hse. Bks. for Young Readers) Random Hse. Children's Bks.

—Here Come the Bubble Guppies! (Bubble Guppies) Tillworth, Mary. 2013. (Friendship Box Ser.). (ENG.). 48p. (J). (-k). bds. 10.99 *(978-0-449-81768-1(7),* Random Hse. Bks. for Young Readers) Random Hse. Children's Bks.

—Hero Story Collection (DC Super Friends) 2012. (Step into Reading Ser.). (ENG.). 160p. (J). (gr. -1-1). pap. 7.99 *(978-0-375-87298-3(1),* Random Hse. Bks. for Young Readers) Random Hse. Children's Bks.

—I Can Be... Story Collection (Barbie) 2013. (Step into Reading Ser.). (ENG.). 160p. (J). (gr. -1-2). 7.99 *(978-0-449-81666-0(4),* Random Hse. Bks. for Young Readers) Random Hse. Children's Bks.

—The Lost Crown of Sodor. Awdry, Wilbert V. 2013. (Pictureback Series.). (ENG.). 24p. (J). (gr. -1-2). 3.99 *(978-0-449-81533-5(1),* Random Hse. Bks. for Young Readers) Random Hse. Children's Bks.

—Monster Madness! (DC Super Friends) Wrecks, Billy. 2011. (Pictureback Ser.). (ENG.). 16p. (J). (gr. -1-2). pap. 3.99 *(978-0-375-87230-3(2),* Random Hse. Bks. for Young Readers) Random Hse. Children's Bks.

—Mutant Origin: Leonardo/Donatello (Teenage Mutant Ninja Turtles) Teitelbaum, Michael. 2012. (Junior Novel Ser.). (ENG.). 128p. (J). (gr. 3-7). 4.99 *(978-0-449-80993-8(5),* RH/Disney) Random Hse. Children's Bks.

—Mutant Origin: Michelangelo/Raphael (Teenage Mutant Ninja Turtles) Teitelbaum, Michael. 2012. (Junior Novel Ser.). (ENG.). 128p. (J). (gr. 3-7). 4.99 *(978-0-449-80994-5(3),* RH/Disney) Random Hse. Children's Bks.

—My Favorite Explorers (Dora the Explorer) Tillworth, Mary. 2013. (Friendship Box Ser.). (ENG.). 48p. (J). (-k). bds. 10.99 *(978-0-449-81763-6(6),* Random Hse. Bks. for Young Readers) Random Hse. Children's Bks.

—A Perfect Christmas. Webster, Christy. 2011. (Step into Reading Ser.). (ENG.). 32p. (J). (gr. -1-1). pap. 3.99 *(978-0-375-86932-7(8),* Random Hse. Bks. for Young Readers) Random Hse. Children's Bks.

—Pink Boots & Ponytails. Man-Kong, Mary & Inches, Alison. 2013. (Pictureback Series.). (ENG.). 16p. (J). (gr. -1-2). 3.99 *(978-0-449-81637-0(0),* Random Hse. Bks. for Young Readers) Random Hse. Children's Bks.

—Pocoyo & Friends (Pocoyo) Depken, Kristen L. 2013. (Friendship Box Ser.). (ENG.). 48p. (J). (— 1). bds. 10.99 *(978-0-449-81341-6(X),* Random Hse. Bks. for Young Readers) Random Hse. Children's Bks.

—Pocoyo Dance (Pocoyo) Depken, Kristen L. 2012. (Pictureback Ser.). (ENG.). 24p. (J). (gr. -1-2). pap. 3.99 *(978-0-307-98096-0(0),* Random Hse. Bks. for Young Readers) Random Hse. Children's Bks.

—The Power of Dragon Flame (Winx Club) Bright, J. E. 2013. (Junior Novel Ser.). (ENG.). 128p. (J). (gr. k-3). 4.99 *(978-0-307-98231-5(9),* Random Hse. Bks. for Young Readers) Random Hse. Children's Bks.

—Princess Charm School. Homberg, Ruth. 2011. (Step into Reading Ser.). (ENG.). 32p. (J). (gr. -1-1). pap. 3.99 *(978-0-375-86931-0(X),* Random Hse. Bks. for Young Readers) Random Hse. Children's Bks.

—Richard Scarry Mr. Paint Pig's ABC's. Scarry, Richard. 2013. (ENG.). 12p. (J). (-k). bds. 5.99 *(978-0-449-81902-9(7),* Random Hse. Bks. for Young Readers) Random Hse. Children's Bks.

—Risky Rails! (Thomas & Friends) Awdry, Wilbert V. 2012. (Pictureback Series.). (ENG.). 24p. (J). (gr. -1-2). pap. 3.99 *(978-0-307-97674-1(2),* Random Hse. Bks. for Young Readers) Random Hse. Children's Bks.

—Scooter Trouble (Pocoyo) Webster, Christy. 2013. (Step into Reading Ser.). (ENG.). 32p. (J). (gr. -1-1). 3.99 *(978-0-449-81541-0(2));* lib. bdg. 12.99 *(978-0-375-97167-9(X))* Random Hse. Children's Bks. (Random Hse. Bks. for Young Readers).

—Search & Rescue! (Thomas & Friends) Awdry, Wilbert V. 2012. (Pictureback with Flaps Ser.). (ENG.). 16p. (J). (gr. -1-2). pap. 4.99 *(978-0-307-93029-3(7),* Random Hse. Bks. for Young Readers) Random Hse. Children's Bks.

—Showdown with Shredder (Teenage Mutant Ninja Turtles) Gilbert, Matthew. 2013. (Junior Novel Ser.). (ENG.). 128p. (J). (gr. 3-7). 4.99 *(978-0-307-98225-4(4),* Random Hse. Bks. for Young Readers) Random Hse. Children's Bks.

—Star Power. Man-Kong, Mary. 2012. (Step into Reading Ser.). (ENG.). 32p. (J). (gr. -1-1). pap. 3.99 *(978-0-307-93196-2(X),* Random Hse. Bks. for Young Readers) Random Hse. Children's Bks.

—Super Friends: Going Bananas. Harper, Ben. 2009. (Step into Reading Ser.). (ENG.). 32p. (J). (gr. -1-1). pap. 3.99 *(978-0-375-85613-6(7),* Random Hse. Bks. for Young Readers) Random Hse. Children's Bks.

—The Super Friends Save Christmas/Race to the North Pole! Wrecks, Billy. 2012. (Deluxe Pictureback Ser.). (ENG.). 32p. (J). (gr. -1-2). pap. 4.99 *(978-0-307-97946-9(6),* Random Hse. Bks. for Young Readers) Random Hse. Children's Bks.

—The Super Friends Save Christmas/Race to the North Pole! Wrecks, Billy. ed. 2012. lib. bdg. 14.75 *(978-0-606-26790-8(5),* Turtleback) Turtleback Bks.

—Surf Princess. Eberly, Chelsea. 2012. (Step into Reading Ser.). (ENG.). 32p. (J). (gr. -1-1). pap. 3.99 *(978-0-307-93004-0(1),* Random Hse. Bks. for Young Readers) Random Hse. Children's Bks.

—Surprise for Pocoyo (Pocoyo) Webster, Christy. 2012. (Step into Reading Ser.). (ENG.). 32p. (J). (gr. -1-1). pap. 3.99 *(978-0-307-98099-1(5),* Random Hse. Bks. for Young Readers) Random Hse. Children's Bks.

—T. Rex Trouble! Wrecks, Billy. 2011. (Step into Reading Ser.). (ENG.). 32p. (J). (gr. -1-1). pap. 3.99 *(978-0-375-86777-4(5),* Random Hse. Bks. for Young Readers) Random Hse. Children's Bks.

—Thomas & Friends Puzzle Book. Awdry, W. & Berrios, Frank. 2010. (Puzzle Book Ser.). (ENG.). 10p. (J). (gr. -1-2). 8.99 *(978-0-375-86168-0(8),* Random Hse. Bks. for Young Readers) Random Hse. Children's Bks.

—Thomas' Big Book of Beginner Books. Awdry, W. 2013. (Beginner Books Ser.). (ENG.). 224p. (J). (gr. -1-1). 15.99 *(978-0-449-81643-1(5),* Random Hse. Bks. for Young Readers) Random Hse. Children's Bks.

—Thomas in Charge/Sodor's Steamworks. Awdry, Wilbert V. 2012. (Deluxe Pictureback Ser.). (ENG.). 32p. (J). (gr. -1-2). pap. 4.99 *(978-0-307-93119-1(6),* Random Hse. Bks. for Young Readers) Random Hse. Children's Bks.

—Thomas Looks up (Thomas & Friends) Awdry, Wilbert V. & Wrecks, Billy. 2012. (ENG.). 16p. (J). (gr. k-k). 7.99 *(978-0-307-93092-7(0),* Random Hse. Bks. for Young Readers) Random Hse. Children's Bks.

—Treasure on the Tracks. Awdry, W. 2013. (Step into Reading Ser.). (ENG.). 32p. (J). (gr. -1-1). lib. bdg. 12.99 *(978-0-375-97168-6(8),* Random Hse. Bks. for Young Readers) Random Hse. Children's Bks.

Random House Staff. Ballet Dreams. Random House Staff. 2013. (Step into Reading Ser.). (ENG.). 32p. (J). (gr. -1-1). pap. 3.99 *(978-0-307-98115-8(0),* Random Hse. Bks. for Young Readers) Random Hse. Children's Bks.

—Bikini Bottom Buddies (SpongeBob SquarePants) Random House Staff. 2013. (Friendship Box Ser.). (ENG.). 48p. (J). (— 1). bds. 10.99 *(978-0-449-81764-3(4),* Random Hse. Bks. for Young Readers) Random Hse. Children's Bks.

—Colors Everywhere! (Bubble Guppies) Random House Staff. 2013. (Bright & Early Board Books Ser.). (ENG.). 24p. (J). (-k). bds. 4.99 *(978-0-449-81782-7(2),* Random Hse. Bks. for Young Readers) Random Hse. Children's Bks.

—Count with Us! (Team Umizoomi) Random House Staff. 2013. (Bright & Early Board Books Ser.). (ENG.). 24p. (J). (-k). bds. 4.99 *(978-0-449-81877-0(2),* Random Hse. Bks. for Young Readers) Random Hse. Children's Bks.

—Dancing with the Star (SpongeBob SquarePants) Random House Staff. 2013. (Step into Reading Ser.). (ENG.). 32p. (J). (gr. -1-1). pap. 3.99 *(978-0-449-81438-3(6),* Random Hse. Bks. for Young Readers) Random Hse. Children's Bks.

Random House Staff. Danger - Dinosaurs! Random House Staff. Carbone, Courtney. 2015. (Step into Reading Ser.). (ENG.). 32p. (J). (gr. -1-1). 4.99 ***(978-0-553-53687-4(7));*** lib. bdg. 12.99 ***(978-0-553-53688-1(5))*** Random Hse. Children's Bks. (Random Hse. Bks. for Young Readers).

Random House Staff. Dora & the Unicorn King (Dora the Explorer) Random House Staff. 2013. (Step into Reading Ser.). (ENG.). 24p. (J). (gr. -1-1). pap. 3.99 *(978-0-449-81437-6(8),* Random Hse. Bks. for Young Readers) Random Hse. Children's Bks.

—Dora Goes to the Doctor/Dora Goes to the Dentist (Dora the Explorer) Random House Staff. Roper, Robert. 2013. (Deluxe Pictureback Ser.). (ENG.). 32p. (J). (gr. -1-2). 4.99 *(978-0-449-81771-1(7),* Random Hse. Bks. for Young Readers) Random Hse. Children's Bks.

—Dora Saves the Enchanted Forest/Dora Saves Crystal Kingdom (Dora the Explorer) Random House Staff. 2013. (Deluxe Pictureback Ser.). (ENG.). 32p. (J). (gr. -1-2). pap. 4.99 *(978-0-449-81450-5(5),* Random Hse. Bks. for Young Readers) Random Hse. Children's Bks.

—Dora's Big Birthday Adventure (Dora the Explorer) Random House Staff. 2013. (Pictureback Series.). (ENG.). 24p. (J). (-k). pap. 3.99 *(978-0-449-81445-1(9),* Random Hse. Bks. for Young Readers) Random Hse. Children's Bks.

—Dora's Easter Bunny Adventure (Dora the Explorer) Random House Staff. 2013. (Pictureback Series.). (ENG.). 16p. (J). (-k). pap. 3.99 *(978-0-449-81442-0(4),* Random Hse. Bks. for Young Readers) Random Hse. Children's Bks.

—The Great Train Mystery (SpongeBob SquarePants) Random House Staff. 2013. (Step into Reading Ser.). (ENG.). 32p. (J). (gr. -1-1). pap. 3.99 *(978-0-449-81441-3(6),* Random Hse. Bks. for Young Readers) Random Hse. Children's Bks.

—Happiness to Go! (SpongeBob SquarePants) Random House Staff. 2013. (Pictureback Ser.). (ENG.). 144p. (J). (gr. -1-2). 11.99 *(978-0-449-81479-6(3),* Random Hse. Bks. for Young Readers) Random Hse. Children's Bks.

—I Love Colors (Dora the Explorer) Random House Staff. 2013. (ENG.). 24p. (J). (-k). bds. 4.99 *(978-0-449-81481-9(5),* Random Hse. Bks. for Young Readers) Random Hse. Children's Bks.

—Meet the Fresh Beats! Random House Staff. 2013. (Pictureback Series.). (ENG.). 16p. (J). (gr. -1-2). pap. 3.99 *(978-0-449-81446-8(7),* Random Hse. Bks. for Young Readers) Random Hse. Children's Bks.

—The Mega-Justice Collection (SpongeBob SquarePants) Random House Staff. 2013. (Junior Novel Ser.). (ENG.). 304p. (J). (gr. 3-7). 7.99 *(978-0-449-81827-5(6),* Random Hse. Bks. for Young Readers) Random Hse. Children's Bks.

—Moms Are the Best! (SpongeBob SquarePants) Random House Staff. Wilson, Sarah. 2014. (Step into Reading Ser.). (ENG.). 32p. (J). (gr. -1-1). lib. bdg. 12.99 *(978-0-385-37500-9(X),* Random Hse. Bks. for Young Readers) Random Hse. Children's Bks.

—Railway Adventures. Random House Staff. 2010. (Step into Reading Ser.). (ENG.). 160p. (J). (gr. -1-1). pap. 7.99 *(978-0-375-86653-1(1),* Random Hse. Bks. for Young Readers) Random Hse. Children's Bks.

—Riddle Me This! Random House Staff. 2010. (Pictureback Ser.). (ENG.). 24p. (J). (gr. -1-2). pap. 3.99 *(978-0-375-84747-9(2),* Random Hse. Bks. for Young Readers) Random Hse. Children's Bks.

—SpongeBob's Easter Parade (SpongeBob SquarePants) Random House Staff. 2013. (Pictureback Series.). (ENG.). 24p. (J). (gr. -1-2). pap. 3.99 *(978-0-449-81444-4(0),* Random Hse. Bks. for Young Readers) Random Hse. Children's Bks.

—Surf's Up, Spongebob! - Runaway Roadtrip. Random House Staff. 2013. (Deluxe Pictureback Ser.). (ENG.). 32p. (J). (gr. k-3). 4.99 *(978-0-449-81849-7(7),* Random Hse. Bks. for Young Readers) Random Hse. Children's Bks.

—Swim, Boots, Swim! (Dora the Explorer) Random House Staff. 2013. (Pictureback Series.). (ENG.). 24p. (J). (gr. -1-2). 3.99 *(978-0-449-81850-3(0)*, Random Hse. Bks. for Young Readers) Random Hse. Children's Bks.

Random House Staff. T. Rex: Hunter or Scavenger? (Jurassic World) Random House Staff. Holtz, Thomas R. 2015. (Step into Reading Ser.). (ENG.). 48p. (J). (gr. 2-4). lib. bdg. 12.99 ***(978-1-101-93409-8(3)***, Random Hse. Bks. for Young Readers) Random Hse. Children's Bks.

Random House Staff. Team Power! (Team Umizoomi) Random House Staff. 2013. (3-D Pictureback Ser.). (ENG.). 16p. (J). (gr. -1-2). pap. 4.99 *(978-0-449-81448-2(3)*, Random Hse. Bks. for Young Readers) Random Hse. Children's Bks.

—Thomas & Friends: Percy's Chocolate Crunch & Other Thomas the Tank Engine Stories. Random House Staff. Mitton, David et al, photos by. 2003. (Pictureback Ser.). (ENG.). 32p. (J). (gr. -1-2). pap. 3.99 *(978-0-375-81392-4(6)*, Random Hse. Bks. for Young Readers) Random Hse. Children's Bks.

—Time for School! (Bubble Guppies) Random House Staff. 2013. (3-D Pictureback Ser.). (ENG.). 16p. (J). (gr. -1-2). pap. 4.99 *(978-0-449-81447-5(5)*, Random Hse. Bks. for Young Readers) Random Hse. Children's Bks.

—Traveling Tales. Random House Staff. 2010. (Pictureback Favorites Ser.). (ENG.). 80p. (J). (gr. -1-2). 7.99 *(978-0-375-86087-4(8)*, Random Hse. Bks. for Young Readers) Random Hse. Children's Bks.

—1, 2, 3 under the Sea (SpongeBob SquarePants) Random House Staff. 2013. (ENG.). 24p. (J). (-k). bds. 4.99 *(978-0-449-81480-2(7)*, Random Hse. Bks. for Young Readers) Random Hse. Children's Bks.

Random House Staff & Aikins, Dave. Haunted Houseboat (SpongeBob SquarePants) Random House Staff. 2013. (Pictureback Series.). (ENG.). 24p. (J). (gr. -1-2). 3.99 *(978-0-449-81759-9(8)*, Random Hse. Bks. for Young Readers) Random Hse. Children's Bks.

—I Love My Mami! (Dora the Explorer) Random House Staff. 2013. (Step into Reading Ser.). (ENG.). 24p. (J). (gr. -1-1). pap. 3.99 *(978-0-449-81439-0(4))*; lib. bdg. 12.99 *(978-0-375-97160-0(2))* Random Hse. Children's Bks. (Random Hse. Bks. for Young Readers).

Random House Staff & Aikins, David. UmiCar's Big Race (Team Umizoomi) Random House Staff. 2013. (Pictureback Ser.). (ENG.). 16p. (J). (gr. -1-2). pap. 3.99 *(978-0-449-81386-7(X)*, Random Hse. Bks. for Young Readers) Random Hse. Children's Bks.

Random House Staff & Jackson, Mike. The Best Doghouse Ever! Random House Staff. 2013. (Step into Reading Ser.). (ENG.). 24p. (J). (gr. -1-1). pap. 3.99 *(978-0-449-81388-1(6)*, Random Hse. Bks. for Young Readers) Random Hse. Children's Bks.

Random House Staff & Meurer, Caleb. Pest of the West. Random House Staff. 2013. (Pictureback Ser.). (ENG.). 16p. (J). (gr. -1-2). pap. 3.99 *(978-0-449-81443-7(2)*, Random Hse. Bks. for Young Readers) Random Hse. Children's Bks.

Random House Staff & MJ Illustrations Staff. The Puppy & the Ring (Bubble Guppies) Tillworth, Mary. 2014. (Pictureback(R) Ser.). (ENG.). 24p. (J). (gr. -1-2). 3.99 *(978-0-385-38408-7(4)*, Random Hse. Bks. for Young Readers) Random Hse. Children's Bks.

Random House Staff & Moore, Harry. Party Time! (SpongeBob SquarePants) Random House Staff. 2013. (Step into Reading Ser.). (ENG.). 32p. (J). (gr. -1-1). 3.99 *(978-0-449-81875-6(6)*, Random Hse. Bks. for Young Readers) Random Hse. Children's Bks.

Random House Staff & Nunn, Paul. A Friend at the Zoo (Bubble Guppies) Random House Staff. 2013. (Pictureback(R) Ser.). (ENG.). 16p. (J). (gr. -1-2). pap. 3.99 *(978-0-449-81389-8(4)*, Random Hse. Bks. for Young Readers) Random Hse. Children's Bks.

Random House Staff & O'Connell, Lorraine. Dog Days (Team Umizoomi) Random House Staff. 2013. (Step into Reading Ser.). (ENG.). 24p. (J). (gr. -1-2). pap. 3.99 *(978-0-449-81436-9(X)*, Random Hse. Bks. for Young Readers) Random Hse. Children's Bks.

Random House Staff & Petrossi, Fabrizio. Chase Is on the Case! (Paw Patrol) Random House Staff. 2014. (Step into Reading Ser.). (ENG.). 24p. (J). (gr. -1-1). 3.99 *(978-0-385-38447-6(5)*, Random Hse. Bks. for Young Readers) Random Hse. Children's Bks.

Random House Staff & Riley, Kellee. I Can Be a Ballerina. Webster, Christy. 2011. (Step into Reading Ser.). (ENG.). 32p. (J). (gr. -1-1). pap. 3.99 *(978-0-375-86839-9(9)*, Random Hse. Bks. for Young Readers) Random Hse. Children's Bks.

Random House Staff & Song, Jennifer. Costume Party! (Julius Jr.) Posner-Sanchez, Andrea. 2015. (Pictureback(R) Ser.). (ENG.). 16p. (J). (-k). 4.99 ***(978-0-553-52463-5(1)***, Random Hse. Bks. for Young Readers) Random Hse. Children's Bks.

Random House Staff & Spaziante, Patrick. Monkey Business (Teenage Mutant Ninja Turtles) Random House Staff. 2013. (Pictureback Series.). (ENG.). 16p. (J). (gr. -1-2). 3.99 *(978-0-449-81852-7(7)*, Random Hse. Bks. for Young Readers) Random Hse. Children's Bks.

—Robot Rampage! (Teenage Mutant Ninja Turtles) Random House Staff & Webster, Christy. 2013. (Step into Reading Ser.). (ENG.). 48p. (J). (gr. k-3). pap. 3.99 *(978-0-307-98212-4(2)*, Random Hse. Bks. for Young Readers) Random Hse. Children's Bks.

Random House Staff & Spaziante, Patrick. The T-Machine Turbo Guide (Teenage Mutant Ninja Turtles) Random House Staff. 2015. (Pictureback(R) Ser.). (ENG.). 16p. (J). (gr. -1-2). 4.99 ***(978-0-553-53867-0(5)***, Random Hse. Bks. for Young Readers) Random Hse. Children's Bks.

Random House Staff & Trover, Zachary. The Spring Chicken! (Bubble Guppies) Random House Staff. 2013. (Step into Reading Ser.). (ENG.). 24p. (J). (gr. -1-1). pap. 3.99 *(978-0-449-81440-6(8)*, Random Hse. Bks. for Young Readers) Random Hse. Children's Bks.

Random House Staff, jt. illus. see Golden Books Staff.

Random House Staff, jt. illus. see Random House Editors.

Random House Staff, jt. illus. see RH Disney Staff.

Random House Value Publishing Staff. Barbie - Fashion Fairytale. Man-Kong, Mary. 2010. (Step into Reading Ser.). (ENG.). 32p. (J). (gr. -1-1). pap. 3.99 *(978-0-375-86697-5(3)*, Random Hse. Bks. for Young Readers) Random Hse. Children's Bks.

Random House Value Publishing Staff, jt. illus. see Golden Books Staff.

Randoplh, Grace, jt. illus. see Secchi, Riccardo.

Rane, Walter & Hood, Philip. Kit's World: A Girl's-Eye View of the Great Depression. Brown, Harriet & Witowski, Teri. 2008. 30p. (YA). (gr. 3-18). 24.95 *(978-1-59369-459-3(8))* American Girl Publishing, Inc.

Rane, Walter & McAliley, Susan. Kit's Surprise. Tripp, Valerie. 2004. (American Girls Collection: Bk. 3). (ENG.). 71p. (gr. 2-18). 12.95 *(978-1-58485-021-2(3))* American Girl Publishing, Inc.

Raney, Tom, et al. The Infinity War. 2006. (ENG.). 400p. (J). (gr. 4-17). pap. 29.99 *(978-0-7851-2105-3(6))* Marvel Worldwide, Inc.

Raney, Tom & Bennett, Davis. Thor Vol. 3: Gods on Earth, 3 vols. Jurgens, Dan et al. 2003. (Thor Ser.). 248p. (YA). pap. 21.99 *(978-0-7851-1126-9(3))* Marvel Worldwide, Inc.

Rangel, Fernando. The Panama Canal: The Story of How a Jungle Was Conquered & the World Made Smaller. Mann, Elizabeth. 2006. (Wonders of the World Book Ser.). (ENG.). 48p. (J). (gr. 4-8). pap. 12.95 *(978-1-931414-14-2(9)*, 9781931414142) Mikaya Pr.

Rangel, Mario Hugo. Valores Morales y Buenos Hábitos — Rodríguez, Orlando A. (SPA.). 32p. (J). 2004. *(978-0-311-38596-6(6))*; 2004. *(978-0-311-38597-3(4))*; 2003. *(978-0-311-38595-9(8))* Baptist Spanish Publishing Hse./Casa Bavtista de Publicaciones: Mundo Hispano.

Rangel, Rawderson. The Very Best Toy. Rinker, Gary W. 2010. 28p. (J). (gr. -1). pap. 5.99 *(978-1-59188-881-9(6))* Maverick Bks., Inc.

Rangner, Mike K. The Seed & the Giant Saguaro. Ward, Jennifer. 2003. (ENG.). 32p. (J). (gr. -1-3). 15.95 *(978-0-87358-845-4(2))* Cooper Square Publishing Llc.

Rankin, Bruce H. Long-Lost Relatives. Ivanoff, George. 2004. iv, 36p. (J). pap. *(978-0-7608-6740-2(2))* Sundance/Newbridge Educational Publishing.

Rankin, Joan. Finding Aunt Joan. Hatton, Jenny. 2012. (Lucy Bks.). (ENG.). 32p. (J). (gr. k-2). pap. 6.95 *(978-1-77009-803-9(8))* Jacana Media ZAF. Dist: Independent Pubs. Group.

—A Frog in the Bog. Wilson, Karma. (ENG.). 32p. (J). (gr. -1-3). 2007. pap. 7.99 *(978-1-4169-2727-3(1))*; 2003. 17.99 *(978-0-689-84081-4(0))* McElderry, Margaret K. Bks. (McElderry, Margaret K. Bks.).

—Moving House. Hatton, Jenny. 2012. (Lucy Bks.). (ENG.). 32p. (J). (gr. -1-k). pap. 6.95 *(978-1-4314-0217-5(6))* Jacana Media ZAF. Dist: Independent Pubs. Group.

—Swimming in the Sun. Hatton, Jenny. 2012. (Lucy Bks.). (ENG.). 32p. (J). (gr. -1-k). pap. 6.95 *(978-1-4314-0218-2(4))* Jacana Media ZAF. Dist: Independent Pubs. Group.

—Who's Afraid of the Dark? Stewart, Dianne. 2012. (ENG.). 24p. (J). (gr. k-2). pap. 6.95 *(978-1-4314-0118-5(8))* Jacana Media ZAF. Dist: Independent Pubs. Group.

Rankin, Joan, jt. illus. see Rankin, Joan E.

Rankin, Joan E. A Whiff of Pine, a Hint of Skunk: A Forest of Poems. Ruddell, Deborah. 2009. (ENG.). 40p. (J). (gr. -1-3). 16.99 *(978-1-4169-4211-5(4)*, McElderry, Margaret K. Bks.) McElderry, Margaret K. Bks.

Rankin, Joan E. First Day. Rankin, Joan E. 2007. (ENG.). 32p. (J). (gr. -1-2). 10.99 *(978-1-4169-6848-1(2)*, Simon & Schuster/Paula Wiseman Bks.) Simon & Schuster/Paula Wiseman Bks.

Rankin, Joan E. & Rankin, Joan. Mrs. McTats & Her Houseful of Cats. Capucilli, Alyssa Satin. 2004. (ENG.). 32p. (J). (gr. -1-3). 7.99 *(978-0-689-86991-4(6)*, Simon & Schuster/Paula Wiseman Bks.) Simon & Schuster/Paula Wiseman Bks.

—Today at the Bluebird Café: A Branchful of Birds. Ruddell, Deborah. 2007. (ENG.). 40p. (J). (gr. k-5). 17.99 *(978-0-689-87153-5(8)*, McElderry, Margaret K. Bks.) McElderry, Margaret K. Bks.

Rankin, Kim. Cut & Create! Ocean Life. Tucker, Mary. Mitchell, Judy & Lindeen, Mary, eds. 2007. 80p. (J). pap. 9.95 *(978-1-57310-526-2(0))* Teaching & Learning Co.

—Cut & Create! Spring & Summer. Tucker, Mary. Mitchell, Judy & Lindeen, Mary, eds. 2007. 80p. (J). pap. 9.95 *(978-1-57310-535-4(X))* Teaching & Learning Co.

Rankin, Laura. A Balloon for Isabel. Underwood, Deborah. 2010. (ENG.). 32p. (J). (gr. -1-2). 16.99 *(978-0-06-177987-9(3)*, Greenwillow Bks.) HarperCollins Pubs.

—The Cowgirl Aunt of Harriet Bean. McCall Smith, Alexander. 2006. (Harriet Bean Ser.). (ENG.). 80p. (J). (gr. 2-4). lib. bdg. 9.95 *(978-1-58234-977-0(0)*, Bloomsbury USA Childrens) Bloomsbury USA.

—How to Drive Your Sister Crazy. Shore, Diane Z. (I Can Read Book 2 Ser.). (ENG.). 48p. (J). (gr. k-3). 2012. pap. 3.99 *(978-0-06-052764-8(1))*; 2008. 16.99 *(978-0-06-052762-4(5))* HarperCollins Pubs.

—How to Drive Your Sister Crazy. Shore, Diane Z. ed. 2012. (I Can Read! Level 2 Ser.). lib. bdg. 13.55 *(978-0-606-26869-1(3)*, Turtleback) Turtleback Bks.

—Rabbit Ears. Stewart, Amber. 2006. (ENG.). 32p. (J). (gr. -1-3). 16.95 *(978-1-58234-959-6(2)*, Bloomsbury USA Childrens) Bloomsbury USA.

—Tiptoe Joe. Gibson, Ginger Foglesong. 2013. (ENG.). 32p. (J). (gr. -1-k). 17.99 *(978-0-06-177203-0(8)*, Greenwillow Bks.) HarperCollins Pubs.

Rankin, Laura. Rabbit Ears. Rankin, Laura. Stewart, Amber. 2012. (ENG.). 32p. (J). (gr. -1-1). pap. 8.99 *(978-1-59990-740-6(2)*, Bloomsbury USA Childrens) Bloomsbury USA.

—Ruthie & the (Not So) Teeny Tiny Lie. Rankin, Laura. 2007. (ENG.). 32p. (J). (gr. -1-3). 17.99 *(978-1-59990-010-0(6)*, Bloomsbury USA Childrens) Bloomsbury USA.

—Ruthie & the (Not So) Very Busy Day. Rankin, Laura. 2014. (ENG.). 32p. (J). (gr. -1-1). 17.99 *(978-1-59990-052-0(1)*, Bloomsbury USA Childrens) Bloomsbury USA.

Rankin, Peter. Making Room. Taylor, Joanne. 2004. (ENG.). 24p. (J). (gr. 1-4). 15.95 *(978-0-88776-651-0(X)*, Tundra Bks.) Tundra Bks. CAN. Dist: Penguin Random Hse., LLC.

Rankin, Shelly. Amelia & Gabby: More Than Just Sisters. Marino, Lia. 2005. 31p. (J). 18.95 *(978-1-886057-30-2(3))* Warren Publishing, Inc.

Ransome, Arthur. Swallowdale. Ransome, Arthur. 2010. (Swallows & Amazons Ser.). 431p. (YA). pap. 14.95 *(978-1-56792-421-3(2))* Godine, David R. Pub.

—Swallows & Amazons. Ransome, Arthur. 2010. (Swallows & Amazons Ser.). 351p. (J). pap. 14.95 *(978-1-56792-420-6(4))* Godine, David R. Pub.

Ransome, James. Aunt Flossie's Hats (and Crab Cakes Later) Howard, Elizabeth Fitzgerald. 2015. 32p. pap. 8.00 ***(978-1-61003-491-3(0))*** Center for the Collaborative Classroom.

Ransome, James. Granddaddy's Turn. Bandy, Michael S. & Stein, Eric. 2015. (ENG.). 32p. (J). (gr. 1-4). 16.99 *(978-0-7636-6593-7(2))* Candlewick Pr.

Ransome, James. Just a Lucky So-And-So: The Story of Louis Armstrong. Cline-Ransome, Lesa. 2015. (J). ***(978-0-8234-3428-2(1))*** Holiday Hse., Inc.

Ransome, James. My Name Is Truth: The Life of Sojourner Truth. Turner, Ann. 2015. 40p. (J). (gr. 1-5). (ENG.). 17.99 *(978-0-06-075898-1(8))*; lib. bdg. 18.89 *(978-0-06-075899-8(6))* HarperCollins Pubs.

—This Is the Rope: A Story from the Great Migration. Woodson, Jacqueline. 2013. (ENG.). 32p. (J). (gr. k-3). 16.99 *(978-0-399-23986-1(3)*, Nancy Paulsen Bks.) Penguin Publishing Group.

—Uncle Jed's Barbershop. Mitchell, Margaree King. 2014. 40p. pap. 8.00 *(978-1-61003-368-8(X))* Center for the Collaborative Classroom.

Ransome, James. Visiting Day. Woodson, Jacqueline. 2015. (ENG.). 32p. (J). (gr. k-2). 8.99 ***(978-0-14-751608-4(0)***, Puffin) Penguin Publishing Group.

Ransome, James E. Baby Blessings: A Prayer for the Day You Are Born. Jordan, Deloris. 2010. (ENG.). 32p. (J). 16.99 *(978-1-4169-5362-3(0)*, Simon & Schuster/Paula Wiseman Bks.) Simon & Schuster/Paula Wiseman Bks.

—Benny Goodman & Teddy Wilson: Taking the Stage as the First Black & White Jazz Band in History. Cline-Ransome, Lesa. 2014. (ENG.). 32p. (J). (gr. 3-7). 16.95 *(978-0-8234-2362-0(X))* Holiday Hse., Inc.

—The Christmas Tugboat: How the Rockefeller Center Christmas Tree Came to New York City. Matteson, George & Ursone, Adele. 2012. (ENG.). 48p. (J). (gr. -1-3). 17.99 *(978-0-618-99215-7(4))* Houghton Mifflin Harcourt Publishing Co.

—Freedom Roads: Searching for the Underground Railroad. Hansen, Joyce & McGowan, Gary. 2003. (ENG.). 166p. (J). (gr. 5-9). 18.95 *(978-0-8126-2673-5(7))* Cricket Bks.

—Freedom's School. Cline-Ransome, Lesa. 2015. (ENG.). 32p. (J). (gr. 1-3). 17.99 *(978-1-4231-6103-5(3)*, Jump at the Sun) Hyperion Bks. for Children.

—Helen Keller: The World in Her Heart. Cline-Ransome, Lesa. 2008. 32p. (J). (gr. k-4). lib. bdg. 17.89 *(978-0-06-057075-0(X)*, Collins) HarperCollins Pubs.

—It Is the Wind. Wolff, Ferida. Date not set. (ENG.). 32p. (J). (gr. -1-1). pap. 5.99 *(978-0-06-443530-7(X))* HarperCollins Pubs.

—Light in the Darkness: A Story about How Slaves Learned in Secret. Cline-Ransome, Lesa. 2013. (ENG.). 40p. (J). (gr. k-3). 16.99 *(978-1-4231-3495-4(8)*, Jump at the Sun) Hyperion Bks. for Children.

—Major Taylor, Champion Cyclist. Cline-Ransome, Lesa. 2004. (ENG.). 40p. (J). (gr. 1-5). 18.99 *(978-0-689-83159-1(5)*, Atheneum Bks. for Young Readers) Simon & Schuster Children's Publishing.

—Quilt Alphabet. Cline-Ransome, Lesa. 2005. (ENG.). 48p. (J). (gr. k-3). pap. 8.95 *(978-0-8234-1765-0(4))* Holiday Hse., Inc.

—Satchel Paige. Cline-Ransome, Lesa. 2004. 31p. (J). (gr. k-4). reprint ed. pap. 7.00 *(978-0-7567-7799-9(2))* DIANE Publishing Co.

—Satchel Paige. Cline-Ransome, Lesa. 2003. (ENG.). 40p. (J). (gr. 1-5). 7.99 *(978-0-689-85681-5(4)*, Simon & Schuster/Paula Wiseman Bks.) Simon & Schuster/Paula Wiseman Bks.

—Sky Boys: How They Built the Empire State Building. Hopkinson, Deborah. 2012. (ENG.). 48p. (J). (gr. -1-3). pap. 7.99 *(978-0-375-86541-1(1)*, Dragonfly Bks.) Random Hse. Children's Bks.

—Sky Boys: How They Built the Empire State Building. Hopkinson, Deborah. ed. 2012. lib. bdg. 18.40 *(978-0-606-23847-2(6)*, Turtleback) Turtleback Bks.

—This Is the Dream. Shore, Diane Z. & Alexander, Jessica. 2009. (ENG.). 40p. (J). (gr. k-5). pap. 7.99 *(978-0-06-055521-4(1)*, Amistad) HarperCollins Pubs.

—This Is the Dream. Alexander, Jessica & Shore, Diane Z. 2005. 40p. (J). (gr. k-5). (ENG.). 16.99 *(978-0-06-055519-1(X))*; lib. bdg. 17.89 *(978-0-06-055520-7(3))* HarperCollins Pubs. (Amistad).

—Under the Quilt of Night. Hopkinson, Deborah. 2005. (gr. k-5). 18.00 *(978-0-7569-5077-4(5))* Perfection Learning Corp.

—Under the Quilt of Night. Hopkinson, Deborah. 2005. (ENG.). 40p. (J). (gr. k-5). reprint ed. 7.99 *(978-0-689-87700-1(5)*, Simon & Schuster/Paula Wiseman Bks.) Simon & Schuster/Paula Wiseman Bks.

—What Lincoln Said. Thomson, Sarah L. 2009. 32p. (J). (gr. k-3). lib. bdg. 18.89 *(978-0-06-084820-0(0))* HarperCollins Pubs.

—When Grandmama Sings. Mitchell, Margaree King. 2012. (ENG.). 40p. (J). (gr. k-4). 16.99 *(978-0-688-17563-4(5)*, Amistad) HarperCollins Pubs.

—Words Set Me Free: The Story of Young Frederick Douglass. Cline-Ransome, Lesa. 2012. (ENG.). 32p. (J). (gr. k-4). 17.99 *(978-1-4169-5903-8(3)*, Simon & Schuster/Paula Wiseman Bks.) Simon & Schuster/Paula Wiseman Bks.

—Young Pele: Soccer's First Star. Cline-Ransome, Lesa. 2011. (ENG.). 40p. (J). (gr. -1-3). pap. 7.99 *(978-0-375-87156-6(X)*, Dragonfly Bks.) Random Hse. Children's Bks.

Ransome, James E. Gunner, Football Hero. Ransome, James E. 2010. (ENG.). 32p. (J). (gr. -1-3). 16.95 *(978-0-8234-2053-7(1))* Holiday Hse., Inc.

Ranson, Arthur. X-Factor. Jenson, Jeff. 2003. (X-Men Ser.: Vol. 1). 96p. (YA). pap. 9.99 *(978-0-7851-1016-3(X))* Marvel Worldwide, Inc.

Ranucci, Claudia. ¡Achís! Escrivá, Victoria Pérez. 2010. (Cosas, Cositas y Cacharros Ser.). (SPA.). (J). (gr. k-3). *(978-84-263-7380-9(1))* Vives, Luis Editorial (Edelvives).

—El Camión de Papel. Aliaga, Roberto. 2010. (Librosaurio Ser.). (SPA.). 48p. (J). (gr. k-2). 11.95 *(978-84-7942-388-9(9))* Heinemann Iberia, S.A. ESP. Dist: Independent Pubs. Group.

—¡Cataplof! Cosas, Cositas Y Cacharros. Escrivá, Victoria Pérez. 2010. (Cosas, Cositas y Cacharros Ser.). (SPA.). (J). (gr. k-3). *(978-84-263-7381-6(X))* Vives, Luis Editorial (Edelvives).

—¡Splash! Escrivá, Victoria Pérez. 2010. (Cosas, Cositas y Cacharros Ser.). (SPA.). (J). (gr. k-3). *(978-84-263-7379-3(8))* Vives, Luis Editorial (Edelvives).

Rao, Rohitash. Creature Keepers & the Hijacked Hydro-Hide. Nelson, Peter. 2014. (Creature Keepers Ser.: 1). (ENG.). 384p. (J). (gr. 3-7). 12.99 *(978-0-06-223643-2(1))* HarperCollins Pubs.

Rao, Rohitash. Creature Keepers & the Swindled Soil-Soles. Nelson, Peter. 2015. (Creature Keepers Ser.: 2). (ENG.). 384p. (J). (gr. 3-7). 12.99 ***(978-0-06-223645-6(8))*** HarperCollins Pubs.

Rao, Rohitash. Herbert's Wormhole. Nelson, Peter. (Herbert's Wormhole Ser.: 1). (ENG.). 304p. (J). (gr. 3-7). 2010. pap. 6.99 *(978-0-06-168870-6(3))*; 2009. 12.99 *(978-0-06-168868-3(1))* HarperCollins Pubs.

—Herbert's Wormhole: AeroStar & the 3 1/2-Point Plan of Vengeance. Nelson, Peter. 2013. (Herbert's Wormhole Ser.: 3). (ENG.). 352p. (J). (gr. 3-7). 12.99 *(978-0-06-201220-3(7))* HarperCollins Pubs.

—Herbert's Wormhole: The Rise & Fall of el Solo Libre. Nelson, Peter. 2014. (Herbert's Wormhole Ser.: 2). (ENG.). 336p. (J). (gr. 3-7). pap. 6.99 *(978-0-06-201219-7(3))* HarperCollins Pubs.

—Herbert's Wormhole: AeroStar & the 3 1/2-Point Plan of Vengeance. Nelson, Peter. 2014. (Herbert's Wormhole Ser.: 3). (ENG.). 368p. (J). (gr. 3-7). pap. 6.99 *(978-0-06-201221-0(5))* HarperCollins Pubs.

—The Rise & Fall of el Solo Libre. Nelson, Peter. 2012. (Herbert's Wormhole Ser.: 2). (ENG.). 320p. (J). (gr. 3-7). 12.99 *(978-0-06-201218-0(5))* HarperCollins Pubs.

Raphael, Elaine. Circus Fun. Hillert, Margaret. rev. ed. 2006. (Beginning to Read Ser.). 30p. (J). (gr. -1-3). lib. bdg. 19.93 *(978-1-59953-030-7(9))* Norwood Hse. Pr.

Rappa, Desiree & Brian. Big Red. 2003. (J). 4.95 *(978-0-9722027-0-1(6))* Covered Bridge Bks.

Rappe-Flowers, Hedvig. Spotted Bear: A Rocky Mountain Folktale. Ippisch, Hanneke. Ort, Kathleen, ed. rev. ed. 49p. (J). (gr. 3-4). *(978-0-87842-387-3(7)*, 326) Mountain Pr. Publishing Co., Inc.

Rasch, Patricia. Alligators, 1 vol. Richardson, Adele & Richardson, Adele D. 2005. (World of Reptiles Ser.). (ENG.). 24p. (gr. 2-3). 23.32 *(978-0-7368-4326-3(4)*, Bridgestone Bks.) Capstone Pr., Inc.

—Dolphins, 1 vol. Miller, Connie Colwell. 2005. (World of Mammals Ser.). (ENG.). 24p. (gr. 2-3). 23.32 *(978-0-7368-4310-2(8)*, Bridgestone Bks.) Capstone Pr., Inc.

—Geckos, 1 vol. Velthaus, Sally. 2005. (World of Reptiles Ser.). (ENG.). 24p. (gr. 2-3). 23.32 *(978-0-7368-4328-7(0)*, Bridgestone Bks.) Capstone Pr., Inc.

—Manatees, 1 vol. Miller, Connie Colwell. 2005. (World of Mammals Ser.). (ENG.). 24p. (gr. 2-3). 23.32 *(978-0-7368-4311-9(6)*, Bridgestone Bks.) Capstone Pr., Inc.

Rasche, Shelly. Easter ABCs. Anders, Isabel. 2004. 32p. (J). tchr. ed. 9.49 *(978-0-570-07020-7(1)*, 56-2040) Concordia Publishing Hse.

Rasche, Shelly S. Write Now! Gould, Judith S. & Burke, Mary F. Mitchell, Judith, ed. 2005. 80p. (J). pap. 6.95 *(978-1-57310-449-4(3))* Teaching & Learning Co.

Raschka, Chris. Another Important Book. Brown, Margaret Wise & Brown. 2006. (ENG.). 32p. (J). (gr. -1-k). reprint ed. pap. 6.99 *(978-0-06-443785-1(X))* HarperCollins Pubs.

—Buggy Bug. 2014. (Thingy Things Ser.). (ENG.). 24p. (J). (gr. -1 — 1). 6.95 *(978-1-4197-1200-5(4)*, Abrams Appleseed) Abrams.

—Cowy Cow. 2014. (Thingy Things Ser.). (ENG.). 24p. (J). (gr. -1 — 1). 6.95 *(978-1-4197-1055-1(9)*, Abrams Appleseed) Abrams.

—Crabby Crab. 2014. (Thingy Things Ser.). (ENG.). 24p. (J). (gr. -1 — 1). 6.95 *(978-1-4197-1056-8(7)*, Abrams Appleseed) Abrams.

—The Death of the Hat: A Brief History of Poetry in 50 Objects. Janeczko, Paul B. 2015. (ENG.). 80p. (J). (gr. 3-7). 17.99 *(978-0-7636-6963-8(6))* Candlewick Pr.

—Fishing in the Air. Creech, Sharon. 2003. (ENG.). 32p. (J). (gr. -1-3). pap. 6.99 *(978-0-06-051606-2(2))* HarperCollins Pubs.

—Fishing in the Air. Creech, Sharon. 2003. pap. 9.95 incl. audio *(978-1-59112-223-4(6))*; (J). 25.95 incl. audio *(978-1-59112-225-8(2))*; (J). pap. 37.95 incl. audio *(978-1-59112-226-5(0))*; (J). pap. 39.95 incl. audio compact disk *(978-1-59112-521-1(9))* Live Oak Media.

—A Foot in the Mouth: Poems to Speak, Sing, & Shout. 2009. (ENG.). 64p. (J). (gr. 3-7). 17.99 *(978-0-7636-0663-3(4))* Candlewick Pr.

—A Foot in the Mouth: Poems to Speak, Sing, & Shout. Janeczko, Paul B. 2012. (ENG.). 64p. (J). (gr. 3-7). pap. 8.99 *(978-0-7636-6083-3(3))* Candlewick Pr.

—Fortune Cookies. Bitterman, Albert. 2011. (ENG.). 28p. (J). (gr. -1-k). 14.99 *(978-1-4169-6814-6(8)*, Beach Lane Bks.) Beach Lane Bks.

—Good Sports: Rhymes about Running, Jumping, Throwing, & More. Prelutsky, Jack. (ENG.). 40p. (J). (gr. 1-4). 2011.

pap. 7.99 *(978-0-375-86558-9(6)*, Dragonfly Bks.); 2007. 16.99 *(978-0-375-83700-5(0)*, Knopf Bks. for Young Readers) Random Hse. Children's Bks.

—Granny Torrelli Makes Soup. Creech, Sharon. 2012. (ENG.). 160p. (J). (gr. 3-7). reprint ed. pap. 6.99 *(978-0-06-440960-5(0))* HarperCollins Pubs.

—Granny Torrelli Makes Soup. Creech, Sharon. 2004. (Joanna Cotler Bks.). 141p. (gr. 3-7). 17.00 *(978-0-7569-4604-3(2))* Perfection Learning Corp.

—The Hello, Goodbye Window. Juster, Norton. 2005. (ENG.). 32p. (gr. -1-17). 18.99 *(978-0-7868-0914-1(0)*, di Capua, Michael Bks.) Hyperion Bks. for Children.

—I Pledge Allegiance. Martin, Bill, Jr. & Sampson, Michael. 2004. (ENG.). 40p. (J). (gr. 1-4). reprint ed. pap. 8.99 *(978-0-7636-2527-6(2))* Candlewick Pr.

—If You Were a Dog. Swenson, Jamie A. 2014. (ENG.). 40p. (J). (gr. -1-1). 17.99 *(978-0-374-33530-4(3)*, Farrar, Straus & Giroux (BYR)) Farrar, Straus & Giroux.

—A Kick in the Head: An Everyday Guide to Poetic Forms. (ENG.). 64p. (J). 2009. (gr. 3-7). pap. 9.99 *(978-0-7636-4132-0(4))*; 2005. (gr. 2-5). 17.99 *(978-0-7636-0662-6(6))* Candlewick Pr.

—Lamby Lamb. 2014. (Thingy Things Ser.). (ENG.). 24p. (J). (gr. -1 — 1). 6.95 *(978-1-4197-1057-5(5)*, Abrams Appleseed) Abrams.

—Little Treasures: Endearments from Around the World. Ogburn, Jacqueline. 2012. (ENG.). 32p. (J). (gr. -1-3). 16.99 *(978-0-547-42862-8(6))* Houghton Mifflin Harcourt Publishing Co.

—Moosey Moose. 2014. (Thingy Things Ser.). (ENG.). 24p. (J). (gr. -1 — 1). 6.95 *(978-1-4197-1202-9(0)*, Abrams Appleseed) Abrams.

—Otter & Odder: A Love Story. Howe, James. 2012. (ENG.). 40p. (J). (gr. 1-4). 14.00 *(978-0-7636-4174-0(X))* Candlewick Pr.

—Peter & the Wolf. Prokofiev, Sergei. 2008. (ENG.). 40p. (J). (gr. -1-2). 17.99 *(978-0-689-85652-5(0)*, Atheneum/Richard Jackson Bks.) Simon & Schuster Children's Publishing.

—A Poke in the I: A Collection of Concrete Poems. Janeczko, Paul B., ed. 2005. (ENG.). 48p. (J). (gr. 1-4). reprint ed. pap. 7.99 *(978-0-7636-2376-0(8))* Candlewick Pr.

—A Primer about the Flag. Bell, Marvin. 2011. (ENG.). 32p. (J). (gr. -1-3). 15.99 *(978-0-7636-4991-3(0))* Candlewick Pr.

—Whaley Whale. 2014. (Thingy Things Ser.). (ENG.). 24p. (J). (gr. -1 — 1). 6.95 *(978-1-4197-1058-2(3)*, Abrams Appleseed) Abrams.

—When Lions Roar. Harris, Robie H. 2013. (ENG.). 32p. (J). (gr. -1-k). 16.99 *(978-0-545-11283-3(4)*, Orchard Bks.) Scholastic, Inc.

Raschka, Chris. A Ball for Daisy. Raschka, Chris. (ENG.). (J). (gr. -1-2). 2015. 36p. bds. 8.99 ***(978-0-553-53723-9(7))***; 2011. 32p. 17.99 *(978-0-375-85861-1(X))* Random Hse. Children's Bks. (Schwartz & Wade Bks.).

Raschka, Chris. Daisy Gets Lost. Raschka, Chris. 2013. (ENG.). 32p. (J). (gr. -1-2). 17.99 *(978-0-449-81741-4(5))*; lib. bdg. 20.99 *(978-0-449-81742-1(3))* Random Hse. Children's Bks. (Schwartz & Wade Bks.).

—Everyone Can Learn to Ride a Bicycle. Raschka, Chris. 2013. (ENG.). 32p. (J). (gr. -1-3). 16.99 *(978-0-375-87007-1(5))*; 19.99 *(978-0-375-97007-8(X))* Random Hse. Children's Bks. (Schwartz & Wade Bks.).

—Farmy Farm. Raschka, Chris. 2011. (ENG.). 8p. (J). (gr. -1 — 1). bds. 8.99 *(978-0-545-21981-5(7)*, Orchard Bks.) Scholastic, Inc.

—Five for a Little One. Raschka, Chris. 2006. (ENG.). 48p. (J). (gr. -1-2). 17.99 *(978-0-689-84599-4(5)*, Atheneum/Richard Jackson Bks.) Simon & Schuster Children's Publishing.

—John Coltrane's Giant Steps. Raschka, Chris. pap. 16.95 incl. audio *(978-0-87499-972-3(3))*; pap. incl. audio *(978-0-87499-974-7(X))*; pap. 18.95 incl. audio compact disk *(978-1-59112-416-0(6))*; pap. incl. audio compact disk *(978-1-59112-603-4(7))* Live Oak Media.

—Little Black Crow. Raschka, Chris. 2010. (ENG.). 40p. (J). (gr. -1-2). 16.99 *(978-0-689-84601-4(0)*, Atheneum/Richard Jackson Bks.) Simon & Schuster Children's Publishing.

—Mysterious Thelonious. Raschka, Chris. pap. 18.95 incl. audio compact disk *(978-1-59112-421-4(2))* Live Oak Media.

—New York Is English, Chattanooga Is Creek. Raschka, Chris. 2005. (ENG.). 40p. (J). (gr. -1-2). 17.99 *(978-0-689-84600-7(2)*, Atheneum/Richard Jackson Bks.) Simon & Schuster Children's Publishing.

—Seriously, Norman! Raschka, Chris. (ENG.). 352p. (J). (gr. 5-9). 2014. pap. 8.99 *(978-0-545-29878-0(4))*; 2011. 17.95 *(978-0-545-29877-3(6))* Scholastic, Inc. (Di Capua, Michael).

—Simple Gifts. Raschka, Chris. 2003. pap. 41.95 incl. audio *(978-0-87499-642-5(2))*; pap. 43.95 incl. audio compact disk *(978-1-59112-604-1(5))* Live Oak Media.

—Yo! Yes? Raschka, Chris. 2007. (Scholastic Bookshelf Ser.). (ENG.). 32p. (J). (gr. -1-1). pap. 6.99 *(978-0-439-92185-5(6))* Scholastic, Inc.

Raschka, Christoph. Clammy Clam. Raschka, Chris. 2014. (Thingy Things Ser.). (ENG.). 24p. (J). (gr. -1 — 1). 6.95 *(978-1-4197-1201-2(2)*, Abrams Appleseed) Abrams.

—Doggy Dog. Raschka, Chris. 2014. (Thingy Things Ser.). (ENG.). 24p. (J). (gr. -1 — 1). 6.95 *(978-1-4197-1203-6(9)*, Abrams Appleseed) Abrams.

Raschke, Andrea. Barf's First Flight. Newcomer, Carolyn. 2009. 40p. (J). 14.95 *(978-0-9792583-8-1(3))* White Stag Pr.

Rasemas, Joe. My Favorite Time of Day (Mi Hora Preferida del Dia) Kondrchek, Jamie. Vega, Eida de la, tr. from ENG. 2009. (Day in the Life Ser.). (SPA & ENG.). 32p. (J). (gr. -1-1). lib. bdg. 25.70 *(978-1-58415-837-0(9))* Mitchell Lane Pubs., Inc.

—What It's Like to Be Ryan Howard: Como Es Ser Ryan Howard. Sherman, Patrice & Murica, Rebecca Thatcher. de la Vega, Eida, tr. from ENG. 2009. (What It's Like to Be Ser.). (SPA & ENG.). 32p. (J). (gr. -1-2). 25.70 *(978-1-58415-845-5(X))* Mitchell Lane Pubs., Inc.

Rasemas, Joe. On My Way to School (De Camino a la Escuela) Rasemas, Joe. Kondrchek, Jamie. Vega, Eida de la, tr. 2009. (Day in the Life Ser.). (SPA & ENG.). 32p. (J). (gr. -1-1). 25.70 *(978-1-58415-840-0(9))* Mitchell Lane Pubs., Inc.

—What Day Is It? (Que Dia Es Hoy?) Rasemas, Joe. Kondrchek, Jamie. Vega, Eida de la, tr. 2009. (Day in the Life Ser.). (SPA & ENG.). 32p. (J). (gr. -1-1). 25.70 *(978-1-58415-838-7(7))* Mitchell Lane Pubs., Inc.

—What Should I Wear Today? (Que Ropa Me Pondre Hoy?) Rasemas, Joe. Kondrchek, Jamie. Vega, Eida de la, tr. 2009. (Day in the Life Ser.). (ENG & SPA.). 32p. (J). (gr. -1-1). 25.70 *(978-1-58415-839-4(5))* Mitchell Lane Pubs., Inc.

Rash, Andy. Boy or Beast. Balaban, Bob. (Creature from the 7th Grade Ser.: 1). (ENG.). (J). (gr. 5). 2013. 272p. pap. 7.99 *(978-0-14-242542-8(7)*, Puffin); 2012. 256p. 15.99 *(978-0-670-01271-8(8)*, Viking Juvenile) Penguin Publishing Group.

—Game over, Pete Watson. Schreiber, Joe. 2014. (ENG.). 224p. (YA). (gr. 5-7). 16.99 *(978-0-544-15756-9(7)*, HMH Books For Young Readers) Houghton Mifflin Harcourt Publishing Co.

—Sea Monster & the Bossy Fish. Messner, Kate. 2013. (ENG.). 40p. (J). (gr. -1-k). 16.99 *(978-1-4521-1253-4(3))* Chronicle Bks. LLC.

—Sea Monster's First Day. Messner, Kate. 2011. (ENG.). 36p. (J). (gr. -1-3). 16.99 *(978-0-8118-7564-6(4))* Chronicle Bks. LLC.

Rash, Andy. Archie the Daredevil Penguin. Rash, Andy. 2015. (ENG.). 40p. (J). (gr. -1-3). 16.99 ***(978-0-451-47123-9(7)***, Viking Juvenile) Penguin Publishing Group.

Rash, Andy. Superhero School. Rash, Andy. Reynolds, Aaron. 2009. (ENG.). 32p. (J). (gr. k-2). 17.99 *(978-1-59990-166-4(8)*, Bloomsbury USA Childrens) Bloomsbury USA.

Rasheed, M. The Wicked Witch Pop Quiz. Peace, Bob. 2013. 132p. pap. 12.95 *(978-0-9824741-4-3(8))* Sojourner Publishing, Inc.

Rashid, Abdul. Amanda's Amazing Adventures: The Case of the Missing Pooch, 6 vols., Vol. 1. Cowan, C. C. 2009. 40p. pap. 14.95 *(978-0-9677385-0-5(4))*; 100p. pap. 14.95 *(978-0-9677385-1-2(2))* CCP Publishing & Entertainment.

Rashin. Two Parrots. Rumi. 2014. (ENG.). 32p. (J). (gr. k-3). 17.95 *(978-0-7358-4171-0(3)*, 9780735841710) North-South Bks., Inc.

Raskauskas, Sally. Lyrical Earth Science: Geology. Elda, Doug & Elda, Dorry. 2003. 116p. (YA). (gr. 5-10). pap. 25.50 incl. audio *(978-0-9741635-2-9(X))* Lyrical Learning.

—Lyrical Earth Science: Geology. Elda, Doug & Elda, Dory. 2003. 116p. (YA). (gr. 5-10). pap. 19.95 incl. audio *(978-0-9741635-7-4(0))* Lyrical Learning.

Raskavskas, Sally. Lyrical Earth Science: Geology. Eldon, Doug & Eldon, Dorry. 2003. 116p. (YA). (gr. 5-10). pap. 23.95 incl. audio compact disk *(978-0-9741635-8-1(9))* Lyrical Learning.

Raskin, Ellen. A Child's Christmas in Wales. Thomas, Dylan. 2003. (New Directions Paperbook Ser.: Vol. 972). (ENG.). 32p. reprint ed. pap. 8.00 *(978-0-8112-1560-2(1))* New Directions Publishing Corp.

Raskin, Ellen. Figgs & Phantoms. Raskin, Ellen. 2011. (ENG.). 176p. (J). (gr. 5-18). 6.99 *(978-0-14-241169-8(8)*, Puffin) Penguin Publishing Group.

—The Mysterious Disappearence of Leon. Raskin, Ellen. 2011. (ENG.). 176p. (J). (gr. 3-7). 6.99 *(978-0-14-241700-3(9)*, Puffin) Penguin Publishing Group.

—The Tattooed Potato & Other Clues. Raskin, Ellen. 2011. (ENG.). 176p. (J). (gr. 5-18). 6.99 *(978-0-14-241699-0(1)*, Puffin) Penguin Publishing Group.

Raskin, Lawrie, photos by. 52 Days by Camel: My Sahara Adventure. Raskin, Lawrie. Pearson, Debora. 2008. (Adventure Travel Ser.). (ENG., 88p. (J). (gr. 5-7). 26.95 *(978-1-55451-137-2(2)*, 9781554511372); pap. 14.95 *(978-1-55451-136-5(4)*, 9781554511365) Annick Pr., Ltd. CAN. Dist: Firefly Bks., Ltd.

Rasmussen, Gerry. Crazy about Basketball! Lesynski, Loris. 2013. (ENG.). 32p. (J). (gr. 3-5). 22.95 *(978-1-55451-541-7(6)*, 9781554515417); pap. 12.95 *(978-1-55451-540-0(8)*, 9781554515400) Annick Pr., Ltd. CAN. Dist: Firefly Bks., Ltd.

Rasmussen, Gerry. Crazy about Hockey! Lesynski, Loris. 2015. (ENG.). 32p. (J). (gr. 3-5). pap. 9.95 ***(978-1-55451-711-4(7)***, 9781554517114) Annick Pr., Ltd. CAN. Dist: Firefly Bks., Ltd.

Rasmussen, Gerry. Crazy about Soccer. Lesynski, Loris. 2012. (ENG.). 48p. (J). (gr. 2-5). 22.95 *(978-1-55451-422-9(3)*, 9781554514229); pap. 12.95 *(978-1-55451-421-2(5)*, 9781554514212) Annick Pr., Ltd. CAN. Dist: Firefly Bks., Ltd.

—Sniffy the Beagle. Eagle, Rita. 2007. (ENG.). 44p. per. 13.95 *(978-1-59800-537-0(5))* Outskirts Pr., Inc.

Rasmussen, Jennifer. What Do You See? Mellen, Wynette. 2012. 42p. (J). pap. 9.95 *(978-0-9839957-4-6(5))* Freundship Pr., LLC.

Rasmussen, Liz. Too Fat to Fly. 2007. 32p. (J). 16.95 *(978-0-9793517-0-9(7))* Silver Bells Publishing Hse.

Rasmussen, Wendy. Dear Santa... Pingry, Patricia A. 2005. (ENG.). 24p. (J). (gr. -1-k). bds. 6.95 *(978-0-8249-6618-8(X))* Ideals Pubns.

—Here Comes Peter Cottontail. Nelson, Steve & Rollins, Jack. 2005. (ENG.). 20p. (J). bds. 9.95 *(978-0-8249-6573-0(6))* Ideals Pubns.

—Police Cat. Hinkes, Enid. 2005. (ENG.). 32p. (J). (gr. k-3). per. 6.95 *(978-0-8075-5759-4(5))* Whitman, Albert & Co.

—The Tale of Benjamin Bunny. Potter, Beatrix. 2009. (Classic Tales by Beatrix Potter Ser.). (ENG.). 24p. (J). (gr. k-3). 28.50 *(978-1-60253-292-2(3)*, 200118) Child's World, Inc., The.

—The Tale of Johnny Town-Mouse. Potter, Beatrix & Aesop. 2009. (Classic Tales by Beatrix Potter Ser.). (ENG.). 24p. (J). (gr. k-3). 28.50 *(978-1-60253-293-9(1)*, 200119) Child's World, Inc., The.

—The Tale of Mrs. Tittlemouse. Potter, Beatrix. 2009. (Classic Tales by Beatrix Potter Ser.). (ENG.). 24p. (J). (gr. k-3). 28.50 *(978-1-60253-294-6(X)*, 200120) Child's World, Inc., The.

—The Tale of Peter Rabbit. Potter, Beatrix. 2009. (Classic Tales by Beatrix Potter Ser.). (ENG.). 24p. (J). (gr. k-3). 28.50 *(978-1-60253-295-3(8)*, 200121) Child's World, Inc., The.

—The Tale of Squirrel Nutkin. Potter, Beatrix. 2009. (Classic Tales by Beatrix Potter Ser.). (ENG.). 24p. (J). (gr. k-3). 28.50 *(978-1-60253-296-0(6)*, 200122) Child's World, Inc., The.

—The Tale of the Flopsy Bunnies. Potter, Beatrix. 2009. (Classic Tales by Beatrix Potter Ser.). (ENG.). 24p. (J). (gr. k-3). 28.50 *(978-1-60253-297-7(4)*, 200123) Child's World, Inc., The.

Rasmussen, Wendy. Marvelous Max, the Mansion Mouse. Rasmussen, Wendy, tr. Rowland, Patty. 2003. 32p. (J). 17.95 *(978-0-9649934-4-0(9))* Norfleet Pr., Inc.

Rassmuss, Jens. Good Dragon, Bad Dragon. Nostlinger, Christine. 2014. (ENG.). 32p. (J). 18.95 *(978-0-7358-4181-9(0))* North-South Bks., Inc.

Rath, Robert. Bug Feats of Montana. Oberbillig, Deborah Richie. 2009. 48p. (J). 7.95 *(978-1-56037-444-2(6))* Farcountry Pr.

—First Dog: Unleashed in the Montana Capital. Solberg, Jessica. 2007. 40p. (J). (gr. 2-4). 17.95 *(978-1-56037-425-1(X))* Farcountry Pr.

—First Dog: Unleashed in the Montana Capitol. Solberg, Jessica L. 2007. (J). 11.95 *(978-1-56037-419-0(5))* Farcountry Pr.

—Fish Do WHAT in the Water? The Secret Lives of Marine Animals. Patterson, Caroline. 2012. 48p. (J). 14.95 *(978-1-56037-519-7(1))* Farcountry Pr.

—Saluting Grandpa: Celebrating Veterans & Honor Flight, 1 vol. Metivier, Gary. 2012. (ENG.). 32p. (J). (gr. k-3). 16.99 *(978-1-4556-1748-7(2))* Pelican Publishing Co., Inc.

—Storm Chasers! on the Trail of Twisters. Davies, Jon & Reed, Jim, photos by. Davies, Jon. 2007. 48p. (J). (gr. 3-7). pap. 12.95 *(978-1-56037-407-7(1))* Farcountry Pr.

—Until Daddy Comes Home, 1 vol. Metivier, Gary. 2014. (ENG.). 32p. (J). (gr. k-3). 16.99 *(978-1-4556-1890-3(X))* Pelican Publishing Co., Inc.

—Who Pooped in the Black Hills? Scats & Tracks for Kids. Robson, Gary D. 2006. (Who Pooped in the Park? Ser.). 48p. (J). (gr. 3-7). pap. 11.95 *(978-1-56037-387-2(3))* Farcountry Pr.

—Who Pooped in the Park? Scat & Tracks for Kids. Robson, Gary D. 2008. 48p. (J). (gr. 3-7). pap. 9.95 *(978-1-56037-403-9(9))* Farcountry Pr.

—Who Pooped in the Park? Acadia National Park. Robson, Gary D. 2006. (Who Pooped in the Park? Ser.). 48p. (J). (gr. -1-3). pap. 11.95 *(978-1-56037-338-4(5))* Farcountry Pr.

—Who Pooped in the Park? Great Smoky Mountains National Park. Kemp, Steve. 2005. (J). pap. 11.95 *(978-1-56037-321-6(0))* Farcountry Pr.

—Who Pooped in the Park? Red Rock Canyon National Conservation Area: Scats & Tracks for Kids. Robson, Gary D. 2005. (Who Pooped in the Park? Ser.). 48p. (J). (gr. -1-3). pap. 9.95 *(978-1-56037-371-1(7))* Farcountry Pr.

—Who Pooped in the Park? Shenandoah National Park: Scats & Tracks for Kids. Robson, Gary D. 2006. (Who Pooped in the Park? Ser.). 48p. (J). (gr. -1-3). pap. *(978-1-56037-339-1(3))* Farcountry Pr.

—Who Pooped in the Sonoran Desert? Scats & Tracks for Kids. Robson, Gary D. 2006. (Who Pooped in the Park? Ser.). 48p. (J). (gr. -1-3). pap. 11.95 *(978-1-56037-349-0(0))* Farcountry Pr.

—Who Pooped in the Zoo? Exploring the Weirdest, Wackiest, Grossest, & Most Surprising Facts about Zoo Poop. Patterson, Caroline. 2011. 40p. (J). 14.95 *(978-1-56037-504-3(3))* Farcountry Pr.

—Who Pooped in the Zoo? San Diego Zoo: Exploring the Weirdest, Wackiest, Grossest & Most Surprising Facts about Zoo Poo. Patterson, Caroline. 2007. (Farcountry Explorer Bks.). 41p. (J). (gr. 3-7). pap. 14.95 *(978-1-56037-421-3(7))* Farcountry Pr.

—Who Pooped on the Colorado Plateau? Scat & Tracks for Kids. Robson, Gary D. 2008. (Who Pooped in the Park? Ser.). 48p. (J). (gr. 1-7). pap. 11.95 *(978-1-56037-430-5(6))* Farcountry Pr.

Rath, Robert. Go Wild for Puzzles Glacier National Park. Rath, Robert. 2008. 32p. (J). (gr. k-3). pap. 5.95 *(978-1-56037-428-2(4))* Farcountry Pr.

Rath, Robert & Wilson, Phil. Digging up Dinosaurs. Horner, Jack. 2007. 49p. (J). (gr. 3-7). pap. 14.95 *(978-1-56037-396-4(2))* Farcountry Pr.

Rather, Sherri. Upside down Danny, 1 vol. Rather, Sherri. 2009. 27p. pap. 24.95 *(978-1-61582-924-8(5))* America Star Bks.

Rathke, Kathryn. Lewis Carroll's Alice in Wonderland. Hautzig, Deborah. 2010. (Penguin Young Readers, Level 4 Ser.). (ENG.). 48p. (J). (gr. 3-4). mass mkt. 3.99 *(978-0-448-45269-2(3)*, Warne, Frederick Pubs.) Penguin Bks., Ltd. GBR. Dist: Penguin Random Hse., LLC.

Rathmann, Peggy. Buenas Noches, Gorila. Rathmann, Peggy. 2004. (SPA & ENG.). 34p. (J). (gr. -1 — 1). bds. 7.99 *(978-0-399-24300-4(3)*, Putnam Juvenile) Penguin Publishing Group.

—The Day the Babies Crawled Away. Rathmann, Peggy. 2003. (ENG.). 40p. (J). (gr. -1-k). 17.99 *(978-0-399-23196-4(X)*, Putnam Juvenile) Penguin Publishing Group.

—Good Night, Gorilla. Rathmann, Peggy. 2004. (ENG.). 34p. (J). (gr. -1 — 1). bds. 14.99 *(978-0-399-24260-1(0)*, Putnam Juvenile) Penguin Publishing Group.

Ratnayake, Kumari/Keiko. Monsieur Bagel's War. Ratnayake, Kumari/Keiko. 2007. 25p. (J). spiral bd. 15.00 net. *(978-0-9797015-1-1(1))* Augustana College Geology Dept. Pr.

Ratner, Phillip. The Passover Zoo Seder, 1 vol. Guttman, S. Daniel. 2011. (ENG.). 32p. (J). (gr. k-3). 16.99 *(978-1-58980-972-7(6))* Pelican Publishing Co., Inc.

Ratto, Cinzia. Jack & the Beanstalk. Arengo, Sue. 2006. (ENG.). 24p. 5.50 *(978-0-19-422538-0(0))* Oxford Univ. Pr. GBR. Dist: Oxford Univ. Pr., Inc.

Ratyna, Linda. Max Goes to Kindy. Lamaro, Glenda. 2009. 36p. pap. 16.44 *(978-1-4251-8830-6(3))* Trafford Publishing.

Rau, Dinah M. Ted E. Bear the Labradoodle. Rau-Tobin, Joanna. 2013. 32p. 19.95 *(978-1-59299-849-4(6))*; pap. 12.95 *(978-1-59299-850-0(X))* Inkwater Pr.

Rauchwerger, Lisa. Holy Days, Holy Ways. Halper, Sharon D. 2004. (gr. k-3). stu. ed. 8.95 *(978-0-8074-0793-6(3)*, 102073) URJ Pr.

Rauchwerger, Lisa. Chocolate Chip Challah. Rauchwerger, Lisa. 2004. (gr. k-3). pap., act. bk. ed. 9.95 *(978-0-8074-0736-3(4)*, 104035) URJ Pr.

—Chocolate Chip Challah: And Other Twists on the Jewish Holiday Table. Rauchwerger, Lisa. 2004. 127p. (J). (gr. k-3). pap. 17.95 *(978-0-8074-0700-4(3)*, 510606) URJ Pr.

—P: Winter, Spring & Summer Holidays. Rauchwerger, Lisa. 2004. (gr. k-3). pap., act. bk. ed. 9.95 *(978-0-8074-0775-2(5)*, 104036) URJ Pr.

Raude, Karina. The Traitors' Gate. Avi. (ENG.). 368p. (J). (gr. 5-8). 2010. pap. 6.99 *(978-0-689-85336-4(X)*, Atheneum Bks. for Young Readers); 2007. 17.99 *(978-0-689-85335-7(1)*, Atheneum/Richard Jackson Bks.) Simon & Schuster Children's Publishing.

Raúl, III. Low Riders in Space. Camper, Cathy. 2014. (ENG & SPA.). 112p. (J). (gr. 3-7). pap. 9.99 *(978-1-4521-2869-6(3))*;Bk. 1. 22.99 *(978-1-4521-2155-0(9))* Chronicle Bks. LLC.

—Otto Es un Rinoceronte. 2003. (SPA.). 102p. (J). (gr. 3-5). pap. 12.95 *(978-958-24-0179-5(6))* Santillana USA Publishing Co., Inc.

—Todo Cambio con Jakob. Boie, Kirsten. 2003. (SPA.). 166p. (J). (gr. 3-5). pap. 8.95 *(978-84-204-4764-3(1))* Santillana USA Publishing Co., Inc.

Rauner, Michael, photos by. The Visionary State: A Journey Through California's Spiritual Landscape. Davis, Erik. 2006. (ENG., 272p. (gr. 8-17). 40.00 *(978-0-8118-4835-0(3))* Chronicle Bks. LLC.

Ravaglia, Paola, et al. 365 Awesome Facts & Records about Everything. Davies, Gill. McRae, Anne, ed. 2008. (365 Awesome Facts & Records Ser.). (ENG.). 176p. (J). (gr. 1-18). 19.95 *(978-88-6098-001-4(1))* McRae Bks. Srl ITA. Dist: Independent Pubs. Group.

Ravanelli, Terry. Sportsercise: A School Story about Exercise-Induced Asthma. Gosselin, Kim. 2nd ed. 2004. (Children's Asthma Ser.). (J). per. 9.95 *(978-1-891383-25-0(6))* JayJo Bks., LLC.

Ravenhill, John A., jt. illus. see Fitzpatrick, Meg.

Rawal, Ishita. Sandy & Mitzi: Off to the Zoo. Crofoot, Nancy. 2013. 48p. pap. 24.95 *(978-1-62709-868-7(2))* America Star Bks.

Rawat, Tania. Christmas in the Barn, 1 vol. Crofoot, Nancy. 2009. 37p. pap. 24.95 *(978-1-61582-585-1(1))* America Star Bks.

—Sandy & Mitzi: Their First Adventure, 1 vol. Crofoot, Nancy. 2009. 31p. pap. 24.95 *(978-1-60836-707-8(X))* America Star Bks.

Rawcliffe, Lee. The Grumpy Troll, 1 vol. Manci, Arlene. 2009. 25p. pap. 19.95 *(978-1-4489-2456-1(1))* PublishAmerica, Inc.

Rawlings, Darren. The Silver Six. Lieberman, A. J. 2013. (ENG.). 192p. (J). (gr. 3-7). 22.99 *(978-0-545-37097-4(3)*, Graphix) Scholastic, Inc.

Rawlings, Louise. Al Final del Dia. Rock, Lois. (Coleccion Luz de Noche). (SPA.). (J). (gr. k-3). *(978-84-236-5039-2(1))* Edebé ESP. Dist: Lectorum Pubns., Inc.

—La Estrella Que Brilló. Rock, Lois. (Coleccion Luz de Noche). (SPA.). 32p. (J). (gr. k-3). *(978-84-236-4915-0(6))* Edebé ESP. Dist: Lectorum Pubns., Inc.

—La Gran Noticia. Rock, Lois. (Coleccion Luz de Noche). (SPA.). (J). (gr. k-3). *(978-84-236-4917-4(2))* Edebé ESP. Dist: Lectorum Pubns., Inc.

—Todos los Dias Contigo. Rock, Lois. (Coleccion Luz de Noche). (SPA.). (J). (gr. k-3). *(978-84-236-4916-7(4))* Edebé ESP. Dist: Lectorum Pubns., Inc.

Rawlins, Donna. Across the Dark Sea. Orr, Wendy. 2006. (Making Tracks Ser.). (ENG.). 64p. (J). (gr. 1-4). pap. 9.95 *(978-1-876944-45-2(5))* National Museum of Australia AUS. Dist: Independent Pubs. Group.

—River Boy. Edwards, Hazel et al. 2006. (Making Tracks Ser.). (ENG.). 72p. (J). (gr. 2-4). pap. 9.95 *(978-1-876944-39-1(0))* National Museum of Australia AUS. Dist: Independent Pubs. Group.

—Seven More Sleeps. Wild, Margaret. 2004. 32p. (J). pap. *(978-1-876288-60-0(4))* Working Title Pr.

Rawlins, Donna. Big & Little. Rawlins, Donna. 2007. (ENG.). 32p. (J). (gr. k-k). pap. 8.99 *(978-1-74166-117-0(X))* Random Hse. Australia AUS. Dist: Independent Pubs. Group.

Rawson, Maurice. James Monroe, Good Neighbor Boy: Childhood of Famous Americans Series. Widdemer, Mabel Cleland. 2011. 200p. 44.95 *(978-1-258-07964-2(X))* Literary Licensing, LLC.

Ray, Christie Jones. Eliz. Ray, Christie Jones. 2012. 28p. pap. 15.00 *(978-0-9853223-1-1(4))* Rose Water Cottage Pr.

—Eliza & a Cottage Door. Ray, Christie Jones. 2012. 40p. pap. 15.00 *(978-0-9853223-0-4(6))* Rose Water Cottage Pr.

—Eliza Celebrates a Royal Wedding. Ray, Christie Jones. 2012. 48p. pap. 15.00 *(978-0-9853223-6-6(5))* Rose Water Cottage Pr.

—Eliza Has a Cousin. Ray, Christie Jones. 2012. 32p. pap. 15.00 *(978-0-9853223-5-9(7))* Rose Water Cottage Pr.

—Eliza Will Not Be Afraid. Ray, Christie Jones. 2012. 24p. pap. 12.00 *(978-0-9853223-7-3(3))* Rose Water Cottage Pr.

—Fox Family of Franklin. Ray, Christie Jones. 2012. 16p. pap. 10.00 *(978-0-9853223-3-5(0))* Rose Water Cottage Pr.

—Goat's Milk & Gardening. Ray, Christie Jones. 2013. 42p. pap. 15.00 *(978-0-9853223-9-7(X))* Rose Water Cottage Pr.

—Pick-A-Pick-a-Pumpkin. Ray, Christie Jones. 2012. 36p. pap. 12.00 *(978-0-9853223-4-2(9))* Rose Water Cottage Pr.

Ray, Dale Marie & Ray, Joli. Moody Mae. Ray, Dale Marie. 2013. 22p. (J). pap. 7.95 *(978-1-935018-86-5(8))* International Localization Network.

Ray, Deborah Kogan. Flying Eagle. Bardhan-Quallen, Sudipta. 2009. (ENG.). 32p. (J). (gr. k-3). 15.95 *(978-1-57091-671-7(3))* Charlesbridge Publishing, Inc.

—The Seven Good Years: And Other Stories of I. L. Peretz. Peretz, I. L. Hautzig, Esther, tr. 2004. (ENG & YID.). 96p. pap. 9.95 *(978-0-8276-0771-2(7))* Jewish Pubn. Society.

Ray, Deborah Kogan. Dinosaur Mountain: Digging into the Jurassic Age. Ray, Deborah Kogan. 2010. (ENG.). 40p. (J). (gr. 3-7). 16.99 *(978-0-374-31789-8(5)*, Farrar, Straus & Giroux (BYR)) Farrar, Straus & Giroux.

—Down the Colorado: John Wesley Powell, the One-Armed Explorer. Ray, Deborah Kogan. Ray, Deborah K. 2007. (ENG.). 48p. (J). (gr. 3-5). 17.99 *(978-0-374-31838-3(7)*, Farrar, Straus & Giroux (BYR)) Farrar, Straus & Giroux.

—Paiute Princess: The Story of Sarah Winnemucca, 1 vol. Ray, Deborah Kogan. 2012. (ENG.). 48p. (J). (gr. 3-7). 17.99 *(978-0-374-39897-2(6)*, Frances Foster Bks.) Farrar, Straus & Giroux.

Ray, Eric. Tommy's War: A Parent Goes to War, 1. Avery, Pat McGrath. 2003. 36p. (J). per. 5.95 *(978-0-9663276-8-7(3))* Red Engine Pr.

Ray, Jane. Arion y el Delfín. Seth, Vikram. Dieguez Dieguez, Remedios, tr. 2004. (SPA & ENG.). 40p. (J). (gr. 2-4). 14.95 *(978-84-95939-74-6(6))* Blume ESP. Dist: Independent Pubs. Group.

—Classic Fairy Tales: Candlewick Illustrated Classic. 2009. (Candlewick Illustrated Classic Ser.). (ENG.). 224p. (J). (gr. 5-4). pap. 12.99 *(978-0-7636-4212-9(6))* Candlewick Pr.

—Greek Myths. Clayton, Sally Pomme. rev. ed. 2014. (Classics Ser.). (ENG.). 80p. (J). (gr. 3-6). 19.99 *(978-1-84780-508-9(6)*, Frances Lincoln) Quarto Publishing Group UK GBR. Dist: Hachette Bk. Group.

—Stories for a Fragile Planet: Traditional Tales about Caring for the Earth. Steven, Kenneth. (ENG.). 48p. (J). (gr. 1-7). 2012. pap. 10.99 *(978-0-7459-6386-0(2))*; 2011. 16.99 *(978-0-7459-6157-6(6))* Lion Hudson PLC GBR. Dist: Independent Pubs. Group.

—Zeraffa Giraffa. Hofmeyr, Dianne & Quarto Generic Staff. 2014. (ENG.). 40p. (J). (gr. -1-1). 17.99 *(978-1-84780-344-3(X)*, Frances Lincoln) Quarto Publishing Group UK GBR. Dist: Hachette Bk. Group.

Ray, Jane. Adam & Eve & the Garden of Eden. Ray, Jane. 2005. 32p. (J). 17.00 *(978-0-8028-5278-6(5))* Eerdmans, William B. Publishing Co.

—Can You Catch a Mermaid? Ray, Jane. 2003. (ENG.). 32p. (J). (gr. -1-2). pap. 9.95 *(978-0-84121-296-8(2))* Hodder & Stoughton GBR. Dist: Independent Pubs. Group.

—Cinderella. Ray, Jane. 2012. (ENG.). 12p. (J). (gr. k-4). 19.99 *(978-0-7636-6175-5(9))* Candlewick Pr.

—The Dollhouse Fairy. Ray, Jane. 2010. (ENG.). 32p. (J). (gr. -1-2). 16.99 *(978-0-7636-4411-6(0))* Candlewick Pr.

Ray, Joli, jt. illus. see Ray, Dale Marie.

Ray, Michael. When Will I See Aunt Carole? Faircloth, M. L. 2012. (J). 26p. 19.95 *(978-1-61863-326-2(0))*; 28p. pap. 9.99 *(978-1-61863-324-8(4))* Bookstand Publishing.

Ray, Mike. Bad-Luck Basketball, 1 vol. Maddox, Jake. 2014. (Jake Maddox JV Ser.). (ENG.). 96p. (gr. 3-4). 24.65 *(978-1-4342-9156-1(1))* Stone Arch Bks.

—Gridiron Showdown, 1 vol. Maddox, Jake. 2014. (Jake Maddox JV Ser.). (ENG.). 96p. (gr. 3-4). 24.65 *(978-1-4342-9155-4(3))* Stone Arch Bks.

—Jake Maddox JV, 1 vol. Maddox, Jake. 2014. (Jake Maddox JV Ser.). (ENG.). 96p. (gr. 3-4). 98.60 *(978-1-4342-9380-0(7))* Stone Arch Bks.

Ray, Mike. Jake Maddox JV. Maddox, Jake. 2015. (Jake Maddox JV Ser.). (ENG.). 96p. (gr. 3-4). 98.60 ***(978-1-4965-0045-8(8))*** Stone Arch Bks.

Ray, Mike. Outfield Outcast, 1 vol. Maddox, Jake. 2014. (Jake Maddox JV Ser.). (ENG.). 96p. (gr. 3-4). 24.65 *(978-1-4342-9153-0(7))* Stone Arch Bks.

—Picture a Slap Shot: A Hockey Drawing Book, 1 vol. Wacholtz, Anthony. 2013. (Drawing with Sports Illustrated Kids Ser.). (ENG.). 64p. (gr. 5-7). 33.32 *(978-1-4765-3105-2(6))* Capstone Pr., Inc.

—Picture a Touchdown: A Football Drawing Book, 1 vol. Wacholtz, Anthony. 2013. (Drawing with Sports Illustrated Kids Ser.). (ENG.). 64p. (gr. 5-7). 33.32 *(978-1-4765-3104-5(8))* Capstone Pr., Inc.

—Second-Chance Soccer, 1 vol. Maddox, Jake. 2014. (Jake Maddox JV Ser.). (ENG.). 96p. (gr. 3-4). 24.65 *(978-1-4342-9154-7(5))* Stone Arch Bks.

Ray, Mike & Haya, Erwin. Drawing with Sports Illustrated Kids. Wacholtz, Anthony. 2013. (Drawing with Sports Illustrated Kids Ser.). (ENG.). 64p. (gr. 5-7). 133.28 *(978-1-4765-3741-2(0))* Capstone Pr., Inc.

Ray, Mike, jt. illus. see Haya, Erwin.

Ray, Ralph. The Lion's Paw. White, Robb. 2008. 243p. (J). (gr. 4-7). 29.95 *(978-0-9820932-0-7(9))* A. W. Ink, Inc.

Ray, Rex. 10,000 Dresses. Ewert, Marcus. 2008. (ENG.). 32p. (J). (gr. k-4). 14.95 *(978-1-58322-850-0(0))* Seven Stories Pr.

Ray, Satyajit. Satyajit Ray: A Vision of Cinema. Ghosh, Nemai, photos by. Robinson, Andrew. 2005. (ENG.). 360p. 115.00 *(978-1-84511-074-1(9))* I. B. Tauris & Co., Ltd. GBR. Dist: Macmillan.

Rayas, Rubén. Safari Survivor. Smith, Anne & Smith, Owen. 2012. (Twisted Journeys (r) Ser.: 21). (ENG.). 112p. (J). (gr. 4-7). pap. 7.95 *(978-1-57505-943-3(6)*, Graphic Universe) Lerner Publishing Group.

Raye, Rebekah. The Secret Bay, 1 vol. Ridley, Kimberly. 2015. (ENG.). 40p. (J). 17.95 ***(978-0-88448-433-2(5))*** Tilbury Hse. Pubs.

Raye, Rebekah. Thanks to the Animals, 1 vol. Sockabasin, Allen. 2nd ed. 2014. (ENG.). 32p. (J). 17.95 *(978-0-88448-414-1(9))* Tilbury Hse. Pubs.

Raye, Rebekah. Bear-ly There, 1 vol. Raye, Rebekah. 2010. (ENG.). 32p. (J). (gr. 1-5). 16.95 *(978-0-88448-314-4(2))* Tilbury Hse. Pubs.

Rayevsky, Robert. Antonyms, Synonyms & Homonyms. Rayevsky, Kim. 2006. (ENG.). 32p. (J). (gr. -1-3). 16.95 *(978-0-8234-1889-3(8))* Holiday Hse., Inc.

—Bernal & Florinda: A Spanish Tale. Kimmel, Eric A. 2004. 29p. (J). (gr. k-4). reprint ed. 16.00 *(978-0-7567-7906-1(5))* DIANE Publishing Co.

—Hey, You! Poems to Skyscrapers, Mosquitoes, & Other Fun Things. Janeczko, Paul B. 2007. 40p. (J). (gr. 2-5). lib. bdg. 16.89 *(978-0-06-052348-0(4))* HarperCollins Pubs.

—Two Fools & a Horse: An Original Tale, 1 vol. Derby, Sally & Derby. 2003. (ENG.). 32p. (J). (gr. k-3). 16.95 *(978-0-7614-5119-8(6))* Marshall Cavendish Corp.

Rayla, Tim. The Wolf Who Cried Boy. Hartman, Bob. ed. 2004. (J). (gr. 1-3). spiral bd. *(978-0-616-14574-6(8))* Canadian National Institute for the Blind/Institut National Canadien pour les Aveugles.

Raymond, Janet Y. Pokey Pig's Picnic. Young, Polly G. 2007. (J). pap. 15.00 *(978-0-8059-7298-6(6))* Dorrance Publishing Co., Inc.

Raymundo, Peter. The Monkey & the Bee. Bloom, C. P. 2015. (Monkey Goes Bananas Ser.). (ENG.). 40p. (J). (gr. -1-2). 14.95 *(978-1-4197-0886-2(4)*, Abrams Bks. for Young Readers) Abrams.

—The Monkey Goes Bananas. Bloom, C. P. 2014. (Monkey Goes Bananas Ser.). (ENG.). 40p. (J). (gr. -1-2). 14.95 *(978-1-4197-0885-5(6)*, Abrams Bks. for Young Readers) Abrams.

Rayner, Catherine. Gobbolino, the Witch's Cat. Williams, Ursula Moray. 2015. (Macmillan Classics Ser.). (ENG.). 256p. (J). (gr. k-2). 16.99 ***(978-1-4472-7303-5(6))*** Pan Macmillan GBR. Dist: Independent Pubs. Group.

Rayner, Catherine. Posy. Newbery, Linda. 2008. (ENG.). 32p. (J). (gr. -1-k). 16.99 *(978-1-4169-7112-2(2)*, Atheneum Bks. for Young Readers) Simon & Schuster Children's Publishing.

Rayner, Catherine. Abigail. Rayner, Catherine. 2013. 32p. (J). 14.99 *(978-1-58925-147-2(4))* Tiger Tales.

—Ernest, the Moose Who Doesn't Fit. Rayner, Catherine. 2010. (ENG.). 32p. (J). (gr. -1-1). 18.99 *(978-0-374-32217-5(1)*, Farrar, Straus & Giroux (BYR)) Farrar, Straus & Giroux.

—Solomon Crocodile. Rayner, Catherine. 2011. (ENG.). 32p. (J). (gr. -1-1). 15.99 *(978-0-374-38064-9(3)*, Farrar, Straus & Giroux (BYR)) Farrar, Straus & Giroux.

Rayner, Olivia. On the Farm: A Barnyard Book. Imperato, Teresa. 2005. 10p. (J). 7.95 *(978-1-58117-270-6(2)*, Intervisual/Piggy Toes) Bendon, Inc.

—On the Go! A Transportation Book. Imperato, Teresa. 2005. 10p. (J). 7.95 *(978-1-58117-271-3(0)*, Intervisual/Piggy Toes) Bendon, Inc.

—World Book Myths & Legends Series, 8 vols., Vol. 8. 2007. (World Book Myths & Legends Ser.). 64p. (gr. 4-8). 239.00 *(978-0-7166-2613-8(6)*, 31020) World Bk., Inc.

Rayner, Shoo. The Big, Bad City. 2015. (Collins Big Cat Ser.). (ENG.). 24p. pap. 6.95 ***(978-0-00-759109-1(8))*** HarperCollins Pubs. Ltd. GBR. Dist: Independent Pubs. Group.

Rayner, Shoo. You Wait till I'm Older Than You! Rosen, Michael. (ENG.). 128p. (J). 7.95 *(978-0-14-038014-9(0))* Penguin Bks., Ltd. GBR. Dist: Trafalgar Square Publishing.

Rayner, Shoo. Cat & Dog Play Hide & Seek. Rayner, Shoo. 2006. (Collins Big Cat Ser.). (ENG.). 16p. (J). pap. 5.99 *(978-0-00-718660-0(6))* HarperCollins Pubs. Ltd. GBR. Dist: Independent Pubs. Group.

—Monster Joke Book. Rayner, Shoo. 2007. (Collins Big Cat Ser.). (ENG.). 32p. (J). pap. 7.99 *(978-0-00-723075-4(3))* HarperCollins Pubs. Ltd. GBR. Dist: Independent Pubs. Group.

—On the Ball. Rayner, Shoo. 2012. (Olympia Ser.: 7). (ENG.). 64p. (J). (gr. 2-4). pap. 7.99 *(978-1-4083-1193-6(3))* Hodder & Stoughton GBR. Dist: Independent Pubs. Group.

—Race for the Stars. Rayner, Shoo. 2012. (Olympia Ser.: 6). (ENG.). 64p. (J). (gr. 2-4). pap. 7.99 *(978-1-4083-1192-9(5))* Hodder & Stoughton GBR. Dist: Independent Pubs. Group.

Raynor, Jackie. Fairytale Mix-up. Smith, Jane. 2005. 12p. (J). (gr. -1-3). per. 10.95 *(978-1-58117-419-9(5)*, Intervisual/Piggy Toes) Bendon, Inc.

Raynor, Maggie. Alan Apostrophe. Cooper, Barbara. 2004. (Meet the Puncs: A Remarkable Punctuation Family Ser.). 32p. (gr. 1-4). lib. bdg. 26.00 *(978-0-8368-4223-4(5)*, Gareth Stevens Learning Library) Stevens, Gareth Publishing LLLP.

—Christopher Comma. Cooper, Barbara. 2004. (Meet the Puncs: A Remarkable Punctuation Family Ser.). 32p. (gr. 1-4). lib. bdg. 26.00 *(978-0-8368-4224-1(3)*, Gareth Stevens Learning Library) Stevens, Gareth Publishing LLLP.

—Emma Exclamation Point. Cooper, Barbara. 2004. (Meet the Puncs: A Remarkable Punctuation Family Ser.). 32p. (gr. 1-4). lib. bdg. 26.00 *(978-0-8368-4225-8(1)*, Gareth Stevens Learning Library) Stevens, Gareth Publishing LLLP.

—Hannah Hyphen-Hyphen. Cooper, Barbara. 2004. (Meet the Puncs: A Remarkable Punctuation Family Ser.). 32p. (gr. 1-4). lib. bdg. 26.00 *(978-0-8368-4226-5(X)*, Gareth Stevens Learning Library) Stevens, Gareth Publishing LLLP.

Raysor, Joan. David & the Phoenix. Ormondroyd, Edward. 2012. (ENG.). 191p. (J). (gr. 3-6). pap. 2.99 *(978-1-930900-58-5(9))* Purple Hse. Pr.

Rayyan, Omar. The Case of the Purloined Professor, 0 vols. Cox, Judy. 2009. (Tails of Frederick & Ishbu Ser.: 0). (ENG.). 256p. (J). (gr. 5-7). 16.99 *(978-0-7614-5544-8(2)*, 9780761455448, Amazon Children's Publishing) Amazon Publishing.

—Castle Avamir. Duey, Kathleen. ed. 2005. 76p. (J). lib. bdg. 15.00 *(978-1-59054-899-8(X))* Fitzgerald Bks.

—Castle Avamir. Duey, Kathleen. 2004. (Unicorn's Secret Ser.). 73p. (gr. 2-5). 15.00 *(978-0-7569-3357-9(9))* Perfection Learning Corp.

—Castle Avamir. Duey, Kathleen. 2003. (Unicorn's Secret Ser.: 7). (ENG.). 80p. (J). (gr. 2-5). pap. 4.99 *(978-0-689-85372-2(6)*, Simon & Schuster/Paula Wiseman Bks.) Simon & Schuster/Paula Wiseman Bks.

—Danger at Snow Hill. Casanova, Mary. 2006. (Dog Watch Ser.: 3). (ENG.). 128p. (J). (gr. 3-7). pap. 4.99 *(978-0-689-86812-2(X)*, Simon & Schuster/Paula Wiseman Bks.) Simon & Schuster/Paula Wiseman Bks.

—Dog-Napped! Casanova, Mary. 2006. (Dog Watch Ser.: 2). (ENG.). 128p. (J). (gr. 3-7). pap. 8.99 *(978-0-689-86811-5(1)*, Simon & Schuster/Paula Wiseman Bks.) Simon & Schuster/Paula Wiseman Bks.

—The Dragon of Never-Was. Downer, Ann. 2008. (ENG.). 320p. (J). (gr. 3-6). pap. 14.99 *(978-1-4169-5453-8(8)*, Atheneum Bks. for Young Readers) Simon & Schuster Children's Publishing.

—Extreme Stunt Dogs. Casanova, Mary. 2007. (Dog Watch Ser.: 5). (ENG.). 144p. (J). (gr. 3-7). pap. 4.99 *(978-1-4169-4782-0(5)*, Simon & Schuster/Paula Wiseman Bks.) Simon & Schuster/Paula Wiseman Bks.

—Good King Wenceslas. Seymour, Jane. 2012. (J). 21.99 *(978-1-60907-143-1(3)*, Shadow Mountain) Shadow Mountain Publishing.

—Hatching Magic. Downer, Ann. 2004. 242p. 16.00 *(978-0-7569-3481-1(8))* Perfection Learning Corp.

—Joha Makes a Wish: A Middle Eastern Tale, 0 vols. Kimmel, Eric A. 2013. (ENG.). 40p. (J). (gr. k-3). pap. 7.99 *(978-1-4778-1687-5(9)*, 9781477816875, Amazon Children's Publishing) Amazon Publishing.

—The Journey Home. Duey, Kathleen. 2003. (Unicorn's Secret Ser.: 8). (ENG.). 80p. (J). (gr. 2-5). pap. 4.99 *(978-0-689-85374-6(2)*, Simon & Schuster/Paula Wiseman Bks.) Simon & Schuster/Paula Wiseman Bks.

—Lords of Trillium: Book Iii of the Nightshade Chronicles. Wagner, Hilary. 2014. (Nightshade Chronicles Ser.: 3). (ENG.). 224p. (J). (gr. 4). 17.95 *(978-0-8234-2413-9(8))* Holiday Hse., Inc.

—Lords of Trillium: Book III of the Nightshade Chronicles. Wagner, Hilary. 2015. (Nightshade Chronicles Ser.: 3). (ENG.). 224p. (J). (gr. 4). pap. 7.95 *(978-0-8234-3306-3(4))* Holiday Hse., Inc.

—The Mountains of the Moon. Duey, Kathleen. ed. 2005. 76p. (J). lib. bdg. 15.00 *(978-1-59054-907-0(4))* Fitzgerald Bks.

—My Kitten's First Year. 2008. (ENG.). 24p. (J). (gr. -1-3). 12.99 *(978-0-8249-5572-4(2)*, Ideals Children's Bks.) Ideals Pubns.

—The Mystery of the Burmese Bandicoot, 1 vol. Cox, Judy. 2007. (Tails of frederick & Ishbu Ser.). (ENG.). 224p. (J). (gr. 5-9). lib. bdg. 16.99 *(978-0-7614-5376-5(8))* Marshall Cavendish Corp.

—Nightshade City. Wagner, Hilary. (Nightshade Chronicles Ser.). (ENG.). 320p. (J). 2011. pap. 7.95 *(978-0-8234-2387-3(5))*; 2010. (gr. 3-7). 17.95 *(978-0-8234-2285-2(2))* Holiday Hse., Inc.

—Possum Summer. Blom, Jen K. 2011. (ENG.). 256p. (J). (gr. 3-7). 17.95 *(978-0-8234-2331-6(X))* Holiday Hse., Inc.

—Ramadan. Ghazi, Suhaib Hamid. (ENG.). 32p. (J). (gr. k-3). pap. 6.95 *(978-0-8234-1275-4(X))* Holiday Hse., Inc.

—The Silver Bracelet. Duey, Kathleen. ed. 2005. 90p. (J). lib. bdg. 15.00 *(978-1-59054-917-9(1))* Fitzgerald Bks.

—The Sunset Gates. Duey, Kathleen. ed. 2005. 76p. (J). lib. bdg. 15.00 *(978-1-59054-918-6(X))* Fitzgerald Bks.

—To Catch a Burglar. Casanova, Mary. 2007. (Dog Watch Ser.: 4). (ENG.). 144p. (J). (gr. 3-7). pap. 4.99 *(978-0-689-86813-9(8)*, Simon & Schuster/Paula Wiseman Bks.) Simon & Schuster/Paula Wiseman Bks.

—Trouble in Pembrook. Casanova, Mary. 2006. (Dog Watch Ser.: 1). (ENG.). 128p. (J). (gr. 3-7). pap. 5.99 *(978-0-689-86810-8(3)*, Simon & Schuster/Paula Wiseman Bks.) Simon & Schuster/Paula Wiseman Bks.

—True Heart. Duey, Kathleen. ed. 2005. 76p. (J). lib. bdg. 15.00 *(978-1-59054-920-9(1))* Fitzgerald Bks.

—True Heart. Duey, Kathleen. 2004. (Unicorn's Secret Ser.). 75p. (gr. 2-5). 15.00 *(978-0-7569-3385-2(4))* Perfection Learning Corp.

—True Heart. Duey, Kathleen. 2003. (Unicorn's Secret Ser.: 6). (ENG.). 80p. (J). (gr. 2-5). pap. 4.99 *(978-0-689-85370-8(X)*, Simon & Schuster/Paula Wiseman Bks.) Simon & Schuster/Paula Wiseman Bks.

—The Turtle-Hatching Mystery. Casanova, Mary. 2008. (Dog Watch Ser.: 6). (ENG.). 144p. (J). (gr. 3-7). pap. 8.99 *(978-1-4169-4783-7(3)*, Simon & Schuster/Paula Wiseman Bks.) Simon & Schuster/Paula Wiseman Bks.

—Waggit Again. Howe, Peter. (Waggit Ser.: 2). (ENG.). (J). (gr. 5). 2010. 320p. pap. 6.99 *(978-0-06-124266-3(7))*; 2009. 304p. 16.99 *(978-0-06-124264-9(0))* HarperCollins Pubs.

—Waggit Forever. Howe, Peter. (Waggit Ser.: 3). (ENG.). (J). (gr. 5). 2011. 288p. pap. 6.99 *(978-0-06-176516-2(3))*; 2010. 272p. 16.99 *(978-0-06-176517-9(1))* HarperCollins Pubs.

—Waggit's Tale. Howe, Peter. (Waggit Ser.: 1). (ENG.). (J). (gr. 5). 2009. 304p. pap. 6.99 *(978-0-06-124263-2(2))*; 2008. 288p. 16.99 *(978-0-06-124261-8(6))* HarperCollins Pubs.

—White Assassin. Wagner, Hilary. 2011. (Nightshade Chronicles Ser.). (ENG.). 304p. (J). 17.95 *(978-0-8234-2333-0(6))* Holiday Hse., Inc.

Rayyan, Omar & Dillon, Julie. The Boggart. Cooper, Susan. 2004. (ENG.). 224p. (J). (gr. 3-7). pap. 7.99 *(978-0-689-86930-3(4)*, McElderry, Margaret K. Bks.) McElderry, Margaret K. Bks.

—The Boggart & the Monster. Cooper, Susan. 2004. (ENG.). 224p. (J). (gr. 3-7). pap. 7.99 *(978-0-689-86931-0(2)*, McElderry, Margaret K. Bks.) McElderry, Margaret K. Bks.

Rayyan, Sheila. Sacred Scars, No. 2. Duey, Kathleen. 2009. (Resurrection of Magic Ser.: 2). (ENG.). 256p. (YA). (gr. 7-18). 18.99 *(978-0-689-84095-1(0)*, Atheneum Bks. for Young Readers) Simon & Schuster Children's Publishing.

Raz, Rachel, photos by. The Colors of Israel. Raz, Rachel. 2015. (ENG., 24p. (J). (gr. -1-2). lib. bdg. 17.99 *(978-1-4677-5539-9(7)*, Kar-Ben Publishing) Lerner Publishing Group.

Razzi, Manuela. Amanite. Rodrigue, Michel. 2012. (Sybil the Backpack Fairy Graphic Novels Ser.: 2). (ENG.). 48p. (J). (gr. 1-5). 11.99 *(978-1-59707-305-9(9))* Papercutz.

Razzi, Manuela, et al. Disney Fairies Graphic Novel #13: Tinker Bell & the Pixie Hollow Games. Orsi, Tea & Panaro, Carlo. 2013. (Disney Fairies Ser.: 13). (ENG.). 64p. (J). (gr. 1-6). 11.99 *(978-1-59707-447-6(0))*; pap. 7.99 *(978-1-59707-446-9(2))* Papercutz.

—Tinker Bell & the Lost Treasure. Orsi, Tea & Panaro, Carlo. 2013. (Disney Fairies Ser.: 12). (ENG.). 64p. (J). (gr. 1-6). 11.99 *(978-1-59707-429-2(2))*; pap. 7.99 *(978-1-59707-428-5(4))* Papercutz.

Razzi, Manuela & Dalena, Antonello. Nina. Rodrigue, Michel. 2011. (Sybil the Backpack Fairy Graphic Novels Ser.: 1). (ENG.). 48p. (J). (gr. 1-5). 10.99 *(978-1-59707-285-4(0))* Papercutz.

Razzi, Manuela, jt. illus. see Dalena, Antonello.

Rchards, Virginia Helen. I Pray the Stations of the Cross. Dateno, Maria Grace. 2006. (J). 4.50 *(978-0-8198-3691-5(5))* Pauline Bks. & Media.

Rea, Ba. Monarch! Come Play with Me. Rea, Ba. 2006. 32p. (J). per. 10.95 *(978-0-9657472-5-7(5))* Bas Relief, LLC.

Ready, D. M. The Opposites. Erickson, Sharon. 2008. 24p. pap. 24.95 *(978-1-60672-551-1(3))* America Star Bks.

Reagan, Mike & Norstrand, Torstein. The Colossus Rises. Lerangis, Peter. 2013. (Seven Wonders Ser.: 1). (ENG.). 368p. (J). (gr. 3-7). 17.99 *(978-0-06-207040-1(1))* HarperCollins Pubs.

Reagan, Mike, jt. illus. see Norstrand, Torstein.

Reagan, Susan. My Sing-Along Bible: 50 Easy-Read Stories + 50 Fun Bible Songs. Elkins, Stephen. 2015. (ENG.). 96p. (J). 12.99 ***(978-1-4964-0543-2(9))*** Tyndale Hse. Pubs.

Reagan, Susan. Randall Reindeer's Naughty & Nice Report. DePrisco, Dorothea. 2011. (ENG.). (J). (gr. -1-3). 24.95 *(978-1-61524-365-5(8)*, Intervisual/Piggy Toes) Bendon, Inc.

—The Something Wonderful: A Christmas Story. Hill, Karen. 2005. 32p. (J). (gr. -1-3). 15.99 *(978-1-58134-732-6(4))* Crossway.

Reagan, Susan. Slipper & Flipper in the Quest for Don Pinguino & the Golden Sun. Reagan, Susan. 2015. (ENG.). 48p. (J). (gr. -1-k). 17.99 *(978-1-4231-6387-9(7))* Disney Publishing Worldwide.

Reagan, Susan Joy. Bitsy's Harvest Party. Carlson, Melody. 2005. 32p. (J). (gr. -1-4). 12.99 *(978-0-8054-2684-7(1))* B&H Publishing Group.

—Forgive Others. Carlson, Melody. 2004. (Just Like Jesus Said Ser.). 32p. (J). (gr. -1-5). 12.99 *(978-0-8054-2385-3(0))* B&H Publishing Group.

—Special Times Bible Prayers for Toddlers. Elkins, Stephen. 2004. (Special Times Ser.). 32p. (J). (gr. -1-18). 9.97 *(978-0-8054-2660-1(4))* B&H Publishing Group.

—Special Times Bible Promises for Toddlers. Elkins, Stephen. 2005. (Special Times Ser.). 32p. (J). (gr. -1-18). 9.97 *(978-0-8054-2678-6(7))* B&H Publishing Group.

—'Twas the Night: The Nativity Story. Carlson, Melody. 2005. 32p. (J). (gr. -1-4). 12.99 *(978-0-8054-2683-0(3))* B&H Publishing Group.

—When the Creepy Things Come Out! Carlson, Melody. 2003. 32p. (J). (gr. -1-5). 12.99 *(978-0-8054-2687-8(6))* B&H Publishing Group.

Ream, Robaire. Shadow on the Moon: A Child's Guide to the Discovery of the Universe. Matejovsky, Char. 2014. (J). *(978-1-59815-151-0(7))* Polebridge Pr.

Reardon, Mary. Snow Treasure. McSwigan, Marie. 2006. (ENG.). 208p. (J). (gr. 3-7). 5.99 *(978-0-14-240224-5(9)*, Puffin) Penguin Publishing Group.

Reasoner, Charles. Bear Hugs. 2015. (J). *(978-1-4795-5944-2(X))* Picture Window Bks.

—A Day at the Zoo. Lee, Howard. 2009. (Inside Outside Board Bks.). 10p. (J). bds. 10.99 *(978-1-934650-55-4(2))* Just For Kids Pr., LLC.

—Honey Bunny. 2015. (J). *(978-1-4795-5945-9(8))* Picture Window Bks.

—I'm Just a Little Pig. Thompson, Kate. 2014. (ENG.). 12p. (gr. -1). *(978-1-78244-590-6(0))* Top That! Publishing PLC.

—Peep! Peep! 2015. (J). *(978-1-4795-5943-5(1))* Picture Window Bks.

—Puppy Love. 2015. (J). *(978-1-4795-5946-6(6))* Picture Window Bks.

—Who's There on Halloween? Beall, Pamela Conn & Nipp, Susan Hagen. 2003. 18p. (J). bds. 4.99 *(978-0-8431-0495-0(3))*; (ENG.). (gr. -1-k). bds. 4.99 *(978-0-8431-0510-0(0))* Penguin Publishing Group. (Price Stern Sloan).

Reasoner, Charles. I'm Just a Bird. Reasoner, Charles. 2007. (I'm Just Book Ser.). 12p. (J). (gr. -1). bds. *(978-1-84666-289-8(3)*, Tide Mill Pr.) Top That! Publishing PLC.

—I'M Just a Crab! Reasoner, Charles. 2007. (I'm Just Book Ser.). (ENG.). 12p. (J). (gr. -1). *(978-1-84666-291-1(5)*, Tide Mill Pr.) Top That! Publishing PLC.

—Inside Jolly Roger's Pirate Ship. Reasoner, Charles. 2007. (Story Book Ser.). 12p. (J). (gr. k). bds. *(978-1-84666-149-5(8)*, Tide Mill Pr.) Top That! Publishing PLC.

—Inside Old Mcdonald's Barn. Reasoner, Charles. 2007. (Story Book Ser.). 12p. (J). (gr. k). bds. *(978-1-84666-287-4(7)*, Tide Mill Pr.) Top That! Publishing PLC.

—Inside Santa's Toy Shop. Reasoner, Charles. 2007. (Story Book Ser.). 12p. (J). (gr. k-3). bds. *(978-1-84666-151-8(X)*, Tide Mill Pr.) Top That! Publishing PLC.

—One Blue Fish: A Colorful Counting Book. Reasoner, Charles. 2010. (ENG.). 26p. (J). (gr. -1 — 1). bds. 9.99 *(978-1-4169-9672-9(9)*, Little Simon) Little Simon.

—Peek-A-Boo Elves, 1 vol. Reasoner, Charles. Wood, Hannah. 2014. (Charles Reasoner Peek-A-Boo Bks.). (ENG.). 10p. (gr. -1 — 1). bds. 12.99 *(978-1-4795-5178-1(3))* Picture Window Bks.

—Peek-A-Boo Reindeer, 1 vol. Reasoner, Charles. Wood, Hannah. 2014. (Charles Reasoner Peek-A-Boo Bks.). (ENG.). 10p. (gr. -1 — 1). bds. 12.99 *(978-1-4795-5179-8(1))* Picture Window Bks.

R

—Peek-A-Boo Santa, 1 vol. Reasoner, Charles. Wood, Hannah. 2014. (Charles Reasoner Peek-A-Boo Bks.). (ENG.). 10p. (gr. -1 — 1). bds. 12.99 *(978-1-4795-5180-4(5))* Picture Window Bks.

—Peek-A-Boo Snowman, 1 vol. Reasoner, Charles. Wood, Hannah. 2014. (Charles Reasoner Peek-A-Boo Bks.). (ENG.). 10p. (gr. -1 — 1). bds. 12.99 *(978-1-4795-5181-1(3))* Picture Window Bks.

—The 3 Blind Mice Inside the Spooky Scary & Creepy Haunted House. Reasoner, Charles. 2007. (Story Book Ser.). 10p. (J). (gr. -1-3). bds. *(978-1-84666-381-9(4),* Tide Mill Pr.) Top That! Publishing PLC.

Reasoner, Charles & Jones, Anna. Winter Friends, 1 vol. Reasoner, Charles. 2013. (Charles Reasoner Holiday Bks.). (ENG.). 10p. (gr. -1 — 1). bds. 4.99 *(978-1-4048-8156-3(5))* Picture Window Bks.

Reasoner, Charles & Reasoner, John. What's Following Us? Cooke, Brandy. 2011. (ENG.). 20p. (J). (gr. -1 — 1). bds. 6.99 *(978-1-4169-9673-6(7),* Little Simon) Little Simon.

Reasoner, John. Best Boat Race Ever! Picou, Lin. 2012. (ENG.). 24p. (gr. 1-2). pap. 7.95 *(978-1-61810-317-8(2));* lib. bdg. 28.50 *(978-1-61810-184-6(6))* Rourke Educational Media.

—Buff Ducks. Mckenzie, Precious. 2012. (ENG.). 24p. (gr. k-1). pap. 7.95 *(978-1-61810-304-8(0));* lib. bdg. 28.50 *(978-1-61810-171-6(4))* Rourke Educational Media.

—Hey Diddle Diddle. 2012. (ENG.). 10p. (gr. -1-k). bds. 5.99 *(978-1-61810-582-0(5))* Rourke Educational Media.

—Hickory Dickory Dock. 2012. (ENG.). 10p. (gr. -1-k). bds. 5.99 *(978-1-61810-060-3(2));* bds. 6.99 *(978-1-61236-976-1(6))* Rourke Educational Media.

—Itsy Bitsy Spider. 2012. (ENG.). 10p. (gr. -1-k). bds. 5.99 *(978-1-61810-062-7(9));* bds. 6.99 *(978-1-61236-978-5(2))* Rourke Educational Media.

—Jack & Jill. 2012. (ENG.). 10p. (gr. -1-k). bds. 5.99 *(978-1-61810-586-8(8))* Rourke Educational Media.

—The Little Tea Pot. 2012. (ENG.). 10p. (gr. -1-k). bds. 5.99 *(978-1-61810-061-0(0))* Rourke Educational Media.

—This Old Man! 2012. (ENG.). 10p. (gr. -1-k). bds. 5.99 *(978-1-61810-587-5(6))* Rourke Educational Media.

—Twinkle Twinkle Little Star. 2012. (ENG.). 10p. (gr. -1-k). bds. 5.99 *(978-1-61810-063-4(7))* Rourke Educational Media.

Reasoner, John, jt. illus. see Reasoner, Charles.

Reasor, Mick. Trabajar y Jugar. Kleinhenz, Sydnie Meltzer. 2006. (Rookie Reader Español Ser.). (SPA.). 23p. (J). (gr. k-2). lib. bdg. 19.50 *(978-0-516-25306-0(9))* Scholastic Library Publishing.

—Work & Play. Meltzer Kleinhenz, Sydnie. 2011. (Rookie Ready to Learn Ser.). 32p. (J). (ENG.). pap. 5.95 *(978-0-531-26829-2(2));* (gr. -1-k). lib. bdg. 23.00 *(978-0-531-27179-7(X))* Scholastic Library Publishing. (Children's Pr.).

Reaugh, Clair. Sammi & Friends - the Great Gidzit Adventure: Sammi & Friends Stories & Adventures. Reaugh, Clair. 2011. (ENG.). 42p. pap. 9.50 *(978-1-4565-8881-6(8))* CreateSpace Independent Publishing Platform.

Reaveley, Trevor. Is Apatosaurus Okay? Nussbaum, Ben. 2005. (Smithsonian's Prehistoric Pals Ser.). (ENG.). (J). (gr. -1-2). 32p. 9.95 *(978-1-59249-510-8(9),* PS2458); 36p. pap. 2.95 *(978-1-59249-509-2(5),* S2458) Soundprints.

—Sabre-Tooth Tiger. Bailey, Gerry. 2011. (Smithsonian Prehistoric Zone Ser.). (ENG.). 32p. (J). (gr. k-3). *(978-0-7787-1801-7(8));* pap. *(978-0-7787-1814-7(X))* Crabtree Publishing Co.

Reavely, Trever. Saber-Tooth Trap. Bentley, Dawn. (Smithsonian's Prehistoric Pals Ser.). (ENG.). 36p. (J). (gr. -1-2). 8.95 *(978-1-59249-455-2(2),* SD2406); 2.95 *(978-1-59249-456-9(0),* S2456) Soundprints.

Reavely, Trevor. Is Apatosaurus Okay? Nussbaum, Ben. 2005. (ENG.). 36p. (J). (gr. -1-2). 8.95 *(978-1-59249-508-5(7),* SD2408); 14.95 *(978-1-59249-506-1(0),* H2408); pap. 6.95 *(978-1-59249-507-8(9),* S2408) Soundprints.

—Saber-Tooth Trap. Bentley, Dawn. 2005. (Smithsonian's Prehistoric Pals Ser.). (ENG.). 36p. (J). (gr. k-2). 14.95 *(978-1-59249-453-8(6),* H2406); pap. 6.95 *(978-1-59249-454-5(4),* S2406) Soundprints.

Reaves, Daniel. Invisible Julian. Hawes, Dorothy. 2011. 24p. pap. 24.95 *(978-1-4560-9583-3(8))* America Star Bks.

Rebecca, Rivard. Ben Has Autism. Ben Is Awesome. Zolty, Meredith. 2011. 32p. (J). lib. bdg. 15.95 *(978-0-944727-40-9(9),* Turtle Bks.) Jason & Nordic Pubs.

Rebels Animation Team. A New Hero. Disney Book Group Staff & Hidalgo, Pablo. 2014. (ENG.). 48p. (J). (gr. 1-3). 17.99 *(978-1-4847-0669-5(2))* Disney Pr.

Rebis, Greg. The Hunchback of Notre Dame, 1 vol. Hugo, Victor. 2006. (Classic Fiction Ser.). (ENG.). 72p. (gr. 2-3). lib. bdg. 26.65 *(978-1-59889-047-1(6),* Graphic Revolve) Stone Arch Bks.

—Journey to the Center of the Earth, 1 vol. Verne, Jules. 2007. (Classic Fiction Ser.). (ENG.). 72p. (gr. 2-3). lib. bdg. 26.65 *(978-1-59889-832-3(9),* Graphic Revolve) Stone Arch Bks.

—Viaje Al Centro de la Tierra, 1 vol. Verne, Jules. Tobon, Sara, tr. from ENG. 2009. (Classic Fiction Ser.). (SPA.). 72p. (gr. 2-3). lib. bdg. 26.65 *(978-1-4342-1687-8(X),* Graphic Revolve en Español) Stone Arch Bks.

Rebman, Renée C. The Articles of Confederation, 1 vol. Rebman, Renée C. 2006. (We the People: Revolution & the New Nation Ser.). (ENG.). 48p. (gr. 5-6). 27.99 *(978-0-7565-1627-7(7),* We the People) Compass Point Bks.

Rebora, Cecilia. Never Let a Ghost Borrow Your Library Book: Book Care Guidelines from the Library Secret Service. Casale, Karen. 2012. 32p. (J). 17.75 *(978-1-60213-061-6(2),* Upstart Bks.) Highsmith Inc.

—Ripple's Effect. Achor, Shawn & Blankson, Amy. O'Malley, Judy, ed. 2012. (ENG.). 36p. (gr. -1-2). 18.95 *(978-0-9829938-7-3(0))* Little Pickle Press LLC.

RéBora, Cecilia. Say Something, Perico. Harris, Trudy. 2011. (Millbrook Picture Books Ser.). (ENG.). 32p. (J). (gr. -1-2). lib. bdg. 16.95 *(978-0-7613-5231-0(7),* Millbrook Pr.) Lerner Publishing Group.

Rébora, Cecilia. Tower of Babel. Gadot, A. S. 2010. (Adult & Young Adult Bks.). (ENG.). 32p. (J). (gr. k-3). pap. 7.95 *(978-0-8225-9952-4(X),* Kar-Ben Publishing) Lerner Publishing Group.

Recher, Andrew. Bats. Vogel, Julia. 2007. (Our Wild World Ser.). (ENG.). 48p. (J). (gr. 2-5). 10.95 *(978-1-55971-968-1(0));* pap. 7.95 *(978-1-55971-969-8(9))* Cooper Square Publishing Llc.

—Butterflies. Stewart, Melissa. 2007. (Our Wild World Ser.). (ENG.). 48p. (J). (gr. 2-5). 10.95 *(978-1-55971-966-7(4));* pap. 7.95 *(978-1-55971-967-4(2))* Cooper Square Publishing Llc.

—Coyotes. Vogel, Julia. 2007. (Our Wild World Ser.). (ENG.). 48p. (J). (gr. 2-5). 10.95 *(978-1-55971-982-7(6))* Cooper Square Publishing Llc.

Rechin, Kevin. Did You Know?, Vol. 2. Winter, Max. l.t. ed. 2005. (Little Books & Big Bks.: Vol. 8). 8p. (gr. k-2). 23.00 net. *(978-0-8215-7517-8(1))* Sadlier, William H. Inc.

—Guess Again! 1,001 Rib-Tickling Riddles from Highlights. 2012. (Laugh Attack! Ser.). (ENG.). 256p. (J). (gr. k). pap. 5.95 *(978-1-59078-919-3(9))* Boyds Mills Pr.

—The Tumbleweed Came Back. Coyle, Carmela Lavigna. 2013. 32p. (J). 15.95 *(978-1-933855-83-7(5),* Rio Nuevo Pubs.) Rio Nuevo Pubs.

Recio, Ricardo. Manana es Domingo y Otras Rimas Infantiles. Puncel, Maria. 2003. (SPA.). 32p. 4.95 *(978-84-372-8021-9(4))* Altea, Ediciones, S.A. - Grupo Santillana ESP. Dist: Santillana USA Publishing Co., Inc.

Record, Adam. Ghost in the House. Paquette, Ammi-Joan. (ENG.). (J). (gr. -1-2). 2015. 20p. 9.99 ***(978-0-7636-7622-3(5));*** 2013. 32p. 15.99 *(978-0-7636-5529-7(5))* Candlewick Pr.

Record, Adam. Kit & Mateo Journey into the Clouds: Learning about Clouds, 1 vol. Meister, Cari. 2013. (Take It Outside Ser.). (ENG.). 24p. (gr. k-2). pap. 7.95 *(978-1-4795-1936-1(7));* lib. bdg. 26.65 *(978-1-4048-8315-4(0))* Picture Window Bks.

—Little Dinos Don't Bite, 1 vol. Dahl, Michael. 2013. (Little Dinos Ser.). (ENG.). 20p. (gr. -1-k). bds. 7.99 *(978-1-4048-7536-4(0))* Picture Window Bks.

—Little Dinos Don't Hit, 1 vol. Dahl, Michael. 2013. (Little Dinos Ser.). (ENG.). 20p. (gr. -1-k). bds. 7.99 *(978-1-4048-7533-3(6))* Picture Window Bks.

—Little Dinos Don't Push, 1 vol. Dahl, Michael. 2013. (Little Dinos Ser.). (ENG.). 20p. (gr. -1-k). bds. 7.99 *(978-1-4048-7534-0(4))* Picture Window Bks.

—Little Dinos Don't Yell, 1 vol. Dahl, Michael. 2013. (Little Dinos Ser.). (ENG.). 20p. (gr. -1-k). bds. 7.99 *(978-1-4048-7912-6(9))* Picture Window Bks.

—Lost Treasure of Larry Longfoot: Learning to Use a Map. Meister, Cari. 2013. (Take It Outside Ser.). (ENG.). 24p. (gr. k-2). 26.65 *(978-1-4048-8305-5(3));* pap. 7.95 *(978-1-4795-1935-4(9))* Picture Window Bks.

Record, Adam. Marvin Redpost #1: Kidnapped at Birth? Sachar, Louis. 2015. (Stepping Stone Book(TM) Ser.). (ENG.). 96p. (J). (gr. 1-4). lib. bdg. 12.99 ***(978-0-553-53540-2(4),*** Random Hse. Bks. for Young Readers) Random Hse. Children's Bks.

—Marvin Redpost #2: Why Pick on Me? Sachar, Louis. 2015. (Stepping Stone Book(TM) Ser.). (ENG.). 96p. (J). (gr. 1-4). lib. bdg. 12.99 ***(978-0-553-53541-9(2),*** Random Hse. Bks. for Young Readers) Random Hse. Children's Bks.

—Marvin Redpost #3: Is He a Girl? Sachar, Louis. 2015. (Stepping Stone Book(TM) Ser.). (ENG.). 96p. (J). (gr. 1-4). lib. bdg. 12.99 ***(978-0-553-53542-6(0),*** Random Hse. Bks. for Young Readers) Random Hse. Children's Bks.

—Marvin Redpost #5: Class President. Sachar, Louis. 2015. (Stepping Stone Book(TM) Ser.). (ENG.). 96p. (J). (gr. 1-4). lib. bdg. 12.99 ***(978-0-553-53543-3(9),*** Random Hse. Bks. for Young Readers) Random Hse. Children's Bks.

—Marvin Redpost #6: a Flying Birthday Cake? Sachar, Louis. 2015. (Stepping Stone Book(TM) Ser.). (ENG.). 96p. (J). (gr. 1-4). lib. bdg. 12.99 ***(978-0-553-53544-0(7),*** Random Hse. Bks. for Young Readers) Random Hse. Children's Bks.

—Marvin Redpost #8: a Magic Crystal? Sachar, Louis. 2015. (Stepping Stone Book(TM) Ser.). (ENG.). 96p. (J). (gr. 1-4). lib. bdg. 12.99 ***(978-0-553-53546-4(3),*** Random Hse. Bks. for Young Readers) Random Hse. Children's Bks.

Record, Adam. Sadie's Seed Adventures: Learning about Seeds, 1 vol. Dybvik, Tina. 2013. (Take It Outside Ser.). (ENG.). 24p. (gr. k-2). 26.65 *(978-1-4048-8316-1(9));* pap. 7.95 *(978-1-4795-1937-8(5))* Picture Window Bks.

—Space Cowboy Caleb & the Night Sky Round-Up: Learning about the Night Sky, 1 vol. Dybvik, Tina. 2013. (Take It Outside Ser.). (ENG.). 24p. (gr. k-2). pap. 7.95 *(978-1-4795-1938-5(3));* lib. bdg. 26.65 *(978-1-4048-8317-8(7))* Picture Window Bks.

Record, Adam. Super Fast, Out of Control. Sachar, Louis. 2015. (Stepping Stone Book(TM) Ser.). (ENG.). 96p. (J). (gr. 1-4). lib. bdg. 12.99 ***(978-0-553-53545-7(5),*** Random Hse. Bks. for Young Readers) Random Hse. Children's Bks.

Record, Adam. Take It Outside. Dybvik, Tina & Meister, Cari. 2013. (Take It Outside Ser.). (ENG.). 24p. (gr. k-2). pap. 31.80 *(978-1-4795-1998-9(7));* lib. bdg. 106.60 *(978-1-4048-8142-6(5))* Picture Window Bks.

Rectenbaugh, Marci. Jonathan Finds True Treasure. Adee, Donna & Adee, Ed. 2004. (Jonathan Ser.: Bk. 2). 344p. (J). per. 10.95 *(978-0-9654272-5-8(0))* Harvest Pubns.

Reczuch, Karen. The Auction, 1 vol. Andrews, Jan. 2nd ed. 2007. (ENG.). 32p. (J). (gr. k-2). pap. 6.95 *(978-0-88899-842-2(2))* Groundwood Bks. CAN. Dist: Perseus-PGW.

—Ghost Cat. Abley, Mark. ed. 2004. (J). (gr. k-3). spiral bd. *(978-0-616-11091-1(X));* spiral bd. *(978-0-616-11092-8(8))* Canadian National Institute for the Blind/Institut National Canadien pour les Aveugles.

—Loon. Griek, Susan Vande. 2011. (ENG.). 48p. (J). (gr. -1-2). 18.95 *(978-1-55498-077-2(1))* Groundwood Bks. CAN. Dist: Perseus-PGW.

—Salmon Creek, 1 vol. LeBox, Annette. 2005. (ENG.). 48p. (J). pap. 12.95 *(978-0-88899-644-2(6))* Groundwood Bks. CAN. Dist: Perseus-PGW.

Reczuch, Karen. West Coast Wild: A Nature Alphabet, 1 vol. Hodge, Deborah. 2015. (ENG.). 48p. (J). (gr. -1-2). 18.95 ***(978-1-55498-440-4(8))*** Groundwood Bks. CAN. Dist: Perseus-PGW.

Red Baklava, photos by. Blackbook Directory & Yearbook 2010-11: Black Business Year in Review, vol. 1. annuals Avista Products. Media Write, ed. aut. collector's ed. 2011. (ENG., 160p. 65.00 *(978-0-9798741-0-9(6))* Avista Products.

Reda, Jaime. The Shummys: Cooking Joy with Every Girl & Boy. Golden, Ryan. 2010. (ENG.). 44p. pap. 9.83 *(978-1-4528-5616-2(8))* CreateSpace Independent Publishing Platform.

Reddy, Sneha. The Ballad of Calvin the Cat. Harpan, Gaile. 2008. 24p. pap. 12.95 *(978-0-9817572-6-1(X))* Peppertree Pr., The.

—The Ballad of Furrio the Cat. Panks, Kristin & Harpan, Gaile. 2008. 24p. pap. 12.95 *(978-0-9822540-4-2(0))* Peppertree Pr., The.

—The Ballad of Omar the Cat. Harpan, Gaile. 2008. 28p. pap. 12.95 *(978-0-9820479-1-0(6))* Peppertree Pr., The.

—The Ballad of Snowball the Cat. Harpan, Gaile. 2009. 24p. pap. 12.95 *(978-1-936051-25-0(7))* Peppertree Pr., The.

—The Ballad of Victor the Cat. Harpan, Gaile. 2008. 20p. pap. 12.95 *(978-0-9814894-4-5(3))* Peppertree Pr., The.

Redel, Nicole. Odessa Bluegill - Out Shovels a Yellow Tractor. Gorman, Suzy, photos by. Session, Garry. Warren, Pamela, ed. 2003. 42p. (J). pap. 9.95 *(978-0-9658006-2-4(8))* Session Family.

Redenbaugh, Vicki. Skar's Picnic ... A Bear's Tale. Redenbaugh, Vicki. 2005. (J). 14.95 *(978-1-59091-034-4(6))* Eastern National.

Redenbaugh, Vicki Jo. Lots of Latkes: A Hanukkah Story. Lanton, Sandy. 2003. (ENG.). 32p. (J). (gr. -1-3). 14.95 *(978-1-58013-091-2(7),* Kar-Ben Publishing) Lerner Publishing Group.

Redenbaugh, Vicki Jo, jt. illus. see Kahn, Katherine Janus.

Redinger, Jacob. In Stitches: More Than 25 Simple & Stylish Sewing Projects. McGuire, Colin, photos by. Butler, Amy. 2006. (ENG.). 176p. (gr. 8-17). 24.95 *(978-0-8118-5159-6(1))* Chronicle Bks. LLC.

Redlich, Ben. The Great Montefiasco. Thompson, Colin. 2004. 40p. (J). (gr. -1 — 1). 16.95 *(978-1-59572-008-5(1))* Star Bright Bks., Inc.

—Octavius O'Malley & the Mystery of the Exploding Cheese. Sunderland, Alan. 2006. 224p. *(978-0-207-20048-9(3))* HarperCollins Pubs. Australia.

—Octavius O'Malley & the Mystery of the Missing Mouse. Sunderland, Alan. 2007. (Octavius O'Malley Investigates Ser.: Bk. 2). 256p. (J). *(978-0-207-20049-6(1))* HarperCollins Pubs. Australia.

Redmon, Angela M. The Adventures of Margaret Mouse: Hide 'n Seek. Wyatt, Cherokee. l.t. ed. 2005. 32p. (J). (gr. k-5). 6.95 *(978-0-9761326-4-6(8))* www.margaretmouse.com publishing co.

—The Adventures of Margaret Mouse: School Days. Wyatt, Cherokee. l.t. ed. 2004. 32p. (J). 6.95 *(978-0-9761326-0-8(5))* www.margaretmouse.com publishing co.

—The Adventures of Margaret Mouse: The Picnic. Wyatt, Cherokee. 2004. 32p. (J). 6.95 *(978-0-9761326-1-5(3))* www.margaretmouse.com publishing co.

Redmond, E. S. Felicity Floo Visits the Zoo. Redmond, E. S. (ENG.). 32p. (J). 2010. (-k). pap. 6.99 *(978-0-7636-4975-3(9));* 2009. (gr. -1-k). 15.99 *(978-0-7636-3444-5(1))* Candlewick Pr.

—The Unruly Queen. Redmond, E. S. 2012. (ENG.). 32p. (J). (gr. -1-2). 15.99 *(978-0-7636-3445-2(X))* Candlewick Pr.

Redondo, Fernando. Dulcita y el Burrito. Reyes, Carlos Jose. 2004. (Primer Acto: Teatro Infantil y Juvenil Ser.). (SPA.). 59p. (J). (gr. -1-7). pap. *(978-958-30-0313-4(1))* Panamericana Editorial.

Redondo, Frank. Mark Twain/the Adventures of Huckleberry Finn. Twain, Mark. 2005. 48p. (gr. 5-8). 25.50 *(978-0-7910-9101-2(5))* Facts On File, Inc.

Redondo, Jesus. Turtle Rescue! Chanda, J-P. 2004. (Teenage Mutant Ninja Turtles Ser.). 32p. (J). (gr. 4-7). 11.65 *(978-0-7569-5371-3(5))* Perfection Learning Corp.

Redondo, Jesus & Ivan & Moxo. Police on Patrol. Auerbach, Annie. 2003. (Matchbox Hero City Ser.). 32p. (J). (gr. -1-3). lib. bdg. 11.25 *(978-0-613-66533-9(3),* Turtleback) Turtleback Bks.

Redondo, Jesus, jt. illus. see Vasquez, Ivan.

Redondo, Nestor. Bram Stoker/Dracula. Stoker, Bram. 2005. 48p. (gr. 5-8). 25.50 *(978-0-7910-9109-8(0))* Facts On File, Inc.

Redpath, Dale. Passages, 1 bk. Hulme, Lucy V. 2005. 40p. (J). 7.95 *(978-0-9769854-0-2(3),* 001) Combs-Hulme Publishing.

Redshaw, Louise. At the Park. Young, Annemarie. 2013. (Start Reading Ser.). (ENG.). 24p. (gr. k-1). pap. 41.94 *(978-1-4765-3207-3(9));* pap. 6.99 *(978-1-4765-3191-5(9))* Capstone Pr., Inc.

—In the Garden. Young, Annemarie. 2013. (Start Reading Ser.). (ENG.). 24p. (gr. k-1). pap. 41.94 *(978-1-4765-3220-2(6));* pap. 6.99 *(978-1-4765-3192-2(7))* Capstone Pr., Inc.

—Let's Go Out. Young, Annemarie. 2013. (Start Reading Ser.). (ENG.). 24p. (gr. k-1). pap. 41.94 *(978-1-4765-3223-3(0));* pap. 6.99 *(978-1-4765-3193-9(5))* Capstone Pr., Inc.

—Our Castle, 1 vol. Young, Annemarie. 2013. (Start Reading Ser.). (ENG.). 24p. (gr. k-1). pap. 6.99 *(978-1-4765-3194-6(3));* pap. 41.94 *(978-1-4765-3228-8(1))* Capstone Pr., Inc.

Reece, James A. Chocolate Puddles. Lovvorn, Ann R. 2010. 36p. pap. 15.49 *(978-1-4520-5158-1(5))* AuthorHouse.

Reece, Maynard. Animals under Your Feet. Green, Ivah E. 2011. 140p. 40.95 *(978-1-258-06244-6(5))* Literary Licensing, LLC.

Reed, Bill. Herbert Hilligan's SeaWorld Adventure. Epner, Paul. 2005. (J). 16.95 *(978-0-9743335-9-5(X))* Imaginative Publishing, Ltd.

—There's a Dachshund in My Bed! Epner, Paul. 2004. 56p. (J). 16.95 *(978-0-9743335-8-8(1))* Imaginative Publishing, Ltd.

Reed, C. W. Jack the Fisherman. Phelps, Elizabeth Stuart. 2005. reprint ed. pap. 15.95 *(978-1-4179-3778-3(5))* Kessinger Publishing, LLC.

Reed, Joel B. Grandpa's New Kitty. Reed, Joel B. 2008. 28p. pap. 12.95 *(978-1-933482-65-1(6))* White Turtle Bks.

Reed, Kyle. Ride the Whale: A Surfer Tall Tale. Apte, Sunita. 2006. 16p. (J). pap. *(978-0-439-74638-0(8))* Scholastic, Inc.

Reed, Linda Davis. Adirondack ABCs. Snavlin, Joyce Burgess. 2009. 32p. (J). 9.95 *(978-1-59531-028-6(2))* North Country Bks., Inc.

Reed, Lisa. Adam Named the Animals from a to Z. Stortz, Diane. 2012. (Roma Downey's Little Angels Ser.). 24p. (J). bds. 7.99 *(978-0-8249-5642-4(7),* Candy Cane Pr.) Ideals Pubns.

—Bob & Larry's Book of Prayers. Schaefer, Peggy. 2014. (VeggieTales Bk Ser.). 32p. (J). bds. 10.99 *(978-0-8249-1929-0(7),* Candy Cane Pr.) Ideals Pubns.

—Everybody Counts. Moore, Karen. 2012. (Roma Downey's Little Angels Ser.). 24p. (J). bds. 7.99 *(978-0-8249-5643-1(5),* Candy Cane Pr.) Ideals Pubns.

—Frosty the Snowman. Rollins, Jack & Nelson, Steve. 2014. 22p. (J). bds. 6.99 *(978-0-8249-1935-1(1))* Ideals Pubns.

—God Made You Special! Fritz, Greg. 2015. (J). *(978-0-8249-1947-4(5))* Ideals Pubns.

—The Great Easter Egg Hunt. Rumbaugh, Melinda. 2014. (VeggieTales Bk Ser.). 16p. (J). 12.99 *(978-0-8249-1928-3(9),* Candy Cane Pr.) Ideals Pubns.

—The Story of Jesus Activity Book. Adams, Michelle Medlock. 2014. 18p. (J). 4.99 *(978-0-8249-5659-2(1),* Ideals Children's Bks.) Ideals Pubns.

—The Story of Noah Activity Book. Adams, Michelle Medlock. 2014. 18p. (J). 4.99 *(978-0-8249-5660-8(5),* Ideals Children's Bks.) Ideals Pubns.

Reed, Lisa & Bennett, Randle Paul. Away in a Manger. Traditional. 2012. (VeggieTales Bk Ser.). 16p. (J). 12.99 *(978-0-8249-1882-8(7),* Candy Cane Pr.) Ideals Pubns.

Reed, Lisa, jt. illus. see Arif, Tasneem.

Reed, Lisa, jt. illus. see Pulley, Kelly.

Reed, Lynn Rowe. Big City Song. Pearson, Debora. 2006. (ENG.). 32p. (J). (gr. -1-3). 16.95 *(978-0-8234-1988-3(6))* Holiday Hse., Inc.

—The Case of the Incapacitated Capitals. Pulver, Robin. 2012. (ENG.). 32p. (J). 16.95 *(978-0-8234-2402-3(2))* Holiday Hse., Inc.

—The Case of the Incapacitated Capitals. Pulver, Robin. 2013. (ENG.). 32p. (J). pap. 7.99 *(978-0-8234-2914-1(8))* Holiday Hse., Inc.

—Happy Endings: A Story about Suffixes. Pulver, Robin. (ENG.). 32p. (J). 2012. pap. 7.95 *(978-0-8234-2434-4(0));* 2011. (gr. -1-3). 16.95 *(978-0-8234-2296-8(8))* Holiday Hse., Inc.

—Happy Endings: A Story about Suffixes. Pulver, Robin. 2013. (ENG.). (J). (gr. 1-3). pap. 44.95 *(978-1-4301-1435-2(5))* Live Oak Media.

—Nouns & Verbs Have a Field Day. Pulver, Robin. 2013. pap. 18.95 incl. audio compact disk *(978-1-4301-1115-3(1))* Live Oak Media.

—Punctuation Takes a Vacation. Pulver, Robin. 2003. (ENG.). (J). (gr. k-3). 36p. tchr. ed. 17.95 *(978-0-8234-1687-5(9));* 32p. reprint ed. pap. 7.99 *(978-0-8234-1820-6(0))* Holiday Hse., Inc.

—Punctuation Takes a Vacation. Pulver, Robin. 2009. (J). (gr. 1-3). 29.95 incl. audio compact disk *(978-1-4301-0708-8(1))* Live Oak Media.

—Silent Letters Loud & Clear. Pulver, Robin. 2010. (ENG.). 32p. (J). (gr. 1-3). pap. 7.99 *(978-0-8234-2309-5(3))* Holiday Hse., Inc.

—A Story with Pictures. Kanninen, Barbara. 2007. (ENG.). 32p. (J). (gr. -1-3). 16.95 *(978-0-8234-2049-0(3))* Holiday Hse., Inc.

Reed, Lynn Rowe. Color Chaos! Reed, Lynn Rowe. 2010. (ENG.). 32p. (J). (gr. -1-3). 16.95 *(978-0-8234-2257-9(7))* Holiday Hse., Inc.

—Fireman Fred. Reed, Lynn Rowe. 2014. (ENG.). 32p. (J). (gr. -1-3). pap. 6.99 *(978-0-8234-3182-3(7))* Holiday Hse., Inc.

—Roscoe & the Pelican Rescue. Reed, Lynn Rowe. 2011. (ENG.). 32p. (J). (gr. -1-3). 14.95 *(978-0-8234-2352-1(2))* Holiday Hse., Inc.

Reed, Mike. Bad to the Bone, 0 vols. Nolan, Lucy. (Down Girl & Sit Ser.: 0). (ENG.). 64p. (J). (gr. 1-4). 2011. pap. 7.99 *(978-0-7614-5834-0(4),* 9780761458340); 2008. 14.99 *(978-0-7614-5439-7(X),* 9780761454397) Amazon Publishing. (Amazon Children's Publishing).

—Catching the Wild Waiyuuzee. Williams-Garcia, Rita. 2007. (ENG.). 32p. (J). (gr. -1-1). 12.99 *(978-1-4169-6141-3(0),* Simon & Schuster/Paula Wiseman Bks.) Simon & Schuster/Paula Wiseman Bks.

—Cowboy Camp. Sauer, Tammi. (ENG.). (J). (gr. -1-k). 2015. 24p. bds. 6.95 *(978-1-4549-1389-4(4));* 2014. 32p. pap. 6.95 *(978-1-4549-1360-3(6));* 2005. 32p. 14.95 *(978-1-4027-2224-0(9))* Sterling Publishing Co., Inc.

—Even Firefighters Hug Their Moms. MacLean, Christine. 2004. (ENG.). 32p. (J). (gr. 3). pap. 5.99 *(978-0-14-240191-0(9),* Puffin) Penguin Publishing Group.

—Home on the Range, 0 vols. Nolan, Lucy. 2010. (Down Girl & Sit Ser.: 0). (ENG.). 64p. (J). (gr. 1-4). 14.99 *(978-0-7614-5649-0(X),* 9780761456490, Amazon Children's Publishing) Amazon Publishing.

—In the Whale. Greenburg, J. C. 2003. (Stepping Stone Book Ser.: Bk. 6). (ENG.). 96p. (J). (gr. 1-4). 3.99 *(978-0-375-82524-8(X),* Random Hse. Bks. for Young Readers) Random Hse. Children's Bks.

—Looking for Luna, 0 vols. Myers, Tim. 2009. (ENG.). 32p. (J). (gr. -1-3). 17.99 *(978-0-7614-5564-6(7),* 9780761455646, Amazon Children's Publishing) Amazon Publishing.

—A Million Dots. Clements, Andrew. 2006. (ENG.). 48p. (J). (gr. -1-3). 17.99 *(978-0-689-85824-6(8)*, Atheneum Bks. for Young Readers) Simon & Schuster Children's Publishing.
—On the Road, 0 vols. Nolan, Lucy. unabr. ed. 2009. (Down Girl & Sit Ser.: 0). (ENG.). 68p. (J). (gr. 1-4). pap. 9.99 *(978-0-7614-5572-1(8)*, 9780761455721, Amazon Children's Publishing) Amazon Publishing.
—Peanut. Kilgras, Heidi. 2003. (Step into Reading Ser.). (ENG.). 32p. (J). (gr. -1-1). pap. 3.99 *(978-0-375-80618-6(0)*, Random Hse. Bks. for Young Readers) Random Hse. Children's Bks.
—Scholastic Children's Thesaurus. Bollard, John K. & Bollard, John. rev. ed. 2006. (ENG.). 240p. (J). (gr. 3-7). 17.99 *(978-0-439-79831-0(0)*, Scholastic Reference) Scholastic, Inc.
—Smarter Than Squirrels, 0 vols. Nolan, Lucy. unabr. ed. 2009. (Down Girl & Sit Ser.: 0). (ENG.). 68p. (J). (gr. 1-4). pap. 9.99 *(978-0-7614-5571-4(X)*, 9780761455714, Amazon Children's Publishing) Amazon Publishing.
—Under Water. Greenburg, J. C. 2003. (Stepping Stone Book Ser.: Bk. 5). (ENG.). 96p. (J). (gr. 1-4). mass mkt. 3.99 *(978-0-375-82523-1(1)*, Random Hse. Bks. for Young Readers) Random Hse. Children's Bks.

Reed, Mike & Gerardi, Jan. On the Reef. Greenburg, J. C. Reed, Mike, tr. 2004. (Stepping Stone Book Ser.: Bk. 7). (ENG.). 96p. (J). (gr. 1-4). 3.99 *(978-0-375-82525-5(8)*, Random Hse. Bks. for Young Readers) Random Hse. Children's Bks.

Reed, Nathan. Beware the Werepup. Sykes, Julie. unabr. ed. 2014. (ENG.). 384p. (J). (gr. 2-4). pap. 8.99 *(978-1-4472-1961-3(9))* Pan Macmillan GBR. Dist: Independent Pubs. Group.
—The Broomstick Collection, Bks 1-4. Friel, Maeve. 2006. (Witch-In-Training Ser.). (ENG.). 368p. (J). (gr. 2-4). 14.95 *(978-0-00-724072-2(4))* HarperCollins Pubs. Ltd. GBR. Dist: Independent Pubs. Group.
—The Buskers of Bremen. 2004. 24p. (J). (POL & ENG.). *(978-1-85269-800-3(4))*; pap. *(978-1-85269-225-4(1))*; pap. *(978-1-85269-765-5(2))*; (ENG & CHI.). pap. *(978-1-85269-767-9(9))*; pap. *(978-1-85269-768-6(7))*; (GER & ENG.). pap. *(978-1-85269-770-9(9))*; pap. *(978-1-85269-771-6(7))*; (CZE & ENG.). pap. *(978-1-85269-773-0(3))*; pap. *(978-1-85269-774-7(1))*; (ENG.). pap. *(978-1-85269-775-4(X))*; pap. *(978-1-85269-776-1(8))*; (ITA & ENG.). pap. *(978-1-85269-777-8(6))*; (ENG & SPA.). pap. *(978-1-85269-778-5(4))*; pap. *(978-1-85269-779-2(2))*; (TUR & ENG.). pap. *(978-1-85269-780-8(6))* Mantra Lingua.
—The Buskers of Bremen. Barkow, Henriette. 2004. (ENG & PAN.). 24p. (J). pap. *(978-1-85269-772-3(5))* Mantra Lingua.
—Buskers of Bremen: Big Book English Only. 2004. (BEN & ENG.). (J). *(978-1-84444-301-7(9))* Mantra Lingua.
—The Last Task. Friel, Maeve. 2006. (Witch-In-Training Ser.). (ENG.). 96p. (J). (gr. 4-7). pap. 7.50 *(978-0-00-718527-6(8)*, HarperCollins Children's Bks.) HarperCollins Pubs. Ltd. GBR. Dist: Independent Pubs. Group.
—Moonlight Mischief. Friel, Maeve. 2005. (Witch-In-Training Ser.). (ENG.). 96p. (J). per. 7.50 *(978-0-00-718526-9(X))* HarperCollins Pubs. Ltd. GBR. Dist: Independent Pubs. Group.
—Pigwitchery. Weatherly, Lee. ed. 2008. (ENG.). 32p. (J). *(978-1-4050-9234-0(3)*, Macmillan Children's Bks.) Pan Macmillan.

Reed, Nathan, jt. illus. see Barkow, Henriette.

Reed, Neil. The Adventures of Tom Sawyer. Twain, Mark. 2008. (Puffin Classics Ser.). (ENG.). 352p. (J). (gr. 3-7). 5.99 *(978-0-14-132110-3(5)*, Puffin) Penguin Publishing Group.
—Nelson Mandela: The Life of an African Statesman. Shone, Rob. 2007. (Graphic Nonfiction Biographies Ser.). (ENG.). 48p. (J). (gr. 4-7). lib. bdg. 31.95 *(978-1-4042-0860-5(7))*; (gr. 5-8). pap. 14.05 *(978-1-4042-0923-7(9))* Rosen Publishing Group, Inc., The.

Reed, Rebecca. The Train to Maine. Spencer, Jamie. 2008. (ENG.). 32p. (J). (gr. -1-3). 15.95 *(978-0-89272-767-4(5))* Down East Bks.

Reed, Rebecca Harrison, jt. illus. see Sollers, Jim.

Reed, Rosemary & Seto, Lillian. Snow Painting: Chinese Brush Painting, 1 book. Brekke, Robert, photos by. Reed, Rosemary. Brekke, Robert & James, Midge, eds. 2006. 88p. 32.95 *(978-1-929170-15-9(7)*, PDG) Publishers Design Group, Inc.

Reed, Stephen. BMO's Day Out, No. 1. Brallier, Max. 2013. (Adventure Time Ser.). (ENG.). 128p. (J). (gr. 3-7). pap. 4.99 *(978-0-8431-7327-7(0)*, Price Stern Sloan) Penguin Publishing Group.

Reed, Stephen. Gumball's Summer Journal That He Definitely Finished All on His Own. Luper, Eric. 2015. (Amazing World of Gumball Ser.). (ENG.). 112p. (J). (gr. 3-7). 8.99 ***(978-0-8431-8282-8(2))*** Penguin Publishing Group.

Reed, Stephen. SpongeBob, Soccer Star! Lewman, David. 2010. (SpongeBob SquarePants Ser.). (ENG.). 24p. (J). (gr. -1-3). pap. 3.99 *(978-1-4169-9445-9(9)*, Simon Spotlight/Nickelodeon) Simon Spotlight/Nickelodeon.
—Tales from the Land of Ooo. Brallier, Max. 2013. (Adventure Time Ser.). (ENG.). 64p. (J). (gr. 3-7). pap. 5.99 *(978-0-8431-7270-6(3)*, Price Stern Sloan) Penguin Publishing Group.
—Which Way, Dude? - Jake Goes Bananas, No. 2. Brallier, Max. 2013. (Adventure Time Ser.). (ENG.). 128p. (J). (gr. 3-7). 4.99 *(978-0-8431-7526-4(5)*, Price Stern Sloan) Penguin Publishing Group.

Reed, Susan. Up up Up. Oldfield, Rachel. 2011. (ENG.). 24p. (J). (gr. 1-4). pap. 9.99 *(978-1-84686-550-3(6))* Barefoot Bks., Inc.

Reed, Susan, jt. illus. see McDonald, Jill.

Reel FX Inc. Staff. Bet on It. Evans, Cordelia. 2014. (Book of Life Ser.). (ENG.). 16p. (J). (gr. -1-3). pap. 5.99 *(978-1-4814-2564-3(1)*, Simon Spotlight) Simon Spotlight.

Reel FX Inc. Staff, et al. A Hero's Journey. Pendergrass, Daphne. 2014. (Book of Life Ser.). (ENG.). 24p. (J). (gr. -1-3). pap. 3.99 *(978-1-4814-2349-6(5)*, Simon Spotlight) Simon Spotlight.
—A Tale of Two Friends. 2014. (Book of Life Ser.). (ENG.). 32p. (J). (gr. k-2). pap. 3.99 *(978-1-4814-2573-5(0)*, Simon Spotlight) Simon Spotlight.

Rees, Mary. The Gordon Star. Patterson, Rebecca. 2006. (ENG.). 32p. (J). (gr. k-2). 17.95 *(978-0-86264-893-0(9))* Andersen Pr. GBR. Dist: Independent Pubs. Group.
—Little Brother & the Cough. Oram, Hiawyn. 32p. (J). (gr. -1-1). 10.99 *(978-0-7112-0844-5(1)*, Frances Lincoln) Quarto Publishing Group UK GBR. Dist: Perseus-PGW.

Reese, Amy. Illustrated Psalms of Praise: Psalmos de Albanza Ilustrados. 2005. (SPA & ENG.). 64p. (J). 16.95 *(978-1-56854-561-5(4))* Liturgy Training Pubns.

Reese, Bob. Camping Out. Steinkraus, Kyla. 2011. (ENG.). 24p. (gr. 2-3). 28.50 *(978-1-61741-827-3(7))*; pap. 7.95 *(978-1-61236-031-7(9))* Rourke Educational Media.
—Do I Have To ... Picou, Lin. 2011. (ENG.). 24p. (gr. 1-2). 28.50 *(978-1-61741-816-7(1))* Rourke Educational Media.
—Do I Have To... Picou, Lin. ed. 2011. (ENG.). 24p. (gr. 1-2). pap. 7.95 *(978-1-61236-020-1(3))* Rourke Educational Media.
—Fish Stories. Robbins, Maureen & Steinkraus, Kyla. ed. 2011. (ENG.). 24p. (gr. 2-3). pap. 7.95 *(978-1-61236-035-5(1))* Rourke Educational Media.
—Gator's Out, Said the Trout. Spaht-Gill, Janie. (J). (gr. k-2). 5.95 *(978-0-89868-305-9(X))* ARO Publishing Co.
—Habitat for Bats. Robbins, Maureen. ed. 2011. (ENG.). 24p. (gr. 2-3). pap. 7.95 *(978-1-61236-037-9(8))* Rourke Educational Media.
—Monster Stew. Spaht-Gill, Janie. (J). 5.95 *(978-0-89868-307-3(6))* ARO Publishing Co.
—Ouch! Stitches. Karapetkova, Holly & Picou, Lin. ed. 2011. (ENG.). 24p. (gr. 1-2). pap. 7.95 *(978-1-61236-023-2(8))* Rourke Educational Media.
—Puppy Trouble. Moreta, Gladys & Picou, Lin. ed. 2011. (ENG.). 24p. (gr. 1-2). pap. 7.95 *(978-1-61236-018-8(1))* Rourke Educational Media.
—Ready, Set, Race! Robbins, Maureen & Steinkraus, Kyla. ed. 2011. (ENG.). 24p. (gr. 2-3). pap. 7.95 *(978-1-61236-033-1(5))* Rourke Educational Media.
—Stop Arguing! Karapetkova, Holly & Moreta, Gladys. 2011. (ENG.). 24p. (gr. 2-3). 28.50 *(978-1-61741-832-7(3))* Rourke Educational Media.
—Stop Arguing! Karapetkova, Holly & Robins, Maureen. ed. 2011. (ENG.). 24p. (gr. 2-3). pap. 7.95 *(978-1-61236-032-4(7))* Rourke Educational Media.
—Stop Arguing! Steinkraus, Kyla & Moreta, Gladys. ed. 2011. (ENG.). 24p. (gr. 2-3). pap. 7.95 *(978-1-61236-036-2(X))* Rourke Educational Media.
—Too Much Tv! Picou, Lin & Moreta, Gladys. ed. 2011. (ENG.). 24p. (gr. 1-2). pap. 7.95 *(978-1-61236-019-5(X))* Rourke Educational Media.
—The Tree Fort. Steinkraus, Kyla. ed. 2011. (ENG.). 24p. (gr. 2-3). pap. 7.95 *(978-1-61236-038-6(6))* Rourke Educational Media.
—The Trouble with Trading. Steinkraus, Kyla. ed. 2011. (ENG.). 24p. (gr. 2-3). pap. 7.95 *(978-1-61236-034-8(3))* Rourke Educational Media.

Reese, Brandon. Print Writing: A Creepy-Crawly Alphabet. Flash Kids Editors, ed. 2012. (ENG.). 112p. (J). (gr. k-2). pap. 5.95 *(978-1-4114-6344-8(7)*, Spark Publishing Group) Sterling Publishing Co., Inc.

Reese, Brandon. Draw Me Healthy! Reese, Brandon. 2012. 32p. (J). 7.99 *(978-0-8280-2680-2(7))* Review & Herald Publishing Assn.

Reese, Erica. My Almighty Daddy. 2007. 16p. (J). 10.00 *(978-0-9720773-3-0(2))* Christiangela Productions.

Reese, Jonathan. In the Ocean. Taylor, Trace et al. 2006. (1-3Y Ecosystems Ser.). (ENG.). 16p. (J). (gr. k-1). pap. 6.50 *(978-1-59301-438-4(4))* American Reading Co.

Reese, Rick. Class Clown Academy. Mooser, Stephen. 2013. (ENG.). 108p. pap. 5.99 *(978-0-615-75102-3(4))* Class Clown Academy.
—Dream Town. Markel, Michelle. 2006. (J). 15.95 *(978-1-59714-022-5(8))* Heyday.

Reeve, Philip. The Snail Patrol. d'Lacey, Chris. 2005. 123p. (J). (gr. 2-5). per. 5.95 *(978-1-903015-30-8(8))* Barn Owl Bks, London GBR. Dist: Independent Pubs. Group.

Reeve, Philip. Esa Condenada Mala Suerte. Reeve, Philip. Poskitt, Kjartan. (SPA.). 176p. (YA). (gr. 5-8). pap. *(978-84-272-2091-1(X))* Molino, Editorial ESP. Dist: Lectorum Pubns., Inc.
—Esas Exasperantes Medidas de Longitud, Area y Volumen. Reeve, Philip. Poskitt, Kjartan. (SPA.). 178p. (YA). (gr. 5-8). *(978-84-272-2069-0(3))* Molino, Editorial ESP. Dist: Lectorum Pubns., Inc.
—Mas Mortiferas Mates. Reeve, Philip. Poskitt, Kjartan. (SPA.). 159p. (YA). (gr. 5-8). pap. *(978-84-272-2060-7(X))* Molino, Editorial ESP. Dist: Lectorum Pubns., Inc.

Reeve, Rosie. Mondays at Monster School. Symes, Ruth Louise. 2009. (ENG.). 32p. (J). (gr. -1-k). pap. 11.99 *(978-1-84255-536-1(7)*, Orion Children's Bks.) Hachette Children's Group GBR. Dist: Independent Pubs. Group.
—My Friend Fred. Oram, Hiawyn. 2012. (J). *(978-1-58925-105-2(9))* Tiger Tales.
—Not Again, Annie!, Vol. 2. Payne, Jan & Payne, Tony. 2004. (Annie Ser.). (ENG.). 80p. (J). (gr. 2-4). pap. 11.95 *(978-1-84255-158-5(2)*, Dolphin Paperbacks) Orion Publishing Group, Ltd. GBR. Dist: Independent Pubs. Group.

Reeve, Rosie. Lullaby Moon. Reeve, Rosie. 2010. (ENG.). 20p. (J). (gr. k — 1). bds. 8.99 *(978-0-545-21146-8(8)*, Cartwheel Bks.) Scholastic, Inc.

Reeve, Tony. Esas Geniales Peliculas. Reeve, Tony, tr. Oliver, Martin. (Coleccion Esa Gran Cultura).Tr. of Groovy Movies. (SPA.). 160p. (YA). (gr. 5-8). 7.96 *(978-84-272-2133-8(9))* Molino, Editorial ESP. Dist: Lectorum Pubns., Inc.

Reeves, Jeni. Anansi & the Box of Stories. Krensky, Stephen. 2008. (On My Own Folklore Ser.). (ENG.). 48p. (gr. 2-4). pap. 6.95 *(978-0-8225-6745-5(8)*, First Avenue Editions) Lerner Publishing Group.
—Enrique Esparza & the Battle of the Alamo. Brown, Susan Taylor. 2010. (History Speaks: Picture Books Plus Reader's Theater Ser.). (ENG.). 48p. (gr. 2-4). pap. 9.95 *(978-0-7613-3942-7(6))*; lib. bdg. 27.93 *(978-0-8225-8566-4(9)*, Millbrook Pr.) Lerner Publishing Group.
—George Washington & the Story of the U. S. Constitution. Ransom, Candice. 2011. (History Speaks: Picture Books Plus Reader's Theater Ser.). 48p. pap. 56.72 *(978-0-7613-7632-3(1))*; (ENG.). (gr. 2-4). 27.93 *(978-0-7613-5877-0(3)*, Millbrook Pr.) Lerner Publishing Group.
—The Lion & the Hare. Krensky, Stephen. 2008. (On My Own Folklore Ser.). (ENG.). 48p. (gr. 2-4). lib. bdg. 25.26 *(978-0-8225-7546-7(9)*, Millbrook Pr.) Lerner Publishing Group.
—Mike Fink. Krensky, Stephen. 2006. (On My Own Folklore Ser.). (ENG.). 48p. (gr. 2-4). lib. bdg. 25.26 *(978-1-57505-891-7(X)*, Millbrook Pr.) Lerner Publishing Group.
—Mike Fink. Krensky, Stephen. 2007. (On My Own Folklore Ser.). (ENG.). 48p. (gr. 2-4). per. 6.95 *(978-0-8225-6478-2(5)*, First Avenue Editions) Lerner Publishing Group.
—La Niña Que Ponchó a Babe Ruth. Patrick, Jean L. S. Translations.com Staff, tr. from ENG. 2007. (Yo Solo: Historia (on My Own History) Ser.).Tr. of Girl Who Struck Out Babe Ruth. (SPA.). 48p. (gr. 2-4). lib. bdg. 25.26 *(978-0-8225-7785-0(2)*, Ediciones Lerner) Lerner Publishing Group.
—Passover. Fishman, Cathy Goldberg. 2006. (On My Own Holidays Ser.). (ENG.). 48p. (gr. 2-4). per. 6.95 *(978-1-57505-695-1(X)*, First Avenue Editions) Lerner Publishing Group.
—Ramadan. Douglass, Susan L. 2003. (On My Own Holidays Ser.). (ENG.). 48p. (gr. 2-4). pap. 6.95 *(978-1-57505-584-8(8))* Lerner Publishing Group.
—Willie McLean & the Civil War Surrender. Ransom, Candice. 2004. (On My Own History Ser.). (ENG.). 48p. (gr. 2-4). 25.26 *(978-1-57505-588-6(0))*; pap. 6.95 *(978-1-57505-698-2(4))* Lerner Publishing Group.

Reeves, Jeni, jt. illus. see Marshall, Ann.

Reeves, Louise. The Talking Animals Part 2: Magic. Ohanian, Armineh. 2011. (ENG.). 68p. pap. 14.95 *(978-1-4637-4470-0(6))* CreateSpace Independent Publishing Platform.

Reeves, Rick. United No More! Stories of the Civil War. Rappaport, Doreen & Verniero, Joan C. 2006. 144p. (J). (gr. 3-7). lib. bdg. 17.89 *(978-0-06-050600-1(8))* HarperCollins Pubs.

Reeves, Ruth. Tal, His Marvelous Adventures with Noom-Zor-Noom. Cooper, Paul Fenimore. 80th ed. 2009. 305p. (J). pap. 12.95 *(978-1-930900-41-7(4))* Purple Hse. Pr.

Reeves, Sue. The Ultimate Sleepover Pack. Goldsack, Gaby. 24p. (J). 79.60 *(978-0-7641-7662-3(5))* Barron's Educational Series, Inc.

Regan, Dana. Away Went the Farmer's Hat: A Book about an Adventure. Moncure, Jane Belk. 2013. (Magic Castle Readers: Language Arts Ser.). (ENG.). 32p. (J). (gr. -1-2). 25.64 *(978-1-62323-572-7(3)*, 206309) Child's World, Inc., The.
—Brains vs. Brawn. Hoena, Blake. 2014. (Jess & Jaylen Ser.). (ENG.). 48p. (J). (gr. 1-4). 27.07 *(978-1-63143-436-5(5)*, 208260) Child's World, Inc., The.
—El Closet de Bessey, la Desordenada. McKissack, Patricia C. & McKissack, Fredrick L. 2003. (Rookie Reader Español Ser.).Tr. of Messy Bessey's Closet. (SPA.). 32p. (J). (gr. k-2). pap. 4.95 *(978-0-516-27796-7(0)*, Children's Pr.) Scholastic Library Publishing.
—Coming Clean. Hoena, Blake. 2014. (Jess & Jaylen Ser.). (ENG.). 48p. (J). (gr. 1-4). 27.07 *(978-1-63143-437-2(3)*, 208261) Child's World, Inc., The.
—Don't Let the Bedbugs Bite. Hawley, Greg. 2004. (J). *(978-0-9657612-7-7(4))* Paddle Wheel Publishing.
—A Dragon in a Wagon: A Book about Ways to Travel. Moncure, Jane Belk. 2013. (Magic Castle Readers: Language Arts Ser.). (ENG.). 32p. (J). (gr. -1-2). 25.64 *(978-1-62323-573-4(1)*, 206307) Child's World, Inc., The.
—Even the Sound Waves Obey Him: Bible Stories Brought to Life with Science. Kennedy, Nancy B. 2005. (CPH Teaching Resource Ser.). (ENG.). 64p. pap. 10.99 *(978-0-7586-0985-4(X))* Concordia Publishing Hse.
—Haiku on Your Shoes. Berry, Eileen M. 2005. 56p. (J). (gr. -1-3). per. 7.49 *(978-1-59166-374-4(1))* BJU Pr.
—Halloween Scream. Hoena, Blake. 2014. (Jess & Jaylen Ser.). (ENG.). 48p. (J). (gr. 1-4). 27.07 *(978-1-63143-438-9(1)*, 208262) Child's World, Inc., The.
—I Can Learn Bible Stories. Ellis, Gwen. 2006. 10p. (J). spiral bd. 10.99 *(978-0-8254-5530-8(8))* Kregel Pubns.
—I Love Bathtime. Berry, Joy. 2010. (Teach Me About Ser.). (ENG.). 20p. (J). (gr. k — 1). pap. 5.99 *(978-1-60577-013-0(2))* Berry, Joy Enterprises.
—I Love Bedtime. Berry, Joy. 2010. (Teach Me About Ser.). (ENG.). 20p. (J). (gr. k — 1). pap. 5.99 *(978-1-60577-004-8(3))* Berry, Joy Enterprises.
—I Love Being Healthy. Berry, Joy. 2010. (Teach Me About Ser.). (ENG.). 20p. (J). (gr. k — 1). pap. 5.99 *(978-1-60577-005-5(1))* Berry, Joy Enterprises.
—I Love Brothers & Sisters. Berry, Joy. 2010. (Teach Me About Ser.). (ENG.). 20p. (J). (gr. k — 1). pap. 5.99 *(978-1-60577-002-4(7))* Berry, Joy Enterprises.
—I Love Daycare. Berry, Joy. 2010. (Teach Me About Ser.). (ENG.). 20p. (J). (gr. k — 1). bds. 5.99 *(978-1-60577-016-1(7))* Berry, Joy Enterprises.
—I Love Getting Dressed. Berry, Joy. 2010. (Teach Me About Ser.). (ENG.). 20p. (J). (gr. k — 1). bds. 5.99 *(978-1-60577-014-7(0))* Berry, Joy Enterprises.
—I Love Grandmas & Grandpas. Berry, Joy. 2010. (Teach Me About Ser.). (ENG.). 40p. (J). (gr. k — 1). pap. 5.99 *(978-1-60577-003-1(5))* Berry, Joy Enterprises.
—I Love Mealtime. Berry, Joy. 2010. (Teach Me About Ser.). (ENG.). 20p. (J). (gr. k — 1). pap. 5.99 *(978-1-60577-006-2(X))* Berry, Joy Enterprises.
—I Love Mommies & Daddies. Berry, Joy. 2010. (Teach Me About Ser.). (ENG.). 20p. (J). (gr. k — 1). pap. 5.99 *(978-1-60577-001-7(9))* Berry, Joy Enterprises.
—I Love My Friends. Berry, Joy. 2010. (Teach Me About Ser.). (ENG.). 20p. (J). (gr. k — 1). bds. 5.99 *(978-1-60577-017-8(5))* Berry, Joy Enterprises.
—I Love Preschool. Berry, Joy. 2010. (Teach Me About Ser.). (ENG.). 20p. (J). (gr. k — 1). bds. 5.99 *(978-1-60577-015-4(9))* Berry, Joy Enterprises.
—Let's Talk Tails. English, June. 2004. 14p. (J). (gr. k-4). reprint ed. 4.00 *(978-0-7567-7832-3(8))* DIANE Publishing Co.
—Messy Bessey Vol. 2: Messy Bessey's Closet - Messy Bessey's Family Reunion - Messy Bessey's Garden. McKissack, Patricia C. & McKissack, Fredrick L. 2008. (Rookie Reader Ser.). (ENG.). 96p. (J). (gr. k-2). 9.95 *(978-0-516-25301-5(8)*, Children's Pr.) Scholastic Library Publishing.
—Mr. Doodle Had a Poodle: A Book about Fun Activities. Moncure, Jane Belk. 2013. (Magic Castle Readers: Language Arts Ser.). (ENG.). 32p. (J). (gr. -1-2). 25.64 *(978-1-62323-574-1(X)*, 206310) Child's World, Inc., The.
—Museum Mystery. Hoena, Blake. 2014. (Jess & Jaylen Ser.). (ENG.). 48p. (J). (gr. 1-4). 27.07 *(978-1-63143-439-6(X)*, 208263) Child's World, Inc., The.
—My Little Easter Book. Steigemeyer, Julie. 2008. 20p. (J). (gr. -1-k). bds. 6.49 *(978-0-7586-1444-5(6))* Concordia Publishing Hse.
—A New Home for Truman. Hapka, Catherine. 2015. (Pet Rescue Club Ser.: 1). (ENG.). 128p. (J). (gr. 1-3). pap. 5.99 *(978-0-7944-3312-3(X))*; lib. bdg. 16.99 *(978-0-7944-3351-2(0))* Studio Fun International.
—No Time for Hallie. Hapka, Catherine. 2015. (Pet Rescue Club Ser.: 2). (ENG.). 128p. (J). (gr. 1-3). pap. 5.99 *(978-0-7944-3313-0(8))*; lib. bdg. 16.99 *(978-0-7944-3352-9(9))* Studio Fun International.
—Polka-Dot Puppy: A Just-for-Fun Book. Moncure, Jane Belk. 2013. (Magic Castle Readers: Language Arts Ser.). (ENG.). 32p. (J). (gr. -1-2). 25.64 *(978-1-62323-575-8(8)*, 206311) Child's World, Inc., The.
—School Bus Bully. Hoena, Blake. 2014. (Jess & Jaylen Ser.). (ENG.). 48p. (J). (gr. 1-4). 27.07 *(978-1-63143-440-2(3)*, 208264) Child's World, Inc., The.
—Skateboard Scare. Hoena, Blake. 2014. (Jess & Jaylen Ser.). (ENG.). 48p. (J). (gr. 1-4). 27.07 *(978-1-63143-441-9(1)*, 208265) Child's World, Inc., The.
—Trouble with Cheating. Hoena, Blake. 2014. (Jess & Jaylen Ser.). (ENG.). 48p. (J). (gr. 1-4). 27.07 *(978-1-63143-442-6(X)*, 208266) Child's World, Inc., The.
—Video Game Zombie. Hoena, Blake. 2014. (Jess & Jaylen Ser.). (ENG.). 48p. (J). (gr. 1-4). 27.07 *(978-1-63143-443-3(8)*, 208267) Child's World, Inc., The.
—When I Am/Cuando Estoy. Rosa-Mendoza, Gladys. (English Spanish Foundations Ser.). 20p. (gr. -1-k). 2007. pap. 19.95 *(978-1-931398-83-1(6))*; 2004. (SPA & ENG.). (J). bds. 6.95 *(978-1-931398-12-1(7))* Me+Mi Publishing.
—A Wish-For Dinosaur: A Just-for-Fun Book. Moncure, Jane Belk. 2013. (Magic Castle Readers: Language Arts Ser.). (ENG.). 32p. (J). (gr. -1-2). 25.64 *(978-1-62323-576-5(6)*, 206308) Child's World, Inc., The.
—5 Steps to Drawing Dogs & Cats. StJohn, Amanda. 2011. (5 Steps to Drawing Ser.). (ENG.). 32p. (J). (gr. k-3). lib. bdg. 27.07 *(978-1-60973-196-0(4)*, 201103) Child's World, Inc., The.

Regan, Laura. A Is for Anaconda: A Rainforest Alphabet. Fredericks, Anthony D. 2009. (Science Ser.). (ENG.). 40p. (J). (gr. 1-5). 17.95 *(978-1-58536-317-9(0))* Sleeping Bear Pr.
—Mama Mama - Papa Papa. Marzollo, Jean. 2003. (Flip Boardbks.). (ENG.). 32p. (J). (gr. -1 — 1). bds. 7.99 *(978-0-06-051915-5(0)*, HarperFestival) HarperCollins Pubs.
—Pierre the Penguin. Marzollo, Jean. 2010. (ENG.). 32p. (J). (gr. -1-2). 15.95 *(978-1-58536-485-5(1))* Sleeping Bear Pr.

Regan, Lisa. Seek & Find Fairy: Find a Charm Book. Elliot, Rachel. 2014. (Seek & Find Ser.). (ENG.). 32p. (J). (gr. -1-1). 9.99 *(978-0-7641-6696-9(4))* Barron's Educational Series, Inc.
—Seek & Find Princess: Find a Charm Book. Elliot, Rachel. 2014. (Seek & Find Ser.). (ENG.). 32p. (J). (gr. -1-1). 9.99 *(978-0-7641-6697-6(2))* Barron's Educational Series, Inc.

Reger, Rob. El Libro Secreto de las Cosas Extranas. Reger, Rob. 2006. (Emily the Strange (Spanish) Ser.). (SPA.). 64p. reprint ed. 19.95 *(978-1-59497-189-1(7))* Public Square Bks.

Reger, Rob & Brooks, Brian. Emily the Strange, Vol. 1. Reger, Rob. 2006. (Emily the Strange (Spanish) Ser.). (SPA.). 64p. 19.95 *(978-1-59497-188-4(9))* Public Square Bks.

Reger, Rob & Parker, Buzz. Dark Times. Reger, Rob & Gruner, Jessica. 2011. (Emily the Strange Ser.: 3). (ENG.). 248p. (YA). (gr. 8). pap. 8.99 *(978-0-06-145237-6(8))* HarperCollins Pubs.
—Emily the Strange: Piece of Mind. Reger, Rob & Gruner, Jessica. 2011. (Emily the Strange Ser.: 4). (ENG.). 280p. (YA). (gr. 8). 17.99 *(978-0-06-145238-3(6))* HarperCollins Pubs.
—The Lost Days. Reger, Rob & Gruner, Jessica. (Emily the Strange Ser.: 1). (ENG.). (gr. 8). 2010. 264p. (YA). pap. 8.99 *(978-0-06-145231-4(9))*; 2009. 256p. (J). 16.99 *(978-0-06-145229-1(7))* HarperCollins Pubs.
—Piece of Mind. Reger, Rob & Gruner, Jessica. 2013. (Emily the Strange Ser.: 4). (ENG.). 288p. (YA). (gr. 8). pap. 9.99 *(978-0-06-145240-6(8))* HarperCollins Pubs.
—Stranger & Stranger. Reger, Rob & Gruner, Jessica. 2010. (Emily the Strange Ser.: 2). (ENG.). 272p. (YA). (gr. 8). pap. 9.99 *(978-0-06-145234-5(3))* HarperCollins Pubs.

Register, J. R. Tiny Paul the Tarantula Takes a Walk, 1 vol. Simpon, Tj. 2010. 70p. pap. 19.95 *(978-1-60703-117-8(5))* America Star Bks.

Reiach, Margaret Amy. El Ciclo de Vida de la Mariposa. Kalman, Bobbie. 2005. (Serie Ciclos de Vida Ser.). (SPA.). 32p. (J). (gr. 1-4). pap. *(978-0-7787-8708-2(7))* Crabtree Publishing Co.

R

Reiach, Margaret Amy & Crabtree, Marc. Goldfish. Crabtree, Marc, photos by. MacAulay, Kelley & Kalman, Bobbie. 2004. (Pet Care Ser.). (ENG.). 32p. (J). pap. *(978-0-7787-1791-1(7))*; lib. bdg. *(978-0-7787-1759-1(3))* Crabtree Publishing Co.

Reibeling, Brandon. Awesome Air. Korb, Rena. 2007. (Science Rocks Ser.). 32p. (gr. -1-4). 28.50 *(978-1-60270-036-9(2)*, Looking Glass Library-Nonfiction) Magic Wagon.

—Busy Buzzers: Bees in Your Backyard. Loewen, Nancy. 2003. (Backyard Bugs Ser.). (ENG.). 24p. (gr. -1-3). 25.99 *(978-1-4048-0143-1(X)*, Nonfiction Picture Bks.) Picture Window Bks.

—Crazy about Clouds. Korb, Rena. 2007. (Science Rocks Ser.). 32p. (gr. -1-4). 28.50 *(978-1-60270-037-6(0)*, Looking Glass Library- Nonfiction) Magic Wagon.

—Digging on Dirt. Korb, Rena. 2007. (Science Rocks Ser.). 32p. (gr. -1-4). 28.50 *(978-1-60270-038-3(9)*, Looking Glass Library- Nonfiction) Magic Wagon.

—Groovy Gravity. Korb, Rena. 2007. (Science Rocks Ser.). 32p. (gr. -1-4). 28.50 *(978-1-60270-039-0(7)*, Looking Glass Library- Nonfiction) Magic Wagon.

—Hungry Hoppers: Grasshoppers in Your Backyard. Loewen, Nancy. 2003. (Backyard Bugs Ser.). (ENG.). 24p. (gr. -1-3). per. 7.95 *(978-1-4048-0448-7(X)*, Nonfiction Picture Bks.) Picture Window Bks.

—Living Lights: Fireflies in Your Backyard. Loewen, Nancy. 2003. (Backyard Bugs Ser.). (ENG.). 24p. (gr. -1-3). 25.99 *(978-1-4048-0145-5(6))*; per. 7.95 *(978-1-4048-0447-0(1))* Picture Window Bks. (Nonfiction Picture Bks.).

—Missy Swiss. Slater, David Michael. 2007. (Missy Swiss & More Ser.). 32p. (gr. -1-4). 28.50 *(978-1-60270-010-9(9)*, Looking Glass Library) ABDO Publishing Co.

—Night Fliers: Moths in Your Backyard. Loewen, Nancy. 2003. (Backyard Bugs Ser.). (ENG.). 24p. (gr. -1-3). 25.99 *(978-1-4048-0144-8(8)*, Nonfiction Picture Bks.) Picture Window Bks.

—Radical Rocks. Korb, Rena. 2007. (Science Rocks Ser.). 32p. (gr. -1-4). 28.50 *(978-1-60270-040-6(0)*, Looking Glass Library- Nonfiction) Magic Wagon.

—Science Rocks! CD + Book Set. Korb, Rena. 2008. (Science Rocks! (CD+Book) Ser.). (J). (gr. 3). lib. bdg. 324.84 *(978-1-60270-210-3(1))* ABDO Publishing Co.

—The Sharpest Tool in the Shed. Slater, David Michael. 2007. (Missy Swiss & More Ser.). 32p. (gr. -1-4). 28.50 *(978-1-60270-013-0(3)*, Looking Glass Library) ABDO Publishing Co.

—The Wild Water Cycle. Korb, Rena. 2007. (Science Rocks Ser.). 32p. (gr. -1-4). 28.50 *(978-1-60270-041-3(9)*, Looking Glass Library- Nonfiction) Magic Wagon.

Reibeling, Brandon & Nichols, Garry. School Daze: A Book of Riddles about School, 1 vol. Dahl, Michael. 2003. (Read-It! Joke Bks.). (ENG.). 24p. (gr. k-3). 19.99 *(978-1-4048-0231-5(2)*, Easy Readers) Picture Window Bks.

Reibeling, Brandon, jt. illus. see Haberstroh, Anne.

Reich, Ashley. Izzy Lizzy. Reich, Ashley. 2005. 32p. (J). per. 16.00 *(978-0-9754298-3-9(3)*, Ithaca Pr.) Authors & Artists Publishers of New York, Inc.

Reich, Carin. Shining Stars: A Colors Book. Robinson, Alise. 2005. (Space Craze Ser.). 16p. (J). (gr. -1-k). per., bds. 6.95 *(978-1-58117-392-5(X)*, Intervisual/Piggy Toes) Bendon, Inc.

Reich, Kass. Up Hamster, down Hamster, 1 vol. 2015. (ENG.). 24p. (J). (gr. -1-k). bds. 9.95 ***(978-1-4598-1013-6(9))*** Orca Bk. Pubs. USA.

Reich, Robert E. Harry MacFly's the Old Mill Adventure. Reich, Robert E. 2013. (ENG.). 28p. (J). pap. 9.95 *(978-0-9895323-1-0(3))* Black Creek Publishing Group.

Reid, Barbara. The Night Before Christmas. Moore, Clement C. 2014. (ENG.). 32p. (J). (gr. -1-2). 16.99 *(978-0-8075-5625-2(4))* Whitman, Albert & Co.

—El Ternero Recien Nacido. Newlin-Chase, Edith. (SPA.). 32p. (J). (gr. -1-1). pap. 4.99 *(978-0-590-46106-1(0)*, SO30492) Scholastic, Inc.

Reid, Barbara. Fox Walked Alone. Reid, Barbara. 2009. (ENG.). 32p. (J). (gr. k-2). 16.99 *(978-0-8075-2548-7(0))* Whitman, Albert & Co.

—Perfect Snow. Reid, Barbara. 2011. (ENG.). 32p. (J). (gr. 1-4). 16.99 *(978-0-8075-6492-9(3))* Whitman, Albert & Co.

—Picture a Tree. Reid, Barbara. 2013. (ENG.). 32p. (J). (gr. -1-2). 16.99 *(978-0-8075-6526-1(1))* Whitman, Albert & Co.

—The Subway Mouse. Reid, Barbara. 2005. (J). *(978-0-439-77430-7(6))* Scholastic, Inc.

Reid, Fiona. Mammals. Alden, Peter C. 2nd ed. 2013. (Peterson Field Guide Color-In Bks.). (ENG.). 64p. (J). 8.95 *(978-0-544-03254-5(3))* Houghton Mifflin Harcourt Publishing Co.

Reid, Michael. Wicked Catch! Childs, Rob. 2003. (Corgi Pups Ser.). (ENG.). 64p. (J). pap. 7.99 *(978-0-552-54792-5(1))* Transworld Publishers Ltd. GBR. Dist: Independent Pubs. Group.

Reid, Mick. Boomerang Bob. Dale, Jenny. 2003. 105p. (J). *(978-0-439-45348-6(8))* Scholastic, Inc.

—Forever Sam. Dale, Jenny. 2003. 104p. (J). *(978-0-439-33801-1(8))* Scholastic, Inc.

—Homeward Bound. Dale, Jenny. 2003. 110p. (J). *(978-0-439-45354-7(2))* Scholastic, Inc.

—How Can I Get a Pet? Williams, Rozanne Lanczak. 2006. (Learn to Write Ser.). 8p. (J). (gr. k-2). pap. *(978-1-59198-290-6(1)*, 6184) Creative Teaching Pr., Inc.

—How Can I Get a Pet? Williams, Rozanne Lanczak. Maio, Barbara & Faulkner, Stacey, eds. 2006. (J). per. 6.99 *(978-1-59198-363-7(0))* Creative Teaching Pr., Inc.

—Husky Hero. Dale, Jenny. 2003. 108p. (J). *(978-0-439-54361-3(4))* Scholastic, Inc.

—If I Were a Cowboy, 1 vol. Braun, Eric. 2010. (Dream Big! Ser.). (ENG.). 24p. (gr. k-3). lib. bdg. 25.99 *(978-1-4048-5531-1(9)*, Nonfiction Picture Bks.) Picture Window Bks.

—If I Were a Firefighter, 1 vol. Troupe, Thomas Kingsley. 2010. (Dream Big! Ser.). (ENG.). 24p. (gr. k-3). lib. bdg. 25.99 *(978-1-4048-5535-9(1)*, Nonfiction Picture Bks.) Picture Window Bks.

—Jake's Progress. Dale, Jenny. 2003. 110p. (J). *(978-0-439-54365-1(7))* Scholastic, Inc.

—Jingle Belle. Dale, Jenny. 2003. 107p. (J). *(978-0-439-54366-8(5))* Scholastic, Inc.

—Little Star. Dale, Jenny. 2003. 109p. (J). *(978-0-439-54363-7(0))* Scholastic, Inc.

—Milly's Triumph. Dale, Jenny & Rowe, Michael. 2003. 102p. (J). *(978-0-439-45346-2(1))* Scholastic, Inc.

—Murphy's Mystery. Dale, Jenny. 2003. 110p. (J). *(978-0-439-54364-4(9))* Scholastic, Inc.

—The Puppy Express. Dale, Jenny. 2003. 108p. (J). *(978-0-439-45355-4(0))* Scholastic, Inc.

—Puppy Power. Dale, Jenny. 2003. 105p. (J). *(978-0-439-45351-6(8))* Scholastic, Inc.

—Signing Around Town: Sign Language for Kids, 1 vol. Clay, Kathryn. 2013. (Time to Sign Ser.). (ENG.). 32p. (gr. 1-2). 26.65 *(978-1-62065-053-0(3)*, Aplus Bks.) Capstone Pr., Inc.

—Top Dog! Dale, Jenny. 2003. 107p. (J). *(978-0-439-54360-6(6))* Scholastic, Inc.

—Wait for Me! Gerver, Jane E. (My First Reader Ser.). (J). (gr. k-1). 2005. (ENG.). 32p. pap. 3.95 *(978-0-516-25116-5(3))*; 2004. 31p. 18.50 *(978-0-516-24676-5(3))* Scholastic Library Publishing. (Children's Pr.).

Reid, Mike. A Night of Nonsense. Arlington, Jane. 2006. 20p. (J). *(978-1-59939-103-8(1)*, Reader's Digest Young Families, Inc.) Studio Fun International.

Reiff, Chris & Trevas, Chris. Darth Vader: A 3-D Reconstruction Log. Wallace, Daniel. 2011. (Star Wars Ser.). (ENG.). 24p. (J). bds. 19.99 *(978-0-545-31215-8(9))* Scholastic, Inc.

Reilly, Joan & Katz, Avi. Bar Mitzvah, Bat Mitzvah: The Ceremony, the Party, & How the Day Came to Be. Metter, Bert & Metter, Bertram. 2007. (ENG.). 80p. (J). (gr. 5-7). pap. 8.95 *(978-0-618-76773-1(8))* Houghton Mifflin Harcourt Publishing Co.

Reilly, Meghan M. What's Wrong with the New Girl? Jacques, Taryn Elise. 2004. 33p. pap. 24.95 *(978-1-4137-1999-4(6))* PublishAmerica, Inc.

Reilly, Michelle. In My Own Backyard. Larsen, Donna R. 2011. 30p. (J). *(978-0-615-52915-8(1))* DeuxRay Productions.

Reim, Melanie. The Cold War. Gottfried, Ted. 2003. (Rise & Fall of the Soviet Union Ser.). (ENG.). 160p. (gr. 7-12). lib. bdg. 29.20 *(978-0-7613-2560-4(3)*, Twenty-First Century Bks.) Lerner Publishing Group.

Reimer, Jackie. No Thanks, but I'd Love to Dance! Choosing to Live Smoke Free. Reimer, Jackie. 2010. (ENG.). 32p. (J). (gr. 2-4). 14.95 *(978-1-60443-027-1(3))* American Cancer Society, Inc.

Reingold, Alan. Liberty on 23rd Street. Glasthal, Jacqueline B. 2006. (Adventures in America Ser.). (gr. 4). 14.95 net. *(978-1-893110-45-8(1))* Silver Moon Pr.

Reinhardt, Jennifer Black. Footer Davis Probably Is Crazy. Vaught, Susan. 2015. (ENG.). 240p. (J). (gr. 5-9). 16.99 *(978-1-4814-2276-5(6)*, Simon & Schuster Bks. For Young Readers) Simon & Schuster Bks. For Young Readers.

—The Inventor's Secret: What Thomas Edison Told Henry Ford. Slade, Suzanne. 2015. (ENG.). 48p. (J). (gr. 1-4). lib. bdg. 16.95 *(978-1-58089-667-2(7))* Charlesbridge Publishing, Inc.

—Rabbi Benjamin's Buttons. McGinty, Alice B. 2014. (J). pap. *(978-1-58089-433-3(X))*; (ENG.). 32p. (gr. -1-3). lib. bdg. 17.95 *(978-1-58089-432-6(1))* Charlesbridge Publishing, Inc.

Reinhart, Larry. Frank & the Balloon: Sapi y el Globo. Ross, Dev & Canetti, Yanitzia. 2010. (SPA & ENG.). 41p. (J). *(978-1-60115-041-7(5))* Treasure Bay, Inc.

—Los dos leemos-el Mejor Truco de Zorro. Ross, Dev. 2006. (We Both Read Ser.). (SPA.). 48p. (J). (gr. -1-3). 7.99 *(978-1-891327-87-2(9))* Treasure Bay, Inc.

—Los dos leemos-el Mejor Truco de Zorro: Nivel 1. Ross, Dev. 2006. (We Both Read Ser.). (SPA.). 48p. (J). (gr. -1-3). pap. 3.99 *(978-1-891327-88-9(7))* Treasure Bay, Inc.

—Los dos leemos-Los Zapatos Perdidos de Lola. Blankenship, Paula. Canetti, Yanitzia James, tr. 2006. (We Both Read Ser.). (SPA.). 48p. (J). (gr. -1-2). pap. 3.99 *(978-1-891327-78-0(X))* Treasure Bay, Inc.

—Los dos leemos-Los Zapatos Perdidos de Lola: Nivel K-1. Blankenship, Paula. 2006. (We Both Read Ser.). (SPA.). 48p. (J). (gr. -1-2). 7.99 *(978-1-891327-77-3(1))* Treasure Bay, Inc.

—Los dos leemos-Sapi y el Gigante. Ross, Dev. 2006. (We Both Read Ser.). (SPA.). 48p. (J). (gr. -1-2). 7.99 *(978-1-891327-73-5(9))* Treasure Bay, Inc.

—Los dos leemos-Sapi y el Gigante. Ross, Dev. Canetti, Yanitzia James, tr. 2006. (We Both Read Ser.). (SPA.). 48p. (J). (gr. -1-2). pap. 3.99 *(978-1-891327-74-2(7))* Treasure Bay, Inc.

—We Both Read Bilingual Edition-Frank & the Giant/Sapi y el Globo. Ross, Dev. ed. 2011. (ENG & SPA.). 44p. (J). pap. 5.99 *(978-1-60115-042-4(3))* Treasure Bay, Inc.

—We Both Read-Fox's Best Trick Ever: Level 1. Ross, Dev. 2006. (We Both Read Ser.). 44p. (J). (gr. -1-3). 7.99 *(978-1-891327-69-8(0))* Treasure Bay, Inc.

—We Both Read-Frank & the Balloon: Level K-1. Ross, Dev. (We Both Read Ser.). 44p. (J). (gr. -1-2). 2008. per. 5.99 *(978-1-60115-012-7(1))*; 2007. 7.99 *(978-1-60115-011-0(3))* Treasure Bay, Inc.

—We Both Read-Frank & the Giant (Picture Book) Ross, Dev. 2007. (We Both Read Ser.). 44p. (J). (gr. -1-2). lib. bdg. 14.95 *(978-1-60115-006-6(7))* Treasure Bay, Inc.

—We Both Read-Frank & the Tiger. Ross, Dev. 44p. (J). 2012. pap. 5.99 *(978-1-60115-260-2(4))*; 2011. 9.95 *(978-1-60115-259-6(0))* Treasure Bay, Inc.

—We Both Read-Lulu's Lost Shoes. Blankenship, Paula. 2005. (We Both Read Ser.). 44p. (J). (gr. k-1). 7.99 *(978-1-891327-55-1(0))*; pap. 5.99 *(978-1-891327-56-8(9))* Treasure Bay, Inc.

—We Both Read-Lulu's Lost Shoes Big Book: Lulu's Lost Shoes Big Book. Blankenship, Paula. 2005. 44p. (J). (gr. k-1). 29.95 *(978-1-891327-90-2(9))* Treasure Bay, Inc.

—We Both Read-Lulu's Wild Party. Blankenship, Paula. 2009. (We Both Read Ser.). 44p. (J). 9.95 *(978-1-60115-231-2(0))*; pap. 5.99 *(978-1-60115-232-9(9))* Treasure Bay, Inc.

—We Read Phonics-Matt & Sid. McKay, Sindy. 2010. 32p. (J). 9.95 *(978-1-60115-315-9(5))*; pap. 4.99 *(978-1-60115-316-6(3))* Treasure Bay, Inc.

Reinhart, Matthew. No Biting, Louise. Palatini, Margie. 2007. 32p. (J). (gr. -1-3). 16.99 *(978-0-06-052627-6(0))*; lib. bdg. 17.89 *(978-0-06-052628-3(9))* HarperCollins Pubs. (Tegen, Katherine Bks).

Reinhart, Matthew. The Ark: A Pop-up Book. Reinhart, Matthew. 2006. 12p. (J). (gr. k-4). reprint ed. 17.00 *(978-1-4223-5673-9(6))* DIANE Publishing Co.

—Cinderella: A Pop-Up Fairy Tale. Reinhart, Matthew. 2005. (ENG.). 12p. (J). (gr. -1-3). 29.99 *(978-1-4169-0501-1(4)*, Little Simon) Little Simon.

—The Jungle Book: A Pop-Up Adventure. Reinhart, Matthew. 2006. (ENG.). 12p. (J). 34.99 *(978-1-4169-1824-0(8)*, Little Simon) Little Simon.

Reinhart, Matthew. Marvel's the Avengers - Age of Ultron: A Pop-Up Book. Reinhart, Matthew. 2015. (ENG.). 10p. (J). (gr. 1-17). 14.99 ***(978-0-316-34086-1(3))*** Little, Brown Bks. for Young Readers.

Reinhart, Matthew. Nursery Rhymes. Reinhart, Matthew. 2009. (ENG.). 12p. (J). (gr. -1-3). 29.99 *(978-1-4169-1825-7(6)*, Little Simon) Little Simon.

Reinhart, Matthew & Sabuda, Robert. Dragons & Monsters. Reinhart, Matthew & Sabuda, Robert. 2011. (Encyclopedia Mythologica Ser.). (ENG.). 12p. (J). (gr. k-4). 29.99 *(978-0-7636-3173-4(6))* Candlewick Pr.

—Encyclopedia Mythologica: Dragons & Monsters. Reinhart, Matthew & Sabuda, Robert. ed. 2011. (Encyclopedia Mythologica Ser.). (ENG.). 12p. (J). (gr. k-4). 250.00 *(978-0-7636-3476-6(X))* Candlewick Pr.

—Encyclopedia Prehistorica Dinosaurs. Reinhart, Matthew & Sabuda, Robert. 2005. (Encyclopedia Prehistorica Ser.: 1). (ENG.). 12p. (J). (gr. k-4). 29.99 *(978-0-7636-2228-2(1))* Candlewick Pr.

—Encyclopedia Prehistorica Sharks & Other Sea Monsters. Reinhart, Matthew & Sabuda, Robert. 2006. (Encyclopedia Prehistorica Ser.: 2). (ENG.). 12p. (J). (gr. k-4). 29.99 *(978-0-7636-2229-9(X))* Candlewick Pr.

—Gods & Heroes. Reinhart, Matthew & Sabuda, Robert. 2010. (Encyclopedia Mythologica Ser.: 2). (ENG.). 12p. (J). (gr. k-4). 29.99 *(978-0-7636-3171-0(X))*; 250.00 *(978-0-7636-3486-5(7))* Candlewick Pr.

Reinhart, Matthew, jt. illus. see Sabuda, Robert.

Reiniger, Lotte. King Arthur & His Knights of the Round Table. Green, Roger Lancelyn. 2008. (Puffin Classics Ser.). (ENG.). 416p. (J). (gr. 3-7). 5.99 *(978-0-14-132101-1(6)*, Puffin) Penguin Publishing Group.

Reinoso, Carlos. Little Ducky Jr. & the Whirlwind Storm: A Tale of Loss, Hope,and Renewal. Reinoso, Carlos. l.t. ed. 2005. 50p. (J). 8.99 *(978-0-9777672-0-5(5))* Behavioral Health & Human Development Ctr.

Reis, Erica, et al. Princess Ai: Rumors from the Other Side. Armand, Villavert. Schilling, Christine & Kim, Hyun-Joo, trs. from JPN. 2008. (Princess Ai Ser.: Vol. 1). 192p. (gr. 8-18). pap. 9.99 *(978-1-4278-0822-6(8))* TOKYOPOP, Inc.

Reis, Ivan, et al. Dark Passage, Vol. 2. Pulido, Brian. 2004. (Lady Death Ser.: Vol. 2). 160p. (YA). pap. 9.95 *(978-1-59314-054-0(1))* CrossGeneration Comics, Inc.

Reisberg, Mira. Baby Rattlesnake. Ata, Te. 2013. (ENG.). 32p. (J). (gr. -1). pap. 10.95 *(978-0-89239-216-2(9))* Lee & Low Bks., Inc.

—Baby Rattlesnake. Ata, Te et al. 2013. (ENG.). 32p. (J). (gr. -1-18). pap. 9.95 *(978-0-89239-049-6(2))* Lee & Low Bks., Inc.

—Baby Rattlesnake. Ata, Te. Alarcón, Francisco X., tr. 2003. (SPA & ENG.). 32p. (J). pap. 7.95 *(978-0-89239-188-2(X))* Lee & Low Bks., Inc.

—Just Like Home: Como en Mi Tierra. Miller, Elizabeth I. Mlawer, Teresa, tr. 2004. (ENG.). 32p. (J). (gr. 1-3). pap. 6.99 *(978-0-8075-4069-5(2))* Whitman, Albert & Co.

—Uncle Nacho's Hat. Flor Ada, Alma & Zubizarreta, Rosalma, trs. 2013.Tr. of El Sombrero Del Tío Nacho. (ENG & SPA.). 32p. (J). (gr. 1-18). pap. 8.95 *(978-0-89239-043-4(3)*, CBP0433S) Lee & Low Bks., Inc.

—Uncle Nacho's Hat: El Sombrero Del to Nacho. Rohmer, Harriet. Flor Ada, Alma & Zubizarreta, Rosalma, trs. 2013. (ENG & SPA.). 32p. (J). (gr. k-18). pap. 9.95 *(978-0-89239-112-7(X))* Lee & Low Bks., Inc.

—Where Fireflies Dance: Ahí, Donde Bailan Las Luciernagas. Corpi, Lucha. 2013. (ENG & SPA.). 32p. (J). (gr. 1-18). pap. 8.95 *(978-0-89239-177-6(4)*, Children's Book Press) Lee & Low Bks., Inc.

Reisch, Jesse. Bed in Summer. Stevenson, Robert Louis. 2011. (Poetry for Children Ser.). (ENG.). 24p. (J). (gr. k-3). 27.07 *(978-1-60973-151-9(4)*, 201180) Child's World, Inc., The.

—The Drum Circle. Todd, Traci N. 2006. (J). *(978-1-58987-023-9(9))* Kindermusik International.

—I Am the Desert. Fredericks, Anthony D. 2012. (J). *(978-1-933855-73-8(8))* Rio Nuevo Pubs.

—The Shortest Day: Celebrating the Winter Solstice. Pfeffer, Wendy. (ENG.). 40p. (J). (gr. 1). 2014. 8.99 *(978-0-14-751284-0(0)*, Puffin); 2003. 17.99 *(978-0-525-46968-1(0)*, Dutton Juvenile) Penguin Publishing Group.

Reisch, Jessie. Ebony & Ivory: Discovering 10 Keys to Racial Harmony. Elkins, Stephen. 2003. 32p. (J). (gr. k-18). 14.99 incl. audio compact disk *(978-0-8054-2674-8(4))* B&H Publishing Group.

—Know God, No Fear. Elkins, Stephen. 2003. 32p. (J). (gr. k-5). 14.99 *(978-0-8054-2658-8(2))* B&H Publishing Group.

Reisenauer, Cynthia Mauro. Emerita. Reisenauer, Cynthia Mauro. 2007. 48p. (J). 18.95 *(978-0-9726487-5-2(5))* Puddle Jump Pr., Ltd.

Reiser, Lynn. Hardworking Puppies. Reiser, Lynn. 2006. (ENG.). 40p. (J). (gr. -1-3). 16.99 *(978-0-15-205404-5(9))* Houghton Mifflin Harcourt Publishing Co.

—My Way(A Mi Manera) A Margaret & Margarita Story(Un Cuento de Margarita y Margaret) Reiser, Lynn. 2007. (ENG & SPA.). 32p. (J). (gr. -1-k). 16.99 *(978-0-06-084101-0(X)*, Greenwillow Bks.) HarperCollins Pubs.

Reiss, William, jt. illus. see Greenblatt, C. H.

Reitmeyer, Shannon. The Proud Inchworm. Reitmeyer, Shannon. 2013. 24p. pap. 12.00 *(978-1-61286-161-6(X))* Avid Readers Publishing Group.

Reitze, Glenn Logan. Ernie the Easter Hippopotamus: A Comic Adventure for Anytime. Reitze, Glenn Logan. 2007. (ENG.). 48p. (J). lib. bdg. 19.95 *(978-0-88265-040-1(8)*, Fine Art Editions) North American International.

Reitze, Glenn Logan. Ernie the Easter Hippotamus: A Comic Adventure for Anytime. Reitze, Glenn Logan, text. 2007. (J). pap. *(978-0-88265-041-8(6))* North American International.

Rejent, Renee. How High Can You Fly? DeVos, Janie. l.t. ed. 2005. 32p. 16.95 *(978-0-9663276-2-5(4))* Red Engine Pr.

Relf, Adam. Can Kittens Take a Catnap? Palfreman-Bunker, Claire. 2007. (J). pap. *(978-0-545-02595-9(8))* Scholastic, Inc.

—Sharks: Information for Young Readers - Level 1. Clarke, Catriona. 2007. (Usborne Beginners Ser.). 32p. (J). (gr. -1-3). 4.99 *(978-0-7945-1581-2(9)*, Usborne) EDC Publishing.

Reller, Marcia Mattingly. Growing up in Wisdom: A Story of Jesus as a Baby & a Young Boy. Watson, Donn, ed. 2nd ed. 2011. 40p. (J). 14.95 *(978-0-9801975-4-9(6))* Blake-Virostko, Pamela.

Relyea, C. M. Caps & Capers: A Story of Boarding-School Life. Jackson, Gabrielle E. 2008. 136p. pap. *(978-1-4099-4255-9(4))* Dodo Pr.

—Caps & Capers: A Story of Boarding School Life (1901) Jackson, Gabrielle Emilie Snow. 284p. 2010. 35.16 *(978-1-164-31862-0(4))*; 2010. pap. 23.16 *(978-1-164-12697-3(0))*; 2008. 43.95 *(978-1-4366-0917-3(8))*; 2008. (ENG.). per. 28.95 *(978-0-548-82612-6(9))* Kessinger Publishing, LLC.

Relyea, Charles M. Catcher Craig. Mathewson, Christy. 2011. 360p. 51.95 *(978-1-258-06942-1(3))* Literary Licensing, LLC.

Rem. Vampire Kisses - Blood Relatives, Vol. II. Schreiber, Ellen. 2008. (Vampire Kisses: Blood Relatives Ser.: Vol. 2). (ENG.). 192p. (YA). (gr. 8-18). pap. 9.99 *(978-0-06-134082-6(0)*, Tegen, Katherine Bks) HarperCollins Pubs.

Rem, jt. illus. see Kwon, Elisa.

Rembert, Winfred. Don't Hold Me Back: My Life & Art. Rembert, Winfred. 2003. (ENG.). 48p. (J). 19.95 *(978-0-8126-2703-9(2))* Cricket Bks.

Remey, Grace Anne. Lion's Pride: A Tail of Deployment. Remey, Grace Anne. 2012. (ENG.). 38p. pap. 12.95 *(978-0-9855445-0-8(3))* Remey, Lisa.

Remkiewicz, jt. illus. see Remkiewicz, Frank.

Remkiewicz, F., jt. illus. see Remkiewicz, Frank.

Remkiewicz, Frank. Arithme-Tickle: An Even Number of Odd Riddle-Rhymes. Lewis, J. Patrick. 2007. (ENG.). 32p. (J). (gr. 1-4). pap. 6.99 *(978-0-15-205848-7(6))* Houghton Mifflin Harcourt Publishing Co.

—Down by the Station. Riggs Vetter, Jennifer. 2009. (ENG.). 32p. (J). (gr. -1-2). 15.99 *(978-1-58246-243-1(7)*, Tricycle Pr.) Ten Speed Pr.

—Froggy Builds a Tree House. London, Jonathan. 2011. (Froggy Ser.). (ENG.). 32p. (J). (gr. -1-k). 16.99 *(978-0-670-01222-0(X)*, Viking Juvenile) Penguin Publishing Group.

—Froggy Eats Out. London, Jonathan. 2003. (Froggy Ser.). (ENG.). 32p. (J). (gr. -1-k). pap. 6.99 *(978-0-14-250061-3(5)*, Puffin) Penguin Publishing Group.

—Froggy Eats Out. London, Jonathan. 2003. (Froggy Ser.). 13.65 *(978-0-7569-1464-6(7))* Perfection Learning Corp.

—Froggy Gets a Doggy. London, Jonathan. (Froggy Ser.). (ENG.). 32p. (J). (gr. -1-k). 2015. 6.99 *(978-0-14-242230-4(4)*, Puffin); 2014. 16.99 *(978-0-670-01428-6(1)*, Viking Juvenile) Penguin Publishing Group.

—Froggy Gets Dressed, 1 vol. London, Jonathan. 2007. (Froggy Ser.). (ENG.). 15p. (J). (gr. -1-k). 9.99 *(978-0-14-240870-4(0)*, Puffin) Penguin Publishing Group.

—Froggy Goes to Camp. London, Jonathan. 2010. (Froggy Ser.). (ENG.). 32p. (J). (gr. -1-k). pap. 6.99 *(978-0-14-241604-4(5)*, Puffin) Penguin Publishing Group.

—Froggy Goes to Hawaii. London, Jonathan. (Froggy Ser.). (ENG.). 32p. (J). (gr. -1-k). 2012. pap. 6.99 *(978-0-14-242119-2(7)*, Puffin); 2011. 15.99 *(978-0-670-01221-3(1)*, Viking Juvenile) Penguin Publishing Group.

—Froggy Goes to School. London, Jonathan. 2006. (Froggy Ser.). 28p. (gr. -1-1). 16.00 *(978-0-7569-6986-8(7))* Perfection Learning Corp.

—Froggy Goes to the Doctor. London, Jonathan. 2004. (Froggy Ser.). (ENG.). 32p. (J). (gr. -1-k). pap. 6.99 *(978-0-14-240193-4(5)*, Puffin) Penguin Publishing Group.

—Froggy Is the Best. London, Jonathan. 2015. (Froggy Ser.). (ENG.). 32p. (J). (gr. 1-2). pap. 3.99 *(978-0-448-48380-1(7)*, Warne, Frederick Pubs.) Penguin Bks., Ltd. GBR. Dist: Penguin Publishing Group.

—Froggy Plays in the Band. London, Jonathan. 2004. (Froggy Ser.). (J). (gr. -1-3). 13.65 *(978-0-7569-2955-8(5))* Perfection Learning Corp.

—Froggy Rides a Bike. London, Jonathan. 2006. (Froggy Ser.). (ENG.). 32p. (J). (gr. -1-k). 15.99 *(978-0-670-06099-3(2)*, Viking Juvenile) Penguin Publishing Group.

—Froggy's Baby Sister. London, Jonathan. 2005. (Froggy Ser.). (ENG.). 32p. (J). (gr. -1-k). pap. 6.99

(978-0-14-240342-6(3), Puffin) Penguin Publishing Group.

—Froggy's Best Babysitter. London, Jonathan. 2011. (Froggy Ser.). (ENG.). 32p. (J). (gr. -1-k). pap. 5.99 (978-0-14-241899-4(4), Puffin) Penguin Publishing Group.

—Froggy's Birthday Wish. London, Jonathan. 2015. (Froggy Ser.). (ENG.). 32p. (J). (gr. -1-k). 16.99 (978-0-670-01572-6(5), Viking Juvenile) Penguin Publishing Group.

—Froggy's Day with Dad. London, Jonathan. 2006. (Froggy Ser.). (ENG.). 32p. (J). (gr. -1-k). pap. 5.99 (978-0-14-240634-2(1), Puffin) Penguin Publishing Group.

—Froggy's Halloween. London, Jonathan. 2010. lib. bdg. 16.10 (978-0-7569-8999-6(X)) Penguin Publishing Group.

—Froggy's Sleepover. London, Jonathan. 2007. (Froggy Ser.). (ENG.). 32p. (J). (gr. -1-k). pap. 6.99 (978-0-14-240750-9(X), Puffin) Penguin Publishing Group.

—Froggy's Worst Playdate. London, Jonathan. (Froggy Ser.). (ENG.). 32p. (J). (gr. -1-k). 2015. 6.99 (978-0-14-242229-8(0), Puffin); 2013. 16.99 (978-0-670-01427-9(3), Viking Juvenile) Penguin Publishing Group.

Remkiewicz, Frank, et al. Horrible Harry & the Dead Letters. Kline, Suzy. 2009. (Horrible Harry Ser.). (ENG.). 80p. (J). (gr. 2-4). 3.99 (978-0-14-241457-6(3), Puffin) Penguin Publishing Group.

Remkiewicz, Frank. Horrible Harry & the Dragon War. Kline, Suzy. 2003. (Horrible Harry Ser.). (ENG.). 64p. (J). (gr. 2-4). 3.99 (978-0-14-250166-5(2), Puffin) Penguin Publishing Group.

—Horrible Harry & the Goog. Kline, Suzy. 2006. (Horrible Harry Ser.). 56p. (gr. 2-5). 14.00 (978-0-7569-6948-6(4)) Perfection Learning Corp.

—Horrible Harry & the Holidaze. Kline, Suzy. 2004. (Horrible Harry Ser.). (ENG.). 80p. (J). (gr. 2-4). 3.99 (978-0-14-240205-4(2), Puffin) Penguin Publishing Group.

—Horrible Harry & the Locked Closet. Kline, Suzy. 2005. (Horrible Harry Ser.). (ENG.). 80p. (J). (gr. 2-4). 3.99 (978-0-14-240451-5(9), Puffin) Penguin Publishing Group.

—Horrible Harry & the Locked Closet. Kline, Suzy. 2005. (Horrible Harry Ser.). 68p. (gr. 2-5). 14.00 (978-0-7569-5825-1(3)) Perfection Learning Corp.

—Horrible Harry & the Mud Gremlins. Kline, Suzy. (Horrible Harry Ser.). (ENG.). 64p. (J). (gr. 2-4). 2004. 3.99 (978-0-14-240123-1(4), Puffin); 2003. 14.99 (978-0-670-03617-2(X), Viking Juvenile) Penguin Publishing Group.

—Horrible Harry & the Mud Gremlins. Kline, Suzy. 2004. (Horrible Harry Ser.). 50p. (gr. 2). 14.00 (978-0-7569-2815-5(X)) Perfection Learning Corp.

—Horrible Harry & the Triple Revenge. Kline, Suzy. (Horrible Harry Ser.). (ENG.). 64p. (J). (gr. 2-4). 2008. 3.99 (978-0-14-241081-3(0), Puffin); 2006. 13.99 (978-0-670-06077-1(1), Viking Juvenile) Penguin Publishing Group.

—Horrible Harry Cracks the Code. Kline, Suzy. 2008. (Horrible Harry Ser.). (ENG.). 80p. (J). (gr. 2-4). 3.99 (978-0-14-241247-3(3), Puffin) Penguin Publishing Group.

—Horrible Harry Goes to Sea: Puffine Chapters. Kline, Suzy. 2003. (Horrible Harry Ser.). (ENG.). 64p. (J). (gr. 2-4). 3.99 (978-0-14-250002-6(X), Puffin) Penguin Publishing Group.

—Horrible Harry Takes the Cake. Kline, Suzy. 2007. (Horrible Harry Ser.). (ENG.). 64p. (J). (gr. 2-4). 3.99 (978-0-14-240939-8(1), Puffin) Penguin Publishing Group.

—Horrible Harry Takes the Cake. Kline, Suzy. 2007. (Horrible Harry Ser.). 45p. (gr. 2-5). 14.00 (978-0-7569-8158-7(1)) Perfection Learning Corp.

—Joe & Sparky Get New Wheels. Michalak, Jamie. 2013. (Candlewick Sparks Ser.). (ENG.). 48p. (J). (gr. k-4). pap. 3.99 (978-0-7636-6641-5(6)) Candlewick Pr.

—Joe & Sparky Go to School. Michalak, Jamie. (Candlewick Sparks Ser.). (ENG.). 48p. (J). (gr. k-4). 2014. pap. 3.99 (978-0-7636-7181-5(9)); 2013. 15.99 (978-0-7636-6278-3(X)) Candlewick Pr.

—Joe & Sparky, Superstars! Michalak, Jamie. (Candlewick Sparks Ser.). (ENG.). 48p. (J). (gr. k-4). 2013. pap. 3.99 (978-0-7636-6642-2(4)); 2011. 15.99 (978-0-7636-4578-6(8)) Candlewick Pr.

—Less Than Zero. Murphy, Stuart J. 2003. (MathStart 3 Ser.: Vol. 49). (ENG.). 40p. (J). (gr. 2-18). pap. 5.99 (978-0-06-000126-1(7)) HarperCollins Pubs.

—Piggy & Dad Play Big Book: Brand New Readers. Martin, David Lozell. 2009. (Brand New Readers Ser.). (ENG.). 48p. (J). (gr. -1-3). pap. 24.99 (978-0-7636-4455-0(2)) Candlewick Pr.

—Seaweed Soup. Murphy, Stuart J. 2003. (Mathstart Ser.). 31p. (J). (gr. -1-3). pap. (978-0-7398-6790-7(3)) Steck-Vaughn.

—The Twelve Days of Christmas in Florida. 2008. (Twelve Days of Christmas in America Ser.). (ENG.). 32p. (J). (gr. k). 12.95 (978-1-4027-3817-3(X)) Sterling Publishing Co., Inc.

Remkiewicz, Frank. Froggy Plays T-Ball. Remkiewicz, Frank. London, Jonathan. 2009. (Froggy Ser.). (ENG.). 32p. (J). (gr. -1-k). pap. 6.99 (978-0-14-241304-3(6), Puffin) Penguin Publishing Group.

Remkiewicz, Frank & Frank, Remkiewicz. Froggy Plays in the Band. London, Jonathan. 2004. (Froggy Ser.). (ENG.). 32p. (J). (gr. -1-k). 6.99 (978-0-14-240051-7(3), Puffin) Penguin Publishing Group.

—Horrible Harry & the Goog. Kline, Suzy. 2006. (Horrible Harry Ser.). (ENG.). 64p. (J). (gr. 2-4). pap. 3.99 (978-0-14-240728-8(3), Puffin) Penguin Publishing Group.

Remkiewicz, Frank & Remkiewicz. Horrible Harry Bugs the Three Bears. Kline, Suzy & Remkiewicz, Frank. 2009. (Horrible Harry Ser.). (ENG.). 80p. (J). (gr. 2-4). 3.99 (978-0-14-241295-4(3), Puffin) Penguin Publishing Group.

Remkiewicz, Frank & Remkiewicz, F. Froggy Rides a Bike. London, Jonathan & Remkiewicz, Frank. 2008. (Froggy Ser.). (ENG.). 32p. (J). (gr. -1-k). pap. 5.99 (978-0-14-241067-7(5), Puffin) Penguin Publishing Group.

Remkiewicz, Frank & Wummer, Amy. Horrible Harry on the Ropes. Kline, Suzy. 2011. (Horrible Harry Ser.). (ENG.). 80p. (J). (gr. 2-4). 3.99 (978-0-14-241695-2(9), Puffin) Penguin Publishing Group.

Rempel, Jennifer. Lavi the Lion Finds His Pride. 2005. (J). 15.95 (978-0-9744715-2-5(6), Towers Maguire Publishing) Local History Co., The.

Remphry, Martin. A Gift for the King. Harvey, Damian. 2005. (Reading Corner Ser.). 24p. (J). (gr. k-3). lib. bdg. 22.80 (978-1-59771-013-8(X)) Sea-To-Sea Pubns.

—Miss Pell Never Misspells: More Cool Ways to Remember Stuff. Martin, Steve. 2013. (ENG.). 128p. (J). (gr. 5-9). 9.99 (978-0-545-49477-9(X), Scholastic Reference) Scholastic, Inc.

Remphry, Martin. The Mud Monster. Billam, Rosemary. 2008. (Reading Corner Ser.). (ENG.). 24p. (J). (gr. k-2). pap. 6.99 **(978-0-7496-7695-7(7))** Hodder & Stoughton GBR. Dist: Independent Pubs. Group.

Remphry, Martin. William Shakespeare. Fischel, Emma. 2010. (Famous People, Famous Lives Ser.). (KOR.). 46p. (J). (978-89-491-8826-3(0)) Biryongso Publishing Co.

—Wizard Balloon, 1 vol. Cassidy, Anne. 2013. (Start Reading Ser.). (ENG.). 24p. (gr. k-1). pap. 6.99 (978-1-4765-4145-7(0)) Capstone Pr., Inc.

—Wizard Woof, 1 vol. Cassidy, Anne. 2013. (Start Reading Ser.). (ENG.). 24p. (gr. k-1). pap. 6.99 (978-1-4765-4147-1(7)) Capstone Pr., Inc.

Renaud, Joanne. Runaway Train: Saved by Belle of the Mines & Mountains. Coleman, Wim & Perrin, Pat. 2015. (Setting the Stage for Fluency Ser.). (ENG.). 40p. (gr. 3-5). lib. bdg. 27.93 **(978-1-939656-71-1(0))** Red Chair Pr.

Renda, Joseph, jt. illus. see Colson, A. W.

Renda, Lori Epstein, photos by. 1776: A New Look at Revolutionary Williamsburg. Kostyal, Karen & Colonial Williamsburg Foundation Staff. 2009. (ENG., 48p. (J). (gr. 3-7). 17.95 (978-1-4263-0517-7(6)); 27.90 (978-1-4263-0518-4(4)) National Geographic Society. (National Geographic Children's Bks.).

Rendeiro, Charlene. Been to Yesterdays: Poems of a Life. Hopkins, Lee Bennett. 2007. 64p. (gr. 3-7). 21.45 (978-0-7569-7966-9(8)) Perfection Learning Corp.

Rendon, Daniel. Identity Theft. Lobdell, Scott. 2005. (Hardy Boys Undercover Brothers Ser.). 88p. (gr. 3-8). 24.21 (978-1-59961-062-7(0)) Spotlight.

—Mad House. Lobdell, Scott. 2005. (Hardy Boys Undercover Brothers Ser.). 88p. (gr. 3-7). 24.21 (978-1-59961-063-4(9)) Spotlight.

—The Ocean of Osyria. Lobdell, Scott. 2005. (Hardy Boys Undercover Brothers Ser.). 88p. (gr. 3-7). 24.21 (978-1-59961-061-0(2)) Spotlight.

Rendon, Daniel, et al. The Opposite Numbers. Lobdell, Scott. 2006. 111p. (J). (978-1-4156-9815-0(5)) Papercutz.

Rendon, Joel. La Invencion de Los Canibales. Navarrete, Federico. rev. ed. 2006. (Otra Escalera Ser.). (ENG.). 56p. (J). (gr. k-2). pap. 12.95 (978-970-20-0774-6(7)) Castillo, Ediciones, S. A. de C. V. MEX. Dist: Macmillan.

Rene, Perez. No Bones about It. Heller, Andrew. I.t. ed. 2003. 12p. (J). 7.99 (978-0-9722038-5-2(0)) Mr Do It All, Inc.

Renfroe, Leisa. A Whale Set Sail. Trechsel, Kelli. 2011. 28p. (J). pap. 14.95 (978-1-936085-42-2(9)) Decent Hill Pubs. LLC.

Renier, Aaron. The Adventures of Sir Balin the Ill-Fated. Morris, Gerald. (Knights' Tales Ser.). (ENG.). 112p. (J). (gr. 1-4). 2013. pap. 5.99 (978-0-544-10488-4(9)); 2012. 14.99 (978-0-547-68085-9(6)) Houghton Mifflin Harcourt Publishing Co.

—The Adventures of Sir Gawain the True. Morris, Gerald. 2013. (Knights' Tales Ser.: 3). (ENG.). 128p. (J). (gr. 1-4). pap. 4.99 (978-0-544-02264-5(5)) Houghton Mifflin Harcourt Publishing Co.

—The Adventures of Sir Givret the Short. Morris, Gerald. 2009. (Knights' Tales Ser.: 2). (ENG.). 112p. (J). (gr. 1-4). pap. 8.95 (978-0-547-24818-9(0)) Houghton Mifflin Harcourt Publishing Co.

Renier, Aaron. The Unsinkable Walker Bean. Renier, Aaron. 2010. (Unsinkable Walker Bean Ser.: 1). (ENG.). 208p. (J). (gr. 4-9). pap. 14.99 (978-1-59643-453-0(8), First Second Bks.) Roaring Brook Pr.

Renn, Chantal. Fairies: Interactive Fun with Fold-Out Play Scene, Reusable Stickers, & Punch-out, Stand-up Figures! Walter Foster Custom Creative Team. 2014. (Sticker, Punch-Out, & Play! Ser.). (ENG.). 12p. (J). (gr. -1-1). pap. 6.99 (978-1-60058-720-7(8)) Quarto Publishing Group USA.

Renne, Philip K. Allosaurus vs. Brachiosaurus: Might Against Height. O'Hearn, Michael. 2010. (Dinosaur Wars Ser.). (ENG.). 32p. (gr. 3-4). lib. bdg. 27.32 (978-1-4296-3935-4(0), Edge Bks.) Capstone Pr., Inc.

—Deinonychus vs. Styracosaurus: When Claws & Spikes Collide, 1 vol. O'Hearn, Michael. 2010. (Dinosaur Wars Ser.). (ENG.). 32p. (gr. 3-4). lib. bdg. 27.32 (978-1-4296-4757-1(4), Edge Bks.) Capstone Pr., Inc.

—Dilophosaurus vs. Ankylosaurus: Weapons Against Armor, 1 vol. O'Hearn, Michael. 2010. (Dinosaur Wars Ser.). (ENG.). 32p. (gr. 3-4). lib. bdg. 27.32 (978-1-4296-4756-4(6), Edge Bks.) Capstone Pr., Inc.

—Spinosaurus vs. Giganotosaurus: Battle of the Giants, 1 vol. O'Hearn, Michael. 2010. (Dinosaur Wars Ser.). (ENG.). 32p. (gr. 3-4). lib. bdg. 27.32 (978-1-4296-3936-1(9), Edge Bks.) Capstone Pr., Inc.

—Triceratops vs. Stegosaurus: When Horns & Plates Collide. O'Hearn, Michael. 2010. (Dinosaur Wars Ser.). (ENG.). 32p. (gr. 3-4). lib. bdg. 27.32 (978-1-4296-3938-5(5), Edge Bks.) Capstone Pr., Inc.

—Tyrannosaurus Rex vs. Velociraptor: Power Against Speed. O'Hearn, Michael. 2010. (Dinosaur Wars Ser.). (ENG.). 32p. (gr. 3-4). lib. bdg. 27.32 (978-1-4296-3937-8(7), Edge Bks.) Capstone Pr., Inc.

Renooy, "Cosmic" Ray. Rodney's SsssSolution - Big Book. Myracle, Lauren. 2003. (J). spiral bd. (978-1-884272-88-2(6)) Premier Schl. Agendas.

Renouf, Michael. Malpas the Dragon. Cattanach, Ann. 2007. (ENG.). 28p. (J). (gr. 3-7). per. (978-1-84310-572-5(1)) Kingsley, Jessica Ltd.

Renteria, Justin, jt. illus. see Gutierez, Francisco.

Renthrope, Damon. All Around Town. Wendel, Gretchen Schomel et al. 2007. (ENG.). 32p. (J). (gr. -1-3). 11.99 (978-1-933754-10-9(9)) Waterside Publishing.

—All Around Town. Wendel, Gretchen Schomer & Schomer, Adam Anthony. 2009. (Becka & the Big Bubble Ser.). 32p. (J). (gr. -1-2). lib. bdg. 22.60 (978-1-60754-104-2(1)) Windmill Bks.

—Becka Goes to Chicago. Wendel, Gretchen Schomer & Schomer, Adam Anthony. 2008. (ENG.). 36p. (J). (gr. -1-3). 11.99 (978-1-933754-52-9(4)) Waterside Publishing.

—Becka Goes to India. Wendel, Gretchen Schomer & Schomer, Adam Anthony. 2009. (Becka & the Big Bubble Ser.). 32p. (J). (gr. -1-2). lib. bdg. 22.60 (978-1-60754-110-3(6)) Windmill Bks.

—Becka Goes to India. Wendel, Gretchen Schomel et al. 2007. (ENG.). 32p. (J). 11.99 (978-1-933754-13-0(3)) Waterside Publishing.

—Becka Goes to San Diego. Wendel, Gretchen Schomer & Schomer, Adam Anthony. 2008. (ENG.). 32p. (J). (gr. -1-3). 11.99 (978-1-933754-51-2(6)) Waterside Publishing.

—Becka Goes to San Francisco. Wendel, Gretchen Schomel et al. 2007. (ENG.). 32p. (J). 11.99 (978-1-933754-12-3(5)) Waterside Publishing.

—Becka Goes to the North Pole. Wendel, Gretchen Schomel et al. 2007. (ENG.). 28p. (J). 11.99 (978-1-933754-11-6(7)) Waterside Publishing.

—Becka Goes to the North Pole. Wendel, Gretchen Schomer & Schomer, Adam Anthony. 2009. (Becka & the Big Bubble Ser.). 32p. (J). (gr. -1-2). lib. bdg. 22.60 (978-1-60754-116-5(5)) Windmill Bks.

Rentta, Sharon. Charlie, the Home-Alone Kitten. Nolan, Tina. 2008. 96p. (J). (gr. 1-5). 3.99 (978-1-56148-648-9(5), Good Bks.) Skyhorse Publishing Co., Inc.

—Honey the Unwanted Puppy. Nolan, Tina. 2008. 96p. (J). (gr. 1-5). 3.99 (978-1-56148-649-6(3), Good Bks.) Skyhorse Publishing Co., Inc.

Reny, Todd, jt. illus. see Snider, Sharon.

Repetto, Laurie. A Dog Named Munson Finds the Missing Game Ball. Thomas, Charlene. 2012. 38p. (J). 14.95 (978-1-62086-054-0(6)) Mascot Bks., Inc.

Reppel, Phyllis. Henriette Delille: Rebellious Saint, 1 vol. Martinez, Elsie & Stelly, Colette. 2010. (ENG.). 200p. (J). (gr. 3-7). 19.95 (978-1-58980-839-3(8)) Pelican Publishing Co., Inc.

Rescek, Sanja. Animal Exercises: Poems to Keep Fit. Mandy Ross. 2006. (Poems for the Young Ser.). (ENG.). 32p. (J). (gr. -1-2). pap. (978-1-84643-044-2(5)) Child's Play International Ltd.

—A Bedtime Prayer. 2013. (ENG.). 24p. (gr. -1). bds. 8.95 (978-1-58925-606-4(9)) Tiger Tales.

—Bounce & Jiggle. 2007. (Baby Gym Ser.). (ENG.). 12p. (J). (gr. -1). bds. (978-1-84643-131-9(X)) Child's Play International Ltd.

—Calm & Soothe. 2007. (Baby Gym Ser.). (ENG.). 12p. (J). (gr. -1). bds. (978-1-84643-133-3(6)) Child's Play International Ltd.

—A Christmas Prayer. Tiger Tales, ed. 2014. 22p. (J). (gr. -1-k). bds. 8.95 (978-1-58925-596-8(8)) Tiger Tales.

—Easter Bunny's Helpers. 2009. (ENG.). 12p. (J). 6.95 (978-1-58117-870-8(0), Intervisual/Piggy Toes) Bendon, Inc.

—A Gift for Baby's Christening. Rock, Lois. 2014. (ENG.). 48p. (J). (— 1). 9.99 (978-0-7459-6490-4(7)) Lion Hudson PLC GBR. Dist: Independent Pubs. Group.

—A Gift for Baby's Dedication. Rock, Lois. 2014. (ENG.). 48p. (J). (— 1). 9.99 (978-0-7459-6491-1(5)) Lion Hudson PLC GBR. Dist: Independent Pubs. Group.

—Hickory, Dickory, Dock: And Other Favorite Nursury Rhymes. Tiger Tales Staff, ed. 2006. 22p. (J). bds. 7.95 (978-1-58925-786-3(3)) Tiger Tales.

—I Do Not Want To. Schulz, Kathy. 2011. (Rookie Ready to Learn Ser.). 40p. (J). pap. 5.95 (978-0-531-26707-3(5)); (gr. -1-k). lib. bdg. 23.00 (978-0-531-26525-3(0)) Scholastic Library Publishing. (Children's Pr.).

—I'm a Little Vampire. Fry, Sonali. 2014. (ENG.). 16p. (J). (gr. -1 — 1). bds. 5.99 (978-1-4814-0504-1(7), Little Simon) Little Simon.

—The Itsy Bitsy Pumpkin. Fry, Sonali. 2014. (ENG.). 16p. (J). (gr. -1 — 1). bds. 5.99 (978-1-4814-0505-8(5), Little Simon) Little Simon.

Rescek, Sanja, et al. Itsy Bitsy Spider & Other Clap-along Rhymes. 2004. (Clap-Alongs Ser.). (ENG.). 36p. (J). (gr. -1-k). 12.95 (978-1-59249-522-1(2), 1D025) Soundprints.

Rescek, Sanja. Mr. Fox's Socks. Harvey, Damian. 2004. (ENG.). 16p. (J). lib. bdg. 23.65 (978-1-59646-678-4(2)) Dingles & Co.

—My Guardian Angel. Piper, Sophie. 2014. (ENG.). 48p. (J). (gr. -1-k). 9.99 (978-0-7459-6397-6(8)) Lion Hudson PLC GBR. Dist: Independent Pubs. Group.

—One Elephant Went Out to Play. (Classic Books with Holes Big Book Ser.). (ENG.). (J). (gr. -1-1). 2009. 16p. (978-1-84643-209-5(X)); 2009. 16p. (978-1-84643-258-3(8)); 2007. 16p. pap. (978-1-84643-107-4(7)); 2007. 14p. bds. (978-1-84643-111-1(5)) Child's Play International Ltd.

—Prayers for Baby's Christening. Rock, Lois. 2008. (ENG.). 48p. (J). (gr. k — 1). 7.95 (978-0-7459-6044-9(8)) Lion Hudson PLC GBR. Dist: Independent Pubs. Group.

—Tim Feels Scared. Slater, Teddy. 2011. (J). (978-0-545-35179-9(0)) Scholastic, Inc.

—Touch & Tickle. 2007. (Baby Gym Ser.). (ENG.). 12p. (J). (gr. -1). bds. (978-1-84643-130-2(1)) Child's Play International Ltd.

—Twinkle, Twinkle Little Star: And Other Favorite Bedtime Rhymes. Tiger Tales Staff, ed. 2006. 22p. (J). bds. 7.95 (978-1-58925-787-0(1)) Tiger Tales.

—Wiggle & Move. 2007. (Baby Gym Ser.). (ENG.). 12p. (J). (gr. -1). bds. (978-1-84643-132-6(8)) Child's Play International Ltd.

Rescek, Sanja, jt. illus. see Richards, Kirsten.

Rescek, Sanja, jt. illus. see Slater, Teddy.

Reschofsky, Jean. The Colors of Christmas: A Christmas Poem for Young & Old. Goff-Tuttle, Marie Jaume. 2013. (ENG.). 16p. (J). 12.95 (978-1-939621-09-2(7)) ORO Editions.

Research & Education Association Editors & Leigh, Rob. Batman & the Monster Men. Wagner, Matt. rev. ed. 2006. (ENG.). 144p. (YA). pap. 14.99 (978-1-4012-1091-5(0)) DC Comics.

Research & Education Association Editors & Starkings, Richard. When in Rome. Loeb, Jeph & Sale, Tim. rev. ed. 2007. (Catwoman Ser.). (ENG.). 160p. pap. 14.99 (978-1-4012-0717-5(0)) DC Comics.

Ressler-Horst, Lara. The World Is a Beautiful Place. Augsburger, A. Don. 2007. 48p. per. 14.95 (978-1-934246-44-3(1)) Peppertree Pr., The.

Restelli, Grazia. We're Sailing to Galapagos: A Week in the Pacific. Krebs, Laurie. (ENG.). 32p. (J). 2007. (gr. -1-3). pap. 7.99 (978-1-84686-102-4(0)); 2005. 16.99 (978-1-84148-902-5(6)) Barefoot Bks., Inc.

Rethi, Lili. Marie Curie. McKown, Robin. 2012. 128p. 40.95 (978-1-258-23532-1(3)); pap. 25.95 (978-1-258-24675-4(9)) Literary Licensing, LLC.

Rettenmund, Tamara, jt. illus. see Charlip, Remy.

Retwick, Roy. Opinions about Themes in Science Fiction: Two Stories about Veronica Logan, Interstellar Troubleshooter. Wood, Greg V. & Benchmark Education Co., LLC. 2014. (Text Connections Ser.). (J). (gr. 3). (978-1-4509-9665-5(5)) Benchmark Education Co.

Retz, Zac. Too Much Glue. Lefebvre, Jason. 2013. (ENG.). 32p. (J). (gr. k-2). 16.95 (978-1-936261-27-7(6)) Flashlight Pr.

Retzlaff, Shay. Annie the Texas Ranch Dog - Danger at Lost Maples. Shafer, Patty. 2012. (ENG.). 96p. (J). pap. 9.95 (978-1-61899-009-9(8), Tadpole Pr. 4 Kids) Smooth Sailing Pr., LLC.

—Annie the Texas Ranch Dog - Injured Hero. Shafer, Patty. 2012. 96p. (J). pap. 9.95 (978-1-61899-008-2(X), Tadpole Pr. 4 Kids) Smooth Sailing Pr., LLC.

—Annie the Texas Ranch Dog - New Life in Utopia. Shafer, Patty. 2012. 96p. (J). pap. 9.95 (978-1-61899-007-5(1), Tadpole Pr. 4 Kids) Smooth Sailing Pr., LLC.

Reuben, Borgen & Jenny, Lindley, photos by. God Loves You So Much... Learn As You Grow. 2010. (ENG., 24p. (J). 12.95 (978-0-9824652-3-3(8)) Learn As You Grow, L.L.C.

Reul, Sarah Lynne. The Smith Family Secret: Book 1. Potoma, Alison. 2013. 122p. pap. 6.25 (978-1-940602-00-4(9)) Potoma, Alison Elise.

Reusch, Mister, jt. illus. see Kasunick, Heather.

Reusswig, William. What Does an Animal Eat? Lowery, Lawrence F. 2012. (ENG.). 40p. (J). pap. 11.95 (978-1-936959-46-4(1)) National Science Teachers Assn.

Revell, Cindy. Bouki Cuts Wood: A Haitian Folktale. StJohn, Amanda. 2011. (Folktales from Around the World Ser.). (ENG.). 24p. (J). (gr. k-3). 28.50 (978-1-60973-135-9(2), 201140) Child's World, Inc., The.

—Me & My Robot. West, Tracey. 2003. (Penguin Young Readers, Level 2 Ser.). (ENG.). 32p. (J). (gr. 1-2). mass mkt. 3.99 (978-0-448-42895-6(4), Warne, Frederick Pubs.) Penguin Bks., Ltd. GBR. Dist: Penguin Random Hse., LLC.

—Room Enough for Daisy, 1 vol. Waldman, Debby & Feutl, Rita. 2011. (ENG.). 32p. (J). (gr. -1-3). 19.95 (978-1-55469-255-2(5)) Orca Bk. Pubs. USA.

—A Sack Full of Feathers, 1 vol. Waldman, Debby. 2007. (ENG.). 32p. (J). (gr. -1-3). 9.95 (978-1-55143-863-4(1)) Orca Bk. Pubs. USA.

Revell, Cindy. Where Do Babies Come From? Our First Talk about Birth, 1 vol. Roberts, Jillian. 2015. (Just Enough Ser.). (ENG.). 32p. (J). (gr. k-1). 19.95 **(978-1-4598-0942-0(4))** Orca Bk. Pubs. USA.

Revels, Robert, jt. illus. see Mori, Midori.

REVILLE, TONI-ANN. Freddie the Frog & Friends. Signoretti, Brenda. 2011. 32p. pap. 12.99 (978-1-4634-4633-8(0)) AuthorHouse.

Revoir, Joyce. Austin Alligator: I'll See You Guys Later. Foust, Cindy G. 2003. (J). 12.95 (978-0-9749220-0-3(5)) Alpha-kidZ.

—Benny Bear: Having A Baby Sister Isn't Fair. Foust, Cindy G. 2004. (J). 12.95 (978-0-9749220-1-0(3)) Alpha-kidZ.

Revoy, Antoine. Anubis Speaks! A Guide to the Afterlife by the Egyptian God of the Dead. Shecter, Vicky Alvear. 2013. (Secrets of the Ancient Gods Ser.). (ENG.). 128p. (J). (gr. 4-6). 16.95 (978-1-59078-995-7(4)) Boyds Mills Pr.

Revoy, Antoine, jt. illus. see Murphy, Kelly.

Revutsky, Helen Ross. Aimee's a Book: El Libro a de Aimee. Zocchi, Judith Mazzeo et al. 2005. (J). (978-1-59646-421-6(6)) Dingles & Co.

—Bebe's "B" Book: El Libro "B" de Bibi. Zocchi, Judith Mazzeo et al. 2005. (SPA.). (J). (978-1-59646-427-8(5)) Dingles & Co.

—Delia's D Book: El Libro D de Delia. Zocchi, Judith Mazzeo et al. 2005. (SPA.). (J). (978-1-59646-439-1(9)) Dingles & Co.

—Uri's "U" Book. Zocchi, Judith Mazzeo. 2007. (J). (978-1-59646-538-1(7)) Dingles & Co.

—Xavia's "X" Book: El Libro "X" de Xavia. Zocchi, Judith Mazzeo et al. 2005. (SPA.). (978-1-59646-559-6(X)) Dingles & Co.

—Yola's "Y" Book. Zocchi, Judith Mazzeo. 2007. (J). (978-1-59646-562-6(X)) Dingles & Co.

R

—Zach's "Z" Book: El Libro "Z" de Zach. Zocchi, Judith Mazzeo et al. 2005. (SPA & ENG.). (J). *(978-1-59646-571-8(9))* Dingles & Co.

Rew, Jen. Game Over. Hunter, Alex. 2012. 126p. pap. *(978-1-78176-771-9(8))* FeedARead.com.

Rex, Adam. Big on Plans. Kelly, Katy. 2007. (Lucy Rose Ser.). (ENG.). 192p. (J). (gr. 3-7). per. 6.99 *(978-0-440-42027-9(X)*, Yearling) Random Hse. Children's Bks.

—Billy Twitters & His Blue Whale Problem. Barnett, Mac. 2009. (ENG.). 48p. (J). (gr. -1-2). 16.99 *(978-0-7868-4958-1(4))* Hyperion Pr.

—Busy Like You Can't Believe. Kelly, Katy. 2007. (Lucy Rose Ser.). (ENG.). 160p. (J). (gr. 3-7). per. 6.99 *(978-0-440-42108-5(X)*, Yearling) Random Hse. Children's Bks.

—The Case of Mistaken Identity. Barnett, Mac. (Brixton Brothers Ser.: 1). (ENG.). (J). (gr. 3-7). 2010. 208p. pap. 7.99 *(978-1-4169-7816-9(X))*; 2009. 192p. 15.99 *(978-1-4169-7815-2(1))* Simon & Schuster Bks. For Young Readers. (Simon & Schuster Bks. For Young Readers).

—Chloe & the Lion. Barnett, Mac. 2012. (ENG.). 48p. (J). (gr. -1-3). 16.99 *(978-1-4231-1334-8(9))* Hyperion Pr.

—Chu's Day. Gaiman, Neil. (ENG.). (J). (gr. -1-3). 2014. 40p. pap. 6.99 *(978-0-06-201783-3(7))*; 2013. 32p. 17.99 *(978-0-06-201781-9(0))* HarperCollins Pubs.

—Chu's Day at the Beach. Gaiman, Neil. 2015. (ENG.). 32p. (J). (gr. -1-3). 17.99 *(978-0-06-222399-9(2))* HarperCollins Pubs.

—Chu's Day Board Book. Gaiman, Neil. 2014. (ENG.). 36p. (J). (gr. -1 — 1). bds. 7.99 *(978-0-06-234746-6(2)*, HarperFestival) HarperCollins Pubs.

—Chu's First Day of School. Gaiman, Neil. 2014. (ENG.). 32p. (J). (gr. -1-3). 17.99 *(978-0-06-222397-5(6))* HarperCollins Pubs.

—Chu's First Day of School Board Book. Gaiman, Neil. 2015. (ENG.). 36p. (J). (gr. -1 — 1). bds. 7.99 *(978-0-06-237149-2(5)*, HarperFestival) HarperCollins Pubs.

—The Dirty Cowboy. Timberlake, Amy. 2003. (ENG.). 32p. (J). (gr. -1-3). 17.99 *(978-0-374-31791-1(7)*, Farrar, Straus & Giroux (BYR)) Farrar, Straus & Giroux.

—The Ghostwriter Secret. Barnett, Mac. (Brixton Brothers Ser.: 2). (ENG.). (J). (gr. 3-7). 2011. 256p. pap. 6.99 *(978-1-4169-7818-3(6))*; 2010. 160p. 14.99 *(978-1-4169-7817-6(8))* Simon & Schuster Bks. For Young Readers. (Simon & Schuster Bks. For Young Readers).

—Guess Again! Barnett, Mac. 2009. (ENG.). 32p. (J). (gr. -1-3). 17.99 *(978-1-4169-5566-5(6)*, Simon & Schuster Bks. For Young Readers) Simon & Schuster Bks. For Young Readers.

—Here's the Thing about Me. Kelly, Katy. 2006. (Lucy Rose Ser.). (ENG.). 160p. (J). (gr. 3-7). reprint ed. per. 6.99 *(978-0-440-42026-2(1)*, Yearling) Random Hse. Children's Bks.

Rex, Adam. How This Book Was Made: Based on a True Story. Barnett, Mac. 2016. (J). ***(978-1-4231-5220-0(4))*** Disney Pr.

Rex, Adam. It Happened on a Train. Barnett, Mac. (Brixton Brothers Ser.: 3). (ENG.). (J). (gr. 3-7). 2012. 304p. pap. 6.99 *(978-1-4169-7820-6(8))*; 2011. 288p. 17.99 *(978-1-4169-7819-0(4))* Simon & Schuster Bks. For Young Readers. (Simon & Schuster Bks. For Young Readers).

Rex, Adam. Funny Business. Rex, Adam. Scieszka, Jon et al. 2010. (Guys Read Ser.: 1). (ENG.). 288p. (J). (gr. 3-7). 16.99 *(978-0-06-196374-2(7))*; pap. 6.99 *(978-0-06-196373-5(9))* HarperCollins Pubs. (Walden Pond Pr.).

—Moonday. Rex, Adam. 2013. (ENG.). 40p. (J). (gr. -1-2). 16.99 *(978-1-4231-1920-3(7))* Disney Pr.

—Smek for President! Rex, Adam. 2015. (Smek Smeries Ser.). (ENG.). 272p. (J). (gr. 3-7). 16.99 *(978-1-4847-0951-1(9))* Hyperion Bks. for Children.

—The True Meaning of Smekday. Rex, Adam. ed. 2015. (ENG.). 432p. (J). (gr. 3-7). pap. 7.99 ***(978-1-4847-2946-5(3))*** Hyperion Bks. for Children.

Rex, Adam. The True Meaning of Smekday. Rex, Adam. 2009. (ENG.). 432p. (J). (gr. 3-7). pap. 7.99 *(978-0-7868-4901-7(0))* Hyperion Pr.

Rex, Adam & Myers, Matthew. Mysterious Case of Cases: The Case of the Mistaken Identity - The Ghostwriter Secret - It Happened on a Train - Danger Goes Berserk. Barnett, Mac. ed. 2013. (Brixton Brothers Ser.). (ENG.). 1024p. (J). (gr. 3-7). pap. 25.99 *(978-1-4424-9818-1(8)*, Simon & Schuster Bks. For Young Readers) Simon & Schuster Bks. For Young Readers.

Rex, Adam, jt. illus. see Teplin, Scott.

Rex, Annmarie. Black's Adventure in the Big, Scary, Hairy World. Rex, Annmarie. 2007. 46p. (J). (gr. -1-3). per. 15.99 *(978-1-59879-364-2(0)*, Lifevest) Lifevest Publishing, Inc.

Rex, Michael. Jack the Builder. Murphy, Stuart J. 2006. (MathStart 1 Ser.). (ENG.). 40p. (J). (gr. -1-3). pap. 5.99 *(978-0-06-055775-1(3))* HarperCollins Pubs.

—My Dog Jack Is Fat, 0 vols. Bunting, Eve. 2011. (ENG.). 32p. (J). (gr. -1-3). 16.99 *(978-0-7614-5809-8(3)*, 9780761458098, Amazon Children's Publishing) Amazon Publishing.

—Sunshine Makes the Seasons. Branley, Franklyn M. 2005. (Let's-Read-And-Find-Out Science 2 Ser.). (ENG.). 40p. (J). (gr. k-4). pap. 5.99 *(978-0-06-059205-9(2)*, Collins) HarperCollins Pubs.

—Sunshine Makes the Seasons. Branley, Franklyn Mansfield. 2005. (Let's-Read-and-Find-Out-Science Ser.). (ENG.). 40p. (J). (gr. -1 — 1). 15.99 *(978-0-06-059203-5(6))* HarperCollins Pubs.

Rex, Michael. The Egg of Misery: Fangbone, Third Grade Barbarian. Rex, Michael. 2012. (Fangbone! Third Grade Barbarian Ser.: 2). (ENG.). 128p. (J). (gr. 2-4). 5.99 *(978-0-399-25522-9(2)*, Putnam Juvenile) Penguin Publishing Group.

—The End of the World. Rex, Michael. 2013. (Stepping Stone Book(TM) Ser.). (ENG.). 128p. (J). (gr. 1-4). 4.99 *(978-0-307-93169-6(2)*, Random Hse. Bks. for Young Readers) Random Hse. Children's Bks.

—Fangbone! Third-Grade Barbarian. Rex, Michael. 2012. (Fangbone! Third Grade Barbarian Ser.: 1). (ENG.). 128p. (J). (gr. 2-4). 5.99 *(978-0-399-25521-2(4)*, Putnam Juvenile) Penguin Publishing Group.

—Firefighter. Rex, Michael. 2003. (Word-by-Word First Reader Ser.). (ENG.). 32p. (J). (gr. -1-k). pap. 3.99 *(978-0-439-52785-9(6))* Scholastic, Inc.

—Furious George Goes Bananas: A Primate Parody. Rex, Michael. 2010. (ENG.). 32p. (J). (gr. k-3). 15.99 *(978-0-399-25433-8(1)*, Putnam Juvenile) Penguin Publishing Group.

—Goodnight Goon: A Petrifying Parody. Rex, Michael. (ENG.). (J). (gr. -1 — 1). 2012. 30p. bds. 6.99 *(978-0-399-26011-7(0))*; 2008. 32p. 15.99 *(978-0-399-24534-3(0))* Penguin Publishing Group. (Putnam Juvenile).

—Icky Ricky #3: the Dead Disco Raccoon. Rex, Michael. 2014. (Stepping Stone Book(TM) Ser.). (ENG.). 128p. (J). (gr. 1-4). 4.99 *(978-0-307-93171-9(4)*, Random Hse. Bks. for Young Readers) Random Hse. Children's Bks.

—Toilet Paper Mummy. Rex, Michael. 2013. (Stepping Stone Book Ser.). (ENG.). 128p. (J). (gr. 1-4). pap. 4.99 *(978-0-307-93167-2(6))* Random Hse., Inc.

—Truck Duck. Rex, Michael. 2008. (ENG.). 26p. (J). (gr. -1 — 1). bds. 7.99 *(978-0-399-25092-7(1)*, Putnam Juvenile) Penguin Publishing Group.

Rexroad, Susan. Whiz Tanner & the Phony Masterpiece: A Tanner-Dent Mystery. Rexroad, Fred. 2009. (ENG.). 192p. (J). pap. 9.95 *(978-0-9817742-2-0(9)*, Rexroad International) Rexroad, Frederick.

Rey, H. A. & Rey, Margret. Curious George's 1 to 10 & Back Again. 2003. (J). bds. 9.95 *(978-0-618-27711-7(0))* Houghton Mifflin Harcourt Trade & Reference Pubs.

—Curious George's ABCs. 2003. (J). bds. 9.95 *(978-0-618-27708-7(0))* Houghton Mifflin Harcourt Trade & Reference Pubs.

—Curious George's Are You Curious? 2003. (J). bds. 9.95 *(978-0-618-27710-0(2))* Houghton Mifflin Harcourt Trade & Reference Pubs.

—Curious George's Opposites. 2003. (J). bds. 9.95 *(978-0-618-27709-4(9))* Houghton Mifflin Harcourt Trade & Reference Pubs.

Rey, Luis. Dinosaurs in the Sea. Staunton, Joseph & Flinthart, Dirk. 2011. (Inside Crime Ser.). 48p. (YA). (gr. 5-9). 34.25 *(978-1-59920-393-5(6))* Black Rabbit Bks.

—Famous Dinosaurs of Africa. Chinsamy-Turan, Anusuya. 2008. 64p. pap. 13.95 *(978-1-77007-588-7(7))* Struik Pubs. ZAF. Dist: International Publishers Marketing.

—Meat Eating Dinosaurs. Staunton, Joseph & Flinthart, Dirk. 2011. (Inside Crime Ser.). 48p. (YA). (gr. 5-9). 34.25 *(978-1-59920-395-9(2))* Black Rabbit Bks.

Rey, Luis & Trotter, Stuart. The Usborne Book of Dinosaurs. Mayes, Susan. rev. ed. 2005. 32p. (J). pap., pap. 6.95 *(978-0-7945-0849-4(9)*, Usborne) EDC Publishing.

Rey, Luis, jt. illus. see Staunton, Joseph.

Rey, Luis V. The Big Golden Book of Dinosaurs. Bakker, Robert T. 2013. (ENG.). 64p. (J). (gr. -1-2). 16.99 *(978-0-375-85958-8(6))*; lib. bdg. 19.99 *(978-0-375-96679-8(X))* Random Hse. Children's Bks. (Golden Bks.).

—Dino Babies! Bakker, Robert T. 2010. (Pictureback Books Series). (ENG.). 24p. (J). (gr. -1-2). pap. 3.99 *(978-0-375-86330-1(3)*, Random Hse. Bks. for Young Readers) Random Hse. Children's Bks.

—Dinosaurs! Bakker, Robert T. 2005. (Pictureback Books Series). (ENG.). 24p. (J). (gr. -1-2). pap. 3.99 *(978-0-375-83141-6(X)*, Random Hse. Bks. for Young Readers) Random Hse. Children's Bks.

—Dinosaurs: The Most Complete, Up-to-Date Encyclopedia for Dinosaur Lovers of All Ages. Holtz, Thomas R. 2007. (ENG.). 432p. (J). (gr. 3-7). 38.99 *(978-0-375-82419-7(7)*, Random Hse. Bks. for Young Readers) Random Hse. Children's Bks.

—Dinosaurs: in Your Face!, 3 vols. Bakker, Robert T. 2012. (ENG.). 76p. (J). (gr. -1-2). 9.99 *(978-0-307-97692-5(0)*, Random Hse. Bks. for Young Readers) Random Hse. Children's Bks.

—The Usborne Internet-Linked World Atlas of Dinosaurs. Davidson, Susanna et al. 2003. 144p. (J). *(978-0-439-81840-7(0))* Scholastic, Inc.

Rey, Margret. Curious George Makes Pancakes. Rey, H. A. 2008. (Curious George Ser.). (ENG.). 24p. (gr. -1-3). lib. bdg. 24.21 *(978-1-59961-417-5(0))* Spotlight.

Rey, Margret, jt. illus. see Rey, H. A.

Reyes, Arlene. Carter Goes to a Funeral, 1 vol. Zorka, Shawna. 2009. 47p. pap. 24.95 *(978-1-60836-785-6(1))* America Star Bks.

Reyes, Glendalys. The Three Little Explorers, 1 vol. Kittredge, James M. 2010. 16p. pap. 24.95 *(978-1-4489-8973-7(6))* PublishAmerica, Inc.

Reyes, Maria Margarita. La Selva Maravillosa/the Wonderful Jungle. Aristizabal, Nora. 2005. (Bilingual Collection). (SPA.). 31p. (J). *(978-958-30-1966-1(6))* Panamericana Editorial.

Reynish, Jenny. Pumpkin Butterfly: Poems from the Other Side of Nature. Mordhorst, Heidi. 2009. (ENG.). 32p. (J). (gr. 4-7). 16.95 *(978-1-59078-620-8(3)*, Wordsong) Boyds Mills Pr.

Reynolds, Adrian. Bear Flies High. Rosen, Michael. 2009. (ENG.). 32p. (J). (gr. -1-1). 16.99 *(978-1-59990-386-6(5)*, Bloomsbury USA Childrens) Bloomsbury USA.

—Bear's Day Out. Rosen, Michael. (ENG.). (J). 2009. 24p. (gr. -1 — 1). bds. 7.99 *(978-1-59990-391-0(1))*; 2007. 32p. (gr. k-3). 16.95 *(978-1-59990-007-0(6))* Bloomsbury USA. (Bloomsbury USA Childrens).

Reynolds, Adrian. Big Blue Train. Jarman, Julia. 2008. (Ben & Bella Ser.). (ENG.). 32p. (J). (-k). pap. 10.99 ***(978-1-84616-436-1(2))*** Hodder & Stoughton GBR. Dist: Independent Pubs. Group.

Reynolds, Adrian. Canterbury Tales: Little Brother Tale. Ryan, Margaret & Reynolds, Ruth. 2003. (Canterbury Tales Ser.). (ENG.). 64p. (J). pap. 7.99 *(978-0-340-71451-5(4))* Hodder & Stoughton GBR. Dist: Independent Pubs. Group.

—Elephants Can't Jump. Willis, Jeanne. 2015. (ENG.). 32p. (J). (gr. -1-3). 16.99 *(978-1-4677-6316-5(0))* Lerner Publishing Group.

—Elephants Can't Jump! Willis, Jeanne. 2015. (J). *(978-1-4677-6320-2(9))* Lerner Publishing Group.

—Harry & the Bucketful of Dinosaurs. Whybrow, Ian. 2010. (Harry & the Dinosaurs Ser.). (ENG.). 32p. (J). (gr. -1-2). pap. 7.99 *(978-0-375-85119-3(4)*, Dragonfly Bks.) Random Hse. Children's Bks.

Reynolds, Adrian. Harry & the Dinosaurs Go to School. Whybrow, Ian. 2015. (ENG.). 32p. (J). (gr. -1-2). 7.99 ***(978-0-553-53400-9(9)***, Dragonfly Bks.) Random Hse. Children's Bks.

Reynolds, Adrian. I'M Sure I Saw a Dinosaur. Willis, Jeanne. 2011. (Andersen Press Picture Books Ser.). 16.95 *(978-0-7613-8093-1(0))* Andersen Pr. GBR. Dist: Lerner Publishing Group.

—The Pets You Get. Taylor, Thomas. 2013. 32p. (gr. -1-3). 16.95 *(978-1-4677-1143-2(8))* Andersen Pr. GBR. Dist: Lerner Publishing Group.

—That's Not Funny! Willis, Jeanne. 2010. (Andersen Press Picture Bks). (ENG.). 32p. (J). (gr. -1-3). 16.95 *(978-0-7613-6445-0(5))* Lerner Publishing Group.

—Upside down Babies. Willis, Jeanne. 2014. (ENG.). 32p. (J). (gr. -1-3). 16.95 *(978-1-4677-3424-0(1))* Lerner Publishing Group.

—What's Naughty? Oram, Hiawyn. 32p. (J). pap. 11.99 *(978-0-340-75447-4(8))* Hodder & Stoughton GBR. Dist: Trafalgar Square Publishing.

—Who's in the Loo? Willis, Jeanne. 2013. (ENG.). 32p. (J). (gr. -1-k). pap. 11.99 *(978-1-84270-698-5(5))* Andersen Pr. GBR. Dist: Independent Pubs. Group.

Reynolds, Doris. Beth & Seth. Varble, Rachel McBrayer. 2012. 208p. 44.95 *(978-1-258-25079-9(9))*; pap. 29.95 *(978-1-258-25542-8(1))* Literary Licensing, LLC.

Reynolds, Emily C. S. Discovering Nature's Laws: A Story about Isaac Newton. Reynolds, Emily C. S., tr. Salas, Laura Purdie. 2003. (Creative Minds Biographies Ser.). (ENG.). 64p. (J). (gr. 4-8). pap. 8.95 *(978-1-57505-606-7(2))*; lib. bdg. 22.60 *(978-1-57505-183-3(4))* Lerner Publishing Group.

Reynolds, Jan, photos by. Celebrate! Connections among Cultures, 1 vol. Reynolds, Jan. 2006. (ENG., 32p. (J). pap. 8.95 *(978-1-60060-452-2(8))* Lee & Low Bks., Inc.

—Cycle of Rice, Cycle of Life: A Story of Sustainable Farming. Reynolds, Jan. 2009. (ENG., 48p. (J). (gr. 2-7). 19.95 *(978-1-60060-254-2(1))* Lee & Low Bks., Inc.

—Only the Mountains Do Not Move: A Maasai Story of Culture & Conservation. Reynolds, Jan. 2011. (ENG., 40p. (J). pap. 9.95 *(978-1-60060-844-5(2))*; (gr. 1-6). pap. 18.95 *(978-1-60060-333-4(5))* Lee & Low Bks., Inc.

Reynolds, Pat. The Boy at the Park. Reilly, Carmel. 2009. 24p. pap. 10.67 *(978-1-4190-5517-1(8))* Rigby Education.

Reynolds, Paul A. & Reynolds, Peter. Sydney & Simon: To the Moon & Beyond! 2016. (J). lib. bdg. ***(978-1-58089-679-5(0))*** Charlesbridge Publishing, Inc.

Reynolds, Peter. Huck Runs Amuck! Taylor, Sean. 2011. (ENG.). 48p. (J). (gr. k-3). 16.99 *(978-0-8037-3261-2(9)*, Dial) Penguin Publishing Group.

—Judy Moody & Stink: La Loca, Loca Busqueda del Tesoro. McDonald, Megan. 2011. (SPA.). 256p. (J). (gr. 2-5). pap. 14.95 *(978-1-61605-137-2(X))* Ediciones Alfaguara ESP. Dist: Perseus Distribution.

—Olivia Kidney. Potter, Ellen. 2004. (ENG.). 176p. (J). (gr. 3-7). reprint ed. 6.99 *(978-0-14-240234-4(6)*, Puffin) Penguin Publishing Group.

Reynolds, Peter, jt. illus. see Reynolds, Paul A.

Reynolds, Peter, jt. illus. see Reynolds, Peter H.

Reynolds, Peter H. Around the World in 8 1/2 Days. McDonald, Megan. 2010. (Judy Moody Ser.: 7). (ENG.). 176p. (J). (gr. 1-4). 15.99 *(978-0-7636-4864-0(7))*;Bk. 7. pap. 5.99 *(978-0-7636-4863-3(9))* Candlewick Pr.

—The Doctor Is In! McDonald, Megan. 2010. (Judy Moody Ser.: 5). (ENG.). 176p. (J). (gr. 1-4). 15.99 *(978-0-7636-4862-6(0))*; pap. 5.99 *(978-0-7636-4861-9(2))* Candlewick Pr.

—Doctora Judy Moody. McDonald, Megan. 2005. (SPA.). 74p. (J). (gr. 3-5). per. 7.95 *(978-1-59820-034-8(8))* Ediciones Alfaguara ESP. Dist: Perseus Distribution.

—Girl Detective. McDonald, Megan. (Judy Moody Ser.: 9). (ENG.). 192p. (J). (gr. 1-4). 2011. pap. 5.99 *(978-0-7636-4349-2(1))*; Bk. 9. 2010. 15.99 *(978-0-7636-3450-6(6))* Candlewick Pr.

—Going Places. Reynolds, Paul A. 2014. (ENG.). 40p. (J). (gr. -1-3). 15.99 *(978-1-4424-6608-1(1)*, Atheneum Bks. for Young Readers) Simon & Schuster Children's Publishing.

—The Holly Joliday. McDonald, Megan. 2008. (Judy Moody Ser.: No. 1). (ENG.). 96p. (J). (gr. k-3). pap. 6.99 *(978-0-7636-4113-9(8))* Candlewick Pr.

Reynolds, Peter H. I Am Yoga. Verde, Susan. 2015. (ENG.). 32p. (J). (gr. -1-3). 14.95 ***(978-1-4197-1664-5(6)***, Abrams Bks. for Young Readers) Abrams.

Reynolds, Peter H. The Incredible Shrinking Kid. McDonald, Megan. 2013. (Stink Ser.: 1). (ENG.). (J). (gr. 1-4). 112p. 12.99 *(978-0-7636-6388-9(3))*; 128p. pap. 4.99 *(978-0-7636-6426-8(X))* Candlewick Pr.

—Judy Moody. McDonald, Megan. 2012. (Judy Moody Ser.: Bks. 7-9). (ENG.). (J). (gr. 1-4). pap. 17.97 *(978-0-7636-5410-8(8))* Candlewick Pr.

—The Judy Moody - Uber Awesome Collection, 9 vols., Bks. 1-9. McDonald, Megan. 2011. (Judy Moody Ser.). (ENG.). 1488p. (J). (gr. 1-4). pap. 48.00 *(978-0-7636-5411-5(6)*, Nosy Crow) Candlewick Pr.

—Judy Moody - Was in a Mood. McDonald, Megan. 2010. (Judy Moody Ser.: 1). (ENG.). 160p. (J). (gr. 1-4). 15.99 *(978-0-7636-4850-3(7))* Candlewick Pr.

—Judy Moody Advina el Futuro. McDonald, Megan. 2004. (SPA.). 74p. (J). (gr. 3-5). pap. 7.95 *(978-1-59437-837-9(1))* Ediciones Alfaguara ESP. Dist: Perseus Distribution.

—Judy Moody & Stink: The Mad, Mad, Mad, Mad Treasure Hunt. McDonald, Megan. 2009. (Judy Moody Ser.: No. 2). (ENG.). 128p. (J). (gr. 1-4). 14.99 *(978-0-7636-3962-4(1))* Candlewick Pr.

—Judy Moody & Stink: the Big Bad Blackout. McDonald, Megan. 2015. (Judy Moody Ser.). (ENG.). 144p. (J). (gr. 1-4). pap. 6.99 *(978-0-7636-7665-0(9))* Candlewick Pr.

Reynolds, Peter H. Judy Moody & Stink: the Wishbone Wish. McDonald, Megan. 2015. (Judy Moody Ser.). (ENG.). 128p. (J). (gr. 1-4). 14.99 ***(978-0-7636-7206-5(8))*** Candlewick Pr.

Reynolds, Peter H. Judy Moody & the Bad Luck Charm. McDonald, Megan. 2012. (Judy Moody Ser.: 11). (ENG.). 176p. (J). (gr. 1-4). 15.99 *(978-0-7636-3451-3(4))* Candlewick Pr.

—Judy Moody & the Bad Luck Charm (Book #11) McDonald, Megan. 2013. (Judy Moody Ser.: 11). (ENG.). 176p. (J). (gr. 1-4). pap. 5.99 *(978-0-7636-4348-5(3))* Candlewick Pr.

—Judy Moody & the Not Bummer Summer. McDonald, Megan. movie tie-in ed. (Judy Moody Ser.: Bk. 10). (ENG.). (J). (gr. 1-4). 2011. 128p. pap. 5.99 *(978-0-7636-5351-4(9))*; Bk. 10. 2012. 208p. 15.99 *(978-0-7636-5711-6(5))*; Bk. 10. 2012. 208p. pap. 5.99 *(978-0-7636-5710-9(7))* Candlewick Pr.

—Judy Moody Declares Independence. McDonald, Megan. 2010. (Judy Moody Ser.: 6). (ENG.). 160p. (J). (gr. 1-4). 15.99 *(978-0-7636-4852-7(3))*; pap. 5.99 *(978-0-7636-4851-0(5))* Candlewick Pr.

—Judy Moody Esta de Mal Humor, de Muy Mal Humor. McDonald, Megan. Mendoza Garcia, Isabel, tr. 2004. (SPA.). 160p. (J). (gr. 3-5). pap. 7.95 *(978-1-59437-816-4(9))* Ediciones Alfaguara ESP. Dist: Perseus Distribution.

—Judy Moody Gets Famous! McDonald, Megan. 2010. (Judy Moody Ser.: 2). (ENG.). 144p. (J). (gr. 1-4). 15.99 *(978-0-7636-4854-1(X))*; pap. 5.99 *(978-0-7636-4853-4(1))* Candlewick Pr.

—Judy Moody Goes to College, Bk. 8. McDonald, Megan. 2010. (Judy Moody Ser.: 8). (ENG.). (J). (gr. 1-4). 144p. 15.99 *(978-0-7636-4856-5(6))*; 160p. pap. 5.99 *(978-0-7636-4855-8(8))* Candlewick Pr.

—The Judy Moody Mood Journal. McDonald, Megan. 2009. (Judy Moody Ser.). (ENG.). 128p. (J). (gr. 3-7). 8.99 *(978-0-7636-2736-2(4))* Candlewick Pr.

—Judy Moody, Mood Martian. McDonald, Megan. 2014. (Judy Moody Ser.: 12). (ENG.). 208p. (J). (gr. 1-4). 15.99 *(978-0-7636-6698-9(X))* Candlewick Pr.

—Judy Moody Predicts the Future. McDonald, Megan. 2010. (Judy Moody Ser.: 4). (ENG.). 160p. (J). (gr. 1-4). 15.99 *(978-0-7636-4858-9(2))*; pap. 5.99 *(978-0-7636-4857-2(4))* Candlewick Pr.

—Judy Moody Salva el Planeta. McDonald, Megan. 2005. (SPA.). 74p. (J). (gr. 3-5). pap. 7.95 *(978-1-59437-838-6(X))* Ediciones Alfaguara ESP. Dist: Perseus Distribution.

—Judy Moody Saves the World! McDonald, Megan. 2004. (Judy Moody Ser.: Bk. 3). 144p. (J). (gr. 1-5). 13.65 *(978-0-7569-2588-8(6))* Perfection Learning Corp.

—Judy Moody Saves the World! McDonald, Megan. 2010. (Judy Moody Ser.: 3). (ENG.). 160p. (J). (gr. 1-4). 15.99 *(978-0-7636-4860-2(4))*;Bk. 3. pap. 5.99 *(978-0-7636-4859-6(0))* Candlewick Pr.

—Judy Moody se Vuelve Famosa! McDonald, Megan. Mendoza Garcia, Isabel, tr. 2004. (SPA.). 340p. (J). (gr. 3-5). pap. 7.95 *(978-1-59437-817-1(7))* Alfaguara S.A. de Ediciones ARG. Dist: Perseus Distribution.

—Judy Moody va a la Universidad. McDonald, Megan. Rozarena, P., tr. 2009. (SPA.). 512p. (J). (gr. 3-5). pap. 7.95 *(978-1-60396-629-0(3))* Alfaguara S.A. de Ediciones ARG. Dist: Perseus Distribution.

—Judy Moody y Stink: ¡Felices Fiestas! McDonald, Megan. Rozarena, P., tr. 2009. (SPA.). 328p. (J). (gr. 2-5). pap. 13.95 *(978-1-60396-631-3(5))* Ediciones Alfaguara ESP. Dist: Perseus Distribution.

—Judy Moody's Best Mood Ever Coloring & Activity Book. McDonald, Megan. 2011. (Judy Moody Ser.). (ENG.). 32p. (J). (gr. -1-2). pap. 3.99 *(978-0-7636-5707-9(7))* Candlewick Pr.

—Judy Moody's Double-Rare Way-Not-Boring Book of Fun Stuff to Do. McDonald, Megan. 2009. (Judy Moody Ser.). (ENG.). 96p. (J). (gr. 2-5). pap. 5.99 *(978-0-7636-4431-4(5))* Candlewick Pr.

—Judy Moody's Mini-Mysteries & Other Sneaky Stuff for Super-Sleuths. McDonald, Megan. 2012. (Judy Moody Ser.). (ENG.). 96p. (J). (gr. 1-4). pap. 4.99 *(978-0-7636-5941-7(X))* Candlewick Pr.

—Judy Moody's Way Wacky Uber Awesome Book of More Fun Stuff to Do. McDonald, Megan. 2010. (Judy Moody Ser.). (ENG.). 96p. (J). (gr. 1-4). pap. 5.99 *(978-0-7636-4309-6(2))* Candlewick Pr.

—Little Boy. McGhee, Alison. 2008. (ENG.). 40p. (J). (gr. -1-3). 16.99 *(978-1-4169-5872-7(X)*, Atheneum Bks. for Young Readers) Simon & Schuster Children's Publishing.

—Little Miss, Big Sis. Rosenthal, Amy Krouse. 2015. (ENG.). 40p. (J). (gr. -1-3). 17.99 *(978-0-06-230203-8(5))* HarperCollins Pubs.

—The Mad, Mad, Mad, Mad Treasure Hunt. McDonald, Megan. 2010. (Judy Moody Ser.: Bk. 2). (ENG.). 128p. (J). (gr. 1-4). pap. 6.99 *(978-0-7636-4351-5(3))* Candlewick Pr.

Reynolds, Peter H. Mood Martian. McDonald, Megan. 2015. (Judy Moody Ser.). (ENG.). 208p. (J). (gr. 1-4). pap. 5.99 ***(978-0-7636-8015-2(X))*** Candlewick Pr.

Reynolds, Peter H. More Super-Stinky Stuff from A to Z. McDonald, Megan. 2010. (Stink Ser.). (ENG.). 144p. (J). (gr. k-4). pap. 5.99 *(978-0-7636-4558-8(3))* Candlewick Pr.

—The Museum. Verde, Susan. 2013. (ENG.). 32p. (J). (gr. -1-2). 16.95 *(978-1-4197-0594-6(6))*, Abrams Bks. for Young Readers) Abrams.

—Off the Path Math with Tobbs, Vol. 1. O'Brien, Thomas C. 2003. 59p. (J). 14.50 *(978-1-891405-09-9(8))* FableVision Pr.

—Olivia Kidney Stops for No One. Potter, Ellen. 2007. (ENG.). 272p. (J). (gr. 3-7). 8.99 *(978-0-14-240772-1(0)*, Puffin) Penguin Publishing Group.
—Plant a Kiss. Rosenthal, Amy Krouse. 2011. (ENG.). 40p. (J). (gr. -1-3). 14.99 *(978-0-06-198675-8(5))* HarperCollins Pubs.
—The Shark Sleepover, Bk. 9. McDonald, Megan. 2015. (Stink Ser.: 9). (ENG.). 176p. (J). (gr. 1-4). pap. 4.99 *(978-0-7636-7678-0(0))* Candlewick Pr.
—Solar System Superhero. McDonald, Megan. 2013. (Stink Ser.: 5). (ENG.). (J). (gr. 1-4). 144p. pap. 4.99 *(978-0-7636-6425-1(1))*;Bk. 5. 128p. 12.99 *(978-0-7636-6392-6(1))* Candlewick Pr.
—Someday. McGhee, Alison. 2007. (ENG.). 32p. (J). (gr. -1-3). 16.99 *(978-1-4169-2811-9(1)*, Atheneum Bks. for Young Readers) Simon & Schuster Children's Publishing.
—Someday. McGhee, Alison. 2008. (J). (gr. -1-2). 27.95 incl. audio *(978-0-8045-6975-0(4))*; 29.95 incl. audio compact disk *(978-0-8045-4200-5(7))* Spoken Arts, Inc.
—Spf 40. FableVision. 2013. (Zebrafish Ser.). (ENG.). 128p. (J). (gr. 5-9). 19.99 *(978-1-4169-9708-5(3)*, Atheneum Bks. for Young Readers) Simon & Schuster Children's Publishing.
—Spf 40. FableVision Staff. 2013. (Zebrafish Ser.). (ENG.). 128p. (J). (gr. 5-9). pap. 9.99 *(978-1-4169-9709-2(1)*, Atheneum Bks. for Young Readers) Simon & Schuster Children's Publishing.
—Star Bright: A Christmas Story. 2014. (ENG.). 40p. (J). (gr. -1-3). 16.99 *(978-1-4169-5858-1(4)*, Atheneum Bks. for Young Readers) Simon & Schuster Children's Publishing.
—Stationery Studio Writing Collection Deluxe CD-ROM Single Computer License: The Irresistible Tool to Encourage Writing. Stearns, Peggy Healy. 2003. 112p. (J). 69.95 incl. cd-rom *(978-1-891405-07-5(1))* FableVision Pr.
—Stink - The Super-Incredible Collection, Bks. 1-3. McDonald, Megan. 2013. (Stink Ser.). (ENG.). 352p. (J). (gr. k-3). pap. 14.97 *(978-0-7636-6831-0(1))* Candlewick Pr.
—Stink & the Freaky Frog Freakout. McDonald, Megan. 2013. (Stink Ser.: 8). (ENG.). 160p. (J). (gr. 1-4). 12.99 *(978-0-7636-6140-3(6))* Candlewick Pr.
—Stink & the Great Guinea Pig Express, Bk. 4. McDonald, Megan. 2013. (Stink Ser.: 4). (ENG.). (J). (gr. 1-4). 128p. 12.99 *(978-0-7636-6391-9(3))*; 144p. pap. 4.99 *(978-0-7636-6421-3(9))* Candlewick Pr.
—Stink & the Incredible Super-Galactic Jawbreaker. McDonald, Megan. 2013. (Stink Ser.: 2). (ENG.). (J). (gr. 1-4). 144p. pap. 4.99 *(978-0-7636-6420-6(0))*;Bk. 2. 128p. 12.99 *(978-0-7636-6389-6(1))* Candlewick Pr.
—Stink & the Midnight Zombie Walk. McDonald, Megan. 2013. (Stink Ser.: 7). (ENG.). 160p. (J). (gr. 1-4). 12.99 *(978-0-7636-6394-0(8))*; pap. 4.99 *(978-0-7636-6422-0(7))* Candlewick Pr.
—Stink & the Shark Sleepover. McDonald, Megan. 2014. (Stink Ser.: 9). (ENG.). 176p. (J). (gr. 1-4). 12.99 *(978-0-7636-6474-9(X))* Candlewick Pr.
—Stink & the Ultimate Thumb-Wrestling Smackdown. McDonald, Megan. 2013. (Stink Ser.: 6). (ENG.). 144p. (J). (gr. 1-4). pap. 4.99 *(978-0-7636-6423-7(5))*;Bk. 6. 12.99 *(978-0-7636-6393-3(X))* Candlewick Pr.
—Stink & the World's Worst Super-Stinky Sneakers, Bk. 3. McDonald, Megan. 2013. (Stink Ser.: 3). (ENG.). 144p. (J). (gr. 1-4). pap. 4.99 *(978-0-7636-6424-4(3))*;Bk. 3. 12.99 *(978-0-7636-6390-2(5))* Candlewick Pr.
—Stink It Up! A Guide to the Gross, the Bad, & the Smelly. McDonald, Megan. 2013. (Stink Ser.). (ENG.). 128p. (J). (gr. 1-4). pap. 5.99 *(978-0-7636-5942-4(8))* Candlewick Pr.
—Stink-O-Pedia Vol. 2: Super Stink-Y Stuff from A to Zzzzz. McDonald, Megan. 2009. (Stink Ser.). (ENG.). 144p. (J). (gr. k-4). pap. 5.99 *(978-0-7636-3963-1(X))* Candlewick Pr.
—Stink: the Absolutely Astronomical Collection: Books 4-6. McDonald, Megan. 2013. (Stink Ser.). (ENG.). 256p. (J). (gr. k-3). pap. 14.97 *(978-0-7636-6830-3(3))* Candlewick Pr.
—Stink y el Gran Expreso del Cobaya. McDonald, Megan. Rozarena, P., tr. 2009. (SPA.). 176p. (J). (gr. 2-5). pap. 7.95 *(978-1-60396-630-6(7))* Ediciones Alfaguara ESP. Dist: Perseus Distribution.
—Tess's Tree. Brallier, Jess M. 2010. (JPN.). 28p. (J). *(978-4-07-269392-6(8))* Shufunotomo Company, Limited.
—Twice as Moody. McDonald, Megan. 2011. (Judy Moody Ser.). (ENG.). 304p. (J). (gr. 1-4). pap. 8.99 *(978-0-7636-5740-6(9))* Candlewick Pr.
—Was in a Mood. McDonald, Megan. 2010. (Judy Moody Ser.: 1). (ENG.). 176p. (J). (gr. 1-4). pap. 5.99 *(978-0-7636-4849-7(3))* Candlewick Pr.
—What to Do If an Elephant Stands on Your Foot. Robinson, Michelle. 2012. (ENG.). 32p. (J). (gr. -1-k). 16.99 *(978-0-8037-3398-5(4)*, Dial) Penguin Publishing Group.
—You & Me. Verde, Susan. 2015. (ENG.). 32p. (J). (gr. k-17). 14.95 *(978-1-4197-1197-8(0)*, Abrams Bks. for Young Readers) Abrams.
Reynolds, Peter H. The Best Kid in the World: A SugarLoaf Book. Reynolds, Peter H. 2012. (ENG.). 48p. (J). (gr. -1-2). pap. 22.99 *(978-1-4424-7178-8(6)*, Atheneum Bks. for Young Readers) Simon & Schuster Children's Publishing.
—The Dot. Reynolds, Peter H. 2005. 34p. (J). bds. 19.95 *(978-0-9769313-0-0(3))* BrailleInk.
—The Dot. Reynolds, Peter H. 2003. (Creatrilogy Ser.). (ENG.). 32p. (J). (gr. k-12). 14.00 *(978-0-7636-1961-9(2)*, 53509533) Candlewick Pr.
—The Dot: Make Your Mark Kit. Reynolds, Peter H. 2013. (Creatrilogy Ser.). (ENG.). (J). (gr. k-4). 24.99 *(978-0-7636-6978-2(4))* Candlewick Pr.
—Guyku: A Year of Haiku for Boys. Reynolds, Peter H. Raczka, Bob. 2010. (ENG.). 48p. (J). (gr. -1-3). 14.99 *(978-0-547-24003-9(1))* Houghton Mifflin Harcourt Publishing Co.
—I'm Here. Reynolds, Peter H. 2011. (ENG.). 32p. (J). (gr. -1-3). 16.99 *(978-1-4169-9649-1(4)*, Atheneum Bks. for Young Readers) Simon & Schuster Children's Publishing.
—Ish. Reynolds, Peter H. unabr. ed. 2005. (J). (gr. -1-4). 24.95 incl. audio *(978-0-439-80428-8(0)*, WHRA676) Scholastic, Inc.
—Ish. Reynolds, Peter H. 2005. (J). (gr. -1-4). 29.95 *(978-0-439-80429-5(9)*, WHCD676) Weston Woods Studios, Inc.
—My Very Big Little World. Reynolds, Peter H. 2006. (ENG.). 40p. (J). (gr. -1-3). 17.99 *(978-0-689-87621-9(1)*, Atheneum Bks. for Young Readers) Simon & Schuster Children's Publishing.
—The North Star. Reynolds, Peter H. 2009. (ENG.). 64p. (J). (gr. -1-2). 16.99 *(978-0-7636-3677-7(0))* Candlewick Pr.
—Rose's Garden. Reynolds, Peter H. 2009. (ENG.). 40p. (J). (gr. k-12). 15.99 *(978-0-7636-4641-7(5))* Candlewick Pr.
—Sky Color. Reynolds, Peter H. 2012. (Creatrilogy Ser.). (ENG.). 32p. (J). (gr. k-12). 14.00 *(978-0-7636-2345-6(8))* Candlewick Pr.
Reynolds, Peter H. The Smallest Gift of Christmas. Reynolds, Peter H. (ENG.). 40p. (J). (gr. -1-2). 2015. 10.00 ***(978-0-7636-7981-1(X))***; 2013. 14.00 *(978-0-7636-6103-8(1))* Candlewick Pr.
Reynolds, Peter H. So Few of Me. Reynolds, Peter H. 2006. (ENG.). 32p. (J). (gr. k-12). 14.00 *(978-0-7636-2623-5(6))* Candlewick Pr.
Reynolds, Peter H. & Candlewick Press Staff. Judy Moody Goes to Hollywood: Behind the Scenes with Judy Moody & Friends. McDonald, Megan. ed. 2011. (Judy Moody Ser.). (ENG.). 160p. (J). (gr. 1-4). 14.99 *(978-0-7636-5551-8(1))* Candlewick Pr.
—The Poop Picnic. McDonald, Megan & Michalak, Jamie. ed. 2011. (Judy Moody Ser.). (ENG.). 48p. (J). (gr. k-3). pap. 3.99 *(978-0-7636-5553-2(8))* Candlewick Pr.
Reynolds, Peter H. & Fable Vision Studios Staff. Charlie & Kiwi: An Evolutionary Adventure. New York Hall of Science Staff. 2011. (ENG.). 48p. (J). (gr. -1-3). 16.99 *(978-1-4424-2112-7(6)*, Atheneum Bks. for Young Readers) Simon & Schuster Children's Publishing.
Reynolds, Peter H. & Kurilla, Renee. Zebrafish. Emerson, Sharon. 2012. (Zebrafish Ser.). (ENG.). 128p. (J). (gr. 5-9). pap. 7.99 *(978-1-4169-9707-8(5)*, Atheneum Bks. for Young Readers) Simon & Schuster Children's Publishing.
Reynolds, Peter H. & Reynolds, Peter. Ish. Reynolds, Peter H. & Reynolds, Peter. 2004. (Creatrilogy Ser.). (ENG.). 32p. (J). (gr. k-12). 14.00 *(978-0-7636-2344-9(X))* Candlewick Pr.
Reynolds, Peter H., jt. illus. see FableVision Studios Staff.
Reynolds, Rhonda. What Kind of War Was It, Anyhow? Reynolds, Rhonda, tr. Ekberg, Nancy. 2003. 45p. (J). pap. 8.95 *(978-1-58838-085-2(8)*, Junebug Bks.) NewSouth, Inc.
Reynolds, Sarah. Aunt Debra & My Favorite Things Poster. Pedrow, Debra A. Karper, Deborah, ed. 2003. 40p. (J). 15.95 *(978-1-928681-09-0(3))* Gladstone Publishing.
Reznicek, Curtis. Harold Discovers Santa's Secret: A Very Long Dog with a Very Big Heart. Witt, Janice. 2013. 40p. pap. 11.99 *(978-1-63022-442-4(1))* Speedy Publishing LLC.
RH Disney Staff. An Adventure in Arendelle. Berrios, Frank. 2014. (Big Coloring Book Ser.). (ENG.). 48p. (J). (gr. -1-2). pap. 6.99 *(978-0-7364-3099-9(7)*, Golden/Disney) Random Hse. Children's Bks.
RH Disney Staff, et al. Anna & Elsa - A Warm Welcome. David, Erica. 2015. (Stepping Stone Book(TM) Ser.). (ENG.). 128p. (J). (gr. 1-4). 9.99 *(978-0-7364-3289-4(2)*, RH/Disney) Random Hse. Children's Bks.
RH Disney Staff. Ariel's Dolphin Adventure - Snow White's New Friend. Posner-Sanchez, Andrea. 2010. (Deluxe Pictureback Ser.). (ENG.). 32p. (J). (gr. -1-2). pap. 4.99 *(978-0-7364-2654-1(X)*, RH/Disney) Random Hse. Children's Bks.
—As Big As a Whale (Disney Junior: Doc Mcstuffins) Posner-Sanchez, Andrea. 2014. (Little Golden Book Ser.). (ENG.). 24p. (J). (-k). 3.99 *(978-0-7364-3087-6(3)*, Golden/Disney) Random Hse. Children's Bks.
—Beauty the Sleepiest Kitty. Redbank, Tennant. 2014. (Stepping Stone Book(TM) Ser.). (ENG.). 64p. (J). (gr. 1-4). lib. bdg. 12.99 *(978-0-7364-8163-2(X)*, RH/Disney) Random Hse. Children's Bks.
—Before the Bell. Thorpe, Kiki. 2015. (Never Girls Ser.: 9). (ENG.). 128p. (J). (gr. 1-4). lib. bdg. 12.99 *(978-0-7364-8167-0(2))*; 5.99 *(978-0-7364-3304-4(X))* Random Hse. Children's Bks. (RH/Disney).
RH Disney Staff. Best in Show! (Disney Princess: Palace Pets) Carbone, Courtney. 2015. (Big Coloring Book Ser.). (ENG.). 48p. (J). (gr. -1-2). pap. 6.99 ***(978-0-7364-3372-3(4)***, Golden/Disney) Random Hse. Children's Bks.
RH Disney Staff. Big Friend, Little Friend. Lagonegro, Melissa. 2010. (Step into Reading Ser.). (ENG.). 32p. (J). (gr. k-3). pap. 3.99 *(978-0-7364-2644-2(2)*, RH/Disney) Random Hse. Children's Bks.
—Big-Screen Blockbusters! (Disney/Pixar) Berrios, Frank. 2014. (Color Plus 1,000 Stickers Ser.). (ENG.). 64p. (J). (gr. -1-2). pap. 9.99 *(978-0-7364-3176-7(4)*, Golden/Disney) Random Hse. Children's Bks.
—Blondie: Rapunzel's Royal Pony. Redbank, Tennant. 2014. (Stepping Stone Book(TM) Ser.). (ENG.). 64p. (J). (gr. 2-5). 5.99 *(978-0-7364-3267-2(1)*, RH/Disney) Random Hse. Children's Bks.
—Blondie the Royal Pony. Redbank, Tennant. 2014. (Stepping Stone Book(TM) Ser.). (ENG.). 64p. (J). (gr. 1-4). lib. bdg. 12.99 *(978-0-7364-8164-9(8)*, RH/Disney) Random Hse. Children's Bks.
—Boomer Gets His Bounce Back (Disney Junior: Doc Mcstuffins) Posner-Sanchez, Andrea. 2013. (Little Golden Book Ser.). (ENG.). 24p. (J). (-k). 3.99 *(978-0-7364-3143-9(8)*, Golden/Disney) Random Hse. Children's Bks.
—Bow-Bot Robot (Disney Junior: Minnie's Bow Toons) Posner-Sanchez, Andrea & Weinberg, Jennifer Liberts. 2014. (Little Golden Book Ser.). (ENG.). 24p. (J). (-k). 3.99 *(978-0-7364-3078-4(4)*, Golden/Disney) Random Hse. Children's Bks.
—Bubble-Rific! Posner-Sanchez, Andrea. 2014. (Little Golden Book Ser.). (ENG.). 24p. (J). (-k). 3.99 *(978-0-7364-3236-8(1)*, Golden/Disney) Random Hse. Children's Bks.
—Bunny Magic! (Disney Junior: Sofia the First) Posner-Sanchez, Andrea. 2014. (Little Golden Book Ser.). (ENG.). 24p. (J). (-k). 3.99 *(978-0-7364-3085-2(7)*, Golden/Disney) Random Hse. Children's Bks.
—The Bunny Surprise (Disney/Pixar Toy Story) Jordan, Apple. 2012. (Step into Reading Ser.). (ENG.). 32p. (J). (gr. -1-1). pap. 3.99 *(978-0-7364-2857-6(7)*, RH/Disney) Random Hse. Children's Bks.
—Car Crazy! (Disney/Pixar Cars) Berrios, Frank. 2012. (Super Jumbo Coloring Book Ser.). (ENG.). 416p. (J). (gr. -1-2). pap. 10.99 *(978-0-7364-3023-4(7)*, Golden/Disney) Random Hse. Children's Bks.
—Cars Little Golden Book Library (Disney/Pixar Cars), 5 vols. 2012. (ENG.). 24p. (J). (gr. -1-2). 19.95 *(978-0-7364-3008-1(3)*, Golden/Disney) Random Hse. Children's Bks.
—The Cars Story Collection. 2011. (Step into Reading Ser.). (ENG.). 160p. (J). (gr. k-3). pap. 7.99 *(978-0-7364-2813-2(5)*, RH/Disney) Random Hse. Children's Bks.
—The Christmas Party. Posner-Sanchez, Andrea. 2014. (Step into Reading Ser.). (ENG.). 24p. (J). (gr. -1-1). lib. bdg. 12.99 *(978-0-7364-8219-6(9)*, RH/Disney) Random Hse. Children's Bks.
—Christmas Toys (Disney/Pixar Toy Story) Weinberg, Jennifer Liberts. 2012. (Step into Reading Ser.). (ENG.). 32p. (J). (gr. -1-1). pap. 3.99 *(978-0-7364-2884-2(4)*, RH/Disney) Random Hse. Children's Bks.
—Cinderella (Diamond) Step into Reading (Disney Princess) Lagonegro, Melissa. 2012. (Step into Reading Ser.). (ENG.). 32p. (J). (gr. -1-1). pap. 3.99 *(978-0-7364-2888-0(7)*, RH/Disney) Random Hse. Children's Bks.
RH Disney Staff, et al. Cinderella Is My Babysitter (Disney Princess) RH Disney Staff & Posner-Sanchez, Andrea. 2015. (Little Golden Book Ser.). (ENG.). 24p. (J). (-k). 3.99 *(978-0-7364-3324-2(4)*, Golden/Disney) Random Hse. Children's Bks.
RH Disney Staff. Cuddly Princess Pals. Posner-Sanchez, Andrea. 2014. (Pictureback(R) Ser.). (ENG.). 24p. (J). (gr. -1-k). 3.99 *(978-0-7364-3135-4(7)*, RH/Disney) Random Hse. Children's Bks.
RH Disney Staff. Cute, Sweet, & Petite! (Disney Princess: Palace Pets) Sky Koster, Amy. 2015. (Big Golden Book Ser.). (ENG.). 64p. (J). (gr. -1-2). 9.99 ***(978-0-7364-3412-6(7)***, Golden/Disney) Random Hse. Children's Bks.
RH Disney Staff. Deputy Mater Saves the Day! (Disney/Pixar Cars) Berrios, Frank. 2013. (Little Golden Book Ser.). (ENG.). 24p. (J). (-k). 3.99 *(978-0-7364-2979-5(4)*, Golden/Disney) Random Hse. Children's Bks.
—Disney Infinity: the Ultimate Fan Book! (Disney Infinity) Berrios, Frank. 2014. (Full-Color Activity Book with Stickers Ser.). (ENG.). 32p. (J). (gr. -1-2). pap. 5.99 *(978-0-7364-3271-9(X)*, Golden/Disney) Random Hse. Children's Bks.
—Disney Junior: Nine Favorite Tales (Disney Mixed Property) 2014. (Little Golden Book Treasury Ser.). (ENG.). 224p. (J). (-k). 11.99 *(978-0-7364-3257-3(4)*, Golden/Disney) Random Hse. Children's Bks.
RH Disney Staff, et al. Disney Princess Joke Book (Disney Princess) Carbone, Courtney. 2015. (Stepping Stone Book(TM) Ser.). (ENG.). 64p. (J). (gr. 1-2). 5.99 ***(978-0-7364-3414-0(3)***, RH/Disney) Random Hse. Children's Bks.
RH Disney Staff. Disney/Pixar Little Golden Book Library (Disney/Pixar), 5 vols. 2014. (ENG.). 24p. (J). (-k). 19.95 *(978-0-7364-3163-7(2)*, Golden/Disney) Random Hse. Children's Bks.
RH Disney Staff. Doc Mcstuffins Little Golden Book Library (Disney Junior: Doc Mcstuffins), 5 vols. 2015. (ENG.). 120p. (J). (-k). 19.95 ***(978-0-7364-3407-2(0)***, Golden/Disney) Random Hse. Children's Bks.
RH Disney Staff. Driving School (Disney/Pixar Cars) Depken, Kristen L. 2013. (Step into Reading Ser.). (ENG.). 24p. (J). (gr. -1-1). 3.99 *(978-0-7364-2982-5(4)*, RH/Disney) Random Hse. Children's Bks.
RH Disney Staff. Drop Zone! (Disney Planes) Berrios, Frank. 2015. (Deluxe Stickerific Ser.). (ENG.). 64p. (J). (gr. -1-2). pap. 5.99 ***(978-0-7364-3409-6(7)***, Golden/Disney) Random Hse. Children's Bks.
RH Disney Staff. Dusty Flies High. Amerikaner, Susan. 2013. (Step into Reading Ser.). (ENG.). 32p. (J). (gr. -1-1). pap. 3.99 *(978-0-7364-3018-0(0)*, RH/Disney) Random Hse. Children's Bks.
—The Easter Buggy (Disney/Pixar Cars) Berrios, Frank. 2014. (Pictureback Series.). (ENG.). 16p. (J). (gr. -1-2). 4.99 *(978-0-7364-3139-2(X)*, RH/Disney) Random Hse. Children's Bks.
RH Disney Staff. Exciting! Awesome! Infinite! (Disney Infinity) Belle, Sebastian. 2015. (Color Plus 1,000 Stickers Ser.). (ENG.). 64p. (J). (gr. -1-2). pap. 9.99 ***(978-0-7364-3400-3(3)***, Golden/Disney) Random Hse. Children's Bks.
—A Fairy's Gift (Disney: the Never Girls) Thorpe, Kiki. 2015. (Disney Chapters Ser.). (ENG.). 224p. (J). (gr. 1-4). 14.99 ***(978-0-7364-3278-8(7)***, RH/Disney) Random Hse. Children's Bks.
RH Disney Staff. Far from Shore. Thorpe, Kiki. 2015. (Never Girls Ser.: No. 8). (ENG.). 128p. (J). (gr. 1-4). lib. bdg. 12.99 *(978-0-7364-8166-3(4)*, RH/Disney) Random Hse. Children's Bks.
—The Fast Lane. Berrios, Frank. 2010. (Super Coloring Book Ser.). (ENG.). 96p. (J). (gr. -1-2). pap. 3.99 *(978-0-7364-2748-7(1)*, Golden/Disney) Random Hse. Children's Bks.
—Five Classic Tales (Disney Classics) 2014. (Step into Reading Ser.). (ENG.). 160p. (J). (gr. -1-1). 7.99 *(978-0-7364-3180-4(2)*, RH/Disney) Random Hse. Children's Bks.
—Five Disney/Pixar Tales (Disney/Pixar) 2014. (Step into Reading Ser.). (ENG.). 160p. (J). (gr. -1-1). pap. 7.99 *(978-0-7364-3171-2(3)*, RH/Disney) Random Hse. Children's Bks.
—Five Toy Tales (Disney/Pixar Toy Story) 2012. (Step into Reading Ser.). (ENG.). 160p. (J). (gr. -1-1). pap. 7.99 *(978-0-7364-2845-3(3)*, RH/Disney) Random Hse. Children's Bks.
—Flying Colors. Callahan, Patricia. 2014. (Deluxe Paint Box Book Ser.). (ENG.). 128p. (J). (gr. -1-2). pap. 7.99 *(978-0-7364-3037-1(7)*, Golden/Disney) Random Hse. Children's Bks.
—Forever a Princess (Disney Princess) Carbone, Courtney. 2014. (Color Plus Chunky Crayons Ser.). (ENG.). 48p. (J). (gr. -1-2). pap. 3.99 *(978-0-7364-3194-1(2)*, Golden/Disney) Random Hse. Children's Bks.
—Friends Forever. Arps, Melissa & Lagonegro, Melissa. 2009. (Step into Reading Ser.). (ENG.). 32p. (J). (gr. k-3). pap. 3.99 *(978-0-7364-2597-1(7)*, RH/Disney) Random Hse. Children's Bks.
—Full Throttle (Disney/Pixar Cars) Berrios, Frank. 2011. (Deluxe Chunky Crayon Book Ser.). (ENG.). 128p. (J). (gr. -1-2). pap. 7.99 *(978-0-375-87172-6(1)*, Golden/Disney) Random Hse. Children's Bks.
RH Disney Staff. Fur-Ever Friends! (Disney Princess: Palace Pets) Berrios, Frank. 2015. (Giant Coloring Book Ser.). (ENG.). 40p. (J). (gr. -1-2). pap. 9.99 ***(978-0-7364-3292-4(2)***, Golden/Disney) Random Hse. Children's Bks.
RH Disney Staff, et al. The Great Ice Engine. David, Erica. 2015. (Stepping Stone Book(TM) Ser.). (ENG.). 128p. (J). (gr. 1-4). 9.99 *(978-0-7364-3431-7(3)*, RH/Disney) Random Hse. Children's Bks.
RH Disney Staff. Happy Birthday, Mike! (Disney/Pixar Monsters, Inc.) Weinberg, Jennifer Liberts. 2014. (Step into Reading Ser.). (ENG.). 32p. (J). (gr. -1-1). 3.99 *(978-0-7364-3198-9(5)*, RH/Disney) Random Hse. Children's Bks.
—Happy Easter, Princess! Carbone, Courtney. 2014. (Full-Color Activity Book with Stickers Ser.). (ENG.). 32p. (J). (gr. -1-2). pap. 4.99 *(978-0-7364-3129-3(2)*, Golden/Disney) Random Hse. Children's Bks.
—Heavy Metal Mater & Other Tall Tales. Berrios, Frank. 2010. (Pictureback Favorites Ser.). (ENG.). 80p. (J). (gr. -1-2). 7.99 *(978-0-7364-2722-7(8)*, RH/Disney) Random Hse. Children's Bks.
—Hello, Olaf! (Disney Frozen) Posner-Sanchez, Andrea. 2015. (Step into Reading Ser.). (ENG.). 24p. (J). (gr. -1-1). lib. bdg. 12.99 *(978-0-7364-8240-0(7)*, RH/Disney) Random Hse. Children's Bks.
—Heroes of the Sky/High-Flying Friends (Disney Planes: Fire & Rescue) Berrios, Frank. 2014. (Jumbo Coloring Book Ser.). (ENG.). 224p. (J). (gr. -1-2). pap. 5.99 *(978-0-7364-3231-3(0)*, Golden/Disney) Random Hse. Children's Bks.
—High Gear! (Disney/Pixar Cars) Berrios, Frank. 2012. (3-D Coloring Book Ser.). (ENG.). 32p. (J). (gr. -1-2). pap. 4.99 *(978-0-7364-2862-0(3)*, Golden/Disney) Random Hse. Children's Bks.
—High-Speed Adventures. Berrios, Frank. 2010. (Jumbo Coloring Book Ser.). (ENG.). 224p. (J). (gr. -1-2). pap. 5.99 *(978-0-7364-2712-8(0)*, Golden/Disney) Random Hse. Children's Bks.
—Holiday Hearts (Disney Princess) Carbone, Courtney. 2013. (Jumbo Coloring Book Ser.). (ENG.). 224p. (J). (gr. -1-2). pap. 5.99 *(978-0-7364-3054-8(7)*, Golden/Disney) Random Hse. Children's Bks.
—A Horse & a Hero. Alberto, Daisy. 2011. (Step into Reading Ser.). (ENG.). 32p. (J). (gr. k-3). pap. 3.99 *(978-0-7364-2746-3(5)*, RH/Disney) Random Hse. Children's Bks.
RH Disney Staff. How to Be a Princess (Disney Princess) Carbone, Courtney. 2015. (Ultimate Handbook Ser.). (ENG.). 64p. (J). (gr. 1-4). 9.99 ***(978-0-7364-3415-7(1)***, RH/Disney) Random Hse. Children's Bks.
RH Disney Staff. I Am Buzz Lightyear (Disney/Pixar Toy Story) Hashimoto, Meika & Tillworth, Mary. 2011. (Shaped Board Book Ser.). (ENG.). 12p. (J). (— 1). bds. 4.99 *(978-0-7364-2821-7(6)*, Golden/Disney) Random Hse. Children's Bks.
—The Ice Box. Carbone, Courtney. 2014. (Friendship Box Ser.). (ENG.). 48p. (J). (-k). bds. 10.99 *(978-0-7364-3128-6(4)*, RH/Disney) Random Hse. Children's Bks.
—In the Game! (Disney Infinity) Carbone, Courtney. 2014. (Super Deluxe Pictureback Ser.). (ENG.). 24p. (J). (gr. -1-2). 5.99 *(978-0-7364-3269-6(8)*, Golden/Disney) Random Hse. Children's Bks.
—In the Lead! (Disney Planes) Wrecks, Billy. 2014. (3-D Pictureback Ser.). (ENG.). 16p. (J). (gr. -1-2). 4.99 *(978-0-7364-2992-4(1)*, RH/Disney) Random Hse. Children's Bks.
RH Disney Staff. Jake & the Never Land Pirates LGB Favorites (Jake & the Never Land Pirates) Posner-Sanchez, Andrea. 2015. (Little Golden Book Favorites Ser.). (ENG.). 80p. (J). (-k). 7.99 ***(978-0-7364-3404-1(6)***, Golden/Disney) Random Hse. Children's Bks.
RH Disney Staff. Jewels for a Princess (Disney Princess) Homberg, Ruth. 2012. (Step into Reading Ser.). (ENG.). 32p. (J). (gr. -1-1). pap. 3.99 *(978-0-7364-2908-5(5)*, RH/Disney) Random Hse. Children's Bks.
RH Disney Staff. Joy's in Charge! Berrios, Frank. 2015. (Color Plus Crayons & Sticker Ser.). (ENG.). 48p. (J). (gr. -1-2). pap. 4.99 ***(978-0-7364-3464-5(X)***, Golden/Disney) Random Hse. Children's Bks.
—Just Wing It! (Disney Planes) Berrios, Frank. 2015. (Pictureback Ser.). (ENG.). 16p. (J). (gr. -1-2). 4.99 ***(978-0-7364-3410-2(0)***, RH/Disney) Random Hse. Children's Bks.
RH Disney Staff. A Knight in Sticky Armor (Disney Junior: Doc Mcstuffins) Posner-Sanchez, Andrea. 2012. (Little Golden Book Ser.). (ENG.). 24p. (J). (-k). 3.99 *(978-0-7364-3030-2(X)*, Golden/Disney) Random Hse. Children's Bks.

R

—Lady & the Tramp. Capozzi, Suzy & Finnegan, Delphine. 2012. (Step into Reading Ser.). (ENG.). 32p. (J). (gr. -1-1). pap. 3.99 *(978-0-7364-3026-5(1)*, RH/Disney) Random Hse. Children's Bks.

—Lightning Loves Racing! (Disney/Pixar Cars) Berrios, Frank. 2013. (Pictureback Series.). (ENG.). 16p. (J). (gr. -1-2). 4.99 *(978-0-7364-3138-5(1)*, RH/Disney) Random Hse. Children's Bks.

—The Little Mermaid Junior Novelization (Disney Princess) Lagonegro, Melissa. 2013. (Junior Novel Ser.). (ENG.). 128p. (J). (gr. 3-7). 4.99 *(978-0-7364-2983-2(2)*, RH/Disney) Random Hse. Children's Bks.

—The Little Mermaid Step into Reading (Disney Princess) Homberg, Ruth. 2013. (Step into Reading Ser.). (ENG.). 32p. (J). (gr. -1-1). 3.99 *(978-0-7364-8128-1(1)*, RH/Disney) Random Hse. Children's Bks.

—Mater & the Little Tractors. Eberly, Chelsea. 2012. (Step into Reading Ser.). (ENG.). 32p. (J). (gr. -1-1). pap. 3.99 *(978-0-7364-2886-6(0)*, RH/Disney) Random Hse. Children's Bks.

—Mater Takes off! (Disney/Pixar Cars) Shealy, Dennis. 2014. (Deluxe Reusable Sticker Book Ser.). (ENG.). 24p. (J). (gr. -1-2). pap. 6.99 *(978-0-7364-3055-5(5)*, Golden/Disney) Random Hse. Children's Bks.

—Mater to the Rescue! (Disney/Pixar Cars) Berrios, Frank. 2012. (Pictureback with Flaps Ser.). (ENG.). 16p. (J). (gr. -1-2). pap. 4.99 *(978-0-7364-2863-7(1)*, RH/Disney) Random Hse. Children's Bks.

—Mater's Amazin' Adventures (Disney/Pixar Cars) Berrios, Frank. 2012. (Full-Color Activity Book with Stickers Ser.). (ENG.). 32p. (J). (gr. -1-2). pap. 3.99 *(978-0-7364-2872-9(0)*, Golden/Disney) Random Hse. Children's Bks.

—Mater's Birthday Surprise (Disney/Pixar Cars) Lagonegro, Melissa. 2012. (Step into Reading Ser.). (ENG.). 32p. (J). (gr. -1-1). pap. 3.99 *(978-0-7364-2858-3(5)*, RH/Disney) Random Hse. Children's Bks.

—Meet the Princesses (Disney Princess) Posner-Sanchez, Andrea. 2013. (ENG.). 16p. (J). (-k). bds. 7.99 *(978-0-7364-3146-0(2)*, RH/Disney) Random Hse. Children's Bks.

—Merry Christmas, Woody (Disney/Pixar Toy Story) Depken, Kristen L. 2013. (Pictureback Series.). (ENG.). 16p. (J). (gr. -1-2). 3.99 *(978-0-7364-3070-8(9)*, RH/Disney) Random Hse. Children's Bks.

—Monster Games. Lagonegro, Melissa. 2013. (Step into Reading Ser.). (ENG.). 32p. (J). (gr. -1-1). 3.99 *(978-0-7364-3106-4(3)*, RH/Disney) Random Hse. Children's Bks.

—Monster Mania! Carbone, Courtney. 2014. (Color & Paint Plus Stickers Ser.). (ENG.). 128p. (J). (gr. -1-2). pap. 9.99 *(978-0-7364-3131-6(4)*, Golden/Disney) Random Hse. Children's Bks.

—Monster Truck Mater (Disney/Pixar Cars) Berrios, Frank. 2011. (3-D Pictureback Ser.). (ENG.). 16p. (J). (gr. -1-2). pap. 4.99 *(978-0-7364-2784-5(8)*, Golden/Disney) Random Hse. Children's Bks.

—Monsters Get Scared of the Dark, Too (Disney/Pixar Monsters, Inc.) Lagonegro, Melissa. 2013. (Glow-In-the-Dark Pictureback Ser.). (ENG.). 16p. (J). (gr. -1-2). 4.99 *(978-0-7364-3056-2(3)*, RH/Disney) Random Hse. Children's Bks.

—Monsters in a Box (Disney/Pixar Monsters University) Posner-Sanchez, Andrea. 2013. (Friendship Box Ser.). (ENG.). 48p. (J). (-k). bds. 10.99 *(978-0-7364-2989-4(1)*, RH/Disney) Random Hse. Children's Bks.

—Nemo's Big Adventure (Disney/Pixar Finding Nemo) 2012. (3-D Pictureback Ser.). (ENG.). 16p. (J). (gr. -1-2). pap. 4.99 *(978-0-7364-2968-9(9)*, RH/Disney) Random Hse. Children's Bks.

—The Never Girls Collection, 4 vols. 2013. (ENG.). 128p. (J). (gr. 1-4). 23.96 *(978-0-7364-3141-5(1)*, RH/Disney) Random Hse. Children's Bks.

—A New Reindeer Friend (Disney Frozen) Julius, Jessica. 2015. (Little Golden Book Ser.). (ENG.). 24p. (J). (-k). 3.99 *(978-0-7364-3351-8(1)*, Golden/Disney) Random Hse. Children's Bks.

—Off-Road Racers!/Crash Course! Auerbach, Annie & Berrios, Frank. 2010. (Deluxe Pictureback Ser.). (ENG.). 32p. (J). (gr. -1-2). pap. 4.99 *(978-0-7364-2650-3(7)*, RH/Disney) Random Hse. Children's Bks.

—Oh, Brother! Jordan, Apple. 2012. (Step into Reading Ser.). (ENG.). 32p. (J). (gr. -1-1). pap. 3.99 *(978-0-7364-2887-3(9)*, RH/Disney) Random Hse. Children's Bks.

—Once upon a Dream. Man-Kong, Mary. 2010. (Big Coloring Book Ser.). (ENG.). 48p. (J). (gr. -1-2). pap. 6.99 *(978-0-7364-2715-9(5)*, Golden/Disney) Random Hse. Children's Bks.

—Overdrive! Shealy, Dennis. 2009. (Hologramatic Sticker Book Ser.). (ENG.). 48p. (J). (gr. -1-2). pap. 3.99 *(978-0-375-84598-7(4)*, Golden Bks.) Random Hse., Inc.

RH Disney Staff. Palace Pets Ultimate Handbook (Disney Princess: Palace Pets) Posner-Sanchez, Andrea. 2015. (Ultimate Handbook Ser.). (ENG.). 64p. (J). (gr. -1-2). 9.99 ***(978-0-7364-3421-8(6)***, RH/Disney) Random Hse. Children's Bks.

RH Disney Staff. Party Central (Disney/Pixar Monsters University) Depken, Kristen L. 2014. (Pictureback(R) Ser.). (ENG.). 24p. (J). (gr. -1-2). 3.99 *(978-0-7364-3179-8(9)*, RH/Disney) Random Hse. Children's Bks.

—The Perfect Tea Party (Disney Junior: Sofia the First) Posner-Sanchez, Andrea. 2013. (Little Golden Book Ser.). (ENG.). 24p. (J). (-k). 3.99 *(978-0-7364-3109-5(8)*, Golden/Disney) Random Hse. Children's Bks.

RH Disney Staff. Petite's Winter Wonderland. Sky Koster, Amy. 2015. (Glitter Picturebook Ser.). (ENG.). 16p. (J). (gr. -1-2). 5.99 ***(978-0-7364-3355-6(4)***, RH/Disney) Random Hse. Children's Bks.

RH Disney Staff, et al. Picture Perfect. RH Disney Staff & Knowles, Heather. 2010. (Deluxe Paint Box Book Ser.). (ENG.). 128p. (J). (gr. -1-2). pap. 7.99 *(978-0-7364-2737-1(6)*, Golden/Disney) Random Hse. Children's Bks.

RH Disney Staff. The Pirate Games. Posner-Sanchez, Andrea. 2012. (Little Golden Book Ser.). (ENG.). 24p. (J). (-k). 3.99 *(978-0-7364-3028-9(8)*, Golden/Disney) Random Hse. Children's Bks.

—Planes: Fire & Rescue the Junior Novelization (Disney Planes: Fire & Rescue) Francis, Suzanne. 2014. (Junior Novel Ser.). (ENG.). 128p. (J). (gr. 3-7). 5.99 *(978-0-7364-3230-6(2)*, Golden/Disney) Random Hse. Children's Bks.

RH Disney Staff. Playful Pets! (Disney Princess: Palace Pets) Berrios, Frank. 2015. (Color Plus 1,000 Stickers Ser.). (ENG.). 64p. (J). (gr. -1-2). pap. 9.99 ***(978-0-7364-3413-3(5)***, Golden/Disney) Random Hse. Children's Bks.

RH Disney Staff. Power Play! (Disney Infinity) Berrios, Frank. 2014. (Deluxe Reusable Sticker Book Ser.). (ENG.). 24p. (J). (gr. -1-2). pap. 9.99 *(978-0-7364-3268-9(X)*, Golden/Disney) Random Hse. Children's Bks.

RH Disney Staff. Pretty As a Picture! (Disney Princess) Berrios, Frank. 2015. (Color Plus Wall Decals Ser.). (ENG.). 48p. (J). (gr. -1-2). pap. 6.99 ***(978-0-7364-3411-9(9)***, Golden/Disney) Random Hse. Children's Bks.

RH Disney Staff, et al. A Princess Can! (Disney Princess) Jordan, Apple. 2015. (Step into Reading Ser.). (ENG.). 24p. (J). (gr. -1-1). 4.99 *(978-0-7364-3341-9(4)*, RH/Disney) Random Hse. Children's Bks.

RH Disney Staff, et al. Pumpkin: Cinderella's Dancing Pup (Disney Princess: Palace Pets) Redbank, Tennant. 2015. (Disney Chapters Ser.). (ENG.). 64p. (J). (gr. 1-4). 5.99 ***(978-0-7364-3423-2(2)***, RH/Disney) Random Hse. Children's Bks.

RH Disney Staff. Puppy Problems! Lagonegro, Melissa. 2014. (Deluxe Pictureback Ser.). (ENG.). 32p. (J). (gr. -1-2). 4.99 *(978-0-7364-3127-9(6)*, RH/Disney) Random Hse. Children's Bks.

—Racing for Good (Disney/Pixar Cars) Homberg, Ruth. 2014. (Step into Reading Ser.). (ENG.). 32p. (J). (gr. -1-1). 3.99 *(978-0-7364-3217-7(5)*, RH/Disney) Random Hse. Children's Bks.

—Radiator Springs 500. Berrios, Frank. deluxe ed. 2015. (Deluxe Pictureback Ser.). (ENG.). 24p. (J). (gr. -1-2). 4.99 *(978-0-7364-3281-8(7)*, RH/Disney) Random Hse. Children's Bks.

—Ready for Action! (Disney/Pixar Cars) Berrios, Frank. 2012. (Color Plus Card Stock Ser.). (ENG.). 48p. (J). (gr. -1-2). pap. 3.99 *(978-0-7364-2949-8(2)*, Golden/Disney) Random Hse. Children's Bks.

—Rescue Buddies! (Disney Planes: Fire & Rescue) Carbone, Courtney. 2015. (Friendship Box Ser.). (ENG.). 48p. (J). (-k). bds. 10.99 *(978-0-7364-3333-4(3)*, RH/Disney) Random Hse. Children's Bks.

RH Disney Staff, et al. A Royal Easter (Disney Princess) Posner-Sanchez, Andrea. 2014. (Pictureback Series.). (ENG.). 16p. (J). (gr. -1-2). 4.99 *(978-0-7364-3084-5(9)*, RH/Disney) Random Hse. Children's Bks.

RH Disney Staff. A Royal Pet Problem. Posner-Sanchez, Andrea. 2015. (Little Golden Book Ser.). (ENG.). 24p. (J). (-k). 3.99 *(978-0-7364-3308-2(2)*, Golden/Disney) Random Hse. Children's Bks.

—Royal Runway! (Disney Princess) Carbone, Courtney. 2014. (Deluxe Reusable Sticker Book Ser.). (ENG.). 24p. (J). (gr. -1-2). pap. 9.99 *(978-0-7364-3195-8(0)*, Golden/Disney) Random Hse. Children's Bks.

—School Daze/Monster Party! (Disney/Pixar Monsters, Inc.; Disney/Pixar Monsters University) Carbone, Courtney. 2013. (Jumbo Coloring Book Ser.). (ENG.). 224p. (J). (gr. -1-2). pap. 5.99 *(978-0-7364-3058-6(X)*, Golden/Disney) Random Hse. Children's Bks.

—Secret Agent Mater. Lagonegro, Melissa. 2011. (Step into Reading Ser.). (ENG.). 32p. (J). (gr. k-3). pap. 3.99 *(978-0-7364-8095-6(1)*, RH/Disney) Random Hse. Children's Bks.

—Shadow Play! Posner-Sanchez, Andrea. 2014. (Little Golden Book Ser.). (ENG.). 24p. (J). (-k). 3.99 *(978-0-7364-3086-9(5)*, Golden/Disney) Random Hse. Children's Bks.

—Shake Your Tail Feathers (Disney Junior: Doc Mcstuffins) Posner-Sanchez, Andrea. 2015. (Little Golden Book Ser.). (ENG.). 24p. (J). (-k). 3.99 *(978-0-7364-3274-0(4)*, Golden/Disney) Random Hse. Children's Bks.

RH Disney Staff, et al. Sharing & Caring. Lagonegro, Melissa et al. 2014. (Pictureback(R) Ser.). (ENG.). 16p. (J). (gr. -1-2). 4.99 *(978-0-7364-3334-1(1)*, RH/Disney) Random Hse. Children's Bks.

RH Disney Staff. Shop with Minnie. Posner-Sanchez, Andrea. 2012. (Little Golden Book Ser.). (ENG.). 24p. (J). (gr. k-k). 3.99 *(978-0-7364-3031-9(8)*, Golden/Disney) Random Hse. Children's Bks.

—Sisters Forever (Disney Frozen) Berrios, Frank. 2014. (Color & Paint Plus Stickers Ser.). (ENG.). 128p. (J). (gr. -1-2). pap. 9.99 *(978-0-7364-3297-9(3)*, Golden/Disney) Random Hse. Children's Bks.

—Sleeping Beauty Step into Reading (Disney Princess) Man-Kong, Mary. 2014. (Step into Reading Ser.). (ENG.). 32p. (J). (gr. -1-1). 3.99 *(978-0-7364-3226-9(4)*, RH/Disney) Random Hse. Children's Bks.

—Snow Princesses (Disney Princess) Trimble, Irene. 2012. (Glitter Board Book Ser.). (ENG.). 12p. (J). (gr. -1-2). bds. 6.99 *(978-0-7364-3004-3(0)*, RH/Disney) Random Hse. Children's Bks.

—Snuggle Buddies. Carbone, Courtney. 2014. (Step into Reading Ser.). (ENG.). 32p. (J). (gr. -1-1). 3.99 *(978-0-7364-3155-2(1)*, Golden/Disney); lib. bdg. 12.99 *(978-0-7364-8158-8(3)*, RH/Disney) Random Hse. Children's Bks.

—Sofia the Second (Disney Junior: Sofia the First) Posner-Sanchez, Andrea. 2014. (Little Golden Book Ser.). (ENG.). 24p. (J). (-k). 3.99 *(978-0-7364-3238-2(8)*, Golden/Disney) Random Hse. Children's Bks.

—A Spooky Adventure (Disney/Pixar Toy Story) Jordan, Apple. 2011. (Step into Reading Ser.). (ENG.). 32p. (J). (gr. k-3). pap. 3.99 *(978-0-7364-2777-7(5)*, RH/Disney) Random Hse. Children's Bks.

RH Disney Staff. The Sword in the Stone (Disney) Merriling, Carl. 2015. (Little Golden Book Ser.). (ENG.). 24p. (J). (-k). 4.99 ***(978-0-7364-3374-7(0)***, Golden/Disney) Random Hse. Children's Bks.

RH Disney Staff. Take to the Sky! Berrios, Frank. 2014. (Big Coloring Book Ser.). (ENG.). 48p. (J). (gr. -1-2). pap. 6.99 *(978-0-7364-3095-1(4)*, Golden/Disney) Random Hse. Children's Bks.

—This Little Piggy (Disney Junior: Minnie's Bow-Toons) Weinberg, Jennifer Liberts. 2014. (Little Golden Book Ser.). (ENG.). 24p. (J). (-k). 3.99 *(978-0-7364-3234-4(5)*, Golden/Disney) Random Hse. Children's Bks.

—Thrills & Chills! Carbone, Courtney & Hands, Cynthia. 2013. (Deluxe Paint Box Book Ser.). (ENG.). 128p. (J). (gr. -1-2). pap. 7.99 *(978-0-7364-3063-0(6)*, Golden/Disney) Random Hse. Children's Bks.

—Time Travel Mater (Disney/Pixar Cars) Berrios, Frank. 2013. (Pictureback Ser.). (ENG.). 16p. (J). (gr. -1-2). 3.99 *(978-0-7364-3107-1(1)*, RH/Disney) Random Hse. Children's Bks.

—Tow Truck Trouble-Lights Out! Berrios, Frank. 2010. (Deluxe Pictureback Ser.). (ENG.). 32p. (J). (gr. -1-2). pap. 4.99 *(978-0-7364-2713-5(9)*, RH/Disney) Random Hse. Children's Bks.

—Toy Box Heroes! Webster, Christy. 2014. (Step into Reading Ser.). (ENG.). 32p. (J). (gr. -1-1). 4.99 *(978-0-7364-3270-2(1)*, RH/Disney) Random Hse. Children's Bks.

RH Disney Staff, et al. Toy to Toy. RH Disney Staff & Redbank, Tennant. 2010. (Step into Reading Ser.). (ENG.). 32p. (J). (gr. k-3). pap. 3.99 *(978-0-7364-2665-7(5)*, RH/Disney) Random Hse. Children's Bks.

RH Disney Staff. Toys That Go Bump in the Night (Disney/Pixar Toy Story) Depken, Kristen L. 2014. (Pictureback Ser.). (ENG.). 24p. (J). (gr. -1-2). 3.99 *(978-0-7364-2980-1(8)*, RH/Disney) Random Hse. Children's Bks.

—Tractor Trouble (Disney/Pixar Cars) Berrios, Frank. 2011. (Little Golden Book Ser.). (ENG.). 24p. (J). (gr. -1-2). 3.99 *(978-0-7364-2831-6(3)*, Golden/Disney) Random Hse. Children's Bks.

RH Disney Staff, et al. Travel Like a Princess (Disney Princess) Lagonegro, Melissa. 2014. (Step into Reading Ser.). (ENG.). 24p. (J). (gr. -1-1). 3.99 *(978-0-7364-3089-0(X)*, RH/Disney) Random Hse. Children's Bks.

—Treasure: Ariel's Curious Kitten (Disney Princess: Palace Pets) Redbank, Tennant. 2015. (Stepping Stone Book(TM) Ser.). (ENG.). 64p. (J). (gr. 1-4). 5.99 *(978-0-7364-3346-4(5)*, RH/Disney) Random Hse. Children's Bks.

RH Disney Staff. Troll Magic. Carbone, Courtney & Hands, Cynthia. 2013. (Color Plus Chunky Crayons Ser.). (ENG.). 48p. (J). (gr. -1-2). pap. 3.99 *(978-0-7364-3062-3(8)*, Golden/Disney) Random Hse. Children's Bks.

—Undersea Friends (Disney Princess) Posner-Sanchez, Andrea. 2013. (Friendship Box Ser.). (ENG.). 48p. (J). (-k). bds. 10.99 *(978-0-7364-3123-1(3)*, RH/Disney) Random Hse. Children's Bks.

—A Very Mater Christmas (Disney/Pixar Cars) Berrios, Frank. 2011. (Glitter Board Book Ser.). (ENG.). 12p. (J). (— 1). bds. 6.99 *(978-0-7364-2793-7(7)*, RH/Disney) Random Hse. Children's Bks.

—Vote for Mater! (Disney/Pixar Cars) Berrios, Frank. 2012. (Color Plus Chunky Crayons Ser.). (ENG.). 48p. (J). (gr. -1-2). pap. 3.99 *(978-0-7364-2963-4(8)*, Golden/Disney) Random Hse. Children's Bks.

RH Disney Staff, et al. A Warm Welcome, No. 3. David, Erica. 2015. (Stepping Stone Book(TM) Ser.). (ENG.). 128p. (J). (gr. 1-4). lib. bdg. 12.99 *(978-0-7364-8247-9(4)*, RH/Disney) Random Hse. Children's Bks.

RH Disney Staff. Welcome to Radiator Springs. Berrios, Frank. 2010. (Paint Box Book Ser.). (ENG.). 48p. (J). (gr. -1-2). pap. 3.99 *(978-0-7364-2749-4(X)*, Golden/Disney) Random Hse. Children's Bks.

—Where's Woody? (Disney/Pixar Toy Story) Depken, Kristen L. 2012. (Pictureback with Flaps Ser.). (ENG.). 16p. (J). (gr. -1-2). pap. 4.99 *(978-0-7364-2850-7(X)*, RH/Disney) Random Hse. Children's Bks.

—Wild West Showdown! Depken, Kristen L. 2011. (Pictureback Ser.). (ENG.). 24p. (J). (gr. -1-2). pap. 3.99 *(978-0-7364-2741-8(4)*, RH/Disney) Random Hse. Children's Bks.

—Wish upon a Star (Disney Princess) Posner-Sanchez, Andrea. 2013. (Glow-In-the-Dark Pictureback Ser.). (ENG.). 16p. (J). (gr. -1-2). pap. 4.99 *(978-0-7364-3046-3(6)*, RH/Disney) Random Hse. Children's Bks.

—101 Dalmatians (Disney 101 Dalmatians) Bobowicz, Pamela. 2015. (Step into Reading Ser.). (ENG.). 32p. (J). (gr. -1-1). 3.99 *(978-0-7364-3182-8(9)*, RH/Disney) Random Hse. Children's Bks.

RH Disney Staff. Action Figures. RH Disney Staff. 2010. (Jumbo Coloring Book Ser.). (ENG.). 224p. (J). (gr. -1-2). pap. 5.99 *(978-0-7364-2729-6(5)*, Golden/Disney) Random Hse. Children's Bks.

—Adventures in Andy's Room. RH Disney Staff. 2010. (Deluxe Coloring Book Ser.). (ENG.). 96p. (J). (gr. -1-2). pap. 3.99 *(978-0-7364-2642-8(6)*, Golden/Disney) Random Hse. Children's Bks.

—Air Power! RH Disney Staff. 2014. (Color Plus 1,000 Stickers Ser.). (ENG.). 64p. (J). (gr. -1-2). pap. 9.99 *(978-0-7364-3133-0(0)*, Golden/Disney) Random Hse. Children's Bks.

—Alice in Wonderland. RH Disney Staff. 2010. (Little Golden Book Ser.). (ENG.). 24p. (J). (gr. -1-2). 3.99 *(978-0-7364-2670-1(1)*, Golden/Disney) Random Hse. Children's Bks.

—Amazing Ariel! (Disney Princess) RH Disney Staff. 2013. (3-D Pictureback Ser.). (ENG.). 16p. (J). (gr. -1-2). 4.99 *(978-0-7364-2994-8(8)*, RH/Disney) Random Hse. Children's Bks.

RH Disney Staff. Anna Is Our Babysitter (Disney Frozen) RH Disney Staff. 2015. (Big Golden Book Ser.). (ENG.). 32p. (J). (gr. -1-2). 9.99 ***(978-0-7364-3405-8(4)***, Golden/Disney) Random Hse. Children's Bks.

—Anna's Birthday Surprise. RH Disney Staff. Julius, Jessica. 2015. (Pictureback(R) Ser.). (ENG.). 24p. (J). (gr. -1-2). 4.99 ***(978-0-7364-3439-3(9)***, RH/Disney) Random Hse. Children's Bks.

RH Disney Staff. Anna's Icy Adventure. RH Disney Staff. 2013. (Golden First Chapters Ser.). (ENG.). 80p. (J). (gr. 1-4). 4.99 *(978-0-7364-8132-8(X))*; lib. bdg. 12.99 *(978-0-7364-3115-6(2))* Random Hse. Children's Bks. (Golden/Disney).

—Arcade Brigade. RH Disney Staff. Hands, Cynthia. 2012. (Deluxe Coloring Book Ser.). (ENG.). 96p. (J). (gr. -1-2). pap. 3.99 *(978-0-7364-2955-9(7)*, Golden/Disney) Random Hse. Children's Bks.

—Ariel's Royal Wedding/Aurora's Royal Wedding (Disney Princess) RH Disney Staff. 2014. (Deluxe Pictureback Ser.). (ENG.). 32p. (J). (gr. -1-2). 4.99 *(978-0-7364-3167-5(5)*, RH/Disney) Random Hse. Children's Bks.

—Ariel's Undersea Adventures (Disney Princess) RH Disney Staff. 2013. (Deluxe Coloring Book Ser.). (ENG.). 96p. (J). (gr. -1-2). pap. 3.99 *(978-0-7364-2986-3(7)*, Golden/Disney) Random Hse. Children's Bks.

—Be My Princess. RH Disney Staff. 2011. (Full-Color Activity Book with Stickers Ser.). (ENG.). 32p. (J). (gr. -1-2). pap. 3.99 *(978-0-7364-2861-3(5)*, Golden/Disney) Random Hse. Children's Bks.

—Best Dad in the Sea. RH Disney Staff. Tyler, Amy J. 2003. (Step into Reading Ser.). (ENG.). 32p. (J). (gr. k-3). pap. 3.99 *(978-0-7364-2131-7(9)*, RH/Disney) Random Hse. Children's Bks.

—The Big Battle. RH Disney Staff. 2014. (Step into Reading Ser.). (ENG.). 32p. (J). (gr. k-3). 4.99 *(978-0-7364-3245-0(0)*, RH/Disney) Random Hse. Children's Bks.

—Big Bear, Little Bear. RH Disney Staff. 2012. (Step into Reading Ser.). (ENG.). 32p. (J). (gr. -1-1). pap. 3.99 *(978-0-7364-2915-3(8)*, RH/Disney) Random Hse. Children's Bks.

—Big Hero 6. RH Disney Staff. 2014. (Little Golden Book Ser.). (ENG.). 24p. (J). (-k). 3.99 *(978-0-7364-3168-2(3)*, Golden/Disney) Random Hse. Children's Bks.

—Big Hero 6 Big Golden Book (Disney Big Hero 6) RH Disney Staff. 2014. (Big Golden Book Ser.). (ENG.). 48p. (J). (gr. k-4). 9.99 *(978-0-7364-3186-6(1)*, Golden Bks.) Random Hse. Children's Bks.

—Big Hero 6 Chapter Book (Disney Big Hero 6) RH Disney Staff. 2014. (Stepping Stone Book(TM) Ser.). (ENG.). 80p. (J). (gr. 1-4). lib. bdg. 12.99 *(978-0-7364-8154-0(0)*, RH/Disney) Random Hse. Children's Bks.

—Big Hero 6 Junior Novelization (Disney Big Hero 6) RH Disney Staff. Trimble, Irene. 2014. (Junior Novel Ser.). (ENG.). 128p. (J). (gr. 4-7). 5.99 *(978-0-7364-3188-0(8)*, RH/Disney) Random Hse. Children's Bks.

—Big Monster, Little Monster. RH Disney Staff. Tillworth, Mary. 2014. (Step into Reading Ser.). (ENG.). 24p. (J). (gr. -1-1). 3.99 *(978-0-7364-3094-4(6)*, RH/Disney) Random Hse. Children's Bks.

—Big Monsters on Campus. RH Disney Staff. 2013. (Giant Coloring Book Ser.). (ENG.). 40p. (J). (gr. -1-2). pap. 9.99 *(978-0-7364-3033-3(4)*, Golden/Disney) Random Hse. Children's Bks.

—The Big Race. RH Disney Staff. 2011. (Big Coloring Book Ser.). (ENG.). 48p. (J). (gr. -1-2). pap. 6.99 *(978-0-7364-2806-4(2)*, Golden/Disney) Random Hse. Children's Bks.

—Big Snowman, Little Snowman. RH Disney Staff. Rabe, Tish. 2013. (Step into Reading Ser.). (ENG.). 32p. (J). (gr. -1-1). 3.99 *(978-0-7364-3119-4(5)*, RH/Disney) Random Hse. Children's Bks.

—Brave - A Mother's Love. RH Disney Staff. 2012. (Step into Reading Ser.). (ENG.). 32p. (J). (gr. -1-1). pap. 3.99 *(978-0-7364-2916-0(6)*, RH/Disney) Random Hse. Children's Bks.

—Brave - A Twist of Fate. RH Disney Staff. 2012. (Reusable Sticker Book Ser.). (ENG.). 12p. (J). (gr. -1-2). pap. 6.99 *(978-0-7364-2913-9(1)*, Golden/Disney) Random Hse. Children's Bks.

—Brave Big Golden Book (Disney/Pixar Brave) RH Disney Staff. 2012. (Big Golden Book Ser.). (ENG.). 64p. (J). (gr. -1-2). 9.99 *(978-0-7364-2918-4(2)*, Golden/Disney) Random Hse. Children's Bks.

—Brave Chunky Crayon Book (Disney/Pixar Brave) RH Disney Staff. 2012. (Color Plus Chunky Crayons Ser.). (ENG.). 48p. (J). (gr. -1-2). pap. 3.99 *(978-0-7364-2902-3(6)*, Golden/Disney) Random Hse. Children's Bks.

—Brave Junior Novelization (Disney/Pixar Brave) RH Disney Staff. Trimble, Irene. 2012. (Junior Novel Ser.). (ENG.). 128p. (J). (gr. 3-7). 4.99 *(978-0-7364-2912-2(3)*, RH/Disney) Random Hse. Children's Bks.

—Brave Little Golden Book (Disney/Pixar Brave) RH Disney Staff. 2012. (Little Golden Book Ser.). (ENG.). 24p. (J). (gr. k-k). 3.99 *(978-0-7364-2901-6(8)*, Golden/Disney) Random Hse. Children's Bks.

—Buzz Off! - Showtime! RH Disney Staff. 2011. (Deluxe Pictureback Ser.). (ENG.). 32p. (J). (gr. -1-2). pap. 4.99 *(978-0-7364-2841-5(0)*, RH/Disney) Random Hse. Children's Bks.

—Buzz's Space Adventure/Sunnyside Boot Camp (Disney/Pixar Toy Story) RH Disney Staff. 2012. (Deluxe Pictureback Ser.). (ENG.). 32p. (J). (gr. -1-2). pap. 4.99 *(978-0-7364-2899-6(2)*, RH/Disney) Random Hse. Children's Bks.

—Cars 2 Little Golden Book (Disney/Pixar Cars 2) RH Disney Staff. 2011. (Little Golden Book Ser.). (ENG.). 24p. (J). (gr. -1-2). 3.99 *(978-0-7364-2781-4(3)*, Golden/Disney) Random Hse. Children's Bks.

—Christmas on Wheels! (Disney/Pixar Cars) RH Disney Staff. 2011. (Color Plus Chunky Crayons Ser.). (ENG.). 48p. (J). (gr. -1-2). pap. 3.99 *(978-0-7364-2868-2(2)*, Golden/Disney) Random Hse. Children's Bks.

—Cinderella's Dream Wedding/Tiana's Royal Wedding (Disney Princess) RH Disney Staff. 2012. (Deluxe Pictureback Ser.). (ENG.). 32p. (J). (gr. -1-2). pap. 4.99 *(978-0-7364-2910-8(7)*, RH/Disney) Random Hse. Children's Bks.

—Cute & Cuddly (Disney Princess) RH Disney Staff. 2012. (Deluxe Stickerific Ser.). (ENG.). 64p. (J). (gr. -1-2). pap. 5.99 *(978-0-7364-2869-9(0)*, Golden/Disney) Random Hse. Children's Bks.

—Cute Curls & Lovely Locks (Disney Princess) RH Disney Staff. 2015. (Color Plus Hair Extension Ser.). (ENG.). 48p. (J). (gr. -1-2). pap. 5.99 *(978-0-7364-3344-0(9)*, Golden/Disney) Random Hse. Children's Bks.

—Dancing Cinderella/Belle of the Ball. RH Disney Staff. 2009. (Deluxe Pictureback Ser.). (ENG.). 32p. (J). (gr. -1-2). pap. 4.99 *(978-0-7364-2560-5(8)*, RH/Disney) Random Hse. Children's Bks.

—A Day at the Races/Night Vision. RH Disney Staff. 2009. (Deluxe Pictureback Ser.). (ENG.). 32p. (J). (gr. -1-2). pap. 4.99 *(978-0-7364-2561-2(6)*, RH/Disney) Random Hse. Children's Bks.

—Dino Fun (Disney/Pixar Toy Story) RH Disney Staff. 2011. (Paint Box Book Ser.). (ENG.). 48p. (J). (gr. -1-2). pap. 3.99 *(978-0-7364-2839-2(9)*, Golden/Disney) Random Hse. Children's Bks.

—Disney Frozen: Special Edition Junior Novelization (Disney Frozen) RH Disney Staff. 2014. (Junior Novel Ser.). (ENG.). 128p. (J). (gr. 3-7). 12.99 *(978-0-7364-3296-2(5)*, RH/Disney) Random Hse. Children's Bks.

—Disney Infinity Game Atlas (Disney Infinity) RH Disney Staff. 2014. (Deluxe Reusable Sticker Book Ser.). (ENG.). 24p. (J). (gr. -1-2). pap. 6.99 *(978-0-7364-3330-3(9)*, Golden/Disney) Random Hse. Children's Bks.

—Disney Planes. RH Disney Staff. 2013. (Big Golden Book Ser.). (ENG.). 64p. (J). (gr. -1-2). 9.99 *(978-0-7364-3019-7(9)*, Golden/Disney) Random Hse. Children's Bks.

—Disney Planes the Junior Novelization. RH Disney Staff. novel ed. 2013. (Junior Novel Ser.). (ENG.). 128p. (J). (gr. 3-7). 4.99 *(978-0-7364-3047-0(4)*, RH/Disney) Random Hse. Children's Bks.

—Disney/Pixar Story Collection. RH Disney Staff. 2008. (Step into Reading Ser.). (ENG.). 160p. (J). (gr. k-3). pap. 7.99 *(978-0-7364-2554-4(3)*, RH/Disney) Random Hse. Children's Bks.

RH Disney Staff. Dress-Up in Arendelle. RH Disney Staff. 2015. (Deluxe Reusable Sticker Book Ser.). (ENG.). 24p. (J). (-k). pap. 9.99 ***(978-0-7364-3417-1(8)***, Golden/Disney) Random Hse. Children's Bks.

RH Disney Staff. Dusty to the Rescue (Disney Planes: Fire & Rescue) RH Disney Staff. 2014. (Pictureback Series.). (ENG.). 24p. (J). (gr. -1-2). 4.99 *(978-0-7364-3255-9(8)*, RH/Disney) Random Hse. Children's Bks.

—Fast! RH Disney Staff. 2013. (Disney Chapters Ser.). (ENG.). 80p. (J). (gr. 1-4). 4.99 *(978-0-7364-3017-3(2)*, RH/Disney) Random Hse. Children's Bks.

—Fast Kart, Slow Kart. RH Disney Staff. Jordan, Apple. 2013. (Step into Reading Ser.). (ENG.). 24p. (J). (gr. -1-1). pap. 3.99 *(978-0-7364-2978-8(6))*; lib. bdg. 12.99 *(978-0-7364-8125-0(7))* Random Hse. Children's Bks. (RH/Disney).

—Fearsome Friends. RH Disney Staff. 2014. (Big Coloring Book Ser.). (ENG.). 48p. (J). (gr. -1-2). pap. 6.99 *(978-0-7364-3151-4(9)*, Golden/Disney) Random Hse. Children's Bks.

—Fight to the Finish! RH Disney Staff. 2014. (Step into Reading Ser.). (ENG.). 48p. (J). (gr. k-3). 3.99 *(978-0-7364-3189-7(6)*, RH/Disney) Random Hse. Children's Bks.

—Finding Nemo Big Golden Book (Disney/Pixar Finding Nemo) RH Disney Staff. 2012. (Big Golden Book Ser.). (ENG.). 64p. (J). (gr. -1-2). 9.99 *(978-0-7364-2922-1(0)*, Golden/Disney) Random Hse. Children's Bks.

—Fire Crew! (Disney Planes: Fire & Rescue) RH Disney Staff. Berrios, Frank. 2015. (Step into Reading Ser.). (ENG.). 24p. (J). (gr. -1-1). lib. bdg. 12.99 *(978-0-7364-8224-0(5)*, RH/Disney) Random Hse. Children's Bks.

—Five Tales from the Road (Disney/Pixar Cars) RH Disney Staff. 2013. (Step into Reading Ser.). (ENG.). 160p. (J). (gr. -1-1). pap. 7.99 *(978-0-7364-3108-8(X)*, RH/Disney) Random Hse. Children's Bks.

—Flight to the Finish. RH Disney Staff. O'Hara, Ellen. 2013. (Giant Coloring Book Ser.). (ENG.). 40p. (J). (gr. -1-2). pap. 9.99 *(978-0-7364-3020-3(2)*, Golden/Disney) Random Hse. Children's Bks.

—A Friend for Merida. RH Disney Staff. 2012. (Pictureback(R) Ser.). (ENG.). 24p. (J). (gr. -1-2). pap. 3.99 *(978-0-7364-2904-7(2)*, RH/Disney) Random Hse. Children's Bks.

—Friends to the Finish. RH Disney Staff. 2011. (Deluxe Coloring Book Ser.). (ENG.). 96p. (J). (gr. -1-2). pap. 3.99 *(978-0-7364-2805-7(4)*, Golden/Disney) Random Hse. Children's Bks.

—Frozen - Big Snowman, Little Snowman. RH Disney Staff. Rabe, Tish. 2013. (Step into Reading Ser.). (ENG.). 32p. (J). (gr. -1-1). lib. bdg. 12.99 *(978-0-7364-8130-4(3)*, RH/Disney) Random Hse. Children's Bks.

—Frozen Big Golden Book (Disney Frozen) RH Disney Staff. 2013. (Big Golden Book Ser.). (ENG.). 64p. (J). (gr. -1-2). 9.99 *(978-0-7364-3065-4(2)*, Golden/Disney) Random Hse. Children's Bks.

RH Disney Staff. Frozen Fever. RH Disney Staff. Saxon, Victoria. deluxe ed. 2015. (Junior Novel Ser.). (ENG.). 96p. (J). (gr. 3-7). 9.99 ***(978-0-7364-3440-9(2)***, RH/Disney) Random Hse. Children's Bks.

RH Disney Staff. Frozen Junior Novelization (Disney Frozen) RH Disney Staff. 2013. (Junior Novel Ser.). (ENG.). 128p. (J). (gr. 3-7). 4.99 *(978-0-7364-3118-7(7)*, RH/Disney) Random Hse. Children's Bks.

RH Disney Staff. Frozen Story Collection (Disney Frozen) RH Disney Staff. 2015. (Step into Reading Ser.). (ENG.). 160p. (J). (gr. -1-2). pap. 7.99 ***(978-0-7364-3435-5(6)***, RH/Disney) Random Hse. Children's Bks.

RH Disney Staff. A Girl & a Dragon. RH Disney Staff. 2013. (Hologramatic Sticker Book Ser.). (ENG.). 48p. (J). (gr. -1-2). pap. 3.99 *(978-0-7364-3113-2(6)*, Golden/Disney) Random Hse. Children's Bks.

—Give Us a Roar! RH Disney Staff. 2013. (Super Color with Stickers Ser.). (ENG.). 96p. (J). (gr. -1-2). pap. 3.99 *(978-0-7364-3040-1(7)*, Golden/Disney) Random Hse. Children's Bks.

—Go, Team! RH Disney Staff. 2013. (Deluxe Paint Box Book Ser.). (ENG.). 128p. (J). (gr. -1-2). pap. 7.99 *(978-0-7364-3039-5(3)*, Golden/Disney) Random Hse. Children's Bks.

—Good Night, Lightning (Disney/Pixar Cars) RH Disney Staff. 2013. (Glow-In-the-Dark Board Book Ser.). (ENG.). 12p. (J). (gr. -1-2). bds. 6.99 *(978-0-7364-2976-4(X)*, RH/Disney) Random Hse. Children's Bks.

—Gorgeous Gems & Royal Crowns Kit (Disney Princess) RH Disney Staff. 2012. (Fun Kit Ser.). (ENG.). 64p. (J). (gr. -1-2). 9.99 *(978-0-7364-2726-5(0)*, Golden/Disney) Random Hse. Children's Bks.

—The Great Toy Escape. RH Disney Staff. Richards, Kitty. 2010. (Step into Reading Ser.). (ENG.). 32p. (J). (gr. k-3). pap. 3.99 *(978-0-7364-2662-6(0)*, RH/Disney) Random Hse. Children's Bks.

—High Score! RH Disney Staff. Hands, Cynthia. 2012. (Color Plus Chunky Crayons Ser.). (ENG.). 48p. (J). (gr. -1-2). pap. 3.99 *(978-0-7364-2956-6(5)*, Golden/Disney) Random Hse. Children's Bks.

—Hiro to the Rescue! RH Disney Staff. 2014. (Stepping Stone Book(TM) Ser.). (ENG.). 80p. (J). (gr. 1-4). 4.99 *(978-0-7364-3243-6(4)*, RH/Disney) Random Hse. Children's Bks.

—Hotshots! (Disney Planes: Fire & Rescue) RH Disney Staff. 2015. (Big Coloring Book Ser.). (ENG.). 48p. (J). (gr. -1-2). pap. 6.99 *(978-0-7364-3192-7(6)*, Golden/Disney) Random Hse. Children's Bks.

—Inside My Mind: A Book about Me! RH Disney Staff. 2015. (Disney Chapters Ser.). (ENG.). 128p. (J). (gr. 1-4). 6.99 *(978-0-7364-3286-3(8)*, RH/Disney) Random Hse. Children's Bks.

—Inside Out Big Golden Book (Disney/Pixar Inside Out) RH Disney Staff. 2015. (Big Golden Book Ser.). (ENG.). 64p. (J). (gr. -1-2). 9.99 *(978-0-7364-3313-6(9)*, RH/Disney) Random Hse. Children's Bks.

—Inside Out Full-Color C&a Plus Cardstock (Disney/Pixar Inside Out) RH Disney Staff. 2015. (Full Color Activity Book with Cardstock Ser.). (ENG.). 32p. (J). (gr. -1-2). pap. 4.99 *(978-0-7364-3288-7(4)*, Golden/Disney) Random Hse. Children's Bks.

—Inside Out Junior Novelization (Disney/Pixar Inside Out) RH Disney Staff. 2015. (Junior Novel Ser.). (ENG.). 128p. (J). (gr. 4-7). 5.99 *(978-0-7364-3312-9(0)*, Random Hse. Bks. for Young Readers) Random Hse. Children's Bks.

—Jasmine & Aladdin. RH Disney Staff. 2015. (Color Plus Chunky Crayons Ser.). (ENG.). 48p. (J). (gr. -1-2). pap. 4.99 *(978-0-7364-3049-4(0)*, Golden/Disney) Random Hse. Children's Bks.

—Jasmine & the Star of Persia (Disney Princess) RH Disney Staff. 2015. (Pictureback(R) Ser.). (ENG.). 16p. (J). (gr. -1-2). pap. 4.99 *(978-0-7364-3048-7(2)*, RH/Disney) Random Hse. Children's Bks.

—Jet Set! RH Disney Staff. Carbone, Courtney. 2014. (Friendship Box Ser.). (ENG.). 48p. (J). (-k). 10.99 *(978-0-7364-2990-0(5)*, RH/Disney) Random Hse. Children's Bks.

—Journey into the Mind. RH Disney Staff. 2015. (Step into Reading Ser.). (ENG.). 32p. (J). (gr. -1-1). 4.99 *(978-0-7364-3316-7(3)*, RH/Disney) Random Hse. Children's Bks.

—Jumbo Movie Mix! (Disney/Pixar) RH Disney Staff. 2014. (Jumbo Coloring Book Ser.). (ENG.). 224p. (J). (gr. -1-2). pap. 5.99 *(978-0-7364-3137-8(3)*, Golden/Disney) Random Hse. Children's Bks.

—Kind & Caring (Disney Princess) RH Disney Staff. 2012. (Coloring Book Ser.). (ENG.). 64p. (J). (gr. -1-2). pap. 5.99 *(978-0-7364-2877-4(1)*, Golden/Disney) Random Hse. Children's Bks.

RH Disney Staff. Let's Stick Together! (Disney Frozen) RH Disney Staff. 2015. (Color Plus 1,000 Stickers Ser.). (ENG.). 64p. (J). (gr. -1-2). pap. 9.99 ***(978-0-7364-3354-9(6)***, Golden/Disney) Random Hse. Children's Bks.

RH Disney Staff. The Little Mermaid Big Golden Book (Disney Princess) RH Disney Staff. 2013. (Big Golden Book Ser.). (ENG.). 64p. (J). (gr. -1-2). 9.99 *(978-0-7364-2988-7(3)*, Golden/Disney) Random Hse. Children's Bks.

—Look Out for Mater! RH Disney Staff. 2009. (Little Golden Book Ser.). (ENG.). 24p. (J). (gr. -1-2). 3.99 *(978-0-7364-2582-7(9)*, Golden/Disney) Random Hse. Children's Bks.

—Lucky Fin! (Disney/Pixar Finding Nemo) RH Disney Staff. 2012. (Super Color with Stickers Ser.). (ENG.). 96p. (J). (gr. -1-2). pap. 3.99 *(978-0-7364-2921-4(2)*, Golden/Disney) Random Hse. Children's Bks.

—M Is for Monster (Disney/Pixar Monsters, Inc.) RH Disney Staff. 2014. (Little Golden Book Ser.). (ENG.). 24p. (J). (-k). 3.99 *(978-0-7364-3170-5(5)*, Golden/Disney) Random Hse. Children's Bks.

—Mater's Big Mission. RH Disney Staff. 2011. (Deluxe Paint Box Book Ser.). (ENG.). 128p. (J). (gr. -1-2). pap. 7.99 *(978-0-7364-2786-9(4)*, Golden/Disney) Random Hse. Children's Bks.

—Mater's Tall Tales. RH Disney Staff. 2009. (ENG.). 80p. (J). (gr. -1-2). 7.99 *(978-0-7364-2638-1(8)*, RH/Disney) Random Hse. Children's Bks.

—Maximum Power. RH Disney Staff. 2014. (Coloring Book Ser.). (ENG.). 128p. (J). (gr. -1-2). pap. 5.99 *(978-0-7364-3187-3(X)*, Golden/Disney) Random Hse. Children's Bks.

RH Disney Staff. Meet the Emotions. RH Disney Staff. 2015. (Glitter Board Book Ser.). (ENG.). 12p. (J). (gr. -1-2). bds. 8.99 ***(978-0-7364-3438-6(0)***, RH/Disney) Random Hse. Children's Bks.

RH Disney Staff. Mega Movie Mix. RH Disney Staff. 2009. (Coloring Book Ser.). (ENG.). 224p. (J). (gr. -1-2). pap. 5.99 *(978-0-7364-2626-8(4)*, Golden/Disney) Random Hse. Children's Bks.

—Merida's Challenge. RH Disney Staff. 2012. (Deluxe Coloring Book Ser.). (ENG.). 96p. (J). (gr. -1-2). pap. 3.99 *(978-0-7364-2903-0(4)*, Golden/Disney) Random Hse. Children's Bks.

—Mermaid Magic (Disney Princess) RH Disney Staff. 2013. (Color Plus Chunky Crayons Ser.). (ENG.). 48p. (J). (gr. -1-2). pap. 3.99 *(978-0-7364-2987-0(5)*, Golden/Disney) Random Hse. Children's Bks.

—Merry Princesses (Disney Princess) RH Disney Staff. 2014. (Big Coloring Book Ser.). (ENG.). 48p. (J). (gr. -1-2). pap. 6.99 *(978-0-7364-3165-1(9)*, Golden/Disney) Random Hse. Children's Bks.

—Monster Hide-and-Seek. RH Disney Staff. 2013. (Glow-In-the-Dark Board Book Ser.). (ENG.). 12p. (J). (-k). 6.99 *(978-0-7364-3032-6(6)*, Golden/Disney) Random Hse. Children's Bks.

—Monsters in Training. RH Disney Staff. 2013. (Color Plus Chunky Crayons Ser.). (ENG.). 48p. (J). (gr. -1-2). pap. 3.99 *(978-0-7364-3042-5(3)*, Golden/Disney) Random Hse. Children's Bks.

—Monsters, Inc. Big Golden Book (Disney/Pixar Monsters, Inc.) RH Disney Staff. 2012. (Big Golden Book Ser.). (ENG.). 64p. (J). (gr. -1-2). 9.99 *(978-0-7364-2855-2(0)*, Golden/Disney) Random Hse. Children's Bks.

—Monsters, Inc. Little Golden Book (Disney/Pixar Monsters, Inc.) RH Disney Staff. 2012. (Little Golden Book Ser.). (ENG.). 24p. (J). (-k). 3.99 *(978-0-7364-2799-9(6)*, Golden/Disney) Random Hse. Children's Bks.

—Monsters University Big Golden Book (Disney/Pixar Monsters University) RH Disney Staff. 2013. (Big Golden Book Ser.). (ENG.). 64p. (J). (gr. k-3). 9.99 *(978-0-7364-3043-2(1)*, Golden/Disney) Random Hse. Children's Bks.

—Monsters University Little Golden Book (Disney/Pixar Monsters University) RH Disney Staff. 2013. (Little Golden Book Ser.). (ENG.). 24p. (J). (-k). 3.99 *(978-0-7364-3034-0(2)*, Golden/Disney) Random Hse. Children's Bks.

—My Hero. RH Disney Staff. 2008. (Step into Reading Ser.). (ENG.). 32p. (J). (gr. k-3). pap. 3.99 *(978-0-375-84812-4(6)*, RH/Disney) Random Hse. Children's Bks.

—A Night to Sparkle (Disney Princess) RH Disney Staff. 2012. (Deluxe Coloring Book Ser.). (ENG.). 96p. (J). (gr. -1-2). pap. 3.99 *(978-0-7364-3006-7(7)*, Golden/Disney) Random Hse. Children's Bks.

—Ocean of Color. RH Disney Staff. 2012. (Deluxe Paint Box Book Ser.). (ENG.). 128p. (J). (gr. -1-2). pap. 7.99 *(978-0-307-97965-0(2)*, Golden/Disney) Random Hse. Children's Bks.

—Ocean's Treasures (Disney Princess) RH Disney Staff. 2013. (Deluxe Paint Box Book Ser.). (ENG.). 128p. (J). (gr. -1-2). pap. 7.99 *(978-0-7364-2985-6(9)*, Golden/Disney) Random Hse. Children's Bks.

—Olaf's 1-2-3. RH Disney Staff. 2013. (Glitter Board Book Ser.). (ENG.). 12p. (J). (— 1). bds. 6.99 *(978-0-7364-3064-7(4)*, Golden/Disney) Random Hse. Children's Bks.

—Once upon a Lily Pad. RH Disney Staff. Hands, Cynthia. 2009. (Color Plus Chunky Crayons Ser.). (ENG.). 48p. (J). (gr. -1-2). pap. 3.99 *(978-0-7364-2615-2(9)*, Golden/Disney) Random Hse. Children's Bks.

—Palace Designs (Disney Princess) RH Disney Staff. 2014. (Rub-On Patterns C&a Ser.). (ENG.). 128p. (J). (gr. -1-2). pap. 8.99 *(978-0-7364-3148-4(9)*, Golden/Disney) Random Hse. Children's Bks.

—Palace Paintings (Disney Princess) RH Disney Staff. 2012. (Deluxe Paint Box Book Ser.). (ENG.). 128p. (J). (gr. -1-2). pap. 7.99 *(978-0-7364-2896-5(8)*, Golden/Disney) Random Hse. Children's Bks.

—Pedal to the Metal. RH Disney Staff. 2008. (Super Stickerific Ser.). (ENG.). 64p. (J). (gr. -1-2). pap. 12.99 *(978-0-7364-2555-1(1)*, Golden/Disney) Random Hse. Children's Bks.

—Perfect Princesses. RH Disney Staff. 2009. (Jumbo Coloring Book Ser.). (ENG.). 224p. (J). (gr. -1-2). pap. 5.99 *(978-0-7364-2641-1(8)*, Golden/Disney) Random Hse. Children's Bks.

—Peter Pan Step into Reading (Disney Peter Pan) RH Disney Staff. 2013. (Step into Reading Ser.). (ENG.). 32p. (J). (gr. -1-1). 3.99 *(978-0-7364-3114-9(4)*, RH/Disney) Random Hse. Children's Bks.

—Planes: Fire & Rescue (Disney Planes: Fire & Rescue) RH Disney Staff. 2014. (Little Golden Book Ser.). (ENG.). 24p. (J). (-k). 3.99 *(978-0-7364-3166-8(7)*, Golden/Disney) Random Hse. Children's Bks.

—Pretty Princess Paintings. RH Disney Staff. 2009. (Deluxe Paint Box Book Ser.). (ENG.). 128p. (J). (gr. -1-2). pap. 7.99 *(978-0-7364-2566-7(7)*, Golden/Disney) Random Hse. Children's Bks.

—Princess Adventures (Disney Princess) RH Disney Staff. 2014. (Big Coloring Book Ser.). (ENG.). 48p. (J). (gr. -1-2). pap. 6.99 *(978-0-7364-3150-7(0)*, Golden/Disney) Random Hse. Children's Bks.

—The Princess & the Frog. RH Disney Staff. 2009. (Little Golden Book Ser.). (ENG.). 24p. (J). (gr. -1-2). 3.99 *(978-0-7364-2628-2(0)*, Golden/Disney) Random Hse. Children's Bks.

—Princess Brides (Disney Princess) RH Disney Staff. 2013. (Color Plus Card Stock Ser.). (ENG.). 48p. (J). (gr. -1-2). pap. 3.99 *(978-0-449-81383-6(5)*, Golden/Disney) Random Hse. Children's Bks.

—Princess Puzzlers (Disney Princess) RH Disney Staff. 2011. (Color Plus Tattoos Ser.). (ENG.). 48p. (J). (gr. -1-2). pap. 3.99 *(978-0-7364-2844-6(5)*, Golden/Disney) Random Hse. Children's Bks.

—Race Around the World. RH Disney Staff. 2011. (Step into Reading Ser.). (ENG.). 32p. (J). (gr. k-3). pap. 3.99 *(978-0-7364-2808-8(9)*, RH/Disney) Random Hse. Children's Bks.

—Racing Rivals. RH Disney Staff. 2011. (Pictureback Ser.). (ENG.). 24p. (J). (gr. -1-2). pap. 3.99 *(978-0-7364-2779-1(1)*, RH/Disney) Random Hse. Children's Bks.

—Racing Through the Snow. RH Disney Staff. 2009. (Deluxe Paint Box Book Ser.). (ENG.). 128p. (J). (gr. -1-2). pap. 7.99 *(978-0-7364-2625-1(6)*, Golden/Disney) Random Hse. Children's Bks.

—Rainbow of Emotions. RH Disney Staff. 2015. (Color Plus Rainbow Pencil Ser.). (ENG.). 128p. (J). (gr. -1-2). pap. 7.99 *(978-0-7364-3287-0(6)*, Golden/Disney) Random Hse. Children's Bks.

—Rapunzel's Royal Wedding/Belle's Royal Wedding (Disney Princess) RH Disney Staff. 2013. (Deluxe Pictureback Ser.). (ENG.). 32p. (J). (gr. -1-2). 4.99 *(978-0-7364-2993-1(X)*, RH/Disney) Random Hse. Children's Bks.

—Rapunzel's Wedding Day (Disney Princess) RH Disney Staff. 2012. (Pictureback Series.). (ENG.). 24p. (J). (gr. -1-2). pap. 3.99 *(978-0-7364-2970-2(0)*, RH/Disney) Random Hse. Children's Bks.

—Razzle-Dazzle! (Disney Princess: Palace Pets) RH Disney Staff. 2015. (Hologramatic Sticker Book Ser.). (ENG.). 64p. (J). (gr. -1-2). pap. 4.99 *(978-0-7364-3337-2(6)*, Golden/Disney) Random Hse. Children's Bks.

—Rescue Racers! (Disney Planes: Fire & Rescue) RH Disney Staff. 2014. (Color Plus Crayons & Sticker Ser.). (ENG.). 48p. (J). (gr. -1-2). pap. 4.99 *(978-0-7364-3193-4(4)*, Golden/Disney) Random Hse. Children's Bks.

—Roaring Rivals. RH Disney Staff. 2013. (Pictureback Ser.). (ENG.). 24p. (J). (gr. -1-2). 3.99 *(978-0-7364-3041-8(5)*, RH/Disney) Random Hse. Children's Bks.

—Royal & Regal (Disney Princess) RH Disney Staff. 2013. (Deluxe Reusable Sticker Book Ser.). (ENG.). 24p. (J). (gr. -1-2). pap. 6.99 *(978-0-7364-3066-1(0)*, Golden/Disney) Random Hse. Children's Bks.

—Scares & Surprises! (Disney/Pixar Toy Story) RH Disney Staff. 2014. (Color Plus Glow Stickers Ser.). (ENG.). 48p. (J). (gr. -1-2). pap. 3.99 *(978-0-7364-3073-9(3)*, Golden/Disney) Random Hse. Children's Bks.

—Scaring All-Stars (Disney/Pixar Monsters, Inc.) RH Disney Staff. 2014. (Color Plus Card Stock Ser.). (ENG.). 48p. (J). (gr. -1-2). pap. 3.99 *(978-0-7364-3197-2(7)*, Golden/Disney) Random Hse. Children's Bks.

—Scaring Lessons. RH Disney Staff. 2013. (Step into Reading Ser.). (ENG.). 32p. (J). (gr. -1-1). 3.99 *(978-0-7364-3035-7(0)*, RH/Disney) Random Hse. Children's Bks.

—Shape up! (Disney/Pixar Toy Story) RH Disney Staff. 2013. (Color Plus Stencil Ser.). (ENG.). 64p. (J). (gr. -1-2). pap. 5.99 *(978-0-307-98206-3(8)*, Golden/Disney) Random Hse. Children's Bks.

—Shapes, Colors, Counting & More! RH Disney Staff. 2014. (Friendship Box Ser.). (ENG.). 48p. (J). (-k). bds. 10.99 *(978-0-7364-3126-2(8)*, RH/Disney) Random Hse. Children's Bks.

—Shapes, Colors, Counting & More! (Disney/Pixar Cars) RH Disney Staff. Berrios, Frank. 2013. (Friendship Box Ser.). (ENG.). 48p. (J). (gr. -1-2). bds. 10.99 *(978-0-7364-3105-7(5)*, RH/Disney) Random Hse. Children's Bks.

—Shifting Gears! RH Disney Staff. Berrios, Frank. 2013. (Color & Paint Plus Stickers Ser.). (ENG.). 128p. (J). (gr. -1-2). pap. 9.99 *(978-0-7364-3144-6(6)*, Golden/Disney) Random Hse. Children's Bks.

RH Disney Staff. Sister Time! (Disney Frozen) RH Disney Staff. 2015. (Color Plus Wall Decals Ser.). (ENG.). 48p. (J). (-k). pap. 6.99 ***(978-0-7364-3418-8(6)***, Golden/Disney) Random Hse. Children's Bks.

RH Disney Staff. Sleeping Beauty Big Golden Book (Disney Princess) RH Disney Staff. 2014. (Big Golden Book Ser.). (ENG.). 64p. (J). (gr. -1-2). 9.99 *(978-0-7364-3233-7(7)*, Golden/Disney) Random Hse. Children's Bks.

—Snow Days! RH Disney Staff. 2013. (Reusable Sticker Book Ser.). (ENG.). 12p. (J). (gr. -1-2). pap. 6.99 *(978-0-7364-3116-3(0)*, Golden/Disney) Random Hse. Children's Bks.

—Sparkle & Shine (Disney Princess) RH Disney Staff. 2012. (Color Plus Chunky Crayons Ser.). (ENG.). 48p. (J). (gr. -1-2). pap. 3.99 *(978-0-7364-2898-9(4)*, Golden/Disney) Random Hse. Children's Bks.

RH Disney Staff. Sparkle Magic! (Disney Frozen) RH Disney Staff. 2015. (Pictureback(R) Ser.). (ENG.). 16p. (J). (gr. -1-2). 5.99 ***(978-0-7364-3366-2(X)***, RH/Disney) Random Hse. Children's Bks.

RH Disney Staff. Stuck on You (Disney/Pixar Toy Story) RH Disney Staff. 2012. (Deluxe Stickerific Ser.). (ENG.). 64p. (J). (gr. -1-2). pap. 5.99 *(978-0-7364-2890-3(9)*, Golden/Disney) Random Hse. Children's Bks.

—Sugar Rush. RH Disney Staff. 2012. (Pictureback(R) Ser.). (ENG.). 24p. (J). (gr. -1-2). pap. 3.99 *(978-0-7364-2959-7(X)*, RH/Disney) Random Hse. Children's Bks.

—Super Princess Art Party (Disney Princess) RH Disney Staff. 2013. (Color & Paint Plus Stickers Ser.). (ENG.). 128p. (J). (gr. -1-2). pap. 9.99 *(978-0-7364-3147-7(0)*, Golden/Disney) Random Hse. Children's Bks.

—Super Spies. RH Disney Staff. 2011. (Step into Reading Ser.). (ENG.). 32p. (J). (gr. k-3). pap. 3.99 *(978-0-7364-2807-1(0)*, RH/Disney) Random Hse. Children's Bks.

—Taking the Lead. RH Disney Staff. 2011. (Puzzle Book Ser.). (ENG.). 8p. (J). (gr. -1-2). 7.99 *(978-0-7364-2822-4(4)*, RH/Disney) Random Hse. Children's Bks.

—A Tale of Two Sisters. RH Disney Staff. Lagonegro, Melissa. 2013. (Step into Reading Ser.). (ENG.). 32p. (J). (gr. -1-1). lib. bdg. 12.99 *(978-0-7364-8131-1(1)*, RH/Disney) Random Hse. Children's Bks.

—Team Lightning (Disney/Pixar Cars) RH Disney Staff. 2014. (Nifty Lift-And-Look Ser.). (ENG.). 12p. (J). (-k). bds. 5.99 *(978-0-7364-3052-4(0)*, RH/Disney) Random Hse. Children's Bks.

—Team Up! RH Disney Staff. 2014. (Pictureback Ser.). (ENG.). 24p. (J). (gr. -1-2). 4.99 *(978-0-7364-3244-3(2)*, RH/Disney) Random Hse. Children's Bks.

R

—Thomas' Mixed-Up Day - Thomas Puts the Brakes On. RH Disney Staff. Awdry, Wilbert V. 2010. (Deluxe Pictureback Ser.). (ENG.). 32p. (J). (gr. -1-2). pap. 4.99 *(978-0-375-85919-9(5)*, Random Hse. Bks. for Young Readers) Random Hse. Children's Bks.

—Time to Play. RH Disney Staff. 2010. (Deluxe Paint Box Book Ser.). (ENG.). 128p. (J). (gr. -1-2). pap. 7.99 *(978-0-375-85734-8(6)*, Golden/Disney) Random Hse. Children's Bks.

—Too Fast! RH Disney Staff. 2011. (Friendship Box Ser.). (ENG.). 48p. (J). (— 1). bds. 10.99 *(978-0-7364-2787-6(2)*, RH/Disney) Random Hse. Children's Bks.

—Totally Tiaras! (Disney Princess) RH Disney Staff. 2015. (Color Plus Cardstock & Stickers Ser.). (ENG.). 32p. (J). (gr. -1-2). pap. 5.99 *(978-0-7364-3347-1(3)*, Golden/Disney) Random Hse. Children's Bks.

—A Toy Christmas (Disney/Pixar Toy Story) RH Disney Staff. 2011. (Glitter Sticker Book Ser.). (ENG.). 64p. (J). (gr. -1-2). pap. 4.99 *(978-0-7364-2842-2(9)*, Golden/Disney) Random Hse. Children's Bks.

—Toy Story. RH Disney Staff. (Fun Kit Ser.). (ENG.). (J). (gr. -1-2). 2010. 64p. 9.99 *(978-0-7364-2699-2(X)*, Golden/Disney); 2009. 24p. 3.99 *(978-0-7364-2596-4(9)*, RH/Disney) Random Hse. Children's Bks.

—Toy Story/Toy Story 2. RH Disney Staff. 2010. (Deluxe Pictureback Ser.). (ENG.). 32p. (J). (gr. -1-2). pap. 4.99 *(978-0-7364-2640-4(X)*, RH/Disney) Random Hse. Children's Bks.

—Tricks, Treats, & Toys (Disney/Pixar Toy Story) RH Disney Staff. 2012. (Color Plus Tattoos Ser.). (ENG.). 48p. (J). (gr. -1-2). pap. 3.99 *(978-0-7364-2920-7(4)*, Golden/Disney) Random Hse. Children's Bks.

—Triplet Trouble! RH Disney Staff. 2012. (Deluxe Paint Box Book Ser.). (ENG.). 128p. (J). (gr. -1-2). pap. 7.99 *(978-0-7364-2905-4(0)*, Golden/Disney) Random Hse. Children's Bks.

—Up. RH Disney Staff. 2009. (Little Golden Book Ser.). (ENG.). 24p. (J). (gr. -1-2). 3.99 *(978-0-7364-2581-0(0)*, Golden/Disney) Random Hse. Children's Bks.

—Welcome to Headquarters. RH Disney Staff. 2015. (Step into Reading Ser.). (ENG.). 32p. (J). (gr. -1-1). 4.99 *(978-0-7364-3318-1(X)*, RH/Disney) Random Hse. Children's Bks.

—Wishes & Dreams. RH Disney Staff. 2014. (Color Plus 1,000 Stickers Ser.). (ENG.). 64p. (J). (gr. -1-2). pap. 9.99 *(978-0-7364-3134-7(9)*, Golden/Disney) Random Hse. Children's Bks.

—Wonderful Princess World. RH Disney Staff. Golden Books Staff. 2007. (Super Stickerific Ser.). (ENG.). 64p. (J). (gr. -1-2). pap. 12.99 *(978-0-375-84171-2(7)*, Golden/Disney) Random Hse. Children's Bks.

—A World of Caring. RH Disney Staff. 2010. (Deluxe Chunky Crayon Book Ser.). (ENG.). 128p. (J). (gr. -1-2). pap. 7.99 *(978-0-7364-2657-2(4)*, Golden/Disney) Random Hse. Children's Bks.

—World's Greatest Racers (Disney/Pixar Cars) RH Disney Staff. 2013. (ENG.). 16p. (J). (-k). bds. 7.99 *(978-0-7364-3145-3(4)*, RH/Disney) Random Hse. Children's Bks.

—Wreck-It Ralph (Disney Wreck-It Ralph) RH Disney Staff. 2012. (Big Golden Book Ser.). (ENG.). 64p. (J). (gr. -1-2). 9.99 *(978-0-7364-2954-2(9)*, Golden/Disney) Random Hse. Children's Bks.

RH Disney Staff & An, Jiyoung. I Can Be a Horse Rider (Barbie) Man-Kong, Mary. 2012. (Step into Reading Ser.). (ENG.). 32p. (J). (gr. -1-1). pap. 3.99 *(978-0-375-97030-6(4)*, Random Hse. Bks. for Young Readers) Random Hse. Children's Bks.

RH Disney Staff & Cohee, Ron. Mater's Awesome Easter (Disney/Pixar Cars) Berrios, Frank. 2012. (Deluxe Paint Box Book Ser.). (ENG.). 128p. (J). (gr. -1-2). pap. 7.99 *(978-0-7364-2871-2(2)*, Golden/Disney) Random Hse. Children's Bks.

—Shakin' in My Tires! Berrios, Frank. 2011. (Glow-In-the-Dark Sticker Book Ser.). (ENG.). 48p. (J). (gr. -1-2). pap. 3.99 *(978-0-7364-2803-3(8)*, Golden/Disney) Random Hse. Children's Bks.

RH Disney Staff & DiCicco, Sue. Sleepy Time with Aurora (Disney Princess) Posner-Sanchez, Andrea. 2015. (Big Bright & Early Board Book Ser.). (ENG.). 24p. (J). (-k). bds. 6.99 *(978-0-7364-3311-2(2)*, RH/Disney) Random Hse. Children's Bks.

RH Disney Staff & DiCicco, Sue. Teacup to the Rescue! (Disney Princess: Palace Pets) Posner-Sanchez, Andrea. 2015. (Little Golden Book Ser.). (ENG.). 24p. (J). (-k). 4.99 ***(978-0-7364-3364-8(3)***, Golden/Disney) Random Hse. Children's Bks.

RH Disney Staff & DiCicco, Sue. Treasure's Day at Sea (Disney Princess: Palace Pets) RH Disney Staff & Posner-Sanchez, Andrea. 2015. (Little Golden Book Ser.). (ENG.). 24p. (J). (-k). 3.99 *(978-0-7364-3335-8(X)*, Golden/Disney) Random Hse. Children's Bks.

RH Disney Staff & Disney Pixar Staff. Play Day! RH Disney Staff & Disney Pixar Staff. 2010. (Reusable Sticker Book Ser.). (ENG.). 12p. (J). (gr. -1-2). pap. 6.99 *(978-0-7364-2672-5(8)*, Golden/Disney) Random Hse. Children's Bks.

RH Disney Staff & Disney Storybook Art Team Staff. Olaf's Perfect Day (Disney Frozen) Posner-Sanchez, Andrea & Julius, Jessica. 2015. (Little Golden Book Ser.). (ENG.). 24p. (J). (-k). 4.99 ***(978-0-7364-3356-3(2)***, Golden/Disney) Random Hse. Children's Bks.

RH Disney Staff & Disney Storybook Artists Staff. Wings Around the Globe. RH Disney Staff & Scollon, Bill. 2013. (Pictureback Series.). (ENG.). 24p. (J). (gr. -1-2). pap. 3.99 *(978-0-7364-3016-6(4)*, RH/Disney) Random Hse. Children's Bks.

RH Disney Staff & Doescher, Erik. Ready to Play! (Disney Infinity) Saxon, Victoria. 2015. (Step into Reading Ser.). (ENG.). 32p. (J). (gr. k-3). 4.99 ***(978-0-7364-3427-0(5)***, RH/Disney) Random Hse. Children's Bks.

RH Disney Staff & Egan, Caroline. The Pet Problem (Disney/Pixar Toy Story) RH Disney Staff & Depken, Kristen L. 2011. (Little Golden Book Ser.). (ENG.). 24p. (J). (gr. -1-2). 3.99 *(978-0-7364-2698-5(1)*, Golden/Disney) Random Hse. Children's Bks.

RH Disney Staff & Fruchter, Jason. Toby the Cowsitter (Disney Junior: Sheriff Callie's Wild West) Posner-Sanchez, Andrea. 2015. (Little Golden Book Ser.). (ENG.). 24p. (J). (-k). 3.99 *(978-0-7364-3299-3(X)*, Golden/Disney) Random Hse. Children's Bks.

RH Disney Staff & Golden Books Staff. Cars 2 Big Golden Book. RH Disney Staff. 2011. (Big Golden Book Ser.). (ENG.). 64p. (J). (gr. -1-2). 9.99 *(978-0-7364-2780-7(5)*, RH/Disney) Random Hse. Children's Bks.

RH Disney Staff & Holtsclaw, Josh. A Roaring Adventure (Disney/Pixar Toy Story) Depken, Kristen L. 2012. (Little Golden Book Ser.). (ENG.). 24p. (J). (gr. k-k). 3.99 *(978-0-7364-2907-8(7)*, Golden/Disney) Random Hse. Children's Bks.

RH Disney Staff & Laguna, Fabio. Toy Box Trouble! RH Disney Staff & Weingartner, Amy. 2015. (Stepping Stone Book(TM) Ser.). (ENG.). 80p. (J). (gr. 1-4). 4.99 *(978-0-7364-3326-6(0)*, RH/Disney) Random Hse. Children's Bks.

—Treasure Hunt! RH Disney Staff & Weingartner, Amy. 2015. (Stepping Stone Book Ser.). (ENG.). 80p. (J). (gr. 1-4). 4.99 *(978-0-7364-3327-3(9)*, Random Hse. Bks. for Young Readers) Random Hse. Children's Bks.

RH Disney Staff & Legramandi, Francesco. A Merry & Magical Christmas. RH Disney Staff. 2010. (Glitter Sticker Book Ser.). (ENG.). 64p. (J). (gr. -1-2). pap. 4.99 *(978-0-7364-2731-9(7)*, Golden/Disney) Random Hse. Children's Bks.

—Princess Hearts (Disney Princess) Weinberg, Jennifer Liberts. 2012. (Step into Reading Ser.). (ENG.). 32p. (J). (gr. -1-1). pap. 3.99 *(978-0-7364-3013-5(X)*, RH/Disney) Random Hse. Children's Bks.

RH Disney Staff & Molina, Adrian H. Toy Story 3. RH Disney Staff & Auerbach, Annie. 2010. (Little Golden Book Ser.). (ENG.). 24p. (J). (gr. -1-2). 3.99 *(978-0-7364-2668-8(X)*, Golden/Disney) Random Hse. Children's Bks.

RH Disney Staff & Random House Staff. I Can Be a Pastry Chef/I Can Be a Lifeguard (Barbie) Man-Kong, Mary et al. 2012. (Deluxe Pictureback Ser.). (ENG.). 32p. (J). (gr. -1-2). pap. 4.99 *(978-0-307-93114-6(5)*, Random Hse. Bks. for Young Readers) Random Hse. Children's Bks.

RH Disney Staff & Robinson, Bill. All Hail the Queen. David, Erica. 2015. (Stepping Stone Book(TM) Ser.). (ENG.). 128p. (J). (gr. 1-4). lib. bdg. 12.99 *(978-0-7364-8216-5(4)*, RH/Disney) Random Hse. Children's Bks.

RH Disney Staff & Robinson, William E. Memory & Magic. David, Erica. 2015. (Stepping Stone Book(TM) Ser.). (ENG.). 128p. (J). (gr. 1-4). 9.99 *(978-0-7364-3285-6(X)*, RH/Disney) Random Hse. Children's Bks.

RH Disney Staff & Storino, Sara. A Princess Halloween (Disney Princess) Posner-Sanchez, Andrea. 2011. (Glow-In-the-Dark Sticker Book Ser.). (ENG.). 48p. (J). (gr. -1-2). pap. 3.99 *(978-0-7364-2802-6(X)*, Golden/Disney) Random Hse. Children's Bks.

RH Disney Staff & Studio IBOIX Staff. Two Princesses & a Baby (Disney Junior: Sofia the First) Posner-Sanchez, Andrea. 2015. (Little Golden Book Ser.). (ENG.). 24p. (J). (-k). 4.99 ***(978-0-7364-3358-7(9)***, Golden/Disney) Random Hse. Children's Bks.

RH Disney Staff & Tyminski, Lori. Simply Sadness/Joy's Greatest Joy. RH Disney Staff & Glum, Felicity. 2015. (Pictureback(R) Ser.). (ENG.). 24p. (J). (gr. -1-2). 4.99 *(978-0-7364-3314-3(7)*, RH/Disney) Random Hse. Children's Bks.

RH Disney Staff & Walt Disney Studios Staff. Little Man of Disneyland (Disney Classic) RH Disney Staff. 2015. (Little Golden Book Ser.). (ENG.). 24p. (J). (-k). 4.99 ***(978-0-7364-3485-0(2)***, Golden/Disney) Random Hse. Children's Bks.

RH Disney Staff, jt. illus. see Christy, Jana.

RH Disney Staff, jt. illus. see Disney Global Artists Staff.

RH Disney Staff, jt. illus. see Disney Storybook Artists Staff.

RH Disney Staff, jt. illus. see Golden Books Staff.

RH Disney Staff, jt. illus. see Tilley, Scott.

RH Disney Staff, jt. illus. see Walt Disney Company Staff.

Rhead, Louis. Treasure Island. Stevenson, Robert Louis. 2015. (J). pap. ***(978-1-4677-7821-3(4)***, First Avenue Editions) Lerner Publishing Group.

Rheberg, Judy. The Hunting Safari. Matthews, T. J. 2003. (East African Adventures Ser.). 166p. (J). per. 11.95 *(978-0-938978-34-3(9))* Wycliffe Bible Translators.

Rheburg, Judy. The Canoeing Safari. Matthews, T. J. 2004. (J). *(978-0-938978-35-0(7))* Wycliffe Bible Translators.

—The Village Safari. Matthews, T. J. 2005. (J). *(978-0-938978-36-7(5))* Wycliffe Bible Translators.

Rhine, Karen C. Princess Aisha & the Cave of Judgment. Taylor, Kay Lovelace. 2007. 32p. (J). 19.95 *(978-0-9799119-0-3(7))* KLT & Assocs.

—San Agustin (St Augustine) Lilly, Melinda. 2005. (Lecturas Historicas Norteamericanas (Reading American Histor Ser.). 24p. (J). (gr. 3-7). lib. bdg. 22.79 *(978-1-59515-637-2(2))* Rourke Educational Media.

Rhodes, Katie. Becky Bunny. Powell, Richard. 2004. (Fuzzy Friends Ser.). 10p. (J). 7.95 *(978-1-58925-723-8(5))* Tiger Tales.

—Leo Lion. Powell, Richard. 2004. (Fuzzy Friends Ser.). 10p. (J). 7.95 *(978-1-58925-719-1(7))* Tiger Tales.

—Lucy Lamb. Powell, Richard. 2004. (Fuzzy Friends Ser.). 8p. (J). 7.95 *(978-1-58925-724-5(3))* Tiger Tales.

—Mandy Monkey. Powell, Richard. 2004. (Fuzzy Friends Ser.). 10p. (J). 7.95 *(978-1-58925-720-7(0))* Tiger Tales.

—Peter Panda. Powell, Richard. 2004. (Fuzzy Friends Ser.). 10p. (J). 7.95 *(978-1-58925-721-4(9))* Tiger Tales.

—Timmy Tiger. Powell, Richard. 2004. (Fuzzy Friends Ser.). 10p. (J). 7.95 *(978-1-58925-722-1(7))* Tiger Tales.

Riano, Carlos. Koku-Yo, Mensajero del Sol. Espriella, Leopoldo Berdella De La. 2003. (Literatura Juvenil (Panamericana Editorial) Ser.). (SPA.). 90p. (YA). (gr. -1-7). per. *(978-958-30-0344-8(1))* Panamericana Editorial.

Ribas, Meritxell. Frankenstein by Mary Shelley. Sierra, Sergio A. & Shelley, Mary. 2012. (Dark Graphic Novels Ser.). 96p. (J). (gr. 5-9). 31.94 *(978-0-7660-4084-7(2))* Enslow Pubs., Inc.

Ribeira, Lili, jt. illus. see Graham, Andrew S.

Ribera, Terry. Fingerprints of You. Madonia, Kristen-Paige. 2012. (ENG.). 272p. (YA). (gr. 9). 16.99 *(978-1-4424-2920-8(8)*, Simon & Schuster Bks. For Young Readers) Simon & Schuster Bks. For Young Readers.

Ribic, Esad & Peterson, Brandon. Ultimate Comics Ultimates, Vol. 1. Hickman, Jonathan. 2012. (ENG.). 136p. (YA). (gr. 8-17). pap. 19.99 *(978-0-7851-5718-2(2))* Marvel Worldwide, Inc.

Ricahrdson, Brittany. Metal Mike. Ricahrdson, Larry. 2010. 24p. (J). pap. 9.95 *(978-1-935706-26-7(8))* Wiggles Pr.

Ricceri, David, jt. illus. see Klossner, John.

Ricci, Andrés. Down for the Count. Riley, Zach. 2012. (Zach Riley Ser.). 80p. (J). (gr. 3-6). lib. bdg. 27.07 *(978-1-61783-533-9(1))* Magic Wagon.

—Quarterback Crisis. Riley, Zach. 2012. (Zach Riley Ser.). 80p. (J). (gr. 3-6). lib. bdg. 27.07 *(978-1-61783-534-6(X))* Magic Wagon.

—Sacred Stick. Riley, Zach. 2012. (Zach Riley Ser.). 80p. (J). (gr. 3-6). lib. bdg. 27.07 *(978-1-61783-535-3(8))* Magic Wagon.

—Surprise Kick. Riley, Zach. 2012. (Zach Riley Ser.). 80p. (J). (gr. 3-6). lib. bdg. 27.07 *(978-1-61783-536-0(6))* Magic Wagon.

Ricci, Andres Martinez. Electricity Is Everywhere. Higgins, Nadia. 2008. (Science Rocks Ser.). 32p. (gr. -1-4). 28.50 *(978-1-60270-276-9(4)*, 1287324, Looking Glass Library-Nonfiction) Magic Wagon.

—Marvelous Motion. Higgins, Nadia. 2008. (Science Rocks Ser.). 32p. (gr. -1-4). 28.50 *(978-1-60270-278-3(0)*, 1287326, Looking Glass Library- Nonfiction) Magic Wagon.

—Mighty Magnets. Higgins, Nadia. 2008. (Science Rocks Ser.). 32p. (gr. -1-4). 28.50 *(978-1-60270-279-0(9)*, 1287327, Looking Glass Library- Nonfiction) Magic Wagon.

—Stupendous Sound. Higgins, Nadia. 2008. (Science Rocks Ser.). 32p. (gr. -1-4). 28.50 *(978-1-60270-280-6(2)*, 1287328, Looking Glass Library- Nonfiction) Magic Wagon.

—Super Shadows. Higgins, Nadia. 2008. (Science Rocks Ser.). 32p. (gr. -1-4). 18.95 *(978-1-60270-281-3(0)*, Looking Glass Library- Nonfiction) Magic Wagon.

—A Wrench in the Works. Slater, David Michael. 2009. (David Michael Slater Set 2 Ser.). 32p. (gr. -1-4). 28.50 *(978-1-60270-660-6(3)*, Looking Glass Library) ABDO Publishing Co.

Ricci, Andrés Martinez. Zap! Wile E. Coyote Experiments with Energy, 1 vol. Slade, Suzanne. 2014. (Wile E. Coyote, Physical Science Genius Ser.). (ENG.). 32p. (gr. 3-4). 29.99 *(978-1-4765-4223-2(6))*; pap. 7.95 *(978-1-4765-5214-9(2))* Capstone Pr., Inc.

Ricci, Andrés Martinez, jt. illus. see Cornia, Christian.

Riccio, Frank. Baseball for Breakfast: The Story of a Boy Who Hated to Wait. Myers, Bill. 2005. 29p. (J). (gr. 4-8). reprint ed. 15.00 *(978-0-7567-9248-0(7))* DIANE Publishing Co.

—The Little Soul & the Earth: A Children's Parable Adapted from Conversations with God. Walsch, Neale Donald. 2005. (ENG.). 32p. (J). 20.00 *(978-1-57174-451-7(7))* Hampton Roads Publishing Co., Inc.

—Milton's Secret: An Adventure of Discovery Through Then, When & the Power of Now. Tolle, Eckhart & Friedman, Robert S. 2008. (ENG.). 40p. (J). (gr. 3-7). 18.95 *(978-1-57174-577-4(7))* Hampton Roads Publishing Co., Inc.

Rice, Ashley. Girls Rule: A Very Special Book Created Especially for Girls. Rice, Ashley. 64p. (J). pap. 9.95 *(978-0-88396-627-3(1)*, Blue Mountain Pr.) Blue Mountain Arts Inc.

Rice, Doug. The Magic Is Me. Rice, Donna. 2012. 34p. (J). mass mkt. 15.99 *(978-1-936497-16-4(6))* Searchlight Pr.

Rice, James. Country Music Night Before Christmas, 1 vol. Turner, Thomas N. 2003. (Night Before Christmas Ser.). (ENG.). 32p. (J). (gr. k-3). 16.99 *(978-1-58980-148-6(2))* Pelican Publishing Co., Inc.

Rice, James. Gaston Joins the Circus. 2015. (ENG.). 32p. (J). (gr. k-3). pap. 9.95 ***(978-1-4556-2092-0(0))*** Pelican Publishing Co., Inc.

Rice, James. An Irish Night Before Christmas Coloring Book, 1 vol. Blazek, Sarah. 2009. (Night Before Christmas Ser.). (ENG.). 32p. (J). (gr. k-3). pap. 3.95 *(978-1-58980-704-4(9))* Pelican Publishing Co., Inc.

—Nurse's Night Before Christmas, 1 vol. Davis, David. 2003. (Night Before Christmas Ser.). (ENG.). 32p. (J). (gr. k-3). 16.99 *(978-1-58980-152-3(0))* Pelican Publishing Co., Inc.

—Ozark Night Before Christmas, 1 vol. McWilliams, Amanda & Moore, Clement C. 2004. (Night Before Christmas Ser.). (ENG.). 32p. (J). (gr. k-3). 16.99 *(978-1-58980-056-4(7))* Pelican Publishing Co., Inc.

—The Principal's Night Before Christmas, 1 vol. Layne, Steven. 2004. (Night Before Christmas Ser.). (ENG.). 32p. (J). (gr. k-3). 16.99 *(978-1-58980-252-0(7))* Pelican Publishing Co., Inc.

Rice, James. Gaston(r) Goes to Texas, 1 vol. Rice, James. 2007. (Gaston(r) Ser.). (ENG.). 32p. (J). (gr. 1-3). 16.99 *(978-1-58980-531-6(3))* Pelican Publishing Co., Inc.

—Gaston Lays an Offshore Pipeline, 1 vol. Rice, James. 2007. (Gaston(r) Ser.). (ENG.). 32p. (J). (gr. k-3). 16.99 *(978-1-58980-510-1(0))* Pelican Publishing Co., Inc.

Rice, James, Jr. Lyn & the Fuzzy, 1 vol. Rice, James, Jr. 2007. (ENG.). 40p. (J). (gr. k-3). 17.99 *(978-1-58980-508-8(9))* Pelican Publishing Co., Inc.

Rice, James. Santa's Revenge, 1 vol. Rice, James. 2005. (ENG.). 32p. (J). (gr. k-3). 16.99 *(978-1-58980-250-6(0))* Pelican Publishing Co., Inc.

—Too Tall Thomas Rides the Grub Line, 1 vol. Rice, James. 2004. (ENG.). 32p. (J). (gr. k-3). 16.99 *(978-1-58980-177-6(6))* Pelican Publishing Co., Inc.

Rice, James. Trail Boss: J. M. Daugherty. Rice, James, tr. 2003. (J). *(978-1-57168-769-2(6)*, Eakin Pr.) Eakin Pr.

Rice, John. How Dogs Came from Wolves: And Other Explorations of Science in Action. Myers, Jack. 2004. (ENG.). 64p. (J). (gr. 4-6). pap. 10.95 *(978-1-59078-278-1(X))* Boyds Mills Pr.

—On Top of Mount Everest: And Other Explortions of Science in Action. Myers, Jack. 2005. (ENG.). 64p. (J). (gr. 4-7). 17.95 *(978-1-59078-252-1(6))* Boyds Mills Pr.

—The Puzzle of the Platypus: And Other Explorations of Science in Action. Myers, Jack. 2008. (ENG.). 64p. (J). (gr. 4-7). 17.95 *(978-1-59078-556-0(8))* Boyds Mills Pr.

Rice, Kaleb & Deasey, Kevin. The Day Kyle Met Nuf. Porrata, Mayra. 2013. 28p. pap. 12.95 *(978-0-9825480-2-8(8))* Sunny Day Publishing, LLC.

Rich, Anna. Blacksmith's Song. Steenwyk, Elizabeth Van. 2012. (J). *(978-1-56145-580-5(6))* Peachtree Pubs.

—Coretta Scott King: Dare to Dream. Medearis, Angela Shelf. 2014. (Women of Our Time Ser.). (ENG.). 96p. (J). (gr. 3-7). 7.99 *(978-0-14-751363-2(4)*, Puffin) Penguin Publishing Group.

—Joshua's Masai Mask. Hru, Dakari. 2013. (ENG.). 32p. (J). (gr. -1-5). pap. 8.95 *(978-1-880000-32-8(6))* Lee & Low Bks., Inc.

—Only the Stars. Scholastic, Inc. Staff & Boyd, Dee. 2004. (Just for You Ser.). (ENG.). 32p. pap. 3.99 *(978-0-439-56862-3(5)*, Teaching Resources) Scholastic, Inc.

—Saturday at the New You. Barber, Barbara E. 2013. (ENG.). 32p. (J). (gr. -1-3). reprint ed. pap. 9.95 *(978-1-880000-43-4(1))* Lee & Low Bks., Inc.

—Under the Night Sky, 1 vol. Lundebrek, Amy. 2008. (ENG.). 32p. (J). (gr. -1-3). 16.95 *(978-0-88448-297-0(9))* Tilbury Hse. Pubs.

Rich, Bobbie. The Running Nose Book. Rich, Carol Bak. 2013. (ENG.). 41p. (J). pap. 9.95 *(978-1-4787-0062-3(9))* Outskirts Pr., Inc.

Richa Kinra. Debra Meets Her Best Friend in Kindergarten. Debra Maymon. 2009. 36p. pap. 15.49 *(978-1-4389-6261-0(4))* AuthorHouse.

Richard, Ilene. The Author with the Fancy Purple Pen. Williams, Rozanne Lanczak. (Learn to Write Ser.). 16p. (J). 2007. (gr. -1-3). pap. 8.99 *(978-1-59198-346-0(0))*; 2006. (gr. k-2). pap. 2.99 *(978-1-59198-299-9(5)*, 6189) Creative Teaching Pr., Inc.

—Here Comes the Parade. Mishica, Clare. 2005. (Rookie Readers Ser.). (ENG.). 24p. (J). (gr. k-2). lib. bdg. 19.50 *(978-0-516-24857-8(X)*, Children's Pr.) Scholastic Library Publishing.

—Let My People Go! Balsley, Tilda. 2008. (ENG.). 32p. (J). (gr. k-3). per. 7.95 *(978-0-8225-7241-1(9)*, Kar-Ben Publishing) Lerner Publishing Group.

—Luke & Leo Build a Limerick. Mataya, Marybeth. 2011. (Poetry Builders Ser.). 32p. (J). (gr. 2-4). lib. bdg. 25.27 *(978-1-59953-436-7(3))* Norwood Hse. Pr.

—The Queen Who Saved Her People. Balsley, Tilda & Balsley, Tilda. 2011. (ENG.). 32p. (J). (gr. 3-5). pap. 7.95 *(978-0-7613-5093-4(4)*, Kar-Ben Publishing) Lerner Publishing Group.

—The Teacher with the Alligator Purse, Vol. 4259. Williams, Rozanne Lanczak. 2005. (Reading for Fluency Ser.). 16p. (J). pap. 3.49 *(978-1-59198-159-6(X))* Creative Teaching Pr., Inc.

Richard, Keisha Luana. The Travels of Kui, the African Spurred Tortoise. Lynch, Stephen D. 2007. 36p. per. 24.95 *(978-1-4137-1802-7(7))* America Star Bks.

Richard, Laurent & Owlkids Books Inc. Staff. Earth & Sky: A Lift-the-Flap Guide to Our World & Solar System. Hédelin, Pascale. 2009. (Lift the Flap & Learn Ser.). (ENG.). 38p. (J). (gr. k). spiral bd. 19.95 *(978-1-897349-68-7(8))* Owlkids Bks. Inc. CAN. Dist: Perseus-PGW.

Richard, P. M. Animals Animales: A Bilingual ABC Book for all Readers. Stanton, Laura. 2014. 32p. (J). 9.95 *(978-0-9860734-0-3(7))* Echo Valley Pr.

—Squirt the Otter: The True Story of an Orphaned Otter who Finds Friendship & Happiness. Mikowski, Tracy L. 2013. 32p. (J). 16.95 *(978-0-9860287-0-0(3))* Talking Crow Publishing.

Richarde. The Big Bad Wolf Strikes It Rich! Fairy Tale Wall Street Memoirs. Richarde. Russin, Nicole. 2013. (ENG.). 176p. pap. 9.99 *(978-0-615-72487-4(6))* Three Legged Toad Pr.

Richards, C. E. King Arthur. 2010. (Classic Fiction Ser.). 72p. 4.75 *(978-1-4342-2603-7(4)*, Graphic Revolve) Stone Arch Bks.

Richards, Charles. Bardolph Bedivere Wolf Returns. Richards, Pat. 2007. 42p. (J). *(978-0-9790796-4-1(0))* PJR Assocs., Ltd.

Richards, Chuck. The Critter Sitter. Richards, Chuck. 2008. (ENG.). 32p. (YA). (gr. k-3). 16.99 *(978-0-8027-9595-3(1))* Walker & Co.

Richards, Jon. Cosmo: A Cautionary Tale. Arkin, Alan. 2005. 40p. (J). 19.95 *(978-1-929115-12-9(1))* Azro Pr., Inc.

Richards, Kirsten. Big Brothers Are the Best, 1 vol. Manushkin, Fran. 2012. (Fiction Picture Bks.). (ENG.). 24p. (gr. -1 — 1). 6.95 *(978-1-4048-7224-0(8))*; lib. bdg. 21.32 *(978-1-4048-7137-3(3)*, Fiction Picture Bks.) Picture Window Bks.

—Big Sisters Are the Best, 1 vol. Manushkin, Fran. 2012. (Fiction Picture Bks.). (ENG.). 24p. (gr. -1 — 1). 6.95 *(978-1-4048-7225-7(6))*; lib. bdg. 21.32 *(978-1-4048-7138-0(1)*, Fiction Picture Bks.) Picture Window Bks.

—Easter Parade! Karr, Lily. 2013. (ENG.). 24p. (J). (gr. -1-k). pap. 4.99 *(978-0-545-45824-5(2)*, Cartwheel Bks.) Scholastic, Inc.

—The Littlest Elf. Dougherty, Brandi. 2012. (ENG.). 24p. (J). (gr. -1-k). pap. 4.99 *(978-0-545-43654-0(0))* Scholastic, Inc.

—The Littlest Pilgrim. Dougherty, Brandi. 2008. (ENG.). 32p. (J). (gr. -1-k). pap. 3.99 *(978-0-545-05372-3(2)*, Cartwheel Bks.) Scholastic, Inc.

—Magical Mermaids. Trowell, Michelle. Top That Publishing Staff, ed. 2008. (Magnetic Story & Play Scene Ser.). 9p. (J). (gr. -1). *(978-1-84666-442-7(X)*, Tide Mill Pr.) Top That! Publishing PLC.

—My Little Beauty Shop: A Girly Girl Book. 2009. (ENG.). 12p. (J). bds. 6.95 *(978-1-58117-857-9(3)*, Intervisual/Piggy Toes) Bendon, Inc.

—My Pets, 1 vol. Dale, Jay. 2012. (Wonder Words Ser.). (ENG.). 32p. (gr. k-2). pap. 5.99 *(978-1-4296-8886-4(6)*, Engage Literacy) Capstone Pr., Inc.

—Tina Cocolina: Queen of the Cupcakes. Cartaya, Pablo & Howard, Martin. 2010. (ENG.). 48p. (J). (gr. -1-2). 16.99 *(978-0-375-85891-8(1))* Random Hse., Inc.

—Woodland Fairies. Ranson, Erin. Top That Publishing Staff, ed. 2008. (Magnetic Story & Play Scene Ser.). 9p. (J). (gr. -1). bds. *(978-1-84666-440-3(3)*, Tide Mill Pr.) Top That! Publishing PLC.

Richards, Kirsten & Rescek, Sanja. The Littlest Christmas Star. Dougherty, Brandi. 2010. (ENG.). 32p. (J). (gr. -1-3). pap. 3.99 *(978-0-545-21415-5(7)*, Cartwheel Bks.) Scholastic, Inc.

Richards, Kris. Rusty's Gift. Springer, Audrey. 2012. 28p. 24.95 *(978-1-4626-6589-1(6))* America Star Bks.

Richards, Kristen. The Littlest Elf. Dougherty, Brandi. 2012. (J). pap. ***(978-0-545-48978-2(4)***, WestBow Pr.) Scholastic, Inc.

Richards, Lucy. Animal Antics (with Header Card) 2004. (Cuddly Cuffs Ser.: No. 5). 10p. (J). tchr. ed. 5.95 *(978-1-58925-729-0(4))* Tiger Tales.

—Busy Bugs (W/Header Card) 2004. (Cuddly Cuffs Ser.: 6). 12p. (J). tchr. ed. 5.95 *(978-1-58925-730-6(8))* Tiger Tales.

—Jumping Jungle (W/Hang Tag) 2004. (Cuddly Cuffs Ser.: No. 7). 12p. (J). tchr. ed. 5.95 *(978-1-58925-727-6(8))* Tiger Tales.

—Jumping Jungle (W/Header Card) 2004. (Cuddly Cuffs Ser.: 7). 6p. (J). tchr. ed. 5.95 *(978-1-58925-731-3(6))* Tiger Tales.

—Mairi's Mermaid. Morpurgo, Michael. 2003. (Blue Bananas Ser.). (ENG.). 48p. (J). (gr. k-2). pap. 5.99 *(978-1-4052-0950-2(X))* Egmont Bks., Ltd. GBR. Dist: Independent Pubs. Group.

—Night Monkey, Day Monkey. Donaldson, Julia. 2012. (ENG.). 32p. (J). (gr. -1-k). pap. 10.99 *(978-0-7497-4893-7(1))* Egmont Bks., Ltd. GBR. Dist: Independent Pubs. Group.

Richards, Lucy. I Can Do It! Richards, Lucy. Hunter, Jana Novotny & Quarto Generic Staff. 2007. (ENG.). 32p. (J). (gr. -1-1). pap. 8.99 *(978-1-84507-586-6(2)*, Frances Lincoln) Quarto Publishing Group UK GBR. Dist: Hachette Bk. Group.

Richards, Lucy & Finn, Rebecca. Silly Sea (W/Hang Tag) 2004. (Cuddly Cuffs Ser.: No. 8). 10p. (J). tchr. ed. 5.95 *(978-1-58925-728-3(6))* Tiger Tales.

—Silly Sea (W/Header Card) 2004. (Cuddly Cuffs Ser.: 8). 10p. (J). tchr. ed. 5.95 *(978-1-58925-732-0(4))* Tiger Tales.

Richards, Lucy, jt. illus. see Parsons, Gary.

Richards, Tanya. Let's Bake a Family. Paulin, Chrita. Burns, Rosalyn, ed. 2009. (ENG.). 32p. (J). pap. 12.95 *(978-0-9763400-1-0(1))* Coal Under Pressure Pubns.

Richards, Theodora. Gus & Me: The Story of My Granddad & My First Guitar. Richards, Keith. 2014. (ENG.). 32p. (J). (gr. -1-1). 18.00 *(978-0-316-32065-8(X))* Little, Brown Bks. for Young Readers.

Richards, Virginia Helen. The Beatitudes Coloring & Activity Book. Halpin, D. Thomas. 2006. (J). 1.95 *(978-0-8198-2359-5(7))* Pauline Bks. & Media.

—Feast Days & Holy Days: Dias Festivos de la Iglesia. Tebo, Mary Elizabeth. 2007. 32p. (J). lab manual ed. 1.95 *(978-0-8198-2682-4(0))* Pauline Bks. & Media.

—Holy Eucharist. Halpin, D. Thomas. 2005. 32p. (J). (gr. 4-7). 1.95 *(978-0-8198-3387-7(8)*, 332-425) Pauline Bks. & Media.

—No Room for Francie. MacDonald, Maryann. 2010. 64p. (J). (gr. 1-3). pap. 6.95 *(978-0-8198-5168-0(X))* Pauline Bks. & Media.

—Spotlight on Saints! A Year of Funny Readers Theater for Today's Catholic Kids. Jenkins, Diana R. 2009. 180p. (J). (gr. 4-7). pap. 18.95 *(978-0-8198-7119-0(2))* Pauline Bks. & Media.

—Starring Francie O'Leary. MacDonald, Maryann. 2010. 64p. (J). (gr. 1-3). pap. 6.95 *(978-0-8198-7132-9(X))* Pauline Bks. & Media.

—The Stations of the Cross for Children. Dateno, Maria Grace. Pompei, Maria Teresa, tr. 2006. (SPA.). 24p. (J). 1.25 *(978-0-8198-7095-7(1))* Pauline Bks. & Media.

Richards, Virginia Helen & Dick, Regina Frances. I Pray the Rosary! Scarfi, Margaret Rose. 2005. 47p. (J). (gr. -1-3). pap. 4.95 *(978-0-8198-3689-2(3)*, 332-141) Pauline Bks. & Media.

Richards, Virginia Helen & Halpin, D. Thomas. Blessed Miguel Pro. 2011. (J). pap. 2.95 *(978-0-8198-1192-9(0))* Pauline Bks. & Media.

—My Christmas Picture Book. 2005. 14p. (J). 4.95 *(978-0-8198-4829-1(8)*, 332-220) Pauline Bks. & Media.

—The Ten Commandments. Richards, Virginia Helen. 2007. (J). 1.95 *(978-0-8198-7420-7(5))* Pauline Bks. & Media.

Richards, Virginia Helen, jt. illus. see Halpin, D. Thomas.

Richardson, Cathie. The Christmas Tin. Eismann, Sheila F. & Putz, Ali F. 2013. 40p. pap. 9.95 *(978-0-9897133-8-2(5))* Desert Sage Pr.

Richardson, Doris, jt. illus. see Byj, Charlot.

Richardson, Frederick. Best-Loved Children's Stories. 2013. (ENG.). 168p. (J). (gr. -1-2). 16.95 *(978-1-4549-0979-8(X)*, Fall River) Sterling Publishing Co., Inc.

—East O' the Sun & West O' the Moon. Thorne-Thomsen, Gudrun. 2009. 148p. pap. 8.95 *(978-1-59915-337-7(8))* Yesterday's Classics.

—Mother Goose: A Classic Collection of Children's Nursery Rhymes. 2008. (ENG.). 24p. (J). 19.95 *(978-1-58117-687-2(2)*, Intervisual/Piggy Toes) Bendon, Inc.

—My Animal Story Book: A Treasury of Sunshine Stories for Children. Maltby, Ethel H. 2004. reprint ed. pap. 15.95 *(978-1-4191-7300-4(6))* Kessinger Publishing, LLC.

—Queen Zixi of Ix: Or the Story of the Magic Cloak. Baum, L. Frank. 2011. (Dover Children's Classics Ser.). (ENG.). 256p. (J). (gr. 3-8). reprint ed. pap. 10.95 *(978-0-486-22691-0(3))* Dover Pubns., Inc.

—Reading-Literature Second Reader. Treadwell, Harriette Taylor & Free, Margaret. 2008. 200p. pap. 9.95 *(978-1-59915-266-0(5))* Yesterday's Classics.

—Reading-Literature the Primer (Yesterday's Classics) Treadwell, Harriette Taylor & Free, Margaret. 2006. (J). per. 8.95 *(978-1-59915-129-8(4))* Yesterday's Classics.

—Reading-Literature Third Reader. Treadwell, Harriette Taylor & Free, Margaret. 2008. 264p. pap. 10.95 *(978-1-59915-267-7(3))* Yesterday's Classics.

Richardson, Frederick & Becker, Charlotte. The Flying Ship: Fairy Tales from the World Over. Faulkner, Georgene. 2011. 100p. 39.95 *(978-1-258-10171-8(8))* Literary Licensing, LLC.

—The Snow Maiden: Fairy Tales from the World Over. Faulkner, Georgene. 2011. 104p. 39.95 *(978-1-258-10524-2(1))* Literary Licensing, LLC.

—Squeaky & the Scare Box: Fairy Tales from the World Over. Faulkner, Georgene. 2011. 96p. 38.95 *(978-1-258-10158-9(0))* Literary Licensing, LLC.

Richardson-Jones, Tessa. Noah's Ark. Umansky, Kaye. 2012. *(978-0-88734-071-0(7))* Players Pr., Inc.

—Y Ddihangfa Anhygoel! Llyfr Drysfa Beiblaidd. Stowell, Gordon. Davies, Aled, ed. Wyn, Delyth, tr. 2005. (WEL.). 12p. *(978-1-85994-469-1(8))* Cyhoeddiadau'r Gair.

Richardson, Kara. The Adventures of NanaCat & Her Children: Moving In. Moon, Catherine R. & Everette, Maureen C. 2003. 32p. (J). 6.95 *(978-0-930507-06-0(1))* GRAND Media, LLC.

—The Adventures of NanaCat & Her Children: Someone New. Moon, Catherine R. & Everette, Maureen C. 2004. 32p. (J). per. 6.95 *(978-0-930507-02-2(9))* GRAND Media, LLC.

—Simon & Barklee in Egypt. Scherer, Catherine W. 2006. (Another Country Calling Ser.). 65p. (J). per. 15.00 *(978-0-9714502-3-3(4)*, Explorer Media) Simon & Barklee, Inc./ExplorerMedia.

—Simon & Barklee in West Africa. Scherer, Catherine W. 2006. (Another Country Calling Ser.). 80p. (J). per. 15.00 *(978-0-9714502-4-0(2)*, Explorer Media) Simon & Barklee, Inc./ExplorerMedia.

Richardson, Kayla. Skip & Marty. Richardson, Levae. 2007. 20p. per. 24.95 *(978-1-4241-8469-9(X))* America Star Bks.

Richardson, Linda. Sea Treasure. Evans, Sally. 2004. (J). 16.95 *(978-1-59094-073-0(3)*, 1590940733, Jawbreakers for Kids) Jawbone Publishing Corp.

Richardson, Mike. Grandma's Crazy Chickens. Snyder, Susan E. 2012. 34p. (J). 14.95 *(978-0-9846428-8-5(9))* FireFly Publishings & Entertainment LLC.

Richardson, Owen. Unnaturals: The Battle Begins. Hughes, Devon. 2015. (Unnaturals Ser.: 1). (ENG.). 352p. (J). (gr. 3-7). 16.99 ***(978-0-06-225754-3(4))*** HarperCollins Pubs.

Richardson, Owen. Warriors - The New Prophecy, Vol. 1-6. Hunter, Erin. 2015. (Warriors: the New Prophecy Ser.). (ENG.). 2176p. (J). (gr. 3-7). pap. 39.99 *(978-0-06-236715-0(3))* HarperCollins Pubs.

Richardson, Owen & Douglas, Allen. Fading Echoes. Hunter, Erin. (Warriors: Omen of the Stars Ser.: 2). (ENG.). (J). (gr. 3-7). 2011. 368p. pap. 6.99 *(978-0-06-155514-5(2))*; 2010. 352p. 16.99 *(978-0-06-155512-1(6))* HarperCollins Pubs.

—The Forgotten Warrior. Hunter, Erin. (Warriors: Omen of the Stars Ser.: 5). (ENG.). (J). (gr. 3-7). 2012. 384p. pap. 6.99 *(978-0-06-155526-8(6))*; 2011. 368p. 16.99 *(978-0-06-155522-0(3))* HarperCollins Pubs.

—The Fourth Apprentice. Hunter, Erin. (Warriors: Omen of the Stars Ser.: 1). (ENG.). (J). (gr. 3-7). 2010. 368p. pap. 6.99 *(978-0-06-155511-4(8))*; 2009. 352p. 16.99 *(978-0-06-155509-1(6))* HarperCollins Pubs.

—The Last Hope. Hunter, Erin. (Warriors: Omen of the Stars Ser.: 6). (J). (gr. 3-7). 2013. (ENG.). 400p. pap. 7.99 *(978-0-06-155529-9(0))*; 2012. (ENG.). 384p. 16.99 *(978-0-06-155527-5(4))*; 2012. 384p. lib. bdg. 17.89 *(978-0-06-155528-2(2))* HarperCollins Pubs.

—Night Whispers. Hunter, Erin. (Warriors: Omen of the Stars Ser.: 3). (ENG.). (J). (gr. 3-7). 2011. 368p. pap. 6.99 *(978-0-06-155517-6(7))*; 2010. 352p. 16.99 *(978-0-06-155515-2(0))* HarperCollins Pubs.

—Sign of the Moon. Hunter, Erin. (Warriors: Omen of the Stars Ser.: 4). (J). (gr. 3-7). 2011. (ENG.). 352p. 16.99 *(978-0-06-155518-3(5))*; 2011. 352p. lib. bdg. 17.89 *(978-0-06-155520-6(7))*; No. 4. 2012. (ENG.). 368p. pap. 6.99 *(978-0-06-155521-3(5))* HarperCollins Pubs.

Richardson, Owen & Stevenson, Dave. A Dangerous Path. Hunter, Erin. 2015. (Warriors: the Prophecies Begin Ser.: 5). (ENG.). 368p. (J). (gr. 3-7). pap. 6.99 *(978-0-06-236700-6(5))* HarperCollins Pubs.

—The Darkest Hour. Hunter, Erin. 2015. (Warriors: the Prophecies Begin Ser.: 6). (ENG.). 368p. (J). (gr. 3-7). pap. 6.99 *(978-0-06-236701-3(3))* HarperCollins Pubs.

—Dawn. Hunter, Erin. 2015. (Warriors: the New Prophecy Ser.: 3). (ENG.). 400p. (J). (gr. 3-7). pap. 6.99 *(978-0-06-236704-4(8))* HarperCollins Pubs.

—Fire & Ice. Hunter, Erin. 2015. (Warriors: the Prophecies Begin Ser.: 2). (ENG.). 368p. (J). (gr. 3-7). pap. 6.99 *(978-0-06-236697-9(1))* HarperCollins Pubs.

—Forest of Secrets. Hunter, Erin. 2015. (Warriors: the Prophecies Begin Ser.: 3). (ENG.). 368p. (J). (gr. 3-7). pap. 6.99 *(978-0-06-236698-6(X))* HarperCollins Pubs.

—Into the Wild. Hunter, Erin. 2015. (Warriors: the Prophecies Begin Ser.: 1). (ENG.). 320p. (J). (gr. 3-7). pap. 6.99 *(978-0-06-236696-2(3))* HarperCollins Pubs.

—Midnight. Hunter, Erin. 2015. (Warriors: the New Prophecy Ser.: 1). (ENG.). 352p. (J). (gr. 3-7). pap. 6.99 *(978-0-06-236702-0(1))* HarperCollins Pubs.

—Moonrise. Hunter, Erin. 2015. (Warriors: the New Prophecy Ser.: 2). (ENG.). 336p. (J). (gr. 3-7). pap. 6.99 *(978-0-06-236703-7(X))* HarperCollins Pubs.

—Rising Storm. Hunter, Erin. 2015. (Warriors: the Prophecies Begin Ser.: 4). (ENG.). 368p. (J). (gr. 3-7). pap. 6.99 *(978-0-06-236699-3(8))* HarperCollins Pubs.

—Starlight. Hunter, Erin. 2015. (Warriors: the New Prophecy Ser.: 4). (ENG.). 368p. (J). (gr. 3-7). pap. 6.99 *(978-0-06-236705-1(6))* HarperCollins Pubs.

—Sunset. Hunter, Erin. 2015. (Warriors: the New Prophecy Ser.: 6). (ENG.). 352p. (J). (gr. 3-7). pap. 6.99 *(978-0-06-236707-5(2))* HarperCollins Pubs.

—Twilight. Hunter, Erin. 2015. (Warriors: the New Prophecy Ser.: 5). (ENG.). 368p. (J). (gr. 3-7). pap. 6.99 *(978-0-06-236706-8(4))* HarperCollins Pubs.

Richardson, Owen, jt. illus. see Barry, James L.

Richardson, Peter. Solving Crimes with Trace Evidence. Jeffrey, Gary. 2008. (Graphic Forensic Science Ser.). (ENG.). 48p. (gr. 5-8). per. 14.05 *(978-1-4042-1432-3(1))*; (YA). lib. bdg. 31.95 *(978-1-4042-1431-6(3))* Rosen Publishing Group, Inc., The.

Richmond, Bob, jt. illus. see Gowens, Kyle.

Richmond, Jake. The CrossRoads of Eternity RPG: Core Rule Book. 2005. per. 24.99 *(978-0-9769951-0-4(7))* Arcadiam Games.

Richmond, Jamea. Grandma's Biscuits. Little, Robert. 2004. 32p. (J). (gr. -1-7). 15.95 *(978-0-9701863-5-5(5))* Relde Publishing.

Richmond, Marianne. Big Boys Go Potty. Richmond, Marianne. 2012. (ENG.). 32p. (J). 9.99 *(978-1-4022-6659-1(6)*, Sourcebooks Jabberwocky) Sourcebooks, Inc.

—Big Girls Go Potty. Richmond, Marianne. 2012. (ENG.). 32p. (J). 9.99 *(978-1-4022-6662-1(6)*, Sourcebooks Jabberwocky) Sourcebooks, Inc.

—The Night Night Book. Richmond, Marianne. 2011. (Marianne Richmond Ser.: 0). (ENG.). 24p. (J). (gr. -1-3). bds. 7.95 *(978-1-934082-90-4(2)*, Sourcebooks Jabberwocky) Sourcebooks, Inc.

Richoll, Stephanie. Mrs. Mumford's Missing. DeLong, Lucianne. 2013. (Saloman Sawdust's Snappy Stories Ser.). (ENG.). 24p. (J). 4.99 *(978-0-9833237-5-4(5))* Krullstone Publishing, LLC.

Richter, Bernd. Listen to Alaskas Animals. Richter, Bernd. Richter, Susan. 12p. 2006. (J). act. bk. ed. 12.95 *(978-1-931353-25-0(5))*; 2003. bds. 12.95 *(978-1-931353-12-0(3))* Saddle Pal Creations, Inc.

Richter, Cheryl R., photos by. From Clay to Bricks. Taus-Bolstad, Stacy. 2003. (Start to Finish Ser.). (ENG., 24p. (gr. k-3). lib. bdg. 19.93 *(978-0-8225-4663-4(9))* Lerner Publishing Group.

Richter, Hank. Little Critters. Sio, Betsy Menson. 2003. (Books for Young Learners). (ENG.). 16p. (J). 5.75 net. *(978-1-57274-532-2(0)*, 2458, Bks. for Young Learners) Owen, Richard C. Pubs., Inc.

Richter, Jeff, photos by. White Deer: Ghost of the Forest. 2007. 96p. pap. 19.95 *(978-0-9741883-1-7(X))* Nature's Pr.

Rickenbaker, Becky Hyatt. Would You Salute? One Child's Story of the Holocaust. Steele, D. Kelley. 2006. 48p. (J). (gr. 4-6). 22.95 *(978-0-9711534-2-4(6))* Hidden Path Pubn., Inc.

Rickerty, Simon. I Am Not a Copycat! Bonwill, Ann. 2013. (ENG.). 32p. (J). (gr. -1-1). 15.99 *(978-1-4424-8053-7(X))* Simon & Schuster Children's Publishing.

—I Don't Want to Be a Pea! Bonwill, Ann. 2012. (ENG.). 32p. (J). (gr. -1-1). 14.99 *(978-1-4424-3614-5(X)*, Atheneum Bks. for Young Readers) Simon & Schuster Children's Publishing.

Rickerty, Simon. Ug-a-Lug: Four Cavemen & a Prehistoric Pencil. Lewis, Jill. 2014. (ENG.). 32p. (J). 16.99 ***(978-1-4711-1728-2(6))*** Simon & Schuster, Ltd. GBR. Dist: Simon & Schuster, Inc.

—The Yoga Ogre. Bently, Peter. 2012. (ENG.). 32p. (J). 15.99 ***(978-1-84738-902-2(3))*** Simon & Schuster, Ltd. GBR. Dist: Simon & Schuster, Inc.

Rickerty, Simon. The Crayon: A Colorful Tale about Friendship. Rickerty, Simon. 2014. (ENG.). 32p. (J). (gr. -1-2). 15.99 *(978-1-4814-0475-4(X)*, Simon & Schuster/Paula Wiseman Bks.) Simon & Schuster/Paula Wiseman Bks.

—The Peanut: A Nutty Tale about Sharing. Rickerty, Simon. 2013. (ENG.). 40p. (J). (gr. -1-2). 15.99 *(978-1-4424-8364-4(4)*, Simon & Schuster/Paula Wiseman Bks.) Simon & Schuster/Paula Wiseman Bks.

Ricketts, William. Teenage Winter Sports Stories. Owen, Frank, ed. 2011. 254p. 46.95 *(978-1-258-10167-1(X))* Literary Licensing, LLC.

Ricks, Melissa. Planting More Than Pansies: A Fable about Love. Bess, Stacey. 2003. (J). 14.95 *(978-1-57008-893-3(4)*, Shadow Mountain) Shadow Mountain Publishing.

Ricks, Sam. Don't Throw It to Mo! Adler, David A. 2015. (Mo Jackson Ser.). (ENG.). 32p. (J). (gr. 1-2). 14.99 *(978-0-670-01631-0(4))* Penguin Bks., Ltd. GBR. Dist: Penguin Random Hse., LLC.

—Eerie Elementary #1: the School Is Alive! (a Branches Book) Chabert, Jack. 2014. (Eerie Elementary Ser.: 1). (ENG.). 96p. (J). (gr. 1-3). pap. 4.99 *(978-0-545-62392-6(8))* Scholastic, Inc.

—Eerie Elementary #2: the Locker Ate Lucy! (a Branches Book) Chabert, Jack. 2014. (Eerie Elementary Ser.: 2). (ENG.). 96p. (J). (gr. 1-3). pap. 4.99 *(978-0-545-62395-7(2))* Scholastic, Inc.

—Locker Ate Lucy! Chabert, Jack. 2014. (Eerie Elementary Ser.: 2). (ENG.). 96p. (J). (gr. 1-3). 15.99 *(978-0-545-62396-4(0))* Scholastic, Inc.

—The School Is Alive! Chabert, Jack. 2014. (Eerie Elementary Ser.: 1). (ENG.). 96p. (J). (gr. 1-3). 15.99 *(978-0-545-62393-3(6))* Scholastic, Inc.

Riddell, Chris. Castle Diary: The Journal of Tobias Burgess. Platt, Richard. 2003. (ENG.). 128p. (J). (gr. 4-7). 6.99 *(978-0-7636-2164-3(1))* Candlewick Pr.

Riddell, Chris. A Great Big Cuddle: Poems for the Very Young. Rosen, Michael. 2015. (ENG.). 80p. (J). (gr. -1-2). 19.99 ***(978-0-7636-8116-6(4))*** Candlewick Pr.

Riddell, Chris. Jonathan Swift's Gulliver: Candlewick Illustrated Classic. Swift, Jonathan. 2010. (Candlewick Illustrated Classic Ser.). (ENG.). 144p. (J). (gr. 2-5). pap. 12.99 *(978-0-7636-4740-7(3))* Candlewick Pr.

—Little Bit of Winter. Stewart, Paul. 2013. (Rabbit & Hedgehog Ser.). (ENG.). 32p. (J). (gr. -1-k). pap. 9.99 *(978-0-86264-998-2(6))* Andersen Pr. GBR. Dist: Independent Pubs. Group.

—Pirate Diary: The Journal of Jake Carpenter. Platt, Richard. (ENG.). (J). (gr. 4-7). 2014. 128p. pap. 6.99 *(978-0-7636-7361-1(7))*; 2005. 64p. per. 7.99 *(978-0-7636-2865-9(4))* Candlewick Pr.

—Un Poquito de Invierno. Stewart, Paul & Stewart, Paul. 2003. (SPA.). 30p. (J). (gr. k-2). *(978-84-348-6839-7(3)*, SM30933) SM Ediciones ESP. Dist: Lectorum Pubns., Inc.

—Un Regalo de Cumpleanos. Stewart, Paul. (SPA.). 30p. (J). (gr. k-2). *(978-84-348-6840-3(7)*, SM30935) SM Ediciones ESP. Dist: Lectorum Pubns., Inc.

Riddell, Chris. The Sleeper & the Spindle. Gaiman, Neil. 2015. (ENG.). 64p. (YA). (gr. 8). 19.99 ***(978-0-06-239824-6(5))*** HarperCollins Pubs.

—The Nameless One. Stewart, Paul. 2015. (Edge Chronicles Ser.: 11). (ENG.). 368p. (J). (gr. 4-6). 8.99 ***(978-0-552-56757-2(4))*** Transworld Publishers Ltd. GBR. Dist: Independent Pubs. Group.

Riddell, Chris. Until I Met Dudley: How Everyday Things Really Work. McGough, Roger. 2012. (ENG.). 32p. (J). (gr. -1-2). pap. 8.99 *(978-1-84780-350-4(4)*, Frances Lincoln) Quarto Publishing Group UK GBR. Dist: Hachette Bk. Group.

Riddell, Chris. Counting Sheep: A Bedtime Adventure! Riddell, Chris. Cave, Kathryn. 2013. (ENG.). 32p. (J). (gr. -1-2). pap. 8.99 *(978-1-84780-480-8(2)*, Frances Lincoln) Quarto Publishing Group UK GBR. Dist: Littlehampton Bk Services, Ltd.

—Dragon's Hoard. Riddell, Chris. Stewart, Paul. 2014. (Knight's Story Ser.: 3). (ENG.). 144p. (J). (gr. 2-6). pap. 13.99 *(978-1-4814-2890-3(X)*, Atheneum Bks. for Young Readers) Simon & Schuster Children's Publishing.

—Joust of Honor. Riddell, Chris. Stewart, Paul. 2014. (Knight's Story Ser.: 2). (ENG.). 144p. (J). (gr. 2-6). pap. 13.99 *(978-1-4814-2889-7(6)*, Atheneum Bks. for Young Readers) Simon & Schuster Children's Publishing.

—Lake of Skulls. Riddell, Chris. Stewart, Paul. 2014. (Knight's Story Ser.: 1). (ENG.). 144p. (J). (gr. 2-6). pap. 13.99 *(978-1-4814-2888-0(8)*, Atheneum Bks. for Young Readers) Simon & Schuster Children's Publishing.

—Mr Underbed. Riddell, Chris. (ENG.). 32p. (J). (gr. -1-k). 2012. pap. 10.99 *(978-1-84270-942-9(9))*; 2010. 19.99 *(978-1-84270-821-7(X))* Andersen Pr. GBR. Dist: Independent Pubs. Group.

—Ottoline & the Yellow Cat. Riddell, Chris. (Ottoline Ser.). 176p. (J). (gr. 3-7). 2009. pap. 8.99 *(978-0-06-144881-2(8))*; 2008. (ENG.). 12.99 *(978-0-06-144879-9(6))* HarperCollins Pubs.

—Ottoline Goes to School. Riddell, Chris. 2009. (Ottoline Ser.). 176p. (J). (gr. 3-7). 12.99 *(978-0-06-144900-0(8))* HarperCollins Pubs.

Riddle, Scott. Arctic Mall Adventure. Stratton, Bart. 2010. 28p. pap. 15.95 *(978-1-60844-558-5(5))* Dog Ear Publishing, LLC.

Riddle, Sue. Gotta Go! Gotta Go! Swope, Sam. 2004. (ENG.). 32p. (J). (gr. -1-1). reprint ed. pap. 7.99 *(978-0-374-42786-3(0))* Square Fish.

Riddle, Tohby. The Word Snoop. Dubosarsky, Ursula. 2009. (ENG.). 272p. (J). (gr. 5-18). 16.99 *(978-0-8037-3406-7(9)*, Dial) Penguin Publishing Group.

Riddle, Tohby. Irving the Magician. Riddle, Tohby. 2005. 32p. (J). *(978-0-670-89649-3(7))* Penguin Publishing Group.

Ridgell, Earl W., Jr. I Like Birthdays! Interactive Book about Me. Bye, K. A. 2008. 30p. (J). (gr. -1-3). 13.95 *(978-1-934490-02-0(4))* Boys Town Pr.

Ridges, Kedrick. Lehi & His Dream. Bruderer, Brooke. 2005. (J). bds. 10.95 *(978-1-58958-096-1(6))* Kofford, Greg Books, Inc.

Ridley, Alice. Lyra & the Adventure of the Flying Fish. Emina, Peter. 2013. (ENG.). 48p. (J). (gr. k-4). 17.99 *(978-1-907912-01-6(0))* Phoenix Yard Bks. GBR. Dist: Independent Pubs. Group.

Ridley, Sharon. My Wildflower Friends. Phillips, Marilyn, photos by. 2006. (J). *(978-0-9786168-0-9(4))* Rio Wildflower Pubns.

Riecks Goss, Carol. The Adventures of Giggles & Owen: A True Story. Holdman, Shirley Terrill. 2010. 26p. pap. 14.95 *(978-1-60844-490-8(2))* Dog Ear Publishing, LLC.

Rieder, Floor. The Mystery of Life: How Nothing Became Everything. Schutten, Jan Paul. Watkinson, Laura, tr. from DUT. 2015. (ENG.). 240p. (YA). (gr. 5-9). 15.99 ***(978-1-58270-525-5(9)***, Simon & Schuster/Paula Wiseman Bks.) Simon & Schuster/Paula Wiseman Bks.

Rieger, Linda. A Good Heart. Rieger, Linda. 2007. 20p. (J). *(978-0-9779427-4-9(0))* Pathways into Science.

Riegle, Janet. Piping Plover Summer. Riegle, Janet. 2008. 32p. (J). (gr. 1-2). 18.95 *(978-0-9794202-9-0(6))*; pap. 12.95 *(978-0-9801045-4-7(8))* Raven Productions, Inc.

Ries, Alex. Zoobots: Wild Robots Inspired by Real Animals, 0 vols. Kids Can Press Staff & Becker, Helaine. 2014. (ENG.). 32p. (J). 17.95 *(978-1-55453-971-0(4))* Kids Can Pr., Ltd. CAN. Dist: Univ. of Toronto Pr.

Riette, Susanne. Rockafella Jones & the Hidden Treasure. Conroe, Lindy. 2011. 108p. (J). pap. 10.95 *(978-1-935199-00-7(5))* Blue Mustang Pr.

Rietz, Kathleen. ABECE de Yoga para Ninos. Power, Teresa Anne. 2011. 32p. (J). pap. 8.95 *(978-0-9822587-4-3(7))* Stafford House.

—El árbol Que Trepó el Oso, 1 vol. Berkes, Marianne. 2012. (SPA.). 32p. (J). (gr. -1-3). 17.95 (978-1-60718-679-3(9)) Arbordale Publishing.

—Champ's Story: Dogs Get Cancer Too!, 1 vol. North, Sherry. 2010. (ENG.). 32p. (J). (gr. -1-4). 16.95 (978-1-60718-077-7(4)); pap. 8.95 (978-1-60718-088-3(X)) Arbordale Publishing.

—Desert Baths, 1 vol. Pattison, Darcy. 2012. (SPA & ENG.). 32p. (J). (gr. -1-3). 17.95 (978-1-60718-525-3(3)); pap. 9.95 (978-1-60718-534-5(2)) Arbordale Publishing.

—La Historia de Campeona: ¡a Los Perros También les Da Cáncer!, 1 vol. North, Sherry. 2012. (SPA & ENG.). 32p. (J). (gr. -1-4). 17.95 (978-1-60718-681-6(0)) Arbordale Publishing.

—Las Duchas en el Desierto, 1 vol. Pattison, Darcy. 2012. (SPA & ENG.). 32p. (J). (gr. -1-3). 17.95 (978-1-60718-676-2(4)) Arbordale Publishing.

—Little Black Ant on Park Street. Halfmann, Janet. 2009. (ENG.). 32p. 9.95 (978-1-60727-006-5(4)); 10.95 (978-1-60727-008-9(0)); 19.95 (978-1-60727-005-8(6)); (J). pap. 6.95 (978-1-60727-003-4(X)) Soundprints.

—Prairie Storms, 1 vol. Pattison, Darcy. 2011. (ENG.). 32p. (J). (gr. -1-4). 16.95 (978-1-60718-129-3(0)); pap. 8.95 (978-1-60718-139-2(8)) Arbordale Publishing.

—The Tree That Bear Climbed, 1 vol. Berkes, Marianne. 32p. (J). (gr. -1-3). 2014. (SPA.). pap. 9.95 (978-1-62855-426-7(6)); 2012. (ENG & SPA.). 17.95 (978-1-60718-528-4(8)); 2012. (ENG & SPA.). pap. 9.95 (978-1-60718-537-6(7)) Arbordale Publishing.

Rifa, Fina. Barcelona, Tell Us about Gaudi. Cormand, Bernat. Kliczkowski, H., ed. 80p. (978-84-89439-29-0(X)) A. Asppan, S.L. Distribuidora Internacional de Libros y Revistas.

Rife, Ann Hollis. Daddy's Love. Leland, Debbie. ed. 2006. (J). 15.95 (978-0-9667086-4-6(4)) Wildflower Run.

Riffey, Rebecca. Got Dementia? Pritchard, Heather. 2012. (Incredible Kid Ser.: Vol. 2). (ENG.). 16p. (J). (gr. -1-3). pap. 8.99 (978-1-62147-635-1(9)) Tate Publishing & Enterprises, LLC.

Rift. The Wise Little Butterfly, 1 vol. Rift. 2009. 39p. pap. 19.95 (978-1-61546-493-7(X)) PublishAmerica, Inc.

Rigano, Giovanni. The Arctic Incident. Colfer, Eoin & Donkin, Andrew. 2nd ed. 2009. (ENG.). 128p. (J). (gr. 5-9). pap. 12.99 (978-1-4231-1407-9(8)) Hyperion Pr.

Rigano, Giovanni & Lamanna, Paolo. Artemis Fowl. Colfer, Eoin & Donkin, Andrew. 2007. (Artemis Fowl Ser.). (ENG.). 112p. (J). (gr. 5-9). 18.99 (978-0-7868-4881-2(2)); pap. 12.99 (978-0-7868-4882-9(0)) Hyperion Pr.

—Artemis Fowl the Opal Deception Graphic Novel. Colfer, Eoin & Donkin, Andrew. 2014. (Artemis Fowl Ser.: 4). (ENG.). 112p. (J). (gr. 5-9). pap. 12.99 (978-1-4231-4549-3(6)) Hyperion Bks. for Children.

—The Eternity Code. Colfer, Eoin & Donkin, Andrew. 2013. (Artemis Fowl Ser.: 3). (ENG.). 112p. (J). (gr. 5-9). 19.99 (978-1-4231-4527-1(5)) Hyperion Pr.

—Eternity Code. Colfer, Eoin & Donkin, Andrew. 2013. (Artemis Fowl Ser.: 3). (ENG.). 112p. (J). (gr. 5-9). pap. 12.99 (978-1-4231-4577-6(1)) Hyperion Pr.

—The Supernaturalist. Colfer, Eoin & Donkin, Andrew. 2012. (Supernaturalist Ser.). (ENG.). 128p. (J). (gr. 5-9). 19.99 (978-0-7868-4879-9(0)); pap. 9.99 (978-0-7868-4880-5(4)) Hyperion Pr.

Rigaudie, Mylene. Hello, I Am Lily from New York City. Husar, Jaco & Husar, Stephane. 2014. (AV2 Fiction Readalong Ser.: Vol. 129). (ENG.). 32p. (J). (gr. -1-3). lib. bdg. 34.28 (978-1-4896-2259-4(4), AV2 by Weigl) Weigl Pubs., Inc.

—Navani from Delhi. Benoit-Renard, Anne. 2014. (AV2 Fiction Readalong Ser.: Vol. 133). (ENG.). 32p. (J). (gr. -1-3). lib. bdg. 34.28 (978-1-4896-2271-6(3), AV2 by Weigl) Weigl Pubs., Inc.

Rigby, Deborah. The Mermaid & the Star. Baxter, Nicola. 2014. 14p. (J). bds. (978-1-84322-907-0(2), Armadillo) Anness Publishing.

—The Noisy Parrot. Scott, Janine. 2009. (Treasure Chest Readers Ser.). 24p. (J). (gr. -1-2). pap. 8.15 (978-1-60754-680-1(9)); lib. bdg. 22.60 (978-1-60754-679-5(5)) Windmill Bks.

—Stop That Stew! Mahy, Margaret. 2009. (Treasure Chest Readers Ser.). 24p. (J). (gr. -1-2). pap. 8.15 (978-1-60754-683-2(3)); lib. bdg. 22.60 (978-1-60754-682-5(5)) Windmill Bks.

Riger, Bob. Riders of the Pony Express. Moody, Ralph. 2004. (ENG.). 184p. pap. 14.95 (978-0-8032-8305-3(9), MOORIX, Bison Bks.) Univ. of Nebraska Pr.

Riggio, Anita. Secret Signs: An Escape Through the Underground Railroad. Riggio, Anita. 2003. (ENG.). 32p. (J). (gr. -1-3). pap. 11.95 (978-1-59078-072-5(8)) Boyds Mills Pr.

Riggs, Jenna. Finding Fairyland: A Picture Riddle Book. Engelman Berner, Beth. 2005. 12p. (J). 9.95 (978-1-58117-386-4(5), Intervisual/Piggy Toes) Bendon, Inc.

—What's in My Dresser?, 1 vol. Rizzi, Kathleen. 2013. (ENG.). 32p. (J). bds. 7.99 (978-1-59572-165-5(7)) Star Bright Bks., Inc.

Riggs, Ransom. Hollow City. Riggs, Ransom. 2014. (ENG.). 352p. (YA). (gr. 9). 18.99 (978-1-59474-612-3(5)) Quirk Bks.

Riggs, Ransom. Hollow City. Riggs, Ransom. 2015. lib. bdg. 22.10 (978-0-606-36394-5(7)) Turtleback Bks.

Right, Mike. Kid Pickers: How to Turn Junk into Treasure. Wolfe, Mike & Sprengelmeyer, Lily. 2013. (ENG.). 128p. (J). (gr. 2-7). 19.99 (978-1-250-00848-0(4)); pap. 14.99 (978-1-250-01930-1(3)) Feiwel & Friends.

Righter, Kate. Perry the Great Leaping Bullfrog of Orleans Parish. Sibley, Paul & Sibley, Paul. 2011. (ENG.). 24p. pap. 9.99 (978-1-4679-1383-6(9)) CreateSpace Independent Publishing Platform.

Riglietti, Serena. The Boy & the Spell. Ravel, Maurice et al. 2007. (Musical Stories Ser.). (ENG.). 36p. (J). (gr. 2-4). 16.95 (978-0-9646010-4-8(4)) Pumpkin Hse., Ltd.

—Fauna Mayor. d'Aquino, Alfonso. 2005. (SPA.). (J). (gr. k-2). pap. 10.95 (978-968-494-100-7(5)) Centro de Informacion y Desarrollo de la Comunicacion y la Literatura MEX. Dist: Iaconi, Mariuccia Bk. Imports.

—How Big Is a Million? Milbourne, Anna. Doherty, Gillian, ed. 2008. (Picture Books Ser.). 32p. (J). (gr. -1-3). 10.99 (978-0-7945-1924-7(5), Usborne) EDC Publishing.

—How Big Is a Million? Milbourne, Anna. 2008. (J). (978-0-545-11519-3(1)) Scholastic, Inc.

—How Deep Is the Sea? Milbourne, Anna. 2010. (Picture Bks). 24p. (J). 10.99 (978-0-7945-2311-4(0)) EDC Publishing.

—How High Is the Sky? Milbourne, Anna. 2009. (Picture Bks). 24p. (J). (gr. -1). 10.99 (978-0-7945-2273-5(4), Usborne) EDC Publishing.

—The Magician's Boy. Cooper, Susan. 2006. (ENG.). 112p. (J). (gr. 3-7). pap. 9.99 (978-1-4169-1555-3(9), McElderry, Margaret K. Bks.) McElderry, Margaret K. Bks.

—Under the Ground. Milbourne, Anna. 2006. 24p. (J). (gr. -1-3). 9.99 (978-0-7945-1264-4(X), Usborne) EDC Publishing.

Rigo, L. Little Bunny. 2012. (Mini Look at Me Bks.). (ENG.). 10p. (J). bds. 4.99 (978-0-7641-6509-2(7)) Barron's Educational Series, Inc.

—Little Dinosaur. (Mini Look at Me Bks.). (ENG.). 10p. (J). (gr. -1 — 1). 2014. bds. 4.99 (978-0-7641-6730-0(8)); 2010. bds. 7.99 (978-0-7641-6356-2(6)) Barron's Educational Series, Inc.

—Little Duckling. (Mini Look at Me Bks.). 10p. (J). 2012. (ENG.). bds. 4.99 (978-0-7641-6510-8(0)); 2011. bds. 7.99 (978-0-7641-6425-5(2)) Barron's Educational Series, Inc.

—Little Elephant. 2011. (Look at Me Bks.). 10p. (J). bds. 7.99 (978-0-7641-6426-2(0)) Barron's Educational Series, Inc.

—Little Lamb. (Mini Look at Me Bks.). 10p. (J). 2012. (ENG.). bds. 4.99 (978-0-7641-6511-5(9)); 2011. (gr. -1). bds. 7.99 (978-0-7641-6427-9(9)) Barron's Educational Series, Inc.

—Little Monkey. 2011. (Look at Me Bks.). 10p. (J). bds. 7.99 (978-0-7641-6428-6(7)) Barron's Educational Series, Inc.

—Little Panda. 2010. (Look at Me Bks.). (ENG.). 10p. (J). (gr. -1-k). 7.99 (978-0-7641-6339-5(6)) Barron's Educational Series, Inc.

—Little Panda Bear. 2014. (Mini Look at Me Bks.). (ENG.). 10p. (J). (gr. -1 — 1). bds. 4.99 (978-0-7641-6739-3(1)) Barron's Educational Series, Inc.

—Little Penguin. 2010. (Look at Me Bks.). (ENG.). 10p. (J). (gr. -1-k). bds. 7.99 (978-0-7641-6353-1(1)) Barron's Educational Series, Inc.

—Little Pig. 2010. (Look at Me Bks.). (ENG.). 10p. (J). (gr. -1-k). bds. 7.99 (978-0-7641-6355-5(8)) Barron's Educational Series, Inc.

—Little Polar Bear. 2010. (Look at Me Bks.). (ENG.). 10p. (J). (gr. -1-k). bds. 7.99 (978-0-7641-6325-8(6)) Barron's Educational Series, Inc.

—Little Pony. 2014. (Mini Look at Me Bks.). (ENG.). 10p. (J). (gr. -1 — 1). bds. 4.99 (978-0-7641-6733-1(2)) Barron's Educational Series, Inc.

—Little Puppy. 2012. (Mini Look at Me Bks.). (ENG.). 10p. (J). bds. 4.99 (978-0-7641-6512-2(7)) Barron's Educational Series, Inc.

—Little Reindeer. 2014. (Mini People Shape Bks.). (ENG.). 10p. (J). (gr. -1-2). bds. 4.99 (978-0-7641-6736-2(7)) Barron's Educational Series, Inc.

Rigo, L. Little Penguin. Rigo, L. 2014. (Mini Look at Me Bks.). (ENG.). 10p. (J). (gr. -1 — 1). bds. 4.99 (978-0-7641-6731-7(6)) Barron's Educational Series, Inc.

Rigo, L. & Caviezel, Giovanni. Little Bunny. 2010. (Look at Me Bks.). (ENG.). 10p. (J). (gr. -1-k). bds. 7.99 (978-0-7641-6322-7(1)) Barron's Educational Series, Inc.

—Little Puppy. 2010. (Look at Me Bks.). (ENG.). 10p. (J). (gr. -1-k). bds. 7.99 (978-0-7641-6324-1(8)) Barron's Educational Series, Inc.

—Little Tiger. 2010. (Look at Me Bks.). (ENG.). 10p. (J). (gr. -1-k). bds. 7.99 (978-0-7641-6326-5(4)) Barron's Educational Series, Inc.

Rigo, L. & Pagnoni, Roberta. Little Elf. 2010. (ENG.). 10p. (J). (gr. -1-2). bds. 7.99 (978-0-7641-6380-7(9)) Barron's Educational Series, Inc.

Rigo, L., jt. illus. see Barron's Educational Series Staff.

Rigo, Laura. A Day at the Firehouse. Caviezel, Giovanni. 2012. (Day At... Bks.). (ENG.). 10p. (J). (gr. -1-k). bds. 6.99 (978-0-7641-6548-1(8)) Barron's Educational Series, Inc.

—Easter Egg Party. Lorini, Andrea. 2014. (ENG.). 8p. (J). (gr. -1 — 1). bds. 6.99 (978-0-7641-6716-4(2)) Barron's Educational Series, Inc.

—Santa's Toyshop. Caviezel, Giovanni. 2012. (ENG.). 10p. (J). (gr. -1-k). bds. 6.99 (978-0-7641-6546-7(1)) Barron's Educational Series, Inc.

Rigo, Laura, jt. illus. see Pagnoni, Roberta.

Rigol, Francesc. Dan & Din Learn Colors. 2009. (Learning with Dan & Din Ser.). 12p. (J). (gr. -1-k). bds. 11.40 (978-1-60754-401-2(6)) Windmill Bks.

—Dan & Din Learn Numbers. 2009. (Learning with Dan & Din Ser.). 12p. (J). (gr. -1-k). bds. 11.40 (978-1-60754-402-9(4)) Windmill Bks.

—Dan & Din Learn Opposites. 2009. (Learning with Dan & Din Ser.). 12p. (J). (gr. -1-k). bds. 11.40 (978-1-60754-403-6(2)) Windmill Bks.

—Dan & Din Learn Shapes. 2009. (Learning with Dan & Din Ser.). 12p. (J). (gr. -1-k). bds. 11.40 (978-1-60754-400-5(8)) Windmill Bks.

—Pooh's Leaf Pile. Gaines, Isabel & Milne, A. A. 2012. (J). (978-1-4351-4190-2(3)) Disney Pr.

Riley, David. Freedom Train. Coleman, Evelyn. 2008. (ENG.). 160p. (J). (gr. 3-7). 17.99 (978-0-689-84716-5(5), McElderry, Margaret K. Bks.) McElderry, Margaret K. Bks.

—President Lincoln, Willie Kettles, & the Telegraph Machine. Figley, Marty Rhodes. 2010. (History Speaks: Picture Books Plus Reader's Theater Ser.). (ENG.). 48p. (gr. 2-4). pap. 9.95 (978-0-7613-6131-2(6)) Lerner Publishing Group.

Riley, Jon. Room 13 & Inside the Worm. Swindells, Robert. 2008. (ENG.). 352p. (YA). (gr. 7). pap. 12.99 (978-0-552-55591-3(6)) Transworld Publishers Ltd. GBR. Dist: Independent Pubs. Group.

—Timesnatch. Swindells, Robert. 2008. (ENG.). 176p. (YA). (gr. 7). pap. 11.99 (978-0-552-55592-0(4), Corgi) Transworld Publishers Ltd. GBR. Dist: Independent Pubs. Group.

Riley, Kellee. Before the Beginning Began. Cavalli, Frank. 2006. 56p. (J). (gr. -1-3). 19.95 (978-0-9766662-0-2(0)) Star Dome Publishing, LLC.

—Behold the Power of Gargamel! Gallo, Tina. 2011. (Smurfs Movie Ser.). (ENG.). 24p. (J). (gr. -1-3). pap. 6.99 (978-1-4424-2395-4(1), Simon Spotlight) Simon Spotlight.

—The Big Boat Race! (Team Umizoomi) Golden Books. 2012. (Hologramatic Sticker Book Ser.). (ENG.). 48p. (J). (gr. -1-2). pap. 3.99 (978-0-375-86215-1(3), Golden Bks.) Random Hse. Children's Bks.

—A Boo-Tiful Halloween! Man-Kong, Mary. 2013. (Glow-In-the-Dark Pictureback Ser.). (ENG.). 16p. (J). (gr. -1-2). 4.99 (978-0-449-81860-2(8), Random Hse. Bks. for Young Readers) Random Hse. Children's Bks.

—An Egg-Cellent Easter! (Barbie) Frazer, Rebecca. 2012. (Pictureback Series.). (ENG.). 16p. (J). (gr. -1-2). pap. 3.99 (978-0-307-93025-5(4), Random Hse. Bks. for Young Readers) Random Hse. Children's Bks.

Riley, Kellee, et al. Find the Dinosaurs! (Team Umizoomi) Golden Books Staff. 2012. (Little Golden Book Ser.). (ENG.). 24p. (J). (gr. -1-2). 3.99 (978-0-307-92995-2(7), Golden Bks.) Random Hse., Inc.

Riley, Kellee. Happy Birthday, Barbie! Random House & Man-Kong, Mary. 2014. (Pictureback Series.). (ENG.). 24p. (J). (gr. -1-2). 5.99 (978-0-385-37320-3(1), Random Hse. Bks. for Young Readers) Random Hse. Children's Bks.

—Happy Halloween, Kai-lan! A Lift-the-Flap Story. 2010. (Ni Hao, Kai-Lan Ser.). (ENG.). 16p. (J). pap. 6.99 (978-1-4424-0178-5(8), Simon Spotlight/Nickelodeon) Simon Spotlight/Nickelodeon.

—I Can Be... A Zoo Vet/I Can Be... A Cheerleader. Random House Staff. 2011. (Deluxe Pictureback Ser.). (ENG.). 32p. (J). (gr. -1-2). pap. 4.99 (978-0-375-87265-5(5), Random Hse. Bks. for Young Readers) Random Hse. Children's Bks.

—I Can Be President. Webster, Christy. 2012. (Step into Reading Ser.). (ENG.). 32p. (J). (gr. -1-1). pap. 3.99 (978-0-307-93122-1(6), Random Hse. Bks. for Young Readers) Random Hse. Children's Bks.

—I Can Be President. Webster, Christy. ed. 2012. (Barbie Step into Reading Ser.). lib. bdg. 13.55 (978-0-606-26549-2(X), Turtleback) Turtleback Bks.

—I Only Have Eye for You. Nuhfer, Heather. 2014. (Monster High Ser.). (ENG.). 112p. (J). (gr. 3-7). pap. 10.00 (978-0-316-28286-4(3)) Little, Brown Bks. for Young Readers.

—Little Bunny Bedtime. Golden Books Staff. 2010. (Super Color with Stickers Ser.). (ENG.). 96p. (J). (gr. -1-2). pap. 3.99 (978-0-375-85780-5(X), Golden Bks.) Random Hse. Children's Bks.

—Penny & Pepper. Betancourt, Jeanne. 2011. (Scholastic Reader Level 3 Ser.). (ENG.). 48p. (J). (gr. 1-4). pap. 3.99 (978-0-545-11508-7(6), Cartwheel Bks.) Scholastic, Inc.

—Sisters on Safari (Barbie) Random House. 2014. (Pictureback Series.). (ENG.). 16p. (J). (gr. -1-2). 4.99 (978-0-385-37410-1(0), Random Hse. Bks. for Young Readers) Random Hse. Children's Bks.

—Tolee's Rhyme Time. 2009. (Ni Hao, Kai-Lan Ser.). (ENG.). 24p. (J). pap. 3.99 (978-1-4169-9024-6(0), Simon Spotlight/Nickelodeon) Simon Spotlight/Nickelodeon.

—Wedding Party! (Barbie) Man-Kong, Mary. 2013. (Pictureback Series.). (ENG.). 16p. (J). (gr. -1-2). pap. 3.99 (978-0-307-93116-0(1), Random Hse. Bks. for Young Readers) Random Hse. Children's Bks.

Riley, Kellee, jt. illus. see Golden Books Staff.

Riley, Kellee, jt. illus. see Random House Staff.

Riley, Kellee, jt. illus. see Spaziante, Patrick.

Riley, Kevin. Inky Winky Spider 1,2,3,4. Makeeff, Cyndi Sue. 2006. 32p. (J). pap. 7.99 (978-0-9778310-1-2(9)) New Vision Entertainment, LLC.

—Inky Winky Spider ABC's. Makeeff, Cyndi Sue. 2006. 32p. (J). pap. 7.99 (978-0-9778310-0-5(0)) New Vision Entertainment, LLC.

—Inky Winky Spider Colors by the Bay. Makeeff, Cyndi Sue. 2006. 32p. (J). pap. 7.99 (978-0-9778310-2-9(7)) New Vision Entertainment, LLC.

Riley, Larry. Kiwi Phonics: Level 1: Basic Vowels & Consonants, 15 vols. Deighton-O'Flynn, Heather et al. 2004. 141p. 45.00 (978-1-877276-69-9(3)) Otago University Pr. NZL. Dist: Independent Pubs. Group.

—Kiwi Phonics: Level 2: Consonant Clusters, 10 vols. Deighton-O'Flynn, Heather et al. 2004. 181p. 45.00 (978-1-877276-70-5(7)) Otago University Pr. NZL. Dist: Independent Pubs. Group.

—Kiwi Phonics: Level 3: Complex Code, 20 vols. Deighton-O'Flynn, Heather et al. 2005. 280p. 85.00 (978-1-877276-71-2(5)) Otago University Pr. NZL. Dist: Independent Pubs. Group.

Riley, Melanie Ellis. Catie the Caterpillar: A Story to Help Break the Silence of Sexual Abuse. Schamburg, Tracy M. 2006. 31p. (J). (gr. -1). pap. 6.95 (978-0-7648-1434-1(6)) Liguori Pubns.

Riley, Scott, jt. illus. see Darroch, Jane.

Riley, Terry. African Myths. Jeffrey, Gary & Newport, Kate. 2006. (Graphic Mythology Ser.). (ENG.). 48p. (J). (gr. 4-7). lib. bdg. 31.95 (978-1-4042-0798-1(8)) Rosen Publishing Group, Inc., The.

—Allosaurus: The Strange Lizard. Shone, Rob. 2009. (Graphic Dinosaurs Ser.). (ENG.). 32p. (J). pap. 12.30 (978-1-4358-8592-9(9)); (gr. 2-5). 26.50 (978-1-4358-8588-2(0)) Rosen Publishing Group, Inc., The. (PowerKids Pr.).

—Autopsies: Pathologists at Work. Jeffrey, Gary. 2008. (Graphic Forensic Science Ser.). (ENG.). 48p. (gr. 5-8). per. 14.05 (978-1-4042-1447-7(X)); (YA). lib. bdg. 31.95 (978-1-4042-1446-0(1)) Rosen Publishing Group, Inc., The.

—Bob Marley: The Life of a Musical Legend. Jeffrey, Gary. 2007. (Graphic Nonfiction Biographies Ser.). (ENG.). 48p. (YA). (gr. 4-7). lib. bdg. 31.95 (978-1-4042-0854-4(2)) Rosen Publishing Group, Inc., The.

—Brachiosaurus: The Long-Limbed Dinosaur. Shone, Rob. 2009. (Graphic Dinosaurs Ser.). (ENG.). 32p. (J). pap. 12.30 (978-1-4358-8600-1(3)); (gr. 2-5). 26.50 (978-1-4358-8589-9(9)) Rosen Publishing Group, Inc., The. (PowerKids Pr.).

—Defying Death at Sea. Jeffrey, Gary. 2010. (Graphic Survival Stories Ser.). 48p. (YA). 58.50 (978-1-61532-897-0(1)); (ENG.). pap. 14.05 (978-1-61532-863-5(7)); (gr. 5-8). 31.95 (978-1-4358-3530-6(1)) Rosen Publishing Group, Inc., The. (Rosen Reference).

—Elasmosaurus: The Long-Necked Swimmer. Jeffrey, Gary. (Graphic Dinosaurs Ser.). (ENG.). 32p. 2009. (gr. 2-5). pap. 12.30 (978-1-4042-7715-1(3), PowerKids Pr.); 2008. (J). 50.50 (978-1-61532-138-4(1), PowerKids Pr.); 2008. (J). (gr. 2-5). lib. bdg. 26.50 (978-1-4358-2505-5(5)) Rosen Publishing Group, Inc., The.

—The Explorations of Lewis & Clark. Jeffrey, Gary. 2012. (Graphic History of the American West Ser.). (ENG.). 24p. (J). (gr. 3-8). pap. 8.15 (978-1-4339-6737-5(5), Gareth Stevens Learning Library); (gr. 4-7). lib. bdg. 23.95 (978-1-4339-6735-1(9)) Stevens, Gareth Publishing LLLP.

—Ghosts & Poltergeists: Stories of the Supernatural. West, David. 2006. (Graphic Mysteries Ser.). (ENG.). 48p. (YA). (gr. 5-8). lib. bdg. 31.95 (978-1-4042-0608-3(6)) Rosen Publishing Group, Inc., The.

—Giganotosaurus: The Giant Southern Lizard. Shone, Rob. (Graphic Dinosaurs Ser.). (ENG.). 32p. 2009. (gr. 2-5). pap. 12.30 (978-1-4042-7712-0(9), PowerKids Pr.); 2008. (J). 50.50 (978-1-61532-135-3(7), PowerKids Pr.); 2008. (J). (gr. 2-5). lib. bdg. 26.50 (978-1-4358-2502-4(0)) Rosen Publishing Group, Inc., The.

—Hadrosaurus: The Duck-Billed Dinosaur. Shone, Rob. 2009. (Graphic Dinosaurs Ser.). (ENG.). 32p. (J). pap. 12.30 (978-1-4358-8598-1(8)); (gr. 2-5). 26.50 (978-1-4358-8591-2(0)) Rosen Publishing Group, Inc., The. (PowerKids Pr.).

—I, Houdini. Banks, Lynne Reid. 2003. (ENG.). 126p. (J). (gr. 3-7). pap. 5.99 (978-0-440-41924-2(7), Yearling) Random Hse. Children's Bks.

—Medical Breakthroughs. Jeffrey, Gary. 2008. (Graphic Discoveries Ser.). (ENG.). 48p. (YA). (gr. 5-9). lib. bdg. 31.95 (978-1-4042-1086-8(5)) Rosen Publishing Group, Inc., The.

—Oprah Winfrey: The Life of a Media Superstar. Jeffrey, Gary. 2007. (Graphic Nonfiction Biographies Ser.). (ENG.). 48p. (YA). (gr. 4-7). lib. bdg. 31.95 (978-1-4042-0862-9(3)) Rosen Publishing Group, Inc., The.

—The Pony Express. Jeffrey, Gary. 2012. (Graphic History of the American West Ser.). (ENG.). 24p. (J). (gr. 3-8). pap. 8.15 (978-1-4339-6749-8(9), Gareth Stevens Learning Library); (gr. 4-7). lib. bdg. 23.95 (978-1-4339-6747-4(2)) Stevens, Gareth Publishing LLLP.

—Secret Agents. Jeffrey, Gary. 2008. (Graphic Careers Ser.). (ENG.). 48p. (gr. 5-8). per. 14.05 (978-1-4042-1465-1(8)); (YA). lib. bdg. 31.95 (978-1-4042-1464-4(X)) Rosen Publishing Group, Inc., The.

—Tornadoes & Superstorms. Jeffrey, Gary. 2007. (Graphic Natural Disasters Ser.). (ENG.). 48p. (gr. 5-8). pap. 14.05 (978-1-4042-1985-4(4)); (J). lib. bdg. 31.95 (978-1-4042-1993-9(5)) Rosen Publishing Group, Inc., The.

—Volcanoes. Shone, Rob. 2007. (Graphic Natural Disasters Ser.). (ENG.). 48p. (J). (gr. 5-9). lib. bdg. 31.95 (978-1-4042-1988-5(9)) Rosen Publishing Group, Inc., The.

Riley, Terry & Ball, Geoff. Pteranodon: Giant of the Sky. West, David. 2007. (Graphic Dinosaurs Ser.). (ENG.). 32p. (J). (gr. 2-5). lib. bdg. 26.50 (978-1-4042-3895-4(6)) Rosen Publishing Group, Inc., The.

—Triceratops: The Three Horned Dinosaur. Shone, Rob. 2007. (Graphic Dinosaurs Ser.). (ENG.). 32p. (J). (gr. 2-5). lib. bdg. 26.50 (978-1-4042-3896-1(4)) Rosen Publishing Group, Inc., The.

Riley, Terry, jt. illus. see Jeffrey, Gary.

Riley-Webb, Charlotte. Around Our Way on Neighbors' Day. Brown, Tameka Fryer. 2010. (ENG.). 32p. (J). (gr. -1-3). 16.95 (978-0-8109-8971-9(9), Abrams Bks. for Young Readers) Abrams.

—Rent Party Jazz. Miller, William. (ENG.). 32p. (J). 2013. (gr. 1-5). 16.95 (978-1-58430-025-0(6)); 2011. pap. 8.95 (978-1-60060-344-0(0)) Lee & Low Bks., Inc.

—Seed Magic, 1 vol. Buchanan, Jane. 2012. (ENG.). 32p. (J). 16.95 (978-1-56145-622-2(5)) Peachtree Pubs.

—Sweet Potato Pie. Lindsey, Kathleen D. 2003. (J). 16.95 (978-1-58430-061-8(2)); (ENG.). 32p. pap. 8.95 (978-1-60060-277-1(0)) Lee & Low Bks., Inc.

Rim, Sujean. Birdie's Big-Girl Shoes. 2009. (Birdie Ser.). (ENG.). 40p. (J). (gr. -1-1). 17.00 (978-0-316-04470-7(9)) Little, Brown Bks. for Young Readers.

—Project Paris. Barham, Lisa. 2007. (Fashion-Forward Adventures of Imogene Ser.). (ENG.). 224p. (YA). (gr. 7-12). pap. 10.99 (978-1-4169-1444-0(7), Simon Pulse) Simon Pulse.

—The Secret Ingredient. Schaefer, Laura. (ENG.). 240p. (J). (gr. 4-8). 2012. pap. 6.99 (978-1-4424-1960-5(1)); 2011. 15.99 (978-1-4424-1959-9(8)) Simon & Schuster/Paula Wiseman Bks. (Simon & Schuster/Paula Wiseman Bks.).

—The Teashop Girls. Schaefer, Laura. (ENG.). (J). 2009. 272p. (gr. 4-9). pap. 6.99 (978-1-4169-6794-1(X)); 2008. 240p. (gr. 3-9). 15.99 (978-1-4169-6793-4(1)) Simon & Schuster/Paula Wiseman Bks. (Simon & Schuster/Paula Wiseman Bks.).

Rimes, Nicole. Puppy Tales. Lattak, Cheryl. 2011. 28p. pap. 24.95 (978-1-4560-2720-9(4)) America Star Bks.

Rimland, Mark. The Secret Night World of Cats. 2008. 32p. (YA). 15.00 (978-0-9740360-6-9(4)) Autism Research Institute.

Rimmington, Natasha. The Wolf & the Seven Little Kids. 2014. (Flip-Up Fairy Tales Ser.). (ENG.). 24p. (J). (978-1-84643-656-7(7)) Child's Play International Ltd.

Rinaldi, Angelo. The Gladiator's Victory. Hulme-Cross, Benjamin. 2015. (ENG.). 160p. (J). (978-0-7787-1764-5(X)) Crabtree Publishing Co.

Rinaldi, Angelo. Horse. Doyle, Malachy. 2008. (ENG.). 32p. (J). (gr. k-4). 17.99 *(978-1-4169-2467-8(1)*, McElderry, Margaret K. Bks.) McElderry, Margaret K. Bks.

Rinaldi, Angelo. The Knight's Enemies. Hulme-Cross, Benjamin. 2015. (ENG.). 160p. (J). ***(978-0-7787-1765-2(8))*** Crabtree Publishing Co.

—The Samurai's Assassin. Hulme-Cross, Benjamin. 2015. (ENG.). 160p. (J). ***(978-0-7787-1766-9(6))*** Crabtree Publishing Co.

—The Viking's Revenge. Hulme-Cross, Benjamin. 2015. (ENG.). 160p. (J). ***(978-0-7787-1767-6(4))*** Crabtree Publishing Co.

Rinaldo, Luana. Butterphants & Eleflies. Froeb, Lori C. 2010. (Sliding Surprise Ser.). (ENG.). 10p. (J). bds. 7.99 *(978-0-7944-1932-5(1))* Reader's Digest Assn., Inc., The.

—Clackers: Penguin. Nash, C. 2011. (ENG.). 14p. (J). (— 1). bds. 5.99 *(978-0-375-87121-4(7)*, Robin Corey Bks.) Random Hse. Children's Bks.

—Feliz Cumpleanos, Tengo 1. Faglia, Matteo. 2006. (Happy Birthday Ser.). (SPA & ENG.). 16p. (J). (gr. -1). bds. 6.95 *(978-1-933605-14-2(6)*, Libros del Mundo) Kane Miller.

—God's Creation, 1 vol. Froeb, Lori C. 2008. 12p. (J). bds. 7.99 *(978-0-8254-5545-2(6))* Kregel Pubns.

—Matching Puzzle Cards - Colors. 2012. (ENG.). 36p. (J). (gr. k-12). 9.99 *(978-1-60905-220-1(X))* Blue Apple Bks.

—Noah's Ark, 1 vol. Froeb, Lori C. 2008. 12p. (J). bds. 7.99 *(978-0-8254-5546-9(4))* Kregel Pubns.

Rincon, Fernando. Los Papeles de Miguela. Nino, Jairo Anibal. 2003. (Literatura Juvenil (Panamericana Editorial) Ser.). (SPA.). 78p. (J). (gr. -1-7). pap. *(978-958-30-0336-3(0)*, PV30462) Centro de Informacion y Desarrollo de la Comunicacion y la Literatura MEX. Dist: Lectorum Pubns., Inc.

Ringgold, Faith. Bronzeville Boys & Girls. Brooks, Gwendolyn. 48p. (J). 2015. (ENG.). (gr. -1-3). pap. 6.99 *(978-0-06-443772-1(8)*, Amistad); 2007. (gr. 2-5). 18.89 *(978-0-06-029506-6(6))* HarperCollins Pubs.

—Bronzeville Boys & Girls. Brooks, Gwendolyn & Brooks. 2006. (ENG.). 48p. (J). (gr. -1-3). 16.99 *(978-0-06-029505-9(8)*, Amistad) HarperCollins Pubs.

—O Holy Night: Christmas with the Boys Choir of Harlem. Boys Choir of Harlem Staff. 2004. 40p. (J). 19.89 *(978-0-06-051819-6(7))* HarperCollins Pubs.

—O Holy Night: Christmas with the Boys Choir of Harlem. 2006. 30p. (J). (gr. 4-8). 19.00 *(978-1-4223-5512-1(8))* DIANE Publishing Co.

—The Three Witches. Hurston, Zora Neale. 2006. 32p. (J). (gr. 1-5). 16.89 *(978-0-06-000650-1(1))* HarperCollins Pubs.

—The Three Witches. Hurston, Zora Neale & Thomas, Joyce Carol. 2006. (ENG.). 32p. (J). (gr. 1-5). 15.99 *(978-0-06-000649-5(8))* HarperCollins Pubs.

Ringgold, Faith. Cassie's Word Quilt. Ringgold, Faith. 2004. (ENG.). 32p. (J). (gr. -1-2). pap. 6.99 *(978-0-553-11233-7(3)*, Dragonfly Bks.) Random Hse. Children's Bks.

—Harlem Renaissance. Ringgold, Faith. 2015. (ENG.). 40p. (J). (gr. -1-3). 17.99 *(978-0-06-057911-1(0)*, Amistad) HarperCollins Pubs.

—Henry Ossawa Tanner: His Boyhood Dream Comes True. Ringgold, Faith. 2011. (ENG.). 32p. (J). (gr. 1-3). 17.50 *(978-1-59373-092-5(6))* Bunker Hill Publishing, Inc.

—If a Bus Could Talk: The Story of Rosa Parks. Ringgold, Faith. 2003. (ENG.). 32p. (J). (gr. k-4). pap. 7.99 *(978-0-689-85676-1(8)*, Simon & Schuster/Paula Wiseman Bks.) Simon & Schuster/Paula Wiseman Bks.

Ringler, J. S. The Family Guide to Classic Movies. Ringler, J. S. 3rd ed. 2005. 354p. spiral bd. 11.95 *(978-0-9660286-0-7(0))* OSS Publishing Co.

Rink, Cynthia A. Where Does the Wind Blow? 2004. (Sharing Nature with Children Book Ser.). 32p. (J). pap. 7.95 *(978-1-58469-040-5(2))* Dawn Pubns.

Rink, Cynthia A. Where Does the Wind Blow? Rink, Cynthia A. 2004. (Sharing Nature with Children Book Ser.). 32p. (J). (gr. k-5). 16.95 *(978-1-58469-041-2(0))* Dawn Pubns.

Rinkel, Ken. Giant Machines. 2003. 12p. (J). (gr. k-3). 20.00 *(978-0-7567-6653-5(2))* DIANE Publishing Co.

Rino. Buzz Buzz, 1, Vol. 1. Rino. 2006. (Bambi Ser.: Vol. 1). 176p. (YA). per. 9.95 *(978-1-59697-012-0(X))* Infinity Studios LLC.

Rio, Adam del & Arroyo, David. Vines of the Earth. Rio, Adam del & Arroyo, David. 2006. (SPA & ENG.). 27p. *(978-0-9772852-7-3(8))*; pap. *(978-0-9772852-6-6(X))* Lectura Bks.

Rio, Adam del & Noel III. Teo & the Brick. Rio, Adam del & Noel III. 2006. (SPA & ENG.). 28p. *(978-0-9772852-4-2(3))*; *(978-0-9772852-5-9(1))* Lectura Bks.

Rios, Emma. In Pursuit of Flight Vol. 1, Vol. 1. Deconnick, Kelly Sue. 2013. (ENG.). 136p. (YA). (gr. 8-17). pap. 14.99 *(978-0-7851-6549-1(5))* Marvel Worldwide, Inc.

—Osborn: Evil Incarcerated. 2011. (ENG.). 120p. (J). (gr. 8-17). pap. 16.99 *(978-0-7851-5175-3(3))* Marvel Worldwide, Inc.

Rioux, Jo. The Golden Twine. Rioux, Jo. 2012. (Cat's Cradle Ser.: 1). (ENG.). 112p. (J). 9.95 *(978-1-55453-637-5(5))*; 17.95 *(978-1-55453-636-8(7))* Kids Can Pr., Ltd. CAN. Dist: Univ. of Toronto Pr.

Rioux, Jo-Anne. Lake Monster Mix-Up. Labatt, Mary. 2009. (Sam & Friends Mystery Ser.). (ENG.). 96p. (J). (gr. 2-5). 7.95 *(978-1-55337-302-5(2))*; 16.95 *(978-1-55337-822-8(9))* Kids Can Pr., Ltd. CAN. Dist: Univ. of Toronto Pr.

—Mummy Mayhem. Labatt, Mary. 2010. (Sam & Friends Mystery Ser.). (ENG.). 96p. (J). (gr. 2-5). 16.95 *(978-1-55453-470-8(4))*; pap. 7.95 *(978-1-55453-471-5(2))* Kids Can Pr., Ltd. CAN. Dist: Univ. of Toronto Pr.

—Sword Quest. Fan, Nancy Yi. (Swordbird Ser.). (J). (gr. 3-7). 2009. (ENG.). 304p. pap. 6.99 *(978-0-06-124337-0(X))*; 2008. 288p. lib. bdg. 16.89 *(978-0-06-124336-3(1))* HarperCollins Pubs.

—Sword Quest. Fan, Nancy Y. 2008. (Swordbird Ser.). 176p. (J). (gr. 3-7). 15.99 *(978-0-06-124335-6(3))* HarperCollins Pubs.

—Witches' Brew. Labatt, Mary. 2011. (Sam & Friends Mystery Ser.). (ENG.). 96p. (J). (gr. 2-5). 16.95 *(978-1-55453-472-2(0))*; pap. 7.95 *(978-1-55453-473-9(9))* Kids Can Pr., Ltd. CAN. Dist: Univ. of Toronto Pr.

Riphagen, Loes. Animals Home Alone. 2011. (ENG.). 32p. (J). (gr. -1-3). 15.95 *(978-1-934734-55-1(1))* Seven Footer Pr.

Ripper, Georgie. Abigail the Breeze Fairy. Meadows, Daisy. 2006. (Weather Fairies Ser.: 2). (ENG.). 80p. (J). (gr. -1-3). 4.99 *(978-0-439-81386-0(7)*, Scholastic Paperbacks) Scholastic, Inc.

—Amber the Orange Fairy. Meadows, Daisy. 2005. (Rainbow Magic Ser.: 2). (ENG.). 80p. (J). (gr. -1-3). pap. 4.99 *(978-0-439-74465-2(2))* Scholastic, Inc.

—Amy the Amethyst Fairy. Meadows, Daisy. 2007. (Jewel Fairies Ser.: 5). (ENG.). 80p. (Orig.). (J). (gr. -1-3). pap. 4.99 *(978-0-439-93532-6(6)*, Scholastic Paperbacks) Scholastic, Inc.

—Bella the Bunny Fairy. Meadows, Daisy. 2008. (Pet Fairies Ser.: 2). (ENG.). 80p. (J). (gr. -1-3). 4.99 *(978-0-545-04185-0(6)*, Scholastic Paperbacks) Scholastic, Inc.

—Bella the Bunny Fairy. Meadows, Daisy. ed. 2008. (Rainbow Magic — the Pet Fairies Ser.). 65p. (gr. 7). lib. bdg. 14.75 *(978-1-4178-2996-5(6)*, Turtleback) Turtleback Bks.

—Chloe the Topaz Fairy. Meadows, Daisy. 2007. (Jewel Fairies Ser.: 4). (ENG.). 80p. (Orig.). (J). (gr. -1-3). 4.99 *(978-0-439-93531-9(8))* Scholastic, Inc.

—Crystal the Snow Fairy. Meadows, Daisy. 2006. (Weather Fairies Ser.: 1). (ENG.). 80p. (Orig.). (J). (gr. -1-3). mass mkt. 4.99 *(978-0-439-81387-7(5)*, Scholastic Paperbacks) Scholastic, Inc.

—Emily the Emerald Fairy. Meadows, Daisy. 2007. (Jewel Fairies Ser.: 3). (ENG.). 80p. (Orig.). (J). (gr. -1-3). 4.99 *(978-0-439-93530-2(X))* Scholastic, Inc.

Ripper, Georgie. Emily, the Emerald Fairy. Meadows, Daisy. 2005. 65p. (J). pap. ***(978-0-545-01190-7(6))*** Scholastic, Inc.

Ripper, Georgie. Evie the Mist Fairy. Meadows, Daisy. 2006. (Weather Fairies Ser.: 5). (ENG.). 80p. (Orig.). (J). (gr. -1-3). 4.99 *(978-0-439-81390-7(5)*, Scholastic Paperbacks) Scholastic, Inc.

—Fairy Friends. Meadows, Daisy & Scholastic, Inc. Staff. 2007. (Rainbow Magic Ser.). (ENG.). 12p. (J). (gr. -1-3). pap. 6.99 *(978-0-439-93046-8(4))* Scholastic, Inc.

—Fern the Green Fairy. Meadows, Daisy. 2005. (Rainbow Magic Ser.: 4). (ENG.). 80p. (Orig.). (J). (gr. 2-5). 4.99 *(978-0-439-74467-6(9)*, Scholastic Paperbacks) Scholastic, Inc.

—Georgia the Guinea Pig Fairy. Meadows, Daisy. 2008. (Pet Fairies Ser.: 3). (ENG.). 80p. (J). (gr. -1-3). 4.99 *(978-0-545-04186-7(4)*, Scholastic Paperbacks) Scholastic, Inc.

—Georgia the Guinea Pig Fairy. Meadows, Daisy. ed. 2008. (Rainbow Magic — the Pet Fairies Ser.). 65p. (gr. 3). lib. bdg. 14.75 *(978-1-4178-2997-2(4)*, Turtleback) Turtleback Bks.

—Goldie the Sunshine Fairy. Meadows, Daisy. 2006. (Weather Fairies Ser.: 4). (ENG.). 80p. (Orig.). (J). (gr. -1-3). 4.99 *(978-0-439-81389-1(1)*, Scholastic Paperbacks) Scholastic, Inc.

—Harriet the Hamster Fairy. Meadows, Daisy. ed. 2008. (Rainbow Magic — the Pet Fairies Ser.). 67p. (gr. -1-3). lib. bdg. 14.75 *(978-1-4178-3007-7(7)*, Turtleback) Turtleback Bks.

—Hayley the Rain Fairy. Meadows, Daisy. 2007. (Weather Fairies Ser.: 7). (ENG.). 80p. (Orig.). (J). (gr. -1-3). pap. 4.99 *(978-0-439-81392-1(1)*, Scholastic Paperbacks) Scholastic, Inc.

—Heather the Violet Fairy. Meadows, Daisy. 2006. (Rainbow Magic Ser.: 7). (ENG.). 80p. (J). (gr. -1-3). 4.99 *(978-0-439-74686-1(8)*, Scholastic Paperbacks) Scholastic, Inc.

—Holly the Christmas Fairy. Meadows, Daisy. 2007. (Rainbow Magic Ser.). (ENG.). 176p. (Orig.). (J). (gr. -1-3). pap. 6.99 *(978-0-439-92880-9(X)*, Scholastic Paperbacks) Scholastic, Inc.

—Holly the Christmas Fairy. Meadows, Daisy. ed. 2007. (Rainbow Magic — Special Edition Ser.). 159p. (Orig.). (gr. -1-3). lib. bdg. 17.20 *(978-1-4178-1771-9(2)*, Turtleback) Turtleback Bks.

—India the Moonstone Fairy. Meadows, Daisy. 2007. (Jewel Fairies Ser.: 1). (ENG.). 80p. (Orig.). (J). (gr. -1-3). 4.99 *(978-0-439-93528-9(8))* Scholastic, Inc.

—Inky the Indigo Fairy. Meadows, Daisy. 2006. (Rainbow Magic Ser.: 6). (ENG.). 80p. (J). (gr. -1-3). per. 4.99 *(978-0-439-74685-4(X)*, Scholastic Paperbacks) Scholastic, Inc.

—Joy the Summer Vacation Fairy. Meadows, Daisy. 2007. (Rainbow Magic Ser.). (ENG.). 192p. (J). (gr. -1-3). 6.99 *(978-0-439-93442-8(7)*, Scholastic Paperbacks) Scholastic, Inc.

—Joy the Summer Vacation Fairy. Meadows, Daisy. ed. 2007. (Rainbow Magic — Special Edition Ser.). 177p. (gr. -1-3). lib. bdg. 17.20 *(978-1-4177-7081-6(3)*, Turtleback) Turtleback Bks.

—Katie the Kitten Fairy. Meadows, Daisy. 2008. (J). (Pet Fairies Ser.: 1). (ENG.). 80p. (gr. -1-3). pap. 4.99 *(978-0-545-02816-5(7)*, Scholastic Paperbacks); 65p. pap. *(978-0-545-13320-3(3))* Scholastic, Inc.

—Katie the Kitten Fairy. Meadows, Daisy. ed. 2008. (Rainbow Magic — the Pet Fairies Ser.). 65p. (gr. 1-4). lib. bdg. 14.75 *(978-1-4178-2999-6(0)*, Turtleback) Turtleback Bks.

—Kylie the Carnival Fairy. Meadows, Daisy. ed. 2008. (Rainbow Magic Ser.). (ENG.). 192p. (J). (gr. -1-3). pap. 6.99 *(978-0-545-05475-1(3)*, Scholastic Paperbacks) Scholastic, Inc.

—Lauren the Puppy Fairy. Meadows, Daisy. 2008. (Pet Fairies Ser.: 4). (ENG.). 80p. (J). (gr. -1-3). pap. 4.99 *(978-0-545-04187-4(2)*, Scholastic Paperbacks) Scholastic, Inc.

—Lucy the Diamond Fairy. Meadows, Daisy. 2008. (Jewel Fairies Ser.: 7). (ENG.). 80p. (Orig.). (J). (gr. -1-3). pap. 4.99 *(978-0-439-93534-0(2)*, Scholastic Paperbacks) Scholastic, Inc.

—Molly the Goldfish Fairy. Meadows, Daisy. 2008. (Pet Fairies Ser.: 6). (ENG.). 80p. (J). (gr. -1-3). pap. 4.99 *(978-0-545-04189-8(9)*, Scholastic Paperbacks) Scholastic, Inc.

—Molly the Goldfish Fairy. Meadows, Daisy. ed. 2008. (Rainbow Magic — the Pet Fairies Ser.). 68p. (gr. -1-3). lib. bdg. 14.75 *(978-1-4178-3001-5(8)*, Turtleback) Turtleback Bks.

—Pearl the Cloud Fairy. Meadows, Daisy. 2006. (Weather Fairies Ser.: 3). (ENG.). 80p. (Orig.). (J). (gr. -1-3). 4.99 *(978-0-439-81388-4(3)*, Scholastic Paperbacks) Scholastic, Inc.

—Ruby the Red Fairy. Meadows, Daisy. 2005. (Rainbow Magic Ser.: 1). (ENG.). 80p. (Orig.). (J). (gr. -1-3). pap. 4.99 *(978-0-439-73861-3(X))* Scholastic, Inc.

—Saffron the Yellow Fairy. Meadows, Daisy. 2004. (Rainbow Magic Ser.). 69p. (Orig.). (J). *(978-0-439-69195-6(8))* Scholastic, Inc.

—Scarlett the Garnet Fairy. Meadows, Daisy. 2007. (Jewel Fairies Ser.: 2). (ENG.). 80p. (Orig.). (J). (gr. -1-3). 4.99 *(978-0-439-93529-6(6))* Scholastic, Inc.

—Sky the Blue Fairy. Meadows, Daisy. 2005. (Rainbow Magic Ser.: 5). (ENG.). 80p. (Orig.). (J). (gr. -1-3). per. 4.99 *(978-0-439-74684-7(1)*, Scholastic Paperbacks) Scholastic, Inc.

—Stella the Star Fairy. Meadows, Daisy. ed. 2008. (Rainbow Magic Ser.). (ENG.). 192p. (J). (gr. -1-3). pap. 6.99 *(978-0-545-06776-8(6)*, Scholastic Paperbacks) Scholastic, Inc.

—Storm the Lightning Fairy. Meadows, Daisy. 2007. (Weather Fairies Ser.: 6). (ENG.). 80p. (Orig.). (J). (gr. -1-3). pap. 4.99 *(978-0-439-81391-4(3)*, Scholastic Paperbacks) Scholastic, Inc.

—Sunny the Yellow Fairy. Meadows, Daisy. 2005. (Rainbow Magic Ser.: 3). (ENG.). 80p. (J). (gr. 2-5). pap. 4.99 *(978-0-439-74466-9(0)*, Little Apple Bks) Scholastic Canada, Ltd. CAN. Dist: Scholastic, Inc.

Ripper, Peter. Hullo Sun. Hodgson, Joan. 2003. 32p. (gr. -1-3). 8.95 *(978-0-85487-072-1(5))* White Eagle Publishing Trust GBR. Dist: DeVorss & Co.

—Our Father. Hodgson, Joan. 2003. 24p. (gr. k-7). 5.95 *(978-0-85487-040-0(7))* White Eagle Publishing Trust GBR. Dist: DeVorss & Co.

Rippin, Sally. Mannie & the Long Brave Day. Murray, Martine. 2010. (ENG.). 32p. (J). (gr. -1-k). 17.99 *(978-1-74175-886-3(6))* Allen & Unwin AUS. Dist: Independent Pubs. Group.

—Meditation Is an Open Sky: Mindfulness for Kids. Stewart, Whitney. 2015. (ENG.). 32p. (J). (gr. -1-2). 16.99 *(978-0-8075-4908-7(8))* Whitman, Albert & Co.

Rippin, Sally. Where Is Baby? Rippin, Sally. 2009. (ENG.). 12p. (J). (gr. k — 1). bds. 7.99 *(978-1-74175-386-8(4))* Allen & Unwin AUS. Dist: Independent Pubs. Group.

Rippin, Sally & Abos, Regine. The Race for the Chinese Zodiac. Wang, Gabrielle. 2013. (ENG.). 32p. (J). (gr. k-4). 14.99 *(978-0-7636-6778-8(1))* Candlewick Pr.

Rippon, Jor-El. Princess, the Future Queen: A Mother's Guidance. Harris, Kandi. l.t. ed. 2006. 32p. (J). bds. 12.99 *(978-0-9770331-1-9(2))* Harris, K Publishing, Inc.

Ripps, Robert A., photos by. She's Out There! Essays by 35 Young Women Who Aspire to Lead the Nation - The Next Generation of Presidential Candidates. Sewell, Amy & Ogilvie, Heather. 2009. (ENG., 224p. 25.00 *(978-0-9816368-4-9(5))* LifeTime Media, Inc.

Risch, Christopher. In Mommy's Garden: A Book to Help Explain Cancer to Young Children. Ammary, Neyal J. 2004. 34p. (J). per. 10.95 *(978-0-9754221-0-6(3))* Canyon Beach Visual Communications.

Rising Star Studios. Auto-B-Good - Citizen Miles: A Lesson in Citizenship. Walton, Phillip. 2010. 48p. (J). pap. 7.95 *(978-1-936086-52-8(2))*; lib. bdg. 14.95 *(978-1-936086-46-7(8))* Rising Star Studios, LLC.

Risley, Jacqueline & Tim. Alpha's ABC's Games: Spanish & English Ages 2-6. Risley, Jacqueline & Tim. 2007.Tr. of Alfa y sus Juegos de la A a la Z. (SPA & ENG.). 32p. (J). 6.99 *(978-0-9791680-0-0(7))* Alpha Learning World, Inc.

Rissing, Karen. Snickerdoodle! a Tall Tale about a Powerful Pee-Wee! Grosgebauer, Clare Ham. 3rd ed. 2005. 40p. (J). (gr. -1-3). 12.99 *(978-0-9741888-2-9(4))* Small Wonders Enterprises.

—Snickerdoodle & the Roller-Skating Horse! Grosgebauer, Clare Ham. 3rd ed. 2005. 36p. (J). (gr. -1-3). 12.99 *(978-0-9741888-4-3(0))* Small Wonders Enterprises.

—Snickerdoodle's Star-Spangled Fourth of July! Grosgebauer, Clare Ham. 4th ed. 2005. 36p. (J). (gr. -1-3). 12.99 *(978-0-9741888-6-7(7))* Small Wonders Enterprises.

Ristow, Trevor. Drawing a Blank: Or How I Tried to Solve a Mystery, End a Feud, & Land the Girl of My Dreams. Ehrenhaft, Daniel. 2009. (ENG.). 352p. (J). pap. 8.99 *(978-0-06-075254-5(8)*, HarperTeen) HarperCollins Pubs.

Ritchie, Alex. Babies Are Boring. Ritchie, Jon. 2008. 40p. (J). *(978-0-9809970-0-2(3))* Purple Possum Publishing Inc.

Ritchie, Fern J. & Ritchie, Ralph W., photos by. Weaving with Rags & Leftovers: The Best of Recycling. Ritchie, Fern J. & Ritchie, Ralph W. 2005. 177p. (YA). cd-rom 14.95 *(978-0-939656-86-8(8)*, 0-939656-86-8) Ritchie Unlimited Pubns.

Ritchie, Ralph W., jt. photos by see Ritchie, Fern J.

Ritchie, Scot. I'm Only Three¿ & Look at All the Things That I Can Do! Graves, Harmon. 2013. 30p. pap. 13.95 *(978-1-4349-3729-2(1))* Dorrance Publishing Co., Inc.

—My Class & Me: Kindergarten. Leatherdale, Mary Beth & Leatherdale, Mary. 2003. (Memory Scrapbook for Kids Ser.). (ENG.). 32p. (J). (gr. k-3). 5.95 *(978-1-55337-129-8(1))* Kids Can Pr., Ltd. CAN. Dist: Univ. of Toronto Pr.

—See Saw Saskatchewan. Heidbreder, Robert. 2005. (ENG.). 32p. (J). 7.95 *(978-1-55337-968-3(3))* Kids Can Pr., Ltd. CAN. Dist: Univ. of Toronto Pr.

—Slowpoke. Pearce, Emily Smith. 2010. (ENG.). 40p. (J). (gr. 2-4). 16.95 *(978-1-59078-705-2(6))* Boyds Mills Pr.

Ritchie, Scot. Follow That Map! Ritchie, Scot. 2009. (ENG.). 32p. (J). (gr. -1-2). 16.95 *(978-1-55453-274-2(4))* Kids Can Pr., Ltd. CAN. Dist: Univ. of Toronto Pr.

—Look at That Building: A First Book of Structures. Ritchie, Scot. 2011. (ENG.). 32p. (J). 16.95 *(978-1-55453-696-2(0))* Kids Can Pr., Ltd. CAN. Dist: Univ. of Toronto Pr.

—Up, up & Away! Ritchie, Scot. 2005. 32p. pap. *(978-1-921049-01-9(4))* Little Hare Bks. AUS. Dist: HarperCollins Pubs. Australia.

Ritchie, Scot & Owlkids Books Inc. Staff. Why? The Best Ever Question & Answer Book about Nature, Science & the World Around You. Ripley, Catherine. 2nd ed. 2010. (ENG.). 192p. (J). (gr. -1-2). 19.95 *(978-1-926818-00-9(8))* Owlkids Bks. Inc. CAN. Dist: Perseus-PGW.

Riti, Marsha. All about Ellie. Barkley, Callie. 2013. (Critter Club Ser.: Bk. 2). (ENG.). 128p. (J). (gr. k-2). 15.99 *(978-1-4424-5789-8(9))*; pap. 5.99 *(978-1-4424-5788-1(0))* Little Simon. (Little Simon).

—Amy & the Missing Puppy. Barkley, Callie. 2013. (Critter Club Ser.: Bk. 1). (ENG.). 128p. (J). (gr. k-2). 15.99 *(978-1-4424-5770-6(8))*; pap. 5.99 *(978-1-4424-5769-0(4))* Little Simon. (Little Simon).

—Amy Meets Her Stepsister. Barkley, Callie. 2013. (Critter Club Ser.: 5). (ENG.). 128p. (J). (gr. k-2). 15.99 *(978-1-4424-8216-6(8))*; pap. 5.99 *(978-1-4424-8215-9(X))* Little Simon. (Little Simon).

—The Critter Club: Amy & the Missing Puppy; All about Ellie; Liz Learns a Lesson. Barkley, Callie. 2014. (Critter Club Ser.). (ENG.). 368p. (J). (gr. k-4). pap. 8.99 *(978-1-4814-2770-8(9)*, Little Simon) Little Simon.

—Ellie & the Good-Luck Pig. Barkley, Callie. 2015. (Critter Club Ser.: 10). (ENG.). 128p. (J). (gr. k-4). pap. 5.99 *(978-1-4814-2402-8(5)*, Little Simon) Little Simon.

—Ellie's Lovely Idea. Barkley, Callie. 2013. (Critter Club Ser.: 6). (ENG.). 128p. (J). (gr. k-2). 15.99 *(978-1-4424-8219-7(2))*; pap. 5.99 *(978-1-4424-8218-0(4))* Little Simon. (Little Simon).

Riti, Marsha. Liz & the Sand Castle Contest. Barkley, Callie. 2015. (Critter Club Ser.: 11). (ENG.). 128p. (J). (gr. k-4). pap. 5.99 ***(978-1-4814-2405-9(X)***, Little Simon) Little Simon.

Riti, Marsha. Liz at Marigold Lake. Barkley, Callie. 2014. (Critter Club Ser.: 7). (ENG.). 128p. (J). (gr. k-4). pap. 5.99 *(978-1-4424-9525-8(1)*, Little Simon) Little Simon.

—Liz Learns a Lesson. Barkley, Callie. 2013. (Critter Club Ser.: 3). (ENG.). 128p. (J). (gr. -1-2). 15.99 *(978-1-4424-6770-5(3))*; pap. 5.99 *(978-1-4424-6768-2(1))* Little Simon. (Little Simon).

—Marion Strikes a Pose. Barkley, Callie. 2014. (Critter Club Ser.: 8). (ENG.). 128p. (J). (gr. k-4). 15.99 *(978-1-4424-9529-6(4)*, Little Simon) Little Simon.

—Marion Takes a Break. Barkley, Callie. 2013. (Critter Club Ser.: 4). (ENG.). 128p. (J). (gr. k-2). 15.99 *(978-1-4424-6773-6(8))*; pap. 5.99 *(978-1-4424-6772-9(X))* Little Simon. (Little Simon).

Riti, Marsha. Marion Takes Charge. Barkley, Callie. 2015. (Critter Club Ser.: Bk. 12). (ENG.). 128p. (J). (gr. k-4). pap. 5.99 ***(978-1-4814-2408-0(4)***, Little Simon) Little Simon.

Riti, Marsha. The Picky Little Witch, 1 vol. Brokamp, Elizabeth. 2011. (ENG.). 32p. (J). (gr. k-3). 16.99 *(978-1-58980-882-9(7))* Pelican Publishing Co., Inc.

Ritter, Adam. Old Mo. Hsu, Stacey W. 2011. (Rookie Ready to Learn Ser.). 40p. (J). pap. 5.95 *(978-0-531-26699-1(0))*; (gr. -1-k). lib. bdg. 23.00 *(978-0-531-26418-8(1))* Scholastic Library Publishing. (Children's Pr.).

Rittmueller, Jeanne. Christopher's Bedtime Story. Haave, Meghan. 2012. 32p. (J). pap. 9.95 *(978-1-59530-459-9(2))* Hallmark Card, Inc.

Ritz, Karen. Ian's Walk: A Story about Autism. Lears, Laurie. 2004. (ENG.). 32p. (J). (gr. k-4). pap. 6.99 *(978-0-8075-3481-6(1))* Whitman, Albert & Co.

—Kate Shelley y el Tren de Medianoche. Wetterer, Margaret K. Translations.com Staff, tr. 2005. (Yo Solo: Historia (on My Own History) Ser.).Tr. of Kate Shelley & the Midnight Express. (SPA.). 48p. (gr. 2-4). lib. bdg. 25.26 *(978-0-8225-3096-1(1)*, Ediciones Lerner) Lerner Publishing Group.

—Martha Washington. Ransom, Candice. 2003. (On My Own Biography Ser.). (ENG.). 48p. (gr. 2-4). per. 6.95 *(978-0-87614-107-6(6)*, Carolrhoda Bks.) Lerner Publishing Group.

—Max Talks to Me. Buchwald, Claire. 2007. (Sit! Stay! Read! Ser.). (ENG.). 24p. (J). (gr. k-2). 16.95 *(978-0-940719-03-3(7))* Gryphon Pr., The.

—Snowboarding on Monster Mountain. Bunting, Eve. 2003. (ENG.). 64p. (J). 15.95 *(978-0-8126-2704-6(0))* Cricket Bks.

Ritzmann, Mary B. L. I. B. B. Y. The Green Dog. Riachi, Ghassan Diab & Mitchell, Anna B. RJI Publishing, ed. 2011.Tr. of L. I. B. B. Y. , el Perro Verde. 32p. (J). mass mkt. 9.95 *(978-1-885184-11-5(5))* RJI Publishing.

Rius, Maria. La Castanera. Combel Editorial Staff & catalán, Cuento popular. 2005. (Caballo Alado Clásicos-Al Trote Ser.). (SPA & ENG.). 24p. (J). (gr. -1-k). 7.95 *(978-84-7864-868-9(2))* Combel Editorial, S.A. ESP. Dist: Independent Pubs. Group.

—Los Tres Cerditos. Orihuela, Luz et al. 2004. (Caballo Alado Clásico Series-Al Paso Ser.). (SPA & ENG.). 24p. (J). (gr. -1-k). 7.95 *(978-84-7864-765-1(1))* Combel Editorial, S.A. ESP. Dist: Independent Pubs. Group.

—Los Tres Cerditos (The Three Little Pigs) Sarfatti, Esther, tr. from ENG. 2006. (Bilingual Tales Ser.). (SPA.). 24p. (J). (gr. -1-3). pap. 3.99 *(978-0-439-77382-9(2)*, Scholastic en Espanol) Scholastic, Inc.

Rius, Roser. ¡No Quiero Dormir! Trévol, S. A. & Produccions Editorials, Trèvol. 2005. (Cucú Ser.). (SPA & ENG.). 16p. (J). (gr. -1-k). 6.95 *(978-84-7864-842-9(9))* Combel Editorial, S.A. ESP. Dist: Independent Pubs. Group.

Rius, Roser. Ruth es un Torbellino. Rius, Roser. Rius Camps, Roser. Terzi, Marinella, tr. 2008. (SPA.). 24p. (J). *(978-84-675-2422-2(7))* SM Ediciones.

Rivard, Rebecca. Ben Has Autism. Ben Is Awesome. Zolty, Meredith. 2011. 32p. (J). pap. 9.95 *(978-0-944727-41-6(7)*, Turtle Bks.) Jason & Nordic Pubs.

R

Rivas, Victor. Caperucita Roja. Andersen, Hans Christian & Stone Arch Books Staff. 2010. (Graphic Spin en Español Ser.). (SPA & ENG.). 40p. (gr. 1-3). pap. 5.95 *(978-1-4342-2315-9(9),* Graphic Spin en Español) Stone Arch Bks.

—Caperucita Roja. Andersen, Hans Christian & Capstone Press Staff. 2010. (Graphic Spin en Español Ser.). (SPA.). 40p. (gr. 1-3). lib. bdg. 23.99 *(978-1-4342-1903-9(8),* Graphic Spin en Español) Stone Arch Bks.

—John Henry vs. the Mighty Steam Drill, 1 vol. Meister, Cari. 2014. (American Folk Legends Ser.). (ENG.). 32p. (gr. k-2). 26.65 *(978-1-4795-5430-0(8))* Picture Window Bks.

—Red Riding Hood: The Graphic Novel. 2008. (Graphic Spin Ser.). (ENG.). 40p. (gr. 1-3). 23.99 *(978-1-4342-0769-2(2),* Graphic Revolve) Stone Arch Bks.

—Red Riding Hood: The Graphic Novel, 1 vol. Stone Arch Books Staff. 2008. (Graphic Spin Ser.). (ENG.). 40p. (gr. 1-3). pap. 5.95 *(978-1-4342-0865-1(6),* Graphic Revolve) Stone Arch Bks.

—Zorgamazoo. Weston, Robert Paul. 2008. (ENG.). 288p. (J). (gr. 3-7). 15.99 *(978-1-59514-199-6(5),* Razorbill) Penguin Publishing Group.

—100% Wolf. Lyons, Jayne. (ENG.). 256p. (J). (gr. 2-7). 2010. pap. 6.99 *(978-1-4424-0252-2(0));* 2009. 16.99 *(978-1-4169-7474-1(1))* Simon & Schuster Children's Publishing. (Atheneum Bks. for Young Readers).

Rivera, Alba Marina. El Contador de Cuentos. Saki. Canales, Veronica & Guix, Juan Gabriel Lopez, trs. 2008. (SPA.). (J). (gr. 5-8). pap. 20.99 *(978-84-936504-3-8(9))* Ekaré Europa S.L. ESP. Dist: Lectorum Pubns., Inc.

Rivera, Diego. My Papá Diego & Me (Mi Papa Diego y Yo) Memories of My Father & His Art (Recuerdos de Mi Padre y Su Arte) Marin, Guadalupe Rivera. 2013. (SPA & ENG.). 32p. (J). (gr. k-5). 18.95 *(978-0-89239-228-5(2))* Lee & Low Bks., Inc.

Rivera, Hanae. Kodoku. Justice, William E. 2012. (ENG.). 32p. (J). 16.95 *(978-1-59714-173-4(9))* Heyday.

Rivera, Paolo Manuel. Spider-Man: One Moment in Time. 2011. (ENG.). 162p. (J). (gr. 4-17). pap. 19.99 *(978-0-7851-4620-9(2))* Marvel Worldwide, Inc.

Rivera, Rafael, et al. Baseball on Mars/Béisbol en Marte. Rivera, Rafael et al. 2009.Tr. of Béisbol en Marte. (SPA & ENG.). 32p. (J). (gr. -1-3). 16.95 *(978-1-55885-521-2(1))* Arte Publico Pr.

Rivera, Roberta. Missing Treasure Means Trouble. Krapp, JoAnn Vergona. 2012. 66p. (J). (gr. 3-5). pap. 12.95 *(978-0-9722576-3-3(2))* JoAnn Vergona Krapp & Gene Zaner.

Rivero, Marcos Almada. Copo de Algodon. Esperon, Maria Garcia. 2010. (SPA.). 136p. (YA). (gr. 6-8). pap. *(978-607-7661-17-7(1))* Ediciones El Naranjo Sa De Cv.

Rivers, Ruth. Bugs: Level 1. Bowman, Lucy. 2007. (Beginners Nature Ser.). 32p. (J). 4.99 *(978-0-7945-1705-2(6),* Usborne) EDC Publishing.

—The Donkey That Went Too Fast. Orme, David. 2005. 32p. (J). lib. bdg. 9.00 *(978-1-4242-0890-6(4))* Fitzgerald Bks.

—It's Not Worth Making a Tzimmes Over! Rosenthal, Betsy R. 2006. 32p. (J). (gr. k-3). lib. bdg. 16.99 *(978-0-8075-3677-3(6))* Whitman, Albert & Co.

—Mary Had a Dinosaur. Browne, Eileen. 2009. (Get Ready (Windmill Books) Ser.). 32p. (J). (gr. k-2). lib. bdg. 22.60 *(978-1-60754-262-9(5))* Windmill Bks.

—Snowshoe the Hare. White, Kathryn. 2005. (Red Go Bananas Ser.). (ENG.). 48p. (J). (gr. 2-3). *(978-0-7787-2699-9(1),* 1253648); lib. bdg. *(978-0-7787-2677-7(0),* 1253648) Crabtree Publishing Co.

Rix, Fred, jt. illus. see Fredericks, Karen.

Rizal, Clarissa, jt. illus. see Koch, Nobu.

Rizvi, Farah. Amazing Biome Projects. Latham, Donna. 2009. (Build It Yourself Ser.). (ENG.). 128p. (J). (gr. 3-7). 21.95 *(978-1-934670-40-8(5))* Nomad Pr.

—Amazing Biome Projects: You Can Build Yourself. Latham, Donna. 2009. (Build It Yourself Ser.). (ENG.). 128p. (J). (gr. 3-7). pap. 15.95 *(978-1-934670-39-2(1))* Nomad Pr.

—Inca: Discover the Culture & Geography of a Lost Civilization with 25 Projects. Kovacs, Lawrence. 2013. (Build It Yourself Ser.). (ENG.). 128p. (J). (gr. 3-7). 21.95 *(978-1-61930-141-2(5));* pap. 15.95 *(978-1-61930-140-5(7))* Nomad Pr.

—Planet Earth: 25 Environmental Projects You Can Build Yourself. Reilly, Kathleen M. 2008. (Build It Yourself Ser.). (ENG.). 128p. (J). (gr. 3-7). 21.95 *(978-1-934670-05-7(7));* pap. 15.95 *(978-1-934670-04-0(9))* Nomad Pr.

—Seven Wonders of the World: Discover Amazing Monuments to Civilization with 20 Projects. Van Vleet, Carmella. 2011. (Build It Yourself Ser.). (ENG.). 128p. (J). (gr. 3-7). 21.95 *(978-1-934670-82-8(0));* pap. 15.95 *(978-1-936313-73-0(1))* Nomad Pr.

Rizvi, Farah, jt. illus. see Carbaugh, Samuel.

Rizy, Brock. Emily Edison: Volume 1. 2006. 139p. (gr. 8-18). pap. 12.95 *(978-0-9777883-2-3(6))* Viper Comics.

Rizzo, Jerry. Fifty-Seven Stories of Saints. Heffernan, Eileen. 2003. (J). 552p. pap. 16.95 *(978-0-8198-2674-9(X),* 332-094); 549p. *(978-0-8198-2675-6(8))* Pauline Bks. & Media.

—57 Stories of Saints. Heffernan, Anne Eileen. 3rd ed. 2006. 531p. (J). pap. 16.95 *(978-0-8198-2681-7(2))* Pauline Bks. & Media.

Roach, David & Offredi, James. A Christmas Carol. Dickens, Charles. Howell, Keith, tr. 2008. (ENG.). 144p. (Orig.). (gr. 4-18). pap. 16.95 *(978-1-906332-51-8(7));* pap. 16.95 *(978-1-906332-52-5(5))* Classical Comics GBR. (Classical Comics, Ltd.). Dist: Perseus-PGW.

Roach-Langille, Nancy. Fiddle Fantasy: A Selection of Fiddle Tunes by Maritime Composers. Roach-Langille, Nancy. Mitchell, Francis G. Mitchell, Francis G., ed. 2nd ed. 2004. (ENG.). 6p. pap. *(978-1-895814-28-6(6),* NWP103) New World Publishing.

Roba, Jean. Friends First. Roba, Jean. 2012. (ENG.). 48p. (J). (gr. 3-12). pap. 11.95 *(978-1-84918-124-2(1))* CineBook GBR. Dist: National Bk. Network.

Robaard, Jedda. A Little Book about Me & My Dad. 2014. (ENG.). 24p. (J). (gr. 1-5). 7.99 *(978-0-7641-6672-3(7))* Barron's Educational Series, Inc.

—A Little Book about Me & My Mom. 2014. (ENG.). 24p. (J). (gr. 1-5). 7.99 *(978-0-7641-6671-6(9))* Barron's Educational Series, Inc.

Robaard, Jedda. Milo & Millie. Robaard, Jedda. 2014. (ENG.). 32p. (J). (-k). 14.99 *(978-0-7636-6783-2(8))* Candlewick Pr.

Robare, Jay. Pets in Heaven Activity Book: Children's Companion Book to: Do Pets & Other Animals Go to Heaven? 2003. 86p. (J). per. 12.95 *(978-0-9726363-1-5(5),* 6315) Brite Bks.

Robb, Jonathan. Doby's First Christmas. Wilkins, Nalini. 2012. 28p. pap. 12.50 *(978-1-62212-777-1(3),* Strategic Bk. Publishing) Strategic Book Publishing & Rights Agency (SBPRA).

Robberecht, Thierry. Perdí mi Sonrisa. Robberecht, Thierry. Goossens, Philippe. (SPA.). 28p. (J). (gr. k-3). 14.95 *(978-970-29-0667-4(9))* Santillana USA Publishing Co., Inc.

Robbins, Ashley. The Legend of Red Leaf. Watson, Don. l.t. ed. 2005. 125p. (J). pap. 9.95 *(978-0-9714358-6-5(3))* Longhorn Creek Pr.

Robbins, Carrie. Who Was Wolfgang Amadeus Mozart? McDonough, Yona Zeldis. 2003. (Who Was... ? Ser.). (ENG.). 112p. (J). (gr. 3-7). pap. 5.99 *(978-0-448-43104-8(1),* Grosset & Dunlap) Penguin Publishing Group.

Robbins, Kathryn. That's What's Different about Me: Helping Children Understand Autism Spectrum Disorders. McKracken, Heather. 2006. (J). pap. 59.95 *(978-1-931282-96-3(X))* Autism Asperger Publishing Co.

—That's What's Different about Me! Helping Children Understand Autism Spectrum Disorders - Story & Coloring BK. Mccracken, Heather. 2006. (J). pap. 3.00 *(978-1-931282-97-0(8))* Autism Asperger Publishing Co.

Robbins, Ken. Fireflies at Midnight. Singer, Marilyn. 2003. (ENG.). 32p. (J). (gr. k-4). 17.99 *(978-0-689-82492-0(0),* Atheneum Bks. for Young Readers) Simon & Schuster Children's Publishing.

Robbins, Ken. For Good Measure: The Ways We Say How Much, How Far, How Heavy, How Big, How Old. Robbins, Ken. 2010. (ENG.). 48p. (J). (gr. -1-3). 17.99 *(978-1-59643-344-1(2))* Roaring Brook Pr.

—Seeds. Robbins, Ken. 2005. (ENG.). 32p. (J). (gr. 1-4). 17.99 *(978-0-689-85041-7(7),* Atheneum Bks. for Young Readers) Simon & Schuster Children's Publishing.

—Thunder on the Plains: The Story of the American Buffalo. Robbins, Ken. 2009. (ENG.). 36p. (J). (gr. 2-5). pap. 10.99 *(978-1-4169-9536-4(6),* Atheneum Bks. for Young Readers) Simon & Schuster Children's Publishing.

—Trucks: Giants of the Highway. Robbins, Ken. 2013. (ENG.). 32p. (J). (gr. -1-3). pap. 16.99 *(978-1-4814-0164-7(5),* Atheneum Bks. for Young Readers) Simon & Schuster Children's Publishing.

Robbins, Ken, photos by. Apples. Robbins, Ken. 2013. (ENG., 32p. (J). (gr. 1-4). pap. 16.99 *(978-1-4814-0165-4(3),* Atheneum Bks. for Young Readers) Simon & Schuster Children's Publishing.

Roberson, Ibraim, jt. illus. see Bradshaw, Nick.

Roberson, Ron. White Cloud: A Little Boy's Dream. Irwin, Esther. Puett, Gayle, ed. 2006. 61p. (J). spiral bd. 10.00 *(978-0-9778462-0-7(2))* Irwin, Esther L.

Robert, Bruno. A Cookie for Santa. Shaw, Stephanie. 2014. (ENG.). 32p. (J). (gr. 1-4). 15.99 *(978-1-58536-883-9(0),* 203675) Sleeping Bear Pr.

—Joey the Juggler, 1 vol. Dolan, Penny. 2013. (Start Reading Ser.). (ENG.). 24p. (gr. k-1). pap. 6.99 *(978-1-4765-4109-9(4))* Capstone Pr., Inc.

—Lola Fanola, 1 vol. Dolan, Penny. 2013. (Start Reading Ser.). (ENG.). 24p. (gr. k-1). pap. 6.99 *(978-1-4765-4113-6(2))* Capstone Pr., Inc.

—Princess Rani, 1 vol. Dolan, Penny. 2013. (Start Reading Ser.). (ENG.). 24p. (gr. k-1). pap. 6.99 *(978-1-4765-4131-0(0))* Capstone Pr., Inc.

—Rabbit Cooks up a Cunning Plan! Peters, Andrew Fusek. 2007. (Traditional Tales with a Twist Ser.). (ENG.). 32p. (J). (gr. -1-3). pap. *(978-1-84643-097-8(6))* Child's Play International Ltd.

Robert, J. Martin. I Want You to Know, Son. Fink, Thad. 2007. 26p. (J). (gr. -1-3). per. 11.99 *(978-1-59879-260-7(1))* Lifevest Publishing, Inc.

Robert, Marstall & Marstall, Bob. Crows! Strange & Wonderful. Pringle, Laurence. 2010. (Strange & Wonderful Ser.). (ENG.). 32p. (J). (gr. 2-4). pap. 9.95 *(978-1-59078-724-3(2))* Boyds Mills Pr.

Robert, Peters. Da Goodie Monsta. Robert, Peters. 2010. 30p. (J). pap. 9.95 *(978-0-9823906-4-1(5))* Wiggles Pr.

Robert, Yannick. Hello, I Am Charlie from London. Husar, Stephane. 2014. (AV2 Fiction Readalong Ser.: Vol. 127). (ENG.). 32p. (J). (gr. -1-3). lib. bdg. 34.28 *(978-1-4896-2256-3(X),* AV2 by Weigl) Weigl Pubs., Inc.

—The King of Spring. Page, Nick & Page, Claire. 2006. (Read with Me (Make Believe Ideas) Ser.). 31p. (J). (gr. k-2). *(978-1-84610-169-4(7))* Make Believe Ideas.

Roberti, Alessandra. Little Pony. Milbourne, Anna. 2009. (Picture Bks.). 24p. (J). (gr. -1). 9.99 *(978-0-7945-2198-1(3),* Usborne) EDC Publishing.

—On the Farm. Milbourne, Anna. 2006. 24p. (J). (gr. -1-3). 9.99 *(978-0-7945-1282-8(8),* Usborne) EDC Publishing.

Roberton, Fiona. Wanted: The Perfect Pet. Roberton, Fiona. 2010. (ENG.). 40p. (J). (gr. k-3). 16.99 *(978-0-399-25461-1(7),* Putnam Juvenile) Penguin Publishing Group.

Roberts, Bruce, photos by. Ghosts of the Wild West. Roberts, Nancy. 2nd fac. ed. 2008. 110p. (J). (gr. 3-7). 24.95 *(978-1-57003-731-3(0))* Univ. of South Carolina Pr.

—Ghosts of the Wild West: Enlarged Edition Including Five Never-Before-Published Stories. Roberts, Nancy. 2nd enl. ed. 2008. (ENG.). 120p. (gr. 3-7). pap. 13.95 *(978-1-57003-732-0(9))* Univ. of South Carolina Pr.

Roberts, Bruno. Rabbit Cooks up a Cunning Plan! Peters, Andrew. 2010. (Traditional Tales with a Twist Ser.). (ENG.). 32p. (J). (gr. -1-2). *(978-1-84643-349-8(5))* Child's Play International Ltd.

Roberts, Curt & Traylor, Waverley. The Story of Scruffy of Smithfield, Virginia. Roberts, Curt. Traylor, Waverley, ed. l.t. ed. 2005. 14p. (J). (gr. k-6). pap. 3.95 *(978-0-9715068-4-8(1))* Traylor, Waverley Publishing.

Roberts, David. Crazy Party at the House of Fun. Blake, Jon. 2007. (House of Fun Ser.: 2). (ENG.). 128p. (J). (gr. 2-4). pap. 7.95 *(978-0-340-88460-7(6))* Hachette Children's Group GBR. Dist: Independent Pubs. Group.

—Dear Tabby. Crimi, Carolyn. 2011. (ENG.). 32p. (J). (gr. -1-3). 16.99 *(978-0-06-114245-1(X))* HarperCollins Pubs.

—Dirty Bertie: Burp! Macdonald, Alan. 2008. 96p. (J). (gr. 1-5). 3.99 *(978-1-56148-644-1(2),* Good Bks.) Skyhorse Publishing Co., Inc.

—Dirty Bertie: Worms! Macdonald, Alan. 2008. 96p. (J). (gr. 4-7). 3.99 *(978-1-56148-645-8(0),* Good Bks.) Skyhorse Publishing Co., Inc.

—Don't Say That, Willy Nilly!, 1 vol. Powell, Anna. 2005. (ENG.). 28p. (J). (gr. k-2). pap. 16.00 *(978-1-56148-488-1(1),* Good Bks.) Skyhorse Publishing Co., Inc.

—The Dumpster Diver. Wong, Janet S. 2007. (ENG.). 32p. (J). (gr. k-3). 16.99 *(978-0-7636-2380-7(6))* Candlewick Pr.

—The Dunderheads. Fleischman, Paul. 2012. (ENG.). 56p. (J). (gr. 1-4). pap. 6.99 *(978-0-7636-5239-5(3))* Candlewick Pr.

—The Dunderheads Behind Bars. Fleischman, Paul. 2012. (ENG.). 48p. (J). (gr. 1-4). 16.99 *(978-0-7636-4543-4(5))* Candlewick Pr.

—Fangs!, 1 vol. MacDonald, Alan. 2012. (Dirty Bertie Ser.). (ENG.). 112p. (gr. 1-3). pap. 4.95 *(978-1-4342-4267-9(6));* 23.99 *(978-1-4342-4601-1(9))* Stone Arch Bks.

—Fleas!, 1 vol. MacDonald, Alan. 2013. (Dirty Bertie Ser.). (ENG.). 112p. (gr. 1-3). pap. 4.95 *(978-1-4342-4822-0(4));* lib. bdg. 23.99 *(978-1-4342-4618-9(3))* Stone Arch Bks.

—Frightfully Friendly Ghosties. King, Daren. 2013. (ENG.). 128p. (J). (gr. k-3). 12.95 *(978-1-62365-026-1(7),* Quercus) Quercus NA.

—Frightfully Friendly Ghosties: School of Meanies. King, Daren. 2014. (ENG.). 128p. (J). (gr. k-3). 12.99 *(978-1-62365-349-1(5),* Quercus) Quercus NA.

—Germs!, 1 vol. MacDonald, Alan. 2012. (Dirty Bertie Ser.). (ENG.). 112p. (gr. 1-3). pap. 4.95 *(978-1-4342-4266-2(8));* 23.99 *(978-1-4342-4600-4(0))* Stone Arch Bks.

—Happy Birthday, Madame Chapeau. Beaty, Andrea. 2014. (ENG.). 32p. (J). (gr. -1-3). 16.95 *(978-1-4197-1219-7(5),* Abrams Bks. for Young Readers) Abrams.

—Holiday Mania at the House of Fun. Blake, Jon. 2007. (House of Fun Ser.: 4). (ENG.). 128p. (J). (gr. 2-4). pap. 6.95 *(978-0-340-93129-5(9))* Hachette Children's Group GBR. Dist: Independent Pubs. Group.

—House of Fun. Blake, Jon. 2007. (House of Fun Ser.: 1). (ENG.). 128p. (J). (gr. 2-4). pap. 6.95 *(978-0-340-88459-1(2))* Hachette Children's Group GBR. Dist: Independent Pubs. Group.

—Iggy Peck, Architect. Beaty, Andrea. 2007. (ENG.). 32p. (J). (gr. k-17). 16.95 *(978-0-8109-1106-2(X),* Abrams Bks. for Young Readers) Abrams.

—Iggy Peck, Architect. Beaty, Andrea. 2010. (ENG.). 32p. (J). (gr. k-17). pap. 7.95 *(978-0-8109-8928-3(X))* UK Abrams Bks. for Young Readers.

—Mrs. Crump's Cat. Smith, Linda. 2006. 32p. (J). (gr. -1-3). 17.89 *(978-0-06-443551-2(2))* HarperCollins Pubs.

—Operation Bunny. Gardner, Sally. 2014. (Wings & Co Ser.: 1). (ENG.). 192p. (J). (gr. 2-5). 12.99 *(978-0-8050-9892-1(5),* Holt, Henry & Co. Bks. For Young Readers) Holt, Henry & Co.

—Operation Bunny. Gardner, Sally. 2014. (Wings & Co Ser.: 1). (ENG.). 208p. (J). (gr. 2-5). pap. 5.99 *(978-1-250-05053-3(7))* Square Fish.

—Peace & Love Thing. Blake, Jon. 2008. (House of Fun Ser.: 5). (ENG.). 128p. (J). (gr. 2-4). pap. 6.95 *(978-0-340-94480-6(3))* Hodder & Stoughton GBR. Dist: Independent Pubs. Group.

—Rapunzel: A Groovy Fairy Tale. Roberts, Lynn. 2003. (ENG.). 32p. (J). (gr. -1-3). 17.95 *(978-0-8109-4242-4(9))* Abrams.

—Rosie Revere, Engineer. Beaty, Andrea. 2013. (ENG.). 32p. (J). (gr. k-17). 16.95 *(978-1-4197-0845-9(7),* Abrams Bks. for Young Readers) Abrams.

—Samantha Cardigan & the Genie's Revenge. Sutherland, David. 2005. (Red Bananas Ser.). (ENG.). 48p. (J). lib. bdg. *(978-0-7787-1070-7(X))* Crabtree Publishing Co.

—Samantha Cardigan & the Ghastly Twirling Sickness. Sutherland, David. 2005. (Red Bananas Ser.). (ENG.). 48p. (J). lib. bdg. *(978-0-7787-1069-1(6))* Crabtree Publishing Co.

—Siriol Llywelyn A'R Salwch Chwyrlio Erchyll. Sutherland, David et al. 2005. (WEL.). 48p. pap. *(978-1-85596-679-6(4))* Dref Wen.

—Tales of Terror from the Black Ship. Priestley, Chris. 2008. (Tales of Terror Ser.: 1). (ENG.). 256p. (J). (gr. 3-6). 12.99 *(978-1-59990-290-6(7),* Bloomsbury USA Childrens) Bloomsbury USA.

—Tales of Terror from the Tunnel's Mouth. Priestley, Chris. 2010. (Tales of Terror Ser.). (ENG.). 272p. (J). (gr. 7). 17.99 *(978-1-4088-0014-0(4),* Bloomsbury USA Childrens) Bloomsbury USA.

—Three Pickled Herrings: Book Two. Gardner, Sally. 2014. (Wings & Co Ser.: 2). (ENG.). 192p. (J). (gr. 2-5). 12.99 *(978-0-8050-9914-0(X),* Holt, Henry & Co. Bks. For Young Readers) Holt, Henry & Co.

—Uncle Montague's Tales of Terror. Priestley, Chris. 2007. (Tales of Terror Ser.). (ENG.). 192p. (J). (gr. 3-7). 12.95 *(978-1-59990-118-3(8),* Bloomsbury USA Childrens) Bloomsbury USA.

—The Vanishing of Billy Buckle. Gardner, Sally. 2015. (Wings & Co Ser.: 3). (ENG.). 240p. (J). (gr. 2-5). 13.99 *(978-0-8050-9915-7(8),* Holt, Henry & Co. Bks. For Young Readers) Holt, Henry & Co.

—The Wind in the Willows. Grahame, Kenneth. 2013. (ENG.). 256p. (J). (gr. 5). 24.99 *(978-0-7636-6526-5(6))* Candlewick Pr.

—Worms!, 1 vol. MacDonald, Alan. 2013. (Dirty Bertie Ser.). (ENG.). 112p. (gr. 1-3). pap. 4.95 *(978-1-4342-4823-7(2));* lib. bdg. 23.99 *(978-1-4342-4619-6(1))* Stone Arch Bks.

Roberts, David. Those Magnificent Sheep in Their Flying Machines. Roberts, David. Bently, Peter. 2014. 32p. (J). (gr. -1-3). 16.95 *(978-1-4677-4935-0(4))* Lerner Publishing Group.

Roberts, David & Fletcher, Corina. Ghoul School. 2003. 10p. (J). (gr. k-4). reprint ed. 18.00 *(978-0-7567-7028-0(9))* DIANE Publishing Co.

Roberts, Ean, jt. illus. see Roberts, Sara.

Roberts, Gaylia. Felix's Fabulous Feathers, 1 vol. Bishop, Rhonda. 2009. 23p. pap. 24.95 *(978-1-60836-890-7(4))* America Star Bks.

Roberts, Gill. Josh in the Jungle. Lewis, Siân. 2005. (ENG.). 32p. pap. 12.95 *(978-1-84323-462-3(9))* Beekman Bks., Inc.

Roberts, J. P. Rock & Rhino Learn Responsibility. Lisbona, Margie Taylor. 2011. 48p. pap. *(978-1-77067-530-8(2))* FriesenPress.

Roberts, Jennifer, photos by. Party in a Jar: 16 Kid-Friendly Jar Projects for Parties, Holidays& Special Occasions, 1 vol. Coppola, Vanessa Rodriguez. 2014. (ENG., 48p. pap. 9.99 *(978-1-4236-3405-8(5))* Gibbs Smith, Publisher.

Roberts, Jeremy. Batman - The Penguin's Arctic Adventure. Lemke, Donald. 2014. (ENG.). 24p. (J). (gr. -1-3). pap. 3.99 *(978-0-06-221000-5(9),* HarperFestival) HarperCollins Pubs.

—The Fate of Krypton. Sazaklis, John. 2013. (Man of Steel Ser.). (ENG.). 24p. (J). (gr. -1-3). pap. 3.99 *(978-0-06-223593-0(1),* HarperFestival) HarperCollins Pubs.

—Superman Saves Smallville. Sazaklis, John. 2013. (Man of Steel Ser.). (ENG.). 24p. (J). (gr. -1-3). pap. 3.99 *(978-0-06-223603-6(2),* HarperFestival) HarperCollins Pubs.

Roberts, Jeremy, jt. illus. see Grosvenor, Charles.

Roberts, Joel. Lenney the Lightning Bug. Williams Jr., Floyd. 2013. 20p. pap. 9.50 *(978-1-4276-1898-6(4))* Witty Publishing.

Roberts, Ley Honor. George Saves the World by Lunchtime. Readman, Jo. 2006. (ENG.). 32p. (J). (gr. k-2). pap. 15.99 *(978-1-903919-50-7(9))* Transworld Publishers Ltd. GBR. Dist: Independent Pubs. Group.

—My Bike Ride: Band 02A/Red A. Kelly, Maoliosa. 2006. (Collins Big Cat Ser.). (ENG.). 16p. (J). pap. 5.99 *(978-0-00-718661-7(4))* HarperCollins Pubs. Ltd. GBR. Dist: Independent Pubs. Group.

Roberts, Maggy. Billy Jones Dog Star. Roberts, Maggy, tr. Lewis, Siân. 2003. (ENG.). 56p. pap. 11.95 *(978-1-84323-169-1(7))* Beekman Bks., Inc.

Roberts, Marilyn. The Boy Who was President. Larichev, Andrei Borisovich. Moresco, Jamie, ed. 2004. 24p. (J). 9.95 *(978-0-9724386-0-5(2),* 2002096236) BlueSky Publishing.

Roberts, Mary Jo. The Pumpkin Fairy. Boyd, William T. 2003. 32p. (J). (gr. k-1). 14.95 *(978-0-9718161-0-7(7))* Wyatt Pr.

Roberts, Mary Sue, photos by. Down by the Shore. Crow, Marilee. 2011. 30p. 19.95 *(978-1-61633-087-3(2))* Guardian Angel Publishing, Inc.

Roberts, MarySue, photos by. Down by the Shore. Crow, Marilee. 2008. 28p. pap. 10.95 *(978-1-933090-39-9(1))* Guardian Angel Publishing, Inc.

—Gifts from God. Reeg, Cynthia. 2007. (J). 28p. 10.95 *(978-1-933090-33-7(2));* 30p. E-Book 5.00 incl. cd-rom *(978-1-933090-34-4(0))* Guardian Angel Publishing, Inc.

—Wicky Wacky Things that Go! Airplanes 1. Burch, Lynda S. 2004. 28p. (J). E-Book 9.95 incl. cd-rom *(978-1-933090-07-8(3))* Guardian Angel Publishing, Inc.

—Wicky Wacky Things that Go! Hot Air Balloons. Burch, Lynda S. 2004. 28p. (J). E-Book 9.95 incl. cd-rom *(978-1-933090-08-5(1))* Guardian Angel Publishing, Inc.

Roberts, MarySue, jt. photos by see Burch, Lynda S.

Roberts, Miranda. The Kid in My Closet. Meyer, Linda. 2008. (ENG.). 32p. (J). pap. 12.95 *(978-1-887542-94-4(9))* Book Pubs. Network.

Roberts, Pam. The Hawk & the Turtles. Moses, Albert. 2011. 16p. pap. 24.95 *(978-1-4626-4261-8(6))* America Star Bks.

Roberts, Ramona. A Cat's Tale. Alexander, Troas. 2007. 36p. per. 14.95 *(978-1-59858-371-7(9))* Dog Ear Publishing, LLC.

Roberts, Rebecca. Sunshine, the Golden Unicorn. Pigg, Theresa. 2011. 20p. pap. 24.95 *(978-1-4626-0733-4(0))* America Star Bks.

Roberts, Sara & Roberts, Ean. The Maylee Adventures: Facing the Sea Serpent. Roberts, Olivia. 2011. (ENG.). 50p. pap. 6.99 *(978-1-4610-7035-1(X))* CreateSpace Independent Publishing Platform.

—The Maylee Adventures: the Adventure Begins. Roberts, Olivia. 2011. (ENG.). 50p. pap. 6.99 *(978-1-4538-5096-1(1))* CreateSpace Independent Publishing Platform.

Roberts, Smith. A House for a Mouse. Roberts, Smith. 2003. 56p. (J). per. 16.00 *(978-0-9727315-3-9(9))* Prospero's Pr.

Roberts, Steve. Animals. Hodge, Susie. 2010. (Let's Draw Ser.). (ENG.). 32p. (gr. 3-5). 22.60 *(978-1-61533-269-4(3));* pap. 10.55 *(978-1-61533-270-0(7))* Windmill Bks.

—Bugs. Regan, Lisa. 2010. (Let's Draw Ser.). (ENG.). 32p. (J). (gr. 3-5). pap. 10.55 *(978-1-61533-268-7(5));* lib. bdg. 22.60 *(978-1-61533-265-6(0))* Windmill Bks.

—Crocodiles. Parker, Steve. 2010. (I Love Animals Ser.). (ENG.). 24p. (J). (gr. 1-5). 22.60 *(978-1-61533-247-2(2));* pap. 8.15 *(978-1-61533-255-7(3))* Windmill Bks.

—Dinosaurs. Hodge, Susie. 2010. (Let's Draw Ser.). (ENG.). 32p. (gr. 3-5). 22.60 *(978-1-61533-264-9(2))* Windmill Bks.

—How to Draw Animals. Hodge, Susie. 2008. (How to Draw Ser.). 47p. (J). (gr. 4-7). *(978-1-84810-005-3(1))* Miles Kelly Publishing, Ltd.

—How to Draw Baby Animals. Regan, Lisa. 2008. (How to Draw Ser.). 47p. (J). (gr. 4-7). *(978-1-84810-066-4(3))* Miles Kelly Publishing, Ltd.
—How to Draw Bugs. Regan, Lisa. 2008. (How to Draw Ser.). 47p. (J). (gr. -1-3). *(978-1-84810-065-7(5))* Miles Kelly Publishing, Ltd.
—How to Draw Dinosaurs. Hodge, Susie. 2008. (How to Draw Ser.). 47p. (J). (gr. 4-7). *(978-1-84810-006-0(X))* Miles Kelly Publishing, Ltd.
—10 Things You Should Know about Crocodiles. Parker, Steve. Gallagher, Belinda & Borton, Paula, eds. 2004. (10 Things You Should Know Ser.). 24p. (J). 6.99 *(978-1-84236-121-4(X))* Miles Kelly Publishing, Ltd. GBR. Dist: Independent Pubs. Group.
Roberts, Temple. Aspen Cat: Adventurer Extraordinaire. Brand, Mary. 2009. 44p. pap. 24.95 *(978-1-60749-165-1(6))* America Star Bks.
Robertson, Catherine. The Christmas Story As Told by Assellus the Christmas Donkey. Duggan, Janet. 2009. (ENG.). 44p. *(978-0-9563389-1-4(7))* Janet Duggan.
Robertson, Chris. My Yellow Umbrella. Robertson, Chris. 2013. 32p. pap. 9.99 *(978-1-62395-543-4(2))* Xist Publishing.
Robertson, Darick, jt. illus. see Capullo, Greg.
Robertson, Elysia Hill. Betsy Book: She Is A Smile. Robertson, Elysia Hill. 2005. 26p. (J). per. 6.95 *(978-0-9764444-7-3(X))* E. J. Publishing.
—Do Fish Cry ? Robertson, Elysia Hill. 2005. 116p. (J). per. 12.95 *(978-0-9764444-1-1(0)*, EJWV-002) E. J. Publishing.
—Dottie Goes to School. Robertson, Elysia Hill. 2005. 30p. (J). per. 6.95 *(978-0-9764444-8-0(8))* E. J. Publishing.
—Toley's Sleep over Learning Party. Robertson, Elysia Hill. 2005. 118p. (J). per. 12.95 *(978-0-9764444-4-2(5)*, EJWV-005) E. J. Publishing.
—Tool of Life My Pink School Books. Robertson, Elysia Hill. 2005. 112p. (J). per. 12.95 *(978-0-9764444-3-5(7)*, EJWV-004) E. J. Publishing.
Robertson, Elysia Hill & Bruce, Cindy. D. J.'s Sneakers. Robertson, Elysia Hill. 2005. 104p. (J). per. 12.95 *(978-0-9764444-2-8(9)*, EJWV-003) E. J. Publishing.
—We Make the World A Special Place. Robertson, Elysia Hill. 2005. 100p. (J). per. 12.95 *(978-0-9764444-0-4(2)*, EJWV-001) E. J. Publishing.
Robertson, Laura. Gordon the Goblin in Oh My! Is That a Pork Pie? Kurd, Tariq. 2012. 36p. pap. *(978-1-907762-10-9(8))* Malt Publishing.
Robertson, M. P. Frank N Stan. Quarto Generic Staff. 2012. (ENG.). 32p. (J). (gr. k-3). 17.99 *(978-1-84780-130-2(7)*, Frances Lincoln) Quarto Publishing Group UK GBR. Dist: Hachette Bk. Group.
—The Great Dragon Rescue. 2009. (ENG.). 32p. (J). (gr. -1-2). pap. 8.95 *(978-1-84507-379-4(7)*, Frances Lincoln) Quarto Publishing Group UK GBR. Dist: Hachette Bk. Group.
Robertson, Michael. Go to Bed, Blue. Bader, Bonnie. 2014. (Penguin Young Readers, Level 1 Ser.). (ENG.). 32p. (J). (gr. k-1). pap. 3.99 *(978-0-448-48219-4(3)*, Warne, Frederick Pubs.) Penguin Bks., Ltd. GBR. Dist: Penguin Random Hse., LLC.
—Grandma Died & Mommy Really, Really Cried: Death - Dying. Frink-Hunter, Chene I. (J). (gr. -1-6). *(978-0-9654185-1-5(0))* Hunter Pubns.
—Play with Blue. Bader, Bonnie. 2013. (Penguin Young Readers, Level 1 Ser.). (ENG.). 32p. (J). (gr. k-1). 14.99 *(978-0-448-46506-7(X))*; mass mkt. 3.99 *(978-0-448-46254-7(0))* Penguin Bks., Ltd. GBR. (Warne, Frederick Pubs.). Dist: Penguin Random Hse., LLC.
Robertson, R. H. The Mystery Key at Camp Green Meadow. Gundel, Jean. 2011. (J). pap. 14.95 *(978-1-59571-730-6(7))* Word Association Pubs.
Robertson, Susan. Little Bunny. 2005. (Bedtime Babies Ser.). 8p. (J). (gr. -1). per., bds. 6.99 *(978-1-57755-503-2(1))* Flying Frog Publishing, Inc.
—Little Puppy. 2005. (Bedtime Babies Ser.). 8p. (J). (gr. -1). per., bds. 6.99 *(978-1-57755-501-8(5))* Flying Frog Publishing, Inc.
Robin, Gulack. While You Were Gone Year Two. Garcia, Justine Marie. 2012. 26p. pap. 12.95 *(978-0-9836913-5-8(5))* Rose Bud Publishing Co. LLC.
Robin, Thierry. Happy Halloween, Li'l Santa. Trondheim, Lewis & Robin, Thierry. 2003. (ENG.). 48p. 14.95 *(978-1-56163-361-6(5))* NBM Publishing Co.
Robins, Arthur. The Amazing Adventures of Chilly Billy. Mayle, Peter. 2013. 72p. pap. *(978-1-908191-69-4(4))* Escargot Bks. Online, Ltd.
—Eco-Wolf & the Three Pigs, 1 vol. Anholt, Laurence. 2004. (Seriously Silly Stories Ser.). (ENG.). 64p. (gr. 3-5). 15.99 *(978-0-7565-0630-8(1)*, CPB Grades 4-8) Compass Point Bks.
—My Granny Is a Pirate. McDermid, Val. 2012. (ENG.). 32p. (J). (gr. -1-k). pap. 10.00 *(978-1-4083-0927-8(0))* Hodder & Stoughton GBR. Dist: Independent Pubs. Group.
—Small Knight & George & the Pirates. Armitage, Ronda. 2013. (Small Knight & George Ser.). (ENG.). 32p. (J). (-k). pap. 10.99 *(978-1-4083-1274-2(3))* Hodder & Stoughton GBR. Dist: Independent Pubs. Group.
Robins, James. What's That Bird? Getting to Know the Birds Around You, Coast to Coast. Vezo, Tom, photos by. Choiniere, Joseph & Golding, Claire Mowbray. 2005. (ENG.). 128p. (J). pap. 14.95 *(978-1-58017-554-8(6)*, 67554) Storey Publishing, LLC.
Robins, Jim. Astronauts. West, David. 2008. (Graphic Careers Ser.). 48p. (gr. 5-8). per. 14.05 *(978-1-4042-1462-0(3))*; (YA). lib. bdg. 31.95 *(978-1-4042-1461-3(5))* Rosen Publishing Group, Inc., The.
Robinson, Alan James. Here Is the Arctic Winter. Dunphy, Madeleine. 2007. (Web of Life Ser.). (ENG.). 32p. (J). (gr. -1-3). 16.95 *(978-0-9777539-1-8(3))*; pap. 9.95 *(978-0-9777539-0-1(5))* Web of Life Children's Bks.
Robinson, Andrew, et al. Where Did Dinosaurs Go? Unwin, Mike. 2006. (Usborne Starting Point Science Ser.). 24p. (J). (gr. 1-4). pap. 4.99 *(978-0-7945-1410-5(3)*, Usborne) EDC Publishing.
Robinson, Anthony, photos by. Street Children. Robinson, Anthony. Allan, June. 2015. 40p. (J). pap. 9.99 ***(978-1-84780-598-0(1)***, Frances Lincoln) Quarto Publishing Group UK GBR. Dist: Littlehampton Bk Services, Ltd.
Robinson, Barbara J. Blue Turtle Moon Queen: The September Book. Biotnick, Elihu. 2009. (ENG.). 114p. (J). (gr. 6-12). pap. 7.25 *(978-0-915090-20-4(1)*, California Street) Firefall Editions.
—The Fog Line. Blotnick, Elihu. 2009. (Mr. Blot Ser.: No. 3). (ENG.). 56p. (YA). (gr. 6-18). pap. 9.00 *(978-0-915090-12-9(0)*, California Street) Firefall Editions.
Robinson, Bill. Penny of the Pyramids (Mr. Peabody & Sherman) Berrios, Frank. 2014. (Step into Reading Ser.). (ENG.). 32p. (J). (gr. -1-1). 3.99 *(978-0-385-37143-8(8)*, Random Hse. Bks. for Young Readers) Random Hse. Children's Bks.
Robinson, Bill, jt. illus. see RH Disney Staff.
Robinson, Charles. The Big Book of Nursery Rhymes. Jerrold, Walter, ed. 2012. (Calla Editions Ser.). (ENG.). 352p. (gr. -1). 40.00 *(978-1-60660-030-6(3))* Dover Pubns., Inc.
—A Child's Garden of Verses: A Collection of Scriptures, Prayers & Poems. Stevenson, Robert Louis. 2009. (ENG.). 100p. (J). (gr. 4-7). pap. 15.95 *(978-1-59583-350-1(1)*, 9781595833501, Green Tiger Pr.) Laughing Elephant.
—Classic Tales of Oscar Wilde. Wilde, Oscar. 2014. (ENG.). 96p. (J). (gr. k-3). 19.99 *(978-1-4052-6423-5(3))* Egmont Bks., Ltd. GBR. Dist: Independent Pubs. Group.
—Floramel & Esteban. Buchwald, Emilie. 2009. (ENG.). 80p. (J). (gr. 1-6). 16.95 *(978-1-57131-688-2(4))* Milkweed Editions.
—Lullaby Land: Songs of Childhood. Field, Eugene. 2006. 236p. per. 20.99 *(978-1-4255-1951-3(2))* Michigan Publishing.
—The Secret Garden. Burnett, Frances Hodgson. 2011. 304p. (J). *(978-1-4351-3344-0(7))* Barnes & Noble, Inc.
—The Secret Garden. Burnett, Frances Hodgson. 2014. (ENG.). 336p. (J). (gr. 2-4). 24.99 *(978-1-4052-6740-3(2))* Egmont Bks., Ltd. GBR. Dist: Independent Pubs. Group.
Robinson-Chavez, Kathryn A. & Madzel, D. E. Emma's House of Sound. Hayes, Mj. 2012. 80p. pap. 12.95 *(978-0-9819634-4-0(7))* St. Augustine Pr.
Robinson, Christian. The Dead Bird. Brown, Margaret Wise. 2016. 32p. (J). (gr. -1-3). 17.99 *(978-0-06-028931-7(7))* HarperCollins Pubs.
—Gaston. DiPucchio, Kelly. 2014. (ENG.). 40p. (J). (gr. -1-3). 17.99 *(978-1-4424-5102-5(5)*, Atheneum Bks. for Young Readers) Simon & Schuster Children's Publishing.
—Harlem's Little Blackbird. Watson, Renée. 2012. (ENG.). 40p. (J). (gr. -1-2). 17.99 *(978-0-375-86973-0(5))*; lib. bdg. 20.99 *(978-0-375-96973-7(X))* Random Hse. Children's Bks.
—Josephine: The Dazzling Life of Josephine Baker. Powell, Patricia Hruby. 2014. (ENG.). 104p. (J). (gr. 2-5). 17.99 *(978-1-4521-0314-3(3))* Chronicle Bks. LLC.
—Last Stop on Market Street. De la Peña, Matt. 2015. (ENG.). 32p. (J). (gr. -1-k). 16.99 *(978-0-399-25774-2(8)*, Putnam Juvenile) Penguin Publishing Group.
—Leo: A Ghost Story. Barnett, Mac. 2015. (ENG.). 52p. (J). (gr. -1-k). 16.99 *(978-1-4521-3156-6(2))* Chronicle Bks. LLC.
—Queer: The Ultimate LGBT Guide for Teens. Bieschke, Marke & Belge, Kathy. 2011. (ENG.). 208p. (YA). (gr. 9-18). pap. 14.99 *(978-0-9819733-4-0(5))* Zest Bks.
—Rain! Ashman, Linda. 2013. (ENG.). 32p. (J). (gr. -1-3). 16.99 *(978-0-547-73395-1(X))* Houghton Mifflin Harcourt Publishing Co.
Robinson, Cindy. Baby Baobab. Robinson, Cindy. 2010. (ENG.). 32p. (J). (gr. k-2). pap. 9.00 *(978-1-77009-671-4(X))* Jacana Media ZAF. Dist: Independent Pubs. Group.
Robinson, Don. Daddy, What Is Love? Shapiro, Jane. 2008. (ENG.). 28p. (J). (gr. -1-3). *(978-1-59700-244-8(5))* Island Heritage Publishing.
—G Is for Gecko: An Alphabet Adventure in Hawai'i. Gillespie, Jane. 2013. (ENG.). 26p. (gr. -1). 12.95 *(978-1-933067-51-3(9))* Beachhouse Publishing, LLC.
—Kamehameha: The Boy Who Became a Warrior King. Crowe, Ellie. rev. ed. 2008. (ENG.). 62p. (J). (gr. k-k). pap. *(978-1-59700-591-3(6))* Island Heritage Publishing.
—Little Malia's Big Poi Idea. Calma, Jocelyn. 2009. 28p. (J). 12.99 *(978-1-59524-328-7(3))* Giddy Up, LLC.
—Mr. Miyataki's Marvelous Machine. Newsome, Tandy. 2004. 28p. (J). (gr. -1-3). 12.95 *(978-0-931548-68-0(3))* Island Heritage Publishing.
—Too Many Mangos. Paikai, Tammy. 2009. 28p. (J). (gr. -1). 11.95 *(978-1-59700-758-0(7))* Island Heritage Publishing.
Robinson, Don Leonard. G Is for Gecko: An Alphabet Adventure in Hawaii. 2006. (J). *(978-1-933067-18-6(7))* Beachhouse Publishing, LLC.
Robinson, Fiona. The Abominables. Ibbotson, Eva. 2013. (ENG.). 272p. (J). (gr. 3-7). 16.95 *(978-1-4197-0789-6(2)*, Amulet Bks.) Abrams.
—The Abominables. Ibbotson, Eva. 2014. (ENG.). 288p. (J). (gr. 3-7). pap. 8.95 *(978-1-4197-1215-9(2)*, Amulet Bks.) Abrams.
Robinson, Gordon. Alice's Adventures in Wonderland. Carroll, Lewis. 2009. 118p. (gr. 3-18). pap. 4.50 *(978-1-60450-761-4(6)*, Serenity Pubs.) Arc Manor.
Robinson, Hilda. Didn't We Have Fun! Robinson, Hilda. Kunkel, Jeff. 2012. 48p. (J). 19.95 *(978-1-933987-17-0(0)*, Crickhollow Bks.) Great Lakes Literary, LLC.
Robinson, Jayme. The Unfortunate Tale of Kachuva the Tortoise: As Told by Chukwa Sulcata. Sapre, Reshme. 2012. (ENG.). 40p. 16.95 *(978-0-9829362-0-7(6))* Hathi Chiti Bks. for Kids.
Robinson, Katherine. Confirming Faith: Candidate Book. Faith Development Program for High School Students Preparing to Celebrate the Sacrament of Confirmation with the Support of the Entire Faith Community. Sawyer, Kieran & Amodei, Michael. rev. ed. 2003. (Confirming Faith Ser.). 152p. (gr. 9-12). stu. ed. 8.95 *(978-0-87793-549-0(1))* Ave Maria Pr.
—Confirming Faith: Director's Manual... Faith Development Program for High School Students Preparing to Celebrate the Sacrament of Confirmation with the Support of the Entire Faith Community. Sawyer, Kieran & Amodei, Michael. rev. ed. 2003. (Confirming Faith Ser.). 232p. tchr. ed., spiral bd. 26.95 *(978-0-87793-548-3(3))* Ave Maria Pr.
Robinson, Keith. Speed Machines: A Pop-up Book with Moving Gears. Imperato, Teresa. 2005. 8p. (J). 14.95 *(978-1-58117-323-9(7)*, Intervisual/Piggy Toes) Bendon, Inc.
Robinson, Laura. Batley Needs Glasses, 10 vols., Vol. 12. Sargent, Dave & Sargent, Pat. 2004. (Learn to Read Ser.: 10).Tr. of Batley Necesita Anteojos. 18p. (J). pap. 10.95 *(978-1-56763-820-2(1))* Ozark Publishing.
—Batley Needs Glasses, 10 vols., Vol. 12. Sargent, Dave & Sargent, Pat. 2004. (Learn to Read Ser.: 10). 18p. (J). lib. bdg. 20.95 *(978-1-56763-819-6(8))* Ozark Publishing.
—Bo Bo's Big Imagination, 10 vols., Vol. 13. Sargent, Dave & Sargent, Pat. 2004. (Learn to Read Ser.: 10).Tr. of Gran Imaginacion de Bo Bo. 18p. (J). pap. 10.95 *(978-1-56763-822-6(8))* Ozark Publishing.
—Bo Bo's Big Imagination/la Gran Imaginación de Bo Bo, 10 vols., Vol. 13. Sargent, Dave & Sargent, Pat. 2004. (Learn to Read Ser.: 10). (ENG & SPA.). 18p. (J). pap. 10.95 *(978-1-56763-986-5(0))* Ozark Publishing.
—Cat Who Barked, 10 vols., Vol. 18. Sargent, Dave & Sargent, Pat. 2004. (Learn to Read Ser.: 10). 18p. (J). pap. 10.95 *(978-1-56763-832-5(5))*; lib. bdg. 20.95 *(978-1-56763-831-8(7))* Ozark Publishing.
—Cat Who Barked/el gato que Ladró, 10. Sargent, Dave & Sargent, Pat. 2004. (Learn to Read Ser.: 10). (ENG & SPA.). 18p. (J). 18. pap. 9.95 *(978-1-56763-996-4(8))*; Vol. 18. lib. bdg. 20.95 *(978-1-56763-995-7(X))* Ozark Publishing.
—Do All Ducks Quack?, 10 vols., Vol. 14. Sargent, Dave & Sargent, Pat. 2004. (Learn to Read Ser.: 10). 18p. (J). lib. bdg. 20.95 *(978-1-56763-823-3(6))*; lib. bdg. 10.95 *(978-1-56763-824-0(4))* Ozark Publishing.
—Do All Ducks Quack?/¿Granznan todos los Patos?, 10 vols., Vol. 14. Sargent, Dave & Sargent, Pat. 2004. (Learn to Read Ser.: 10). (ENG & SPA.). 18p. (J). pap. 10.95 *(978-1-56763-988-9(7))*; lib. bdg. 20.95 *(978-1-56763-987-2(9))* Ozark Publishing.
—Do Frogs Have Tails?, 10 vols., Vol. 15. Sargent, Dave & Sargent, Pat. 2004. (Learn to Read Ser.: 10).Tr. of Tienen Colas las Ranas?. 18p. (J). pap. 10.95 *(978-1-56763-826-4(0))*; lib. bdg. 20.95 *(978-1-56763-825-7(2))* Ozark Publishing.
—Do Frogs Have Tails?/Tienen Colas las Ranas?, 10 vols. Sargent, Dave & Sargent, Pat. 2004. (Learn to Read Ser.: 10).Tr. of Tienen Colas las Ranas?. (ENG & SPA.). 18p. (J). lib. bdg. 20.95 *(978-1-56763-989-6(5))*;15. pap. 9.95 *(978-1-56763-990-2(9))* Ozark Publishing.
—Fuzzy Bunny, 10 vols., Vol. 19. Sargent, Dave & Sargent, Pat. 2004. (Learn to Read Ser.: 10). 18p. (J). lib. bdg. 20.95 *(978-1-56763-833-2(3))*; lib. bdg. 10.95 *(978-1-56763-834-9(1))* Ozark Publishing.
—Fuzzy Bunny/el conejito Velloso, 10 vols., Vol. 19. Sargent, Dave & Sargent, Pat. 2004. (Learn to Read Ser.: 10). (ENG & SPA.). 18p. (J). pap. 10.95 *(978-1-56763-998-8(4))*; lib. bdg. 20.95 *(978-1-56763-997-1(6))* Ozark Publishing.
—I Can Read, Too/Puedo Leer, Tambien, 10 vols. Sargent, Dave & Sargent, Pat. 2003. (Puedo Leer Ser.). (SPA.). 24p. (J). Vol. 1. lib. bdg. 20.95 *(978-1-56763-943-8(7))*; Vol. 3. pap. 10.95 *(978-1-56763-948-3(8))*; Vol. 3. lib. bdg. 20.95 *(978-1-56763-947-6(X))*; Vol. 4. pap. 10.95 *(978-1-56763-950-6(X))*; Vol. 5. lib. bdg. 20.95 *(978-1-56763-951-3(8))*; Vol. 6. pap. 6.95 *(978-1-56763-954-4(2))*; Vol. 6. lib. bdg. 20.95 *(978-1-56763-953-7(4))*; Vol. 7. pap. 6.95 *(978-1-56763-956-8(9))*; Vol. 8. pap. 10.95 *(978-1-56763-958-2(5))*; Vol. 9. pap. 10.95 *(978-1-56763-960-5(7))*; Vol. 9. lib. bdg. 20.95 *(978-1-56763-959-9(3))*; Vol. 10. pap. 10.95 *(978-1-56763-962-9(3))*; Vol. 10. lib. bdg. 20.95 *(978-1-56763-961-2(5))* Ozark Publishing.
—Little Big Cat, 10 vols., Vol. 16. Sargent, Dave & Sargent, Pat. 2004. (Learn to Read Ser.: 10). 18p. (J). pap. 10.95 *(978-1-56763-828-8(7))*; lib. bdg. 20.95 *(978-1-56763-827-1(9))* Ozark Publishing.
—Little Big Cat/Gato pequeño y Grande, 10 vols., Vol. 16. Sargent, Dave & Sargent, Pat. 2004. (Learn to Read Ser.: 10). (ENG & SPA.). 18p. (J). pap. 10.95 *(978-1-56763-992-6(5))* Ozark Publishing.
—Little Big Cat/Gato Pequeño y Grande, 10 vols., Vol. 16. Sargent, Dave & Sargent, Pat. 2004. (Learn to Read Ser.: 10).Tr. of Gato Pequeno y Grande. (ENG & SPA.). 18p. (J). (gr. k-2). lib. bdg. 20.95 *(978-1-56763-991-9(7))* Ozark Publishing.
—Little Tadpole, 10. Sargent, Dave & Sargent, Pat. 2004. (Learn to Read Ser.: 10). 18p. (J). 20. lib. bdg. 9.95 *(978-1-56763-836-3(8))*; Vol. 20. lib. bdg. 20.95 *(978-1-56763-835-6(X))* Ozark Publishing.
—Little Tadpole/el Renacuajo Pequeño, 10 vols. Sargent, Dave & Sargent, Pat. 2004. (Learn to Read Ser.: 10). (ENG & SPA.). 18p. (J). pap. 10.95 *(978-1-56763-567-6(9))*; lib. bdg. 20.95 *(978-1-56763-999-5(2))* Ozark Publishing.
—Lizzy Lightning Bug, 10 vols., Vol. 17. Sargent, Dave & Sargent, Pat. 2004. (Learn to Read Ser.: 10). 18p. (J). lib. bdg. 20.95 *(978-1-56763-829-5(5))*; lib. bdg. 10.95 *(978-1-56763-830-1(9))* Ozark Publishing.
—Lizzy Lightning Bug/Lizzy la Luciérnaga, 10 vols. Sargent, Dave & Sargent, Pat. 2004. (Learn to Read Ser.: 10). (ENG & SPA.). 18p. (J). pap. 10.95 *(978-1-56763-994-0(1))* Ozark Publishing.
—Lizzy Lightning Bug/Lizzy la Luciérnaga, 10 vols., Vol. 17. Sargent, Dave & Sargent, Pat. 2004. (Learn to Read Ser.: 10).Tr. of Lizzy la Luciernaga. (ENG & SPA.). 18p. (J). (gr. k-2). lib. bdg. 20.95 *(978-1-56763-993-3(3))* Ozark Publishing.
—A Puppy for Bobby/un cachorro para Robertito, 10 vols. Sargent, Dave & Sargent, Pat. 2004. (Learn to Read Ser.: 10). (ENG & SPA.). 18p. (J). pap. 10.95 *(978-1-56763-982-7(8))* Ozark Publishing.
—Puppy for Bobby/un cachorro para Robertito, 10, 11. Sargent, Dave & Sargent, Pat. 2004. (Learn to Read Ser.: 10). (ENG & SPA.). 18p. (J). lib. bdg. 19.95 *(978-1-56763-981-0(X))* Ozark Publishing.
Robinson, Lenord. Brighton One Star's Journey to Shine. Speicher, Diane Carty. 2005. 84p. (J). 19.95 *(978-0-9749806-0-7(9))* Shine On Pubns.
Robinson, Linda. Lazar, the Good Deed Dog. Shanker, Myrna Gelman. 2010. (J). *(978-0-9829273-0-4(4))* IGI Pr.
Robinson, Marcus. My Life By: D. D. Duck. Branen, Kathy. 2012. 24p. pap. 12.95 *(978-0-9845904-1-4(2))* Joshua Tree Publishing.
Robinson, Michael. Little Lion Goes to School. Magnus, Kellie. l.t. ed. 2003. 16p. (J). 9.99 *(978-0-9744211-0-0(3))* Media Magic New York.
Robinson, Nicola. Peter Pan: With Three-Dimensional Pop-Up Scenes. Barrie, J. M. 2013. (Fairytale Pop-Ups Ser.). (ENG.). 24p. (J). (gr. -1). 24.99 *(978-1-85707-828-2(4))* Tango Bks. GBR. Dist: Independent Pubs. Group.
Robinson, Nicola. The Monster Machine. Robinson, Nicola. 2013. (ENG.). 32p. (J). (gr. -1-k). pap. 8.99 *(978-1-84365-200-7(5)*, Pavilion) Pavilion Bks. GBR. Dist: Independent Pubs. Group.
Robinson, Nicola L. Orchestra! Safran, Sheri. 2011. (ENG.). 14p. (J). (gr. -1-2). 26.99 *(978-1-85707-810-7(1))* Tango Bks. GBR. Dist: Independent Pubs. Group.
Robinson, Robin. L. Frank Baum's Wizard of Oz. 2013. (Penguin Young Readers, Level 4 Ser.). (ENG.). 48p. (J). (gr. 3-4). 14.99 *(978-0-448-46508-1(6))*; mass mkt. 3.99 *(978-0-448-45588-4(9))* Penguin Bks., Ltd. GBR. (Warne, Frederick Pubs.). Dist: Penguin Random Hse., LLC.
Robinson, Roger, jt. illus. see Eaton, Scot.
Robinson, Susan. The Captain & Harry: A Trembling Tail of Thieves. Langley, Jan. 2006. 30p. (J). (gr. 4-7). pap. 10.95 *(978-1-892384-23-2(X))* Avery Color Studios, Inc.
—One Little Balsam Fir: A Northwoods Counting Book. DuTemple, Leslie A. 2006. 32p. (J). per. *(978-1-892384-37-9(X))* Avery Color Studios, Inc.
Robinson, Susan G. The Good Neighbors' Cheese Feast: A Cheesy Mouse Tale of Subtraction with Regrouping. Ramsay, Mark. 2010. (ENG.). 32p. pap. 8.95 *(978-0-9842863-1-7(4))* Strategic Educational Tools.
—The Good Neighbors Store an Award: A Cheesy Mouse Tale of Addition with Regrouping. Ramsay, Mark. 2010. (ENG.). 32p. pap. 8.95 *(978-0-9842863-0-0(6))* Strategic Educational Tools.
Robinson, T. H. A Child's Book of Saints. Canton, William. 2013. 268p. pap. 12.75 *(978-1-936639-22-9(X))* St. Augustine Academy Pr.
—The Heroes. Kingsley, Charles. 2009. 240p. pap. 10.95 *(978-1-59915-291-2(6))* Yesterday's Classics.
Robinson, Tanya. Sir up & Sir Down: The Story of Cakes Made in Pans with Syrup. Merrick, Daniel. l.t. ed. 2010. (ENG.). 24p. pap. 11.97 *(978-1-4538-8760-8(1))* CreateSpace Independent Publishing Platform.
Robinson, Tim. Christmas Sing-Along Car-I-Oke. Schiller, David. 2005. (ENG.). 64p. (J). (gr. -1-3). bds. 15.95 *(978-0-7611-3984-3(2)*, 13984) Workman Publishing Co., Inc.
—King George: What Was His Problem? - The Whole Hilarious Story of the American Revolution. Sheinkin, Steve. 2009. (ENG.). 208p. (J). (gr. 5-9). pap. 9.99 *(978-1-59643-518-6(6))* Square Fish.
—Two Miserable Presidents: The Amazing, Terrible, & Totally True Story of the Civil War. Sheinkin, Steve. 2009. (ENG.). 256p. (J). (gr. 5-9). pap. 9.99 *(978-1-59643-519-3(4))* Square Fish.
Robinson, William & Legramandi, Francesco. Anna & Elsa #5: the Polar Bear Piper (Disney Frozen) David, Erica. 2015. (Stepping Stone Book(TM) Ser.). (ENG.). 128p. (J). (gr. 1-4). 9.99 ***(978-0-7364-3436-2(4)***, RH/Disney) Random Hse. Children's Bks.
Robinson, William E., jt. illus. see RH Disney Staff.
Robison Gamble Creative, photos by. Dan & Louie Vol. 1: The Greatest Stories Ever Told, Robison Gamble Creative, des. deluxe ed. 2005. (J). 89.95 incl. audio compact disk *(978-1-933497-00-6(9))* Robison Gamble Creative.
Robledo, Emilia. The Birthday Party, 1 vol. Dale, Jay. 2012. (Engage Literacy Magenta Ser.). (ENG.). 32p. (gr. k-2). pap. 5.99 *(978-1-4296-8866-6(1)*, Engage Literacy) Capstone Pr., Inc.
—Cooking in Class, 1 vol. Dale, Jay. 2012. (Wonder Words Ser.). (ENG.). 32p. (gr. k-2). pap. 5.99 *(978-1-4296-8922-9(6)*, Engage Literacy) Capstone Pr., Inc.
Robledo, Honorio. ¡El Cucuy! A Bogeyman Cuento in English & Spanish. Hayes, Joe. 2003. (ENG & SPA.). 40p. (J). (gr. k-2). pap. 7.95 *(978-0-938317-78-4(4))* Cinco Puntos Pr.
—The Dog Child. Black, Simon. 2006. (ENG.). 32p. (J). (gr. -1-3). 17.95 *(978-0-938317-42-5(3))* Consortium Bk. Sales & Distribution.
Robledo Tapia, Honorio. La Supemina del Cilantro. Herrera, Juan Felipe & Herrera, Juan. 2003.Tr. of Super Cilantro Girl. (ENG & SPA.). 32p. (J). 16.95 *(978-0-89239-187-5(1))* Lee & Low Bks., Inc.
Robson, Matthew. Planes. Kelleher, Damian. 2008. (ENG.). 30p. (J). (gr. 3-7). pap., act. bk. ed. 8.95 *(978-1-84425-465-1(8)*, 1844254658) Haynes Publishing PLC GBR. Dist: Hachette Bk. Group.
Roca, François. Life of Jesus for Children. Paterson, Katherine. 2008. (J). *(978-0-545-01173-0(6)*, Levine, Arthur A. Bks.) Scholastic, Inc.
—Soar, Elinor! Brown, Tami Lewis. 2010. (ENG.). 40p. (J). (gr. -1-3). 16.99 *(978-0-374-37115-9(6)*, Farrar, Straus & Giroux (BYR)) Farrar, Straus & Giroux.
—Twenty-One Elephants & Still Standing. Prince, April Jones. 2005. (ENG.). 32p. (J). (gr. -1-3). 17.99 *(978-0-618-44887-6(X))* Houghton Mifflin Harcourt Publishing Co.

R

Rocco & Dorémus, Gaëtan. Half & Half-Swimming with Dolphins. Gillot, Laurence & Sebaoun, Elisabeth. 2010. 32p. (J). 9.95 *(978-1-60115-215-2(9))*; pap. 4.99 *(978-1-60115-216-9(7))* Treasure Bay, Inc.

Rocco, Joe. Halloween Motel. Diviny, Sean. Date not set. 32p. (J). (gr. -1-3). 5.25 hd 5.99 *(978-0-06-443651-9(9))* HarperCollins Pubs.

Rocco, John. Beep! Beep! Go to Sleep! Tarpley, Todd. 2015. (ENG.). 40p. (J). (gr. -1-1). 17.00 ***(978-0-316-25443-4(6))*** Little, Brown Bks. for Young Readers.

Rocco, John. Boy, Were We Wrong about the Solar System! Kudlinski, Kathleen V. 2008. (ENG.). 32p. (J). (gr. 1-3). 16.99 *(978-0-525-46979-7(6)*, Dutton Juvenile) Penguin Publishing Group.

—The Flint Heart. Paterson, Katherine & Paterson, John B. 2012. (ENG.). 304p. (J). (gr. 2-5). pap. 9.99 *(978-0-7636-6243-1(7))* Candlewick Pr.

—The Flint Heart. Paterson, Katherine & Paterson, John. 2011. (ENG.). 304p. (J). (gr. 2-5). 19.99 *(978-0-7636-4712-4(8))* Candlewick Pr.

—How to Train a Train. Eaton, Jason Carter. 2013. (ENG.). 48p. (J). (gr. -1-3). 16.99 *(978-0-7636-6307-0(7))* Candlewick Pr.

—The Kane Chronicles Box Set. Riordan, Rick. 2013. (Kane Chronicles Ser.). (ENG.). 1472p. (J). (gr. 3-7). pap. 26.99 *(978-1-4231-9962-5(6))* Hyperion Bks. for Children.

—The Legend Thief. Patten, E. J. (Hunter Chronicles Ser.: 2). (ENG.). 384p. (J). (gr. 3-7). 2014. pap. 7.99 *(978-1-4424-2036-6(7))*; 2013. 16.99 *(978-1-4424-2035-9(9))* Simon & Schuster Bks. For Young Readers. (Simon & Schuster Bks. For Young Readers).

—Percy Jackson & the Olympians 3 Book Paperback Boxed Set with New Covers. Riordan, Rick. 2014. (Percy Jackson & the Olympians Ser.). (ENG.). (J). (gr. 5-9). pap. 19.99 *(978-1-4847-2147-6(0))* Hyperion Bks. for Children.

—Percy Jackson's Greek Gods. Riordan, Rick. 2014. (ENG.). 336p. (J). (gr. 3-7). 24.99 *(978-1-4231-8364-8(9))* Hyperion Bks. for Children.

Rocco, John. Percy Jackson's Greek Heroes. Riordan, Rick. 2015. (ENG.). 416p. (J). (gr. 3-7). 24.99 ***(978-1-4231-8365-5(7))*** Hyperion Bks. for Children.

Rocco, John. Return to Exile. Patten, E. J. (Hunter Chronicles Ser.: 1). (ENG.). 512p. (J). (gr. 3-7). 2013. pap. 7.99 *(978-1-4424-2033-5(2))*; 2011. 16.99 *(978-1-4424-2032-8(4))* Simon & Schuster Bks. For Young Readers. (Simon & Schuster Bks. For Young Readers).

Rocco, John. Blackout. Rocco, John. 2011. (ENG.). 40p. (J). (gr. -1-k). 17.99 *(978-1-4231-2190-9(2))* Hyperion Pr.

—Blizzard. Rocco, John. 2014. (ENG.). 40p. (J). (gr. -1-k). 17.99 *(978-1-4231-7865-1(3))* Disney Pr.

—Fu Finds the Way. Rocco, John. 2009. (ENG.). 40p. (J). (gr. -1-2). 16.99 *(978-1-4231-0965-5(1))* Hyperion Pr.

—Super Hair-O & the Barber of Doom. Rocco, John. 2013. (ENG.). 32p. (J). (gr. -1-4). 16.99 *(978-1-4231-2189-3(9))* Disney Pr.

—Swim That Rock. Rocco, John. Primiano, Jay. 2014. (ENG.). 304p. (J). (gr. 7). 16.99 *(978-0-7636-6905-8(9))* Candlewick Pr.

Roche, Denis. Can You Count Ten Toes? Count to 10 in 10 Different Languages. Evans, Lezlie. 2004. (J). (gr. -1-3). 13.60 *(978-0-7569-5182-5(8))* Perfection Learning Corp.

—Can You Count Ten Toes? Count to 10 in 10 Different Languages. Evans, Lezlie. 2004. (ENG.). 32p. (J). (gr. -1-3). pap. 5.95 *(978-0-618-49487-3(1))* Houghton Mifflin Harcourt Publishing Co.

—Can You Greet the Whole Wide World? 12 Common Phrases in 12 Different Languages. Evans, Lezlie. 2010. 32p. (J). (gr. k-3). pap. *(978-0-618-81519-7(8))* Houghton Mifflin Harcourt Trade & Reference Pubs.

—A Plane Goes Ka-Zoom! London, Jonathan. 2010. (ENG.). 32p. (J). (gr. -1-k). 15.99 *(978-0-8050-8970-7(5)*, Holt, Henry & Co. Bks. For Young Readers) Holt, Henry & Co.

Roche, Jackie. The Derby Ram. 2010. (First Steps in Music Ser.). (ENG.). 32p. (J). (gr. -1-k). 16.95 *(978-1-57999-783-0(X))* G I A Pubns., Inc.

Roche, Maite. The Beautiful Story of Jesus. Roche, Maite. 2010.Tr. of belle histoire de Jesus. 64p. (J). (gr. k-2). 14.95 *(978-0-8198-1177-6(7))* Pauline Bks. & Media.

—The First Noel. Roche, Maite. 2009.Tr. of plus belle histoire de Noël. 48p. (J). (gr. -1-1). 16.95 *(978-0-8198-2687-9(1))* Pauline Bks. & Media.

Rocheleau, Paul, jt. photos by see McLaughlin, David.

Rochester, Andre. The Sunflower & Rose. 2010. (ENG.). 36p. (J). 22.95 *(978-0-9817291-1-4(8))* Metaphors 4 Life.

Rock, Howard. Neeluk: An Eskimo Boy in the Days of the Whaling Ships. Kittredge, Frances. 2005. 88p. (J). (gr. 3-7). 18.95 *(978-0-88240-545-2(4))* Graphic Arts Ctr. Publishing Co.

Rockefeller, Matt. Brain Quest Workbook: Grade 5. Heos, Bridget. 2015. (ENG.). 320p. (J). (gr. 5-5). pap. 12.95 *(978-0-7611-8278-8(0))* Workman Publishing Co., Inc.

Rockfield, Darryl. A Leopard Is More Than His Spots. Beeson, Lea Ann. Popovich, Richard E., ed. l.t. ed. 2005. 51p. (J). lib. bdg. 19.95 *(978-0-9604876-1-5(1))* REP Pubs.

Rockford, Nancy. The Story of Lucia. Surace, Joan. 2006. (YA). pap. 8.00 *(978-0-8059-7062-3(2))* Dorrance Publishing Co., Inc.

Rockhill, Dennis. Polar Slumber. Rockhill, Dennis. 2007. (ENG.). 32p. (J). (gr. -1-3). 16.95 *(978-0-9741992-8-3(1)*, Raven Tree Pr.,Csi) Continental Sales, Inc.

—Polar Slumber/Sueño Polar. Rockhill, Dennis. Raven Tree Press Staff, ed. de la Vega, Eida, tr. 2004.Tr. of Sueño Polar. (SPA & ENG.). 32p. (J). (gr. -1-3). 16.95 *(978-0-9724973-1-2(5)*, 1234791, Raven Tree Pr.,Csi) Continental Sales, Inc.

Rocks, Tim. Bathroom Jokes: For Kids of All Ages. 2006. 288p. pap. *(978-1-58173-601-4(0))* Sweetwater Pr.

—Gross-Out Jokes: For Kids of All Ages. 2006. 288p. pap. *(978-1-58173-602-1(9))* Sweetwater Pr.

—Knock-Knock Jokes: For Kids of All Ages. 2006. 288p. pap. *(978-1-58173-600-7(2))* Sweetwater Pr.

Rockwell, Anne F. At the Firehouse. Rockwell, Anne F. 2003. 40p. (J). (gr. -1-1). 16.89 *(978-0-06-029816-6(2))* HarperCollins Pubs.

—My Preschool. Rockwell, Anne F. 2008. (ENG.). 32p. (J). (gr. -1-k). 16.95 *(978-0-8050-7955-5(6)*, Holt, Henry & Co. Bks. For Young Readers) Holt, Henry & Co.

—Welcome to Kindergarten. Rockwell, Anne F. 2004. (ENG.). 32p. (J). (gr. -1-1). pap. 7.99 *(978-0-8027-7664-8(7))* Walker & Co.

Rockwell, Anne F. & Rockwell, Harlow. The Toolbox. Rockwell, Anne F. & Rockwell, Harlow. 2006. (ENG.). 24p. (J). (gr. -1-k). bds. 7.99 *(978-0-8027-9609-7(5))* Walker & Co.

Rockwell, Barry. Amazing Grace. Douglas, Babette. 2006. (Kiss a Me Teacher Creature Stories Ser.). (J). (gr. 3-7). 9.99 *(978-1-890343-33-0(1))* Kiss A Me Productions, Inc.

—Kiss a Me: A Little Whale Watching. Douglas, Babette. 2006. (Kiss a Me Teacher Creature Stories Ser.). (J). (gr. 3-7). 9.99 *(978-1-890343-08-8(0))* Kiss A Me Productions, Inc.

—Kiss a Me Goes to School. Douglas, Babette. 2006. (Kiss a Me Teacher Creature Stories Ser.). (J). (gr. -1-3). 9.99 *(978-1-890343-09-5(9))* Kiss A Me Productions, Inc.

—Kiss a Me to the Rescue. Douglas, Babette. 2006. (Kiss a Me Teacher Creature Stories Ser.). (J). (gr. -1-3). 9.99 *(978-1-890343-11-8(0))* Kiss A Me Productions, Inc.

—Oscarpus. Douglas, Babette. 2006. (Kiss a Me Teacher Creature Stories Ser.). (J). (gr. -1-3). 9.99 *(978-1-890343-30-9(7))* Kiss A Me Productions, Inc.

Rockwell, Eve. Make Your Own Christmas Cards. 2012. (Christmas Ser.). (ENG.). 8p. pap. 8.95 *(978-1-59583-452-2(4))* Laughing Elephant.

Rockwell, Harlow. My Spring Robin. Rockwell, Anne. 2015. (ENG.). 24p. (J). (gr. -1-3). 16.99 *(978-1-4814-1137-0(3)*, Simon & Schuster/Paula Wiseman Bks.) Simon & Schuster/Paula Wiseman Bks.

Rockwell, Harlow & Rockwell, Lizzy. At the Beach. Rockwell, Anne F. 2014. (ENG.). 24p. (J). (gr. -1-3). 14.99 *(978-1-4814-1133-2(0)*, Simon & Schuster/Paula Wiseman Bks.) Simon & Schuster/Paula Wiseman Bks.

Rockwell, Harlow, jt. illus. see Rockwell, Anne F.

Rockwell, Joanna. Toasters Are Easy, School Not So Much. Souliere, Lisa. 2012. 20p. pap. 10.95 *(978-1-60976-654-2(7)*, Strategic Bk. Publishing) Strategic Book Publishing & Rights Agency (SBPRA).

Rockwell, Lizzy. Apples & Pumpkins. Rockwell, Anne F. (ENG.). 24p. (J). (gr. -1-3). 2012. 5.99 *(978-1-4424-7656-1(7))*; 2011. 14.99 *(978-1-4424-0350-5(0))* Simon & Schuster/Paula Wiseman Bks. (Simon & Schuster/Paula Wiseman Bks.).

—Apples & Pumpkins. Rockwell, Anne. 2014. (Classic Board Bks.). (ENG.). 28p. (J). (gr. -1-k). bds. 7.99 *(978-1-4424-9977-5(X)*, Little Simon) Little Simon.

—Cedric of Jamaica. Angelou, Maya. 2005. (Random House Pictureback Book Ser.). (J). *(978-0-375-83269-7(6))* Random Hse., Inc.

—Father's Day. Rockwell, Anne F. 2005. 40p. (J). (gr. -1-1). lib. bdg. 15.89 *(978-0-06-051378-8(0))* HarperCollins Pubs.

—First Day of School. Rockwell, Anne F. (ENG.). 40p. (J). (gr. -1-3). 2013. pap. 6.99 *(978-0-06-050193-8(6))*; 2011. 16.99 *(978-0-06-050191-4(X))* HarperCollins Pubs.

—Mary Clare Likes to Share: A Math Reader. Hulme, Joy N. 2006. (Step into Reading Ser.: Vol. 2). (ENG.). 32p. (J). (gr. -1-1). pap. 3.99 *(978-0-375-83421-9(4)*, Random Hse. Bks. for Young Readers) Random Hse. Children's Bks.

Rockwell, Lizzy. A Nest Full of Eggs. Jenkins, Priscilla Belz. 2015. (Let's-Read-And-Find-Out Science 1 Ser.). (ENG.). 32p. (J). (gr. -1-3). pap. 6.99 ***(978-0-06-238193-4(8))*** HarperCollins Pubs.

Rockwell, Lizzy. Presidents' Day. Rockwell, Anne F. 2009. (ENG.). 40p. (J). (gr. -1-1). pap. 6.99 *(978-0-06-050196-9(0))* HarperCollins Pubs.

—Presidents' Day. Rockwell, Anne F. 2007. (ENG.). 40p. (J). (gr. -1-1). 16.99 *(978-0-06-050194-5(4))* HarperCollins Pubs.

—St. Patrick's Day. Rockwell, Anne F. 2010. 40p. (J). (gr. -1-3). (ENG.). 14.99 *(978-0-06-050197-6(9))*; lib. bdg. 15.89 *(978-0-06-050198-3(7))* HarperCollins Pubs.

—Who Lives in an Alligator Hole? Rockwell, Anne F. & Rockwell. 2006. (Let's-Read-and-Find-Out Science Ser.). (ENG.). 40p. (J). (gr. k-4). 15.99 *(978-0-06-028530-2(3))*; pap. 5.99 *(978-0-06-445200-7(X)*, Collins) HarperCollins Pubs.

—Who Lives in an Alligator Hole? Rockwell, Anne F. 2006. (Let's-Read-and-Find-Out Science Ser.). 33p. (gr. k-4). 16.00 *(978-0-7569-6953-0(0))* Perfection Learning Corp.

—100 School Days. Rockwell, Anne F. & Rockwell. 2004. (ENG.). 40p. (J). (gr. -1-3). pap. 6.99 *(978-0-06-443727-1(2))* HarperCollins Pubs.

Rockwell, Lizzy. A Bird Is a Bird. Rockwell, Lizzy. 2015. (ENG.). 32p. (J). (gr. -1-2). 16.95 *(978-0-8234-3042-0(1))* Holiday Hse., Inc.

—The Busy Body Book: A Kid's Guide to Fitness. Rockwell, Lizzy. (ENG.). 40p. (J). (gr. -1-2). 2008. pap. 7.99 *(978-0-553-11374-7(7)*, Dragonfly Bks.); 2004. 15.95 *(978-0-375-82203-2(8)*, Crown Books For Young Readers) Random Hse. Children's Bks.

—Good Enough to Eat: A Kid's Guide to Food & Nutrition. Rockwell, Lizzy. 2009. (ENG.). 40p. (J). (gr. k-4). pap. 6.99 *(978-0-06-445174-1(7)*, Collins) HarperCollins Pubs.

—Plants Feed Me. Rockwell, Lizzy. 2015. (ENG.). 32p. (J). (gr. -1-1). 6.99 *(978-0-8234-3307-0(2))* Holiday Hse., Inc.

Rockwell, Lizzy, jt. illus. see Rockwell, Harlow.

Rockwell, Norman. Deck the Halls. Public Domain Staff. 2008. (ENG.). 32p. (J). (gr. k). 16.99 *(978-1-4169-1771-7(3)*, Atheneum Bks. for Young Readers) Simon & Schuster Children's Publishing.

Rockwell, Richard. The Improv Workshop Handbook: Creative Movement & Verbal Interaction for Students K-8: The Object Is Teamwork. Polsky, Milton & Gilead, Jack. Cordero, Chris, ed. l.t. ed. 2003. 112p. (J). (gr. k-8). pap. 15.00 *(978-0-88734-691-0(X))* Players Pr., Inc.

Rockwell, Scott. Uncle Scrooge, Vol. 345. Barks, Carl. Clark, John, ed. 2005. (Walt Disney's Uncle Scrooge Ser.). 64p. (YA). pap. 6.95 *(978-0-911903-88-1(7))* Gemstone Publishing, Inc.

Rocque, Rose. A Madcap Mother Goose. Mosher, Geraldine. 2003. pap. 9.95 *(978-0-9726311-4-3(3))* Top Quality Pubns.

Rodanas, Kristina. Flamingo Sunset, 0 vols. London, Jonathan. 2013. (ENG.). 33p. (J). (gr. k-3). pap. 9.99 *(978-1-4778-1674-5(7)*, 9781477816745, Amazon Children's Publishing) Amazon Publishing.

—Little Swan, 0 vols. London, Jonathan. 2009. (ENG.). 32p. (J). (gr. -1-3). 17.99 *(978-0-7614-5523-3(X)*, 9780761455233, Amazon Children's Publishing) Amazon Publishing.

—Yonder Mountain: A Cherokee Legend, 1 vol. 2005. (ENG.). 32p. (J). (gr. k-3). 16.95 *(978-0-7614-5113-6(7))* Marshall Cavendish Corp.

Rodanas, Kristina. The Blind Hunter, 1 vol. Rodanas, Kristina. 2003. (ENG.). 32p. (J). (gr. 1-4). 16.95 *(978-0-7614-5132-7(3))* Marshall Cavendish Corp.

Rodenberg, Charlotte Vivian. Bronto, Friend of Ceratops: Friend of Ceratops. Rodenberg, Charlotte Vivian. 2013. (ENG.). 32p. (J). 14.99 *(978-0-9844422-9-4(4))* Craigmore Creations.

Rodgers, Frank. The Huge Bag of Worries. Ironside, Virgina & Ironside, Virginia. 2004. (ENG.). 32p. (J). (gr. -1-k). pap. 11.99 *(978-0-340-90317-9(1))* Hodder & Stoughton GBR. Dist: Independent Pubs. Group.

Rodgers, Frank. Little T & Lizard the Wizard, 1 vol. Rodgers, Frank. 2006. (Read-It! Chapter Bks.). (ENG.). 52p. (gr. 2-4). lib. bdg. 21.32 *(978-1-4048-2725-7(0)*, Chapter Readers) Picture Window Bks.

—Little T & the Royal Roar, 1 vol. Rodgers, Frank. 2006. (Read-It! Chapter Bks.). (ENG.). 52p. (gr. 2-4). lib. bdg. 21.32 *(978-1-4048-2728-8(5)*, Chapter Readers) Picture Window Bks.

—Mr. Croc's Silly Sock, 1 vol. Rodgers, Frank. 2006. (Read-It! Chapter Bks.). (ENG.). 52p. (gr. 2-4). lib. bdg. 21.32 *(978-1-4048-2730-1(7)*, Chapter Readers) Picture Window Bks.

—Mr. Croc's Walk, 1 vol. Rodgers, Frank. 2006. (Read-It! Chapter Bks.). (ENG.). 52p. (gr. 2-4). lib. bdg. 21.32 *(978-1-4048-2729-5(3)*, Chapter Readers) Picture Window Bks.

Rodgers, John. I Is for Indy. King, Mike. 2006. 48p. (J). (gr. 4-18). 18.95 *(978-1-891390-21-0(X))* Witness Productions.

Rodgers, Phillip W. The D Word: Divorce. Cook, Julia. 2011. (ENG.). (J). (gr. 2-7). pap. 9.95 *(978-1-931636-76-6(1))* National Ctr. For Youth Issues.

Rodrigue. Black Moon. Groot, De. Spear, Luke, tr. from FRE. 2007. (ENG.). 48p. (J). (gr. 4-7). pap. 9.99 *(978-1-905460-30-4(9))* CineBook GBR. Dist: National Bk. Network.

—Jade Vol. 5. Groot, Bob de. 2008. (ENG.). 48p. pap. 11.95 *(978-1-905460-52-6(X))* CineBook GBR. Dist: National Bk. Network.

Rodriguez, Albert G. Jewish Alphabet, 1 vol. Clement, Janet. 2006. (ENG.). 32p. (J). (gr. k-3). 16.99 *(978-1-58980-414-2(7))* Pelican Publishing Co., Inc.

Rodriguez, Artemio. The King of Things/el Rey de Las Cosas. Rodriguez, Artemio. 2006. (SPA & ENG.). 32p. (J). (gr. -1-3). 12.95 *(978-0-938317-97-5(0))* Consortium Bk. Sales & Distribution.

Rodriguez, Béatrice. Fox & Hen Together. 2011. (Stories Without Words Ser.). (ENG.). 32p. (J). (gr. -1-3). 14.95 *(978-1-59270-109-4(4))* Enchanted Lion Bks., LLC.

Rodriguez, Beatrix. Gingerbread Man. Folk Tale Staff. 2012. (ENG.). 32p. (J). (gr. -1-3). 17.95 *(978-0-7358-4086-7(5))* North-South Bks., Inc.

Rodriguez Braojos, Alberto, et al. Toothtime with Chomper. Friden, Chris. 2008. (J). *(978-0-9801849-3-8(2))* Haydenburn Lane.

Rodriguez, Christina. Boon the Raccoon & Easel the Weasel. Jackson, Bobby L. 2004. 32p. (J). pap. 11.95 *(978-1-884242-03-8(0)*, BREW2NED); 19.95 *(978-1-884242-02-1(2)*, BREW2NED) Multicultural Pubns.

—Un Dia con Mis Tias: A Day with My Aunts. Bernardo, Anilu. 2006. (ENG & SPA.). 32p. (J). (gr. -1-2). 16.95 *(978-1-55885-374-4(X)*, Piñata Books) Arte Publico Pr.

—Mayte & the Bogeyman/Mayte y el Cuco. Gonzalez, Ada Acosta. 2006. (ENG & SPA.). 32p. (J). (gr. -1-2). 16.95 *(978-1-55885-442-0(8)*, Piñata Books) Arte Publico Pr.

—Storm Codes. Maurer, Tracy. 2007. 40p. (J). pap. 8.95 *(978-0-89317-064-6(X)*, WW-064X); (gr. 1-7). lib. bdg. 17.95 *(978-0-89317-063-9(1)*, WW-0631) Finney Co., Inc. (Windward Publishing).

—The Wishing Tree. Redman, Mary. 2008. (ENG.). 32p. (J). 15.95 *(978-1-934617-02-1(4)*, Elva Resa) Elva Resa Publishing, LLC.

Rodriguez, Christina Ann. ¡A Bailar! / Let's Dance! Cofer, Judith Ortiz. 2011. (ENG & SPA.). (J). 16.95 *(978-1-55885-698-1(6)*, Piñata Books) Arte Publico Pr.

Rodriguez, Christina Ann, et al. I Want to Be... Troupe, Thomas Kingsley. 2015. (I Want to Be... Ser.). (ENG.). 24p. (gr. k-3). 103.96 ***(978-1-4795-8006-4(6))*** Picture Window Bks.

Rodriguez, Christina Ann. I Want to Be a Bald Eagle. Troupe, Thomas Kingsley. 2015. (I Want to Be... Ser.). (ENG.). 24p. (gr. k-3). lib. bdg. 25.99 ***(978-1-4795-6858-1(9))*** Capstone Pr., Inc.

Rodriguez, Christina E. We Are Cousins/Somos Primos. Bertrand, Diane Gonzales. 2007. (SPA & ENG.). 32p. (J). (gr. -1-k). 16.95 *(978-1-55885-486-4(X)*, Piñata Books) Arte Publico Pr.

Rodriguez, Cristian. The Adventures of Señorita Rita: Running of the Bulls. Jones, Karen. 2011. (ENG.). 32p. pap. 9.99 *(978-1-4538-3804-4(X))* CreateSpace Independent Publishing Platform.

Rodriguez, Dave. Bella Wishes. May, Tessa. 2004. 35p. pap. 13.95 incl. audio compact disk *(978-0-9759325-0-6(0))* CarLou Interactive Media & Publishing.

Rodriguez, Edarissa. The Girl Who Took a Shower. Rodriguez, Edarissa. Santiago, Claribel, ed. 2003. (J). pap. 13.99 *(978-0-9744726-0-7(3))* Santiago, Claribel.

Rodriguez, Edel. Chike & the River. Achebe, Chinua. 2011. (ENG.). 96p. (J). pap. 10.00 *(978-0-307-47386-8(4)*, Anchor) Knopf Doubleday Publishing Group.

Rodriguez, Edel. Sonia Sotomayor. Winter, Jonah. 2015. 40p. pap. 8.00 ***(978-1-61003-616-0(6))*** Center for the Collaborative Classroom.

Rodriguez, Edel. Sonia Sotomayor: A Judge Grows in the Bronx. Winter, Jonah. Ziegler, Argentina Palacios, tr. from SPA. 2009. (ENG & SPA.). 32p. (J). (gr. -1-3). 17.99 *(978-1-4424-0303-1(9)*, Atheneum Bks. for Young Readers) Simon & Schuster Children's Publishing.

Rodriguez, Edel, jt. illus. see Jenkins, Steve.

Rodriguez, Gonzalo. Serafin Es un Diablo. Arciniegas, Triunfo. 2003. (Literatura Juvenil (Panamericana Editorial) Ser.). (SPA.). 109p. (YA). (gr. 5-7). per. *(978-958-30-0477-3(4))* Panamericana Editorial.

Rodriguez Howard, Pauline. Remembering Grandma / Recordando a Abuela. Armas, Teresa. Ventura, Gabriela Baeza, tr. from ENG. 2003. (ENG & SPA.). 32p. (J). 16.95 *(978-1-55885-344-7(8)*, Piñata Books) Arte Publico Pr.

Rodriguez Howard, Pauline & Howard, Pauline Rodriguez. Icy Watermelon/Sandia Fria. Galindo, Mary Sue. 2008. (J). (gr. -1-2). pap. 7.95 *(978-1-55885-307-2(3)*, Piñata Books) Arte Publico Pr.

Rodriguez, Ingrid. The Lion Who Saw Himself in the Water. Shah, Idries. 2005. (Sounds of Afghanistan Ser.). (J). (gr. -1-3). 28.95 incl. audio compact disk *(978-1-883536-71-8(5)*, LIWCB1, Hoopoe Bks.) I S H K.

—The Lion Who Saw Himself in the Water/el Leon Que Se Vio en el Aqua. Shah, Idries. 2003. (SPA & ENG.). (J). 18.00 *(978-1-883536-31-2(6)*, LIWS3); 6.95 *(978-1-883536-32-9(4)*, LIWS4) I S H K. (Hoopoe Bks.).

Rodriguez, Leonardo. Home-Field Advantage. Tuck, Justin. 2011. (ENG.). 40p. (J). (gr. -1-3). 16.99 *(978-1-4424-0369-7(1)*, Simon & Schuster Bks. For Young Readers) Simon & Schuster Bks. For Young Readers.

Rodriguez, Lorenzo. Huckleberry Finn. Rodriguez, Lorenzo, tr. Imbernón, Teresa & Twain, Mark. 2003. (Timeless Classics Ser.). (SPA.). 95p. (J). (gr. 5-8). pap. 12.95 *(978-84-204-5779-6(5))* Santillana USA Publishing Co., Inc.

Rodriguez, Manny. The Crazy Kids Guide to Cooking for Your Pet: Recipes, Jokes, Pet Care Tips & Fun Things to Do with Your Pet Featuring the Back Bones of Character. Denzer, Barbara & Denzer, Missy. 2004. 64p. (J). (gr. k-7). 12.95 *(978-0-9744749-0-8(8))* Crazy Pet Pr., The.

Rodriguez, Marc. Shelly Goes to the Zoo. Martin, Kentrell. 2013. 32p. pap. 8.50 *(978-0-9851845-1-3(5))* Shelly's Adventures LLC.

Rodriguez, Mari. Le Comieron la Lengua los Ratones. Molina, Silvia & Silvia, Molina. 2005. (Montana Encantada Ser.). (SPA.). 96p. (YA). (gr. 3-5). pap. 9.50 *(978-84-241-8557-2(9))* Everest Editora ESP. Dist: Lectorum Pubns., Inc.

Rodriguez, Mary. El Beso Mas Largo del Mundo(The Longest Kiss in the World) Castaneda, Ricardo Chavez. rev. ed. 2006. (Castillo de la Lectura Verde Ser.). (SPA & ENG.). 111p. (J). (gr. 2-4). pap. 7.95 *(978-970-20-0356-4(3))* Castillo, Ediciones, S. A. de C. V. MEX. Dist: Macmillan.

Rodriguez, Paul. Don't Do Drugs! Do Dance! Character Education/Prevention. Rodriguez, Paul. 2003. 32p. (J). lib. bdg. 15.99 *(978-0-9744770-1-5(X))* Rodro.

—Let's All Play! Character Education/ Anti-Bullying. Rodriguez, Paul. 2003. 32p. (J). lib. bdg. 15.99 *(978-0-9744770-0-8(1))* Rodro.

—What Color Are You? Rodriguez, Paul. 2003. 32p. (J). lib. bdg. 15.99 *(978-0-9744770-2-2(8))* Rodro.

Rodriguez, Pedro. How the Camel Got His Hump: The Graphic Novel, 1 vol. Kipling, Rudyard. 2012. (Graphic Spin Ser.). (ENG.). 40p. (gr. 1-3). pap. 5.95 *(978-1-4342-3879-5(2))*; lib. bdg. 22.65 *(978-1-4342-3202-1(6))* Stone Arch Bks. (Graphic Revolve).

—How the Elephant Got His Trunk: The Graphic Novel, 1 vol. Kipling, Rudyard. 2012. (Graphic Spin Ser.). (ENG.). 40p. (gr. 1-3). pap. 5.95 *(978-1-4342-3880-1(6))*; lib. bdg. 22.65 *(978-1-4342-3222-9(0))* Stone Arch Bks. (Graphic Revolve).

—How the Leopard Got His Spots. Kipling, Rudyard. 2012. (Graphic Spin Ser.). (ENG.). 40p. (gr. 1-3). lib. bdg. 22.65 *(978-1-4342-3223-6(9)*, Graphic Revolve) Stone Arch Bks.

—How the Leopard Got His Spots: The Graphic Novel, 1 vol. Kipling, Rudyard. 2012. (Graphic Spin Ser.). (ENG.). 40p. (gr. 1-3). pap. 5.95 *(978-1-4342-3881-8(4)*, Graphic Revolve) Stone Arch Bks.

Rodriguez, Pedro. How the Rhinoceros Got His Skin: The Graphic Novel, 1 vol. Kipling, Rudyard. 2012. (Graphic Spin Ser.). (ENG.). 40p. (gr. 1-3). lib. bdg. 22.65 *(978-1-4342-3025-6(2)*, Graphic Revolve) Stone Arch Bks.

Rodriguez, Pedro. How the Rhinoceros Got His Skin: The Graphic Novel, 1 vol. Kipling, Rudyard. 2012. (Graphic Spin Ser.). (ENG.). 40p. (gr. 1-3). pap. 5.95 *(978-1-4342-3882-5(2)*, Graphic Revolve) Stone Arch Bks.

Rodriguez, Pedro. Just So Comics: Tales of the World's Wildest Beasts. Kipling, Rudyard. 2013. (Graphic Spin Ser.). (ENG.). 144p. (gr. 3-6). pap. 12.95 *(978-1-4342-4880-0(1))* Stone Arch Bks.

Rodriguez, Perfecto. Tina Springs into Summer/Tina Se Lanza Al Verano. Bevin, Teresa. 2005. (ENG & SPA.). 114p. (J). pap. 21.00 *(978-1-928589-28-0(6))* Gival Pr., LLC.

Rodriguez, Robert. Max's Journal: The Adventures of Shark Boy & Lava Girl. Toader, Alex. 2005. 128p. (J). *(978-1-933104-03-4(1))* Troublemaker Publishing, LP.

Rodriguez, Tina. Adelita & the Veggie Cousins / Adelita y las primas Verduritas. Rodriguez, Tina. Bertrand, Diane Gonzales & Ventura, Gabriela Baeza. 2011. (SPA.). (J). 16.95 *(978-1-55885-699-8(4),* Piñata Books) Arte Publico Pr.

Rodriguez, Tom. The Littlest Camel: And the Journey of the Three Kings. Aguiar, Judy Lee. 2008. 176p. (J). per. *(978-0-9725231-2-7(X))* Turnapaige & Reed Moore.

Rodriguez, Pedro. The Elves & the Shoemaker: A Grimm Graphic Novel, 1 vol. Grimm, Jacob et al. 2011. (Graphic Spin Ser.). (ENG.). 40p. (gr. 1-3). lib. bdg. 23.99 *(978-1-4342-2553-5(4),* Graphic Revolve) Stone Arch Bks.

—Hot Iron: The Adventures of a Civil War Powder Boy. Burgan, Michael. 2007. (Historical Fiction Ser.). (ENG.). 56p. (gr. 2-3). pap. 6.25 *(978-1-59889-406-6(4),* Graphic Flash) Stone Arch Bks.

Rodstrom, Terri. Moondancer's Adventures. Morneau, Ronald E. 2011. 28p. pap. 24.95 *(978-1-4626-2590-1(8))* America Star Bks.

Rodwell, Timothy. The Elephant Scientist. Rodwell, Timothy, photos by. O'Connell, Caitlin, photos by. O'Connell, Caitlin & Jackson, Donna M. 2011. (Scientists in the Field Ser.). (ENG.). 80p. (J). (gr. 5-7). 18.99 *(978-0-547-05344-8(4))* Houghton Mifflin Harcourt Publishing Co.

Rodwell, Timothy, jt. illus. see O'Connell, Caitlin.

Roe, David. Attack of the Leaping Lizards: Library Edition. Aber, Linda Williams. 2012. (Chiller Thrillers Ser.). (ENG.). 96p. (J). (gr. 4-6). 14.99 *(978-0-7944-2729-0(4))* Reader's Digest Assn., Inc., The.

—The Chiller Thrillers: Attack of the Leaping Lizards. Aber, Linda. 2012. (Chiller Thrillers Ser.). (ENG.). 96p. (J). (gr. 4-6). pap. 7.99 *(978-0-7944-2566-1(6))* Reader's Digest Assn., Inc., The.

—The Secret of Spider Motel. Gilden, Mel. ltd. ed. 2012. (Chiller Thrillers Ser.). (ENG.). 96p. (J). (gr. 4-6). 14.99 *(978-0-7944-2728-3(6))* Reader's Digest Assn., Inc., The.

—The Secret of the Spider Motel. Gilden, Mel. 2012. (Chiller Thrillers Ser.). (ENG.). 96p. (J). (gr. 4-6). pap. 7.99 *(978-0-7944-2565-4(8))* Reader's Digest Assn., Inc., The.

Roe, Monika. The Official Book of Me: Tips for a Lifestyle of Health, Happiness & Wellness. Wallach, Marlene. 2014. (ENG.). 176p. (J). (gr. 4-8). pap. 9.99 *(978-1-4424-9479-4(4),* Simon & Schuster/Paula Wiseman Bks.) Simon & Schuster/Paula Wiseman Bks.

Roeder, Virginia. Jane Long: Texas Journey. Wade, Mary Dodson. 2009. (ENG.). 64p. (J). (gr. 4-7). 16.95 *(978-1-933979-39-7(9),* e90c463d-875c-4dc8-af1d-f58f210b12e6) Bright Sky Pr.

Roeder, Virginia M. Phoebe Clappsaddle for Sheriff, 1 vol. Chrismer, Melanie. 2003. (ENG.). 32p. (J). (gr. k-3). 16.99 *(978-1-58980-127-1(X))* Pelican Publishing Co., Inc.

—Phoebe Clappsaddle Has a Tumbleweed Christmas, 1 vol. Chrismer, Melanie. 2004. (ENG.). 32p. (J). (gr. k-3). 16.99 *(978-1-58980-241-4(1))* Pelican Publishing Co., Inc.

Roeder, Virginia Marsh. Jane Long: Choosing Texas. Wade, Mary Dodson. 2009. (ENG.). 24p. (J). (gr. k-2). 16.95 *(978-1-933979-38-0(0),* 05baad2b-c909-449b-8dfe-7ba8ad733f21) Bright Sky Pr.

Roederer, Charlotte. Animal Fables, 4 bks., Set. Grimm, Jacob et al. 2007. (Abbeville Classic Fairy Tales Ser.). (ENG.). 112p. (J). (gr. 1-2). 19.95 *(978-0-7892-0951-1(9))* Abbeville Pr., Inc.

—Goig. Echerique, Alfredo Bryce & Duenas, Ana Maria. (Literary Encounters Ser.). (SPA.). (J). (gr. 3-5). pap. *(978-968-494-065-9(3),* CI7706) Centro de Informacion y Desarrollo de la Comunicacion y la Literatura MEX. Dist: Lectorum Pubns., Inc.

Roehler, Yvonne Fetig. Good Night, Grandma. Washburn, Sandi. 2009. (ENG.). 16p. (J). 17.95 *(978-1-934367-09-4(5))* Growing Art Pr.

Rofé, April. The SENSEsational Alphabet: See-Read, Touch-Feel, Scratch & Smell, Hear-Learn, Have Fun! 2006. (J). *(978-0-9779189-1-1(2))* Waldenhouse Pubs., Inc.

Roffe, Michael. The Boer War. Wilkinson-Latham, Christopher. 2011. (Men-at-Arms Ser.: 62). (ENG.). 48p. pap. *(978-0-85045-257-0(0),* Osprey Publishing) Bloomsbury Publishing Plc.

Roffey, Maureen. 1 2 3 Count with Me! 2014. (ENG.). 26p. (J). (gr. -1 — 1). bds. 5.99 *(978-0-7944-3016-0(3))* Reader's Digest Assn., Inc., The.

Rog&eacute. The French Fry King. Rog&eacute. 2012. (ENG.). 32p. (J). (gr. -1-1). 17.95 *(978-1-77049-350-6(6),* Tundra Bks.) Tundra Bks. CAN. Dist: Penguin Random Hse., LLC.

Rogalski, Robert. Mrs. Murphy's Marvelous Mansion. Roberts, Emma Perry. 2006. 32p. (J). (gr. -1-3). 15.95 *(978-0-9740190-4-8(6),* 888-210-8216) Illumination Arts Publishing Co., Inc.

Rogé. Roger Gets Carried Away. Todd, Barbara. 2005. (ENG.). 32p. (J). (gr. -1-2). pap. 7.95 *(978-1-55037-898-6(8),* 9781550378986) Annick Pr., Ltd. CAN. Dist: Firefly Bks., Ltd.

—Taming Horrible Harry. Chartrand, Lili. Ouriou, Susan, tr. from FRE. 2006. (ENG.). 32p. (J). (gr. -1-3). 16.95 *(978-0-88776-772-2(9),* Tundra Bks.) Tundra Bks. CAN. Dist: Penguin Random Hse., LLC.

Rogers, Carol. Adventures of the American Colonies. McCall, Edith S. 2011. 126p. 40.95 *(978-1-258-06470-9(7))* Literary Licensing, LLC.

Rogers, Christopher M. Homer the Helicopter Grand Canyon Adventures. 2007. 72p. (J). 18.95 *(978-0-9786352-3-7(X))* Buscher, Julie W.

Rogers, David, jt. illus. see Speer, Julie.

Rogers, Denny. The Little Rock & Other Stories: And Other Stories. Hasling, Jack. 2003. (ENG.). 32p. (Orig.). (J). (gr. 1-6). pap. 9.95 *(978-1-878044-51-8(6),* Wild Rose) Mayhaven Publishing, Inc.

—The Peanut Butter Kid. Stonesifer, Gertrude. 2003. (ENG.). 32p. (J). (gr. 1-4). pap. 9.95 *(978-1-878044-44-0(3))* Mayhaven Publishing, Inc.

—The Wellness Tree. Cox, Judith. 2003. 32p. (J). (gr. k-4). (ENG.). 19.95 *(978-1-878044-29-7(X));* pap. 2.95 *(978-1-878044-35-8(4))* Mayhaven Publishing, Inc.

Rogers, Gregory. Chew Bee or Not Chew Bee. Chatterton, Martin. 2012. (Willy Waggledagger Ser.: 3). (ENG.). 174p. (J). (gr. 4-7). pap. 12.99 *(978-1-921541-31-5(8))* Little Hare Bks. AUS. Dist: Independent Pubs. Group.

—Future Knight. Davis, Tony. 2009. 129p. (J). Non-ISBN Publisher.

—High Hopes on Sea. Wagner, Jenny. 2005. (UQP Children's Fiction Ser.). 80p. (Orig.). (J). pap. *(978-0-7022-3525-2(3))* Univ. of Queensland Pr.

Rogers, Gregory. Pigeon Problems. Watts, Frances. 2015. (Sword Girl Ser.: 6). (ENG.). 124p. (J). (gr. 2-4). 9.99 ***(978-1-74331-322-0(5))*** Allen & Unwin AUS. Dist: Independent Pubs. Group.

Rogers, Gregory. The Poison Plot. Watts, Frances. 2015. (Sword Girl Ser.: 2). (ENG.). 112p. (J). (gr. 2-4). 9.99 *(978-1-74237-792-6(0))* Allen & Unwin AUS. Dist: Independent Pubs. Group.

—Roland Wright: at the Joust. Davis, Tony. 2011. (ENG.). 144p. (J). (gr. 1-4). 6.99 *(978-0-375-87328-7(7),* Yearling) Random Hse. Children's Bks.

—Roland Wright: Brand-New Page. Davis, Tony. 2011. (Roland Wright Ser.). (ENG.). 144p. (J). (gr. 1-4). 6.99 *(978-0-385-73803-3(X),* Yearling) Random Hse. Children's Bks.

—Roland Wright: Future Knight. Davis, Tony. 2010. (Roland Wright Ser.). (ENG.). 160p. (J). (gr. 1-4). 6.99 *(978-0-385-73801-9(3),* Yearling) Random Hse. Children's Bks.

—The Secret of the Swords. Watts, Frances. 2015. (Sword Girl Ser.: 1). (ENG.). 96p. (J). (gr. 2-4). 9.99 *(978-1-74237-728-5(9))* Allen & Unwin AUS. Dist: Independent Pubs. Group.

—The Secrets of Flamant Castle: The Complete Adventures of Sword Girl & Friends. Watts, Frances. ed. 2014. (Sword Girl Ser.). (ENG.). 576p. (J). (gr. 2-4). 15.99 *(978-1-74331-954-3(1))* Allen & Unwin AUS. Dist: Independent Pubs. Group.

Rogers, Gregory. The Terrible Trickster. Watts, Frances. 2015. (Sword Girl Ser.: 5). (ENG.). 126p. (J). (gr. 2-4). 9.99 ***(978-1-74331-321-3(7))*** Allen & Unwin AUS. Dist: Independent Pubs. Group.

Rogers, Gregory. What's Wrong with the Wobbegong? Gwynne, Phillip. 2013. (ENG.). 32p. (J). (gr. -1-k). 22.99 *(978-1-921714-96-2(4))* Little Hare Bks. AUS. Dist: Independent Pubs. Group.

Rogers, Gregory. The Hero of Little Street. Rogers, Gregory. 2012. (ENG.). 32p. (J). (gr. k-3). 17.99 *(978-1-59643-729-6(4))* Roaring Brook Pr.

Rogers, Jacqueline. Alvin & the Chipmunks: Alvin Gets an A. Mayer, Kirsten. 2012. (I Can Read Book 2 Ser.). (ENG.). 32p. (J). (gr. -1-3). pap. 3.99 *(978-0-06-208603-7(0))* HarperCollins Pubs.

—A Big Spooky House: Picture Book. Washington, Donna L. & Washington, Donna. 2006. (ENG.). 32p. (J). (gr. k-4). 4.99 *(978-0-7868-1231-8(1))* Hyperion Pr.

—Calvin Coconut: Man Trip. Salisbury, Graham. 2013. (Calvin Coconut Ser.). (ENG.). 144p. (J). (gr. 2-5). pap. 6.99 *(978-0-375-86507-7(1),* Delacorte Pr) Random House Publishing Group.

—Calvin Coconut: Rocket Ride. Salisbury, Graham. 2013. (Calvin Coconut Ser.). (ENG.). 160p. (J). (gr. 2-5). pap. 6.99 *(978-0-375-86508-4(X),* Delacorte Pr) Random House Publishing Group.

—Calvin Coconut: Zoo Breath. Salisbury, Graham. 2010. (Calvin Coconut Ser.). (ENG.). 160p. (J). (gr. 3-7). lib. bdg. 15.99 *(978-0-385-90642-5(0),* Delacorte Pr) Random House Publishing Group.

—Calvin Coconut: Dog Heaven. Salisbury, Graham. 2011. (Calvin Coconut Ser.). (ENG.). 160p. (J). (gr. 3-7). 6.99 *(978-0-375-84602-1(6),* Yearling) Random Hse. Children's Bks.

—Calvin Coconut: Man Trip. Salisbury, Graham. 2012. (Calvin Coconut Ser.). (ENG.). 144p. (J). (gr. 2-5). lib. bdg. 15.99 *(978-0-385-90798-9(2),* Lamb, Wendy) Random Hse. Children's Bks.

—Calvin Coconut: Rocket Ride. Salisbury, Graham. 2012. (Calvin Coconut Ser.). (ENG.). 160p. (J). (gr. 2-5). 12.99 *(978-0-385-73965-8(6),* Lamb, Wendy) Random Hse. Children's Bks.

—Calvin Coconut: Zoo Breath. Salisbury, Graham. 2011. (Calvin Coconut Ser.). (ENG.). 160p. (J). (gr. 3-7). 6.99 *(978-0-375-84603-8(4),* Yearling) Random Hse. Children's Bks.

—Dixie & the Best Day Ever. Gilman, Grace. 2014. (I Can Read Book 1 Ser.). (ENG.). 32p. (J). (gr. -1-3). pap. 3.99 *(978-0-06-208609-9(X))* HarperCollins Pubs.

—Dixie & the Class Treat. Gilman, Grace. 2012. (I Can Read Book 1 Ser.). (ENG.). 32p. (J). (gr. -1-3). 16.99 *(978-0-06-208606-8(5));* pap. 3.99 *(978-0-06-208605-1(7))* HarperCollins Pubs.

—Dixie Wins the Race. Gilman, Grace. 2012. (I Can Read Book 1 Ser.). (ENG.). 32p. (J). (gr. -1-3). 16.99 *(978-0-06-208618-1(9));* pap. 3.99 *(978-0-06-208614-3(6))* HarperCollins Pubs.

—The Enormous Turnip: Classic Tales Edition. Smith, Carrie. 2011. (Classic Tales Ser.). (J). *(978-1-936258-70-3(6))* Benchmark Education Co.

—Even More Short & Shivery: Thirty Spine-Tingling Tales. San Souci, Robert D. 2003. (ENG.). 176p. (J). (gr. 3-7). pap. 5.99 *(978-0-440-41877-1(1),* Yearling) Random Hse. Children's Bks.

—Even More Short & Shivery: Thirty Spine-Tingling Tales. San Souci, Robert D. ed. 2003. 162p. (gr. 5-7). lib. bdg. 16.00 *(978-0-613-72191-2(8),* Turtleback) Turtleback Bks.

—Extra Famous. Salisbury, Graham. (Calvin Coconut Ser.). (ENG.). 176p. (J). (gr. 2-5). 2014. pap. 6.99 *(978-0-307-93075-0(0));* 2013. 12.99 *(978-0-385-74220-7(7))* Random House Publishing Group. (Delacorte Pr).

—Five Bouncing Bunnies. Karr, Lily. 2013. (ENG.). 10p. (J). (gr. -1 — 1). bds. 6.99 *(978-0-545-45825-2(0),* Cartwheel Bks.) Scholastic, Inc.

—The Gingerbread Man: Classic Tales Edition. Adams, Alison. 2011. (Classic Tales Ser.). (J). *(978-1-936258-67-3(6))* Benchmark Education Co.

—Goosed! Wallace, Bill. 2004. (ENG.). 128p. (J). (gr. 2-4). pap. 6.99 *(978-0-689-86681-4(X),* Simon & Schuster/Paula Wiseman Bks.) Simon & Schuster/Paula Wiseman Bks.

—Hero of Hawaii. Salisbury, Graham. 2012. (Calvin Coconut Ser.). (ENG.). 160p. (J). (gr. 2-5). pap. 6.99 *(978-0-375-86505-3(5),* Delacorte Pr) Random House Publishing Group.

—Hero of Hawaii. Salisbury, Graham. 2011. (Calvin Coconut Ser.). (ENG.). 160p. (J). (gr. 3-7). 12.99 *(978-0-385-73962-7(1),* Lamb, Wendy) Random Hse. Children's Bks.

—Kung Fooey. Salisbury, Graham. 2012. (Calvin Coconut Ser.). (ENG.). 144p. (J). (gr. 2-5). 6.99 *(978-0-375-86506-0(3),* Delacorte Pr) Random House Publishing Group.

—Little Scraggly Hair: A Dog on Noah's Ark. Cullen, Lynn. 2003. (ENG.). 32p. (J). (gr. k-3). tchr. ed. 16.95 *(978-0-8234-1772-8(7))* Holiday Hse., Inc.

—The Littles Have a Happy Valentine's Day. Peterson, John & Slater, Teddy. 2003. (Littles First Readers Ser.: No. 11). (ENG.). 32p. (J). (gr. k-2). pap. 3.99 *(978-0-439-42499-8(2),* Scholastic Paperbacks) Scholastic, Inc.

—The Littlest Christmas Tree. Herman, R. A. 2007. (ENG.). 32p. (J). (gr. -1-3). pap. 3.99 *(978-0-439-54007-0(0))* Scholastic, Inc.

—One Tractor. Siy, Alexandra. 2008. (ENG.). 32p. (J). (gr. -1-k). pap. 6.95 *(978-0-8234-2188-6(0))* Holiday Hse., Inc.

—One Tractor: A Counting Book. Siy, Alexandra. 2008. (ENG.). 32p. (J). (gr. -1-k). 16.95 *(978-0-8234-1923-4(1))* Holiday Hse., Inc.

—Princess for a Week. Wright, Betty Ren. (ENG.). 160p. (J). (gr. 4-7). 2007. pap. 6.95 *(978-0-8234-2111-4(2));* 2006. 16.95 *(978-0-8234-1945-6(2))* Holiday Hse., Inc.

—Stone Soup: Classic Tales Edition. Smith, Carrie. 2011. (Classic Tales Ser.). (J). *(978-1-936258-72-7(2))* Benchmark Education Co.

—Trouble Magnet. Salisbury, Graham. 2010. (Calvin Coconut Ser.). (ENG.). 160p. (J). (gr. 3-7). pap. 6.99 *(978-0-375-84600-7(X),* Delacorte Pr) Random House Publishing Group.

—The Ugly Duckling: Classic Tales Edition. Smith, Carrie. 2011. (Classic Tales Ser.). (J). *(978-1-936258-63-5(3))* Benchmark Education Co.

—The Zippy Fix. Salisbury, Graham. (Calvin Coconut Ser.). (ENG.). 176p. (J). (gr. 3-7). 2010. pap. 6.99 *(978-0-375-84601-4(8));* 2009. 12.99 *(978-0-385-73702-9(5))* Random House Publishing Group. (Delacorte Pr).

Rogers, Jacqueline. Cars: A Holiday House Reader, Level 2. Rogers, Jacqueline, tr. Levinson, Nancy Smiler. 2004. (ENG.). 32p. (J). (gr. k-3). tchr. ed. 14.95 *(978-0-8234-1614-1(3))* Holiday Hse., Inc.

Rogers, Jacqueline & Parlagreco, Aurora M. Just for Me: My Ramona Quimby Journal. Cleary, Beverly. 2013. (ENG.). 144p. (J). (gr. 3-7). 11.99 *(978-0-06-223049-2(2))* HarperCollins Pubs.

Rogers, Jacqueline, jt. illus. see Darling, Louis.

Rogers, Jacqueline, jt. illus. see Dockray, Tracy.

Rogers, Jacqueline, jt. illus. see Peterson, Joel.

Rogers, Jacqueline, jt. illus. see Rogers, Jaqueline.

Rogers, Jacqueline, jt. illus. see Tiegreen, Alan.

Rogers, Jacqueline, jt. illus. see Zelinsky, Paul O.

Rogers, Jaqueline & Rogers, Jacqueline. Turkeys Together. Wallace, Carol. 2005. (Holiday House Readers: Level 2 Ser.). (ENG.). 40p. (J). (gr. k-3). 15.95 *(978-0-8234-1895-4(2))* Holiday Hse., Inc.

Rogers, Joe. Fun Days. Hillert, Margaret. 2008. (Beginning-to-Read Ser.). 32p. (J). (gr. -1-3). lib. bdg. 19.93 *(978-1-59953-148-9(8))* Norwood Hse. Pr.

Rogers, Madalyn V. Your Own Little Silly Mcgilly. Liner, Robin. 2013. 38p. pap. 9.99 *(978-0-9910342-0-8(1))* East Stream Group, LLC.

Rogers, Melissa & Heran, Michelle. The Plot Thickens... Harry Potter Investigated by Fans for Fans. Waters, Galadriel, ed. 2005. 300p. (YA). pap. 18.95 *(978-0-9723936-3-8(3))* Wizarding World Pr.

Rogers, Paul. Forever Young. Dylan, Bob. 2008. (ENG.). 40p. (J). (gr. -1-4). 17.99 *(978-1-4169-5808-6(8),* Atheneum Bks. for Young Readers) Simon & Schuster Children's Publishing.

—Jazz A-B-Z: An A to Z Collection of Jazz Portraits. Marsalis, Wynton. 2005. (ENG.). 76p. (J). (gr. 4-7). 24.99 *(978-0-7636-2135-3(8))* Candlewick Pr.

—Squeak, Rumble, Whomp! Whomp! Whomp! Marsalis, Wynton. 2012. (ENG.). 40p. (J). (gr. -1-3). 15.99 *(978-0-7636-3991-4(5))* Candlewick Pr.

Rogers, Ruth W., et al. Bible Stories in Pictures. Beck, William F. 2nd ed. 2003.Tr. of Bible Stories in Pictures. (ALB, SPA & SWE.). 376p. pap. 10.65 *(978-1-931891-08-0(7))* Multi-Language Pubns.

—Histori Biblike Me Llustrime: Nga Knjimi Ne Kishen e Hershme. Beck, William F. 2003.Tr. of Bible Stories in Pictures. (ALB, SPA & SWE.). 374p. (J). pap. 10.65 *(978-1-931891-07-3(9),* 38-7378) Multi-Language Pubns.

Rogers, Sherry. Burro's Tortillas, 1 vol. Fields, Terri. 2007. (ENG.). 32p. (J). (gr. -1-3). 15.95 *(978-0-9768823-9-8(6))* Arbordale Publishing.

—¡Clasifícalo!, 1 vol. Mariconda, Barbara. 2012.Tr. of Sort it Out!. (SPA.). 32p. (J). (gr. k-4). 17.95 *(978-1-60718-695-3(0))* Arbordale Publishing.

—La Dama de Los Pingüinos, 1 vol. Cole, Carol A. 2012. (SPA & ENG.). 32p. (J). (gr. -1-3). 17.95 *(978-1-60718-697-7(7))* Arbordale Publishing.

Rogers, Sherry. The Deductive Detective, 1 vol. Rock, Brian. 2014. (SPA.). 32p. (J). (gr. -1-2). pap. 9.95 ***(978-1-62855-347-5(2))*** Arbordale Publishing.

Rogers, Sherry. Hey Diddle Diddle: A Food Chain Tale, 1 vol. Kapchinske, Pam. 2011. (ENG.). 32p. (J). (gr. -1-3). 16.95 *(978-1-60718-130-9(4));* pap. 8.95 *(978-1-60718-140-8(1))* Arbordale Publishing.

—If You Were a Parrot, 1 vol. Rawson, Katherine. 2006. (ENG.). 32p. (J). (gr. -1-3). 15.95 *(978-0-9764943-9-3(6))* Arbordale Publishing.

—Kersplatypus, 1 vol. Mitchell, Susan K. 2008. (ENG.). 32p. (J). (gr. -1-2). 16.95 *(978-1-934359-07-5(6));* pap. 8.95 *(978-1-934359-23-5(8))* Arbordale Publishing.

—Moose & Magpie, 1 vol. Restrepo, Bettina. 2009. (ENG.). 32p. (J). (gr. -1-3). pap. 8.95 *(978-1-60718-042-5(1))* Arbordale Publishing.

—Newton & Me. Mayer, Lynne. 2010. 32p. (J). (gr. -1-3). 16.95 *(978-1-60718-067-8(7))* Arbordale Publishing.

—Paws, Claws, Hands, & Feet, 1 vol. Hutmacher, Kimberly. 2009. (ENG.). 32p. (J). (gr. -1-2). 16.95 *(978-1-934359-88-4(2));* pap. 8.95 *(978-1-934359-98-3(X))* Arbordale Publishing.

Rogers, Sherry. The Penguin Lady, 1 vol. Cole, Carol A. 32p. (J). (gr. -1-3). 2014. (SPA.). pap. 9.95 ***(978-1-62855-420-5(7));*** 2012. (ENG.). 17.95 *(978-1-60718-527-7(X));* 2012. (ENG.). pap. 9.95 *(978-1-60718-536-9(9))* Arbordale Publishing.

Rogers, Sherry. Sort It Out!, 1 vol. Mariconda, Barbara. 2008. (ENG.). 32p. (J). (gr. k-4). 16.95 *(978-1-934359-11-2(4));* pap. 8.95 *(978-1-934359-32-7(7))* Arbordale Publishing.

Rogers, Sherry. El Detective Deductivo, 1 vol. Rogers, Sherry. Rock, Brian. 2013. (SPA.). 32p. (J). (gr. -1-2). 17.95 *(978-1-60718-708-0(6))* Arbordale Publishing.

Rogers, Suzanne, photos by. My Mother Can Do Anything. Rogers, Suzanne. 2011. (ENG., 40p. pap. 11.99 *(978-1-4611-2039-1(X))* CreateSpace Independent Publishing Platform.

Rogers, Terry. Androcles & the Lion: A Roman Legend. 2003. (Dominie Collection of Myths & Legends). (SPA.). 20p. (J). pap. *(978-0-7685-2122-1(X));* lib. bdg. *(978-0-7685-2419-2(9))* Dominie Pr., Inc.

Rogers, Walter S. Little Woodcrafters' Fun on the Farm. Roy, Lillian Elizabeth. 2011. 232p. 46.95 *(978-1-258-09314-3(6))* Literary Licensing, LLC.

Rogge, Rachel. Nature's Yucky! 2: The Desert Southwest. Landstrom, Lee Ann & Shragg, Karen. 2007. (Nature's Yucky Ser.). 48p. (J). (gr. k-7). pap. 12.00 *(978-0-87842-529-7(2))* Mountain Pr. Publishing Co., Inc.

—Nature's Yucky! 3: The Eastern United States. Landstrom, Lee Ann & Shragg, Karen I. 2013. 48p. (J). pap. 12.00 *(978-0-87842-601-0(9))* Mountain Pr. Publishing Co., Inc.

Roguez, Jesus. The Littlest Smoke Detector. Brozman, Dave. 2006. (ENG.). 32p. per. 21.99 *(978-1-4259-6096-4(0))* AuthorHouse.

Roher, Michael. My New Granny. Steinkellner, Elisabeth. 2012. (ENG.). 32p. (J). (gr. -1-3). pap. 16.95 *(978-1-62087-223-9(4),* 620223, Sky Pony Pr.) Skyhorse Publishing Co., Inc.

Rohmann, Eric. Bulldozer's Big Day. Fleming, Candace. 2015. (ENG.). 40p. (J). (gr. -1-2). 17.99 ***(978-1-4814-0097-8(5),*** Atheneum Bks. for Young Readers) Simon & Schuster Children's Publishing.

Rohmann, Eric. Go Sleep in Your Own Bed. Fleming, Candace. 2016. (J). *(978-0-375-86648-7(5),* Schwartz & Wade Bks.) Random Hse. Children's Bks.

—Oh, No! Fleming, Candace. 2012. (ENG.). 40p. (J). (gr. -1-2). 17.99 *(978-0-375-84271-9(3),* Schwartz & Wade Bks.) Random Hse. Children's Bks.

Rohmann, Eric. Bone Dog. Rohmann, Eric. 2011. (ENG.). 32p. (J). (gr. -1-3). 16.99 *(978-1-59643-150-8(4))* Roaring Brook Pr.

—My Friend Rabbit. Rohmann, Eric. 2011. (ENG.). 34p. (J). (gr. -1-3). bds. 7.99 *(978-1-59643-641-1(7))* Roaring Brook Pr.

—My Friend Rabbit. Rohmann, Eric. 2007. (ENG.). 32p. (J). (gr. -1-3). per. 7.99 *(978-0-312-36752-7(X))* Square Fish.

Rohmann, Eric, jt. illus. see Lowry, Lois.

Rohner, Dorothia. Effie's Image. 2006. 32p. (J). (gr. -1-3). 17.95 *(978-0-9759829-5-2(8))* Prairieland Pr.

—Numbers in a Row: An Iowa Number Book. Patricia Pierce. 2006. (Count Your Way Across the U. S. A. Ser.). (ENG.). 40p. (J). (gr. -1-3). 17.95 *(978-1-58536-164-9(X))* Sleeping Bear Pr.

Röhr, Stéphanie. The Bad Easter Bunny. Atherton, Isabel. 2013. (ENG.). 32p. (J). (gr. -1-1). 12.95 *(978-1-62087-500-1(4),* 620500, Sky Pony Pr.) Skyhorse Publishing Co., Inc.

—Count the Sheep to Sleep. Rae, Philippa. 2012. (ENG.). 28p. (J). (gr. -1-k). 12.95 *(978-1-61608-660-2(2),* 608660, Sky Pony Pr.) Skyhorse Publishing Co., Inc.

Rohrbach, Sophie. Sherlock Holmes & a Scandal in Bohemia. Shaw, Murray & Cosson, M. J. 2010. (On the Case with Holmes & Watson Ser.: 1). (ENG.). 48p. (J). (gr. 4-6). pap. 6.95 *(978-0-7613-6197-8(9),* Graphic Universe) Lerner Publishing Group.

—Sherlock Holmes & a Scandal in Bohemia. Doyle, Arthur. 2010. (On the Case with Holmes & Watson Ser.: 1). (ENG.). 48p. (J). (gr. 4-6). lib. bdg. 27.93 *(978-0-7613-6185-5(5))* Lerner Publishing Group.

—Sherlock Holmes & the Adventure at the Abbey Grange. Shaw, Murray & Cosson, M. J. 2010. (On the Case with Holmes & Watson Ser.: 2). (ENG.). 48p. (J). (gr. 4-6). pap. 6.95 *(978-0-7613-6200-5(2),* Graphic Universe) Lerner Publishing Group.

—Sherlock Holmes & the Adventure at the Abbey Grange. Doyle, Arthur. 2010. (On the Case with Holmes & Watson Ser.: 2). (ENG.). 48p. (J). (gr. 4-6). lib. bdg. 27.93 *(978-0-7613-6189-3(8))* Lerner Publishing Group.

—Sherlock Holmes & the Adventure of the Blue Gem. Shaw, Murray & Cosson, M. J. 2010. (On the Case with Holmes & Watson Ser.: 3). (ENG.). 48p. (J). (gr. 4-6). pap. 6.95 *(978-0-7613-6202-9(9),* Graphic Universe) Lerner Publishing Group.

—Sherlock Holmes & the Adventure of the Blue Gem. Doyle, Arthur. 2010. (On the Case with Holmes & Watson Ser.: 3). (ENG.). 48p. (J). (gr. 4-6). lib. bdg. 27.93 *(978-0-7613-6190-9(1))* Lerner Publishing Group.

—Sherlock Holmes & the Adventure of the Dancing Men. Shaw, Murray & Cosson, M. J. 2010. (On the Case with Holmes & Watson Ser.: 4). (ENG.). 48p. (J). (gr. 4-6). pap. 6.95 *(978-0-7613-6199-2(5),* Graphic Universe) Lerner Publishing Group.

—Sherlock Holmes & the Adventure of the Dancing Men. Doyle, Arthur. 2010. (On the Case with Holmes & Watson

R

Ser.: 4). (ENG.). 48p. (J). (gr. 4-6). lib. bdg. 27.93 *(978-0-7613-6188-6(X))* Lerner Publishing Group.

—Sherlock Holmes & the Adventure of the Speckled Band. Shaw, Murray & Cosson, M. J. 2010. (On the Case with Holmes & Watson Ser.: 5). (ENG.). 48p. (J). (gr. 4-6). 27.93 *(978-0-7613-6186-2(3))*; pap. 6.95 *(978-0-7613-6198-5(7),* Graphic Universe) Lerner Publishing Group.

—Sherlock Holmes & the Adventure of the Sussex Vampire. Shaw, Murray & Cosson, M. J. 2010. (On the Case with Holmes & Watson Ser.: 6). (ENG.). 48p. (J). (gr. 4-6). pap. 6.95 *(978-0-7613-6201-2(0),* Graphic Universe) Lerner Publishing Group.

—Sherlock Holmes & the Adventure of the Sussex Vampire. Doyle, Arthur. 2010. (On the Case with Holmes & Watson Ser.: 6). (ENG.). 48p. (J). (gr. 4-6). lib. bdg. 27.93 *(978-0-7613-6187-9(1))* Lerner Publishing Group.

Rohrbach, Sophie & Morrow, J. T. Sherlock Holmes & the Adventure of Black Peter. Doyle, Arthur. 2012. (On the Case with Holmes & Watson Ser.: 11). (ENG.). 48p. (J). (gr. 4-6). lib. bdg. 27.93 *(978-0-7613-7092-5(7))* Lerner Publishing Group.

—Sherlock Holmes & the Adventure of Black Peter. Doyle, Arthur. 2012. (On the Case with Holmes & Watson Ser.). 48p. (J). (gr. 4-6). pap. 39.62 *(978-0-7613-9274-3(2))*; (ENG.). pap. 6.95 *(978-0-7613-7100-7(1))* Lerner Publishing Group. (Graphic Universe).

—Sherlock Holmes & the Adventure of the Cardboard Box. Doyle, Arthur. 2012. (On the Case with Holmes & Watson Ser.: 12). (ENG.). 48p. (J). (gr. 4-6). lib. bdg. 27.93 *(978-0-7613-7090-1(0))* Lerner Publishing Group.

—Sherlock Holmes & the Adventure of the Cardboard Box. Doyle, Arthur. 2012. (On the Case with Holmes & Watson Ser.). 48p. (J). (gr. 4-6). pap. 39.62 *(978-0-7613-9275-0(0))*; (ENG.). pap. 6.95 *(978-0-7613-7098-7(6))* Lerner Publishing Group. (Graphic Universe).

—Sherlock Holmes & the Adventure of the Three Garridebs. Doyle, Arthur. 2012. (On the Case with Holmes & Watson Ser.). 48p. (J). (gr. 4-6). pap. 39.62 *(978-0-7613-9276-7(9))*; (ENG.). pap. 6.95 *(978-0-7613-7099-4(4))* Lerner Publishing Group. (Graphic Universe).

—Sherlock Holmes & the Boscombe Valley Mystery. Doyle, Arthur. 2011. (On the Case with Holmes & Watson Ser.: 10). (ENG.). 48p. (J). (gr. 4-6). 27.93 *(978-0-7613-7089-5(7))*; pap. 6.95 *(978-0-7613-7097-0(8))* Lerner Publishing Group. (Graphic Universe).

—Sherlock Holmes & the Gloria Scott. Doyle, Arthur. 2012. (On the Case with Holmes & Watson Ser.: 14). (ENG.). 48p. (J). (gr. 4-6). lib. bdg. 27.93 *(978-0-7613-7093-2(5))* Lerner Publishing Group.

—Sherlock Holmes & the Gloria Scott. Doyle, Arthur. 2012. (On the Case with Holmes & Watson Ser.). 48p. (J). (gr. 4-6). pap. 39.62 *(978-0-7613-9277-4(7))*; (ENG.). pap. 6.95 *(978-0-7613-7101-4(X))* Lerner Publishing Group. (Graphic Universe).

—Sherlock Holmes & the Three Garridebs. Doyle, Arthur. 2012. (On the Case with Holmes & Watson Ser.: 13). (ENG.). 48p. (J). (gr. 4-6). lib. bdg. 27.93 *(978-0-7613-7091-8(9))* Lerner Publishing Group.

Rohrbach, Sophie & Morrow, Jt. #07 Sherlock Holmes & the Redheaded League. Doyle, Arthur. 2011. (On the Case with Holmes & Watson Set II Ser.). pap. 39.62 *(978-0-7613-7609-5(7),* Graphic Universe) Lerner Publishing Group.

—#08 Sherlock Holmes & the Adventure at the Copper Beeches. Doyle, Arthur. 2011. (On the Case with Holmes & Watson Set II Ser.). (J). pap. 39.62 *(978-0-7613-7610-1(0),* Graphic Universe) Lerner Publishing Group.

—#09 Sherlock Holmes & the Adventure of the Six Napoleons. Doyle, Arthur. 2011. (On the Case with Holmes & Watson Set II Ser.). pap. 39.62 *(978-0-7613-7611-8(9),* Graphic Universe) Lerner Publishing Group.

—#10 Sherlock Holmes & the Boscombe Valley Mystery. Doyle, Arthur. 2011. (On the Case with Holmes & Watson Set II Ser.). pap. 39.62 *(978-0-7613-7612-5(7),* Graphic Universe) Lerner Publishing Group.

Rohrer, Neal. Rohrer's Fun Coloring & Games. Rohrer, Neal. 2003. 28p. 3.95 *(978-0-9721138-0-9(0))* Rohrer Design.

Roitman, Tanya. Do You Wear Diapers? 2012. (ENG.). 12p. (J). (gr. k — 1). 6.99 *(978-1-60905-257-7(9))* Blue Apple Bks.

—Draw + Learn - Animals. Ziefert, Harriet. 2011. (ENG.). 96p. (J). (gr. k-k). pap. 8.99 *(978-1-60905-094-8(0))* Blue Apple Bks.

—Draw + Learn - Faces. Ziefert, Harriet. 2011. (ENG.). 96p. (J). (gr. k-k). pap. 8.99 *(978-1-60905-095-5(9))* Blue Apple Bks.

—Draw + Learn - People. Ziefert, Harriet. 2012. (ENG.). 96p. (J). (gr. -1-2). pap. 8.99 *(978-1-60905-218-8(8))* Blue Apple Bks.

—Draw + Learn - Places. Ziefert, Harriet. 2012. (ENG.). 96p. (J). (gr. -1-2). pap. 8.99 *(978-1-60905-217-1(X))* Blue Apple Bks.

—I'm Going to New York to Visit the Lions. Linn, Margot. 2005. (I'm Going to Read(r) Ser.: Level 2). (ENG.). 32p. (J). (gr. k-1). pap. 3.95 *(978-1-4027-2099-4(8))* Sterling Publishing Co., Inc.

—I'm Going to Washington to Visit the President. Ziefert, Harriet. 2006. (I'm Going to Read(r) Ser.). (ENG.). 24p. (J). (gr. -1-k). pap. 3.95 *(978-1-4027-3408-3(5))* Sterling Publishing Co., Inc.

—Long Vowels. Ziefert, Harriet. 2007. (I'm Going to Read(r) Ser.). (ENG.). 64p. (J). (gr. -1-1). pap. 5.95 *(978-1-4027-5057-1(9))* Sterling Publishing Co., Inc.

—The More We Are Together. 2009. (Rookie Toddler: Sing along Toddler Ser.). (ENG.). 12p. (J). (gr. -1). bds. 6.95 *(978-0-531-24547-7(0))* Scholastic Library Publishing.

—Short Vowels. Ziefert, Harriet. 2007. (I'm Going to Read(r) Ser.). (ENG.). 64p. (J). (gr. -1-1). pap. 5.95 *(978-1-4027-5056-4(0))* Sterling Publishing Co., Inc.

—Sight Words. Ziefert, Harriet. 2007. (I'm Going to Read(r) Ser.). (ENG.). 64p. (J). (gr. -1-1). pap. 5.95 *(978-1-4027-5058-8(7))* Sterling Publishing Co., Inc.

Rojankovsky, Feodor. The Three Bears. Little Golden Books Staff. 2012. (Little Golden Book Ser.). (ENG.). 24p. (J). (gr. k-k). 3.99 *(978-0-307-02140-3(8),* Golden Bks.) Random Hse. Children's Bks.

Rojankovsky, Feodor & Gergely, Tibor. Little Golden Book Farm Favorites. McGinley, Phyllis et al. 2012. (Little Golden Book Favorites Ser.). (ENG.). 80p. (J). (gr. k-k). 6.99 *(978-0-307-93020-0(3),* Golden Bks.) Random Hse., Inc.

Rojas, Clare. We Need a Horse. Heti, Sheila. 2011. (ENG.). 32p. (J). (gr. k-6). 16.95 *(978-1-936365-40-1(5))* McSweeney's Publishing.

Rojas, Jessica. Abecedarium Latinum. Sipes, Peter. 2011.Tr. of Latin Alphabet. 36p. (J). pap. 8.95 *(978-1-937847-00-5(4))* Pluteo Pleno.

Rojas, Mary. Before I Sleep I Say Thank You. Ekster, Carol Gordon. 2015. (J). 14.95 *(978-0-8198-1225-4(0))* Pauline Bks. & Media.

—Siempre Tú: Un Libro Sobre Tu Cuerpo y Tu Alma. Lataif, Nicole. Pérez, Karen H., tr. from ENG. 2014.Tr. of Forever You: a Book about Your Body & Soul. (SPA.). (J). pap. 9.95 *(978-0-8198-9009-2(X))* Pauline Bks. & Media.

Rojas, Mary & Grayson, Rick. Everyone's a Star. Allen, Margaret. Hults, Alaska, ed. 2003. (J). pap. 13.99 *(978-1-59198-008-7(9),* CTP2258) Creative Teaching Pr., Inc.

Rojas, Mary & Vangsgard, Amy. Jingle Jangles Vol. 2256: Fun, Interactive Reading Selections for Fluency Practice. Allen, Margaret. Walter, LaDawn, ed. 2004. 128p. (J). (gr. k-2). pap. 14.99 *(978-1-59198-048-3(8),* 2256) Creative Teaching Pr., Inc.

Rojas, Mary & Willardson, David. Leap into Literacy Spring. Geiser, Traci Ferguson & Boylan, Maureen McCourt. Cernek, Kim, ed. 2003. 160p. (J). (gr. k-2). pap. 17.99 *(978-1-57471-959-8(9),* 3375) Creative Teaching Pr., Inc.

Rojas, Mary Galan. Mrs. E's Extraordinary Number Activities. Etringer, Kathy. Mitchell, Judy & Sussman, Ellen, eds. 2006. 128p. (J). pap. 13.95 *(978-1-57310-506-4(6))* Teaching & Learning Co.

Rojas, Saul Oscar. Había una Vez una Casa. Montes, Graciela. 2005. (Pictocuentos Ser.). (SPA.). 24p. (J). 8.95 *(978-1-59820-212-0(X),* Alfaguara) Santillana USA Publishing Co., Inc.

Rojo, Sara. Baba Yaga: the Flying Witch. 2008. (Usborne First Reading: Level 4 Ser.). 48p. (J). 8.99 *(978-0-7945-2078-6(2),* Usborne) EDC Publishing.

—La Cigarra y la Hormiga: Versión de la Fábula de Esopo, 1 vol. White, Mark. Abello, Patricia, tr. 2006. (Read-It! Readers en Español: Fábulas Ser.).Tr. of Ant & the Grasshopper - A Retelling of Aesop's Fable. (SPA.). 24p. (gr. k-3). 19.99 *(978-1-4048-1614-5(3),* Easy Readers) Picture Window Bks.

—Why the Sea Is Salty. 2009. (First Reading Level 4 Ser.). 48p. (J). 6.99 *(978-0-7945-2308-4(0),* Usborne) EDC Publishing.

Roland, Harry, et al. Cesar Chavez: Fighting for Farmworkers, 1 vol. Braun, Eric. 2005. (Graphic Biographies Ser.). (ENG.). 32p. (gr. 3-4). 29.99 *(978-0-7368-4631-8(X),* Graphic Library) Capstone Pr., Inc.

Roland, Timothy. Monkey Me #1: Monkey Me & the Golden Monkey (a Branches Book) Roland, Timothy. 2014. (Monkey Me Ser.). (ENG.). 96p. (J). (gr. 1-3). pap. 4.99 *(978-0-545-55976-8(6))* Scholastic, Inc.

—Monkey Me & the New Neighbor. Roland, Timothy. 2014. (Monkey Me Ser.: 3). (ENG.). 96p. (J). (gr. 1-3). pap. 4.99 *(978-0-545-55984-3(7))* Scholastic, Inc.

—Monkey Me & the School Ghost. Roland, Timothy. 2014. (Monkey Me Ser.: 4). (ENG.). 96p. (J). (gr. 1-3). 15.99 *(978-0-545-55990-4(1))* Scholastic, Inc.

Roldan, Patrict. The Hero: It's up to You. Burns, Judith. (Reader Friendly Bks.). (YA). (gr. 5-12). pap. 9.95 *(978-0-9726099-9-9(7))* BurnsBooks.

Rolf, Heidi. Hey I'm Alex. Pellegrin, Leeann. 2012. 26p. pap. 12.95 *(978-1-61244-049-1(5))* Halo Publishing International.

—My Pet Dinosaur. Elefritz, Erin. 2012. 24p. pap. 11.95 *(978-1-61244-117-7(3))* Halo Publishing International.

Rolland, Leonard Le. Animal Jokes. Howell, Laura, ed. 2004. (Jokes Ser.). 96p. (J). pap. 6.95 *(978-0-7945-0655-1(0),* Usborne) EDC Publishing.

—The Usborne Encyclopedia of World Religions: Internet-Linked. Hickman, Clare & Meredith, Sue. Rogers, Kirsteen, ed. rev. ed. 2006. (Usborne Encyclopedia of World Religions Ser.). 128p. (J). (gr. 5-9). per. 14.95 *(978-0-7945-1059-6(0),* Usborne) EDC Publishing.

Rolland, Will. Brolga. Reilly, Pauline. (Picture Roo Bks.). 32p. (J). pap. *(978-0-86417-719-3(4),* Kangaroo Pr.) Simon & Schuster Australia.

Rolling, Beanic. Paper Boy Two: Over Whelming 0005. Veremiah, Omari. 2004. 74p. (YA). (gr. 7-12). pap. 12.99 *(978-1-929188-10-9(2))* Morton Bks.

Rollinger, Marsha. Starlight Blue: A New Baby. Klingensmith, Ryan Lee & Klingensmith, Sherri Ann. 2012. 32p. pap. 24.95 *(978-1-4626-8219-5(7))* America Star Bks.

Rollins, Berni. Paper Boy Four: L. O. E. P. S. Worst Nightmare. Jeremiah, Omari. 2007. 96p. (YA). (gr. 7-12). pap. 12.99 *(978-1-929188-15-4(3))* Morton Bks.

Rollins, Bernic. Paper Boy. Jeremiatt, Omani. 2003. 40p. (J). (gr. 6-8). pap. 10.00 *(978-1-929188-09-3(9))* Morton Bks.

Rollins, Bernie. Paperboy 3: The School of Doom. Jeremiah, Omari. 2006. 75p. pap. 12.99 *(978-1-929188-13-0(7))* Morton Bks.

Rollins, Joe. Timmy the Turtle Learns to Swim. Crays, Lettie L. 2011. 44p. (J). pap. 11.95 *(978-1-937089-06-1(1))* Truth Bk. Pubs.

Rolseth, Ruthie. Tommie Turtle's Secret. Hicks, Robert Z. 2007. (ENG.). 40p. (J). 16.95 *(978-0-9792031-0-7(4))* R.Z. Enterprises of Florida.

Rolston, Steve. The Great Motion Mission: A Surprising Story of Physics in Everyday Life. Lee, Cora. 2009. (ENG.). 112p. (J). (gr. 4-6). 24.95 *(978-1-55451-185-3(2),* 9781554511853); pap. 14.95 *(978-1-55451-184-6(4),* 9781554511846) Annick Pr., Ltd. CAN. Dist: Firefly Bks., Ltd.

—In My House. Torres, J. 4th ed. 2007. (Degrassi the Next Generation Ser.). (ENG.). 120p. (J). pap. *(978-1-55168-303-4(2))* Fenn, H. B. & Co., Ltd.

—Seeing Red: The True Story of Blood. Kyi, Tanya Lloyd. 2012. (ENG.). 122p. (J). (gr. 4-12). pap. 14.95 *(978-1-55451-384-0(7),* 9781554513840) Annick Pr., Ltd. CAN. Dist: Firefly Bks., Ltd.

Roma, Ursula. Maccabee Meals: Food & Fun for Hanukkah. Groner, Judyth Saypol & Wikler, Madeline. 2012. (Hanukkah Ser.). (ENG.). 64p. (J). (gr. 2-5). pap. 8.95 *(978-0-7613-5144-3(2),* Kar-Ben Publishing) Lerner Publishing Group.

Romagna, Karen. Voyage. Collins, Billy. 2014. (ENG.). 32p. (J). (gr. 1-2). 16.95 *(978-1-59373-154-0(X))* Bunker Hill Publishing, Inc.

Romain, Trevor. How to Do Homework Without Throwing Up. Romain, Trevor. Verdick, Elizabeth, ed. 2005. (Laugh & Learn Ser.). (ENG.). 72p. (J). (gr. 3-8). pap. 8.95 *(978-1-57542-011-0(2),* FS424) Free Spirit Publishing, Inc.

—Stress Can Really Get on Your Nerves! Romain, Trevor. Verdick, Elizabeth. 2005. (Laugh & Learn Ser.). (ENG.). 104p. (J). (gr. 3-8). pap. 8.95 *(978-1-57542-078-3(3))* Free Spirit Publishing, Inc.

Roman, Dave. Astronaut Academy - Re-Entry. Roman, Dave. 2013. (Astronaut Academy Ser.: 2). (ENG.). 192p. (J). (gr. 5-9). pap. 9.99 *(978-1-59643-621-3(2),* First Second Bks.) Roaring Brook Pr.

—Zero Gravity. Roman, Dave. 2011. (Astronaut Academy Ser.: 1). (ENG.). 192p. (J). (gr. 5-9). 17.99 *(978-1-59643-756-2(1))*; pap. 9.99 *(978-1-59643-620-6(4))* Roaring Brook Pr. (First Second Bks.).

Roman, Santi. Dibuja y Pinta. Lenam, Salva. 2005. (Kiko Ser.). (SPA & ENG.). 10p. (J). (gr. -1-k). 3.95 *(978-84-95761-78-1(5))* Ediciones Norte, Inc.

—¡Hoy Empieza la Escuela!. Kiko. Lenam, Salva. 2005. (Kiko Ser.). (SPA & ENG.). 10p. (J). (gr. -1-k). 3.95 *(978-84-95761-76-7(9))* Ediciones Norte, Inc.

—A Kiko le Pican los Ojitos. Lenam, Salva. 2005. (Kiko Ser.). (SPA & ENG.). 10p. (J). (gr. -1-k). 3.95 *(978-84-95761-82-8(3))* Ediciones Norte, Inc.

—Kiko No Quiere Comer. Lenam, Salva. 2005. (Kiko Ser.). (SPA & ENG.). 10p. (J). (gr. -1-k). 3.95 *(978-84-95761-77-4(7))* Ediciones Norte, Inc.

—Kiko Ya Se Viste Solo. Lenam, Salva. 2005. (Kiko Ser.). (SPA & ENG.). 10p. (J). (gr. -1-k). 3.95 *(978-84-95761-80-4(7))* Ediciones Norte, Inc.

Romanenko, Vasilisa, jt. illus. see Romanenko, Vitaliy.

Romanenko, Vitaliy & Romanenko, Vasilisa. A Car That Goes Far. Mermelstein, Yael. Rosenfeld, Dina, ed. 2009. 30p. (J). (gr. 1-3). 12.95 *(978-1-929628-47-6(1))* Hachai Publishing.

Romanet, Caroline. Rumplestiltskin. Longstaff, Abie. 2015. (Collins Big Cat Ser.). (ENG.). 24p. pap. 7.95 *(978-0-00-759117-6(9))* HarperCollins Pubs. Ltd. GBR. Dist: Independent Pubs. Group.

Romango, Jim. Rhymes for Teens: Poems Older Students Can Enjoy. Catalano, Tom. 2004. 80p. (YA). per. 9.95 *(978-1-882646-48-7(7))* Wordsmith Bks.

Romberger, James, et al. Something Wicca This Way Comes, No. 7. Lansdale, John L. et al. 7th ed. 2009. (Tales from the Crypt Graphic Novels Ser.: 7). (ENG.). 96p. (J). (gr. 5-12). 12.95 *(978-1-59707-151-2(X))* Papercutz.

Rombough, John. Caribou Song, 1 vol. Highway, Tomson. 2013. (ENG & CRE.). 32p. (J). 19.95 *(978-1-897252-61-1(7))* Fifth Hse. Pubs. CAN. Dist: Ingram Pub. Services.

Romendik, Irena. The Musical Muffin Man. 2003. (Rub a Dub Books Ser.). 8p. (J). (gr. -1-k). vinyl bd. 7.00 *(978-1-883043-45-2(X))* Straight Edge Pr., The.

Romendik, Irene. I've Been Working on the Railroad: Musical Book. 2003. (J). 6.49 *(978-1-883043-48-3(4))* Straight Edge Pr., The.

Romero, Enric Badia. The Puppet Master. O'Donnell, Peter. 2006. (Modesty Blaise Ser.). (ENG.). 96p. per. 19.95 *(978-1-84023-867-9(4))* Titan Bks. Ltd. GBR. Dist: Random Hse., Inc.

Romero, Gina. Claude, the Clumsy Clydesdale. Altieri, Marion. 2011. (Alpha Mare Ser.: Vol. 1). 42p. (J). 16.47 *(978-0-9840418-0-0(X))*; pap. 14.47 *(978-0-9840418-1-7(8))* Caballo Pr. of Ann Arbor. (Caballito Children's Bks.).

Romita, John, et al. The Amazing Spider-Man, Vol. 6. Lee, Stan et al. Youngquist, Jeff, ed. 2011. (ENG.). 576p. (J). (gr. -1-17). pap. 19.99 *(978-0-7851-1365-2(7))* Marvel Worldwide, Inc.

—The Amazing Spider-Man: Origin of the Hobgoblin. 2011. (ENG.). 256p. (J). (gr. 4-17). pap. 29.99 *(978-0-7851-5854-7(5))* Marvel Worldwide, Inc.

Romita, John. Avengers by Brian Michael Bendis Volume 1. 2011. (ENG.). 112p. (J). (gr. 4-17). pap. 19.99 *(978-0-7851-4501-1(X))* Marvel Worldwide, Inc.

Romita, John, Jr. The Book of Ezekiel, Vol. 7. Straczynski, J. Michael. 2004. (Spider-Man Ser.). 144p. (YA). pap. 12.99 *(978-0-7851-1525-0(0))* Marvel Worldwide, Inc.

Romita, John. Daredevil: The Man Without Fear. 2010. (ENG.). 224p. (YA). (gr. 8-17). pap. 19.99 *(978-0-7851-3479-4(4))* Marvel Worldwide, Inc.

—Essential Daredevil, Vol. 1. Lee, Stan. ed. 2012. (ENG.). 544p. (J). (gr. -1-17). pap. 19.99 *(978-0-7851-6420-3(0))* Marvel Worldwide, Inc.

—The Marvel Art of John Romita Jr. 2011. (ENG.). 240p. (YA). (gr. 8-17). 49.99 *(978-0-7851-5535-5(X))* Marvel Worldwide, Inc.

Romita, John, et al. Marvel Masterworks. 2014. (ENG.). 240p. (J). (gr. -1-17). pap. 24.99 *(978-0-7851-8807-0(X))* Marvel Worldwide, Inc.

—Origins of Marvel Comics. 2011. (ENG.). 272p. (YA). (gr. 8-17). pap., pap. 24.99 *(978-0-7851-5615-4(1))* Marvel Worldwide, Inc.

Romita, John, Jr., et al. Spider-Man, Vol. 10. O'Neil, Denny & Fleisher, Michael. 2011. (ENG.). 504p. (J). (gr. 4-17). pap. 19.99 *(978-0-7851-5747-2(6))* Marvel Worldwide, Inc.

Romita, John, et al. Thor by Dan Jurgens & John Romita Jr., Vol. 4. 2010. (ENG.). 248p. (YA). (gr. 8-17). pap. 29.99 *(978-0-7851-4927-9(9))* Marvel Worldwide, Inc.

Romita, John, Jr. Typhoid Mary, 4 vols. Nocenti, Ann. 2003. (Daredevil Legends Ser.: Vol. 4). 224p. (YA). pap. 19.99 *(978-0-7851-1041-5(0))* Marvel Worldwide, Inc.

Romita, John, Jr., et al. X-Men: Ghosts. 2013. (ENG.). 360p. (J). (gr. 4-17). pap. 34.99 *(978-0-7851-8449-2(X))* Marvel Worldwide, Inc.

Romita, John & Ditko, Steve. X-Men - The Hidden Year, Vol. 2. 2012. (ENG.). 304p. (J). (gr. 4-17). pap. 34.99 *(978-0-7851-6055-7(8))* Marvel Worldwide, Inc.

Romita, John & Lieber, Larry. The Amazing Spider-Man, Vol. 6. Lee, Stan et al. 2011. (ENG.). 296p. (J). (gr. -1-17). pap. 24.99 *(978-0-7851-5054-1(4))* Marvel Worldwide, Inc.

Romita, John, Jr. & Romita, John, Sr. Happy Birthday. Straczynski, J. Michael. 2004. (Amazing Spider-Man Ser.). 100p. lib. bdg. 24.35 *(978-1-4176-6025-4(2),* Turtleback) Turtleback Bks.

Romita, John & Windsor-Smith, Barry. X-Men, Vol. 6. 2007. (ENG.). 656p. (J). (gr. -1-17). pap. 19.99 *(978-0-7851-1727-8(X))* Marvel Worldwide, Inc.

Romita, John, Jr., jt. illus. see Cho, Frank.

Romita, John, Sr., jt. illus. see Romita, John, Jr.

Romo, Adriana. Felicia's Favorite Story. Newman, Lesléa. 2003. 24p. (J). pap. 9.95 *(978-0-9674468-5-1(6))* Two Lives Publishing.

Ron Frazier, photos by. Colleen Goes to the Farmer's Market. Janice Turner & Colleen Connelly. 2009. 20p. pap. 12.49 *(978-1-4389-6085-2(9))* AuthorHouse.

Ronald, Robrahn. Steven the Vegan. Bodenstein, Dan. 2012. 38p. (J). pap. 12.99 *(978-0-9843228-9-3(2))* Totem Tales Publishing.

Ronchi, Susanna. One Snowy Night. Harwood, Beth. 2005. 12p. (J). *(978-1-84011-627-4(7))* Templar Publishing.

Ronda Eden. The Brothers Foot: A Hare Raising Story. Steve Cormey. 2009. 56p. pap. 21.99 *(978-1-4389-4269-8(9))* AuthorHouse.

Ronda, Gilger. Lyssa Lamb. Bell, Debora. 2005. 32p. (J). 4.95 *(978-0-9768465-0-5(0))* Frontier Pr.

Rong, Yap Kun. Dragon Theft Auto, 1 vol. Dahl, Michael. 2010. (Dragonblood Ser.). (ENG.). 40p. (gr. 1-3). pap. 6.25 *(978-1-4342-2310-4(8),* Zone Bks.) Stone Arch Bks.

Rong, Yap Kun & Kun Rong, Yap. It Screams at Night, 1 vol. Dahl, Michael. 2010. (Dragonblood Ser.). (ENG.). 40p. (gr. 1-3). pap. 6.25 *(978-1-4342-2311-1(6),* Zone Bks.) Stone Arch Bks.

Rong, Yu. Tracks of a Panda. Dowson, Nick. 2007. (ENG.). 32p. (J). (gr. k-3). 16.99 *(978-0-7636-3146-8(9))* Candlewick Pr.

—Tracks of a Panda: Read & Wonder. Dowson, Nick. 2010. (Read & Wonder Ser.). (ENG.). 32p. (J). (gr. -1-3). pap. 6.99 *(978-0-7636-4737-7(3))* Candlewick Pr.

Ronney, David. Tommy the Theatre Cat. Potter, Maureen. 3rd rev. ed. 2005. (ENG.). 80p. (J). pap. 10.95 *(978-0-86278-919-0(2))* O'Brien Pr., Ltd., The. IRL. Dist: Dufour Editions, Inc.

Ronney, Ronnie. Apes Find Shapes: A Book about Recognizing Shapes. Moncure, Jane Belk. 2013. (Magic Castle Readers: Math Ser.). (ENG.). 32p. (J). (gr. -1-2). 25.64 *(978-1-62323-577-2(4),* 206312) Child's World, Inc., The.

—The Smart Kid's Guide to Manners. Petersen, Christine. 2014. (Smart Kid's Guide to Everyday Life Ser.). (ENG.). 32p. (J). (gr. 2-5). 28.50 *(978-1-62687-344-5(5),* 207184) Child's World, Inc., The.

Ronnquist, Debby. Child Out of Place: A Story for New England. Wall, Patricia Q. 2003. 116p. (J). (gr. 6-9). pap. 12.00 *(978-0-9742185-0-2(2))* Fall Rose Bks.

Rood, Brian. The Art of Brian Rood. 2003. 48p. (YA). (gr. 11-18). pap. *(978-0-86562-066-7(0))* Anabas Marketing, Ltd.

—Star Wars: a New Hope Read-Along Storybook & CD. Disney Book Group Staff & Thornton, Randy. 2015. (Read-Along Storybook & CD Ser.). (ENG.). 32p. (J). (gr. 1-3). pap. 6.99 *(978-1-4847-0667-1(6),* Disney Lucasfilm Press) Disney Publishing Worldwide.

Rood, Phil. Mom's Backyard Zoo. Ferris, Susan. 2011. (ENG.). 32p. pap. 9.13 *(978-1-4610-0095-2(5))* CreateSpace Independent Publishing Platform.

Roode, Daniel. Cookie Meets Peanut. Frankel, Bethenny. 2014. (ENG.). 32p. (J). (gr. -1-1). 17.00 *(978-0-316-36843-8(1))* Little Brown & Co.

—Dini Dinosaur. Beaumont, Karen. 2012. (ENG.). 32p. (J). (gr. -1-k). 14.99 *(978-0-06-207299-3(4),* Greenwillow Bks.) HarperCollins Pubs.

—Glasses to Go. Eliot, Hannah. 2014. (ENG.). 16p. (J). (gr. -1-k). bds. 7.99 *(978-1-4814-1791-4(6),* Little Simon) Little Simon.

—Moustache Up! A Playful Game of Opposites. Ainsworth, Kimberly. 2013. (ENG.). 18p. (J). (gr. -1-k). bds. 7.99 *(978-1-4424-7526-7(9),* Little Simon) Little Simon.

Roode, Daniel. Little Bea. Roode, Daniel. 2011. (ENG.). 32p. (J). (gr. -1-3). 12.99 *(978-0-06-199392-3(1),* Greenwillow Bks.) HarperCollins Pubs.

—Little Bea & the Snowy Day. Roode, Daniel. 2011. (ENG.). 32p. (J). (gr. -1-k). 12.99 *(978-0-06-199395-4(6),* Greenwillow Bks.) HarperCollins Pubs.

Rooke, Veronica. Who Dresses God? ... for God's house is this world we share & God Is in it Everywhere. Raffa-Mulligan, Teena. 2012. 32p. (J). pap. *(978-1-921883-28-6(6))* Pick-a-Woo Woo Pubs.

Rooney, David. Saint Patrick: Ireland's Patron Saint. Simms, George Otto. 3rd rev. ed. 2004. (Exploring Ser.). (ENG.). 104p. pap. 8.95 *(978-0-86278-749-3(1))* O'Brien Pr., Ltd., The. IRL. Dist: Dufour Editions, Inc.

Rooney, Ronnie. Alimenta Tu Cuerpo. Tourville, Amanda Doering. 2011. (Cómo Mantenemos Saludables/How to Be Healthy Ser.).Tr. of Fuel the Body. (SPA, MUL & ENG.). 24p. (gr. k-2). 25.99 *(978-1-4048-6890-8(9))* Picture Window Bks.
—Basic Manners. Ingalls, Ann. 2012. (Good Manners Ser.). (ENG.). 24p. (J). (gr. -1-2). 27.07 *(978-1-61473-223-5(X)*, 204918) Child's World, Inc., The.
—Batter Up! You Can Play Softball, 1 vol. Fauchald, Nick. 2005. (Game Day Ser.). (ENG.). 24p. (gr. k-3). lib. bdg. 25.99 *(978-1-4048-1152-2(4)*, Nonfiction Picture Bks.) Picture Window Bks.
—Being a Good Guest. Ingalls, Ann. 2012. (Good Manners Ser.). (ENG.). 24p. (J). (gr. -1-2). 27.07 *(978-1-61473-224-2(8)*, 204919) Child's World, Inc., The.
—The Best Mud Pie. Quinn, Lin. 2011. (Rookie Ready to Learn Ser.). 40p. (J). (gr. -1-k). pap. 5.95 *(978-0-531-26650-2(8))*; lib. bdg. 23.00 *(978-0-531-26425-6(4))* Scholastic Library Publishing. (Children's Pr.).
—The Biggest Snowball of All: A Book about Sizes. Moncure, Jane Belk. 2013. (Magic Castle Readers: Math Ser.). (ENG.). 32p. (J). (gr. -1-2). 25.64 *(978-1-62323-578-9(2)*, 206315) Child's World, Inc., The.
—Brush, Floss, & Rinse: Caring for Your Teeth & Gums, 1 vol. Tourville, Amanda Doering. 2008. (How to Be Healthy! Ser.). (ENG.). 24p. (gr. k-2). 25.99 *(978-1-4048-4805-4(3)*, Nonfiction Picture Bks.) Picture Window Bks.
—Camiones Amigos/Truck Buddies, 1 vol. Crow, Melinda Melton. Heck, Claudia M., tr. from ENG. 2012. (Camiones Amigos/Truck Buddies Ser.). (ENG, SPA & MUL.). 32p. (gr. -1-1). pap. 5.05 *(978-1-4342-3913-6(6))*; lib. bdg. 21.32 *(978-1-4342-3774-3(5))* Stone Arch Bks. (Bilingual Stone Arch Readers).
—Carrera en la Carretera. Crow, Melinda Melton. Heck, Claudia M., tr. 2012. (Camiones Amigos/Truck Buddies Ser.).Tr. of Road Race. (ENG, SPA & MUL.). 32p. (gr. -1-1). pap. 5.05 *(978-1-4342-3915-0(2))*; lib. bdg. 21.32 *(978-1-4342-3776-7(1))* Stone Arch Bks. (Bilingual Stone Arch Readers).
—Cepíllate, Usa Hilo Dental y Enjuágate. Tourville, Amanda Doering. 2011. (Cómo Mantenemos Saludables/How to Be Healthy Ser.).Tr. of Brush, Floss, & Rinse. (SPA, MUL & ENG.). 24p. (gr. k-2). 25.99 *(978-1-4048-6889-2(5))* Picture Window Bks.
—The Christmas Baby. Kramer, Janice. 2008. (Arch Bks.). 16p. (J). (gr. k-4). pap. 1.99 *(978-0-7586-1454-4(3))* Concordia Publishing Hse.
—Comin' Through. Slater, David Michael. 2007. (Missy Swiss & More Ser.). 32p. (gr. -1-4). 28.50 *(978-1-60270-008-6(7)*, Looking Glass Library) ABDO Publishing Co.
—Evan & Erin Build an Essay. St. John, Amanda. 2012. 32p. (J). lib. bdg. 25.27 *(978-1-59953-508-1(4))* Norwood Hse. Pr.
—Fuel the Body: Eating Well, 1 vol. Tourville, Amanda Doering. 2008. (How to Be Healthy! Ser.). (ENG.). 24p. (gr. k-2). 25.99 *(978-1-4048-4814-6(2)*, Nonfiction Picture Bks.) Picture Window Bks.
—Funky Chicken Enchiladas: And Other Mexican Dishes, 1 vol. Fauchald, Nick. 2009. (Kids Dish Ser.). (ENG.). 32p. (gr. 1-3). lib. bdg. 26.65 *(978-1-4048-5189-4(5)*, Nonfiction Picture Bks.) Picture Window Bks.
—Get up & Go: Being Active, 1 vol. Tourville, Amanda Doering. 2008. (How to Be Healthy! Ser.). (ENG.). 24p. (gr. k-2). 25.99 *(978-1-4048-4811-5(8)*, Nonfiction Picture Bks.) Picture Window Bks.
—Go Wash Up: Keeping Clean, 1 vol. Tourville, Amanda Doering. 2008. (How to Be Healthy! Ser.). (ENG.). 24p. (gr. k-2). 25.99 *(978-1-4048-4808-5(8)*, Nonfiction Picture Bks.) Picture Window Bks.
—Good Manners During Special Occasions. Ingalls, Ann. 2012. (Good Manners Ser.). (ENG.). 24p. (J). (gr. -1-2). 27.07 *(978-1-61473-229-7(9)*, 204921) Child's World, Inc., The.
—Good Manners in Public. Ingalls, Ann. 2012. (Good Manners Ser.). (ENG.). 24p. (J). (gr. -1-2). 27.07 *(978-1-61473-226-6(4)*, 204922) Child's World, Inc., The.
—Good Manners on the Phone. Ingalls, Ann. 2012. (Good Manners Ser.). (ENG.). 24p. (J). (gr. -1-2). 27.07 *(978-1-61473-228-0(0)*, 204923) Child's World, Inc., The.
—Good Manners with Family. Ingalls, Ann. 2012. (Good Manners Ser.). (ENG.). 24p. (J). (gr. -1-2). 27.07 *(978-1-61473-227-3(2)*, 204924) Child's World, Inc., The.
—Good Table Manners. Ingalls, Ann. 2012. (Good Manners Ser.). (ENG.). 24p. (J). (gr. -1-2). 27.07 *(978-1-61473-230-3(2)*, 204925) Child's World, Inc., The.
—How Many Ways Can You Cut a Pie? A Book about Math. Moncure, Jane Belk. 2013. (Magic Castle Readers: Math Ser.). (ENG.). 32p. (J). (gr. -1-2). 25.64 *(978-1-62323-579-6(0)*, 206313) Child's World, Inc., The.
—How the Camel Got Its Hump, 1 vol. Jones, Christianne C. 2011. (My First Classic Story Ser.). (ENG.). 32p. (gr. k-3). pap. 7.10 *(978-1-4048-7358-2(9)*, My First Classic Story) Picture Window Bks.
—How the Camel Got Its Hump, 1 vol. Jones, Christianne C. & Kipling, Rudyard. 2010. (My First Classic Story Ser.). (ENG.). 32p. (gr. k-3). lib. bdg. 21.32 *(978-1-4048-6075-9(4)*, My First Classic Story) Picture Window Bks.
—If I Were a Movie Star, 1 vol. Lyons, Shelly. 2010. (Dream Big! Ser.). (ENG.). 24p. (gr. k-3). lib. bdg. 25.99 *(978-1-4048-6162-6(9))*; pap. 7.95 *(978-1-4048-6398-9(2))* Picture Window Bks. (Nonfiction Picture Bks.).
—If I Were a Veterinarian, 1 vol. Lyons, Shelly. 2010. (Dream Big! Ser.). (ENG.). 24p. (gr. k-3). pap. 7.95 *(978-1-4048-6399-6(0)*, Nonfiction Picture Bks.) Picture Window Bks.
—Lávate. Tourville, Amanda Doering. 2011. (Cómo Mantenemos Saludables/How to Be Healthy Ser.).Tr. of Go Wash Up. (SPA, MUL & ENG.). 24p. (gr. k-2). 25.99 *(978-1-4048-6892-2(5))* Picture Window Bks.
—Líos en el Lodo. Crow, Melinda Melton. Heck, Claudia M., tr. from ENG. 2012. (Camiones Amigos/Truck Buddies Ser.).Tr. of Mud Mess. (MUL & SPA.). 32p. (gr. -1-1). pap. 5.05 *(978-1-4342-3916-7(0))*; lib. bdg. 21.32 *(978-1-4342-3777-4(X))* Stone Arch Bks. (Bilingual Stone Arch Readers).
—Líos en la Nieve. Crow, Melinda Melton. Heck, Claudia M., tr. from ENG. 2012. (Camiones Amigos/Truck Buddies Ser.).Tr. of Snow Trouble. (MUL & SPA.). 32p. (gr. -1-1). pap. 5.05 *(978-1-4342-3914-3(4))*; lib. bdg. 21.32 *(978-1-4342-3775-0(3))* Stone Arch Bks. (Bilingual Stone Arch Readers).
—The Magic Moon Machine: A Counting Adventure. Moncure, Jane Belk. 2013. (Magic Castle Readers: Math Ser.). (ENG.). 32p. (J). (gr. -1-2). 25.64 *(978-1-62323-580-2(4)*, 206316) Child's World, Inc., The.
—Mud Mess, 1 vol. Crow, Melinda Melton. 2009. (Truck Buddies Ser.). (ENG.). 32p. (gr. -1-1). 21.32 *(978-1-4342-1622-9(5))*; pap. 6.25 *(978-1-4342-1753-0(1))* Stone Arch Bks.
—Muévete. Tourville, Amanda Doering. 2011. (Cómo Mantenemos Saludables/How to Be Healthy Ser.).Tr. of Get up & Go. (ENG, SPA & MUL.). 24p. (gr. k-2). 25.99 *(978-1-4048-6893-9(3))* Picture Window Bks.
—November. Kesselring, Mari. 2009. (Months of the Year Ser.). 24p. (gr. -1-2). 27.07 *(978-1-60270-638-5(7)*, Looking Glass Library- Nonfiction) Magic Wagon.
—October. Kesselring, Mari. 2009. (Months of the Year Ser.). 24p. (gr. -1-2). 27.07 *(978-1-60270-637-8(9)*, Looking Glass Library- Nonfiction) Magic Wagon.
—On-the-Go Schwarmas: And Other Middle-Eastern Dishes. Fauchald, Nick. 2009. (Kids Dish Ser.). (ENG.). 32p. (gr. 1-3). lib. bdg. 26.65 *(978-1-4048-5192-4(5)*, Nonfiction Picture Bks.) Picture Window Bks.
—One Tricky Monkey up on Top: A Counting Adventure. Moncure, Jane Belk. 2013. (Magic Castle Readers: Math Ser.). (ENG.). 32p. (J). (gr. -1-2). 25.64 *(978-1-62323-581-9(2)*, 206314) Child's World, Inc., The.
—Road Race, 1 vol. Crow, Melinda Melton. 2009. (Truck Buddies Ser.). (ENG.). 32p. (gr. -1-1). 21.32 *(978-1-4342-1623-6(3))*; pap. 6.25 *(978-1-4342-1754-7(X))* Stone Arch Bks.
—Roly-Poly Ravioli: And Other Italian Dishes, 1 vol. Fauchald, Nick. 2009. (Kids Dish Ser.). (ENG.). 32p. (gr. 1-3). lib. bdg. 26.65 *(978-1-4048-5186-3(0)*, Nonfiction Picture Bks.) Picture Window Bks.
—Ruth & Naomi. Sanders, Karen Nordberg. 2007. 16p. (J). (gr. k-4). 1.99 *(978-0-7586-1283-0(4))* Concordia Publishing Hse.
—September. Kesselring, Mari. 2009. (Months of the Year Ser.). 24p. (gr. -1-2). 27.07 *(978-1-60270-636-1(0)*, Looking Glass Library- Nonfiction) Magic Wagon.
—The Smart Kid's Guide to Divorce. Petersen, Christine. 2014. (Smart Kid's Guide to Everyday Life Ser.). (ENG.). 32p. (J). (gr. 2-5). 28.50 *(978-1-62687-340-7(2)*, 207180) Child's World, Inc., The.
—The Smart Kid's Guide to Feeling Sad or Angry. Cosson, J. 2014. (Smart Kid's Guide to Everyday Life Ser.). (ENG.). 32p. (J). (gr. 2-5). 28.50 *(978-1-62687-341-4(0)*, 207181) Child's World, Inc., The.
—The Smart Kid's Guide to Friendships. Cosson, J. 2014. (Smart Kid's Guide to Everyday Life Ser.). (ENG.). 32p. (J). (gr. 2-5). 28.50 *(978-1-62687-342-1(9)*, 207182) Child's World, Inc., The.
—The Smart Kid's Guide to Knowing What to Say. Cosson, J. 2014. (Smart Kid's Guide to Everyday Life Ser.). (ENG.). 32p. (J). (gr. 2-5). 28.50 *(978-1-62687-343-8(7)*, 207183) Child's World, Inc., The.
—The Smart Kid's Guide to Losing a Pet. Petersen, Christine. 2014. (Smart Kid's Guide to Everyday Life Ser.). (ENG.). 32p. (J). (gr. 2-5). 28.50 *(978-1-62687-346-9(1)*, 207186) Child's World, Inc., The.
—The Smart Kid's Guide to Moving. Petersen, Christine. 2014. (Smart Kid's Guide to Everyday Life Ser.). (ENG.). 32p. (J). (gr. 2-5). 28.50 *(978-1-62687-345-2(3)*, 207185) Child's World, Inc., The.
—The Smart Kid's Guide to Using the Internet. Cosson, J. 2014. (Smart Kid's Guide to Everyday Life Ser.). (ENG.). 32p. (J). (gr. 2-5). 28.50 *(978-1-62687-347-6(X)*, 207187) Child's World, Inc., The.
—Snow Trouble, 1 vol. Crow, Melinda Melton. 2009. (Truck Buddies Ser.). (ENG.). 32p. (gr. -1-1). 21.32 *(978-1-4342-1624-3(1))*; pap. 6.25 *(978-1-4342-1755-4(8))* Stone Arch Bks.
—Truck Buddies, 1 vol. Crow, Melinda Melton. 2009. (Truck Buddies Ser.). (ENG.). 32p. (gr. -1-1). 21.32 *(978-1-4342-1625-0(X))*; pap. 6.25 *(978-1-4342-1756-1(6))* Stone Arch Bks.
—Wrap-N-Bake Egg Rolls: And Other Chinese Dishes. Fauchald, Nick. 2009. (Kids Dish Ser.). (ENG.). 32p. (gr. 1-3). lib. bdg. 26.65 *(978-1-4048-5183-2(6)*, Nonfiction Picture Bks.) Picture Window Bks.
Rooney, Ronnie. Thanksgiving Recipes, 1 vol. Rooney, Ronnie. 2011. (Thanksgiving Ser.). (ENG.). 24p. (gr. 1-2). lib. bdg. 26.65 *(978-1-4048-6283-8(8)*, Nonfiction Picture Bks.) Picture Window Bks.
—There Was a Crooked Man. Rooney, Ronnie. 2011. (Favorite Mother Goose Rhymes Ser.). (ENG.). 16p. (J). (gr. -1-2). lib. bdg. 25.64 *(978-1-60954-283-2(5)*, 200235) Child's World, Inc., The.
Rooney, Ronnie & Peterson, Shauna. Busy Truck, 1 vol. Calder, C. J. 2012. (Truck Buddies Ser.). (ENG.). 16p. (gr. -1-k). bds. 7.95 *(978-1-4342-4388-1(5))* Stone Arch Bks.
—Fast Truck. Calder, C. J. 2012. (Truck Buddies Ser.). (ENG.). 16p. (gr. -1-k). bds. 7.95 *(978-1-4342-4389-8(3))* Stone Arch Bks.
—Muddy Truck, 1 vol. Calder, C. J. 2012. (Truck Buddies Ser.). (ENG.). 16p. (gr. -1-k). bds. 7.95 *(978-1-4342-4390-4(7))* Stone Arch Bks.
—Snow Truck, 1 vol. Calder, C. J. 2012. (Truck Buddies Ser.). (ENG.). 16p. (gr. -1-k). bds. 7.95 *(978-1-4342-4391-1(5))* Stone Arch Bks.
Rooney, Sandra. Ally M. & Ally G. Young, Lauren. 2006. 20p. (J). 9.95 *(978-1-4120-8518-2(7))* Trafford Publishing.
Roos, Maryn. Alphabetical Sleepy Sheep. Zuckerman, Rory. 2004. (J). bds. 12.95 *(978-0-9749305-3-4(9))* Castle Pacific Publishing.
—Alphabetical Sleepy Sheep. Zuckerman, Rory. 2007. (Sleepy Sheep Ser.). (J). (gr. -1-k). bds. 7.95 incl. audio compact disk *(978-0-9796393-1-9(X))* Little Lion Pr.
—Colorful Sleepy Sheep. Zuckerman, Rory. 2004. (J). bds. 12.95 *(978-0-9749305-1-0(2))* Castle Pacific Publishing.
—Colorful Sleepy Sheep. Zuckerman, Rory. 2007. (Sleepy Sheep Ser.). (J). (gr. -1). bds. 7.95 incl. audio compact disk *(978-0-9796393-2-6(8))* Little Lion Pr.
—Counting Sleepy Sheep. Zuckerman, Rory. 2004. (J). bds. 12.95 *(978-0-9749305-0-3(4))* Castle Pacific Publishing.
—Counting Sleepy Sheep. Zuckerman, Rory. 2007. (Sleepy Sheep Ser.). 16p. (J). (gr. -1). bds. 7.95 incl. audio compact disk *(978-0-9796393-3-3(6))* Little Lion Pr.
—Dancing Diva. Goldberg, Whoopi. 2012. (ENG.). 160p. (J). (gr. 1-5). pap. 4.99 *(978-0-7868-5265-9(8)*, Jump at the Sun) Hyperion Bks. for Children.
—How to Fish for Trouble. Wesley, Valerie Wilson. 2004. 89p. (J). lib. bdg. 15.00 *(978-1-4242-0643-8(X))* Fitzgerald Bks.
—Jump at the Sun Bible Classics David & Goliath. Schall, Jane. 2007. (ENG.). (J). (gr. -1-2). pap. 3.50 *(978-0-7868-5517-9(7)*, Jump at the Sun) Hyperion Bks. for Children.
—Jump at the Sun Bible Classics Jonah & the Whale. Schall, Jane. 2007. (ENG.). (J). (gr. -1-2). pap. 3.50 *(978-0-7868-5518-6(5)*, Jump at the Sun) Hyperion Bks. for Children.
—Perfectly Prima, No. 3. Goldberg, Whoopi. 2010. (ENG.). 160p. (J). (gr. 1-17). pap. 4.99 *(978-0-7868-5262-8(3)*, Jump at the Sun) Hyperion Bks. for Children.
—Shapely Sleepy Sheep. Zuckerman, Rory. 2004. (J). bds. 12.95 *(978-0-9749305-2-7(0))* Castle Pacific Publishing.
—Shapely Sleepy Sheep. Zuckerman, Rory. 2007. (Sleepy Sheep Ser.). (J). (gr. -1). bds. 7.95 incl. audio compact disk *(978-0-9796393-4-0(4))* Little Lion Pr.
—Sugar Plum to the Rescue! Goldberg, Whoopi. 2011. (ENG.). 160p. (J). (gr. 1-5). pap. 4.99 *(978-0-7868-5264-2(X)*, Jump at the Sun) Hyperion Bks. for Children.
—Terrible Terrel. Goldberg, Whoopi. 2010. (ENG.). 160p. (J). (gr. 1-17). pap. 4.99 *(978-0-7868-5263-5(1)*, Jump at the Sun) Hyperion Bks. for Children.
—Toeshoe Trouble. Goldberg, Whoopi. 2009. (ENG.). 160p. (J). (gr. 1-17). pap. 4.99 *(978-0-7868-5261-1(5)*, Jump at the Sun) Hyperion Bks. for Children.
—Who Do I Look Like? Schulte, Mary. 2006. (Rookie Reader Skill Set Ser.). (ENG.). 32p. (J). (gr. k-2). pap. 4.95 *(978-0-516-24758-8(1)*, Children's Pr.) Scholastic Library Publishing.
Roos, Maryn, jt. illus. see Cato, Nancy.
Roosevelt, Michele Chopin. Gray Squirrel at Pacific Avenue. Harrington, Geri. 2011. (Smithsonian's Backyard Ser.). (ENG.). 32p. (J). (gr. -1-3). 19.95 *(978-1-60727-638-8(0))* Soundprints.
Roosevelt, Theodore. Simply Father: Life with Theodore Roosevelt As Seen through the Eyes of His Children. Selda, Toby. 2007. 28p. (J). 7.95 *(978-1-59091-030-6(3))* Eastern National.
Root, Barry. The Birthday Tree. Fleischman, Paul. 2008. (ENG.). 40p. (J). (gr. -1-3). 16.99 *(978-0-7636-2604-4(X))* Candlewick Pr.
—By My Brother's Side. Barber, Tiki & Barber, Ronde. 2004. (ENG.). 32p. (J). (gr. 1-5). 17.99 *(978-0-689-86559-6(7)*, Simon & Schuster/Paula Wiseman Bks.) Simon & Schuster/Paula Wiseman Bks.
—Christmas Farm. Ray, Mary Lyn. (ENG.). 40p. (J). (gr. -1-3). 2008. 17.00 *(978-0-15-216290-0(9))*; 2013. 6.99 *(978-0-544-10509-6(5))* Houghton Mifflin Harcourt Publishing Co.
—Dream Big: Michael Jordan & the Pursuit of Excellence. Jordan, Deloris. 2014. (ENG.). 32p. (J). (gr. -1-3). 7.99 *(978-1-4424-1270-5(4)*, Simon & Schuster/Paula Wiseman Bks.) Simon & Schuster/Paula Wiseman Bks.
—Dream Big: Michael Jordan & the Pursuit of Olympic Gold. Jordan, Deloris. 2012. (ENG.). 32p. (J). (gr. -1-3). 16.99 *(978-1-4424-1269-9(0)*, Simon & Schuster/Paula Wiseman Bks.) Simon & Schuster/Paula Wiseman Bks.
—Game Day. Barber, Tiki & Barber, Ronde. 2005. (ENG.). 32p. (J). (gr. k-5). 16.95 *(978-1-4169-0093-1(4)*, Simon & Schuster/Paula Wiseman Bks.) Simon & Schuster/Paula Wiseman Bks.
—Giant Peach Yodel, 1 vol. Peck, Jan. 2012. (ENG.). 32p. (J). (gr. k-3). 16.99 *(978-1-58980-980-2(7))* Pelican Publishing Co., Inc.
Root, Barry. An Invisible Thread Christmas Story: A True Story Based on the New York Times Bestseller. Schroff, Laura & Tresniowski, Alex. 2015. (ENG.). 32p. (J). (gr. -1-3). 17.99 ***(978-1-4814-1930-7(7)***, Little Simon) Little Simon.
Root, Barry. Messenger, Messenger. Burleigh, Robert. 2011. (ENG.). 32p. (J). (gr. -1-3). pap. 16.99 *(978-1-4424-5335-7(4)*, Atheneum Bks. for Young Readers) Simon & Schuster Children's Publishing.
—Passing the Music Down. Sullivan, Sarah. 2011. (ENG.). 32p. (J). (gr. k-3). 16.99 *(978-0-7636-3753-8(X))* Candlewick Pr.
—Teammates. Barber, Tiki & Barber, Ronde. (ENG.). 32p. (J). (gr. 1-5). 2011. 6.99 *(978-1-4424-1262-0(3))*; 2006. 16.95 *(978-1-4169-2489-0(2))* Simon & Schuster/Paula Wiseman Bks. (Simon & Schuster/Paula Wiseman Bks.).
Root, Barry, jt. illus. see Root, Kimberly Bulcken.
Root, Jeff & Runcorn, Scott. The Woollyhoodwinks: Vs. the Dark Patch. Dumesnil, Phil & Sanchez, Asa. 2008. (ENG.). 36p. (J). (gr. -1-3). 15.95 *(978-1-59702-012-1(5))* Immedium.
Root, Kimberly Bulcken. Born & Bred in the Great Depression. Winter, Jonah. 2011. (ENG.). 40p. (J). (gr. k-4). 17.99 *(978-0-375-86197-0(1)*, Schwartz & Wade Bks.) Random Hse. Children's Bks.
—Dadblamed Union Army Cow. Fletcher, Susan. 2007. (ENG.). 32p. (J). (gr. k-3). 16.99 *(978-0-7636-2263-3(X))* Candlewick Pr.
—Don't Forget Winona. Peterson, Jeanne Whitehouse. 2004. 32p. (J). (gr. -1-3). lib. bdg. 15.89 *(978-0-06-027198-5(1))* HarperCollins Pubs.
Root, Kimberly Bulcken & Root, Barry. Whatever Happened to the Pony Express? Kay, Verla. 2010. (ENG.). 32p. (J). (gr. k-3). 16.99 *(978-0-399-24483-4(2)*, Putnam Juvenile) Penguin Publishing Group.
Rooth, Mike. Beware the Vikings. Boyd, David. 2007. 48p. (J). lib. bdg. 23.08 *(978-1-4242-1624-6(9))* Fitzgerald Bks.
—Cave of Secrets. Low, Vicki. 2007. (Timeline Ser.). 48p. pap. 8.99 *(978-1-4190-4391-8(9))* Steck-Vaughn.
—A Time for Evron. Smillie, Bryan. 2004. 190p. 11.95 *(978-0-9689516-0-6(0))* Shabrya Publishing CAN. Dist: Hushion Hse. Publishing, Ltd.
—United Force. O'Donnell, Liam. 2007. 44p. (J). lib. bdg. 23.08 *(978-1-4242-1633-8(8))* Fitzgerald Bks.
Roots, Adrian, jt. illus. see Johnson, Staz.
Roper, Bob. Dora's Lift-And-Look Book (Dora the Explorer) Random House. 2014. (Nifty Lift-And-Look Ser.). (ENG.). 12p. (J). (— 1). bds. 5.99 *(978-0-385-38514-5(5)*, Random Hse. Bks. for Young Readers) Random Hse. Children's Bks.
—Egg Surprise. Golden Books Staff. 2003. (Paint Box Book Ser.). (ENG.). 32p. (J). (gr. -1-2). pap. 3.99 *(978-0-307-10043-6(X)*, Golden Bks.) Random Hse. Children's Bks.
—You Be the Jury: Courtroom Collection. Miller, Marvin. 2005. 361p. pap. *(978-0-439-77480-2(2))* Scholastic, Inc.
Roper, Clyde F. E., photos by. Giant Squid: Searching for a Sea Monster, 1 vol. Cerullo, Mary M. 2012. (Smithsonian Ser.). (ENG., 48p. (gr. 4-5). pap. 8.95 *(978-1-4296-8023-3(7))*; lib. bdg. 26.86 *(978-1-4296-7541-3(1))* Capstone Pr., Inc.
Roper, Robert. ¡A nadar, Boots! (Swim, Boots, Swim!) Beinstein, Phoebe. 2009. (Dora la Exploradora Ser.). (SPA.). 24p. (J). pap. 3.99 *(978-1-4169-7939-5(5)*, Libros Para Ninos) Libros Para Ninos.
—At the Carnival. Valdes, Leslie. 2005. (Dora the Explorer Ser.). (ENG.). 24p. (J). pap. 3.99 *(978-0-689-85841-3(8)*, Simon Spotlight/Nickelodeon) Simon Spotlight/Nickelodeon.
—Dolls of Danger. ed. 2005. 32p. (J). lib. bdg. 15.00 *(978-1-59054-989-6(9))* Fitzgerald Bks.
—Dora & the Baby Crab. Larsen, Kirsten. 2008. (Dora the Explorer Ser.: 17). (ENG.). 24p. (J). (gr. -1-1). pap. 3.99 *(978-1-4169-5451-4(1)*, Simon Spotlight/Nickelodeon) Simon Spotlight/Nickelodeon.
—Dora & the Stuck Truck. Beinstein, Phoebe. 2008. (Dora the Explorer Ser.: 25). (ENG.). 24p. (J). (gr. -1-2). pap. 3.99 *(978-1-4169-4799-8(X)*, Simon Spotlight/Nickelodeon) Simon Spotlight/Nickelodeon.
—Dora Goes to School. Valdes, Leslie. ed. 2005. (Dora the Explorer Ser.: 8). 22p. (J). lib. bdg. 15.00 *(978-1-59054-791-5(8))* Fitzgerald Bks.
—Dora Goes to School. 2004. (Dora the Explorer Ser.: Vol. 8). (ENG.). 24p. (J). pap. 3.99 *(978-0-689-86494-0(9)*, Simon Spotlight/Nickelodeon) Simon Spotlight/Nickelodeon.
—Dora in the Deep Sea. Ricci, Christine. 2003. (Dora the Explorer Ser.: Vol. 3). (ENG.). 24p. (J). pap. 3.99 *(978-0-689-85845-1(0)*, Simon Spotlight/Nickelodeon) Simon Spotlight/Nickelodeon.
—Dora y la Aventura de Cumpleaños. Dominguez, Adriana, tr. 2010. (Dora la Exploradora Ser.). (SPA.). 24p. (J). 6.99 *(978-1-4424-0286-7(5)*, Libros Para Ninos) Libros Para Ninos.
—Happy Birthday, Dora! 2010. (Dora the Explorer Ser.). (ENG.). 14p. (J). (gr. -1-k). bds. 6.99 *(978-1-4424-0333-8(0)*, Simon Spotlight/Nickelodeon) Simon Spotlight/Nickelodeon.
—The Little Flower Seed. Fisch, Sarah. 2007. (J). pap. *(978-0-439-90899-3(X))* Scholastic, Inc.
—Los Deseos de Dora. Beinstein, Phoebe. Ziegler, Argentina Palacios, tr. from ENG. 2008. (Dora la Exploradora Ser.).Tr. of Dora's Bedtime Wishes. (ENG.). 14p. (J). (gr. -1). bds. 4.99 *(978-1-4169-5036-3(2)*, Libros Para Ninos) Libros Para Ninos.
—La Mochila de Dora. Willson, Sarah. 2003. (Dora the Explorer Ser.).Tr. of Dora's Backpack. (SPA.). 24p. (J). pap. 3.99 *(978-0-689-86306-6(3)*, Libros Para Ninos) Libros Para Ninos.
—Show Me Your Smile! Ricci, Christine. ed. 2005. (Dora the Explorer Ser.: 11). 22p. (J). lib. bdg. 15.00 *(978-1-59054-800-4(0))* Fitzgerald Bks.
—Swim, Boots, Swim! Beinstein, Phoebe. 2009. (Dora the Explorer Ser.: 29). (ENG.). 24p. (J). (gr. -1-2). pap. 3.99 *(978-1-4169-7195-5(5)*, Simon Spotlight/Nickelodeon) Simon Spotlight/Nickelodeon.
Roper, Robert, jt. illus. see Angle, Scott.
Roper, Robert, jt. illus. see Hall, Susan.
Roraback, Robin. Fall Fun for Kit. Hoffmann, Sara E. 2013. (My Reading Neighborhood: Kindergarten Sight Word Stories Ser.). (ENG.). 16p. (gr. -1-1). pap. 5.95 *(978-1-4677-1165-4(9))* Lerner Publishing Group.
—Nan Swims. Hoffmann, Sara E. 2013. (My Reading Neighborhood: Kindergarten Sight Word Stories Ser.). (ENG.). 16p. (gr. -1-1). pap. 5.95 *(978-1-4677-1166-1(7))* Lerner Publishing Group.
—A Picnic with Kit. Hoffmann, Sara E. 2013. (My Reading Neighborhood: Kindergarten Sight Word Stories Ser.). (ENG.). 16p. (gr. -1-1). pap. 5.95 *(978-1-4677-1168-5(3))* Lerner Publishing Group.
Ros, Rafael. Entonces? Ros, Rafael. Crowther, Kitty & Crowther. 2007. (SPA.). 32p. (J). (gr. -1-k). 14.99 *(978-84-8470-249-8(9))* Corimbo, Editorial S.L. ESP. Dist: Lectorum Pubns., Inc.
Rosa, Don, jt. illus. see Mebberson, Amy.
Rosa, Marrisa, photos by. Come the Morning. Harris, Mark Jonathan. 2nd ed. 2005. (Landscapes of Childhood Ser.). (ENG., 220p. (gr. 5-9). per. 25.95 *(978-0-8143-3241-2(2)*, 1366) Wayne State Univ. Pr.
Rosado, Michael. The Wishing Flower, 1 vol. Townsan, Judy. 2009. 13p. pap. 24.95 *(978-1-61546-179-0(5))* America Star Bks.
Rosado, Puig. Le Gentil Petit Diable: Et Autres Contes de la Rue Broca. Gripari, Pierre. 2007. (Folio Junior Ser.). 142p. (J). per. *(978-2-07-061255-0(4))* National Round Table on the Environment & the Economy (NRTEE)/Table ronde nationale sur l'environnement et l'economie (TRNEE).

R

Rosado, Rafael. Dragons Beware! Aguirre, Jorge. 2015. (Chronicles of Claudette Ser.). (ENG.). 160p. (J). (gr. 2-5). pap. 14.99 *(978-1-59643-878-1(9)*, First Second Bks.) Roaring Brook Pr.

—Giants Beware! Aguirre, Jorge. 2012. (Chronicles of Claudette Ser.). (ENG.). 208p. (J). (gr. 2-5). pap. 14.99 *(978-1-59643-582-7(8)*, First Second Bks.) Roaring Brook Pr.

Rosado, Will, et al. Silken Ghost. Dixon, Chuck. 2004. 160p. (YA). pap. 9.95 *(978-1-59314-036-6(3))* CrossGeneration Comics, Inc.

Rosanbalm, Sunny. A Gift for Baby. 2009. (SPA & ENG.). 15.95 *(978-0-9685754-7-5(1))* Natural Child Project Society, The CAN. Dist: Consortium Bk. Sales & Distribution.

Rosario, Joann. Bitty Witty Witty Witty Witty Monkey! Rosario, Joann. 2004. 10p. (J). pap. 10.00 *(978-0-9758746-9-1(1)*, 1246169) J.G.R. Enterprises.

—Double Diddley WHaaat! Rosario, Joann. 2004. (J). pap. *(978-0-9758746-8-4(3))* J.G.R. Enterprises.

—Happy- Go -Lucky Giraffe!! Rosario, Joann. 2004. 20p. (J). (gr. k-5). pap. 10.00 *(978-0-9758746-7-7(5)*, 1246169) J.G.R. Enterprises.

—Joey & His Famous Fish! Rosario, Joann. 2004. 20p. (J). (gr. -1-5). pap. 10.00 *(978-0-9758746-2-2(4)*, 1246169) J.G.R. Enterprises.

—The PenguinThat Boom- Booms to a Ferret That Zoom-Zoomed. Rosario, Joann. 2004. 28p. (J). (gr. -1-5). pap. 10.00 *(978-0-9758746-4-6(0)*, 1246169) J.G.R. Enterprises.

—Puddy Cat & the Chick Muck. Rosario, Joann. 2004. 15p. (J). (gr. -1-5). pap. 10.00 *(978-0-9758746-3-9(2)*, 1246169) J.G.R. Enterprises.

—Swiggly Swiggly Do! Rosario, Joann. 2004. 5p. (J). (gr. -1-5). pap. 10.00 *(978-0-9758746-6-0(7)*, 1246169) J.G.R. Enterprises.

—The Trick That Turned into Poop! Rosario, Joann. 2004. 20p. (J). (gr. -1-13). pap. 10.00 *(978-0-9758746-5-3(9)*, 1246169) J.G.R. Enterprises.

—Where Did Sabrina Go? Rosario, Joann. 2004. 13p. (J). (gr. -1-5). pap. 10.00 *(978-0-9758746-1-5(6))* J.G.R. Enterprises.

Rosario, Sherwin. Meet the Letters. 2005. 26p. (J). 9.99 *(978-0-9767008-0-7(8))* Preschool Prep Co.

—Meet the Numbers Lift the Flap Book. 2005. 12p. (J). bds. 9.99 *(978-0-9767008-1-4(6))* Preschool Prep Co.

—Meet the Numbers One to Ten. 2005. 10p. (J). bds. 7.99 *(978-0-9767008-3-8(2))* Preschool Prep Co.

—Meet the Vowels. 2005. 12p. (J). bds. 7.99 *(978-0-9767008-2-1(4))* Preschool Prep Co.

Rosas, Heather. ABC What Will I Be? Rosas, Heather. 2008. (ENG.). 16p. (J). 12.95 *(978-1-58117-681-0(3)*, Intervisual/Piggy Toes) Bendon, Inc.

Roscoe Robinson. Teddy's Bear, 1 vol. Robinson, Marquita E. 2009. 15p. pap. 24.95 *(978-1-60749-249-8(0))* America Star Bks.

Rose, Carolyn Maree. Pick-a-WooWoo - Angel Steps: Love You, Miss You, 16 vols., Vol. 10. Pretreger, Lidija. 2010. 32p. pap. *(978-0-9803669-9-0(2))* Pick-a-Woo Woo Pubs.

—Pick-a-WooWoo - My Angels Advice: A Story about Love, 16 vols., Vol. 3. Harper, Julie-Ann. 2009. 32p. pap. *(978-0-9803669-2-1(5))* Pick-a-Woo Woo Pubs.

—Pick-a-WooWoo -Frolicking with the Fairies: Two Enchanting Fairytales, 16 vols., Vol. 1. Harper, Julie-Ann. 2008. (ENG.). 32p. (J). pap. *(978-0-9803669-0-7(9))* Pick-a-Woo Woo Pubs.

Rose, Drew. Baby Beluga. Pingry, Patricia A. 2006. (SeaWorld Library: Vol. 6). 26p. (J). (gr. -1-k). bds. 6.95 *(978-0-8249-6643-0(0)*, Candy Cane Pr.) Ideals Pubns.

—Baby Manatee. Pingry, Patricia A. 2006. (SeaWorld Library: Vol. 5). 24p. (J). (gr. -1-k). bds. 6.95 *(978-0-8249-6644-7(9)*, Candy Cane Pr.) Ideals Pubns.

—Baby Sea Otter. Seaworld, photos by. Pingry, Patricia A. 2006. (SeaWorld Library: Vol. 7). 26p. (J). (gr. -1-k). bds. 6.95 *(978-0-8249-6646-1(5)*, Candy Cane Pr.) Ideals Pubns.

—Baby Sea Turtle. Pingry, Patricia A. 2006. (SeaWorld Library: Vol. 8). 26p. (J). (gr. -1-k). bds. 6.95 *(978-0-8249-6645-4(7)*, Candy Cane Pr.) Ideals Pubns.

—Brava OLIVIA. Gallo, Tina. 2009. (Olivia TV Tie-In Ser.). (ENG.). 32p. (J). (gr. -1-1). 4.99 *(978-1-4169-8521-1(2)*, Simon Scribbles) Simon Scribbles.

—Frosty the Snowman Returns. Ritchie, Joseph R. 2006. 14p. (J). (gr. -1-k). bds. 9.95 *(978-0-8249-6670-6(8)*, Candy Cane Pr.) Ideals Pubns.

—God's Heroes. 2005. (Bible Activity Bks.). 94p. (J). (gr. -1-3). 2.99 *(978-0-7814-4313-5(X)*, 078144313X) Cook, David C.

—God's Son, Jesus. 2005. (Bible Activity Bks.). 94p. (J). (gr. -1-3). 2.99 *(978-0-7814-4314-2(8)*, 0781443148) Cook, David C.

—God's World. 2005. (Bible Activity Bks.). 94p. (J). (gr. -1-3). 2.99 *(978-0-7814-4312-8(1)*, 0781443121) Cook, David C.

—John Henry. 2003. (Tall Tales Ser.). (ENG.). 32p. (gr. 3-5). 27.32 *(978-0-7565-0457-1(0)*, CPB Grades 4-8) Compass Point Bks.

—Knock, Knock, Who's There? Ritchie, Joseph R. 2005. (ENG.). 12p. (J). bds. 7.95 *(978-0-8249-6613-3(9))* Ideals Pubns.

—Lost & Found. Poland, Pitch & Poland, Inglan. 2013. 30p. (J). *(978-0-9853430-0-2(1))* Little P Pr. Co.

—Noses & Toes. Pingry, Patricia A. 2005. (J). *(978-0-8249-6594-5(9)*, Candy Cane Pr.) Ideals Pubns.

—OLIVIA & the Christmas Party. Gallo, Tina. 2011. (Olivia TV Tie-In Ser.). (ENG.). 32p. (J). (gr. -1-1). 4.99 *(978-1-4424-3070-9(2)*, Simon Scribbles) Simon Scribbles.

—OLIVIA in the Park. Gallo, Tina. 2010. (Olivia TV Tie-In Ser.). (ENG.). 48p. (J). (gr. -1-1). 5.99 *(978-1-4169-9887-7(X)*, Simon Scribbles) Simon Scribbles.

—Opposites. DeGrie, Eve. 2008. (ENG.). 12p. (J). bds. 6.95 *(978-0-8249-6559-4(0))* Ideals Pubns.

—Sounds. Pingry, Patricia A. 2005. (J). *(978-0-8249-6596-9(5)*, Candy Cane Pr.) Ideals Pubns.

—Tennis Court Conjunctions. Fisher, Doris & Gibbs, D. L. 2008. (Grammar All-Stars Ser.). 32p. (J). (gr. 2-5). lib. bdg. 26.00 *(978-0-8368-8905-5(3)*, Gareth Stevens Learning Library) Stevens, Gareth Publishing LLLP.

—Thomas Jefferson & the Ghostriders. Goldsmith, Howard. 2008. (Ready-To-read COFA Ser.). (ENG.). 32p. (J). (gr. k-2). pap. 3.99 *(978-1-4169-2692-4(5))*; lib. bdg. 13.89 *(978-1-4169-2749-5(2))* Simon Spotlight. (Simon Spotlight).

Rose, Drew, jt. illus. see Childrens Books Staff.

Rose, Heidi. Squishy, Squishy: A Book about My Five Senses. Stihler, Cherie B. 2005. 23p. (J). pap. 5.95 *(978-0-8198-7078-0(1)*, 332-374) Pauline Bks. & Media.

—When Should I Pray? Pharr, Nancy Elizabeth. 2003. 40p. (J). pap. 8.95 *(978-0-8198-8304-9(2)*, 332-412) Pauline Bks. & Media.

Rose, Hilda. Freddy's Day at the Races, 1 vol. Browne, Susan Chalker. 2008. (ENG.). 32p. (J). (gr. 1-8). 10.95 *(978-1-897174-36-4(5))* Creative Bk. Publishing CAN. Dist: Orca Bk. Pubs. USA.

—Freddy's Hockey Hero, 1 vol. Browne, Susan Chalker. 2010. (ENG.). 32p. (J). (gr. k-3). 10.95 *(978-1-897174-62-3(4)*, Tuckamore Bks) Creative Bk. Publishing CAN. Dist: Orca Bk. Pubs. USA.

—Hey Freddy! It's Canada's Birthday!, 1 vol. Browne, Susan Chalker. 2009. (ENG.). 32p. (J). (gr. k-5). 10.95 *(978-1-897174-39-5(X)*, Tuckamore Bks) Creative Bk. Publishing CAN. Dist: Orca Bk. Pubs. USA.

—Johnny & the Gypsy Moth, 1 vol. Sullivan-Fraser, Deannie. 2009. (ENG.). 32p. (J). (gr. k-5). 10.95 *(978-1-897174-40-1(3)*, Tuckamore Bks) Creative Bk. Publishing CAN. Dist: Orca Bk. Pubs. USA.

—What If Your Mom Made Raisin Buns?, 1 vol. Safer, Catherine Hogan. 2007. (ENG.). 32p. (J). (gr. -1-2). pap. 8.95 *(978-1-897174-03-6(9)*, Tuckamore Bks) Creative Bk. Publishing CAN. Dist: Orca Bk. Pubs. USA.

Rose, Julianna. Go Out & Play! Favorite Outdoor Games from KaBOOM! KaBOOM!. 2012. (ENG.). 104p. (J). (gr. k-4). pap. 11.99 *(978-0-7636-5530-3(9))* Candlewick Pr.

Rose, Melanie. A Is for Algonquin: An Ontario Alphabet. Gorman, Lovenia. rev. ed. 2005. (Discover Canada Province by Province Ser.). (ENG.). 40p. (J). (gr. k-5). 17.95 *(978-1-58536-263-9(8))* Sleeping Bear Pr.

—B Is for Big Ben: An England Alphabet. Edwards, Pamela Duncan. 2008. (Discover the World Ser.). (ENG.). 40p. (J). (gr. -1-3). 17.95 *(978-1-58536-305-6(7))* Sleeping Bear Pr.

—E Is for Extreme: An Extreme Sports Alphabet. Herzog, Brad. rev. ed. 2007. (Sports Ser.). (ENG.). 40p. (J). (gr. -1-3). 17.95 *(978-1-58536-310-0(3))* Sleeping Bear Pr.

—The Gift of the Inuksuk. Ulmer, Mike. rev. ed. 2004. (ENG.). 32p. (J). (gr. k-6). 17.95 *(978-1-58536-214-1(X))* Sleeping Bear Pr.

—H Is for Home Run: A Baseball Alphabet. Herzog, Brad. (Alphabet-Sports Ser.). (ENG.). 40p. 2009. (gr. k-6). pap. 7.95 *(978-1-58536-475-6(4))*; 2004. (J). (gr. -1-5). 16.95 *(978-1-58536-219-6(0))* Sleeping Bear Pr.

—Hat Tricks Count: A Hockey Number Book. Napier, Matt. rev. ed. 2005. (Sports Ser.). (ENG.). 40p. (J). (gr. k-5). 16.95 *(978-1-58536-163-2(1))* Sleeping Bear Pr.

—Hockey Numbers. Napier, Matt. (Numbers & Counting Ser.). (ENG.). 2009. 14p. 11.75 *(978-1-58536-495-4(9))*; 2007. 22p. (J). (gr. -1-1). 7.99 *(978-1-58536-346-9(4))* Sleeping Bear Pr.

—A Is for Amazing Moments: A Sports Alphabet. Herzog, Brad. 2008. (Sports Ser.). (ENG.). 40p. (J). (gr. -1-5). 17.95 *(978-1-58536-360-5(X))* Sleeping Bear Pr.

—A Is for Axel: An Ice Skating Alphabet. Browning, Kurt. rev. ed. 2005. (Sports Ser.). (ENG.). 40p. (J). (gr. -1-5). 17.95 *(978-1-58536-280-6(8))* Sleeping Bear Pr.

—K Is for Kick: A Soccer Alphabet. Herzog, Brad. rev. ed. (Sports Ser.). (ENG.). 40p. (J). (gr. -1-3). 2006. pap. 7.95 *(978-1-58536-339-1(1))*; 2003. 16.95 *(978-1-58536-130-4(5))* Sleeping Bear Pr.

—Loonies & Toonies: A Canadian Number Book. Ulmer, Mike. rev. ed. 2006. (ENG.). 40p. (J). (gr. k-6). 18.95 *(978-1-58536-239-4(5))* Sleeping Bear Pr.

—M Is for Maple: A Canadian Alphabet. Ulmer, Mike & Ulmer, Michael. rev. abr. ed. 2007. (Discover the World Ser.). (ENG.). 34p. (J). (gr. -1-1). 7.99 *(978-1-58536-345-2(6)*, 202380) Sleeping Bear Pr.

—M Is for Maple Leafs. Ulmer, Michael. 2014. (ENG.). 32p. (J). 19.95 *(978-1-77049-798-6(6))* Tundra Bks. CAN. Dist: Random Hse., Inc.

—P Is for Passport: A World Alphabet. Scillian, Devin. 2003. (Discover the World Ser.). (ENG.). 56p. (J). (gr. 1-3). 19.95 *(978-1-58536-157-1(7)*, 202017) Sleeping Bear Pr.

—W Is for Wind: A Weather Alphabet. Michaels, Pat. rev. ed. (Science Ser.). (ENG.). 40p. (J). 2006. (gr. -1-3). pap. 7.95 *(978-1-58536-330-8(8))*; 2005. 16.95 *(978-1-58536-237-0(9))* Sleeping Bear Pr.

—Z Is for Zamboni: A Hockey Alphabet. Napier, Matt. rev. ed. 2006. (Sports Alphabet Ser.). (ENG.). 38p. (J). (gr. -1-1). 8.99 *(978-1-58536-303-2(0)*, 202286) Sleeping Bear Pr.

Rose, Melanie. Z Is for Zamboni: A Hockey Alphabet. Rose, Melanie. Napier, Matt. rev. ed. 2003. (Sports Alphabet Ser.). (ENG.). 40p. (J). (gr. -1-1). pap. 7.95 *(978-1-58536-238-7(7)*, 202277) Sleeping Bear Pr.

Rose, Melanie, jt. illus. see Megahan, John.

Rose, Nathalie. Nathalie's Socks. Jeanne, Diana. 2004. 51p. (J). mass mkt. 7.95 *(978-0-9727583-9-0(9))* Taylor-Dth Publishing.

Rose, Patricia M. The Curious Polka-Dot Present. Hallwood, Cheri L. 2007. (ENG.). 32p. (J). 16.99 *(978-0-9774422-1-8(7))* Forever Young Pubs.

—Winter's First Snowflake. Hallwood, Cheri L. l.t. ed. 2006. (ENG.). 32p. (J). 15.99 *(978-0-9774422-0-1(9))* Forever Young Pubs.

Rose-Popp, Melanie. M Is for Maple: A Canadian Alphabet. Ulmer, Mike. rev. ed. 2004. (Discover the World Ser.). (ENG.). 48p. (J). (gr. -1-1). pap. 8.95 *(978-1-58536-235-6(2)*, 202276) Sleeping Bear Pr.

Rose, Thorina. Starring Celia. Kenny, Allison. 2013. (Glitter & Razz Presents... Ser.). (ENG.). 148p. pap. 9.99 *(978-0-615-77472-5(5))* Glitter & Razz Productions LLC.

Rosely, Rose. New Friends, True Friends, Stuck-Like-Glue Friends. Kroll, Virginia L. 2004. 32p. (J). (gr. -1-3). pap. 8.00 *(978-0-8028-5202-1(5))* Eerdmans, William B. Publishing Co.

Rosen, Anne. Good Night Colorado. Gamble, Adam & Mackey, Bill. 2012. (Good Night Our World Ser.). (ENG.). 20p. (J). (gr. k — 1). bds. 9.95 *(978-1-60219-055-9(0))* Our World of Books.

—Good Night Connecticut. Vrba, Christina. 2009. (Good Night Our World Ser.). (ENG.). 20p. (J). (gr. k — 1). bds. 9.95 *(978-1-60219-035-1(6))* Our World of Books.

—Good Night Florida Keys. Jasper, Mark. 2008. (Good Night Our World Ser.). (ENG.). 20p. (J). (gr. k — 1). bds. 9.95 *(978-1-60219-020-7(8))* Our World of Books.

—Good Night Israel. Jasper, Mark. 2010. (Good Night Our World Ser.). (ENG.). 28p. (J). (gr. k — 1). bds. 9.95 *(978-1-60219-043-6(7))* Our World of Books.

—Good Night Martha's Vineyard. Adams, Megan Weeks & Gamble, Adam. 2007. (Good Night Our World Ser.). (ENG.). 18p. (J). (gr. k — 1). bds. 9.95 *(978-1-60219-011-5(9))* Our World of Books.

—Good Night Michigan. Gamble, Adam. 2011. (Good Night Our World Ser.). (ENG.). 20p. (J). (gr. k — 1). bds. 9.95 *(978-1-60219-054-2(2))* Our World of Books.

—Good Night Nantucket. Gamble, Adam. 2007. (Good Night Our World Ser.). (ENG.). 20p. (J). (gr. k — 1). bds. 9.95 *(978-1-60219-013-9(5))* Our World of Books.

—Good Night New Hampshire. Gamble, Adam. 2009. (Good Night Our World Ser.). (ENG.). 20p. (J). (gr. k — 1). bds. 9.95 *(978-1-60219-037-5(2))* Our World of Books.

—Good Night North Carolina. Gamble, Adam. 2009. (Good Night Our World Ser.). (ENG.). 20p. (J). (gr. k — 1). bds. 9.95 *(978-1-60219-033-7(X))* Our World of Books.

—Good Night Rhode Island. Gamble, Adam. 2008. (Good Night Our World Ser.). (ENG.). 20p. (J). (gr. k — 1). bds. 9.95 *(978-1-60219-024-5(0))* Our World of Books.

Rosen, Anne & Hart, Jason. Good Night Utah. Gamble, Adam & Jasper, Mark. 2012. (Good Night Our World Ser.). (ENG.). 20p. (J). (gr. k — 1). bds. 9.95 *(978-1-60219-059-7(3))* Our World of Books.

Rosen, Anne & Jasper, Mark. Good Night Country Store. Gamble, Adam. 2010. (Good Night Our World Ser.). (ENG.). 20p. (J). (gr. k — 1). bds. 9.95 *(978-1-60219-044-3(5))* Our World of Books.

Rosen, Anne & Veno, Joe. Good Night Georgia. Gamble, Adam. 2009. (Good Night Our World Ser.). (ENG.). 20p. (J). (gr. k — 1). bds. 9.95 *(978-1-60219-032-0(1))* Our World of Books.

—Good Night Nevada. Gamble, Adam & Jasper, Mark. 2012. (Good Night Our World Ser.). (ENG.). 20p. (J). (gr. k — 1). bds. 9.95 *(978-1-60219-060-3(7))* Our World of Books.

Rosen, Anne, jt. illus. see Veno, Joe.

Rosen, Barry & Bell, Greg. Do You Know What a Stranger Is? Rosen, Barry. 2003. 34p. (J). pap. 7.25 *(978-0-9625593-4-1(2))* B.R. Publishing Co.

Rosen, Ellis J., jt. illus. see Rosen, Lev Ac.

Rosen, Gary. Appleblossom the Possum. Sloan, Holly Goldberg. 2015. (ENG.). 288p. (J). (gr. 3-7). 16.99 *(978-0-8037-4133-1(2)*, Dial) Penguin Publishing Group.

Rosen, Kim. 10 Plants That Shook the World. Richardson, Gillian. 2013. (World of Tens Ser.). (ENG.). 132p. (J). (gr. 5-7). 24.95 *(978-1-55451-445-8(2)*, 9781554514458); pap. 14.95 *(978-1-55451-444-1(4)*, 9781554514441) Annick Pr., Ltd. CAN. Dist: Firefly Bks., Ltd.

Rosen, Kim. 10 Rivers That Shaped the World. Peters, Marilee. 2015. (World of Tens Ser.). (ENG.). 132p. (J). (gr. 4-7). pap. 14.95 ***(978-1-55451-738-1(9)***, 9781554517381) Annick Pr., Ltd. CAN. Dist: Firefly Bks., Ltd.

—10 Ships That Rocked the World. Richardson, Gillian. 2015. (World of Tens Ser.). (ENG.). 176p. (J). (gr. 4-7). pap. 14.95 ***(978-1-55451-781-7(8)***, 9781554517817) Annick Pr., Ltd. CAN. Dist: Firefly Bks., Ltd.

Rosen, Lev Ac & Rosen, Ellis J. Woundabout. Rosen, Lev Ac & Rosen, Ellis J. 2015. (ENG.). 288p. (J). (gr. 3-7). 17.00 *(978-0-316-37078-3(9))* Little Brown & Co.

Rosen, Michael & Oxenbury, Helen. Chung Ta Di Sian Gau. 2004. Orig. Title: We're Going on a Bear Hunt. 33p. (J). *(978-1-85269-722-8(9))* Mantra Lingua.

Rosenbaum, Andria Warmflash & Gill, Deirdre. Trains Don't Sleep. Rosenbaum, Andria Warmflash & Gill, Deirdre. 2016. (J). ***(978-0-544-38074-5(6))*** Harcourt.

Rosenberg, Amye. My First Learn & Do Jewish Holiday Book. Gootel, Rifka. 64p. (J). (gr. k-2). pap. 4.95 *(978-0-87441-475-2(X))* Behrman Hse., Inc.

Rosenberg, Natascha. Bake, Mice, Bake! Seltzer, Eric. 2012. (Penguin Young Readers, Level 1 Ser.). (ENG.). 32p. (J). (gr. k-1). mass mkt. 3.99 *(978-0-448-45763-5(6)*, Warne, Frederick Pubs.) Penguin Bks., Ltd. GBR. Dist: Penguin Random Hse., LLC.

Rosenberg, Rachelle, jt. illus. see Lim, Ron.

Rosenberry, Akiko & Rosenberry, Susan. Spectacular Journey. Donaki & Rosenberry, Donald. 2006. (J). per. 20.00 *(978-0-9771482-6-4(2)*, Ithaca Pr.) Authors & Artists Publishers of New York, Inc.

Rosenberry, Susan, jt. illus. see Rosenberry, Akiko.

Rosenberry, Vera. Baya, Baya, Lulla-By-a. McDonald, Megan. 2014. (ENG.). 32p. (J). (gr. -1-1). 16.99 *(978-1-4814-2533-9(1)*, Atheneum Bks. for Young Readers) Simon & Schuster Children's Publishing.

—Enviarme a Ti, Level 2. Guthrie, Woody. Flor Ada, Alma, tr. 2003. (Dejame Leer Ser.). (SPA.). 8p. (J). (gr. -1-1). 6.50 *(978-0-673-36301-5(5)*, Good Year Bks.) Celebration Pr.

—Monster Mischief. Jane, Pamela. 2014. (ENG.). 32p. (J). (gr. -1-2). 16.99 *(978-1-4814-2535-3(8)*, Atheneum Bks. for Young Readers) Simon & Schuster Children's Publishing.

Rosenberry, Vera. When Vera Was Sick, 4 bks., Set. Rosenberry, Vera. unabr. ed. 2006. (Picture Book Readalong Ser.). (J). (gr. -1-3). pap. 37.95 incl. audio *(978-1-59519-652-1(8))*; pap. 39.95 incl. audio compact disk *(978-1-59519-653-8(6))* Live Oak Media.

Rosendahl, Melissa M. Ebenezer Flea & the Right Thing to Do, 1 vol. Budic, Hannah Purdy. 2008. (ENG.). 30p. 24.95 *(978-1-60441-750-0(1))* America Star Bks.

Rosenfelder, Cheryl. Neddy the Nutty Acorn. Vos, Sharon. 2008. 40p. per. 24.95 *(978-1-60441-232-1(1))* America Star Bks.

Rosenthal, Amy Krouse & Lichtenheld, Tom. The OK Book. Rosenthal, Amy Krouse & Lichtenheld, Tom. 2007. 40p. (J). (gr. -1-3). lib. bdg. 14.89 *(978-0-06-115256-6(0))* HarperCollins Pubs.

—The Ok Book. Rosenthal, Amy Krouse & Lichtenheld, Tom. 2007. (ENG.). 40p. (J). (gr. -1-2). 12.99 *(978-0-06-115255-9(2))* HarperCollins Pubs.

Rosenthal, Marc. Bobo the Sailor Man! Rosenthal, Eileen. 2013. (ENG.). 40p. (J). (gr. -1-1). 15.99 *(978-1-4424-4443-0(6))* Simon & Schuster Children's Publishing.

—Dig! Zimmerman, Andrea & Clemesha, David. 2014. (ENG.). 30p. (J). (— 1). bds. 7.99 *(978-0-544-17388-0(0)*, HMH Books For Young Readers) Houghton Mifflin Harcourt Publishing Co.

—I Must Have Bobo! Rosenthal, Eileen. 2011. (ENG.). 40p. (J). (gr. -1-1). 14.99 *(978-1-4424-0377-2(2)*, Atheneum Bks. for Young Readers) Simon & Schuster Children's Publishing.

—I'll Save You Bobo! Rosenthal, Eileen. 2012. (ENG.). 40p. (J). (gr. -1-1). 14.99 *(978-1-4424-0378-9(0)*, Atheneum Bks. for Young Readers) Simon & Schuster Children's Publishing.

—Making a Friend. McGhee, Alison. 2011. (ENG.). 40p. (J). (gr. -1-3). 16.99 *(978-1-4169-8998-1(6)*, Atheneum Bks. for Young Readers) Simon & Schuster Children's Publishing.

—Mogie: The Heart of the House. Appelt, Kathi. 2014. (ENG.). 40p. (J). (gr. -1-3). 17.99 *(978-1-4424-8054-4(8)*, Atheneum Bks. for Young Readers) Simon & Schuster Children's Publishing.

Rosenthal, Marc. Archie & the Pirates. Rosenthal, Marc. 2009. (ENG.). 40p. (J). (gr. -1-3). 16.99 *(978-0-06-144164-6(3))* HarperCollins Pubs.

—Phooey! Rosenthal, Marc. 2007. 40p. (J). (gr. -1-3). lib. bdg. 17.89 *(978-0-06-075249-1(1)*, Cotler, Joanna Books) HarperCollins Pubs.

Rosenthal, Marc. Dig! Rosenthal, Marc, tr. Zimmerman, Andrea Griffing & Clemesha, David. 2004. (ENG.). 32p. (J). (gr. -1-3). 16.00 *(978-0-15-216785-1(4))* Houghton Mifflin Harcourt Publishing Co.

Rosenwasser, Robert. Biting Sun. Kitrilakis, Thalia. Rosenwasser, Rena, ed. 2011. 48p. (J). pap. 5.00 *(978-0-932716-17-0(2))* Kelsey Street Pr.

Rosenzweig, Sharon. The Comic Torah: Reimagining the Very Good Book. Rosenzweig, Sharon. Freeman, Aaron. 2010. (ENG.). 128p. pap. 19.95 *(978-1-934730-54-6(8))* Yehuda, Ben Pr.

Rosewarne, Graham. Alligator. Johnson, Jinny. 2007. (Zoo Animals in the Wild Ser.). 32p. (J). (gr. -1-3). lib. bdg. 28.50 *(978-1-58340-902-2(5))* Black Rabbit Bks.

—Brachiosaurus & Other Dinosaur Giants. Johnson, Jinny. 2009. (Dinosaurs Alive! Ser.). 32p. (J). (gr. 4-7). pap. 7.95 *(978-1-59920-182-5(8))* Black Rabbit Bks.

—Chimpanzee. Johnson, Jinny. 2007. (Zoo Animals in the Wild Ser.). 32p. (J). (gr. -1-3). lib. bdg. 28.50 *(978-1-58340-900-8(9))* Black Rabbit Bks.

—Dandelion. Johnson, Jinny. 2010. (J). 28.50 *(978-1-59920-351-5(0))* Black Rabbit Bks.

Rosewarne, Graham, et al. Discover the Amazing World of Animals. 87p. (J). *(978-1-902272-27-6(7))* Tucker Slingsby, Ltd.

Rosewarne, Graham. Elephant. Johnson, Jinny. 2005. (Zoo Animals in the Wild Ser.). 32p. (J). (gr. 2-5). lib. bdg. 27.10 *(978-1-58340-643-4(3))* Black Rabbit Bks.

—Fox. Johnson, Jinny. 2010. (J). 28.50 *(978-1-59920-354-6(5))* Black Rabbit Bks.

—Frog. Johnson, Jinny. 2010. (J). 28.50 *(978-1-59920-355-3(3))* Black Rabbit Bks.

—Iguanodon & Other Plant-Eating Dinosaurs. Johnson, Jinny. (Dinosaurs Alive! Ser.). 32p. (J). (gr. 4-7). 2009. pap. 7.95 *(978-1-59920-184-9(4))*; 2007. lib. bdg. 28.50 *(978-1-59920-067-5(8))* Black Rabbit Bks.

—Oak Tree. Johnson, Jinny. 2010. (J). 28.50 *(978-1-59920-356-0(1))* Black Rabbit Bks.

—Polar Bear. Johnson, Jinny. 2007. (Zoo Animals in the Wild Ser.). 32p. (J). (gr. -1-3). lib. bdg. 28.50 *(978-1-58340-901-5(7))* Black Rabbit Bks.

—Pteranodon & Other Flying Reptiles. Johnson, Jinny. (Dinosaurs Alive! Ser.). 32p. (J). (gr. 4-7). 2009. pap. 7.95 *(978-1-59920-185-6(2))*; 2007. lib. bdg. 28.50 *(978-1-59920-068-2(6))* Black Rabbit Bks.

—Triceratops & Other Horned & Armored Dinosaurs. Johnson, Jinny. 2009. (Dinosaurs Alive! Ser.). 32p. (J). (gr. 4-7). pap. 7.95 *(978-1-59920-181-8(X))* Black Rabbit Bks.

—Triceratops & Other Horned & Armored Dinosaurs. Johnson, Jinny. 2007. (Dinosaurs Alive! Ser.). 32p. (J). (gr. -1-3). lib. bdg. 28.50 *(978-1-59920-064-4(3))* Black Rabbit Bks.

—Tyrannosaurus & Other Mighty Hunters. Johnson, Jinny. (Dinosaurs Alive! Ser.). 32p. (J). 2009. (gr. 4-7). pap. 7.95 *(978-1-59920-180-1(1))*; 2007. (gr. -1-3). lib. bdg. 28.50 *(978-1-59920-063-7(5))* Black Rabbit Bks.

—Velociraptor & Other Speedy Killers. Johnson, Jinny. (Dinosaurs Alive! Ser.). 32p. (J). (gr. 4-7). 2009. pap. 7.95 *(978-1-59920-183-2(6))*; 2007. lib. bdg. 28.50 *(978-1-59920-066-8(X))* Black Rabbit Bks.

Rosinski. Thorgal Vol. 14: Giants. Hamme, Van. 2013. (ENG.). 48p. pap. 11.95 *(978-1-84918-156-3(X))* CineBook GBR. Dist: National Bk. Network.

—The Three Elders of Aran. Van Hamme, Jean. 2007. (ENG.). 96p. (J). (gr. 4-7). pap. 14.99 *(978-1-905460-31-1(7))* CineBook GBR. Dist: National Bk. Network.

Rosinski, Adolf. Child of the Stars. Rosinski & Van Hamme, Jean. 2007. (Thorgal Ser.). (ENG.). 96p. per. 14.99 *(978-1-905460-23-6(6))* CineBook GBR. Dist: National Bk. Network.

Rosinski, Grzegorz. Beyond the Shadows. Van Hamme, Jean. 2008. (ENG.). 96p. pap. 19.95 *(978-1-905460-45-8(7))* CineBook GBR. Dist: National Bk. Network.

—The Brand of the Exiles. Van Hamme, Jean. 2013. (ENG.). 48p. (J). (gr. 7-12). pap. 11.95 *(978-1-84918-136-5(5))* CineBook GBR. Dist: National Bk. Network.

—The Guardian of the Keys. Van Hamme, Jean. 2010. (ENG.). 48p. pap. 11.95 *(978-1-84918-050-4(4))* CineBook GBR. Dist: National Bk. Network.

—The Invisible Fortress. Van Hamme, Jean. 2012. (ENG.). 48p. (YA). (gr. 6-17). pap. 11.95 *(978-1-84918-103-7(9))* CineBook GBR. Dist: National Bk. Network.

—Mas alla de las Sombras, Vol. 5. Van Hamme, Jean. 2005. Orig. Title: Thorgal Vol. 5: Au-dela des Ombres. (SPA.). 48p. pap. 16.95 *(978-1-59497-010-8(6))* Public Square Bks.

—Siobhan. Dufaux, Jean. 2014. (ENG.). 64p. pap. 15.95 *(978-1-84918-169-3(1))* CineBook GBR. Dist: National Bk. Network.

—Thorgal: La Isla de los Mares Helados, , Vol. 2. Van Hamme, Jean. 2004. Orig. Title: Thorgal vol. 2: L' Ile des Mers Gelees. (SPA.). 48p. pap. 16.95 *(978-1-59497-007-8(6))* Public Square Bks.

—Thorgal: La Maga Traicionada. Van Hamme, Jean. 2004. Orig. Title: Thorgal vol. 1: la Magicienne Trahie. (SPA.). 48p. pap. 16.95 *(978-1-59497-006-1(8))* Public Square Bks.

—Thorgal Vol. 4: La Galera Negra. Van Hamme, Jean. 2004. Orig. Title: Thorgal: la Galere Negra. (SPA.). 48p. pap. 16.95 *(978-1-59497-009-2(2))* Public Square Bks.

—Thorgal - City of the Lost God. van Hamme, Jean. 2009. (ENG.). 96p. pap. 19.95 *(978-1-84918-001-6(6))* CineBook GBR. Dist: National Bk. Network.

—Thorgal Vol. 13: Ogotai's Crown. Van Hamme, Jean. 2013. (ENG.). 48p. pap. 11.95 *(978-1-84918-142-6(X))* CineBook GBR. Dist: National Bk. Network.

Rosinsky, Natalie M. California Ranchos, 1 vol. Rosinsky, Natalie M. 2006. (We the People: Expansion & Reform Ser.). (ENG.). 48p. (gr. 5-6). 27.99 *(978-0-7565-1633-8(1),* We the People) Compass Point Bks.

Roski, Gayle Garner. Endeavour's Long Journey. Olivas, John D. 2013. (J). *(978-0-9856237-2-2(1))* East West Discovery Pr.

—Endeavour's Long Journey: Celebrating 19 Years of Space Exploration. Olivas, John D. 2013. (J). pap. *(978-0-9856237-3-9(X))* East West Discovery Pr.

—Mystery of the Giant Mask of Sanxingdui. Smith, Icy. 2015. (J). *(978-0-9913454-8-9(7))* East West Discovery Pr.

—Thomas the T. Rex: The Journey of a Young Dinosaur to Los Angeles. Smith, Michael. 2011. (J). *(978-0-9832278-4-7(5));* 44p. (gr. 3-5). 19.95 *(978-0-9821675-3-3(9))* East West Discovery Pr.

Roski, Gayle Garner. Thomas the T. Rex: The Journey of a Young Dinosaur to Los Angeles. Roski, Gayle Garner. Smith, Michael. 2011. (SPA & ENG.). (J). *(978-0-9832278-2-3(9))* East West Discovery Pr.

Roskifte, Kristin. Animal Beauty. 2015. 50p. (J). ***(978-0-8028-5454-4(0),*** Eerdmans Bks For Young Readers) Eerdmans, William B. Publishing Co.

Roskinski, Grzegorz. Los Tres Ancianos del pais de Aran, Vol. 3. Van Hamme, Jean. 2004. Orig. Title: Thorgal Vol. 3: les Trois Vieillards du Pays d'Aran. (SPA.). 48p. pap. 16.95 *(978-1-59497-008-5(4))* Public Square Bks.

Roslyn, Jacquelyn. The Peanut Pickle: A Story about Peanut Allergy. Ureel, Jessica & Jacobs, Jessica. 2012. (ENG.). 48p. (J). (gr. k-3). 14.95 *(978-1-61608-672-5(6),* 608672, Sky Pony Pr.) Skyhorse Publishing Co., Inc.

Ross, Adam. Winston, the Polite St Bernard. Wainwright, Joann M. 2009. 28p. pap. 14.99 *(978-1-4389-2704-6(5))* AuthorHouse.

Ross, Alex. Marvels. Busiek, Kurt. Youngquist, Jeff, ed. 10th anniv. ed. 2004. (Marvel Heroes Ser.). 400p. (YA). 49.99 *(978-0-7851-1388-1(6))* Marvel Worldwide, Inc.

Ross, Alex & Braithwaite, Doug. Paradise X, 5 vols., Vol. 4. Kruger, Jim. 2003. (Universe X Ser.). 304p. (YA). pap. 29.99 *(978-0-7851-1120-7(4))* Marvel Worldwide, Inc.

Ross, Andrea. Turtles Go Slow. Ross, Andrea. 2003. 25p. (J). (gr. 1-3). pap. 7.95 *(978-1-887683-45-6(3))* Storybook Pr. & Productions.

Ross, C. Spooks. Dorison, Xavier & Nury, Fabian. 2012. (ENG.). 56p. (J). (gr. 10-12). pap. 13.95 *(978-1-84918-129-7(2))* CineBook GBR. Dist: National Bk. Network.

Ross, Christine. Molly Whuppie & the Giant: Band 13/Topaz. Booth, David. 2007. (Collins Big Cat Ser.). (ENG.). 24p. (J). pap. 8.99 *(978-0-00-722874-4(0))* HarperCollins Pubs. Ltd. GBR. Dist: Independent Pubs. Group.

—A Quick Picnic, 6 pack. Holden, Pam. 2009. (Red Rocket Readers Ser.). 16p. (gr. -1-3). pap. *(978-1-877363-22-1(7),* Red Rocket Readers) Flying Start Bks.

—Weather: KinderConcepts Individual Title Six-Packs. Wallace, Jessica. (Kinderstarters Ser.). 8p. (gr. -1-1). 21.00 *(978-0-7635-8725-3(7))* Rigby Education.

Ross, Damon, photos by. Odd Jobs: The Wackiest Jobs You've Never Heard Of. Weiss, Ellen. 2012. (ENG., 80p. (J). (gr. 4-6). pap. 33.99 *(978-0-689-82934-5(5),* Simon & Schuster/Paula Wiseman Bks.) Simon & Schuster/Paula Wiseman Bks.

Ross, Daniel Vaughn. The Fake Heir. Petrucha, Stefan et al. 2006. (J). *(978-1-59707-060-7(2))* Papercutz.

Ross, Dave. The Not-so-Scary Monster Handbook: Halloween. Ross, Dave. 2003. (J). 135.44 *(978-0-06-055492-7(4))* HarperCollins Pubs.

Ross, Dave, jt. illus. see Scott, Greg.

Ross, Deborah. Ny Alay Ako: Ako the Aye-Aye. Jolly, Alison. Rasamimanana, Hantanirina, tr. 2005. (MLA & ENG.). (J). 20.00 *(978-0-9766009-0-9(0))* Lemur Conservation Foundation.

Ross, Gary. Nature Walks & Sunday Drives 'Round Edmonton, Vol. 1. Edmonton Natural History Club. 2nd rev. ed. 2003. (ENG.). 88p. pap. *(978-0-9698507-2-4(7))* Edmonton Natural History Club CAN. Dist: Lone Pine Publishing.

Ross, Gary & Nordhagen, Ted. Birds of Oregon. Burrows, Roger & Gilligan, Jeff. rev. ed. 2003. (ENG.). 384p. (J). (gr. 4). pap. *(978-1-55105-374-5(8))* Lone Pine Publishing USA.

Ross, Graham. Alphabetter, 1 vol. Bar-el, Dan. 2007. (ENG.). 32p. (J). (gr. -1-3). 8.95 *(978-1-55143-861-0(5))* Orca Bk. Pubs. USA.

Ross, Graham. And the Stink Spectacular. Sharpe, Luke. 2015. (Billy Sure Kid Entrepreneur Ser.: 2). (ENG.). 160p. (J). (gr. 3-7). 17.99 ***(978-1-4814-3951-0(0),*** Simon Spotlight) Simon Spotlight.

—Billy Sure, Kid Entrepreneur. Sharpe, Luke. 2015. (Billy Sure Kid Entrepreneur Ser.: 1). (ENG.). 160p. (J). (gr. 3-7). pap. 6.99 ***(978-1-4814-3947-3(2),*** Simon Spotlight) Simon Spotlight.

Ross, Graham. By a Thread, 1 vol. Dickens, Ned. 2005. (ENG.). 32p. (J). (gr. -1-3). 16.95 *(978-1-55143-325-7(7))* Orca Bk. Pubs. USA.

—Cheetah, 1 vol. Lewis, Wendy A. 2007. (Orca Echoes Ser.). (ENG.). 64p. (J). (gr. 2-3). per. 6.95 *(978-1-55143-465-0(2))* Orca Bk. Pubs. USA.

—The Paper Wagon. Attema, Martha. 2005. 61p. (J). lib. bdg. 20.00 *(978-1-4242-1260-6(X))* Fitzgerald Bks.

—The Paper Wagon, 1 vol. Attema, Martha. 2005. (Orca Echoes Ser.). (ENG.). 64p. (J). (gr. 2-3). per. 6.95 *(978-1-55143-356-1(7))* Orca Bk. Pubs. USA.

—Rhyme Stones, 1 vol. Skene, Pat. 2007. (Orca Echoes Ser.). (ENG.). 64p. (J). (gr. 2-3). per. 6.95 *(978-1-55143-636-4(1))* Orca Bk. Pubs. USA.

Ross, Graham. The Stink Drink. Sharpe, Luke. 2015. (Billy Sure Kid Entrepreneur Ser.: 2). (ENG.). 160p. (J). (gr. 3-7). pap. 6.99 ***(978-1-4814-3950-3(2),*** Simon Spotlight) Simon Spotlight.

Ross, Graham. Timberwolf Prey, 1 vol. Brouwer, Sigmund. ed. 2010. (Orca Echoes Ser.). (ENG.). 64p. (J). (gr. 2-3). pap. 6.95 *(978-1-55469-109-8(5))* Orca Bk. Pubs. USA.

—Timberwolf Rivals, 1 vol. Brouwer, Sigmund. 2009. (Orca Echoes Ser.). (ENG.). 64p. (J). (gr. 2-3). pap. 6.95 *(978-1-55469-107-4(9))* Orca Bk. Pubs. USA.

—Timberwolf Tracks, 1 vol. Brouwer, Sigmund. 2009. (Orca Echoes Ser.). (ENG.). 64p. (J). (gr. 2-3). pap. 6.95 *(978-1-55143-734-7(1))* Orca Bk. Pubs. USA.

—What a Hippopota-Mess!, 1 vol. Skene, Pat. 2006. (Orca Echoes Ser.). (ENG.). 64p. (J). (gr. 2-3). per. 4.99 *(978-1-55143-402-5(4))* Orca Bk. Pubs. USA.

Ross, Graham T. Monster Lunch, 1 vol. Skene, Pat. 2008. (Orca Echoes Ser.). (ENG.). 64p. (J). (gr. 2-3). pap. 6.95 *(978-1-55143-941-9(7))* Orca Bk. Pubs. USA.

Ross, Heather. Crafty Chloe. DiPucchio, Kelly. 2012. (Crafty Chloe Ser.). (ENG.). 40p. (J). (gr. -1-3). 16.99 *(978-1-4424-2123-3(1),* Atheneum Bks. for Young Readers) Simon & Schuster Children's Publishing.

—Dress-Up Mess-Up. DiPucchio, Kelly. 2013. (Crafty Chloe Ser.). (ENG.). 40p. (J). (gr. -1-3). 16.99 *(978-1-4424-2124-0(X))* Simon & Schuster Children's Publishing.

—Hot Diggity Dogs. Calmenson, Stephanie & Cole, Joanna. 2015. (Ready, Set, Dogs! Ser.: 2). (ENG.). 112p. (J). (gr. 1-4). 14.99 *(978-0-8050-9649-1(3),* Holt, Henry & Co. Bks. For Young Readers) Holt, Henry & Co.

—How to Behave at a Dog Show. Rosenberg, Madelyn. 2015. (ENG.). 32p. (J). (gr. -1-3). 17.99 *(978-0-06-227927-9(0))* HarperCollins Pubs.

—How to Behave at a Tea Party. Rosenberg, Madelyn. 2014. (ENG.). 32p. (J). (gr. -1-3). 17.99 *(978-0-06-227926-2(2),* Tegen, Katherine Bks) HarperCollins Pubs.

—Iva Honeysuckle Meets Her Match. Ransom, Candice. 2014. (Iva Honeysuckle Book Ser.). (ENG.). 192p. (J). (gr. 1-3). pap. 4.99 *(978-1-4231-3516-6(4))* Hyperion Bks. for Children.

—Iva Honeysuckle Meets Her Match. Ransom, Candice. 2013. (Iva Honeysuckle Book Ser.). (ENG.). 192p. (J). (gr. 2-5). 14.99 *(978-1-4231-3514-2(8))* Hyperion Pr.

—Mo Wren, Lost & Found. Springstubb, Tricia. 2011. (Fox Street Ser.: 2). (ENG.). 256p. (J). (gr. 3-7). 15.99 *(978-0-06-199039-7(6))* HarperCollins Pubs.

—No Dogs Allowed. Calmenson, Stephanie & Cole, Joanna. 2013. (Ready, Set, Dogs! Ser.: 1). (ENG.). 128p. (J). (gr. 1-4). 14.99 *(978-0-8050-9645-3(0),* Holt, Henry & Co. Bks. For Young Readers) Holt, Henry & Co.

—No Dogs Allowed. Calmenson, Stephanie & Cole, Joanna. 2014. (Ready, Set, Dogs! Ser.: 1). (ENG.). 144p. (J). (gr. 1-4). pap. 5.99 *(978-1-250-04414-3(6))* Square Fish.

—Teacher's Pets. Calmenson, Stephanie & Cole, Joanna. 2014. (Ready, Set, Dogs! Ser.: 2). (ENG.). 128p. (J). (gr. 1-4). 14.99 *(978-0-8050-9647-7(7),* Holt, Henry & Co. Bks. For Young Readers) Holt, Henry & Co.

—Teacher's Pets. Calmenson, Stephanie & Cole, Joanna. 2015. (Ready, Set, Dogs! Ser.: 2). (ENG.). 144p. (J). (gr. 1-4). pap. 5.99 *(978-1-250-05705-1(1))* Square Fish.

—What Happened on Fox Street. Springstubb, Tricia. (Fox Street Ser.: 1). (J). (gr. 3-7). 2011. 240p. pap. 6.99 *(978-0-06-198636-9(4));* 2010. 224p. 15.99 *(978-0-06-198635-2(6))* HarperCollins Pubs.

Ross, Julie. The Door in the Floor. Pimot, Karen Hutchins. 2009. 24p. pap. 12.95 *(978-0-9823002-6-8(3))* Peppertree Pr., The.

—Sam's Perfect Plan. Pimot, Karen Hutchins. 2008. 32p. pap. 12.95 *(978-0-9814894-8-3(6))* Peppertree Pr., The.

Ross Kennedy. Revenge of the Cannibal Chickens. Lihou, Gavin. 2013. 74p. pap. 10.50 *(978-1-62212-484-8(7),* Strategic Bk. Publishing) Strategic Book Publishing & Rights Agency (SBPRA).

Ross, M. T. Animal Children: The Friends of the Forest & the Plain. Kirkwood, Edith Brown. 2007. 100p. per. *(978-1-4065-2907-4(9))* Dodo Pr.

—Bird Children. Gordon, Elizabeth. 2011. (ENG.). (J). (gr. -1-3). 14.95 *(978-1-55709-083-6(1))* Applewood Bks.

—Bird Children: The Little Playmates of the Flower Children. Gordon, Elizabeth. 2008. (ENG.). 96p. (J). (gr. -1-3). pap. 14.95 *(978-1-55709-087-4(4))* Applewood Bks.

—Flower Children: The Little Cousins of the Field & Garden. Gordon, Elizabeth. 2008. (ENG.). 96p. (J). (gr. -1-3). pap. 14.95 *(978-1-55709-086-7(6))* Applewood Bks.

Ross, Melissa. Scriptures for Kids. Arbo, Barbara. 2013. 24p. 19.95 *(978-1-61633-402-4(9));* pap. 10.95 *(978-1-61633-403-1(7))* Guardian Angel Publishing, Inc.

Ross, Melissa. Today I Am a Penguin. Ross, Melissa. 2012. 24p. pap. 10.95 *(978-1-61633-306-5(5))* Guardian Angel Publishing, Inc.

Ross, Sharon & Bergman, Shannon. Cookie Crisis! Willson, Sarah. ed. 2005. 32p. (J). lib. bdg. 15.00 *(978-1-59054-981-0(3))* Fitzgerald Bks.

Ross, Sylvia. Lion Singer. Ross, Sylvia. 2005. 33p. (J). (gr. 3-7). 12.95 *(978-1-59714-009-6(0),* Great Valley Bks.) Heyday.

Ross, Tony. Ámbar en Cuarto y Sin Su Amigo, Level 3.7. Danziger, Paula. 2003.Tr. of Amber Brown Goes Fourth. (SPA.). 136p. (J). (gr. 3-5). pap. 10.95 *(978-84-204-4412-3(X),* SAN412X) Ediciones Alfaguara ESP. Dist: Santillana USA Publishing Co., Inc.

—Amber Brown Goes Fourth. Danziger, Paula. 2007. (Amber Brown Ser.: No. 3). 101p. (gr. 2-5). 15.00 *(978-0-7569-8197-6(2))* Perfection Learning Corp.

—Amber Brown Goes Fourth. Danziger, Paula. 2007. (Amber Brown Ser.: 3). (ENG.). 128p. (J). (gr. 2-5). 5.99 *(978-0-14-240901-5(4),* Puffin) Penguin Publishing Group.

—Amber Brown Is Green with Envy. Danziger, Paula. 2004. (Amber Brown Ser.: No. 9). 151p. (J). (gr. 2-5). 12.65 *(978-0-7569-2978-7(4))* Perfection Learning Corp.

—Amber Brown Is Not a Crayon. Danziger, Paula. 2006. (Amber Brown Ser.: 1). (ENG.). 96p. (J). (gr. 2-5). 5.99 *(978-0-14-240619-9(8),* Puffin) Penguin Publishing Group.

—Amber Brown Is Tickled Pink. Danzinger, Paula. 2012. 152p. pap. 14.99 *(978-1-101-58155-1(7))* Penguin Publishing Group.

—Amber Brown Is Tickled Pink. Danziger, Paula et al. 2013. (Amber Brown Ser.: 10). (ENG.). 176p. (J). (gr. 2-5). pap. 5.99 *(978-0-14-242757-6(8),* Puffin) Penguin Publishing Group.

—Amber Brown Wants Extra Credit. Danziger, Paula. 2008. (Amber Brown Ser.: 4). (ENG.). 144p. (J). (gr. 2-5). 5.99 *(978-0-14-241049-3(7),* Puffin) Penguin Publishing Group.

—Las Aventuras de Ulises. McCaughrean, Geraldine. Barroso, Paz, tr. 2005. (Mythology Series Collection Mitos Ser.).Tr. of Odysseus. (SPA.). 48p. (J). (gr. 2-3). 9.95 *(978-84-348-6426-9(6))* SM Ediciones ESP. Dist: Iaconi, Mariuccia Bk. Imports.

—Boa's Bad Birthday. Willis, Jeanne. 2014. (ENG.). 32p. (J). (gr. -1-3). 16.95 *(978-1-4677-3450-9(0))* Lerner Publishing Group.

—Bob the Bursting Bear. Rosen, Michael. (ENG.). 32p. (J). (gr. -1-k). 2014. pap. 9.99 *(978-1-84939-687-5(6));* 2013. 17.99 *(978-1-84939-440-6(7))* Andersen Pr. GBR. Dist: Independent Pubs. Group.

—Bravo, Max! Grindley, Sally. 2007. (ENG.). 160p. (J). (gr. 1-4). pap. 8.99 *(978-1-4169-3645-9(9),* Simon & Schuster/Paula Wiseman Bks.) Simon & Schuster/Paula Wiseman Bks.

—Burping Bertha. Rosen, Michael. 2004. (ENG.). 80p. (J). (gr. k-2). per. 7.50 *(978-1-84270-351-9(X))* Andersen Pr. GBR. Dist: Independent Pubs. Group.

—Burping Bertha. Rosen, Michael. 2012. (ENG.). 64p. (J). (gr. -1-2). pap. 8.99 *(978-1-84939-406-2(7))* Andersen Pr. GBR. Dist: Independent Pubs. Group.

—El Caballo de Madera. McCaughrean, Geraldine. Barroso, Paz, tr. 2005. (Mythology Series Collection Mitos Ser.).Tr. of Wooden Horse (Pandora's Box). (SPA.). 50p. (J). (gr. 2-3). 9.95 *(978-84-348-6432-0(0))* SM Ediciones ESP. Dist: Iaconi, Mariuccia Bk. Imports.

—Caterpillar Dreams. Willis, Jeanne. 2013. (ENG.). 32p. (J). (gr. -1-k). pap. 8.99 *(978-1-84939-025-5(8))* Andersen Pr. GBR. Dist: Independent Pubs. Group.

Ross, Tony. The Chocolate Monster. Page, Jan. 2014. (ENG.). 80p. (J). (gr. k-2). pap. 7.99 ***(978-0-552-56889-0(9))*** Transworld Publishers Ltd. GBR. Dist: Independent Pubs. Group.

Ross, Tony. Class Six & the Very Big Rabbit. Waddell, Martin. 2005. (Collins Big Cat Ser.). (ENG.). 32p. (J). pap. 7.99 *(978-0-00-718629-7(0))* HarperCollins Pubs. Ltd. GBR. Dist: Independent Pubs. Group.

—Cottonball Colin. Willis, Jeanne. 2008. 26p. (J). (gr. -1-4). 16.00 *(978-0-8028-5331-8(5),* Eerdmans Bks For Young Readers) Eerdmans, William B. Publishing Co.

—Daft Bat. Willis, Jeanne. 2007. (ENG.). 32p. (J). (gr. k-2). 16.95 *(978-1-84270-476-9(1))* Transworld Publishers Ltd. GBR. Dist: Independent Pubs. Group.

—Dear Max. Grindley, Sally & Lucas, D J. 2007. (ENG.). 144p. (J). (gr. 1-4). pap. 6.99 *(978-1-4169-3443-1(X),* Simon & Schuster/Paula Wiseman Bks.) Simon & Schuster/Paula Wiseman Bks.

—Deathwood Damian Strikes Again. Townson, Hazel. 2008. (Deathwood Letters Ser.). (ENG.). 60p. (J). (gr. 4-6). pap. 9.95 *(978-1-84270-707-4(8))* Andersen Pr. GBR. Dist: Independent Pubs. Group.

—Dédalo e Ícaro: El Rey Midas. McCaughrean, Geraldine. Barroso, Paz, tr. 2nd ed. 2005. (Mythology Series Collection Mitos Ser.).Tr. of Daedalus & Icarus (King Midas). (SPA.). 48p. (J). (gr. 2-3). 9.95 *(978-84-348-6431-3(2))* SM Ediciones ESP. Dist: Iaconi, Mariuccia Bk. Imports.

—Los Doce Trabajos de Hércules: Eco y Narciso. McCaughrean, Geraldine. Barroso, Paz, tr. 2005. (Mythology Series Collection Mitos Ser.).Tr. of Twelve Labours of Heracles. (SPA.). 48p. (J). (gr. 2-3). 9.95 *(978-84-348-6429-0(0))* SM Ediciones ESP. Dist: Iaconi, Mariuccia Bk. Imports.

—Dr Xargle's Book of Earth Hounds. Willis, Jeanne. 2012. (ENG.). 28p. (J). (gr. -1-k). pap. 10.99 *(978-1-84270-170-6(3))* Andersen Pr. GBR. Dist: Independent Pubs. Group.

—Dr Xargle's Book of Earth Relations. Willis, Jeanne. (ENG.). 32p. (J). pap. 9.99 *(978-1-84270-307-6(2))* Andersen Pr. GBR. Dist: Trafalgar Square Publishing.

—Dr Xargle's Book of Earth Tiggers. Willis, Jeanne. 2012. (ENG.). 28p. (J). (gr. -1-k). pap. 10.99 *(978-1-84939-297-6(8))* Andersen Pr. GBR. Dist: Independent Pubs. Group.

—Dr Xargle's Book of Earthlets. Willis, Jeanne. 2012. (ENG.). 28p. (J). (gr. -1-k). pap. 12.99 *(978-1-84939-292-1(7))* Andersen Pr. GBR. Dist: Independent Pubs. Group.

—Es Dia de Feria, Ambar Dorado. Danziger, Paula. 2007. (de Ambar / a Is for Amber Easy-To-Read Ser.).Tr. of It's a Fair Day, Amber Brown. (SPA.). 48p. (gr. k-3). pap. 8.95 *(978-1-59820-596-1(X))* Santillana USA Publishing Co., Inc.

—Flabby Cat & Slobby Dog. Willis, Jeanne. 2009. (Andersen Press Picture Bks). (ENG.). 32p. (J). (gr. -1-3). 16.95 *(978-0-7613-5151-1(5),* Carolrhoda Bks.) Lerner Publishing Group.

—Fly, Chick, Fly! Willis, Jeanne. 2012. (Andersen Press Picture Bks). (ENG.). 32p. (J). (gr. -1-3). 16.95 *(978-1-4677-0314-7(1))* Lerner Publishing Group.

—Get Ready for Second Grade, Amber Brown. Danziger, Paula. 2003. (Is for Amber Ser.). (ENG.). 48p. (J). (gr. 1-3). mass mkt. 3.99 *(978-0-14-250081-1(X),* Warne, Frederick Pubs.) Penguin Bks., Ltd. GBR. Dist: Penguin Random Hse., LLC.

—Get Ready for Second Grade, Amber Brown. Danziger, Paula. 2004. (A Is for Amber Ser.). 48p. (gr. k-2). 14.00 *(978-0-7569-2177-4(5))* Perfection Learning Corp.

—Get Ready for Second Grade, Amber Brown. Danzinger, Paula. 2003. pap. 31.95 incl. audio compact disk *(978-1-59112-562-4(6));* (J). 25.95 incl. audio *(978-1-59112-234-0(1));* (J). pap. 29.95 incl. audio *(978-1-59112-235-7(X))* Live Oak Media.

—Grill Pan Eddy. Willis, Jeanne. 2008. (ENG.). 32p. (J). (gr. k — 1). pap. 13.99 *(978-1-84270-711-1(6))* Andersen Pr. GBR. Dist: Independent Pubs. Group.

—Harry the Poisonous Centipede Goes to Sea. Banks, Lynne Reid. 2006. 203p. (J). (gr. 3-7). lib. bdg. 16.89 *(978-0-06-077549-0(1))* HarperCollins Pubs.

—Helping Hercules. Simon, Francesca. 2014. (ENG.). 128p. (J). (gr. 2-4). pap. 8.99 *(978-1-84255-153-0(1),* Orion Children's Bks.) Hachette Children's Group GBR. Dist: Independent Pubs. Group.

—Hippospotamus. Willis, Jeanne. 2012. (Andersen Press Picture Bks). (ENG.). 32p. (J). (gr. -1-3). 16.95 *(978-1-4677-0316-1(8))* Lerner Publishing Group.

—Horrid Henry. Simon, Francesca. 2009. (J). Non-ISBN Publisher.

—Horrid Henry. Simon, Francesca. 2009. (Horrid Henry Ser.: 0). (ENG.). 112p. (J). (gr. 2-5). pap. 5.99 *(978-1-4022-1775-3(7),* Sourcebooks Jabberwocky) Sourcebooks, Inc.

—Horrid Henry. Simon, Francesca. 2012. (Horrid Henry Ser.). 112p. (J). (gr. 2-5). lib. bdg. 24.21 *(978-1-59961-185-3(6))* Spotlight.

—Horrid Henry & the Abominable Snowman. Simon, Francesca. 2010. (Horrid Henry Ser.: 0). (ENG.). 112p. (J). (gr. 2-5). pap. 5.99 *(978-1-4022-4256-4(5),* Sourcebooks Jabberwocky) Sourcebooks, Inc.

—Horrid Henry & the Abominable Snowman. Simon, Francesca. 2012. (Horrid Henry Ser.). 112p. (J). (gr. 2-5). lib. bdg. 24.21 *(978-1-59961-186-0(4))* Spotlight.

—Horrid Henry & the Mega-Mean Time Machine. Simon, Francesca. 2009. (Horrid Henry Ser.: 0). (ENG.). 112p. (J). (gr. 2-5). pap. 5.99 *(978-1-4022-1780-7(3),* Sourcebooks Jabberwocky) Sourcebooks, Inc.

—Horrid Henry & the Mega-Mean Time Machine. Simon, Francesca. 2012. (Horrid Henry Ser.). 112p. (J). (gr. 2-5). lib. bdg. 24.21 *(978-1-59961-187-7(2))* Spotlight.

—Horrid Henry & the Mummy's Curse. Simon, Francesca. 2009. (Horrid Henry Ser.: 0). (ENG.). 112p. (J). (gr. 2-5). pap. 5.99 *(978-1-4022-1776-0(5),* Sourcebooks Jabberwocky) Sourcebooks, Inc.

—Horrid Henry & the Scary Sitter. Simon, Francesca. 2009. (Horrid Henry Ser.: 0). (ENG.). 112p. (J). (gr. 2-5). pap. 5.99 *(978-1-4022-1781-4(1),* Sourcebooks Jabberwocky) Sourcebooks, Inc.

—Horrid Henry & the Scary Sitter. Simon, Francesca. 2012. (Horrid Henry Ser.). 112p. (J). (gr. 2-5). lib. bdg. 24.21 *(978-1-59961-188-4(0))* Spotlight.

—Horrid Henry & the Soccer Fiend. Simon, Francesca. 2009. (Horrid Henry Ser.: 0). (ENG.). 112p. (J). (gr. 2-5). pap. 5.99 *(978-1-4022-1778-4(1),* Sourcebooks Jabberwocky) Sourcebooks, Inc.

—Horrid Henry & the Soccer Fiend. Simon, Francesca. 2012. (Horrid Henry Ser.). 112p. (J). (gr. 2-5). lib. bdg. 24.21 *(978-1-59961-189-1(9))* Spotlight.

—Horrid Henry & the Zombie Vampire. Simon, Francesca. 2012. (Horrid Henry Ser.: 0). (ENG.). 112p. (J). (gr. 2-5). pap. 5.99 *(978-1-4022-6785-7(1),* Sourcebooks Jabberwocky) Sourcebooks, Inc.

—Horrid Henry Robs the Bank. Simon, Francesca. 2013. (Horrid Henry Ser.: 0). (ENG.). 112p. (J). (gr. 2-5). pap. 5.99 *(978-1-4022-7995-9(7),* Sourcebooks Jabberwocky) Sourcebooks, Inc.

—Horrid Henry Rocks. Simon, Francesca. 2011. (Horrid Henry Ser.: 0). (ENG.). 112p. (J). (gr. 2-5). pap. 5.99 *(978-1-4022-5674-5(4),* Sourcebooks Jabberwocky) Sourcebooks, Inc.

—Horrid Henry Rocks. Simon, Francesca. 2012. (Horrid Henry Ser.). 112p. (J). (gr. 2-5). lib. bdg. 24.21 *(978-1-59961-190-7(2))* Spotlight.

—Horrid Henry Tricks the Tooth Fairy. Simon, Francesca. 2009. 90p. (J). Non-ISBN Publisher.

—Horrid Henry Tricks the Tooth Fairy. Simon, Francesca. 2009. (Horrid Henry Ser.: 0). (ENG.). 112p. (J). (gr. 2-5). pap. 5.99 *(978-1-4022-2275-7(0),* Sourcebooks Jabberwocky) Sourcebooks, Inc.

—Horrid Henry Tricks the Tooth Fairy. Simon, Francesca. 2012. (Horrid Henry Ser.). 112p. (J). (gr. 2-5). lib. bdg. 24.21 *(978-1-59961-191-4(0))* Spotlight.

—Horrid Henry Wakes the Dead. Simon, Francesca. 2011. (Horrid Henry Ser.: 0). (ENG.). 112p. (J). (gr. 2-5). pap. 4.99 *(978-1-4022-5934-0(4),* Sourcebooks Jabberwocky) Sourcebooks, Inc.

—Horrid Henry Wakes the Dead. Simon, Francesca. 2012. (Horrid Henry Ser.). 112p. (J). (gr. 2-5). lib. bdg. 24.21 *(978-1-59961-192-1(9))* Spotlight.

R

—Horrid Henry's Christmas. Simon, Francesca. 2009. (Horrid Henry Ser.: 0). (ENG.). 112p. (J). (gr. 2-5). pap. 5.99 (978-1-4022-1782-1(X), Sourcebooks Jabberwocky) Sourcebooks, Inc.

—Horrid Henry's Joke Book. Simon, Francesca. 2010. (Horrid Henry Ser.: 0). (ENG.). 112p. (J). (gr. 2-5). pap. 4.99 (978-1-4022-4425-4(8), Sourcebooks Jabberwocky) Sourcebooks, Inc.

—Horrid Henry's Monster Movie. Simon, Francesca. 2012. (Horrid Henry Ser.: 0). (ENG.). 112p. (J). (gr. 2-5). pap. 4.99 (978-1-4022-7737-5(7), Sourcebooks Jabberwocky) Sourcebooks, Inc.

—Horrid Henry's Stinkbomb. Simon, Francesca. 2009. (Horrid Henry Ser.: 0). (ENG.). 112p. (J). (gr. 2-5). pap. 5.99 (978-1-4022-1779-1(X), Sourcebooks Jabberwocky) Sourcebooks, Inc.

—Horrid Henry's Underpants. Simon, Francesca. 2009. 112p. (J). (gr. 2-5). (Horrid Henry Ser.: 0). (ENG.). pap. 5.99 (978-1-4022-3825-3(8)); pap. 4.99 (978-1-4022-1777-7(3)) Sourcebooks, Inc. (Sourcebooks Jabberwocky).

—I, Amber Brown. Danziger, Paula. 2011. (Amber Brown Ser.: 8). (ENG.). 160p. (J). (gr. 2-5). 5.99 (978-0-14-241965-6(6), Puffin) Penguin Publishing Group.

—I Don't Want to Go to Hospital. 2013. (ENG.). 32p. (J). (gr. -1-3). 16.95 (978-1-4677-1155-5(1)) Lerner Publishing Group.

—I Feel Sick! 2015. (J). (978-1-4677-5798-0(5)) Andersen Pr.

—I Feel Sick! 2015. (ENG.). 32p. (J). (gr. -1-3). 16.99 (978-1-4677-5797-3(7)) Andersen Pr. GBR. Dist: Lerner Publishing Group.

—In Control, Ms. Wiz?, 0 vols. Blacker, Terence. (ENG.). 64p. (gr. 1-4). 2013. pap. 9.99 (978-1-4778-1086-6(2), 9781477810866); 2009. 12.99 (978-0-7614-5557-8(4), 9780761455578) Amazon Publishing. (Amazon Children's Publishing).

—In Jail, Ms. Wiz?, 0 vols. Blacker, Terence. 2009. (ENG.). 64p. (gr. 2-5). 12.99 (978-0-7614-5556-1(6), 9780761455561, Amazon Children's Publishing) Amazon Publishing.

—Is Green with Envy. Danziger, Paula & Mazer, Anne. 2004. (Amber Brown Ser.: 9). (ENG.). 160p. (J). (gr. 2-5). pap. 4.99 (978-0-439-07171-0(2), Scholastic Paperbacks) Scholastic, Inc.

—It's a Fair Day, Amber Brown. Danziger, Paula. 2003. pap. 31.95 incl. audio compact disk (978-1-59112-564-8(2)); (J). 25.95 incl. audio (978-1-59112-246-3(5)); (J). pap. 29.95 incl. audio (978-1-59112-247-0(3)); (J). (gr. -1-2). audio compact disk 28.95 (978-1-59112-565-5(0)) Live Oak Media.

—It's a Fair Day, Amber Brown. Danziger, Paula. 2003. (Is for Amber Ser.). (ENG.). 32p. (J). (gr. 1-3). pap. 3.99 (978-0-698-11982-6(7), Puffin) Penguin Publishing Group.

—It's Justin Time, Amber Brown. Danziger, Paula. (Amber Brown Ser.). 9.95 (978-1-59112-294-4(5)) Live Oak Media.

—Jack & the Broomstick: From a Jack to a King. Lawrence, Michael. 2012. (Pair of Jacks Ser.: 2). (ENG.). 128p. (J). (gr. 2-4). pap. 7.99 (978-1-4083-0775-5(8)) Hodder & Stoughton GBR. Dist: Independent Pubs. Group.

—Jack & the Giant Killer / Jackwitch. Lawrence, Michael. 2012. (Pair of Jacks Ser.: 1). (ENG.). 128p. (J). (gr. 2-4). pap. 7.99 (978-1-4083-0774-8(X)) Hodder & Stoughton GBR. Dist: Independent Pubs. Group.

—Jack Four's Jackdaws & Jack of the Gorgons. Lawrence, Michael. 2012. (Pair of Jacks Ser.: 4). (ENG.). 128p. (J). (gr. 2-4). pap. 7.99 (978-1-4083-0777-9(4)) Hodder & Stoughton GBR. Dist: Independent Pubs. Group.

—Jack in the Box? And Tall-Tale Jack. Lawrence, Michael. 2012. (Pair of Jacks Ser.: 3). (ENG.). 128p. (J). (gr. 2-4). pap. 7.99 (978-1-4083-0776-2(6)) Hodder & Stoughton GBR. Dist: Independent Pubs. Group.

—Jason y el Vellocino de Oro: Aracne, la Tejedora. McCaughrean, Geraldine. Barroso, Paz, tr. 2005. (Mythology Series Collection Mitos Ser.).Tr. of Jason & the Golden Fleece. (SPA.). 48p. (J). (gr. 2-3). 9.95 (978-84-348-6425-2(8)) SM Ediciones ESP. Dist: Iaconi, Mariuccia Bk. Imports.

—Justo a Tiempo, Ambar Dorado. Danziger, Paula. 2007. (Amber Brown Ser.). (SPA.). 48p. (gr. k-3). per. 8.95 (978-1-59820-595-4(1), Alfaguara) Santillana USA Publishing Co., Inc.

—Lista para Segundo Grado, Ambar Dorado. Danziger, Paula. 2007. (de Ámbar / a Is for Amber Easy-To-Read Ser.).Tr. of Get Ready for Second Grade, Amber Brown. (SPA.). 48p. (gr. k-3). pap. 8.95 (978-1-59820-593-0(5)) Santillana USA Publishing Co., Inc.

—Little Wolf, Terror of the Shivery Sea. Whybrow, Ian. 2004. (Little Wolf Adventures Ser.). (ENG.). 144p. (J). (gr. 3-6). 14.95 (978-1-57505-629-6(1)) Lerner Publishing Group.

—Lobito Aprende a Ser Malo. Whybrow, Ian. Azaola, Miguel, tr. from ENG. 2007. (Ediciones Lerner Single Titles Ser.). (SPA.). 136p. (J). (gr. 3-6). per. 6.95 (978-0-8225-8644-9(4), Ediciones Lerner) Lerner Publishing Group.

—Malicia para Principiantes: Una Aventura de Lobito y Apestosito. Whybrow, Ian. Quintana, Joela, tr. 2005. (Libros Ilustrados (Picture Bks.)). (SPA.). 32p. (J). (gr. k-2). 16.95 (978-0-8225-3211-8(5), Ediciones Lerner) Lerner Publishing Group.

—Mammoth Pie. Willis, Jeanne. (ENG.). 32p. (J). (gr. -1-k). 2013. pap. 8.99 (978-1-84270-757-9(4)); 2008. 19.99 (978-1-84270-659-6(4)) Andersen Pr. GBR. Dist: Independent Pubs. Group.

—Mayfly Day. Ross, Melanie H. & Willis, Jeanne. 2012. (ENG.). 32p. (J). (gr. -1-k). pap. 10.99 (978-1-84270-606-0(3)) Andersen Pr. GBR. Dist: Independent Pubs. Group.

—Michael. Bradman, Tony. 2009. (ENG.). 32p. (J). (gr. k-2). pap. 11.99 (978-1-84270-911-5(9)) Andersen Pr. GBR. Dist: Independent Pubs. Group.

—Mind the Door! Skidmore, Steve & Barlow, Steve. 2006. (Mad Myths Ser.). 121p. (J). (gr. 2-4). per. 6.95 (978-1-903015-49-0(9)) Barn Owl Bks, London GBR. Dist: Independent Pubs. Group.

—Miss Dirt the Dustman's Daughter. Ahlberg, Allan. (ENG.). 24p. (J). pap. 6.95 (978-0-14-037882-5(0)) Penguin Bks., Ltd. GBR. Dist: Trafalgar Square Publishing.

—El Nino Que Perdio el Ombligo. Willis, Jeanne. (SPA.). (J). 8.95 (978-958-04-5632-2(1)) Norma S.A. COL. Dist: Distribuidora Norma, Inc., Lectorum Pubns., Inc.

—Old Dog. Willis, Jeanne. 2011. (ENG.). 32p. (J). (gr. -1-k). pap. 8.99 (978-1-84270-880-4(5)) Andersen Pr. GBR. Dist: Independent Pubs. Group.

—Orange You Glad It's Halloween, Amber Brown?, 4 bks., Set. Danziger, Paula. 2007. (Amber Brown Ser.). (J). (gr. 1-3). pap. 29.95 incl. audio (978-1-4301-0080-5(X)) Live Oak Media.

—Orange You Glad It's Halloween, Amber Brown? Danziger, Paula. 2007. (Is for Amber Ser.). (ENG.). 48p. (J). (gr. 1-3). 3.99 (978-0-14-240809-4(3), Puffin) Penguin Publishing Group.

—Orange You Glad It's Halloween, Amber Brown? Danziger, Paula. 2007. (Amber Brown Ser.). 48p. (J). (gr. k-3). 11.65 (978-0-7569-8154-9(9)) Perfection Learning Corp.

—The Orchard Book of Goblins Ghouls & Ghosts & Other Magical Stories. Waddell, Martin. 2006. (ENG.). 128p. (J). (gr. 2-4). 22.99 (978-1-84121-922-6(3)) Hodder & Stoughton GBR. Dist: Independent Pubs. Group.

—Pablo Diablo Y la Cangura Fantasma. Simon, Francesca. 2005. (Pablo Diablo Ser.).Tr. of Horrid Harry & the Kangaroo Ghost. (SPA.). (J). (gr. 2-3). pap. 8.95 (978-84-348-9684-0(2)) SM Ediciones ESP. Dist: Iaconi, Mariuccia Bk. Imports.

—Pablo Diablo Y Los Piojos. Simon, Francesca. 2005. (Pablo Diablo Ser.).Tr. of Horrid Harry & the Lice. (SPA.). (J). (gr. 2-3). pap. 8.95 (978-84-348-8673-5(1)) SM Ediciones ESP. Dist: Iaconi, Mariuccia Bk. Imports.

—Perseo y la Gorgona Medisa. McCaughrean, Geraldine. Barroso, Paz, tr. 2005. (Mythology Series Collection Mitos Ser.).Tr. of Perseus & the Gorgon Medusa. (SPA.). 48p. (J). (gr. 2-3). 9.95 (978-84-348-6430-6(4)) SM Ediciones ESP. Dist: Iaconi, Mariuccia Bk. Imports.

—Pippi in the South Seas. Lindgren, Astrid. Turner, Marianne, tr. from SWE. ed. 2006. 128p. pap. (978-0-19-275481-3(5)) Oxford Univ. Pr.

—Por Que? Camp, Lindsay. (SPA.). 32p. (978-84-233-3053-9(2), DS0265) Ediciones Destino ESP. Dist: Lectorum Pubns., Inc.

—Prince Charmless. Willis, Jeanne. 2014. (ENG.). 32p. (J). (gr. -1-k). pap. 9.99 (978-1-84939-778-0(3)) Andersen Pr. GBR. Dist: Independent Pubs. Group.

—Que Viaje, Ambar Dorado! Danziger, Paula. 2007. (de Ámbar / a Is for Amber Easy-To-Read Ser.).Tr. of What a Trip, Amber Brown. (SPA.). 48p. (gr. k-3). pap. 8.95 (978-1-59820-592-3(7)) Santillana USA Publishing Co., Inc.

—Querido Max. Grindley, Sally & Max, Querido. rev. ed. 2006. (Castillo de la Lectura Naranja Ser.). (ENG.). 120p. (J). pap. 7.95 (978-970-20-0854-5(9)) Castillo, Ediciones, S. A. de C. V. MEX. Dist: Macmillan.

—The Really Rude Rhino. Willis, Jeanne. 2007. (ENG.). 32p. (J). (gr. -1-k). per. 10.99 (978-1-84270-571-1(7)) Andersen Pr. GBR. Dist: Independent Pubs. Group.

—Rita's Rhino. 2015. (J). (978-1-4677-6319-6(5)) Lerner Publishing Group.

—Second Grade Rules, Amber Brown. Danziger, Paula. 2005. (Is for Amber Ser.). (ENG.). 48p. (J). (gr. 1-3). mass mkt. 3.99 (978-0-14-240421-8(7), Warne, Frederick Pubs.) Penguin Bks., Ltd. GBR. Dist: Penguin Random Hse., LLC.

—Second Grade Rules, Amber Brown. Danziger, Paula. 2005. (Amber Brown Ser.). 48p. (gr. k-2). 14.00 (978-0-7569-5521-2(1)) Perfection Learning Corp.

—Segundo Grado Es Increible, Ambar Dorado. Danziger, Paula. 2007. (de Ámbar / a Is for Amber Easy-To-Read Ser.).Tr. of Second Grade Rules, Amber Brown. (SPA.). 48p. (gr. k-3). pap. 8.95 (978-1-59820-594-7(3)) Santillana USA Publishing Co., Inc.

—El Senor Browser y los Afilacerebros. Curtis, Philip. (SPA.). 112p. (YA). (gr. 5-8). (978-84-239-2754-8(7), EC2750) Espasa Calpe, S.A. ESP. Dist: Lectorum Pubns., Inc.

—Sir Gadabout. Beardsley, Martyn. 2nd ed. 2007. (Sir Gadabout Ser.: 1). (ENG.). 96p. (J). (gr. 4-7). pap. 6.95 (978-1-85881-055-3(8)) Orion Publishing Group, Ltd. GBR. Dist: Independent Pubs. Group.

Ross, Tony. Slug Needs a Hug! Willis, Jeanne. 2015. (ENG.). 32p. (J). (gr. -1-3). 17.99 (978-1-4677-9309-4(4)) Lerner Publishing Group.

Ross, Tony. Stone Me! Barlow, Steve & Skidmore, Steve. 2005. (Mad Myths Ser.). 122p. (J). pap. 5.95 (978-1-903015-43-8(X)) Barn Owl Bks, London GBR. Dist: Independent Pubs. Group.

—Super Dooper Jezebel. 32p. (J). pap. 9.99 (978-1-84270-096-9(0)) Andersen Pr. GBR. Dist: Trafalgar Square Publishing.

—Tadpole's Promise. Willis, Jeanne. 2005. (ENG.). 32p. (J). (gr. -1-k). pap. 12.99 (978-1-84270-426-4(5)) Andersen Pr. GBR. Dist: Independent Pubs. Group.

—A Touch of Wind! Barlow, Steve & Skidmore, Steve. 2006. (Mad Myths Ser.). 96p. (J). pap. 6.95 (978-1-903015-56-8(1)) Barn Owl Bks, London GBR. Dist: Independent Pubs. Group.

—Why? Camp, Lindsay. 2008. (ENG.). 32p. (J). (gr. -1-k). pap. 12.99 (978-1-84270-607-7(1)) Andersen Pr. GBR. Dist: Independent Pubs. Group.

—The Wind in the Wallows. Willis, Jeanne. 2013. (ENG.). 32p. (J). (gr. -1-k). pap. 9.99 (978-1-84939-453-6(9)) Andersen Pr. GBR. Dist: Independent Pubs. Group.

—You Can't Eat Your Chicken Pox, Amber Brown. Danziger, Paula. 2006. (Amber Brown Ser.: No. 2). 100p. (gr. 2-5). 15.00 (978-0-7569-6756-7(2)) Perfection Learning Corp.

—You Can't Eat Your Chicken Pox, Amber Brown. Danziger, Paula. 2006. (Amber Brown Ser.: 2). (ENG.). 128p. (J). (gr. 2-5). 5.99 (978-0-14-240629-8(5), Puffin) Penguin Publishing Group.

Ross, Tony. Centipede's One Hundred Shoes. Ross, Tony. rev. ed. 2003. (ENG.). 32p. (J). (gr. -1-3). 18.99 (978-0-8050-7298-3(5), Holt, Henry & Co. Bks. For Young Readers) Holt, Henry & Co.

—Don't Do That! Ross, Tony. 2011. (ENG.). 32p. (J). (gr. k — 1). pap. 12.99 (978-1-84270-936-8(4)) Andersen Pr. GBR. Dist: Independent Pubs. Group.

—I Want a Cat! Ross, Tony. 2008. (ENG.). 32p. (J). (gr. -1-k). pap. 10.99 (978-1-84270-691-6(8)) Andersen Pr. GBR. Dist: Independent Pubs. Group.

—I Want a Party! Ross, Tony. 2011. (Andersen Press Picture Books Ser.). (J). 16.95 (978-0-7613-8089-4(2)) Andersen Pr. GBR. Dist: Lerner Publishing Group.

—I Want My Light On! Ross, Tony. 2010. (Andersen Press Picture Bks). (ENG.). 32p. (J). (gr. -1-3). 16.95 (978-0-7613-6443-6(9)) Lerner Publishing Group.

—I Want My Mom! Ross, Tony. 2012. (Andersen Press Picture Bks). (ENG.). 32p. (J). (gr. -1-3). 16.95 (978-1-4677-0318-5(4)) Lerner Publishing Group.

—I Want My Pacifier. Ross, Tony. 2004. 28p. (J). pap. 4.95 (978-1-929132-65-2(4)) Kane Miller.

—I Want to Do It Myself! Ross, Tony. 2011. (Andersen Press Picture Bks). (ENG.). 32p. (J). (gr. -1-3). 16.95 (978-0-7613-7412-1(4)) Lerner Publishing Group.

—I Want to Go Home! Ross, Tony. 2014. 32p. (J). (gr. -1-3). 16.95 (978-1-4677-5095-0(6)) Lerner Publishing Group.

—I Want to Win! Ross, Tony. 2012. (Andersen Press Picture Bks). (ENG.). 32p. (J). (gr. -1-3). 16.95 (978-0-7613-8993-4(8)) Lerner Publishing Group.

—I Want Two Birthdays! Ross, Tony. 2010. (ENG.). 32p. (J). (gr. -1-3). 16.95 (978-0-7613-5495-6(6)) Lerner Publishing Group.

—Is It Because... ? Ross, Tony. 2006. (ENG.). 32p. (J). (gr. -1-k). pap. 11.99 (978-1-84270-581-0(4)) Andersen Pr. GBR. Dist: Independent Pubs. Group.

—My Favourite Fairy Tales. Ross, Tony. (ENG.). 96p. (J). (gr. -1-k). 2012. pap. 16.99 (978-1-84939-211-2(0)); 2011. 23.95 (978-1-84270-980-1(1)) Andersen Pr. GBR. Dist: Independent Pubs. Group.

—Naughty Nigel. Ross, Tony. 2010. (ENG.). 32p. (J). (gr. k-k). pap. 10.99 (978-1-84270-744-9(2)) Andersen Pr. GBR. Dist: Independent Pubs. Group.

—Oscar Got the Blame. Ross, Tony. 2004. (ENG.). 32p. (J). (-k). pap. 10.99 (978-1-84270-359-5(5)) Andersen Pr. GBR. Dist: Independent Pubs. Group.

—Paisajes. Ross, Tony. Delafosse, Claude & Jeunesse, Gallimard. (Coleccion Mundo Maravilloso). (SPA.). 168p. (J). (gr. 3-5). (978-84-348-4450-6(8)) SM Ediciones.

—Three Little Kittens & Other Favorite Nursery Rhymes. Ross, Tony. 2009. (ENG.). 96p. (J). (gr. -1-1). 16.95 (978-0-8050-8885-4(7), Holt, Henry & Co. Bks. For Young Readers) Holt, Henry & Co.

—Wash Your Hands! Ross, Tony. 2006. 28p. (J). (gr. -1-1). pap. 4.95 (978-1-933605-03-6(0)) Kane Miller.

Rossell, Judith. The House of 12 Bunnies. Stills, Caroline & Stills-Blott, Sarcia. 2012. (ENG.). 24p. (J). 16.95 (978-0-8234-2422-1(7)) Holiday Hse., Inc.

—Me & You. Holmes, Janet A. 2009. (ENG.). 32p. (J). (gr. -1-3). 14.95 (978-0-7358-2250-4(6)) North-South Bks., Inc.

—Merry Christmas, Mr. Snowman! Hanel, Wolfram. 2011. (ENG.). 32p. (J). (gr. -1-3). 16.95 (978-0-7358-4045-4(8)) North-South Bks., Inc.

—Mice Mischief: Math Facts in Action. Stills, Caroline. 2014. (ENG.). 24p. (J). (gr. -1-1). 16.95 (978-0-8234-2947-9(4)) Holiday Hse., Inc.

—My Little Library - Me & You. Holmes, Janet A. 2014. (My Little Library). (ENG.). 24p. (J). (-k). 12.99 (978-1-921541-58-2(X)) Little Hare Bks. AUS. Dist: Independent Pubs. Group.

—To Get to Me. Kerr, Eleanor. 2013. (ENG.). 32p. (J). (gr. -1-k). 18.99 (978-1-74275-883-1(5)) Random Hse. Australia AUS. Dist: Independent Pubs. Group.

—You Are a Star! Parker, Michael & Wiedmer, Caroline. 2012. (ENG.). 40p. (J). (gr. k-3). 17.89 (978-0-8027-2842-5(1)); 16.99 (978-0-8027-2841-8(3)) Walker & Co.

Rossell, Judith. I Spy with Inspector Stilton. Rossell, Judith. 2003. 32p. (Orig.). pap., act. bk. ed. (978-1-877003-29-5(8)) Little Hare Bks. AUS. Dist: HarperCollins Pubs. Australia.

—Inspector Stilton & the Missing Jewels. Rossell, Judith. 2005. 32p. pap. (978-1-921049-09-5(X)) Little Hare Bks. AUS. Dist: HarperCollins Pubs. Australia.

—Oliver. Rossell, Judith. 2012. (ENG.). 32p. (J). (gr. -1-2). 16.99 (978-0-06-202210-3(5)) HarperCollins Pubs.

—Ruby & Leonard & the Great Big Surprise. Rossell, Judith. 2011. (ENG.). 24p. (J). (gr. -1-k). pap. 8.99 (978-1-921541-59-9(8)) Little Hare Bks. AUS. Dist: Independent Pubs. Group.

Rossi, Andrea. Allison Marisa Burbank Gets into Trouble. Korobov, Kristine. Mahanov, Tanya, ed. 2008. 172p. 26.90 (978-1-4251-8976-1(8)) Trafford Publishing.

Rossi, Christian. El Santero Vol. 3: Spooks. Dorison, Xavier & Nury, Fabien. 2014. (ENG.). 56p. pap. 13.95 (978-1-84918-170-9(5)) CineBook GBR. Dist: National Bk. Network.

Rossi, Francesca. Aladdin. 2015. (Fairy Tale Adventures Ser.). (ENG.). 64p. (J). (gr. 2-6). 7.95 (978-1-4549-1506-5(4)) Sterling Publishing Co., Inc.

—Beauty & the Beast. 2015. (Fairy Tale Adventures Ser.). (ENG.). 64p. (J). (gr. 2-6). 7.95 (978-1-4549-1507-2(2)) Sterling Publishing Co., Inc.

—Cinderella. 2015. (Fairy Tale Adventures Ser.). (ENG.). 64p. (J). (gr. 2-6). 7.95 (978-1-4549-1508-9(0)) Sterling Publishing Co., Inc.

—The Little Mermaid. 2015. (Fairy Tale Adventures Ser.). (ENG.). 64p. (J). (gr. 2-6). 7.95 (978-1-4549-1509-6(9)) Sterling Publishing Co., Inc.

—Little Red Riding Hood. 2015. (Fairy Tale Adventures Ser.). (ENG.). 64p. (J). (gr. 2-6). 7.95 (978-1-4549-1510-2(2)) Sterling Publishing Co., Inc.

—Rapunzel. 2015. (Fairy Tale Adventures Ser.). (ENG.). 64p. (J). (gr. 2-6). 7.95 (978-1-4549-1511-9(0)) Sterling Publishing Co., Inc.

—The Sleeping Beauty. 2015. (Fairy Tale Adventures Ser.). (ENG.). 64p. (J). (gr. 2-6). 7.95 (978-1-4549-1512-6(9)) Sterling Publishing Co., Inc.

—Snow White. 2015. (Fairy Tale Adventures Ser.). (ENG.). 64p. (J). (gr. 2-6). 7.95 (978-1-4549-1513-3(7)) Sterling Publishing Co., Inc.

Rossi, Joe. Ariel Bradley, Spy for General Washington. Oelschlager, Vanita & Durrant, Lynda. 2013. (ENG.). 56p. (J). (gr. 1-5). 9.99 (978-0-9832904-9-0(0)) VanitaBooks.

—Knees: The Mixed up World of a Boy with Dyslexia. Oelschlager, Vanita. 2012. (ENG.). 128p. (J). (gr. k-5). pap. 9.95 (978-0-9826366-9-5(5)) VanitaBooks.

Rossi, Joe, photos by. Minnesota's Hidden Alphabet. 2010. (ENG., 48p. (J). (gr. -1-1). 16.95 (978-0-87351-808-6(X)) Minnesota Historical Society Pr.

Rossi, Pamela. Grandmother's Song. Bauer, Marion Dane. 2007. (ENG.). 32p. (J). (gr. -1-3). 10.99 (978-1-4169-6849-8(0), Simon & Schuster/Paula Wiseman Bks.) Simon & Schuster/Paula Wiseman Bks.

Rossi, Rich. Ouch! Ziefert, Harriet. 2006. (I'm Going to Read(r) Ser.). (ENG.). 32p. (J). (gr. 1-2). pap. 3.95 (978-1-4027-3424-3(7)) Sterling Publishing Co., Inc.

—Pillow Fight. 2005. (I'm Going to Read(r) Ser.). (ENG.). 32p. (J). (gr. k-1). per. 3.95 (978-1-4027-2719-1(4)) Sterling Publishing Co., Inc.

Rossi, Richard. The Twelve Days of Christmas in New Jersey. Woollatt, Margaret. 2008. (Twelve Days of Christmas in America Ser.). (ENG.). 32p. (J). (gr. k). 12.95 (978-1-4027-3816-6(1)) Sterling Publishing Co., Inc.

Rosteck, Rachel. The Road Home. Speaker, Cathy. 2012. (ENG.). 45p. (J). pap. 15.95 (978-1-4327-9146-9(X)) Outskirts Pr., Inc.

Roswell, Stacey. Garden Stories: Rosemarie's Garden, Rosemarie's Roof Garden & Rosemarie Returns to Her Garden. Alexander, Carmen. 2006. 60p. (J). pap. 14.99 (978-1-886383-55-5(3)) Blue Forge Pr.

—Rosemarie Returns to Her Garden. Alexander, Carmen. 2009. (ENG.). 44p. (J). (gr. -1-4). pap. 10.99 (978-1-886383-68-5(5)) Blue Forge Pr.

—Rosemarie's Garden. Alexander, Carmen. 2009. 44p. (J). (gr. -1-4). pap. 10.99 (978-1-886383-66-1(9)) Blue Forge Pr.

—Rosemarie's Roof Garden. Alexander, Carmen. 2009. 44p. (J). (gr. -1-4). pap. 10.99 (978-1-886383-67-8(7)) Blue Forge Pr.

Roszel, Karen. The Diamond Button. l.t. ed. 2005. 32p. (J). bds. 14.95 (978-0-9709630-7-9(6)) Coal Hole Productions.

Roth, David, photos by. Grill Pan Cookbook: Great Recipes for Stovetop Grilling. Ruth, Jamee. 2006. (ENG., 108p. (gr. 8-17). pap. 16.95 (978-0-8118-5352-1(7)) Chronicle Bks. LLC.

Roth, Judith L. & Rothshank, Brooke. Julia's Words. 2008. (J). (gr. -1-3). pap. 12.99 (978-0-8361-9417-3(9)) Herald Pr.

Roth, Judy Langemo. Sun Rays: Tales for Children of Every Age. Livingston, Joshua. 2011. 136p. pap. 17.00 (978-1-61097-261-1(9), Resource Pubns.(OR)) Wipf & Stock Pubs.

Roth, Justin. Baltazar & the Flying Pirates. Chin, Oliver. 2009. (ENG.). 36p. (J). (gr. -1-3). 15.95 (978-1-59702-018-3(4)) Immedium.

—The Year of the Rabbit: Tales from the Chinese Zodiac. Chin, Oliver Clyde. 2010. (Tales from the Chinese Zodiac Ser.). (ENG.). 36p. (J). (gr. -1-3). 15.95 (978-1-59702-023-7(0)) Immedium.

—The Year of the Tiger: Tales from the Chinese Zodiac. Chin, Oliver. 2010. (Tales from the Chinese Zodiac Ser.). (ENG.). 36p. (J). (gr. -1-3). 15.95 (978-1-59702-020-6(6)) Immedium.

Roth, R. G. Busing Brewster. Michelson, Richard. 2010. (ENG.). 32p. (J). (gr. -1-2). 16.99 (978-0-375-83334-2(X), Knopf Bks. for Young Readers) Random Hse. Children's Bks.

Roth, R G. Everybody Gets the Blues. Staub, Leslie. 2012. (ENG.). 32p. (J). (gr. -1-3). 16.99 (978-0-15-206300-9(5)) Houghton Mifflin Harcourt Publishing Co.

—This Jazz Man. Ehrhardt, Karen. 2006. (ENG.). 32p. (J). (gr. -1-3). 17.99 (978-0-15-205307-9(7)) Houghton Mifflin Harcourt Publishing Co.

Roth, R. G. This Jazz Man. Ehrhardt, Karen. 2010. (J). (gr. 1-5). 28.95 incl. audio compact disk (978-1-4301-0740-8(5)) Live Oak Media.

Roth, Robert. Journey of the Nightly Jaguar. Albert, Burton. 2007. (ENG.). 32p. (J). (gr. k-3). 10.99 (978-1-4169-7092-7(4), Simon & Schuster/Paula Wiseman Bks.) Simon & Schuster/Paula Wiseman Bks.

Roth, Roger. The American Story: 100 True Tales from American History. Armstrong, Jennifer. 2006. (ENG.). 368p. (gr. 3-7). 34.99 (978-0-375-81256-9(3), Knopf Bks. for Young Readers) Random Hse. Children's Bks.

—The Giraffe That Walked to Paris. Milton, Nancy. 2013. (ENG.). 32p. (J). (gr. -1-3). 18.95 (978-1-930900-67-7(8)) Purple Hse. Pr.

Roth, Roger, Sr. Roanoke, the Lost Colony: An Unsolved Mystery from History. Yolen, Jane & Stemple, Heidi E. Y. 2003. (Unsolved Mystery from History Ser.). (ENG.). 32p. (J). (gr. 1-5). 17.99 (978-0-689-82321-3(5), Simon & Schuster Bks. For Young Readers) Simon & Schuster Bks. For Young Readers.

—The Salem Witch Trials: An Unsolved Mystery from History. Yolen, Jane & Stemple, Heidi E. Y. 2004. (Unsolved Mystery from History Ser.). (ENG.). 32p. (J). (gr. 1-5). 17.99 (978-0-689-84620-5(7), Simon & Schuster Bks. For Young Readers) Simon & Schuster Bks. For Young Readers.

Roth, Roger. Star of the Week: A Story of Love, Adoption, & Brownies with Sprinkles. Friedman, Darlene. 2009. (ENG.). 32p. (J). (gr. k-3). 17.99 (978-0-06-114136-2(4)) HarperCollins Pubs.

Roth, Ruby. That's Why We Don't Eat Animals: A Book about Vegans, Vegetarians, & All Living Things. Roth, Ruby. 2009. (ENG.). 48p. (J). (gr. 1-4). 16.95 (978-1-55643-785-4(4)) North Atlantic Bks.

—V Is for Vegan: The ABCs of Being Kind. Roth, Ruby. 2013. (ENG.). 32p. (J). (gr. -1-2). 12.95 *(978-1-58394-649-7(7))* North Atlantic Bks.
—Vegan Is Love: Having Heart & Taking Action. Roth, Ruby. 2012. (ENG.). 44p. (J). (gr. 2-5). 16.95 *(978-1-58394-354-0(4))* North Atlantic Bks.
Roth, Ruchela. Who Am I? Schon, Ruchy. 2006. 26p. (J). (gr. -1-k). 14.99 *(978-1-58330-889-9(X))* Feldheim Pubs.
Roth Sisson, Stephanie. A Pocketful of Princess Posey: First Grade Parade-Perfect Present-Next-Door Dog. Greene, Stephanie. 2014. (Princess Posey, First Grader Ser.). (ENG.). 288p. (J). (gr. k-3). 8.99 *(978-0-14-751472-1(X)*, Puffin) Penguin Publishing Group.
—Princess Posey & the First Grade Ballet. Greene, Stephanie. 2014. (Princess Posey, First Grader Ser.: 9). (ENG.). 96p. (J). (gr. k-3). pap. 4.99 *(978-0-14-751292-5(1)*, Puffin) Penguin Publishing Group.
—Princess Posey & the First Grade Parade, Bk. 1. Greene, Stephanie. 2010. (Princess Posey, First Grader Ser.: 1). (ENG.). 96p. (J). (gr. k-3). 12.99 *(978-0-399-25167-2(7)*, Putnam Juvenile) Penguin Publishing Group.
Roth Sisson, Stephanie. Star Stuff: Carl Sagan & the Mysteries of the Cosmos. Roth Sisson, Stephanie. 2014. (ENG.). 40p. (J). (gr. -1-3). 17.99 *(978-1-59643-960-3(2))* Roaring Brook Pr.
Roth, Stacy Schulstrom. It's Raining Outside & I'm Gonna Be Bored! Fenton, Karen B. 2006. (J). lib. bdg. 16.82 *(978-0-9778196-4-5(7))* Harbour Arts, LLC.
Roth, Stephanie. The Perfect Cat-Sitter. Nagda, Ann Whitehead. 2007. (ENG.). 96p. (J). (gr. 4-7). 15.95 *(978-0-8234-2112-1(0))* Holiday Hse., Inc.
—Third Grade Wedding Bells? O'Shaughnessy McKenna, Colleen. 2006. (Third Grade Ser.). (ENG.). 160p. (J). (gr. 2-5). 15.95 *(978-0-8234-1943-2(6))* Holiday Hse., Inc.
—Two Christmas Mice. Demas, Corinne. 2005. (ENG.). 32p. (J). (gr. -1-3). 16.95 *(978-0-8234-1785-8(9))* Holiday Hse., Inc.
—The Valentine Cat. Nagda, Ann Whitehead. 2008. (ENG.). 32p. (J). (gr. 2-5). 16.95 *(978-0-8234-2123-7(6))* Holiday Hse., Inc.
Roth, Susan L. Dream Something Big: The Story of the Watts Towers. Aston, Dianna Hutts. 2011. (ENG.). 40p. (J). (gr. k-3). 17.99 *(978-0-8037-3245-2(7)*, Dial) Penguin Publishing Group.
—Hecho en Mexico. Laufer, Peter. Reyes, Victor, tr. 2008. (SPA.). 32p. (J). (gr. 3-7). 16.95 *(978-1-4263-0364-7(5))* National Geographic Society.
—Listen to the Children: The Story of Dr. Greg & Stones into Schools. Mortenson, Greg & Husain, Farzana. 2011. (ENG.). 32p. (J). (gr. 1-3). 17.99 *(978-0-8037-3593-4(6)*, Dial) Penguin Publishing Group.
—Nothing but Miracles. Whitman, Walt. 2003. (ENG.). 32p. (J). (gr. -1-3). 15.95 *(978-0-7922-6143-8(7))* National Geographic Society.
—Pass the Fritters, Critters. Chapman, Cheryl. 2007. (ENG.). 40p. (J). (gr. -1-2). 11.99 *(978-1-4169-6160-4(7)*, Simon & Schuster/Paula Wiseman Bks.) Simon & Schuster/Paula Wiseman Bks.
Roth, Susan L. Prairie Dog Song: How One Small Animal Helps North America's Grasslands. Trumbore, Cindy. 2016. (J). *(978-1-62014-245-5(7))* Lee & Low Bks., Inc.
Roth, Susan L. Do Re Mi: If You Can Read Music, Thank Guido D'Arezzo. Roth, Susan L. Roth, Susan. 2007. (ENG.). 40p. (J). (gr. -1-3). 17.00 *(978-0-618-46572-9(3))* Houghton Mifflin Harcourt Publishing Co.
—Hands Around the Library: Protecting Egypt's Treasured Books. Roth, Susan L. Abouraya, Karen Leggett. 2012. (ENG.). 32p. (J). (gr. -1-k). 16.99 *(978-0-8037-3747-1(5)*, Dial) Penguin Publishing Group.
—Listen to the Wind: The Story of Dr. Greg & Three Cups of Tea. Roth, Susan L. Mortenson, Greg. 2009. (ENG.). 32p. (J). (gr. 1-3). 16.99 *(978-0-8037-3058-8(6)*, Dial) Penguin Publishing Group.
—The Mangrove Tree: Planting Trees to Feed Families. Roth, Susan L. Trumbore, Cindy. 2011. (ENG.). 40p. (J). (gr. 1-6). 19.95 *(978-1-60060-459-1(5))* Lee & Low Bks., Inc.
Roth, Werner, et al. Essential X-Men, Vol. 2. 2006. (ENG.). 640p. (J). (gr. 4-17). pap. 19.99 *(978-0-7851-2116-9(1))* Marvel Worldwide, Inc.
—Marvel Masterworks. 2013. (ENG.). 304p. (J). (gr. -1-17). pap. 24.99 *(978-0-7851-5909-4(6))* Marvel Worldwide, Inc.
Rothan, Ann. Miranda's Magic Garden. Atnip, Linda. 2004. 32p. (gr. -1-7). 19.95 *(978-1-885394-21-7(7))* Amber Lotus Publishing.
—Twice Blessed: the Special Life of Twins. Cheviot, Patrice. 2013. (ENG.). 28p. (J). (gr. k-5). 16.95 *(978-1-939116-48-2(1))* Waterside Productions, Inc.
—Who Can Help Me Sleep? Fox, Sabrina. 2004. 32p. (gr. -1-3). 16.95 *(978-1-885394-36-1(5))* Amber Lotus Publishing.
Rothan, Ann. ¿Quién Puede Ayudarme a Dormir? Rothan, Ann, tr. Fox, Sabrina & FOX, SABRINA. Pérez Galván, Ana, tr. 2004. (SPA.). 32p. *(978-84-9777-018-7(8))* Obelisco, Ediciones S.A.
Rothenberg, Joan. Matzah Ball Soup. Rothenberg, Joan. 2005. 29p. (J). (gr. -1-2). reprint ed. 15.00 *(978-0-7567-8930-5(3))* DIANE Publishing Co.
Rothenberg, Joani. Shabbat Angels. Sigal, Maxine Handelman. 2003. (gr. k-3). 13.95 *(978-0-8074-0865-0(4)*, 164051) URJ Pr.
Rothenberg, Joani Keller. Adam & Eve's First Sunset: God's New Day. Sasso, Sandy Eisenberg. 2003. (ENG.). 32p. (gr. -1-3). 17.95 *(978-1-58023-177-0(2)*, Jewish Lights Publishing) LongHill Partners, Inc.
—Adam & Eve's New Day. Sasso, Sandy Eisenberg. 2006. (ENG.). 24p. (gr. -1). bds. 7.99 *(978-1-59473-205-8(1)*, Skylight Paths Publishing) LongHill Partners, Inc.
—Butterflies under Our Hats. Sasso, Sandy Eisenberg. (ENG.). 32p. 2014. (J). (gr. k-5). pap. 15.99 *(978-1-61261-583-7(X))*; 2006. (gr. -1-3). 16.95 *(978-1-55725-474-0(5))* Paraclete Pr., Inc.
—The Shema in the Mezuzah: Listening to Each Other. Sasso, Sandy Eisenberg. 2012. (ENG.). 32p. (J). 18.99 *(978-1-58023-506-8(9)*, Jewish Lights Publishing) LongHill Partners, Inc.
Rothenberger, Boyd & Bays, Gail. Kara's Kapers with Katy Pillar. Rothenberger, Charlene. 2006. 64p. per. 9.99 *(978-0-9776260-6-9(7))* Bearhead Publishing, LLC.
Rothero, Chris. Strawberry Fair. 2004. 96p. (gr. 1-6). 14.95 *(978-0-7136-2676-6(3)*, A & C Black) Bloomsbury Publishing Plc GBR. Dist: Consortium Bk. Sales & Distribution.
Rothero, Chris. Noah's Ark. Rothero, Chris. 2005. 20p. (J). 5.95 *(978-965-483-007-2(8)*, Devora Publishing) Simcha Media Group.
Rothman, Michael. At Home with the Gopher Tortoise: The Story of a Keystone Species. Dunphy, Madeleine. 2010. (ENG.). 32p. (J). (gr. k-4). 16.95 *(978-0-9777539-6-3(4))*; pap. 9.95 *(978-0-9777539-5-6(6))* Web of Life Children's Bks.
—Giant Lizards. Clarke, Ginjer L. 2005. (Penguin Young Readers, Level 3 Ser.). (ENG.). 48p. (J). (gr. 1-3). mass mkt. 3.99 *(978-0-448-43120-8(3)*, Grosset & Dunlap) Penguin Publishing Group.
—Here Is the Tropical Rain Forest. Dunphy, Madeleine. 2006. (Web of Life Ser.). (ENG.). 32p. (J). (gr. -1-3). 16.95 *(978-0-9773795-1-4(5))*; pap. 9.95 *(978-0-9773795-0-7(7))* Web of Life Children's Bks.
Rothshank, Brooke. Cups Held Out. 2006. 40p. (J). (gr. -1-3). per. 12.99 *(978-0-8361-9316-9(4))* Herald Pr.
—Plant a Seed of Peace. Selling, Rebecca. 2007. 115p. (J). (gr. 3-7). per. 15.99 *(978-0-8361-9397-8(0))* Faith & Life Pr.
Rothshank, Brooke, jt. illus. see Roth, Judith L.
Rotman, Jeffrey L. City Fish, Country Fish, 1 vol. Rotman, Jeffrey L., photos by. Cerullo, Mary M. 2012. (ENG.). 32p. (J). 16.95 *(978-0-88448-323-6(1))* Tilbury Hse. Pubs.
—Journey to Shark Island: A Shark Photographer's Close Encounters, 1 vol. Rotman, Jeffrey L., photos by. Cerullo, Mary M. 2014. (Shark Expedition Ser.). (ENG.). 40p. (gr. 5-7). lib. bdg. 31.32 *(978-0-7565-4887-2(X))* Compass Point Bks.
—Seeking Giant Sharks: A Shark Diver's Quest for Whale Sharks, Basking Sharks, & Manta Rays, 1 vol. Rotman, Jeffrey L., photos by. Cerullo, Mary M. 2014. (Shark Expedition Ser.). (ENG.). 40p. (gr. 5-7). lib. bdg. 31.32 *(978-0-7565-4885-8(3))* Compass Point Bks.
—Sharks of the Deep: A Shark Photographer's Search for Sharks at the Bottom of the Sea, 1 vol. Rotman, Jeffrey L., photos by. Cerullo, Mary M. 2014. (Shark Expedition Ser.). (ENG.). 40p. (gr. 5-7). lib. bdg. 31.32 *(978-0-7565-4886-5(1))* Compass Point Bks.
Rotman, Jeffrey L., photos by. Searching for Great White Sharks: A Shark Diver's Quest for Mr. Big, 1 vol. Cerullo, Mary M. 2014. (Shark Expedition Ser.). (ENG., 40p. (gr. 5-7). lib. bdg. 31.32 *(978-0-7565-4884-1(5))* Compass Point Bks.
—Shark Expedition, 1 vol. Cerullo, Mary M. 2014. (Shark Expedition Ser.). (ENG., 40p. (gr. 5-7). 125.28 *(978-0-7565-4888-9(8)*, CPB Grades 4-8) Compass Point Bks.
—Shark Expedition: A Shark Photographer's Close Encounters. Cerullo, Mary M. 2015. (ENG., 144p. (gr. 5-7). pap. 12.95 *(978-1-62370-156-7(2))* Capstone Pr., Inc.
Rotner, Shelley. Whose Eye Am I? 2016. (J). *(978-0-8234-3558-6(X))* Holiday Hse., Inc.
Rotner, Shelley. Nature Spy. Rotner, Shelley. Kreisler, Ken. 2014. (ENG.). 32p. (J). (gr. -1-1). pap. 13.99 *(978-1-4814-5042-3(5)*, Atheneum Bks. for Young Readers) Simon & Schuster Children's Publishing.
Rotner, Shelley, photos by. Garbage Helps Our Garden Grow: A Compost Story. Glaser, Linda. 2010. (ENG., 32p. (gr. k-3). lib. bdg. 25.26 *(978-0-7613-4911-2(1))* Lerner Publishing Group.
Rotner, Shelley, photos by. De Muchas Maneras: Como las Familias Practican Sus Creencias y Religiones. Rotner, Shelley. Kelly, Sheila M. 2006. (Spanish Picture Bks.). (SPA., 32p. (J). (gr. k-3). lib. bdg. 15.95 *(978-0-8225-6506-2(4)*, Ediciones Lerner) Lerner Publishing Group.
—Different Kinds of Good-Byes, 1 vol. Rotner, Shelley. 2013. (Shelley Rotner's World Ser.). (ENG., 32p. (gr. 1-2). pap. 8.10 *(978-1-62065-750-8(3))*; lib. bdg. 26.65 *(978-1-62065-066-0(5))* Capstone Pr., Inc.
—Families. Rotner, Shelley. Kelly, Sheila M. 2015. (ENG., 32p. (J). (gr. -1-1). 17.95 *(978-0-8234-3053-6(7))* Holiday Hse., Inc.
—Feeling Thankful, 1 vol. Rotner, Shelley. 2013. (Shelley Rotner's World Ser.). (ENG., 24p. (gr. 1-2). pap. 8.10 *(978-1-62065-752-2(X))*; lib. bdg. 26.65 *(978-1-62065-068-4(1))* Capstone Pr., Inc. (Aplus Bks.).
—Home. Rotner, Shelley. Goldblas, Amy. 2010. (Shelley Rotner's Early Childhood Library). (ENG., 32p. (gr. -1-2). lib. bdg. 25.26 *(978-0-7613-4605-0(8)*, Millbrook Pr.) Lerner Publishing Group.
—I'm Adopted! Rotner, Shelley. Kelly, Sheila M. 2012. (ENG., 32p. (J). pap. 6.95 *(978-0-8234-2430-6(8))* Holiday Hse., Inc.
—Lots of Feelings. Rotner, Shelley. Kelly, Sheila. 2003. (Shelley Rotner's Early Childhood Library). (ENG., 32p. (gr. k-3). pap. 7.95 *(978-0-7613-2377-8(5)*, Millbrook Pr.) Lerner Publishing Group.
—Lots of Grandparents. Rotner, Shelley. Kelly, Sheila M. 2003. (Shelley Rotner's Early Childhood Library: Vol. 3). (ENG., 32p. (gr. k-3). pap. 7.95 *(978-0-7613-1896-5(8)*, Millbrook Pr.) Lerner Publishing Group.
—Many Ways: How Families Practice Their Beliefs & Religions. Rotner, Shelley. Kelly, Sheila M. (Shelley Rotner's Early Childhood Library). (ENG., 32p. (gr. k-3). 2010. pap. 7.95 *(978-0-7613-6531-0(1)*, First Avenue Editions); 2005. lib. bdg. 22.60 *(978-0-7613-2873-5(4)*, Millbrook Pr.) Lerner Publishing Group.
—Senses at the Seashore. Rotner, Shelley. (Shelley Rotner's Early Childhood Library). (ENG., 32p. (gr. -1-2). 2010. pap. 7.95 *(978-0-7613-6530-3(3)*, First Avenue Editions); 2006. lib. bdg. 22.60 *(978-0-7613-2897-1(1)*, Millbrook Pr.) Lerner Publishing Group.
—Senses in the City. Rotner, Shelley. 2008. (Shelley Rotner's Early Childhood Library). (ENG., 32p. (gr. -1-2). lib. bdg. 23.93 *(978-0-8225-7502-3(7)*, Millbrook Pr.) Lerner Publishing Group.
—Shades of People. Rotner, Shelley. Kelly, Sheila M. 2009. (ENG., 32p. (J). (gr. -1-k). 17.95 *(978-0-8234-2191-6(0))* Holiday Hse., Inc.
—We All Do Something Well, 1 vol. Rotner, Shelley. 2013. (Shelley Rotner's World Ser.). (ENG., 24p. (gr. 1-2). pap. 8.10 *(978-1-62065-754-6(6))*; lib. bdg. 26.65 *(978-1-62065-067-7(3))* Capstone Pr., Inc. (Aplus Bks.).
—What's Love?, 1 vol. Rotner, Shelley. Kelly, Sheila M. 2013. (Shelley Rotner's World Ser.). (ENG., 32p. (gr. 1-2). pap. 8.10 *(978-1-62065-756-0(2))*; lib. bdg. 26.65 *(978-1-62065-069-1(X))* Capstone Pr., Inc.
—Yummy! Rotner, Shelley. Kelly, Sheila M. 2013. (ENG., 32p. (J). 16.95 *(978-0-8234-2426-9(X))* Holiday Hse., Inc.
Rotner, Shelley & White, David A. Body Actions. Rotner, Shelley, photos by. 2012. (ENG.). 32p. (J). 16.95 *(978-0-8234-2366-8(2))* Holiday Hse., Inc.
Rottinger, Amy. Bailey's Heartstrings. Chicatelli, Joy. 2011. 28p. pap. 12.95 *(978-1-935268-96-3(1))* Halo Publishing International.
—Charlie's Gingerbread House. Staehli, Melissa. 2012. 24p. pap. 11.95 *(978-1-61244-063-7(0))* Halo Publishing International.
—My Mommy's Sweater. Torres, Veronica Hilda. 2013. 24p. pap. 12.95 *(978-1-61244-203-7(X))* Halo Publishing International.
—The Owl Who Couldn't Whoo. Kail, Leanna. 2013. 24p. pap. 11.95 *(978-1-61244-129-0(7))* Halo Publishing International.
—Skydive to Hive. Phelan, Anne. 2012. 24p. pap. 11.95 *(978-1-61244-098-9(3))* Halo Publishing International.
—Swanee Day. Consugar, Beth. 2013. 24p. pap. 12.95 *(978-1-61244-176-4(9))* Halo Publishing International.
—The Ticker That Needed a Fixer. Gibson, Donovan. 2011. 28p. pap. 12.95 *(978-1-935268-46-8(5))* Halo Publishing International.
—Tommy Gets Lost! Turner, Darlene. 2012. 24p. pap. 12.95 *(978-1-61244-064-4(9))* Halo Publishing International.
—When the Monsters Are Quiet. Lloyd, Alicia. 2013. 26p. pap. 11.95 *(978-1-61244-219-8(6))* Halo Publishing International.
Round, Graham. Dot-to-Dot Book: Combined Volume. Bryant-Mole, Karen & Tyler, Jenny. 2004. (Dot to Dot Ser.). 168p. (J). pap. 12.95 *(978-0-7945-0699-5(2)*, Usborne) EDC Publishing.
—Dot-to-Dot Machines. Bryant-Mole, Karen. Tyler, Jenny, ed. rev. ed. 2006. (Dot to Dot Ser.). 22p. (J). (gr. -1-2). pap. 3.99 *(978-0-7945-1495-2(2)*, Usborne) EDC Publishing.
—Dot-to-Dot on Seashore. Bryant-Mole, Karen. 2003. 24p. (J). pap. 3.99 *(978-0-7945-0494-6(9)*, Usborne) EDC Publishing.
Round, Graham, et al. How to Draw Cartoons & Caricatures. Tatchell, Judy. 2007. 40p. (J). (gr. 4). lib. bdg. 13.99 *(978-1-58086-895-2(9)*, Usborne) EDC Publishing.
Round, Graham. 42 Bible Stories for Little Ones: From Creation to Pentecost. Word Among Us Editorial Staff. 2008. 96p. pap. 13.95 *(978-1-59325-138-3(6))* Word Among Us Pr.
Rounds, Glen. A Wild Goose Tale. Gage, Wilson. 2012. 114p. 39.95 *(978-1-258-25188-8(4))*; pap. 24.95 *(978-1-258-25729-3(7))* Literary Licensing, LLC.
Rountree, Harry. Alice's Adventures in Wonderland. Carroll, Lewis. 2011. (Calla Editions Ser.). (ENG.). 248p. (gr. 3). 40.00 *(978-1-60660-014-6(1))* Dover Pubns., Inc.
Rouse, Andy, photos by. Busy Gorillas. Schindel, John. 2010. (Busy Book Ser.). (ENG., 20p. (J). (— 1). bds. 6.99 *(978-1-58246-352-0(2)*, Tricycle Pr.) Ten Speed Pr.
Rouse, Bonna. Les Arts Martiaux. Levigne, Heather. Briere, Marie-Josee, tr. from ENG. 2007. (Sans Limites Ser.). (FRE.). 32p. (J). pap. 9.95 *(978-2-89579-168-3(6))* Bayard Canada Livres CAN. Dist: Crabtree Publishing Co.
—El Ciclo de Vida de la Rana. Kalman, Bobbie & Smithyman, Kathryn. 2005. (Serie Ciclos de Vida Ser.). (SPA.). 32p. (J). (gr. 1-4). pap. *(978-0-7787-8709-9(5))* Crabtree Publishing Co.
—Les Grenouilles. Kalman, Bobbie & Smithyman, Kathryn. Briere, Marie-Josee, tr. from ENG. 2006. (Petit Monde Vivant Ser.). (FRE.). 32p. (J). (gr. -1-3). pap. 9.95 *(978-2-89579-080-8(9))* Bayard Canada Livres CAN. Dist: Crabtree Publishing Co.
—Porristas en Acción. Crabtree, Marc, photos by. Crossingham, John. 2005. (Deportes en Acción Ser.). (SPA & ENG.). 32p. (J). (gr. 3-4). lib. bdg. *(978-0-7787-8575-0(0))*; (gr. 6-9). pap. *(978-0-7787-8621-4(8))* Crabtree Publishing Co.
Rouse, Bonna, jt. illus. see Crabtree, Marc.
Roush, April. My Baby Book. Wolf, Jackie. 2003. 10p. (J). (gr. -1-18). bds. 5.99 *(978-1-57151-712-8(X))* Playhouse Publishing.
—Picture Me One: Baby's First Year in Photos. D'Andrea, Deborah. 2004. (Picture Me Developmental Ser.). 10p. (J). (gr. -1-18). bds. 5.99 *(978-1-57151-736-4(7))* Playhouse Publishing.
—Picture Me Three Vol. 3: Child's Third Year in Photos. D'Andrea, Deborah. 2004. (Picture Me Developmental Ser.). 10p. (J). (gr. -1-18). bds. 5.99 *(978-1-57151-738-8(3))* Playhouse Publishing.
—Picture Me to the Rescue. Hapka, Cathy. 2003. (Role Play Ser.). 10p. (J). (gr. -1-18). bds. 6.99 *(978-1-57151-567-4(4))* Playhouse Publishing.
—Picture Me Two Vol. 2: Toddler's Second Year in Photos. D'Andrea, Deborah. 2004. (Picture Me Developmental Ser.). 10p. (J). (gr. -1-18). bds. 5.99 *(978-1-57151-737-1(5))* Playhouse Publishing.
Roush, April, jt. illus. see Hill, Heather C.
Rousseau, Craig. The Invincible Iron Man: An Origin Story. Thomas, Rich. 2012. (Marvel Origins Ser.). 48p. (J). (gr. -1-4). lib. bdg. 24.21 *(978-1-61479-010-5(8))* Spotlight.
—Souljacker: #2. McCool, Ben. 2012. (Captain America: the Korvac Saga Ser.). 24p. (J). (gr. 3-5). lib. bdg. 24.21 *(978-1-61479-020-4(5))* Spotlight.
—The Star Lord: #4. McCool, Ben. 2012. (Captain America: the Korvac Saga Ser.). 24p. (J). (gr. 3-5). lib. bdg. 24.21 *(978-1-61479-022-8(1))* Spotlight.
—Strange Days: #1. McCool, Ben. 2012. (Captain America: the Korvac Saga Ser.). 24p. (J). (gr. 3-5). lib. bdg. 24.21 *(978-1-61479-019-8(1))* Spotlight.
—The Traveler: #3. McCool, Ben. 2012. (Captain America: the Korvac Saga Ser.). 24p. (J). (gr. 3-5). lib. bdg. 24.21 *(978-1-61479-021-1(3))* Spotlight.
Roussey, Christine. Brave as Can Be: A Book of Courage. Witek, Jo. 2015. (Growing Hearts Ser.). (ENG.). 32p. (J). (gr. -1 — 1). 16.95 *(978-1-4197-1923-3(8)*, Abrams Appleseed) Abrams.
Roussey, Christine. Hello in There! A Big Sister's Book of Waiting. Witek, Jo. 2013. (Growing Hearts Ser.). (ENG.). 28p. (J). (gr. -1 — 1). 16.95 *(978-1-4197-0371-3(4)*, Abrams Appleseed) Abrams.
—In My Heart: A Book of Feelings. Witek, Jo. 2014. (Growing Hearts Ser.). (ENG.). 32p. (J). (gr. -1 — 1). 16.95 *(978-1-4197-1310-1(8)*, Abrams Appleseed) Abrams.
—My Beastly Book of Tangled Tinsel: 140 Ways to Doodle, Scribble, Color & Draw. 2012. (My Beastly Book Ser.). (ENG.). 144p. (J). (gr. -1). pap. 12.95 *(978-1-926973-55-5(0)*, Owlkids) Owlkids Bks. Inc. CAN. Dist: Perseus-PGW.
Roux, Stephane, jt. illus. see Disney Book Group Staff.
Rovira, Francesc. Caperucita Roja. Grimm, Jacob et al. 2005. (Caballo Alado Clásico Series-Al Paso Ser.). (SPA & ENG.). 24p. (J). (gr. -1-k). 7.95 *(978-84-7864-851-1(8))* Combel Editorial, S.A. ESP. Dist: Independent Pubs. Group.
—Caperucita Roja. Sarfatti, Esther, tr. 2006. (Bilingual Tales Ser.). (SPA & ENG.). 24p. (J). (gr. -1-3). pap. 3.99 *(978-0-439-77375-1(X)*, Scholastic en Espanol) Scholastic, Inc.
Rovner, Michal. The Hug. Grossman, David. Schoffman, Stuart, tr. 2013. (ENG.). 32p. (gr. 4-13). 19.95 *(978-1-4683-0273-8(6)*, 460273) Overlook Pr., The.
Rovollo, Jimothy. The Friendliest Ballerina. Knapman, Tim. 2012. (Marvelous Manners Ser.). (ENG.). 24p. (J). (gr. -1-1). 15.99 *(978-1-60992-268-9(9))* QEB Publishing Inc.
—The Princesses Love to Share! Knapman, Tim. 2012. (Marvelous Manners Ser.). (ENG.). 24p. (J). (gr. -1-1). 15.99 *(978-1-60992-267-2(0))* QEB Publishing Inc.
Row, Richard. The Kugel Valley Klezmer Band. Stuchner, Joan Betty. 2005. 30p. (J). (gr. 2-6). reprint ed. 16.00 *(978-0-7567-8605-2(3))* DIANE Publishing Co.
—The Kugel Valley Klezmer Band. Stuchner, Joan Betty. 2009. (PJ Library). (ENG.). 32p. (J). (gr. -1-3). pap. 7.95 *(978-1-56656-782-4(3)*, Crocodile Bks.) Interlink Publishing Group, Inc.
Rowe, Alan. Cracking Christmas. Locke, Ian. 21st ed. 2003. (ENG.). 64p. (J). pap. 3.99 *(978-0-330-37504-7(0)*, Pan) Pan Macmillan GBR. Dist: Trafalgar Square Publishing.
Rowe, Anne Burgess. The Newest Angel. 2015. (J). pap. *(978-1-63293-039-2(0))* Sunstone Pr.
Rowe, Eric F. Robin Hood. Rowe, Eric F. Sutton, Rosalind & Rosalind, Sutton. 4th ed. (Coleccion Clasicos en Accion). (SPA.). 80p. (YA). (gr. 5-8). 15.95 *(978-84-241-5782-1(6)*, EV1455) Everest Editora ESP. Dist: Lectorum Pubns., Inc.
Rowe, Harriet. I Don't Care! Said Claire. Hodgson, Karen J. 2010. (ENG.). 32p. (J). (gr. -1-2). pap. 9.99 *(978-1-907432-05-7(1))* Hogs Back Bks. GBR. Dist: Independent Pubs. Group.
Rowe, Jeannette. YoYo Goes Next Door. Rowe, Jeannette. 2003. 16p. (J). 5.95 *(978-1-58925-368-1(X))* Tiger Tales.
—YoYo Goes to the Park. Rowe, Jeannette. 2003. 12p. (J). pap. 5.95 *(978-1-58925-369-8(8))* Tiger Tales.
Rowe, John. I Wonder. Harris, Annaka. 2013. (ENG.). 32p. (J). 16.95 *(978-1-940051-04-8(5))* Four Elephants Pr.
—The Jungle Book. Kipling, Rudyard & Landolf, Diane Wright. 2008. (Stepping Stone Book Ser.). (ENG.). 112p. (J). (gr. 1-4). per. 3.99 *(978-0-375-84276-4(4))* Random Hse., Inc.
Rowe, Louise. Hansel & Gretel. Grimm, Jacob et al. 2nd ed. 2014. (Fairytale Pop-Ups Ser.). (ENG.). 16p. (J). (gr. k-2). 27.99 *(978-1-85707-858-9(6))* Tango Bks. GBR. Dist: Independent Pubs. Group.
—Sleeping Beauty: A Pop-Up Book. 2012. (Fairytale Pop-Ups Ser.). (ENG.). 14p. (J). (gr. k-2). 18.99 *(978-1-85707-826-8(8))* Tango Bks. GBR. Dist: Independent Pubs. Group.
Rowe, Michael Langham. Wild Cats. Batten, Mary. 2004. (Step into Reading Ser.). (ENG.). 48p. (J). (gr. 2-4). pap. 3.99 *(978-0-375-82551-4(7)*, Random Hse. Bks. for Young Readers) Random Hse. Children's Bks.
Rowell, Coralynn. The Gknobin. King, M. 2011. (ENG.). 72p. pap. 14.99 *(978-1-4611-4510-3(4))* CreateSpace Independent Publishing Platform.
Rowland, Andrew. Hank Hammer, 1 vol. Klein, Adria F. 2011. (Tool School Ser.). (ENG.). 32p. (gr. 1-2). pap. 6.25 *(978-1-4342-3385-1(5))*; lib. bdg. 21.32 *(978-1-4342-3043-0(0))* Stone Arch Bks.
—Hank Hammer & the Puppy, 1 vol. Klein, Adria F. 2012. (Tool School Ser.). (ENG.). 32p. (gr. 1-3). pap. 6.25 *(978-1-4342-4233-4(1))*; lib. bdg. 21.32 *(978-1-4342-4020-0(7))* Stone Arch Bks.
—Journey into the Bible. Rock, Lois. 2011. (ENG.). 48p. (J). (gr. 1-7). 14.99 *(978-0-7459-6088-3(X))* Lion Hudson PLC GBR. Dist: Independent Pubs. Group.
—Limericks. Cleary, Brian P. 2015. (Poetry Adventures Ser.). (ENG.). 32p. (J). (gr. 2-5). lib. bdg. 26.60 *(978-1-4677-2044-1(5)*, Millbrook Pr.) Lerner Publishing Group.
—Little Lizards. Crow, Melinda Melton. 2013. (Little Lizards Ser.). (ENG.). 32p. (gr. -1-1). 170.56 *(978-1-4342-8840-0(4))* Stone Arch Bks.
—Little Lizard's Big Party, 1 vol. Crow, Melinda Melton. 2010. (Little Lizards Ser.). (ENG.). 32p. (gr. -1-1). lib. bdg. 21.32 *(978-1-4342-2007-3(9))* Stone Arch Bks.
—Little Lizard's Family Fun, 1 vol. Crow, Melinda Melton. 2010. (Little Lizards Ser.). (ENG.). 32p. (gr. -1-1). lib. bdg. 21.32 *(978-1-4342-2006-6(0))* Stone Arch Bks.

R

—Little Lizard's First Day, 1 vol. Crow, Melinda Melton. 2010. (Little Lizards Ser.). (ENG.). 32p. (gr. -1-1). lib. bdg. 21.32 *(978-1-4342-2005-9(2))* Stone Arch Bks.
—Little Lizard's New Baby, 1 vol. Crow, Melinda Melton. 2011. (Little Lizards Ser.). (ENG.). 32p. (gr. -1-1). pap. 6.25 *(978-1-4342-3047-8(3))*; lib. bdg. 21.32 *(978-1-4342-2510-8(0))* Stone Arch Bks.
—Little Lizard's New Bike, 1 vol. Crow, Melinda Melton. 2010. (Little Lizards Ser.). (ENG.). 32p. (gr. -1-1). lib. bdg. 21.32 *(978-1-4342-2008-0(7))* Stone Arch Bks.
—Little Lizard's New Friend, 1 vol. Crow, Melinda Melton. 2011. (Little Lizards Ser.). (ENG.). 32p. (gr. -1-1). pap. 6.25 *(978-1-4342-3048-5(1))*; lib. bdg. 21.32 *(978-1-4342-2507-8(0))* Stone Arch Bks.
—Little Lizard's New Pet, 1 vol. Crow, Melinda Melton. 2011. (Little Lizards Ser.). (ENG.). 32p. (gr. -1-1). pap. 6.25 *(978-1-4342-3049-2(X))*; lib. bdg. 21.32 *(978-1-4342-2508-5(9))* Stone Arch Bks.
—Little Lizard's New Shoes, 1 vol. Crow, Melinda Melton. 2011. (Little Lizards Ser.). (ENG.). 32p. (gr. -1-1). pap. 6.25 *(978-1-4342-3050-8(3))*; lib. bdg. 21.32 *(978-1-4342-2509-2(7))* Stone Arch Bks.
—Sammy Saw, 1 vol. Klein, Adria F. 2011. (Tool School Ser.). (ENG.). 32p. (gr. 1-2). pap. 6.25 *(978-1-4342-3387-5(1))*; lib. bdg. 21.32 *(978-1-4342-3045-4(7))* Stone Arch Bks.
—Sammy Saw & the Campout, 1 vol. Klein, Adria F. 2012. (Tool School Ser.). (ENG.). 32p. (gr. 1-3). pap. 6.25 *(978-1-4342-4234-1(X))*; lib. bdg. 21.32 *(978-1-4342-4022-4(3))* Stone Arch Bks.
Rowland, Andrew. Snow White Sees the Light. Wallace, Karen. 2015. (ENG.). 32p. (J). *(978-0-7787-1931-1(6))* Crabtree Publishing Co.
Rowland, Andrew. Something Sure Smells Around Here: Limericks. Cleary, Brian P. 2015. (Poetry Adventures Ser.). (ENG.). 32p. (gr. 2-5). pap. 6.95 *(978-1-4677-6035-5(8)*, Millbrook Pr.) Lerner Publishing Group.
—Sophie Screwdriver, 1 vol. Klein, Adria F. 2011. (Tool School Ser.). (ENG.). 32p. (gr. 1-2). pap. 6.25 *(978-1-4342-3386-8(3))*; lib. bdg. 21.32 *(978-1-4342-3044-7(9))* Stone Arch Bks.
—Sophie Screwdriver & the Classroom, 1 vol. Klein, Adria F. 2012. (Tool School Ser.). (ENG.). 32p. (gr. 1-3). pap. 6.25 *(978-1-4342-4235-8(8))*; lib. bdg. 21.32 *(978-1-4342-4021-7(5))* Stone Arch Bks.
—Tia Tape Measure, 1 vol. Klein, Adria F. 2011. (Tool School Ser.). (ENG.). 32p. (gr. 1-2). pap. 6.25 *(978-1-4342-3388-2(X))*; lib. bdg. 21.32 *(978-1-4342-3046-1(5))* Stone Arch Bks.
—Tia Tape Measure & the Move, 1 vol. Klein, Adria F. 2012. (Tool School Ser.). (ENG.). 32p. (gr. 1-3). pap. 6.25 *(978-1-4342-4236-5(6))*; lib. bdg. 21.32 *(978-1-4342-4023-1(1))* Stone Arch Bks.
—Tool School. Klein, Adria F. 2013. (Tool School Ser.). (ENG.). 32p. (gr. -1-1). 170.56 *(978-1-4342-8842-4(0))* Stone Arch Bks.
—Viaje Por la Biblia. Rock, Lois. Pimentel, Alejandro, tr. 2011. (SPA.). 47p. (J). (gr. 4-7). 13.50 *(978-1-55883-030-1(8))* Libros Desafio.
Rowland, Andrew & Rowlands, Andy. Little Lizard's Big Party. Crow, Melinda Melton. 2010. (Little Lizards Ser.). (ENG.). 32p. (gr. -1-1). pap. 6.25 *(978-1-4342-2791-1(X))* Stone Arch Bks.
—Little Lizard's Family Fun. Crow, Melinda Melton. 2010. (Little Lizards Ser.). (ENG.). 32p. (gr. -1-1). pap. 6.25 *(978-1-4342-2790-4(1))* Stone Arch Bks.
—Little Lizard's First Day. Crow, Melinda Melton. 2010. (Little Lizards Ser.). (ENG.). 32p. (gr. -1-1). pap. 6.25 *(978-1-4342-2789-8(8))* Stone Arch Bks.
—Little Lizard's New Bike. Crow, Melinda Melton. 2010. (Little Lizards Ser.). (ENG.). 32p. (gr. -1-1). pap. 6.25 *(978-1-4342-2792-8(8))* Stone Arch Bks.
Rowland, Andy. Bow-Tie Pasta: Acrostic Poems. Cleary, Brian P. 2015. (ENG.). 32p. (gr. 2-5). 26.65 *(978-1-4677-2046-5(1)*, Millbrook Pr.) Lerner Publishing Group.
—Collins Big Cat - One Potato. Rickards, Lynne. 2015. (Collins Big Cat Ser.). (ENG.). 24p. pap. 6.95 *(978-0-00-759102-2(0))* HarperCollins Pubs. Ltd. GBR. Dist: Independent Pubs. Group.
Rowland, Andy. Esther's Hanukkah Disaster. Sutton, Jane. 2013. 32p. 17.95 *(978-1-4677-1638-3(3))*; (ENG.). (J). (gr. -1-3). 7.95 *(978-0-7613-9044-2(8)*, Kar-Ben Publishing) Lerner Publishing Group.
—Little Nelly's Big Book. Goodhart, Pippa. 2012. (ENG.). 32p. (J). (gr. -1-3). 16.99 *(978-1-59990-779-6(8)*, Bloomsbury USA Childrens) Bloomsbury USA.
—Ode to a Commode: Concrete Poems. Cleary, Brian. 2014. (Poetry Adventures Ser.). 32p. (gr. 2-5). pap. 6.95 *(978-1-4677-4454-6(9)*, Millbrook Pr.) Lerner Publishing Group.
Rowland-Hill, Hugo. Bosco - The Dog Who Was Once Afraid of the Dark. Broz, Jon. 2011. (ENG.). 34p. pap. 10.00 *(978-1-4563-5245-5(8))* CreateSpace Independent Publishing Platform.
Rowland, Jada. Miss Tizzy. Gray, Libba Moore. 2014. 40p. pap. 8.00 *(978-1-61003-356-5(6))* Center for the Collaborative Classroom.
Rowland, Lauri. Grandma's Just Not Herself. Richards, Josie Aleardi. 2010. 36p. pap. 13.95 *(978-1-60911-236-3(9)*, Eloquent Bks.) Strategic Book Publishing & Rights Agency (SBPRA).
Rowland, Michael J. An Irish Tale: Tom Moore & the Seal Woman. Kasony_O'Malley, Michael R. 2007. (J). lib. bdg. 19.95 incl. audio compact disk *(978-0-9776170-3-6(3))* Green Igric Pr.
Rowlands, Andy, jt. illus. see Rowland, Andrew.
Rowles, Charles G., 3rd & Rowles, Steve. The Gods of Arr-Kelaan: Going Home (Book 2) Rowles, Charles G., 3rd. Pezzino, Martha, ed. 2005. 200p. (YA). per. 14.95 *(978-0-9748960-2-1(0))* Drunk Duck Comics.
Rowles, Chuck, et al. Drunk & Disorderly Vol. 2: The Drunk Duck Collection. Rowles, Chuck et al. 2004. (YA). per. 14.95 *(978-0-9748960-1-4(2))* Drunk Duck Comics.
Rowles, Steve, jt. illus. see Rowles, Charles G., 3rd.
Rowley, Alexandra, photos by. The Confetti Cakes Cookbook: Spectacular Cookies, Cakes, & Cupcakes from New York City's Famed Bakery. Strauss, Elisa & Matheson, Christie. 2007. (ENG.). 224p. 29.99 *(978-0-316-11307-6(7))* Bulfinch.
Rowley, Jillian. The Tree & Annly el Árbol y Annly. Saavedra, Eusebio. 2011. 8p. (J). 7.00 *(978-0-9742432-9-0(9))* Flying Scroll Publishing, LLC.
Rowton, Caitlin. My Best Friend. Pruett, Nichole Lee. 2013. (ENG.). 46p. (J). pap. 14.95 *(978-1-936578-15-3(8))* 5 Fold Media LLC.
Roxas, Isabel. Boo-la-La Witch Spa. Berger, Samantha. 2015. (ENG.). 32p. (J). (gr. -1-k). 16.99 *(978-0-8037-3886-7(2)*, Dial) Penguin Publishing Group.
—The Case of the Missing Donut. McGhee, Alison. 2013. (ENG.). 32p. (J). (gr. -1-k). 16.99 *(978-0-8037-3925-3(7)*, Dial) Penguin Publishing Group.
Roxas, Isabel. Let Me Finish! Lê, Minh. 2016. (J). *(978-1-4847-2173-5(X))* Disney Pr.
Roy, Indrapramit. Euripides' Hippolytos. Euripides. 2006. (ENG.). 28p. 25.00 *(978-0-89236-864-8(0))* Oxford Univ. Pr., Inc.
—The Very Hungry Lion: A Folktale. Wolf, Gita. 2006. (ENG.). 24p. 20.95 *(978-81-86211-02-1(0))* Tara Publishing IND. Dist: Consortium Bk. Sales & Distribution.
Roy, Karen. A Royal Little Pest, 1 vol. Reynolds MacArthur, Anita. 2008. (ENG.). 32p. (J). (gr. k-2). 17.95 *(978-0-9810575-0-7(0))* Pollywog Bog Bks. CAN. Dist: Ingram Pub. Services.
Roy, Katherine. Buried Beneath Us: Discovering the Ancient Cities of the Americas. Aveni, Anthony. 2013. (ENG.). 96p. (J). (gr. 4-8). 18.99 *(978-1-59643-567-4(4))* Roaring Brook Pr.
—The Expeditioners & the Secret of King Triton's Lair. Taylor, S. S. 2014. (ENG.). 320p. (gr. 4-9). 22.00 *(978-1-940450-20-9(9))* McSweeney's Publishing.
—The Expeditioners & the Treasure of Drowned Man's Canyon. Taylor, S. S. 2013. (ENG.). 384p. pap. 12.95 *(978-1-938073-71-7(1))* McSweeney's Publishing.
Roy, Katherine. Neighborhood Sharks: Hunting with the Great Whites of California's Farallon Islands. Roy, Katherine. 2014. (ENG.). 48p. (J). (gr. 2-6). 17.99 *(978-1-59643-874-3(6)*, Macaulay, David Studio) Roaring Brook Pr.
Roy, Kelsey. Nemanee. Roy, Kelsey. 2011. (ENG.). 40p. pap. 15.00 *(978-1-4635-7125-2(9))* CreateSpace Independent Publishing Platform.
Royal British Columbia Museum Staff, photos by. Safari Beneath the Sea: The Wonder World of the North Pacific Coast. Swanson, Diane. (ENG.). 64p. (J). pap. 12.95 *(978-1-55110-441-6(5))* Whitecap Bks., Ltd. CAN. Dist: Graphic Arts Ctr. Publishing Co.
Royce Conant, Jan. Children of Light. Royce Conant, Jan. 2005. (J). per. 20.00 *(978-0-9740683-7-4(3)*, Ithaca Pr.) Authors & Artists Publishers of New York, Inc.
Roydon, Michael. B Is for Beaver: An Oregon Alphabet. Smith, Marie & Smith, Roland. 2003. (Discover America State by State Ser.). (ENG.). 40p. (J). 17.95 *(978-1-58536-071-0(6))* Sleeping Bear Pr.
Royo-Horodynska, Irena. Mnie Stworzye Bog - Ciebie Euolucya. Royo-Horodynska, Irena. 2004.Tr. of I am Created by God - Mov: By Evolution. (POL.). 160p. (YA). pap. *(978-83-88214-58-5(6))* Edytor, Wydawnictwo, Grzywacz, Halina | Franciszek.
Royo, Luis. The Ice Dragon. Martin, George R. R. 2014. (ENG.). 128p. (YA). (gr. 7-12). 14.99 *(978-0-7653-7877-4(9)*, Tor Teen) Doherty, Tom Assocs., LLC.
Royse, Jane. Moozie's Cow Wisdom for Loving to the "Uddermost" Morton, Jane & Dreier, Ted. 2003. (J). pap. 4.95 *(978-0-9662268-3-6(6))* Children's Kindness Network.
Roytman, Arkady. Extreme Sports. 2008. (Dover Coloring Bks.). (ENG.). 32p. (J). (gr. k-5). pap. 3.99 *(978-0-486-46688-0(4))* Dover Pubns., Inc.
Rozelaar, Angie. Don't Call Me Sweet! Prasadam-Halls, Smriti. 2015. (ENG.). 32p. (J). (gr. -1-1). 18.99 *(978-1-4088-3881-5(8)*, Bloomsbury USA Childrens) Bloomsbury USA.
Rozinski, Bob, jt. photos by see Shattil, Wendy.
Ruano, Alfonso. The Composition, 1 vol. Skármeta, Antonio & Skarmeta, Antonio. 2003. (ENG.). 32p. (J). (gr. 3-18). pap. 7.95 *(978-0-88899-550-6(4))* Groundwood Bks. CAN. Dist: Perseus-PGW.
—El Triciclo, 1 vol. Amado, Elisa. 2007. (SPA.). 32p. (J). (gr. k-4). 17.95 *(978-0-88899-613-8(6))* Groundwood Bks. CAN. Dist: Perseus-PGW.
Rubbino, Salvatore. Just Ducks! Davies, Nicola. 2012. (ENG.). 32p. (J). (gr. k-4). 15.99 *(978-0-7636-5936-3(3))* Candlewick Pr.
Rubbino, Salvatore. A Walk in London. Rubbino, Salvatore. 2011. (ENG.). 40p. (J). (gr. k-3). 16.99 *(978-0-7636-5272-2(5))* Candlewick Pr.
—A Walk in New York. Rubbino, Salvatore. 2009. (ENG.). 40p. (J). (gr. -1-3). 16.99 *(978-0-7636-3855-9(2))* Candlewick Pr.
—A Walk in Paris. Rubbino, Salvatore. 2014. (ENG.). 40p. (J). (gr. -1-3). 16.99 *(978-0-7636-6984-3(9))* Candlewick Pr.
Rubel, Doris. Esa Eres Tu y Este Soy Yo. Caballero, D., tr. 2006. (Junior (Silver Dolphin) Ser.). (SPA.). 16p. (J). (gr. -1). 9.95 *(978-970-718-346-9(2))* Baker & Taylor Publishing Group.
Rubel, Nicole. Best in Show for Rotten Ralph. Gantos, Jack. 2005. (Rotten Ralph Rotten Readers Ser.: 4). (ENG.). 48p. (J). (gr. 1-3). 16.99 *(978-0-374-36358-1(7)*, Farrar, Straus & Giroux (BYR)) Farrar, Straus & Giroux.
—Best in Show for Rotten Ralph. Gantos, Jack. 2008. (Rotten Ralph Rotten Readers Ser.). (J). 25.95 incl. audio *(978-1-4301-0448-3(1))*; 28.95 incl. audio compact disk *(978-1-4301-0451-3(1))* Live Oak Media.
—Dino Riddles. Hall, Katy & Eisenberg, Lisa. 2003. (Easy-to-Read Ser.). 40p. (J). (gr. -1-3). 11.65 *(978-0-7569-2823-0(0))* Perfection Learning Corp.
—The Nine Lives of Rotten Ralph. Gantos, Jack. 2009. (ENG.). 32p. (J). (gr. -1-3). 16.00 *(978-0-618-80046-9(8))* Houghton Mifflin Harcourt Publishing Co.
—Practice Makes Perfect for Rotten Ralph. Gantos, Jack. 2009. (Rotten Ralph Rotten Readers Ser.: 2). (ENG.). 48p. (J). (gr. 1-3). pap. 7.99 *(978-0-374-40002-6(4))* Square Fish.
—Rotten Ralph Feels Rotten. Gantos, Jack. 2007. (Rotten Ralph Ser.). (J). (gr. -1-3). 28.95 incl. audio compact disk *(978-1-4301-0098-0(2))* Live Oak Media.
—Rotten Ralph Helps Out. Gantos, Jack. unabr. ed. 2006. (Readalongs for Beginning Readers Ser.). (J). (gr. -1-3). 24.95 incl. audio *(978-1-59519-678-1(1))*; 28.95 incl. audio compact disk *(978-1-59519-679-8(X))* Live Oak Media.
—Rotten Ralph Helps Out. Gantos, Jack. (Rotten Ralph Rotten Readers Ser.: 1). (ENG.). 48p. (J). (gr. 1-3). 2012. 15.99 *(978-0-312-64172-6(9))*; 2012. pap. 3.99 *(978-0-312-67281-2(0))*; 2004. pap. 6.99 *(978-0-374-46355-7(7))* Square Fish.
—Rotten Ralph's Rotten Family. Gantos, Jack. 2014. (Rotten Ralph Rotten Readers Ser.: 6). (ENG.). 48p. (J). (gr. 1-3). 16.99 *(978-0-374-36353-6(6)*, Farrar, Straus & Giroux (BYR)) Farrar, Straus & Giroux.
—Three Strikes for Rotten Ralph. Gantos, Jack. 2011. (Rotten Ralph Rotten Readers Ser.: 5). (ENG.). 48p. (J). (gr. 1-3). 16.99 *(978-0-374-36354-3(4)*, Farrar, Straus & Giroux (BYR)) Farrar, Straus & Giroux.
Rubel, Nicole. Rotten Ralph Feels Rotten. Rubel, Nicole, tr. Gantos, Jack. 2004. (Rotten Ralph Rotten Readers Ser.: 3). (ENG.). 48p. (J). (gr. 1-3). 16.99 *(978-0-374-36357-4(9)*, Farrar, Straus & Giroux (BYR)) Farrar, Straus & Giroux.
Ruben, Paul L., photos by. Scream Machines: All about Roller Coasters. Karr, Susan Schott. 2004. 32p. (J). *(978-0-7652-3264-9(2))* Celebration Pr.
Ruben, Ruben. The Three Musketeers. Dumas, Alexandre. 2011. (Classics Illustrated Deluxe Graphic Nove Ser.: 6). (ENG.). 192p. (J). (gr. 3-9). 21.99 *(978-1-59707-253-3(2))* Papercutz.
Rubenstein, Reva. The Thankyou Twins. Finkelstein, Ruth. 2006. 24p. (J). *(978-0-9628157-5-1(6))* Finkelstein, Ruth.
Rubin, David. The Rise of Aurora West. Pope, Paul & Petty, J. T. 2014. (Battling Boy Ser.). (ENG.). 160p. (J). (gr. 5-12). 17.99 *(978-1-62672-268-2(4))*; pap. 9.99 *(978-1-62672-009-1(6))* Roaring Brook Pr. (First Second Bks.).
Rubin, Sean. The Rogue Crew. Jacques, Brian. 2011. (Redwall Ser.). (ENG.). 400p. (J). (gr. 5-18). 23.99 *(978-0-399-25416-1(1)*, Philomel) Penguin Publishing Group.
Rubine. Safari Survivor. Smith, Owen & Smith, Anne. 2012. (Twisted Journeys (r) Ser.: 21). (ENG.). 112p. (J). (gr. 4-7). lib. bdg. 27.93 *(978-0-7613-6727-7(6)*, Graphic Universe) Lerner Publishing Group.
Rubinger, Ami. Dog Number 1, Dog Number 10. 2011. (ENG.). 28p. (J). (gr. k-k). 13.95 *(978-0-7892-1066-1(5)*, Abbeville Kids) Abbeville Pr., Inc.
Rubinger, Ami. Big Cat, Small Cat. Rubinger, Ami. Baltner, Ray, tr. from HEB. 2009. (ENG.). 28p. (J). (gr. -1-k). 13.95 *(978-0-7892-1029-6(0)*, Abbeville Kids) Abbeville Pr., Inc.
—I Dream of an Elephant. Rubinger, Ami. 2010. (ENG.). 23p. (J). (gr. k-k). 13.95 *(978-0-7892-1058-6(4)*, Abbeville Kids) Abbeville Pr., Inc.
Rubino, Alisa A. Bella: The Crooked Hat Witch. Serafin, Jordan. 2004. (J). *(978-0-932991-57-7(2))* Place In The Woods, The.
—Goldie, the Homeless Calico Cat. Stryker, Robin. 2005. (J). pap. *(978-0-932991-35-5(1))* Place In The Woods, The.
Rubino, Alisa A., jt. illus. see Brudos, Susan E.
Rubio, Adrian, jt. illus. see Benatar, Raquel.
Rubio, Gabriela. He Decidido Llamarme Max. Smadja, Bridgette & Brigitte, Smadja. (SPA.). 96p. (J). *(978-84-392-8669-1(4))* Gaviota Ediciones ESP. Dist: Lectorum Pubns., Inc.
—Los Milagros de Max. Miracles, Max & Brigitte, Smadja. (SPA.). 84p. (J). *(978-84-392-8700-1(3))* Gaviota Ediciones ESP. Dist: Lectorum Pubns., Inc.
Ruble, Eugene. A Brainy Refrain: The Sum of Our Parts Book 4. Kirk, Bill. 2012. 24p. pap. 10.95 *(978-1-61633-231-0(X))* Guardian Angel Publishing, Inc.
—Circulation Celebration: The Sum of Our Parts Series. Kirk, Bill. 2010. 24p. pap. 10.95 *(978-1-61633-019-4(8))* Guardian Angel Publishing, Inc.
—Earthquake! Berger, Susan J. 28p. 2013. 19.95 *(978-1-61633-430-7(4))*; 2009. pap. 11.95 *(978-1-933090-66-5(9))* Guardian Angel Publishing, Inc.
—Gatsby's Grand Adventure: Book 2 Renoir's the Apple Seller. Cairn, Barbara. 2013. 16p. pap. 9.95 *(978-1-61633-387-4(1))* Guardian Angel Publishing, Inc.
—Gatsby's Grand Adventures: Book 1 Winslow Homer's Snap the Whip. Cairns, Barbara. 2012. 16p. pap. 9.95 *(978-1-61633-350-8(2))* Guardian Angel Publishing, Inc.
—Great Gobs of Gustation- the Sum of Our Parts. Kirk, Bill. 2013. 24p. pap. 10.95 *(978-1-61633-358-4(8))* Guardian Angel Publishing, Inc.
—A Horse of Course. Lyle-Soffe, Shari. 2009. 20p. pap. 10.95 *(978-1-935137-82-5(4))* Guardian Angel Publishing, Inc.
—The Ins & Outs of Air: The Sum of Our Parts Series. Kirk, Bill. 2013. 24p. pap. 10.95 *(978-1-61633-391-1(X))* Guardian Angel Publishing, Inc.
—Liddil Gets Her Light. Cox, Tracey M. 2011. 16p. pap. 9.95 *(978-1-61633-151-1(8))* Guardian Angel Publishing, Inc.
—Little Shepherd. Malandrinos, Cheryl C. 2010. 16p. pap. 9.95 *(978-1-61633-085-9(6))* Guardian Angel Publishing, Inc.
—Muscles Make Us Move. Kirk, Bill. 2011. 32p. pap. 10.95 *(978-1-61633-134-4(8))* Guardian Angel Publishing, Inc.
—My Tooth Is Loose: The Sum of Our Parts. Kirk, Bill. 2012. 20p. pap. 10.95 *(978-1-61633-258-7(1))* Guardian Angel Publishing, Inc.
—Secret Service Saint. Collins, Janet Ann. 2009. 16p. pap. 9.95 *(978-1-935137-98-6(0))* Guardian Angel Publishing, Inc.
—The Skin We're In: The Sum of Our Parts Series. Kirk, Bill. 2012. 24p. pap. 10.95 *(978-1-61633-296-9(4))* Guardian Angel Publishing, Inc.
—The Soggy Town of Hilltop. McNamee, Kevin. 2010. 20p. pap. 10.95 *(978-1-61633-041-5(4))* Guardian Angel Publishing, Inc.
—Tales from Indi: Character Counts! RESPECT. Vishpriya. 2009. 24p. pap. 10.95 *(978-1-933090-57-3(X))* Guardian Angel Publishing, Inc.
—Tissue Tantra: The Sum of Our Parts Series Book 9. Kirk, Bill. 2013. 28p. pap. 10.95 *(978-1-61633-448-2(7))* Guardian Angel Publishing, Inc.
Ruble, Eugene. Counting 1 to 10 with Professor Hoot. Ruble, Eugene. 2008. 24p. pap. 10.95 *(978-1-935137-47-4(6))* Guardian Angel Publishing, Inc.
—Learning the Basics of Color. Ruble, Eugene. 2010. 16p. pap. 9.95 *(978-1-61633-063-7(5))* Guardian Angel Publishing, Inc.
Ruble, Stephanie. Ewe & Aye. Ryan, Candace. 2014. (ENG.). 40p. (J). (gr. -1-k). 17.99 *(978-1-4231-7591-9(3))* Hyperion Bks. for Children.
Rucker, Georgia, jt. illus. see Bove, Neysa.
Rudd, Benton. The Heart of a Christmas Tree. Adair, Tammi. 2013. 32p. 16.99 *(978-0-9886409-1-7(0))* Mindstir Media.
—The Itty Bitty It. Ferguson, Scott. 2012. 26p. pap. 9.99 *(978-0-9858398-1-9(3))* Mindstir Media.
—The Poodle Tales: Book Eight. Faber, Toni Tuso. 2013. 24p. 16.99 *(978-0-9897168-0-2(5))*; pap. 10.99 *(978-0-9897168-1-9(3))* Mindstir Media.
—The Poodle Tales: Book Five. Faber, Toni Tuso. 2013. 24p. 16.99 *(978-0-9892711-0-3(2))*; pap. 10.99 *(978-0-9892711-1-0(0))* Mindstir Media.
—The Poodle Tales: Book Four. Faber, Toni Tuso. 2013. 24p. 16.99 *(978-0-9890288-9-9(5))*; pap. 10.99 *(978-0-9890288-8-2(7))* Mindstir Media.
—The Poodle Tales: Book Nine. Faber, Toni Tuso. 2013. 24p. 16.99 *(978-0-9897168-2-6(1))* Mindstir Media.
—The Poodle Tales: Book One. Faber, Toni Tuso. 2012. 26p. (-18). 16.99 *(978-0-9883162-9-4(3))* Mindstir Media.
—The Poodle Tales: Book Seven. Faber, Toni Tuso. 2013. 26p. 16.99 *(978-0-9894748-6-3(0))*; pap. 10.99 *(978-0-9894748-7-0(9))* Mindstir Media.
—The Poodle Tales: Book Six. Faber, Toni Tuso. 2013. 24p. 16.99 *(978-0-9892711-2-7(9))*; pap. 10.99 *(978-0-9892711-3-4(7))* Mindstir Media.
—The Poodle Tales: Book Ten. Faber, Toni Tuso. 2013. 24p. 16.99 *(978-0-9910324-1-9(1))* Mindstir Media.
—The Poodle Tales: Book Three. Faber, Toni Tuso. 2012. 24p. 16.99 *(978-0-9886409-3-1(7))*; pap. 10.99 *(978-0-9886409-8-6(8))* Mindstir Media.
—The Poodle Tales: Book Twelve. Faber, Toni Tuso. 2013. 24p. pap. 10.99 *(978-0-9913190-8-4(7))* Mindstir Media.
—The Poodle Tales: Book Two. Faber, Toni Tuso. 2012. 24p. 16.99 *(978-0-9885180-9-4(0))*; pap. 10.99 *(978-0-9885180-8-7(2))* Mindstir Media.
Ruddy, Limner. Bonnie & Clyde's First Christmas. Rose, Wendy. l.t. ed. 2011. (ENG.). 24p. pap. 12.95 *(978-1-4680-5589-4(5))* CreateSpace Independent Publishing Platform.
Rude, Steve. Captain America Legends: What Price Glory. Jones, Bruce. 2003. (Captain America Ser.). 96p. (YA). pap. 9.99 *(978-0-7851-1227-3(8))* Marvel Worldwide, Inc.
Rudge, Leila. Duck for a Day. McKinlay, Meg. 2012. (ENG.). 96p. (J). (gr. 2-4). 12.99 *(978-0-7636-5784-0(0))* Candlewick Pr.
—No Bears. McKinlay, Meg. 2012. (ENG.). 32p. (J). (gr. -1-2). 15.99 *(978-0-7636-5890-8(1))* Candlewick Pr.
Rudge, Leila. A Perfect Place for Ted. Rudge, Leila. 2014. (ENG.). 32p. (J). (gr. -1-2). 16.99 *(978-0-7636-6781-8(1))* Candlewick Pr.
Rudkin, Tracy. Gift of Love, Vol. 2. Polk, James G. Rudkin, Shawn, ed. (YA). *(978-0-9727753-1-1(5))* New Wave Bks. & CD.
Rudnicki, Richard. A Christmas Dollhouse, 1 vol. ed. 2012. (ENG.). 32p. (J). (gr. -1-3). 18.95 *(978-1-55109-868-5(7))* Nimbus Publishing, Ltd. CAN. Dist: Orca Bk. Pubs. USA.
—Gracie: The Public Gardens Duck, 1 vol. Meyrick, Judith. 2008. (ENG.). 32p. (J). (gr. -1-3). 10.95 *(978-1-55109-645-2(5))* Nimbus Publishing, Ltd. CAN. Dist: Orca Bk. Pubs. USA.
—I Spy a Bunny, 1 vol. Dudar, Judy. ed. 2009. (ENG.). 32p. (J). (gr. -1-2). 17.95 *(978-1-55109-700-8(1))* Nimbus Publishing, Ltd. CAN. Dist: Orca Bk. Pubs. USA.
—I Spy a Bunny (pb), 1 vol. Dudar, Judy. ed. 2013. (ENG.). 32p. (J). (gr. -1-3). pap. 12.95 *(978-1-55109-942-2(X))* Nimbus Publishing, Ltd. CAN. Dist: Orca Bk. Pubs. USA.
—Making Contact! Marconi Goes Wireless. Kulling, Monica. 2013. (Great Idea Ser.). (ENG.). 32p. (J). (gr. k-3). 17.95 *(978-1-77049-378-0(6))* Tundra Bks. CAN. Dist: Random Hse., Inc.
—Tecumseh, 1 vol. Laxer, James. 2012. (ENG.). 56p. (J). (gr. 3). 19.95 *(978-1-55498-123-6(9))* Groundwood Bks. CAN. Dist: Perseus-PGW.
Rudnicki, Richard & Junaid, Bushra. Viola Desmond Won't Be Budged, 1 vol. Warner, Jody Nyasha. 2010. (ENG.). 32p. (J). (gr. k-4). 18.95 *(978-0-88899-779-1(5))* Groundwood Bks. CAN. Dist: Perseus-PGW.
Rudolph, Ellen K., photos by. Willi Gets a History Lesson: In Virginia's Historic Triangle. Rudolph, Ellen K. 2007. (ENG., 80p. pap. 24.00 *(978-0-9791348-0-7(3))* EKR Pubns.
Rudy, Carol-Ann. Crossing to Freedom. Rudy, Carol-Ann. George, Paul S., ed. Date not set. (Hometown Heritage Ser.). 48p. (Orig.). (J). (gr. 2-4). pap. 4.95 *(978-1-889300-02-3(0))* Dormouse Productions, Inc.
Rudy, Maggie. I Wish I Had a Pet. Rudy, Maggie. 2014. (ENG.). 40p. (J). (gr. -1-3). 15.99 *(978-1-4424-5332-6(X)*, Beach Lane Bks.) Beach Lane Bks.
Ruebartsch, John, photos by. All about Wisconsin: Todo Acerca de Wisconsin. 2007.Tr. of Todo Acerca de Wisconsin. (ENG & SPA., 84p. (J). pap. 16.00 *(978-0-9770816-3-9(X))* SHARP Literacy, Inc.
—Friends & Neighbors: We Love to Learn. Cole, Kenneth. 2005. (J). pap. 9.95 *(978-0-9770816-1-5(3))* SHARP Literacy, Inc.

—Friends & Neighbors: We Love to Learn. Cole, Kenneth. ed. 2005. (J). 16.95 *(978-0-9770816-0-8(5))* SHARP Literacy, Inc.

Rueda, Claudia. Celebra el Dia de Accion de Gracias con Beto y Gaby. Flor Ada, Alma. 2006. (Cuentos para Celebrar / Stories to Celebrate Ser.). (SPA.). 30p. (gr. k-6). per. 11.95 *(978-1-59820-121-5(2),* Alfaguara) Santillana USA Publishing Co., Inc.

—Celebrate Thanksgiving Day with Beto & Gaby. Flor Ada, Alma. Hayes, Joe & Franco, Sharon, trs. 2006. (Cuentos para Celebrar / Stories to Celebrate Ser.). 30p. (gr. k-6). per. 11.95 *(978-1-59820-133-8(6))* Santillana USA Publishing Co., Inc.

—Eency Weency Spider. Wang, Margaret. 2006. (ENG.). (J). 12p. bds. 5.95 *(978-1-58117-505-9(1));* 22p. (gr. -1-3). bds. 10.95 *(978-1-58117-418-2(7))* Bendon, Inc. (Intervisual/Piggy Toes).

—Here Comes Santa Cat. Underwood, Deborah. 2014. (ENG.). 88p. (J). (gr. -1-k). 16.99 *(978-0-8037-4100-3(6),* Dial) Penguin Publishing Group.

—Here Comes the Easter Cat. Underwood, Deborah. 2014. (ENG.). 80p. (J). (gr. -1-k). 16.99 *(978-0-8037-3939-0(7),* Dial) Penguin Publishing Group.

—I Know an Old Lady Who Swallowed a Fly. 2005. 14p. (J). 12.95 *(978-1-58117-267-6(2),* Intervisual/Piggy Toes) Bendon, Inc.

Ruell, L J. Is That Funny? Patrick, B. & Schotz, Leo D. 2006. (ENG.). 32p. (J). (gr. -1-3). 15.95 *(978-0-9741319-6-2(2))* 4N Publishing LLC.

Ruelle, Karen Gray. Bark Park, 1 vol. Ruelle, Karen Gray. (ENG.). 32p. (J). (gr. -1-1). 2014. pap. 7.95 *(978-1-56145-773-1(6));* 2008. 15.95 *(978-1-56145-434-1(6))* Peachtree Pubs.

—The Crunchy, Munchy Christmas Tree. Ruelle, Karen Gray. 2003. (Holiday House Readers Ser.). (ENG.). 32p. (J). (gr. k-3). tchr. ed. 14.95 *(978-0-8234-1787-2(5))* Holiday Hse., Inc.

—Dear Tooth Fairy. Ruelle, Karen Gray. 2006. (Harry & Emily Adventure Ser.). (ENG.). 32p. (J). (gr. k-3). 4.95 *(978-0-8234-1984-5(3))* Holiday Hse., Inc.

—Dear Tooth Fairy: A Harry & Emily Adventure. Ruelle, Karen Gray. 2006. (Holiday House Readers: Level 2 Ser.). (ENG.). 32p. (J). (gr. 5-8). 14.95 *(978-0-8234-1929-6(0))* Holiday Hse., Inc.

—Easter Egg Disaster: A Harry & Emily Adventure. Ruelle, Karen Gray. 2003. (Holiday House Readers Ser.). (ENG.). 32p. (J). (gr. k-3). pap. 4.95 *(978-0-8234-1823-7(5))* Holiday Hse., Inc.

—Great Groundhogs! A Harry & Emily Adventure. Ruelle, Karen Gray. 2005. (Holiday House Readers: Level 2 Ser.). (ENG.). 32p. (J). (gr. k-3). 14.95 *(978-0-8234-1930-2(4))* Holiday Hse., Inc.

—Just in Time for New Year's! A Harry & Emily Adventure. Ruelle, Karen Gray. 2004. (Holiday House Readers Ser.). (ENG.). 32p. (J). pap. 4.95 *(978-0-8234-1842-8(1))* Holiday Hse., Inc.

—The Monster in Harry's Backyard. Ruelle, Karen Gray. 2003. (Holiday House Readers Ser.). (ENG.). 32p. (J). (gr. k-3). 4.95 *(978-0-8234-1783-4(2))* Holiday Hse., Inc.

—The Thanksgiving Beast Feast Level 2: A Holiday House Reader. Ruelle, Karen Gray. (ENG.). 32p. (J). (gr. k-3). tchr. ed. 15.95 *(978-0-8234-1511-3(2))* Holiday Hse., Inc.

Ruff, Jim, jt. illus. see Ruff, Zeata P.

Ruff, Zeata P. & Ruff, Jim. The Gumdrop Tree. Ruff, Zeata P. 2013. 34p. 16.95 *(978-1-937449-25-4(4))* YAV.

Ruffenach, France, photos by. The Country Cooking of France. Willan, Anne. 2007. (ENG., 392p. (gr. 8-17). 50.00 *(978-0-8118-4646-2(6))* Chronicle Bks. LLC.

—Cupcakes! Klivans, Elinor. 2005. (ENG., 144p. (gr. 8-17). pap. 16.95 *(978-0-8118-4545-8(1))* Chronicle Bks. LLC.

—Everyday Celebrations: Savoring Food, Family & Life at Home. Maggipinto, Donata. 2005. (ENG., 180p. (gr. 8-17). pap. 24.95 *(978-0-8118-4487-1(0))* Chronicle Bks. LLC.

—Tartine. Prueitt, Elisabeth M. & Robertson, Chad. 2006. (ENG., 224p. (gr. 8-17). 35.00 *(978-0-8118-5150-3(8))* Chronicle Bks. LLC.

Ruffin, Aurzella. Have You Ever Made Mud Pies on a Hot Summer Day? This Is a Bitty Book. Stevenson-Spurgon, Barbara J. 2006. 36p. (J). (gr. -1-4). per. 19.95 *(978-1-60002-234-0(0),* 4073) Mountain Valley Publishing, LLC.

Ruffins, Reynold. Koi & the Kola Nuts. Gleeson, Brian. 2007. (Rabbit Ears: A Classic Tale Ser.). 36p. (gr. k-3). 25.65 *(978-1-59961-310-9(7))* Spotlight.

—Marco's Run. Cartier, Wesley. ed. 2003. (Green Light Readers Level 2 Ser.). (ENG.). 24p. (J). (gr. -1-3). pap. 3.95 *(978-0-15-204828-0(6))* Houghton Mifflin Harcourt Publishing Co.

—Marco's Run. Cartier, Wesley. ed. 2003. (Green Light Readers — Level 2 Ser.). (J). (gr. -1-3). lib. bdg. 13.50 *(978-0-613-64442-6(5),* Turtleback) Turtleback Bks.

Ruffle, Mark. The Big Countdown. Rockett, Paul. 2015. (Big Countdown Ser.). (ENG.). 32p. (gr. 3-5). 175.92 ***(978-1-4109-6881-4(2),*** Raintree Perspectives) Heinemann-Raintree.

Ruffle, Mark. Seven Quintillion, Five Hundred Quadrillion Grains of Sand on Planet Earth. Rockett, Paul. 2015. (Big Countdown Ser.). (ENG.). 32p. (gr. 3-5). 29.32 *(978-1-4109-6880-7(4))* Heinemann-Raintree.

—Ten Thousand, Eight Hundred & Twenty Endangered Species in the Animal Kingdom. Rockett, Paul. 2015. (Big Countdown Ser.). (ENG.). 32p. (gr. 3-5). 29.32 *(978-1-4109-6879-1(0))* Heinemann-Raintree.

—30 Million Different Insects in the Rain Forest. Rockett, Paul. 2015. (Big Countdown Ser.). (ENG.). 32p. (gr. 3-5). 29.32 *(978-1-4109-6876-0(6))* Heinemann-Raintree.

—70 Thousand Million, Million, Million Stars in Space. Rockett, Paul. 2015. (Big Countdown Ser.). (ENG.). 32p. (gr. 3-5). 29.32 *(978-1-4109-6875-3(8))* Heinemann-Raintree.

—100 Trillion Good Bacteria Living in the Human Body. Rockett, Paul. 2015. (Big Countdown Ser.). (ENG.). 32p. (gr. 3-5). 29.32 *(978-1-4109-6877-7(4))* Heinemann-Raintree.

Ruffle, Mark & Bernstein, Galia. Build the Shark. Taylor, Barbara. 2013. (Build It Ser.). (ENG.). 32p. (J). (gr. k). 19.95 *(978-1-60710-414-8(8),* Silver Dolphin Bks.) Baker & Taylor Publishing Group.

Ruffle, Mark, jt. illus. see Bernstein, Galia.

Ruffolo, Rob, jt. illus. see Milne, Alex.

Rugg, Jim. Head, Vol. 1. Seagle, Steven T. rev. ed. 2006. (American Virgin Ser.). (ENG.). 112p. pap. 9.99 *(978-1-4012-1065-6(1),* Vertigo) DC Comics.

Ruggiero, Lorenzo. Reasons to Be Cheerful. Carey, Mike. rev. ed. 2007. (John Constantine, Hellblazer Ser.). (ENG.). 144p. pap. 14.99 *(978-1-4012-1251-3(4),* Vertigo) DC Comics.

Ruhl, Greg. The Buried City of Pompeii: What It Was Like When Vesuvius Exploded. Christopher, Peter, photos by. Tanaka, Shelley. 2003. 48p. (J). (gr. 4-9). reprint ed. 17.00 *(978-0-7567-6722-8(9))* DIANE Publishing Co.

—The Buried City of Pompeii: What It Was Like When Vesuvius Exploded. Tanaka, Shelley. 2010. (I Was There Ser.). (ENG.). 48p. (J). (gr. k-2). pap. 9.95 *(978-1-897330-61-6(8))* Madison Pr. Bks. CAN. Dist: Independent Pubs. Group.

—Lost Temple of the Aztecs: What It Was Like When the Spaniards Invaded Mexico. Tanaka, Shelley. 2010. (I Was There Ser.). (ENG.). 48p. (J). (gr. k-2). pap. 10.95 *(978-1-897330-59-3(6))* Madison Pr. Bks. CAN. Dist: Independent Pubs. Group.

Rui, Paolo. Galileo's Journal, 1609-1610. Pettenati, Jeanne. 2006. (ENG.). 32p. (J). (gr. 1-4). pap. 7.95 *(978-1-57091-880-3(5))* Charlesbridge Publishing, Inc.

Ruis, Maria. Mi Gato. Sánchez, Isidro. (Coleccion Mis Animales Preferidos).Tr. of My Cat. (SPA.). 32p. (J). (gr. k-3). 6.36 *(978-84-342-1127-8(0),* PR0482) Parramon Ediciones S.A. ESP. Dist: Lectorum Pubns., Inc.

—Mi Hamster. Sánchez, Isidro. (Coleccion Mis Animales Preferidos).Tr. of My Hamster. (SPA.). 32p. (J). (gr. k-3). 6.36 *(978-84-342-1129-2(7),* PR0485) Parramon Ediciones S.A. ESP. Dist: Lectorum Pubns., Inc.

—Mi Pajaro. Sánchez, Isidro. (Coleccion Mis Animales Preferidos).Tr. of My Bird. (SPA.). 32p. (J). (gr. k-3). 6.36 *(978-84-342-1128-5(9),* PR0483) Parramon Ediciones S.A. ESP. Dist: Lectorum Pubns., Inc.

—Mi Perro. Sánchez, Isidro. (Coleccion Mis Animales Preferidos).Tr. of My Dog. (SPA.). 32p. (J). (gr. k-3). *(978-84-342-1126-1(2),* PR0481) Parramon Ediciones S.A. ESP. Dist: Lectorum Pubns., Inc.

Ruiz Abello, Margarita, jt. illus. see Ruiz, Margarita.

Ruiz, Alfonso. Drácula. Stoker, Bram. Schuler, Susan, tr. (Classic Fiction Ser.). 72p. (gr. 2-3). 2010. (ENG & SPA.). pap. 7.15 *(978-1-4342-2277-0(2));* 2009. (SPA.). lib. bdg. 26.65 *(978-1-4342-1686-1(1))* Stone Arch Bks. (Graphic Revolve en Español).

—Dracula. Stoker, Bram. Schuler, Susan, tr. 2010. (Classic Fiction Ser.). 72p. pap. 0.90 *(978-1-4342-2985-4(8),* Graphic Revolve) Stone Arch Bks.

—Full Court Pressure, 1 vol. Gunderson, Jessica & Gonzalez, Jorge. 2010. (Sports Illustrated Kids Graphic Novels Ser.). (ENG.). 56p. (gr. 2-3). pap. 7.19 *(978-1-4342-2291-6(8));* 25.32 *(978-1-4342-1911-4(9))* Stone Arch Bks.

—La Guerra de los Mundos. Protobunker Studio Staff & Wells, H. G. 2010. (Classic Fiction Ser.). (SPA.). 72p. (gr. 2-3). 26.65 *(978-1-4342-2322-7(1),* Graphic Revolve en Español) Stone Arch Bks.

—Kickoff Blitz. Hoena, Blake A. & Gonzalez, Jorge. 2010. (Sports Illustrated Kids Graphic Novels Ser.). 56p. pap. 0.50 *(978-1-4342-3205-2(0));* (ENG.). (gr. 2-3). pap. 7.19 *(978-1-4342-2292-3(6));* (ENG.). (gr. 2-3). 25.32 *(978-1-4342-1909-1(7))* Stone Arch Bks.

—Pinocchio, 1 vol. Gonzalez, Jorge & Collodi, Carlo. 2009. (Classic Fiction Ser.).Tr. of Avventure di Pinocchio. (ENG.). 72p. (gr. 2-3). lib. bdg. 26.65 *(978-1-4342-1583-3(0),* Graphic Revolve) Stone Arch Bks.

Ruiz, Ana, jt. illus. see Gonzalez, Ralfka.

Ruiz, Aristides. The Cat in the Hat's. Seuss, Dr. 2014. (Great Big Board Book Ser.). (ENG.). 12p. (J). (gr. k — 1). bds. 12.99 *(978-0-679-89360-8(1),* Random Hse. Bks. for Young Readers) Random Hse. Children's Bks.

—From Army Ants to Zebrafish: Animals That Hop, Fly & Swish! (Dr. Seuss/Cat in the Hat) Golden Books. 2013. (Deluxe Stickerific Ser.). (ENG.). 64p. (J). (gr. -1-2). pap. 5.99 *(978-0-449-81432-1(7),* Golden Bks.) Random Hse. Children's Bks.

—Going Buggy! Insects & Spiders to Paint. Golden Books Staff. 2011. (Deluxe Paint Box Book Ser.). (ENG.). 128p. (J). (gr. -1-2). pap. 7.99 *(978-0-375-87215-0(9),* Golden Bks.) Random Hse. Children's Bks.

Ruiz, Aristides, et al. How to Help the Earth-By the Lorax. Rabe, Tish. 2012. (Step into Reading Ser.). (ENG.). 48p. (J). (gr. k-3). lib. bdg. 12.99 *(978-0-375-96977-5(2))* Random Hse., Inc.

—How to Help the Earth-By the LORAX. Rabe, Tish. 2012. (Step into Reading Ser.). (ENG.). 48p. (J). (gr. k-3). pap. 3.99 *(978-0-375-86977-8(8))* Random Hse., Inc.

Ruiz, Aristides. I See Seeds! Golden Books. 2013. (Color Plus Chunky Crayons Ser.). (ENG.). 48p. (J). (gr. -1-2). pap. 3.99 *(978-0-307-98209-4(2),* Golden Bks.) Random Hse. Children's Bks.

—If I Ran the Rain Forest: All about Tropical Rain Forests. Worth, Bonnie. 2003. (Cat in the Hat's Learning Library). (ENG.). 48p. (J). (gr. -1-3). 8.99 *(978-0-375-81097-8(8),* Random Hse. Bks. for Young Readers) Random Hse. Children's Bks.

—Inside Your Outside! All about the Human Body. Rabe, Tish. 2003. (Cat in the Hat's Learning Library). (ENG.). 48p. (J). (gr. -1-3). 8.99 *(978-0-375-81100-5(1),* Random Hse. Bks. for Young Readers) Random Hse. Children's Bks.

Ruiz, Aristides, et al. Look for the Lorax. Rabe, Tish & Seuss, Dr. 2012. (Step into Reading Ser.). (ENG.). 32p. (J). (gr. -1-1). pap. 3.99 *(978-0-375-86999-0(9))* Random Hse., Inc.

Ruiz, Aristides. Oh, Give Me a Home! Rabe, Tish. 2011. (Color Plus Chunky Crayons Ser.). (ENG.). 48p. (J). (gr. -1-2). pap. 3.99 *(978-0-375-87343-0(0),* Golden Bks.) Random Hse. Children's Bks.

—Oh Say Can You Say What's the Weather Today? All about Weather. Rabe, Tish. 2004. (Cat in the Hat's Learning Library). (ENG.). 48p. (J). (gr. -1-3). 8.99 *(978-0-375-82276-6(3),* Random Hse. Bks. for Young Readers) Random Hse. Children's Bks.

—Oh, the Things Spring Brings! Golden Books Staff. 2013. (Color Plus Stencil Ser.). (ENG.). 64p. (J). (-k). pap. 5.99 *(978-0-307-98123-3(1),* Golden Bks.) Random Hse. Children's Bks.

—Oh, the Things You Can Do That Are Good for You! All about Staying Healthy. Rabe, Tish. 2015. (Cat in the Hat's Learning Library). (ENG.). 64p. (J). (gr. k-3). lib. bdg. 13.99 *(978-0-375-91098-2(0),* Random Hse. Bks. for Young Readers) Random Hse. Children's Bks.

—Out of This World! (Dr. Seuss/Cat in the Hat) Golden Books. 2013. (Big Coloring Book Ser.). (ENG.). 48p. (J). (-k). pap. 6.99 *(978-0-449-81433-8(5),* Golden Bks.) Random Hse. Children's Bks.

—Wings & Paws & Fins & Claws. Rabe, Tish. 2010. (Deluxe Coloring Book Ser.). (ENG.). 96p. (J). (gr. -1-2). pap. 3.99 *(978-0-375-85928-1(4),* Golden Bks.) Random Hse. Children's Bks.

Ruiz, Aristides & Giles, Mike. Comic Book Heroes. Thomas, Jim. ed. 2005. 32p. (J). lib. bdg. 15.00 *(978-1-59054-990-2(2))* Fitzgerald Bks.

Ruiz, Aristides & Mathieu, Joe. Can You See a Chimpanzee? All about Primates. Rabe, Tish. 2014. (Cat in the Hat's Learning Library). (ENG.). 48p. (J). (gr. k-3). 9.99 *(978-0-375-87074-3(1));* lib. bdg. 13.99 *(978-0-375-97074-0(6))* Random Hse. Children's Bks. (Random Hse. Bks. for Young Readers).

—Chasing Rainbows. Rabe, Tish. 2012. (3-D Pictureback Ser.). (ENG.). 16p. (J). (gr. -1-2). pap. 4.99 *(978-0-375-87124-5(1),* Random Hse. Bks. for Young Readers) Random Hse. Children's Bks.

—Clam-I-Am! All about the Beach. Rabe, Tish. 2005. (Cat in the Hat's Learning Library). (ENG.). 48p. (J). (gr. -1-3). 9.99 *(978-0-375-82280-3(1),* Random Hse. Bks. for Young Readers) Random Hse. Children's Bks.

—Hark! a Shark! All about Sharks. Worth, Bonnie. 2013. (Cat in the Hat's Learning Library). (ENG.). 48p. (J). (gr. k-3). 8.99 *(978-0-375-87073-6(3),* Random Hse. Bks. for Young Readers) Random Hse. Children's Bks.

—How Wet Can You Get? Cat in the Hat Knows a Lot about That! Rabe, Tish. 2011. (Pictureback Ser.). (ENG.). 16p. (J). (gr. -1-2). pap. 3.99 *(978-0-375-86517-6(9),* Random Hse. Bks. for Young Readers) Random Hse. Children's Bks.

—I Can Name 50 Trees Today! All about Trees. Worth, Bonnie. 2006. (Cat in the Hat's Learning Library). (ENG.). 48p. (J). (gr. -1-3). 8.99 *(978-0-375-82277-3(1),* Random Hse. Bks. for Young Readers) Random Hse. Children's Bks.

—I Love the Nightlife! Rabe, Tish. 2010. (Pictureback Ser.). (ENG.). 16p. (J). (gr. -1-2). pap. 3.99 *(978-0-375-86354-7(0),* Random Hse. Bks. for Young Readers) Random Hse. Children's Bks.

—Ice Is Nice! All about the North & South Poles. Worth, Bonnie. 2010. (Cat in the Hat's Learning Library). (ENG.). 48p. (J). (gr. -1-3). 8.99 *(978-0-375-82885-0(0))* Random Hse., Inc.

—If I Ran the Dog Show: All about Dogs. Rabe, Tish. 2012. (Cat in the Hat's Learning Library). (ENG.). 48p. (J). (gr. k-3). 8.99 *(978-0-375-86682-1(5),* Random Hse. Bks. for Young Readers) Random Hse. Children's Bks.

—If I Ran the Horse Show: All about Horses. Worth, Bonnie. 2012. (Cat in the Hat's Learning Library). (ENG.). 48p. (J). (gr. k-3). 8.99 *(978-0-375-86683-8(3))* Random Hse., Inc.

—A Long Winter's Nap. Rabe, Tish. 2011. (Deluxe Pictureback Ser.). (ENG.). 32p. (J). (gr. -1-2). pap. 4.99 *(978-0-375-87279-2(5),* Random Hse. Bks. for Young Readers) Random Hse. Children's Bks.

—Miles & Miles of Reptiles: All about Reptiles. Rabe, Tish. 2009. (Cat in the Hat's Learning Library). (ENG.). 48p. (J). (gr. -1-3). 8.99 *(978-0-375-82884-3(2))* Random Hse., Inc.

—My, Oh My — A Butterfly! All about Butterflies. Rabe, Tish. 2007. (Cat in the Hat's Learning Library). (ENG.). 48p. (J). (gr. -1-3). 8.99 *(978-0-375-82882-9(6),* Random Hse. Bks. for Young Readers) Random Hse. Children's Bks.

—Night Lights (Dr. Seuss/Cat in the Hat) Rabe, Tish. 2014. (Glow-In-the-Dark Pictureback Ser.). (ENG.). 16p. (J). (gr. -1-2). pap. 4.99 *(978-0-385-37116-2(0),* Random Hse. Bks. for Young Readers) Random Hse. Children's Bks.

—Oh, the Pets You Can Get! All about Our Animal Friends. Rabe, Tish. 2005. (Cat in the Hat's Learning Library). (ENG.). 48p. (J). (gr. -1-3). 8.99 *(978-0-375-82278-0(X),* Random Hse. Bks. for Young Readers) Random Hse. Children's Bks.

—Oh, the Things They Invented! All about Great Inventors. Worth, Bonnie. 2015. (Cat in the Hat's Learning Library). (ENG.). 48p. (J). (gr. k-3). 9.99 *(978-0-449-81497-0(1))* Random Hse., Inc.

—Safari, So Good! All about African Wildlife. Worth, Bonnie. 2011. (Cat in the Hat's Learning Library). (ENG.). 48p. (J). (gr. -1-3). 8.99 *(978-0-375-86681-4(7))* Random Hse., Inc.

—Thump!/The Lost Egg (Cat in the Hat/Seuss) Rabe, Tish. 2013. (Pictureback Series.). (ENG.). 32p. (J). (gr. -1-2). pap. 4.99 *(978-0-307-98063-2(4),* Random Hse. Bks. for Young Readers) Random Hse. Children's Bks.

—Trick-or-Treat!/Aye-Aye! Rabe, Tish. 2012. (Deluxe Pictureback Ser.). (ENG.). 32p. (J). (gr. -1-2). pap. 4.99 *(978-0-307-93056-9(4),* Random Hse. Bks. for Young Readers) Random Hse. Children's Bks.

—A Whale of a Tale! All about Porpoises, Dolphins, & Whales. Worth, Bonnie. 2006. (Cat in the Hat's Learning Library). (ENG.). 48p. (J). (gr. -1-3). 8.99 *(978-0-375-82279-7(8),* Random Hse. Bks. for Young Readers) Random Hse. Children's Bks.

—What Cat Is That? All about Cats. Rabe, Tish. 2013. (Cat in the Hat's Learning Library). (ENG.). 48p. (J). (gr. k-3). 8.99 *(978-0-375-86640-1(X));* lib. bdg. 12.99 *(978-0-375-96640-8(4))* Random Hse. Children's Bks. (Random Hse. Bks. for Young Readers).

—Why Oh Why Are Deserts Dry? All about Deserts. Rabe, Tish. 2011. (Cat in the Hat's Learning Library). (ENG.). 48p. (J). (gr. -1-3). 8.99 *(978-0-375-85868-0(7))* Random Hse., Inc.

Ruiz, Aristides & Mathieu, Joseph. One Cent, Two Cents, Old Cent, New Cent: All about Money. Worth, Bonnie. 2008. (Cat in the Hat's Learning Library). (ENG.). 48p. (J). (gr. -1-3). 8.99 *(978-0-375-82881-2(8))* Random Hse., Inc.

—Would You Rather Be a Pollywog? All about Pond Life. Worth, Bonnie. 2010. (Cat in the Hat's Learning Library). (ENG.). 48p. (J). (gr. -1-3). 9.99 *(978-0-375-82883-6(4))* Random Hse., Inc.

Ruiz, Aristides, jt. illus. see Mathieu, Joe.

Ruiz, Fernando. Laugh Your Rabbids Off! A Rabbids Joke Book. McCarthy, Rebecca. 2014. (Rabbids Invasion Ser.). (ENG.). 48p. (J). (gr. 2-5). pap. 3.99 *(978-1-4814-0040-4(1),* Simon Spotlight) Simon Spotlight.

Ruiz, Jorge. ¡Quiero Chocolate! Velasquez, Leonor Bravo. 2015. 24p. (J). (gr. -1-2). pap. 12.95 ***(978-9942-19-153-3(4),*** Alfaguara Infantil) Santillana Ecuador ECU. Dist: Santillana USA Publishing Co., Inc.

Ruiz, Jose Alfonso Ocampo & Smith, Tod. Dracula, 1 vol. Fuentes, Benny & Stoker, Bram. 2008. (Classic Fiction Ser.). (ENG.). 72p. (gr. 2-3). lib. bdg. 26.65 *(978-1-4342-0448-6(0),* 1278680, Graphic Revolve) Stone Arch Bks.

Ruiz, Jose Alfonso Ocampo & Woodman, Ned. The Last Rider: The Final Days of the Pony Express. Gunderson, J. 2007. (Historical Fiction Ser.). (ENG.). 56p. (gr. 2-3). pap. 6.25 *(978-1-59889-407-2(2),* Graphic Flash) Stone Arch Bks.

Ruiz, Margarita. Ali Baba y Los Cuarenta Ladrones. Combel Editorial Staff & árabe, Cuento popular. 2004. (Troquelados Clásicos Ser.). (SPA & ENG.). 16p. (J). (gr. -1-k). pap. 3.95 *(978-84-7864-736-1(8))* Combel Editorial, S.A. ESP. Dist: Independent Pubs. Group.

—Amahal y los tres Reyes. Combel Editorial Staff & Menotti, Gian Carlo. 2004. (Troquelados Clásicos Ser.). (SPA & ENG.). 16p. (J). (gr. -1-k). pap. 3.95 *(978-84-7864-735-4(X))* Combel Editorial, S.A. ESP. Dist: Independent Pubs. Group.

—La Boda del Ratón y la Ratita. 2006. (Troquelados Del Mundo Ser.). (SPA & ENG.). 16p. (J). (gr. -1-k). pap. 3.95 *(978-84-7864-972-3(7))* Combel Editorial, S.A. ESP. Dist: Independent Pubs. Group.

—El Cuento de la Lechera. Combel Editorial Staff et al. 2003. (Troquelados Clásicos Ser.). (SPA & ENG.). 16p. (J). (gr. -1-k). pap. 3.95 *(978-84-7864-676-0(0))* Combel Editorial, S.A. ESP. Dist: Independent Pubs. Group.

—Historia de un Conejito. catalán, Cuento popular. 2005. (Troquelados Clásicos Ser.). (SPA & ENG.). 16p. (J). (gr. -1-k). pap. 3.95 *(978-84-7864-898-6(4))* Combel Editorial, S.A. ESP. Dist: Independent Pubs. Group.

—El Indio Errante. 2006. (Troquelados Del Mundo Ser.). (SPA & ENG.). 16p. (J). (gr. -1-k). pap. 3.95 *(978-84-7864-971-6(9))* Combel Editorial, S.A. ESP. Dist: Independent Pubs. Group.

—Pinocho. (SPA & ENG.). (J). (gr. -1-5). pap. 5.95 incl. audio compact disk *(978-88-8148-253-5(3))* EMC/Paradigm Publishing.

—El Rey Midas. griego, Mito. 2005. (Troquelados Clásicos Ser.). (SPA & ENG.). 16p. (J). (gr. -1-k). pap. 3.95 *(978-84-7864-895-5(X))* Combel Editorial, S.A. ESP. Dist: Independent Pubs. Group.

Ruiz, Margarita & Ruiz Abello, Margarita. Pedrito y el Rey Gloton. Combel Editorial Staff. 2004. (Troquelados Clásicos Ser.). (SPA & ENG.). 16p. (J). (gr. -1-k). pap. 3.95 *(978-84-7864-738-5(4))* Combel Editorial, S.A. ESP. Dist: Independent Pubs. Group.

—El Pez de Oro. 2005. (Troquelados Clásicos Ser.). (SPA & ENG.). 16p. (J). (gr. -1-k). pap. 3.95 *(978-84-7864-897-9(6))* Combel Editorial, S.A. ESP. Dist: Independent Pubs. Group.

—Una Princesa de Verdad. Combel Editorial Staff. 2003. (Troquelados Clásicos Ser.). (SPA & ENG.). 16p. (J). (gr. -1-k). pap. 3.95 *(978-84-7864-677-7(9))* Combel Editorial, S.A. ESP. Dist: Independent Pubs. Group.

—El Ruisenor. Combel Editorial Staff. 2004. (Troquelados Clásicos Ser.). (SPA & ENG.). 16p. (J). (gr. -1-k). pap. 3.95 *(978-84-7864-737-8(6))* Combel Editorial, S.A. ESP. Dist: Independent Pubs. Group.

—El Sastrecillo Valiente. 2005. (Troquelados Clásicos Ser.). (SPA & ENG.). 16p. (J). (gr. -1-k). pap. 3.95 *(978-84-7864-896-2(8))* Combel Editorial, S.A. ESP. Dist: Independent Pubs. Group.

—La Vendedora de Fósforos. Combel Editorial Staff. 2003. (Troquelados Clásicos Ser.). (ENG & SPA.). 16p. (J). (gr. -1-k). pap. 3.95 *(978-84-7864-675-3(2))* Combel Editorial, S.A. ESP. Dist: Independent Pubs. Group.

—Los Zapatos Bailarines. Combel Editorial Staff. 2003. (Troquelados Clásicos Ser.). (SPA & ENG.). 16p. (J). (gr. -1-k). pap. 3.95 *(978-84-7864-678-4(7))* Combel Editorial, S.A. ESP. Dist: Independent Pubs. Group.

Ruiz Navarro, Jose. Rafael Alberti y los Niños. Ruiz Navarro, Jose. González, Lola et al. 2007. (SPA.). 50p. (J). (gr. 4-5). 23.99 *(978-84-241-2728-2(5))* Everest Editora ESP. Dist: Lectorum Pubns., Inc.

Ruiz, Pedro. Una Noche en el Tejado. Ruiz, Clarisa & Reyes, Yolanda. 2004. (Primer Acto: Teatro Infantil y Juvenil Ser.). (SPA.). 63p. (J). (gr. -1-7). pap. *(978-958-30-0320-2(4))* Panamericana Editorial.

Rujin, Ma, jt. illus. see She, Liu.

Rukl, Antonin, jt. illus. see Tirion, Wil.

Rumble, Chris. Stink Trek: The Adventures of Uncle Stinky #2. Rumble, Chris. 2004. (ENG.). 96p. (J). (gr. 1-4). pap. 6.99 *(978-1-58246-123-6(6),* Tricycle Pr.) Ten Speed Pr.

Rumford, James. From the Good Mountain: How Gutenberg Changed the World. Rumford, James. 2012. (ENG.). 36p. (J). (gr. -1-3). 17.99 *(978-1-59643-542-1(9))* Roaring Brook Pr.

—Silent Music: A Story of Baghdad. Rumford, James. 2008. (ENG.). 32p. (J). (gr. -1-3). 17.99 *(978-1-59643-276-5(4))* Roaring Brook Pr.

Rumford, James. Beowulf: A Hero's Tale Retold. Rumford, James, retold by. 2006. (J). *(978-0-399-24391-2(7))* Penguin Publishing Group.

R

Ruminski, Jeff. Taking Care of Pets. Mullican, Judy. l.t. ed. 2004. (HRL Big Book Ser.). 8p. (J). (gr. -1-1). pap. 10.95 *(978-1-57332-278-2(4))*; pap. 10.95 *(978-1-57332-279-9(2))* Carson-Dellosa Publishing, LLC. (HighReach Learning, Incorporated).

Runcorn, Scott, jt. illus. see Root, Jeff.

Runnells, Patricia & Runnells, Treesha. Pig-a-Boo! A Farmyard Peekaboo Book. DePrisco, Dorothea. 2009. (ENG.). 14p. (J). (gr. -1-k). 7.99 *(978-1-4169-7226-6(9))*, Little Simon) Little Simon.

Runnells, Treesha. Pat Them Gently. O'Brien, Melanie. 2006. (ENG.). 10p. (J). (gr. -1-3). bds. 8.95 *(978-1-58117-462-5(4))*, Intervisual/Piggy Toes) Bendon, Inc.

Runnells, Treesha. Afraid of the Dark? Runnells, Treesha. 2005. (Stories to Share Ser.). 14p. (J). (gr. -1-2). 10.95 *(978-1-58117-107-5(2))*, Intervisual/Piggy Toes) Bendon, Inc.

—Forest Friends: A Fold-Out Fun Book. Runnells, Treesha. 2005. (Fold-Out Fun Ser.). 10p. (J). 4.95 *(978-1-58117-275-1(3))*, Intervisual/Piggy Toes) Bendon, Inc.

—Safari Friends: Fold-Out Fun. Runnells, Treesha. 2005. (Fold-Out Fun Ser.). 10p. (J). 4.95 *(978-1-58117-276-8(1))*, Intervisual/Piggy Toes) Bendon, Inc.

Runnells, Treesha, jt. illus. see Runnells, Patricia.

Runnentrom, Bengt-Arne. La Niña y la Anguila. Zak, Monica. Orea, Lucia, tr. 2009. (SPA.). 32p. (J). (gr. 1-3). pap. 13.95 *(978-99922-1-325-4(6))* Piedra Santa, Editorial GTM. Dist: Libros Sin Fronteras.

Runnerstrom, Bengt-Arne. Salven Mi Selva. Zak, Monica. (SPA.). 29p. (J). (gr. 3-18). pap. 12.95 *(978-968-6048-23-0(5))* volcano pr.

Runton, Andy. Owly & Wormy, Bright Lights & Starry Nights. Runton, Andy. 2012. (ENG.). 40p. (J). (gr. -1-2). 15.99 *(978-1-4169-5775-1(8))*, Atheneum Bks. for Young Readers) Simon & Schuster Children's Publishing.

—Owly & Wormy, Friends All Aflutter! Runton, Andy. 2011. (ENG.). 40p. (J). (gr. -1-2). 16.99 *(978-1-4169-5774-4(X))*, Atheneum Bks. for Young Readers) Simon & Schuster Children's Publishing.

Runyen, Elizabeth. Watch Me Draw Disney's Mickey Mouse Clubhouse. 2012. (J). *(978-1-936309-74-0(2))* Quarto Publishing Group USA.

Runyon, Anne Marshall. The Sheltering Cedar. Runyon, Anne Marshall. 2007. 32p. (J). pap. 16.99 *(978-1-933454-02-3(4))* Portal Pr.

Ruocco, Paul. Madison's Journey. Amarone, Morgan. 2011. 30p. (J). pap. 16.99 *(978-0-9841934-5-5(6))* Bryson Taylor Publishing.

Rupert, Chris, et al. Kitty Treats Cookbook. Bledsoe, Michele. 2010. (ENG.). 15p. (gr. 6). bds. 10.95 *(978-0-9753883-8-9(X))* Come & Get It Publishing.

Rupp, Kristina. Bats & Birds. Fleischer, Jayson. 2012. (1G Science Ser.). (ENG.). 32p. (J). pap. 8.50 *(978-1-61406-173-1(4))* American Reading Co.

—The Gorilla Family. Fleischer, Jayson & Lynch, Michelle. 2012. (2G Animals Ser.). (ENG.). 40p. (J). pap. 8.50 *(978-1-61406-203-5(X))* American Reading Co.

Ruppelius, Conrad. Conrad's Hiking Adventure. Ruppelius, Conrad. Ruppelius, Jeffrey. 2006. (J). per. 12.95 *(978-0-9774143-3-8(7))* Little Dog Pubns.

Ruppert, Larry. Freddie & Flossie & the Leaf Monster. Hope, Laura Lee. 2005. (Bobbsey Twins Ser.). (ENG.). 32p. (J). (gr. -1-k). pap. 13.99 *(978-1-4169-0271-3(6))*, Simon Spotlight) Simon Spotlight.

Rusan Jeffers. McDuff & the Baby. Rosemary Wells. 2014. 28p. pap. 9.99 *(978-1-61003-384-8(1))* Center for the Collaborative Classroom.

Ruse, Jill, jt. illus. see Long, John.

Rush, Peter. Return to Sula, 1 vol. Derwent, Lavinia. 2003. (Kelpies Ser.). (ENG.). 128p. 10.00 *(978-0-86315-424-9(7))* Floris Bks. GBR. Dist: SteinerBooks, Inc.

Rusky, Ann G. Mac's Mackinac Island Adventure. Vachon, Mary Beth. 2005. 216p. (J). pap. 17.95 *(978-0-9766104-1-0(8))* Arbutus Pr.

Russ Cardona. My Name Is Jeromy. 1. Jewell, Beverly. 2004. 28p. (J). 11.95 *(978-0-9701519-1-9(8))* All Gold Publishing Co.

Russell, Carol. No Eat Not Food: The Search for Intelligent Food on Planet Earth. Sanger, Rick. l.t. ed. 2006. 48p. (J). 15.95 *(978-0-9653149-2-3(8))* Mountain Path Pr.

Russell, Elaine. Savannah Dreams. Stewart, Lolla. 2011. (ENG.). 30p. (J). (gr. -1-k). 24.99 *(978-1-921714-03-0(4))* Little Hare Bks. AUS. Dist: Independent Pubs. Group.

Russell, Elaine. The Shack That Dad Built. Russell, Elaine. 2005. (ENG.). 32p. (J). (gr. k-2). 10.95 *(978-1-877003-94-3(8))* Little Hare Bks. AUS. Dist: Independent Pubs. Group.

Russell, Fletch, photos by. I Like Rocks! Russell, Carol & Russell, Tally. 2011. 32p. pap. 12.95 *(978-1-4634-3271-3(2))* AuthorHouse.

Russell, Gayle. Kangaroo. Reilly, Pauline. (Picture Roo Bks.). 32p. (J). pap. *(978-0-86417-538-0(8))*, Kangaroo Pr.) Simon & Schuster Australia.

Russell, Harriet. Is It Still Cheating If I Don't Get Caught? Weinstein, Bruce D. 2009. (ENG.). 160p. (J). (gr. 5-9). pap. 14.99 *(978-1-59643-306-9(X))* Roaring Brook Pr.

Russell, Joyce. The Key of the Kingdom: A Book of Stories & Poems for Children. Gmeyner, Elizabeth. 2004. 100p. (J). pap. 15.00 *(978-0-88010-549-1(6))*, Bell Pond Bks.) SteinerBooks, Inc.

Russell, Kay. Murphy Moose & Garrett Goose. Macy-Mills, Phyllis. 2003. (J). spiral bd. *(978-1-932303-48-3(0))*, Llumina Pr.) Aeon Publishing Inc.

Russell, Kerri G. Get Ready... Get Set... Read!, 5 sets (35 bks.) Foster, Kelli C. & Erickson, Gina Clegg. (J). lib. bdg. 418.25Set. lib. bdg. 418.25 *(978-1-56674-920-6(4))* Forest Hse. Publishing Co., Inc.

Russell, Lyndsay & Hanson, Tippi. Rainbow Weaver. Russell, Lyndsay & Hanson, Tippi. 2007. (ENG.). 48p. (J). (gr. k-2). 13.99 *(978-1-84243-229-7(X))* Oldcastle Bks., Ltd. GBR. Dist: Independent Pubs. Group.

Russell, Natalie. Donkey's Busy Day. Russell, Natalie. 2009. (ENG.). 32p. (J). (gr. k-k). pap. 11.95 *(978-0-7475-9547-2(X))* Bloomsbury Publishing Plc GBR. Dist: Independent Pubs. Group.

—Lost for Words, 1 vol. Russell, Natalie. 2014. (ENG.). 32p. (J). (gr. -1-3). 16.95 *(978-1-56145-739-7(6))* Peachtree Pubs.

Russell, P. Craig. Buffy the Vampire Slayer: Tales of the Slayers: Tales of the Slayers. Sale, Tim et al. 2004. (Buffy the Vampire Slayer Ser.). (ENG.). 96p. pap. 14.95 *(978-1-56971-605-2(6))* Dark Horse Comics.

—Coraline. Gaiman, Neil. 2008. (ENG.). 192p. (J). (gr. 3-7). 18.99 *(978-0-06-082543-0(X))* HarperCollins Pubs.

—Coraline Graphic Novel. Gaiman, Neil. 2009. (ENG.). 192p. (J). (gr. 3-7). pap. 9.99 *(978-0-06-082545-4(6))* HarperCollins Pubs.

—Coraline Novela Grafica. Gaiman, Neil. Isern, Carol, tr. 2010. (SPA.). 186p. (YA). (gr. 5-8). pap. 20.95 *(978-84-9918-067-0(1))* Roca Editorial De Libros ESP. Dist: Spanish Pubs., LLC.

—The Fairy Tales of Oscar Wilde Vol. 4: The Devoted Friend, The Nightengale, & the Rose, Vol. 4. Wilde, Oscar. 2004. (Fairy Tales of Oscar Wilde Ser.: 4). (ENG.). 32p. 16.99 *(978-1-56163-391-3(7))* NBM Publishing Co.

—Fairy Tales of Oscar Wilde: the Complete Hardcover Set 1-5. Wilde, Oscar. 2014. (Fairy Tales of Oscar Wilde Ser.). (ENG.). 192p. (J). (gr. 4-7). 79.99 *(978-1-56163-890-1(0))* NBM Publishing Co.

—The Fairy Tales of Oscar Wilde: the Happy Prince Signed & Numbered. Wilde, Oscar. 2012. (Fairy Tales of Oscar Wilde Ser.). (ENG.). 32p. (J). (gr. 4-7). 49.99 *(978-1-56163-687-7(8))*; 50.00 *(978-1-56163-629-7(0))* NBM Publishing Co.

Russell, P. Craig. The Devoted Friend, the Nightengale, & the Rose. Russell, P. Craig. Wilde, Oscar. 2004. (Fairy Tales of Oscar Wilde Ser.: 4). (ENG.). 48p. pap. 8.99 *(978-1-56163-392-0(5))* NBM Publishing Co.

—Fairy Tales of Oscar Wilde: The Selfish Giant & the Star Child, Vol. 1. Russell, P. Craig. 2003. (Fairy Tales of Oscar Wilde Ser.: 1). (ENG.). 1111p. pap. 9.99 *(978-1-56163-375-3(5))* NBM Publishing Co.

—The Graveyard Book Graphic Novel. Russell, P. Craig. Gaiman, Neil. 2014. (ENG.). (J). (gr. 3-7). Vol. 1. 192p. 19.99 *(978-0-06-219481-7(X))*; Vol. 2. 176p. 19.99 *(978-0-06-219483-1(6))* HarperCollins Pubs.

Russell, P. Craig & Barreto, Eduardo. Gotham by Gaslight. Augustyn, Brian. rev. ed. 2006. (Batman Ser.). (ENG.). 112p. (YA). pap. 12.99 *(978-1-4012-1153-0(4))* DC Comics.

Russell, Rachel Renée. Dork Diaries, Set. Russell, Rachel Renée. ed. 2013. (Dork Diaries: Nos. 4-6). (ENG.). 1056p. (J). (gr. 4-8). 41.99 *(978-1-4424-9859-4(5))*, Simon & Schuster/Paula Wiseman Bks.) Simon & Schuster/Paula Wiseman Bks.

—Dork Diaries Set, Set. Russell, Rachel Renée. ed. 2011. (Dork Diaries: Nos. 1-3). (ENG.). 928p. (J). (gr. 4-8). 41.99 *(978-1-4424-2662-7(4))*, Simon & Schuster/Paula Wiseman Bks.) Simon & Schuster/Paula Wiseman Bks.

—How to Dork Your Diary. Russell, Rachel Renée. 2011. (Dork Diaries: No. 3.5). (ENG.). 288p. (J). (gr. 4-8). 13.99 *(978-1-4424-2233-9(5))*, Simon & Schuster/Paula Wiseman Bks.) Simon & Schuster/Paula Wiseman Bks.

—OMG!:All about Me Diary! Russell, Rachel Renée. 2013. (Dork Diaries). (ENG.). 272p. (J). (gr. 4-8). 12.99 *(978-1-4424-8771-0(2))*, Simon & Schuster/Paula Wiseman Bks.) Simon & Schuster/Paula Wiseman Bks.

Russell, Rachel Renée. Tales from a Not-So-Dorky Drama Queen. Russell, Rachel Renée. 2015. (Dork Diaries: Bk. 9). (ENG.). 352p. (J). (gr. 4-8). 13.99 ***(978-1-4424-8769-7(0))***, Aladdin Paperbacks) Simon & Schuster Children's Publishing.

Russell, Rachel Renée. Tales from a Not-So-Fabulous Life. Russell, Rachel Renée. 2009. (Dork Diaries: 1). (ENG.). 288p. (J). (gr. 4-8). 13.99 *(978-1-4169-8006-3(7))*, Simon & Schuster/Paula Wiseman Bks.) Simon & Schuster/Paula Wiseman Bks.

—Tales from a Not-So-Glam TV Star. Russell, Rachel Renée. 2014. (Dork Diaries: 7). (ENG.). 336p. (J). (gr. 4-8). 13.99 *(978-1-4424-8767-3(4))*, Simon & Schuster/Paula Wiseman Bks.) Simon & Schuster/Paula Wiseman Bks.

—Tales from a Not-So-Graceful Ice Princess. Russell, Rachel Renée. 2012. (Dork Diaries: 4). (ENG.). 368p. (J). (gr. 4-8). 13.99 *(978-1-4424-1192-0(9))*, Simon & Schuster/Paula Wiseman Bks.) Simon & Schuster/Paula Wiseman Bks.

—Tales from a Not-So-Happy Heartbreaker. Russell, Rachel Renée. 2013. (Dork Diaries: 6). (ENG.). 352p. (J). (gr. 4-8). 13.99 *(978-1-4424-4963-3(2))*, Simon & Schuster/Paula Wiseman Bks.) Simon & Schuster/Paula Wiseman Bks.

—Tales from a Not-So-Popular Party Girl. Russell, Rachel Renée. 2010. (Dork Diaries: 2). (ENG.). 288p. (J). (gr. 4-8). 13.99 *(978-1-4169-8008-7(3))*, Simon & Schuster/Paula Wiseman Bks.) Simon & Schuster/Paula Wiseman Bks.

—Tales from a Not-So-Smart Miss Know-It-All. Russell, Rachel Renée. 2012. (Dork Diaries: 5). (ENG.). 336p. (J). (gr. 4-8). 13.99 *(978-1-4424-4961-9(6))*, Simon & Schuster/Paula Wiseman Bks.) Simon & Schuster/Paula Wiseman Bks.

—Tales from a Not-So-Talented Pop Star. Russell, Rachel Renée. 2011. (Dork Diaries: 3). (ENG.). 320p. (J). (gr. 4-8). 13.99 *(978-1-4424-1190-6(2))*, Simon & Schuster/Paula Wiseman Bks.) Simon & Schuster/Paula Wiseman Bks.

Russell, Terry. Three Best Friends. Leonard, Mary T. 2004. 96p. (J). per. 12.00 *(978-0-9740683-8-1(1))* Authors & Artists Publishers of New York, Inc.

Russik, Michael. Moon over the Mountain. Polette, Keith. 2010. (ENG.). 32p. (J). (gr. -1-3). pap. 7.95 *(978-1-934960-08-0(X))*, Raven Tree Pr.,Csi) Continental Sales, Inc.

Russo, Blythe. My Daughters Are Smart! D Is for Daughters & S Is for Smart. Adhikary, Anita B. 2014. (ENG.). 24p. (J). (gr. -1-3). 14.95 *(978-1-62086-429-6(0))* Mascot Bks., Inc.

Russo, David Anson. Around the World: The Great Treasure Hunt. Russo, David Anson. 2011. (ENG.). 28p. (J). (gr. 4-6). pap. 14.99 *(978-1-4424-4343-3(X))*, Simon & Schuster Bks. For Young Readers) Simon & Schuster Bks. For Young Readers.

—The Great Treasure Hunt. Russo, David Anson. 2011. (ENG.). 28p. (J). (gr. k-3). pap. 14.99 *(978-1-4424-4342-6(1))*, Simon & Schuster Bks. For Young Readers) Simon & Schuster Bks. For Young Readers.

Russo, Marisabina. Peter Is Just a Baby. 2012. (J). 16.00 *(978-0-8028-5384-4(6))*, Eerdmans Bks For Young Readers) Eerdmans, William B. Publishing Co.

Russo, Marisabina. Always Remember Me: How One Family Survived World War II. Russo, Marisabina. 2005. (ENG.). 48p. (J). (gr. 1-5). 19.99 *(978-0-689-86920-4(7))*, Atheneum Bks. for Young Readers) Simon & Schuster Children's Publishing.

—The Bunnies Are Not in Their Beds. Russo, Marisabina. 2013. (ENG.). 40p. (J). (gr. -1-2). pap. 7.99 *(978-0-307-98126-4(6))*, Dragonfly Bks.) Random Hse. Children's Bks.

—Sophie Sleeps Over. Russo, Marisabina. 2014. (ENG.). 32p. (J). (gr. -1-2). 16.99 *(978-1-59643-933-7(5))* Roaring Brook Pr.

—The Trouble with Baby. Russo, Marisabina. 2003. 32p. (J). (gr. -1-18). 16.89 *(978-0-06-008925-2(3))* HarperCollins Pubs.

—A Very Big Bunny. Russo, Marisabina. 2010. (ENG.). 40p. (J). (gr. -1-3). 17.99 *(978-0-375-84463-8(5))*, Schwartz & Wade Bks.) Random Hse. Children's Bks.

Russon, Anne E., jt. photos by see Smith, Dale.

Rust, Graham. A Little Princess: The Story of Sara Crewe. Burnett, Frances Hodgson. (J). pap. 22.95 *(978-0-590-24079-6(X))* Scholastic, Inc.

Ruta, Angelo, et al. Christmas Around the World. Sims, Lesley. 2006. (Young Reading Series 1 Gift Bks.). 47p. (J). (gr. -1-3). 8.99 *(978-0-7945-1132-6(5))*, Usborne) EDC Publishing.

Ruta, Angelo. My First Holy Communion. Piper, Sophie. 2010. (ENG.). 64p. (J). (gr. 1-4). 14.99 *(978-1-55725-696-6(9))* Paraclete Pr., Inc.

—The Plan: How God Got the World Ready for Jesus. Ferguson, Sinclair B. 2009. (Colour Bks.). (ENG.). 40p. (J). 9.99 *(978-1-84550-451-9(8))* Christian Focus Pubns. GBR. Dist: Send The Light Distribution LLC.

—The Story of Jesus. Skevington, Andrea. 2008. (ENG.). 128p. (J). (gr. 2-4). pap. 16.95 *(978-0-7459-6121-7(5))* Lion Hudson PLC GBR. Dist: Independent Pubs. Group.

Ruth, Annie. I Can Read. Ruth, Annie. l.t. ed. 2005. 32p. (J). (gr. -1-3). pap. 10.00 *(978-0-9656306-7-2(6))* Ruth, A Creations.

Ruth, Greg. City of Orphans. Avi. (ENG.). 368p. (J). (gr. 5-9). 2012. pap. 7.99 *(978-1-4169-7108-5(4))*, Atheneum Bks. for Young Readers); 2011. 17.99 *(978-1-4169-7102-3(5))*, Atheneum/Richard Jackson Bks.) Simon & Schuster Children's Publishing.

—Our Enduring Spirit: President Barack Obama's First Words to America. Obama, Barack. 2009. 48p. lib. bdg. 18.89 *(978-0-06-183456-1(4))* HarperCollins Pubs.

—A Pirate's Guide to First Grade. Preller, James. 2013. (ENG.). 48p. (J). (gr. -1-1). 6.99 *(978-1-250-02721-4(7))* Square Fish.

—A Pirate's Guide to Recess. Preller, James. 2013. (ENG.). 36p. (J). (gr. -1-1). 16.99 *(978-1-250-00515-1(9))* Feiwel & Friends.

—Red Kite, Blue Kite. Jiang, Ji-Li. 2013. (ENG.). 32p. (J). (gr. 1-3). 17.99 *(978-1-4231-2753-6(6))* Hyperion Pr.

—The Sea Wolves Bk. 2. Golden, Christopher & Lebbon, Tim. 2012. (Secret Journeys of Jack London Ser.: 2). (ENG.). 400p. (YA). (gr. 8). 16.99 *(978-0-06-186320-2(3))* HarperCollins Pubs.

—The Wild. Golden, Christopher & Lebbon, Tim. (Secret Journeys of Jack London Ser.: 1). (ENG.). (YA). (gr. 5). 2012. 400p. pap. 6.99 *(978-0-06-186319-6(X))*; 2011. 368p. 15.99 *(978-0-06-186317-2(3))* HarperCollins Pubs.

Ruth, Greg. Coming Home. Ruth, Greg. 2014. (ENG.). 32p. (J). (gr. -1-2). 16.99 *(978-1-250-05547-7(4))* Feiwel & Friends.

Rutherford, Alexa. B Is for Bagpipes: A Scotland Alphabet. Kiehm, Eve Begley. 2010. (Discover the World Ser.). (ENG.). 40p. (J). 17.95 *(978-1-58536-453-3(4))* Sleeping Bear Pr.

Rutherford, James. Ancient Rome Student Book: Questions for the Thinker. Rutherford, Fran. 2006. (ENG.). 161p. (YA). spiral bd. 34.90 *(978-0-9773990-8-6(7))* Mother's Hse. Publishing.

Rutherford, Meg. Brave Lion, Scared Lion. Stimson, Joan. Rubio, Esther, tr. (J). (gr. k-1). pap. *(978-0-590-90985-3(1))*, SO3690) Scholastic, Inc.

Rutherford, Peter. Baby's Bible Stories: Noah's Ark. 2015. (ENG.). 24p. bds. 6.99 *(978-1-86147-644-9(2))*, Armadillo) Anness Publishing GBR. Dist: National Bk. Network.

—A Claddagh Ring for Nuala, 1 vol. Crosbie, Duncan. gif. ed. 2003. (ENG.). 16p. (J). (gr. k-3). 7.95 *(978-1-58980-175-2(X))* Pelican Publishing Co., Inc.

—Giant Fun-to-Find Puzzles Busy Animals: Search for Pictures in Eight Exciting Scenes. 2015. (ENG.). 24p. pap. 6.99 *(978-1-86147-460-5(1))*, Armadillo) Anness Publishing GBR. Dist: National Bk. Network.

Rutland, Jarrett. The Best Parade Day. Spatz. Fair, Sherry. 2006. (Spatz Ser.). 40p. (J). (gr. -1-5). 18.95 *(978-1-57736-375-0(2))* Providence Hse Pubs.

—The Scratching Sound: Spatz. Fair, Sherry W. 2005. 28p. (J). (gr. -1-7). 16.98 *(978-1-57736-348-4(5))* Providence Hse Pubs.

Rutten, Nicole. Not yet, Rose. Hill, Susanna Leonard. 2009. 34p. (J). (gr. -1-3). 16.50 *(978-0-8028-5326-4(9))*, Eerdmans Bks For Young Readers) Eerdmans, William B. Publishing Co.

—Sleepy Time Blessings. Conan, Sally Anne. 2009. 12p. (J). (gr. -1). 7.99 *(978-0-8028-5350-9(1))* Eerdmans, William B. Publishing Co.

RUZICKA, Carol. The Butterfly. Baker, Bill. 2012. 46p. pap. 15.00 *(978-0-9859132-0-5(7))* Asbury Heritage Publishing.

Ruzicka, Delores F. The Star That Sparkled. Zachmeyer, Mary L. Date not set. 26p. (J). pap. 5.00 *(978-0-9646864-1-0(4))* Zachmeyer, Mary L.

Ruzzier, Sergio. Broom, Zoom! Cohen, Caron Lee. 2010. (ENG.). 32p. (J). (gr. -1-3). 14.99 *(978-1-4169-9113-7(1))*, Simon & Schuster Bks. For Young Readers) Simon & Schuster Bks. For Young Readers.

—Have You Seen My New Blue Socks? Bunting, Eve. 2013. (ENG.). 32p. (J). (gr. -1-3). 16.99 *(978-0-547-75267-9(9))* Houghton Mifflin Harcourt Publishing Co.

—Tweak Tweak. Bunting, Eve. 2011. (ENG.). 40p. (J). (gr. -1-3). 14.99 *(978-0-618-99851-7(9))* Houghton Mifflin Harcourt Publishing Co.

—Whose Shoe? Bunting, Eve. 2015. (ENG.). 32p. (J). (gr. -1-3). 16.99 *(978-0-544-30210-5(9))* Houghton Mifflin Harcourt Publishing Co.

Ruzzier, Sergio. Bear & Bee. Ruzzier, Sergio. 2013. (Bear & Bee Ser.). (ENG.). 48p. (J). (gr. -1-k). 14.99 *(978-1-4231-5957-5(8))* Hyperion Pr.

—Too Busy. Ruzzier, Sergio. 2014. (Bear & Bee Ser.). (ENG.). 48p. (J). (gr. -1-k). 14.99 *(978-1-4231-5961-2(6))* Disney Pr.

Ryan & Marie, Anne. Top Dog. Ryan, Ann Marie. 2011. (My Phonics Readers: Level 1 Ser.). 24p. (J). (gr. -1-1). 24.25 *(978-1-84898-505-6(3))* Sea-To-Sea Pubns.

Ryan, Ann. The Little Wannabee. Ryan, Ann. 2006. (ENG.). 24p. (J). 16.95 *(978-1-933660-31-8(7))*, Tadpole Pr. 4 Kids) Smooth Sailing Pr., LLC.

Ryan, Ashley. The Legend of Athlon. Hall, Melissa. 2011. (ENG.). 32p. pap. 10.00 *(978-0-615-43583-1(1))* Willow Mountain Publishing.

Ryan, John. Pugwash the Smuggler. fac. ed. 2009. (ENG.). 32p. (J). (gr. -1-2). 16.95 *(978-1-84507-889-8(6))*, Frances Lincoln) Quarto Publishing Group UK GBR. Dist: Perseus-PGW.

Ryan, Mary C. Twitcher Mcgee & the Wonderful Tree. Ryan, Mary C., text. 2008. 12p. (J). 4.95 *(978-0-9678115-3-6(8))* Dragonseed Pr.

Ryan, Michael. Dead End Kids. 2009. (ENG.). 152p. (YA). (gr. 8-17). pap. 15.99 *(978-0-7851-3459-6(X))* Marvel Worldwide, Inc.

Ryan, Michael & Azaceta, Paul. Crazy Like a Fox, Vol. 3. David, Peter. Youngquist, Jeff, ed. 2004. (Captain Marvel Ser.). 136p. pap. 14.99 *(978-0-7851-1340-9(1))* Marvel Worldwide, Inc.

Ryan, Nellie. Beautiful Doodles: Over 100 Pictures to Complete & Create. 2008. (ENG.). 128p. (J). (gr. -1). pap. 12.95 *(978-0-7624-3298-1(5))* Running Pr. Bk. Pubs.

—Designer Doodles: Over 100 Designs to Complete & Create. 2009. (ENG.). 128p. (J). pap. 12.95 *(978-0-7624-3761-0(8))* Running Pr. Bk. Pubs.

—Fabulous Doodles: Over 100 Pictures to Complete & Create. Running Press Staff. 2009. (ENG.). 128p. (J). pap. 12.95 *(978-0-7624-3653-8(0))* Running Pr. Bk. Pubs.

—The Girls' Book of Secrets. Scholastic, Inc. Staff & Bailey, Ellen. 2011. (Best at Everything Ser.). (ENG.). 128p. (J). (gr. 3-7). pap. 7.99 *(978-0-545-37356-2(5))* Scholastic, Inc.

Ryan, Nellie. Fabulous Fashion. Ryan, Nellie. 2014. (ENG.). 160p. (J). (gr. 3-7). 12.99 *(978-1-907151-84-2(2))* O'Mara, Michael Bks., Ltd. GBR. Dist: Independent Pubs. Group.

Ryan, Nellie & Jackson, Lisa. The Girls' Summer Book. Bailey, Ellen. 2011. (ENG.). 96p. (J). (gr. 1-3). pap. 6.99 *(978-0-8431-9853-9(2))*, Price Stern Sloan) Penguin Publishing Group.

Ryan, Nellie, jt. illus. see Davies, Hannah.

Ryan, Paul, et al. Iron Man Epic Collection: War Games. 2014. (ENG.). 504p. (J). (gr. 4-17). pap. 39.99 *(978-0-7851-8550-5(X))* Marvel Worldwide, Inc.

—Squadron Supreme. 2013. (ENG.). 368p. (J). (gr. 4-17). pap. 34.99 *(978-0-7851-8469-0(4))* Marvel Worldwide, Inc.

Ryan, Rob. The Gift. Duffy, Carol Ann. 2009. 32p. (J). *(978-1-84686-354-7(6))* Barefoot Bks., Inc.

Ryan, Rob. The Gift. Ryan, Rob. Duffy, Carol Ann. 2010. (ENG.). 32p. (J). (gr. 3-18). 16.99 *(978-1-84686-355-4(4))* Barefoot Bks., Inc.

Ryan, Susannah. Coming to America. Maestro, Betsy. 2015. 40p. pap. 9.00 ***(978-1-61003-543-9(7))*** Center for the Collaborative Classroom.

Ryan, Victoria & Alley, R. W. When Your Pet Dies: A Healing Handbook for Kids. Ryan, Victoria. 2003. (Elf-Help Books for Kids). 32p. (J). per. 7.95 *(978-0-87029-376-4(1))* Abbey Pr.

Rycroft, Nina. Ballroom Bonanza: A Hidden Pictures ABC Book. Harris, Stephen. 2010. (ENG.). 40p. (J). (gr. -1-3). 16.95 *(978-0-8109-8842-2(9))*, Abrams Bks. for Young Readers) Abrams.

—Boom Bah! Cummings, Phil. 2010. (ENG.). 32p. (J). (gr. -1-3). 10.99 *(978-1-935279-22-8(X))* Kane Miller.

—No More Kisses. Wild, Margaret. 2012. (ENG.). 21p. (J). (gr. -1-k). pap. 9.99 *(978-1-921714-28-3(X))* Little Hare Bks. AUS. Dist: Independent Pubs. Group.

—No More Kisses! Wild, Margaret. 2011. (ENG.). 24p. (J). (gr. -1-k). 14.99 *(978-1-921541-52-0(0))* Little Hare Bks. AUS. Dist: Independent Pubs. Group.

Rydberg, Viktor. Our Fathers' Godsaga: Retold for the Young. Rydberg, Viktor. Reeves, William P. 2003. 223p. 25.95 *(978-0-595-66097-1(5))* iUniverse, Inc.

Ryder, Michael/Todd. Twins. 2012. 32p. (J). pap. 12.00 *(978-0-9847836-0-1(1))* Celtic Cat Publishing.

Rylant, Cynthia. Give Me Grace: A Child's Daybook of Prayers. Rylant, Cynthia. ed. 2005. (ENG.). 32p. (J). (gr. -1-k). 7.99 *(978-0-689-87885-5(0))*, Little Simon) Little Simon.

Ryley, David. Joshua/Rahab Flip-Over Book. Kovacs, Victoria. 2015. (Little Bible Heroes(tm) Ser.). (ENG.). 32p. (J). (gr. k-2). pap. 3.99 ***(978-1-4336-8716-7(X))***, B&H Kids) B&H Publishing Group.

S

Ryley, David, jt. illus. see Krome, Mike.

Rymer, Alta M. Stars of Obron: Chambo Returns. Rymer, Alta M. (Tales of Planet Artembo Ser.: Bk. 3). 56p. (Orig.). (J). (gr. 5-7). pap. 20.00 *(978-0-9600792-3-0(8))* Rymer Bks.

—Up from Uzam. Rymer, Alta M. (Tharma Lo Fairyland Ser.: Story 1). 28p. (Orig.). (J). (gr. 2-4). pap. 20.00 *(978-0-9600792-8-5(9))* Rymer Bks.

Ryniak, Christopher. The Word Eater. Amato, Mary. 2004. (ENG.). 151p. (J). (gr. 3-7). reprint ed. pap. 7.99 *(978-0-8234-1940-1(1))* Holiday Hse., Inc.

Ryser, Nicolas. The Championship! Richard, Laurent. Gauvin, Edward, tr. 2014. 64p. (J). (gr. 2-5). pap. 6.95 *(978-1-4677-4459-1(X))*; (Tao, the Little Samurai Ser.: 4). (ENG.). lib. bdg. 29.27 *(978-1-4677-2097-7(6))* Lerner Publishing Group. (Graphic Universe).

—Clowns & Dragons! Richard, Laurent. Gauvin, Edward, tr. from FRE. 2014. (Tao, the Little Samurai Ser.: 3). (ENG.). 56p. (J). (gr. 2-5). lib. bdg. 29.27 *(978-1-4677-2096-0(8)*, Graphic Universe) Lerner Publishing Group.

—Ninjas & Knock Outs! Richard, Laurent. Gauvin, Edward, tr. from FRE. 2014. (Tao, the Little Samurai Ser.: 2). (ENG.). 64p. (J). (gr. 2-5). lib. bdg. 29.27 *(978-1-4677-3272-7(9)*, Graphic Universe) Lerner Publishing Group.

—Pranks & Attacks! Richard, Laurent. Gauvin, Edward, tr. from FRE. 2014. (Tao, the Little Samurai Ser.: 1). (ENG.). 64p. (J). (gr. 2-5). lib. bdg. 29.27 *(978-1-4677-2095-3(X)*, Graphic Universe) Lerner Publishing Group.

—Wild Animals! Richard, Laurent. Gauvin, Edward, tr. from FRE. 2014. (Tao, the Little Samurai Ser.: 5). (ENG.). 64p. (J). (gr. 2-5). lib. bdg. 29.27 *(978-1-4677-2098-4(4)*, Graphic Universe) Lerner Publishing Group.

Ryskind, Sam. Los Santos Valientes de los Caballeros de Columbus. Drake, Tim. Alvarado, Tomas, tr. 2003.Tr. of Courageous Saints of the Knights of Columbus. (SPA.). (J). 5.00 *(978-0-9747571-1-7(X))* Catholic World Mission.

Rzasa, Jennifer, et al. Drawing Fun Fashions. Bolte, Mari. 2013. (Drawing Fun Fashions Ser.). (ENG.). 32p. (gr. 3-4). lib. bdg. 163.92 *(978-1-62065-040-0(1)*, Snap Bks.) Capstone Pr., Inc.

Rzasa, Jennifer. Skater Chic Style: Fun Fashions You Can Sketch, 1 vol. Bolte, Mari. 2013. (Drawing Fun Fashions Ser.). (ENG.). 32p. (gr. 3-4). lib. bdg. 27.32 *(978-1-62065-038-7(X)*, Snap Bks.) Capstone Pr., Inc.

S

S., Bijan, jt. illus. see Mukherjee, Aiswarya.

S. I. Artists Staff. Fisher Price Little People Curious Little Chicks. Mitter, Matt. 2012. (Lift-The-Flap Ser.: 1). (ENG.). 18p. (J). (gr. -1-k). bds. 12.99 *(978-0-7944-2567-8(4))* Reader's Digest Assn., Inc., The.

—Fisher-Price Little People Let's Go to School. Reader's Digest Staff & Tomaselli, Doris. 2009. (Lift-The-Flap Ser.). (ENG.). 10p. (J). (gr. -1-k). bds. 9.99 *(978-0-7944-1877-9(5))* Reader's Digest Assn., Inc., The.

—Fun & Games. 2003. 40p. (J). 3.95 *(978-0-9729026-1-8(9))* Midwest Cylinder Management, Inc.

—Fun & Games. 2003. (J). per. *(978-1-57657-854-4(2))* Paradise Pr., Inc.

Saaf, Donald. The ABC Animal Orchestra. Saaf, Donald. 2015. (ENG.). 40p. (J). (gr. -1 — 1). 16.99 *(978-0-8050-9072-7(X)*, Holt, Henry & Co. Bks. For Young Readers) Holt, Henry & Co.

Saavedra, Anthony. Justin's Very Own Drum. Cox, Steven. 2009. 24p. pap. 24.95 *(978-1-60749-553-6(8))* America Star Bks.

Sabado, Joe. Mommy Teach Us to Pray. Fujii, Jason, photos by. l.t. ed. 2006. 31p. (J). 15.95 *(978-1-59879-122-8(2))* Lifevest Publishing, Inc.

Sabaka, Donna. Seashells in My Pocket: AMC's Family Guide to Exploring the Coast from Maine to Florida. Hansen, Judith. 3rd ed. 2008. (ENG.). 160p. (gr. 3-7). per. 14.95 *(978-1-929173-61-7(X))* Appalachian Mountain Club Bks.

Sabanski, Helen. The Very Best Friend There Ever Could Be. Fedderesen, Jill. 2004. 8p. pap. 5.73 *(978-1-4116-0898-6(4))* Lulu Enterprises Inc.

Sabatini, Marie. Joseph's Hands. Sabatini, Kety. 2007. (ENG.). 36p. (J). per. 12.99 *(978-0-9792258-8-8(4))* Bezalel Bks.

Sabatino, Chris. The Imitation of Christ for Children: A Guide to Following Jesus. Ficocelli, Elizabeth. 2006. 49p. (J). (gr. 3-7). per. 9.95 *(978-0-8091-6733-3(6)*, 6733-6) Paulist Pr.

Sabbagh, Tatiana. Lebanon A to Z: A Middle Eastern Mosaic. Boutros, Jill et al. 2006. (ENG.). 40p. (J). (gr. -1-3). 25.00 *(978-0-9744803-4-3(7))* PublishingWorks.

Sabella, Elisa. Please Explain "Anxiety" to Me! Simple Biology & Solutions for Children & Parents. Zelinger, Laurie E. & Zelinger, Jordan. 2014. (J). pap. 15.95 *(978-1-61599-216-4(2))* Loving Healing Pr., Inc.

—Please Explain Anxiety to Me! Simple Biology & Solutions for Children & Parents. Zelinger, Laurie & Zelinger, Jordan. 2010. 38p. 32.95 *(978-1-61599-051-1(8))*; 40p. pap. 21.95 *(978-1-61599-029-0(1))* Loving Healing Pr., Inc.

Sabiston, Susan. The Bluff, 1. Gunther, Joseph. l.t. ed. 2006. 28p. (J). 14.95 *(978-0-9789525-0-1(2))* Young Readers Publications.

Sable, Katherine. Hello Goldy! Aryal, Aimee. 2004. 24p. (J). 19.95 *(978-0-9743442-4-9(9))* Mascot Bks., Inc.

Sabnani, Nina. The Boy Who Loved Colour. Shukla, Subir. 2004. (ENG & HIN.). (J). 8.50 *(978-81-8146-042-4(1))* Tulika Pubs.

—My Mother's Sari. Rao, Sandhya. 2009. (ENG.). 24p. (J). (gr. -1-3). 7.95 *(978-0-7358-2233-7(6))* North-South Bks., Inc.

Sabol, Elizabeth. Day Is Done: A Lullaby. l.t. ed. 2004. 26p. (J). pap. incl. audio compact disk *(978-0-9747382-0-8(4))* LeDor Publishing.

Sabuda, Robert. Chanukah Lights. Rosen, Michael J. 2011. (ENG.). 16p. (J). (gr. k-4). 34.99 *(978-0-7636-5533-4(3))* Candlewick Pr.

—I Hear America Singing. Whitman, Walt. 2004. 30p. (J). (gr. k-4). reprint ed. 15.00 *(978-0-7567-8097-5(7))* DIANE Publishing Co.

—Peter Pan: A Pop-Up Adaptation of J. M. Barrie's Original Tale. 2008. (ENG.). 16p. (J). 29.99 *(978-0-689-85364-7(5)*, Little Simon) Little Simon.

Sabuda, Robert. America the Beautiful. Sabuda, Robert. 2004. (ENG.). 12p. (J). (gr. -1-3). 35.00 *(978-0-689-84744-8(0)*, Little Simon) Little Simon.

—Beauty & the Beast: A Pop-Up Adaptation of the Classic Tale. Sabuda, Robert. 2010. (ENG.). 12p. (J). (gr. -1-2). 29.99 *(978-1-4169-6079-9(1)*, Little Simon) Little Simon.

—The Little Mermaid. Sabuda, Robert. 2013. (ENG.). 12p. (J). (gr. 1). 29.99 *(978-1-4169-6080-5(5))*; 250.00 *(978-1-4424-5086-8(X))* Little Simon. (Little Simon).

—Uh-Oh, Leonardo! The Adventures of Providence Traveler. Sabuda, Robert. 2007. (ENG.). 48p. (J). (gr. k-3). 12.99 *(978-1-4169-6164-2(X)*, Simon & Schuster/Paula Wiseman Bks.) Simon & Schuster/Paula Wiseman Bks.

—Winter in White: A Mini Pop-Up Treat. Sabuda, Robert. 2007. (ENG.). 18p. (J). (gr. -1-3). 17.99 *(978-0-689-85365-4(3)*, Little Simon) Little Simon.

—The 12 Days of Christmas. Sabuda, Robert. 10th anniv. ed. 2006. (ENG.). 14p. (J). (gr. -1-3). 34.99 *(978-1-4169-2792-1(1)*, Little Simon) Little Simon.

Sabuda, Robert & Reinhart, Matthew. Encyclopedia Prehistorica Mega-Beasts. Sabuda, Robert & Reinhart, Matthew. ed. 2007. (Encyclopedia Prehistorica Ser.). (ENG.). 12p. (J). (gr. k-4). 250.00 *(978-0-7636-3204-5(X))* Candlewick Pr.

Sabuda, Robert, jt. illus. see Reinhart, Matthew.

Saccheri, Briana. The Secret to Easter Eggs. Saccheri, Josephine. 2008. 28p. pap. 24.95 *(978-1-60474-210-7(0))* America Star Bks.

Sacco, Joe. One Flew over the Cuckoo's Nest. Kesey, Ken. 2007. (Penguin Classics Deluxe Edition Ser.). (ENG.). 320p. (gr. 12-18). 17.00 *(978-0-14-310502-2(7)*, Penguin Classics) Penguin Publishing Group.

Sachs, Barry. Ghost Train to Freedom: An Adventure on the Underground Railroad. Reese Martin, Faith. 2012. (JMP Mystery Ser.: Bk. 3). (ENG.). 416p. (YA). pap. 14.99 *(978-1-60800-014-2(1)*, American Literary Publishing) LifeReloaded Specialty Publishing LLC.

Sachs, Bernard & Anderson, Murphy. Justice League of America, Vol. 3. Fox, Gardner et al. 2007. (Showcase Presents Ser.). (ENG.). 528p. (YA). (gr. 4). pap. 16.99 *(978-1-4012-1718-1(4))* DC Comics.

Sachse, Dina. My Body: 12 Lift-N-Learn Flashcards about the Human Body, 12 vols. 2013. (Early Start Singles Ser.). (ENG.). 12p. (J). *(978-1-77132-070-2(2))* SpiceBox Products Ltd.

—My Clothes: 12 Lift-N-Learn Flashcards about Clothes, 26 vols. 2013. (Early Start Singles Ser.). (ENG.). 12p. (J). *(978-1-77132-101-3(6))* SpiceBox Products Ltd.

—My Food: 12 Lift-N-Learn Flashcards about Food!, 26 vols. 2013. (Early Start Singles Ser.). (ENG.). 12p. (J). *(978-1-77132-102-0(4))* SpiceBox Products Ltd.

Sacui, Alexandru. Leni the Pug: The Comet Christmas Caper. Fiore, Keith M. 2006. 95p. per. 29.50 *(978-0-9785773-0-8(2))* Brownstone Monkey Productions, Inc.

Sada, Margarita. La Enfermedad del Beso. Ruiz, Maria Emilia Beyer. rev. ed. 2006. (Otra Escalera Ser.). (SPA & ENG.). 36p. (J). (gr. 5). pap. 9.95 *(978-968-5920-82-7(6))* Castillo, Ediciones, S. A. de C. V. MEX. Dist: Macmillan.

—Forajidos: Historia y Poesia en Siete Corridos Mexicanos. Flores, Enrique. 2006. (SPA & ENG.). 48p. (J). (gr. 4). pap. 10.95 *(978-968-5920-75-9(3))* Castillo, Ediciones, S. A. de C. V. MEX. Dist: Macmillan.

—Guacamole: A Cooking Poem, 1 vol. Argueta, Jorge & Amado, Elisa. 2012. (Bilingual Cooking Poems Ser.). (ENG & SPA.). 32p. (J). (gr. -1-2). 18.95 *(978-1-55498-133-5(6))* Groundwood Bks. CAN. Dist: Perseus-PGW.

—Oloyou. Cardenas, Teresa. Amado, Elisa, tr. from SPA. 2008. (ENG & SPA.). 32p. (J). (gr. -1-2). 18.95 *(978-0-88899-795-1(7))* Groundwood Bks. CAN. Dist: Perseus-PGW.

—Yo, Claudia. Arciniegas, Triunfo. rev. ed. 2006. (Castillo de la Lectura Preschool Ser.). (ENG.). 36p. (J). pap. 6.95 *(978-970-20-0845-3(X))* Castillo, Ediciones, S. A. de C. V. MEX. Dist: Macmillan.

Sada, Margarita, jt. illus. see Mateo, Rosario.

Sadamoto, Yoshiyuki. Neon Genesis Evangelion. Sadamoto, Yoshiyuki. (Neon Genesis Evangelion Ser.). (ENG.). 184p. 2nd ed. 2004. pap. 9.95 *(978-1-59116-400-5(1))*; Vol. 2. 2nd ed. 2004. pap. 9.95 *(978-1-59116-390-9(0))*; Vol. 3. 2nd ed. 2004. pap. 9.95 *(978-1-59116-401-2(X))*; Vol. 4. 2nd ed. 2004. pap. 9.95 *(978-1-59116-402-9(8))*; Vol. 5. 2nd ed. 2004. pap. 9.95 *(978-1-59116-403-6(6))*; Vol. 6. 2nd ed. 2004. pap. 9.95 *(978-1-59116-404-3(4))*; Vol. 7. 2nd ed. 2004. pap. 9.95 *(978-1-59116-405-0(2))*; Vol. 8. 2004. pap. 9.95 *(978-1-59116-415-9(X))*; Vol. 9. 2004. pap. 9.99 *(978-1-59116-707-5(8))*; Vol. 10. 2007. pap. 9.99 *(978-1-4215-1160-3(6))* Viz Media.

Sadeghian, Alireza. Everyone Prays: Celebrating Faith Around the World. York Lumbard, Alexis. 2014. (ENG.). 28p. (J). (gr. -1-3). 17.95 *(978-1-937786-19-9(6)*, Wisdom Tales) World Wisdom, Inc.

—The Knight, the Princess, & the Magic Rock: A Classic Persian Tale. 2012. (ENG.). 32p. (J). (gr. -1-3). 15.95 *(978-1-937786-01-4(3))* World Wisdom, Inc.

Sadig bai Afshar & Beg, Sadiqi. Two Crafty Jackals: The Animal Fables of Kalilah & Dimnah. Laird, Elizabeth. 2014. (ENG.). 64p. (J). 19.95 ***(978-0-9919928-1-2(4))*** Aga Khan Museum CAN. Dist: Ingram Pub. Services.

Sadler, Dale. More Than a Stove. Fussell, Bonnie. l.t. ed. 2004. 32p. (J). pap. 7.99 *(978-0-615-12702-6(9))* Blackberry Pubs.

Sadler, Sonia Lynn. MaDear's Old Green House. Patrick, Denise Lewis. 2004. 32p. (J). (gr. k-3). 16.95 *(978-0-940975-55-2(6)*, Sankofa Bks.) Just Us Bks., Inc.

—Seeds of Change. Johnson, Jen Cullerton. 2013. (ENG.). 40p. (J). (gr. 1-6). 18.95 *(978-1-60060-367-9(X))* Lee & Low Bks., Inc.

Sadowski, Jeff. Cherry Pie Charlie & More Poems for Children. Tully, Sandra M. 2007. (J). 15.00 *(978-1-933556-86-4(2))* Publishers' Graphics, L.L.C.

Sadowski, Stephen, jt. illus. see Bair, M.

Saenger, Stefanie. Grow Healthy Little One. 2007. 24p. (J). pap. 16.95 *(978-0-9796010-0-2(2))* Johnston, Ann.

Saez, Fernando. Don Quijote de la Mancha. de Cervantes, Miguel. 2010. (Grandes Libros Ser.). (SPA.). 260p. (J). (gr. k-2). 24.95 *(978-84-8426-596-2(X))* Susaeta Ediciones, S.A. ESP. Dist: Independent Pubs. Group.

Saez, Javier. Animalario Universal. Murugarren, Miguel. 2003. (Los Especials de A la Orilla Del Viento Ser.). (SPA.). 40p. (J). (gr. -1-3). 12.99 *(978-968-16-7048-1(5))* Fondo de Cultura Economica USA.

Saez, Sofia. Una Carta de Delke. De Matos, Isabel Freire. 2004. (SPA.). 32p. (gr. k-3). pap. 8.95 *(978-1-57581-573-2(7))* Santillana USA Publishing Co., Inc.

—Una Carta de Monica. De Matos, Isabel Freire. 2004. (SPA.). 32p. (gr. k-3). pap. 8.95 *(978-1-57581-574-9(5))* Santillana USA Publishing Co., Inc.

Safar, Lina. The Forgotten Ornament. Shein, Erik Daniel & Reker, Martin. 2010. (J). pap. 11.95 *(978-0-578-05938-9(X))* Ark Watch Holdings LLC.

—The Forgotten Ornament. Shein, Erik Daniel. Reker, Martin, ed. 2010. 32p. (J). pap. 16.95 *(978-0-9765358-2-9(3))* Ark Watch Holdings LLC.

—How Did I Get Here? Maillis, Nicole. 2011. 4p. (J). 7.95 *(978-1-60131-086-6(2))* Big Tent Bks.

—Pink Fire Trucks. Barberi, Gladys. 2013.Tr. of Los Camiones de Bomberos de Color Rosado. 30p. (J). 16.95 *(978-1-60131-145-0(1))* Big Tent Bks.

Safarewicz, Evie. World of Ballet. Tatchell, Judy. Miles, Lisa, ed. 2006. (Kid Kits Ser.). 64p. (J). (gr. 5). lib. bdg. 17.95 *(978-1-58086-514-2(3))* EDC Publishing.

Safarewicz, Evie & Smith, Guy. The World of Ballet: Internet-Linked. Tatchell, Judy. Miles, Lisa, ed. rev. ed. 2007. (World of Ballet Ser.). 64p. (J). (gr. 4-7). per. 9.99 *(978-0-7945-1060-2(4)*, Usborne) EDC Publishing.

Safran, Sheri. The Magic Carousel: A Book & Removable 3-D Play Carousel. Safran, Sheri. 2011. (ENG.). 6p. (J). (gr. -1-k). 24.99 *(978-1-85707-800-8(4))* Tango Bks. GBR. Dist: Independent Pubs. Group.

Saga-Whyte. Why the Naiads Dance: Book One of the Naiad Legends, 8 vols., Vol. 1. Saga-Whyte. 2007. 25p. (J). 18.20 *(978-90-8885-018-9(6))* Saga-Whyte Pr. NLD. Dist: AtlasBooks Distribution.

Sagasti, Miriam. The Leaves Are Falling One by One. Metzger, Steve. 2007. (J). *(978-0-439-02444-0(7))* Scholastic, Inc.

—Thank You, Ruth & Naomi. Lundy, Charlotte. Waldrep, Evelyn L., ed. 2004. 32p. (J). (gr. k-4). 15.95 *(978-0-9741817-0-7(6))* Bay Light Publishing.

—We Like Puddles. Kolodny, Cynthia. 2004. (ENG.). 12p. (gr. k-1). pap. 5.95 *(978-1-57874-040-6(1))* Kaeden Corp.

Sage, Molly. Christmas Fairy Cooking. Allman, Howard, photos by. Pratt, Leonie & Atkinson, Catherine. 2006. (Usborne Activities Ser.). (ENG.). 32p. (J). (gr. -1-3). pap. 8.99 *(978-0-7945-1118-0(X)*, Usborne) EDC Publishing.

—Things to Make & Do with Paper. Gulliver, Amanda & Turnbull, Stephanie. 2004. (Activity Books). 32p. (J). pap. 6.95 *(978-0-7945-0674-2(7)*, Usborne) EDC Publishing.

Sage, Molly. At the Beach. Sage, Molly. 2007. (ENG.). 6p. (J). (gr. k — 1). 6.99 *(978-1-85602-497-6(0))* Pavilion Bks. GBR. Dist: Independent Pubs. Group.

Sage, Molly & Larkum, Adam. Little Children's Cookbook. Allman, Howard, photos by. Gilpin, Rebecca. 2005. (ENG.). 96p. (J). (gr. 4-7). 7.95 *(978-0-7945-1113-5(9)*, Usborne) EDC Publishing.

Sage, Molly, jt. illus. see Cartwright, Stephen.

Sage, Trina. Sarah's Most Perfect Day. Krohn, Kathryn T. 2007. 24p. (J). 13.99 *(978-1-59879-325-3(X))*, Lifevest Lifevest Publishing, Inc.

Sager, Michelle. Detective Sniffer & the Mysterious Case of the Sphinx's Beard. Delaney, Lawrence. 2011. (ENG.). 86p. pap. 17.18 *(978-1-4611-0130-7(1))* CreateSpace Independent Publishing Platform.

Sah, Anup, photos by. The Tiger. Ledu-Frattini, Stephanie. Uhlig, Elizabeth, tr. from FRE. 2004. (Animal Close-Ups Ser.). 28p. (J). pap. 6.95 *(978-1-57091-373-0(0))* Charlesbridge Publishing, Inc.

Sahai, Supriya. We've Got Your Number. Patel, Mukul. 2013. (ENG.). 96p. (J). (gr. 5-8). 14.99 *(978-0-7534-7072-5(1)*, Kingfisher) Roaring Brook Pr.

Saichann, Alberto. A Dream for a Princess. Lagonegro, Melissa & RH Disney Staff. 2005. (Step into Reading Ser.). (ENG.). 32p. (J). (gr. k-3). pap. 3.99 *(978-0-7364-2340-3(0)*, RH/Disney) Random Hse. Children's Bks.

Saidens, Amy. Lovers' Massage: Soothing Touch for Two. Zeer, Darrin. 2006. (ENG.). 96p. (gr. 8-17). 9.95 *(978-0-8118-4944-9(9))* Chronicle Bks. LLC.

Saijyo, Shinji. Iron Wok Jan!, Vol. 12. Saijyo, Shinji. 2005. (Iron Wok Jan! Ser.). (ENG.). 200p. (YA). pap. 9.95 *(978-1-58899-303-8(5))* DrMaster Pubns. Inc.

Saikia, Mayur. Anansi & His Children. 2010. (J). *(978-1-60617-139-4(9))* Teaching Strategies, Inc.

Saillard, Remi. Funny Machines for George the Sheep: A Children's Book Inspired by Leonardo Da Vinci. 2014. (ENG.). 32p. 14.95 *(978-3-7913-7166-5(5))* Prestel Publishing.

Saincilus, Larimer. Rita & the Parrot. Jeune, Marie Carole. 2010. (HAT.). 32p. (J). pap. 16.95 *(978-1-60195-317-9(8))* International Step by Step Assn.

Sainsilus, Ismer. A Mango for Grandpa. Hudicourt, Caroline. 2007. 32p. (J). (ARA & ENG.). pap. 14.95 *(978-1-60195-085-7(3))*; (POL.). pap. 14.95 *(978-1-60195-093-2(4))* International Step by Step Assn.

Saint-James, Synthia. Dream a World: A Child's Journey to Self-Discovery Dreamer's Activity Kit. Hull, Bunny. 2004. 24p. (J). 16.95 incl. cd-rom *(978-0-9721478-3-5(7))* BrassHeart Music.

Saint James, Synthia. Enduring Wisdom: Sayings from American Indians. Sneve, Virginia Driving Hawk. 2003. (ENG.). 32p. (J). (gr. k-3). tchr. ed. 16.95 *(978-0-8234-1455-0(8))* Holiday Hse., Inc.

—Hallelujah! A Christmas Celebration. Nikola-lisa, W. & Nikola-lisa, W. 2009. (ENG.). 36p. (J). (gr. -1-3). 10.99 *(978-1-4424-0224-9(5)*, Atheneum Bks. for Young Readers) Simon & Schuster Children's Publishing.

Saint-James, Synthia. Happy, Happy Kwanzaa: Kwanzaa for the World. Hull, Bunny. 2003. 24p. (J). (gr. k-5). pap. 16.95 incl. audio compact disk *(978-0-9721478-1-1(0)*, KCC/HHKCD810, Kid's Creative Classics) BrassHeart Music.

Saint James, Synthia. No Mirrors in My Nana's House: Musical CD & Book. Barnwell, Ysaye M. 2005. (ENG.). 32p. (J). (gr. -1-3). reprint ed. 10.99 *(978-0-15-205243-0(7))* Houghton Mifflin Harcourt Publishing Co.

Saito, Chiho. Revolutionary Girl Utena: The Adolesence of Utena. Saito, Chiho. 2004. (Revolutionary Girl Utena Ser.). (ENG.). 192p. (YA). pap. 9.95 *(978-1-59116-500-2(8))* Viz Media.

—Revolutionary Girl Utena: To Till, Vol. 1. Saito, Chiho. 2nd ed. 2003. (Revolutionary Girl Utena Ser.: Vol. 1). (ENG.). 200p. (YA). pap. 9.95 *(978-1-56931-964-2(2))* Viz Media.

Saito, Ioe. The Adventure of Momotaro, the Peach Boy, 1 vol. McCarthy, Ralph F. 2013. (Kodansha Children's Bilingual Classics Ser.). (ENG.). 48p. 9.95 *(978-1-56836-528-2(4))* Kodansha America, Inc.

Saito, Kazu, photos by. Shiki O Wataru Kaze. Pace, Teruko, tr. 2003. (JPN.). (YA). pap. 20.00 *(978-0-9743474-0-0(X))* Zuiho.

Saito, Masamitsu. Beach Feet. Konagaya, Kiyomi. 2012. (Being in the World Ser.). (ENG.). 32p. (J). (gr. k-k). 14.95 *(978-1-59270-121-6(3))* Enchanted Lion Bks., LLC.

Saitou, Chiho. The World Exists for Me, Vol. 1. Be-Papas. 2005. 200p. per. 9.99 *(978-1-59816-034-5(6)*, Tokyopop Adult) TOKYOPOP, Inc.

Sakai, Komako. In the Meadow. Kato, Yukiko. 2011. (Being in the World Ser.). (ENG.). 32p. (J). (gr. k-k). 14.95 *(978-1-59270-108-7(6))* Enchanted Lion Bks., LLC.

—Wait! Wait! Nakawaki, Hatsue. 2013. (ENG.). 24p. (J). 14.95 *(978-1-59270-138-4(8))* Enchanted Lion Bks., LLC.

Sakai, Komako. Mad at Mommy. Sakai, Komako. 2010. (ENG.). 40p. (J). (gr. -1-3). 16.99 *(978-0-545-21209-0(X)*, Levine, Arthur A. Bks.) Scholastic, Inc.

Sakai, Stan. Usagi Yojimbo Saga Volume 3. Sakai, Stan. 2015. (ENG.). 616p. (J). pap. 24.99 *(978-1-61655-611-2(0))* Dark Horse Comics.

—Usagi Yojimbo Saga Volume 3 Ltd. Ed. Sakai, Stan. 2015. (ENG.). 618p. (J). 79.99 *(978-1-61655-673-0(0))* Dark Horse Comics.

Sakakura, Yoshinobu & Mitsui, Eiichi. A Treasury of Japanese Folktales. Yasuda, Yuri & Yasuda, Yuri Old tales of Japan. Matsunari, Yumi & Yamaguchi, Yumi, trs. ed. 2010. (ENG & JPN.). 112p. (J). (gr. k-8). 19.95 *(978-4-8053-1079-3(0))* Tuttle Publishing.

Sakamoto, Miki. The Boat Noah Built. Froeb, Lori C. 2014. (Pop & Play Ser.: 3). (ENG.). 10p. (J). (gr. -1-1). 12.99 *(978-0-7944-3156-3(9))* Reader's Digest Assn., Inc., The.

—Every Day's a Dog's Day: A Year in Poems. Singer, Marilyn. 2012. (ENG.). 32p. (J). (gr. -1-k). 16.99 *(978-0-8037-3715-0(7)*, Dial) Penguin Publishing Group.

—I Am McKinley, Level 2. Froeb, Lori. 2015. (Rescue Readers Ser.: 1). (ENG.). 32p. (J). (gr. k-3). lib. bdg. 16.99 *(978-0-7944-3349-9(9))*; (gr. 1-2). pap. 3.99 *(978-0-7944-3310-9(3))* Studio Fun International.

—I'm Like You, You're Like Me: A Book about Understanding & Appreciating Each Other. Gainer, Cindy. (ENG.). 48p. (J). (gr. -1-3). 2013. pap. 9.99 *(978-1-57542-436-1(3))*; 2011. 14.99 *(978-1-57542-383-8(9))* Free Spirit Publishing, Inc.

—My First Garden. Lewison, Wendy Cheyette. 2009. (Little Green Bks.). (ENG.). 16p. (J). (gr. -1-1). 6.99 *(978-1-4169-6767-5(2)*, Little Simon) Little Simon.

—We Go Together! Dunn, Todd. 2013. (ENG.). 22p. (J). (— 1). bds. 6.95 *(978-1-4549-0023-8(7))* Sterling Publishing Co., Inc.

—We're Going on a Leaf Hunt. Metzger, Steve. (J). 2008. (ENG.). 32p. (gr. -1-3). pap. 6.99 *(978-0-439-87377-2(0)*, Cartwheel Bks.); 2005. pap. *(978-0-439-77361-4(X))* Scholastic, Inc.

—What I Like about Me! Zobel-Nolan, Allia. 2009. (What I Like about Me Ser.). (ENG.). 14p. (J). (gr. -1-2). 6.99 *(978-0-7944-1945-5(3))* Reader's Digest Assn., Inc., The.

—What I Like about Me! Zobel-Nolan, Allia. 2005. (What I Like about Me Ser.). (ENG.). 16p. (J). (gr. k-3). tchr. ed., per. 19.99 *(978-0-7944-1016-2(2))* Reader's Digest Assn., Inc., The.

Saker, Linda. Nana Star. Sills, Elizabeth & Patrice, Elena. 32p. (J). (gr. -1-3). 2007. 15.95 *(978-0-9753843-5-0(X))*; 2004. 17.99 *(978-0-9753843-0-5(9))* ee publishing & productions, inc.

—Nana Star & the Moonman. Sills, Elizabeth & Patrice, Elena. 2008. 32p. (J). (gr. -1-3). 15.95 *(978-0-9753843-6-7(8))* ee publishing & productions, inc.

Sakevich, C. J. Sister-Brother Adoption Day: Updated Edition. Sakevich, Linda & C. J. 2010. (ENG.). 32p. pap. 11.95 *(978-1-4505-4432-0(0))* CreateSpace Independent Publishing Platform.

—Sister-Sister Adoption Day: Updated Edition. Sakevich, Linda & C. J. 2010. (ENG.). 32p. pap. 11.95 *(978-1-4505-4425-2(8))* CreateSpace Independent Publishing Platform.

Sakhavarz, Nazy. Orff Explorations: Classroom Projects in Music, Movement & Poetry. Brass, Alice. 2010. (ENG.). 80p. spiral bd. 20.00 *(978-1-896941-34-9(6))* Brass, Robin Studio, Inc. CAN. Dist: Midpoint Trade Bks., Inc.

Sakkai, Yohei. Dinosaur King. Sakkai, Yohei. 2010. (Dinosaur King Ser.: 1). (ENG.). 192p. (J). Vol. 1. (gr. 3-6). pap. 7.99 *(978-1-4215-3253-0(0))*; Vol. 2. pap. 7.99 *(978-1-4215-3254-7(9))* Viz Media.

Sakmar-Sullivan, Eva M. Kangaroo's Out of This World Restaurant, 1 vol. Sakmar-Sullivan, Eva M. 2013. (ENG.). 32p. (J). 14.99 *(978-0-7643-4519-7(2))* Schiffer Publishing, Ltd.

Sakprayoonpong, Worachet Boon. Innovators in Action! Leonardo Da Vinci Gets a Do-Over. Friedlander, Mark P., Jr. 2014. (Innovators in Action Ser.: 1). (ENG.). 208p. (J). (gr. 5-9). pap. 12.95 *(978-0-9678020-6-0(7))* Science, Naturally!.

Sakura, Ken-Ichi. Dragon Drive, Volume 5. Sakura, Ken-Ichi. 2007. (Dragon Drive Ser.). 17.55 *(978-1-4177-9904-6(8),* Turtleback) Turtleback Bks.

Sakuragi, Yukiya. Inubaka - Crazy for Dogs Vol. 1. Sakuragi, Yukiya. 2007. (Inubaka: Crazy for Dogs Ser.). (ENG.). 208p. pap. 9.99 *(978-1-4215-1149-8(5))* Viz Media.

Sakurakoji, Kanoko. Black Bird. Sakurakoji, Kanoko. 2010. (Black Bird Ser.: 4). (ENG.). 200p. pap. 9.99 *(978-1-4215-2767-3(7))*; pap. 9.99 *(978-1-4215-2766-6(9))* Viz Media.

Sala, Richard. Cat Burglar Black. Sala, Richard. 2009. (ENG.). 128p. (J). (gr. 6-9). pap. 16.99 *(978-1-59643-144-7(X),* First Second Bks.) Roaring Brook Pr.

Salamunic, Tim, et al. Who Was Andy Warhol? Anderson, Kirsten. 2014. (Who Was...? Ser.). (ENG.). 112p. (J). (gr. 3-7). 4.99 *(978-0-448-48242-2(8),* Grosset & Dunlap) Penguin Publishing Group.

Salan, Felipe Lopez. Jack & the Beanstalk. 2006. (ENG.). 32p. (J). (gr. -1). 15.95 *(978-1-933327-11-2(1))* Purple Bear Bks., Inc.

Salanitro, Robert. Pizza Friday. Benhamu, Margaret. 2009. (Slide-Out Book Ser.). 9p. (J). 7.99 *(978-1-60436-025-7(9))* Educational Publishing LLC.

—A Surprise in the Mail! Rosenberg, Amye. 2009. (Discovery Ser.). (ENG.). 12p. (J). 7.99 *(978-1-60436-018-9(6))* Educational Publishing LLC.

Salariya, David & Scrace, Carolyn. The X-Ray Picture Book of Incredible Creatures. Legg, Gerald. 2004. 48p. (J). (gr. 4-8). pap. 9.00 *(978-0-7567-7406-6(3))* DIANE Publishing Co.

Salazar, Riana. Pink Hat's Adventure with Kites. Roller, John, photos by. Roller, Pat Kellogg. 2009. 36p. pap. 10.95 *(978-1-59858-957-3(1))* Dog Ear Publishing, LLC.

Salazar, Souther. Destined for Dizzyness. Salazar, Souther. 2005. 48p. pap. 5.95 *(978-0-9766848-1-7(0))* Buenaventura Pr.

Salazar, Vivian. Santa Revisits His Secret Little Helper. Bass, William E. 2012. 26p. 24.95 *(978-1-4626-5396-6(0))* America Star Bks.

Salazar, Vivian Rose. A Gift for Sant. Bass, William E. 2012. 36p. pap. 24.95 *(978-1-4626-6731-4(7))* America Star Bks.

Sale, Graham. What Is Right? Bortzer, Etan. l.t. ed. 2005. (What Is? Ser.). 40p. (J). (gr. k-5). pap. 6.95 *(978-0-9762743-0-8(2))*; *(978-0-9762743-1-5(0))* Lane, Veronica Bks.

Sale, Tim. Blue. Loeb, Jeph. 2003. (Spider-Man Ser.). 160p. (YA). 21.99 *(978-0-7851-1062-0(3))* Marvel Worldwide, Inc.

—Yellow. Loeb, Jeph. 2011. (ENG.). 168p. (YA). (gr. 8-17). pap. 19.99 *(978-0-7851-0969-3(2))* Marvel Worldwide, Inc.

Salem, Iosi. The Great Friday Clean-up (French Flap) Fridman, Sashi. 2009. 32p. 12.95 *(978-1-934440-77-3(9),* Pitspopany Pr.) Simcha Media Group.

—The Great Friday Clean-up (Hard Cover) Fridman, Sashi. 2009. 32p. 17.95 *(978-1-934440-93-3(0),* Pitspopany Pr.) Simcha Media Group.

—The Mr. Mentch Coloring Book. 2008. (J). (gr. -1-3). 6.95 *(978-1-934440-37-7(X),* Pitspopany Pr.) Simcha Media Group.

Salenas, Bobbi. Cinderella Latina - Cinicienta Latina. Salenas, Bobbi. La Madrid, Enriquee, tr. 2003. (SPA.). (YA). (gr. 3-12). 19.95 *(978-0-934925-06-8(2))* Pinata Pubns.

Salerno, John. I've Got Mail! Messinger, Robert. 2003. 40p. (J). 12.95 *(978-1-893237-01-8(X))* Little Mai Pr.

Salerno, Steven. Bebé Goes Shopping. Elya, Susan Middleton. 2008. (ENG.). 36p. (J). (gr. -1-3). pap. 6.99 *(978-0-15-206142-5(8))* Houghton Mifflin Harcourt Publishing Co.

—Brothers at Bat: The True Story of an Amazing All-Brother Baseball Team. Vernick, Audrey. 2012. (ENG.). 40p. (J). (gr. -1-3). 17.99 *(978-0-547-38557-0(9))* Houghton Mifflin Harcourt Publishing Co.

—Counting Our Way to the 100th Day! Franco, Betsy. 2004. (ENG.). 48p. (J). (gr. -1-3). 17.99 *(978-0-689-84793-6(9),* McElderry, Margaret K. Bks.) McElderry, Margaret K. Bks.

—The Dirty Little Boy, 1 vol. Brown, Margaret Wise. 2005. (ENG.). 32p. (J). (gr. -1-1). pap. 5.95 *(978-0-7614-5180-8(3))* Marshall Cavendish Corp.

—Mrs. Wow Never Wanted a Cow. Freeman, Martha. 2006. (Beginner Books(R) Ser.). (ENG.). 48p. (J). (gr. -1-2). 8.99 *(978-0-375-83418-9(4),* Random Hse. Bks. for Young Readers) Random Hse. Children's Bks.

Salerno, Steven. Wild Child. 2015. (ENG.). 32p. (J). (gr. -1-3). 16.95 ***(978-1-4197-1662-1(X),*** Abrams Bks. for Young Readers) Abrams.

Salerno, Steven. Go-Go Baby!, 1 vol. Salerno, Steven, tr. Orgill, Roxane & Orgill. 2004. (ENG.). 32p. (J). 14.95 *(978-0-7614-5157-0(9))* Marshall Cavendish Corp.

Sales, Jordi. No, No y No. García, César Fernández. 2007. (Primeros Lectores Ser.). (ENG.). 48p. (J). (gr. k-2). pap. 7.95 *(978-84-8343-008-8(8),* Bambu, Editorial) Combel Editorial, S.A. ESP. Dist: Independent Pubs. Group.

Salesse, Alain. Kung Fu Panda 3-D Puzzle Book. Chihak, Sheena. 2008. 10p. (J). 9.99 *(978-0-696-23485-9(8))* Meredith Bks.

Salg, Bert. Andy Blake's Comet Coaster. Edwards, Leo. 2011. 274p. 47.95 *(978-1-258-06587-4(8))* Literary Licensing, LLC.

—Bill Darrow's Victory. Heyliger, William. 2011. 202p. 44.95 *(978-1-258-07262-9(9))* Literary Licensing, LLC.

—Jerry Hicks, Explorer. Heyliger, William. 2011. 210p. 44.95 *(978-1-258-08964-1(5))* Literary Licensing, LLC.

—Jerry Hicks, Ghost Hunter. Heyliger, William. 2011. 210p. 44.95 *(978-1-258-08870-5(3))* Literary Licensing, LLC.

—The Lonesome Swamp Mystery: A Hal Keen Mystery Story. Lloyd, Hugh. 2011. 278p. 47.95 *(978-1-258-10174-9(2))* Literary Licensing, LLC.

—The Lost Mine of the Amazon. Lloyd, Hugh. 2011. 232p. 46.95 *(978-1-258-10175-6(0))* Literary Licensing, LLC.

—Poppy Ott Hits the Trail. Edwards, Leo. 2011. 218p. 44.95 *(978-1-258-10146-6(7))* Literary Licensing, LLC.

Salinas, Alex. James' Night of Terror. Martin, Bob. 2010. 120p. (gr. 4-6). 20.95 *(978-1-4502-6500-3(6))*; pap. 10.95 *(978-1-4502-6498-3(0))* iUniverse, Inc.

Salmaso, Valentina. Goldilocks & the Three Bears, 1 vol. Piumini, Roberto. 2009. (Storybook Classics Ser.). (ENG.). 32p. (gr. 3-4). lib. bdg. 25.32 *(978-1-4048-5499-4(1),* Fiction Picture Bks.) Picture Window Bks.

Salmeron Lopez, Rafael, jt. illus. see Salmeron, Rafael.

Salmeron, Rafael. El Cernicalo Porque. Narváez, Concha López & Concha, López Narváez. (Pajaros de Cuento Coleccion). (SPA.). 84p. (YA). (gr. 5-8). *(978-84-241-7927-4(7))* Everest Editora ESP. Dist: Lectorum Pubns., Inc.

Salmeron, Rafael & Salmeron Lopez, Rafael. De la A A la Z con Mozart y la Musica. Cruz-Contarini, Rafael & Rafael, Cruz-Contarini. 2005. (Montana Encantada Ser.). (SPA.). 36p. (J). (gr. 1-3). pap., pap. 8.50 incl. audio compact disk *(978-84-241-1697-2(6))* Everest Editora ESP. Dist: Lectorum Pubns., Inc.

Salmieri, Daniel. Big Bad Bubble. Rubin, Adam. 2014. (ENG.). 40p. (J). (gr. -1-3). 16.99 *(978-0-544-04549-1(1))* Houghton Mifflin Harcourt Publishing Co.

—Dragons Love Tacos. Rubin, Adam. 2012. (ENG.). 40p. (J). (gr. -1-2). 16.99 *(978-0-8037-3680-1(0),* Dial) Penguin Publishing Group.

—Meet the Dullards. Pennypacker, Sara. 2015. (ENG.). 32p. (J). (gr. -1-3). 17.99 *(978-0-06-219856-3(4))* HarperCollins Pubs.

—Secret Pizza Party. Rubin, Adam. 2013. (ENG.). 40p. (J). (gr. -1-2). 16.99 *(978-0-8037-3947-5(8),* Dial) Penguin Publishing Group.

—Those Darn Squirrels! Rubin, Adam. (ENG.). 32p. (J). (gr. -1-3). 2011. pap. 6.99 *(978-0-547-57681-7(1))*; 2008. 17.99 *(978-0-547-00703-8(5))* Houghton Mifflin Harcourt Publishing Co.

—Those Darn Squirrels & the Cat Next Door. Rubin, Adam. 2011. (ENG.). 32p. (J). (gr. -1-3). 17.99 *(978-0-547-42922-9(3))* Houghton Mifflin Harcourt Publishing Co.

—Those Darn Squirrels Fly South. Rubin, Adam. 2012. (ENG.). 32p. (J). (gr. -1-3). 17.99 *(978-0-547-67823-8(1))* Houghton Mifflin Harcourt Publishing Co.

Salom, Ivette. When the Anger Ogre Visits. Salom, Andree. 2015. (ENG.). 40p. (J). 18.95 *(978-1-61429-166-4(7))* Wisdom Pubns.

Salopek, Kirk. I Can Be: A Child's Whimsical Introduction to Yoga. Sumner, Christine. 2008. 32p. (J). 8.95 *(978-0-615-16566-0(4))* Q & J Bird Pr., LLC.

Salter, Safaya. Aesop's Fables. Handford, S. A. 2003. (Chrysalis Childrens Classics Ser.). 111p. (YA). pap. *(978-1-84365-035-5(5),* Pavilion Children's Books) Pavilion Bks.

—Just So Stories Set: For Little Children. Kipling, Rudyard. 2003. (Chrysalis Childrens Classics Ser.). 125p. (YA). pap. *(978-1-84365-036-2(3),* Pavilion Children's Books) Pavilion Bks.

Saltzberg, Barney. All Around the Seasons. Saltzberg, Barney. 2010. (ENG.). 32p. (J). (gr. -1-k). 11.99 *(978-0-7636-3694-4(0))* Candlewick Pr.

—Chengdu Could Not, Would Not, Fall Asleep. Saltzberg, Barney. 2014. (Chengdu Ser.). (ENG.). 48p. (J). (gr. -1-k). 16.99 *(978-1-4231-6721-1(X))* Hyperion Bks. for Children.

—Cornelius P. Mud, Are You Ready for Baby? Saltzberg, Barney. 2009. (ENG.). 32p. (J). (gr. -1-k). 15.99 *(978-0-7636-3596-1(0))* Candlewick Pr.

—Crazy Hair Day. Saltzberg, Barney. 2008. (ENG.). 32p. (J). (gr. k-3). pap. 6.99 *(978-0-7636-2464-4(0))* Candlewick Pr.

—Crazy Hair Day. Saltzberg, Barney. 2011. (J). (gr. k-3). 29.95 *(978-0-545-13450-7(1))* Weston Woods Studios, Inc.

—Crazy Hair Day Big Book. Saltzberg, Barney. 2008. (ENG.). 32p. (J). (gr. k-3). pap. 24.99 *(978-0-7636-3969-3(9))* Candlewick Pr.

—Star of the Week. Saltzberg, Barney. 2010. (ENG.). 32p. (J). (gr. k-3). pap. 6.99 *(978-0-7636-3076-8(4))* Candlewick Pr.

—Tea with Grandpa. Saltzberg, Barney. 2014. (ENG.). 40p. (J). (gr. -1-2). 15.99 *(978-1-59643-894-1(0))* Roaring Brook Pr.

Salus, Diane. Understanding Katie: A Day in the Life Of. Do, Elisa Shipon-Blum. 2003. 28p. (J). (gr. -1-18). pap. *(978-0-9714800-3-2(6))* Selective Mutism Anxiety Research & Treatment Ctr.

Salvador, Martin. George Washington. Leighton, Marian. 2005. (Heroes of America Ser.). 239p. (gr. 3-8). 27.07 *(978-1-59679-262-3(0),* Abdo & Daughters) ABDO Publishing Co.

Salvas, Jay Peter. Gentlemen, Start Your Ovens: Killer Recipes for Guys. Beisch, Leigh, photos by. Shaw, Tucker. 2007. (ENG.). 192p. (gr. 8-17). pap. 16.95 *(978-0-8118-5206-7(7))* Chronicle Bks. LLC.

Salvatus III, Mark Ramsel N., jt. illus. see Salvatus, Mark.

Salvatus, Mark & Salvatus III, Mark Ramsel N. Pan de Sal Saves the Day: A Filipino Children's Story. Olizon-Chikiamco, Norma et al. 2009. (ENG.). 24p. (J). (gr. k-3). 12.95 *(978-0-8048-4078-1(4))* Tuttle Publishing.

Salvucci, Richard J. Construction Vehicles. Joachim, Jean C. 2006. (Dot-to-Dot Ser.). (ENG.). 80p. (J). (gr. 1-4). per. 5.95 *(978-1-4027-1276-0(6))* Sterling Publishing Co., Inc.

Salyer, Adam Ernest. My Shadow. Salyer, Jennifer Marie. 2011. 32p. pap. *(978-1-77067-642-8(2))* FriesenPress.

Salzberg, Helen. What Is an Angel? Falzon, Adrienne. 2012. 32p. 18.99 *(978-0-9855562-2-8(6))* Blue Note Pubns.

Sam, Ackerman. Language Quest Spanish B Blue. 2nd ed. 2008. (SPA & ENG.). (J). pap. *(978-0-9744691-1-9(4))* Language Quest Corp.

Sam, Hundley. There Goes a Mermaid - A NorFolktale. Suhay, Lisa. 2004. 32p. (J). pap. 7.95 *(978-0-9648308-2-0(5))* Virginian Pilot.

Sam, Joe. The Invisible Hunters (Los Cazadores Invisibles) (YA). (gr. 1-18). 25.95 incl. audio *(978-0-89239-036-6(0))* Lee & Low Bks., Inc.

Sam, Kagan. Mr. Duz Goes to the Doctor. Patrick, Wellman. 2007. 24p. (J). 5.95 *(978-0-9796226-6-3(2))* MrDuz.com.

—Mr. Duz Solves a Mystery. 2007. 24p. (J). 5.95 *(978-0-9796226-0-1(3))* MrDuz.com.

—Mr. Duz Trick or Treat. Patrick, Wellman. 2007. 24p. (J). 5.95 *(978-0-9796226-4-9(6))* MrDuz.com.

Samantha May Cerney. The Three Little Green Pigs, Llc: A Recycling Pig Tale. Oldenburg, Richard. 2013. 28p. 23.50 *(978-1-62516-753-8(9),* Strategic Bk. Publishing) Strategic Book Publishing & Rights Agency (SBPRA).

Samantha Nowak. Adam B Brave. Jessica Hoel. 2009. 20p. pap. 12.49 *(978-1-4389-3240-8(5))* AuthorHouse.

Sami. Bear in Underwear - Color & Draw. Doodler, Todd H. 2013. (ENG.). 72p. (J). (gr. -1-3). act. bk. ed. 7.99 *(978-1-60905-397-0(4))* Blue Apple Bks.

—Colors - Shapes. 2013. (ENG.). 20p. (J). (gr. -1-2). 12.99 *(978-1-60905-227-0(7))* Blue Apple Bks.

—Yum! 2013. (ENG.). 16p. (J). (— 1). bds. 6.99 *(978-1-60905-337-6(0))* Blue Apple Bks.

SAMI Staff. The Big, Bigger, Biggest Book. 2008. (ENG.). 24p. (J). (gr. k-k). 14.95 *(978-1-934706-39-8(6))* Blue Apple Bks.

Samol, Nanette & Prosofsky, Merle, photos by. The British Columbia Seasonal Cookbook: History, Folklore & Recipes with a Twist. Ogle, Jennifer et al. rev. ed. 2007. (ENG.). 160p. pap. *(978-1-55105-584-8(8))* Lone Pine Publishing.

Sampar. Did You Know? Crocodiles!, 1 vol. Bergeron, Alain M. & Quintin, Michel. 2013. (ENG.). 64p. (J). *(978-1-55455-304-4(0))* Fitzhenry & Whiteside, Ltd.

—Did You Know? Spiders!, 1 vol. Bergeron, Alain M. & Quintin, Michel. 2013. (ENG.). 64p. (J). *(978-1-55455-302-0(4))* Fitzhenry & Whiteside, Ltd.

—Did You Know? Toads!, 1 vol. Bergeron, Alain M. & Quintin, Michel. 2013. (ENG.). 64p. (J). *(978-1-55455-303-7(2))* Fitzhenry & Whiteside, Ltd.

—Did You Know Chameleons?, 1 vol. Bergeron, Alain M. & Quintin, Michel. 2013. (ENG.). 64p. (J). *(978-1-55455-299-3(0))* Fitzhenry & Whiteside, Ltd.

—Do You Know Crows?, 1 vol. Bergeron, Alain M. & Quintin, Michel. 2014. (ENG.). 64p. (J). pap. *(978-1-55455-320-4(2))* Fitzhenry & Whiteside, Ltd.

—Do You Know Dinosaurs?, 1 vol. Bergeron, Alain M. 2014. (Do You Know? Ser.). (ENG.). 64p. (J). pap. 9.95 *(978-1-55455-336-5(9))* Fitzhenry & Whiteside, Ltd. CAN. Dist: Midpoint Trade Bks., Inc.

—Do You Know Hyenas?, 1 vol. Bergeron, Alain M. 2014. (Do You Know? Ser.). (ENG.). 64p. (J). pap. 9.95 *(978-1-55455-338-9(5))* Fitzhenry & Whiteside, Ltd. CAN. Dist: Midpoint Trade Bks., Inc.

—Do You Know Komodo Dragons?, 1 vol. Bergeron, Alain M. 2014. (Do You Know? Ser.). (ENG.). 64p. (J). pap. 9.95 *(978-1-55455-339-6(3))* Fitzhenry & Whiteside, Ltd. CAN. Dist: Midpoint Trade Bks., Inc.

—Do You Know Leeches?, 1 vol. Bergeron, Alain M. & Quintin, Michel. 2014. (ENG.). 64p. (J). pap. *(978-1-55455-318-1(0))* Fitzhenry & Whiteside, Ltd.

—Do You Know Porcupines?, 1 vol. Bergeron, Alain M. & Quintin, Michel. 2014. (ENG.). 64p. (J). pap. *(978-1-55455-321-1(0))* Fitzhenry & Whiteside, Ltd.

—Do You Know Praying Mantises?, 1 vol. Bergeron, Alain M. 2014. (Do You Know? Ser.). (ENG.). 64p. (J). pap. 9.95 *(978-1-55455-337-2(7))* Fitzhenry & Whiteside, Ltd. CAN. Dist: Midpoint Trade Bks., Inc.

—Do You Know Rats?, 1 vol. Bergeron, Alain M. & Quintin, Michel. 2014. (ENG.). 64p. (J). pap. *(978-1-55455-319-8(9))* Fitzhenry & Whiteside, Ltd.

—Do You Know Rhinoceros?, 1 vol. Quintin, Michel et al. Messier, Solange, tr. from FRE. 2015. (Do You Know? Ser.). (ENG.). 64p. (J). pap. 9.95 *(978-1-55455-354-9(7))* Fitzhenry & Whiteside, Ltd. CAN. Dist: Midpoint Trade Bks., Inc.

—Do You Know Tigers?, 1 vol. Quintin, Michel & Bergeron, Alain. Messier, Solange, tr. from FRE. 2015. (Do You Know? Ser.). (ENG.). 64p. (J). pap. 9.95 *(978-1-55455-355-6(5))* Fitzhenry & Whiteside, Ltd. CAN. Dist: Midpoint Trade Bks., Inc.

Sample, Matthew & Sample, Matthew. Grandma's Moving In! Cone, Stephanie M. 2013. (Learning to Care Ser.). (ENG.). (J). 18.00 *(978-1-937460-68-6(1))* Vision Forum, Inc., The.

Sample, Matthew, jt. illus. see Sample, Matthew.

Sample, Matthew II. God's Great Plan. Cutrera, Melissa. 2013. 28p. (J). *(978-1-936908-81-3(6))*; *(978-1-936908-83-7(2))*; *(978-1-936908-82-0(4))* Shepherd Pr. Inc.

Sampson, Ajpril. Margarita y la Mariposa. Sampson, Ajpril. 2006. (SPA.). (J). 7.95 *(978-0-9774822-5-2(1))* Crosam Pr.

Sampson, April. Hallo, Mallo & Pallo: The Ostracized Ostrich Family. Stockton, Lucille. ed. 2005. 31p. (J). 19.95 *(978-1-59408-511-6(0))* Cork Hill Pr.

Sampson, Jody. Abby. Russo, Anthony. 2003. 18p. (J). 7.95 *(978-1-59466-006-1(9),* Little Ones) Port Town Publishing.

—Tony the Pony. Kelly, Theresa. l.t. ed. 2003. 12p. (J). 5.95 *(978-1-59466-003-0(4))* Port Town Publishing.

—Tony the Pony: Bugs Are Not Bad. Kelly, Theresa. 2005. (J). per. 7.95 *(978-1-59466-030-6(1))* Port Town Publishing.

Sampson, Kathleen. Penelope's Piggies. Abbruzzi, Danielle. 2012. 42p. 24.95 *(978-1-4626-6264-7(1))* America Star Bks.

Sams, B. B. All about the ABC's. Gaydos, Nora. 2006. (ENG.). 112p. (J). (gr. -1-1). 16.99 *(978-1-58476-410-6(4),* IKIDS) Innovative Kids.

—Look Around! Gaydos, Nora. 2003. (NIR! Leveled Readers Ser.). (ENG.). 128p. (J). (gr. -1-2). 16.99 *(978-1-58476-167-9(9))* Random Hse. Children's Bks.

—Now I'm Reading! - My World. Gaydos, Nora. 2004. (NIR! Leveled Readers Ser.). (ENG.). 128p. (J). (gr. -1-2). 16.99 *(978-1-58476-263-8(2))* Random Hse. Children's Bks.

—Playful Pals, Level 1. Gaydos, Nora. 2003. (Now I'm Reading!). 128p. (J). (gr. -1-2). 14.99 *(978-1-58476-243-0(8))* Innovative Kids.

—Playful Pals. Gaydos, Nora. 2003. (NIR! Leveled Readers Ser.). (ENG.). 128p. (J). (gr. -1-3). 16.99 *(978-1-58476-203-4(9))* Random Hse. Children's Bks.

—Snack Attack, Level 2. Gaydos, Nora. 2004. (NIR! Leveled Readers Ser.). (ENG.). 128p. (J). (gr. -1-3). 16.99 *(978-1-58476-264-5(0))* Random Hse. Children's Bks.

Sams, Carl R., II & Stoick, Jean, photos by. Happy Bird Day! Sams, Carl R., II & Stoick, Jean. 2012. (ENG., 14p. (J). bds. 7.95 *(978-0-9827625-2-3(6))* Sams, II, Carl R. Photography, Inc.

—Lost in the Woods: A Photographic Fantasy. 2004. (ENG., 48p. (J). 19.95 *(978-0-9671748-8-4(0))* Sams, II, Carl R. Photography, Inc.

Sams, Carl R., 2nd & Stoick, Jean, photos by. One Child, One Planet: Inspiration for the Young Conservationist. Llewellyn, Bridget McGovern. 2009. 48p. (J). 19.95 *(978-0-9841880-0-0(2))* Emerald Shamrock Pr. LLC.

Sams, Carl R., II & Stoick, Jean, photos by. Winter Friends. Sams, Carl R., II & Stoick, Jean. McDiarmid, Karen, ed. 2003. (ENG., 14p.). (J). bds. 7.95 *(978-0-9671748-5-3(6))* Sams, II, Carl R. Photography, Inc.

Sams, Carl R., II, jt. photos by see Stoick, Jean.

Sams II, Carl R. & Stoick, Jean, photos by. When Snowflakes Fall. 2009. (ENG., 14p. bds. 7.95 *(978-0-9770108-9-9(9))* Sams, II, Carl R. Photography, Inc.

Sams II, Carl R., jt. photos by see Stoick, Jean.

Samuel, Dot. The Tale of Jacob's Journey. Woodruff, Ellen Larkin. 2012. 36p. pap. 9.99 *(978-1-935354-66-6(3))* Amethyst Moon Publishing and Services.

Samuel, Janet. Bible Prayers for Teddy & Me. Goodings, Christina. ed. 2014. (ENG.). 64p. (J). (gr. -1-k). 12.99 *(978-0-7459-6452-2(4))* Lion Hudson PLC GBR. Dist: Independent Pubs. Group.

Samuel, Janet. Guess Who's at the Zoo. Mumme, Sarah. 2015. (Guess Who's... Bks.). (ENG.). 10p. (J). (gr. -1 — 1). 5.99 ***(978-0-7641-6801-7(0))*** Barron's Educational Series, Inc.

—Guess Who's My Pet. Mumme, Sarah. 2015. (Guess Who's... Bks.). (ENG.). 10p. (J). (gr. -1 — 1). 5.99 ***(978-0-7641-6800-0(2))*** Barron's Educational Series, Inc.

—Guess Who's on the Farm. Mumme, Sarah. 2015. (Guess Who's... Bks.). (ENG.). 10p. (J). (gr. -1 — 1). 5.99 ***(978-0-7641-6802-4(9))*** Barron's Educational Series, Inc.

—Guess Who's under the Sea. Mumme, Sarah. 2015. (Guess Who's... Bks.). (ENG.). 10p. (J). (gr. -1 — 1). 5.99 ***(978-0-7641-6803-1(7))*** Barron's Educational Series, Inc.

Samuel, Janet. Imagine That! McKendry, Sam. 2007. (ENG.). 12p. (gr. -1-k). 9.95 *(978-1-58117-484-7(5),* Intervisual/Piggy Toes) Bendon, Inc.

—Jingle Bells. Pierpont, James Lord. 2014. 24p. (J). bds. 6.99 *(978-0-8249-1941-2(6),* Candy Cane Pr.) Ideals Pubns.

—The Night Before Christmas. Moore, Clement C. 2012. (ENG.). 24p. (J). bds. 6.99 *(978-0-8249-1884-2(3))* Ideals Pubns.

—Noah's Big Boat. Hartman, Bob. 2007. (ENG.). 32p. (J). (gr. -1-k). pap. 9.95 *(978-0-7459-4995-6(9))* Lion Hudson PLC GBR. Dist: Independent Pubs. Group.

—One Sneaky Sheep: A Touch-and-Feel Fluffy Tale. 2007. (ENG.). 20p. (gr. -1). 14.95 *(978-1-58117-560-8(4),* Intervisual/Piggy Toes) Bendon, Inc.

—One Sneaky Sheep: The Sheep Who Didn't Want to Get Sheared. 2009. (ENG.). 20p. (J). 9.95 *(978-1-58117-841-8(7),* Intervisual/Piggy Toes) Bendon, Inc.

—The Ten Commandments for Little Ones. Nolan, Allia Zobel. 2009. 32p. (J). 14.99 *(978-0-7369-2545-7(7))* Harvest Hse. Pubs.

Samuel, Janet. Where, Oh Where Is Huggle Buggle Bear? Sully, Katherine. 2013. (J). ***(978-1-4351-4776-8(6))*** Barnes & Noble, Inc.

Samuel, Karen. Why Transfer Day, Anyway? Sewer, Anecia. 2007. 16p. (J). 15.99 *(978-0-9752986-0-2(7))* Research Institute Pr., The.

Samuel, Karen L. The Lesson Box. Roach, Tregenza A. 2012. (J). *(978-1-934370-25-4(8))* Editorial Campana.

Samuels, Barbara. Someday Angeline. Sachar, Louis. 2005. (Avon Camelot Bks.). (ENG.). 192p. (J). (gr. 3-7). pap. 5.99 *(978-0-380-83444-0(8))* HarperCollins Pubs.

Samuels, Barbara. Fred's Beds. Samuels, Barbara. 2014. (ENG.). 40p. (J). (gr. -1-3). 16.99 *(978-0-374-31813-0(1),* Farrar, Straus & Giroux (BYR)) Farrar, Straus & Giroux.

—The Trucker. Samuels, Barbara. 2010. (ENG.). 40p. (J). (gr. -1-1). 16.99 *(978-0-374-37804-2(5),* Farrar, Straus & Giroux (BYR)) Farrar, Straus & Giroux.

Samuels, Linda Nissen. Cuando Elly Fue a la Reserva Ecologica. Samuels, Linda Nissen. 2013. 40p. pap. *(978-0-9511751-8-7(1))* Samuels, Linda Y.

—Elly e il Parco Degli Animali. Samuels, Linda Nissen. 2013. 40p. pap. *(978-0-9511751-7-0(3))* Samuels, Linda Y.

—When Elly Went to the Animal Park... Samuels, Linda Nissen. 2013. 40p. pap. *(978-0-9511751-5-6(7))* Samuels, Linda Y.

Samuels, Ryan. No One Told Me I Could Be Presient. W, Maurice. 2012. 28p. (J). 16.95 *(978-1-62407-818-7(4))* PlatyPr.

Samura, Hiroaki. Last Blood. Samura, Hiroaki. Lewis, Dana & Smith, Toren, trs. 2005. (Blade of the Immortal Ser.). per. 30.15 *(978-1-4176-5923-4(8),* Turtleback) Turtleback Bks.

San Diego Zoo Staff, photos by. Cheetah. Pingry, Patricia A. 2005. (San Diego Zoo Animal Library: Vol. 12). (ENG., 24p. (J). bds. 6.95 *(978-0-8249-6579-2(5),* 1242115) Ideals Pubns.

San Diego Zoological Society Staff, photos by. A Pair of Polar Bears: Twin Cubs Find a Home at the San Diego Zoo. Ryder, Joanne. 2006. (ENG.). 32p. (J). (gr. -1-3). 17.99 *(978-0-689-85871-0(X)*, Simon & Schuster Bks. For Young Readers) Simon & Schuster Bks. For Young Readers.

San Francisco Bay Area Staff. Exactly: Ten Beavers, Nine Fairies, Eight Dreams, Seven Knights, Six Princesses, Five Dogs, Four Otters, Three Old Men, Two Robots, One Traveling Shoe & Everything Else It Takes to Make a Great Children's Story Book. Students of Wallenberg Traditional High School Staff. 2007. (ENG.). 256p. (J). (gr. 3-18). 28.00 *(978-0-9790073-2-3(1))* 826 Valencia.

San Francisco School. Do I Bug You? A Who Am I? Book. Moog, Bob. 2006. (Spinner Books for Kids Ser.). (ENG.). 32p. (J). (gr. -1-12). 9.95 *(978-1-57528-898-7(2))* Univ. Games.

San Jorge, José. Variedades Poéticas. San Jorge, José. Hernández, René Mario, ed. l.t. ed. 2003. (SPA.). 154p. (YA). pap. *(978-1-931481-49-6(0))* LiArt-Literature & Art.

San Souci, Daniel. The Flying Canoe: A Christmas Story. Kimmel, Eric A. 2011. (ENG.). 32p. (J). 16.95 *(978-0-8234-1730-8(1))* Holiday Hse., Inc.

—Yosemite's Songster: One Coyote's Story. Wadsworth, Ginger. 2013. (ENG.). 32p. (J). (gr. -1-2). 15.95 *(978-1-930238-34-3(7))* Yosemite Assn.

San Souci, Daniel, jt. illus. see San Souci, Robert D.

San Souci, Robert D. & San Souci, Daniel. Sister Tricksters: Rollicking Tales of Clever Females. 2006. (ENG.). 70p. (J). (gr. 3-7). 19.95 *(978-0-87483-791-9(X))* August Hse. Pubs., Inc.

San Vicente, Luis. The Festival of Bones / el Festival de Las Calaveras. 2014. (ENG.). 32p. (J). 7.95 *(978-1-941026-03-8(6))* Cinco Puntos Pr.

Sananmuang, Chatree. 20 Umbrellas. Pujari, M. Nathalie. 2007. (J). *(978-0-9715865-0-5(0))* Abuzz Bks.

Sanborn, Casey. Close-Up: Forensic Photography, 5 vols. McIntosh, Kenneth. 2007. (Crime Scene Club Ser.: Bk. 5). 144p. (YA). (gr. 9-12). lib. bdg. 24.95 *(978-1-4222-0251-7(8))* Mason Crest.

—Dinosaur. Rader, Mark. 2008. (J). *(978-1-4127-9359-9(9))* Publications International, Ltd.

—Over the Edge: Forensic Accident Reconstruction, 2 vols. McIntosh, Kenneth. 2007. (Crime Scene Club Ser.: Bk. 2). 144p. (YA). (gr. 9-12). lib. bdg. 24.95 *(978-1-4222-0248-7(8))* Mason Crest.

Sanborn, F. C. & Railton, Fanny. More Mother Stories. Lindsay, Maud. 2008. 160p. pap. 9.95 *(978-1-59915-168-7(5))* Yesterday's Classics.

SanCartier, Emma. The World Is Your Oyster. James, Tamara. 2010. (ENG.). 50p. (J). (gr. -1-3). 16.95 *(978-1-897476-22-2(1))* Simply Read Bks. CAN. Dist: Ingram Pub. Services.

Sanchez Almara, Dono & Almara, Dono Sanchez. A Christmas Carol. Dickens, Charles. 2015. (Graphic Revolve: Common Core Editions Ser.). (ENG.). 72p. (gr. 2-3). lib. bdg. 26.65 ***(978-1-4965-0370-1(8))*** Stone Arch Bks.

Sánchez, Alvaro Iglesias, jt. illus. see Lokus, Rex.

Sanchez, Andres & Arte Y Diseno, Tane. Acoyani: El Nino y el Poeta. Peredo, Roberto. 2nd rev. ed. 2006. (Castillo de la Lectura Naranja Ser.). (SPA & ENG.). 166p. (J). (gr. 4-7). pap. 7.95 *(978-970-20-0146-1(3))* Castillo, Ediciones, S. A. de C. V. MEX. Dist: Macmillan.

Sanchez, Andres & Tagle. El Cinturón. Abodehman, Ahmed. Lovillo, Pilar Ortiz, tr. 2006. (la Orilla del Viento Ser.). (SPA.). 121p. (J). per. 8.50 *(978-968-16-6670-5(4))* Fondo de Cultura Economica USA.

—Sarah de Cordoba. Soci Et E de La Faune Et Des Parcs Du Qu Ebec. 2003. (la Orilla del Viento Ser.). (SPA.). 136p. (J). per. 8.50 *(978-968-16-7020-7(5))* Fondo de Cultura Economica USA.

Sanchez, Edmundo. Caleb's Birthday Wish. Villanueva, David. 2006. 40p. (J). (gr. -1-3). per. 17.95 *(978-0-9771971-8-7(2))* Better Be Write Pub., A.

Sanchez, Enrique O. Abuela's Weave. Castañeda, Omar S. 2013. (ENG.). 75p. (J). (gr. -1-18). pap. 8.95 *(978-1-880000-20-5(2))* Lee & Low Bks., Inc.

—Botas Negras. Gonzalez Jensen, Margarita. (SPA.). (J). (gr. 2-4). 3.96 net. *(978-0-590-26842-4(2))* Scholastic, Inc.

—Confeti: Poemas para Ninos, 1 vol. Mora, Pat. Mora, Pat & Fernandez, Queta, trs. 2006. (SPA.). 32p. (J). (gr. -1-5). pap. 9.95 *(978-1-58430-270-4(4))* Lee & Low Bks., Inc.

—Estela en el Mercado de Pulgas. O'Neill, Alexis. de la Vega, Eida, tr. from ENG. 2005. (SPA.). 32p. (J). (gr. -1-k). pap. 9.95 *(978-1-58430-246-9(1))* Lee & Low Bks., Inc.

—Estela en el Mercado de Pulgas. de la Vega, Eida, tr. from ENG. 2005. (SPA.). 32p. (J). (gr. -1-k). 16.95 *(978-1-58430-245-2(3))* Lee & Low Bks., Inc.

—La Flor de Oro: Un Mito Taino de Puerto Rico. Jaffe, Nina. Ventura, Gabriela Baeza, tr. from ENG. 2006. (SPA.). 32p. (J). (gr. -1-3). 16.95 *(978-1-55885-463-5(0)*, Piñata Books) Arte Publico Pr.

—The Golden Flower: A Taino Myth from Puerto Rico. Jaffe, Nina. 2005. 32p. (J). (gr. -1-3). 16.95 *(978-1-55885-452-9(5)*, Piñata Books) Arte Publico Pr.

—Una Muneca para el Dia de Reyes. Santiago, Esmeralda. Torres-Vidal, Nina, tr. from ENG. 2005.Tr. of Doll for Navidades. (SPA & ENG.). 32p. (J). (gr. -1-3). per. 5.99 *(978-0-439-75510-8(7))* Scholastic, Inc.

Sanchez, Evan. The Snail with Two Slippers. Shonka, Maria. 2011. 40p. pap. 24.95 *(978-1-60836-786-3(X))* America Star Bks.

Sanchez, Israel. The Dinosaur Tooth Fairy. Brockenbrough, Martha. 2013. (ENG.). 32p. (J). (gr. -1-3). 16.99 *(978-0-545-24466-4(8)*, Levine, Arthur A. Bks.) Scholastic, Inc.

Sanchez, Javier G. Un Rey sin Corona. Monkman, Olga. 2003. (SPA.). 39p. (J). (gr. k-3). pap. 7.95 *(978-950-511-368-2(4))* Santillana USA Publishing Co., Inc.

Sanchez, Jimena. Snow White & the Seven Robots. Simonson, Louise. 2015. (Far Out Fairy Tales Ser.). (ENG.). 40p. (gr. 3-4). lib. bdg. 23.99 *(978-1-4342-9648-1(2))* Stone Arch Bks.

Sanchez, Maria. Jose. Lazaro, Georgina. 2007. (J). 14.99 *(978-1-933032-08-5(1))* Lectorum Pubns., Inc.

Sanchez, Sara. Monkey in the Mirror. Zur Muehlen, Nersel. 2012. 56p. pap. 14.95 *(978-0-9829224-2-2(6))* BPM Research LLC.

Sánchez, Sergio García. Lost in NYC: A Subway Adventure. Spiegelman, Nadja. 2015. (ENG.). 52p. (J). (gr. 2-7). 16.95 *(978-1-935179-81-8(0))* TOON Books / RAW Junior, LLC.

Sánchez, Sonia. Here I Am, 1 vol. Kim, Patti. 2013. (ENG.). 40p. (gr. k-5). 14.95 *(978-1-62370-036-2(1))* Capstone Young Readers.

—Here I Am, 1 vol. Kim, Patti. (ENG.). 40p. (gr. k-5). 2015. pap. 7.95 *(978-1-4795-1931-6(6))*; 2013. 27.32 *(978-1-4048-8299-7(5))* Picture Window Bks.

—Sister Day! Mantchev, Lisa. 2016. (J). *(978-1-4814-3795-0(X)*, Simon & Schuster Bks. For Young Readers) Simon & Schuster Bks. For Young Readers.

Sanchez Vigil, Luis Gerardo & VandenBroeck, Fabricio. Ahi Viene el Lobo Gris. Romeu, Emma. 2003. (Colección Animales de América / Animals of the Americas Ser.). (SPA.). 32p. (gr. 3-5). pap. 11.95 *(978-970-29-0512-7(5))* Santillana USA Publishing Co., Inc.

—Mi amigo el manatí. Romeu, Emma. 2003. (Colección Animales de América / Animals of the Americas Ser.). (SPA.). 24p. (gr. 3-5). pap. 11.95 *(978-970-29-0513-4(3))* Santillana USA Publishing Co., Inc.

—Las Patas del Flamenco. Romeu, Emma. 2004. (Colección Animales de América / Animals of the Americas Ser.). (SPA.). 28p. (gr. 3-5). pap. 11.95 *(978-970-29-0514-1(1))* Santillana USA Publishing Co., Inc.

Sancton, Sylvaine, photos by. Some Birds ..., 1 vol. Sancton, Sylvaine. 2013. (ENG., 40p. (J). (gr. k-3). pap. 14.99 *(978-1-4556-1863-7(2))* Pelican Publishing Co., Inc.

Sanda-Ebosh, Mary. The Unfroggettable Fiona Fayetta Froggee: A Green Pond Memoir. Merriweather-Beech, Myrtle. 2009. 52p. pap. 24.99 *(978-1-4389-2585-1(9))* AuthorHouse.

Sandall, Diane. Small Graces. Sandall, Anne. 2004. (J). *(978-0-9741620-1-0(9))* Solsidan Hse.

Sandall, Ellie. Copycat Bear! Sandall, Ellie. 2013. (ENG.). 32p. (J). (gr. -1-k). 14.99 *(978-1-58925-120-5(2))* Tiger Tales.

—Daisy Plays Hide-and-Seek. Sandall, Ellie. (ENG.). 32p. (J). (gr. -1-k). 2012. pap. 8.99 *(978-1-4052-5457-1(2))*; 2011. 17.99 *(978-1-4052-5419-9(X))* Egmont Bks., Ltd. GBR. Dist: Independent Pubs. Group.

Sande, Ana. El Patito Feo. 2006. (Coleccion Libros para Sonar Ser.). (J). (gr. -1-3). *(978-84-96388-21-5(2))* Kalandraka Editora, S.L.

Sandemose, Iben. Gracie & Grandma. Sandemose, Iben. 2008. (Gracie & Grandma Ser.). 36p. (J). (gr. -1-1). 14.95 *(978-0-9790347-3-2(6))* Mackenzie Smiles, LLC.

—Gracie & Grandma & the Itsy, Bitsy Seed. Sandemose, Iben. Vetleseter, Tonje, tr. from NOR. 2008. (Gracie & Grandma Ser.). 40p. (J). (gr. -1-1). 14.95 *(978-0-9790347-5-6(2))* Mackenzie Smiles, LLC.

Sanders, Brian. Titanic. Jenkins, Martin. 2012. (ENG.). 32p. (J). (gr. 3-7). pap. 6.99 *(978-0-7636-6034-5(5))* Candlewick Pr.

Sanders, Martin B., et al. Super Dentist Guy: Attack of the Yukkies. Xavier, Imbeus & Sanders, Martin B. 2003. 52p. 7.99 *(978-0-9708523-0-4(4))* DeMosi Publishing.

Sanders, Martin B. Super Dentist Guy: Attack of the Yukkies. Sanders, Martin B. Xavier, Imbeus. 2003. 64p. lib. bdg. 11.99 *(978-0-9708523-2-8(0))* DeMosi Publishing.

Sanderson, Constance. The Frog & the Fly. Webb, Heather. 2008. 29p. pap. 24.95 *(978-1-60441-380-9(8))* America Star Bks.

Sanderson, Jessica B. Global Heart Warming: Dream Believe Achieve Series. Symington, Martha M. 2009. 36p. pap. *(978-1-897435-34-2(7))* Agio Publishing Hse.

Sanderson, Ruth. Bell's Star. Hart, Alison. 2009. (Horse Diaries: No. 2). (ENG.). 144p. (J). (gr. 3-7). pap. 7.99 *(978-0-375-85204-6(2))* Random Hse. Children's Bks.

—Darcy. Sanderson, Whitney. 2013. (Horse Diaries). (ENG.). 160p. (J). (gr. 3-7). pap. 6.99 *(978-0-307-97635-2(1))*; lib. bdg. 12.99 *(978-0-375-97121-1(1))* Random Hse., Inc.

—Golden Sun. Sanderson, Whitney. 2010. (Horse Diaries). (ENG.). 160p. (J). (gr. 3-7). pap. 7.99 *(978-0-375-86194-9(7))*; lib. bdg. 12.99 *(978-0-375-96194-6(1))* Random Hse., Inc.

—Horse Diaries - Koda. Hermes, Patricia. 2009. (Horse Diaries: No. 3). (ENG.). 160p. (J). (gr. 3-7). pap. 5.99 *(978-0-375-85199-5(2))* Random Hse., Inc.

Sanderson, Ruth. Horse Diaries #12: Luna. Hapka, Catherine. 2015. (Horse Diaries). (ENG.). 160p. (J). (gr. 3-7). lib. bdg. 12.99 ***(978-0-553-53371-2(1)**,* Random Hse. Bks. for Young Readers) Random Hse. Children's Bks.

Sanderson, Ruth. Hush, Little Horsie. Yolen, Jane. 2010. (ENG.). 32p. (J). (gr. -1-2). 16.99 *(978-0-375-85853-6(9))* Random Hse., Inc.

—Jingle Bells (Horse Diaries Special Edition) Hapka, Catherine. 2014. (Horse Diaries). (ENG.). 208p. (J). (gr. 3-7). pap. 7.99 *(978-0-385-38484-1(X))*; lib. bdg. 12.99 *(978-0-385-38485-8(8))* Random Hse. Children's Bks. (Random Hse. Bks. for Young Readers).

—Maestoso Petra. Kendall, Jane F. 2010. (Horse Diaries: No. 4). (ENG.). 160p. (J). (gr. 3-7). pap. 5.99 *(978-0-375-85842-0(3))* Random Hse., Inc.

—Risky Chance. Hart, Alison. 2011. (Horse Diaries). (ENG.). 176p. (J). (gr. 3-7). pap. 7.99 *(978-0-375-86833-7(X))* Random Hse., Inc.

—Summer Pony. Doty, Jean Slaughter. 2008. (Stepping Stone Book Ser.). (ENG.). 144p. (J). (gr. 1-4). pap. 3.99 *(978-0-375-84709-7(X))* Random Hse. Children's Bks.

—Summer Pony. Doty, Jean Slaughter. 2008. (Stepping Stones: A Chapter Book: Fiction Ser.). 139p. (J). (gr. 1-4). 13.55 *(978-1-4178-1929-4(4)*, Turtleback) Turtleback Bks.

—Where Have the Unicorns Gone? Yolen, Jane. 2003. (ENG.). 32p. (J). (gr. -1-3). 7.99 *(978-0-689-86359-2(4)*, Simon & Schuster/Paula Wiseman Bks.) Simon & Schuster Bks. For Young Readers.

—Winter Pony. Doty, Jean Slaughter. 2008. (Stepping Stone Book(TM) Ser.). (ENG.). 144p. (J). (gr. 1-4). 3.99 *(978-0-375-84710-3(3))* Random Hse., Inc.

—Yatimah. Hapka, Catherine. 2011. (Horse Diaries). (ENG.). 176p. (J). (gr. 3-7). pap. 7.99 *(978-0-375-86719-4(8))*; lib. bdg. 12.99 *(978-0-375-96719-1(2))* Random Hse., Inc.

Sanderson, Ruth. More Saints: Lives & Illuminations. Sanderson, Ruth. 2007. 40p. (J). (gr. 1). 20.00 *(978-0-8028-5272-4(6)*, Eerdmans Bks For Young Readers) Eerdmans, William B. Publishing Co.

—Saints: Lives & Illuminations. Sanderson, Ruth. 2010. 160p. (YA). (gr. 3-18). 15.99 *(978-0-8028-5365-3(X)*, Eerdmans Bks For Young Readers); 2004. 40p. 20.00 *(978-0-8028-5220-5(3))* Eerdmans, William B. Publishing Co.

Sanderson, Ruth, jt. illus. see Griffin-Scott, Janet.

Sanderson, Sean. Time for Bed Little Red. Scand, Sandra. 2009. 20p. pap. 10.00 *(978-1-934925-36-2(5)*, Eloquent Bks.) Strategic Book Publishing & Rights Agency (SBPRA).

Sandford, Barbara. Grandma's Day. Anderson, P. G. 2013. 32p. 16.00 *(978-1-61170-133-3(3))* Robertson Publishing.

Sandford, John. Argyle. Wallace, Barbara Brooks. (ENG.). 32p. (J). 2007. (gr. k-2). 8.95 *(978-1-59078-245-3(3))*; 2004. (gr. -1-3). 9.95 *(978-1-56397-043-6(0))* Boyds Mills Pr.

—The Leprechaun in the Basement. Tucker, Kathy. 2004. (ENG.). 32p. (J). (gr. k-3). pap. 6.95 *(978-0-8075-4451-8(5))* Whitman, Albert & Co.

—The Terrible Hodag & the Animal Catchers. Arnold, Caroline. 2006. (ENG.). 34p. (J). (gr. k-7). 15.95 *(978-1-59078-166-1(X))* Boyds Mills Pr.

—Woolies & Worms. MacNeil, Stephen. 2007. (ENG.). 192p. (J). (gr. 1-5). 16.95 *(978-0-8126-2751-0(2))* Cricket Bks.

Sandford, John. Little House Hotel. Sandford, John. 24p. (J). 2.99 *(978-1-59445-000-6(5))* Dogs in Hats Children's Publishing Co.

Sandham, Henry. Editha's Burglar. Burnett, Frances Hodgson. 2005. reprint ed. pap. 15.95 *(978-1-4179-0135-7(7))* Kessinger Publishing, LLC.

Sandheim, May. The Golden Heart, & Other Fairy Stories. Jacob, Violet. 2011. 168p. pap. *(978-1-84921-098-0(5))* Kennedy & Boyd.

Sandiford, Ted. Counting St. Lucian Style: A delightfully illustrated counting rhyme set in the Caribbean island of St. Lucia. Bousquet, Anthea. 2011. 16p. (J). pap. *(978-976-8238-01-6(1))* Maryli Pubs.

—Lucy's St. Lucian Alphabet: The ABCs of Caribbean Culture in Upbeat Rhyming Verse. Bousquet, Anthea. 2012. 20p. (J). pap. *(978-976-8238-02-3(X))* Maryli Pubs.

Sandland, Reg. Good Friday. Ulmer, Louise. 2004. (Arch Bks.). (ENG.). 16p. (J). 1.99 *(978-0-7586-0638-9(9))* Concordia Publishing Hse.

Sandler, Martin W. America's Great Disasters. Sandler, Martin W. 2003. 96p. (J). (gr. 3-18). 17.99 *(978-0-06-029107-5(9))* HarperCollins Pubs.

Sandon, Gina. The Princes of Pleasant Valley: A Day in the Life of Zyler & Xavier, 1 vol. Proulx, Roxanna Darling. 2010. 46p. 24.95 *(978-1-4489-7641-6(3))* PublishAmerica, Inc.

Sandoval, Gerardo. BMX Breakthrough, 1 vol. Bowen, Carl & Fuentes, Benny. 2011. (Sports Illustrated Kids Graphic Novels Ser.). (ENG.). 56p. (gr. 2-3). pap. 7.19 *(978-1-4342-3401-8(0))*; lib. bdg. 25.32 *(978-1-4342-2240-4(3))* Stone Arch Bks.

—End Zone Thunder, 1 vol. Ciencin, Scott & Fuentes, Benny. 2010. (Sports Illustrated Kids Graphic Novels Ser.). (ENG.). 56p. (gr. 2-3). 25.32 *(978-1-4342-2010-3(9))*; pap. 7.19 *(978-1-4342-2784-3(7))* Stone Arch Bks.

—Full Court Flash, 1 vol. Ciencin, Scott & Fuentes, Benny. 2011. (Sports Illustrated Kids Graphic Novels Ser.). (ENG.). 56p. (gr. 2-3). pap. 7.19 *(978-1-4342-3074-4(0))*; lib. bdg. 25.32 *(978-1-4342-2225-1(X))* Stone Arch Bks.

—Jason & the Golden Fleece, 1 vol. Yomtov, Nel et al. 2009. (Mythology Ser.). (ENG.). 72p. (gr. 2-3). pap. 7.15 *(978-1-4342-1385-3(4))*; lib. bdg. 26.65 *(978-1-4342-1172-9(X))* Stone Arch Bks. (Graphic Revolve).

—Quarterback Scramble, 1 vol. Terrell, Brandon & Fuentes, Benny. 2011. (Sports Illustrated Kids Graphic Novels Ser.). (ENG.). 56p. (gr. 2-3). pap. 7.19 *(978-1-4342-3070-6(8))*; lib. bdg. 25.32 *(978-1-4342-2220-6(9))* Stone Arch Bks.

—Reality Check, 1 vol. Yomtov, Nel & Fuentes, Benny. 2010. (Sports Illustrated Kids Graphic Novels Ser.). (ENG.). 56p. (gr. 2-3). pap. 7.19 *(978-1-4342-2294-7(2))*; 25.32 *(978-1-4342-1912-1(7))* Stone Arch Bks.

—Sack Attack!, 1 vol. Fuentes, Benny & Hoena, Blake A. 2011. (Sports Illustrated Kids Graphic Novels Ser.). (ENG.). 56p. (gr. 2-3). pap. 7.19 *(978-1-4342-3404-9(5))*; lib. bdg. 25.32 *(978-1-4342-2243-5(8))* Stone Arch Bks.

—Skateboard Breakdown, 1 vol. Fein, Eric & Fuentes, Benny. 2010. (Sports Illustrated Kids Graphic Novels Ser.). (ENG.). 56p. (gr. 2-3). 25.32 *(978-1-4342-2011-0(7))*; pap. 7.19 *(978-1-4342-2785-0(5))* Stone Arch Bks.

—Skateboard Sonar, 1 vol. Stevens, Eric & Fuentes, Benny. 2010. (Sports Illustrated Kids Graphic Novels Ser.). (ENG.). 56p. (gr. 2-3). pap. 7.19 *(978-1-4342-2295-4(0))*; 25.32 *(978-1-4342-1910-7(0))* Stone Arch Bks.

—Spotlight Striker, 1 vol. Hoena, Blake A. & Fuentes, Benny. 2010. (Sports Illustrated Kids Graphic Novels Ser.). (ENG.). 56p. (gr. 2-3). 25.32 *(978-1-4342-2128-5(8))*; pap. 7.19 *(978-1-4342-2787-4(1))* Stone Arch Bks.

—The Swiss Family Robinson. Wyss, Johann D. & Fuentes, Benny. 2008. (Classic Fiction Ser.). (ENG.). 72p. (gr. 2-3). 26.65 *(978-1-4342-0756-2(0)*, Graphic Revolve) Stone Arch Bks.

—Wild Pitch, 1 vol. Fein, Eric & Fuentes, Benny. 2011. (Sports Illustrated Kids Graphic Novels Ser.). (ENG.). 56p. (gr. 2-3). pap. 7.19 *(978-1-4342-3073-7(2))*; lib. bdg. 25.32 *(978-1-4342-2221-3(7))* Stone Arch Bks.

Sandoval, Migs. Beauty & the Beast: Level 3: Learn Chinese Mandarin Through Fairy Tales. 2006. (Learn Chinese Through Fairy Tales Ser.). (ENG & CHI.). 29p. (J). (gr. -1-3). pap. 14.95 incl. audio compact disk *(978-1-891888-91-5(9))* Slangman Publishing.

—Beauty & the Beast: Level 3: Learn French Through Fairy Tales. Burke, David. 2006. (Learn French Through Fairy Tales Ser.). (ENG & FRE.). 29p. (J). (gr. -1-3). pap. 14.95 incl. audio compact disk *(978-1-891888-87-8(0))* Slangman Publishing.

—Beauty & the Beast: Level 3: Learn German Through Fairy Tales. Burke, David. 2006. (Learn German Through Fairy Tales Ser.). (ENG & GER.). 29p. (J). (gr. -1-3). pap. 14.95 incl. audio compact disk *(978-1-891888-88-5(9))* Slangman Publishing.

—Beauty & the Beast: Level 3: Learn Spanish Through Fairy Tales. Burke, David. 2006. (Learn Spanish Through Fairy Tales Ser.). (ENG & SPA.). 29p. (J). (gr. -1-3). pap. 14.95 incl. audio compact disk *(978-1-891888-86-1(2))* Slangman Publishing.

—La Bella y la Bestia: Nivel 3: Aprende Ingles con Cuentos de Hadas. Burke, David. Redoles, Marcela, tr. 2006. (Slangman para Ninos: Nivel 3 Ser.). (SPA & ENG.). 29p. (J). (gr. -1-3). pap. 14.95 incl. audio compact disk *(978-1-891888-97-7(8))* Slangman Publishing.

—La Cenicienta: Nivel 1: Aprende Ingles con Cuentos de Hadas. Burke, David. Bobrick, Julie, ed. Redoles, Marcela, tr. 2006. (Slangman para Ninos: Nivel 1 Ser.). (SPA & ENG.). 29p. pap. 14.95 incl. cd-rom *(978-1-891888-95-3(1))* Slangman Publishing.

—Cinderella: Level 1: Learn French Through Fairy Tales. 2006. (Learn French Through Fairy Tales Ser.). (ENG & FRE.). 29p. (J). (gr. -1-3). pap. 14.95 incl. audio compact disk *(978-1-891888-75-5(7))* Slangman Publishing.

—Cinderella: Level 1: Learn German Through Fairy Tales. Burke, David. Bobrick, Julie, ed. Deese, Teut & Wirth, Petra, trs. 2006. (Learn German Through Fairy Tales Ser.). (ENG & GER.). 29p. pap. 14.95 incl. audio compact disk *(978-1-891888-76-2(5))* Slangman Publishing.

—Cinderella: Level 1: Learn Hebrew Through Fairy Tales. Burke, David. Obejas, Ofra, tr. 2006. (Slangman Kids: Level 1 Ser.). (ENG & HEB.). 29p. pap. 14.95 incl. audio compact disk *(978-1-891888-92-2(7))* Slangman Publishing.

—Cinderella: Level 1: Learn Italian Through Fairy Tales. Burke, David. Bobrick, Julie, ed. Filippi, Alessio, tr. 2006. (Learn Italian Through Fairy Tales Ser.). (ENG & ITA.). 29p. pap. 14.95 incl. audio compact disk *(978-1-891888-77-9(3))* Slangman Publishing.

—Cinderella: Level 1: Learn Japanese Through Fairy Tales. Burke, David. Bobrick, Julie, ed. Bird, Mariko, tr. 2006. (Slangman Kids: Level 1 Ser.). (ENG & JPN.). 29p. pap. 14.95 incl. audio compact disk *(978-1-891888-78-6(1))* Slangman Publishing.

—Cinderella: Level 1: Learn Mandarin Chinese Through Fairy Tales. Bobrick, Julie, ed. Peters, Li Li & Tao, Ming, trs. 2006. (Learn Chinese Through Fairy Tales Ser.). (ENG & CHI.). 29p. pap. 14.95 incl. audio compact disk *(978-1-891888-79-3(X))* Slangman Publishing.

—Cinderella: Level 1: Learn Spanish Through Fairy Tales. Burke, David. Bobrick, Julie, ed. Redoles, Marcela, tr. 2006. (Learn Spanish Through Fairy Tales Ser.). (ENG & SPA.). 29p. pap. 14.95 incl. audio compact disk *(978-1-891888-74-8(9))* Slangman Publishing.

—Goldilocks & the 3 Bears: Level 2: Learn French Through Fairy Tales. 2006. (Learn French Through Fairy Tales Ser.). (ENG & FRE.). 29p. (J). (gr. -1-3). pap. 14.95 incl. audio compact disk *(978-1-891888-81-6(1))* Slangman Publishing.

—Goldilocks & the 3 Bears: Level 2: Learn Hebrew Through Fairy Tales. Burke, David. 2006. (Slangman Kids: Level 2 Ser.). (ENG & HEB.). 29p. (J). (gr. -1-3). pap. 14.95 incl. audio compact disk *(978-1-891888-93-9(5))* Slangman Publishing.

—Goldilocks & the 3 Bears: Level 2: Learn Japanese Through Fairy Tales. Burke, David. 2006. (Slangman Kids: Level 2 Ser.). (ENG & JPN.). 29p. (J). (gr. -1-3). pap. 14.95 incl. audio compact disk *(978-1-891888-84-7(6))* Slangman Publishing.

—Goldilocks & the 3 Bears: Level 2: Learn Spanish Through Fairy Tales. Burke, David. 2006. (Learn Spanish Through Fairy Tales Ser.). (ENG & SPA.). 29p. (J). (gr. -1-3). pap. 14.95 incl. audio compact disk *(978-1-891888-80-9(3))* Slangman Publishing.

Sandoval, Rafa. Ultimate Comics Doomsday. 2011. (ENG.). 304p. (YA). (gr. 8-17). pap. 34.99 *(978-0-7851-4777-0(2))* Marvel Worldwide, Inc.

Sandoval, Sam. Beaver Steals Fire: A Salish Coyote Story. Confederated Salish and Kootenai Tribes Staff. 2008. (ENG.). 64p. (YA). (gr. k-3). pap. 14.95 *(978-0-8032-1640-2(8)*, Bison Bks.) Univ. of Nebraska Pr.

Sandoval, Sergio & Peris, Nuria. Gear School, Vol. 1. Gallardo, Adam. 2007. (ENG.). 96p. (gr. 4-9). pap. 7.95 *(978-1-59307-854-6(4))* Dark Horse Comics.

Sandoz, Matt. Doggie Bets. Howard, Assuanta. 2013. 32p. pap. 7.99 *(978-1-934947-76-0(8))* Asta Publications, LLC.

Sandstrom, Karen. Weird? (Me, Too!) Let's Be Friends. Holbrook, Sara E. 2011. (ENG.). 56p. (J). (gr. 4-6). 16.95 *(978-1-59078-821-9(4)*, Wordsong) Boyds Mills Pr.

—Zombies! Evacuate the School. Holbrook, Sara E. 2010. (ENG.). 56p. (J). (gr. 4-6). 16.95 *(978-1-59078-820-2(6)*, Wordsong) Boyds Mills Pr.

—Zombies! Evacuate the School! Holbrook, Sara. 2014. (ENG.). 56p. (J). (gr. 3-6). pap. 7.95 *(978-1-62979-110-4(5)*, Wordsong) Boyds Mills Pr.

Sandu, Anca. Churchill's Tale of Tails, 1 vol. Sandu, Anca. 2013. (ENG.). 32p. (J). (gr. -1-3). 16.95 *(978-1-56145-738-0(8))* Peachtree Pubs.

Sandy, J. P. Bizarre Vehicles. Rosen, Michael J. & Kassoy, Ben. 2013. (No Way! Ser.). (ENG.). 32p. (gr. 3-5). lib. bdg. 26.60 *(978-0-7613-8985-9(7)*, Millbrook Pr.) Lerner Publishing Group.

—Miss Pell Would Never Misspell & Other Painless Tricks for Memorizing How to Spell & Use Wily Words. Cleary, Brian P. 2011. (Adventures in Memory Ser.). (ENG.). 48p. (gr.

4-6). lib. bdg. 26.60 *(978-0-8225-7822-2(0)*, Millbrook Pr.) Lerner Publishing Group.

—Mrs. Riley Bought Five Itchy Aardvarks & Other Painless Tricks for Memorizing Science Facts. Cleary, Brian P. 2008. (Adventures in Memory Ser.). (ENG.). 48p. (gr. 4-6). 26.60 *(978-0-8225-7819-2(0)*, Millbrook Pr.) Lerner Publishing Group.

—Rhyme & Punishment: Adventures in Wordplay. Cleary, Brian P. 2006. (ENG.). 48p. (gr. 4-6). 26.60 *(978-1-57505-849-8(9)*, Millbrook Pr.) Lerner Publishing Group.

—Super-Hungry Mice Eat Onions & Other Painless Tricks for Memorizing Geography Facts. Cleary, Brian P. 2009. (Adventures in Memory Ser.). (ENG.). 48p. (gr. 4-6). 26.60 *(978-0-8225-7820-8(4)*, Millbrook Pr.) Lerner Publishing Group.

—Washing Adam's Jeans & Other Painless Tricks for Memorizing Social Studies Facts. Cleary, Brian P. 2010. (Adventures in Memory Ser.). (ENG.). 48p. (gr. 4-6). lib. bdg. 26.60 *(978-0-8225-7821-5(2)*, Millbrook Pr.) Lerner Publishing Group.

Sandy, John. The Laugh Stand: Adventures in Humor. Cleary, Brian P. 2008. (Exceptional Reading & Language Arts Titles for Intermediate Grades Ser.). (ENG.). 48p. (gr. 4-6). lib. bdg. 16.95 *(978-0-8225-7849-9(2))* Lerner Publishing Group.

Sandy, Pat. Odd Medical Cures. Rosen, Michael J. & Kassoy, Ben. 2013. (No Way! Ser.). (ENG.). 32p. (gr. 3-5). lib. bdg. 26.60 *(978-0-7613-8987-3(3)*, Millbrook Pr.) Lerner Publishing Group.

—Weird Jobs. Rosen, Michael J. & Kassoy, Ben. 2013. (No Way! Ser.). (ENG.). 32p. (gr. 3-5). lib. bdg. 26.60 *(978-0-7613-8983-5(0)*, Millbrook Pr.) Lerner Publishing Group.

Sane, Justin. Heart of a Corpse; an Undead Engagement Part One. Sane, Justin. 2012. 34p. pap. 5.95 *(978-1-59362-243-5(0)*, Slave Labor Graphics) Slave Labor Bks.

Saneshige, Norio. Wu-lung & I-lung: Color Edition. 2004. 33p. (J). pap. 16.50 *(978-0-9759251-0-2(5)*, FortuneChild) Forest Hill Publishing, LLC.

—Wu-lung & I-lung: Deluxe Edition. deluxe l.t. ed. 2004. 33p. (J). 24.50 *(978-0-9759251-1-9(3)*, FortuneChild) Forest Hill Publishing, LLC.

Sanfilippo, Simona. Beauty & the Pea. Robinson, Hilary. 2013. (ENG.). 32p. (J). *(978-0-7787-1155-1(2))*; pap. *(978-0-7787-1159-9(5))* Crabtree Publishing Co.

—Cinderella & the Beanstalk. Robinson, Hilary. 2013. (ENG.). 32p. (J). pap. *(978-0-7787-1161-2(7))* Crabtree Publishing Co.

—The Elves & the Emperor. Robinson, Hilary. 2012. (ENG.). 32p. (J). *(978-0-7787-8025-0(2))*; pap. *(978-0-7787-8036-6(8))* Crabtree Publishing Co.

—Goldilocks & the Wolf. Robinson, Hilary. 2012. (ENG.). 32p. (J). *(978-0-7787-8023-6(6))*; pap. *(978-0-7787-8034-2(1))* Crabtree Publishing Co.

—The Grumpy Queen. Wilding, Valerie. 2011. (ENG.). 32p. (J). (gr. -1-k). pap. *(978-1-84089-637-4(X))* Zero to Ten, Ltd.

—Hansel, Gretel, & the Ugly Duckling. Robinson, Hilary. 2013. (ENG.). 32p. (J). *(978-0-7787-1157-5(9))*; pap. *(978-0-7787-1166-7(8))* Crabtree Publishing Co.

—Rapunzel. 2009. (Flip-Up Fairy Tales Ser.). (ENG.). 24p. (J). (gr. -1-2). pap. *(978-1-84643-249-1(9))* Child's Play International Ltd.

—Rapunzel & the Billy Goats. Robinson, Hilary. 2013. (ENG.). 32p. (J). pap. *(978-0-7787-1158-2(7))* Crabtree Publishing Co.

—Snow White & the Enormous Turnip. Robinson, Hilary. 2012. (ENG.). 32p. (J). *(978-0-7787-8024-3(4))*; pap. *(978-0-7787-8035-9(X))* Crabtree Publishing Co.

—Three Pigs & a Gingerbread Man. Robinson, Hilary. 2012. (ENG.). 32p. (J). *(978-0-7787-8026-7(0))*; pap. *(978-0-7787-8037-3(6))* Crabtree Publishing Co.

Sanford, Lori Hood. Teach Them to Your Children: An Alphabet of Biblical Poems, Verses, & Stories. Wean, Sarah. 2006. 56p. (J). 17.00 *(978-0-9787559-5-9(2))* Vision Forum, Inc., The.

Sang-Sun, Park. Les Bijoux, Vol. I. Eun-Ha, Jo. 2004. 200p. pap. 14.99 *(978-1-59182-690-3(X)*, Tokyopop Adult) TOKYOPOP, Inc.

—Les Bijoux, 6 vols., Vol. 2. Eun-Ha, Jo. Lee, Seung-Ah, tr. from KOR. rev. ed. 2004. 200p. pap. 14.99 *(978-1-59182-691-0(8)*, Tokyopop Adult) TOKYOPOP, Inc.

—Les Bijoux, 6 vols., Vol. 3. Eun-Ha, Jo. rev. ed. 2004. 200p. pap. 14.99 *(978-1-59182-692-7(6)*, Tokyopop Adult) TOKYOPOP, Inc.

Sanger, Amy Wilson. Yum Yum Dim Sum. Sanger, Amy Wilson. 2003. (ENG.). 22p. (J). (gr. k — 1). bds. 6.99 *(978-1-58246-108-3(2)*, Tricycle Pr.) Ten Speed Pr.

Sangha Mitra, Ms Janice. Golden Bear: The Story of a Flowering Heart. Sangha Mitra, Ms Janice. 4th ed. 2013. (ENG.). 38p. pap. *(978-0-9805945-2-2(9))* Little Bear Values.

Sangregorio, Fernando, et al. Pictodiccionario: Diccionario en Im Genes. Santillana. 2003. (SPA.). 144p. (gr. k-3). 29.95 *(978-1-58105-973-1(6))* Santillana USA Publishing Co., Inc.

Sanjo, Riku. Beet the Vandel Buster, Vol. 9. Sanjo, Riku. Inada, Koji. 2006. (Beet the Vandel Buster Ser.). (ENG.). 208p. pap. 7.99 *(978-1-4215-0270-0(4))* Viz Media.

—Beet the Vandel Buster, Vol. 12. Sanjo, Riku. Inada, Koji. Kawasaki, Beth, ed. 2007. (Beet the Vandel Buster Ser.: 12). (ENG.). 184p. pap. 7.99 *(978-1-4215-1406-2(0))* Viz Media.

Sankaranarayanan, Ayswarya. The Story & the Song. Subramaniam, Manasi. 2013. (ENG.). 32p. (J). (gr. k). pap. 9.95 *(978-81-8190-273-3(4))* Karadi Tales Co. Pvt. Ltd. IND. Dist: Consortium Bk. Sales & Distribution.

Sankey, Tom. Camilla Gryski's Favorite String Games. Gryski, Camilla. 2005. 48p. *(978-0-439-77939-5(1))* Scholastic, Inc.

Sanne, Don. Lighthouse Mouse Meets Simon the Cat. Coons, Susan Anderson. 2012. 52p. pap. 10.03 *(978-1-4669-1223-6(5))* Trafford Publishing.

Sanrio Company, Ltd Staff. Hello Kitty Super-Sweet Stencils. Becker and Mayer! Books Staff. 2013. (ENG.). 24p. (J). (gr. 2-6). spiral bd. 14.95 *(978-1-4197-0631-8(4)*, Abrams Bks. for Young Readers) Abrams.

Sansevero, Tony. Just for Now: Kids & the People of the Court. Morris, Kimberly & Burke, Kathleen. 2007. 48p. (J). (gr. k-4). 16.95 *(978-0-9754953-9-1(9))* Child Advocates, Inc.

—Short Boat on a Long River. Cockrum, James L. 2013. 180p. (YA). pap. 14.95 *(978-0-9768586-1-4(4))* Pangloss Publishing.

—The World According to Rock. Wermund, Jerry. 2005. 48p. (J). pap. *(978-0-9726255-1-7(8))* Rockon Publishing.

Sansom, Fiona. Daisy & the First Wish. Williams, Suzanne. 2009. (Fairy Blossoms Ser.: No. 5). (ENG.). 96p. (J). (gr. 2-5). pap. 4.99 *(978-0-06-113942-0(4))* HarperCollins Pubs.

—Egyptian Myths. Elgin, Kathy. 2009. (Myths from Many Lands Ser.). 48p. (YA). (gr. 2-6). pap. 12.85 *(978-1-60754-222-3(6))*; (gr. 4-7). 29.25 *(978-1-60754-221-6(8))* Windmill Bks.

—Fairy Blossoms: Daisy & the Magic Lesson. Williams, Suzanne. 2008. (Fairy Blossoms Ser.: No. 1). 128p. (J). (gr. 2-5). pap. 4.99 *(978-0-06-113938-3(6))* HarperCollins Pubs.

—Greek Myths. Claybourne, Anna. 2009. (Myths from Many Lands Ser.). 48p. (YA). (gr. 2-6). pap. 12.85 *(978-1-60754-225-4(0))*; (gr. 4-7). 29.25 *(978-1-60754-224-7(2))* Windmill Bks.

—Roman Myths. Elgin, Kathy. 2009. (Myths from Many Lands Ser.). 48p. (YA). (gr. 2-6). pap. 12.85 *(978-1-60754-231-5(5))*; (J). (gr. 4-7). 29.25 *(978-1-60754-230-8(7))* Windmill Bks.

Sansom, Fiona & Kennedy, Graham. African Myths. Morris, Neil. 2009. (Myths from Many Lands Ser.). 48p. (YA). (gr. 4-7). 29.25 *(978-1-60754-215-5(3))* Windmill Bks.

Santa, Carlos Piedra. Los Animales Mensajeros. 2010. (SPA.). 16p. (J). (gr. -1-1). 10.95 *(978-99922-1-358-2(2))* Piedra Santa, Editorial GTM. Dist: Libros Sin Fronteras.

—Zico Perico. Zea, Amilcar. 2009. (SPA.). 16p. (J). (gr. -1-1). pap. 7.95 *(978-99922-1-345-2(0))* Piedra Santa, Editorial GTM. Dist: Libros Sin Fronteras.

Santacruz, Juan. Ego: The Loving Planet. Parker, Jeff. 2012. (Avengers Set 3 Ser.). 24p. (J). (gr. 2-6). lib. bdg. 24.21 *(978-1-61479-014-3(0))* Spotlight.

—High Serpent Society. Parker, Jeff. 2012. (Avengers Set 3 Ser.). 24p. (J). (gr. 2-6). lib. bdg. 24.21 *(978-1-61479-015-0(9))* Spotlight.

—Medieval Women. Parker, Jeff. 2012. (Avengers Set 3 Ser.). 24p. (J). (gr. 2-6). lib. bdg. 24.21 *(978-1-61479-016-7(7))* Spotlight.

—A Not-So-Beautiful Mind. Parker, Jeff. 2012. (Avengers Set 3 Ser.). 24p. (J). (gr. 2-6). lib. bdg. 24.21 *(978-1-61479-017-4(5))* Spotlight.

Santana, Andrea. Los Gatos en la Luna/the Cats on the Moon. Castelli, Jeanette. 2005. (Bilingual Collection). (SPA.). 51p. (J). (gr. k-2). *(978-958-30-1767-4(1))* Panamericana Editorial.

Santanach, Tino. The Mask of Power. Beakman, Onk. 2013. (Skylanders Universe Ser.). (ENG.). 160p. (J). (gr. 3-7). pap. 5.99 *(978-0-448-46355-1(5)*, Grosset & Dunlap) Penguin Publishing Group.

—Ride along the Countryside. Golden Books Staff. 2004. (Paint Box Book Ser.). (ENG.). 32p. (J). (gr. -1-2). pap. 3.99 *(978-0-375-82820-1(6)*, Golden Bks.) Random Hse. Children's Bks.

—Travel with Thomas. Golden Books Staff. 2007. (Deluxe Coloring Book Ser.). (ENG.). 96p. (J). (gr. -1-2). pap. 3.99 *(978-0-375-83953-5(4)*, Golden Bks.) Random Hse. Children's Bks.

Santat, Dan. The Adventures of Nanny Piggins. Spratt, R. A. 2012. (Nanny Piggins Ser.: 1). (ENG.). 272p. (J). (gr. 3-7). pap. 7.00 *(978-0-316-06818-5(7))* Little, Brown Bks. for Young Readers.

—Attack of the Fluffy Bunnies. Beaty, Andrea. 2010. (Fluffy Bunnies Ser.). (ENG.). 192p. (YA). (gr. 3-7). 13.95 *(978-0-8109-8416-5(4)*, Amulet Bks.) Abrams.

—Because I'm Your Dad. Zappa, Ahmet. 2013. (ENG.). 32p. (J). (gr. -1-k). 15.99 *(978-1-4231-4774-9(X))* Disney Pr.

—Bobby the Brave (Sometimes) Yee, Lisa. 2012. (ENG.). 160p. (J). (gr. 2-5). pap. 5.99 *(978-0-545-05595-6(4)*, Levine, Arthur A. Bks.) Scholastic, Inc.

—Bobby vs. Girls (Accidentally) Yee, Lisa. 2010. (ENG.). 176p. (J). (gr. 2-5). pap. 5.99 *(978-0-545-05593-2(8)*, Levine, Arthur A. Bks.) Scholastic, Inc.

—Born to Drive. Perlman, Rhea. 2006. (Otto Undercover Ser.). 127p. (J). (gr. 4-7). 14.99 *(978-0-06-075496-9(6)*, Tegen, Katherine Bks) HarperCollins Pubs.

—Canyon Catastrophe. Perlman, Rhea. 2006. (Otto Undercover Ser.). 128p. (J). (gr. 4-7). 14.99 *(978-0-06-075498-3(2))* HarperCollins Pubs.

—Chicken Dance. Sauer, Tammi. (ENG.). (J). (gr. -1-2). 2015. 40p. pap. 6.95 *(978-1-4549-1477-8(7))*; 2009. 36p. 14.95 *(978-1-4027-5366-4(7))* Sterling Publishing Co., Inc.

—The Christmas Genie. Gutman, Dan. (ENG.). (J). (gr. 3-7). 2010. 174p. pap. 5.99 *(978-1-4169-9002-4(X))*; 2009. 112p. 16.99 *(978-1-4169-9001-7(1))* Simon & Schuster Bks. For Young Readers. (Simon & Schuster Bks. For Young Readers).

—Crankenstein. Berger, Samantha. 2013. (ENG.). 40p. (J). (gr. -1-1). 16.99 *(978-0-316-12656-4(X))* Little Brown & Co.

—Crankenstein. Berger, Samantha. 2014. (ENG.). 24p. (J). (gr. -1 — 1). bds. 8.99 *(978-0-316-28232-1(4))* Little, Brown Bks. for Young Readers.

—A Crankenstein Valentine. Berger, Samantha. 2014. (ENG.). 40p. (J). (gr. -1-1). 17.00 *(978-0-316-37638-9(8))* Little, Brown Bks. for Young Readers.

—Dog in Charge. Going, K. L. 2012. (ENG.). 40p. (J). (gr. -1-k). 16.99 *(978-0-8037-3479-1(4)*, Dial) Penguin Publishing Group.

—Dylan's Pets from A to Z. Marsoli, Lisa Ann. 2005. (J). bds. 14.99 *(978-0-9767325-1-8(3))* Toy Quest.

—Fire! Fuego! Brave Bomberos. Elya, Susan Middleton. ed. 2012. (ENG & SPA.). 40p. (J). (gr. -1-1). lib. bdg. 17.89 *(978-1-59990-759-8(3)*, Bloomsbury USA Childrens) Bloomsbury USA.

—Fluffy Bunnies 2: The Schnoz of Doom. Beaty, Andrea. 2015. (Fluffy Bunnies Ser.). (ENG.). 192p. (J). (gr. 3-7). 12.95 *(978-1-4197-1051-3(6)*, Amulet Bks.) Abrams.

—The Ghosts of Luckless Gulch. Isaacs, Anne. 2008. (ENG.). 48p. (J). (gr. k-3). 18.99 *(978-1-4169-0201-0(5)*, Atheneum Bks. for Young Readers) Simon & Schuster Children's Publishing.

—The Griffin's Riddle. Selfors, Suzanne. 2015. (Imaginary Veterinary Ser.: 5). (ENG.). 240p. (J). (gr. 2-7). 17.00 *(978-0-316-28690-9(7))* Little, Brown Bks. for Young Readers.

—Kel Gilligan's Daredevil Stunt Show. Buckley, Michael. 2012. (ENG.). 40p. (J). (gr. -1-2). 17.95 *(978-1-4197-0379-9(X)*, Abrams Bks. for Young Readers) Abrams.

—The Lonely Lake Monster. Selfors, Suzanne. 2013. (Imaginary Veterinary Ser.: 2). (ENG.). 224p. (J). (gr. 2-7). 16.00 *(978-0-316-22567-0(3))* Little Brown & Co.

—The Lonely Lake Monster. Selfors, Suzanne. 2014. (Imaginary Veterinary Ser.: 2). (ENG.). 240p. (J). (gr. 2-7). pap. 7.00 *(978-0-316-22561-8(4))* Little, Brown Bks. for Young Readers.

—Mighty Robot vs. the Mecha-Monkeys from Mars. Pilkey, Dav. 2014. (Ricky Ricotta Ser.: 4). (ENG.). 144p. (J). (gr. -1-3). pap. 5.99 *(978-0-545-63012-2(6))* Scholastic, Inc.

—Mighty Robot vs. the Mutant Mosquitoes from Mercury. Pilkey, Dav. 2014. (Ricky Ricotta Ser.: 2). (ENG.). 128p. (J). (gr. -1-3). pap. 5.99 *(978-0-545-63010-8(X))* Scholastic, Inc.

—Mighty Robot vs. the Stupid Stinkbugs from Saturn. 2015. (Ricky Ricotta Ser.: 6). (ENG.). 128p. (J). (gr. -1-3). 15.99 *(978-0-545-63121-1(1))* Scholastic, Inc.

—Ninja Red Riding Hood. Schwartz, Corey Rosen. 2014. (ENG.). 40p. (J). (gr. k-3). 16.99 *(978-0-399-16354-8(9)*, Putnam Juvenile) Penguin Publishing Group.

—Oh No! Or How My Science Project Destroyed the World. Barnett, Mac. 2010. (ENG.). 40p. (J). (gr. -1-2). 16.99 *(978-1-4231-2312-5(3))* Hyperion Pr.

—Oh No! Not Again! Or How I Built a Time Machine to Save History - Or at Least My History Grade. Barnett, Mac. 2012. (Oh No! Picture Book Ser.). (ENG.). 40p. (J). (gr. -1-k). 17.99 *(978-1-4231-4912-5(2))* Hyperion Pr.

—The Order of the Unicorn. Selfors, Suzanne. 2014. 197p. (J). *(978-0-316-32339-0(X))* Little Brown & Co.

—The Order of the Unicorn: The Imaginary Veterinary. Selfors, Suzanne. 2014. (Imaginary Veterinary Ser.: 4). (ENG.). 208p. (J). (gr. 2-7). 16.00 *(978-0-316-36406-5(1))* Little, Brown Bks. for Young Readers.

—Picture Day Perfection. Diesen, Deborah. 2013. (ENG.). 32p. (J). (gr. -1-3). 17.95 *(978-1-4197-0844-2(9)*, Abrams Bks. for Young Readers) Abrams.

—Ricky Ricotta's Mighty Robot. Pilkey, Dav. 2014. (Ricky Ricotta Ser.: 1). (ENG.). 112p. (J). (gr. -1-3). pap. 5.99 *(978-0-545-63009-2(6))*; lib. bdg. 15.99 *(978-0-545-63106-8(8))* Scholastic, Inc.

—Ricky Ricotta's Mighty Robot vs. the Jurassic Jackrabbits from Jupiter. Pilkey, Dav. 2014. (Ricky Ricotta Ser.: 5). (ENG.). 128p. (J). (gr. -1-3). pap. 5.99 *(978-0-545-63013-9(4))* Scholastic, Inc.

—The Sasquatch Escape. Selfors, Suzanne. (Imaginary Veterinary Ser.: 1). (ENG.). (J). (gr. 2-7). 2014. 240p. pap. 7.00 *(978-0-316-22569-4(X))*; 2013. 224p. 16.00 *(978-0-316-20934-2(1))* Little, Brown Bks. for Young Readers.

—The Sports Pages. Scieszka, Jon et al. 2012. (Guys Read Ser.: 3). (ENG.). 272p. (J). (gr. 3-7). 16.99 *(978-0-06-196378-0(X))*; pap. 6.99 *(978-0-06-196377-3(1))* HarperCollins Pubs. (Walden Pond Pr.).

—Stupid Stinkbugs from Saturn. 2015. (Ricky Ricotta Ser.: 6). (ENG.). 128p. (J). (gr. -1-3). pap. 5.99 *(978-0-545-63014-6(2))* Scholastic, Inc.

—The Three Ninja Pigs. Schwartz, Corey Rosen. 2012. (ENG.). 40p. (J). (gr. k-3). 16.99 *(978-0-399-25514-4(1)*, Putnam Juvenile) Penguin Publishing Group.

—The Voodoo Vultures from Venus. Pilkey, Dav. 2014. (Ricky Ricotta Ser.: 3). (ENG.). 128p. (J). (gr. -1-3). pap. 5.99 *(978-0-545-63011-5(8))* Scholastic, Inc.

—Water Balloon Doom. Perlman, Rhea. 2006. (Otto Undercover Ser.: No. 3). 124p. (J). (gr. 2-6). 14.99 *(978-0-06-075500-3(8)*, Tegen, Katherine Bks) HarperCollins Pubs.

Santat, Dan, jt. illus. see Dantat, Dan.

Santat, Dan, jt. illus. see Newman, Jeff.

Santat, Dan, jt. illus. see Stone, Kyle M.

Santella, Andrew. The Library of Congress, 1 vol. Santella, Andrew. 2006. (We the People: Expansion & Reform Ser.). (ENG.). 48p. (gr. 5-6). lib. bdg. 27.99 *(978-0-7565-1631-4(5)*, We the People) Compass Point Bks.

Santiago, Rose Mary. The Clever Boy & the Terrible, Dangerous Animal. Shah, Idries. 2005. 32p. (J). (gr. -1 — 1). pap. 6.99 *(978-1-883536-51-0(0)*, Hoopoe Bks.) I S H K.

—The Clever Boy & the Terrible, Dangerous Animal/el Muchachito Listo y el Terrible y Peligroso Animal. Shah, Idries. Wirkala, Rita, tr. 2005. 32p. (J). (gr. -1-3). 18.00 *(978-1-883536-39-8(1))*; pap., per. 6.95 *(978-1-883536-40-4(5))* I S H K. (Hoopoe Bks.).

—The Farmer's Wife. Shah, Idries. 2005. (Sounds of Afghanistan Ser.). 32p. (J). (gr. -1-3). 28.95 incl. audio compact disk *(978-1-883536-67-1(7)*, FAWCB1); pap., pap. 6.99 *(978-1-883536-49-7(9))* I S H K. (Hoopoe Bks.).

—The Farmer's Wife (La Esposa del Granjero) Shah, Idries. 2005. (ENG & SPA.). (J). (gr. -1-18). pap. 18.95 incl. audio compact disk *(978-1-883536-70-1(7)*, FAWCB4, Hoopoe Bks.) I S H K.

—The Farmer's Wife/la Esposa Del Granjero. Shah, Indries. 2003. (SPA & ENG.). (J). 6.95 *(978-1-883536-34-3(0)*, FAWI3, Hoopoe Bks.) I S H K.

—The Farmer's Wife/la Esposa Del Granjero. Shah, Idries. 2003. (SPA & ENG.). (J). 18.00 *(978-1-883536-33-6(2)*, FAWI2, Hoopoe Bks.) I S H K.

—The Farmer's Wife/la Esposa del Granjero. Shah, Idries. de Gonzales, Angelica Villagran, tr. 2005. (ENG & SPA.). 32p. (J). (gr. 4-7). 28.95 incl. audio compact disk *(978-1-883536-69-5(3)*, FAWCB3, Hoopoe Bks.) I S H K.

—The Man with Bad Manners. Shah, Idries. 2005. (Sounds of Afghanistan Ser.). (J). (gr. -1-3). 28.95 incl. audio compact disk *(978-1-883536-75-6(8)*, Hoopoe Bks.) I S H K.

Santiago, Rose Mary. The Man with Bad Manners. Santiago, Rose Mary, tr. Shah, Idries. 2003. 32p. (J). 18.00 *(978-1-883536-30-5(8)*, MABM1, Hoopoe Bks.) I S H K.

Santiago, Tony. A Greyhound's Tale: Running for Glory, Walking for Home. 2006. 40p. (J). 15.00 *(978-0-9762564-2-7(8))* Ideate Prairie.

—A Greyhound's Tale: Running for Glory, Walking for Home. Pierce, Craig. 2004. (J). per. 15.00 *(978-0-9762564-0-3(1)*, American Dog) Ideate Prairie.

—A Labrador's Tale: An Eye for Heroism. Pierce, Craig. 2006. 30p. (J). 15.00 *(978-0-9762564-3-4(6)*, American Dog) Ideate Prairie.

—A Labrador's Tale 2: The Incredible Thank You Gift, 1. Pierce, Craig. 2006. 34p. (J). 15.00 *(978-0-9762564-4-1(4)*, 2500, American Dog) Ideate Prairie.

—Sit. Stay. Work. Play: All Dogs Have Their Day. Pierce, Craig. 2008. 40p. (J). per. 5.95 *(978-0-9762564-5-8(2))* Ideate Prairie.

Santillan, Jorge. Alphabet of Music. Schwaeber, Barbie Heit. 2008. (ENG.). 40p. (J). (gr. k-2). 15.95 *(978-1-59249-770-6(5))* Soundprints.

—Drawing Baby Animals. Eason, Sarah. 2013. (Learn to Draw Ser.). 32p. (J). (gr. 2-5). pap. 63.00 *(978-1-4339-9526-2(3))* Stevens, Gareth Publishing LLLP.

—Drawing Dinosaurs. Eason, Sarah. 2013. (Learn to Draw Ser.). 32p. (J). (gr. 2-5). pap. 63.00 *(978-1-4339-9530-9(1))*; pap. 10.50 *(978-1-4339-9529-3(8))* Stevens, Gareth Publishing LLLP.

—Drawing Dragons. Eason, Sarah. 2013. (Learn to Draw Ser.). 32p. (J). (gr. 2-5). pap. 63.00 *(978-1-4339-9534-7(4))*; pap. 10.50 *(978-1-4339-9533-0(6))* Stevens, Gareth Publishing LLLP.

—Drawing Fairies, Mermaids, & Unicorns. Eason, Sarah. 2013. (Learn to Draw Ser.). 32p. (J). (gr. 2-5). pap. 63.00 *(978-1-4339-9538-5(7))*; pap. 10.50 *(978-1-4339-9537-8(9))* Stevens, Gareth Publishing LLLP.

—Drawing Knights & Castles. Eason, Sarah. 2013. (Learn to Draw Ser.). 32p. (J). (gr. 2-5). pap. 63.00 *(978-1-4339-9542-2(5))*; pap. 10.50 *(978-1-4339-9541-5(7))* Stevens, Gareth Publishing LLLP.

—Drawing Pirates & Pirate Ships. Eason, Sarah. 2013. (Learn to Draw Ser.). 32p. (J). (gr. 2-5). pap. 63.00 *(978-1-4339-9546-0(8))*; pap. 10.50 *(978-1-4339-9545-3(X))* Stevens, Gareth Publishing LLLP.

—Learn to Draw. Eason, Sarah. 2013. (Learn to Draw Ser.). 32p. (J). (gr. 2-5). 159.60 *(978-1-4339-9682-5(0))* Stevens, Gareth Publishing LLLP.

Santillan, Jorge & Clark, Debbie. Alphabet of Music. Schwaeber, Barbie Heit. 2011. (Alphabet Bks.). (ENG.). 40p. (J). (gr. -1-3). 9.95 *(978-1-60727-445-2(0))* Soundprints.

Santillan, Jorge H. Beach Volleyball Is No Joke, 1 vol. Yasuda, Anita. 2011. (Sports Illustrated Kids Victory School Superstars Ser.). (ENG.). 56p. (gr. 1-3). pap. 5.95 *(978-1-4342-3393-6(6))*; lib. bdg. 25.32 *(978-1-4342-2232-9(2))* Stone Arch Bks.

—Cheerleading Really Is a Sport, 1 vol. Gassman, Julie A. 2010. (Sports Illustrated Kids Victory School Superstars Ser.). (ENG.). 56p. (gr. 1-3). 25.32 *(978-1-4342-2130-8(X))*; pap. 5.95 *(978-1-4342-2809-3(6))* Stone Arch Bks.

—Don't Break the Balance Beam!, 1 vol. Gunderson, Jessica. 2010. (Sports Illustrated Kids Victory School Superstars Ser.). (ENG.). 56p. (gr. 1-3). 25.32 *(978-1-4342-2057-8(5))*; pap. 5.95 *(978-1-4342-2807-9(X))* Stone Arch Bks.

—Don't Wobble on the Wakeboard!, 1 vol. Kreie, Chris. 2011. (Sports Illustrated Kids Victory School Superstars Ser.). (ENG.). 56p. (gr. 1-3). lib. bdg. 25.32 *(978-1-4342-2235-0(7))* Stone Arch Bks.

—Five Fouls & You're Out!, 1 vol. Priebe, Val. 2011. (Sports Illustrated Kids Victory School Superstars Ser.). (ENG.). 56p. (gr. 1-3). pap. 5.95 *(978-1-4342-3075-1(9))*; lib. bdg. 25.32 *(978-1-4342-2228-2(4))* Stone Arch Bks.

—I Am on Strike Against Softball, 1 vol. Gassman, Julie A. 2012. (Sports Illustrated Kids Victory School Superstars Ser.). (ENG.). 56p. (gr. 1-3). pap. 5.95 *(978-1-4342-3870-2(9))*; lib. bdg. 25.32 *(978-1-4342-2247-3(0))* Stone Arch Bks.

—I Broke into Gymnastics Camp, 1 vol. Gunderson, Jessica. 2012. (Sports Illustrated Kids Victory School Superstars Ser.). (ENG.). 56p. (gr. 1-3). pap. 5.95 *(978-1-4342-3869-6(5))*; lib. bdg. 25.32 *(978-1-4342-2245-9(4))* Stone Arch Bks.

—I Could Be a One-Man Relay, 1 vol. Nickel, Scott. 2012. (Sports Illustrated Kids Victory School Superstars Ser.). (ENG.). 56p. (gr. 1-3). pap. 5.95 *(978-1-4342-3867-2(9))*; lib. bdg. 25.32 *(978-1-4342-2246-6(2))* Stone Arch Bks.

—I Couldn't Land a Bunny Hop, 1 vol. Kreie, Chris. 2012. (Sports Illustrated Kids Victory School Superstars Ser.). (ENG.). 56p. (gr. 1-3). pap. 5.95 *(978-1-4342-3865-8(2))*; lib. bdg. 25.32 *(978-1-4342-3762-0(1))* Stone Arch Bks.

—I Don't Want to Live on the Tennis Court, 1 vol. Priebe, Val. 2012. (Sports Illustrated Kids Victory School Superstars Ser.). (ENG.). 56p. (gr. 1-3). pap. 5.95 *(978-1-4342-3868-9(7))*; lib. bdg. 25.32 *(978-1-4342-3761-3(3))* Stone Arch Bks.

—I Just Have to Ride the Halfpipe! Gunderson, Jessica. 2011. (Sports Illustrated Kids Victory School Superstars Ser.). (ENG.). 56p. (gr. 1-3). pap. 5.95 *(978-1-4342-3397-4(9))*; lib. bdg. 25.32 *(978-1-4342-2236-7(5))* Stone Arch Bks.

—I Only Surf Online, 1 vol. Priebe, Val. 2011. (Sports Illustrated Kids Victory School Superstars Ser.). (ENG.).

56p. (gr. 1-3). pap. 5.95 *(978-1-4342-3394-3(4))*; lib. bdg. 25.32 *(978-1-4342-2233-6(0))* Stone Arch Bks.

—It's a Wrestling Mat, Not a Dance Floor, 1 vol. Nickel, Scott. 2011. (Sports Illustrated Kids Victory School Superstars Ser.). (ENG.). 56p. (gr. 1-3). pap. 5.95 *(978-1-4342-3076-8(7))*; lib. bdg. 25.32 *(978-1-4342-2227-5(6))* Stone Arch Bks.

—It's Hard to Dribble with Your Feet, 1 vol. Priebe, Val. 2010. (Sports Illustrated Kids Victory School Superstars Ser.). (ENG.). 56p. (gr. 1-3). 25.32 *(978-1-4342-2016-5(8))*; pap. 5.95 *(978-1-4342-2782-9(0))* Stone Arch Bks.

—I've Got the No-Skateboard Blues, 1 vol. Yasuda, Anita. 2012. (Sports Illustrated Kids Victory School Superstars Ser.). (ENG.). 56p. (gr. 1-3). pap. 5.95 *(978-1-4342-3866-5(0))*; lib. bdg. 25.32 *(978-1-4342-2244-2(6))* Stone Arch Bks.

—Nobody Wants to Play with a Ball Hog, 1 vol. Gassman, Julie A. 2010. (Sports Illustrated Kids Victory School Superstars Ser.). (ENG.). 56p. (gr. 1-3). 25.32 *(978-1-4342-2056-1(7))*; pap. 5.95 *(978-1-4342-2806-2(1))* Stone Arch Bks.

—A Running Back Can't Always Rush, 1 vol. LeBoutillier, Nate. 2010. (Sports Illustrated Kids Victory School Superstars Ser.). (ENG.). 56p. (gr. 1-3). 25.32 *(978-1-4342-2055-4(9))*; pap. 5.95 *(978-1-4342-2805-5(3))* Stone Arch Bks.

—Skating Is Hard When You're Homesick, 1 vol. Gassman, Julie A. 2011. (Sports Illustrated Kids Victory School Superstars Ser.). (ENG.). 56p. (gr. 1-3). pap. 5.95 *(978-1-4342-3398-1(7))*; lib. bdg. 25.32 *(978-1-4342-2237-4(3))* Stone Arch Bks.

—Skiing Has Its Ups & Downs, 1 vol. Nickel, Scott. 2011. (Sports Illustrated Kids Victory School Superstars Ser.). (ENG.). 56p. (gr. 1-3). pap. 5.95 *(978-1-4342-3395-0(2))*; lib. bdg. 25.32 *(978-1-4342-2234-3(9))* Stone Arch Bks.

—There Are No Figure Eights in Hockey, 1 vol. Kreie, Chris. 2010. (Sports Illustrated Kids Victory School Superstars Ser.). (ENG.). 56p. (gr. 1-3). 25.32 *(978-1-4342-2071-4(0))*; pap. 5.95 *(978-1-4342-2808-6(8))* Stone Arch Bks.

—There's a Hurricane in the Pool!, 1 vol. Gunderson, Jessica. 2011. (Sports Illustrated Kids Victory School Superstars Ser.). (ENG.). 56p. (gr. 1-3). 25.32 *(978-1-4342-2230-5(6))* Stone Arch Bks.

—There's No Crying in Baseball, 1 vol. Yasuda, Anita. 2011. (Sports Illustrated Kids Victory School Superstars Ser.). (ENG.). 56p. (gr. 1-3). pap. 5.95 *(978-1-4342-3077-5(5))*; lib. bdg. 25.32 *(978-1-4342-2226-8(8))* Stone Arch Bks.

—Who Wants to Play Just for Kicks?, 1 vol. Kreie, Chris. 2011. (Sports Illustrated Kids Victory School Superstars Ser.). (ENG.). 56p. (gr. 1-3). pap. 5.95 *(978-1-4342-3079-9(1))*; lib. bdg. 25.32 *(978-1-4342-2229-9(2))* Stone Arch Bks.

—You Can't Spike Your Serves, 1 vol. Gassman, Julie A. 2011. (Sports Illustrated Kids Victory School Superstars Ser.). (ENG.). 56p. (gr. 1-3). pap. 5.95 *(978-1-4342-3080-5(5))*; lib. bdg. 25.32 *(978-1-4342-2231-2(4))* Stone Arch Bks.

Santillan, Mariano. My Jewish Friend: A Young Catholic Learns about Judaism. Sirois, Celia. 2008. 47p. (J). (gr. 5-7). 15.95 *(978-0-8198-4857-4(3))* Pauline Bks. & Media.

—Trouble on the Blue Planet. Edison, Richard E. 2012. 47p. (J). 4.99 *(978-0-8280-2655-0(6))* Review & Herald Publishing Assn.

Santilli Wolfinger, Lorrie. Trouble in Treeville. Santilli, Shirley. 2013. 42p. 19.99 *(978-0-9910962-0-6(7))* Aperture Pr., LLC.

Santillo, LuAnn. At the Beach, 6 vols. Santillo, LuAnn. 2003. (Half-Pint Kids Readers Ser.). 42p. (J). (gr. -1-1). pap. 6.95 *(978-1-59256-084-4(9))* Half-Pint Kids, Inc.

—At the Circus, 6 vols. Santillo, LuAnn. 2003. (Half-Pint Kids Readers Ser.). 42p. (J). (gr. -1-1). pap. 6.95 *(978-1-59256-112-4(8))* Half-Pint Kids, Inc.

—The Bad Crab. Santillo, LuAnn. 2003. (Half-Pint Kids Readers Ser.). 7p. (J). (gr. -1-1). pap. 1.00 *(978-1-59256-094-3(6))* Half-Pint Kids, Inc.

—The Ball. Santillo, LuAnn. 2003. (Half-Pint Kids Readers Ser.). 7p. (J). (gr. -1-1). pap. 1.00 *(978-1-59256-081-3(4))* Half-Pint Kids, Inc.

—Barnyard Buddies, 6 vols. Santillo, LuAnn. 2003. (Half-Pint Kids Readers Ser.). 42p. (J). (gr. -1-1). pap. 6.95 *(978-1-59256-063-9(6))* Half-Pint Kids, Inc.

—Bee. Santillo, LuAnn. 2003. (Half-Pint Kids Readers Ser.). 7p. (J). (gr. -1-1). pap. *(978-1-59256-108-7(X))* Half-Pint Kids, Inc.

—The Best Show. Santillo, LuAnn. 2003. (Half-Pint Kids Readers Ser.). 7p. (J). (gr. -1-1). pap. 1.00 *(978-1-59256-117-9(9))* Half-Pint Kids, Inc.

—The Best Tricks. Santillo, LuAnn. 2003. (Half-Pint Kids Readers Ser.). 7p. (J). (gr. -1-1). pap. 1.00 *(978-1-59256-082-0(2))* Half-Pint Kids, Inc.

—The Big Hunt. Santillo, LuAnn. 2003. (Half-Pint Kids Readers Ser.). 7p. (J). (gr. -1-1). pap. 1.00 *(978-1-59256-076-9(8))* Half-Pint Kids, Inc.

—The Big Job. Santillo, LuAnn. 2003. (Half-Pint Kids Readers Ser.). 7p. (J). (gr. -1-1). pap. *(978-1-59256-044-8(X))* Half-Pint Kids, Inc.

—The Big Top. Santillo, LuAnn. 2003. (Half-Pint Kids Readers Ser.). 7p. (J). (gr. -1-1). pap. 1.00 *(978-1-59256-113-1(6))* Half-Pint Kids, Inc.

—Blends & Ends - Level B, 36 vols. Santillo, LuAnn. 2003. (Half-Pint Kids Readers Ser.). 7p. (J). (gr. -1-1). pap. 39.95 *(978-1-59256-127-8(6))* Half-Pint Kids, Inc.

—Bluejay. Santillo, LuAnn. 2003. (Half-Pint Kids Readers Ser.). 7p. (J). (gr. -1-1). pap. 1.00 *(978-1-59256-110-0(1))* Half-Pint Kids, Inc.

—Buzz. Santillo, LuAnn. 2003. (Half-Pint Kids Readers Ser.). 7p. (J). (gr. -1-1). pap. 1.00 *(978-1-59256-046-2(6))* Half-Pint Kids, Inc.

—The Cat. Santillo, LuAnn. 2003. (Half-Pint Kids Readers Ser.). 7p. (J). (gr. -1-1). pap. 1.00 *(978-1-59256-066-0(0))* Half-Pint Kids, Inc.

—The Chick. Santillo, LuAnn. 2003. (Half-Pint Kids Readers Ser.). 7p. (J). (gr. -1-1). pap. 1.00 *(978-1-59256-059-2(8))* Half-Pint Kids, Inc.

—Chip. Santillo, LuAnn. 2003. (Half-Pint Kids Readers Ser.). 7p. (J). (gr. -1-1). pap. *(978-1-59256-075-2(X))* Half-Pint Kids, Inc.

—Community Helpers, 6 vols. Santillo, LuAnn. 2003. (Half-Pint Kids Readers Ser.). 42p. (J). (gr. -1-1). pap. 6.95 *(978-1-59256-119-3(5))* Half-Pint Kids, Inc.

—The Cop. Santillo, LuAnn. 2003. (Half-Pint Kids Readers Ser.). 7p. (J). (gr. -1-1). pap. 1.00 *(978-1-59256-122-3(5))* Half-Pint Kids, Inc.

—The Dentist. Santillo, LuAnn. 2003. (Half-Pint Kids Readers Ser.). 7p. (J). (gr. -1-1). pap. 1.00 *(978-1-59256-120-9(9))* Half-Pint Kids, Inc.

—Digging for Clams. Santillo, LuAnn. 2003. (Half-Pint Kids Readers Ser.). 7p. (J). (gr. -1-1). pap. *(978-1-59256-092-9(X))* Half-Pint Kids, Inc.

—Dip & Sip. Santillo, LuAnn. 2003. (Half-Pint Kids Readers Ser.). 7p. (J). (gr. -1-1). pap. 1.00 *(978-1-59256-051-6(2))* Half-Pint Kids, Inc.

—The Doctor. Santillo, LuAnn. 2003. (Half-Pint Kids Readers Ser.). 7p. (J). (gr. -1-1). pap. 1.00 *(978-1-59256-121-6(7))* Half-Pint Kids, Inc.

—The Dog. Santillo, LuAnn. 2003. (Half-Pint Kids Readers Ser.). 7p. (J). (gr. -1-1). pap. 1.00 *(978-1-59256-065-3(2))* Half-Pint Kids, Inc.

—Down on the Farm, 6 vols. Santillo, LuAnn. 2003. (Half-Pint Kids Readers Ser.). 42p. (J). (gr. -1-1). pap. 6.95 *(978-1-59256-056-1(3))* Half-Pint Kids, Inc.

—The Duck. Santillo, LuAnn. 2003. (Half-Pint Kids Readers Ser.). 7p. (J). (gr. -1-1). pap. 1.00 *(978-1-59256-069-1(5))* Half-Pint Kids, Inc.

—The Eggs. Santillo, LuAnn. 2003. (Half-Pint Kids Readers Ser.). 7p. (J). (gr. -1-1). pap. *(978-1-59256-061-5(X))* Half-Pint Kids, Inc.

—Family Fun, 6 vols. Santillo, LuAnn. 2003. (Half-Pint Kids Readers Ser.). 42p. (J). (gr. -1-1). pap. 6.95 *(978-1-59256-098-1(9))* Half-Pint Kids, Inc.

—The Fire Fighter. Santillo, LuAnn. 2003. (Half-Pint Kids Readers Ser.). 7p. (J). (gr. -1-1). pap. 1.00 *(978-1-59256-124-7(1))* Half-Pint Kids, Inc.

—Fishing. Santillo, LuAnn. 2003. (Half-Pint Kids Readers Ser.). 7p. (J). (gr. -1-1). pap. 1.00 *(978-1-59256-093-6(8))* Half-Pint Kids, Inc.

—Flap. Santillo, LuAnn. 2003. (Half-Pint Kids Readers Ser.). 7p. (J). (gr. -1-1). pap. 1.00 *(978-1-59256-096-7(2))* Half-Pint Kids, Inc.

—Flipper. Santillo, LuAnn. 2003. (Half-Pint Kids Readers Ser.). 7p. (J). (gr. -1-1). pap. 1.00 *(978-1-59256-095-0(4))* Half-Pint Kids, Inc.

—Fred & Ed. Santillo, LuAnn. 2003. (Half-Pint Kids Readers Ser.). 7p. (J). (gr. -1-1). pap. 1.00 *(978-1-59256-074-5(1))* Half-Pint Kids, Inc.

—A Fun Trip. Santillo, LuAnn. 2003. (Half-Pint Kids Readers Ser.). 7p. (J). (gr. -1-1). pap. 1.00 *(978-1-59256-085-1(7))* Half-Pint Kids, Inc.

—Fun with Phonemes. Santillo, LuAnn. 2004. (Half-Pint Readers Ser.). 36p. (J). (gr. -1-1). pap. 11.95 *(978-1-59256-129-2(2))* Half-Pint Kids, Inc.

—Funny Clowns. Santillo, LuAnn. 2003. (Half-Pint Kids Readers Ser.). 7p. (J). (gr. -1-1). pap. 1.00 *(978-1-59256-116-2(0))* Half-Pint Kids, Inc.

—Go West. Santillo, LuAnn. 2003. (Half-Pint Kids Readers Ser.). 7p. (J). (gr. -1-1). pap. 1.00 *(978-1-59256-071-4(7))* Half-Pint Kids, Inc.

—Good Food. Santillo, LuAnn. 2003. (Half-Pint Kids Readers Ser.). 7p. (J). (gr. -1-1). pap. 1.00 *(978-1-59256-118-6(7))* Half-Pint Kids, Inc.

—Gum. Santillo, LuAnn. 2003. (Half-Pint Kids Readers Ser.). 7p. (J). (gr. -1-1). pap. 1.00 *(978-1-59256-087-5(3))* Half-Pint Kids, Inc.

—I Have Fun. Santillo, LuAnn. 2003. (Half-Pint Kids Readers Ser.). 7p. (J). (gr. -1-1). pap. 1.00 *(978-1-59256-055-4(5))* Half-Pint Kids, Inc.

—In the Meadow, 6 vols. Santillo, LuAnn. 2003. (Half-Pint Kids Readers Ser.). 42p. (J). (gr. -1-1). pap. 6.95 *(978-1-59256-105-6(5))* Half-Pint Kids, Inc.

—Jack. Santillo, LuAnn. 2003. (Half-Pint Kids Readers Ser.). 7p. (J). (gr. -1-1). pap. 1.00 *(978-1-59256-062-2(8))* Half-Pint Kids, Inc.

—Jake's Big Day. Santillo, LuAnn. 2003. (Half-Pint Kids Readers Ser.). 7p. (J). (gr. -1-1). pap. 1.00 *(978-1-59256-104-9(7))* Half-Pint Kids, Inc.

—Jane. Santillo, LuAnn. 2003. (Half-Pint Kids Readers Ser.). 7p. (J). (gr. -1-1). pap. 1.00 *(978-1-59256-099-8(7))* Half-Pint Kids, Inc.

—Jim & the Thug. Santillo, LuAnn. 2003. (Half-Pint Kids Readers Ser.). 7p. (J). (gr. -1-1). pap. 1.00 *(978-1-59256-078-3(4))* Half-Pint Kids, Inc.

—The King. Santillo, LuAnn. 2003. (Half-Pint Kids Readers Ser.). 7p. (J). (gr. -1-1). pap. 1.00 *(978-1-59256-050-9(4))* Half-Pint Kids, Inc.

—The Kiss. Santillo, LuAnn. 2003. (Half-Pint Kids Readers Ser.). 7p. (J). (gr. -1-1). pap. 1.00 *(978-1-59256-053-0(9))* Half-Pint Kids, Inc.

—Level A- Take Home Readers. Santillo, LuAnn. 2004. (Half-Pint Readers Ser.). 36p. (J). (gr. -1-1). pap. 79.95 *(978-1-59256-132-2(2))* Half-Pint Kids, Inc.

—Level B Take Home Readers. Santillo, LuAnn. 2004. (Half-Pint Readers Ser.). 36p. (J). (gr. -1-1). pap. 79.95 *(978-1-59256-133-9(0))* Half-Pint Kids, Inc.

—Level C - Take Home Readers. Santillo, LuAnn. 2004. (Half-Pint Readers Ser.). 36p. (J). (gr. -1-1). pap. 79.95 *(978-1-59256-134-6(9))* Half-Pint Kids, Inc.

—Lift-Off. Santillo, LuAnn. 2003. (Half-Pint Kids Readers Ser.). 7p. (J). (gr. -1-1). pap. 1.00 *(978-1-59256-043-1(1))* Half-Pint Kids, Inc.

—The Lion Tamer. Santillo, LuAnn. 2003. (Half-Pint Kids Readers Ser.). 7p. (J). (gr. -1-1). pap. 1.00 *(978-1-59256-115-5(2))* Half-Pint Kids, Inc.

—Liz. Santillo, LuAnn. 2003. (Half-Pint Kids Readers Ser.). 7p. (J). (gr. -1-1). pap. 1.00 *(978-1-59256-083-7(0))* Half-Pint Kids, Inc.

—Look at Me. Santillo, LuAnn. 2003. (Half-Pint Kids Readers Ser.). 7p. (J). (gr. -1-1). pap. 1.00 *(978-1-59256-052-3(0))* Half-Pint Kids, Inc.

—Lots More Fun with Phonemes. Santillo, LuAnn. 2004. (Half-Pint Readers Ser.). 36p. (J). (gr. -1-1). pap. 11.95 *(978-1-59256-131-5(4))* Half-Pint Kids, Inc.

—The Mailman. Santillo, LuAnn. 2003. (Half-Pint Kids Readers Ser.). 7p. (J). (gr. -1-1). pap. *(978-1-59256-125-4(X))* Half-Pint Kids, Inc.

—Medieval Magic, 6 vols. Santillo, LuAnn. 2003. (Half-Pint Kids Readers Ser.). 42p. (J). (gr. -1-1). pap. 6.95 *(978-1-59256-049-3(0))* Half-Pint Kids, Inc.

—Mike. Santillo, LuAnn. 2003. (Half-Pint Kids Readers Ser.). 7p. (J). (gr. -1-1). pap. 1.00 *(978-1-59256-100-1(4))* Half-Pint Kids, Inc.

—Mole. Santillo, LuAnn. 2003. (Half-Pint Kids Readers Ser.). 7p. (J). (gr. -1-1). pap. *(978-1-59256-111-7(X))* Half-Pint Kids, Inc.

—More Fun with Phonemes. Santillo, LuAnn. 2004. (Half-Pint Readers Ser.). 36p. (J). (gr. -1-1). pap. 11.95 *(978-1-59256-130-8(6))* Half-Pint Kids, Inc.

—Moving A-Long Level C, 36 vols. Santillo, LuAnn. 2003. (Half-Pint Kids Readers Ser.). 7p. (J). (gr. -1-1). pap. 39.95 *(978-1-59256-128-5(4))* Half-Pint Kids, Inc.

—Outerspace, 6 vols. Santillo, LuAnn. 2003. (Half-Pint Kids Readers Ser.). 42p. (J). (gr. -1-1). pap. 6.95 *(978-1-59256-042-4(3))* Half-Pint Kids, Inc.

—Packing. Santillo, LuAnn. 2003. (Half-Pint Kids Readers Ser.). 7p. (J). (gr. -1-1). pap. 1.00 *(978-1-59256-072-1(5))* Half-Pint Kids, Inc.

—The Picnic. Santillo, LuAnn. 2003. (Half-Pint Kids Readers Ser.). 7p. (J). (gr. -1-1). pap. 1.00 *(978-1-59256-090-5(3))* Half-Pint Kids, Inc.

—The Pig. Santillo, LuAnn. 2003. (Half-Pint Kids Readers Ser.). 7p. (J). (gr. -1-1). pap. 1.00 *(978-1-59256-064-6(4))* Half-Pint Kids, Inc.

—Pioneer Days, 6 vols. Santillo, LuAnn. 2003. (Half-Pint Kids Readers Ser.). 42p. (J). (gr. -1-1). pap. 6.95 *(978-1-59256-070-7(9))* Half-Pint Kids, Inc.

—Rags. Santillo, LuAnn. 2003. (Half-Pint Kids Readers Ser.). 7p. (J). (gr. -1-1). pap. 1.00 *(978-1-59256-073-8(3))* Half-Pint Kids, Inc.

—Rose. Santillo, LuAnn. 2003. (Half-Pint Kids Readers Ser.). 7p. (J). (gr. -1-1). pap. 1.00 *(978-1-59256-101-8(2))* Half-Pint Kids, Inc.

—Running Fox. Santillo, LuAnn. 2003. (Half-Pint Kids Readers Ser.). 7p. (J). (gr. -1-1). pap. 1.00 *(978-1-59256-079-0(2))* Half-Pint Kids, Inc.

—The Seeds. Santillo, LuAnn. 2003. (Half-Pint Kids Readers Ser.). 7p. (J). (gr. -1-1). pap. 1.00 *(978-1-59256-109-4(8))* Half-Pint Kids, Inc.

—Shag. Santillo, LuAnn. 2003. (Half-Pint Kids Readers Ser.). 7p. (J). (gr. -1-1). pap. 1.00 *(978-1-59256-068-4(7))* Half-Pint Kids, Inc.

—A Sights & Sounds - Level, 36 vols. Santillo, LuAnn. 2003. (Half-Pint Kids Readers Ser.). 7p. (J). (gr. -1-1). pap. 39.95 *(978-1-59256-126-1(8))* Half-Pint Kids, Inc.

—Six Jobs. Santillo, LuAnn. 2003. (Half-Pint Kids Readers Ser.). 7p. (J). (gr. -1-1). pap. *(978-1-59256-058-5(X))* Half-Pint Kids, Inc.

—The Snack Shack. Santillo, LuAnn. 2003. (Half-Pint Kids Readers Ser.). 7p. (J). (gr. -1-1). pap. 1.00 *(978-1-59256-086-8(5))* Half-Pint Kids, Inc.

—Snail. Santillo, LuAnn. 2003. (Half-Pint Kids Readers Ser.). 7p. (J). (gr. -1-1). pap. 1.00 *(978-1-59256-106-3(3))* Half-Pint Kids, Inc.

—Steve & Pete. Santillo, LuAnn. 2003. (Half-Pint Kids Readers Ser.). 7p. (J). (gr. -1-1). pap. 1.00 *(978-1-59256-103-2(9))* Half-Pint Kids, Inc.

—Stop Hopping. Santillo, LuAnn. 2003. (Half-Pint Kids Readers Ser.). 7p. (J). (gr. -1-1). pap. 1.00 *(978-1-59256-054-7(7))* Half-Pint Kids, Inc.

—Stubs. Santillo, LuAnn. 2003. (Half-Pint Kids Readers Ser.). 7p. (J). (gr. -1-1). pap. 1.00 *(978-1-59256-097-4(0))* Half-Pint Kids, Inc.

—The Sun. Santillo, LuAnn. 2003. (Half-Pint Kids Readers Ser.). 7p. (J). (gr. -1-1). pap. 1.00 *(978-1-59256-047-9(4))* Half-Pint Kids, Inc.

—The Suntan. Santillo, LuAnn. 2003. (Half-Pint Kids Readers Ser.). 7p. (J). (gr. -1-1). pap. 1.00 *(978-1-59256-088-2(1))* Half-Pint Kids, Inc.

—Ted's Job. Santillo, LuAnn. 2003. (Half-Pint Kids Readers Ser.). 7p. (J). (gr. -1-1). pap. 1.00 *(978-1-59256-060-8(1))* Half-Pint Kids, Inc.

—The Tight Rope. Santillo, LuAnn. 2003. (Half-Pint Kids Readers Ser.). 7p. (J). (gr. -1-1). pap. 1.00 *(978-1-59256-114-8(4))* Half-Pint Kids, Inc.

—Toad. Santillo, LuAnn. 2003. (Half-Pint Kids Readers Ser.). 7p. (J). (gr. -1-1). pap. 1.00 *(978-1-59256-107-0(1))* Half-Pint Kids, Inc.

—The Tracks. Santillo, LuAnn. 2003. (Half-Pint Kids Readers Ser.). 7p. (J). (gr. -1-1). pap. 1.00 *(978-1-59256-080-6(6))* Half-Pint Kids, Inc.

—The Trip. Santillo, LuAnn. 2003. (Half-Pint Kids Readers Ser.). 7p. (J). (gr. -1-1). pap. 1.00 *(978-1-59256-057-8(1))* Half-Pint Kids, Inc.

—Trot, Trot. Santillo, LuAnn. 2003. (Half-Pint Kids Readers Ser.). 7p. (J). (gr. -1-1). pap. 1.00 *(978-1-59256-067-7(9))* Half-Pint Kids, Inc.

—The Tune. Santillo, LuAnn. 2003. (Half-Pint Kids Readers Ser.). 7p. (J). (gr. -1-1). pap. 1.00 *(978-1-59256-102-5(0))* Half-Pint Kids, Inc.

—The UFO. Santillo, LuAnn. 2003. (Half-Pint Kids Readers Ser.). 7p. (J). (gr. -1-1). pap. 1.00 *(978-1-59256-045-5(8))* Half-Pint Kids, Inc.

—Under the Sea, 6 vols. Santillo, LuAnn. 2003. (Half-Pint Kids Readers Ser.). 42p. (J). (gr. -1-1). pap. 6.95 *(978-1-59256-091-2(1))* Half-Pint Kids, Inc.

—The Vet. Santillo, LuAnn. 2003. (Half-Pint Kids Readers Ser.). 7p. (J). (gr. -1-1). pap. 1.00 *(978-1-59256-123-0(3))* Half-Pint Kids, Inc.

—The Wet Dock. Santillo, LuAnn. 2003. (Half-Pint Kids Readers Ser.). 7p. (J). (gr. -1-1). pap. *(978-1-59256-089-9(X))* Half-Pint Kids, Inc.

—Wild West, 6 vols. Santillo, LuAnn. 2003. (Half-Pint Kids Readers Ser.). 42p. (J). (gr. -1-1). pap. 6.95 *(978-1-59256-077-6(6))* Half-Pint Kids, Inc.

—The Wish. Santillo, LuAnn. 2003. (Half-Pint Kids Readers Ser.). 7p. (J). (gr. -1-1). pap. 1.00 *(978-1-59256-048-6(2))* Half-Pint Kids, Inc.

Santini, Debrah L. Abby's Chairs. Santucci, Barbara. 2004. 32p. 16.00 *(978-0-8028-5205-2(X))* Eerdmans, William B. Publishing Co.

Santitoro, Theresa & Tumminello, Giovanna. It's Elementary, Funny Things Kids Say in School. Isler, Linda Germano. 2010. 32p. pap. 9.95 *(978-1-936343-00-3(2))* Peppertree Pr., The.

Santolaya, Antonia. La Aventura Del Zorro. Santolaya, Antonia, tr. Alonso, Manuel L. & Alonso Gómez, Manuel L. 2008. (SPA.). 72p. (J). pap. 10.99 *(978-84-207-4354-7(2))* Lectorum Pubns., Inc.

Santomauro, Fabio. The Whispering Town. Elvgren, Jennifer. 2014. (Holocaust Ser.). (ENG.). 32p. (J). (gr. 2-5). 17.95 *(978-1-4677-1194-4(2))*; 7.95 *(978-1-4677-1195-1(0))* Lerner Publishing Group. (Kar-Ben Publishing).

Santora, Bud. Wise Bear William: A New Beginning. Wooten, Arthur. 2012. 44p. pap. 12.99 *(978-0-9850529-1-1(0))* Galaxias Productions.

Santora, Maureen Crethan. The Day the Towers Fell: The Story of September 11, 2001. Santora, Maureen Crethan. 2008. 32p. (J). 31.99 *(978-1-4257-7872-9(0))* Xlibris Corp.

Santore, Charles. C'Etait la Veille de Noel. Moore, Clement C. 2012. (FRE.). 48p. (J). 18.95 *(978-1-60433-300-8(6)*, Applesauce Pr.) Cider Mill Pr. Bk. Pubs., LLC.

Santore, Charles. The Classic Tale of Mr. Jeremy Fisher. Potter, Beatrix. 2015. (ENG.). 22p. (J). bds. 8.95 ***(978-1-60433-548-4(3)***, Applesauce Pr.) Cider Mill Pr. Bk. Pubs., LLC.

Santore, Charles. The Classic Tale of Peter Rabbit: And Other Cherished Stories. Potter, Beatrix. 2013. (ENG.). 68p. (J). 19.95 *(978-1-60433-376-3(6)*, Applesauce Pr.) Cider Mill Pr. Bk. Pubs., LLC.

Santore, Charles. The Classic Tale of the Flopsy Bunnies. Potter, Beatrix. 2015. (ENG.). 22p. (J). bds. 8.95 ***(978-1-60433-551-4(3)***, Applesauce Pr.) Cider Mill Pr. Bk. Pubs., LLC.

Santore, Charles. Cuento de Nochebuena. Moore, Clement C. 2013. (ENG.). 24p. (J). bds. 9.95 *(978-1-60433-451-7(7)*, Applesauce Pr.) Cider Mill Pr. Bk. Pubs., LLC.

—The Little Mermaid. Anderson, Hans Christian. 2013. Orig. Title: Lille havfrue. (ENG.). 48p. (J). 16.95 *(978-1-60433-377-0(4)*, Applesauce Pr.) Cider Mill Pr. Bk. Pubs., LLC.

—The Night Before Christmas. 2011. (Classic Edition Ser.). (ENG.). 32p. (J). (gr. -1). 19.95 *(978-1-60433-237-7(9)*, Applesauce Pr.) Cider Mill Pr. Bk. Pubs., LLC.

—The Night Before Christmas, Set. Moore, Clement C. gif. ed. 2013. (ENG.). 48p. (J). 14.95 *(978-1-60433-437-1(1)*, Applesauce Pr.) Cider Mill Pr. Bk. Pubs., LLC.

—The Night Before Christmas: Or, a Visit from St. Nicholas. Moore, Clement C. 2011. 41p. (J). *(978-1-60464-033-5(2))* Appleseed Pr. Bk. Pub. LLC.

—Night Before Christmas Board Book: The Classic Edition. Moore, Clement C. 2013. (ENG.). 26p. (J). bds. 8.95 *(978-1-60433-438-8(X)*, Applesauce Pr.) Cider Mill Pr. Bk. Pubs., LLC.

—The Night Before Christmas Mini Edition. Moore, Clement C. 2011. (Little Seedling Edition Ser.: 1). (ENG.). 32p. (J). 5.95 *(978-1-60433-244-5(1)*, Applesauce Pr.) Cider Mill Pr. Bk. Pubs., LLC.

—Paul Revere's Ride: The Landlord's Tale. Longfellow, Henry Wadsworth. Encarnacion, Elizabeth, ed. 2014. (ENG.). 40p. (J). 17.95 *(978-1-60433-493-7(2)*, Applesauce Pr.) Cider Mill Pr. Bk. Pubs., LLC.

—Paul Revere's Ride: The Landlord's Tale. Longfellow, Henry Wadsworth. 2005. 28p. (J). (gr. 4-8). reprint ed. 17.00 *(978-0-7567-9202-2(9))* DIANE Publishing Co.

—Paul Revere's Ride: The Landlord's Tale. Longfellow, Henry Wadsworth. 2003. 40p. (J). lib. bdg. 17.89 *(978-0-06-623747-3(5))* HarperCollins Pubs.

—Snow White: A Tale from the Brothers Grimm. Grimm, Jacob & Grimm, Wilhelm. 2010. (ENG.). 48p. (J). (gr. 1-5). 16.95 *(978-1-4027-7157-6(6))* Sterling Publishing Co., Inc.

—The Velveteen Rabbit: Or How Toys Become Real. Williams, Margery. 2013. (Classic Edition Ser.). (ENG.). 48p. (J). 16.95 *(978-1-60433-277-3(8)*, Applesauce Pr.) Cider Mill Pr. Bk. Pubs., LLC.

—The Velveteen Rabbit: Or, How Toys Become Real. Williams, Margery. Encarnacion, Liz, ed. 2014. (ENG.). 24p. (J). bds. 8.95 *(978-1-60433-461-6(4)*, Applesauce Pr.) Cider Mill Pr. Bk. Pubs., LLC.

—William the Curious: Knight of the Water Lilies. 2012. (J). *(978-1-60464-034-2(0))* Appleseed Pr. Bk. Pub. LLC.

Santore, Charles. William the Curious: Knight of the Water Lilies. Santore, Charles. 2014. (ENG.). 44p. (J). (gr. -1). 16.95 *(978-1-60433-474-6(6))* Cider Mill Pr. Bk. Pubs., LLC.

Santoro. My Secret Place: A Simply Gorjuss Journal. Santoro. 2014. (Gorjuss Ser.). (ENG.). 128p. (J). (gr. 2-4). 12.99 *(978-0-7636-7453-3(2))* Candlewick Pr.

Santoro, Christopher. Bang! Boom! Roar! A Busy Crew of Dinosaurs. Evans, Nate & Brown, Stephanie Gwyn. 2012. (ENG.). 40p. (J). (gr. -1-2). 15.99 *(978-0-06-087960-0(2))* HarperCollins Pubs.

—Bears Are Curious. Milton, Joyce. 2015. (Step into Reading Ser.). (ENG.). 32p. (J). (gr. -1-1). pap. 3.99 *(978-0-679-85301-5(4)*, Random Hse. Bks. for Young Readers) Random Hse. Children's Bks.

—Dinosaur ABC. Evans, Nate & Brown, Stephanie Gwyn. 2011. (J). lib. bdg. 16.89 *(978-0-06-087962-4(9))* HarperCollins Pubs.

—Old MacDonald Had a Dragon, 0 vols. Baker, Ken. 2012. (ENG.). 32p. (J). (gr. k-3). 16.99 *(978-0-7614-6175-3(2)*, 9780761461753, Amazon Children's Publishing) Amazon Publishing.

—Peter Cottontail. Stephens, Amanda. 2008. (ENG.). (J). (gr. -1-3). 58p. 9.95 *(978-0-545-05248-1(3))*; 60p. 18.95 *(978-0-545-05250-4(5))* Scholastic, Inc.

Santoro, Scott. Which Way to Witch School? Santoro, Scott. (ENG.). 32p. (J). (gr. -1-2). 2012. pap. 5.99 *(978-0-06-078183-5(1))*; 2010. 16.99 *(978-0-06-078181-1(5))* HarperCollins Pubs.

Santos, Carriel Ann. A Straw Hat So Big. Bortnick, Lori. 2013. 52p. pap. 11.95 *(978-0-9851492-6-0(4))* Flying Turtle Publishing.

Santos, Ma Jesus. El Color de la Arena. O'Callaghan, Elena. 2010. (SPA.). 48p. (J). (gr. 4-6). *(978-84-263-5921-6(3))* Vives, Luis Editorial (Edelvives).

Santoso, Charles. The Best Friend Battle. Eyre, Lindsay. 2015. (Sylvie Scruggs Ser.: 1). (ENG.). 160p. (J). (gr. 2-5). 16.99 *(978-0-545-62027-7(9))* Scholastic, Inc.

—I Don't Like Koala. Ferrell, Sean. 2015. (ENG.). 40p. (J). (gr. -1-3). 17.99 *(978-1-4814-0068-8(1)*, Atheneum Bks. for Young Readers) Simon & Schuster Children's Publishing.

Santoso, Charles. Peanut Butter & Brains. McGee, Joe. 2015. (ENG.). 32p. (J). (gr. -1-3). 16.95 ***(978-1-4197-1247-0(0)***, Abrams Bks. for Young Readers) Abrams.

Santoso, Charles. Spy Guy: The Not-So-Secret Agent. Young, Jessica. 2015. (ENG.). 40p. (J). (gr. -1-3). 16.99 *(978-0-544-20859-9(5)*, HMH Books For Young Readers) Houghton Mifflin Harcourt Publishing Co.

Santy, Elizabeth & Fisher, Jessie. I Believe in You: A Mother's Message to Her Son with Learning Differences. Debeer, Kristen. 2012. 32p. pap. 12.97 *(978-1-61897-802-8(0)*, Strategic Bk. Publishing) Strategic Book Publishing & Rights Agency (SBPRA).

Sanz, Jesús. Charlie y el Gran Ascensor de Cristal. Sanz, Jesús, tr. Dahl, Roald. 27th ed. 2005.Tr. of Charlie & the Great Glass Elevator. (SPA.). 208p. (J). (gr. 5-8). pap. 11.95 *(978-84-204-6573-9(9)*, Alfaguara) Santillana USA Publishing Co., Inc.

—Charlie y la Fabrica de Chocolate. Sanz, Jesús, tr. Dahl, Roald. 51st ed.Tr. of Charlie & the Chocolate Factory. (SPA.). 172p. (J). (gr. 5-8). pap. 9.95 *(978-84-204-6450-3(3))* Santillana USA Publishing Co., Inc.

Sanzi, Desiderio. An Ant. Johnson, Jinny. 2015. (J). pap. ***(978-1-68152-073-5(7))*** Amicus Educational.

Sanzi, Desiderio. What's It Like to Be... Ant? Johnson, Jinny. 2011. (What's It Like to Be... ? Ser.). 24p. (J). (gr. -1-k). 25.65 *(978-1-60753-183-8(6))* Amicus Educational.

—What's It Like to Be... Bee? Ganeri, Anita & Johnson, Jinny. 2011. (What's It Like to Be... ? Ser.). 24p. (J). (gr. -1-k). 25.65 *(978-1-60753-184-5(4))* Amicus Educational.

—What's It Like to Be... Butterfly? Johnson, Jinny. 2011. (What's It Like to Be... ? Ser.). 24p. (J). (gr. -1-k). 25.65 *(978-1-60753-185-2(2))* Amicus Educational.

—What's It Like to Be... Dragonfly? Ganeri, Anita & Johnson, Jinny. 2011. (What's It Like to Be... ? Ser.). 24p. (J). (gr. -1-k). 25.65 *(978-1-60753-186-9(0))* Amicus Educational.

—What's It Like to Be... Grasshopper? Martineau, Susan & Jinny, Johnson. 2011. (What's It Like to Be... ? Ser.). 24p. (J). (gr. -1-k). 25.65 *(978-1-60753-193-7(3))* Amicus Educational.

Sao, Jennifer. Summer Daze: The Brush Fire. Cecca, John. Tick, David, ed. 2011. (ENG.). 94p. pap. 8.95 *(978-1-4679-1734-6(6))* CreateSpace Independent Publishing Platform.

Saphin, Wendy. Rosie's Box: A Box Full of Surprises. Saphin, Wendy. 2012. 20p. pap. 10.95 *(978-1-62212-457-2(X)*, Strategic Bk. Publishing) Strategic Book Publishing & Rights Agency (SBPRA).

Saponaro, Dominick. The Guns of Tortuga. Strickland, Brad & Fuller, Thomas E. 2003. (ENG.). 208p. (J). (gr. 3-7). pap. 10.99 *(978-0-689-85297-8(5)*, Simon & Schuster/Paula Wiseman Bks.) Simon & Schuster/Paula Wiseman Bks.

Saport, Linda. Circles of Hope. Williams, Karen Lynn. 2005. 32p. (J). 16.00 *(978-0-8028-5276-2(9))* Eerdmans, William B. Publishing Co.

Saport, Linda. Before You Were Born. Saport, Linda. Carlstrom, Nancy White. 2004. 32p. (J). (gr. -1-k). 17.00 *(978-0-8028-5185-7(1))* Eerdmans, William B. Publishing Co.

Sapp, Allen. Nokum: Ma Voix et Mon Coeur, 1 vol. Bouchard, David. 2006. (CRE & FRE.). 32p. (J). (gr. -1). 24.95 *(978-0-88995-383-3(X))* Red Deer Pr. CAN. Dist: Ingram Pub. Services.

—Nokum Is My Teacher, 1 vol. Bouchard, David & Bouchard, David. 2006. (CRE & ENG.). 32p. (J). (gr. -1). 24.95 *(978-0-88995-367-3(8)*, 0889953678) Red Deer Pr. CAN. Dist: Midpoint Trade Bks., Inc.

Sapp, Karen. Barnaby the Bedbug Detective. Stier, Catherine. 2013. (ENG.). 32p. (J). (gr. -1-2). 16.99 *(978-0-8075-0904-3(3))* Whitman, Albert & Co.

—Christmas Is... 2010. (ENG.). 24p. (J). (gr. -1-k). 8.99 *(978-0-00-730375-5(0))* HarperCollins Pubs. Ltd. GBR. Dist: Independent Pubs. Group.

—Counting on the Farm. Top That Publishing Staff, ed. 2007. (Magnetic Fun Ser.). 16p. (J). (gr. -1). *(978-1-84666-270-6(2)*, Tide Mill Pr.) Top That! Publishing PLC.

—Ed's Egg. Bedford, David. 2010. (Storytime Ser.). (ENG.). 24p. (J). (gr. -1-1). lib. bdg. 15.99 *(978-1-59566-859-2(4))* QEB Publishing Inc.

—Ellie's Christmas. 2013. (J). *(978-1-4351-4835-2(5))* Barnes & Noble, Inc.

Sappington, Ray. Ben the Flying Cat, 1 vol. Randolph, Robert. 2009. 30p. pap. 24.95 *(978-1-60749-088-3(9))* America Star Bks.

Sapulich, Joseph. Day by Day Begin-to-Read Bible. Henley, Karyn. 2007. (ENG.). 448p. (J). (gr. -1-2). 14.99 *(978-1-4143-0934-7(1))* Tyndale Hse. Pubs.

Saraceni, Claudia. Chinese Myths. Shone, Rob. 2006. (Graphic Mythology Ser.). (ENG.). 48p. (J). (gr. 4-7). lib. bdg. 31.95 *(978-1-4042-0799-8(6))* Rosen Publishing Group, Inc., The.

—Crime Scene Investigators. Shone, Rob. 2008. (Graphic Forensic Science Ser.). (ENG.). 48p. (YA). (gr. 5-8). lib. bdg. 31.95 *(978-1-4042-1443-9(7))* Rosen Publishing Group, Inc., The.

—Spectacular Shipwrecks. Jeffrey, Gary. 2008. (Graphic Nonfiction Ser.). (ENG.). 48p. (gr. 3-8). pap. 14.05 *(978-1-4042-9597-1(6))*; (J). (gr. 5-9). lib. bdg. 31.95 *(978-1-4042-1091-2(1))* Rosen Publishing Group, Inc., The.

Sarago-Kendrick, Delphine. Djomi Dream Child. Fry, Christopher. 2004. (ENG.). 32p. (J). (gr. k-7). pap. 13.95 *(978-1-875641-82-6(3))* Magabala Bks. AUS. Dist: Independent Pubs. Group.

Sarago-Kendrick, Delphine. Nana's Land. Sarago-Kendrick, Delphine. 2004. 44p. (J). pap. *(978-1-875641-90-1(4))* Magabala Bks.

Saraniti, Carlos. La Polilla del Baul. Carvajal, Mario. 2003. (SPA.). 32p. (J). (gr. k-3). pap. 8.95 *(978-968-19-0483-8(4))* Santillana USA Publishing Co., Inc.

Sarcone-Roach, Julia. Incredible Inventions. Hopkins, Lee Bennett. 2009. 32p. (J). (gr. k-5). (ENG.). 17.99 *(978-0-06-087245-8(4))*; lib. bdg. 18.89 *(978-0-06-087246-5(2))* HarperCollins Pubs. (Greenwillow Bks.).

Sardinha, Rick. The Land of the Silver Apples. Farmer, Nancy. 2007. (ENG.). 512p. (J). (gr. 5-9). 18.99 *(978-1-4169-0735-0(1)*, Atheneum/Richard Jackson Bks.) Simon & Schuster Children's Publishing.

Sarecky, Melody. Apples, Bubbles, & Crystals: Your Science ABCs. Bennett, Andrea T. & Kessler, James H. 2004. (J). *(978-0-8412-3944-9(4))* American Chemical Society.

—Sunlight, Skyscrapers, & Soda-Pop: The Wherever-You-Look Science Book. Bennett, Andrea T. & Kessler, James H. 2003. (J). 12.95 *(978-0-8412-3870-1(7))* American Chemical Society.

Sargent, Claudia Karabaic. Nice Vine, Quite Fine, Vol. 2. Goldish, Meish. l.t. ed. 2005. (Little Books & Big Bks.: Vol. 7). 8p. (gr. k-2). 23.00 net. *(978-0-8215-7516-1(3))* Sadlier, William H. Inc.

Sargent, Shannon Marie. My Little One: A Mother's Lullaby. Wilt, Gerri Ann et al. 2008. (J). *(978-0-87839-299-5(8))* North Star Pr. of St. Cloud.

Sari. The Pink Maple House. Govan, Christine Noble. 2013. 292p. pap. 13.95 *(978-1-61427-443-8(6))* Martino Publishing.

—The Surprising Summer. Govan, Christine Noble. 2013. 178p. pap. 9.95 *(978-1-61427-449-0(5))* Martino Publishing.

Sariola, Eulalia. El Libro de Las Mil y una Noches: Relatos de Hoy y Siempre. Castells, Margarita. 2006. (SPA & ENG.). 72p. (J). (gr. 4-7). pap. 15.00 *(978-84-666-1335-4(8))* Ediciones B ESP. Dist: Independent Pubs. Group.

Sarkar, Soumitro. Monkey's Drum. Moorthy, Anita. 2003. (ENG.). 24p. pap. 3.99 *(978-81-86211-15-1(2))* Penguin Publishing Group.

Sarl Aky-Aka Creations & Golden Books Staff. Wedding Bells. Golden Books Staff. 2008. (Holographic Sticker Book Ser.). (ENG.). 48p. (J). (gr. -1-2). pap. 3.99 *(978-0-375-84285-6(3)*, Golden Bks.) Random Hse. Children's Bks.

Sarna, Billy. Where Do Raindrops Go? Champagne, Elena. l.t. ed. 2006. 24p. (J). (gr. -1-3). per. 10.99 *(978-1-59879-233-1(4))* Lifevest Publishing, Inc.

Saroff, Phyllis. Belle: The Amazing, Astonishingly Magical Journey of an Artfully Painted Lady. Corlett, Mary Lee. 12th ed. 2011. (ENG.). 52p. (J). (gr. 3-7). pap. 25.00 *(978-1-59373-084-0(5))* Bunker Hill Publishing, Inc.

—Dear Tree. Weber, Rivka Doba. Rosenfeld, D. L., ed. 2010. 24p. (YA). 10.95 *(978-1-929628-48-3(X))* Hachai Publishing.

—Jesus, I Feel Close to You. Stuckey, Denise. 2005. 32p. (J). 10.95 *(978-0-8091-6718-0(2)*, 6718-2) Paulist Pr.

—Saving the Whooping Crane. Goodman, Susan E. 2008. (On My Own Science Ser.). (ENG.). 48p. (gr. 2-4). pap. 6.95 *(978-0-8225-6751-6(2)*, First Avenue Editions) Lerner Publishing Group.

—Signal's Airport Adventure. Friday, Stormy. 2006. (J). 14.95 *(978-0-9717047-5-6(9))* Bay Media, Inc.

Saroff, Phyllis. Sounds of the Savanna, 1 vol. Jennings, Terry Catasús. 2015. 32p. (J). (gr. k-3). (ENG.). pap. 9.95 ***(978-1-62855-637-7(4))***; (SPA & ENG.). pap. 9.95 ***(978-1-62855-642-1(0))*** Arbordale Publishing.

Saroff, Phyllis. Time & the Tapestry. Plotz, John. 2014. (ENG.). 192p. (YA). 18.50 *(978-1-59373-145-8(0))* Bunker Hill Publishing, Inc.

Saroff, Phyllis V. A Journey into an Estuary. Johnson, Rebecca L. 2004. (Biomes of North America Ser.). (ENG.). 48p. (gr. 3-6). lib. bdg. 23.93 *(978-1-57505-592-3(9))* Lerner Publishing Group.

—A Journey into the Ocean. Johnson, Rebecca L. 2004. (Biomes of North America Ser.). (ENG.). 48p. (gr. 3-6). pap. 8.95 *(978-0-8225-2046-7(X)*, I); lib. bdg. 23.93 *(978-1-57505-591-6(0))* Lerner Publishing Group.

—Saving the Whooping Crane. Goodman, Susan E. 2007. (On My Own Science Ser.). (ENG.). 48p. (gr. 2-4). lib. bdg. 25.26 *(978-0-8225-6748-6(2)*, Millbrook Pr.) Lerner Publishing Group.

—Teeth. Collard, Sneed B., III. 2008. (ENG.). 32p. (J). (gr. k-3). per. 7.95 *(978-1-58089-121-9(7))* Charlesbridge Publishing, Inc.

Sarrazin, Jean-charles. El Mas Bonito de Todos los Regalos del Mundo. Teulade, Pascale. (SPA.). 40p. (J). (gr. k-1). 15.95 *(978-84-95150-27-1(1)*, COR30367) Corimbo, Editorial S.L. ESP. Dist: Lectorum Pubns., Inc.; Distribooks, Inc.

Sarrazin, Marisol. A Friend for Sam. Labatt, Mary. 2003. (Kids Can Read Ser.). (ENG.). 32p. (J). (gr. k-3). 14.95 *(978-1-55337-374-2(X))*; pap. 3.95 *(978-1-55337-375-9(8))* Kids Can Pr., Ltd. CAN. Dist: Univ. of Toronto Pr.

—Lizards Don't Wear Lip Gloss. Wiebe, Trina. 2004. (Abby & Tess Pet-Sitters Ser.). 91p. 15.95 *(978-0-7569-3425-5(7))* Perfection Learning Corp.

—Pizza for Sam. Labatt, Mary. 2003. (Kids Can Read Ser.). (ENG.). 32p. (J). (gr. k-3). 3.95 *(978-1-55337-331-5(6))*; 14.95 *(978-1-55337-329-2(4))* Kids Can Pr., Ltd. CAN. Dist: Univ. of Toronto Pr.

—Sam at the Seaside. Labatt, Mary. 2006. (Kids Can Read Ser.). (ENG.). 32p. (J). (gr. k-1). pap. 3.95 *(978-1-55337-877-8(6))* Kids Can Pr., Ltd. CAN. Dist: Univ. of Toronto Pr.

—Sam Finds a Monster. Butcher, Kristin & Labatt, Mary. 2003. (Kids Can Read Ser.). (ENG.). 32p. (J). (gr. k-3). 3.95 *(978-1-55337-352-0(9))* Kids Can Pr., Ltd. CAN. Dist: Univ. of Toronto Pr.

—Sam Finds a Monster. Labatt, Mary. 2003. 32p. (J). pap. *(978-0-439-58742-6(5))* Scholastic, Inc.

—Sam Goes Next Door. Labatt, Mary. 2006. (Kids Can Read Ser.). (ENG.). 32p. (J). (gr. k-1). 3.95 *(978-1-55337-879-2(2))* Kids Can Pr., Ltd. CAN. Dist: Univ. of Toronto Pr.

—Sam's First Halloween. Labatt, Mary. 2003. (Kids Can Read Ser.). (ENG.). 32p. (J). (gr. k-3). pap. 3.95 *(978-1-55337-356-8(1))* Kids Can Pr., Ltd. CAN. Dist: Univ. of Toronto Pr.

—Sam's Snowy Day. Labatt, Mary. 2005. (Kids Can Start to Read Ser.). (ENG.). 32p. (J). (gr. k-1). 14.95 *(978-1-55337-789-4(3))*; pap. 3.95 *(978-1-55337-790-0(7))* Kids Can Pr., Ltd. CAN. Dist: Univ. of Toronto Pr.

Sarrazin, Marisol. Sam Goes to School. Sarrazin, Marisol, tr. Labatt, Mary. 2004. (Kids Can Read Ser.: Vol. 1). (ENG.). 32p. (J). (gr. k-3). 3.95 *(978-1-55337-565-4(3))* Kids Can Pr., Ltd. CAN. Dist: Univ. of Toronto Pr.

Sartor, Amanda. Fighting for Equal Rights: A Story about Susan B. Anthony. Sartor, Amanda, tr. Weidt, Maryann N. 2003. (Creative Minds Biographies Ser.). (ENG.). 64p. (gr. 4-8). pap. 8.95 *(978-1-57505-609-8(7))* Lerner Publishing Group.

Sartore, Joel. Face to Face with Grizzlies. Sartore, Joel. 2007. (Face to Face with Animals Ser.). (ENG.). 32p. (J). (gr. 2-5). 16.95 *(978-1-4263-0050-9(6))*; lib. bdg. 25.90 *(978-1-4263-0051-6(4))* National Geographic Society. (National Geographic Children's Bks.).

Sasaki, Chie. Someone Took Vanessa's Bike. Moran, Maggie A. 2003. 28p. (J). lib. bdg. 14.95 *(978-1-931642-03-3(6))* New Voices Publishing Co.

Sasaki, Ellen Joy. Gus, the Pilgrim Turkey. Bateman, Teresa. 2008. (ENG.). 32p. (J). (gr. 1-3). 16.99 *(978-0-8075-1266-1(4))* Whitman, Albert & Co.

Saseen, Sharon. Patience & the Flower Girl. 2004. *(978-0-9748425-0-9(8))* Saseen, Sharon.

Sasheva, Iva. Helen Thayer's Arctic Adventure: A Woman & a Dog Walk to the North Pole. Isaacs, Sally Senzell. 2016. (J). pap. ***(978-1-4914-8045-8(9))*** Capstone Pr., Inc.

Sasic, Natasha. Love Potion. Banks, Steven. ed. 2005. (Adventures of Jimmy Neutron Ser.: 7). 24p. (J). lib. bdg. 15.00 *(978-1-59054-784-7(5))* Fitzgerald Bks.

Sassin, Eva. Be a Survivor. Oxlade, Chris. 2015. (Go Wild Ser.). (ENG.). 32p. (J). (gr. 3-6). 26.65 ***(978-1-4677-6356-1(X))*** Lerner Publishing Group.

—Be a Tracker. Oxlade, Chris. 2015. (Go Wild Ser.). (ENG.). 32p. (J). (gr. 3-6). pap. 7.99 ***(978-1-4677-7650-9(5)***, Lerner Pubns.) Lerner Publishing Group.

—Be an Adventurer. Oxlade, Chris. 2015. (Go Wild Ser.). (ENG.). 32p. (J). (gr. 3-6). pap. 7.99 ***(978-1-4677-7647-9(5)***, Lerner Pubns.) Lerner Publishing Group.

Sassin, Eva. My Two Dogs. Crow, Melinda Melton. 2013. (My Two Dogs Ser.). (ENG.). 32p. (gr. 1-3). lib. bdg. 170.56 *(978-1-4342-6069-7(0))*; lib. bdg. 85.28 *(978-1-4342-6068-0(2))* Stone Arch Bks.

—Rocky & Daisy & the Birthday Party. Crow, Melinda Melton. 2013. (My Two Dogs Ser.). (ENG.). 32p. (gr. 1-3). pap. 29.70 *(978-1-4342-6296-7(0))*; (gr. 2-3). pap. 5.95 *(978-1-4342-6205-9(7))*; (gr. 2-3). lib. bdg. 21.32 *(978-1-4342-6011-6(9))* Stone Arch Bks.

—Rocky & Daisy Go to the Vet. Crow, Melinda Melton. 2013. (My Two Dogs Ser.). (ENG.). 32p. (gr. 1-3). pap. 29.70 *(978-1-4342-6297-4(9))*; (gr. 2-3). pap. 5.95 *(978-1-4342-6203-5(0))*; (gr. 2-3). lib. bdg. 21.32 *(978-1-4342-6009-3(7))* Stone Arch Bks.

—Rocky & Daisy Take a Vacation. Crow, Melinda Melton. 2013. (My Two Dogs Ser.). (ENG.). 32p. (gr. 1-3). pap. 29.70 *(978-1-4342-6298-1(7))*; (gr. 2-3). lib. bdg. 21.32 *(978-1-4342-6008-6(9))* Stone Arch Bks.

—Rocky & Daisy Wash the Van. Crow, Melinda Melton. 2013. (My Two Dogs Ser.). (ENG.). 32p. (gr. 1-3). pap. 29.70 *(978-1-4342-6299-8(5))*; (gr. 2-3). pap. 5.95 *(978-1-4342-6204-2(9))*; (gr. 2-3). lib. bdg. 21.32 *(978-1-4342-6010-9(0))* Stone Arch Bks.

Sasso. Coloured Pictures. Bannerji, Himani. Date not set. 80p. pap. *(978-0-920813-86-7(0))* Sister Vision Pr.

—How the East Pond Got Its Flowers. Trotman, Althea. Date not set. 88p. (J). (gr. 3-7). pap. *(978-0-920813-85-0(2))* Sister Vision Pr.

Sassone, Richard. Galangous. Sassone, Richard. 2009. 62p. pap. 14.95 *(978-1-936051-14-4(1))* Peppertree Pr., The.

Sato, Anna & Sato, Eriko. My First Japanese Kanji Book: Learning Kanji the Fun & Easy Way! Sato, Anna & Sato, Eriko. 2009. (JPN & ENG.). 64p. (J). (gr. 2-6). 19.95 *(978-4-8053-1037-3(5))* Tuttle Publishing.

Sato, Eriko, jt. illus. see Sato, Anna.

Sato, Kunio. The Restaurant of Many Colors. Miyazawa, Kenji. 2005. 31p. (J). 17.95 *(978-4-902216-24-0(8))* R.I.C. Publications Asia Co, Inc. JPN. Dist: Continental Enterprises Group, Inc. (CEG).

Sato, Yuki. Sherlock Bones, Vol. 1. Ando, Yuma. 2013. (ENG.). 200p. pap. 10.99 *(978-1-61262-444-0(8))* Kodansha America, Inc.

Satoru, Akahori. Sorcerer Hunter, Vol. 13. Satoru, Akahori. 13th rev. ed. 2003. 192p. (gr. 11-18). pap. 12.99 *(978-1-59182-066-6(9))* TOKYOPOP, Inc.

Satoshi, Yamamoto. Pokémon Adventures Vol. 3: Diamond & Pearl - Platinum. Kusaka, Hidenori. 2011. (Pokemon Ser.: 3). (ENG.). 208p. (J). pap. 9.99 *(978-1-4215-3818-1(0))* Viz Media.

Sattler, Jennifer. Uh-Oh, Dodo! Sattler, Jennifer. 2013. (ENG.). 32p. (J). (gr. -1-k). 15.95 *(978-1-59078-929-2(6))* Boyds Mills Pr.

Sattler, Jennifer Gordon. A Chick 'n' Pug Christmas. 2014. (J). *(978-1-61963-463-3(5))* Bloomsbury Pr.

—Pig Kahuna Pirates! 2014. (J). *(978-1-61963-203-5(9))* Bloomsbury Pr.

Saules, Tony de. Esa Repugnante Digestion. Saules, Tony de. Arnold, Nick. 2003. (Coleccion Esa Horrible Ciencia). (SPA.). 156p. (YA). pap. *(978-84-272-2057-7(X)*, ML4090) Molino, Editorial ESP. Dist: Lectorum Pubns., Inc.

—Esos Insoportables Sonidos. Saules, Tony de. Arnold, Nick. (SPA.). 160p. (YA). (gr. 5-8). *(978-84-272-2058-4(8))* Molino, Editorial ESP. Dist: Lectorum Pubns., Inc.

Saull, Eve. A Child's Garden: Introducing Your Child to the Joys of the Garden. Muse, Elizabeth St. Cloud. 2007. 45p. reprint ed. 15.00 *(978-1-4223-6638-7(3))* DIANE Publishing Co.

Sauls, Lynn B. Gabriel Goes to Washington: Through Big Brown Eyes; the Adventures of Gabriel the Poodle. Sauls, Lynn B. 2013. 26p. pap. 9.99 *(978-0-9893216-1-7(4))* Sauls, Lynn.

Saumell, Marina, jt. illus. see Papeo, Maria Eugenia.

Saunders, Katie. Brandon's Birthday Surprise. Bullard, Lisa. 2012. (Holidays & Special Days Ser.). 24p. (gr. k-2). (J). pap. 39.62 *(978-0-7613-9246-0(7)*, Millbrook Pr.); (ENG.). pap. 6.95 *(978-0-7613-8578-3(9)*, Millbrook Pr.); (ENG.). lib. bdg. 23.93 *(978-0-7613-5085-9(3))* Lerner Publishing Group.

—Carter's Christmas. Bullard, Lisa. 2012. (Cloverleaf Books (tm) — Fall & Winter Holidays Ser.). (ENG.). 24p. (gr. k-2). 6.95 *(978-0-7613-8584-4(3))*; lib. bdg. 23.93 *(978-0-7613-5074-3(8))* Lerner Publishing Group. (Millbrook Pr.).

—Chelsea's Chinese New Year. Bullard, Lisa. 2012. (Holidays & Special Days Ser.). 24p. (gr. k-2). (J). pap. 39.62 *(978-0-7613-9247-7(5)*, Millbrook Pr.); (ENG.). pap. 6.95 *(978-0-7613-8579-0(7)*, Millbrook Pr.); (ENG.). lib. bdg. 23.93 *(978-0-7613-5078-1(0))* Lerner Publishing Group.

—Cloverleaf Books#8482; - Holidays & Special Days: 6Pack Set. Bullard, Lisa. 2012. (Holidays & Special Days Ser.). 24p. (J). (gr. k-2). pap. 237.69 *(978-0-7613-9252-1(1)*, Millbrook Pr.) Lerner Publishing Group.

—Cloverleaf Books#8482; - Holidays & Special Days: Single Copy Set. Bullard, Lisa. 2012. (Holidays & Special Days Ser.). 24p. (J). (gr. k-2). pap. 39.62 *(978-0-7613-9251-4(3)*, Millbrook Pr.) Lerner Publishing Group.

—Finger Friends Tickle Monsters. Bicknell, Joanna & Page, Nick. 2007. (Finger Puppet Books Ser.). 12p. (gr. -1). bds. *(978-1-84610-427-5(0))* Make Believe Ideas.

—Grace's Thanksgiving. Bullard, Lisa. 2012. (Cloverleaf Books (tm) — Fall & Winter Holidays Ser.). (ENG.). 24p. (gr. k-2). 6.95 *(978-0-7613-8589-9(4))*; lib. bdg. 23.93 *(978-0-7613-5076-7(4))* Lerner Publishing Group. (Millbrook Pr.).

—Little Reindeer. 2012. 10p. (J). *(978-1-4351-4314-2(0))* Barnes & Noble, Inc.

—Read with Me Three Billy Goats Gruff: Sticker Activity Book. Page, Nick & Page, Claire. 2006. (Read with Me (Make Believe Ideas) Ser.). 12p. (J). (gr. k-2). pap. *(978-1-84610-181-6(6))* Make Believe Ideas.

—Toddler Treasury: 5 Lively Sections for Toddlers on the Move. 2012. (Toddler Bks.). (ENG.). 50p. (J). (gr. -1-k). 9.99 *(978-0-7641-6562-7(3))* Barron's Educational Series, Inc.

Saunders, Katie. Color Fun! An Abacus Book. Saunders, Katie. Little Bee Books Staff. 2015. (Baby Steps Ser.). (ENG.). 14p. (J). (gr. -1 — 1). bds. 7.99 *(978-1-4998-0006-7(1))* Little Bee Books Inc.

—Counting Fun! An Abacus Book. Saunders, Katie. Little Bee Books Staff. 2015. (Baby Steps Ser.). (ENG.). 14p. (J). (gr. -1 — 1). bds. 7.99 *(978-1-4998-0005-0(3))* Little Bee Books Inc.

Saunders, M. D. Harry Meets Mathilda, 5 bks., Bk.1. Wisdom, Eileen Mary. 2007. 36p. (J). pap. 20.00 *(978-0-9771102-2-3(2))* Pelican Pr.

Saunders, Mike. You Can Draw Birds! Dicker, Katie. 2013. (Draw Your Pet! Ser.). 32p. (gr. 3-5). 26.60 *(978-1-4339-8723-6(6))*; pap. 10.50 *(978-1-4339-8724-3(4))* Stevens, Gareth Publishing LLLP. (Gareth Stevens Learning Library).

—You Can Draw Cats! Dicker, Katie. 2013. (Draw Your Pet! Ser.). 32p. (gr. 3-5). 26.60 *(978-1-4339-8727-4(9))*; pap. 10.50 *(978-1-4339-8728-1(7))* Stevens, Gareth Publishing LLLP. (Gareth Stevens Learning Library).

—You Can Draw Dogs! Dicker, Katie. 2013. (Draw Your Pet! Ser.). 32p. (J). (gr. 3-5). pap. 10.50 *(978-1-4339-8732-8(5))*; lib. bdg. 26.60 *(978-1-4339-8731-1(7))* Stevens, Gareth Publishing LLLP.

—You Can Draw Exotic Pets! Dicker, Katie. 2013. (Draw Your Pet! Ser.). 32p. (gr. 3-5). 26.60 *(978-1-4339-8735-9(X))*; pap. 10.50 *(978-1-4339-8736-6(8))* Stevens, Gareth Publishing LLLP. (Gareth Stevens Learning Library).

—You Can Draw Fish! Dicker, Katie. 2013. (Draw Your Pet! Ser.). 32p. (gr. 3-5). 26.60 *(978-1-4339-8739-7(2))*; pap. 10.50 *(978-1-4339-8740-3(6))* Stevens, Gareth Publishing LLLP. (Gareth Stevens Learning Library).

—You Can Draw Horses! Dicker, Katie. 2013. (Draw Your Pet! Ser.). 32p. (gr. 3-5). 26.60 *(978-1-4339-8743-4(0))*; pap. 10.50 *(978-1-4339-8744-1(9))* Stevens, Gareth Publishing LLLP. (Gareth Stevens Learning Library).

Saunders-Smith, Gail. Cool Soccer Facts, 1 vol. Czeskleba, Abby. 2011. (Cool Sports Facts Ser.). (ENG.). 24p. (gr. k-1). pap. 7.29 *(978-1-4296-7394-5(X))*; pap. 41.70 *(978-1-4296-7397-6(4))* Capstone Pr., Inc. (Pebble Plus).

Saunders, Zina. Dora Loves Boots. Inches, Alison & Weiner, Eric. 2004. (SPA & ENG.). (J). *(978-0-7383-3858-3(3)*, Simon Spotlight/Nickelodeon) Simon Spotlight/Nickelodeon.

—Dora Quiere Mucho a Boots. Inches, Alison. 2005. (Dora the Explorer Ser.). (SPA.). 24p. (J). (gr. -1-2). pap. 3.99 *(978-1-4169-0620-9(7)*, Libros Para Ninos) Libros Para Ninos.

—Dora's Costume Party! Ricci, Christine. 2005. (Dora the Explorer Ser.). (ENG.). 24p. (J). (gr. -1-2). pap. 3.99 *(978-1-4169-0010-8(1)*, Simon Spotlight/Nickelodeon) Simon Spotlight/Nickelodeon.

The check digit for ISBN-10 appears in parentheses after the full ISBN-13

—¿Qué Voy a Ser? Beinstein, Phoebe. 2007. (Dora la Exploradora Ser.).Tr. of What Will I Be?. (ENG & SPA.). 14p. (J). (gr. -1). bds. 4.99 *(978-1-4169-3366-3(2)*, Libros Para Ninos) Libros Para Ninos.

—Say Please! A Book about Manners. 2006. (Backyardigans Ser.). (ENG.). 24p. (J). (gr. -1-2). pap. 3.99 *(978-1-4169-1386-3(6)*, Simon Spotlight/Nickelodeon) Simon Spotlight/Nickelodeon.

—SpongeBob Goes to the Doctor. Banks, Steven. 2005. (SpongeBob SquarePants Ser.: 9). (ENG.). 24p. (J). pap. 3.99 *(978-1-4169-0359-8(3)*, Simon Spotlight/Nickelodeon) Simon Spotlight/Nickelodeon.

—Spongebob Goes to the Doctor. Banks, Steven. 2005. 22p. (J). lib. bdg. 15.00 *(978-1-4242-0976-7(5))* Fitzgerald Bks.

—Trouble at the Krusty Krab! 2004. (SpongeBob SquarePants Ser.). (ENG.). 32p. (J). pap. 3.99 *(978-0-689-86838-2(3)*, Simon Spotlight/Nickelodeon) Simon Spotlight/Nickelodeon.

—U. S. Presidents: Feats & Foul-Ups. Fuqua, Nell & Jankowki, Dan. 2003. 48p. (J). pap. *(978-0-439-54081-0(X))* Lemondrop Pr.

—UFO! (SpongeBob SquarePants) Beechen, Adam. 2005. (SpongeBob SquarePants Ser.). (ENG.). 32p. (J). pap. 3.99 *(978-0-689-87202-0(X)*, Simon Spotlight/Nickelodeon) Simon Spotlight/Nickelodeon.

Saunderson, Chris. Climb up the Tree with Zacchaeus. Lane, Leena. Reynolds, Annette, ed. ed. 2007. (Action Rhymes Ser.). (ENG.). 16p. (J). (gr. -1-2). pap. 4.99 *(978-0-9789056-2-0(8))* New Day Publishing, Inc.

—Come into the Ark with Noah. Jeffs, Stephanie. Reynolds, Annette, ed. ed. 2007. (Action Rhymes Ser.). (ENG.). 16p. (J). (gr. -1-2). pap. 4.99 *(978-0-9789056-6-8(0))* New Day Publishing, Inc.

—Come to the Party with Jesus. Lane, Leena. Reynolds, Annette, ed. ed. 2007. (Action Rhymes Ser.). (ENG.). 16p. (J). (gr. -1-2). pap. 4.99 *(978-0-9789056-5-1(2))* New Day Publishing, Inc.

—Follow the Star with the Wise Men. Jeffs, Stephanie. Reynolds, Annette, ed. ed. 2007. (Action Rhymes Ser.). (ENG.). 16p. (J). (gr. -1-3). per. 4.99 *(978-0-9789056-3-7(6))* New Day Publishing, Inc.

—March Round the Walls with Joshua. Jeffs, Stephanie. Reynolds, Annette, ed. ed. 2007. (Action Rhymes Ser.). (ENG.). 16p. (J). (gr. -1-2). pap. 4.99 *(978-0-9789056-7-5(9))* New Day Publishing, Inc.

—Sail in the Boat with Jesus. Lane, Leena. Reynolds, Annette, ed. ed. 2007. (Action Rhymes Ser.). (ENG.). 16p. (J). (gr. -1-2). pap. 4.99 *(978-0-9789056-0-6(1))* New Day Publishing, Inc.

—Share Out the Food with Jesus. Jeffs, Stephanie. Reynolds, Annette, ed. ed. 2007. (Action Rhymes Ser.). (ENG.). 16p. (J). (gr. -1-2). pap. 4.99 *(978-0-9789056-1-3(X))* New Day Publishing, Inc.

—Stand up & Walk with Jesus. Lane, Leena. Reynolds, Annette, ed. 2007. (Action Rhymes Ser.). (ENG.). 16p. (J). (gr. -1-2). pap. 4.99 *(978-0-9789056-4-4(4))* New Day Publishing, Inc.

Sautai, Raoul. Castle under Seige. Fuhr, Ute. 2013. (ENG.). 36p. (J). (gr. -1-k). 12.99 *(978-1-85103-414-7(5))* Moonlight Publishing, Ltd. GBR. Dist: Independent Pubs. Group.

—Let's Look at Castles. Fuhr, Ute. 2012. (ENG.). 38p. (J). (gr. k-3). pap. 11.99 *(978-1-85103-286-0(X))* Moonlight Publishing, Ltd. GBR. Dist: Independent Pubs. Group.

—Let's Look at the Ocean Depths. Fuhr, UteSautai & Allaire, Caroline. 2012. (ENG.). 38p. (J). (gr. 1-4). pap. 11.99 *(978-1-85103-363-8(7))* Moonlight Publishing, Ltd. GBR. Dist: Independent Pubs. Group.

—Let's Look at the Pond. Moonlight Publishing Ltd Staff et al. 2012. (ENG.). 38p. (J). (gr. 1-4). pap. 11.99 *(978-1-85103-338-6(6))* Moonlight Publishing, Ltd. GBR. Dist: Independent Pubs. Group.

—Let's Look at the Rainforest. Fuhr, Ute & Allaire, Caroline. 2012. (ENG.). 38p. (J). (gr. 1-4). pap. 11.99 *(978-1-85103-360-7(2))* Moonlight Publishing, Ltd. GBR. Dist: Independent Pubs. Group.

Sautai, Raoul. La Abeja. Sautai, Raoul. Fhur, Ute et al. Fhur, Ute & Barroso, Paz, trs. 3rd ed. (Coleccion Mundo Maravilloso). (SPA.). 40p. (J). (gr. 2-4). *(978-84-348-4036-2(7)*, SM5786) SM Ediciones ESP. Dist: Lectorum Pubns., Inc.

Sautai, Raoul, jt. illus. see Fuhr, Ute.

Sauvageot, Claude, photos by. Poland. Sein, Dominique. (Countries of the World Ser.: No. 27). 83p. (J). lib. bdg. 14.95 *(978-0-8288-3938-9(7))* French & European Pubns., Inc.

Sauve, Gordon. Car Smarts: Hot Tips for the Car Crazy. Edmonston, Phil & Sawa, Maureen. 2003. (ENG.). 80p. (J). (gr. 4-7). pap. 15.95 *(978-0-88776-646-6(3))* Tundra Bks. CAN. Dist: Random Hse., Inc.

Savadier, Elivia. I Love Saturdays y Domingos. Flor Ada, Alma. 2004. (ENG.). 32p. (J). (gr. -1-3). reprint ed. 7.99 *(978-0-689-87409-3(X)*, Atheneum Bks. for Young Readers) Simon & Schuster Children's Publishing.

—Me Encantan los Saturdays y los Domingos. Flor Ada, Alma. 2004.Tr. of I Love Saturdays y Domingos. (SPA.). 36p. (gr. k-3). pap. 11.95 *(978-1-59437-576-7(3)*, AF33204) Santillana USA Publishing Co., Inc.

Savage, Bridgette Z. Fly Like the Wind. Savage, Bridgette Z. Savage, Charles J., photos by. Savage, Charles J., ed. 2005. (ENG.). 112p. (YA). (gr. 5). per. 16.99 *(978-0-9771494-0-7(4))* Buckbeech Studios.

Savage, Joshua. JogNog: The Story of How a Small Creature Made a Big Difference & Everyone Got Smarter. Smith, Stephen. 2011. (ENG.). 34p. pap. 6.99 *(978-1-4663-8227-5(9))* CreateSpace Independent Publishing Platform.

Savage, Stephen. The Fathers Are Coming Home. Brown, Margaret Wise. 2010. (ENG.). 32p. (J). (gr. -1-k). 16.99 *(978-0-689-83345-8(8)*, McElderry, Margaret K. Bks.) McElderry, Margaret K. Bks.

—Polar Bear Morning. Thompson, Lauren. 2013. (ENG.). 32p. (J). (gr. -1-k). 16.99 *(978-0-439-69885-6(5)*, Scholastic Pr.) Scholastic, Inc.

—Polar Bear Night. Thompson, Lauren. (ENG.). (J). (gr. -1 — 1). 2013. 36p. bds. 8.99 *(978-0-545-48558-6(4)*, Cartwheel Bks.); 2004. 32p. 17.99 *(978-0-439-49524-0(5)*, Scholastic Pr.) Scholastic, Inc.

Savage, Stephen. Little Tug. Savage, Stephen. 2015. (ENG.). 34p. (J). (gr. -1-1). 7.99 *(978-1-62672-124-1(6))* Roaring Brook Pr.

—Supertruck. Savage, Stephen. 2015. (ENG.). 32p. (J). (gr. -1-1). 12.99 *(978-1-59643-821-7(5))* Roaring Brook Pr.

—Where's Walrus? Savage, Stephen. 2011. (ENG.). 32p. (J). (gr. -1-k). 16.99 *(978-0-439-70049-8(3)*, Scholastic Pr.) Scholastic, Inc.

Savage, Virginia, jt. illus. see Peterson, Roger Tory.

Save, Ken. Dunamis Heroes: Issue #1: the Lost Kingdom. Bateman, Jordan. 2007. 120p. (J). per. *(978-0-9781953-0-4(2))* Dunamis Media.

Saville, Kathy Dee. Dance of the Eggshells: Baile de los Cascarones. Aragón, Carla et al. 2010. (SPA & ENG.). 32p. (J). (gr. 1). 18.95 *(978-0-8263-4770-1(3))* Univ. of New Mexico Pr.

Savitsky, Steve, et al. Bug Hunt. Ricci, Christine & Golden Books Staff. 2008. (Color Plus Chunky Crayons Ser.). (ENG.). 48p. (J). (gr. -1-2). pap. 3.99 *(978-0-375-84298-6(5)*, Golden Bks.) Random Hse. Children's Bks.

Savitsky, Steve. Dora Had a Little Lamb. Risco, Elle D. 2007. (Dora the Explorer Ser.). (J). (gr. -1-2). 11.65 *(978-0-7569-8294-2(4))* Perfection Learning Corp.

—Dora's Pirate Treasure Hunt. 2010. (Dora the Explorer Ser.). (ENG.). 12p. (J). (gr. -1-1). 6.99 *(978-1-4169-9927-0(2)*, Simon Spotlight/Nickelodeon) Simon Spotlight/Nickelodeon.

Savitsky, Steven. Dónde Está Boots? - Cuento para Levantar la Tapita. Thorpe, Kiki. 2005. (Dora the Explorer Ser.).Tr. of Where Is Boots? - A Lift-the-Flap Story. (SPA.). 16p. (J). pap. 5.99 *(978-1-4169-0621-6(5)*, Libros Para Ninos) Libros Para Ninos.

—Dora Had a Little Lamb. 2007. (Dora the Explorer Ser.: 23). (ENG.). 24p. (J). (gr. -1-2). pap. 3.99 *(978-1-4169-3368-7(9)*, Simon Spotlight/Nickelodeon) Simon Spotlight/Nickelodeon.

—Dora y el Día lluvioso. Echeverria, Jessica. 2009. (Dora la Exploradora Ser.). Orig. Title: Dora & the Rainy Day. (SPA.). 26p. (J). (gr. -1). bds. 5.99 *(978-1-4169-7186-3(6)*, Libros Para Ninos) Libros Para Ninos.

—Dora's Chilly Day. Thorpe, Kiki. ed. 2005. (Dora the Explorer Ser.: No. 10). 22p. (J). lib. bdg. 15.00 *(978-1-59054-794-6(2))* Fitzgerald Bks.

—Dora's Chilly Day. Thorpe, Kiki. 2004. (Dora the Explorer Ser.). (ENG.). 24p. (J). pap. 3.99 *(978-0-689-86795-8(6)*, Simon Spotlight/Nickelodeon) Simon Spotlight/Nickelodeon.

—Dora's Halloween Adventure. Willson, Sarah. 2003. (Dora the Explorer Ser.). (ENG.). 14p. (J). bds. 5.99 *(978-0-689-85844-4(2)*, Simon Spotlight/Nickelodeon) Simon Spotlight/Nickelodeon.

—The Magical Mermaid Crown. Golden Books Staff. 2007. (Holographic Sticker Book Ser.). (ENG.). 48p. (J). (gr. -1-2). pap. 3.99 *(978-0-375-84213-9(6)*, Golden Bks.) Random Hse. Children's Bks.

—Say Cheese! Ricci, Christine. ed. 2005. 22p. (J). lib. bdg. 15.00 *(978-1-59054-975-9(9))* Fitzgerald Bks.

—Say Cheese! Ricci, Christine. 2004. (Dora the Explorer Ser.). (ENG.). 24p. (J). pap. 3.99 *(978-0-689-86496-4(5)*, Simon Spotlight/Nickelodeon) Simon Spotlight/Nickelodeon.

Savitt, Sam. Buffalo Bill: Wild West Showman. Davidson, Mary Richmond. 2011. 80p. 37.95 *(978-1-258-01669-2(9))* Literary Licensing, LLC.

Sawada, Hajime. Orphen, Vol. 3. Akita, Yoshinobu. 2005. (Orphen Ser.). 192p. (gr. 8-12). pap. 9.99 *(978-1-4139-0268-6(5))* ADV Manga.

Sawai, Yoshio. Bobobo-Bo Bo-Bobo. Sawai, Yoshio. 2010. (Bobobo-Bo Bo-bobo Ser.: 4). (ENG.). 192p. pap. 9.99 *(978-1-4215-3128-1(3))*; (gr. 8-18). pap. 9.99 *(978-1-4215-3127-4(5))* Viz Media.

Sawyer-Aitch, Anne. Nalah & the Pink Tiger. Sawyer-Aitch, Anne. 2013. (ENG.). 40p. pap. 13.95 *(978-1-938063-00-8(7)*, Mighty Media Kids) Mighty Media Pr.

Sawyer, Darren, photos by. Guinea Pig. Rayner, Matthew. 2007. (I Am Your Pet Ser.). 32p. (gr. k-4). lib. bdg. 26.00 *(978-0-8368-8385-5(3)*, Gareth Stevens Learning Library) Stevens, Gareth Publishing LLLP.

—Rat. Rayner, Matthew. 2007. (I Am Your Pet Ser.). 32p. (gr. k-4). lib. bdg. 26.00 *(978-0-8368-8386-2(1)*, Gareth Stevens Learning Library) Stevens, Gareth Publishing LLLP.

Sawyer, Jocelyn. Slinky Slithertail & the Talent Show. Lorenzen, Margaret. 2004. 96p. (J). per. 12.50 *(978-0-9708053-9-3(X))* Authors & Artists Publishers of New York, Inc.

Sawyer, Judith L. This Is How I Pray. Sawyer, Judith L. 2008. 24p. (J). pap. *(978-1-926585-11-6(9)*, CCB Publishing) CCB Publishing.

Sawyer, Odessa. At the Edge of the Woods, 1 vol. Bracken, Beth & Fraser, Kay. 2013. (Faerieground Ser.). (ENG.). 96p. (gr. 1-3). lib. bdg. 22.65 *(978-1-4342-4489-5(X))* Stone Arch Bks.

—Believe, 1 vol. Bracken, Beth & Fraser, Kay. 2014. (Faerieground Ser.). (ENG.). 288p. (gr. 4-8). 12.95 *(978-1-62370-113-0(9))* Capstone Young Readers.

—Bloodfate, 1 vol. Bracken, Beth & Fraser, Kay. 2012. (Faerieground Ser.). (ENG.). 96p. (gr. 1-3). lib. bdg. 22.65 *(978-1-4342-3305-9(7)*, Faerieground) Stone Arch Bks.

—Faerieground, 1 vol. Bracken, Beth & Fraser, Kay. (Faerieground Ser.). (ENG.). 96p. (gr. 1-3). 2014. 90.60 *(978-1-4342-9465-4(X))*; 2013. 181.20 *(978-1-4342-6049-9(6))*; 2013. 90.60 *(978-1-4342-6050-5(X))* Stone Arch Bks. (Faerieground).

—Fate of the Willow Queen. Bracken, Beth & Fraser, Kay. 2013. (Faerieground Ser.). (ENG.). 96p. (gr. 1-3). 22.65 *(978-1-4342-4492-5(X)*, Faerieground) Stone Arch Bks.

—The Hidden Things, 1 vol. Bracken, Beth & Fraser, Kay. 2014. (Faerieground Ser.). (ENG.). 96p. (gr. 1-3). 22.65 *(978-1-4342-9185-1(5)*, Faerieground) Stone Arch Bks.

—Hope, 1 vol. Bracken, Beth & Fraser, Kay. 2013. (Faerieground Ser.). (ENG.). 288p. (gr. 4-8). 12.95 *(978-1-62370-010-2(8))* Capstone Young Readers.

—A Murder of Crows, 1 vol. Bracken, Beth & Fraser, Kay. 2013. (Faerieground Ser.). (ENG.). 96p. (gr. 1-3). lib. bdg. 22.65 *(978-1-4342-4491-8(1))* Stone Arch Bks.

—The Seventh Kingdom, 1 vol. Bracken, Beth & Fraser, Kay. 2014. (Faerieground Ser.). (ENG.). 96p. (gr. 1-3). 22.65 *(978-1-4342-9186-8(3)*, Faerieground) Stone Arch Bks.

—The Shadows, 1 vol. Bracken, Beth & Fraser, Kay. 2012. (Faerieground Ser.). (ENG.). 96p. (gr. 1-3). lib. bdg. 22.65 *(978-1-4342-3306-6(5)*, Faerieground) Stone Arch Bks.

—Two Mothers. Bracken, Beth & Fraser, Kay. 2013. (Faerieground Ser.). (ENG.). 96p. (gr. 1-3). 22.65 *(978-1-4342-4490-1(3)*, Faerieground) Stone Arch Bks.

—The Willow Queen's Gate, 1 vol. Bracken, Beth & Fraser, Kay. 2012. (Faerieground Ser.). (ENG.). 96p. (gr. 1-3). lib. bdg. 22.65 *(978-1-4342-3304-2(9)*, Faerieground) Stone Arch Bks.

—Wish, 1 vol. Bracken, Beth & Fraser, Kay. 2013. (Faerieground Ser.). (ENG.). 304p. (gr. 4-8). 12.95 *(978-1-62370-003-4(5))* Stone Arch Bks.

—A Wish in the Woods, 1 vol. Bracken, Beth & Fraser, Kay. 2012. (Faerieground Ser.). (ENG.). 96p. (gr. 1-3). lib. bdg. 22.65 *(978-1-4342-3303-5(0)*, Faerieground) Stone Arch Bks.

Sawyer, Peter, jt. illus. see Burney, Laura.

Saxton, Brenda. Reading Pals: Alphabet Recognition Gr. Pre K-K. 2007. (J). per. 6.99 *(978-1-59198-435-1(1))* Creative Teaching Pr., Inc.

Saxton, Patricia. A Book of Fairies. Saxton, Patricia. 2009. (ENG.). 32p. (J). (gr. 1-5). 14.95 *(978-1-934860-01-4(8))* Shenanigan Bks.

—The Book of Mermaids. Saxton, Patricia. 2006. (ENG.). 32p. (J). (gr. 1-5). 14.95 *(978-0-9726614-6-1(8))* Shenanigan Bks.

Say, Allen. Drawing from Memory. Say, Allen. 2011. (ENG.). 64p. (J). (gr. 5-18). 17.99 *(978-0-545-17686-6(7)*, Scholastic Pr.) Scholastic, Inc.

—The Favorite Daughter. Say, Allen. 2013. (ENG.). 32p. (J). (gr. -1-3). 17.99 *(978-0-545-17662-0(X)*, Levine, Arthur A. Bks.) Scholastic, Inc.

—Grandfather's Journey. Say, Allen. 2008. (ENG.). 32p. (J). (gr. -1-3). 7.99 *(978-0-547-07680-5(0))* Houghton Mifflin Harcourt Publishing Co.

—Tea with Milk. Say, Allen. 2009. (ENG.). 32p. (J). (gr. -1-3). pap. 7.99 *(978-0-547-23747-3(2))* Houghton Mifflin Harcourt Publishing Co.

—Tree of Cranes. Say, Allen. 2009. (ENG.). 32p. (J). (gr. -1-3). pap. 7.99 *(978-0-547-24830-1(X))* Houghton Mifflin Harcourt Publishing Co.

Sayers, Myrna. Pound a Poem: The Winning Entries from the National Schools Poetry Competition. John Blake Publishing Staff. 2007. (ENG.). 256p. 19.95 *(978-1-84454-436-3(2))* Blake, John Publishing, Ltd. GBR. Dist: Independent Pubs. Group.

Sayers, Rachel. Nibbles. Heeney, Bronwyn. 2011. 26p. pap. 13.50 *(978-1-60860-278-0(8)*, Eloquent Bks.) Strategic Book Publishing & Rights Agency (SBPRA).

Sayler, Machelle. Folkeminnevitskap II. 2004. 144p. *(978-0-9744422-1-1(6))* Erickson, Rakel L.

Sayles, Elizabeth. Anne Frank's Chestnut Tree. Kohuth, Jane. 2013. (Step into Reading Ser.). (ENG.). 48p. (J). (gr. k-3). 3.99 *(978-0-307-97579-9(7))*; 12.99 *(978-0-449-81255-6(3))* Random Hse., Inc.

—How Does Sleep Come? Blackmore, Jeanne C. 2012. (ENG.). 32p. (J). (-3). 16.99 *(978-1-4022-7105-2(0)*, Sourcebooks Jabberwocky) Sourcebooks, Inc.

—I Already Know I Love You. Crystal, Billy. (J). 2008. (ENG.). 32p. (gr. -1-3). bds. 7.99 *(978-0-06-145057-0(X)*, HarperFestival); 2007. (ENG.). 40p. (gr. -1-3). pap. 6.99 *(978-0-06-059393-3(8))*; 2004. (ENG.). 40p. 16.99 *(978-0-06-059391-9(1))*; 2004. 40p. lib. bdg. 17.89 *(978-0-06-059392-6(X))* HarperCollins Pubs.

—Moon Child. Krilanovich, Nadia. 2010. (ENG.). 32p. (J). (gr. -1-2). 15.99 *(978-1-58246-325-4(5)*, Tricycle Pr.) Ten Speed Pr.

—The Rainbow Tulip. Mora, Pat. 2003. (ENG.). 32p. (J). (gr. k-3). 6.99 *(978-0-14-250009-5(7)*, Puffin) Penguin Publishing Group.

—The Very Little Princess: Rose's Story. Bauer, Marion Dane. 2012. (Stepping Stone Book(TM) Ser.). (ENG.). 128p. (J). (gr. 1-4). pap. 4.99 *(978-0-375-85694-5(3))* Random Hse., Inc.

Sayles, Elizabeth, jt. illus. see Dooling, Michael.

Sayles, John. The Girl Who Reached for the Star. Lyons, Wendy Ackerman. 2007. (J). *(978-0-696-23982-3(5))* Meredith Bks.

Sayre, April Pulley. Go, Go, Grapes! A Fruit Chant. Sayre, April Pulley. 2012. (ENG.). 32p. (J). (gr. -1-3). 17.99 *(978-1-4424-3390-8(6)*, Beach Lane Bks.) Beach Lane Bks.

—Let's Go Nuts! Seeds We Eat. Sayre, April Pulley. 2013. (ENG.). 32p. (J). (gr. -1-3). 16.99 *(978-1-4424-6728-6(2)*, Beach Lane Bks.) Beach Lane Bks.

Sayre, April Pulley, photos by. Rah, Rah, Radishes! A Vegetable Chant. Sayre, April Pulley. 2011. (ENG., 32p. (J). (gr. -1-3). 16.99 *(978-1-4424-2141-7(X)*, Beach Lane Bks.) Beach Lane Bks.

—Rah, Rah, Radishes! A Vegetable Chant. Sayre, April Pulley. 2014. (Classic Board Bks.). (ENG., 34p. (J). (gr. -1 — 1). bds. 7.99 *(978-1-4424-9927-0(3)*, Little Simon) Little Simon.

—Raindrops Roll. Sayre, April Pulley. 2015. (ENG., 40p. (J). (gr. -1-3). 17.99 *(978-1-4814-2064-8(X)*, Beach Lane Bks.) Beach Lane Bks.

Sayre, Tamara. Guide to Freshwater Animals Without Backbones. DeStrulle, Arlene & Johnson, Tora. Date not set. (Orig.). (J). (gr. 4-6). pap. 10.95 *(978-0-9616712-6-6(2))* Catskill Ctr. for Conservation & Development, Inc.

Sazaklis, John. The Lizard's Legacy. McVeigh, Mark W. 2009. (Spider-Man Ser.). 64p. (J). (gr. 2-5). pap. 4.99 *(978-0-06-162627-2(9)*, HarperFestival) HarperCollins Pubs.

—The Secret Life of Black Cat. Teitelbaum, Michael. 2009. (Spider-Man Ser.). 64p. (J). (gr. 2-5). pap. 4.99 *(978-0-06-162626-5(0)*, HarperFestival) HarperCollins Pubs.

Sazaklis, John, jt. illus. see Merkel, Joe F.

Scadden, Kathryn. Mr. Munson's Itvice on Bullying. Nolan, Nancy. 2015. (J). 16.95 ***(978-1-59298-907-2(1))*** Beaver's Pond Pr., Inc.

Scala, Susan. Captain Nathaniel Brown Palmer. Sanford, Candace. 2007. 96p. (YA). pap. 14.95 *(978-0-9773725-9-1(6))* Flat Hammock Pr.

Scales, Simon. Monsters, Mind Your Manners! Spurr, Elizabeth. 2012. (J). 34.28 *(978-1-61913-124-8(2))* Weigl Pubs., Inc.

—Monsters, Mind Your Manners! Spurr, Elizabeth. 2011. (ENG.). 24p. (J). (gr. -1-2). 15.99 *(978-0-8075-5251-3(8))* Whitman, Albert & Co.

Scalf, Chris. Spinosaurus in the Storm. Nussbaum, Ben. (Smithsonian's Prehistoric Pals Ser.). (ENG.). 36p. (J). (gr. -1-2). 9.95 *(978-1-59249-462-0(5)*, PS2457) Soundprints.

—Spinosaurus in the Storm. Nussbaum, Ben & McIntosh, G. B. 2005. (Smithsonian's Prehistoric Pals Ser.). (ENG.). 36p. (J). (gr. -1-2). 2.95 *(978-1-59249-461-3(7)*, S2457) Soundprints.

—Spinosaurus in the Storm. Nussbaum, Ben. 2005. (ENG.). 36p. (J). (gr. -1-2). 8.95 *(978-1-59249-460-6(9)*, SD2407) Soundprints.

Scalf, Chris & McIntosh, Gabe. Spinosaurus. Bailey, Gerry. 2011. (Smithsonian Prehistoric Zone Ser.). (ENG.). 32p. (J). (gr. k-3). *(978-0-7787-1802-4(6))*; pap. *(978-0-7787-1815-4(8))* Crabtree Publishing Co.

Scalf, Christopher. Spinosaurus in the Storm. Nussbaum, Ben. 2005. (Smithsonian's Prehistoric Pals Ser.). (ENG.). 36p. (J). (gr. -1 — 1). pap. 6.95 *(978-1-59249-459-0(5)*, S2407) Soundprints.

Scalf, Christopher & McIntosh, Gabe. Spinosaurus in the Storm. Nussbaum, Ben. 2005. (Smithsonian's Prehistoric Pals Ser.). (ENG.). 36p. (J). (gr. 2-2). 14.95 *(978-1-59249-458-3(7)*, H2407) Soundprints.

Scamihorn, Aaron. Extraordinary People. Hearst, Michael. 2015. (ENG.). 112p. (J). (gr. 3-7). 16.99 *(978-1-4521-2709-5(3))* Chronicle Bks. LLC.

Scandella, Alessandra. Maria Callas. Capriolo, Paola. 2009. (SPA.). 116p. (YA). (gr. 7-18). 27.95 *(978-84-8483-351-2(8))* Ediciones del Laberinto ESP. Dist: Ediciones Universal.

Scanlon, Michael. Best Friends: A Chock-a-Block Book. Seiss, Ellie. 2010. (Yo Gabba Gabba! Ser.). (ENG.). 12p. (J). 5.99 *(978-1-4424-0970-5(3)*, Simon Spotlight) Simon Spotlight.

—A Mystery in Gabba Land. McDoogle, Farrah. 2010. (Yo Gabba Gabba! Ser.). (ENG.). 24p. (J). (gr. -1-k). pap. 3.99 *(978-1-4424-0652-0(6)*, Simon Spotlight) Simon Spotlight.

Scanlon, Michael, jt. illus. see Little Airplane Productions.

Scanziani, Emanuele. To Market! to Market! 2013. (ENG.). 24p. (J). (gr. -1). 8.95 *(978-81-923171-3-7(7))* Tara Books Agency IND. Dist: Perseus-PGW.

Scarborough, Casey. Cindy Lou Ella: A Country Fairy Tale. Ondrias, Rachel. 2007. (ENG.). 56p. (J). 18.95 *(978-1-933660-28-8(7)*, Tadpole Pr. 4 Kids) Smooth Sailing Pr., LLC.

—Kolby, the Skating Bear: A Kalamazoo Christmas. Ondrias, Rachel. 2007. (ENG.). 32p. (J). 16.95 *(978-1-933660-29-5(5)*, Tadpole Pr. 4 Kids) Smooth Sailing Pr., LLC.

—The Pumpkin Gift. Hollis, Ginger. 2006. (ENG.). 28p. (J). 16.95 *(978-1-933660-04-2(X)*, Tadpole Pr. 4 Kids) Smooth Sailing Pr., LLC.

—There's a Pig in My Fridge. Ondrias, Rachel. 2006. (ENG.). 28p. (J). 16.95 *(978-1-933660-30-1(9)*, Tadpole Pr. 4 Kids) Smooth Sailing Pr., LLC.

Scarborough, Rob. Brothers of the Fire Star. Arvidson, Douglas. 2012. 207p. (YA). pap. 15.95 *(978-1-890109-91-2(6)*, Cross Time) Crossquarter Publishing Group.

Scardina, Tom. The Leaf That Was Afraid to Fall, 1 vol. Nunnery, Donna. 2010. 26p. 24.95 *(978-1-4489-5927-3(6))* PublishAmerica, Inc.

—Old Billy, the Bike. England, Don. 2011. 24p. pap. 24.95 *(978-1-4560-3049-0(3))* America Star Bks.

Scarpa, Daniel. Bugs. Courtauld, Sarah. 2008. (Usborne First Reading: Level 3 Ser.). 47p. (J). 8.99 *(978-0-7945-1938-4(5)*, Usborne) EDC Publishing.

Scarpulla, Caren. Super Kids: Ordinary Kids Who Have Done Extraordinary Things. Fitterman, Lisa. 2005. 96p. (J). (gr. 3-7). *(978-1-59258-136-8(6))* Hylas Publishing.

Scarrone, Gustavo. Insomnios. Villarreal, Francisco, photos by. Villalba Casas, Consuelo, I.t. ed. 2003. (SPA.). 100p. (YA). pap. *(978-1-931481-18-2(0))* LiArt-Literature & Art.

Scarry, Huck. Cake Soup. Scarry, Richard & Farber, Erica. 2011. (Richard Scarry's Great Big Schoolhouse Ser.). (ENG.). 24p. (J). (gr. -1-k). 12.95 *(978-1-4027-8446-0(5))*; pap. 3.95 *(978-1-4027-7317-4(X))* Sterling Publishing Co., Inc.

—Go, Huckle, Go! Scarry, Richard & Farber, Erica. 2011. (Richard Scarry's Great Big Schoolhouse Ser.). (ENG.). 24p. (J). (gr. -1-k). pap. 3.95 *(978-1-4027-7316-7(1))* Sterling Publishing Co., Inc.

—Ice Cream for Breakfast. Scarry, Richard & Farber, Erica. 2011. (Richard Scarry's Great Big Schoolhouse Ser.). (ENG.). 24p. (J). (gr. 1-2). 12.95 *(978-1-4027-8449-1(X))* Sterling Publishing Co., Inc.

—Kooky Campout. Farber, Erica. 2015. (Richard Scarry's Great Big Schoolhouse Ser.). (ENG.). 24p. (J). (gr. 1-2). 12.95 *(978-1-4027-9914-3(4))* Sterling Publishing Co., Inc.

—Richard Scarry's Readers (Level 1): Get That Hat! Farber, Erica. 2015. (Richard Scarry's Great Big Schoolhouse Ser.). (ENG.). 24p. (J). (gr. -1-k). pap. 3.95 *(978-1-4027-9919-8(5))* Sterling Publishing Co., Inc.

—Richard Scarry's Readers (Level 1): Snow Dance. Farber, Erica. 2014. (Richard Scarry's Great Big Schoolhouse Ser.). (ENG.). 24p. (J). (gr. -1 — 1). pap. 3.95 (978-1-4027-9896-2(2)); 12.95 (978-1-4027-9895-5(4)) Sterling Publishing Co., Inc.

—Richard Scarry's Readers (Level 2): One, Two, AH-CHOO! Farber, Erica. 2014. (Richard Scarry's Great Big Schoolhouse Ser.). (ENG.). 24p. (J). (gr. k-1). 12.95 (978-1-4549-0380-2(5)) Sterling Publishing Co., Inc.

—Richard Scarry's Readers (Level 3): Spooky Campout. Farber, Erica. 2015. (Richard Scarry's Great Big Schoolhouse Ser.). (ENG.). 24p. (J). (gr. 1-2). pap. 3.95 (978-1-4027-9915-0(2)) Sterling Publishing Co., Inc.

—A Smelly Story, Level 2. Scarry, Richard & Farber, Erica. 2011. (Richard Scarry's Great Big Schoolhouse Ser.). (ENG.). 24p. (J). (gr. k-1). 12.95 (978-1-4027-8445-3(7)) Sterling Publishing Co., Inc.

Scarry, Richard. The Animals' Merry Christmas. Jackson, Kathryn. 2005. (ENG.). 72p. (J). (gr. -1-2). 15.99 (978-0-375-83341-0(2), Golden Bks.) Random Hse. Children's Bks.

—The Bunny Book. Scarry, Patricia M. & Scarry, Patsy. 2005. (Little Golden Book Ser.). (ENG.). 24p. (J). (gr. -1-2). 3.99 (978-0-375-83224-6(6), Golden Bks.) Random Hse. Children's Bks.

—Counting to Ten Jigsaw Book: With Six 24-Piece Jigsaws Inside. 2004. 12p. (J). bds. (978-1-74124-406-9(4)) Five Mile Pr. Pty Ltd. The.

—The Gingerbread Man. Nolte, Nancy. 2004. (Big Little Golden Book Ser.). (ENG.). 32p. (J). (gr. -1-2). 8.99 (978-0-375-82589-7(4), Golden Bks.) Random Hse. Children's Bks.

—I Am a Bunny. Risom, Ole. 2004. (Golden Sturdy Book Ser.). (ENG.). 26p. (J). (gr. k — 1). bds. 5.99 (978-0-375-82778-5(1), Golden Bks.) Random Hse. Children's Bks.

—Richard Scarry's Best Little Golden Books Ever! Scarry, Patsy et al. 2014. (Little Golden Book Treasury Ser.). (ENG.). 224p. (J). (-k). 11.99 (978-0-385-37912-0(9), Golden Bks.) Random Hse. Children's Bks.

—Richard Scarry's Good Night, Little Bear. Scarry, Patsy. 2014. (Big Golden Book Ser.). (ENG.). 32p. (J). (-k). 9.99 (978-0-385-38729-3(6), Golden Bks.) Random Hse. Children's Bks.

—Richard Scarry's the Bunny Book. Scarry, Patsy. 2015. (Big Golden Book Ser.). (ENG.). 32p. (J). (-k). 9.99 (978-0-385-39090-3(4), Golden Bks.) Random Hse. Children's Bks.

Scarry, Richard. Richard Scarry's the Gingerbread Man. Nolte, Nancy. 2015. (Little Golden Book Ser.). (ENG.). 24p. (J). (-k). 4.99 (978-0-385-37619-8(7), Golden Bks.) Random Hse. Children's Bks.

Scarry, Richard. Biggest, Busiest Storybook Ever. Scarry, Richard. 2009. (Picture Book Ser.). (ENG.). 184p. (J). (gr. -1-2). 27.99 (978-0-375-85483-5(5), Golden Bks.) Random Hse. Children's Bks.

Scarry, Richard. Busy, Busy World. Scarry, Richard. 2015. (ENG.). 96p. (J). (gr. -1-2). 15.99 (978-0-385-38480-3(7), Golden Bks.) Random Hse. Children's Bks.

Scarry, Richard. Christmas Mice. Scarry, Richard. 2014. (Little Golden Book Ser.). (ENG.). 24p. (J). (-k). 4.99 (978-0-385-38421-6(1), Golden Bks.) Random Hse. Children's Bks.

—A Day at the Police Station. Scarry, Richard. Scarry, Huck. 2004. (Look-Look Ser.). (ENG.). 24p. (J). (gr. -1-2). pap. 3.99 (978-0-375-82822-5(2), Golden Bks.) Random Hse. Children's Bks.

—Mi Casa. Scarry, Richard. 2003. (Richard Scarry Ser.).Tr. of My Home. (SPA.). (J). (gr. -1-3). pap. (978-970-690-845-2(5)) Planeta Mexicana Editorial S. A. de C. V.

—The Night Before the Night Before Christmas! Scarry, Richard. 2014. (ENG.). 48p. (J). (gr. -1-2). 14.99 (978-0-385-38804-7(7), Golden Bks.) Random Hse. Children's Bks.

—Pie Rats Ahoy! Scarry, Richard. 2014. (Step into Reading Ser.). (ENG.). 32p. (J). (gr. -1-1). lib. bdg. 12.99 (978-0-679-94760-8(4)); per. 3.99 (978-0-679-84760-1(X)) Random Hse. Children's Bks. (Random Hse. Bks. for Young Readers).

—Richard Scarry's Be Careful, Mr. Frumble! Scarry, Richard. 2015. (Step into Reading Ser.). (ENG.). 32p. (J). (gr. -1-1). lib. bdg. 12.99 (978-0-375-97346-8(X), Random Hse. Bks. for Young Readers) Random Hse. Children's Bks.

—Richard Scarry's Best Bunny Book Ever! Scarry, Richard. 2014. (Little Golden Book Favorites Ser.). (ENG.). 80p. (J). (-k). 6.99 (978-0-385-38467-4(X), Golden Bks.) Random Hse. Children's Bks.

—Richard Scarry's Best Counting Book Ever. Scarry, Richard. 2004. (SPA, ENG & MUL.). 40p. (J). (gr. -1-2). 14.95 (978-0-87358-875-1(4)); pap. 8.95 (978-0-87358-876-8(2)) Cooper Square Publishing Llc.

—Richard Scarry's Best Word Book Ever. Scarry, Richard. 2004. (SPA, ENG & MUL.). 64p. (J). (gr. -1-2). pap. 10.95 (978-0-87358-874-4(6)) Cooper Square Publishing Llc.

Scarry, Richard. Richard Scarry's Boats. Scarry, Richard. 2015. (ENG.). 24p. (J). (— 1). bds. 4.99 (978-0-385-39269-3(9), Golden Bks.) Random Hse. Children's Bks.

Scarry, Richard. Richard Scarry's Books on the Go. Scarry, Richard. 2015. (ENG.). 24p. (J). (gr. k — 1). bds. 19.96 (978-0-375-87522-9(0), Golden Bks.) Random Hse. Children's Bks.

—Richard Scarry's Bunnies. Scarry, Richard. 2014. (ENG.). 26p. (J). (-k). bds. 8.99 (978-0-385-38518-3(8), Golden Bks.) Random Hse. Children's Bks.

—Richard Scarry's Good Night, Little Bear: With Stickers! Scarry, Richard. 2015. (Pictureback(R) Ser.). (ENG.). 24p. (J). (-k). pap. 4.99 (978-0-385-39272-3(9), Random Hse. Bks. for Young Readers) Random Hse. Children's Bks.

—Richard Scarry's Just Right Word Book! Scarry, Richard. 2015. (ENG.). 24p. (J). (— 1). bds. 7.99 (978-0-553-50902-1(0), Random Hse. Bks. for Young Readers) Random Hse. Children's Bks.

—Richard Scarry's Lowly Worm Word Book. Scarry, Richard. 2014. (Chunky Book Ser.). (ENG.). 28p. (J). (gr. -1 — 1). bds. 3.99 (978-0-394-84728-3(8), Random Hse. Bks. for Young Readers) Random Hse. Children's Bks.

—Richard Scarry's Pig Will & Pig Won't. Scarry, Richard. 2014. (Pictureback(R) Ser.). (ENG.). 24p. (J). (gr. -1-2). 4.99 (978-0-385-38337-0(1), Random Hse. Bks. for Young Readers) Random Hse. Children's Bks.

Scarry, Richard. Richard Scarry's Planes. Scarry, Richard. 2015. (ENG.). 24p. (J). (— 1). bds. 4.99 (978-0-385-39270-9(2), Golden Bks.) Random Hse. Children's Bks.

Scarry, Richard. Richard Scarry's Postman Pig & His Busy Neighbors. Scarry, Richard. 2015. (Pictureback(R) Ser.). (ENG.). 32p. (J). (gr. -1-2). pap. 4.99 (978-0-385-38419-3(X), Random Hse. Bks. for Young Readers) Random Hse. Children's Bks.

—Richard Scarry's Smokey the Fireman. Scarry, Richard. 2015. (Step into Reading Ser.). (ENG.). 32p. (J). (gr. -1-1). 12.99 (978-0-375-97363-5(X)) Random Hse., Inc.

Scarry, Richard & Golden Books Staff. Little Golden Book Favorites. Golden Books Staff. 2008. (Little Golden Book Favorites Ser.). (ENG.). 80p. (J). (gr. -1-2). 5.99 (978-0-375-84580-2(1), Golden Bks.) Random Hse., Inc.

Scauzillo, Tony. WonderChess - Chess Kit for Kids: Featuring unique, prize-fillable pieces & 3D illustrated lesson Book. Thyrion, Marie-Noelle, photos by. Alvarez, Michel J. 2004. 54p. (J). pap. 19.95 (978-0-9771787-0-4(6)) Wonder Chess LLC.

—WonderChess - Chess Kit for Kids - Deluxe Edition in Tin: Featuring, unique prize fillable pieces & 3D illustrated lesson Book, 1. Thyrion, Marie-Noelle, photos by. Alvarez, Michel J. 2005. 54p. (J). 29.95 (978-0-9771787-1-1(4)) Wonder Chess LLC.

Schacher, Tracey. The Greatest Marriage Ever. Powell, Joyce. 2011. 26p. pap. 11.95 (978-1-4575-0215-6(1)) Dog Ear Publishing, LLC.

Schachner, Judy, et al. Knock, Knock! Schachner, Judy. 2007. (ENG.). 32p. (J). (gr. -1-3). 16.99 (978-0-8037-3152-3(3), Dial) Penguin Publishing Group.

Schachner, Judy. Color Crazy. Schachner, Judy. 2007. (Skippyjon Jones Ser.). (ENG.). 12p. (J). (gr. -1 — 1). bds. 6.99 (978-0-525-47782-2(9), Dutton Juvenile) Penguin Publishing Group.

Schachner, Judy. Dewey Bob. Schachner, Judy. 2015. (ENG.). 32p. (J). (gr. -1-k). 17.99 (978-0-8037-4120-1(0), Dial) Penguin Publishing Group.

Schachner, Judy. Get Busy with Skippyjon Jones! Schachner, Judy. 2013. (Skippyjon Jones Ser.). (ENG.). 16p. (J). (gr. -1-k). 6.99 (978-0-448-47783-1(1), Grosset & Dunlap) Penguin Publishing Group.

—Skippydoodle-Do & Draw! Schachner, Judy. 2014. (Skippyjon Jones Ser.). (ENG.). 32p. (J). (gr. -1-k). 6.99 (978-0-448-48024-4(7), Grosset & Dunlap) Penguin Publishing Group.

—Skippyjon Jones. Schachner, Judy. (Skippyjon Jones Ser.). (ENG.). 32p. (J). 2003. (gr. -1-k). 17.99 (978-0-525-47134-9(0), Dutton Juvenile); 2005. (gr. k-k). reprint ed. pap. 6.99 (978-0-14-240403-4(9), Puffin) Penguin Publishing Group.

—Skippyjon Jones Book & Toy Set, Set. Schachner, Judy. 2007. (Skippyjon Jones Ser.). (ENG.). 32p. (J). (gr. -1-k). 16.99 (978-0-525-47774-7(8), Dutton Juvenile) Penguin Publishing Group.

—Skippyjon Jones in Mummy Trouble. Schachner, Judy. 2006. (Skippyjon Jones Ser.). (ENG.). 32p. (J). (gr. -1-k). 16.99 (978-0-525-47754-9(3), Dutton Juvenile) Penguin Publishing Group.

—Skippyjon Jones in the Doghouse. Schachner, Judy. 2007. (Skippyjon Jones Ser.). (ENG.). 32p. (J). (gr. -1-k). pap. 6.99 (978-0-14-240749-3(6), Puffin) Penguin Publishing Group.

—Skippyjon Jones in the Doghouse. Schachner, Judy. Wilhelm, James J., ed. 2005. (Skippyjon Jones Ser.). (ENG.). 32p. (J). (gr. -1-18). 16.99 (978-0-525-47297-1(5), Dutton Juvenile) Penguin Publishing Group.

—Skippyjon Jones Keepin' Busy Kit. Schachner, Judy. 2014. (Skippyjon Jones Ser.). (ENG.). 14p. (J). (gr. -1-k). 16.99 (978-0-448-48145-6(6), Grosset & Dunlap) Penguin Publishing Group.

—Skippyjon Jones, Lost in Spice. Schachner, Judy. 2009. (Skippyjon Jones Ser.). (ENG.). 32p. (J). (gr. -1-k). 17.99 (978-0-525-47965-9(1), Dutton Juvenile) Penguin Publishing Group.

—Up & Down. Schachner, Judy. 2007. (Skippyjon Jones Ser.). (ENG.). 12p. (J). (gr. -1 — 1). bds. 6.99 (978-0-525-47807-2(8), Dutton Juvenile) Penguin Publishing Group.

Schaefer, Nikki. The Potty Train. Schaefer, Nikki. 2010. 24p. pap. 10.95 (978-1-61633-043-9(0)) Guardian Angel Publishing, Inc.

Schaeffer, Bob. Peppy Learns to Play Baseball. Heller, Pete. Kinsey, Thomas D., ed. (Peppy Learns to Play Ser.). 32p. (J). (gr. k-5). pap. 3.95 (978-0-932423-00-9(3)) Summa Bks.

Schaerer, Kathrin. Fox in the Library. Pauli, Lorenz. 2013. (ENG.). 32p. (J). (gr. -1-3). 17.95 (978-0-7358-4150-5(0)) North-South Bks., Inc.

Schafer, Holden J. Blue Tooth Sleuth. Steininger-Moore, Cheryl A. 2013. 26p. 16.50 (978-1-61314-141-0(6)); (J). pap. 9.99 (978-1-61314-142-7(4), Innovo Pr.) Innovo Publishing, LLC.

Schafer, Rick, photos by. Cooking with the Seafood Steward: Taking the Mystery Out of Seafood Preparation. Puetz, Gary Rainer. 2008. (ENG., 198p. 24.95 (978-0-9801942-5-8(3)) ACS, LLC Amica Creative Services.

—The Vintner's Kitchen: Celebrating the Wines of Oregon. King, William. 2008. (Chef's Bounty Ser.). (ENG., 187p. 29.95 (978-0-9794771-3-3(1)) ACS, LLC Amica Creative Services.

Schafrath, Ty. Feet. McCullough, Myrina D. 2013. 28p. pap. 15.00 (978-0-9847740-1-2(7)) Systems Group, Inc., The.

Schallmo, Carolyn. Ryan the Lion Finds His Roar. Lamb, Jim. 2011. 32p. 22.95 (978-1-60844-880-7(0)); pap. 12.95 (978-1-60844-879-1(7)) Dog Ear Publishing, LLC.

Schanck, Agnes. The Flower Pot Bunnies: Not A Good Place For A Nest. Rehm, Carolyn. 2004. 48p. (J). bds. 12.99 (978-0-9755390-1-9(9)) Fifth Ave Pr.

Schandy, Rosita & Wooten, Neal. Spencer the Spring Chicken & Other Stories. Mitchell, Malinda. 2007. 88p. pap. 23.95 (978-0-9800675-0-7(2)) Mirror Publishing.

Schanzer, Olivia. B'chol L'vavcha: With All Your Heart. rev. ed. 2004. (ENG & HEB.). xxiv, 261p. (gr. 7-9). pap. 14.00 (978-0-8074-0777-6(1), 142611) URJ Pr.

Schanzer, Rosalyn. The True-or-False Book of Dogs. Lauber, Patricia. 2003. (ENG.). 32p. (J). 15.99 (978-0-06-029767-1(0)) HarperCollins Pubs.

Schanzer, Rosalyn. How Ben Franklin Stole the Lightning. Schanzer, Rosalyn. 2003. 40p. (J). lib. bdg. 18.89 (978-0-688-16994-7(5)) HarperCollins Pubs.

Schärer, Kathrin. The Fox in the Library. Pauli, Lorenz. 2015. (ENG.). 32p. (J). pap. 7.95 (978-0-7358-4213-7(2)) North-South Bks., Inc.

—You Call That Brave? Pauli, Lorenz. 2014. (ENG.). 32p. (J). 17.95 (978-0-7358-4182-6(9)) North-South Bks., Inc.

Scharschmidt, Sherry. Tuck Me In! Hacohen, Dean. 2010. (ENG.). 40p. (J). (gr. -1 — 1). 9.99 (978-0-7636-4728-5(4)) Candlewick Pr.

Scharschmidt, Sherry. Who's Hungry? Hacohen, Dean. 2015. (ENG.). 40p. (J). (— 1). 9.99 (978-0-7636-6586-9(X)) Candlewick Pr.

Schartup, Adam. Hello, Beaker! Morehead State University. Aryal, Naren. 2013. (ENG.). (J). 14.95 (978-1-62086-151-6(8)) Mascot Bks., Inc.

—The Secret Society of the Palos Verdes Lizards. Milani, Joan. 2013. (ENG.). (J). 14.95 (978-1-62086-346-6(4)) Mascot Bks., Inc.

Schatell, Brian. On the First Night of Chanukah. Kaiser, Cecily. 2007. (ENG.). 24p. (J). (gr. -1-3). pap. 3.99 (978-0-439-75802-4(5), Cartwheel Bks.) Scholastic, Inc.

Schaub, Stephen, photos by. Through a Glass Darkly: Photographs by Stephen M. Schaub. 2004. (ENG & FRE., 60p. 65.00 (978-0-9669079-1-9(4)) Indian Hill Gallery of Fine Photography.

Schauer, Jane. Fantasy Park Book 1: The Doorman. Schauer, Jane. 2008. 36p. pap. (978-0-9804633-2-3(7)) KREAV Publishing.

Schedeen, Minnie. Bleep Blop Bloop, 1. Arthur, Clint. 2006. 24p. (J). per. 8.99 net. (978-1-4276-0218-3(2)) Aardvark Global Publishing.

Scheffler, Axel. Axel Scheffler's Noisy Jungle. ed. 2014. (ENG.). 400p. (J). (gr. -1-k). 19.99 (978-1-4472-4634-3(9)) Pan Macmillan GBR. Dist: Independent Pubs. Group.

—Charlie Cook's Favorite Book. Donaldson, Julia. (ENG.). 32p. (J). (gr. -1-k). 2008. pap. 6.99 (978-0-14-241138-4(8), Puffin); 2006. 17.99 (978-0-8037-3142-4(6), Dial) Penguin Publishing Group.

—Christmas Poems. Morgan, Gaby. unabr. ed. 2014. (ENG.). 400p. (J). pap. 9.99 (978-1-4472-5463-8(5)) Pan Macmillan GBR. Dist: Independent Pubs. Group.

—The Fish Who Cried Wolf. Donaldson, Julia. 2008. (J). pap. (978-0-545-03454-8(X), Levine, Arthur A. Bks.) Scholastic, Inc.

—Flip Flap Farm. Crow, Nosy. 2014. (ENG.). 26p. (J). (gr. -1-2). 11.99 (978-0-7636-7067-2(7), Nosy Crow) Candlewick Pr.

—Flip Flap Safari. Nosy Crow. 2015. (ENG.). 28p. (J). (gr. -1-2). 11.99 (978-0-7636-7605-6(5), Nosy Crow) Candlewick Pr.

—A Gold Star for Zog. Donaldson, Julia. 2012. (ENG.). 32p. (J). (gr. -1-3). 16.99 (978-0-545-41724-2(4), Levine, Arthur A. Bks.) Scholastic, Inc.

—El Grufalo. Donaldson, Julia. 2003. (SPA.). 32p. (J). (gr. k-2). 7.96 (978-84-233-3145-1(8), DS4478) Ediciones Destino ESP. Dist: Lectorum Pubns., Inc.

—The Gruffalo. Donaldson, Julia. (ENG.). (J). (gr. -1-2). 2006. 32p. pap. 6.99 (978-0-14-240387-7(3), Puffin); 2005. 24p. bds. 6.99 (978-0-8037-3047-2(0), Dial) Penguin Publishing Group.

—The Gruffalo. Donaldson, Julia. 2005. (ENG.). 32p. (J). (gr. -1-2). 16.99 (978-0-8037-3109-7(4), Dial) Penguin Publishing Group.

—The Gruffalo (Al Gharfoul) Donaldson, Julia. Fouda, Nadia, tr. 2010. (ENG & ARA.). 32p. (J). (gr. -1-k). pap. 8.99 (978-99921-42-12-7(X)) Bloomsbury USA.

—The Gruffalo Theatre, 1. Donaldson, Julia. ed. 2008. (ENG.). 18p. (gr. 2-5). 34.95 (978-0-230-53179-6(2), Macmillan) Pan Macmillan GBR. Dist: Trans-Atlantic Pubns., Inc.

—The Gruffalo's Child. Donaldson, Julia. 2007. (ENG.). 32p. (J). (gr. -1-2). pap. 6.99 (978-0-14-240754-7(2), Puffin) Penguin Publishing Group.

—The Highway Rat. Donaldson, Julia. 2013. (ENG.). 32p. (J). (gr. -1-3). 16.99 (978-0-545-47758-1(1), Levine, Arthur A. Bks.) Scholastic, Inc.

—Katie the Kitten. ed. (Buggy Buddies Ser.). (ENG.). (J). (— 1). 2015. 12p. bds. 7.99 (978-0-230-75615-1(8)); 2014. 10p. 13.99 (978-1-4472-6805-5(9)) Pan Macmillan GBR. Dist: Independent Pubs. Group.

—Lizzy the Lamb. ed. 2015. (Buggy Buddies Ser.). (ENG.). 12p. (J). (— 1). bds. 7.99 (978-0-230-75616-8(6)) Pan Macmillan GBR. Dist: Independent Pubs. Group.

—Mother Goose's Bedtime Rhymes, 2 vols. Collins, Mark et al. 2008. (ENG.). 32p. (J). (gr. 2-6). 19.95 (978-0-230-70842-6(0), Macmillan) Pan Macmillan GBR. Dist: Trans-Atlantic Pubns., Inc.

—Mother Goose's Nursery Rhymes: And How She Came to Tell Them. Green, Alison. ed. 2006. (ENG.). 128p. (978-0-333-96136-0(6), Macmillan Children's Bks.) Pan Macmillan.

—Noisy Farm. Prasadam-Halls, Smriti. ed. 2014. (ENG.). 10p. (J). (gr. -1-k). 19.99 (978-0-230-76680-8(3)) Pan Macmillan GBR. Dist: Independent Pubs. Group.

—Pip & Posy: the Bedtime Frog. Crow, Nosy. 2014. (Pip & Posy Ser.). (ENG.). 32p. (J). (-k). 12.99 (978-0-7636-7068-9(5), Nosy Crow) Candlewick Pr.

—Pip & Posy: the Little Puddle. Nosy Crow. 2011. (Pip & Posy Ser.). (ENG.). 32p. (J). (gr. k-k). 12.99 (978-0-7636-5878-6(2), Nosy Crow) Candlewick Pr.

—Pip & Posy: the Scary Monster. Nosy Crow. 2012. (Pip & Posy Ser.). (ENG.). 32p. (J). (gr. k-k). 12.99 (978-0-7636-5918-9(5), Nosy Crow) Candlewick Pr.

—Pip & Posy: the Scary Monster. Crow, Nosy. 2014. (Pip & Posy Ser.). (ENG.). 24p. (J). (-k). bds. 6.99 (978-0-7636-7231-7(9), Nosy Crow) Candlewick Pr.

—Pip & Posy: the Super Scooter. Nosy Crow. (Pip & Posy Ser.). (ENG.). (J). (-k). 2013. 24p. bds. 6.99 (978-0-7636-6609-5(2)); 2011. 32p. 12.99 (978-0-7636-5877-9(4)) Candlewick Pr. (Nosy Crow).

—Pip the Puppy. ed. 2015. (Buggy Buddies Ser.). (ENG.). 12p. (J). (— 1). bds. 7.99 (978-0-230-75617-5(4)) Pan Macmillan GBR. Dist: Independent Pubs. Group.

—Rhyming Stories: Pip the Dog & Freddy the Frog. ed. 2015. (ENG.). 20p. (J). (— 1). bds. 9.99 (978-1-4472-6824-6(5)) Pan Macmillan GBR. Dist: Independent Pubs. Group.

—Rhyming Stories Bk. 2: Katie the Kitten; Lizzy the Lamb. ed. 2015. (ENG.). 20p. (J). (— 1). bds. 9.99 (978-1-4472-6828-4(8)) Pan Macmillan GBR. Dist: Independent Pubs. Group.

—Room on the Broom. Donaldson, Julia. 2003. (ENG.). 32p. (J). (gr. -1-2). pap. 6.99 (978-0-14-250112-2(3), Puffin) Penguin Publishing Group.

Scheffler, Axel. Room on the Broom Big Activity Book. Donaldson, Julia. 2015. (ENG.). 48p. (J). (gr. -1-3). pap. 10.99 (978-0-448-48944-5(9), Grosset & Dunlap) Penguin Publishing Group.

Scheffler, Axel. The Scarecrows' Wedding. Donaldson, Julia. 2014. (ENG.). 32p. (J). (gr. -1-3). 17.99 (978-0-545-72606-1(9), Levine, Arthur A. Bks.) Scholastic, Inc.

—The Snail & the Whale. Donaldson, Julia. (ENG.). 32p. (J). (gr. -1-2). 2004. 18.99 (978-0-8037-2922-3(7), Dial); 2006. reprint ed. pap. 6.99 (978-0-14-240580-2(9), Puffin) Penguin Publishing Group.

—The Spiffiest Giant in Town. Donaldson, Julia. 2005. (ENG.). 32p. (J). (gr. -1-2). reprint ed. pap. 6.99 (978-0-14-240275-7(3), Puffin) Penguin Publishing Group.

—Stick Man. Donaldson, Julia. 2009. (ENG.). 32p. (J). (gr. -1-3). 16.99 (978-0-545-15761-2(7), Levine, Arthur A. Bks.) Scholastic, Inc.

—Superworm. Donaldson, Julia. 2014. (ENG.). 32p. (J). (gr. -1-3). 16.99 (978-0-545-59176-8(7), Levine, Arthur A. Bks.) Scholastic, Inc.

—Tabby McTat: The Musical Cat. Donaldson, Julia. 2012. (ENG.). 32p. (J). (gr. -1-3). 17.99 (978-0-545-45168-0(X), Levine, Arthur A. Bks.) Scholastic, Inc.

—Where's My Mom? Donaldson, Julia. 2008. (ENG.). 32p. (J). (gr. -1-2). 18.99 (978-0-8037-3228-5(7), Dial) Penguin Publishing Group.

Scheffler, Axel. Freddy the Frog. Scheffler, Axel. ed. 2014. (Noisy Bath Bks.). (ENG.). 10p. (J). (— 1). 13.99 (978-1-4472-6804-8(0)) Pan Macmillan GBR. Dist: Independent Pubs. Group.

—Pip & Posy: the Big Balloon. Scheffler, Axel. 2013. (Pip & Posy Ser.). (ENG.). 32p. (J). (-k). 12.99 (978-0-7636-6372-8(7), Nosy Crow) Candlewick Pr.

—Pip & Posy: the Little Puddle. Scheffler, Axel. 2013. (Pip & Posy Ser.). (ENG.). 24p. (J). (-k). bds. 6.99 (978-0-7636-6161-8(9), Nosy Crow) Candlewick Pr.

—Pip & Posy: the Snowy Day. Scheffler, Axel. Nosy Crow Staff. 2013. (Pip & Posy Ser.). (ENG.). 32p. (J). (-k). 12.99 (978-0-7636-6607-1(6), Nosy Crow) Candlewick Pr.

Scheibe, Nancy. Clara & Mr. Twiddles: The Magical Adventures of Clara the Cleaning Lady. Murray-Gibson, Lynnette A. 2010. (ENG.). 40p. pap. 15.95 (978-1-58985-123-8(4)) Five Star Pubns., Inc.

—Loon & Moon: And Other Animal Stories. Strauss, Kevin. 2005. 48p. (J). (gr. 4-6). per. 12.95 (978-0-9766264-3-5(8)) Raven Productions, Inc.

Scheie, Jesse. Kisses to Heaven, 1 vol. Scheie, Jesse. 2009. 16p. pap. 24.95 (978-1-61582-707-7(2)) America Star Bks.

Scheinberg, Shepsil. Out of the Woods. Lazewnik, Libby. 2011. 320p. (J). (978-1-4226-1176-0(0)) Mesorah Pubns., Ltd.

Scheiner, A. & Wenckebach, L. W. R. The Nutcracker & the Mouse King. Hoffmann, E. T. A. 2013. Orig. Title: Nutcracker & the King of the Mice. 88p. pap. (978-1-909115-77-4(0)) Planet, The.

Schellenbach, Pete. The Easter Bunny Visits Easterville. Kissane, sheela. Lavery, Breanne, ed. 2010. (ENG.). 28p. pap. 10.99 (978-1-4515-4155-7(4)) CreateSpace Independent Publishing Platform.

Schellpeper, Kathy, photos by. The Community of Lincoln. Manton, Charlotte. Stanley, Karen & Bornemeier, Pam, eds. 116p. (J). (gr. 3-6). pap. 10.50 (978-0-9671920-0-0(5)) Lincoln Public Schls.

Schenker, Hilary. Same Sun Here. House, Silas & Vaswani, Neela. (ENG.). (J). 2013. 304p. (gr. 4-7). pap. 7.99 (978-0-7636-6451-0(0)); 2012. 288p. (gr. 5). 15.99 (978-0-7636-5684-3(4)) Candlewick Pr.

Scherberger, Patrick & Wegener, Scott. Earth's Mightiest Heroes Avengers, Vol. 2. Marvel Comics Staff. 2012. (ENG.). 32p. (J). (gr. -1-17). pap. 3.99 (978-0-7851-5364-1(0)) Marvel Worldwide, Inc.

—Marvel Universe Avengers Earth's Mightiest Comic Reader 4. Yost, Christopher. 2012. (ENG.). 32p. (J). (gr. -1-17). 3.99 (978-0-7851-5375-7(6)) Marvel Worldwide, Inc.

Scherberger, Patrick, jt. illus. see Wegener, Scott.

Scherer, Donovan Harold. Fear & Sunshine. Scherer, Donovan Harold. 2009. 248p. (J). pap. 14.95 (978-0-9841746-1-4(3)) Studio Moonfall.

Schettle, Jane. Mad Maddie Maxwell, 1 vol. Maslyn, Stacie K. B. & Maslyn, Stacie K. 2007. (I Can Read! Ser.). (ENG.). 32p. (J). (gr. -1-1). pap. 3.99 (978-0-310-71467-5(2)) Zonderkidz.

Scheuer, Lauren. Mini Mysteries: 20 Tricky Tales to Untangle. Walton, Rick. American Girl Editorial Staff & Magruder, Trula, eds. 2004. (ENG.). 80p. (gr. 4-18). pap. 7.95 (978-1-58485-871-3(0)) American Girl Publishing, Inc.

—Mini Mysteries 2: 20 More Tricky Tales to Untangle. Walton, Rick. 2006. 87p. (J). *(978-1-4156-6869-6(8)*, American Girl) American Girl Publishing, Inc.

—Mini Mysteries 3: 20 More Tricky Tales to Untangle. Walton, Rick. 2007. (ENG.). 80p. (gr. 4-7). pap. 7.95 *(978-1-59369-281-0(1))* American Girl Publishing, Inc.

—A Smart Girl's Guide to Staying Home Alone. Raymer, Dottie. 2009. (ENG.). 64p. (J). pap. 9.95 *(978-1-59369-487-6(3))* American Girl Publishing, Inc.

—A Smart Girl's Guide to Understanding Her Family: Feelings, Fighting & Figuring It Out. Lynch, Amy. 2009. (ENG.). 64p. (J). (gr. 3-18). pap. 9.95 *(978-1-59369-617-7(5))* American Girl Publishing, Inc.

Schexnayder, Paul. The Kajun Kween. 2003. (ENG.). 100p. (J). per. 22.00 *(978-0-9650977-1-0(4))* Border Pr.

—Mr. Tootles & the Polka-Dot Lollypops. Clement, Maryceleste. 2005. (Tootle Tales Ser.: Vol. 2). 32p. (J). 14.95 *(978-0-9721706-1-1(8))* Tootle Time Publishing Co.

Scheyder, Jacob P. One More Thing. Scheyder, S. Jane. 2013. 42p. pap. 7.99 *(978-0-9830318-6-4(X))* Andres & Blanton.

Schiavello, Arlene, photos by. My Chosen Path: A Poetic Reflection of Teenage Emotions. Schiavello, Kira. 2005. 108p. (YA). 14.00 *(978-0-9761513-4-0(0))* ADR Inc.

Schick, Joel. The Jungle Book: A Story about Loyalty. 2006. (J). 6.99 *(978-1-59939-023-9(X))* Cornerstone Pr.

—The Magic School Bus in the Haunted Museum: A Book about Sound. Beech, Linda Ward. Duchesne, Lucie, tr. (Magic School Bus Ser.). (FRE.). 32p. (J). (gr. 1-4). pap. 5.99 *(978-0-590-24657-6(7))* Scholastic, Inc.

—Max Can Fix That. Albee, Sarah. 2006. (Step-By-Step Readers Ser.). (J). pap. *(978-1-59939-055-0(8)*, Reader's Digest Young Families, Inc.) Studio Fun International.

Schick, Joel & McCauley, Adam. Wayside School Gets a Little Stranger. Sachar, Louis. 2003. (Wayside School Ser.). (ENG.). 176p. (J). (gr. 3-7). pap. 5.99 *(978-0-380-72381-2(6))* HarperCollins Pubs.

Schickle, Ian. Behind the Door of Timothy Moore. Cameron, Kristy. 2013. 28p. pap. *(978-0-9859790-1-0(1))* LP Publishing.

Schiebold, Olivia, jt. illus. see Thomas, Leanne.

Schieldt, Jodi. Somebody's Gotta Get Rid of That Vacuum. Schieldt, Corine. 2008. 24p. per. 24.95 *(978-1-4241-9121-5(1))* America Star Bks.

Schifferli, Paul Phillip. Darryl's Daring Deed. Schifferli, Paul Phillip. 2006. (J). 9.95 *(978-0-9765304-7-3(3))* Windsor Media Enterprises, Inc.

Schiffman, Jessica. The Doll Maker's Gift. Fridman, Sashi. 2011. 36p. 14.95 *(978-0-8266-0040-0(9))* Kehot Pubn. Society.

—Sybil Ludington: Freedom's Brave Rider. 2005. 32p. (J). pap. *(978-0-7367-2931-4(3))* Zaner-Bloser, Inc.

Schigiel, Gregg. The Deadly Dream Machine. Bright, J. E. & Loughridge, Lee. (Superman Ser.). (ENG.). 56p. (gr. 2-3). 2014. pap. 4.95 *(978-1-4342-2759-1(6))*; 2010. lib. bdg. 25.32 *(978-1-4342-1978-7(X))* Stone Arch Bks. (DC Super Heroes).

—Feel the Love (SpongeBob SquarePants) Golden Books Staff. 2013. (Pictureback Series.). (ENG.). 16p. (J). (gr. -1-2). 4.99 *(978-0-449-81956-2(6)*, Random Hse. Bks. for Young Readers) Random Hse. Children's Bks.

—Mad Hatter's Movie Madness, 1 vol. Lemke, Donald B. & Loughridge, Lee. (Batman Ser.). (ENG.). 56p. (gr. 2-3). 2014. pap. 4.95 *(978-1-4342-1675-5(6))*; 2010. lib. bdg. 25.32 *(978-1-4342-2131-5(8))* Stone Arch Bks. (DC Super Heroes).

—My Frozen Valentine, 1 vol. Fein, Eric & Loughridge, Lee. (Batman Ser.). (ENG.). 56p. (gr. 2-3). 2013. pap. 4.95 *(978-1-4342-1731-8(0))*; 2009. 25.32 *(978-1-4342-1564-2(4))* Stone Arch Bks. (DC Super Heroes).

—The Shrinking City, 1 vol. Dahl, Michael & Loughridge, Lee. 2009. (Superman Ser.). (ENG.). 56p. (gr. 2-3). 25.32 *(978-1-4342-1569-7(5)*, DC Super Heroes) Stone Arch Bks.

—Shrinking City. Dahl, Michael & Loughridge, Lee. 2013. (Superman Ser.). (ENG.). 56p. (gr. 2-3). pap. 4.95 *(978-1-4342-1735-6(3)*, DC Super Heroes) Stone Arch Bks.

—SpongeBob LovePants. Pass, Erica. 2006. (Ready-to-Read Ser.). (ENG.). 32p. (J). (gr. k-2). pap. 3.99 *(978-1-4169-1758-8(6)*, Simon Spotlight/Nickelodeon) Simon Spotlight/Nickelodeon.

Schigiel, Gregg. Bat-Mite's Big Blunder, 1 vol. Schigiel, Gregg. Kupperberg, Paul & Loughridge, Lee. (Batman Ser.). (ENG.). 56p. (gr. 2-3). 2013. pap. 4.95 *(978-1-4342-2255-8(1))*; 2010. lib. bdg. 25.32 *(978-1-4342-1877-3(5))* Stone Arch Bks. (DC Super Heroes).

—Five Riddles for Robin, 1 vol. Schigiel, Gregg. Dahl, Michael & Loughridge, Lee. (Batman Ser.). (ENG.). 56p. (gr. 2-3). 2013. pap. 4.95 *(978-1-4342-1366-2(8))*; 2009. lib. bdg. 25.32 *(978-1-4342-1151-4(7))* Stone Arch Bks. (DC Super Heroes).

—The Revenge of Clayface, 1 vol. Schigiel, Gregg. Stevens, Eric & Loughridge, Lee. (Batman Ser.). (ENG.). 56p. (gr. 2-3). 2013. pap. 4.95 *(978-1-4342-1369-3(2))*; 2009. lib. bdg. 25.32 *(978-1-4342-1149-1(5))* Stone Arch Bks. (DC Super Heroes).

—Robin's First Flight. Schigiel, Gregg. Greenberger, Robert & Loughridge, Lee. (Batman Ser.). (ENG.). 56p. (gr. 2-3). 2013. pap. 4.95 *(978-1-4342-2262-6(4))*; 2010. lib. bdg. 25.32 *(978-1-4342-1879-7(1))* Stone Arch Bks. (DC Super Heroes).

Schigiel, Gregg, jt. illus. see Beavers, Ethen.

Schilling, Deborah. Sago, A Very Special Service Dog: N/a. Davis, Beth. 2011.Tr. of N/a. 28p. (J). 15.00 *(978-0-9822974-9-0(1))*; lib. bdg. 24.00 *(978-0-9822974-8-3(3))* Rolemommy.

Schimler, Amy. What Do You See? A Lift-the-Flap Book about Endangered Animals. Krensky, Stephen. 2009. (Little Green Bks.). (ENG.). 16p. (J). (gr. -1-k). 6.99 *(978-1-4169-7123-8(8)*, Little Simon) Little Simon.

Schimler, Amy. Splish Splash! A Touch & Hear Book. Schimler, Amy. 2011. (ENG.). 14p. (J). (gr. -1 — 1). bds. 6.99 *(978-1-4424-1354-2(9)*, Little Simon) Little Simon.

Schimmel, Beth. Abigail's New Home. Taylor, Dorothy L. (Valley View Farm Tales Ser.). 20p. (J). (gr. k-3). 7.50 *(978-0-9610640-0-6(5))* Taylor, Dorothy Loring.

Schimmel, David. Dear Dragon Goes to the Library. Hillert, Margaret. 2008. (Beginning to Read Ser.). 32p. (J). (gr. k-3). lib. bdg. 19.93 *(978-1-59953-160-1(7))* Norwood Hse. Pr.

—Dear Dragon's A Is for Apple. Hillert, Margaret. 2008. (Beginning-to-Read Bks.). 32p. (J). (gr. k-3). lib. bdg. 19.93 *(978-1-59953-158-8(5))* Norwood Hse. Pr.

—Dear Dragon's Day with Father. Hillert, Margaret. 2008. (Beginning to Read Ser.). 32p. (J). (gr. k-3). lib. bdg. 19.93 *(978-1-59953-162-5(3))* Norwood Hse. Pr.

—What's in the Sky, Dear Dragon? Hillert, Margaret. 2013. (ENG.). 32p. (J). pap. 10.60 *(978-1-60357-416-7(6))* Norwood Hse. Pr.

Schimmel, Schim. Magic Planet: Pop-Up Fun. 2003. 12p. (J). (gr. k-5). 20.00 *(978-0-7567-6651-1(6))* DIANE Publishing Co.

—Our Precious World Stationery Set. Book Company Staff. 2003. (Stationery Ser.). (J). pap. 15.95 *(978-1-74047-215-9(2))* Book Co. Publishing Pty, Ltd., The AUS. Dist: Penton Overseas, Inc.

Schimmell, David. Dear Dragon Eats Out. Hillert, Margaret. rev. ed. 2014. (Beginning-To-Read: New Dear Dragon Ser.). (ENG.). 32p. (J). (gr. k-2). pap. 10.60 *(978-1-60357-637-6(1))*; lib. bdg. 21.27 *(978-1-59953-629-3(3))* Norwood Hse. Pr.

—Dear Dragon Goes Camping. Hillert, Margaret. 2010. (Dear Dragon Ser.). 32p. (J). (gr. k-3). lib. bdg. 19.93 *(978-1-59953-345-2(6))* Norwood Hse. Pr.

—Dear Dragon Goes to the Bank. Hillert, Margaret. 2012. 32p. (J). lib. bdg. 21.27 *(978-1-59953-502-9(5))* Norwood Hse. Pr.

—Dear Dragon Goes to the Carnival. Hillert, Margaret. 2010. (Dear Dragon Ser.). 32p. (J). (gr. k-3). lib. bdg. 19.93 *(978-1-59953-346-9(4))* Norwood Hse. Pr.

—Dear Dragon Goes to the Dentist. Hillert, Margaret. rev. ed. 2014. (Beginning-To-Read: New Dear Dragon Ser.). (ENG.). 32p. (J). (gr. k-2). lib. bdg. 21.27 *(978-1-59953-577-7(7))* Norwood Hse. Pr.

—Dear Dragon Goes to the Firehouse. Hillert, Margaret. 2010. (Dear Dragon Ser.). 32p. (J). (gr. k-3). lib. bdg. 19.93 *(978-1-59953-375-9(8))* Norwood Hse. Pr.

—Dear Dragon Goes to the Hospital. Hillert, Margaret. rev. ed. 2014. (Beginning-To-Read: New Dear Dragon Ser.). (ENG.). 32p. (J). (gr. k-2). pap. 10.60 *(978-1-60357-422-8(0))*; lib. bdg. 21.27 *(978-1-59953-581-4(5))* Norwood Hse. Pr.

—Dear Dragon Goes to the Market. Hillert, Margaret. 2010. (Dear Dragon Ser.). 32p. (J). (gr. k-3). lib. bdg. 19.93 *(978-1-59953-347-6(2))* Norwood Hse. Pr.

—Dear Dragon Goes to the Zoo. Hillert, Margaret. 2010. (Dear Dragon Ser.). 32p. (J). (gr. k-3). lib. bdg. 19.93 *(978-1-59953-348-3(0))* Norwood Hse. Pr.

—Dear Dragon Grows a Garden. Hillert, Margaret. rev. ed. 2014. (Beginning-To-Read: New Dear Dragon Ser.). (ENG.). 32p. (J). (gr. k-2). pap. 10.60 *(978-1-60357-414-3(X))*; lib. bdg. 21.27 *(978-1-59953-578-4(X))* Norwood Hse. Pr.

—Dear Dragon's Colors 1,2,3. Hillert, Margaret. 2010. (Dear Dragon Ser.). 32p. (J). (gr. k-3). lib. bdg. 19.93 *(978-1-59953-376-6(6))* Norwood Hse. Pr.

—Dear Dragon's Colors 123. Hillert, Margaret. 2012. 32p. (J). pap. 7.95 net. *(978-1-60357-100-5(0))* Norwood Hse. Pr.

—Dear Dragon's Fun with Shapes. Hillert, Margaret. del Risco, Eida, tr. 2013. 32p. (J). pap. 21.27 *(978-1-60357-447-1(6))* Norwood Hse. Pr.

—Dear Dragon's Fun with Shapes. Hillert, Margaret. 2012. 32p. (J). lib. bdg. 21.27 *(978-1-59953-544-9(0))* Norwood Hse. Pr.

—¿Dónde Está Querido Dragón? Where Is Dear Dragon? Hillert, Margaret. Fernandez, Queta, tr. from ENG. 2014.Tr. of Where Is Dear Dragon?. (SPA & ENG.). 32p. (J). lib. bdg. 21.27 *(978-1-59953-615-6(3))* Norwood Hse. Pr.

—Es Hora de Ir a la Cama, Querido Dragón: It's Bedtime, Dear Dragon. Hillert, Margaret. Fernandez, Queta, tr. 2014.Tr. of It's Bedtime, Dear Dragon. (ENG & SPA.). 32p. (J). lib. bdg. 21.27 *(978-1-59953-612-5(9))* Norwood Hse. Pr.

—Es primavera, querido dragón/It's Spring, Dear Dragon. Hillert, Margaret. del Risco, Eida, tr. from ENG. 2011. (Dear Dragon = Querido Dragon Ser.). 32p. (J). (gr. k-3). lib. bdg. 27.93 *(978-1-59953-471-8(1))* Norwood Hse. Pr.

—Es Primavera, Querido Dragón/It's Spring, Dear Dragon. Hillert, Margaret. 2013. 32p. (J). pap. 21.27 *(978-1-60357-555-3(3))* Norwood Hse. Pr.

—Es un Buen Juego, Querido Dragon/It's a Good Game, Dear Dragon. Hillert, Margaret. Del Risco, Eida, tr. from ENG. 2010. (Dear Dragon Ser.). (SPA & ENG.). 32p. (J). (gr. k-3). lib. bdg. 19.93 *(978-1-59953-362-9(6))* Norwood Hse. Pr.

—Es un Buen Juego, Querido Dragón/It's a Good Game, Dear Dragon. Hillert, Margaret. 2013. 32p. (J). pap. 21.27 *(978-1-60357-550-8(2))* Norwood Hse. Pr.

—Happy Hanukkah, Dear Dragon. Hillert, Margaret. 2008. (Beginning to Read Ser.). 32p. (J). (gr. k-3). lib. bdg. 19.93 *(978-1-59953-159-5(3))* Norwood Hse. Pr.

—I Did It, Dear Dragon. Hillert, Margaret. 2009. (Dear Dragon Ser.). 32p. (J). (gr. k-3). lib. bdg. 19.95 *(978-1-59953-295-0(6))* Norwood Hse. Pr.

—It's a Good Game, Dear Dragon. Hillert, Margaret. 2009. (Dear Dragon Ser.). 32p. (J). (gr. k-3). lib. bdg. 19.95 *(978-1-59953-293-6(X))* Norwood Hse. Pr.

—It's Bedtime Dear Dragon. Hillert, Margaret. 2012. 32p. (J). lib. bdg. 21.27 *(978-1-59953-503-6(3))* Norwood Hse. Pr.

—It's Fall, Dear Dragon. Hillert, Margaret. 2009. (Dear Dragon Ser.). 32p. (J). (gr. k-3). lib. bdg. 19.93 *(978-1-59953-311-7(1))* Norwood Hse. Pr.

—It's Ground Hog Day Dear Dragon. Hillert, Margaret. 2012. 32p. (J). lib. bdg. 21.27 *(978-1-59953-504-3(1))* Norwood Hse. Pr.

—It's Spring, Dear Dragon. Hillert, Margaret. 2009. (Dear Dragon Ser.). 32p. (J). (gr. k-3). lib. bdg. 19.93 *(978-1-59953-312-4(X))* Norwood Hse. Pr.

—It's St. Patrick's Day, Dear Dragon. Hillert, Margaret. del Risco, Eida, tr. 2013. 32p. (J). pap. 21.27 *(978-1-60357-086-2(1))* Norwood Hse. Pr.

—It's St. Patrick's Day, Dear Dragon. Hillert, Margaret. 2008. (Beginning-to-Read Bks.). 32p. (J). (gr. k-3). lib. bdg. 19.93 *(978-1-59953-161-8(5))* Norwood Hse. Pr.

—It's Summer, Dear Dragon. Hillert, Margaret. 2009. (Dear Dragon Ser.). 32p. (J). (gr. k-3). lib. bdg. 19.93 *(978-1-59953-313-1(8))* Norwood Hse. Pr.

—It's Winter, Dear Dragon. Hillert, Margaret. 2009. (Dear Dragon Ser.). 32p. (J). (gr. k-3). lib. bdg. 19.93 *(978-1-59953-314-8(6))* Norwood Hse. Pr.

—Juega, Juega, Juega, Querido Dragon/Play, Play, Play, Dear Dragon. Hillert, Margaret. Del Risco, Eida, tr. from ENG. 2010. (Dear Dragon Ser.). (SPA & ENG.). 32p. (J). (gr. k-3). lib. bdg. 19.93 *(978-1-59953-363-6(4))* Norwood Hse. Pr.

—Juega, Juega, Juega, Querido Dragón/Play, Play, Play, Dear Dragon. Hillert, Margaret. del Risco, Eida, tr. 2013. 32p. (J). pap. 21.27 *(978-1-60357-551-5(0))* Norwood Hse. Pr.

—Play, Play, Play Dear Dragon. Hillert, Margaret. 2009. (Dear Dragon Ser.). 32p. (J). (gr. k-3). lib. bdg. 19.95 *(978-1-59953-294-3(8))* Norwood Hse. Pr.

—¿Qué Hay en el Bosque, Querido Dragon? What's in the Woods, Dear Dragon? Hillert, Margaret & Fernández, Queta. 2014.Tr. of What's in the Woods, Dear Dragon?. (ENG & SPA.). 32p. (J). lib. bdg. 21.27 *(978-1-59953-609-5(9))* Norwood Hse. Pr.

—¿Qué Hay en el Cielo, Querido Dragón? What's in the Sky, Dear Dragon? Hillert, Margaret. Fernandez, Queta, tr. from ENG. 2014.Tr. of What's in the Sky, Dear Dragon?. (ENG & SPA.). 32p. (J). lib. bdg. 21.27 *(978-1-59953-610-1(2))* Norwood Hse. Pr.

—¿Qué Hay en el Estanque, Querido Dragón? What's in the Pond, Dear Dragon? Hillert, Margaret. Fernandez, Queta, tr. 2014.Tr. of What's in the Pond, Dear Dragon?. (ENG & SPA.). 32p. (J). lib. bdg. 21.27 *(978-1-59953-608-8(0))* Norwood Hse. Pr.

—¿Qué Tengo en el Bolsillo, Querido Dragón? What's in My Pocket, Dear Dragon? Hillert, Margaret. Fernandez, Queta, tr. 2014.Tr. of What's in My Pocket, Dear Dragon?. (ENG & SPA.). 32p. (J). lib. bdg. 21.27 *(978-1-59953-611-8(0))* Norwood Hse. Pr.

—Querido dragón, los colores y 1, 2, 3 /Dear Dragon's Colors 1, 2, 3. Hillert, Margaret. del Risco, Eida, tr. from ENG. 2011. (Dear Dragon = Querido Dragon Ser.). 32p. (J). (gr. k-3). lib. bdg. 27.93 *(978-1-59953-470-1(3))* Norwood Hse. Pr.

—Querido Dragón, Los Colores y 1, 2, 3 /Dear Dragon's Colors 1, 2, 3. Hillert, Margaret. del Risco, Eida, tr. 2013. 32p. (J). pap. 21.27 *(978-1-60357-554-6(5))* Norwood Hse. Pr.

—Querido Dragon Pasa el Dia con Papa/Dear Dragon's Day with Father. Hillert, Margaret. Del Risco, Eida, tr. from ENG. 2010. (Dear Dragon Ser.). (SPA & ENG.). 32p. (J). (gr. k-3). lib. bdg. 19.93 *(978-1-59953-360-5(X))* Norwood Hse. Pr.

—Querido Dragón Quiere Ayudar: Dear Dragon Helps Out. Hillert, Margaret. Fernandez, Queta, tr. 2014.Tr. of Dear Dragon Helps Out. (ENG & SPA.). 32p. (J). lib. bdg. 21.27 *(978-1-59953-613-2(7))* Norwood Hse. Pr.

—Querido Dragon Va a la Biblioteca/Dear Dragon Goes to the Library. Hillert, Margaret. Del Risco, Eida, tr. from ENG. 2010. (Dear Dragon Ser.). (SPA & ENG.). 32p. (J). (gr. k-3). lib. bdg. 19.93 *(978-1-59953-361-2(8))* Norwood Hse. Pr.

—Querido Dragón Va a la Biblioteca/Dear Dragon Goes to the Library. Hillert, Margaret. del Risco, Eida, tr. 2013. 32p. (J). pap. 21.27 *(978-1-60357-549-2(9))* Norwood Hse. Pr.

—Querido Dragón Va a la Estación de Bomberos/Dear Dragon Goes to the Firehouse. Hillert, Margaret. de', Eida, tr. 2013. 32p. (J). pap. 21.27 *(978-1-60357-552-2(9))* Norwood Hse. Pr.

—Querido Dragón Va Al Banco: Dear Dragon Goes to the Bank. Hillert, Margaret. Fernandez, Queta, tr. 2014.Tr. of Dear Dragon Goes to the Bank. (ENG & SPA.). 32p. (J). lib. bdg. 21.27 *(978-1-59953-614-9(5))* Norwood Hse. Pr.

—Querido dragón va al cuartel de bomberos/Dear Dragon Goes to the Firehouse. Hillert, Margaret. del Risco, Eida, tr. from ENG. 2011. (Dear Dragon = Querido Dragon Ser.). 32p. (J). (gr. k-3). lib. bdg. 21.27 *(978-1-59953-468-8(1))* Norwood Hse. Pr.

—Querido dragón va al mercado/Dear Dragon Goes to the Market. Hillert, Margaret. del Risco, Eida, tr. from ENG. 2011. (Dear Dragon = Querido Dragon Ser.). (SPA.). 32p. (J). (gr. k-3). lib. bdg. 21.27 *(978-1-59953-469-5(X))* Norwood Hse. Pr.

—Querido Dragón Va Al Mercado/Dear Dragon Goes to the Market. Hillert, Margaret. 2013. 32p. (J). pap. 21.27 *(978-1-60357-553-9(7))* Norwood Hse. Pr.

—Touchdown! Dear Dragon. Hillert, Margaret. 2009. (Dear Dragon Ser.). 32p. (J). (gr. k-3). lib. bdg. 19.95 *(978-1-59953-296-7(4))* Norwood Hse. Pr.

—Up, up, up, Dear Dragon. Hillert, Margaret. 2012. 32p. (J). lib. bdg. 21.27 *(978-1-59953-545-6(9))* Norwood Hse. Pr.

—We Can Help, Dear Dragon. Hillert, Margaret. 2012. 32p. (J). lib. bdg. 21.27 *(978-1-59953-505-0(X))* Norwood Hse. Pr.

—What's in My Pocket, Dear Dragon? Hillert, Margaret. 2013. (ENG.). 32p. (J). pap. 10.60 *(978-1-60357-415-0(8))*; lib. bdg. 21.27 *(978-1-59953-579-1(3))* Norwood Hse. Pr.

—What's in the Pond, Dear Dragon? Hillert, Margaret. 2013. (ENG.). 32p. (J). pap. 10.60 *(978-1-60357-601-7(0))*; lib. bdg. 21.27 *(978-1-59953-607-1(2))* Norwood Hse. Pr.

—What's in the Sky, Dear Dragon? Hillert, Margaret. 2013. (ENG.). 32p. (J). lib. bdg. 21.27 *(978-1-59953-580-7(7))* Norwood Hse. Pr.

—What's in the Woods, Dear Dragon? Hillert, Margaret. 2013. (ENG.). 32p. (J). pap. 10.60 *(978-1-60357-599-7(5))*; lib. bdg. 21.27 *(978-1-59953-606-4(4))* Norwood Hse. Pr.

—Where Is Dear Dragon? Hillert, Margaret. 2012. 32p. (J). lib. bdg. 21.27 *(978-1-59953-546-3(7))* Norwood Hse. Pr.

Schimmelman, Alex. Buster & Snoopy. Zsikai-Spiker, Lisa Marie. 2012. 24p. 24.95 *(978-1-4626-7112-0(8))* America Star Bks.

Schindelman, Joseph, jt. illus. see Brunetti, Ivan.

Schindler, Roslyn. Zeon. Schindler, Roslyn. 2013. 28p. pap. 13.95 *(978-0-61493-192-8(5))* Peppertree Pr., The.

Schindler, S. D. Are We There Yet, Daddy? Walters, Virginia. 2005. 27p. (J). (gr. k-4). reprint ed. 16.00 *(978-0-7567-9708-9(X))* DIANE Publishing Co.

—Bat in the Dining Room, 1 vol. Dragonwagon, Crescent. 2005. (ENG.). 32p. (J). pap. 5.95 *(978-0-7614-5146-4(3))* Marshall Cavendish Corp.

—Ben Franklin's Big Splash: The Mostly True Story of His First Invention. Rosenstock, Barb. 2014. (ENG.). 32p. (J). (gr. 3). 16.95 *(978-1-62091-446-5(6)*, Calkins Creek) Boyds Mills Pr.

—A Big Cheese for the White House: The True Tale of a Tremendous Cheddar. Fleming, Candace. 2004. (ENG.). 32p. (J). (gr. -1-3). reprint ed. pap. 8.99 *(978-0-374-40627-1(8))* Square Fish.

—Boy, Were We Wrong about Dinosaurs! Kudlinski, Kathleen V. (ENG.). 32p. (J). (gr. 1-3). 2008. pap. 6.99 *(978-0-14-241193-3(0)*, Puffin); 2005. 15.99 *(978-0-525-46978-0(8)*, Dutton Juvenile) Penguin Publishing Group.

—Catwings. Le Guin, Ursula K. 2003. (Catwings Ser.: No. 1). (ENG.). 48p. (J). (gr. -1-3). 4.99 *(978-0-439-55189-2(7))* Scholastic, Inc.

—Catwings Return. Le Guin, Ursula K. 2003. (Catwings Ser.: No. 2). (ENG.). 56p. (J). (gr. -1-3). 4.99 *(978-0-439-55190-8(0))* Scholastic, Inc.

—The Cod's Tale. Kurlansky, Mark. 2014. (ENG.). 48p. (J). (gr. 2). 8.99 *(978-0-14-751277-2(8)*, Puffin) Penguin Publishing Group.

—Don't Know Much about the Pilgrims. Davis, Kenneth C. 2006. (Don't Know Much About Ser.). (ENG.). 48p. (J). (gr. 1-4). pap. 6.99 *(978-0-06-446228-0(5)*, Collins) HarperCollins Pubs.

—Honey in a Hive. Rockwell, Anne F. & Rockwell. 2005. (Let's-Read-And-Find-Out Science 2 Ser.). (ENG.). 40p. (J). (gr. k-4). pap. 5.99 *(978-0-06-445204-5(2)*, Collins) HarperCollins Pubs.

—Hornbooks & Inkwells. Kay, Verla. 2011. (ENG.). 32p. (J). (gr. -1-3). 16.99 *(978-0-399-23870-3(0)*, Putnam Juvenile) Penguin Publishing Group.

—How Santa Lost His Job. Krensky, Stephen. 2004. (ENG.). 32p. (J). (gr. -1-3). 7.99 *(978-0-689-87147-4(3)*, Simon & Schuster Bks. For Young Readers) Simon & Schuster Bks. For Young Readers.

—Jane on Her Own. Le Guin, Ursula K. 2003. (Catwings Ser.: No. 4). (ENG.). 48p. (J). (gr. -1-3). 4.99 *(978-0-439-55192-2(7))* Scholastic, Inc.

—Magnus Maximus, a Marvelous Measurer. Pelley, Kathleen T. 2010. (ENG.). 32p. (J). (gr. -1-3). 17.99 *(978-0-374-34725-3(5)*, Farrar, Straus & Giroux (BYR)) Farrar, Straus & Giroux.

—Monster Mess! Cuyler, Margery. 2008. (ENG.). 32p. (J). (gr. -1-1). 14.99 *(978-0-689-86405-6(1)*, McElderry, Margaret K. Bks.) McElderry, Margaret K. Bks.

Schindler, S. D., et al. Off to First Grade. Borden, Louise. 2008. (ENG.). 40p. (J). (gr. -1-3). 17.99 *(978-0-689-87395-9(6)*, McElderry, Margaret K. Bks.) McElderry, Margaret K. Bks.

Schindler, S. D. Skeleton Hiccups. Cuyler, Margery. 2005. (ENG.). 32p. (J). (gr. -1-3). reprint ed. 7.99 *(978-1-4169-0276-8(7)*, McElderry, Margaret K. Bks.) McElderry, Margaret K. Bks.

—The Snow Globe Family. O'Connor, Jane. 2008. (ENG.). 40p. (J). (gr. 1-3). pap. 6.99 *(978-0-14-241242-8(2)*, Puffin) Penguin Publishing Group.

Schindler, S. D. Spinning Spiders. Berger, Melvin. 2015. 40p. pap. 6.00 ***(978-1-61003-617-7(4))*** Center for the Collaborative Classroom.

Schindler, S. D. Spinning Spiders. Berger, Melvin. 2003. 40p. (J). (gr. k-4). (Let's-Read-and-Find-Out Science Ser.). (ENG.). 15.99 *(978-0-06-028696-5(2))*; (Let's-Read-And-Find-Out Science 2 Ser.). (ENG.). pap. 5.99 *(978-0-06-445207-6(7)*, Collins); (Let's-Read-and-Find-Out-Science Ser.: Vol. 2). lib. bdg. 16.89 *(978-0-06-028697-2(0))* HarperCollins Pubs.

—Spinning Spiders. Berger, Melvin. 2003. (Let's-Read-and-Find-Out Science Ser.). 33p. (gr. k-4). 16.00 *(978-0-7569-1449-3(3))* Perfection Learning Corp.

—The Story of Salt. Kurlansky, Mark. (ENG.). 48p. (J). (gr. -1-3). 2014. 8.99 *(978-0-14-751166-9(6)*, Puffin); 2006. 17.99 *(978-0-399-23998-4(7)*, Putnam Juvenile) Penguin Publishing Group.

—Those Amazing Ants. Demuth, Patricia Brennan. 2012. (ENG.). 32p. (J). (gr. -1-3). pap. 16.99 *(978-1-4424-5932-8(8)*, Simon & Schuster Bks. For Young Readers) Simon & Schuster Bks. For Young Readers.

—Tricking the Tallyman. Davies, Jacqueline. 2014. (ENG.). 40p. (J). (gr. k-3). 7.99 *(978-0-385-75519-1(8)*, Knopf Bks. for Young Readers) Random Hse. Children's Bks.

—The Tyrannosaurus Game, 0 vols. Kroll, Steven. 2010. (ENG.). 32p. (J). (gr. -1-3). 17.99 *(978-0-7614-5603-2(1)*, 9780761456032, Amazon Children's Publishing) Amazon Publishing.

—The Unforgettable Season: Joe Dimaggio, Ted Williams & the Record-Setting Summer of 1941. Bildner, Phil. 2011. (ENG.). 32p. (J). (gr. 2-4). 16.99 *(978-0-399-25501-4(X)*, Putnam Juvenile) Penguin Publishing Group.

—We're Going on a Ghost Hunt, 0 vols. Pearson, Susan. 2012. (ENG.). 32p. (J). (gr. -1-3). 16.99 *(978-0-7614-6307-8(0)*, 9780761463078, Amazon Children's Publishing) Amazon Publishing.

—Whittington. Armstrong, Alan W. 2007. 191p. (gr. 3-7). 17.00 *(978-0-7569-7768-9(1))* Perfection Learning Corp.

S

—Wonderful Alexander & the Catwings. Le Guin, Ursula K. 2003. (Catwings Ser.: No. 3). (ENG.). 48p. (J). (gr. -1-3). 4.99 *(978-0-439-55191-5(9))* Scholastic, Inc.

Schirack, Timm. The Night the Animals Spoke. Beres, Nancy. 2012. (J). 12.95 *(978-0-9752801-3-3(9))* Beres, Nancy.

Schirmer, Susan. A Little Dab of Paint. Frazin, Julian. 2012. 32p. (J). 22.95 *(978-0-9838846-5-1(X))* Berwick Court Publishing.

Schiti, Valerio. Donatello. Lynch, Brian & Waltz, Tom. 2015. (J). ***(978-1-61479-338-0(7))*** Spotlight.

Schlabach, Amy. Times of Trial: Poem Stories of Anabaptist Martyrs for Children. Schlabach, Amy. 2011. 46p. (J). (gr. 1-5). 14.99 *(978-1-933753-19-5(6))* Carlisle Pr.- Walnut Creek.

Schlafman, Dave. The Beast with 1000 Eyes. Dower, Laura. 2009. (Monster Squad Ser.: 3). (ENG.). 144p. (J). (gr. 2-4). pap. 5.99 *(978-0-448-44914-2(5)*, Grosset & Dunlap) Penguin Publishing Group.

—Return of Mega Mantis, 2 vols. Dower, Laura. 2009. (Monster Squad Ser.: 2). (ENG.). 144p. (J). (gr. 2-4). pap. 5.99 *(978-0-448-44913-5(7)*, Grosset & Dunlap) Penguin Publishing Group.

—They Came from Planet Q. Dower, Laura. 2010. (Monster Squad Ser.: 4). (ENG.). 144p. (J). (gr. 2-4). pap. 5.99 *(978-0-448-44915-9(3)*, Grosset & Dunlap) Penguin Publishing Group.

Schlechter, Annie, photos by. Celebrations: Easy Entertaining for Every Occasion. Rains, Valerie & Real Simple Magazine Staff. rev. ed. 2006. (ENG., 192p. (gr. 8-17). 27.95 *(978-1-933405-18-6(X)*, People Bks.) Time Inc. Bks.

Schleich, Mary B. Adventures on the Farm. Heisinger, Denise. 2010. (ENG.). 24p. pap. 12.99 *(978-1-4536-1335-1(8))* CreateSpace Independent Publishing Platform.

Schleihs, Kristin. Link & Rosie's Pets. Hubbard, Sharron/Y. 2007. (J). bds. *(978-0-9762434-3-4(1))* Link & Rosie Pr.

—Rosie's New Bike. Hubbard, Sharron/Y. 2006. (J). bds. 7.95 *(978-0-9762434-1-0(5))* Link & Rosie Pr.

Schleihs, Krostin. Link & Rosie Pick Berries. Hubbard, Sharron/Y. 2007. (J). bds. 7.95 *(978-0-9762434-2-7(3))* Link & Rosie Pr.

Schley, Cheri & Champagne, Heather. The Adventures of Hip Hop: Hip Hop & the Yellow Hat. Marshall, Denise. 2011. 36p. pap. 14.75 *(978-1-60976-342-8(4)*, Eloquent Bks.) Strategic Book Publishing & Rights Agency (SBPRA).

Schlingman, Dana. The Night Before Christmas in Ski Country. Brown, Suzanne. 2013. 32p. (J). 17.95 *(978-1-56579-658-4(6))* Westcliffe Pubs.

Schlitt, RaRa. Two Little Birds. Hayton, Althea. 2012. 38p. pap. *(978-0-9557808-1-3(0))* Wren Pubns.

Schloesser, Natalie. The Donkey's Ear. 2005. 34p. (J). 10.00 *(978-0-9743850-1-3(8))* O'Brien, Gerard.

Schloss, E. Songs to Share. Goldstein, Rose B. (ENG & HEB.). 64p. (J). (gr. -1-5). 2.95 *(978-0-8381-0720-1(6)*, 10-720) United Synagogue of America Bk. Service.

Schlossberg, Elizabeth. On the Way to Kindergarten. Kroll, Virginia. 2008. (ENG.). 32p. (J). (gr. -1-k). pap. 6.99 *(978-0-14-241144-5(2)*, Puffin) Penguin Publishing Group.

Schluenderfritz, Ted. Darby O'Gill & the Crocks of Gold: And Other Irish Tales. Kavanagh, Herminie Templeton. 2003. ix, 155p. (J). pap. 14.95 *(978-1-928832-85-0(7))* Sophia Institute Pr.

Schluenderfritz, Theodore. Alvin Fernald, Foreign Trader. Hicks, Clifford B. 2007. (Alvin Fernald Mysteries Ser.). 181p. (J). (gr. 4). per. 11.95 *(978-1-883937-74-4(4))* Bethlehem Bks.

—Alvin Fernald, Mayor for a Day. Hicks, Clifford B. 2007. (Secret Panel Mysteries Ser.). 142p. (J). (gr. 8-12). pap. 11.95 *(978-1-883937-98-0(1))* Bethlehem Bks.

Schlueter, Rachel. The Tree That Loved the Eagle. Pappas, Charles. 2013. 56p. (J). 19.95 *(978-1-58790-175-1(7))* Regent Pr.

Schlund, Mackenzie. Evelyn's Special Eggs. Mcinnes, Lisa. Duersch, Gretchen, ed. 2011. 32p. pap. *(978-1-77067-394-6(6))* FriesenPress.

Schmid, Paul. My Dog Is the Best. Thompson, Laurie Ann. 2015. (ENG.). 40p. (J). (gr. -1-1). 17.99 *(978-0-374-30051-7(8)*, Farrar, Straus & Giroux (BYR)) Farrar, Straus & Giroux.

—Peanut & Fifi Have a Ball. de Seve, Randall. 2013. (ENG.). 40p. (J). (gr. -1-k). 15.99 *(978-0-8037-3578-1(2)*, Dial) Penguin Publishing Group.

—The Wonder Book. Rosenthal, Amy Krouse. 2010. (ENG.). 80p. (J). (gr. -1-3). 17.99 *(978-0-06-142974-3(0))* HarperCollins Pubs.

Schmid, Paul. Hugs from Pearl. Schmid, Paul. 2011. (ENG.). 40p. (J). (gr. -1-2). 14.99 *(978-0-06-180434-2(7))* HarperCollins Pubs.

—Oliver & His Alligator. Schmid, Paul. 2013. (ENG.). 40p. (J). (gr. -1-k). 15.99 *(978-1-4231-7437-0(2))* Disney Pr.

—Oliver & His Egg. Schmid, Paul. 2014. (ENG.). 40p. (J). (gr. -1-k). 15.99 *(978-1-4231-7573-5(5))* Hyperion Bks. for Children.

—Perfectly Percy. Schmid, Paul. 2013. (ENG.). 40p. (J). (gr. -1-3). 17.99 *(978-0-06-180436-6(3))* HarperCollins Pubs.

—A Pet for Petunia. Schmid, Paul. 2011. (ENG.). 40p. (J). (gr. -1-2). 12.99 *(978-0-06-196331-5(3))* HarperCollins Pubs.

—Petunia Goes Wild. Schmid, Paul. 2012. (ENG.). 40p. (J). (gr. -1-2). 12.99 *(978-0-06-196334-6(8))* HarperCollins Pubs.

Schmid, Paul & Cordell, Matthew. Forgive Me, I Meant to Do It: False Apology Poems. Levine, Gail Carson. 2012. 80p. (J). (gr. 3-7). (ENG.). 16.99 *(978-0-06-178725-6(6))*; lib. bdg. 16.89 *(978-0-06-178726-3(4))* HarperCollins Pubs.

Schmidt, Caleb & Schmidt, Carter. The Wonderful Adventures of Bradley the Bat. Paulding, Steve. 2013. 70p. pap. 18.95 *(978-0-615-74591-6(1))* Slow on the Draw Productions.

Schmidt, Carter, jt. illus. see Schmidt, Caleb.

Schmidt, Dennis. Our Federal Constitution, Our Michigan Constitution. Schmidt, Dennis, ed. Schmidt, Alex J. & Schmidt, Steven L. rev. ed. 2009. 72p. 8.00 *(978-1-892291-01-1(0))* AJS Pubns., Inc.

—Our Federal Constitution, Our Missouri Constitution. Schmidt, Dennis, ed. Schmidt, Alex & Schmidt, Steve. rev. ed. 2010. 72p. pap. 8.00 *(978-1-892291-00-4(2))* AJS Pubns., Inc.

—Our Federal Constitution, Our New Jersey Constitution. Schmidt, Dennis, ed. Schmidt, Alex & Schmidt, Steve. 2006. 72p. (YA). stu. ed. 8.00 *(978-1-892291-02-8(9))* AJS Pubns., Inc.

—Our Federal Constitution, Our Texas Constitution. Schmidt, Dennis, ed. Schmidt, Alex & Schmidt, Steve. rev. ed. 2008. 72p. pap. 8.00 *(978-1-892291-06-6(1))* AJS Pubns., Inc.

—Our Federal Constitution, Our Wisconsin Constitution. Schmidt, Dennis, ed. Schmidt, Alex & Schmidt, Steve. rev. ed. 2010. (ENG.). 72p. (YA). pap. 8.00 *(978-1-892291-04-2(5))* AJS Pubns., Inc.

Schmidt, Erica Lyn. Dinosaur Discovery: Everything You Need to Be a Paleontologist. McGowan, Chris. 2011. (ENG.). 48p. (J). (gr. 2-6). 17.99 *(978-1-4169-4764-6(7)*, Simon & Schuster Bks. For Young Readers) Simon & Schuster Bks. For Young Readers.

Schmidt, Jacqueline. Patchwork Helps a Friend. Greiner, Gail. 2013. (ENG.). 40p. (J). (gr. -1-2). 17.95 *(978-1-57687-642-8(X)*, powerHouse Bks.) powerHouse Cultural Entertainment, Inc.

Schmidt, Karenlee. The Jungle Baseball Game. Paxton, Tom. 2005. 30p. (J). (gr. -1-2). reprint ed. 16.00 *(978-0-7567-8932-9(X))* DIANE Publishing Co.

Schmidt, Katen. Max & Jax Plant a Garden. Nolen, Jerdine. Date not set. (J). 14.00 *(978-0-15-201672-2(4)*, Silver Whistle) Harcourt Children's Bks. CAN. Dist: Harcourt Trade Pubs.

Schmidt, Nathan. Zoey & the Zones: Coloring Book, 2. 2003. 0.99 *(978-0-9718120-7-9(1))* HealthSprings, LLC.

Schmidt, Ron, photos by. Dog-Gone School. Schmidt, Amy. 2013. (ENG., 40p. (J). (gr. -1-2). 16.99 *(978-0-375-86974-7(3)*, Random Hse. Bks. for Young Readers) Random Hse. Children's Bks.

Schmitt, Louis J. Goodnight Nola: An Endearing Bedtime Book for All Ages. Landry, Cornell P. 2009. (ENG.). 36p. (J). 16.95 *(978-0-9818126-4-9(3)*, Ampersand) Ampersand, Inc.

Schmitt, Nannette Toups & Endres, Sharlene Duggan. Remember Last Island. Schmitt, Nannette Toups. Gorman, Carolyn Portier, ed. 2003. 206p. (YA). pap. 19.95 *(978-0-9740901-0-8(7)*, 11-May) Orage Publishing.

Schmitz, Cecile & Mouchet, Klutt. Father Damien Hawaii's Saint. 2009. 32p. (J). (gr. 4). pap. 14.95 *(978-1-57306-307-4(X))* Bess Pr., Inc.

Schmitz, Tamara. Back to School, Mallory. Friedman, Laurie. (Mallory Ser.: 2). (ENG.). 176p. (J). (gr. 2-5). 2005. per. 5.95 *(978-1-57505-865-8(0))*; 2004. 15.95 *(978-1-57505-658-6(5))* Lerner Publishing Group.

—A Clases Otra Vez, Mallory. Friedman, Laurie. Anaya, Josefina, tr. from ENG. 2008. (Mallory en Español (Mallory in Spanish) Ser.).Tr. of Back to School, Mallory. (SPA & ENG.). 176p. (J). (gr. 2-5). pap. 5.95 *(978-0-7613-3904-5(3)*, Ediciones Lerner) Lerner Publishing Group.

—Happy Birthday, Mallory! Friedman, Laurie. 2006. (Mallory Ser.: 4). (ENG.). 160p. (J). (gr. 2-5). per. 5.95 *(978-0-8225-6502-4(1)*, First Avenue Editions) Lerner Publishing Group.

—Mallory on the Move. Friedman, Laurie. 2005. (Mallory Ser.: 1). (ENG.). 160p. (J). (gr. 2-5). per. 5.95 *(978-1-57505-831-3(6))* Lerner Publishing Group.

—Mallory vs. Max. Friedman, Laurie. (Mallory Ser.: 3). (ENG.). 160p. (J). (gr. 2-5). 2006. per. 5.95 *(978-1-57505-863-4(4)*, First Avenue Editions); 2005. 15.95 *(978-1-57505-795-8(6))* Lerner Publishing Group.

—Playtime Devotions: Sharing Bible Moments with Your Baby or Toddler. Tangvald, Christine Harder. 2006. (Heritage Builders Ser.). 36p. (J). 15.99 *(978-0-7847-1361-7(6)*, 04024) Standard Publishing.

Schmitz, Tamara. Standing on My Own Two Feet: A Child's Affirmation of Love in the Midst of Divorce. Schmitz, Tamara. 2008. (ENG.). 32p. (J). (gr. -1-2). 12.99 *(978-0-8431-3221-2(3)*, Price Stern Sloan) Penguin Publishing Group.

Schmitz, Tamara. Mallory on the Move. Schmitz, Tamara, tr. Friedman, Laurie. 2004. (Mallory Ser.: 1). (ENG.). 160p. (J). (gr. 2-5). 15.95 *(978-1-57505-538-1(4))* Lerner Publishing Group.

Schmolze, Ian. The Adventure of Paperman - Journey into Night. Larner, Eric. 2013. 194p. pap. 16.99 *(978-1-883651-68-8(9))* Winters Publishing.

Schneid, Frances E. Janey Junkfood's Fresh Adventure! Making Good Eating Great Fun! Storper, Barbara. 2008. 32p. (J). (gr. 3-7). 15.95 *(978-0-9642858-5-9(1))* FoodPlay Productions.

Schneider, Barbara Hoss. Remembering Pets: A Book for Children Who Have Lost a Special Friend. Berman, Gina Dalpra. 2010. (ENG.). 30p. (gr. -1-3). 14.95 *(978-1-885003-68-3(4))* Reed, Robert D. Pubs.

Schneider, Cheryl. Bunnaby Bunny (L) Toddler Reader. Schneider, Cheryl. Olson, Carole. deluxe ed. 2006. 20p. (J). bds. 10.00 *(978-0-9712816-5-3(3))* Third Week Bks.

Schneider, Christine. My Food, Your Food. Bullard, Lisa. 2015. (Cloverleaf Books (tm) — Alike & Different Ser.). (ENG.). 24p. (gr. k-2). (J). lib. bdg. 23.99 *(978-1-4677-4903-9(6))*; pap. 6.99 ***(978-1-4677-6031-7(5))*** Lerner Publishing Group. (Millbrook Pr.).

—Under Construction: A Moving Track Book. Perez, Jessica. 2005. (ENG.). 12p. (J). 12.95 *(978-1-58117-272-0(9)*, Intervisual/Piggy Toes) Bendon, Inc.

—Who Stole the Cookie from the Cookie Jar? Wang, Margaret. 2006. (ENG.). (J). 22p. bds. 10.95 *(978-1-58117-383-3(0))*; 12p. (gr. -1-3). 4.95 *(978-1-58117-429-8(2))* Bendon, Inc. (Intervisual/Piggy Toes).

—The World Is a Rainbow. Scelsa, Greg. Faulkner, Stacey, ed. 2006. (J). pap. 2.99 *(978-1-59198-319-4(3))* Creative Teaching Pr., Inc.

—Writing about Books. Williams, Rozanne Lanczak. 2006. (Learn to Write Ser.). 8p. (J). (gr. k-2). pap. 3.49 *(978-1-59198-289-0(8)*, 6183) Creative Teaching Pr., Inc.

—Writing about Books. Williams, Rozanne Lanczak. Maio, Barbara & Faulkner, Stacey, eds. 2006. (J). per. 6.99 *(978-1-59198-340-8(1))* Creative Teaching Pr., Inc.

Schneider, Christine M. Lily Learns about Wants & Needs. Bullard, Lisa. 2013. (Cloverleaf Books — Money Basics Ser.). (ENG.). 24p. (gr. k-2). pap. 6.95 *(978-1-4677-1509-6(3))*; lib. bdg. 23.93 *(978-1-4677-0764-0(3))* Lerner Publishing Group. (Millbrook Pr.).

—My Learn to Read Bible: Stories in Words & Pictures, 1 vol. Harrast, Tracy L. 2013. (ENG.). 240p. (J). 19.99 *(978-0-310-72740-8(5))* Zonderkidz.

—Shanti Saves Her Money. Bullard, Lisa. 2013. (Cloverleaf Books — Money Basics Ser.). (ENG.). 24p. (gr. k-2). pap. 6.95 *(978-1-4677-1513-3(1))*; lib. bdg. 23.93 *(978-1-4677-0765-7(1))* Lerner Publishing Group. (Millbrook Pr.).

Schneider, Christine M. What Is It Made Of? Noticing Types of Materials. Rustad, Martha E. H. 2015. (ENG.). 24p. (J). (gr. k-2). 25.32 ***(978-1-4677-8561-7(X)***, Millbrook Pr.) Lerner Publishing Group.

—Why Do Puddles Disappear? Noticing Forms of Water. Rustad, Martha E. H. 2015. (ENG.). 24p. (gr. k-2). 25.32 ***(978-1-4677-8562-4(8)***, Millbrook Pr.) Lerner Publishing Group.

Schneider, Claude. Vegetable Dreams/Huerto Sonado. Jeffers, Dawn. de la Vega, Eida, tr. 2006. (SPA & ENG.). 32p. (J). (gr. -1-3). 16.95 *(978-0-9741992-9-0(X)*, 626999); per. 7.95 *(978-0-9770906-0-0(4)*, 626999) Continental Sales, Inc. (Raven Tree Pr.,Csi).

Schneider, Hank, photos by. Look What You Can Make with Boxes: Creative Crafts from Everyday Objects. Siomades, Lorianne, ed. 2013. (Look What You Can Make Ser.). (ENG., 48p. (J). (gr. k-7). pap. 6.95 *(978-1-56397-704-6(4))* Boyds Mills Pr.

—Look What You Can Make with Paper Bags: Creative Crafts from Everyday Objects. Burke, Judy, ed. 2013. (Look What You Can Make Ser.). (ENG., 48p. (J). (gr. -1-7). pap. 6.95 *(978-1-56397-717-6(6))* Boyds Mills Pr.

—Look What You Can Make with Paper Plates: Creative Crafts from Everyday Objects. Highlights for Children Editorial Staff & Boyds Mills Press Staff. Richmond, Margie Hayes, ed. 2013. (Look What You Can Make Ser.). (ENG., 48p. (J). (gr. k-7). pap., stu. ed. 6.95 *(978-1-56397-643-8(9))* Boyds Mills Pr.

—Look What You Can Make with Plastic Bottles & Tubs: Over 80 Pictured Crafts & Dozens of Other Ideas. Ross, Kathy. 2003. (ENG., 48p. (YA). (gr. -1-7). pap. 5.95 *(978-1-56397-567-7(X))* Boyds Mills Pr.

—Look What You Can Make with Tubes: Creative Crafts from Everyday Objects. Boyds Mills Press Staff. Richmond, Margie Hayes, ed. 2013. (Look What You Can Make Ser.). (ENG., 48p. (J). (gr. k-9). pap., stu. ed. 6.95 *(978-1-56397-677-3(3))* Boyds Mills Pr.

Schneider, Hank & Filipski, J. W., photos by. Look What You Can Make with Craft Sticks. Halls, Kelly Milner. Halls, Kelly Milner, ed. 2013. (Look What You Can Make Ser.). (ENG., 48p. (J). (gr. k-7). pap. 6.95 *(978-1-56397-997-2(7))* Boyds Mills Pr.

—Look What You Can Make with Egg Cartons. Boyds Mills Press Staff. Ochester, Betsy, ed. 2013. (Look What You Can Make Ser.). (ENG., 48p. (J). (gr. k-7). pap. 6.95 *(978-1-56397-906-4(3))* Boyds Mills Pr.

—Look What You Can Make with Plastic Containers. Highlights for Children Editorial Staff. 2013. (Look What You Can Make Ser.). (ENG., 48p. (J). (gr. k). pap. 6.95 *(978-1-62091-533-2(2))* Boyds Mills Pr.

—Look What You Can Make with Recycled Paper. Ross, Kathy. 2013. (Look What You Can Make Ser.). (ENG., 48p. (J). (gr. k). pap. 6.95 *(978-1-62091-534-9(0))* Boyds Mills Pr.

Schneider, Josh. Tales for Very Picky Eaters. Schneider, Josh. 2011. (ENG.). 48p. (J). (gr. 1-4). 15.99 *(978-0-547-14956-1(5))* Houghton Mifflin Harcourt Publishing Co.

Schneider, Katy. I Didn't Do It. MacLachlan, Patricia & Charest, Emily MacLachlan. 2010. (ENG.). 32p. (J). (gr. -1-3). 16.99 *(978-0-06-135833-9(3)*, Tegen, Katherine Bks) HarperCollins Pubs.

—Once I Ate a Pie. MacLachlan, Patricia & Charest, Emily MacLachlan. 40p. (J). (gr. -1-3). 2010. (ENG.). pap. 6.99 *(978-0-06-073533-3(3))*; 2006. 18.89 *(978-0-06-073532-6(5))*; 2006. (ENG.). 17.99 *(978-0-06-073531-9(7))* HarperCollins Pubs.

—Painting the Wind. MacLachlan, Patricia & MacLachlan, Emily. 2006. (Joanna Cotler Bks.). (ENG.). 40p. (J). (gr. -1-3). reprint ed. pap. 7.99 *(978-0-06-443825-4(2))* HarperCollins Pubs.

Schneider, Rex. Tree House in a Storm. Burk, Rachelle. 2009. 42p. (J). pap. 11.95 *(978-0-88045-169-7(6))*; 16.95 *(978-0-916144-23-4(2))* Stemmer Hse. Pubs.

Schneider, Rex. Alice's Adventures in Wonderland: With a Discussion of Imagination. Schneider, Rex, tr. Carroll, Lewis. 2003. (J). *(978-1-59203-046-0(7))* Learning Challenge, Inc.

Schneider, Robin. Balloons for Grandpa, 1 vol. Smith-Eubanks, Jennifer. 2010. 20p. pap. 24.95 *(978-1-4489-5282-3(4))* PublishAmerica, Inc.

—Zoe the Zebra. Weaver, Amy Garrett. 2009. 33p. pap. 24.95 *(978-1-60749-552-9(X))* PublishAmerica, Inc.

schneider, Sandra. Secrets of the Symbols: Advanced Phonics Book including 54 skill Cards. schneider, Sandra. Hoppe, Gail, ed. 2008. 76p. (J). 18.00 *(978-0-9761987-5-8(4))* Magic Penny Reading.

Schneller, Lisa. The Five Keys to Wellness. Mather, Kelly. 2006. 46p. *(978-0-9787179-8-8(8))* Harmony Healing Hse.

Schoen-Smith, Sieglinde. Mother Earth & Her Children: A Quilted Fairy Tale. von Olfers, Sibylle. Zipes, Jack, tr. from GER. 2007. (ENG.). 32p. (J). (gr. -1-2). 17.95 *(978-1-933308-18-0(4))* Breckling Pr.

Schoenberg-Lam, Dahlia. My Synagogue Scrapbook. Person, Hara & Lewy, Faye Tillis. 2006. pap. 11.95 *(978-0-8074-0990-9(1)*, 164065) URJ Pr.

Schoenberg, Richard, photos by. Boot Camp - A Marine Legacy. Schoenberg, Richard. 2008. 100p. (YA). 129.95 *(978-0-9748208-3-5(0))* Schoenberg & Assocs.

Schoene, Kerstin. Monsters Aren't Real. Schoene, Kerstin. ed. 2012. (Picture Book Ser.). (ENG.). 44p. (J). 9.99 *(978-1-61067-073-9(6))* Kane Miller.

Schoene, Kerstin & Gunetsreiner, Nina. Milo Is Not a Dog Today. Schoene, Kerstin & Gunetsreiner, Nina. 2014. (ENG.). 32p. (J). (gr. -1-2). 16.99 *(978-0-8075-4793-9(X))* Whitman, Albert & Co.

Schoenfeld, Wayne, photos by. American Photo Mission to India: Portrait of a Volunteer Surgical Team in Action. Weiner, Rex. 2006. 125p. 34.95 *(978-0-9727696-6-2(8)*, SWC Editions) Wayne, Steven Co.

Schoenherr, Ian. The Apothecary. Meloy, Maile. 2011. (Apothecary Ser.: 1). (ENG.). 368p. (J). (gr. 5-18). 16.99 *(978-0-399-25627-1(X)*, Putnam Juvenile) Penguin Publishing Group.

—The Apprentices. Meloy, Maile. (Apothecary Ser.: 2). (ENG.). (J). (gr. 5). 2014. 432p. pap. 8.99 *(978-0-14-242598-5(2)*, Puffin); 2013. 448p. 16.99 *(978-0-399-16245-9(3)*, Putnam Juvenile) Penguin Publishing Group.

—Bitterblue. Cashore, Kristin. (ENG.). (YA). (gr. 9). 2013. 608p. pap. 10.99 *(978-0-14-242601-2(6)*, Puffin); 2012. 576p. 19.99 *(978-0-8037-3473-9(5)*, Dial) Penguin Publishing Group.

—Castaways of the Flying Dutchman. Jacques, Brian. 2003. (ENG.). 336p. (J). (gr. 3-7). pap. 9.99 *(978-0-14-250118-4(2)*, Puffin) Penguin Publishing Group.

—Little Raccoon's Big Question. Schlein, Miriam. 2004. (ENG.). 32p. (J). (gr. -1-3). 16.99 *(978-0-06-052116-5(3)*, Greenwillow Bks.) HarperCollins Pubs.

—Sunrise, Sunset. Harnick, Sheldon. 2005. 32p. (J). (gr. -1-1). lib. bdg. 16.89 *(978-0-06-051527-0(9))* HarperCollins Pubs.

—The Twistrose Key. Almhjell, Tone. (ENG.). (J). (gr. 5). 2014. 384p. pap. 8.99 *(978-0-14-242345-5(9)*, Puffin); 2013. 368p. 16.99 *(978-0-8037-3895-9(1)*, Dial) Penguin Publishing Group.

Schoenherr, Ian. Cat & Mouse. Schoenherr, Ian. 2008. 40p. (J). (gr. -1). lib. bdg. 17.89 *(978-0-06-136314-6(6)*, Greenwillow Bks.) HarperCollins Pubs.

—Don't Spill the Beans! Schoenherr, Ian. 2010. 32p. (J). (gr. -1 — 1). (ENG.). 16.99 *(978-0-06-172457-2(2))*; lib. bdg. 17.89 *(978-0-06-172458-9(0))* HarperCollins Pubs. (Greenwillow Bks.).

—Pip & Squeak. Schoenherr, Ian. 32p. (J). (gr. -1-k). 2007. 18.89 *(978-0-06-087254-0(3))*; 2006. (ENG.). 16.99 *(978-0-06-087253-3(5)*, Greenwillow Bks.) HarperCollins Pubs.

—Read It, Don't Eat It! Schoenherr, Ian. 2009. 32p. (J). (gr. -1 — 1). (ENG.). 17.99 *(978-0-06-172455-8(6))*; lib. bdg. 18.89 *(978-0-06-178034-9(0))* HarperCollins Pubs. (Greenwillow Bks.).

Schoenherr, Ian, jt. illus. see Elliot, David.

Schoenherr, John. Gentle Ben. Morey, Walt. l.t. ed. 2004. (LRS Large Print Cornerstone Ser.). 264p. (J). lib. bdg. 33.95 *(978-1-58118-119-7(1))* LRS.

—Gentle Ben. Morey, Walt. 2006. (ENG.). 192p. (J). (gr. 3-7). 6.99 *(978-0-14-240551-2(5)*, Puffin) Penguin Publishing Group.

—Julie of the Wolves. George, Jean Craighead. 2003. (Julie of the Wolves Ser.). (ENG.). 208p. (J). (gr. 8-18). pap. 8.99 *(978-0-06-054095-1(8)*, HarperTeen) HarperCollins Pubs.

—Pigs in the Mud in the Middle of the Rud. Plourde, Lynn. ed. 2006. (ENG.). 32p. (J). (gr. -1-17). 15.95 *(978-0-89272-719-3(5))* Down East Bks.

Schoening, Dan. Attack of the Cheetah, 1 vol. Mason, Jane B. 2013. (Wonder Woman Ser.). (ENG.). 56p. (gr. 2-3). pap. 4.95 *(978-1-4342-2254-1(3)*, DC Super Heroes) Stone Arch Bks.

—Battle of the Blue Lanterns, 1 vol. Acampora, Michael V. 2011. (Green Lantern Ser.). (ENG.). 56p. (gr. 2-3). pap. 4.95 *(978-1-4342-3085-0(6))*; lib. bdg. 25.32 *(978-1-4342-2608-2(5))* Stone Arch Bks. (DC Super Heroes).

—Beware Our Power! Sonneborn, Scott. 2011. (J). lib. bdg. (ENG.). 56p. (gr. 2-3). 25.32 *(978-1-4342-2607-5(7)*, DC Super Heroes); (ENG.). 56p. (gr. 2-3). pap. 4.95 *(978-1-4342-3086-7(4)*, DC Super Heroes) Stone Arch Bks.

—Catwoman's Classroom of Claws. Sonneborn, Scott. (Batman Ser.). (ENG.). 56p. (gr. 2-3). 2013. pap. 4.95 *(978-1-4342-1732-5(9))*; 2009. lib. bdg. 25.32 *(978-1-4342-1565-9(2))* Stone Arch Bks. (DC Super Heroes).

—Clock King's Time Bomb, 1 vol. Tulien, Sean et al. 2011. (Flash Ser.). (ENG.). 56p. (gr. 2-3). pap. 4.95 *(978-1-4342-3412-4(6))*; lib. bdg. 25.32 *(978-1-4342-2626-6(3))* Stone Arch Bks. (DC Super Heroes).

—Creature of Chaos. Stephens, Sarah Hines. (Wonder Woman Ser.). (ENG.). 56p. (gr. 2-3). 2013. pap. 4.95 *(978-1-4342-2256-5(X))*; 2010. lib. bdg. 25.32 *(978-1-4342-1885-8(6))* Stone Arch Bks. (DC Super Heroes).

—Crime Wave! (DC Super Friends) Wrecks, Billy. 2012. (Step into Reading Ser.). (ENG.). 32p. (J). (gr. -1-1). pap. 3.99 *(978-0-375-86898-6(4))*; lib. bdg. 12.99 *(978-0-375-96898-3(9))* Random Hse. Children's Bks. (Random Hse. Bks. for Young Readers).

—Deep Space Hijack. Sonneborn, Scott. (Superman Ser.). (ENG.). 56p. (gr. 2-3). 2013. pap. 4.95 *(978-1-4342-2257-2(8))*; 2010. lib. bdg. 25.32 *(978-1-4342-1880-3(5))* Stone Arch Bks. (DC Super Heroes).

Schoening, Dan, et al. Deepwater Disaster. Bright, J. E. 2011. (DC Super Heroes Ser.). (ENG.). 56p. (gr. 2-3). 25.32 *(978-1-4342-3317-2(0),* DC Super Heroes) Stone Arch Bks.

Schoening, Dan. Dr. Psycho's Circus of Crime, 1 vol. Kupperberg, Paul. 2014. (Wonder Woman Ser.). (ENG.). 56p. (gr. 2-3). pap. 4.95 *(978-1-4342-2761-4(8),* DC Super Heroes) Stone Arch Bks.

—Escape from the Orange Lanterns, 1 vol. Acampora, Michael Vincent. 2011. (Green Lantern Ser.). (ENG.). 56p. (gr. 2-3). lib. bdg. 25.32 *(978-1-4342-2622-8(0),* DC Super Heroes) Stone Arch Bks.

—Escape from the Orange Lanterns, 1 vol. Acampora, Michael V. 2011. (Green Lantern Ser.). (ENG.). 56p. (gr. 2-3). pap. 4.95 *(978-1-4342-3408-7(8),* DC Super Heroes) Stone Arch Bks.

—Fear the Shark, 1 vol. Sutton, Laurie S. 2011. (Green Lantern Ser.). (ENG.). 56p. (gr. 2-3). pap. 4.95 *(978-1-4342-3406-3(1));* lib. bdg. 25.32 *(978-1-4342-2620-4(4))* Stone Arch Bks. (DC Super Heroes).

—Flower Power! (DC Super Friends) Carbone, Courtney. 2014. (Little Golden Book Ser.). (ENG.). 24p. (J). (-k). 3.99 *(978-0-385-37396-8(1),* Golden Bks.) Random Hse. Children's Bks.

—The Fruit of All Evil. Crawford, Philip & Crawford, Philip Charles. 2014. (Wonder Woman Ser.). (ENG.). 56p. (gr. 2-3). pap. 4.95 *(978-1-4342-2766-9(9),* DC Super Heroes) Stone Arch Bks.

—Guardian of Earth, 1 vol. Dahl, Michael. 2011. (Green Lantern Ser.). (ENG.). 56p. (gr. 2-3). pap. 4.95 *(978-1-4342-3081-2(3));* lib. bdg. 25.32 *(978-1-4342-2611-2(5))* Stone Arch Bks. (DC Super Heroes).

—Harley Quinn's Shocking Surprise, 1 vol. Hoena, Blake A. (Batman Ser.). (ENG.). 56p. (gr. 2-3). 2013. pap. 4.95 *(978-1-4342-1729-5(9));* 2009. lib. bdg. 25.32 *(978-1-4342-1562-8(8))* Stone Arch Bks. (DC Super Heroes).

—High-Tech Terror, 1 vol. Steele, Michael A. 2011. (Green Lantern Ser.). (ENG.). 56p. (gr. 2-3). pap. 4.95 *(978-1-4342-3084-3(8));* lib. bdg. 25.32 *(978-1-4342-2609-9(3))* Stone Arch Bks. (DC Super Heroes).

—The Last Super Hero, 1 vol. Dahl, Michael. 2011. (Green Lantern Ser.). (ENG.). 56p. (gr. 2-3). pap. 4.95 *(978-1-4342-3082-9(1));* lib. bdg. 25.32 *(978-1-4342-2612-9(3))* Stone Arch Bks. (DC Super Heroes).

—The Light King Strikes!, 1 vol. Sutton, Laurie S. 2011. (Green Lantern Ser.). (ENG.). 56p. (gr. 2-3). pap. 4.95 *(978-1-4342-3083-6(X));* lib. bdg. 25.32 *(978-1-4342-2610-5(7))* Stone Arch Bks. (DC Super Heroes).

—Livewire! Hoena, B. A. 2010. (J). pap. 34.99 *(978-1-4342-1766-0(3))* Stone Arch Bks.

—Livewire!, 1 vol. Hoena, Blake A. & Hoena, B. A. 2013. (Superman Ser.). (ENG.). 56p. (gr. 2-3). pap. 4.95 *(978-1-4342-1733-2(7),* DC Super Heroes) Stone Arch Bks.

—Livewire!, 1 vol. Hoena, Blake A. 2009. (Superman Ser.). (ENG.). 56p. (gr. 2-3). lib. bdg. 25.32 *(978-1-4342-1566-6(0),* DC Super Heroes) Stone Arch Bks.

—The Man Behind the Mask, 1 vol. Dahl, Michael. (Batman Ser.). (ENG.). 56p. (gr. 2-3). 2013. pap. 4.95 *(978-1-4342-1730-1(2));* 2009. 25.32 *(978-1-4342-1563-5(6))* Stone Arch Bks. (DC Super Heroes).

—Monster Magic, 1 vol. Simonson, Louise. (Wonder Woman Ser.). (ENG.). 56p. (gr. 2-3). 2013. pap. 4.95 *(978-1-4342-2260-2(8));* 2010. lib. bdg. 25.32 *(978-1-4342-1884-1(8))* Stone Arch Bks. (DC Super Heroes).

—The Museum Monsters. Dahl, Michael. (Superman Ser.). (ENG.). 56p. (gr. 2-3). 2013. pap. 4.95 *(978-1-4342-1372-3(2));* 2009. lib. bdg. 25.32 *(978-1-4342-1157-6(6))* Stone Arch Bks. (DC Super Heroes).

—Prisoner of the Ring, 1 vol. Sonneborn, Scott. 2011. (Green Lantern Ser.). (ENG.). 56p. (gr. 2-3). pap. 4.95 *(978-1-4342-3410-0(X));* lib. bdg. 25.32 *(978-1-4342-2624-2(7))* Stone Arch Bks. (DC Super Heroes).

—Red Lanterns' Revenge, 1 vol. Acampora, Michael Vincent. 2011. (Green Lantern Ser.). (ENG.). 56p. (gr. 2-3). lib. bdg. 25.32 *(978-1-4342-2623-5(9),* DC Super Heroes) Stone Arch Bks.

—Red Lanterns' Revenge, 1 vol. Acampora, Michael V. 2011. (Green Lantern Ser.). (ENG.). 56p. (gr. 2-3). pap. 4.95 *(978-1-4342-3409-4(6),* DC Super Heroes) Stone Arch Bks.

—Rumble in the Rainforest, 1 vol. Stephens, Sarah Hines & Hines-Stephens, Sarah. (Wonder Woman Ser.). (ENG.). 56p. (gr. 2-3). 2014. pap. 4.95 *(978-1-4342-2765-2(0));* 2010. 25.32 *(978-1-4342-1992-3(5))* Stone Arch Bks. (DC Super Heroes).

—Savage Sands, 1 vol. Bright, J. E. 2011. (Green Lantern Ser.). (ENG.). 56p. (gr. 2-3). pap. 4.95 *(978-1-4342-3405-6(3));* lib. bdg. 25.32 *(978-1-4342-2619-8(0))* Stone Arch Bks. (DC Super Heroes).

—Skyscraper Showdown. Wrecks, Billy. 2012. (3-D Pictureback Ser.). (ENG.). 16p. (J). (gr. -1-2). pap. 4.99 *(978-0-375-87299-0(X),* Random Hse. Bks. for Young Readers) Random Hse. Children's Bks.

—Sword of the Dragon, 1 vol. Sutton, Laurie S. (Wonder Woman Ser.). (ENG.). 56p. (gr. 2-3). 2014. pap. 4.95 *(978-1-4342-2760-7(X));* 2010. 25.32 *(978-1-4342-1979-4(8))* Stone Arch Bks. (DC Super Heroes).

—Trial of the Amazons, 1 vol. Dahl, Michael. 2010. (Wonder Woman Ser.). (ENG.). 56p. (gr. 2-3). lib. bdg. 25.32 *(978-1-4342-1883-4(X),* DC Super Heroes) Stone Arch Bks.

—Under the Red Sun, 1 vol. Hoena, Blake A. (Superman Ser.). (ENG.). 56p. (gr. 2-3). 2013. pap. 4.95 *(978-1-4342-1375-4(7));* 2009. lib. bdg. 25.32 *(978-1-4342-1159-0(2))* Stone Arch Bks. (DC Super Heroes).

—Web of Doom, 1 vol. Steele, Michael Anthony. 2011. (Green Lantern Ser.). (ENG.). 56p. (gr. 2-3). pap. 4.95 *(978-1-4342-3407-0(X),* DC Super Heroes) Stone Arch Bks.

—Web of Doom, 1 vol. Steele, Michael A. 2011. (Green Lantern Ser.). (ENG.). 56p. (gr. 2-3). lib. bdg. 25.32 *(978-1-4342-2621-1(2),* DC Super Heroes) Stone Arch Bks.

Schoening, Dan & Beavers, Ethen. Batman! (DC Super Friends) Wrecks, Billy. 2012. (Little Golden Book Ser.). (ENG.). 24p. (J). (gr. k-k). 3.99 *(978-0-307-93103-0(X),* Golden Bks.) Random Hse. Children's Bks.

Schofield, Angela. Why Is There Money? A Facinating Journey Through the Evolution of Money. Nourigat, Paul. 2011. (ENG.). 36p. (J). pap. 11.29 *(978-1-936872-00-8(5))* FarBeyond Publishing LLC.

Schofield, Christina Diane. Mrs. Rosey Posey & the Fine China Plate, 1 vol. Gunn, Robin Jones. 2008. (I Can Read! Ser.). (ENG.). 32p. (J). (gr. -1-3). pap. 3.99 *(978-0-310-71578-8(4))* Zondervan.

Schofield-Farmer, Twila. A Deaf Boy Meets Jesus. Entinger, Chad. 2011. 42p. (J). 10.00 *(978-1-59799-082-0(5))* Deaf Missions.

Scholastic, Inc. Staff. Animals on the Farm. Hernandez, Christopher. 2012. (ENG.). 10p. (J). (gr. -1-k). bds. 9.99 *(978-0-545-38250-2(5),* Cartwheel Bks.) Scholastic, Inc.

—Emmet's Awesome Day. Holmes, Anna. 2014. (LEGO: the LEGO Movie Ser.). (ENG.). 32p. (J). (gr. 1-3). pap. 3.99 *(978-0-545-79539-5(7))* Scholastic, Inc.

—Emmet's Guide to Being Awesome. Landers, Ace. 2014. (LEGO: the LEGO Movie Ser.). (ENG.). 128p. (J). (gr. 2-5). 9.99 *(978-0-545-79532-6(X))* Scholastic, Inc.

—Face Off: Makuro's Secret Guidebook. Farshtey, Greg. 2013. (LEGO Hero Factory Ser.). (ENG.). 140p. (J). (gr. 3-7). pap. 7.99 *(978-0-545-55235-6(4))* Scholastic, Inc.

—Power Rangers Megaforce: Robo Knight! Landers, Ace. 2014. (ENG.). 24p. (J). (gr. -1-3). pap. 3.99 *(978-0-545-62899-0(7))* Scholastic, Inc.

—Star Wars: Science Fair Book. Margles, Samantha. 2013. (Star Wars Ser.). (ENG.). 128p. (J). (gr. 5-9). pap. 9.99 *(978-0-545-52099-7(1))* Scholastic, Inc.

Scholastic, Inc. Staff. Peppa's Windy Fall Day. Scholastic, Inc. Staff. 2015. (Peppa Pig Ser.). (ENG.). 24p. (J). (gr. -1-k). 3.99 ***(978-0-545-84818-3(0))*** Scholastic, Inc.

—Welcome to Shopville. Scholastic, Inc. Staff. Simon, Jenne. 2015. (Shopkins Ser.). (ENG.). 24p. (J). (gr. -1-3). pap. 3.99 ***(978-0-545-84228-0(X))*** Scholastic, Inc.

Scholastic, Inc. Staff & Alcadia SNC Staff. A Haunted Halloween. Howard, Lee. 2011. (Scooby-Doo Comic Storybook Ser.: 1). (ENG.). 32p. (J). (gr. -1-3). pap. 3.99 *(978-0-545-36864-3(2))* Scholastic, Inc.

Scholten, Cheri. Ganz Gleich Mit Wem Wir Zusammen Sind. Vescio, Robert. Beer, Michele, tr. from ENG. 2013.Tr. of No Matter Who We're With. (GER.). 36p. pap. *(978-1-922120-48-9(0),* IP Kidz) Interactive Pubns. Pty, Ltd.

—No Matter Who We're With. Vescio, Robert. 2012. 32p. *(978-1-922120-21-2(9),* IP Kidz) Interactive Pubns. Pty, Ltd.

Scholz, Barbara. Der Abc-Duden. 2nd ed. (Duden Ser.). (GER.). 96p. (J). *(978-3-411-70772-0(0))* Bibliographisches Institut & F. A. Brockhaus AG DEU. Dist: International Bk. Import Service, Inc.

Schon, Nick. Alien Swap. Cullimore, Stan. 2005. (ENG.). 24p. (J). lib. bdg. 23.65 *(978-1-59646-744-6(4))* Dingles & Co.

—The Amazing Adventures of Batbird. Clarke, Jane. Moon, Cliff, ed. 2005. (Collins Big Cat Ser.). (ENG.). 32p. (J). pap. 7.99 *(978-0-00-718637-2(1))* HarperCollins Pubs. Ltd. GBR. Dist: Independent Pubs. Group.

Schönberg, John. Yussuf the Guide or the Mountain Bandits: Being the Strange Story of the Travels in Asia Minor of Burne the Lawyer, Preston the Professor, & Lawren. Fenn, George. 2007. 424p. 26.95 *(978-0-9776786-6-2(0))* Salem Ridge Press LLC.

—Yussuf the Guide or the Mountain Bandits: Being the Strange Story of the Travels in Asia Minor of Burne the Lawyer, Preston the Professor, & Lawrenc. Fenn, George Manville. 2008. 432p. pap. 16.95 *(978-1-934671-20-7(7))* Salem Ridge Press LLC.

Schonfeld, Shaya. Touched by a Story: For Children. Spero, Yechiel. 2004. (ArtScroll Youth Ser.). 48p. (J). *(978-1-57819-436-0(9))* Mesorah Pubns., Ltd.

Schongut, Emanuel. Christmas Eve Blizzard, 1 vol. Vlahakis, Andrea. 2005. (ENG.). 32p. (J). (gr. k-4). 15.95 *(978-0-9764943-3-1(7))* Arbordale Publishing.

—Turtles in My Sandbox, 1 vol. Curtis, Jennifer Keats. 2006. (ENG.). 32p. (J). (gr. 1-5). 16.95 *(978-0-9768823-7-4(X))* Arbordale Publishing.

Schons, Chris. Teen Angst? Naaah... A Quasi-Autobiography. Vizzini, Ned. 2004. 240p. (J). (gr. 8-18). pap. 12.95 *(978-1-57542-084-4(8))* Free Spirit Publishing, Inc.

School, Liberty. The Amazing City of Arbella Lamore. Webb, Dirk. 2011. (ENG.). 40p. pap. 10.00 *(978-1-4679-8978-7(9))* CreateSpace Independent Publishing Platform.

Schoonmaker, Christina. Lucas & Leroy, 1 vol. Farrow, Nancy L. 2009. 32p. pap. 24.95 *(978-1-60836-232-5(9))* America Star Bks.

Schoonmaker, Elizabeth. Square Cat. Schoonmaker, Elizabeth. 2011. (ENG.). 32p. (J). (gr. -1-3). 15.99 *(978-1-4424-0619-3(4),* Simon & Schuster/Paula Wiseman Bks.) Simon & Schuster/Paula Wiseman Bks.

Schoonmaker, Gail. Do You Want a Friend? Piper, Noël. 2009. 32p. (J). (gr. -1-2). 12.99 *(978-1-4335-0621-5(1))* Crossway.

Schoonover, Brent. Ropes of Revolution: The Boston Tea Party, 1 vol. Gunderson, J. 2008. (Historical Fiction Ser.). (ENG.). 56p. (gr. 2-3). pap. 6.25 *(978-1-4342-0492-9(6),* Graphic Flash) Stone Arch Bks.

—Standoff: Remembering the Alamo, 1 vol. Trumbauer, Lisa. 2008. (Historical Fiction Ser.). (ENG.). 56p. (gr. 2-3). pap. 6.25 *(978-1-4342-0849-1(4),* Graphic Flash) Stone Arch Bks.

Schoonover, Brent, jt. illus. see Martin, Cynthia.

Schories, Pat. Biscuit. Capucilli, Alyssa Satin. (My First I Can Read Bks.). (ENG.). 32p. (J). (gr. -1-k). 2007. pap. 24.99 *(978-0-06-111973-6(3),* HarperFestival); ed. 2006. reprint ed. pap. 3.99 *(978-0-06-444212-1(8));* 10th anniv. ed. 2006. 16.99 *(978-0-06-026197-9(8))* HarperCollins Pubs.

—Biscuit & the Baby. Capucilli, Alyssa Satin. 2005. (My First I Can Read Ser.). 32p. (J). (gr. -1 — 1). (ENG.). pap. 3.99 *(978-0-06-009461-4(3));* (ENG.). 16.99 *(978-0-06-009459-1(1));* lib. bdg. 17.89 *(978-0-06-009460-7(5))* HarperCollins Pubs.

—Biscuit & the Little Pup. Capucilli, Alyssa Satin. 2007. (My First I Can Read Ser.). (ENG.). 32p. (J). (gr. -1 — 1). 16.99 *(978-0-06-074170-9(8))* HarperCollins Pubs.

—Biscuit & the Little Pup. Capucilli, Alyssa Satin. ed. 2008. (Biscuit: I Can Read! Ser.). 29p. (gr. -1-3). lib. bdg. 13.55 *(978-1-4178-1002-4(5),* Turtleback) Turtleback Bks.

—Biscuit & the Lost Teddy Bear. Capucilli, Alyssa Satin. 2011. (My First I Can Read Ser.). (ENG.). 32p. (J). (gr. -1 — 1). 16.99 *(978-0-06-117751-4(2));* pap. 3.99 *(978-0-06-117753-8(9))* HarperCollins Pubs.

Schories, Pat. Biscuit Feeds the Pets. Capucilli, Alyssa Satin. 2016. (My First I Can Read Ser.). 32p. (J). (gr. -1-3). pap. 3.99 ***(978-0-06-223696-8(2))*** HarperCollins Pubs.

Schories, Pat. Biscuit Gives a Gift. Capucilli, Alyssa Satin. 2004. (ENG.). 16p. (J). (gr. -1-3). bds. 4.99 *(978-0-06-009467-6(2),* HarperFestival) HarperCollins Pubs.

—Biscuit Goes Camping. Capucilli, Alyssa Satin. 2015. (My First I Can Read Ser.). (ENG.). 32p. (J). (gr. -1-3). pap. 3.99 *(978-0-06-223693-7(8))* HarperCollins Pubs.

—Biscuit Goes to School. Capucilli, Alyssa Satin. 2003. (My First I Can Read Ser.). (ENG.). 32p. (J). (gr. -1-3). pap. 3.99 *(978-0-06-443616-8(0))* HarperCollins Pubs.

—Biscuit Goes to School. Capucilli, Alyssa Satin. ed. 2003. (Biscuit: I Can Read! Ser.). 21p. (gr. -1-3). lib. bdg. 13.55 *(978-0-613-66941-2(X),* Turtleback) Turtleback Bks.

—Biscuit in the Garden. Capucilli, Alyssa Satin. 2013. (My First I Can Read Ser.). (ENG.). 32p. (J). (gr. -1-3). 16.99 *(978-0-06-193505-3(0));* pap. 3.99 *(978-0-06-193504-6(2))* HarperCollins Pubs.

—Biscuit Is Thankful. Capucilli, Alyssa Satin. 2003. (Biscuit Ser.). (ENG.). 16p. (J). (gr. -1-1). bds. 4.99 *(978-0-694-01519-1(9),* HarperFestival) HarperCollins Pubs.

—Biscuit Loves School. Capucilli, Alyssa Satin. 2003. (ENG.). 12p. (J). (gr. -1-1). pap. 9.99 *(978-0-06-009454-6(0),* HarperFestival) HarperCollins Pubs.

—Biscuit Loves the Library. Capucilli, Alyssa Satin. 2014. (My First I Can Read Ser.). (ENG.). 32p. (J). (gr. -1-3). 16.99 *(978-0-06-193507-7(7));* pap. 3.99 *(978-0-06-193506-0(9))* HarperCollins Pubs.

—Biscuit Meets the Class Pet. Capucilli, Alyssa Satin. 2009. (My First I Can Read Ser.). (ENG.). 32p. (J). (gr. -1-3). 16.99 *(978-0-06-117747-7(4));* pap. 3.99 *(978-0-06-117749-1(0))* HarperCollins Pubs.

—Biscuit Phonics Fun. Capucilli, Alyssa Satin. 2008. (My First I Can Read Ser.). (ENG.). 100p. (J). (gr. -1 — 1). pap. 12.99 *(978-0-06-143204-0(0))* HarperCollins Pubs.

—Biscuit Plays Ball. Capucilli, Alyssa Satin. 2012. (My First I Can Read Ser.). (ENG.). 32p. (J). (gr. -1-2). 16.99 *(978-0-06-193503-9(4));* pap. 3.99 *(978-0-06-193502-2(6))* HarperCollins Pubs.

—Biscuit Storybook Collection. Capucilli, Alyssa Satin. 2004. (Biscuit Ser.). (ENG.). 192p. (J). (gr. -1-3). 11.99 *(978-0-06-075904-9(6),* HarperFestival) HarperCollins Pubs.

—Biscuit Takes a Walk. Capucilli, Alyssa Satin. 2009. (My First I Can Read Ser.). (ENG.). 32p. (J). (gr. -1 — 1). 16.99 *(978-0-06-117745-3(8));* pap. 3.99 *(978-0-06-117746-0(6))* HarperCollins Pubs.

—Biscuit Visits the Big City. Capucilli, Alyssa Satin. (My First I Can Read Ser.). (ENG.). 32p. (J). (gr. -1 — 1). 2007. pap. 3.99 *(978-0-06-074166-2(X));* 2006. 16.99 *(978-0-06-074164-8(3))* HarperCollins Pubs.

—Biscuit Visits the Big City. Capucilli, Alyssa Satin. 2007. (Biscuit Ser.). 28p. (gr. -1-k). lib. bdg. 14.00 *(978-0-7569-8109-9(3))* Perfection Learning Corp.

—Biscuit Visits the Farm. 2012. (J). *(978-1-4351-4383-8(3),* HarperFestival) HarperCollins Pubs.

—Biscuit Visits the Pumpkin Patch. Capucilli, Alyssa Satin. 2004. (Biscuit Ser.). (ENG.). 16p. (J). (gr. -1-3). bds. 4.99 *(978-0-06-009466-9(4),* HarperFestival) HarperCollins Pubs.

—Biscuit Wins a Prize. Capucilli, Alyssa Satin. (My First I Can Read Ser.). 32p. (J). (gr. -1-3). 2005. (ENG.). pap. 3.99 *(978-0-06-009458-4(3));* 2003. (ENG.). 16.99 *(978-0-06-009455-3(9));* 2003. lib. bdg. 17.89 *(978-0-06-009457-7(5))* HarperCollins Pubs.

—Biscuit's ABCs. Capucilli, Alyssa Satin. 2011. (Biscuit Ser.). (ENG.). 16p. (J). (gr. -1-1). 6.99 *(978-0-06-162518-3(3),* HarperFestival) HarperCollins Pubs.

—Biscuit's Big Field Trip. Capucilli, Alyssa Satin. 2008. (Biscuit Ser.). 32p. (J). pap. 3.99 *(978-0-06-112844-8(9),* HarperFestival) HarperCollins Pubs.

—Biscuit's Big Friend. Capucilli, Alyssa Satin. 2003. (My First I Can Read Ser.). 32p. (J). (gr. -1 — 1). (ENG.). pap. 3.99 *(978-0-06-444288-6(8));* (ENG.). 16.99 *(978-0-06-029167-9(2));* lib. bdg. 17.89 *(978-0-06-029168-6(0))* HarperCollins Pubs.

—Biscuit's Birthday. Capucilli, Alyssa Satin. 2005. (Biscuit Ser.). (ENG.). 24p. (J). (gr. -1-1). pap. 3.99 *(978-0-06-057845-9(9),* HarperFestival) HarperCollins Pubs.

—Biscuit's Christmas Eve. Capucilli, Alyssa Satin. 2007. (Biscuit Ser.). (ENG.). 20p. (J). (gr. -1-1). pap. 6.99 *(978-0-06-112836-3(8),* HarperFestival) HarperCollins Pubs.

—Biscuit's Christmas Storybook Collection. Capucilli, Alyssa Satin. 2013. (ENG.). 192p. (J). (gr. -1-3). 11.99 *(978-0-06-228842-4(3),* HarperFestival) HarperCollins Pubs.

—Biscuit's Day at the Farm. Capucilli, Alyssa Satin. 2007. (My First I Can Read Ser.). 32p. (J). (gr. -1 — 1). (ENG.). pap. 3.99 *(978-0-06-074169-3(4));* (ENG.). 16.99 *(978-0-06-074167-9(8));* lib. bdg. 17.89 *(978-0-06-074168-6(6))* HarperCollins Pubs.

—Biscuit's First Beach Day. Capucilli, Alyssa Satin. 2010. (Biscuit Ser.). (ENG.). 24p. (J). (gr. -1-3). pap. 3.99 *(978-0-06-162515-2(9),* HarperFestival) HarperCollins Pubs.

—Biscuit's Fourth of July. 2005. (J). *(978-1-4156-0311-6(1),* HarperFestival) HarperCollins Pubs.

—Biscuit's Graduation Day. 2005. (J). *(978-1-4155-9660-9(3),* HarperFestival) HarperCollins Pubs.

—Bizcocho Encuentra un Amigo. Capucilli, Alyssa Satin. Pastemac, Susana, tr. 2008. (My First I Can Read Ser.).Tr. of Biscuit Finds a Friend. (SPA.). 32p. (J). (gr. -1 — 1). pap. 4.99 *(978-0-06-143526-3(0),* Rayo) HarperCollins Pubs.

—Forest, What Would You Like? O'Garden, Irene. 2013. (ENG.). 32p. (J). 16.95 *(978-0-8234-2322-4(0))* Holiday Hse., Inc.

—Meet Biscuit! Capucilli, Alyssa Satin. 2005. (Biscuit Ser.). (ENG.). 24p. (J). (gr. -1-1). pap. 3.99 *(978-0-06-057846-6(7),* HarperFestival) HarperCollins Pubs.

—Reading Is Fun with Biscuit: Biscuit; Biscuit Wants to Play; Biscuit Finds a Friend. Capucilli, Alyssa Satin. 2003. (My First I Can Read Ser.). (J). (gr. -1 — 1). pap. 11.99 *(978-0-06-058933-2(7))* HarperCollins Pubs.

Schories, Pat. Biscuit & the Little Pup. Schories, Pat. Capucilli, Alyssa Satin. 2007. (My First I Can Read Ser.). (ENG.). 32p. (J). (gr. -1 — 1). pap. 3.99 *(978-0-06-074172-3(4))* HarperCollins Pubs.

—Pants for Chuck. Schories, Pat. 2014. (ENG.). 24p. (J). (gr. -1-3). 14.95 *(978-0-8234-3066-6(9))* Holiday Hse., Inc.

Schories, Pat & Berlin, Rose Mary. Biscuit's 123. Capucilli, Alyssa Satin. 2012. (Biscuit Ser.). (ENG.). 16p. (J). (gr. -1-1). pap. 6.99 *(978-0-06-162523-7(X),* HarperFestival) HarperCollins Pubs.

—Biscuit's First Sleepover. Capucilli, Alyssa Satin. 2008. (Biscuit Ser.). (ENG.). 24p. (J). (gr. -1-1). pap. 3.99 *(978-0-06-112842-4(2),* HarperFestival) HarperCollins Pubs.

Schories, Pat & Young, Mary O'Keefe. Biscuit Loves Father's Day. Capucilli, Alyssa Satin. 2004. (ENG.). 20p. (J). (gr. -1-1). pap. 6.99 *(978-0-06-009463-8(X),* HarperFestival) HarperCollins Pubs.

—Biscuit Loves Mother's Day. Capucilli, Alyssa Satin. 2004. (ENG.). 20p. (J). (gr. -1-1). pap. 6.99 *(978-0-06-009462-1(1),* HarperFestival) HarperCollins Pubs.

—Biscuit's Hanukkah. Capucilli, Alyssa Satin. 2005. (Biscuit Ser.). (ENG.). 16p. (J). (gr. -1-3). bds. 4.99 *(978-0-06-009469-0(9),* HarperFestival) HarperCollins Pubs.

—Biscuit's Pet & Play Christmas. Capucilli, Alyssa Satin. 2006. (Biscuit Ser.). (ENG.). 12p. (J). (gr. -1-1). bds. 6.99 *(978-0-06-009470-6(2),* HarperFestival) HarperCollins Pubs.

—Biscuit's Show & Share Day. Capucilli, Alyssa Satin. 2007. (Biscuit Ser.). (ENG.). 24p. (J). (gr. -1-1). pap. 3.99 *(978-0-06-112832-5(5),* HarperFestival) HarperCollins Pubs.

—Biscuit's Snowy Day. Capucilli, Alyssa Satin. 2005. (Biscuit Ser.). (ENG.). 16p. (J). (gr. -1-3). bds. 4.99 *(978-0-06-009468-3(0),* HarperFestival) HarperCollins Pubs.

—Mind Your Manners, Biscuit! Capucilli, Alyssa Satin. 2007. (Biscuit Ser.). (ENG.). 24p. (J). (gr. -1-1). pap. 3.99 *(978-0-06-112835-6(X),* HarperFestival) HarperCollins Pubs.

Schories, Pat, jt. illus. see Andreasen, Dan.

Schories, Pat, jt. illus. see Berlin, Rose Mary.

Schories, Pat, jt. illus. see Wenzel, David T.

Schories, Pat, jt. illus. see Young, Mary O'Keefe.

Schorr, Bill. Red Roger to the Rescue. Riegelman, Rianna. 2012. (ENG.). 28p. (J). (gr. -1-3). 16.99 *(978-1-4494-2189-2(X))* Andrews McMeel Publishing.

Schott, Elizabeth. Jake & Sam at the Empty Abbey. 2006. 96p. (J). per. 9.95 *(978-0-9724421-1-4(1))* Fountain Square Publishing.

Schpitalnik, Vladimir. Sasha & Babushka: A Story of Russia. Evans, Connie. (Make Friends Around the World Ser.). (ENG.). 32p. (J). (gr. k-3). 8.95 *(978-1-59249-446-0(3),* SC8007) Soundprints.

Schrader, Kimberly. Green Knee-High Farm. Schrader, Margaret. 2009. 28p. pap. 12.95 *(978-1-60844-000-9(1))* Dog Ear Publishing, LLC.

Schrader, Mark. Don't Take Monkeys Home to Lunch. Furlong, Michelle. 2011. (ENG.). 30p. pap. 9.99 *(978-1-4664-4537-6(8))* CreateSpace Independent Publishing Platform.

Schrader, Racheal. Doodlebugs: Trouble On Moss Farm. Schrader, Racheal. 2008. 156p. (YA). per. 7.99 *(978-0-9815274-0-6(X))* Schrader, Racheal.

Schrey, Sophie. I Love Louis. Schrey, Sophie. Buster Books Staff. 2013. (I Love One Direction Ser.). (ENG.). 96p. (J). (gr. 3-7). pap. 7.99 *(978-1-78055-215-6(7))* O'Mara, Michael Bks., Ltd. GBR. Dist: Independent Pubs. Group.

Schrier, Alfred. Arizona. McHugh, Erin. 2007. (ENG.). 48p. (J). (gr. -1-17). 9.95 *(978-1-57912-701-5(0),* 81701, Black Dog & Leventhal Pubs. Inc.) Hachette Bks.

—New Jersey. McHugh, Erin. 2010. (ENG.). 52p. (J). (gr. -1-17). 9.95 *(978-1-57912-820-3(3),* 81820, Black Dog & Leventhal Pubs. Inc.) Hachette Bks.

—Ohio. McHugh, Erin. 2007. (ENG.). 48p. (J). (gr. -1-17). 9.95 *(978-1-57912-702-2(9),* 81702, Black Dog & Leventhal Pubs. Inc.) Hachette Bks.

—Pennsylvania. McHugh, Erin. 2010. (ENG.). 52p. (J). (gr. -1-17). 9.95 *(978-1-57912-821-0(1),* 81821, Black Dog & Leventhal Pubs. Inc.) Hachette Bks.

Schroder, Mark. Casey Jones. Krensky, Stephen. 2006. (On My Own Folklore Ser.). (ENG.). 48p. (gr. 2-4). lib. bdg. 25.26 *(978-1-57505-890-0(1))*, Millbrook Pr.) Lerner Publishing Group.

—Casey Jones. Krensky, Stephen. 2007. (On My Own Folklore Ser.). (ENG.). 48p. (gr. 2-4). per. 6.95 *(978-0-8225-6476-8(9))*, First Avenue Editions) Lerner Publishing Group.

—Cesar Chavez. Wadsworth, Ginger. 2005. (On My Own Biography Ser.). (ENG.). 48p. (gr. 2-4). pap. 6.95 *(978-1-57505-826-9(X))* Lerner Publishing Group.

—César Chávez. Wadsworth, Ginger. Fitzpatrick, Julia, tr. from ENG. 2005. (Yo Solo: Biografías (on My Own Biographies) Ser.). (SPA.). 48p. (gr. 2-4). lib. bdg. 25.26 *(978-0-8225-3124-1(0))*, Ediciones Lerner) Lerner Publishing Group.

—Juneteenth. Nelson, Vaunda Micheaux & Nelson, Drew. 2006. (On My Own Holidays Ser.). (ENG.). 48p. (gr. 2-4). per. 6.95 *(978-0-8225-5974-0(9))*, First Avenue Editions) Lerner Publishing Group.

Schroeder, Binette. Sir Lofty & Sir Tubb. Schroeder, Binette. 2009. (ENG.). 36p. (J). (gr. -1-3). 17.95 *(978-0-7358-2251-1(4))* North-South Bks., Inc.

Schroeder, Binette, jt. illus. see Hager, Christian.

Schroeder, Binnette, jt. illus. see Mogensen, Jan.

Schroeder, Erin. Oh no! it's the helpful hound... & the days of the Week. Schroeder, Erin, . 2006. (FRE, JPN, SPA & GER.). 27p. (J). per. 7.95 *(978-0-9779155-0-7(6))* Erinsillart.

Schroeder, Louise. The BLUES Go Birding Across America. Malnor, Carol L. & Fuller, Sandy F. 2010. 36p. (J). (gr. k-4). 16.95 *(978-1-58469-124-2(7))*; pap. 8.95 *(978-1-58469-125-9(5))* Dawn Pubns.

—The BLUES Go Birding at Wild America's Shores. Malnor, Carol L. & Fuller, Sandy F. 2010. 36p. (J). 16.95 *(978-1-58469-131-0(X))*; pap. 8.95 *(978-1-58469-132-7(8))* Dawn Pubns.

—The BLUES Go Extreme Birding. Malnor, Carol & Fuller, Sandy F. 2011. 36p. (J). (gr. k-4). 16.95 *(978-1-58469-133-4(6))*; pap. 8.95 *(978-1-58469-134-1(4))* Dawn Pubns.

Schrom, Garren. Pepe & Lupita & the Great Yawn Jar. Lacy, Sandy Allbee. 2013. 36p. pap. 10.95 *(978-1-60494-923-0(8))* Wheatmark.

Schrotter, Gustav. Robert Boyle, Founder of Modern Chemistry. Sootin, Harry. 2011. 142p. 40.95 *(978-1-258-00545-0(X))* Literary Licensing, LLC.

Schubert, Dieter. Opposites. Schubert, Dieter. 2013. (ENG.). 32p. (J). (gr. -1). 17.95 *(978-1-935954-26-2(1))*, 9781935954262) Lemniscaat USA.

Schubert, Jan. The Sun Seed. Schubert, Jan. 2007. 28p. (J). (gr. -1-k). lib. bdg. *(978-0-88010-585-9(2))*, Bell Pond Bks.) SteinerBooks, Inc.

Schubert, Karin. Extrano, Muy Extrano. Alonso, Manuel L. 2003. (SPA.). 124p. (J). (gr. 3-5). pap. 10.95 *(978-84-204-4906-7(7))* Santillana USA Publishing Co., Inc.

Schuck, Jenna, photos by. Fashionable Clothing from the Sears Catalogs: Early 1940s. Skinner, Tina. 2003. (Schiffer Book for Collectors Ser.). (ENG.). 160p. (gr. 10-13). pap. 29.95 *(978-0-7643-1755-2(5))* Schiffer Publishing, Ltd.

Schuepbach, Lynnette. Can You See Me Now? Dwyer, Cynthia. 2006. 24p. (J). 12.95 *(978-0-9677685-8-8(6))* Grannie Annie Family Story Celebration, The.

—Four-Eyed Philip. Dwyer, Cynthia. 2007. (J). 14.95 *(978-0-9793296-0-9(4))* Grannie Annie Family Story Celebration, The.

Schuepbach, Lynnette. Froggy Hollow. Schuepbach, Lynnette. l.t. ed. 2004. 32p. (J). 7.00 net. *(978-0-9759613-0-8(6))* Creative Sources.

—Shhhh!!! Schuepbach, Lynnette. l.t. ed. 2004. (ENG.). 32p. (J). pap. 12.95 *(978-0-9759613-1-5(4))* Creative Sources.

Schuett, Stacey. Alex & the Wednesday Chess Club. Wong, Janet S. 2004. (ENG.). 40p. (J). (gr. -1-3). 17.99 *(978-0-689-85890-1(6))*, McElderry, Margaret K. Bks.) McElderry, Margaret K. Bks.

—America Is... Borden, Louise. 2005. (ENG.). 40p. (J). (gr. 1-4). 7.99 *(978-1-4169-0286-7(4))*, McElderry, Margaret K. Bks.) McElderry, Margaret K. Bks.

—Are Trees Alive? Miller, Debbie S. 2003. (ENG.). 32p. (J). (gr. -1-3). 16.95 *(978-0-8027-8801-6(7))* Walker & Co.

—Grandmother's Dreamcatcher, 1 vol. McCain, Becky Ray. 2004. (ENG.). 32p. (J). (gr. k-3). pap. 6.99 *(978-0-8075-3032-0(8))* Whitman, Albert & Co.

—Halloween Howls: Holiday Poetry. Hopkins, Lee Bennett. 2005. (I Can Read Bks.). 32p. (J). (gr. k-3). 15.99 *(978-0-06-008060-0(4))*; lib. bdg. 16.89 *(978-0-06-008061-7(2))* HarperCollins Pubs.

—Hanukkah in Alaska. Brown, Barbara. 2013. (ENG.). 32p. (J). (gr. -1-3). 16.99 *(978-0-8050-9748-1(1))*, Holt, Henry & Co. Bks. For Young Readers) Holt, Henry & Co.

—I Love to Write! Williams, Rozanne Lanczak. 2006. (Learn to Write Ser.). 8p. (J). (gr. k-2). pap. 3.49 *(978-1-59198-283-8(9))*, 6177) Creative Teaching Pr., Inc.

—I Love to Write! Williams, Rozanne Lanczak. Maio, Barbara & Faulkner, Stacey, eds. 2006. (J). per. 6.99 *(978-1-59198-334-7(7))* Creative Teaching Pr., Inc.

—Liberty's Voice: The Story of Emma Lazarus. Silverman, Erica. 2011. (ENG.). 32p. (J). (gr. 1-3). 17.99 *(978-0-525-47859-1(0))*, Dutton Juvenile) Penguin Publishing Group.

—Liberty's Voice the Story of Emma Lazarus. Silverman, Erica. 2014. (ENG.). 32p. (J). (gr. 1-3). 8.99 *(978-0-14-751174-4(7))*, Puffin) Penguin Publishing Group.

—Marching with Aunt Susan: Susan B. Anthony & the Fight for Women's Suffrage, 1 vol. Murphy, Claire Rudolf. 2011. (ENG.). 36p. (J). (gr. 1-5). 16.95 *(978-1-56145-593-5(8))*, Peachtree Junior) Peachtree Pubs.

—Oh, Theodore! Guinea Pig Poems. Katz, Susan. 2007. (ENG.). 48p. (J). (gr. -1-3). 16.00 *(978-0-618-70222-0(9))* Houghton Mifflin Harcourt Publishing Co.

—Out of This World: Poems & Facts about Space. Sklansky, Amy. 2012. (ENG.). 40p. (J). (gr. k-4). 17.99 *(978-0-375-86459-9(8))*, Knopf Bks. for Young Readers) Random Hse. Children's Bks.

—Outside the Window. Smucker, Anna. 2005. 32p. (J). reprint ed. per. 7.95 *(978-1-891852-40-4(X))* Quarrier Pr.

—Pleasing the Ghost. Creech, Sharon. 2013. (Trophy Bk.). 112p. (J). (gr. 3-7). reprint ed. pap. 5.99 *(978-0-06-440686-4(5))* HarperCollins Pubs.

—Prairie Friends. Levinson, Nancy Smiler. 2003. (I Can Read Bks.). 64p. (J). (gr. k-3). 16.89 *(978-0-06-028002-4(6))*; 15.99 *(978-0-06-028001-7(8))* HarperCollins Pubs.

—Purple Mountain Majesties: The Story of Katharine Lee Bates & America the Beautiful. Younger, Barbara. 2005. 29p. (J). reprint ed. 16.00 *(978-0-7567-8984-8(2))* DIANE Publishing Co.

—Winter Candle. Ashford, Jeron. 2014. (ENG.). 28p. (J). (gr. -1-6). 16.95 *(978-1-939547-10-1(5))* Creston Bks.

Schuett, Stacey, jt. illus. see Gustavson, Adam.

Schulbaum, Michael. Jyoti Meditation for Children. Singh, Rajinder. 2011. 24p. (J). (gr. -1-3). 10.00 *(978-0-918224-81-1(0))* Radiance Pubs.

Schultz, Ashlee. Electrical Circuits: Harnessing Electricity, 1 vol. Dreier, David. 2007. (Exploring Science: Physical Science Ser.). (ENG.). 48p. (gr. 6-7). lib. bdg. 28.65 *(978-0-7565-3267-3(1))*, Exploring Science) Compass Point Bks.

—Food Webs: Interconnecting Food Chains, 1 vol. Gray, Susan H. 2008. (Exploring Science: Life Science Ser.). (ENG.). 48p. (gr. 6-7). lib. bdg. 28.65 *(978-0-7565-3261-1(2))*, Exploring Science) Compass Point Bks.

—Igneous Rocks: From Fire to Stone, 1 vol. Stille, Darlene R. 2008. (Exploring Science: Earth Science Ser.). (ENG.). 48p. (gr. 6-7). lib. bdg. 28.65 *(978-0-7565-3252-9(3))*, Exploring Science) Compass Point Bks.

—Metamorphic Rocks: Recycled Rock, 1 vol. Stille, Darlene R. 2008. (Exploring Science: Earth Science Ser.). (ENG.). 48p. (gr. 6-7). lib. bdg. 28.65 *(978-0-7565-3255-0(8))*, Exploring Science) Compass Point Bks.

—Sedimentary Rocks: A Record of Earth's History, 1 vol. Stille, Darlene R. 2008. (Exploring Science: Earth Science Ser.). (ENG.). 48p. (gr. 6-7). lib. bdg. 28.65 *(978-0-7565-3258-1(2))*, Exploring Science) Compass Point Bks.

Schultz, Ashlee, jt. illus. see Hossain, Farhana.

Schultz, Barbara, jt. illus. see Martin, Cynthia.

Schultz, Gary, photos by. Tundra Food Webs. Fleisher, Paul. 2007. (Early Bird Food Webs Ser.). (ENG., 48p. (gr. 2-5). lib. bdg. 26.60 *(978-0-8225-6727-1(X))*, Lerner Pubns.) Lerner Publishing Group.

Schultz, Jolene. Albert Einstein: Scientist & Genius. Slade, Suzanne. 2007. (Biographies Ser.). (ENG.). 24p. (gr. k-3). 25.99 *(978-1-4048-3730-0(2))*, Nonfiction Picture Bks.) Picture Window Bks.

Schultz, Michael. Mom, I Love Spaghetti. Fort, Gary W. 2011. 86p. pap. 24.00 *(978-1-60911-562-3(7))*, Eloquent Bks.) Strategic Book Publishing & Rights Agency (SBPRA).

Schulz, Barbara. The Curse of King Tut's Tomb, 1 vol. Burgan, Michael. 2005. (Graphic History Ser.). (ENG.). 32p. (gr. 3-4). per. 8.10 *(978-0-7368-5244-9(1))*, Graphic Library) Capstone Pr., Inc.

—Getting to the Bottom of Global Warming: An Isabel Soto Investigation. Collins, Terry et al. 2010. (Graphic Expeditions Ser.). (ENG.). 32p. (gr. 3-4). lib. bdg. 29.99 *(978-1-4296-3972-9(5))*, Graphic Library) Capstone Pr., Inc.

Schulz, Barbara & Kurth, Steve. Demeter & Persephone: Spring Held Hostage. Fontes, Justine & Fontes, Ron. 2007. (Graphic Myths & Legends Ser.). (ENG.). 48p. (gr. 4-8). lib. bdg. 27.93 *(978-0-8225-5966-5(8))* Lerner Publishing Group.

Schulz, Barbara, jt. illus. see Kurth, Steve.

Schulz, Barbara, jt. illus. see Lohse, Otha Zackariah Edward.

Schulz, Barbara, jt. illus. see Martin, Cynthia.

Schulz, Barbara, jt. illus. see Purcell, Gordon.

Schulz, Barbara, jt. illus. see Seeley, Tim.

Schulz, Charles M. Christmas Is Together-Time. Schulz, Charles M. 2006. (Peanuts(r) Ser.). (ENG.). 72p. 6.95 *(978-1-933662-37-4(9))* Cider Mill Pr. Bk. Pubs., LLC.

Schulz, Janet. Will y Orv. Schulz, Walter A. Translations.com Staff, tr. from ENG. 2006. (Yo Solo: Historia (on My Own History) Ser.). (SPA.). 48p. (gr. 2-4). lib. bdg. 25.26 *(978-0-8225-6263-4(4))*, Ediciones Lerner) Lerner Publishing Group.

Schulze, Marc-Alexander. A Child Is Born: The Nativity Story. 2010. (ENG.). 32p. (gr. -1). 16.95 *(978-0-7358-2321-1(9))* North-South Bks., Inc.

Schumaker, Ward. A Kids Guide to Giving. Zeiler, Freddi. 2006. (ENG.). 208p. (J). (gr. 7-17). 9.99 *(978-1-58476-489-2(9))*, IKIDS) Innovative Kids.

Schuna, Ramona. Aristotle: the Firefly's Message. Brown, Elizabeth. 2007. (ENG.). 40p. per. 19.95 *(978-1-59800-557-8(X))* Outskirts Pr., Inc.

Schuna, Sam, jt. illus. see Merrell, Patrick.

Schunemann, Ryan. Gabriel's Magic Ornament. Bush, Randall B. 2003. 120p. (gr. 5-8). pap. 11.95 *(978-0-9716633-0-5(0))* Pristine Pubs., Inc.

Schuppert, David. What Do Roots Do? Kudlinski, Kathleen V. (ENG.). 32p. (J). (gr. k-3). 2007. pap. 7.95 *(978-1-55971-980-3(X))*; 2005. 15.95 *(978-1-55971-896-7(X))* Cooper Square Publishing Llc.

Schuster, Rob. Super Basketball Infographics. Savage, Jeff. 2015. (Super Sports Infographics Ser.). (ENG.). 32p. (J). (gr. 3-5). pap. 8.99 *(978-1-4677-7575-5(4))*; lib. bdg. 26.65 *(978-1-4677-5233-6(9))* Lerner Publishing Group. (Lerner Pubns.).

Schutzer, Dena. 3 Kids Dreamin' England, Linda. 2011. (ENG.). 32p. (J). (gr. 4-6). 6.99 *(978-1-4424-2944-4(5))*, McElderry, Margaret K. Bks.) McElderry, Margaret K. Bks.

Schuurmans, Hilde. Sidney Won't Swim. Schuurmans, Hilde. pap. 6.95 *(978-1-57091-515-4(6))* Charlesbridge Publishing, Inc.

Schwab, Jordan. Pages, the Book-Maker Elf. Delrusso, Diana. 2008. 68p. pap. 23.49 *(978-1-4343-9844-4(7))* AuthorHouse.

Schwake, Rainer, photos by. Art Lab for Kids: 52 Creative Adventures in Drawing, Painting, Printmaking, Paper, & Mixed Media - For Budding Artists of All Ages. Schwake, Susan. 2012. (Lab Ser.). (ENG., 144p. pap. 22.99 *(978-1-59253-765-5(0))*, 1592537650, Quarry Bks.) Quarto Publishing Group USA.

—3D Art Lab for Kids: 32 Hands-On Adventures in Sculpture & Mixed Media - Including Fun Projects Using Clay, Plaster, Cardboard, Paper, Fiber Beads & More! Schwake, Susan. 2013. (Lab Ser.). (ENG., 144p. pap. 24.99 *(978-1-59253-815-7(0))*, 1592538150, Quarry Books) Quarto Publishing Group USA.

Schwalm, Claudia, photos by. Folk Art of Mexico Book & Game. Schwalm, Claudia. Martinez Aydelott, Carmen, tr. 2005. (SPA., pap. 25.00 *(978-1-57371-050-3(4))* Cultural Connections.

Schwaner, Lynne. Sparkle Purse. Hapka, Cathy. Date not set. 10p. (J). 5.99 *(978-0-9986300-7-6(1))* Playhouse Publishing.

Schwark, Mike. Van Von Hunter. 2005. Vol. 1. 184p. pap. 9.99 *(978-1-59532-692-8(8))*; Vol. 2. 192p. per. 9.99 *(978-1-59532-693-5(6))* TOKYOPOP, Inc.

Schwartz, Amy. A Little Kitty. Feder, Jane. 2009. (ENG.), 14p. (J). (— 1). bds. 4.99 *(978-0-7636-2650-1(3))* Candlewick Pr.

—A Little Puppy. Feder, Jane. 2009. (ENG.). 14p. (J). (— 1). bds. 4.99 *(978-0-7636-2651-8(1))* Candlewick Pr.

—The Night Flight. Ryder, Joanne. 2014. (ENG.). 32p. (J). (gr. k-2). 16.99 *(978-1-4814-2521-6(8))*, Simon & Schuster Bks. For Young Readers) Simon & Schuster Bks. For Young Readers.

Schwartz, Amy. Polka Dots. 2016. (J). ***(978-0-8234-3431-2(1))*** Holiday Hse., Inc.

Schwartz, Amy. 100 Things That Make Me Happy. 2014. (ENG.). 40p. (J). (gr. -1-1). 16.95 *(978-1-4197-0518-2(0))*, Abrams Appleseed) Abrams.

Schwartz, Amy. Begin at the Beginning: A Little Artist Learns about Life. Schwartz, Amy. 2005. 40p. (J). (gr. -1-2). lib. bdg. 16.89 *(978-0-06-000112-4(7))* HarperCollins Pubs.

—The Boys Team. Schwartz, Amy. 2014. (ENG.). 40p. (J). (gr. -1-1). 19.99 *(978-1-4814-2534-6(X))*, Atheneum Bks. for Young Readers) Simon & Schuster Children's Publishing.

—Dee Dee & Me. Schwartz, Amy. 2014. (ENG.). 32p. (J). (gr. -1-3). pap. 6.99 *(978-0-8234-3178-6(9))* Holiday Hse., Inc.

—A Glorious Day. Schwartz, Amy. 2010. (ENG.). 32p. (J). (gr. -1-k). 16.99 *(978-1-4424-2190-5(8))*, Atheneum Bks. for Young Readers) Simon & Schuster Children's Publishing.

—Oscar: The Big Adventure of a Little Sock Monkey. Schwartz, Amy. Marcus, Leonard S. 2006. 32p. (J). (gr. -1-2). 16.99 *(978-0-06-072622-5(9))*, Tegen, Katherine Bks) HarperCollins Pubs.

—What James Likes Best. Schwartz, Amy. 2014. (ENG.). 32p. (J). (gr. -1-k). 16.99 *(978-1-4814-2536-0(6))*, Atheneum Bks. for Young Readers) Simon & Schuster Children's Publishing.

Schwartz, Carol. Best Friends: The True Story of Owen & Mzee. Edwards, Roberta. 2007. (Penguin Young Readers, Level 2 Ser.). (ENG.). 32p. (J). (gr. 1-3). mass mkt. 3.99 *(978-0-448-44567-0(0))*, Grosset & Dunlap) Penguin Publishing Group.

—Best Friends: The True Story of Owen & Mzee. Edwards, Roberta. 2007. (All Aboard Science Reader Ser.). 32p. (J). (gr. -1-3). 14.00 *(978-0-7569-8167-9(0))* Perfection Learning Corp.

—Emperor Penguins. Edwards, Roberta. 2007. (Penguin Young Readers, Level 3 Ser.). (ENG.). 48p. (J). (gr. 1-3). mass mkt. 3.99 *(978-0-448-44664-6(2))*, Grosset & Dunlap) Penguin Publishing Group.

—Fireflies. Bryant, Megan E. 2008. (Penguin Young Readers, Level 3 Ser.). (ENG.). 48p. (J). (gr. 1-3). mass mkt. 3.99 *(978-0-448-44834-3(3))*, Grosset & Dunlap) Penguin Publishing Group.

—How Does a Seed Sprout? And Other Questions about Plants. Stewart, Melissa. 2014. (Good Question! Ser.). (ENG.). 32p. (J). (gr. 1). 12.95 *(978-1-4549-0670-4(7))*; pap. 5.95 *(978-1-4549-0671-1(5))* Sterling Publishing Co., Inc.

—How Strong Is an Ant? And Other Questions about Bugs & Insects. Carson, Mary Kay. 2014. (Good Question! Ser.). (ENG.). 32p. (J). (gr. 1). 12.95 *(978-1-4549-0684-1(7))* Sterling Publishing Co., Inc.

—Shelley, the Hyperactive Turtle. Moss, Deborah. 2nd ed. 2006. 20p. (J). (gr. -1-2). pap. *(978-1-890627-75-1(5))* Woodbine Hse.

—Whales. Norman, Kim & American Museum of Natural History Staff. 2012. (Storytime Stickers Ser.). (ENG.). 16p. (J). (gr. k-2). pap. 5.95 *(978-1-4027-7350-1(1))* Sterling Publishing Co., Inc.

—What If There Were No Bees? A Book about the Grassland Ecosystem, 1 vol. Slade, Suzanne. 2010. (Food Chain Reactions Ser.). (ENG.). 24p. (gr. 2-4). lib. bdg. 25.99 *(978-1-4048-6019-3(3))*; pap. 8.95 *(978-1-4048-6394-1(X))* Picture Window Bks. (Nonfiction Picture Bks.).

—What If There Were No Gray Wolves? A Book about the Temperate Forest Ecosystem, 1 vol. Slade, Suzanne. 2010. (Food Chain Reactions Ser.). (ENG.). 24p. (gr. 2-4). lib. bdg. 25.99 *(978-1-4048-6020-9(7))*; pap. 8.95 *(978-1-4048-6395-8(8))* Picture Window Bks. (Nonfiction Picture Bks.).

—What If There Were No Lemmings? A Book about the Tundra Ecosystem, 1 vol. Slade, Suzanne. 2010. (Food Chain Reactions Ser.). (ENG.). 24p. (gr. 2-4). lib. bdg. 25.99 *(978-1-4048-6021-6(5))*; pap. 8.95 *(978-1-4048-6396-5(6))* Picture Window Bks. (Nonfiction Picture Bks.).

—What If There Were No Sea Otters? A Book about the Ocean Ecosystem, 1 vol. Slade, Suzanne. 2010. (Food Chain Reactions Ser.). (ENG.). 24p. (gr. 2-4). lib. bdg. 25.99 *(978-1-4048-6018-6(5))*; pap. 8.95 *(978-1-4048-6397-2(4))* Picture Window Bks. (Nonfiction Picture Bks.).

—Wild Fibonacci: Nature's Secret Code Revealed. Hulme, Joy N. 2010. (ENG.). 32p. (J). (gr. -1-2). pap. 7.99 *(978-1-58246-324-7(7))*, Tricycle Pr.) Ten Speed Pr.

Schwartz, Carol. Emperor Penguins. Schwartz, Carol. Edwards, Roberta. 2007. (All Aboard Science Reader Ser.). 48p. (J). (gr. 1-3). 14.00 *(978-0-7569-8174-7(3))* Perfection Learning Corp.

—Old Mother Hubbard. Schwartz, Carol. 2010. (Favorite Mother Goose Rhymes Ser.). (ENG.). 16p. (J). (gr. -1-2). 25.64 *(978-1-60253-538-1(8))*, 200242) Child's World, Inc., The.

Schwartz, Marty. Changing Statements to Questions Fun Deck: Fd55. Webber, Sharon. 2003. (J). 11.95 *(978-1-58650-248-5(4))* Super Duper Pubns.

—What Makes Sense? Fun Deck: Fd60. 2003. (J). 11.95 *(978-1-58650-268-3(9))* Super Duper Pubns.

Schwartz, Marty, jt. illus. see Ink, Bruce.

Schwartz, Robert, jt. illus. see Schwartz, Suzanne.

Schwartz, Roslyn. The Complete Adventures of the Mole Sisters. Schwartz, Roslyn. 2004. (Mole Sisters Ser.). (ENG.). 168p. (J). (gr. -1-k). 19.95 *(978-1-55037-883-2(X))*, 9781550378832) Annick Pr., Ltd. CAN. Dist: Firefly Bks., Ltd.

—The Mole Sisters & the Fairy Ring. Schwartz, Roslyn. 2003. (Mole Sisters Ser.). (ENG.). 32p. (J). (gr. -1-k). 14.95 *(978-1-55037-819-1(8))*, 9781550378191); pap. 5.95 *(978-1-55037-818-4(X))*, 9781550378184) Annick Pr., Ltd. CAN. Dist: Firefly Bks., Ltd.

—The Mole Sisters & the Way Home. Schwartz, Roslyn. 2003. (Mole Sisters Ser.). (ENG.). 32p. (J). (gr. -1-k). 14.95 *(978-1-55037-821-4(X))*, 9781550378214); pap. 5.95 *(978-1-55037-820-7(1))*, 9781550378207) Annick Pr., Ltd. CAN. Dist: Firefly Bks., Ltd.

—Tales from Parc la Fontaine. Schwartz, Roslyn. 2006. (Parc la Fontaine Ser.). (ENG.). 48p. (J). (gr. -1-1). 19.95 *(978-1-55451-044-3(9))*, 9781554510443) Annick Pr., Ltd. CAN. Dist: Firefly Bks., Ltd.

Schwartz, Roslyn & Owlkids Books Inc. Staff. The Vole Brothers. Schwartz, Roslyn. 2011. (ENG.). 32p. (J). (gr. -1-k). 15.95 *(978-1-926818-83-2(0))* Owlkids Bks. Inc. CAN. Dist: Perseus-PGW.

Schwartz, Suzanne & Schwartz, Robert. The Christmas Palm Tree: A Storybook to Color. Schwartz, Suzanne & Schwartz, Robert. l.t. ed. 2005. 22p. (J). spiral bd. 3.99 *(978-0-9764152-3-7(2))* Seascay Productions.

—Hibby's Coloring Book. 2005. 24p. (J). spiral bd. 3.95 *(978-0-9764152-1-3(6))* Seascay Productions.

—My Friend Hibby: A Tropical Adventure. Schwartz, Suzanne & Schwartz, Robert. 2005. 20p. (J). spiral bd. 6.00 *(978-0-9764152-0-6(8))* Seascay Productions.

Schwartz, Wendy. The Winged Pony. Beloat, Betty. 2005. 32p. (J). (gr. k-5). pap. 5.99 *(978-0-9701008-8-7(4))* Bicast, Inc.

Schwarz, Manuela. I Think, I Am! Teaching Kids the Power of Affirmations. Hay, Louise L. & Tracy, Kristina. 2008. (ENG.). 32p. (gr. -1-2). 15.99 *(978-1-4019-2208-5(2))* Hay Hse., Inc.

Schwarz, Renee. Birdfeeders. Schwarz, Renee. 2005. (Kids Can Do It Ser.). (ENG.). 40p. (J). (gr. 4-7). 6.95 *(978-1-55337-700-9(1))* Kids Can Pr., Ltd. CAN. Dist: Univ. of Toronto Pr.

—Birdhouses. Schwarz, Renee. 2005. (Kids Can Do It Ser.). (ENG.). 40p. (J). (gr. 3-18). 6.95 *(978-1-55337-550-0(5))* Kids Can Pr., Ltd. CAN. Dist: Univ. of Toronto Pr.

—Funky Junk: Cool Stuff to Make with Hardware. Schwarz, Renee. 2003. (Kids Can Do It Ser.). (ENG.). 40p. (J). (gr. 4-6). 5.95 *(978-1-55337-388-9(X))* Kids Can Pr., Ltd. CAN. Dist: Univ. of Toronto Pr.

—Wind Chimes & Whirligigs. Schwarz, Renee. 2007. (Kids Can Do It Ser.). (ENG.). 40p. (J). (gr. 3-18). 12.95 *(978-1-55337-868-6(7))*; pap. 6.95 *(978-1-55337-870-9(9))* Kids Can Pr., Ltd. CAN. Dist: Univ. of Toronto Pr.

Schwarz, Thies & Style Guide, Style. Tip's Tips on Friendship. 2015. (Home Ser.). (ENG.). 32p. (J). (gr. k-2). 16.99 *(978-1-4814-2611-4(7))*, Simon Spotlight) Simon Spotlight.

Schwarz, Thies, jt. illus. see Style Guide, Style.

Schwarz, Viviane. Cheese Belongs to You! Deacon, Alexis. 2013. (ENG.). 32p. (J). (gr. -1-1). 15.99 *(978-0-7636-6608-8(4))* Candlewick Pr.

Schwarz, Viviane. I Am Henry Finch. Deacon, Alexis. 2015. (ENG.). 40p. (J). (gr. k-3). 16.99 ***(978-0-7636-7812-8(0))*** Candlewick Pr.

Schwarz, Viviane. A Place to Call Home. Deacon, Alexis. 2011. (ENG.). 40p. (J). (gr. -1-2). 16.99 *(978-0-7636-5360-6(8))* Candlewick Pr.

—Welcome to Your Awesome Robot. 2013. (ENG.). 32p. (J). (gr. -1). pap. 13.95 *(978-1-909263-00-0(1))* Flying Eye Bks. GBR. Dist: Consortium Bk. Sales & Distribution.

Schwarz, Viviane. Is There a Dog in This Book? Schwarz, Viviane. 2014. (ENG.). 32p. (J). (gr. -1-2). 16.99 *(978-0-7636-6991-1(1))* Candlewick Pr.

Schweitzer-Johnson, Betty. How Meg Changed Her Mind. Coffey, Ethel. 2014. (ENG.). 32p. pap. 11.95 *(978-1-4525-8377-8(3))*, Balboa Pr.) Author Solutions, Inc.

Schweltzer, Patty. The Fox, the Badger, & the Bunny: A Dales Tale. Wolcott, P. A. Wolcott, K. Hannah, ed. 2009. 20p. pap. 24.95 *(978-1-60749-525-3(2))* America Star Bks.

Schweninger, Ann. Amanda Pig & Her Big Brother Oliver. Van Leeuwen, Jean. (Oliver Pig Ser.). 56p. (J). (gr. k-2). pap. 3.99 *(978-0-8072-1341-4(1))*, Listening Library) Random Hse. Audio Publishing Group.

—Amanda Pig & the Awful, Scary Monster. Van Leeuwen, Jean. 2004. (Oliver & Amanda Ser.). (ENG.). 48p. (J). (gr. 1-3). mass mkt. 3.99 *(978-0-14-240203-0(6))*, Warne, Frederick Pubs.) Penguin Bks., Ltd. GBR. Dist: Penguin Random Hse., LLC.

—Amanda Pig & the Really Hot Day. Van Leeuwen, Jean. 2007. (Oliver & Amanda Ser.). (ENG.). 48p. (J). (gr. 1-3). pap. 3.99 *(978-0-14-240775-2(5))*, Warne, Frederick Pubs.) Penguin Bks., Ltd. GBR. Dist: Penguin Publishing Group.

—Amanda Pig & the Really Hot Day. Van Leeuwen, Jean. 2007. (Oliver & Amanda Pig Bks.). 47p. (J). (gr. -1-3). 11.65 *(978-0-7569-8152-5(2))* Perfection Learning Corp.

—Amanda Pig & the Wiggly Tooth. Van Leeuwen, Jean. 2009. (Oliver & Amanda Ser.). (ENG.). 48p. (J). (gr. 1-3). mass mkt. 3.99 *(978-0-14-241290-9(2),* Puffin) Penguin Publishing Group.

—Amanda Pig, First Grader. Van Leeuwen, Jean. (Oliver & Amanda Ser.). (J). 2009. (ENG.). 48p. (gr. 1-3). mass mkt. 3.99 *(978-0-14-241276-3(7),* Puffin); 2007. 40p. *(978-1-4287-4781-4(8),* Dial) Penguin Publishing Group.

—Tales of Oliver Pig. Van Leeuwen, Jean. (Oliver Pig Ser.). 64p. (J). (gr. k-2). pap. 3.99 *(978-0-8072-1334-6(9),* Listening Library) Random Hse. Audio Publishing Group.

Schwortz, Anna M. A B C Rhymetime. Schwortz, Anna M. Schwortz, Anna M., ed. 2005. 48p. (J). (gr. k-3). pap. *(978-0-9769719-0-0(9))* AnnArt Pr.

Sciarrone, Claudio. Paint the Town! (Dora & Friends) Golden Books. 2014. (Deluxe Paint Box Book Ser.). (ENG.). 128p. (J). (gr. -1-2). pap. 7.99 *(978-0-385-37441-5(0),* Golden Bks.) Random Hse. Children's Bks.

—Welcome to the City! (Dora & Friends) Golden Books. 2014. (Color Plus Chunky Crayons Ser.). (ENG.). 48p. (J). (gr. -1-2). pap. 3.99 *(978-0-385-38412-4(2),* Golden Bks.) Random Hse. Children's Bks.

Sciarrone, Claudio, jt. illus. see Golden Books Staff.

Sciascia, Salvatore. Papá Guillermo y los Pájaros. Sartori, Gloria. Brignole, Giancarla, tr. rev. ed. 2007. (Fabulas De Familia Ser.). (SPA & ENG.). 32p. (J). pap. 6.95 *(978-970-20-0256-7(7))* Castillo, Ediciones, S. A. de C. V. MEX. Dist: Macmillan.

Sciulli, Erika. No Andy No! Brant, Dennis, Jr. 2008. 18p. pap. 24.95 *(978-1-60703-203-8(1))* America Star Bks.

Sciuto, Alex. Energy & Waves Through Infographics. Rowell, Rebecca. 2013. (Super Science Infographics Ser.). (ENG.). 32p. (gr. 3-5). pap. 8.95 *(978-1-4677-1590-4(5));* lib. bdg. 26.60 *(978-1-4677-1290-3(6),* Lerner Pubns.) Lerner Publishing Group.

—Natural Disasters Through Infographics. Higgins, Nadia. 2013. (Super Science Infographics Ser.). (ENG.). 32p. (gr. 3-5). pap. 8.95 *(978-1-4677-1593-5(X));* lib. bdg. 26.60 *(978-1-4677-1287-3(6),* Lerner Pubns.) Lerner Publishing Group.

—US Government Through Infographics. Higgins, Nadia. 2014. (Super Social Studies Infographics Ser.). 32p. (gr. 3-5). (J). lib. bdg. 26.60 *(978-1-4677-3463-9(2),* Lerner Pubns.); pap. 8.95 *(978-1-4677-4567-3(7))* Lerner Publishing Group.

Scobie, Andrea. Black & White Animals Color the World. Yontz-Oetting, Carolyn. 2011. (ENG.). 46p. pap. 10.50 *(978-1-4536-9037-6(9))* CreateSpace Independent Publishing Platform.

—Erica from America & the Start of the Gang of Four. Waldman, Alan/A. 2013. 44p. pap. *(978-0-9840514-2-7(2))* Roxby Media Ltd.

Scoggins, Jocelyn. Jocelyn's Theatre. Achilles, Carole. 2011. 20p. pap. 24.95 *(978-1-4560-8333-5(3))* America Star Bks.

Scorey, John, jt. illus. see Shackell, John.

Scott, A. O. Treasure Trove of Pirate Stories: A Collection of Best Pirate Stories for Young People. Kessler, Ramon Wilke. 2011. 294p. 48.95 *(978-1-258-05706-0(9))* Literary Licensing, LLC.

Scott, Angela, jt. illus. see Scott, Jonathan.

Scott, Ann. Isaac & the Red Jumper. Seyderhelm, Amanda. 2013. 26p. pap. *(978-0-9572146-1-3(8))* HARK Pubns.

Scott, Bob. Happiness Is a Warm Blanket, Charlie Brown! Schulz, Charles M. & Pastis, Stephan. 2011. (Peanuts Ser.). (ENG.). 96p. (gr. 3). pap. 9.99 *(978-1-60886-681-6(5));* (J). 19.99 *(978-1-60886-682-3(3))* Boom! Studios.

Scott, Brandon James. Justin Time: the Big Pet Story. 2013. (Justin Time Ser.). (ENG.). 36p. (J). (gr. -1-3). 15.95 *(978-1-59702-041-1(9))* Immedium.

—The Pancake Express. 2012. (Justin Time Ser.). (ENG.). 36p. (J). (gr. -1-3). 15.95 *(978-1-59702-035-0(4))* Immedium.

Scott, Chelsey. Ah-Choo - God Bless You. Jahn, Benny. 2009. 24p. pap. 11.95 *(978-1-60844-178-5(4))* Dog Ear Publishing, LLC.

Scott, Christopher L. I'm Mommy's Little Helper. Pendleton, Claudette M. 2012. 46p. 24.95 *(978-1-4626-9303-0(2));* 48p. pap. 24.95 *(978-1-4626-7427-5(5))* America Star Bks.

Scott, Concetta C. Move over, Mother Goose! Finger Plays, Action Verses & Funny Rhymes. Dowell, Ruth I. Charner, Kathleen, ed. 2004. 126p. (Orig.). (gr. -1-1). pap. 12.95 *(978-0-87659-113-0(6),* 10006) Gryphon Hse., Inc.

Scott, Damion. Here There Be the Monsters, Vol. 3. Jenkins, Paul. 2004. (Spider-Man Ser.). 144p. (YA). 9.99 *(978-0-7851-1333-1(9))* Marvel Worldwide, Inc.

Scott-Daniel, Toni. The Adventures of Super T: The Missing Blanket. Jackson, Gwendolyn. 2004. 32p. (J). lib. bdg. 15.95 *(978-0-9753434-0-1(8))* LeTay Publishing.

Scott, E. I Want My Kitty Cat Tv! Lee, G. 2012. 24p. pap. 24.95 *(978-1-4626-6610-2(8))* America Star Bks.

Scott, Gavin. Cuddle Bear. Freedman, Claire. 2013. 28p. (J). 12.99 *(978-1-61067-081-4(7))* Kane Miller.

—Lost Little Penguin, 1 vol. Corderoy, Tracey. 2014. (ENG.). 32p. (gr. -1-2). 14.95 *(978-1-62370-116-1(3))* Capstone Young Readers.

—My Precious Little Bear. Freedman, Claire. 2011. (ENG.). 20p. (J). (gr. k — 1). bds. 8.99 *(978-0-545-27432-6(X),* Cartwheel Bks.) Scholastic, Inc.

—You're My Little Bunny. Freedman, Claire. 2010. (ENG.). 20p. (J). (gr. k — 1). bds. 8.99 *(978-0-545-20721-8(5),* Cartwheel Bks.) Scholastic, Inc.

Scott, Greg. X Isle, Vol.1. Cosby, Andrew & Nelson, Michael Alan. 2007. (ENG.). 128p. per. 14.99 *(978-1-934506-09-7(5))* Boom! Studios.

Scott, Greg & Ross, Dave. Captain America by Dan Jurgens, Vol. 2. Scott, Greg. 2011. (ENG.). 280p. (YA). (gr. 8-17). pap. 29.99 *(978-0-7851-5540-9(6))* Marvel Worldwide, Inc.

Scott, Jane Beecher. The Amazing Mosquito Bridge Secret. Scott, Jane Beecher, photos by. Scott, Jane Beecher. Scott, Jane Beecher, ed. 5th ed. 2004. 32p. (J). (gr. k-12). 12.95 *(978-0-9763077-0-9(7))* Beecher Scott.

Scott, Jane Wooster. Mitzi's World: Seek & Discover More Than 150 Details in 15 Works of Folk Art. Raffin, Deborah. 2009. (ENG.). 32p. (J). (gr. -1-3). 18.95 *(978-0-8109-8004-4(5),* Abrams Bks. for Young Readers) Abrams.

Scott, Jennifer. The Clumsiest Spider. Harney Jr., Robert. 2011. 44p. pap. 24.95 *(978-1-4626-2166-8(X))* America Star Bks.

Scott, Jonathan. Big Cat Babies. Scott, Johnathan & Scott, Angela. Moon, Cliff, ed. 2005. (Collins Big Cat Ser.). (ENG.). 24p. (J). pap. 6.99 *(978-0-00-718594-8(4))* HarperCollins Pubs. Ltd. GBR. Dist: Independent Pubs. Group.

Scott, Jonathan & Scott, Angela. Africa's Big Three. Scott, Jonathan & Scott, Angela. 2006. (Collins Big Cat Ser.). (ENG.). 24p. (J). pap. 6.99 *(978-0-00-718693-8(2))* HarperCollins Pubs. Ltd. GBR. Dist: Independent Pubs. Group.

—Kings of the Wild. Scott, Jonathan & Scott, Angela. 2007. (Collins Big Cat Ser.). (ENG.). 384p. (J). pap. 8.99 *(978-0-00-723085-3(0))* HarperCollins Pubs. Ltd. GBR. Dist: Independent Pubs. Group.

—Living Dinosaurs. Scott, Jonathan & Scott, Angela. 2007. (Collins Big Cat Ser.). (ENG.). 48p. (J). pap. 6.99 *(978-0-00-718673-0(8))* HarperCollins Pubs. Ltd. GBR. Dist: Independent Pubs. Group.

—The Masai: Tribe of Warriors. Scott, Jonathan & Scott, Angela. 2007. (Collins Big Cat Ser.). (ENG.). 48p. (J). pap. 8.99 *(978-0-00-723097-6(4))* HarperCollins Pubs. Ltd. GBR. Dist: Independent Pubs. Group.

Scott, Judy. Can Daddy Stay Home & Play? Floyd, Gina. 2011. 28p. pap. 12.99 *(978-1-4567-1373-7(6))* AuthorHouse.

Scott, Julie. The Little Creek. Ward, Jennifer. 2005. 28p. (J). (gr. 3-7). pap. 7.95 *(978-1-58369-057-4(3))* Western National Parks Assn.

Scott, Katie. Animalium. Broom, Jenny. 2014. (ENG.). 112p. (J). (gr. 3-7). 35.00 *(978-0-7636-7508-0(3),* Big Picture Press) Candlewick Pr.

Scott, Kimberley. Cinderella: A Wheel-Y Silly Fairy Tale. Gallo, Tina. 2011. (Little Simon Sillies Ser.). (ENG.). 14p. (J). (gr. -1-1). lib. bdg. 5.99 *(978-1-4424-2106-6(1),* Little Simon) Little Simon.

—Rise & Shine: A Challah-Day Tale. Ostrove, Karen. 2013. (Shabbat Ser.). (ENG.). 24p. (J). (gr. -1-3). 7.95 *(978-0-7613-7500-5(7));* lib. bdg. 17.95 *(978-0-7613-7499-2(X))* Lerner Publishing Group. (Kar-Ben Publishing).

—The Terrible Time Without Tilly. McKay, Hilary. 2014. (Red Bananas Ser.). (ENG.). 48p. (J). (gr. k-2). pap. 5.99 *(978-1-4052-6080-0(7))* Egmont Bks., Ltd. GBR. Dist: Independent Pubs. Group.

—Wipe-Clean First Math. 2014. (ENG.). (J). (gr. k-4). pap. 7.99 *(978-0-7945-3354-0(X),* Usborne) EDC Publishing.

—Wipe-Clean First Words. 2014. (ENG.). (J). (gr. k-2). pap. 7.99 *(978-0-7945-3331-1(0),* Usborne) EDC Publishing.

—Wipe-Clean Telling the Time. Greenwell, Jessica. 2013. (Usborne Wipe-Clean Ser.). (ENG.). 20p. (J). (gr. -1-3). pap. 7.99 *(978-0-7945-3403-5(1),* Usborne) EDC Publishing.

Scott, Kimberley, jt. illus. see Francis, John.

Scott, Kimberley G., jt. illus. see Shaw, Mick.

Scott, Kimberly & Dean, Venetia. Make It Boom!, 1 vol. Claybourne, Anna. 2014. (Whiz Kid Science Ser.). (ENG.). 32p. (gr. 2-4). 29.32 *(978-1-4109-6745-9(X),* Read Me!) Heinemann-Raintree.

—Make It Change!, 1 vol. Claybourne, Anna. 2014. (Whiz Kid Science Ser.). (ENG.). 32p. (gr. 2-4). 29.32 *(978-1-4109-6746-6(8),* Read Me!) Heinemann-Raintree.

—Make It Glow!, 1 vol. Claybourne, Anna. 2014. (Whiz Kid Science Ser.). (ENG.). 32p. (gr. 2-4). 29.32 *(978-1-4109-6747-3(6),* Read Me!) Heinemann-Raintree.

—Make It Grow!, 1 vol. Claybourne, Anna. 2014. (Whiz Kid Science Ser.). (ENG.). 32p. (gr. 2-4). 29.32 *(978-1-4109-6748-0(4),* Read Me!) Heinemann-Raintree.

—Make It Splash!, 1 vol. Claybourne, Anna. 2014. (Whiz Kid Science Ser.). (ENG.). 32p. (gr. 2-4). 29.32 *(978-1-4109-6749-7(2),* Read Me!) Heinemann-Raintree.

—Make It Zoom!, 1 vol. Claybourne, Anna. 2014. (Whiz Kid Science Ser.). (ENG.). 32p. (gr. 2-4). 29.32 *(978-1-4109-6750-3(6),* Read Me!) Heinemann-Raintree.

—Whiz Kid Science, 1 vol. Claybourne, Anna. 2014. (Whiz Kid Science Ser.). (ENG.). 32p. (gr. 2-4). 175.92 *(978-1-4109-6751-0(4),* Read Me!) Heinemann-Raintree.

Scott, Korey. The Energy Bus for Kids: A Story about Staying Positive & Overcoming Challenges. Gordon, Jon. 2012. (ENG.). 48p. (J). 17.00 *(978-1-118-28735-4(5),* Wiley) Wiley, John & Sons, Inc.

—Eric & the Enchanted Leaf: A Night with Echo. Frontiera, Deborah. 2007.Tr. of Eric y la hojita encantada: una noche con Eco. (SPA.). 32p. (J). *(978-0-9795474-2-3(3))* KAM Publishing.

—Eric & the Enchanted Leaf: The First Adventure, Frontiera, Deborah K. 2nd I.t. ed. 2004. 32p. (J). pap. 16.95 *(978-0-9753410-0-1(6))* Jade Enterprises.

—Eric & the Enchanted Leaf / Eric y la Hoja Encantada: A Visit with Canis Lupis / una Visita con Canis Lupis. Frontiera, Deborah K. Santilian-Cruz, Silvia R., tr. 2nd I.t. ed. 2005. (SPA & ENG.). 32p. (J). lib. bdg. 16.95 *(978-0-9663629-8-5(5))* By Grace Enterprises.

—How Do We Stay on Earth? A Gravity Mystery, 1 vol. Hansen, Amy S. 2011. (First Graphics: Science Mysteries Ser.). (ENG.). 24p. (gr. 1-2). pap. 6.29 *(978-1-4296-7174-3(2));* pap. 35.70 *(978-1-4296-7178-1(5));* lib. bdg. 23.32 *(978-1-4296-6097-6(X))* Capstone Pr., Inc.

—A Sharefish Tale: A Story about Learning to Share. Osterkamp, Ole. 2011. (ENG.). 32p. pap. 11.11 *(978-1-4609-7307-3(0))* CreateSpace Independent Publishing Platform.

—Where Does the Sun Go at Night? An Earth Science Mystery, 1 vol. Hansen, Amy S. 2011. (First Graphics: Science Mysteries Ser.). (ENG.). 24p. (gr. 1-2). pap. 6.29 *(978-1-4296-7176-7(9));* pap. 35.70 *(978-1-4296-7180-4(7));* lib. bdg. 23.32 *(978-1-4296-6098-3(8))* Capstone Pr., Inc.

Scott, Korey & McDee, Katie. First Graphics: Science Mysteries. Hansen, Amy S. & Olien, Rebecca. 2011. (First Graphics: Science Mysteries Ser.). (ENG.). 24p. (gr. 1-2). lib. bdg. 93.28 *(978-1-4296-6099-0(6))* Capstone Pr., Inc.

—First Graphics: Science Mysteries: A Science Mystery. Hansen, Amy S. & Olien, Rebecca. 2011. (First Graphics: Science Mysteries Ser.). (ENG.). 24p. (gr. 1-2). pap. 25.16 *(978-1-4296-7181-1(5));* pap. 142.80 *(978-1-4296-7182-8(3))* Capstone Pr., Inc.

Scott, Larry. Patsy Goes to a New Home: The Patsy Adventures Volume 1. Russell, Peggy. 2008. 16p. pap. 24.95 *(978-1-60703-799-6(8))* America Star Bks.

Scott, Marc. We Both Read-the Oprah Winfrey Story. McKay, Sindy. 2009. 44p. (J). (gr. 1-5). 9.95 *(978-1-60115-241-1(8))* Treasure Bay, Inc.

Scott, Maren J. The Christmas Pageant. Heno, Christy C. 2007. 32p. (J). (gr. -1-3). 17.00 *(978-0-687-46630-6(X))* Abingdon Pr.

Scott, Peter. Birds Lift-the-Flap. Khan, Sarah. 2004. (Luxury Lift-the-Flap Ser.). 16p. (J). (gr. 1-18). 11.95 *(978-0-7945-0714-5(X),* Usborne) EDC Publishing.

—Creepy Crawlies Lift-the-Flap. Khan, Sarah. 2005. (Luxury Lift-the-Flap Learners Ser.). 16p. (J). (gr. 1-18). 11.95 *(978-0-7945-0763-3(8),* Usborne) EDC Publishing.

—Los Dinosaurios Con Cuatro Puzzles Sencillos. Turnbull, Stephanie. 2004. (Titles in Spanish Ser.). (SPA.). 6p. (J). 8.95 *(978-0-7460-6109-1(9),* Usborne) EDC Publishing.

—Dinosaurs. Greenwell, Jessica. 2010. (Lift & Look Board Bks.). 12p. (J). bds. 9.99 *(978-0-7945-2585-9(7),* Usborne) EDC Publishing.

—Dragons Jigsaw Book. Tatchell, Judy & Rogers, Kirsteen. 2005. (Usborne Jigsaw Bks.). 12p. (J). (gr. -1-3). bds. 14.95 *(978-0-7945-1117-3(1),* Usborne) EDC Publishing.

—Dragons Lift-the-flap. Tatchell, Judy. 2005. 16p. (J). (gr. 1-18). 11.99 *(978-0-7945-0968-2(1),* Usborne) EDC Publishing.

—See Inside the World of Dinosaurs. Frith, Alex. 2007. 16p. (J). bds. 13.99 *(978-0-7945-1436-5(7),* Usborne) EDC Publishing.

—Under the Sea Jigsaw Book. Rogers, Kirsteen. 2007. (Luxury Jigsaw Bks.). 14p. (J). bds. 14.99 *(978-0-7945-1330-6(1),* Usborne) EDC Publishing.

—Unicorns. Clarke, Phillip. 2006. (Luxury Lift-the-Flap Learners Ser.). 16p. (J). (gr. -1-3). 11.99 *(978-0-7945-1280-4(1),* Usborne) EDC Publishing.

Scott, Peter & JessT, Grant. Clarissa the Clown. Segal, Andrew. 2007. 32p. per. *(978-1-905823-20-8(7))* Panoma Pr. Ltd.

—Roberto the Robot. Segal, Andrew. 2007. 32p. per. *(978-1-905823-26-0(6))* Panoma Pr. Ltd.

Scott, Peter & Justine, Torode. Box of Bugs. 2005. 6p. (J). 11.95 *(978-0-7945-1023-7(X),* Usborne) EDC Publishing.

Scott, Peter David. The A to Z Book of Wild Animals: An Alphabet Adventure. 2012. (ENG.). 64p. (J). (gr. -1). 16.95 *(978-1-60710-592-3(6),* Silver Dolphin Bks.) Baker & Taylor Publishing Group.

—Amazing Animals: A Nature Adventure. 2015. (Peter David Scott Ser.). (ENG.). 64p. (J). (gr. -1). 16.95 *(978-1-62686-323-1(7),* Silver Dolphin Bks.) Baker & Taylor Publishing Group.

—Creepy Crawlies. Kahn, Sarah. 2006. (J). *(978-0-439-78702-4(5))* Scholastic, Inc.

—Dinosaur. 2006. 31p. (J). *(978-0-7607-7524-0(9))* backpackbooks.

—Dinosaurs. Smith, Alastair & Tatchell, Judy. 2005. (J). *(978-0-439-68903-8(1))* Scholastic, Inc.

—Sharks. Clarke, Phillip & Furnival, Keith. 2005. (J). *(978-0-439-86358-2(9))* Scholastic, Inc.

—Under the Sea. Smith, Alastair & Tachell, Judy. 2007. (J). *(978-0-545-03305-3(5))* Scholastic, Inc.

Scott, Peter David & Furnival, Keith. Dragons. Tatchell, Judy. 2006. (J). *(978-0-439-82790-4(6))* Scholastic, Inc.

Scott, Richard, jt. illus. see Denham, Gemma.

Scott, Rose Marie. Gentle Ones. Scott, Rose Marie. 2003. 60p. (J). lib. bdg. 22.95 *(978-1-59098-395-9(5))* Wooster Bk. Co., The.

Scott, Rosseau. The Snow That Just Wouldn't Stop. Ivan, Benson. 2008. 24p. (J). pap. 8.95 *(978-0-9774754-4-5(1))* Spiritbuilding.

Scott, Sarah C. Why Dogs Bark: & Other Tall Tales. Day, Ed D. 2006. 50p. (J). per. 12.95 *(978-1-933002-20-0(4))* PublishingWorks.

Scott, Sarah Chamberlin. Don't Slam the Door. Green, Holly G. 2005. (ENG.). 39p. (J). (gr. 2-7). 19.95 *(978-0-9744803-7-4(1))* PublishingWorks.

Scott, Steve. Even a Hawkeye Can Cry. Parker, Jeff. 2014. (Avengers Set 4 Ser.). (ENG.). 24p. (J). (gr. 9-14). lib. bdg. 24.21 *(978-1-61479-296-3(8))* Spotlight.

—Indiana Jones & the Tomb of the Gods, 2 vols., Vol. 2. Williams, Rob. 2010. (Indiana Jones Ser.: No. 2). 24p. (J). (gr. 5-9). 24.21 *(978-1-59961-658-2(0))* Spotlight.

—Parrot in the Oven. Martinez, Victor. rev. ed. 2004. (ENG.). 240p. (YA). (gr. 8-18). pap. 8.99 *(978-0-06-447186-2(1),* Rayo) HarperCollins Pubs.

Scott, Susan. An Amazing Adventure Back in Time. Cohen-Spence, Susan. 2013. 32p. pap. 14.99 *(978-0-9886360-4-0(2))* Kids At Heart Publishing & Bks.

—Gypsy. O'Connell, Isabel. 2012. 24p. pap. 12.99 *(978-0-9855202-8-1(0))* Kids At Heart Publishing & Bks.

Scott, Trevor. My Life in Miniature. Simone, Gail. rev. ed. 2007. (All New Atom Ser.). (ENG.). 160p. (YA). pap. 14.99 *(978-1-4012-1325-1(1))* DC Comics.

Scott-Waters, Marilyn, jt. illus. see Everett, J. H.

Scotton, Rob. Back to School, Splat! Scotton, Rob. 2011. (Splat the Cat Ser.). (ENG.). 24p. (J). (gr. -1-3). pap. 3.99 *(978-0-06-197851-7(5),* HarperFestival) HarperCollins Pubs.

—The Big Helper. Scotton, Rob. 2015. (Splat the Cat Ser.). (ENG.). 24p. (J). (gr. -1-3). pap. 3.99 *(978-0-06-229427-2(X),* HarperFestival) HarperCollins Pubs.

—Doodle & Draw. Scotton, Rob. 2013. (Splat the Cat Ser.). (ENG.). 64p. (J). (gr. -1-3). pap. 6.99 *(978-0-06-211607-9(X),* HarperFestival) HarperCollins Pubs.

—Funny Valentine. Scotton, Rob. 2012. (Splat the Cat Ser.). (ENG.). 16p. (J). (gr. -1-3). pap. 6.99 *(978-0-06-197862-3(0),* HarperFestival) HarperCollins Pubs.

—I Scream for Ice Cream. Scotton, Rob. 2015. (I Can Read Book 1 Ser.). (ENG.). 32p. (J). (gr. -1-3). 16.99 *(978-0-06-229419-7(9))* HarperCollins Pubs.

—Love, Splat. Scotton, Rob. (Splat the Cat Ser.). (ENG.). 40p. (J). (gr. -1-2). 2011. 9.99 *(978-0-06-207776-9(7));* 2008. 16.99 *(978-0-06-083157-8(X))* HarperCollins Pubs.

—Merry Christmas, Splat. Scotton, Rob. (Splat the Cat Ser.). 40p. (J). (gr. -1-2). 2013. (ENG.). 9.99 *(978-0-06-212450-0(1));* 2009. (ENG.). 16.99 *(978-0-06-083160-8(X));* 2009. lib. bdg. 17.89 *(978-0-06-083161-5(8))* HarperCollins Pubs.

—The Name of the Game. Scotton, Rob. 2012. (I Can Read Book 1 Ser.). (ENG.). 32p. (J). (gr. -1-3). 16.99 *(978-0-06-209015-7(1))* HarperCollins Pubs.

—On with the Show. Scotton, Rob. 2013. (Splat the Cat Ser.). (ENG.). 24p. (J). (gr. -1-3). pap. 3.99 *(978-0-06-209010-2(0),* HarperFestival) HarperCollins Pubs.

—Oopsie-Daisy. Scotton, Rob. 2014. (Splat the Cat Ser.). (ENG.). 24p. (J). (gr. -1-3). pap. 4.99 *(978-0-06-211585-0(5),* HarperFestival) HarperCollins Pubs.

—The Perfect Present for Mom & Dad. Scotton, Rob. 2012. (Splat the Cat Ser.). (ENG.). 24p. (J). (gr. k-3). pap. 4.99 *(978-0-06-210009-2(2),* HarperFestival) HarperCollins Pubs.

—The Rain Is a Pain. Scotton, Rob. 2012. (I Can Read Book 1 Ser.). (ENG.). 32p. (J). (gr. -1-3). pap. 3.99 *(978-0-06-209017-1(8))* HarperCollins Pubs.

—Russell & the Lost Treasure. Scotton, Rob. 2006. (ENG.). 32p. (J). (gr. -1-2). 15.99 *(978-0-06-059851-8(4))* HarperCollins Pubs.

Scotton, Rob. Russell the Sheep. Scotton, Rob. (ENG.). (J). (gr. -1-3). 2015. 32p. pap. 5.99 ***(978-0-06-239243-5(3),*** HarperFestival); 2011. 32p. pap. 6.99 *(978-0-06-059850-1(6));* 2009. 32p. bds. 7.99 *(978-0-06-170996-8(4),* HarperFestival); 2007. 16p. 9.99 *(978-0-06-128434-2(3));* 2005. 32p. 17.99 *(978-0-06-059848-8(4))* HarperCollins Pubs.

Scotton, Rob. Russell's Christmas Magic. Scotton, Rob. 2007. 32p. (J). (gr. -1-2). lib. bdg. 17.89 *(978-0-06-059855-6(7))* HarperCollins Pubs.

Scotton, Rob. Scaredy-Cat, Splat! Scotton, Rob. (Splat the Cat Ser.). 40p. (J). (gr. -1-3). 2015. (ENG.). 9.99 ***(978-0-06-236897-3(4));*** 2010. (ENG.). 16.99 *(978-0-06-117760-6(1));* 2010. lib. bdg. 17.89 *(978-0-06-117761-3(X))* HarperCollins Pubs.

Scotton, Rob. Secret Agent Splat! Scotton, Rob. 2012. (Splat the Cat Ser.). 40p. (J). (gr. -1-2). (ENG.). 16.99 *(978-0-06-197871-5(X));* lib. bdg. 17.89 *(978-0-06-197872-2(8))* HarperCollins Pubs.

—Sings Flat. Scotton, Rob. 2011. (I Can Read Book 1 Ser.). (ENG.). 32p. (J). (gr. -1-3). 16.99 *(978-0-06-197854-8(X))* HarperCollins Pubs.

—Splat & the Cool School Trip. Scotton, Rob. 2013. (Splat the Cat Ser.). (ENG.). 40p. (J). (gr. -1-3). 17.99 *(978-0-06-213386-1(1))* HarperCollins Pubs.

—Splat Says Thank You! Scotton, Rob. 2012. (Splat the Cat Ser.). (ENG.). 40p. (J). (gr. -1-3). 16.99 *(978-0-06-197874-6(4))* HarperCollins Pubs.

—Splat the Cat. Scotton, Rob. 2008. (Splat the Cat Ser.). 40p. (J). (gr. -1-3). (ENG.). 16.99 *(978-0-06-083154-7(5));* lib. bdg. 17.89 *(978-0-06-083155-4(3))* HarperCollins Pubs.

—Splat the Cat: A Whale of a Tale. Scotton, Rob. 2013. (I Can Read Book 1 Ser.). (ENG.). 32p. (J). (gr. -1-3). 16.99 *(978-0-06-209024-9(0))* HarperCollins Pubs.

—Splat the Cat: And the Snowy Day Surprise. Scotton, Rob. 2014. (Splat the Cat Ser.). (ENG.). 16p. (J). (gr. -1-3). pap. 6.99 *(978-0-06-197864-7(7),* HarperFestival) HarperCollins Pubs.

—Splat the Cat: Big Reading Collection. Scotton, Rob. 2012. (I Can Read Book 1 Ser.). (ENG.). 100p. (J). (gr. k-3). pap. 16.99 *(978-0-06-209029-4(1))* HarperCollins Pubs.

—Splat the Cat: Blow, Snow, Blow. Scotton, Rob. 2013. (I Can Read Book 1 Ser.). (ENG.). 32p. (J). (gr. -1-3). 16.99 *(978-0-06-209026-3(7));* pap. 3.99 *(978-0-06-209027-0(5))* HarperCollins Pubs.

—Splat the Cat: Splat & Seymour, Best Friends Forevermore. Scotton, Rob. 2014. (I Can Read Book 1 Ser.). (ENG.). 32p. (J). (gr. -1-3). pap. 3.99 *(978-0-06-211601-7(0))* HarperCollins Pubs.

Scotton, Rob. Splat the Cat: Twice the Mice. Scotton, Rob. 2015. (I Can Read Book 1 Ser.). (ENG.). 32p. (J). (gr. -1-3). pap. 3.99 ***(978-0-06-229421-0(0))*** HarperCollins Pubs.

Scotton, Rob. Splat the Cat: Up in the Air at the Fair. Scotton, Rob. 2014. (I Can Read Book 1 Ser.). (ENG.). 32p. (J). (gr. -1-3). pap. 3.99 *(978-0-06-211595-9(2))* HarperCollins Pubs.

—Splat the Cat: What Was That? Scotton, Rob. deluxe ed. 2013. (Splat the Cat Ser.). (ENG.). 16p. (J). (gr. k-3). pap. 6.99 *(978-0-06-197863-0(9),* HarperFestival) HarperCollins Pubs.

—Splat the Cat - Fishy Tales. Scotton, Rob. 2012. (Splat the Cat Ser.). (ENG.). 24p. (J). (gr. -1-3). pap. 3.99 *(978-0-06-197852-4(3),* HarperFestival) HarperCollins Pubs.

—Splat the Cat - I Scream for Ice Cream. Scotton, Rob. 2015. (I Can Read Book 1 Ser.). (ENG.). 32p. (J). (gr. -1-3). pap. 3.99 *(978-0-06-229418-0(0))* HarperCollins Pubs.

—Splat the Cat - Sticker Fun. Scotton, Rob. 2013. (Splat the Cat Ser.). (ENG.). 100p. (J). (gr. -1-3). pap. 12.99 *(978-0-06-211594-2(4),* HarperFestival) HarperCollins Pubs.

—Splat the Cat - The Rain Is a Pain. Scotton, Rob. 2012. (I Can Read Book 1 Ser.). (ENG.). 32p. (J). (gr. -1-3). 16.99 *(978-0-06-209018-8(6))* HarperCollins Pubs.

S

Scotton, Rob. Splat the Cat - Twice the Mice. Scotton, Rob. 2015. (I Can Read Book 1 Ser.). (ENG.). 32p. (J). (gr. -1-3). 16.99 ***(978-0-06-229422-7(9))*** HarperCollins Pubs.

Scotton, Rob. Splat the Cat & the Duck with No Quack. Scotton, Rob. 2011. (I Can Read Book 1 Ser.). (ENG.). 32p. (J). (gr. k-3). 16.99 *(978-0-06-197858-6(2))*; pap. 3.99 *(978-0-06-197857-9(4))* HarperCollins Pubs.

—Splat the Cat & the Hotshot. Scotton, Rob. 2015. (I Can Read Book 1 Ser.). (ENG.). 32p. (J). (gr. -1-3). pap. 3.99 *(978-0-06-229415-9(6))* HarperCollins Pubs.

—Splat the Cat & the Pumpkin-Picking Plan. Scotton, Rob. 2014. (Splat the Cat Ser.). (ENG.). 24p. (J). (gr. -1-3). pap. 4.99 *(978-0-06-211586-7(3))* HarperCollins Pubs.

—Splat the Cat Dreams Big. Scotton, Rob. 2013. (Splat the Cat Ser.). (ENG.). 24p. (J). (gr. -1-3). pap. 3.99 *(978-0-06-209012-6(7))*, HarperFestival) HarperCollins Pubs.

—Splat the Cat Goes to the Doctor. Scotton, Rob. 2014. (Splat the Cat Ser.). (ENG.). 24p. (J). (gr. -1-3). pap. 4.99 *(978-0-06-211588-1(X))*, HarperFestival) HarperCollins Pubs.

—Splat the Cat Makes Dad Glad. Scotton, Rob. 2014. (I Can Read Book 1 Ser.). (ENG.). 32p. (J). (gr. -1-3). 16.99 *(978-0-06-211599-7(5))*; pap. 3.99 *(978-0-06-211597-3(9))* HarperCollins Pubs.

—Splat the Cat Sings Flat. Scotton, Rob. 2011. (I Can Read Book 1 Ser.). (ENG.). 32p. (J). (gr. -1-3). pap. 3.99 *(978-0-06-197853-1(1))* HarperCollins Pubs.

—Splat the Cat Storybook Collection. Scotton, Rob. 2013. (Splat the Cat Ser.). (ENG.). 192p. (J). (gr. -1-3). 11.99 *(978-0-06-213383-0(7))* HarperCollins Pubs.

—Splat the Cat Takes the Cake. Scotton, Rob. 2012. (I Can Read Book 1 Ser.). (ENG.). 32p. (J). (gr. k-3). 16.99 *(978-0-06-197860-9(4))*; pap. 3.99 *(978-0-06-197859-3(0))* HarperCollins Pubs.

—Splat the Cat Treasure Box. Scotton, Rob. 2011. (Splat the Cat Ser.). (ENG.). (J). (gr. k-3). pap. 15.99 *(978-0-06-210010-8(6))* HarperCollins Pubs.

—Splat the Cat with a Bang & a Clang. Scotton, Rob. 2013. (I Can Read Book 1 Ser.). (ENG.). 32p. (J). (gr. -1-3). 16.99 *(978-0-06-209021-8(6))* HarperCollins Pubs.

—Splish, Splash, Splat! Scotton, Rob. 2011. (Splat the Cat Ser.). 40p. (J). (gr. -1-3). (ENG.). 16.99 *(978-0-06-197868-5(X))*; lib. bdg. 17.89 *(978-0-06-197869-2(8))* HarperCollins Pubs.

—Up in the Air at the Fair. Scotton, Rob. 2014. (I Can Read Book 1 Ser.). (ENG.). 32p. (J). (gr. -1-3). 16.99 *(978-0-06-211596-6(0))* HarperCollins Pubs.

—A Whale of a Tale. Scotton, Rob. 2013. (I Can Read Book 1 Ser.). (ENG.). 32p. (J). (gr. -1-3). pap. 3.99 *(978-0-06-209022-5(4))* HarperCollins Pubs.

—Where's the Easter Bunny? Scotton, Rob. 2011. (Splat the Cat Ser.). (ENG.). 16p. (J). (gr. -1-1). pap. 6.99 *(978-0-06-197861-6(2))*, HarperFestival) HarperCollins Pubs.

Scotton, Rob & Eberz, Robert. Good Night, Sleep Tight. Scotton, Rob. 2011. (I Can Read Book 1 Ser.). (ENG.). 32p. (J). (gr. -1-3). pap. 3.99 *(978-0-06-197855-5(8))* HarperCollins Pubs.

—Splat the Cat: Good Night, Sleep Tight. Scotton, Rob. 2011. (I Can Read Book 1 Ser.). (ENG.). 32p. (J). (gr. -1-3). 16.99 *(978-0-06-197856-2(6))* HarperCollins Pubs.

Scottorosano, Deborah. The Gift of Rainbows. Columbro, Judy. 2011. 24p. pap. 24.95 *(978-1-4626-0355-8(6))* PublishAmerica, Inc.

—The Gift That Grows. Columbro, Judy. 2011. 28p. pap. 24.95 *(978-1-4626-1800-2(6))* America Star Bks.

Scrace, Carolyn, jt. illus. see Salariya, David.

Scrambly, Crab. The Floods #2: School Plot. Thompson, Colin. 2008. (Floods Ser.). (J). (ENG.). 224p. 15.99 *(978-0-06-113861-4(4))*; 256p. lib. bdg. 16.89 *(978-0-06-113855-3(X))* HarperCollins Pubs.

—Good Neighbors. Thompson, Colin. 2008. (Floods Ser.: No. 1). 214p. (J). (gr. 3-7). 15.99 *(978-0-06-113196-7(2))* HarperCollins Pubs.

Scratchmann, Max. The Teeth. Durant, Alan. 2014. (Collins Big Cat Progress Ser.). (ENG.). 32p. (J). pap. 7.99 *(978-0-00-751933-0(8))* HarperCollins Pubs. Ltd. GBR. Dist: Independent Pubs. Group.

Scribner, Carol A., photos by. To Life in the Small Corners, Scribner, Carol A. 2005. 232p. 48.00 *(978-0-9752936-0-7(5))* Butterfly Productions, LLC.

Scribner, Joanne & Pham, LeUyen. A Father Like That. Zolotow, Charlotte. 2007. (ENG.). 40p. (J). (gr. -1-3). 16.99 *(978-0-06-027864-9(1))* HarperCollins Pubs.

Scribner, Peter. Bennie & Thomas & the Rescue at Razor's Edge: Volume I. Scribner, Don. 2012. 44p. pap. 24.95 *(978-1-4626-8957-6(4))* America Star Bks.

—Bennie & Thomas & the Rescue at Razor's Edge: Volume II. Scribner, Don. 2012. 48p. pap. 24.95 *(978-1-4626-9472-3(1))* America Star Bks.

Scruggs, Trina. Pinky & Peanut: The Adventure Begins. Cook, Deena & McIntosh, Cherie. 2007. 78p. (J). per. 4.99 *(978-0-9797020-0-6(3))* P & P Publishing LLC.

Scruton, Clive. Dead Trouble. Gray, Keith. 90p. (J). pap. 7.50 *(978-0-7497-4556-1(8))* Egmont Bks., Ltd. GBR. Dist: Trafalgar Square Publishing.

—Zack Can Fix It!, Vol. 4. Goldish, Meish. l.t. ed. 2005. (Sadlier Phonics Reading Program). 8p. (gr. -1-1). 23.00 net. *(978-0-8215-7359-4(4))* Sadlier, William H. Inc.

Scull, Marie-Louise. The Skit Book: 101 Skits from Kids. MacDonald, Margaret. 2006. (ENG.). 160p. (J). (gr. -1-12). per. 17.95 *(978-0-87483-785-8(5))* August Hse. Pubs., Inc.

Seabaugh, Jan. Where Does the Water Come From? Shookuhi, Aminjon. Khodjibaev, Karim & Khodjibaeva, Moukhabbat, trs. 2009. 88p. (J). pap. 15.95 *(978-0-9740551-2-1(3))* Smith, Viveca Publishing.

Seabaugh, Jan. Doctor Ouch. Seabaugh, Jan, tr. Chukovsky, Kornei. 2004. (Children's International Ser.: 1). Orig. Title: Aibolit. 43p. (J). pap. 6.99 *(978-0-9740551-0-7(7))* Smith, Viveca Publishing.

Seabrooks, Lydia. The ed up Platypus. Young, Elizabeth. 2011. 20p. pap. 24.95 *(978-1-4560-7028-1(2))* America Star Bks.

Seager, Maryann, et al. Sara Safety, School Safety: Kid's Activity Book. LaBerge, Margaret M. 2004. (J). pap. 9.95 *(978-0-9755561-1-5(8))* Reading Resc.

Seahorse, Risa. In the Swamp, Oh Yeah, in the Swamp. Ryan, Ruth. 2012. 54p. pap. *(978-1-55483-922-3(X))* Insomniac Pr.

Seaman, Paul. Feng Suey's Special Garden. Bell, Frank. 2004. 24p. pap. 7.00 *(978-1-84161-071-9(2))* Ravette Publishing, Ltd. GBR. Dist: Parkwest Pubns., Inc.

—How Slip Slap Slop Got His Name. Bell, Frank. 2004. 24p. pap. 7.00 *(978-1-84161-069-6(0))* Ravette Publishing, Ltd. GBR. Dist: Parkwest Pubns., Inc.

—Ma Jong & the Magic Carpet. Bell, Frank. 2004. 24p. pap. 7.00 *(978-1-84161-070-2(4))* Ravette Publishing, Ltd. GBR. Dist: Parkwest Pubns., Inc.

—Panda Patrol Go on Holiday. Bell, Frank & Bowler, Colin. 2004. 24p. pap. 7.00 *(978-1-84161-083-2(6))* Ravette Publishing, Ltd. GBR. Dist: Parkwest Pubns., Inc.

—Panda Patrol to the Rescue. Bell, Frank. 2004. 24p. pap. 7.00 *(978-1-84161-068-9(2))* Ravette Publishing, Ltd. GBR. Dist: Parkwest Pubns., Inc.

—Panda Power. Bell, Frank & Bowler, Colin. 2004. 24p. pap. 7.00 *(978-1-84161-084-9(4))* Ravette Publishing, Ltd. GBR. Dist: Parkwest Pubns., Inc.

Seamans, Amanda. Endangered Species & Friends in the U. S. A. Scott, Karen. unabr. ed. Date not set. (J). (gr. -1-6). 16.95 *(978-1-889667-00-3(5))* Second Ark Pubns.

Seapics.com Staff, photos by. Out of the Blue: A Journey Through the World's Oceans. Horsman, Paul. 2005. (ENG., 160p. (gr. 17). 32.00 *(978-0-262-08341-6(8))*, 026208341B) MIT Pr.

Searle, Ken. Australians All: A History of Growing up from the Ice Age to the Apology. Wheatley, Nadia. 2013. (ENG.). 280p. (J). (gr. 5-7). 45.99 *(978-1-74114-637-0(2))* Allen & Unwin AUS. Dist: Independent Pubs. Group.

—Playground: Listening to Stories from Country & from Inside the Heart. Wheatley, Nadia. 2010. (ENG.). 96p. (J). (gr. 3-7). 34.95 *(978-1-74237-097-2(7))* Allen & Unwin AUS. Dist: Independent Pubs. Group.

Searle, Ronald. Beast Friends Forever. Forbes, Robert L. 2013. (ENG.). 80p. (gr. 4-13). 19.95 *(978-1-59020-808-3(0))*, 902808) Overlook Pr., The.

—Beastly Feasts! A Mischievous Menagerie in Rhyme. Forbes, Robert L. 2007. (ENG.). 96p. (gr. 4-13). 19.95 *(978-1-58567-929-4(1))*, 856929) Overlook Pr., The.

—Let's Have a Bite! A Banquet of Beastly Rhymes. Forbes, Robert. 2010. (ENG.). 96p. (gr. 4-13). 19.95 *(978-1-59020-409-2(3))*, 902409) Overlook Pr., The.

Sears, Bart, et al. Blood on Snow, Vol. 2. Marz, Ron. 2003. (Path Ser.: Vol. 2). 160p. (YA). (gr. 7-18). pap. 15.95 *(978-1-931484-60-2(0))* CrossGeneration Comics, Inc.

—Death & Dishonor, Vol. 3. Marz, Ron. 2004. (Path Traveler Ser.: Vol. 3). 160p. (YA). pap. 9.95 *(978-1-59314-059-5(2))* CrossGeneration Comics, Inc.

—The Path, Vol. 3. Marz, Ron. 2003. (Path Ser.: Vol. 3). 160p. (YA). pap. 15.95 *(978-1-931484-88-6(0))* CrossGeneration Comics, Inc.

Sears, Bart. Sabretooth: Open Season. Way, Daniel. 2005. (Wolverine Ser.). 96p. pap. 9.99 *(978-0-7851-1507-6(2))* Marvel Worldwide, Inc.

Sears, Bart & Pennington, Mark. Crisis of Faith. Marz, Ron. 2003. (Path Traveler Ser.: Vol. 1). 192p. (YA). (gr. 7-18). pap. 9.95 *(978-1-59314-016-8(9))* CrossGeneration Comics, Inc.

Sears, Dovid. Rabbi Riddle Says... Look Who Dropped in for Yom Tov. Estrin, Leibel. 2005. (J). 10.95 *(978-1-931681-74-2(0))* Israel Bookshop Pubns.

Sears, Mary A. Vaulting: The Art of Gymnastics on Horseback. Sears, Mary A. Pakizer, Debi. Anderson, Julia & Barnette, Jackie, eds. 24p. (Orig.). (J). (gr. k-6). pap. 5.00 *(978-0-9639785-6-5(X))* Sears, M.A.

Seatter, Pamela. Dancer Girl M. C's Story: One Step at a Time. Douglass Thom, Kara. 2014. (Go! Go! Sports Girls Ser.). (ENG.). 32p. (J). (gr. k-2). pap. 4.99 *(978-1-940731-02-5(X))*, Go! Go! Sports Girls) Dream Big Toy Co.

—Gymnastics Girl Maya's Story: Becoming Brave. Douglass Thom, Kara. 2014. (Go! Go! Sports Girls Ser.). (ENG.). 32p. (J). (gr. k-2). pap. 4.99 *(978-1-940731-01-8(1))*, Go! Go! Sports Girls) Dream Big Toy Co.

—Soccer Girl Cassie's Story: Teamwork Is the Goal. Douglass Thom, Kara. 2014. (Go! Go! Sports Girls Ser.). (ENG.). 32p. (J). (gr. k-2). pap. 4.99 *(978-1-940731-00-1(3))*, Go! Go! Sports Girls) Dream Big Toy Co.

Seaver Keith, Emily. A Home for Webby. Seaver Keith, Emily. 2008. 23p. (J). (gr. -1-3). 16.95 *(978-0-9728646-1-9(X))* Bangzoom Pubs.

Seaworld, Chris, jt. illus. see Sharp, Chris.

Seay, Christina. Silly Sally Sometime. Savannah. 2007. 188p. per. 24.95 *(978-1-60441-451-6(0))* America Star Bks.

Seay, Dave. Baxter's Big Teeth, Counce, Betty. 2011. (ENG.). 34p. (J). 16.95 *(978-0-9833155-0-6(7))* Keepworthy Creations LLC.

Sebastian. The Abc's of Character. Cabanillas, Laura Sabin. 2009. 60p. pap. 12.95 *(978-0-9818488-2-2(6))* Ajoyin Publishing, Inc.

Sebastian Quigley, Sebastian. The Glow in the Dark Book of Space: The Book You Can Read in the Dark! Harris, Nicholas. 2013. (ENG.). 32p. (J). (gr. -1-2). 17.99 *(978-1-84780-417-4(9))*, Frances Lincoln) Quarto Publishing Group UK GBR. Dist: Hachette Bk. Group.

Sebastián, Soledad. Cantaba la Rana. Ruesga, Rita Rosa & Scholastic, Inc. Staff. ed. 2011. (SPA.). 32p. (J). (gr. -1-3). pap. 6.99 *(978-0-545-27357-2(9))*, Scholastic en Espanol) Scholastic, Inc.

Sebe, Masayuki. Let's Count to 100! Sebe, Masayuki. 2011. (ENG.). 24p. (J). (gr. -1-2). 16.95 *(978-1-55453-661-0(8))* Kids Can Pr., Ltd. CAN. Dist: Univ. of Toronto Pr.

—100 Animals on Parade! Sebe, Masayuki. 2013. (ENG.). 24p. (J). 16.95 *(978-1-55453-871-3(8))* Kids Can Pr., Ltd. CAN. Dist: Univ. of Toronto Pr.

—100 Hungry Monkeys!, 0 vols. Sebe, Masayuki. 2014. (ENG.). 24p. (J). 16.95 *(978-1-77138-045-4(4))* Kids Can Pr., Ltd. CAN. Dist: Univ. of Toronto Pr.

Sebern, Brian. Little Tree: A Story for Children with Serious Medical Illness. Mills, Joyce C. 2nd ed. 2003. 32p. (J). pap. 9.95 *(978-1-59147-042-7(0))*; 14.95 *(978-1-59147-041-0(2))* American Psychological Assn. (Magination Pr.).

Secchi, Riccardo. Ultraheroes Vol. 1: Save the World. Ghiglione, Marco. 2010. (Disney's Hero Squad Ser.). (ENG.). 112p. (J). pap. 9.99 *(978-1-60886-543-7(6))* Boom! Studios.

Secchi, Riccardo & Randoplh, Grace. Ultraheroes: Save the World. Ghiglione, Marco & Randolph, Grace. 2010. (Disney's Hero Squad Ser.: 1). (ENG.). 112p. (J). pap. 24.99 *(978-1-60886-552-9(5))* Boom! Studios.

Secheret, Jessica. Art-Rageous. Young, Jessica. 2015. (Finley Flowers Ser.). (ENG.). 128p. (gr. 2-3). 8.95 ***(978-1-4795-5960-2(1))*** Picture Window Bks.

Secheret, Jessica. Dolls of the World Coloring Book. 2012. (ENG.). 56p. (J). (gr. 1-4). 9.99 *(978-1-60905-264-5(1))* Blue Apple Bks.

—Kokeshi Dolls Coloring Book. 2012. (ENG.). 56p. (J). (gr. 1-4). 9.99 *(978-1-60905-222-5(6))* Blue Apple Bks.

—Nature Calls. Young, Jessica. 2015. (Finley Flowers Ser.). (ENG.). 128p. (gr. 2-3). 8.95 *(978-1-4795-5879-7(6))*, Finley Flowers) Picture Window Bks.

Secheret, Jessica. New & Improved. Young, Jessica. 2015. (Finley Flowers Ser.). (ENG.). 128p. (gr. 2-3). 8.95 ***(978-1-4795-5959-6(8))*** Picture Window Bks.

Secheret, Jessica. Original Recipe. Young, Jessica. 2015. (Finley Flowers Ser.). (ENG.). 128p. (gr. 2-3). 8.95 *(978-1-4795-5878-0(8))*, Finley Flowers) Picture Window Bks.

Seckel, Al. 50 Optical Illusions. Taplin, Sam. 2010. (Activity Cards Ser.). 50p. (J). 9.99 *(978-0-7945-2664-1(0))*, Usborne) EDC Publishing.

Second Story Press Staff, jt. illus. see Ammirati, Christelle.

Second Story Press Staff, jt. illus. see Benoit, Renne.

Second Story Press Staff, jt. illus. see Côté, Geneviève.

Second Story Press Staff, jt. illus. see Jovanovic, Vanja Vuleta.

Second Story Press Staff, jt. illus. see Leng, Qin.

Second Story Press Staff, jt. illus. see Newland, Gillian.

Second Story Press Staff, jt. illus. see Steele-Card, Adrianna.

Second Story Press Staff, jt. illus. see Thurman, Mark.

Seda, Alison. Dino Manners: Some Prehistoric Lessons Featuring Our Friends from the Cretaceous Period. Finch, Susan M. 2009. 32p. pap. 16.50 *(978-1-4490-5102-0(2))* AuthorHouse.

Sedalia, Rajan. In Search of Yourself Word Search Puzzles: Explorations into the Black Experience. Dunn, Kevin Ikim. 2005. (ENG.). 92p. per. 9.95 *(978-0-9767337-0-6(6))* Invision Pubns.

Seddon, Viola Anne. The Sleeping Beauty Ballet Theatre. Mahoney, Jean. 2007. (ENG.). 32p. (J). (gr. 1-4). 24.99 *(978-0-7636-3467-4(0))* Candlewick Pr.

—Swan Lake Ballet Theatre. Mahoney, Jean. 2009. (ENG.). 16p. (J). (gr. 1-4). 24.99 *(978-0-7636-4396-6(3))* Candlewick Pr.

Seder, Rufus Butler. Waddle! Seder, Rufus Butler. 2009. 12p. (J). *(978-0-7611-5720-5(4))* Workman Publishing Co., Inc.

Seeberger, Beverley. Razzle Dazzler. 2007. (J). per. 15.00 *(978-0-9713589-8-0(2))* Ubaviel's Gifts.

Seeger, Laura Vaccaro. Bully. Seeger, Laura Vaccaro. 2013. (ENG.). 36p. (J). (gr. -1-3). 16.99 *(978-1-59643-630-5(1))* Roaring Brook Pr.

—Dog & Bear: Three to Get Ready. Seeger, Laura Vaccaro. 2009. (Dog & Bear Ser.). (ENG.). 32p. (J). (gr. -1-2). 12.99 *(978-1-59643-396-0(5))* Roaring Brook Pr.

—Dog & Bear: Tricks & Treats. Seeger, Laura Vaccaro. 2014. (Dog & Bear Ser.). (ENG.). 32p. (J). (gr. -1-3). 14.99 *(978-1-59643-632-9(8))* Roaring Brook Pr.

—Dog & Bear: Two Friends, Three Stories. Seeger, Laura Vaccaro. 2007. (Dog & Bear Ser.). (ENG.). 32p. (J). (gr. -1-3). 14.99 *(978-1-59643-053-2(2))* Roaring Brook Pr.

—Dog & Bear: Two's Company. Seeger, Laura Vaccaro. 2008. (Dog & Bear Ser.). (ENG.). 32p. (J). (gr. -1-2). 12.95 *(978-1-59643-273-4(X))* Roaring Brook Pr.

—Dog & Bear, Level 2: Two Friends, Three Stories. Seeger, Laura Vaccaro. 2012. (My Readers Ser.). (ENG.). 32p. (J). (gr. k-2). pap. 3.99 *(978-0-312-54799-8(4))* Square Fish.

—First the Egg. Seeger, Laura Vaccaro. 2007. (ENG.). 32p. (J). (gr. -1-1). 15.99 *(978-1-59643-272-7(1))* Roaring Brook Pr.

—Green. Seeger, Laura Vaccaro. 2012. (ENG.). 36p. (J). (gr. -1-1). 16.99 *(978-1-59643-397-7(3))* Roaring Brook Pr.

—Lemons Are Not Red. Seeger, Laura Vaccaro. rev. ed. 2004. (ENG.). 32p. (J). (gr. -1-k). 16.99 *(978-1-59643-008-2(7))* Roaring Brook Pr.

—Lemons Are Not Red. Seeger, Laura Vaccaro. 2006. (ENG.). 32p. (J). (gr. -1-k). pap. 8.99 *(978-1-59643-195-9(4))* Square Fish.

—One Boy. Seeger, Laura Vaccaro. 2008. (ENG.). 48p. (J). (gr. -1-1). 18.99 *(978-1-59643-274-1(8))* Roaring Brook Pr.

—Walter Was Worried. Seeger, Laura Vaccaro. 2006. (ENG.). 40p. (J). (gr. -1-3). pap. 8.99 *(978-1-59643-196-6(2))* Square Fish.

—What If? Seeger, Laura Vaccaro. 2010. (ENG.). 32p. (J). (gr. -1-2). 15.99 *(978-1-59643-398-4(1))* Roaring Brook Pr.

Seeley, Douglas A. Sun & Ponies, Wind & Sky. Lidard, Kelly, photos by. Seeley, Bonnie L. 2004. 32p. (J). lib. bdg. 11.95 *(978-0-9728380-1-6(5))* Seelcraft Publishing.

Seeley, Douglas A., jt. illus. see Lidard, Kelly.

Seeley, Laura L. Un Colchón de Plumas para Ágata, 1 vol. Deedy, Carmen Agra. De la Torre, Cristina, tr. from ENG. 2007. (SPA.). 32p. (J). (gr. k-3). 15.95 *(978-1-56145-426-6(5))*; pap. 7.95 *(978-1-56145-404-4(4))* Peachtree Pubs.

Seeley, Scott & Potts, Sam. The 82NYC Review. New York City Students Staff. 2008. (826NYC Review Ser.: 3). (ENG.). 256p. (J). (gr. 3-12). pap. 14.00 *(978-0-9790073-6-1(4))* 826 Valencia.

Seeley, Terre Lamb. The Little Black Dog Buccaneer. Spooner, J. B. 2011. (Little Black Dog Ser.). (ENG.). 32p. (J). (gr. k-1). 16.95 *(978-1-61145-000-2(4))*, 611000, Arcade Publishing) Skyhorse Publishing Co., Inc.

—The Story of the Little Black Dog. Spooner, J. B. & Seaver, Richard. 2011. (Little Black Dog Ser.). (ENG.). 32p. (J). (gr. k-1). 16.95 *(978-1-61145-001-9(2))*, 611001, Arcade Publishing) Skyhorse Publishing Co., Inc.

Seeley, Terre Lamb. The Little Black Dog Has Puppies. Seeley, Terre Lamb. Spooner, J. B. 2011. (Little Black Dog Ser.). (ENG.). 32p. (J). (gr. k-1). 16.95 *(978-1-61145-006-4(3))*, 611006, Arcade Publishing) Skyhorse Publishing Co., Inc.

Seeley, Tim & Schulz, Barbara. Jason: Quest for the Golden Fleece, a Greek Myth. Limke, Jeff. 2008. (Graphic Myths & Legends Ser.). (ENG.). 48p. (gr. 4-8). per. 8.95 *(978-0-8225-6571-0(4))* Lerner Publishing Group.

Seelig, Renate. Mein Kleiner Brockhaus: Erste Woerter. 28p. (J). (gr. -1-18). *(978-3-7653-2561-8(9))* Brockhaus, F. A., GmbH DEU. Dist: International Bk. Import Service, Inc.

—Mein Kleiner Brockhaus: Jahreszeiten. (GER.). 28p. (J). (gr. -1-18). *(978-3-7653-2571-7(6))* Brockhaus, F. A., GmbH DEU. Dist: International Bk. Import Service, Inc.

Seely, Tim, et al. Jennifer's Body. Spears, Rick. 2009. (ENG.). 112p. 24.99 *(978-1-60886-501-7(0))* Boom! Studios.

Sefcik, Wendy. Gallery Eleven Twenty-Two. Brown, Tiffany M. 2013. 30p. 17.99 *(978-0-9854423-0-9(1))*; pap. 9.99 *(978-0-9854423-1-6(X))* Brewster Moon.

—J Mac Is the Freestyle King! Thomas, Terri. 2010. 38p. pap. 20.00 *(978-1-60844-453-3(8))* Dog Ear Publishing, LLC.

Segal, John. Sleepyhead. Wilson, Karma. 2012. (Classic Board Bks.). (ENG.). 32p. (J). (gr. -1 — 1). bds. 7.99 *(978-1-4424-3433-2(3))*, Little Simon) Little Simon.

—Sleepyhead. Wilson, Karma. 2006. (ENG.). 32p. (J). (gr. -1-2). 16.99 *(978-1-4169-1241-5(X))*, McElderry, Margaret K. Bks.) McElderry, Margaret K. Bks.

Segal, John. Alistair & Kip's Great Adventure! Segal, John. 2008. (ENG.). 32p. (J). (gr. -1-3). 17.99 *(978-1-4169-0280-5(5))*, McElderry, Margaret K. Bks.) McElderry, Margaret K. Bks.

—Carrot Soup. Segal, John. 2006. (ENG.). 32p. (J). (gr. -1-3). 17.99 *(978-0-689-87702-5(1))*, McElderry, Margaret K. Bks.) McElderry, Margaret K. Bks.

—Pirates Don't Take Baths. Segal, John. 2011. (ENG.). 32p. (J). (gr. -1-k). 16.99 *(978-0-399-25425-3(0))*, Philomel) Penguin Publishing Group.

Segarra, Angelo M. Coca Finds a Shell. Segarra, Angelo M. Segarra, Kirstie, ed. 2004. 24p. (J). 14.95 *(978-0-9752664-0-3(3))* Segarra, Angelo.

Segawa, Michael. Mackenzie Blue. Wells, Tina. 2009. (Mackenzie Blue Ser.: 1). (ENG.). 224p. (J). (gr. 3-7). 12.99 *(978-0-06-158308-7(1))* HarperCollins Pubs.

—Mackenzie Blue Vol. 5: Double Trouble. Wells, Tina. 2014. (Mackenzie Blue Ser.: 5). (ENG.). 224p. (J). (gr. 3-7). pap. 6.99 *(978-0-06-224412-3(4))* HarperCollins Pubs.

—The Secret Crush. Wells, Tina. 2009. (Mackenzie Blue Ser.: 2). (ENG.). 240p. (J). (gr. 3-7). 10.99 *(978-0-06-158311-7(1))* HarperCollins Pubs.

Segawa, Yasuo. Peek-A-Boo. Matsutani, Miyoko. 2006. 20p. (J). (gr. -1). 10.95 *(978-1-74126-047-2(7))* R.I.C. Pubns. AUS. Dist: SCB Distributors.

Segner, Ellen. The Wild Dog of Edmonton. Grew, David. 2011. 208p. 44.95 *(978-1-258-09902-2(0))* Literary Licensing, LLC.

Segovia, Carmen. Brownie Groundhog & the February Fox. Blackaby, Susan. 2011. (ENG.). 32p. (J). (gr. -1-2). 14.95 *(978-1-4027-4336-8(X))* Sterling Publishing Co., Inc.

—Brownie Groundhog & the Wintry Surprise. Blackaby, Susan. 2013. (ENG.). 32p. (J). (gr. -1). 14.95 *(978-1-4027-9836-8(9))* Sterling Publishing Co., Inc.

Segovia, Stephen, et al. Silver Surfer Devolution. 2011. (ENG.). 200p. (YA). (gr. 8-17). pap. 14.99 *(978-0-7851-5665-9(8))* Marvel Worldwide, Inc.

Seibold, J. Otto. Mind Your Manners, B. B. Wolf. Sierra, Judy. 2007. (ENG.). 40p. (J). (gr. -1-2). 16.99 *(978-0-375-83532-2(6))*, Knopf Bks. for Young Readers) Random Hse. Children's Bks.

—Mind Your Manners, B. B. Wolf. Sierra, Judy. 2012. (ENG.). 40p. (J). (gr. -1-3). pap. 7.99 *(978-0-307-93101-6(3))*, Dragonfly Bks.) Random Hse. Children's Bks.

—Seamore, the Very Forgetful Porpoise. Edgemon, Darcie. 2008. 48p. (J). (gr. -1-3). lib. bdg. 17.89 *(978-0-06-085076-0(0))* HarperCollins Pubs.

—Tell the Truth, B. B. Wolf. Sierra, Judy. 2010. (ENG.). 40p. (J). (gr. -1-2). 16.99 *(978-0-375-85620-4(X))* Knopf, Alfred A. Inc.

Seibold, J. Otto & Vivian, Siobhan. Vunce upon a Time. Chronicle Books Staff. 2008. (ENG.). 40p. (J). (gr. -1-3). 16.99 *(978-0-8118-6271-4(2))* Chronicle Bks. LLC.

Seiden, Art. Howdy Doody in Funland. Kean, Edward. 2011. 30p. 35.95 *(978-1-258-02315-7(6))* Literary Licensing, LLC.

—Howdy Doody in the Wild West. Kean, Edward. 2011. 34p. 35.95 *(978-1-258-02316-4(4))* Literary Licensing, LLC.

—Howdy Doody's Animal Friends. Daly, Kathleen. 2011. 26p. 35.95 *(978-1-258-02771-1(2))* Literary Licensing, LLC.

—My ABC Book. Grosset and Dunlap Staff. 2015. (G&d Vintage Ser.). (ENG.). 24p. (J). (gr. -1-k). 7.99 *(978-0-448-48215-6(0))*, Grosset & Dunlap) Penguin Publishing Group.

—The Noisy Clock Shop. Berg, Jean Horton. 2015. (G&d Vintage Ser.). (ENG.). 32p. (J). (gr. -1-k). 7.99 *(978-0-448-48216-3(9))*, Grosset & Dunlap) Penguin Publishing Group.

—Tom Glazer's Treasury of Songs for Children. Glazer, Tom. 2nd ed. 2003. 256p. (J). (gr. 3-6). pap. 20.00 *(978-1-58690-003-8(X))* Empire Publishing Service.

Seiders, Marian. Mommy, Am I A ? Ali, Anila & Gottlieb, Karen. 2010. 28p. pap. 11.95 *(978-1-935105-45-9(0))* Avid Readers Publishing Group.

Seiler, Jason & Farley, Jason. The Christmas Train. Bannister, Barbara. 2007. 61p. (J). (gr. 3-7). per. 7.95 *(978-0-940895-54-6(4))* Cornerstone Pr. Chicago.

Seitler, Travis. Mickey Mouse Adventures, Vol. 9. Erickson, Byron et al. Clark, John & Kolberg, Sue, eds. 2006. 128p. (YA). (gr. -1-3). pap. 7.95 *(978-1-888472-10-3(3))* Gemstone Publishing, Inc.

Seitzinger, Victoria. The Oz Odyssey. Baum, Roger S. 2006. 176p. (J). 19.95 *(978-1-57072-299-8(4))* Overmountain Pr.

—Toto of Oz & the Surprise Party. Baum, Roger S. 2004. (ENG.). 32p. (J). 13.95 *(978-1-57072-284-4(6)*, 1233723) Overmountain Pr.

Selwright, Leonard. Rudy the Shy Car. Landy, Adrienne. 2009. 48p. pap. 13.75 *(978-1-935125-43-3(5))* Robertson Publishing.

Seki, Sunny. The Tale of the Lucky Cat. Moon, Josephine. 2008. (KOR & ENG.). 32p. (J). *(978-0-9799339-1-2(9))* East West Discovery Pr.

Seki, Sunny. The Tale of the Lucky Cat. Seki, Sunny. 2008. (ENG & SPA.). 32p. (J). 18.95 *(978-0-9669437-9-5(1))* East West Discovery Pr.

Seki, Sunny. The Tale of the Lucky Cat. Seki, Sunny, retold by. 32p. (J). 2008. *(978-0-9669437-6-4(7))*; 2007. (JPN & ENG.). 18.95 *(978-0-9669437-5-7(9))* East West Discovery Pr.

Sekowsky, Mike. Justice League of America. Fox, Gardner. rev. ed. 2007. (Showcase Presents Ser.). (ENG.). 560p. (YA). pap. 16.99 *(978-1-4012-1203-2(4))* DC Comics.

—Justice League of America. Fox, Gardner & DC Comics Staff. Kahan, Bob, ed. rev. ed. 2006. (Justice League of America Archives Ser.: Vol. 3). (ENG.). 256p. (YA). 49.99 *(978-1-56389-159-5(X))* DC Comics.

Selby, Shannon. Lynnie Leonardson & the Weeping Willow. Coffey, Joe. 2011. 44p. pap. 24.95 *(978-1-4560-6487-7(8))* America Star Bks.

Sellaro, Brendan. Lily & Nana. Hamilton, Lily & Myers, Barbara. 2010. (J). *(978-0-929915-38-8(0))* Headline Bks., Inc.

—Lily Goes to School. Hamilton, Lily & Myers, Barbara. 2012. (ENG.). 32p. (J). 17.95 *(978-0-938467-59-5(X))* Headline Bks., Inc.

Sellers, Amy. Believe I-Can. Gallucci, Susie. 2006. (J). *(978-0-9776074-1-9(0))* Pounce To Success International, Inc.

—Dream I-Can. Gallucci, Susie. 2006. (J). *(978-0-9776074-2-6(9))* Pounce To Success International, Inc.

—Harry Spotter: The Incontinent Puppy. Hanson, Paige & Hanson, Jon. I.t. ed. 2005. 44p. (J). per. 20.00 *(978-0-9721146-1-5(0))* Monroe Educational Media.

Selover, Arthur, jt. illus. see Selover, Lisa.

Selover, Lisa & Selover, Arthur. Lynn Can Fly, 1 vol. Linkowski, Tami Leli. 2009. 15p. pap. 24.95 *(978-1-60749-611-3(9))* America Star Bks.

Seltzer, Eric. Doodle Dog. Seltzer, Eric. 2005. (Ready-To-Reads Ser.). (ENG.). 32p. (J). (gr. -1-1). pap. 3.99 *(978-0-689-85910-6(4)*, Simon Spotlight) Simon Spotlight.

—Granny Doodle Day. Seltzer, Eric. 2006. (Ready-To-Reads Ser.). (ENG.). 32p. (J). (gr. -1-1). pap. 3.99 *(978-0-689-85911-3(2)*, Simon & Schuster/Paula Wiseman Bks.) Simon & Schuster/Paula Wiseman Bks.

Seltzer, Jerry. Hannah the Magic Shelter Dog. Bogardus, Ray & Bogardus, Karin. 2005. 143p. (J). pap. 14.99 *(978-1-932864-30-4(X))* Masthof Pr.

—Hover for a Day. Collins, Charles. 2006. (ENG.). 56p. (J). 19.95 *(978-1-60131-004-0(8)*, Castlebridge Bks.) Big Tent Bks.

—A Pet for Me. Abbott, Rosalind. 2013. 24p. (J). 16.95 *(978-1-60131-155-9(9)*, Castlebridge Bks.) Big Tent Bks.

—500 Presents for Penelope Potts. Yaldezian, Lisa M. 2006. (J). 16.95 *(978-1-60131-005-7(6))* Big Tent Bks.

Seltzer, Jerry Joe. A Bump in the Road. Abbott, Roz. 2013. 26p. (J). 16.95 *(978-1-60131-179-5(6))* Big Tent Bks.

Seltzer, Jerry Joe. There Are Fairies in My Tub. Seltzer, Jerry Joe. 2013. 20p. (J). 12.95 *(978-1-60131-175-7(3)*, Castlebridge Bks.) Big Tent Bks.

Selway, Martina. Little Yoga: A Toddler's First Book of Yoga. Whitford, Rebecca. 2005. (ENG.). 28p. (J). (gr. -1 — 1). 11.99 *(978-0-8050-7879-4(7)*, Holt, Henry & Co. Bks. For Young Readers) Holt, Henry & Co.

—Sleepy Little Yoga. Whitford, Rebecca. 2007. (ENG.). 28p. (J). (gr. -1 — 1). 13.99 *(978-0-8050-8193-0(3)*, Holt, Henry & Co. Bks. For Young Readers) Holt, Henry & Co.

Selznick, Brian. The Dinosaurs of Waterhouse Hawkins: An Illuminating History of Mr. Warehouse Hawkins, Artist & Lecturer. Kerley, Barbara. 2011. (J). (gr. 2-5). 18.95 *(978-0-545-19703-8(1))*; 29.95 *(978-0-545-19697-0(3))* Weston Woods Studios, Inc.

—The Doll People, Set. Martin, Ann M. & Godwin, Laura. 2014. (Doll People Ser.: Bk. 1). (ENG.). 944p. (J). (gr. 3-7). pap. 24.99 *(978-1-4847-1299-3(4))* Hyperion Bks. for Children.

—The Doll People. Martin, Ann M. & Godwin, Laura. 2003. (Doll People Ser.: Bk. 1). (ENG.). 288p. (J). (gr. 3-7). pap. 7.99 *(978-0-7868-1240-0(0))* Hyperion Pr.

Selznick, Brian. The Doll People. Martin, Ann M. & Godwin, Laura. pap. ***(978-0-439-05648-9(9))*** Scholastic, Inc.

Selznick, Brian. The Doll People. Martin, Ann M. & Godwin, Laura. ed. 2003. (Doll People Ser.: Bk. 1). (J). (gr. 3-6). lib. bdg. 18.40 *(978-0-613-49623-0(X)*, Turtleback) Turtleback Bks.

—The Dulcimer Boy. Seidler, Tor. 2003. 160p. (J). (gr. 3-7). lib. bdg. 16.89 *(978-0-06-623610-0(X))* HarperCollins Pubs.

—The Dulcimer Boy. Seidler, Tor. 2004. 153p. (gr. 5-7). 17.00 *(978-0-7569-3520-7(2))* Perfection Learning Corp.

—Frindle. Clements, Andrew. 105p. (J). (gr. 3-5). pap. 4.50 *(978-0-8072-1522-7(8)*, Listening Library) Random Hse. Audio Publishing Group.

—Head of the Class: Frindle - The Landry News - The Janitor's Boy. Clements, Andrew. 2007. (ENG.). 416p. (J). (gr. 3-7). 20.99 *(978-1-4169-4974-9(7)*, Atheneum Bks. for Young Readers) Simon & Schuster Children's Publishing.

—The Last Holiday Concert. Clements, Andrew. 2004. (ENG.). 192p. (J). (gr. 3-7). 17.99 *(978-0-689-84516-1(2)*, Atheneum Bks. for Young Readers) Simon & Schuster Children's Publishing.

—Lunch Money. Clements, Andrew. (ENG.). 224p. (J). (gr. 3-7). 2007. pap. 6.99 *(978-0-689-86685-2(2))*; 2005. 17.99 *(978-0-689-86683-8(6))* Simon & Schuster Children's Publishing. (Atheneum Bks. for Young Readers).

—Marly's Ghost. Levithan, David. 2007. (ENG.). 208p. (YA). (gr. 7-18). 7.99 *(978-0-14-240912-1(X))* Penguin Publishing Group.

—The Meanest Doll in the World. Martin, Ann M. & Godwin, Laura. 2005. (Doll People Ser.: Bk. 2). (ENG.). 304p. (J). (gr. 3-7). pap. 7.99 *(978-0-7868-5297-0(6))* Hyperion Pr.

—El Periodico Landry. Clements, Andrew. 2004.Tr. of Landry News. (SPA.). (YA). pap. 9.99 *(978-84-241-7886-4(6))* Everest Editora ESP. Dist: Lectorum Pubns., Inc.

—The Runaway Dolls. Martin, Ann M. & Godwin, Laura. (Doll People Ser.: Bk. 3). (ENG.). 352p. (J). (gr. 3-7). 2010. pap. 7.99 *(978-0-7868-5585-8(1))*; 2008. 17.99 *(978-0-7868-5584-1(3))* Hyperion Pr.

—The Runaway Dolls. Martin, Ann M. & Godwin, Laura. ed. 2010. (Doll People Ser.: 03). lib. bdg. 18.40 *(978-0-606-13987-8(7)*, Turtleback) Turtleback Bks.

—Walt Whitman: Words for America. Kerley, Barbara. 2004. (ENG.). 56p. (J). (gr. 2-5). 17.99 *(978-0-439-35791-3(8)*, Scholastic Pr.) Scholastic, Inc.

—When Marian Sang: The True Recital of Marian Anderson. Ryan, Pam Muñoz. pap. 16.95 incl. audio *(978-1-59112-943-1(5))*; pap. incl. audio *(978-1-59112-945-5(1))*; pap. 18.95 incl. audio compact disk *(978-1-59112-947-9(8))*; pap. incl. audio compact disk *(978-1-59112-949-3(4))*; 2004. (J). 28.95 incl. audio compact disk *(978-1-59112-948-6(6))* Live Oak Media.

Selznick, Brian. The Houdini Box. Selznick, Brian. 2008. (ENG.). 80p. (J). (gr. 2-5). 19.99 *(978-1-4169-6878-8(4)*, Atheneum Bks. for Young Readers) Simon & Schuster Children's Publishing.

—The Invention of Hugo Cabret. Selznick, Brian. 2007. (ENG.). 544p. (J). (gr. 3-7). 24.99 *(978-0-439-81378-5(6)*, Scholastic Pr.); 534p. *(978-1-4071-0348-8(2))* Scholastic, Inc.

—Wonderstruck. Selznick, Brian. 2011. (ENG.). 640p. (J). (gr. 3-7). 29.99 *(978-0-545-02789-2(6)*, Scholastic Pr.); (gr. 5-9). 300.00 *(978-0-545-38985-3(2))* Scholastic, Inc.

Semeiks, Val. The Courageous Captain America: An Origin Story. Thomas, Rich. 2012. (Marvel Origins Ser.). 48p. (J). (gr. -1-4). lib. bdg. 24.21 *(978-1-61479-008-2(6))* Spotlight.

—The Incredible Hulk: An Origin Story. Thomas, Rich. 2012. (Marvel Origins Ser.). 48p. (J). (gr. -1-4). lib. bdg. 24.21 *(978-1-61479-009-9(4))* Spotlight.

Semeiks, Val, jt. illus. see Disney Book Group Staff.

Semerad, Johnnie. Josh W. Time Out. Semerad, Johnnie. Semerad, Emma. 2003. 32p. (J). 15.00 *(978-0-9744251-0-8(9))* Quiet Man.

Semionov, Vladimir. Chinese Dragons. Montgomery, R. A. 2009. (Choose Your Own Adventure Ser.: No. 30). 144p. (J). (gr. 2-7). pap. 6.99 *(978-1-933390-30-7(1))* Chooseco LLC.

—Moon Quest. Montgomery, Anson. 2008. (Choose Your Own Adventure Ser.: No. 26). 144p. (J). (gr. 2-7). pap. 6.99 *(978-1-933390-26-0(3))* Chooseco LLC.

—Silver Wings. 2007. (Choose Your Own Adventure Ser.: No. 23). 107p. (J). (gr. 4-7). pap. 6.99 *(978-1-933390-23-9(9))* Chooseco LLC.

Semionov, Vladimir & Cannella, Marco. Project UFO. Montgomery, R. A. 2008. 144p. (J). (gr. 4-7). pap. 6.99 *(978-1-933390-27-7(1))* Chooseco LLC.

Semionov, Vladimir & Louie, Wes. Forecast from Stonehenge. 2007. (Choose Your Own Adventure Ser.: No. 19). 127p. (J). (gr. 4-7). pap. 6.99 *(978-1-933390-19-2(0))* Chooseco LLC.

Sempé, Jean-Jacques. Nicholas. Goscinny, René & Bell, Anthea. 2011. (ENG.). 136p. (J). (gr. 7-17). pap. 9.95 *(978-0-7148-6115-9(4))* Phaidon Pr., Inc.

—Nicholas. Goscinny, Ren&eacute. Bell, Anthea, tr. from FRE. rev. ed. 2005. (ENG.). 132p. (J). (gr. 8-17). 19.95 *(978-0-7148-4529-6(9))* Phaidon Pr. Ltd. GBR. Dist: Hachette Bk. Group.

—Nicholas Again. Goscinny, René. Bell, Anthea, tr. from FRE. rev. ed. 2006. (ENG.). 120p. (J). (gr. 8-17). 19.95 *(978-0-7148-4564-7(7))* Phaidon Pr., Inc.

—Nicholas & the Gang. Goscinny, René. Bell, Anthea, tr. from FRE. 2011. (ENG.). 120p. (J). (gr. 4-7). pap. 9.95 *(978-0-7148-6226-2(6))* Phaidon Pr., Inc.

—Nicholas in Trouble. Bell, Anthea, tr. from FRE. 2008. (ENG.). 128p. (J). (gr. 1-4). 19.95 *(978-0-7148-4813-6(1))* Phaidon Pr., Inc.

—Nicholas on Vacation. Goscinny, René. Bell, Anthea, tr. 2013. (ENG.). 136p. (J). (gr. 1-4). pap. 9.95 *(978-0-7148-6224-8(X))* Phaidon Pr., Inc.

—Nicholas on Vacation. Goscinny, René. Bell, Anthea, tr. from FRE. rev. ed. 2006. (ENG.). 132p. (J). (gr. 8-17). 19.95 *(978-0-7148-4678-1(3))* Phaidon Pr., Inc.

Sempé, Jean-Jacques. Everything Is Complicated. Sempé, Jean-Jacques. Bell, Anthea, tr. from FRE. rev. ed. 2006. (ENG.). 144p. (gr. 8-17). 24.95 *(978-0-7148-4542-5(6))* Phaidon Pr., Inc.

—Mixed Messages. Sempé, Jean-Jacques. Bell, Anthea, tr. from FRE. rev. ed. 2006. (ENG.). 104p. (gr. 8-17). 24.95 *(978-0-7148-4543-2(4))* Phaidon Pr., Inc.

—Nothing Is Simple. Sempé, Jean-Jacques. Bell, Anthea, tr. from FRE. rev. ed. 2006. (ENG.). 148p. (gr. 8-17). 24.95 *(978-0-7148-4483-1(7))* Phaidon Pr., Inc.

—Sunny Spells. Sempé, Jean-Jacques. Bell, Anthea, tr. from FRE. rev. ed. 2006. (ENG.). 104p. (gr. 8-17). 24.95 *(978-0-7148-4544-9(2))* Phaidon Pr., Inc.

Sempill. The Pulp7 Quartereader, Bk. 2. Storm, Michael. I.t. ed. 2005. Orig. Title: Pulp7. 265p. (YA). per. *(978-0-9744929-1-9(4))* Leeway Pubs.

Semple, Dave. The Fearless Four: Braced for Battle. Richards, Lynne. 2009. (ENG.). 24p. (J). (gr. 1-17). pap. 3.99 *(978-1-58476-814-2(2))* Innovative Kids.

—Phonics Comics: the Fearless Four - Level 2. Bergen, Lara Rice. 2007. (ENG.). 24p. (J). (gr. 1-17). per. 3.99 *(978-1-58476-564-6(X))* Innovative Kids.

Semple, David. Rory's Lost His Voice. Doyle, Malachy. 2005. (ENG.). 24p. (J). lib. bdg. 23.65 *(978-1-59646-714-9(2))* Dingles & Co.

—There Was a Crooked Man. Punter, Russell. 2010. (First Reading Level 2 Ser.). 32p. (J). 6.99 *(978-0-7945-2682-5(9)*, Usborne) EDC Publishing.

Sendak, Maurice. Los Amigos de Osito. Minarik, Else Holmelund. Benavides, Rosa, tr. 2nd ed. (Infantil Alfaguara Ser.: 32).Tr. of Little Bear's Friends. (SPA.). 64p. (J). 7.95 *(978-84-204-3049-2(8))* Santillana USA Publishing Co., Inc.

—Bears. Krauss, Ruth. 2005. (ENG.). 24p. (J). 19.99 *(978-0-06-027994-3(X))* HarperCollins Pubs.

—Bears. Krauss, Ruth. 2005. 24p. (J). *(978-0-00-720662-9(3)*, HarperCollins Children's Bks.) HarperCollins Pubs. Ltd.

—The Bee-Man of Orn. Stockton, Frank Richard. 2005. (Sendak Reissues Ser.). (ENG.). 56p. (J). (gr. 1-18). 15.95 *(978-0-06-029729-9(8))* HarperCollins Pubs.

—Un Beso para Osito. Minarik, Else Holmelund. Benavides, Rosa, tr. 2003. (Infantil Alfaguara Ser.: 31).Tr. of Kiss for Little Bear. (SPA.). 36p. (J). (gr. k-3). 11.95 *(978-84-204-3050-8(1)*, AF1633) Ediciones Alfaguara ESP. Dist: Lectorum Pubns., Inc., Santillana USA Publishing Co., Inc.

—Brundibar. Kushner, Tony. 2003. (ENG.). 56p. (J). (gr. 1-17). 24.99 *(978-0-7868-0904-2(3)*, di Capua, Michael Bks.) Hyperion Bks. for Children.

—Dear Mili. Grimm, Wilhelm K. Manheim, Ralph, tr. 2013. (ENG.). 40p. (J). (gr. k-2). pap. 8.99 *(978-1-250-03512-7(0))* Square Fish.

—The Griffin & the Minor Canon. Stockton, Frank R. & Stockton. 2005. (Sendak Reissues Ser.). (ENG.). 56p. (J). 15.95 *(978-0-06-029731-2(X))* HarperCollins Pubs.

—The Happy Rain. Sendak, Jack & Sendak, J. 2004. (Sendak Reissues Ser.). (ENG.). 48p. (J). reprint ed. 13.95 *(978-0-06-028785-6(3))* HarperCollins Pubs.

—In Grandpa's House. Sendak, Philip. 2003. (Sendak Reissues Ser.). (ENG.). 48p. (J). reprint ed. 16.95 *(978-0-06-028787-0(X))* HarperCollins Pubs.

—The Juniper Tree: And Other Tales from Grimm. Segal, Lore et al. Segal, Lore & Jarrell, Randall, trs. from GER. 2003. (ENG.). 352p. (J). (gr. 2-7). 24.99 *(978-0-374-33971-5(6)*, Farrar, Straus & Giroux (BYR)) Farrar, Straus & Giroux.

—Little Bear. Minarik, Else Holmelund. 2003. (I Can Read Book 1 Ser.). (ENG.). 64p. (J). (gr. k-3). pap. 3.99 *(978-0-06-444004-2(4))* HarperCollins Pubs.

—Little Bear's Visit. Minarik, Else Holmelund. (J). pap. 12.95 incl. audio Weston Woods Studios, Inc.

—Lullabies & Night Songs. Engvick, William. 2004. (Sendak Reissues Ser.). 80p. (J). 40.00 *(978-0-06-029733-6(6))* HarperCollins Pubs.

—Mommy? Yorinks, Arthur. 2006. (ENG.). 6p. (J). (gr. -1-2). 24.95 *(978-0-439-88050-3(5))* Scholastic, Inc.

—The Moon Jumpers. Udry, Janice May. 2013. (Sendak Reissues Ser.). (ENG.). 32p. (J). (gr. -1-3). 17.95 *(978-0-06-028460-2(9))* HarperCollins Pubs.

—No Fighting, No Biting! Minarik, Else Holmelund. 2004. 63p. (J). (gr. k-4). reprint ed. pap. 17.00 *(978-0-7567-7235-2(4))* DIANE Publishing Co.

—The Nutcracker. Hoffmann, E. T. A. Manheim, Ralph, tr. from GER. 2012. (ENG.). 120p. 24.99 *(978-0-385-34864-5(9)*, Crown) Crown Publishing Group.

—Osito. Minarik, Else Holmelund. Aguilar, Joaquina, tr. 2003. (Infantil Alfaguara Ser.: 25).Tr. of Little Bear. (SPA.). 60p. (J). (gr. k-3). pap. 8.95 *(978-84-204-3044-7(7)*, AF1346) Santillana USA Publishing Co., Inc.

—El Oso Que No Es Era. Minarik, Else Holmelund & Tashlin, Frank. 2003. (Infantil Ser.).Tr. of Bear That Wasn't. (SPA.). 62p. (J). (gr. k-3). pap. 8.95 *(978-958-24-0002-6(1))* Santillana USA Publishing Co., Inc.

—Papa Oso Vuelve a Casa. Minarik, Else Holmelund. Benavides, Rosa, tr. 2nd ed. 2003. (Infantil Alfaguara Ser.: 29).Tr. of Father Bear Comes Home. (SPA.). 63p. (J). (gr. -1-3). pap. *(978-84-204-3048-5(X)*, AF1359) Ediciones Alfaguara ESP. Dist: Santillana USA Publishing Co., Inc.

—Pleasant Fieldmouse. Wahl, Jan. 2007. (Sendak Reissues Ser.). (ENG.). 72p. (J). 15.95 *(978-0-06-029725-1(5))* HarperCollins Pubs.

—Sarah's Room. Orgel, Doris. 2005. 47p. (J). (gr. k-4). reprint ed. 15.00 *(978-0-7567-9683-9(0))* DIANE Publishing Co.

—Sarah's Room. Orgel, Doris. 2003. (Sendak Reissues Ser.). (ENG.). 48p. (J). (gr. -1-3). 15.95 *(978-0-06-029727-5(1))* HarperCollins Pubs.

—La Visita de Osito. Minarik, Else Holmelund. Puncel, Maria, tr. 2006. (Osito / Little Bear Ser.).Tr. of Little Bear's Visit. (SPA.). 64p. (gr. k-3). pap. 8.95 *(978-968-19-0623-8(3)*, AF1060) Santillana USA Publishing Co., Inc.

—What Do You Say, Dear? Joslin, Sesyle. (J). (gr. k-2). 14.45 incl. audio *(978-0-8045-6525-7(2)*, SAC 6525) Spoken Arts, Inc.

Sendak, Maurice. Alligators All Around Board Book: An Alphabet. Sendak, Maurice. 2075. (ENG.). 32p. (J). (gr. -1-3). bds. 7.99 *(978-0-06-233245-5(7)*, HarperFestival) HarperCollins Pubs.

—Bumble-Ardy. Sendak, Maurice. 2011. (ENG.). 40p. (J). 17.95 *(978-0-06-205198-1(9))* HarperCollins Pubs.

—Chicken Soup with Rice Board Book: A Book of Months. Sendak, Maurice. 2075. (ENG.). 32p. (J). (gr. -1-3). bds. 7.99 *(978-0-06-233246-2(5)*, HarperFestival) HarperCollins Pubs.

—La Cocina de Noche. Sendak, Maurice. 2003. (Picture Books Collection). (SPA.). 40p. (J). (gr. k-3). 10.95 *(978-84-204-4570-0(3))* Ediciones Alfaguara ESP. Dist: Santillana USA Publishing Co., Inc.

—Kenny's Window. Sendak, Maurice. 2004. 54p. (J). (gr. k-4). reprint ed. 14.00 *(978-0-7567-7767-8(4))* DIANE Publishing Co.

—Kenny's Window. Sendak, Maurice. 2004. (Trophy Picture Bks.). (ENG.). 64p. (J). (gr. 3-6). pap. 11.95 *(978-0-06-443209-2(2))* HarperCollins Pubs.

—My Brother's Book. Sendak, Maurice. 2013. (ENG.). 32p. 18.95 *(978-0-06-223489-6(7))* HarperCollins Pubs.

—One Was Johnny Board Book: A Counting Book. Sendak, Maurice. 2075. (ENG.). 46p. (J). (gr. -1-3). bds. 7.99 *(978-0-06-233247-9(3)*, HarperFestival) HarperCollins Pubs.

—Pierre Board Book: A Cautionary Tale in Five Chapters & a Prologue. Sendak, Maurice. 2075. (ENG.). 38p. (J). (gr. -1-3). bds. 7.99 *(978-0-06-233248-6(1)*, HarperFestival) HarperCollins Pubs.

—Very Far Away. Sendak, Maurice. 2005. (Sendak Reissues Ser.). (ENG.). 56p. (J). 19.99 *(978-0-06-029723-7(9))* HarperCollins Pubs.

—Where the Wild Things Are. Sendak, Maurice. 25th anniv. ed. 2012. (ENG.). 48p. (J). (gr. -1-3). 18.99 *(978-0-06-025492-6(0))*; pap. 8.99 *(978-0-06-443178-1(9))* HarperCollins Pubs.

—Where the Wild Things Are Collector's Edition. Sendak, Maurice. 2012. (ENG.). 48p. (J). (gr. -1-3). 24.95 *(978-0-06-226573-9(3))* HarperCollins Pubs.

Sendak, Maurice. Un Beso para Osito. Sendak, Maurice, tr. Minarik, Else Holmelund.Tr. of Kiss for Little Bear. (SPA.). 34p. (J). (gr. k-3). pap. 8.95 *(978-84-204-4827-5(3))* Santillana USA Publishing Co., Inc.

Sendelbach, Brian. My Tooth Is Loose, Dr. Moose! Johnston, Teresa. 2012. (ENG.). 32p. (J). (gr. -1-3). 3.99 *(978-0-545-28910-8(6))* Scholastic, Inc.

Sendelbach, Brian. The Underpants Zoo. Sendelbach, Brian. 2011. (ENG.). 32p. (J). (gr. -1-3). 16.99 *(978-0-545-24935-5(X)*, Orchard Bks.) Scholastic, Inc.

Senisi, Ellen B., photos by. Friend Power. Marx, Trish. 2011. (J). (gr. k-5). 17.95 *(978-1-60060-233-7(9))* Lee & Low Bks., Inc.

—Kindergarten Day USA & China. Marx, Trish. 2010. (ENG., 48p. (J). (gr. -1-3). pap. 7.95 *(978-1-58089-220-9(5))* Charlesbridge Publishing, Inc.

Senisi, Ellen B., photos by. Berry Smudges & Leaf Prints: Finding & Making Colors from Nature. Senisi, Ellen B. 2005. 40p. (J). (gr. 4-8). reprint ed. 17.00 *(978-0-7567-9707-2(1))* DIANE Publishing Co.

Senkel, Nicholas. Celia & the Witches. Teare, Nellie. 2008. 24p. (J). 13.95 *(978-0-9820852-0-2(6))* Harmon Creek Pr.

Senner, Katja. Abre, Cierra y Aprende! Cuno, Sabine. Caballero, D., tr. 2007. 14p. (J). (gr. -1). *(978-970-718-489-3(2)*, Silver Dolphin en Español) Advanced Marketing, S. de R. L. de C. V.

Senning, Susan. A Sergeant in the House. Turnbull, Betty J. 2013. 44p. pap. 14.95 *(978-1-61153-060-5(1))* Light Messages Publishing.

—A Sergeant in the House. Turnbull, Betty. 2013. 44p. (J). 19.95 *(978-1-61153-059-9(8))* Light Messages Publishing.

Senopati, Erik, et al. The Moto Mutants, Vol. 1. Smith, Brian. 2013. (Monsuno Ser.: 1). (ENG.). 96p. (J). pap. 7.99 *(978-1-4215-4941-5(7))* Viz Media.

Senturk, Burak. The Princess & Her Pony, 1 vol. Redmond, Shirley Raye. 2007. (Read-It! Readers Ser.). (ENG.). 24p. (gr. -1-3). lib. bdg. 19.99 *(978-1-4048-3142-1(8)*, Easy Readers) Picture Window Bks.

Seo, Hong-Seock. Dragon Hunter, Vol. 13. Seo, Hong-Seock. 13th rev. ed. 2005. (Dragon Hunter Ser.). 176p. per. 9.99 *(978-1-59532-649-2(9))* TOKYOPOP, Inc.

Seo, Kaila Eunhye. Fred. 2015. (ENG.). (J). 15.99 *(978-1-4413-1731-5(7)*, 9781441317315) Peter Pauper Pr. Inc.

Seock Seo, Hong. Dragon Hunter, Vol. 12. Im, Hye-Young, tr. rev. ed. 2005. 176p. pap. 9.99 *(978-1-59182-960-7(7))* TOKYOPOP, Inc.

Seon, JeongHyeon. Zippy the Runner. Kim, JiYu. rev. ed. 2014. (MySELF Bookshelf: Social & Emotional Learning/Self-Worth Ser.). (ENG.). 32p. (J). (gr. k-2). pap. 11.94 *(978-1-60357-656-7(8))*; lib. bdg. 22.60 *(978-1-59953-647-7(1))* Norwood Hse. Pr.

Serafini, Frank. The Garden. Serafini, Frank. 2008. (Looking Closely Ser.). (ENG.). 40p. (J). (gr. -1-2). 16.95 *(978-1-55453-210-0(8))* Kids Can Pr., Ltd. CAN. Dist: Univ. of Toronto Pr.

—Looking Closely Across the Desert. Serafini, Frank. 2008. (Looking Closely Ser.). (ENG.). 40p. (J). (gr. -1-2). 16.95 *(978-1-55453-211-7(6))* Kids Can Pr., Ltd. CAN. Dist: Univ. of Toronto Pr.

—Looking Closely along the Shore. Serafini, Frank. 2008. (Looking Closely Ser.). (ENG.). 40p. (J). (gr. 4-7). 16.95 *(978-1-55453-141-7(1))* Kids Can Pr., Ltd. CAN. Dist: Univ. of Toronto Pr.

—Looking Closely in the Rain Forest. Serafini, Frank. 2010. (Looking Closely Ser.). (ENG.). 40p. (J). (gr. -1-2). 16.95 *(978-1-55337-543-2(2))* Kids Can Pr., Ltd. CAN. Dist: Univ. of Toronto Pr.

—Looking Closely Through the Forest, 0 vols. Serafini, Frank. (ENG.). 40p. (J). 2014. pap. 7.95 *(978-1-77138-118-5(3))*; 2008. (gr. 4-7). 16.95 *(978-1-55453-212-4(4))* Kids Can Pr., Ltd. CAN. Dist: Univ. of Toronto Pr.

Sereda, Maja. A Kite's Flight. Gumede, William. 2011. (ENG.). 32p. (J). (gr. k-2). pap. 11.00 *(978-1-77009-804-6(6))* Jacana Media ZAF. Dist: Independent Pubs. Group.

Seredy, Kate. Winterbound. Bianco, Margery Williams. 2014. (ENG.). 256p. (J). (gr. 5). pap. 5.99 *(978-0-486-49290-2(7))* Dover Pubns., Inc.

Seredy, Kate. Philomena. Seredy, Kate. 2008. 93p. (J). pap. 11.95 *(978-1-932350-19-7(5))* Bethlehem Bks.

—A Tree for Peter. Seredy, Kate. 2004. 112p. (J). reprint ed. 19.95 *(978-1-930900-26-4(0))* Purple Hse. Pr.

Serfass, Jim. The Little Motorcycle. Link, C. Edward. 2004. (J). 9.95 *(978-0-9749615-0-7(7))* Roadracing World Publishing, Inc.

Sergeyeva, Marina. Nikki & Nick Are Great Friends to Pick. Sergeyeva, Marina. 2012. 34p. 19.95 *(978-0-9834735-4-1(4))* Leo Publishing.

Serizawa, Naoki. Samurai Man, Vol.2. Serizawa, Naoki. 2005. 192p. (YA). pap. 9.99 *(978-1-58655-693-8(2)*, AWNOV-0562) Media Blasters, Inc.

Seroya, Tea. The Adventures of Weezy, the One-Eyed Pug: Book 1: How Weezy Lost His Eye & Came to His Senses. Lefkowits, John. 2013. (Adventures of Weezy, the One-Eyed Pug Ser.). (ENG.). 24p. pap. 9.99 *(978-0-615-76239-5(5))* Lefkowits,, John Ph.D.

—Cassandra Gets Her Smile Back: Teaching Children to Care for Their Teeth. Alpert, Sherri. 2010. (Let's Talk Ser.). (ENG.). 48p. (J). (gr. -1-4). pap. 8.95 *(978-0-88282-314-0(0))* New Horizon Pr. Pubs., Inc.

—David & Jacko. Downie, David. Tatsi, Andreanna, tr. 2012. 52p. pap. *(978-1-922159-15-1(8))*; pap. *(978-1-922159-24-3(7))* Blue Peg Publishing.

—David & Jacko. Downie, David. Ivanova, Kalina, tr. 2012. 52p. pap. *(978-1-922159-01-4(8))* Blue Peg Publishing.

—David & Jacko. Downie, David. 2012. 52p. pap. *(978-1-922159-99-1(9))* Blue Peg Publishing.

—Horrible Stories My Dad Told Me. Downie, David. Tatsi, Andreanna, tr. 2012. 44p. pap. *(978-1-922159-95-3(6))* Blue Peg Publishing.

—Horrible Stories My Dad Told Me. Downie, David. M, Akiko, tr. 2012. 44p. pap. *(978-1-922159-94-6(8))* Blue Peg Publishing.

—Horrible Stories My Dad Told Me. Downie, David. Ivanova, Kalina, tr. 2012. 42p. pap. *(978-1-922159-96-0(4))* Blue Peg Publishing.

—Horrible Stories My Dad Told Me. Downie, David. Nanevych, Julia, tr. 2012. 44p. pap. *(978-1-922159-97-7(2))* Blue Peg Publishing.

—Horrible Stories My Dad Told Me. Downie, David. Nanevich, Julia, tr. 2012. 44p. pap. *(978-1-922159-90-8(5))* Blue Peg Publishing.

—Horrible Stories My Dad Told Me. Downie, David. 2012. 42p. pap. *(978-0-9873501-0-7(2))* Blue Peg Publishing.

—The Tale of the Teeny, Tiny Black Ant: Helping Children Learn Persistence. Allen, Teresa R. 2011. (Let's Talk Ser.). (ENG.). 48p. (J). (gr. -1-2). pap. 9.95 *(978-0-88282-351-5(5))* New Horizon Pr. Pubs., Inc.

Serpentelli, John. OUCH or AHHH - The Choice IS Easy!, 1 vol. Kelso, Susan. 2009. 47p. pap. 24.95 *(978-1-61546-148-6(5))* America Star Bks.

Serra, Alexander, jt. illus. see Greene, Sanford.

Serra, Armando. La Familia de Nieve. Romero, Sensi. 2004. (Cuentos con miga Ser.). 47p. (J). (gr. 1-5). pap. 11.00 *(978-84-95895-22-6(6))* Editorial Brief ESP. Dist: Independent Pubs. Group.

Serra, Sebastià. Boy, Were We Wrong about the Weather! Kudlinski, Kathleen V. 2015. (ENG.). 32p. (J). (gr. -1-3). 16.99 *(978-0-8037-3793-8(9),* Dial) Penguin Publishing Group.

Serra, Sebastia. The Dog Who Loved the Moon. García, Cristina. 2011. (ENG.). 32p. (J). (gr. -1-3). 16.99 *(978-1-4424-3089-1(3),* Atheneum Bks. for Young Readers) Simon & Schuster Children's Publishing.

—Garbancito. Grimm, Jacob et al. 2005. (Caballo Alado Clásico Series-Al Paso Ser.). (SPA & ENG.). 24p. (J). (gr. -1-k). 7.95 *(978-84-7864-853-5(4))* Combel Editorial, S.A. ESP. Dist: Independent Pubs. Group.

—A Mango in the Hand: A Story Told Through Proverbs. Sacre, Antonio. 2011. (ENG.). 32p. (J). (gr. -1-3). 16.95 *(978-0-8109-9734-9(7),* Abrams Bks. for Young Readers) Abrams.

Serra, Sebastià. A Pirate's Night Before Christmas. Yates, Philip. (ENG.). 32p. (J). (gr. -1-1). 2014. pap. 6.95 *(978-1-4549-1357-3(6))*; 2008. 14.95 *(978-1-4027-4257-6(5))* Sterling Publishing Co., Inc.

Serra, Sebastià. A Pirate's Twelve Days of Christmas. Yates, Philip. 2012. (ENG.). 32p. (J). (gr. -1-1). 14.95 *(978-1-4027-9225-0(5))* Sterling Publishing Co., Inc.

Serra, Sebastia. The Runaway Wok: A Chinese New Year Tale. Compestine, Ying Chang. 2011. (ENG.). 32p. (J). (gr. 1-3). 16.99 *(978-0-525-42068-2(1),* Dutton Juvenile) Penguin Publishing Group.

Serrano, Alfonso. Born from the Heart. Serrano, Berta. 2013. (ENG.). 40p. (J). (gr. -1). 14.95 *(978-1-4549-1144-9(1))* Sterling Publishing Co., Inc.

Serrano, Javier. ¡¡¡Lambertooo!!! Serrano, Javier, tr. Sierra I. Fabra, Jordi & Sierra i Fabra, Jordi. 9th ed. 2004. (SPA.). 136p. (J). (gr. 6-12). pap. 14.99 *(978-84-207-2975-6(2))* Grupo Anaya, S.A. ESP. Dist: Lectorum Pubns., Inc.

Serrano, Javier U. Dias de Reyes Magos. Pascual, Emilio. 4th ed. 2003. (SPA.). 158p. *(978-84-207-9079-4(6),* GS4140) Grupo Anaya, S.A. ESP. Dist: Lectorum Pubns., Inc.

Serrano, Pablo. La Malinche: The Princess Who Helped Cortés Conquer the Aztec Empire, 1 vol. Serrano, Francisco. Ouriou, Susan, tr. from SPA. 2012. (ENG.). 40p. (J). (gr. 3-7). 18.95 *(978-1-55498-111-3(5))* Groundwood Bks. CAN. Dist: Perseus-PGW.

—Mi Mano. Ramos, Maria Cristina. 2007. (SPA.). 18p. (J). 11.95 *(978-968-494-213-4(3))* Centro de Informacion y Desarrollo de la Comunicacion y la Literatura MEX. Dist: Lectorum Pubns., Inc.

—The Poet King of Tezcoco: A Great Leader of Ancient Mexico, 1 vol. Serrano, Francisco. Balch, Trudy & Engelbert, Jo Anne, trs. from SPA. 2007. (ENG.). 48p. (J). (gr. 3-6). 18.95 *(978-0-88899-787-6(6))* Groundwood Bks. CAN. Dist: Perseus-PGW.

Serratosa, Miquel. Dark Graphic Tales by Edgar Allan Poe. Despeyroux, Denise & Poe, Edgar Allen. 2012. (Dark Graphic Novels Ser.). 96p. (J). (gr. 5-9). 31.94 *(978-0-7660-4086-1(0))* Enslow Pubs., Inc.

Serrurier, Jane. The Adventures of the Little Tin Tortoise: A Self-Esteem Story with Activities for Teachers, Parents & Carers. Plummer, Deborah. 2005. (ENG.). 144p. per. *(978-1-84310-406-3(7))* Kingsley, Jessica Ltd.

Servello, Joe. Trouble in Bugland: A Collection of Inspector Mantis Mysteries. Kotzwinkle, William. 2012. (Godine Storyteller Ser.). (ENG.). 190p. (gr. 4-7). reprint ed. pap. 14.95 *(978-1-56792-070-3(5))* Godine, David R. Pub.

Serwacki, Kevin & Pallace, Chris. Joey & Johnny - The Ninjas - Get Mooned. Serwacki, Kevin & Pallace, Chris. 2015. (Joey & Johnny, the Ninjas Ser.: 1). (ENG.). 320p. (J). (gr. 3-7). 12.99 *(978-0-06-229933-8(6))* HarperCollins Pubs.

Seth. File Under - 13 Suspicious Incidents. Snicket, Lemony. 2014. (ENG.). 272p. (J). (gr. 3-17). 12.00 *(978-0-316-28403-5(3))* Little, Brown Bks. for Young Readers.

—Shouldn't You Be in School? Snicket, Lemony. 2014. (All the Wrong Questions Ser.: 3). (ENG.). (J). (gr. 3-17). 336p. 16.00 *(978-0-316-12306-8(4))*; 352p. 18.00 *(978-0-316-40968-1(5))* Little, Brown Bks. for Young Readers.

—When Did You See Her Last? Snicket, Lemony. (All the Wrong Questions Ser.: 2). (ENG.). (J). (gr. 3-17). 2014. 304p. pap. 7.00 *(978-0-316-33684-0(X))*; 2013. 288p. 16.00 *(978-0-316-12305-1(6))*; 2013. 304p. 18.00 *(978-0-316-23993-6(3))* Little, Brown Bks. for Young Readers.

—Who Could That Be at This Hour? Snicket, Lemony. (All the Wrong Questions Ser.: 1). (ENG.). (J). (gr. 3-17). 2014. 288p. pap. 7.00 *(978-0-316-33547-8(9))*; 2012. 272p. 15.99 *(978-0-316-12308-2(0))* Little, Brown Bks. for Young Readers.

Seto, Lillian, jt. illus. see Reed, Rosemary.

Seton, Ernest Thompson. The Trail of the Sandhill Stag. Seton, Ernest Thompson. 2007. 94p. (YA). pap. 16.95 *(978-1-60355-055-0(0))* Juniper Grove.

—Two Little Savages: The Adventures of Two Boys Who Lived As American Indians. Seton, Ernest Thompson. 2010. (ENG.). 313p. (J). (gr. 4-7). pap. 18.00 *(978-1-60419-033-5(7))* Axios Pr.

Seton-Thompson, Grace Gallatin. Biography of a Grizzly. Seton, Ernest Thompson. 2008. 72p. pap. *(978-1-4099-1427-3(5))* Dodo Pr.

Seung-Man, Hwang. Zippy Ziggy, Vol. 2. Eun-Jeong, Kim. 2005. (Zippy Ziggy Ser.: Vol. 2). 192p. (YA). pap. 9.95 *(978-1-59697-162-2(2))* Infinity Studios LLC.

Seuss, Dr. Green Eggs & Ham Cookbook. Frankeny, Frankie, photos by. Brennan, Georgeanne. 2006. (ENG.). 64p. (J). (gr. k-12). 16.95 *(978-0-679-88440-8(8),* Random Hse. Bks. for Young Readers) Random Hse. Children's Bks.

Seuss, Dr. Oh, Baby, the Places You'll Go! Rabe, Tish. 2015. (ENG.). 32p. (J). (gr. k-12). 9.99 ***(978-0-553-52057-6(1),*** Random Hse. Bks. for Young Readers) Random Hse. Children's Bks.

Seuss, Dr. Poisson Un - Poisson Deux - Poisson Rouge - Poisson Bleu. 2011. (FRE & ENG.). 64p. (J). (gr. -1-3). 12.95 *(978-1-61243-029-4(5))* Ulysses Pr.

Seuss, Dr. Do You Like Green Eggs & Ham? Seuss, Dr. 2010. (Dr. Seuss Nursery Collection). (ENG.). 14p. (J). (—1). 9.99 *(978-0-375-85960-1(8),* Random Hse. Bks. for Young Readers) Random Hse. Children's Bks.

—Gerald McBoing Boing. Seuss, Dr. 2004. (Little Golden Book Ser.). (ENG.). 24p. (J). (gr. -1-2). 4.99 *(978-0-375-82721-1(8),* Golden Bks.) Random Hse. Children's Bks.

—How the Grinch Stole Christmas! Seuss, Dr. 50th ed. 2007. (ENG.). 64p. pap. *(978-0-00-725860-4(7),* HarperCollins) HarperCollins Pubs. Ltd.

—How the Grinch Stole Christmas! Seuss, Dr. Jonaitis, Alice, ed. deluxe ed. 2014. (Classic Seuss Ser.). (ENG.). 64p. (J). (gr. k-4). 25.99 *(978-0-679-89153-6(6),* Random Hse. Bks. for Young Readers) Random Hse. Children's Bks.

—The Lorax. Seuss, Dr. ed. 2010. (ENG.). 24p. bds. *(978-0-00-732618-1(1),* HarperCollins Children's Bks.) HarperCollins Pubs. Ltd.

Seuss, Dr. Come Over to My House. Seuss, Dr., tr. Date not set. (J). lib. bdg. 11.99 *(978-0-679-98255-5(8))*; (gr. -1-3). 7.99 *(978-0-679-88255-8(3))* Random Hse. Children's Bks. (Random Hse. Bks. for Young Readers).

Seuss, Dr. & McKie, Roy. Would You Rather Be a Bullfrog? Seuss, Dr. 2008. (Bright & Early Books(R) Ser.). (ENG.). 36p. (J). (gr. -1-k). 8.99 *(978-0-394-83128-2(4),* Random Hse. Bks. for Young Readers) Random Hse. Children's Bks.

Seva. The Last Pair of Shoes. Fridman, Sashi. 2006. 32p. (J). 13.95 *(978-0-8266-0031-8(X))* Merkos L'Inyonei Chinuch.

—A Touch of the High Holidays: A Touch & Feel Book. Glazer, Devorah. 2006. 16p. (J). bds. 7.95 *(978-0-8266-0020-2(4))* Merkos L'Inyonei Chinuch.

Severance, Lyn. Pig. Older, Jules. 2004. (ENG.). 32p. (J). (gr. k-3). 16.95 *(978-0-88106-109-3(3))* Charlesbridge Publishing, Inc.

—Pig. Older, Jules et al. 2004. (ENG.). 32p. (J). (gr. k-3). pap. 7.95 *(978-0-88106-110-9(7))* Charlesbridge Publishing, Inc.

Severin, Marie. Fraggle Rock Classics Volume 1. Kay, Stan. Christy, Stephen et al, eds. 2011. (Fraggle Rock Ser.: 1). (ENG.). 96p. (J). (gr. 4). pap. 9.95 *(978-1-936393-22-0(0))* Boom Entertainment, Inc.

—X-Men, Magneto's Master Plan. Gallagher, Michael. 24p. (YA). (gr. k-18). 12.95 *(978-0-9627001-6-3(9))* Futech Educational Products, Inc.

—X-Men, Scourge of the Savage Land. Gallagher, Michael. 24p. (YA). (gr. k-18). 12.95 *(978-0-9627001-7-0(7))* Futech Educational Products, Inc.

Severino, Philip. Getting Your First Allowance. Burke, Patrick J. 2008. 28p. pap. 24.95 *(978-1-60441-882-8(6))* America Star Bks.

Sevigny, Eric. As Good as New. 2012. (Ecology Club Ser.). (ENG.). 24p. (J). (gr. -1-1). pap. 5.99 *(978-2-89450-832-9(8))* Éditions Chouette CAN. Dist: Perseus-PGW.

Sévigny, Eric. Caillou: Accidents Happen. 2014. (ENG.). 24p. (J). (gr. -1-1). pap. 3.99 *(978-2-89718-120-8(6))* Éditions Chouette CAN. Dist: Perseus-PGW.

—Caillou: Happy Halloween. 2nd ed. 2012. (Clubhouse Ser.). (ENG.). 24p. (J). (gr. -1-1). pap. 4.99 *(978-2-89450-932-6(4))* Éditions Chouette CAN. Dist: Perseus-PGW.

—Caillou: Storybook Treasury. Chouette Publishing Staff. 2014. (ENG.). 240p. (J). (gr. -1-k). 15.99 *(978-2-89718-149-9(4))* Éditions Chouette CAN. Dist: Perseus-PGW.

—Caillou: The Birthday Party. 2014. (ENG.). 24p. (J). (gr. -1-1). pap. 4.99 *(978-2-89718-122-2(2))* Éditions Chouette CAN. Dist: Perseus-PGW.

Sevigny, Eric. Caillou: The Magic of Compost. Johanson, Sarah Margaret. 2011. (Ecology Club Ser.). (ENG.). 24p. (J). (gr. -1-1). pap. 5.99 *(978-2-89450-773-5(9))* Éditions Chouette CAN. Dist: Perseus-PGW.

Sévigny, Eric. Caillou: Watches Rosie. rev. ed. 2008. (Playtime Ser.). (ENG.). 24p. (J). (gr. -1-1). pap. 4.95 *(978-2-89450-635-6(X))* Éditions Chouette CAN. Dist: Perseus-PGW.

Sevigny, Eric. Caillou: When I Grow Up ... Chouette Publishing Staff. 2011. (Pop Up Ser.). (ENG.). 10p. (J). (gr. -1-1). 6.95 *(978-2-89450-760-5(7))* Éditions Chouette CAN. Dist: Perseus-PGW.

—Caillou - The Best Day Ever! Paradis, Anne. 2013. (Caillou (Board Books) Ser.). (ENG.). 24p. (J). (gr. -1-1). bds. 9.99 *(978-2-89718-097-3(8))* Éditions Chouette CAN. Dist: Perseus-PGW.

—Caillou - The Little Artist. Chouette Publishing Staff. 2011. (Coloring & Activity Book Ser.). (ENG.). 96p. (J). (gr. -1-1). 7.95 *(978-2-89450-809-1(3))* Éditions Chouette CAN. Dist: Perseus-PGW.

Sévigny, Éric. Caillou - Training Wheels. 2010. (Clubhouse Ser.). (ENG.). 24p. (J). (gr. -1-1). pap. 3.99 *(978-2-89450-746-9(1))* Éditions Chouette CAN. Dist: Perseus-PGW.

Sévigny, Eric. Caillou & the Rain. 2012. (Clubhouse Ser.). (ENG.). 24p. (J). (gr. -1-1). pap. 3.99 *(978-2-89450-870-1(0))* Éditions Chouette CAN. Dist: Perseus-PGW.

Sevigny, Eric. Caillou Around Town. Paradis, Anne. 2nd ed. 2013. (Coloring & Activity Book Ser.). (ENG.). 16p. (J). (gr. -1-1). bds. 9.99 *(978-2-89718-045-4(5))* Éditions Chouette CAN. Dist: Perseus-PGW.

Sévigny, Eric. Caillou Borrows a Book. 2014. (Clubhouse Ser.). (ENG.). 24p. (J). (gr. -1 — 1). pap. 3.99 *(978-2-89718-141-3(9))* Éditions Chouette CAN. Dist: Perseus-PGW.

—Caillou Dances with Grandma. 2013. (Clubhouse Ser.). (ENG.). 24p. (J). (gr. -1-1). 3.99 *(978-2-89718-062-1(5))* Éditions Chouette CAN. Dist: Perseus-PGW.

Sévigny, Eric. Caillou, Emma's Extra Snacks: Living with Diabetes. 2015. (Playtime Ser.). (ENG.). 24p. (J). (gr. -1-1). pap. 4.99 ***(978-2-89718-205-2(9))*** Éditions Chouette CAN. Dist: Perseus-PGW.

Sévigny, Eric. Caillou: Family Fun Story Box, 4 vols. 2014. (ENG.). 40p. (J). (gr. -1-k). 12.99 *(978-2-89718-123-9(0))* Éditions Chouette CAN. Dist: Perseus-PGW.

Sevigny, Eric. Caillou Gets the Hiccups! 2013. (Clubhouse Ser.). (ENG.). 24p. (J). (gr. -1-1). 3.99 *(978-2-89718-063-8(3))* Éditions Chouette CAN. Dist: Perseus-PGW.

Sévigny, Eric. Caillou Goes Apple Picking. 2014. (Clubhouse Ser.). (ENG.). 24p. (J). (gr. -1 — 1). pap. 3.99 *(978-2-89718-145-1(1))* Éditions Chouette CAN. Dist: Perseus-PGW.

—Caillou Gone Fishing. 2015. (Clubhouse Ser.). (ENG.). 24p. (J). (gr. -1-1). 3.99 *(978-2-89718-183-3(4))* Éditions Chouette CAN. Dist: Perseus-PGW.

—Caillou Is Sick. 2012. (Clubhouse Ser.).Tr. of Caillou Est Malade. (ENG.). 24p. (J). (gr. -1-1). pap. 3.99 *(978-2-89450-865-7(4))* Éditions Chouette CAN. Dist: Perseus-PGW.

—Caillou Makes a Snowman. ed. 2014. (Clubhouse Ser.). (ENG.). 24p. (J). (gr. -1 — 1). pap. 3.99 *(978-2-89718-143-7(5))* Éditions Chouette CAN. Dist: Perseus-PGW.

—Caillou: My First Sticker Book: Includes 400 Fun Stickers. 2015. (Coloring & Activity Book Ser.). (ENG.). 64p. (J). (gr. -1-1). 9.99 *(978-2-89718-179-6(6))* Éditions Chouette CAN. Dist: Perseus-PGW.

—Caillou: Mystery Valentine. 2014. (Clubhouse Ser.). (ENG.). 24p. (gr. -1-1). pap. 4.99 *(978-2-89718-181-9(8))* Éditions Chouette CAN. Dist: Perseus-PGW.

Sevigny, Eric. Caillou Plants a Tree. 2012. (Ecology Club Ser.). (ENG.). 24p. (J). (gr. -1-1). pap. 5.99 *(978-2-89450-834-3(4))* Éditions Chouette CAN. Dist: Perseus-PGW.

—Caillou, Search & Count: Fun Adventures! Paradis, Anne. 2013. (Coloring & Activity Book Ser.). (ENG.). 16p. (J). (gr. -1-1). bds. 9.99 *(978-2-89718-034-8(X))* Éditions Chouette CAN. Dist: Perseus-PGW.

Sévigny, Eric. Caillou: the Doodle Artist. 2014. (ENG.). 128p. (J). (gr. -1-1). 7.95 *(978-2-89718-126-0(5))* Éditions Chouette CAN. Dist: Perseus-PGW.

Sevigny, Eric. Caillou: the Little Christmas Artist. Paradis, Anne. 2013. (Coloring & Activity Book Ser.). (ENG.). 64p. (J). (gr. -1-1). 8.99 *(978-2-89718-065-2(X))* Éditions Chouette CAN. Dist: Perseus-PGW.

—Every Drop Counts. 2011. (Ecology Club Ser.). (ENG.). 24p. (J). (gr. -1-1). pap. 5.99 *(978-2-89450-772-8(0))* Éditions Chouette CAN. Dist: Perseus-PGW.

—In the Garden. 2005. (Playtime Ser.). (ENG.). 24p. (J). (gr. -1-1). pap. 4.99 *(978-2-89450-383-6(0))* Éditions Chouette CAN. Dist: Perseus-PGW.

Sévigny, Eric. The Missing Sock. rev. ed. 2003. (Clubhouse Ser.). (ENG.). 24p. (J). (gr. -1-1). pap. 3.99 *(978-2-89450-445-1(4))* Éditions Chouette CAN. Dist: Perseus-PGW.

—The Phone Call. 2003. (Clubhouse Ser.). (ENG.). 24p. (J). (gr. -1-1). pap. 3.99 *(978-2-89450-446-8(2))* Éditions Chouette CAN. Dist: Perseus-PGW.

Sevigny, Eric & Sévigny, Eric. My Imaginary Friend. 2003. (Clubhouse Ser.). (ENG.). 24p. (J). (gr. -1-1). pap. 3.95 *(978-2-89450-478-9(0))* Éditions Chouette CAN. Dist: Perseus-PGW.

Sévigny, Eric, jt. illus. see Brignaud, Pierre.

Sévigny, Eric, jt. illus. see Sevigny, Eric.

Sewall, Marcia. Sable. Hesse, Karen. 2010. (ENG.). 96p. (J). (gr. 2-5). pap. 6.99 *(978-0-312-37610-9(3))* Square Fish.

—Stone Fox. Gardiner, John Reynolds. 25th anniv. ed. 2005. (ENG.). 96p. (J). (gr. 2-6). 16.99 *(978-0-690-03983-2(2))* HarperCollins Pubs.

Sewall, Marcia & Hargreaves, Greg. Stone Fox. Gardiner, John Reynolds. 30th anniv. ed. 2010. (Trophy Bk.). (ENG.). 96p. (J). (gr. 2-6). pap. 5.99 *(978-0-06-440132-6(4))* HarperCollins Pubs.

Seward, Daniel. Hide & Seek, No Ticks Please. Fox, Nancy. 2014. (Morgan James Kids Ser.). (ENG.). 42p. (gr. k-6). pap. 9.95 *(978-1-61448-705-0(7))* Morgan James Publishing.

Seward, Prudence. Voyage to Tasmani. Parker, Richard. 2011. 128p. 40.95 *(978-1-258-08572-8(0))* Literary Licensing, LLC.

Sewell, Byron W. Snarkmaster: A Destiny in Eight Fits. a Tale Inspired by Lewis Carroll's the Hunting of the Snark. Sewell, Byron W. 2012. 138p. pap. *(978-1-78201-002-9(5))* Evertype.

Sewell, Helen. Away Goes Sally. Coatsworth, Elizabeth. 2004. 118p. (J). pap. 10.95 *(978-1-883937-83-6(3))* Bethlehem Bks.

—The Fair American. Coatsworth, Elizabeth Jane. 2005. (Sally (Bethlehem Books) Ser.). 137p. (J). pap. 11.95 *(978-1-883937-85-0(X))* Bethlehem Bks.

—Five Bushel Farm. Coatsworth, Elizabeth. 2004. 143p. (J). pap. 10.95 *(978-1-883937-84-3(1))* Bethlehem Bks.

—Old John. Cregan, Mairin. 2012. 198p. 44.95 *(978-1-258-23306-8(1))*; pap. 29.95 *(978-1-258-24727-0(5))* Literary Licensing, LLC.

—The White Horse. Coatsworth, Elizabeth. 2006. (Sally (Bethlehem Books) Ser.). 169p. (J). (gr. 5-7). per. 11.95 *(978-1-883937-86-7(8))* Bethlehem Bks.

—The Wonderful Day. Coatsworth, Elizabeth. 2006. (Sally (Bethlehem Books) Ser.). 139p. (J). (gr. -1). pap. 11.95 *(978-1-883937-87-4(6))* Bethlehem Bks.

Sexton, Brenda. Five Shiny Apples. Fleming, Maria. 2005. (Number Tales Ser.). (ENG.). 16p. (J). (gr. -1-1). pap. 2.99 *(978-0-439-69014-0(5))* Scholastic, Inc.

—Have a Silly Easter! 2009. (Mad Libs Junior Ser.). (ENG.). 32p. (J). (gr. -1-k). 5.99 *(978-0-8431-3125-3(X),* Price Stern Sloan) Penguin Publishing Group.

—Little Jackie Rabbit. 2008. (ENG.). 10p. (J). (gr. -1). 14.99 *(978-0-8249-6732-1(1),* Candy Cane Pr.) Ideals Pubns.

—Little Sleepy Eyes. 2008. (ENG.). 10p. (J). 14.99 *(978-0-8249-6733-8(X),* Candy Cane Pr.) Ideals Pubns.

—Monkey's Missing Bananas. Charlesworth, Liza & Scholastic, Inc. Staff. 2005. (Number Tales Ser.). (ENG.). 16p. (J). (gr. -1-1). pap. 2.99 *(978-0-439-69032-4(3))* Scholastic, Inc.

—Rainbow of Colors. Scelsa, Greg. Faulkner, Stacey, ed. 2006. (J). pap. 2.99 *(978-1-59198-351-4(7))* Creative Teaching Pr., Inc.

—Reading Pals: Rhyming Words Using Blends & Digraphs Gr. K-1. Allen, Margaret. Taylor, Jennifer, ed. 2007. (J). per. 6.99 *(978-1-59198-437-5(8))* Creative Teaching Pr., Inc.

—Reading Pals: Short & Long Vowels Gr. K-1. Abrams, Majella. Taylor, Jennifer, ed. 2007. (J). per. 6.99 *(978-1-59198-436-8(X))* Creative Teaching Pr., Inc.

—Reading Pals: Sight Words Gr. K-1. Allen, Molly. Taylor, Jennifer, ed. 2007. (J). per. 6.99 *(978-1-59198-438-2(6))* Creative Teaching Pr., Inc.

—1+1=5: And Other Unlikely Additions. LaRochelle, David. 2010. (ENG.). 32p. (J). (gr. k). 14.95 *(978-1-4027-5995-6(9))* Sterling Publishing Co., Inc.

Sexton, Brenda. You Can Draw Fairies & Princesses, 1 vol. Sexton, Brenda. 2011. (You Can Draw Ser.). (ENG.). 24p. (gr. 1-2). lib. bdg. 25.99 *(978-1-4048-6808-3(9),* Nonfiction Picture Bks.) Picture Window Bks.

—You Can Draw Pets, 1 vol. Sexton, Brenda. 2011. (You Can Draw Ser.). (ENG.). 24p. (gr. 1-2). lib. bdg. 25.99 *(978-1-4048-6277-7(3),* Nonfiction Picture Bks.) Picture Window Bks.

—You Can Draw Planes, Trains, & Other Vehicles, 1 vol. Sexton, Brenda. Bruning, Matt. 2011. (You Can Draw Ser.). (ENG.). 24p. (gr. 1-2). lib. bdg. 25.99 *(978-1-4048-6278-4(1),* Nonfiction Picture Bks.) Picture Window Bks.

Sexton, Brenda & Ho, Jannie. Easy-To-Draw Animals: A Step-By-Step Drawing Book. Sexton, Brenda & Ho, Jannie. 2014. (You Can Draw Ser.). (ENG.). 64p. (gr. 1-2). pap. 6.95 *(978-1-4795-5511-6(8))* Picture Window Bks.

Sexton, Brenda, jt. illus. see Cerato, Mattia.

Sexton, Brenda, jt. illus. see Ho, Jannie.

Sexton, Brenton. The Little Golden Bible Storybook. Simeon, S. & Golden Books Staff. 2005. (Padded Board Book Ser.). (ENG.). 36p. (J). (gr. -1 — 1). bds. 6.99 *(978-0-375-83549-0(0),* Golden Inspirational) Random Hse. Children's Bks.

Sexton, Jessa R., photos by. Mobert's Irish Experience. Sexton, Jessa R. 2012. 34p. pap. 10.00 *(978-0-9860150-3-8(2))* O'More Publishing.

Sexton, Kris. Because You Teach: A Dynamic Musical Resource for Innovative Staff Development. Hunt-Ullock, Kathy et al. Norris, Jill, ed. 2006. (ENG.). 144p. (gr. -1-12). pap. 24.99 incl. audio compact disk *(978-0-86530-227-3(8),* IP NO. 140-2) Incentive Pubns., Inc.

—Middle School Matters: Innovative Classroom Activities. Hunt-Ullock, Kathy et al. Norris, Jill, ed. 2007. (ENG.). 144p. (gr. 4-8). pap. 24.99 *(978-0-86530-228-0(6),* 140-3) Incentive Pubns., Inc.

—Punctuation Power. Forte, Imogene. Norris, Jill, ed. 2006. (ENG.). 128p. (gr. 5-9). pap. 14.99 *(978-0-86530-031-6(3),* IP 31-3) Incentive Pubns., Inc.

Sexton, Richard, photos by. In the Victorian Style. 2006. (ENG., 192p. (gr. 8-17). 40.00 *(978-0-8118-5360-6(8))* Chronicle Bks. LLC.

—New Orleans: Elegance & Decadence. rev. ed. 2003. (ENG., 224p. (gr. 8-17). 45.00 *(978-0-8118-4131-3(6))* Chronicle Bks. LLC.

Seymour, Arlene. The Moon Book: A Lunar Pop-up Celebration. Seymour, Arlene. 2004. 14p. (YA). (gr. k-4). reprint ed. 22.00 *(978-0-7567-7645-9(7))* DIANE Publishing Co.

Sfar, Joann. The Little Prince Graphic Novel. Saint-Exupéry, Antoine de. ed. 2013. (Little Prince Ser.). (ENG.). 112p. (J). (gr. 5-7). 12.99 *(978-0-547-33800-2(7))* Houghton Mifflin Harcourt Publishing Co.

—Le Petit Prince Graphic Novel. de Saint-Exupéry, Antoine. 2010. (FRE & ENG.). 112p. (J). (gr. 5-7). 22.00

(978-0-547-44330-0(7)) Houghton Mifflin Harcourt Publishing Co.
—Sardine in Outer Space 6. Guibert, Emmanuel. 2008. (Sardine in Outer Space Ser.: 6). (ENG.). 96p. (J). (gr. 1-5). pap. 16.99 *(978-1-59643-424-0(4)*, First Second Bks.) Roaring Brook Pr.
—Space Pirate Sardine vs. the Brainwashing Machine. Guibert, Emmanuel. 2008. (ENG.). 64p. (J). (gr. 1-5). pap. 6.99 *(978-0-312-38445-6(9))* Square Fish.
Sfar, Joann. Sardine in Outer Space, Vol. 4. Sfar, Joann. Guibert, Emmanuel. Gauvin, Edward, tr. from FRE. 4th rev. ed. 2007. (Sardine in Outer Space Ser.: 4). (ENG.). 112p. (J). (gr. 1-5). pap. 15.99 *(978-1-59643-129-4(6)*, First Second Bks.) Roaring Brook Pr.
Sfar, Joann & Pezzali, Walter. Sardine in Outer Space. Guibert, Emmanuel & Sfar, Joann. Watson, Sasha, tr. from FRE. 2006. (Sardine in Outer Space Ser.: 1). (ENG.). 128p. (J). (gr. 1-5). deluxe ed. pap. 16.99 *(978-1-59643-126-3(1))*; Vol. 2. 2nd rev. ed. pap. 16.99 *(978-1-59643-127-0(X))* Roaring Brook Pr. (First Second Bks.).
—Sardine in Outer Space, Vol. 3. Guibert, Emmanuel & Sfar, Joann. Brizzi, Elisabeth & Siegel, Alexis, trs. from FRE. 3rd rev. ed. 2007. (Sardine in Outer Space Ser.: 3). (ENG.). 112p. (J). (gr. 1-5). pap. 17.99 *(978-1-59643-128-7(8)*, First Second Bks.) Roaring Brook Pr.
Sfar, Joann, jt. illus. see Pezzali, Walter.
Sgouros, Yorgos. My Toddler Bible. James, Bethan. 2008. (ENG.). 36p. (J). (gr. -1-k). 12.99 *(978-1-4143-2013-7(2))* Tyndale Hse. Pubs.
Sgroi, Tony. Annie Oakley in the Ghost Town Secret. Schroeder, Doris. 2011. 280p. 47.95 *(978-1-258-06482-2(0))* Literary Licensing, LLC.
Shachat, Andrew. Stop That Pickle! Armour, Peter. 2005. (ENG.). 32p. (J). (gr. -1-3). 6.99 *(978-0-618-54889-7(0))* Houghton Mifflin Harcourt Publishing Co.
Shackelford, David. One Christmas Night. Henderson, Richard. 2008. 32p. (J). 15.95 *(978-0-615-17629-1(1))* St. Clair Publishing.
Shackell, John. French Dictionary for Beginners. Davies, Helen. Irving, Nicole, ed. 2006. (Beginner's Dictionaries Ser.). (FRE.). 128p. (J). (gr. 4). lib. bdg. 20.95 *(978-1-58086-475-6(9))* EDC Publishing.
—German Dictionary for Beginners. Davies, Helen. Irving, Nicole, ed. 2006. (Beginner's Dictionaries Ser.). (GER.). 128p. (J). (gr. 4). lib. bdg. 20.95 *(978-1-58086-487-9(2))* EDC Publishing.
—Italian Dictionary for Beginners. Davies, Helen. Irving, Nicole, ed. 2006. (Beginner's Dictionaries Ser.). (ITA.). 128p. (J). (gr. 4). lib. bdg. 20.95 *(978-1-58086-555-5(0))* EDC Publishing.
—Spanish Dictionary for Beginners. Davies, Helen. Irving, Nicole, ed. 2003. (Beginner's Dictionaries Ser.). (SPA.). 128p. lib. bdg. 20.99 *(978-1-58086-488-6(0))* EDC Publishing.
—Where Does Electricity Come From? Mayes, Susan. 2006. (Usborne Starting Point Science Ser.). 23p. (J). (gr. 4-7). lib. bdg. 12.99 *(978-1-58086-938-6(6)*, Usborne) EDC Publishing.
Shackell, John & Scorey, John. Where Does Electricity Come From? Mayes, Susan. 2006. (Usborne Starting Point Science Ser.). 23p. (J). (gr. 1-4). pap. 4.99 *(978-0-7945-1411-2(1)*, Usborne) EDC Publishing.
Shafer, Anders C. The Fantastic Journey of Pieter Bruegel. Shafer, Anders C. 2005. 38p. (J). 19.00 *(978-0-7567-9540-5(0))* DIANE Publishing Co.
Shaffer, Bren. Black Beauty. Sewell, Anna. 2013. 206p. (J). pap. 14.95 *(978-1-937004-85-9(6))* Old Line Publishing, LLC.
Shaffer, Dale E. Marbles: A Forgotten Part of Salem History. 2 vols. Shaffer, Dale E. 2nd rev. ed. 2004. 38p. (Orig.). (YA). (gr. 3-18). mass mkt. 8.00 *(978-0-915060-34-4(5))* Shaffer, Dale E.
Shafran, Nigel & Davies, Richard, photos by. Ron Arad Talks to Matthew Collings about Designing Chairs, Vases, Buildings And... Collings, Matthew. rev. ed. 2004. (ENG.). 248p. (gr. 8-17). 69.95 *(978-0-7148-4310-0(5))* Phaidon Pr. Ltd. GBR. Dist: Hachette Bk. Group.
Shah, Nupur. In the Woods. Shah, Nupur. rev. ed. 2011. (1-3Y Ecosystems Ser.). (ENG.). 12p. (J). (gr. k-1). pap. 6.50 *(978-1-61541-458-1(4))* American Reading Co.
Shahan, Sherry. Feeding Time at the Zoo. Shahan, Sherry. 2014. (Step into Reading Ser.). (ENG.). 32p. (J). (gr. -1-1). lib. bdg. 12.99 *(978-0-375-97190-7(4)*, Random Hse. Bks. for Young Readers) Random Hse. Children's Bks.
—The Little Butterfly. Shahan, Sherry. 2015. (Step into Reading Ser.). (ENG.). 32p. (J). (gr. -1-1). lib. bdg. 12.99 *(978-0-375-97189-1(0)*, Random Hse. Bks. for Young Readers) Random Hse. Children's Bks.
Shahan, Sherry, photos by. Dashing Through the Snow: The Story of the Jr. Iditarod. 2nd ed. 2006. (J). pap. *(978-1-59336-714-5(7))* Mondo Publishing.
Shahn, Ben. A Boy of Old Prague. Ish-Kishor, Sulamith. 2008. (Dover Children's Classics Ser.). (ENG.). 96p. (J). (gr. 3-5). pap. 3.99 *(978-0-486-46766-5(X))* Dover Pubns., Inc.
—Ounce, Dice, Trice. Reid, Alastair. 2009. (ENG.). 64p. (J). (gr. k-4). 15.95 *(978-1-59017-320-6(1)*, NYR Children's Collection) New York Review of Bks., Inc., The.
Shakir, Susie. I Want to Potty. Neis, Izzy. 2005. 10p. (J). 9.95 *(978-1-58117-422-9(5)*, Intervisual/Piggy Toes) Bendon, Inc.
—My First Big Book Numbers. Poitier, Anton. ed. 2012. (Novelty Ser.). (ENG.). 16p. (J). 9.99 *(978-1-61067-090-6(6))* Kane Miller.
—One to Ten... & Back Again. Schwartz, Betty Ann. 2009. 24p. bds. 12.99 *(978-0-8249-1436-3(8)*, Candy Cane Pr.) Ideals Pubns.
Shalaby, Asharaf. Resilient. Vanasse, Patricia. 2013. (ENG.). 328p. (YA). pap. 13.99 *(978-0-9860373-2-0(X))* Pants On Fire Pr.
Shalansky, Len. Aesop's Opposites: Interactive Aesop Fables. Enderle, Dotti. Mitchell, Judy, ed. 2004. 64p. (J). pap. 9.95 *(978-1-57310-424-1(8))* Teaching & Learning Co.
—100 Little Reading Comprehension Lessons, Grade 1-4: Fun-To-Read Stories with Skill-Building Exercises. Brinton, Margaret. 2004. (ENG.). 112p. pap. 12.95 *(978-1-57310-425-8(6))* Teaching & Learning Co.
Shaloshvili, Natasha. Not What I Expected. Friedman, Laurie B. 2015. (ENG.). 176p. (J). (gr. 5-9). 17.95 ***(978-1-4677-8588-4(1))*** Lerner Publishing Group.
Shalvey, Declan, et al. Sweeney Todd: The Demon Barber of Fleet Street. Bryant, Clive, ed. 2012. (ENG.). 176p. pap. 16.95 *(978-1-907127-10-6(0)*, Classical Comics, Ltd.); pap. 16.95 *(978-1-907127-09-0(7)*, Classical Comics, Ltd.); (gr. 9). lib. bdg. 24.95 *(978-1-907127-82-3(8))* Classical Comics GBR. Dist: Perseus-PGW.
Shalvey, Declan & Walker, Kev. Shadowland: Thunderbolts. 2011. (ENG.). 128p. (YA). (gr. 8-17). pap. 15.99 *(978-0-7851-5219-4(9))* Marvel Worldwide, Inc.
Shalvey, Declan, jt. illus. see Walker, Kev.
Shames, Stephen, photos by. Transforming Lives: Turning Uganda's Forgotten Children into Leaders. Shames, Stephen. 2009. 40p. (YA). pap. 12.95 *(978-1-59572-213-3(0))* Star Bright Bks., Inc.
Shamp, Danielle. When I Wished ... Tabor, Stephen A. 2009. 31p. pap. 24.95 *(978-1-60836-086-4(5))* America Star Bks.
Shamshirsaz, Shahab. Tatter Wings. McRae, J. R. 2014. 48p. pap. 20.99 *(978-1-62746-113-9(2))* Tate Publishing & Enterprises, LLC.
Shanahan, Danny. The Bus Ride That Changed History: The Story of Rosa Parks. Edwards, Pamela Duncan. 2009. (ENG.). 32p. (J). (gr. -1-3). pap. 6.99 *(978-0-547-07674-4(6))* Houghton Mifflin Harcourt Publishing Co.
Shanahan, Sue. Sarah the Best Bridesmaid: Paper Doll Storybook. Rubins, Diane Teitel. 2004. (Dover Paper Dolls Ser.). (ENG.). 24p. (J). (gr. 2-5). pap. 5.95 *(978-0-486-43531-2(8))* Dover Pubns., Inc.
Shannon, Ben. Cliques: Using What You Have Inside, 1 vol. Mototsune, Kat. 2010. (Lorimer Deal with It Ser.). (ENG.). 32p. (J). (gr. 4-6). pap. 12.95 *(978-1-55277-544-8(5))*; lib. bdg. 24.95 *(978-1-55277-545-5(3))* Lorimer, James & Co., Ltd., Pubs. CAN. Dist: Casemate Pubs. & Bk. Distributors, LLC.
—Gaming: Before It Outplays You, 1 vol. Peters, Diane. 2010. (Lorimer Deal with It Ser.). (ENG.). 32p. (YA). (gr. 4-6). 24.95 *(978-1-55277-490-8(2))* Lorimer, James & Co., Ltd., Pubs. CAN. Dist: Casemate Pubs. & Bk. Distributors, LLC.
—Gaming: Deal with It Before It Outplays You, 1 vol. Peters, Diane. 2010. (Lorimer Deal with It Ser.). (ENG.). 32p. (YA). (gr. 4-6). pap. 12.95 *(978-1-55277-434-2(1))* Lorimer, James & Co., Ltd., Pubs. CAN. Dist: Casemate Pubs. & Bk. Distributors, LLC.
—Image: Deal with It from the Inside Out, 1 vol. Mototsune, Kat. 2007. (Lorimer Deal with It Ser.). (ENG.). 32p. (J). (gr. 4-6). pap. 12.95 *(978-1-55028-994-7(2))* Lorimer, James & Co., Ltd., Pubs. CAN. Dist: Casemate Pubs. & Bk. Distributors, LLC.
—Morgan & the Money, 1 vol. Staunton, Ted. ed. 2008. (Formac First Novels Ser.). (ENG.). 64p. (J). (gr. 1-5). 4.95 *(978-0-88780-774-9(7))* Formac Publishing Co., Ltd. CAN. Dist: Casemate Pubs. & Bk. Distributors, LLC.
—Peer Pressure: Deal with It Without Losing Your Cool, 1 vol. Slavens, Elaine. 2004. (Lorimer Deal with It Ser.). (ENG.). 32p. (J). (gr. 4-6). 12.95 *(978-1-55028-815-5(6))* Lorimer, James & Co., Ltd., Pubs. CAN. Dist: Casemate Pubs. & Bk. Distributors, LLC.
Shannon, Ben, jt. illus. see Slavin, Bill.
Shannon, David. Alice the Fairy. 2004. (ENG.). 40p. (J). (gr. -1-k). 17.99 *(978-0-439-49025-2(1)*, Blue Sky Pr., The) Scholastic, Inc.
Shannon, David, et al. All Around Trucktown. Harper, Benjamin & Scieszka, Jon. 2008. (Jon Scieszka's Trucktown Ser.). (ENG.). 32p. (J). (gr. -1-1). 3.99 *(978-1-4169-4194-1(0)*, Simon Scribbles) Simon Scribbles.
Shannon, David. The Bunyans. Wood, Audrey. 2006. (Scholastic Bookshelf Ser.). (ENG.). 32p. (J). (gr. -1-3). 6.99 *(978-0-439-81214-6(3)*, Scholastic Paperbacks) Scholastic, Inc.
Shannon, David, et al. A Christmas Surprise. Mason, Tom & Danko, Dan. 2011. (Jon Scieszka's Trucktown Ser.). (ENG.). 12p. (J). (gr. -1-k). 7.99 *(978-1-4169-4193-4(2)*, Simon & Schuster Bks. For Young Readers) Simon & Schuster Bks. For Young Readers.
—Dizzy Izzy. Scieszka, Jon. (Jon Scieszka's Trucktown Ser.). (ENG.). 24p. (J). (gr. -1-1). 2014. 16.99 *(978-1-4814-1460-9(7))*; 2010. lib. bdg. 14.99 *(978-1-4169-4156-9(8))* Simon Spotlight. (Simon Spotlight).
—Easter Egg Dash! A Lift-The-Flap Book with Stickers. Sander, Sonia. 2010. (Jon Scieszka's Trucktown Ser.). (ENG.). 12p. (J). (gr. -1-k). bds. 7.99 *(978-1-4169-4183-5(5)*, Little Simon) Little Simon.
—The Great Truck Rescue. Scieszka, Jon. 2010. (Jon Scieszka's Trucktown Ser.). (ENG.). 40p. (J). (gr. -1-3). pap. 3.99 *(978-1-4424-0932-3(0)*, Simon & Schuster Bks. For Young Readers) Simon & Schuster Bks. For Young Readers.
Shannon, David. Hiawatha & the Peacemaker. Robertson, Robbie. 2015. (ENG.). 48p. (J). (gr. -1-3). 19.95 ***(978-1-4197-1220-3(9))***, Abrams Bks. for Young Readers) Abrams.
Shannon, David, et al. Honk That Horn! Mason, Tom et al. 2011. (Jon Scieszka's Trucktown Ser.). (ENG.). 24p. (J). (gr. -1-k). pap. 3.99 *(978-1-4169-4184-2(3)*, Simon & Schuster Bks. For Young Readers) Simon & Schuster Bks. For Young Readers.
Shannon, David. How I Became a Pirate. Long, Melinda. 2003. (ENG.). 44p. (J). (gr. -1-3). 16.99 *(978-0-15-201848-1(4))* Houghton Mifflin Harcourt Publishing Co.
—How I Became A Pirate. Long, Melinda. 2004. (J). *(978-0-439-66474-5(8)*, Scholastic) Scholastic, Inc.
Shannon, David, et al. Junkyard Dig! Building from A to Z. Auerbach, Annie. 2010. (Jon Scieszka's Trucktown Ser.). (ENG.). 26p. (J). (gr. -1-k). bds. 5.99 *(978-1-4169-4187-3(8)*, Little Simon) Little Simon.
—Kat's Maps. Scieszka, Jon. 2011. (Jon Scieszka's Trucktown Ser.). (ENG.). 24p. (J). (gr. -1-1). pap. 3.99 *(978-1-4169-4148-4(7)*, Simon Spotlight) Simon Spotlight.
—Kat's Mystery Gift. Scieszka, Jon. (Jon Scieszka's Trucktown Ser.). (ENG.). 24p. (J). (gr. -1-1). 2013. 16.99 *(978-1-4814-1459-3(3))*; 2009. lib. bdg. 14.99 *(978-1-4169-4154-5(1))* Simon Spotlight. (Simon Spotlight).
—Let's Dig It! Bergen, Lara. 2010. (Jon Scieszka's Trucktown Ser.). (ENG.). 12p. (J). (gr. -1-k). bds. 5.99 *(978-1-4169-4190-3(8)*, Little Simon) Little Simon.
—Max's Big Show. Testa, Maggie. 2010. (Jon Scieszka's Trucktown Ser.). (ENG.). 32p. (J). (gr. -1-1). 4.99 *(978-1-4169-4191-0(6)*, Simon Scribbles) Simon Scribbles.
—Meet Jack Truck! McKown, Hunter. 2008. (Jon Scieszka's Trucktown Ser.). (ENG.). 14p. (J). (gr. -1-1). 5.99 *(978-1-4169-4173-6(8)*, Little Simon) Little Simon.
—Melvin's Valentine. Scieszka, Jon. (Jon Scieszka's Trucktown Ser.). (ENG.). 24p. (J). (gr. -1-1). 2014. 16.99 *(978-1-4814-1458-6(5))*; 2009. pap. 3.99 *(978-1-4169-4144-6(4))*; 2009. lib. bdg. 15.99 *(978-1-4169-4155-2(X))* Simon Spotlight. (Simon Spotlight).
—On the Move! Teitelbaum, Michael & Scieszka, Jon. 2009. (Jon Scieszka's Trucktown Ser.). (ENG.). 10p. (J). (gr. -1-k). 6.99 *(978-1-4169-4178-1(9)*, Little Simon) Little Simon.
Shannon, David. Pirates Activity Book. Long, Melinda. 2010. (ENG.). 24p. (J). (gr. -1-3). pap. 6.99 *(978-0-547-31490-7(6))* Houghton Mifflin Harcourt Publishing Co.
—Pirates Don't Change Diapers. Long, Melinda. 2007. (ENG.). 44p. (J). (gr. -1-3). 16.99 *(978-0-15-205353-6(0))* Houghton Mifflin Harcourt Publishing Co.
Shannon, David, et al. Playtime in Trucktown. Rao, Lisa. 2008. (Jon Scieszka's Trucktown Ser.). (ENG.). 24p. (J). (gr. -1-1). 5.99 *(978-1-4169-4197-2(5)*, Simon Scribbles) Simon Scribbles.
Shannon, David. Robot Zot! Scieszka, Jon. 2009. (ENG.). 40p. (J). (gr. -1-2). 17.99 *(978-1-4169-6394-3(4)*, Simon & Schuster Bks. For Young Readers) Simon & Schuster Bks. For Young Readers.
—Robot Zot! Scieszka, Jon. 2011. (J). (gr. -1-2). 29.95 *(978-0-545-32739-8(3))* Weston Woods Studios, Inc.
Shannon, David, et al. Sand Castle Bash: Counting from 1 To 10. McKown, Hunter. 2009. (Jon Scieszka's Trucktown Ser.). (ENG.). 26p. (J). (gr. -1-k). 5.99 *(978-1-4169-4179-8(7)*, Little Simon) Little Simon.
—Scoop That Snow! Parker, Sydney. 2009. (Jon Scieszka's Trucktown Ser.). (ENG.). 12p. (J). (gr. -1-k). bds. 7.99 *(978-1-4169-4182-8(7)*, Little Simon) Little Simon.
—Smash! Crash! Scieszka, Jon. 2008. (Jon Scieszka's Trucktown Ser.). (ENG.). 42p. (J). (gr. -1-2). 16.99 *(978-1-4169-4133-0(9)*, Simon & Schuster Bks. For Young Readers) Simon & Schuster Bks. For Young Readers.
—Smash That Trash! Sander, Sonia & Scieszka, Jon. 2009. (Jon Scieszka's Trucktown Ser.). (ENG.). 14p. (J). (gr. -1-k). 7.99 *(978-1-4169-4180-4(0)*, Little Simon) Little Simon.
—The Spooky Tire. Scieszka, Jon. 2009. (Jon Scieszka's Trucktown Ser.). (ENG.). 24p. (J). (gr. -1-k). lib. bdg. 15.99 *(978-1-4169-4153-8(3))*; pap. 3.99 *(978-1-4169-4142-2(8))* Simon Spotlight. (Simon Spotlight).
—Steer the Wheel! Teitelbaum, Michael. 2011. (Jon Scieszka's Trucktown Ser.). (ENG.). 12p. (J). (gr. -1-1). bds. 7.99 *(978-1-4169-4185-9(1)*, Simon & Schuster Bks. For Young Readers) Simon & Schuster Bks. For Young Readers.
—Trucks Line Up. Scieszka, Jon. 2011. (Jon Scieszka's Trucktown Ser.). (ENG.). 24p. (J). (gr. -1-1). 16.99 *(978-1-4169-4158-3(4)*, Simon Spotlight) Simon Spotlight.
—Trucksgiving. Scieszka, Jon. 2010. (Jon Scieszka's Trucktown Ser.). (ENG.). 24p. (J). (gr. -1-1). 16.99 *(978-1-4169-4157-6(6))*; pap. 3.99 *(978-1-4169-4146-0(0))* Simon Spotlight. (Simon Spotlight).
—Uh-Oh, Max. Scieszka, Jon. (Jon Scieszka's Trucktown Ser.). (ENG.). 24p. (J). (gr. -1-1). 2014. 16.99 *(978-1-4814-1461-6(5))*; 2009. pap. 3.99 *(978-1-4169-4141-5(X))* Simon Spotlight. (Simon Spotlight).
—Welcome to Trucktown! Scieszka, Jon. 2010. (Jon Scieszka's Trucktown Ser.). (ENG.). 40p. (J). (gr. -1-3). pap. 3.99 *(978-1-4424-1271-2(2)*, Simon & Schuster Bks. For Young Readers) Simon & Schuster Bks. For Young Readers.
—Who's That Truck? Mason, Tom et al. 2008. (Jon Scieszka's Trucktown Ser.). (ENG.). 14p. (J). (gr. -1-1). 7.99 *(978-1-4169-4175-0(4)*, Little Simon) Little Simon.
—Zoom! Boom! Bully. Scieszka, Jon. 2008. (Jon Scieszka's Trucktown Ser.). (ENG.). 24p. (J). (gr. -1-k). lib. bdg. 13.89 *(978-1-4169-4150-7(9))*; pap. 3.99 *(978-1-4169-4139-2(8))* Simon Spotlight. (Simon Spotlight).
Shannon, David. Alice the Fairy. Shannon, David. (ENG.). (J). 2009. (gr. -1-k). pap. 9.95 incl. audio compact disk *(978-0-545-11758-6(5))*; 2004. *(978-0-439-69379-0(9)*, Blue Sky Pr., The) Scholastic, Inc.
—A Bad Case of Stripes. Shannon, David. (ENG.). (J). (gr. -1-3). 2007. 9.99 *(978-0-439-92494-8(4))*; 2004. 32p. reprint ed. pap. 6.99 *(978-0-439-59838-5(9)*, Scholastic Paperbacks) Scholastic, Inc.
—Bugs in My Hair! Shannon, David. 2013. (ENG.). 40p. (J). (gr. -1-3). 17.99 *(978-0-545-14313-4(6)*, Blue Sky Pr., The) Scholastic, Inc.
—David Smells! Shannon, David. 2005. (David Smells! Ser.). (ENG.). 12p. (J). (gr. -1-k). bds. 6.99 *(978-0-439-69138-3(9)*, Blue Sky Pr., The) Scholastic, Inc.
—Good Boy, Fergus! Shannon, David. 2006. (ENG.). 40p. (J). (gr. -1-k). 17.99 *(978-0-439-49027-6(8)*, Blue Sky Pr., The) Scholastic, Inc.
—How Georgie Radbourn Saved Baseball. Shannon, David. 2012. (ENG.). 32p. (J). (gr. -1-3). 17.99 *(978-0-545-38178-9(9)*, Blue Sky Pr., The) Scholastic, Inc.
—It's Christmas, David! Shannon, David. 2010. (ENG.). 32p. (J). (gr. -1-3). 17.99 *(978-0-545-14311-0(X)*, Blue Sky Pr., The) Scholastic, Inc.
—Jangles: A Big Fish Story. Shannon, David. 2012. (ENG.). 32p. (J). (gr. -1-3). 17.99 *(978-0-545-14312-7(8)*, Blue Sky Pr., The) Scholastic, Inc.
—Oh, David! A Diaper David Book. Shannon, David. 2005. (Oh, David! Ser.). (ENG.). 12p. (J). (gr. -1-k). bds. 6.99 *(978-0-439-68881-9(7)*, Blue Sky Pr., The) Scholastic, Inc.
—Oops! A Diaper David Book. Shannon, David. 2005. (Oops! Ser.). (ENG.). 12p. (J). (gr. -1-k). bds. 6.99 *(978-0-439-68882-6(5)*, Blue Sky Pr., The) Scholastic, Inc.
—Too Many Toys. Shannon, David. (ENG.). (J). (gr. -1-3). 2011. 9.99 *(978-0-545-35393-9(9))*; 2008. 32p. 16.99 *(978-0-439-49029-0(4))* Scholastic, Inc.
—Uh-Oh, David! A David Sticker Book. Shannon, David. 2013. (ENG.). 16p. (J). (gr. -1-k). 6.99 *(978-0-545-43768-4(7)*, Cartwheel Bks.) Scholastic, Inc.
Shannon, Doug. The Anxiety Survival Guide for Teens: CBT Skills to Overcome Fear, Worry, & Panic. Shannon, Jennifer. 2015. (Instant Help Solutions Ser.). (ENG.). 256p. (YA). (gr. 5-12). pap. 16.95 ***(978-1-62625-243-1(2))*** New Harbinger Pubns.
Shannon, Kate. Freddie, Bill & Irving. Bennett, Paul. 2009. 112p. (gr. 2-2). pap. 25.16 *(978-1-4251-7692-1(5))* Trafford Publishing.
—The Magical Adventures of Tara & the Talking Kitten. Cooper, Diana. 2011. (Tara & Ash-Ting Ser.). (ENG.). 80p. (J). (gr. k-4). 8.95 *(978-1-84409-550-6(9))* Findhorn Pr. GBR. Dist: Perseus-PGW.
—Tara & Her Talking Kitten Meet a Mermaid. Cooper, Diana. 2012. (Tara & Ash-Ting Ser.). (ENG.). 80p. (J). (gr. k-4). 8.95 *(978-1-84409-580-3(0))* Findhorn Pr. GBR. Dist: Perseus-PGW.
—Tara & the Talking Kitten Meet a Unicorn. Cooper, Diana. 2011. (Tara & Ash-Ting Ser.). (ENG.). 80p. (J). (gr. k-4). 8.95 *(978-1-84409-557-5(6))* Findhorn Pr. GBR. Dist: Perseus-PGW.
—Tara & the Talking Kitten Meet Angels & Fairies. Cooper, Diana. 2011. (Tara & Ash-Ting Ser.). (ENG.). 80p. (J). (gr. k-4). 8.95 *(978-1-84409-551-3(7))* Findhorn Pr. GBR. Dist: Perseus-PGW.
Shannon, Kenyon. The How & Why Wonder Book of Rocks & Minerals. Hyler, Nelson W. Blackwood, Paul E., ed. 2011. 52p. 36.95 *(978-1-258-10482-5(2))* Literary Licensing, LLC.
Shanower, Eric. The Living House of Oz. Einhorn, Edward. 2005. 239p. (J). 27.95 *(978-1-929527-08-3(X))* Hungry Tiger Pr.
Shanower, Eric. Adventures in Oz. Shanower, Eric. 2007. 256p. (J). (gr. 5-7). 75.00 *(978-1-60010-071-0(6))* Idea & Design Works, LLC.
—Betrayal, Pt. 1, Vol. 3. Shanower, Eric. 2007. (Age of Bronze Ser.: Vol. 3A). 176p. (YA). (gr. 10-18). 27.99 *(978-1-58240-845-3(9))* Image Comics.
—The Salt Sorcerer of Oz & Other Stories. Shanower, Eric. 2003. (Oz Ser.). 288p. (J). 24.95 *(978-1-929527-06-9(3))* Hungry Tiger Pr.
Shapiro, Alison Bonds. Just for Today. Phillips, Jan. 2005. (ENG.). 32p. (J). (gr. -1-5). 15.95 *(978-1-932073-07-2(8))* Kramer, H.J. Inc.
Shapiro, Alla. Tales from the Frog Forest. Lopatina, Irina. Lopatin, Dmitry, tr. 2012. (ENG.). 48p. (J). 18.00 *(978-1-61153-022-3(9))* Light Messages Publishing.
Shapiro, Deborah & Daniel, Alan. Letters from the Sea. Bjelke, Rolf, photos by. Shapiro, Deborah & Daniel, Lea. 2010. (ENG.). 96p. (J). (gr. 4-7). pap. 9.95 *(978-0-939837-03-8(X))* Paradise Cay Pubns.
Shapiro, Michelle. The Hanukkah Mice, 0 vols. Kroll, Steven. 2012. (ENG.). 40p. (J). (gr. -1-3). pap. 7.99 *(978-0-7614-5988-0(X)*, 9780761459880, Amazon Children's Publishing) Amazon Publishing.
—Happy Hanukkah Lights. Jules, Jacqueline. 2010. (Hanukkah Ser.). (ENG.). 12p. (J). (gr. -1 — 1). bds. 5.95 *(978-0-7613-5120-7(5)*, Kar-Ben Publishing) Lerner Publishing Group.
—Rebecca's Journey Home. Sugarman, Brynn Olenberg. 2014. (Life Cycle Ser.). (ENG.). 32p. (J). (gr. k-4). 8.95 *(978-1-4677-4937-4(0)*, Kar-Ben Publishing) Lerner Publishing Group.
Shapiro, Neil. The Amazing Menorah of Mazeltown. Dresner, Hal. 2009. (ENG.). 32p. (J). (gr. -1-3). 16.95 *(978-1-933176-28-4(8))* Red Rock Pr., Inc.
Shapiro, Pepper. The Journey of the Coconut. Meyer, Kim Shapiro. 2012. 34p. 24.95 *(978-1-4626-5576-2(9))*; 36p. pap. 24.95 *(978-1-4626-6641-4(9))* America Star Bks.
Shapiro, Rebecca. The Worry Worm. Brody, Lazer. 2007. 26p. (J). 26.95 *(978-0-9797530-1-5(5))* Kalcorn Publishing.
Share, Brian. There's a Dinosaur in My Room. Sharfe, Elaine. 2005. 20p. (J). pap. 7.95 *(978-1-894601-05-4(X))* Chestnut Publishing Group CAN. Dist: Hushion Hse. Publishing, Ltd.
Sharkey, Niamh. Dreams of Old Ireland. (J). *(978-1-84148-481-5(4))* Barefoot Bks., Inc.
—The Gigantic Turnip. Tolstoy, Aleksei. 2005. (ENG.). 40p. (J). (gr. -1-2). 8.99 *(978-1-905236-58-9(1))* Barefoot Bks., Inc.
—Tales from Old Ireland. Doyle, Malachy. 2008. (ENG.). 96p. (J). 21.99 *(978-1-84686-241-0(8))* Barefoot Bks., Inc.
—Tales of Wisdom & Wonder. Lupton, Hugh. (ENG.). 64p. (J). 2008. 19.99 *(978-1-84686-243-4(4))*; 2006. (gr. -1-3). pap. 15.99 *(978-1-905236-84-8(0))* Barefoot Bks., Inc.
—Tales of Wisdom & Wonder. 2005. 64p. (J). *(978-1-84148-231-6(5))* Barefoot Bks., Inc.

S

Sharkey, Niamh. I'm a Happy Hugglewug: Laugh & Play the Hugglewug Way. Sharkey, Niamh. 2008. (ENG.). 34p. (J). (gr. k-k). bds. 6.99 (978-0-7636-3981-5(8)) Candlewick Pr.

—Jack & the Beanstalk. Sharkey, Niamh. Walker, Richard. 2006. (ENG.). 40p. (J). (gr. 4-7). pap. 9.99 (978-1-905236-69-5(7)) Barefoot Bks., Inc.

—Santasaurus. Sharkey, Niamh. (ENG.). 32p. (J). (gr. -1-2). 2008. pap. 3.99 (978-0-7636-3890-0(0)); 2005. 15.99 (978-0-7636-2671-6(6)) Candlewick Pr.

Sharma, Lalit Kumar. In Defense of the Realm: Graphic Novel. Deshpande, Sanjay. 2011. (Campfire Graphic Novels Ser.). (ENG.). 104p. (gr. 3-7). pap. 12.99 (978-93-80028-64-4(4), Campfire) Kalyani Navyug Media Pty. Ltd. IND. Dist: Random Hse., Inc.

—Muhammad Ali: The King of the Ring. Helfand, Lewis. 2012. (Campfire Graphic Novels Ser.). (ENG.). 92p. (gr. 5). pap. 12.99 (978-93-80741-23-9(5), Campfire) Kalyani Navyug Media Pty. Ltd. IND. Dist: Random Hse., Inc.

—World War One, 1914-1918. Cowsill, Alan. 2014. (Campfire Graphic Novels Ser.). (ENG.). 114p. (J). (gr. 7). pap. 12.99 (978-93-80741-85-7(5), Campfire) Kalyani Navyug Media Pty. Ltd. IND. Dist: Random Hse., Inc.

Sharmat, Mitchell & Weston, Martha. Nate the Great on the Owl Express. Sharmat, Marjorie Weinman. 2004. (Nate the Great Ser.: No. 24). (ENG.). 80p. (J). (gr. 1-4). 5.99 (978-0-440-41927-3(1), Yearling) Random Hse. Children's Bks.

Sharp, Alice & Sharp, Paul. ¿Adivina Que? Historias de la Biblia, 1 vol. Harrast, Tracy. 2005. (SPA.). 192p. (J). (gr. 1-5). 13.99 (978-0-8297-4448-4(7)) Vida Pubs.

Sharp, Anne. Pop-up Dinosaur Danger! ed. 2007. (ENG.). 10p. 28.95 (978-1-4050-5332-7(1), Macmillan) Pan Macmillan GBR. Dist: Trans-Atlantic Pubns., Inc.

Sharp, Anne, jt. illus. see Denchfield, Nick.

Sharp, Chris. All Aboard! Charlie the Can-Do Choo Choo. Berry, Ron & Mead, David. 2009. (ENG.). 8p. 12.99 (978-0-8249-1420-2(1), Candy Cane Pr.) Ideals Pubns.

—Baby Flamingo. Pingry, Patricia A. 2004. (San Diego Zoo Animal Library: Vol. 8). (ENG.). 26p. (J). bds. 6.95 (978-0-8249-6557-0(4)) Ideals Pubns.

—Baby Hippopotamus. Pingry, Patricia A. 2004. 26p. (J). bds. 6.95 (978-0-8249-6554-9(X)) Ideals Pubns.

—Baby Orca. Seaworld, photos by. Shively, Julie. 2005. (Seaworld Animal Library). 24p. (J). (gr. -1-3). bds. 6.95 (978-0-8249-6615-7(5)) Ideals Pubns.

—Baby Panda. Pingry, Patricia A. 2004. (San Diego Zoo Animal Library: Vol. 7). (ENG.). 26p. (J). bds. 6.95 (978-0-8249-6555-6(8)) Ideals Pubns.

—Baby Zebra. Pingry, Patricia A. 2004. (San Diego Zoo Animal Library: Vol. 6). (ENG.). 26p. (J). bds. 6.95 (978-0-8249-6556-3(6)) Ideals Pubns.

—Beware the Haunted House. Berry, Ron. 2008. (ENG.). 12p. (J). (gr. -1-k). bds. 12.99 (978-0-8249-1815-6(0), Ideals Children's Bks.) Ideals Pubns.

—Can You Make Peter Rabbit Giggle? Berry, Ron. 2012. 10p. (J). bds. 10.99 (978-0-8249-1418-9(X)) Ideals Pubns.

—Can You Make the Monster Giggle? A Halloween Self-Scare Book! Mead, David & Berry, Ron. 2011. 16p. (J). 10.99 (978-0-8249-1526-1(7), Ideals Children's Bks.) Ideals Pubns.

—Can You Roar Like a Lion? Berry, Ron. 2009. (ENG.). 14p. bds. 10.99 (978-0-8249-1433-2(3), Candy Cane Pr.) Ideals Pubns.

—Charlie the Can-Do Choo-Choo! Berry, Ron. 2006. (ENG.). 7p. (J). (gr. -1). bds. 12.95 (978-0-8249-6678-2(3), Candy Cane Pr.) Ideals Pubns.

—David & Goliath: A Story about Courage. Smart Kids Publishing Staff. 2006. (I Can Read the Bible Ser.). (ENG.). 12p. (J). (gr. -1-3). 14.95 (978-0-8249-6659-1(7), Candy Cane Pr.) Ideals Pubns.

—The Forgetful Little Leprechaun. Mead, David. 2011. 18p. (J). (gr. -1-1). bds. 10.99 (978-0-8249-1509-4(7)) Ideals Pubns.

—God, Please Send Fire. Lashbrook, Marilyn. 2012. 32p. (J). pap. 8.00 (978-1-935014-42-3(0)) Hutchings, John Pubs.

—How Do I Kiss You? Weimer, Heidi R. 2008. (ENG.). 18p. (J). (gr. -1-k). bds. 12.99 (978-0-8249-1814-9(2), Ideals Children's Bks.) Ideals Pubns.

—It Was a Dark Dark Night. Berry, Ron. 2012. 14p. (J). bds. 12.99 (978-0-8249-1602-2(6)) Ideals Pubns.

—Jonah & the Whale: A Story about Responsibility. Smart Kids Publishing Staff. 2006. (I Can Read the Bible Ser.). (ENG.). 12p. (J). (gr. -1-3). 14.95 (978-0-8249-6661-4(9), Candy Cane Pr.) Ideals Pubns.

—Joy to the World. Mead, David. 2010. 16p. (J). (gr. -1-1). 10.99 (978-0-8249-1470-7(8)) Ideals Pubns.

—Little Abe Lincoln Learns a Lesson in Honesty: Honesty. Mead, David. 2003. (American Virtues for Kids Ser.). (J). bds. 6.95 (978-0-9746440-0-4(5)) Ideals Pubns.

—Little Ben Franklin Learns a Lesson in Generosity: Generosity. Mead, David. 2003. (American Virtues for Kids Ser.). (J). bds. 6.95 (978-0-9746440-2-8(1)) Ideals Pubns.

—The Little Drummer Boy. Berry, Ron & Mead, David. 2009. (ENG.). 16p. 12.99 (978-0-8249-1429-5(5), Candy Cane Pr.) Ideals Pubns.

—Little George Washington Learns about Responsibility: Responsibility. Mead, David. 2004. (American Virtues for Kids Ser.). (J). bds. 6.95 (978-0-9746440-1-1(3)) Ideals Pubns.

—Little Teddy Roosevelt Learns a Lesson in Courage: Courage. Mead, David. 2003. (American Virtues for Kids Ser.). (J). bds. 6.95 (978-0-9746440-3-5(X)) Ideals Pubns.

—Look for the Rainbow! Berry, Ron. 2009. (ENG.). 18p. bds. 10.99 (978-0-8249-1428-8(7), Candy Cane Pr.) Ideals Pubns.

—Me 'n Mom: A Keepsake Scrapbook Journal. Barry, Ron & Fitzgerald, Paula. 2009. (ENG.). 33p. pap. 14.99 (978-0-8249-1435-6(X), Ideals Children's Bks.) Ideals Pubns.

—My First Family Photo Album. Berry, Ron. 2008. (ENG.). 12p. (J). bds. 8.99 (978-0-8249-6722-2(4), Ideals Children's Bks.) Ideals Pubns.

—My Guardian Angel. Berry, Ron. 2008. 12p. (J). (gr. -1-k). bds. 12.99 (978-0-8249-1819-4(3), Ideals Children's Bks.) Ideals Pubns.

—Rise & Shine! Berry, Ron. 2008. 14p. (J). bds. 12.99 (978-0-8249-6735-2(6), Ideals Children's Bks.) Ideals Pubns.

—Silent Night. Mead, David. 2010. 16p. (J). (gr. -1-1). 10.99 (978-0-8249-1427-1(9)) Ideals Pubns.

—The Silly Safari Bus! Berry, Ron. 2008. (ENG.). 12p. (J). bds. 12.99 (978-0-8249-6736-9(4), Ideals Children's Bks.) Ideals Pubns.

—We Wish You a Merry Christmas. Berry, Ron. 2011. 16p. (J). 10.99 (978-0-8249-1464-6(3), Candy Cane Pr.) Ideals Pubns.

—What's That Sound. Smart Kids Publishing Staff. 2005. 10p. (J). (gr. -1-k). 12.95 (978-0-8249-6624-9(4), Candy Cane Pr.) Ideals Pubns.

—You're My Little Love Bug. Weimer, Heidi. 2008. (ENG.). 16p. (J). bds. 12.99 (978-0-8249-6589-1(2)) Ideals Pubns.

—The 123s of How I Love You. Berry, Ron. 2012. 24p. (J). bds. 12.99 (978-0-8249-1601-5(8)) Ideals Pubns.

—131 Fun-Damental Facts for Catholic Kids: Liturgy, Litanies, Rituals, Rosaries, Symbols, Sacraments & Sacred Scripture. Synder, Bernadette. 2006. (Liguori's Fun Facts Ser.). 144p. (J). (gr. 3-7). per. 12.99 (978-0-7648-1502-7(4)) Liguori Pubns.

Sharp, Chris & Currant, Gary. It's Bedtime. Berry, Ron & Sharp, Chris. 2003. (It's Time to Ser.). (ENG.). 14p. (J). (gr. -1-k). bds. 6.95 (978-1-891100-61-1(0)) Smart Kidz Media, Inc.

Sharp, Chris & Seaworld, Chris. Baby Dolphin. Seaworld, Chris, photos by. Shivley, Julie. 2005. (Seaworld Animal Library: Vol. 4). 26p. (J). (gr. -1-k). bds. 6.95 (978-0-8249-6614-0(7)) Ideals Pubns.

—Baby Seal. Seaworld, Chris, photos by. Shivley, Julie. 2005. (Seaworld Animal Library: Vol. 3). 26p. (J). (gr. -1-k). bds. 6.95 (978-0-8249-6617-1(1)) Ideals Pubns.

Sharp, Craig. Mummy's Happy Tears. Bishop, Michele. 2013. 18p. pap. (978-1-78148-186-8(5)) Grosvenor Hse. Publishing Ltd.

Sharp, Gene. Please, Wind? Greene, Carol. 2011. (Rookie Ready to Learn - First Science Ser.). 40p. (J). (gr. -1-k). lib. bdg. 23.00 (978-0-531-26502-4(1), Children's Pr.) Scholastic Library Publishing.

—Too Many Balloons. Matthias, Catherine. 2011. (Rookie Ready to Learn Ser.). 40p. (J). (gr. -1-k). pap. 5.95 (978-0-531-26749-3(0)); lib. bdg. 23.00 (978-0-531-26449-2(1)) Scholastic Library Publishing. (Children's Pr.).

Sharp, Gene. Demasiados Globos. Sharp, Gene. Matthias, Catherine. 2011. (Rookie Ready to Learn Español Ser.). (SPA.). 40p. (J). pap. 5.95 (978-0-531-26792-9(X)); lib. bdg. 23.00 (978-0-531-26124-8(7)) Scholastic Library Publishing. (Children's Pr.).

Sharp, Kelley. Thisbe's Promise. Scott, Laurian. 2008. (ENG.). 32p. (J). 16.99 (978-0-9816642-0-0(2)) ETS Publishing.

SHARP Literacy Students. The American Dream. SHARP Literacy Students, . 2008.Tr. of gran sueño Americano. (ENG & SPA.). 84p. pap. (978-0-9770816-6-0(4)) SHARP Literacy, Inc.

Sharp, Melanie. Bedtime & New School. Cunningham, Anna. 2012. (Talk a Story Ser.). (ENG.). 16p. (J). (-k). pap. 7.99 (978-1-4451-0667-0(1)) Hodder & Stoughton GBR. Dist: Independent Pubs. Group.

Sharp, Melanie. In the Garden. Cronick, Mitch. 2005. (Collins Big Cat Ser.). (ENG.). 16p. (J). pap. 5.99 (978-0-00-718538-2(3)) HarperCollins Pubs. Ltd. GBR. Dist: Independent Pubs. Group.

—In the Garden. Collins Educational Staff & Cronick, Mitch. 2012. (Collins Big Cat Ser.). (ENG.). 16p. (J). pap., wbk. ed. 4.99 (978-0-00-747489-9(X)) HarperCollins Pubs. Ltd. GBR. Dist: Independent Pubs. Group.

Sharp, Paul. My Little Doctor Bag Book. Hapka, Cathy. 2005. (J). (978-1-57151-754-8(5)) Playhouse Publishing.

—Paul the Pitcher. 2011. (Rookie Ready to Learn Ser.). 40p. (J). pap. 5.95 (978-0-531-26651-9(6)); (gr. -1-k). lib. bdg. 23.00 (978-0-531-26426-3(2)) Scholastic Library Publishing. (Children's Pr.).

—Snow Joe. Greene, Carol. 2011. (Rookie Ready to Learn Ser.). 40p. (J). (ENG.). pap. 5.95 (978-0-531-26804-9(7)); (gr. -1-k). lib. bdg. 23.00 (978-0-531-25644-2(8)) Scholastic Library Publishing. (Children's Pr.).

Sharp, Paul. Pablo el Lanzador. Sharp, Paul. 2011. (Rookie Ready to Learn Español Ser.). (SPA.). 40p. (J). pap. 5.95 (978-0-531-26781-3(4)); lib. bdg. 23.00 (978-0-531-26113-2(1)) Scholastic Library Publishing. (Children's Pr.).

Sharp, Paul, jt. illus. see Sharp, Alice.

Sharp, Todd. Tom Tuff to the Rescue. Edgar, Robert. 2013. 26p. pap. (978-0-9874832-0-1(X)) MoshPit Publishing.

—Who Caught the Yawn? & Where Did the Sneeze Go? Mosher, Jennifer. 2013. 38p. pap. (978-0-9874832-3-2(4)) MoshPit Publishing.

Sharpe, Jim, jt. illus. see Spector, Joel.

Sharpe, Roseanne. First Farm in the Valley: Anna's Story. Pellowski, Anne. 2008. 194p. (J). pap. 12.95 (978-1-932350-24-1(1)) Bethlehem Bks.

—Stairstep Farm: Anna Rose's Story. Pellowski, Anne. 2011. 182p. (J). pap. 12.95 (978-1-932350-40-1(3)) Bethlehem Bks.

Sharpley, Kate. The Fantastic Christmas. Hughes, Julie. 2013. 34p. pap. (978-0-9868344-9-3(1)) Yodoki Inc.

Sharpnack, Joe. The Magic Music Shop. Brenner, Vida. Sharp, Mary, ed. 2013. 102p. pap. 12.95 (978-1-57216-094-1(2)) Penfield Bks.

Sharrat, Nick. Just Imagine. Goodhart, Pippa. 2014. 32p. (J). 12.99 (978-1-61067-343-3(3)) Kane Miller.

Sharratt, Nick. Animal Music. Donaldson, Julia. (ENG.). 24p. (J). ed. 2014. (— 1). pap. 9.99 (978-1-4472-1095-5(6)); 2nd ed. 2013. (gr. -1-k). 16.99 (978-0-330-51230-5(7)) Pan Macmillan GBR. Dist: Independent Pubs. Group.

—Best Friends. Wilson, Jacqueline. 2009. (ENG.). 256p. (J). (gr. 4-7). pap. 8.99 (978-0-312-58144-2(0)) Square Fish.

Sharratt, Nick. Billy Bonkers. Andreae, Giles. 2006. (Billy Bonkers Ser.). (ENG.). 128p. (J). (gr. 2-4). pap. 7.99 (978-1-84616-151-3(7)) Hodder & Stoughton GBR. Dist: Independent Pubs. Group.

Sharratt, Nick. Candyfloss. Wilson, Jacqueline. 2008. (ENG.). 352p. (J). (gr. 4-7). pap. 9.99 (978-0-312-38418-0(1)) Square Fish.

—Chocolate Mousse for Greedy Goose, 2. Donaldson, Julia. 2006. (ENG.). 24p. (J). (gr. -1-k). pap. 8.99 (978-1-4050-2190-6(X)) Macmillan Pubs., Ltd. GBR. Dist: Independent Pubs. Group.

—Cookie. Wilson, Jacqueline. 2010. (ENG.). 352p. (J). (gr. 4-7). pap. 11.99 (978-0-312-64290-7(3)) Square Fish.

—Daisy & the Trouble with Sports Day. Gray, Kes. 2014. (Daisy Ser.). (ENG.). 320p. (J). (gr. 2-4). pap. 7.99 (978-1-78295-285-5(3), Red Fox) Random House Children's Books GBR. Dist: Independent Pubs. Group.

—Goat Goes to Playgroup. Donaldson, Julia. ed. (ENG.). (J). 2014. 26p. bds. 9.99 (978-1-4472-5484-3(8)); 2012. 32p. (gr. -1). 16.99 (978-0-330-51228-2(5)); 8. 2013. 24p. (gr. -1-k). pap. 9.99 (978-1-4472-1094-8(8)) Pan Macmillan GBR. Dist: Independent Pubs. Group.

—Hippo Has a Hat. Donaldson, Julia. ed. 2007. (ENG.). 24p. (J). (gr. k-k). pap. 8.99 (978-1-4050-2192-0(6)) Macmillan Pubs., Ltd. GBR. Dist: Independent Pubs. Group.

—Hippo Has a Hat, 1. Donaldson, Julia. ed. 2010. (ENG.). 20p. (J). (gr. k-k). bds. 7.99 (978-0-230-71145-7(6)) Macmillan Pubs., Ltd. GBR. Dist: Independent Pubs. Group.

—The Indoor Pirates on Treasure Island. Strong, Jeremy. (ENG.). 96p. (J). 7.95 (978-0-14-038637-0(8)) Penguin Bks., Ltd. GBR. Dist: Trafalgar Square Publishing.

—Mixed up Fairy Tales. Robinson, Hilary. 2007. (ENG.). 32p. (J). (gr. k-2). pap. 11.95 (978-0-340-87558-2(5)) Hachette Children's Group GBR. Dist: Independent Pubs. Group.

—Never Shake a Rattlesnake, 1. Morgan, Michaela. ed. 2012. (ENG.). 32p. (J). (gr. -1-k). pap. 8.99 (978-0-330-51229-9(3)) Macmillan Pubs., Ltd. GBR. Dist: Independent Pubs. Group.

—One Mole Digging a Hole. Donaldson, Julia. ed. 2012. (ENG.). 24p. (J). (gr. k-k). bds. 8.99 (978-0-230-75049-4(4)) Macmillan Pubs., Ltd. GBR. Dist: Independent Pubs. Group.

—One Mole Digging a Hole, 2. Donaldson, Julia. ed. 2010. (ENG.). 32p. (J). (gr. k-k). pap. 8.99 (978-0-230-70647-7(9)) Macmillan Pubs., Ltd. GBR. Dist: Independent Pubs. Group.

—Shuffle & Squelch. Donaldson, Julia. 2015. (ENG.). 32p. (J). (-k). pap. 11.99 (978-1-4472-7681-4(7)) Pan Macmillan GBR. Dist: Independent Pubs. Group.

—The Story of Tracy Beaker. Wilson, Jacqueline. 2004. (ENG.). 133p. 16.00 (978-0-7569-3205-3(X)) Perfection Learning Corp.

—Toddle Waddle. Donaldson, Julia. ed. 2012. (ENG.). 32p. (J). (— 1). bds. 8.99 (978-0-230-75751-6(0)) Pan Macmillan GBR. Dist: Independent Pubs. Group.

—When a Monster Is Born. Taylor, Sean. 2011. (ENG.). 32p. (J). (gr. -1-1). pap. 6.99 (978-0-312-55348-7(X)) Square Fish.

—Whose Toes Are Those? Symes, Sally. 2012. (ENG.). 22p. (J). (gr. k-12). bds. 7.99 (978-0-7636-6274-5(7)) Candlewick Pr.

—Wriggle & Roar! Donaldson, Julia. 2015. (ENG.). 32p. (J). (gr. -1-1). pap. 9.99 (978-1-4472-7665-4(5)) Pan Macmillan GBR. Dist: Independent Pubs. Group.

—Wriggle & Roar! Rhymes to Join in With. Donaldson, Julia. 2nd ed. 2005. (ENG.). 32p. (J). (gr. k-k). pap. 10.99 (978-1-4050-2166-1(7)) Macmillan Pubs., Ltd. GBR. Dist: Independent Pubs. Group.

—Yawn. Symes, Sally. 2011. (ENG.). 24p. (J). (gr. -1-2). bds. 7.99 (978-0-7636-5725-3(5)) Candlewick Pr.

Sharratt, Nick. What's in the Witch's Kitchen? Sharratt, Nick. 2011. (ENG.). 20p. (J). (gr. -1-2). 12.99 (978-0-7636-5224-1(5)) Candlewick Pr.

Sharratt, Nick & Heap, Sue. Double Act. Wilson, Jacqueline. 2006. (ENG.). 192p. (J). (gr. 4-7). pap. 14.95 (978-0-440-86759-3(2)) Transworld Publishers Ltd. GBR. Dist: Independent Pubs. Group.

Sharratt, Nick & Parsons, Garry. Daisy & the Trouble with Burglars. Gray, Kes. 2014. (Daisy Ser.: 8). (ENG.). 236p. (J). (gr. 2-4). pap. 7.99 (978-1-84941-681-8(8), Red Fox) Random House Children's Books GBR. Dist: Independent Pubs. Group.

—Daisy & the Trouble with Coconuts. Gray, Kes. 2013. (Daisy Ser.). (ENG.). 272p. (J). (gr. 2-4). pap. 7.99 (978-1-84941-678-8(8), Red Fox) Random House Children's Books GBR. Dist: Independent Pubs. Group.

—Daisy & the Trouble with Giants. Gray, Kes. 2010. (Daisy Ser.: 10). (ENG.). 240p. (J). (gr. 2-4). pap. 7.99 (978-1-86230-495-6(5), Red Fox) Random House Children's Books GBR. Dist: Independent Pubs. Group.

—Daisy & the Trouble with Kittens. Gray, Kes. 2010. (Daisy Ser.). (ENG.). 256p. (J). (gr. 2-4). pap. 7.99 (978-1-86230-834-3(9), Red Fox) Random House Children's Books GBR. Dist: Independent Pubs. Group.

—Daisy & the Trouble with Life. Gray, Kes. 2007. (Daisy Ser.: 12). (ENG.). 224p. (J). (gr. 2-4). pap. 11.95 (978-1-86230-167-2(0), Red Fox) Random House Children's Books GBR. Dist: Independent Pubs. Group.

—Daisy & the Trouble with Maggots, No. 6. Gray, Kes. 2010. (Daisy Ser.: 6). (ENG.). 240p. (J). (gr. 2-4). pap. 8.99 (978-1-86230-846-6(2), Red Fox) Random House Children's Books GBR. Dist: Independent Pubs. Group.

Shaskan, Stephen. Art Panels, BAM! Speech Bubbles, POW! Writing Your Own Graphic Novel, 1 vol. Shaskan, Trisha Speed. 2010. (Writer's Toolbox Ser.). (ENG.). 32p. (gr. 2-4). pap. 8.95 (978-1-4048-6393-4(1), Nonfiction Picture Bks.) Picture Window Bks.

Shaskan, Stephen. The Three Triceratops Tuff. Shaskan, Stephen. 2013. (ENG.). 32p. (J). (gr. -1-2). 16.99 (978-1-4424-4397-6(9), Beach Lane Bks.) Beach Lane Bks.

Shattil, Wendy, et al, photos by. Sierra Babies. 2013. 26p. (J). 8.95 (978-1-56037-557-9(4)) Farcountry Pr.

Shattil, Wendy & Rozinski, Bob, photos by. The Wildlife Detectives: How Forensic Scientists Fight Crimes Against Nature. Jackson, Donna M. 2005. (Scientists in the Field Ser.). 47p. (gr. 3-7). 20.00 (978-0-7569-5191-7(7)) Perfection Learning Corp.

Shaughnessy, Mara. Downpour. Martin, Emily. 2013. (ENG.). 32p. (J). (gr. -1-k). 14.95 (978-1-62087-545-2(4), 620545, Sky Pony Pr.) Skyhorse Publishing Co., Inc.

Shavell, Lauren. Reflexology Deck: 50 Healing Techniques. Dreyfuss, Katy. 2004. (ENG.). 50p. (gr. 8-17). 14.95 (978-0-8118-4176-4(6)) Chronicle Bks. LLC.

Shaw, Brian. Cuenta con el Beisbol. Shaw, Brian. McGrath, Barbara Barbieri. Canetti, Yanitzia, tr. from SPA. 2005. (ENG & SPA.). 32p. (J). (gr. -1-2). pap. 7.95 (978-1-57091-608-3(X)) Charlesbridge Publishing, Inc.

Shaw, Charles. Baxter Barret Brown's Bass Fiddle. McKenzie, Tim A. 2004. (ENG.). 24p. (J). (gr. 2-4). 19.95 (978-1-931721-06-6(8)) Bright Sky Pr.

—Big Cat Trouble. Smalley, Roger. 2005. (J). (978-1-933248-13-4(0)) World Quest Learning.

—Gorilla Guardian. Smalley, Roger. 2005. (J). (978-1-933248-14-1(9)) World Quest Learning.

—Horned Toad Canyon. Roach, Joyce Gibson. 2003. (ENG.). 48p. (J). (gr. 2-4). 17.95 (978-1-931721-01-1(7), c2d211ff-dcbc-4d55-8600-9edaa91d316d) Bright Sky Pr.

Shaw, Daniel. Journey to Pansophigus. ed. 2005. (J). per. 9.95 (978-0-9772168-0-2(2)) Water Lily Pr., Inc.

Shaw, David. The Brave Little Tailor: A Retelling of the Grimm's Fairy Tale, 1 vol. Blair, Eric. 2011. (My First Classic Story Ser.). (ENG.). 32p. (gr. k-3). pap. 7.10 (978-1-4048-7357-5(0), My First Classic Story) Picture Window Bks.

—The Brave Little Tailor: A Retelling of the Grimm's Fairy Tale, 1 vol. Blair, Eric et al. 2010. (My First Classic Story Ser.). (ENG.). 32p. (gr. k-3). lib. bdg. 21.32 (978-1-4048-6074-2(6), My First Classic Story) Picture Window Bks.

—Rumpelstiltskin. Blair, Eric. Abello, Patricia, tr. from ENG. 2006. (Read-It! Readers en Español: Cuentos de Hadas Ser.). (SPA.). 32p. (gr. k-3). 19.99 (978-1-4048-1637-4(2), Easy Readers) Picture Window Bks.

—Rumpelstiltskin: A Retelling of the Grimm's Fairy Tale, 1 vol. Blair, Eric. 2013. (My First Classic Story Ser.). (ENG.). 32p. (gr. k-3). pap. 7.10 (978-1-4795-1850-0(6), My First Classic Story) Picture Window Bks.

Shaw, Hannah. The Complete Critter Capers Set: The Great Hamster Massacre; The Great Rabbit Rescue; The Great Cat Conspiracy; The Great Dog Disaster. Davies, Katie. ed. 2013. (Great Critter Capers Ser.). (ENG.). 864p. (J). (gr. 3-7). 51.99 (978-1-4424-9990-4(7), Beach Lane Bks.) Beach Lane Bks.

—Crocodiles Are the Best Animals of All! Taylor, Sean. 2009. (Time to Read Ser.). (ENG.). 32p. (J). (gr. -1-k). 16.95 (978-1-84507-904-8(3), Frances Lincoln) Quarto Publishing Group UK GBR. Dist: Perseus-PGW.

—The Great Cat Conspiracy. Davies, Katie. 2012. (Great Critter Capers Ser.). (ENG.). 224p. (J). (gr. 3-7). 12.99 (978-1-4424-4513-0(0), Beach Lane Bks.) Beach Lane Bks.

—The Great Dog Disaster. Davies, Katie. 2013. (Great Critter Capers Ser.). (ENG.). 208p. (J). (gr. 3-7). 12.99 (978-1-4424-4517-8(3), Beach Lane Bks.) Beach Lane Bks.

—The Great Hamster Massacre. Davies, Katie. 2011. (Great Critter Capers Ser.). (ENG.). 208p. (J). (gr. 3-7). 12.99 (978-1-4424-2062-5(6), Beach Lane Bks.) Beach Lane Bks.

—The Great Rabbit Rescue. Davies, Katie. 2011. (Great Critter Capers Ser.). (ENG.). 224p. (J). (gr. 3-7). 12.99 (978-1-4424-2064-9(2), Beach Lane Bks.) Beach Lane Bks.

—Grizzly Bear with the Frizzly Hair. Taylor, Sean & Quarto Generic Staff. 2011. (Time to Read Ser.). (ENG.). 32p. (J). (gr. -1-1). pap. 8.95 (978-1-84780-144-9(7), Frances Lincoln) Quarto Publishing Group UK GBR. Dist: Hachette Bk. Group.

—We Have Lift-Off! Taylor, Sean & Quarto Generic Staff. 2013. (Time to Read Ser.). (ENG.). 32p. (J). (gr. -1-2). 17.99 (978-1-84780-322-1(9), Frances Lincoln) Quarto Publishing Group UK GBR. Dist: Hachette Bk. Group.

Shaw, Hannah. Crocodiles Are the Best Animals of All! Shaw, Hannah. Taylor, Sean & Quarto Generic Staff. rev. ed. 2014. (Time to Read Ser.). (ENG.). 32p. (J). (gr. -1-1). pap. 6.99 (978-1-84780-476-1(4), Frances Lincoln) Quarto Publishing Group UK GBR. Dist: Hachette Bk. Group.

—The Grizzly Bear with the Frizzly Hair. Shaw, Hannah. Taylor, Sean & Quarto Generic Staff. rev. ed. 2014. (Time to Read Ser.). (ENG.). 32p. (J). (gr. -1-2). pap. 6.99 (978-1-84780-475-4(6), Frances Lincoln) Quarto Publishing Group UK GBR. Dist: Hachette Bk. Group.

—We Have Lift-Off! Shaw, Hannah. Taylor, Sean & Quarto Generic Staff. rev. ed. 2014. (Time to Read Ser.). (ENG.). 32p. (J). (gr. -1-2). pap. 6.99 (978-1-84780-477-8(2), Frances Lincoln Children's Bks.) Quarto Publishing Group UK GBR. Dist: Hachette Bk. Group.

—Who Ate Auntie Iris? Shaw, Hannah. Taylor, Sean et al. rev. ed. 2014. (Time to Read Ser.). (ENG.). 32p. (J). (gr. -1-2). pap. 6.99 (978-1-84780-478-5(0), Frances Lincoln) Quarto Publishing Group UK GBR. Dist: Hachette Bk. Group.

Shaw, Mick & Scott, Kimberley G. Tilly & the Dragon: Red Banana. McKay, Hilary. 2014. (Red Bananas Ser.). (ENG.). 48p. (J). pap. 7.99 (978-1-4052-6721-2(6)) Egmont Bks., Ltd. GBR. Dist: Independent Pubs. Group.

Shaw, Peter. Hop, Little Hare! Wild, Margaret. 2006. (ENG.). 24p. (J). (gr. -1-2). 19.95 (978-1-877003-95-0(6)) Little Hare Bks. AUS. Dist: Independent Pubs. Group.

Shaw-Peterson, Kimberly. A Baby Brother! Oh No! Hakala, Joann. 2006. 32p. (J). (gr. -1). per. 10.95 (978-1-59298-152-6(6)) Beaver's Pond Pr., Inc.

—The Crayon Kids' Art Adventure. Ruprecht, Jennifer L. 2007. (ENG.). 32p. (J). per. 9.95 (978-1-933916-10-1(9)) Nelson Publishing & Marketing.

S

—Darcy Daisy & the Firefly Festival: Learning about Bipolar Disorder & Community. Lewandowski, Lisa & Trost, Shannon. 2005. 32p. (J). (gr. -1-9). pap. 9.95 *(978-0-9785075-2-7(5)*, Ferne Pr.) Nelson Publishing & Marketing.

Shaw, Sarah. Davey the Detective: A Bird Brain Book. Chand, Emlyn. l.t. ed. 2012. (ENG.). 42p. (gr. k-1). pap. 10.95 *(978-1-62253-119-6(1))*; 21.95 *(978-1-62253-107-3(8))* Evolved Publishing.

—Honey the Hero: A Bird Brain Book. Chand, Emlyn. ed. 2012. (ENG.). 44p. (gr. k-1). (J). 21.95 *(978-1-62253-106-6(X))*; pap. 10.95 *(978-1-62253-118-9(3))* Evolved Publishing.

—Poppy the Proud: A Bird Brain Book. Chand, Emlyn. ed. 2012. 3. (ENG.). 44p. (gr. k-3). 21.95 *(978-1-62253-108-0(6))*; pap. 10.95 *(978-1-62253-120-2(5))* Evolved Publishing.

Shaw-Smith, Emma. Bread Is for Eating. Gershator, David & Gershator, Phillis. 2003. (ENG & SPA.). 25p. (J). (gr. k-4). reprint ed. 16.00 *(978-0-7567-9033-2(6))* DIANE Publishing Co.

Shaw, Stan. Oscar Wilde, Vol. 16. Wilde, Oscar et al. Pomplun, Tom, ed. 2009. (Graphic Classics Ser.: Vol. 16). 144p. (YA). pap. 11.95 *(978-0-9787919-6-4(7))* Eureka Productions.

Shaw, Yvonne. Priscilla & the Big Red Ball, 1 vol. Shaw, Laura. 2009. 19p. pap. 24.95 *(978-1-60749-523-9(6))* America Star Bks.

She, Liu & Rujin, Ma. Chinese Fables & Folktales (I) Ma, Zheng & Li, Zheng. 2010. (ENG.). 48p. (J). (gr. -1-2). 16.95 *(978-1-60220-962-6(6))* BetterLink Pr., Inc.

She, Liu & Xiaoqing, Pan. Stories Behind Chinese Idioms (III) Ma, Zheng & Li, Zheng. 2010. (ENG.). 48p. (J). (gr. 3-6). 16.95 *(978-1-60220-967-1(7))* BetterLink Pr., Inc.

Shea, Bob. Gilbert Goldfish Wants a Pet. DiPucchio, Kelly. 2011. (ENG.). 32p. (J). (gr. -1-k). 16.99 *(978-0-8037-3394-7(1)*, Dial) Penguin Publishing Group.

—I Will Chomp You! John, Jory. 2015. (ENG.). 40p. (J). (gr. -1-2). 20.99 *(978-0-385-38987-7(6)*, Random Hse. Bks. for Young Readers) Random Hse. Children's Bks.

Shea, Bob. I'm No Monster! John, Jory. 2016. (J). ***(978-0-385-38990-7(6))*** Random Hse., Inc.

Shea, Bob. Me Want Pet! Sauer, Tammi. 2012. (ENG.). 40p. (J). (gr. -1-3). 16.99 *(978-1-4424-0810-4(3)*, Simon & Schuster/Paula Wiseman Bks.) Simon & Schuster/Paula Wiseman Bks.

—Wedgieman: A Hero Is Born. Harper, Charise Mericle. ed. 2012. (Step into Reading Level 3 Ser.). lib. bdg. 13.55 *(978-0-606-26807-3(3)*, Turtleback) Turtleback Bks.

—Wedgieman & the Big Bunny Trouble. Harper, Charise Mericle. 2014. (Step into Reading Ser.). (ENG.). 48p. (J). (gr. k-3). 3.99 *(978-0-307-93073-6(4)*, Random Hse. Bks. for Young Readers) Random Hse. Children's Bks.

Shea, Bob. Ballet Cat: The Totally Secret Secret. Shea, Bob. 2015. (Ballet Cat Ser.). (ENG.). 56p. (J). (gr. 1-3). 9.99 *(978-1-4847-1378-5(8))* Disney Pr.

—Cheetah Can't Lose. Shea, Bob. 2013. (ENG.). 40p. (J). (gr. -1-3). 17.99 *(978-0-06-173083-2(1))* HarperCollins Pubs.

—Dinosaur vs. Bedtime. Shea, Bob. (Dinosaur vs. Book Ser.). (ENG.). (J). (gr. -1-k). 2011. 30p. bds. 6.99 *(978-1-4231-3788-7(4))*; 2008. 40p. 15.99 *(978-1-4231-1335-5(7))* Hyperion Pr.

—Dinosaur vs. Mommy. Shea, Bob. 2015. (Dinosaur vs. Book Ser.). (ENG.). 40p. (J). (gr. -1-k). 16.99 *(978-1-4231-6086-1(X))* Hyperion Bks. for Children.

—Dinosaur vs. Santa. Shea, Bob. 2014. (Dinosaur vs. Book Ser.). (ENG.). 30p. (J). (gr. -1-k). bds. 7.99 *(978-1-4231-6824-9(0))* Hyperion Bks. for Children.

—Dinosaur vs. School. Shea, Bob. 2014. (Dinosaur vs. Book Ser.). (ENG.). 40p. (J). (gr. -1-k). 16.99 *(978-1-4231-6087-8(8))* Hyperion Bks. for Children.

—Dinosaur vs. the Library. Shea, Bob. 2011. (ENG.). 40p. (J). (gr. -1-1). 15.99 *(978-1-4231-3338-4(2))* Hyperion Pr.

—Dinosaur vs. the Potty. Shea, Bob. (ENG.). (J). (gr. -1-1). 2012. 30p. bds. 6.99 *(978-1-4231-5179-1(8))*; 2010. 40p. 15.99 *(978-1-4231-3339-1(0))* Hyperion Pr.

—I'm a Shark. Shea, Bob. 2011. (ENG.). 40p. (J). (gr. -1-1). 16.99 *(978-0-06-199846-1(X))* HarperCollins Pubs.

—Oh, Daddy! Shea, Bob. 2010. (ENG.). 40p. (J). (gr. -1-1). 16.99 *(978-0-06-173080-1(7))* HarperCollins Pubs.

—Race You to Bed. Shea, Bob. 2010. (ENG.). 40p. (J). (gr. -1-2). 16.99 *(978-0-06-170417-8(2)*, Tegen, Katherine Bks) HarperCollins Pubs.

—Unicorn Thinks He's Pretty Great. Shea, Bob. 2013. (ENG.). 40p. (J). (gr. -1-k). 15.99 *(978-1-4231-5952-0(7))* Hyperion Pr.

Shea, Chris. That's How Much God Loves You! Shea, Chris. 2008. (HarperBlessings Ser.). (ENG.). 24p. (J). (gr. -1-3). pap. 7.99 *(978-0-06-083876-8(0)*, HarperFestival) HarperCollins Pubs.

Shea, Denise. Altas y Bajas, Blancas y Grises: Un Libro Sobre las Nubes. Meachen Rau, Dana & Picture Window Books Staff. Robledo, Sol, tr. from ENG. 2007. (Ciencia Asombrosa: Exploremos el Espacio Ser.). (SPA.). 24p. (gr. k-4). 25.99 *(978-1-4048-3216-9(5))* Picture Window Bks.

—Caliente y Brillante: Un Libro Sobre el Sol, 1 vol. Meachen Rau, Dana & Picture Window Books Staff. Robledo, Sol, tr. 2007. (Ciencia Asombrosa: Exploremos el Espacio Ser.). (SPA.). 24p. (gr. k-4). 25.99 *(978-1-4048-3218-3(1))* Picture Window Bks.

—Cut, Chop, & Stop: A Book about Wedges, 1 vol. Dahl, Michael. 2006. (Amazing Science: Simple Machines Ser.). (ENG.). 24p. (gr. k-4). lib. bdg. 25.99 *(978-1-4048-1307-6(1)*, 1253207, Nonfiction Picture Bks.) Picture Window Bks.

—Eye of the Storm: A Book about Hurricanes, 1 vol. Thomas, Rick & Picture Window Books Staff. 2005. (Amazing Science: Weather Ser.). (ENG.). 24p. (gr. -1-3). per. 7.95 *(978-1-4048-1845-3(6)*, Nonfiction Picture Bks.) Picture Window Bks.

—Giran en el Espacio: Un Libro Sobre Los Planetas. Meachen Rau, Dana & Picture Window Books Staff. Robledo, Sol, tr. from ENG. 2007. (Ciencia Asombrosa: Exploremos el Espacio Ser.). (SPA.). 24p. (gr. k-4). 25.99 *(978-1-4048-3231-2(9))* Picture Window Bks.

—¡Juush! ¡Ruum! Un Libro Sobre Tornados. Thomas, Rick & Picture Window Books Staff. Robledo, Sol, tr. from ENG. 2007. (Ciencia Asombrosa: el Tiempo Ser.). (SPA.). 24p. (gr. -1-3). 25.99 *(978-1-4048-3237-4(8))* Picture Window Bks.

—Luz de Noche: Un Libro Sobre la Luna, 1 vol. Meachen Rau, Dana & Picture Window Books Staff. Robledo, Sol, tr. from ENG. 2007. (Ciencia Asombrosa: Exploremos el Espacio Ser.). (SPA.). 24p. (gr. k-4). 25.99 *(978-1-4048-3223-7(8))* Picture Window Bks.

—Night Light: A Book about the Moon, 1 vol. Meachen Rau, Dana. 2005. (Amazing Science: Exploring the Sky Ser.). (ENG.). 24p. (gr. k-4). lib. bdg. 25.99 *(978-1-4048-1136-2(2)*, Nonfiction Picture Bks.) Picture Window Bks.

—El Ojo de la Tormenta: Un Libro Sobre Huracanes, 1 vol. Thomas, Rick & Picture Window Books Staff. Robledo, Sol, tr. from ENG. 2007. (Ciencia Asombrosa: el Tiempo Ser.). (SPA.). 24p. (gr. -1-3). 25.99 *(978-1-4048-3214-5(9))* Picture Window Bks.

—Pull, Lift, & Lower: A Book about Pulleys, 1 vol. Dahl, Michael. 2006. (Amazing Science: Simple Machines Ser.). (ENG.). 24p. (gr. k-4). lib. bdg. 25.99 *(978-1-4048-1305-2(5)*, 1253208, Nonfiction Picture Bks.) Picture Window Bks.

—Puntos de Luz: Un Libro Sobre las Estrellas. Meachen Rau, Dana & Picture Window Books. Robledo, Sol, tr. 2007. (Ciencia Asombrosa: Exploremos el Espacio Ser.). (SPA.). 24p. (gr. k-4). 25.99 *(978-1-4048-3233-6(5))* Picture Window Bks.

—¡Rambum! ¡Pum! Un Libro Sobre Tormentas. Thomas, Rick & Picture Window Books Staff. Robledo, Sol, tr. from ENG. 2007. (Ciencia Asombrosa: el Tiempo Ser.). (SPA.). 24p. (gr. -1-3). 25.99 *(978-1-4048-3227-5(0))* Picture Window Bks.

—Scoop, Seesaw, & Raise: A Book about Levers, 1 vol. Dahl, Michael. 2006. (Amazing Science: Simple Machines Ser.). (ENG.). 24p. (gr. k-4). lib. bdg. 25.99 *(978-1-4048-1303-8(9)*, Nonfiction Picture Bks.) Picture Window Bks.

—Space Leftovers: A Book about Comets, Asteroids, & Meteoroids, 1 vol. Meachen Rau, Dana. 2005. (Amazing Science: Exploring the Sky Ser.). (ENG.). 24p. (gr. k-4). lib. bdg. 25.99 *(978-1-4048-1137-9(0)*, Nonfiction Picture Bks.) Picture Window Bks.

—Spots of Light: A Book about Stars, 1 vol. Meachen Rau, Dana. 2005. (Amazing Science: Exploring the Sky Ser.). (ENG.). 24p. (gr. k-4). lib. bdg. 25.99 *(978-1-4048-1139-3(7)*, Nonfiction Picture Bks.) Picture Window Bks.

—Twist, Dig, & Drill: A Book about Screws, 1 vol. Dahl, Michael. 2006. (Amazing Science: Simple Machines Ser.). (ENG.). 24p. (gr. k-4). lib. bdg. 25.99 *(978-1-4048-1306-9(3)*, 1253212, Nonfiction Picture Bks.) Picture Window Bks.

—Twisters: A Book about Tornadoes, 1 vol. Thomas, Rick. 2005. (Amazing Science: Weather Ser.). (ENG.). 24p. (gr. -1-3). 25.99 *(978-1-4048-0930-7(9)*, Nonfiction Picture Bks.) Picture Window Bks.

Shea, Denise, jt. illus. see Alderman, Derrick.

Shea, Gary. Trading Places. Roller, Ellen. 2008. (J). pap. 11.95 *(978-0-9792645-0-4(2))* Edgewood Publishing, LLC.

Shea, Shawn. In Search of the Perfect Pumpkin. Evangelista, Gloria. 2008. (ENG.). 32p. (J). pap. 7.95 *(978-1-55591-697-8(X))* Fulcrum Publishing.

Shea, Therese. Soccer Stars. Shea, Therese. 2007. (Sports Stars Ser.). (ENG.). 48p. (J). (gr. 4-7). pap. 6.95 *(978-0-531-18705-0(5))* Scholastic Library Publishing.

Shearing, Leonie. It's Fall! Ringler, Matt. 2006. 28p. (J). pap. *(978-0-439-87146-4(8))* Scholastic, Inc.

Shearing, Leonie. Guess Who Says Moo? Shearing, Leonie. 2011. (ENG.). 16p. (J). (gr. k — 1). 8.99 *(978-1-921541-68-1(7))* Little Hare Bks. AUS. Dist: Independent Pubs. Group.

Sheban, Chris. Brooklyn Bridge. Hesse, Karen. 2011. (ENG.). 256p. (J). (gr. 5-9). pap. 8.99 *(978-0-312-67428-1(7))* Square Fish.

—Christmas at Stony Creek. Greene, Stephanie. 2007. 96p. (gr. -1-3). lib. bdg. 15.89 *(978-0-06-121487-5(6))* HarperCollins Pubs.

—Firstborn. Seidler, Tor. 2015. (J). Non-ISBN Publisher.

—Firstborn. Seidler, Tor. 2015. (ENG.). 240p. (J). (gr. 4-9). 16.99 *(978-1-4814-1017-5(2)*, Atheneum Bks. for Young Readers) Simon & Schuster Children's Publishing.

—I Met a Dinosaur. Wahl, Jan. 2015. (ENG.). 32p. (J). (gr. 1-3). 16.99 *(978-1-56846-233-2(6)*, Creative Editions) Creative Co., The.

—Immortal Max. Clifton, Lutricia. 2014. (ENG.). 192p. (J). (gr. 3-7). 16.95 *(978-0-8234-3041-3(3))* Holiday Hse., Inc.

Sheban, Chris, et al. It's Milking Time. Alsdurf, Phyllis. 2012. (ENG.). 40p. (J). (gr. k-3). 16.99 *(978-0-375-86911-2(5)*, Random Hse. Bks. for Young Readers) Random Hse. Children's Bks.

Sheban, Chris. Job Wanted. Bateman, Teresa. 2015. (ENG.). 32p. (J). (gr. k-3). 16.95 ***(978-0-8234-3391-9(9))*** Holiday Hse., Inc.

Sheban, Chris. The Lonely Book. Bernheimer, Kate. 2012. (ENG.). 40p. (J). (gr. -1-3). 17.99 *(978-0-375-86226-7(9)*, Schwartz & Wade Bks.) Random Hse. Children's Bks.

—A Night on the Range. Frisch, Aaron. (ENG.). 32p. (J). 2013. (gr. -1-17). pap. 7.99 *(978-0-89812-829-1(3)*, Creative Paperbacks); 2010. (gr. 1-3). 19.99 *(978-1-56846-205-9(0)*, Creative Editions) Creative Co., The.

—Red Fox at McCloskey's Farm. Heinz, Brian J. 2006. 32p. (J). (gr. -1-3). 17.95 *(978-1-56846-195-3(X)*, Creative Editions) Creative Co., The.

—The Tiger Rising. DiCamillo, Kate. 2006. 144p. (J). (gr. 5). pap. 5.99 *(978-0-7636-2916-8(2))* Candlewick Pr.

Sheckels, Astrid. Black Cloud. Hermes, Patricia. 2012. (Horse Diaries). (ENG.). 176p. (J). (gr. 3-7). lib. bdg. 12.99 *(978-0-375-96881-5(4))*; No. 8. pap. 6.99 *(978-0-375-86881-8(X))* Random Hse. Children's Bks. (Random Hse. Bks. for Young Readers).

—The Fish House Door. Baldwin, Robert F. ed. 2010. (ENG.). 36p. (J). 16.95 *(978-1-934031-30-8(5)*, 10b511a5-c2dc-4bc7-8d33-85991c0a158b) Islandport Pr., Inc.

—Nic & Nellie, 1 vol. 2013. (ENG.). 36p. (gr. 1-4). 17.95 *(978-1-934031-52-0(6)*, 789d27ec-dbc2-4d0b-a5ab-282ac65dc0d5) Islandport Pr., Inc.

—The Scallop Christmas. Freeberg, Jane. ed. 2009. (ENG.). 36p. (J). 16.95 *(978-1-934031-25-4(9))* Islandport Pr., Inc.

—Tennessee Rose. Kendall, Jane F. 2012. (Horse Diaries). (ENG.). 160p. (J). (gr. 3-7). pap. 6.99 *(978-0-375-87006-4(7))*; lib. bdg. 12.99 *(978-0-375-97006-1(1))* Random Hse., Inc.

Shed, Greg. I Loved You Before You Were Born. Bowen, Anne M. 2004. (ENG.). 32p. (J). (gr. -1-3). reprint ed. pap. 6.99 *(978-0-06-443631-1(4))* HarperCollins Pubs.

—The Secret of Saying Thanks. Wood, Douglas. 2005. (ENG.). 32p. (J). (gr. -1-3). 17.99 *(978-0-689-85410-1(2)*, Simon & Schuster Bks. For Young Readers) Simon & Schuster Bks. For Young Readers.

—Squanto's Journey: The Story of the First Thanksgiving. Bruchac, Joseph. 2007. (ENG.). 32p. (J). (gr. -1-3). pap. 6.99 *(978-0-15-206044-2(8))* Houghton Mifflin Harcourt Publishing Co.

—The Turning of the Year. Martin, Bill, Jr. 2007. (ENG.). 28p. (J). (gr. -1-3). pap. 6.00 *(978-0-15-204555-5(4))* Houghton Mifflin Harcourt Publishing Co.

Shed, Greg & Pham, LeUyen. Aunt Mary's Rose. Wood, Douglas. 2010. (ENG.). 32p. (J). (gr. -1-3). 16.99 *(978-0-7636-1090-6(9))* Candlewick Pr.

Shedd, Blair. Amazing Kitchen Chemistry Projects. Brown, Cynthia Light. 2008. (Build It Yourself Ser.). (ENG.). 128p. (J). (gr. 3-7). 21.95 *(978-1-934670-06-4(5))* Nomad Pr.

Shedd, Blair & Kim, Alex. Explore Ancient Greece! 25 Great Projects, Activities, Experiments. Van Vleet, Carmella. 2008. (Explore Your World Ser.). (ENG.). 96p. (J). (gr. k-4). pap. 12.95 *(978-1-934670-11-8(1))* Nomad Pr.

Sheehan, Monica. Be Happy! Sheehan, Monica. 2014. (ENG.). 68p. (J). (gr. -1-3). 14.99 *(978-1-4424-9857-0(9)*, Little Simon) Little Simon.

—Love Is You & Me. Sheehan, Monica. (ENG.). (J). (gr. -1-3). 2013. 48p. 14.99 *(978-1-4424-3607-7(7))*; 2010. 38p. bds. 7.99 *(978-1-4424-0765-7(4))* Little Simon. (Little Simon).

Sheehan, Peter. Charlie Burr & the Great Shed Invasion. Morgan, Sally et al. 2011. (ENG.). 128p. (J). (gr. 3-7). pap. 13.99 *(978-1-921714-05-4(0))* Little Hare Bks. AUS. Dist: Independent Pubs. Group.

—Send Simon Savage: Return of the Black Death. Measday, Stephen. 2012. (ENG.). 200p. (J). (gr. 4-8). pap. 15.99 *(978-1-921541-91-9(1))* Little Hare Bks. AUS. Dist: Independent Pubs. Group.

Sheehan, Peter, jt. illus. see Ottley, Matt.

Sheehy, Shawn. Welcome to the Neighborwood. Sheehy, Shawn. 2015. (ENG.). 18p. (J). (gr. -1-3). 29.99 *(978-0-7636-6594-4(0))* Candlewick Pr.

Sheely, Tiffany. Captain William Clark's Great Montana Adventure. 2003. 32p. (J). mass mkt. 3.95 *(978-0-9711667-0-7(6))* Outlook Publishing, Inc.

Sheesley, Brian. The Trouble with Fuzzwonker Fizz. Carman, Patrick. 2016. (Fizzopolis Ser.: 1). 160p. (J). (gr. 3-7). 12.99 ***(978-0-06-239390-6(1))*** HarperCollins Pubs.

Sheets, Leslie. Brave Just Like Me. Ruff, Kimberly & Venturi-Pickett, Stacy. 2011. 32p. pap. 9.99 *(978-1-60888-106-2(7))* Nimble Bks. LLC.

Shefelman, Janice J. & Shefelman, Tom. Son of Spirit Horse. 2004. 74p. (J). *(978-1-57168-833-0(1)*, Eakin Pr.) Eakin Pr.

Shefelman, Janice Jordan & Shefelman, Tom. I, Vivaldi. Shefelman, Janice Jordan & Shefelman, Tom. Shefelman, Janice. 2008. 32p. (J). (gr. 2-6). 18.00 *(978-0-8028-5318-9(8))* Eerdmans, William B. Publishing Co.

Shefelman, Tom, jt. illus. see Shefelman, Janice Jordan.

Shefelman, Tom, jt. illus. see Shefelman, Janice J.

Sheffler, Axel. Room on the Broom Board Book. Donaldson, Julia. 2012. (ENG.). 24p. (J). bds. 6.99 *(978-0-8037-3841-6(2)*, Dial) Penguin Publishing Group.

Shefrin, Sima Elizabeth. Abby's Birds, 1 vol. Schwartz, Ellen. 2007. (ENG.). 32p. (J). (gr. 1-4). 16.95 *(978-1-896580-86-9(6))* Tradewind Bks. CAN. Dist: Orca Bk. Pubs. USA.

—Jewish Fairy Tale Feasts: A Literary Cookbook. Yolen, Jane & Stemple, Heidi E. Y. 2013. (ENG.). 200p. (J). 25.00 *(978-1-56656-909-5(5)*, Crocodile Bks.) Interlink Publishing Group, Inc.

—Once upon a Bathtime, 1 vol. Goss, Shelia M. & Hughes, Vi. 2011. (ENG.). 32p. (J). (gr. -1-k). 17.95 *(978-1-896580-54-8(8))* Tradewind Bks. CAN. Dist: Orca Bk. Pubs. USA.

Shehan, Terece. Mad about Miller. Thompson, Shannon Raines. Stone, Kathrine Thompson, ed. 2006. 24p. (YA). 12.95 *(978-1-59971-853-8(7))* Aardvark Global Publishing.

—Nuts about Neal. Thompson, Shannon Raines. Stone, Kathrine Thompson, ed. 2006. 24p. (YA). 12.95 *(978-1-59971-852-1(9))* Aardvark Global Publishing.

Shekailo, Pamela. Meet Angel & All Her Friends. Edwards-Wright, Tracy. 2012. 48p. pap. 24.95 *(978-1-4512-8280-1(X))* America Star Bks.

Sheldon, David. Guess Who? Namm, Diane. 2004. (My First Reader Ser.). (ENG.). 32p. (J). (gr. k-1). pap. 3.95 *(978-0-516-25503-3(7)*, Children's Pr.) Scholastic Library Publishing.

—The Little Golden Book of Jokes & Riddles. Brown, Peggy. 2013. (Little Golden Book Ser.). (ENG.). 24p. (J). (-k). 3.99 *(978-0-307-97916-2(4)*, Golden Bks.) Random Hse. Children's Bks.

—Matzo Frogs. Rosenthal, Sally. 2014. (ENG.). 32p. (J). 17.95 *(978-1-58838-302-0(4)*, NewSouth Bks.) NewSouth, Inc.

—Way down below Deep, 1 vol. Day, Nancy. 2014. (ENG.). 32p. (J). (gr. k-3). 16.99 *(978-1-4556-1945-0(0))* Pelican Publishing Co., Inc.

Sheldon, David. Barnum Brown: Dinosaur Hunter. Sheldon, David. 2006. (ENG.). 32p. (J). (gr. -1-3). 16.95 *(978-0-8027-9602-8(8))* Walker & Co.

Sheldon, Ian. Bugs of Ontario. Acorn, John Harrison. rev. ed. 2003. (ENG.). 160p. (J). (gr. 4). pap. *(978-1-55105-287-8(3))* Lone Pine Publishing USA.

—Bugs of the Rockies. Acorn, John. 2005. (ENG.). 160p. (gr. 4). pap. *(978-1-55105-313-4(6))* Lone Pine Publishing.

Sheldon, Ian. Seashore of Southern California. Sheldon, Ian. rev. ed. 2007. (Lone Pine Field Guides). (ENG.). 216p. per. 12.95 *(978-1-55105-232-8(6))* Lone Pine Publishing USA.

Sheldon, Kristin. The Martha Is Mine: An Almost True Story. Hicks, Greg & Foster, Rick. 2007. 56p. (J). 16.95 *(978-0-9790709-0-7(2))* Foster, Hicks & Assocs.

Sheldon, Tamia. The Zebra Said Shhh. Nelson, M. R. 2013. 44p. pap. 9.99 *(978-1-62395-440-6(1))* Xist Publishing.

Sheldon, Tamia. What Is a Family? Sheldon, Tamia. 2013. 36p. pap. 9.99 *(978-1-62395-527-4(0))* Xist Publishing.

Sheldrake, Missy. Nothing's Too Hard for Me. Peine, Jan. 2013. 28p. (J). 7.00 *(978-0-9754575-4-2(3))* Ashway Pr.

Shell-Aurora, Callie, photos by. TIME: President Obama: The Path to the White House. Ignatius, Adi et al, eds. 2009. 95p. (J). (gr. 5-13). 30.60 *(978-0-7613-5034-7(9))* Time Inc. Bks.

Shelley, Jeff. I Can Do It All. Pearson, Mary E. 2011. (Rookie Ready to Learn Ser.). 32p. (J). (gr. -1-k). pap. 5.95 *(978-0-531-26654-0(0))*; lib. bdg. 23.00 *(978-0-531-26429-4(7)*, Children's Pr.) Scholastic Library Publishing.

Shelley, John. Bella Baxter & the Lighthouse Mystery. Mason, Jane B. & Stephens, Sarah Hines. 2006. (Bella Baxter Ser.: 3). (ENG.). 80p. (J). (gr. 1-4). pap. 6.99 *(978-0-689-86282-3(2)*, Simon & Schuster/Paula Wiseman Bks.) Simon & Schuster/Paula Wiseman Bks.

—The Boat in the Tree. Wynne-Jones, Tim. 2007. (ENG.). 40p. (J). (gr. 2-4). 17.95 *(978-1-932425-49-9(7)*, Front Street) Boyds Mills Pr.

—Crinkle, Crackle, Crack: It's Spring! Bauer, Marion Dane. 2015. (ENG.). 32p. (J). (gr. -1-3). 16.95 *(978-0-8234-2952-3(0))* Holiday Hse., Inc.

—Family Reminders. Danneberg, Julie. (ENG.). 112p. (J). (gr. 3-7). 2013. pap. 6.95 *(978-1-58089-321-3(X))*; 2009. 14.95 *(978-1-58089-320-6(1))* Charlesbridge Publishing, Inc.

—The Halloween Forest. Bauer, Marion Dane. 2012. (ENG.). 32p. (J). 16.95 *(978-0-8234-2324-8(7))* Holiday Hse., Inc.

—MVP. Evans, Douglas. (ENG.). 232p. (J). (gr. 4-6). 2008. pap. 9.95 *(978-1-59078-625-3(4)*, Front Street); 2004. 16.95 *(978-1-932425-13-0(6)*, Lemniscaat) Boyds Mills Pr.

—Stone Giant: Michelangelo's David & How He Came to Be. Sutcliffe, Jane. 2014. (J). (ENG.). 32p. (gr. 1-4). lib. bdg. 16.95 *(978-1-58089-295-7(7))*; pap. *(978-1-58089-296-4(5))* Charlesbridge Publishing, Inc.

Shellly, Jeff, jt. illus. see LaPadula, Tom.

Shelly, Jeff. Alfred's Kid's Drum Course. Black, Dave & Houghton, Steve. 2004. (Kid's Drum Course Ser.: Bk 1). (ENG.). 48p. pap. 17.99 *(978-0-7390-3609-9(2)*, 23182) Alfred Publishing Co., Inc.

Shelly, Jeff, Sr. Dillan Mcmillan, Please Eat Your Peas. Schneider, David. 2015. (ENG.). 36p. (J). 14.95 *(978-0-9744446-4-2(2))* All About Kids Publishing.

Shelly, Jeff. The Easiest Guitar Method Ever! Vol. 2. Manus, Ron & Harnsberger, L. C. 2005. (Kid's Guitar Course Ser.). (ENG.). 48p. pap. 15.99 *(978-0-88284-987-4(5))* Alfred Publishing Co., Inc.

—Goodnight, Little Bug. Perez, Jessica. 2005. (J). bds. 14.99 *(978-0-9767325-2-5(1))* Toy Quest.

—Hubert Invents the Wheel. Montgomery, Claire & Montgomery, Monte. 2005. (ENG.). 192p. (J). (gr. 4-7). 16.95 *(978-0-8027-8990-7(0))* Walker & Co.

—Kid's Guitar Course 1: The Easiest Guitar Method Ever! Manus, Ron & Harnsberger, L. C. 2003. (Kid's Guitar Course Ser.). (ENG.). 48p. pap. 15.99 *(978-0-88284-989-8(1)*, 18451) Alfred Publishing Co., Inc.

—Learn to Draw Cars & Trucks. 2012. (J). *(978-1-936309-49-8(1))* Quarto Publishing Group USA.

—Learn to Draw Dinosaurs. 2012. (J). *(978-1-936309-48-1(3))* Quarto Publishing Group USA.

—A Plump & Perky Turkey, 0 vols. Bateman, Teresa. 2013. (ENG.). 32p. (J). (gr. k-4). pap. 9.99 *(978-0-7614-5188-4(9)*, 9780761451884, Amazon Children's Publishing) Amazon Publishing.

Shelly, Jeff. Puedo Hacer de Todo. Shelly, Jeff. Pearson, Mary E. 2011. (Rookie Ready to Learn Español Ser.). Tr. of I Can Do It All. (SPA.). 40p. (J). pap. 5.95 *(978-0-531-26787-5(3))*; lib. bdg. 23.00 *(978-0-531-26119-4(0))* Scholastic Library Publishing. (Children's Pr.).

Shelly, Jeff, jt. illus. see Fisher, Diana.

Shelly, Jeff, jt. illus. see LaPadula, Tom.

sheltrown, karen. The Adventures of AJ & Hunter: Lost in the Back Yard. Jones, Rachel. 2011. (ENG.). 24p. pap. 6.99 *(978-1-4681-0130-0(7))* CreateSpace Independent Publishing Platform.

Shems, Ed. Ancient Science: 40 Time-Traveling, World-Exploring, History-Making Activities for Kids. Wiese, Jim. 2003. (ENG.). 128p. (J). pap. 16.00 *(978-0-471-21595-0(3)*, Wiley) Wiley, John & Sons, Inc.

—Easy First Puzzles. Hovanec, Helene. 2011. (First Puzzles Ser.). (ENG.). 64p. (J). pap. 4.95 *(978-1-4027-7810-0(4))* Sterling Publishing Co., Inc.

—First Word Search: Phonics, Phonics, Phonics! 2011. (First Word Search Ser.). (ENG.). 64p. (J). (gr. -1-1). pap. 4.95 *(978-1-4027-7805-6(8))* Sterling Publishing Co., Inc.

—Letter Fun. Hovanec, Helene. 2008. (My First Puzzles Ser.). (ENG.). 64p. (J). (gr. -1). per. 3.95 *(978-1-4027-4631-4(8))* Sterling Publishing Co., Inc.

—Reading Games. Hovanec, Helene. 2008. (My First Puzzles Ser.). (ENG.). 64p. (J). (gr. k-1). per. 3.95 *(978-1-4027-4632-1(6))* Sterling Publishing Co., Inc.

—Silly Jokes & Giggles. Yates, Philip & Rissinger, Matt. 2010. (ENG.). 96p. (J). (gr. 1-4). pap. 4.95 *(978-1-4027-7855-1(4))* Sterling Publishing Co., Inc.

Shems, Ed. Weird Science: 40 Strange-Acting, Bizarre-Looking, & Barely Believable Activities for Kids. Shems, Ed. Wiese, Jim. 2004. (ENG.). 132p. (J). pap. 14.95 *(978-0-471-46229-3(2),* Wiley) Wiley, John & Sons, Inc.

Shene, Prescott. Mandy - The Alpha Dog: The Chronicles of the K-9 Boys & Girls on Locus Street. Shene, Paula. 2009. 36p. pap. 24.95 *(978-1-60836-710-8(X))* America Star Bks.

Shepard, Ernest H. ABC. Milne, A. A. 2004. (Winnie-The-Pooh Ser.). (ENG.). 26p. (J). (gr. -1-k). bds. 8.99 *(978-0-525-47280-3(0),* Dutton Juvenile) Penguin Publishing Group.

—Dream Days. Grahame, Kenneth. 2004. reprint ed. pap. 21.95 *(978-1-4179-0979-7(X))* Kessinger Publishing, LLC.

—Giant. Milne, A. A. 2009. (Winnie-The-Pooh Ser.). (ENG.). 5p. (J). (gr. -1-k). bds. 9.99 *(978-0-525-42088-0(6),* Dutton Juvenile) Penguin Publishing Group.

—An Gwyns I'n Helyk. Grahame, Kenneth & Williams, Nicholas. 2013. (COR.). 202p. pap. *(978-1-78201-029-6(7))* Evertype.

—The House at Pooh Corner. Milne, A. A. deluxe ed. 2009. (Winnie-The-Pooh Ser.). (ENG.). 192p. (J). (gr. 3-7). 19.99 *(978-0-525-47856-0(6),* Dutton Juvenile) Penguin Publishing Group.

—The House at Pooh Corner, Set. Milne, A. A. (J). incl. audio *(978-1-57375-653-2(9),* 71524) Audioscope.

—In Which a House Is Built at Pooh Corner for Eeyore. Milne, A. A. unabr. ed. (Classic Pooh Treasury Ser.). (J). incl. audio *(978-1-57375-527-6(3),* 71394) Audioscope.

—In Which Christopher Robin Gives Pooh a Party. Milne, A. A. unabr. ed. (Winnie-the-Pooh Ser.). (J). incl. audio *(978-1-57375-046-2(8),* 70554) Audioscope.

—In Which Everyone Has a Birthday & Gets Two Presents. Milne, A. A. unabr. ed. (Winnie-the-Pooh Ser.). (J). incl. audio *(978-1-57375-015-8(8),* 70134) Audioscope.

—In Which It Is Shown That Tiggers Don't Climb Trees. Milne, A. A. unabr. ed. (Classic Pooh Treasury Ser.). (J). incl. audio *(978-1-57375-529-0(X),* 71414) Audioscope.

—In Which Piglet Meets a Heffalump. Milne, A. A. unabr. ed. (Winnie-the-Pooh Ser.). (J). incl. audio *(978-1-57375-014-1(X),* 70124) Audioscope.

—In Which Pooh Goes Visiting & Gets into a Tight Place & in Which Pooh & Piglet Go Hunting & Nearly Catch a Woozle. Milne, A. A. unabr. ed. (Winnie-the-Pooh Ser.). (J). incl. audio *(978-1-57375-001-1(8),* 70014) Audioscope.

—In Which Tigger Is Unbounced. Milne, A. A. unabr. ed. (Classic Pooh Treasury Ser.). (J). incl. audio *(978-1-57375-528-3(1),* 71404) Audioscope.

—In Which We Are Introduced to Winnie the Pooh & Some Bees, & the Stories Begin. Milne, A. A. unabr. ed. (Winnie-the-Pooh Ser.). (J). incl. audio *(978-1-57375-000-4(X),* 70004) Audioscope.

—Now We Are Six. Milne, A. A. deluxe ed. 2008. (Winnie-The-Pooh Ser.). (ENG.). 128p. (J). (gr. 3-7). 19.99 *(978-0-525-47929-1(5),* Dutton Juvenile) Penguin Publishing Group.

—Positively Pooh: Timeless Wisdom from Pooh. Milne, A. A. 2008. (Winnie-The-Pooh Ser.). (ENG.). 120p. (J). (gr. 3-7). 22.00 *(978-0-525-47931-4(7),* Dutton Juvenile) Penguin Publishing Group.

—The Reluctant Dragon. Grahame, Kenneth. 2013. (ENG.). 64p. (J). 2nd ed. pap. 6.95 *(978-0-8234-2821-2(4));* 75th ed. 16.95 *(978-0-8234-2820-5(6))* Holiday Hse., Inc.

—A Smackerel of Pooh: Ten Favorite Stories & Poems. Milne, A. A. 2006. 79p. (J). (gr. k-4). 16.00 *(978-1-4223-5283-0(8))* DIANE Publishing Co.

—Tigger Tales. Milne, A. A. 2006. 36p. (J). (gr. k-4). reprint ed. 15.00 *(978-1-4223-5453-7(9))* DIANE Publishing Co.

—When We Were Very Young. Milne, A. A. deluxe ed. 2009. (Winnie-The-Pooh Ser.). (ENG.). 128p. (J). (gr. 3-7). 19.99 *(978-0-525-47930-7(9),* Dutton Juvenile) Penguin Publishing Group.

—The Wind in the Willows. Grahame, Kenneth. 2007. 259p. (J). (gr. 5-6). reprint ed. lib. bdg. 22.95 *(978-0-88411-877-0(0))* Amereon LTD.

—Winnie Ille Pu: A Latin Edition of Winnie-the-Pooh, 16 vols. Milne, A. A. & Soman, David. Lenard, Alexander, tr. 2015. (ENG.). (J). (gr. 7-18). 207.84 *(978-0-525-43007-0(5),* Dutton Adult) Penguin Publishing Group.

—Winnie Puh. Milne, A. A. Meddemmen, John, tr.Tr. of Winnie the Pooh. (ITA.). 164p. pap. 29.95 *(978-88-7782-278-9(3))* Salani ITA. Dist: Distribooks, Inc.

—Winnie-the-Pooh. Milne, A. A. 2005. (Winnie-The-Pooh Ser.). (ENG.). 176p. (J). (gr. 3-7). 6.99 *(978-0-14-240467-6(5),* Puffin) Penguin Publishing Group.

—Winnie-the-Pooh. Milne, A. A. 80th anniv. ed. 2009. (Winnie-The-Pooh Ser.). (ENG.). 176p. (J). (gr. 3-7). 19.99 *(978-0-525-47768-6(3),* Dutton Juvenile) Penguin Publishing Group.

—Winnie the Pooh & When We Were Young. Milne, A. A. 32p. (J). Boxed set. pap. incl. audio compact disk *(978-1-57375-583-2(4),* 71512); Set. pap. incl. audio *(978-1-57375-652-5(0),* 71514) Audioscope.

—The Winnie-the-Pooh Cookbook. Ellison, Virginia H. 2010. (ENG.). 120p. (J). (gr. 3-7). 19.99 *(978-0-525-42359-1(1),* Dutton Juvenile) Penguin Publishing Group.

—Winnie the Pooh Tells Time. Milne, A. A. 2009. (Winnie-The-Pooh Ser.). (ENG.). 9p. (J). (gr. -1-k). bds. 6.99 *(978-0-525-42142-9(4),* Dutton Juvenile) Penguin Publishing Group.

—Winnie the Pooh's 1,2,3. Milne, A. A. 2009. (Winnie-The-Pooh Ser.). (ENG.). 18p. (J). (gr. -1 — 1). bds. 6.99 *(978-0-525-42084-2(3),* Dutton Juvenile) Penguin Publishing Group.

—Winnie the Pooh's Colors. Milne, A. A. 2009. (Winnie-The-Pooh Ser.). (ENG.). 9p. (J). (gr. -1 — 1). bds. 6.99 *(978-0-525-42083-5(5),* Dutton Juvenile) Penguin Publishing Group.

—The World of Pooh: The Complete Winnie-the-Pooh & the House at Pooh Corner. Milne, A. A. 2010. (Winnie-The-Pooh Ser.). (ENG.). 384p. (J). (gr. 3-7). 25.99 *(978-0-525-44447-3(5),* Dutton Juvenile) Penguin Publishing Group.

Shepard, Mary. Mary Poppins. Travers, P. L. 2006. (Mary Poppins Ser.: No. 1). (ENG.). 224p. (J). (gr. 5-7). 16.99 *(978-0-15-205810-4(9))* Houghton Mifflin Harcourt Publishing Co.

—Mary Poppins: 80th Anniversary Collection. Travers, P. L. 2014. (ENG.). 1024p. (J). (gr. 5-7). 24.99 *(978-0-544-34047-3(7),* HMH Books For Young Readers) Houghton Mifflin Harcourt Publishing Co.

—Mary Poppins & Mary Poppins Comes Back. Travers, P. L. 2007. (Mary Poppins Ser.: No 1 and 2). (ENG.). 368p. (J). (gr. 5-7). 19.99 *(978-0-15-205922-4(9))* Houghton Mifflin Harcourt Publishing Co.

—Mary Poppins Comes Back. Travers, P. L. 2006. (Mary Poppins Ser.: No. 2). (ENG.). 336p. (J). (gr. 5-7). 16.99 *(978-0-15-205816-6(8))* Houghton Mifflin Harcourt Publishing Co.

—Mary Poppins from A to Z. Travers, P. L. 2006. (Mary Poppins Ser.). (ENG.). 64p. (J). (gr. 5-7). 16.99 *(978-0-15-205834-0(6))* Houghton Mifflin Harcourt Publishing Co.

—Mary Poppins in the Kitchen: A Cookery Book with a Story. Travers, P. L. 2006. (Mary Poppins Ser.: No. 6). (ENG.). 88p. (J). (gr. 5-7). 16.99 *(978-0-15-206080-0(4))* Houghton Mifflin Harcourt Publishing Co.

—Mary Poppins in the Park. Travers, P. L. (Mary Poppins Ser.). (ENG.). (J). (gr. 5-7). 2015. 272p. pap. 6.99 *(978-0-544-51384-6(3),* HMH Books For Young Readers); 2006. 304p. 16.99 *(978-0-15-205828-9(1))* Houghton Mifflin Harcourt Publishing Co.

Shepard, Mary & Sims, Agnes. Mary Poppins Opens the Door. Travers, P. L. 2015. (Mary Poppins Ser.). (ENG.). 256p. (J). (gr. 5-7). pap. 6.99 *(978-0-544-43958-0(9),* HMH Books For Young Readers) Houghton Mifflin Harcourt Publishing Co.

Shepard, Mary, jt. illus. see Sims, Agnes.

Shepherd, Amanda. Mouse House Tales. Pearson, Susan. 2013. (ENG.). 56p. (J). (gr. -1-3). 17.99 *(978-1-60905-050-4(9))* Blue Apple Bks.

Shepherd, J. A. Old Hendrik's Tales - 13 South African Folk Tales. 2013. 198p. pap. *(978-1-909302-15-0(5))* Abela Publishing.

Shepherd, Keith D. Kumba & Kambili: A Tale from Mali. 2013. (Tales of Honor Ser.). (ENG.). 32p. (J). (gr. 1-4). pap. 8.95 *(978-1-937529-58-1(4))* Red Chair Pr.

—Walking Home to Rosie Lee. LaFaye, A. 2011. (ENG.). 32p. (J). (gr. 1-6). 16.95 *(978-1-933693-97-2(5))* Cinco Puntos Pr.

Shepherd, Keith D. Kumba & Kambili: A Tale from Mali. Shepherd, Keith D., retold by. 2013. (Tales of Honor (Red Chair Press) Ser.). (ENG.). 32p. (J). (gr. 1-4). lib. bdg. 26.60 *(978-1-937529-74-1(6))* Red Chair Pr.

Shepherd, Rosalie M. Women Who Fly, 1 vol. Homan, Lynn M. & Reilly, Thomas. 2004. (ENG.). 104p. (J). (gr. 3-7). 14.95 *(978-1-58980-160-8(1))* Pelican Publishing Co., Inc.

Shepherd, Rosalie M. Girls Fly!, 1 vol. Shepherd, Rosalie M., tr. Homan, Lynn M. & Reilly, Thomas. 2003. (ENG.). 32p. (J). (gr. k-3). 16.99 *(978-1-58980-154-7(7))* Pelican Publishing Co., Inc.

Shepherd, Rosalie M., jt. illus. see Lauve, Celia.

Shepherd, Wendy & Hershenson, Ken, photos by. Ernie's Special Summer Day: An Ernie the Sock Monkey Adventure. Shepherd, Wendy & Hershenson, Ken. 2011. (ENG., 32p. pap. 9.49 *(978-1-4609-8157-3(X))* CreateSpace Independent Publishing Platform.

Sheppard, Kate. Keeper's Ball. Childs, Rob. 2005. (Corgi Pups Ser.). (ENG.). 64p. (J). pap. 7.50 *(978-0-552-55030-7(2))* Transworld Publishers Ltd. GBR. Dist: Independent Pubs. Group.

Sheppard, Kate. Yo Ho Ho! Newman, Marjorie. 2014. (Colour First Reader Ser.). (ENG.). 80p. (J). (gr. k-2). pap. 9.99 ***(978-0-552-56897-5(X))*** Transworld Publishers Ltd. GBR. Dist: Independent Pubs. Group.

Shepperson, Claude A. The Diary of a Goose Girl. Wiggin, Kate Douglas. 2004. reprint ed. pap. 20.95 *(978-1-4179-1501-9(3))* Kessinger Publishing, LLC.

Shepperson, Rob. Annika Riz, Math Whiz. Mills, Claudia. 2014. (Franklin School Friends Ser.: 2). (ENG.). 128p. (J). (gr. 2-5). 15.99 *(978-0-374-30335-8(5),* Farrar, Straus & Giroux (BYR)) Farrar, Straus & Giroux.

—The Big House. Coman, Carolyn. 2004. (ENG.). 224p. (J). (gr. 4-6). 16.95 *(978-1-932425-09-3(8),* Lemniscaat) Boyds Mills Pr.

—Can I Just Take a Nap? Rauss, Ron. 2012. (ENG.). 32p. (J). (gr. -1-1). 15.99 *(978-1-4424-3497-4(X),* Simon & Schuster/Paula Wiseman Bks.) Simon & Schuster/Paula Wiseman Bks.

—Don't Know Much about Abraham Lincoln, Vol. 4. Davis, Kenneth C. 2003. (Don't Know Much About Ser.). 144p. (J). (gr. 3-7). pap. 4.99 *(978-0-06-442127-0(9))* HarperCollins Pubs.

—Don't Know Much about Abraham Lincoln Abraham Lincoln, Vol. 4. Davis, Kenneth C. 2004. (Don't Know Much About Ser.). 144p. (J). (gr. 2-5). 15.89 *(978-0-06-028820-4(5))* HarperCollins Pubs.

—Don't Know Much about George Washington. Davis, Kenneth C. 2003. (Don't Know Much About Ser.). 128p. (J). (gr. 3). pap. 4.99 *(978-0-06-442124-9(4))* HarperCollins Pubs.

—Don't Know Much about Thomas Jefferson. Davis, Kenneth C. 2005. (Don't Know Much About Ser.). 128p. (J). (gr. 2-5). pap. 4.99 *(978-0-06-442128-7(7))* HarperCollins Pubs.

—Izzy Barr, Running Star. Mills, Claudia. 2015. (Franklin School Friends Ser.: 3). (ENG.). 144p. (J). (gr. 2-5). 15.99 *(978-0-374-33578-6(8),* Farrar, Straus & Giroux (BYR)) Farrar, Straus & Giroux.

—Kelsey Green, Reading Queen, 1 vol. Mills, Claudia. 2013. (Franklin School Friends Ser.: 1). (ENG.). 128p. (J). (gr. 2-5). 15.99 *(978-0-374-37485-3(6),* Farrar, Straus & Giroux (BYR)) Farrar, Straus & Giroux.

—Kelsey Green, Reading Queen. Mills, Claudia. 2014. (Franklin School Friends Ser.: 1). (ENG.). 144p. (J). (gr. 2-5). pap. 5.99 *(978-1-250-03405-2(1))* Square Fish.

—Lilly & the Pirates. Root, Phyllis. (ENG.). (J). 2013. 180p. (gr. 3-7). pap. 8.95 *(978-1-62091-027-6(6));* 2010. 116p. (gr. 4-6). 16.95 *(978-1-59078-583-6(5),* Front Street) Boyds Mills Pr.

—The Memory Bank. Coman, Carolyn. 2010. (J). 263p. pap. *(978-0-545-21067-6(4));* (ENG.). 288p. (gr. 3-7). 16.99 *(978-0-545-21066-9(6))* Scholastic, Inc. (Levine, Arthur A. Bks.).

—Sneaking Suspicions. Coman, Carolyn. 2007. (ENG.). 204p. (J). (gr. 4-6). 16.95 *(978-1-59078-491-4(X),* Front Street) Boyds Mills Pr.

—Thunderboom! Poems for Everyone. Pomerantz, Charlotte. (ENG.). 48p. (J). 2012. (gr. 2-5). pap. 7.95 *(978-1-59078-909-4(1),* Wordsong); 2006. (gr. -1). 17.95 *(978-1-932425-40-6(3),* Lemniscaat) Boyds Mills Pr.

—Tummies on the Run. White, Andrea & Mimi, Vance. 2012. 32p. pap. 11.95 *(978-1-60898-134-2(7))* namelos llc.

—Under the Kissletoe: Christmastime Poems. Lewis, J. Patrick. 2007. (ENG.). 32p. (J). (gr. 2-4). 16.95 *(978-1-59078-438-9(3),* Wordsong) Boyds Mills Pr.

—Vacation: We're Going to the Ocean. Harrison, David L. 2009. (ENG.). 64p. (J). (gr. 2-4). 16.95 *(978-1-59078-568-3(1),* Wordsong) Boyds Mills Pr.

Sherman, Shandel. Something for Nothing. Early, Kelly. l.t. ed. 2007. 13p. (J). per. 8.95 *(978-1-59879-100-6(1));* (gr. -1-3). 14.95 *(978-1-59879-131-0(1))* Lifevest Publishing, Inc.

Sherrard, Laura. Silky: The Dog That Saved the Day. Innis-Weisseneder, Emma May. 2008. (ENG.). 65p. pap. 9.00 *(978-1-894372-43-5(3))* DreamCatcher Publishing CAN. Dist: Univ. of Toronto Pr.

Sherrell, Craig. Thando Rocker. Kowen, Dorothy. 2012. (ENG.). 24p. (J). (gr. k-2). pap. 7.95 *(978-1-4314-0087-4(4))* Jacana Media ZAF. Dist: Independent Pubs. Group.

Sherrill, Rusty. Kid Nitro & the Sinister Slorp. Sherrill, Rusty. Miers, Doug. Sherrill, Cathy, ed. 2007. 273p. (YA). per. 14.95 *(978-0-9787729-0-1(3))* RS Art Studio.

Sherup. Tales of the Golden Corpse: Tibetan Folk Tales. Benson, Sandra. 2006. (ENG.). 224p. (gr. 9-18). per. 15.00 *(978-1-56656-632-2(0))* Interlink Publishing Group, Inc.

Sherwood, Stewart. Legends in Their Time: Young Heroes & Victims of Canada. Sherwood, George. 2006. (ENG.). 272p. pap. 19.95 *(978-1-897045-10-7(7))* Natural Heritage/Natural History, Inc. CAN. Dist: Ingram Pub. Services.

Shetterly, Robert. The Pond God & Other Stories. Keyser, Samuel Jay & Boyds Mills Press Staff. 2003. (ENG.). 96p. (J). (gr. 6-9). 14.95 *(978-1-886910-96-6(0),* Lemniscaat) Boyds Mills Pr.

Shetty, Lakshmi. Tales of Toy World. Shetty, Lalitha A. 2010. 48p. pap. 12.00 *(978-1-60911-157-1(5),* Eloquent Bks.) Strategic Book Publishing & Rights Agency (SBPRA).

Sheuer, Lauren. The Pop Quiz Book: Tons of Trivia! Seip, Shannon Payette. 2008. (American Girl Library). (ENG.). 80p. (gr. 3-7). spiral bd. 7.95 *(978-1-58485-844-7(3),* American Girl) American Girl Publishing, Inc.

Shibamoto, Thores. Attack on Titan: Before the Fall (Novel) Kyklo. Suzukaze, Ryo. 2015. (Attack on Titan Ser.). (ENG.). 298p. (J). (gr. 7). pap. 14.95 ***(978-1-939130-87-7(5))*** Vertical, Inc.

Shibley, Joe. Standards-Based Language Arts Graphic Organizers & Rubrics. Forte, Imogene & Schurr, Sandra. Bosarge, Charlotte, ed. 2003. (Standards-Based Graphic Organizers & Rub Ser.). (ENG.). 128p. (gr. 1-5). per. 15.99 *(978-0-86530-627-1(3))* Incentive Pubns., Inc.

—Standards-Based Math Graphic Organizers & Rubrics. Forte, Imogene & Schurr, Sandra. Bosarge, Charlotte, ed. 2003. (Standards-Based Graphic Organizers & Rub Ser.). (ENG.). 128p. (gr. 1-5). per. 15.99 *(978-0-86530-629-5(X))* Incentive Pubns., Inc.

—Standards-Based Social Studies Graphic Organizers & Rubrics. Forte, Imogene & Schurr, Sandra. Bosarge, Charlotte, ed. 2003. (Standards-Based Graphic Organizers & Rub Ser.). (ENG.). 128p. (gr. 1-5). per. 15.99 *(978-0-86530-630-1(3))* Incentive Pubns., Inc.

Shickle, Ian. The Adventures of Herb the Wild Turkey - Herb Goes Camping. Cameron, Kristy. 2012. 38p. pap. *(978-0-9859790-0-3(3))* LP Publishing.

Shiei. Amazing Agent Luna Omnibus 1. DeFilippis, Nunzio & Weir, Christina. 2008. (Amazing Agent Luna Ser.: 1). (ENG.). 496p. pap. 14.99 *(978-1-933164-74-8(3))* Seven Seas Entertainment, LLC.

—Aoi House Omnibus 2, 2 vols. Arnold, Adam. 2008. (Aoi House Ser.: 2). (ENG.). 352p. pap. 13.99 *(978-1-934876-26-8(7))* Seven Seas Entertainment, LLC.

—The Warlock Diaries Omnibus. Roberts, Rachel. 2010. (Avalon: Web of Magic Ser.). (ENG.). 304p. (J). (gr. 3-6). pap. 11.99 *(978-1-934876-88-6(7))* Seven Seas Entertainment, LLC.

Shiei & Shiei, Shiei. Aoi House Omnibus 1, 2 vols. Arnold, Adam. 2008. (Aoi House Ser.: 1). (ENG.). 352p. (gr. 11). pap. 11.99 *(978-1-933164-73-1(5))* Seven Seas Entertainment, LLC.

Shiei, Shiei, jt. illus. see Shiei.

Shields, Bonnie. Jasper: A Christmas Caper. Hodges, Meredith. 2004. 85p. (J). 24.95 *(978-1-928624-20-2(0))* Lucky 3 Ranch, Inc.

—Jasper: A Fabulous Fourth. Hodges, Meredith. 2006. 83p. (J). *(978-1-928624-24-0(3))* Lucky 3 Ranch, Inc.

—Jasper: The Story of a Mule. Hodges, Meredith. 2003. 245p. (J). (gr. k-7). 39.95 *(978-0-9702309-8-0(2))* Lucky 3 Ranch, Inc.

Shields, Chris, et al. Creepy Crawlies. Kilpatrick, Cathy. Jacquemier, Sue, ed. rev. ed. 2006. (First Nature Ser.). 24p. (J). pap. 4.99 *(978-0-7945-1494-5(4),* Usborne) EDC Publishing.

Shields, Chris, jt. illus. see Gower, Jeremy.

Shields, Erik P., jt. illus. see Petersen, Darla.

Shields, Laurie. Burned & Beautiful. Tartakoff, Katy. 54p. (Orig.). (J). stu. ed. 14.95 *(978-0-9629365-1-7(0))* Children's Legacy.

—Let Me Show You My World. Tartakoff, Katy. 54p. (Orig.). (J). stu. ed. 14.95 *(978-0-9629365-2-4(9))* Children's Legacy.

Shields, Ruth. Il Goatino. Zyrro, Roggen. 2004. 32p. (J). 16.95 *(978-0-9762580-0-1(5))* Zyrro, Roggen.

Shields, Sue. Chameleons Are Cool. Jenkins, Martin. 2015. 32p. pap. 7.00 ***(978-1-61003-406-7(6))*** Center for the Collaborative Classroom.

Shields, Sue. Clever Cleo. Ross, Stewart. 32p. pap. 9.99 *(978-0-7502-2853-4(9))* Hodder & Stoughton GBR. Dist: Trafalgar Square Publishing.

Shields, Susan. Don't Say No to Flo: The Story of Florence Nightingale. Ross, Stewart. 32p. (J). pap. *(978-0-7502-3273-9(0),* Wayland) Hachette Children's Group.

—Sink the Armada! Sir Francis Drake & the Spanish Armada of 1588. Ross, Stewart. 62p. (J). pap. *(978-0-237-51959-9(3))* Evans Brothers, Ltd.

—Will's Dream. Ross, Stewart. 28p. pap. 9.99 *(978-0-7502-2965-4(9))* Hodder & Stoughton GBR. Dist: Trafalgar Square Publishing.

Shiffman, Lena. A Second Chance for Tina. Snyder, Marilyn. 2003. (Hello Reader! Ser.). (J). *(978-0-439-44154-4(4))* Scholastic, Inc.

Shigeno, Shuichi. Initial D, 20 vols., Vol. 5. Shigeno, Shuichi. Hagihara, Rie, tr. from JPN. rev. ed. 2003. 232p. (gr. 8-18). pap. 14.99 *(978-1-59182-038-3(3),* Tokyopop Adult) TOKYOPOP, Inc.

—Initial D, 23 vols. Shigeno, Shuichi. Vol. 9. rev. ed. 2003. 200p. pap. 14.99 *(978-1-59182-109-0(6));* Vol. 10. rev. ed. 2004. 192p. pap. 14.99 *(978-1-59182-110-6(X));* Vol. 16. rev. ed. 2005. 240p. pap. 14.99 *(978-1-59182-992-8(5));* Vol. 18. rev. ed. 2005. 192p. pap. 14.99 *(978-1-59182-994-2(1));* Vol. 19. 19th rev. ed. 2005. 240p. pap. 14.99 *(978-1-59182-995-9(X));* Vol. 20. 20th rev. ed. 2005. 192p. pap. 14.99 *(978-1-59182-996-6(8))* TOKYOPOP, Inc. (Tokyopop Adult).

—Initial D: Volume 17, Vol. 17. Shigeno, Shuichi. 2005. (Initial D Ser.). 212p. lib. bdg. 20.90 *(978-1-4176-5264-8(0),* Turtleback) Turtleback Bks.

—Initial D: Volume 6. Shigeno, Shuichi. 2003. (Initial D Ser.). 210p. lib. bdg. 20.90 *(978-1-4176-5259-4(4),* Turtleback) Turtleback Bks.

Shigeno, Shuichi. Initial D, Vol. 17. Shigeno, Shuichi, creator. rev. ed. 2005. 240p. (YA). pap. 14.99 *(978-1-59182-993-5(3),* Tokyopop Adult) TOKYOPOP, Inc.

Shih, Lin. Santa's Christmas Train. Caro, Joe. 2005. 32p. pap. *(978-0-9628078-2-4(6))* Cowboy Collector Pubns.

—Santa's Christmas Train Coloring Book. Caro, Joe. 2005. 32p. pap. *(978-0-9628078-5-5(0))* Cowboy Collector Pubns.

Shiina, Karuho. From Me to You. Shiina, Karuho. 2014. (Kimi ni Todoke: from Me to You Ser.: 18). (ENG.). 176p. pap. 9.99 *(978-1-4215-5917-9(X))* Viz Media.

—Kimi Ni Todoke Vol. 5: From Me to You. Shiina, Karuho. 2010. (Kimi ni Todoke Ser.: 5). (ENG.). 192p. pap. 9.99 *(978-1-4215-2787-1(1))* Viz Media.

—Kimi Ni Todoke Vol. 10: From Me to You. Shiina, Karuho. 2010. (Kimi ni Todoke Ser.: 3). (ENG.). 216p. (gr. 8-18). pap. 9.99 *(978-1-4215-2757-4(X));* Vol. 6. 184p. pap. 9.99 *(978-1-4215-2788-8(X))* Viz Media.

—Kimi Ni Todoke - From Me to You. Shiina, Karuho. 2010. (Kimi ni Todoke Ser.: 4). (ENG.). 208p. pap. 9.99 *(978-1-4215-2786-4(3))* Viz Media.

Shilliam, Jo-Anne. Will I Live Forever? Nystrom, Carolyn. 2006. 32p. (J). (gr. -1-3). 11.99 *(978-0-8254-7306-7(3),* Candle Bks.) Lion Hudson PLC GBR. Dist: Kregel Pubns.

Shiloh, Ramon. The Otter, the Spotted Frog & the Great Flood: A Creek Indian Story. Hausman, Gerald. 2013. (ENG.). 36p. (J). (gr. k-3). pap. 17.95 *(978-1-937786-12-0(9),* Wisdom Tales) World Wisdom, Inc.

Shiloh, Ramon. Guidance Through an Illustrative Alphabet: Written & Illustrated by Ramon Shiloh. Shiloh, Ramon. 2006. 64p. (J). per. 29.95 *(978-1-4259-5132-0(5))* AuthorHouse.

Shimabukuro, Mitsutoshi. Toriko, Vol. 1. Shimabukuro, Mitsutoshi. 2010. (Toriko Ser.: 1). (ENG.). 208p. (gr. 8-18). pap. 9.99 *(978-1-4215-3509-8(2))* Viz Media.

Shimano, Chie. BioGraphic Novel: Che Guevara. 2008. (JPN.). 192p. (YA). pap. 14.95 *(978-0-9817543-2-1(5))* Emotional Content, LLC.

Shimin, Symeon. Zeely. Hamilton, Virginia. 2006. (ENG.). 128p. (J). (gr. 3-7). pap. 6.99 *(978-1-4169-1413-6(7),* Simon & Schuster/Paula Wiseman Bks.) Simon & Schuster/Paula Wiseman Bks.

Shimizu, Aki. Qwan, Vol. 2. Kiefl, Mike, tr. from JPN. rev. ed. 2005. 192p. (YA). pap. 9.99 *(978-1-59532-535-8(2))* TOKYOPOP, Inc.

Shimizu, Aki. Qwan, Vol. 1. Shimizu, Aki, creator. 2005. 192p. (YA). pap. 9.99 *(978-1-59532-534-1(4))* TOKYOPOP, Inc.

Shimizu, Yuko. Barbed Wire Baseball. Moss, Marissa. 2013. (ENG.). 48p. (J). (gr. 1-5). 19.95 *(978-1-4197-0521-2(0),* Abrams Bks. for Young Readers) Abrams.

—Guardian of the Darkness. Uehashi, Nahoko & Hirano, Cathy. 2009. (Moribito Ser.: No. 2). (J). pap. *(978-0-545-10874-4(8),* Levine, Arthur A. Bks.) Scholastic, Inc.

—Guardian of the Darkness. Uehashi, Nahoko. Hirano, Cathy, tr. 2009. (Moribito Ser.: 2). (ENG.). 272p. (J). (gr. 7-18). 17.99 *(978-0-545-10295-7(2),* Levine, Arthur A. Bks.) Scholastic, Inc.

—Guardian of the Spirit. Uehashi, Nahoko. Hirano, Cathy, tr. 2009. (Moribito Ser.: 1). (ENG.). 288p. (J). (gr. 7). pap. 8.99 *(978-0-545-00543-2(4),* Levine, Arthur A. Bks.) Scholastic, Inc.

Shimmen, Cathy. Five Teddy Bears. Adeney, Anne. 2008. (Tadpoles Ser.). (ENG.). 24p. (J). (gr. -1-k). pap. *(978-0-7787-3884-8(1));* lib. bdg. *(978-0-7787-3853-4(1))* Crabtree Publishing Co.

The check digit for ISBN-10 appears in parentheses after the full ISBN-13

—Five Teddy Bears. Adeney, Anne. 2008. (Tadpoles Ser.). 23p. (gr. -1-k). 17.15 (978-1-4178-0926-4(4), Turtleback) Turtleback Bks.

—The Loaves & Fishes. Page, Nick & Page, Claire. 2006. (Read with Me (Make Believe Ideas) Ser.). 30p. (J). (gr. k-2). (978-1-84610-175-5(1)) Make Believe Ideas.

—Under the Sea. Milbourne, Anna. 2007. (Picture Bks). 32p. (J). 9.99 (978-0-7945-1801-1(X), Usborne) EDC Publishing.

—The Winter Prince. Page, Nick & Page, Claire. 2006. (Read with Me (Make Believe Ideas) Ser.). 31p. (J). (gr. k-2). (978-1-84610-172-4(7)) Make Believe Ideas.

Shimon, Diana. The Pilgrim Book of Bible Stories. Water, Mark. 2003. 320p. (J). 22.50 (978-0-8298-1487-3(6)) Pilgrim Pr., The/United Church Pr.

Shimony, Yaniv. Macbeth. Plaisted, Caroline. 2012. (Tales from Shakespeare Ser.). (ENG.). 48p. (J). (gr. 2-6). 14.99 (978-1-60992-239-9(5)) QEB Publishing Inc.

—A Midsummer Night's Dream. Plaisted, Caroline. 2012. (Tales from Shakespeare Ser.). (ENG.). 48p. (J). (gr. 2-6). 14.99 (978-1-60992-237-5(9)) QEB Publishing Inc.

—Romeo & Juliet. Plaisted, Caroline. 2012. (Tales from Shakespeare Ser.). (ENG.). 48p. (J). (gr. 2-6). 14.99 (978-1-60992-236-8(0)) QEB Publishing Inc.

Shin, Hayoung. Thanksgiving Then & Now, 1 vol. Gunderson, Jessica. 2011. (Thanksgiving Ser.). (ENG.). 24p. (gr. 1-2). lib. bdg. 26.65 (978-1-4048-6286-9(2)); pap. 7.95 (978-1-4048-6723-9(6)) Picture Window Bks. (Nonfiction Picture Bks.).

Shin, Hwan. Threads of Time, Vol. 3. Noh, Mi Young. rev. ed. 2005. 192p. pap. 9.99 (978-1-59532-034-6(2)) TOKYOPOP, Inc.

Shin, Ji-Soo. So Lonely. Kim, Young-Ah. 2012. 32p. (J). (978-1-4338-1287-3(8)); pap. (978-1-4338-1288-0(6)) American Psychological Assn. (Magination Pr.).

Shin, Simone. Insults Aren't Funny: What to Do about Verbal Bullying. Doering, Amanda. 2015. (No More Bullies Ser.). (ENG.). 24p. (gr. k-3). lib. bdg. 25.32 **(978-1-4795-6942-7(9))** Picture Window Bks.

—No More Bullies. Doering, Amanda F. & Higgins, Melissa. 2015. (No More Bullies Ser.). (ENG.). 24p. (gr. k-3). 101.28 **(978-1-4795-8007-1(4))** Picture Window Bks.

—Pushing Isn't Funny: What to Do about Physical Bullying. Higgins, Melissa. 2015. (No More Bullies Ser.). (ENG.). 24p. (gr. k-3). lib. bdg. 25.32 **(978-1-4795-6941-0(0))** Picture Window Bks.

—The Red Bicycle: The Extraordinary Story of One Ordinary Bicycle. Isabella, Jude. 2015. (CitizenKid Ser.). (ENG.). 32p. (J). (gr. 3-7). 18.95 **(978-1-77138-023-2(3))** Kids Can Pr., Ltd. CAN. Dist: Univ. of Toronto Pr.

—Sometimes Jokes Aren't Funny: What to Do about Hidden Bullying. Doering, Amanda. 2015. (No More Bullies Ser.). (ENG.). 24p. (gr. k-3). lib. bdg. 25.32 **(978-1-4795-6943-4(7))** Picture Window Bks.

—Teasing Isn't Funny: What to Do about Emotional Bullying. Higgins, Melissa. 2015. (No More Bullies Ser.). (ENG.). 24p. (gr. k-3). lib. bdg. 25.32 **(978-1-4795-6940-3(2))** Picture Window Bks.

Shindo, Hikaru & Obata, Takeshi. Hikaru No Go. Hotta, Yumi & Shindo, Hikaru. 2008. (Hikaru No Go Ser.: 13). (ENG.). 210p. pap. 7.95 (978-1-4215-1509-0(1)) Viz Media.

Shine, Andrea. Family Reunion. Quattlebaum, Mary. 2004. 32p. (J). 16.00 (978-0-8028-5237-3(8)) Eerdmans, William B. Publishing Co.

—Loon Summer. Santucci, Barbara. 2004. 32p. (J). (gr. k-3). 16.00 (978-0-8028-5182-6(7)) Eerdmans, William B. Publishing Co.

—Nellie Bishop. Clark, Clara. 2003. (ENG.). 128p. (YA). (gr. 4-6). pap. 12.95 (978-1-56397-642-1(0)) Boyds Mills Pr.

—The Summer My Father Was Ten. Brisson, Pat. 2014. 32p. pap. 8.00 (978-1-61003-366-4(3)) Center for the Collaborative Classroom.

Shingle, Jude. Christopher Counts the Constellation, bks. 500, bk. 500. Moodey, Mary. 500th l.t. ed. 2012. (ENG.). 37p. 16.99 (978-0-9853579-0-0(8)) MarMooWorks,LLC.

Shinjo, Mayu. Sensual Phrase. Shinjo, Mayu. (Sensual Phrase Ser.). (ENG.). 5. 2004. 192p. pap. 9.95 (978-1-59116-560-6(1)); Vol. 3. 2004. 192p. pap. 9.95 (978-1-59116-449-4(4)); Vol. 4. 2004. 192p. (YA). pap. 9.95 (978-1-59116-411-1(7)); Vol. 6. 2005. 184p. pap. 9.99 (978-1-59116-671-9(3)); Vol. 7. 2005. 200p. (YA). pap. 9.99 (978-1-59116-734-1(5)); Vol. 9. 2005. 200p. pap. 9.99 (978-1-59116-867-6(8)); Vol. 11. 2005. 192p. pap. 9.99 (978-1-4215-0107-9(4)); Vol. 13. 2006. 208p. pap. 9.99 (978-1-4215-0395-0(6)) Viz Media.

Shinjo, Shelly. Ghosts for Breakfast. Terasaki, Stanley Todd. 2013. (ENG.). 32p. (J). (gr. k-4). 16.95 (978-1-58430-046-5(9)) Lee & Low Bks., Inc.

Shinohara, Chie. Red River. Shinohara, Chie. (Red River Ser.). (ENG.). 2005. 192p. (YA). pap. 9.95 (978-1-59116-780-8(9)); 3. 2004. 200p. (YA). pap. 9.95 (978-1-59116-431-9(1)); Vol. 1. 2004. 200p. (YA). pap. 9.95 (978-1-59116-429-6(X)); Vol. 2. 2004. 200p. (YA). pap. 9.95 (978-1-59116-430-2(3)); Vol. 4. 2004. 200p. (YA). pap. 9.95 (978-1-59116-432-6(X)); Vol. 5. 2005. 192p. (YA). pap. 9.95 (978-1-59116-433-3(8)); Vol. 7. 2005. 192p. (YA). pap. 9.95 (978-1-59116-847-8(3)); Vol. 8. 2005. 200p. pap. 9.99 (978-1-59116-988-8(7)); Vol. 9. 2005. 192p. pap. 9.99 (978-1-4215-0066-9(3)); Vol. 11. 2006. 208p. pap. 9.99 (978-1-4215-0327-1(1)); Vol. 14. 2006. 208p. pap. 9.99 (978-1-4215-0556-5(8)) Viz Media.

Shiozaki, Yuji. Battle Vixens, Vol. 6. Shiozaki, Yuji. rev. ed. 2005. (Battle Vixens Ser.). 168p. pap. 9.99 (978-1-59182-948-5(8)) TOKYOPOP, Inc.

Shipe, Becky. Bend & Stretch: Learning about Your Bones & Muscles. Nettleton, Pamela Hill. 2004. (Amazing Body Ser.). (ENG.). 24p. (gr. k-3). per. 7.95 (978-1-4048-0507-1(9), Nonfiction Picture Bks.) Picture Window Bks.

—Breathe in, Breathe Out: Learning about Your Lungs. Nettleton, Pamela Hill. 2004. (Amazing Body Ser.). (ENG.). 24p. (gr. k-3). 25.99 (978-1-4048-0254-4(1), Nonfiction Picture Bks.) Picture Window Bks.

—Gurgles & Growls: Learning about Your Stomach. Nettleton, Pamela Hill. 2004. (Amazing Body Ser.). (ENG.). 24p. (gr. k-3). 25.99 (978-1-4048-0253-7(3)); per. 7.95 (978-1-4048-0504-0(4)) Picture Window Bks. (Nonfiction Picture Bks.).

—Look, Listen, Taste, Touch, & Smell: Learning about Your Five Senses. Nettleton, Pamela Hill. 2004. (Amazing Body Ser.). (ENG.). 24p. (gr. k-3). per. 7.95 (978-1-4048-0508-8(7), Nonfiction Picture Bks.) Picture Window Bks.

—Out & about at the Post Office. Shea, Kitty. 2004. (Field Trips Ser.). (ENG.). 24p. (gr. -1-3). 26.65 (978-1-4048-0294-0(0), Nonfiction Picture Bks.) Picture Window Bks.

—Out & about at the Science Center. Shea, Kitty. 2004. (Field Trips Ser.). (ENG.). 24p. (gr. -1-3). 26.65 (978-1-4048-0297-1(5), Nonfiction Picture Bks.) Picture Window Bks.

—Think, Think, Think: Learning about Your Brain. Nettleton, Pamela Hill. 2004. (Amazing Body Ser.). (ENG.). 24p. (gr. k-3). per. 7.95 (978-1-4048-0503-3(6), Nonfiction Picture Bks.) Picture Window Bks.

Shipley, Marie. The Lion & the Lamb. Skoor, Susan. 2003. (ENG.). (J). pap. 12.95 (978-0-8309-1068-7(9)) Herald Publishing Hse.

Shipman, Gary. Pakkins' Land: Tavitah, 4. 2003. (Pakkins' Land: 4). 128p. pap. 16.95 (978-0-9700241-4-5(2)) Pakkins Presents.

Shipman, Josie. Where's the Gold. Kruse, Donald W. 2012. 50p. pap. 12.95 (978-1-59663-857-0(5), Castle Keep Pr.) Rock, James A. & Co. Pubs.

Shipman, Talitha. You Are My Little Cupcake. Sklansky, Amy E. 2011. (ENG.). 16p. (J). (gr. -1-17). bds. 6.99 (978-0-316-07818-4(2)) Little, Brown Bks. for Young Readers.

Shirasu, Nori. Solar System Song. Nono, Auntie. 2004. (J). bds. 1.25 (978-0-9754098-0-0(8)) Accordian Bks.

Shireen, Nadia. The Baby That Roared. Puttock, Simon. 2012. (ENG.). 32p. (J). (gr. -1-2). 15.99 (978-0-7636-5903-5(7), Nosy Crow) Candlewick Pr.

Shireen, Nadia. Yeti & the Bird. Shireen, Nadia. 2015. (ENG.). 32p. (J). (gr. -1-3). 17.99 (978-1-4814-0389-4(3), Atheneum Bks. for Young Readers) Simon & Schuster Children's Publishing.

Shirley, Alice. The Gentle Lion & the Little Owlet. Shirley, Alice. 2013. Orig. Title: Owlet & Pussycat. (ENG.). 32p. (J). (gr. -1-k). pap. 8.99 (978-1-84365-199-4(8), Pavilion) Pavilion Bks. GBR. Dist: Independent Pubs. Group.

Shirley, Hoskins. Letters from Scamper. Mary, Mize. 2012. 32p. pap. 10.00 (978-0-9832514-3-9(6)) Gypsy Heart Pr.

Shirley, John. Build Your Own Cars Sticker Book. Tudhope, Simon. 2013. (ENG.). 23p. (J). (gr. -1-3). 8.99 (978-0-7945-3379-3(5), Usborne) EDC Publishing.

Shirley-Smith, Sanette. A Donkey Is Not Stupid, a Donkey Can Think. Smith, Pieter Ernst. 2011. 24p. pap. 11.50 (978-1-61204-039-4(X), Eloquent Bks.) Strategic Book Publishing & Rights Agency (SBPRA).

Shivack, Nadia. Inside Out: Portrait of an Eating Disorder. Shivack, Nadia. 2007. (ENG.). 64p. (YA). (gr. 7-12). 17.99 (978-0-689-85216-9(9), Atheneum Bks. for Young Readers) Simon & Schuster Children's Publishing.

Shively, Julie. What Belongs? Baby Looney Tunes. Kurtz, John. 2004. 12p. bds. 6.95 (978-0-8249-6560-0(4)) Ideals Pubns.

Shlichta, Joe. Eleven Nature Tales: A Multicultural Journey. DeSpain, Pleasant. 2005. (ENG.). 96p. (J). (gr. k-17). pap. 9.95 (978-0-87483-458-1(9)) August Hse. Pubs., Inc.

—Strongheart Jack & the Beanstalk. 2005. (ENG.). 32p. (J). (gr. k-3). 15.95 (978-0-87483-414-7(7)) August Hse. Pubs., Inc.

—Thirty-Three Multicultural Tales to Tell. DeSpain, Pleasant. 2005. (American Storytelling Ser.). (ENG.). 126p. (J). (gr. 2-5). pap. 16.95 (978-0-87483-266-2(7), AH2667) August Hse. Pubs., Inc.

Shneiderman, Ben, photos by. David Seymour (Chim) Beck, Tom. rev. ed. 2005. (55s Ser.). (ENG., 128p. (gr. 8-17). 27.95 (978-0-7148-4276-9(1)) Phaidon Pr., Inc.

Shoals, Melinda, jt. illus. see Worthington, Jennifer.

Shoemaker, Kathryn. Floyd the Flamingo: And His Flock of Friends, 1 vol. Stone, Tiffany. 2004. (ENG.). 64p. (J). (gr. 2-5). per. 7.95 (978-1-896580-58-6(0)) Tradewind Bks. CAN. Dist: Orca Bk. Pubs. USA.

—My Animal Friends, 1 vol. Stephens, R. David. 2003. (ENG.). 32p. (J). (gr. k-3). pap. 6.95 (978-1-896580-74-6(2)) Tradewind Bks. CAN. Dist: Orca Bk. Pubs. USA.

Shoemaker, Kathryn E. Good-Bye Marianne: A Story of Growing up in Nazi Germany. Watts, Irene N. 2008. (ENG.). 128p. (J). (gr. 4-7). pap. 12.95 (978-0-88776-830-9(X)) Tundra Bks. CAN. Dist: Random Hse., Inc.

—A Telling Time, 1 vol. Watts, Irene N. 2004. (ENG.). 32p. (J). (gr. 2-5). 17.95 (978-1-896580-39-5(4)); pap. 7.95 (978-1-896580-72-2(6)) Tradewind Bks. CAN. Dist: Orca Bk. Pubs. USA.

Shoemaker, Terry, et al. Dr. Strange: Strange Tales. Gillis, Peter & Alexander, Larry. 2011. (ENG.). 240p. (J). (gr. 4-17). pap. 29.99 (978-0-7851-5549-2(X)) Marvel Worldwide, Inc.

—Evolutionary War. Simonson, Louise & Engelhart, Steve. 2011. (ENG.). 472p. (J). (gr. 4-17). 74.99 (978-0-7851-5547-8(3)) Marvel Worldwide, Inc.

Shogakukan & Mitsui-Kids. Duel Masters Vol. 3: The Champion of Tomorrow. 2004. (Teen Ser.). 96p. pap. 14.99 (978-1-59532-065-0(2), Tokyopop Kids) TOKYOPOP, Inc.

Sholto, Walker. Molly & the Giant. Jarman, Julia. 2005. (ENG.). 24p. (J). lib. bdg. 23.65 (978-1-59646-746-0(0)) Dingles & Co.

Shondeck, Betty. Liking Myself. Palmer, Pat. 2010. 102p. (J). pap. 12.99 (978-0-9622834-2-0(8)) Uplift Pr.

—The Mouse, the Monster & Me: Assertiveness for Young People. Palmer, Pat. rev. ed. 2010. 100p. (J). pap. 12.99 (978-0-9622834-3-7(6)) Uplift Pr.

Shone, Rob. Harriet Tubman: The Life of an African-American Abolitionist. Ganeri, Anita. 2005. (Graphic Biographies Ser.). (ENG.). 48p. (gr. 5-8). pap. 14.05 (978-1-4042-5172-4(3)) Rosen Publishing Group, Inc., The.

Shone, Rob & Field, James. Diplodocus: The Whip-Tailed Dinosaur. 2009. (Graphic Dinosaurs Ser.). (ENG.). 32p. (gr. 2-5). pap. 12.30 (978-1-4042-7714-4(5)) Rosen Publishing Group, Inc., The.

Shonkwiler, Martha. The Power of Self Ralph Waldo Emerson's Wonder Filled Life. Miller, Ruth L. 2013. 66p. pap. 12.00 (978-0-945385-85-1(4)) WiseWoman Pr.

Shoop, Johanna. The Big Black Dog & the Big Blue Se. Lindeman, Craig. 2009. 40p. pap. 15.95 (978-1-60844-047-4(8)) Dog Ear Publishing, LLC.

Shoopik, Marina. Jessie's Big Move. Wilson, Nathaniel. 2010. (ENG.). 54p. (J). 16.95 (978-0-9744935-7-2(0)) AllWrite Advertising & Publishing.

Shooter, Howard, photos by. DK Children's Cookbook. Dorling Kindersley Publishing Staff & Ibbs, Katharine. 2004. (ENG., 128p. (J). (gr. 3-7). 17.99 (978-0-7566-0597-1(0), 1235962) Dorling Kindersley Publishing, Inc.

—Kids' Fun & Healthy Cookbook. Graimes, Nicola. 2007. (ENG., 128p. (J). (gr. 2-5). 17.99 (978-0-7566-2916-8(0)) Dorling Kindersley Publishing, Inc.

Shore, Judie. Naturaleza Divertida. Hickman, Pamela & Federation of Ontario Naturalists. (SPA.). 92p. (978-84-9754-095-7(6), 87821) Ediciones Oniro S.A.

—La Naturaleza y Tú. Hickman, Pamela & Federation of Ontario Naturalists. (SPA.). 63p. (978-84-9754-106-0(5), 87822) Ediciones Oniro S.A.

Shore, Stephen, photos by. The Nature of Photographs. Shore, Stephen. 2nd rev. ed. 2007. (ENG., 136p. (gr. 8-17). 39.95 (978-0-7148-4585-2(X)) Phaidon Pr., Inc.

Short, Gregory T. Safety Sam, I Am: How to Avoid A Sticky Jelly Jam. Weathers, Regina Lorick. 2004. (J). per. 7.95 (978-0-9665909-6-8(1)) Kalawantis Publishing Services, Inc.

Short, Kasey. Betsy Beansprout Adventure Guide. Elmore, Amber. 2011. (J). pap. 15.99 (978-0-9822632-8-0(7)) ShadeTree Publishing, LLC.

Short, Robbie. Hiro Dragon Warrior: Battle at Mount Kamado. Weiss, Bobbi & Weiss, David. 2008. (ENG.). 24p. (J). (gr. 1-17). pap. 3.99 (978-1-58476-721-3(9)) Innovative Kids.

—Hiro: Dragon Warrior: Level 2. Weiss, Bobbi & Weiss, David. 2007. (ENG.). 24p. (J). (gr. 1-4). per. 3.99 (978-1-58476-616-2(6), IKIDS) Innovative Kids.

—I Want One Too! Ehrmantraut, Brenda. 2003. (J). lib. bdg. 16.95 (978-0-9729833-1-0(7)); per. 9.95 (978-0-9729833-0-3(9)) Bubble Gum Pr.

—I Want One Too! 2003. 32p. (J). lib. bdg. 12.95 (978-0-9729833-2-7(5)) Bubble Gum Pr.

Shortall, Leonard. Encyclopedia Brown & the Case of the Dead Eagles. Sobol, Donald J. 2015. 96p. (J). **(978-1-61479-308-3(5))** ABDO Publishing Co.

—Encyclopedia Brown & the Case of the Secret Pitch. Sobol, Donald J. 2015. 96p. (J). **(978-1-61479-310-6(7))** ABDO Publishing Co.

—Encyclopedia Brown, Boy Detective. Sobol, Donald J. 2015. 88p. (J). **(978-1-61479-320-5(4))** ABDO Publishing Co.

—Encyclopedia Brown Finds the Clues. Sobol, Donald J. 2015. 96p. (J). **(978-1-61479-311-3(5))** ABDO Publishing Co.

—Encyclopedia Brown Gets His Man. Sobol, Donald J. 2015. 96p. (J). **(978-1-61479-312-0(3))** ABDO Publishing Co.

—Encyclopedia Brown Keeps the Peace. Sobol, Donald J. 2015. 96p. (J). **(978-1-61479-313-7(1))** ABDO Publishing Co.

—Encyclopedia Brown Lends a Hand. Sobol, Donald J. 2015. 96p. (J). **(978-1-61479-314-4(X))** ABDO Publishing Co.

—Encyclopedia Brown Saves the Day. Sobol, Donald J. 2015. 96p. (J). **(978-1-61479-315-1(8))** ABDO Publishing Co.

—Encyclopedia Brown Shows the Way. Sobol, Donald J. 2015. 96p. (J). **(978-1-61479-316-8(6))** ABDO Publishing Co.

—Encyclopedia Brown Solves Them All. Sobol, Donald J. 2015. 96p. (J). **(978-1-61479-317-5(4))** ABDO Publishing Co.

—Encyclopedia Brown Takes the Case. Sobol, Donald J. 2015. 96p. (J). **(978-1-61479-318-2(2))** ABDO Publishing Co.

—Encyclopedia Brown Tracks Them Down. Sobol, Donald J. 2015. 96p. (J). **(978-1-61479-319-9(0)**, 1383123) ABDO Publishing Co.

Shortall, Leonard W. Encyclopedia Brown, 4 vols., Set. Sobol, Donald J. 2007. (Encyclopedia Brown Ser.). (ENG.). 384p. (J). (gr. 2-18). 19.96 (978-0-14-240985-5(5), Puffin) Penguin Publishing Group.

—Encyclopedia Brown & the Case of the Dead Eagles. Sobol, Donald J. 2008. (Encyclopedia Brown Ser.: 12). (ENG.). 96p. (J). (gr. 3-7). 4.99 (978-0-14-241135-3(3), Puffin) Penguin Publishing Group.

—Encyclopedia Brown & the Case of the Secret Pitch. Sobol, Donald J. 2007. (Encyclopedia Brown Ser.: 2). (ENG.). 96p. (J). (gr. 3-7). 4.99 (978-0-14-240889-6(1), Puffin) Penguin Publishing Group.

—Encyclopedia Brown, Boy Detective. Sobol, Donald J. 2007. (Encyclopedia Brown Ser.: 1). (ENG.). 96p. (J). (gr. 3-7). 4.99 (978-0-14-240888-9(3), Puffin) Penguin Publishing Group.

—Encyclopedia Brown, Boy Detective. Sobol, Donald J. 2009. (Encyclopedia Brown Ser.). 88p. lib. bdg. 15.00 (978-1-60686-386-2(X)) Perfection Learning Corp.

—Encyclopedia Brown, Boy Detective. Sobol, Donald J. ed. 2007. (Encyclopedia Brown Ser.: 1). 88p. (J). (gr. 4-7). 14.75 (978-1-4177-8622-0(1), Turtleback) Turtleback Bks.

—Encyclopedia Brown Finds the Clues. Sobol, Donald J. 2007. (Encyclopedia Brown Ser.: 3). (ENG.). 96p. (J). (gr. 3-7). 4.99 (978-0-14-240890-2(5), Puffin) Penguin Publishing Group.

—Encyclopedia Brown Finds the Clues. Sobol, Donald J. 2008. (Encyclopedia Brown Ser.). 96p. (J). (gr. 4-7). 15.00 (978-0-7569-8846-3(2)) Perfection Learning Corp.

—Encyclopedia Brown Gets His Man. Sobol, Donald J. 2007. (Encyclopedia Brown Ser.: 4). (ENG.). 96p. (J). (gr. 3-7). 4.99 (978-0-14-240891-9(3), Puffin) Penguin Publishing Group.

—Encyclopedia Brown Gets His Man. Sobol, Donald J. 2009. (Encyclopedia Brown Ser.). 96p. lib. bdg. 15.00 (978-1-60686-464-7(5)) Perfection Learning Corp.

—Encyclopedia Brown Keeps the Peace. Sobol, Donald J. 2008. (Encyclopedia Brown Ser.: 6). (ENG.). 96p. (J). (gr. 3-7). 4.99 (978-0-14-240950-3(2), Puffin) Penguin Publishing Group.

—Encyclopedia Brown Lends a Hand. Sobol, Donald J. 2008. (Encyclopedia Brown Ser.: 11). (ENG.). 96p. (J). (gr. 3-7). 4.99 (978-0-14-241105-6(1), Puffin) Penguin Publishing Group.

—Encyclopedia Brown Saves the Day. Sobol, Donald J. 2008. (Encyclopedia Brown Ser.: 7). (ENG.). 96p. (J). (gr. 3-7). 4.99 (978-0-14-240921-3(9), Puffin) Penguin Publishing Group.

—Encyclopedia Brown Shows the Way. Sobol, Donald J. 2008. (Encyclopedia Brown Ser.: 9). (ENG.). 96p. (J). (gr. 3-7). 4.99 (978-0-14-241086-8(1), Puffin) Penguin Publishing Group.

—Encyclopedia Brown Shows the Way. Sobol, Donald J. 2008. (Encyclopedia Brown Ser.). 96p. (J). (gr. 2-5). 12.65 (978-0-7569-8937-8(X)) Perfection Learning Corp.

—Encyclopedia Brown Solves Them All. Sobol, Donald J. 2008. (Encyclopedia Brown Ser.: 5). (ENG.). 96p. (J). (gr. 3-7). 4.99 (978-0-14-240920-6(0), Puffin) Penguin Publishing Group.

—Encyclopedia Brown Takes the Case. Sobol, Donald J. 2008. (Encyclopedia Brown Ser.: 10). (ENG.). 96p. (J). (gr. 3-7). 4.99 (978-0-14-241085-1(3), Puffin) Penguin Publishing Group.

—Encyclopedia Brown Takes the Case. Sobol, Donald J. 2008. (Encyclopedia Brown Ser.). 96p. (J). (gr. 3-7). 12.65 (978-0-7569-9078-7(5)) Perfection Learning Corp.

—Encyclopedia Brown Tracks Them Down. Sobol, Donald J. 2008. (Encyclopedia Brown Ser.: No. 8). (ENG.). 96p. (J). (gr. 3-7). 4.99 (978-0-14-240951-0(0), Puffin) Penguin Publishing Group.

—Secret Agents Four. Sobol, Donald J. 2003. (Adventure Library). 133p. (J). pap. 10.95 (978-1-883937-65-2(5)) Bethlehem Bks.

Shortell, Stephen. Itchy Lee & Itchy Dee Mcgee. Rowe, Papa. Wilkins, Kevan & Mason, Shannon, eds. ed. 2006. (J). 15.99 (978-0-9778858-0-0(1)) WowZee Works Inc.

Shortley, Michele. Malarkey & the Big Trap. Krensky, Stephen. 2011. 29p. (J). pap. (978-0-7680-3487-5(6)) SAE Intl.

—Once upon a Time in the Woods. Krensky, Stephen. 2011. (J). pap. (978-0-7680-3488-2(4)) SAE Intl.

—The Three Little Pigs' Sledding Adventure. Krensky, Stephen. 2011. 28p. (J). pap. (978-0-7680-3486-8(8)) SAE Intl.

Shoup, Andrew J. Andy & Elmer's Apple Dumpling Adventure Coloring & Activity Book. Shoup, Andrew J. 2007. 36p. (J). 3.95 (978-0-9720436-2-5(4)) TokoBooks, LLC.

Shoutarou, Harada. Na Na Na Na. Shoutarou, Harada. 2006. 208p. (YA). Vol. 3. (Café Au Cult Ser.: 3). per. 9.95 (978-1-59697-103-5(7)); Vol. 4. (Na Na Na Na Ser.: Vol. 4). per. 9.95 (978-1-59697-104-2(5)) Infinity Studios LLC.

Showalter, Kristin. When Dogs Dream. Olsen, S. R. 2013. 48p. pap. 13.95 (978-0-9842560-2-0(4)) Sleepy Dog Publishing.

Showalter, Sarah Evelyn. Animals of the Bible from A to Z. 2007. (J). (gr. -1-3). 16.95 (978-0-87946-331-1(7)) ACTA Pubns.

Shreder, Etienne & Aubin, Antoine. The Curse of the 30 Pieces of Silver, Vol. 14, Pt. 2. Van Hamme, Jean. 2012. (ENG.). 64p. (J). (gr. 5-12). pap. 15.95 (978-1-84918-130-3(6)) CineBook GBR. Dist: National Bk. Network.

Shrestha, Anuj. Hello Big Jay! Aryal, Aimee. 2004. 24p. (J). 14.95 (978-1-932888-41-6(1)) Mascot Bks., Inc.

—Hello Herbie Husker! Aryal, Aimee. 2004. 24p. (J). 14.95 (978-1-932888-43-0(8)) Mascot Bks., Inc.

—Hello Otto! Aryal, Aimee. 2004. 22p. (J). 19.95 (978-0-9743442-2-5(2)) Mascot Bks., Inc.

—Let's Go Hoosiers! Aryal, Aimee. 2004. 24p. (J). 19.95 (978-1-932888-32-4(2)) Mascot Bks., Inc.

—Lets Go Illini! Aryal, Aimee. 2004. 24p. (J). lib. bdg. 19.95 (978-1-932888-21-8(7)) Mascot Bks., Inc.

—Let's Go Irish! Aryal, Aimee. 2004. 24p. (J). 19.95 (978-0-9743442-5-6(7)) Mascot Bks., Inc.

Shrestha, Romio, jt. illus. see Shrestha, Sophie.

Shrestha, Sophie & Shrestha, Romio. In Search of the Thunder Dragon. Shrestha, Sophie & Shrestha, Romio. 2007. (ENG.). 32p. (J). (gr. 3). 16.95 (978-1-60109-100-0(1)) Mandala Publishing.

Shreve, Steve. The Adventures of Charlie: Bigfoot or the Value of a Smelly Friend. Shreve, Steve. 2010. (Adventures of Charlie Ser.). 32p. pap. (978-0-237-54284-9(6)) Evans Brothers, Ltd.

—The Bogey Man: Or a Good Argument for Not Picking Your Nose. Shreve, Steve. 2010. (Adventures of Charlie Ser.). 32p. pap. (978-0-237-54287-0(0)) Evans Brothers, Ltd.

—Monkey Island: Or the Advantage of Opposable Thumbs. Shreve, Steve. 2010. (Adventures of Charlie Ser.). 32p. pap. (978-0-237-54288-7(9)) Evans Brothers, Ltd.

—Pirates: Or the Truth about Life on the High Seas. Shreve, Steve. 2010. (Adventures of Charlie Ser.). 32p. pap. (978-0-237-54286-3(2)) Evans Brothers, Ltd.

Shroades, John. The Dragon in the Driveway. Klimo, Kate. (Dragon Keepers Ser.). (ENG.). 176p. (J). (gr. 3-7). 2010. pap. 6.99 (978-0-375-85590-0(4), Yearling); 2009. lib. bdg. 17.99 (978-0-375-95589-1(5), Random Hse. Bks. for Young Readers) Random Hse. Children's Bks.

—The Dragon in the Sock Drawer. Klimo, Kate. 2009. (Dragon Keepers Ser.). (ENG.). 192p. (J). (gr. 3-7). 6.99 (978-0-375-85588-7(2), Yearling) Random Hse. Children's Bks.

—Dragon Keepers #3: the Dragon in the Library. Klimo, Kate. 2011. (Dragon Keepers Ser.). (ENG.). 240p. (J). (gr. 3-7).

S

6.99 *(978-0-375-85592-4(0)*, Yearling) Random Hse. Children's Bks.
—Dragon Keepers #4: the Dragon in the Volcano. Klimo, Kate. 2012. (Dragon Keepers Ser.). (ENG.). 256p. (J). (gr. 3-7). 6.99 *(978-0-375-86688-3(4)*, Yearling) Random Hse. Children's Bks.
—Dragon Keepers #5: the Dragon in the Sea. Klimo, Kate. 2013. (Dragon Keepers Ser.). (ENG.). 224p. (J). (gr. 3-7). 6.99 *(978-0-375-87116-0(0)*, Yearling) Random Hse. Children's Bks.
—Dragon Keepers #6: the Dragon at the North Pole. Klimo, Kate. (Dragon Keepers Ser.). (ENG.). 176p. (J). (gr. 3-7). 2014. 6.99 *(978-0-375-87117-7(9)*, Yearling); 2013. 15.99 *(978-0-375-87066-8(0)*, Random Hse. Bks. for Young Readers); 2013. lib. bdg. 18.99 *(978-0-375-97066-5(5)*, Random Hse. Bks. for Young Readers) Random Hse. Children's Bks.
—Magical Creatures. Torpie, Kate. 2007. (ENG.). 24p. (J). (gr. 2-7). 19.99 *(978-1-58476-619-3(0)*, IKIDS) Innovative Kids.
—Tyrannoclaus. Lawler, Janet & Moore, Clement C. 2009. (ENG.). 32p. (J). (gr. -1-2). 16.99 *(978-0-06-117054-6(2))* HarperCollins Pubs.
Shroades, John / W. The Great Grand Canyon Time Train. Lowell, Susan. 2011. 32p. (J). 15.95 *(978-1-933855-63-9(0))* Rio Nuevo Pubs.
Shropshire, Sandy. Bone Head: Story of the Longhorn. Webber, Desiree Morrison. 2003. 74p. (J). 16.95 *(978-1-57168-763-0(7))*; pap. 9.95 *(978-1-57168-750-0(5))* Eakin Pr. (Eakin Pr.).
Shrum, Edgar. When I Was Little. Cortez, Linda. 2009. 44p. pap. 19.99 *(978-1-4389-5934-4(6))* AuthorHouse.
Shubin, Jon. The Fairytale Fracas: A Shubin Cousins Adventure. Shubin, Masha. 2012. 200p. pap. 7.95 *(978-0-9792145-8-5(0))* Anno Domini.
Shuler, Curtis. Safiya's Garden. Shuler, Melissa. 2010. (ENG.). 66p. pap. 20.00 *(978-1-4538-2180-0(5))* CreateSpace Independent Publishing Platform.
Shulevitz, Uri. Dusk. Shulevitz, Uri. 2013. (ENG.). 32p. (J). (gr. -1-3). 17.99 *(978-0-374-31903-8(0)*, Farrar, Straus & Giroux (BYR)) Farrar, Straus & Giroux.
—How I Learned Geography. Shulevitz, Uri. 2008. (ENG.). 32p. (J). (gr. -1-3). 17.99 *(978-0-374-33499-4(4)*, Farrar, Straus & Giroux (BYR)) Farrar, Straus & Giroux.
—One Monday Morning. Shulevitz, Uri. 2003. (ENG.). 48p. (J). (gr. -1-1). reprint ed. pap. 7.99 *(978-0-374-45648-1(8))* Square Fish.
—Rain Rain Rivers. Shulevitz, Uri. 2006. (ENG.). 32p. (J). (gr. -1-3). reprint ed. pap. 8.99 *(978-0-374-46195-9(3))* Square Fish.
—Snow, 1 vol. Shulevitz, Uri. 2012. (ENG.). 36p. (J). (gr. -1-2). bds. 7.99 *(978-0-374-37093-0(1)*, Farrar, Straus & Giroux (BYR)) Farrar, Straus & Giroux.
—Snow. Shulevitz, Uri. 2004. (ENG.). 32p. (J). (gr. -1-2). reprint ed. pap. 7.99 *(978-0-374-46862-0(1))* Square Fish.
—Snow Storytime Set. Shulevitz, Uri. unabr. ed. 2013. (ENG.). (J). 12.99 *(978-1-4272-4370-6(0))* Macmillan Audio.
Shulman, Dee. Silly Sausage & the Little Visitor, 1 vol. Morgan, Michaela. 2006. (Read-It! Chapter Bks.). (ENG.). 52p. (gr. 2-4). lib. bdg. 21.32 *(978-1-4048-2735-6(8)*, Chapter Readers) Picture Window Bks.
—Silly Sausage & the Spooks, 1 vol. Morgan, Michaela. 2006. (Read-It! Chapter Bks.). (ENG.). 52p. (gr. 2-4). lib. bdg. 21.32 *(978-1-4048-2736-3(6)*, Chapter Readers) Picture Window Bks.
—Silly Sausage in Trouble, 1 vol. Morgan, Michaela. 2006. (Read-It! Chapter Bks.). (ENG.). 52p. (gr. 2-4). lib. bdg. 21.32 *(978-1-4048-2737-0(4)*, Chapter Readers) Picture Window Bks.
Shulman, Mark. Fillmore & Geary Take Off! Fickling, Phillip. 2003. 40p. (J). lib. bdg. *(978-1-58717-258-8(5)*, SeaStar Bks.) Chronicle Bks. LLC.
Shulte, Sara. Sandy's Aunt. Shulte, Sharon. 2004. (J). per. 12.00 *(978-0-9747147-5-2(5))* MK Publishing.
Shultz, Kirsten, photos by. Mermaid Cookbook, 1 vol. Beery, Barbara. 2008. (ENG., 64p. (J). (gr. 1). spiral bd. 14.99 *(978-1-4236-0417-4(2))* Gibbs Smith, Publisher.
Shupe, Bobbi & Crum, Anna-Maria. Spiders: Read Well Level K Unit 1 Storybook. Sprick, Marilyn et al. 2003. (Read Well Level K Ser.). 20p. (J). *(978-1-57035-673-5(4))* Cambium Education, Inc.
—Spiders: Unit 1 Read Well Level K Teacher's Storybook. Sprick, Marilyn et al. 2003. (Read Well Level K Ser.). 20p. (J). *(978-1-57035-696-4(3))* Cambium Education, Inc.
Shurei, Kouyu. Return to Labyrinth, 4 vols., Vol. 2. Forbes, Jake T. & Jake, T. F. 2007. (Return to Labyrinth Ser.). 192p. pap. 9.99 *(978-1-59816-726-9(X))* TOKYOPOP, Inc.
Shurei, Kouyu. Alichino. Shurei, Kouyu. 2005. Vol. 1. 164p. pap. 14.99 *(978-1-59532-478-8(X))*; Vol. 2. rev. ed. 160p. pap. 14.99 *(978-1-59532-479-5(8))*; Vol. 3. 3rd rev. ed. 160p. per. 14.99 *(978-1-59532-480-1(1))* TOKYOPOP, Inc. (Tokyopop Kids).
Shurtliff, William. Today Someone I Love Passed Away. Ahern, Dianne. 2008. (J). *(978-0-9679437-4-9(4))* Aunt Dee's Attic, Inc.
Shusterman, Brendan. Challenger Deep. Shusterman, Neal. 2015. (ENG.). 320p. (YA). (gr. 9). 17.99 *(978-0-06-113411-1(2))* HarperCollins Pubs.
Shusterman, Danielle. Chimps Use Sticks. Cline, Gina. 2014. (1B Animal Behaviors Ser.). (ENG.). 32p. (J). pap. 8.50 *(978-1-61406-689-7(2))* American Reading Co.
Shute, A. B. With Washington in the West or A Soldier Boy's Battles in the Wilderness. Stratemeyer, Edward. 2004. reprint ed. pap. 30.95 *(978-1-4179-2977-1(4))* Kessinger Publishing, LLC.
Shute, A. B. & Fitterling, Michael A. Fighting for the Right. Optic, Oliver. 2005. (Blue & Gray Ser.). (ENG.). 365p. (J). (gr. 4-7). reprint ed. pap. 14.95 *(978-1-890623-12-8(1))* Lost Classic Bks.
Shute, Linda. Captain John Smith's Big & Beautiful Bay, 1 vol. Jones, Rebecca C. 2011. (ENG.). 32p. (J). 14.99 *(978-0-7643-3869-4(2)*, Schiffer Publishing Ltd) Schiffer Publishing, Ltd.
Shuttlewood, Anna. Stork's Landing. Lehman-Wilzig, Tami. 2014. 32p. (J). (gr. -1-2). 17.95 *(978-1-4677-1395-5(3)*, Kar-Ben Publishing) Lerner Publishing Group.
Shuttleworth, Cathie. The Bunny Tales Collection: Twelve Lively Stories of Rascally Rabbits. Baxter, Nicola. 2014. (ENG.). 80p. (J). (gr. -1-3). pap. 9.99 *(978-1-84322-934-6(X)*, Armadillo) Anness Publishing GBR. Dist: National Bk. Network.
—Celtic Tales & Legends. Baxter, Nicola. 2012. (ENG.). 80p. (J). (gr. 2-7). pap. 9.99 *(978-1-84322-950-6(1))* Anness Publishing GBR. Dist: National Bk. Network.
—The Children's Classic Poetry Collection: 60 Poems by the World's Greatest Writers. Baxter, Nicola. 2013. (ENG.). 96p. (J). (gr. 3-8). pap. 9.99 *(978-1-84322-983-4(8)*, Armadillo) Anness Publishing GBR. Dist: National Bk. Network.
—The Children's Treasury of Classic Poetry. 176p. (J). pap. *(978-1-84322-143-2(8))* Bookmart Ltd.
—Classic Collection of Fairy Tales & Poems, 2 vols. 2014. (ENG.). 192p. (J). (gr. 2-12). 19.99 *(978-1-84322-972-8(2)*, Armadillo) Anness Publishing GBR. Dist: National Bk. Network.
—Classic Fairy Tales from Hans Christian Andersen. Baxter, Nicola. 2012. (ENG.). 96p. (J). (gr. 2-7). pap. 9.99 *(978-1-84322-875-2(0))* Anness Publishing GBR. Dist: National Bk. Network.
—Classic Fairy Tales from the Brothers Grimm. Baxter, Nicola. 2012. (ENG.). 96p. (J). (gr. 2-7). pap. 9.99 *(978-1-84322-874-5(2))* Anness Publishing GBR. Dist: National Bk. Network.
—Classic Nursery Rhymes. Baxter, Nicola. 2012. (ENG.). 80p. (J). (gr. -1-k). 9.99 *(978-1-84322-837-0(8))* Anness Publishing GBR. Dist: National Bk. Network.
—Classic Poetry for Children. Baxter, Nicola. 2013. (ENG.). 80p. (J). (gr. k-4). pap. 9.99 *(978-1-84322-820-2(3))* Anness Publishing GBR. Dist: National Bk. Network.
—Little Tales for Toddlers: 35 Stories about Adorable Teddy Bears, Puppies & Bunnies. 2013. (ENG.). 256p. pap. 14.99 *(978-1-84322-925-4(0))* Anness Publishing GBR. Dist: National Bk. Network.
—My Book of Magical Pony Tales: 12 Beautifully Illustrated Stories. Baxter, Nicola. 2013. (ENG.). 80p. (J). (gr. -1-12). pap. 9.99 *(978-1-84322-965-0(X))* Anness Publishing GBR. Dist: National Bk. Network.
—The Puppy Tales Collection: Twelve Silly Stories from Houndsville. Baxter, Nicola. 2014. (ENG.). 80p. (J). (gr. k-5). pap. 9.99 *(978-1-84322-935-3(8)*, Armadillo) Anness Publishing GBR. Dist: National Bk. Network.
—Rhymes for Playtime Fun. Baxter, Nicola. 2013. (ENG.). 80p. (J). (gr. -1-k). pap. 9.99 *(978-1-84322-921-6(8))* Anness Publishing GBR. Dist: National Bk. Network.
—Tales from the Farmyard: 12 Stories of Grunting Pigs, Quacking Ducks, Clucking Hens, Neighing Horses, Bleating Sheep & Other Animals. Baxter, Nicola. 2013. (ENG.). 80p. (J). (gr. 1-8). pap. 9.99 *(978-1-84322-899-8(8))* Anness Publishing GBR. Dist: National Bk. Network.
—Traditional Fairy Tales from Hans Christian Andersen & the Brothers Grimm. Baxter, Nicola. 2013. (ENG.). 192p. (J). (gr. 1-7). pap. 14.99 *(978-1-84322-971-1(4))* Anness Publishing GBR. Dist: National Bk. Network.
Shuttleworth, Cathy. The Classic Collection of Fairy Tales. Grimm, Jacob & Grimm, Wilhelm. 2011. (ENG.). 192p. (J). (gr. -1-12). 9.99 *(978-1-84322-787-8(8))* Anness Publishing GBR. Dist: National Bk. Network.
—Classic Poems for Children: Classic Verse from the Great Poets, Including Lewis Carroll, John Keats & Walt Whitman. 2011. (ENG.). 192p. (J). (gr. -1-12). 9.99 *(978-1-84322-788-5(6))* Anness Publishing GBR. Dist: National Bk. Network.
Shyam. Kumari Loves a Monster: Kumariyin Ratcaca Katalan. Devadasan, Rashmi Ruth. 2010. (TAM & ENG.). 52p. pap. 17.95 *(978-93-80636-01-6(6))* Blaft Pubns.
Shyam, Bhajju. Alone in the Forest. Wolf, Gita & Anastasio, Andrea. 2013. (ENG.). 40p. (J). (gr. -1). 16.95 *(978-81-923171-5-1(3))* Tara Books Agency IND. Dist: Perseus-PGW.
—The London Jungle Book. 2nd ed. 2014. (ENG.). 48p. 19.95 *(978-81-923171-2-0(9))* Tara Books Agency IND. Dist: Perseus-PGW.
SI Artists Staff. Cars, Trucks, Planes, & Trains. Rindone, Nancy L. 2011. (Lift-The-Flap Ser.). (ENG.). 10p. (J). (gr. -1-k). bds. 9.99 *(978-0-7944-2180-9(6))* Reader's Digest Assn., Inc., The.
—Christmastime Is Here! Weiss, Ellen. 2012. (Lift-The-Flap Ser.: 4). (ENG.). 10p. (J). (gr. -1-k). bds. 9.99 *(978-0-7944-2718-4(9))* Reader's Digest Assn., Inc., The.
—Farm Friends. Froeb, Lori C. 2011. (Boardbooks - Board Book Ser.). (ENG.). 10p. (J). (— 1). bds. 9.99 *(978-0-7944-2124-3(5))* Reader's Digest Assn., Inc., The.
—Fisher Price Little People Noah & the Animals. Froeb, Lori C. 2011. (Lift-The-Flap Ser.). (ENG.). 10p. (J). (gr. -1-k). bds. 9.99 *(978-0-7944-2471-8(6))* Studio Fun International.
—Fisher-Price Little People Valentine's Day Is Here! Reader's Digest Editors. 2012. (Lift-The-Flap Ser.). (ENG.). 10p. (J). (gr. -1-k). bds. 9.99 *(978-0-7944-2731-3(6))* Reader's Digest Assn., Inc., The.
—Follow Me to the Farm. Reader's Digest Editors & Mitter, Matt. 2012. (Lift-The-Flap Ser.). (ENG.). 18p. (J). (gr. -1 — 1). bds. 6.99 *(978-0-7944-2523-4(2))* Reader's Digest Assn., Inc., The.
—Let's Go to the Zoo! Weiss, Ellen. 2011. (Lift-The-Flap Ser.). (ENG.). 10p. (J). (gr. -1-k). bds. 9.99 *(978-0-7944-2276-9(4))* Reader's Digest Assn., Inc., The.
—School Trip. Reader's Digest Editors & Mitter, Matt. 2012. (Boardbooks - Board Book Ser.). (ENG.). 18p. (J). (gr. -1 — 1). bds. 6.99 *(978-0-7944-2524-1(0))* Reader's Digest Assn., Inc., The.
—To the Rescue. Packard, Mary. 2011. (Boardbooks - Board Book Ser.). (ENG.). 18p. (J). (— 1). bds. 6.99 *(978-0-7944-2103-8(2))* Reader's Digest Assn., Inc., The.
—Worlds of Adventure. Mitter, Matt & Reader's Digest Editors. 2008. (Look-Inside Ser.). (ENG.). 20p. (J). (gr. -1-k). bds. 9.99 *(978-0-7944-1446-7(X))* Reader's Digest Assn., Inc., The.
SI Illustrators. To the Rescue! Schoberle, Cecile. 2003. (Ready-to-Read Ser.). 31p. (J). (gr. k-3). lib. bdg. 9.02 *(978-0-613-66550-6(3)*, Turtleback) Turtleback Bks.
Sias, Ryan. Are You Eating Something Green? Blue Apple Staff. 2010. (ENG.). 36p. (J). (— 1). 9.99 *(978-1-60905-010-8(X))* Blue Apple Bks.
—Are You Eating Something Red? Blue Apple Staff. 2010. (ENG.). 12p. (J). (— 1). 7.99 *(978-1-60905-018-4(5))* Blue Apple Bks.
—Zoe & Robot, Let's Pretend! 2011. (ENG.). 40p. (J). (gr. 1-4). 10.99 *(978-1-60905-063-4(0))* Blue Apple Bks.
Siau, John. Retrieving with Evie. Harp, Susan. 2007. (ENG.). 24p. (J). lib. bdg. 12.95 *(978-1-932439-67-0(6))* M.T. Publishing Co., Inc.
Siau, Jon. Evie Goes Clean & Green. Harp, Susan. 2013. 24p. (J). lib. bdg. 14.95 *(978-1-938730-09-2(7))* M.T. Publishing Co., Inc.
Sibbick, John. My Favorite Dinosaurs. Ashby, Ruth. 2005. 32p. (J). (gr. 1-3). 16.95 *(978-0-689-03921-8(2))* ibooks, Inc.
Sibert, Stephanie Grace. A Royal Tea. Boyce, Catherine & Boyce, Peter. 2006. 32p. (J). per. 16.95 *(978-0-9778420-1-8(0))* Semper Studio.
—Tea with the Queen. Boyce, Catherine & Boyce, Peter. 2006. 32p. (J). per. 16.95 net. incl. audio compact disk *(978-0-9778420-0-1(2)*, 10,000) Semper Studio.
Sichel, Harold. Captain Billie: Leads the way to the land of I don't want To. Gates, Josephine Scribner. 2007. 96p. (J). lib. bdg. 59.00 *(978-1-60304-019-8(6))* Dollworks.
Sickler, Jonas & Pixton, Kaaren. Frere Jacques: Hey Baby! Look Where Jacques is Sleeping — and Dreaming — in Paris! Sickler, Jonas & Pixton, Amy. 2011. (Indestructibles Ser.). (ENG.). 12p. (J). (gr. k — 1). pap. 4.95 *(978-0-7611-5923-0(1)*, 15923) Workman Publishing Co., Inc.
Siculan, Dan. The Little Cowboy & the Big Cowboy. Hillert, Margaret. 2008. 32p. (J). lib. bdg. 19.93 *(978-1-59953-187-8(9))* Norwood Hse. Pr.
—Why We Have Thanksgiving. Hillert, Margaret. rev. exp. ed. 2006. (Beginning to Read Ser.). 32p. (J). (gr. -1-3). lib. bdg. 19.93 *(978-1-59953-049-9(X))* Norwood Hse. Pr.
Siddell, Thomas. Gunnerkrigg Court - Reason Vol. 3, Vol. 3. Siddell, Thomas. 2011. (Gunnerkrigg Court Ser.: 3). (ENG.). 280p. (YA). (gr. 2). 26.95 *(978-1-936393-23-7(9))* Boom Entertainment, Inc.
—Orientation, Vol. 1. Siddell, Thomas. 2009. (Gunnerkrigg Court Ser.: 1). (ENG.). 296p. (J). (gr. 2-18). 26.95 *(978-1-932386-34-9(3))* Boom Entertainment, Inc.
—Research, Vol. 2. Siddell, Thomas. 2010. (Gunnerkrigg Court Ser.: 2). (ENG.). 296p. (YA). (gr. 2). 26.95 *(978-1-932386-77-6(7)*, Archaia Entertainment) Boom! Studios.
Siddiqa, Juma. My Arabic Words Book. 2007. (ARA & ENG.). 30p. (J). (gr. -1-6). 18.00 *(978-1-879402-33-1(5))* Tahrike Tarsile Quran, Inc.
Sido, Barbi. The Cardboard Box Book. Priddy, Roger & Powell, Sarah. 2014. (ENG.). 48p. (J). (gr. k-3). 12.99 *(978-0-312-51738-0(6)*, Priddy Bks.) St. Martin's Pr.
Sidwell, Kathy. Ethan Goes Green. Bell, Holly. 2009. 32p. pap. 12.99 *(978-1-4389-0115-2(1))* AuthorHouse.
Siebel, Fritz. Amelia Bedelia. Parish, Peggy. 50th ed. 2012. (I Can Read Book 2 Ser.). (ENG.). 64p. (J). (gr. k-3). pap. 3.99 *(978-0-06-444155-1(5)*, Greenwillow Bks.) HarperCollins Pubs.
—A Fly Went By. McClintock, Mike. 2007. (Beginner Ser.). (ENG.). 68p. pap. *(978-0-00-722482-1(6)*, HarperCollins Children's Bks.) HarperCollins Pubs. Ltd.
Siebel, Fritz, jt. illus. see Sweat, Lynn.
Siebold, J. Otto. The Pig in the Spigot. Wilbur, Richard. 2004. (J). reprint ed. pap. 7.00 *(978-0-15-525066-6(3)*, Voyager Books/Libros Viajeros) Harcourt Children's Bks. CAN. Dist: Allen, Thomas & Son, Ltd.
Siebold, Kim. Starry Night, Hold Me Tight. Sagendorph, Jean. 2015. (ENG.). 18p. (J). (— 1). bds. 6.95 ***(978-0-7624-5853-0(4)***, Running Pr. Kids) Running Pr. Bk. Pubs.
Siegel, Mark. Boogie Knights. Wheeler, Lisa. 2008. (ENG.). 40p. (J). (gr. -1-3). 16.99 *(978-0-689-87639-4(4)*, Atheneum/Richard Jackson Bks.) Simon & Schuster Children's Publishing.
—How to Read a Story. Messner, Kate. 2015. (ENG.). 32p. (J). (gr. k-3). 16.99 *(978-1-4521-1233-6(9))* Chronicle Bks. LLC.
Siegel, Mark. Oskar & the Eight Blessings. Simon, Tanya & Simon, Richard. 2015. (ENG.). 40p. (J). (gr. -1-3). 17.99 ***(978-1-59643-949-8(1))*** Roaring Brook Pr.
Siegel, Mark. Seadogs: An Epic Ocean Operetta. Wheeler, Lisa. 2006. (ENG.). 40p. (J). (gr. 2-5). reprint ed. 7.99 *(978-1-4169-4103-3(7)*, Atheneum Bks. for Young Readers) Simon & Schuster Children's Publishing.
—To Dance: A Ballerina's Graphic Novel. Siegel, Siena Cherson. 2006. (ENG.). 64p. (J). (gr. 3-9). 19.99 *(978-0-689-86747-7(6)*, Atheneum/Richard Jackson Bks.); pap. 9.99 *(978-1-4169-2687-0(9)*, Atheneum Bks. for Young Readers) Simon & Schuster Children's Publishing.
Siegel, Mark. Long Night Moon. Siegel, Mark. Rylant, Cynthia. 2004. (ENG.). 40p. (J). (gr. -1-3). 17.99 *(978-0-689-85426-2(9)*, Simon & Schuster Bks. For Young Readers) Simon & Schuster Bks. For Young Readers.
Siegel, Melanie. ¡Eres Increible! 10 Formas de Permitir Que Tu Grandeza Brille a Traves de Ti. Dyer, Wayne W. & Tracy, Kristina. 2007.Tr. of Incredible You! 10 Ways to Let Your Greatness Shine Through. (SPA & ENG.). 32p. 14.95 *(978-1-4019-1700-5(3))* Hay Hse., Inc.
—Incredible You! 10 Ways to Let Your Greatness Shine Through. Dyer, Wayne W. & Tracy, Kristina. 2005. (ENG.). 32p. (gr. -1-3). 15.99 *(978-1-4019-0782-2(2))* Hay Hse., Inc.
—Isabella & Ivan Build an Interview. Ingalls, Ann. 2012. 32p. (J). lib. bdg. 25.27 *(978-1-59953-509-8(2))* Norwood Hse. Pr.
Siegel, Melanie. I Brought My Rat for Show-and-Tell. Siegel, Melanie, tr. Horton, Joan. 2004. (Penguin Young Readers, Level 3 Ser.). (ENG.). 48p. (J). (gr. 1-3). mass mkt. 3.99 *(978-0-448-43364-6(8)*, Grosset & Dunlap) Penguin Publishing Group.
Siegel, William. The Jumping-off Place. McNeely, Marian Hurd. 2008. 321p. (J). 15.95 *(978-0-9798940-4-6(2)*, South Dakota State Historical Society Pr.) South Dakota State Historical Society Pr.
Siegrist, Wes. Realm of the Panther: A Story of South Florida's Forests. Costello, Emily. 2005. (Habitat Ser.). (ENG.). 32p. (J). (gr. 1-4). 15.95 *(978-1-56899-847-3(3))*; pap. 6.95 *(978-1-56899-848-0(1))* Soundprints.
Sienkiewicz, Bill, jt. illus. see Janson, Klaus.
Sierra, Holly. Cinabrio y la Isla de las Sombras, Bk. 7. Sweet, J. H. et al. Rabascall, Iolanda, tr. 2009. (SPA.). 124p. (J). (gr. 3-5). 11.95 *(978-84-92691-43-2(3))* Roca Editorial De Libros ESP. Dist: Spanish Pubs., LLC.
—Just Like Mom. Hiris, Monica. 2005. (ENG.). 8p. (gr. k-1). pap. 4.95 *(978-1-57874-088-8(6))* Kaeden Corp.
—Snapdragon & the Odyssey of Élan. Sweet, J. H. 2009. (J). Non-ISBN Publisher.
Sierra, Juan. El Pirata de la Pata de Palo. Arciniegas, Triunfo. 2003. (Primer Acto: Teatro Infantil y Juvenil Ser.). (SPA.). 51p. (J). (gr. -1-7). pap. *(978-958-30-0321-9(2))* Panamericana Editorial.
Sierra, Juan Ramon. El Intripido Simon: Aventuras del Libertador. Bastidas Padilla, Carlos. 2004. (Literatura Juvenil (Panamericana Editorial) Ser.). (SPA.). 252p. (YA). (gr. -1-7). pap. *(978-958-30-0354-7(9))* Panamericana Editorial.
—Razzgo, Indo y Zaz. Nino, Jairo Anibal. 2004. (Literatura Juvenil (Panamericana Editorial) Ser.). (SPA.). 128p. (YA). (gr. 4-7). pap. *(978-958-30-0292-2(5))* Panamericana Editorial.
Sieveking, Anthea, photos by. Young Gardener. Buczacki, Stefan & Buczacki, Beverley. 2009. (ENG., 125p. (J). (gr. 2-5). pap. 12.95 *(978-1-84780-000-8(9)*, Frances Lincoln) Quarto Publishing Group UK GBR. Dist: Hachette Bk. Group.
—Young Gardener. Buczacki, Stefan & Buczacki, Beverly. 2006. (ENG., 120p. (J). (gr. 1-17). 19.95 *(978-1-84507-295-7(2)*, Frances Lincoln) Quarto Publishing Group UK GBR. Dist: Hachette Bk. Group.
Sievers, Lee. Beebear 2. Follett, Ross C. 2013. (ENG.). 52p. (J). (gr. -1-3). 15.95 *(978-0-9881748-0-1(4)*, OddInt Media) Greenwood Hill Pr.
Sievert, Claus. The Lion & the Puppy: And Other Stories for Children. Tolstoy, Leo & Riordan, James. Riordan, James, tr. from RUS. 2012. (ENG.). 76p. (J). (gr. 4-7). 16.95 *(978-1-61608-484-4(7)*, 608484, Sky Pony Pr.) Skyhorse Publishing Co., Inc.
Siewart, Pauline. Look What I Can Do! 2009. (Watch This! Ser.). 32p. (J). (gr. -1-k). 22.60 *(978-1-60754-452-4(0))*; pap. 10.55 *(978-1-60754-453-1(9))* Windmill Bks.
—Look What I Can Make! 2009. (Watch This! Ser.). 32p. (J). (gr. -1-k). 22.60 *(978-1-60754-446-3(6))*; pap. 10.55 *(978-1-60754-447-0(4))* Windmill Bks.
—Look What I Can Play! 2009. (Watch This! Ser.). 32p. (J). (gr. -1-k). 22.60 *(978-1-60754-458-6(X))*; pap. 10.55 *(978-1-60754-586-6(1))* Windmill Bks.
—See What I Can Do! 2009. (Watch This! Ser.). 32p. (J). (gr. -1-k). 22.60 *(978-1-60754-455-5(5))*; pap. 10.55 *(978-1-60754-456-2(3))* Windmill Bks.
—See What I Can Make! 2009. (Watch This! Ser.). 32p. (J). (gr. -1-k). 22.60 *(978-1-60754-449-4(0))*; pap. 10.55 *(978-1-60754-450-0(4))* Windmill Bks.
—See What I Can Play! 2009. (Watch This! Ser.). 32p. (J). (gr. -1-k). 22.60 *(978-1-60754-461-6(X))*; pap. 10.55 *(978-1-60754-462-3(8))* Windmill Bks.
—3-Minute Sleepytime Stories. Baxter, Nicola. 2013. (ENG.). 80p. (J). (gr. -1-3). pap. 9.99 *(978-1-84322-977-3(3)*, Armadillo) Anness Publishing GBR. Dist: National Bk. Network.
Siewert, Pauline. God Is Always with You. Adams, Michelle Medlock. 2014. (Peek-A-Boo Promises Ser.). 16p. (J). bds. 8.99 *(978-0-8249-1907-8(6)*, Candy Cane Pr.) Ideals Pubns.
—It's Valentine's Day! A Valentine Book & Activity Kit. 2005. 10p. (J). bds. 9.95 *(978-1-58117-377-2(6)*, Intervisual/Piggy Toes) Bendon, Inc.
Siewert, Pauline. Jingle Bells. Pierpont, James Lord. 2015. (ENG.). 14p. (J). (— 1). 12.99 ***(978-0-7636-8197-5(0))*** Candlewick Pr.
Siewert, Pauline. The Very First Christmas - Changing Pictures, 1 vol. David, Juliet. 2010. (ENG.). 14p. (J). 11.99 *(978-1-85985-870-7(8)*, Candle Bks.) Lion Hudson PLC GBR. Dist: Kregel Pubns.
Sif, Birgitta. Miss Hazeltine's Home for Shy & Fearful Cats. Potter, Alicia. 2015. (ENG.). 40p. (J). (gr. k-3). 16.99 *(978-0-385-75334-0(9))*; lib. bdg. 19.99 *(978-0-385-75335-7(7))* Random Hse. Children's Bks. (Knopf Bks. for Young Readers).
Sif, Birgitta. Frances Dean Who Loved to Dance & Dance. Sif, Birgitta. 2014. (ENG.). 32p. (J). (gr. -1-3). 15.99 *(978-0-7636-7306-2(4))* Candlewick Pr.
—Oliver. Sif, Birgitta. 2012. (ENG.). 40p. (J). (gr. -1-3). 16.99 *(978-0-7636-6247-9(X))* Candlewick Pr.
Signorino, Slug. I Know an Old Lady Who Swallowed a Fly: A Traditional Rhyme. 2004. 16p. (J). (gr. k-4). reprint ed. pap. 10.00 *(978-0-7567-9066-0(2))* DIANE Publishing Co.
Sikoryak, Bob, jt. illus. see Davis, Guy.
Siku. The Filth Licker. Burne, Cristy. 2012. (ENG.). 208p. (J). (gr. 3-7). pap. 8.99 *(978-1-84780-136-4(6)*, Frances Lincoln) Quarto Publishing Group UK GBR. Dist: Hachette Bk. Group.
—Takeshita Demons. Burne, Cristy. 2010. (ENG.). 128p. (J). (gr. 3-7). pap. 8.95 *(978-1-84780-115-9(3)*, Frances Lincoln) Quarto Publishing Group UK GBR. Dist: Hachette Bk. Group.
Silas, Thony, et al. Ends of the Earth. Slott, Dan & Caselli, Stefano. 2013. (ENG.). 192p. (J). (gr. 4-17). pap. 24.99 *(978-0-7851-6006-9(X))* Marvel Worldwide, Inc.

Silberberg, Alan. The Awesome, Almost 100% True Adventures of Matt & Craz. Silberberg, Alan. (ENG.). 336p. (J). (gr. 4-8). 2014. pap. 7.99 *(978-1-4169-9433-6(5))*; 2013. 16.99 *(978-1-4169-9432-9(7))* Simon & Schuster/Paula Wiseman Bks. (Simon & Schuster/Paula Wiseman Bks.).

—Milo: Sticky Notes & Brain Freeze. Silberberg, Alan. (ENG.). 288p. (J). (gr. 4-8). 2011. pap. 7.99 *(978-1-4169-9431-2(9))*; 2010. 15.99 *(978-1-4169-9430-5(0))* Simon & Schuster/Paula Wiseman Bks. (Simon & Schuster/Paula Wiseman Bks.).

Silin-Palmer, Pamela. Unicorn Wings. Loehr, Mallory. 2006. (Step into Reading Ser.: Vol. 1). (ENG.). 32p. (J). (gr. -1-1). per. 3.99 *(978-0-375-83117-1(7)*, Random Hse. Bks. for Young Readers) Random Hse. Children's Bks.

Sill, Cathryn P. & Sill, John. About Arachnids: A Guide for Children, 1 vol. Sill, Cathryn P. & Sill, John. Sill, Cathryn. 2003. (About...Ser.). (ENG.). 40p. (J). (gr. k-3). 16.95 *(978-1-56145-038-1(3))* Peachtree Pubs.

—About Hummingbirds, 1 vol. Sill, Cathryn P. & Sill, John. 2011. (ENG.). 48p. (J). (gr. -1-2). 16.95 *(978-1-56145-588-1(1))* Peachtree Pubs.

Sill, Cathryn P. & Sill, John. About Mammals: A Guide for Children = Sobre Los Mamíferos: Una Guía para Niños. Torre, Cristina de la. 2014. (SPA & ENG.). (J). ***(978-1-56145-815-8(5)***, Peachtree Junior) Peachtree Pubs.

Sill, John. About Amphibians: A Guide for Children, 1 vol. Sill, Cathryn. 2004. (ENG.). 48p. (J). (gr. k-3). pap. 16.95 *(978-1-56145-312-2(9))* Peachtree Pubs.

—About Arachnids: A Guide for Children, 1 vol. Sill, Cathryn. 2006. (About... Ser.). (ENG.). 40p. (J). (gr. k-3). pap. 7.95 *(978-1-56145-364-1(1))* Peachtree Pubs.

—About Birds: A Guide for Children, 1 vol. Sill, Cathryn. 2nd rev. ed. 2013. (About ... Ser.). (ENG.). 40p. (J). (gr. -1-2). 16.95 *(978-1-56145-688-8(8))*; 7.95 *(978-1-56145-699-4(3))* Peachtree Pubs.

—About Birds: A Guide for Children / Sobre Los Pajaros: una Guia para Niños, 1 vol. Sill, Cathryn. ed. 2014. (About Ser.). (SPA & ENG.). 40p. (J). (gr. -1-2). pap. 8.95 *(978-1-56145-783-0(3))* Peachtree Pubs.

—About Crustaceans: A Guide for Children, 1 vol. Sill, Cathryn. 2007. (ENG.). 40p. (J). (gr. k-3). pap. 7.95 *(978-1-56145-405-1(2))* Peachtree Pubs.

—About Fish: A Guide for Children, 1 vol. Sill, Cathryn. 2005. (ENG.). 40p. (J). (gr. k-3). pap. 7.95 *(978-1-56145-335-1(8))* Peachtree Pubs.

Sill, John. About Habitats: Polar Regions, 1 vol. Sill, Cathryn. 2015. (About Habitats Ser.). (ENG.). 48p. (J). (gr. -1-2). 16.95 ***(978-1-56145-832-5(5))*** Peachtree Pubs.

Sill, John. About Habitats-Deserts, 1 vol. Sill, Cathryn. 2007. (About Habitats Ser.). (ENG.). 48p. (J). (gr. k-3). 16.95 *(978-1-56145-390-0(0))* Peachtree Pubs.

—About Habitats: Deserts. Sill, Cathryn. 2012. (About Habitats Ser.). (ENG.). (J). (gr. 4-7). 16.95 *(978-1-56145-641-3(1))* Peachtree Pubs.

—About Habitats-Grasslands, 1 vol. Sill, Cathryn P. 2011. (About Habitats Ser.). (ENG.). 48p. (J). (gr. -1-3). 16.95 *(978-1-56145-559-1(8))* Peachtree Pubs.

—About Habitats-Oceans, 1 vol. Sill, Cathryn. 2012. (ENG.). 48p. (J). 16.95 *(978-1-56145-618-5(7))* Peachtree Pubs.

—About Habitats-Wetlands, 1 vol. Sill, Cathryn. 2008. (About... Ser.). (ENG.). 48p. (J). (gr. k-3). 15.95 *(978-1-56145-432-7(X))* Peachtree Pubs.

—About Hummingbirds: A Guide for Children, 1 vol. Sill, Cathryn. 2015. (About... Ser.). (ENG.). 48p. (J). (gr. -1-2). pap. 7.95 *(978-1-56145-837-0(6))* Peachtree Pubs.

Sill, John. About Insects: A Guide for Children, 1 vol. Sill, Cathryn. rev. ed. 2015. (About... Ser.). (ENG.). 48p. (J). (gr. -1-2). 16.95 ***(978-1-56145-881-3(3))*** Peachtree Pubs.

—About Insects / Sobre Los Insectos: A Guide for Children / una Guia para Niños, 1 vol. Sill, Cathryn. rev. ed. 2015. (About... Ser.). (ENG & SPA.). 48p. (J). (gr. -1-2). pap. 8.95 ***(978-1-56145-883-7(X))*** Peachtree Pubs.

—About Mammals: A Guide for Children, 1 vol. Sill, Cathryn. rev. ed. 2014. (About ... Ser.). (ENG.). 48p. (J). (gr. -1-2). 16.95 ***(978-1-56145-757-1(4))*** Peachtree Pubs.

Sill, John. About Marsupials: A Guide for Children, 1 vol. Sill, Cathryn. (ENG.). 48p. (J). 2009. pap. 7.95 *(978-1-56145-407-5(9))*; 2006. 15.95 *(978-1-56145-358-0(7))* Peachtree Pubs.

—About Mollusks: A Guide for Children, 1 vol. Sill, Cathryn. 2008. (About... Ser.). (ENG.). 40p. (J). (gr. k-3). pap. 7.95 *(978-1-56145-406-8(0))* Peachtree Pubs.

—About Penguins: A Guide for Children, 1 vol. Sill, Cathryn P. 2009. (ENG.). 48p. (J). (gr. -1-2). 15.95 *(978-1-56145-488-4(5))* Peachtree Pubs.

—About Penguins: a Guide for Children: A Guide for Children, 1 vol. Sill, Cathryn. 2nd rev. ed. 2013. (About ... Ser.). (ENG.). 48p. (J). (gr. -1-2). 7.95 *(978-1-56145-741-0(8))*; 16.95 *(978-1-56145-743-4(4))* Peachtree Pubs.

—About Raptors: A Guide for Children, 1 vol. Sill, Cathryn. 2010. (ENG.). 48p. (J). (gr. -1-2). 16.95 *(978-1-56145-536-2(9))* Peachtree Pubs.

—About Reptiles: A Guide for Children, 1 vol. Sill, Cathryn P. & Sill, Cathryn. 2003. (About...Ser.). (ENG.). 40p. (J). (gr. k-3). pap. 7.95 *(978-1-56145-233-0(5))* Peachtree Pubs.

—Birds. Alden, Peter C. & Peterson, Roger Tory. Peterson, Roger Tory, ed. 2nd ed. 2013. (Peterson Field Guide Color-In Bks.). (ENG.). 64p. (J). 8.95 *(978-0-544-02692-6(6))* Houghton Mifflin Harcourt Publishing Co.

—Wetlands, 1 vol. Sill, Cathryn. 2013. (ENG.). 48p. (J). (gr. -1-2). 7.95 *(978-1-56145-689-5(6))* Peachtree Pubs.

Sill, John. About Mollusks: A Guide for Children, 1 vol. Sill, John. Sill, Cathryn. 2005. (ENG.). 40p. (J). (gr. k-3). 15.95 *(978-1-56145-331-3(5))* Peachtree Pubs.

Sill, John & Sill, John. About Crustaceans: A Guide for Children, 1 vol. Sill, Cathryn. 2004. (ENG.). 40p. (J). (gr. k-3). 16.95 *(978-1-56145-301-6(3))* Peachtree Pubs.

—About Habitats-Mountains, 1 vol. Sill, Cathryn P. & Sill, Cathryn P. 2009. (About Habitats Ser.). (ENG.). 48p. (J). (gr. -1-2). 16.95 *(978-1-56145-469-3(9))* Peachtree Pubs.

Sill, John, jt. illus. see Bond, Higgins.

Sill, John, jt. illus. see Sill, Cathryn P.

Sill, John, jt. illus. see Sill, John.

Siller, Germin. Los Frutos del Sol. Fuentes, Claudia Luna & Fuente, Claudia Luna. rev. ed. 2006. (Otra Escalera Ser.). (SPA & ENG.). 14p. (J). (gr. k). pap. 7.95 *(978-968-5920-54-4(0))* Castillo, Ediciones, S. A. de C. V. MEX. Dist: Macmillan.

Silva, Augusto Alves da. Trisba & Sula: A Miskitu Folktale from Nicaragua (Una Leyenda de los Miskitos de Nicaragua) MacCracken, Joan. Macdonald, Isabel et al, trs. 2005. (ENG & SPA.). 16.95 *(978-0-9646018-2-6(6))* Tiffin Pr. of Maine.

Silva, David, jt. illus. see Gomez, Marcela.

Silva, Eliseo Art. Let's Cook Adobo!, 1 vol. Montoya, Carina Monica. 2010. 22p. pap. 24.95 *(978-1-4489-9022-1(X))* PublishAmerica, Inc.

Silva, Erika. Como a Raposinha Salvou Sua Pele: How the Little Fox Saved Her Coat. Close, Rosa. Tsibana, Rosana, tr. l.t. ed. 2012. (POR.). 48p. pap. 13.98 *(978-0-615-68421-5(1))* Misha Foundation.

Silva, Simon. La Mariposa. Jiménez, Francisco. 2004. 38p. (J). (gr. k-4). reprint ed. pap. 14.00 *(978-0-7567-8433-1(6))* DIANE Publishing Co.

Silva, Tom, jt. illus. see Hahn, Beverly.

Silver, Jago. Mr. Aesop's Story Shop. 2011. (ENG.). 48p. (J). (gr. 1-4). 14.99 *(978-0-7459-6915-2(1))* Lion Hudson PLC GBR. Dist: Independent Pubs. Group.

—Oh No, Jonah! Balsley, Tilda. 2012. (Bible Ser.). (ENG.). 32p. (J). (gr. k-4). lib. bdg. 17.95 *(978-0-7613-5139-9(6)*, Kar-Ben Publishing) Lerner Publishing Group.

Silver, Jane. Sister Sun, Brother Storm. Matsakis, Cynthia. 2012. 32p. 24.95 *(978-1-4575-0768-7(4))* Dog Ear Publishing, LLC.

Silver, Maggie & Mayer, Uwe. How Flowers Grow. Helbrough, Emma. (Beginners Nature Ser.). 32p. (J). 2007. (gr. -1-3). 4.99 *(978-0-7945-1340-5(9)*, Usborne); 2006. (gr. 4-7). lib. bdg. 12.95 *(978-1-58086-508-1(9))* EDC Publishing.

Silver, Pattie. Kitty's Barn. 2005. 12p. (J). bds. 9.95 *(978-1-58117-385-7(7)*, Intervisual/Piggy Toes) Bendon, Inc.

Silver-Thompson, Pattie. Postcards from Kitty. Wang, Margaret. 2005. 12p. (J). (gr. -1-3). 9.95 *(978-1-58117-427-4(6)*, Intervisual/Piggy Toes) Bendon, Inc.

Silverberg-Kiss, Esti. Solomon & the Trees. Biers-Ariel, Matt. 2004. (J). (gr. k-3). 13.95 *(978-0-8074-0749-3(6)*, 101055) URJ Pr.

Silveria, Gordon. The Greedy Triangle. Burns, Marilyn. 2008. (Scholastic Bookshelf Ser.). (ENG.). 32p. (J). (gr. -1-3). pap. 6.99 *(978-0-545-04220-8(6)*, Scholastic Paperbacks) Scholastic, Inc.

Silverman, Dianne. Annie Oakley, 1 vol. Blair, Eric. (My First Classic Story Ser.). (ENG.). 32p. (J). (gr. k-3). 2013. pap. 7.10 *(978-1-4795-1846-3(8))*; 2011. lib. bdg. 21.32 *(978-1-4048-6577-8(2))* Picture Window Bks. (My First Classic Story).

—Belling the Cat: A Retelling of Aesop's Fable, 1 vol. Blair, Eric. 2013. (My First Classic Story Ser.). (ENG.). 24p. (gr. k-3). pap. 7.10 *(978-1-4795-1854-8(9)*, My First Classic Story) Picture Window Bks.

—Belling the Cat: A Retelling of Aesop's Fable, 1 vol. Blair, Eric & Aesop Enterprise Inc. Staff. 2011. (My First Classic Story Ser.). (ENG.). 24p. (gr. k-3). lib. bdg. 21.32 *(978-1-4048-6504-4(7)*, My First Classic Story) Picture Window Bks.

—The Boy Who Cried Wolf, 1 vol. Blair, Eric. 2011. (My First Classic Story Ser.). (ENG.). 24p. (gr. k-3). pap. 7.10 *(978-1-4048-7364-3(3)*, My First Classic Story) Picture Window Bks.

—The Boy Who Cried Wolf: A Retelling of Aesop's Fable, 1 vol. Blair, Eric & Aesop Enterprise Inc. Staff. 2011. (My First Classic Story Ser.). (ENG.). 24p. (gr. k-3). lib. bdg. 21.32 *(978-1-4048-6507-5(1)*, My First Classic Story) Picture Window Bks.

—The Country Mouse & the City Mouse: A Retelling of Aesop's Fable, 1 vol. Blair, Eric. 2013. (My First Classic Story Ser.). (ENG.). 24p. (gr. k-3). pap. 7.10 *(978-1-4795-1858-6(1)*, My First Classic Story) Picture Window Bks.

—The Country Mouse & the City Mouse: A Retelling of Aesop's Fable, 1 vol. Blair, Eric & Aesop Enterprise Inc. Staff. 2011. (My First Classic Story Ser.). (ENG.). 24p. (gr. k-3). lib. bdg. 21.32 *(978-1-4048-6510-5(1)*, My First Classic Story) Picture Window Bks.

—El Cuervo y la Jarra: Versión de la Fábula de Esopo. Blair, Eric. Abello, Patricia, tr. 2006. (Read-It! Readers en Español: Fábulas Ser.).Tr. of Crow & the Pitcher - A Retelling of Aesop's Fable. (SPA.). 24p. (gr. k-3). 19.99 *(978-1-4048-1618-3(6)*, Easy Readers) Picture Window Bks.

—The Donkey in the Lion's Skin: A Retelling of Aesop's Fable, 1 vol. Blair, Eric. 2013. (My First Classic Story Ser.). (ENG.). 24p. (gr. k-3). pap. 7.10 *(978-1-4795-1855-5(7)*, My First Classic Story) Picture Window Bks.

—The Donkey in the Lion's Skin: A Retelling of Aesop's Fable, 1 vol. Blair, Eric & Aesop Enterprise Inc. Staff. 2011. (My First Classic Story Ser.). (ENG.). 24p. (gr. k-3). lib. bdg. 21.32 *(978-1-4048-6506-8(3)*, My First Classic Story) Picture Window Bks.

—El Pastorcito Mentiroso: Versión de la Fábula de Esopo. Blair, Eric. Abello, Patricia, tr. from ENG. 2006. (Read-It! Readers en Español: Fábulas Ser.).Tr. of Boy Who Cried Wolf - A Retelling of Aesop's Fable. (SPA.). 24p. (gr. k-3). 19.99 *(978-1-4048-1616-9(X)*, Easy Readers) Picture Window Bks.

—El Raton de Campo y el Raton de Ciudad: Versión de la Fábula de Esopo. Blair, Eric. Abello, Patricia, tr. from ENG. 2006. (Read-It! Readers en Español: Fábulas Ser.).Tr. of Country Mouse & the City Mouse - A Retelling of Aesop's Fable. (SPA.). 24p. (gr. k-3). 19.99 *(978-1-4048-1617-6(8)*, Easy Readers) Picture Window Bks.

Silverstein, Grant. Davey Mcgravy. Mason, David. 2015. (ENG.). 120p. (J). (gr. k). pap. 14.95 *(978-1-58988-099-3(4))* Dry, Paul Bks., Inc.

Silverstein, Shel. Different Dances. Silverstein, Shel. 25th anniv. ed. 2004. (ENG.). 224p. 35.00 *(978-0-06-055430-9(4))* HarperCollins Pubs.

—Don't Bump the Glump! And Other Fantasies. Silverstein, Shel. 2014. (ENG.). 64p. (J). (gr. -1-3). 17.99 *(978-0-06-149338-6(4))* HarperCollins Pubs.

—Every Thing on It. Silverstein, Shel. 2011. 208p. (J). (gr. -1-3). (ENG.). 19.99 *(978-0-06-199816-4(8))*; lib. bdg. 20.89 *(978-0-06-199817-1(6))* HarperCollins Pubs.

—Falling Up: Poems & Drawings. Silverstein, Shel. ed. 2006. (ENG.). 184p. (J). (gr. -1-3). 19.99 *(978-0-06-024802-4(5))* HarperCollins Pubs.

—Falling up Special Edition. Silverstein, Shel. 2015. (ENG.). 200p. (J). (gr. -1-3). 19.99 *(978-0-06-232133-6(1))* HarperCollins Pubs.

—A Giraffe & a Half. Silverstein, Shel. 40th anniv. ed. 2014. (ENG.). 48p. (J). (gr. -1-3). 16.99 *(978-0-06-025655-5(9))* HarperCollins Pubs.

—The Giving Tree. Silverstein, Shel. 64p. 2003. (J). (gr. -1-3). lib. bdg. 17.89 *(978-0-06-025666-1(4))*; anniv. ed. 2014. (ENG.). (J). (gr. -1-3). 19.99 *(978-0-06-058675-1(3))*; gif. ed. 2007. 16.99 *(978-0-06-124001-0(X))*; 50th anniv. ed. 2014. (ENG.). (J). (gr. -1-3). 16.99 *(978-0-06-025665-4(6)*, HC5567) HarperCollins Pubs.

—Lafcadio, the Lion Who Shot Back. Silverstein, Shel. 2013. (ENG.). 112p. (J). (gr. -1-3). 16.99 *(978-0-06-025675-3(3))* HarperCollins Pubs.

—A Light in the Attic. Silverstein, Shel. ed. (ENG.). (J). (gr. -1-3). 2009. 192p. 19.99 *(978-0-06-190585-8(2))*; 2005. 176p. 19.99 *(978-0-06-025673-9(7))* HarperCollins Pubs.

—The Missing Piece. Silverstein, Shel. Silverstein. 30th anniv. ed. 2006. (Ursula Nordstrom Bk.). (ENG.). 112p. (J). (gr. -1-3). 17.99 *(978-0-06-025671-5(0))* HarperCollins Pubs.

—The Missing Piece Meets the Big O. Silverstein, Shel. ed. 2006. (ENG.). 104p. (J). (gr. -1-3). 16.99 *(978-0-06-025657-9(5))* HarperCollins Pubs.

—Runny Babbit: A Billy Sook. Silverstein, Shel. (ENG.). 96p. (J). (gr. -1-3). 2015. 18.99 *(978-0-06-025653-1(2))*; 2006. 22.99 *(978-0-06-113047-2(8))* HarperCollins Pubs.

—Shel Silverstein Pop-up Treasury. Silverstein, Shel. 2008. 16p. (J). 29.99 *(978-0-06-147269-5(7))* HarperCollins Pubs.

—Where the Sidewalk Ends: Poems & Drawings. Silverstein, Shel. (J). (gr. -1-3). 2014. (ENG.). 176p. 19.99 *(978-0-06-025667-8(2))*; 30th anniv. ed. 2014. (ENG.). 192p. 18.99 *(978-0-06-057234-1(5))*; 30th anniv. ed. 2004. 192p. lib. bdg. 19.89 *(978-0-06-058653-9(2))* HarperCollins Pubs.

—Who Wants a Cheap Rhinoceros? Silverstein, Shel. 50th anniv. ed. 2014. (ENG.). 64p. (J). (gr. -1-3). 17.99 *(978-1-4814-1593-4(X)*, Simon & Schuster Bks. For Young Readers) Simon & Schuster Bks. For Young Readers.

Silverthorne, Sandy. Surviving When You're Home Alone: How to Avoid Being Grounded for Life. Silverthorne, Sandy. 2006. 96p. (YA). (gr. 3-6). pap. 5.99 *(978-0-7847-1434-8(7)*, 42176) Standard Publishing.

—Surviving Zits: How to Cope with Your Changing Self. Silverthorne, Sandy. 2006. 96p. (YA). (gr. 3-6). pap. 5.99 *(978-0-7847-1435-5(5)*, 42177) Standard Publishing.

Silvestri, Marc, et al. Bad Ideas Collected!!!, Vol. 1. Waid, Mark & Chinsang, Wayne. collector's ed. 2005. 128p. pap. 12.99 *(978-1-58240-531-5(X))* Image Comics.

—Essential X-Factor Volume 4. 2012. (ENG.). 520p. (J). (gr. 4-17). pap. 19.99 *(978-0-7851-6285-8(2))* Marvel Worldwide, Inc.

—X-Men, Vol. 1. Claremont, Chris & Austin, Terry. 2011. (ENG.). 728p. (J). (gr. 4-17). 125.00 *(978-0-7851-5822-6(7))* Marvel Worldwide, Inc.

—X-Men vs. Avengers/Fantastic Four. 2011. (ENG.). 272p. (J). (gr. 4-17). pap. 24.99 *(978-0-7851-5727-4(1))* Marvel Worldwide, Inc.

Silvey, Allen, jt. illus. see Silvey, Joan.

Silvey, Joan & Silvey, Allen. Help Me Learn: Counting 1 - 10 in American Language. Silvey, Joan. Silvey, Allen, ed. l.t. ed. 2005. (Help Me Learn Ser.: Vol. 1). 24p. (J). per. 5.95 *(978-0-9762446-0-8(8))* Silvey Bk. Publishing.

Sim, David. Bear Boar. Robinson, Michelle. 2012. (ENG.). 12p. (J). (gr. -1-k). bds. 10.99 *(978-1-4088-1704-9(7)*, 38575, Bloomsbury USA Childrens) Bloomsbury USA.

—Driving My Tractor. Dobbins, Jan & Songs, Steve. 2011. (ENG.). 30p. (J). pap. 9.99 *(978-1-84686-664-7(2))* Barefoot Bks., Inc.

—Driving My Tractor. Dobbins, Jan. 2009. (ENG.). 32p. (J). (gr. -1-3). 16.99 incl. audio compact disk *(978-1-84686-358-5(9))* Barefoot Bks., Inc.

—Driving My Tractor Puzzle. Dobbins, Jan. 2011. (ENG.). n/ap. (J). 14.99 *(978-1-84686-573-2(5))* Barefoot Bks., Inc.

—Jungle School. Laird, Elizabeth & Davison, Roz. 2006. (Green Bananas Ser.). (ENG.). 48p. (J). (gr. -1-3). *(978-0-7787-1042-4(4))*; lib. bdg. *(978-0-7787-1026-4(2))* Crabtree Publishing Co.

—Jungle School. Laird, Elizabeth & Davison, Roz. 2006. (Green Bananas Ser.). (ENG.). 48p. (J). (gr. k-2). pap. 5.99 *(978-1-4052-1919-8(X))* Egmont Bks., Ltd. GBR. Dist: Independent Pubs. Group.

—The Shape Song Singalong. SteveSongs Staff. 2011. (ENG.). 36p. (J). 16.99 *(978-1-84686-671-5(5))* Barefoot Bks., Inc.

—Shape Song Singalong. SteveSongs Staff. 2011. (ENG.). 36p. (J). pap. 9.99 *(978-1-84686-679-1(0))* Barefoot Bks., Inc.

—Space Song Rocket Ride. Scribens, Sunny et al. 24p. pap. 9.99 *(978-1-78285-098-4(8))* Barefoot Bks., Inc.

—Yak Yuk. Robinson, Michelle. 2012. (ENG.). 12p. (J). (gr. -1-k). bds. 10.99 *(978-1-4088-1703-2(9)*, 38574, Bloomsbury USA Childrens) Bloomsbury USA.

Sim, David. Jump Freddy, Jump! Sim, David. 2007. (ENG.). 12p. (J). (gr. -1-k). 12.99 *(978-1-85707-659-2(1))* Tango Bks. GBR. Dist: Independent Pubs. Group.

—Matt's Hat: A Find the Hat Color Book, 2 bks. Sim, David. 2003. 10p. (J). 7.95 *(978-1-58117-197-6(8)*, Intervisual/Piggy Toes) Bendon, Inc.

—Matt's Mat: A Touch & Feel Counting Book, 2 vols. Sim, David. 2003. 10p. (J). 7.95 *(978-1-58117-198-3(6)*, Intervisual/Piggy Toes) Bendon, Inc.

—Panda's Pants. Sim, David. 2006. (ENG.). 20p. (J). (gr. -1-k). 16.99 *(978-1-85707-663-9(X))* Tango Bks. GBR. Dist: Independent Pubs. Group.

Simard, Remy. Bus Ride Bully, 1 vol. Meister, Cari. (My First Graphic Novel Ser.). (ENG.). 32p. (gr. k-2). 2011. pap. 6.25 *(978-1-4342-3101-7(1))*; 2010. 23.32 *(978-1-4342-2059-2(1))* Stone Arch Bks. (My First Graphic Novel).

—Busy Day Coloring Storybook. 2003. (Rainbow Fish & Friends Ser.). 24p. (J). mass mkt. 2.99 *(978-1-59014-132-8(6))* Night Sky Bks.

—The Cat That Disappeared, 1 vol. Mortensen, Lori. 2010. (My First Graphic Novel Ser.). (ENG.). 32p. (gr. k-2). pap. 6.25 *(978-1-4342-2282-4(9))*; lib. bdg. 23.32 *(978-1-4342-1887-2(2))* Stone Arch Bks. (My First Graphic Novel).

—Clues in the Attic, 1 vol. Meister, Cari. 2010. (My First Graphic Novel Ser.). (ENG.). 32p. (gr. k-2). pap. 6.25 *(978-1-4342-2283-1(7))*; lib. bdg. 23.32 *(978-1-4342-1889-6(9))* Stone Arch Bks. (My First Graphic Novel).

—Duped! True Stories of the World's Best Swindlers. Schroeder, Andreas. 2011. (It Actually Happened Ser.). (ENG.). 158p. (J). (gr. 4-7). 21.95 *(978-1-55451-351-2(0)*, 9781554513512); pap. 12.95 *(978-1-55451-350-5(2)*, 9781554513505) Annick Pr., Ltd. CAN. Dist: Firefly Bks., Ltd.

—Favorite Places Coloring Storybook. 2003. (Rainbow Fish & Friends Ser.). 24p. (J). mass mkt. 2.99 *(978-1-59014-133-5(4))* Night Sky Bks.

—First Day, No Way!, 1 vol. Mortensen, Lori. (My First Graphic Novel Ser.). (ENG.). 32p. (gr. k-2). 2011. pap. 6.25 *(978-1-4342-3102-4(X))*; 2010. 23.32 *(978-1-4342-2015-8(X))* Stone Arch Bks. (My First Graphic Novel).

Simard, Rémy. Hocus Pocus. Desrosiers, Sylvie. 2011. (ENG.). 32p. (J). 16.95 *(978-1-55453-577-4(8))* Kids Can Pr., Ltd. CAN. Dist: Univ. of Toronto Pr.

Simard, Remy. Horrendo's Curse: The Graphic Novel. Fienberg, Anna. 2013. (ENG.). 104p. (J). (gr. 3-5). 24.95 *(978-1-55451-549-3(1)*, 9781554515493); pap. 14.95 *(978-1-55451-548-6(3)*, 9781554515486) Annick Pr., Ltd. CAN. Dist: Firefly Bks., Ltd.

—It's My Birthday!/Es Mi Cumpleanos! Rosa-Mendoza, Gladys. 2006. (Englishspanish Foundations Ser.). (ENG & SPA.). 20p. (J). (gr. -1-k). bds. 6.95 *(978-1-931398-17-6(8))* Me+Mi Publishing.

—The Lost Lunch, 1 vol. Mortensen, Lori. (My First Graphic Novel Ser.). (ENG.). 32p. (gr. k-2). 2011. pap. 6.25 *(978-1-4342-3103-1(8))*; 2010. 23.32 *(978-1-4342-2014-1(1))* Stone Arch Bks. (My First Graphic Novel).

—Mazes. School Zone Interactive Staff. rev. ed. 2006. (ENG.). 64p. (J). (gr. 1-2). wbk. ed. 7.99 *(978-1-58947-300-3(0))* School Zone Publishing Co.

—Meet the Sparkplugs, Level 3. Richards, Kitty. 2006. (ENG.). 24p. (J). (gr. 1-17). per. 3.99 *(978-1-58476-419-9(8)*, IKIDS) Innovative Kids.

—The Missing Monster Card, 1 vol. Mortensen, Lori. 2010. (My First Graphic Novel Ser.). (ENG.). 32p. (gr. k-2). pap. 6.25 *(978-1-4342-2284-8(5))*; lib. bdg. 23.32 *(978-1-4342-1888-9(0))* Stone Arch Bks. (My First Graphic Novel).

—Morning Mystery, 1 vol. Jones, Christianne C. 2010. (My First Graphic Novel Ser.). (ENG.). 32p. (gr. k-2). lib. bdg. 23.32 *(978-1-4342-1890-2(2)*, My First Graphic Novel) Stone Arch Bks.

—My Brain. Korb, Rena B. & Weinhaus, Anthony J. 2010. (My Body Ser.). 32p. (J). (gr. k-3). 28.50 *(978-1-60270-805-1(3))* Magic Wagon.

—My Mouth. Korb, Rena B. & Weinhaus, Anthony J. 2010. (My Body Ser.). 32p. (J). (gr. k-3). 28.50 *(978-1-60270-806-8(1))* Magic Wagon.

—My Muscles. Korb, Rena B. & Weinhaus, Anthony J. 2010. (My Body Ser.). 32p. (J). (gr. k-3). 28.50 *(978-1-60270-807-5(X))* Magic Wagon.

—My Nose. Korb, Rena B. & Weinhaus, Anthony J. 2010. (My Body Ser.). 32p. (J). (gr. k-3). 28.50 *(978-1-60270-808-2(8))* Magic Wagon.

—My Spine. Korb, Rena B. & Weinhaus, Anthony J. 2010. (My Body Ser.). 32p. (J). (gr. k-3). 28.50 *(978-1-60270-809-9(6))* Magic Wagon.

—My Stomach. Korb, Rena B. & Weinhaus, Anthony J. 2010. (My Body Ser.). 32p. (J). (gr. k-3). 28.50 *(978-1-60270-810-5(X))* Magic Wagon.

—Polly's Pen Pal. Murphy, Stuart J. 2005. (MathStart 3 Ser.). (ENG.). 40p. (J). (gr. 2-18). pap. 5.99 *(978-0-06-053170-6(3))* HarperCollins Pubs.

—Robbers! True Stories of the World's Most Notorious Thieves. Schroeder, Andreas. 2012. (It Actually Happened Ser.). (ENG.). 166p. (J). (gr. 4-7). pap. 12.95 *(978-1-55451-440-3(1)*, 9781554514403) Annick Pr., Ltd. CAN. Dist: Firefly Bks., Ltd.

—Shark in the Library!, 1 vol. Meister, Cari. (My First Graphic Novel Ser.). (ENG.). 32p. (gr. k-2). 2011. pap. 6.25 *(978-1-4342-3104-8(6))*; 2010. 23.32 *(978-1-4342-2058-5(3))* Stone Arch Bks. (My First Graphic Novel).

—Top Secret. Hall, Kirsten. 2003. 64p. (J). *(978-0-439-50133-0(4))* Scholastic, Inc.

Simatoribus, Alessandra. Baby Whiskers. Patacrúa. 2007. (ENG.). 36p. (J). 17.95 *(978-84-96788-90-9(3))* OQO, Editora ESP. Dist: Baker & Taylor Bks.

Simcic, Christina. We're Three: A Story About Families & The Only Child. Cameron-Gallo, Vivian. 2009. 28p. (J). (gr. -1). pap. 10.96 *(978-1-4251-7215-2(6))* Trafford Publishing.

Siminovich, Lorena. In My Barn. Gillingham, Sara. 2012. (ENG.). 12p. (J). (gr. -1 — 1). bds. 8.99 *(978-1-4521-0641-0(X))* Chronicle Bks. LLC.

—In My Den. Gillingham, Sara. 2009. (ENG.). 12p. (J). (gr. -1 — 1). bds. 8.99 *(978-0-8118-7053-5(7))* Chronicle Bks. LLC.

—In My Flower. Gillingham, Sara & Chronicle Books Staff. 2009. (ENG.). 12p. (J). (gr. -1 — 1). bds. 8.99 *(978-0-8118-7339-0(0))* Chronicle Bks. LLC.

—In My Forest. Gillingham, Sara. 2010. (ENG.). 12p. (J). (gr. -1 — 1). bds. 8.99 *(978-0-8118-7566-0(0))* Chronicle Bks. LLC.

—In My Jungle. Gillingham, Sara. 2011. (ENG.). 12p. (J). (gr. -1 — 1). bds. 8.99 *(978-0-8118-7716-9(7))* Chronicle Bks. LLC.

—In My Meadow. Gillingham, Sara & Chronicle Books Staff. 2009. (ENG.). 12p. (J). (gr. -1 — 1). bds. 8.99 *(978-0-8118-7338-3(2))* Chronicle Bks. LLC.

—In My Nest. Gillingham, Sara. 2009. (ENG.). 12p. (J). (gr. -1 — 1). bds. 8.99 *(978-0-8118-6555-5(X))* Chronicle Bks. LLC.

—In My Ocean. Gillingham, Sara. 2011. (ENG.). 12p. (J). (gr. -1 — 1). bds. 8.99 *(978-0-8118-7717-6(5))* Chronicle Bks. LLC.

—In My Patch. Simi, Gillingham & Gillingham, Sara. 2010. (ENG.). 12p. (J). (gr. -1 — 1). bds. 8.99 *(978-0-8118-7567-7(9))* Chronicle Bks. LLC.

—In My Pond. Gillingham, Sara. 2009. (ENG.). 12p. (J). (gr. -1 — 1). bds. 8.99 *(978-0-8118-6556-2(8))* Chronicle Bks. LLC.

—My Favorite Things Flash Cards. Chronicle Books Staff. 2010. (ENG.). 26p. (J). (gr. -1 — 1). 14.95 *(978-0-8118-6799-3(4))* Chronicle Bks. LLC.

—On My Beach. Gillingham, Sara. 2015. (ENG.). 12p. (J). (gr. -1 — 1). bds. 8.99 *(978-1-4521-0640-3(1))* Chronicle Bks. LLC.

—On My Leaf. Gillingham, Sara. 2012. (ENG.). 12p. (J). (gr. -1 — 1). bds. 8.99 *(978-1-4521-0813-1(7))* Chronicle Bks. LLC.

—You Are My Baby - Farm. 2013. (ENG.). 10p. (J). (gr. -1 — 1). bds. 8.99 *(978-1-4521-0643-4(6))* Chronicle Bks. LLC.

—You Are My Baby - Safari. 2013. (ENG.). 10p. (J). (gr. -1 — 1). bds. 8.99 *(978-1-4521-0642-7(8))* Chronicle Bks. LLC.

—You Are My Baby: Garden. 2014. (ENG.). 10p. (J). (gr. -1 — 1). bds. 8.99 *(978-1-4521-2649-4(6))* Chronicle Bks. LLC.

—You Are My Baby: Meadow. 2015. (ENG.). 10p. (J). (gr. -1 — 1). bds. 8.99 *(978-1-4521-4011-7(1))* Chronicle Bks. LLC.

—You Are My Baby: Ocean. 2014. (ENG.). 10p. (J). (gr. -1 — 1). bds. 8.99 *(978-1-4521-2650-0(X))* Chronicle Bks. LLC.

—You Are My Baby: Pets. 2014. (ENG.). 10p. (J). (gr. -1 — 1). bds. 8.99 *(978-1-4521-3430-7(8))* Chronicle Bks. LLC.

—You Are My Baby: Woodland. 2014. (ENG.). 10p. (J). (gr. -1 — 1). bds. 8.99 *(978-1-4521-3431-4(6))* Chronicle Bks. LLC.

Siminovich, Lorena. Alex & Lulu: Two of a Kind. Siminovich, Lorena. 2009. (ENG.). 32p. (J). (gr. -1-3). 14.99 *(978-0-7636-4423-9(4),* Templar) Candlewick Pr.

—I Like Bugs. Siminovich, Lorena. 2010. (Petit Collage Ser.). (ENG.). 10p. (J). (gr. k-12). bds. 6.99 *(978-0-7636-4802-2(7),* Templar) Candlewick Pr.

—I Like Toys. Siminovich, Lorena. 2011. (Petit Collage Ser.). (ENG.). 10p. (J). (— 1). bds. 6.99 *(978-0-7636-5074-2(9),* Templar) Candlewick Pr.

Simione, Allen. Mike the Microbe. Simione, Ruth. Date not set. 38p. (J). (gr. 4-8). pap. 14.70 *(978-1-877960-23-9(3))* Kemtec Educational Corp.

Simkins, Ed. The Human Body. Richards, Jon. 2013. (World in Infographics Ser.). (ENG.). 32p. (J). (gr. 3-7). 15.95 *(978-1-926973-93-7(3))* Owlkids Bks. Inc. CAN. Dist: Perseus-PGW.

—The Human World. Richards, Jon. 2013. (World in Infographics Ser.). (ENG.). 32p. (J). (gr. 3-7). 15.95 *(978-1-926973-94-4(1))* Owlkids Bks. Inc. CAN. Dist: Perseus-PGW.

—The Natural World. Richards, Jon. 2013. (World in Infographics Ser.). (ENG.). 32p. (J). (gr. 3-7). 15.95 *(978-1-926973-74-6(7))* Owlkids Bks. Inc. CAN. Dist: Perseus-PGW.

—Planet Earth. Richards, Jon. 2013. (World in Infographics Ser.). (ENG.). 32p. (J). (gr. 3-7). 15.95 *(978-1-926973-75-3(5))* Owlkids Bks. Inc. CAN. Dist: Perseus-PGW.

Simko, Danielle. The Master Potter: KK Makes a Choice. Martinez, Genevieve. 2010. (ENG.). 46p. pap. 13.95 *(978-1-4515-3733-8(6))* CreateSpace Independent Publishing Platform.

Simko, Joe. Big Billy & the Ice Cream Truck That Wouldn't Stop, 1 vol. Consiglio, Joe. 2012. (ENG.). 48p. (J). 16.99 *(978-0-7643-4067-3(0))* Schiffer Publishing, Ltd.

—Spirit, No. 1. Baldwin, Stephen. 2006. (ENG.). 208p. (gr. 8-12). per. 9.99 *(978-0-8054-4357-8(6))* B&H Publishing Group.

Simko, Joe. The Sweet Rot Book 3: The Purple Meltdown, 1 vol. Simko, Joe. 2012. (ENG.). 32p. 19.99 *(978-0-7643-3977-6(X))* Schiffer Publishing, Ltd.

Simko, Joe & Tidwell, Jeral. Spirit Warriors: Number Two. Baldwin, Stephen & Rosato, Bruno. 2007. (Spirit Warriors Ser.). 208p. (YA). per. 9.99 *(978-0-8054-4355-4(X))* B&H Publishing Group.

Simmans, Sean. The War of the Worlds. Wells, H. G. 2005. 220p. (YA). per. *(978-0-9737282-1-7(3))* Coscom Entertainment.

Simmonds, Frank H. The Tale of Strawberry Snow, 1 vol. Caudle, P. L. 2012. (ENG.). 48p. (J). 16.99 *(978-0-7643-4076-5(X))* Schiffer Publishing, Ltd.

Simmonds, Posy. Baker Cat. Simmonds, Posy. 2015. (ENG.). 32p. (J). (gr. -1-k). pap. 11.99 ***(978-1-78344-105-1(4))*** Andersen Pr. GBR. Dist: Independent Pubs. Group.

Simmons, Ann. Jojo the Dappled Dachshund. Jones, Cheryl & Joseph, Rahzheena. 2013. 30p. pap. 15.95 *(978-1-4787-0560-4(4))* Outskirts Pr., Inc.

Simmons, Bethany. Spy Recruit, 1 vol. Osborne, Erin. 2010. (ENG.). 216p. (J). (gr. 3-6). pap. 8.95 *(978-1-58980-782-2(0))* Pelican Publishing Co., Inc.

Simmons, Jane. Matty in a Mess! Moss, Miriam. 2010. (Matty & Milly Ser.). (ENG.). 32p. (J). (gr. k-k). pap. 9.99 *(978-1-84270-946-7(1))* Andersen Pr. GBR. Dist: Independent Pubs. Group.

—Matty Takes Off! Moss, Miriam. 2009. (Matty & Milly Ser.). (ENG.). 32p. (J). (gr. k-k). pap. 9.99 *(978-1-84270-758-6(2))* Andersen Pr. GBR. Dist: Independent Pubs. Group.

Simmons, Jane. Ship's Cat Doris. Simmons, Jane. 2012. (ENG.). 176p. (J). (gr. 2-4). pap. 8.99 *(978-1-4083-0896-7(7))* Hodder & Stoughton GBR. Dist: Independent Pubs. Group.

Simmons, Mark. Nickolas Flux History Chronicles, 1 vol. Collins, Terry et al. 2014. (Nickolas Flux History Chronicles Ser.). (ENG.). 32p. (gr. 3-4). 119.96 *(978-1-4914-0255-9(5),* Graphic Library) Capstone Pr., Inc.

—Titanic Disaster! Nickolas Flux & the Sinking of the Great Ship. Yomtov, Nelson. 2015. (Nickolas Flux History Chronicles Ser.). (ENG.). 32p. (gr. 3-4). lib. bdg. 29.99 *(978-1-4914-2070-6(7))* Capstone Pr., Inc.

Simmons, Mark. Trapped in Antarctica! Nickolas Flux & the Shackleton Expedition. Yomtov, Nelson. 2015. (Nickolas Flux History Chronicles Ser.). (ENG.). 32p. (gr. 3-4). lib. bdg. 29.99 ***(978-1-4914-2069-0(3))*** Capstone Pr., Inc.

Simmons, Mark, jt. illus. see Foster, Brad W.

Simmons, Robert. The Wind & Little Cloud. Hancock, Susan G. 2006. (J). (ENG.). 40p. spiral bd. 17.95 *(978-0-9741743-3-4(5));* 48p. (gr. -1-3). per. 10.95 *(978-0-9741743-0-3(0))* Perlycross Pubs.

Simmons, Russell. Hannah's Homework. Mayer, Nicole & Mayer, Ryan. 2012. 36p. (J). 14.95 *(978-0-9849293-0-6(4))* Beaner Bks.

Simon, Annette. Robot Zombie Frankenstein! Simon, Annette. 2012. (ENG.). 40p. (J). (gr. -1-3). 16.99 *(978-0-7636-5124-4(9))* Candlewick Pr.

Simon, Eric M. The Story of Mozart. Kaufmann, Helen L. Meadowcroft, Enid Lamonte, ed. 2011. 190p. 42.95 *(978-1-258-06631-4(9))* Literary Licensing, LLC.

Simon, Loris. Sirol. Salum, Rose Mary. 2005. (J). *(978-0-9770287-0-2(4))* Literal Publishing Inc.

Simon, Madeline Gerstein. Voyage to Shelter Cove. Nunez, Ralph da Costa & Ellison, Jesse Andrews. 2005. (J). pap. 5.00 *(978-0-9724425-3-4(7))* Homes for the Homeless Institute, Inc.

Simon, Romain. Forest Animals. 2011. 90p. 38.95 *(978-1-258-10284-5(6))* Literary Licensing, LLC.

Simon, Seymour. Cats. Simon, Seymour. (J). 2009. (ENG.). 32p. (gr. k-4). pap. 6.99 *(978-0-06-446254-9(4),* Collins); 2004. 40p. (gr. -1-3). lib. bdg. 17.89 *(978-0-06-028941-6(4))* HarperCollins Pubs.

—Dogs. Simon, Seymour. 2009. (ENG.). 32p. (J). (gr. k-4). pap. 6.99 *(978-0-06-446255-6(2),* Collins) HarperCollins Pubs.

—Horses. Simon, Seymour. Date not set. 32p. (J). (gr. -1-1). pap. 6.99 *(978-0-06-446256-3(0))* HarperCollins Pubs.

Simon, Sue A., et al. Big Keep Books- Spanish Emergent Reader 1: Mira como Juego; ¡Curitas!; Los Animales del Zoológico; Construyendo una Casa; la Alberca; ¡Agua y Jabón!; Me Visto; Mi Gato, 8 bks., Set. Estice, Rose Mary & Fried, Mary. Elías, Annette, tr. 2005.Tr. of Emergent Reader 1. (SPA.). 8p. (J). 20.00 *(978-1-893986-42-8(X))* Keep Bks.

—Health & Safety 1: Gym Class; Shopping for Lunch; Good for You; My Happy Heart; Just Like Me; Staying Safe; Always Brush Your Teeth; A Visit to the Doctor, 8 bks. Cicola, Amanda et al. ed. 2005. (ENG.). 8p. (J). pap. 120.00 *(978-1-893986-26-8(8))* Keep Bks.

—Health & Safety 2: Safety First; Don't Be a Couch Potato; Birthday Shots; Just in Case; Time Out; Home Sick; the Eye Doctor; the Big Race, 8 bks., Set. Pinnell, Gay Su et al. ed. 2005. (ENG.). 8p. (J). pap. 120.00 *(978-1-893986-27-5(6))* Keep Bks.

Simon, Susan. No Rules for Michael. Rouss, Sylvia A. 2004. (ENG.). 24p. (J). (gr. -1-1). pap. 6.95 *(978-1-58013-044-8(5),* Kar-Ben Publishing) Lerner Publishing Group.

Simon, Ute. Albert Einstein. Norwich, Grace. 2012. (I Am Ser.). (ENG.). 128p. (J). (gr. 3-7). pap. 5.99 *(978-0-545-40575-1(0),* Scholastic Paperbacks) Scholastic, Inc.

—I Am Harriet Tubman. Norwich, Grace. 2013. 127p. (J). *(978-0-545-61344-6(2))* Scholastic, Inc.

Simonet, Evan. Jake & the Sailing Tree. 2009. (J). *(978-1-60108-019-6(0))* Red Cygnet Pr.

Simonis, Cheryl, jt. illus. see Lind, Kathleen.

Simonnet, Aurore. Why Can't I Jump Very High? A Book about Gravity. Prasad, Kamal S. 2004. 32p. (J). lib. bdg. 14.95 *(978-0-9740861-5-6(0))* Science Square Publishing.

Simons, Marijke. Who's a Scaredy Cat! A Story of the Halifax Explosion, 1 vol. Simons, Marijke, tr. Payzant, Joan M. 2005. (ENG.). 85p. (J). (gr. 4-7). pap. 11.95 *(978-1-55109-456-4(8))* Nimbus Publishing, Ltd. CAN. Dist: Orca Bk. Pubs. USA.

Simons, Sally. Plants Grow Almost Anywhere. Walker, Colin. 2012. (Concept Science: Plants Ser.). (ENG.). 16p. (J). (gr. k-3). pap. 8.50 *(978-0-8136-7331-8(3))* Modern Curriculum Pr.

Simonson, Louise, et al. Meltdown, 3 vols. Simonson, Walter. 2003. (Wolverine Legends Ser.: Vol. 2). 200p. (YA). pap. 19.99 *(978-0-7851-1048-4(8))* Marvel Worldwide, Inc.

Simont, Marc. Un Arbol es Hermoso. Udry, Janice May & Udry, Janice M. Fiol, Maria A., tr. 2006.Tr. of Tree Is Nice. (SPA.). 32p. (J). (gr. -1-3). pap. 7.99 *(978-0-06-088708-7(7),* Rayo) HarperCollins Pubs.

—The Backward Day. Krauss, Ruth. 2007. (ENG.). 40p. (J). (gr. -1-2). 14.95 *(978-1-59017-237-7(X),* NYR Children's Collection) New York Review of Bks., Inc., The.

—In the Year of the Boar & Jackie Robinson. Lord, Bette Bao. 2003. (ENG.). 176p. (J). (gr. 3-7). pap. 5.99 *(978-0-06-440175-3(8))* HarperCollins Pubs.

—Nate the Great. Sharmat, Marjorie Weinman. (Nate the Great Ser.: No. 1). 48p. (J). (gr. 1-4). pap. 4.50 *(978-0-8072-1351-3(9),* Listening Library) Random Hse. Audio Publishing Group.

—Nate the Great & the Halloween Hunt. Sharmat, Marjorie Weinman. (Nate the Great Ser.: No. 12). 48p. (J). (gr. 1-4). pap. 4.50 *(978-0-8072-1283-7(0),* Listening Library) Random Hse. Audio Publishing Group.

—Nate the Great & the Missing Key. Sharmat, Marjorie Weinman. (Nate the Great Ser.: No. 6). 48p. (J). (gr. 1-4). pap. 4.50 *(978-0-8072-1335-3(7),* Listening Library) Random Hse. Audio Publishing Group.

—Nate the Great Goes Undercover. Sharmat, Marjorie Weinman. (Nate the Great Ser.: No. 2). 48p. (J). (gr. 1-4). pap. 4.50 *(978-0-8072-1284-4(9));* 2004. pap. 17.00 incl. audio *(978-0-8072-0201-2(0),* FTR172SP) Random Hse. Audio Publishing Group. (Listening Library).

—The Wonderful O. Thurber, James. 2009. (ENG.). 80p. (J). (gr. 2-5). 14.95 *(978-1-59017-309-1(0),* NYR Children's Collection) New York Review of Bks., Inc., The.

—The 13 Clocks. Thurber, James. 2008. (ENG.). 136p. (J). (gr. 3-7). 14.95 *(978-1-59017-275-9(2),* NYR Children's Collection) New York Review of Bks., Inc., The.

Simont, Marc. El Perro Vagabundo. Simont, Marc. 2003.Tr. of Stray Dog. (SPA.). 32p. (J). (gr. -1-3). pap. 6.99 *(978-0-06-052274-2(7),* Rayo) HarperCollins Pubs.

—The Stray Dog. Simont, Marc. 2003. (ENG.). 32p. (J). (gr. -1-3). pap. 6.99 *(978-0-06-443669-4(1))* HarperCollins Pubs.

—The Stray Dog. Simont, Marc. 2004. (gr. -1-3). 17.00 *(978-0-7569-1912-2(6))* Perfection Learning Corp.

Simonton, Tom. Hoops & Me. Furr, L. David. 2005. (ENG.). 16p. (J). 5.75 *(978-1-57274-751-7(X),* 2746, Bks. for Young Learners) Owen, Richard C. Pubs., Inc.

—Jeepers. Rondinone, Craig. 2005. (ENG.). 16p. (J). 5.75 *(978-1-57274-755-5(2),* 2750, Bks. for Young Learners) Owen, Richard C. Pubs., Inc.

—The Stone Hat. Hood, Douglas. 2005. (ENG.). 16p. (J). 5.75 *(978-1-57274-754-8(4),* 2784, Bks. for Young Learners) Owen, Richard C. Pubs., Inc.

Simpkins, Iravis. One Sunny Day. Buzzy. Martin, John, ed. 2003. 52p. (J). (gr. -1-2). pap. 7.99 *(978-0-9719054-1-2(X))* Buzzy's Bks.

Simpson, Howard. Afro-Bets Quotes for Kids: Words for Kids to Live By. Hudson, Katura J. 2004. (Afro-Bets Ser.). 64p. (J). (gr. k-4). pap. 5.95 *(978-0-940975-89-7(0),* Sankofa Bks.) Just Us Bks., Inc.

—Book of Opposites. Hudson, Cheryl Willis. (Afro-Bets Ser.). (J). pap. 4.95 *(978-0-940975-11-8(4))* Just Us Bks., Inc.

—Book of Seasons. Hudson, Cheryl Willis. (Afro-Bets Ser.). (J). pap. 4.95 *(978-0-940975-15-6(7))* Just Us Bks., Inc.

—Kim & Jones Investigations: Welcome to Elm City. Foster, William H. 2009. (ENG.). 48p. (YA). per. 14.95 *(978-0-9740212-4-9(5))* Cedar Grove Bks.

—Through Loona's Door: A Tammy & Owen Adventure with Carter G. Woodson. 2009. 80p. (J). per. 14.95 *(978-0-9740212-2-5(9),* Sapling Bks.) Cedar Grove Bks.

Simpson, Howard, jt. illus. see Blair, Culverson.

Simpson, Mary. America Vol. 3: Art Activities about Lewis & Clark, Pioneers, & Plains Indians. Merrill, Yvonne Y. 2009. (Hands-On Ser.: 3). (ENG.). 82p. (gr. k-10). pap. 25.00 *(978-0-9778797-1-7(2))* KITS Publishing.

—Ancient People: Art Activities about Mesopotamia, Egypt, & Islam. Merrill, Yvonne Y. 2003. (Hands-On Ser.). (ENG.). 88p. (J). (gr. 4-7). pap. 20.00 *(978-0-9643177-8-9(8))* KITS Publishing.

—Ancient People Vol. 2: Art Activities about Minoans, Mycenaeans, Trojans, Ancient Greeks, Etruscans, & Romans. Merrill, Yvonne Y. 2nd ed. 2004. (Hands-On Ser.). (ENG.). 88p. (J). (gr. 3-7). pap. 20.00 *(978-0-9643177-9-6(6))* KITS Publishing.

Simpson, Steve. Billy Bully. Galan, Alvaro. 2009. (ENG.). 32p. (J). (gr. -1-3). pap. 3.99 *(978-0-545-11012-9(2))* Scholastic, Inc.

—Chinese New Year Activity Book. Jones, Karl. 2014. (ENG.). 16p. (J). (gr. 1-3). pap. 9.99 *(978-0-8431-8079-4(X),* Price Stern Sloan) Penguin Publishing Group.

—Day of the Dead Activity Book. Jones, Karl. 2013. (ENG.). 16p. (J). (gr. 1-4). 9.99 *(978-0-8431-7300-0(9),* Price Stern Sloan) Penguin Publishing Group.

—The Farmer in the Dell. 2009. (J). *(978-0-545-06702-7(2))* Scholastic, Inc.

Simpson, Sue. Grave Tales: A Mother Goose Spoof. Sonnenberg, Lois. 2011. (ENG.). 48p. pap. 9.95 *(978-1-4637-9526-9(2))* CreateSpace Independent Publishing Platform.

Simpson, William. Pirates, Bats, & Dragons. Davis, Mike. 2004. 174p. (J). 15.95 *(978-0-9747078-2-2(1))* Perceval Pr.

Sims, Agnes & Shepard, Mary. Mary Poppins Opens the Door. Travers, P. L. 2006. (Mary Poppins Ser.: No. 3). (ENG.). 288p. (J). (gr. 5-7). 16.99 *(978-0-15-205822-7(2))* Houghton Mifflin Harcourt Publishing Co.

Sims, Agnes, jt. illus. see Shepard, Mary.

Sims, Blanche. Abracadabra: Magia para Niños: 50 Divertido Trucos Mágicos. Charney, Steve. 2004. (SPA.). 144p. (gr. 3-4). *(978-84-9754-111-4(1),* 87442) Ediciones Oniro S.A.

—Bugged! Knudsen, Michelle. 2008. (Science Solves It! Ser.). 32p. (J). (gr. -1-3). pap. 5.95 *(978-1-57565-259-7(5))* Kane Pr., Inc.

—Check It Out! Walker, Nan. 2006. (Social Studies Connects). 32p. (J). (gr. -1-3). pap. 5.95 *(978-1-57565-166-8(1))* Kane Pr., Inc.

—The Cupcake Thief. Jackson, Ellen. 2007. (Social Studies Connects). 32p. (J). (gr. -1-3). pap. 5.95 *(978-1-57565-247-4(1))* Kane Pr., Inc.

—Lila the Fair. Driscoll, Laura. 2005. (Social Studies Connects). 32p. (J). pap. 5.95 *(978-1-57565-148-4(3))* Kane Pr., Inc.

—The Longest Yawn. Dussling, Jennifer A. 2005. (Science Solves It! Ser.). 32p. (J). (gr. -1-3). pap. 5.95 *(978-1-57565-160-6(2))* Kane Pr., Inc.

—Pete for President! Alberto, Daisy. 2004. (Social Studies Connects). 32p. (J). (gr. 1-3). pap. 5.95 *(978-1-57565-142-2(4))* Kane Pr., Inc.

—Sidewalk Chalk: Outdoor Fun & Games. McGillian, Jamie Kyle. 2006. 80p. (J). (gr. k-4). reprint ed. 18.00 *(978-1-4223-5580-0(2))* DIANE Publishing Co.

—Soccer Song. Giff, Patricia Reilly. 2008. (Green Light Readers Level 2 Ser.). (ENG.). 24p. (J). (gr. k-2). pap. 3.95 *(978-0-15-206565-2(2))* Houghton Mifflin Harcourt Publishing Co.

—Who Needs It? May, Eleanor. 2009. (Social Studies Connects Ser.). 32p. (J). (gr. 1-3). pap. 5.95 *(978-1-57565-281-8(1))* Kane Pr., Inc.

—Who Needs It? May, Eleanor. 2009. (Social Studies Connects (r) Ser.). (ENG.). (gr. 1-3). pap. 33.92 *(978-0-7613-4804-7(2))* Lerner Publishing Group.

Sims, Kathy C. Louisiana Potpourri from A to Z. Sims, Kathy C., text. 2004.Tr. of Potpourri Louisianais d' A à Z. (FRE.). 64p. (YA). lib. bdg. 24.95 *(978-0-9753435-0-0(5))* Louisiana Ladybug Pr.

Simson, Dana. Dreamland. Simson, Dana. Book Company Staff. 2003. (Pop-up Bks.). 14p. (J). 15.95 *(978-1-74047-211-1(X))* Book Co. Publishing Pty, Ltd., The AUS. Dist: Penton Overseas, Inc.

Sinclair, Alex, jt. illus. see Williams, Scott.

Sinclair, Bella. Ava's Secret Tea Party. Shepherd, Donna J. 2012. 24p. 19.95 *(978-1-61633-285-3(9));* pap. 11.95 *(978-1-61633-286-0(7))* Guardian Angel Publishing, Inc.

—Lulu & the Witch Baby. O'Connor, Jane. 2014. (I Can Read Book 2 Ser.). (ENG.). 48p. (J). (gr. -1-3). pap. 3.99 *(978-0-06-230516-9(6))* HarperCollins Pubs.

—Lulu Goes to Witch School. O'Connor, Jane. 2013. (I Can Read Book 2 Ser.). (ENG.). 48p. (J). (gr. -1-3). 16.99 *(978-0-06-223351-6(3));* pap. 3.99 *(978-0-06-223350-9(5))* HarperCollins Pubs.

Sinclair, James. Hellboy: Despierta al Demonio, Mignola, Mike. Abuli, Enrique Sanchez, tr. from ENG. 2004. Orig. Title: Hellboy: Wake the Devil. (SPA.). 144p. pap. 22.95 *(978-1-59497-027-6(0))* Public Square Bks.

Sinclair, Jeff. Mental Magic: Surefire Tricks to Amaze Your Friends. Gardner, Martin. 2010. (Dover Children's Activity Bks.). (ENG.). 96p. (J). (gr. 3-5). pap. 4.99 *(978-0-486-47495-3(X))* Dover Pubns., Inc.

—Monster Jokes. Pellowski, Michael J. 2011. (ENG.). 96p. (J). pap. 4.95 *(978-1-4027-8478-1(3))* Sterling Publishing Co., Inc.

Sinclair, Peter. Grandpa's Crooked Smile: A Story of Stroke Survival. Reeves, Barbara. 2007. (J). *(978-1-4276-2013-2(X))* Aardvark Global Publishing.

Singer, Rhona Stein. There Can't Bee Two Queens in the Same Hive. Singer, Rhona Stein. l.t. ed. 2004. 32p. (J). pap. *(978-0-9687946-2-3(9))* Stone Woman Warrior Pr.

Singer, Ryan. Johonaa'ei: Bringer of Dawn. Tsinajinnie, Veronica. Thomas, Peter A., tr. from NAV. 2007. (ENG & NAV.). 32p. (J). (gr. -1-3). 17.95 *(978-1-893354-54-8(7))* Salina Bookshelf Inc.

Singh, Jen. Cheap Psychological Tricks for Parents: 62 Sure-Fire Secrets & Solutions for Successful Parenting, 1 vol. Buffington, Perry W. 2003. (ENG.). 160p. pap. 9.95 *(978-1-56145-204-0(1))* Peachtree Pubs.

—It Can't Be Done, Nellie Bly! A Reporter's Race Around the World, 1 vol. Butcher, Nancy. 2003. (ENG.). 144p. (J). (gr. 2-5). 12.95 *(978-1-56145-289-7(0))* Peachtree Pubs.

Singh, Lalit Kumar. 400 BC: The Story of the Ten Thousand. Helfand, Lewis. 2011. (Campfire Graphic Novels Ser.). (ENG.). 72p. (gr. 3-7). pap. 9.99 *(978-93-80028-61-3(X),* Campfire) Kalyani Navyug Media Pty. Ltd. IND. Dist: Random Hse., Inc.

Singh, Nikhil. Salem Brownstone: All along the Watchtowers. Singh, Nikhil. Dunning, John Harris. 2010. (ENG.). 96p. (YA). (gr. 7-18). 18.99 *(978-0-7636-4735-3(7))* Candlewick Pr.

Singh, Raghubir, photos by. River of Colour the India of Raghubir Singh. Singh, Raghubir. Singh, Devika. 2nd rev. ed. 2006. (ENG., 168p. (gr. 8-17). 55.00 *(978-0-7148-4602-6(3))* Phaidon Pr., Inc.

Singh, Sara. Wuthering Heights. Brontë, Emily. 2012. (Classic Lines Ser.). (ENG.). 368p. (J). pap. 8.95 *(978-1-4027-8736-2(7))* Sterling Publishing Co., Inc.

Sinha, Rhea. Latte's Vacation. Sinha, Rhea. 2011. 20p. pap. 7.50 *(978-1-61170-045-9(0))* Robertson Publishing.

Siniard, Ricky. Joel's Adventure at Sea. Fenton, Geleta. 2013. 50p. (J). mass mkt. 9.95 *(978-0-9824433-2-3(3))* Octopus Publishing Co.

Sink, Cynthia. The Nautical Road: A Straight Forward Approach to Learning the Navigation Rules. Pritchard, Herman S. Helwig, Teresa L., ed. 2nd rev. l.t. ed. 2004. 176p. (YA). 29.95 *(978-0-9716479-3-0(3))* Selby Dean Ventures, Inc.

Sinker, Alice. Franklin Stays Up. Bourgeois, Paulette & Clark, Brenda. 2003. (Kids Can Read Ser.). (ENG.). 32p. (J). (gr. k-3). 14.95 *(978-1-55337-371-1(5))* Kids Can Pr., Ltd. CAN. Dist: Univ. of Toronto Pr.

Sinkovec, Igor. Blood Shark! Dahl, Michael. 2015. (J). lib. bdg. ***(978-1-4965-0456-2(9))*** Stone Arch Bks.

Sinkovec, Igor. How Long? Wacky Ways to Compare Length, 1 vol. Gunderson, Jessica. 2013. (Wacky Comparisons Ser.). (ENG.). 24p. (gr. -1-2). 27.32 *(978-1-4048-8324-6(X));* pap. 7.95 *(978-1-4795-1914-9(6))* Picture Window Bks.

—How Tall? Wacky Ways to Compare Height, 1 vol. Weakland, Mark. 2013. (Wacky Comparisons Ser.). (ENG.). 24p. (gr. -1-2). 27.32 *(978-1-4048-8323-9(1));* pap. 7.95 *(978-1-4795-1913-2(8))* Picture Window Bks.

Sinkovec, Igor. A Jar of Eyeballs. Dahl, Michael. 2015. (J). lib. bdg. ***(978-1-4965-0455-5(0))*** Stone Arch Bks.

—Ooze Is It? Dahl, Michael. 2015. (J). lib. bdg. ***(978-1-4965-0457-9(7))*** Stone Arch Bks.

—Werewolf Skin. Dahl, Michael. 2015. (J). lib. bdg. ***(978-1-4965-0458-6(5))*** Stone Arch Bks.

Sinkovec, Igor, jt. illus. see Bolton, Bill.

Sinnott, Adrian C. Grasshopper Pie & Other Poems. Sinnott, Adrian C., tr. Steinberg, D. J. 2004. (Penguin Young Readers, Level 3 Ser.). (ENG.). 48p. (J). (gr. 1-3). pap. 3.99 *(978-0-448-43347-9(8),* Warne, Frederick Pubs.) Penguin Bks., Ltd. GBR. Dist: Penguin Random Hse., LLC.

Sinnott, Joe, et al. The Fantastic Four, Vol. 5. 2006. (ENG.). 568p. (J). (gr. 4-17). pap. 19.99 *(978-0-7851-2162-6(5))* Marvel Worldwide, Inc.

Siobhan, Bell. We All Go Traveling By. Sheena, Roberts & Roberts, Sheena. 2003. (ENG.). 24p. (J). pap. 6.99 *(978-1-84148-595-9(0))* Barefoot Bks., Inc.

Siomades, Lorianne. Cuckoo Can't Find You. Siomades, Lorianne. 2003. (ENG.). 32p. (J). (gr. -1-18). 12.95 *(978-1-56397-778-7(8))* Boyds Mills Pr.

Siple, Greg & Jenne, Ed. Fly Fishing for the Compleat Idiot: A No-Nonsense Guide to Fly Casting. Rutter, Michael. Ort, Kathleen, ed. rev. ed. 194p. (Orig.). (J). (gr. 4). pap. 15.00 *(978-0-87842-313-2(3)*, 316) Mountain Pr. Publishing Co., Inc.

Sipple, Dan. Funny Fill-In - My Space Adventure. Krieger, Emily. 2013. (ENG.). 48p. (J). (gr. 3-7). pap. 4.99 *(978-1-4263-1354-7(3)*, National Geographic Children's Bks.) National Geographic Society.

—National Geographic Kids Funny Fill-In: My Dinosaur Adventure. Krieger, Emily. 2014. (ENG.). 48p. (J). (gr. 3-7). pap. 4.99 *(978-1-4263-1481-0(7)*, National Geographic Children's Bks.) National Geographic Society.

Siravo, Christina E. An Orphan's Promise: A Christmas Story. Davis, Dan. Davis, Jan, ed. 2006. 96p. (J). 14.95 *(978-0-9725977-5-3(1))* Second Star Creations.

Sirrell, Terri. Power Reading: Chapter Books/Wizard of OZ. Cole, Bob. 2004. 94p. (J). (gr. 3-4). vinyl bd. 39.95 *(978-1-883186-64-7(1)*, PPCL1) National Reading Styles Institute, Inc.

—Power Reading: Chapter/Sci-Fi/Dr. Little. Cole, Bob. 2004. 25p. (J). (gr. 3-4). vinyl bd. 39.95 *(978-1-883186-63-0(3)*, PPSF1) National Reading Styles Institute, Inc.

—Power Reading: Comic Book/Dr. Little. Cole, Bob. 2005. 36p. (J). (gr. 2-4). vinyl bd. *(978-1-883186-77-7(3)*, PPSFC1) National Reading Styles Institute, Inc.

—Power Reading: Comic Book/Wizard of OZ. Cole, Bob. 2005. 60p. (J). (gr. 3-4). vinyl bd. 39.95 *(978-1-883186-80-7(3)*, PPCLC1) National Reading Styles Institute, Inc.

Sirrell, Terry. I Love Trees. Meister, Cari. 2011. (Rookie Ready to Learn Ser.). 40p. (J). pap. 5.95 *(978-0-531-26733-2(4))*; (gr. -1-k). lib. bdg. 23.00 *(978-0-531-26501-7(3))* Scholastic Library Publishing. (Children's Pr.).

—Oh, Yikes! History's Grossest, Wackiest Moments. Masoff, Joy. 2006. (ENG.). 320p. (J). (gr. 3-7). pap. 14.95 *(978-0-7611-3684-2(3)*, 13684) Workman Publishing Co., Inc.

Sirrell, Terry. Me Fascinan Los Arboles. Sirrell, Terry. Meister, Cari. 2005. (Rookie Reader Español Ser.). (ENG & SPA.). 32p. (J). (gr. k-2). 19.50 *(978-0-516-25253-7(4)*, Children's Pr.) Scholastic Library Publishing.

—Me Fascinan Los árboles. Sirrell, Terry. Meister, Cari. 2011. (Rookie Ready to Learn Español Ser.). (SPA.). 40p. (J). lib. bdg. 23.00 *(978-0-531-26118-7(2)*, Children's Pr.) Scholastic Library Publishing.

—Me Fascinan los Àrboles. Sirrell, Terry. Meister, Cari. 2011. (Rookie Ready to Learn Español Ser.). (SPA.). 40p. (J). pap. 5.95 *(978-0-531-26786-8(5)*, Children's Pr.) Scholastic Library Publishing.

Sís, Peter. A Collection of Rudyard Kipling's Just So Stories. Kipling, Rudyard. 2004. (ENG.). 128p. (J). (gr. k-12). 22.99 *(978-0-7636-2629-7(5))* Candlewick Pr.

—The Dream Stealer. Fleischman, Sid. (ENG.). (J). 2011. 128p. pap. 5.99 *(978-0-06-178729-4(9))*; 2009. 96p. (gr. 4-18). 16.99 *(978-0-06-175563-7(X))* HarperCollins Pubs. (Greenwillow Bks.).

—The Dreamer. Ryan, Pam Muñoz. (ENG.). (J). 2012. 400p. (gr. 5-9). pap. 8.99 *(978-0-439-26998-8(9)*, Scholastic Paperbacks); 2010. 384p. (gr. 3-7). 19.99 *(978-0-439-26970-4(9)*, Scholastic Pr.) Scholastic, Inc.

—The Ghost in the Noonday Sun. Fleischman, Sid. 2007. (ENG.). 256p. (J). (gr. 3-7). per. 5.99 *(978-0-06-134502-9(4)*, Greenwillow Bks.) HarperCollins Pubs.

—The Little Wing Giver. Taravant, Jacques. Ignatowicz, Nina, tr. from FRE. 2004. 30p. (J). (gr. k-4). reprint ed. 15.00 *(978-0-7567-7970-2(7))* DIANE Publishing Co.

—The Magician's Apprentice. Banks, Kate. 2012. (ENG.). 224p. (J). (gr. 5-9). 16.99 *(978-0-374-34716-1(6)*, Farrar, Straus & Giroux (BYR)) Farrar, Straus & Giroux.

—The Midnight Horse. Fleischman, Sid. 2004. (ENG.). 96p. (J). (gr. 3-7). pap. 5.99 *(978-0-06-072216-6(9)*, Greenwillow Bks.) HarperCollins Pubs.

—Scranimals. Prelutsky, Jack. 2006. (ENG.). 48p. (J). (gr. -1-3). reprint ed. pap. 6.99 *(978-0-06-075368-9(4)*, Greenwillow Bks.) HarperCollins Pubs.

—El Soñador. Ryan, Pam Muñoz. 2010. (SPA.). 368p. (J). (gr. 3-7). pap. 8.99 *(978-0-545-17600-2(X)*, Scholastic en Espanol) Scholastic, Inc.

—The Whipping Boy. Fleischman, Sid. 2003. (HarperClassics Ser.). (ENG.). 96p. (J). (gr. 3-8). pap. 5.99 *(978-0-06-052122-6(8)*, Greenwillow Bks.) HarperCollins Pubs.

—The 13th Floor: A Ghost Story. Fleischman, Sid. 2007. (ENG.). 240p. (J). (gr. 3-7). per. 6.99 *(978-0-06-134503-6(2)*, Greenwillow Bks.) HarperCollins Pubs.

Sís, Peter. Dinosaur! Sís, Peter. 2005. (ENG.). 28p. (J). (gr. -1-1). bds. 7.99 *(978-0-06-075967-4(4)*, Greenwillow Bks.) HarperCollins Pubs.

—Fire Truck. Sís, Peter. 2004. (ENG.). 28p. (J). (gr. -1-1). bds. 6.99 *(978-0-06-056259-5(5)*, Greenwillow Bks.) HarperCollins Pubs.

—Follow the Dream: The Story of Christopher Columbus. Sís, Peter. 2003. (ENG.). 40p. (J). (gr. -1-2). 15.95 *(978-0-679-80628-8(8)*, Knopf Bks. for Young Readers) Random Hse. Children's Bks.

—Madlenka. Sís, Peter. 2010. (ENG.). 48p. (J). (gr. -1-3). pap. 8.99 *(978-0-312-65912-7(1))* Square Fish.

—The Pilot & the Little Prince: The Life of Antoine de Saint-Exupéry. Sís, Peter. 2014. (ENG.). 48p. (J). (gr. k-3). 18.99 *(978-0-374-38069-4(4)*, Farrar, Straus & Giroux (BYR)) Farrar, Straus & Giroux.

—Play, Mozart, Play! Sís, Peter. 2006. 32p. (J). (gr. -1-3). 16.99 *(978-0-06-112181-4(9)*, Greenwillow Bks.) HarperCollins Pubs.

—The Train of States. Sís, Peter. 2004. 64p. (J). (gr. 1-18). 17.99 *(978-0-06-057838-1(6))* HarperCollins Pubs.

—The Tree of Life: Charles Darwin. Sís, Peter. 2003. (ENG.). 44p. (J). (gr. k-3). 21.99 *(978-0-374-45628-3(3)*, Farrar, Straus & Giroux (BYR)) Farrar, Straus & Giroux.

—Trucks Trucks Trucks. Sís, Peter. 2004. (ENG.). 28p. (J). (gr. -1-1). bds. 7.99 *(978-0-06-056258-8(7)*, Greenwillow Bks.) HarperCollins Pubs.

—The Wall: Growing up Behind the Iron Curtain. Sís, Peter. 2007. (ENG.). 56p. (J). (gr. 3-7). 19.99 *(978-0-374-34701-7(8)*, Farrar, Straus & Giroux (BYR)) Farrar, Straus & Giroux.

Sisk, Clay & Gilpin, Stephen. Even Firefighters Go to the Potty: A Potty Training Lift-the-Flap Story. Wax, Wendy & Wax, Naomi. 2008. (ENG.). 22p. (J). (gr. -1-k). 7.99 *(978-1-4169-2720-4(4)*, Little Simon) Little Simon.

Sisneros, Shawn. Shelby. Nyikos, Stacy. 2006. 32p. (J). (gr. -1-3). 15.95 *(978-0-9764199-1-4(2))* Stonehorse Publishing, LLC.

—Squirt. Nyikos, Stacy Ann. l.t. ed. 2005. 32p. (J). lib. bdg. 15.95 *(978-0-9764199-0-7(4))* Stonehorse Publishing, LLC.

Sisson, Mark, et al. Alaskan Railroad Adventure: Messy Macie Where Have You Been Today? Sisson, Mark & Sisson, Wesley. l.t. ed. 2010. (ENG.). 30p. pap. 12.95 *(978-1-4564-1137-4(3))* CreateSpace Independent Publishing Platform.

Sisson, Stéphanie Roth. Persuading Miss Doover. Pulver, Robin. 2015. (J). ***(978-0-8234-3426-8(5))*** Holiday Hse., Inc.

Sisson, Stephanie Roth. Princess Posey & the Christmas Magic. Greene, Stephanie. 2013. (Princess Posey, First Grader Ser.: 7). (ENG.). 96p. (J). (gr. k-3). 13.99 *(978-0-399-16363-0(8)*, Putnam Juvenile) Penguin Publishing Group.

—Princess Posey & the First-Grade Boys. Greene, Stephanie. 2014. (Princess Posey, First Grader Ser.: 8). (ENG.). 96p. (J). (gr. k-3). pap. 4.99 *(978-0-14-242735-4(7)*, Puffin) Penguin Publishing Group.

—Princess Posey & the First Grade Parade, Bk. 1. Greene, Stephanie. 2011. (Princess Posey, First Grader Ser.: 1). (ENG.). 96p. (J). (gr. k-3). 4.99 *(978-0-14-241827-7(7)*, Puffin) Penguin Publishing Group.

—Princess Posey & the Monster Stew. Greene, Stephanie. 2012. (Princess Posey, First Grader Ser.: 4). (ENG.). 96p. (J). (gr. k-3). 12.99 *(978-0-399-25464-2(1)*, Putnam Juvenile); pap. 4.99 *(978-0-14-242105-5(7)*, Puffin) Penguin Publishing Group.

—Princess Posey & the New First Grader. Greene, Stephanie. 2013. (Princess Posey, First Grader Ser.: 6). (ENG.). 96p. (J). pap. 4.99 *(978-0-14-242763-7(2)*, Puffin) Penguin Publishing Group.

—Princess Posey & the Next-Door Dog, 3 vols. Greene, Stephanie. 2011. (Princess Posey, First Grader Ser.: 3). (ENG.). 96p. (J). (gr. k-3). 4.99 *(978-0-14-241939-7(7)*, Puffin); 12.99 *(978-0-399-25463-5(3)*, Putnam Juvenile) Penguin Publishing Group.

—Princess Posey & the Perfect Present, Bk. 2. Greene, Stephanie. 2011. (Princess Posey, First Grader Ser.: 2). (ENG.). 96p. (J). (gr. k-3). 4.99 *(978-0-14-241828-4(5)*, Puffin); 12.99 *(978-0-399-25462-8(5)*, Putnam Juvenile) Penguin Publishing Group.

—Princess Posey & the Tiny Treasure. Greene, Stephanie. 2013. (Princess Posey, First Grader Ser.: 5). (ENG.). 96p. (J). (gr. k-3). pap. 4.99 *(978-0-14-242415-5(3)*, Puffin) Penguin Publishing Group.

Sisson, Stéphanie Roth. The Sunhat. Ward, Jennifer. 2013. (ENG.). (J). 15.95 *(978-1-933855-78-3(9)*, Rio Nuevo Pubs.) Rio Nuevo Pubs.

—Thank You, Miss Doover. Pulver, Robin. 2010. (ENG.). 32p. (J). (gr. k-3). 16.95 *(978-0-8234-2046-9(9))* Holiday Hse., Inc.

Sister Mary of the Compassion. Saint John Masias: Marvelous Dominican Gatekeeper of Lima, Peru. Windeatt, Mary F. 2009. Orig. Title: Warrior in White. (ENG.). 156p. (J). (gr. 3-9). pap. 11.95 *(978-0-89555-428-4(3))* TAN Bks.

Sistig, Heike. The Prince Who Was Just Himself. Schnee, Silke. 2015. (ENG.). 32p. (J). (gr. -1-4). 16.00 ***(978-0-87486-682-7(0))*** Plough Publishing Hse.

Sisung, Peter. Do You Know the Way to Find an A? A Rhyming ABC Book. Wildman, Dale. 2006. 24p. (J). per. 2.99 *(978-1-59958-002-9(0))* Journey Stone Creations, LLC.

—Nicholas Knows: Big Brother Nicholas Knows It All! Wildman, Dale. 2006. 24p. (J). per. 2.99 *(978-1-59958-005-0(5))* Journey Stone Creations, LLC.

Sitaraman, Soumya. Chachaji's Cup. Krishnaswami, Uma. 2013. (ENG.). 32p. (J). (gr. 1-18). 16.95 *(978-0-89239-178-3(2))* Lee & Low Bks., Inc.

Sites, Jennifer. Chloe, the Very Special Goat. Glover, Rosanne Harper. 2012. (ENG.). 48p. (J). 16.95 *(978-0-938467-53-3(0))* Headline Bks., Inc.

Siwinski, Deborah. The Adventures of Teddy & Freddy Summer Safari. Siwinski, Deborah. l.t. ed. 2006. 41p. (J). per. 8.95 *(978-1-59879-097-9(8))* Lifevest Publishing, Inc.

Sizemore, Carmen. 10 Busy Bumble Bees, 1 vol. Pitman, Sandra. 2009. 20p. pap. 24.95 *(978-1-60749-683-0(6))* America Star Bks.

Sjostrom, Nicole & Iseminger, Jonathan. Lucky. Carey-Costa, Denise. 2011. 34p. pap. 12.99 *(978-1-61170-035-0(3))* Robertson Publishing.

Sjostrom, Nicole & Iseminger, Jonathon. A Tale of Three Tails. Carey-Costa, Denise. 2009. 81p. 10.99 *(978-1-4251-8492-6(8))* Trafford Publishing.

Skalak, Daniel. All Summer's Fun. Skalak, Daniel. 2006. 32p. (J). (gr. -1-3). 15.95 *(978-1-60108-000-4(X))* Red Cygnet Pr.

Skardarasy, Doreen L. Gerry the Grape. Hereford, L. F. 2005. (J). pap. *(978-0-9728969-9-3(6))* Acorn Publishing.

Skeens, Matthew. Ancient Coins Were Shaped Like Hams: And Other Freaky Facts about Coins, Bills, & Counterfeiting. Seuling, Barbara. 2008. (Freaky Facts Ser.). (ENG.). 40p. (gr. 3-5). pap. 5.29 *(978-1-4048-3755-3(8)*, Nonfiction Picture Bks.) Picture Window Bks.

—The Bald Eagle, 1 vol. Pearl, Norman. 2007. (American Symbols Ser.). (ENG.). 24p. (gr. 1-2). 8.95 *(978-1-4048-2645-8(9))*; lib. bdg. 25.99 *(978-1-4048-2642-7(4))* Picture Window Bks. (Nonfiction Picture Bks.).

—The Bill of Rights, 1 vol. Pearl, Norman. 2007. (American Symbols Ser.). (ENG.). 24p. (gr. 1-2). 8.95 *(978-1-4048-2219-1(4)*, Nonfiction Picture Bks.) Picture Window Bks.

—The Bill of Rights, 1 vol. Pearl, Norman & Picture Window Books Staff. 2007. (American Symbols Ser.). (ENG.). 24p. (gr. 1-2). 25.99 *(978-1-4048-2213-9(5)*, Nonfiction Picture Bks.) Picture Window Bks.

—Celebrate America: A Guide to America's Greatest Symbols. Firestone, Mary et al. 2010. (American Symbols Ser.). (ENG.). 208p. (gr. 1-2). pap. 14.95 *(978-1-4048-6170-1(X)*, Nonfiction Picture Bks.) Picture Window Bks.

—Cows Sweat Through Their Noses: And Other Freaky Facts about Animal Habits, Characteristics, & Homes. Seuling, Barbara. 2008. (Freaky Facts Ser.). (ENG.). 40p. (gr. 3-5). pap. 5.29 *(978-1-4048-3754-6(X)*, Nonfiction Picture Bks.) Picture Window Bks.

—Cows Sweat Through Their Noses [Dollar General]: And Other Freaky Facts about Animal Habits, Charac. Seuling, Barbara. 2010. (Freaky Facts Ser.). 40p. pap. 0.50 *(978-1-4048-6200-5(5)*, Nonfiction Picture Bks.) Picture Window Bks.

—The Declaration of Independence, 1 vol. Mortensen, Lori. 2009. (American Symbols Ser.). (ENG.). 24p. (gr. 1-2). lib. bdg. 25.99 *(978-1-4048-5165-8(8)*, Nonfiction Picture Bks.) Picture Window Bks.

—Earth Is Like a Giant Magnet: And Other Freaky Facts about Planets, Oceans. Seuling, Barbara. 2008. (Freaky Facts Ser.). 40p. (gr. 3-5). pap. 3.00 *(978-1-4048-5289-1(1)*, Nonfiction Picture Bks.) Picture Window Bks.

—Earth Is Like a Giant Magnet: And Other Freaky Facts about Planets, Oceans, & Volcanoes. Seuling, Barbara. 2008. (Freaky Facts Ser.). (ENG.). 40p. (gr. 3-5). pap. 5.29 *(978-1-4048-3757-7(4)*, Nonfiction Picture Bks.) Picture Window Bks.

—Earth Is Like a Giant Magnet [Dollar General]: And Other Freaky Facts about Planets, Oceans, And. Seuling, Barbara. 2010. (Freaky Facts Ser.). 40p. pap. 0.50 *(978-1-4048-6202-9(1)*, Nonfiction Picture Bks.) Picture Window Bks.

—Ellis Island, 1 vol. Mortensen, Lori. 2008. (American Symbols Ser.). (ENG.). 24p. (gr. 1-2). 25.99 *(978-1-4048-4705-7(7)*, Nonfiction Picture Bks.) Picture Window Bks.

—The Great Seal of the United States. Pearl, Norman. 2006. (American Symbols Ser.). (ENG.). 24p. (gr. 1-2). lib. bdg. 25.99 *(978-1-4048-2214-6(3))*; per. 8.95 *(978-1-4048-2220-7(8))* Picture Window Bks. (Nonfiction Picture Bks.).

—The Liberty Bell, 1 vol. Firestone, Mary. 2007. (American Symbols Ser.). (ENG.). 24p. (gr. 1-2). 8.95 *(978-1-4048-3467-5(2)*, Nonfiction Picture Bks.) Picture Window Bks.

—The Liberty Bell, 1 vol. Firestone, Mary & Picture Window Books Staff. 2007. (American Symbols Ser.). (ENG.). 24p. (gr. 1-2). 25.99 *(978-1-4048-3101-8(0)*, Nonfiction Picture Bks.) Picture Window Bks.

—The Lifeguard, 1 vol. Jones, Christianne C. 2006. (Read-It! Readers Ser.). (ENG.). 32p. (gr. -1-3). 19.99 *(978-1-4048-1584-1(8)*, Easy Readers) Picture Window Bks.

—The Lincoln Memorial, 1 vol. Firestone, Mary. 2007. (American Symbols Ser.). (ENG.). 24p. (gr. 1-2). lib. bdg. 25.99 *(978-1-4048-3718-8(3)*, Nonfiction Picture Bks.) Picture Window Bks.

—Mount Rushmore, 1 vol. Troupe, Thomas Kingsley. 2009. (American Symbols Ser.). (ENG.). 24p. (gr. 1-2). lib. bdg. 25.99 *(978-1-4048-5168-9(2)*, Nonfiction Picture Bks.) Picture Window Bks.

—One President Was Born on Independence Day: And Other Freaky Facts about the 26th Through 43rd Presidents. Seuling, Barbara. 2008. (Freaky Facts Ser.). (ENG.). 48p. (gr. 3-5). lib. bdg. 25.32 *(978-1-4048-4118-5(0)*, Nonfiction Picture Bks.) Picture Window Bks.

—Our American Flag, 1 vol. Firestone, Mary. 2006. (American Symbols Ser.). (ENG.). 24p. (gr. 1-2). 8.95 *(978-1-4048-2218-4(6)*, 1258436, Nonfiction Picture Bks.) Picture Window Bks.

—Our National Anthem. Pearl, Norman. 2006. (American Symbols Ser.). (ENG.). 24p. (gr. 1-2). lib. bdg. 25.99 *(978-1-4048-2215-3(1)*, Nonfiction Picture Bks.) Picture Window Bks.

—Our National Anthem, 1 vol. Pearl, Norman. 2006. (American Symbols Ser.). (ENG.). 24p. (gr. 1-2). 8.95 *(978-1-4048-2221-4(6)*, Nonfiction Picture Bks.) Picture Window Bks.

—Our U. S. Capitol, 1 vol. Firestone, Mary. 2007. (American Symbols Ser.). (ENG.). 24p. (gr. 1-2). lib. bdg. 25.99 *(978-1-4048-3719-5(1)*, Nonfiction Picture Bks.) Picture Window Bks.

—The Pledge of Allegiance, 1 vol. Pearl, Norman. 2007. (American Symbols Ser.). (ENG.). 24p. (gr. 1-2). 8.95 *(978-1-4048-2647-2(5)*, Nonfiction Picture Bks.) Picture Window Bks.

—The Pledge of Allegiance, 1 vol. Pearl, Norman & Picture Window Books Staff. 2007. (American Symbols Ser.). (ENG.). 24p. (gr. 1-2). 25.99 *(978-1-4048-2644-1(0)*, Nonfiction Picture Bks.) Picture Window Bks.

—The Statue of Liberty, 1 vol. Firestone, Mary. 2006. (American Symbols Ser.). (ENG.). 24p. (gr. 1-2). 8.95 *(978-1-4048-2222-1(4)*, Nonfiction Picture Bks.) Picture Window Bks.

—The U. S. Constitution, 1 vol. Pearl, Norman. 2006. (American Symbols Ser.). (ENG.). 24p. (gr. 1-2). 8.95 *(978-1-4048-2646-5(7))*; lib. bdg. 25.99 *(978-1-4048-2643-4(2))* Picture Window Bks. (Nonfiction Picture Bks.).

—The U. S. Supreme Court, 1 vol. Suen, Anastasia. 2008. (American Symbols Ser.). (ENG.). 24p. (gr. 1-2). 25.99 *(978-1-4048-4707-1(3)*, Nonfiction Picture Bks.) Picture Window Bks.

—The White House, 1 vol. Firestone, Mary. 2006. (American Symbols Ser.). (ENG.). 24p. (gr. 1-2). 8.95 *(978-1-4048-2223-8(2))*; lib. bdg. 25.99 *(978-1-4048-2217-7(8))* Picture Window Bks. (Nonfiction Picture Bks.).

—Your Skin Weighs More Than Your Brain: And Other Freaky Facts about Your Skin, Skeleton, & Other Body Parts. Seuling, Barbara. 2008. (Freaky Facts Ser.). (ENG.). 40p. (gr. 3-5). per. 5.29 *(978-1-4048-3756-0(6)*, Nonfiction Picture Bks.) Picture Window Bks.

Skehan, Krista. Alphabetica: Odes to the Alphabet. Spieker, Diana. 2009. (ENG.). 26p. 16.95 *(978-0-9797491-0-0(7))* Personify Pr.

Skelton, J. R. Our Empire Story. Marshall, H. E. 2012. 402p. *(978-1-78139-188-4(2))* Benediction Classics.

Skelton, J. R., et al. Scotland's Story (Yesterday's Classics) Marshall, H. E. 2005. 552p. (J). per. 17.95 *(978-1-59915-056-7(5))* Yesterday's Classics.

Skerry, Brian, photos by. Adventure Beneath the Sea: Living in an Underwater Science Station. Mallory, Kenneth. 2010. (ENG., 48p. (J). (gr. 4-6). 18.95 *(978-1-59078-607-9(6))* Boyds Mills Pr.

—Ocean Counting. Lawler, Janet. 2013. (ENG., 32p. (J). (-k). 16.95 *(978-1-4263-1116-1(8))*; lib. bdg. 25.90 *(978-1-4263-1117-8(6))* National Geographic Society. (National Geographic Children's Bks.).

Skewes, John. Portland ABC. 2014. (Larry Gets Lost Ser.). (ENG.). 32p. (J). (gr. -1-k). 14.99 *(978-1-57061-920-5(4))* Sasquatch Bks.

Skewes, John. Elliott the Otter: The Totally Untrue Story of Elliott Bay. Skewes, John. Ode, Eric. 2015. (ENG.). 32p. (J). (gr. -1-2). 16.99 *(978-1-57061-952-6(2)*, Little Bigfoot) Sasquatch Bks.

—Larry Gets Lost in Alaska. Skewes, John. Mullin, Michael. (Larry Gets Lost Ser.). (ENG.). 32p. (J). (gr. -1-2). 2013. pap. 10.99 *(978-1-57061-859-8(3))*; 2011. 16.99 *(978-1-57061-728-7(7))* Sasquatch Bks.

—Larry Gets Lost in Boston. Skewes, John. Mullin, Michael. 2013. (Larry Gets Lost Ser.). (ENG.). 32p. (J). (gr. -1-2). 16.99 *(978-1-57061-793-5(7))* Sasquatch Bks.

—Larry Gets Lost in Chicago. Skewes, John. Mullin, Michael. 2010. (Larry Gets Lost Ser.). (ENG.). 32p. (J). (gr. -1-2). 16.99 *(978-1-57061-619-8(1))* Sasquatch Bks.

—Larry Gets Lost in Los Angeles. Skewes, John. Mullin, Michael. 2009. (Larry Gets Lost Ser.). (ENG.). 32p. (J). (gr. -1-2). 16.99 *(978-1-57061-568-9(3))* Sasquatch Bks.

—Larry Gets Lost in New York City. Skewes, John. Mullin, Michael. 2010. (Larry Gets Lost Ser.). (ENG.). 32p. (J). (gr. -1-2). 16.99 *(978-1-57061-620-4(5))* Sasquatch Bks.

—Larry Gets Lost in Philadelphia. Skewes, John. Mullin, Michael. 2013. (Larry Gets Lost Ser.). (ENG.). 32p. (J). (gr. -1-2). 16.99 *(978-1-57061-792-8(9))* Sasquatch Bks.

—Larry Gets Lost in Portland. Skewes, John. Mullin, Michael. 2012. (Larry Gets Lost Ser.). (ENG.). 32p. (J). (gr. -1-2). 16.99 *(978-1-57061-679-2(5))* Sasquatch Bks.

—Larry Gets Lost in Prehistoric Times: From Dinosaurs to the Stone Age. Skewes, John. Fox, Andrew. 2013. (Larry Gets Lost Ser.). (ENG.). 32p. (J). (gr. -1-2). 16.99 *(978-1-57061-862-8(3))* Sasquatch Bks.

—Larry Gets Lost in San Francisco. Skewes, John. Mullin, Michael. 2009. (Larry Gets Lost Ser.). (ENG.). 32p. (J). (gr. -1-2). 16.99 *(978-1-57061-567-2(5))* Sasquatch Bks.

—Larry Gets Lost in Texas. Skewes, John. Mullin, Michael. 2010. (Larry Gets Lost Ser.). (ENG.). 32p. (J). (gr. -1-2). 16.99 *(978-1-57061-680-8(9))* Sasquatch Bks.

—Larry Gets Lost in the Twin Cities. Skewes, John. Mullin, Michael. 2012. (Larry Gets Lost Ser.). (ENG.). 32p. (J). (gr. -1-2). 16.99 *(978-1-57061-754-6(6))* Sasquatch Bks.

—Larry Gets Lost in Washington, D. C. Skewes, John. Fox, Andrew. 2014. (Larry Gets Lost Ser.). (ENG.). 32p. (J). (gr. -1-2). 16.99 *(978-1-57061-899-4(2))* Sasquatch Bks.

—Larry Gets Lost under the Sea. Skewes, John. Ode, Eric. 2015. (Larry Gets Lost Ser.). (ENG.). 32p. (J). (gr. -1-2). 16.99 *(978-1-57061-925-0(5)*, Little Bigfoot) Sasquatch Bks.

—Larry Loves Chicago! Skewes, John. 2014. (Larry Gets Lost Ser.). (ENG.). 20p. (J). (— 1). bds. 9.99 *(978-1-57061-913-7(1))* Sasquatch Bks.

—Larry Loves New York City! Skewes, John. 2014. (Larry Gets Lost Ser.). (ENG.). 20p. (J). (— 1). bds. 9.99 *(978-1-57061-936-6(0))* Sasquatch Bks.

—Larry Loves Portland! Skewes, John. 2014. (Larry Gets Lost Ser.). (ENG.). 20p. (J). (— 1). bds. 9.99 *(978-1-57061-935-9(2))* Sasquatch Bks.

—Larry Loves San Francisco! Skewes, John. 2014. (Larry Gets Lost Ser.). (ENG.). 20p. (J). (— 1). bds. 9.99 *(978-1-57061-912-0(3))* Sasquatch Bks.

—Seattle ABC. Skewes, John. Schwartz, Robert. 2009. (Larry Gets Lost Ser.). (ENG.). 32p. (J). (gr. -1-2). 16.99 *(978-1-57061-590-0(X))* Sasquatch Bks.

Skewes, John & Mullin, Michael. Larry Gets Lost in Seattle. Skewes, John & Schwartz, Robert. 2007. (Larry Gets Lost Ser.). (ENG.). 32p. (J). (gr. -1-2). 16.99 *(978-1-57061-483-5(0))* Sasquatch Bks.

Skiadas, Melissa & Skiadas, Stephanie. The Forest of the Leprechauns. McMachan, Susan K. 2008. 36p. pap. 15.95 *(978-1-4389-1325-4(7))* AuthorHouse.

Skiadas, Stephanie, jt. illus. see Skiadas, Melissa.

Skiles, Janet. Thru-the-Bible Coloring Pages, (Ages 3-6) Standard Publishing Staff. 2005. (HeartShaper(r) Resources — Early Childhood Ser.). 240p. (J). (gr. -1-3). 16.99 *(978-0-7847-1783-7(4)*, 02272) Standard Publishing.

—Thru-the-Bible Coloring Pages, Ages 6-8. Standard Publishing Staff. 2005. (HeartShaper(r) Resources —

Elementary Ser.). 240p. (J). (gr. -1-3). 16.99 *(978-0-7847-1785-1(0),* 02274) Standard Publishing.

Skiles, Janet, jt. illus. see Armbrust, Janet.

Skinner, Gayle. Cinnamon the Adventurous Guinea Pig Goes to Devil's Island. Turner, Daniel. 2013. (ENG.). 48p. (J). pap. 10.95 *(978-1-4787-1753-9(X))* Outskirts Pr., Inc.

Skinner, Michael. The Sinking Castle. Heidhausen, Bud. 2011. (ENG.). 36p. pap. 5.95 *(978-0-615-48856-1(0))* Heidhausen, Eric.

Skirvan, Ted, 3rd. The Bad Day. Skirvan, Pamela. 2003. 12p. (J). (gr. k-6). pap. 4.95 *(978-0-9742943-0-8(6))* Skirvan, Pamela.

Sklar, Andy. Undercover Kid: The Comic Book King. Kidd, Ronald. 2007. (All Aboard Mystery Reader Ser.). (ENG.). 48p. (J). pap. 3.99 *(978-0-448-44438-3(0),* Grosset & Dunlap) Penguin Publishing Group.

Skon, Sandy. Bianca the Dancing Crocodile. Lamb. 2008. 30p. pap. 24.95 *(978-1-60563-447-0(6))* America Star Bks.

Skorpen, Neal. Oregon Is Fun! Rain or Sun! Klug, Kirsten. 2011. 20p. (J). pap. 7.95 *(978-0-9798173-3-5(1))* Bamboo River Pr.

Skortcheva, Rossitza. Elijah's Tears: Stories for the Jewish Holidays, 1 vol. Pearl, Sydelle. 2004. (ENG.). 80p. (J). (gr. 3-7). 14.95 *(978-1-58980-178-3(4))* Pelican Publishing Co., Inc.

Skou, Nick. Fanakapan & the Fairies - a Children's Fairy Story. Jordan, Claire. 2013. 52p. pap. *(978-1-78148-648-1(4))* Grosvenor Hse. Publishing Ltd.

Skrbic, Melissa. Touch of Christmas. Murnaugh, Lene. l.t. ed. 2003. 28p. per. 9.95 *(978-1-932344-19-6(5))* Thornton Publishing, Inc.

Skrepnick, Michael. Raptor Pack. Bakker, Robert T. 2003. (Step into Reading Ser.). (ENG.). 48p. (J). (gr. 2-4). pap. 3.99 *(978-0-375-82303-9(4),* Random Hse. Bks. for Young Readers) Random Hse. Children's Bks.

—T. Rex: Hunter or Scavenger? Holtz, Thomas R. & Random House Staff. 2015. (Step into Reading Ser.). (ENG.). 48p. (J). (gr. 2-4). pap. 3.99 *(978-0-375-81297-2(0),* Random Hse. Bks. for Young Readers) Random Hse. Children's Bks.

Skrepnick, Michael W. Descubriendo Dinosaurios con un Cazador de Fsiles. Williams, Judith. 2008. (I Like Science! Bilingual Ser.).Tr. of Discovering Dinosaurs with a Fossil Hunter. (SPA & ENG.). 24p. (J). (gr. 3-7). lib. bdg. 22.60 *(978-0-7660-2978-1(6),* Enslow Elementary) Enslow Pubs., Inc.

Skrepnick, Michael William. Baby Dinosaurs: Eggs, Nests, & Recent Discoveries. Holmes, Thom & Holmes, Laurie. 2003. (Dinosaur Library). 104p. (J). (gr. 6-12). lib. bdg. 26.60 *(978-0-7660-2074-0(6))* Enslow Pubs., Inc.

—Discovering Dinosaurs with a Fossil Hunter. Williams, Judith. 2004. (I Like Science! Ser.). 24p. (J). lib. bdg. 22.60 *(978-0-7660-2267-6(6))* Enslow Pubs., Inc.

—Great Dinosaur Expeditions & Discoveries: Adventures with the Fossil Hunters. Holmes, Thom & Holmes, Laurie. 2003. (Dinosaur Library). 112p. (J). lib. bdg. 26.60 *(978-0-7660-2078-8(9))* Enslow Pubs., Inc.

—Prehistoric Flying Reptiles: The Pterosaurs. Holmes, Thom & Holmes, Laurie. 2003. (Dinosaur Library). 104p. (J). (gr. 6-12). lib. bdg. 26.60 *(978-0-7660-2072-6(X))* Enslow Pubs., Inc.

Skrepnick, Michael William. Diplodocus — Gigantic Long-Necked Dinosaur. Skrepnick, Michael William. 2005. (I Like Dinosaurs! Ser.). 24p. (J). lib. bdg. 22.60 *(978-0-7660-2622-3(1),* Enslow Elementary) Enslow Pubs., Inc.

—Triceratops — Mighty Three-Horned Dinosaur. Skrepnick, Michael William. 2005. (I Like Dinosaurs! Ser.). 24p. (J). lib. bdg. 22.60 *(978-0-7660-2620-9(5),* Enslow Elementary) Enslow Pubs., Inc.

—Tyrannosaurus Rex — Fierce King of the Dinosaurs. Skrepnick, Michael William. 2005. (I Like Dinosaurs! Ser.). 24p. (J). lib. bdg. 22.60 *(978-0-7660-2621-6(3),* Enslow Elementary) Enslow Pubs., Inc.

Skroce, Steve, et al. X-Man: Dance with the Devil. Kavanagh, Terry et al. 2013. (ENG.). 344p. (J). (gr. 4-17). pap. 39.99 *(978-0-7851-6289-6(5))* Marvel Worldwide, Inc.

Skye, Obert. Katfish. Skye, Obert. 2014. (Creature from My Closet Ser.: 4). (ENG.). 256p. (J). (gr. 4-7). 13.99 *(978-0-8050-9690-3(6),* Holt, Henry & Co. Bks. For Young Readers) Holt, Henry & Co.

—Pinocula. Skye, Obert. 2013. (Creature from My Closet Ser.: 3). (ENG.). 256p. (J). (gr. 4-7). 12.99 *(978-0-8050-9689-7(2),* Holt, Henry & Co. Bks. For Young Readers) Holt, Henry & Co.

—Potterwookiee. Skye, Obert. 2012. (Creature from My Closet Ser.: 2). (ENG.). 256p. (J). (gr. 4-7). 13.99 *(978-0-8050-9451-0(2),* Holt, Henry & Co. Bks. For Young Readers) Holt, Henry & Co.

—Wonkenstein. Skye, Obert. 2011. (Creature from My Closet Ser.: 1). (ENG.). 240p. (J). (gr. 4-7). 12.99 *(978-0-8050-9268-4(4),* Holt, Henry & Co. Bks. For Young Readers) Holt, Henry & Co.

—Wonkenstein. Skye, Obert. 2015. (Creature from My Closet Ser.: 1). (ENG.). 256p. (J). (gr. 4-7). pap. 6.99 *(978-1-250-01022-3(5))* Square Fish.

Slack, Alex. Sneakermania. Poulter, J. R. 2014. 42p. pap. 12.99 *(978-1-62563-915-8(5))* Tate Publishing & Enterprises, LLC.

Slack, Michael. Edgar Allan Poe's Pie: Math Puzzlers in Classic Poems. Lewis, J. Patrick. 2012. (ENG.). 40p. (J). (gr. 1-4). 16.99 *(978-0-547-51338-6(0))* Houghton Mifflin Harcourt Publishing Co.

—How Do You Burp in Space? And Other Tips Every Space Tourist Needs to Know. Goodman, Susan E. 2013. (ENG.). 80p. (J). (gr. 3-6). 17.89 *(978-1-59990-934-9(0),* Bloomsbury USA Childrens) Bloomsbury USA.

—Nugget & Fang: Friends Forever - Or Snack Time? Sauer, Tammi. 2013. (ENG.). 40p. (J). (gr. -1-3). 16.99 *(978-0-547-85285-0(1))* Houghton Mifflin Harcourt Publishing Co.

—Nugget & Fang: Friends Forever — Or Snack Time? Sauer, Tammi. 2015. (ENG.). 40p. (J). (gr. -1-3). 6.99 *(978-0-544-48171-8(2),* HMH Books For Young Readers) Houghton Mifflin Harcourt Publishing Co.

—Pass It On! Sadler, Marilyn. 2012. (ENG.). 40p. (J). (gr. -1-3). 16.99 *(978-1-60905-188-4(2))* Blue Apple Bks.

—Scapegoat: The Story of a Goat Named Oat & a Chewed-Up Coat. Hale, Dean. 2011. (ENG.). 32p. (J). (gr. -1-3). 16.99 *(978-1-59990-468-9(3),* Bloomsbury USA Childrens) Bloomsbury USA.

—Scapegoat: The Story of a Goat Named Oat & a Chewed-Up Coat. Hale, Dean & Hale, Shannon. 2011. (ENG.). 32p. (J). (gr. -1-3). lib. bdg. 17.89 *(978-1-59990-469-6(1),* Bloomsbury USA Childrens) Bloomsbury USA.

Slack, Michael. Elecopter. Slack, Michael. 2013. (ENG.). 32p. (J). (gr. -1 — 1). 15.99 *(978-0-8050-9304-9(4),* Holt, Henry & Co. Bks. For Young Readers) Holt, Henry & Co.

Slack, Michael H. Clot & Scab: Gross Stuff about Your Scrapes, Bumps, & Bruises. Lew, Kristi. 2009. (Gross Body Science Ser.). (ENG.). 48p. (gr. 3-5). lib. bdg. 29.27 *(978-0-8225-8965-5(6))* Lerner Publishing Group.

—Crust & Spray: Gross Stuff in Your Eyes, Ears, Nose, & Throat. Larsen, C. S. 2009. (Gross Body Science Ser.). (ENG.). 48p. (gr. 3-5). lib. bdg. 29.27 *(978-0-8225-8964-8(8))* Lerner Publishing Group.

—Hawk & Drool: Gross Stuff in Your Mouth. Donovan, Sandy. 2009. (Gross Body Science Ser.). (ENG.). 48p. (gr. 3-5). lib. bdg. 29.27 *(978-0-8225-8966-2(4))* Lerner Publishing Group.

—How Do You Burp in Space? And Other Tips Every Space Tourist Needs to Know. Goodman, Susan E. 2013. (ENG.). 80p. (J). (gr. 3-6). pap. 16.99 *(978-1-59990-068-1(8),* Bloomsbury USA Childrens) Bloomsbury USA.

—Itch & Ooze: Gross Stuff on Your Skin. Lew, Kristi & Lewandowski, Laura C. 2009. (Gross Body Science Ser.). (ENG.). 48p. (gr. 3-5). lib. bdg. 29.27 *(978-0-8225-8963-1(X))* Lerner Publishing Group.

—My Life as a Chicken. Kelley, Ellen A. 2007. (ENG.). 40p. (J). (gr. -1-3). 16.00 *(978-0-15-205306-2(9))* Houghton Mifflin Harcourt Publishing Co.

—Rumble & Spew: Gross Stuff in Your Stomach & Intestines. Donovan, Sandy. 2009. (Gross Body Science Ser.). (ENG.). 48p. (gr. 3-5). lib. bdg. 29.27 *(978-0-8225-8899-3(4))* Lerner Publishing Group.

Slack, Michael H. & Slack, Mike. Monkey Truck. Slack, Michael H. & Slack, Mike. 2011. (ENG.). 32p. (J). (gr. -1 — 1). 12.99 *(978-0-8050-8878-6(4),* Holt, Henry & Co. Bks. For Young Readers) Holt, Henry & Co.

Slack, Mike, jt. illus. see Slack, Michael H.

Slade, Christian. Aliens in Disguise. Smith, Clete Barrett. 2013. (Intergalactic Bed & Breakfast Ser.). (ENG.). 240p. (J). (gr. 3-7). 16.99 *(978-1-4231-6598-9(5))* Disney Pr.

—Aliens on Vacation. Smith, Clete Barrett. 2012. (Intergalactic Bed & Breakfast Ser.). (ENG.). 272p. (J). (gr. 3-7). pap. 6.99 *(978-1-4231-5723-6(0))* Hyperion Pr.

—Angel of God, My Guardian Dear. Tebo, Mary Elizabeth. 2008. 14p. (J). (gr. -1). 8.95 *(978-0-8198-0784-7(2))* Pauline Bks. & Media.

—Music Star. Hannigan, Paula & Accord Publishing Staff. 2011. (ENG.). 16p. (J). (gr. -1-3). 14.99 *(978-1-4494-0173-3(2))* Andrews McMeel Publishing.

—What Does Mrs. Claus Do? Wharton, Kate. 2008. (ENG.). 32p. (J). (gr. -1-2). 15.99 *(978-1-58246-164-9(3),* Tricycle Pr.) Ten Speed Pr.

—Where Do Diggers Sleep at Night? Sayres, Brianna Caplan. 2014. (ENG.). 26p. (J). (-k). bds. 7.99 *(978-0-385-37415-6(1),* Random Hse. Bks. for Young Readers) Random Hse. Children's Bks.

—Where Do Diggers Sleep at Night? Sayres, Brianna Caplan. 2012. (ENG.). 32p. (J). (gr. k-k). 16.99 *(978-0-375-86848-1(8))* Random Hse., Inc.

Slade-Robinson, Nikki. The Seven Stars of Matariki. Rolleston-Cummins, Toni. 28p. pap. 12.00 *(978-1-86969-327-5(2))* Huia Pubs. NZL. Dist: Univ. of Hawaii Pr.

Slaghekke, Harry. Meet Nancy Bird Walton. Atwood, Grace. 2015. 32p. (J). (gr. k). 22.99 ***(978-0-85798-387-9(3))*** Random Hse. Australia AUS. Dist: Independent Pubs. Group.

Slane, Andrea & Chen, Kuo Kang. Weather. Clarke, Catriona. 2006. (Beginners Science: Level 2 Ser.). 32p. (J). (gr. 1-3). 4.99 *(978-0-7945-1253-8(4),* Usborne) EDC Publishing.

Slater, Jean M. The Adventures of Hopper. Slater, Jean M. 2003. 8p. (J). bds. 16.00 *(978-0-9743149-3-8(5))* Slater Software, Inc.

—Mixed up Morning. Slater, Jean M. 2003. 13p. (J). bds. 16.00 *(978-0-9743149-2-1(7))* Slater Software, Inc.

—Monkey Business: At the Market. Slater, Jean M. 2003. 10p. (J). bds. 16.00 *(978-0-9743149-4-5(3))* Slater Software, Inc.

—Wonderful Snow! Slater, Jean M. 2003. 9p. (J). bds. 16.00 *(978-0-9743149-1-4(9))* Slater Software, Inc.

Slater, Kate. ABC London. Dunn, James. 2015. 40p. (J). 6.99 ***(978-1-84780-678-9(3),*** Frances Lincoln) Quarto Publishing Group UK GBR. Dist: Littlehampton Bk Services, Ltd.

Slater, Kate. ABC London. Dunn, James & Quarto Generic Staff. rev. ed. 2014. (ENG.). 40p. (J). (gr. k-3). pap. 8.99 *(978-1-84780-495-2(0),* Frances Lincoln) Quarto Publishing Group UK GBR. Dist: Hachette Bk. Group.

—After the River the Sun. Calhoun, Dia. 2013. (ENG.). 368p. (J). (gr. 4-7). 16.99 *(978-1-4424-3985-6(8))* Simon & Schuster Children's Publishing.

—Eva of the Farm. Calhoun, Dia. (ENG.). (J). (gr. 4-7). 2013. 272p. pap. 6.99 *(978-1-4424-1701-4(3));* 2012. 256p. 16.99 *(978-1-4424-1700-7(5))* Simon & Schuster Children's Publishing. (Atheneum Bks. for Young Readers).

—Goldilocks & the Three Bears. Bateson-Hill, Margaret. 2015. (J). *(978-1-84686-890-0(4))* Barefoot Bks., Inc.

—The Little Red Hen. Finch, Mary & Messing, Debra. 2013. (ENG.). 32p. (J). 16.99 *(978-1-84686-575-6(1));* pap. 9.99 *(978-1-84686-751-4(7));* pap. 7.99 *(978-1-78285-041-0(4))* Barefoot Bks., Inc.

Slater, Kate. La Gallinita Roja. Slater, Kate. Finch, Mary. 2013. (SPA.). 32p. (J). pap. 7.99 *(978-1-84686-753-8(3))* Barefoot Bks., Inc.

—Magpie's Treasure. Slater, Kate. 2012. (ENG.). 32p. (J). (gr. -1 — 1). pap. 10.99 *(978-1-84939-075-0(4))* Andersen Pr. GBR. Dist: Independent Pubs. Group.

Slater, Nicola. Chihuawolf: A Tail of Mystery & Horror. Ganny, Charlee. 2011. (ENG.). 144p. (J). (gr. 4-6). pap. 6.99 *(978-1-4022-5940-1(9),* Sourcebooks Jabberwocky) Sourcebooks, Inc.

—Clumsies Make a Mess of the Big Show. Anderson, Sorrel. 2011. (ENG.). 112p. (J). (gr. 2-4). 6.99 *(978-0-00-733936-5(4))* HarperCollins Pubs. Ltd. GBR. Dist: Independent Pubs. Group.

—My Dog. Joy, Angela. 2005. 14p. (J). 12.95 *(978-1-58925-759-7(6))* Tiger Tales.

—We're Bored. 2005. 12p. (J). 12.95 *(978-1-58117-384-0(9),* Intervisual/Piggy Toes) Bendon, Inc.

Slater, Teddy & Rescek, Sanja. I Can Say Please. 2012. (J). *(978-0-545-47249-4(0))* Scholastic, Inc.

Slaughter, Tom. ABC X 3: English - Espanol - Francais. Jocelyn, Marthe. 2005. (ENG, SPA & FRE.). 32p. (J). (gr. k-k). 12.95 *(978-0-88776-707-4(9),* Tundra Bks.) Tundra Bks. CAN. Dist: Penguin Random Hse., LLC.

—Boat Works. 2012. (ENG.). 20p. (J). (gr. -1-k). 13.99 *(978-1-60905-215-7(3))* Blue Apple Bks.

—Do You Know Which Ones Will Grow? Shea, Susan A. 2011. (ENG.). 38p. (J). (gr. -1-3). 16.99 *(978-1-60905-062-7(2))* Blue Apple Bks.

—Eats. Jocelyn, Marthe. (ENG.). (J). (gr. k-k). 2010. 16p. bds. 7.95 *(978-0-88776-988-7(8));* 2007. 24p. 15.95 *(978-0-88776-820-0(2))* Tundra Bks. CAN. (Tundra Bks.). Dist: Penguin Random Hse., LLC.

—One Some Many. Jocelyn, Marthe. (ENG.). (J). (gr. k-k). 2006. 16p. bds. 7.95 *(978-0-88776-789-0(3));* 2004. 32p. 11.95 *(978-0-88776-675-6(7))* Tundra Bks. CAN. (Tundra Bks.). Dist: Penguin Random Hse., LLC.

—Over Under. Jocelyn, Marthe. (ENG.). (J). (gr. k-k). 2006. 16p. bds. 7.95 *(978-0-88776-790-6(7));* 2005. 24p. 15.95 *(978-0-88776-708-1(7))* Tundra Bks. CAN. (Tundra Bks.). Dist: Penguin Random Hse., LLC.

—Same Same. Jocelyn, Marthe. (ENG.). (J). (gr. k-k). 2010. 16p. bds. 7.95 *(978-0-88776-987-0(X));* 2009. 24p. 15.95 *(978-0-88776-885-9(7))* Tundra Bks. CAN. (Tundra Bks.). Dist: Penguin Random Hse., LLC.

—What Is Part This, Part That? Ziefert, Harriet. 2013. (ENG.). 40p. (J). (gr. 1-4). 17.99 *(978-1-60905-309-3(5))* Blue Apple Bks.

—Which Way? Jocelyn, Marthe. 2010. (ENG.). 24p. (J). (gr. k-k). 15.95 *(978-0-88776-970-2(5),* Tundra Bks.) Tundra Bks. CAN. Dist: Penguin Random Hse., LLC.

Slaughter, Tom. 1 2 3. Slaughter, Tom. 2006. (FRE.). 24p. (J). (gr. k-k). pap. 7.95 *(978-0-88776-802-6(4),* Livres Tundra) Tundra Bks. CAN. Dist: Random Hse., Inc.

Slavens, Rick, photos by. Growing Pains: A Childhood on Bear Creek. Rieken, Ethel Plaep. Zander, Julie McDonald, ed. 2004. 140p. (YA). per. 23.00 *(978-0-9740348-2-9(7),* Special Editions — Customized Biographies) Slavens Enterprises, LLC.

Slavin, Bill. Adventures in Ancient China. Bailey, Linda. 2008. (Good Times Travel Agency Ser.). (ENG.). 48p. (J). (gr. 4-6). 8.95 *(978-1-55337-454-1(1))* Kids Can Pr., Ltd. CAN. Dist: Univ. of Toronto Pr.

—Adventures in the Ice Age. Bailey, Linda. 2004. (Good Times Travel Agency Ser.). (ENG.). 48p. (J). (gr. 3-7). 8.95 *(978-1-55337-504-3(1))* Kids Can Pr., Ltd. CAN. Dist: Univ. of Toronto Pr.

—All Aboard! Elijah McCoy's Steam Engine. Kulling, Monica. (Great Idea Ser.). (ENG.). 32p. (J). (gr. k-3). 2013. pap. 7.95 *(978-1-77049-514-2(2));* 2010. 17.95 *(978-0-88776-945-0(4),* Tundra Bks.) Tundra Bks. CAN. Dist: Random Hse., Inc., Penguin Random Hse., LLC.

—The Bone Talker, 1 vol. Leedahl, Shelley A. 2005. (ENG.). 32p. (J). pap. 8.95 *(978-1-55041-350-2(3),* 1550413503) Fitzhenry & Whiteside, Ltd. CAN. Dist: Midpoint Trade Bks., Inc.

—Caedmon's Song. Ashby, Ruth. 2006. 32p. (J). (gr. k). 16.00 *(978-0-8028-5241-0(6),* Eerdmans Bks For Young Readers) Eerdmans, William B. Publishing Co.

—Campfire Morgan, 1 vol. Staunton, Ted. 2007. (Formac First Novels Ser.). (ENG.). 64p. (J). (gr. 2-5). 4.95 *(978-0-88780-721-3(6));* 14.95 *(978-0-88780-725-1(9))* Formac Publishing Co., Ltd. CAN. Dist: Orca Bk. Pubs. USA, Casemate Pubs. & Bk. Distributors, LLC.

—Discover Space. Nicolson, Cynthia. 2005. 32p. (J). lib. bdg. 15.38 *(978-1-4242-1193-7(X))* Fitzgerald Bks.

—Discover Space. Nicolson, Cynthia Pratt. 2005. (Kids Can Read Ser.). (ENG.). 32p. (J). (gr. 1-3). 3.95 *(978-1-55337-824-2(5))* Kids Can Pr., Ltd. CAN. Dist: Univ. of Toronto Pr.

—Discover Space Rocks. Nicolson, Cynthia Pratt & Nicolson, Cynthia. 2006. (Kids Can Read Ser.). (ENG.). 32p. (J). (gr. 1-3). 3.95 *(978-1-55337-901-0(2))* Kids Can Pr., Ltd. CAN. Dist: Univ. of Toronto Pr.

—Discover Space Rocks. Nicolson, Cynthia. 2006. 32p. (J). lib. bdg. 15.38 *(978-1-4242-1195-1(6))* Fitzgerald Bks.

—Discover the Planets. Nicolson, Cynthia. 2005. 32p. (J). lib. bdg. 15.38 *(978-1-4242-1194-4(8))* Fitzgerald Bks.

—Discover the Stars. Nicolson, Cynthia. 2006. 32p. (J). lib. bdg. 15.38 *(978-1-4242-1196-8(4))* Fitzgerald Bks.

Slavin, Bill, et al. Drumheller Dinosaur Dance. Heidbreder, Robert. 2006. (ENG.). 32p. (J). (gr. -1-1). pap. 7.95 *(978-1-55337-982-9(9))* Kids Can Pr., Ltd. CAN. Dist: Univ. of Toronto Pr.

Slavin, Bill. The Faceless Fiend: Being the Tale of a Criminal Mastermind, His Masked Minions & a Princess with a Butter Knife, Involving Explosives & a Certain Amount of Pushing & Shoving. Whitehouse, Howard. 2007. (Mad Misadventures of Emmaline & Rubberbones Ser.). (ENG.). 272p. (J). (gr. 4-7). 7.95 *(978-1-55453-180-6(2))* Kids Can Pr., Ltd. CAN. Dist: Univ. of Toronto Pr.

—The Farm Team. Bailey, Linda. (ENG.). 32p. (J). (gr. -1-2). 2008. pap. 7.95 *(978-1-55453-317-6(1));* 2006. 16.95 *(978-1-55337-850-1(4))* Kids Can Pr., Ltd. CAN. Dist: Univ. of Toronto Pr.

—Gonzalo Grabs the Good Life. Levy, Janice. 2009. 34p. (J). (gr. k-4). 17.50 *(978-0-8028-5328-8(5),* Eerdmans Bks For Young Readers) Eerdmans, William B. Publishing Co.

—Great Play, Morgan. Staunton, Ted. 2008. (First Novel Ser.). (ENG.). 64p. (J). (gr. 2-6). *(978-0-88780-772-5(0))* Formac Publishing Co., Ltd. CAN. Dist: Casemate Pubs. & Bk. Distributors, LLC.

—The Island of Mad Scientists: Being an Excursion to the Wilds of Scotland, Involving Many Marvels of Experimental Invention, Pirates, a Heroic Cat, a Mechanical Man & a Monkey. Whitehouse, Howard. 2008. (Mad Misadventures of Emmaline & Rubberbones Ser.). (ENG.). 264p. (J). (gr. 4-7). pap. 7.95 *(978-1-55453-237-7(X))* Kids Can Pr., Ltd. CAN. Dist: Univ. of Toronto Pr.

—It's a Snap! George Eastman's First Photograph. Kulling, Monica. (Great Idea Ser.). (ENG.). 32p. (J). (gr. k-3). 2013. pap. 7.95 *(978-1-77049-513-5(4));* 2009. 17.95 *(978-0-88776-881-1(4),* Tundra Bks.) Tundra Bks. CAN. Dist: Random Hse., Inc., Penguin Random Hse., LLC.

—Little Chicken Duck. Beiser, Tim. 2013. (ENG.). 24p. (J). (gr. -1-2). 17.95 *(978-1-77049-392-6(1))* Tundra Bks. CAN. Dist: Random Hse., Inc.

—Morgan & the Dune Racer. Staunton, Ted. 2011. (Formac First Novels Ser.). (ENG.). (J). (gr. 2-3). 60p. 14.95 *(978-0-88780-966-8(9));* 64p. pap. 5.95 *(978-0-88780-965-1(0))* Formac Publishing Co., Ltd. CAN. Dist: Casemate Pubs. & Bk. Distributors, LLC.

—Morgan & the Money. Staunton, Ted. 2008. (First Novel Ser.). (ENG.). 64p. (J). (gr. 1-5). *(978-0-88780-776-3(3))* Formac Publishing Co., Ltd.

—Morgan Makes a Deal. Staunton, Ted. 2005. 60p. (J). lib. bdg. 12.00 *(978-1-4242-1205-7(7))* Fitzgerald Bks.

—Morgan Makes a Deal. Staunton, Ted. 2005. (Formac First Novels Ser.: 33). (ENG.). 64p. (J). (gr. 2-5). 14.95 *(978-0-88780-667-4(8))* Formac Publishing Co., Ltd. CAN. Dist: Casemate Pubs. & Bk. Distributors, LLC.

—Morgan Makes a Splash. Staunton, Ted. 2004. (Formac First Novels Ser.: 28). (ENG.). 64p. (J). (gr. 1-5). 14.95 *(978-0-88780-623-0(6))* Formac Publishing Co., Ltd. CAN. Dist: Casemate Pubs. & Bk. Distributors, LLC.

—Morgan on Ice, 1 vol. Staunton, Ted. 2013. (Formac First Novels Ser.). (ENG.). (J). (gr. 2-3). 60p. 14.95 *(978-1-4595-0289-5(2));* 56p. pap. 5.95 *(978-1-4595-0290-1(6))* Formac Publishing Co., Ltd. CAN. Dist: Casemate Pubs. & Bk. Distributors, LLC.

—Morgan's Pet Plot. Staunton, Ted. 2003. (Formac First Novels Ser.: 24). (ENG.). 64p. (J). (gr. 1-5). 14.95 *(978-0-88780-588-2(4))* Formac Publishing Co., Ltd. CAN. Dist: Casemate Pubs. & Bk. Distributors, LLC.

—Music by Morgan, 1 vol. Staunton, Ted. 2010. (Formac First Novels Ser.). (ENG.). 64p. (J). (gr. 1-4). pap. 5.95 *(978-0-88780-926-2(X))* Formac Publishing Co., Ltd. CAN. Dist: Casemate Pubs. & Bk. Distributors, LLC.

—Pandemic Survival: It's Why You're Alive. Drake, Jane & Love, Ann. 2013. (ENG.). 128p. (J). (gr. 4-7). 22.95 *(978-1-77049-268-4(2))* Tundra Bks. CAN. Dist: Penguin Random Hse., LLC.

—Pucker up, Morgan, 1 vol. Staunton, Ted. 2008. (Formac First Novels Ser.). (ENG.). 64p. (J). (gr. 2-3). 5.95 *(978-0-88780-744-2(5));* 14.95 *(978-0-88780-746-6(1))* Formac Publishing Co., Ltd. CAN. Dist: Casemate Pubs. & Bk. Distributors, LLC.

—Shapes in Math, Science & Nature: Squares, Triangles & Circles. Ross, Catherine Sheldrick. 2014. (ENG.). 192p. (J). 24.95 *(978-1-77138-124-6(8))* Kids Can Pr., Ltd. CAN. Dist: Univ. of Toronto Pr.

—Le Soleil. Bourgeois, Paulette.Tr. of Destination Univers: Le Soleil. (FRE.). 40p. (J). pap. 8.99 *(978-0-590-16019-3(2))* Scholastic, Inc.

—Something to Tell the Grandcows. Spinelli, Eileen. 2004. 32p. (J). 16.00 *(978-0-8028-5236-6(X));* (gr. -1-3). 8.00 *(978-0-8028-5304-2(8),* Eerdmans Bks For Young Readers) Eerdmans, William B. Publishing Co.

—Stanley at Sea. Bailey, Linda. 2008. (ENG.). 32p. (J). (gr. -1-3). 16.95 *(978-1-55453-193-6(4))* Kids Can Pr., Ltd. CAN. Dist: Univ. of Toronto Pr.

—Stanley's Beauty Contest. Bailey, Linda. 2009. (ENG.). 32p. (J). (gr. -1-2). 17.95 *(978-1-55453-318-3(X))* Kids Can Pr., Ltd. CAN. Dist: Univ. of Toronto Pr.

—Stanley's Little Sister. Bailey, Linda. 2010. (ENG.). 32p. (J). (gr. -1-2). 17.95 *(978-1-55453-487-6(9))* Kids Can Pr., Ltd. CAN. Dist: Univ. of Toronto Pr.

—Stanley's Party. Bailey, Linda. (ENG.). 32p. (J). 2004. (gr. 1-2). pap. 7.95 *(978-1-55337-768-9(0));* 2003. (gr. k-3). 16.95 *(978-1-55337-382-7(0))* Kids Can Pr., Ltd. CAN. Dist: Univ. of Toronto Pr.

—Stanleys Wild Ride. Bailey, Linda. (ENG.). 32p. (J). (gr. -1-2). 2008. pap. 7.95 *(978-1-55453-254-4(X));* 2006. 16.95 *(978-1-55337-960-7(8))* Kids Can Pr., Ltd. CAN. Dist: Univ. of Toronto Pr.

—The Strictest School in the World: Being the Tale of a Clever Girl, a Rubber Boy & a Collection of Flying Machines, Mostly Broken. Whitehouse, Howard. 2006. (Mad Misadventures of Emmaline & Rubberbones Ser.). (ENG.). 256p. (J). (gr. 4-7). 16.95 *(978-1-55337-882-2(2))* Kids Can Pr., Ltd. CAN. Dist: Univ. of Toronto Pr.

—Super Move, Morgan! Staunton, Ted. 2006. (Formac First Novels Ser.: 35). (ENG.). 64p. (J). (gr. 2-5). 14.95 *(978-0-88780-704-6(6));* 4.95 *(978-0-88780-702-2(X))* Formac Publishing Co., Ltd. CAN. Dist: Casemate Pubs. & Bk. Distributors, LLC.

—Talking Tails: The Incredible Connection Between People & Their Pets. Love, Ann & Drake, Jane. 2010. (ENG.). 80p. (J). (gr. 4-7). 22.95 *(978-0-88776-884-2(9))* Tundra Bks. CAN. Dist: Penguin Random Hse., LLC.

Slavin, Bill. Big Top Otto. Slavin, Bill. Melo, Esperanca. 2013. (Elephants Never Forget Ser.). (ENG.). 88p. (J). 16.95 *(978-1-55453-806-5(8));* Vol. 2. pap. 7.95 *(978-1-55453-807-2(6))* Kids Can Pr., Ltd. CAN. Dist: Univ. of Toronto Pr.

—The Stone Lion, 1 vol. Slavin, Bill. 2003. (ENG.). 32p. (J). (gr. k-3). pap. 9.95 *(978-0-88995-154-9(3))* Red Deer Pr. CAN. Dist: Ingram Pub. Services.

—Transformed: How Everyday Things Are Made. Slavin, Bill. (ENG.). 160p. (J). (gr. 3-7). 2007. pap. 16.95 *(978-1-55453-244-5(2))*; 2005. 24.95 *(978-1-55337-179-3(8))* Kids Can Pr., Ltd. CAN. Dist: Univ. of Toronto Pr.

Slavin, Bill & Melo, Esperanca. The Seven Seas. Jackson, Ellen B. 2011. 36p. (J). (gr. -1-3). 15.99 *(978-0-8028-5341-7(2))*, Eerdmans Bks For Young Readers) Eerdmans, William B. Publishing Co.

Slavin, Bill & Shannon, Ben. Great Play, Morgan!, 1 vol. Staunton, Ted. ed. 2008. (Formac First Novels Ser.). (ENG.). 64p. (J). (gr. 1-5). 5.95 *(978-0-88780-770-1(4))* Formac Publishing Co., Ltd. CAN. Dist: Casemate Pubs. & Bk. Distributors, LLC.

—Morgan Makes a Deal, 1 vol. Staunton, Ted. 2005. (Formac First Novels Ser.: 33). (ENG.). 64p. (J). (gr. 2-5). 4.95 *(978-0-88780-666-7(X))* Formac Publishing Co., Ltd. CAN. Dist: Casemate Pubs. & Bk. Distributors, LLC.

—Morgan Makes a Splash, 1 vol. Staunton, Ted. 2004. (Formac First Novels Ser.: 28). (ENG.). 64p. (J). (gr. 1-5). 4.95 *(978-0-88780-622-3(8))* Formac Publishing Co., Ltd. CAN. Dist: Casemate Pubs. & Bk. Distributors, LLC.

—Morgan's Pet Plot, 1 vol. Staunton, Ted. 2003. (Formac First Novels Ser.: 24). (ENG.). 64p. (J). (gr. 1-5). 4.95 *(978-0-88780-587-5(6))* Formac Publishing Co., Ltd. CAN. Dist: Casemate Pubs. & Bk. Distributors, LLC.

Slavin, Bill, jt. illus. see Nicolson, Cynthia Pratt.

Slegers, Liesbet. Andy & Sam. Slegers, Liesbet. 2010. (ENG.). 28p. (J). (gr. -1-1). 10.99 *(978-1-935279-35-8(1))* Kane Miller.

—The Child in the Manger. Slegers, Liesbet. 2010. (ENG.). 30p. (J). (gr. k — 1). 15.95 *(978-1-60537-084-2(3))* Clavis Publishing.

—Guess What I Feel. Slegers, Liesbet. 2009. (Guess Ser.). (ENG.). 26p. (J). (gr. k — 1). 7.95 *(978-1-60537-036-1(3))* Clavis Publishing.

—Guess What I Hear. Slegers, Liesbet. 2009. (Guess Ser.). (ENG.). 26p. (J). (gr. k — 1). 7.95 *(978-1-60537-034-7(7))* Clavis Publishing.

—Guess Who Eats What. Slegers, Liesbet. 2009. (Guess Ser.). (ENG.). 30p. (J). (gr. k — 1). 8.95 *(978-1-60537-045-3(2))* Clavis Publishing.

—Happy Easter! Slegers, Liesbet. 2012. (ENG.). 30p. (J). (gr. k — 1). 15.95 *(978-1-60537-114-6(9))* Clavis Publishing.

—Happy Halloween! Slegers, Liesbet. 2011. (ENG.). 32p. (J). (gr. -1-k). 15.95 *(978-1-60537-101-6(7))* Clavis Publishing.

—Katie Discovers Summer. Slegers, Liesbet. 2009. (Kevin & Katie Ser.). (ENG.). 24p. (J). (gr. -1-k). 12.95 *(978-1-60537-030-9(4))* Clavis Publishing.

—Katie Discovers Winter. Slegers, Liesbet. 2009. (Kevin & Katie Ser.). (ENG.). 30p. (J). (gr. k — 1). 12.95 *(978-1-60537-054-5(1))* Clavis Publishing.

—Katie Goes to the Doctor. Slegers, Liesbet. 2011. (Kevin & Katie Ser.). (ENG.). 30p. (J). (gr. k — 1). 12.95 *(978-1-60537-076-7(2))* Clavis Publishing.

—Katie Helps Mom. Slegers, Liesbet. 2010. (Kevin & Katie Ser.). (ENG & DUT.). 30p. (J). (gr. k — 1). 12.95 *(978-1-60537-066-8(5))* Clavis Publishing.

—Kevin Discovers Autumn. Slegers, Liesbet. 2010. (Kevin & Katie Ser.). (ENG.). 30p. (J). (gr. k — 1). 12.95 *(978-1-60537-064-4(9))* Clavis Publishing.

—Kevin Discovers Spring. Slegers, Liesbet. 2009. (Kevin & Katie Ser.). (ENG.). 24p. (J). (gr. -1-k). 12.95 *(978-1-60537-029-3(0))* Clavis Publishing.

—Kevin Goes to School. Slegers, Liesbet. 2009. (Kevin & Katie Ser.). (ENG.). 30p. (J). (gr. -1-k). 12.95 *(978-1-60537-043-9(6))* Clavis Publishing.

—Kevin Goes to the Hospital. Slegers, Liesbet. 2012. (Kevin & Katie Ser.). (ENG.). 24p. (J). (— 1). 12.95 *(978-1-60537-125-2(4))* Clavis Publishing.

—Kevin Goes to the Library. Slegers, Liesbet. 2011. (Kevin & Katie Ser.). (ENG.). 30p. (J). (gr. k — 1). 12.95 *(978-1-60537-075-0(4))* Clavis Publishing.

—Kevin Helps Dad. Slegers, Liesbet. 2010. (Kevin & Katie Ser.). (ENG & DUT.). 30p. (J). (gr. k — 1). 12.95 *(978-1-60537-065-1(7))* Clavis Publishing.

—Kevin's Big Book of the Five Senses. Slegers, Liesbet. 2012. (Kevin & Katie Ser.). (ENG.). 56p. (J). (gr. k — 1). 17.95 *(978-1-60537-124-5(6))* Clavis Publishing.

—Kevin's Christmas. Slegers, Liesbet. 2011. (Kevin & Katie Ser.). (ENG.). 30p. (J). (gr. k — 1). 12.95 *(978-1-60537-104-7(1))* Clavis Publishing.

—A Puppy for Kevin. Slegers, Liesbet. 2013. (Kevin & Katie Ser.). (ENG.). 32p. (J). (— 1). 13.95 *(978-1-60537-144-3(0))* Clavis Publishing.

Sleva, Michael. 303 Kid-Approved Exercises & Active Games. Wechsler, Kimberly. 2013. (SmartFun Activity Bks.). (ENG.). (gr. k-3). 144p. pap. 14.95 *(978-0-89793-619-4(1))*; 168p. spiral bd. 19.95 *(978-0-89793-624-8(8))* Turner Publishing Co. (Hunter Hse.).

—303 Preschooler-Approved Exercises & Active Games. Wechsler, Kimberly. 2013. (SmartFun Activity Bks.). (ENG.). 168p. (gr. k-k). pap. 14.95 *(978-0-89793-618-7(3))*; spiral bd. 19.95 *(978-0-89793-623-1(X))* Turner Publishing Co. (Hunter Hse.).

—303 Tween-Approved Exercises & Active Games. Wechsler, Kimberly. 2013. (SmartFun Activity Bks.). (ENG.). 168p. (gr. 3-6). pap. 14.95 *(978-0-89793-620-0(5))*; spiral bd. 19.95 *(978-0-89793-625-5(6))* Turner Publishing Co. (Hunter Hse.).

Slim, Lillian, et al. Subsistence Adventures. Slim, Lillian et al. 2006. (Adventure Story Collection Ser.). 28p. (J). (gr. 2-6). pap. 10.00 *(978-1-58084-252-5(6))* Lower Kuskokwim Schl. District.

Slimp, Gwen H. The Winter Sleep: A Story of Hibernation. Rice, Joan W. 2004. 48p. (J). (gr. k-3). *(978-0-9755573-0-3(0))* Coastal Publishing, LLC.

Sloan, Michael. Glendale: Nashville's Magical Park. Lane, Andy. 2009. 88p. (J). 22.95 *(978-1-57736-408-5(2))* Providence Hse Pubs.

—My Anxious Mind: A Teen's Guide to Managing Anxiety & Panic. Tompkins, Michael A. & Martinez, Katherine A. 2009. 128p. (YA). (gr. 7-12). pap. 14.95 *(978-1-4338-0450-2(6))*, Magination Pr.) American Psychological Assn.

Sloan, Monty, photos by. Wolves: For the Earliest Reader. Hillert, Margaret. Starfall Education, ed. 2005. (ENG.). 32p. (J). *(978-1-59577-037-0(2))*; pap. *(978-1-59577-038-7(0))* Starfall Education.

Sloan, Peter. Alice in Wonderland Made Simple for Kids. Carroll, Lewis. 2007. 126p. (J). per. 19.95 net. *(978-0-923891-91-6(9))* Ishi Pr. International.

Sloane, Eric. An Age of Barns: An Illustrated Review of Classic Barn Styles & Construction. Sloane, Eric. rev. ed. 2005. (ENG.). 94p. (gr. 10-18). pap. 16.95 *(978-0-89658-565-2(4))*, 0896585654, Voyageur Pr) Quarto Publishing Group USA.

Sloane, Roxy. Blueberry Pie: The Adventures of Blueberry Bear & Her Friends. Erin, K. c. 2009. 40p. pap. 16.99 *(978-1-4389-7592-4(9))* AuthorHouse.

Sloat, Teri. Dance on a Sealskin. Winslow, Barbara. 2015. (ENG.). 32p. (J). pap. 8.99 ***(978-1-941821-80-0(4))***, Alaska Northwest Bks.) Graphic Arts Ctr. Publishing Co.

Sloat, Teri. How the Bear Lost This Tail. Alexie, Oscar. 2004. (J). pap. 14.00 *(978-1-58084-222-8(4))* Lower Kuskokwim Schl. District.

—My Bug Box. Blanchard, Patricia & Suhr, Joanne. 2003. (Books for Young Learners). 12p. (J). pap. 15.00 *(978-1-57274-701-2(3))*, BB2473, Bks. for Young Learners) Owen, Richard C. Pubs., Inc.

Sloat, Teri. I'm a Duck! Sloat, Teri. 2008. (ENG.). 32p. (J). (gr. -1-k). pap. 6.99 *(978-0-14-241062-2(4))*, Puffin) Penguin Publishing Group.

Slobodkin, Louis. The Hundred Dresses. Estes, Eleanor. anniv. ed. 2004. (ENG.). 96p. (J). (gr. 1-4). 16.99 *(978-0-15-205170-9(8))*; pap. 7.99 *(978-0-15-205260-7(7))* Houghton Mifflin Harcourt Publishing Co.

Slobodkina, Esphyr. Caps for Sale. Slobodkina, Esphyr. 75th ed. 2015. (Reading Rainbow Bks.). (ENG.). 32p. (J). (gr. -1-3). bds. 8.99 *(978-0-06-147453-8(3))*, HarperFestival) HarperCollins Pubs.

—Caps for Sale: A Tale of a Peddler, Some Monkeys & Their Monkey Business. Slobodkina, Esphyr. Slobodkina. 2015. (Young Scott Bks.). (ENG.). 48p. (J). (gr. -1-3). 17.99 *(978-0-201-09147-2(X))* HarperCollins Pubs.

—Caps for Sale: A Tale of a Peddler, Some Monkeys & Their Monkey Business. Slobodkina, Esphyr. 2008. (Young Scott Bks.). 48p. (J). (gr. -1-3). lib. bdg. 17.89 *(978-0-06-025778-1(4))* HarperCollins Pubs.

—Caps for Sale: A Tale of a Peddler, Some Monkeys & Their Monkey Business. Slobodkina, Esphyr. Slobodkina. 75th ed. 2015. (Reading Rainbow Bks.). (ENG.). 48p. (J). (gr. -1-3). pap. 6.99 *(978-0-06-443143-9(6))* HarperCollins Pubs.

—Circus Caps for Sale. Slobodkina, Esphyr. 2004. 40p. (J). (gr. -1-2). reprint ed. 17.00 *(978-0-7567-8345-7(3))* DIANE Publishing Co.

—Circus Caps for Sale. Slobodkina, Esphyr. Slobodkina. 2004. (ENG.). 48p. (J). (gr. -1-3). reprint ed. pap. 7.99 *(978-0-06-443793-6(0))* HarperCollins Pubs.

Slobodkina, Esphyr. More Caps for Sale: Another Tale of Mischievous Monkeys. Slobodkina, Esphyr. Sayer, Ann Marie Mulhearn. 2015. (ENG.). 40p. (J). (gr. -1-3). 18.99 ***(978-0-06-240545-6(4))*** HarperCollins Pubs.

Slocum, Bradley. A Tale of Too Many Cities - Egypt. Wax, Wendy & Weiss, Bobbi. Vargus, Nanci, ed. 2008. (ENG.). 24p. (J). (gr. 1-17). pap. 3.99 *(978-1-58476-722-0(7))* Innovative Kids.

Slonim, David. Bed Hog, 0 vols. Noullet, Georgette. 2011. (ENG.). 24p. (J). (gr. -1-3). 12.99 *(978-0-7614-5823-4(9))*, 9780761458234, Amazon Children's Publishing) Amazon Publishing.

Slonim, David. Believe It or Not, My Brother Has a Monster! Nesbitt, Kenn. 2015. (ENG.). 32p. (J). (gr. k-2). 16.99 ***(978-0-545-65059-5(3))***, Cartwheel Bks.) Scholastic, Inc.

Slonim, David. The Deer Watch. Collins, Pat Lowery. 2013. (ENG.). 32p. (J). (gr. -1-2). 15.99 *(978-0-7636-4890-9(6))* Candlewick Pr.

—Digger, Dozer, Dumper. Vestergaard, Hope. 2013. (ENG.). 32p. (J). (gr. -1-3). 15.99 *(978-0-7636-5078-0(1))* Candlewick Pr.

—How to Teach a Slug to Read, 0 vols. Pearson, Susan. 2011. (ENG.). 32p. (J). (gr. k-3). 16.99 *(978-0-7614-5805-0(0))*, 9780761458050, Amazon Children's Publishing) Amazon Publishing.

—I Know an Old Lady Who Swallowed a Dreidel. Yacowitz, Caryn. 2014. (ENG.). 32p. (J). (gr. -1-3). 17.99 *(978-0-439-91530-4(9))*, Levine, Arthur A. Bks.) Scholastic, Inc.

—It's a Dog's Life: How Man's Best Friend Sees, Hears, & Smells the World. Goodman, Susan E. 2012. (ENG.). 32p. (J). (gr. 1-4). 16.99 *(978-1-59643-448-6(1))* Roaring Brook Pr.

—Moishe's Miracle: A Hanukkah Story. Melmed, Laura Krauss. 2005. (ENG.). 32p. (J). (gr. -1-7). 6.95 *(978-0-8118-5234-0(2))* Chronicle Bks. LLC.

—Silly Tilly, 0 vols. Spinelli, Eileen. 2012. (ENG.). 32p. (J). (gr. -1-2). pap. 7.99 *(978-0-7614-5990-3(1))*, 9780761459903, Amazon Children's Publishing) Amazon Publishing.

—Slugger, 0 vols. Pearson, Susan. 2013. (ENG.). 32p. (J). (gr. -1-2). 14.99 *(978-1-4778-1641-7(0))*, 9781477816417, Amazon Children's Publishing) Amazon Publishing.

—A Sweet Passover. Newman, Lesléa. 2012. (ENG.). 40p. (J). (gr. -1-3). 17.95 *(978-0-8109-9737-0(1))*, Abrams Bks. for Young Readers) Abrams.

—Who Swallowed Harold? And Other Poems about Pets, 0 vols. Pearson, Susan. 2013. (ENG.). 31p. (J). (gr. k-4). pap. 9.99 *(978-1-4778-1595-3(3))*, 9781477815953, Amazon Children's Publishing) Amazon Publishing.

—Who Swallowed Harold? And Other Poems about Pets, 1 vol. Pearson, Susan & Pearson. 2005. (ENG.). 32p. (J). (gr. k-4). 16.95 *(978-0-7614-5193-8(5))* Marshall Cavendish Corp.

—You Think It's Easy Being the Tooth Fairy? Bell-Rehwoldt, Sheri. 2007. (ENG.). 32p. (J). (gr. -1-3). 15.99 *(978-0-8118-5460-3(4))* Chronicle Bks. LLC.

—10 Turkeys in the Road, 0 vols. Sturgis, Brenda Reeves. 2011. (ENG.). 32p. (J). (gr. -1-1). 16.99 *(978-0-7614-5847-0(6))*, 9780761458470, Amazon Children's Publishing) Amazon Publishing.

Slonim, David. He Came with the Couch. Slonim, David. 2005. (ENG.). 36p. (J). (gr. -1-3). 15.99 *(978-0-8118-4430-7(7))* Chronicle Bks. LLC.

—I Loathe You. Slonim, David. 2012. (ENG.). 24p. (J). (gr. -1-2). 15.99 *(978-1-4424-2244-5(0))*, Simon & Schuster/Paula Wiseman Bks.) Simon & Schuster/Paula Wiseman Bks.

—Oh, Ducky! A Chocolate Calamity. Slonim, David. 2006. 28p. (J). (gr. k-4). 16.00 *(978-1-4223-5259-5(5))* DIANE Publishing Co.

—Patch. Slonim, David. 2013. (ENG.). 32p. (J). (gr. k-2). 15.99 *(978-1-59643-643-5(3))* Roaring Brook Pr.

Slutz, Stephani. Ko 'Eku Tohi Lau Maau. Thompson, Richard & Thompson, Ofa. l.t. ed. 2005. (TON.). 16p. (J). (gr. -1-18). 5.00 *(978-0-9678979-4-3(7))* Friendly Isles Pr.

—Ko 'Eku Tohi 'oe Fanga Manu. Thompson, Richard & Thompson, Ofa. l.t. ed. 2004. (TON.). 16p. (J). (gr. -1-18). 5.00 *(978-0-9678979-2-9(0))* Friendly Isles Pr.

Sluzhaev, Viktor. The Lute Player: A Tale from Russia. 2013. (Tales of Honor Ser.). (ENG.). 32p. (J). (gr. 1-4). pap. 8.95 *(978-1-937529-59-8(2))*; lib. bdg. 26.60 *(978-1-937529-75-8(4))* Red Chair Pr.

Smale, Denise L & Blowars, Ryan. What If the Sun Didn't Rise. Smale, Denise L. 2011. 32p. pap. 24.95 *(978-1-4560-5032-0(X))* America Star Bks.

Small, David. Catch That Cookie! Durand, Hallie. 2014. (ENG.). 32p. (J). (gr. -1-k). 17.99 *(978-0-525-42835-0(6))*, Dial) Penguin Publishing Group.

—Elsie's Bird. Yolen, Jane. 2010. (ENG.). 40p. (J). (gr. k-3). 17.99 *(978-0-399-25292-1(4))*, Philomel) Penguin Publishing Group.

—The Essential Worldwide Monster Guide. Ashman, Linda. 2010. (ENG.). 40p. (J). (gr. -1-3). 13.99 *(978-1-4424-1436-5(7))*, Simon & Schuster Bks. For Young Readers) Simon & Schuster Bks. For Young Readers.

—The Gardener. Stewart, Sarah. 2003. (J). (gr. -1-2). 28.95 incl. audio compact disk *(978-1-59112-531-0(6))* Live Oak Media.

—The Gardener. Stewart, Sarah. 2007. (ENG.). 40p. (J). (gr. -1-2). per. 7.99 *(978-0-312-36749-7(X))* Square Fish.

—Glamourpuss. Weeks, Sarah. 2015. (ENG.). 40p. (J). (gr. -1-k). 16.99 *(978-0-545-60954-8(2))*, Scholastic Pr.) Scholastic, Inc.

—The Huckabuck Family: And How They Raised Popcorn in Nebraska & Quit & Came Back. Sandburg, Carl. 2006. 30p. (J). (gr. k-4). reprint ed. 16.00 *(978-1-4223-5854-2(2))* DIANE Publishing Co.

—The Journey. Stewart, Sarah. 2006. (ENG.). 40p. (J). (gr. k-4). reprint ed. pap. 8.99 *(978-0-374-40010-1(5))* Square Fish.

—The Library. Stewart, Sarah. pap. 35.95 incl. audio compact disk *(978-1-59519-010-9(4))*; 2004. (J). (gr. -1-2). 28.95 incl. audio compact disk *(978-1-59519-011-6(2))* Live Oak Media.

—My Senator & Me: A Dog's-Eye View of Washington, D. C. Kennedy, Edward M. 2006. (ENG.). 56p. (J). (gr. -1-3). 16.99 *(978-0-439-65077-9(1))*, Scholastic) Scholastic, Inc.

—My Senator & Me: A Dog's-Eye View of Washington, D. C. Kennedy, Edward M. 2011. (J). (gr. 2-5). 29.95 *(978-0-545-04379-3(4))* Weston Woods Studios, Inc.

—My Senator & Me: A Dog's-Eye View of Washington, D. C. Kennedy, Edward. 2010. (ENG.). (J). (gr. -1-3). 9.99 *(978-0-545-24952-2(X))* Scholastic, Inc.

—Once upon a Banana. Armstrong, Jennifer. (ENG.). 48p. (J). (gr. -1-3). 2013. 6.99 *(978-0-689-85951-9(1))*; 2006. 17.99 *(978-0-689-84251-1(1))* Simon & Schuster/Paula Wiseman Bks. (Simon & Schuster/Paula Wiseman Bks.).

—One Cool Friend. Buzzeo, Toni. 2012. (ENG.). 32p. (J). (gr. k-3). 17.99 *(978-0-8037-3413-5(1))*, Dial) Penguin Publishing Group.

Small, David. One Cool Friend. Buzzeo, Toni. 2015. DVD 59.95 ***(978-0-545-67553-6(7))*** Scholastic, Inc.

Small, David. The Princess Says Goodnight. Howland, Naomi. 2010. 32p. (J). (gr. -1-2). (ENG.). 16.99 *(978-0-06-145525-4(3))*; lib. bdg. 17.89 *(978-0-06-145526-1(1))* HarperCollins Pubs.

—The Quiet Place, 1 vol. Stewart, Sarah. 2012. (ENG.). 44p. (J). (gr. k-4). 16.99 *(978-0-374-32565-7(0))*, Farrar, Straus & Giroux (BYR)) Farrar, Straus & Giroux.

—So You Want to Be an Inventor? St. George, Judith. 2005. (ENG.). 56p. (J). (gr. 2-5). pap. 7.99 *(978-0-14-240460-7(8))*, Puffin) Penguin Publishing Group.

—So You Want to Be President? St. George, Judith. 2004. (J). (gr. 1-6). 29.95 *(978-1-55592-132-3(9))* Weston Woods Studios, Inc.

—So You Want to Be President? St. George, Judith. rev. ed. 2004. (ENG.). 56p. (J). (gr. 2-5). 17.99 *(978-0-399-24317-2(8))*, Philomel) Penguin Publishing Group.

—That Book Woman. Henson, Heather. 2008. (ENG.). 40p. (J). (gr. -1-3). 17.99 *(978-1-4169-0812-8(9))*, Atheneum Bks. for Young Readers) Simon & Schuster Children's Publishing.

—That Book Woman. Henson, Heather. 2011. (J). (gr. 2-4). 29.95 *(978-0-545-23715-4(7))* Weston Woods Studios, Inc.

—The Underneath. Appelt, Kathi. 2010. (KOR.). 395p. (YA). pap. *(978-89-527-5767-8(X))* Sigongsa Co., Ltd.

—The Underneath. Appelt, Kathi. (ENG.). (J). (gr. 5-9). 2010. 336p. pap. 8.99 *(978-1-4169-5059-2(1))*; 2008. 320p. 17.99 *(978-1-4169-5058-5(3))* Simon & Schuster Children's Publishing. (Atheneum Bks. for Young Readers).

—When Dinosaurs Came with Everything. Broach, Elise. 2007. (ENG.). 40p. (J). (gr. -1-3). 17.99 *(978-0-689-86922-8(3))*, Atheneum Bks. for Young Readers) Simon & Schuster Children's Publishing.

Small, David. Eulalie & the Hopping Head. Small, David. 2003. pap. 35.95 incl. audio compact disk *(978-1-59112-520-4(0))*; (J). pap. 33.95 incl. audio *(978-1-59112-218-0(X))* Live Oak Media.

Small, Jan. Juni B. Dicello, Bob. 2013. 36p. 25.95 *(978-1-61493-157-7(7))* Peppertree Pr., The.

Smallfield, Graeme. The Bedtime Treasury of Real Fairy Tales. Smallfield, Jane. 2005. 96p. 17.95 *(978-0-689-03923-2(9))*, Milk & Cookies) ibooks, Inc.

Smallman, Steve. Benjamin Bear Stencil Book, 1 vol. Freedman, Claire. 2010. (ENG.). 12p. (J). bds. 11.99 *(978-0-8254-7427-9(2))*, Candle Bks.) Lion Hudson PLC GBR. Dist: Kregel Pubns.

—Read & Share Bible: More Than 200 Best-Loved Bible Stories, 1 vol. Ellis, Gwen. 2007. (Read & Share (Tommy Nelson) Ser.). (ENG.). 440p. (J). (gr. k-3). 16.99 *(978-1-4003-0853-8(4))* Nelson, Thomas Inc.

—The Story of Easter, 1 vol. Ellis, Gwen. 2008. (Read & Share (Tommy Nelson) Ser.). (ENG.). 32p. (J). (gr. -1-2). 7.99 *(978-1-4003-0855-2(0))* Nelson, Thomas Inc.

Smallman, Steve. Super Ben. Smallman, Steve. 2007. (Collins Big Cat Ser.). (ENG.). 16p. (J). pap. 5.99 *(978-0-00-718656-3(8))* HarperCollins Pubs. Ltd. GBR. Dist: Independent Pubs. Group.

Smalls, David. The Journey. Stewart, Sarah. pap. 16.95 incl. audio *(978-0-87499-922-8(7))*; pap. incl. audio *(978-0-87499-924-2(3))*; pap. 18.95 incl. audio compact disk *(978-1-59112-344-6(5))*; pap. incl. audio compact disk *(978-1-59112-556-3(1))* Live Oak Media.

Smallwood, Sally. Sweet as a Strawberry. Smallwood, Sally. 2005. (Things I Eat Ser.: 1). (ENG.). 24p. (J). (gr. -1-k). *(978-1-84089-419-6(9))* Zero to Ten, Ltd.

Smart, Andy. The Adventures of Wormie Wormington Book Three: Wormie & the Snowball. Brown, Adam. 2013. 48p. pap. *(978-0-9919196-3-5(7))* Beckon Creative.

—The Adventures of Wormie Wormington Book Two: Wormie & the Kite. Brown, Adam. 2013. 48p. pap. *(978-0-9919196-2-8(9))* Beckon Creative.

Smart, Andy. The Adventures of Wormie Wormington Book One: Wormie & the Fish. Smart, Andy. Brown, Adam. 2013. 50p. pap. *(978-0-9919196-0-4(2))* Beckon Creative.

—Bob'n Joe Book One: Lunch Time. Smart, Andy. 2013. 42p. (J). pap. *(978-0-9919196-1-1(0))* Beckon Creative.

Smart, George. Pupitukaar. Shield, Sophie. 2004. (J). pap. 10.00 *(978-1-58084-220-4(8))* Lower Kuskokwim Schl. District.

Smart Kids Publishing Staff. My Snuggle up Bedtime Book. Smart Kids Publishing Staff. 2007. 16p. 14.99 *(978-0-8249-6695-9(3))* Ideals Pubns.

Smart, Ross. Free to Be. Turner, Dale. Summer, Angel, ed. 2003. 112p. (J). (gr. k-5). 16.95 *(978-1-892696-28-1(2))* High Tide Pr.

Smarto, Luke. A Donde Te Vas? 2003. 16p. (J). per. 0.75 *(978-0-930201-05-0(1))* Frontline Pr.

Smath, Jerry. All Aboard! Skinner, Daphne. 2007. (Math Matters Ser.). 32p. (J). (gr. -1-3). pap. 5.95 *(978-1-57565-239-9(0))* Kane Pr., Inc.

—Apaguen las Luces! Penner, Lucille Recht. 2007. (Math Matters (Kane Press Spanish) Ser.). (SPA.). (J). (gr. -1-3). pap. 5.95 *(978-1-57565-241-2(2))* Kane Pr., Inc.

—Bible Stories of Boys & Girls. Ditchfield, Christin. 2010. (Little Golden Book Ser.). (ENG.). 24p. (J). (gr. -1-2). 3.99 *(978-0-375-85461-3(4))*, Golden Bks.) Random Hse. Children's Bks.

—Buried in the Backyard. Herman, Gail. 2003. (Science Solves It! Ser.). 32p. (J). pap. 5.95 *(978-1-57565-126-2(2))* Kane Pr., Inc.

—Buried in the Backyard. Herman, Gail. 2003. (Science Solves It! Ser.). 32p. (J). (gr. -1-3). lib. bdg. 13.00 *(978-0-613-79274-5(2))*, Turtleback) Turtleback Bks.

—Butterfly Fever. Haskins, Lori. 2004. 31p. (J). lib. bdg. 20.00 *(978-1-4242-1087-9(9))* Fitzgerald Bks.

—Enterrado en el Jardin. Herman, Gail. 2008. (Science Solves It! en Espanol Ser.). (SPA.). 32p. (J). (gr. -1-3). pap. 5.95 *(978-1-57565-262-7(5))* Kane Pr., Inc.

—La feria musical de Matematicas: Math Matters en Espanol. Kassirer, Sue. 2005. 32p. (J). pap. 5.95 *(978-1-57565-153-8(X))* Kane Pr., Inc.

—The Ghost Town Mystery. Larsen, Kirsten. 2008. (Social Studies Connects Ser.). 32p. (J). (gr. -1-3). pap. 5.95 *(978-1-57565-257-3(9))* Kane Pr., Inc.

—Locura por las Mariposas. Haskins, Lori & Ramirez, Alma. 2009. (Science Solves It! en Espanol Ser.). (SPA.). 32p. (J). (gr. 1-3). pap. 5.95 *(978-1-57565-284-9(6))* Kane Pr., Inc.

—Locura Por Las Marisposas (Butterfly Fever) Haskins, Lori. 2009. (Science Solves It! (r) en Espanol Ser.). (SPA.). (gr. 1-3). pap. 33.92 *(978-0-7613-4799-6(2))* Lerner Publishing Group.

—Mac & the Messmaker. Hudson, Iris. 2005. (Social Studies Connects). 32p. (J). (gr. k-2). pap. 5.95 *(978-1-57565-158-3(0))* Kane Pr., Inc.

—The Messiest Room on the Planet. Kulling, Monica & Walker, Nan. 2009. (Social Studies Connects Ser.). 32p. (J). (gr. k-2). pap. 5.95 *(978-1-57565-282-5(X))* Kane Pr., Inc.

—Miracles of Jesus. Broughton, Pamela & Watson, Jane Werner. 2009. (Little Golden Book Ser.). (ENG.). 24p. (J). (gr. -1-2). 3.99 *(978-0-375-85623-5(4))*, Golden Inspirational) Random Hse. Children's Bks.

—My Brother, the Knight. Driscoll, Laura. 2004. (Social Studies Connects). 32p. (J). (gr. 1-3). pap. 5.95 *(978-1-57565-140-8(8))* Kane Pr., Inc.

—No Rules for Rex! Alberto, Daisy. 2005. (Social Studies Connects). 32p. (J). pap. 5.95 *(978-1-57565-146-0(7))* Kane Pr., Inc.

—Palapalooza. Skinner, Daphne. 2006. (Social Studies Connects). 32p. (J). (gr. -1-3). pap. 5.95 *(978-1-57565-163-7(7))* Kane Pr., Inc.

—The Secret of the Circle-K Cave. Hays, Anna Jane. 2006. (Science Solves It! Ser.). 32p. (J). (gr. -1-3). pap. 5.95 *(978-1-57565-189-7(0))* Kane Pr., Inc.

—Seven Little Hippos. Thaler, Mike. 2014. (ENG.). 36p. (J). (gr. -1-1). 16.99 *(978-1-4814-2541-4(2))*, Simon &

S

Schuster Bks. For Young Readers) Simon & Schuster Bks. For Young Readers.
—The Story of Jesus. Watson, Jane Werner. 2007. (Little Golden Book Ser.). (ENG.). 24p. (J). (gr. -1-k). 4.99 *(978-0-375-83941-2(0),* Golden Inspirational) Random Hse. Children's Bks.
—The Taming of Lola: A Shrew Story. Weiss, Ellen. 2010. (ENG.). 32p. (J). (gr. -1-3). 15.95 *(978-0-8109-4066-6(3),* Abrams Bks. for Young Readers) Abrams.
—Tanya Tinker & the Gizmo Gang. Marks, Burton. 2003. 20p. (J). (gr. -1-3). reprint ed. 22.00 *(978-0-7567-6760-0(1))* DIANE Publishing Co.
Smedley, Chris. Pongwiffy. Umansky, Kaye. 2007. (ENG.). 192p. (J). (gr. 3-7). pap. 10.95 *(978-1-4169-6832-0(6),* Simon & Schuster/Paula Wiseman Bks.) Simon & Schuster/Paula Wiseman Bks.
Smee, Nicola. The Lion Little Book of Bedtime Stories. Pasquali, Elena. 2014. (ENG.). 96p. (J). (gr. -1-k). 9.99 *(978-0-7459-6459-1(1))* Lion Hudson PLC GBR. Dist: Independent Pubs. Group.
—My Big Rainy Day Activity Book. Dann, Penny. 2004. 96p. (J). act. bk. ed. 7.99 *(978-1-85854-554-7(4))* Brimax Books Ltd. GBR. Dist: Byeway Bks.
—Two-Minute Bedtime Stories. 2010. (Two-Minute Stories Ser.). (ENG.). 48p. (J). (gr. -1-k). 12.99 *(978-0-7459-6079-1(0))* Lion Hudson PLC GBR. Dist: Independent Pubs. Group.
—Two-Minute Bible Stories. Pasquali, Elena. 2009. (Two-Minute Stories Ser.). (ENG.). 44p. (J). (gr. -1-k). 12.99 *(978-0-7459-6053-1(7),* Lion Children's) Lion Hudson PLC GBR. Dist: Independent Pubs. Group.
Smee, Nicola. Sleepyhead. Smee, Nicola. 2004. (ENG & BEN.). 10p. (J). bds. *(978-1-85269-095-3(X));* bds. *(978-1-85269-097-7(6))* Mantra Lingua.
Smekhov, Zely. Seven Delightful Stories for Every Day. Elkins, Dov Peretz. 2005. 48p. (J). 16.95 *(978-1-930143-02-9(8),* Devora Publishing) Simcha Media Group.
Smerek, Kim. What Is Zazu?, 1 bk. Smerek, Kim. 2003. 24p. (J). bds. 7.95 *(978-0-9745116-0-3(9))* Sunshine Bks. for Children.
Smiley, Mary Anne. Sam's Birthmark. Griffin, Martha & Griffin, Grant. 2013. (ENG.). 24p. (J). (gr. -1-3). 18.95 *(978-0-692-01920-7(0))* Griffin Group Publishing LLC.
Smileyworld Ltd. Staff. Where's Smiley? Smileyworld Ltd. Staff. 2010. (SmileyWorld Ser.). (ENG.). 34p. (J). (gr. k-3). 9.99 *(978-1-4424-0756-5(5),* Little Simon) Little Simon.
Smishliaev, Anatoli. Grapette, the Runaway Who Rolled Away: A Timeless Tale of Love & Family: A Child Discovering the World. Konnikova, Svetlana. 2007. (Grapette's Adventures Ser.). (ENG.). 32p. (J). (gr. k-2). 15.95 *(978-0-9791758-0-0(1))* Aurora Pubs., Inc.
Smit, Noelle. Snail's Birthday Wish. Rempt, Fiona. 2007. (ENG.). 32p. (J). (gr. -1-1). 14.95 *(978-1-905417-52-0(7))* Boxer Bks., Ltd. GBR. Dist: Sterling Publishing Co., Inc.
Smith, Abby. The Mysterious Money Tree: Little Tommy Learns a Lesson in Giving. Toombs, Tom. 2012. 28p. (J). pap. 12.95 *(978-1-61314-033-8(9),* Innovo Pr.) Innovo Publishing, LLC.
Smith, Alastair. On the Farm. Tatchell, Judy. 2004. (Lift-the-Flap Learners Ser.). (ENG.). 1p. (J). (gr. 1-18). pap. 8.95 *(978-0-7460-2775-2(3))* EDC Publishing.
Smith, Alex. Home. Smith, Alex. 2011. 32p. pap. 7.95 *(978-1-58925-433-6(3))* Tiger Tales.
Smith, Alex T. Eliot Jones Midnight Superhero. Cottringer, Anne. 2009. 24p. (J). (gr. -1-2). pap. 7.95 *(978-1-58925-416-9(3))* Tiger Tales.
Smith, Alex T. The Great Brain Robbery. Kemp, Anna. 2013. (ENG.). 288p. (J). pap. 6.99 ***(978-0-85707-996-1(4))*** Simon & Schuster, Ltd. GBR. Dist: Simon & Schuster, Inc.
—Little Red & the Very Hungry Lion. 2016. (J). ***(978-0-545-91438-3(8),*** Scholastic Pr.) Scholastic, Inc.
Smith, Alex T. My Mom Has X-Ray Vision. McAllister, Angela. 2011. 32p. (J). (gr. -1-2). 15.95 *(978-1-58925-097-0(4));* pap. 7.95 *(978-1-58925-428-2(7))* Tiger Tales.
Smith, Alex T. Claude at the Beach, 1 vol. Smith, Alex T. 2014. (Claude Ser.). (ENG.). 96p. (J). (gr. 1-3). 12.95 *(978-1-56145-703-8(5))* Peachtree Pubs.
—Claude at the Circus, 1 vol. Smith, Alex T. 2013. (Claude Ser.). (ENG.). 96p. (J). (gr. 2-4). 12.95 *(978-1-56145-702-1(7))* Peachtree Pubs.
—Claude in the City, 1 vol. Smith, Alex T. (Claude Ser.). (ENG.). 96p. (J). (gr. 2-4). 2015. pap. 7.95 *(978-1-56145-843-1(0));* 2013. 12.95 *(978-1-56145-697-0(7))* Peachtree Pubs.
—Foxy & Egg: Starring Vivien Vixen As Foxy Dubois - Introducing Edward l'Ouef As Egg. Smith, Alex T. 2011. 32p. (J). (gr. -1-3). 17.95 *(978-0-8234-2330-9(1))* Holiday Hse., Inc.
Smith, Alice. I'm So over Fairies: Really - I Hate Them. Smith, Alice. Smith, James. 2007. (ENG.). 32p. (J). (gr. k-2). pap. 5.99 *(978-1-84255-542-2(1),* Orion Children's Bks.) Hachette Children's Group GBR. Dist: Independent Pubs. Group.
Smith, Alison. Trading Faces. DeVillers, Julia & Roy, Jennifer Rozines. 2009. (Mix Ser.). (ENG.). 320p. (J). (gr. 4-8). pap. 7.99 *(978-1-4169-6168-0(2),* Simon & Schuster/Paula Wiseman Bks.) Simon & Schuster/Paula Wiseman Bks.
Smith, Andy. Attack of the Toyman. Sazaklis, John & Farley, John. 2012. (ENG.). 24p. (J). (gr. -1-3). pap. 3.99 *(978-0-06-188535-8(5),* HarperFestival) HarperCollins Pubs.
Smith, Andy, et al. The First, Vol. 5. Kesel, Barbara. 2003. (First Ser.: Vol. 5). 192p. (YA). pap. 15.95 *(978-1-59314-002-1(9))* CrossGeneration Comics, Inc.
—The First: Ragnarok, Vol. 6. Kesel, Barbara. 2004. (First Ser.). 160p. (YA). pap. 15.95 *(978-1-59314-035-9(5))* CrossGeneration Comics, Inc.
Smith, Andy. Superman: Day of Doom. Sazaklis, John & Vancata, Brad. 2013. 29p. (YA). *(978-1-4844-0620-5(6))* Harper & Row Ltd.
—Superman vs. the Silver Banshee. Lemke, Donald. 2013. (I Can Read Book 2 Ser.). (ENG.). 32p. (J). (gr. -1-3). pap. 3.99 *(978-0-06-188524-2(X))* HarperCollins Pubs.
Smith, Andy & Vancata, Brad. Battle - Battle in Metropolis. Sazaklis, John. 2013. (ENG.). 24p. (J). (gr. -1-3). pap. 3.99 *(978-0-06-188537-2(1),* HarperFestival) HarperCollins Pubs.
—I Am Aquaman. Mayer, Kirsten. 2013. (I Can Read Book 2 Ser.). (ENG.). 32p. (J). (gr. -1-3). pap. 3.99 *(978-0-06-221003-6(3))* HarperCollins Pubs.
—Partners in Peril. Sonneborn, Scott. 2013. (ENG.). 24p. (J). (gr. -1-3). pap. 3.99 *(978-0-06-221007-4(6),* HarperFestival) HarperCollins Pubs.
—Superman Classic - Day of Doom. Sazaklis, John. 2013. (I Can Read Book 2 Ser.). (ENG.). 32p. (J). (gr. -1-3). pap. 3.99 *(978-0-06-221001-2(7))* HarperCollins Pubs.
Smith, Andy, jt. illus. see Farley, Rick.
Smith, Andy J. Attack of the Mutant Lunch Lady. Nickel, Scott. 2008. (Graphic Sparks Ser.). (ENG.). 40p. (gr. 1-3). per. 5.95 *(978-1-4342-0501-8(0),* Graphic Sparks) Stone Arch Bks.
—Attack of the Mutant Lunch Lady: A Buzz Beaker Brainstorm, 1 vol. Nickel, Scott. 2008. (Buzz Beaker Brainstorm Ser.). (ENG.). 40p. (gr. 1-3). lib. bdg. 22.65 *(978-1-4342-0451-6(0),* Graphic Sparks) Stone Arch Bks.
—Backyard Bug Battle: A Buzz Beaker Brainstorm, 1 vol. Nickel, Scott. 2006. (Buzz Beaker Brainstorm Ser.). (ENG.). 40p. (gr. 1-3). lib. bdg. 22.65 *(978-1-59889-054-9(9));* per. 5.95 *(978-1-59889-224-6(X))* Stone Arch Bks. (Graphic Sparks).
—Billions of Bats. Nickel, Scott. 2007. (Graphic Sparks Ser.). (ENG.). 40p. (gr. 1-3). per. 5.95 *(978-1-59889-408-0(0),* Graphic Sparks) Stone Arch Bks.
—Buzz Beaker vs Dracula: A Buzz Beaker Brainstorm, 1 vol. Nickel, Scott. 2009. (Buzz Beaker Brainstorm Ser.). (ENG.). 40p. (gr. 1-3). lib. bdg. 22.65 *(978-1-4342-1191-0(6),* Graphic Sparks) Stone Arch Bks.
—Robot Rampage: A Buzz Beaker Brainstorm. Nickel, Scott. 2006. (Graphic Sparks Ser.). (ENG.). 40p. (gr. 1-3). per. 5.95 *(978-1-59889-227-7(4),* Graphic Sparks) Stone Arch Bks.
—Wind Power Whiz Kid: A Buzz Beaker Brainstorm, 1 vol. Nickel, Scott. 2008. (Buzz Beaker Brainstorm Ser.). (ENG.). 40p. (gr. 1-3). 22.65 *(978-1-4342-0758-6(7));* pap. 5.95 *(978-1-4342-0854-5(0))* Stone Arch Bks. (Graphic Sparks).
Smith, Andy J. Fang Fairy, 1 vol. Smith, Andy J. 2007. (Jeremy Kreep Ser.). (ENG.). 40p. (gr. 1-3). lib. bdg. 22.65 *(978-1-59889-835-4(3),* Graphic Sparks) Stone Arch Bks.
Smith, Anne. Japan: Panorama Pops. Candlewick Press, Candlewick. 2015. (Panorama Pops Ser.). (ENG.). 30p. (J). (gr. k-4). 8.99 *(978-0-7636-7504-2(0))* Candlewick Pr.
—Ox, House, Stick: The History of Our Alphabet. Robb, Don. 2007. (Junior Library Guild Selection (Charlesbridge Paper) Ser.). (ENG.). 48p. (J). (gr. 3-7). pap. 7.95 *(978-1-57091-610-6(1))* Charlesbridge Publishing, Inc.
—The Whale Whisperers, 1 vol. Smith, John D. H. 2009. 17p. pap. 24.95 *(978-1-60749-211-5(3))* America Star Bks.
Smith, Ashley. Gooey Gummy Geese. Holzer, Angela. 2008. (ENG.). (J). lib. bdg. 8.99 *(978-0-9821563-1-5(6))* Good Sound Publishing.
Smith, Barry. The Odyssey, Vol. 4. Redmond, Diane. unabr. ed. 2003. (Curtain Up Ser.: Vol. 4). (ENG.). 48p. (J). (gr. 1-4). pap. 15.00 *(978-0-7136-4628-3(4),* A & C Black) Bloomsbury Publishing Plc GBR. Dist: Players Pr., Inc.
—The Odyssey. Redmond, Diane. 2012. *(978-0-88734-067-3(9))* Players Pr., Inc.
Smith, Bart, photos by. The Appalachian Trail: Calling Me Back to the Hills. 2007. (ENG., 128p. (YA). 39.95 *(978-0-9795659-0-8(1))* Shaffer, Earl Foundation, Inc.
Smith, Brenda. When Boo Boo Wakes Up!, 1 vol. Sister Flowers. 2009. 36p. pap. 24.95 *(978-1-61546-250-6(3))* America Star Bks.
Smith, Brian. Grow Up!, 4 vols., No. 4. Steinberg, D. J. 2010. (Daniel Boom Aka Loud Boy Ser.: 4). (ENG.). 96p. (J). (gr. 1-4). pap. 6.99 *(978-0-448-44701-8(0),* Grosset & Dunlap) Penguin Publishing Group.
—Mac Attack!, No. 2. Steinberg, D. J. 2008. (Daniel Boom Aka Loud Boy Ser.: 2). (ENG.). 96p. (J). (gr. 1-4). pap. 6.99 *(978-0-448-44699-8(5),* Grosset & Dunlap) Penguin Publishing Group.
Smith, Brock R. & Smith, Raissa B. Where Did Mommy Go? A Spiritual Tool to Help Children Grow from Grief to Peace. Smith, Brenda J. Smith, Brenda J. & Cloud, Olivia, eds. 2004. Orig. Title: Listed Above. 52p. (gr. 3-12). pap. 16.95 *(978-0-9744549-0-0(7))* Tall Through Bks.
Smith, Brody. A Cat Named Friend. Barbre, Mark. 2008. 18p. (J). pap. 9.95 *(978-0-615-20414-7(7))* Edgar Road Publishing.
Smith, Bron. Explorers of the New World Time Line. Fisher, Ann Richmond. Mitchell, Judy & Lindeen, Mary, eds. 2007. 112p. (J). pap. 12.95 *(978-1-57310-523-1(6))* Teaching & Learning Co.
—Language Fundamentals. Myers, R. E. Mitchell, Judith, ed. 2005. 96p. (J). Bk. 1. pap. 11.95 *(978-1-57310-450-0(7));* Bk. 2. pap. 11.95 *(978-1-57310-451-7(5))* Teaching & Learning Co.
Smith, Buckley. Moonsailors. Smith, Buckley. 2007. (ENG.). 40p. (J). (gr. -1-7). 14.95 *(978-0-937822-95-1(7))* WoodenBoat Pubns.
Smith, Cat Bowman. Boom Town. Levitin, Sonia. 2004. 30p. (J). (gr. -1-3). 14.65 *(978-0-7569-3185-8(1))* Perfection Learning Corp.
—Feliciana Feydra Leroux: A Cajun Tall Tale, 1 vol. Thomassie, Tynia. 2005. (ENG.). 32p. (J). (gr. k-3). 16.99 *(978-1-58980-286-5(1))* Pelican Publishing Co., Inc.
—Feliciana Meets d'Loup Garou: A Cajun Tall Tale, 1 vol. Thomassie, Tynia. 2005. (ENG.). 32p. (J). (gr. k-3). 16.99 *(978-1-58980-287-2(X))* Pelican Publishing Co., Inc.
—Joshua the Giant Frog, 1 vol. Thomas, Peggy. 2005. (ENG.). 32p. (J). (gr. k-3). 16.99 *(978-1-58980-267-4(5))* Pelican Publishing Co., Inc.
—The Rosie Stories. Voigt, Cynthia. 2003. (ENG.). 48p. (J). (gr. k-3). tchr. ed. 16.95 *(978-0-8234-1625-7(9))* Holiday Hse., Inc.
—The Trouble with Twins. Freeman, Martha. 2007. (ENG.). 112p. (J). (gr. 2-6). 16.95 *(978-0-8234-2025-4(6))* Holiday Hse., Inc.
Smith, Cat Bowman & Smith, Catharine Bowman. General Butterfingers. Gardiner, John Reynolds. 2007. (ENG.). 96p. (J). (gr. 5-7). 7.95 *(978-0-618-75922-4(0))* Houghton Mifflin Harcourt Publishing Co.
Smith, Catharine Bowman, jt. illus. see Smith, Cat Bowman.
Smith, Charles R., Jr. My People. Hughes, Langston. 2009. (ENG.). 40p. (J). (gr. -1-3). 17.99 *(978-1-4169-3540-7(1),* Atheneum Bks. for Young Readers) Simon & Schuster Children's Publishing.
Smith, Charles R., Jr. Pick-Up Game: A Full Day of Full Court. Smith, Charles R., Jr., ed. Aronson, Marc, ed. (ENG.). 176p. (YA). (gr. 9). 2012. pap. 6.99 *(978-0-7636-6068-0(X));* 2011. 15.99 *(978-0-7636-4562-5(1))* Candlewick Pr.
Smith, Charles R., Jr., photos by. If: A Father's Advice to His Son. Kipling, Rudyard. 2007. (ENG., 40p. (J). (gr. 1-5). 15.99 *(978-0-689-87799-5(4),* Atheneum Bks. for Young Readers) Simon & Schuster Children's Publishing.
Smith, Charlie E. T. The Farmer & His Animals. MacNeil, Ben. 2013. 26p. pap. *(978-1-927625-02-6(5))* Quarter Castle Publishing.
Smith, Claire. Annie Elf Meets Mitty Mouse. Smith, Gloria. 2012. 24p. 29.95 *(978-1-62709-398-9(2));* pap. 24.95 *(978-1-4626-8151-8(4))* America Star Bks.
Smith, Clara Batton. Elliott & Anastaci. Smith, Clara Batton. 2012. 16p. pap. 9.95 *(978-1-61633-233-4(6))* Guardian Angel Publishing, Inc.
Smith, Craig. Algunos Secretos Nunca Deben Guardarse. Sanders, Jayneen. abr. ed. 2013.Tr. of Some Secrets Should Never. (SPA.). 34p. (J). pap. *(978-0-9871860-2-7(7))* UpLoad Publishing Pty, Ltd.
—The Boy Who Built the Boat. Mueller, Ross. 2007. (ENG.). 32p. (J). (gr. -1-k). 14.95 *(978-1-74114-393-5(4))* Allen & Unwin AUS. Dist: Independent Pubs. Group.
—Cat. Dumbleton, Mike. 2008. (ENG.). 32p. (J). (gr. -1-3). 10.99 *(978-1-933605-73-9(1))* Kane Miller.
—Clown's Pants. Eggleton, Jill. 2003. (Rigby Sails Early Ser.). (ENG.). 16p. (gr. 1-2). pap. 6.95 *(978-0-7578-8723-9(6))* Houghton Mifflin Harcourt Publishing Co.
—Clown's Party. Eggleton, Jill. 2003. (Rigby Sails Early Ser.). (ENG.). 16p. (gr. 1-2). pap. 6.95 *(978-0-7578-8669-0(8))* Houghton Mifflin Harcourt Publishing Co.
—Emily Eyefinger & the Balloon Bandits. Ball, Duncan. 7th ed. 2003. 112p. *(978-0-207-19940-0(X))* HarperCollins Pubs. Australia.
—Emily Eyefinger & the City in the Sky. Ball, Duncan. 2006. 112p. *(978-0-207-20067-0(X))* HarperCollins Pubs. Australia.
—Emily Eyefinger & the Ghost Ship. Ball, Duncan. 2004. 112p. (Orig.). *(978-0-207-19869-4(1))* HarperCollins Pubs. Australia.
—Emily Eyefinger & the Puzzle in the Jungle. Ball, Duncan. 2005. 112p. (Orig.). *(978-0-207-19903-5(5))* HarperCollins Pubs. Australia.
—Grandma Joins the All Blacks. McKinlay, Helen. 2007. 32p. pap. *(978-1-86950-640-7(5))* HarperCollins Pubs. Australia.
—Heather Fell in the Water. MacLeod, Doug. 2013. (ENG.). 32p. (J). (gr. -1-k). 19.99 *(978-1-74237-648-6(7))* Allen & Unwin AUS. Dist: Independent Pubs. Group.
—Hush Baby Hush. Rippin, Sally. 2009. (ENG.). 12p. (J). (gr. k — 1). bds. 7.99 *(978-1-74175-387-5(2))* Allen & Unwin AUS. Dist: Independent Pubs. Group.
—The Joker. Condon, Bill. 2004. iv, 36p. (J). pap. *(978-0-7608-6742-6(9))* Sundance/Newbridge Educational Publishing.
—Some Secrets Should Never Be Kept. Sanders, Jayneen. 2nd ed. 2013. (ENG.). 34p. (J). pap. *(978-0-9871860-1-0(9))* UpLoad Publishing Pty, Ltd.
Smith, Craig. The Baseball Card Kid. Smith, Craig. Osterweil, Adam. 2009. (ENG.). 199p. (J). (gr. 3-7). 17.95 *(978-1-59078-526-3(6),* Front Street) Boyds Mills Pr.
Smith, Crystal & Lin, Albert. Questions for Kids: A Book to Discover a Child's Imagination & Knowledge. Smith, Michael. 2003. 209p. (J). (gr. k-4). 13.95 *(978-0-9669437-3-3(2))* East West Discovery Pr.
Smith, Crystal, jt. illus. see Lin, Albert.
Smith, Dale & Russon, Anne E., photos by. What the Orangutan Told Alice: A Rain Forest Adventure. Smith, Dale. 2003. 192p. (gr. 6-12). pap. 15.95 *(978-0-9651452-8-2(X))* Deer Creek Publishing.
Smith, Dan. Portable Adventures: 8th Grade. Smith, Dan, ed. Nickoloff, Michael, ed. 2003. (YA). bds. 12.95 *(978-0-9728526-2-3(X))* Third World Games, Inc.
—Portable Adventures: Lair of the Rat King. Smith, Dan, ed. Nickoloff, Michael, ed. 2003. (YA). bds. 12.95 *(978-0-9728526-1-6(1))* Third World Games, Inc.
Smith, David. The Prehistoric Adventures of Dinosaur George: Jurassic Tigers. Blasing, George & Blasing, George. 2007. 16p. (J). 4.95 *(978-0-9797304-0-5(6))* Raining Popcorn Media.
Smith, David Preston. Anne of Green Gables, 1 vol. Kessler, Deirdre & Montgomery, L. M. ed. 2008. (ENG.). 46p. (J). (gr. k-5). pap. 10.95 *(978-1-55109-662-9(5))* Nimbus Publishing, Ltd. CAN. Dist: Orca Bk. Pubs. USA.
—Joe Howe to the Rescue, 1 vol. Bawtree, Michael. 2004. (ENG.). 152p. (J). (gr. 4-7). pap. 12.95 *(978-1-55109-495-3(9))* Nimbus Publishing, Ltd. CAN. Dist: Orca Bk. Pubs. USA.
—Tommy's New Block Skates, 1 vol. Vaughan, Garth. 2007. (ENG.). 32p. (J). (gr. -1-3). pap. 12.95 *(978-1-55109-620-9(X))* Nimbus Publishing, Ltd. CAN. Dist: Orca Bk. Pubs. USA.
Smith, Devin. The Real-Life Princess. Dunning, Rebecca. Rohman, Stefanie & Ritchie, Mary, eds. 2010. (ENG.). 40p. (J). pap. 13.99 *(978-0-9826670-0-2(0))* Awen Hse. Publishing.
Smith, Diana, jt. illus. see Last, Ian.
Smith, Dietrich. Crisis Intervention. Winick, Judd et al. rev. ed. 2006. (Outsiders Ser.: Vol. 4). (ENG.). 128p. (YA). pap. 12.99 *(978-1-4012-0973-5(4))* DC Comics.
Smith, Donald A. Enemies of Slavery. Adler, David A. 2004. (ENG.). 32p. (J). (gr. k-3). lib. bdg., tchr. ed. 16.95 *(978-0-8234-1596-0(1))* Holiday Hse., Inc.
—Heroes of the Revolution. Adler, David A. 2006. (ENG.). 32p. (J). (gr. 1-4). 7.99 *(978-0-8234-2017-9(5))* Holiday Hse., Inc.
Smith, Duane. Mama's Window. Rubright, Lynn. 2005. 89p. (J). 16.95 *(978-1-57480-160-6(0))* Lee & Low Bks., Inc.
—Mama's Window. Rubright, Lynn. 2008. 89p. (J). (gr. 3-7). 19.60 *(978-1-4178-1567-8(1),* Turtleback) Turtleback Bks.
—Seven Miles to Freedom: The Robert Smalls Story. Halfmann, Janet. 2008. 40p. (J). (gr. 1-6). 17.95 *(978-1-60060-232-0(0))* Lee & Low Bks., Inc.
Smith, Duane A. Night Journey to Vicksburg. Masters, Susan Rowan. Kilcoyne, Hope L., ed. 2003. (Adventures in America Ser.). 74p. (gr. 4). 14.95 *(978-1-893110-30-4(3))* Silver Moon Pr.
Smith, Duncan. People Are So Different! Clarke, Ann. 2008. 24p. 16.95 *(978-0-9787235-0-7(3))* Precious Little Bks.
Smith, Duriel. The Myths of the Lechuza. Alexander, David E. Date not set. 78p. (Orig.). (J). pap. 12.95 *(978-0-9623078-5-0(8))* Alexander Pubns.
Smith, Dwight. The Leaping Grasshopper. Archambault, Jeanne. 2006. 32p. (J). bds. 15.95 *(978-0-9763031-2-1(4))* Jitterbug Bks.
Smith, E. Boyd. In the Days of Giants. Brown, Abbie Farwell. 2008. 204p. per. 9.95 *(978-1-59915-044-4(1))* Yesterday's Classics.
—The Tortoise & the Geese & Other Fables of Bidpai. Dutton, Maude Barrows. 2008. 104p. pap. 7.95 *(978-1-59915-249-3(5))* Yesterday's Classics.
Smith, Elise & Smith, Kimanne. The Missing Trumpet Blues. 2004. 56p. (J). *(978-0-7652-3276-2(6))* Celebration Pr.
Smith, Elwood. See How They Run: Campaign Dreams, Election Schemes, & the Race to the White House. Goodman, Susan E. 2nd rev. ed. 2012. (ENG.). 96p. (J). (gr. 3-12). pap. 9.99 *(978-1-59990-897-7(2),* Bloomsbury USA Childrens) Bloomsbury USA.
—Señor Pancho Had a Rancho. Laínez, René Colato. 2014. (ENG & SPA.). 32p. (J). (gr. -1-1). 6.99 *(978-0-8234-3173-1(8))* Holiday Hse., Inc.
Smith, Elwood. How to Draw with Your Funny Bone. Smith, Elwood. 2015. (ENG.). 40p. (J). (gr. 1-3). 17.99 *(978-1-56846-243-1(3),* Creative Editions) Creative Co., The.
—I'm Not a Pig in Underpants. Smith, Elwood. 2013. (ENG.). 40p. (J). (gr. 1-3). 18.99 *(978-1-56846-229-5(8),* Creative Editions) Creative Co., The.
Smith, Elwood H. Catfish Kate & the Sweet Swamp Band. Weeks, Sarah. 2009. (ENG.). 32p. (J). (gr. -1-3). 17.99 *(978-1-4169-4026-5(X),* Atheneum Bks. for Young Readers) Simon & Schuster Children's Publishing.
—Hot Diggity Dog: The History of the Hot Dog. Sylver, Adrienne. 2010. (ENG.). 32p. (J). (gr. k-3). 16.99 *(978-0-525-47897-3(3),* Dutton Juvenile) Penguin Publishing Group.
—Señor Pancho Had a Rancho & Old MacDonald Had a Farm. Laínez, René Colato. 2013. (ENG.). 32p. (J). 16.95 *(978-0-8234-2632-4(7))* Holiday Hse., Inc.
—Stalling. Katz, Alan. 2010. (ENG.). 40p. (J). (gr. -1-2). 16.99 *(978-1-4169-5567-2(4),* McElderry, Margaret K. Bks.) McElderry, Margaret K. Bks.
—The Truth about Poop & Pee: All the Facts on the Ins & Outs of Bodily Functions. Goodman, Susan E. 2014. (ENG.). 144p. (J). (gr. 3-7). 6.99 *(978-0-14-751037-2(6),* Puffin) Penguin Publishing Group.
—Zoo Ah-Choooo. Mandel, Peter. 2012. (ENG.). 32p. (J). 16.95 *(978-0-8234-2317-0(4))* Holiday Hse., Inc.
Smith, Eric. The Blue Moon Effect. Freidman, Mel. gif. ed. 2005. (Extreme Monsters Ser.). 96p. (J). (gr. 2-5). per. 3.99 *(978-1-57791-178-4(4))* Brighter Minds Children's Publishing.
—Mr. Rabbit the Farmer. Chandler, Pauline. 2005. (ENG.). 24p. (J). lib. bdg. 23.65 *(978-1-59646-736-1(3))* Dingles & Co.
—Mummy's Little Monkey! Faulkner, Keith. 2006. 12p. (J). *(978-0-86461-700-2(3),* Koala Books) Scholastic Australia.
Smith, Eric, et al. This Little Piggy: And Other Favorite Rhymes. 2005. (Mother Goose Rhymes Ser.). (ENG.). 36p. (J). (gr. -1-k). 12.95 *(978-1-59249-466-8(8),* 1D013) Soundprints.
Smith, Eric. Water Views. Warren, Marion E., photos by. Carr, Stephen. 2003. 37.00 *(978-1-884878-08-4(3))* Annapolis Publishing Co.
Smith, Graham. Captain Ross & the Old Sea Ferry, 1 vol. Dale, Jay. 2012. (Engage Literacy Green Ser.). (ENG.). 32p. (gr. k-2). pap. 5.99 *(978-1-4296-9016-4(X),* Engage Literacy) Capstone Pr., Inc.
Smith, Guy, jt. illus. see Chen, Kuo Kang.
Smith, Guy, jt. illus. see Safarewicz, Evie.
Smith, Helen. A Home for Virginia. St. John, Patricia. 2005. (ENG.). 24p. (J). (gr. 4-7). 9.99 *(978-1-85792-961-4(6))* Christian Focus Pubns. GBR. Dist: Send The Light Distribution LLC.
—Princess Stories. Baxter, Nicola. 2013. (ENG.). 80p. (J). (gr. k-4). pap. 9.99 *(978-1-84322-954-4(4))* Anness Publishing GBR. Dist: National Bk. Network.
Smith, Hope Anita. Mother Poems. Smith, Hope Anita. 2009. (ENG.). 80p. (J). (gr. 5-8). 16.95 *(978-0-8050-8231-9(X),* Holt, Henry & Co. Bks. For Young Readers) Holt, Henry & Co.
Smith, Huhana. Haere: Farewell, Jack, Farewell. Tipene, Tim. 2006. 32p. (J). (gr. -1-3). pap. 12.00 *(978-1-86969-104-2(0))* Huia Pubs. NZL. Dist: Univ. of Hawaii Pr.
Smith, Iain. Angel Fish: A Pull & Lift Book. Smith, Iain. 2005. (Stories to Share Ser.). 12p. (J). 10.95 *(978-1-58117-084-9(X),* Intervisual/Piggy Toes) Bendon, Inc.
Smith, Ian. Rooster's Alarm. Smith, Ian. Julian, Sean. 2009. (Tadpoles Ser.). (ENG.). 24p. (J). (gr. -1-2). pap. *(978-0-7787-3905-0(8));* (gr. k-2). lib. bdg. *(978-0-7787-3874-9(4))* Crabtree Publishing Co.

Smith, Jack K. Huey P. Long: Talker & Doer, 1 vol. Collins, David R. 2003. (ENG.). 32p. (J). (gr. k-3). 16.99 *(978-1-56554-913-5(9))* Pelican Publishing Co., Inc.

Smith, Jacquelyn & Kalafatis, John. Pitty the City Kitty; Tokyo. Smith, Jacquelyn. 2009. 32p. (J). 15.99 *(978-1-935479-01-7(6))* A.M. Green Publishing.

Smith, Jacqui. The Rainbow Jars. Lincoln, James. 2013. 28p. (J). pap. 14.95 *(978-1-60131-153-5(2),* Castlebridge Bks.) Big Tent Bks.

Smith, James Noel. The Book of a Thousand Days. Hale, Shannon. 2007. (ENG.). 320p. (YA). (gr. 7-12). 17.95 *(978-1-59990-051-3(3),* Bloomsbury USA Childrens) Bloomsbury USA.

Smith, Jamie. The Case of the Four-Leaf Clover. Barbo, Maria S. & Preller, James. 2008. 104p. (J). pap. *(978-0-545-03837-9(5))* Scholastic, Inc.

—Home Safe Home. Slater, Teddy. 2010. 16p. (J). *(978-0-545-24606-4(7))* Scholastic, Inc.

—Martin Luthur King, Jr. Bauer, Marion Dane. 2009. (My First Biography Ser.). (ENG.). 32p. (J). (gr. -1-3). pap. 3.99 *(978-0-545-14233-5(4))* Scholastic, Inc.

—Mystery at the Aquarium (a Nightlight Detective Book) Orloff, Karen Kaufman. 2014. (ENG.). 26p. (J). 12.99 *(978-1-4413-1615-8(9),* 9781441316158) Peter Pauper Pr. Inc.

—Nightlight Detective: Big Top Circus Mystery. Orloff, Karen Kaufman. 2013. 42p. spiral bd. 12.99 *(978-1-4413-1227-3(7))* Peter Pauper Pr. Inc.

—Nightlight Detective: Mystery at the Museum. Orloff, Karen Kaufman. 2013. 42p. spiral bd. 12.99 *(978-1-4413-1228-0(5))* Peter Pauper Pr. Inc.

—Safety in the Bus. Slater, Teddy. 2010. 16p. (J). *(978-0-545-24602-6(4))* Scholastic, Inc.

—Street Safety. Slater, Teddy. 2010. 16p. (J). *(978-0-545-24604-0(0))* Scholastic, Inc.

Smith, Jamie & Alley, R. W. The Case of the Groaning Ghost. Preller, James. 2008. (Jigsaw Jones Mysteries Ser.: Bk. 32). 89p. (gr. 1-5). 15.00 *(978-0-7569-8302-4(9))* Perfection Learning Corp.

Smith, Jan. Apple Countdown. Holub, Joan. 2012. (J). *(978-1-61913-117-0(X))* Weigl Pubs., Inc.

—Apple Countdown. Holub, Joan. 2009. (ENG.). 32p. (J). (gr. -1-2). 16.99 *(978-0-8075-0398-0(3))* Whitman, Albert & Co.

—Dot to Dot Coloring & Stickers, 1 vol., 2. David, Juliet. 2008. (Candle Activity Fun Ser.). 24p. (J). (gr. 4-7). pap. 6.99 *(978-0-8254-7361-6(6),* Candle Bks.) Lion Hudson PLC GBR. Dist: Kregel Pubns.

—Dot to Dot Coloring & Stickers Bk. 1, 1 vol., 1. David, Juliet. 2008. (Candle Activity Fun Ser.). 24p. (J). (gr. 4-7). pap. 6.99 *(978-0-8254-7360-9(8),* Candle Bks.) Lion Hudson PLC GBR. Dist: Kregel Pubns.

—Pumpkin Countdown. Holub, Joan. 2012. (ENG.). 32p. (J). (gr. -1-2). 16.99 *(978-0-8075-6660-2(8))* Whitman, Albert & Co.

Smith, Jane. Five Silly Pumpkins: A Pop-up Halloween Book. Seal, Kerry. 2009. 10p. (J). 5.95 *(978-1-58117-908-8(1),* Intervisual/Piggy Toes) Bendon, Inc.

Smith, Jay F. A Day to Remember: A Sam & Coco Story. Smith, Jay F. 2005. 32p. (J). *(978-0-9764719-0-5(6))* MiceWorks.

Smith, Jeff. The Boy Who Wouldn't Sit Still!, Vol. 2. Lester, Sharon. 2nd ed. 2011. 40p. (J). 15.95 *(978-0-9802302-2-2(5))* Privileged Communications, LLC.

—Quest for the Spark. Sniegoski, Tom. (Bone Ser.). (ENG.). (J). (gr. 3-7). 2012. 240p. pap. 10.99 *(978-0-545-14104-8(4))*; Bk. 2. 2012. 240p. 26.99 *(978-0-545-14103-1(6))*; Bk. 3. 2013. 288p. pap. 10.99 *(978-0-545-14106-2(0))*; No. 3. 2013. 288p. 22.99 *(978-0-545-14105-5(2))* Scholastic, Inc. (Graphix).

Smith, Jeff. Crown of Horns. Smith, Jeff. 2009. (Bone Ser.: 9). (ENG.). 224p. (J). (gr. 4-7). 26.99 *(978-0-439-70631-5(9))*; pap. 10.99 *(978-0-439-70632-2(7))* Scholastic, Inc. (Graphix).

—The Dragonslayer. Smith, Jeff. 2006. (Bone Ser.: 4). (ENG.). 176p. (J). (gr. 3-7). 26.99 *(978-0-439-70626-1(2))*; pap. 12.99 *(978-0-439-70637-7(8))* Scholastic, Inc. (Graphix).

—Out from Boneville. Smith, Jeff. 2005. (Bone Ser.: 1). (ENG.). 144p. (J). pap. 26.99 *(978-0-439-70623-0(8),* Graphix) Scholastic, Inc.

—Quest for the Spark, Bk. 1. Smith, Jeff. Sniegoski, Tom. 2011. (BONE: Quest for the Spark Ser.: 1). (ENG.). 224p. (J). (gr. 3-7). 22.99 *(978-0-545-14101-7(X))*; pap. 10.99 *(978-0-545-14102-4(8))* Scholastic, Inc. (Graphix).

—Tall Tales. Smith, Jeff. Sniegoski, Tom. 2010. (Bone Ser.). (ENG.). 128p. (J). (gr. 4-7). 22.99 *(978-0-545-14095-9(1),* Graphix) Scholastic, Inc.

—Tall Tales. Smith, Jeff. Sniegoski, Tom. 2010. (Bone Ser.). (ENG.). 128p. (J). (gr. 4-7). pap. 12.99 *(978-0-545-14096-6(X),* Graphix) Scholastic, Inc.

Smith, Jeff & Hamaker, Steve. Eyes of the Storm. Smith, Jeff. 2006. (Bone Ser.: 3). (ENG.). 192p. (J). (gr. 3-7). 26.99 *(978-0-439-70625-4(4))*; pap. 12.99 *(978-0-439-70638-4(6))* Scholastic, Inc. (Graphix).

—Ghost Circles. Smith, Jeff. 2008. (Bone Ser.: 7). (ENG.). 160p. (J). (gr. 4-7). 26.99 *(978-0-439-70629-2(7))*; pap. 12.99 *(978-0-439-70634-6(3))* Scholastic, Inc. (Graphix).

—The Great Cow Race. Smith, Jeff. 2005. (Bone Ser.: 2). (ENG.). 144p. (J). (gr. 4-7). 26.99 *(978-0-439-70624-7(6))*; pap. 12.99 *(978-0-439-70639-1(4))* Scholastic, Inc. (Graphix).

—Old Man's Cave. Smith, Jeff. 2007. (Bone Ser.: 6). (ENG.). 128p. (J). (gr. 4-7). 26.99 *(978-0-439-70628-5(9))*; pap. 12.99 *(978-0-439-70635-3(1))* Scholastic, Inc.

—Out from Boneville. Smith, Jeff. 2005. (Bone Ser.: 1). (ENG.). 144p. (J). pap. 12.99 *(978-0-439-70640-7(8),* Graphix) Scholastic, Inc.

—Rock Jaw: Master of the Eastern Border. Smith, Jeff. 2007. (Bone Ser.: 5). (ENG.). 128p. (J). (gr. 4-7). pap. 12.99 *(978-0-439-70636-0(X),* Graphix) Scholastic, Inc.

Smith, Jeff, jt. illus. see Hamaker, Steve.

Smith, Jeffrey. Peachboy. Metaxas, Eric. 2005. (Rabbit Ears Ser.). 36p. (gr. k-6). 25.65 *(978-1-59679-227-2(2))* Spotlight.

Smith, Jen. Big Ted's Guide to Tapping: Positive EFT Emotional Freedom Techniques for Children. Kent, Alex. 2013. 26p. pap. *(978-1-908269-40-9(5))* DragonRising Publishing.

Smith, Jenni. The Inspired ABC's. Branch, Jennifer. 2008. 60p. (J). per. 16.99 *(978-0-615-18948-2(2))* Laughing Baby Pubns.

Smith, Jeremy. Zoo Force: Dear Eniko. Thomas, John Ira. 2003. 68p. per. 6.95 *(978-0-9743147-1-6(4))* Candle Light Pr.

Smith, Jerry. The Adventures of Inka the Feline. Janowski, Alice. 2010. 36p. pap. 14.00 *(978-1-60844-576-9(3))* Dog Ear Publishing, LLC.

Smith, Jessie Willcox. The Children of Dickens. Crothers, Samuel McChord. 2005. (ENG.). 150p. (gr. 4-7). pap. 14.95 *(978-0-89733-475-4(2),* Academy Chicago Pubs., Ltd.) Chicago Review Pr., Inc.

—A Child's Book of Stories. Coussens, Penrhyn W. 2008. 608p. pap. 19.95 *(978-1-59915-248-6(7))* Yesterday's Classics.

—Twas the Night Before Christmas: A Visit from St. Nicholas. Moore, Clement C. 2015. (J). pap. *(978-1-4677-7805-3(2),* First Avenue Editions) Lerner Publishing Group.

Smith, Jessie Willcox. 'Twas the Night Before Christmas. Smith, Jessie Willcox. Moore, Clement C. 2005. (ENG.). 32p. (J). (gr. -1-3). 6.99 *(978-0-618-61510-0(5))*; 14.00 *(978-0-618-61682-4(9))* Houghton Mifflin Harcourt Publishing Co.

Smith, Jim. How to Be a Detective. Waddell, Dan. 2012. (ENG.). 24p. (J). (gr. 2-4). 19.99 *(978-0-7636-6142-7(2))* Candlewick Pr.

Smith, Jim W. W., jt. illus. see Loxton, Daniel.

Smith, Jonathan. Comanche 1800-74. Meed, Douglas V. 2003. (Warrior Ser.: 75). (ENG.). 64p. pap. *(978-1-84176-587-7(2),* Osprey Publishing) Bloomsbury Publishing Plc.

Smith, Jordyn. Rich the Itch. McHaney, Eric & McHaney, Mandy. l.t. ed. 2005. 20p. (J). *(978-0-9769086-0-9(3))* RTI Publishing, LLC.

Smith, Jos. A. Bandit's Moon. Fleischman, Sid. 2008. (ENG.). 192p. (J). (gr. 3-7). pap. 6.99 *(978-0-06-145096-9(0),* Greenwillow Bks.) HarperCollins Pubs.

Smith, Jos. A. Gregor Mendel: The Friar Who Grew Peas. Bardoe, Cheryl. (ENG.). (J). (gr. k-4). 2015. 32p. pap. 9.95 ***(978-1-4197-1840-3(1))***; 2006. 40p. 21.95 *(978-0-8109-5475-5(3))* Abrams. (Abrams Bks. for Young Readers).

Smith, Jos. A. Jim Ugly. Fleischman, Sid. 2003. (ENG.). 144p. (J). (gr. 3-7). pap. 6.99 *(978-0-06-052121-9(X),* Greenwillow Bks.) HarperCollins Pubs.

—The Witch's Child. Yorinks, Arthur. 2007. (ENG.). 34p. (J). (gr. 1-4). 17.95 *(978-0-8109-9349-5(X),* Abrams Bks. for Young Readers) Abrams.

Smith, Keith. Dibe Lizhini Jiliigo Bee Shanah IDLI/Proud to Be a Blacksheep. John, Roberta. Thomas, Peter A., tr. from ENG. 2007. (NAV & ENG.). 32p. (J). (gr. 4-7). 17.95 *(978-1-893354-05-0(9))* Salina Bookshelf Inc.

—Little Prankster Girl: At'Eed Adilahi Yazhi. Blue, Martha. Ruffenach, Jessie, ed. Thomas, Peter, tr. from NAV. 2008. (NAV & ENG.). 32p. (J). (gr. -1-3). 17.95 *(978-1-893354-36-4(9))* Salina Bookshelf Inc.

Smith, Keri. Tear up This Book! The Sticker, Stencil, Stationery, Games, Crafts, Doodle, & Journal Book for Girls! Smith, Keri. Magruder, Trula, ed. 2005. (ENG.). 96p. (J). (gr. 3-7). spiral bd. 10.95 *(978-1-58485-977-2(6),* American Girl) American Girl Publishing, Inc.

Smith, Kim. Abuela's Birthday. Jules, Jacqueline. 2015. (Sofia Martinez Ser.). (ENG.). 32p. (gr. k-2). lib. bdg. 19.99 *(978-1-4795-5775-2(7),* Sofia Martinez) Picture Window Bks.

—Kaugjakjuk. Lewis, Marion. 2011. (ENG.). 40p. (J). (gr. 1-3). 13.95 *(978-1-926569-39-0(3))* Inhabit Media Inc. CAN. Dist: Independent Pubs. Group.

—The Marigold Mess. Jules, Jacqueline. 2015. (Sofia Martinez Ser.). (ENG.). 32p. (gr. k-2). lib. bdg. 19.99 *(978-1-4795-5776-9(5,* Sofia Martinez) Picture Window Bks.

—The Missing Mouse. Jules, Jacqueline. 2015. (Sofia Martinez Ser.). (ENG.). 32p. (gr. k-2). lib. bdg. 19.99 *(978-1-4795-5774-5(9),* Sofia Martinez) Picture Window Bks.

—My Family Adventure. Jules, Jacqueline. 2015. (Sofia Martinez Ser.). (ENG.). 96p. (gr. k-2). pap. 4.95 *(978-1-4795-5790-5(0),* Sofia Martinez) Picture Window Bks.

—Picture Perfect. Jules, Jacqueline. 2015. (Sofia Martinez Ser.). (ENG.). 32p. (gr. k-2). lib. bdg. 19.99 *(978-1-4795-5773-8(0),* Sofia Martinez) Picture Window Bks.

—A Ticket Around the World. Diaz, Natalia & Owens, Melissa. 2015. (ENG.). 32p. (J). (gr. k-3). 16.95 *(978-1-77147-051-3(8))* Owlkids Bks. Inc. CAN. Dist: Perseus-PGW.

Smith, Kimanne. Demanding Justice: A Story about Mary Ann Shadd Cary. Ferris, Jeri Chase. 2003. (Creative Minds Biographies Ser.). (ENG.). 64p. (gr. 4-8). 22.60 *(978-1-57505-177-2(X))*; pap. 8.95 *(978-0-87614-928-7(X),* Carolrhoda Bks.) Lerner Publishing Group.

Smith, Kimanne, jt. illus. see Smith, Elise.

Smith, Kuleigh. ¿Chili Texano? ¡Ay Dios! Vermillion, Patricia. Guadalupe, Jezabel, tr. from ENG. 2013. (SPA & ENG.). 40p. 21.95 *(978-0-87565-584-0(X))* Texas Christian Univ. Pr.

—Texas Chili? Oh My! Vermillion, Patricia. 2013. (ENG.). 40p. 21.95 *(978-0-87565-568-0(8))* Texas Christian Univ. Pr.

Smith, Landa. Not Again, Mr. Cat! Johnson, Kimberly P. 2003. 36p. (J). (gr. k-3). 14.95 *(978-1-57197-362-7(1),* Ivy House Publishing Group) Pentland Pr., Inc.

Smith, Lane. Baloney (Henry P.) Scieszka, Jon. 2005. (gr. -1-3). 17.00 *(978-0-7569-5494-9(0))* Perfection Learning Corp.

—Baloney (Henry P.) Scieszka, Jon. 2005. (ENG.). 40p. (J). (gr. k-k). pap. 6.99 *(978-0-14-240430-0(6),* Puffin) Penguin Publishing Group.

—Los Caballeros de la Mesa de la Cocina. Scieszka, Jon. (SPA.). (J). (gr. 5-8). 7.95 *(978-958-04-3400-9(X),* NR4516) Norma S.A. COL. Dist: Distribuidora Norma, Inc., Lectorum Pubns., Inc.

—The Good, the Bad, & the Goofy. Scieszka, Jon. 2004. (Time Warp Trio Ser.: 3). (ENG.). 80p. (J). (gr. 2-4). pap. 4.99 *(978-0-14-240046-3(7),* Puffin) Penguin Publishing Group.

—The Good, the Bad, & the Goofy. Scieszka, Jon. 2005. (Time Warp Trio Ser.: No. 3). 70p. (gr. 4-7). 15.00 *(978-0-7569-5876-3(8))* Perfection Learning Corp.

—It's All Greek to Me, No. 8. Scieszka, Jon. 2004. (Time Warp Trio Ser.: 8). (ENG.). 96p. (J). (gr. 2-4). pap. 4.99 *(978-0-14-240116-3(1),* Puffin) Penguin Publishing Group.

—It's All Greek to Me. Scieszka, Jon. 2006. (Time Warp Trio Ser.: No. 8). 71p. (gr. 4-7). 15.00 *(978-0-7569-6780-2(5))* Perfection Learning Corp.

—Kid Sheriff & the Terrible Toads. Shea, Bob. 2014. (ENG.). 32p. (J). (gr. -1-3). 17.99 *(978-1-59643-975-7(0))* Roaring Brook Pr.

—Lulu & the Brontosaurus. Viorst, Judith. (ENG.). 128p. (J). (gr. 1-5). 2012. pap. 7.99 *(978-1-4169-9962-1(0))*; 2010. 17.99 *(978-1-4169-9961-4(2))* Simon & Schuster Children's Publishing. (Atheneum Bks. for Young Readers).

—Lulu Walks the Dogs. Viorst, Judith. (ENG.). (J). (gr. 1-5). 2014. 176p. pap. 7.99 *(978-1-4424-3580-3(1))*; 2012. 160p. 16.99 *(978-1-4424-3579-7(8))* Simon & Schuster Children's Publishing. (Atheneum Bks. for Young Readers).

—Lulu's Mysterious Mission. Viorst, Judith. 2015. (ENG.). 192p. (J). (gr. 1-5). pap. 7.99 *(978-1-4424-9747-4(5))* Simon & Schuster Children's Publishing.

—Math Curse. Scieszka, Jon. 2011. (J). (gr. 1-4). 29.95 *(978-0-545-13458-3(7))* Weston Woods Studios, Inc.

—El Pirata Barbanegra. Scieszka, Jon. (SPA.). (J). (gr. 5-8). 7.95 *(978-958-04-3401-6(8),* NR8584) Norma S.A. COL. Dist: Distribuidora Norma, Inc., Lectorum Pubns., Inc.

—Princess Hyacinth. Heide, Florence Parry. 2009. (ENG.). 48p. (J). (gr. -1-3). 17.99 *(978-0-375-84501-7(1),* Schwartz & Wade Bks.) Random Hse. Children's Bks.

—Science Verse. Scieszka, Jon. 2004. (ENG.). 40p. (J). (gr. 2-5). 17.99 *(978-0-670-91057-1(0),* Viking Juvenile) Penguin Publishing Group.

—Seen Art? Scieszka, Jon. 2005. (ENG.). 48p. (J). (gr. -1-2). 16.99 *(978-0-670-05986-7(2),* Viking Juvenile) Penguin Publishing Group.

—Squids Will Be Squids: Fresh Morals, Beastly Fables. Scieszka, Jon. 2003. (ENG.). 48p. (J). (gr. 3-7). pap. 7.99 *(978-0-14-250040-8(2),* Puffin) Penguin Publishing Group.

—Summer Reading Is Killing Me! Scieszka, Jon. 2004. (Time Warp Trio Ser.: 7). (ENG.). 80p. (J). (gr. 2-4). pap. 4.99 *(978-0-14-240115-6(3),* Puffin) Penguin Publishing Group.

—Summer Reading Is Killing Me! Scieszka, Jon. 2004. (Time Warp Trio Ser.: No. 7). 73p. (J). (gr. 4-7). 12.65 *(978-0-7569-6781-9(3))* Perfection Learning Corp.

—The True Story of the 3 Little Pigs. Scieszka, Jon. 2011. (J). (gr. -1-3). 29.95 *(978-0-545-09457-3(7))*; 18.95 *(978-0-545-09459-7(3))* Weston Woods Studios, Inc.

—The True Story of the 3 Little Pigs! Scieszka, Jon. 25th anniv. ed. 2014. (ENG.). 32p. (J). (gr. k-3). 17.99 *(978-0-451-47195-6(4),* Viking Juvenile) Penguin Publishing Group.

—Tu Mama Era Neanderthal. Scieszka, Jon. (SPA.). (J). (gr. 5-8). 7.95 *(978-958-04-5045-0(5),* NR3076) Norma S.A. COL. Dist: Distribuidora Norma, Inc., Lectorum Pubns., Inc.

—Tut, Tut, No. 6. Scieszka, Jon. 2004. (Time Warp Trio Ser.: 6). (ENG.). 96p. (J). (gr. 2-4). pap. 4.99 *(978-0-14-240047-0(5),* Puffin) Penguin Publishing Group.

—Tut, Tut. Scieszka, Jon. 2004. (Time Warp Trio Ser.: No. 6). 74p. (gr. 4-7). 15.00 *(978-0-7569-4050-8(8))* Perfection Learning Corp.

—Your Mother Was a Neanderthal. Scieszka, Jon. 2004. (Time Warp Trio Ser.: 4). (ENG.). 80p. (J). (gr. 2-4). pap. 4.99 *(978-0-14-240048-7(3),* Puffin) Penguin Publishing Group.

—Your Mother Was a Neanderthal. Scieszka, Jon. 2006. (Time Warp Trio Ser.: No. 4). 78p. (gr. 4-7). 15.00 *(978-0-7569-6782-6(1))* Perfection Learning Corp.

—Your Mother Was a Neanderthal. Scieszka, Jon. ed. 2004. (Time Warp Trio Ser.: 4). 78p. (J). 14.75 *(978-1-4176-3603-7(3))* Turtleback Bks.

—2095. Scieszka, Jon. 2004. (Time Warp Trio Ser.: 5). (ENG.). 80p. (J). (gr. 2-4). pap. 4.99 *(978-0-14-240044-9(0),* Puffin) Penguin Publishing Group.

—2095. Scieszka, Jon. 2005. (Time Warp Trio Ser.: No. 5). 72p. (gr. 4-7). 15.00 *(978-0-7569-5989-0(6))* Perfection Learning Corp.

Smith, Lane. Abe Lincoln's Dream. Smith, Lane. 2012. (ENG.). 32p. (J). (gr. k-4). 16.99 *(978-1-59643-608-4(5))* Roaring Brook Pr.

—Cowboy & Octopus. Smith, Lane. Scieszka, Jon. 2007. (ENG.). 40p. (J). (gr. k-k). 16.99 *(978-0-670-91058-8(9),* Viking Juvenile) Penguin Publishing Group.

—Grandpa Green. Smith, Lane. 2011. (ENG.). 32p. (J). (gr. k-4). 16.99 *(978-1-59643-607-7(7))* Roaring Brook Pr.

—Inaho Kitab. Smith, Lane. 2015.Tr. of It's a Book. (ARA & ENG.). 32p. pap. 8.95 *(978-99921-95-52-9(5),* 232851) Bloomsbury Qatar Foundation Publishing QAT. Dist: Macmillan.

—It's a Book. Smith, Lane. 2010. (ENG.). 32p. (J). (gr. 1-5). 12.99 *(978-1-59643-606-0(9))* Roaring Brook Pr.

—John, Paul, George & Ben. Smith, Lane. 2006. (ENG.). 40p. (J). (gr. -1 — 1). 17.99 *(978-0-7868-4893-5(6))* Hyperion Pr.

—Madam President. Smith, Lane. 2008. (ENG.). 40p. (J). (gr. -1-k). 16.99 *(978-1-4231-0846-7(9))* Hyperion Pr.

Smith, Lawrence Beall. Me & Caleb. Meyer, Franklyn E. 2006. (J). kivar 16.95 *(978-0-9789388-0-2(1))* Hester Publishing.

Smith, Lesley. Little Red Hen & the Wheat. Andrews, Jackie. 2012. (ENG.). 32p. pap. 6.50 *(978-1-84135-190-2(3))* Award Pubns. Ltd. GBR. Dist: Parkwest Pubns., Inc.

—My Big Book of Rhymes. 2012. (ENG.). 96p. (J). 13.50 *(978-1-84135-134-6(2))* Award Pubns. Ltd. GBR. Dist: Parkwest Pubns., Inc.

—Three Little Kittens. Andrews, Jackie. 2012. (ENG.). 32p. (J). pap. 6.50 *(978-1-84135-197-1(0))* Award Pubns. Ltd. GBR. Dist: Parkwest Pubns., Inc.

Smith, Lisa. Little Troll. Dolan, Penny. 2008. (Tadpoles Ser.). (ENG.). 24p. (J). (gr. -1-3). lib. bdg. *(978-0-7787-3856-5(6))* Crabtree Publishing Co.

—Plip & Plop. Dolan, Penny. 2004. (Read-It! Readers Ser.). (J). lib. bdg. 18.60 *(978-1-4048-0551-4(6))* Picture Window Bks.

Smith, Lurs Schwarz. Sing a Song with Baby, 2 vol. Thienes-Schunemann, Mary. 2003. 50p. (J). 21.95 incl. audio compact disk *(978-0-9708397-5-6(8))* Naturally You Can Sing.

Smith, Maggie. Daddy Is a Cozy Hug. Greene, Rhonda Gowler. 2010. (ENG.). 32p. (J). (gr. -1-1). 14.99 *(978-0-8027-9728-5(8))* Walker & Co.

—Feet Go to Sleep. Bottner, Barbara. 2015. (ENG.). 32p. (J). (gr. -1-2). 16.99 *(978-0-449-81325-6(8),* Knopf Bks. for Young Readers) Random Hse. Children's Bks.

—Good Thing You're Not an Octopus! Markes, Julie & Markes. 2006. (ENG.). 40p. (J). (gr. -1-3). pap. 6.99 *(978-0-06-443586-4(5))* HarperCollins Pubs.

—Let's Talk about Being Away from Your Parents. Berry, Joy. 2010. (Let's Talk About Ser.). (ENG.). 32p. (J). (gr. -1-k). pap. 4.99 *(978-1-60577-202-8(X))* Berry, Joy Enterprises.

—Let's Talk about Being Patient. Berry, Joy. 2010. (Let's Talk About Ser.). (ENG.). 32p. (J). (gr. -1-k). pap. 4.99 *(978-1-60577-209-7(7))* Berry, Joy Enterprises.

—Let's Talk about Being Shy. Berry, Joy. 2010. (Let's Talk About Ser.). (ENG.). 32p. (J). (gr. -1-k). pap. 4.99 *(978-1-60577-220-2(8))* Berry, Joy Enterprises.

—Let's Talk about Feeling Afraid. Berry, Joy. 2010. (Let's Talk About Ser.). (ENG.). 32p. (J). (gr. -1-k). pap. 4.99 *(978-1-60577-205-9(4))* Berry, Joy Enterprises.

—Let's Talk about Feeling Angry. Berry, Joy. 2010. (Let's Talk About Ser.). (ENG.). 32p. (J). (gr. -1-k). pap. 4.99 *(978-1-60577-207-3(0))* Berry, Joy Enterprises.

—Let's Talk about Feeling Disappointed. Berry, Joy. 2010. (Let's Talk About Ser.). (ENG.). 32p. (J). (gr. -1-k). pap. 4.99 *(978-1-60577-204-2(6))* Berry, Joy Enterprises.

—Let's Talk about Feeling Jealous. Berry, Joy. 2010. (Let's Talk About Ser.). (ENG.). 32p. (J). (gr. -1-k). pap. 4.99 *(978-1-60577-223-3(2))* Berry, Joy Enterprises.

—Let's Talk about Feeling Sad. Berry, Joy. 2010. (Let's Talk About Ser.). (ENG.). 32p. (J). (gr. -1-k). pap. 4.99 *(978-1-60577-206-6(2))* Berry, Joy Enterprises.

—Let's Talk about Feeling Worried. Berry, Joy. 2010. (Let's Talk About Ser.). (ENG.). 32p. (J). (gr. -1-k). pap. 4.99 *(978-1-60577-221-9(6))* Berry, Joy Enterprises.

—Let's Talk about Getting Hurt. Berry, Joy. 2010. (Let's Talk About Ser.). (ENG.). 32p. (J). (gr. -1-k). pap. 4.99 *(978-1-60577-203-5(8))* Berry, Joy Enterprises.

—Let's Talk about Needing Attention. Berry, Joy. 2010. (Let's Talk About Ser.). (ENG.). 32p. (J). (gr. -1-k). pap. 4.99 *(978-1-60577-222-6(4))* Berry, Joy Enterprises.

—¡Libro! George, Kristine O'Connell. 2008. (SPA & ENG.). 30p. (J). (gr. k — 1). bds. 5.95 *(978-0-547-15406-0(2))* Houghton Mifflin Harcourt Publishing Co.

—Mommy Is a Soft, Warm Kiss. Greene, Rhonda Gowler. 2010. (ENG.). 32p. (J). (gr. -1-1). 14.99 *(978-0-8027-9729-2(6))* Walker & Co.

—Our Library. Bunting, Eve. 2008. (ENG.). 32p. (J). (gr. -1-3). 16.00 *(978-0-618-49458-3(8))* Houghton Mifflin Harcourt Publishing Co.

—What Does Bunny See? A Book of Colors & Flowers. Park, Linda Sue. 2005. (ENG.). 32p. (J). (gr. -1-3). 15.00 *(978-0-618-23485-1(3))* Houghton Mifflin Harcourt Publishing Co.

Smith, Mandy M. Evan & Cassie Go on a Train Meet, 1 vol. Smith, B. M. 2009. 35p. pap. 24.95 *(978-1-60836-552-4(2))* America Star Bks.

Smith, Marcelle. Jasmine Finds a Doctor. Smith, Leone. 2011. 30p. pap. 12.50 *(978-1-61204-042-4(X),* Strategic Bk. Publishing) Strategic Book Publishing & Rights Agency (SBPRA).

Smith, Mary Ann Free. Come Follow Me: A Child's Guide to Faith, Hope, & Charity. Newell, Karmel H. 2003. (J). 16.95 *(978-1-57008-809-4(8),* Bookcraft, Inc.) Deseret Bk. Co.

Smith, Mary C. A Day in the Life of William Bray Goat. Smith, Mary C. Date not set. (J). 16.95 *(978-1-889668-11-6(7))* Smith & Daniel.

Smith, Mary Claire. Nightspinners. Petty, Kate. 2003. (ENG.). 32p. (J). (gr. k-2). 14.99 *(978-1-85881-836-8(2),* Orion Children's Bks.) Hachette Children's Group GBR. Dist: Independent Pubs. Group.

—The Nightspinners. Petty, Kate. 2004. 32p. (J). pap. 8.99 *(978-1-84255-105-9(1),* Dolphin Paperbacks) Orion Publishing Group, Ltd. GBR. Dist: Trafalgar Square Publishing.

Smith, Mary Elizabeth. Coffee with Orange Sherbert: Friendship Can Be Found Where Eyes & Hearts Are Open. Shell, S. E. 2012. (ENG.). 42p. (J). pap. 14.99 *(978-0-9885461-2-7(4))* Osherbert Bks., LLC.

Smith, Matt. All God's Bugs. Derico, Laura. 2013. (Happy Day Ser.). (ENG.). 16p. (J). pap. 2.49 *(978-1-4143-9295-0(8))* Tyndale Hse. Pubs.

Smith, Matt. All God's Bugs. Derico, Laura Ring. 2015. (Faith That Sticks Ser.). (ENG.). 30p. (J). pap. 3.99 ***(978-1-4964-0317-9(7))*** Tyndale Hse. Pubs.

Smith, Matt. Lenny Cyrus, School Virus. Schreiber, Joe. (ENG.). 288p. (gr. 5-7). 2014. (YA). pap. 6.99 *(978-0-544-33628-5(3),* HMH Books For Young Readers); 2013. (J). 15.99 *(978-0-547-89315-0(9))* Houghton Mifflin Harcourt Publishing Co.

Smith, Matt. Barbarian Lord. Smith, Matt. 2014. (ENG.). 176p. (YA). (gr. 7-12). 17.99 *(978-0-547-85906-4(6))* Houghton Mifflin Harcourt Publishing Co.

Smith, Matthew, et al. Enemies & Allies, Vol. 4. Marz, Ron. 2004. (Path Ser.: Vol. 4). 160p. (YA). pap. 15.95 *(978-1-59314-052-6(5))* CrossGeneration Comics, Inc.

Smith, Mavis. Fluffy's Happy Halloween. McMullan, Kate. 2004. (Fluffy, the Classroom Guinea Pig Ser.). 40p. (J). lib. bdg. 15.00 *(978-1-59054-464-8(1))* Fitzgerald Bks.

Smith, Mindy. Little H 2 O: A Story about the Rain Cycle. Holladay, Shirley. 2011. (ENG.). 24p. pap. 10.00 *(978-1-4538-9295-4(8))* CreateSpace Independent Publishing Platform.

Smith-Moore, J. J. The Adventures of Lulu. Hay, Louise L. 2005. (ENG.). 96p. per. 12.95 *(978-1-4019-0553-8(6))* Hay Hse., Inc.

Smith, Naniloa. The Children are Happy CD with Animals from the Southwest. Smith, Naniloa. 2004. (J). cd-rom 5.00 *(978-0-9744005-2-5(1))* In the Desert.

Smith, Nathan. Little Flathead & the Black Pearl. Wakefield, Nelida. 2009. 36p. pap. 12.99 *(978-1-59858-828-6(1))* Dog Ear Publishing, LLC.

Smith, Nial. The Lord's Prayer: Explained for Children. Steven, Kenneth C. 2006. (ENG.). 32p. 12.99 *(978-1-904325-19-2(X))* Saint Andrew Pr., Ltd. GBR. Dist: Westminster John Knox Pr.

Smith, Nina & Nelson, Thea. Swute's Stories: The Circle Must Grow. Nelson, Thea. 2011. (ENG.). 92p. pap. 9.00 *(978-1-4538-8628-1(1))* CreateSpace Independent Publishing Platform.

Smith, Owen. Magnus at the Fire. Armstrong, Jennifer. 2005. (ENG.). 32p. (J). (gr. k-3). 17.99 *(978-0-689-83922-1(7))*, Simon & Schuster Bks. For Young Readers) Simon & Schuster Bks. For Young Readers.

—This Is the Game. Shore, Diane ZuHone & Alexander, Jessica. 2011. (ENG.). 32p. (J). (gr. -1-3). 16.99 *(978-0-06-055522-1(X))* HarperCollins Pubs.

Smith, P. Athene. Captive Birds in Health & Disease: A Practical Guide for Those Who Keep Gamebirds, Raptors, Parrots, Waterfowl & Other Species. Smith, P. Athene, tr. Cooper, John E., tr. 2003. 132p. 34.95 *(978-0-88839-538-2(8))* Hancock Hse. Pubs.

Smith, Paul, et al. Avengers: Falcon. 2014. (ENG.). 216p. (J). (gr. 4-17). pap. 24.99 *(978-0-7851-8826-1(6))* Marvel Worldwide, Inc.

Smith, Paul & Byrne, John. Alpha Flight. Claremont, Chris et al. 2011. (ENG.). 280p. (J). (gr. 4-17). 34.99 *(978-0-7851-5513-3(9))* Marvel Worldwide, Inc.

Smith, Paul, jt. illus. see Wieringo, Mike.

Smith, Phil. How Does a Plant Grow? Lowery, Lawrence F. (J). 2013. *(978-1-936959-60-0(7))*; 2012. (ENG.). 40p. pap. *(978-1-936959-47-1(X))* National Science Teachers Assn.

—How Tall Was Milton? Lowery, Lawrence F. 2012. (ENG.). 40p. (J). pap. *(978-1-936959-43-3(7))* National Science Teachers Assn.

—Rubber vs. Glass: I Wonder Why. Lowery, Lawrence F. 2014. (ENG.). 36p. (J). pap. 11.95 *(978-1-938946-50-9(2))* National Science Teachers Assn.

Smith, R. M. An A to Z Walk in the Park (Animal Alphabet Book) Smith, R. M. 2008. (ENG.). 32p. (J). per. 7.95 *(978-0-615-19572-8(5))* Clarence-Henry Bks.

Smith, Rachael. Flying Solo. Stephas, Kristi. 2005. 40p. (J). 16.95 *(978-0-9764983-2-2(4))* Toy Truck Publishing.

Smith, Rachel. A Purple Hippopotamus Pillow & Pink Penguin Sheets. Maurer, Amy J. 2006. 52p. (J). 19.99 *(978-1-59879-239-3(3))*; per. 15.99 *(978-1-59879-167-9(2))* Lifevest Publishing, Inc.

Smith, Raissa B., jt. illus. see Smith, Brock R.

Smith, Raven, et al. God Loves to Color Too! Smith, Scott. l.t. ed. 2011. (ENG.). 42p. pap. 12.99 *(978-1-4538-1994-4(0))* CreateSpace Independent Publishing Platform.

Smith, Raven, photos by. Making Stuff for Kids. Waley, Safiya & Woodcock, Victoria. 2007. (ENG., 160p. pap. 24.95 *(978-1-906155-00-1(3))* Black Dog Publishing Ltd. GBR. Dist: Perseus Distribution.

Smith, Richard. The Trouble with Adam's Heart. Bancroft, Myles. Brouillette, Peter, ed. 2004. (YA). per. 19.99 *(978-0-9760419-4-8(4))* ThatsMyLife Co.

Smith, Richard G. The Princess of Booray. Murphy, Emily. 2005. (J). *(978-0-9742891-2-0(4))* Marriwell Publishing.

Smith, Richard Shirley. The Prettiest Love Letters in the World: Letters Between Lucrezia Borgia & Pietro Bembo 1503 to 1519. Shankland, Hugh, tr. 2005. 111p. (YA). reprint ed. pap. 17.00 *(978-0-7567-9495-8(1))* DIANE Publishing Co.

Smith, Robin Wayne. If You Got It, a Truck Brought It. Smith, Robin Wayne. 2012. 20p. pap. 6.00 *(978-0-615-63721-1(3))* Bright Tyke Creations LLC.

Smith, Sandra. Come Follow Me Bk. 1: Understanding One's Worth: Color Orange. Allgood, Jean. l.t. ed. 2004. 23p. (J). 14.95 *(978-0-9741627-3-7(6))* Write Designs, Ltd.

Smith, Sarah. Where's My Mommy? 2009. (J). *(978-0-7607-8404-4(3))* Barnes & Noble, Inc.

Smith, Shane W. The Lesser Evil, Book 3 Comic Book. Smith, Shane W. 2012. 114p. pap. *(978-1-927384-04-6(4))* Zeta Comics.

Smith, Simon. Eggs, Legs, Wings: A Butterfly Life Cycle, 1 vol. Knudsen, Shannon. 2011. (First Graphics: Nature Cycles Ser.). (ENG.). 24p. (gr. 1-2). lib. bdg. 23.32 *(978-1-4296-5367-1(1))*; pap. 6.29 *(978-1-4296-6228-4(X))*; pap. 35.70 *(978-1-4296-6397-7(9))* Capstone Pr., Inc.

—Out-Of-This-World Aliens: Hidden Picture Puzzles, 1 vol. Kalz, Jill. 2013. (Seek It Out Ser.). (ENG.). 32p. (gr. 1-2). 25.99 *(978-1-4048-7942-3(0))* Picture Window Bks.

Smith, Simon, et al. Poet in You, 1 vol. Fandel, Jennifer et al. 2014. (Poet in You Ser.). (ENG.). 32p. (gr. 2-4). lib. bdg. 106.60 *(978-1-4795-3358-9(0))* Picture Window Bks.

Smith, Simon. Seed, Sprout, Fruit: An Apple Tree Life Cycle, 1 vol. Knudsen, Shannon. 2011. (First Graphics: Nature Cycles Ser.). (ENG.). 24p. (gr. 1-2). lib. bdg. 23.32 *(978-1-4296-5366-4(3))*; pap. 6.29 *(978-1-4296-6230-7(1))*; pap. 35.70 *(978-1-4296-6399-1(5))* Capstone Pr., Inc.

Smith, Simon, et al. Tickles, Pickles, & Floofing Persnickles: Reading & Writing Nonsense Poems, 1 vol. Miller, Connie Colwell et al. 2014. (Poet in You Ser.). (ENG.). 32p. (gr. 2-4). pap. 8.95 *(978-1-4795-2949-0(4))*; lib. bdg. 26.65 *(978-1-4795-2198-2(1))* Picture Window Bks.

—Trust, Truth, & Ridiculous Goofs: Reading & Writing Friendship Poems, 1 vol. Fandel, Jennifer et al. 2014. (Poet in You Ser.). (ENG.). 32p. (gr. 2-4). lib. bdg. 26.65 *(978-1-4795-2199-9(X))* Picture Window Bks.

Smith, Simon & Chiacchiera, Moreno. Zoo Hideout: Hidden Picture Puzzles, 1 vol. Kalz, Jill. 2012. (Seek It Out Ser.). (ENG.). 32p. (gr. 1-2). 9.95 *(978-1-4048-7730-6(4))*; lib. bdg. 25.99 *(978-1-4048-7497-8(6))* Picture Window Bks.

Smith, Simon & Epstein, Len. Seek It Out. Kalz, Jill. 2013. (Seek It Out Ser.). (ENG.). 32p. (gr. 1-2). 59.70 *(978-1-4048-8081-8(X))*; 19.90 *(978-1-4048-8080-1(1))*; lib. bdg. 51.98 *(978-1-4048-7944-7(7))* Picture Window Bks.

Smith, Simon, jt. illus. see Epstein, Len.

Smith, Sindy. Charlie the Chipmunk & the Lost Goldmine. Smith, Sindy. 2012. 38p. 29.95 *(978-1-4626-9865-3(4))* America Star Bks.

—Dadu the Dolphin. Smith, Sindy. 2012. 24p. 29.95 *(978-1-4626-9862-2(X))* America Star Bks.

—Indy the Unicorn Prince. Smith, Sindy. 2012. 46p. 29.95 *(978-1-4626-9864-6(6))* America Star Bks.

—Little Lucy Lou. Smith, Sindy. 2012. 38p. 29.95 *(978-1-4489-3350-1(1))* America Star Bks.

—Mr. Minko. Smith, Sindy. 2012. 38p. 29.95 *(978-1-4626-9863-9(8))* America Star Bks.

—Rosie the Rottweiler. Smith, Sindy. 2012. 26p. 29.95 *(978-1-4626-9860-8(3))* America Star Bks.

Smith, Stephan. The Day of the Sandwich. Salzman, Jeremiah. 2010. (Very Small Adventures of Daisie Pup! Ser.). 48p. (J). pap. 8.99 *(978-0-9842632-8-8(4))* Salzman Bks. LLC.

—Mike's Adventure Packs: England. Salzman, Jeremiah. 2010. (Mike's Adventure Packs Ser.). 144p. (J). pap. 16.95 *(978-0-9842632-5-7(X))* Salzman Bks. LLC.

Smith, Stephen, photos by. Choosing a Dance School: What Every Parent Should Consider. 2008. (ENG., 113p. (YA). spiral bd. 15.00 *(978-0-9801919-2-9(0))* Thacker Hse. Enterprises.

Smith, Sue Millar. Raspberry & Turner. Reid, Joy. 2004. 32p. pap. 17.50 *(978-1-4120-2927-8(9))* Trafford Publishing.

Smith, Sydney. The Dread Crew: Pirates of the Backwoods, 1 vol. Inglis, Kate. ed. 2010. (ENG.). 196p. (J). (gr. 3-7). pap. 12.95 *(978-1-55109-775-6(3))* Nimbus Publishing, Ltd. CAN. Dist: Orca Bk. Pubs. USA.

—Mabel Murple, 1 vol. Fitch, Sheree. ed. 2014. (ENG.). 24p. (J). (gr. -1-3). pap. 12.95 *(978-1-55109-859-3(8))* Nimbus Publishing, Ltd. CAN. Dist: Orca Bk. Pubs. USA.

—Music Is for Everyone, 1 vol. Barber, Jill. 2014. (ENG.). 32p. (J). (gr. -1-3). 19.95 *(978-1-77108-150-4(3))* Nimbus Publishing, Ltd. CAN. Dist: Orca Bk. Pubs. USA.

—Pit Pony: The Picture Book. Barkhouse, Joyce & Barkhouse, Janet. 2012. (ENG.). 32p. (J). (gr. -1-2). 14.95 *(978-1-4595-0143-0(8))* Formac Publishing Co., Ltd. CAN. Dist: Casemate Pubs. & Bk. Distributors, LLC.

—There Were Monkeys in My Kitchen, 1 vol. Fitch, Sheree. 2014. (ENG.). 32p. (J). (gr. -1-3). pap. 12.95 *(978-1-55109-994-1(2))* Nimbus Publishing, Ltd. CAN. Dist: Orca Bk. Pubs. USA.

—Toes in My Nose: And Other Poems, 1 vol. Fitch, Sheree. ed. 2014. (ENG.). 32p. (J). (gr. -1-3). 19.95 *(978-1-55109-939-2(X))* Nimbus Publishing, Ltd. CAN. Dist: Orca Bk. Pubs. USA.

Smith, Tammy. Apples: And How They Grow. Driscoll, Laura. 2003. (Penguin Young Readers, Level 2 Ser.). (ENG.). 32p. (J). (gr. 1-2). mass mkt. 3.99 *(978-0-448-43275-5(7))*, Warne, Frederick Pubs.) Penguin Bks., Ltd. GBR. Dist: Penguin Random Hse., LLC.

Smith, Tim. Custer's Last Stand. Dunn, Joeming W. 2008. (Graphic History Ser.). 32p. 28.50 *(978-1-60270-181-6(4))*, Graphic Planet- Nonfiction) ABDO Publishing Co.

—The Oregon Trail. Dunn, Joeming W. 2008. (Graphic History Ser.). 32p. 28.50 *(978-1-60270-183-0(0))*, Graphic Planet- Nonfiction) ABDO Publishing Co.

Smith, Tod. The Explosive World of Volcanoes with Max Axiom, Super Scientist, 1 vol. Harbo, Christopher L. (Graphic Science Ser.). (ENG.). 32p. (gr. 3-4). 2008. pap. 8.10 *(978-1-4296-1770-3(5))*; 2007. 29.99 *(978-1-4296-0144-3(2))* Capstone Pr., Inc. (Graphic Library).

—How to Draw Amazing Motorcycles, 1 vol. Sautter, Aaron. 2007. (Drawing Cool Stuff Ser.). (ENG.). 32p. (gr. 3-4). 27.32 *(978-1-4296-0073-6(X))*, Edge Bks.) Capstone Pr., Inc.

—La Maquina del Tiempo. Wells, H. G. 2010. (Classic Fiction Ser.).Tr. of Time Machine. (SPA.). 72p. (gr. 2-3). 26.65 *(978-1-4342-2326-5(4))*, Graphic Revolve en Español) Stone Arch Bks.

—20,000 Leguas de Viaje Submarino, 1 vol. Verne, Jules & Fuentes, Benny. 2010. (Classic Fiction Ser.). (SPA.). 72p. (gr. 2-3). 26.65 *(978-1-4342-2324-1(8))*, Graphic Revolve en Español) Stone Arch Bks.

Smith, Tod & Smith, Tod G. The Legend of Sleepy Hollow, 1 vol. Gutierrez, Dave & Irving, Washington. 2008. (Classic Fiction Ser.). (ENG.). 72p. (gr. 2-3). lib. bdg. 26.65 *(978-1-4342-0446-2(4))*, Graphic Revolve) Stone Arch Bks.

Smith, Tod, jt. illus. see Ocampo Ruiz, Jose Alfonso.

Smith, Tod, jt. illus. see Ruiz, Jose Alfonso Ocampo.

Smith, Tod G. Around the World in 80 Days. Verne, Jules & Lokus, Rex. 2015. (Graphic Revolve: Common Core Editions Ser.). (ENG.). 72p. (gr. 2-3). pap. 6.95 *(978-1-4965-0381-7(3))* Stone Arch Bks.

Smith, Tod G., et al. The Buffalo Soldiers & the American West. Glaser, Jason. 2005. (Graphic History Ser.). (ENG.). 32p. (gr. 3-4). 29.99 *(978-0-7368-4966-1(1))*, Graphic Library) Capstone Pr., Inc.

Smith, Tod G. Dead Man's Map, 1 vol. Peschke, Marci. 2008. (Vortex Bks.). (ENG.). 112p. (gr. 2-3). pap. 7.19 *(978-1-59889-921-4(X))*, 1271328, Vortex Bks.) Stone Arch Bks.

—Explorar Ecosistemas con Max Axiom, Supercientífico. Biskup, Agnieszka. Strictly Spanish Translation Services Staff, tr. from ENG. 2012. (Ciencia Gráfica Ser.). (SPA.). 32p. (gr. 3-4). 29.99 *(978-1-4296-9238-0(3))* Capstone Pr., Inc.

—Exploring Ecosystems with Max Axiom, Super Scientist, 1 vol. Biskup, Agnieszka. 2007. (Graphic Science Ser.). (ENG.). 32p. (gr. 3-4). per. 8.10 *(978-0-7368-7894-4(7))*, Graphic Library) Capstone Pr., Inc.

—Johann Gutenberg & the Printing Press, 1 vol. Olson, Kay Melchisedech. 2006. (Inventions & Discovery Ser.). (ENG.). 32p. (gr. 3-4). 29.99 *(978-0-7368-6482-4(2))*; pap. 8.10 *(978-0-7368-9644-3(9))* Capstone Pr., Inc. (Graphic Library).

—Lecciones Sobre la Seguridad en el Trabajo Científico. Lemke, Donald B. et al. 2013. (Ciencia Gráfica Ser.). (SPA.). 32p. (gr. 3-4). lib. bdg. 29.99 *(978-1-62065-183-4(1))* Capstone Pr., Inc.

—Lessons in Science Safety with Max Axiom, Super Scientist, 1 vol. Lemke, Donald B. et al. 2007. (Graphic Science Ser.). (ENG.). 32p. (gr. 3-4). per. 8.10 *(978-0-7368-7887-6(4))*, Graphic Library) Capstone Pr., Inc.

—La Leyenda Del Jinete Sin Cabeza, 1 vol. Irving, Washington & Gutierrez, Dave. Tobon, Sara, tr. from ENG. 2009. (Classic Fiction Ser.). (SPA.). 72p. (gr. 2-3). lib. bdg. 26.65 *(978-1-4342-1688-5(8))*, Graphic Revolve en Español) Stone Arch Bks.

Smith, Tod G., et al. Molly Pitcher: Young American Patriot, 1 vol. Glaser, Jason. 2006. (Graphic Biographies Ser.). (ENG.). 32p. (gr. 3-4). 29.99 *(978-0-7368-5486-3(X))*, Graphic Library) Capstone Pr., Inc.

Smith, Tod G. El Mundo Explosivo de los Volcanes con Max Axiom, Supercientífico. Harbo, Christopher L. Strictly Spanish, LLC., tr. 2012. (Ciencia Gráfica Ser.). (SPA & ENG.). 32p. (gr. 3-4). lib. bdg. 29.99 *(978-1-4296-9237-3(5))* Capstone Pr., Inc.

Smith, Tod G., et al. Samuel Adams: Patriot & Statesman. Doeden, Matt. 2006. (Graphic Biographies Ser.). (ENG.). 32p. (gr. 3-4). 29.99 *(978-0-7368-6500-5(4))*, Graphic Library) Capstone Pr., Inc.

Smith, Tod G. Theseus & the Minotaur, 1 vol. Yomtov, Nel et al. (Mythology Ser.). (ENG.). 72p. (gr. 2-3). 2010. pap. 7.15 *(978-1-4342-1387-7(0))*; 2009. lib. bdg. 26.65 *(978-1-4342-1171-2(1))* Stone Arch Bks. (Graphic Revolve).

Smith, Tod G. & Milgram, Al. The Earth-Shaking Facts about Earthquakes with Max Axiom, Super Scientist, 1 vol. Krohn, Katherine. 2008. (Graphic Science Ser.). (ENG.). 32p. (gr. 3-4). per. 8.10 *(978-1-4296-1759-8(4))*, Graphic Library) Capstone Pr., Inc.

—Investigating the Scientific Method with Max Axiom, Super Scientist, 1 vol. Lemke, Donald B. 2008. (Graphic Science Ser.). (ENG.). 32p. (gr. 3-4). per. 8.10 *(978-1-4296-1760-4(8))*, Graphic Library) Capstone Pr., Inc.

Smith, Tod G. & Milgrom, Al. The Earth-Shaking Facts about Earthquakes with Max Axiom, Super Scientist. Krohn, Katherine E. 2008. (Graphic Science Ser.). (ENG.). 32p. (gr. 3-4). 29.99 *(978-1-4296-1328-6(9))*, Graphic Library) Capstone Pr., Inc.

—Investigating the Scientific Method with Max Axiom, Super Scientist, 1 vol. Lemke, Donald B. 2008. (Graphic Science Ser.). (ENG.). 32p. (gr. 3-4). 29.99 *(978-1-4296-1329-3(7))*, Graphic Library) Capstone Pr., Inc.

—Steve Jobs, Steve Wozniak, & the Personal Computer, 1 vol. Lemke, Donald B. 2006. (Inventions & Discovery Ser.). (ENG.). 32p. (gr. 3-4). 29.99 *(978-0-7368-6488-6(1))*, Graphic Library) Capstone Pr., Inc.

Smith, Tod G., jt. illus. see Anderson, Bill.

Smith, Tod G., jt. illus. see Milgrom, Al.

Smith, Tod G., jt. illus. see Smith, Todd Aaron.

Smith, Tod G., jt. illus. see Smith, Tod.

Smith, Todd Aaron. The Average Monkey. Smith, Todd Aaron. 2003. (Higby the Monkey Ser.). 32p. (J). pap. 4.97 *(978-1-58660-857-6(6))* Barbour Publishing, Inc.

—Higby Throws a Fit. Smith, Todd Aaron. 2003. (Higby the Monkey Ser.). 32p. (J). pap. 4.97 *(978-1-58660-858-3(4))* Barbour Publishing, Inc.

Smith, Todd Aaron & Smith, Tod G. Exploring Ecosystems with Max Axiom, Super Scientist, 1 vol. Biskup, Agnieszka. 2007. (Graphic Science Ser.). (ENG.). 32p. (gr. 3-4). 29.99 *(978-0-7368-6842-6(9))*, Graphic Library) Capstone Pr., Inc.

Smith, Tracy. Mommy Has 1 Foot: Learning about Numbers - Learning about People. Derke, Connie Butterfield. 2003. (Kayla's Learning Books). 24p. (J). (gr. 1-6). pap. 5.95 *(978-0-9747063-0-6(2))* Derke, Connie.

Smith, Wendy. Red Fox at Hickory Lane. Hollenbeck, Kathleen M. 2005. (Smithsonian's Backyard Ser.). (ENG.). 32p. (J). (gr. -1-2). 8.95 *(978-1-59249-117-9(0))*, SC5025); 19.95 *(978-1-59249-116-2(2))*, BC5025); 9.95 *(978-1-59249-120-9(0))*, PB5075); 4.95 *(978-1-59249-114-8(6))*, B5075) Soundprints.

—We Both Read Bilingual Edition-About Bats/Acerca de Los Murcielagos. McKay, Sindy. Canetti, Yanitzia, tr. 2014. (We Both Read - Level K-1 (Quality) Ser.). (ENG & SPA.). 44p. (J). (gr. k-1). pap. 5.99 *(978-1-60115-060-8(1))* Treasure Bay, Inc.

Smith, Wendy. Red Fox at Hickory Lane. Smith, Wendy, tr. Hollenbeck, Kathleen M. 2005. (Smithsonian's Backyard Ser.). (ENG.). 32p. (J). (gr. -1-2). 15.95 *(978-1-59249-113-1(8))*, B5025); pap. 6.95 *(978-1-59249-115-5(4))*, S5025) Soundprints.

Smith, Wendy, jt. illus. see Hunt, Judith.

Smith, William. Alby's Letters to Henry: Written from Isle of Mull. Tennant Iain Staff. 2007. (ENG.). 176p. (J). pap. 15.99 *(978-1-903071-14-4(3))* Bene Factum Publishing, Ltd. GBR. Dist: Independent Pubs. Group.

Smith, William E. Hank & Kale Visit the Aquarium. Snowden, Gary. 2012. 24p. pap. 8.99 *(978-1-938768-05-7(1))* Gypsy Pubns.

Smithers, J. Megan. Emma: An Interactive Storybook. 2nd ed. 2005. 60p. (J). (gr. k-4). pap. 9.00 *(978-0-9713342-6-7(9))* B V Wespat.

Smitherton, Jeb. Dinos are Big Babies & Dylan's Pets. Marsoli, Lisa Ann. 2005. (J). bds. 19.99 *(978-0-9767325-7-0(2))* Toy Quest.

—Dinosaurs are Big Babies. Marsoli, Lisa Ann. 2005. (J). bds. 14.99 *(978-0-9767325-0-1(5))* Toy Quest.

—Let's Go to the Zoo. Marsoli, Lisa Ann. 2005. (J). bds. 14.99 *(978-0-9767325-4-9(8))* Toy Quest.

—Let's Go to the Zoo & Leaping Lilly. Marsoli, Lisa Ann. 2005. (J). bds. 19.99 *(978-0-9767325-6-3(4))* Toy Quest.

Smithwick, Margo, photos by. Point to Happy: A Book for Kids on the Autism Spectrum. Smith, Miriam & Fraser, Afton. 2011. (ENG., 20p. (J). 19.95 *(978-0-7611-5715-1(8))*, 15715) Workman Publishing Co., Inc.

Smits, Josh. The Grumble Rumble Mumbler. Drewery, Melanie. 36p. pap. 13.00 *(978-1-86969-284-1(5))* Univ. of Hawaii Pr.

Smoak, I. W. & Washington, C. E. Brave Enough: The Story of Rob Sanford, Vermont Pioneer Boy. Washington, Ida H. 2003. vii, 128p. (J). (gr. 4-6). pap. 12.95 *(978-0-9666832-7-1(7))* Cherry Tree Bks.

Smollin, Michael. Another Monster at the End of This Book. Stone, Jon. 2012. (ENG.). 32p. (J). (gr. k-k). 8.99 *(978-0-375-86984-6(0))*, Golden Bks.) Random Hse., Inc.

—The Monster at the End of This Book. Stone, Jon. (Little Golden Board Book Ser.). (ENG.). (J). 2015. 26p. (— 1). bds. 7.99 *(978-0-553-50873-4(3))*; 2004. 32p. (gr. -1-2). 8.99 *(978-0-375-82913-0(X))* Random Hse. Children's Bks. (Golden Bks.).

Smouse, Phil A. Jesus Wants All of Me: Based on the Classic Devotional My Utmost for His Highest. Chambers, Oswald. ltd. ed. 2003. 384p. (J). pap. 4.99 *(978-1-58660-841-5(X))* Barbour Publishing, Inc.

Smy, Pam. Butter-Finger. Cattell, Bob & Agard, John. 2006. (ENG.). 128p. (J). (gr. 2-17). per. 7.95 *(978-1-84507-376-3(2))*, Frances Lincoln) Quarto Publishing Group UK GBR. Dist: Hachette Bk. Group.

—Follow the Swallow. Donaldson, Julia. ed. 2008. (ENG.). 32p. (J). (gr. -1-2). pap. 9.95 *(978-1-4052-1788-0(X))* Egmont Bks., Ltd. GBR. Dist: Independent Pubs. Group.

—Hush, Baby, Hush! Lullabies from Around the World. Henderson, Kathy & Quarto Generic Staff. 2011. (MUL & ENG.). 40p. (J). (gr. -1 — 1). 17.95 *(978-1-84507-967-3(1))*, Frances Lincoln) Quarto Publishing Group UK GBR. Dist: Hachette Bk. Group.

—Shine on, Butter-Finger. Cattell, Bob & Agard, John. 2007. (ENG.). 96p. (J). (gr. 2-7). per. 7.95 *(978-1-84507-626-9(5))*, Frances Lincoln) Quarto Publishing Group UK GBR. Dist: Hachette Bk. Group.

Smyth, Bambi. Favourite Nursery Rhymes. 15p. (J). bds. *(978-1-86503-636-6(6))* Five Mile Pr. Pty Ltd. The.

Smyth, Fiona. Sex Is a Funny Word: A Book about Bodies, Relationships, & YOU. Silverberg, Cory. 2015. (ENG.). 162p. (J). (gr. 2-5). 23.95 *(978-1-60980-606-4(9))*, Triangle Square) Seven Stories Pr.

—What Makes a Baby. Silverberg, Cory. 2013. (ENG.). 36p. (YA). (gr. -1-2). 16.95 *(978-1-60980-485-5(6))* Seven Stories Pr.

Smyth, Iain. The Eye of the Pharaoh: A Pop-up Whodunit. Smyth, Iain. 2005. 12p. (J). (gr. 4-8). reprint ed. pap. 17.00 *(978-0-7567-8840-7(4))* DIANE Publishing Co.

Smyth, Iain, jt. illus. see Goulding, June.

Smythe, Theresa. Chester's Colorful Easter Eggs. Smythe, Theresa. 2013. (ENG.). 24p. (J). (gr. -1-k). 12.99 *(978-0-8050-9326-1(5))*, Holt, Henry & Co. Bks. For Young Readers) Holt, Henry & Co.

Snader, Gregory. Sadie. Krone, Thelma Smith. 2008. 6p. (J). pap. 7.95 *(978-1-934696-02-6(1))*, Shooting Star Edition) American Literary Pr.

Snaith, Andy, photos by. Lift & Learn 123. Donoghue, Stella. 2006. 24p. (gr. -1). per., bds. *(978-1-84610-030-7(5))* Make Believe Ideas.

—Lift & Learn ABC. Phillips, Sarah. 2006. 24p. (gr. -1). per., bds. *(978-1-84610-029-1(1))* Make Believe Ideas.

—Lift & Learn Colors. Gordon, Bob. 2006. 24p. (gr. -1 — 1). per., bds. *(978-1-84610-028-4(3))* Make Believe Ideas.

—Lift & Learn Opposites. Holmen, Lene. 2006. 24p. (gr. -1 — 1). per., bds. *(978-1-84610-031-4(3))* Make Believe Ideas.

—Look at Me! I'm a Ballerina! Bicknell, Joanna & Page, Nick. 2005. 23p. (J). (gr. -1-3). *(978-1-905051-72-4(7))* Make Believe Ideas.

Snape, Jenny. Charlie's Harmonica. Robertson, J. Jean. 2012. (ENG.). 24p. (gr. 1-2). pap. 7.95 *(978-1-61810-312-3(1))*; lib. bdg. 28.50 *(978-1-61810-179-2(X))* Rourke Educational Media.

—Now or Later Alligator. Mckenzie, Precious. 2012. (ENG.). 24p. (gr. k-1). pap. 7.95 *(978-1-61810-305-5(9))*; lib. bdg. 28.50 *(978-1-61810-172-3(2))* Rourke Educational Media.

—Who Stole the Veggies from the Veggie Patch? Mckenzie, Precious. 2012. (ENG.). 24p. (gr. k-1). pap. 7.95 *(978-1-61810-298-0(2))*; lib. bdg. 28.50 *(978-1-61810-165-5(X))* Rourke Educational Media.

Snape, Juliet. A-Maze-Ing Minotaur. Rix, Juliet. 2014. (ENG.). 32p. (J). (gr. k-4). 17.99 *(978-1-84780-431-0(4))*, Frances Lincoln) Quarto Publishing Group UK GBR. Dist: Hachette Bk. Group.

Snare, Todd Tariq. KIDS CAN PLAY HIP HOP DRUMS! Book Series: Volume One: the Snare Drum. Snare, Todd Tariq. 2012. 60p. (J). pap. 16.00 *(978-1-62050-977-7(6))* PlatyPr.

Sneed, Brad. Big Bad Wolves at School. Krensky, Stephen. 2007. (ENG.). 32p. (J). (gr. -1-3). 17.99 *(978-0-689-83799-9(2))*, Simon & Schuster Bks. For Young Readers) Simon & Schuster Bks. For Young Readers.

—The Boy Who Was Raised by Librarians, 1 vol. Morris, Carla. 2007. (ENG.). 32p. (J). (gr. k-3). 16.95 *(978-1-56145-391-7(9))* Peachtree Pubs.
—Cock-A-Doodle Doo, Creak, Pop-Pop, Moo. Aylesworth, Jim. 2013. (ENG.). 32p. (J). pap. 7.99 *(978-0-8234-2754-3(4))* Holiday Hse., Inc.
—Cock-a-Doodle-Doo, Creak, Pop-Pop, Moo. Aylesworth, Jim. 2012. (ENG.). 32p. (J). 16.96 *(978-0-8234-2356-9(5))* Holiday Hse., Inc.
—Johnny Kaw: A Tall Tale. Scillian, Devin. 2013. (ENG.). 32p. (J). (gr. 1-4). 15.95 *(978-1-58536-791-7(5)*, 202353) Sleeping Bear Pr.
—Mr. President Goes to School, 1 vol. Walton, Rick. 2010. (ENG.). 32p. (J). (gr. -1-3). 15.95 *(978-1-56145-538-6(5))* Peachtree Pubs.
—Wash Day. Bunting, Eve. 2014. (ENG.). 32p. (J). (gr. -1-3). 16.95 *(978-0-8234-2868-7(0))* Holiday Hse., Inc.
—When the Wind Blows. Clark, Stacy. 2015. (ENG.). 32p. (J). (gr. -1-3). 16.95 *(978-0-8234-3069-7(3))* Holiday Hse., Inc.
Sneed, Brad. The Boy Who Was Raised by Librarians. Sneed, Brad. 2008. (J). (gr. k-3). 27.95 incl. audio *(978-0-8045-6965-1(7))* Spoken Arts, Inc.
—Thumbelina. Sneed, Brad. Andersen, Hans Christian. 2004. (ENG.). 40p. (J). (gr. -1-3). 17.99 *(978-0-8037-2812-7(3)*, Dial) Penguin Publishing Group.
Sneed, Patty. Hailey's Dream. Kuhns, Jennifer. 2013. 32p. pap. 13.95 *(978-0-9846811-8-1(3))* Shalako Pr.
Snellenberger, Bonita, jt. illus. see Snellenberger, Earl.
Snellenberger, Earl & Snellenberger, Bonita. Noah's Ark Pre-School Activity Book. Snellenberger, Earl & Snellenberger, Bonita. 2014. (ENG.). 98p. (J). (gr. -1-3). pap. 8.99 *(978-0-89051-832-8(7))* Master Bks.
—The Wonders of God's World Dinosaur Activity Book. Snellenberger, Earl & Snellenberger, Bonita. 2008. 128p. (J). (gr. -1). per. 8.99 *(978-0-89051-515-0(8))* Master Bks.
Snerling, Tina. Peas in a Pod. McCartney, Tania. 2015. (ENG.). 32p. (J). (gr. -1-2). 17.99 ***(978-1-921966-71-2(8))*** Exisle Publishing Ltd. NZL. Dist: Hachette Bk. Group.
—Tottie & Dot. McCartney, Tania. 2015. (ENG.). 32p. (J). (gr. -1-2). 17.99 ***(978-1-921966-49-1(1))*** Exisle Publishing Ltd. NZL. Dist: Hachette Bk. Group.
Snider, Jackie. Eight Legs Are Great! Charlesworth, Liza & Scholastic Canada Ltd. Staff. 2005. (Number Tales Ser.). (ENG.). 16p. (J). (gr. -1-1). pap. 2.99 *(978-0-439-69019-5(6))* Scholastic, Inc.
—My Family. Cifuentes, Carolina. 2010. (My World Ser.). (ENG.). 24p. (J). (gr. -1-1). lib. bdg. 22.60 *(978-1-60754-946-8(8))* Windmill Bks.
—My Family. Cifuentes, Carolina, ed. 2010. (My World Ser.). (ENG.). 24p. (J). (gr. -1-1). pap. 8.15 *(978-1-61533-025-6(9))* Windmill Bks.
—My Family & I. Rosa-Mendoza, Gladys. Cifuentes, Carolina, ed. 2004. (English-Spanish Foundations Ser.: Vol. 4).Tr. of Mi Familia y Yo. (ENG & SPA.). 20p. (J). (gr. -1-4). bds. 6.95 *(978-0-9679748-4-2(4))* Me+Mi Publishing.
—My Family & I/Mi Familia y Yo. Rosa-Mendoza, Gladys. 2007. (English Spanish Foundations Ser.). 20p. (gr. -1-k). pap. 19.95 *(978-1-931398-80-0(1))* Me+Mi Publishing.
—The Perfect Pet. Baker, Courtney. 2003. (Hello Reader! Ser.). (J). pap. *(978-0-439-47111-4(7))* Scholastic, Inc.
—Silly Riddles to Make You Giggle. Horsfall, Jacqueline. 2010. (ENG.). 96p. (J). pap. 4.95 *(978-1-4027-7848-3(1))* Sterling Publishing Co., Inc.
—Wild & Wacky Pet Jokes & Riddles. Pellowski, Michael J. 2010. (ENG.). 108p. (J). pap. 4.95 *(978-1-4027-7859-9(7))* Sterling Publishing Co., Inc.
Snider, K. C. The Adventures of Andy & Spirit: Book 1. Kelso, Mary Jean. 2010. 64p. pap. 9.95 *(978-1-61633-069-9(4))* Guardian Angel Publishing, Inc.
—Andy & Spirit Go to the Fair. Kelso, Mary Jean. 2008. 24p. pap. 10.95 *(978-1-935137-03-0(4))* Guardian Angel Publishing, Inc.
—Andy & Spirit in the Big Rescue. Kelso, Mary Jean. 2009. 24p. pap. 10.95 *(978-1-935137-67-2(0))* Guardian Angel Publishing, Inc.
—Andy & Spirit Meet the Rodeo Queen. Kelso, Mary Jean. 2010. 24p. pap. 10.95 *(978-1-61633-031-6(7))* Guardian Angel Publishing, Inc.
—Baby Jesus Is Missing. Phillips, Dixie. 2009. 16p. pap. 9.95 *(978-1-61633-000-2(7))* Guardian Angel Publishing, Inc.
—A Bad Mad Sad Day for Mama Bear. Calvani, Mayra. 2013. 24p. 19.95 *(978-1-61633-434-5(7))* Guardian Angel Publishing, Inc.
—Benjamin Jay Was a Bully. Glover, Emma M. 2012. 16p. pap. 9.95 *(978-1-61633-327-0(8))* Guardian Angel Publishing, Inc.
—Cartwheel Annie. Crow, Marilee. 2009. 24p. pap. 10.95 *(978-1-935137-71-9(9))* Guardian Angel Publishing, Inc.
—The Christmas Angel. Kelso, Mary Jean. 2007. 32p. (J). 11.95 *(978-1-933090-58-0(8))* Guardian Angel Publishing, Inc.
—Cowboy James. Kelso, Mary Jean. 2011. 24p. pap. 10.95 *(978-1-61633-174-0(7))*; 19.95 *(978-1-61633-178-8(X))* Guardian Angel Publishing, Inc.
—Does Heaven Get Mail? Crow, Marilee. 2008. 24p. pap. 10.95 *(978-1-935137-12-2(3))* Guardian Angel Publishing, Inc.
—God Loves You Whoever You Are. Reece, Colleen L. & DeMarco, Julie Reece. 2011. 20p. pap. 10.95 *(978-1-61633-183-2(6))* Guardian Angel Publishing, Inc.
—The Milk Horse. Luce, Catherine. 2011. 20p. pap. 10.95 *(978-1-61633-168-9(2))* Guardian Angel Publishing, Inc.
—Monster Maddie. Stephenson, Susan. 2010. 20p. pap. 10.95 *(978-1-61633-027-9(9))* Guardian Angel Publishing, Inc.
—One Family's Christmas. Kelso, Mary Jean. 24p. 2012. 19.95 *(978-1-61633-308-9(1))*; 2008. pap. 10.95 *(978-1-935137-05-4(0))* Guardian Angel Publishing, Inc.
—A Pocketful of Manners. Crow, Marilee. 2011. 16p. pap. 9.95 *(978-1-61633-176-4(3))* Guardian Angel Publishing, Inc.
—Preston, the Not-So-Perfect-Pig. Robinson, Janie. 2009. 20p. pap. 10.95 *(978-1-935137-84-9(0))* Guardian Angel Publishing, Inc.
—Ruthie & the Hippo's Fat Behind. Finke, Margot. 2010. 16p. pap. 10.95 *(978-1-61633-059-0(7))* Guardian Angel Publishing, Inc.
—Rv Mouse. Kelso, Mary Jean. 2010. 24p. pap. 10.95 *(978-1-61633-025-5(2))* Guardian Angel Publishing, Inc.
—A Short Tale about a Long Tail. Crow, Marilee. 2010. 16p. pap. 10.95 *(978-1-61633-067-5(8))* Guardian Angel Publishing, Inc.
—So Silly. Crow, Marilee. 2013. 28p. pap. 10.95 *(978-1-61633-443-7(6))* Guardian Angel Publishing, Inc.
—The Town of Masquerade. Samuels, Jack. 2012. 20p. pap. 9.95 *(978-1-61633-329-4(4))* Guardian Angel Publishing, Inc.
—What Is That Thing? McNamee, Kevin. 2011. 16p. pap. 9.95 *(978-1-61633-141-2(0))* Guardian Angel Publishing, Inc.
Snider, Kc. Andy & Spirit in Search & Rescue. Kelso, Mary Jean. 2013. 28p. 19.95 *(978-1-61633-410-9(X))*; pap. 10.95 *(978-1-61633-408-6(8))* Guardian Angel Publishing, Inc.
—Powder Monkey. McDine, Donna M. 2013. 24p. 19.95 *(978-1-61633-384-3(7))*; pap. 10.95 *(978-1-61633-385-0(5))* Guardian Angel Publishing, Inc.
Snider, Kc. Silence. Snider, Kc. 2013. 28p. 19.95 *(978-1-61633-437-6(1))* Guardian Angel Publishing, Inc.
Snider, Sharon. Responza the Bull Learns the Ropes of Friendship. Dunlap, Sonya. 2009. 32p. pap. 17.95 *(978-0-9815245-8-0(3))* Accelerator Bks.
Snider, Sharon & Reny, Todd. Yummy Yummy Nummy Nummy, Should I Put This in My Tummy? MacGregor, Kim. Ioannou, Gregory Phillip, ed. 2004. 24p. *(978-0-9731301-0-2(5))* Beautiful Beginnings Youth, Inc.
Snook, Randy, photos by. Many Ideas Open the Way: A Collection of Hmong Proverbs. 2003. 32p. (J). 16.95 *(978-1-885008-23-7(6)*, Shen's Bks.) Lee & Low Bks., Inc.
Snortum, Marty, photos by. Pink Princess Cookbook, 1 vol. Beery, Barbara. 2006. (ENG.). 64p. (J). (gr. -1-3). spiral bd. 14.99 *(978-1-4236-0173-9(4))* Gibbs Smith, Publisher.
Snow, Alan. Here's What You Do When You Can't Find Your Shoe: Ingenious Inventions for Pesky Problems. Perry, Andrea J. & Perry, Andrea. 2003. (ENG.). 40p. (J). (gr. -1-3). 18.99 *(978-0-689-83067-9(X)*, Atheneum Bks. for Young Readers) Simon & Schuster Children's Publishing.
—On a Tall, Tall Cliff. Murray, Andrew. (ENG.). 32p. (J). (gr. k-2). 2005. 19.99 *(978-0-00-712155-7(5))*; 2004. pap. 11.95 *(978-0-00-712156-4(3))* HarperCollins Pubs. Ltd. GBR. Dist: Independent Pubs. Group.
—The Snack Smasher: And Other Reasons Why It's Not My Fault. Perry, Andrea. 2007. (ENG.). 40p. (J). (gr. -1-3). 17.99 *(978-0-689-85469-9(2)*, Atheneum Bks. for Young Readers) Simon & Schuster Children's Publishing.
—A Spell Behind Bars. Bowvayne. 2006. (Misadventures of Danny Cloke Ser.). (J). 207p. per. 4.99 *(978-0-7945-1293-4(3))*; 208p. (gr. 6). lib. bdg. 12.99 *(978-1-58086-926-3(2))* EDC Publishing. (Usborne).
—A Turn in the Grave. Bowvayne. 2006. (Misadventures of Danny Cloke Ser.). 143p. (J). per. 4.99 *(978-0-7945-1292-7(5)*, Usborne) EDC Publishing.
Snow, Alan. Here Be Monsters! Snow, Alan. (Ratbridge Chronicles Ser.: 1). (ENG.). 544p. (J). (gr. 3-9). 2007. per. 9.99 *(978-0-689-87048-4(5))*; 2006. 17.95 *(978-0-689-87047-7(7))* Simon & Schuster Children's Publishing. (Atheneum Bks. for Young Readers).
—How Dinosaurs Really Work! Snow, Alan. 2013. (ENG.). 32p. (J). (gr. -1-3). 17.99 *(978-1-4424-8294-4(X)*, Atheneum Bks. for Young Readers) Simon & Schuster Children's Publishing.
—How Kids Really Work. Snow, Alan. 2013. (ENG.). 40p. (J). (gr. -1-5). 16.99 *(978-0-689-85818-5(3)*, Atheneum Bks. for Young Readers) Simon & Schuster Children's Publishing.
—How Santa Really Works. Snow, Alan. 2007. (ENG.). 48p. (J). (gr. -1-3). 7.99 *(978-1-4169-5000-4(1)*, Atheneum Bks. for Young Readers) Simon & Schuster Children's Publishing.
—Worse Things Happen at Sea! A Tale of Pirates, Poison, & Monsters. Snow, Alan. (Ratbridge Chronicles Ser.: 2). (ENG.). 352p. (J). (gr. 3-9). 2014. pap. 9.99 *(978-0-689-87050-7(7))*; 2013. 17.99 *(978-0-689-87049-1(3))* Simon & Schuster Children's Publishing. (Atheneum Bks. for Young Readers).
Snow, Jeff. Beasts in the Closet. Snow, Jeff. 2006. 32p. (J). 17.95 *(978-1-932362-11-4(8))* Snowbound Pr., Inc.
Snow, Philip. Animals of the Bible. Snow, Philip. 2005. (Bible Discover & Colour Ser.). 32p. (J). (gr. -1-7). 4.00 *(978-1-903087-88-6(0))* DayOne Pubns. GBR. Dist: Send The Light Distribution LLC.
—Birds of the Bible. Snow, Philip. 2005. (Bible Discover & Colour Ser.). 32p. (J). (gr. -1-7). 4.00 *(978-1-903087-89-3(9))* DayOne Pubns. GBR. Dist: Send The Light Distribution LLC.
—Places of the Bible. Snow, Philip. 2005. (Bible Discover & Colour Ser.). 32p. (J). (gr. -1-7). 4.00 *(978-1-903087-90-9(2))* DayOne Pubns. GBR. Dist: Send The Light Distribution LLC.
—Plants of the Bible. Snow, Philip. 2005. (Bible Discover & Colour Ser.). 32p. (J). (gr. -1-7). 4.00 *(978-1-903087-91-6(0))* DayOne Pubns. GBR. Dist: Send The Light Distribution LLC.
Snow, Ravay L. Hildegarde & the Great Green Shirt Factory. Snow, Ravay L. 2005. (Hildegarde Ser.). 32p. (J). 16.95 *(978-1-932362-10-7(X))* Snowbound Pr., Inc.
Snow, Sarah. These Bees Count! Formento, Alison. 2012. (These Things Count! Ser.). (ENG.). 32p. (J). (gr. -1-2). 16.99 *(978-0-8075-7868-1(1))* Whitman, Albert & Co.
—These Rocks Count! Formento, Alison. 2014. (These Things Count! Ser.). (ENG.). 32p. (J). (gr. -1-2). 16.99 *(978-0-8075-7870-4(3))* Whitman, Albert & Co.
—This Tree Counts!, 1 vol. Formento, Alison. 2010. (These Things Count! Ser.). (ENG.). 32p. (J). (gr. -1-2). 16.99 *(978-0-8075-7890-2(8))* Whitman, Albert & Co.
Snow, Scott. In the Eye of the Storm. Kimmel, Elizabeth Cody. 2003. (Adventures of Young Buffalo Bill Ser.). 144p. (J). (gr. 3-7). lib. bdg. 16.89 *(978-0-06-029116-7(8))* HarperCollins Pubs.
—In the Eye of the Storm. Kimmel, E. Cody. 2003. (Adventures of Young Buffalo Bill Ser.). (ENG.). 144p. (J). (gr. 3-7). 15.99 *(978-0-06-029115-0(X))* HarperCollins Pubs.
—West on the Wagon Train. Kimmel, E. Cody. 2003. (Adventures of Young Buffalo Bill Ser.). (ENG.). 160p. (J). 15.99 *(978-0-06-029113-6(3))* HarperCollins Pubs.
Snowden, Linda. Uncle Moishy Visits Torah Island. Safran, Faigy. (J). pap. 5.99 *(978-0-89906-806-0(5)*, UM1P) Mesorah Pubns., Ltd.
Snure, Roger. The Dragon Slayers: Essential Training Guide for Young Dragon Fighters. Denham, Joyce. 2011. (ENG.). 224p. (J). (gr. 5-6). pap. 23.99 *(978-1-55725-584-3(5))* Paraclete Pr., Inc.
Snyder, Anthony. Qbee Wants to Bee a Dolphin Trainer. Trivelli, John. 2013. (Qbee Wants To Bee Ser.). 39p. (J). 14.95 *(978-1-61888-052-9(7))*; pap. 9.95 *(978-1-61888-051-2(9))* Mother's Hse. Publishing.
—Qbee Wants to Bee a Fighterfighter. Trivelli, John. 2013. (Qbee Wants To Bee Ser.). 39p. (J). 14.95 *(978-1-61888-046-8(2))*; pap. 9.95 *(978-1-61888-045-1(4))* Mother's Hse. Publishing.
—Qbee Wants to Bee a Homebuilder. Trivelli, John. 2013. (Qbee Wants To Bee Ser.). 39p. (J). 14.95 *(978-1-61888-042-0(X))* Mother's Hse. Publishing.
—Qbee Wants to Bee a Pilot. Trivelli, John. 2013. (Qbee Wants To Bee Ser.). 41p. (J). 14.95 *(978-1-61888-056-7(X))*; pap. 9.95 *(978-1-61888-055-0(1))* Mother's Hse. Publishing.
—Qbee Wants to Bee a Racecar Driver. Trivelli, John. 2013. (Qbee Wants To Bee Ser.). 39p. (J). 14.95 *(978-1-61888-044-4(6))* Mother's Hse. Publishing.
—Qbee Wants to Bee a Rock Star. Trivelli, John. 2013. (Qbee Wants To Bee Ser.). 37p. 14.95 *(978-1-61888-048-2(9))*; 41p. pap. 9.95 *(978-1-61888-047-5(0))* Mother's Hse. Publishing.
—Qbee Wants to Bee a School Teacher. Trivelli, John. 2013. (Qbee Wants To Bee Ser.). 41p. (J). 14.95 *(978-1-61888-054-3(3))*; pap. 9.95 *(978-1-61888-053-6(5))* Mother's Hse. Publishing.
—Qbee Wants to Bee a Soldier. Trivelli, John. 2013. (Qbee Wants To Bee Ser.: 9). (ENG.). 44p. (J). pap. 9.95 *(978-1-61888-073-4(X))* Mother's Hse. Publishing.
—Qbee Wants to Bee an Author. Trivelli, John. 2013. (Qbee Wants To Bee Ser.). (J). 37p. 14.95 *(978-1-61888-050-5(0))*; 41p. pap. 9.95 *(978-1-61888-049-9(7))* Mother's Hse. Publishing.
Snyder, Betsy E. Don't Throw That Away! A Lift-the-Flap Book about Recycling & Reusing. Bergen, Lara. 2009. (Little Green Bks.). (ENG.). 14p. (J). (gr. -1-1). bds. 6.99 *(978-1-4169-7517-5(9)*, Little Simon) Little Simon.
—I Can Dance. 2015. (ENG.). 14p. (J). (gr. -1 — 1). bds. 8.99 *(978-1-4521-2929-7(0))* Chronicle Bks. LLC.
—I Can Play. 2015. (ENG.). 14p. (J). (gr. -1 — 1). bds. 8.99 *(978-1-4521-2905-1(3))* Chronicle Bks. LLC.
—Lily's Potty. 2010. 16p. (J). bds. *(978-1-60906-001-5(6))* Begin Smart LLC.
—Peanut Butter & Jellyfishes: A Very Silly Alphabet Book. Cleary, Brian P. 2007. (ENG.). 32p. (J). (gr. -1-2). 15.95 *(978-0-8225-6188-0(3)*, Millbrook Pr.) Lerner Publishing Group.
—Tons of Trucks. Fliess, Sue. 2012. (ENG.). 18p. (J). (gr. k — 1). 13.99 *(978-0-547-44927-2(5))* Houghton Mifflin Harcourt Publishing Co.
Snyder, Betsy E. Haiku Baby. Snyder, Betsy E. 2008. (ENG.). 14p. (J). (gr. k — 1). bds. 6.99 *(978-0-375-84395-2(7)*, Random Hse. Bks. for Young Readers) Random Hse. Children's Bks.
Snyder, Diana, jt. illus. see Sun Star, Elan.
Snyder, Don, photos by. Swatches. La Prade, Erik. 2008. (ENG., 26p. pap. 10.00 *(978-0-9817678-1-9(8))* Poets Wear Prada.
Snyder, Harold E. A Frontier Girl of New York. Curtis, Alice Turner. 2011. 282p. 48.95 *(978-1-258-01096-6(8))* Literary Licensing, LLC.
Snyder, Iii, jt. illus. see Snyder, Max.
Snyder, Joe. Pokey & the Rooster. Helsel, Sandra. 2009. 28p. pap. 9.95 *(978-0-9818488-1-5(8))* Ajoyin Publishing, Inc.
Snyder, Joel. Fawn at Woodland Way. Zoehfeld, Kathleen Weidner. 2011. (Smithsonian's Backyard Ser.). (ENG.). 32p. (J). (gr. -1-3). 19.95 *(978-1-60727-637-1(2))* Soundprints.
—Good News for Naaman. Konzen, Lisa M. 2004. (ENG.). 16p. (J). 1.99 *(978-0-570-07573-8(4))* Concordia Publishing Hse.
—Joshua James Likes Trucks. Petrie, Catherine. 2011. (Rookie Ready to Learn Ser.). 32p. (J). (ENG.). pap. 5.95 *(978-0-531-26827-8(6))*; (gr. -1-k). lib. bdg. 23.00 *(978-0-531-27177-3(3))* Scholastic Library Publishing. (Children's Pr.).
—Martin Luther King, Jr. Day. Trueit, Trudi Strain. 2013. (Holidays & Celebrations Ser.). (ENG.). 32p. (J). (gr. k-3). 27.07 *(978-1-62323-509-3(X)*, 206283) Child's World, Inc., The.
—Opossum at Sycamore Road. Walker, Sally M. 2011. (Smithsonian's Backyard Ser.). (ENG.). 32p. (J). (gr. -1-3). 8.95 *(978-1-60727-640-1(2))* Soundprints.
—Screech Owl at Midnight Hollow. Lamm, C. Drew. 2011. (Smithsonian's Backyard Ser.). (ENG.). 32p. (J). (gr. -1-3). 19.95 *(978-1-60727-643-2(7))* Soundprints.
—St. Patrick's Day. Heinrichs, Ann. 2013. (Holidays & Celebrations Ser.). (ENG.). 32p. (J). (gr. k-3). 27.07 *(978-1-62323-512-3(X)*, 206285) Child's World, Inc., The.
—Timothy Joins Paul. Rottmann, Erik. 2005. (ENG.). 16p. (J). 1.99 *(978-0-7586-0506-1(4))* Concordia Publishing Hse.
Snyder, Max & Snyder, Iii. The King with No Kingdom. Snyder, Max. 2013. 42p. 18.99 *(978-0-9911512-9-5(1))* Mindstir Media.
Snyder, Peter Etril. Winterberries & Apple Blossoms: Reflections & Flavors of a Mennonite Year. Forler, Nan. 2011. (ENG.). 40p. (J). (gr. k-12). 22.95 *(978-1-77049-254-7(2)*, Tundra Bks.) Tundra Bks. CAN. Dist: Penguin Random Hse., LLC.
Snyder, Robert. Up on the Housetop. Hanby, Benjamin Russell. 2007. (ENG.). 26p. (J). (gr. -1-3). bds. 12.99 *(978-0-8249-6714-7(3)*, Candy Cane Pr.) Ideals Pubns.
Snyder, Robert. Itsy Bitsy Spider. Snyder, Robert. 2009. (ENG.). 20p. (J). 12.99 *(978-0-8249-1821-7(5)*, Candy Cane Pr.) Ideals Pubns.
Snyder, Ronda. The Kingdom of Wish & Why. Milliner, Donna L. 2013. 30p. pap. 11.95 *(978-1-938743-06-1(7))* Reimann Bks.
Snyder, Sally. Hold the Fort. Snyder, Sally. 2003. 45p. (J). 20.00 *(978-1-882203-99-4(2))* Orange Frazer Pr.
Snyder, Suzanne. Sing Alleluia! An Easter Story for Children. Flegal, Daphna. 2004. 32p. (J). (gr. -1-3). pap. 5.00 *(978-0-687-05369-8(2))* Abingdon Pr.
So, Meilo. El Agua Rueda, el Agua Sube. Mora, Pat & Dominguez, Adriana. 2014.Tr. of Water Rolls, Water Rises. (SPA & ENG.). 32p. (J). 17.95 *(978-0-89239-325-1(4))* Lee & Low Bks., Inc.
—Alex the Parrot: No Ordinary Bird. Spinner, Stephanie. 2012. (ENG.). 48p. (J). (gr. 3-7). 17.99 *(978-0-375-86846-7(1)*, Knopf Bks. for Young Readers) Random Hse. Children's Bks.
—Brush of the Gods. Look, Lenore. 2013. (ENG.). 40p. (J). (gr. -1-3). 17.99 *(978-0-375-87001-9(6)*, Schwartz & Wade Bks.) Random Hse. Children's Bks.
—By Day, by Night. Gibson, Amy. 2014. (ENG.). 32p. (J). (gr. -1). 16.95 *(978-1-59078-991-9(1))* Boyds Mills Pr.
—Fairy Tales. Cummings, E. E. Firmage, George James, ed. 2004. (ENG.). 48p. 17.95 *(978-0-87140-658-3(6)*, 40658) Liveright Publishing Corp.
—Hurry & the Monarch. O Flatharta, Antoine. 2009. (ENG.). 40p. (J). (gr. k-3). pap. 7.99 *(978-0-385-73719-7(X)*, Dragonfly Bks.) Random Hse. Children's Bks.
—It's Simple, Said Simon. Hoberman, Mary Ann. 2003. (ENG.). 40p. (J). (gr. -1-2). pap. 6.99 *(978-0-440-41772-9(4)*, Dragonfly Bks.) Random Hse. Children's Bks.
—My Mom Is a Foreigner, but Not to Me. Moore, Julianne. 2013. (ENG.). 40p. (J). (gr. k-3). 16.99 *(978-1-4521-0792-9(0))* Chronicle Bks. LLC.
—Noodle Magic. Thong, Roseanne Greenfield. 2014. (ENG.). 32p. (J). (gr. -1-3). 17.99 *(978-0-545-52167-3(X))* Scholastic, Inc.
—Pale Male: Citizen Hawk of New York City. Schulman, Janet. 2008. (ENG.). 40p. (J). (gr. -1-2). 16.99 *(978-0-375-84558-1(5)*, Knopf Bks. for Young Readers) Random Hse. Children's Bks.
—Read a Rhyme, Write a Rhyme. (ENG.). 32p. (J). (gr. 1-4). 2009. pap. 7.99 *(978-0-385-73727-2(0)*, Dragonfly Bks.); 2005. 16.95 *(978-0-375-82286-5(0)*, Knopf Bks. for Young Readers) Random Hse. Children's Bks.
—Water Sings Blue: Ocean Poems. Coombs, Kate. 2012. (ENG.). 36p. (J). (gr. -1-3). 16.99 *(978-0-8118-7284-3(X))* Chronicle Bks. LLC.
So, Meilo. Water Rolls, Water Rises, 1 vol. So, Meilo. Mora, Pat & Dominguez, Adriana. 2014. (SPA & ENG.). 32p. (J). *(978-1-60060-899-5(X))* Lee & Low Bks., Inc.
So, Patty. So Simple Sightwords at-Home Volume 3. So, Patty. 2008. 117p. (J). spiral bd. *(978-0-9772158-4-3(9))* So Simple Learning.
So, Sungwan, photos by. C Is for China. So, Sungwan. Quarto Generic Staff. 2004. (World Alphabets Ser.). (ENG., 32p. (J). (gr. k-3). pap. 8.95 *(978-1-84507-318-3(5)*, Frances Lincoln) Quarto Publishing Group UK GBR. Dist: Hachette Bk. Group.
So-Young, Lee. Model, Vol. 5. So-Young, Lee. rev. ed. 2005. 192p. pap. 9.99 *(978-1-59532-007-0(5))* TOKYOPOP, Inc.
Soares, Maria Fernanda, jt. photos by see Butefish, Jennifer.
Sobol, Laurel Marie. Nez Perce Nimiipuu Stories & Legends. Sobol, Laurel Marie. 2011. (ENG.). 58p. pap. 13.99 *(978-1-4679-0760-6(X))* CreateSpace Independent Publishing Platform.
Sobol, Richard. Breakfast in the Rainforest: A Visit with Mountain Gorillas. Sobol, Richard. 2008. (Traveling Photographer Ser.). (ENG.). 48p. (J). (gr. 3-7). 18.99 *(978-0-7636-2281-7(8))* Candlewick Pr.
—The Story of Silk: From Worm Spit to Woven Scarves. Sobol, Richard. 2012. (Traveling Photographer Ser.). (ENG.). 40p. (J). (gr. 1-4). 17.99 *(978-0-7636-4165-8(0))* Candlewick Pr.
Sobol, Richard, photos by. Construction Zone. Hudson, Cheryl Willis. 2006. (ENG., 32p. (J). (gr. -1-3). 15.99 *(978-0-7636-2684-6(8))* Candlewick Pr.
—An Elephant in the Backyard. 2004. (J). *(978-0-525-46970-4(2)*, Dutton Juvenile) Penguin Publishing Group.
Sobol, Richard, photos by. Breakfast in the Rainforest: A Visit with Mountain Gorillas. Sobol, Richard. 2010. (Traveling Photographer Ser.). (ENG., 48p. (J). (gr. 1-4). pap. 7.99 *(978-0-7636-5134-3(6))* Candlewick Pr.
—The Life of Rice: From Seedling to Supper. Sobol, Richard. 2010. (Traveling Photographer Ser.: 2). (ENG., 40p. (J). (gr. k-3). 17.99 *(978-0-7636-3252-6(X))* Candlewick Pr.
Sochor, Lesia. A Moose's Morning. Love, Pamela. ed. 2007. (ENG.). 32p. (J). (gr. -1-3). 15.95 *(978-0-89272-733-9(0))* Down East Bks.
Soda, Masahito. Firefighter! Soda, Masahito. (Firefighter Ser.: Vol. 12). (ENG.). 2005. 200p. pap. 9.95 *(978-1-59116-980-2(1))*; 2003. 200p. pap. 9.95 *(978-1-56931-991-8(X))*; 2003. 192p. pap. 9.95 *(978-1-56931-881-2(6))* Viz Media.
—Firefighter: Daigo of Fire Company M. Soda, Masahito. 2004. (Firefighter Ser.: Vol. 7). (ENG.). 200p. pap. 9.95 *(978-1-59116-315-2(3))* Viz Media.
—Firefighter! Daigo of Fire Company M. Soda, Masahito. (Firefighter Ser.: Vol. 11). (ENG.). 2005. 200p. pap. 9.95 *(978-1-59116-795-2(7))*; 2004. 200p. pap. 9.95 *(978-1-59116-464-7(8))*; 2003. 192p. pap. 9.95 *(978-1-59116-093-9(6))* Viz Media.
—Firefighter! Vol. 10: Daigo of Fire Company M. Soda, Masahito. 2005. (Firefighter Ser.: Vol. 10). (ENG.). 208p. pap. 9.95 *(978-1-59116-635-1(7))* Viz Media.

—Privileged to Kill. Soda, Masahito. 2004. (Firefighter Ser.: Vol. 9). (ENG.). 200p. pap. 9.95 *(978-1-59116-634-4(9))* Viz Media.

Soderlund, Birgit. Pacific Halibut Flat or Fiction?, 1. Sadorus, Lauri. 2005. 24p. (J). per. *(978-0-9776931-0-8(4))* International Pacific Halibut Commission.

Sodré, Julie. Baby Farm Animals. Grimm, Sandra. 2012. (ENG.). 20p. (J). (gr. -1-1). 12.95 *(978-1-61608-654-1(8),* 608654, Sky Pony Pr.) Skyhorse Publishing Co., Inc.

Soentpiet, Chris K. Amazing Faces. Hopkins, Lee Bennett. 2011. (ENG.). 40p. (J). (gr. 1-18). 18.95 *(978-1-60060-334-1(3))* Lee & Low Bks., Inc.

—Coolies. Yin. 2003. (ENG.). 40p. (J). (gr. 2-5). 7.99 *(978-0-14-250055-2(0),* Puffin) Penguin Publishing Group.

—Coolies. Yin. 2003. (gr. k). 18.00 *(978-0-7569-1545-2(7))* Perfection Learning Corp.

—Happy Birthday to You! The Mystery Behind the Most Famous Song in the World. Raven, Margot Theis. 2008. (ENG.). 37p. (J). (gr. k-6). 17.95 *(978-1-58536-169-4(0))* Sleeping Bear Pr.

—My Brother Martin: A Sister Remembers Growing up with the Rev. Dr. Martin Luther King Jr. Farris, Christine King. 2003. (ENG.). 32p. (J). (gr. 1-6). 19.99 *(978-0-689-84387-7(9),* Simon & Schuster Bks. For Young Readers) Simon & Schuster Bks. For Young Readers.

—My Brother Martin: A Sister Remembers Growing up with the Rev. Dr. Martin Luther King Jr. Farris, Christine King. 2006. (ENG.). 40p. (J). (gr. 1-6). 7.99 *(978-0-689-84388-4(7),* Simon & Schuster/Paula Wiseman Bks.) Simon & Schuster/Paula Wiseman Bks.

—My Brother Martin: A Sister Remembers Growing up with the Rev. Dr. Martin Luther King Jr. King Farris, Christine. 2005. 35p. (J). (gr. 4-7). 15.65 *(978-0-7569-6552-5(7))* Perfection Learning Corp.

—Saturdays & Teacakes, 1 vol. Laminack, Lester L. (ENG.). 32p. (J). 2009. 19.95 *(978-1-56145-513-3(X));* 2004. 16.95 *(978-1-56145-303-0(X))* Peachtree Pubs.

—So Far from the Sea. Bunting, Eve. 2009. (ENG.). 32p. (J). (gr. 5-7). pap. 7.99 *(978-0-547-23752-7(9))* Houghton Mifflin Harcourt Publishing Co.

Soffritti, Donald. Double Duck. Enna, Bruno. 2010. (ENG.). 112p. (J). pap. 9.99 *(978-1-60886-545-1(2))* Boom! Studios.

Sofilas, Mark. Hello, I Am Fiona from Scotland. Graham, Mark. 2014. (AV2 Fiction Readalong Ser.: Vol. 128). (ENG.). 32p. (J). (gr. -1-3). lib. bdg. 34.28 *(978-1-4896-2253-2(5),* AV2 by Weigl) Weigl Pubs., Inc.

—Hello, I Am Max from Sydney. Husar, Stephane. 2014. (AV2 Fiction Readalong Ser.: Vol. 130). (ENG.). 32p. (J). (gr. -1-3). lib. bdg. 34.28 *(978-1-4896-2250-1(0),* AV2 by Weigl) Weigl Pubs., Inc.

Sogabe, Aki. The Origami Master. Lachenmeyer, Nathaniel. 2008. (ENG.). 32p. (J). (gr. 2-4). 16.99 *(978-0-8075-6134-8(7))* Whitman, Albert & Co.

Sohn, Jeana. Laffy the Lamb. Bee, Granny. Werthiemer, Beverly, ed. 2006. 32p. (J). 16.95 *(978-1-932367-00-3(4))* BookBound Publishing.

Sohn, Tonia. Socks! Sohn, Tonia. 2014. (ENG.). 32p. (J). 9.99 *(978-1-61067-244-3(5))* Kane Miller.

Soileau, Hodges. The Black Widow Spider Mystery. 2004. (Boxcar Children Special Ser.). 130p. (gr. 2-7). 15.50 *(978-0-7569-3266-4(1))* Perfection Learning Corp.

—The Comic Book Mystery. 2003. (Boxcar Children Ser.). 106p. (gr. 4-7). 15.00 *(978-0-7569-1611-4(9))* Perfection Learning Corp.

—The Great Shark Mystery. 2003. (Boxcar Children Mystery & Activities Specials Ser.: 20). (ENG.). 160p. (J). (gr. 2-5). pap. 5.99 *(978-0-8075-5532-3(0))* Whitman, Albert & Co.

—The Great Shark Mystery. 2003. (Boxcar Children Special Ser.). 130p. (gr. 4-7). 15.50 *(978-0-7569-1616-9(X))* Perfection Learning Corp.

—The Mystery at Skeleton Point. 2003. (Boxcar Children Ser.). 120p. (gr. 4-7). 15.00 *(978-0-7569-1609-1(7))* Perfection Learning Corp.

—The Mystery in the Fortune Cookie. 2003. (Boxcar Children Ser.: No. 96). (ENG.). 128p. (J). (gr. 2-5). pap. 4.99 *(978-0-8075-5540-8(1))* Whitman, Albert & Co.

—The Mystery of the Haunted Boxcar. 2004. (Boxcar Children Ser.: No. 100). (ENG.). 128p. (J). (gr. 2-5). mass mkt. 4.99 *(978-0-8075-5554-5(1))* Whitman, Albert & Co.

—The Mystery of the Runaway Ghost. Warner, Gertrude Chandler. 2004. (Boxcar Children Ser.). 135p. (J). 12.65 *(978-0-7569-3264-0(5))* Perfection Learning Corp.

—The Mystery of the Runaway Ghost. 2004. (Boxcar Children Mysteries Ser.: 98). (ENG.). 144p. (J). (gr. 2-5). pap. 5.99 *(978-0-8075-5551-4(7))* Whitman, Albert & Co.

—The Radio Mystery. 2003. (Boxcar Children Ser.: No. 97). (ENG.). 128p. (J). (gr. 2-5). mass mkt. 4.99 *(978-0-8075-5547-7(9))* Whitman, Albert & Co.

Sokol, Bill. Alvin Fernald, Mayor for a Day. Hicks, Clifford B. 2015. (J). pap. ***(978-1-930900-86-8(4))*** Purple Hse. Pr.

—Alvin's Secret Code. Hicks, Clifford B. 2015. (J). pap. ***(978-1-930900-85-1(6))*** Purple Hse. Pr.

Sokolava, Valerie. Cinderella. McFadden, Deanna. 2013. (Silver Penny Stories Ser.). (ENG.). 40p. (J). (gr. -1-1). 4.95 *(978-1-4027-8333-3(7))* Sterling Publishing Co., Inc.

—Thumbelina. Olmstead, Kathleen et al. 2013. (Silver Penny Stories Ser.). (ENG.). 40p. (J). (gr. -1-1). 4.95 *(978-1-4027-8352-4(3))* Sterling Publishing Co., Inc.

Sokoloff, David. The Queen of Persia. Moscowitz, Moshe & Resnick, Yael. 2004. 107p. *(978-1-930925-09-0(3),* Shazak Productions) Torah Excel.

Sokolova, Valerie. Bella Basset Ballerina. Gam, Laura Aimee. 2006. 32p. (J). (gr. -1-3). 15.95 *(978-0-9759378-0-8(4))* Pretty Please Pr., Inc.

—Elijah & King Ahab, 1 vol. Bowman, Crystal. 2012. (I Can Read! / Bible Stories Ser.). (ENG.). 32p. (J). pap. 3.99 *(978-0-310-72675-3(1))* Zonderkidz.

—Jesus Feeds the Five Thousand, 1 vol. Bowman, Crystal. 2011. (I Can Read! / Bible Stories Ser.). (ENG.). 32p. (J). (gr. -1-2). pap. 3.99 *(978-0-310-72157-4(1))* Zonderkidz.

—Jesus Raises Lazarus, 1 vol. Bowman, Crystal. 2011. (I Can Read! / Bible Stories Ser.). (ENG.). 32p. (J). (gr. -1-2). pap. 3.99 *(978-0-310-72158-1(X))* Zonderkidz.

—Joshua Crosses the Jordan, 1 vol. Bowman, Crystal. 2011. (I Can Read! / Bible Stories Ser.). (ENG.). 32p. (J). (gr. -1-2). pap. 3.99 *(978-0-310-72156-7(3))* Zonderkidz.

—The Magic of Merlin. Spinner, Stephanie. 2004. (Stepping Stones: A Chapter Book: Fantasy Ser.). 42p. (J). 11.65 *(978-0-7569-0905-5(8))* Perfection Learning Corp.

—The Prodigal Son, 1 vol. Bowman, Crystal. 2011. (I Can Read! / Bible Stories Ser.). (ENG.). 32p. (J). (gr. -1-2). pap. 3.99 *(978-0-310-72155-0(5))* Zonderkidz.

—Thankful Together. Davis, Holly. 2006. 36p. (J). 5.99 *(978-0-7847-1436-2(3),* 04077) Standard Publishing.

Solana, Javier. Poesias para Todos los Dias: Versos Fritos. Solana, Javier, tr. Fuertes, Gloria. 2003. (SPA.). 126p. *(978-84-305-7805-4(6),* SU4857) Susaeta Ediciones, S.A. ESP. Dist: Lectorum Pubns., Inc.

Solbert, Ronni. The Elephant Who Liked to Smash Small Cars. Merrill, Jean. 2015. (ENG.). 40p. (J). (gr. -1-2). 14.95 *(978-1-59017-872-0(6),* NYR Children's Collection) New York Review of Bks., Inc., The.

—The Pushcart War. Merrill, Jean. 50th anniv. ed. 2014. (ENG.). 232p. (J). (gr. 3-7). 15.95 *(978-1-59017-819-5(X),* NYR Children's Collection) New York Review of Bks., Inc., The.

Sole, Francisco. El Senor del Cero. Molina, Maria Isabel. 2003. (SPA.). 153p. (J). (gr. 5-8). pap. 10.95 *(978-968-19-0388-6(9))* Santillana USA Publishing Co., Inc.

Solé, Francisco. La Isla del Tesoro. Solé, Francisco, tr. Ruiz, Celia & Stevenson, Robert Louis. 3rd ed. 2003. (Timeless Classics Ser.). (SPA.). 92p. (J). (gr. 5-8). pap. 12.95 *(978-84-204-5729-1(9))* Santillana USA Publishing Co., Inc.

Soleilhac, Aude. Around the World in 80 Days. Verne, Jules. 2011. (Classics Illustrated Deluxe Graphic Nove Ser.: 7). (ENG.). 144p. (J). (gr. 3-9). 17.99 *(978-1-59707-284-7(2))* Papercutz.

Soleiman, Serg & Parks, Phil. The Mothman's Shadow, 1 vol. Strange, Jason. 2011. (Jason Strange Ser.). (ENG.). 72p. (gr. 2-3). lib. bdg. 23.99 *(978-1-4342-2965-6(3))* Stone Arch Bks.

—Zombie Winter, 1 vol. Strange, Jason. 2011. (Jason Strange Ser.). (ENG.). 72p. (gr. 2-3). lib. bdg. 23.99 *(978-1-4342-2964-9(5))* Stone Arch Bks.

Soley, Liesel. Can You Be an Artist? Soley, Liesel. 2011. 28p. (J). (gr. -1-3). 16.95 *(978-1-935359-69-2(X))* Book Pubs. Network.

Solheim, Kermit. Callie Cow. Hogan, Jayne. Reiter, Cheryl, ed. (J). (gr. -1). mass mkt. 12.99 *(978-1-887327-55-8(X))* TOMY International, Inc.

Soli, Tina. When Two Are Angry at Each Other. Bringsvaerd, Tor Age. Vetleseter, Tonje, tr. from NOR. 2008. 32p. (J). (gr. -1-1). 14.95 *(978-0-9790347-8-7(7))* Mackenzie Smiles, LLC.

—When Two Get Up. Bringsvaerd, Tor Age. 2009. (When Two Ser.). 36p. (J). (gr. -1-1). 14.95 *(978-0-9815761-4-5(1))* Mackenzie Smiles, LLC.

—When Two Say Goodnight. Bringsvaerd, Tor Age. 2009. (When Two Ser.). 36p. (J). (gr. -1-1). 14.95 *(978-0-9815761-3-8(3))* Mackenzie Smiles, LLC.

—When Two Take a Bath. Bringsvaerd, Tor Age. 2009. (When Two Ser.). 36p. (J). (gr. -1-3). 14.95 *(978-0-9815761-1-4(7))* Mackenzie Smiles, LLC.

Solid, Silas, photos by. The Creatures, Creation, & Creator at the Galapagos Islands. Jaime, Catherine. 2011. (ENG., 40p. pap. 11.50 *(978-1-4610-7700-8(1))* CreateSpace Independent Publishing Platform.

Sollers, Jim. Beau Beaver Goes to Town. Bloxam, Frances. ed. 2009. (ENG.). 32p. (J). (gr. -1-3). 16.95 *(978-0-89272-792-6(6))* Down East Bks.

—The First Feud: Between the Mountain & the Sea. Plourde, Lynn. 2003. (ENG.). 30p. (J). (gr. k-17). 15.95 *(978-0-89272-611-0(3))* Down East Bks.

Sollers, Jim & Reed, Rebecca Harrison. Only Cows Allowed!, 1 vol. Plourde, Lynn. 2011. (ENG.). 32p. (gr. -1-3). 16.95 *(978-0-89272-790-2(X))* Down East Bks.

Solly, Gloria, jt. illus. see Cruzan, Patricia.

Solly, Gloria D. Max Does It Again. Cruzan, Patricia. 2005. 116p. (J). pap. 14.00 *(978-1-4120-6581-8(X))* Trafford Publishing.

Solner Heimer, Patricia. Li'l Earth. Solner Heimer, Patricia. 2010. 32p. (J). (gr. k-4). 15.99 *(978-0-9844453-0-1(7))* Maple Road Publishing, Inc.

Solomon, Debra. How Come? Every Kid's Science Questions Explained. Wollard, Kathy. ed. 2014. (ENG.). 416p. (J). pap. 16.95 *(978-0-7611-7978-8(X),* 17978) Workman Publishing Co., Inc.

—How Come? in the Neighborhood. Wollard, Kathy. 2007. (ENG.). 292p. (J). (gr. 4-7). pap. 12.95 *(978-0-7611-4429-8(3),* 14429) Workman Publishing Co., Inc.

Solomon, Debra. El Libro de Los Porqués 2: Las Preguntas Más Difíciles y Las Respuestas Más Fáciles Sobre Las Personas, Los Animales y Las Cosas. Solomon, Debra. Wollard, Kathy. 2004. (SPA.). 208p. 28.99 *(978-84-9754-047-6(6),* 87432) Ediciones Oniro S.A. ESP. Dist: Lectorum Pubns., Inc.

Solomon, Harry. The Day Silver Snowed. Solomon, Harry. 2009. 112p. 80.00 *(978-0-9630376-1-9(7))* Figure 8 Pr.

Solomon, Heather. Ugly Pie. Wheeler, Lisa. (ENG.). 32p. (J). (gr. -1-3). 2014. pap. 6.99 *(978-0-544-23961-6(X),* HMH Books For Young Readers); 2010. 16.99 *(978-0-15-216754-7(4))* Houghton Mifflin Harcourt Publishing Co.

Solomon, Heather M. Clever Beatrice. Willey, Margaret. 2004. (ENG.). 40p. (J). (gr. -1-3). reprint ed. 7.99 *(978-0-689-87068-2(X),* Atheneum Bks. for Young Readers) Simon & Schuster Children's Publishing.

—Clever Beatrice & the Best Little Pony. Willey, Margaret. 2004. (ENG.). 40p. (J). (gr. -1-3). 17.99 *(978-0-689-85339-5(4),* Atheneum Bks. for Young Readers) Simon & Schuster Children's Publishing.

—A Clever Beatrice Christmas. Willey, Margaret. 2006. (ENG.). 40p. (J). (gr. -1-2). 17.99 *(978-0-689-87017-0(5),* Atheneum Bks. for Young Readers) Simon & Schuster Children's Publishing.

—If I Were a Lion. Weeks, Sarah. (ENG.). 40p. (J). (gr. -1-2). 2007. 7.99 *(978-1-4169-3837-8(0));* 2004. 17.99 *(978-0-689-84836-0(6))* Simon & Schuster Children's Publishing. (Atheneum Bks. for Young Readers).

—The Secret-Keeper. Coombs, Kate. 2006. (ENG.). 32p. (J). (gr. -1-3). 17.99 *(978-0-689-83963-4(4),* Atheneum Bks. for Young Readers) Simon & Schuster Children's Publishing.

—Willa & the Wind, 1 vol. Del Negro, Janice M. & Del Negro. 2005. (ENG.). 32p. (J). (gr. k-3). 16.95 *(978-0-7614-5232-4(X))* Marshall Cavendish Corp.

—The 3 Bears & Goldilocks. Willey, Margaret. 2008. (ENG.). 32p. (J). (gr. -1-3). 17.99 *(978-1-4169-2494-4(9),* Atheneum Bks. for Young Readers) Simon & Schuster Children's Publishing.

Solomon, Rosiland. Mammals: Hairy, Milk-Making Animals. Salas, Laura Purdie. 2009. (Amazing Science: Animal Classification Ser.). (ENG.). 24p. (gr. k-3). lib. bdg. 25.32 *(978-1-4048-5525-0(4),* Nonfiction Picture Bks.) Picture Window Bks.

—Reptiles: Scaly-Skinned Animals. Salas, Laura Purdie. 2009. (Amazing Science: Animal Classification Ser.). (ENG.). 24p. (gr. k-3). lib. bdg. 25.32 *(978-1-4048-5526-7(2),* Nonfiction Picture Bks.) Picture Window Bks.

Solotareff, Gregoire. El Rey Cocodrilo. Solotareff, Gregoire. Solotareff, Ros, Rafael, tr. 2006. (SPA.). (J). *(978-84-8470-224-5(3))* Corimbo, Editorial S.L.

Soltero, Emilio. A Very Special Athlete. Flynn, Dale Bachm. 2004. 32p. (J). lib. bdg. 14.95 *(978-0-9741332-1-8(3),* 1237268) Pearl Pr.

Soltero, Emilio. Draw the Line. Soltero, Emilio, text. 2003. 128p. (YA). per. 15.95 *(978-0-9741332-0-1(5))* Pearl Pr.

Soltz, Sheri. Finn Learns to Surf. Soltz, Sheri. Soltz, Sheri. l.t. ed. 2011. (ENG.). 30p. pap. 9.25 *(978-0-615-48117-3(5))* Soltz, Sheri.

Solway, Jeff. Maritime Monsters, 1 vol. Vernon, Steve. ed. 2010. (ENG.). 32p. (J). (gr. 3-7). 12.95 *(978-1-55109-727-5(3))* Nimbus Publishing, Ltd. CAN. Dist: Orca Bk. Pubs. USA.

Soman, David. The Amazing Adventures of Bumblebee Boy. Davis, Jacky. 2011. (Ladybug Girl Ser.). (ENG.). 40p. (J). (gr. -1-k). 16.99 *(978-0-8037-3418-0(2),* Dial) Penguin Publishing Group.

—Do You Like These Boots? Davis, Jacky. 2014. (Ladybug Girl Ser.). (ENG.). 32p. (J). (gr. k-1). pap. 3.99 *(978-0-448-46503-6(5),* Warne, Frederick Pubs.) Penguin Bks., Ltd. GBR. Dist: Penguin Random Hse., LLC.

Soman, David. Ladybug Girl & the Best Ever Playdate. Davis, Jacky. 2015. (Ladybug Girl Ser.). (ENG.). 40p. (J). (gr. -1-k). 17.99 ***(978-0-8037-4030-3(1),*** Dial) Penguin Publishing Group.

Soman, David. Ladybug Girl Ready for Snow. Davis, Jacky. 2014. (Ladybug Girl Ser.). (ENG.). 12p. (J). (gr. -1-k). bds. 5.99 *(978-0-8037-4137-9(5),* Dial) Penguin Publishing Group.

—My Big Sister's First Day of School. Heller, Maryellen. 2009. (J). *(978-0-8037-3246-9(5),* Dial) Penguin Publishing Group.

Soman, David. Doodle All Day with Ladybug Girl. Soman, David. Davis, Jacky. 2014. (Ladybug Girl Ser.). (ENG.). 32p. (J). (gr. -1-k). 6.99 *(978-0-448-47859-3(5),* Grosset & Dunlap) Penguin Publishing Group.

—Happy Halloween, Ladybug Girl! Soman, David. Davis, Jacky. 2014. (Ladybug Girl Ser.). (ENG.). 16p. (J). (gr. -1-k). 6.99 *(978-0-448-47860-9(9),* Grosset & Dunlap) Penguin Publishing Group.

—Happy Holidays, Ladybug Girl! Gift Set. Soman, David. Davis, Jacky. 2014. (Ladybug Girl Ser.). (ENG.). 14p. (J). (gr. -1-k). 16.99 *(978-0-448-47861-6(7),* Grosset & Dunlap) Penguin Publishing Group.

—Ladybug Girl. Soman, David. Davis, Jacky. 2008. (Ladybug Girl Ser.). (ENG.). 40p. (J). (gr. -1-k). 16.99 *(978-0-8037-3195-0(7),* Dial) Penguin Publishing Group.

—Ladybug Girl & Bingo. Soman, David. Davis, Jacky. 2012. (Ladybug Girl Ser.). (ENG.). 40p. (J). (gr. -1-k). 16.99 *(978-0-8037-3582-8(0),* Dial) Penguin Publishing Group.

—Ladybug Girl & Bumblebee Boy. Soman, David. Davis, Jacky. 2009. (Ladybug Girl Ser.). (ENG.). 40p. (J). (gr. -1-k). 16.99 *(978-0-8037-3339-8(9),* Dial) Penguin Publishing Group.

—Ladybug Girl & Her Mama. Soman, David. Davis, Jacky. 2013. (Ladybug Girl Ser.). (ENG.). 14p. (J). (gr. -1-k). bds. 5.99 *(978-0-8037-3891-1(9),* Dial) Penguin Publishing Group.

—Ladybug Girl & the Big Snow. Soman, David. Davis, Jacky. 2013. (Ladybug Girl Ser.). (ENG.). 40p. (J). (gr. -1-k). 17.99 *(978-0-8037-3583-5(9),* Dial) Penguin Publishing Group.

—Ladybug Girl & the Bug Squad. Soman, David. Davis, Jacky. 2011. (Ladybug Girl Ser.). (ENG.). 40p. (J). (gr. -1-k). 16.99 *(978-0-8037-3419-7(0),* Dial) Penguin Publishing Group.

—Ladybug Girl & the Dress-Up Dilemma. Soman, David. Davis, Jacky. 2014. (Ladybug Girl Ser.). (ENG.). 40p. (J). (gr. -1-k). 17.99 *(978-0-8037-3584-2(7),* Dial) Penguin Publishing Group.

—Ladybug Girl at the Beach. Soman, David. Davis, Jacky. 2010. (Ladybug Girl Ser.). (ENG.). 36p. (J). (gr. -1-k). 17.99 *(978-0-8037-3416-6(6),* Dial) Penguin Publishing Group.

—Ladybug Girl Book & Doll Set. Soman, David. Davis, Jacky. 2011. (Ladybug Girl Ser.). (ENG.). 32p. (J). (gr. -1-k). 16.99 *(978-0-8037-3444-9(1),* Dial) Penguin Publishing Group.

—Ladybug Girl Dresses Up! Soman, David. Davis, Jacky. 2010. (Ladybug Girl Ser.). (ENG.). 14p. (J). (gr. -1-k). bds. 5.99 *(978-0-448-45373-6(8),* Grosset & Dunlap) Penguin Publishing Group.

—Ladybug Girl Feels Happy. Soman, David. Davis, Jacky. 2012. (Ladybug Girl Ser.). (ENG.). 12p. (J). (gr. -1-k). bds. 5.99 *(978-0-8037-3890-4(0),* Dial) Penguin Publishing Group.

—Ladybug Girl Loves... Soman, David. Davis, Jacky. 2010. (Ladybug Girl Ser.). (ENG.). 12p. (J). (gr. -1-k). bds. 5.99 *(978-0-448-45374-3(6),* Grosset & Dunlap) Penguin Publishing Group.

—Ladybug Girl Loves... Gift Set. Soman, David. Davis, Jacky. 2013. (Ladybug Girl Ser.). (ENG.). 1p. (J). (gr. -1-k). 16.99 *(978-0-448-47785-5(8),* Grosset & Dunlap) Penguin Publishing Group.

—Ladybug Girl Makes Friends. Soman, David. Davis, Jacky. 2012. (Ladybug Girl Ser.). (ENG.). 12p. (J). (gr. -1-k). bds. 5.99 *(978-0-448-45764-2(4),* Grosset & Dunlap) Penguin Publishing Group.

—Ladybug Girl Plays. Soman, David. Davis, Jacky. 2013. (Ladybug Girl Ser.). (ENG.). 14p. (J). (gr. -1-k). bds. 5.99 *(978-0-8037-3892-8(7),* Dial) Penguin Publishing Group.

—Ladybug Girl Says Good Night. Soman, David. Davis, Jacky. 2014. (Ladybug Girl Ser.). (ENG.). 12p. (J). (gr. -1-k). bds. 5.99 *(978-0-8037-3893-5(5),* Dial) Penguin Publishing Group.

—Ladybug Girl Visits the Farm. Soman, David. Davis, Jacky. 2011. (Ladybug Girl Ser.). (ENG.). 16p. (J). (gr. -1-k). pap. 6.99 *(978-0-448-45598-3(6),* Grosset & Dunlap) Penguin Publishing Group.

—Little Box of Ladybug Girl, 4 vols. Soman, David. Davis, Jacky. 2013. (Ladybug Girl Ser.). (ENG.). 12p. (J). (gr. -1 — 1). bds., bds., bds. 23.96 *(978-0-8037-4102-7(2),* Dial) Penguin Publishing Group.

—Play All Day with Ladybug Girl. Soman, David. Davis, Jacky. 2013. (Ladybug Girl Ser.). (ENG.). 16p. (J). (gr. -1-k). 6.99 *(978-0-448-46686-6(4),* Grosset & Dunlap) Penguin Publishing Group.

—Super Catarina y los Super Insectos. Soman, David. Davis, Jacky. 2012. (Ladybug Girl Ser.).Tr. of Ladybug Girl & the Bug Squad. (ENG.). 40p. (J). (gr. -1-k). mass mkt. 6.99 *(978-0-14-242582-4(6),* Puffin) Penguin Publishing Group.

—Three Bears in a Boat. Soman, David. 2014. (ENG.). 40p. (J). (gr. -1-k). 17.99 *(978-0-8037-3993-2(1),* Dial) Penguin Publishing Group.

—Who Can Play? Soman, David. Davis, Jacky. 2013. (Ladybug Girl Ser.). (ENG.). 32p. (J). (gr. k-1). 14.99 *(978-0-448-46502-9(7));* pap. 3.99 *(978-0-448-46501-2(9))* Penguin Bks., Ltd. GBR. (Warne, Frederick Pubs.). Dist: Penguin Publishing Group.

Somers, Kevin. 123 Boston. Puck. 2010. (Cool Counting Bks.). (ENG.). 22p. (J). (gr. k — 1). bds. 8.95 *(978-0-9825295-1-5(1))* Duo Pr. LLC.

—123 California. Puck. 2008. (Cool Counting Bks.). (ENG.). 22p. (J). (gr. k — 1). bds. 7.95 *(978-0-9796213-3-8(X))* Duo Pr. LLC.

—123 Chicago. Puck. 2009. (Cool Counting Bks.). (ENG.). 22p. (J). (gr. k — 1). bds. 8.95 *(978-0-9796213-5-2(6))* Duo Pr. LLC.

—123 Philadelphia. Puck. 2010. (Cool Counting Bks.). (ENG.). 22p. (J). (gr. k — 1). bds. 8.95 *(978-0-9796213-9-0(9))* Duo Pr. LLC.

—123 San Francisco. Puck. 2009. (Cool Counting Bks.). (ENG.). 22p. (J). (gr. k — 1). bds. 8.95 *(978-0-9796213-8-3(0))* Duo Pr. LLC.

—123 Texas. Puck. 2009. (Cool Counting Bks.). (ENG.). 22p. (J). (gr. k — 1). bds. 8.95 *(978-0-9796213-6-9(4))* Duo Pr. LLC.

—123 USA: A Cool Counting Book. Puck. 2008. (Cool Counting Bks.). (SPA & ENG.). 22p. (J). (gr. k — 1). bds. 7.95 *(978-0-9796213-1-4(3))* Duo Pr. LLC.

Somers, Kevin. 1 2 3 New York. Somers, Kevin. Puck. ed. 2008. (Cool Counting Bks.). (ENG.). 22p. (J). (gr. k — 1). bds. 7.95 *(978-0-9796213-0-7(5))* Duo Pr. LLC.

Somervill, Barbara A. William Penn: Founder of Pennsylvania, 1 vol. Somervill, Barbara A. 2006. (Signature Lives: Colonial America Ser.). (ENG.). 112p. (gr. 6-7). lib. bdg. 35.32 *(978-0-7565-1598-0(X),* Signature Lives) Compass Point Bks.

Somerville, Charles C. E Is for Egypt. Somerville, Charles C. 2015. (Is for Alphabet Ser.). (ENG.). 32p. (J). (gr. -1-3). pap. 9.99 ***(978-1-907432-15-6(9))*** Hogs Back Bks. GBR. Dist: Independent Pubs. Group.

—F Is for Football. Somerville, Charles C. Elliott, Ned. 2014. (ENG.). 32p. (J). (gr. -1-3). pap. 9.99 ***(978-1-907432-16-3(7))*** Hogs Back Bks. GBR. Dist: Independent Pubs. Group.

Somerville, Sheila. The Adventures of Walter the Weremouse; the Adventures of Mishka the Mousewere. Dashney, John. 2005. 202p. (J). pap. *(978-0-9633236-7-5(9))* Storm Peak Pr.

—The Pig That Bethlehem Never Knew. Copeland, Colene. 2003. 56p. (J). 14.95 *(978-0-939810-26-0(3),* Q) Jordan Valley Heritage Hse.

Somerville/ Lampstand Press, David. South America: The Continent & Its Countries. Rohwer/Lampstand Press, Lauren. 2008. (ENG.). 56p. (J). pap. 8.95 *(978-1-935301-01-1(2))* Lampstand Pr., Ltd.

Son, Eugene, jt. illus. see Mosier, Scott.

Son, Hee-Joon. Phantasy Degree, Vol. 4. Son, Hee-Joon. rev. ed. 2005. (PhD: Phantasy Degree Ser.). 192p. pap. 9.99 *(978-1-59532-322-4(8))* TOKYOPOP, Inc.

Sona & Jacob. Counting. Singhal, Sheetal. 2007.Tr. of Ginti. (ENG, HIN, GUJ & PAN.). 24p. (J). pap. 8.00 *(978-0-9773645-8-9(5))* MeeraMasi, Inc.

—Diwali: A Festival of Lights & Fun. Kumar, Monica & Kumar, Manisha. 2006.Tr. of Diwali: Khushiyon Ka Tyohaar. (ENG & HIN.). 32p. (J). 11.00 *(978-0-9773645-7-2(7))* MeeraMasi, Inc.

—Jay & Juhi: Taj Mahal Kee Saahsik Khoj. Kumar, Monica. Aggarwal, Madhu, tr. 2008.Tr. of Jay & Juhi: the Taj Mahal Adventure. (HIN & ENG.). 32p. (J). pap. 14.99 *(978-0-9797191-4-1(3))* MeeraMasi, Inc.

—Opposites. Singhal, Sheetal. 2007.Tr. of Vipareet Shabdh. (ENG, HIN, GUJ & PAN.). 24p. (J). pap. 8.00 *(978-0-9773645-9-6(3))* MeeraMasi, Inc.

—Vamamala Geet. 2006. (HIN & ENG.). 3p. (J). 12.00 *(978-0-9773645-6-5(9))* MeeraMasi, Inc.

Sona and Jacob. Hide-n-seek Monday. Darling, Helen. Glickstein, Jennifer, ed. 2007. (J). 10.00 *(978-0-9797674-0-1(7))* My Darling-Tots Pubns.

Song, Aram. Annie's Solo Mission. Kelman, Marcy. 2007. (Disney's Little Einsteins Ser.). (J). (gr. -1-1). 12.90 *(978-1-4177-9664-9(2),* Turtleback) Turtleback Bks.

Song, Danielle, jt. illus. see Payne, Rachel.

Song, Jennifer, jt. illus. see Random House Staff.

Song, Jennifer, jt. illus. see Random House.

Songs, Steve. Knick Knack Paddy Whack. Engel, Christiane. 2009. (ENG.). 24p. (J). pap. 6.99 *(978-1-84686-305-9(8))* Barefoot Bks., Inc.

Soni, Parwinder Singh. Little Red Riding Hood. 2010. (J). *(978-1-60617-132-5(1))* Teaching Strategies, Inc.

Sonishi, Kenji. Leave It to PET! Sonishi, Kenji. (Leave It to PET! Ser.: 3). (ENG.). (J). 2009. 192p. pap. 7.99 *(978-1-4215-2651-5(4));* 2009. 196p. pap. 7.99 *(978-1-4215-2650-8(6));* Vol. 4. 2010. 192p. pap. 7.99 *(978-1-4215-2652-2(2))* Viz Media.

Sonkin, Jessica. Standing for Socks. Weissman, Elissa Brent. (ENG.). 224p. (J). (gr. 3-7). 2010. pap. 6.99 *(978-1-4169-9777-1(6));* 2009. 15.99 *(978-1-4169-4801-8(5))* Simon & Schuster Children's Publishing. (Atheneum Bks. for Young Readers).

Sonnemair, Jan. Cowboy Up! Ride the Navajo Rodeo. Flood, Nancy Bo. 2013. (ENG.). 48p. (J). (gr. 3-7). 17.95 *(978-1-59078-893-6(1),* Wordsong) Boyds Mills Pr.

Sonoda, Konami. Choco Mimi. Sonoda, Konami. (Choco Mimi Ser.: 3). (ENG.). (J). 2010. 184p. pap. 7.99 *(978-1-4215-2760-4(X));* Vol. 2. 2009. 200p. pap. 7.99 *(978-1-4215-2759-8(6))* Viz Media.

—Chocomimi. Sonoda, Konami. (ENG.). 2010. (ChocoMimi Ser.: 4). 184p. (YA). pap. 9.99 *(978-1-4215-2900-4(9));* 2009. (Choco Mimi Ser.: 1). 176p. (J). pap. 9.99 *(978-1-4215-2758-1(8))* Viz Media.

—ChocoMimi , Vol. 5. Sonoda, Konami. 2010. (Choco Mimi Ser.: 5). (ENG.). 185p. (J). pap. 9.99 *(978-1-4215-3667-5(6))* Viz Media.

Sonsky, Kim. Stamp It! Brush-Free Art Prints & Paint Projects. Sonsky, Kim. Garry-McCord, Kathleen. 2006. 48p. (J). *(978-0-439-81340-2(9))* Scholastic, Inc.

Soo, Kean. The Baker's Run. 2015. (March Grand Prix Ser.). (ENG.). 48p. (gr. 1-3). lib. bdg. 31.99 ***(978-1-4342-9640-5(7))*** Stone Arch Bks.

—The Great Desert Rally. 2015. (March Grand Prix Ser.). (ENG.). 48p. (gr. 1-3). lib. bdg. 31.99 ***(978-1-4342-9641-2(5))*** Stone Arch Bks.

—March Grand Prix: The Fast & the Furriest. 2015. (March Grand Prix Ser.). (ENG.). 144p. (gr. 1-3). pap. 14.95 ***(978-1-62370-171-0(6))*** Stone Arch Bks.

—The Race at Harewood. 2015. (March Grand Prix Ser.). (ENG.). 48p. (gr. 1-3). lib. bdg. 31.99 ***(978-1-4342-9639-9(3))*** Stone Arch Bks.

Soos, Eva, photos by. Songs of Life: Psalm Meditations from the Catholic Community at Stanford. Greenfield, Anne. 2004. 191p. 55.00 *(978-0-9745206-1-2(6))* Blackfairs Pr.

Soper, Vernon. The Magic Walking Stick & Stories from the Arabian Nights. Buchan, John. 2007. 336p. per. 19.95 *(978-0-9791702-8-7(1))* Capricorn Hse. Publishing.

Soprano, Sophie. Laughing All the Way. 2008. (J). *(978-1-59811-642-7(8))* Covenant Communications.

Sorba, Richard. Getting to Know Your Emotional Needs. Dombrower, Jan. Date not set. (J). *(978-1-55864-021-4(5))* Kidsrights.

Sorel, Edward. Jack & the Beanstalk. Metaxas, Eric. 2005. (Rabbit Ears: A Classic Tale Ser.). 36p. (gr. 2-7). 25.65 *(978-1-59679-345-3(7))* Spotlight.

Sorensen, Heather. Bugs, Bugs, Bugs! Davies, Kathern. 2010. 24p. pap. 12.99 *(978-1-4520-1624-5(0))* AuthorHouse.

Sorensen, Henri. Christmas in the Trenches, 1 vol. McCutcheon, John. 2006. (ENG.). 32p. (J). (gr. 1-5). 18.95 *(978-1-56145-374-0(9))* Peachtree Pubs.

—Daddy Played Music for the Cows. Weidt, Maryann N. 2nd ed. 2004. 32p. (J). pap. 7.95 *(978-0-89317-060-8(7),* WW-0607, Windward Publishing) Finney Co., Inc.

—My Love Will Be with You. Melmed, Laura Krauss. 2009. (ENG.). 24p. (J). (gr. -1-2). 17.99 *(978-0-06-155260-1(7))* HarperCollins Pubs.

Sørensen, Henri. O! Bloo's Boogie-Woogie Band & Blues Ensemble, 1 vol. Huling, Jan. 2010. (ENG.). 32p. (J). (gr. 1-5). 16.95 *(978-1-56145-436-5(2))* Peachtree Pubs.

Sorensen, Henri. Poetry for Young People: Robert Frost. Schmidt, Gary D., ed. 2014. (ENG.). 48p. (J). (gr. 3). 14.95 *(978-1-4549-0288-1(4))* Sterling Publishing Co., Inc.

Sørensen, Henri. The Printer, 1 vol. Uhlberg, Myron. 2009. (ENG.). 32p. (J). (gr. -1-3). pap. 8.95 *(978-1-56145-483-9(4))* Peachtree Pubs.

Sorensen, Henri. Robert Frost. Schmidt, Gary D., ed. 2008. (Poetry for Young People Ser.). (ENG.). 48p. (J). (gr. 3). pap. 6.95 *(978-1-4027-5475-3(2))* Sterling Publishing Co., Inc.

—Wishes for You. Tobias, Tobi. 40p. (J). (gr. -1-2). 2005. pap. 6.99 *(978-0-06-443730-1(2));* 2003. 16.99 *(978-0-688-10838-0(5))* HarperCollins Pubs.

Sorensen, Henri. The Printer, 1 vol. Sorensen, Henri, tr. Uhlberg, Myron. 2003. (ENG.). 32p. (J). (gr. k-3). 16.95 *(978-1-56145-221-7(1))* Peachtree Pubs.

Sorensen, Peter, jt. illus. see Liss, Ira.

Sorenson, Vanessa. The Secret Life of a Snowflake: An up-Close Look at the Art & Science of Snowflakes. Libbrecht, Kenneth. 2010. (ENG.). 48p. (J). (gr. 1-17). 17.00 *(978-0-7603-3676-2(8),* 0760336768, Voyageur Pr) Quarto Publishing Group USA.

Sorra, Kristin. Groundhog Weather School. Holub, Joan. 2009. (ENG.). 32p. (J). (gr. k-3). 16.99 *(978-0-399-24659-3(2),* Putnam Juvenile) Penguin Publishing Group.

—Groundhog Weather School: Fun Facts about Weather & Groundhogs. Holub, Joan. 2013. (ENG.). 32p. (J). (gr. k-3). 6.99 *(978-0-14-750945-1(9),* Puffin) Penguin Publishing Group.

—King o' the Cats. Shepard, Aaron. 2010. (ENG.). 32p. (J). (gr. -1-3). 11.99 *(978-1-4424-1256-9(9),* Atheneum Bks. for Young Readers) Simon & Schuster Children's Publishing.

—Mi Amiga Tiene Dislexia. Tourville, Amanda Doering. Translations.com Staff, tr. 2012. (Amigos con Discapacidades/Friends with Disabilities Ser.).Tr. of My Friend Has Dyslexia. (MUL & SPA.). 24p. (gr. k-3). lib. bdg. 25.32 *(978-1-4048-7314-8(7))* Picture Window Bks.

—My Friend Has ADHD, 1 vol. Tourville, Amanda Doering. 2010. (Friends with Disabilities Ser.). (ENG.). 24p. (gr. k-3). lib. bdg. 25.32 *(978-1-4048-5749-0(4),* Nonfiction Picture Bks.) Picture Window Bks.

—My Friend Has ADHD, 1 vol. Doering Tourville, Amanda. 2010. (Friends with Disabilities Ser.). (ENG.). 24p. (gr. k-3). pap. 7.49 *(978-1-4048-6108-4(4),* Nonfiction Picture Bks.) Picture Window Bks.

—My Friend Has ADHD [Readers World]. Doering Tourville, Amanda. 2010. (Friends with Disabilities Ser.). 24p. pap. 6.00 *(978-1-4048-6701-7(5),* Nonfiction Picture Bks.) Picture Window Bks.

—My Friend Has Autism, 1 vol. Tourville, Amanda Doering. 2010. (Friends with Disabilities Ser.). (ENG.). 24p. (gr. k-3). lib. bdg. 25.32 *(978-1-4048-5750-6(8),* Nonfiction Picture Bks.) Picture Window Bks.

—My Friend Has Autism, 1 vol. Doering Tourville, Amanda. 2010. (Friends with Disabilities Ser.). (ENG.). 24p. (gr. k-3). pap. 7.49 *(978-1-4048-6109-1(2),* Nonfiction Picture Bks.) Picture Window Bks.

—My Friend Has Autism [Readers World]. Doering Tourville, Amanda. 2010. (Friends with Disabilities Ser.). 24p. pap. 6.00 *(978-1-4048-6702-4(3),* Nonfiction Picture Bks.) Picture Window Bks.

—My Friend Has down Syndrome, 1 vol. Doering Tourville, Amanda. 2010. (Friends with Disabilities Ser.). (ENG.). 24p. (gr. k-3). pap. 7.49 *(978-1-4048-6110-7(6),* Nonfiction Picture Bks.) Picture Window Bks.

—My Friend Has down Syndrome, 1 vol. Tourville, Amanda Doering. 2010. (Friends with Disabilities Ser.). (ENG.). 24p. (gr. k-3). lib. bdg. 25.32 *(978-1-4048-5751-3(6),* Nonfiction Picture Bks.) Picture Window Bks.

—My Friend Has down Syndrome [Readers World]. Doering Tourville, Amanda. 2010. (Friends with Disabilities Ser.). 24p. pap. 6.00 *(978-1-4048-6703-1(1),* Nonfiction Picture Bks.) Picture Window Bks.

—My Friend Has Dyslexia, 1 vol. Tourville, Amanda Doering. 2010. (Friends with Disabilities Ser.). (ENG.). 24p. (gr. k-3). lib. bdg. 25.32 *(978-1-4048-5752-0(4),* Nonfiction Picture Bks.) Picture Window Bks.

—My Friend Has Dyslexia, 1 vol. Doering Tourville, Amanda. 2010. (Friends with Disabilities Ser.). (ENG.). 24p. (gr. k-3). pap. 7.49 *(978-1-4048-6111-4(4),* Nonfiction Picture Bks.) Picture Window Bks.

—My Friend Has Dyslexia [Readers World]. Doering Tourville, Amanda. 2010. (Friends with Disabilities Ser.). 24p. pap. 6.00 *(978-1-4048-6704-8(X),* Nonfiction Picture Bks.) Picture Window Bks.

—Scarlett the Cat to the Rescue: Fire Hero, 1 vol. Loewen, Nancy. 2014. (Animal Heroes Ser.). (ENG.). 32p. (gr. k-2). 27.99 *(978-1-4795-5464-5(2))* Picture Window Bks.

Sorra, Kristin. Mi Amiga Tiene Sindrome de Down. Sorra, Kristin. Tourville, Amanda Doering. Translations.com Staff, tr. from ENG. 2012. (Amigos con Discapacidades/Friends with Disabilities Ser.). (MUL & SPA.). 24p. (gr. k-3). lib. bdg. 25.32 *(978-1-4048-7313-1(9))* Picture Window Bks.

—Mi Amigo Tiene ADHD. Sorra, Kristin. Tourville, Amanda Doering. Translations.com Staff, tr. from ENG. 2012. (Amigos con Discapacidades/Friends with Disabilities Ser.).Tr. of My Friend Has ADHD. (SPA & MUL.). 24p. (gr. k-3). lib. bdg. 25.32 *(978-1-4048-7311-7(2))* Picture Window Bks.

—Mi Amigo Tiene Autismo. Sorra, Kristin. Tourville, Amanda Doering. Translations.com Staff, tr. 2012. (Amigos con Discapacidades/Friends with Disabilities Ser.).Tr. of My Friend Has Autism. (MUL, SPA & ENG.). 24p. (gr. k-3). lib. bdg. 25.32 *(978-1-4048-7312-4(0))* Picture Window Bks.

Sorrentino, Alessandra. Mi Monstruo Burrufu. Corral, Alberto. 2013. (SPA.). 108p. pap. 8.95 *(978-0-615-80250-3(8))* Petite Grande Idée.

Sorrentino, Michela. The Edible Alphabet: 26 Reasons to Love the Farm. Watterson, Carol. 2011. (ENG.). 48p. (J). (gr. k-3). 16.99 *(978-1-58246-421-3(9),* Tricycle Pr.) Ten Speed Pr.

Sorrow, Casey. The Cats of Copenhagen. Joyce, James. 2012. (ENG.). 32p. (J). 19.99 *(978-1-4767-0894-2(0),* Scribner) Scribner.

Sosa, Hernan. Armando & the Blue Tarp School, 1 vol. Fine, Edith Hope & Josephson, Judith Pinkerton. 2007. (ENG.). 32p. (J). (gr. -1-3). lib. bdg. 16.95 *(978-1-58430-278-0(X))* Lee & Low Bks., Inc.

—Armando y la Escuela de Lona Azul. Fine, Edith Hope & Josephson, Judith Pinkerton. 2015.Tr. of Armando & the Blue Tarp School. (SPA & ENG.). 32p. (J). (gr. k-4). pap. 8.95 *(978-1-60060-449-2(8))* Lee & Low Bks., Inc.

—Mimi's Parranda/la Parranda de Mimi. Gil, Lydia M. 2007. (SPA & ENG.). 32p. (J). (gr. -1-2). 16.95 *(978-1-55885-477-2(0),* Piñata Books) Arte Publico Pr.

Sosebee, Cheryl. Bobby's Dove. Hamilton, Matthew. 2005. (J). bds. 9.99 *(978-1-4183-0061-6(6))* Christ Inspired, Inc.

Sosnowski, Tiffany. Ace's Wish for a Forever Home. Written By Kimberly M Sosnowski; Illustr. 2011. 28p. pap. 24.95 *(978-1-4626-3031-8(6))* America Star Bks.

Sotirovski, Aleksandar. Earthquakes!, 1 vol. Gray-Wilburn, Renée. 2012. (First Graphics: Wild Earth Ser.). (ENG.). 24p. (gr. 1-2). pap. 6.29 *(978-1-4296-7950-3(6));* pap. 35.70 *(978-1-4296-8370-8(8));* lib. bdg. 23.32 *(978-1-4296-7605-2(1))* Capstone Pr., Inc.

—First Graphics: Wild Earth. Aboff, Marcie & Gray-Wilburn, Renée. 2012. (First Graphics: Wild Earth Ser.). (ENG.). 24p. (gr. 1-2). pap. 142.80 *(978-1-4296-8375-3(9));* pap. 25.16 *(978-1-4296-8374-6(0));* lib. bdg. 93.28 *(978-1-4296-8146-9(2))* Capstone Pr., Inc.

—Hurricanes!, 1 vol. Aboff, Marcie. 2012. (First Graphics: Wild Earth Ser.). (ENG.). 24p. (gr. 1-2). pap. 6.29 *(978-1-4296-7951-0(4));* pap. 35.70 *(978-1-4296-8371-5(6));* lib. bdg. 23.32 *(978-1-4296-7607-6(8))* Capstone Pr., Inc.

—Tornadoes!, 1 vol. Aboff, Marcie. 2012. (First Graphics: Wild Earth Ser.). (ENG.). 24p. (gr. 1-2). pap. 6.29 *(978-1-4296-7952-7(2));* pap. 35.70 *(978-1-4296-8372-2(4));* lib. bdg. 23.32 *(978-1-4296-7608-3(6))* Capstone Pr., Inc.

—Volcanoes!, 1 vol. Gray-Wilburn, Renée & Beehive Illustrations Staff. 2012. (First Graphics: Wild Earth Ser.). (ENG.). 24p. (gr. 1-2). pap. 6.29 *(978-1-4296-7953-4(0))* Capstone Pr., Inc.

—Volcanoes! Gray-Wilburn, Renée. 2012. (First Graphics: Wild Earth Ser.). (ENG.). 24p. (gr. 1-2). pap. 35.70 *(978-1-4296-8373-9(2));* lib. bdg. 23.32 *(978-1-4296-7606-9(X))* Capstone Pr., Inc.

Sotnik, Katherine. Choir of Angels Coloring Book. 2012. (Holy Imitation Ser.). (ENG.). 72p. (J). (gr. -1-3). 4.95 *(978-1-58617-588-7(2))* Ignatius Pr.

Soud. Abraham Lincoln: 16th U. S. President. Hall, Margaret. 2008. (Beginner Biographies Ser.). 32p. (gr. -1-3). 28.50 *(978-1-60270-250-9(0),* Looking Glass Library-Nonfiction) Magic Wagon.

—George Washington: 1st U. S. President. Cosson, Jody. 2008. (Beginner Biographies Ser.). 32p. (gr. -1-3). 28.50 *(978-1-60270-253-0(5),* Looking Glass Library-Nonfiction) Magic Wagon.

—Jane Goodall: Friend of the Apes. Lindeen, Mary. 2008. (Beginner Biographies Ser.). 32p. (gr. -1-3). 28.50 *(978-1-60270-249-3(7),* Looking Glass Library-Nonfiction) Magic Wagon.

—Kate, the Ghost Dog: Coping with the Death of a Pet. Wilson, Wayne L. 2009. 48p. (J). (gr. 3-8). 14.95 *(978-1-4338-0554-7(5));* pap. 9.95 *(978-1-4338-0555-4(3))* American Psychological Assn. (Magination Pr.).

—Marie Curie: Scientist. Lindeen, Mary. 2008. (Beginner Biographies Ser.). 32p. (gr. -1-3). 28.50 *(978-1-60270-248-6(9),* Looking Glass Library-Nonfiction) Magic Wagon.

—Martin Luther King, Jr. Civil Rights Leader. Hall, M. C. 2008. (Beginner Biographies Ser.). 32p. (gr. -1-3). 28.50 *(978-1-60270-251-6(9),* Looking Glass Library-Nonfiction) Magic Wagon.

—Sacagawea: Indian Guide. Cosson, Jody. 2008. (Beginner Biographies Ser.). 32p. (gr. -1-3). 28.50 *(978-1-60270-252-3(7),* Looking Glass Library-Nonfiction) Magic Wagon.

Souhami, Jessica. Foxy! 2013. (ENG.). 32p. (J). (gr. -1-2). 17.99 *(978-1-84780-218-7(4),* Frances Lincoln) Quarto Publishing Group UK GBR. Dist: Hachette Bk. Group.

—King Pom & the Fox. 2009. (ENG.). 36p. (J). (gr. -1-2). pap. 7.95 *(978-1-84507-365-7(7),* Frances Lincoln) Quarto Publishing Group UK GBR. Dist: Hachette Bk. Group.

—Piglet's Picnic: A Story about Food & Counting. 2010. (ENG.). 28p. (J). (gr. -1-1). 16.95 *(978-1-84507-976-5(0),* Frances Lincoln Children's Bks.) Quarto Publishing Group UK GBR. Dist: Hachette Bk. Group.

Souleiman, Serg. The Golden Book of Death. Dahl, Michael. 2008. (Library of Doom Ser.). (ENG.). 40p. (gr. 1-3). lib. bdg. 22.65 *(978-1-4342-0487-5(1));* per. 6.25 *(978-1-4342-0547-6(9))* Stone Arch Bks. (Zone Bks.).

Soulier, Daniel. Pateando Lunas. Berocay, Roy. 2003. (SPA.). 166p. (J). (gr. 3). pap. 12.95 *(978-9974-590-63-2(9))* Santillana S. A. URY. Dist: Santillana USA Publishing Co., Inc.

Soumagnac, Virginie. Zero Kisses for Me. Monari, Manuela. 2010. (ENG.). 24p. (J). (gr. -1-1). 12.95 *(978-1-77049-208-0(9),* Tundra Bks.) Tundra Bks. CAN. Dist: Penguin Random Hse., LLC.

Sourdais, Clémentine. Little Red Riding Hood. Grimm, Jacob & Grimm, Wilhelm. 2014. (ENG.). 28p. (J). 16.95 *(978-3-89955-723-7(9))* Die Gestalten Verlag DEU. Dist: Prestel Publishing.

Sourwine, David. The Dragon Prince. Blum, Vicki. 2005. (ENG.). 160p. pap. *(978-0-439-95668-0(4))* Scholastic Canada, Ltd.

Sousa, Jay, photos by. How to Build a California Mission: Santa Barbara, 20 vols. Campodonica, Carol A. Wardup, Shirley et al, eds. Date not set. (How to Build a California Mission Ser.). (J). (gr. 4-5). pap. *(978-0-9648488-3-2(X))* Buzzard Pr. International.

Southard, Jan. Ookie! Stoll, Emily. 2012. 28p. pap. 12.00 *(978-1-4575-0859-2(1))* Dog Ear Publishing, LLC.

Southerland, Taylor. The Savvy Cyber Kids at Home: The Defeat of the Cyber Bully. Halpert, Ben. 2011. (J). 22.99 *(978-0-9827968-4-9(6))* Savvy Cyber Kids, Inc.

Southern, Shelley. Franklin's Pumpkin. Bourgeois, Paulette & Clark, Brenda. 2004. (Kids Can Read Ser.). (ENG.). 32p. (J). (gr. 1-2). 14.95 *(978-1-55337-495-4(9))* Kids Can Pr., Ltd. CAN. Dist: Univ. of Toronto Pr.

Southern, Shelley. Franklin's Nickname. Southern, Shelley, tr. Bourgeois, Paulette & Clark, Brenda. 2004. (Franklin TV Storybook Ser.). (ENG.). 32p. (J). 4.95 *(978-1-55337-490-9(8));* (gr. -1-3). 10.95 *(978-1-55337-489-3(4))* Kids Can Pr., Ltd. CAN. Dist: Univ. of Toronto Pr.

Souto, Jose. Chusco the Stray Dog. Ibarrola, Begonia. 2013. (ENG.). 32p. (J). *(978-84-95923-99-8(8))* Primera Persona.

Souza, Paul. Roy Rogers & the Desert Treasure. Sankey, Alice. 2011. 26p. 35.95 *(978-1-258-03927-1(3))* Literary Licensing, LLC.

Sovak, Jean-Marc Superville. Deadly. Chibbaro, Julie. (ENG.). 304p. (YA). (gr. 7). 2012. pap. 10.99 *(978-0-689-85739-3(X));* 2011. 16.99 *(978-0-689-85738-6(1))* Simon & Schuster Children's Publishing. (Atheneum Bks. for Young Readers).

Sowards, Ben. Christmas Oranges. 2004. 32p. 17.95 *(978-1-59156-098-2(5))* Covenant Communications, Inc.

—The Eyes of the Want. Skye, Obert. 2008. (Leven Thumps Ser.: 3). (ENG.). 416p. (J). (gr. 3-7). pap. 9.99 *(978-1-4169-4719-6(1),* Simon & Schuster/Paula Wiseman Bks.) Simon & Schuster/Paula Wiseman Bks.

—The Gateway. Skye, Obert. 2006. (Leven Thumps Ser.: 1). (ENG.). 400p. (J). (gr. 3-7). pap. 8.99 *(978-1-4169-2806-5(5),* Simon & Schuster/Paula Wiseman Bks.) Simon & Schuster/Paula Wiseman Bks.

—He Took My Lickin' for Me: A Classic Folk Tale. 2003. 32p. (J). (gr. 3-7). 16.95 *(978-1-57008-953-4(1),* Shadow Mountain) Shadow Mountain Publishing.

—Penny's Christmas Jar Party. Wright, Jason F. 2009. 32p. (J). 17.95 *(978-1-60641-167-4(5),* Shadow Mountain) Shadow Mountain Publishing.

—The Ruins of Alder. Skye, Obert. 2010. (Leven Thumps Ser.: 5). (ENG.). 416p. (J). (gr. 4-9). pap. 8.99 *(978-1-4169-9093-2(3),* Simon & Schuster/Paula Wiseman Bks.) Simon & Schuster/Paula Wiseman Bks.

—The Whispered Secret. Skye, Obert. 2007. (Leven Thumps Ser.: 2). (ENG.). 464p. (J). (gr. 3-7). pap. 8.99 *(978-1-4169-4718-9(3),* Simon & Schuster/Paula Wiseman Bks.) Simon & Schuster/Paula Wiseman Bks.

—The Wrath of Ezra. Skye, Obert. 2009. (Leven Thumps Ser.: 4). (ENG.). 464p. (J). (gr. 4-9). pap. 9.99 *(978-1-4169-9092-5(5),* Simon & Schuster/Paula Wiseman Bks.) Simon & Schuster/Paula Wiseman Bks.

—You Are Priceless: The Parable of the Bicycle. Robinson, Stephen Edward. 2004. 32p. (J). (gr. -1-3). 18.95 *(978-1-59038-361-2(3),* Shadow Mountain) Shadow Mountain Publishing.

Sowards, Ben. Asleep on the Hay: A Dust Bowl Christmas. Sowards, Ben. 2015. (J). 17.99 ***(978-1-62972-067-8(4),*** Ensign Peak) Deseret Bk. Co.

Sowerby, Githa & Sowerby, Millicent. Cinderella. 2012. (J). *(978-1-59583-458-4(3))* Laughing Elephant.

Sowerby, Millicent, jt. illus. see Sowerby, Githa.

Sozapato. Monstruos. Williams, Ricardo. 2015. 24p. (J). (gr. -1-2). pap. 14.95 ***(978-9942-19-154-0(2),*** Alfaguara Infantil) Santillana Ecuador ECU. Dist: Santillana USA Publishing Co., Inc.

Spachner, Karen D. Volcano Adventures of Keikilani. Jackson, Kimberly. 2009. 32p. pap. 8.95 *(978-0-9643512-1-9(8))* Mouse! Publishing.

Spackman, Jeff. Boo! Halloween Poems & Limericks, 1 vol. Hubbell, Patricia & Hubbell. 2005. (ENG.). 32p. (YA). pap. 5.95 *(978-0-7614-5151-8(X))* Marshall Cavendish Corp.

Spadaccini, Cheryl. Where Will We Fly. Seymour, Marysue. 2013. 20p. pap. 9.95 *(978-1-61633-417-8(7))* Guardian Angel Publishing, Inc.

Spafford, Suzy. My Little Book of Prayers. gif. ed. 2005. 32p. 9.99 *(978-0-7369-1495-6(1))* Harvest Hse. Pubs.

Spafford, Suzy. Helping-Out Day? Hooray! Spafford, Suzy. 2003. (Tales from Duckport Ser.). (ENG.). 40p. (J). (gr. k-3). pap. 3.99 *(978-0-439-38358-5(7))* Scholastic, Inc.

Spagnol, Estelle Billon. Ah! Collet, Géraldine. 2015. (ENG.). 32p. (J). (gr. -1-k). 16.95 *(978-0-8234-3199-1(1))* Holiday Hse., Inc.

Spagnol, Estelle Billon. Little Benguin. Spagnol, Estelle Billon. 2014. (ENG.). 32p. (J). (gr. -1-1). 16.95 *(978-0-8234-2934-9(2))* Holiday Hse., Inc.

Spahn, Jerrold. Pearl Harbor: A Day of Infamy. White, Steve D. 2007. (Graphic Battles of World War II Ser.). (ENG.). 48p. (YA). (gr. 4-7). lib. bdg. 31.95 *(978-1-4042-0785-1(6))* Rosen Publishing Group, Inc., The.

Spahn, Jerrold & Erskine, Gary. Day of Infamy: Attack on Pearl Harbor. White, Steve. 2007. (Graphic History Ser.: 1). (ENG.). 48p. (YA). (gr. 2-4). pap. *(978-1-84603-059-8(5),* Osprey Publishing) Bloomsbury Publishing Plc.

Spalenka, Greg. The Eyes of the Unicorn. Bateman, Teresa. 2007. (ENG.). 32p. (J). (gr. 1-5). 17.95 *(978-0-8234-1728-5(X))* Holiday Hse., Inc.

Spalinski, Amanda. El circo llega al Pueblo: Version de Lectura Temprana. Scalzo, Linda V. Torres, Marcela H., tr. l.t. ed. 2005. (SPA.). 24p. per. 9.99 *(978-0-9753724-2-5(4))* Carazona Creations LLC.

—The Circus Is coming to Town: Early Reader Version. Scalzo, Linda V. l.t. ed. 2005. 24p. (J). per. 9.99 *(978-0-9753724-1-8(6))* Carazona Creations LLC.

Spang, Janine, photos by. Number Fun with Riley. Ferone, Jen. l.t. ed. 2011. (ENG., 24p. pap. 10.95 *(978-1-4662-2484-1(3))* CreateSpace Independent Publishing Platform.

Spangler, Brie. We Both Read-the Mystery of Pirate's Point. 2007. (We Both Read Ser.). 40p. (J). (gr. 1-5). 7.99 *(978-1-60115-009-7(1))* Treasure Bay, Inc.

—We Both Read-The Mystery of Pirate's Point: Level 3. 2008. (We Both Read Ser.). 40p. (J). (gr. 1-5). per. 4.99 *(978-1-60115-010-3(5))* Treasure Bay, Inc.

Spanjer, Kendra. All Me, All the Time: The Authorized Art-O-Biography Of... Oceanak, Karla. 2012. (Aldo Zelnick Comic Novel Ser.). (ENG.). 80p. (J). (gr. 3-7). pap. 7.95 *(978-1-934649-20-6(1))* Bailiwick Pr.

—Cahoots. Oceanak, Karla. 2011. (Aldo Zelnick Comic Novel Ser.). (ENG.). 151p. (J). (gr. 3-7). 12.95 *(978-1-934649-08-4(2))* Bailiwick Pr.

—Dumbstruck. Oceanak, Karla. 2011. (Aldo Zelnick Comic Novel Ser.). (ENG.). 160p. (J). (gr. 3-7). 12.95 *(978-1-934649-16-9(3))* Bailiwick Pr.

—Egghead. Oceanak, Karla. 2012. (ENG.). 160p. (gr. 1-8). 12.95 *(978-1-934649-17-6(1))* Bailiwick Pr.

—Finicky. Oceanak, Karla. 2012. (Aldo Zelnick Comic Novel Ser.). (ENG.). 160p. (J). (gr. 3-7). 12.95 *(978-1-934649-24-4(4))* Bailiwick Pr.

—Glitch. Oceanak, Karla. 2012. (Aldo Zelnick Comic Novel Ser.). (ENG.). 160p. (J). (gr. 3-7). 12.95 *(978-1-934649-25-1(2))* Bailiwick Pr.

—Hotdogger. Oceanak, Karla. 2013. (Aldo Zelnick Comic Novel Ser.). (ENG.). 160p. (J). (gr. 3-7). 12.95 *(978-1-934649-37-4(6))* Bailiwick Pr.

—Ignoramus. Oceanak, Karla. 2013. (Aldo Zelnick Comic Novel Ser.). (ENG.). 160p. (J). (gr. 3-7). 12.95 *(978-1-934649-41-1(4))* Bailiwick Pr.

Spanyol, Jessica. Keith & His Super-Stunt Rally Racer. Spanyol, Jessica. 2008. (Mini Bugs Ser.). (ENG.). 24p. (J). (gr. k-k). 5.99 *(978-0-7636-3742-2(4))* Candlewick Pr.

—Little Neighbors on Sunnyside Street. Spanyol, Jessica. 2007. (ENG.). 64p. (J). (gr. -1-2). 16.99 *(978-0-7636-2986-1(3))* Candlewick Pr.

Sparks, Beverly, photos by. Busy Doggies. Schindel, John. 2003. (Busy Book Ser.). (ENG., 20p. (J). (— 1). bds. 6.99 *(978-1-58246-090-1(6),* Tricycle Pr.) Ten Speed Pr.

S

Sparks, David. Flat-Top Sam & the Junkyard Elephant. Sparks, David. 2008. 36p. pap. 12.95 *(978-1-59858-587-2(8))* Dog Ear Publishing, LLC.

Sparks, Jolene. Mr. Squirrel. Sparks, Joanne. 2009. 29p. pap. 24.95 *(978-1-61546-375-6(5))* America Star Bks.

Sparks, Michal. The Sweetest Story Ever Told: A New Christmas Tradition for Families. TerKeurst, Lysa. 2003. 32p. 9.99 *(978-0-8024-7094-2(7))* Moody Pubs.

—The Sweetest Story Ever Told Activity Kit. TerKeurst, Lysa. 2003. 14.99 *(978-0-8024-7093-5(9))* Moody Pubs.

Sparling, Bren M. Through the Fairy Door. Reintjes, Susan B. 2012. 128p. (J). pap. 16.95 *(978-1-59715-085-9(1))* Chapel Hill Press, Inc.

Spartels, Stephanie. The Best Party Ever. Rippin, Sally. 2014. (ENG.). 48p. (J). pap. 4.99 *(978-1-61067-261-0(5))* Kane Miller.

—The Bumpy Ride: Hey Jack! Rippin, Sally. 2014. (ENG.). 48p. (J). pap. 4.99 *(978-1-61067-187-3(2))* Kane Miller.

—The Circus Lesson. Rippin, Sally. 2013. 41p. (J). *(978-1-61067-236-8(4))* Kane Miller.

—The Circus Lesson: Hey Jack! Rippin, Sally. 2014. (ENG.). 48p. (J). pap. 4.99 *(978-1-61067-186-6(4))* Kane Miller.

—The Crazy Cousins. Rippin, Sally. (J). 2013. (ENG.). 48p. pap. 4.99 *(978-1-61067-121-7(X))*; 2012. 42p. *(978-1-61067-135-4(X))* Kane Miller.

—The New Friend: Hey Jack! Rippin, Sally. 2014. (ENG.). 48p. (J). pap. 4.99 *(978-1-61067-125-5(2))* Kane Miller.

—The Playground Problem. Rippin, Sally. 2015. (ENG.). 48p. (J). pap. 4.99 *(978-1-61067-260-3(7))* Kane Miller.

—The Robot Blues. Rippin, Sally. 2014. (ENG.). 48p. (J). pap. 4.99 *(978-1-61067-124-8(4))* Kane Miller.

—The Scary Solo. Rippin, Sally. (J). 2013. (ENG.). 48p. pap. 4.99 *(978-1-61067-122-4(8))*; 2012. 43p. *(978-1-61067-136-1(8))* Kane Miller.

—The Top Team. Rippin, Sally. 2014. 42p. (J). *(978-1-61067-293-1(3))* Kane Miller.

—The Winning Goal. Rippin, Sally. (J). 2013. (ENG.). 48p. pap. 4.99 *(978-1-61067-123-1(6))*; 2012. 43p. *(978-1-61067-137-8(6))* Kane Miller.

—The Worry Monsters. Rippin, Sally. 2014. (ENG.). 48p. (J). pap. 4.99 *(978-1-61067-126-2(0))* Kane Miller.

—The Worst Sleepover: Hey Jack! Rippin, Sally. 2014. (ENG.). 48p. (J). pap. 4.99 *(978-1-61067-185-9(6))* Kane Miller.

Spatrisano, Kimberly, jt. illus. see Lawson, Robert.

Spay, Anthony & Campbell, Alex. Louis Armstrong. Holland, Gini & O'Hern, Kerri. 2007. (Biografías Gráficas (Graphic Biographies) Ser.). (SPA.). 32p. (gr. 5-8). lib. bdg. 27.00 *(978-0-8368-7878-3(7))* Stevens, Gareth Publishing LLLP.

—Louis Armstrong. O'Hern, Kerri & Holland, Gini. 2007. (Biografías Gráficas (Graphic Biographies) Ser.). (SPA.). 32p. (gr. 5-8). pap. 10.50 *(978-0-8368-7885-1(X))* Stevens, Gareth Publishing LLLP.

Spay, Anthony, jt. illus. see Campbell, Alex.

Spay, Anthony, jt. illus. see Floor, Guus.

Spaziante, Patrick. Blackout! Peterson, Scott. ed. 2005. (Teenage Mutant Ninja Turtles Ser.: Garden & No. 6). 24p. (J). lib. bdg. 15.00 *(978-1-59054-831-8(0))* Fitzgerald Bks.

—Case File #1 First Contact. Lewman, David. 2014. (Rabbids Invasion Ser.). (ENG.). 96p. (J). (gr. 2-5). pap. 4.99 *(978-1-4814-0037-4(1))*, Simon Spotlight) Simon Spotlight.

—Case File #4 Rabbids Go Viral. Lewman, David. 2015. (Rabbids Invasion Ser.). (ENG.). 96p. (J). (gr. 2-5). 16.99 *(978-1-4814-2766-1(0))*, Simon Spotlight) Simon Spotlight.

—Double-Team! (Teenage Mutant Ninja Turtles) Webster, Christy. 2014. (Step into Reading Ser.). (ENG.). 48p. (J). (gr. 2-4). 3.99 *(978-0-385-37434-7(8))*, Random Hse. Bks. for Young Readers) Random Hse. Children's Bks.

—Dude-It-Yourself Adventure Journal. Mayer, Kirsten. 2012. (Adventure Time Ser.). (ENG.). 112p. (J). (gr. 2-5). 7.99 *(978-0-8431-7244-7(4))*, Price Stern Sloan) Penguin Publishing Group.

—Green Team! (Teenage Mutant Ninja Turtles) Webster, Christy. 2012. (Step into Reading Ser.). (ENG.). 48p. (J). (gr. k-3). pap. 3.99 *(978-0-307-98070-0(7))*, Random Hse. Bks. for Young Readers) Random Hse. Children's Bks.

—Look Out! It's Turtle Titan! 2004. (Teenage Mutant Ninja Turtles Ser.). 24p. (J). (gr. -1-3). lib. bdg. 11.80 *(978-0-613-83491-9(7))*, Turtleback) Turtleback Bks.

—The Lost Scrolls: Fire. Mason, Tom & Danko, Dan. 2006. (Avatar Ser.). (ENG.). 64p. (J). pap. 4.99 *(978-1-4169-1880-6(9))*, Simon Spotlight/Nickelodeon) Simon Spotlight/Nickelodeon.

—Meet Casey Jones. ed. 2005. (Teenage Mutant Ninja Turtles Ser.: No. 1). 24p. (J). lib. bdg. 15.00 *(978-1-59054-836-3(1))* Fitzgerald Bks.

—Meet Leatherhead. Wax, Wendy. 2005. 22p. (J). lib. bdg. 15.00 *(978-1-4242-0972-9(2))* Fitzgerald Bks.

—The Might of Doom. Shealy, Dennis. ed. 2012. (Step into Reading Level 3 Ser.). lib. bdg. 13.55 *(978-0-606-23737-6(2))*, Turtleback) Turtleback Bks.

—Mikey's Monster (Teenage Mutant Ninja Turtles) Smith, James J. & James, Hollis. 2013. (Step into Reading Ser.). (ENG.). 48p. (J). (gr. k-3). 3.99 *(978-0-449-81826-8(8))*, Random Hse. Bks. for Young Readers) Random Hse. Children's Bks.

—New Developments, No. 2. Lewman, David. 2014. (Rabbids Invasion Ser.). (ENG.). 96p. (J). (gr. 2-5). pap. 4.99 *(978-1-4814-0204-0(8))*, Simon Spotlight) Simon Spotlight.

Spaziante, Patrick. Ninjas on Ice! (Teenage Mutant Ninja Turtles) Random House. 2015. (Glitter Picturebook Ser.). (ENG.). 16p. (J). (gr. -1-1). 5.99 ***(978-0-553-52272-3(8))***, Random Hse. Bks. for Young Readers) Random Hse. Children's Bks.

Spaziante, Patrick. Olivia Acts Out. 2009. (Olivia TV Tie-In Ser.). (ENG.). 24p. (J). (gr. -1-1). 16.99 *(978-1-4169-8571-6(9))*, Simon Spotlight) Simon Spotlight.

—OLIVIA & Her Alien Brother. 2014. (Olivia TV Tie-In Ser.). (ENG.). 24p. (J). (gr. -1-2). pap. 3.99 *(978-1-4424-9749-8(1))*, Simon Spotlight) Simon Spotlight.

—OLIVIA & Her Favorite Things. Testa, Maggie. 2013. (Olivia TV Tie-In Ser.). (ENG.). 12p. (J). (gr. -1-1). bds. 5.99 *(978-1-4424-6587-9(5))*, Simon Spotlight) Simon Spotlight.

—OLIVIA & the Butterfly Adventure. Shaw, Natalie. 2012. (Olivia TV Tie-In Ser.). (ENG.). 36p. (J). (gr. -1-2). bds. 10.99 *(978-1-4424-3601-5(8))*, Simon Spotlight) Simon Spotlight.

—OLIVIA & the Fashion Show. 2011. (Olivia TV Tie-In Ser.). (ENG.). 16p. (J). (gr. -1-1). pap. 5.99 *(978-1-4424-2028-1(6))*, Simon Spotlight) Simon Spotlight.

—Olivia & the Haunted Hotel. Shepherd, Jodie. 2010. (Olivia TV Tie-In Ser.). (ENG.). 24p. (J). (gr. -1-2). pap. 4.99 *(978-1-4424-0182-2(6))*, Simon Spotlight) Simon Spotlight.

—OLIVIA & the Kite Party. 2012. (Olivia TV Tie-In Ser.). (ENG.). 24p. (J). (gr. -1-1). 16.99 *(978-1-4424-4650-2(1))*; pap. 3.99 *(978-1-4424-4649-6(8))* Simon Spotlight. (Simon Spotlight).

—OLIVIA & the Kite Party. Harvey, Alex. ed. 2012. (Olivia Ready-To-Read Ser.). lib. bdg. 13.55 *(978-0-606-26360-3(8))*, Turtleback) Turtleback Bks.

—OLIVIA & the Puppy Wedding. Gallo, Tina. 2012. (Olivia TV Tie-In Ser.). (ENG.). 24p. (J). (gr. -1-2). pap. 3.99 *(978-1-4424-5315-9(X))*, Simon Spotlight) Simon Spotlight.

—OLIVIA & the Sea Lions. McDoogle, Farrah. 2013. (Olivia TV Tie-In Ser.). (ENG.). 16p. (J). (gr. -1-1). pap. 5.99 *(978-1-4424-7364-5(9))*, Simon Spotlight) Simon Spotlight.

—OLIVIA Dances for Joy. Shaw, Natalie. 2012. (Olivia TV Tie-In Ser.). (ENG.). 24p. (J). (gr. -1-1). pap. 16.99 *(978-1-4424-5257-2(9))*, Simon Spotlight) Simon Spotlight.

—OLIVIA Learns to Surf. 2010. (Olivia TV Tie-In Ser.). (ENG.). 12p. (J). (gr. -1-1). bds. 6.99 *(978-1-4424-0330-7(6))*, Simon Spotlight) Simon Spotlight.

—Olivia Plans a Tea Party: From the Fancy Keepsake Collection. 2011. (Olivia TV Tie-In Ser.). (ENG.). 28p. (J). (gr. -1-2). 6.99 *(978-1-4423-3962-0(4))*, Simon Spotlight) Simon Spotlight.

—OLIVIA Says Good Night. McDoogle, Farrah & Pulliam, Gabe. 2011. (Olivia TV Tie-In Ser.). (ENG.). 24p. (J). (gr. -1-1). bds. 16.99 *(978-1-4424-2947-5(X))*, Simon Spotlight) Simon Spotlight.

—OLIVIA Sells Cookies. 2013. (Olivia TV Tie-In Ser.). (ENG.). 24p. (J). (gr. -1-2). pap. 3.99 *(978-1-4424-5965-6(4))*, Simon Spotlight) Simon Spotlight.

—Olivia Takes Ballet: From the Fancy Keepsake Collection. Evans, Cordelia. 2013. (Olivia TV Tie-In Ser.). (ENG.). 28p. (J). (gr. -1-2). 6.99 *(978-1-4424-7394-2(0))*, Simon Spotlight) Simon Spotlight.

—Olivia the Ballerina. McDoogle, Farrah. 2013. (Olivia TV Tie-In Ser.). (ENG.). 24p. (J). (gr. -1-1). 16.99 *(978-1-4424-8515-0(9))*, Simon Spotlight) Simon Spotlight.

—OLIVIA Vende Galletas (OLIVIA Sells Cookies) Romay, Alexis, tr. 2013. (Olivia TV Tie-In Ser.). (SPA.). 24p. (J). (gr. -1-2). pap. 3.99 *(978-1-4424-5967-0(0))*, Libros Para Ninos) Libros Para Ninos.

—Pizza Party! (Teenage Mutant Ninja Turtles) Random House. 2014. (Step into Reading Ser.). (ENG.). 24p. (J). (gr. -1-1). 3.99 *(978-0-385-38506-0(4))*, Random Hse. Bks. for Young Readers) Random Hse. Children's Bks.

—Red Alert! (Teenage Mutant Ninja Turtles) Random House. 2015. (Pictureback(R) Ser.). (ENG.). 16p. (J). (gr. -1-2). 4.99 *(978-0-553-50901-4(2))*, Random Hse. Bks. for Young Readers) Random Hse. Children's Bks.

—The Santa Snatcher. Gerver, Jane E. 2004. 32p. (J). lib. bdg. 15.00 *(978-1-4242-0959-0(5))* Fitzgerald Bks.

—Show Your Colors! (Teenage Mutant Ninja Turtles) Random House. 2015. (Bright & Early Board Books Ser.). (ENG.). 24p. (J). (— 1). bds. 4.99 *(978-0-553-49776-2(6))*, Random Hse. Bks. for Young Readers) Random Hse. Children's Bks.

—Sokka, the Sword Master. 2008. (Avatar Ser.: 1). (ENG.). 32p. (J). (gr. 1-3). pap. 3.99 *(978-1-4169-5491-0(0))*, Simon Spotlight/Nickelodeon) Simon Spotlight/Nickelodeon.

—Sonic Genesis. Flynn, Ian & Sonic Scribes Staff. 2012. (ENG.). 144p. (J). (gr. 4-7). pap. 14.99 *(978-1-936975-08-2(4))*, Archie Comics) Archie Comic Pubns., Inc.

—Sonic the Hedgehog Archives 18. Flynn, Ian & Sonic Scribes Staff. 2012. (Sonic the Hedgehog Archives Ser.: 18). (ENG.). 112p. (J). (gr. 4-7). 7.99 *(978-1-936975-07-5(6))*, Archie Comics) Archie Comic Pubns., Inc.

Spaziante, Patrick. Star Wars: Revenge of the Sith (Star Wars) Smith, Geof. 2015. (Little Golden Book Ser.). (ENG.). 24p. (J). (-k). 4.99 ***(978-0-7364-3540-6(9))***, Golden Bks.) Random Hse. Children's Bks.

Spaziante, Patrick. Strength in Numbers! (Teenage Mutant Ninja Turtles) Random House. 2015. (Bright & Early Board Books Ser.). (ENG.). 24p. (J). (— 1). bds. 4.99 *(978-0-553-49777-9(4))*, Random Hse. Bks. for Young Readers) Random Hse. Children's Bks.

—Super Slam Turtles! Thomas, Jim. 2005. 22p. (J). lib. bdg. 15.00 *(978-1-4242-0971-2(4))* Fitzgerald Bks.

—Tale of Zuko. Teitelbaum, Michael. 2008. (Avatar Ser.). (ENG.). 96p. (J). (gr. 2-6). pap. 5.99 *(978-1-4169-4984-8(4))*, Simon Spotlight/Nickelodeon) Simon Spotlight/Nickelodeon.

—This Is Olivia. Sambar, Syma. 2009. (Olivia TV Tie-In Ser.). (ENG.). 12p. (J). (gr. -1-2). 7.99 *(978-1-4169-8709-3(6))*, Simon Spotlight) Simon Spotlight.

Spaziante, Patrick & Giles, Mike. Dino Disaster! Mattern, Joanne. ed. 2005. (Adventures of Jimmy Neutron Ser.: 9). 24p. (J). lib. bdg. 15.00 *(978-1-59054-782-3(9))* Fitzgerald Bks.

Spaziante, Patrick & Riley, Kellee. Crushed, Bk. 5. Black, Allyson. 2011. (Scarlett & Crimson Ser.). (ENG.). 112p. (J). pap. 6.99 *(978-1-4169-9648-4(6))*, Simon Spotlight) Simon Spotlight.

Spaziante, Patrick, jt. illus. see Golden Books Staff.

Spaziante, Patrick, jt. illus. see Laguna, Fabio.

Spaziante, Patrick, jt. illus. see Random House Editors.

Spaziante, Patrick, jt. illus. see Random House Staff.

Spaziante, Patrick Spaz. The Hedgehog, Vol. 1. Bates, Ben et al. 2011. (Sonic the Hedgehog: Legacy Ser.: 1). (ENG.). 512p. (J). (gr. 4-7). pap. 14.95 *(978-1-879794-88-7(8))*, Archie Comics) Archie Comic Pubns., Inc.

—Knuckles the Echidna Archives, Vol. 1. Flynn, Ian & Sonic Scribes Staff. 2011. (Knuckles Archives Ser.: 1). (ENG.). 160p. (J). (gr. 4-7). pap. 9.95 *(978-1-879794-81-8(0))*, Archie Comics) Archie Comic Pubns., Inc.

—Sonic Select, Bk. 3. Flynn, Ian & Sonic Scribes Staff. 2011. (Sonic Select Ser.: 3). (ENG.). 128p. (J). (gr. 4-7). pap. 11.95 *(978-1-879794-62-7(4))*, Archie Comics) Archie Comic Pubns., Inc.

Spaziante, Patrick 'Spaz'. Sonic Select, Bk. 5. Sonic Scribes Staff. 2012. (Sonic Select Ser.: 5). (ENG.). 128p. (J). (gr. 4-7). pap. 11.99 *(978-1-936975-05-1(X))*, Archie Comics) Archie Comic Pubns., Inc.

Spaziante, Patrick Spaz. Sonic Select, Vol. 1. Gallagher, Mike et al. 2008. (Sonic Select Ser.: 1). (ENG.). 128p. (J). (gr. 4-7). pap. 11.95 *(978-1-879794-29-0(2))*, Archie Comics) Archie Comic Pubns., Inc.

—Sonic the Hedgehog Archives. Flynn, Ian & Sonic Scribes Staff. 2011. (Sonic the Hedgehog Archives Ser.: 15). (ENG.). 112p. (J). (gr. 4-7). pap. 7.95 *(978-1-879794-70-2(5))*, Archie Comics) Archie Comic Pubns., Inc.

Spear, Kevin. What's a Bathtub Doing in My Church? Fifteen Questions Kids Ask about Baptism, Salvation & Snorkels. Spear, Kevin. 2006. (ENG.). 32p. (J). per. 5.99 *(978-1-59317-155-1(2))* Warner Pr. Pubs.

Spearing, Craig J. Our Texas. Hopkins, Jackie Mims. 2010. (ENG.). 44p. (J). (gr. 1-4). pap. 8.95 *(978-1-57091-726-4(4))* Charlesbridge Publishing, Inc.

Spearman, Davidx & Spearman, Terry. What Will I Grow up to Be?, 1 vol. Spearman, David. 2009. 34p. pap. 24.95 *(978-1-60749-728-8(X))* America Star Bks.

Spearman, Terry, jt. illus. see Spearman, Davidx.

Spears, Ashley, jt. illus. see Clayton, Sean.

Spears, Ashley E. Cloudy. Stover, Anne Long. 2005. 20p. (J). *(978-0-9762389-0-4(X))* Trent's Prints.

—The Piggle. Shams, K. l.t. ed. 2004. 20p. (J). 9.99 *(978-0-9728872-9-8(6))* Trent's Prints.

—Young Eagle, Pretty Flower. Forester, MaMa Eagle. 2004. 16p. (J). 7.95 *(978-0-9762389-4-2(2))* Trent's Prints.

Spears, Rick. Alien Investigation: Searching for the Truth about UFOs & Aliens. Halls, Kelly Milner. 2012. (Single Titles Ser.). (ENG.). 64p. (gr. 5-12). lib. bdg. 20.95 *(978-0-7613-6204-3(5))*, Millbrook Pr.) Lerner Publishing Group.

—Dinosaur Parade: A Spectacle of Prehistoric Proportions. Halls, Kelly Milner. 2008. (ENG.). 32p. (J). (gr. 4-7). 12.95 *(978-1-60059-267-6(8))* Lark Bks.

Spears, Sheri. Pee Wee Pickle Goes to Kinder-Garden. Schmitt, H. D. 2008. 20p. pap. 24.95 *(978-1-60672-731-7(1))* America Star Bks.

Speas, Joann. Meet Mister Muttley. Leduc-Lenmark, MaryAlice. 2004. 25p. (J). 16.95 *(978-0-9760733-0-7(7))* Heartstrings Publishing.

Specht, Jessica. Call Me Charly. Michaels, Joanna. 2012. 92p. pap. 10.95 *(978-1-61493-102-7(X))* Peppertree Pr., The.

Specialty Publishing Company. Fearless Faith: And the New School. Newmark, Rachel J. 2006. (J). pap. 7.95 *(978-0-9755199-4-3(8))* Specialty Publishing Co.

Spector, Joel. And Still They Bloom: A Family's Journey of Loss & Healing. Rovere, Amy. 2012. (ENG.). 48p. (J). (gr. 4-7). 14.95 *(978-1-60443-036-3(2))* American Cancer Society, Inc.

—The Story of Me. Jones, Stan & Jones, Brenna. ed. 2007. (God's Design for Sex Ser.: 1). (ENG.). 48p. (Orig.). 10.99 *(978-1-60006-013-7(7))* NavPress Publishing Group.

Spector, Joel & Sharpe, Jim. Poetry for Young People: Rudyard Kipling. Gillooly, Eileen, ed. 2010. (Poetry for Young People Ser.). (ENG.). 48p. (J). (gr. 3). pap. 6.95 *(978-1-4027-7293-1(9))* Sterling Publishing Co., Inc.

Spee, Gitte. Detective Gordon - The First Case. Nilsson, Ulf. 2015. (Detective Gordon Ser.). (ENG.). 96p. (J). (gr. k-5). 16.99 ***(978-1-927271-49-0(5))*** Gecko Pr. NZL. Dist: Lerner Publishing Group.

Speer, Julie & Davis, Christopher Owen. Farmer Dillo Paints His Barn. Adams, Jesse. 2007. (J). (gr. -1-1). 21p. *(978-1-59166-481-9(0))*; pap. 12.95 *(978-1-59166-808-4(5))* BJU Pr.

Speer, Julie & Polhamus, Bruce. Farmer Dillo Shapes Things Up. Adams, Jesse. 2009. 24p. (gr. -1-1). pap. 7.99 *(978-1-59166-865-7(4))* BJU Pr.

Speer, Julie & Rogers, David. Farmer Dillo Counts His Chickens. Adams, Jesse. 2008. 22p. (gr. -1-1). pap. 7.99 *(978-1-59166-868-8(9))* BJU Pr.

Speidel, Sandra. Before I Was Born. Nystrom, Carolyn. rev. ed. 2007. (God's Design for Sex Ser.: 2). (ENG.). 40p. 10.99 *(978-1-60006-014-4(5))* NavPress Publishing Group.

—What's Happening to Grandpa? Shriver, Maria. 2004. (ENG.). 48p. (J). (gr. -1-1). 18.00 *(978-0-316-00101-4(5))* Little, Brown Bks. for Young Readers.

—What's Heaven. Shriver, Maria. 2007. (ENG.). 32p. (gr. -1-3). 15.99 *(978-0-312-38241-4(3))*, Golden Bks. Adult Publishing Group) St. Martin's Pr.

Speigel, Beth. Samantha Jane's Missing Smile: A Story about Coping with the Loss of a Parent. Pincus, Donna & Kaplow, Julie. 2007. 32p. (J). (gr. -1-3). 14.95 *(978-1-59147-808-9(1))*; per. 9.95 *(978-1-59147-809-6(X))* American Psychological Assn. (Magination Pr.).

Speir, Nancy. Check It Out! Reading, Finding, Helping, 0 vols. Hubbell, Patricia. 2011. (ENG.). 32p. (J). (gr. -1-3). 16.99 *(978-0-7614-5803-6(4))*, 9780761458036, Amazon Children's Publishing) Amazon Publishing.

—Eliza's Kindergarten Pet, 0 vols. McGinty, Alice B. 2010. (ENG.). 32p. (J). (gr. k-3). 15.99 *(978-0-7614-5702-2(X))*, 9780761457022, Amazon Children's Publishing) Amazon Publishing.

—Eliza's Kindergarten Surprise, 0 vols. McGinty, Alice B. 2013. (ENG.). 34p. (J). (gr. k-3). pap. 9.99 *(978-1-4778-1683-7(6))*, 9781477816837, Amazon Children's Publishing) Amazon Publishing.

—My First Airplane Ride, 0 vols. Hubbell, Patricia. 2013. (ENG.). 36p. (J). (gr. -1-2). pap. 9.99 *(978-1-4778-1675-2(5))*, 9781477816752, Amazon Children's Publishing) Amazon Publishing.

—Teacher! Sharing, Helping, Caring, 0 vols. Hubbell, Patricia. 2009. (ENG.). 32p. (J). (gr. -1-3). 16.99 *(978-0-7614-5574-5(4))*, 9780761455745, Amazon Children's Publishing) Amazon Publishing.

Speirs, John. Amazing Magnetism. Carmi, Rebecca. 2003. (Magic School Bus Science Chapter Bks.). 76p. (gr. 2-4). 15.00 *(978-0-7569-1576-6(7))* Perfection Learning Corp.

—Food Chain Frenzy. Capeci, Anne. 2004. (Magic School Bus Science Chapter Bks.). 91p. (gr. 2-5). 15.00 *(978-0-7569-2206-1(2))* Perfection Learning Corp.

—Food Chain Frenzy. Capeci, Anne. 2004. (Magic School Bus Ser.). (ENG.). 96p. (J). (gr. 2-5). pap. 4.99 *(978-0-439-56050-4(0))* Scholastic, Inc.

—It's about Time! Murphy, Stuart J. 2005. (MathStart Ser.). 40p. (J). 16.99 *(978-0-06-055768-3(0))*; (ENG.). (gr. -1). pap. 5.99 *(978-0-06-055769-0(9))* HarperCollins Pubs.

—It's about Time! Murphy, Stuart J. 2005. (Mathstart Ser.). 33p. (gr. -1-3). 16.00 *(978-0-7569-5224-2(7))* Perfection Learning Corp.

—Twister Trouble. Schreiber, Ann. 2010. (Magic School Bus Science Chapter Bks.). (KOR.). 82p. (J). *(978-89-491-5320-9(3))* Biryongso Publishing Co.

—Voyage to the Volcano. Stamper, Judith Bauer. 2003. (Magic School Bus Ser.: 15). (ENG.). 96p. (J). (gr. -1-3). mass mkt. 4.99 *(978-0-439-42935-1(8))* Scholastic, Inc.

—Voyage to the Volcano. Stamper, Judith. 2010. (Magic School Bus Science Chapter Bks.). (KOR.). 101p. (J). *(978-89-491-5322-3(X))* Biryongso Publishing Co.

—Voyage to the Volcano. Stamper, Judith. 2003. (Magic School Bus Science Chapter Bks.). 87p. (gr. 3-6). 15.00 *(978-0-7569-1581-0(3))* Perfection Learning Corp.

Speirs, John. Best Halloween Hunt Ever. Speirs, John. 2008. (ENG.). 32p. (J). (gr. -1-3). pap. 4.99 *(978-0-545-06867-3(3))*, Cartwheel Bks.) Scholastic, Inc.

Speirs, John. Animal Tracks: Wild Poems to Read Aloud. Speirs, John, tr. Ghigna, Charles. 2004. (ENG.). 36p. (J). (gr. -1-1). 14.95 *(978-0-8109-4841-9(9))* Abrams.

Spellman, Susan. Bright Easter Day. Stiegemeyer, Julie. 2005. 32p. (J). 10.49 *(978-0-7586-0818-5(7))* Concordia Publishing Hse.

—Every Turtle Counts. Hunter, Sara Hoagland. 2014. (ENG.). 36p. (J). 16.95 *(978-1-931807-25-8(6))* Randall, Peter E. Pub.

—How Timbo & Trevor Got Together. Towle, Barbara E. 2007. (ENG.). 38p. (J). (gr. -1-3). 19.95 *(978-1-933002-21-7(2))* PublishingWorks.

—Hurricane Mia: A Caribbean Adventure. Seim, Donna Marie. 2010. 168p. (J). (gr. 3-7). pap. 12.95 *(978-0-9826911-0-6(6))*, Peapod Pr.) PublishingWorks.

—Pinky & Bubs' Stinky Night Out. Spellman, Frankie. 2005. (ENG.). 32p. (J). (gr. -1-3). per. 12.95 *(978-1-933002-16-3(6))* PublishingWorks.

Spence, Bob. The One & Only Sam: A Story Explaining Idioms for Children with Asperger Syndrome & Other Communication Difficulties. Stalker, Aileen. 2009. (ENG.). 64p. (J). (gr. 1-3). *(978-1-84905-040-1(6))* Kingsley, Jessica Ltd.

Spence, Jim. Joseph & the Dream: Based on Genesis 37/46:7. Pingry, Patricia A. 2005. (Stories from the Bible Ser.). (ENG.). 26p. (J). (gr. -1-k). bds. 6.95 *(978-0-8249-6625-6(2))* Ideals Pubns.

Spence, Thomas. Jackie Robinson: Hero & Athlete, 1 vol. Slade, Suzanne. 2008. (Biographies Ser.). (ENG.). 24p. (gr. k-3). 25.99 *(978-1-4048-3978-6(X))*, Nonfiction Picture Bks.) Picture Window Bks.

—Wendell the Worrier, 1 vol. Donahue, Jill Urban. 2006. (Read-It! Readers Ser.). (ENG.). 24p. (gr. -1-3). lib. bdg. 19.99 *(978-1-4048-2425-6(1))*, Easy Readers) Picture Window Bks.

Spenceley, Annabel. Beauty & the Beast. 2013. (ENG.). 48p. (J). (gr. -1-4). pap. 7.99 *(978-1-84322-789-2(4))*, Armadillo) Anness Publishing GBR. Dist: National Bk. Network.

—First Prayers for Baby. Piper, Sophie. 2014. (ENG.). 48p. (J). (— 1). 8.99 *(978-0-7459-6407-9(2))* Lion Hudson PLC GBR. Dist: Independent Pubs. Group.

—Jesus in Pictures for Little Eyes. Taylor, Kenneth N. ed. 2003. (Leading Young Hearts & Minds to God Ser.). (ENG.). 128p. (J). (gr. k-3). 9.99 *(978-0-8024-3059-5(7))* Moody Pubs.

—The New Bible in Pictures for Little Eyes. Taylor, Kenneth N. gif. ed. 2004. (Leading Young Hearts & Minds to God Ser.). (ENG.). 384p. (J). 24.99 *(978-0-8024-3078-6(3))* Moody Pubs.

—Puzzle Journey through Time. Heddle, Rebecca. 2003. 32p. (J). pap. 6.95 *(978-0-7945-0440-3(X))*, Usborne) EDC Publishing.

—A Storyteller Book: Cinderella. Perrault, Charles. 2014. (ENG.). 48p. (J). (gr. k-5). pap. 7.99 *(978-1-84322-883-7(1))* Anness Publishing GBR. Dist: National Bk. Network.

—Who Is New York's Prettiest Princess? Elliot, Rachel. 2012. (ENG.). 32p. (J). (-3). 9.99 *(978-1-4022-8221-8(4))*, Sourcebooks Jabberwocky) Sourcebooks, Inc.

Spenceley, Annabel & Chen, Kuo Kang. What Makes You Ill? Unwin, Mike & Woodward, Kate. Meredith, Susan, ed. rev. ed. 2006. (Starting Point Science Ser.). 24p. (J). (gr. -1-3). pap. 4.99 *(978-0-7945-1624-6(6))*, Usborne) EDC Publishing.

—Why Do People Eat? Needham, Kate. rev. ed. 2007. (Starting Point Science Ser.). 24p. (J). (gr. 1-4). pap. 4.99 *(978-0-7945-1623-9(8))*, Usborne) EDC Publishing.

Spencer, Alison. Cinders. Stewart, Maddie. 2007. (Panda Cubs Ser.: 05). (ENG.). 48p. (J). pap. 9.95 *(978-1-84717-027-9(7))* O'Brien Pr., Ltd., The IRL. Dist: Dufour Editions, Inc.

Spencer, Chip. Porka-Bella-Snu & the Mystery of the Letters. Hays, Phillip. 2013. 54p. pap. 6.95 *(978-1-938679-05-6(9))* Written World Communications.

Spencer, Kay Kincannon. Sleigh Ride with Santa. Spencer, John Nicholas. 2012. (ENG.). 26p. (J). pap. 14.95 *(978-1-61296-140-8(1))* Black Rose Writing.

S

Spencer, Mariko Ando. Cheetah Cubs & Beetle Grubs: The Wacky Ways We Name Young Animals. Swanson, Diane. 2007. (ENG.). 24p. (J). (gr. k-2). 19.95 *(978-1-55451-084-9(8)*, 9781554510849); pap. 7.95 *(978-1-55451-083-2(X)*, 9781554510832) Annick Pr., Ltd. CAN. Dist: Firefly Bks., Ltd.

Spencer, Monica. The Bell That Wouldn't Ring. Kline, Karen E. 2008. 16p. pap. 24.95 *(978-1-60672-497-2(5))* PublishAmerica, Inc.

Spencer, Trevor. Teddy Mars: Almost a World Record Breaker. Burnham, Molly B. 2015. (Teddy Mars Ser.: 1). (ENG.). 224p. (J). (gr. 3-7). 16.99 *(978-0-06-227810-4(X))* HarperCollins Pubs.

Spender, Nick. Ancient Treasures. Shone, Rob. 2008. (Graphic Nonfiction Ser.). (ENG.). 48p. (gr. 3-8). pap. 14.05 *(978-1-4042-9593-3(3))*; (YA). (gr. 5-9). lib. bdg. 31.95 *(978-1-4042-1089-9(X))* Rosen Publishing Group, Inc., The.

—The Battle of the Alamo. Jeffrey, Gary. 2012. (Graphic History of the American West Ser.). (ENG.). 24p. (J). (gr. 3-8). pap. 8.15 *(978-1-4339-6729-0(4)*, Gareth Stevens Learning Library); (gr. 4-7). lib. bdg. 23.95 *(978-1-4339-6727-6(8))* Stevens, Gareth Publishing LLLP.

—The Battle of the Little Bighorn. Jeffrey, Gary. 2012. (Graphic History of the American West Ser.). (ENG.). 24p. (J). (gr. 3-8). pap. 8.15 *(978-1-4339-6733-7(2)*, Gareth Stevens Learning Library); (gr. 4-7). lib. bdg. 23.95 *(978-1-4339-6731-3(6))* Stevens, Gareth Publishing LLLP.

—Bigfoot & Other Strange Beasts. Shone, Rob. 2006. (Graphic Mysteries Ser.). (ENG.). 48p. (YA). (gr. k-3). lib. bdg. 31.95 *(978-1-4042-0793-6(7))* Rosen Publishing Group, Inc., The.

—Corpses & Skeletons: The Science of Forensic Anthropology. Shone, Rob. 2008. (Graphic Forensic Science Ser.). (ENG.). 48p. (gr. 5-8). per. 14.05 *(978-1-4042-1441-5(0))*; (YA). lib. bdg. 31.95 *(978-1-4042-1440-8(2))* Rosen Publishing Group, Inc., The.

—Defying Death in the Mountains. Shone, Rob. 2010. (Graphic Survival Stories Ser.). 48p. (YA). 58.50 *(978-1-61532-901-4(3)*, Rosen Reference) Rosen Publishing Group, Inc., The.

—Earthquakes. Shone, Rob. 2007. (Graphic Natural Disasters Ser.). (ENG.). 48p. (YA). (gr. 5-9). lib. bdg. 31.95 *(978-1-4042-1989-2(7))* Rosen Publishing Group, Inc., The.

—Muhammad Ali: The Life of a Boxing Hero. Shone, Rob. 2007. (Graphic Nonfiction Biographies Ser.). (ENG.). 48p. (J). (gr. 4-7). lib. bdg. 31.95 *(978-1-4042-0856-8(9))*; (gr. 5-8). pap. 14.05 *(978-1-4042-0919-0(0))* Rosen Publishing Group, Inc., The.

—Rosa Parks: The Life of a Civil Rights Heroine. Shone, Rob. 2007. (Graphic Nonfiction Biographies Ser.). (ENG.). 48p. (J). (gr. 4-7). lib. bdg. 31.95 *(978-1-4042-0864-3(X))* Rosen Publishing Group, Inc., The.

—Solving Crimes Through Criminal Profiling. Shone, Rob. 2008. (Graphic Forensic Science Ser.). (ENG.). 48p. (gr. 5-8). per. 14.05 *(978-1-4042-1438-5(0))*; (YA). lib. bdg. 31.95 *(978-1-4042-1437-8(2))* Rosen Publishing Group, Inc., The.

Spender, Nik. Bigfoot & Other Strange Beasts. Shone, Rob. 2006. (Graphic Mysteries Ser.). (ENG.). 48p. (gr. 5-8). pap. 14.05 *(978-1-4042-0804-9(6))* Rosen Publishing Group, Inc., The.

—Defying Death at the North & South Poles. Jeffrey, Gary & Shone, Rob. 2010. (Graphic Survival Stories Ser.). 48p. (YA). (gr. 5-8). 31.95 *(978-1-4358-3527-6(1)*, Rosen Reference) Rosen Publishing Group, Inc., The.

—Defying Death in the Mountains. Shone, Rob. 2010. (Graphic Survival Stories Ser.). 48p. (YA). (ENG.). pap. 14.05 *(978-1-61532-866-6(1))*; (gr. 5-8). 31.95 *(978-1-4358-3532-0(8))* Rosen Publishing Group, Inc., The. (Rosen Reference).

—Rosa Parks: The Life of a Civil Rights Heroine. Shone, Rob. 2007. (Graphic Biographies Ser.). (ENG.). 48p. (gr. 5-8). pap. 14.05 *(978-1-4042-0927-5(1))* Rosen Publishing Group, Inc., The.

—The Soviet War in Afghanistan. Jeffrey, Gary. 2013. (ENG.). 48p. (J). *(978-0-7787-1235-0(4))*; pap. *(978-0-7787-1239-8(7))* Crabtree Publishing Co.

Spender, Nik & Moulder, Bob. The Loch Ness Monster & Other Lake Mysteries. Jeffrey, Gary. 2006. (Graphic Mysteries Ser.). (ENG.). 48p. (YA). (gr. 5-8). lib. bdg. 31.95 *(978-1-4042-0796-7(1))* Rosen Publishing Group, Inc., The.

Spender, Nik, jt. illus. see Jeffrey, Gary.

Spender, Nik, jt. illus. see West, David.

Spengler, Kenneth. Mountain Night Mountain Day. Fredericks, Anthony D. 2014. (ENG.). 32p. (J). 15.95 *(978-1-933855-98-1(3)*, Rio Nuevo Pubs.) Rio Nuevo Pubs.

—Oh My, Pumpkin Pie! Ghigna, Charles. 2005. (Step into Reading Ser.). (ENG.). 32p. (J). (gr. -1-1). pap. 3.99 *(978-0-375-82945-1(8)*, Random Hse. Bks. for Young Readers) Random Hse. Children's Bks.

Spengler, Kenneth. Whose Tail on the Trail at Grand Canyon. Stephenson, Midji. 2012. (J). ***(978-1-934656-55-6(0))*** Grand Canyon Assn.

Spengler, Kenneth. Hotel Jungle. Spengler, Kenneth, tr. Napoli, Donna Jo & Johnston, Shelagh. 2004. 33p. (J). 15.95 *(978-1-59336-002-3(9))*; pap. *(978-1-59336-003-0(7))* Mondo Publishing.

Spengler, Kenneth J. Buster. Sudduth, Brent H. 2003. 32p. (J). 15.95 *(978-1-59034-478-1(2))* Mondo Publishing.

—Campfire for Cowboy Billy. Ulmer, Wendy K. 2011. (ENG.). 32p. (gr. -1-3). pap. 8.95 *(978-1-58979-605-8(5))* Taylor Trade Publishing.

—Desert Night Desert Day. Fredericks, Anthony D. 2011. 32p. (J). 15.95 *(978-1-933855-70-7(3))* Rio Nuevo Pubs.

—Way up in the Arctic. Ward, Jennifer. 2007. (SPA & ENG.). 32p. (J). (gr. -1-3). 15.95 *(978-0-87358-928-4(9))* Cooper Square Publishing Llc.

Spengler, Margaret. Animal Strike at the Zoo - It's True! Wilson, Karma. 2006. (ENG.). 32p. (J). (gr. -1-1). 16.99 *(978-0-06-057502-1(6))* HarperCollins Pubs.

—One, Two, Buckle My Shoe. 2004. (J). bds. 6.99 *(978-1-890647-12-4(8))* TOMY International, Inc.

—See Through Safari. Hawksley, Gerald. 2005. (J). bds. *(978-1-890647-15-5(2))* TOMY International, Inc.

—Storm Is Coming! Tekavec, Heather. 2004. (ENG.). 32p. (J). (gr. -1-3). reprint ed. pap. 6.99 *(978-0-14-240070-8(X)*, Puffin) Penguin Publishing Group.

Spengler, Margaret. Little Loon & Papa. Spengler, Margaret, tr. Buzzeo, Toni. 2004. (ENG.). 32p. (J). (gr. -1-2). 16.99 *(978-0-8037-2958-2(8)*, Dial) Penguin Publishing Group.

Spengler, Margaret L. Noah & the Mighty Ark, 1 vol. Greene, Rhonda Gowler. 2014. (ENG.). 32p. (J). 9.99 *(978-0-310-73217-4(4))* Zonderkidz.

Sper, Emily. The Kids' Fun Book of Jewish Time. Sper, Emily. 2006. (HEB & ENG.). 24p. (J). (gr. -1-1). 16.99 *(978-1-58023-311-8(2)*, 1260461, Jewish Lights Publishing) LongHill Partners, Inc.

Sperling, Alia, jt. illus. see Sperling, Karima.

Sperling, Karima & Sperling, Alia. Links of Light: The Golden Chain: A Child's Version of the Naqshbandi Sufi Way. Kabbani, Shaykh Muhammad & Kabbani, Muhammad Hisham. 2009. xi, 217p. (J). *(978-1-930409-68-2(0))* Islamic Supreme Council of America.

Sperling, S. David, jt. illus. see Mantell, Ahuva.

Sperling, Thomas. Chicken Licken. 2005. (J). *(978-0-7664-1050-3(1))* Abrams.

—Let's Celebrate Columbus Day. DeRubertis, Barbara. 2014. (Holidays & Heroes Ser.). 32p. (J). (gr. 1-3). pap. 7.95 *(978-1-57565-634-2(5))* Kane Pr., Inc.

—Let's Celebrate Thanksgiving Day. DeRubertis, Barbara. 2013. (Holidays & Heroes Ser.). 32p. (J). (gr. 1-3). pap. 7.95 *(978-1-57565-636-6(1))* Kane Pr., Inc.

—Let's Celebrate Thanksgiving Day. deRubertis, Barbara. 2014. (Holidays & Heroes Ser.). 32p. (gr. 1-3). lib. bdg. 25.26 *(978-1-57565-723-3(6))* Kane Pr., Inc.

—The Little Red Hen. 2005. (J). *(978-0-7664-1052-7(8))* Abrams.

—Little Red Riding Hood. 2005. (J). *(978-0-7664-1055-8(2))* Abrams.

—Stone Cheese. 2005. (J). *(978-0-7664-1053-4(6))* Abrams.

—The Three Billy Goats Gruff. Asbjørnsen, Peter Christen. 2005. (J). *(978-0-7664-1054-1(4))* Abrams.

—The Three Little Pigs. 2005. (J). *(978-0-7664-1051-0(X))* Abrams.

Sperling, Tom. The First Independence Day Celebration, 1 vol. Allen, Kathy. 2010. (Our American Story Ser.). (ENG.). 32p. (gr. 1-3). lib. bdg. 26.65 *(978-1-4048-5542-7(4)*, Nonfiction Picture Bks.) Picture Window Bks.

Sperry, Armstrong. Wagons Westward: The Old Trail to Santa Fe. Sperry, Armstrong. 2005. 200p. (YA). (gr. 6-11). reprint ed. pap. 15.00 *(978-0-7567-9693-8(8))* DIANE Publishing Co.

Speth, Brandilyn. Some Secrets Hurt: A Story of Healing. Garner, Linda. 2009. 64p. (J). (gr. 1). 15.95 *(978-1-60641-135-3(7))* Deseret Bk. Co.

Spetter, Jung-Hee. Bye, Bye! Kaufmann, Nancy. 2004. (ENG.). 32p. (J). (gr. -1-1). 14.95 *(978-1-886910-95-9(2)*, Lemniscaat) Boyds Mills Pr.

Spicer, Bridgett. Earl Joins the Circus. Scheber, George. l.t. ed. 2005. (Adventures of Earl the Squirrel Ser.). 32p. (J). (gr. -1-3). 12.95 *(978-1-878847-01-0(5))* Make Me A Story Pr.

—Earl the Squirrel. Scheber, George. l.t. ed. 2005. (Adventures of Earl the Squirrel Ser.). 32p. (J). (gr. -1-2). 12.95 *(978-1-878847-00-3(7))* Make Me A Story Pr.

Spiegel, Beth. First Grade Stinks!, 1 vol. Rodman, Mary Ann. (ENG.). 32p. (J). (gr. k-3). 2008. pap. 8.95 *(978-1-56145-462-4(1))*; 2006. 15.95 *(978-1-56145-377-1(3))* Peachtree Pubs.

—Rosa's Room, 1 vol. Bottner, Barbara. 2014. (ENG.). 32p. (J). (gr. -1-3). pap. 7.95 *(978-1-56145-776-2(0))* Peachtree Pubs.

—Will It Be a Baby Brother? Bunting, Eve. 2010. (ENG.). 32p. (J). (gr. -1-1). 16.95 *(978-1-59078-439-6(1))* Boyds Mills Pr.

Spiegel, Beth. Rosa's Room, 1 vol. Spiegel, Beth, tr. Bottner, Barbara. 2004. (ENG.). 32p. (J). (gr. k-3). 15.95 *(978-1-56145-302-3(1))* Peachtree Pubs.

Spiegelman, Art & Mouly, Françoise. It Was a Dark & Silly Night... Spiegelman, Art & Mouly, Françoise. 2003. (Little Lit Ser.: Vol. 3). 48p. (J). (gr. 1-18). 19.99 *(978-0-06-028628-6(8))* HarperCollins Pubs.

Spieler, Leah. ThumBie Character Kit. Spieler, Leah. 2004. (J). pap. 29.95 *(978-0-9761408-2-5(9))* Creative Marketing Concepts, Inc.

Spier, Jo. The Story of Louis Pasteur. Malkus, Alida Sims. Meadowcroft, Enid Lamonte, ed. 2011. 190p. 42.95 *(978-1-258-05476-2(0))* Literary Licensing, LLC.

Spier, Peter. The Fox Went Out on a Chilly Night. unabr. ed. 2006. (J). (gr. -1-3). pap. 16.95 incl. audio *(978-1-59112-440-5(9))*;Set. pap. 37.95 incl. audio *(978-1-59112-442-9(5))*;Set. pap. 39.95 incl. audio compact disk *(978-1-59112-443-6(3))* Live Oak Media.

Spiker, Sue Ann. The Day the Snapdragons Snapped Back. Chambers, Melinda. 2007. 32p. (J). 16.95 *(978-0-929915-72-2(0))* Headline Bks., Inc.

—We Are Whoooo We Are. Chambers, Melinda. 2006. 32p. (J). 16.95 *(978-0-929915-46-3(1))* Headline Bks., Inc.

Spiker, Sue Ann Maxwell. Tails, Trails & Pies: An Appalachian Cattle Drive. Hedrick, Helen Groves. 2008. 32p. 15.95 *(978-0-929915-87-6(9))* Headline Bks., Inc.

Spikes, Leon, Jr. Taffey Pop Kids Presents the Adventures of Lemmon Head & Mudd Duck: What to Do if Someone Tries to Grab YOU!!! Spikes, James L. 2007. 32p. (J). 14.95 *(978-0-9771438-0-1(5))* Taffey Pop Kids Publishing.

Spillane, Lisa. Six Healing Sounds with Lisa & Ted: Qigong for Children. Spillane, Lisa. 2011. (ENG.). 32p. (J). *(978-1-84819-051-1(4)*, Singing Dragon) Kingsley, Jessica Ltd.

Spiller, Michael. The Sandman. Milligan, Domino. 2008. 16p. pap. 24.95 *(978-1-60703-728-6(9))* America Star Bks.

Spina Dixon, Debra, jt. illus. see Dixon, Debra Spina.

Spinelli, Patti. Alphabet Book with Mackenzie & Emma. Spinelli, Patti. 2003. 32p. (Orig.). (J). (gr. k-4). pap. 11.95 *(978-1-892066-00-8(9))* Nicolin Fields Publishing, Inc.

—Mackenzie & Emma Visit York Beach. Spinelli, Patti. 2003. (J). *(978-0-9742328-0-5(7))* Spinelli, Patti.

Spinks, Scott. Mommy, Am I Strong? Lazurek, Michelle S. 2015. (J). pap. ***(978-0-8198-4948-9(0))*** Pauline Bks. & Media.

Spinks, Stefphany (Snider). When the Moon Was Born, 1 vol. Eubanks-Adkison, Eufa. 2010. 16p. 24.95 *(978-1-4512-1367-6(0))* PublishAmerica, Inc.

Spino, Bonnie. Wild about Manners. Lorraine, Loria. 2013. 36p. pap. 11.95 *(978-0-9881889-0-7(2))* Piccolo Tales.

Spiotto, Joey. Attack! Boss! Cheat Code! A Gamer's Alphabet. Barton, Chris. 2014. (ENG.). 32p. (J). (gr. 1-4). 14.95 *(978-1-57687-701-2(9)*, powerHouse Bks.) powerHouse Cultural Entertainment, Inc.

Spires, Ashley. C'mere, Boy! Jennings, Sharon. 2010. (ENG.). 32p. (J). (gr. -1-2). 16.95 *(978-1-55453-440-1(2))* Kids Can Pr., Ltd. CAN. Dist: Univ. of Toronto Pr.

—Ella's Umbrellas. Lloyd, Jennifer. 2010. (ENG.). 32p. (J). (gr. -1-3). 16.95 *(978-1-897476-23-9(X))* Simply Read Bks. CAN. Dist: Ingram Pub. Services.

—My Mom Loves Me More Than Sushi. Gomes, Filomena. 2006. 24p. (J). pap. *(978-1-897187-13-5(0))* Second Story Pr.

—My Mom Loves Me More Than Sushi, 1 vol. Gomes, Filomena. 2006. (ENG.). 32p. (J). (gr. -1-3). 15.95 *(978-1-897187-09-8(2))* Second Story Pr. CAN. Dist: Orca Bk. Pubs. USA.

—The Red Shoes. Glass, Eleri. 2008. (ENG.). 36p. (J). (gr. -1-3). 16.95 *(978-1-894965-78-1(7))* Simply Read Bks. CAN. Dist: Ingram Pub. Services.

—Scary Science: 25 Creepy Experiments. Levine, Shar & Johnstone, Leslie. 2011. (ENG.). 64p. (J). (gr. 3-7). pap. 6.99 *(978-0-545-32406-9(8)*, Scholastic Paperbacks) Scholastic, Inc.

Spires, Ashley. Binky: License to Scratch. Spires, Ashley. 2013. (Binky Adventure Ser.). (ENG.). 64p. (J). 16.95 *(978-1-55453-963-5(3))*; pap. 8.95 *(978-1-55453-964-2(1))* Kids Can Pr., Ltd. CAN. Dist: Univ. of Toronto Pr.

—Binky Takes Charge. Spires, Ashley. 2012. (Binky Adventure Ser.: 4). (ENG.). 64p. (J). 8.95 *(978-1-55453-768-6(1))*; 16.95 *(978-1-55453-703-7(7))* Kids Can Pr., Ltd. CAN. Dist: Univ. of Toronto Pr.

—Binky the Space Cat. Spires, Ashley. 2009. (Binky Adventure Ser.). (ENG.). 64p. (J). (gr. 2-5). 8.95 *(978-1-55453-419-7(4))*; 16.95 *(978-1-55453-309-1(0))* Kids Can Pr., Ltd. CAN. Dist: Univ. of Toronto Pr.

—Binky to the Rescue. Spires, Ashley. 2010. (Binky Adventure Ser.). (ENG.). 64p. (J). (gr. 2-5). 8.95 *(978-1-55453-597-2(2))*; 16.95 *(978-1-55453-502-6(6))* Kids Can Pr., Ltd. CAN. Dist: Univ. of Toronto Pr.

—Larf. Spires, Ashley. 2012. (ENG.). 32p. (J). 16.95 *(978-1-55453-701-3(0))* Kids Can Pr., Ltd. CAN. Dist: Univ. of Toronto Pr.

—Small Saul. Spires, Ashley. 2011. (ENG.). 32p. (J). (gr. -1-2). 16.95 *(978-1-55453-503-3(4))* Kids Can Pr., Ltd. CAN. Dist: Univ. of Toronto Pr.

Spiridellis, Evan, jt. illus. see Spiridellis, Gregg.

Spiridellis, Gregg & Spiridellis, Evan. Grumpy Santa. Moore, Clement C. 2003. (ENG.). (J). *(978-0-439-53039-2(3)*, Orchard Bks.) Scholastic, Inc.

Spirin, Gennady. Frog Song. Guiberson, Brenda Z. 2013. (ENG.). 40p. (J). (gr. -1-3). 17.99 *(978-0-8050-9254-7(4)*, Holt, Henry & Co. Bks. For Young Readers) Holt, Henry & Co.

—The Greatest Dinosaur Ever. Guiberson, Brenda Z. 2013. (ENG.). 32p. (J). (gr. -1-3). 17.99 *(978-0-8050-9625-5(6)*, Holt, Henry & Co. Bks. For Young Readers) Holt, Henry & Co.

—La Hija del Rey de los Mares. Shepard, Aaron. (SPA.). 32p. (J). (gr. 3-5). *(978-84-264-3725-9(7)*, LM5051) Editorial Lumen ESP. Dist: Lectorum Pubns., Inc.

—Jesus, 0 vols. Cuyler, Margery. 2010. (ENG.). 36p. (gr. 3-7). 21.00 *(978-0-7614-5630-8(9)*, 9780761456308, Amazon Children's Publishing) Amazon Publishing.

—Life in the Boreal Forest. Guiberson, Brenda Z. 2009. (ENG.). 40p. (J). (gr. k-4). 18.99 *(978-0-8050-7718-6(9)*, Holt, Henry & Co. Bks. For Young Readers) Holt, Henry & Co.

—The Most Amazing Creature in the Sea. Guiberson, Brenda Z. 2015. (ENG.). 32p. (J). (gr. -1-3). 17.99 *(978-0-8050-9961-4(1)*, Holt, Henry & Co. Bks. For Young Readers) Holt, Henry & Co.

—The Night Before Christmas, 0 vols. ltd. ed. 2006. (ENG.). 32p. (J). (gr. -1-3). 16.99 *(978-0-7614-5298-0(2)*, 9780761452980, Amazon Children's Publishing) Amazon Publishing.

—Perceval: King Arthur's Knight of the Holy Grail, 1 vol. Perkins, John. 2007. (ENG.). 40p. (J). (gr. 3-7). 16.99 *(978-0-7614-5339-0(3))* Marshall Cavendish Corp.

—Simeon's Gift. Andrews, Julie & Hamilton, Emma Walton. 2006. 30p. (J). (gr. 4-8). reprint ed. 17.00 *(978-1-4223-5855-9(0))* DIANE Publishing Co.

—Simeon's Gift. Andrews, Julie & Hamilton, Emma Walton. 2003. (Julie Andrews Collection). 40p. (J). 17.89 *(978-0-06-008915-3(6)*, Julie Andrews Collection) HarperCollins Pubs.

—Simeon's Gift. Andrews, Julie et al. 2003. (Julie Andrews Collection). 40p. (J). (gr. k-4). 19.99 *(978-0-06-008914-6(8))* HarperCollins Pubs.

—The Velveteen Rabbit, 0 vols. Williams, Margery. 2011. (ENG.). 48p. (gr. 3-7). 17.99 *(978-0-7614-5848-7(4)*, 9780761458487, Amazon Children's Publishing) Amazon Publishing.

Spirin, Gennady. Martha. Spirin, Gennady. 2005. (ENG.). 32p. (J). (gr. -1-3). 16.99 *(978-0-399-23980-9(4)*, Philomel) Penguin Publishing Group.

—The Twelve Days of Christmas, 0 vols. Spirin, Gennady. 2009. (ENG.). 32p. (J). (gr. -1-3). 16.99 *(978-0-7614-5551-6(5)*, 9780761455516, Amazon Children's Publishing) Amazon Publishing.

—The Twelve Days of Christmas. Spirin, Gennady. ltd. ed. 2009. 32p. (J). (gr. -1-3). 16.99 *(978-0-7614-5607-0(4))* Marshall Cavendish Corp.

Spirin, Ilya. Ice Bears. Guiberson, Brenda Z. 2014. (ENG.). 40p. (J). (gr. k-3). 7.99 *(978-1-250-04061-9(2))* Square Fish.

—Little Lost Tiger, 0 vols. London, Jonathan. 2012. (ENG.). 32p. (J). (gr. k-3). 17.99 *(978-0-7614-6130-2(2)*, 9780761461302, Amazon Children's Publishing) Amazon Publishing.

Spizzirri, Peter M. Prehistoric Birds. Spizzirri, Linda, ed. 32p. (J). (gr. 1-8). pap. 4.98 incl. audio *(978-0-86545-023-3(4))* Spizzirri Pr., Inc.

—Space Craft. Spizzirri, Linda, ed. 32p. (J). (gr. 1-8). pap. 4.98 incl. audio *(978-0-86545-036-3(6))* Spizzirri Pr., Inc.

Splho, Michal. Repair for Teens: A Program for Recovery from Incest & Childhood Sexual Abuse. McKinnon, Margie. 2012. 138p. (J). 28.95 *(978-1-61599-127-3(1))*; pap. 16.95 *(978-1-61599-126-6(3))* Loving Healing Pr., Inc.

Splink, jt. illus. see Loki.

Spoerl, Amber. Dee Dee's First Shot, 1 vol. Dusablon, David. 2009. 17p. pap. 24.95 *(978-1-60749-113-2(3))* America Star Bks.

—The Dentist, 1 vol. Dusablon, David. 2009. 11p. pap. 24.95 *(978-1-60836-186-1(1))* America Star Bks.

Spohn, David. The Creation Story: In Words & Sign Language. Audia, John P. 2007. (ENG.). 16p. (gr. 3-7). 9.95 *(978-0-8146-3174-4(6))* Liturgical Pr.

Spohn, Kate. Turtle & Snake's Day at the Beach. Spohn, Kate. 2004. (Penguin Young Readers, Level 2 Ser.). (ENG.). 32p. (J). (gr. 1-2). mass mkt. 3.99 *(978-0-14-240157-6(9)*, Puffin) Penguin Publishing Group.

—Turtle & Snake's Day at the Beach. Spohn, Kate. 2004. (Puffin Easy-to-Read Ser.). 32p. (gr. k-3). 14.00 *(978-0-7569-2826-1(5))* Perfection Learning Corp.

—Turtle & Snake's Spooky Halloween. Spohn, Kate. 2003. (Easy-to-Read Ser.). 32p. (J). (gr. -1-3). 11.65 *(978-0-7569-1949-8(5))* Perfection Learning Corp.

Spohn, Onna J. Faerywood. Walley, Judith L. & Faith, Virginia T. 2011. (ENG.). 134p. pap. 14.95 *(978-1-4637-8030-2(3))* CreateSpace Independent Publishing Platform.

Sponaugle, Kim. Angel Eyes. Phillips, Dixie. 2008. 24p. pap. 10.95 *(978-1-933090-74-0(X))* Guardian Angel Publishing, Inc.

—Benny & Marshmallow. Matulewicz, Elisabeth Ann. 2008. 31p. (J). pap. 15.00 *(978-0-9786211-7-9(4)*, Ithaca Pr.) Authors & Artists Publishers of New York, Inc.

—Grandma Kathy Has Cancer. Buckley, Colleen. 2007. 24p. per. 11.50 *(978-1-59858-422-6(7))* Dog Ear Publishing, LLC.

—Just a Quilt? Keys, Dalen. 2nd ed. 2012. (ENG.). 32p. (J). 16.00 *(978-1-886068-56-8(9))* Fruitbearer Publishing, LLC.

—One Noble Journey. Phillips, Dixie. 2009. 16p. pap. 9.95 *(978-1-935137-86-3(7))* Guardian Angel Publishing, Inc.

—Seymour the Semi- Space Truckin' Spoonmore, Scott. 2012. 24p. 19.95 *(978-1-61633-282-2(4))*; pap. 11.95 *(978-1-61633-283-9(2))* Guardian Angel Publishing, Inc.

—Sweet Sweet Carabee. Gresham, Evelyn. 2013. 24p. pap. 11.95 *(978-1-61244-233-4(1))* Halo Publishing International.

Spong, Clive. Let's Look on the Move. Rutherford, Peter. 2015. (ENG.). 24p. (J). (gr. -1-2). bds. 6.99 *(978-1-86147-414-8(8)*, Armadillo) Anness Publishing GBR. Dist: National Bk. Network.

—Rapunzel. McCafferty, Catherine. 2008. (Keepsake Stories Ser.). (ENG & SPA.). 32p. (gr. -1-3). pap. 3.99 *(978-0-7696-5418-8(5))* Carson-Dellosa Publishing, LLC.

Sponheimer, Katheryne. The Sun Tea Fish. Callahan, Ann Marie. 2008. 16p. pap. 24.95 *(978-1-60672-160-5(7))* America Star Bks.

Spookytooth, T. S. Bone by Bone: Comparing Animal Skeletons. Levine, Sara. 2013. (ENG.). 32p. (J). (gr. k-4). lib. bdg. 26.60 *(978-0-7613-8464-9(2)*, Millbrook Pr.) Lerner Publishing Group.

Spookytooth, T. S. Tooth by Tooth. Levine, Sara (Veterinarian). 2015. (J). ***(978-1-4677-5215-2(0)***, Millbrook Pr.) Lerner Publishing Group.

—Tooth by Tooth: Comparing Fangs, Tusks, & Chompers. Levine, Sara. 2015. (J). ***(978-1-4677-9727-6(8)***, Millbrook Pr.) Lerner Publishing Group.

Spooner, Joe. Max's Moving Adventure: A Coloring Book for Kids on the Move. Till, Danelle. 2006. 52p. (J). 8.95 *(978-0-912301-64-8(3))* First Bks.

Spooner, Joe. The Elephant Walk. Spooner, Joe. McCann, Michelle, ed. 2005. (ENG.). 36p. (J). (gr. -1-3). 15.00 *(978-0-9745686-3-8(5))* ACS, LLC Amica Creative Services.

Spooner, Luke. Emlyn & the Gremlin: Emlyn & the Gremlin Series. Kneff, Steff F. l.t. ed. 2014. 1. (ENG.). 52p. (gr. k-3). 26.95 *(978-1-62253-399-2(2))*; pap. 10.95 *(978-1-62253-398-5(4))* Evolved Publishing.

Spoor, Mike. Alice's Birthday Pig. Kennemore, Tim. 2008. 54p. (J). (gr. 2-5). 12.00 *(978-0-8028-5335-6(8))* Eerdmans, William B. Publishing Co.

—Alice's World Record. Kennemore, Tim. 2008. 85p. (J). (gr. 4-7). 12.00 *(978-0-8028-5336-3(6))* Eerdmans, William B. Publishing Co.

—Benjamin the Bear: A Tale of Selfishness. Law, Felicia. 2010. (Animal Fair Values Ser.). (ENG.). 32p. (J). (gr. -1-3). pap. 10.55 *(978-1-60754-915-4(8))*; lib. bdg. 22.60 *(978-1-60754-905-5(0))* Windmill Bks.

—Blackbeard's Sword: The Pirate King of the Carolinas. O'Donnell, Liam. 2007. (Historical Fiction Ser.). (ENG.). 56p. (gr. 2-3). pap. 6.25 *(978-1-59889-404-2(8)*, Graphic Flash) Stone Arch Bks.

—Desperate Measures: Units of Measurement in Action. 2010. (Mandrill Mountain Math Mysteries Ser.). (ENG.). 32p. (J). (gr. 2-6). pap. 10.55 *(978-1-60754-925-3(5))* Windmill Bks.

—Desperate Measures: Units of Measurement in Action. 2010. (Mandrill Mountain Math Mysteries Ser.). (ENG.).

32p. (J). (gr. 2-6). lib. bdg. 22.60 *(978-1-60754-920-8(4))* Windmill Bks.

—The Emperor's Guards: Concepts of Time. 2010. (Mandrill Mountain Math Mysteries Ser.). (ENG.). 32p. (J). (gr. 2-6). pap. 10.55 *(978-1-60754-927-7(1))*; lib. bdg. 22.60 *(978-1-60754-922-2(0))* Windmill Bks.

—The Emperor's Last Command: Problem-solving in Action. 2010. (Mandrill Mountain Math Mysteries Ser.). (ENG.). 32p. (J). (gr. 2-6). pap. 10.55 *(978-1-60754-928-4(X))* Windmill Bks.

—The Emperor's Last Command: Problem-Solving in Action. 2010. (Mandrill Mountain Math Mysteries Ser.). (ENG.). 32p. (J). (gr. 2-6). lib. bdg. 22.60 *(978-1-60754-923-9(9))* Windmill Bks.

—Farmer Ham. Sillifant, Alec. import ed. 2004. 24p. *(978-1-904511-93-9(7))* Meadowside Children's Bks.

—The Hidden Valley: Reasoning in Action. 2010. (Mandrill Mountain Math Mysteries Ser.). (ENG.). 32p. (J). (gr. 2-6). pap. 10.55 *(978-1-60754-924-6(7))*; lib. bdg. 22.60 *(978-1-60754-919-2(0))* Windmill Bks.

—Lightning Flash: Probability in Action. 2010. (Mandrill Mountain Math Mysteries Ser.). (ENG.). 32p. (J). (gr. 2-6). pap. 10.55 *(978-1-60754-926-0(3))*; lib. bdg. 22.60 *(978-1-60754-921-5(2))* Windmill Bks.

—Monster under the Stairs. Dhami, Narinder. 2005. (ENG.). 24p. (J). lib. bdg. 23.65 *(978-1-59646-718-7(5))* Dingles & Co.

—The Mystery of the Vampire Boy: Dare You Peek Through the Pop-Up Windows? Taylor, Dereen. 2014. (ENG.). 12p. (J). (gr. k-5). 16.99 *(978-1-86147-410-0(5)*, Armadillo) Anness Publishing GBR. Dist: National Bk. Network.

—Olivia the Orangutan: A Tale of Helpfulness. Law, Felicia. 2010. (Animal Fair Values Ser.). (ENG.). 32p. (J). (gr. -1-3). pap. 10.55 *(978-1-60754-917-8(4))*; lib. bdg. 22.60 *(978-1-60754-906-2(9))* Windmill Bks.

Spoor, Mike & Mostyn, David. Crocodile Teeth: Geometric Shapes in Action. Law, Felicia & Way, Steve. 2010. (Mandrill Mountain Math Mysteries Ser.). 32p. (J). (gr. 2-6). 22.60 *(978-1-60754-816-4(X))*; pap. 10.55 *(978-1-60754-821-8(6))* Windmill Bks.

—Mirage in the Mist: Measurement in Action. Law, Felicia & Way, Steve. 2010. (Mandrill Mountain Math Mysteries Ser.). 32p. (J). (gr. 2-6). pap. 10.55 *(978-1-60754-823-2(2))* Windmill Bks.

—Mirage in the Mist: Measurements in Action. Law, Felicia & Way, Steve. 2010. (Mandrill Mountain Math Mysteries Ser.). 32p. (J). (gr. 2-6). 22.60 *(978-1-60754-818-8(6))* Windmill Bks.

—The Mystery of Nine: Number Place & Value in Action. Law, Felicia & Way, Steve. 2010. (Mandrill Mountain Math Mysteries Ser.). 32p. (J). (gr. 2-6). 22.60 *(978-1-60754-819-5(4))*; pap. 10.55 *(978-1-60754-824-9(0))* Windmill Bks.

—A Storm at Sea: Sorting, Mapping, & Grids in Action. Law, Felicia & Way, Steve. 2010. (Mandrill Mountain Math Mysteries Ser.). 32p. (J). (gr. 2-6). 22.60 *(978-1-60754-815-7(1))*; pap. 10.55 *(978-1-60754-820-1(8))* Windmill Bks.

Spowart, Robin. Baby Day. O'Keefe, Susan Heyboer. 2006. (ENG.). 32p. (J). (gr. -1-k). 15.95 *(978-1-56397-981-1(0))* Boyds Mills Pr.

Spowart, Robin. Oh, What a Beautiful Day! A Counting Book. Spowart, Robin. Modesitt, Jeanne. 2009. (ENG.). 32p. (J). (gr. -1-1). 16.95 *(978-1-56397-409-0(6))* Boyds Mills Pr.

Spradlin, Leslie. H Is for Heaven; The Bible Alphabet Book. Gilbert, Drexel. 2011. 36p. (J). pap. *(978-0-9818464-3-9(2))* Gilbert, Drexel Enterprises, Inc.

Sprague, Dean. The Adventure of Pushy Octopus & His Friends. Trimble, Marcia. 2005. 18p. (J). (gr. k-2). 4.95 *(978-1-891577-61-1(1)*, SAN2994844) Images Pr.

Sprague, Lois. The Sandal Artist, 1 vol. Pelley, Kathleen. 2012. (ENG.). 32p. (J). (gr. k-3). 16.99 *(978-1-58980-910-9(6))* Pelican Publishing Co., Inc.

Sprague, Lois Rosio. The Goodnight Thing. Hurst, Rich. 2006. 25p. (J). (gr. 4-7). 10.99 *(978-0-9763770-1-6(2))* Red Door Pr.

Spreen, Kathe. Ann Paints & Plays. Kalar, Bonnie. Date not set. 12p. (J). (gr. -1-2). pap. *(978-1-891619-40-3(3))* Corona Pr.

—At Dawn. Kalar, Bonnie. Date not set. 8p. (J). (gr. -1-2). pap. *(978-1-891619-24-3(1))* Corona Pr.

—At the Lake. Kalar, Bonnie. Date not set. 12p. (J). (gr. -1-2). pap. *(978-1-891619-34-2(9))* Corona Pr.

—At the Pond. Kalar, Bonnie. Date not set. 8p. (J). (gr. -1-2). pap. *(978-1-891619-07-6(1))* Corona Pr.

—At the Zoo. Kalar, Bonnie. Date not set. 8p. (J). (gr. -1-2). pap. *(978-1-891619-18-2(7))* Corona Pr.

—Beth & Thad. Kalar, Bonnie. Date not set. 12p. (J). (gr. -1-2). pap. *(978-1-891619-17-5(9))* Corona Pr.

—The Bird & the Shirt. Kalar, Bonnie. Date not set. 12p. (J). (gr. -1-2). pap. *(978-1-891619-30-4(6))* Corona Pr.

—Burt. Kalar, Bonnie. Date not set. 8p. (J). (gr. -1-2). pap. *(978-1-891619-31-1(4))* Corona Pr.

—Chuck & the Chick. Kalar, Bonnie. Date not set. 8p. (J). (gr. -1-2). pap. *(978-1-891619-16-8(0))* Corona Pr.

—Clair at Home. Kalar, Bonnie. Date not set. 12p. (J). (gr. -1-2). pap. *(978-1-891619-44-1(6))* Corona Pr.

—The Clown. Kalar, Bonnie. Date not set. 12p. (J). (gr. -1-2). pap. *(978-1-891619-22-9(5))* Corona Pr.

—The Cook & the Crook. Kalar, Bonnie. Date not set. 12p. (J). (gr. -1-2). pap. *(978-1-891619-29-8(2))* Corona Pr.

—The Crows. Kalar, Bonnie. Date not set. 8p. (J). (gr. -1-2). pap. *(978-1-891619-28-1(4))* Corona Pr.

—A Dream. Kalar, Bonnie. Date not set. 12p. (J). (gr. -1-2). pap. *(978-1-891619-23-6(3))* Corona Pr.

—Fran & the Doll. Kalar, Bonnie. Date not set. 8p. (J). (gr. -1-2). pap. *(978-1-891619-09-0(8))* Corona Pr.

—Fred. Kalar, Bonnie. Date not set. 8p. (J). (gr. -1-2). pap. *(978-1-891619-10-6(1))* Corona Pr.

—Gail Sails. Kalar, Bonnie. Date not set. 12p. (J). (gr. -1-2). pap. *(978-1-891619-20-5(9))* Corona Pr.

—Gay & Jay Play. Kalar, Bonnie. Date not set. 8p. (J). (gr. -1-2). pap. *(978-1-891619-19-9(5))* Corona Pr.

—A Good Day. Kalar, Bonnie. Date not set. 12p. (J). (gr. -1-2). pap. *(978-1-891619-41-0(1))* Corona Pr.

—Jack. Kalar, Bonnie. Date not set. 12p. (J). (gr. -1-2). pap. *(978-1-891619-13-7(6))* Corona Pr.

—Joan's Coat. Kalar, Bonnie. Date not set. 12p. (J). (gr. -1-2). pap. *(978-1-891619-21-2(7))* Corona Pr.

—Josh & the Fish. Kalar, Bonnie. Date not set. 8p. (J). (gr. -1-2). pap. *(978-1-891619-14-4(4))* Corona Pr.

—Kirk & the Deer. Kalar, Bonnie. Date not set. 12p. (J). (gr. -1-2). pap. *(978-1-891619-43-4(8))* Corona Pr.

—Lew & His New Cap. Kalar, Bonnie. Date not set. 8p. (J). (gr. -1-2). pap. *(978-1-891619-27-4(6))* Corona Pr.

—Mark at the Farm. Kalar, Bonnie. Date not set. 12p. (J). (gr. -1-2). pap. *(978-1-891619-25-0(X))* Corona Pr.

—Mike. Kalar, Bonnie. Date not set. 8p. (J). (gr. -1-2). pap. *(978-1-891619-35-9(7))* Corona Pr.

—Miss Lane's Class. Kalar, Bonnie. Date not set. 12p. (J). (gr. -1-2). pap. *(978-1-891619-38-0(1))* Corona Pr.

—Neal Camps Out. Kalar, Bonnie. Date not set. 12p. (J). (gr. -1-2). pap. *(978-1-891619-39-7(X))* Corona Pr.

—Rose & the Mole. Kalar, Bonnie. Date not set. 12p. (J). (gr. -1-2). pap. *(978-1-891619-36-6(5))* Corona Pr.

—The Scouts. Kalar, Bonnie. Date not set. 8p. (J). (gr. -1-2). pap. *(978-1-891619-26-7(8))* Corona Pr.

—The Sheep & the Bee. Kalar, Bonnie. Date not set. 8p. (J). (gr. -1-2). pap. *(978-1-891619-15-1(2))* Corona Pr.

—Stan & His Sled. Kalar, Bonnie. Date not set. 8p. (J). (gr. -1-2). pap. *(978-1-891619-08-3(X))* Corona Pr.

—The Trip. Kalar, Bonnie. Date not set. 8p. (J). (gr. -1-2). pap. *(978-1-891619-11-3(X))* Corona Pr.

—A Trip to the Beach. Kalar, Bonnie. Date not set. 12p. (J). (gr. -1-2). pap. *(978-1-891619-42-7(X))* Corona Pr.

Spremulli, Pam. Woof! Markey, Neil. 2011. (ENG.). 34p. (J). (gr. k-k). 14.00 *(978-1-935557-77-7(7))* PublishingWorks.

Springer, Sally. Fun on the Farm. Stamper, Judith Bauer & Keyes, Joan Ross. 2005. (Oxford Picture Dictionary for Kids Ser.). (ENG.). 16p. 6.94 *(978-0-19-430935-6(5))* Oxford Univ. Pr., Inc.

—Hide & Seek. Stamper, Judith Bauer & Ross Keyes, Joan. 2005. (Oxford Picture Dictionary for Kids Ser.). (ENG.). 15p. 6.94 *(978-0-19-430926-4(6))* Oxford Univ. Pr., Inc.

—Patty & the Pink Princesses. Slater, Teddy. 2007. (J). pap. *(978-0-439-89707-5(6))* Scholastic, Inc.

—The Shapes of My Jewish Year. Gold-Vukson, Marji. 2003. (Very First Board Bks.). (ENG.). 12p. (J). (gr. -1 — 1). bds. 5.95 *(978-1-58013-049-3(6)*, Kar-Ben Publishing) Lerner Publishing Group.

—What's for Breakfast? Stamper, Judith Bauer & Keyes, Joan Ross. 2005. (Oxford Picture Dictionary for Kids Ser.). (ENG.). 16p. 6.94 *(978-0-19-430934-9(7))* Oxford Univ. Pr., Inc.

Springett, Isobel, photos by. Kate & Pippin: An Unlikely Love Story. Springett, Martin. 2012. (ENG.). 32p. (J). (gr. -1-3). 16.99 *(978-0-8050-9487-9(3)*, Holt, Henry & Co. Bks. For Young Readers) Holt, Henry & Co.

Springett, Martin. Come Like Shadows. Katz, Welwyn W. 2005. 318p. (gr. 7-12). 7.95 *(978-1-55050-170-4(4))* Coteau Bks. CAN. Dist: Fitzhenry & Whiteside, Ltd.

—The Follower, 1 vol. Thompson, Springett & Thompson, Richard. 2003. (ENG.). 32p. (J). pap. 7.95 *(978-1-55041-880-4(7)*, 1550418807) Fitzhenry & Whiteside, Ltd. CAN. Dist: Midpoint Trade Bks., Inc.

SpringSprang Studio Staff. Madame Blue's Easter Hullabaloo: A Veggie Tales Book. Poth, Karen. 2011. 16p. (J). (gr. -1-k). bds. 12.99 *(978-0-8249-1856-9(8)*, Candy Cane Pr.) Ideals Pubns.

Sprunger, Reed. Eleanor Roosevelt: First Lady & Civil Rights Activist. Stille, Darlene R. 2013. (Beginner Biographies Set 2 Ser.). 32p. (J). (gr. -1-4). 28.50 *(978-1-61641-941-7(5))* Magic Wagon.

Spudvilas, Anne. A Certain Music. Walters, Celeste. 2nd ed. 2013. (ENG.). 138p. (J). (gr. 4-7). 8.99 *(978-1-74275-740-7(5))* Random Hse. Australia AUS. Dist: Independent Pubs. Group.

—The Silver Donkey. Hartnett, Sonya. 2004. viii, 193p. (J). *(978-0-670-04240-1(4)*, Viking Adult) Penguin Publishing Group.

Spurgeon, Aaron. Dinosaurs Live On! And Other Fun Facts. DiSiena, Laura Lyn & Eliot, Hannah. 2015. (Did You Know? Ser.). (ENG.). 32p. (J). (gr. -1-3). pap. 6.99 *(978-1-4814-2424-0(6)*, Little Simon) Little Simon.

Spurgeon, Aaron, jt. illus. see Oswald, Pete.

Spurll, Barbara. Ashley's Elephant: The Pond Hockey Challenge. Zaretsky, Evan. 2005. (ENG.). 32p. (gr. 1-2). pap. 7.25 *(978-1-57874-095-6(9)*, Kaeden Bks.) Kaeden Corp.

—Crow Said No. Haight, Angela. 2006. (ENG.). 36p. (gr. 1-2). pap. 7.25 *(978-1-57874-107-6(6))* Kaeden Corp.

—The Easter Bunny Is Missing! Metzger, Steve. 2007. (J). pap. *(978-0-439-92959-2(8))* Scholastic, Inc.

—Emma at the Fair, 1 vol. Ruurs, Margriet. 2007. (ENG.). 32p. (J). (gr. -1-3). per. *(978-1-55005-127-8(X))* Fitzhenry & Whiteside, Ltd.

—Emma's Cold Day, 1 vol. Ruurs, Margriet. 2003. (ENG.). 24p. (J). pap. 8.95 *(978-1-55005-076-9(1)*, 1550050761) Fitzhenry & Whiteside, Ltd. CAN. Dist: Midpoint Trade Bks., Inc.

—Theodora Bear, 1 vol. Jones, Carolyn. 2007. (Orca Echoes Ser.). (ENG.). 64p. (J). (gr. 2-5). per. 4.99 *(978-1-55143-496-4(2))* Orca Bk. Pubs. USA.

Spusta, Marq. All the Way to the Ocean. Harper, Joel. 2006. (J). 14.95 *(978-0-9714254-1-5(8))* Harper, Joel D.

Squier, Robert. Aphrodite: Goddess of Love & Beauty. Temple, Teri. 2012. (Greek Mythology Ser.). (ENG.). 32p. (J). (gr. 2-5). 29.93 *(978-1-61473-253-2(1)*, 204926) Child's World, Inc., The.

—Apollo: God of the Sun, Healing, Music, & Poetry. Temple, Teri. 2012. (Greek Mythology Ser.). (ENG.). 32p. (J). (gr. 2-5). 29.93 *(978-1-61473-254-9(X)*, 204927) Child's World, Inc., The.

—Ares: God of War. Temple, Teri. 2012. (Greek Mythology Ser.). (ENG.). 32p. (J). (gr. 2-5). 29.93 *(978-1-61473-255-6(8)*, 204928) Child's World, Inc., The.

—Artemis: Goddess of Hunting & Protector of Animals. Temple, Teri. 2012. (Greek Mythology Ser.). (ENG.). 32p. (J). (gr. 2-5). 29.93 *(978-1-61473-256-3(6)*, 204929) Child's World, Inc., The.

—Athena: Goddess of Wisdom, War, & Crafts. Temple, Teri. 2012. (Greek Mythology Ser.). (ENG.). 32p. (J). (gr. 2-5). 29.93 *(978-1-61473-257-0(4)*, 204930) Child's World, Inc., The.

—Eros: God of Love. Temple, Teri. 2012. (Greek Mythology Ser.). (ENG.). 32p. (J). (gr. 2-5). 29.93 *(978-1-61473-258-7(2)*, 204931) Child's World, Inc., The.

—Follow the Drinking Gourd: An Underground Railroad Story, 1 vol. 2012. (Night Sky Stories Ser.). (ENG.). 24p. (gr. 2-3). pap. 7.95 *(978-1-4048-7714-6(2))* Picture Window Bks.

—Follow the Drinking Gourd: An Underground Railroad Story, 1 vol. Capstone Press Staff. 2012. (Night Sky Stories Ser.). (ENG.). 24p. (gr. 2-3). lib. bdg. 25.99 *(978-1-4048-7375-9(9))* Picture Window Bks.

—Hades: God of the Underworld. Temple, Teri. 2012. (Greek Mythology Ser.). (ENG.). 32p. (J). (gr. 2-5). 29.93 *(978-1-61473-259-4(0)*, 204932) Child's World, Inc., The.

—Hephaestus: God of Fire, Metalwork, & Building. Temple, Teri. 2012. (Greek Mythology Ser.). (ENG.). 32p. (J). (gr. 2-5). 29.93 *(978-1-61473-260-0(4)*, 204933) Child's World, Inc., The.

—Hera: Queen of the Gods, Goddess of Marriage. Temple, Teri. 2012. (Greek Mythology Ser.). (ENG.). 32p. (J). (gr. 2-5). 29.93 *(978-1-61473-261-7(2)*, 204934) Child's World, Inc., The.

—Hermes: God of Travels & Trade. Temple, Teri. 2012. (Greek Mythology Ser.). (ENG.). 32p. (J). (gr. 2-5). 29.93 *(978-1-61473-262-4(0)*, 204935) Child's World, Inc., The.

—Independence Day. Heinrichs, Ann. 2013. (Holidays & Celebrations Ser.). (ENG.). 32p. (J). (gr. k-3). 27.07 *(978-1-62323-508-6(1)*, 206282) Child's World, Inc., The.

—The Lost Sheep. Berendes, Mary. 2011. (Parables Ser.). (ENG.). 24p. (J). (gr. k-3). lib. bdg. 28.50 *(978-1-60954-392-1(0)*, 201187) Child's World, Inc., The.

—Poseidon: God of the Sea & Earthquakes. Temple, Teri. 2012. (Greek Mythology Ser.). (ENG.). 32p. (J). (gr. 2-5). 29.93 *(978-1-61473-263-1(9)*, 204936) Child's World, Inc., The.

—The Prodigal Son. Berendes, Mary. 2011. (Parables Ser.). (ENG.). 24p. (J). (gr. k-3). lib. bdg. 28.50 *(978-1-60954-393-8(9)*, 201188) Child's World, Inc., The.

—The Sower & the Seeds. Berendes, Mary. 2011. (Parables Ser.). (ENG.). 24p. (J). (gr. k-3). lib. bdg. 28.50 *(978-1-60954-394-5(7)*, 201189) Child's World, Inc., The.

—Spinosaurus. Gray, Susan H. 2009. (Introducing Dinosaurs Ser.). (ENG.). 24p. (J). (gr. -1-2). 27.07 *(978-1-60253-241-0(9)*, 200377) Child's World, Inc., The.

—The Story of Cassiopeia: A Roman Constellation Myth, 1 vol. 2012. (Night Sky Stories Ser.). (ENG.). 24p. (gr. 2-3). pap. 7.95 *(978-1-4048-7716-0(9))* Picture Window Bks.

—The Story of Cassiopeia: A Roman Constellation Myth, 1 vol. Capstone Press Staff. 2012. (Night Sky Stories Ser.). (ENG.). 24p. (gr. 2-3). lib. bdg. 25.99 *(978-1-4048-7376-6(7))* Picture Window Bks.

—The Ten Bridesmaids. Berendes, Mary. 2011. (Parables Ser.). (ENG.). 24p. (J). (gr. k-3). lib. bdg. 28.50 *(978-1-60954-395-2(5)*, 201190) Child's World, Inc., The.

—Triceratops. Gray, Susan H. 2009. (Introducing Dinosaurs Ser.). (ENG.). 24p. (J). (gr. -1-2). 27.07 *(978-1-60253-243-4(5)*, 200379) Child's World, Inc., The.

—The Truth about Elves, 1 vol. Troupe, Thomas Kingsley. 2010. (Fairy-Tale Superstars Ser.). (ENG.). 32p. (gr. 1-3). lib. bdg. 26.65 *(978-1-4048-6047-6(9)*, Nonfiction Picture Bks.) Picture Window Bks.

—The Truth about Witches, 1 vol. Braun, Eric. 2011. (Fairy-Tale Superstars Ser.). (ENG.). 32p. (gr. 1-3). lib. bdg. 26.65 *(978-1-4048-6160-2(2)*, Nonfiction Picture Bks.) Picture Window Bks.

—The Unmerciful Servant. Berendes, Mary. 2011. (Parables Ser.). (ENG.). 24p. (J). (gr. k-3). lib. bdg. 28.50 *(978-1-60954-396-9(3)*, 201191) Child's World, Inc., The.

—Yankee Doodle. Bangs, Edward. 2010. (Favorite Children's Songs Ser.). (ENG.). 16p. (J). (gr. -1-2). 25.64 *(978-1-60253-534-3(5)*, 200116) Child's World, Inc., The.

—Your Sensational Sense of Hearing. Vogel, Julia. 2011. (Sensational Senses Ser.). (ENG.). 32p. (J). (gr. k-3). lib. bdg. 27.07 *(978-1-60954-286-3(X)*, 200815) Child's World, Inc., The.

—Your Sensational Sense of Sight. Vogel, Julie. 2011. (Sensational Senses Ser.). (ENG.). 32p. (J). (gr. k-3). lib. bdg. 27.07 *(978-1-60954-287-0(8)*, 200816) Child's World, Inc., The.

—Your Sensational Sense of Smell. Vogel, Julie & Vogel, Julia. 2011. (Sensational Senses Ser.). (ENG.). 32p. (J). (gr. k-3). lib. bdg. 27.07 *(978-1-60954-288-7(6)*, 200817) Child's World, Inc., The.

—Your Sensational Sense of Taste. Vogel, Julie & Vogel, Julia. 2011. (Sensational Senses Ser.). (ENG.). 32p. (J). (gr. k-3). lib. bdg. 27.07 *(978-1-60954-289-4(4)*, 200818) Child's World, Inc., The.

—Your Sensational Sense of Touch. Vogel, Julie & Vogel, Julia. 2011. (Sensational Senses Ser.). (ENG.). 32p. (J). (gr. k-3). lib. bdg. 27.07 *(978-1-60954-290-0(8)*, 200819) Child's World, Inc., The.

—Zeus: King of the Gods, God of Sky & Storms. Temple, Teri. 2012. (Greek Mythology Ser.). (ENG.). 32p. (J). (gr. 2-5). 29.93 *(978-1-61473-264-8(7)*, 204937) Child's World, Inc., The.

Squier, Robert & Harrison, Nancy. Who Was Davy Crockett? Herman, Gail. 2013. (Who Was...? Ser.). (ENG.). 112p. (J). (gr. 3-7). 5.99 *(978-0-448-46704-7(6)*, Grosset & Dunlap) Penguin Publishing Group.

—Who Was Frederick Douglass? Prince, April Jones. 2014. (Who Was...? Ser.). (ENG.). 112p. (J). (gr. 3-7). 5.99 *(978-0-448-47911-8(7)*, Grosset & Dunlap) Penguin Publishing Group.

Squier, Robert, jt. illus. see Anderson, Scott.

Squier, Robert, jt. illus. see Johnson, Pamela.

Squillace, Elisa. Aladdin. 2007. (Flip-Up Fairy Tales Ser.). (ENG.). 24p. (J). (gr. -1-2). *(978-1-84643-154-8(9))*; (gr. 2-2). *(978-1-84643-113-5(1))* Child's Play International Ltd.

—Aladdin: Flip-up Fairy Tales. 2008. (Flip-Up Fairy Tales Ser.). (ENG.). 24p. (J). *(978-1-84643-193-7(X))* Child's Play International Ltd.

—Down in the Jungle. (Classic Books with Holes Big Book Ser.). (ENG.). (J). (gr. -1-3). 2006. 16p. *(978-1-84643-009-1(7))*; 2005. 14p. bds. *(978-1-904550-61-7(4))* Child's Play International Ltd.

—Down in the Jungle. (Classic Books with Holes Ser.). (ENG.). 16p. 2013. (gr. -1). pap. incl. audio compact disk *(978-1-84643-623-9(0))*; 2005. (J). pap. *(978-1-904550-32-7(0))* Child's Play International Ltd.

—Three Wishes. 2009. (First Reading Level 1 Ser.). 32p. (J). (gr. 2). 6.99 *(978-0-7945-2278-0(5)*, Usborne) EDC Publishing.

Squire, M H & Mars, E. Heroes of Greek Mythology. Kingsley, Charles. 2006. (Dover Children's Classics Ser.). (ENG.). 240p. (YA). (gr. 3-12). per. 9.95 *(978-0-486-44854-1(1))* Dover Pubns., Inc.

Squire, Maud Hunt. Hindu Stories. Williston, Teresa Peirce. 2011. 110p. 39.95 *(978-1-258-02581-6(7))* Literary Licensing, LLC.

—Hindu Tales. Williston, Teresa Peirce. 2011. 86p. 37.95 *(978-1-258-02582-3(5))* Literary Licensing, LLC.

Squire, Stan. Sent to Sydney, 1 vol. Thompson, Lisa. 2006. (Read-It! Chapter Books: SWAT Ser.). (ENG.). 80p. (gr. 2-4). 21.32 *(978-1-4048-1671-8(2)*, Chapter Readers) Picture Window Bks.

Srinivasan, Divya. Little Owl's 1-2-3. Srinivasan, Divya. 2015. (ENG.). 18p. (J). (— 1). bds. 5.99 ***(978-0-451-47454-4(6)***, Viking Juvenile) Penguin Publishing Group.

—Little Owl's Colors. Srinivasan, Divya. 2015. (ENG.). 18p. (J). (— 1). bds. 5.99 ***(978-0-451-47456-8(2)***, Viking Juvenile) Penguin Publishing Group.

Srinivasan, Divya. Little Owl's Day. Srinivasan, Divya. 2014. (ENG.). 32p. (J). (gr. -1-k). 16.99 *(978-0-670-01650-1(0)*, Viking Juvenile) Penguin Publishing Group.

Srivi. Hanuman's Adventures in the Nether World: A 600 Year Old Classic Retold. Mahadevan, Madhavi S. 2005. (J). *(978-81-89020-30-9(7))* Katha.

Ssebulime, John. Dragon Baked Bread. Cohen, Warren Lee. 2005. 32p. (J). *(978-1-902636-70-2(8))* Clairview Bks.

St. Angelo, Ron, photos by. Princess Bible, 1 vol. Hitzges, Norm. 2007. (Compact Kids Ser.). (ENG.), 1152p. pap. 24.99 *(978-1-4003-0987-0(5))* Nelson, Thomas Inc.

St Anthony, Gus. Tutti Frutti. Marcucci, Vince. 2005. 32p. (J). (gr. -1-3). pap. 8.99 *(978-0-9769198-0-3(X))* Chick Light Publishing.

St. Aubin, Bruno. Corre, Nicolas, Corre! Tibo, Gilles. Rioja, Alberto Jiménez, tr. from FRE. 2009. (SPA & ENG.). 32p. (J). (gr. 2-4). pap. 6.99 *(978-1-933032-57-3(X))* Lectorum Pubns., Inc.

St-Aubin, Bruno. Fred & the Mysterious Letter. Croteau, Marie-Danielle. 2005. 61p. (J). lib. bdg. 12.00 *(978-1-4242-1199-9(9))* Fitzgerald Bks.

—Fred & the Mysterious Letter. Croteau, Marie-Danielle. Cummins, Sarah, tr. from FRE. 2005. (Formac First Novels Ser.). (ENG.). 64p. (J). (gr. 2-5). 14.95 *(978-0-88780-689-6(9))*; 4.95 *(978-0-88780-688-9(0))* Formac Publishing Co., Ltd. CAN. Dist: Casemate Pubs. & Bk. Distributors, LLC.

—Fred & the Pig Race. Croteau, Marie-Danielle. Cummins, Sarah, tr. from FRE. 2007. (Formac First Novels Ser.). (ENG.). 64p. (gr. 2-5). 14.95 *(978-0-88780-733-6(X))*; 4.95 *(978-0-88780-731-2(3))* Formac Publishing Co., Ltd. CAN. Dist: Casemate Pubs. & Bk. Distributors, LLC.

St. Aubin, Bruno. La Petite Reine au Nez Rouge. Croteau, Marie-Danielle. 2004. (Premier Roman Ser.). (FRE.). 64p. (J). (gr. 1-4). pap. *(978-2-89021-706-5(X))* Diffusion du livre Mirabel (DLM).

St-Aubin, Bruno. The Several Lives of Orphan Jack, 1 vol. Ellis, Sarah. 2005. (ENG.). 88p. (J). pap. 8.95 *(978-0-88899-618-3(7))* Groundwood Bks. CAN. Dist: Perseus-PGW.

St. Aubin, Claude. Captured off Guard: The Attack on Pearl Harbor, 1 vol. Lemke, Donald B. & Pattison, Ronda. 2008. (Historical Fiction Ser.). (ENG.). 56p. (gr. 2-3). pap. 6.25 *(978-1-4342-0493-6(6))*; lib. bdg. 25.32 *(978-1-4342-0443-1(X))* Stone Arch Bks. (Graphic Flash).

—A Totally True Princess Story. Patton, Chris. Wellman, Mike, ed. 2009. 72p. 12.99 *(978-0-615-27602-1(4))* Atomic Basement.

St. George, Carolyn. Vine & Branches. Hakowski, Maryann. 2003. (Resources for Youth Retreats Ser.: Vol. 1). 160p. (YA). (gr. 7-12). spiral bd. 24.95 *(978-0-88489-255-7(7))* St. Mary's Pr. of MN.

—Vine & Branches, Vol. 2. Hakowski, Maryann. Stamschror, Robert P., ed. 2003. (Resources for Youth Retreats Ser.: Vol. 2). 168p. (YA). (gr. 7-12). spiral bd. 24.95 *(978-0-88489-278-6(6))* St. Mary's Pr. of MN.

St. John Taylor, Jeannie, jt. illus. see Taylor, Jeannie St. John.

Staake, Bob. Bugs Galore. Stein, Peter. (ENG.). 32p. (J). 2013. (— 1). bds. 6.99 *(978-0-7636-6220-2(8))*; 2012. (gr. -1-3). 15.99 *(978-0-7636-4754-4(3))* Candlewick Pr.

—Cars Galore. Stein, Peter. (ENG.). (J). (gr. -1-3). 2012. 30p. bds. 6.99 *(978-0-7636-6148-9(1))*; 2011. 32p. 15.99 *(978-0-7636-4743-8(8))* Candlewick Pr.

Staake, Bob, et al. Favorites: I'm a Truck/The Happy Man & His Dump Truck/I'm a Monster Truck. Shealy, Dennis & Miryam. 2011. (Little Golden Book Favorites Ser.). (ENG.). 80p. (J). (gr. -1-2). 6.99 *(978-0-375-86549-7(7)*, Golden Bks.) Random Hse. Children's Bks.

—Hot Summer Fun, Cool Summer Stars. Thomas, Stephen, ed. Date not set. 28p. (Orig.). (J). (gr. 3-7). pap. *(978-1-886749-26-9(4))* Sports Illustrated For Kids.

Staake, Bob. I'm a Monster Truck. Shealy, Dennis & Little Golden Books Staff. 2011. (Little Golden Book Ser.). (ENG.). 24p. (J). (gr. -1-2). 3.99 *(978-0-375-86132-1(7)*, Golden Bks.) Random Hse. Children's Bks.

—I'm a Truck. Shealy, Dennis. 2006. (Little Golden Book Ser.). (ENG.). 24p. (J). (gr. -1-2). 3.99 *(978-0-375-83263-5(7)*, Golden Bks.) Random Hse. Children's Bks.

—Robots, Robots Everywhere! Fliess, Sue. 2013. (Little Golden Book Ser.). (ENG.). 24p. (J). (-k). 3.99

(978-0-449-81079-8(8), Golden Bks.) Random Hse. Children's Bks.
—Robots, Robots Everywhere. Fliess, Sue. 2014. (Little Golden Board Book Ser.). (ENG.). 26p. (J). (-k). bds. 7.99 (978-0-385-38924-2(8), Random Hse. Bks. for Young Readers) Random Hse. Children's Bks.
—Sputter, Sputter, Sput! Bell, Babs. 2008. 32p. (J). (gr. -1-k). lib. bdg. 17.89 (978-0-06-056223-6(4)) HarperCollins Pubs.
—Toys Galore. Stein, Peter. 2013. (ENG.). 32p. (J). (gr. -1-3). 15.99 (978-0-7636-6254-7(2)) Candlewick Pr.
—We Planted a Tree. Muldrow, Diane. 2010. (ENG.). 40p. (J). (gr. -1-2). 17.99 (978-0-375-86432-2(6), Golden Bks.) Random Hse. Children's Bks.
Staake, Bob. The Donut Chef. Staake, Bob. (ENG.). 40p. (J). (gr. -1-2). 2013. 7.99 (978-0-385-36992-3(1), Dragonfly Bks.); 2008. 14.99 (978-0-375-84403-4(1), Golden Bks.) Random Hse. Children's Bks.
—The First Pup: The Real Story of How Bo Got to the White House. Staake, Bob. 2010. (ENG.). 40p. (J). (gr. k-3). 16.99 (978-0-312-61346-4(6)) Feiwel & Friends.
—The Red Lemon. Staake, Bob. 2012. (ENG.). 32p. (J). (gr. -1-3). pap. 7.99 (978-0-307-97846-2(X), Random Hse. Bks. for Young Readers) Random Hse. Children's Bks.
—This Is Not a Pumpkin. Staake, Bob. 2007. (ENG.). 32p. (J). (gr. -1 — 1). bds. 6.99 (978-1-4169-3353-3(0), Little Simon) Little Simon.
Staake, Bob, jt. illus. see Truesdell, Sue.
Stabile, Nicolette. Why Am I Brown? A Child's View of Multi-cultural Adoption, 1 vol. Meissner, Jacqueline. 2009. 22p. pap. 24.95 (978-1-60836-234-9(5)) America Star Bks.
Stacey, Alan. Round Up: A Texas Number Book. Crane, Carol. 2003. (America by the Numbers Ser.). (ENG.). 40p. (J). (gr. k-6). 16.95 (978-1-58536-133-5(X)) Sleeping Bear Pr.
Stacey, Mark. Wizards: From Merlin to Faust. McIntee, David. 2014. (Myths & Legends Ser.: 9). (ENG.). 80p. pap. (978-1-4728-0339-9(6), Osprey Publishing) Bloomsbury Publishing Plc.
Stacey, W. The Martyr's Victory: A Story of Danish England. Leslie, Emma. 2007. 300p. 24.95 (978-1-934671-08-5(8)); per. 14.95 (978-1-934671-09-2(6)) Salem Ridge Press LLC.
Stacey, W. S., jt. illus. see Hymper, W.
Stack, Jocelyn. P Is for Potato: An Idaho Alphabet. Steiner, Stan et al. 2005. (Discover America State by State Ser.). (ENG.). 40p. (J). 17.95 (978-1-58536-155-7(0)) Sleeping Bear Pr.
Stacy, Alan. Alaskan Night Before Christmas, 1 vol. Brown, Tricia. 2008. (Night Before Christmas Ser.). (ENG.). 32p. (gr. 1-3). 16.99 (978-1-58980-554-5(2)) Pelican Publishing Co., Inc.
—Discover Texas, 2 bks. Crane, Carol. 2003. (ENG.). 40p. (J). 27.95 (978-1-58536-227-1(1)) Sleeping Bear Pr.
—G Is for Galaxy: An Out of This World Alphabet. Collison, Cathy & Campbell, Janis. (World/Country Alphabet Ser.). (ENG.). 40p. (J). (gr. k-5). 2005. 16.95 (978-1-58536-255-4(7)); 2006. pap. 7.95 (978-1-58536-335-3(9)) Sleeping Bear Pr.
—Pennsylvania Dutch Alphabet, 1 vol. Williamson, Chet. 2007. (ENG.). 32p. (J). (gr. k-3). 16.99 (978-1-58980-496-8(1)) Pelican Publishing Co., Inc.
—Texas Zeke & the Longhorn, 1 vol. Davis, David. 2006. (ENG.). 32p. (J). (gr. k-3). 16.99 (978-1-58980-348-0(5)) Pelican Publishing Co., Inc.
Stacy, Alan & Braught, Mark. T Is for Touchdown: A Football Alphabet. Herzog, Brad. 2004. (Sports Ser.). (ENG.). 40p. (J). (gr. -1-5). 16.95 (978-1-58536-233-2(6)) Sleeping Bear Pr.
Stacy, Alan F. Ross the Reader & the Great Balloon Race. Dailey, Reid. 2011. 46p. pap. 13.95 (978-1-4575-0154-8(6)) Dog Ear Publishing, LLC.
Stacy, Dorothy. Erie Canal Cousins. Stacy, Dorothy. 2007. 110p. (J). per. 9.95 (978-0-9792947-0-9(3)) Blackberry Hill Pr.
—Three Weeks in Utica. Stacy, Dorothy. 2008. 120p. (J). pap. 9.95 (978-0-9792947-1-6(1)) Blackberry Hill Pr.
Stader, Kristina & Stroede, Paul. Frog on my Head. Stadler, Kristina. 2011. 24p. (J). lib. bdg. 11.95 (978-1-59598-138-7(1), Goblin Fern Pr.) HenschelHAUS Publishing.
Stadler, John. Catilda. Stadler, John. 2010. (ENG.). 32p. (J). (gr. -1-k). 16.99 (978-1-4424-2939-0(9), Atheneum Bks. for Young Readers) Simon & Schuster Children's Publishing.
Stadther, Michael. Secrets of the Alchemist Dar. Stadther, Michael. 2006. (Treasure's Trove Ser.). (ENG.). 144p. (J). 21.99 (978-1-4169-2653-5(4)); 39.99 (978-1-4169-2661-0(5)) Treasure Trove, Inc.
—101 New Puzzles Clues, Maps, Tantalizing Tales: And Stories of Real Treasure. Stadther, Michael. 2006. (Treasure's Trove Ser.). (ENG.). 112p. (J). pap. 12.99 (978-1-4169-2655-9(0)) Treasure Trove, Inc.
Stadtlander, Becca. Many Hands: A Farm Prepares for Winter. Doyle, Eugenie. 2015. (J). **(978-1-4521-2901-3(0))** Chronicle Bks. LLC.
Stadtlander, Becca. On the Wing. Elliott, David. 2014. (ENG.). 32p. (J). (gr. -1-2). 16.99 (978-0-7636-5324-8(1)) Candlewick Pr.
Stafford, Jordan. The Legend of the Sweet Potato Pie. Mitchell, Shirley Lipscomb. Tombers, Monica, ed. 2012. 40p. (-18). pap. 12.95 (978-0-9851996-0-9(1)) HMSI, Inc.
—Poetino Piccolino Saves the Day. Gambini, Josephine. 2011. (ENG.). (J). pap. 19.95 (978-0-9829496-3-4(4)) Giusti-Gambini, J.M. Publishing, LLC.
Stafford, Rosalee. Wood's New Collar. Salyers, Rita. 2006. (J). per. 11.95 (978-0-9760129-3-1(6)) The Publishing Place LLC.
Staggenborg, Kim. Stories of the Saints V1, 4 vols. Woodfield, Elaine. 2009. (J). pap. 13.95 (978-0-9788376-8-6(1)) Catholic Heritage Curricula.
—Stories of the Saints V2, 4 vols. Woodfield, Elaine. 2009. (J). pap. 0.00 (978-0-9788376-9-3(X)) Catholic Heritage Curricula.
Stagno, Laura. Yo Tenia 10 Perritos. Anónimo. 2004. (SPA.). 24p. (J). (gr. k-18). pap. 6.50 (978-980-257-277-9(2)) Ekare, Ediciones VEN. Dist: Lectorum Pubns., Inc.
Stahl, Miriam Klein. Rad American Women A-Z: Rebels, Trailblazers, & Visionaries Who Shaped Our History ... & Our Future! Schatz, Kate. 2015. (City Lights/Sister Spit Ser.). (ENG.). 64p. (J). (gr. 2-11). 14.95 (978-0-87286-683-6(1)) City Lights Bks.
Stahlberg, Carina. Lucia Morning in Sweden. Rydaker, Ewa. Lewis, Anne Gillespie, ed. 2014. (ENG.). 35p. (J). (gr. -1-3). pap. 8.99 (978-1-935666-65-3(7)) Nodin Pr.
—A Perfect Tree for Christmas. Lewis, Anne G. 2013. (ENG.). (J). pap. 7.99 (978-1-935666-55-4(X)) Nodin Pr.
Staige, Pat & Stanton, Janet. Farmer Carpenter's Barn & the Cow's Saturday Night Dance. Banicki, Patsy & Staige, Pat. Date not set. (Orig.). (J). (gr. k-4). pap. (978-0-9641375-1-6(8)) Staige Productions.
Staino, Franco. The Adventures of Pinocchio. 2012. 312p. (978-88-492-2206-7(8)) Gangemi.
Staino, Franco & Innocenti, Roberto. The Adventures of Pinocchio. Collodi, Carlo. rev. ed. 2004. (ENG.). 192p. (J). (gr. 1-3). 35.00 (978-1-56846-190-8(9)) Creative Co., The.
Stalio, Ivan. The Human Body. Starry Dog Books. 2007. (Back to Basics Ser.). 31p. (J). lib. bdg. (978-88-6098-050-2(X)) McRae Bks. Srl.
Stallop, Christy. There's a Yak in my Bed. Pluta, K. 2007. (ENG.). 32p. (J). (gr. -1 — 1). 16.95 (978-0-9769417-4-3(0)) Blooming Tree Pr.
Stalsjo, Eva. Goldie at the Farm. Sandwall-Bergstrom, Martha. 24p. 17.95 (978-0-86315-485-0(9)) Floris Bks. GBR. Dist: SteinerBooks, Inc.
Stålsjö, Eva. Goldie at the Orphanage. Sandwall-Bergström, Martha. 2004. 24p. (J). 16.95 (978-0-86315-443-0(3)) Floris Bks. GBR. Dist: SteinerBooks, Inc.
Sta.Maria, Ian & Blanden, Neale. Edgar Allan Poe's Tales of Mystery. Caputo, Antonella et al. Pomplun, Tom, ed. 2011. (Graphic Classics Ser.: 21). 144p. (YA). pap. 17.95 (978-0-9825630-2-1(7)) Eureka Productions.
Stammen, Jo Ellen McAllister. Hero Cat, 0 vols. Spinelli, Eileen. 2011. (ENG.). 32p. (J). (gr. -1-3). pap. 9.99 (978-0-7614-5837-1(9), 9780761458371, Amazon Children's Publishing) Amazon Publishing.
Stammen, JoEllen McAllister. Wild Fox: A True Story. Mason, Cherie. 2013. (ENG.). 56p. 14.99 (978-1-60893-212-2(5)) Down East Bks.
Stan, Jaskiel. Dumplings are Delicious Learning & Activity Guide. Deb, Capone. 2007. 20p. (J). 9.95 (978-0-9728666-9-8(8)) As Simple As That Publishing.
—Families are Forever Learning & Activity Guide. 2007. 20p. (J). 9.95 (978-0-9728666-2-0(0)) As Simple As That Publishing.
Stanbridge, Joanne. The Extraordinary Music of Mr. Ives: The True Story of a Famous American Composer. Stanbridge, Joanne. 2012. (ENG.). 32p. (J). (gr. -1-3). 16.99 (978-0-547-23866-1(5)) Houghton Mifflin Harcourt Publishing Co.
Standingdeer, John, Jr. & Goshorn, Shan. The Origin of the Milky Way & Other Living Stories of the Cherokee. Duncan, Barbara, ed. 2008. (ENG.). 144p. (gr. 4-18). pap. 15.95 (978-0-8078-5930-8(3)) Univ. of North Carolina Pr.
Standley, Peter & Chalk, Gary. Taggerung. Jacques, Brian. 2003. (Redwall Ser.). (ENG.). 448p. (J). (gr. 5-18). pap. 8.99 (978-0-14-250154-2(9), Puffin) Penguin Publishing Group.
Stanek, Joyce Huntington. Sarah 'n' Dippity. Stanek, Gerald. 2004. (ENG.). 28p. (J). 14.95 (978-0-9747417-0-3(1)) Shiver Hill Bks.
Stanek, Mary Beth. The Fire Keepers: Mystery at Manitou Beach. Stanek, Mary Beth. Stanek, Linda, photos by. 2003. (J). pap. 20.00 (978-0-9747556-0-1(5)) Stanek, Mary Beth.
Stanek, Robert, pseud. The Kingdoms & the Elves of the Reaches. Stanek, Robert. alt. gif. ed. 2004. 176p. (YA). pap. 10.99 (978-1-57545-501-3(3), Reagent Pr. Echo) RP Media.
—The Kingdoms & the Elves of the Reaches II. Stanek, Robert. alt. gif. ed. 2004. (ENG.). 180p. (YA). pap. 10.99 (978-1-57545-502-0(1), Reagent Pr. Echo) RP Media.
—The Kingdoms & the Elves of the Reaches III. Stanek, Robert. alt. gif. ed. 2004. (ENG.). 172p. (YA). pap. 10.99 (978-1-57545-503-7(X), Reagent Pr. Echo) RP Media.
—The Kingdoms & the Elves of the Reaches IV. Stanek, Robert. alt. gif. ed. 2005. 172p. (YA). pap. 10.99 (978-1-57545-504-4(8), Reagent Pr. Echo) RP Media.
Staniland, C. Gytha's Message: A Tale of Saxon England. Leslie, Emma. 2007. 256p. 22.95 (978-1-934671-11-5(8)) Salem Ridge Press LLC.
Stankiewicz, Steven. Economics Through Infographics. Kenney, Karen. 2014. (Super Social Studies Infographics Ser.). 32p. (gr. 3-5). (J). lib. bdg. 26.60 (978-1-4677-3460-8(8), Lerner Pubns.); pap. 8.95 (978-1-4677-4564-2(2)) Lerner Publishing Group.
Stanley, Amanda. The Search for Young Niclas: Young Niclas Disappears & His Magical Friends Witch Hilga & Jackie the Ghost Help to Find Him. Morgan, Randolph & Morgan, Niclas. 2011. (ENG.). 36p. pap. 9.99 (978-1-4611-2747-5(5)) CreateSpace Independent Publishing Platform.
Stanley, Anne. Listen in Addition. 2007. (ENG.). 16p. (J). 16.99 (978-0-9796150-0-9(3)) Jandie Jams Music LLC.
Stanley, Christopher Heath & Parsons, Arielle. The Castle Rock Critter. Stanley, Phillip Orin, 2nd. l.t. ed. 2004. 16p. (J). 8.00 (978-0-9761355-0-0(7)) Floodgate Publishing.
Stanley, Diane. The Giant & the Beanstalk. Stanley, Diane. 2004. 32p. (J). (gr. k-3). (ENG.). 17.99 (978-0-06-000010-3(4)); lib. bdg. 18.89 (978-0-06-000011-0(2)) HarperCollins Pubs.
—Goldie & the Three Bears. Stanley, Diane. 2007. (ENG.). 40p. (J). (gr. k-3). pap. 7.99 (978-0-06-113611-5(5)) HarperCollins Pubs.
—Michelangelo. Stanley, Diane. 2003. (ENG.). 48p. (J). (gr. 2-18). pap. 6.99 (978-0-06-052113-4(9)) HarperCollins Pubs.
—Mozart: The Wonder Child - A Puppet Play in Three Acts. Stanley, Diane. 2009. (ENG.). 48p. (J). (gr. 3-7). 17.99 (978-0-06-072674-4(1), Collins) HarperCollins Pubs.
—Raising Sweetness, 4 bks. Stanley, Diane. 2003. (J). pap. 37.95 incl. audio (978-1-59112-267-8(8)) Live Oak Media.
—The Trouble with Wishes. Stanley, Diane. 2007. 32p. (J). (gr. k-3). lib. bdg. 17.89 (978-0-06-055452-1(5)) HarperCollins Pubs.
Stanley, Mandy. Baby Blessings Baby's Bible. 2005. 6p. (YA). (gr. -1 — 1). 15.99 (978-0-7847-1739-4(7), 04382) Standard Publishing.
—Christmas Blessings Baby's Holiday Photo Album. Davidson, Alice Joyce. 2005. (Baby Blessings Ser.). 10p. (YA). (gr. -1-k). 15.99 (978-0-7847-1771-4(0), 04723) Standard Publishing.
—Daddy Loves Me. Moore, Karen. gif. ed. 2005. 10p. (J). (gr. -1-1). per., bds. 6.99 (978-1-57791-183-8(0)) Brighter Minds Children's Publishing.
—Good Puppy. Hawksley, Gerald. 2005. (J). (978-1-890647-14-8(4)) TOMY International, Inc.
—Jack & Jill & Other Nursery Favourites. 2010. (Time for a Rhyme Ser.). (ENG.). 24p. (J). (gr. k — 1). 6.99 (978-0-00-731564-2(3)) HarperCollins Pubs. Ltd. GBR. Dist: Independent Pubs. Group.
—Lift & Look Daniel. 2005. 8p. (J). (gr. -1-k). 7.99 (978-0-7847-1751-6(6), 04377) Standard Publishing.
—Mommy Loves Me. Moore, Karen. gif. ed. 2005. 10p. (J). (gr. -1-1). per., bds. 6.99 (978-1-57791-182-1(2)) Brighter Minds Children's Publishing.
—Twinkle, Twinkle, Little Star & Other Nursery Favourites. 2009. (Time for a Rhyme Ser.). (ENG.). 24p. (J). (gr. k — 1). 6.99 (978-0-00-731563-5(5), HarperCollins Children's Bks.) HarperCollins Pubs. Ltd. GBR. Dist: HarperCollins Pubs.
Stanley, Mandy. The Birthday Party. Stanley, Mandy. ed. 2011. (ENG.). 32p. (J). (gr. -1-k). pap. 9.95 (978-0-00-718409-5(3), HarperCollins Children's Bks.) HarperCollins Pubs. Ltd. GBR. Dist: HarperCollins Pubs.
—The Fairy Ball. Stanley, Mandy. ed. 2010. (Lettice Ser.). (ENG.). 32p. (J). (gr. -1-k). pap. 9.95 (978-0-00-720195-2(8), HarperCollins Children's Bks.) HarperCollins Pubs. Ltd. GBR. Dist: HarperCollins Pubs.
—Who Do You Love? Stanley, Mandy. 2007. (ENG.). 24p. (J). (gr. -1 — 1). bds. 8.99 (978-1-4169-3929-0(6), Little Simon) Little Simon.
—Who Tickled Tilly? Stanley, Mandy. 2011. (ENG.). 32p. (J). (gr. -1-k). pap. 7.99 (978-1-84365-192-5(0), Pavilion Children's Books) Pavilion Bks. GBR. Dist: Independent Pubs. Group.
Stanley, Sanna. Amistad: The Story of a Slave Ship. McKissack, Patricia C. 2005. (Penguin Young Readers, Level 4 Ser.). (ENG.). 48p. (J). (gr. 3-4). mass mkt. 3.99 (978-0-448-43900-6(X), Grosset & Dunlap) Penguin Publishing Group.
Stanley, Stephen. Kanga Santa. Stanley, David. 2015. 24p. (J). pap. **(978-1-326-21343-5(1))** Stanley, Stephen.
Stanley, Susan. Marv the Moose Is on the Loose. Scaling, Sam T. 2012. 32p. (J). (978-0-9798806-4-3(5)) STS Publishing.
Stanton, Brandon, photos by. Little Humans. Stanton, Brandon. 2014. (ENG.). 40p. (J). (gr. -1-1). 17.99 **(978-0-374-37456-3(2)**, Farrar, Straus & Giroux (BYR)) Farrar, Straus & Giroux.
Stanton, Brian. Color Dog. Stanton, Brian, photos by. Van Fleet, Matthew. 2015. (ENG.). 22p. (J). (gr. -1-k). 19.99 **(978-1-4814-4986-1(9)**, Simon & Schuster Bks. For Young Readers) Simon & Schuster Bks. For Young Readers.
Stanton, Brian, photos by. Cat. Van Fleet, Matthew. 2009. (ENG., 20p. (J). (gr. -1-2). 17.99 (978-1-4169-7800-8(3), Simon & Schuster/Paula Wiseman Bks.) Simon & Schuster/Paula Wiseman Bks.
—Dog. Van Fleet, Matthew. 2007. (ENG., 20p. (J). (gr. -1-2). 18.99 (978-1-4169-4137-8(1), Simon & Schuster/Paula Wiseman Bks.) Simon & Schuster/Paula Wiseman Bks.
—Moo. Van Fleet, Matthew. 2011. (ENG., 18p. (J). (gr. -1-1). 17.99 (978-1-4424-3503-2(8), Simon & Schuster/Paula Wiseman Bks.) Simon & Schuster/Paula Wiseman Bks.
—Van Fleet Animal Trio: Moo; Cat; Dog. Van Fleet, Matthew. ed. 2013. (ENG., 58p. (J). (gr. -1-2). 51.99 (978-1-4424-8450-4(0), Simon & Schuster/Paula Wiseman Bks.) Simon & Schuster/Paula Wiseman Bks.
Stanton, Elizabeth Rose. Henny. Stanton, Elizabeth Rose. 2014. (ENG.). 40p. (J). (gr. -1-3). 16.99 (978-1-4424-8436-8(5), Simon & Schuster/Paula Wiseman Bks.) Simon & Schuster/Paula Wiseman Bks.
Stanton, Janet, jt. illus. see Staige, Pat.
Stanton, Karen. Monday, Wednesday, & Every Other Weekend. Stanton, Karen. 2014. (ENG.). 40p. (J). (gr. -1-1). 16.99 (978-1-250-03489-2(2)) Feiwel & Friends.
Stanton, Martin. Kristen's Bears. Stanton, Ilene. 2013. (ENG.). 26p. pap. 5.99 (978-0-615-82206-8(1)) Stanton, Ilene J.
Stanton, Philip. Got Geography! Hopkins, Lee Bennett. 2006. (ENG.). 32p. (J). (gr. k-5). 16.99 (978-0-06-055601-3(3), Greenwillow Bks.) HarperCollins Pubs.
Staples, Val. Trucks. Balaban, Mariah, ed. 2007. (Tonka Ser.). (ENG.). 8p. (J). (gr. -1-k). bds. 7.99 (978-0-439-89464-7(6)) Scholastic, Inc.
Stapley, Craig. I Believe in Jesus Too. Nielson, Mark S. 2011. (J). 17.99 (978-1-60908-741-8(0)) Deseret Bk. Co.
Star, Brenda. Grandpa's Magical Accordion. Errico, Jessica / C. 2007. 28p. (J). pap. 17.95 incl. cd-rom (978-0-9800577-0-6(1)) Three Part Harmony LLC.
Starace, Tom. Easter Fun. Knudsen, Michelle. 2006. (ENG.). 12p. (J). bds. 4.99 (978-0-689-87894-7(X), Little Simon) Little Simon.
Starbuck-McMillan, Elizabeth. The Little Ferry Travels with Virginia Bk. 6: The Little Ferry Goes to Yorktown. Briggs, Martha Wren. 2007. (The Little Ferry Travels with Virginia Ser.: Vol. 6). 30p. (YA). (gr. 5-8). pap. 6.95 (978-0-9633240-8-5(X)) Dory Pr.
Starfall Education, photos by. Pumpkin, Pumpkin: For the Earliest Reader. Hillert, Margaret. 2005. (ENG., 32p. (J). (978-1-59577-035-6(6)); pap. (978-1-59577-036-3(4)) Starfall Education.
Stargeon, Bobbi. Haunted Doghouse II: Halloween Night, 3 vols., bk. 2. Johnson, Sandi et al. Durant, Sybrina, ed. l.t. ed. 2014. (ENG.). 36p. (J). (gr. k-5). pap. 12.99 (978-1-929063-27-7(X), 351) Moons & Stars Publishing For Children.

S

Stark, jt. illus. see Stark, Ken.
Stark, Ken. Marching to Appomattox: The Footrace That Ended the Civil War. Stark, Ken. 2015. (ENG.). 48p. (J). (gr. 4-7). 8.99 (978-0-14-751449-3(5), Puffin) Penguin Publishing Group.
Stark, Ken & Stark. Marching to Appomattox: The Footrace That Ended the Civil War. Stark, Ken. 2009. (ENG.). 48p. (J). (gr. 4-7). 17.99 (978-0-399-24212-0(0), Putnam Juvenile) Penguin Publishing Group.
Stark, Mindy C. A Is for Alligator. Bringhurst, Nancy J. 2004. 32p. (J). 17.95 (978-1-883991-96-8(X)) White Cloud Pr.
Stark, Regina. Meghan's World: The Story of One Girl's Triumph Over Sensory Processing Disorder. Renna, Diane M. 2007. 32p. (J). 17.95 (978-0-9788339-0-9(2)) Indigo Impressions.
Stark, Ryan. We Like to Invent! Dunham, Bandhu Scott. 2010. (J). pap. (978-1-935387-13-8(8)) Hohm Pr.
Starkey, Fiona. The Amazing Adventure of Tiptoe & the Yellow Balloon. White, June. 2011. 32p. pap. (978-0-7552-1345-0(9)) Authors OnLine, Ltd.
Starkings, Richard, jt. illus. see Norman, Justin.
Starkings, Richard, jt. illus. see Research & Education Association Editors.
Starlin, Jim. Thanos Vol. 3: Marvel Universe - The End, 3 vols. Starlin, Jim. 2003. (Marvel Heroes Ser.). 160p. (YA). (gr. 7-18). pap. 16.99 (978-0-7851-1116-0(6)) Marvel Worldwide, Inc.
—Thanos Vol. 4: Epiphany. Starlin, Jim. Youngquist, Jeff, ed. 2004. (Marvel Heroes Ser.). 144p. pap. 14.99 (978-0-7851-1355-3(X)) Marvel Worldwide, Inc.
Starmer, Anika & Wertz, Michael. Bliss Live It! Bliss Give It! Thomas, Wendy Russell & Ruchman, Laura. 2010. 60p. (YA). (978-0-88441-754-5(9)) Girl Scouts of the USA.
Starr, Branka. Quimble Wood. Bodecker, N. M. 2004. (ENG.). 32p. (J). reprint ed. (978-1-931561-97-6(4)) MacAdam/Cage Publishing, Inc.
Starr, Branka, jt. illus. see Blegvad, Erik.
Starr, Lisa. Paddy the Penguin's Adventure. McGuinness, Jeff. l.t. ed. 2006. 33p. (J). 27.95 (978-1-59879-231-7(8)); (gr. -1-3). per. 15.95 (978-1-59879-229-4(6)) Lifevest Publishing, Inc.
Starr Taylor, Bridget. Old MacDonald's Funny Farm, Vol. 4261. Williams, Rozanne Lanczak. 2005. (Reading for Fluency Ser.). 16p. (J). pap. 3.49 (978-1-59198-161-9(1), 4261) Creative Teaching Pr., Inc.
Stasiak, Krystyna. Four Good Friends. Hillert, Margaret. rev. exp. ed. 2006. (Beginning to Read Ser.). 32p. (J). (gr. -1-3). lib. bdg. 14.95 (978-1-59953-047-5(3)) Norwood Hse. Pr.
—The Purple Pussycat. Hillert, Margaret. rev. exp. ed. 2006. (Beginning to Read Ser.). 32p. (J). (gr. -1-3). lib. bdg. 14.95 (978-1-59953-044-4(9)) Norwood Hse. Pr.
—The Witch Who Went for a Walk. Hillert, Margaret. 2008. 32p. (J). lib. bdg. 19.93 (978-1-59953-186-1(0)) Norwood Hse. Pr.
Stasiuk, Max. Anastasia Rose Sleeps in Her Own Room, 1 vol. Kopczynski, Megan. 2010. 26p. pap. 24.95 (978-1-4489-4923-6(8)) PublishAmerica, Inc.
Stasolla, Mario. The Bright Blue Button & the Button-Hole. Peck, Judith. 2004. 28p. (J). 18.95 (978-0-9746119-5-2(6)) Imagination Arts Pubns.
Stassen. Deogratias: A Tale of Rwanda. Stassen. Siegel, Alexis, tr. from FRE. deluxe rev. ed. 2006. (ENG.). 96p. (YA). (gr. 9-13). pap. 18.99 (978-1-59643-103-4(2), First Second Bks.) Roaring Brook Pr.
Stasuyk, Max. Daddy's Picture. Levine, Karen R. 2013. 24p. pap. 14.95 (978-1-57258-794-6(6), Aspect Bk.) TEACH Services, Inc.
Stasyuk, Max. The Blue Wizard. Edwards, Garth. 2011. (Adventures of Titch & Mitch Ser.). (J). pap. 6.99 (978-0-9567449-9-0(0)) Inside Pocket Publishing, Ltd. GBR. Dist: Lerner Publishing Group.
—The King of the Castle. Edwards, Garth. 2011. (Adventures of Titch & Mitch Ser.). (J). pap. 6.99 (978-0-9567449-7-5(4)) Inside Pocket Publishing, Ltd. GBR. Dist: Lerner Publishing Group.
—The Magic Boots. Edwards, Garth. 2011. (Adventures of Titch & Mitch Ser.). (J). pap. 6.99 (978-0-9567449-8-2(2)) Inside Pocket Publishing, Ltd. GBR. Dist: Lerner Publishing Group.
—The Trolls of Sugar Loaf Wood. Edwards, Garth. 2011. (Adventures of Titch & Mitch Ser.). (J). pap. 6.99 (978-0-9567449-6-8(6)) Inside Pocket Publishing, Ltd. GBR. Dist: Lerner Publishing Group.
—#01 Shipwrecked! Edwards, Garth. 2011. (Adventures of Titch & Mitch, the Ser.). (J). pap. 39.84 (978-0-7613-8421-2(9)) Inside Pocket Publishing, Ltd. GBR. Dist: Lerner Publishing Group.
—The #02 Trolls of Sugar Loaf Wood. Edwards, Garth. 2011. (Adventures of Titch & Mitch, the Ser.). (J). pap. 39.84 (978-0-7613-8422-9(7)) Inside Pocket Publishing, Ltd. GBR. Dist: Lerner Publishing Group.
—The #03 King of the Castle. Edwards, Garth. 2011. (Adventures of Titch & Mitch, the Ser.). (J). pap. 39.84 (978-0-7613-8423-6(5)) Inside Pocket Publishing, Ltd. GBR. Dist: Lerner Publishing Group.
—The #04 Magic Boots. Edwards, Garth. 2011. (Adventures of Titch & Mitch, the Ser.). (J). pap. 39.84 (978-0-7613-8424-3(3)) Inside Pocket Publishing, Ltd. GBR. Dist: Lerner Publishing Group.
—The #05 Blue Wizard. Edwards, Garth. 2011. (Adventures of Titch & Mitch, the Ser.). (J). pap. 39.84 (978-0-7613-8425-0(1)) Inside Pocket Publishing, Ltd. GBR. Dist: Lerner Publishing Group.

States, Anna. The Unordinary Elephant. Yamada, Rikako. 2005.Tr. of Chisana mimi no Kozou. (JPN.). 26p. (J). per. 14.99 *(978-0-9761606-0-1(9))* WonderToast.
Staton, Joe, jt. illus. see Brizuela, Dario.
Staub, Frank J., photos by. America's Forests & Woodlands. 2006. 48p. (J). pap. *(978-1-59034-806-2(0))* Mondo Publishing.
Staub, Frank J., photos by. Running Free: America's Wild Horses. Staub, Frank J. 2006. (Prime (Elementary) Ser.). 48p. (J). (gr. 3-4). lib. bdg. 25.27 *(978-0-7660-2670-4(1))* Enslow Pubs., Inc.
Staub, Leslie. Mama's Nightingale: A Story of Immigration & Separation. Danticat, Edwidge. 2015. (ENG.). 32p. (J). (gr. k-3). 17.99 *(978-0-525-42809-1(7),* Dial) Penguin Publishing Group.
Staub, Leslie. Whoever You Are. Fox, Mem. 2007.Tr. of Sé de¿ït Mak Ó. (ENG.). 28p. (J). (gr. -1 — 1). bds. 6.95 *(978-0-15-206066-4(9))* Houghton Mifflin Harcourt Publishing Co.
—Whoever You Are (Quienquiera Que Seas) Fox, Mem. Flor Ada, Alma & Campoy, F. Isabel, trs. 2007. (ENG & SPA.). 28p. (J). (gr. k — 1). bds. 6.95 *(978-0-15-205891-3(5))* Houghton Mifflin Harcourt Publishing Co.
Stauffer, Lori. Let's Talk about Safety Skills for Kids: A Personal Safety Activity Book for Children. Stauffer, Lori. Deblinger, Esther. 2004. 32p. (J). (gr. k-6). 5.00 *(978-0-9676489-3-4(9))* Hope for Families, Inc.
Stauffer, Lori. Let's Talk about Coping & Safety Skills: A Workbook about Taking Care of Me! Stauffer, Lori, photos by. Deblinger, Esther. 2005. (J). (gr. k-6). pap. 10.00 *(978-0-9676489-4-1(7))* Hope for Families, Inc.
—Let's Talk about Taking Care of Me: An Educational Book about Body Safety for Young Children. Stauffer, Lori, photos by. Deblinger, Esther. 2004. 64p. (J). (gr. -1-1). pap. 12.00 *(978-0-9676489-2-7(0))* Hope for Families, Inc.
Stauffer, Lori & Moyer, Brett. Let's Talk about Taking Care of Me: An Educational Book about Body Safety. Stauffer, Lori & Deblinger, Esther. 2nd rev. ed. 2003. 96p. (J). (gr. k-6). pap. 18.00 *(978-0-9676489-1-0(2))* Hope for Families, Inc.
Staunton, Joseph & Rey, Luis. Plant-Eating Dinosaurs. Hynson, Colin. 2011. (Inside Crime Ser.). 48p. (YA). (gr. 5-9). 34.25 *(978-1-59920-396-6(0))* Black Rabbit Bks.
Staunton, Mathew. I Met a Man from Artikelly: Verse for the Young & Young at Heart. Rosenstock, Gabriel. 2013. 96p. pap. *(978-1-78201-032-6(7))* Evertype.
Stayte, James. Forces & Motion: Investigating a Car Crash, 1 vol. Graham, Ian. 2013. (Anatomy of an Investigation Ser.). (ENG.). 56p. (gr. 7-8). 33.50 *(978-1-4329-7602-6(8))*; pap. 9.49 *(978-1-4329-7608-8(7))* Heinemann-Raintree.
—Human Body: Investigating an Unexplained Death. Solway, Andrew. 2013. (Anatomy of an Investigation Ser.). (ENG.). 56p. (gr. 7-8). 33.50 *(978-1-4329-7604-0(4))*; pap. 9.49 *(978-1-4329-7610-1(9))* Heinemann-Raintree.
Steacy, Ken. Bessie Coleman: Daring Stunt Pilot, 1 vol. Robbins, Trina. 2007. (Graphic Biographies Ser.). (ENG.). 32p. (gr. 3-4). per. 8.10 *(978-0-7368-7903-3(X),* Graphic Library) Capstone Pr., Inc.
Stead, April-Nicole. If I Called You a Hippopotamus! Stevens, Gary J. 2010. 24p. pap. 11.50 *(978-1-60911-280-6(6),* Eloquent Bks.) Strategic Book Publishing & Rights Agency (SBPRA).
Stead, Erin E. And Then It's Spring. Fogliano, Julie. 2012. (ENG.). 32p. (J). (gr. -1-2). 16.99 *(978-1-59643-624-4(7))* Roaring Brook Pr.
—Bear Has a Story to Tell. Stead, Philip C. 2012. (ENG.). 32p. (J). (gr. -1-1). 16.99 *(978-1-59643-745-6(6))* Roaring Brook Pr.
—If You Want to See a Whale. Fogliano, Julie. 2013. (ENG.). 32p. (J). (gr. -1-2). 16.99 *(978-1-59643-731-9(6))* Roaring Brook Pr.
—Indama Marada Al Am Nooh. Stead, Philip C. 2014.Tr. of Sick Day for Amos McGee. (ARA & ENG.). 32p. pap. 8.95 *(978-99921-95-51-2(7),* 232855, Bloomsbury Academic) Bloomsbury Publishing Plc GBR. Dist: Macmillan.
—A Sick Day for Amos McGee. Stead, Philip C. 2010. (ENG.). 32p. (J). (gr. -1-1). 17.99 *(978-1-59643-402-8(3))* Roaring Brook Pr.
Stead, Judy. Best Friend on Wheels. Shirley, Debra. 2008. (ENG.). 32p. (J). (gr. k-3). lib. bdg. 16.99 *(978-0-8075-8868-0(7))* Whitman, Albert & Co.
—Isabel's Car Wash. Bair, Sheila. 2012. (J). 34.28 *(978-1-61913-118-7(8))* Weigl Pubs., Inc.
—Isabel's Car Wash. Bair, Sheila. 2011. (ENG.). 32p. (J). (gr. 1-4). 6.99 *(978-0-8075-3653-7(9))* Whitman, Albert & Co.
—Mister Sun. 2006. (J). *(978-1-58987-097-0(2))* Kindermusik International.
—The Pink Party, 0 vols. MacDonald, Maryann. 2011. (ENG.). 32p. (J). (gr. -1-3). 16.99 *(978-0-7614-5814-2(X),* 9780761458142, Amazon Children's Publishing) Amazon Publishing.
—Snowy, Blowy Winter, 1 vol. Raczka, Bob. 2008. (ENG.). 32p. (J). (gr. -1-1). 16.99 *(978-0-8075-7526-0(7))* Whitman, Albert & Co.
—Summer Wonders. Raczka, Bob. 2012. (J). 34.28 *(978-1-61913-125-5(0))* Weigl Pubs., Inc.
—What a Way to Start a New Year! A Rosh Hashanah Story. Jules, Jacqueline. 2013. (High Holidays Ser.). (ENG.). 24p. (J). (gr. -1-2). 7.95 *(978-0-7613-8117-4(1))*; lib. bdg. 16.95 *(978-0-7613-8116-7(3))* Lerner Publishing Group. (Kar-Ben Publishing).
Stead, Judy. The Twelve Days of Christmas in North Carolina. Stead, Judy. 2009. (Twelve Days of Christmas in America Ser.). (ENG.). 32p. (J). (gr. k). 12.95 *(978-1-4027-4467-9(6))* Sterling Publishing Co., Inc.
Stead, Kevin, jt. illus. see Lewis, Kimberly.
Stead, Philip C. Creamed Tuna Fish & Peas on Toast. Stead, Philip C. 2009. (ENG.). 32p. (J). (gr. -1-1). 16.99 *(978-1-59643-401-1(5))* Roaring Brook Pr.
—Hello, My Name Is Ruby. Stead, Philip C. 2013. (ENG.). 36p. (J). (gr. -1-1). 16.99 *(978-1-59643-809-5(6))* Roaring Brook Pr.
—A Home for Bird. Stead, Philip C. 2012. (ENG.). 32p. (J). (gr. -1-3). 16.99 *(978-1-59643-711-1(1))* Roaring Brook Pr.
—Jonathan & the Big Blue Boat. Stead, Philip C. 2011. (ENG.). 32p. (J). (gr. -1-2). 16.99 *(978-1-59643-562-9(3))* Roaring Brook Pr.
—Sebastian & the Balloon. Stead, Philip C. 2014. (ENG.). 40p. (J). (gr. -1-2). 17.99 *(978-1-59643-930-6(0))* Roaring Brook Pr.
Steadman, Barbara. Russian Picture Word Book: Learn over 500 Commonly Used Russian Words Through Pictures. Rogers, Svetlana. 2003. (Dover Children's Language Activity Bks.). (ENG.). 32p. (J). (gr. 1-5). pap. 3.99 *(978-0-486-42671-6(8))* Dover Pubns., Inc.
Steadman, Ralph. Alice in Wonderland. Carroll, Lewis. 2010. (ENG.). 128p. pap. 19.95 *(978-1-55407-203-3(4),* 9781554072033) Firefly Bks., Ltd.
—Big Red Squirrel & the Little Rhinoceros. Damjan, Mischa. 2010. (ENG.). 32p. (J). (gr. -1-k). 15.99 *(978-1-84365-130-7(0),* Pavilion Children's Books) Pavilion Bks. GBR. Dist: Independent Pubs. Group.
—The False Flamingoes. Damjan, Mischa. 32p. (J). (gr. -1-3). 13.95 *(978-0-87592-016-0(0))* Scroll Pr., Inc.
—Fly Away Peter. Dickens, Frank. 2009. (ENG.). 32p. (J). (gr. -1-k). 9.99 *(978-1-84365-122-2(X))* Pavilion Bks. GBR. Dist: Independent Pubs. Group.
Steadman, Ralph. The Jelly Book. Steadman, Ralph. 32p. (J). (gr. -1-3). 14.95 *(978-0-87592-026-9(8))* Scroll Pr., Inc.
Stearns, Forest. The Wonderful Adventures of Ozzie Sea Otter (Spanish) Dohlke, Nora. 2009. (ENG.). 98p. 19.95 *(978-0-9822046-2-7(0))* Bay Publishing.
—The Wonderful Adventures of Ozzie the Sea Otter. Dohlke, Nora. 2009. 98p. (J). 19.95 *(978-0-9822046-0-3(4))* Bay Publishing.
—The Wonderful Adventures of Ozzie the Sea Otter (Book & CD) Dohlke, Nora. 2009. (ENG.). 98p. 26.95 *(978-0-9822046-1-0(2))* Bay Publishing.
Stebakova, Elena. I Am a Rainbow Child Coloring-Story Book. Yacoubou, Jeanne. 2005. 16p. (J). *(978-0-9788737-4-5(2))* Alaafia Kids Co.
—Wanna Play? Coloring-Story Book. Yacoubou, Jeanne. 2005. 16p. (J). *(978-0-9788737-5-2(0))* Alaafia Kids Co.
—What's My Heritage? Coloring-Story Book. Yacoubou, Jeanne. 2006. 24p. (J). *(978-0-9788737-2-1(6))* Alaafia Kids Co.
Steccati, Eve. The Secret of Stoneship Woods. Barba, Rick. 2006. (Spy Gear Adventures Ser.: 1). (ENG.). 160p. (J). (gr. 3-7). pap. 8.99 *(978-1-4169-0887-6(0),* Simon & Schuster/Paula Wiseman Bks.) Simon & Schuster/Paula Wiseman Bks.
Steck, Jim. Flipping Out! How to Draw Flip Animation. Bellen-Berthézène, Cyndie. 2005. 48p. (J). *(978-0-439-81335-8(2))* Scholastic, Inc.
Steckel, Michele, jt. illus. see Steckel, Richard.
Steckel, Michele, jt. photos by see Steckel, Richard.
Steckel, Richard, et al. Wise at Heart: Children & Adults Share Words of Wisdom. Steckel, Richard et al. 2011. (ENG.). 72p. (J). (gr. 2-18). 18.95 *(978-1-55453-630-6(8))* Kids Can Pr., Ltd. CAN. Dist: Univ. of Toronto Pr.
Steckel, Richard & Steckel, Michele. Faith. Steckel, Richard & Steckel, Michele, photos by. 2012. (ENG.). 36p. (J). 17.95 *(978-1-55453-750-1(9))* Kids Can Pr., Ltd. CAN. Dist: Univ. of Toronto Pr.
Steckel, Richard & Steckel, Michele, photos by. Happy Birthday! Stromberg, Betsy & Steckel, Richard. Steckel, Michele. 2007. (Milestones Project Chewables Ser.). (ENG., 20p. (J). (gr. k — 1). bds. 6.99 *(978-1-58246-210-3(0),* Tricycle Pr.) Ten Speed Pr.
—My Teeth. 2008. (Milestones Project Chewables Ser.). (ENG., 20p. (J). (gr. k — 1). bds. 6.99 *(978-1-58246-212-7(7),* Tricycle Pr.) Ten Speed Pr.
Steckler, Elaine. Bella the Dragon. Nick, Barbara. 2013. 36p. pap. 11.75 *(978-1-938078-05-7(5))* Catto Creations, LLC.
Steckler, Kerren Barbas. Ready, Set, Draw... under the Sea! Conlon, Mara. 2009. (Activity Bks). 40p. (J). spiral bd. 15.99 *(978-1-59359-837-2(8))* Peter Pauper Pr. Inc.
—Water Magic. Paulding, Barbara. 2009. (Young Artist Ser.). 24p. (J). (gr. -1). 15.99 *(978-1-59359-842-6(4))* Peter Pauper Pr. Inc.
Steckler, Megan. Boots. Roman, Lisa. 2009. 24p. pap. 24.95 *(978-1-60749-329-7(2))* America Star Bks.
—Finding the Perfect Fit. Ayres, S. C. 2011. 28p. pap. 24.95 *(978-1-4560-0912-0(5))* America Star Bks.
—Krissy & the Indians, 1 vol. Fitzsimmons, Christy. 2009. 28p. pap. 24.95 *(978-1-61546-206-3(6))* America Star Bks.
Steedman, Judith. Snowy & Chinook. Mitchell, Robin. 2005. (ENG.). 22p. (J). (gr. -1-3). 15.95 *(978-0-9688768-9-3(7))* Simply Read Bks. CAN. Dist: Ingram Pub. Services.
Steege, Joanna. Hooray! I'm Catholic. Cole, Hana. 2010. 32p. (J). 14.95 *(978-0-8091-6746-3(8),* Ambassador Bks.) Paulist Pr.
Steel, John. Roy Rogers' Surprise for Donnie. Sankey, Alice. 2011. 32p. pap. 35.95 *(978-1-258-03591-4(X))* Literary Licensing, LLC.
Steele, Andrea M. Princess Zoe & the Mer-Bird. Brower, Sandra Shane. 2013. 46p. pap. 10.95 *(978-1-936688-77-7(8),* Compass Flower Pr.) AKA:yoLa.
—Zoe & the Cocoa-Brown Tutu. Brower. 2nd ed. 2013. 56p. pap. 10.95 *(978-1-936688-79-1(4))* AKA:yoLa.
Steele, Andrew & Clement, Devyn. The Paperweight. Young, Francis Kerr. 2008. 39p. pap. 24.95 *(978-1-60610-034-9(3))* America Star Bks.
Steele-Card, Adrianna & Second Story Press Staff. Sandy's Incredible Shrinking Footprint, 1 vol. Handy, Femida & Carpenter, Carole H. 2010. (ENG.). 24p. (J). (gr. 3 — 1). 15.95 *(978-1-897187-69-2(6))* Second Story Pr. CAN. Dist: Orca Bk. Pubs. USA.
Steele, Gregory D. The Adventures of Maximillian P. Dogg - Rescue Dog: Max Finds a New Home. Tveite, William P. 2012. (ENG.). 30p. (J). pap. 12.95 *(978-1-61863-289-0(2))* Bookstand Publishing.
Steele, Kris. Journey to Cahokia. Steele, Kris. 32p. (Orig.). (J). (gr. 4-6). pap. 4.95 *(978-1-881563-02-0(2))* Cahokia Mounds Museum Society.
Steele-Morgan, Alex. Tashlich at Turtle Rock. Schnur, Susan & Schnur-Fishman, Anna. 2010. (High Holidays Ser.). (ENG.). 32p. (J). (gr. k-3). pap. 7.95 *(978-0-7613-4510-7(8),* Kar-Ben Publishing) Lerner Publishing Group.
—Touch & Feel Bible Animal Friends. Nolan, Allia Zobel. 2004. (Touch & Feel Ser.). 12p. (J). bds. 10.99 *(978-0-8254-5512-4(X))* Kregel Pubns.
Steele-Morgan, Alexandra. A Star for Me, 1 vol. Fischer, Jean & Thomas Nelson Publishing Staff. 2014. (ENG.). 32p. (J). pap. 14.99 *(978-0-529-11212-5(4))* Nelson, Thomas Inc.
Steele, Paul. The Bonsai Coloring Book. Baran, Robert J. 2005. 5.95 net. *(978-0-9659913-5-3(0))* Pyramid Dancer Pubns.
Steele, Robert. Lily's Victory Garden. Wilbur, Helen. 2010. (Tales of Young Americans Ser.). (ENG.). 32p. (J). (gr. 2-4). 16.95 *(978-1-58536-450-3(9))* Sleeping Bear Pr.
Steelhammer, Ilona. Storybook Readers, 5 bks. Cosgrove, Stephen. (J). lib. bdg. 73.75 *(978-1-56674-921-3(2))* Forest Hse. Publishing Co., Inc.
Steen, Rob. Flanimals Pop-up. Gervais, Ricky. 2010. (ENG.). 14p. (J). (gr. k-4). 19.99 *(978-0-7636-4781-0(0))* Candlewick Pr.
Steenholdt, Jeff. Come, Ye Children: A Bible Storybook for Young Children. Hoeksema, Gertrude. 3rd ed. 2010. (ENG.). 599p. (J). reprint ed. 47.95 *(978-0-916206-27-7(0))* Reformed Free Publishing Assn.
Steers, Billy. Tractor Mac Learns to Fly. 2007. (J). 7.95 *(978-0-9788496-2-7(0))* Tractor Mac Inc.
Steers, Billy. Tractor Mac Farmers Market: Farmer's Market. Steers, Billy. 2009. (ENG.). (J). 7.95 *(978-0-9826870-1-7(X))* Tractor Mac Inc.
Steever, Sarah. The New Colorful Creatures. Porras, Nikki Jo & Hix, Jax. 2013. (ENG.). 28p. pap. 10.00 *(978-0-615-72878-0(2))* Dreaming Dragon Publishing LLC.
Steffen, Jennifer. The Wonder of a Summer Day. Becker, Laura. 2008. (ENG.). 40p. (J). (gr. -1-3). lib. bdg. *(978-1-934363-25-6(1))* Zoe Life Publishing.
Steffen, Jeremy. What Hurricane? My Solar-Powered History on a Supply Ship to the Jamestown Colony. Terry, Alana. 2013. 136p. pap. 12.99 *(978-1-937848-05-7(1))* Do Life Right, Inc.
—What, No Sushi? Terry, Alana. 2013. 116p. pap. 7.99 *(978-1-937848-04-0(3))* Do Life Right, Inc.
Steffen, Randy. Roy Rogers & the Sure 'Nough Cowpoke. Beecher, Elizabeth. 2011. 32p. pap. 35.95 *(978-1-258-03587-7(1))* Literary Licensing, LLC.
Steffensmeier, Alexander. Millie in the Snow. Steffensmeier, Alexander. 2008. (Millie's Misadventures Ser.). (ENG.). 32p. (J). (gr. -1-3). 16.99 *(978-0-8027-9800-8(4))* Walker & Co.
—Millie Waits for the Mail. Steffensmeier, Alexander. 2007. (Millie's Misadventures Ser.). (ENG.). 32p. (J). (gr. -1-2). 16.95 *(978-0-8027-9662-2(1))* Walker & Co.
Steffibauer, Thomas. Queen Nzinga. Panev, Aleksandar. 2007. 48p. (J). lib. bdg. 23.08 *(978-1-4242-1641-3(9))* Fitzgerald Bks.
Stegall, Joel E. I'm Happy Being Me. Johns, Isabel G. 2012. 32p. pap. 14.95 *(978-1-61493-093-8(7))* Peppertree Pr., The.
Steggall, Susan. Red Car, Red Bus. 2012. (ENG.). 32p. (J). (gr. -1-1). 17.99 *(978-1-84780-184-5(6),* Frances Lincoln) Quarto Publishing Group UK GBR. Dist: Hachette Bk. Group.
Stegman, Ryan. The Return of Anti-Venom. Slott, Dan. 2011. (ENG.). 120p. (YA). (gr. 8-17). 19.99 *(978-0-7851-5108-1(7))* Marvel Worldwide, Inc.
Stegos, Daniel. Canada Goose at Cat Tail Lane. Halfmann, Janet. 2006. (ENG.). 32p. (J). (gr. -1-2). 9.95 *(978-1-59249-499-6(4),* PB5079) Soundprints.
—Penguins Family: Story of a Humboldt Penguin Hardcover. Hollenbeck, Kathleen. 2005. (ENG.). 32p. (J). (gr. -1-2). 19.95 *(978-1-59249-349-4(1),* BC4027) Soundprints.
—Penguin's Family: The Story of a Humboldt Penguin. Hollenbeck, Kathleen. 2005. (ENG.). 32p. (J). (gr. -1-2). 9.95 *(978-1-59249-351-7(3),* PB4027); 15.95 *(978-1-59249-346-3(7),* B4027) Soundprints.
—Penguins Family: The Story of a Humboldt Penguin. Hollenbeck, Kathleen. 2005. (ENG.). 32p. (J). (gr. -1-2). 4.95 *(978-1-59249-348-7(3),* B4077); pap. 6.95 *(978-1-59249-347-0(5),* S4027) Soundprints.
—Red Bat at Sleep Hollow Lane. Halfmann, Janet. 2005. (ENG.). 32p. (J). (gr. -1-2). 19.95 *(978-1-59249-343-2(2),* BC5027); 15.95 *(978-1-59249-340-1(8),* B5027); 4.95 *(978-1-59249-342-5(4),* B5077) Soundprints.
—Red Bat at Sleepy Hollow Lane. Halfmann, Janet. 2005. (Smithsonian's Backyard Ser.). (ENG.). 32p. (J). (gr. -1-2). pap. 6.95 *(978-1-59249-341-8(6),* S5027) Soundprints.
—Swordfish Returns. Korman, Susan. (ENG.). 32p. (J). 2005. (gr. -1-2). 9.95 *(978-1-59249-132-2(4),* PB4075); 2005. (gr. -1-2). 4.95 *(978-1-59249-126-1(X),* B4075); 2004. (gr. 2-2). pap. 6.95 *(978-1-59249-127-8(8),* S4025); 2003. (gr. -1-2). 8.95 *(978-1-59249-129-2(4),* SC4025); 2003. (gr. -1-2). 19.95 *(978-1-59249-128-5(6),* BC4025) Soundprints.
Stegos, Daniel J. Canada Goose at Cattail Lane. Halfmann, Janet. (Smithsonian's Backyard Ser.). (ENG.). 32p. (J). 2011. (gr. -1-3). 19.95 *(978-1-60727-632-6(1))*; 2011. (gr. -1-3). pap. 8.95 *(978-1-60727-633-3(X))*; 2006. (gr. -1-2). 8.95 *(978-1-59249-498-9(6),* SC5029); 2006. (gr. -1-2). pap. 6.95 *(978-1-59249-495-8(1),* S5029); 2006. (gr. k-2). 19.95 *(978-1-59249-497-2(8),* BC5029); 2005. (gr. k-2). 15.95 *(978-1-59249-494-1(3),* B5029) Soundprints.
—Penguin's Family: The Story of a Humboldt Penguin. Hollenbeck, Kathleen M. 2008. (ENG.). 32p. (J). (gr. -1-3). 19.95 *(978-1-59249-765-2(9))* Soundprints.
—Swordfish Returns. Korman, Susan. (Smithsonian Oceanic Collection Ser.). (ENG.). 32p. (J). 2011. (gr. -1-3). 8.95 *(978-1-60727-666-1(6))*; 2011. (gr. -1-3). 19.95 *(978-1-60727-665-4(8))*; 2003. (gr. 2-2). 15.95 *(978-1-59249-125-4(1),* B4025) Soundprints.
Steig, William. Abel's Island. Steig, William. 2007. (ENG.). 128p. (J). (gr. 3-7). per. 6.99 *(978-0-312-37143-2(8))* Square Fish.
—The Amazing Bone. Steig, William. 2011. (ENG.). 32p. (J). (gr. k-3). pap. 7.99 *(978-0-312-56421-6(X))* Square Fish.
—Amos & Boris. Steig, William. 2009. (ENG.). 32p. (J). (gr. k-3). pap. 7.99 *(978-0-312-53566-7(X))* Square Fish.
—Brave Irene. Steig, William. unabr. ed. 2013. (ENG.). (J). (gr. -1-3). 12.99 *(978-1-4272-3780-4(8))* Macmillan Audio.
—Brave Irene. Steig, William. 2011. (ENG.). 32p. (J). (gr. -1-3). pap. 7.99 *(978-0-312-56422-3(8))* Square Fish.
—C D B! Steig, William. 2003. (ENG.). 48p. (J). (gr. k-3). pap. 7.99 *(978-0-689-85706-5(3),* Simon & Schuster/Paula Wiseman Bks.) Simon & Schuster/Paula Wiseman Bks.
—C D C ? Steig, William. 2008. (ENG.). 64p. (J). (gr. 1-4). pap. 8.99 *(978-0-312-38012-0(7))* Square Fish.
—Doctor de Soto. Steig, William. 2010. (ENG.). 32p. (J). (gr. -1-3). pap. 7.99 *(978-0-312-61189-7(7))* Square Fish.
—Doctor de Soto Book & CD Storytime Set, 1 vol. Steig, William. unabr. ed. 2012. (ENG.). (J). (gr. k-3). 12.99 *(978-1-4272-3219-9(9))* Macmillan Audio.
—Dominic. Steig, William. 2007. (ENG.). 160p. (J). (gr. 3-7). per. 6.99 *(978-0-312-37144-9(6))* Square Fish.
—Farmer Palmer's Wagon Ride. Steig, William. 2014. (ENG.). 32p. (J). (gr. -1-3). 6.99 *(978-1-250-05791-4(4))* Square Fish.
—Grown-Ups Get to Do All the Driving. Steig, William. gif. ed. 2003. (ENG.). 48p. (J). (gr. k-3). 10.95 *(978-1-57505-617-3(8))* Lerner Publishing Group.
—Pete's a Pizza. Steig, William. 2003. (ENG.). 34p. (J). (gr. -1 — 1). bds. 7.99 *(978-0-06-052754-9(4),* HarperFestival) HarperCollins Pubs.
—The Real Thief. Steig, William. 2007. (ENG.). 64p. (J). (gr. 2-5). per. 7.99 *(978-0-312-37145-6(4))* Square Fish.
—Shrek! Steig, William. 20th anniv. ed. 2010. (ENG.). 40p. (J). (gr. -1-3). 16.99 *(978-0-374-36879-1(1),* Farrar, Straus & Giroux (BYR)) Farrar, Straus & Giroux.
—Shrek! Steig, William. 2003. (J). (gr. -1-2). pap. 35.95 incl. audio compact disk *(978-1-59112-551-8(0))* Live Oak Media.
—Shrek!, Set. Steig, William. unabr. ed. 2009. (ENG.). (J). (gr. -1-3). 9.99 *(978-1-4272-0827-9(1))* Macmillan Audio.
—Shrek! Steig, William. 2008. (ENG.). 32p. (J). (gr. -1-3). pap. 7.99 *(978-0-312-38449-4(1))* Square Fish.
—Spinky Sulks. Steig, William. 2011. (ENG.). 32p. (J). (gr. -1-3). pap. 7.99 *(978-0-312-67246-1(2))* Square Fish.
—Sylvester & the Magic Pebble. Steig, William. 2012. (ENG.). 32p. (J). (gr. -1-2). pap. 9.99 *(978-1-4424-3560-5(7),* Little Simon) Little Simon.
—Sylvester & the Magic Pebble. Steig, William. 2005. (ENG.). 42p. (J). (gr. -1-3). 17.99 *(978-1-4169-0206-5(6),* Simon & Schuster Bks. For Young Readers) Simon & Schuster Bks. For Young Readers.
—Sylvester & the Magic Pebble. Steig, William. 2006. (Stories to Go! Ser.). 32p. (J). (gr. -1-3). 4.99 *(978-1-4169-1857-8(4),* Simon & Schuster/Paula Wiseman Bks.) Simon & Schuster/Paula Wiseman Bks.
—When Everybody Wore a Hat. Steig, William. 40p. (J). 2003. (gr. k-5). lib. bdg. 18.89 *(978-0-06-009701-1(9),* Cotler, Joanna Books); 2005. (ENG.). (gr. -1-3). reprint ed. pap. 8.99 *(978-0-06-009702-8(7))* HarperCollins Pubs.
Steimle, Robert. Tinkertoy Building Manual: Graphic Instructions for 37 World-Famous Designs. Dawson, Dylan. 2007. (ENG.). 144p. (J). (gr. 3-7). pap. 9.95 incl. audio compact disk *(978-1-4027-5078-6(1))* Sterling Publishing Co., Inc.
Stein, David Ezra. Because Amelia Smiled. Stein, David Ezra. 2012. (ENG.). 40p. (J). (gr. -1-2). 16.99 *(978-0-7636-4169-6(3))* Candlewick Pr.
—Cowboy Ned & Andy. Stein, David Ezra. (ENG.). 32p. (J). (gr. -1-1). 2011. 6.99 *(978-1-4424-3619-0(0))*; 2006. 15.99 *(978-1-4169-0041-2(1))* Simon & Schuster/Paula Wiseman Bks. (Simon & Schuster/Paula Wiseman Bks.).
—Dinosaur Kisses. Stein, David Ezra. (ENG.). (J). (-k). 2014. 34p. bds. 6.99 *(978-0-7636-7389-5(7))*; 2013. 32p. 15.99 *(978-0-7636-6104-5(X))* Candlewick Pr.
—I'm My Own Dog. Stein, David Ezra. 2014. (ENG.). 32p. (J). (gr. -1-3). 15.99 *(978-0-7636-6139-7(2))* Candlewick Pr.
—Interrupting Chicken. Stein, David Ezra. 2010. (ENG.). 40p. (J). (gr. -1-3). 16.99 *(978-0-7636-4168-9(5))* Candlewick Pr.
—Leaves. Stein, David Ezra. (ENG.). (J). (gr. -1 — 1). 2010. 30p. bds. 6.99 *(978-0-399-25497-0(8))*; 2007. 32p. 15.99 *(978-0-399-24636-4(3))* Penguin Publishing Group. (Putnam Juvenile).
—Love, Mouserella. Stein, David Ezra. 2011. (ENG.). 32p. (J). (gr. -1-k). 15.99 *(978-0-399-25410-9(2),* Nancy Paulsen Bks.) Penguin Publishing Group.
—The Nice Book. Stein, David Ezra. 2013. (ENG.). 32p. (J). (gr. -1 — 1). bds. 6.99 *(978-0-399-16534-4(7),* Nancy Paulsen Bks.) Penguin Publishing Group.
—Ol' Mama Squirrel. Stein, David Ezra. 2013. (ENG.). 32p. (J). (gr. -1-k). 16.99 *(978-0-399-25672-1(5),* Nancy Paulsen Bks.) Penguin Publishing Group.
—Pouch! Stein, David Ezra. (ENG.). 32p. (J). (gr. -1 — 1). 2012. bds. 6.99 *(978-0-399-25738-4(1),* Nancy Paulsen Bks.); 2009. 15.99 *(978-0-399-25051-4(4),* Putnam Juvenile) Penguin Publishing Group.
—Tad & Dad. Stein, David Ezra. 2015. (ENG.). 40p. (J). (gr. -1-k). 16.99 *(978-0-399-25671-4(7))* Penguin Publishing Group.
Stein, Harve. Young Cowboys at the Broken Arrow. Bell, Marion R. & Geyer, Donna M. 2011. 256p. 47.95 *(978-1-258-10205-0(6))* Literary Licensing, LLC.
Stein, Laurie. Fred's Wish for Fish. Landman, Yael & Hill, Barbara. 2009. 8p. (J). *(978-0-545-16144-2(4))* Scholastic, Inc.
Steinbach, Coreen. My Dad Is an Ironman. Hoese, Ray. 2004. (ENG.). 32p. (J). 15.00 *(978-1-891369-51-3(2))* Breakaway Bks.
Steinbach, Hans. A Midnight Opera: Act 2, Vol. 2. Steinbach, Hans. 2006. 176p. per. 14.99 *(978-1-59816-471-8(6),* Tokyopop Adult) TOKYOPOP, Inc.

Steinbauer, Larry. Tommy the Timid Turtle. Swartz, Neva. 2004. (ENG.). 24p. (J). 19.95 *(978-1-878044-75-4(3))* Mayhaven Publishing, Inc.

Steiner, Elke. Bella's Brazilian Football. Steiner, Elke. Guillain, Adam. 2007. (Bella Balistica Ser.). (ENG.). 32p. (J). (gr. k-2). pap. 8.95 *(978-1-84059-488-1(8))* Milet Publishing.

Steiner, Joan. Look-Alikes: The More You Look, the More You See! Steiner, Joan. Lindley, Thomas, photos by. rev. ed. 2003. (ENG.). 32p. (J). (gr. -1-1). 16.00 *(978-0-316-71348-1(1))* Little, Brown Bks. for Young Readers.

—Look-Alikes Christmas: The More You Look, the More You See! Steiner, Joan. 2003. (ENG.). 32p. (J). (gr. -1-1). 14.95 *(978-0-316-81187-3(4),* 51394553) Little, Brown Bks. for Young Readers.

—Look-Alikes Jr. The More You Look, the More You See! Steiner, Joan. rev. ed. 2003. (ENG.). 32p. (J). (gr. -1-1). 16.00 *(978-0-316-71347-4(3))* Little, Brown Bks. for Young Readers.

Steiner, Maria. God Gave Us Fathers & Mothers. Newswanger, Rebecca. 2009. (Little Jewel Book Ser.). 24p. (J). (gr. 2). pap. 2.70 *(978-0-7399-2408-2(7))* Rod & Staff Pubs., Inc.

Steinhardt, Marge. Letters to Antonio Andrew Anderson from His Mother. Mills Inc. 2011. 36p. pap. 35.95 *(978-1-258-10331-6(1))* Literary Licensing, LLC.

Steinke, Aron Nels. The Super Crazy Cat Dance. 2010. (ENG.). 40p. (J). (gr. 1-4). 10.99 *(978-1-60905-035-1(5))* Blue Apple Bks.

—The Super Duper Dog Park. 2011. (ENG.). 40p. (J). (gr. 1-4). 11.99 *(978-1-60905-093-1(2))* Blue Apple Bks.

—The Zoo Box. Cohn, Ariel. 2014. (ENG.). 48p. (J). (gr. k-2). 17.99 *(978-1-62672-052-7(5),* First Second Bks.) Roaring Brook Pr.

Steinlage, Kelly. Frollica & Frenzi: New York City Friends. Ramsey, Charmaine J. 2009. 36p. pap. 15.49 *(978-1-4490-0487-3(3))* AuthorHouse.

Steinmark, Sharyl. Marvin Mallard & the Magic Medallion. Riva, Jim. 2004. 64p. (YA). pap. 14.95 *(978-1-891262-03-6(3))* Soaring Sparrow Pr.

Steinmeyer, Petra. Los Musicos de Bremen. Combel Editorial Staff. 2004. (Caballo Alado Clásicos-Al Galope Ser.). (SPA & ENG.). 24p. (J). (gr. k-2). 7.95 *(978-84-7864-783-5(X))* Combel Editorial, S.A. ESP. Dist: Independent Pubs. Group.

Steinwart, Coe. The Elf on the Shelf: Spanish Boy Dark Elf. Aebersold, Carol V. & Bell, Chanda. 2012. 32p. (J). lib. bdg. 15.00 net. *(978-0-9769907-5-8(X))* CCA & B, LLC.

—The Elf on the Shelf: Spanish Girl Dark Elf. Aebersold, Carol V. & Chanda, Bell. 2012. (J). lib. bdg. 29.95 *(978-0-9843651-6-6(8))* CCA & B, LLC.

—The Elf on the Shelf - a Christmas Tradition: Boy Light. Bell, Chanda & Aebersold, Carol. 2009. 32p. (J). lib. bdg. 29.95 *(978-0-9769907-0-3(9))* CCA & B, LLC.

—The Elf on the Shelf - a Christmas Tradition: Girl Dark. Aebersold, Carol V. & Bell, Chanda. 2012. (J). lib. bdg. 29.95 *(978-0-9843651-5-9(X))* CCA & B, LLC.

Steltzer, Ulli, photos by. Building an Igloo. Steltzer, Ulli. (ENG., 100p. (J). (gr. -1-2). *(978-0-88899-118-8(5))* Groundwood Bks.

Stemen, Jeffrey. Critter Giggles. 2006. (J). *(978-1-58987-035-2(2))* Kindermusik International.

Stemple, Jason. Count Me a Rhyme: Animal Poems by the Numbers. Stemple, Jason, photos by. Yolen, Jane. 2006. (ENG.). 32p. (J). (gr. 5-7). 18.95 *(978-1-59078-345-0(X),* Wordsong) Boyds Mills Pr.

—An Egret's Day. Stemple, Jason, photos by. Yolen, Jane. 2010. (ENG.). 32p. (J). (gr. 4-6). 17.95 *(978-1-59078-650-5(5),* Wordsong) Boyds Mills Pr.

Stemple, Jason, photos by. Birds of a Feather. Yolen, Jane. 2011. (ENG., 32p. (J). (gr. 4-6). 17.95 *(978-1-59078-830-1(3),* Wordsong) Boyds Mills Pr.

—Bug Off! Creepy, Crawly Poems. Yolen, Jane. 2012. (ENG., 32p. (J). (gr. k). 16.95 *(978-1-59078-862-2(1),* Wordsong) Boyds Mills Pr.

—Color Me a Rhyme: Nature Poems for Young People. Yolen, Jane. 2003. (ENG., 32p. (J). (gr. 4-6). pap. 6.95 *(978-1-59078-172-2(4))* Boyds Mills Pr.

—Count Me a Rhyme: Animal Poems by the Numbers. Yolen, Jane. 2014. (ENG., 32p. (J). (gr. 1-5). pap. 6.95 *(978-1-62091-733-6(5),* Wordsong) Boyds Mills Pr.

—A Mirror to Nature: Poems about Reflection. Yolen, Jane. 2009. (ENG., 32p. (J). (gr. 5-7). 17.95 *(978-1-59078-624-6(6),* Wordsong) Boyds Mills Pr.

—On the Slant. Yolen, Jane. 2009. (ENG., 56p. (J). pap. 8.00 *(978-1-57274-978-8(4),* Author at Work) Owen, Richard C. Pubs., Inc.

—Once upon Ice: And Other Frozen Poems. Yolen, Jane. (ENG., 40p. (YA). (gr. 4-6). pap. 9.95 *(978-1-59078-174-6(0))* Boyds Mills Pr.

—Snow, Snow: Winter Poems for Children. Yolen, Jane. 2005. (ENG., 32p. (J). (gr. 4-6). pap. 12.95 *(978-1-59078-346-7(8))* Boyds Mills Pr.

—Water Music: Poems for Children. Yolen, Jane. 2003. (ENG., 40p. (J). (gr. 5-7). pap. 11.95 *(978-1-59078-251-4(8))* Boyds Mills Pr.

Stenberg, Dick. Not My Fault. Kristiansson, Leif. 2006. (ENG.). 32p. (J). (gr. 4-7). 11.95 *(978-0-9762056-6-1(1))* Heryin Publishing Corp.

Stengel, Michelle, photos by. Terror in the Darkness (Confessions of a Stalked Fan) Darnell, Yolanda. 2005. 260p. (YA). (gr. 9-18). pap. 14.99 *(978-1-884429-28-6(9),* B-104) Papilion Pr.

Stensaas, Martin & Strasburg, Sunny. Gingerbread Jimmi: Magical Storybook. Holbrook, John Robert. Scott, Catherine, ed. 2004. (J). 19.95 *(978-0-9762440-0-4(4))* Holbrook Studios.

Stensen, Cindy. I Never Get Scared. Knutson, Eric. 2010. (J). *(978-1-930596-99-3(5))* Amherst Pr.

Stenton, Murray. Miss Popular Steals the Show: Girls in Wheelchairs Rule! Kats, Jewel. 2014. (J). pap. 14.95 *(978-1-61599-236-2(7))* Loving Healing Pr., Inc.

Stephen, Lib. Finger Phonics Big Books 1-7 Vol. 7: Set of 7 Big Books (precursive Letters), 7 vols., Set. Lloyd, Sue & Wernham, Sara. 2005. 16p. pap. 124.95 *(978-1-870946-94-0(4))* Jolly Learning, Ltd. GBR. Dist: American International Distribution Corp.

—Jolly Phonics Activity Book 4: Ai, J, Oa, Ie, Ee, Or, 7 vols. Wernham, Sara & Lloyd, Sue. 2010. 7p. (J). pap. *(978-1-84414-156-2(X))* Jolly Learning, Ltd.

—Jolly Phonics Letter Sound Strips (Print Letters), 30 vols. Lloyd, Sue. 2003. (Jolly Phonics Ser.). (J). (gr. k-2). pap. 13.00 *(978-1-84414-030-5(X))* Jolly Learning, Ltd. GBR. Dist: American International Distribution Corp.

—Jolly Phonics Sound Stories (US Ed, in Print Letters) Lloyd, Sue & Wernham, Sara. 2008. 80p. (J). pap. 29.50 *(978-1-84414-081-7(4))* Jolly Learning, Ltd. GBR. Dist: American International Distribution Corp.

—Jolly Readers Level 2 Complete Set: Pack of 18 Books, 18 vols. Wernham, Sara. 2008. (J). pap. *(978-1-84414-091-6(1))* Jolly Learning, Ltd.

—Jolly Readers Level 2 Inky & Friends Level 2: Pack of 6 Books, 6 vols. Wernham, Sara. 2003. (Jolly Phonics Ser.). 12p. (J). pap. 12.50 *(978-1-903619-86-5(6),* JL866) Jolly Learning, Ltd. GBR. Dist: American International Distribution Corp.

—Jolly Readers Level 3 Inky & Friends: Pack Of 6, Vol. 3. Wernham, Sara. 2005. (J). pap. 14.00 *(978-1-84414-008-4(3))* Jolly Learning, Ltd. GBR. Dist: American International Distribution Corp.

—Jolly Readers Level 4 - General Fiction: Pack of 6 Books, Vol. 4. Wernham, Sara. 2008. (ENG.). (J). pap. 14.00 *(978-1-84414-061-9(X))* Jolly Learning, Ltd. GBR. Dist: American International Distribution Corp.

—Jolly Readers Level 4 - Non-Fiction: Set of 6 Books, Vol. 4. Wernham, Sara. 2008. (ENG.). (J). pap. 14.00 *(978-1-84414-068-8(7))* Jolly Learning, Ltd. GBR. Dist: American International Distribution Corp.

—Jolly Songs (US Print Letters) Book & CD. Fyke, Laurie & Sinclair, Kerrie. 2005. (J). audio compact disk 17.50 *(978-1-84414-079-4(2))* Jolly Learning, Ltd. GBR. Dist: American International Distribution Corp.

Stephen, Marchesi, jt. illus. see Pukac, Michael.

Stephens, Helen. Betsy Goes to School. 2014. (Betsy First Experiences Ser.). (ENG.). 32p. (J). 11.99 *(978-1-4052-6823-3(9))* Egmont Bks., Ltd. GBR. Dist: Independent Pubs. Group.

—Betsy Makes a Splash. 2014. (Betsy First Experiences Ser.). (ENG.). 32p. (J). 11.99 *(978-1-4052-6822-6(0))* Egmont Bks., Ltd. GBR. Dist: Independent Pubs. Group.

—Jo-Jo the Melon Donkey. Morpurgo, Michael. 2014. (ENG.). 40p. (J). (gr. -1-k). pap. 10.99 *(978-1-4052-6353-5(9))* Egmont Bks., Ltd. GBR. Dist: Independent Pubs. Group.

Stephens, Helen. Mimi & the Mountain Dragon. Morpurgo, Michael. 2015. (ENG.). 48p. (J). (gr. 2-4). 9.99 ***(978-1-4052-6934-6(0))*** Egmont Bks., Ltd. GBR. Dist: Independent Pubs. Group.

Stephens, Helen. The Big Adventure of the Smalls. Stephens, Helen. 2012. (ENG.). 32p. (J). (gr. -1-3). 15.99 *(978-1-4424-5058-5(4),* Simon & Schuster/Paula Wiseman Bks.) Simon & Schuster/Paula Wiseman Bks.

—How to Hide a Lion. Stephens, Helen. 2013. (ENG.). 32p. (J). (gr. -1-3). 16.99 *(978-0-8050-9834-1(8),* Holt, Henry & Co. Bks. For Young Readers) Holt, Henry & Co.

—Witchety Sticks & the Magic Buttons. Stephens, Helen. 2010. (ENG.). 32p. (J). (gr. -1-k). pap. 8.99 *(978-1-4169-1107-4(3))* Simon & Schuster, Ltd. GBR. Dist: Simon & Schuster, Inc.

Stephens, Jay. Eat It Up! Lip-Smacking Recipes for Kids. de Mariaffi, Elisabeth. 2004. 88p. 15.95 *(978-2-89507-549-3(2))* Bayard Canada Livres CAN. Dist: Univ. of Toronto Pr.

Stephens, Joan Wilson. Wethechildren, Future Leaders - Patriotic 123. Catalani, Dorothy Kon & Catalani, Jim. 2010. 16p. pap. 10.95 *(978-1-936343-19-5(3))* Peppertree Pr., The.

Stephens, Pat. Animal Groups: How Animals Live Together. Kaner, Etta. 2004. (Animal Behavior Ser.). (ENG.). 40p. (J). (gr. 4-6). 7.95 *(978-1-55337-338-4(3))* Kids Can Pr., Ltd. CAN. Dist: Univ. of Toronto Pr.

—Animals & Their Mates: How Animals Attract, Fight for & Protect Each Other. Hickman, Pamela. 2004. (Animal Behavior Ser.). (ENG.). 40p. (J). (gr. 2-6). 5.95 *(978-1-55337-546-3(7))* Kids Can Pr., Ltd. CAN. Dist: Univ. of Toronto Pr.

—Animals & Their Young: How Animals Produce & Care for Their Babies. Hickman, Pamela. 2003. (Animal Behavior Ser.). (ENG.). 40p. (J). (gr. 4-6). 5.95 *(978-1-55337-062-8(7))* Kids Can Pr., Ltd. CAN. Dist: Univ. of Toronto Pr.

—Animals Hibernating: How Animals Survive Extreme Conditions. Hickman, Pamela. 2005. (Animal Behavior Ser.). (ENG.). 40p. (J). (gr. 2-6). 6.95 *(978-1-55337-663-7(3))* Kids Can Pr., Ltd. CAN. Dist: Univ. of Toronto Pr.

—Animals Migrating: How, When, Where & Why Animals Migrate. Kaner, Etta. 2005. (Animal Behavior Ser.). (ENG.). 40p. (J). (gr. 2-6). 6.95 *(978-1-55337-548-7(3))* Kids Can Pr., Ltd. CAN. Dist: Univ. of Toronto Pr.

—Desert Animals. Hodge, Deborah. 2008. (Who Lives Here? Ser.). (ENG.). 24p. (J). (gr. -1-3). 14.95 *(978-1-55453-047-2(4));* pap. 5.95 *(978-1-55453-048-9(2))* Kids Can Pr., Ltd. CAN. Dist: Univ. of Toronto Pr.

—Forest Animals. Hodge, Deborah. 2009. (Who Lives Here? Ser.). (ENG.). 24p. (J). (gr. -1-2). 5.95 *(978-1-55453-071-7(7));* 14.95 *(978-1-55453-070-0(9))* Kids Can Pr., Ltd. CAN. Dist: Univ. of Toronto Pr.

—How Animals Defend Themselves. Kaner, Etta. 2006. (Kids Can Read Ser.). (ENG.). 32p. (J). (gr. -1-3). 14.95 *(978-1-55337-904-1(7))* Kids Can Pr., Ltd. CAN. Dist: Univ. of Toronto Pr.

—How Animals Eat. Hickman, Pamela. 2007. (Kids Can Read Ser.). (ENG.). 32p. (J). (gr. 1-3). 3.95 *(978-1-55453-032-8(6));* 14.95 *(978-1-55453-031-1(8))* Kids Can Pr., Ltd. CAN. Dist: Univ. of Toronto Pr.

—How Animals Move. Hickman, Pamela. 2007. (Kids Can Read Ser.). (ENG.). 32p. (J). (gr. 1-3). 3.95 *(978-1-55453-030-4(X));* 14.95 *(978-1-55453-029-8(6))* Kids Can Pr., Ltd. CAN. Dist: Univ. of Toronto Pr.

—How Animals Use Their Senses. Hickman, Pamela. 2006. (Kids Can Read Ser.). (ENG.). 32p. (J). (gr. 1-3). 3.95 *(978-1-55337-903-4(9));* 14.95 *(978-1-55337-902-7(0))* Kids Can Pr., Ltd. CAN. Dist: Univ. of Toronto Pr.

—Looking at Bears. Hodge, Deborah. 2008. (Kids Can Read Ser.). (ENG.). 32p. (J). (gr. -1-3). pap. 3.95 *(978-1-55453-250-6(7))* Kids Can Pr., Ltd. CAN. Dist: Univ. of Toronto Pr.

—Polar Animals. Hodge, Deborah. 2008. (Who Lives Here? Ser.). (ENG.). 24p. (J). (gr. -1-2). 14.95 *(978-1-55453-043-4(1));* pap. 5.95 *(978-1-55453-044-1(X))* Kids Can Pr., Ltd. CAN. Dist: Univ. of Toronto Pr.

—Rain Forest Animals. Hodge, Deborah. 2008. (Who Lives Here? Ser.). (ENG.). 24p. (J). (gr. -1-2). 14.95 *(978-1-55453-041-0(5));* pap. 5.95 *(978-1-55453-042-7(3))* Kids Can Pr., Ltd. CAN. Dist: Univ. of Toronto Pr.

—Savanna Animals. Hodge, Deborah. 2009. (Who Lives Here? Ser.). (ENG.). 24p. (J). (gr. -1-3). 5.95 *(978-1-55453-073-1(3));* 14.95 *(978-1-55453-072-4(5))* Kids Can Pr., Ltd. CAN. Dist: Univ. of Toronto Pr.

—Wetland Animals. Hodge, Deborah. 2008. (Who Lives Here? Ser.). (ENG.). 24p. (J). 14.95 *(978-1-55453-045-8(8));* (gr. -1-2). pap. 5.95 *(978-1-55453-046-5(6))* Kids Can Pr., Ltd. CAN. Dist: Univ. of Toronto Pr.

—Wild Dogs: Wolves, Coyotes & Foxes. Hodge, Deborah. unabr. ed. 2009. (Kids Can Press Wildlife Ser.). (ENG.). 32p. (J). (gr. -1-3). 6.95 *(978-1-55074-420-0(8))* Kids Can Pr., Ltd. CAN. Dist: Univ. of Toronto Pr.

Stephens, Sherry & Finnell, Cyndy. Don't You See It? Jungle Edition, 1 vol. Argo, Sandi & Argo, Kaitlyn. 2009. 39p. pap. 19.95 *(978-1-61546-322-0(4))* PublishAmerica, Inc.

Stephenson, Kristina. The Angel & the Dove: A Story for Easter. Piper, Sophie. 2010. (ENG.). 28p. (J). (gr. -1-k). 12.99 *(978-0-7459-6123-1(1))* Lion Hudson PLC GBR. Dist: Independent Pubs. Group.

—The Angel & the Lamb: A Story for Christmas. Piper, Sophie. 2009. (ENG.). 32p. (J). (gr. -1-k). bds. 12.95 *(978-0-7459-6115-6(0))* Lion Hudson PLC GBR. Dist: Independent Pubs. Group.

—Baby Boy Bible, 1 vol. 2007. (ENG.). 159p. (J). pap. 16.99 *(978-1-56148-570-3(5),* Good Bks.) Skyhorse Publishing Co., Inc.

—Baby Girl Bible, 1 vol. 2007. (ENG.). 159p. (J). pap. 16.99 *(978-1-56148-569-7(1),* Good Bks.) Skyhorse Publishing Co., Inc.

—Baby Prayers, 1 vol. Toulmin, Sarah. 2008. (ENG.). 63p. (J). pap. 12.99 *(978-1-56148-623-6(X),* Good Bks.) Skyhorse Publishing Co., Inc.

—Baby's Little Bible. Toulmin, Sarah. gif. ed. 2011. (ENG.). 160p. (J). (gr. k — 1). 13.99 *(978-0-7459-6038-8(3))* Lion Hudson PLC GBR. Dist: Independent Pubs. Group.

—Baby's Tiny Bible & Prayers, 2 vols., Set. Toulmin, Sarah. 2013. (ENG.). 224p. (J). (— 1). 14.99 *(978-0-7459-6205-4(X))* Lion Hudson PLC GBR. Dist: Independent Pubs. Group.

—From the Day You Were Born. Piper, Sophie. 2014. (ENG.). 24p. (J). (— 1). bds. 6.99 *(978-0-7459-6237-5(8))* Lion Hudson PLC GBR. Dist: Independent Pubs. Group.

—New Kid in Town, 1 vol. Freedman, Claire. 2006. (ENG.). 28p. (J). (gr. -1-2). pap. 16.00 *(978-1-56148-547-5(0),* Good Bks.) Skyhorse Publishing Co., Inc.

—The Time-for-Bed Angel. Stromberg, Ronica. (ENG.). 32p. (J). (gr. -1-k). 2010. pap. 9.99 *(978-0-7459-6066-1(9));* 2008. 14.95 *(978-0-7459-6073-9(1))* Lion Hudson PLC GBR. Dist: Independent Pubs. Group.

Stephenson, Kristina. Sir Charlie Stinky Socks & the Terrible Secret. Stephenson, Kristina. 2011. (Sir Charlie Stinky Socks Ser.: 4). (ENG.). 32p. (J). (gr. -1-k). pap. 9.99 *(978-1-4052-5397-0(5))* Egmont Bks., Ltd. GBR. Dist: Independent Pubs. Group.

—Sir Charlie Stinkysocks & the Really Big Adventure. Stephenson, Kristina. 2007. (Sir Charlie Stinky Socks Ser.: 1). (ENG.). 32p. (J). (gr. -1-k). pap. 9.99 *(978-1-4052-2803-9(2))* Egmont Bks., Ltd. GBR. Dist: Independent Pubs. Group.

Stephenson, Kristina, jt. illus. see Sweet, Melissa.

Steptoe, Javaka. All of the Above. Pearsall, Shelley. 2008. (ENG.). 256p. (J). (gr. 3-7). per. 8.00 *(978-0-316-11526-1(6))* Little, Brown Bks. for Young Readers.

—All of the Above. Pearsall, Shelley. 2007. 234p. (gr. 3-7). 18.00 *(978-0-7569-8144-0(1))* Perfection Learning Corp.

—In Daddy's Arms I Am Tall: African Americans Celebrating Fathers. Schoeder, Alan. 2013. (ENG.). 32p. (J). pap. 8.95 *(978-1-58430-016-8(7))* Lee & Low Bks., Inc.

—Jimi: Sounds Like a Rainbow - A Story of the Young Jimi Hendrix. Golio, Gary. 2010. (ENG.). 32p. (J). (gr. 1-4). 17.99 *(978-0-618-85279-6(4))* Houghton Mifflin Harcourt Publishing Co.

Steptoe, John. She Come Bringing Me That Little Baby Girl. Greenfield, Eloise. 2014. 32p. pap. 7.00 *(978-1-61003-336-7(1))* Center for the Collaborative Classroom.

Steranko. Magnus, Robot Fighter, Vol. 1. Simonson, Louise & Hendricks, Damion. 2005. (ENG.). 48p. pap. 6.95 *(978-1-59687-833-4(9))* IBks., Inc.

Steranko, Jim. Compliments of the Domino Lady. Anderson, Lars. Harvey, Rich, ed. 2004. 96p. per. 14.95 *(978-0-9712246-6-7(8))* Bold Venture Pr.

Stergulz, Richard. Barack Obama: 44th U.S. President. Stille, Darlene R. 2013. (Beginner Biographies Set 2 Ser.). 32p. (J). (gr. -1-4). 28.50 *(978-1-61641-939-4(3))* Magic Wagon.

—Jackie Robinson: Amazing Athlete & Activist. Stille, Darlene R. 2013. (Beginner Biographies Set 2 Ser.). 32p. (J). (gr. -1-4). 28.50 *(978-1-61641-940-0(7))* Magic Wagon.

Sterling, Zack. Pixel Princesses, Vol. 2. Corsetto, Danielle. 2013. (Adventure Time Ser.: 2). (ENG.). 160p. (J). (gr. 3). pap. 11.99 *(978-1-60886-329-7(8))* Boom! Studios.

Stern, Marie Simchow. Favorite Psalms for Children. 2011. 40p. pap. 35.95 *(978-1-258-07228-5(9))* Literary Licensing, LLC.

Sternberg, Kate. The Year My Mother Was Bald. Speltz, Ann. 2003. 64p. (J). (gr. 4-7). lib. bdg. 17.60 *(978-0-613-61137-4(3),* Turtleback) Turtleback Bks.

Sternberg, Kate. Oh, Brother! Growing up with a Special Needs Sibling. Sternberg, Kate, tr. Hale, Natalie. 2004. 48p. (J). 14.95 *(978-1-59147-060-1(9));* pap. 9.95 *(978-1-59147-061-8(7))* American Psychological Assn. (Magination Pr.).

Sterne, René & De Spiegeleer, Chantal. The Curse of the 30 Pieces of Silver, Pt. 1. Van Hamme, Jean. 2012. (ENG.). 62p. (J). (gr. 5-12). pap. 15.95 *(978-1-84918-125-9(X))* CineBook GBR. Dist: National Bk. Network.

Sternhagen, Mimi. The Beatitudes for Children. Gortler, Rosemarie & Piscitelli, Donna. 2009. 64p. (J). (gr. -1-3). pap. 6.95 *(978-1-59276-545-4(9))* Our Sunday Visitor, Publishing Div.

—Just Like Mary. Gorler, Rosemarie & Piscitelli, Donna. 2003. 48p. (J). 5.95 *(978-1-931709-79-8(3))* Our Sunday Visitor, Publishing Div.

—Living the 10 Commandments for Children. Piscitelli, Donna & Gortler, Rosemarie. 2006. 48p. (J). pap. 6.95 *(978-1-59276-231-6(X))* Our Sunday Visitor, Publishing Div.

—The Mass Book for Children. Gortler, Rosemarie & Piscitelli, Donna. 2004. 48p. per. 5.95 *(978-1-59276-075-6(9))* Our Sunday Visitor, Publishing Div.

Sterns, Megan. Amazing Africa Projects. Mooney, Carla. 2010. (Build It Yourself Ser.). (ENG.). 128p. (J). (gr. 3-7). pap. 15.95 *(978-1-934670-41-5(3))* Nomad Pr.

Sterrett, Virginia. Tanglewood Tales. Hawthorne, Nathaniel. 2012. (Calla Editions Ser.). (ENG.). 304p. (gr. 4). 40.00 *(978-1-60660-026-9(5))* Dover Pubns., Inc.

Sterrett, Virginia Frances. Old French Fairy Tales. Segur, Sophie. 2010. (ENG.). 296p. (gr. -1-3). pap. 19.95 *(978-1-4290-1186-0(6))* Applewood Bks.

Stetz, Ken. Christmas Tails. Leeds, Robert X. rev. ed. 2005. 55p. (J). 16.95 *(978-0-9674025-7-4(3))* EPIC Publishing Co.

—Words of Promise: A Story about James Weldon Johnson. Shull, Jodie A. 2005. (Creative Minds Biographies Ser.). (ENG.). 64p. (gr. 4-8). lib. bdg. 22.60 *(978-1-57505-755-2(7),* Carolrhoda Bks.) Lerner Publishing Group.

—Words of Promise: A Story about James Weldon Johnson. Shull, Jodie. 2006. (Creative Minds Biographies Ser.). (ENG.). 64p. (gr. 4-8). pap. 8.95 *(978-0-8225-3089-3(9))* Lerner Publishing Group.

Steuerwald, Joy. One Christmas Story. Harper, Stephan J. 2003. 32p. (J). lib. bdg. 16.95 *(978-0-9741800-0-7(9))* Inspire Press, Inc.

Stevanovic, Ivica. Jack & the Wild Life. Doan, Lisa. (Berenson Schemes Ser.: 2). (ENG.). 144p. (J). (gr. 4-6). 2015. pap. 6.95 ***(978-1-4677-2476-0(9),*** Darby Creek); 2014. 17.95 *(978-1-4677-1077-0(6))* Lerner Publishing Group.

Stevanovic, Ivica. Jack at the Helm. Doan, Lisa. 2015. (J). *(978-1-4677-7787-2(0));* (Berenson Schemes Ser.: 3). (ENG.). 152p. (gr. 4-6). 17.95 *(978-1-4677-1078-7(4))* Lerner Publishing Group.

—Jack the Castaway. Doan, Lisa. 2014. (Berenson Schemes Ser.: 1). (ENG.). 152p. (J). (gr. 4-6). 17.95 *(978-1-4677-1076-3(8),* Darby Creek) Lerner Publishing Group.

—Monsters Can Mosey: Understanding Shades of Meaning, 1 vol. Olson, Gillia M. 2013. (Language on the Loose Ser.). (ENG.). 24p. (gr. 2-4). 27.32 *(978-1-4048-8320-8(7));* pap. 7.95 *(978-1-4795-1919-4(7))* Picture Window Bks.

—The Royal Treasure Measure. Harris, Trudy. 2012. (Math Is Fun! Ser.). (ENG.). 32p. (gr. k-2). lib. bdg. 16.95 *(978-0-7613-6806-9(X),* Millbrook Pr.) Lerner Publishing Group.

—Scarlett & Sam: Escape from Egypt. Kimmel, Eric A. 2015. (J). *(978-1-4677-6207-6(5));* (ENG.). 168p. (gr. 1-3). lib. bdg. 15.95 *(978-1-4677-3850-7(6))* Lerner Publishing Group. (Kar-Ben Publishing).

—Where's My Tushy? Aronson, Deborah. 2014. (ENG.). 24p. (J). (gr. -1-3). 17.95 *(978-1-4677-1197-5(7),* Carolrhoda Bks.) Lerner Publishing Group.

Steve, Lavigne. Shine Like a Lighhouse. Janis, Tim. 2nd ed. 2007. (J). 12.95 *(978-0-9773335-1-6(5))* Janis, Tim Ensemble, Inc.

Stevens. From Bobcat to Wolf: The Story of Den Seven, Pack Four. Gardner, L. S. 2011. 192p. 42.95 *(978-1-258-04225-7(8))* Literary Licensing, LLC.

Stevens, Angie. My Daddy Says. Smith, Justine. ed. 2014. (ENG.). 16p. (J). (-k). bds. 9.99 *(978-1-4472-6121-6(6))* Pan Macmillan GBR. Dist: Independent Pubs. Group.

—My Mummy Says. Doodlemum & Smith, Justine. ed. 2014. (Families & Friends Ser.). (ENG.). 16p. (J). (-k). bds. 9.99 *(978-1-4472-6097-4(X))* Pan Macmillan GBR. Dist: Independent Pubs. Group.

Stevens, arthur. The Sharing Circle: Stories about First Nations Culture, 1 vol. Meuse, Theresa. 2003. (ENG.). 52p. (J). (gr. k-3). pap. 11.95 *(978-1-55109-450-2(9))* Nimbus Publishing, Ltd. CAN. Dist: Orca Bk. Pubs. USA.

Stevens, Chris & Udon. G. I. Joe Master & Apprentice vol II. Jerwa, Brandon. 2006. (YA). per. 14.95 *(978-1-932796-45-2(2))* Devil's Due Publishing, Inc.

Stevens, Daniel. Can't & Able: An Inspirational Story. Fabian, Cynthia. 2012. 28p. pap. 12.50 *(978-1-61204-327-2(5),* Strategic Bk. Publishing) Strategic Book Publishing & Rights Agency (SBPRA).

—Orchestra in Our Brain: The Story of a Child with Epilepsy. Fabian, Cynthia. 2011. 20p. pap. 10.95 *(978-1-60976-783-9(7),* Eloquent Bks.) Strategic Book Publishing & Rights Agency (SBPRA).

Stevens, David S. Stepping Stones for Boys & Girls. Stevens, Margaret M. 2003. 32p. (gr. 5-18). 5.95 *(978-0-87516-248-5(7))* DeVorss & Co.

S

—Stepping Stones for Little Feet. Stevens, Margaret M. 2003. 31p. (gr. 4-6). 4.50 *(978-0-87516-202-7(9)*, Devorss Pubns.) DeVorss & Co.

Stevens, Debra. Whos' Riley? Van Kersen, Elizabeth. l.t. ed. 2006. 23p. (J). 15.99 *(978-1-59879-173-0(7))* Lifevest Publishing, Inc.

Stevens, Helen. Healthy Foods from Healthy Soils: A Hands-On Resource for Teachers, 1 vol. Patten, Elizabeth & Lyons, Kathy. 2005. (ENG.). 192p. (J). (gr. k-6). pap. 19.95 *(978-0-88448-242-0(1))* Tilbury Hse. Pubs.

—Moose Eggs: Or, Why Moose Has Flat Antlers. Beckhorn, Susan Williams. ed. 2007. (ENG.). 32p. (J). (gr. -1-3). 15.95 *(978-0-89272-689-9(X))* Down East Bks.

—Spirit of the Snowpeople. Keyes, Diane. ed. 2008. (ENG.). 32p. (J). (gr. -1-3). 15.95 *(978-0-89272-710-0(1))* Down East Bks.

Stevens, Janet. Anansi & the Magic Stick. 2005. (ENG.). 32p. (J). (gr. k-3). 7.99 *(978-0-8234-1763-6(8))* Holiday Hse., Inc.

—Anansi & the Magic Stick. Kimmel, Eric A. 2003. (J). 25.95 incl. audio *(978-1-59112-482-5(4))*; pap. 37.95 incl. audio *(978-1-59112-483-2(2))*; pap. 39.95 incl. audio compact disk *(978-1-59112-519-8(7))* Live Oak Media.

—Anansi Series. Kimmel, Eric A. 2003. pap. 68.95 incl. audio compact disk *(978-1-59112-840-3(4))*;Set. (J). pap. 61.95 incl. audio *(978-0-87499-469-8(1))* Live Oak Media.

—Anansi's Party Time. Kimmel, Eric A. (ENG.). 32p. (J). (gr. -1-3). 2009. pap. 6.95 *(978-0-8234-2241-8(0))*; 2008. 16.95 *(978-0-8234-1922-7(3))* Holiday Hse., Inc.

—Epossumondas Plays Possum. Salley, Coleen. 2009. (ENG.). 40p. (J). (gr. -1-3). 16.00 *(978-0-15-206420-4(6))* Houghton Mifflin Harcourt Publishing Co.

—Epossumondas Saves the Day. Salley, Coleen. 2006. (ENG.). 48p. (J). (gr. -1-3). 16.00 *(978-0-15-205701-5(3))* Houghton Mifflin Harcourt Publishing Co.

—Tumbleweed Stew. Crummel, Susan Stevens. 2003. (Green Light Readers Level 2 Ser.). (ENG.). 32p. (J). (gr. -1-3). pap. 3.95 *(978-0-15-204830-3(8))* Houghton Mifflin Harcourt Publishing Co.

—The Weighty Word Book. Levitt, Paul M. et al. 3rd ed. 2009. (ENG.). 96p. (J). 21.95 *(978-0-8263-4555-4(7))* Univ. of New Mexico Pr.

—Why Epossumondas Has No Hair on His Tail. Salley, Coleen. 2004. (ENG.). 40p. (J). (gr. -1-3). 16.00 *(978-0-15-204935-5(5))* Houghton Mifflin Harcourt Publishing Co.

—Wild about Us! Beaumont, Karen. 2015. (ENG.). 40p. (J). (gr. -1-3). 16.99 *(978-0-15-206294-1(7))*, HMH Books For Young Readers) Houghton Mifflin Harcourt Publishing Co.

Stevens, Janet. Find a Cow Now! Stevens, Janet. Crummel, Susan Stevens. 2012. (ENG.). 32p. (J). 16.95 *(978-0-8234-2218-0(6))* Holiday Hse., Inc.

—Help Me, Mr. Mutt! Expert Answers for Dogs with People Problems. Stevens, Janet. Crummel, Susan Stevens. 2008. (ENG.). 56p. (J). (gr. -1-3). 17.00 *(978-0-15-204628-6(3))* Houghton Mifflin Harcourt Publishing Co.

—The Little Red Pen. Stevens, Janet. Crummel, Susan Stevens. 2011. (ENG.). 56p. (J). (gr. 1-4). 17.99 *(978-0-15-206432-7(X))* Houghton Mifflin Harcourt Publishing Co.

—My Big Dog. Stevens, Janet. Stevens Crummel, Susan. 2009. (Golden Classic Ser.). (ENG.). 40p. (J). (gr. -1-2). pap. 6.99 *(978-0-375-85103-2(8)*, Dragonfly Bks.) Random Hse. Children's Bks.

—Plaidypus Lost. Stevens, Janet. Crummel, Susan Stevens. 2013. (ENG.). 40p. (J). pap. 7.99 *(978-0-8234-2753-6(6))* Holiday Hse., Inc.

—Tumbleweed Stew/Sopa de Matojos. Stevens, Janet. Crummel, Susan Stevens. Flor Ada, Alma & Campoy, F. Isabel, trs. from ENG. 2009. (Green Light Readers Level 2 Ser.). (SPA & ENG.). 36p. (J). (gr. -1-3). pap. 3.99 *(978-0-547-25261-2(7))* Houghton Mifflin Harcourt Publishing Co.

Stevens, Judy. Stories of the Saints. Denham, Joyce. 2003. 48p. (J). pap. 11.99 *(978-0-7459-4637-5(2)*, Lion Books) Lion Hudson PLC GBR. Dist: Trafalgar Square Publishing.

—Stories of the Saints. Denham, Joyce. 2007. (ENG.). 48p. (J). (gr. 4-7). pap. 9.95 *(978-1-55725-534-1(2))* Paraclete Pr., Inc.

Stevens, Larry. Clown Games. 2005. (I'm Going to Read(r) Ser.). (ENG.). 32p. (J). (gr. -1-k). per. 3.95 *(978-1-4027-2723-8(2))* Sterling Publishing Co., Inc.

Stevens, Mary. The Gatehouse Mystery. Campbell, Julie. ed. 2003. (Trixie Belden Ser.: No. 3). (ENG.). 272p. (J). (gr. 3-7). 6.99 *(978-0-375-82579-8(7)*, Random Hse. Bks. for Young Readers) Random Hse. Children's Bks.

—Good Old Archibald. Parkinson, Ethelyn. 2014. 145p. (J). pap. 14.95 *(978-1-932350-42-5(X))* Bethlehem Bks.

—Palace Wagon Family: A True Story of the Donner Party. Sutton, Margaret. 2011. 224p. 44.95 *(978-1-258-00668-6(5))* Literary Licensing, LLC.

—The Red Trailer Mystery. Campbell, Julie. 2003. (Trixie Belden Ser.: No. 2). (ENG.). 272p. (J). (gr. 3-7). 6.99 *(978-0-375-82411-1(1)*, Random Hse. Bks. for Young Readers) Random Hse. Children's Bks.

—The Secret of the Mansion. Campbell, Julie. 2003. (Trixie Belden Ser.: No. 1). (ENG.). 272p. (J). (gr. 3-7). 6.99 *(978-0-375-82412-8(X)*, Random Hse. Bks. for Young Readers) Random Hse. Children's Bks.

Stevens-Marzo, Bridget. The Big Book of Shapes. Cocagne, Marie-Pascale. 2009. (ENG.). 60p. (J). (gr. -1-3). 15.95 *(978-1-85437-851-4(1))* Tate Publishing, Ltd. GBR. Dist: Abrams.

Stevens, Matt. Encountering Chupacabra & Other Cryptids: Eyewitness Accounts, 1 vol. Peterson, Megan Cooley & Rustad, Martha E. H. 2014. (Eyewitness to the Unexplained Ser.). (ENG.). 32p. (gr. 3-4). 29.99 *(978-1-4914-0242-9(3))* Capstone Pr., Inc.

Stevens, Tim. Brother Aelred's Feet. Cross, Gillian. 2007. (Collins Big Cat Ser.). (ENG.). 544p. (J). pap. 8.99 *(978-0-00-723093-8(1))* HarperCollins Pubs. Ltd. GBR. Dist: Independent Pubs. Group.

Stevens, Tim & Wyatt, David. Troll Blood. Langrish, Katherine. 2008. 352p. (gr. 5-8). (ENG.). (J). 16.99 *(978-0-06-111674-2(2))*; (YA). lib. bdg. 17.89 *(978-0-06-111675-9(0)*, Eos) HarperCollins Pubs.

Stevens, Tracey. Chalice of the Goddess. Stevens, Tracey. Snowden, Susan, ed. 2004. 313p. (YA). per. 17.95 *(978-0-9719628-4-2(7))* Amazing Dreams Publishing.

Stevenson, Daryl. Flossie Crums & the Enchanted Cookie Tree: A Flossie Crums Baking Adventure. Nathan, Helen. 2012. (Flossie Crums Ser.). (ENG.). 56p. (J). (gr. k-2). pap. 8.99 *(978-1-84365-197-0(1)*, Pavilion Children's Books) Pavilion Bks. GBR. Dist: Independent Pubs. Group.

—Flossie Crums & the Fairies' Cupcake Ball. Nathan, Helen. 2012. (Flossie Crums Ser.). (ENG.). 56p. (J). (gr. k-2). pap. 8.99 *(978-1-84365-196-3(3)*, Pavilion Children's Books) Pavilion Bks. GBR. Dist: Independent Pubs. Group.

—Flossie Crums & the Royal Spotty Dotty Cake. Nathan, Helen. 2012. (Flossie Crums Ser.). (ENG.). 56p. (J). (gr. k-2). 14.99 *(978-1-84365-188-8(2)*, Pavilion Children's Books) Pavilion Bks. GBR. Dist: Independent Pubs. Group.

Stevenson, Dave. A Dangerous Path. Hunter, Erin. (Warriors: the Prophecies Begin Ser.: 5). (ENG.). 336p. (J). (gr. 3-7). 2005. pap. 6.99 *(978-0-06-052565-1(7))*; 2004. 16.99 *(978-0-06-000006-6(6))* HarperCollins Pubs.

—The Darkest Hour. Hunter, Erin. (Warriors: the Prophecies Begin Ser.: 6). (ENG.). 336p. (J). (gr. 3-7). 2005. pap. 6.99 *(978-0-06-052585-9(1))*; 2004. 17.99 *(978-0-06-000007-3(4))* HarperCollins Pubs.

—Dawn. Hunter, Erin. (Warriors: the New Prophecy Ser.: 3). (ENG.). 352p. (J). (gr. 3-7). 2006. pap. 6.99 *(978-0-06-074457-1(X))*; 2005. 16.99 *(978-0-06-074455-7(3))* HarperCollins Pubs.

—Fire & Ice. Hunter, Erin. (Warriors: the Prophecies Begin Ser.: 2). (ENG.). 336p. (J). (gr. 3-7). 2004. pap. 6.99 *(978-0-06-052559-0(2))*; 2003. 16.99 *(978-0-06-000003-5(1))* HarperCollins Pubs.

—Forest of Secrets. Hunter, Erin. (Warriors: the Prophecies Begin Ser.: 3). 336p. (J). (gr. 3-7). 2004. (ENG.). pap. 6.99 *(978-0-06-052561-3(4))*; 2003. (ENG.). 16.99 *(978-0-06-000004-2(X))*; 2003. lib. bdg. 17.89 *(978-0-06-052560-6(6))* HarperCollins Pubs.

—Into the Wild. Hunter, Erin. (Warriors: the Prophecies Begin Ser.: 1). (ENG.). 288p. (J). (gr. 3-7). 2004. pap. 6.99 *(978-0-06-052550-7(9))*; 2003. 16.99 *(978-0-06-000002-8(3))* HarperCollins Pubs.

—Midnight. Hunter, Erin. (Warriors: the New Prophecy Ser.: 1). (ENG.). (J). (gr. 3-7). 2006. 336p. pap. 6.99 *(978-0-06-074451-9(0))*; 2005. 320p. 16.99 *(978-0-06-074449-6(9))* HarperCollins Pubs.

—Moonrise. Hunter, Erin. (Warriors: the New Prophecy Ser.: 2). (J). (gr. 3-7). 2006. (ENG.). 320p. pap. 6.99 *(978-0-06-074454-0(5))*; 2005. (ENG.). 304p. 16.99 *(978-0-06-074452-6(9))*; 2005. 304p. lib. bdg. 17.89 *(978-0-06-074453-3(7))* HarperCollins Pubs.

—Rising Storm. Hunter, Erin. (Warriors: the Prophecies Begin Ser.: 4). 336p. (J). (gr. 3-7). 2005. (ENG.). pap. 6.99 *(978-0-06-052563-7(0))*; 2004. (ENG.). 16.99 *(978-0-06-000005-9(8))*; 2004. lib. bdg. 17.89 *(978-0-06-052562-0(2))* HarperCollins Pubs.

—Starlight. Hunter, Erin. (Warriors: the New Prophecy Ser.: 4). (ENG.). (J). (gr. 3-7). 2007. 320p. pap. 6.99 *(978-0-06-082762-5(9))*; 2006. 336p. 16.99 *(978-0-06-082758-8(0))* HarperCollins Pubs.

—Sunset. Hunter, Erin. (Warriors: the New Prophecy Ser.: 6). (ENG.). 320p. (J). (gr. 3-7). 2007. pap. 6.99 *(978-0-06-082771-7(8))*; 2006. 16.99 *(978-0-06-082769-4(6))* HarperCollins Pubs.

—Twilight. Hunter, Erin. (Warriors: the New Prophecy Ser.: 5). (ENG.). (J). (gr. 3-7). 2007. 352p. pap. 6.99 *(978-0-06-082767-0(X))*; 2006. 336p. 16.99 *(978-0-06-082764-9(5))* HarperCollins Pubs.

Stevenson, Dave. The Vanishing Island. Wolverton, Barry. 2015. (Chronicles of the Black Tulip Ser.: 1). (ENG.). 352p. (J). (gr. 3-7). 16.99 ***(978-0-06-222190-2(6)***, Waldon Pond Pr.) HarperCollins Pubs.

Stevenson, Dave, jt. illus. see Richardson, Owen.

Stevenson, Emma. Eggs. Singer, Marilyn. 2008. (ENG.). 32p. (J). (gr. 1-5). 16.95 *(978-0-8234-1727-8(1))* Holiday Hse., Inc.

—Killer Ants. Nirgiotis, Nicholas. 2009. (ENG.). 32p. (J). (gr. 1-5). 17.95 *(978-0-8234-2034-6(5))* Holiday Hse., Inc.

—Mysterious Bones: The Story of Kennewick Man. Kirkpatrick, Katherine. 2011. (ENG.). 64p. (J). (gr. 3-7). 18.95 *(978-0-8234-2187-9(2))* Holiday Hse., Inc.

Stevenson, Emma. Hide-and-Seek Science: Animal Camouflage. Stevenson, Emma. 2014. (ENG.). 32p. (J). (gr. 1-5). 7.99 *(978-0-8234-3187-8(8))* Holiday Hse., Inc.

Stevenson, Geoff. The Invisible String. Karst, Patrice. 2003. 36p. (J). 16.95 *(978-0-87516-734-3(9)*, Devorss Pubns.) DeVorss & Co.

Stevenson, Harvey. Coal Country Christmas. Brown, Elizabeth Ferguson & Boyds Mills Press Staff. 2003. (ENG.). 32p. (J). (gr. 1-7). 15.95 *(978-1-59078-020-6(5))* Boyds Mills Pr.

—Wilhe'mina Miles: After the Stork Night. Carter, Dorothy. 2005. 30p. (J). (gr. k-4). reprint ed. 16.00 *(978-0-7567-9421-7(8))* DIANE Publishing Co.

Stevenson, Harvey. Looking at Liberty. Stevenson, Harvey. 2003. 40p. (J). (gr. -1-2). 17.89 *(978-0-06-000101-8(1))* HarperCollins Pubs.

Stevenson, James, et al. The Big Green Book of Beginner Books. Seuss, Dr. 2009. (Beginner Books Ser.). (ENG.). 256p. (J). (gr. -1-2). 15.99 *(978-0-375-85807-9(5)*, Random Hse. Bks. for Young Readers) Random Hse. Children's Bks.

Stevenson, James. Cool Zone with the Pain & the Great One. Blume, Judy. 2009. (ENG.). 128p. (J). (gr. 3-7). 5.99 *(978-0-440-42093-4(8)*, Yearling) Random Hse. Children's Bks.

—Friend or Fiend? With the Pain & the Great One. Blume, Judy. 2009. (ENG.). 128p. (J). (gr. 3-7). 12.99 *(978-0-385-73308-3(9)*, Delacorte Bks. for Young Readers) Random Hse. Children's Bks.

—Friend or Fiend? with the Pain & the Great One. Blume, Judy. 2010. (ENG.). 128p. (J). (gr. 3-7). 5.99 *(978-0-440-42095-8(4)*, Yearling) Random Hse. Children's Bks.

—Going, Going, Gone! with the Pain & the Great One. Blume, Judy. 2010. (ENG.). 128p. (J). (gr. 3-7). 5.99 *(978-0-440-42094-1(6)*, Yearling) Random Hse. Children's Bks.

—It's Raining Pigs & Noodles. Prelutsky, Jack. 2012. (ENG.). 160p. (J). (gr. k-5). reprint ed. pap. 9.99 *(978-0-06-076390-9(6)*, Greenwillow Bks.) HarperCollins Pubs.

—My Dog May Be a Genius. Prelutsky, Jack. 2008. 160p. (J). (gr. k-5). (ENG.). 18.99 *(978-0-06-623862-3(5))*; lib. bdg. 19.89 *(978-0-06-623863-0(3))* HarperCollins Pubs. (Greenwillow Bks.).

—The New Kid on the Block. Prelutsky, Jack. 2013. (ENG.). 160p. (J). (gr. k-5). pap. 9.99 *(978-0-06-223950-1(3)*, Greenwillow Bks.) HarperCollins Pubs.

—Something Big Has Been Here. Prelutsky, Jack. 2010. (ENG.). 160p. (J). (gr. k-5). pap. 9.99 *(978-0-06-185775-1(0)*, Greenwillow Bks.) HarperCollins Pubs.

—Soupy Saturdays with the Pain & the Great One. Blume, Judy. 2009. (ENG.). 128p. (J). (gr. 3-7). 5.99 *(978-0-440-42092-7(X)*, Yearling) Random Hse. Children's Bks.

Stevenson, James. Flying Feet: A Mud Flat Story. Stevenson, James. 2004. 48p. (J). 15.99 *(978-0-06-051975-9(4))* HarperCollins Pubs.

Stevenson, John & Davidson, Dawn. The Twig Pencil: A Story of Perseverance. Stevenson, Paula. 2010. (ENG.). 44p. pap. 12.95 *(978-1-4528-5722-0(9))* CreateSpace Independent Publishing Platform.

Stevenson, Noelle. Nimona. Stevenson, Noelle. 2015. (ENG.). 272p. (YA). (gr. 8). 17.99 *(978-0-06-227823-4(1))*; pap. 12.99 *(978-0-06-227822-7(3))* HarperCollins Pubs. (HarperTeen).

Stevenson, Peter. Catholic Baby's Bedtime Bible Stories. Zobel-Nolan, Allia. 2006. (First Bible Collection). (gr. -1-k). bds. 15.95 *(978-0-88271-067-9(2))* Regina Pr., Malhame & Co.

Stevenson, Robert, photos by. Already Legends: Stevenson Studios Sports Photo Journal. 2005. 160p. per. 29.95 *(978-0-9753434-5-6(9))* LeTay Publishing.

Stevenson, Robert Louis & Timothy, Hamilton Baird. Treasure Island. Stevenson, Robert Louis. 2005. (ENG.). 176p. (J). (gr. 3-7). 10.99 *(978-0-14-240470-6(5)*, Puffin) Penguin Publishing Group.

Stevenson, Seline. The Street Cats of Marrakech. Tóth-Jones, Dee S. 2013. 34p. pap. *(978-1-908794-08-6(9))* Chiaroscuro Bks.

Stevenson, Suçie. Annie & Snowball & the Book Bugs Club. Rylant, Cynthia. (Annie & Snowball Ser.: 9). (ENG.). 40p. (J). (gr. k-2). 2012. pap. 3.99 *(978-1-4169-7201-3(3))*; 2011. 16.99 *(978-1-4169-7199-3(8))* Simon Spotlight. (Simon Spotlight).

—Annie & Snowball & the Cozy Nest. Rylant, Cynthia. (Annie & Snowball Ser.: 5). (ENG.). 40p. (J). (gr. k-2). 2010. pap. 3.99 *(978-1-4169-3947-4(4))*; 2009. 16.99 *(978-1-4169-3943-6(1))* Simon Spotlight. (Simon Spotlight).

—Annie & Snowball & the Dress-Up Birthday. Rylant, Cynthia. (Annie & Snowball Ser.: 1). (ENG.). 40p. (J). (gr. k-2). 2008. pap. 3.99 *(978-1-4169-1459-4(5))*; 2007. 16.99 *(978-1-4169-0938-5(9))* Simon Spotlight. (Simon Spotlight).

—Annie & Snowball & the Grandmother Night. Rylant, Cynthia. (Annie & Snowball Ser.: 12). (ENG.). 40p. (J). (gr. k-2). 2013. pap. 3.99 *(978-1-4169-7204-4(8))*; 2012. 15.99 *(978-1-4169-7203-7(X))* Simon Spotlight. (Simon Spotlight).

—Annie & Snowball & the Magical House. Rylant, Cynthia. (Annie & Snowball Ser.: 7). (ENG.). 40p. (J). (gr. k-2). 2011. pap. 3.99 *(978-1-4169-3949-8(0))*; 2010. 15.99 *(978-1-4169-3945-0(8))* Simon Spotlight. (Simon Spotlight).

—Annie & Snowball & the Pink Surprise. Rylant, Cynthia. (Annie & Snowball Ser.: 4). (ENG.). 40p. (J). (gr. k-2). 2010. pap. 3.99 *(978-1-4169-1462-4(5))*; 2008. 16.99 *(978-1-4169-0941-5(9))* Simon Spotlight. (Simon Spotlight).

—Annie & Snowball & the Prettiest House. Rylant, Cynthia. (Annie & Snowball Ser.: 2). (ENG.). 40p. (J). (gr. k-2). 2008. pap. 3.99 *(978-1-4169-1460-0(9))*; 2007. 16.99 *(978-1-4169-0939-2(7))* Simon Spotlight. (Simon Spotlight).

—Annie & Snowball & the Shining Star. Rylant, Cynthia. (Annie & Snowball Ser.: 6). (ENG.). 40p. (J). (gr. k-2). 2010. pap. 3.99 *(978-1-4169-3950-4(4))*; 2009. 15.99 *(978-1-4169-3946-7(6))* Simon Spotlight. (Simon Spotlight).

—Annie & Snowball & the Surprise Day. Rylant, Cynthia. (Annie & Snowball Ser.: 11). (ENG.). 40p. (J). (gr. k-2). 2013. pap. 3.99 *(978-1-4169-3948-1(2))*; 2012. 16.99 *(978-1-4169-3944-3(X))* Simon Spotlight. (Simon Spotlight).

—Annie & Snowball & the Teacup Club. Rylant, Cynthia. (Annie & Snowball Ser.: 3). (ENG.). (J). (gr. k-2). 2009. 40p. pap. 3.99 *(978-1-4169-1461-7(7))*; 2008. 32p. 16.99 *(978-1-4169-0940-8(0))* Simon Spotlight. (Simon Spotlight).

—Annie & Snowball & the Thankful Friends. Rylant, Cynthia. (Annie & Snowball Ser.: 10). (ENG.). 40p. (J). (gr. k-2). 2012. pap. 3.99 *(978-1-4169-7202-0(1))*; 2011. 15.99 *(978-1-4169-7200-6(5))* Simon Spotlight. (Simon Spotlight).

—Annie & Snowball & the Wedding Day. Rylant, Cynthia. 2014. (Annie & Snowball Ser.: 13). (ENG.). 40p. (J). (gr. k-2). 16.99 *(978-1-4169-7485-7(7)*, Simon Spotlight) Simon Spotlight.

—Annie & Snowball & the Wedding Day: The Thirteenth Book of Their Adventures. Rylant, Cynthia. 2015. (Annie & Snowball Ser.: 13). (ENG.). 40p. (J). (gr. k-2). pap. 3.99 *(978-1-4169-7486-4(5)*, Simon Spotlight) Simon Spotlight.

—Annie & Snowball & the Wintry Freeze. Rylant, Cynthia. (Annie & Snowball Ser.: 8). (ENG.). 40p. (J). (gr. k-2). 2011. pap. 3.99 *(978-1-4169-7206-8(4))*; 2010. 16.99 *(978-1-4169-7205-1(6))* Simon Spotlight. (Simon Spotlight).

—Family Stories You Can Relate To: A Reading Rainbow Reader. Rylant, Cynthia. 2004. 64p. (J). (gr. 1-4). reprint ed. 15.00 *(978-0-7567-7150-8(1))* DIANE Publishing Co.

—Henry & Mudge & a Very Merry Christmas. Rylant, Cynthia. 2005. (Henry & Mudge Ser.). 40p. (gr. -1-3). 14.00 *(978-0-7569-5816-9(4))* Perfection Learning Corp.

—Henry & Mudge & a Very Merry Christmas. Rylant, Cynthia. (Henry & Mudge Ser.: 25). (ENG.). 40p. (J). (gr. k-2). 2005. pap. 3.99 *(978-0-689-83448-6(9))*; 2004. 16.99 *(978-0-689-81168-5(3))* Simon Spotlight. (Simon Spotlight).

—Henry & Mudge & the Big Sleepover. Rylant, Cynthia. 2007. (Henry & Mudge Ser.). 40p. (gr. k-2). lib. bdg. 14.00 *(978-0-7569-8117-4(4))* Perfection Learning Corp.

—Henry & Mudge & the Big Sleepover, Bk. 28. Rylant, Cynthia. 2007. (Henry & Mudge Ser.: 28). (ENG.). 40p. (J). (gr. k-2). pap. 3.99 *(978-0-689-83451-6(9)*, Simon Spotlight) Simon Spotlight.

—Henry & Mudge & the Big Sleepover. Rylant, Cynthia. ed. 2007. (Henry & Mudge Ready-To-Read Ser.: 28). 40p. (gr. -1-3). lib. bdg. 13.55 *(978-1-4177-8140-9(8)*, Turtleback) Turtleback Bks.

—Henry & Mudge & the Great Grandpas. Rylant, Cynthia. 2006. (Henry & Mudge Ser.). 40p. (gr. k-2). 14.00 *(978-0-7569-6793-2(7))* Perfection Learning Corp.

—Henry & Mudge & the Great Grandpas. Rylant, Cynthia. 2006. (Henry & Mudge Ser.: 26). (ENG.). 40p. (J). (gr. k-2). pap. 3.99 *(978-0-689-83447-9(0)*, Simon Spotlight) Simon Spotlight.

—Henry & Mudge Get the Cold Shivers. Rylant, Cynthia. (Henry & Mudge Ser.). 9.95 *(978-1-59112-290-6(2))* Live Oak Media.

—Henry & Mudge Ready-To-Read Value Pack #2: Henry & Mudge & the Long Weekend; Henry & Mudge & the Bedtime Thumps; Henry & Mudge & the Big Sleepover; Henry & Mudge & the Funny Lunch; Henry & Mudge & the Great Grandpas; Henry & Mudge & the Tall Tree House. Rylant, Cynthia. 2013. (Henry & Mudge Ser.). (ENG.). 240p. (J). (gr. k-2). pap. 15.96 *(978-1-4424-9441-1(7)*, Simon Spotlight) Simon Spotlight.

—Puppy Mudge Finds a Friend. Rylant, Cynthia. (Puppy Mudge Ser.). (ENG.). 32p. (J). (gr. -1-k). 2005. pap. 3.99 *(978-1-4169-0369-7(0))*; 2004. 16.99 *(978-0-689-83982-5(0))* Simon Spotlight. (Simon Spotlight).

—Puppy Mudge Wants to Play. Rylant, Cynthia. (Puppy Mudge Ser.). (ENG.). 32p. (J). (gr. -1-k). 2006. pap. 3.99 *(978-1-4169-1556-0(7))*; 2005. 16.99 *(978-0-689-83984-9(7))* Simon Spotlight. (Simon Spotlight).

Stevenson, Suçie & Stevenson, Suçie. Henry & Mudge & the Big Sleepover. Rylant, Cynthia. 2006. (Henry & Mudge Ser.: 28). (ENG.). 40p. (J). (gr. k-2). 16.99 *(978-0-689-81171-5(3)*, Simon Spotlight) Simon Spotlight.

—Henry & Mudge & the Great Grandpas. Rylant, Cynthia. 2005. (Henry & Mudge Ser.: 26). (ENG.). 40p. (J). (gr. k-2). 15.99 *(978-0-689-81170-8(5)*, Simon Spotlight) Simon Spotlight.

Stevenson, Suçie, jt. illus. see Stevenson, Suçie.

Stewart, Carolyn. Children's Phonology Sourcebook. Flynn, Lesley et al. ed. 232p. spiral bd. *(978-0-86388-412-2(1)*, 002-3077) Speechmark Publishing Ltd.

Stewart, Chantal. Dependable Dan. Zail, Suzy. 2004. iv, 36p. (J). pap. *(978-0-7608-6747-1(X))* Sundance/Newbridge Educational Publishing.

—Diary Disaster. Smith Dinbergs, Holly. 2005. (Girlz Rock! Ser.). (J). pap. *(978-1-59336-700-8(7))* Mondo Publishing.

—Hair Scare. Dinbergs, Holly Smith. 2005. (Girlz Rock! Ser.). (J). pap. *(978-1-59336-702-2(3))* Mondo Publishing.

—The Princess & the Pea Vol. 9: Band 15/Emerald. Abela, Donna. 2007. (Collins Big Cat Ser.). (ENG.). 32p. (J). pap. 8.99 *(978-0-00-722866-9(X))* HarperCollins Pubs. Ltd. GBR. Dist: Independent Pubs. Group.

—To the Light. Flynn, Pat. 2005. 120p. (Orig.). (YA). pap. *(978-0-7022-3492-7(3))* Univ. of Queensland Pr.

—Tortoise Soup! 2009. 24p. pap. 10.67 *(978-1-4190-5523-2(2))* Rigby Education.

Stewart, Dave. Conquerer Worm. Mignola, Mike, Allie, Scott, ed. 2004. (Hellboy Ser.: Vol. 5). (ENG.). 144p. pap. 17.99 *(978-1-59307-092-2(6))* Dark Horse Comics.

Stewart, David. World of Gods & Goddesses. Morley, Jacqueline. 2013. (World Of Ser.). (ENG.). 61p. (J). lib. bdg. *(978-1-908973-92-4(7))* Book Hse.

Stewart, Don. Blessed Pier Giorgio Frassati: Journey to the Summit. Vazquez, Ana Maria & Dean, Jennings. 2004. (Encounter Ser.: 18). 144p. (J). pap. 5.95 *(978-0-8198-1165-3(3)*, 332-028) Pauline Bks. & Media.

Stewart, Edgar. They Dance in the Sky: Native American Star Myths. Williamson, Ray A. & Monroe, Jean Guard. 2007. (ENG.). 144p. (J). (gr. 5-7). pap. 8.95 *(978-0-618-80912-7(0))* Houghton Mifflin Harcourt Publishing Co.

Stewart, Fion. On the Way Home. Chen, Julia. 2009. (J). *(978-0-9787550-6-5(5))* Heryin Publishing Corp.

Stewart, James. Guitar Method for Young Beginners, Book 1. Turner, Gary. 2006. (Young Beginner Giant Coloring Bks.). 36p. pap. incl. audio compact disk *(978-1-86469-096-5(8))* LearnToPlayMusic.com Pty Ltd.

—Keyboard Method for Young Beginners, Book 1. Turner, Gary. 2006. (Young Beginner Giant Coloring Bks.). 48p. pap. incl. audio compact disk *(978-1-86469-097-2(6))* LearnToPlayMusic.com Pty Ltd.

—Piano Method for Young Beginners, Book 1. Turner, Gary. 2006. (Young Beginner Giant Coloring Bks.). 44p. pap. incl. audio compact disk *(978-1-86469-098-9(4))* LearnToPlayMusic.com Pty Ltd.

—Recorder Method for Young Beginners, Book 1. Turner, Gary. 2006. (Young Beginner Giant Coloring Bks.). 36p.

S

pap. *(978-1-86469-099-6(2))* LearnToPlayMusic.com Pty Ltd.

Stewart, Joel. The Cow Tripped over the Moon: a Nursery Rhyme Emergency. Willis, Jeanne. 2015. (ENG.). 32p. (J). (gr. -1-2). 15.99 *(978-0-7636-7402-1(8))* Candlewick Pr.

—Red Ted & the Lost Things. Rosen, Michael. 2009. (ENG.). 40p. (J). (gr. -1-2). pap. 8.99 *(978-0-7636-4624-0(5))* Candlewick Pr.

—Shark & Lobster's Amazing Undersea Adventure. Schwarz, Viviane. 2006. 34p. (J). *(978-1-4156-8140-4(6))* Candlewick Pr.

—Tales of Hans Christian Andersen. Andersen, Hans Christian. 2010. (Candlewick Illustrated Classic Ser.). (ENG.). 208p. (J). (gr. 3-7). pap. 12.99 *(978-0-7636-4892-3(2))* Candlewick Pr.

Stewart, Joel. Addis Berner Bear Forgets. Stewart, Joel. 2008. (ENG.). 32p. (J). (gr. -1-1). 16.95 *(978-0-374-30036-4(4)*, Farrar, Straus & Giroux (BYR)) Farrar, Straus & Giroux.

—Dexter Bexley & the Big Blue Beastie. Stewart, Joel. 2007. (ENG.). 32p. (J). (gr. -1-3). 16.95 *(978-0-8234-2068-1(X))* Holiday Hse., Inc.

Stewart, K. L. Happy the Hippo: Eats Healthy Food. Hoyes, Amy & Reimann, A. J. 2013. 24p. pap. 9.99 *(978-1-938743-08-5(3))* Reimann Bks.

Stewart, Lisa. Jam for Nana. Kelly, Deborah. 2014. 32p. (J). (gr. k-2). 9.99 *(978-0-85798-001-4(7))* Random Hse. Australia AUS. Dist: Independent Pubs. Group.

Stewart, Michael G. Noises from under the Rug: The Barry Louis Polisar Songbook. Polisar, Barry Louis. rev. ed. 2006. (ENG.). 32p. (gr. 4-7). per. 7.95 *(978-0-938663-24-9(0))* Rainbow Morning Music Alternatives.

Stewart, Muriel. My Mommy's Getting Married. Chambers, Pamela G. 2009. 32p. (gr. -1-3). 17.95 *(978-0-9799487-0-1(3))* Infinity Publishing Co.

Stewart, Pat, jt. illus. see Kerr, George.

Stewart, Pat Ronson, jt. illus. see Cady, Harrison.

Stewart, Pat Ronson, jt. illus. see Kerr, George.

Stewart, Roger. Captured by Pirates! An Isabel Soto History Adventure, 1 vol. Biskup, Agnieszka. 2012. (Graphic Expeditions Ser.). (ENG.). 32p. (gr. 3-4). pap. 8.10 *(978-1-4296-7991-6(3))*; pap. 47.70 *(978-1-4296-8471-2(2))*; lib. bdg. 29.99 *(978-1-4296-7545-1(4))* Capstone Pr., Inc. (Graphic Library).

—Egypt's Mysterious Pyramids: An Isabel Soto Archaeology Adventure. Biskup, Agnieszka. 2012. (Graphic Expeditions Ser.). (ENG.). 32p. (gr. 3-4). pap. 47.70 *(978-1-4296-8472-9(0)*, Graphic Library) Capstone Pr., Inc.

—Graphic Expeditions. Biskup, Agnieszka. 2012. (Graphic Expeditions Ser.). (ENG.). 32p. (gr. 3-4). pap. 111.30 *(978-1-4296-8473-6(9))*; pap. 667.80 *(978-1-4296-8474-3(7))*; pap. 15.90 *(978-1-4296-9511-4(0))*; lib. bdg. 419.86 *(978-1-4296-8176-6(4))*; lib. bdg. 59.98 *(978-1-4296-8174-2(8))* Capstone Pr., Inc. (Graphic Library).

Stewart, Scott. Robo Monster. Black, Jake & Meredith Books Staff. 2008. 22p. (J). pap. 3.99 *(978-0-696-23957-1(4))* Meredith Bks.

Stewart, Yale. Alien Superman!, 1 vol. Stewart, Yale. 2014. (Amazing Adventures of Superman! Ser.). (ENG.). 32p. (gr. k-2). lib. bdg. 23.99 *(978-1-4795-5733-2(1))* Picture Window Bks.

—The Amazing Adventures of Superman, 1 vol. Stewart, Yale. 2014. (Amazing Adventures of Superman! Ser.). (ENG.). 32p. (gr. k-2). 95.96 *(978-1-4795-5816-2(8)*, DC Super Heroes) Stone Arch Bks.

—Battle of the Super Heroes!, 1 vol. Stewart, Yale. 2014. (Amazing Adventures of Superman! Ser.). (ENG.). 32p. (gr. k-2). 23.99 *(978-1-4795-5731-8(5))* Picture Window Bks.

—Creatures from Planet X!, 1 vol. Stewart, Yale. 2014. (Amazing Adventures of Superman! Ser.). (ENG.). 32p. (gr. k-2). lib. bdg. 23.99 *(978-1-4795-5734-9(X))* Picture Window Bks.

—Escape from Future World!, 1 vol. Stewart, Yale. 2014. (Amazing Adventures of Superman! Ser.). (ENG.). 32p. (gr. k-2). lib. bdg. 23.99 *(978-1-4795-5732-5(3))* Picture Window Bks.

Steyert, Bill. Queen Esther's New Coloring Book. Brodsky, Irene. 2011. 39p. pap. 17.95 *(978-1-4327-6771-6(2))* Outskirts Pr., Inc.

Stich, Carolyn R. The Barefoot Boys of Fayette. Henry, Regene. 2005. 180p. (J). (gr. 4-7). pap. 9.95 *(978-0-9749412-3-3(9))* EDCO Publishing, Inc.

—Water Words Rhymed & Defined. McKinney, Barbara Shaw. 2007. 30p. (J). (gr. 4-7). 19.95 *(978-0-9712692-8-6(9))* EDCO Publishing, Inc.

Stich, Carolyn R. Atsa & Ga: A Story from the High Desert. Stroschin, Jane H. 2005. 32p. (J). (gr. k-6). *(978-1-883960-29-2(0))* Henry Quill Pr.

Stickland, Paul. Dinosaur More! A First Book of Dinosaur Facts. Stickland, Henrietta. 2009. (ENG.). 32p. (J). (gr. -1-2). 9.95 *(978-1-4027-6494-3(4))* Sterling Publishing Co., Inc.

Stickland, Shadra. A Place Where Hurricanes Happen. Watson, Renée. 2014. (ENG.). 40p. (J). (gr. k-4). 7.99 *(978-0-385-37668-6(5)*, Dragonfly Bks.) Random Hse. Children's Bks.

Stickland, Shadra. White Water. Bandy, Michael S. & Stein, Eric. 2015. (ENG.). 40p. (J). (gr. k-3). 7.99 ***(978-0-7636-7945-3(3))*** Candlewick Pr.

Stickley, Kelly. Little Train! Mysak, Mary. 2004. 16p. (J). 7.50 *(978-0-9762274-0-3(1))* Helping Hands Children's Bks.

Stieber, Joel. Secret of the Tree: Marcus Speer's Ecosentinel. MacDonald, Tom. 2009. 300p. 28.95 *(978-0-595-51985-9(7))*; pap. 18.95 *(978-0-595-52402-0(8))* iUniverse, Inc.

Stietencron, Bettina. Hut in the Forest, 1 vol. Grimm, Jacob & Grimm, Wilhelm K. Lawson, Polly, tr. from GER. 2007. (Grimm's Fairy Tales Ser.). (ENG.). 28p. (J). *(978-0-86315-615-1(0))* Floris Bks.

Stiffler, Michael. You Are a Twisting Tornado. Malavolti, Angela. 2011. 28p. (J). 16.99 *(978-0-9834092-0-5(X))* Jungle Wagon Pr.

Stigler, Marilyn. Into the Hidden Lands: A Castle Rose Adventure. Franz, Kevin. 2004. 112p. (J). per. 7.99 *(978-0-9747774-0-5(4))* Starbell Bks.

—The Princess Sisters & the Underwater City. Franz, Kevin. 2004. 112p. (J). per. 7.99 *(978-0-9747774-1-2(2))* Starbell Bks.

Stiglich, Tom. Goin' to the Zoo / Vamos Al Zoologico. Adams, William J. 2007. (ENG & SPA.). 58p. (J). pap. 10.95 *(978-0-9772757-2-4(8))* Mandy & Andy Bks., Inc.

—Goin' to the Zoo Coloring Book: Vamos Al Zoologico. Adams, William J. 2007. (ENG & SPA.). (J). pap. 3.95 *(978-0-9772757-3-1(6))* Mandy & Andy Bks., Inc.

—Hate that Thunder. Adams, William J. 2005. 24p. (J). pap. 8.95 *(978-0-9772757-0-0(1))* Mandy & Andy Bks., Inc.

—Hate That Thunder/Odio Ese Trueno, 1 vol. Adams, William J. 2007. (Mandy & Andy Bks.). (ENG & SPA.). 49p. (J). (gr. k-2). per. 10.95 *(978-0-9772757-1-7(X))* Mandy & Andy Bks., Inc.

—Visiting the Farm / Visitando la Granja. Adams, William J. 2008. (ENG & SPA.). (J). pap. 10.95 *(978-0-9772757-4-8(4))* Mandy & Andy Bks., Inc.

—Visiting the Farm / Visitando la Granja Coloring Book. Adams, William J. 2008. (ENG & SPA.). 26p. (J). pap. 3.95 *(978-0-9772757-5-5(2))* Mandy & Andy Bks., Inc.

—Woe Is I Jr. The Younger Grammarphobe's Guide to Better English in Plain English. O'Conner, Patricia T. 2007. (ENG.). 176p. (J). (gr. 3-7). 16.99 *(978-0-399-24331-8(3)*, Putnam Juvenile) Penguin Publishing Group.

Stileman, Kali. Big Book of My World. 2012. 48p. (J). *(978-1-58925-114-4(8))* Tiger Tales.

Stiles, Tim. William Penn: Founder of Pennsylvania. Jacobson, Ryan. 2006. (Graphic Biographies Ser.). (ENG.). 32p. (gr. 3-4). 29.99 *(978-0-7368-6501-2(2)*, Graphic Library) Capstone Pr., Inc.

Still, Wayne A. A Salute to African American Architects: Learning Activities. Chandler, Alton. Chapman, Loring F., ed. 24p. (Orig.). (J). (gr. 3-8). pap. 1.75 *(978-1-877804-16-8(9))* Chandler/White Publishing Co.

—A Salute to African American in Medicine: Learning. Chandler, Alton. Chapman, L., ed. 24p. (Orig.). (J). (gr. 3-8). pap. 1.75 *(978-1-877804-17-5(7))* Chandler/White Publishing Co.

—A Salute to Black Inventors Vol. 2: Coloring Learning Activities. Howell, Ann C. & Chandler, Alton. Chapman, L., ed. 96p. (J). (gr. 3-8). pap. 6.95 *(978-1-877804-19-9(3))* Chandler/White Publishing Co.

Still, Wayne A. & Hayden, Seitu. A Salute to Black Inventor, Dr. Georde Washington Carver: The Peanut Wizard. Chandler, Alton. Chapman, L., ed. 24p. (Orig.). (J). (gr. 3-8). pap. 1.75 *(978-1-877804-15-1(0))* Chandler/White Publishing Co.

Stille, Darlene R. Anne Hutchinson: Puritan Protester, 1 vol. Stille, Darlene R. 2006. (Signature Lives: Colonial America Ser.). (ENG.). 112p. (gr. 6-7). lib. bdg. 35.32 *(978-0-7565-1577-5(7)*, Signature Lives) Compass Point Bks.

Stille, Ljuba. Mia's Thumb. Stille, Ljuba. Mundt, Anja. 2014. (ENG.). 32p. (J). (gr. -1-k). 16.95 *(978-0-8234-3067-3(7))* Holiday Hse., Inc.

Stillerman, Robbie. Make Your Own Laptop: Color & Build Your Own Computer! Pearlstein, Don. 2011. (Dover Children's Activity Bks.). (ENG.). 12p. (J). (gr. -1-2). 9.99 *(978-0-486-48532-4(3))* Dover Pubns., Inc.

Stillview, photos by. Mini Temporary Tattoos. Top That! Team Staff. 2005. 51p. (J). (gr. 4-8). reprint ed. pap. 8.00 *(978-0-7567-9417-0(X))* DIANE Publishing Co.

Stillwell, Heath. The Haunted Dog House. Johnson, Sandi. Brundige, Britt & Durant, Sybrina, eds. 2014. (Spooky Ser.). 32p. (J). (gr. -1-6). pap. 12.99 *(978-1-929063-50-5(4)*, 149) Moons & Stars Publishing For Children.

Stillwell, Jennifer. The I Love You Mom Coupon Book: 28 Ways to Show Mom You Appreciate Her Every Day, 4. Loveland-Coen, Victoria. 2007. (Give a Little Love Ser.: 4). 62p. (J). pap. 5.95 *(978-0-9644765-8-5(4))* Love & Blessings.

Stimpson, Colin. Germs! Howard, Martin. 2012. (ENG.). 32p. (J). (gr. k-3). 16.99 *(978-1-84365-119-2(X)*, Pavilion Children's Books) Pavilion Bks. GBR. Dist: Independent Pubs. Group.

—Germs! An Epic Tale on a Tiny Scale! Howard, Martin. 2013. (ENG.). 32p. (J). (gr. k-3). pap. 8.99 *(978-1-84365-185-7(8)*, Pavilion) Pavilion Bks. GBR. Dist: Independent Pubs. Group.

—How to Cook Children: A Grisly Recipe Book for Gruesome Witches. Howard, Martin. 2011. (ENG.). 80p. (J). (gr. 4-7). pap. 9.99 *(978-1-84365-179-6(3)*, Pavilion Children's Books) Pavilion Bks. GBR. Dist: Independent Pubs. Group.

—The White Wand. Howard, Martin. 2011. (Witches at War! Ser.: 2). (ENG.). 204p. (J). (gr. 3-7). 12.99 *(978-1-84365-134-5(3)*, Pavilion Children's Books) Pavilion Bks. GBR. Dist: Independent Pubs. Group.

—The Wild Winter. Howard, Martin. 2012. (Witches at War! Ser.: 3). (ENG.). 214p. (J). (gr. 3-7). 12.99 *(978-1-84365-180-2(7)*, Pavilion Children's Books) Pavilion Bks. GBR. Dist: Independent Pubs. Group.

Stimpson, Colin. Jack & the Baked Beanstalk. Stimpson, Colin. 2012. (ENG.). 40p. (J). (gr. -1-2). 15.99 *(978-0-7636-5563-1(5)*, Templar) Candlewick Pr.

Stimson, James. The Bully Goat Grim: A Maynard Moose Tale. 2012. (ENG.). 32p. (J). (gr. 2-6). 18.95 *(978-0-87483-952-4(1))* August Hse. Pubs., Inc.

—The Little Moose Who Couldn't Go to Sleep. Claflin, Willy. 2014. (ENG.). 36p. 18.95 *(978-1-939160-67-6(7))* August Hse. Pubs., Inc.

—Rapunzel & the Seven Dwarfs: A Maynard Moose Tale. Claflin, Willy. 2011. (ENG.). 32p. (J). (gr. -1-3). 18.95 *(978-0-87483-914-2(9))* August Hse. Pubs., Inc.

—The Uglified Ducky. Claflin, Willy. 2011. (ENG.). 32p. (J). (gr. -1-3). 9.95 *(978-0-87483-953-1(X))* August Hse. Pubs., Inc.

Stimson, James. Thirteen O'Clock. Stimson, James. 2005. (ENG.). 40p. (J). (gr. -1-2). 15.95 *(978-0-8118-4839-8(6))* Chronicle Bks. LLC.

Stislow, John. Baby-Gami: Baby Wrapping for Beginners. Milne, Bill, photos by. Sarvady, Andrea et al. 2005. (ENG.). 96p. (gr. 8-17). 16.95 *(978-0-8118-4764-3(0))* Chronicle Bks. LLC.

Stites, Theresa. Wolf. Porter, Harry. 2012. 28p. pap. 14.99 *(978-0-9838018-5-6(1))* 4RV Publishing, LLC.

Stitt, Sue. Big Book of Things to Do: Combined Volume. Gibson, Ray. 2004. (What Shall I Do Today? Ser.). 192p. (J). pap. 18.95 *(978-0-7945-0442-7(6)*, Usborne) EDC Publishing.

—Who Built the Pyramids? Chisholm, Jane & Reid, Straun. 2004. (Starting Point History Ser.). 32p. (J). (gr. 1). lib. bdg. 12.95 *(978-1-58086-629-3(8)*, Usborne) EDC Publishing.

Stiver, Megan. The Great Bellybutton Cover-Up. 2011. 32p. *(978-0-9810634-7-8(0))* Susan Ross (self publishing).

—Say Please to the Honeybees. 2010. 33p. *(978-0-9810634-3-0(8))* Susan Ross (self publishing).

sto. The Chess Set in the Mirror. Bontempelli, Massimo. Gilson, Estelle, tr. from ITA. 2007. (Nautilus Ser.). (ENG.). 114p. (J). (gr. 7-9). per. 9.95 *(978-1-58988-031-3(5))* Dry, Paul Bks., Inc.

Stock, Catherine. After the Kill. Lunde, Darrin P. 2011. (ENG.). 32p. (J). (gr. 1-4). 16.95 *(978-1-57091-743-1(4))*; pap. 7.95 *(978-1-57091-744-8(2))* Charlesbridge Publishing, Inc.

—The Daring Miss Quimby. Whitaker, Suzanne George. 2009. (ENG.). 32p. (J). (gr. -1-3). 16.95 *(978-0-8234-1996-8(7))* Holiday Hse., Inc.

—Emily & Carlo. Figley, Marty Rhodes. 2012. (ENG.). 32p. (J). (gr. k-3). 15.95 *(978-1-58089-274-2(4))* Charlesbridge Publishing, Inc.

Stock, Catherine. Galimoto. Williams, Karen Lynn. 2015. 32p. pap. 7.00 ***(978-1-61003-604-7(2))*** Center for the Collaborative Classroom.

Stock, Catherine. Justin & the Best Biscuits in the World. Walter, Mildred Pitts. 2010. (ENG.). 144p. (J). (gr. 3-7). pap. 5.99 *(978-0-06-195891-5(3)*, Amistad) HarperCollins Pubs.

Stock, Catherine. Karl, Get Out of the Garden! Carolus Linnaeus & the Naming of Everything. Sanchez, Anita. 2016. (J). lib. bdg. ***(978-1-58089-606-1(5))*** Charlesbridge Publishing, Inc.

Stock, Catherine. My Name Is Sangoel. Mohammed, Khadra & Williams, Karen Lynn. 2009. 36p. (J). (gr. 1-5). 17.00 *(978-0-8028-5307-3(2)*, Eerdmans Bks For Young Readers) Eerdmans, William B. Publishing Co.

—Ready & Waiting for You. Moreillon, Judi. 2013. 32p. 17.00 *(978-0-8028-5355-4(2)*, Eerdmans Bks For Young Readers) Eerdmans, William B. Publishing Co.

—Vinnie & Abraham. FitzGerald, Dawn. 2007. (ENG.). 48p. (J). (gr. k-3). lib. bdg. 16.95 *(978-1-57091-658-8(6))* Charlesbridge Publishing, Inc.

Stock, Rose. Catfish & Spaghetti. Freeman, Marcia S. 2013. (Maupin House Ser.). (ENG.). 48p. (gr. 3-5). pap. 4.50 *(978-0-929895-21-5(5))* Maupin Hse. Publishing.

Stockdale, Susan. Bring on the Birds, 1 vol. Stockdale, Susan. (ENG.). (J). (gr. -1 — 1). 2013. 22p. bds. 6.95 *(978-1-56145-692-5(6))*; 2011. 32p. 16.95 *(978-1-56145-560-7(1))* Peachtree Pubs.

—Carry Me! Animal Babies on the Move, 1 vol. Stockdale, Susan. (ENG.). 32p. (J). (gr. k-1). 2008. pap. 7.95 *(978-1-56145-449-5(4))*; 2005. 15.95 *(978-1-56145-328-3(5))* Peachtree Pubs.

—Fabulous Fishes, 1 vol. Stockdale, Susan. 2008. (ENG.). 32p. (J). (gr. k-1). 15.95 *(978-1-56145-429-7(X))* Peachtree Pubs.

—Spectacular Spots, 1 vol. Stockdale, Susan. 2015. (ENG.). 32p. (J). (gr. 1-1). 15.95 *(978-1-56145-817-2(1))* Peachtree Pubs.

—Stripes of All Types, 1 vol. Stockdale, Susan. 2013. (About Habitats Ser.). (ENG.). 32p. (J). (gr. -1-1). 16.95 *(978-1-56145-695-6(0))* Peachtree Pubs.

—Stripes of All Types / Rayas de Todas Las Tallas, 1 vol. Stockdale, Susan. ed. 2014. (SPA & ENG.). 32p. (J). (gr. -1-1). pap. 8.95 *(978-1-56145-793-9(0))* Peachtree Pubs.

Stockelbach, Ed. The Little Girl Who Did... What?!!! Dupuy, Diane. 2004. 32p. 12.95 *(978-0-9730736-0-7(8))* Beyond Light CAN. Dist: Hushion Hse. Publishing, Ltd.

Stockham, Jess. Baby Sitter. 2009. (First Time Ser.). (ENG.). 24p. (J). (gr. -1-k). *(978-1-84643-279-8(0))* Child's Play International Ltd.

—Beauty & the Beast. 2007. (Flip-Up Fairy Tales Ser.). (ENG.). 24p. (J). (gr. -1-2). *(978-1-84643-155-5(7))*; *(978-1-84643-114-2(X))* Child's Play International Ltd.

—Beauty & the Beast: Flip up Fairy Tales. 2008. (Flip-Up Fairy Tales Ser.). (ENG.). 24p. (J). *(978-1-84643-194-4(8))* Child's Play International Ltd.

—Big Day Out. 2009. (First Time Ser.). (ENG.). 24p. (J). (gr. -1-k). *(978-1-84643-282-8(0))* Child's Play International Ltd.

—The Boy Who Cried Wolf. 2011. (Flip-Up Fairy Tales Ser.). (ENG.). 24p. (J). *(978-1-84643-368-9(1))*; *(978-1-84643-407-5(6))* Child's Play International Ltd.

—Cinderella. (Classic Fairy Tales Ser.). (ENG.). 24p. (J). 2011. *(978-1-84643-440-2(8))*; 2011. *(978-1-84643-455-6(6))*; 2007. (gr. -1-2). *(978-1-84643-091-6(7))*; 2005. (gr. -1-k). *(978-1-904550-46-4(0))* Child's Play International Ltd.

—The Cockerel, the Mouse & the Little Red Hen. (Flip-Up Fairy Tales Ser.). (ENG.). 24p. (J). 2007. (gr. -1-2). *(978-1-84643-092-3(5))*; 2006. (gr. -1-2). *(978-1-904550-75-4(4))*; 2005. *(978-1-904550-47-1(9))* Child's Play International Ltd.

—The Ding-Dong Bag. Peters, Polly. 2006. (Child's Play Library). (ENG.). 32p. (J). (gr. -1-3). *(978-1-84643-015-2(1))* Child's Play International Ltd.

—Down by the Station. Twinn, A. 2007. (Classic Books with Holes 8x8 with CD Ser.). (ENG.). 16p. (J). (gr. -1-1). *(978-1-904550-68-6(1))* Child's Play International Ltd.

—Feeling Great!/Sentirse Bien! 2013. (Just Like Me! Ser.). (ENG & SPA.). 12p. (gr. -1). bds. *(978-1-84643-561-4(7))* Child's Play International Ltd.

Stockham, Jess, et al. The Frog Prince. 2007. (Flip-Up Fairy Tales Ser.). (ENG.). 24p. (J). pap. *(978-1-84643-077-0(1))* Child's Play International Ltd.

Stockham, Jess. The Frog Prince. 2007. (Flip-Up Fairy Tales Ser.). (ENG.). 24p. (J). *(978-1-84643-143-2(3))* Child's Play International Ltd.

—It's Raining, It's Pouring, We're Exploring. Peters, Polly. 2007. (Child's Play Library). (ENG.). 32p. (J). (gr. -1-3). pap. *(978-1-84643-117-3(4))* Child's Play International Ltd.

—Little Red Riding Hood. (Classic Fairy Tales Ser.). (ENG.). 24p. (J). 2011. *(978-1-84643-439-6(4))*; 2011. *(978-1-84643-458-7(0))*; 2007. (gr. -1-2). *(978-1-84643-088-6(7))* Child's Play International Ltd.

—Looking Good!/Lucir Bien! 2013. (Just Like Me! Ser.). (ENG & SPA.). 12p. (gr. -1). bds. *(978-1-84643-560-7(9))* Child's Play International Ltd.

—Moving House! 2011. (Helping Hands Ser.). 24p. (J). *(978-1-84643-414-3(9))* Child's Play International Ltd.

—Nursery. 2009. (First Time Ser.). (ENG.). 24p. (J). (gr. -1-k). *(978-1-84643-281-1(2))* Child's Play International Ltd.

—Oh Baby! 2006. (Blanket Babies Ser.). (ENG.). 12p. (J). (gr. -1-k). bds. *(978-1-904550-87-7(8))* Child's Play International Ltd.

—On the Go!/a Moverse! 2013. (Just Like Me! Ser.). (ENG & SPA.). 12p. (gr. -1). bds. *(978-1-84643-563-8(3))* Child's Play International Ltd.

—Party! 2011. (Helping Hands Ser.). (ENG.). 24p. (J). *(978-1-84643-413-6(0))* Child's Play International Ltd.

—Peekaboo- Forest. 2011. (Child's Play Library). (ENG.). 10p. (J). bds. *(978-1-84643-454-9(8))* Child's Play International Ltd.

—Peekaboo- Ocean. 2011. (Child's Play Library). (ENG.). 10p. (J). bds. *(978-1-84643-453-2(X))* Child's Play International Ltd.

—Peekaboo- Safari. 2011. (Child's Play Library). (ENG.). 10p. (J). bds. *(978-1-84643-452-5(1))* Child's Play International Ltd.

—Peekaboo-Jungle. 2011. (Child's Play Library). (ENG.). 10p. (J). bds. *(978-1-84643-451-8(3))* Child's Play International Ltd.

—Peep-O! 2006. (Blanket Babies Ser.). (ENG.). 12p. (J). (gr. -1-k). bds. *(978-1-904550-88-4(6))* Child's Play International Ltd.

—The Princess & the Pea. 2010. (Flip-Up Fairy Tales Ser.). (ENG.). 24p. (J). (gr. -1-2). *(978-1-84643-332-0(0))* Child's Play International Ltd.

—Puss in Boots. 2012. (Classic Fairy Tales Ser.). (ENG.). 24p. (J). *(978-1-84643-441-9(6))* Child's Play International Ltd.

—Recycling! 2011. (Helping Hands Ser.). (ENG.). 24p. (J). *(978-1-84643-415-0(7))* Child's Play International Ltd.

—Shopping! 2011. (Helping Hands Ser.). (ENG.). 24p. (J). *(978-1-84643-412-9(2))* Child's Play International Ltd.

—Sleep Tight! Baker, Sue & Stockham, Jessica. 2006. (Blanket Babies Ser.). (ENG.). 12p. (J). (gr. -1-k). bds. *(978-1-904550-90-7(8))* Child's Play International Ltd.

—Sleepover. 2009. (First Time Ser.). (ENG.). 24p. (J). (gr. -1-k). *(978-1-84643-280-4(4))* Child's Play International Ltd.

—The Steadfast Tin Soldier. 2012. (Flip-Up Fairy Tales Ser.). (ENG.). 24p. (J). *(978-1-84643-516-4(1))*; *(978-1-84643-477-8(7))* Child's Play International Ltd.

—Stone Soup. (Flip-Up Fairy Tales Ser.). (ENG.). 24p. (J). (gr. -1-2). 2007. *(978-1-84643-094-7(1))*; 2006. pap. *(978-1-84643-021-3(6))* Child's Play International Ltd.

—Town Mouse, Country Mouse. 2012. (Flip-Up Fairy Tales Ser.). (ENG.). 24p. (J). *(978-1-84643-518-8(8))*; *(978-1-84643-479-2(3))* Child's Play International Ltd.

—Wash Day! Baker, Sue & Stockham, Jessica. 2006. (Blanket Babies Ser.). (ENG.). 12p. (J). (gr. -1-k). bds. *(978-1-904550-89-1(4))* Child's Play International Ltd.

Stockham, Jessica. Little Red Riding Hood. 2005. (Flip-Up Fairy Tales Ser.). (ENG.). 24p. (J). pap. *(978-1-904550-22-8(3))* Child's Play International Ltd.

—Princess & the Pea. 2009. (Flip-Up Fairy Tales Ser.). (ENG.). 24p. (J). (gr. -1-2). pap. *(978-1-84643-326-9(6))* Child's Play International Ltd.

—Visiting the Dentist. 2011. (First Time Ser.). (ENG.). 24p. (J). pap. *(978-1-84643-335-1(5))* Child's Play International Ltd.

—Visiting the Doctor. 2011. (First Time Ser.). (ENG.). 24p. (J). pap. *(978-1-84643-334-4(7))* Child's Play International Ltd.

—Visiting the Hospital. 2011. (First Time Ser.). (ENG.). 24p. (J). pap. *(978-1-84643-336-8(3))* Child's Play International Ltd.

—Visiting the Vet. 2011. (First Time Ser.). (ENG.). 24p. (J). pap. *(978-1-84643-337-5(1))* Child's Play International Ltd.

Stockham, Jessica. Down by the Station. Stockham, Jessica, tr. 2003. (Classic Books with Holes 8x8 Ser.). (ENG.). 16p. (J). *(978-0-85953-132-0(5))* Child's Play International Ltd.

Stockley, Gerry. Mac, Information Detective, in the Curious Kids... - Digging for Answers: A Storybook Approach to Introducing Research Skills, 2 vols. Arnone, Marilyn P. & Coatney, Sharon. 2006. 104p. 35.00 *(978-1-59158-397-4(7)*, LU3977) Libraries Unlimited, Inc.

Stockman, Jack. Benjamin's Box: The Story of the Resurrection Eggs, 1 vol. Carlson, Melody. rev. ed. 2008. (ENG.). 40p. (J). (gr. -1-3). 7.99 *(978-0-310-71505-4(9))* Zonderkidz.

Stockton, Frank. World Without Fish. Kurlansky, Mark. (ENG.). (J). 2014. 208p. (gr. 5). pap. 14.95 *(978-0-7611-8500-0(3))*; 2011. 192p. (gr. 4-7). 16.95 *(978-0-7611-5607-9(0)*, 15607) Workman Publishing Co., Inc.

Stockton, Greta & Philbrick, Katie. Goddesses of Legend & Myth: A Coloring Book Celebrating the Heroines of Ancient Europe. Toutz-Hager, Tanya. Date not set. 40p. (YA). (gr. 4-12). pap. 8.95 *(978-0-9672107-0-4(4))* MoonStar Pr.

Stockton, Kevin. Silly Kitty! Joke & Coloring Book. Batcher, Jack. 2011. (ENG.). 34p. pap. 7.95 *(978-1-4664-7465-9(3))* CreateSpace Independent Publishing Platform.

Stockwell, Pel. Fandango: The Key to the Wind. Stockwell, Jeff. 2007. 58p. (YA). per. 22.50 *(978-0-9785594-0-3(1))* Stockwell Publishing.

Stoddard, Jeff. The Garden Wall: A Story of Love Based on I Corinthians 13. Bishop, Jennie. 2006. (ENG.). 32p. (J). (gr. 2-7). 12.99 *(978-1-59317-168-1(4))* Warner Pr. Pubs.

Stoddard, Jeffery. Pete & Pillar: A Story of Friendship Based on John 15:13: the Big Rain. Stoddard, Jeffery. 2007. (Pete & Pillar Ser.). (ENG.). 32p. (J). (gr. -1-2). 12.99 *(978-1-59317-203-9(6))* Warner Pr. Pubs.

—Skid & the Too Tiny Tunnel: A Story of Courage Based on Deuteronomy 31:6. Stoddard, Jeffery. Fogle, Robin & Rhodes, Karen, eds. 2009. (ENG.). 32p. (J). (gr. -1-2). 12.99 *(978-1-59317-355-5(5))* Warner Pr. Pubs.

Stodden, Lindsay. Our Cat Hogan - Could He Be Part Dog? Powell, Anthony. 2012. 24p. (J). 19.95 *(978-1-61863-358-3(9))* Bookstand Publishing.

Stoeke, Janet Morgan. Letting Go. Stoeke, Janet Morgan. 2015. (Loopy Coop Hens Ser.). (ENG.). 32p. (J). (gr. 1-2). pap. 3.99 *(978-0-448-48458-7(7)*, Warne, Frederick Pubs.) Penguin Bks., Ltd. GBR. Dist: Penguin Publishing Group.

—The Loopy Coop Hens. Stoeke, Janet Morgan. 2013. (Loopy Coop Hens Ser.). (ENG.). 32p. (J). (gr. 1-2). mass mkt. 3.99 *(978-0-448-46272-1(9)*, Warne, Frederick Pubs.) Penguin Bks., Ltd. GBR. Dist: Penguin Random Hse., LLC.

—Minerva Louise on Christmas Eve. Stoeke, Janet Morgan. 2009. (ENG.). 32p. (J). (gr. -1-k). pap. 6.99 *(978-0-14-241449-1(2)*, Puffin) Penguin Publishing Group.

—Minerva Louise on Halloween. Stoeke, Janet Morgan. 2009. (ENG.). 24p. (J). (gr. -1-k). 16.99 *(978-0-525-42149-8(1)*, Dutton Juvenile) Penguin Publishing Group.

—Pip's Trip. Stoeke, Janet Morgan. 2014. (Loopy Coop Hens Ser.). (ENG.). 32p. (J). (gr. 1-2). pap. 3.99 *(978-0-448-48133-3(2)*, Warne, Frederick Pubs.) Penguin Bks., Ltd. GBR. Dist: Penguin Random Hse., LLC.

Stoffel, Dominique, jt. photos by see Amann, Remy.

Stoh, Judy. Roger Meets Sam. Stoh, Emily. 2009. 24p. pap. 9.95 *(978-1-935105-41-1(8))* Avid Readers Publishing Group.

Stoick, Jean & Sams, Carl R., II, photos by. First Snow in the Woods. 2007. (ENG., 49p. (J). (gr. -1-3). 19.95 *(978-0-9770108-6-8(4))* Sams, II, Carl R. Photography, Inc.

Stoick, Jean & Sams II, Carl R., photos by. Stranger in the Woods: Snowflake Edition. 2010. (ENG., 48p. 21.95 *(978-0-9827625-0-9(X))* Sams, II, Carl R. Photography, Inc.

Stoick, Jean, jt. photos by see Sams, Carl R., II.

Stoick, Jean, jt. photos by see Sams, Carl R., 2nd.

Stoick, Jean, jt. photos by see Sams, Carl R., II.

Stoick, Jean, jt. photos by see Sams II, Carl R.

Stojanova, Elena. Oranges for Everyone. Zake, Daiga. 2007. 32p. (J). (ARA.). pap. 12.95 *(978-1-60195-306-3(2))*; (POL & ENG.). pap. 12.95 *(978-1-60195-104-5(3))* International Step by Step Assn.

Stojanovic, Laura & Frankeny, Frankie, photos by. Mini Bar - Rum: Little Book of Big Drinks. Hellmich, Mittie. 2007. (ENG., 80p. (gr. 8-17). 7.95 *(978-0-8118-5438-2(8))* Chronicle Bks. LLC.

Stojic, Manya. Baby Goes Too. Roddie, Shen. 2003. 32p. (YA). *(978-1-85602-460-0(1)*, Pavilion Children's Books) Pavilion Bks.

—Weather Report. Collins Educational Staff & Hawes, Alison. 2012. (Collins Big Cat Ser.). (ENG.). 16p. (J). pap., wbk. ed. 4.99 *(978-0-00-747290-1(0))* HarperCollins Pubs. Ltd. GBR. Dist: Independent Pubs. Group.

—Weather Report: Band 02a/Red A. Hawes, Alison. 2007. (Collins Big Cat Ser.). (ENG.). 16p. (J). pap. 5.99 *(978-0-00-718655-6(X))* HarperCollins Pubs. Ltd. GBR. Dist: Independent Pubs. Group.

Stojic, Manya. Rain. Stojic, Manya. 2009. (ENG.). 32p. (J). (gr. -1-2). pap. 7.99 *(978-0-385-73729-6(7)*, Dragonfly Bks.) Random Hse. Children's Bks.

Stojic, Manya & Hamilton, Allen. Happy Cat, Me! A Slide-the-Spot Book of Animals. Wilson-Max, Ken. 2005. 10p. (J). (gr. k-4). reprint ed. 10.00 *(978-0-7567-9364-7(5))* DIANE Publishing Co.

Stokes, John. The Importance of Being Earnest. Wilde, Oscar. Bryant, Clive, ed. 2014. (ENG.). 136p. (gr. 5). pap. 16.95 *(978-1-907127-31-1(3))* Classical Comics GBR. Dist: Perseus-PGW.

—The Importance of Being Earnest the Graphic Novel Quick Text: (American English) Wilde, Oscar. 2012. 144p. (J). pap. *(978-1-907127-32-8(1)*, Classical Comics, Ltd.) Classical Comics.

Stoll, Annie. Star Wars Rebels: Sabine My Rebel Sketchbook. Wallace, Daniel. 2015. (ENG.). 96p. (J). (gr. 1-5). 9.99 *(978-0-7944-3289-8(1))* Studio Fun International.

Stollinger, Heide. Donkeys. Dahiméne, Adelheid. 2014. (ENG.). 48p. (J). (gr. k-3). 17.95 *(978-0-7358-4160-4(8))* North-South Bks., Inc.

Stoloff, Maxene. Maxy Poppinz: A Contemporary Tale about a Girl & Her New Nanny. Stoloff, Maxene. 2011. (ENG.). 32p. pap. 11.95 *(978-1-4664-3859-0(2))* CreateSpace Independent Publishing Platform.

Stoltenberg, Nathan. Lily Hates Goodbyes. Marler, Jerilyn. 2012. 32p. pap. 6.95 *(978-1-936214-78-5(4))* Wyatt-MacKenzie Publishing.

Stomann, Allan. Selby Santa. Ball, Duncan. ed. 2007. 192p. *(978-0-7322-8679-8(4))* HarperCollins Pubs. Australia.

—Selby Scrambled. Ball, Duncan. 2004. 208p. *(978-0-207-19911-0(6))* HarperCollins Pubs. Australia.

—Selby Screams. Ball, Duncan. 2004. 192p. *(978-0-207-20023-6(8))* HarperCollins Pubs. Australia.

—Selby Shattered. Ball, Duncan. 2006. 192p. *(978-0-207-20066-3(1))* HarperCollins Pubs. Australia.

—Selby Snaps. Ball, Duncan. 2004. 208p. (Orig.). *(978-0-207-20020-5(3))* HarperCollins Pubs. Australia.

—Selby Snowbound. Ball, Duncan. 2004. 192p. (Orig.). *(978-0-207-20019-9(X))* HarperCollins Pubs. Australia.

—Selby Sorcerer. Ball, Duncan. 2003. 208p. *(978-0-207-19861-8(6))* HarperCollins Pubs. Australia.

—Selby Spacedog. Ball, Duncan. 2003. 176p. *(978-0-207-20006-9(8))* HarperCollins Pubs. Australia.

—Selby Speaks. Ball, Duncan. 2004. 176p. *(978-0-207-20024-3(6))* HarperCollins Pubs. Australia.

—Selby Splits. Ball, Duncan. 2004. 224p. *(978-0-207-20025-0(4))* HarperCollins Pubs. Australia.

—Selby Supersnoop. Ball, Duncan. 2003. 176p. *(978-0-207-20005-2(X))* HarperCollins Pubs. Australia.

—Selby Surfs. Ball, Duncan. 2003. 208p. *(978-0-207-20003-8(3))* HarperCollins Pubs. Australia.

—Selby's Secret. Ball, Duncan. 2003. 160p. *(978-0-207-20004-5(1))* HarperCollins Pubs. Australia.

—Selby's Selection. Ball, Duncan. 2006. 192p. *(978-0-207-20040-3(8))* HarperCollins Pubs. Australia.

—Selby's Shemozzle. Ball, Duncan. 2005. 192p. (J). *(978-0-207-20030-4(0))* HarperCollins Pubs. Australia.

—Selby's Side-Splitting Joke Book. Ball, Duncan. 2006. 160p. *(978-0-207-20041-0(6))* HarperCollins Pubs. Australia.

—Selby's Stardom. Ball, Duncan. 2004. 192p. *(978-0-207-20021-2(1))* HarperCollins Pubs. Australia.

Stone, A. R. Lion in the Living Room. McKinna, Caelaach. 2008. 24p. (J). pap. 14.99 *(978-0-9797513-4-9(9))* 4RV Publishing, LLC.

Stone-Barker, Holly. The Biggest Pumpkin, 1 vol. Horning, Sandra. 2014. 32p. (J). 16.99 *(978-1-4556-1925-2(6))* Pelican Publishing Co., Inc.

—Blue Frog: The Legend of Chocolate, 1 vol. De Las Casas, Dianne. 2011. (ENG.). 32p. (J). (gr. k-3). 16.99 *(978-1-4556-1459-2(9))* Pelican Publishing Co., Inc.

—The House That Santa Built, 1 vol. De Las Casas, Dianne. 2013. (ENG.). 32p. (J). (gr. -1-k). 16.99 *(978-1-4556-1750-0(4))* Pelican Publishing Co., Inc.

—The House That Witchy Built, 1 vol. De Las Casas, Dianne. 2011. (ENG.). 32p. (J). (gr. k-k). 16.99 *(978-1-58980-965-9(3))* Pelican Publishing Co., Inc.

—The Little Read Hen, 1 vol. de Las Casas, Dianne. 2013. (ENG.). 32p. (J). (gr. -1-k). 16.99 *(978-1-4556-1702-9(4))* Pelican Publishing Co., Inc.

—Mama's Bayou, 1 vol. de Las Casas, Dianne. 2010. (ENG.). 32p. (J). (gr. k-k). 16.99 *(978-1-58980-787-7(1))* Pelican Publishing Co., Inc.

Stone, Bryan. Explore Colonial America! 25 Great Projects, Activities, Experiments. Fisher, Verna. 2009. (Explore Your World Ser.). (ENG.). 96p. (J). (gr. k-4). pap. 12.95 *(978-1-934670-37-8(5))* Nomad Pr.

—Explore Electricity! With 25 Great Projects. Van Vleet, Carmella. 2013. (Explore Your World Ser.). (ENG.). 96p. (J). (gr. k-4). pap. 13.95 *(978-1-61930-180-1(6))* Nomad Pr.

—Explore Flight! With 25 Great Projects. Yasuda, Anita. 2013. (Explore Your World Ser.). (ENG.). 96p. (J). (gr. k-4). pap. 13.95 *(978-1-61930-176-4(8))* Nomad Pr.

—Explore Gravity! With 25 Great Projects. Blobaum, Cindy. 2013. (Explore Your World Ser.). (ENG.). 96p. (J). (gr. k-4). pap. 13.95 *(978-1-61930-207-5(1))* Nomad Pr.

—Explore Honey Bees! With 25 Great Projects. Blobaum, Cindy. 2015. (Explore Your World Ser.). (ENG.). 96p. (J). (gr. 1-5). 19.95 *(978-1-61930-286-0(1))* Nomad Pr.

—Explore Life Cycles! 25 Great Projects, Activities, Experiments. Reilly, Kathleen M. 2011. (Explore Your World Ser.). (ENG.). 96p. (J). (gr. k-4). pap. 12.95 *(978-1-934670-80-4(4))* Nomad Pr.

—Explore Night Science! With 25 Great Projects. Blobaum, Cindy. 2012. (Explore Your World Ser.). (ENG.). 96p. (J). (gr. k-4). pap. 12.95 *(978-1-61930-156-6(3))* Nomad Pr.

—Explore Poetry! With 25 Great Projects. Diehn, Andi. 2015. (Explore Your World Ser.). (ENG.). 96p. (gr. 1-5). 19.95 *(978-1-61930-279-2(9))* Nomad Pr.

—Explore Rivers & Ponds! With 25 Great Projects. Mooney, Carla. 2012. (Explore Your World Ser.). (ENG.). 96p. (J). (gr. k-4). pap. 12.95 *(978-1-936749-80-5(7))* Nomad Pr.

—Explore Rocks & Minerals! 20 Great Projects, Activities, Experiments. Brown, Cynthia Light & Brown, Nick. 2010. (Explore Your World Ser.). (ENG.). 96p. (J). (gr. k-4). pap. 12.95 *(978-1-934670-61-3(8))* Nomad Pr.

—Explore Solids & Liquids! With 25 Great Projects. Reilly, Kathleen M. 2014. (Explore Your World Ser.). (ENG.). 96p. (J). (gr. 1-5). 19.95 *(978-1-61930-171-9(7))* Nomad Pr.

—Explore Water! 25 Great Projects, Activities, Experiments. Yasuda, Anita. 2011. (Explore Your World Ser.). (ENG.). 96p. (J). (gr. k-4). pap. 12.95 *(978-1-936313-42-6(1))* Nomad Pr.

—Explore Weather & Climate! With 25 Great Projects. Reilly, Kathleen M. 2012. (Explore Your World Ser.). (ENG.). 96p. (J). (gr. k-4). pap. 12.95 *(978-1-936313-84-6(7))* Nomad Pr.

—Music: Investigate the Evolution of American Sound. Latham, Donna. 2013. (Inquire & Investigate Ser.). (ENG.). 128p. (YA). (gr. 6-10). 21.95 *(978-1-61930-199-3(7))*; pap. 16.95 *(978-1-61930-203-7(9))* Nomad Pr.

Stone, Bryan. Explore the Solar System! 25 Great Projects, Activities, Experiments. Stone, Bryan. Yasuda, Anita. 2009. (Explore Your World Ser.). (ENG.). 96p. (J). (gr. k-4). pap. 12.95 *(978-1-934670-36-1(7))* Nomad Pr.

Stone, Bryan, jt. illus. see Kim, Alex.

Stone, David. The Mystery of Arroyo Seco. Ryan, Jessica. 2011. 186p. 42.95 *(978-1-258-08470-7(8))* Literary Licensing, LLC.

—The Secret of the Old Coach Inn. Evatt, Harriet. 2011. 190p. 42.95 *(978-1-258-08239-0(X))* Literary Licensing, LLC.

Stone, Diane. My Autism. Evangelista, Colette. 2012. 24p. pap. 10.99 *(978-0-615-62256-9(9))* Toot and Moo.

Stone, Helen. Little Witch. Bennett, Anna Elizabeth. 60th anniv. ed. 2013. (ENG.). 128p. (J). (gr. k-3). pap. 12.95 *(978-1-61608-964-1(4)*, 608964, Sky Pony Pr.) Skyhorse Publishing Co., Inc.

Stone, John. The Amazing Adventures of Andy Owl: A Children's Guide to Understanding Music. Russell, D. Z. 2003. 34p. (J). per. 7.95 *(978-0-9725398-0-7(8))* World Famous Children's Bks.

Stone, Jonny. The Kitty Who Found His Meeooww. Salter, Michelle Lewis. 2011. 40p. pap. 24.95 *(978-1-4560-5953-8(X))* America Star Bks.

Stone, Joyce M., jt. illus. see Stone, Kelly P.

Stone, Kate. ABC Train. 2013. (ENG.). 20p. (J). bds. 10.99 *(978-1-4494-3157-0(7))* Andrews McMeel Publishing.

—Colors. Andrews McMeel Publishing, LLC Staff. 2015. (ENG.). 12p. (J). bds. 10.99 *(978-1-4494-5587-3(5))* Andrews McMeel Publishing.

—Heads & Tails. 2013. (ENG.). 20p. (J). bds. 10.99 *(978-1-4494-3246-1(8))* Andrews McMeel Publishing.

Stone, Kazuko G. Cool Melons-Turn to Frogs! The Life & Poems of Issa, 1 vol. Gollub, Matthew. 2013. (ENG.). 32p. (J). (gr. 1-6). pap. 10.95 *(978-1-58430-241-4(0))* Lee & Low Bks., Inc.

—Ten Oni Drummers. Gollub, Matthew. 2013. (JPN & ENG.). 32p. (J). (gr. -1-3). 16.95 *(978-1-58430-011-3(6))* Lee & Low Bks., Inc.

Stone, Kelly P. & Stone, Joyce M. What Do Pets Do When They Go up to Heaven?, 1 vol. Stone, Kelly P. 2009. 13p. pap. 24.95 *(978-1-61546-212-4(0))* America Star Bks.

Stone, Kyle M. Please Bury Me in the Library. Lewis, J. Patrick. 2005. (ENG.). 32p. (J). (gr. -1-3). 16.99 *(978-0-15-216387-7(5))* Houghton Mifflin Harcourt Publishing Co.

Stone, Kyle M. & Santat, Dan. Tom's Tweet. Esbaum, Jill. 2011. (ENG.). 32p. (J). (gr. -1-2). 16.99 *(978-0-375-85171-1(2))* Knopf, Alfred A. Inc.

Stone, Lyn. The Fairy Midnight Surprise Party. Taylor, Dereen. 2012. (ENG.). 12p. (J). (gr. 1-6). 16.99 *(978-1-84322-763-2(0))* Anness Publishing GBR. Dist: National Bk. Network.

—Rosie Rides to the Rescue: Peek Inside the Pop-Up Windows! Taylor, Dereen. 2015. (ENG.). 12p. 16.99 *(978-1-86147-488-9(1)*, Armadillo) Anness Publishing GBR. Dist: National Bk. Network.

Stone, Lynn M., photos by. Box Turtles. Stone, Lynn M. 2007. (Nature Watch Ser.). (ENG., 48p. (gr. 4-8). lib. bdg. 27.93 *(978-1-57505-869-6(3)*, Lerner Pubns.) Lerner Publishing Group.

—Grizzlies. Stone, Lynn M. rev. ed. 2007. (Nature Watch Ser.). (ENG., 48p. (gr. 4-8). lib. bdg. 27.93 *(978-0-8225-6601-4(X)*, Lerner Pubns.) Lerner Publishing Group.

Stone, Natalie. Monkey in a Tree Counts 1-2-3. Stone, Natalie. 2013. (ENG.). 28p. (J). 16.95 *(978-1-922036-67-4(6))* Brolga Publishing AUS. Dist: Midpoint Trade Bks., Inc.

Stone, Phoebe. In God's Name. Sasso, Sandy Eisenberg. 2004. (ITA, SPA & ENG.). 32p. (J). (gr. -1-7). 18.99 *(978-1-879045-26-2(5)*, Jewish Lights Publishing) LongHill Partners, Inc.

Stone, Sandra, et al, photos by. The Alaska We Love. Stone, Sandra & Stone, James. 2007. 70p. *(978-0-9800019-0-7(0))* Blue Skies Above Texas Co.

Stone, Steve. Warriors Verses Warriors. Stone, Steve. 2009. (ENG.). 64p. (J). (gr. 5-9). 19.99 *(978-0-7534-1916-8(5)*, Kingfisher) Roaring Brook Pr.

Stone, Wendy. Beatrice's Dream: Life in an African Slum. Williams, Karen Lynn. 2013. (ENG.). 32p. (J). (gr. 4-7). pap. 8.99 *(978-1-84780-418-1(7)*, Frances Lincoln) Quarto Publishing Group UK GBR. Dist: Hachette Bk. Group.

Stoner, Alexis. Especially Me! Gerbracht, Edie. 2012. 34p. pap. 11.77 *(978-0-9843855-5-3(X))* aBASK Publishing.

Stooke, Andrew. Bafana Bafana: A Story of Soccer, Magic & Mandela. Blacklaws, Troy. 2010. (ENG.). 64p. pap. 24.00 *(978-1-77009-718-6(X))* Jacana Media ZAF. Dist: Independent Pubs. Group.

Stoop, Naoko. All Creatures Great & Small. 2012. (ENG.). 22p. (J). (gr. k — 1). bds. 6.95 *(978-1-4027-8581-8(X))* Sterling Publishing Co., Inc.

—Noah's Ark. Collins Thoms, Susan. 2013. (ENG.). 22p. (J). (— 1). bds. 6.95 *(978-1-4027-8549-8(6))* Sterling Publishing Co., Inc.

Storch, Ellen N. At the Circus. Muench-Williams, Heather. l.t. ed. 2005. (HRL Board Book Ser.). 10p. (J). (gr. -1-1). bds. 10.95 *(978-1-57332-285-0(7)*, HighReach Learning, Incorporated) Carson-Dellosa Publishing, LLC.

—Building a Sand Castle. Mullican, Judy & Williams, Heather L. l.t. ed. 2004. (HRL Big Book Ser.). (J). (gr. -1). pap. 10.95 *(978-1-57332-297-3(0))*; pap. 10.95 *(978-1-57332-298-0(9))* Carson-Dellosa Publishing, LLC. (HighReach Learning, Incorporated).

—Caillou & the Storyteller. Mullican, Judy. l.t. ed. 2006. (HRL Board Book Ser.). (J). (gr. k-18). pap. 10.95 *(978-1-57332-330-7(6)*, HighReach Learning, Incorporated) Carson-Dellosa Publishing, LLC.

—Caillou Finds a Caterpillar. Jarrell, Pamela R. l.t. ed. 2005. (HRL Board Book Ser.). (J). (gr. -1-1). pap. 10.95 *(978-1-57332-292-8(X)*, HighReach Learning, Incorporated) Carson-Dellosa Publishing, LLC.

—Caillou's Community. Vonthron, Satanta C. l.t. ed. 2006. (HRL Board Book Ser.). (J). (gr. k-18). pap. 10.95 *(978-1-57332-332-1(2)*, HighReach Learning, Incorporated) Carson-Dellosa Publishing, LLC.

—Caillou's Hiking Adventure. Muench-Williams, Heather & Jarrell, Pamela R. l.t. ed. 2005. (HRL Board Book Ser.). (J). (gr. k-18). pap. 10.95 *(978-1-57332-329-1(2)*, HighReach Learning, Incorporated) Carson-Dellosa Publishing, LLC.

—Caillov Learns about Space. Williams, Heather L. & Muench-Williams, Heather. l.t. ed. 2005. (HRL Board Book Ser.). (J). (gr. -1-k). bds. 10.95 *(978-1-57332-308-6(X)*, HighReach Learning, Incorporated) Carson-Dellosa Publishing, LLC.

—Caillov Visits the Circus. Hensley, Sarah M. l.t. ed. 2005. (HRL Board Book Ser.). (J). (gr. -1-k). pap. 10.95 *(978-1-57332-309-3(8)*, HighReach Learning, Incorporated) Carson-Dellosa Publishing, LLC.

—Down at the Shore. Vonthron, Satanta C. l.t. ed. 2005. (HRL Board Book Ser.). (J). (gr. -1-k). pap. 10.95 *(978-1-57332-306-2(3)*, HighReach Learning, Incorporated) Carson-Dellosa Publishing, LLC.

—In the Kitchen. Vonthron, Satanta C. l.t. ed. 2004. (HRL Big Book Ser.). (J). (gr. -1-k). pap. 10.95 *(978-1-57332-316-1(0))*; pap. 10.95 *(978-1-57332-317-8(9))* Carson-Dellosa Publishing, LLC. (HighReach Learning, Incorporated).

—Mary & Marsha Make Cookies. Mullican, Judy. l.t. ed. 2005. 18p. (J). (gr. -1-k). pap. 10.95 *(978-1-57332-346-8(2)*, HighReach Learning, Incorporated) Carson-Dellosa Publishing, LLC.

—What's at the Beach? Heady, Heather. l.t. ed. 2005. 10p. (J). (gr. -1-k). pap. 10.95 *(978-1-57332-355-0(1)*, HighReach Learning, Incorporated) Carson-Dellosa Publishing, LLC.

Storch, Ellen N. Here We Go! Storch, Ellen N. l.t. ed. 2005. (HRL Board Book Ser.). (J). (gr. -1-k). pap. 10.95 *(978-1-57332-322-2(5)*, HighReach Learning, Incorporated) Carson-Dellosa Publishing, LLC.

Storch, Ellen N. & Gillen, Lisa P. Someone New in the Neighborhood. Mullican, Judy. l.t. ed. 2005. 20p. (J). (gr. -1-k). pap. 10.95 *(978-1-57332-356-7(X)*, HighReach Learning, Incorporated) Carson-Dellosa Publishing, LLC.

Storer, Florence. Christmas Tales & Christmas Verse. Field, Eugene. 2007. 100p. per. *(978-1-4065-2387-4(9))* Dodo Pr.

Storey, Jim. Animal Art, 6 vols. Holden, Pam. 2009. (Red Rocket Readers Ser.). 16p. (gr. 1-3). pap. *(978-1-877419-73-7(7)*, Red Rocket Readers) Flying Start Bks.

—Huff & Puff!, 6 pack. Holden, Pam. 2009. (Red Rocket Readers Ser.). 16p. (gr. 2-4). pap. *(978-1-877363-58-0(8)*, Red Rocket Readers) Flying Start Bks.

—The Long, Long Ride, 6 pack. Holden, Pam. 2009. (Red Rocket Readers Ser.). 16p. (gr. 2-5). pap. *(978-1-877363-76-4(6))* Flying Start Bks.

—Sailor Sam in Trouble. Eggleton, Jill. 2004. (Rigby Sails Early Ser.). (ENG.). 16p. (gr. 1-2). pap. 6.95 *(978-0-7578-9295-0(7))* Houghton Mifflin Harcourt Publishing Co.

—Sally Snip Snap's Party, 6 pack. Holden, Pam. 2009. (Red Rocket Readers Ser.). 16p. (gr. 2-4). pap. *(978-1-877363-57-3(X)*, Red Rocket Readers) Flying Start Bks.

—Sneaky Spider, 6 pack. Holden, Pam. 2009. (Red Rocket Readers Ser.). 16p. (gr. 2-5). pap. *(978-1-877363-83-2(9))* Flying Start Bks.

—Three Little Pigs, 6 pack. Holden, Pam. 2009. (Red Rocket Readers Ser.). 16p. (gr. -1-2). pap. *(978-1-877363-11-5(1)*, Red Rocket Readers) Flying Start Bks.

Storey, Jim & Hawley, Kelvin. Dinosaur Hunters, 6 pack. Holden, Pam. 2009. (Red Rocket Readers Ser.). 16p. (gr. 2-4). pap. *(978-1-877363-59-7(6)*, Red Rocket Readers) Flying Start Bks.

Storey, Lela Belle. The Mystery of the Vanishing Chickens. Lozzi, Annette. 2013. 32p. pap. *(978-1-922120-68-7(5))* Interactive Pubns. Pty, Ltd.

Storey, Linda & Nielson, Doug. Angie the Aviator. Carlson, Glenn E. Robinson, Helen, ed. l.t. ed. 2004. 55p. (J). (gr. 2-9). 21.95 *(978-0-9611954-4-1(4))* Watosh Publishing.

Storino, Sara & Zanotta, Roberta. Tinker Bell & the Great Fairy Rescue. Hilgenberg, Bob & Muir, Roberto. movie tie-in ed. 2010. (Disney Fairies Ser.). (ENG.). 56p. (J). (gr. 1-6). 9.99 *(978-1-59707-232-8(X))* Papercutz.

Storino, Sara, jt. illus. see RH Disney Staff.

Storms, Patricia. Edward & the Eureka Lucky Wish Company. Todd, Barbara. 2009. (ENG.). 32p. (J). (gr. -1-2). 16.95 *(978-1-55453-264-3(7))* Kids Can Pr., Ltd. CAN. Dist: Univ. of Toronto Pr.

—Kid Confidential: An Insider's Guide to Grown-Ups. Montgomery, Monte. 2012. (ENG.). 160p. (J). (gr. 3-6). pap. 8.99 *(978-0-8027-2353-6(5)*, 226294) Walker & Co.

—Saints of Note: The Comic Collection. Jenkins, Diana R. 2009. 93p. (J). (gr. 2-5). pap. 9.95 *(978-0-8198-7120-6(6))* Pauline Bks. & Media.

Storms, Patricia & Owlkids Books Inc. Staff. The Pirate & the Penguin. Storms, Patricia. 2009. (ENG.). 32p. (J). (gr. -1-3). 16.95 *(978-1-897349-67-0(X))* Owlkids Bks. Inc. CAN. Dist: Perseus-PGW.

Storr, Nicola. Grandma's Basket. Sims, Janice. 2010. 28p. pap. *(978-1-904408-68-0(0))* Bank House Bks.

Story Rhyme Staff. Self-Esteem: Stories, Poetry & Activity Pages. Story Rhyme Staff. Date not set. 28p. (YA). (gr. 4-9). ring bd. 19.95 *(978-1-56820-107-8(9))* Story Time Stories That Rhyme.

Stossel, Sage. Season of Angels. Wile, Mary Lee. 2013. *(978-0-88028-367-0(X))* Forward Movement Pubns.

Stott, Apryl. Daddy, Am I Beautiful? Lazurek, Michelle S. 2015. (J). pap. *(978-0-8198-1905-5(0))* Pauline Bks. & Media.

Stott, Apryll. Historias de la Biblia para Los Pequeñitos. Monchamp, Genny. 2014.Tr. of Bible Stories for Little Ones. (SPA.). (J). 16.95 *(978-0-8198-3443-0(2))* Pauline Bks. & Media.

Stott, Dorothy. Bunny Loves Others. Simon, Mary Manz. 2006. (First Virtues for Toddlers Ser.). 20p. (J). 5.99 *(978-0-7847-1409-6(6)*, 04037) Standard Publishing.

—Hannah Is a Big Sister. Capucilli, Alyssa Satin. 2014. (Hannah & Henry Ser.). (ENG.). 32p. (J). (gr. -1-k). 5.99 *(978-0-7641-6750-8(2))* Barron's Educational Series, Inc.

—Henry Is a Big Brother. Capucilli, Alyssa Satin. 2014. (Hannah & Henry Ser.). (ENG.). 32p. (J). (gr. -1-k). 5.99 *(978-0-7641-6749-2(9))* Barron's Educational Series, Inc.

—Little Jesus, Little Me, 1 vol. Rikkers, Doris. 2008. (ENG.). 14p. (J). (gr. -1-k). bds. 4.99 *(978-0-310-71651-8(9))* Zondervan.

—Piglet Tells the Truth. Simon, Mary Manz. 2006. (First Virtues for Toddlers Ser.). 20p. (J). 5.99 *(978-0-7847-1407-2(X)*, 04035) Standard Publishing.

—Ten in the Bed. 2010. (Padded Board Book W/CD Ser.). 8p. (J). (gr. k-2). bds. 10.99 incl. audio compact disk *(978-1-59922-578-4(6))* Twin Sisters IP, LLC.

Stotts, Jasmyn & Jayda. When I Learned to Read. Toles-Stotts, LaShunda. l.t. ed. 2005. 36p. (J). per. 11.99 *(978-1-59879-071-9(4))* Lifevest Publishing, Inc.

Stouch, Ryan. Bailey & Friends. Klick, Lisa. 2008. 40p. pap. 14.95 *(978-1-59858-743-2(9))* Dog Ear Publishing, LLC.

Stout, William. Abu & the 7 Marvels. Matheson, Richard. 2003. 128p. (YA). pap. 21.95 *(978-1-887368-49-0(3))* Gauntlet, Inc.

—The Emerald Wand of Oz. Smith, Sherwood. 2007. 262p. (J). 17.00 *(978-1-4223-6710-0(X))* DIANE Publishing Co.

—The Emerald Wand of Oz. Smith, Sherwood. 2005. (ENG.). 272p. (J). (gr. -1-17). 16.99 *(978-0-06-029607-0(0))* HarperCollins Pubs.

—The Emerald Wand of Oz. Smith, Sherwood. 2008. (ENG.). 262p. (gr. 3-18). lib. bdg. 17.89 *(978-0-06-029608-7(9))* IBks., Inc.

Stover, Beth. Busy Little Beaver. Bentley, Dawn. 2003. (ENG.). 32p. (J). (gr. -1-1). pap. 3.95 *(978-1-59249-011-0(5),* S2029); 12.95 *(978-1-59249-012-7(3),* PS2079) Soundprints.

—The Prickly Porcupine. Bentley, Dawn. 2003. (Soundprints' Read-and-Discover Ser.). (ENG.). 32p. (J). (gr. -1-3). 12.95 *(978-1-59249-014-1(X),* PS2065); pap. 3.95 *(978-1-59249-013-4(1),* S2015) Soundprints.

—Wake up, Black Bear! Bentley, Dawn. 2003. (ENG.). 32p. (J). (gr. -1-17). pap. 4.35 *(978-1-59249-007-3(7),* S2020); 12.95 *(978-1-59249-008-0(5),* PS2070) Soundprints.

—Welcome Back, Puffin! Bentley, Dawn. 2003. (Soundprints' Read-and-Discover Ser.). (ENG.). 32p. (J). (gr. -1-k). 12.95 *(978-1-59249-010-3(7),* PS2064); pap. 3.95 *(978-1-59249-009-7(3),* S2014) Soundprints.

Stow, Jenny. The Coming of Night: A Yoruba Creation Myth from West Africa. Riordan, James. 2011. (ENG.). 32p. (J). (gr. k-3). pap. 8.95 *(978-1-84780-276-7(1),* Frances Lincoln) Quarto Publishing Group UK GBR. Dist: Hachette Bk. Group.

Stowell, Charlotte. God's Wonderful World, 3 vols. 2003. 20p. (J). bds. 6.99 *(978-0-8254-7269-5(5),* Candle Bks.) Lion Hudson PLC GBR. Dist: Kregel Pubns.

Stower, Adam. Children's English History in Verse. Baker, Kenneth, ed. 2007. 289p. pap. 20.00 *(978-1-4223-9012-2(8))* DIANE Publishing Co.

—Fear Itself. Clements, Andrew. 2011. (Benjamin Pratt & the Keepers of the School Ser.: 2). (ENG.). (J). (gr. 2-5). 240p. pap. 6.99 *(978-1-4169-3908-5(3));* 176p. 14.99 *(978-1-4169-3887-3(7))* Simon & Schuster Children's Publishing. (Atheneum Bks. for Young Readers).

—In Harm's Way. Clements, Andrew. (Benjamin Pratt & the Keepers of the School Ser.: 4). (ENG.). (J). (gr. 2-5). 2014. 240p. pap. 6.99 *(978-1-4169-3910-8(5));* 2013. 224p. 14.99 *(978-1-4169-3889-7(3))* Simon & Schuster Children's Publishing. (Atheneum Bks. for Young Readers).

—Legends of the Shadow World: The Secret Country; the Shadow World; Dragon's Fire. Johnson, Jane. 2010. (ENG.). 1120p. (J). (gr. 3-7). pap. 14.99 *(978-1-4169-9082-6(8),* Simon & Schuster Bks. For Young Readers) Simon & Schuster Bks. For Young Readers.

—Mrs. Noodlekugel. Pinkwater, Daniel M. (Mrs. Noodlekugel Ser.). (ENG.). 80p. (J). (gr. k-4). 2013. pap. 5.99 *(978-0-7636-6452-7(9));* 2012. 14.99 *(978-0-7636-5053-7(6))* Candlewick Pr.

—Mrs. Noodlekugel & Drooly the Bear. Pinkwater, Daniel M. 2015. (ENG.). 96p. (J). (gr. k-4). 14.99 *(978-0-7636-6645-3(9))* Candlewick Pr.

—Mrs. Noodlekugel & Four Blind Mice. Pinkwater, Daniel M. (Mrs. Noodlekugel Ser.). (ENG.). 96p. (J). (gr. k-4). 2015. pap. 5.99 *(978-0-7636-7658-2(6));* 2013. 14.99 *(978-0-7636-5054-4(4))* Candlewick Pr.

—The Secret Country. Johnson, Jane. 2007. (Eidolon Chronicles Ser.: 1). (ENG.). 336p. (J). (gr. 3-7). per. 15.99 *(978-1-4169-3815-6(X),* Simon & Schuster Bks. For Young Readers) Simon & Schuster Bks. For Young Readers.

—This Side of Magic. Jones, Marcia Thornton & Dadey, Debbie. 2009. (Keyholders Ser.: 1). (ENG.). 144p. (J). (gr. 2-5). 3.99 *(978-0-7653-5982-7(0),* Starscape) Doherty, Tom Assocs., LLC.

—Walls Within Walls. Sherry, Maureen. (ENG.). 368p. (J). (gr. 3-7). 2012. pap. 6.99 *(978-0-06-176703-6(4));* 2010. 16.99 *(978-0-06-176700-5(X))* HarperCollins Pubs. (Tegen, Katherine Bks).

—We Hold These Truths. Clements, Andrew. 2013. (Benjamin Pratt & the Keepers of the School Ser.: 5). (ENG.). 272p. (J). (gr. 2-5). 14.99 *(978-1-4169-3890-3(7),* Atheneum Bks. for Young Readers) Simon & Schuster Children's Publishing.

—We the Children. Clements, Andrew. 2010. (Benjamin Pratt & the Keepers of the School Ser.: 1). (ENG.). 128p. (J). (gr. 2-5). 14.99 *(978-1-4169-3886-6(9),* Atheneum Bks. for Young Readers) Simon & Schuster Children's Publishing.

—The Whites of Their Eyes. Clements, Andrew. (Benjamin Pratt & the Keepers of the School Ser.: 3). (ENG.). (J). (gr. 2-5). 2013. 240p. pap. 6.99 *(978-1-4169-3909-2(1));* 2012. 224p. 14.99 *(978-1-4169-3888-0(5))* Simon & Schuster Children's Publishing. (Atheneum Bks. for Young Readers).

Stower, Adam. Naughty Kitty! Stower, Adam. 2014. (ENG.). 40p. (J). (gr. -1-k). 16.99 *(978-0-545-57604-8(0),* Orchard Bks.) Scholastic, Inc.

—Silly Doggy! Stower, Adam. 2012. (ENG.). 40p. (J). (gr. -1-k). 16.99 *(978-0-545-37323-4(9),* Orchard Bks.) Scholastic, Inc.

Stower, Adam. Troll & the Oliver. Stower, Adam. 2015. (ENG.). 40p. (J). (gr. -1-2). 16.99 ***(978-0-7636-7956-9(9),*** Templar) Candlewick Pr.

Stowers, B. J., photos by. Hal Stowers & the Art of Life Blending: How to Keep Your Creative Juices Flowing, 2 vols., 1 bk, Stowers, B. J. Stowers, Hal. 2004. (Life Blending Ser.: Vols. 1-2). 276p. 90.00 *(978-0-9749832-0-2(9))* Walking Tree, Inc.

Strahm, Jake. The Island of Beginnings. Strahm, Luke. 2011. (ENG.). 116p. pap. 6.50 *(978-1-4680-0192-1(2))* CreateSpace Independent Publishing Platform.

Straker, Bethany. Boo's Beard. Mannering, Rose. 2015. (ENG.). 32p. (J). (gr. -1-k). 16.99 ***(978-1-63450-207-8(8),*** Sky Pony Pr.) Skyhorse Publishing Co., Inc.

Straker, Bethany. A Curious Robot on Mars! Duffett-Smith, James. 2013. (ENG.). 32p. (J). (gr. -1-1). 14.95 *(978-1-62087-994-8(8),* 620994, Sky Pony Pr.) Skyhorse Publishing Co., Inc.

—The Funny Bunny Fly. 2014. (ENG.). 32p. (J). (gr. -1-k). 14.95 *(978-1-62914-610-2(2),* Sky Pony Pr.) Skyhorse Publishing Co., Inc.

—Pierre the French Bulldog Recycles. Ormand, Kate & Louise, Kate. 2015. (ENG.). 32p. (J). (gr. -1-k). 14.99 *(978-1-63220-411-0(8),* Sky Pony Pr.) Skyhorse Publishing Co., Inc.

—Ruby Moo's Deep-Sea Adventure! Atherton, Isabel. 2014. (ENG.). 32p. (J). (gr. -1-k). 14.95 *(978-1-62914-625-6(0),* Sky Pony Pr.) Skyhorse Publishing Co., Inc.

—Smelly Ghost. Atherton, Isabel. 2013. (ENG.). 32p. (J). (gr. -1-1). 14.95 *(978-1-62087-989-4(1),* 620989, Sky Pony Pr.) Skyhorse Publishing Co., Inc.

—The Spotty Dotty Daffodil. Mannering, Rose. 2014. (ENG.). 32p. (J). (gr. -1-k). 16.95 *(978-1-62636-346-5(3),* Sky Pony Pr.) Skyhorse Publishing Co., Inc.

—Stella & Steve Travel Through Space! Duffett-Smith, James. 2014. (ENG.). 32p. (J). (gr. -1-k). 14.95 *(978-1-62873-815-5(4),* Sky Pony Pr.) Skyhorse Publishing Co., Inc.

Straker, Bethany. Springy Chicken. Straker, Bethany. Atherton, Isabel. 2014. (ENG.). 32p. (J). (gr. -1-k). 14.95 *(978-1-62636-161-4(4),* Sky Pony Pr.) Skyhorse Publishing Co., Inc.

Strambini, Karla. The Extraordinary Mr. Qwerty. Strambini, Karla. 2014. (ENG.). 32p. (J). (gr. k-3). 16.99 *(978-0-7636-7324-6(2))* Candlewick Pr.

Strand, Vivian. I Am Utterly Unique: Celebrating the Strengths of Children with Asperger Syndrome & High-Functioning Autism. Larson, Elaine M. et al. 2006. 56p. (J). (gr. -1-3). 18.95 *(978-1-931282-89-5(7))* Autism Asperger Publishing Co.

—The Kaleidoscope Kid: Focusing on the Strengths of Children with Asperger Syndrome & High-Functioning Autism. Larson, Elaine Marie. 2007. 35p. 17.95 *(978-1-931282-41-3(2))* Autism Asperger Publishing Co.

Strange, Katie. Ana & the Pet Show. Hoffmann, Sara E. 2013. (My Reading Neighborhood: First-Grade Sight Word Stories Ser.). (ENG.). 16p. (gr. -1-1). pap. 5.95 *(978-1-4677-1170-8(5))* Lerner Publishing Group.

—Ana & the Rainy Day. Hoffmann, Sara E. 2013. (My Reading Neighborhood: First-Grade Sight Word Stories Ser.). (ENG.). 16p. (gr. -1-1). pap. 5.95 *(978-1-4677-1174-6(8))* Lerner Publishing Group.

—Nia Bakes Cookies. Hoffmann, Sara E. 2013. (My Reading Neighborhood: First-Grade Sight Word Stories Ser.). (ENG.). 16p. (gr. -1-1). pap. 5.95 *(978-1-4677-1172-2(1))* Lerner Publishing Group.

Strapec, Amy. The Garbage Grandma. Silverman, Toby. 2005. 23p. (J). 9.50 *(978-0-9793475-0-4(5))* Silverman, Toby.

Strasburg, Sunny, jt. illus. see Stensaas, Martin.

Strassburg, Brian. More-If You Had to Choose, What Would You Do? Humphrey, Sandra McLeod & Barker, Dan. 2003. (ENG.). 132p. (J). (gr. 4-7). pap. 14.99 *(978-1-59102-077-6(8),* Pyr Bks.) Prometheus Bks., Pubs.

Strasser, Susanne. Mr. Happy & Miss Grimm. Schneider, Antonie & Maccarone, Grace. 2015. (ENG.). 32p. (J). (gr. -1-3). 16.95 *(978-0-8234-3198-4(3))* Holiday Hse., Inc.

Stratford, Stevan. Allah Gave Me a Nose to Smell. Qamaruddin, Rizwana. 2015. (ENG.). 32p. (J). 8.95 ***(978-0-86037-333-9(9))*** Kube Publishing Ltd. GBR. Dist: Consortium Bk. Sales & Distribution.

Stratman, Kay. The Christmas Crown. Martin, Maria G. 2010. 20p. pap. 10.95 *(978-1-60911-442-8(6),* Eloquent Bks.) Strategic Book Publishing & Rights Agency (SBPRA).

Stratton, Helen. The Princess & Curdie. MacDonald, George. 2003. 162p. pap. 12.99 *(978-1-57646-634-6(5))* Quiet Vision Publishing.

Strecker, Darren. Leelah at the Lake. Fettig, Pamela. 2010. 28p. pap. 9.99 *(978-1-60844-697-1(2))* Dog Ear Publishing, LLC.

Street, James. Santa's Elves & the Tickets. Garner, Ellen. 2012. 56p. pap. 12.99 *(978-0-615-55920-9(4))* EG Bks.

Street Level Studio. Math & Stories, Grades K-3. Bartch, Marian. 2007. 173p. per. 17.95 *(978-1-59647-222-8(7))* Good Year Bks.

Streich, Michel. Grumpy Little King. Streich, Michel. 2012. (ENG.). 32p. (J). (gr. k-3). 19.99 *(978-1-74237-572-4(3))* Allen & Unwin AUS. Dist: Independent Pubs. Group.

Stremanos, A. M. Rosemary's Taken over My Potatoes. 2008. 20p. (J). 5.00 *(978-0-9801372-0-0(9))* Benedetti, Jef.

Strevens-Marzo, Bridget. Daddy Does the Cha Cha Cha! Bedford, David. 2010. (ENG.). 32p. (J). (gr. -1-k). pap. 8.99 *(978-1-921541-16-2(4))* Little Hare Bks. AUS. Dist: Independent Pubs. Group.

—How Do You Make a Baby Smile? Sturges, Philemon. 2007. 24p. (J). (gr. -1-k). lib. bdg. 17.89 *(978-0-06-076073-1(7))* HarperCollins Pubs.

—Hush, Hush! Wild, Margaret. (ENG.). 24p. (J). (gr. -1-1). 2014. bds. 8.99 *(978-1-921541-92-6(X));* 2010. 14.99 *(978-1-921272-86-8(4))* Little Hare Bks. AUS. Dist: Independent Pubs. Group.

—Kiss Kiss! Wild, Margaret. 2004. 26p. pap. *(978-1-877003-51-6(4))* Little Hare Bks. AUS. Dist: HarperCollins Pubs. Australia.

—Kiss Kiss! Wild, Margaret. 2004. (ENG.). 24p. (J). (gr. -1-1). 12.95 *(978-0-689-86279-3(2),* Simon & Schuster Bks. For Young Readers) Simon & Schuster Bks. For Young Readers.

—Kiss, Kiss! Wild, Margaret. 2008. 24p. bds. *(978-1-921272-33-2(3))* Little Hare Bks. AUS. Dist: HarperCollins Pubs. Australia.

—Kiss Kiss! Wild, Margaret. ed. 2006. (J). *(978-1-921049-24-8(3))* Little Hare Bks. AUS. Dist: HarperCollins Pubs. Australia.

—Mini Racer. Dempsey, Kristy. 2011. (ENG.). 32p. (J). (gr. -1-k). 16.99 *(978-1-59990-170-1(6));* 17.89 *(978-1-59990-591-4(4))* Bloomsbury USA. (Bloomsbury USA Childrens).

Strickland, Shadra. The Diary of B. B. Bright, Possible Princess. Randall, Alice & Williams, Caroline Randall. 2012. (ENG.). 192p. (J). (gr. 2-6). 19.95 *(978-1-61858-015-3(9))* Turner Publishing Co.

—Eliza's Freedom Road: An Underground Railroad Diary. Nolen, Jerdine. 2011. (ENG.). 160p. (J). (gr. 3-7). 14.99 *(978-1-4169-5814-7(2),* Simon & Schuster/Paula Wiseman Bks.) Simon & Schuster/Paula Wiseman Bks.

—A Place Where Hurricanes Happen. Watson, Renée. 2010. (ENG.). 40p. (J). (gr. k-4). 17.99 *(978-0-375-85609-9(9))* Random Hse., Inc.

—Please, Louise. Morrison, Toni & Morrison, Slade. 2014. (ENG.). 32p. (J). (gr. -1-3). 17.99 *(978-1-4169-8338-5(4),* Simon & Schuster Bks. For Young Readers) Simon & Schuster Bks. For Young Readers.

—Sunday Shopping, 1 vol. Derby, Sally. 2015. (ENG.). 32p. (J). 17.95 *(978-1-60060-438-6(2),* 9781600000000) Lee & Low Bks., Inc.

—White Water. Bandy, Michael S. & Stein, Eric. 2011. (ENG.). 40p. (J). (gr. k-3). 16.99 *(978-0-7636-3678-4(9))* Candlewick Pr.

Stride, Lottie. Meerkat Mischief. Stride, Lottie. 2012. (ENG.). 64p. (J). (gr. 1-4). pap., act. bk. ed. 7.99 *(978-1-78055-009-1(X))* O'Mara, Michael Bks., Ltd. GBR. Dist: Independent Pubs. Group.

Stringer, Karen. The Light of Stars. Glowatsky, Phyllis. 2003. 32p. (J). 19.95 *(978-1-931650-18-2(7))* Coastal Publishing Carolina, Inc.

Stringer, Lauren. Deer Dancer. Ray, Mary Lyn. 2014. (ENG.). 40p. (J). (gr. -1-3). 17.99 *(978-1-4424-3421-9(X),* Beach Lane Bks.) Beach Lane Bks.

—Fold Me a Poem. George, Kristine O'Connell. 2005. (ENG.). 56p. (J). (gr. 1-4). 16.99 *(978-0-15-202501-4(4))* Houghton Mifflin Harcourt Publishing Co.

—Our Family Tree: An Evolution Story. Peters, Lisa Westberg. 2003. (ENG.). 48p. (J). (gr. -1-3). 17.99 *(978-0-15-201772-9(0))* Houghton Mifflin Harcourt Publishing Co.

—The Princess & Her Panther. Orr, Wendy. 2010. (ENG.). 40p. (J). (gr. -1-3). 16.99 *(978-1-4169-9780-1(6),* Beach Lane Bks.) Beach Lane Bks.

—Red Rubber Boot Day. Ray, Mary Lyn. 2005. (ENG.). 32p. (J). (gr. -1-3). pap. 6.99 *(978-0-15-205398-7(0))* Houghton Mifflin Harcourt Publishing Co.

—Scarecrow. Rylant, Cynthia. 2014. 32p. pap. 7.00 *(978-1-61003-181-3(4))* Center for the Collaborative Classroom.

—Snow. Rylant, Cynthia. 2008. (ENG.). 40p. (J). (gr. -1-3). 17.99 *(978-0-15-205303-1(4))* Houghton Mifflin Harcourt Publishing Co.

—Tell Me about Your Day Today. Fox, Mem. 2012. (ENG.). 40p. (J). (gr. -1-3). 17.99 *(978-1-4169-9006-2(2),* Beach Lane Bks.) Beach Lane Bks.

Stringer, Margaret. Googus, the Toothless Alligator. Shaffert, Charles. l.t. ed. 2003. 30p. (J). per. 7.95 *(978-1-932338-27-0(6))* Lifevest Publishing, Inc.

—Googus to the Rescue. Shaffert, Charles F. l.t. ed. 2005. 31p. (J). per. 10.00 *(978-1-59879-043-6(9))* Lifevest Publishing, Inc.

Stringfield, Joni. Circle of Three: Enough Friendship to Go Around? Brokamp, Elizabeth. 2008. 44p. (J). (gr. 3-7). 14.95 *(978-1-4338-0321-5(6));* pap. 9.95 *(978-1-4338-0322-2(4))* American Psychological Assn. (Magination Pr.).

Stringle, Sam, jt. illus. see Duncan, Karen.

Stroede, Paul. The Dog Days of Christmas. Rogala, Judy. 2012. 32p. (J). 12.95 *(978-1-59598-219-3(1),* Goblin Fern Pr.) HenschelHAUS Publishing.

Stroede, Paul, jt. illus. see Stader, Kristina.

Strom, Maria Diaz. Joe Arco Iris y Yo. Strom, Maria Diaz. 2008.Tr. of Rainbow Joe & Me. (SPA.). 32p. (J). (gr. -1-3). pap. 8.95 *(978-1-60060-278-8(9))* Lee & Low Bks., Inc.

Stroman, Larry. Peter David, 4 vols., Vol. 1. 2005. (ENG.). 136p. (J). (gr. 4-17). pap. 15.99 *(978-0-7851-1872-5(1))* Marvel Worldwide, Inc.

Stromoski, Rick. Bats in My Attic. Meltzer Kleinhenz, Sydnie. 2005. (Rookie Readers Ser.). (ENG.). 32p. (J). (gr. k-2). lib. bdg. 19.50 *(978-0-516-24865-3(0),* Children's Pr.) Scholastic Library Publishing.

—Chairs, Chairs, Chairs! Cappetta, Cynthia. 2004. (Rookie Readers Ser.). 31p. (gr. k-3). 14.95 *(978-0-7569-3639-6(X))* Perfection Learning Corp.

—Willie's Word World. Curry, Don L. 2011. (Rookie Ready to Learn Ser.). 40p. (J). (gr. -1-k). pap. 5.95 *(978-0-531-26679-3(6));* lib. bdg. 23.00 *(978-0-531-26374-7(6))* Scholastic Library Publishing. (Children's Pr.).

Strong, Melodee. You Are Beautiful. Snow, Todd. 2007. (You Are Important Ser.). (ENG.). 24p. (J). (gr. -1-k). bds. 7.99 *(978-1-934277-10-2(X))* Marn Green Publishing, Inc.

—You Are Friendly. Snow, Todd. 2007. (You Are Important Ser.). (ENG.). 24p. (J). (gr. -1-k). bds. 7.99 *(978-1-934277-09-6(6))* Marn Green Publishing, Inc.

—You Are Helpful. Snow, Todd. 2008. (You Are Important Ser.). (ENG.). 24p. (J). (gr. -1-3). pap. 8.99 *(978-1-934277-23-2(1))* Marn Green Publishing, Inc.

—You Are Important. Snow, Todd. 2007. (You Are Important Ser.). (ENG.). 24p. (J). (gr. -1-k). bds. 7.99 *(978-1-934277-06-5(1))* Marn Green Publishing, Inc.

Stroniarz, Christina V. Let's Sing & Celebrate! 105 Original Songs for Seasons & Festivals. 2003. 224p. pap. 24.95 *(978-0-9720913-9-8(4))* Songbird Pr.

Stroud, Brenda. The Thursday Surprise: A Story about Kids & Autism. Ennis, Ryan R. 2011. 86p. pap. 9.95 *(978-0-9843426-7-9(2))* G Publishing LLC.

Stroud, Brenda D. A Proper Place for Boogers. Finley, Ucal P. 2011. 54p. pap. 12.95 *(978-0-9834307-0-4(5))* G Publishing LLC.

Stroud, David Wayne. Wiggles the White Blood Cell. Stroud, David Wayne. 2005. (J). 14.95 *(978-0-9762835-1-5(4))* Shooting Star Publishing.

Stroud, Joanne. 365 Silly Jokes for Kids. West, Tracey. West, Simon, ed. 2013. 100p. pap. *(978-1-910094-05-1(6))* Magic Oxygen.

Strugnell, Ann. Julian, Dream Doctor. Cameron, Ann. ed. 2003. (Julian's Stories Ser.). 62p. (gr. 4-7). lib. bdg. 14.75 *(978-0-8335-4929-7(4),* Turtleback) Turtleback Bks.

Strunk, Peter. Two Inch Hero: The Adventures of Lorenzo Lizard, Strunk, Peter, creator. 2006. (J). 17.95 *(978-0-9785961-0-1(2))* Smile Time Publishing.

Stryk, Suzanne, jt. illus. see Hooper, Hadley.

Stryker, Dale, jt. illus. see Stryker, Stephanie.

Stryker, Stephanie & Stryker, Dale. Speech Illustrated Numero Uno: Pictured Nouns & Verbs. Stryker, Stephanie & Stryker, Dale. 2008.Tr. of Numero uno -Sustantivos Imaginados y Verbos. (SPA.). 48p. 24.95 net. *(978-0-9821038-7-6(5))* Stryker Illustrations.

Stuart, B. S. One day in Betty,s Life. Gates, Josephine Scribner. 2007. 58p. (J). lib. bdg. 59.00 *(978-1-60304-018-1(8))* Dollworks.

Stuart, Jon. Collins Big Cat - What's for Breakfast? Shipton, Paul. 2006. (Collins Big Cat Ser.). (ENG.). 16p. (J). pap. 5.99 *(978-0-00-718668-6(1))* HarperCollins Pubs. Ltd. GBR. Dist: Independent Pubs. Group.

—What Is CGI? Band 06/Orange. Sage, Alison. 2007. (Collins Big Cat Ser.). (ENG.). 24p. (J). pap. 6.99 *(978-0-00-718667-9(3))* HarperCollins Pubs. Ltd. GBR. Dist: Independent Pubs. Group.

Stuart, Mitchell. The Curious Adventures of India Sophia. Stewart, Angela. 2004. (Juvenile Novel Ser.). 176p. (J). (gr. 4-6). pap. 9.95 *(978-1-895836-78-3(6))* River Bks. CAN. Dist: Fitzhenry & Whiteside, Ltd.

Stuart, Walter. Little Walrus Warning. Young, Carol. (Smithsonian Oceanic Collection). (J). 2009. 24.95 incl. audio compact disk *(978-1-59249-667-9(9));* 2005. (ENG.). 32p. (gr. -1-2). 8.95 *(978-1-59249-070-7(0),* SC4009); 2005. (ENG.). 32p. (gr. -1-3). 6.95 *(978-1-56899-937-1(2),* S4009) Soundprints.

Stubbing, Lori. Little Hero's Frown. Rjk. 2012. 36p. pap. 24.95 *(978-1-4626-7786-3(X))* America Star Bks.

Stubbs, Robert Earl. Fearfully & Wonderfully Made: A Christian Health & Puberty Guide for Preteen Boys & Girls. Stubbs, Lori. 2nd ed. 2005. 40p. (J). (gr. -1 — 1). pap. 10.00 *(978-1-58597-174-9(X))* Leathers Publishing.

Stubbs, Tommy. The Birthday Express! Awdry, W. 2014. (ENG.). 48p. (J). (gr. -1-2). pap. 4.99 *(978-0-385-37531-3(X),* Golden Bks.) Random Hse. Children's Bks.

—Blue Mountain Mystery. Awdry, Wilbert V. 2012. (Big Golden Book Ser.). (ENG.). 48p. (J). (gr. -1-2). 9.99 *(978-0-307-93149-8(8),* Golden Bks.) Random Hse. Children's Bks.

—Blue Train, Green Train. Awdry, Wilbert V. & Awdry, W. 2007. (Bright & Early Board Books Ser.). (ENG.). 24p. (J). (— 1). bds. 4.99 *(978-0-375-83984-9(4),* Random Hse. Bks. for Young Readers) Random Hse. Children's Bks.

—Blue Train, Green Train. Awdry, Wilbert V. 2006. (Bright & Early Books Ser.). (ENG.). 36p. (J). (gr. k-k). 8.99 *(978-0-375-83463-9(X),* Random Hse. Bks. for Young Readers) Random Hse. Children's Bks.

—Busy, Busy Thomas. Awdry, W. 2013. (Nifty Lift-And-Look Ser.). (ENG.). 12p. (J). (— 1). bds. 5.99 *(978-0-449-81642-4(7),* Random Hse. Bks. for Young Readers) Random Hse. Children's Bks.

—A Crack in the Track. 2004. (Bright & Early Board Books Ser.). (ENG.). 24p. (J). bds. 4.99 *(978-0-375-82755-6(2),* Random Hse. Bks. for Young Readers) Random Hse. Children's Bks.

—Day of the Diesels. Awdry, Wilbert V. 2011. (Big Golden Book Ser.). (ENG.). 48p. (J). (gr. -1-2). 9.99 *(978-0-375-87181-8(0),* Golden Bks.) Random Hse. Children's Bks.

—Fast Train, Slow Train. Awdry, Wilbert V. 2009. (Bright & Early Books Ser.). (ENG.). 36p. (J). (gr. -1-2). 8.99 *(978-0-375-85689-1(7))* Random Hse. Children's Bks.

—The Fearsome Footprints/Thomas the Brave (Thomas & Friends) Random House. 2014. (Pictureback(R) Ser.). (ENG.). 24p. (J). (gr. -1-2). 4.99 *(978-0-385-37392-0(9),* Random Hse. Bks. for Young Readers) Random Hse. Children's Bks.

—Go, Train, Go! Awdry, Wilbert V. & Terrill, Elizabeth. 2005. (Beginner Books(R) Ser.). (ENG.). 48p. (J). (gr. -1-1). 8.99 *(978-0-375-83177-5(0),* Random Hse. Bks. for Young Readers) Random Hse. Children's Bks.

—Go, Train, Go! Awdry, Wilbert V. 2006. (Bright & Early Board Books(TM) Ser.). (ENG.). 24p. (J). (gr. k — 1). bds. 4.99 *(978-0-375-83461-5(3),* Random Hse. Bks. for Young Readers) Random Hse. Children's Bks.

—King of the Railway. Awdry, W. 2013. (Big Golden Book Ser.). (ENG.). 48p. (J). (gr. -1-2). 9.99 *(978-0-449-81661-5(3),* Golden Bks.) Random Hse. Children's Bks.

—Lost at Sea! Hit Entertainment. 2010. (Pictureback Ser.). (ENG.). 24p. (J). (gr. -1-2). pap. 3.99 *(978-0-375-84754-7(5),* Golden Bks.) Random Hse. Children's Bks.

—May the Best Engine Win! Courtney, Richard, photos by. Golden Books Staff. 2008. (Little Golden Book Ser.). (ENG.). 24p. (J). (gr. -1-2). 3.99 *(978-0-375-84381-5(7),* Golden Bks.) Random Hse. Children's Bks.

—The Missing Christmas Tree. Awdry, Wilbert Were. 2013. (Glitter Board Book Ser.). (ENG.). 12p. (J). (— 1). bds. 6.99 *(978-0-449-81713-1(X),* Golden Bks.) Random Hse. Children's Bks.

—My Red Railway Book Box. Awdry, Wilbert V. 2008. (Bright & Early Board Books(TM) Ser.). (ENG.). 96p. (J). (gr. k —

S

1). bds. 14.99 *(978-0-375-84322-8(1)*, Random Hse. Bks. for Young Readers) Random Hse. Children's Bks.

—Ride the Rails with Thomas (Thomas & Friends) Awdry, W. 2015. (Pictureback Ser.). (ENG.). 24p. (J). (gr. -1-2). 5.99 *(978-0-385-38538-1(2)*, Random Hse. Bks. for Young Readers) Random Hse. Children's Bks.

—Runaway Engine! Awdry, W. 2011. (3-D Pictureback Ser.). (ENG.). 16p. (J). (gr. -1-2). pap. 4.99 *(978-0-375-87253-2(1)*, Random Hse. Bks. for Young Readers) Random Hse. Children's Bks.

—Steam Team! Awdry, W. 2011. (Reusable Sticker Book Ser.). (ENG.). 12p. (J). (gr. -1-2). pap. 6.99 *(978-0-375-87162-7(4)*, Golden Bks.) Random Hse. Children's Bks.

—Tale of the Brave (Thomas & Friends) Awdry, W. 2014. (Big Golden Book Ser.). (ENG.). 48p. (J). (gr. -1-2). 9.99 *(978-0-385-37915-1(3)*, Golden Bks.) Random Hse. Children's Bks.

—Thomas & Friends Little Golden Book Library (Thomas & Friends), 5 vols. 2013. (ENG.). 120p. (J). (-k). 19.95 *(978-0-449-81482-6(3)*, Golden Bks.) Random Hse. Children's Bks.

—Thomas & the Great Discovery. Hooke, R. Schuyler. 2009. (Little Golden Book Ser.). (ENG.). 24p. (J). (gr. -1-2). 3.99 *(978-0-375-85153-7(4)*, Golden Bks.) Random Hse. Children's Bks.

Stubbs, Tommy. Thomas & the Lost Pirate / The Sunken Treasure, 2 Bks. in 1. Random House. 2015. (Pictureback(R) Ser.). (ENG.). 24p. (J). (gr. -1-2). 4.99 ***(978-0-553-52078-1(4)***, Random Hse. Bks. for Young Readers) Random Hse. Children's Bks.

Stubbs, Tommy. Thomas' Favorite Places & Faces. Awdry, Wilbert V. 2014. (Reusable Sticker Book Ser.). (ENG.). 24p. (J). (gr. -1-2). pap. 6.99 *(978-0-449-81712-4(1)*, Golden Bks.) Random Hse. Children's Bks.

—Thomas Saves Easter! Awdry, Wilbert V. 2013. (Glitter Board Book Ser.). (ENG.). 12p. (J). (-k). 6.99 *(978-0-307-98158-5(4)*, Golden Bks.) Random Hse. Children's Bks.

—Thomas's Christmas Delivery. Awdry, W. 2004. (Sparkle Storybook Ser.). (ENG.). 32p. (J). (gr. -1-2). 8.99 *(978-0-375-82877-5(X)*, Random Hse. Bks. for Young Readers) Random Hse. Children's Bks.

—Trains, Cranes & Troublesome Trucks. Awdry, Wilbert V. 2008. (Beginner Books Ser.). (ENG.). 36p. (J). (gr. -1-1). 8.99 *(978-0-375-84977-0(7)*, Random Hse. Bks. for Young Readers) Random Hse. Children's Bks.

Stubbs, Tommy, jt. illus. see Carbajal, Richard.

Stubbs, Tommy, jt. illus. see Courtney, Richard.

Stubbs, Tommy, jt. illus. see Durk, Jim.

Stuby, Tim. Extreme Monsters Joke Book. Bataille Lange, Nikki. gif. ed. 2005. 95p. (J). (gr. 2-5). per. 3.99 *(978-1-57791-181-4(4))* Brighter Minds Children's Publishing.

Stucki, Ron. Edgar & the Tattle-Tale Heart. Adams, Jennifer. 2014. (ENG.). 32p. (J). 16.99 *(978-1-4236-3766-0(6))* Gibbs Smith, Publisher.

—Edgar Gets Ready for Bed, 1 vol. Adams, Jennifer. ed. 2014. (ENG.). 32p. (J). 16.99 *(978-1-4236-3528-4(0))* Gibbs Smith, Publisher.

Students, Shelton Intermediate School Art & Weir, Susan. The Yellow Dog with One Bad Eye. Gelderman, Robert G. 2010. (ENG.). 44p. pap. 9.99 *(978-1-4505-2921-1(6))* CreateSpace Independent Publishing Platform.

Studio, Gau Family. Toodle's Big Race: Interactive for Children That Don't Like to Sit Still! Jusino, Cindy M. 2013. 44p. 20.00 *(978-0-9888003-2-8(2))* Sensational Pubns.

Studio IBOIX. Aurora: The Perfect Party. Loggia, Wendy. 2012. (Disney Princesses Set 2 Ser.). 96p. (J). (gr. 2-6). lib. bdg. 24.21 *(978-1-59961-181-5(3))* Spotlight.

—Jasmine: The Missing Coin. Nathan, Sarah. 2012. (Disney Princesses Set 2 Ser.). 96p. (J). (gr. 2-6). lib. bdg. 24.21 *(978-1-59961-182-2(1))* Spotlight.

—Rapunzel: A Day to Remember. Perelman, Helen. 2012. (Disney Princesses Set 2 Ser.). 96p. (J). (gr. 2-6). lib. bdg. 24.21 *(978-1-59961-183-9(X))* Spotlight.

Studio IBOIX & Disney Storybook Artists Staff. Rapunzel & the Golden Rule/Jasmine & the Two Tigers (Disney Princess) Bazaldua, Barbara & Bergen, Lara. 2011. (Deluxe Pictureback Ser.). (ENG.). 32p. (J). (gr. -1-2). pap. 4.99 *(978-0-7364-2829-3(1)*, RH/Disney) Random Hse. Children's Bks.

Studio Iboix Staff, jt. illus. see Cagol, Andrea.

Studio Iboix Staff, jt. illus. see Disney Storybook Art Team.

Studio Iboix Staff, jt. illus. see Disney Storybook Artists Staff.

Studio IBOIX Staff, jt. illus. see RH Disney Staff.

Studio Stalio. Abejas: Por Dentro y Por Fuera. Houghton, Gillian. Velazquez De Leon, Mauricio, tr. 2004. (Explora la Naturaleza (Getting into Nature) Ser.). (SPA.). 32p. (YA). (gr. 3-6). lib. bdg. 25.25 *(978-1-4042-2862-7(4))* Rosen Publishing Group, Inc., The.

—Aranas: Por Dentro y Por Fuera. Houghton, Gillian. Gonzalez, Tomas, tr. 2004. (Explora la Naturaleza (Getting into Nature) Ser.). (SPA.). 27p. (YA). (gr. 3-6). lib. bdg. 25.25 *(978-1-4042-2867-2(5))* Rosen Publishing Group, Inc., The.

—Buhos: Por Dentro y Por Fuera. Houghton, Gillian. Gonzalez, Tomas, tr. 2004. (Explora la Naturaleza (Getting into Nature) Ser.). (SPA.). 27p. (YA). (gr. 3-6). lib. bdg. 25.25 *(978-1-4042-2866-5(7))* Rosen Publishing Group, Inc., The.

—Tortugas: Por Dentro y Por Fuera. Houghton, Gillian. Gonzalez, Tomas, tr. 2004. (Explora la Naturaleza (Getting into Nature) Ser.). (SPA.). 32p. (J). (gr. k-5). lib. bdg. 25.25 *(978-1-4042-2869-6(1))* Rosen Publishing Group, Inc., The.

Studio, Xian Nu, jt. illus. see Ota, Yuko.

Studios, A&J. Dora's Starry Christmas. Ricci, Christine. 2005. 24p. (J). lib. bdg. 9.00 *(978-1-4242-0980-4(3))* Fitzgerald Bks.

Studios, Arcana. Braving the Lake. Falligant, Erin. 2010. (ENG.). 120p. (YA). (gr. 3-18). pap. 8.95 *(978-1-59369-757-0(0))* American Girl Publishing, Inc.

—Dive Right In. Hart, Alison. 2011. (ENG.). 120p. (J). pap. 8.95 *(978-1-59369-909-3(3))* American Girl Publishing, Inc.

—Fork in the Trail. Calkhoven, Laurie. 2010. (ENG.). 120p. (J). (gr. 3-18). pap. 8.95 *(978-1-59369-758-7(9))* American Girl Publishing, Inc.

—Into the Spotlight. Falligant, Erin. 2011. (ENG.). 120p. (YA). (gr. 3-18). pap. 8.95 *(978-1-59369-835-5(6))* American Girl Publishing, Inc.

—A Surprise Find. Falligant, Erin. 2011. (ENG.). 120p. (J). pap. 8.95 *(978-1-59369-908-6(5))* American Girl Publishing, Inc.

—Taking the Reins. Hart, Alison. 2010. (ENG.). 120p. (YA). (gr. 3-18). pap. 8.95 *(978-1-59369-760-0(0))* American Girl Publishing, Inc.

—A Winning Goal. Calkhoven, Laurie. 2011. (ENG.). 120p. (YA). (gr. 3-18). pap. 8.95 *(978-1-59369-836-2(4))* American Girl Publishing, Inc.

Stuhmer, Bob. Don't Be a Schwoe: Fitness. Mauzy, Barbara E. 2013. (ENG.). 64p. (J). 16.99 *(978-0-7643-4295-0(9))* Schiffer Publishing, Ltd.

Sturcke, Otto. A Heart That Finds His Way: More on the Line. List, Gloria A. 2005. 18p. (J). pap. 7.95 *(978-0-9709861-0-8(6))* Fingerprint Bks.

Sturgen, Bobbi. Black Ridge Mountain. Johnson, Sandi. Durant, Sybrina, ed. 2014. (ENG.). 34p. (J). (gr. k-5). pap. 12.99 *(978-1-929063-66-6(0)*, 165) Moons & Stars Publishing For Children.

—Chip Dude from Outer Space. Johnson, Sandi. Johnson, Britt, ed. l.t. ed. 2014. (ENG.). 28p. (J). (gr. k-5). pap. 12.99 *(978-1-929063-81-9(4)*, 254) Moons & Stars Publishing For Children.

—Dittle's Christmas Wish. Johnson, Sandi. Durant, Sybrina, ed. 2014. 40p. (J). (gr. k-5). pap. 12.99 *(978-1-929063-65-9(2)*, 164) Moons & Stars Publishing For Children.

—My Teacher Is an Alien. Johnson, Sandi. Durant, Sybrina, ed. 2014. (ENG.). 30p. (J). (gr. k-5). pap. 12.99 *(978-1-929063-75-8(X)*, 285) Moons & Stars Publishing For Children.

—White Wolf at Dawn. Johnson, Sandi. Johnson, Britt, ed. 2014. (ENG.). 30p. (J). (gr. k-5). pap. 12.99 *(978-1-929063-72-7(5)*, 171) Moons & Stars Publishing For Children.

Sturgeon, Bobbi. Harold the Hopping Hamster. Johnson, Sandi. Johnson, Britt, ed. l.t. ed. 2003. (ENG.). 34p. (J). (gr. k-5). pap. 12.99 *(978-1-929063-91-8(1)*, 322) Moons & Stars Publishing For Children.

—Lost Island. Johnson, Sandi. Johnson, Britt & Durant, Sybrina, eds. l.t. ed. 2014. 28p. (J). (gr. k-5). pap. 12.99 *(978-1-929063-69-7(5)*, 168) Moons & Stars Publishing For Children.

Sturgeon, Bobbi, jt. illus. see Brundige, Britt.

Sturgeon, Brad. The Wonder of Keys for Kids. Cruz-Martinez, George. 2006. 43p. (J). *(978-1-55452-013-8(4))* Essence Publishing.

Sturm, Ellen. Floating & Sinking, 1 vol. Niz, Ellen S. 2006. (Our Physical World Ser.). (ENG.). 24p. (gr. 1-2). 24.65 *(978-0-7368-5401-6(0)*, First Facts) Capstone Pr., Inc.

Sturm, James. Characters in Action! Sturm, James. Arnold, Andrew & Frederick-Frost, Alexis. 2013. (Adventures in Cartooning Ser.). (ENG.). 64p. (J). (gr. 1-5). pap. 9.99 *(978-1-59643-732-6(4)*, First Second Bks.) Roaring Brook Pr.

—Christmas Special! Sturm, James. Arnold, Andrew & Frederick-Frost, Alexis. 2012. (Adventures in Cartooning Ser.). (ENG.). 64p. (J). (gr. 1-5). pap. 9.99 *(978-1-59643-730-2(8)*, First Second Bks.) Roaring Brook Pr.

Stutz, Chris. Lady, 1 vol. Depucci, Diana M. 2009. 25p. pap. 24.95 *(978-1-61546-677-1(0))* America Star Bks.

—My Mom Inside My Pocket, 1 vol. Barr, Barbara Jean. 2010. 16p. 24.95 *(978-1-4489-5704-0(4))* America Star Bks.

—Never Never Be a Bully. Pam, Miss. 2011. 24p. pap. 24.95 *(978-1-4626-4325-7(6))* America Star Bks.

—The Story of Chris Moose, 1 vol. McArthur, Cathy E. 2009. 24p. pap. 24.95 *(978-1-4489-0928-5(7))* America Star Bks.

Stutzman, Laura. B Is for Blue Crab: A Maryland Alphabet. Menendez, Shirley. 2004. (Discover America State by State Ser.). (ENG.). 40p. (J). (gr. 1-3). 17.95 *(978-1-58536-160-1(7)*, 202020) Sleeping Bear Pr.

—The Happy Prince. Wilde, Oscar & Grodin, Elissa. rev. ed. 2006. (ENG.). 48p. (J). (gr. k-6). 17.95 *(978-1-58536-264-6(6))* Sleeping Bear Pr.

Style Guide, jt. illus. see Style Guide Staff.

Style Guide Staff. All about the Dragons. Katschke, Judy. 2014. (How to Train Your Dragon 2 Ser.). (ENG.). 32p. (J). (gr. k-2). 16.99 *(978-1-4814-0486-0(5)*, Simon Spotlight) Simon Spotlight.

—A Busy Day in Busytown. Shaw, Natalie. 2010. (Busytown Mysteries Ser.). (ENG.). 14p. (J). (gr. -1-k). bds. 5.99 *(978-1-4424-0968-2(1)*, Simon Spotlight) Simon Spotlight.

—Christmas in Gabba Land. Jameson, Louise. (Yo Gabba Gabba! Ser.). (ENG.). 12p. (J). (gr. -1-k). 2013. bds. 5.99 *(978-1-4424-8596-9(5))*; 2009. bds. 7.99 *(978-1-4169-9167-0(0))* Simon Spotlight. (Simon Spotlight).

—Dragon Race! Evans, Cordelia. 2014. (How to Train Your Dragon 2 Ser.). (ENG.). 24p. (J). (gr. -1-2). pap. 6.99 *(978-1-4814-0474-7(1)*, Simon Spotlight) Simon Spotlight.

—Everyone Is Different: Why Being Different Is Great! 2012. (Yo Gabba Gabba! Ser.). (ENG.). 24p. (J). (gr. -1-2). pap. 3.99 *(978-1-4424-5443-9(1)*, Simon Spotlight) Simon Spotlight.

—Feel Better, Toodee! 2011. (Yo Gabba Gabba! Ser.). (ENG.). 14p. (J). (gr. -1-k). bds. 5.99 *(978-1-4424-1251-4(8)*, Simon Spotlight) Simon Spotlight.

—Gift of the Night Fury. 2014. (How to Train Your Dragon TV Ser.). (ENG.). 24p. (J). (gr. -1-2). pap. 3.99 *(978-1-4814-0436-5(9)*, Simon Spotlight) Simon Spotlight.

—Good Po, Bad Po. 2014. (Kung Fu Panda TV Ser.). (ENG.). 24p. (J). (gr. -1-2). pap. 3.99 *(978-1-4814-0001-5(0)*, Simon Spotlight) Simon Spotlight.

—Goodnight, Daniel Tiger. Santomero, Angela C. 2014. (Daniel Tiger's Neighborhood Ser.). (ENG.). 26p. (J). (gr. -1-2). 12.99 *(978-1-4814-0048-0(7)*, Simon Spotlight) Simon Spotlight.

—Hilda Hippo's Big Surprise! Shaw, Natalie. 2010. (Busytown Mysteries Ser.). (ENG.). 14p. (J). (gr. -1-k). bds. 5.99 *(978-1-4424-0969-9(X)*, Simon Spotlight) Simon Spotlight.

—Home: The Chapter Book. 2015. (Home Ser.). (ENG.). 96p. (J). (gr. 2-5). pap. 5.99 *(978-1-4814-2606-0(0)*, Simon Spotlight) Simon Spotlight.

—I'm Thankful for You! 2014. (Yo Gabba Gabba! Ser.). (ENG.). 12p. (J). (gr. -1-k). bds. 5.99 *(978-1-4814-1723-5(1)*, Simon Spotlight) Simon Spotlight.

—Kung Fu to the Rescue! 2014. (Kung Fu Panda TV Ser.). (ENG.). 96p. (J). (gr. 2-5). pap. 5.99 *(978-1-4814-0511-9(X)*, Simon Spotlight) Simon Spotlight.

—Legendary Legends. Testa, Maggie. 2014. (Kung Fu Panda TV Ser.). (ENG.). 16p. (J). (gr. -1-2). 5.99 *(978-1-4424-9998-0(2)*, Simon Spotlight) Simon Spotlight.

—Let's Put on a Show! Gallo, Tina. 2010. (Yo Gabba Gabba! Ser.). (ENG.). 16p. (J). (gr. -1-1). pap. 5.99 *(978-1-4169-9535-7(8)*, Simon Scribbles) Simon Scribbles.

—Meet the Neighbors! Shaw, Natalie. 2014. (Daniel Tiger's Neighborhood Ser.). (ENG.). 16p. (J). (gr. -1-k). bds. 7.99 *(978-1-4424-9837-2(4)*, Simon Spotlight) Simon Spotlight.

—The Missing Apple Mystery. 2010. (Busytown Mysteries Ser.). (ENG.). 24p. (J). (gr. -1-2). pap. 3.99 *(978-1-4424-0227-0(X)*, Simon Spotlight) Simon Spotlight.

—Oh, Barnacles! SpongeBob's Handbook for Bad Days. Lewman, David. 2005. (SpongeBob SquarePants Ser.). (ENG.). 48p. (J). pap. 3.99 *(978-1-4169-0641-4(X)*, Simon Spotlight/Nickelodeon) Simon Spotlight/Nickelodeon.

—Po's Secret Move. 2014. (Kung Fu Panda TV Ser.). (ENG.). 32p. (J). (gr. k-2). pap. 3.99 *(978-1-4424-9995-9(8)*, Simon Spotlight) Simon Spotlight.

—A Ride Through the Neighborhood. Testa, Maggie. 2014. (Daniel Tiger's Neighborhood Ser.). (ENG.). 12p. (J). (gr. -1-1). bds. 6.99 *(978-1-4424-9839-6(0)*, Simon Spotlight) Simon Spotlight.

—Snack Attack! Shaw, Natalie. 2013. (Cloudy with a Chance of Meatballs Movie Ser.). (ENG.). 16p. (J). (gr. -1-2). pap. 5.99 *(978-1-4424-9737-5(8)*, Simon Spotlight) Simon Spotlight.

—SpongeBob SpookyPants. Silverhardt, Lauryn. 2004. (SpongeBob SquarePants Ser.). (ENG.). 16p. (J). bds. 5.99 *(978-0-689-87320-1(4)*, Simon Spotlight/Nickelodeon) Simon Spotlight/Nickelodeon.

—SpongeBob's Backpack Book. 2003. (SpongeBob SquarePants Ser.). (ENG.). 16p. (J). bds. 6.99 *(978-0-689-85648-8(2)*, Simon Spotlight/Nickelodeon) Simon Spotlight/Nickelodeon.

—Two to Kung Fu. 2014. (Kung Fu Panda TV Ser.). (ENG.). 96p. (J). (gr. 2-5). pap. 4.99 *(978-1-4424-9992-8(3)*, Simon Spotlight) Simon Spotlight.

Style Guide Staff & Fruchter, Jason. Daniel Goes to School. 2014. (Daniel Tiger's Neighborhood Ser.). (ENG.). 24p. (J). (gr. -1-7). pap. 3.99 *(978-1-4814-0318-4(4)*, Simon Spotlight) Simon Spotlight.

—Happy Halloween, Daniel Tiger! Santomero, Angela C. 2014. (Daniel Tiger's Neighborhood Ser.). (ENG.). 14p. (J). (gr. -1-2). bds. 6.99 *(978-1-4814-0429-7(6)*, Simon Spotlight) Simon Spotlight.

Style Guide Staff & Garwood, Gord. Thank You Day. 2014. (Daniel Tiger's Neighborhood Ser.). (ENG.). 24p. (J). (gr. -1-k). pap. 3.99 *(978-1-4424-9833-4(1)*, Simon Spotlight) Simon Spotlight.

—Welcome to the Neighborhood! Friedman, Becky. 2014. (Daniel Tiger's Neighborhood Ser.). (ENG.). 24p. (J). (gr. -1-1). pap. 3.99 *(978-1-4424-9741-2(6)*, Simon Spotlight) Simon Spotlight.

Style Guide Staff & Style Guide. Patricks Backpack Book. 2003. (SpongeBob SquarePants Ser.). (ENG.). 16p. (J). bds. 6.99 *(978-0-689-85649-5(0)*, Simon Spotlight/Nickelodeon) Simon Spotlight/Nickelodeon.

Style Guide Staff, jt. illus. see Giles, Mike.

Style Guide, Style. The Furry & the Furious. 2014. (Kung Fu Panda TV Ser.). (ENG.). 96p. (J). (gr. 2-5). pap. 4.99 *(978-1-4814-1703-7(7)*, Simon Spotlight) Simon Spotlight.

—Guide to the Dragons. Testa, Maggie. 2014. (How to Train Your Dragon TV Ser.: 1). (ENG.). 24p. (J). (gr. -1-2). pap. 8.99 *(978-1-4814-1936-9(6)*, Simon Spotlight) Simon Spotlight.

—The Knightly Campout. 2014. (Mike the Knight Ser.). (ENG.). 24p. (J). (gr. -1-1). pap. 3.99 *(978-1-4814-0418-1(0)*, Simon Spotlight) Simon Spotlight.

—Lovely, Love My Family. 2011. (Yo Gabba Gabba! Ser.). (ENG.). 14p. (J). (gr. -1-1). bds. 5.99 *(978-1-4424-2134-9(7)*, Simon Spotlight) Simon Spotlight.

—Meet the Penguins! Pendergrass, Daphne. 2014. (Penguins of Madagascar Ser.). (ENG.). 24p. (J). (gr. -1-3). pap. 3.99 *(978-1-4814-3734-9(8)*, Simon Spotlight) Simon Spotlight.

—School Is Awesome! 2014. (Yo Gabba Gabba! Ser.). (ENG.). 24p. (J). (gr. -1-1). pap. 3.99 *(978-1-4814-0930-8(1)*, Simon Spotlight) Simon Spotlight.

Style Guide, Style & Fruchter, Jason. Friends Are the Best! Testa, Maggie. 2014. (Daniel Tiger's Neighborhood Ser.). (ENG.). 12p. (J). (gr. -1-k). bds. 5.99 *(978-1-4424-9547-0(2)*, Simon Spotlight) Simon Spotlight.

Style Guide, Style & Schwarz, Thies. Tip's Tips on Friendship. 2015. (Home Ser.). (ENG.). 32p. (J). (gr. k-2). pap. 3.99 *(978-1-4814-2610-7(9)*, Simon Spotlight) Simon Spotlight.

Style Guide, Style, jt. illus. see Schwarz, Thies.

Styles, Emily. One Humpy Grumpy Camel. Johnson, Julia. Stacey International Staff, ed. 2005. (ENG.). 32p. (J). (gr. 3-6). 16.95 *(978-1-900988-75-9(5)*, Stacey International) Stacey Publishing GBR. Dist: Casemate Academic.

Stylou, Georgia. Cloud City: A Child's Journey Through Bereavement. Spergel, Heather. 2013. (ENG.). 40p. (J). 15.95 *(978-1-938501-45-6(4))* Turn the Page Publishing.

Su, Keren, photos by. Giant Pandas. Stone, Lynn M. 2003. (Nature Watch Ser.). (ENG., 48p. (gr. 4-8). 27.93 *(978-1-57505-343-1(8)*, Carolrhoda Bks.) Lerner Publishing Group.

Su, Keren, et al, photos by. Global Babies. Global Fund for Children Staff. 2007. (Global Fund for Children Ser.). (ENG., 16p. (J). (gr. -1 — 1). bds. 6.95 *(978-1-58089-174-5(8))* Charlesbridge Publishing, Inc.

—Global Babies (Bebes del Mundo) Global Fund for Children Staff. 2009. (ENG & SPA., 16p. (J). (gr. -1 — 1). bds. 6.95 *(978-1-58089-250-6(7))* Charlesbridge Publishing, Inc.

Su, Lucy. Children of Lir Jigsaw Book. 2005. 12p. (J). 24.95 *(978-0-7171-3942-2(5))* Gill & MacMillan, Ltd. IRL. Dist: Dufour Editions, Inc.

—Irish Legends for Children, 1 vol. Carroll, Yvonne. 2004. (ENG.). 64p. (J). (gr. k-3). 18.99 *(978-1-58980-278-0(0))* Pelican Publishing Co., Inc.

Su, Lucy. Make a Picnic. Su, Lucy. 2003. (Kitten & Baby Kitten Ser.). 32p. (YA). *(978-1-85602-445-7(8)*, Pavilion Children's Books) Pavilion Bks.

—Make Cards. Su, Lucy. 2003. (Kitten & Baby Kitten Ser.). 32p. (YA). *(978-1-85602-446-4(6)*, Pavilion Children's Books) Pavilion Bks.

—Play Dressing Up. Su, Lucy. 2003. (Kitten & Baby Kitten Ser.). 24p. (J). bds. *(978-1-85602-463-1(6)*, Pavilion Children's Books) Pavilion Bks.

—Play Hide & Seek. Su, Lucy. 2003. (Kitten & Baby Kitten Ser.). 42p. (J). pap. *(978-1-85602-538-6(1)*, Pavilion Children's Books) Pavilion Bks.

—Say Good Morning. Su, Lucy. 2003. (Kitten & Baby Kitten Ser.). 42p. (J). bds. *(978-1-85602-466-2(0)*, Pavilion Children's Books) Pavilion Bks.

—Say Good Night. Su, Lucy. 2003. (Kitten & Baby Kitten Ser.). 42p. (J). bds. *(978-1-85602-537-9(3)*, Pavilion Children's Books) Pavilion Bks.

Su, Qin. At Home in This World: A China Adoption Story. MacLeod, Jean. 2nd ed. 2004. 32p. 15.95 *(978-0-9726244-1-1(4))* EMK Pr.

Suad, Laura. The Great Chapatti Chase. Dolan, Penny. 2015. (Collins Big Cat Ser.). (ENG.). 32p. pap. 7.95 ***(978-0-00-759121-3(7))*** HarperCollins Pubs. Ltd. GBR. Dist: Independent Pubs. Group.

Suarez, Maribel. Dreams. Santillana USA. (Rowing Frog's Rhymes Ser.). 16p. (J). (gr. k-3). 7.95 *(978-1-59437-842-3(8))* Santillana USA Publishing Co., Inc.

—Este Soy Yo. Robleda, Margarita. 2006. (Rana, Rema, Rimas Ser.). (SPA.). 12p. (J). (gr. -1-k). 7.95 *(978-1-59820-207-6(3)*, Alfaguara) Santillana USA Publishing Co., Inc.

—Here, Kitty, Kitty! (Ven, Gatita, Ven!) Mora, Pat. 2008. (My Family: Mi Familia Ser.). (SPA & ENG.). 24p. (J). (gr. 4-7). lib. bdg. 15.89 *(978-0-06-085045-6(0)*, Rayo) HarperCollins Pubs.

—Here Kitty Kitty!/Ven Gatita Ven! Mora, Pat. 2008. (My Family: Mi Familia Ser.). (SPA & ENG.). 24p. (J). (gr. -1-1). 14.99 *(978-0-06-085044-9(2)*, Rayo) HarperCollins Pubs.

—Jugando con Las Vocales. Robleda, Margarita. 2006. (Rana, Rema, Rimas Ser.).Tr. of Playing with Vowels. (SPA.). 12p. (J). (gr. -1-k). 7.95 *(978-1-59820-210-6(3)*, Alfaguara) Santillana USA Publishing Co., Inc.

—Let's Eat! - ¡A Comer! Mora, Pat. 2008. (My Family: Mi Familia Ser.). (SPA & ENG.). 24p. (J). (gr. -1-3). 12.99 *(978-0-06-085038-8(8)*, Rayo) HarperCollins Pubs.

—Muneca de Trapo. Robleda, Margarita. 2006. (Rana, Rema, Rimas Ser.). (SPA.). 12p. (J). (gr. -1-k). 7.95 *(978-1-59820-209-0(X)*, Alfaguara) Santillana USA Publishing Co., Inc.

—Patito, Donde Estas? Robleda, Margarita. 2006. (Rana, Rema, Rimas Ser.).Tr. of Where Are You Little Ducky?. (SPA.). 12p. (J). (gr. -1-k). 7.95 *(978-1-59820-208-3(1)*, Alfaguara) Santillana USA Publishing Co., Inc.

—Ramon & His Mouse. (Rowing Frog's Rhymes Ser.). 16p. (J). (gr. k-3). 7.95 *(978-1-59437-839-3(8))* Santillana USA Publishing Co., Inc.

—Ramon y Su Raton. Robleda, Margarita. (Rana, Rema, Rimas Ser.). (SPA.). 16p. (J). (gr. k-3). 7.95 *(978-1-59437-818-8(5))* Santillana USA Publishing Co., Inc.

—Rebeca. Robleda, Margarita. (Rana, Rema, Rimas Ser.).Tr. of Rebecca. (SPA.). 16p. (J). (gr. k-3). 7.95 *(978-1-59437-819-5(3))* Santillana USA Publishing Co., Inc.

—Rebecca. (Rowing Frog's Rhymes Ser.). 16p. (J). (gr. k-3). 7.95 *(978-1-59437-840-9(1))* Santillana USA Publishing Co., Inc.

—Sana Ranita, Sana. Robleda, Margarita. (Rana, Rema, Rimas Ser.). (SPA.). 16p. (J). (gr. k-3). 7.95 *(978-1-59437-820-1(7))* Santillana USA Publishing Co., Inc.

—Suenos. Robleda, Margarita. (Rana, Rema, Rimas Ser.). (SPA.). 16p. (J). (gr. k-3). 7.95 *(978-1-59437-821-8(5))* Santillana USA Publishing Co., Inc.

—Sweet Dreams/Dulces Suenos. Mora, Pat. 2008. (My Family: Mi Familia Ser.). (SPA & ENG.). 24p. (J). (gr. -1-1). 12.99 *(978-0-06-085041-8(8)*, Rayo) HarperCollins Pubs.

—Wiggling Pockets (Los Bolsillos Saltarines) Mora, Pat. 2009. (My Family: Mi Familia Ser.). (SPA & ENG.). 24p. (J). (gr. -1-1). 12.99 *(978-0-06-085047-0(7)*, Rayo) HarperCollins Pubs.

Suarez, Maribel. Pick a Pet. Suarez, Maribel, tr. Namm, Diane. 2004. (My First Reader Ser.). (ENG.). 31p. (J). 18.50 *(978-0-516-24417-4(5)*, Children's Pr.) Scholastic Library Publishing.

Suarez, Nora. Noah's Moon. Peirce-Bale, Mary. 2006. (ENG.). 28p. (J). pap. 10.90 *(978-0-9773990-2-4(8))* Mother's Hse. Publishing.

Suarez, Rosa Virginia Urdaneta, photos by. Un Caballo en la Ciudad. Pantin, Yolanda. 2003. (Playco's Best Collection). (SPA., 36p. (J). (gr. 2-7). *(978-980-6437-40-1(3))* Playco Editores, C.A.

Suarez, Sergio Lopez. Huakala! a los Miedos. Suarez, Sergio Lopez. 2003. (SPA.). 32p. (J). (gr. k-3). 9.95 *(978-968-19-0556-9(3))* Aguilar, Altea, Taurus, Alfaguara, S.A. de C.V MEX. Dist: Santillana USA Publishing Co., Inc.

Suber, Melissa. Milo the Really Big Bunny. Krensky, Stephen. 2010. (ENG.). 32p. (J). (gr. -1-1). 11.99 *(978-1-4424-1434-1(0),* Simon & Schuster Bks. For Young Readers) Simon & Schuster Bks. For Young Readers.

Suber, Melissa. Tough Chicks. Suber, Melissa. Meng, Cece. 2009. (ENG.). 32p. (J). (gr. -1-3). 16.00 *(978-0-618-82415-1(4))* Houghton Mifflin Harcourt Publishing Co.

Subi. Las Aventuras de Don Quijote. Palacio, Carla, tr. 2005. (SPA.). 32p. *(978-84-264-1492-2(3))* Editorial Lumen.

—Stegosaurus: the Friendliest Dinosaur. Obiols, Anna. 2012. (Dinosaur Bks.). (ENG.). 36p. (J). (gr. -1-1). pap. 6.99 *(978-1-4380-0107-4(X))* Barron's Educational Series, Inc.

—Triceratops: the Strongest Dinosaur. Obiols, Anna. 2012. (Dinosaur Bks.). (ENG.). 36p. (J). (gr. -1-1). pap. 6.99 *(978-1-4380-0108-1(8))* Barron's Educational Series, Inc.

—Tyrannosaurus Rex: the King of the Dinosaurs. Obiols, Anna. 2012. (Dinosaur Bks.). (ENG.). 36p. (J). (gr. -1-1). pap. 6.99 *(978-1-4380-0109-8(6))* Barron's Educational Series, Inc.

Subirana, Joan. El León y el Ratón. Bailer, Darice et al. 2007. (SPA & ENG.). 28p. (J). *(978-0-545-02449-5(8))* Scholastic, Inc.

Sudo, Kumiko. Coco-Chan's Kimono. Sudo, Kumiko. 2010. (ENG.). 32p. (J). (gr. k-2). 16.95 *(978-1-933308-26-5(5))* Breckling Pr.

Sudyka, Diana. The Extraordinary Education of Nicholas Benedict. Stewart, Trenton Lee. (Mysterious Benedict Society Ser.). (ENG.). (J). (gr. 3-7). 2013. 496p. pap. 8.99 *(978-0-316-17620-0(6))*; 2012. 480p. 17.99 *(978-0-316-17619-4(2))* Little, Brown Bks. for Young Readers.

—Mr. Benedict's Book of Perplexing Puzzles, Elusive Enigmas, & Curious Conundrums. Stewart, Trenton Lee. 2011. (Mysterious Benedict Society Ser.). (ENG.). 176p. (J). (gr. 3-7). 12.99 *(978-0-316-18193-8(5))* Little, Brown Bks. for Young Readers.

—The Mysterious Benedict Society & the Perilous Journey. Stewart, Trenton Lee. 2009. (Mysterious Benedict Society Ser.: 2). (ENG.). 464p. (J). (gr. 3-7). pap. 8.00 *(978-0-316-03673-3(0))* Little Brown & Co.

—The Mysterious Benedict Society & the Perilous Journey. Stewart, Trenton Lee. 2008. (Mysterious Benedict Society Ser.: 2). (ENG.). 448p. (J). (gr. 3-7). 18.00 *(978-0-316-05780-6(0))* Little, Brown Bks. for Young Readers.

—Mysterious Benedict Society & the Prisoner's Dilemma. Stewart, Trenton Lee. Tingley, Megan, ed. 2010. (Mysterious Benedict Society Ser.: 3). (ENG.). 400p. (J). (gr. 3-7). pap. 8.00 *(978-0-316-04550-6(0))* Little, Brown Bks. for Young Readers.

—Mysterious Benedict Society & the Prisoner's Dilemma. Stewart, Trenton Lee. 2009. (Mysterious Benedict Society Ser.: 3). (ENG.). 400p. (J). (gr. 3-7). 17.99 *(978-0-316-04552-0(7))* Little, Brown Bks. for Young Readers.

Suekane, Kumiko. Afterschool Charisma. Suekane, Kumiko. 2010. (Afterschool Charisma Ser.: 1). (ENG.). 208p. pap. 12.99 *(978-1-4215-3397-1(9))* Viz Media.

Suenobu, Keiko. Life, Vol. 1. Suenobu, Keiko. 2006. (Life (Tokyopop) Ser.). 200p. (YA). pap. 14.99 *(978-1-59532-931-8(5),* Tokyopop Adult) TOKYOPOP, Inc.

Sugarman, S. Allan. The Heroes of Masada. Rosenfield, Geraldine. 38p. (J). (gr. 6-10). pap. 1.50 *(978-0-8381-0733-1(8),* 10-732) United Synagogue of America Bk. Service.

Suggs, Aisha. The Boy Who Did Not Want to Read, 1 vol. Williams, Tova. 2010. 36p. pap. 24.95 *(978-1-4489-5705-7(2))* PublishAmerica, Inc.

Suggs, Margaret. Blue, Where Are You? Magee, Wes. 2007. (Flyers Ser.: 16). (ENG.). 64p. (J). pap. 9.95 *(978-1-84717-009-5(9))* O'Brien Pr., Ltd., The IRL. Dist: Dufour Editions, Inc.

Sugisaki, Yukiru. Brain Powered, 3 vols., Vol. 3. Tomino, Yoshiyuki. rev. ed. 2003. 192p. pap. 9.99 *(978-1-59182-391-9(9))* TOKYOPOP, Inc.

—Brain Powered, 4 vols., Vol. 4. Tomino, Yoshiyuki. Matsunaga, Aya, tr. from JPN. rev. ed. 2004. 192p. pap. 9.99 *(978-1-59182-392-6(7))* TOKYOPOP, Inc.

Sugisaki, Yukiru. D. N. Angel, Vol. 6. Sugisaki, Yukiru. Nibley, Alethea & Nibley, Athena, trs. from JPN. rev. ed. 2005. 176p. (YA). pap. 9.99 *(978-1-59182-955-3(0))* TOKYOPOP, Inc.

—D. N. Angel. Sugisaki, Yukiru. 2005. Vol. 7. 7th rev. ed. 176p. pap. 9.99 *(978-1-59182-956-0(9))*; Vol. 8. rev. ed. 192p. (YA). pap. 9.99 *(978-1-59182-957-7(7))* TOKYOPOP, Inc.

—Rizelmine, Vol. 1. Sugisaki, Yukiru. 2005. 144p. per. 9.99 *(978-1-59532-901-1(3),* Tokyopop Adult) TOKYOPOP, Inc.

Sugita, Yataka. Good Morning-Sun's Up. Beach, Stewart. 32p. (J). (gr. -1-3). 13.95 *(978-0-87592-021-4(7))* Scroll Pr., Inc.

Sugita, Yutaka. Goodnight, One, Two, Three. Sugita, Yutaka. 32p. (J). (gr. -1-2). 14.95 *(978-0-87592-022-1(5))* Scroll Pr., Inc.

Suhr, James W. Like a Cat: Creep, Sleep, Pounce, & Peek. . . Donlon, Diane Youngblood. 2003. 32p. (J). 16.95 *(978-0-9720427-2-7(5))* OLLY Publishing Co.

—Tippee Tippee Tiptoe. Donlon, Diane Youngblood. 2003. (J). 16.95 *(978-0-9720427-0-3(9))* OLLY Publishing Co.

Suits, Rosella. Leggys in Number-land. Ostrom, Gladys. 2011. 40p. (J). pap. 12.95 *(978-0-9841721-6-0(5))* Open Door Publishers, Inc.

Sukanada, I. Gusti Made. Gecko's Complaint: A Balinese Folktale. Bowler, Ann Martin & Bowler, Anna. ed. 2009. (ENG & IND.). 32p. (J). (gr. k-3). 14.95 *(978-0-7946-0484-4(6))* Tuttle Publishing.

Suker, Ashlee. Crocheting for Fun! Bullard, Lisa. 2008. (For Fun!: Crafts Ser.). (ENG.). 48p. (gr. 3-6). 26.65 *(978-0-7565-3861-3(0),* For Fun!) Compass Point Bks.

SukWon, Sa. Bubbly & Grumpy. SungJa, Cho. rev. ed. 2014. (MySELF Bookshelf: Social & Emotional Learning/Social Awareness Ser.). (ENG.). 32p. (J). (gr. k-2). pap. 11.94 *(978-1-60357-660-4(6))*; lib. bdg. 22.60 *(978-1-59953-651-4(X))* Norwood Hse. Pr.

Suleman, Shilo Shiv. The Bookworm. R. N., Lavanya. 2013. (ENG.). 32p. (J). (gr. k). pap. 9.95 *(978-81-8190-180-4(0))* Karadi Tales Co. Pvt, Ltd. IND. Dist: Consortium Bk. Sales & Distribution.

—Tak-Tak! Ranade, Soumitra. 2013. (ENG.). 32p. (J). (gr. k). pap. 9.95 *(978-81-8190-183-5(5))* Karadi Tales Co. Pvt, Ltd. IND. Dist: Consortium Bk. Sales & Distribution.

Sullivan, Carolyn Rose. The Music Box: Songs, Rhymes, & Games for Young Children, 1 box. 2006. 200p. (J). 49.95 *(978-0-9772717-1-9(4))* ELZ Publishing.

Sullivan, Dana. Bob Books: First Stories. Kertell, Lynn Maslen. 2015. (ENG.). (J). (gr. k-2). 16.99 ***(978-0-545-73409-7(6))*** Scholastic, Inc.

Sullivan, Dana. Digger & Daisy Go on a Picnic. Young, Judy. 2014. (I Am a Reader: Digger & Daisy Ser.). (ENG.). 32p. (J). (gr. k-1). 9.99 *(978-1-58536-843-3(1),* 203006) Sleeping Bear Pr.

—Digger & Daisy Go to the Doctor. Young, Judy. 2014. (I AM a READER!: Digger & Daisy Ser.). (ENG.). 32p. (J). (gr. k-2). 9.99 *(978-1-58536-845-7(8),* 203674); pap. 4.99 *(978-1-58536-846-4(6),* 203728) Sleeping Bear Pr.

—Rhyming Words. Kertell, Lynn Maslen. 2013. (Bob Bks.). (ENG.). 16p. (J). (gr. -1-k). 16.99 *(978-0-545-51322-7(7))* Scholastic, Inc.

Sullivan, Dana. Ozzie & the Art Contest. Sullivan, Dana. 2013. (ENG.). 15.99 *(978-1-58536-820-4(2))* Sleeping Bear Pr.

Sullivan, Derek. Party Croc! A Folktale from Zimbabwe. MacDonald, Margaret Read. 2015. (ENG.). 32p. (J). (gr. -1-2). 16.99 *(978-0-8075-6320-5(X))* Whitman, Albert & Co.

Sullivan, Don. The Adventures of Max the Minnow. Boniface, William. 2015. (ENG.). 26p. (J). (gr.). bds. 9.99 *(978-1-4494-6490-5(4))* Andrews McMeel Publishing.

—El Tronco de Arbol, Level 1. Forbes, Chris. Flor Ada, Alma, tr. 2003. (Dejame Leer Ser.). (SPA.). 8p. (J). (gr. -1-k). 6.50 *(978-0-673-36300-8(7),* Good Year Bks.) Celebration Pr.

Sullivan, Elizabeth. Hannah y Molly. Schiller Brenz, Jeanne. 2011. (ENG.). 46p. pap. 12.99 *(978-1-4611-8129-3(1))* CreateSpace Independent Publishing Platform.

Sullivan, James Kevin. What Went Right Today? Journal: WWRT Journal. 2007. 72p. (J). spiral bd. 12.95 *(978-0-9766990-1-9(X))* Buz-Land Presentations, Inc.

Sullivan, Kate. On Linden Square. Sullivan, Kate. 2013. (ENG.). 40p. 15.99 *(978-1-58536-832-7(6))* Sleeping Bear Pr.

Sullivan, Mary. Bella's Boat Surprise, 1 vol. Jones, Christianne C. (My First Graphic Novel Ser.). (ENG.). 32p. (gr. k-2). 2010. pap. 6.25 *(978-1-4342-2287-9(X))*; 2009. 23.32 *(978-1-4342-1617-5(9))* Stone Arch Bks. (My First Graphic Novel).

—Bree's Bike Jump, 1 vol. Mortensen, Lori. 2009. (My First Graphic Novel Ser.). (ENG.). 32p. (gr. k-2). 23.32 *(978-1-4342-1620-5(9),* My First Graphic Novel) Stone Arch Bks.

—The End Zone, 1 vol. Mortensen, Lori. 2009. (My First Graphic Novel Ser.). (ENG.). 32p. (gr. k-2). pap. 6.25 *(978-1-4342-1408-9(7))*; lib. bdg. 23.32 *(978-1-4342-1289-4(0))* Stone Arch Bks. (My First Graphic Novel).

—Every Which Way to Pray, 1 vol. Meyer, Joyce. 2012. (Everyday Zoo Ser.). (ENG.). 40p. (J). 15.99 *(978-0-310-72317-2(5))* Zonderkidz.

—Hidden Pictures. School Zone Interactive Staff. rev. ed. 2006. (ENG.). 64p. (J). (gr. 1-2). 7.99 *(978-1-58947-301-0(9))* School Zone Publishing Co.

—Joy's Journey Home. Connolly, Timothy. 2012. (ENG.). 92p. (J). 17.95 *(978-0-9859986-2-2(8))*; pap. 8.95 *(978-0-9859986-1-5(X))* Nectar Pubns.

—The Lunchroom Fight. Sateren, Shelley Swanson. 2013. (Max & Zoe Ser.). (ENG.). 32p. (gr. k-2). lib. bdg. 19.99 *(978-1-4048-7199-1(3))* Picture Window Bks.

—Max & Zoe. Sateren, Shelley Swanson. (Max & Zoe Ser.). (ENG.). 32p. (gr. k-2). 2014. pap. 19.80 *(978-1-4795-5043-2(4))*; 2013. 239.88 *(978-1-4795-1695-7(3))*; 2013. 79.96 *(978-1-4795-1694-0(5))*; 2013. pap. 19.80 *(978-1-4048-8064-1(X))* Picture Window Bks. (Max & Zoe).

—Max & Zoe at Recess, 1 vol. Sateren, Shelley Swanson. 2012. (Max & Zoe Ser.). (ENG.). 32p. (gr. k-2). lib. bdg. 19.99 *(978-1-4048-7200-4(0))* Picture Window Bks.

—Max & Zoe at School, 1 vol. Sateren, Shelley Swanson. (Max & Zoe Ser.). (ENG.). 32p. (gr. k-2). 2013. pap. 5.19 *(978-1-4048-8059-7(3))*; 2011. lib. bdg. 19.99 *(978-1-4048-6211-1(0))* Picture Window Bks. (Max & Zoe).

—Max & Zoe at Soccer Practice, 1 vol. Sateren, Shelley Swanson. 2012. (Max & Zoe Ser.). (ENG.). 32p. (gr. k-2). lib. bdg. 19.99 *(978-1-4048-6213-5(7),* Max & Zoe) Picture Window Bks.

—Max & Zoe at the Dentist, 1 vol. Sateren, Shelley Swanson. (Max & Zoe Ser.). (ENG.). 32p. (gr. k-2). 2013. pap. 5.19 *(978-1-4048-8057-3(7))*; 2011. lib. bdg. 19.99 *(978-1-4048-6206-7(4))* Picture Window Bks. (Max & Zoe).

—Max & Zoe at the Doctor, 1 vol. Sateren, Shelley Swanson. (Max & Zoe Ser.). (ENG.). 32p. (gr. k-2). 2013. pap. 5.19 *(978-1-4048-8060-3(7))*; 2011. lib. bdg. 19.99 *(978-1-4048-6212-8(9))* Picture Window Bks. (Max & Zoe).

—Max & Zoe at the Library, 1 vol. Sateren, Shelley Swanson. (Max & Zoe Ser.). (ENG.). 32p. (gr. k-2). 2013. pap. 5.19 *(978-1-4048-8058-0(5))*; 2011. lib. bdg. 19.99 *(978-1-4048-6210-4(2))* Picture Window Bks. (Max & Zoe).

—Max & Zoe Celebrate Mother's Day, 1 vol. Sateren, Shelley Swanson. 2012. (Max & Zoe Ser.). (ENG.). 32p. (gr. k-2). lib. bdg. 19.99 *(978-1-4048-6214-2(5))* Picture Window Bks.

—Max & Zoe: the Lunchroom Fight, 1 vol. Sateren, Shelley Swanson. 2013. (Max & Zoe Ser.). (ENG.). 32p. (gr. k-2). pap. 5.19 *(978-1-4795-2328-3(3),* Max & Zoe) Picture Window Bks.

—Max & Zoe: the Science Fair, 1 vol. Sateren, Shelley Swanson. 2013. (Max & Zoe Ser.). (ENG.). 32p. (gr. k-2). pap. 5.19 *(978-1-4795-2330-6(5),* Max & Zoe) Picture Window Bks.

—Max & Zoe: the Very Best Art Project, 1 vol. Sateren, Shelley Swanson. 2013. (Max & Zoe Ser.). (ENG.). 32p. (gr. k-2). pap. 5.19 *(978-1-4795-2329-0(1),* Max & Zoe) Picture Window Bks.

—Max & Zoe: Too Many Tricks, 1 vol. Sateren, Shelley Swanson. 2013. (Max & Zoe Ser.). (ENG.). 32p. (gr. k-2). pap. 5.19 *(978-1-4795-2327-6(5),* Max & Zoe) Picture Window Bks.

—Oliver's Must-Do List. Brown, Susan Taylor. 2005. (ENG.). 32p. (J). (gr. -1-1). 15.95 *(978-1-59078-198-2(8))* Boyds Mills Pr.

—Phonics Comics: Clara the Klutz - Level 2. Wax, Wendy. 2007. (ENG.). 24p. (J). (gr. 1-17). per. 3.99 *(978-1-58476-565-3(8))* Innovative Kids.

—The School Concert. Sateren, Shelley Swanson. 2012. (Max & Zoe Ser.). (ENG.). 32p. (gr. k-2). lib. bdg. 19.99 *(978-1-4048-7198-4(5))* Picture Window Bks.

—The Science Fair. Sateren, Shelley Swanson. 2013. (Max & Zoe Ser.). (ENG.). 32p. (gr. k-2). lib. bdg. 19.99 *(978-1-4048-7202-8(7))* Picture Window Bks.

—Secret Scooter, 1 vol. Jones, Christianne C. 2009. (My First Graphic Novel Ser.). (ENG.). 32p. (gr. k-2). 23.32 *(978-1-4342-1619-9(5),* My First Graphic Novel) Stone Arch Bks.

—Too Many Tricks. Sateren, Shelley Swanson. 2013. (Max & Zoe Ser.). (ENG.). 32p. (gr. k-2). lib. bdg. 19.99 *(978-1-4048-7197-7(7))* Picture Window Bks.

—The Very Best Art Project. Sateren, Shelley Swanson. 2013. (Max & Zoe Ser.). (ENG.). 32p. (gr. k-2). lib. bdg. 19.99 *(978-1-4048-7201-1(9))* Picture Window Bks.

—Word Play: Sight Words. Gaydos, Nora. 2008. (NIR! Leveled Readers Ser.). (ENG.). 120p. (J). (gr. -1-2). 16.99 *(978-1-58476-725-1(1))* Random Hse. Children's Bks.

Sullivan, Mary & Gray, Steve. Clever Critters. Gaydos, Nora. 2008. (NIR! Leveled Readers Ser.). (ENG.). 128p. (J). (gr. -1-3). 16.99 *(978-1-58476-666-7(2))* Random Hse. Children's Bks.

Sullivan, Mary C. Bugs! a Counting Book. Sullivan, Mary C. 2013. 32p. 18.95 *(978-0-9859986-6-0(0))* Nectar Pubns.

Sullivan, Sarah & Tusa, Tricia. Once upon a Baby Brother. Sullivan, Sarah. 2010. (ENG.). 32p. (J). (gr. k-3). 16.99 *(978-0-374-34635-5(6),* Farrar, Straus & Giroux (BYR)) Farrar, Straus & Giroux.

Sullivan, Simon. Clara Barton: Spirit of the American Red Cross. Lakin, Patricia. 2004. (Ready-To-read SOFA Ser.). (ENG.). 48p. (J). (gr. 1-3). pap. 3.99 *(978-0-689-86513-8(9),* Simon Spotlight) Simon Spotlight.

—Clara Barton Spirit of the American Red Cross. Lakin, Patricia. ed. 2005. (Ready-to-Read Ser.). 48p. (J). lib. bdg. 15.00 *(978-1-59054-958-2(9))* Fitzgerald Bks.

—The Dog That Dug for Dinosaurs. Redmond, Shirley Raye & Redmond, Shirley Raye. 2004. (Ready-To-Reads Ser.). (ENG.). 32p. (J). (gr. 1-3). pap. 3.99 *(978-0-689-85708-9(X),* Simon Spotlight) Simon Spotlight.

Sullivan, Sonja. I Am A Kumeyaay. Sullivan, Sonja. Stanley, Barbara, ed. 2007. 29p. (J). *(978-0-9790951-1-5(5))* Sycuan Pr.

Sullivan, Troy. Scribble & Grin: 53 Rhymes for Inspiring Times. Giuffre, Mary & Clark, Paul L. 2013. 142p. *(978-0-9919101-0-6(9))* inspirtainment ink.

Suman, Surendra. Classic Collection: 22 Short Stories. Menon, Geeta. 2005. 143p. (J). *(978-81-7011-970-8(7))* Children's Bk. Trust.

Sumberac, Manuel. The Snow Queen. Andersen, Hans Christian. 2014. (J). ***(978-1-4351-5587-9(4))*** Barnes & Noble, Inc.

Sumberac, Manuel. The Snow Queen: The Hans Christian Andersen Classic Story. Woodward, Kay & Andersen, Hans Christian. 2014. (ENG.). 28p. (J). (gr. 3). 19.95 *(978-1-78312-015-4(0))* Carlton Bks., Ltd. GBR. Dist: Sterling Publishing Co., Inc.

Sumberac, Manuel, jt. illus. see Basic, Zdenko.

Sume, Lori Anne. Sorry, Sorry, Sorry: Learning to Choose the Right. 2004. (J). bds. 9.95 *(978-1-59156-298-6(8))* Covenant Communications, Inc.

Sumichrast, Jozef. The Funny Ride. Hillert, Margaret. 2008. (Beginning-to-Read Ser.). 32p. (J). (gr. -1-3). lib. bdg. 19.93 *(978-1-59953-149-6(6))* Norwood Hse. Pr.

Summerhayes, Roger, photos by. Whatever Happened to Baby Harry: The True Story of the First Child Born to an Officer's Family at Camp Apache, Arizona Territory. Ruffner, Melissa. 2003. 19p. (YA). pap. 12.95 *(978-0-9673171-1-3(8))* Primrose Pr.

Summers, Dana. Run, Dogs, Run! Higdon, Hal. 2003. 56p. (J). *(978-0-9636346-3-4(1))* Roadrunner Pr.

Summers, Mark. Pirates at the Plate. Frisch, Aaron. 2012. (ENG.). 32p. (J). (gr. 1-3). 17.99 *(978-1-56846-210-3(7),* Creative Editions) Creative Co., The.

Summy, Margaret A. Imagine Me... Love My Body. I.t. ed. 2005. 60p. per. *(978-1-880292-96-9(3))* LangMarc Publishing.

Sumner, William. Saving the Baghdad Zoo: A True Story of Hope & Heroes. Sumner, William. Halls, Kelly Milner. 2010. 64p. (J). lib. bdg. 18.89 *(978-0-06-177200-9(3))*; (ENG.). (gr. 3-18). 17.99 *(978-0-06-177202-3(X),* Greenwillow Bks.) HarperCollins Pubs.

Sumpter, Rachell. InStyle Getting Gorgeous: The Step-by-Step Guide to Your Best Hair, Makeup & Skin. Tung, Jennifer. rev. ed. 2004. (ENG.). 192p. (gr. 8-17). 27.95 *(978-1-932273-55-7(7))* Time Inc. Bks.

—The Wizard of Oz: And Other Wonderful Books of Oz - The Emerald City of Oz & Glinda of Oz. Baum, L. Frank. deluxe ed. 2012. (Penguin Classics Deluxe Edition Ser.). (ENG.). 432p. (gr. 12). pap. 16.00 *(978-0-14-310663-0(5),* Penguin Classics) Penguin Publishing Group.

Sun, Antuanette. Pat-A-Cake, Pat-a-Cake... We Made a Mistake! Dellas, Melanie & Woodworth, John. 2012. 24p. pap. 9.95 *(978-0-9830163-2-8(1))* Dellas, Melanie.

Sun, Jun. The Musical. Chen, Bill. 2013. (J). ***(978-0-9845523-1-3(6))*** Heryin Publishing Corp.

Sun Rise Illustration and Computer Animation Staff. Zagros & Nature Force: Coloring Book. Esmaili, Roza. Date not set. 74p. (J). (gr. k-8). pap. 2.49 *(978-0-9656185-1-9(X))* Esmaili, Inc.

Sun, Ru & Long, Ethan. You & Me: We're Opposites. Ziefert, Harriet. 2009. (ENG.). 32p. (J). (gr. -1-3). 12.99 *(978-1-934706-48-0(5))* Blue Apple Bks.

Sun Star, Elan & Snyder, Diana. Megan... A Child of God I Am. Chauvin, Belinda N. 2008. 40p. (J). 14.75 *(978-0-9801675-2-8(3))* Robertson Publishing.

Sundaravej, Sittisan & Barchus, Nathan. Terror on the Titanic. Wallace, Jim. 2007. (Choose Your Own Adventure Ser.: No. 24). (ENG.). 122p. (J). (gr. 4-7). pap. 6.99 *(978-1-933390-24-6(7))* Chooseco LLC.

Sundaravej, Sittisan & Thongmoon, Kriangsak. House of Danger. 2006. (Choose Your Own Adventure Ser.: No. 6). 108p. (J). (gr. 4-7). per. 6.99 *(978-1-933390-06-2(9),* CHCL06) Chooseco LLC.

—Race Forever. 2006. (Choose Your Own Adventure Ser.: No. 7). 122p. (J). (gr. 4-7). per. 6.99 *(978-1-933390-07-9(7),* CHCL07) Chooseco LLC.

—Return to Atlantis. 2007. (Choose Your Own Adventure Ser.: No. 18). 119p. (J). (gr. 4-7). per. 6.99 *(978-1-933390-18-5(2),* CHCL18) Chooseco LLC.

Sundberg, Angela M., et al. The Pottamus Family & the Unhappy Pottamus. Sundberg, Angela M. et al. 2007. (J). pap. 16.00 *(978-0-8059-7478-2(4))* Dorrance Publishing Co., Inc.

Sundblom, Haddon H. The Night Before Christmas: A Family Treasury of Songs, Poems, & Stories. 2007. 32p. (J). (gr. -1-3). 7.98 *(978-1-4127-8961-5(3))* Publications International, Ltd.

Sundermann, Elke. Wow! Ancient Asia! Sundermann, Elke. I.t. ed. 2011. (ENG.). 48p. pap. 10.99 *(978-1-4563-1330-2(4))* CreateSpace Independent Publishing Platform.

Sundram, Steve. Three Whales: Who Won the Heart of the World. Kita, Suzanne. 2010. (ENG.). 40p. (J). (gr. 3). *(978-1-59700-761-0(7))* Island Heritage Publishing.

Sundstrom, Mary. El Becerrito en Valle Grande. Hunter, Skillman "Kim". Ritthaler, Sarah Pilcher, tr. 2006.Tr. of Little Cow in Valle Grande. (SPA & ENG.). 32p. (J). (gr. -1-k). 16.95 *(978-0-8263-4044-3(X))* Univ. of New Mexico Pr.

Sundy, Jonathan. El Conejito de Pascua: El Cuento de un Dia Extraordinario. Benoist, Cathy & Gilmore, Cathy. 2014. (SPA.). 40p. (J). (gr. 4-7). 16.99 *(978-0-7648-2456-2(2),* Libros Liguori) Liguori Pubns.

—Easter Bunny's AMAZING Day. Gilmore, Cathy & Benoist, Carol. 2011. (ENG.). 40p. 15.99 *(978-0-9847656-1-4(1))* I.H.S. Pubs.

Sunn, Dionny. Betty Duck's Adventures in Paradise. Sunn, Dionny. 2013. (ENG.). 40p. pap. 10.00 *(978-0-615-83261-6(X))* Czerwonka, Larry Co., The.

Sunni Brannan, jt. illus. see Phil Brannan.

Sunset Producciones & Producciones, Sunset. El Huevo Azul. Cordero, Silvia Jaeger & Cordero, Silvia Jaegar. rev. ed. 2005. (Castillo de la Lectura Verde Ser.). (SPA & ENG.). 136p. (J). (gr. -1-7). pap. 7.95 *(978-970-20-0127-0(7))* Castillo, Ediciones, S. A. de C. V. MEX. Dist: Macmillan.

Sunshine, Mary Lou. Happy Days: Book 1. Orth, Jack. 2013. 50p. (J). pap. 9.95 *(978-1-61863-545-7(X))* Bookstand Publishing.

—Happy Days: Book 2. Orth, Jack. 2013. 50p. (J). pap. 9.95 *(978-1-61863-546-4(8))* Bookstand Publishing.

—Happy Days: Book 3. Orth, Jack. 2013. 50p. (J). pap. 9.95 *(978-1-61863-547-1(6))* Bookstand Publishing.

Suomalainen, Sami. Bola de Mugre. Munsch, Robert. Lopez, Jose M., tr. from ENG. 2004. (SPA.). 32p. (J). (gr. -1-2). pap. 5.95 *(978-1-55037-873-3(2),* 9781550378733) Annick Pr., Ltd. CAN. Dist: Firefly Bks., Ltd.

Suorsa, Michael. Puppy Stew. Gregory, Caroline. 2009. (ENG.). 28p. (J). pap. 8.99 *(978-0-9772025-9-1(3))* Sortis Publishing.

Super Duper Inc. Staff, photos by. Artic Photos Fun Deck S Blends: Ap04. 2003. (J). 11.99 *(978-1-58650-283-6(2))* Super Duper Pubns.

Surber, Shawn-Michelle. Hope, 1. Surber, Shawn-Michelle. collector's ed. 2007. 35p. (J). 19.99 *(978-0-9763534-0-9(7),* Mornin'Light Media) Mornin' Light Media.

Suriano, Andy & Davis, Dan W. Menace of the Time Thief, 1 vol. Wayne, Matt. 2012. (Batman: the Brave & the Bold Ser.). (ENG.). 32p. (gr. 2-3). lib. bdg. 21.27 *(978-1-4342-4548-9(9))* Stone Arch Bks.

—Panic of the Composite Creatures. Wayne, Matt. 2012. (Batman: the Brave & the Bold Ser.). (ENG.). 32p. (gr. 2-3). lib. bdg. 21.27 *(978-1-4342-4545-8(4))* Stone Arch Bks.

—President Batman, 1 vol. Wayne, Matt. 2012. (Batman: the Brave & the Bold Ser.). (ENG.). 32p. (gr. 2-3). lib. bdg. 21.27 *(978-1-4342-4547-2(0))* Stone Arch Bks.

Suriano, Andy, jt. illus. see Davis, Dan.

Surojegin, Pirkko-Liisa. The Kalevala: Tales of Magic & Adventure. Mäkinen, Kirsti. Brooks, Kaarina, tr. from FIN. 2009. (ENG.). 214p. (YA). (gr. 4-18). 24.95 *(978-1-897476-00-0(0))* Simply Read Bks. CAN. Dist: Ingram Pub. Services.

Surovec, Yasmine. A Bed for Kitty. Surovec, Yasmine. 2014. (ENG.). 40p. (J). (gr. -1-1). 16.99 *(978-1-59643-863-7(0))* Roaring Brook Pr.

—I See Kitty. Surovec, Yasmine. (ENG.). (J). (gr. -1-1). 2015. 34p. bds. 7.99 *(978-1-62672-093-0(2))*; 2013. 36p. 15.99 *(978-1-59643-862-0(2))* Roaring Brook Pr.

Surplice, Holly. Guinea Pig Party. Surplice, Holly. (ENG.). (J). 2015. 24p. (— 1). bds. 7.99 *(978-0-7636-7604-9(7))*; 2012. 32p. (gr. -1-k). 14.99 *(978-0-7636-6269-1(0))* Candlewick Pr. (Nosy Crow).

—Peek-a-Boo Bunny. Surplice, Holly. 2014. (ENG.). 32p. (J). (gr. -1-3). 9.99 *(978-0-06-224265-5(2))* HarperCollins Pubs.

Surrey, Michael. Cool It Frida! Hamer, Ron. 2008. 40p. pap. 11.95 *(978-1-59858-654-1(8))* Dog Ear Publishing, LLC.

—Move It Milton! Hamer, Ron. 2009. 36p. pap. 11.95 *(978-1-59858-738-8(2))* Dog Ear Publishing, LLC.

—Suck It up Tate! Hamer, Ron. 2008. 36p. pap. 11.95 *(978-1-59858-512-4(6))* Dog Ear Publishing, LLC.

Susan, Lisbin. Mommy, What's an MRI? Soloway, Cindy. Steve, Sumner, ed. 2006. (J). mass mkt. *(978-0-9765060-2-7(5))* TouchSmart Publishing, LLC.

Susan, Paradis. Edna. Susan, Paradis. 2013. 32p. pap. 11.95 *(978-1-60898-153-3(3))* namelos llc.

Susan, Turnbull. The Raccoon & the Bee Tree. Eastman, Charles A. & Eastman, Elaine Goodale. 2013. 32p. (J). *(978-0-9860355-4-8(8))* South Dakota State Historical Society Pr.

Sutanto, Tommy. Friends in the Garden. Gopinath, Karin Ursula. 2008. 34p. (J). per. 19.95 *(978-0-9800637-0-7(1))* Lotus Art Works Inc.

Sutcliff, Rosemary, jt. illus. see Lee, Alan.

Suteski, Monika. Secret Lives of the Civil War: What Your Teachers Never Told You about the War Between the States. O'Brien, Cormac. 2007. (Secret Lives Ser.). (ENG.). 320p. (gr. 9-18). pap. 16.95 *(978-1-59474-138-8(7))* Quirk Bks.

Sutherland, Dianne. Rashiecoat: A Story in Scots for Young Readers. 16p. pap. 6.95 *(978-1-899827-19-0(6))* Scottish Children's Pr. GBR. Dist: Wilson & Assocs.

Sutherland, Eileen & Sutherland, Maggie. Mom & the Polka-Dot Boo-Boo: A Gentle Story Explaining Breast Cancer to a Young Child. Sutherland, Eileen. 2007. (ENG.). 24p. (J). (gr. -1-k). 14.95 *(978-0-944235-87-4(5)*, 9780944235874) American Cancer Society, Inc.

Sutherland, James. The Tale of the Miserous Mip. Sutherland, James. 2011. (ENG.). 150p. pap. 6.99 *(978-1-4610-2992-2(9))* CreateSpace Independent Publishing Platform.

Sutherland, Leah. For Girls Only! Devotions. Larsen, Carolyn. 2009. (ENG.). 256p. (J). pap. 9.99 *(978-1-4143-2209-4(7)*, Tyndale Kids) Tyndale Hse. Pubs.

Sutherland, Maggie, jt. illus. see Sutherland, Eileen.

Sutherland, Marc. The Waiting Place. Sutherland, Marc. 2004. 24p. (J). (gr. k-4). reprint ed. 15.00 *(978-0-7567-8382-2(8))* DIANE Publishing Co.

Sutherland, Nicholas. Snuffley. Shumate, Robert O. 2008. 28p. pap. 24.95 *(978-1-60610-707-2(0))* America Star Bks.

Sutphin, Joe. Dr. Critchlore's School for Minions: Book 1. Grau, Sheila. 2015. (Dr. Critchlore's School for Minions Ser.). (ENG.). 288p. (J). (gr. 3-7). 14.95 *(978-1-4197-1370-5(1)*, Amulet Bks.) Abrams.

Suttie, Alan, jt. illus. see Jackson, Ian.

Sutton, Emily. Tiny Creatures: The World of Microbes. Davies, Nicola. 2014. (ENG.). 40p. (J). (gr. k-3). 15.99 *(978-0-7636-7315-4(3))* Candlewick Pr.

Sutton, George Miksch. The Burgess Seashore Book for Children. Burgess, Thornton W. 2005. (Dover Children's Classics Ser.). (ENG.). 288p. (J). (gr. -1-8). per. 11.95 *(978-0-486-44253-2(5))* Dover Pubns., Inc.

Sutula, Hollie. Uncle Bills Farm: True Stories of His Crazy Farm Animals. Susedik, Tina & Rearry, Alli. 2014. 29p. (J). pap. 10.00 ***(978-0-9667527-6-2(7))*** Maple Lane Writing & Desktop Publishing.

Suwannakit, Tul. How the Tooth Mouse Met the Tooth Fairy. Vries, Lizzette de & Vries, Cecile de. 2010. (J). 19.95 *(978-0-86715-507-5(8))* Quintessence Publishing Co., Inc.

Suzan, Gerardo. Jardin del Mar. Bracho, Coral. 2005. (SPA.). (J). (gr. k-2). pap. 10.95 *(978-968-494-055-0(6)*, CI6078) Centro de Informacion y Desarrollo de la Comunicacion y la Literatura MEX. Dist: Iaconi, Mariuccia Bk. Imports, Lectorum Pubns., Inc.

—My New Town. Hall, Kirsten. 2005. (My First Reader Ser.). (ENG.). 32p. (J). (gr. k-1). lib. bdg. 18.50 *(978-0-516-24877-6(4)*, Children's Pr.) Scholastic Library Publishing.

Suzuki, Mary. Miss Patch's Learn-To-Sew Book. Meyer, Carolyn. 2014. (ENG.). 96p. (J). (gr. 1-4). pap. 9.99 *(978-0-544-33905-7(3)*, HMH Books For Young Readers) Houghton Mifflin Harcourt Publishing Co.

Svensson, Richard. The Sweeet Old Lady Coloring & Activity Book. Killam, Catherine D. 2013. 62p. pap. 6.99 *(978-0-9910700-4-6(6))* Enchanted Forest Publishing.

—The Sweeet Old Lady down the Street. Killam, Catherine D. 2013. 42p. pap. 9.99 *(978-0-9910700-2-2(X))* Enchanted Forest Publishing.

Svetlin. Don Quijote. de Cervantes, Miguel. 2005. 159p. (J). (gr. 6-8). per. 14.99 *(978-84-316-7637-7(X))* Vicens-Vives, Editorial, S.A. ESP. Dist: Lectorum Pubns., Inc.

Swaab, Neil. Big Fat Liar. Patterson, James & Papademetriou, Lisa. 2014. (Middle School Ser.: Bk. 3). (ENG.). 304p. (J). (gr. 3-7). 13.99 *(978-0-316-32203-4(2))* Little Brown & Co.

—The Immortal Fire. Ursu, Anne. 2010. (Cronus Chronicles Ser.: 3). (ENG.). 528p. (J). (gr. 3-7). pap. 7.99 *(978-1-4169-0592-9(8)*, Atheneum Bks. for Young Readers) Simon & Schuster Children's Publishing.

—My Brother Is a Big, Fat Liar. Patterson, James & Papademetriou, Lisa. 2013. (Middle School Ser.: Bk. 3). (ENG.). 304p. (J). (gr. 3-7). 15.99 *(978-0-316-20754-6(3))* Little Brown & Co.

Swaab, Neil, jt. illus. see Fortune, Eric.

Swaab, Neil, jt. illus. see Park, Laura.

Swaim. The King & the Queen & the Jelly Bean. Crichton, Julie. l.t. ed. 2005. (SPA.). 24p. (J). bds. 7.95 *(978-0-9761990-0-7(9))* Bean Bk. Publishing.

Swaim, Michael. The Adventures of Rodger Dodger Dog. Britland, Jan. 2009. 40p. pap. 15.95 *(978-1-936051-23-6(0))* Peppertree Pr., The.

—The Adventures of Rodger Dodger Dog: A Christmas Story. Britland, Jan. 2009. 52p. pap. 18.95 *(978-1-936051-48-9(6))* Peppertree Pr., The.

—The Story Shell: A Tale of Friendship Bog. Repp, Gloria. 2011. (ENG.). 122p. pap. 5.99 *(978-1-4609-1810-4(X))* CreateSpace Independent Publishing Platform.

Swaim, Mike. The Adventures of Rodger Dodger Dog: A Christmas Story. Britland, Jan. l.t. ed. 2011. (ENG.). 52p. pap. 12.95 *(978-1-4637-3712-2(2))* CreateSpace Independent Publishing Platform.

—The Adventures of Rodger Dodger Dog: First Adventure. Britland, Jan. l.t. ed. 2012. (ENG.). 38p. pap. 10.95 *(978-1-4637-1559-5(5))* CreateSpace Independent Publishing Platform.

—The Adventures of Rodger Dodger Dog: Rodger Meets Dr. Glee. Britland, Jan. l.t. ed. 2010. (ENG.). 50p. pap. 12.95 *(978-1-4495-9362-9(3))* CreateSpace Independent Publishing Platform.

—The Adventures of Rodger Dodger Dog: Rodger Saves Bunny. Britland, Jan. l.t. ed. 2011. (ENG.). 50p. pap. 12.95 *(978-1-4565-3403-5(3))* CreateSpace Independent Publishing Platform.

—I Wonder What a Fish Would Wish For? Clish, Marian L. 2009. 29p. pap. 24.95 *(978-1-60836-289-9(2))* America Star Bks.

—Noodles - a Lunchtime Adventure. MacDonald, Alysha. 2012. 28p. pap. *(978-0-9735526-8-3(9))* Cold Rock Publishing.

Swaim, Ramon. El rey y la reina y el frijolito de Goma. Crichton, Julie. l.t. ed. 2005. 24p. (J). bds. 7.95 *(978-0-9761990-1-4(7))* Bean Bk. Publishing.

Swain, Alison Campbell. Bobby the Bush Pilot. Baker, Kane. 2003. (J). pap. *(978-1-932046-02-1(X))* Pastime Pr.

Swain, Holly. The King Who Wouldn't Sleep. Singleton, Debbie. 2012. (Andersen Press Picture Bks). (ENG.). 32p. (J). (gr. -1-3). 16.95 *(978-0-7613-8997-2(0))* Lerner Publishing Group.

—Miss Fox. Puttock, Simon. rev. ed. 2014. (Time to Read Ser.). (ENG.). 32p. (J). (gr. -1-2). pap. 6.99 *(978-1-84780-545-4(0)*, Frances Lincoln) Quarto Publishing Group UK GBR. Dist: Hachette Bk. Group.

—The Perfect Baby. Bradman, Tony. 2010. (ENG.). 32p. (J). (gr. k — 1). pap. 8.99 *(978-1-4052-2755-1(9))* Egmont Bks., Ltd. GBR. Dist: Independent Pubs. Group.

Swain, Wilson. A Nutty Nutcracker Christmas. Covert, Ralph & Mills, G. Riley. 2009. (ENG.). 40p. (J). (gr. -1-2). 18.99 *(978-0-8118-6111-3(2))* Chronicle Bks. LLC.

—The Misfits, Level 3. MacDonald, Kimber. 2006. (ENG.). 24p. (J). (gr. 1-17). per. 3.99 *(978-1-58476-421-2(X)*, IKIDS) Innovative Kids.

Swan, Angela. Chocolate Wishes #1. Bentley, Sue. 2013. (Magic Bunny Ser.: 1). (ENG.). 128p. (J). (gr. 1-3). pap. 4.99 *(978-0-448-46727-6(5)*, Grosset & Dunlap) Penguin Publishing Group.

—Circus Surprise #7. Bentley, Sue. 2014. (Magic Ponies Ser.: 7). (ENG.). 128p. (J). (gr. 1-3). 4.99 *(978-0-448-46734-4(8)*, Grosset & Dunlap) Penguin Publishing Group.

—Classroom Princess #9. Bentley, Sue. 2013. (Magic Puppy Ser.: 9). (ENG.). 128p. (J). (gr. 1-3). 4.99 *(978-0-448-46732-0(1)*, Grosset & Dunlap) Penguin Publishing Group.

—Firelight Friends #10. Bentley, Sue. 2014. (Magic Kitten Ser.: 10). (ENG.). 128p. (J). (gr. 1-3). 4.99 *(978-0-448-46788-7(7)*, Grosset & Dunlap) Penguin Publishing Group.

—Friendship Forever #10. Bentley, Sue. 2013. (Magic Puppy Ser.: 10). (ENG.). 128p. (J). (gr. 1-3). 4.99 *(978-0-448-46733-7(X)*, Grosset & Dunlap) Penguin Publishing Group.

—A Glittering Gallop, No. 8. Bentley, Sue. 2013. (Magic Kitten Ser.: 8). (ENG.). 128p. (J). (gr. 1-3). 4.99 *(978-0-448-46730-6(5)*, Grosset & Dunlap) Penguin Publishing Group.

—Magic Reindeer: a Christmas Wish. Bentley, Sue. 2013. (ENG.). 128p. (J). (gr. 2-4). 6.99 *(978-0-448-46736-8(4)*, Grosset & Dunlap) Penguin Publishing Group.

—A New Friend, No. 1. Bentley, Sue. 2013. (Magic Ponies Ser.: 1). (ENG.). 128p. (J). (gr. 1-3). pap. 4.99 *(978-0-448-46205-9(2)*, Grosset & Dunlap) Penguin Publishing Group.

—Pony Camp #8. Bentley, Sue. 2014. (Magic Ponies Ser.: 8). (ENG.). 128p. (J). (gr. 1-3). 4.99 *(978-0-448-46787-0(9)*, Grosset & Dunlap) Penguin Publishing Group.

—Riding Rescue #6. Bentley, Sue. 2013. (Magic Ponies Ser.: 6). (ENG.). 128p. (J). (gr. 1-3). 4.99 *(978-0-448-46735-1(6)*, Grosset & Dunlap) Penguin Publishing Group.

—Seaside Mystery #9. Bentley, Sue. 2013. (Magic Kitten Ser.: 9). (ENG.). 128p. (J). (gr. 1-3). 4.99 *(978-0-448-46731-3(3)*, Grosset & Dunlap) Penguin Publishing Group.

—Show-Jumping Dreams #4. Bentley, Sue. 2013. (Magic Ponies Ser.: 4). (ENG.). 128p. (J). (gr. 1-3). pap. 4.99 *(978-0-448-46208-0(7)*, Grosset & Dunlap) Penguin Publishing Group.

—Snowy Wishes. Bentley, Sue. 2013. (Magic Puppy Ser.). (ENG.). 128p. (J). (gr. 1-3). 4.99 *(978-0-448-46737-5(2)*, Grosset & Dunlap) Penguin Publishing Group.

—A Special Wish, No. 2. Bentley, Sue. 2013. (Magic Ponies Ser.: 2). (ENG.). 128p. (J). (gr. 1-3). pap. 4.99 *(978-0-448-46206-6(0)*, Grosset & Dunlap) Penguin Publishing Group.

—A Splash of Magic #3. Bentley, Sue. 2013. (Magic Bunny Ser.: 3). (ENG.). 128p. (J). (gr. 1-3). pap. 4.99 *(978-0-448-46729-0(1)*, Grosset & Dunlap) Penguin Publishing Group.

—A Twinkle of Hooves #3. Bentley, Sue. 2013. (Magic Ponies Ser.: 3). (ENG.). 128p. (J). (gr. 1-3). pap. 4.99 *(978-0-448-46207-3(9)*, Grosset & Dunlap) Penguin Publishing Group.

—Vacation Dreams #2. Bentley, Sue. 2013. (Magic Bunny Ser.: 2). (ENG.). 128p. (J). (gr. 1-3). pap. 4.99 *(978-0-448-46728-3(3)*, Grosset & Dunlap) Penguin Publishing Group.

—Winter Wonderland #5. Bentley, Sue. 2013. (Magic Ponies Ser.: 5). (ENG.). 128p. (J). (gr. 1-3). 4.99 *(978-0-448-46786-3(0)*, Grosset & Dunlap) Penguin Publishing Group.

Swan, Angela & Farley, Andrew. A Christmas Surprise. Bentley, Sue. 2008. (Magic Kitten Ser.). (ENG.). 128p. (J). (gr. 1-3). pap. 4.99 *(978-0-448-45001-8(1)*, Grosset & Dunlap) Penguin Publishing Group.

—Classroom Capers #4. Bentley, Sue. 2014. (Magic Bunny Ser.: 4). (ENG.). 128p. (J). (gr. 1-3). 4.99 *(978-0-448-46792-4(5)*, Grosset & Dunlap) Penguin Publishing Group.

—Classroom Chaos, 2 vols. Bentley, Sue. 2008. (Magic Kitten Ser.: 2). (ENG.). 128p. (J). (gr. 1-3). pap. 4.99 *(978-0-448-44999-9(4)*, Grosset & Dunlap) Penguin Publishing Group.

—Cloud Capers, 3 vols. Bentley, Sue. 2009. (Magic Puppy Ser.: 3). (ENG.). 128p. (J). (gr. 1-3). pap. 4.99 *(978-0-448-45046-9(1)*, Grosset & Dunlap) Penguin Publishing Group.

—Dancing Days #5. Bentley, Sue. 2014. (Magic Bunny Ser.: 5). (ENG.). 128p. (J). (gr. 1-3). 4.99 *(978-0-448-46793-1(3)*, Grosset & Dunlap) Penguin Publishing Group.

—Magic Puppy: Books 1-3. Bentley, Sue. 2014. (Magic Puppy Ser.). (ENG.). 368p. (J). (gr. 1-3). 7.99 *(978-0-448-48460-0(9)*, Grosset & Dunlap) Penguin Publishing Group.

—Moonlight Mischief #5, 5 vols. Bentley, Sue. 2009. (Magic Kitten Ser.: 5). (ENG.). 128p. (J). (gr. 1-3). pap. 4.99 *(978-0-448-45061-2(5)*, Grosset & Dunlap) Penguin Publishing Group.

—Muddy Paws, No. 2. Bentley, Sue. 2009. (Magic Puppy Ser.: 2). (ENG.). 128p. (J). (gr. 1-3). pap. 4.99 *(978-0-448-45045-2(3)*, Grosset & Dunlap) Penguin Publishing Group.

—New Beginning, No. 1. Bentley, Sue. 2009. (Magic Puppy Ser.: 1). (ENG.). 128p. (J). (gr. 1-3). pap. 4.99 *(978-0-448-45044-5(5)*, Grosset & Dunlap) Penguin Publishing Group.

—The Perfect Secret #14. Bentley, Sue. 2014. (Magic Puppy Ser.: 14). (ENG.). 128p. (J). (gr. 1-3). 4.99 *(978-0-448-46799-3(2)*, Grosset & Dunlap) Penguin Publishing Group.

—Picture Perfect #13. Bentley, Sue. 2014. (Magic Kitten Ser.: 13). (ENG.). 128p. (J). (gr. 1-3). 4.99 *(978-0-448-46796-2(8)*, Grosset & Dunlap) Penguin Publishing Group.

—A Puzzle of Paws #12. Bentley, Sue. 2014. (Magic Kitten Ser.: 12). (ENG.). 128p. (J). (gr. 1-3). 4.99 *(978-0-448-46795-5(X)*, Grosset & Dunlap) Penguin Publishing Group.

—A Shimmering Splash #11. Bentley, Sue. 2014. (Magic Kitten Ser.: 11). (ENG.). 128p. (J). (gr. 1-3). 4.99 *(978-0-448-46789-4(5)*, Grosset & Dunlap) Penguin Publishing Group.

—Sparkling Skates #13. Bentley, Sue. 2014. (Magic Puppy Ser.: 13). (ENG.). 128p. (J). (gr. 1-3). 4.99 *(978-0-448-46798-6(4)*, Grosset & Dunlap) Penguin Publishing Group.

—Spellbound at School #11. Bentley, Sue. 2014. (Magic Puppy Ser.: 11). (ENG.). 128p. (J). (gr. 1-3). 4.99 *(978-0-448-46790-0(9)*, Grosset & Dunlap) Penguin Publishing Group.

—A Splash of Forever #14. Bentley, Sue. 2014. (Magic Kitten Ser.: 14). (ENG.). 128p. (J). (gr. 1-3). 4.99 *(978-0-448-46797-9(6)*, Grosset & Dunlap) Penguin Publishing Group.

—Star Dreams, 3 vols. Bentley, Sue. 2008. (Magic Kitten Ser.: 3). (ENG.). 128p. (J). (gr. 1-3). pap. 4.99 *(978-0-448-45000-1(3)*, Grosset & Dunlap) Penguin Publishing Group.

—Star of the Show, 4 vols. Bentley, Sue. 2009. (Magic Puppy Ser.: 4). (ENG.). 128p. (J). (gr. 1-3). pap. 4.99 *(978-0-448-45047-6(X)*, Grosset & Dunlap) Penguin Publishing Group.

—A Summer Spell. Bentley, Sue. 2008. (Magic Kitten Ser.: 1). (ENG.). 128p. (J). (gr. 1-3). pap. 4.99 *(978-0-448-44998-2(6)*, Grosset & Dunlap) Penguin Publishing Group.

—Sunshine Shimmers #12. Bentley, Sue. 2014. (Magic Puppy Ser.: 12). (ENG.). 128p. (J). (gr. 1-3). 4.99 *(978-0-448-46791-7(7)*, Grosset & Dunlap) Penguin Publishing Group.

Swan, Angela, jt. illus. see Farley, Andrew.

Swan, Curt. Showcase Presents Superman, Vol. 2. Coleman, Jerry et al. rev. ed. 2006. (Showcase Presents Ser.: Vol. 2). (ENG.). 560p. (YA). pap. 16.99 *(978-1-4012-1041-0(4))* DC Comics.

Swan, Curt & Giordano, Dick. Superman in the Seventies. Maggin, Elliot et al. rev. ed. 2010. (Superman Ser.). (ENG.). 224p. (YA). pap. 19.99 *(978-1-56389-638-5(9))* DC Comics.

Swan, Gloria. Mama Grizzly Bear. Finke, Margot. 2012. 16p. (-18). pap. 9.95 *(978-1-61633-304-1(9))* Guardian Angel Publishing, Inc.

Swan, Shawn. Pigboy: The Legend of a Wildchild. Swan, Kenneth. 2011. (ENG.). 180p. pap. 9.95 *(978-1-4564-1073-5(3))* CreateSpace Independent Publishing Platform.

Swan, Susan. Cheers for a Dozen Ears: A Summer Crop of Counting. Chernesky, Felicia Sanzari. 2014. (ENG.). 32p. (J). (gr. -1-2). 16.99 *(978-0-8075-1130-5(7))* Whitman, Albert & Co.

—A Dollar Bill's Journey, 1 vol. Slade, Suzanne. 2011. (Follow It! Ser.). (ENG.). 24p. (gr. 1-3). lib. bdg. 25.99 *(978-1-4048-6265-4(X))*; pap. 7.49 *(978-1-4048-6709-3(0))* Picture Window Bks. (Nonfiction Picture Bks.).

—Guess Who's in the Desert. Profin, Charline. 2013. (J). *(978-1-933855-79-0(7))* Rio Nuevo Pubs.

—It's Fall! Glaser, Linda. 2003. (Celebrate the Seasons Ser.). (ENG.). 32p. (gr. k-3). pap. 7.95 *(978-0-7613-1342-7(7)*, First Avenue Editions) Lerner Publishing Group.

—It's Spring! Glaser, Linda. 2003. (Celebrate the Seasons Ser.). (ENG.). 32p. (gr. k-3). pap. 7.95 *(978-0-7613-1345-8(1)*, First Avenue Editions) Lerner Publishing Group.

—A Monarch Butterfly's Journey, 1 vol. Slade, Suzanne. 2011. (Follow It! Ser.). (ENG.). 24p. (gr. 1-3). pap. 7.49 *(978-1-4048-7029-1(6))*; lib. bdg. 25.99 *(978-1-4048-6655-3(8))* Picture Window Bks. (Nonfiction Picture Bks.).

—Pick a Circle, Gather Squares: A Fall Harvest of Shapes. Chernesky, Felicia Sanzari. 2013. (ENG.). 32p. (J). (gr. -1-2). 16.99 *(978-0-8075-6538-4(5))* Whitman, Albert & Co.

—Sugar White Snow & Evergreens: A Winter Wonderland of Color. Chernesky, Felicia Sanzari. 2014. (ENG.). 32p. (J). (gr. -1-2). 16.99 *(978-0-8075-7234-4(9))* Whitman, Albert & Co.

—Sun above & Blooms Below: A Springtime of Opposites. Chernesky, Felicia Sanzari. 2015. (ENG.). 32p. (J). (gr. -1-2). 16.99 *(978-0-8075-3632-2(6))* Whitman, Albert & Co.

—When Autumn Falls. Nidey, Kelli. 2004. (ENG.). 32p. (J). (gr. -1-1). 16.99 *(978-0-8075-0490-1(4))* Whitman, Albert & Co.

Swann, Mary. A Fearsome Day. Swann, Mary. 2007. 56p. (J). (gr. 1-3). 19.95 *(978-0-932616-87-6(9))* BrickHouse Bks., Inc.

Swann, Stefan. Tales of Pig Isle. Swann, Joyce. 2010. (ENG.). 72p. pap. 7.99 *(978-1-4564-7248-1(8))* CreateSpace Independent Publishing Platform.

Swanson, Karl. John Muir & Stickeen: An Alaskan Adventure. Koehler-Pentacoff, Elizabeth. 2003. (Single Titles Ser.). (ENG.). 32p. (J). (gr. 4-8). lib. bdg. 15.95 *(978-0-7613-2769-1(X)*, Millbrook Pr.) Lerner Publishing Group.

Swanson, Maggie. The Bunny Hop. Albee, Sarah. 2004. (Big Bird's Favorites Board Bks.). (ENG.). 24p. (J). (gr. k — 1). bds. 4.99 *(978-0-375-82693-1(9)*, Random Hse. Bks. for Young Readers) Random Hse. Children's Bks.

—Chocolate Cakes & Cookie Bakes! Muldrow, Diane. 2009. (Storytime Stickers Ser.). (ENG.). 16p. (J). (gr. -1-1). pap. 5.95 *(978-1-4027-6128-7(7))* Sterling Publishing Co., Inc.

—Elmo! Allen, Constance. 2009. (ENG.). 12p. (J). (gr. k — 1). 9.99 *(978-0-375-85080-6(5)*, Random Hse. Bks. for Young Readers) Random Hse. Children's Bks.

—Elmo Can... Taste! Touch! Smell! See! Hear! (Sesame Street) Muntean, Michaela. 2013. (Big Bird's Favorites Board Bks.). (ENG.). 24p. (J). (— 1). bds. 4.99 *(978-0-307-98078-6(2)*, Random Hse. Bks. for Young Readers) Random Hse. Children's Bks.

—Elmo's 12 Days of Christmas. Albee, Sarah. 2003. (Big Bird's Favorites Board Bks.). (ENG.). 24p. (J). (gr. k — 1). bds. 4.99 *(978-0-375-82506-4(1)*, Random Hse. Bks. for Young Readers) Random Hse. Children's Bks.

—Elmo's Tricky Tongue Twisters. Albee, Sarah. 2011. (Big Bird's Favorites Board Bks.). (ENG.). 24p. (J). (gr. k — 1). bds. 4.99 *(978-0-375-87249-5(3)*, Random Hse. Bks. for Young Readers) Random Hse. Children's Bks.

—Goldilocks & the Three Bears: A Tale about Respecting Others. 2006. (J). 6.99 *(978-1-59939-006-2(X))* Cornerstone Pr.

—My Name Is Elmo (Sesame Street) Allen, Constance. 2013. (Little Golden Book Ser.). (ENG.). 24p. (J). (-k). 3.99 *(978-0-449-81066-8(6)*, Golden Bks.) Random Hse. Children's Bks.

—Shake a Leg! Allen, Constance. 2010. (Big Bird's Favorites Board Bks.). (ENG.). 24p. (J). (gr. k — 1). bds. 4.99 *(978-0-375-85424-8(X)*, Random Hse. Bks. for Young Readers) Random Hse. Children's Bks.

—St. Francis & the Animals. Davidson, Alice Joyce. 2006. 24p. (J). 7.95 *(978-0-88271-003-7(6))* Regina Pr., Malhame & Co.

—St. Therese: the Little Flower. Davidson, Alice Joyce. 2006. 24p. (J). 7.95 *(978-0-88271-214-7(4))* Regina Pr., Malhame & Co.

—The Tale of Two Bad Mice. 2006. (J). 6.99 *(978-1-59939-030-7(2))* Cornerstone Pr.

—Time for Bed, Elmo! (Sesame Street) Albee, Sarah. 2014. (Little Golden Book Ser.). (ENG.). 24p. (J). (-k). 3.99 *(978-0-385-37138-4(1)*, Golden Bks.) Random Hse. Children's Bks.

Swanson, Maggie. My First Christmas. Swanson, Maggie. 2006. 10p. (gr. -1). bds. 7.95 *(978-0-88271-707-4(3))* Regina Pr., Malhame & Co.

Swanson, Maggie. The Kitten's Christmas Lullaby. Swanson, Maggie, retold by. 2007. (J). (gr. -1-3). 8.95 *(978-0-88271-064-8(8))* Regina Pr., Malhame & Co.

Swanson, Maggie. Grow, Tree, Grow! Swanson, Maggie, tr. Dreyer, Ellen. 2003. (Hello Reader! Ser.). (J). *(978-0-439-43964-0(7))* Scholastic, Inc.

Swanson, Maggie & Ewers, Joe. Elmo's Little Golden Book Favorites (Sesame Street) Allen, Constance & Albee, Sarah. 2014. (Little Golden Book Favorites Ser.). (ENG.). 80p. (J). (gr. -1-2). 6.99 *(978-0-385-37196-4(9)*, Golden Bks.) Random Hse. Children's Bks.

Swanson, Maggie & Leigh, Tom. Elmo's Little Library (Sesame Street) Albee, Sarah et al. 2013. (ENG.). 24p. (J). (— 1). bds. 14.99 *(978-0-449-81740-7(7)*, Random Hse. Bks. for Young Readers) Random Hse. Children's Bks.

Swanson, Peter Joseph. Tedoul. Bond, Alan. 2009. 28p. pap. 8.95 *(978-1-60076-137-9(2))* StoneGarden.net Publishing.

Swanson, Tom. Twas the Night Before Christmas. ed. 2011. (Recordable Bks). 12p. (J). ring bd. 24.99 *(978-1-60130-261-8(4)*, Usborne) EDC Publishing.

Swanson, Weldon. My Backpack! Scholastic, Inc. Staff. 2013. (ENG.). 12p. (J). (— 1). bds. 6.99 *(978-0-545-49749-7(3)*, Cartwheel Bks.) Scholastic, Inc.

—Who's Hiding? Zuravicky, Orli & Scholastic Canada Ltd. Staff. 2012. (Skip Hop Ser.). (ENG.). 12p. (J). (— 1). bds. 6.99 *(978-0-545-45903-7(6))* Scholastic, Inc.

S

Sward, Adam. The Best Saturday Ever! Cook, Gary. 2013. (Robbie's Big Adventures Ser.). (ENG.). 40p. (J). (gr. k-3). 15.95 *(978-1-938063-25-1(2)*, Mighty Media Kids) Mighty Media Pr.

Swarner, Kristina. The Bedtime Sh'ma: A Good Night Book. 2007. (ENG & HEB.). 40p. (J). 17.95 *(978-0-939144-55-6(7))*; pap. 10.95 *(978-0-939144-54-9(9))* EKS Publishing Co.

—The BEDTIME SH'MA, Book & CD Set. 2007. (ENG & HEB.). 40p. (J). 24.95 incl. audio compact disk *(978-0-939144-58-7(1))* EKS Publishing Co.

—Gathering Sparks. Schwartz, Howard. 2010. (ENG.). 32p. (J). (gr. -1-3). 16.99 *(978-1-59643-280-2(2))* Roaring Brook Pr.

—Good People Everywhere. Gillen, Lynea. 2012. (ENG.). 32p. (J). (gr. -1-2). 15.95 *(978-0-9799289-8-7(2))* Three Pebble Pr., LLC.

—Modeh Ani: A Good Morning Book. 2010. 32p. (J). (HEB.). 17.95 *(978-0-939144-64-8(6))*; pap. 10.95 *(978-0-939144-63-1(8))* EKS Publishing Co.

—The Nutcracker: A Magic Theater Book. McCaughrean, Geraldine & Hoffmann, E. T. A. 2012. (ENG.). 24p. (J). (gr. 1-17). 19.99 *(978-1-4521-0669-4(X))* Handprint Bks.

—One White Wishing Stone: A Beach Day Counting Book. Gayzagian, Doris K. 2006. (ENG.). 32p. (J). (gr. -1-1). 16.95 *(978-0-7922-5110-1(5))* CENGAGE Learning.

—One White Wishing Stone: A Beach Day Counting Book. Gayzagian, Doris K. 2006. (ENG.). 32p. (J). (gr. -1-2). 25.90 *(978-0-7922-5573-4(9)*, National Geographic Children's Bks.) National Geographic Society.

Swarte, Joost. Thrice Told Tales: Three Mice Full of Writing Advice. Lewis, Catherine. 2013. (ENG.). 144p. (YA). (gr. 7). 16.99 *(978-1-4169-5784-3(7))* Simon & Schuster Children's Publishing.

Swearingen, Greg. The Dragons of Ordinary Farm. Williams, Tad & Beale, Deborah. 2009. (ENG.). 416p. (J). (gr. 4-7). 16.99 *(978-0-06-154345-6(4))* HarperCollins Pubs.

—The Giants & the Joneses. Donaldson, Julia. 2008. (ENG.). 224p. (J). (gr. 3-5). pap. 7.99 *(978-0-312-37961-2(7))* Square Fish.

—Is That an Unlucky Leprechaun in Your Lunch? Strasser, Todd. 2009. 184p. (J). *(978-0-545-11034-1(3))* Scholastic, Inc.

—Mr. Worry: A Story about OCD. Niner, Holly L. 2003. (ENG.). 32p. (J). (gr. 2-5). 16.99 *(978-0-8075-5182-0(1))* Whitman, Albert & Co.

—The Outlandish Adventures of Liberty Aimes. Easton, Kelly. 2011. (ENG.). 224p. (J). (gr. 3-7). pap. 6.99 *(978-0-375-83772-2(8)*, Delacorte Pr) Random House Publishing Group.

—Quinny & Hopper. Schanen, Adriana Brad. 2014. (ENG.). 240p. (J). (gr. 3-7). 15.99 *(978-1-4231-7829-3(7))* Hyperion Bks. for Children.

Sweat, Lynn. Amelia Bedelia & the Baby. Parish, Peggy. 2004. (I Can Read Book 2 Ser.). (ENG.). 64p. (J). (gr. k-3). pap. 3.99 *(978-0-06-051105-0(2)*, Greenwillow Bks.) HarperCollins Pubs.

—Amelia Bedelia & the Cat. Parish, Herman. (I Can Read Book 2 Ser.). (ENG.). 48p. (J). (gr. k-3). 2009. pap. 3.99 *(978-0-06-084351-9(9))*; 2008. 16.99 *(978-0-06-084349-6(7))* HarperCollins Pubs. (Greenwillow Bks.).

—Amelia Bedelia Bakes Off. Parish, Herman. 2010. (I Can Read Book 2 Ser.). 64p. (J). (gr. k-3). (ENG.). pap. 3.99 *(978-0-06-084360-1(8))*; (ENG.). 17.99 *(978-0-06-084358-8(6))*; lib. bdg. 18.89 *(978-0-06-084359-5(4))* HarperCollins Pubs. (Greenwillow Bks.).

—Amelia Bedelia, Bookworm. Parish, Herman. (I Can Read Book 2 Ser.). (ENG.). 64p. (J). (gr. k-3). 2005. pap. 3.99 *(978-0-06-051892-9(8))*; 2003. 17.99 *(978-0-06-051890-5(1))* HarperCollins Pubs. (Greenwillow Bks.).

—Amelia Bedelia, Bookworm. Parish, Herman. 2005. (I Can Read Bks.). 63p. (gr. -1-3). 14.00 *(978-0-7569-5766-7(4))* Perfection Learning Corp.

—Amelia Bedelia, Cub Reporter. Parish, Herman. 2012. (I Can Read Book 2 Ser.). (ENG.). 64p. (J). (gr. -1-3). 16.99 *(978-0-06-209510-7(2))*; pap. 3.99 *(978-0-06-209509-1(9))* HarperCollins Pubs. (Greenwillow Bks.).

—Amelia Bedelia Goes Back to School. Parish, Herman. 2004. (Amelia Bedelia Ser.). (ENG.). 20p. (J). (gr. -1-3). pap. 6.99 *(978-0-06-051873-8(1)*, Greenwillow Bks.) HarperCollins Pubs.

—Amelia Bedelia Goes Camping. Parish, Peggy. 2003. (I Can Read Book 2 Ser.). (ENG.). 64p. (J). (gr. k-3). pap. 3.99 *(978-0-06-051106-7(0)*, Greenwillow Bks.) HarperCollins Pubs.

—Amelia Bedelia Helps Out. Parish, Peggy. 2005. (I Can Read Book 2 Ser.). (ENG.). 64p. (J). (gr. k-3). pap. 3.99 *(978-0-06-051111-1(7)*, Harper Trophy) HarperCollins Pubs.

—Amelia Bedelia, Rocket Scientist? Parish, Herman. (I Can Read Book 2 Ser.). 64p. (J). 2007. (ENG.). (gr. k-3). pap. 3.99 *(978-0-06-051889-9(8)*, Greenwillow Bks.); 2005. (gr. 1-18). 15.99 *(978-0-06-051887-5(1))*; 2005. (gr. k-4). lib. bdg. 17.89 *(978-0-06-051888-2(X)*, Greenwillow Bks.) HarperCollins Pubs.

—Amelia Bedelia, Rocket Scientist? Parish, Herman. 2007. (I Can Read Ser.). 64p. 14.00 *(978-0-7569-8058-0(5))* Perfection Learning Corp.

—Amelia Bedelia, Rocket Scientist? Parish, Herman. ed. 2007. (Amelia Bedelia — I Can Read! Ser.: 19). lib. bdg. 13.55 *(978-1-4177-8068-6(1)*, Turtleback) Turtleback Bks.

—Amelia Bedelia Talks Turkey. Parish, Herman. (I Can Read Book 2 Ser.). (ENG.). 64p. (J). (gr. k-3). 2009. pap. 3.99 *(978-0-06-084354-0(3))*; 2008. 16.99 *(978-0-06-084352-6(7))* HarperCollins Pubs. (Greenwillow Bks.).

—Amelia Bedelia under Construction. Parish, Herman. (I Can Read Book 2 Ser.). 64p. (J). (gr. k-3). 2007. (ENG.). pap. 3.99 *(978-0-06-084346-5(2))*; 2006. (ENG.). 15.99 *(978-0-06-084344-1(6))*; 2006. lib. bdg. 16.89 *(978-0-06-084345-8(4))* HarperCollins Pubs. (Greenwillow Bks.).

—Amelia Bedelia under Construction. Parish, Herman. 2007. (I Can Read Bks.). 64p. (gr. k-3). 14.00 *(978-0-7569-8054-2(2))* Perfection Learning Corp.

—Amelia Bedelia's Backpack Bundle. Parish, Herman. 2012. 192p. (J). *(978-1-4351-4392-0(2)*, Greenwillow Bks.) HarperCollins Pubs.

—Amelia Bedelia's Family Album. Parish, Peggy. 2003. (I Can Read Book 2 Ser.). (ENG.). 48p. (J). (gr. k-3). pap. 3.99 *(978-0-06-051116-6(8)*, Greenwillow Bks.) HarperCollins Pubs.

—Amelia Bedelia's Masterpiece. Parish, Herman. (I Can Read Book 2 Ser.). (ENG.). 64p. (J). (gr. k-3). 2008. pap. 3.99 *(978-0-06-084357-1(8))*; 2007. 16.99 *(978-0-06-084355-7(1))* HarperCollins Pubs. (Greenwillow Bks.).

—Be My Valentine, Amelia Bedelia. Parish, Herman. 2004. (Amelia Bedelia Ser.). (ENG.). 20p. (J). (gr. -1-3). pap. 6.99 *(978-0-06-051886-8(3)*, Greenwillow Bks.) HarperCollins Pubs.

—Calling Doctor Amelia Bedelia. Parish, Herman. 2004. (I Can Read Book 2 Ser.). (ENG.). 64p. (J). (gr. k-3). pap. 3.99 *(978-0-06-008780-7(3)*, Greenwillow Bks.) HarperCollins Pubs.

—Calling Doctor Amelia Bedelia. Parish, Herman. 2004. (Amelia Bedelia Ser.). 64p. (J). (gr. -1-2). 14.00 *(978-0-7569-3209-1(2))* Perfection Learning Corp.

—Go West, Amelia Bedelia! Parish, Herman. (I Can Read Book 2 Ser.). 64p. (J). (gr. k-4). 2012. (ENG.). pap. 3.99 *(978-0-06-084363-2(2))*; 2011. (ENG.). 17.99 *(978-0-06-084361-8(6))*; 2011. lib. bdg. 18.89 *(978-0-06-084362-5(4))* HarperCollins Pubs. (Greenwillow Bks.).

—Good Work, Amelia Bedelia. Parish, Peggy. 2003. (I Can Read Book 2 Ser.). (ENG.). 64p. (J). (gr. k-3). pap. 3.99 *(978-0-06-051115-9(X)*, Greenwillow Bks.) HarperCollins Pubs.

—Happy Haunting, Amelia Bedelia. Parish, Herman. (I Can Read Book 2 Ser.). 64p. (J). (gr. k-3). 2006. (ENG.). pap. 3.99 *(978-0-06-051895-0(2))*; 2004. (ENG.). 16.99 *(978-0-06-051893-6(6))*; 2004. lib. bdg. 16.89 *(978-0-06-051894-3(4))* HarperCollins Pubs. (Greenwillow Bks.).

—Teach Us, Amelia Bedelia. Parish, Peggy. 2004. (I Can Read Book 2 Ser.). (ENG.). 64p. (J). (gr. k-3). pap. 3.99 *(978-0-06-051114-2(1)*, Greenwillow Bks.) HarperCollins Pubs.

—Teach Us, Amelia Bedelia. Parish, Peggy. 2005. (Amelia Bedelia Ser.). 58p. (gr. -1-3). 14.00 *(978-0-7569-4804-7(5))* Perfection Learning Corp.

Sweat, Lynn & Siebel, Fritz. An Amelia Bedelia Celebration: Four Stories Tall. Parish, Peggy & Parish, Herman. 2009. (Amelia Bedelia Ser.). (ENG.). 224p. (J). (gr. -1-3). 19.99 *(978-0-06-171030-8(X)*, Greenwillow Bks.) HarperCollins Pubs.

Sweat, Lynn, jt. illus. see Parish, Herman.

Sweeny, Elizabeth Mifflin. Second Hand Cat. Sweeny, Vell. 2013. (ENG.). 48p. (J). (gr. -1-6). 14.95 *(978-0-9816360-2-3(0))* Pink Pig Pr.

Sweet Briar School. Bea's Almost Bad Day. Wolf, Penny et al. 2011. 32p. (J). 8.00 *(978-0-9802015-1-2(9))* Sweetbriar Crafts & Pubns.

Sweet, Darrell & Allen, Douglas. The How & Why Wonder Book of Reptiles & Amphibians. Mathewson, Robert F. 2011. 48p. pap. 35.95 *(978-1-258-09940-4(3))* Literary Licensing, LLC.

Sweet, Glenn. Fuzzy. Sweet, Glenn. 2003. (ENG.). (J). lib. bdg. *(978-0-9766674-0-7(1))* Cactus Publishing, LLC.

Sweet, Melissa. Bat Jamboree. Appelt, Kathi. 2004. 17.00 *(978-0-7569-4074-4(5))* Perfection Learning Corp.

—The Boy Who Drew Birds: A Story of John James Audubon. Davies, Jacqueline. 2004. (ENG.). 32p. (J). (gr. -1-3). tchr. ed. 16.99 *(978-0-618-24343-3(7))* Houghton Mifflin Harcourt Publishing Co.

—Brave Girl: Clara & the Shirtwaist Makers' Strike of 1909. Markel, Michelle. 2013. (ENG.). 32p. (J). (gr. -1-3). 17.99 *(978-0-06-180442-7(8))* HarperCollins Pubs.

—Charlotte in Giverny. Knight, Joan MacPhail. 2007. (Charlotte Ser.: CHAR). (ENG.). 68p. (J). (gr. 3-17). pap. 6.99 *(978-0-8118-5803-8(0))* Chronicle Bks. LLC.

—Charlotte in Paris. Knight, Joan MacPhail. 2003. (Charlotte Ser.: CHAR). (ENG.). 52p. (J). (gr. -1-7). 16.99 *(978-0-8118-3766-8(1))* Chronicle Bks. LLC.

—Christmas Tree. Martin, David Lozell. 2009. (ENG.). 26p. (J). (— 1). bds. 5.99 *(978-0-7636-3030-0(6))* Candlewick Pr.

Sweet, Melissa. Christmas Tree. Martin, David. 2015. (ENG.). 26p. (J). (gr. -1-2). 5.99 ***(978-0-7636-7968-2(2))*** Candlewick Pr.

Sweet, Melissa. Day Is Done. Yarrow, Peter. (ENG.). 24p. (J). (— 1). 2014. bds. 7.95 *(978-1-4549-1147-0(6))*; 2009. 16.95 *(978-1-4027-4806-6(X))* Sterling Publishing Co., Inc.

—A Giant Crush. Choldenko, Gennifer. 2011. (ENG.). 32p. (J). (gr. k-3). 16.99 *(978-0-399-24352-3(6)*, Putnam Juvenile) Penguin Publishing Group.

—Hanukkah Lights. Martin, David Lozell. 2009. (ENG.). 26p. (J). (gr. -1 — 1). bds. 5.99 *(978-0-7636-3029-4(2))* Candlewick Pr.

Sweet, Melissa. Hanukkah Lights. Martin, David. 2015. (ENG.). 26p. (J). (gr. -1-2). 5.99 ***(978-0-7636-7972-9(0))*** Candlewick Pr.

Sweet, Melissa. It's Spring! Berger, Samantha & Chanko, Pamela. 2003. (ENG.). 30p. (J). (gr. -1-3). bds. 6.99 *(978-0-439-44238-1(9)*, Cartwheel Bks.) Scholastic, Inc.

—Little Red Writing. Holub, Joan. 2013. (ENG.). 36p. (J). (gr. k-3). 16.99 *(978-0-8118-7869-2(4))* Chronicle Bks. LLC.

—Love & Kisses. Wilson, Sarah. 2014. (ENG.). 24p. (J). (— 1). bds. 6.99 *(978-0-7636-7391-8(9))* Candlewick Pr.

—Moonlight: The Halloween Cat. Rylant, Cynthia. (ENG.). 32p. (J). (gr. -1-3). 2009. pap. 6.99 *(978-0-06-443814-8(7))*; 2003. 17.99 *(978-0-06-029711-4(5))* HarperCollins Pubs.

—Mrs. Harkness & the Panda. Potter, Alicia. 2012. (ENG.). 40p. (J). (gr. k-3). 16.99 *(978-0-375-84448-5(1)*, Knopf Bks. for Young Readers) Random Hse. Children's Bks.

—The Right Word: Roget & His Thesaurus. Bryant, Jen. 2014. (J). 17.50 *(978-0-8028-5385-1(4)*, Eerdmans Bks For Young Readers) Eerdmans, William B. Publishing Co.

—A River of Words: The Story of William Carlos Williams. Bryant, Jennifer. 2008. 34p. (J). (gr. 4-7). 17.00 *(978-0-8028-5302-8(1)*, Eerdmans Bks For Young Readers) Eerdmans, William B. Publishing Co.

—The Sky's the Limit: Stories of Discovery by Women & Girls. Thimmesh, Catherine. 2005. 73p. (J). (gr. 4-8). reprint ed. 16.00 *(978-0-7567-9631-0(8))* DIANE Publishing Co.

—Sleepy Little Alphabet: A Bedtime Story from Alphabet Town. Sierra, Judy. 2009. (ENG.). 40p. (J). (gr. -1 — 1). 16.99 *(978-0-375-84002-9(8))* Knopf, Alfred A. Inc.

—The Sleepy Little Alphabet: A Bedtime Story from Alphabet Town. Sierra, Judy. 2014. (ENG.). 34p. (J). (— 1). bds. 6.99 *(978-0-385-75400-2(0)*, Knopf Bks. for Young Readers) Random Hse. Children's Bks.

—Spike: The Mixed-Up Monster. Hood, Susan. 2012. (ENG.). 40p. (J). (gr. -1-3). 16.99 *(978-1-4424-0601-8(1)*, Simon & Schuster/Paula Wiseman Bks.) Simon & Schuster/Paula Wiseman Bks.

—A Splash of Red: The Life & Art of Horace Pippin. Bryant, Jennifer. 2013. (ENG.). 40p. (J). (gr. k-3). 17.99 *(978-0-375-86712-5(0))*; lib. bdg. 20.99 *(978-0-375-96712-2(5))* Random Hse. Children's Bks. (Knopf Bks. for Young Readers).

—Won't You Be My Kissaroo? Ryder, Joanne. 2008. (ENG.). 30p. (J). (gr. -1 — 1). bds. 6.95 *(978-0-15-206060-2(X))* Houghton Mifflin Harcourt Publishing Co.

—You Nest Here with Me. Yolen, Jane & Stemple, Heidi. 2015. (ENG.). 40p. (J). (gr. -1-3). 16.95 *(978-1-59078-923-0(7))* Boyds Mills Pr.

Sweet, Melissa & Stephenson, Kristina. Thank You for Me! Bauer, Marion Dane. 2010. (ENG.). 32p. (J). (gr. -1-3). 17.99 *(978-0-689-85788-1(8)*, Simon & Schuster Bks. For Young Readers) Simon & Schuster Bks. For Young Readers.

Sweet, Melissa & Walker, David. First Grade, Here I Come! Johnston, Tony. 2015. (ENG.). 32p. (J). (gr. k-2). 8.99 *(978-0-545-20143-8(8)*, Cartwheel Bks.) Scholastic, Inc.

Sweet, Melissa, jt. illus. see Nap, Dug.

Sweet, Stephen. Cars. Parker, Steve. 2005. (Twenty4Sevens Ser.). 48p. (J). pap. *(978-0-439-78528-0(6))* Scholastic, Inc.

Sweeten, Sami. Snow Dog. Blackman, Malorie. 2014. (ENG.). 80p. (J). (gr. k-2). pap. 7.99 ***(978-0-552-56891-3(0))*** Transworld Publishers Ltd. GBR. Dist: Independent Pubs. Group.

Sweetland, Robert. My Pal Victor. Bertrand, Diane Gonzales. 2010.Tr. of Mi Amigo, Victor. (ENG.). 32p. (J). (gr. 4-7). 16.95 *(978-1-934960-84-4(5)*, Raven Tree Pr.,Csi) Continental Sales, Inc.

Sweetman, Gary W., photos by. Pockets: Book: Nonfiction_Juvenile, The Molly Brave Preschool Series Vol. 1. Deveny, Mary Alice. 2011. 40p. (J). pap. 14.95 *(978-1-61245-000-1(8))* Molly Brave.

Swiatkowska, Gabi. Arrowhawk. Schaefer, Lola M. rev. ed. 2004. (ENG.). 32p. (J). (gr. -1-3). 18.99 *(978-0-8050-6371-4(4)*, Holt, Henry & Co. Bks. For Young Readers) Holt, Henry & Co.

—Arrowhawk: A True Survival Story. Schaefer, Lola M. 2014. (ENG.). 32p. (J). (gr. -1-3). 7.99 *(978-1-250-03988-0(6))* Square Fish.

—The Golden Rule. Cooper, Ilene. (J). (gr. k-4). 2008. 27.95 incl. audio *(978-0-8045-6968-2(1))*; 2007. 29.95 incl. audio compact disk *(978-0-8045-4191-6(4))* Spoken Arts, Inc.

—Infinity & Me. Hosford, Kate. 2012. (Carolrhoda Picture Bks). (ENG.). 32p. (J). (gr. k-4). lib. bdg. 16.95 *(978-0-7613-6726-0(8)*, Carolrhoda Bks.) Lerner Publishing Group.

—Me Llama Yoon. Recorvits, Helen. 2003.Tr. of My Name is Yoon. (SPA.). 32p. (J). (gr. k-3). 17.99 *(978-84-261-3335-9(5))* Juventud, Editorial ESP. Dist: Lectorum Pubns., Inc.

—My Name Is Yoon. Recorvits, Helen. 2003. (ENG.). 32p. (J). (gr. -1-3). 17.99 *(978-0-374-35114-4(7)*, Farrar, Straus & Giroux (BYR)) Farrar, Straus & Giroux.

—My Name Is Yoon. Recorvits, Helen. 2014. (ENG.). 32p. (J). (gr. -1-3). 6.99 *(978-1-250-05711-2(6))* Square Fish.

—The Perfect Cup of Tea. Hosford, Kate. 2014. (J). *(978-1-4677-3904-7(9))* Lerner Publishing Group.

—Please, Papa. Banks, Kate. 2013. (ENG.). 32p. (J). (gr. -1-3). 16.99 *(978-0-374-36002-3(2)*, Farrar, Straus & Giroux (BYR)) Farrar, Straus & Giroux.

—Waiting for Gregory. Holt, Kimberly Willis. rev. ed. 2006. (ENG.). 32p. (J). (gr. -1-2). 16.95 *(978-0-8050-7388-1(4)*, Holt, Henry & Co. Bks. For Young Readers) Holt, Henry & Co.

—Yoon & the Jade Bracelet. Recorvits, Helen & Recorvits, H. 2008. (ENG.). 32p. (J). (gr. -1-3). 18.99 *(978-0-374-38689-4(7)*, Farrar, Straus & Giroux (BYR)) Farrar, Straus & Giroux.

Swiatkowska, Gabi. Queen on Wednesday. Swiatkowska, Gabi. 2014. (ENG.). 36p. (J). (gr. -1-3). 17.99 *(978-0-374-37446-4(5)*, Farrar, Straus & Giroux (BYR)) Farrar, Straus & Giroux.

Swiatoviak, Jeri. Buddy & the Poi Puppy. Gissing, Kathleen. 2012. 24p. pap. 24.95 *(978-1-4626-8089-4(5))* America Star Bks.

Swiatowska, Gabi. The Golden Rule. Cooper, Ilene. 2007. (ENG.). 32p. (J). (gr. -1-3). 17.95 *(978-0-8109-0960-1(X)*, Abrams Bks. for Young Readers) Abrams.

Swiderska, Barbara. The Fisherman's Bride. Swiderska, Barbara. 32p. (J). (gr. -1-3). 12.95 *(978-0-87592-018-4(7))* Scroll Pr., Inc.

Swift, Christine. Croak, Frog! 2014. (Shake, Rattle, Splash Ser.). (ENG.). 8p. (J). (gr. -1 — 1). 6.99 *(978-1-4380-0422-8(2))* Barron's Educational Series, Inc.

—Splash, Dolphin! 2014. (Shake, Rattle, Splash Ser.). (ENG.). 8p. (J). (gr. -1 — 1). 6.99 *(978-1-4380-0421-1(4))* Barron's Educational Series, Inc.

Swift, Gary. The Bug Book. Fleming, Maria. 2004. (Grammar Tales Ser.). (ENG.). 16p. (J). (gr. 3-7). pap. 3.25 *(978-0-439-45818-4(8))* Scholastic, Inc.

—The Fantastic Fruit Group, 1 vol. Aboff, Marcie. 2011. (First Graphics: Myplate & Healthy Eating Ser.). (ENG.). 24p. (gr. 1-2). pap. 6.29 *(978-1-4296-7160-6(2))*; lib. bdg. 23.32 *(978-1-4296-6090-7(2))*; pap. 35.70 *(978-1-4296-7166-8(1))* Capstone Pr., Inc.

—Healthy Snacks, Healthy You!, 1 vol. Lee, Sally. 2011. (First Graphics: Myplate & Healthy Eating Ser.). (ENG.). 24p. (gr. 1-2). pap. 6.29 *(978-1-4296-7162-0(9))*; pap. 35.70 *(978-1-4296-7168-2(8))* Capstone Pr., Inc.

—Healthy Snacks, Healthy You! [Scholastic]. Lee, Sally. 2013. (First Graphics: Myplate & Healthy Eating Ser.). (ENG.). (gr. 1-2). pap. 0.50 *(978-1-4765-3129-8(3))* Capstone Pr., Inc.

—The Powerful Protein Group, 1 vol. Lee, Sally. 2011. (First Graphics: Myplate & Healthy Eating Ser.). (ENG.). 24p. (gr. 1-2). pap. 6.29 *(978-1-4296-7164-4(5))*; lib. bdg. 23.32 *(978-1-4296-6091-4(0))*; pap. 35.70 *(978-1-4296-7170-5(X))* Capstone Pr., Inc.

Swift, Gary, jt. illus. see Poling, Kyle.

Swigelson, Kayce M. The Grand Adventures of Petit Louis. Swigelson, Kayce M. 2013. 54p. 24.95 *(978-0-9889643-1-0(7))* MathisJones Communications, LLC.

Swinford, Charles. Breakfast with Bigfoot. Cotter, Amelia. 2013. 30p. pap. 11.95 *(978-1-61876-017-3(3))* Black Oak Media, Inc.

Swing, Michael. My Florida Facts. Johnson, Russell W. & Johnson, Annie P. 2009. (ENG.). 64p. (J). (gr. 3-7). 14.95 *(978-1-56164-430-8(7))* Pineapple Pr., Inc.

Swingler, Simon. Bad News Birthday. Badger, M. C. 2015. (Super Baddies Ser.: 3). (ENG.). 48p. (J). (gr. k-2). pap. 9.99 *(978-1-921848-44-5(8))* Hardie Grant Egmont Pty Ltd. AUS. Dist: Independent Pubs. Group.

—Baddies vs. Goodies. Badger, M. C. 2014. (Super Baddies Ser.: 1). (ENG.). 48p. (J). (gr. k-2). pap. 9.99 *(978-1-921848-42-1(1))* Hardie Grant Egmont Pty, Ltd. AUS. Dist: Independent Pubs. Group.

—Locked In. Fraillon, Z. 2011. (Monstrum House Ser.: 1). (ENG.). 176p. (J). (gr. 4-7). pap. 8.99 *(978-1-921564-25-3(3))* Hardie Grant Bks. AUS. Dist: Independent Pubs. Group.

—When Robots Go Bad. Badger, M. C. 2014. (Super Baddies Ser.: 2). (ENG.). 48p. (J). (gr. k-2). pap. 9.99 *(978-1-921848-43-8(X))* Hardie Grant Egmont Pty, Ltd. AUS. Dist: Independent Pubs. Group.

Swinks, Judi, photos by. Solo Suppers: Simple Delicious Meals to Cook for Yourself. Goldstein, Joyce Esersky. 2003. (ENG., 156p. (gr. 8-17). pap. 19.95 *(978-0-8118-3620-3(7))* Chronicle Bks. LLC.

Swisher, Elizabeth, et al. Celebrate with Jesus: A Child's Book of the Sacraments. Larkin, Jean, ed. 2007. 32p. pap. 3.95 *(978-1-933178-67-7(1))* Pflaum Publishing Group.

Swisher, Elizabeth. Days of Faith: Student Planner & Assignment Book/Primary Grades 2005-2006. Ward, Hadley & Castano, Marie. Cannizzo, Karen, ed. 2005. (J). spiral bd. 4.99 *(978-1-933178-05-9(1)*, 9806) Pflaum Publishing Group.

—Jesus Walks on the Water. Sanders, Nancy I. 2005. (ENG.). 16p. (J). 1.99 *(978-0-7586-0864-2(0))* Concordia Publishing Hse.

—The Lord Calls Samuel. Susan, Hammond. 2005. (Arch Bks.). 16p. (J). 1.99 *(978-0-7586-0639-6(7))* Concordia Publishing Hse.

Swisher, Michael-Che. Secret along the St. Mary's. Swisher, Michael-Che, tr. Troeger, Virginia B. 2003. (Mysteries in Time Ser.). 92p. (gr. 4). 14.95 *(978-1-893110-35-9(4))* Silver Moon Pr.

Switzer, Bobbi. The Adventures of Pj & Split Pea. Moore, S. D. 2008. 36p. per. 12.95 *(978-1-4327-1288-4(8))* Outskirts Pr., Inc.

—Aidan's Shoes. Sampson, Brent. 2006. (ENG.). 28p. per. 12.95 *(978-1-59800-684-1(3))* Outskirts Pr., Inc.

—Onyx. Barreto, Sonia. 2008. 36p. pap. 13.95 *(978-1-4327-1787-2(1))* Outskirts Pr., Inc.

—Queen Vernita's Visitors. Menge, Dawn. 2008. 36p. pap. 19.95 *(978-1-59800-714-5(9))* Outskirts Pr., Inc.

—When Little Pinkie Gets Her Wings. Elliott, Linda. 2007. 28p. per. 11.95 *(978-1-59800-871-5(4))* Outskirts Pr., Inc.

Switzer, Bobby. Angus & the Triplets. Rhoton, Lesa. 2006. 28p. (J). (gr. -1-3). per. 13.95 *(978-1-58939-852-8(1))* Virtualbookworm.com Publishing, Inc.

Switzer Hutson, Betty. History of the Christian Methodist Episcopal Church for Children. 2010. 48p. (YA). pap. 15.00 *(978-0-615-37424-6(7))* leharperwilliamsdesign group.

Swogger, John-Gordon. Something Different about Dad: How to Live with Your Asperger's Parent. Evans, Kirsti. 2011. (ENG.). 144p. (J). (gr. 3-6). pap. *(978-1-84905-114-9(3))* Kingsley, Jessica Ltd.

Swope, Brenda. The Adventures of Katie Koala: Oops! My Momma Is Lost!, 1 vol. Robinson Ed. D., Shannon R. 2009. 23p. pap. 24.95 *(978-1-60749-733-2(6))* America Star Bks.

—Beethoven. Cardona, Nancy. 2011. 28p. pap. 24.95 *(978-1-4560-0961-8(3))* America Star Bks.

—Bob the Lizard, 1 vol. Ramirez, Iz. 2009. 26p. pap. 24.95 *(978-1-60749-232-0(6))* America Star Bks.

—Bobby & Bun Bun's Afternoon Adventure. Murray, Rosalie. 2012. 32p. pap. 24.95 *(978-1-4560-5090-0(7))* America Star Bks.

—Chicken Church. Mattingly, Robin. 2011. 28p. pap. 24.95 *(978-1-4560-0962-5(1))* America Star Bks.

—Dollop the Cloud & Dee the Bee. Ferry, Ann. 2012. 28p. pap. 24.95 *(978-1-4626-7433-6(X))* America Star Bks.

—Don't Forget about Me. Joseph, Beverly L. 2011. 28p. pap. 24.95 *(978-1-4560-0972-4(9))* America Star Bks.

—Farm Friends. Fass, Amanda L. 2011. 28p. pap. 24.95 *(978-1-4560-0894-9(3))* America Star Bks.

—Gusty the Cloud & Streakie the Snail. Ferry, Ann. 2011. 28p. pap. 24.95 *(978-1-4560-0928-1(1))* America Star Bks.

—Huff the Magicless Dragon, 1 vol. Lawson, Barbara. 2009. 35p. pap. 24.95 *(978-1-61546-419-7(0))* PublishAmerica, Inc.

—I Guess I'll Be, 1 vol. Kelty, Colleen Alyce. 2010. 24p. 24.95 *(978-1-4489-4937-3(8))* PublishAmerica, Inc.

—Little Bird & the Wind. Hart-Plaugher, Teresa. 2011. 28p. pap. 24.95 *(978-1-4512-9102-5(7))* America Star Bks.

—Little John, God, & the Circus. Dubrule, Jackie. 2011. 32p. pap. 24.95 *(978-1-4560-0978-6(8))* America Star Bks.

—Lunie Balloonies. Blace, Maria. 2011. 24p. pap. 24.95 *(978-1-4560-0947-2(8))* America Star Bks.

—Malcolm's Cubby House. Stewart, Mark R. 2011. 28p. pap. 24.95 *(978-1-4560-0958-8(3))* America Star Bks.

—Mi Mi's Mini Tea Party. Kirkland, Kim M. 2011. 28p. pap. 24.95 *(978-1-4512-8099-9(8))* America Star Bks.

—Miranda, God & the Park. Dubrule, Jackie. 2011. 32p. pap. 24.95 *(978-1-4560-0966-3(4))* America Star Bks.

—Mr Mouse Morgan. Seaman, Lucy. 2011. 28p. pap. 24.95 *(978-1-4560-0916-8(8))* America Star Bks.

—My Dad's off to War. Calabrese, Diane Marie. 2011. 28p. pap. 24.95 *(978-1-4560-0942-7(7))* America Star Bks.

—Nine & a Half Dozen, 1 vol. V. 2010. 24p. 24.95 *(978-1-4489-2596-4(7))* PublishAmerica, Inc.

—The Puppy Tree, 1 vol. Emanuel, Lora. 2009. 30p. pap. 24.95 *(978-1-60749-614-4(3))* America Star Bks.

—The Rivers. Trimoglie, Mario. 2012. 26p. 24.95 *(978-1-4560-3907-3(5))* America Star Bks.

—Tree Talkers: A Christmas Story, 1 vol. Doman, Dave. 2009. 32p. pap. 24.95 *(978-1-61546-180-6(9))* America Star Bks.

—Why Santa Claus Comes at Christmas. McDade Jr, Bert M. 2011. 32p. pap. 24.95 *(978-1-4560-0921-2(4))* America Star Bks.

—Zoey Finds a New Home. Wade, Joan. 2011. 28p. pap. 24.95 *(978-1-4560-0899-4(4))* PublishAmerica, Inc.

Sycamore, Hilary & O'Connor, George. Journey into Mohawk Country. Bogaert, Harmen Meyndertsz van den & O'Connor, George. rev. ed. 2006. (ENG.). 144p. (YA). (gr. 7). pap. 19.99 *(978-1-59643-106-5(7),* First Second Bks.) Roaring Brook Pr.

Sycamore, Hilary, jt. illus. see Abadzis, Nick.

Sykes, Shannon. A Cub Explores. Love, Pamela. ed. 2004. (ENG.). 32p. (J). (gr. -1-17). 15.95 *(978-0-89272-593-9(1))* Down East Bks.

Sylvada, Peter. Firefly Mountain, 1 vol. Thomas, Patricia. 2007. (ENG.). 32p. (J). (gr. 1-5). 16.95 *(978-1-56145-360-3(9))* Peachtree Pubs.

—Gleam & Glow. Bunting, Eve. 2005. (ENG.). 32p. (J). (gr. -1-3). reprint ed. pap. 7.00 *(978-0-15-205380-2(8))* Houghton Mifflin Harcourt Publishing Co.

—Yatandou. Whelan, Gloria. rev. ed. 2007. (Tales of the World Ser.). (ENG.). 32p. (J). (gr. -1-3). 17.95 *(978-1-58536-211-0(5))* Sleeping Bear Pr.

Sylvaine, Jenny. The Mouse & the Wizard: A Hindu Folktale. Malaspina, Ann. 2013. (Folktales from Around the World Ser.). (ENG.). 24p. (J). (gr. k-3). 28.50 *(978-1-62323-633-5(9),* 206384) Child's World, Inc., The.

Sylvester, Kevin. And the Crowd Goes Wild! A Global Gathering of Sports Poems. Hoyte, Carol-Ann. Roemer, Heidi Bee, ed. 2012. 80p. pap. *(978-1-77097-953-6(0))* FriesenPress.

Sylvester, Kevin. Baseballogy: Tons of Things You Never Knew. 2015. (ENG.). 72p. (J). (gr. 4-7). pap. 14.95 ***(978-1-55451-707-7(9),*** 9781554517077) Annick Pr., Ltd. CAN. Dist: Firefly Bks., Ltd.

Sylvester, Kevin. Don't Touch That Toad & Other Strange Things Adults Tell You. Rondina, Catherine. 2010. (ENG.). 96p. (J). (gr. 2-5). 14.95 *(978-1-55453-454-8(2))* Kids Can Pr., Ltd. CAN. Dist: Univ. of Toronto Pr.

Sylvester, Kevin. Follow Your Money: Who Gets It, Who Spends It, Where Does It Go? Sylvester, Kevin. Hlinka, Michael. 2013. (ENG.). 60p. (J). (gr. 5-12). 24.95 *(978-1-55451-481-6(9),* 9781554514816); pap. 14.95 *(978-1-55451-480-9(0),* 9781554514809) Annick Pr., Ltd. CAN. Dist: Firefly Bks., Ltd.

—Gold Medal for Weird. Sylvester, Kevin. 2007. (ENG.). 112p. (J). (gr. 2-5). 7.95 *(978-1-55453-021-2(0))* Kids Can Pr., Ltd. CAN. Dist: Univ. of Toronto Pr.

—Neil Flambe & the Aztec Abduction. Sylvester, Kevin. (Neil Flambe Capers Ser.: 2). (ENG.). (J). (gr. 3-7). 2014. 336p. pap. 7.99 *(978-1-4424-4608-3(0));* 2012. 320p. 14.99 *(978-1-4424-4607-6(2))* Simon & Schuster Bks. For Young Readers. (Simon & Schuster Bks. For Young Readers).

—Neil Flambé & the Bard's Banquet. Sylvester, Kevin. 2015. (Neil Flambe Capers Ser.: 5). (ENG.). 320p. (J). (gr. 3-7). 12.99 *(978-1-4814-1038-0(5),* Simon & Schuster Bks. For Young Readers) Simon & Schuster Bks. For Young Readers.

—Neil Flambé & the Crusader's Curse. Sylvester, Kevin. (Neil Flambe Capers Ser.: 3). (ENG.). (J). (gr. 3-7). 2014. 320p. pap. 7.99 *(978-1-4424-4287-0(5));* 2012. 304p. 13.99 *(978-1-4424-4286-3(7))* Simon & Schuster Bks. For Young Readers. (Simon & Schuster Bks. For Young Readers).

—Neil Flambé & the Marco Polo Murders. Sylvester, Kevin. (Neil Flambe Capers Ser.: 1). (ENG.). (J). (gr. 3-7). 2014. 320p. pap. 7.99 *(978-1-4424-4605-2(6));* 2012. 304p. 14.99 *(978-1-4424-4604-5(8))* Simon & Schuster Bks. For Young Readers. (Simon & Schuster Bks. For Young Readers).

—Neil Flambé & the Tokyo Treasure. Sylvester, Kevin. (Neil Flambe Capers Ser.: 4). (ENG.). (J). (gr. 3-7). 2014. 368p. pap. 7.99 *(978-1-4424-4289-4(1));* 2012. 352p. 13.99 *(978-1-4424-4288-7(3))* Simon & Schuster Bks. For Young Readers. (Simon & Schuster Bks. For Young Readers).

—The Neil Flambé Capers Collection: Neil Flambé & the Marco Polo Murders; Neil Flambé & the Aztec Abduction; Neil Flambé & the Crusader's Curse; Neil Flambé & the Tokyo Treasure. Sylvester, Kevin. ed. 2014. (Neil Flambe Capers Ser.). (ENG.). 1344p. (J). (gr. 3-7). pap. 31.99 *(978-1-4814-3238-2(9),* Simon & Schuster Bks. For Young Readers) Simon & Schuster Bks. For Young Readers.

—Sports Hall of Weird. Sylvester, Kevin. 2005. (ENG.). 96p. (J). (gr. 2-18). 8.95 *(978-1-55337-635-4(8))* Kids Can Pr., Ltd. CAN. Dist: Univ. of Toronto Pr.

Sylvester, Suzanne, photos by. Sharkey Helps ChooChoo. Stoltz, Susan. 2011. (ENG., 44p. pap. 11.99 *(978-1-4565-9069-7(3))* CreateSpace Independent Publishing Platform.

Sylvestre, Daniel. Aimez-Vous la Musique? Desrosiers, Sylvie. 2004. (Roman Jeunesse Ser.). (FRE.). 96p. (J). (gr. 4-7). pap. *(978-2-89021-709-6(4))* Diffusion du livre Mirabel (DLM).

—Deux Squelettes au Téléphone. Duggan, Paul. 2004. (Picture Bks.). (FRE.). 32p. (J). (gr. 4). *(978-2-89021-677-8(2))* Diffusion du livre Mirabel (DLM).

—Qui Veut Entrer dans la Legende? Desrosiers, Sylvie. 2003. (Roman Jeunesse Ser.). (FRE.). 96p. (YA). (gr. 4-7). pap. *(978-2-89021-269-5(6))* Diffusion du livre Mirabel (DLM).

Symington, Lindsay. The Children's Hour of Heaven on Earth. McNabb, Vincent. 2007. 48p. per. 21.95 *(978-0-9782985-2-4(7))* Catholic Authors Pr.

Symmons, Sheeres. From Bondage to Freedom: A Tale of the Times of Mohammed. Leslie, Emma. 2007. 308p. 24.95 *(978-1-934671-10-8(X))* Salem Ridge Press LLC.

Synarski, Susan & Johnson, Karen. Cool Tricks for Kids. Gordon, Lynn & Chronicle Books Staff. 2008. (ENG.). 54p. (gr. 8-17). 6.95 *(978-0-8118-6374-2(3))* Chronicle Bks. LLC.

Synarski, Susan, jt. illus. see Johnson, Karen.

Synepolsky, I. & Belomlinsky, M. Volleyball with the Family: Fife Steps to Success. Slupskiy, Leon. 2003. 105/35p. (YA). pap. *(978-0-9728301-3-3(8))* Publishing Hse. Gelany.

Synge, E. M. The Awakening of Europe (Yesterday's Classics) Synge, M. B. l.t. ed. 2006. 268p. (J). per. 11.95 *(978-1-59915-015-4(8))* Yesterday's Classics.

—The Discovery of New Worlds (Yesterday's Classics) Synge, M. B. l.t. ed. 2006. 252p. (J). per. *(978-1-59915-014-7(X))* Yesterday's Classics.

—The Growth of the British Empire (Yesterday's Classics) Synge, M. B. 2006. 284p. (YA). per. 11.95 *(978-1-59915-017-8(4))* Yesterday's Classics.

—On the Shores of the Great Sea (Yesterday's Classics) Synge, M. B. l.t. ed. 2006. 240p. (J). per. 11.95 *(978-1-59915-013-0(1))* Yesterday's Classics.

—The Struggle for Sea Power (Yesterday's Classics) Synge, M. B. l.t. ed. 2006. 276p. (J). per. 11.95 *(978-1-59915-016-1(6))* Yesterday's Classics.

Szafranski, Keith. Barrington Bear Visits the Emperor - the Emperor Penguin That Is. Szafranski, Keith. 2008. (ENG.). 48p. (J). 19.95 *(978-0-9801662-0-0(9))* Small Bear Publishing.

Szegedi, Katalin. Ambrose & the Cathedral Dream. Sorenson, Margo. 2006. (ENG.). 32p. (J). (gr. -1-3). 4.24 *(978-0-8146-3004-4(9))* Liturgical Pr.

—Ambrose & the Princess. Sorenson, Margo. 2005. (ENG.). 32p. (J). (gr. -1-3). 16.95 *(978-0-8146-3043-3(X))* Liturgical Pr.

—El Peso de Una Misa: Un Relato de fe. Nobisso, Josephine. 2003. Orig. Title: The Weight of a Mass a Tale of Faith. (SPA.). 32p. (J). (gr. k-2). pap. 9.95 *(978-0-940112-17-9(5))* Gingerbread Hse.

—El Peso de Una Misa: Un Relato de Fe. Nobisso, Josephine. 2003. Orig. Title: The Weight of a Mass a Tale of Faith. (SPA.). 32p. (J). (gr. k-2). 17.95 *(978-0-940112-15-5(9))* Gingerbread Hse.

—Take It to the Queen: A Tale of Hope. Nobisso, Josephine. 2008. (ENG.). 32p. (J). (gr. k-2). 17.95 *(978-0-940112-19-3(1));* pap. 9.95 *(978-0-940112-21-6(3))* Gingerbread Hse.

—The Weight of a Mass: A Tale of Faith. Nobisso, Josephine. 2005. (ENG.). 32p. (J). (gr. -1 — 1). 17.95 *(978-0-8146-2930-7(X))* Liturgical Pr.

Szegedy, Esther. Isabel & the Hungry Coyote/Isabel y el Coyote Hambriento. Polette, Keith. Raven Tree Press Staff, ed. 2004.Tr. of Isabel y el coyote Hambriento. (SPA & ENG.). 32p. (J). (gr. -1-3). 16.95 *(978-0-9724973-0-5(7),* 626999, Raven Tree Pr.) Continental Sales, Inc.

Szekeres, Cyndy. A Small Child's Book of Prayers. Szekeres, Cyndy. 2010. (ENG.). 24p. (J). (gr. -1-k). bds. 8.99 *(978-0-545-15624-0(6))* Scholastic, Inc.

Szekeres, Cyndy & McElmurry, Jill. When Otis Courted Mama. Appelt, Kathi. 2015. (ENG.). 40p. (J). (gr. -1-3). 16.99 *(978-0-15-216688-5(2),* HMH Books For Young Readers) Houghton Mifflin Harcourt Publishing Co.

Szewczyk, Manda. Messy Penny. Weber, Roopa. 2013. 38p. pap. 11.99 *(978-0-9896966-2-3(6))* Karma Kollection LLC.

Szijgyarto, Cynthia, jt. illus. see Broughton, Ilona.

Szilagyi, Mary. Big & Little. Krauss, Ruth. 2003. (J). pap. 12.95 *(978-0-590-40698-7(1))* Scholastic, Inc.

—Night in the Country. Rylant, Cynthia. 2014. 32p. pap. 7.00 *(978-1-61003-359-6(0))* Center for the Collaborative Classroom.

Szuc, Jeff. Have You Ever Seen a Duck in a Raincoat? Kaner, Etta. 2009. (Have You Ever Seen Ser.). (ENG.). 32p. (J). (gr. -1-2). 14.95 *(978-1-55453-246-9(9))* Kids Can Pr., Ltd. CAN. Dist: Univ. of Toronto Pr.

—Have You Ever Seen a Hippo with Sunscreen? Kaner, Etta. 2010. (Have You Ever Seen Ser.). (ENG.). 32p. (J). (gr. -1-2). 14.95 *(978-1-55453-337-4(6))* Kids Can Pr., Ltd. CAN. Dist: Univ. of Toronto Pr.

—Have You Ever Seen a Stork Build a Log Cabin? Kaner, Etta. 2010. (Have You Ever Seen Ser.). (ENG.). 32p. (J). (gr. -1-2). 14.95 *(978-1-55453-336-7(8))* Kids Can Pr., Ltd. CAN. Dist: Univ. of Toronto Pr.

—Have You Ever Seen an Octopus with a Broom? Kaner, Etta. 2009. (Have You Ever Seen Ser.). (ENG.). 32p. (J). (gr. -1-2). 14.95 *(978-1-55453-247-6(7))* Kids Can Pr., Ltd. CAN. Dist: Univ. of Toronto Pr.

T

T, N. Magic in Us. the Power of Imagination: The Power of Imagination, bks. 1, vol. 2. Tinti, Natalie. ed. 2013. (Sewing a Friendship Ser.). (ENG.). 116p. (J). pap. 12.95 *(978-0-9842625-3-3(9))* Tintinatie Publishing Hse.

T. W. Zimmerman. The Day the Horse Was Free. Dodgson, Y. K. 2004. 16p. (J). 11.95 *(978-0-9748091-0-6(1))* Alaska Avenue Pr.

Taback, Simms. Animals. LePan, Don. 2009. (ENG.). 18p. (J). (-k). bds. 4.99 *(978-1-934706-87-9(6))* Blue Apple Bks.

—Count 4, 5, 6. Blue Apple Staff. 2009. (ENG.). 18p. (J). (-k). bds. 4.99 *(978-1-60905-006-1(1))* Blue Apple Bks.

—Dinosaurs: A Giant Fold-Out Book. 2012. (ENG.). 20p. (J). (gr. -1-k). 13.99 *(978-1-60905-212-6(9))* Blue Apple Bks.

—Do You Have a Tail? 2012. (ENG.). 12p. (J). (gr. k — 1). bds. 6.99 *(978-1-60905-258-4(7))* Blue Apple Bks.

—Simms Taback's City Animals. 2009. (ENG.). 20p. (J). (gr. k-k). 13.99 *(978-1-934706-52-7(3))* Blue Apple Bks.

—Simms Taback's Farm Animals. 2011. (ENG.). 20p. (J). (gr. k-k). 13.99 *(978-1-60905-078-8(9))* Blue Apple Bks.

—Two Little Witches: A Halloween Counting Story. Ziefert, Harriet. 2007. (ENG.). 32p. (J). (gr. k-k). pap. 3.99 *(978-0-7636-3309-7(7))* Candlewick Pr.

—Where Is My Baby? Ziefert, Harriet. 2012. (ENG.). 118p. (J). (gr. k-12). bds. 7.99 *(978-1-60905-280-5(3))* Blue Apple Bks.

—Who Said Moo? Ziefert, Harriet. 2012. (ENG.). 18p. (J). (gr. k-k). 7.99 *(978-1-60905-279-9(X))* Blue Apple Bks.

—Wiggle! Like an Octopus. Ziefert, Harriet. 2011. (ENG.). 12p. (J). (gr. k-12). bds. 8.99 *(978-1-60905-072-6(X))* Blue Apple Bks.

—1, 2, 3. 2009. (ENG.). 18p. (J). (-k). bds. 4.99 *(978-1-934706-89-3(2))* Blue Apple Bks.

Taback, Simms. Colors. Taback, Simms. 2010. (ENG.). 18p. (J). (-k). bds. 4.99 *(978-1-934706-88-6(4))* Blue Apple Bks.

—Joseph Had a Little Overcoat. Taback, Simms. pap. incl. audio compact disk *(978-1-59112-608-9(8))* Live Oak Media.

—Listomania. Taback, Simms. Ziefert, Harriet. 2012. (ENG.). 96p. (J). (gr. 1-4). 12.99 *(978-1-60905-223-2(4))* Blue Apple Bks.

—Mommies & Babies. Taback, Simms. Blue Apple Staff. 2010. (ENG.). 18p. (J). (-k). bds. 4.99 *(978-1-60905-005-4(3))* Blue Apple Bks.

—Peek-A-Boo Who? Taback, Simms. 2nd rev. ed. 2013. (ENG.). 14p. (J). (-k). bds. 8.99 *(978-1-60905-277-5(3))* Blue Apple Bks.

—Postcards from Camp. Taback, Simms. 2011. (ENG.). 40p. (J). (gr. -1-3). 17.99 *(978-0-399-23973-1(1),* Nancy Paulsen Bks.) Penguin Publishing Group.

—Safari Animals. Taback, Simms. 2008. (ENG.). 20p. (J). (gr. k-k). 13.99 *(978-1-934706-19-0(1))* Blue Apple Bks.

—This Is the House That Jack Built. Taback, Simms. 2004. (ENG.). 32p. (J). (gr. k-3). reprint ed. 6.99 *(978-0-14-240200-9(1),* Puffin) Penguin Publishing Group.

—Zoom. Taback, Simms. Blue Apple Staff. 2010. (ENG.). 18p. (J). (-k). bds. 4.99 *(978-1-60905-007-8(X))* Blue Apple Bks.

Tabares, Bridgitt. Monkeys on an Island. Tabares, Veronica. 2012. 32p. (J). pap. 14.50 *(978-1-60916-005-0(3))* Sun Break Publishing.

Tabary. The Grand Vizier Iznogoud, Vol. 9. Goscinny, René. 2012. (ENG.). 52p. (J). (gr. 3-12). pap. 13.95 *(978-1-84918-131-0(4))* CineBook GBR. Dist: National Bk. Network.

—Iznogoud - The Infamous, Vol. 7. Goscinny, René. 2011. (ENG.). 48p. (J). (gr. 3-17). pap. 11.95 *(978-1-84918-074-0(1))* CineBook GBR. Dist: National Bk. Network.

—Iznogoud & the Magic Carpet. Goscinny, René. 2010. (ENG.). 46p. (J). (gr. 3-17). pap. 11.95 *(978-1-84918-044-3(X))* CineBook GBR. Dist: National Bk. Network.

—Rockets to Stardom - Iznogoud, Vol. 8. Goscinny, René. 2011. (ENG.). 48p. pap. 11.95 *(978-1-84918-092-4(X))* CineBook GBR. Dist: National Bk. Network.

Tabary, Armelle. The Wicked Wiles of Iznogoud, Vol. 1. Goscinny, René. 2008. (ENG.). 48p. (J). (gr. -1-12). pap. 13.95 *(978-1-905460-46-5(5))* CineBook GBR. Dist: National Bk. Network.

Tabary, Jean. Iznogoud Vol. 10: Iznogoud the Relentless. Goscinny, René. 2013. (ENG.). 48p. (J). (gr. 3-12). pap. 11.95 *(978-1-84918-181-5(0))* CineBook GBR. Dist: National Bk. Network.

Tabatabaei, Maryam. Stone Soup with Matzoh Balls: A Passover Tale in Chelm. Glaser, Linda. 2014. (ENG.). 32p. (J). (gr. -1-2). 16.99 *(978-0-8075-7620-5(4))* Whitman, Albert & Co.

Tabbutt, Steven. Alphabet of Art. Gates Galvin, Laura. 2011. (ENG.). 40p. (J). 9.95 *(978-1-60727-196-3(6))* Soundprints.

Tablason, Jamie. The Brothers & the Star Fruit Tree: A Tale from Vietnam. Barchers, Suzanne. 2015. (Tales of Honor Ser.). (ENG.). 32p. (gr. 1-3). lib. bdg. 26.60 ***(978-1-939656-83-4(4))*** Red Chair Pr.

Tabler, Marie. One Pea. Tabler, Marie. Meyer, Julia. 2013. 36p. 14.95 *(978-1-62314-139-4(7))* ePub Bud.

Tabor, Nancy Maria Grande. Celebraciones: Dias Feriados de los Estados Unidos y Mexico. Tabor, Nancy Maria Grande. ed. 2004.Tr. of Celebrations - Holidays of the United States of America & Mexico. (SPA & ENG.). 32p. (J). (gr. -1-2). pap. 7.95 *(978-1-57091-550-5(4))* Charlesbridge Publishing, Inc.

—Somos un Arco Iris (We Are a Rainbow) Tabor, Nancy Maria Grande. 2006. (ENG & SPA.). 28p. (gr. -1-3). 17.95 *(978-0-7569-7027-7(X))* Perfection Learning Corp.

Tabor, Nathan. Peekaboo Barn. Sims, Nat. 2014. (Peekaboo Ser.). (ENG.). 22p. (J). (— 1). bds. 7.99 *(978-0-7636-7557-8(1))* Candlewick Pr.

Tachibana, Yutaka. Gatcha Gacha, 8 vols., Vol. 1. Tachibana, Yutaka. Tachibana, Yutaka. 2006. (Gatcha Gacha Ser.). 208p. pap. 9.99 *(978-1-59816-153-3(9))* TOKYOPOP, Inc.

Tackett, Mike. Kai: The Honu Didn't Know He Was Brave. Mora, Ebie. 2005. 24p. (J). 12.95 *(978-1-56647-755-0(7))* Mutual Publishing LLC.

Taddeo, John. ¿Qué le Pasa a la Mamá de Bridget? Los Medikidz Explican el Cáncer de Seno. Chilman-Blair, Kim. 2011. (Medikidz Explain [Cancer XYZ] Ser.). (SPA.). 32p. (J). (gr. 7). 14.95 *(978-1-60443-022-6(2))* American Cancer Society, Inc.

—¿Qué le Pasa a Richard? Los Medikidz Explican la Leucemia. Chilman-Blair, Kim. 2011. (Medikidz Explain [Cancer XYZ] Ser.). (SPA.). 32p. (J). (gr. 7). 14.95 *(978-1-60443-020-2(6))* American Cancer Society, Inc.

—¿Qué le Pasa Jo? Los Medikidz Explican los Tumores Cerebrales. Chilman-Blair, Kim. 2012. (Medikidz Explain [Cancer XYZ] Ser.). (SPA.). 32p. (J). (gr. 7). 14.95 *(978-1-60443-024-0(9))* American Cancer Society, Inc.

—Que le Sucede a Lyndon? Los Medikidz Explican el Osteosarcoma. Chilman-Blair, Kim. 2012. (Medikidz Explain [Cancer XYZ] Ser.). (SPA.). 32p. (J). (gr. 7). 14.95 *(978-1-60443-026-4(5))* American Cancer Society, Inc.

—What's up with Jo? Medikidz Explain Brain Tumors. Chilman-Blair, Kim. 2011. (Medikidz Explain [Cancer XYZ] Ser.). (ENG.). 32p. (J). (gr. 7). 14.95 *(978-1-60443-023-3(0))* American Cancer Society, Inc.

—What's up with Lyndon? Medikidz Explain Osteosarcoma. Chilman-Blair, Kim. 2011. (Medikidz Explain [Cancer XYZ] Ser.). (ENG.). 32p. (J). (gr. 7). 14.95 *(978-1-60443-025-7(7))* American Cancer Society, Inc.

—What's up with Richard? Medikidz Explain Leukemia. Chilman-Blair, Kim. 2010. (Medikidz Explain [Cancer XYZ] Ser.). (ENG.). 32p. (YA). (gr. 7). 14.95 *(978-1-60443-019-6(2))* American Cancer Society, Inc.

Tadgell, Nicole. A Day with Daddy. Scholastic, Inc. Staff & Grimes, Nikki. 2004. (Just for You Ser.). (ENG.). 32p. pap. 3.99 *(978-0-439-56850-0(1),* Teaching Resources) Scholastic, Inc.

—First Peas to the Table: How Thomas Jefferson Inspired a School Garden. Grigsby, Susan. 2012. (ENG.). 32p. (J). (gr. 1-4). 16.99 *(978-0-8075-2452-7(2))* Whitman, Albert & Co.

—Friends for Freedom: The Story of Susan B. Anthony & Frederick Douglass. Slade, Suzanne. 2014. (ENG.). 40p. (J). (gr. 1-4). 16.95 *(978-1-58089-568-2(9))* Charlesbridge Publishing, Inc.

—I'll Do the Right Thing. Elster, Jean Alicia. 2010. (ENG.). 32p. (J). pap. 11.99 *(978-0-8170-1658-6(9))* Judson Pr.

—In the Garden with Doctor Carver. Grigsby, Susan. 2010. (ENG.). 32p. (J). (gr. 2-4). 16.99 *(978-0-8075-3630-8(X))* Whitman, Albert & Co.

—In the Garden with Dr. Carver. Grigsby, Susan. 2012. (J). *(978-1-61913-157-6(9))* Weigl Pubs., Inc.

—Josias, Hold the Book. Elvgren, Jennifer. 2011. (ENG.). 32p. (J). (gr. 2-4). pap. 10.95 *(978-1-59078-856-1(7))* Boyds Mills Pr.

—Lucky Beans. Birtha, Becky. 2012. (J). 34.28 *(978-1-61913-129-3(3))* Weigl Pubs., Inc.

—Lucky Beans. Birtha, Becky. 2010. (ENG.). 32p. (J). (gr. 2-5). 16.99 *(978-0-8075-4782-3(4))* Whitman, Albert & Co.

—No Mush Today, 1 vol. Derby, Sally. 2008. (ENG.). 32p. (J). (gr. -1-3). 17.95 *(978-1-60060-238-2(X))* Lee & Low Bks., Inc.

—With Books & Bricks: How Booker T. Washington Built a School. Slade, Suzanne. 2014. (ENG.). 32p. (J). (gr. 2-5). 16.99 *(978-0-8075-0897-8(7))* Whitman, Albert & Co.

Tadiello, Ed. Rebecca of Sunnybrook Farm. Wiggin, Kate Douglas Smith. Warren, Eliza Gatewood, ed. 2006. 240p. (YA). (gr. 4-8). reprint ed. 10.00 *(978-0-7567-9830-7(2))* DIANE Publishing Co.

Tae-Hyung, Kim. Planet Blood. Tae-Hyung, Kim. Vol. 1. 2005. 200p. pap. 9.99 *(978-1-59532-537-2(9));* Vol. 4. 4th rev. ed. 2006. 184p. per. 9.99 *(978-1-59532-540-2(9))* TOKYOPOP, Inc.

Tafalla, Ortiz. Benjamin Franklin. Kelly, Jack. 2005. (Heroes of America Ser.). 239p. (gr. 3-8). 27.07 *(978-1-59679-257-9(4),* Abdo & Daughters) ABDO Publishing Co.

Tafuri, Nancy. The Big Storm: A Very Soggy Counting Book. Tafuri, Nancy. 2013. (Classic Board Bks.). (ENG.). 34p. (J). (gr. -1 — 1). bds. 7.99 *(978-1-4424-8179-4(X),* Little Simon) Little Simon.

—The Big Storm: A Very Soggy Counting Book. Tafuri, Nancy. 2009. (ENG.). 32p. (J). (gr. -1-2). 17.99 *(978-1-4169-6795-8(8),* Simon & Schuster Bks. For Young Readers) Simon & Schuster Bks. For Young Readers.

—Blue Goose. Tafuri, Nancy. 2010. (Classic Board Bks.). (ENG.). 34p. (J). bds. 7.99 *(978-1-4169-2835-5(9),* Little Simon) Little Simon.

—Blue Goose. Tafuri, Nancy. 2008. (ENG.). 32p. (J). (gr. -1-3). 17.99 *(978-1-4169-2834-8(0),* Simon & Schuster Bks. For Young Readers) Simon & Schuster Bks. For Young Readers.

—The Busy Little Squirrel. Tafuri, Nancy. 2010. (Classic Board Bks.). (ENG.). 34p. (J). (gr. -1 — 1). bds. 7.99 *(978-1-4424-0721-3(2),* Little Simon) Little Simon.

—The Busy Little Squirrel. Tafuri, Nancy. 2007. (ENG.). 32p. (J). (gr. -1-k). 17.99 *(978-0-689-87341-6(7),* Simon & Schuster Bks. For Young Readers) Simon & Schuster Bks. For Young Readers.

—Five Little Chicks. Tafuri, Nancy. 2011. (Classic Board Bks.). (ENG.). 34p. (J). (gr. -1 — 1). bds. 7.99 *(978-1-4424-0722-0(0),* Little Simon) Little Simon.

—Five Little Chicks. Tafuri, Nancy. 2006. (ENG.). 32p. (J). (gr. -1-3). 15.99 *(978-0-689-87342-3(5),* Simon & Schuster Bks. For Young Readers) Simon & Schuster Bks. For Young Readers.

—Have You Seen My Duckling? Tafuri, Nancy. 2007. (gr. -1-k). 17.00 *(978-0-7569-7869-3(6))* Perfection Learning Corp.

—Silly Little Goose. Tafuri, Nancy. 2010. (ENG.). 13p. (J). (gr. k — 1). bds. 8.99 *(978-0-545-15692-9(0)*, Cartwheel Bks.) Scholastic, Inc.
—Whose Chick Are You? Tafuri, Nancy. 2007. (ENG.). 40p. (J). (gr. -1-k). 16.99 *(978-0-06-082514-0(6)*, Greenwillow Bks.) HarperCollins Pubs.
Tageau, Jerry. Who Were the Beatles? Edgers, Geoff. 2006. (Who Was... ? Ser.). 106p. (J). *(978-0-448-43907-5(7)*, Grosset & Dunlap) Penguin Publishing Group.
Tagel, Peggy. Animal Safari. 2003. (Squishy Shapes Ser.). 10p. (J). 12.95 *(978-1-57145-741-7(0)*, Silver Dolphin Bks.) Baker & Taylor Publishing Group.
—Color My World Blue. 2005. (J). *(978-1-58987-101-4(4))* Kindermusik International.
—Dinosaurs. 2003. (Squishy Shapes Ser.). 10p. (J). 12.95 *(978-1-57145-740-0(2)*, Silver Dolphin Bks.) Baker & Taylor Publishing Group.
—The M & M's(r) Brand All-American Parade Book. McGrath, Barbara Barbieri. 2004. 12p. (J). (gr. -1-k). bds. 6.95 *(978-1-57091-430-0(3))* Charlesbridge Publishing, Inc.
—The M & M's(r) Brand Birthday Book. McGrath, Barbara Barbieri. 2004. 12p. (J). (gr. -1-3). bds. 6.95 *(978-1-57091-480-5(X))* Charlesbridge Publishing, Inc.
—The M & M's(r) Brand Easter Egg Hunt. McGrath, Barbara Barbieri. 2004. 12p. (J). (gr. -1-3). bds. 6.95 *(978-1-57091-423-2(0))* Charlesbridge Publishing, Inc.
—The M & M's(r) Brand Valentine Book. McGrath, Barbara Barbieri. 2004. 12p. (J). (gr. -1-k). bds. 6.95 *(978-1-57091-422-5(2))* Charlesbridge Publishing, Inc.
—On the Go. 2003. (Squishy Shapes Ser.). 10p. (J). 12.95 *(978-1-57145-739-4(9)*, Silver Dolphin Bks.) Baker & Taylor Publishing Group.
Taggart, Katy, et al. Workin' on the Railroad: And Other Favorite Rhymes. 2004. (Mother Goose Ser.). (ENG.). 32p. (J). 15.95 *(978-1-59249-385-2(8)*, 1D004) Soundprints.
Tagle, jt. illus. see Sanchez, Andres.
Taglietti, Emanuele. John Calvin. Carr, Simonetta. 2008. (ENG.). 63p. (J). 18.00 *(978-1-60178-055-3(9))* Reformation Heritage Bks.
Taguchi, Masayuki. Battle Royale, 5 vols., Vol. 1. Takami, Koushun. 2003. 192p. pap. 9.99 *(978-1-59182-314-8(5))* TOKYOPOP, Inc.
Tagyos, Paul Rátz de. Maybelle Goes to School. Speck, Katie. 2015. (Maybelle Ser.). (ENG.). 64p. (J). (gr. 2-5). 16.99 *(978-0-8050-9158-8(0)*, Holt, Henry & Co. Bks. For Young Readers) Holt, Henry & Co.
—Maybelle in the Soup / Maybelle Goes to Tea. Speck, Katie. 2009. (Maybelle Ser.). (ENG.). 128p. (J). (gr. 2-4). pap. 6.99 *(978-0-312-53598-8(8))* Square Fish.
Tahleh, Eleykaa. The Legend of Kalikimaka: Alohalani, Kalikimaka Auntie. Westerman, Rob. 2003. 32p. (J). 12.95 *(978-0-9761992-0-5(3))* Gold Boy Music & Pubn.
Taimy Studios. Isobel's New World. Turnbull, Betty Turnbull. 2011. 48p. (J). 11.95 *(978-1-61153-016-2(4))* Light Messages Publishing.
Taixi, Su & Xiaoming, Wang. Stories Behind Chinese Idioms (I) Ma, Zheng & Li, Zheng. 2010. (ENG.). 48p. (J). (gr. 3-6). 16.95 *(978-1-60220-965-7(0))* BetterLink Pr., Inc.
Takabatake, Jun. Hello, Hello. Takeshita, Fumiko. 2006. (ENG.). 28p. (J). (gr. -1-1). pap. *(978-1-933605-11-1(1))* Kane Miller.
Takacs-Moore, Mary. Energy: 25 Projects Investigate Why We Need Power & How We Get It. Takacs-Moore, Mary. Reilly, Kathleen M. 2009. (Build It Yourself Ser.). (ENG.). 128p. (J). (gr. 3-7). pap. 15.95 *(978-1-934670-34-7(0))* Nomad Pr.
Takada, Eriko. Start It Up: The Complete Teen Business Guide to Turning Your Passions into Pay. Naasel, Kenrya R. & Rankin, Kenrya. 2011. (ENG.). 160p. (YA). (gr. 7-18). pap. 14.99 *(978-0-9819733-5-7(3))* Zest Bks.
Takada, Rie. Gaba Kawa, Vol. 1. Takada, Rie. 2008. (Gaba Kawa Ser.: 1). (ENG.). 192p. (gr. 8-18). pap. 8.99 *(978-1-4215-2259-3(4))* Viz Media.
—Happy Hustle High, 5 vols. Takada, Rie. (Happy Hustle High Ser.). (ENG.). 2005. 100p. pap. 9.99 *(978-1-59116-912-3(7))*; Vol. 2. 2005. 200p. pap. 9.99 *(978-1-59116-913-0(5))*; Vol. 4. 2005. 192p. pap. 9.99 *(978-1-4215-0083-6(3))*; Vol. 5. 2006. 200p. pap. 9.99 *(978-1-4215-0323-3(9))* Viz Media.
Takagi, Shigeyoshi. Flower in a Storm. Takagi, Shigeyoshi. 2010. (Flower in a Storm Ser.: 1). (ENG.). 200p. pap. 9.99 *(978-1-4215-3241-7(7))* Viz Media.
Takahashi, Hideko. Eight Is Great. Balsley, Tilda. 2012. (Hanukkah Ser.). (ENG.). 12p. (J). (gr. -1 — 1). bds. 5.95 *(978-0-7613-6523-2(7)*, Kar-Ben Publishing) Lerner Publishing Group.
—Hello, New Baby. 2005. 12p. (J). (gr. -1-18). 9.95 *(978-1-58117-345-1(6)*, Intervisual/Piggy Toes) Bendon, Inc.
Takahashi, Kazuki. Duelist. Takahashi, Kazuki. Wall, Frances, ed. 2007. (Yu-Gi-oh! the Duelist Ser.: 23). (ENG.). 200p. pap. 9.99 *(978-1-4215-1116-0(9))* Viz Media.
—The Millenium Puzzle. Takahashi, Kazuki. Sengupta, Anita, tr. 2003. (Yu-Gi-oh Ser.: Vol. 1). (ENG.). 192p. pap. 9.99 *(978-1-56931-903-1(0))* Viz Media.
—Millennium World. Takahashi, Kazuki. (Yu-Gi-oh! Millennium World Ser.). (ENG.). 2005. 192p. pap. 9.99 *(978-1-59116-878-2(3))*; Vol. 2. 2005. 192p. pap. 9.99 *(978-1-4215-0151-2(1))*; Vol. 3. 2006. 208p. pap. 9.99 *(978-1-4215-0409-4(X))*; Vol. 4. 2006. 208p. pap. 7.95 *(978-1-4215-0693-7(9))*; Vol. 5. 2007. 208p. pap. 7.95 *(978-1-4215-0694-4(7))* Viz Media.
—The Movie Ani-Manga. Takahashi, Kazuki. 2004. (Yu-Gi-oh Ser.). (ENG.). 228p. pap. 13.99 *(978-1-59116-999-4(2))* Viz Media.
—Yu-Gi-Oh! Takahashi, Kazuki. (Yu-Gi-oh! the Duelist Ser.). (ENG.). 2006. 208p. pap. 7.95 *(978-1-4215-0339-4(5))*; 2005. 224p. pap. 9.99 *(978-1-59116-998-7(4))* Viz Media.
—Yu-Gi-Oh! Takahashi, Kazuki. Sengupta, Anita, tr. from JPN. (Yu-Gi-oh Ser.: Vol. 7). (ENG.). 192p. 2004. pap. 9.99 *(978-1-59116-613-9(6))*; 2004. pap. 9.99 *(978-1-59116-471-5(0))*; 2003. pap. 9.99 *(978-1-59116-081-6(2))* Viz Media.
—Yu-Gi-Oh! Takahashi, Kazuki. 2004. (Yu-Gi-oh Ser.). (ENG.). Vol. 4. 192p. pap. 9.99 *(978-1-59116-185-1(1))*; Vol. 5. 208p. pap. 9.99 *(978-1-59116-324-4(2))* Viz Media.
—Yu-Gi-Oh! Duelist. Takahashi, Kazuki. 2005. (Yu-Gi-oh! the Duelist Ser.: Vol. 10). (ENG.). 200p. pap. 7.95 *(978-1-4215-0078-2(7))*; Vol. 5. pap. 7.95 *(978-1-59116-811-9(2))* Viz Media.
—Yu-Gi-Oh! Vol. 2: Duelist. Takahashi, Kazuki. 2005. (Yu-Gi-oh! the Duelist Ser.). (ENG.). 208p. pap. 9.99 *(978-1-59116-716-7(7))* Viz Media.
—Yu-Gi-Oh! Vol. 3: Capsule Monster Chess. Takahashi, Kazuki. Sengupta, Anita, tr. 2003. (Yu-Gi-oh Ser.). (ENG.). 200p. pap. 9.99 *(978-1-59116-179-0(7))* Viz Media.
—Yu-Gi-Oh! Vol. 4: Duelist. Takahashi, Kazuki. 2005. (Yu-Gi-oh! the Duelist Ser.). (ENG.). 208p. pap. 9.99 *(978-1-59116-759-4(0))* Viz Media.
—Yu-Gi-Oh! Vol. 6: Duelist. Takahashi, Kazuki. 2005. (Yu-Gi-oh! the Duelist Ser.). (ENG.). 208p. pap. 7.95 *(978-1-59116-856-0(2))* Viz Media.
—Yu-Gi-Oh! - Duelist. Takahashi, Kazuki. 2005. (Yu-Gi-oh! the Duelist Ser.). (ENG.). 192p. pap. 9.99 *(978-1-4215-0052-2(3))* Viz Media.
—Yu-Gi-Oh! - Duelist! Takahashi, Kazuki. 2005. (Yu-Gi-oh! the Duelist Ser.). (ENG.). 216p. pap. 9.99 *(978-1-59116-614-6(4))* Viz Media.
—Yu-Gi-Oh! - Duelist. Takahashi, Kazuki. (Yu-Gi-oh! the Duelist Ser.). (ENG.). Vol. 11. 2005. 200p. pap. 7.95 *(978-1-4215-0150-5(3))*; Vol. 12. 2006. 208p. pap. 9.99 *(978-1-4215-0207-6(0))* Viz Media.
—Yu-Gi-Oh! - Millennium World. Takahashi, Kazuki. Wall, Frances, ed. 2007. (Yu-Gi-oh! Millennium World Ser.: 6). (ENG.). 208p. pap. 9.99 *(978-1-4215-1328-7(5))* Viz Media.
—Yu-Gi-Oh! Duelist 3. Takahashi, Kazuki. 2005. (Yu-Gi-oh! the Duelist Ser.). (ENG.). 192p. (gr. 8-13). pap. 9.99 *(978-1-59116-771-6(X))* Viz Media.
—Yu-Gi-Oh! the Duelist. Takahashi, Kazuki. 2005. (Yu-Gi-oh! the Duelist Ser.: Vol. 7). (ENG.). 192p. pap. 9.99 *(978-1-59116-877-5(5))* Viz Media.
Takahashi, Rumiko. Intensive Care, Vol. 7. Takahashi, Rumiko. 2nd ed. 2004. (Maison Ikkoku Ser.). (ENG.). 288p. pap. 9.95 *(978-1-59116-485-2(0))* Viz Media.
—Inu Yasha Ani-Manga, Vol. 11. Takahashi, Rumiko. 2005. (Inuyasha Ser.). (ENG.). 216p. pap. 11.99 *(978-1-4215-0022-5(1))* Viz Media.
—Inu-Yasha Ani-Manga: Volume 5. Takahashi, Rumiko. 2004. 206p. 21.35 *(978-1-4176-6422-1(3)*, Turtleback) Turtleback Bks.
—Inuyasha, Set. Takahashi, Rumiko. 2003. (Inuyasha Ser.). (ENG.). 200p. (YA). pap. 39.98 *(978-1-59116-235-3(1)*, Viz Comics) Viz Media.
—Inuyasha Vol. 7: Ani-Manga. Takahashi, Rumiko. 2005. (Inuyasha Ser.). (ENG.). 216p. pap. 11.95 *(978-1-59116-612-2(8))* Viz Media.
—Inuyasha Ani-Manga. Takahashi, Rumiko. (Inuyasha Ser.). (ENG.). Vol. 10. 2005. 216p. pap. 11.99 *(978-1-59116-859-1(7))*; Vol. 14. 2006. 208p. pap. 11.99 *(978-1-4215-0384-4(0))* Viz Media.
—Inuyasha the Movie Ani-Manga: Affections Touching Across Time. Takahashi, Rumiko. 2005. (Inuyasha Ser.). (ENG.). 432p. (YA). pap. 24.99 *(978-1-59116-828-7(7))* Viz Media.
—Maison Ikkoku. Takahashi, Rumiko. (Maison Ikkoku Ser.). (ENG.). Vol. 10. 2nd ed. 2005. 248p. pap. 9.95 *(978-1-59116-729-7(9))*; Vol. 11. 2nd ed. 2005. 232p. pap. 9.95 *(978-1-59116-804-1(X))*; Vol. 12. 2005. 323p. pap. 9.95 *(978-1-59116-869-0(4))*; Vol. 13. 2nd ed. 2005. 232p. pap. 9.95 *(978-1-4215-0141-3(4))*; Vol. 14. 2nd ed. 2005. 240p. pap. 9.95 *(978-1-4215-0142-0(2))*; Vol. 15. 2nd ed. 2006. 208p. pap. 9.95 *(978-1-4215-0279-3(8))* Viz Media.
—Mermaid Saga. Takahashi, Rumiko. 2004. (Mermaid Saga Ser.). (ENG.). (YA). 3. 176p. pap. 9.95 *(978-1-59116-483-8(4))*; Vol. 4. 2nd ed. 192p. pap. 9.99 *(978-1-59116-482-1(6))* Viz Media.
—Rin-Ne, Vol. 2. Takahashi, Rumiko. 2010. (Rin-Ne Ser.: 2). (ENG.). 192p. pap. 9.99 *(978-1-4215-3486-2(X))* Viz Media.
Takahashi, Shin. Saikano. Takahashi, Shin. (Saikano Ser.). (ENG.). (YA). Vol. 2. 2004. 200p. pap. 9.95 *(978-1-59116-474-6(5))*; Vol. 3. 2004. 200p. pap. 9.95 *(978-1-59116-475-3(3))*; Vol. 4. 2005. 248p. pap. 9.95 *(978-1-59116-476-0(1))* Viz Media.
—Saikano: The Last Love Song on This Little Planet. Takahashi, Shin. 2005. (Saikano Ser.: Vol. 5). (ENG.). 248p. pap. 9.95 *(978-1-59116-477-7(X))* Viz Media.
Takamisaki, Ryo. Megaman NT Warrior, 13 vols. Takamisaki, Ryo. 2004. (Megaman NT Warrior Ser.). (ENG.). 192p. (YA). pap. 7.95 *(978-1-59116-465-4(6))* Viz Media.
—Megaman NT Warrior, 13 vols. Takamisaki, Ryo. (ENG.). (J). (gr. 1). 2008. (Megaman Ser.: 13). 184p. pap. 7.99 *(978-1-4215-1785-8(X))*; 2007. (Megaman Ser.: 12). 200p. pap. 7.99 *(978-1-4215-1325-6(0))*; 2006. (Megaman Ser.: Vol. 10). 200p. pap. 7.99 *(978-1-4215-0749-1(8))*; Vol. 2. 2004. (Megaman NT Warrior Ser.). 192p. pap. 7.95 *(978-1-59116-466-1(4))*; Vol. 3. 2004. (Megaman NT Warrior Ser.). 200p. pap. 7.95 *(978-1-59116-414-2(1))* Viz Media.
—Megaman Nt Warrior, 13 vols. Takamisaki, Ryo. (Megaman Ser.). (ENG.). 200p. Vol. 4. 2004. (J). (gr. 1). pap. 7.95 *(978-1-59116-501-9(6))*; Vol. 5. 2005. (YA). pap. 7.95 *(978-1-59116-561-3(X))* Viz Media.
—Megaman NT Warrior, 13 vols. Takamisaki, Ryo. (Megaman Ser.). (ENG.). (J). (gr. 1). Vol. 6. 2005. 200p. pap. 7.99 *(978-1-59116-755-6(8))*; Vol. 7. 2005. 184p. pap. 7.99 *(978-1-4215-0003-4(5))*; Vol. 8. 2005. 192p. pap. 7.99 *(978-1-59116-981-9(X))*; Vol. 9. 2005. 192p. pap. 7.99 *(978-1-4215-0132-1(5))*; Vol. 11. 2007. 184p. pap. 7.99 *(978-1-4215-1141-2(X))* Viz Media.
—Megaman NT Warrior W/Trading Card (no foil Wrap) Takamisaki, Ryo. 2004. (Megaman Nt Warrior Ser.). (ENG.). 192p. (YA). pap. 7.95 *(978-1-59116-827-0(9))* Viz Media.
—The Rise of Darkrai. Takamisaki, Ryo. Viz Media Staff. 2008. (Pokemon Ser.). (ENG.). 192p. (J). (gr. 1). pap. 9.99 *(978-1-4215-2289-0(6))* Viz Media.
Takamiya, Satoru. Heaven's Will. Takamiya, Satoru. 2009. (Heaven's Will Ser.: 1). (ENG.). 200p. (gr. 8-18). pap. 8.99 *(978-1-4215-2258-6(6))* Viz Media.
Takanashi, Mitsuba. Crimson Hero. Takanashi, Mitsuba. (Crimson Hero Ser.). (ENG.). Vol. 1. 2005. 192p. pap. 8.99 *(978-1-4215-0140-6(6))*; Vol. 3. 2006. 208p. pap. 8.99 *(978-1-4215-0577-0(0))*; Vol. 11. 2009. 200p. (gr. 8-18). pap. 8.99 *(978-1-4215-2364-4(7))* Viz Media.
Takara, Marcio. City of Incredibles, Vol. 2. Waid, Mark. 2010. (Incredibles Ser.). (ENG.). 112p. (J). 24.99 *(978-1-60886-529-1(0))* Boom! Studios.
—Family Matters. Waid, Mark. 2009. (Incredibles Ser.). (ENG.). 128p. (J). 24.99 *(978-1-60886-525-3(8))*; pap. 9.99 *(978-1-934506-83-7(4))* Boom! Studios.
—Incorruptible. Waid, Mark. 2012. (ENG.). 128p. Vol. 6. (Incorruptible Ser.: 6). (gr. 10). pap. 16.99 *(978-1-60886-084-5(1))*; Vol. 7. (gr. 9). pap. 16.99 *(978-1-60886-085-2(X))* Boom! Studios.
—The Incredibles: City of Incredibles, Vol. 2. Waid, Mark. 2010. (Incredibles Ser.). (ENG.). 112p. (J). pap. 9.99 *(978-1-60886-503-1(7))* Boom! Studios.
—Revenge from Below. Waid, Mark & Walker, Landry. 2010. (Incredibles Ser.). (ENG.). 112p. (J). (gr. 3-6). pap. 9.99 *(978-1-60886-518-5(5))* Boom! Studios.
—Secrets & Lies. Walker, Landry. 2010. (Incredibles Ser.). 112p. (J). (gr. 3-8). pap. 9.99 *(978-1-60886-583-3(5))* Boom! Studios.
Takase, Naoko. Helen Keller: From Darkness to Light. 2011. (Biographical Comic Ser.). (ENG.). 152p. (J). (gr. 2-6). 18.99 *(978-1-4215-4238-6(2))*; pap. 9.99 *(978-1-4215-4239-3(0))* Shogakukan JPN. Dist: Simon & Schuster, Inc.
Takaya, Natsuki. Fruits Basket, Vol. 7. Takaya, Natsuki. Nibley, Alethea & Nibley, Athena, trs. from JPN. rev. ed. 2005. 208p. (YA). pap. 9.99 *(978-1-59532-402-3(X))* TOKYOPOP, Inc.
—Fruits Basket. Takaya, Natsuki. (Fruits Basket Ser.). 208p. Vol. 10. 10th rev. ed. 2005. pap. 9.99 *(978-1-59532-405-4(4))*; Vol. 13. 13th rev. ed. 2006. pap. 9.99 *(978-1-59532-408-5(9))* TOKYOPOP, Inc.
Takaya, Natsuki. Fruits Basket, Vol. 11. Takaya, Natsuki, creator. rev. ed. 2005. (Fruits Basket Ser.). 208p. pap. 9.99 *(978-1-59532-406-1(2))* TOKYOPOP, Inc.
Takei, Hiroyuki. Kung-Fu Master. Takei, Hiroyuki. Caselman, Lance et al. Olsen, Lillian, tr. 2003. (Shaman King Ser.: Vol. 2). (ENG & JPN.). 200p. pap. 9.99 *(978-1-59116-182-0(7))* Viz Media.
—A Shaman in Tokyo. Takei, Hiroyuki. Caselman, Lance et al. Caselman, Lillian, tr. 2003. (Shaman King Ser.). (ENG & JPN.). 208p. pap. 9.99 *(978-1-56931-902-4(2))* Viz Media.
—Shaman King. Takei, Hiroyuki. 2011. (Shaman King Ser.: 32). (ENG.). 224p. pap. 9.99 *(978-1-4215-2185-5(7))* Viz Media.
—Shaman King. Takei, Hiroyuki. Caselman, Lance et al. 2008. (Shaman King Ser.: 17). (ENG & JPN.). 192p. pap. 9.99 *(978-1-4215-1659-2(4))* Viz Media.
—Shaman King. Takei, Hiroyuki. 2005. (Shaman King Ser.). (ENG & JPN.). 192p. pap. 9.99 *(978-1-59116-996-3(8))* Viz Media.
—Shaman King. Takei, Hiroyuki. Caselman, Lance et al. 2004. (Shaman King Ser.). (ENG & JPN.). 192p. pap. 9.99 *(978-1-59116-252-0(1))* Viz Media.
—Shaman King. Takei, Hiroyuki. 2004. (Shaman King Ser.). (ENG & JPN.). 200p. Vol. 4. pap. 9.99 *(978-1-59116-253-7(X))*; Vol. 5. pap. 7.95 *(978-1-59116-254-4(8))* Viz Media.
—Shaman King Vol. 6. Takei, Hiroyuki. 2005. (Shaman King Ser.). (ENG.). 192p. pap. 9.99 *(978-1-59116-788-4(4))* Viz Media.
—Ultimo. Takei, Hiroyuki. 2010. (Ultimo Ser.: 1). (ENG.). 192p. (gr. 8-18). pap. 9.99 *(978-1-4215-3132-8(1))* Viz Media.
Takeshita, Gene. True Blue Friend. Block, Cheryl. 2006. 32p. (J). 21.95 *(978-0-9761625-2-0(0))* Block Publishing.
Takeuchi, Kana. Death Trance. Takeuchi, Kana. 2005. 152p. (YA). Bk. 2, Vol. 2. pap. 9.99 *(978-1-58655-652-5(5)*, TSNOV-0514); Vol. 3. pap. 9.99 *(978-1-58655-691-4(6)*, TSNOV-0515) Media Blasters, Inc.
Takhar, Jodi & Jones, Paul. Four Seasons of Fun. Takhar, Jodi. 14p. (J). (gr. -1-3). 19.95 *(978-1-886000-02-5(6))* Takhar's, Jodi Spilt Milk Collection.
—What Can I Do Today? Takhar, Jodi. 14p. (J). (gr. -1-3). 19.95 *(978-1-886000-03-2(4))* Takhar's, Jodi Spilt Milk Collection.
Taki, Emiko, photos by. A Taste of Home. Jamison, Heather & Meckenstock, Shay. Marconette, Gennifer, ed. 2008. (ENG., 128p. (YA). 24.95 *(978-0-9794167-2-9(8))* Simple Ink, LLC.
Takken, Sylvia. Aquarius: January 21-February 19. 2014. (Zodiac Sign Bks.). (ENG.). 12p. (J). (gr. -1 — 1). bds. 3.99 *(978-0-7641-6676-1(X))* Barron's Educational Series, Inc.
—Aries: March 21-April 20. 2014. (Zodiac Sign Bks.). (ENG.). 12p. (J). (gr. -1 — 1). bds. 3.99 *(978-0-7641-6678-5(6))* Barron's Educational Series, Inc.
—Cancer. 2014. (Zodiac Sign Bks.). (ENG.). 12p. (J). (gr. -1 — 1). bds. 3.99 *(978-0-7641-6681-5(6))* Barron's Educational Series, Inc.
—Capricorn: December 22-January 20. 2014. (Zodiac Sign Bks.). (ENG.). 12p. (J). (gr. -1 — 1). bds. 3.99 *(978-0-7641-6675-4(1))* Barron's Educational Series, Inc.
—Gemini: May 22-June 21. 2014. (Zodiac Sign Bks.). (ENG.). 12p. (J). (gr. -1 — 1). bds. 3.99 *(978-0-7641-6679-2(4))* Barron's Educational Series, Inc.
—Leo: July 23-August 23. 2014. (Zodiac Sign Bks.). (ENG.). 12p. (J). (gr. -1 — 1). bds. 3.99 *(978-0-7641-6682-2(4))* Barron's Educational Series, Inc.
—Libra: September 24-October 23. 2014. (Zodiac Sign Bks.). (ENG.). 12p. (J). (gr. -1 — 1). bds. 3.99 *(978-0-7641-6684-6(0))* Barron's Educational Series, Inc.
—Pisces: February 20-March 20. 2014. (Zodiac Sign Bks.). (ENG.). 12p. (J). (gr. -1 — 1). bds. 3.99 *(978-0-7641-6677-8(8))* Barron's Educational Series, Inc.
—Sagittarius: November 23-December 21. 2014. (Zodiac Sign Bks.). (ENG.). 12p. (J). (gr. -1 — 1). bds. 3.99 *(978-0-7641-6686-0(7))* Barron's Educational Series, Inc.
—Scorpio: October 24-November 22. 2014. (Zodiac Sign Bks.). (ENG.). 12p. (J). (gr. -1 — 1). bds. 3.99 *(978-0-7641-6685-3(9))* Barron's Educational Series, Inc.
—Taurus: April 21-May 21. 2014. (Zodiac Sign Bks.). (ENG.). 12p. (J). (gr. -1 — 1). bds. 3.99 *(978-0-7641-6680-8(8))* Barron's Educational Series, Inc.
—Virgo: August 24-September 23. 2014. (Zodiac Sign Bks.). (ENG.). 12p. (J). (gr. -1 — 1). bds. 3.99 *(978-0-7641-6683-9(2))* Barron's Educational Series, Inc.
Takvorian, Nadine. Apples, Apples Everywhere! Learning about Apple Harvests, 1 vol. Koontz, Robin Michal. 2010. (Autumn Ser.). (ENG.). 24p. (gr. 1-2). lib. bdg. 25.99 *(978-1-4048-6012-4(6)*, Nonfiction Picture Bks.) Picture Window Bks.
—Apples, Apples Everywhere! Learning about Apple Harvests, 1 vol. Koontz, Robin. 2010. (Autumn Ser.). (ENG.). 24p. (gr. 1-2). pap. 7.95 *(978-1-4048-6388-0(5)*, Nonfiction Picture Bks.) Picture Window Bks.
—Busy Animals: Learning about Animals in Autumn, 1 vol. Bullard, Lisa. 2010. (Autumn Ser.). (ENG.). 24p. (gr. 1-2). lib. bdg. 25.99 *(978-1-4048-6014-8(2))*; pap. 7.95 *(978-1-4048-6389-7(3))* Picture Window Bks. (Nonfiction Picture Bks.).
—Jason & the Argonauts, 1 vol. 2011. (Greek Myths Ser.). (ENG.). 32p. (gr. 4-5). lib. bdg. 27.99 *(978-1-4048-6669-0(8)*, Nonfiction Picture Bks.) Picture Window Bks.
—Leaves Fall Down: Learning about Autumn Leaves, 1 vol. Bullard, Lisa. 2010. (Autumn Ser.). (ENG.). 24p. (gr. 1-2). lib. bdg. 25.99 *(978-1-4048-6013-1(4))*; pap. 7.95 *(978-1-4048-6390-3(7))* Picture Window Bks. (Nonfiction Picture Bks.).
—Odysseus & the Cyclops, 1 vol. 2011. (Greek Myths Ser.). (ENG.). 32p. (gr. 4-5). lib. bdg. 27.99 *(978-1-4048-6666-9(3)*, Nonfiction Picture Bks.) Picture Window Bks.
—Pick a Perfect Pumpkin: Learning about Pumpkin Harvests, 1 vol. Koontz, Robin Michal. 2010. (Autumn Ser.). (ENG.). 24p. (gr. 1-2). lib. bdg. 25.99 *(978-1-4048-6011-7(8)*, Nonfiction Picture Bks.) Picture Window Bks.
—Pick a Perfect Pumpkin: Learning about Pumpkin Harvests, 1 vol. Koontz, Robin. 2010. (Autumn Ser.). (ENG.). 24p. (gr. 1-2). pap. 7.95 *(978-1-4048-6391-0(5)*, Nonfiction Picture Bks.) Picture Window Bks.
—Thanksgiving Crafts, 1 vol. Muehlenhardt, Amy Bailey. 2011. (Thanksgiving Ser.). (ENG.). 24p. (gr. 1-2). lib. bdg. 26.65 *(978-1-4048-6282-1(X))*; pap. 7.95 *(978-1-4048-6721-5(X))* Picture Window Bks. (Nonfiction Picture Bks.).
Talbot, Jim. Whoa! Amusement Park Gone Wild! Lerangis, Peter. 2003. (Abracadabra Ser.: No. 7). (ENG.). 112p. (J). pap. 3.99 *(978-0-439-38938-9(0)*, Scholastic Paperbacks) Scholastic, Inc.
—Wow! Blast from the Past! Lerangis, Peter. 2003. (Abracadabra Ser.: No. 8). (ENG.). 112p. (J). pap. 3.99 *(978-0-439-38939-6(9)*, Scholastic Paperbacks) Scholastic, Inc.
Talbot, Laura. If I Were a French Quarter Rat. Talbot, Sharon. 2010. (ENG.). 44p. pap. 13.95 *(978-1-4515-1324-0(0))* CreateSpace Independent Publishing Platform.
Talbott, Hudson. The Lost Colony of Roanoke. Fritz, Jean. 2004. (ENG.). 64p. (J). (gr. 2-5). 18.99 *(978-0-399-24027-0(6)*, Putnam Juvenile) Penguin Publishing Group.
—Show Way. Woodson, Jacqueline. 2005. (ENG.). 48p. (J). (gr. -1-3). 17.99 *(978-0-399-23749-2(6)*, Putnam Juvenile) Penguin Publishing Group.
Talbott, Hudson. It's All about Me-Ow. Talbott, Hudson. 2012. (ENG.). 32p. (J). (gr. -1-2). 16.99 *(978-0-399-25403-1(X)*, Nancy Paulsen Bks.) Penguin Publishing Group.
—River of Dreams: The Story of the Hudson River. Talbott, Hudson. 2009. (ENG.). 40p. (J). (gr. 1-3). 17.99 *(978-0-399-24521-3(9)*, Putnam Juvenile) Penguin Publishing Group.
—United Tweets of America: 50 State Birds Their Stories, Their Glories. Talbott, Hudson. (ENG.). 64p. (J). (gr. 1-3). 2015. 8.99 *(978-0-14-751557-5(2)*, Puffin); 2008. 17.99 *(978-0-399-24520-6(0)*, Putnam Juvenile) Penguin Publishing Group.
Talbott, Kerry. The Day Roy Riegels Ran the Wrong Way. Gutman, Dan. 2011. (ENG.). 40p. (J). (gr. -1-8). 16.99 *(978-1-59990-494-8(2)*, Bloomsbury USA Childrens) Bloomsbury USA.
—Fingerprints on the Table: The Story of the White House Treaty Table. Trounstine, Connie / Remlinger. 2013. (ENG.). 48p. (J). 16.95 *(978-1-931917-14-8(0))* White Hse. Historical Assn.
Talbott, Sherri. My Mom Has Wheels. Rose, Sandra. 2009. 28p. pap. 24.95 *(978-1-60836-889-1(0))* America Star Bks.
Talib, Binny. The Perfect Flower Girl. Chandab, Taghred. 2012. (ENG.). 32p. (J). (gr. -1-k). 19.99 *(978-1-74237-573-1(1))* Allen & Unwin AUS. Dist: Independent Pubs. Group.
Talkowski, Steve & MJ Illustrations Staff. Fin-Tastic Friends! Tillworth, Mary & Random House Children's Books Staff. 2013. (Glitter Board Book Ser.). (ENG.). 12p. (J). (gr. -1 — 1). bds. 6.99 *(978-0-385-37534-4(4)*, Random Hse. Bks. for Young Readers) Random Hse. Children's Bks.
Tallardy, Laura. The Girls Body Book: Everything You Need to Know for Growing up YOU. Dunham, Kelli. 2013. (ENG.). 116p. (J). pap. 11.95 *(978-1-60433-353-4(7)*, Applesauce Pr.) Cider Mill Pr. Bk. Pubs., LLC.
Tallardy, Laura. The Girl's Body Book: Everything You Need to Know for Growing up You! Dunham, Kelli. 3rd rev. ed. 2015. (ENG.). 132p. (J). pap. 12.95 *(978-1-60433-575-0(0)*, Applesauce Pr.) Cider Mill Pr. Bk. Pubs., LLC.
Tallardy, Laura. Party Girl: How to Throw a Fab Fest. Speregen, Devra Newberger. 2008. 48p. pap. *(978-0-545-04093-8(0))* Scholastic, Inc.

T

—Sophie the Awesome. Bergen, Lara. 2010. (J). (Sophie Ser.: 1). (ENG.). 112p. (gr. 2-5). 4.99 *(978-0-545-14604-3(6),* Scholastic Paperbacks); 99p. *(978-0-545-24231-8(2))* Scholastic, Inc.

—Sophie the Hero. Bergen, Lara. 2010. (Sophie Ser.: 2). (ENG.). 112p. (J). (gr. 2-5). pap. 4.99 *(978-0-545-14605-0(4),* Scholastic Paperbacks) Scholastic, Inc.

Tallarico, Tony & Eagle, Cameron. License Plates Across the States: Travel Puzzles & Games. Tallarico, Tony & Tallarigo, Tony. 2005. (ENG.). 24p. (J). (gr. -1-2). mass mkt. 4.99 *(978-0-8431-7737-4(3),* Price Stern Sloan) Penguin Publishing Group.

Tallec, Olivier. The Bathing Costume. Moundlic, Charlotte. 2013. (ENG.). 40p. (J). (gr. k-3). 15.95 *(978-1-59270-141-4(8))* Enchanted Lion Bks., LLC.

—Big Wolf & Little Wolf. Brun-Cosme, Nadine. Bedrick, Claudia Z., tr. from FRE. 2009. (ENG.). 32p. (J). (gr. -1-2). 16.95 *(978-1-59270-084-4(5))* Enchanted Lion Bks., LLC.

—Big Wolf & Little Wolf: The Little Leaf That Wouldn't Fall. Brun-Cosme, Nadine. 2009. (ENG.). 32p. (J). (gr. -1-2). 16.95 *(978-1-59270-088-2(8))* Enchanted Lion Bks., LLC.

—Big Wolf & Little Wolf, Such a Beautiful Orange! Brun-Cosme, Nadine. 2011. (ENG.). 32p. (J). (gr. -1-3). 16.95 *(978-1-59270-106-3(X))* Enchanted Lion Bks., LLC.

—Gus Is a Fish. Babin, Claire. Bedrick, Claudia Z., tr. from FRE. 2008. (ENG.). 32p. (J). (gr. -1-2). 14.95 *(978-1-59270-101-8(9))* Enchanted Lion Bks., LLC.

—Gus Is a Tree. Babin, Claire. 2009. (ENG.). 32p. (J). (gr. -1-2). 14.95 *(978-1-59270-078-3(0))* Enchanted Lion Bks., LLC.

—The Scar. Moundlic, Charlotte. 2011. (ENG.). 32p. (J). (gr. k-4). 14.99 *(978-0-7636-5341-5(1))* Candlewick Pr.

—Thumbelina of Toulaba. Picouly, Daniel. Bedrick, Claudia Z., tr. from FRE. 2007. (ENG.). 36p. (J). (gr. -1-3). 16.95 *(978-1-59270-069-1(1))* Enchanted Lion Bks., LLC.

Tallent, Alyssa. Danny Calloway & the Puzzle House. Bolger, Z. C. Robinson, Garrett, ed. 2013. 346p. 24.99 *(978-1-939898-01-2(3))* Story Road Publishing, Inc.

Talley, Pam. Two Foals, a Dash of Sprinkles & a Cherry on Top! Bevis, Brittany. 2011. 32p. (J). 18.47 *(978-0-9824766-7-3(1));* pap. 18.47 *(978-0-9824766-8-0(X))* Caballo Pr. of Ann Arbor. (Caballito Children's Bks.).

Tamaki, Jillian. This One Summer. Tamaki, Mariko. 2014. (ENG.). 320p. (YA). (gr. 7). 21.99 *(978-1-62672-094-7(0));* pap. 17.99 *(978-1-59643-774-6(X))* Roaring Brook Pr. (First Second Bks.).

Tamaki, Nozomu. Dance in the Vampire Bund. Tamaki, Nozomu. 2008. (Dance in the Vampire Bund Ser.: 2). (ENG.). 192p. pap. 10.99 *(978-1-933164-81-6(6));* Vol. 3. 208p. pap. 10.99 *(978-1-934876-15-2(1))* Seven Seas Entertainment, LLC.

Tamang, Mayan. The Adventures of Captain Remarkable: Companion chapter book to Captain Remarkable. O'Neal-Thorpe, Rochelle. 2nd ed. 2010. 124p. (J). pap. 10.95 *(978-0-9823906-0-3(2))* Wiggles Pr.

—Captain Remarkable; Girls can be Superheroes Too! 2009. 28p. (J). pap. 10.95 *(978-0-9823906-1-0(0))* Wiggles Pr.

Tamara, Visco. Dinero the Frog Learns to Save Energy. Colon De Mejias, Leticia. 2013. 32p. pap. 7.00 *(978-0-9822168-9-7(0))* Independent Pub.

Tamarin, Nicole. Little Yellow Pear Tomatoes. Yumel, Demain. 2005. 32p. (J). 15.95 *(978-0-9740190-2-4(X))* Illumination Arts Publishing Co., Inc.

Tamayo, Natalia. Paso A Paso. Vasco, Irene. 2003. (Literatura Juvenil (Panamericana Editorial) Ser.). (SPA.). 77p. (YA). (gr. -1-7). pap. *(978-958-30-0374-5(3))* Panamericana Editorial.

Tambellini, Stefano & Owl, William. Sam & Charlie (and Sam Too!) Kimmelman, Leslie. 2013. (ENG.). 48p. (J). (gr. 1-3). 13.99 *(978-0-8075-7213-9(6))* Whitman, Albert & Co.

Tamura, Mitsuhisa. Bakegyamon. Tamura, Mitsuhisa. 2009. (Bakégyamon Ser.: 5). (ENG.). 216p. (J). pap. 7.99 *(978-1-4215-2171-8(7))* Viz Media.

—BakéGyamon. Tamura, Mitsuhisa. 2009. (ENG.). 216p. (J). Vol. 3. (Bakégyamon Ser.: 3). pap. 7.99 *(978-1-4215-1795-7(7));* Vol. 4. (Bakgyamon Ser.: 4). pap. 7.99 *(978-1-4215-1882-4(1))* Viz Media.

Tamura, Yumi. Basara. Tamura, Yumi. 2004. (Basara Ser.). 190p. (YA). (gr. 7-12). 18.75 *(978-0-613-86370-4(4),* Turtleback) Turtleback Bks.

—Basara. Tamura, Yumi. 2006. (Basara Ser.: 17). (ENG.). 208p. pap. 9.99 *(978-1-4215-0391-2(3))* Viz Media.

—Basara. Tamura, Yumi. Olsen, Lillian, tr. 2003. (Basara Ser.: Vol. 1). (ENG.). 200p. (YA). pap. 9.95 *(978-1-56931-974-1(X))* Viz Media.

—Basara. Tamura, Yumi. (Basara Ser.). (ENG.). 9. 2004. 200p. (YA). pap. 9.95 *(978-1-59116-369-5(2));* Vol. 5. 2004. 200p. pap. 9.95 *(978-1-59116-246-9(7));* Vol. 7. 2004. 200p. (YA). pap. 9.95 *(978-1-59116-367-1(6));* Vol. 8. 2004. 200p. pap. 9.95 *(978-1-59116-368-8(4));* Vol. 10. 2005. 200p. (YA). pap. 9.95 *(978-1-59116-628-3(4));* Vol. 11. 2005. 200p. (YA). pap. 9.99 *(978-1-59116-746-4(9));* Vol. 12. 2005. 200p. pap. 9.99 *(978-1-59116-800-3(7));* Vol. 13. 2005. 200p. pap. 9.99 *(978-1-59116-864-5(3));* Vol. 16. 2006. 208p. pap. 9.99 *(978-1-4215-0261-8(5))* Viz Media.

—Book of Justice. Tamura, Yumi. 2003. (Chicago Ser.: Vol. 2). (ENG.). 200p. pap. 15.95 *(978-1-56931-829-4(8))* Viz Media.

—Wild Com. Tamura, Yumi. 2004. (Wild Com Ser.). (ENG.). 192p. (YA). pap. 9.95 *(978-1-59116-559-0(8))* Viz Media.

Tamura, Yumi, jt. illus. see Yuki, Kaori.

Tan, Anthony. Bratz: Super-Bratz. Christine, Peymani. 2008. 96p. pap. 6.99 *(978-1-4278-0789-2(2))* TOKYOPOP, Inc.

Tan, Billy, et al. Thor by Kieron Gillen Ultimate Collection. 2011. (ENG.). 312p. (YA). (gr. 8-17). pap. 34.99 *(978-0-7851-5922-3(3))* Marvel Worldwide, Inc.

Tan, Shaun. Al Aranib (the Rabbits- Arabic Edition) Marsden, John. 2013. (ENG & ARA.). 32p. (J). (gr. -1-3). pap. 12.00 *(978-99921-94-60-7(X),* 227646) Bloomsbury USA.

—Memorial. Crew, Gary. 32p. *(978-0-85091-983-7(5),* Lothian Children's Bks.) Hachette Australia.

—The Viewer. Crew, Gary. 2003. (ENG.). 32p. (J). (gr. 1-6). 16.95 *(978-1-894965-02-6(7))* Simply Read Bks. CAN. Dist: Ingram Pub. Services.

Tan, Shaun. The Arrival. Tan, Shaun. 2007. (ENG.). 128p. (J). (gr. 7-12). 19.99 *(978-0-439-89529-3(4),* Levine, Arthur A. Bks.) Scholastic, Inc.

—Lost & Found. Tan, Shaun. 2011. (ENG.). 128p. (J). (gr. -1-3). 21.99 *(978-0-545-22924-1(3),* Levine, Arthur A. Bks.) Scholastic, Inc.

—Tales from Outer Suburbia. Tan, Shaun. 2009. (ENG.). 96p. (J). (gr. 7-18). 19.99 *(978-0-545-05587-1(3),* Levine, Arthur A. Bks.) Scholastic, Inc.

Tanabe, Yellow. Kekkaishi. Tanabe, Yellow. (Kekkaishi Ser.: 22). (ENG.). 2010. 192p. pap. 9.99 *(978-1-4215-3069-7(4));* 2006. 208p. pap. 9.99 *(978-1-4215-0487-2(1));* 2005. 200p. pap. 9.99 *(978-1-4215-0067-6(1));* Vol. 1. 2005. 192p. pap. 9.99 *(978-1-59116-968-0(2));* Vol. 2. 2005. 192p. pap. 9.99 *(978-1-59116-970-3(4));* Vol. 5. 2006. 208p. pap. 9.99 *(978-1-4215-0486-5(3));* Vol. 23. 2010. 192p. pap. 9.99 *(978-1-4215-3200-4(X))* Viz Media.

—Kekkaishi 24. Tanabe, Yellow. 2011. (Kekkaishi Ser.: 24). (ENG.). 192p. pap. 9.99 *(978-1-4215-3529-6(7))* Viz Media.

Tanaka, Shinsuke. Wings. 2006. (ENG.). 80p. (J). (gr. -1). 14.95 *(978-1-933327-19-8(7))* Purple Bear Bks., Inc.

Tanaka, Suzuki. Menkui!, Vol. 1. Tanaka, Suzuki. 2006. (Menkui! Ser.). 192p. pap. 9.99 *(978-1-59816-358-2(2))* TOKYOPOP, Inc.

Tanaka, Usa. Give Me That! Tanaka, Usa. 2007. (ENG.). 32p. (J). 15.95 *(978-0-9741319-0-0(3))* 4N Publishing LLC.

Tanaka, Yoko. Blanket & Bear, a Remarkable Pair. Kelly, L. J. R. 2013. (ENG.). 32p. (J). (gr. -1-k). 16.99 *(978-0-399-25681-3(4),* Putnam Juvenile) Penguin Publishing Group.

—The Magician's Elephant. DiCamillo, Kate. (ENG.). 208p. (J). (gr. 3-7). 2011. 6.99 *(978-0-7636-5298-2(9));* 2009. 16.99 *(978-0-7636-4410-9(2))* Candlewick Pr.

—One Moon, Two Cats. Godwin, Laura. 2011. (ENG.). 32p. (J). (gr. -1-1). 16.99 *(978-1-4424-1202-6(X),* Atheneum Bks. for Young Readers) Simon & Schuster Children's Publishing.

—Sparrow Girl. Pennypacker, Sara. 2009. (ENG.). 40p. (J). (gr. k-4). 16.99 *(978-1-4231-1187-0(7))* Hyperion Pr.

—Theodosia & the Eyes of Horus. LaFevers, R. L. 2011. (Theodosia Ser.). (ENG.). 384p. (J). (gr. 2-5). pap. 6.99 *(978-0-547-55011-4(1))* Houghton Mifflin Harcourt Publishing Co.

—Theodosia & the Serpents of Chaos. LaFevers, R. L. 2008. (Theodosia Ser.). (ENG.). 352p. (J). (gr. 2-5). pap. 7.99 *(978-0-618-99976-7(0))* Houghton Mifflin Harcourt Publishing Co.

—Theodosia & the Staff of Osiris. LaFevers, R. L. 2009. (Theodosia Ser.). (ENG.). 400p. (J). (gr. 2-5). pap. 7.99 *(978-0-547-24819-6(9))* Houghton Mifflin Harcourt Publishing Co.

—The Witch's Curse. McGowan, Keith. 2013. (ENG.). 304p. (J). (gr. 4-7). 16.99 *(978-0-8050-9324-7(9),* Holt, Henry & Co. Bks. For Young Readers) Holt, Henry & Co.

—The Witch's Curse. McGowan, Keith. 2014. (ENG.). 320p. (J). (gr. 4-7). pap. 7.99 *(978-1-250-04426-6(X))* Square Fish.

—The Witch's Guide to Cooking with Children. McGowan, Keith. 2011. (ENG.). 192p. (J). (gr. 4-7). pap. 6.99 *(978-0-312-67486-1(4))* Square Fish.

Tanchak, Diane. The True Story of Federico Fish & Ana Alligator. Beckenstein, Cara. 2003. 32p. 11.95 *(978-0-9726699-0-0(6))* Laughing Gull Pr.

Tanchez, Plinio. El Viaje de Lucita. Garcia, Elizabeth. 2010. (SPA.). (J). (gr. -1-1). pap. *(978-99922-1-343-8(4))* Piedra Santa, Editorial.

Tanco, Miguel. My Best Buddy. Kim, YeShil. 2015. (MySELF Bookshelf Ser.). (ENG.). 32p. (J). (gr. k-2). pap. 11.94 *(978-1-60357-693-2(2));* lib. bdg. 22.60 *(978-1-59953-658-3(7))* Norwood Hse. Pr.

Tancredi, Sharon. Buddha at Bedtime: Tales of Love & Wisdom for You to Read with Your Child to Enchant, Enlighten & Inspire. Nagaraja, Dharmachari. 2008. (ENG.). 144p. (gr. -1-3). pap. 16.95 *(978-1-84483-623-9(1),* Watkins Publishing) Watkins Media Limited GBR. Dist: Penguin Random Hse., LLC.

Tandoc, Melissa. Andre the Squirrel & the Christmas Gift. Durham, Roy. 2011. (ENG.). 34p. pap. 9.95 *(978-1-4679-0001-0(X))* CreateSpace Independent Publishing Platform.

Tandy, Russell H. The Clue in the Jewel Box, No. 20. Keene, Carolyn. 2005. (Nancy Drew Mystery Stories Ser.). (ENG.). 228p. (J). (gr. 5-9). 17.95 *(978-1-55709-277-9(X))* Applewood Bks.

Tanemura, Arina. The Gentlemen's Alliance + Tanemura, Arina. 2007. (Gentlemen's Alliance + Ser.: Vol. 3). (ENG.). 192p. pap. 8.99 *(978-1-4215-1185-6(1))* Viz Media.

—The Gentlemen's Alliance, Vol. 1. Tanemura, Arina. 2007. (Gentlemen's Alliance + Ser.). (ENG.). 208p. pap. 8.99 *(978-1-4215-1183-2(5))* Viz Media.

—Gentlemen's Alliance Cross. Tanemura, Arina. 2007. (Gentlemen's Alliance + Ser.: 2). (ENG.). 192p. pap. 8.99 *(978-1-4215-1184-9(3))* Viz Media.

—Mistress Fortune. Tanemura, Arina. 2011. (Mistress Fortune Ser.). (ENG.). 200p. pap. 9.99 *(978-1-4215-3881-5(4))* Viz Media.

—O Sagashite, 7 vols. Tanemura, Arina. 2005. (Full Moon Ser.). (ENG.). 192p. pap. 9.99 *(978-1-4215-0036-2(1))* Viz Media.

—O Sagashite Vol. 6, 7 vols. Tanemura, Arina. 2006. (Full Moon Ser.). (ENG.). 208p. pap. 8.99 *(978-1-4215-0397-4(2))* Viz Media.

—Sagashite, 7 vols. Tanemura, Arina. Kimura, Tomo. 2005. (Full Moon Ser.). (ENG.). 192p. pap. 9.99 *(978-1-4215-0125-3(2))* Viz Media.

—Sagashite, 7 vols. Tanemura, Arina. (Full Moon Ser.: Vol. 3). (ENG.). 2005. 176p. pap. 8.99 *(978-1-4215-0059-1(0));* Vol. 1. 2005. 208p. pap. 8.99 *(978-1-59116-928-4(3));* Vol. 5. 2006. 208p. pap. 9.99 *(978-1-4215-0266-3(6))* Viz Media.

Tang, Charles. The Mystery in New York. 2004. (Boxcar Children Special Ser.: No. 13). (ENG.). 121p. (J). (gr. 2-5). 14.99 *(978-0-8075-5459-3(6));* pap. 4.99 *(978-0-8075-5460-9(X))* Whitman, Albert & Co.

Tang, Li Chu. The Chinese Wonder Book: A Classic Collection of Chinese Tales. Pitman, Norman Hinsdale. 2011. (ENG.). 96p. (J). (gr. 4-6). 16.95 *(978-0-8048-4161-0(6))* Tuttle Publishing.

Tang, Sandara. Following Magic. Duey, Kathleen. 2010. (Faeries' Promise Ser.: 2). (ENG.). (J). (gr. 2-5). 96p. 15.99 *(978-1-4169-8459-7(3))* Simon & Schuster/Paula Wiseman Bks. (Simon & Schuster/Paula Wiseman Bks.).

—The Full Moon. Duey, Kathleen. 2011. (Faeries' Promise Ser.: 4). (ENG.). 128p. (J). (gr. 2-5). pap. 4.99 *(978-1-4169-8463-4(1));* lib. bdg. 15.99 *(978-1-4169-8462-7(3))* Simon & Schuster/Paula Wiseman Bks. (Simon & Schuster/Paula Wiseman Bks.).

—Silence & Stone. Duey, Kathleen. 2010. (Faeries' Promise Ser.: 1). (ENG.). 80p. (J). (gr. 2-5). 15.99 *(978-1-4169-8456-6(9));* pap. 4.99 *(978-1-4169-8457-3(7))* Simon & Schuster/Paula Wiseman Bks. (Simon & Schuster/Paula Wiseman Bks.).

—Wishes & Wings. Duey, Kathleen. 2011. (Faeries' Promise Ser.: 3). (ENG.). 128p. (J). (gr. 2-5). 15.99 *(978-1-4169-8460-3(7));* pap. 4.99 *(978-1-4169-8461-0(5))* Simon & Schuster/Paula Wiseman Bks. (Simon & Schuster/Paula Wiseman Bks.).

Tang, You-shan. Striking It Rich: Treasures from Gold Mountain. Yamada, Debbie Leung. l.t. ed. 2004. 128p. (J). (gr. 4-8). pap. 13.95 *(978-1-879965-21-8(6))* Polychrome Publishing Corp.

Tang, Youshan. Abadeha: The Philippine Cinderella. De La Paz, Myrna J. 2014. (ENG.). 32p. (J). (gr. 3-7). 16.95 *(978-1-885008-17-6(1),* Shen's Bks.) Lee & Low Bks., Inc.

—Abadeha: The Philippine Cinderella. de la Paz, Myrna J. 2014. (ENG.). 32p. (J). pap. 8.95 *(978-1-885008-44-2(9),* Shen's Bks.) Lee & Low Bks., Inc.

—Anklet for a Princess: A Cinderella Story from India. Mehta, Lila. 2014. (ENG.). 32p. (J). pap. 8.95 *(978-1-885008-46-6(5),* Shen's Bks.) Lee & Low Bks., Inc.

—The Magical Monkey King: Mischief in Heaven. 2004. (J). (gr. 2-5). 113p. 14.95 *(978-1-885008-24-4(4));* 32p. per. 8.95 *(978-1-885008-25-1(2))* Lee & Low Bks., Inc. (Shen's Bks.).

Tangen, Nick. Trains & Tow Boats. Trombello, William. 2013. 34p. pap. *(978-0-9842998-1-2(5))* Roxby Media Ltd.

Tango-Schurmann, Ann. Olivia Macallister, Who Are You? A Ghost Mystery Set in Maine. Mariotti, Celine Rose. 2004. 85p. (YA). (gr. 3-6). pap. 12.95 *(978-0-9721389-6-3(X))* Rock Village Publishing.

Tanguay, David D., jt. illus. see DeCarlo, Mike.

Tanguy, Elara, jt. illus. see Biggs, Brian.

Tani, Toshihiko. The Deer King. Yamanushi, Toshiko. 2014. (J). 8.95 *(978-1-935523-70-3(8))* World Tribune Pr.

Taniguchi, Tomoko. Aquarium, Vol. 1. Taniguchi, Tomoko. 2nd rev. ed. 2003. 200p. pap. 9.99 *(978-1-58664-900-5(0),* CMX 62801MM, CPM Manga) Central Park Media Corp.

—Call Me Princess. Taniguchi, Tomoko. 2nd rev. ed. 2003. 192p. pap. 9.99 *(978-1-58664-898-5(5),* CMX 61601MM, CPM Manga) Central Park Media Corp.

—Just a Girl, 2 bks., Bk. 1. Taniguchi, Tomoko. Pannone, Frank, ed. Hiroe, Ikoi, tr. from JPN. 2004. 184p. (YA). pap. 9.99 *(978-1-58664-911-1(6),* CMX 64801CG, CPM Manga) Central Park Media Corp.

—Just a Girl 2, 2 vols., Vol. 2. Taniguchi, Tomoko. Pannone, Frank, ed. Hiroe, Ikoi, tr. from JPN. 2004. 168p. pap. 9.99 *(978-1-58664-912-8(4),* CMX 64802G, CPM Manga) Central Park Media Corp.

—Let's Stay Together Forever. Taniguchi, Tomoko. Pannone, Frank, ed. Rose, Julia, tr. from JPN. 2003. 192p. pap. 15.95 *(978-1-58664-881-7(0),* CMX 62701G, CPM Manga) Central Park Media Corp.

—Miss Me? Taniguchi, Tomoko. Pannone, Frank, ed. Hiroe, Ikoi, tr. from JPN. 2004. 184p. pap. 9.99 *(978-1-58664-905-0(1),* CMX 64701G, CPM Manga) Central Park Media Corp.

—Popcorn Romance. Taniguchi, Tomoko. 2003. Orig. Title: Love & Peace in a Cornfield. 192p. pap. 9.99 *(978-1-58664-901-2(9),* CMX 64901G, CPM Manga) Central Park Media Corp.

—Princess Prince. Taniguchi, Tomoko. 2003. 336p. (YA). pap. 15.95 *(978-1-58664-860-2(8),* CMX 62601G, CPM Manhwa) Central Park Media Corp.

Tanis, Joel. Kid's Study Bible, 1 vol. Zondervan Publishing Staff. rev. ed. 2004. (ENG.). 1824p. (J). 27.99 *(978-0-310-70801-8(X))* Zonderkidz.

Tanis, Joel E. Swing! Klein, Pamela. 2006. (ENG.). (J). 15.95 *(978-1-932514-05-6(8))* College of DuPage Pr.

Tank, Daniel, jt. illus. see Pennington, Jack.

Tank, Daniel, jt. illus. see Vitale, Raoul.

Tank, Daniel, jt. illus. see White, John, Jr.

Tankard, Jeremy. Here Comes Destructosaurus! Reynolds, Aaron. 2014. (ENG.). 32p. (J). (gr. -1-k). 16.99 *(978-1-4521-2454-4(X))* Chronicle Bks. LLC.

—It's a Tiger! LaRochelle, David. 2012. (ENG.). 36p. (J). (gr. -1-k). 16.99 *(978-0-8118-6925-6(3))* Chronicle Bks. LLC.

—Piggy Bunny. Vail, Rachel. 2012. (ENG.). 32p. (J). (gr. -1-1). 14.99 *(978-0-312-64988-3(6))* Feiwel & Friends.

—Privacy: Deal with It Like Nobody's Business, 1 vol. Peters, Diane. 2006. (Lorimer Deal with It Ser.). (ENG.). 32p. (J). (gr. 4-6). pap. 12.95 *(978-1-55028-907-7(1))* Lorimer, James & Co., Ltd., Pubs. CAN. Dist: Casemate Pubs. & Bk. Distributors, LLC.

—Procrastination: Deal with It All in Good Time, 1 vol. Peters, Diane. 2006. (Lorimer Deal with It Ser.). (ENG.). 32p. (J). (gr. 4-6). pap. 12.95 *(978-1-55028-947-3(0))* Lorimer, James & Co., Ltd., Pubs. CAN. Dist: Casemate Pubs. & Bk. Distributors, LLC.

Tankard, Jeremy. Boo Hoo Bird. Tankard, Jeremy. 2009. (ENG.). 32p. (J). (gr. -1-k). 14.99 *(978-0-545-06570-2(4),* Scholastic Pr.) Scholastic, Inc.

—Grumpy Bird. Tankard, Jeremy. 2007. (ENG.). 32p. (J). (gr. -1-k). 16.99 *(978-0-439-85147-3(5),* Scholastic Pr.) Scholastic, Inc.

—Me Hungry! Tankard, Jeremy. (ENG.). (J). 2010. 34p. (— 1). bds. 7.99 *(978-0-7636-4780-3(2));* 2008. 40p. (gr. -1-2). 15.99 *(978-0-7636-3360-8(7))* Candlewick Pr.

Tanksley, Ann. The Six Fools. Hurston, Zora Neale. 2006. (ENG.). 40p. (J). (gr. 1-5). 15.99 *(978-0-06-000646-4(3))* HarperCollins Pubs.

—The Six Fools. Hurston, Zora Neale & Thomas, Joyce Carol. 2005. 40p. (J). (gr. 1-5). lib. bdg. 18.89 *(978-0-06-000647-1(1))* HarperCollins Pubs.

Tannehill, Mary Jo. The Little Acorn. Kauble, Christa. Natural Resources Conservation Service (U.S.), ed. 2008. (ENG.). 24p. (gr. -1-4). pap. 5.00 *(978-0-16-081701-4(3),* Forest Service) United States Government Printing Office.

Tannenbaum, Rose. Theo: The Blue Rider Pigeon. Sireau, Christine. 2005. 20p. (J). (gr. -1-3). pap. 15.00 *(978-0-88010-561-3(5))* SteinerBooks, Inc.

Tanner, Jennifer. Robin Hood, 1 vol. Stone Arch Books Staff. Tobon, Sara, tr. from ENG. 2009. (Classic Fiction Ser.). (SPA.). 72p. (gr. 2-3). lib. bdg. 26.65 *(978-1-4342-1689-2(6),* Graphic Revolve en Español) Stone Arch Bks.

—Robin Hood. 2010. (Classic Fiction Ser.). 72p. lib. bdg. 4.95 *(978-1-4342-2604-4(2),* Graphic Revolve) Stone Arch Bks.

—Robin Hood, 1 vol. Stone Arch Books Staff. Tobon, Sara, tr. 2010. (Classic Fiction Ser.). (ENG & SPA.). 72p. (gr. 2-3). pap. 7.15 *(978-1-4342-2275-6(6),* Graphic Revolve en Español) Stone Arch Bks.

Tanner, Stephanie. Sam's Mission Call. Brown, Gary. 24p. (J). 12.95 *(978-0-910523-13-4(4))* Grandin Bk. Co.

Tanner, Suzy-Jane. Nursery Rhymes. 2012. (ENG.). 24p. (J). pap. 9.95 *(978-1-84135-743-0(X))* Award Pubns. Ltd. GBR. Dist: Parkwest Pubns., Inc.

Tanner Voyles. Mickey's Mini Farm. Jean Emily Myers, Emily Myers & Jean Emily Myers. 2009. 32p. pap. 21.99 *(978-1-4389-5544-5(8))* AuthorHouse.

Tans, Adrian. The Emperor's Army, 1 vol. Pilegard, Virginia. 2010. (ENG.). 32p. (J). (gr. k-3). 16.99 *(978-1-58980-690-0(5))* Pelican Publishing Co., Inc.

—Kick the Cowboy, 1 vol. Gribnau, Joe. 2009. (ENG.). 32p. (J). (gr. k-3). 16.99 *(978-1-58980-605-4(0))* Pelican Publishing Co., Inc.

—Pirate Treasure Hunt!, 1 vol. Peck, Jan. 2008. (ENG.). 32p. (J). (gr. k-3). 16.99 *(978-1-58980-549-1(6))* Pelican Publishing Co., Inc.

—Pirates Don't Say Please!, 1 vol. Knowlton, Laurie. 2012. (ENG.). 32p. (J). (gr. k-3). 16.99 *(978-1-58980-982-6(3))* Pelican Publishing Co., Inc.

—Witches' Night Before Halloween, 1 vol. Bannatyne, Lesley Pratt. 2007. (ENG.). 32p. (J). (gr. k-3). 16.99 *(978-1-58980-485-2(6))* Pelican Publishing Co., Inc.

Tanselle, Eve. Virtual Maniac: Silly & Serious Poems for Kids. Ruurs, Margriet. 2013. (Maupin House Ser.). (ENG.). 64p. (gr. 1-1). pap. 20.00 *(978-0-929895-43-7(6))* Maupin Hse. Publishing.

Tansley, Eric. Ajax: Golden Dog of the Australian Bush. Patchett, Mary Elwyn. 2011. 172p. 42.95 *(978-1-258-01103-1(4))* Literary Licensing, LLC.

Tanwar, Rajesh. Goldilocks & the Three Bears. 2010. (J). *(978-1-60617-147-9(X))* Teaching Strategies, Inc.

Tapia, Alfredo. Pounce de Leon, 1 vol. Wynne-Jones, Tim. 2014. (ENG.). 32p. (J). pap. 9.95 *(978-0-88995-510-3(7))* Red Deer Pr. CAN. Dist: Ingram Pub. Services.

Taplinger, Lee, jt. photos by see Florian, Douglas.

Tappin, Christine. Whose Lovely Child Can You Be? Viswanath, Shobha. 2013. (ENG.). 32p. (J). (gr. -1). pap. 9.95 *(978-81-8190-304-4(8))* Karadi Tales Co. Pvt. Ltd. IND. Dist: Consortium Bk. Sales & Distribution.

Tarazona, Oscar. Volando con Alas Propias. l.t. ed. 2004. (SPA.). 116p. (YA). pap. 12.00 *(978-1-931481-88-5(1))* LiArt-Literature & Art.

Tarbett, Debbie. Farmyard Families. Rivers-Moore, Debbie. 2012. (Animal Dioramas Ser.). (ENG.). 8p. (J). bds. 4.99 *(978-0-7641-6463-7(5))* Barron's Educational Series, Inc.

—Five Silly Monkeys. Brooks, Susie. 2009. (ENG.). 14p. (J). (gr. k — 1). bds. 9.99 *(978-0-545-10222-3(7),* Cartwheel Bks.) Scholastic, Inc.

—Garden Games. Rivers-Moore, Debbie. 2012. (Animal Dioramas Ser.). (ENG.). 8p. (J). bds. 4.99 *(978-0-7641-6464-4(3))* Barron's Educational Series, Inc.

—Playful Pets. Rivers-Moore, Debbie. 2012. (Animal Dioramas Ser.). (ENG.). 8p. (J). bds. 4.99 *(978-0-7641-6465-1(1))* Barron's Educational Series, Inc.

—Woodland Adventure. Rivers-Moore, Debbie. 2012. (Animal Dioramas Ser.). (ENG.). 8p. (J). bds. 4.99 *(978-0-7641-6467-5(8))* Barron's Educational Series, Inc.

Tardif, Mandy. Love Me. Perez, Claudia. 2011. (ENG.). 28p. pap. 9.29 *(978-1-4680-3305-2(0))* CreateSpace Independent Publishing Platform.

Tarnowski, Mark. The Sun Stone. Treanor, H. T. 2012. 16p. pap. 10.00 *(978-1-60976-125-7(1),* Strategic Bk. Publishing) Strategic Book Publishing & Rights Agency (SBPRA).

Tarr, Lisa M. Colorado Fun: Activities for on the Road & at Home. Perry, Phyllis J. 2007. 80p. (J). (gr. 1-7). pap. 12.95 *(978-1-55566-402-2(4))* Johnson Bks.

Tarrant, Percy. Tom & Some Other Girls. Vaizey, George de Horne. 2007. 208p. per. *(978-1-4065-4698-9(4))* Dodo Pr.

Tarver, Monroe S. Little Light Shine Bright. Tarver, Monroe S. l.t. ed. 2004. 32p. (J). 6.99 *(978-0-9743568-4-6(0))* Tarver, Monroe.

Tashjian, Jake. Einstein the Class Hamster. Tashjian, Janet. 2013. (Einstein the Class Hamster Ser.: 1). (ENG.). 160p. (J). (gr. 2-5). 12.99 *(978-0-8050-9610-1(8),* Holt, Henry & Co. Bks. For Young Readers) Holt, Henry & Co.

—Einstein the Class Hamster & the Very Real Game Show. Tashjian, Janet. 2014. (Einstein the Class Hamster Ser.: 2). (ENG.). 176p. (J). (gr. 2-5). 12.99 *(978-1-62779-026-0(8),* Holt, Henry & Co. Bks. For Young Readers) Holt, Henry & Co.

Tashjian, Jake. Einstein the Class Hamster Saves the Library. Tashjian, Janet. 2015. (Einstein the Class Hamster Ser.: 3). (ENG.). 192p. (J). (gr. 2-5). 13.99 ***(978-1-62779-061-1(6)***, Holt, Henry & Co. Bks. For Young Readers) Holt, Henry & Co.

Tashjian, Jake. My Life As a Book. Tashjian, Janet. 2010. (My Life Ser.). (ENG.). 224p. (J). (gr. 4-7). 17.99 *(978-0-8050-8903-5(9)*, Holt, Henry & Co. Bks. For Young Readers) Holt, Henry & Co.

—My Life As a Book. Tashjian, Janet. 2011. (My Life Ser.). (ENG.). 240p. (J). (gr. 4-7). pap. 6.99 *(978-0-312-67289-8(6))* Square Fish.

—My Life As a Cartoonist. Tashjian, Janet. 2013. (My Life Ser.). (ENG.). 272p. (J). (gr. 4-7). 13.99 *(978-0-8050-9609-5(4)*, Holt, Henry & Co. Bks. For Young Readers) Holt, Henry & Co.

—My Life As a Gamer. Tashjian, Janet. 2015. (My Life Ser.). (ENG.). 272p. (J). (gr. 4-7). 13.99 *(978-0-8050-9851-8(8)*, Holt, Henry & Co. Bks. For Young Readers) Holt, Henry & Co.

—My Life As a Joke. Tashjian, Janet. 2014. (My Life Ser.). (ENG.). 272p. (J). (gr. 4-7). 13.99 *(978-0-8050-9850-1(X)*, Holt, Henry & Co. Bks. For Young Readers) Holt, Henry & Co.

—My Life as a Stuntboy. Tashjian, Janet. 2011. (My Life Ser.). (ENG.). 272p. (J). (gr. 4-7). 13.99 *(978-0-8050-8904-2(7)*, Holt, Henry & Co. Bks. For Young Readers) Holt, Henry & Co.

—My Life as a Stuntboy. Tashjian, Janet. 2015. (My Life Ser.). (ENG.). 288p. (J). (gr. 4-7). pap. 6.99 *(978-1-250-01038-4(1))* Square Fish.

Taso, Alex. The Wind in the Willows. Grahame, Kenneth. 2006. (ENG.). 240p. (gr. 12-18). 5.95 *(978-0-451-53014-1(4)*, Signet Classics) Penguin Publishing Group.

Tatarnikau, Pavel. Arthur of Albion. Matthews, John & Matthe, John. 2008. (ENG.). 96p. (J). (gr. 4-7). 24.99 *(978-1-84686-049-2(0))* Barefoot Bks., Inc.

Tatarnikov, Pavel. The Snow Queen. Andersen, Hans Christian. 2006.Tr. of ??????? ????????. (ENG.). 48p. (J). (gr. 1). 15.95 *(978-1-933327-22-8(7))*; lib. bdg. 16.50 *(978-1-933327-23-5(5))* Purple Bear Bks., Inc.

Tatcheva, Eva. Witch Zelda's Birthday Cake: A Wild & Wicked Pop-up, Pull-the-Tab Book. Tatcheva, Eva. 2004. 12p. (J). (gr. k-3). reprint ed. 18.00 *(978-0-7567-7225-3(7))* DIANE Publishing Co.

Tate, Don. The Amazing Age of John Roy Lynch. Barton, Chris. 2015. 50p. (J). 17.00 ***(978-0-8028-5379-0(X)***, Eerdmans Bks For Young Readers) Eerdmans, William B. Publishing Co.

Tate, Don. Black All Around! Hubbell, Patricia. 2003. (ENG.). 32p. (J). 16.95 *(978-1-58430-048-9(5))* Lee & Low Bks., Inc.

—The Cart That Carried Martin. Bunting, Eve. 2013. (ENG.). 32p. (J). (gr. 1-4). lib. bdg. 16.95 *(978-1-58089-387-9(2))* Charlesbridge Publishing, Inc.

—Duke Ellington's Nutcracker Suite. Celenza, Anna Harwell. 2011. (ENG.). 32p. (J). (gr. 1-4). 19.95 *(978-1-57091-700-4(0))* Charlesbridge Publishing, Inc.

—The Hidden Feast: A Folktale from the American South. Hamilton, Martha & Weiss, Mitch. 2006. (ENG.). 100p. (J). (gr. k-3). 16.95 *(978-0-87483-758-2(8))* August Hse. Pubs., Inc.

—Hope's Gift. Lyons, Kelly Starling. 2012. (ENG.). 32p. (J). (gr. 1-3). 16.99 *(978-0-399-16001-1(9)*, Putnam Juvenile) Penguin Publishing Group.

—I Am My Grandpa's Enkelin. Wangerin, Walter, Jr. 2008. 30p. (J). (gr. 3-7). 18.95 *(978-1-55725-468-9(0))* Paraclete Pr., Inc.

—It Jes' Happened: When Bill Traylor Started to Draw, 1 vol. Christie, R. Gregory. 2012. (ENG.). (J). 17.95 *(978-1-60060-260-3(6))* Lee & Low Bks., Inc.

—Ron's Big Mission. Blue, Rose et al. 2009. (ENG.). 32p. (J). (gr. 1-3). 16.99 *(978-0-525-47849-2(3)*, Dutton Juvenile) Penguin Publishing Group.

—Say Hey! A Song of Willie Mays. Mandel, Peter. 2004. 30p. (J). (gr. k-2). reprint ed. 16.00 *(978-0-7567-8162-0(0))* DIANE Publishing Co.

Tate, Don, jt. illus. see Vernick, Audrey.

Tate, Lizzy. I Love My Church. Tate, Andy. 2008. 16p. pap. 24.95 *(978-1-60441-419-6(7))* America Star Bks.

Tate, M., photos by. My Little Life: A Cancer Survivor's Story As Told by Nature. Tate, M. 2004. (YA). pap. 10.00 *(978-0-9761969-0-7(5))* Heads First (1st).

Tatsuyama, Sayuri. Happy Happy Clover. Tatsuyama, Sayuri. (Happy Happy Clover Ser.: 4). (ENG.). (J). 2010. 192p. pap. 7.99 *(978-1-4215-2735-2(9))*; 2009. 192p. pap. 7.99 *(978-1-4215-2658-4(1))*; Vol. 1. 2009. 200p. pap. 7.99 *(978-1-4215-2656-0(5))*; Vol. 2. 2009. 192p. pap. 9.99 *(978-1-4215-2657-7(3))*; Vol. 5. 2010. 192p. pap. 7.99 *(978-1-4215-2736-9(7))* Viz Media.

Tattersfield, Jane. Sam Stars at Shakespeare's Globe. Francis, Pauline. 2006. (ENG.). 32p. (J). (gr. -1-3). 15.95 *(978-1-84507-406-7(8)*, Frances Lincoln) Quarto Publishing Group UK GBR. Dist: Hachette Bk. Group.

Taub, Udi. A Chanukah Story. Davis, Linda. 2003. 24p. 12.99 *(978-1-58330-652-9(8))* Feldheim Pubs.

Taulo, Tuija. King Solomon Figures It Out. Steinberg, Sari. 2005. 32p. (J). (gr. k-3). 9.95 *(978-965-465-004-5(5)*, Devora Publishing) Simcha Media Group.

Tauss, Marc. Desiderata: Words to Live By. Ehrmann, Max. 2003. (Desiderata Ser.). (ENG.). 48p. (J). 15.95 *(978-0-439-37293-0(3)*, Scholastic Pr.) Scholastic, Inc.

Tavares, Matt. The Gingerbread Pirates. Kladstrup, Kristin. (ENG.). 32p. (J). (gr. -1-3). 2012. 8.99 *(978-0-7636-6233-2(X))*; 2009. 16.99 *(978-0-7636-3223-6(6))* Candlewick Pr.

—Helen's Big World: The Life of Helen Keller. Rappaport, Doreen. 2012. (Big Words Ser.). (ENG.). 48p. (J). (gr. 1-3). 17.99 *(978-0-7868-0890-8(X))* Hyperion Pr.

—Iron Hans. 2007. (Grimms' Fairy Tales Ser.). (ENG.). 40p. (J). (gr. 1-4). 16.99 *(978-0-7636-2160-5(9))* Candlewick Pr.

—Jack & the Beanstalk. Nesbit, E. 2006. (ENG.). 48p. (J). (gr. -1-2). 16.99 *(978-0-7636-2124-7(2))* Candlewick Pr.

—Lady Liberty: A Biography. Rappaport, Doreen. (Candlewick Biographies Ser.). (ENG.). (J). 2014. 48p. (gr. 3-7). 14.99 *(978-0-7636-7114-3(2))*; 2011. 40p. (gr. 3-7). pap. 8.99 *(978-0-7636-5301-9(2))*; 2008. 40p. (gr. 2-5). 19.99 *(978-0-7636-2530-6(2))* Candlewick Pr.

—Over the River & Through the Wood: The New England Boy's Song about Thanksgiving Day. Child, L. Maria. 2011. (ENG.). 32p. (J). (gr. -1-2). 16.99 *(978-0-7636-2790-4(9))* Candlewick Pr.

—Over the River & Through the Wood: The New England Boy's Song about Thanksgiving Day. Child, L. Maria. 2013. (ENG.). 32p. (J). (gr. -1-2). 8.99 *(978-0-7636-6696-5(3))* Candlewick Pr.

—'Twas the Night Before Christmas. Anonymus. 2006. (ENG.). 32p. (J). (gr. k-12). 8.99 *(978-0-7636-3118-5(3))* Candlewick Pr.

Tavares, Matt. Becoming Babe Ruth. Tavares, Matt. 2013. (ENG.). 40p. (J). (gr. k-3). 16.99 *(978-0-7636-5646-1(1))* Candlewick Pr.

—Growing up Pedro: How the Martinez Brothers Made It from the Dominican Republic All the Way to the Major Leagues. Tavares, Matt. 2015. (ENG.). 40p. (J). (gr. 3-7). 16.99 *(978-0-7636-6824-2(9))* Candlewick Pr.

—Henry Aaron's Dream. Tavares, Matt. (Candlewick Biographies Ser.). (ENG.). (J). (gr. 3-7). 2015. 48p. 14.99 *(978-0-7636-7653-7(5))*; 2012. 40p. pap. 6.99 *(978-0-7636-5820-5(0))*; 2010. 40p. 16.99 *(978-0-7636-3224-3(4))* Candlewick Pr.

—Mudball. Tavares, Matt. 2011. (ENG.). 32p. (J). (gr. 1-4). pap. 6.99 *(978-0-7636-4136-8(7))* Candlewick Pr.

—Oliver's Game. Tavares, Matt. (Tavares Baseball Bks.). (ENG.). 32p. (J). (gr. 1-4). 2009. pap. 6.99 *(978-0-7636-4137-5(5))*; 2004. 15.99 *(978-0-7636-1852-0(7))* Candlewick Pr.

—There Goes Ted Williams: The Greatest Hitter Who Ever Lived. Tavares, Matt. (Candlewick Biographies Ser.). (ENG.). (J). (gr. 1-4). 2015. 48p. 14.99 *(978-0-7636-7655-1(1))*; 2012. 40p. 16.99 *(978-0-7636-2789-8(5))* Candlewick Pr.

—Zachary's Ball. Tavares, Matt. anniv. ed. 2012. (Tavares Baseball Bks.). (ENG.). 32p. (J). (gr. 1-4). 15.99 *(978-0-7636-5033-9(1))*; pap. 6.99 *(978-0-7636-5977-6(0))* Candlewick Pr.

Tavares, Matt & Borgens, Matthew Todd. Jack's Path of Courage: The Life of John F. Kennedy. Rappaport, Doreen. 2010. (Big Words Ser.). (ENG.). 48p. (J). (gr. 1-3). 17.99 *(978-1-4231-2272-2(0))* Hyperion Pr.

Tavares, Victor. Beauty & the Beast. 2007. (Picture Book Classics Ser.). (J). 24p. (gr. -1-3). 9.99 *(978-0-7945-1855-4(9))*; 63p. 8.99 *(978-0-7945-1456-3(1))* EDC Publishing. (Usborne).

—Lin Yi's Lantern: A Moon Festival Tale. Williams, Brenda. 2008. 32p. (J). *(978-1-84686-148-2(9))* Barefoot Bks., Inc.

—The Magical Book. Sims, Lesley. 2007. (Young Reading Series 2 Gift Bks). 64p. (J). (gr. 4-7). 8.99 *(978-0-7945-1703-8(X)*, Usborne) EDC Publishing.

Tavares, Victor. Star Seeker: A Journey to Outer Space. Tavares, Victor. Heine, Theresa. 2006. (ENG.). 32p. (J). (gr. -1-3). 16.99 *(978-1-905236-36-7(0))* Barefoot Bks., Inc.

Tavares, Victore. Three Musketeers. Levene, Rebecca, ed. 2009. (Young Reading 3 Ser.). 64p. (J). (gr. 2). 6.99 *(978-0-7945-1946-9(6)*, Usborne) EDC Publishing.

Tavoularis, Alex. Father of the Constitution: A Story about James Madison. Mitchell, Barbara. 2003. (Creative Minds Biographies Ser.). (ENG.). 64p. (gr. 4-8). 22.60 *(978-1-57505-182-6(6)*, Carolrhoda Bks.); pap. 8.95 *(978-1-57505-607-4(0))* Lerner Publishing Group.

Taxali, Gary. Apple. DePrisco, Dorothea. 2005. (Plush Learning Books Ser.). 10p. (J). bds. 6.95 *(978-1-58117-191-4(9)*, Intervisual/Piggy Toes) Bendon, Inc.

—Lemon. DePrisco, Dorothea. 2005. (Plush Learning Books Ser.). 10p. (J). bds. 6.95 *(978-1-58117-194-5(3)*, Intervisual/Piggy Toes) Bendon, Inc.

—Orange. DePrisco, Dorothea. 2005. (Plush Learning Books Ser.). 10p. (J). bds. 6.95 *(978-1-58117-192-1(7)*, Intervisual/Piggy Toes) Bendon, Inc.

—Pear. DePrisco, Dorothea. 2005. (Plush Learning Books Ser.). 10p. (J). bds. 6.95 *(978-1-58117-193-8(5)*, Intervisual/Piggy Toes) Bendon, Inc.

Tay, Kaiyee. Can I Tell You about Anxiety? A Guide for Friends, Family & Professionals. Willetts, Lucy & Waite, Polly. 2014. (ENG.). 56p. pap. *(978-1-84905-527-7(0))* Kingsley, Jessica Ltd.

Tayal, Amit. Conquering Everest: The Lives of Edmund Hillary & Tenzing Norgay. Helfand, Lewis. 2011. (Campfire Graphic Novels Ser.). (ENG.). 96p. (gr. 3-7). pap. 12.99 *(978-93-80741-24-6(3)*, Campfire) Kalyani Navyug Media Pty. Ltd. IND. Dist: Random Hse., Inc.

Tayal, Amit. Jack & the Beanstalk: An Interactive Fairy Tale Adventure. Hoena, B. A. 2015. (You Choose: Fractured Fairy Tales Ser.). (ENG.). 112p. (gr. 3-4). pap. 6.95 ***(978-1-4914-5930-0(1))*** Capstone Pr., Inc.

Tayal, Amit. No Kidding, Mermaids Are a Joke! The Story of the Little Mermaid As Told by the Prince. Loewen, Nancy. 2013. (Other Side of the Story Ser.). (ENG.). 24p. (gr. 2-3). 9.95 *(978-1-4795-1947-7(2))* Picture Window Bks.

—No Kidding, Mermaids Are a Joke! The Story of the Little Mermaid as Told by the Prince. Loewen, Nancy. 2013. (Other Side of the Story Ser.). (ENG.). 24p. (gr. 2-3). 26.65 *(978-1-4048-8303-1(7))* Picture Window Bks.

—The Swiss Family Robinson. Wyss, Johann David. 2011. (Campfire Graphic Novels Ser.). (ENG.). 88p. (gr. 3-7). pap. 11.99 *(978-93-80028-47-7(4)*, Campfire) Kalyani Navyug Media Pty. Ltd. IND. Dist: Random Hse., Inc.

—The Three Musketeers. Dumas, Alexandre. 2011. (Campfire Graphic Novels Ser.). (ENG.). 104p. (J). (gr. 3-7). pap. 12.99 *(978-93-80028-57-6(1)*, Campfire) Kalyani Navyug Media Pty. Ltd. IND. Dist: Random Hse., Inc.

—Truly, We Both Loved Beauty Dearly! The Story of Sleeping Beauty as Told by the Good & Bad Fairies. Shaskan, Trisha Speed. 2013. (Other Side of the Story Ser.). (ENG.). 24p. (gr. 2-3). 26.65 *(978-1-4048-7940-9(4))* Picture Window Bks.

—Truly, We Both Loved Beauty Dearly! The Story of Sleeping Beauty As Told by the Good & Bad Fairies. Shaskan, Trisha Speed. 2013. (Other Side of the Story Ser.). (ENG.). 24p. (gr. 2-3). 9.95 *(978-1-4795-1945-3(6))* Picture Window Bks.

Tayal, Amit & Alsonso, Denis. No Kidding, Mermaids Are a Joke! The Story of the Little Mermaid, As Told by the Prince. Loewen, Nancy. 2013. (Other Side of the Story Ser.). (ENG.). 24p. (gr. 2-3). pap. 6.95 *(978-1-4795-1951-4(0))* Picture Window Bks.

—Truly, We Both Loved Beauty Dearly! The Story of Sleeping Beauty, As Told by the Good & Bad Fairies. Shaskan, Trisha Speed & Loewen, Nancy. 2013. (Other Side of the Story Ser.). (ENG.). 24p. (gr. 2-3). pap. 6.95 *(978-1-4795-1949-1(9))* Picture Window Bks.

Tayal, Amit, jt. illus. see Alonso, Denis.

Tayama, Thomas. Mother Goose on the Loose in Guam A Chamorro Adaptation of Traditional Nursery Rhymes. Jackson, Marilyn Malloy, ed. 2006. (J). 6.50 net. *(978-0-9790111-5-3(9))* M-m-mauleg Publishing.

Taylor, Adam. The Exasperated Clock. Hickman, Debbie. 2013. 40p. pap. *(978-1-4602-1811-2(6))* FriesenPress.

—Little Red Fire. Heidari, Mahdi. 2012. 40p. (J). pap. 12.99 *(978-0-9838321-8-8(8))* Higher Ground Pr.

—Saving Santa's Seals. Murphy, T. M. 2009. (LeapKids Ser.). (ENG.). 170p. (J). (gr. 1-5). pap. 10.95 *(978-0-9815148-8-8(X))* Leapfrog Pr.

—A Treasure Hunt for Mama & Me: Helping Children Cope with Parental Illness. Le Verrier, Renee & Frank, Samuel. 2013. (Let's Talk Ser.). (ENG.). 48p. (J). (gr. -1-2). 9.95 *(978-0-88282-436-9(8))* New Horizon Pr. Pubs., Inc.

Taylor, Adam. George in the UK: The Unknown Kingdom. Taylor, Adam. West, Jeannette, ed. 2011. 28p. (J). 8.99 *(978-0-9766062-9-1(1))* Higher Ground Pr.

Taylor, Amber. Mommy Does a Lot So I Want to Too, 1 vol. Reyes, S. L. 2010. 30p. 24.95 *(978-1-4489-5420-9(7))* PublishAmerica, Inc.

Taylor, Amber L. I'm Two, So What Should I Do?, 1 vol. Reyes, Shawntie L. 2010. 34p. 24.95 *(978-1-4489-7869-4(6))* PublishAmerica, Inc.

Taylor, Ann Creal. Lydia Ann & Scraggles: The Adventures of a Girl & Her Dog. Taylor, Ann Creal. Creal, Nancy. 2013. 28p. (J). 12.00 *(978-0-9800059-4-3(9))* Taylor, Ann.

Taylor, Bridget Starr. The Truth about Trolls, 1 vol. Troupe, Thomas Kingsley. 2010. (Fairy-Tale Superstars Ser.). (ENG.). 32p. (gr. 1-3). lib. bdg. 26.65 *(978-1-4048-5984-5(5)*, Nonfiction Picture Bks.) Picture Window Bks.

—Why the Stomach Growls. Edwards, Pamela Duncan. 2006. (ENG.). 32p. (J). (gr. k-6). 15.95 *(978-1-58536-298-1(0))* Sleeping Bear Pr.

Taylor, Byron. Ghost Stories from the American South. McNeil, W. K., ed. 2005. (ENG.). 176p. (J). (gr. 4-17). pap. 15.95 *(978-0-935304-84-8(3))* August Hse. Pubs., Inc.

Taylor, Carol. The Pony Princess. Watts, Ana Dearborn & Dearborn, Dorothy. 2008. (ENG.). 32p. pap. 6.00 *(978-1-896543-32-1(4))* DreamCatcher Publishing CAN. Dist: Univ. of Toronto Pr.

Taylor, Carolyn. The Princess & the Garden. Johnson, Esther A. 2012. 34p. pap. 19.99 *(978-1-62419-614-0(4))* Salem Publishing Solutions, Inc.

Taylor, Catherine. Downtown Ducks. Taylor, Douglas. 2005. 62p. (J). per. 22.99 *(978-1-4134-3803-1(2))* Xlibris Corp.

Taylor, Chet. Brother Dragon. Branson, Terri. 2004. (J). 18.99 *(978-0-9755888-5-7(0))* Dragonfly Publishing, Inc.

—Little Lost Leprechaun. Gorgas, Paula Blais. l.t. ed. 2005. 20p. (J). 17.99 *(978-0-9755888-4-0(2))* Dragonfly Publishing, Inc.

—Perky Turkey Finds a Friend. Goodspeed, Judy. l.t. ed. 2006. 24p. (J). pap. 14.99 *(978-0-9765786-6-6(2))* Dragonfly Publishing, Inc.

—Perky Turkey's Perfect Plan. Goodspeed, Judy. 2005. 22p. (J). 18.99 *(978-0-9765786-0-4(3))* Dragonfly Publishing, Inc.

—Pete, the Peacock, Goes to Town. Branson, Terri. l.t. ed. 2005. 22p. (J). lib. bdg. 24.95 *(978-0-9765786-1-1(1))* Dragonfly Publishing, Inc.

—Tyler on the Moon. Branson, Terri. l.t. ed. 24p. (J). 2005. lib. bdg. 24.95 *(978-0-9765786-2-8(X))*; 2004. 18.99 *(978-0-9755888-2-6(6))* Dragonfly Publishing, Inc.

Taylor, Chet. Last, but Not Least. Taylor, Chet. l.t. ed. 2004. 20p. (J). 17.99 *(978-0-9755888-6-4(9))*; lib. bdg. 22.99 *(978-0-9755888-1-9(8))* Dragonfly Publishing, Inc.

Taylor, Clive. Brave Mouse, 3 vols., Pack. Eggleton, Jill. (Sails Literacy Ser.). 24p. (gr. 1-18). 57.00 *(978-0-7578-3205-5(9))* Rigby Education.

—Rabbit & Rooster's Ride: 3-in-1 Package. Eggleton, Jill. (Sails Literacy Ser.). 24p. (gr. k-18). 57.00 *(978-0-7578-8617-1(5))* Rigby Education.

—Rabbit & Rooster's Ride: 6 Small Books. Eggleton, Jill. (Sails Literacy Ser.). 24p. (gr. k-18). 25.00 *(978-0-7578-7727-8(3))* Rigby Education.

—Rabbit & Rooster's Ride: Big Book Only. Eggleton, Jill. (Sails Literacy Ser.). 24p. (gr. k-18). 27.00 *(978-0-7578-6200-7(4))* Rigby Education.

Taylor, Dan. DogFish. Shields, Gillian. 2008. (ENG.). 32p. (J). (gr. -1-2). 16.99 *(978-1-4169-7127-6(0)*, Atheneum Bks. for Young Readers) Simon & Schuster Children's Publishing.

Taylor, David A. Bandit Raccoon. McCorkle, Barbara. l.t. ed. 2006. 39p. (J). 19.95 *(978-1-59879-170-9(2))*; per. 13.99 *(978-1-59879-123-5(0))* Lifevest Publishing, Inc.

—Brutis' New Friend. McCorkle, Barbara. 2007. 30p. (J). 13.99 *(978-1-59879-439-7(6))* Lifevest Publishing, Inc.

Taylor, David W. Christian Kids Explore Biology. Redmond, Stephanie L. 2007. (Christian Kids Explore Ser.). 291p. per. 34.95 *(978-1-892427-05-2(2))* Bright Ideas! Educational Resources.

Taylor, David W., Jr. & Northcutt, Leslie L. Earth & Space. Redmond, Stephanie L. 2006. (Christian Kids Explore Ser.). 363p. (J). (gr. 3-7). per. *(978-1-892427-19-9(2))* Bright Ideas! Educational Resources.

Taylor, Eleanor. Cha-Cha Chimps. Durango, Julia. (ENG.). 32p. (J). (gr. -1-3). 2010. 7.99 *(978-1-4169-9574-6(9))*; 2006. 17.99 *(978-0-689-86456-8(6))* Simon & Schuster Bks. For Young Readers. (Simon & Schuster Bks. For Young Readers).

—The Christmas Tale of Peter Rabbit. Thompson, Emma. 2013. (Peter Rabbit Ser.). (ENG.). 72p. (J). (gr. -1-2). 20.00 *(978-0-7232-7694-4(3)*, Warne) Penguin Publishing Group.

—The Further Tale of Peter Rabbit. Thompson, Emma. 2012. (Peter Rabbit Ser.). (ENG.). 72p. (J). (gr. -1-2). 20.00 *(978-0-7232-6910-6(6)*, Warne) Penguin Publishing Group.

—Go-Go Gorillas. Durango, Julia. 2010. (ENG.). 32p. (J). (gr. -1-1). 15.99 *(978-1-4169-3779-1(X)*, Simon & Schuster Bks. For Young Readers) Simon & Schuster Bks. For Young Readers.

Taylor, Eleanor. Half a Creature from the Sea: A Life in Stories. Almond, David. 2015. (ENG.). 240p. (J). (gr. 7). 16.99 ***(978-0-7636-7877-7(5))*** Candlewick Pr.

Taylor, Eleanor. The Spectacular Tale of Peter Rabbit. Thompson, Emma. 2014. (Peter Rabbit Ser.). (ENG.). 72p. (J). (gr. -1-2). 20.00 *(978-0-7232-7116-1(X)*, Warne) Penguin Publishing Group.

—Whoa, Baby, Whoa! Nichols, Grace. 2012. (ENG.). 32p. (J). (gr. -1-k). 15.99 *(978-1-59990-742-0(9)*, Bloomsbury USA Childrens) Bloomsbury USA.

Taylor, Eleonor. Sgeulachd Eile Mu Pheader Rabaid. Thompson, Emma et al. 2012.Tr. of Further Tale of Peter Rabbit. (GLA.). 80p. (J). *(978-1-907676-12-3(0))* Grace Note Pubns.

Taylor, Erin. The Adventures of the Little Prince. Evans, Rosemary R. 2011. (ENG.). 44p. (J). 16.95 *(978-1-61658-706-2(7))* Independent Pub.

—Go Go Sadie. Lee, Bonnie. 2011. 46p. 24.00 *(978-1-4349-8679-5(9)*, RoseDog Bks.) Dorrance Publishing Co., Inc.

—The Little Princesses Magial Party. Evans, Rosemary R. 2012. 40p. (J). 16.95 *(978-1-60743-759-8(7))* Wink Publishing.

Taylor, Geoff. El Clan de la Foca. Paver, Michelle & Paver, Michelle. Anton de vez, Patricia, tr. 2006. (SPA.). 252p. (J). *(978-84-9836-028-6(6))* Oceano Grupo Editorial, S.A.

—Ghost Hunter. Paver, Michelle. (Chronicles of Ancient Darkness: No. 6). 304p. (J). (gr. 5). 2011. pap. 6.99 *(978-0-06-072842-7(6))*; 2010. 16.99 *(978-0-06-072840-3(X))* HarperCollins Pubs. (Tegen, Katherine Bks).

—Oath Breaker. Paver, Michelle. (Chronicles of Ancient Darkness: No. 5). (J). (gr. 5). 2010. 320p. pap. 6.99 *(978-0-06-072839-7(6))*; 2009. 304p. 16.99 *(978-0-06-072837-3(X))* HarperCollins Pubs. (Tegen, Katherine Bks).

—Outcast. Paver, Michelle. (Chronicles of Ancient Darkness: No. 4). (J). (gr. 5). 2009. 352p. pap. 6.99 *(978-0-06-072836-6(1)*, Tegen, Katherine Bks); 2008. 336p. 16.99 *(978-0-06-072834-2(5))* HarperCollins Pubs.

—Soul Eater. Paver, Michelle. 2008. (Chronicles of Ancient Darkness: No. 3). 352p. (J). (gr. 5). pap. 6.99 *(978-0-06-072833-5(7)*, Tegen, Katherine Bks) HarperCollins Pubs.

—Spirit Walker. Paver, Michelle. (Chronicles of Ancient Darkness: No. 2). (J). (gr. 5-9). 2007. 384p. per. 6.99 *(978-0-06-072830-4(2))*; 2006. 368p. lib. bdg. 17.89 *(978-0-06-072829-8(9))* HarperCollins Pubs. (Tegen, Katherine Bks).

—Wolf Brother. Paver, Michelle. 2006. (Chronicles of Ancient Darkness: No. 1). 320p. (J). (gr. 5-9). reprint ed. per. 6.99 *(978-0-06-072827-4(2)*, Tegen, Katherine Bks) HarperCollins Pubs.

Taylor, Gerad. The Real Story of the Exodus. Maier, Paul L. 2009. 32p. (J). (gr. -1-3). 16.99 *(978-0-7586-1268-7(0))* Concordia Publishing Hse.

Taylor, Gypsy. Pearlie & Great Aunt Garnet. Harmer, Wendy. 2014. (Pearlie Ser.: 7). (ENG.). 48p. (Orig.). (J). (gr. 2-4). pap. 7.99 *(978-1-74166-131-6(5))* Random Hse. Australia AUS. Dist: Independent Pubs. Group.

—Pearlie & Her Pink Shell. Harmer, Wendy. 2014. (Pearlie Ser.: 9). (ENG.). 48p. (J). (gr. 2-4). pap. 7.99 *(978-1-74166-143-9(9))* Random Hse. Australia AUS. Dist: Independent Pubs. Group.

—Pearlie & Sapphire. Harmer, Wendy. 2014. (Pearlie Ser.: 8). (ENG.). 48p. (J). (gr. 2-4). pap. 7.99 *(978-1-74166-137-8(4))* Random Hse. Australia AUS. Dist: Independent Pubs. Group.

—Pearlie & the Cherry Blossom Fairy. Harmer, Wendy. 2014. (Pearlie Ser.: 12). (ENG.). 48p. (J). (gr. 2-4). pap. 7.99 *(978-1-74166-378-5(4))* Random Hse. Australia AUS. Dist: Independent Pubs. Group.

—Pearlie & the Fairy Queen. Harmer, Wendy. 2014. (Pearlie Ser.: 10). (ENG.). 48p. (J). (gr. 2-4). pap. 7.99 *(978-1-74166-149-1(8))* Random Hse. Australia AUS. Dist: Independent Pubs. Group.

—Pearlie & the Flamenco Fairy. Harmer, Wendy. 2015. (Pearlie Ser.: 15). (ENG.). 48p. (J). (gr. 2-4). pap. 7.99 *(978-1-74275-540-3(2))* Random Hse. Australia AUS. Dist: Independent Pubs. Group.

—Pearlie & the Silver Fern Fairy. Harmer, Wendy. 2015. (Pearlie Ser.: 13). (ENG.). 48p. (J). (gr. 2-4). pap. 7.99 *(978-1-74166-379-2(2))* Random Hse. Australia AUS. Dist: Independent Pubs. Group.

—Pearlie Goes to Rio. Harmer, Wendy. 2015. (Pearlie Ser.: 16). (ENG.). 48p. (J). (gr. 2-4). pap. 8.99 *(978-0-85798-216-2(8))* Random Hse. Australia AUS. Dist: Independent Pubs. Group.

—Pearlie in Central Park. Harmer, Wendy. 2014. (Pearlie Ser.: 11). (ENG.). 48p. (J). (gr. 2-4). pap. 7.99 *(978-1-74166-377-8(6))* Random Hse. Australia AUS. Dist: Independent Pubs. Group.

—Pearlie in Paris. Harmer, Wendy. 2015. (Pearlie Ser.: 14). (ENG.). 48p. (J). (gr. 2-4). pap. 7.99 *(978-1-74166-380-8(6))* Random Hse. Australia AUS. Dist: Independent Pubs. Group.

T

Taylor, Gypsy & Zarb, Mike. Pearlie & the Christmas Angel. Harmer, Wendy. 2014. (Pearlie Ser.: 6). (ENG.). 48p. (Orig.). (J). (gr. 2-4). pap. 7.99 *(978-1-74166-077-7(7))* Random Hse. Australia AUS. Dist: Independent Pubs. Group.

Taylor, Gypsy, jt. illus. see Zarb, Mike.

Taylor Harris Photography, photos by. I Believe I'll Testify: A True Story about the Power of Prayer. Harris, Patricia Taylor. 2008. (ENG., 53p. (YA). pap. 18.95 *(978-0-615-24897-4(7))* Blue Scribbles Publishing.

Taylor, Jacqui. Nama Kwa's Garden. Clanahan, Mary. 2005. 72p. (J). (gr. -1-7). 12.95 *(978-1-77007-025-7(7))* Struik Pubs. ZAF. Dist: International Publishers Marketing.

Taylor, Jeannie St. John & St. John Taylor, Jeannie. Who Did It? Mehl, Ron & Taylor, Jeannie St. John. St. John Taylor, Jeannie. 2004. 32p. (J). (gr. k-4). 12.99 *(978-0-8254-3168-5(9))* Kregel Pubns.

Taylor, Jennifer. Frankie Works the Night Shift. Peters, Lisa Westberg. 2010. (ENG.). 32p. (J). (gr. -1-k). 16.99 *(978-0-06-009095-1(2),* Greenwillow Bks.) HarperCollins Pubs.

—The Life of Riley the Cat. Akerson, Julie Chicos. 2005. 28p. (J). 15.50 *(978-1-4120-5858-2(9))* Trafford Publishing.

—The Poisons of Caux. Appelbaum, Susannah. 2010. (Poisons of Caux Ser.). (ENG.). 416p. (J). (gr. 3-7). 7.99 *(978-0-440-42247-1(7),* Yearling) Random Hse. Children's Bks.

—The Rising Star Ball. Rickman, Jeanie Parker. 2006. 32p. per. 17.95 *(978-1-59858-201-7(1))* Dog Ear Publishing, LLC.

—Way down Yonder in the Paw Paw Patch. Clark, Abbie. 2006. 32p. (J). (gr. -1-3). per. 16.95 *(978-1-59858-129-4(5))* Dog Ear Publishing, LLC.

Taylor, Jennifer Louise. The Cookie Crumb Trail. Johnson, Doris M. 2008. (ENG.). 28p. pap. 15.99 *(978-1-4196-9127-0(9))* CreateSpace Independent Publishing Platform.

Taylor, Jenny. Anna the Goanna: And Other Poems. McDougall, Jill. 2009. (ENG.). 48p. (J). (gr. k-6). pap. 17.95 *(978-0-85575-616-1(0))* Aboriginal Studies Pr. AUS. Dist: Independent Pubs. Group.

Taylor, Jill. Little Wolf's Christmas. Hopkins, Suzette. 2004. (Little Wolf & Friends Ser.). 19p. (J). 12.95 *(978-1-932133-72-1(0))* Writers' Collective, The.

Taylor, Jon. Tower of Babel. 2007. 24p. (J). (gr. 4-7). 14.99 *(978-0-89051-487-0(9))* Master Bks.

Taylor, Jonathan. My Creation Bible: Teaching Kids to Trust the Bible from the Very First Verse. Ham, Ken. 2006. 12p. (gr. -1-1). bds. 11.99 incl. audio compact disk *(978-0-89051-462-7(3))* Master Bks.

Taylor, Josephine. Lawrence the Laughing Cookie Jar. Marks, William C. 2003. 16.95 *(978-0-9715541-0-8(2))* MPC Pr. International.

Taylor, Josh. Joshua & the Spider. Blocker, Adam P. 2013. (ENG.). 72p. 17.99 *(978-1-939418-08-1(9))* Writer of the Round Table Pr.

Taylor, Kathleen. Eddie & Bingo: A Friendship Tale. Taylor, Kathleen. 2011. 42p. (J). pap. 21.95 *(978-1-59299-558-5(6))* Inkwater Pr.

Taylor-Kielty, Simon. The Special Christmas Tree. Walters, Catherine. 2012. (J). *(978-1-4351-4315-9(9))* Barnes & Noble, Inc.

Taylor, Kristen Michelle. Tatiana. Mbonu, Ngozi Elizabeth. 2013. (ENG.). (J). 14.95 *(978-1-62086-307-7(3))* Mascot Bks., Inc.

Taylor, Lawrie. Goldilocks & the Three Bears. Andrews, Jackie. 2012. (ENG.). 32p. (J). pap. 6.50 *(978-1-84135-191-9(1))* Award Pubns. Ltd. GBR. Dist: Parkwest Pubns., Inc.

—Great Big Enormous Turnip. Andrews, Jackie. 2012. (ENG.). 32p. (J). pap. 6.50 *(978-1-84135-192-6(X))* Award Pubns. Ltd. GBR. Dist: Parkwest Pubns., Inc.

—Henny Penny. Andrews, Jackie. 2012. (ENG.). 32p. (J). pap. 6.50 *(978-1-84135-194-0(6))* Award Pubns. Ltd. GBR. Dist: Parkwest Pubns., Inc.

Taylor, Linda. Wisdom Weaver/Bina'nitin Bidziilgo Atl'ohi. Johnson, Jann A. Manavi, Lorraine Begay, tr. from ENG. 2006. (ENG.). 32p. (J). (gr. -1-3). 17.95 *(978-1-893354-82-1(2))* Salina Bookshelf Inc.

Taylor, Lori. What to Do When Your Hoof Turns Blue!!! Taylor, Lori. lt. ed. 2006. 28p. (J). pap. 20.99 *(978-1-59879-220-1(2))* Lifevest Publishing, Inc.

Taylor, Maria. Castle Sticker Book: Complete Your Own Mighty, Medieval Fortress! Pipe, Jim. 2014. (ENG.). 40p. (J). (gr. 1). pap. 9.95 *(978-1-78312-013-0(4))* Carlton Bks., Ltd. GBR. Dist: Sterling Publishing Co., Inc.

—Doll's House Sticker Book: Decorate Your Very Own Victorian Home! Pipe, Jim. 2014. (ENG.). 40p. (J). (gr. 1). pap. 9.95 *(978-1-78097-293-0(8))* Carlton Bks., Ltd. GBR. Dist: Sterling Publishing Co., Inc.

—Lift, Look & Learn Castle: Uncover the Secrets of a Medieval Fortress. Pipe, Jim. 2014. (ENG.). 24p. (J). (gr. 1). 19.95 *(978-1-78312-081-9(9))* Carlton Bks., Ltd. GBR. Dist: Sterling Publishing Co., Inc.

—Lift, Look & Learn Doll's House: Uncover the Secrets of a Victorian Home. Pipe, Jim. 2014. (ENG.). 24p. (J). (gr. 1). 19.95 *(978-1-78312-082-6(7))* Carlton Bks., Ltd. GBR. Dist: Sterling Publishing Co., Inc.

Taylor, Marjorie. Challenger. Bricker, Sandra D. Miller, Zachary N., ed. rev. ed. 2003. (Take Ten Ser.). 47p. (J). (gr. 4-18). pap. 4.95 *(978-1-58659-021-5(9))* Artesian Pr.

—The Kuwaiti Oil Fires. Skip Press Staff. Miller, Zachary N., ed. rev. ed. 2003. (Take Ten Ser.). 46p. (J). (gr. 4-18). pap. 4.95 *(978-1-58659-024-6(3))* Artesian Pr.

—The Mount St. Helens Volcano. Bankier, William. Miller, Zachary N., ed. rev. ed. 2003. (Take Ten Ser.). 45p. (J). (gr. 4-12). pap. 4.95 *(978-1-58659-023-9(5))* Artesian Pr.

—The Nuclear Disaster at Chernobyl. Cruise, Robin. rev. ed. 2003. (Take Ten Ser.). 46p. (J). (gr. 4-18). pap. 4.95 *(978-1-58659-022-2(7))* Artesian Pr.

Taylor, Mark. The Tale of Sidney Elderberry - an Ordinary Boy with Extraordinary Bowels. Younge, Cathy. 2013. 32p. pap. *(978-1-78148-838-6(X))* Grosvenor Hse. Publishing Ltd.

Taylor, Mike. Ancient Chinese. Binns, Tristan Boyer. 2006. (Ancient Civilizations Ser.). (ENG.). 32p. (gr. 4-6). lib. bdg. 29.32 *(978-0-7565-1647-5(1),* CPB Grades 4-8) Compass Point Bks.

—Mesoamerican Myths. West, David. 2006. (Graphic Mythology Ser.). (ENG.). 48p. (J). (gr. 4-7). lib. bdg. 31.95 *(978-1-4042-0802-5(0))* Rosen Publishing Group, Inc., The.

Taylor, Mike, photos by. The Secret Galaxy, 1 vol. Hodgkins, Fran. 2014. (ENG., 32p. (J). (gr. 1-5). 16.95 *(978-0-88448-391-5(6))* Tilbury Hse. Pubs.

Taylor, Nate. The Adventures of the Princess & Mr. Whiffle: The Thing Beneath the Bed. Rothfuss, Patrick. 2010. 25.00 *(978-1-59606-313-6(0))* Subterranean Pr.

Taylor, Nicole. Hug-A-Bug Travels to Greece. Church, Anna. 2012. 44p. pap. 12.00 *(978-0-9831449-5-3(8))* Mighty Lion Ventures.

Taylor, Nicole, jt. illus. see Church, Anna.

Taylor, Non, et al. Yummy Little Cookbook. Gilpin, Rebecca & Atkinson, Catherine. rev. ed. 2007. (Children's Cooking Ser.). (ENG.). 96p. (J). (gr. -1-3). 7.99 *(978-0-7945-1655-0(6),* Usborne) EDC Publishing.

Taylor, R. For Merrie England: A Tale of the Weavers of Norfolk. Leslie, Emma. 2010. 168p. 20.95 *(978-1-934671-38-2(X));* pap. 10.95 *(978-1-934671-39-9(8))* Salem Ridge Press LLC.

Taylor, Roger. The Special Birthday. MacKenzie, Carine. 2006. (Bible Art Ser.). (ENG.). 16p. (J). pap., act. bk. ed. 1.99 *(978-1-85792-307-0(3))* Christian Focus Pubns. GBR. Dist: Send The Light Distribution LLC.

Taylor, Sally & van Deelen, Fred. Changeling. Gregory, Philippa. 2012. (Order of Darkness Ser.: 1). (ENG.). 272p. (YA). (gr. 9). 18.99 *(978-1-4424-5344-9(3),* Simon Pulse) Simon Pulse.

Taylor, Sally, jt. illus. see van Deelen, Fred.

Taylor, Stephen. Cakewalk. Helmso, Candy Grant. 2003. (Books for Young Learners). (ENG.). 16p. (J). pap. 5.75 net. *(978-1-57274-250-5(X),* 2727, Bks. for Young Learners) Owen, Richard C. Pubs., Inc.

—Gift Days, 1 vol. Winters, Kari-Lynn. 2012. (ENG.). 32p. (J). 18.95 *(978-1-55455-192-7(7))* Fitzhenry & Whiteside, Ltd. CAN. Dist: Midpoint Trade Bks., Inc.

—Like You, Like Me, 1 vol. Morgan, Cliff. 2010. 20p. 24.95 *(978-1-4489-5140-6(2))* PublishAmerica, Inc.

—Rise of the Golden Cobra. Aubin, Henry T. 2007. (ENG.). 200p. (J). (gr. 6-12). 21.95 *(978-1-55451-060-3(0),* 9781554510603); pap. 11.95 *(978-1-55451-059-7(7),* 9781554510597) Annick Pr., Ltd. CAN. Dist: Firefly Bks., Ltd.

Taylor, Sue. Yarns of Ballpoint II. Olofson, Darrell. 2005. (ENG.). 4p. (J). spiral bd. *(978-1-60225-002-4(2))* Motherhood Printing & Etc.

Taylor, Theodore, III. When the Beat Was Born: DJ Kool Herc & the Creation of Hip Hop. Hill, Laban Carrick. 2013. (ENG.). 32p. (J). (gr. 1-5). 17.99 *(978-1-59643-540-7(2))* Roaring Brook Pr.

Taylor, Thomas. Frankin's Bear. d'Lacey, Chris. 2005. (Red Go Bananas Ser.). (ENG.). 48p. (J). (gr. 2-3). *(978-0-7787-2696-8(7));* lib. bdg. *(978-0-7787-2674-6(6))* Crabtree Publishing Co.

—It's Hard to Hurry When You're a Snail. Stewart, Dorothy M. 2009. (ENG.). 28p. (J). (gr. -1-k). 14.95 *(978-0-7459-6150-7(9))* Lion Hudson PLC GBR. Dist: Independent Pubs. Group.

—The Red Ribbon: A Book about Friendship. Reader's Digest Editors, ed. 2004. (ENG.). 14p. (J). 12.99 *(978-0-7944-0401-7(4),* Reader's Digest Children's Bks.) Studio Fun International.

—Two Times the Fun. Cleary, Beverly. ed. 2005. (ENG.). 96p. (J). (gr. -1-2). 16.99 *(978-0-06-057921-0(8))* HarperCollins Pubs.

Taylor, Trace. Viento. Sánchez, Lucía M. 2012. (1B el Tiempo Ser.). (SPA.). 40p. (J). pap. 8.50 *(978-1-61406-207-3(2))* American Reading Co.

Taylor, Trace. Baseball. Taylor, Trace. 2009. (2G Sports Ser.). (ENG.). 16p. (J). (gr. k-2). pap. 7.50 *(978-1-59301-877-1(0))* American Reading Co.

—Basketball. Taylor, Trace. 2009. (2G Sports Ser.). (ENG.). 12p. (J). (gr. k-2). pap. 7.50 *(978-1-59301-876-4(2))* American Reading Co.

—Bikes. Taylor, Trace. 2008. (1-3Y Moving on Wheels Ser.). (ENG.). 24p. (J). (gr. k-2). pap. 6.50 *(978-1-59301-465-0(1))* American Reading Co.

—Cobras. Taylor, Trace. Lynch, Michelle. 2011. (2G Predator Animals Ser.). (ENG.). 24p. (J). (gr. k-2). pap. 8.50 *(978-1-61541-504-5(1))* American Reading Co.

—Dogtown Diner. Taylor, Trace. 2010. (1G ARC Pres Comics Ser.). (ENG.). 24p. (J). (gr. k-2). pap. 8.50 *(978-1-61541-073-6(2))* American Reading Co.

—Earth Movers. Taylor, Trace. 2008. (1-3Y Moving on Wheels Ser.). (ENG.). 24p. (J). (gr. k-2). pap. 6.50 *(978-1-59301-466-7(X))* American Reading Co.

—Jumping Spiders. Taylor, Trace. 2014. (1-3Y Bugs, Bugs, & More Bugs Ser.). (ENG.). 20p. (J). pap. 6.50 *(978-1-61406-687-3(6))* American Reading Co.

—Lions of Africa. Taylor, Trace. 2007. (1-3Y Wild Animals Ser.). (ENG.). 24p. (J). (gr. k-2). pap. 6.50 *(978-1-59301-654-8(9))* American Reading Co.

—Nile Crocodiles. Taylor, Trace. 2007. (1-3Y Wild Animals Ser.). (ENG.). 24p. (J). (gr. k-2). pap. 6.50 *(978-1-59301-655-5(7))* American Reading Co.

—Soccer. Taylor, Trace. 2009. (2G Sports Ser.). (ENG.). 16p. (J). (gr. k-2). pap. 7.50 *(978-1-59301-878-8(9))* American Reading Co.

—The Tree Truck. Taylor, Trace. 2008. (1-3Y Moving on Wheels Ser.). (ENG.). 24p. (J). (gr. k-2). pap. 6.50 *(978-1-61541-463-6(5))* American Reading Co.

—Wheels. Taylor, Trace. 2012. (1-3Y Moving on Wheels Ser.). (ENG.). 16p. (J). pap. 6.50 *(978-1-61406-201-1(3))* American Reading Co.

—Who Took That Dog? Taylor, Trace. 2008. (1B Graphic Novels Ser.). (ENG.). 32p. (J). (gr. k-2). pap. 8.50 *(978-1-59301-757-6(X))* American Reading Co.

—You Think You Know Giraffes. Taylor, Trace. 2008. (1-3Y Wild Animals Ser.). (ENG.). 20p. (J). (gr. k-2). pap. 6.50 *(978-1-59301-437-7(6))* American Reading Co.

—You Think You Know Hippos. Taylor, Trace. 2008. (1-3Y Wild Animals Ser.). (ENG.). 24p. (J). (gr. k-2). pap. 6.50 *(978-1-59301-267-0(5))* American Reading Co.

Taylor, Trace, jt. illus. see Bianchi, John.

Taylor, Val Paul. Who Is Maria Tallchief? Gourley, Catherine. 2003. (Who Was... ? Ser.). 103p. 15.00 *(978-0-7569-1592-6(9))* Perfection Learning Corp.

Taylor, Yvonne. Hartlie: The Streak. Taylor, Yvonne. (Hartlie: Vol. 1). 32p. (J). 10.99 *(978-0-9709187-0-3(4))* Peaceable Productions.

Tayts, Alexandra. Celeste & the Adorable Kitten. Typaldos, Melanie. 2013. 244p. 14.99 *(978-0-9899847-0-6(2))* Capybara Madness.

Tazzyman, David. Mr Gum & the Biscuit Billionaire. Stanton, Andy. 2015. (Mr Gum Ser.: 2). (ENG.). 192p. (J). (gr. 2-4). pap. 8.99 *(978-1-4052-7493-7(X))* Egmont Bks., Ltd. GBR. Dist: Independent Pubs. Group.

Tazzyman, David. Mr Gum & the Cherry Tree. Stanton, Andy. 2015. (Mr Gum Ser.: 7). (ENG.). 256p. (J). (gr. 2-4). pap. 8.99 ***(978-1-4052-7498-2(0))*** Egmont Bks., Ltd. GBR. Dist: Independent Pubs. Group.

—Mr Gum & the Dancing Bear. Stanton, Andy. 2015. (Mr Gum Ser.: 5). (ENG.). 256p. (J). (gr. 2-4). pap. 8.99 ***(978-1-4052-7496-8(4))*** Egmont Bks., Ltd. GBR. Dist: Independent Pubs. Group.

—Mr. Gum & the Goblins. Stanton, Andy. 2015. (Mr Gum Ser.: 3). (ENG.). 208p. (J). (gr. 2-4). pap. 8.99 ***(978-1-4052-7494-4(8))*** Egmont Bks., Ltd. GBR. Dist: Independent Pubs. Group.

—Mr Gum & the Power Crystals. Stanton, Andy. 2015. (Mr Gum Ser.: 4). (ENG.). 224p. (J). (gr. 2-4). pap. 8.99 ***(978-1-4052-7495-1(6))*** Egmont Bks., Ltd. GBR. Dist: Independent Pubs. Group.

—Mr Gum & the Secret Hideout. Stanton, Andy. 2015. (Mr Gum Ser.: 8). (ENG.). 256p. (J). (gr. 2-4). pap. 8.99 ***(978-1-4052-7499-9(9))*** Egmont Bks., Ltd. GBR. Dist: Independent Pubs. Group.

—What's for Dinner, Mr Gum? Stanton, Andy. 2015. (Mr Gum Ser.: 6). (ENG.). 256p. (J). (gr. 2-4). pap. 8.99 ***(978-1-4052-7497-5(2))*** Egmont Bks., Ltd. GBR. Dist: Independent Pubs. Group.

Tazzyman, David. You're a Bad Man. Stanton, Andy. ed. 2012. (Mr Gum Ser.). (ENG.). 214p. (J). (gr. 1). pap. 12.99 *(978-1-4052-6539-3(6))* Egmont Bks., Ltd. GBR. Dist: Independent Pubs. Group.

—You're a Bad Man, Mr. Gum! Stanton, Andy. 2013. (Mr Gum Ser.: 1). (ENG.). 192p. (J). (gr. 2-5). pap. 7.99 *(978-1-4052-2310-2(3))* Egmont Bks., Ltd. GBR. Dist: Independent Pubs. Group.

—You're a Bad Man, Mr Gum! Stanton, Andy. 2015. (Mr Gum Ser.: 1). (ENG.). 192p. (J). (gr. 2-4). pap. 8.99 *(978-1-4052-7492-0(1))* Egmont Bks., Ltd. GBR. Dist: Independent Pubs. Group.

Tcherevkoff, Michel, jt. illus. see Barrager, Brigette.

Te Loo, Sanne. Pescadito. Te Loo, Sanne. 2007. (SPA & ENG.). 32p. (J). (gr. -1-1). pap. 7.95 *(978-1-933605-39-5(1),* 05395, Libros del Mundo) Kane Miller.

Te Selle, Davis. Whitefoot: A Story from the Center of the World. Berry, Wendell. 2010. (ENG.). 64p. pap. 12.95 *(978-1-58243-640-1(1),* Counterpoint) Counterpoint LLC.

—Whitefoot: A Story from the Center of the World. Berry, Wendell & Rorer, Abigail. 2008. (Port William Ser.). (ENG.). 64p. (gr. 2-7). 22.00 *(978-1-58243-432-2(8))* Counterpoint LLC.

Teagle, Caitlyn. Just Batty. Spalding, Brenda M. 2011. 26p. pap. 12.00 *(978-1-61204-156-8(6),* Strategic Bk. Publishing) Strategic Book Publishing & Rights Agency (SBPRA).

Teague, Mark. ¿Cómo Aprenden los Colores los Dinosaurios? Yolen, Jane. 2006. (How Do Dinosaurs... Ser.).Tr. of How Do Dinosaurs Learn Their Colors?. (SPA.). 12p. (J). (gr. -1-k). bds. 6.99 *(978-0-439-87192-1(1),* Scholastic en Espanol) Scholastic, Inc.

—¿Cómo Comen los Dinosaurios? Yolen, Jane. 2006. (How Do Dinosaurs... Ser.). (SPA.). 40p. (J). (gr. -1-k). pap. 6.99 *(978-0-439-76404-9(1),* Scholastic en Espanol) Scholastic, Inc.

—Como Dicen Estoy Enojado los Dinosaurios? Yolen, Jane. 2014. (SPA.). 40p. (J). (gr. -1-k). pap. 6.99 *(978-0-545-62780-1(X),* Scholastic en Espanol) Scholastic, Inc.

—How Do Dinosaurs Clean Their Rooms? Yolen, Jane. 2004. (How Do Dinosaurs... Ser.). (ENG.). 12p. (J). (gr. -1-k). bds. 6.99 *(978-0-439-64950-6(1),* Blue Sky Pr., The) Scholastic, Inc.

—How Do Dinosaurs Count to Ten? Yolen, Jane. 2004. (How Do Dinosaurs... Ser.). (ENG.). 12p. (J). (gr. -1-k). bds. 6.99 *(978-0-439-64949-0(8),* Blue Sky Pr., The) Scholastic, Inc.

—How Do Dinosaurs Eat Cookies? Yolen, Jane. 2012. (How Do Dinosaurs... Ser.). (ENG.). 14p. (J). (gr. -1-k). bds. 7.99 *(978-0-545-38253-3(X),* Cartwheel Bks.) Scholastic, Inc.

—How Do Dinosaurs Eat Their Food? Yolen, Jane. 2005. (How Do Dinosaurs... Ser.). (ENG.). 40p. (J). (gr. -1-k). 16.99 *(978-0-439-24102-1(2),* Blue Sky Pr., The) Scholastic, Inc.

—How Do Dinosaurs Get Well Soon? Yolen, Jane. 2003. (How Do Dinosaurs... Ser.). (ENG.). 40p. (J). (gr. -1-3). 16.99 *(978-0-439-24100-7(6),* Blue Sky Pr., The) Scholastic, Inc.

—How Do Dinosaurs Go to School? Yolen, Jane. 2007. (How Do Dinosaurs... Ser.). (ENG.). 40p. (J). (gr. -1-k). 16.99 *(978-0-439-02081-7(6))* Scholastic, Inc.

—How Do Dinosaurs Go to School? Yolen, Jane. 2011. (J). (gr. -1-3). 29.95 *(978-0-545-19700-7(7));* 18.95 *(978-0-545-19707-6(4))* Weston Woods Studios, Inc.

—How Do Dinosaurs Laugh Out Loud? Yolen, Jane. 2010. (How Do Dinosaurs... Ser.). (ENG.). 16p. (J). (gr. -1-k). bds. 7.99 *(978-0-545-23652-2(5),* Cartwheel Bks.) Scholastic, Inc.

—How Do Dinosaurs Learn Their Colors? Yolen, Jane. 2006. (How Do Dinosaurs... Ser.). (ENG.). 12p. (J). (gr. -1-k). bds. 6.99 *(978-0-439-85653-9(1),* Blue Sky Pr., The) Scholastic, Inc.

—How Do Dinosaurs Love Their Cats? Yolen, Jane. 2010. (How Do Dinosaurs... Ser.). (ENG.). 6p. (J). (gr. -1-k). bds. 6.99 *(978-0-545-15354-6(9))* Scholastic, Inc.

—How Do Dinosaurs Love Their Dogs? Yolen, Jane. 2010. (How Do Dinosaurs... Ser.). (ENG.). 6p. (J). (gr. -1-k). bds. 6.99 *(978-0-545-15352-2(2))* Scholastic, Inc.

—How Do Dinosaurs Play All Day? Yolen, Jane. 2011. (How Do Dinosaurs... Ser.). (ENG.). 16p. (J). (gr. -1-k). pap. 6.99 *(978-0-545-23653-9(3),* Cartwheel Bks.) Scholastic, Inc.

—How Do Dinosaurs Play with Their Friends? Yolen, Jane. 2006. (How Do Dinosaurs... Ser.). (ENG.). 12p. (J). (gr. -1-k). bds. 6.99 *(978-0-439-85654-6(X),* Blue Sky Pr., The) Scholastic, Inc.

—How Do Dinosaurs Say Good Night? Yolen, Jane. 2008. (How Do Dinosaurs... Ser.). (ENG.). (J). (gr. -1-3). 9.99 *(978-0-545-09319-4(8))* Scholastic, Inc.

—How Do Dinosaurs Say Good Night? Yolen, Jane. 2004. (J). (gr. -1-3). 29.95 *(978-1-55592-138-5(8))* Weston Woods Studios, Inc.

—How Do Dinosaurs Say Happy Birthday? Yolen, Jane. 2011. (How Do Dinosaurs... Ser.). (ENG.). 12p. (J). (gr. -1-k). bds. 6.99 *(978-0-545-15353-9(0),* Blue Sky Pr., The) Scholastic, Inc.

—How Do Dinosaurs Say Happy Chanukah? Yolen, Jane. 2012. (How Do Dinosaurs... Ser.). (ENG.). 40p. (J). (— 1). 16.99 *(978-0-545-41677-1(9),* Blue Sky Pr., The) Scholastic, Inc.

—How Do Dinosaurs Say I Love You? Yolen, Jane. (J). 2011. pap. *(978-0-545-33076-3(9));* 2009. (ENG.). 40p. 16.99 *(978-0-545-14314-1(4),* Blue Sky Pr., The) Scholastic, Inc.

—How Do Dinosaurs Say I'm Mad? Yolen, Jane. 2013. (ENG.). 40p. (J). (gr. -1-k). 16.99 *(978-0-545-14315-8(2),* Blue Sky Pr., The) Scholastic, Inc.

—How Do Dinosaurs Say Merry Christmas? Yolen, Jane. 2012. (How Do Dinosaurs... Ser.). (ENG.). 40p. (J). (— 1). 16.99 *(978-0-545-41678-8(7),* Blue Sky Pr., The) Scholastic, Inc.

—How Do Dinosaurs Stay Safe? Yolen, Jane. 2015. (ENG.). 40p. (J). (gr. -1-k). 16.99 *(978-0-439-24104-5(9),* Blue Sky Pr., The) Scholastic, Inc.

Teague, Mark. Poppleton. Rylant, Cynthia. 2015. 56p. pap. 4.00 ***(978-1-61003-551-4(8))*** Center for the Collaborative Classroom.

Teague, Mark. Poppleton in Spring. Rylant, Cynthia. 2009. (Scholastic Reader Level 3 Ser.). (ENG.). 48p. (J). (gr. -1-3). pap. 3.99 *(978-0-545-07867-2(9),* Cartwheel Bks.) Scholastic, Inc.

—Poppleton in Winter. Rylant, Cynthia. 2008. 48p. (gr. -1-3). 14.00 *(978-0-7569-8910-1(8))* Perfection Learning Corp.

—Poppleton in Winter, Level 3. Rylant, Cynthia. 2008. (Scholastic Reader Level 3 Ser.). (ENG.). 56p. (J). (gr. -1-3). pap. 3.99 *(978-0-545-06823-9(1),* Cartwheel Bks.) Scholastic, Inc.

—Poppleton Se Divierte. Rylant, Cynthia. 2006. (Poppleton Ser.). (SPA.). 48p. pap. 11.73 *(978-0-15-356487-1(3))* Harcourt Children's Bks.

—The Tree House That Jack Built. Verburg, Bonnie. 2014. (ENG.). 40p. (J). (gr. -1-k). 17.99 *(978-0-439-85338-5(9),* Orchard Bks.) Scholastic, Inc.

Teague, Mark. Dear Mrs. LaRue: Letters from Obedience School. Teague, Mark. 2003. (LaRue Bks.). (ENG.). 32p. (J). (gr. -1-3). 17.99 *(978-0-439-20663-1(4),* Scholastic Pr.) Scholastic, Inc.

—Detective LaRue: Letters from the Investigation. Teague, Mark. 2004. (LaRue Bks.). (ENG.). 32p. (J). (gr. -1-3). 17.99 *(978-0-439-45868-9(4),* Scholastic Pr.) Scholastic, Inc.

—The Doom Machine. Teague, Mark. Scholastic, Inc. Staff. 2009. (ENG.). 384p. (J). (gr. 3-7). 17.99 *(978-0-545-15142-9(2),* Blue Sky Pr., The) Scholastic, Inc.

—Firehouse! Teague, Mark. 2013. (ENG.). 32p. (J). (gr. -1 — 1). bds. 6.99 *(978-0-545-49215-7(7),* Cartwheel Bks.) Scholastic, Inc.

—Funny Farm. Teague, Mark. 2009. (ENG.). 32p. (J). (gr. -1-3). 16.99 *(978-0-439-91499-4(X),* Orchard Bks.) Scholastic, Inc.

Tebalan, Helman. El Vaso de Miel. Menchú, Rigoberta & Liano, Dante. 2003. (SPA.). 96p. (J). (gr. 5-8). pap. 13.95 *(978-970-29-0985-9(6))* Santillana USA Publishing Co., Inc.

Tebbit, Jake. Grandpa & the Raccoon. Odom, Rebecca. 2009. 36p. pap. 24.95 *(978-1-60749-912-1(6))* America Star Bks.

—My Sister Sophie. MacKey, Cindy. 2013. 30p. pap. 12.99 *(978-0-9892699-9-5(X))* Cyrano Bks.

Techau, Ashlyn. Rosie: The Patchwork Bunny. Midden, Maribeth Grubb. 2011. 24p. (gr. 1-2). pap. 12.99 *(978-1-4269-5671-3(1))* Trafford Publishing.

Teckentrup, Britta. Big & Small. 2013. (ENG.). 16p. (J). bds. 6.99 *(978-1-84686-951-8(X))* Barefoot Bks., Inc.

—Bumposaurus. McKinlay, Penny. rev. ed. 2014. (Time to Read Ser.). (ENG.). 32p. (J). (gr. -1-1). pap. 6.99 *(978-1-84780-542-3(6),* Frances Lincoln) Quarto Publishing Group UK GBR. Dist: Hachette Bk. Group.

—Busy Bunny Days: In the Town, on the Farm & at the Port. 2014. (ENG.). 56p. (J). (gr. -1-3). 17.99 *(978-1-4521-1700-3(4))* Chronicle Bks. LLC.

—Fast & Slow. 2013. (ENG.). 16p. (J). bds. 6.99 *(978-1-84686-952-5(8))* Barefoot Bks., Inc.

—Fast & Slow Spanish. 2013. (ENG.). 16p. (J). 6.99 *(978-1-78285-035-9(X))* Barefoot Bks., Inc.

—Flabby Tabby. McKinlay, Penny. rev. ed. 2014. (Time to Read Ser.). (ENG.). 32p. (J). (gr. 1-4). pap. 6.99 *(978-1-84780-543-0(4),* Frances Lincoln) Quarto Publishing Group UK GBR. Dist: Hachette Bk. Group.

Teckentrup, Britta. Get Out of My Bath! Nosy Crow. 2015. (ENG.). 24p. (J). (gr. -1-2). 15.99 ***(978-0-7636-8006-0(0),*** Nosy Crow) Candlewick Pr.

Teckentrup, Britta. Grande y Pequeno. 2013. (ENG.). 16p. (J). 6.99 *(978-1-78285-034-2(1))* Barefoot Bks., Inc.

—Playbook Farm. Fletcher, Corina. 2012. (ENG.). 12p. (J). (gr. -1-2). 24.00 *(978-0-7636-6165-6(1),* Nosy Crow) Candlewick Pr.
—Playbook Pirates. Fletcher, Corina. 2013. (ENG.). 12p. (J). (gr. -1-2). 24.00 *(978-0-7636-6606-4(8),* Nosy Crow) Candlewick Pr.
Teckentrup, Britta. The Odd One Out. Teckentrup, Britta. 2014. (ENG.). 32p. (J). (-k). 14.99 *(978-0-7636-7127-3(4),* Big Picture Press) Candlewick Pr.
—Up & Down. Teckentrup, Britta. 2014. (ENG.). 28p. (J). (-k). 17.99 *(978-0-7636-7129-7(0),* Templar) Candlewick Pr.
—Where's the Pair? Teckentrup, Britta. 2015. (ENG.). 32p. (J). (-k). 14.99 *(978-0-7636-7772-5(8),* Big Picture Press) Candlewick Pr.
Ted, Hood, Jr., photos by. The Cardinal Nest: Where the Life Cycle Begins. Dealla, Yancey. 2013. 30p. (J). pap. 9.95 *(978-0-578-05005-8(6))* Four Seasons Publishing.
Tedder, Elizabeth. Alphabet & Numbers in a New Way. 2011. 32p. pap. 35.95 *(978-1-258-06357-3(3))* Literary Licensing, LLC.
—The Three Bears. 2011. 20p. 35.95 *(978-1-258-10100-8(9))* Literary Licensing, LLC.
Teeple, Jackie. Amy Washes Her Hands. Muench-Williams, Heather. l.t. ed. 2004. (HRL Board Book Ser.). (J). (gr. -1-k). pap. 10.95 *(978-1-57332-314-7(4));* pap. 10.95 *(978-1-57332-315-4(2))* Carson-Dellosa Publishing, LLC. (HighReach Learning, Incorporated).
—I Can Be. Hensley, Sarah M. l.t. ed. 2006. 12p. (J). (gr. -1-k). pap. 10.95 *(978-1-57332-339-0(X),* HighReach Learning, Incorporated) Carson-Dellosa Publishing, LLC.
—I Want a Pet. Muench-Williams, Heather. l.t. ed. 2006. 12p. (J). (gr. -1-k). pap. 10.95 *(978-1-57332-353-6(5),* HighReach Learning, Incorporated) Carson-Dellosa Publishing, LLC.
—Loving Our Country. Howard-Parham, Pam. l.t. ed. 2004. (HRL Little Book Ser.). (J). (gr. -1-1). pap. 10.95 *(978-1-57332-302-4(0));* pap. 10.95 *(978-1-57332-301-7(2))* Carson-Dellosa Publishing, LLC. (HighReach Learning, Incorporated).
—Marsy's Perfect Eyesight. Vonthron, Satanta C. l.t. ed. 2005. (J). (gr. -1-k). pap. 10.95 *(978-1-57332-344-4(6));* pap. 10.95 *(978-1-57332-345-1(4))* Carson-Dellosa Publishing, LLC. (HighReach Learning, Incorporated).
—A Nice Cool Drink. Jarrell, Pamela R. l.t. ed. 2005. (J). (gr. -1-k). pap. 10.95 *(978-1-57332-340-6(3));* pap. 10.95 *(978-1-57332-341-3(1))* Carson-Dellosa Publishing, LLC. (HighReach Learning, Incorporated).
—Spending Time Outdoors. Howard-Parham, Pam. l.t. ed. 2005. (HRL Big Book Ser.). (J). (gr. k-18). pap. 10.95 *(978-1-57332-333-8(0));* pap. 10.95 *(978-1-57332-334-5(9))* Carson-Dellosa Publishing, LLC. (HighReach Learning, Incorporated).
Teets, Ashley. Dori's Gift. Wilson, Angie. 2013. (ENG.). 32p. (J). (gr. -1-3). 16.95 *(978-0-938467-85-4(9))* Headline Bks., Inc.
—Robot Rhymes. Teel, Karen. 2013. (ENG.). 31p. (J). (gr. -1-3). 16.95 *(978-0-938467-79-3(4))* Headline Bks., Inc.
—Season of Play. Benedetti, Debra. 2011. 32p. (J). *(978-0-929915-99-9(2))* Headline Bks., Inc.
Teets, Ashley, jt. illus. see McNeal, Drema.
Tegan-Olsen, Sandra. Joey's adventures by the Sea: Jellyfish Everywhere! 2008. 20p. (J). per. 9.95 *(978-0-9801527-0-8(4))* Freefox Publishing.
Teich, Melle. Sly the Fly: The Doctor's Office. Harter, Gage. 2003. 16p. (J). 7.95 *(978-1-59466-009-2(3),* Little Ones) Port Town Publishing.
Teis, Kyra. Read to Me, 1 vol. Moreillon, Judi. (J). 2004. (ENG.). 32p. (J). bds. 6.95 *(978-1-59572-014-6(6));* 2003. 24p. 6.95 *(978-1-932065-49-7(0),* 1-718-784-9112) Star Bright Bks., Inc.
—Speaking of Me... Stepping Stones to a Better Life, 1 vol. Mathers, Beth. 2006. (ENG.). 32p. (YA). (gr. 5-9). pap. 15.95 *(978-1-59572-039-9(1))* Star Bright Bks., Inc.
—Vamos a Leer. Moreillon, Judi. Mercado, Mary M., tr. from ENG.Tr. of Read to Me. (SPA.). 12p. (J). 2005. bds. 6.95 *(978-1-59572-015-3(4));* 2004. 6.95 *(978-1-932065-50-3(4))* Star Bright Bks., Inc.
—Words are like Faces, 1 vol. Baer, Edith. 2007. (ENG.). 32p. (J). 15.95 *(978-1-59572-108-2(8))* Star Bright Bks., Inc.
Teixeira, Doug. Mystery at the O'Reilly Farm. Teixeira, G. Ann. 2010. 30p. pap. 10.00 *(978-1-60911-336-0(5),* Eloquent Bks.) Strategic Book Publishing & Rights Agency (SBPRA).
Tejado, Irene. The Adventures of a Water Drop. Ibarrola, Begonia. 2013. (ENG.). 32p. (J). *(978-84-95923-96-7(3))* Primera Persona.
Tejpar, Iman. A Manual for Marco: Living, Learning, & Laughing with an Autistic Sibling. Abdullah, Shaila. 2015. (J). *(978-1-61599-248-5(0))* Loving Healing Pr., Inc.
Tekenteam. My Favorite Safari. 2011. (My Favorite Vehicles Ser.). (ENG.). 12p. (J). (gr. -1-k). bds. 5.99 *(978-0-7641-6412-5(0))* Barron's Educational Series, Inc.
Tekiela, Stan, photos by. Baby Bear Discovers the World, 1 vol. Bauer, Marion Dane. 2006. 64p. (J). (gr. -1-k). 14.95 *(978-1-59193-165-2(7))* Adventure Pubns., Inc.
—The Cutest Critter, 1 vol. Bauer, Marion Dane. 2010. 44p. (J). (gr. 4-6). 14.95 *(978-1-59193-253-6(X))* Adventure Pubns., Inc.
Tela, Donna L. Squnky's Big Awakening. Tela, Carl M. 2009. 140p. pap. 14.99 *(978-1-4251-8145-1(7))* Trafford Publishing.
Telford, Jane. Tomas Loves... A Rhyming Book about Fun, Friendship - & Autism. Welton, Jude. 2015. (ENG.). 32p. *(978-1-84905-544-4(0))* Kingsley, Jessica Ltd.
Telgemeier, Raina. Claudia & Mean Janine. Martin, Ann M. 2008. (Baby-Sitters Club Graphix Ser.: 4). (ENG.). 176p. (J). (gr. 3-7). pap. 10.99 *(978-0-439-88517-1(5),* Graphix) Scholastic, Inc.
Telgemeier, Raina. Kristy's Great Idea. Martin, Ann M. rev. ed. 2015. (Baby-Sitters Club Graphix Ser.: 1). (ENG.). 192p. (J). (gr. 3-7). 24.99 ***(978-0-545-81386-0(7),*** Graphix) Scholastic, Inc.
—The Truth about Stacey. Martin, Ann M. rev. ed. 2015. (Baby-Sitters Club Graphix Ser.: 2). (ENG.). 144p. (J). (gr. 3-7). 24.99 ***(978-0-545-81388-4(3));*** pap. 10.99 ***(978-0-545-81389-1(1))*** Scholastic, Inc. (Graphix).
Telielska, M. Magdalena. Old Fairy Tales Anew. Doolittle, Eva M. 2008. 88p. (J). *(978-0-9791065-0-7(8))* Vesta Bks., LLC.
Tellekamp, Lynda. Waiting for Ding. McKnight, Alex. 2013. 20p. pap. 24.95 *(978-1-62709-362-0(1))* America Star Bks.
Tello, Jorge. Here Come the Blobbies. Tello, Jorge. 2004. 32p. (J). pap. 15.89 incl. audio compact disk *(978-1-932179-32-3(1))* Pers Publishing.
—Pookie & Tushka Find a Little Piano. Tello, Jorge. 2004. 32p. (J). 15.89 incl. cd-rom *(978-1-932179-23-1(2))* Pers Publishing.
Temairik, Jaime. Alice & Lucy Will Work for Bunk Beds. 2015. (J). *(978-1-4847-0816-3(4))* Disney Publishing Worldwide.
—How to Negotiate Everything. Spellman, David & Lutz, Lisa. 2013. (ENG.). 32p. (J). (gr. -1-3). 16.99 *(978-1-4424-5119-3(X),* Simon & Schuster Bks. For Young Readers) Simon & Schuster Bks. For Young Readers.
Temairik, Jaime. Troll Two — Three — Four. Smallman, Steve. 2014. (J). ***(978-1-4723-2925-7(2))*** Parragon Bk. Service Ltd.
Tempesta, Franco. Angry Birds Playground - Dinosaurs. National Geographic Editors & Esbaum, Jill. 2013. (ENG.). 128p. (J). (gr. -1-3). lib. bdg. 21.90 *(978-1-4263-1325-7(X),* National Geographic Children's Bks.) National Geographic Society.
—Dinosaur Days. Milton, Joyce. 2014. (Step into Reading Ser.). (ENG.). 48p. (J). (gr. k-3). lib. bdg. 12.99 *(978-0-375-97338-3(9),* Random Hse. Bks. for Young Readers) Random Hse. Children's Bks.
—Dinosaurs: A Prehistoric Adventure! National Geographic Editors & Esbaum, Jill. 2013. (ENG.). 128p. (J). (gr. -1-3). 14.95 *(978-1-4263-1324-0(1),* National Geographic Children's Bks.) National Geographic Society.
—National Geographic Kids Ultimate Dinopedia: The Most Complete Dinosaur Reference Ever. Lessem, Don. 2010. (ENG.). 272p. (J). (gr. 2-5). 24.95 *(978-1-4263-0164-3(2));* lib. bdg. 34.90 *(978-1-4263-0165-0(0))* National Geographic Society. (National Geographic Children's Bks.).
—National Geographic Little Kids First Big Book of Dinosaurs. Hughes, Catherine D. 2011. (National Geographic Little Kids First Big Bks.). (ENG.). 128p. (J). (gr. -1-3). 14.95 *(978-1-4263-0846-8(9));* lib. bdg. 21.90 *(978-1-4263-0847-5(7))* National Geographic Society. (National Geographic Children's Bks.).
Temple, Chuck. Brady Brady & the B Team, 12 vols. Shaw, Mary. l.t. ed. 2006. 32p. (J). per. *(978-1-897169-09-4(4))* Brady Brady, Inc.
—Brady Brady & the Ballpark Bark. Shaw, Mary. 2007. (J). *(978-1-897169-10-0(8))* Brady Brady, Inc.
—Brady Brady & the Big Mistake, 11vols. Shaw, Mary. l.t. ed. 2004. 32p. (J). per. *(978-0-9735557-4-5(2))* Brady Brady, Inc.
—Brady Brady & the Cleanup Hitters. Shaw, Mary. 2008. 32p. (J). pap. *(978-1-897169-11-7(6))* Brady Brady, Inc.
—Brady Brady & the Great Exchange, 11 vols. Shaw, Mary. l.t. ed. 2003. 32p. (J). per. *(978-0-9735557-5-2(0))* Brady Brady, Inc.
—Brady Brady & the Great Rink, 11 vols. Shaw, Mary. l.t. ed. 2004. 32p. (J). per. *(978-0-9735557-0-7(X))* Brady Brady, Inc.
—Brady Brady & the Most Important Game, 11 vols. Shaw, Mary. l.t. ed. 2004. 32p. (J). per. *(978-0-9735557-6-9(9))* Brady Brady, Inc.
—Brady Brady & the MVP, 11 vols. Shaw, Mary. l.t. ed. 2004. 32p. (J). per. *(978-0-9735557-7-6(7))* Brady Brady, Inc.
—Brady Brady & the Puck on the Pond, 11 vols. Shaw, Mary. l.t. ed. 2005. 32p. (J). per. *(978-1-897169-07-0(8))* Brady Brady, Inc.
—Brady Brady & the Runaway Goalie, 11 vols. Shaw, Mary. l.t. ed. 2004. 32p. (J). per. *(978-0-9735557-1-4(8))* Brady Brady, Inc.
—Brady Brady & the Singing Tree, 11 vols. Shaw, Mary. l.t. ed. 2004. 32p. (J). per. *(978-0-9735557-3-8(4))* Brady Brady, Inc.
—Brady Brady & the Super Skater, 11 vols. Shaw, Mary. l.t. ed. 2005. 32p. (J). per. *(978-1-897169-06-3(X))* Brady Brady, Inc.
—Brady Brady & the Twirlin' Torpedo, 11 vols. Shaw, Mary. l.t. ed. 2004. 32p. (J). per. *(978-0-9735557-2-1(6))* Brady Brady, Inc.
Templeton, Robyn. Tell Me Why. Templeton, Robyn. Jackson, Sarah. 2004. 32p. (Orig.). (J). pap. *(978-1-875641-96-3(3))* Magabala Bks.
Templeton, Ty. Bill the Boy Wonder: The Secret Co-Creator of Batman. Nobleman, Marc Tyler. 2012. (J). pap. 17.95 *(978-1-58089-290-2(6));* (ENG.). 48p. (gr. 3-7). 17.95 *(978-1-58089-289-6(2))* Charlesbridge Publishing, Inc.
—Target: Deadshot!, 1 vol. Slott, Dan et al. 2013. (Batman Adventures Ser.). (ENG.). 32p. (gr. 2-3). 21.27 *(978-1-4342-6033-8(X))* Stone Arch Bks.
Templeton, Ty. Batman Adventures. Templeton, Ty. Slott, Dan. 2013. (Batman Adventures Ser.). (ENG.). 32p. (gr. 2-3). 148.89 *(978-1-4342-8837-0(4))* Stone Arch Bks.
—Free Man, 1 vol. Templeton, Ty. Slott, Dan. 2012. (Batman Adventures Ser.). (ENG.). 32p. (gr. 2-3). lib. bdg. 21.27 *(978-1-4342-4558-8(6))* Stone Arch Bks.
—Need to Know, 1 vol. Templeton, Ty. Slott, Dan. 2012. (Batman Adventures Ser.). (ENG.). 32p. (gr. 2-3). lib. bdg. 21.27 *(978-1-4342-4560-1(8))* Stone Arch Bks.
—No Asylum, 1 vol. Templeton, Ty. Slott, Dan. 2012. (Batman Adventures Ser.). (ENG.). 32p. (gr. 2-3). lib. bdg. 21.27 *(978-1-4342-4557-1(8))* Stone Arch Bks.
Temporin, Elena. The Gingerbread Man. 2007. (Picture Book Classics Ser.). 24p. (J). 9.99 *(978-0-7945-1786-1(2),* Usborne) EDC Publishing.
—The Paraclete Treasury of Angel Stories. Joslin, Mary. 2008. (ENG.). 48p. (J). (gr. -1-6). 18.95 *(978-1-55725-572-3(5))* Paraclete Pr., Inc.
—Saint Francis of Assisi. Denham, Joyce. 2008. (ENG.). 32p. (J). (gr. k-6). pap. 9.95 *(978-1-55725-571-6(7))* Paraclete Pr., Inc.
—The Snowy Day. Milbourne, Anna. 2005. 24p. (J). (gr. -1-3). 9.99 *(978-0-7945-1147-0(3),* Usborne) EDC Publishing.
—The Snowy Day. Milbourne, Anna. 2007. (J). *(978-0-439-88988-9(X))* Scholastic, Inc.
—The Usborne Book of Christmas Lullabies. 2006. (Christmas Lullabies Ser.). 8p. (J). bds. 14.99 incl. audio compact disk *(978-0-7945-1469-3(3),* Usborne) EDC Publishing.
—Usborne Stories from Shakespeare. Fearn, Laura. 2006. 191p. pap. *(978-0-439-88984-1(7))* Scholastic, Inc.
—The Windy Day. Milbourne, Anna. 2007. (Picture Bks). 24p. (J). (gr. -1-3). 9.99 *(978-0-7945-1616-1(5),* Usborne) EDC Publishing.
ten Cate, Marijke. A Strange Day. Van Der Heide, Iris. 2007. (ENG.). 24p. (J). (gr. -1-3). 16.95 *(978-1-932425-94-9(2),* Lemniscaat) Boyds Mills Pr.
Tenggren, Gustaf. Little Golden Book Poky Little Puppy Tales. Sebring Lowrey, Janette. 2015. (Little Golden Book Favorites Ser.). (ENG.). 80p. (J). (-k). 7.99 ***(978-0-553-51208-3(0),*** Golden Bks.) Random Hse. Children's Bks.
Tenggren, Gustaf. The Poky Little Puppy. Lowrey, Janette Sebring. 2011. (Little Golden Book Ser.). (ENG.). 24p. (J). (-k). bds. 6.99 *(978-0-375-86129-1(7),* Golden Bks.) Random Hse. Children's Bks.
—The Poky Little Puppy. Lowrey, Janette Sebring. 2007. (Little Golden Book Ser.). (ENG.). 26p. (J). (gr. k-k). bds. 4.99 *(978-0-375-83925-2(9),* Golden Bks.) Random Hse. Children's Bks.
—The Poky Little Puppy. Lowrey, Janette Sebring. deluxe ed. Date not set. 23p. (J). (gr. -1-2). reprint ed. *(978-1-929566-56-3(5));* (978-1-929566-50-1(6)) Cronies.
—The Poky Little Puppy. Lowery, Janette Sebring. 65th anniv. ed. 2007. (Special Edition Little Golden Book Ser.). (ENG.). 52p. (J). (gr. k — 1). 8.99 *(978-0-375-83920-7(8),* Golden Bks.) Random Hse. Children's Bks.
—The Saggy Baggy Elephant. Jackson, Kathryn & Jackson, B. deluxe ed. Date not set. (J). (gr. -1-2). reprint ed. *(978-1-929566-60-0(3))* Cronies.
—The Saggy Baggy Elephant: Classic Edition. Jackson, Kathryn & Jackson, B. Date not set. 23p. (J). (gr. -1-1). *(978-1-929566-54-9(9))* Cronies.
—The Shy Little Kitten. Schurr, Cathleen. deluxe ed. Date not set. (J). (gr. -1-2). reprint ed. *(978-1-929566-57-0(3))* Cronies.
—The Shy Little Kitten: Classic Edition. Schurr, Cathleen. Date not set. (J). (gr. -1-1). reprint ed. *(978-1-929566-51-8(4))* Cronies.
—Tawney Scrawny Lion. Jackson, Kathryn. deluxe ed. Date not set. (J). (gr. -1-2). reprint ed. *(978-1-929566-61-7(1))* Cronies.
—Tawny Scrawny Lion: Classic Edition. Jackson, Kathryn. Date not set. 23p. (J). (gr. -1-1). reprint ed. *(978-1-929566-55-6(7))* Cronies.
—Where Is the Poky Little Puppy? Lowrey, Janette Sebring. 2015. (Little Golden Book Ser.). (ENG.). 24p. (J). (-k). 3.99 *(978-0-375-84750-9(2),* Golden Bks.) Random Hse. Children's Bks.
Tenney, Shawna J. C. The Truth about Ogres, 1 vol. Braun, Eric. 2011. (Fairy-Tale Superstars Ser.). (ENG.). 32p. (gr. 1-3). lib. bdg. 26.65 *(978-1-4048-6159-6(9),* Nonfiction Picture Bks.) Picture Window Bks.
—When I Take the Sacrament, I Remember Jesus. Gudmundson, C. J. 2012. (J). *(978-1-62108-020-6(X))* Covenant Communications, Inc.
Tenniel, John. Alilce's Anters in Ferlielann. Carroll, Lewis. McClure, Derrick, tr. from ENG. 2012. (GER.). 144p. pap. *(978-1-78201-016-6(5))* Evertype.
—Ailis's Anterins I the Laun o Ferlies. Carroll, Lewis. McCallum, Andrew, tr. from ENG. 2013. (GER.). 138p. pap. *(978-1-78201-026-5(2))* Evertype.
—Alice in Wonderland Giant Poster & Coloring Book. Carroll, Lewis. 2012. (ENG.). 48p. (gr. -1-17). pap. 12.95 *(978-1-4197-0089-7(8),* Abrams Image) Abrams.
—Alice's Abenteuer im Wunderland. Carroll, Lewis. Zimmermann, Antonie, tr. 2012. (Dover Dual Language German Ser.).Tr. of Alice's Adventures in Wonderland. (GER & ENG.). 192p. (J). reprint ed. pap. 8.95 *(978-0-486-20668-4(8))* Dover Pubns., Inc.
—Alice's Adventirs in Wonderlaand. Carroll, Lewis. Johnson, Laureen, tr. from ENG. 2012. (GER.). 140p. pap. *(978-1-78201-008-1(4))* Evertype.
—Alice's Adventures in Wonderland. Carroll, Lewis. Date not set. 248p. (YA). 14.95 *(978-1-884807-19-0(4))* Blushing Rose Publishing.
—Alice's Adventures in Wonderland. Carroll, Lewis. 2013. (Cambridge Library Collection - Fiction & Poetry Ser.). (ENG.). 210p. 54.00 *(978-1-108-06037-0(4));* pap. 26.99 *(978-1-108-05958-9(9))* Cambridge Univ. Pr.
—Alice's Adventures in Wonderland. Carroll, Lewis. 2007. 204p. (J). 24.95 *(978-1-58218-791-4(6));* (ENG.). (YA). per. 14.95 *(978-1-58218-790-7(8))* Digital Scanning, Inc.
—Alice's Adventures in Wonderland. Carroll, Lewis. 2009. 68p. pap. 14.14 *(978-1-151-46988-5(2))* General Bks. LLC.
—Alice's Adventures in Wonderland, 1. Carroll, Lewis. ed. 2011. (ENG.). 208p. (J). (gr. 2). 26.99 *(978-0-230-75538-3(0))* Pan Macmillan GBR. Dist: Independent Pubs. Group.
—Alice's Adventures in Wonderland: And Other Stories. Carroll, Lewis. 2013. (Leather-Bound Classics Ser.). (ENG.). 544p. 24.95 *(978-1-60710-933-4(6),* Thunder Bay Pr.) Baker & Taylor Publishing Group.
—Alice's Adventures in Wonderland & Through the Looking Glass. Carroll, Lewis. 2008. (Vintage Classics Ser.). (ENG.). 336p. (gr. 4-7). pap. 11.95 *(978-0-09-951207-3(6))* Random Hse. GBR. Dist: Independent Pubs. Group.
—Alice's Adventures in Wonderland & Through the Looking-Glass. Carroll, Lewis & Frith, Barbara. 2013. (ENG.). 288p. *(978-1-907360-36-7(0),* Collector's Library, The) Pan Macmillan.
—Alice's Adventures in Wonderland, & Through the Looking Glass. Carroll, Lewis. Haughton, Hugh & Roberge, Thomas, eds. ed. 2009. (ENG.). 304p. (gr. 12). pap. 14.00 *(978-0-14-311773-5(4))* Penguin Publishing Group.
—Alice's Adventures in Wonderland & Through the Looking-Glass. Carroll, Lewis. Haughton, Hugh, ed. rev. ed. 2003. (ENG.). 400p. (gr. 12-18). pap. 11.00 *(978-0-14-143976-1(9),* Penguin Classics) Penguin Publishing Group.
—Alice's Carränts in Wunnerlan. Carroll, Lewis. Morrison-Smyth, Anne, tr. from ENG. 2nd ed. 2013. 140p. pap. *(978-1-78201-011-1(4))* Evertype.
—La Aventuras de Alisia en la Pais de Mervelias. Carroll, Lewis. Davies, Simon, tr. from ENG. 2012. 136p. pap. *(978-1-904808-88-6(3))* Evertype.
—L' Aventuros d'Alis in Marvoland. Carroll, Lewis. Midgley, Ralph, tr. from ENG. 2013. (GER.). 134p. pap. *(978-1-78201-019-7(X))* Evertype.
—Eachdraidh Ealasaid Ann an Tir Nan Iongantas. Carroll, Lewis. Watson, Moray, tr. from ENG. 2012. 156p. pap. *(978-1-78201-015-9(7))* Evertype.
—Lès-Aventûres D'Alice Ô Pèyis Dès Mèrvèy. Carroll, Lewis. Capron, André, tr. from ENG. 2012. (GER.). 150p. pap. *(978-1-904808-87-9(5))* Evertype.
—Na Hana Kupanaha a Aleka Ma Ka Aina Kamaha'o. Carroll, Lewis. NeSmith, R. Keao, tr. from ENG. 2012. (HAW.). 148p. pap. *(978-1-904808-97-8(2))* Evertype.
—The Nursery Alice. Carroll, Lewis. 2010. 86p. pap. *(978-1-904808-42-8(5))* Evertype.
—The Nursery Alice. Carroll, Lewis. 2013. 74p. (J). pap. 18.58 *(978-1-939652-68-3(5))* Lire Bks.
—The Nursery Alice. Carroll, Lewis. 2009. 56p. *(978-973-88826-8-3(0))* Mediamorphosis.
Tenniel, John. The Nursery Alice. Carroll, Lewis. 2015. (ENG.). 72p. (J). (-k). 19.99 ***(978-1-4472-8711-7(8))*** Pan Macmillan GBR. Dist: Independent Pubs. Group.
Tenniel, John. 'O Tafaoga a 'Alise I Le Nu'o O Mea Ofoofogia. Carroll, Lewis. Simanu-Klutz, Luafata, tr. from ENG. 2013. 152p. pap. *(978-1-78201-023-4(8))* Evertype.
—Sense & Nonsense Stories from Lewis Carroll: Alice, Sylvie & Bruno, & More. Carroll, Lewis. 2009. 672p. pap. 24.95 *(978-1-930585-75-1(6))* Coachwhip Pubns.
—Through the Looking Glass. Carroll, Lewis. 2012. *(978-1-897093-65-8(9))* Qualitas Publishing.
—Through the Looking-Glass, & What Alice Found There, Original Version: Alice Through the Looking Glass. Carroll, Lewis. 2010. (ENG.). 210p. pap. 25.95 *(978-4-87187-304-8(8))* Ishi Pr. International.
—Trans la Spegulo Kaj Kion Alico Trovis Tie. Carroll, Lewis. Broadribb, Donald, tr. from ENG. 2012. 180p. pap. *(978-1-78201-001-2(7))* Evertype.
Tenniel, John & Bickford-Smith, Coralie. Alice's Adventures in Wonderland & Through the Looking Glass. Carroll, Lewis. 2010. (Hardcover Classics Ser.). (ENG.). 448p. (gr. 12). 22.00 *(978-0-14-119246-8(1),* Penguin Classics Hardcover) Penguin Publishing Group.
Tenniel, John & Thomson, E. Gertrude. The Nursery Alice. Carroll, Lewis. 2010. 64p. pap. *(978-1-907900-00-0(7))* English Rose Publishing.
Tenniel, Sir John & Thomson, E. Gertrude. The Nursery Alice. Carroll, Lewis. 2014. 64p. *(978-1-907900-09-3(0))* English Rose Publishing.
Teo, Ali. Barnaby Bennett, 1 vol. Rainforth, Hannah. 2008. (ENG.). 32p. (J). (gr. -1-3). pap. 5.95 *(978-1-59572-156-3(8))* Star Bright Bks., Inc.
—Barnaby Bennett. Rainforth, Hannah. 2007. 32p. (J). (gr. -1-3). pap. 10.00 *(978-1-86969-232-2(2))* Univ. of Hawaii Pr.
Teo, Ali & O'Reilly, John. Kiss! Kiss! Yuck! Yuck!, 1 vol. Mewburn, Kyle. 2008. (ENG.). 32p. (J). (gr. -1-3). 16.95 *(978-1-56145-457-0(5))* Peachtree Pubs.
Teo, Ali, jt. illus. see Jensen, Astrid.
Teplin, Scott & Rex, Adam. The Clock Without a Face. Barnett, Mac et al. 2010. (ENG.). 30p. (gr. 2-18). bds. 19.95 *(978-1-934781-71-5(1))* McSweeney's Publishing.
Tercio, Ricardo. Aesop's Fables. McGovern, Ann. 2013. (ENG.). 80p. (J). (gr. 2-5). 14.99 *(978-0-545-46721-6(7));* pap. 4.99 *(978-0-545-46722-3(5))* Scholastic, Inc.
—Jack & the Beanstalk: The Graphic Novel. 2008. (Graphic Spin Ser.). (ENG.). 40p. (gr. 1-3). 23.99 *(978-1-4342-0766-1(8),* Graphic Revolve) Stone Arch Bks.
—Jack & the Beanstalk: The Graphic Novel, 1 vol. Stone Arch Books Staff. 2008. (Graphic Spin Ser.). (ENG.). 40p. (gr. 1-3). pap. 5.95 *(978-1-4342-0862-0(1),* Graphic Revolve) Stone Arch Bks.
—Jack y los Frijoles Magicos. Andersen, Hans Christian & Stone Arch Books Staff. 2010. (Graphic Spin en Español Ser.). (SPA & ENG.). 40p. (gr. 1-3). pap. 5.95 *(978-1-4342-2272-5(1),* Graphic Spin en Español) Stone Arch Bks.
—Jack y los Frijoles Magicos. Andersen, Hans Christian & Capstone Press Staff. 2010. (Graphic Spin en Español Ser.). (SPA.). 40p. (gr. 1-3). lib. bdg. 23.99 *(978-1-4342-1902-2(X),* Graphic Spin en Español) Stone Arch Bks.
Terrazzini, Daniela Jaglenka. The Call of the Wild. London, Jack. 2011. (Puffin Classics Ser.). (ENG.). 160p. (J). (gr. 3-7). 16.99 *(978-0-14-133654-1(4),* Puffin) Penguin Publishing Group.
—The Seeing Stick. Yolen, Jane. 2009. (ENG.). 32p. (J). (gr. -1-1). 16.95 *(978-0-7624-2048-3(0),* Running Pr.) Running Pr. Bk. Pubs.
—Tales for Great Grandchildren: Folk Tales from India & Nepal. Jackson, John. 2014. (ENG.). 142p. 30.00 *(978-0-9569212-3-9(X))* JJ Bks. GBR. Dist: Casemate Pubs. & Bk. Distributors, LLC.
Terrazzini, Daniela Jaglenka, jt. illus. see Blake, Quentin.
Terrazzini, Daniela Jaglenka, jt. illus. see Hall, Arthur.
Terry, Brian. The Lemonade Crash. Hafer, Tom. 2010. 24p. 16.95 *(978-1-4520-1439-5(6))* AuthorHouse.
Terry, Chris, jt. photos by see Loftus, David.

T

Terry, Michael. Gossipy Parrot Parrot. Roddie, Shen. 2003. (ENG.). 1p. (J). pap. 9.99 *(978-0-7475-6489-8(2))* Bloomsbury Publishing Plc GBR. Dist: Independent Pubs. Group.

—Lonely Giraffe. Blight, Peter. Matthewson, Emma, ed. 2005. (ENG.). 32p. (J). 19.99 *(978-0-7475-6894-0(4))* Bloomsbury Publishing Plc GBR. Dist: Independent Pubs. Group.

—The Lonely Giraffe. Blight, Peter. 2006. (Bloomsbury Paperbacks Ser.). (ENG.). 32p. (J). (gr. -1-3). pap. 12.99 *(978-0-7475-7144-5(9))* Bloomsbury Publishing Plc GBR. Dist: Trafalgar Square Publishing.

—See the Sea! A Book about Colors. Reader's Digest Editors & Zobel-Nolan, Allia. 2004. (Googly Eyes Ser.). (ENG.). 10p. (J). (-1). bds. 7.99 *(978-0-7944-0291-4(7))* Reader's Digest Assn., Inc., The.

—The Selfish Crocodile. Charles, Faustin. 2010. (Selfish Crocodile Ser.). (ENG.). 32p. (J). (gr. -1-k). pap. 9.99 *(978-0-7475-4193-6(0))*, Bloomsbury USA Childrens) Bloomsbury USA.

—The Selfish Crocodile Book of Colours. Charles, Faustin. 2013. (Selfish Crocodile Ser.). (ENG.). 14p. (J). 10.99 *(978-1-4088-1449-9(8))*, 38597, Bloomsbury USA Childrens) Bloomsbury USA.

—The Selfish Crocodile Book of Numbers. Charles, Faustin & Beynon-Davies, Paul. 2012. (Selfish Crocodile Ser.). (ENG.). 14p. (J). (gr. -1-k). pap. 10.99 *(978-1-4088-1451-2(X))*, 38599, Bloomsbury USA Childrens) Bloomsbury USA.

—The Selfish Crocodile Book of Sounds. Charles, Faustin. 2012. (Selfish Crocodile Ser.). (ENG.). 14p. (J). (gr. -1-3). bds. 10.99 *(978-1-4088-1450-5(1))*, 38598, Bloomsbury USA Childrens) Bloomsbury USA.

—The Selfish Crocodile Book of Words. Charles, Faustin. 2012. (Selfish Crocodile Ser.). (ENG.). 12p. (J). (gr. -1-k). bds. 10.99 *(978-1-4088-1452-9(8))*, 38600, Bloomsbury USA Childrens) Bloomsbury USA.

—The Selfish Crocodile Counting Book. Charles, Faustin. l.t. ed. 2008. (ENG.). 12p. (J). (gr. k-k). bds. 8.95 *(978-0-7475-9238-9(1))* Bloomsbury Publishing Plc GBR. Dist: Independent Pubs. Group.

—The Selfish Crocodile Jigsaw Book. Charles, Faustin & Beynon-Davies, Paul. 2012. (Selfish Crocodile Ser.). (ENG.). 14p. (J). (gr. -1-3). 20.99 *(978-1-4088-1453-6(6))*, 38601, Bloomsbury USA Childrens) Bloomsbury USA.

—Who Lives Here? 2012. (ENG.). 12p. (J). (gr. -1-k). 14.99 *(978-1-4088-1943-2(0))*, 43231, Bloomsbury USA Childrens) Bloomsbury USA.

Terry, Michael. Captain Wag & the Big Blue Whale. Terry, Michael. 2008. (Captain Wag Ser.). (ENG.). 32p. (J). (gr. k-k). pap. 13.95 *(978-0-7475-9254-9(3))* Bloomsbury Publishing Plc GBR. Dist: Independent Pubs. Group.

—The Selfish Crocodile Book of Nursery Rhymes. Terry, Michael. Charles, Faustin. 2008. (ENG.). 1p. (J). (gr. -1-k). 25.95 *(978-0-7475-9523-6(2))* Bloomsbury Publishing Plc GBR. Dist: Independent Pubs. Group.

Terry, Michael. The Gossipy Parrot. Terry, Michael, tr. Roddie, Shen. 2004. (ENG.). 32p. (J). (gr. k-2). 20.00 *(978-0-7475-6079-1(X))* Bloomsbury Publishing Plc GBR. Dist: Independent Pubs. Group.

Terry, Roger. How 'Pilly-Pine', the Alpaca, Lost His Quills. Miceli, Mary Anne. 2012. 44p. pap. 20.00 *(978-0-578-10145-3(9))* Miceli, Mary Anne.

Terry, Will. Armadilly Chili. Ketteman, Helen. 2012. (J). *(978-1-61913-143-9(9))* Weigl Pubs., Inc.

—Armadilly Chili. Ketteman, Helen. 2004. (ENG.). 32p. (J). (gr. k-3). pap. 7.95 *(978-0-8075-0458-1(0))* Whitman, Albert & Co.

—Big Heart! A Valentine's Day Tale. Holub, Joan. 2007. (Ant Hill Ser.). (ENG.). 24p. (J). (gr. -1-k). lib. bdg. 13.89 *(978-1-4169-2562-0(7))*, Simon & Schuster/Paula Wiseman Bks.) Simon & Schuster/Paula Wiseman Bks.

—Big Heart! A Valentine's Day Tale. Holub, Joan. 2007. (Ant Hill Ser.). (ENG.). 24p. (J). (gr. -1-k). pap. 3.99 *(978-1-4169-0957-6(5))*, Simon Spotlight) Simon Spotlight.

—The Christmas Troll: Sometimes God's Best Gifts Are the Most Unexpected. Peterson, Eugene H. 2004. (ENG.). 40p. (J). 11.99 *(978-1-57683-581-1(9))* NavPress Publishing Group.

—The Frog with the Big Mouth. 2012. (J). 34.28 *(978-1-61913-146-0(3))* Weigl Pubs., Inc.

—The Frog with the Big Mouth, 1 vol. 2008. (ENG.). 32p. (J). (gr. k-3). 16.99 *(978-0-8075-2621-7(5))* Whitman, Albert & Co.

—Good Luck! A St. Patrick's Day Story. Holub, Joan. 2007. (Ant Hill Ser.). (ENG.). 24p. (J). (gr. -1-k). lib. bdg. 11.89 *(978-1-4169-2560-6(0))*, Aladdin Library) Simon & Schuster Children's Publishing.

—Good Luck! A St. Patrick's Day Story. Holub, Joan. 2007. (Ant Hill Ser.). (ENG.). 24p. (J). (gr. -1-k). pap. 3.99 *(978-1-4169-0955-2(9))*, Simon Spotlight) Simon Spotlight.

—Little Rooster's Diamond Button. 2012. (J). *(978-1-61913-156-9(0))* Weigl Pubs., Inc.

—Little Rooster's Diamond Button. 2013. (ENG.). 32p. (J). (gr. -1-2). pap. 7.99 *(978-0-8075-4645-1(3))* Whitman, Albert & Co.

—Little Rooster's Diamond Button Book & DVD Set, 1 vol. MacDonald, Margaret Read. 2010. (Book & DVD Packages with Nutmeg Media Ser.). (ENG.). 4p. (J). (gr. -1-3). 49.95 *(978-0-8075-9982-2(4))* Whitman, Albert & Co.

—Monster Parade. Corey, Shana. 2009. (Step into Reading Ser.). (ENG.). 24p. (J). (gr. -1-1). 3.99 *(978-0-375-85638-9(2))* Random Hse., Inc.

—More Snacks! A Thanksgiving Play. Holub, Joan. 2006. (Ant Hill Ser.: 1). (ENG.). 24p. (J). (gr. -1-k). pap. 3.99 *(978-1-4169-0954-5(0))*; lib. bdg. 11.89 *(978-1-4169-2559-0(7))* Simon Spotlight. (Simon Spotlight).

—Nasty Bugs. Hopkins, Lee Bennett. 2012. (ENG.). 32p. (J). (gr. 1-3). 17.99 *(978-0-8037-3716-7(5))*, Dial) Penguin Publishing Group.

—Picnic! A Day in the Park. Holub, Joan. 2008. (Ant Hill Ser.). (ENG.). 24p. (J). (gr. -1-k). pap. 3.99 *(978-1-4169-5133-9(4))*, Simon Spotlight) Simon Spotlight.

—Scaredy-Pants! A Halloween Story. Holub, Joan. 2007. (Ant Hill Ser.). (ENG.). 24p. (J). (gr. -1-k). pap. 3.99 *(978-1-4169-0956-9(7))*, Simon Spotlight/Nickelodeon) Simon Spotlight/Nickelodeon.

—Senorita Gordita. Ketteman, Helen. 2012. (ENG.). 32p. (J). (gr. -1-2). 16.99 *(978-0-8075-7302-0(7))* Whitman, Albert & Co.

—Skeleton for Dinner. Cuyler, Margery. 2013. (ENG.). 32p. (J). (gr. -1-2). 16.99 *(978-0-8075-7398-3(1))* Whitman, Albert & Co.

—Snow Day! A Winter Tale. Holub, Joan. 2008. (Ant Hill Ser.). (ENG.). 24p. (J). (gr. -1-k). pap. 3.99 *(978-1-4169-5135-3(0))*, Simon Spotlight) Simon Spotlight.

—Spring Is Here! A Story about Seeds. Holub, Joan. 2008. (Ant Hill Ser.). (ENG.). 24p. (J). (gr. -1-k). lib. bdg. 13.89 *(978-1-4169-5132-2(6))*, Simon & Schuster/Paula Wiseman Bks.) Simon & Schuster/Paula Wiseman Bks.

—Spring Is Here! A Story about Seeds. Holub, Joan. 2008. (Ant Hill Ser.). (ENG.). 24p. (J). (gr. -1-k). pap. 3.99 *(978-1-4169-5131-5(8))*, Simon Spotlight) Simon Spotlight.

—There Once Was a Cowpoke Who Swallowed an Ant. Ketteman, Helen. 2014. (ENG.). 32p. (J). (gr. -1-2). 16.99 *(978-0-8075-7850-6(9))* Whitman, Albert & Co.

—The Three Bully Goats. Kimmelman, Leslie. 2012. (J). *(978-1-61913-136-1(6))* Weigl Pubs., Inc.

—The Three Bully Goats. Kimmelman, Leslie. 2011. (ENG.). 32p. (J). (gr. -1-3). 16.99 *(978-0-8075-7900-8(9))* Whitman, Albert & Co.

—The Three Little Gators. Ketteman, Helen. 2012. (J). 34.28 *(978-1-61913-140-8(4))* Weigl Pubs., Inc.

—The Three Little Gators. Ketteman, Helen. 2009. (ENG.). 32p. (J). (gr. -1-3). 16.99 *(978-0-8075-7824-7(X))* Whitman, Albert & Co.

—The Treasure of Ghostwood Gully: A Southwest Mystery. Vaughan, Marcia. 2004. (ENG.). 32p. (J). (gr. 1-3). 15.95 *(978-0-87358-858-4(4))* Cooper Square Publishing Llc.

Terzian, Alexandria M. The Kids Multicultural Art Book. Terzian, Alexandria M. 2007. (ENG.). 160p. (gr. 1-2). 16.99 *(978-0-8249-6807-6(7))*, Williamson Bks.) Ideals Pubns.

Teskey, Donald. The Táin: Ireland's Epic Adventure. Mac Uistin, Liam. 2012. (ENG.). 112p. (J). pap. 10.95 *(978-1-84717-288-4(1))* O'Brien Pr., Ltd., The IRL. Dist: Dufour Editions, Inc.

—Under the Hawthorn Tree. Conlon-McKenna, Marita. 2003. 160p. pap. 5.95 *(978-0-86278-206-1(6))* O'Brien Pr., Ltd., The IRL. Dist: Independent Pubs. Group.

Tessama, C. Eeny, Meeny, Miney, Moe, Four Alaskan Ravens. Johannes, Avril & Branham, Jan. 2003. 32p. (J). 7.95 *(978-0-9749360-0-0(6))* Icicle Falls Publishing Co.

Tessler, Beth Marie, photos by. Debbie's Eyes. Barry, Debra R. 2011. 32p. pap. 24.95 *(978-1-4560-5272-0(1))* America Star Bks.

Tessler, Daria. Young Henry & the Dragon. Kaufman, Jeanne. 2011. (J). *(978-1-934860-11-3(5))* Shenanigan Bks.

Testa, Fulvio. Aesop's Forgotten Fables. Waters, Fiona. 2014. (ENG.). 96p. (J). (gr. 2-4). 24.99 *(978-1-84939-706-3(6))* Andersen Pr. GBR. Dist: Independent Pubs. Group.

—Pinocchio (illustrated) Collodi, Carlo. Brock, Geoffrey, tr. from ITA. 2012. (ENG.). 184p. (J). (gr. k-4). 24.95 *(978-1-59017-588-0(3))*, NYR Children's Collection) New York Review of Bks., Inc., The.

Testa, Fulvio. Aesop's Fables. Testa, Fulvio. Waters, Fiona & Aesop Staff. 2015. (ENG.). 128p. (J). (gr. 2-4). pap. 16.99 *(978-1-84939-247-1(1))* Andersen Pr. GBR. Dist: Independent Pubs. Group.

—Aesop's Fables. Testa, Fulvio. Aesop Enterprise Inc. Staff. 2011. (ENG.). 128p. (J). (gr. 2-4). 24.99 *(978-1-84939-049-1(5))* Andersen Pr. GBR. Dist: Independent Pubs. Group.

Testar, Sue, jt. illus. see Francis, John.

Tettmar, Jacqueline. The Animals of Farthing Wood. Dann, Colin. ed. 2007. (ENG.). 320p. (J). (gr. 4-7). per. 12.99 *(978-1-4052-2552-6(1))* Egmont Bks., Ltd. GBR. Dist: Independent Pubs. Group.

Teves, Miles. The Dragon Hunter's Handbook. 2008. (J). *(978-1-4351-0204-0(5))* Metro Bks.

Texier, Jean. Alfie Green & the Bee-Bottle Gang. O'Brien, Joe. 2nd rev. ed. 2007. (Alfie Green Ser.). (ENG.). 80p. (J). pap. 10.95 *(978-1-84717-054-5(4))* O'Brien Pr., Ltd., The IRL. Dist: Dufour Editions, Inc.

—Alfie Green & the Conker King. O'Brien, Joe. 2012. (Alfie Green Ser.). (ENG.). 80p. (J). pap. 10.95 *(978-1-84717-283-9(0))* O'Brien Pr., Ltd., The IRL. Dist: Dufour Editions, Inc.

Tezuka, Osamu. Civil War, Vol. 8, Pt. 2. Tezuka, Osamu. 2006. (Phoenix Ser.). (ENG.). 208p. pap. 15.99 *(978-1-4215-0518-3(5))* Viz Media.

—Dawn. Tezuka, Osamu. 2003. (Phoenix Ser.: Vol. 1). (ENG.). 344p. pap. 15.95 *(978-1-56931-868-3(9))* Viz Media.

—Karma. Tezuka, Osamu. 2004. (Phoenix Ser.: Vol. 4). (ENG.). 368p. pap. 15.95 *(978-1-59116-300-8(5))* Viz Media.

—Nextworld. Tezuka, Osamu. 2003. (ENG.). Vol. 1. 168p. pap. 13.95 *(978-1-56971-866-7(0))*; Vol. 2. 152p. pap. 13.95 *(978-1-56971-867-4(9))* Dark Horse Comics.

—Resurrection. Tezuka, Osamu. 2004. (Phoenix Ser.). (ENG.). 200p. pap. 15.95 *(978-1-59116-593-4(8))* Viz Media.

—Yamato/Space, Vol. 3. Tezuka, Osamu. 2003. (Phoenix Ser.). (ENG.). 336p. pap. 15.95 *(978-1-59116-100-4(2))* Viz Media.

Thacker, Becky. The Chorus Kids' Memorial Day Parade. Thacker, Becky. 2006. (J). 10.95 *(978-0-9786276-1-4(X))* Mentzer Printing Ink.

Thalamus. Zebra-Striped Whale Alphabet Book. Donahue, Shari Faden. 2012. (ENG.). 32p. (J). 17.95 *(978-0-9634287-6-9(4))*; (gr. -1-k). pap. 7.95 *(978-0-9634287-7-6(2))* Arimax, Inc.

Thaler, Shmuel, photos by. Bread Comes to Life: A Garden of Wheat & a Loaf to Eat. Levenson, George. 2008. (ENG., 32p. (J). (gr. -1-2). pap. 7.99 *(978-1-58246-273-8(9))*, Tricycle Pr.) Ten Speed Pr.

—Piece = Part = Portion. Gifford, Scott. 2008. (SPA & ENG., 32p. (J). (gr. 1-4). pap. 7.99 *(978-1-58246-261-5(5))*, Tricycle Pr.) Ten Speed Pr.

—Piece = Part = Portion: Fractions = Decimals = Percents. Gifford, Scott. 2003. (ENG., 32p. (J). (gr. 1-4). 15.99 *(978-1-58246-102-1(3))*, Tricycle Pr.) Ten Speed Pr.

Thames, Bob. Hermy the Hermit Crab Goes Shrimping. 2007. 44p. (J). 16.99 *(978-0-933101-05-0(8))* Legacy Pubns.

Thammavongsa, Christine, jt. illus. see Disney Storybook Artists Staff.

Thapar, Bindia. The Magic Raindrop. Dharmarajan, Geeta. 2005. (J). *(978-81-89020-28-6(5))* Katha.

Tharlet, Eve. The Carnival. Luciani, Brigitte. 2014. 32p. (J). 6.95 *(978-1-4677-4204-7(X))*; (ENG.). lib. bdg. 25.26 *(978-1-4677-4203-0(1))*, Graphic Universe) Lerner Publishing Group.

Tharlet, Eve. A Child Is a Child. Weninger, Brigitte. 2004. (ENG.). 32p. (J). (gr. -1-k). 14.99 *(978-0-698-40006-1(2))*, Minedition) Penguin Publishing Group.

—Davy in the Middle. Weninger, Brigitte. 2008. (ENG.). 32p. (J). (gr. -1-3). 6.95 *(978-0-7358-2180-4(1))* North-South Bks., Inc.

—Davy Loves the Baby. Weninger, Brigitte. 2015. (ENG.). 32p. (J). 15.95 *(978-0-7358-4210-6(8))* North-South Bks., Inc.

—Davy, Soccer Star! Weninger, Brigitte. 2010. (ENG.). 40p. (J). (gr. -1-3). pap. 7.95 *(978-0-7358-2287-0(5))* North-South Bks., Inc.

—Happy Easter, Davy! Weninger, Brigitte. 2014. (ENG.). 32p. (J). (gr. k-3). 15.95 *(978-0-7358-4161-1(6))* North-South Bks., Inc.

—How Will We Get to the Beach? Luciani, Brigitte. 2003. (ENG.). 36p. (J). (gr. -1). pap. 7.95 *(978-0-7358-1783-8(9))* North-South Bks., Inc.

—A Hubbub. Luciani, Brigitte. Gauvin, Edward, tr. from FRE. 2010. (Mr. Badger & Mrs. Fox Ser.: 2). (ENG.). 32p. (J). (gr. k-3). pap. 6.95 *(978-0-7613-5632-5(0))*, Graphic Universe);Bk. 2. 25.26 *(978-0-7613-5626-4(6))* Lerner Publishing Group.

—Hugs & Kisses. Loupy, Christophe. 2005. (ENG.). 14p. (J). (gr. 1-18). bds. 6.95 *(978-0-7358-2019-7(8))* North-South Bks., Inc.

—Hugs & Kisses. Loupy, Christophe. James, J. Alison, tr. from GER. 2004. (ENG.). 36p. (J). pap. 6.95 *(978-0-7358-1972-6(6))* North-South Bks., Inc.

—The Meeting. Luciani, Brigitte. Burrell, Carol, tr. from FRE. 2010. (Mr. Badger & Mrs. Fox Ser.: 1). (ENG.). 32p. (J). (gr. k-3). pap. 6.95 *(978-0-7613-5631-8(2))*, Graphic Universe); lib. bdg. 25.26 *(978-0-7613-5625-7(8))* Lerner Publishing Group.

—Merry Christmas Davy. Weninger, Brigitte. 2014. (ENG.). 32p. (J). 15.95 *(978-0-7358-4186-4(1))* North-South Bks., Inc.

—Peace & Quiet. Luciani, Brigitte. Burrell, Carol, tr. 2012. (Mr. Badger & Mrs. Fox Ser.: 4). (ENG.). 32p. (J). (gr. k-3). pap. 6.95 *(978-0-8225-9163-4(4))*; lib. bdg. 25.26 *(978-0-7613-8520-2(7))* Lerner Publishing Group. (Graphic Universe).

—What a Team! Luciani, Brigitte. Gauvin, Edward, tr. from FRE. 2011. (Mr. Badger & Mrs. Fox Ser.: 3). (ENG.). 32p. (J). (gr. k-3). 25.26 *(978-0-7613-5627-1(4))*; pap. 6.95 *(978-0-7613-5633-2(9))*, Graphic Universe) Lerner Publishing Group.

Tharlet, Eve. Puppy Love: A Litter of Puppy Stories. Tharlet, Eve. Loupy, Christophe. 2010. (ENG.). 72p. (J). (gr. -1-3). 17.95 *(978-0-7358-2294-8(8))* North-South Bks., Inc.

Tharp, Jason. Funny Fill-In: My Animal Adventure. Musgrave, Ruth. 2013. (ENG.). 48p. (J). (gr. 3-7). pap. 4.99 *(978-1-4263-1355-4(1))*, National Geographic Children's Bks.) National Geographic Society.

—National Geographic Kids Funny Fill-In: My Pirate Adventure. Bowman, Bianca. 2014. (ENG.). 48p. (J). (gr. 3-7). pap. 4.99 *(978-1-4263-1480-3(9))*, National Geographic Children's Bks.) National Geographic Society.

Tharp, Lauren R. Scary Man. Barlow, C. E. 2009. 44p. pap. 18.99 *(978-1-4269-1060-9(6))* Trafford Publishing.

Tharp, Tricia. I Love You! Lee, Calee M. 2013. 32p. pap. 9.99 *(978-1-62395-471-0(1))* Xist Publishing.

Thayer, Elizabeth. The Trouble with Jeremy Chance. Harrar, George. 2007. (Historical Fiction for Young Readers Ser.). (ENG.). 168p. (J). (gr. 2-8). per. 6.95 *(978-1-57131-669-1(8))* Milkweed Editions.

Thayne, Tamira Ci. Puddles on the Floor. Estep, Lorena. 2008. 24p. 15.95 *(978-0-615-21952-3(7))* Crescent Renewal Resource.

The Artifact Group. Lost in Time. Banks, Steven. 2006. 22p. (J). lib. bdg. 15.00 *(978-1-4242-0977-4(3))* Fitzgerald Bks.

The Artist, Eleven. Spirit Comes to Earth: Fearless Love. The Artist, Eleven. 2007. 128p. lib. bdg. 9.95 *(978-0-9743540-3-3(1))* Peace Love Karma Publishing.

—Spirit Comes to Earth: Renewing Your Heart's Mission. The Artist, Eleven. 2005. 128p. (YA). lib. bdg. 19.95 *(978-0-9743540-2-6(3))* Peace Love Karma Publishing.

The Ciletti Publishing Group. Story Time Cafe Maisy's Blue Bath Set. The Ciletti Publishing Group. 2010. (J). 24.95 *(978-0-917665-71-4(6))* Ciletti Publishing Group, Inc., The.

The de Villiers Family Staff. The Long Shortcut. The de Villiers Family Staff. 2006. (Sprout Growing with God Ser.). (ENG.). 40p. (J). (gr. -1-2). 9.99 *(978-1-4000-7195-1(X))*, WaterBrook Pr.) Doubleday Religious Publishing Group, The.

The Mousekins Staff. Letters from Space. Knaus, Patricia. 2004. 112p. (J). (gr. 3-4). pap. 8.50 *(978-0-9758742-0-2(9))*, 10704) KnausWorks.

The Pope Twins. We Are Proud of You. Kim, YeShil. rev. ed. 2014. (MySELF Bookshelf: Social & Emotional Learning/Self-Worth Ser.). (ENG.). 32p. (J). (gr. k-2). pap. 11.94 *(978-1-60357-651-2(7))*; lib. bdg. 22.60 *(978-1-59953-642-2(0))* Norwood Hse. Pr.

The Storybook Art Group. The Uncanny X-Men: An Origin Story. Thomas, Rich. 2012. (Marvel Origins Ser.). 48p. (J). (gr. -1-4). lib. bdg. 24.21 *(978-1-61479-012-9(4))* Spotlight.

The, Tienny. An Instrument for Eddie. Lee, Karen. 2012. 30p. pap. 12.97 *(978-1-61204-302-9(X))*, Strategic Bk. Publishing) Strategic Book Publishing & Rights Agency (SBPRA).

The Toy Box. Pull the Lever: Who Are You? Wolfe, Jane. 2014. (ENG.). 8p. (J). (gr. -1-2). bds. 6.99 *(978-1-86147-391-2(5))*, Armadillo) Anness Publishing GBR. Dist: National Bk. Network.

Theisen, Patricia. A Magical Mystery Tour of hte Senses: What Does it Mean to be a Human? All about Your Body & You, 1 CD. Theisen, Patricia. l.t. ed. 2007. 160p. (YA). *(978-0-9793076-1-4(9))* Theisen, Patricia.

Thelan, Mary. Little Red Hen Makes Soup. Williams, Rozanne Lanczak. Hamaguchi, Carla, ed. 2003. (Sight Word Readers Ser.). 16p. (J). (gr. k-2). pap. 3.49 *(978-1-57471-969-7(6))*, 3591) Creative Teaching Pr., Inc.

Thelen, Mary. The Jazzy Alphabet. Shahan, Sherry. 2006. 30p. (J). (gr. k-4). reprint ed. 16.00 *(978-1-4223-5730-9(9))* DIANE Publishing Co.

—Postcards from Barney Bear. Williams, Rozanne Lanczak. Maio, Barbara & Faulkner, Stacey, eds. 2006. (Learn to Write Ser.). 8p. (J). pap. 3.49 *(978-1-59198-287-6(1))*, 6181) Creative Teaching Pr., Inc.

Themerson, Franciszka. The Table That Ran Away to the Woods. Themerson, Stefan. 2012. (ENG.). 20p. 10.95 *(978-1-84976-057-7(8))* Tate Publishing, Ltd. GBR. Dist: Abrams.

Theobald, Denise. Baby, the Poodle Cow Dog. Webb, Willyn. 2007. 32p. (J). 13.95 *(978-1-932738-40-7(1))* Western Reflections Publishing Co.

—Toliver in Time: For a Fourth of July Celebration. Hein, Connie L. 2003. 40p. (J). lib. bdg. 19.95 *(978-0-9740855-8-6(8))*; per. 12.95 *(978-0-9740855-9-3(6))* Still Water Publishing.

—Toliver in Time; for a Journey West: History in a Nutshell. Hein, Connie L. l.t. ed. 2005. 28p. (J). lib. bdg. 17.95 *(978-0-9740855-6-2(1))*; per. 9.95 *(978-0-9740855-7-9(X))* Still Water Publishing.

Theobald, Joseph. Collins Big Cat - When Arthur Wouldn't Sleep: Band 06/Orange. Theobald, Joseph. 2006. (Collins Big Cat Ser.). (ENG.). 24p. (J). pap. 6.99 *(978-0-00-718688-4(6))* HarperCollins Pubs. Ltd. GBR. Dist: Independent Pubs. Group.

—Marvin Wanted More! Theobald, Joseph. (ENG.). 32p. (J). (gr. -1-k). 2005. pap. 12.99 *(978-0-7475-6481-2(7))*; 2004. 16.99 *(978-0-7475-5631-2(8))* Bloomsbury Publishing Plc GBR. Dist: Independent Pubs. Group.

Theophilopoulos, Andrew. Junior & Bo's Trip to the Olympics. Panayotis. 2007. 104p. per. 10.95 *(978-1-934246-26-9(3))* Peppertree Pr., The.

Therian, Francis Patrick & Bruha, Victor. Tommy Too. Therian, Francis Patrick. 96p. (J). (gr. 4-6). pap. 5.99 *(978-0-9702944-0-1(9))* Pennywise Pubns., Inc.

Thermes, Jennifer. Bear & Bird. Skofield, James. 2014. (ENG.). 40p. (J). (gr. 1-3). 15.99 *(978-1-58536-835-8(0))*, 203012) Sleeping Bear Pr.

—Beginning Again: Immigrating to America. Kule, Elaine A. 2006. 40p. *(978-1-59137-473-2(1))* Options Publishing.

—Helen Keller's Best Friend Belle. Barry, Holly M. 2013. (ENG.). 32p. (J). (gr. -1-2). 16.99 *(978-0-8075-3198-3(7))* Whitman, Albert & Co.

—The Iciest, Diciest, Scariest Sled Ride Ever! Rule, Rebecca. 2012. (ENG.). 36p. (J). 17.95 *(978-1-934031-88-9(7))*, 7e0b5554-6142-497e-ae8f-c0cb24d9743a) Islandport Pr., Inc.

—Little Author in the Big Woods: A Biography of Laura Ingalls Wilder. McDonough, Yona Zeldis. 2014. (ENG.). 176p. (J). (gr. 3-7). 16.99 *(978-0-8050-9542-5(X))*, Holt, Henry & Co. Bks. For Young Readers) Holt, Henry & Co.

—Maggie & Oliver or a Bone of One's Own. Hobbs, Valerie. 2013. (ENG.). 208p. (J). (gr. 3-7). pap. 6.99 *(978-1-250-01672-0(X))* Square Fish.

—There Are No Moose on This Island, 1 vol. Calmenson, Stephanie. 2013. (ENG.). 32p. (J). 17.95 *(978-1-934031-34-6(8))*, a2b39bfc-ad16-4e21-bc2e-5db5168164a8) Islandport Pr., Inc.

Therrian, John. Why the Hyena Has Short Hind Legs. Kimani, Kamande. 2011. 40p. pap. 24.95 *(978-1-4560-5468-7(6))* America Star Bks.

Theurer, Heather. Thaddeus Macdonald III: Aka the Boss. 2011. (ENG.). 64p. (gr. -1). 16.95 *(978-0-9826137-8-8(4))*, Channel Kids) Channel Photographics.

Thibault, Dominique & Durual, Christophe. Family Favorites, 4 bks., Set. Grimm, Jacob et al. 2007. (Abbeville Classic Fairy Tales Ser.). (ENG.). 112p. (J). (gr. 1-2). 19.95 *(978-0-7892-0952-8(7))* Abbeville Pr., Inc.

Thibert, Art, jt. illus. see Finch, David.

Thibodeaux, Rebecca. Tenan & Colleen: I Don't Want to Go to Bed. Moffett, Elzater. 2010. 36p. 15.49 *(978-1-4490-6633-8(X))* AuthorHouse.

Thiebaux-Heikalo, Tamara. Apples & Butterflies: A Poem for Prince Edward Island, 1 vol. Grant, Shauntay. ed. 2013. (ENG.). 32p. (J). (gr. k-3). 19.95 *(978-1-55109-935-4(7))* Nimbus Publishing, Ltd. CAN. Dist: Orca Bk. Pubs. USA.

Thisdale, Francois. Bird Child. Forler, Nan. 2009. (ENG.). 32p. (J). (gr. k-3). 19.95 *(978-0-88776-894-1(6))*, Tundra Bks.) Tundra Bks. CAN. Dist: Penguin Random Hse., LLC.

—The Stamp Collector, 1 vol. Lanthier, Jennifer. 2015. (ENG.). 32p. (J). (gr. 3-6). 18.95 *(978-1-55455-218-4(4))* Fitzhenry & Whiteside, Ltd. CAN. Dist: Midpoint Trade Bks., Inc.

Thisdale, François. Nini. Thisdale, François. 2011. (ENG.). 40p. (J). (gr. -1-2). 15.95 *(978-1-77049-270-7(4))*, Tundra Bks.) Tundra Bks. CAN. Dist: Penguin Random Hse., LLC.

Thivierge, Claude. Platypus Creek. Giancamilli, Vanessa. 2005. (Soundprints' Amazing Animal Adventures! Ser.). (ENG.). 36p. (J). (gr. -1-2). 19.95 *(978-1-59249-355-5(6),* BC7109); (gr. -1-2). 2.95 *(978-1-59249-354-8(8),* S7159); (gr. -1-2). 9.95 *(978-1-59249-357-9(2),* PS7159); (gr. -1-2). 15.95 *(978-1-59249-352-4(1),* B7109); (gr. -1-2). pap. 6.95 *(978-1-59249-353-1(X),* S7109); (gr. 2-6). 8.95 *(978-1-59249-356-2(4),* SC7109) Soundprints.

Thoburn, Michelle. Tres Mures Caeci. Noe, David C. 2005. (LAT.). 48p. (J). (gr. k-12). 11.99 *(978-0-9714458-1-9(8))* Patrick Henry College Pr.

Tholen, Shane. Groovy Granny. Haynes, Cate. 2003. 32p. (J). pap. 13.50 *(978-1-86368-332-6(1))* Fremantle Pr. AUS. Dist: Independent Pubs. Group.

Thomas, B. K. Logs. Thomas, B. K. 2013. 36p. 24.95 *(978-1-4512-2170-1(3))* America Star Bks.

Thomas, Bill. Asking about Sex & Growing Up: A Question-and-Answer Book for Kids. Cole, Joanna. rev. ed. 2009. (ENG.). 96p. (J). (gr. 3-18). 15.99 *(978-0-06-142987-3(2),* Collins) HarperCollins Pubs.

—Asking about Sex & Growing Up: A Question & Answer Book for Kids. Cole, Joanna. rev. ed. 2009. (ENG.). 96p. (J). (gr. 3-18). pap. 6.99 *(978-0-06-142986-6(4),* Collins) HarperCollins Pubs.

—A Drama-Free Life. Scholastic, Inc. Staff. Bokram, Karen, ed. 2010. (ENG.). 128p. (J). (gr. 5-9). pap. 8.99 *(978-0-545-21493-3(9),* Scholastic Paperbacks) Scholastic, Inc.

—Girls' Life Guide to Being the Most Amazing You. Scholastic, Inc. Staff. Bokram, Karen, ed. 2010. (ENG.). 128p. (J). (gr. 5-9). pap. 8.99 *(978-0-545-21494-0(7),* Scholastic Paperbacks) Scholastic, Inc.

—Girls' Life Ultimate Guide to Surviving Middle School. Bokram, Karen, ed. 2010. (ENG.). 128p. (J). (gr. 3-7). pap. 8.99 *(978-0-545-20235-0(3),* Scholastic Paperbacks) Scholastic, Inc.

—Head-to-Toe Guide to You. Bokram, Karen, ed. 2010. (ENG.). 128p. (J). (gr. 5-9). pap. 8.99 *(978-0-545-20236-7(1),* Scholastic Paperbacks) Scholastic, Inc.

Thomas, Cassia. I Love My Baby Because... Simons, Paullina. 2015. (ENG.). 24p. (J). 17.99 *(978-0-00-810211-1(2),* HarperCollins Children's Bks.) HarperCollins Pubs. Ltd. GBR. Dist: HarperCollins Pubs.

—Lively Elizabeth! What Happens When You Push, 1 vol. Bergman, Mara. 2010. (ENG.). 32p. (J). (gr. -1-2). 16.99 *(978-0-8075-4702-1(6))* Whitman, Albert & Co.

Thomas, Chad. Tricky Coyote Tales. Schweizer, Chris. 2011. (Tricky Journeys Ser.: 1). (ENG.). (J). (gr. 2-4). pap. 39.62 *(978-0-7613-8625-4(4));*No. 1. 64p. pap. 6.95 *(978-0-7613-7859-4(6));*No. 1. 64p. lib. bdg. 27.93 *(978-0-7613-6601-0(6))* Lerner Publishing Group. (Graphic Universe).

—Tricky Monkey Tales. Schweizer, Chris. 2011. (Tricky Journeys Ser.: 6). (ENG.). (J). (gr. 2-4). pap. 39.62 *(978-0-7613-8630-8(0));* 64p. pap. 6.95 *(978-0-7613-7860-0(X));*No. 6. 64p. lib. bdg. 27.93 *(978-0-7613-6611-9(3))* Lerner Publishing Group. (Graphic Universe).

Thomas, Cristine. Can I Catch Cancer? Explaing cancer to Children. Thomas, Cristine. 2007. 44p. (J). 10.95 *(978-0-9778796-9-4(0))* Brittany's Bks.

Thomas, Cristine Leeann. I Can Too! Cancer Kids Can Too African American Series. Thomas, Cristine Leeann. 2006. (J). *(978-0-9778796-4-9(X))* Brittany's Bks.

Thomas, Dylan. Morus Yr Ystlum. Thomas-Christensen, Sheelagh. 2005. (Cyfres Llyfrau Llawen Ser.: Vol. 1). (WEL.). 36p. pap. *(978-0-86243-396-3(7))* Y Lolfa.

Thomas, Eric. Children's Illustrated Bible. Hastings, Selina. 3rd ed. 2004. (ENG.). 320p. (J). (gr. 5-12). 24.99 *(978-0-7566-0261-1(0))* Dorling Kindersley Publishing, Inc.

—The Children's Illustrated Jewish Bible. Brown, Laaren & Dorling Kindersley Publishing Staff. 2007. (ENG.). 192p. (J). (gr. k-3). 19.99 *(978-0-7566-2665-5(X))* Dorling Kindersley Publishing, Inc.

—Delivering Your Mail: A Book about Mail Carriers, 1 vol. Owen, Ann. 2003. (Community Workers Ser.). (ENG.). 24p. (gr. -1-3). per. 7.95 *(978-1-4048-0485-2(4),* Nonfiction Picture Bks.) Picture Window Bks.

—Helping You Heal: A Book about Nurses. Wohlrabe, Sarah C. 2003. (Community Workers Ser.). (ENG.). 24p. (gr. -1-3). 25.99 *(978-1-4048-0086-1(7));* per. 7.95 *(978-1-4048-0480-7(3))* Picture Window Bks. (Nonfiction Picture Bks.).

—Helping You Learn: A Book about Teachers, 1 vol. Wohlrabe, Sarah C. 2003. (Community Workers Ser.). (ENG.). 24p. (gr. -1-3). per. 7.95 *(978-1-4048-0478-4(1),* Nonfiction Picture Bks.) Picture Window Bks.

—Keeping You Healthy: A Book about Doctors. Owen, Ann. 2003. (Community Workers Ser.). (ENG.). 24p. (gr. -1-3). 25.99 *(978-1-4048-0085-4(9),* Nonfiction Picture Bks.) Picture Window Bks.

—Keeping You Healthy: A Book about Doctors, 1 vol. Owen, Ann & Picture Window Books Staff. 2003. (Community Workers Ser.). (ENG.). 24p. (gr. -1-3). per. 7.95 *(978-1-4048-0479-1(X),* Nonfiction Picture Bks.) Picture Window Bks.

—Keeping You Safe: A Book about Police Officers, 1 vol. Owen, Ann. 2003. (Community Workers Ser.). (ENG.). 24p. (gr. -1-3). per. 7.95 *(978-1-4048-0483-8(8),* Nonfiction Picture Bks.) Picture Window Bks.

—Protecting Your Home: A Book about Firefighters, 1 vol. Owen, Ann. 2003. (Community Workers Ser.). (ENG.). 24p. (gr. -1-3). per. 7.95 *(978-1-4048-0482-1(X),* Nonfiction Picture Bks.) Picture Window Bks.

—Taking You Places: A Book about Bus Drivers, 1 vol. Owen, Ann. 2003. (Community Workers Ser.). (ENG.). 24p. (gr. -1-3). per. 7.95 *(978-1-4048-0484-5(6),* Nonfiction Picture Bks.) Picture Window Bks.

Thomas, Erika & Treg, Mccoy. Petey Yikes! A very, very true story about a homeless little blue bird in New York City. 2006. (J). *(978-0-9789642-0-7(9))* Petey, Rock & Roo Children's Pubns.

Thomas, Franselica, jt. illus. see Isabel, Michelle.

Thomas, Glenn. Flights & Chimes & Mysterious Times. Trevayne, Emma. 2014. (ENG.). 320p. (J). (gr. 3-7). 16.99 *(978-1-4424-9877-8(3),* Simon & Schuster Bks. For Young Readers) Simon & Schuster Bks. For Young Readers.

Thomas, Jacqui. The Bible from Beginning to End. Williams, Derek. 2004. 60p. (gr. 4-7). 11.00 *(978-0-687-07605-5(6))* Abingdon Pr.

—If You'd Been There in Bible Times. Jeffs, Stephanie. 2004. 64p. 14.00 *(978-0-687-01507-8(3))* Abingdon Pr.

—Jenny: Coming to Terms with the Death of a Sibling. Jeffs, Stephanie. 2006. 29p. (J). (gr. -1-3). 14.00 *(978-0-687-49709-6(4))* Abingdon Pr.

—What's What in the Bible. Williams, Derek. 2004. 32p. bds. 11.00 *(978-0-687-02654-8(7))* Abingdon Pr.

Thomas, James. The Adventures of Mr. Feeny & Cinnamon. Kesecker, Jennifer. 2012. 20p. pap. 24.95 *(978-1-4626-8858-6(6))* America Star Bks.

—God Loves Me! Traywick-Jones, Andrea. 2003. 24p. (J). *(978-1-55306-459-6(3),* Guardian Bks.) Essence Publishing.

Thomas, Jan. Let's Count Goats! Fox, Mem. 2010. (ENG.). 40p. (J). (gr. -1-1). 16.99 *(978-1-4424-0598-1(8),* Beach Lane Bks.) Beach Lane Bks.

Thomas, Jan. Can You Make a Scary Face? Thomas, Jan. 2009. (ENG.). 40p. (J). (gr. -1-3). 15.99 *(978-1-4169-8581-5(6),* Beach Lane Bks.) Beach Lane Bks.

—The Easter Bunny's Assistant. Thomas, Jan. 2012. (ENG.). 40p. (J). (gr. -1-3). 12.99 *(978-0-06-169286-4(7))* HarperCollins Pubs.

—Here Comes the Big, Mean Dust Bunny! Thomas, Jan. 2009. (ENG.). 40p. (J). (gr. -1-3). 14.99 *(978-1-4169-9150-2(6),* Beach Lane Bks.) Beach Lane Bks.

—Is Everyone Ready for Fun? Thomas, Jan. 2011. (ENG.). 40p. (J). (gr. -1-3). 14.99 *(978-1-4424-2364-0(1),* Beach Lane Bks.) Beach Lane Bks.

—Let's Sing a Lullaby with the Brave Cowboy. Thomas, Jan. 2012. (ENG.). 40p. (J). (gr. -1-3). 12.99 *(978-1-4424-4276-4(X),* Beach Lane Bks.) Beach Lane Bks.

—Pumpkin Trouble. Thomas, Jan. 2011. (ENG.). 40p. (J). (gr. -1-3). 9.99 *(978-0-06-169284-0(0))* HarperCollins Pubs.

—Rhyming Dust Bunnies. Thomas, Jan. 2009. (ENG.). 40p. (J). (gr. -1-3). 14.99 *(978-1-4169-7976-0(X),* Beach Lane Bks.) Beach Lane Bks.

Thomas, Jean, et al. The Magical Scarecrows Special RSPCA Edition: For the Magical Scarecrows Let's Make Magic program with the RSPCA's Million Paws Walk ~ 2010. Altuney, Aldwyn, photos by. Lynn, Auntie. 2010. (ENG.). 108p. pap. 12.95 *(978-1-4495-3647-3(6))* CreateSpace Independent Publishing Platform.

Thomas, John, Jr., jt. illus. see Thomas, Wes.

Thomas, Keith A. Cross-Lengua Coloring Book for Kids. Thomas, Keith A. I.t. ed. 2004. (ENG & SPA.). 22p. (J). (gr. 3-18). pap. *(978-0-9617451-2-7(6))* KALEXT Productions, LLC.

—The Idioms. Thomas, Keith A. (ENG & SPA.). 44p. (J). (gr. 3-18). pap. *(978-0-9617451-4-1(2))* KALEXT Productions, LLC.

Thomas, Laura. Berry Best Friends Journal. Ackelsberg, Amy. 2014. (Strawberry Shortcake Ser.). (ENG.). 112p. (J). (gr. -1-k). 7.99 *(978-0-448-48421-1(8),* Grosset & Dunlap) Penguin Publishing Group.

—The Berry Bitty Princess Pageant. Matheis, Mickie. 2013. (Strawberry Shortcake Ser.). (ENG.). 32p. (J). (gr. -1-k). 16.99 *(978-0-448-46691-0(0),* Grosset & Dunlap) Penguin Publishing Group.

—A Berry Lucky St. Patrick's Day. Matheis, Mickie. 2015. (Strawberry Shortcake Ser.). (ENG.). 24p. (J). (gr. -1-k). 4.99 *(978-0-448-48420-4(X),* Grosset & Dunlap) Penguin Publishing Group.

Thomas, Laura. Berryella & Prince Berry Charming. Matheis, Mickie. 2015. (Strawberry Shortcake Ser.). (ENG.). 24p. (J). (gr. -1-k). 4.99 ***(978-0-448-48706-9(3),*** Grosset & Dunlap) Penguin Publishing Group.

Thomas, Laura. Camp Berry. Matheis, Mickie. 2014. (Strawberry Shortcake Ser.). (ENG.). 32p. (J). (gr. 1-3). pap. 3.99 *(978-0-448-48153-1(7),* Warne, Frederick Pubs.) Penguin Bks., Ltd. GBR. Dist: Penguin Publishing Group.

—A Day at the Apple Orchard. Ackelsberg, Amy. 2013. (Strawberry Shortcake Ser.). (ENG.). 24p. (J). (gr. -1-k). 4.99 *(978-0-448-46752-8(6),* Grosset & Dunlap) Penguin Publishing Group.

—Easter Surprise. Ackelsberg, Amy. 2011. (Strawberry Shortcake Ser.). (ENG.). 24p. (J). (gr. -1-k). mass mkt. 4.99 *(978-0-448-45547-1(1),* Grosset & Dunlap) Penguin Publishing Group.

—Gymnastics Fun. Matheis, Mickie. 2014. (Strawberry Shortcake Ser.). (ENG.). 24p. (J). (gr. -1-k). 4.99 *(978-0-448-46750-4(X),* Grosset & Dunlap) Penguin Publishing Group.

—Love, Raggedy Ann. Pinehurst, Bonnie. 2008. (Raggedy Ann & Me! Ser.). (ENG.). 14p. (J). (gr. -1-k). 7.99 *(978-1-4169-5947-2(5),* Little Simon) Little Simon.

—Makeover Madness. Brooke, Samantha. 2011. (Strawberry Shortcake Ser.). (ENG.). 24p. (J). (gr. -1-k). pap. 4.99 *(978-0-448-45720-8(2),* Grosset & Dunlap) Penguin Publishing Group.

—Merry Christmas, Strawberry Shortcake! Matheis, Mickie. 2014. (Strawberry Shortcake Ser.). (ENG.). 32p. (J). (gr. -1-k). 16.99 *(978-0-448-48212-5(6),* Grosset & Dunlap) Penguin Publishing Group.

—A Picnic Adventure. Gallo, Lisa. 2010. (Strawberry Shortcake Ser.). (ENG.). 32p. (J). (gr. 1-3). mass mkt. 3.99 *(978-0-448-45345-3(2),* Grosset & Dunlap) Penguin Publishing Group.

—Raggedy Ann's Beach Bag. Heller, Alyson. 2009. (Raggedy Ann & Me! Ser.). (ENG.). 10p. (J). (gr. -1-k). 5.99 *(978-1-4169-5546-7(1),* Little Simon) Little Simon.

—The Snow Dance. Ackelsberg, Amy. 2010. (Strawberry Shortcake Ser.). (ENG.). 24p. (J). (gr. -1-k). 4.99 *(978-0-448-45404-7(1),* Grosset & Dunlap) Penguin Publishing Group.

—Strawberry Shortcake's Easter Egg Hunt. Unknown. 2014. (Strawberry Shortcake Ser.). (ENG.). 16p. (J). (gr. -1-k). 6.99 *(978-0-448-48016-9(6),* Grosset & Dunlap) Penguin Publishing Group.

—Welcome to Berry Bitty City. 2009. (Strawberry Shortcake Ser.). (ENG.). 16p. (J). (gr. -1-k). pap. 5.99 *(978-0-448-45254-8(5),* Grosset & Dunlap) Penguin Publishing Group.

Thomas, Leanne & Schiebold, Olivia. Puppylicious. 2010. 96p. (J). ***(978-0-545-26020-6(5))*** Scholastic, Inc.

Thomas, LeSean. Out of the Shadows. David, Peter. 2007. (Teenage Mutant Ninja Turtles Ser.). (ENG.). 96p. pap. 12.95 *(978-1-84576-146-2(4))* Titan Bks. Ltd. GBR. Dist: Random Hse., Inc.

Thomas, Lillie Michelle. When the Carnival Comes to Town. Q., Bev. 2009. 28p. pap. 24.95 *(978-1-60749-682-3(8))* America Star Bks.

Thomas, Marc, jt. illus. see Elder, Jennifer.

Thomas, Meredith. Girl Pirates. Kettle, Shey. 2005. (Girlz Rock! Ser.). (J). pap. *(978-1-59336-701-5(5))* Mondo Publishing.

—Surf Girls. Kettle, Shey. 2005. (Girlz Rock! Ser.). (J). pap. *(978-1-59336-708-4(2))* Mondo Publishing.

Thomas, Michael. The Church Fathers for Young People, , Grube, George. 2007. (ENG.). 35p. (J). pap. 7.95 *(978-1-933654-07-2(4))* Light & Life Publishing Co.

Thomas, Michael Lee. A Father for Me. James-Carde, Genice. 2011. 20p. pap. 24.95 *(978-1-4560-3951-6(2))* America Star Bks.

Thomas, Middy. Gooney Bird & All Her Charms. Lowry, Lois. (Gooney Bird Greene Ser.). (ENG.). 160p. (J). (gr. 1-4). 2015. pap. 5.99 *(978-0-544-45596-2(7),* HMH Books For Young Readers); 2014. 16.99 *(978-0-544-11354-1(3))* Houghton Mifflin Harcourt Publishing Co.

—Gooney Bird & the Room Mother. Lowry, Lois. 2006. (Gooney Bird Ser.: No. 2). (ENG.). 80p. (J). (gr. 3-7). 5.99 *(978-0-440-42133-7(0),* Yearling) Random Hse. Children's Bks.

—Gooney Bird Is So Absurd. Lowry, Lois. (Gooney Bird Greene Ser.). (ENG.). 112p. (J). (gr. 1-4). 2013. pap. 5.99 *(978-0-547-87559-0(2));* 2009. 15.99 *(978-0-547-11967-0(4))* Houghton Mifflin Harcourt Publishing Co.

—Gooney Bird on the Map. Lowry, Lois. (Gooney Bird Greene Ser.). (ENG.). 128p. (J). (gr. 1-4). 2013. pap. 5.99 *(978-0-547-85088-7(3));* 2011. 16.99 *(978-0-547-55622-2(5))* Houghton Mifflin Harcourt Publishing Co.

Thomas, Pamela L. Do I Have to Go to Church Today? Rome, Jacqueline Thomas. 2010. 36p. pap. 14.95 *(978-0-9841899-6-0(3))* PearlStone Publishing, Inc.

Thomas, Richard A. Lucky & Me. Lamuth, Nancy. 2012. 20p. pap. 24.95 *(978-1-4626-0665-8(2))* America Star Bks.

Thomas, Robyn. The Cricket Winter. Holman, Felice. 2006. 91p. (J). (gr. 3-7). 15.00 *(978-0-8028-5289-2(0),* Eerdmans Bks For Young Readers) Eerdmans, William B. Publishing Co.

Thomas, Sonya. Today I Got Saved. 1 book. Magee, Kanika A. M. 2003. 20p. (J). 10.00 net. *(978-0-9748834-0-3(9))* Ebenezer A.M.E. Church.

—Where Is God at Midnight?? Magee, Kanika. 2003. (J). 10.00 net. *(978-0-9748834-1-0(7))* Ebenezer A.M.E. Church.

Thomas, Tamara. ABC Poem Book. Thomas, Tamara. 2004. (YA). (gr. 1-6). pap. *(978-1-930200-28-9(5))* Martell Publishing Co.

Thomas, Tim. Do You Know Where Sea Turtles Go? Lowery, Paul. 2005. (J). lib. bdg. 15.99 *(978-0-9771059-9-1(7))* Thomas Expressions, LLC.

—Fruitman. 2007. 32p. (J). *(978-0-9790487-0-8(2))* J & K Publishing.

—What Happened to Willie? Dixon, Virginia. 2007. 32p. (J). 16.00 *(978-0-9795386-0-5(2))* Grand Productions.

Thomas, Tina & Witter, Rahad. The Night Before Christmas. Moore, Clement C. 2013. 32p. (gr. -1 — 1). pap. 15.00 *(978-0-615-80497-2(7))* Colleton County Memorial Library.

Thomas, Titus V. Everybody Eats Lunch. Azima, Cricket. 2008. (ENG.). 16p. (J). (gr. -1-3). 16.00 *(978-0-9793384-4-1(1))* Glitterati, Inc.

Thomas, Tria M., photos by. The Artful Journey: The Artwork of Andy Thomas. Thomas, Dina M. & Thomas, Andy, eds. I.t. ed. 2003. 122p. 50.00 *(978-0-9742285-0-1(8))* Maze Creek Studio.

Thomas, Wes. Choose to Reuse. Bullard, Lisa. 2011. (Planet Protectors Ser.). pap. 39.62 *(978-0-7613-8651-3(3));* (ENG.). 24p. pap. 6.95 *(978-0-7613-8511-0(8))* Lerner Publishing Group. (Millbrook Pr.).

—Go Easy on Energy. Bullard, Lisa. 2011. (Planet Protectors Ser.). pap. 39.62 *(978-0-7613-8653-7(X));* (ENG.). 24p. pap. 6.95 *(978-0-7613-8513-4(4))* Lerner Publishing Group. (Millbrook Pr.).

—Phil & His Fabulous Feathers, 1 vol. Blazek, Frank. 2005. (ENG.). 32p. (J). (gr. k-3). 16.99 *(978-1-58980-280-3(2))* Pelican Publishing Co., Inc.

—Power up to Fight Pollution. Bullard, Lisa. 2011. (Planet Protectors Ser.). pap. 39.62 *(978-0-7613-8655-1(6),* Millbrook Pr.); (ENG.). 24p. lib. bdg. 23.93 *(978-0-7613-6108-4(1))* Lerner Publishing Group.

—Rally for Recycling. Bullard, Lisa. 2011. (Planet Protectors Ser.). pap. 39.62 *(978-0-7613-8656-8(4),* Millbrook Pr.); (ENG.). 24p. pap. 6.95 *(978-0-7613-8516-5(9),* Millbrook Pr.); (ENG.). 24p. lib. bdg. 23.93 *(978-0-7613-6103-9(0))* Lerner Publishing Group.

Thomas, Wes. Down the Crawfish Hole, 1 vol. Thomas, Wes. 2004. (ENG.). 32p. (J). (gr. k-3). 16.99 *(978-1-58980-163-9(6))* Pelican Publishing Co., Inc.

Thomas, Wes & Thomas, John, Jr. Choose to Reuse. Bullard, Lisa. 2011. (Cloverleaf Books (tm) — Planet Protectors Ser.). (ENG.). 24p. (gr. k-2). lib. bdg. 23.93 *(978-0-7613-6104-6(9))* Lerner Publishing Group.

—Go Easy on Energy. Bullard, Lisa. 2011. (Cloverleaf Books (tm) — Planet Protectors Ser.). (ENG.). 24p. (gr. k-2). lib. bdg. 23.93 *(978-0-7613-6107-7(3))* Lerner Publishing Group.

—Power up to Fight Pollution. Bullard, Lisa. 2011. (Cloverleaf Books (tm) — Planet Protectors Ser.). (ENG.). 24p. (gr. k-2). pap. 6.95 *(978-0-7613-8515-8(0),* Millbrook Pr.) Lerner Publishing Group.

Thomasma, Lanin. Billy's Family. Thomasma, Eric. 2011. (ENG.). 26p. pap. 10.99 *(978-1-4635-1260-6(0))* CreateSpace Independent Publishing Platform.

Thomassen, Hellen. The Featherless Chicken. Nunez, Marisa. 2003. 32p. (J). 14.95 *(978-84-95730-36-7(7))* Kalandraka Catalunya, Edicions, S.L. ESP. Dist: Independent Pubs. Group.

Thomburgh, Rebecca. Alphabet. Connelly, Neil O. 10p. (J). (gr. -1). bds. 3.95 *(978-1-58989-004-6(3))* Thurman Hse., LLC.

—Colors. Connelly, Neil O. 10p. (J). (gr. -1). bds. 3.95 *(978-1-58989-003-9(5))* Thurman Hse., LLC.

—Numbers. Connelly, Neil O. (Cuddly Beasties Ser.). 10p. (J). (gr. -1). bds. 3.95 *(978-1-58989-001-5(9))* Thurman Hse., LLC.

—Shapes. Connelly, Neil O. 10p. (J). (gr. -1). bds. 3.95 *(978-1-58989-002-2(7))* Thurman Hse., LLC.

Thompson, Angie. We Like to Read: A Picture Book for Pre-Readers & Parents. April, Elyse. 2008. (We Like To Ser.). 32p. (J). (gr. 3-7). pap. 9.95 *(978-1-890772-80-2(1))* Hohm Pr.

Thompson, Betsy, jt. illus. see Johnson, Betsy.

Thompson, Brian. The Dyerville Tales. Kozlowsky, M. P. 2014. (ENG.). 336p. (J). (gr. 3-7). 16.99 *(978-0-06-199871-3(0),* Walden Pond Pr.) HarperCollins Pubs.

Thompson Brothers Staff. My Little People Farm (Mi Pequena Granja) Tomaselli, Doris. ed. 2003. (Lift-The-Flap Ser.). (ENG & SPA.). 5p. (J). (gr. -1-k). bds. 8.99 *(978-0-7944-0213-6(5))* Reader's Digest Assn., Inc., The.

Thompson Brothers Studio Staff. Estrellita. Willson, Sarah & Thompson Bros. 2003. (Dora la Exploradora Ser.).Tr. of Little Star. (SPA.). 24p. (J). pap. 3.99 *(978-0-689-86307-3(1),* Libros Para Ninos) Libros Para Ninos.

Thompson, Bryon & Kulihin, Vic. US Culture Through Infographics. Higgins, Nadia. 2014. (Super Social Studies Infographics Ser.). (ENG.). 32p. (gr. 3-5). lib. bdg. 26.60 *(978-1-4677-3464-6(0),* Lerner Pubns.) Lerner Publishing Group.

Thompson, Carol. Hold My Hand: Five Stories of Love & Family. Zolotow, Charlotte. 2003. (ENG.). 64p. (gr. -1-k). 19.99 *(978-0-7868-0518-1(8))* Hyperion Pr.

—Molly & Her Dad. Ormerod, Jan. 2008. 32p. *(978-1-921272-55-4(4))* Little Hare Bks. AUS. Dist: HarperCollins Pubs. Australia.

—My Turtle & Me. Bernstein, Owen. 2012. (ENG.). 10p. (J). (— 1). bds. 9.99 *(978-0-545-43387-7(8))* Scholastic, Inc.

—Thunder-Boomer! Crum, Shutta. 2009. (ENG.). 40p. (J). (gr. -1-3). 17.99 *(978-0-618-61865-1(1))* Houghton Mifflin Harcourt Publishing Co.

—Winners Never Quit! Hamm, Mia. 2006. (ENG.). 32p. (J). (gr. -1-2). pap. 6.99 *(978-0-06-074052-8(3))* HarperCollins Pubs.

Thompson, Carol. Climb! Thompson, Carol. 2013. (Little Movers Ser.). (ENG.). 12p. (J). bds. *(978-1-84643-617-8(6))* Child's Play International Ltd.

—Crawl! Thompson, Carol. 2013. (Little Movers Ser.). (ENG.). 12p. (J). bds. *(978-1-84643-614-7(1))* Child's Play International Ltd.

—Daddy, Papa, & Me. Thompson, Carol. Newman, Lesléa. 2009. (ENG.). 20p. (J). (gr. -1 — 1). bds. 7.99 *(978-1-58246-262-2(3),* Tricycle Pr.) Ten Speed Pr.

—I Like You the Best. Thompson, Carol. 2011. (ENG.). 32p. (J). (gr. -1-1). 16.95 *(978-0-8234-2341-5(7))* Holiday Hse., Inc.

—Jump! Thompson, Carol. 2013. (Little Movers Ser.). (ENG.). 12p. (J). bds. *(978-1-84643-615-4(X))* Child's Play International Ltd.

—Mommy, Mama, & Me. Thompson, Carol. Newman, Lesléa. 2009. (ENG.). 20p. (J). (gr. -1-2). bds. 7.99 *(978-1-58246-263-9(1),* Tricycle Pr.) Ten Speed Pr.

—Run! Thompson, Carol. 2013. (Little Movers Ser.). (ENG.). 12p. (J). bds. *(978-1-84643-616-1(8))* Child's Play International Ltd.

Thompson, Chad. Brave Fire Truck, 1 vol. Crow, Melinda Melton. 2011. (Wonder Wheels Ser.). (ENG.). 32p. (gr. -1-1). pap. 6.25 *(978-1-4342-3384-4(7));* lib. bdg. 21.32 *(978-1-4342-3029-4(5))* Stone Arch Bks.

—Bully Bill. Birky, Joy. 2007. 40p. (J). (gr. 3-7). per. 12.99 *(978-0-8361-9382-4(2))* Herald Pr.

—Busy, Busy Train, 1 vol. Crow, Melinda Melton. 2011. (Wonder Wheels Ser.). (ENG.). 32p. (gr. -1-1). pap. 6.25 *(978-1-4342-3383-7(9));* lib. bdg. 21.32 *(978-1-4342-3028-7(7))* Stone Arch Bks.

—Field Trip for School Bus, 1 vol. Crow, Melinda Melton. 2012. (Wonder Wheels Ser.). (ENG.). 32p. (gr. -1-1). pap. 6.25 *(978-1-4342-4237-2(4));* lib. bdg. 21.32 *(978-1-4342-4019-4(3))* Stone Arch Bks.

—Gluten-Free Me Beckman Goes to School. Bykowski, Christy. 2013. 24p. pap. 11.95 *(978-1-61244-228-0(5))* Halo Publishing International.

—Helpful Tractor, 1 vol. Crow, Melinda Melton. 2011. (Wonder Wheels Ser.). (ENG.). 32p. (gr. -1-1). pap. 6.25 *(978-1-4342-3382-0(0));* lib. bdg. 21.32 *(978-1-4342-3027-0(9))* Stone Arch Bks.

—Let's Paint the Garage!, 1 vol. Crow, Melinda Melton. 2012. (Wonder Wheels Ser.). (ENG.). 32p. (gr. -1-1). pap. 6.25 *(978-1-4342-4238-9(2));* lib. bdg. 21.32 *(978-1-4342-4016-3(9))* Stone Arch Bks.

—Let's Volunteer. Houghton, Jill Zierels. 2013. 28p. pap. 10.95 *(978-1-61244-211-2(0))* Halo Publishing International.

—The Long Train Ride, 1 vol. Crow, Melinda Melton. 2012. (Wonder Wheels Ser.). (ENG.). 32p. (gr. -1-1). pap. 6.25 *(978-1-4342-4239-6(0));* lib. bdg. 21.32 *(978-1-4342-4018-7(5))* Stone Arch Bks.

—Lucky School Bus, 1 vol. Crow, Melinda Melton. 2011. (Wonder Wheels Ser.). (ENG.). 32p. (gr. -1-1). pap. 6.25

T

(978-1-4342-3381-3(2)); lib. bdg. 21.32 *(978-1-4342-3026-3(0))* Stone Arch Bks.
—Milo Finds His Best Friend. Umina, Lisa. 2013. 30p. 15.95 *(978-1-61244-182-5(3))* Halo Publishing International.
—Truck Parade, 1 vol. Crow, Melinda Melton. 2012. (Wonder Wheels Ser.). (ENG.). 32p. (gr. -1-1). pap. 6.25 *(978-1-4342-4240-2(4))*; lib. bdg. 21.32 *(978-1-4342-4017-0(7))* Stone Arch Bks.
Thompson, Colin. The Amazing Illustrated Floodsopedia. Thompson, Colin. 2013. (Floods Ser.). (ENG.). 96p. (J). (gr. 4-7). pap. 16.99 *(978-1-74275-104-7(0))* Random Hse. Australia AUS. Dist: Independent Pubs. Group.
—Barry. Thompson, Colin. (ENG.). 32p. (J). (gr. k-4). 2013. pap. 9.99 *(978-1-86471-884-3(6))*; 2012. 16.99 *(978-1-86471-883-6(8))* Random Hse. Australia AUS. Dist: Independent Pubs. Group.
—Better Homes & Gardens. Thompson, Colin. 2009. (Floods Ser.: 8). (ENG.). 208p. (J). (gr. 3-7). pap. 9.99 *(978-1-74166-255-9(9))* Random Hse. Australia AUS. Dist: Independent Pubs. Group.
—The Big Little Book of Happy Sadness. Thompson, Colin. 2008. (ENG.). 32p. (J). (gr. -1-3). 10.99 *(978-1-933605-90-6(1))* Kane Miller.
—Camelot. Thompson, Colin. 2011. (Dragons Ser.: 1). (ENG.). 234p. (J). (gr. 4-7). 9.99 *(978-1-74166-381-5(4))* Random Hse. Australia AUS. Dist: Independent Pubs. Group.
—Castles. Thompson, Colin. 2007. (ENG.). 32p. (J). (gr. k-2). pap. 14.99 *(978-0-09-943942-4(5)*, Red Fox) Random House Children's Books GBR. Dist: Independent Pubs. Group.
—Disasterchef. Thompson, Colin. 2012. (Floods Ser.: 11). (ENG.). 204p. (J). (gr. 4-7). 12.99 *(978-1-86471-947-5(8))* Random Hse. Australia AUS. Dist: Independent Pubs. Group.
—Excalibur. Thompson, Colin. 2011. (Dragons Ser.: 2). (ENG.). 256p. (J). (gr. 4-7). 9.99 *(978-1-74166-382-2(2))* Random Hse. Australia AUS. Dist: Independent Pubs. Group.
—The Floods Family Files. Thompson, Colin. 2012. (Floods Ser.: 1). (ENG.). 32p. (J). (gr. 4-7). pap. 10.99 *(978-1-86471-942-0(7))* Random Hse. Australia AUS. Dist: Independent Pubs. Group.
—Free to a Good Home. Thompson, Colin. 2012. (ENG.). 32p. (J). (gr. k-2). pap. 9.99 *(978-1-74166-319-8(9))* Random Hse. Australia AUS. Dist: Independent Pubs. Group.
—Home & Away. Thompson, Colin. 2006. (Floods Ser.: 3). (ENG.). 240p. (J). (gr. 3-7). 9.99 *(978-1-74166-032-6(7))* Random Hse. Australia AUS. Dist: Independent Pubs. Group.
—The Last Alchemist. Thompson, Colin. 2003. 30p. (J). (gr. k-3). reprint ed. 17.00 *(978-0-7567-6164-6(6))* DIANE Publishing Co.
—Pictures of Home. Thompson, Colin. 2011. (ENG.). 32p. (J). (gr. -1-k). pap. 15.99 *(978-1-74275-090-3(7))* Random Hse. Australia AUS. Dist: Independent Pubs. Group.
—Playschool. Thompson, Colin. 2006. (Floods Ser.: 2). (ENG.). 224p. (Orig.). (J). (gr. 3-7). 10.99 *(978-1-74166-026-5(2))* Random Hse. Australia AUS. Dist: Independent Pubs. Group.
—Ruby. Thompson, Colin. ed. 2011. (ENG.). 32p. (J). (gr. k-2). pap. 14.99 *(978-1-74275-089-7(3))* Random Hse. Australia AUS. Dist: Independent Pubs. Group.
—Survivor. Thompson, Colin. 2007. (Floods Ser.: 4). (ENG.). 224p. (J). (gr. 3-7). pap. 9.99 *(978-1-74166-129-3(3))* Random Hse. Australia AUS. Dist: Independent Pubs. Group.
—Top Gear. Thompson, Colin. 2008. (Floods Ser.: 7). (ENG.). 208p. (J). (gr. 3-7). pap. 9.99 *(978-1-74166-254-2(0))* Random Hse. Australia AUS. Dist: Independent Pubs. Group.
—Who Wants to Be a Billionaire? Thompson, Colin. 2012. (Floods Ser.: 9). (ENG.). 208p. (J). (gr. 4-7). 10.99 *(978-1-86471-945-1(1))* Random Hse. Australia AUS. Dist: Independent Pubs. Group.
Thompson, Colin W. Was There Really a Gunfight at the O. K. Corral? And Other Questions about the Wild West. Kerns, Ann. 2011. (Is That a Fact? Ser.). (ENG.). 40p. (gr. 4-6). lib. bdg. 26.60 *(978-0-7613-6100-8(6))* Lerner Publishing Group.
Thompson, Del, et al. Tony Salerno's Good News Express. Salerno, Tony et al. 64p. (Orig.). (J). (gr. k-6). pap. *(978-1-881597-00-1(8))* Magination.
Thompson, Egil. Uncle Amel & the Swamp Witch, 1 vol. Lane, Alison Hoffman. 2009. (Uncle Amel Ser.). (ENG.). 32p. (J). (gr. k-3). 16.99 *(978-1-58980-644-3(1))* Pelican Publishing Co., Inc.
Thompson, Elizabeth. Thrill in The 'Ville. Trollinger, Patsi B. 2012. 128p. (J). pap. 6.99 *(978-0-9836106-1-8(4))* Benjamin Pr.
Thompson, George. Vlad the Drac. Jungman, Ann. 2006. (Vlad the Drac Ser.). 124p. (J). (gr. 2-4). per. 6.95 *(978-1-903015-22-3(7))* Barn Owl Bks, London GBR. Dist: Independent Pubs. Group.
—Vlad the Drac Superstar. Jungman, Ann. 2006. (Vlad the Drac Ser.). 122p. (J). (gr. 2-4). pap. 6.95 *(978-1-903015-45-2(6))* Barn Owl Bks, London GBR. Dist: Independent Pubs. Group.
Thompson, Ian, jt. illus. see Moores, Ian.
Thompson, Janet M., jt. illus. see Thompson, Michelle Gormican.
Thompson, Jeffrey. Cesar Chavez: Champion & Voice of Farmworkers. Slade, Suzanne. 2007. (Biographies Ser.). (ENG.). 24p. (gr. k-3). lib. bdg. 25.99 *(978-1-4048-3724-9(8)*, Nonfiction Picture Bks.) Picture Window Bks.
—A Day at the Fire Station. Mortensen, Lori. 2010. (First Graphics: My Community Ser.). (ENG.). 24p. (gr. 1-2). pap. 6.29 *(978-1-4296-5612-2(3))*; pap. 35.70 *(978-1-4296-5613-9(1))* Capstone Pr., Inc.
—Going to the Dentist, 1 vol. Mortensen, Lori. 2010. (First Graphics: My Community Ser.). (ENG.). 24p. (gr. 1-2). 23.32 *(978-1-4296-4507-2(5))*; pap. 35.70 *(978-1-4296-5611-5(5))* Capstone Pr., Inc.
—Thomas Edison: Inventor, Scientist, & Genius, 1 vol. Mortensen, Lori & Picture Window Books Staff. 2007. (Biographies Ser.). (ENG.). 24p. (gr. k-3). 25.99 *(978-1-4048-3105-6(3)*, Nonfiction Picture Bks.) Picture Window Bks.
—Transportation in the City, 1 vol. Tourville, Amanda Doering. 2011. (First Graphics: My Community Ser.). (ENG.). 24p. (gr. 1-2). lib. bdg. 23.32 *(978-1-4296-5370-1(1))* Capstone Pr., Inc.
—Transportation in the City, 1 vol. Doering Tourville, Amanda. 2011. (First Graphics: My Community Ser.). (ENG.). 24p. (gr. 1-2). pap. 6.29 *(978-1-4296-6233-8(6))*; pap. 35.70 *(978-1-4296-6403-5(7))* Capstone Pr., Inc.
—A Visit to the Library, 1 vol. Wohlrabe, Sarah C. 2011. (First Graphics: My Community Ser.). (ENG.). 24p. (gr. 1-2). lib. bdg. 23.32 *(978-1-4296-5371-8(X))*; pap. 6.29 *(978-1-4296-6234-5(4))*; pap. 35.70 *(978-1-4296-6404-2(5))* Capstone Pr., Inc.
—A Visit to the Police Station, 1 vol. Doering Tourville, Amanda. 2011. (First Graphics: My Community Ser.). (ENG.). 24p. (gr. 1-2). lib. bdg. 23.32 *(978-1-4296-5369-5(8))*; pap. 6.29 *(978-1-4296-6235-2(2))*; pap. 35.70 *(978-1-4296-6402-8(9))* Capstone Pr., Inc.
—A Visit to the Vet, 1 vol. Mortensen, Lori. 2010. (First Graphics: My Community Ser.). (ENG.). 24p. (gr. 1-2). 23.32 *(978-1-4296-4509-6(1))*; pap. 6.29 *(978-1-4296-5614-6(X))* Capstone Pr., Inc.
—Working on the Farm, 1 vol. Mortensen, Lori. 2010. (First Graphics: My Community Ser.). (ENG.). 24p. (gr. 1-2). 23.32 *(978-1-4296-4510-2(5))*; pap. 6.29 *(978-1-4296-5616-0(6))*; pap. 35.70 *(978-1-4296-5617-7(4))* Capstone Pr., Inc.
Thompson, Jenean. All in a Day's Play. Thompson, Jenean. l.t. ed. 2005. 40p. (J). 14.95 *(978-1-59879-066-5(8))* Lifevest Publishing, Inc.
Thompson, Jessica. Alvin the Proud Prankster. Burt, Vickie. 2011. 24p. pap. 13.99 *(978-1-937129-10-1(1))* Faithful Life Pubs.
Thompson, Jill. Classics Illustrated #6: the Scarlet Letter. Hawthorne, Nathaniel. 2009. (Classics Illustrated Graphic Novels Ser.: 6). (ENG.). 56p. (J). (gr. 3-9). 9.95 *(978-1-59707-162-8(5))* Papercutz.
Thompson, Jill, et al. Terror Trips. Stine, R. L. 2007. (Goosebumps Graphix Ser.: 2). (ENG.). 144p. (J). (gr. 3-7). pap. 9.99 *(978-0-439-85780-2(5)*, Graphix) Scholastic, Inc.
Thompson, Jill. Magic Trixie. Thompson, Jill. 2008. (ENG.). 96p. (J). (gr. 3-7). pap. 8.99 *(978-0-06-117045-4(3))* HarperCollins Pubs.
—Magic Trixie & the Dragon. Thompson, Jill. 2009. (ENG.). 96p. (J). (gr. 3-7). pap. 7.99 *(978-0-06-117050-8(X))* HarperCollins Pubs.
Thompson, John. Hattie on Her Way. Clark, Clara Gillow. 2005. (ENG.). 208p. (J). (gr. 5-18). 15.99 *(978-0-7636-2286-2(9))* Candlewick Pr.
—Prairie Train. Chall, Marsha Wilson. 2003. 40p. (J). (gr. -1-3). 16.89 *(978-0-688-13434-1(3))* HarperCollins Pubs.
Thompson, Josephine. Big Book of Science Things to Make & Do. Gilpin, Rebecca & Pratt, Leonie. 2008. (Big Book of Science Things to Make & Do Ser.). 95p. (J). (gr. 1). pap. 14.99 *(978-0-7945-1923-0(7)*, Usborne) EDC Publishing.
Thompson, Josephine & Day, Caroline. Big Drawing Book. Watt, Fiona. ed. 2013. (Doodle Bks). 95p. (J). pap. 11.99 *(978-0-7945-3365-6(5)*, Usborne) EDC Publishing.
Thompson, Josephine Et Al. Knights & Castles Things to Make & Do. Pratt, Leonie. 2006. 32p. (J). pap. 6.99 *(978-0-7945-1355-9(7)*, Usborne) EDC Publishing.
Thompson, Karin. The Night the Moon Went Out. Lord, Pia. 2011. 28p. pap. 24.95 *(978-1-4626-0010-6(7))* America Star Bks.
Thompson, Keith. Behemoth. Westerfeld, Scott. (Leviathan Trilogy Ser.). (ENG.). (YA). (gr. 7). 2011. 512p. pap. 11.99 *(978-1-4169-7176-4(9))*; 2010. 496p. 18.99 *(978-1-4169-7175-7(0))* Simon Pulse. (Simon Pulse).
—Behemoth. Westerfeld, Scott. l.t. ed. 2010. (Leviathan Trilogy: Bk. 2). (ENG.). 540p. 23.99 *(978-1-4104-3066-3(9))* Thorndike Pr.
—Darkwing. Oppel, Kenneth. 2007. (Silverwing Ser.: 1). 432p. (J). (gr. 5-9). 17.99 *(978-0-06-085054-8(X))* HarperCollins Pubs.
—Goliath. Westerfeld, Scott. (Leviathan Trilogy Ser.). (ENG.). (YA). (gr. 7). 2012. 576p. pap. 9.99 *(978-1-4169-7178-8(5))*; 2011. 560p. 19.99 *(978-1-4169-7177-1(7))* Simon Pulse. (Simon Pulse).
—Leviathan. Westerfeld, Scott. (Leviathan Trilogy Ser.). (ENG.). (YA). (gr. 7-18). 2010. 464p. pap. 9.99 *(978-1-4169-7174-0(2))*; 2009. 448p. 19.99 *(978-1-4169-7173-3(4))* Simon Pulse. (Simon Pulse).
—Leviathan: Leviathan; Behemoth; Goliath. Westerfeld, Scott. ed. 2012. (Leviathan Trilogy Ser.). (ENG.). 1552p. (YA). (gr. 7). pap. 29.99 *(978-1-4424-8377-4(6)*, Simon Pulse) Simon Pulse.
—The Manual of Aeronautics: An Illustrated Guide to the Leviathan Series. Westerfeld, Scott. 2012. (ENG.). 64p. (YA). (gr. 7). 19.99 *(978-1-4169-7179-5(3)*, Simon Pulse) Simon Pulse.
—Witherwood Reform School. Skye, Obert. 2015. (Witherwood Reform School Ser.: 1). (ENG.). 240p. (J). (gr. 4-7). 16.99 *(978-0-8050-9879-2(8)*, Holt, Henry & Co. Bks. For Young Readers) Holt, Henry & Co.
Thompson, Kim. Farm Animals. Regan, Lisa. 2010. (I Love Animals Ser.). (ENG.). 24p. (J). (gr. 1-5). pap. 8.15 *(978-1-61533-233-5(2))*; lib. bdg. 22.60 *(978-1-61533-227-4(8))* Windmill Bks.
Thompson, Kristi June. Molly, the Good Furry Friend. Thompson, Holly Sue. 2011. 36p. pap. 14.75 *(978-1-60911-431-2(0)*, Eloquent Bks.) Strategic Book Publishing & Rights Agency (SBPRA).
Thompson, Lisa. New York City, 1 vol. Thompson, Lisa. 2006. (Read-It! Chapter Books: SWAT Ser.). (ENG.). 80p. (gr. 2-4). 21.32 *(978-1-4048-1670-1(4)*, Chapter Readers) Picture Window Bks.
Thompson, Lydia. Welby the Worm Who Lost His Wiggle. Hunter, Lee Hargus. 2004. 32p. (J). (gr. -1-1). *(978-1-930093-04-1(7))* Brookfield Reader, Inc., The.
Thompson, Margot. Biomimicry: Inventions Inspired by Nature. Lee, Dora & Palmer, Dora. 2011. (ENG.). 40p. (J). 18.95 *(978-1-55453-467-8(4))* Kids Can Pr., Ltd. CAN. Dist: Univ. of Toronto Pr.
—Planet Ark: Preserving Earth's Biodiversity. Mason, Adrienne. 2013. (CitizenKid Ser.). (ENG.). 32p. (J). 18.95 *(978-1-55453-753-2(3))* Kids Can Pr., Ltd. CAN. Dist: Univ. of Toronto Pr.
—Sea Monsters: A Canadian Museum of Nature Book. Cumbaa, Stephen. 2007. (ENG.). 40p. (J). (gr. 2-5). 7.95 *(978-1-55337-560-9(2))* Kids Can Pr., Ltd. CAN. Dist: Univ. of Toronto Pr.
—Tree of Life: The Incredible Biodiversity of Life on Earth. Strauss, Rochelle. (CitizenKid Ser.). (ENG.). 40p. (J). 2013. pap. 12.95 *(978-1-55453-961-1(7))*; 2004. (gr. 3-18). 18.95 *(978-1-55337-669-9(2))* Kids Can Pr., Ltd. CAN. Dist: Univ. of Toronto Pr.
Thompson, Maria. Exploring the Native Plant World: A Life Science Curriculum, 5th-6th Grade: Adaptations in the Native Plant World. Russell, Margaret. 2004. 63p. (J). (gr. 5-6). per. 14.95 *(978-1-57168-851-4(X)*, Eakin Pr.) Eakin Pr.
Thompson, Michael. Los Otros Osos, 1 vol. Thompson, Michael. 2013. (SPA.). 32p. (J). pap. 6.99 *(978-1-59572-664-3(0))* Star Bright Bks., Inc.
—Los Otros Osos / the Other Bears. Thompson, Michael. 2013. (ENG & SPA.). (J). 16.99 *(978-1-59572-644-5(6))* Star Bright Bks., Inc.
—The Other Bears, 1 vol. Thompson, Michael. 2013.Tr. of Os Outros Ursos. (ENG.). 32p. (J). 16.99 *(978-1-59572-638-4(1))*; pap. 6.99 *(978-1-59572-639-1(X))* Star Bright Bks., Inc.
Thompson, Michelle Gormican & Thompson, Janet M. Wyatt Walker Turbo Talker. Hierl, Christine Gormican. 2004. 28p. *(978-0-9760680-0-6(1))* Cedar Shamrock Publishing.
Thompson, Mike. Chicken Boy & the Wrath of Dr. Dimwad. Thompson, Mike. 2008. 102p. (J). per. 9.95 *(978-0-9799216-0-5(0))* Thompson Original Productions LLC.
Thompson, Richard. Science, Fresh Squeezed! Shields, Carol Diggory. 2003. (ENG.). 64p. (J). (gr. -1-7). 14.95 *(978-1-59354-005-0(1)*, Handprint Bks.) Chronicle Bks. LLC.
Thompson, Samantha. Photographing Greatness: The Story of Karsh. Goodall, Lian. 2007. (Stories of Canada Ser.: 11). (ENG.). 96p. (J). 21.99 *(978-1-894917-34-6(0)*, Napoleon & Co.) Dundurn CAN. Dist: Ingram Pub. Services.
—Sailing for Glory: The Story of Captain Angus Walters & the Bluenose. Janveau, Teri-Lynn & Thompson, Allister. 2006. (Stories of Canada Ser.: 10). (ENG.). 72p. (J). 18.95 *(978-1-894917-09-4(X)*, Napoleon & Co.) Dundurn CAN. Dist: Ingram Pub. Services.
Thompson, Scott M. Color. Lilly, Melinda. 2003. 24p. (J). 22.79 *(978-1-58952-646-4(5))* Rourke Educational Media.
—Dirty & Clean. Lilly, Melinda. 2003. 24p. (J). 22.79 *(978-1-58952-636-5(8))* Rourke Educational Media.
—Gravity. Lilly, Melinda. 2003. (Read & Do Science Ser.). 24p. (J). 22.79 *(978-1-58952-642-6(2))* Rourke Educational Media.
—Make It Grow. Lilly, Melinda. 2003. (Rourke Discovery Library). 24p. (J). 22.79 *(978-1-58952-637-2(6))* Rourke Educational Media.
—Solid, Liquid, & Gas. Lilly, Melinda. 2003. 24p. (J). 20.64 *(978-1-58952-648-8(1))* Rourke Educational Media.
—Sound up & Down. Lilly, Melinda. 2003. 24p. (J). 20.64 *(978-1-58952-644-0(9))* Rourke Educational Media.
Thompson, Scott M., photos by. Energy. Lilly, Melinda. 2005. (Rourke Discovery Library). 24p. (J). (gr. 1-4). lib. bdg. 22.79 *(978-1-59515-401-9(9)*, 1244272) Rourke Educational Media.
—Rocks. Lilly, Melinda. 2005. (Rourke Discovery Library). 24p. (J). (gr. 1-4). lib. bdg. 14.95 *(978-1-59515-404-0(3)*, 1244275) Rourke Educational Media.
—Sun & Moon. Lilly, Melinda. 2005. (Rourke Discovery Library). 24p. (J). (gr. 1-4). lib. bdg. 14.95 *(978-1-59515-405-7(1)*, 1244276) Rourke Educational Media.
Thompson, Sharon. Horse Mad. Wolfer, Dianne. 2005. 62p. (Orig.). (J). 10.95 *(978-1-920731-47-2(4))* Fremantle Pr. AUS. Dist: Independent Pubs. Group.
—The Judas Donkey. Broome, Errol. 2003. 144p. pap. 13.50 *(978-1-920731-18-2(0))* Fremantle Pr. AUS. Dist: Independent Pubs. Group.
—Rainbow Jackets. Forrestal, Elaine. 2003. 64p. (YA). pap. 11.95 *(978-1-920731-67-0(9))* Fremantle Pr. AUS. Dist: Independent Pubs. Group.
—What a Goat! Broome, Errol. 2004. (Annick Chapter Bks.). (ENG.). 72p. (J). (gr. 2-4). 16.95 *(978-1-55037-869-6(4)*, 9781550378696); pap. 4.95 *(978-1-55037-868-9(6)*, 9781550378689) Annick Pr., Ltd. CAN. Dist: Firefly Bks., Ltd.
Thompson, Sunnie R. What's So Great about Silent E? The Thoughts of Sunnie Rae. Thompson, Deanna T. 2010. 28p. pap. 13.99 *(978-1-4490-9274-0(8))* AuthorHouse.
Thoms, Scott. Friction, 1 vol. Niz, Ellen S. 2006. (Our Physical World Ser.). (ENG.). 24p. (gr. 1-2). 24.65 *(978-0-7368-5402-3(9)*, First Facts) Capstone Pr., Inc.
Thomson, Andrew. Who Is Derek Jeter? Herman, Gail. 2015. (Who Was...? Ser.). (ENG.). 112p. (J). (gr. 3-7). 5.99 ***(978-0-448-48697-0(0)***, Grosset & Dunlap) Penguin Publishing Group.
—Who Is Malala Yousafzai? Anastasio, Dina & Brown, Dinah. 2015. (Who Was...? Ser.). (ENG.). 112p. (J). (gr. 3-7). 5.99 ***(978-0-448-48937-7(6)***, Grosset & Dunlap) Penguin Publishing Group.
Thomson, Andrew & Harrison, Nancy. Who Was Genghis Khan? Medina, Nico. 2014. (Who Was...? Ser.). (ENG.). 112p. (J). (gr. 3-7). pap. 4.99 *(978-0-448-48260-6(6)*, Grosset & Dunlap) Penguin Publishing Group.
Thomson, Andrew & Harrison, Nancy. Who Was Woodrow Wilson? Frith, Margaret. 2015. (Who Was...? Ser.). (ENG.). 112p. (J). (gr. 3-7). 5.99 ***(978-0-448-48428-0(5)***, Grosset & Dunlap) Penguin Publishing Group.
Thomson, Bill. Baseball Hour, 0 vols. Nevius, Carol. 2008. (ENG.). 32p. (J). (gr. -1-3). lib. bdg. 16.99 *(978-0-7614-5380-2(6)*, 9780761453802, Amazon Children's Publishing) Amazon Publishing.
—Building with Dad, 0 vols. Nevius, Carol. 2012. (ENG.). 32p. (J). (gr. k-3). pap. 7.99 *(978-0-7614-5984-2(7)*, 9780761459842, Amazon Children's Publishing) Amazon Publishing.
—Karate Hour, 0 vols. Nevius, Carol. 2011. (ENG.). 32p. (J). (gr. -1-2). pap. 7.99 *(978-0-7614-5840-1(9)*, 9780761458401, Amazon Children's Publishing) Amazon Publishing.
—Karate Hour, 0 vols. Nevius, Carol & Nevius, Thomson. 2004. (ENG.). 32p. (J). (gr. -1-2). 14.95 *(978-0-7614-5169-3(2)*, 9780761451693, Amazon Children's Publishing) Amazon Publishing.
—Soccer Hour, 0 vols. Nevius, Carol. 2011. (ENG.). 32p. (J). (gr. -1-3). 16.99 *(978-0-7614-5689-6(9)*, 9780761456896, Amazon Children's Publishing) Amazon Publishing.
Thomson, Bill. Chalk, 0 vols. Thomson, Bill. 2010. (ENG.). 40p. (J). (gr. -1-3). 15.99 *(978-0-7614-5526-4(4)*, 9780761455264, Amazon Children's Publishing) Amazon Publishing.
—Fossil, 0 vols. Thomson, Bill. 2013. (ENG.). 40p. (J). (gr. k-3). 17.99 *(978-1-4778-4700-8(6)*, 9781477847008, Amazon Children's Publishing) Amazon Publishing.
Thomson, E. Gertrude, jt. illus. see Tenniel, John.
Thomson, E. Gertrude, jt. illus. see Tenniel, Sir John.
Thomson, Emma. A Birthday Ball. Thomson, Emma. 2013. (Princess Pearl Ser.). (ENG.). 24p. (J). (gr. -1-2). 8.99 *(978-1-4449-0587-8(2))* Hodder & Stoughton GBR. Dist: Independent Pubs. Group.
—A Fashion Fairytale. Thomson, Emma. 2013. (Princess Pearl Ser.). (ENG.). 24p. (J). (gr. -1-2). 8.99 *(978-1-4449-0585-4(6))* Hodder & Stoughton GBR. Dist: Independent Pubs. Group.
—A Friend to Treasure. Thomson, Emma. 2013. (Princess Pearl Ser.). (ENG.). 24p. (J). (gr. -1-2). 8.99 *(978-1-4449-0584-7(8))* Hodder & Stoughton GBR. Dist: Independent Pubs. Group.
—Princess Pearl & the Underwater Kingdom. Thomson, Emma. 2012. (Princess Pearl Ser.). (ENG.). 28p. (J). (gr. -1-2). 19.99 *(978-0-340-98849-7(5))* Hodder & Stoughton GBR. Dist: Independent Pubs. Group.
—A Royal Ballet. Thomson, Emma. 2013. (Princess Pearl Ser.). (ENG.). 24p. (J). (gr. -1-2). 8.99 *(978-1-4449-0586-1(4))* Hodder & Stoughton GBR. Dist: Independent Pubs. Group.
Thomson, Regan. The Boy in Number Four. Kootstra, Kara. 2014. (ENG.). 32p. (J). (gr. -1-k). 16.99 *(978-0-8037-4167-6(7)*, Dial) Penguin Publishing Group.
Thomson, Tracy. Ahmek. Watson, Patrick. 2011. (ENG.). 168p. pap. 12.95 *(978-1-55278-417-4(7))* McArthur & Co. CAN. Dist: National Bk. Network.
Thongmoon, Kriangsak, jt. illus. see Montgomery, R. A.
Thongmoon, Kriangsak, jt. illus. see Sundaravej, Sittisan.
Thoraval, Carly & Buchanan, Jessie. The Mystical Noise, 1 vol. Belanger, Madeleine. 2010. 40p. 24.95 *(978-1-4512-9062-2(4))* PublishAmerica, Inc.
Thornborrow, Nick. Brain Quest Workbook: Grade 6. Walker, Persephone. 2015. (ENG.). 320p. (J). (gr. 6-7). pap. 12.95 *(978-0-7611-8243-6(8))* Workman Publishing Co., Inc.
Thornburgh, Rebecca. Cuenta con Pablo: Math Matters en Espanol. DeRubertis, Barbara. 2005. 32p. pap. 5.95 *(978-1-57565-151-4(3))* Kane Pr., Inc.
—Frosty the Snowman Sticker Book. Rollins, Jack & Nelson, Steve. 2012. 24p. (J). 5.99 *(978-0-8249-5646-2(X)*, Ideals Children's Bks.) Ideals Pubns.
—Hanukkah. Trueit, Trudi Strain. 2013. (Holidays & Celebrations Ser.). (ENG.). 32p. (J). (gr. k-3). 27.07 *(978-1-62323-511-6(1)*, 206281) Child's World, Inc., The.
—My "a" Sound Box. Moncure, Jane Belk. 2009. (Sound Box Bks.). (ENG.). 32p. (J). (gr. -1-2). 25.64 *(978-1-60253-141-3(2)*, 200822) Child's World, Inc., The.
—My "b" Sound Box. Moncure, Jane Belk. 2009. (Sound Box Bks.). (ENG.). 32p. (J). (gr. -1-2). 25.64 *(978-1-60253-142-0(0)*, 200823) Child's World, Inc., The.
—My "c" Sound Box. Moncure, Jane Belk. 2009. (Sound Box Bks.). (ENG.). 32p. (J). (gr. -1-2). 25.64 *(978-1-60253-143-7(9)*, 200824) Child's World, Inc., The.
—My "d" Sound Box. Moncure, Jane Belk. 2009. (Sound Box Bks.). (ENG.). 32p. (J). (gr. -1-2). 25.64 *(978-1-60253-144-4(7)*, 200825) Child's World, Inc., The.
—My 'e' Sound Box. Moncure, Jane Belk. 2009. (Sound Box Bks.). (ENG.). 32p. (J). (gr. -1-2). 25.64 *(978-1-60253-145-1(5)*, 200826) Child's World, Inc., The.
—My "f" Sound Box. Moncure, Jane Belk. 2009. (Sound Box Bks.). (ENG.). 32p. (J). (gr. -1-2). 25.64 *(978-1-60253-146-8(3)*, 200827) Child's World, Inc., The.
—My 'g' Sound Box. Moncure, Jane Belk. 2009. (Sound Box Bks.). (ENG.). 32p. (J). (gr. -1-2). 25.64 *(978-1-60253-147-5(1)*, 200828) Child's World, Inc., The.
—My 'h' Sound Box. Moncure, Jane Belk. 2009. (Sound Box Bks.). (ENG.). 32p. (J). (gr. -1-2). 25.64 *(978-1-60253-148-2(X)*, 200829) Child's World, Inc., The.
—My "i" Sound Box. Moncure, Jane Belk. 2009. (Sound Box Bks.). (ENG.). 32p. (J). (gr. -1-2). 25.64 *(978-1-60253-149-9(8)*, 200830) Child's World, Inc., The.
—My "j" Sound Box. Moncure, Jane Belk. 2009. (Sound Box Bks.). (ENG.). 32p. (J). (gr. -1-2). 25.64 *(978-1-60253-150-5(1)*, 200831) Child's World, Inc., The.
—My "k" Sound Box. Moncure, Jane Belk. 2009. (Sound Box Bks.). (ENG.). 32p. (J). (gr. -1-2). 25.64 *(978-1-60253-151-2(X)*, 200832) Child's World, Inc., The.
—My "l" Sound Box. Moncure, Jane Belk. 2009. (Sound Box Bks.). (ENG.). 32p. (J). (gr. -1-2). 25.64 *(978-1-60253-152-9(8)*, 200833) Child's World, Inc., The.
—My 'm' Sound Box. Moncure, Jane Belk. 2009. (Sound Box Bks.). (ENG.). 32p. (J). (gr. -1-2). 25.64 *(978-1-60253-153-6(6)*, 200834) Child's World, Inc., The.

—My "n" Sound Box. Moncure, Jane Belk. 2009. (Sound Box Bks.). (ENG.). 32p. (J). (gr. -1-2). 25.64 *(978-1-60253-154-3(4),* 200835) Child's World, Inc., The.
—My 'o' Sound Box. Moncure, Jane Belk. 2009. (Sound Box Bks.). (ENG.). 32p. (J). (gr. -1-2). 25.64 *(978-1-60253-155-0(2),* 200836) Child's World, Inc., The.
—My 'p' Sound Box. Moncure, Jane Belk. 2009. (Sound Box Bks.). (ENG.). 32p. (J). (gr. -1-2). 25.64 *(978-1-60253-156-7(0),* 200837) Child's World, Inc., The.
—My 'q' Sound Box. Moncure, Jane Belk. 2009. (Sound Box Bks.). (ENG.). 32p. (J). (gr. -1-2). 25.64 *(978-1-60253-157-4(9),* 200838) Child's World, Inc., The.
—My "r" Sound Box. Moncure, Jane Belk. 2009. (Sound Box Bks.). (ENG.). 32p. (J). (gr. -1-2). 25.64 *(978-1-60253-158-1(7),* 200839) Child's World, Inc., The.
—My 's' Sound Box. Moncure, Jane Belk. 2009. (Sound Box Bks.). (ENG.). 32p. (J). (gr. -1-2). 25.64 *(978-1-60253-159-8(5),* 200840) Child's World, Inc., The.
—My 't' Sound Box. Moncure, Jane Belk. 2009. (Sound Box Bks.). (ENG.). 32p. (J). (gr. -1-2). 25.64 *(978-1-60253-160-4(9),* 200841) Child's World, Inc., The.
—My "u" Sound Box. Moncure, Jane Belk. 2009. (Sound Box Bks.). (ENG.). 32p. (J). (gr. -1-2). 25.64 *(978-1-60253-161-1(7),* 200842) Child's World, Inc., The.
—My 'v' Sound Box. Moncure, Jane Belk. 2009. (Sound Box Bks.). (ENG.). 32p. (J). (gr. -1-2). 25.64 *(978-1-60253-162-8(5),* 200843) Child's World, Inc., The.
—My "w" Sound Box. Moncure, Jane Belk. 2009. (Sound Box Bks.). (ENG.). 32p. (J). (gr. -1-2). 25.64 *(978-1-60253-163-5(3),* 200844) Child's World, Inc., The.
—My "xyz" Sound Box. Moncure, Jane Belk. 2009. (Sound Box Bks.). (ENG.). 32p. (J). (gr. -1-2). 25.64 *(978-1-60253-164-2(1),* 200845) Child's World, Inc., The.
—Peter Cottontaol's Easter Egg Hunt. Ritchie, Joseph R. 2006. (ENG.). 26p. (J). (gr. -1-k). 12.95 *(978-0-8249-6653-9(8),* Candy Cane Pr.) Ideals Pubns.
—Picture Book & Library Lessons. Hopkins, Jackie Mims. 2004. 32p. (gr. -1-2). 16.95 *(978-1-932146-27-1(X),* K67-39703, Upstart Bks.) Highsmith Inc.
—El problema de 100 Libras: Math Matters en Espanol. Dussling, Jennifer. 2005. 32p. (J). pap. 5.95 *(978-1-57565-154-5(8))* Kane Pr., Inc.
—Rufus & Ryan Celebrate Easter! Bostrom, Kathleen Long. 2014. (Rufus & Ryan Ser.). 20p. (J). bds. 7.99 *(978-0-8249-1919-1(X),* Candy Cane Pr.) Ideals Pubns.
—The Story of Adam & Eve. Pingry, Patricia A. 2003. (ENG.). 24p. (J). bds. 6.95 *(978-0-8249-4229-8(9))* Ideals Pubns.
—The Story of Christmas. Pingry, Patricia A. 2012. 24p. (J). pap. 4.99 *(978-0-8249-5645-5(1),* Ideals Children's Bks.) Ideals Pubns.
—The Story of Jesus. Pingry, Patricia A. 2008. (ENG.). 32p. (J). (gr. -1-3). pap. 3.95 *(978-0-8249-5545-8(5))* Ideals Pubns.
Thornburgh, Rebecca, jt. illus. see Thornburgh, Rebecca McKillip.
Thornburgh, Rebecca McKillip. The Blast off Kid! Driscoll, Laura. 2003. (Math Matters Ser.). 32p. (J). pap. 5.95 *(978-1-57565-130-9(0))* Kane Pr., Inc.
—El Chico del Despegue. Driscoll, Laura. Ramirez, Alma, tr. from ENG. 2009. (Math Matters en Espanol Ser.). (SPA.). 32p. (J). (gr. k-2). pap. 5.95 *(978-1-57565-267-2(6))* Kane Pr., Inc.
—Frosty the Snowman. Rollins, Jack & Nelson, Steve. 2003. (ENG.). 24p. (J). bds. 6.95 *(978-0-8249-6500-6(0))* Ideals Pubns.
—The Little Land. Stevenson, Robert Louis. 2011. (Poetry for Children Ser.). (ENG.). 24p. (J). (gr. k-3). 27.07 *(978-1-60973-153-3(0),* 201184) Child's World, Inc., The.
—Peter Cottontail's Easter Egg Hunt. Ritchie, Joseph R. (J). 2012. 14p. bds. 6.99 *(978-0-8249-1880-4(0),* Candy Cane Pr.); 2004. (ENG.). 12p. (gr. -1-k). bds. 9.95 *(978-0-8249-6522-8(1))* Ideals Pubns.
—Rufus & Ryan Give Thanks. 2014. (Rufus & Ryan Ser.). 20p. (J). bds. 7.99 *(978-0-8249-1936-8(X),* Candy Cane Pr.) Ideals Pubns.
—The Shelf Elf. Hopkins, Jackie Mims. 2004. (J). (gr. k-3). 17.95 *(978-1-932146-16-5(4),* 1237659) Highsmith Inc.
—The Shelf Elf Helps Out. Hopkins, Jackie Mims. 2006. (J). *(978-1-932146-45-5(8),* Upstart Bks.) Highsmith Inc.
—Which Way, Wendy? Dussling, Jennifer. 2005. (Social Studies Connects). 32p. (J). pap. 5.95 *(978-1-57565-147-7(5))* Kane Pr., Inc.
Thornburgh, Rebecca McKillip & Thornburgh, Rebecca. The Story of Easter. Pingry, Patricia A. 2011. 22p. (J). bds. 6.99 *(978-0-8249-1844-6(4),* Candy Cane Pr.) Ideals Pubns.
Thorne, Jenny. Alice Through the Needle's Eye: The Further Adventures of Lewis Carroll's Alice. Adair, Gilbert. 4th ed. 2012. 150p. pap. *(978-1-78201-000-5(9))* Evertype.
—A Child's Treasury of Classic Stories: Charles Dickens, William Shakespeare, Oscar Wilde. Baxter, Nicola. 2012. (ENG.). 240p. (J). (gr. 2-7). 18.99 *(978-1-84322-948-3(X))* Anness Publishing GBR. Dist: National Bk. Network.
Thorne, Jenny. Classic Stories: Charles Dickens, William Shakespeare & Oscar Wilde: a Treasury for Children. Baxter, Nicola, ed. 2015. (ENG.). 240p. 16.99 ***(978-0-85723-756-9(X),*** Armadillo) Anness Publishing GBR. Dist: National Bk. Network.
Thorne, Jenny. A Midsummer Night's Dream & Other Classic Tales of the Plays: Six Illustrated Stories from Shakespeare. Baxter, Nicola, ed. 2015. (ENG.). 80p. pap. 9.99 *(978-1-86147-466-7(0),* Armadillo) Anness Publishing GBR. Dist: National Bk. Network.
—Oliver Twist & Other Classic Tales. Dickens, Charles. 2015. (ENG.). 80p. (J). (gr. -1-12). pap. 9.99 *(978-1-86147-408-7(3),* Armadillo) Anness Publishing GBR. Dist: National Bk. Network.
—The Selfish Giant & Other Classic Tales. Wilde, Oscar. 2014. (ENG.). 96p. (J). (gr. k-5). pap. 9.99 *(978-1-86147-403-2(2),* Armadillo) Anness Publishing GBR. Dist: National Bk. Network.
—A Storyteller Book: The Jungle Book. Kipling, Rudyard. 2014. (ENG.). 48p. (J). (gr. k-5). pap. 7.99 *(978-1-84322-882-0(3),* Armadillo) Anness Publishing GBR. Dist: National Bk. Network.
Thorne, Sean. When Do You Grow? Captain, Tamira. 2003. (J). pap. 6.95 *(978-0-9742288-0-8(X))* Stories From Four Publishing Co.
Thorne-Thomsen, Kathleen. A Shaker's Dozen: Counting Book. Thorne-Thomsen, Kathleen. Rocheleau, Paul, photos by. 2003. 27p. (J). (gr. k-13). reprint ed. 16.00 *(978-0-7567-9041-7(7))* DIANE Publishing Co.
Thornhill, Jan. Over in the Meadow. Thornhill, Jan. rev. ed. 2012. (ENG.). 32p. (J). (gr. -1-1). pap. 7.95 *(978-1-926973-06-7(2))* Owlkids Bks. Inc. CAN. Dist: Perseus-PGW.
—The Wildlife ABC: A Nature Alphabet Book. Thornhill, Jan. 2012. (ENG.). 32p. (J). (gr. -1-k). pap. 7.95 *(978-1-926973-08-1(9))* Owlkids Bks. Inc. CAN. Dist: Perseus-PGW.
Thornton, Barbara. Classroom Times: Charactoons & Rhymes. Stolz, Donald R. 2011. 266p. 76.95 *(978-1-60976-951-2(1),* Strategic Bk. Publishing) Strategic Book Publishing & Rights Agency (SBPRA).
Thornton, Christine. Heading to the Wedding: You're Invited to Join Patrick & Evie on the Great Adventure of Becoming (Almost) Perfect Guests. Shacter, Sara F. 2006. (ENG.). 32p. (J). (gr. -1-3). 18.95 *(978-1-933176-05-5(9))* Red Rock Pr., Inc.
Thornton, Jan. Haunted Fairy Tales - Volume 1. Thornton, Jan. 2011. (ENG.). 184p. pap. 7.95 *(978-1-4662-3520-5(9))* CreateSpace Independent Publishing Platform.
—Spooky Halloween Stories Volume 1. Thornton, Jan. 2011. (ENG.). 184p. pap. 7.95 *(978-1-4663-6266-6(9))* CreateSpace Independent Publishing Platform.
—Spooky Haunted Stories Part 1. Thornton, Jan. 2011. (ENG.). 204p. pap. 7.95 *(978-1-4662-6934-7(0))* CreateSpace Independent Publishing Platform.
Thornton, Peter J. Everybody Brings Noodles. Dooley, Norah. 2005. (ENG.). 40p. (J). (gr. k-3). pap. 6.95 *(978-1-57505-916-7(9))* Lerner Publishing Group.
Thornton, Peter J. Everybody Cooks Rice. Dooley, Norah. 2015. 32p. pap. 7.00 ***(978-1-61003-603-0(4))*** Center for the Collaborative Classroom.
Thornton, Susan Ann. The Adventures of Baby Cat in Cherry Grove: Finding Faith. Thornton, Susan Ann. Steffen, Tim. 2007. 50p. (J). per. 12.00 *(978-0-9779518-1-9(2))* Cardinal Pr.
—The Golden Dragonfly: The Adventures of Baby Cat in Cherry Grove. Thornton, Susan Ann. Steffen, Tim. 2009. 76p. pap. 8.95 *(978-1-4401-4804-0(X))* iUniverse, Inc.
Thornycroft, Rosalind. Kings & Queens. Farjeon, Eleanor & Farjeon, Herbert. 2011. 85p. 16.95 *(978-0-7123-5850-7(1))* British Library, The GBR. Dist: Chicago Distribution Ctr.
Thorp, Cameron. Beat the Clock Sports. Miller, Ray et al. 2007. 48p. (J). *(978-0-439-02189-0(8))* Scholastic, Inc.
—Mwangi: A Young African Boy's Journey of Faith. Ritsi, Renee. 2006. 32p. (J). 17.95 *(978-1-888212-67-9(5))* Conciliar Pr.
Thorpe, Peter. The Amulet of Komondor. Osterweil, Adam. 2003. (ENG.). 112p. (J). (gr. 4-6). 15.95 *(978-1-886910-81-2(2),* Lemniscaat) Boyds Mills Pr.
—The Lost Treasure of Talus Scree. Osterweil, Adam. 2005. (ENG.). 152p. (J). (gr. 4-6). 16.95 *(978-1-932425-30-7(6),* Lemniscaat) Boyds Mills Pr.
Thrall, Gordon & Heflin, Jenifer. Puertas Abiertas Student Workbook Level 1: Open Doors to Spanish. 2003. Orig. Title: Puertas Abiertas. 212p. (J). pap., wbk. ed. 15.00 *(978-0-9723341-1-2(4))* Heflin & Thrall Language Pubns., Inc.
Thrash, Maggie. Honor Girl: A Graphic Memoir. Thrash, Maggie. 2015. (ENG.). 272p. (YA). (gr. 9). 19.99 ***(978-0-7636-7382-6(X))*** Candlewick Pr.
Thrasher, Brian. Wandering Sam. Bowlin, Serina. 2011. 20p. pap. 9.97 *(978-1-61204-280-0(5),* Eloquent Bks.) Strategic Book Publishing & Rights Agency (SBPRA).
Throckmorton, Sylvestra, et al. Star Baby. Throckmorton, Sylvestra. 2006. (ENG & RAJ.). 16p. (J). 14.95 *(978-0-9761723-1-4(3))* Greene, A.S. & Co.
Thuillier, Eleonore. Wolf, Are You There? Learn How to Get Dressed with the Little Wolf. 2012. (ENG.). 14p. (J). (gr. -1). bds. 14.99 *(978-2-7338-1952-4(6))* Auzou, Philippe Editions FRA. Dist: Consortium Bk. Sales & Distribution.
—The Wolf Who Didn't Want to Walk. Lallemand, Orianne. 2012. (My Little Picture Book Ser.). (ENG.). 32p. (J). 6.95 *(978-2-7338-2149-7(0))* Auzou, Philippe Editions FRA. Dist: Consortium Bk. Sales & Distribution.
—The Wolf Who Wanted to Change His Color. Lallemand, Orianne. 2012. (My Little Picture Book Ser.). (ENG.). 32p. (J). pap. 6.95 *(978-2-7338-1945-6(3))* Auzou, Philippe Editions FRA. Dist: Consortium Bk. Sales & Distribution.
—The Wolf Who Wanted to Travel the World. Lallemand, Orianne. 2013. (My Little Picture Book Ser.). (ENG.). 32p. (J). (gr. -1). pap. 6.95 *(978-2-7338-2314-9(0))* Auzou, Philippe Editions FRA. Dist: Consortium Bk. Sales & Distribution.
Thumann, Robin K. Peaceful Thoughts: An Interactive Journey in Positive Thinking for Children & Their Parents. Thumann, Robin K. 2003. 44p. (J). (gr. -1-4). 19.95 *(978-0-9725118-0-3(6))* Peaceful Thoughts Pr.
Thurlby, Paul. Paul Thurlby's Alphabet. Thurlby, Paul. (ENG.). (J). 2013. 26p. (-k). bds. 9.99 *(978-0-7636-6618-7(1));* 2011. 64p. (gr. -1-2). 16.99 *(978-0-7636-5565-5(1))* Candlewick Pr. (Templar).
—Paul Thurlby's Wildlife. Thurlby, Paul. 2013. (ENG.). 32p. (J). (gr. k-4). 17.99 *(978-0-7636-6563-0(0),* Templar) Candlewick Pr.
Thurman, Mark. Alien Invaders: Species That Threaten Our World. Drake, Jane & Love, Ann. (ENG.). 56p. (J). (gr. 4-7). 2013. pap. 8.95 *(978-1-77049-512-8(6));* 2008. 19.95 *(978-0-88776-798-2(2))* Tundra Bks. CAN. Dist: Random Hse., Inc.
—Carrie Loses Her Nerve, 1 vol. Choyce, Lesley. 2003. (Formac First Novels Ser.: 26). (ENG.). 64p. (J). (gr. 1-5). 4.95 *(978-0-88780-591-2(4));* 14.95 *(978-0-88780-592-9(2))* Formac Publishing Co., Ltd. CAN. Dist: Casemate Pubs. & Bk. Distributors, LLC.
—Snow Amazing: Cool Facts & Warm Tales. Drake, Jane & Love, Ann. 2004. (ENG.). 80p. (J). (gr. 4-7). 19.95 *(978-0-88776-670-1(6))* Tundra Bks. CAN. Dist: Random Hse., Inc.
Thurman, Mark & Second Story Press Staff. Franny & the Music Girl, 1 vol. Hearn, Emily. 2005. (ENG.). 24p. (J). (gr. -1-3). pap. 4.95 *(978-0-929005-03-4(1))* Second Story Pr. CAN. Dist: Orca Bk. Pubs. USA.
Thurn, David Ryan, jt. illus. see Thurn, Gwen.
Thurn, Gwen & Thurn, David Ryan. Hong Kong Kitty. Crotty, Martha. 2005. (J). per. 14.00 *(978-0-9766017-0-8(2))* Ironcreek Pr.
Tian, Elli. Silly nursery Rhymes. Tian, Elli. 2007. 12p. (J). 9.49 *(978-0-9798611-5-4(2))* Byte Me! Inc.
Tibbles, Jean-Paul. Clues in the Shadows. Ernst, Kathleen. 2009. (ENG.). 192p. (J). (gr. 4-18). pap. 6.95 *(978-1-59369-478-4(4))* American Girl Publishing, Inc.
—The Cry of the Loon: A Samantha Mystery. Steiner, Barbara. (ENG.). 192p. (gr. 4-18). 2009. (YA). pap. 6.95 *(978-1-59369-480-7(6));* 2006. 10.95 *(978-1-59369-479-1(2))* American Girl Publishing, Inc.
—Josefina Story Collection. Tripp, Valerie. 2008. 420p. pap. 29.95 *(978-1-59369-453-1(9))* American Girl Publishing, Inc.
—The Light in the Cellar: A Molly Mystery. Buckey, Sarah Masters. 2007. (ENG.). 176p. (gr. 4-7). pap. 6.95 *(978-1-59369-158-5(0))* American Girl Publishing, Inc.
—Midnight in Lonesome Hollow: A Kit Mystery. Ernst, Kathleen. 2007. (ENG.). 192p. (gr. 4-7). pap. 6.95 *(978-1-59369-160-8(2),* American Girl) American Girl Publishing, Inc.
—The Runaway Friend. Ernst, Kathleen. 2008. (ENG.). 192p. (gr. 3-7). pap. 6.95 *(978-1-59369-298-8(6))* American Girl Publishing, Inc.
—Shadows on Society Hill: An Addy Mystery. Coleman, Evelyn. 2007. (ENG.). 192p. (gr. 4-7). pap. 6.95 *(978-1-59369-162-2(9),* American Girl) American Girl Publishing, Inc.
—The Tangled Web: A Julie Mystery. Reiss, Kathryn. 2009. (ENG.). 168p. (YA). (gr. 4-18). 10.95 *(978-1-59369-475-3(X));* pap. 6.95 *(978-1-59369-476-0(8))* American Girl Publishing, Inc.
Tibbles, JeanPaul. Danger at the Zoo: A Kit Mystery. Ernst, Kathleen. 2005. (ENG.). 192p. (YA). pap. 6.95 *(978-1-58485-989-5(X),* American Girl) American Girl Publishing, Inc.
—Peril at King's Creek: A Felicity Mystery. Jones, Elizabeth McDavid. 2006. (ENG.). 176p. (gr. 4-7). pap. 6.95 *(978-1-59369-101-1(7),* American Girl) American Girl Publishing, Inc.
—The Puzzle of the Paper Daughter. Reiss, Kathryn. Hirsch, Jennifer, ed. 2010. (ENG.). 192p. (YA). (gr. 4-18). pap. 6.95 *(978-1-59369-658-0(2))* American Girl Publishing, Inc.
—Secrets at Camp Nokomis: A Rebecca Mystery. Greene, Jacqueline. Hirsch, Jennifer, ed. 2010. (ENG.). 192p. (J). (gr. 4-8). pap. 6.95 *(978-1-59369-657-3(4))* American Girl Publishing, Inc.
—A Spy on the Home Front: A Molly Mystery. Hart, Alison. 2005. (ENG.). 176p. (YA). pap. 6.95 *(978-1-58485-988-8(1),* American Girl) American Girl Publishing, Inc.
—The Stolen Sapphire: A Samantha Mystery. Buckey, Sarah Masters. 2006. (ENG.). 192p. (J). (gr. 4-7). pap. 6.95 *(978-1-59369-099-1(1),* American Girl) American Girl Publishing, Inc.
Tibo, Gilles. Pikolo's Night Voyage. Filion, Pierre. 2004. 28p. (J). (gr. k-4). reprint ed. 16.00 *(978-0-7567-7818-7(2))* DIANE Publishing Co.
Tickle, Jack. The Crunching Munching Caterpillar. Cain, Sheridan. (J). 2013. (ENG.). 20p. (gr. -1). 9.99 *(978-1-58925-616-3(6));* 2005. 18p. bds. 6.95 *(978-1-58925-757-3(X))* Tiger Tales.
—Crunching Munching Caterpillar. Cain, Sheridan. 2003. 32p. (J). tchr. ed. 15.95 *(978-1-58925-025-3(7))* Tiger Tales.
—The Crunching Munching Caterpillar Pop-up. Cain, Sheridan. 2006. 16p. (J). 15.95 *(978-1-58925-771-9(5))* Tiger Tales.
—Itsy Bitsy Spider. Chapman, Keith. (Tiger Tales Ser.). (J). 2008. 24p. (gr. -1-2). pap. 6.95 *(978-1-58925-407-7(4));* 2006. 32p. 15.95 *(978-1-58925-055-0(9))* Tiger Tales.
—The Teeny Weeny Tadpole. Cain, Sheridan. 2005. 32p. (J). 15.95 *(978-1-58925-047-5(8))* Tiger Tales.
—The Very Lazy Ladybug. Finn, Isobel. 2005. 16p. (J). bds. 6.95 *(978-1-58925-758-0(8))* Tiger Tales.
—Yummy Yummy! Food for My Tummy. Lloyd, Sam R. 2004. 32p. (J). tchr. ed. 15.95 *(978-1-58925-035-2(4))* Tiger Tales.
Tickle, Jack. The Very Sleepy Sloth. Tickle, Jack, tr. Murray, Andrew. 2003. 32p. (J). tchr. ed. 15.95 *(978-1-58925-033-8(8))* Tiger Tales.
Tidwell, Jeral, jt. illus. see Simko, Joe.
Tidwell, Susan. Three Virtuous Brothers: A Story of the Three Acts of Goodness. Tidwell, Susan. 2012. 47p. (J). pap. 9.95 *(978-1-932293-63-0(9))* Buddha's Light Publishing.
Tiede, Dirk, jt. illus. see Cella, Kristen.
Tiegreen, Alan. Peanut-Butter Pilgrims. Delton, Judy & Pee Wee Scouts Staff. 2007. (Stepping Stone Book Ser.: No. 6). (ENG.). 80p. (J). (gr. 1-4). 4.99 *(978-0-440-40066-0(X),* Yearling) Random Hse. Children's Bks.
Tiegreen, Alan, et al. Ramona & Her Father. Cleary, Beverly. 2013. (Ramona Ser.: 4). (ENG.). 192p. (J). (gr. 3-7). 16.99 *(978-0-688-22114-0(9))* HarperCollins Pubs.
—Ramona & Her Mother. Cleary, Beverly. 2013. (Ramona Ser.: 5). (ENG.). 224p. (J). (gr. 3-7). 16.99 *(978-0-688-22195-9(5))* HarperCollins Pubs.
—Ramona Forever. Cleary, Beverly. 2013. (Ramona Ser.: 7). (ENG.). 208p. (J). (gr. 3-7). 16.99 *(978-0-688-03785-7(2))* HarperCollins Pubs.
—Ramona Quimby, Age 8. Cleary, Beverly. 2014. (Ramona Ser.: 6). (ENG.). 208p. (J). (gr. 3-7). 16.99 *(978-0-688-00477-4(6))* HarperCollins Pubs.
—Ramona the Brave. Cleary, Beverly. 2013. (Ramona Ser.: 3). (ENG.). 208p. (J). (gr. 3-7). 16.99 *(978-0-688-22015-0(0));* pap. 6.99 *(978-0-380-70959-5(7))* HarperCollins Pubs.
—Ramona's World. Cleary, Beverly. 2014. (Ramona Ser.: 8). (ENG.). 240p. (J). (gr. 3-7). 16.99 *(978-0-688-16816-2(7))* HarperCollins Pubs.
Tiegreen, Alan. Yours till Banana Splits: 201 Autograph Rhymes. Cole, Joanna & Calmenson, Stephanie. 2004. 64p. (J). (gr. 6-8). reprint ed. pap. 7.00 *(978-0-7567-7349-6(0))* DIANE Publishing Co.
Tiegreen, Alan & Dockray, Tracy. Mitch & Amy. Cleary, Beverly. 2008. (Cleary Reissue Ser.). (ENG.). 288p. (J). (gr. 3-7). pap. 6.99 *(978-0-380-70925-0(2))* HarperCollins Pubs.
—Muggie Maggie. Cleary, Beverly. 2015. (Cleary Reissue Ser.). (ENG.). 96p. (J). (gr. 3-7). reprint ed. pap. 5.99 *(978-0-380-71087-4(0))* HarperCollins Pubs.
—Socks. Cleary, Beverly. 2015. (Avon Camelot Bks.). (ENG.). 160p. (J). (gr. 3-7). pap. 6.99 *(978-0-380-70926-7(0))* HarperCollins Pubs.
Tiegreen, Alan & Rogers, Jacqueline. Ramona & Her Father. Cleary, Beverly. 2013. (Ramona Ser.: 4). (ENG.). 192p. (J). (gr. 3-7). pap. 6.99 *(978-0-380-70916-8(3))* HarperCollins Pubs.
—Ramona & Her Mother. Cleary, Beverly. 2013. (Ramona Ser.: 5). (ENG.). 224p. (J). (gr. 3-7). reprint ed. pap. 6.99 *(978-0-380-70952-6(X))* HarperCollins Pubs.
—Ramona Forever. Cleary, Beverly. 2013. (Ramona Ser.: 7). (ENG.). 208p. (J). (gr. 3-7). reprint ed. pap. 6.99 *(978-0-380-70960-1(0))* HarperCollins Pubs.
—Ramona Quimby, Age 8. Cleary, Beverly. 2013. (Ramona Ser.: 6). (ENG.). 224p. (J). (gr. 3-7). pap. 6.99 *(978-0-380-70956-4(2))* HarperCollins Pubs.
—Ramona's World. Cleary, Beverly. 2013. (Ramona Ser.: 8). (ENG.). 240p. (J). (gr. 3-7). pap. 6.99 *(978-0-380-73272-2(6))* HarperCollins Pubs.
Tiegren, Alan. Tons of Fun: Over 300 Action Rhymes, Old & New Riddles, Tongue Twisters, & Play Rhymes. Cole, Joanna & Calmenson, Stephanie, eds. 2004. 229p. (J). (gr. k-4). reprint ed. pap. 15.00 *(978-0-7567-8222-1(8))* DIANE Publishing Co.
Tien, Wai. The Land of Os: John Ramsay. Robertson, David. 2014. (Tales from Big Spirit Ser.: 6). (ENG.). 32p. pap. ***(978-1-55379-491-2(5),*** 71d193fb-9d6f-4711-9ca7-63e7716b3ed2, HighWater Pr.) Portage & Main Pr.
—The Slave Woman: Thanadelthur. Robertson, David. 2014. (Tales from Big Spirit Ser.: 6). (ENG.). 32p. pap. ***(978-1-55379-479-0(6),*** 51f7764c-c947-4547-8ce4-63887e0f4e03, HighWater Pr.) Portage & Main Pr.
Tierney, Jim. The Boundless. Oppel, Kenneth. 2014. (ENG.). 336p. (J). (gr. 3-7). 17.99 *(978-1-4424-7288-4(X),* Simon & Schuster Bks. For Young Readers) Simon & Schuster Bks. For Young Readers.
Tiffany, Sean. Backup Goalie, 1 vol. Maddox, Jake. 2008. (Jake Maddox Sports Stories Ser.). (ENG.). 72p. (gr. 2-3). pap. 5.95 *(978-1-4342-0517-9(7));* lib. bdg. 23.99 *(978-1-4342-0467-7(7))* Stone Arch Bks.
—Batter Up!, 1 vol. Maddox, Jake. 2008. (Jake Maddox Sports Stories Ser.). (ENG.). 72p. (gr. 2-3). lib. bdg. 23.99 *(978-1-4342-0465-3(0));* per. 5.95 *(978-1-4342-0515-5(0))* Stone Arch Bks.
—Behind the Plate, 1 vol. Maddox, Jake. 2012. (Jake Maddox Sports Stories Ser.). (ENG.). 72p. (gr. 2-3). pap. 5.95 *(978-1-4342-4205-1(6));* lib. bdg. 23.99 *(978-1-4342-4010-1(X))* Stone Arch Bks.
—Blizzard! A Survive! Story, 1 vol. Maddox, Jake. 2009. (Jake Maddox Sports Stories Ser.). (ENG.). 72p. (gr. 2-3). 23.99 *(978-1-4342-1206-1(8))* Stone Arch Bks.
—BMX Bully, 1 vol. Suen, Anastasia & Maddox, Jake. 2006. (Jake Maddox Sports Stories Ser.). (ENG.). 72p. (gr. 2-3). pap. 5.95 *(978-1-59889-236-9(3));* lib. bdg. 23.99 *(978-1-59889-059-4(X))* Stone Arch Bks.
—BMX Challenge, 1 vol. Maddox, Jake. 2011. (Jake Maddox Sports Stories Ser.). (ENG.). 72p. (gr. 2-3). pap. 5.95 *(978-1-4342-3423-0(1))* Stone Arch Bks.
—Board Rebel. Maddox, Jake. 2007. (Jake Maddox Sports Stories Ser.). (ENG.). 72p. (gr. 2-3). pap. 5.95 *(978-1-59889-414-1(5));* lib. bdg. 23.99 *(978-1-59889-319-9(X))* Stone Arch Bks.
—Cowboy Up, 1 vol. Maddox, Jake. 2011. (Jake Maddox Sports Stories Ser.). (ENG.). 72p. (gr. 2-3). pap. 5.95 *(978-1-4342-3425-4(8));* lib. bdg. 23.99 *(978-1-4342-2989-2(0))* Stone Arch Bks.
—Definición por Penales. Maddox, Jake. Heck, Claudia M., tr. from ENG. 2012. (Jake Maddox en Español Ser.). (SPA.). 72p. (gr. 2-3). 23.99 *(978-1-4342-3814-6(8))* Stone Arch Bks.
—Disc Golf Drive, 1 vol. Maddox, Jake. 2009. (Jake Maddox Sports Stories Ser.). (ENG.). 72p. (gr. 2-3). 23.99 *(978-1-4342-1599-4(7))* Stone Arch Bks.
—Diving off the Edge, 1 vol. Maddox, Jake. 2009. (Jake Maddox Sports Stories Ser.). (ENG.). 72p. (gr. 2-3). lib. bdg. 23.99 *(978-1-4342-1205-4(X))* Stone Arch Bks.
—En la línea de Ataque. Maddox, Jake. Heck, Claudia M., tr. from ENG. 2012. (Jake Maddox en Español Ser.). (SPA.). 72p. (gr. 2-3). 23.99 *(978-1-4342-3813-9(X))* Stone Arch Bks.
—Face-Off, 1 vol. Maddox, Jake. 2006. (Jake Maddox Sports Stories Ser.). (ENG.). 72p. (gr. 2-3). lib. bdg. 23.99 *(978-1-59889-063-1(8))* Stone Arch Bks.
—Face-Off, 1 vol. Maddox, Jake. 2006. (Jake Maddox Sports Stories Ser.). (ENG.). 72p. (gr. 2-3). pap. 5.95 *(978-1-59889-237-6(1))* Stone Arch Bks.
—Free Climb. Maddox, Jake. 2008. (Jake Maddox Sports Stories Ser.). (ENG.). 72p. (gr. 2-3). 23.99 *(978-1-4342-0784-5(6));* pap. 5.95 *(978-1-4342-0880-4(X))* Stone Arch Bks.
—Free Throw, 1 vol. Maddox, Jake. 2006. (Jake Maddox Sports Stories Ser.). (ENG.). 72p. (gr. 2-3). pap. 5.95 *(978-1-59889-238-3(X));* lib. bdg. 23.99 *(978-1-59889-060-0(3))* Stone Arch Bks.
—Geocache Surprise, 1 vol. Maddox, Jake. 2011. (Jake Maddox Sports Stories Ser.). (ENG.). 72p. (gr. 2-3). lib. bdg. 23.99 *(978-1-4342-2600-6(X))* Stone Arch Bks.

T

—Go-Kart Rush. Maddox, Jake. 2007. (Jake Maddox Sports Stories Ser.). (ENG.). 72p. (gr. 2-3). pap. 5.95 *(978-1-59889-415-8(3))* Stone Arch Bks.

—Gridiron Bully, 1 vol. Maddox, Jake. 2009. (Jake Maddox Sports Stories Ser.). (ENG.). 72p. (gr. 2-3). 23.99 *(978-1-4342-1201-6(7))* Stone Arch Bks.

—Hockey. 2008. (Sticker Stories Ser.). (ENG.). 16p. (J). (gr. -1-2). 5.99 *(978-0-448-44902-9(1))* Penguin Publishing Group.

—Hockey Meltdown, 1 vol. Maddox, Jake. 2011. (Jake Maddox Sports Stories Ser.). (ENG.). 72p. (gr. 2-3). pap. 5.95 *(978-1-4342-3426-1(6))*; lib. bdg. 23.99 *(978-1-4342-2990-8(4))* Stone Arch Bks.

—Home-Field Football, 1 vol. Maddox, Jake. 2012. (Jake Maddox Sports Stories Ser.). (ENG.). 72p. (gr. 2-3). pap. 5.95 *(978-1-4342-4206-8(4))*; 23.99 *(978-1-4342-4008-8(8))* Stone Arch Bks.

—Hoop Hotshot, 1 vol. Maddox, Jake. 2009. (Jake Maddox Sports Stories Ser.). (ENG.). 72p. (gr. 2-3). lib. bdg. 23.99 *(978-1-4342-1202-3(5))* Stone Arch Bks.

—The Hunter's Code. Maddox, Jake. 2008. (Jake Maddox Sports Stories Ser.). (ENG.). 72p. (gr. 2-3). 23.99 *(978-1-4342-0782-1(X))*; pap. 5.95 *(978-1-4342-0878-1(8))* Stone Arch Bks.

—Impact Books, 10 bks., Set. Maddox, Jake. 2007. (Jake Maddox Sports Stories Ser.). (ENG.). 72p. (gr. 2-3). 239.90 *(978-1-59889-462-2(5))* Stone Arch Bks.

—Jake Maddox. Maddox, Jake. 2013. (Jake Maddox Sports Stories Ser.). (ENG.). 72p. (gr. 2-3). lib. bdg. 95.96 *(978-1-4342-6051-2(8))* Stone Arch Bks.

—Karate Countdown, 1 vol. Maddox, Jake. 2009. (Jake Maddox Sports Stories Ser.). (ENG.). 72p. (gr. 2-3). lib. bdg. 23.99 *(978-1-4342-1200-9(9))* Stone Arch Bks.

—Kart Crash, 1 vol. Maddox, Jake. 2008. (Jake Maddox Sports Stories Ser.). (ENG.). 72p. (gr. 2-3). 23.99 *(978-1-4342-0777-7(3))*; pap. 5.95 *(978-1-4342-0873-6(7))* Stone Arch Bks.

—Lacrosse Attack. Maddox, Jake. 2008. (Jake Maddox Sports Stories Ser.). (ENG.). 72p. (gr. 2-3). 23.99 *(978-1-4342-0776-0(5))*; pap. 5.95 *(978-1-4342-0872-9(9))* Stone Arch Bks.

—El Lanzador Bajo Presión. Maddox, Jake. Heck, Claudia M., tr. from ENG. 2012. (Jake Maddox en Español Ser.). (SPA.). 72p. (gr. 2-3). 23.99 *(978-1-4342-3815-3(6))* Stone Arch Bks.

—Legend of the Lure, 1 vol. Maddox, Jake. 2008. (Jake Maddox Sports Stories Ser.). (ENG.). 72p. (gr. 2-3). 23.99 *(978-1-4342-0783-8(8))*; pap. 5.95 *(978-1-4342-0879-8(6))* Stone Arch Bks.

—Linebacker Block, 1 vol. Maddox, Jake. 2010. (Team Jake Maddox Sports Stories Ser.). (ENG.). 72p. (gr. 2-3). lib. bdg. 23.99 *(978-1-4342-1635-9(7))*; pap. 5.95 *(978-1-4342-2779-9(0))* Stone Arch Bks.

—Motocross Double-Cross. Maddox, Jake. 2007. (Jake Maddox Sports Stories Ser.). (ENG.). 72p. (gr. 2-3). pap. 5.95 *(978-1-59889-897-2(3))*; lib. bdg. 23.99 *(978-1-59889-845-3(0))* Stone Arch Bks.

—Mountain Bike Hero, 1 vol. Maddox, Jake. 2011. (Jake Maddox Sports Stories Ser.). (ENG.). 72p. (gr. 2-3). lib. bdg. 23.99 *(978-1-4342-2536-8(4))* Stone Arch Bks.

—Mr. Strike Out, 1 vol. Maddox, Jake. 2006. (Jake Maddox Sports Stories Ser.). (ENG.). 72p. (gr. 2-3). 23.99 *(978-1-59889-061-7(1))* Stone Arch Bks.

—Off the Bench, 1 vol. Maddox, Jake. 2010. (Team Jake Maddox Sports Stories Ser.). (ENG.). 72p. (gr. 2-3). pap. 5.95 *(978-1-4342-2278-7(0))*; lib. bdg. 23.99 *(978-1-4342-1922-0(4))* Stone Arch Bks.

—On Guard, 1 vol. Maddox, Jake. 2010. (Team Jake Maddox Sports Stories Ser.). (ENG.). 72p. (gr. 2-3). pap. 5.95 *(978-1-4342-2279-4(9))*; lib. bdg. 23.99 *(978-1-4342-1920-6(8))* Stone Arch Bks.

—On the Line, 1 vol. Maddox, Jake. 2006. (Jake Maddox Sports Stories Ser.). (ENG.). 72p. (gr. 2-3). 23.99 *(978-1-59889-062-4(X))*; pap. 5.95 *(978-1-59889-240-6(1))* Stone Arch Bks.

—On the Speedway, 1 vol. Maddox, Jake. 2011. (Jake Maddox Sports Stories Ser.). (ENG.). 208p. (gr. 3-6). pap. 7.95 *(978-1-4342-3030-0(9))* Stone Arch Bks.

—Paintball Blast. Maddox, Jake. 2007. (Jake Maddox Sports Stories Ser.). (ENG.). 72p. (gr. 2-3). pap. 5.95 *(978-1-59889-417-2(X))*; lib. bdg. 23.99 *(978-1-59889-322-9(X))* Stone Arch Bks.

—Paintball Invasion, 1 vol. Maddox, Jake. 2008. (Jake Maddox Sports Stories Ser.). (ENG.). 72p. (gr. 2-3). lib. bdg. 23.99 *(978-1-4342-0466-0(9))*; per. 5.95 *(978-1-4342-0516-2(9))* Stone Arch Bks.

—Pit Crew Crunch, 1 vol. Maddox, Jake. 2009. (Jake Maddox Sports Stories Ser.). (ENG.). 72p. (gr. 2-3). 23.99 *(978-1-4342-1600-7(4))* Stone Arch Bks.

—Pitcher Pressure, 1 vol. Maddox, Jake. 2009. (Jake Maddox Sports Stories Ser.). (ENG.). 72p. (gr. 2-3). 23.99 *(978-1-4342-1596-3(2))* Stone Arch Bks.

—Playing Forward. Maddox, Jake. 2010. (Team Jake Maddox Sports Stories Ser.). (ENG.). 72p. (gr. 2-3). pap. 5.95 *(978-1-4342-2280-0(2))*; lib. bdg. 23.99 *(978-1-4342-1921-3(6))* Stone Arch Bks.

—Playing Forward. Stevens, Eric & Maddox, Jake. 2010. (Jake Maddox Sports Story Ser.). 72p. pap. 0.60 *(978-1-4342-3206-9(9))*, Impact Bks.) Stone Arch Bks.

—Point Guard Prank, 1 vol. Maddox, Jake. 2012. (Jake Maddox Sports Stories Ser.). (ENG.). 72p. (gr. 2-3). pap. 5.95 *(978-1-4342-4207-5(2))*; 23.99 *(978-1-4342-4009-5(6))* Stone Arch Bks.

—Quarterback Comeback, 1 vol. Maddox, Jake. 2010. (Team Jake Maddox Sports Stories Ser.). (ENG.). 72p. (gr. 2-3). lib. bdg. 23.99 *(978-1-4342-1634-2(9))*; pap. 5.95 *(978-1-4342-2778-2(2))* Stone Arch Bks.

—Quarterback Sneak, 1 vol. Maddox, Jake. 2008. (Jake Maddox Sports Stories Ser.). (ENG.). 72p. (gr. 2-3). lib. bdg. 23.99 *(978-1-4342-0464-6(2))*; per. 5.95 *(978-1-4342-0514-8(2))* Stone Arch Bks.

—Race Car Rival, 1 vol. Maddox, Jake. 2009. (Jake Maddox Sports Stories Ser.). (ENG.). 72p. (gr. 2-3). 23.99 *(978-1-4342-1601-4(2))* Stone Arch Bks.

—El Rebelde de la Patineta, 1 vol. Maddox, Jake. Heck, Claudia, tr. from ENG. 2012. (Jake Maddox en Español Ser.). (SPA.). 72p. (gr. 2-3). 23.99 *(978-1-4342-3816-0(4))* Stone Arch Bks.

—Record Run, 1 vol. Maddox, Jake. 2009. (Jake Maddox Sports Stories Ser.). (ENG.). 72p. (gr. 2-3). 23.99 *(978-1-4342-1598-7(9))* Stone Arch Bks.

—Running Back Dreams, 1 vol. Maddox, Jake. 2010. (Team Jake Maddox Sports Stories Ser.). (ENG.). 72p. (gr. 2-3). lib. bdg. 23.99 *(978-1-4342-1637-3(3))*; pap. 5.95 *(978-1-4342-2781-2(2))* Stone Arch Bks.

—Shark Attack! Maddox, Jake. 2009. (Jake Maddox Sports Stories Ser.). (ENG.). 72p. (gr. 2-3). 23.99 *(978-1-4342-1210-8(6))* Stone Arch Bks.

—Shipwreck! Maddox, Jake. 2009. (Jake Maddox Sports Stories Ser.). (ENG.). 72p. (gr. 2-3). 23.99 *(978-1-4342-1207-8(6))* Stone Arch Bks.

—Skate Park Challenge, 1 vol. Maddox, Jake. 2006. (Jake Maddox Sports Stories Ser.). (ENG.). 72p. (gr. 2-3). 23.99 *(978-1-59889-064-8(6))* Stone Arch Bks.

—Skateboard Save. Maddox, Jake. 2008. (Jake Maddox Sports Stories Ser.). (ENG.). 72p. (gr. 2-3). 23.99 *(978-1-4342-0775-3(7))*; pap. 5.95 *(978-1-4342-0871-2(0))* Stone Arch Bks.

—Skateboard Struggle, 1 vol. Maddox, Jake. 2011. (Jake Maddox Sports Stories Ser.). (ENG.). 72p. (gr. 2-3). pap. 5.95 *(978-1-4342-3424-7(X))*; lib. bdg. 23.99 *(978-1-4342-2987-8(4))* Stone Arch Bks.

—Skatepark Challenge. Maddox, Jake. 2010. (Jake Maddox Sports Story Ser.). 72p. pap. 0.60 *(978-1-4342-3207-6(7))*, Impact Bks.) Stone Arch Bks.

—Slam Dunk Shoes, 1 vol. Maddox, Jake. 2007. (Jake Maddox Sports Stories Ser.). (ENG.). 72p. (gr. 2-3). 23.99 *(978-1-59889-842-2(6))*; per. 5.95 *(978-1-59889-894-1(9))* Stone Arch Bks.

—Snowboard Duel, 1 vol. Maddox, Jake. 2007. (Jake Maddox Sports Stories Ser.). (ENG.). 72p. (gr. 2-3). 23.99 *(978-1-59889-843-9(4))*; pap. 5.95 *(978-1-59889-895-8(7))* Stone Arch Bks.

—Soccer Shootout, 1 vol. Maddox, Jake. 2007. (Jake Maddox Sports Stories Ser.). (ENG.). 72p. (gr. 2-3). 23.99 *(978-1-59889-844-6(2))*; per. 5.95 *(978-1-59889-896-5(5))* Stone Arch Bks.

—Speed Camp, 1 vol. Maddox, Jake. 2009. (Jake Maddox Sports Stories Ser.). (ENG.). 72p. (gr. 2-3). 23.99 *(978-1-4342-1602-1(0))* Stone Arch Bks.

—Speed Receiver, 1 vol. Maddox, Jake. 2010. (Team Jake Maddox Sports Stories Ser.). (ENG.). 72p. (gr. 2-3). lib. bdg. 23.99 *(978-1-4342-1636-6(5))*; pap. 5.95 *(978-1-4342-2780-5(4))* Stone Arch Bks.

—Speedway Switch. Maddox, Jake. 2007. (Jake Maddox Sports Stories Ser.). (ENG.). 72p. (gr. 2-3). pap. 5.95 *(978-1-59889-416-5(1))*; lib. bdg. 23.99 *(978-1-59889-321-2(1))* Stone Arch Bks.

—Stock Car Sabotage, 1 vol. Maddox, Jake. 2009. (Jake Maddox Sports Stories Ser.). (ENG.). 72p. (gr. 2-3). 23.99 *(978-1-4342-1603-8(9))* Stone Arch Bks.

—Striker Assist, 1 vol. Maddox, Jake. 2012. (Jake Maddox Sports Stories Ser.). (ENG.). 72p. (gr. 2-3). pap. 5.95 *(978-1-4342-4208-2(0))*; 23.99 *(978-1-4342-4011-8(8))* Stone Arch Bks.

—Takedown. Maddox, Jake. 2008. (Jake Maddox Sports Stories Ser.). (ENG.). 72p. (gr. 2-3). 23.99 *(978-1-4342-0774-6(9))*; pap. 5.95 *(978-1-4342-0870-5(2))* Stone Arch Bks.

—Tennis Liar, 1 vol. Maddox, Jake. 2009. (Jake Maddox Sports Stories Ser.). (ENG.). 72p. (gr. 2-3). 23.99 *(978-1-4342-1597-0(0))* Stone Arch Bks.

—Tiro Libre, 1 vol. Maddox, Jake. Heck, Claudia M., tr. from ENG. 2012. (Jake Maddox en Español Ser.). (SPA.). 72p. (gr. 2-3). 23.99 *(978-1-4342-3812-2(1))* Stone Arch Bks.

—El Tramposo de BMX, 1 vol. Maddox, Jake. Heck, Claudia M., tr. from ENG. 2012. (Jake Maddox en Español Ser.). (SPA.). 72p. (gr. 2-3). 23.99 *(978-1-4342-3817-7(2))* Stone Arch Bks.

—Volcano! A Survive! Story. Maddox, Jake. 2009. (Jake Maddox Sports Stories Ser.). (ENG.). 72p. (gr. 2-3). 23.99 *(978-1-4342-1208-5(4))* Stone Arch Bks.

—Whitewater Courage, 1 vol. Maddox, Jake. 2011. (Jake Maddox Sports Stories Ser.). (ENG.). 72p. (gr. 2-3). lib. bdg. 23.99 *(978-1-4342-2530-6(5))* Stone Arch Bks.

—Wild Hike. Maddox, Jake. 2008. (Jake Maddox Sports Stories Ser.). (ENG.). 72p. (gr. 2-3). 23.99 *(978-1-4342-0785-2(4))*; pap. 5.95 *(978-1-4342-0881-1(8))* Stone Arch Bks.

—Wildcats Blitz, 1 vol. Maddox, Jake. 2010. (Team Jake Maddox Sports Stories Ser.). (ENG.). 208p. (gr. 3-6). pap. 7.95 *(978-1-4342-2887-1(8))* Stone Arch Bks.

—Wildcats Slam Dunk, 1 vol. Maddox, Jake. 2010. (Team Jake Maddox Sports Stories Ser.). (ENG.). 208p. (gr. 3-6). pap. 7.95 *(978-1-4342-2886-4(X))* Stone Arch Bks.

—Win or Lose. Maddox, Jake. 2010. (Team Jake Maddox Sports Stories Ser.). (ENG.). 72p. (gr. 2-3). pap. 5.95 *(978-1-4342-2281-7(0))*; lib. bdg. 23.99 *(978-1-4342-1919-0(4))* Stone Arch Bks.

—Windsurfing Winner, 1 vol. Maddox, Jake. 2011. (Jake Maddox Sports Stories Ser.). (ENG.). 72p. (gr. 2-3). lib. bdg. 23.99 *(978-1-4342-2535-1(6))* Stone Arch Bks.

Tiffany, Sean. Mr. Strike Out, 1 vol. Tiffany, Sean. Maddox, Jake. 2006. (Jake Maddox Sports Stories Ser.). (ENG.). 72p. (gr. 2-3). per. 5.95 *(978-1-59889-239-0(8))* Stone Arch Bks.

Tigue, Terry & Turner, Diane. The Gift: A Woodsong Story. Mundy, Dawn. 2003. (J). lib. bdg. *(978-1-932139-16-7(8))* DEMDACO.

Tilak, Brian, jt. illus. see Moore, Sasha.

Tilde, photos by. How Does a Seed Grow? A Book with Foldout Pages. Kim, Sue. 2010. (ENG., 14p. (J). (gr. -1-1). bds. 8.99 *(978-1-4169-9435-0(1)*, Little Simon) Little Simon.

—It's Harvest Time! A Book with Foldout Pages. McElroy, Jean. 2010. (ENG., 14p. (J). (gr. -1-1). bds. 7.99 *(978-1-4424-0352-9(7)*, Little Simon) Little Simon.

Tildes, Phyllis L. The Garden Wall. Tildes, Phyllis L. 2005. (J). per. 7.95 *(978-0-9723729-1-6(1))* Imagination Stage, Inc.

Tildes, Phyllis Limbacher. Apples. Farmer, Jacqueline. 2007. (ENG.). 32p. (J). (gr. k-3). 6.95 *(978-1-57091-695-3(0))* Charlesbridge Publishing, Inc.

—Calabazas. Farmer, Jacqueline. DelRisco, Eida, tr. from ENG. 2006. (SPA & ENG.). 32p. (J). (gr. k-3). per. 7.95 *(978-1-57091-696-0(9))* Charlesbridge Publishing, Inc.

—Plant Secrets. Goodman, Emily. 2009. (ENG.). 40p. (J). (gr. -1-3). pap. 7.95 *(978-1-58089-205-6(1))* Charlesbridge Publishing, Inc.

—Pumpkins. Farmer, Jacqueline. 2004. (ENG.). 32p. (J). (gr. k-3). pap. 7.95 *(978-1-57091-558-1(X))* Charlesbridge Publishing, Inc.

Tildes, Phyllis Limbacher. Baby Animals Spots & Stripes. Tildes, Phyllis Limbacher. 2015. (ENG.). 12p. (J). (— 1). bds. 6.95 *(978-1-58089-608-5(1))* Charlesbridge Publishing, Inc.

—Eye Guess: A Foldout Guessing Game. Tildes, Phyllis Limbacher. 2005. (ENG.). 36p. (J). (gr. -1-2). 11.95 *(978-1-57091-650-2(0))* Charlesbridge Publishing, Inc.

—The Magic Babushka. Tildes, Phyllis Limbacher. 2009. (ENG.). 32p. (J). (gr. k-3). pap. 7.95 *(978-1-58089-225-4(6))* Charlesbridge Publishing, Inc.

—Will You Be Mine? A Nursery Rhyme Romance. Tildes, Phyllis Limbacher. 2011. (ENG.). 32p. (J). (gr. -1-2). pap. 7.95 *(978-1-58089-245-2(0))* Charlesbridge Publishing, Inc.

Till, Tom, photos by. Photographing the World: A Guide to Photographing 201 of the Most Beautiful Places on Earth. Till, Tom. Martres, Laurent, ed. 2012. 336p. pap. *(978-0-916189-22-8(8))* Graphic International, Inc.

Tiller, Amy. My Sister Is Like a Baby Bird. Tiller, Amy. 2009. (ENG.). 26p. (J). 12.95 *(978-1-935130-02-4(1))* Grateful Steps.

Tilley, Debbie. Babies Don't Eat Pizza: A Big Kids' Book about Baby Brothers & Baby Sisters. Danzig, Dianne. 2009. (ENG.). 32p. (J). (gr. -1-k). 16.99 *(978-0-525-47441-8(2)*, Dutton Juvenile) Penguin Publishing Group.

—E Is for Elisa. Hurwitz, Johanna. 2003. (Riverside Kids Ser.). (ENG.). 96p. (J). (gr. 1-4). pap. 4.25 *(978-0-06-054374-7(4))* HarperCollins Pubs.

—My Teacher Is an Idiom. Gilson, Jamie. 2015. (ENG.). 144p. (YA). (gr. 1-4). 16.99 *(978-0-544-05680-0(9))* Houghton Mifflin Harcourt Publishing Co.

—Oye, Hormiguita. Hoose, Phillip & Hoose, Hannah. 2004.Tr. of Hey Little Ant!. (SPA.). 32p. (J). (gr. -1-2). pap. 7.99 *(978-1-58246-089-5(2)*, Tricycle Pr.) Ten Speed Pr.

—Spaghetti & Meatballs for All! A Mathematical Story. Burns, Marilyn. 2008. (ENG.). 40p. (J). (gr. -1-3). pap. 6.99 *(978-0-545-04445-5(6)*, Scholastic Paperbacks) Scholastic, Inc.

—Winky Blue Goes Wild! Jane, Pamela. 2003. 64p. (J). 13.95 *(978-1-59034-588-7(6))*; pap. *(978-1-59034-589-4(4))* Mondo Publishing.

Tilley, Scott. The Bing Bong Book. Uyeda, Laura. 2015. (Little Golden Book Ser.). (ENG.). 24p. (J). (-k). 4.99 *(978-0-7364-3321-1(X)*, Golden/Disney) Random Hse. Children's Bks.

—Boo on the Loose (Disney/Pixar Monsters, Inc.) Herman, Gail. 2012. (Step into Reading Ser.). (ENG.). 32p. (J). (gr. -1-1). pap. 3.99 *(978-0-7364-2860-6(7)*, RH/Disney) Random Hse. Children's Bks.

Tilley, Scott & Becker, Ken. Monster Time (Disney/Pixar Monsters, Inc.) Posner-Sanchez, Andrea. 2013. (Nifty Lift-And-Look Ser.). (ENG.). 12p. (J). (-k). bds. 5.99 *(978-0-7364-3060-9(1)*, RH/Disney) Random Hse. Children's Bks.

Tilley, Scott & Orpinas, Jean-Paul. Ratatouille. Saxon, Victoria & RH Disney Staff. 2007. (Little Golden Book Ser.). (ENG.). 24p. (J). (gr. -1-2). 3.99 *(978-0-7364-2423-3(7)*, RH/Disney) Random Hse. Children's Bks.

Tilley, Scott & RH Disney Staff. Finding Nemo. RH Disney Staff. 2003. (Little Golden Book Ser.). (ENG.). 24p. (J). (gr. -1-2). lib. bdg. 3.99 *(978-0-7364-2139-3(4)*, Golden/Disney) Random Hse. Children's Bks.

Tilley, Scott, jt. illus. see Orpinas, Jean-Paul.

Tillis, Carrie. Rudy the Rabbit. Tillis, Doris. 2005. 32p. per. 17.95 *(978-1-58961-410-9(0))* PageFree Publishing, Inc.

Tillman, Nancy. Let There Be Light, 1 vol. Tutu, Desmond. 2014. (ENG.). 30p. (J). bds. 7.99 *(978-0-310-73396-6(0))* Zonderkidz.

Tillman, Nancy. The Crown on Your Head. Tillman, Nancy. (ENG.). (J). (gr. -1-3). 2014. 34p. 7.99 *(978-1-250-04045-9(0))*; 2011. 32p. 16.99 *(978-0-312-64521-2(X))* Feiwel & Friends.

—The Heaven of Animals. Tillman, Nancy. 2014. (ENG.). 32p. (J). (gr. -1-3). 17.99 *(978-0-312-55369-2(2))* Feiwel & Friends.

—I'd Know You Anywhere, My Love. Tillman, Nancy. 2013. (ENG.). 32p. (J). (gr. -1-3). 17.99 *(978-0-312-55368-5(4))* Feiwel & Friends.

—It's Time to Sleep, My Love. Tillman, Nancy. Metaxas, Eric. (ENG.). (J). 2011. 34p. (— 1). bds. 7.99 *(978-0-312-67336-9(1))*; 2008. 32p. (gr. -1 — 1). 16.95 *(978-0-312-38371-8(1))* Feiwel & Friends.

—On the Night You Were Born. Tillman, Nancy. 2006. (ENG.). 32p. (J). (gr. -1 — 1). 16.95 *(978-0-312-34606-5(9))* Feiwel & Friends.

—The Spirit of Christmas. Tillman, Nancy. 2009. (ENG.). 32p. (J). (gr. -1-3). 17.99 *(978-0-312-54965-7(2))* Feiwel & Friends.

—Tumford the Terrible. Tillman, Nancy. (Tumford Ser.). (ENG.). 32p. (J). (gr. -1-1). 2015. bds. 7.99 *(978-1-250-03364-2(0))*; 2011. 16.99 *(978-0-312-36840-1(2))* Feiwel & Friends.

—Tumford's Rude Noises. Tillman, Nancy. 2012. (Tumford Ser.). (ENG.). 32p. (J). (gr. -1-1). 16.99 *(978-0-312-36841-8(0))* Feiwel & Friends.

—Wherever You Are: My Love Will Find You. Tillman, Nancy. (ENG.). 32p. (J). (gr. -1-3). 2012. bds. 7.99 *(978-1-250-01797-0(1))*; 2010. 16.99 *(978-0-312-54966-4(0))* Feiwel & Friends.

—The Wonder of You: A Book for Celebrating Baby's First Year. Tillman, Nancy. 2008. (ENG.). 48p. (J). (— 1). 24.99 *(978-0-312-36839-5(9))* Feiwel & Friends.

Tillotson, Katherine. All Ears, All Eyes. Jackson, Richard. 2015. (J). *(978-1-4814-1571-2(9))* Simon & Schuster Children's Publishing.

—All the Water in the World. Lyon, George Ella. 2011. (ENG.). 40p. (J). (gr. -1-3). 17.99 *(978-1-4169-7130-6(0)*, Atheneum/Richard Jackson Bks.) Simon & Schuster Children's Publishing.

—It's Picture Day Today! McDonald, Megan. 2009. (ENG.). 36p. (J). (gr. -1-3). 16.99 *(978-1-4169-2434-0(5)*, Atheneum/Richard Jackson Bks.) Simon & Schuster Children's Publishing.

—Nice Try, Tooth Fairy. Olson, Mary W. 2003. Orig. Title: Dear Tooth Fairy. (ENG.). 32p. (J). (gr. -1-2). 13.99 *(978-0-689-86141-3(9)*, Simon & Schuster/Paula Wiseman Bks.) Simon & Schuster/Paula Wiseman Bks.

—Shoe Dog. McDonald, Megan. 2014. (ENG.). 40p. (J). (gr. -1-2). 17.99 *(978-1-4169-7932-6(8)*, Atheneum/Richard Jackson Bks.) Simon & Schuster Children's Publishing.

—When the Library Lights Go Out. McDonald, Megan. 2009. (ENG.). 40p. (J). (gr. -1-1). 7.99 *(978-1-4169-8028-5(8)*, Atheneum Bks. for Young Readers) Simon & Schuster Children's Publishing.

Tillotson, Katherine. When the Library Lights Go Out. Tillotson, Katherine, tr. McDonald, Megan. 2005. (ENG.). 40p. (J). (gr. -1-3). 17.99 *(978-0-689-86170-3(2)*, Atheneum/Richard Jackson Bks.) Simon & Schuster Children's Publishing.

Tillson, Linda L. The Moon & the Mouse. Ryan, Christopher. 2011. 32p. pap. 24.95 *(978-1-4626-1586-5(4))* America Star Bks.

Tilton, David. The Tale of Despereaux: The Graphic Novel. Tilton, David. Smith, Matt. 2008. 126p. (J). (gr. 3). 20.85 *(978-1-4178-2948-4(6)*, Turtleback) Turtleback Bks.

Timmers, Leo. All Through My Town. Reidy, Jean. (ENG.). (J). (gr. -1-k). 2015. 26p. bds. 7.99 *(978-1-61963-562-3(3))*; 2013. 32p. 14.99 *(978-1-59990-785-7(2))*; 2013. 32p. lib. bdg. 15.89 *(978-1-61963-029-1(X))* Bloomsbury USA. (Bloomsbury USA Childrens).

Timmers, Leo. Bang. Timmers, Leo. 2013.Tr. of Boem. 48p. (J). (gr. -1-2). 17.95 *(978-1-877579-18-9(1))* Gecko Pr. NZL. Dist: Lerner Publishing Group.

—Crow. Timmers, Leo. 2010. (ENG.). 30p. (J). (gr. -1-k). 16.95 *(978-1-60537-071-2(1))* Clavis Publishing.

—I Am the King. Timmers, Leo. 2008. (ENG.). 32p. (J). (gr. -1-k). 16.95 *(978-1-60537-018-7(5))* Clavis Publishing.

—The Magical Life of Mr. Renny. Timmers, Leo. Nagelkerke, Bill, tr. from DUT. 2012.Tr. of Meneer Rene. (ENG.). 40p. (gr. 2-5). 17.95 *(978-1-877579-20-2(3))* Gecko Pr. NZL. Dist: Lerner Publishing Group.

—Oops! Timmers, Leo. 2011. (ENG.). 32p. (J). (gr. k — 1). 15.95 *(978-1-60537-105-4(X))* Clavis Publishing.

—Who Is Driving? Timmers, Leo. 2014. (ENG.). 30p. (J). (gr. -1-1). bds. 7.99 *(978-1-61963-169-4(5)*, Bloomsbury USA Childrens) Bloomsbury USA.

Timmins, Jeffrey Stewart. Another Whole Nother Story. Soup, Cuthbert. (Whole Nother Story Ser.). (ENG.). 304p. (J). (gr. 3-6). 2012. pap. 7.99 *(978-1-59990-737-6(2))*; 2010. 16.99 *(978-1-59990-436-8(5))* Bloomsbury USA. (Bloomsbury USA Childrens).

—Cenicienta. Andersen, Hans Christian & Capstone Press Staff. Feely, Maria Luisa, tr. 2010. (Graphic Spin en Español Ser.). (SPA.). 40p. (gr. 1-3). lib. bdg. 23.99 *(978-1-4342-1900-8(3)*, Graphic Spin en Español) Stone Arch Bks.

—Cenicienta: La Novela Grafica. Andersen, Hans Christian & Stone Arch Books Staff. 2010. (Graphic Spin en Español Ser.). (SPA & ENG.). 40p. (gr. 1-3). pap. 5.95 *(978-1-4342-2270-1(5)*, Graphic Spin en Español) Stone Arch Bks.

—Cinderella: The Graphic Novel, 1 vol. 2008. (Graphic Spin Ser.). (ENG.). 40p. (gr. 1-3). 23.99 *(978-1-4342-0764-7(1)*, Graphic Revolve) Stone Arch Bks.

—Cinderella: The Graphic Novel, 1 vol. Stone Arch Books Staff. 2008. (Graphic Spin Ser.). (ENG.). 40p. (gr. 1-3). pap. 5.95 *(978-1-4342-0860-6(5)*, Graphic Revolve) Stone Arch Bks.

—The Emperor's New Clothes: The Graphic Novel, 1 vol. Andersen, Hans Christian. 2009. (Graphic Spin Ser.). (ENG.). 40p. (gr. 1-3). pap. 5.95 *(978-1-4342-1744-8(2)*, Graphic Revolve) Stone Arch Bks.

—Last Laughs: Animal Epitaphs. Lewis, J. Patrick & Yolen, Jane. 2012. (ENG.). 32p. (J). (gr. 2-5). 16.95 *(978-1-58089-260-5(4))* Charlesbridge Publishing, Inc.

—Rapunzel. Capstone Press Staff. 2009. (Graphic Spin Ser.). (ENG.). 40p. (gr. 1-3). pap. 5.95 *(978-1-4342-1392-1(7))*; lib. bdg. 23.99 *(978-1-4342-1194-1(0))* Stone Arch Bks. (Graphic Revolve).

—A Whole Nother Story. Soup, Cuthbert. 2009. (Whole Nother Story Ser.). (ENG.). 256p. (J). (gr. 3-7). 16.99 *(978-1-59990-435-1(7)*, Bloomsbury USA Childrens) Bloomsbury USA.

Timmins, William. Wild Bill Hickok & Deputy Marshal Joey. Stone, Ethel B. 2011. 32p. pap. 35.95 *(978-1-258-05913-2(4))* Literary Licensing, LLC.

Timmons, Anne. Florence Nightingale: Lady with the Lamp, 1 vol. Robbins, Trina & Capstone Press Staff. 2007. (Graphic Biographies Ser.). (ENG.). 32p. (gr. 3-4). 29.99 *(978-0-7368-6850-1(X)*, Graphic Library) Capstone Pr., Inc.

—Florence Nightingale: Lady with the Lamp, 1 vol. Robbins, Trina. 2007. (Graphic Biographies Ser.). (ENG.). 32p. (gr. 3-4). per. 8.10 *(978-0-7368-7902-6(1)*, 1264942, Graphic Library) Capstone Pr., Inc.

—How to Draw Faces, 1 vol. Clay, Kathryn. 2009. (Drawing Fun Ser.). (ENG.). 32p. (gr. 3-4). lib. bdg. 27.32 *(978-1-4296-3404-5(9)*, Snap Bks.) Capstone Pr., Inc.

—How to Draw Mythical Creatures, 1 vol. Clay, Kathryn. 2009. (Drawing Fun Ser.). (ENG.). 32p. (gr. 3-4). 27.32 *(978-1-4296-2307-0(1)*, Snap Bks.) Capstone Pr., Inc.

—Pigling: A Cinderella Story [A Korean Tale]. Jolley, Dan. 2009. (Graphic Myths & Legends Ser.). (ENG.). 48p. (gr. 4-8). pap. 8.95 *(978-1-58013-825-3(X))* Lerner Publishing Group.

—Rescue in Antarctica: An Isabel Soto Geography Adventure, 1 vol. Sohn, Emily et al. 2009. (Graphic Expeditions Ser.). (ENG.). 32p. (gr. 3-4). pap. 8.10 *(978-1-4296-3896-8(6))*; lib. bdg. 29.99 *(978-1-4296-3408-3(1))* Capstone Pr., Inc. (Graphic Library).

Timmons, Anne & Oh, Mo. Lily Renée, Escape Artist: From Holocaust Survivor to Comic Book Pioneer. Robbins, Trina. 2011. (Single Titles Ser.). (ENG.). 96p. (J). (gr. 5-8). pap. 7.95 *(978-0-7613-8114-3(7))*; lib. bdg. 29.27 *(978-0-7613-6010-0(7))* Lerner Publishing Group. (Graphic Universe).

Timmons, Anne, jt. illus. see Martin, Cynthia.

Timmons, Bonnie. Amazing Skin from Outside In. Settel, Joanne. 2016. (J). *(978-1-4814-2205-5(7))* Simon & Schuster Children's Publishing.

—Eats, Shoots & Leaves: Why, Commas Really Do Make a Difference! Truss, Lynne. 2006. (ENG.). 32p. (J). (gr. 1-4). 15.99 *(978-0-399-24491-9(3)*, Putnam Juvenile) Penguin Publishing Group.

—The Girl's Like Spaghetti: Why, You Can't Manage Without Apostrophes! Truss, Lynne. 2007. (ENG.). 32p. (J). (gr. 1-4). 16.99 *(978-0-399-24706-4(8)*, Putnam Juvenile) Penguin Publishing Group.

—Twenty-Odd Ducks: Why, Every Punctuation Mark Counts! Truss, Lynne. 2008. (ENG.). 32p. (J). (gr. 1-3). 16.99 *(978-0-399-25058-3(1)*, Putnam Juvenile) Penguin Publishing Group.

Timmons, Gayle. Do You Love Me Best? Schad, Kristine. 2007. 40p. (J). lib. bdg. 23.95 *(978-1-58374-156-6(9))* Chicago Spectrum Pr.

Timmons, Jonathan, jt. illus. see Floor, Guus.

Timmons, Jonathan, jt. illus. see Isaacs, Rebekah.

Timothy, Hamilton Baird, jt. illus. see Stevenson, Robert Louis.

Tina, Dunnier. The Gentle Elephant. Kneisley, Amy. 2013. 24p. pap. 8.99 *(978-1-938768-21-7(3))* Gypsy Pubns.

Tinkelman, Murray. Pigeon Flight. Stolz, Mary. 2012. 62p. 36.95 *(978-1-258-25234-2(1))*; pap. 21.95 *(978-1-258-25387-5(9))* Literary Licensing, LLC.

Tinker, Jason. My Wish, Our Little Oat. Martin, Tamra. 2007. 36p. (J). 21.99 *(978-1-59879-522-6(8)*, Lifevest) Lifevest Publishing, Inc.

Tinling, Molly. Shanie June Jumped over the Moon. Wand, Dana. 2013. 32p. pap. *(978-1-4602-0466-5(2))* FriesenPress.

Tino. La Panza del Tepozteco. Agustin, Jose. 2003. (SPA.). 118p. (J). (gr. 8-12). pap. 12.95 *(978-968-19-0187-5(8))* Santillana USA Publishing Co., Inc.

—Stargirl. Spinelli, Jerry. 2004. (SPA.). 224p. (J). (gr. 5-8). pap. 10.95 *(978-1-59437-815-7(0))* Santillana USA Publishing Co., Inc.

Tinti, Natalie. Magic in Us. the Healing Circle, bks. 2, vol. 2. Tinti, Natalie. ed. 2013. (Sewing a Friendship Ser.). (ENG.). 96p. (J). 25.95 *(978-0-9830884-4-8(6))* Tintinatie Publishing Hse.

—Magic in Us. the Healing Circle: The Healing Circle, bks. 2, vol. 2. Tinti, Natalie. ed. 2013. (Sewing a Friendship Ser.: 3). (ENG.). 96p. (J). pap. 12.95 *(978-0-9830884-0-0(3))* Tintinatie Publishing Hse.

—Magic in Us. the Power of Imagination, bks. 1, vol. 2. Tinti, Natalie. ed. 2013. (Sewing a Friendship Ser.: 2). (ENG.). 116p. (J). 25.95 *(978-0-9830884-1-7(1))* Tintinatie Publishing Hse.

—Sewing a Friendship. Tinti, Natalie. ed. 2009. (Sewing a Friendship Ser.: 1). (ENG.). 88p. (J). pap. 12.95 *(978-0-9842625-1-9(2))* Tintinatie Publishing Hse.

Tintjer, Birgit. Stary's Secret. Wilson, Jessica. 2007. 28p. pap. 24.95 *(978-1-4241-9089-8(4))* America Star Bks.

Tipeo. Caillou: Los Contrarios. Savary, Fabien & Vadeboncoeur, Isabelle. 2004. (Caillou Ser.).Tr. of What's the Difference?. (SPA & ENG.). 12p. (J). (gr. -1-17). 4.95 *(978-1-58728-348-2(4))* Cooper Square Publishing Llc.

—Caillou: Que Falta? Savary, Fabien. 2004. (Caillou Ser.).Tr. of What's Missing?. (SPA & ENG.). 12p. (J). (gr. -1-17). 4.95 *(978-1-58728-349-9(2))* Cooper Square Publishing Llc.

—Caillou: Sorpresa! Savary, Fabien & Vadeboncoeur, Isabelle. 2004. (Caillou Ser.).Tr. of What's Inside?. (SPA & ENG.). 12p. (J). (gr. -1-17). 4.95 *(978-1-58728-390-1(5))* Cooper Square Publishing Llc.

Tipping, Naomi. Bully. Safran, Sheri. 2012. (ENG.). 12p. (J). (gr. -1). 12.99 *(978-1-60887-163-6(0))* Insight Editions LP.

Tirabosco, Tom. Weekend with Purpose. Wazem, Pierre. 2003. 108p. (YA). pap. 9.95 *(978-1-930652-98-9(4))* Humanoids, Inc.

Tirey, Rodney. Coppershoo Saves the Sarge's Saddle! Tirey, Rodney. 2007. 32p. (J). 16.95 *(978-0-9789591-0-4(8))* MirthMarks Publishing.

Tirion, Wil. Stars & Planets: The Most Complete Guide to the Stars, Planets, Galaxies, & the Solar System. Ridpath, Ian. rev. exp. ed. 2008. (Princeton Field Guides). (ENG.). 400p. pap. 19.95 *(978-0-691-13556-4(8))* Princeton Univ. Pr.

Tirion, Wil & Rukl, Antonin. Atlas of the Night Sky. Storm, Dunlop. 2005. (Smithsonian Institution Ser.). 224p. 29.95 *(978-0-06-081891-3(3))* HarperCollins Pubs.

Tiritilli, Robert. Adventures in Sportsand - the Baseball Bully (with accompanying CD) The Baseball Bully. Hellman, Charles. 2008. (Adventures in SportsLand: the Bully Ser.). 32p. pap. 19.95 *(978-0-935938-27-2(3))* LuckySports.

—Adventures in SportsLand - the Basketball Bully (with accompanying CD) Hellman, Charles. 2008. (Adventures in SportsLand: the Bully Ser.). 32p. (J). (gr. -1-3). 19.95 *(978-0-935938-28-9(1))* LuckySports.

—Adventures in SportsLand - the Football Bully (with accompanying CD) Hellman, Charles. 2008. (Adventures in SportsLand: the Bully Ser.). 32p. (J). (gr. -1-3). 19.95 *(978-0-935938-30-2(3))* LuckySports.

—Adventures in SportsLand - the Soccer Bully (with accompanying CD) Hellman, Charles. 2008. (Adventures in SportsLand: the Bully Ser.). 32p. (gr. -1-3). pap. 19.95 *(978-0-935938-26-5(5))* LuckySports.

—Adventures in SportsLand - the Tennis Bully (with accompanying CD) Hellman, Charles. 2008. (Adventures in SportsLand: the Bully Ser.). 32p. (J). (gr. -1-3). 19.95 *(978-0-935938-32-6(X))* LuckySports.

Tiritilli, Robert A. The Baseball Bully. Hellman, Charles S. 2013. 34p. pap. 9.25 *(978-0-935938-19-7(2))* LuckySports.

—The Baseball Challenge: Defenders of Sportsland. Hellman, Charles S. 2013. 54p. pap. 11.25 *(978-0-935938-52-4(4))* LuckySports.

—Discovering Sportsland. Hellman, Charles S. 2013. 44p. pap. 9.49 *(978-0-935938-51-7(6))* LuckySports.

—The Football Bully. Hellman, Charles S. 2013. 34p. pap. 9.25 *(978-0-935938-22-7(2))* LuckySports.

—The Hockey Bully. Hellman, Charles S. 2013. 34p. pap. 9.25 *(978-0-935938-23-4(0))* LuckySports.

—Luckysports Abc's Coloring Book. Hellman, Charles S. 2013. 50p. pap. 5.40 *(978-0-935938-46-3(X))* LuckySports.

—The Volleyball Bully. Hellman, Charles S. 2013. 34p. pap. 9.25 *(978-0-935938-53-1(2))* LuckySports.

Tisdall, Sarah. You're Thinking about Doughnuts. Rosen, Michael. 2006. 90p. (J). (gr. 2-4). per. 6.95 *(978-1-903015-03-2(0))* Barn Owl Bks, London GBR. Dist: Independent Pubs. Group.

Tisdel, L. L. The Incredibly Awesome Adventures of Puggie Liddel, the Graphic Novel. Bryson, Karen Mueller. 2013. 108p. pap. *(978-1-927384-09-1(5))* Zeta Comics.

Titonis, George. The Gift of the Giggles. 2005. 24p. (J). 16.95 *(978-0-9765398-0-3(2))* Bellaboozle Books, Inc.

Titra, Stephen. We'll Ring in God's Name. Thiry, Joan. 2009. (ENG.). 44p. (YA). tchr. ed. 5.00 *(978-0-935046-06-9(2))* Chateau Thierry Pr.

Titus, Gregory. Vampire Hunt. Jolley, Dan. 2008. (Twisted Journeys (r) Ser.: 7). (ENG.). 112p. (J). (gr. 4-7). 27.93 *(978-0-8225-8877-1(3)*, Graphic Universe); pap. 7.95 *(978-0-8225-8879-5(X))* Lerner Publishing Group.

Tiwari, Saral. Abraham Lincoln: The Civil War President. 2004. 48p. (J). 15.95 *(978-0-9742502-0-5(1))* Gossamer Bks., LLC.

—Thirteen Americas: American Revolution & Constitution. Pettinato, Laura. 2004. (J). 18.95 *(978-0-9742502-7-4(9))* Gossamer Bks., LLC.

—Thirteen Americas: The Declaration of Independence. Pettinato, Laura. 2nd ed. 2004. (J). lib. bdg. *(978-0-9742502-6-7(0))* Gossamer Bks., LLC.

Tjia, Sherwin. Black Stars in a White Night Sky. Lawson, JonArno. 2008. (ENG.). 128p. (J). (gr. 6-9). 16.95 *(978-1-59078-521-6(5)*, Wordsong) Boyds Mills Pr.

—Black Stars in a White Night Sky. Lawson, JonArno. 2006. (ENG.). 80p. *(978-1-897141-07-6(6))* Pedlar Pr.

—The Man in the Moon-Fixer's Mask. Lawson, JonArno. 2004. (ENG.). 88p. (J). (gr. 3-7). *(978-0-9732140-9-3(0))* Pedlar Pr.

—The Man in the Moon-Fixer's Mask. Lawson, Jon Arno. 2006. (ENG.). 80p. (J). (gr. 1-7). 14.95 *(978-1-932425-82-6(9)*, Lemniscaat) Boyds Mills Pr.

Tk. The Sea of Monsters, Bk. 2. Riordan, Rick. 2nd rev. ed. 2007. (Percy Jackson & the Olympians Ser.: Bk. 2). (ENG.). 320p. (J). (gr. 5-9). pap. 7.99 *(978-1-4231-0334-9(3))* Disney Publishing Worldwide.

To, Vivienne. The Case of the Time-Capsule Bandit. Rhodes, O. K. & Spencer, Octavia. 2013. (Randi Rhodes, Ninja Detective Ser.: 1). (ENG.). 224p. (J). (gr. 3-7). 16.99 *(978-1-4424-7681-3(8)*, Simon & Schuster Bks. For Young Readers) Simon & Schuster Bks. For Young Readers.

—Clawed! An Up2U Horror Adventure. Enderle, Dotti. 2013. (Up2U Adventures Ser.). 80p. (J). (gr. 2-5). lib. bdg. 27.07 *(978-1-61641-965-3(2)*, Calico Chapter Bks) Magic Wagon.

—Mouseheart. Fiedler, Lisa. (Mouseheart Ser.: 1). (ENG.). (J). (gr. 3-7). 2015. 336p. pap. 6.99 *(978-1-4424-8783-3(6))*; 2014. 320p. 16.99 *(978-1-4424-8781-9(X))* McElderry, Margaret K. Bks. (McElderry, Margaret K. Bks.).

—Really New School: An Up2U Action Adventure. Fields, Jan. 2013. (Up2U Adventures Ser.). 80p. (J). (gr. 2-5). lib. bdg. 27.07 *(978-1-61641-969-1(5)*, Calico Chapter Bks) Magic Wagon.

Toader, Alex. The Day Dreamer. Rodriguez, Robert et al. 2005. (Shark Boy & Lava Girl Adventures Ser.: Bk. 1). 162p. (J). (gr. -1-7). per. *(978-1-933104-04-1(X))* Troublemaker Publishing, LP.

—Shark Boy & Lava Girl Adventures: Return to Planet Drool. Rodriguez, Robert & Roberson, Chris. 2005. (Shark Boy & Lava Girl Adventures Ser.: Book 2). 150p. (J). *(978-1-933104-05-8(8))* Troublemaker Publishing, LP.

—Shark Boy & Lava Girl Adventures: The Deep Sleep. Rodriguez, Robert & Roberson, Chris. 2005. 150p. (J). 10.95 *(978-1-933104-08-9(2))* Troublemaker Publishing, LP.

—Shark Boy & Lava Girl Adventures: The Knight Mare. Rodriguez, Robert & Roberson, Chris. 2005. 150p. (J). 10.95 *(978-1-933104-09-6(0))* Troublemaker Publishing, LP.

Tobar, Jorge. Cuaderno de la Rosa Tomo 4, 8 vols., Vol. 88. Tobar, Malena & Oyola, Milta, eds. 2011.Tr. of Roses-Student Manual. (SPA.). 74p. (J). 7.00 *(978-1-931984-86-7(7)*, 7809-65S1) Faith & Action Team.

Tobar, Malena. Barnabas & His Great Mission for Christ. Jingling, Kathy, ed. 2011. (SPA.). 198p. (J). spiral bd. 7.00 *(978-1-931984-40-9(9)*, 2002-00E1) Faith & Action Team.

—Bernabe y su Gran Mision por Cristo. Jingling, Kathy, ed. Oyola, Milta, tr. from ENG. 2011.Tr. of Barnabas & his Great Mission for Christ. (SPA.). 191p. (J). spiral bd. 7.00 *(978-1-931984-41-6(7)*, 2002-00S1) Faith & Action Team.

—¡Vívelo al extremo! Nivel 1: Lecciones prácticas para aprender de Dios. Brannan, Dara, ed. 2011. 218p. (J). ring bd. 20.00 *(978-1-931984-36-2(0))* Faith & Action Team.

Tobella, Montse. El Grito de la Botella. Albanell, Pep. 2004.Tr. of Scream from the Bottle. (SPA.). (J). pap. 7.99 *(978-84-236-6701-7(4))* Edebé ESP. Dist: Lectorum Pubns., Inc.

—Los Supermusicos. Navarro, Carlos. 2003.Tr. of Super Musicians. (SPA.). 45p. (J). 10.36 *(978-84-7901-701-9(5))* Oasis, Producciones Generales de Comunicacion, S.L. ESP. Dist: Lectorum Pubns., Inc.

Tobia, Lauren. Anna Hibiscus' Song. Atinuke. ed. 2011. (ENG.). 32p. (J). 12.99 *(978-1-61067-040-1(X))* Kane Miller.

—Baby's Got the Blues. Shields, Carol Diggory. 2014. (ENG.). 32p. (J). (gr. -1-2). 16.99 *(978-0-7636-3260-1(0))* Candlewick Pr.

—Good Luck Anna Hibiscus!, Bk. 3. Atinuke. ed. 2011. (ENG.). 112p. (J). (gr. k-4). pap. 5.99 *(978-1-61067-007-4(8))* Kane Miller.

Tobia, Lauren. Happy in Our Skin. Manushkin, Fran. 2015. (ENG.). 32p. (J). (-k). 15.99 ***(978-0-7636-7002-3(2))*** Candlewick Pr.

Tobia, Lauren. Have Fun Anna Hibiscus! Atinuke. 2011. (ENG.). 109p. (J). (gr. k-4). pap. 5.99 *(978-1-61067-008-1(6))* Kane Miller.

—Hooray for Anna Hibiscus! Atinuke. 2010. (ENG.). 112p. (J). (gr. k-4). pap. 5.99 *(978-1-935279-74-7(2))* Kane Miller.

—How to Find a Fruit Bat. Robinson, Michelle. (ENG.). 32p. (J). (-k). 2013. pap. 10.99 *(978-1-4083-0855-4(X))*; 2012. 18.99 *(978-1-4083-0854-7(1))* Hodder & Stoughton GBR. Dist: Independent Pubs. Group.

—Splash, Anna Hibiscus! Atinuke. 2013. (ENG.). 32p. (J). 14.99 *(978-1-61067-173-6(2))* Kane Miller.

Tobias, Tom. Harry Meets a Bully. Tobias, Anne B. 2008. 16p. pap. 9.95 *(978-0-9822540-3-5(2))* Peppertree Pr., The.

—Harry's Problem First Loose Tooth. Tobias, Anne B. 2008. 16p. pap. 9.95 *(978-0-9818683-9-4(8))* Peppertree Pr., The.

Tobin, Jennifer, photos by. ABCs of the BWCAW: A Fun Guide to the Boundary Waters Canoe Area Wilderness. Tobin, Jennifer. Tobin, Adriana. 2003. 60p. (YA). bds. 17.95 *(978-0-9742555-0-7(5))* MyHandiwork.

Tobin, Marc. The Life & Times of Lilly the Lash: The Garden Gathering. Woik, Julie. 2009. (ENG.). 48p. (J). 19.95 *(978-0-9663335-7-2(8))* Snow In Sarasota Publishing.

Tobin, Nancy. Flick a Switch: How Electricity Gets to Your Home. Seuling, Barbara. 2003. (ENG.). 32p. (J). (gr. k-3). tchr. ed. 16.95 *(978-0-8234-1729-2(8))* Holiday Hse., Inc.

Tocchini, Greg, et al. Eye for Eye, Vol. 2. Ciencin, Scott. 2004. 160p. (YA). pap. 12.95 *(978-1-59314-033-5(9))* CrossGeneration Comics, Inc.

Tocco, Douglas. Meet the Gizmos: The First Kids on the International Space Station. Tocco, John V. 2003. 32p. 16.95 *(978-0-9711665-2-3(8))*; per. 9.95 *(978-0-9711665-3-0(6))* Favorite Uncle Bks., LLC.

Toda, Yasunari. Mobile Suit Gundam Seed Astray R, Vol. 4. Chiba, Tomohiro. rev. ed. 2005. (Mobile Suit Gundam Seed (Novels) Ser.). 232p. per. 9.99 *(978-1-59532-997-4(8)*, Tokyopop Adult) TOKYOPOP, Inc.

—Scryed, 5 vols. Kuroda, Yosuke. 2003. Vol. 2. rev. ed. 192p. pap. 9.99 *(978-1-59182-229-5(7))*; Vol. 4. 4th rev. ed. 200p. pap. 9.99 *(978-1-59182-231-8(9))*; Vol. 5. rev. ed. 192p. pap. 9.99 *(978-1-59182-232-5(7))* TOKYOPOP, Inc.

Todd, Chuck. Raccoon Next Door: And Other Creatures of the Urban Wilderness. Bogue, Gary. 2003. 196p. pap. 16.95 *(978-1-890771-71-3(6))* Heyday.

—There's a Hummingbird in My Backyard. Bogue, Gary. 2010. 40p. (J). (gr. -1-3). 15.95 *(978-1-59714-131-4(3))* Heyday.

—There's an Opossum in My Backyard. Bogue, Gary. 2007. 40p. (J). (gr. -1-3). 15.95 *(978-1-59714-059-1(7))* Heyday.

Todd, Justin. Treasure Island. Stevenson, Robert Louis. unabr. ed. 2003. (Chrysalis Childrens Classics Ser.). 208p. (YA). pap. *(978-1-84365-037-9(1)*, Pavilion Children's Books) Pavilion Bks.

Todd, Mark. My Monster Notebook. Harris, John. 2011. (ENG.). 48p. (J). (gr. 3-18). 16.95 *(978-1-60606-050-6(3)*, J. Paul Getty Museum) Getty Pubns.

—Whatcha Mean, What's a Zine? The Art of Making Zines & Mini-Comics. Watson, Esther Pearl. 2006. (ENG.). 112p. (YA). (gr. 7). pap. 12.99 *(978-0-618-56315-9(6))* Houghton Mifflin Harcourt Publishing Co.

Todd, Michelle, jt. illus. see Chiacchiera, Moreno.

Todd, Mort, et al. Tales from the Crypt. Van Lente, Fred et al. Lansdale, John L. et al. 2009. (Tales from the Crypt Graphic Novels Ser.: 6). (ENG.). 96p. (J). (gr. 5-12). 12.95 *(978-1-59707-137-6(4))* Papercutz.

Todd, Sheri. Little Bent Cedar. Speed, Bryan W. 2007. (ENG.). 24p. (J). (gr. 2-4). per. *(978-1-933255-38-5(2))* DNA Pr.

Todd, Sue. Medio Pollito (Half-Chick) A Mexican Folktale. StJohn, Amanda. 2011. (Folktales from Around the World Ser.). (ENG.). 24p. (J). (gr. k-3). 28.50 *(978-1-60973-141-0(7)*, 201144) Child's World, Inc., The.

—Mira & the Big Story. Alary, Laura. 2012. (ENG.). 36p. (J). 12.00 *(978-1-55896-693-2(5)*, Skinner Hse. Bks.) Unitarian Universalist Assn.

—One Last Wish: A Tale from India. 2013. (Tales of Honor (Red Chair Press) Ser.). (ENG.). 32p. (J). (gr. 1-4). lib. bdg. 26.60 *(978-1-937529-76-5(2))* Red Chair Pr.

—One Last Wish: A Tale from India. Barchers, Suzanne I. 2013. (Tales of Honor Ser.). 32p. (gr. 1-3). pap. 8.95 *(978-1-937529-60-4(6))* Red Chair Pr.

Todd, Sue. Steam! Taming the River Monster. Coleman, Wim & Perrin, Pat. 2015. (Setting the Stage for Fluency Ser.). (ENG.). 40p. (gr. 3-5). lib. bdg. 27.93 ***(978-1-939656-74-2(5))*** Red Chair Pr.

Toddy, Irving. D Is for Drum: A Native American Alphabet. Shoulders, Michael & Shoulders, Debbie. rev. ed. 2006. (ENG.). 40p. (J). (gr. k-6). 16.95 *(978-1-58536-274-5(3))* Sleeping Bear Pr.

—Desert Digits: An Arizona Number Book. Gowan, Barbara. 2006. (Count Your Way Across the U. S. A. Ser.). (ENG.). 40p. (J). (gr. -1-3). 17.95 *(978-1-58536-162-5(3))* Sleeping Bear Pr.

—Little Woman Warrior Who Came Home. Parsons Yazzie, Evangeline. Ruffenach, Jessie, ed. 2005. (NAV & ENG.). 32p. (J). (gr. 4-7). 17.95 *(978-1-893354-55-5(5))* Salina Bookshelf Inc.

—A Summer's Trade/Shiigo Na'iini' Trotter, Deborah W. 2007. (ENG & NAV.). 32p. (J). (gr. -1-3). 17.95 *(978-1-893354-71-5(7))* Salina Bookshelf Inc.

Todo Color. Biblia Ilustrada para Ninos. Winkler, Jude. 2007. 172p. (J). (gr. -1-3). 12.99 *(978-0-89942-636-5(0))* Catholic Bk. Publishing Corp.

Toft, Kim Michelle. The World That We Want. Toft, Kim Michelle. 2005. 32p. (J). pap. *(978-0-7022-3482-8(6))* Univ. of Queensland Pr.

Tofte, Mavis. Doogie Dork & the Storm. Tofte, Mavis. 2006. 64p. (J). per. 6.75 *(978-0-9709906-5-5(0))* Creative Quill Publishing, Inc.

—Doogie Dork's Wish. Tofte, Mavis. 2003. (J). per. 5.75 *(978-0-9709906-2-4(6))* Creative Quill Publishing, Inc.

Tofts, Hannah. One Cool Watermelon. Tofts, Hannah. 2008. (Things I Eat Ser.). (ENG.). 24p. (J). (gr. -1-k). *(978-1-84089-555-1(1))* Zero to Ten, Ltd.

Togashi, Yoshihiro. Hunter X Hunter. Togashi, Yoshihiro. Olsen, Lillian, tr. from JPN. 2005. (Hunter X Hunter Ser.: Vol. 2). (ENG.). 192p. pap. 9.99 *(978-1-59116-785-3(X))* Viz Media.

—Hunter X Hunter. Togashi, Yoshihiro. (Hunter X Hunter Ser.). (ENG.). Vol. 1. 2005. 184p. pap. 9.99 *(978-1-59116-753-2(1))*; Vol. 3. 2005. 192p. pap. 9.99 *(978-1-59116-849-2(X))*; Vol. 4. 2005. 192p. pap. 9.99 *(978-1-59116-992-5(5))*; Vol. 5. 2005. 192p. pap. 9.99 *(978-1-4215-0184-0(8))*; Vol. 6. 2006. 208p. pap. 9.99 *(978-1-4215-0185-7(6))*; Vol. 7. 2006. 208p. pap. 9.99 *(978-1-4215-0332-5(8))*; Vol. 9. 2006. 208p. pap. 9.99 *(978-1-4215-0644-9(0))* Viz Media.

—Yu Yu Hakusho. Togashi, Yoshihiro. (YuYu Hakusho Ser.). (ENG.). Vol. 3. 2004. 192p. pap. 9.99 *(978-1-59116-183-7(5))*; Vol. 4. 2004. 192p. pap. 9.99 *(978-1-59116-325-1(0))*; Vol. 5. 2004. 200p. pap. 7.95 *(978-1-59116-521-7(0))*; Vol. 6. 2005. 208p. pap. 9.99 *(978-1-59116-668-9(3))* Viz Media.

—Yu Yu Hakusho: Lonesome Ghosts, 2. Togashi, Yoshihiro. Olsen, Lillian, tr. 2003. (YuYu Hakusho Ser.: Vol. 2). (ENG.). 200p. pap. 9.99 *(978-1-59116-082-3(0))* Viz Media.

—YuYu Hakusho. Togashi, Yoshihiro. (YuYu Hakusho Ser.: 13). (ENG.). 2007. 192p. pap. 7.95 *(978-1-4215-1119-1(3))*; Vol. 1. 2003. 208p. pap. 9.99 *(978-1-56931-904-8(9))* Viz Media.

—Yuyu Hakusho. Togashi, Yoshihiro. (YuYu Hakusho Ser.). (ENG.). Vol. 7. 2005. 200p. pap. 7.95 *(978-1-59116-812-6(0))*; Vol. 8. 2005. 192p. pap. 9.99 *(978-1-4215-0026-3(4))*; Vol. 9. 2006. 208p. pap. 9.99 *(978-1-4215-0278-6(X))* Viz Media.

Toka, Yumie. Jimi's Book of Japanese: A Motivating Method to Learn Japanese (Extra Spicy Super Crunchy Edition) Takahashi, Peter X. ltd. ed. 2006. 172p. (J). pap. 34.95 *(978-0-9723247-1-7(2)*, PB&J OmniMedia) Takahashi & Black.

—Jimi's Book of Japanese: A Motivating Method to Learn Japanese (Hiragana) Takahashi, Peter X. 2003. (JPN & ENG.). 72p. reprint ed. pap. 18.95 *(978-0-9723247-0-0(4)*, PB&J OmniMedia) Takahashi & Black.

—Jimi's Book of Japanese: A Motivating Method to Learn Japanese (Kanji) Takahashi, Peter X. Moto, Mikki, ed. 2006. (J). pap. 24.95 *(978-0-9723247-5-5(5)*, PB&J OmniMedia) Takahashi & Black.

—Jimi's Book of Japanese: A Motivating Method to Learn Japanese (Katakana) Takahashi, Peter X. Moto, Mikki, ed. 2005. (JPN & ENG.). 76p. (J). pap. 18.95 *(978-0-9723247-2-4(0)*, PB&J OmniMedia) Takahashi & Black.

—Jimi's Book of Japanese: A Motivating Method to Learn Japanese (Some of My Best Friends Are Monkeys Edition), 2 vols. Takahashi, Peter X. Moto, Mikki, ed. ltd. ed. 2005. 146p. pap. 36.95 *(978-0-9723247-4-8(7)*, PB&J OmniMedia) Takahashi & Black.

—Jimi's Sumo Stack: A Motivating Method to Memorize Japanese. Takahashi, Peter X. 2006. pap. 19.95 *(978-0-9723247-8-6(X)*, PB&J OmniMedia) Takahashi & Black.

Toki, Wilfred. Grandpa, What's a Humuhumu? Toki, Wilfred. Hoover, John J., photos by. 2004. 64p. (J). pap. 8.95 *(978-0-9729905-9-2(3))* Beachhouse Publishing, LLC.

—Hana & the Honu. Toki, Wilfred. 2004. 32p. (J). 12.95 *(978-0-9729905-8-5(5))* Beachhouse Publishing, LLC.

—Moku & the Heoe of Waimea. Toki, Wilfred. 2004. 32p. (J). 12.95 *(978-0-9729905-7-8(7))* Beachhouse Publishing, LLC.

Tokunbo, Dimitrea. Amadi's Snowman. Saint-Lot, Katia Novet. 2008. 32p. (J). (gr. -1-3). 16.95 *(978-0-88448-298-7(7))* Tilbury Hse. Pubs.

—Has Anybody Lost a Glove? Johnson, G. Francis. 2004. (ENG.). 32p. (J). (gr. k-2). 15.95 *(978-1-59078-041-1(8))* Boyds Mills Pr.

Tokyopop Staff. Rave Master: The Sound of Thunder, Vol. 3. 2005. 96p. (J). pap. 7.99 *(978-1-59532-791-8(6))* TOKYOPOP, Inc.

Tokyopop Staff. Passion Fruit: Sweat & Honey, 3 vols., Vol. 1. Tokyopop Staff. ltd. ed. 2005. 208p. pap. 19.99 *(978-1-59182-796-2(5))* TOKYOPOP, Inc.

Toland, Darrell. Edsel Mcfarlan's New Car. Holechek, Max. 2010. 52p. (J). *(978-1-935359-40-1(1))* Book Pubs. Network.

Toledano, Connie. Mardi Gras Abcs. Toledano, Connie. 2013. 56p. pap. 11.99 *(978-0-615-79138-8(7))* Irma's Bks.

Toledo, Francisco. Light Foot (Pies Ligeros) Toledo, Natalia. Amado, Elisa, tr. from CAI. 2007. (ENG & SPA.). 56p. (J). (gr. k-7). 17.95 *(978-0-88899-789-0(2))* Groundwood Bks. CAN. Dist: Perseus-PGW.

Tolford, Joshua. Blitz. Beatty, Hetty Burlingame. 2012. 124p. 40.95 *(978-1-258-25354-7(2))*; pap. 25.95 *(978-1-258-25430-8(1))* Literary Licensing, LLC.

T

Tolkien, J. R. R. The Hobbit. Tolkien, J. R. R. 70th anniv. ed. 2011. (ENG.). 400p. mass mkt. ***(978-0-261-10221-7(4))*** HarperCollins Pubs. Ltd.

Tolkien, J. R. R. The Hobbit. Tolkien, J. R. R. 75th anniv. ed. 2007. (ENG.). 320p. (gr. 7). 25.00 *(978-0-618-96863-3(6))* Houghton Mifflin Harcourt Publishing Co.

Tolman, Marije. Intercambio Magico. Heide, Iris van der. De Sterck, Goedele, tr. 2009. (Los Especiales de A la Orilla del Viento Ser.). (SPA.). 28p. (J). (gr. -1-3). *(978-968-16-8565-2(2))* Fondo de Cultura Economica.

—Our Very Own Christmas. Langen, Annette. 2012. (ENG.). 32p. (J). (gr. -1-3). 17.95 *(978-0-7358-4088-1(1))* North-South Bks., Inc.

—Wolf & Dog. Vanden Heede, Sylvia. Nagelkerke, Bill, tr. from DUT. 2013. 96p. 16.95 *(978-1-877579-47-9(5))* Gecko Productions, Inc.

Tolman, Marije & Tolman, Ronald. The Tree House. Tolman, Marije. 2012. (ENG.). 32p. (J). pap. 6.99 *(978-99921-787-5-1(2)*, 134923) Bloomsbury Qatar Foundation Publishing QAT. Dist: Macmillan.

Tolman, Ronald, jt. illus. see Tolman, Marije.

Tolman, Tom. Little One. Reid, Pamela Carrington. 2010. (J). *(978-1-59811-574-1(X))* Covenant Communications.

Tolson, Scott. If You Want My Advice- Owens, L. L. 2004. 25p. *(978-1-57021-030-3(6))* Comprehensive Health Education Foundation.

—The Longest Car Ride Ever. Owens, L. L. 2004. 28p. *(978-1-57021-032-7(2))* Comprehensive Health Education Foundation.

—The New Girl. Owens, L. L. 2004. 27p. *(978-1-57021-029-7(2))* Comprehensive Health Education Foundation.

Tolstikova, Dasha. The Jacket. Hall, Kirsten. 2014. (ENG.). 48p. (J). (gr. -1-3). 17.95 *(978-1-59270-168-1(X))* Enchanted Lion Bks., LLC.

Tom, Darcy. Advantage Reading Grade 3, Vol. 8114. Morss, Martha. Hamaguchi, Carla, ed. 2004. (Advantage Workbook Ser.). 112p. 8.99 *(978-1-59198-024-7(0)*, CTP 8114) Creative Teaching Pr., Inc.

—Down on the Farm. Jordano, Kimberly & Corcoran, Tebra. Fisch, Teri L., ed. 2003. (Stepping into Standards Theme Ser.). 64p. (J). (gr. k-2). pap. 10.99 *(978-1-57471-947-5(5)*, 2475) Creative Teaching Pr., Inc.

—Going Buggy! Jordano, Kimberly & Corcoran, Tebra. Fisch, Teri L., ed. 2003. (Stepping into Standards Theme Ser.). 64p. (J). (gr. k-2). pap. 10.99 *(978-1-57471-949-9(1)*, 2477) Creative Teaching Pr., Inc.

—Native American Peoples. Jennett, Pamela. Rous, Sheri, ed. 2003. (Stepping into Standards Theme Ser.). 64p. (J). (gr. 2-4). pap. 10.99 *(978-1-59198-003-2(8)*, CTP2485) Creative Teaching Pr., Inc.

—Rain Forest Adventures. Jordano, Kimberly & Corcoran, Tebra. Fisch, Teri L., ed. 2003. (Stepping into Standards Theme Ser.). 64p. (J). (gr. k-2). pap. 10.99 *(978-1-57471-945-1(9)*, 2473) Creative Teaching Pr., Inc.

—Reading First: Unlock the Secrets to Reading Success with Research-Based Strategies, Vol. 2259. Hults, Alaska. Hamaguchi, Carla, ed. 2003. 176p. per. 13.99 *(978-1-59198-009-4(7)*, CTP2259) Creative Teaching Pr., Inc.

—Rocks & Minerals. Shiotsu, Vicky. Rous, Sheri, ed. 2003. (Stepping into Standards Theme Ser.). 64p. (J). (gr. 2-4). pap. 10.99 *(978-1-59198-005-6(4)*, CTP2487) Creative Teaching Pr., Inc.

—Solar System. Cernek, Kim et al. Rous, Sheri & Hamaguchi, Carla, eds. 2003. (Stepping into Standards Theme Ser.). 64p. (J). (gr. 2-4). pap. 10.99 *(978-1-59198-001-8(1)*, 2483) Creative Teaching Pr., Inc.

—Super Senses. Jordano, Kimberly & Corcoran, Tebra. Fisch, Teri L., ed. 2003. (Stepping into Standards Theme Ser.). 64p. (J). (gr. k-2). pap. 10.99 *(978-1-57471-951-2(3)*, 2479) Creative Teaching Pr., Inc.

Tom, Darcy. Habitats. Tom, Darcy, ed. Phillips, Heather. Jennett, Pamela & Rous, Sheri, eds. 2003. (Stepping into Standards Theme Ser.). 64p. (J). (gr. 2-4). pap. 10.99 *(978-1-59198-007-0(0)*, CTP2489) Creative Teaching Pr., Inc.

Tom, Darcy & Grayson, Rick. Bookmaking Bonanza, Vol. 2234. Jordano, Kimberly & Adsit, Kim. Cernek, Kim, ed. 2004. 80p. (J). (gr. k-1). pap. 11.99 *(978-1-59198-049-0(6))* Creative Teaching Pr., Inc.

Tom, Darcy & Mathis, Teresa. Kid Concoctions, Creations & Contraptions. Eagan, Robynne. 2005. (ENG.). 224p. pap. 18.95 *(978-1-57310-455-5(8))* Teaching & Learning Co.

Tom, Darcy, jt. illus. see Campbell, Jenny.

Tom, LaBaff. Fractions & Decimals Made Easy. Wingard-Nelson, Rebecca. 2005. (Making Math Easy Ser.). 48p. (J). (gr. 2-4). lib. bdg. 25.27 *(978-0-7660-2513-4(6)*, Enslow Elementary) Enslow Pubs., Inc.

—Science Fair Projects about the Properties of Matter Using Marbles, Water, Balloons, & More. Gardner, Robert. 2004. (Physics! Best Science Projects Ser.). 128p. (J). lib. bdg. 27.94 *(978-0-7660-2128-0(9))* Enslow Pubs., Inc.

Tomasek, Dean. The Christmas Tree That Cried. Marshall, Jane Garrett. 2013. 106p. pap. 24.99 *(978-0-9896247-0-1(6))* WRB Pub.

Tomasello, Sam. Gardening with Children. Hanneman, Monika et al. 2011. (BBG Guides for a Greener Planet Ser.). (ENG.). 120p. pap. 12.95 *(978-1-889538-78-5(7))* Brooklyn Botanic Garden.

Tomes, Margot. Homesick: My Own Story. Fritz, Jean. 2007. (Puffin Modern Classics Ser.). (ENG.). 176p. (J). (gr. 3-7). 6.99 *(978-0-14-240761-5(5)*, Puffin) Penguin Publishing Group.

—I Saw Three Ships. Goudge, Elizabeth. 2008. (ENG.). 64p. (J). 15.95 *(978-1-56792-369-8(0))* Godine, David R. Pub.

—Little Sister & the Month Brothers, 0 vols. De Regniers, Beatrice Schenk. 2009. (ENG.). 48p. (J). (gr. -1-3). 17.99 *(978-0-7614-5546-2(9)*, 9780761455462, Amazon Children's Publishing) Amazon Publishing.

Tomic, Tomislav. The Fairy Tale Handbook. Hamilton, Libby. 2014. (ENG.). 20p. (J). (gr. k-4). 22.99 *(978-0-7636-7130-3(4)*, Templar) Candlewick Pr.

Tomita, Kuni, jt. illus. see Perilli, Marilena.

Tomita, Sukehiro & Yazawa, Nao. Wedding Peach, Vol. 1. Tomita, Sukehiro. 2003. (Wedding Peach Ser.). (ENG.). 192p. (YA). pap. 9.95 *(978-1-59116-076-2(6))* Viz Media.

Tomizawa, Hitoshi. Alien Nine: Emulators. Tomizawa, Hitoshi. Pannone, Frank, ed. Jackson, Laura & Kobayashi, Yoko, trs. from JPN. 2004. 248p. pap. 9.99 *(978-1-58664-924-1(8)*, CMX 65004G, CPM Manga) Central Park Media Corp.

—Alien Nine 1, Vol. 1. Tomizawa, Hitoshi. Pannone, Frank, ed. Jackson, Laura & Kobayashi, Yoko, trs. from JPN. 2003. 224p. (gr. 11-18). pap. 15.95 *(978-1-58664-891-6(8)*, CMX 64201G, CPM Manga) Central Park Media Corp.

—Alien Nine 2, Vol. 2. Tomizawa, Hitoshi. Pannone, Frank, ed. Jackson, Laura & Kobayashi, Yoko, trs. from JPN. 2003. 224p. (gr. 11-18). pap. 15.95 *(978-1-58664-892-3(6)*, CMX 64202G, CPM Manga) Central Park Media Corp.

—Treasure Hunter 1: Eternal Youth, 3 vols., Vol. 1. Tomizawa, Hitoshi. Pannone, Frank, ed. Kobayashi, Mayumi, tr. from JPN. 2004. Orig. Title: Hizenya Jyubei 2. 200p. pap. 9.99 *(978-1-58664-921-0(3)*, CMX 65101G, CPM Manga) Central Park Media Corp.

—Treasure Hunter 2: Figurehead of Souls, 3 vols., Vol. 2. Tomizawa, Hitoshi. Pannone, Frank, ed. Kobayashi, Mayumi, tr. from JPN. 2004. Orig. Title: Hizenya Jyubei 2. 200p. pap. 9.99 *(978-1-58664-922-7(1)*, CMX 65102G, CPM Manga) Central Park Media Corp.

—Treasure Hunter 3: The Last Crusade, 3 vols., Vol. 3. Tomizawa, Hitoshi. Pannone, Frank, ed. Kobayashi, Mayumi, tr. from JPN. 2004. Orig. Title: Hizenya Jyubei 2. 216p. pap. 9.99 *(978-1-58664-923-4(X)*, CMX 65103G, CPM Manga) Central Park Media Corp.

Tomkins, Jasper. Nimby: An Extraordinary Cloud Who Meets a Remarkable Friend. 2011. (ENG.). 60p. 15.95 *(978-1-59583-428-7(1)*, 9781595834287, Green Tiger Pr.) Laughing Elephant.

Tomkinson, Tim. What Was the Gold Rush? Holub, Joan. 2013. (What Was... ? Ser.). (ENG.). (J). (gr. 3-7). 128p. 15.99 *(978-0-448-46577-7(9))*; 112p. pap. 5.99 *(978-0-448-46289-9(3))* Penguin Publishing Group. (Grosset & Dunlap).

—What Was the March on Washington? Krull, Kathleen. 2013. (What Was... ? Ser.). (ENG.). (J). (gr. 3-7). 128p. 15.99 *(978-0-448-46578-4(7))*; 112p. pap. 5.99 *(978-0-448-46287-5(7))* Penguin Publishing Group. (Grosset & Dunlap).

Tomkinson, Tim, jt. illus. see Mantha, John.

Tomlins, Karen. Winston Churchill. Daynes, Katie. 2006. (Usborne Famous Lives Gift Bks.). 64p. (J). (gr. 2-5). 8.99 *(978-0-7945-1258-3(5)*, Usborne) EDC Publishing.

Tommer, Sarah. Sidney the Silly Who Only Eats 6. Penn, M. W. 2007. 32p. (J). *(978-0-9784047-2-7(6))* Pays et Terroirs.

—Sidney the Silly Who Only Eats 6. Penn, Mw. 2013. 36p. pap. 13.95 *(978-0-9840425-7-9(1))* MathWord Pr., LLC.

Tomos, Angharad. Rala Rwdins. Tomos, Angharad. 2005. (WEL.). 48p. pap. 1.95 *(978-0-86243-065-8(8))* Y Lolfa GBR. Dist: Dufour Editions, Inc.

Tomos, Morgan. Welsh Folk Stories. Edwards, Meinir Wyn. 2012. (WEL & ENG.). 128p. (J). pap. 9.95 *(978-1-84771-358-2(0))* Y Lolfa GBR. Dist: Dufour Editions, Inc.

Tonatiuh, Duncan. Salsa: Un Poema Para Cocinar / a Cooking Poem, 1 vol. Argueta, Jorge. Amado, Elisa, tr. ed. 2015. (Bilingual Cooking Poems Ser.). (ENG & SPA.). 32p. (J). (gr. -1-2). 18.95 *(978-1-55498-442-8(4))* Groundwood Bks. CAN. Dist: Perseus-PGW.

Tonel. Drum, Chavi, Drum! Dole, Mayra L. 2013.Tr. of ¡Toca, Chavi, Toca!. (ENG & SPA.). 32p. (J). pap. 8.95 *(978-0-89239-302-2(5)*, Children's Book Press) Lee & Low Bks., Inc.

—Toca, Chavi, Toca! Dole, Mayra L. 2003.Tr. of Drum, Chavi, Drum!. (ENG & SPA.). 32p. (J). 16.95 *(978-0-89239-186-8(3))* Lee & Low Bks., Inc.

Tonel, jt. illus. see Pedlar, Elaine.

Tong, Andie. Batman - Nightmare in Gotham City. Lemke, Donald. 2015. (ENG.). 24p. (J). (gr. -1-3). pap. 3.99 *(978-0-06-234486-1(2)*, HarperFestival) HarperCollins Pubs.

—Batman Classic - Eternal Enemies. Sazaklis, John. 2013. (ENG.). 24p. (J). (gr. -1-3). pap. 3.99 *(978-0-06-220997-9(3)*, HarperFestival) HarperCollins Pubs.

—Batman Versus Bane. Huelin, Jodi. 2012. (I Can Read Book 2 Ser.). (ENG.). 32p. (J). (gr. -1-3). pap. 3.99 *(978-0-06-213224-6(5))* HarperCollins Pubs.

—Convergence. Lee, Stan & Moore, Stuart. 2015. (Zodiac Legacy Ser.). (ENG.). 480p. (J). (gr. 3-7). 16.99 *(978-1-4231-8085-2(2))* Disney Pr.

—Day of the Undead. Sazaklis, John & Merkel, Joe F. 2013. (ENG.). 24p. (J). (gr. -1-3). pap. 3.99 *(978-0-06-220999-3(X)*, HarperFestival) HarperCollins Pubs.

—Superman's Superpowers. Rosen, Lucy. 2013. (I Can Read Book 2 Ser.). (ENG.). 32p. (J). (gr. -1-3). pap. 3.99 *(978-0-06-223597-8(4))* HarperCollins Pubs.

Tong, Kevin. The Earth Machine. Tong, Kevin. 2007. 32p. (J). (gr. -1-3). 15.95 *(978-1-60108-001-1(8))* Red Cygnet Pr.

Tong-Li, Candace. Tales of Titans: Timeless Dinosaur Stories. Tong-Li, Candace. 2011. (ENG.). 126p. pap. 12.99 *(978-1-4637-5023-7(4))* CreateSpace Independent Publishing Platform.

Tong, Paul. A Little at a Time. Adler, David A. 2010. (ENG.). 32p. (J). (gr. -1-3). 16.95 *(978-0-8234-1739-1(5))* Holiday Hse., Inc.

—Mama, Will It Snow Tonight? Carlstrom, Nancy White. 2009. (ENG.). 32p. (J). (gr. k-3). 16.95 *(978-1-59078-562-1(2))* Boyds Mills Pr.

—The Night of the Hurricane's Fury. Ransom, Candice. (On My Own History Ser.). 48p. 2011. (J). pap. 39.62 *(978-0-7613-7621-7(6)*, First Avenue Editions); 2011. (ENG.). (gr. 2-4). pap. 6.95 *(978-0-7613-3940-3(X)*, First Avenue Editions); 2009. (ENG.). (gr. 2-4). 25.26 *(978-0-8225-7893-2(X))* Lerner Publishing Group.

—Pecos Bill. Krensky, Stephen. 2007. (On My Own Folklore Ser.). (ENG.). 48p. (gr. 2-4). per. 6.95 *(978-0-8225-6475-1(0)*, First Avenue Editions) Lerner Publishing Group.

Toni, Alessandra. Where's My Mommy? Hao, K. T. 2008. (ENG.). 32p. (J). (gr. -1). 15.95 *(978-1-933327-40-2(5))* Purple Bear Bks., Inc.

—Where's My Mommy? Hao, K. T. 2008. (ENG.). 32p. (J). (gr. -1). 16.50 *(978-1-933327-41-9(3))* Purple Bear Bks., Inc.

Tonk, Ernest. Pirate of the North. McCracken, Harold. 2011. 224p. 44.95 *(978-1-258-09631-1(5))* Literary Licensing, LLC.

Toohey, Eileen N. 365 Knock-Knock Jokes. Myers, Robert. 2006. (ENG.). 128p. (J). (gr. 1-4). per. 4.95 *(978-1-4027-4108-1(1))* Sterling Publishing Co., Inc.

Tooke, Susan. Brave Jack & the Unicorn. McNaughton, Janet. 2005. (ENG.). 32p. (J). (gr. k-3). 15.95 *(978-0-88776-677-0(3)*, Tundra Bks.) Tundra Bks. CAN. Dist: Penguin Random Hse., LLC.

—The City Speaks in Drums, 1 vol. Grant, Shauntay. ed. 2010. (ENG.). 32p. (J). (gr. -1-12). 19.95 *(978-1-55109-758-9(3))* Nimbus Publishing, Ltd. CAN. Dist: Orca Bk. Pubs. USA.

—F Is for Fiddlehead: A New Brunswick Alphabet. Lohnes, Marilyn. rev. ed. 2007. (Discover Canada Province by Province Ser.). (ENG.). 40p. (J). (gr. 1-7). 17.95 *(978-1-58536-318-6(9))* Sleeping Bear Pr.

—A Fiddle for Angus. Wilson, Budge. 2006. (ENG.). 32p. (J). (gr. 1-4). pap. 13.95 *(978-0-88776-785-2(0)*, Random Hse. Puzzles & Games) Tundra Bks. CAN. Dist: Penguin Random Hse., LLC.

—Free As the Wind, 1 vol. Bastedo, Jamie. 2010. (ENG.). 32p. (J). pap. 10.95 *(978-0-88995-446-5(1))* Red Deer Pr. CAN. Dist: Ingram Pub. Services.

—Lasso the Wind: Aurelia's Verses & Other Poems, 1 vol. Clarke, George Elliott. 2014. (ENG.). 66p. (J). (gr. 3-6). 24.95 *(978-1-77108-050-7(7))* Nimbus Publishing, Ltd. CAN. Dist: Orca Bk. Pubs. USA.

—A Seaside Alphabet. Grassby, Donna. 2009. (ABC Our Country Ser.). (ENG.). 32p. (J). (gr. 1-4). pap. 7.95 *(978-0-88776-938-2(1)*, Tundra Bks.) Tundra Bks. CAN. Dist: Penguin Random Hse., LLC.

—Up Home, 1 vol. Grant, Shauntay. ed. (ENG.). (J). (gr. k-5). 2012. 32p. pap. 12.95 *(978-1-55109-911-8(X))*; 2009. 34p. 19.95 *(978-1-55109-660-5(9))* Nimbus Publishing, Ltd. CAN. Dist: Orca Bk. Pubs. USA.

Tooke, Susan. B Is for Bluenose: A Nova Scotia Alphabet. Tooke, Susan. 2008. (Discover Canada Province by Province Ser.). (ENG.). 40p. (J). 17.95 *(978-1-58536-362-9(6))* Sleeping Bear Pr.

Toothman, Lindsey. I'm Okay, Mommy. Toothman, Sherry. 2007. 20p. per. 24.95 *(978-1-4241-8733-1(8))* America Star Bks.

Topaz, Ksenia. Jodie's Hanukkah Dig. Levine, Anna. 2008. (Hanukkah Ser.). (ENG.). 32p. (J). (gr. k-3). 17.95 *(978-0-8225-7391-3(1))*; pap. 7.95 *(978-0-8225-7402-6(0))* Lerner Publishing Group. (Kar-Ben Publishing).

—Jodie's Passover Adventure. Levine, Anna. 2012. (Passover Ser.). (ENG.). 32p. (J). (gr. k-3). pap. 7.95 *(978-0-7613-5642-4(8))*; lib. bdg. 17.95 *(978-0-7613-5641-7(X))* Lerner Publishing Group. (Kar-Ben Publishing).

—Jodie's Shabbat Surprise. Levine, Anna. 2015. (J). (gr. k-3). (ENG.). 32p. lib. bdg. 17.95 *(978-1-4677-3465-3(9))*; *(978-1-4677-6204-5(0))* Lerner Publishing Group. (Kar-Ben Publishing).

—Zvuvi's Israel. Lehman-Wilzig, Tami. 2009. (Israel Ser.). (ENG.). 32p. (J). (gr. -1-2). 16.95 *(978-0-8225-8759-0(9))*; pap. 7.95 *(978-0-8225-8760-6(2))* Lerner Publishing Group. (Kar-Ben Publishing).

Topla, Beegee. Winnie's Journal. Myracle, Lauren. Yoskowitz, Lisa, ed. 2010. (Winnie Years Ser.). (ENG.). 144p. (J). (gr. 5-18). 8.99 *(978-0-525-42398-0(2)*, Dutton Juvenile) Penguin Publishing Group.

Toppenberg, Lily. Delta & Dawn: Mother & Baby Whales' Journey. Cruz, Stefanie. 2007. 32p. (J). lib. bdg. 15.95 *(978-0-9791233-2-0(1))* Big Tomato Pr.

Toppi, Sergio. Pope John Paul II. Pagotto, Toni. 2006. (Comic Book Ser.). 64p. (J). pap. 7.95 *(978-0-8198-5957-0(5))* Pauline Bks. & Media.

Torbert, Wayne E. Twelve for Thebes, a Tale of Ancient Greece. Torbert, Wayne E. 2009. 82p. pap. 8.95 *(978-1-936051-73-1(7))* Peppertree Pr., The.

Torcida, María Luisa. 125 Refranes Infantiles. Herrera, J. Ignacio. (SPA.). (J). (gr. 3-5). 12.76 *(978-84-305-9180-0(X)*, SU6580) Susaeta Ediciones, S.A. ESP. Dist: Lectorum Pubns., Inc.

Torcida, María Luisa. Poesías de Animales: La Selva en Verso. Torcida, María Luisa. Fuertes, Gloria. 2003. (SPA.). 126p. *(978-84-305-7804-7(8)*, SU4856) Susaeta Ediciones, S.A. ESP. Dist: Lectorum Pubns., Inc.

Torey Fuller. Taylor's Strawberry. Fuller, Taneka. 2014. 28p. pap. 8.99 *(978-1-62994-504-0(8))* Tate Publishing & Enterprises, LLC.

Torgeson, Sarah. Hello, Cy! Delashmutt, Amy. 2007. 24p. (J). lib. bdg. 14.95 *(978-1-932888-53-9(5))* Mascot Bks., Inc.

Toriyama, Akira. Cowa! Toriyama, Akira. 2008. (Cowa! Ser.). (ENG.). 208p. (gr. 2). pap. 7.99 *(978-1-4215-1805-3(8))* Viz Media.

—Dr. Slump. Toriyama, Akira. 2009. (Dr. Slump Ser.: 17). (ENG.). 210p. (gr. 8-18). pap. 7.99 *(978-1-4215-1999-9(2))* Viz Media.

—Dr. Slump, Vol. 1. Toriyama, Akira. Akira, Shouko. 2005. (Dr. Slump Ser.). (ENG.). 192p. pap. 9.99 *(978-1-59116-950-5(X))* Viz Media.

—Dr. Slump. Toriyama, Akira. (Dr. Slump Ser.). (ENG.). Vol. 2. 2005. 192p. pap. 9.99 *(978-1-59116-951-2(8))*; Vol. 4. 2005. 200p. pap. 9.99 *(978-1-4215-0165-9(1))*; Vol. 5. 2006. 200p. pap. 9.99 *(978-1-4215-0173-4(2))*; Vol. 6. 2006. 208p. pap. 7.99 *(978-1-4215-0174-1(0))*; Vol. 8. 2006. 208p. pap. 9.99 *(978-1-4215-0632-6(7))* Viz Media.

—Dragon Ball. Toriyama, Akira. (Dragon Ball Ser.: 3). (ENG.). (Orig.). 2009. 568p. (gr. 2). pap. 19.99 *(978-1-4215-2061-2(3))*; 2nd ed. 2003. 200p. pap. 9.99 *(978-1-56931-921-5(9))*; Vol. 1. 2nd ed. 2003. 192p. pap. 9.99 *(978-1-56931-920-8(0))* Viz Media.

—Dragon Ball, Vol. 3. Toriyama, Akira. Morimoto, Mari, tr. from JPN. 2nd ed. 2003. (Dragon Ball Ser.: Vol. 3). (ENG.). 192p. (Orig.). pap. 9.99 *(978-1-56931-922-2(7))* Viz Media.

—Dragon Ball. Toriyama, Akira. (Dragon Ball Ser.). (ENG.). (Orig.). Vol. 4. 2nd ed. 2003. 192p. pap. 7.95 *(978-1-56931-923-9(5))*; Vol. 5. 2nd ed. 2003. 192p. pap. 9.99 *(978-1-56931-924-6(3))*; Vol. 6. 2010. 80p. (J). pap. 4.99 *(978-1-4215-3122-9(4))* Viz Media.

—Dragon Ball. Toriyama, Akira. Morimoto, Mari, tr. from JPN. 2nd ed. 2003. (Dragon Ball Ser.: Vol. 6). (ENG.). 192p. (Orig.). Vol. 6. pap. 9.99 *(978-1-56931-925-3(1))*; Vol. 7. pap. 9.99 *(978-1-56931-926-0(X))* Viz Media.

—Dragon Ball. Toriyama, Akira. 2nd ed. 2003. (Dragon Ball Ser.). (ENG.). 192p. (Orig.). Vol. 8. pap. 9.99 *(978-1-56931-927-7(8))*; Vol. 9. pap. 9.99 *(978-1-56931-928-4(6))*; Vol. 10. pap. 9.99 *(978-1-56931-929-1(4))* Viz Media.

—Dragon Ball, Vol. 11. Toriyama, Akira. Morimoto, Mari, tr. from JPN. 2003. (Dragon Ball Ser.). (ENG.). 192p. (Orig.). pap. 9.99 *(978-1-56931-919-2(7))* Viz Media.

—Dragon Ball. Toriyama, Akira. (Dragon Ball Ser.). (ENG.). (Orig.). Vol. 12. 2003. 200p. pap. 9.99 *(978-1-59116-155-4(X))*; Vol. 13. 2003. 192p. pap. 9.99 *(978-1-59116-148-6(7))*; Vol. 14. 2004. 192p. pap. 9.99 *(978-1-59116-169-1(X))* Viz Media.

—Dragon Ball, 42 vols., Vol. 16. Toriyama, Akira. Morimoto, Mari, tr. 2004. (Dragon Ball Ser.). (ENG.). 216p. (Orig.). pap. 9.99 *(978-1-59116-457-9(5))* Viz Media.

—Dragon Ball Z. Toriyama, Akira. 2009. (Dragon Ball Z Ser.: 5). (ENG.). 576p. (gr. 8-18). pap. 19.99 *(978-1-4215-2068-1(0))* Viz Media.

—Dragon Ball Z. Toriyama, Akira. Jones, Gerard. (Dragon Ball Z Ser.). (ENG.). 2004. 192p. pap. 9.99 *(978-1-59116-186-8(X))*; 2003. 192p. pap. 9.99 *(978-1-59116-180-6(0))*; 2003. 200p. pap. 9.99 *(978-1-56931-986-4(3))* Viz Media.

—Dragon Ball Z. Toriyama, Akira. Jones, Gerard. Olsen, Lillian, tr. from JPN. 2nd ed. 2003. (Dragon Ball Z Ser.: Vol. 8). (ENG.). 192p. pap. 9.99 *(978-1-56931-937-6(5))*; pap. 9.99 *(978-1-56931-931-4(6))*; pap. 9.99 *(978-1-56931-936-9(7))* Viz Media.

—Dragon Ball Z, Vol. 1. Toriyama, Akira. 2008. (Dragon Ball Z Ser.: 1). (ENG.). 528p. (gr. 4-7). pap. 19.99 *(978-1-4215-2064-3(8))* Viz Media.

—Dragon Ball Z. Toriyama, Akira. Jones, Gerard. 2nd ed. 2003. (Dragon Ball Z Ser.). (ENG.). 192p. Vol. 1. pap. 9.99 *(978-1-56931-930-7(8))*; Vol. 3. pap. 9.99 *(978-1-56931-932-1(4))* Viz Media.

—Dragon Ball Z, Vol. 4. Toriyama, Akira. Jones, Gerard. Olsen, Lillian, tr. from JPN. 2nd ed. 2003. (Dragon Ball Z Ser.: Vol. 4). (ENG.). 192p. pap. 9.99 *(978-1-56931-933-8(2))* Viz Media.

—Dragon Ball Z. Toriyama, Akira. Jones, Gerard. 2003. (Dragon Ball Z Ser.). (ENG.). 192p. Vol. 5. 2nd ed. pap. 9.99 *(978-1-56931-934-5(0))*; Vol. 6. pap. 9.99 *(978-1-56931-935-2(9))*; Vol. 9. 2nd ed. pap. 9.99 *(978-1-56931-938-3(3))*; Vol. 10. pap. 9.99 *(978-1-56931-939-0(1))*; Vol. 11. pap. 9.99 *(978-1-56931-807-2(7))*; Vol. 12. pap. 9.99 *(978-1-56931-985-7(5))* Viz Media.

—Dragon Ball Z, Vol. 15. Toriyama, Akira. 2004. (Dragon Ball Ser.). (ENG.). 192p. pap. 9.99 *(978-1-59116-297-1(1))* Viz Media.

—Dragon Ball Z. Toriyama, Akira. Jones, Gerard. 2004. (Dragon Ball Z Ser.). (ENG.). 192p. Vol. 16. pap. 9.99 *(978-1-59116-328-2(5))*; Vol. 17. pap. 9.99 *(978-1-59116-505-7(9))* Viz Media.

—Dragon Ball Z, Vol. 18. Toriyama, Akira. 2004. (Dragon Ball Z Ser.). (ENG.). 192p. pap. 9.99 *(978-1-59116-637-5(3))* Viz Media.

—Dragon Ball Z. Toriyama, Akira. Jones, Gerard. 2005. (Dragon Ball Z Ser.). (ENG.). Vol. 20. 192p. pap. 9.99 *(978-1-59116-808-9(2))*; Vol. 21. 200p. pap. 9.99 *(978-1-59116-873-7(2))* Viz Media.

—Dragon Ball Z. Toriyama, Akira. (Dragon Ball Z Ser.). (ENG.). Vol. 22. 2005. 192p. pap. 9.99 *(978-1-4215-0051-5(5))*; Vol. 24. 2006. 192p. pap. 9.99 *(978-1-4215-0273-1(9))*; Vol. 25. 2006. 240p. pap. 9.99 *(978-1-4215-0404-9(9))*; Vol. 26. 2006. 248p. pap. 9.99 *(978-1-4215-0636-4(X))* Viz Media.

—Dragon Ball Z, Vol. 8 (VIZBIG Edition) Toriyama, Akira. 2010. (Dragon Ball Z Ser.: 8). (ENG.). 560p. pap. 19.99 *(978-1-4215-2071-1(0))* Viz Media.

—Fight to the Finish! Toriyama, Akira. 2010. (Dragon Ball Ser.: 8). (ENG.). 80p. (J). pap. 4.99 *(978-1-4215-3124-3(0))* Viz Media.

—Is This the End? Vol. 9. Toriyama, Akira. 2010. (Dragon Ball Ser.). (ENG.). 80p. (J). pap. 4.99 *(978-1-4215-3125-0(9))* Viz Media.

—Let the Tournament Begin! Toriyama, Akira. 2010. (Dragon Ball Ser.: 7). (ENG.). 80p. (J). pap. 4.99 *(978-1-4215-3123-6(2))* Viz Media.

—One Enemy, One Goal. Toriyama, Akira. 2009. (Dragon Ball Ser.: 5). (ENG.). 80p. (J). pap. 4.99 *(978-1-4215-3121-2(6))* Viz Media.

—Sand Land. Toriyama, Akira. 2003. (Sand Land Ser.). (ENG.). 224p. pap. 7.95 *(978-1-59116-181-3(9))* Viz Media.

—Strongest under the Heavens. Toriyama, Akira. 2010. (Dragon Ball Ser.). (ENG.). 80p. (J). pap. 4.99 *(978-1-4215-3126-7(7))* Viz Media.

—Yami No Matsuei, Vol. 23. Toriyama, Akira. 2005. (Dragon Ball Z Ser.: Vol. 23). (ENG.). 192p. pap. 9.99 *(978-1-4215-0148-2(1))* Viz Media.

Toriyama, Akira, jt. illus. see Inagaki, Riichiro.

Tormey, Carlotta. A Soldier in Disguise. McDonnell, Peter. 2005. 16p. (J). pap. *(978-0-7367-2909-3(7))* Zaner-Bloser, Inc.

Tornatore, Carol. Earthquake Surprise: A Bailey Fish Adventure. Salisbury, Linda. 2012. 192p. (J). pap. 8.95 *(978-1-881539-65-0(2))* Tabby Hse. Bks.

—Trouble in Contrary Woods: A Bailey Fish Adventure. Salisbury, Linda G. 2009. (J). 8.85 *(978-1-881539-46-9(6))* Tabby Hse. Bks.

Törnqvist, Marit. A Calf for Christmas. Lindgren, Astrid. Lawson, Polly, tr. from SWE. 2010. (ENG.). 36p. (J). (gr. -1-2). 17.95 *(978-0-86315-785-1(8))* Floris Bks. GBR. Dist: SteinerBooks, Inc.

Tornqvist, Marit. The Red Bird. Lindgren, Astrid & Crampton, Patricia. 2005. (J). 5.99 *(978-0-439-62797-9(4)*, Levine, Arthur A. Bks.) Scholastic, Inc.

Torode, Justine. On the Farm Lift-the-Flap. Smith, Alastair. 2004. (Luxury Lift-the-Flap Ser.). 16p. (J). (gr. 1-18). 11.95 *(978-0-7945-0508-0(2)*, Usborne) EDC Publishing.

Torode, Sam. Everyday Graces: Child's Book of Good Manners. Santorum, Karen. 2003. (Foundations Ser.). 407p. (J). 25.00 *(978-1-932236-09-5(0))* ISI Bks.

Toron, Eli. Gifts to Treasure. Greenberger, Tehilla. 2007. (Fun to Read Book). 224p. (J). per. 10.95 *(978-1-929628-32-2(3))* Hachai Publishing.

—Parsha with Rabbi Juravel: Bereishis. Juravel, Rabbi. 2005. (J). 26.95 *(978-1-931681-83-4(X))* Israel Bookshop Pubns.

—Parsha with Rabbi Juravel: Shemos. Juravel, Rabbi. 2006. (J). 27.95 *(978-1-60091-002-9(5))* Israel Bookshop Pubns.

Toron, Eli & Graybar, Shmuel. Eight Chanukah Tales. Mindel, Nissan. 2007. 78p. (J). 10.95 *(978-0-8266-0039-4(5))* Kehot Pubn. Society.

Torre, Attilio. Blob's Odd Jobs. Patrick, B. 2006. (ENG.). 48p. (J). (gr. -1-3). 16.95 *(978-0-9741319-3-1(8))* 4N Publishing LLC.

Torrecilla, Pablo. I Kick the Ball: Pateo el Balón. Zepeda, Gwendolyn. Ventura, Gabriela Baeza, tr. 2011. (SPA & ENG.). 32p. (J). (gr. -1-3). 16.95 *(978-1-55885-688-2(9)*, Piñata Books) Arte Publico Pr.

—Level up / Paso de Nivel. Zepeda, Gwendolyn. Baeza Ventura, Gabriela, tr. from ENG. 2012. (J). (gr. 5-9). 16.95 *(978-1-55885-747-6(8)*, Piñata Books) Arte Publico Pr.

—Looking for Uncle Louie on the Fourth of July. Whitehead, Kathy. 2005. (ENG.). 32p. (J). (gr. -1-3). 15.95 *(978-1-59078-061-9(2))* Boyds Mills Pr.

—The Road to Santiago. Figueredo, D. H. 2003. (ENG.). 32p. (J). 16.95 *(978-1-58430-059-5(0))* Lee & Low Bks., Inc.

Torrecilla, Pablo, jt. illus. see Benatar, Raquel.

Torrecilla, Pablo, jt. illus. see Caraballo, Samuel.

Torres, Diana. How Did Nonnie Get to Heaven? Bronstein, Arlene. 2013. (J). 48p. 19.95 *(978-1-60131-158-0(3))*; 54p. pap. 13.95 *(978-1-60131-159-7(1))* Big Tent Bks. (Castlebridge Bks.).

Torres, Dottie. Jacob & His Magical Flying Bears. Sobel, Gerrie. 2009. 32p. pap. 12.95 *(978-1-936051-16-8(8))* Peppertree Pr., The.

—Jacob & His Magical Flying Bears, a Halloween Story. Sobel, Gerrie. 2009. 32p. pap. 12.95 *(978-1-936051-42-7(7))* Peppertree Pr., The.

Torres, Elena. Habia una Vez una Princesa. Montes, Graciela. 2006. (Alfaguara Infantil Ser.). 26p. (J). 8.95 *(978-1-59820-215-1(4)*, Alfaguara) Santillana USA Publishing Co., Inc.

Torres, German. The Werewolf Chase: A Mystery about Adaptations. Beauregard, Lynda. 2012. (Summer Camp Science Mysteries Ser.: 4). (ENG.). 48p. (gr. 3-6). pap. 39.62 *(978-0-7613-9271-2(8)*, Graphic Universe); pap. 6.95 *(978-0-7613-8542-4(8)*, Graphic Universe); lib. bdg. 29.27 *(978-0-7613-5691-2(6))* Lerner Publishing Group.

—The Whispering Lake Ghosts: A Mystery about Sound. Beauregard, Lynda. 2013. (Summer Camp Science Mysteries Ser.: 6). (ENG.). 48p. (gr. 3-6). pap. 6.95 *(978-1-4677-0734-3(1))*; lib. bdg. 29.27 *(978-1-4677-0168-6(8))* Lerner Publishing Group. (Graphic Universe).

—The Yucky Duck Rescue: A Mystery about Pollution. Beauregard, Lynda. 2013. (Summer Camp Science Mysteries Ser.: 8). (ENG.). 48p. (gr. 3-6). pap. 6.95 *(978-1-4677-0736-7(8))*; lib. bdg. 29.27 *(978-1-4677-0170-9(X))* Lerner Publishing Group. (Graphic Universe).

Torres, German, jt. illus. see Barón, Lara.

Torres, German, jt. illus. see BaróN, Lara.

Torres, Irving. Matt the Rat & His Magic Cloud / Raton Mateo y Su Nube Magica: A Day at School / un Dia de Escuela. Liberto, Lorenzo. Gomez, Rocio, ed. 2003. (Matt the Rat Ser. / La Serie de Ratón Mateo). (ENG & SPA.). 32p. (J). lib. bdg. 20.00 *(978-0-9743668-0-7(3))* Harvest Sun Pr., LLC.

—Matt the Rat & His Sister Maggie (Raton Mateo y Su Hermana Maggie) When I Grow Up (Cuando Yo Crezca) Liberto, Lorenzo. Gomez, Rocio, ed. 2003. (Matt the Rat Ser. / La Serie de Ratón Mateo). (SPA & ENG.). 40p. (J). lib. bdg. 20.00 *(978-0-9743668-1-4(1))* Harvest Sun Pr., LLC.

—Matt the Rat Fights Back / Ratón Mateo se Defiende. Liberto, Lorenzo. Gomez, Rocio, tr. from ENG. 2005. (Matt the Rat Ser. / La Serie de Ratón Mateo). (ENG & SPA.). 32p. (J). lib. bdg. 20.00 *(978-0-9743668-4-5(6))* Harvest Sun Pr., LLC.

—Save the Planet / Salva el Planeta. Liberto, Lorenzo. Gomez, Rocio, tr. 2005. (Matt the Rat Ser. / La Serie de Ratón Mateo). (ENG & SPA.). 32p. (J). lib. bdg. 20.00 *(978-0-9743668-5-2(4))* Harvest Sun Pr., LLC.

Torres, Irving. Matt the Rat's Incredible Creations / Las Creaciones Increíbles de Ratón Mateo. Torres, Irving. Liberto, Lorenzo & Gomez, Rocio. 2004. (ENG & SPA.). 32p. (J). lib. bdg. 20.00 *(978-0-9743668-3-8(8))* Harvest Sun Pr., LLC.

—Practice Makes Perfect / la Práctica Hace al Maestro. Torres, Irving. Liberto, Lorenzo & Gomez, Rocio. 2004. (ENG & SPA.). 32p. (J). lib. bdg. 20.00 *(978-0-9743668-2-1(X))* Harvest Sun Pr., LLC.

Torres, Jickie. Watch Me Draw Robots. Walter Foster Publishing & Berry, Bob. 2014. (ENG.). 24p. (J). (gr. k-2). lib. bdg. 23.93 *(978-1-939581-38-9(9))* Quarto Publishing Group USA.

Torres, Marina. El bibliobus Magico. Fernandez, Cesar. 2004. 88p. pap. 10.00 *(978-84-931888-1-8(6))* Editorial Brief ESP. Dist: Independent Pubs. Group.

Torres, Nora Estela. Travesuras del Tio Conejo. Espriella, Leopoldo Berdella De La. 2004. (Relato Ser.). (SPA.). 76p. (J). (gr. -1-7). per. *(978-958-30-0302-8(6))* Panamericana Editorial.

Torres, Nora Estela & Jaime, Daniel. Historia en Cuentos 3: Todo Por un Florero/el Cometa Llanero/el Zapatero Soldado. Caballero, Eduardo. 2004. (Literatura Juvenil (Panamericana Editorial) Ser.). (SPA.). 78p. (YA). (gr. -1-7). pap. *(978-958-30-0369-1(7))* Panamericana Editorial.

—Historia en Cuentos 4: El Almirante Nino/el Caballito de Bolivar/el Sargento de Doce Anos. Calderon, Eduardo Caballero. 2003. (Literatura Juvenil (Panamericana Editorial) Ser.). (SPA.). 75p. (YA). (gr. -1-7). per. *(978-958-30-0370-7(0))* Panamericana Editorial.

Torres, Raul Vazquez. Otra Vez Ese Tal Principito! Ordonez, Paulino. rev. ed. 2006. (Castillo de la Lectura Naranja Ser.). (SPA & ENG.). 152p. (J). (gr. 4-7). pap. 7.95 *(978-970-20-0178-2(1))* Castillo, Ediciones, S. A. de C. V. MEX. Dist: Macmillan.

Torres, Walter. Celebra la Navidad y el Dia de Los Reyes Magos con Pablo y Carlitos. Flor Ada, Alma. 2006. (Cuentos para Celebrar / Stories to Celebrate Ser.). (SPA.). 30p. (gr. k-6). per. 11.95 *(978-1-59820-124-6(7)*, Alfaguara) Santillana USA Publishing Co., Inc.

—Celebrate Christmas & Three Kings Day with Pablo & Carlitos. Flor Ada, Alma. 2006. (Cuentos para Celebrar / Stories to Celebrate Ser.). 30p. (gr. k-6). per. 11.95 *(978-1-59820-136-9(0))* Santillana USA Publishing Co., Inc.

—El Pececito Magico. De Matos, Isabel Freire. 2004. (SPA.). 22p. (J). pap. 6.95 *(978-1-57581-578-7(8))* Santillana USA Publishing Co., Inc.

—Viaje a Isla de Mona. Montero, Mayra. 2009. (SPA.). 111p. (J). (gr. 4-7). pap. 8.95 *(978-1-934801-64-2(X))* Ediciones SM.

—¡Viva la Tortuga! León, Georgina Lázaro. (SPA.). 30p. (J). (gr. 3-5). 12.95 *(978-1-57581-605-0(9))* Santillana USA Publishing Co., Inc.

Torrey Balsara, Andrea. Jellybean Mouse. Roy, Philip. 2014. (ENG.). 32p. 11.95 ***(978-1-55380-344-7(2))*** Ronsdale Pr. CAN. Dist: SPD-Small Pr. Distribution.

Torrey Balsara, Andrea. Mouse Tales. Roy, Philip. 2014. (ENG.). 32p. pap. 9.95 *(978-1-55380-262-4(4))* Ronsdale Pr. CAN. Dist: SPD-Small Pr. Distribution.

Torrey, Jesse, photos by. Squeeze: Poems from a Juicy Universe. Mordhorst, Heidi. 2005. (ENG., 32p. (J). (gr. 3-7). 16.95 *(978-1-59078-292-7(5))* Boyds Mills Pr.

Torrey, Michele & Newman, Barbara Johansen. The Case of the Gasping Garbage. Torrey, Michele. 2009. (Doyle & Fossey, Science Detectives Ser.: 1). (ENG.). 96p. (J). (gr. 4-7). pap. 6.95 *(978-1-4027-4960-5(0))* Sterling Publishing Co., Inc.

—The Case of the Mossy Lake Monster. Torrey, Michele. 2009. (Doyle & Fossey, Science Detectives Ser.: 2). (ENG.). 96p. (J). (gr. 4-7). pap. 6.95 *(978-1-4027-4962-9(7))* Sterling Publishing Co., Inc.

Torrey, Rich. The Runaway Soccer Ball. Stiles, Amanda. 2010. 16p. (J). pap. *(978-0-545-24819-8(1))* Scholastic, Inc.

—Splat! Pérez-Mercado, Mary Margaret. 2011. (Rookie Ready to Learn Ser.). 40p. (J). pap. 5.95 *(978-0-531-26678-6(8))*; (gr. -1-k). lib. bdg. 23.00 *(978-0-531-26373-0(8))* Scholastic Library Publishing. (Children's Pr.).

Torrey, Rich. ¡Zas! Torrey, Rich. Pérez-Mercado, Mary Margaret. 2011. (Rookie Ready to Learn Español Ser.). (SPA.). 40p. (J). lib. bdg. 23.00 *(978-0-531-26120-0(4)*, Children's Pr.) Scholastic Library Publishing.

Torrey, Richard. Almost. Torrey, Richard. 2009. (ENG.). 40p. (J). (gr. -1-3). 17.99 *(978-0-06-156166-5(5))* HarperCollins Pubs.

—A Baseball Story. Torrey, Richard. 2013. (ENG.). 36p. (J). 10.99 *(978-1-61067-054-8(X))* Kane Miller.

—A Basketball Story. Torrey, Richard. 2014. (ENG.). 36p. (J). 10.99 *(978-1-61067-286-3(0))* Kane Miller.

—Because. Torrey, Richard. 2011. (ENG.). 40p. (J). (gr. -1-3). 16.99 *(978-0-06-156173-3(8))* HarperCollins Pubs.

—A Football Story. Torrey, Richard. 2014. (ENG.). 36p. (J). 10.99 *(978-1-61067-055-5(8))* Kane Miller.

—A Hockey Story. Torrey, Richard. ed. 2011. (ENG.). 32p. (J). 10.99 *(978-1-61067-053-1(1))* Kane Miller.

—Moe Is Best. Torrey, Richard. 2014. (ENG.). 24p. (J). (gr. -1-3). 14.95 *(978-0-8234-2837-3(0))* Holiday Hse., Inc.

—Why? Torrey, Richard. 2010. (ENG.). 40p. (J). (gr. -1-3). 16.99 *(978-0-06-156170-2(3))* HarperCollins Pubs.

Torrey, Richard L. ¡Zas! Pérez-Mercado, Mary Margaret. 2011. (Rookie Ready to Learn Español Ser.). (SPA.). 40p. (J). pap. 5.95 *(978-0-531-26788-2(1)*, Children's Pr.) Scholastic Library Publishing.

Torrey, Richard L. Beans Baker's Best Shot. Torrey, Richard L. 2006. (Step into Reading Ser.: Vol. 3). (ENG.). 48p. (J). (gr. k-3). per. 3.99 *(978-0-375-82839-3(7)*, Random Hse. Bks. for Young Readers) Random Hse. Children's Bks.

Torrijos, Eduardo. Papalotes: Tecnicas de Armado y Vuelo. Torrijos, Eduardo. Garcia, Gretel. 2004. (SPA.). 157p. (J). pap. *(978-970-643-734-1(7))* Selector, S.A. de C.V. MEX. Dist: Lectorum Pubns., Inc.

Torseter, Øyvind. My Father's Arms Are a Boat. Lunde, Stein Erik. Dickson, Kari, tr. from NOR. 2013. (ENG.). 40p. (J). (gr. -1). 15.95 *(978-1-59270-124-7(8))* Enchanted Lion Bks., LLC.

Tortop, Anil. Mary Bea Says Why Is for Yog. Hogan, Tamara Anne. 2013. 28p. pap. *(978-1-922204-06-6(4))* Vivid Publishing.

Tortosa, Wilson. Critical Strike. Bowen, Carl & Fuentes, Benny. 2014. (Shadow Squadron Ser.). (ENG.). 224p. (gr. 4-8). pap. 8.95 *(978-1-62370-109-3(0))* Capstone Young Readers.

—Dark Agent, 1 vol. Bowen, Carl & Fuentes, Benny. 2014. (Shadow Squadron Ser.). (ENG.). 112p. (gr. 4-8). 25.32 *(978-1-4342-9170-7(7))* Stone Arch Bks.

Tortosa, Wilson. Dragon Teeth. Bowen, Carl & Fuentes, Benny. 2015. (Shadow Squadron Ser.). (ENG.). 112p. (gr. 4-8). lib. bdg. 25.32 ***(978-1-4965-0383-1(X))*** Stone Arch Bks.

Tortosa, Wilson. Eagle Down, 1 vol. Bowen, Carl & Fuentes, Benny. 2013. (Shadow Squadron Ser.). (ENG.). 112p. (gr. 4-8). lib. bdg. 25.32 *(978-1-4342-4606-6(X))* Stone Arch Bks.

—Elite Infantry. Bowen, Carl & Fuentes, Benny. 2013. (Shadow Squadron Ser.). (ENG.). 224p. pap. 8.95 *(978-1-62370-032-4(9))* Capstone Young Readers.

Tortosa, Wilson. Guardian Angel. Bowen, Carl & Fuentes, Benny. 2015. (Shadow Squadron Ser.). (ENG.). 112p. (gr. 4-8). lib. bdg. 25.32 ***(978-1-4965-0382-4(1))*** Stone Arch Bks.

—Long Shadow. Bowen, Carl & Fuentes, Benny. 2015. (Shadow Squadron Ser.). (ENG.). 112p. (gr. 4-8). pap. 5.95 ***(978-1-4965-0388-6(0))*** Stone Arch Bks.

Tortosa, Wilson. Phantom Sun, 1 vol. Bowen, Carl & Fuentes, Benny. 2014. (Shadow Squadron Ser.). (ENG.). 112p. (gr. 4-8). 25.32 *(978-1-4342-6399-5(1))* Stone Arch Bks.

—Recharged, Vol. 12. Terrell, Brandon. 2013. (Tony Hawk's 900 Revolution Ser.). (ENG.). 128p. (gr. 3-4). lib. bdg. 25.32 *(978-1-4342-3843-6(1))* Stone Arch Bks.

—Recharged: Volume Twelve, 1 vol. Terrell, Brandon. 2013. (Tony Hawk's 900 Revolution Ser.). (ENG.). 128p. (gr. 3-4). pap. 7.19 *(978-1-4342-4896-1(8)*, Tony Hawk's 900 Revolution) Stone Arch Bks.

Tortosa, Wilson. Rogue Agent. Bowen, Carl & Fuentes, Benny. 2015. (Shadow Squadron Ser.). (ENG.). 224p. (gr. 4-8). pap. 8.95 ***(978-1-62370-296-0(8))*** Capstone Young Readers.

Tortosa, Wilson. Sand Spider, 1 vol. Bowen, Carl & Fuentes, Benny. 2014. (Shadow Squadron Ser.). (ENG.). 112p. (gr. 4-8). 25.32 *(978-1-4342-9169-1(3))* Stone Arch Bks.

—Sea Demon, 1 vol. Bowen, Carl & Fuentes, Benny. 2013. (Shadow Squadron Ser.). (ENG.). 112p. (gr. 4-8). lib. bdg. 25.32 *(978-1-4342-4604-2(3))* Stone Arch Bks.

—Sniper Shield, 1 vol. Bowen, Carl & Fuentes, Benny. 2013. (Shadow Squadron Ser.). (ENG.). 112p. (gr. 4-8). lib. bdg. 25.32 *(978-1-4342-4607-3(8))* Stone Arch Bks.

Tortosa, Wilson. Steel Hammer. Bowen, Carl & Fuentes, Benny. 2015. (Shadow Squadron Ser.). (ENG.). 112p. (gr. 4-8). lib. bdg. 25.32 ***(978-1-4965-0385-5(6))*** Stone Arch Bks.

Tortosa, Wilson. Unearthed, Vol. 10. Terrell, Brandon. 2013. (Tony Hawk's 900 Revolution Ser.). (ENG.). 128p. (gr. 3-4). lib. bdg. 25.32 *(978-1-4342-3841-2(5))* Stone Arch Bks.

—Unearthed: Volume Ten, 1 vol. Terrell, Brandon. 2013. (Tony Hawk's 900 Revolution Ser.). (ENG.). 128p. (gr. 3-4). pap. 7.19 *(978-1-4342-4897-8(6)*, Tony Hawk's 900 Revolution) Stone Arch Bks.

—White Needle, 1 vol. Bowen, Carl & Fuentes, Benny. 2014. (Shadow Squadron Ser.). (ENG.). 112p. (gr. 4-8). 25.32 *(978-1-4342-6398-8(3))* Stone Arch Bks.

Tortosa, Wilson & Fuentes, Benny. Black Anchor, 1 vol. Bowen, Carl. 2013. (Shadow Squadron Ser.). (ENG.). 112p. (gr. 4-8). lib. bdg. 25.32 *(978-1-4342-4605-9(1))* Stone Arch Bks.

Tortosa, Wilson, jt. illus. see Dal Bello, Thiago.

Toth, Shannon. Laika the Space Dog: First Hero in Outer Space, 1 vol. Wittrock, Jeni. 2014. (Animal Heroes Ser.). (ENG.). 32p. (gr. k-2). 27.99 *(978-1-4795-5463-8(4))*; pap. 7.95 *(978-1-4795-5467-6(7))* Picture Window Bks.

Totire, Valerie, et al. Carla Tiene Gafas Nuevas. Coulton, Mia. 2006.Tr. of Carla's New Glasses. (ENG.). 32p. (gr. 1-2). pap. 7.25 *(978-1-57874-108-3(4))* Kaeden Corp.

Totire, Valerie. Carla's New Glasses. Coulton, Mia. 2005. (ENG.). 16p. (gr. k-2). pap. 5.95 *(978-1-57874-092-5(4))* Kaeden Corp.

—People Do Silly Things. Worthington, Lisa & Moon, Susan. 2003. (ENG.). 16p. (gr. k-2). pap. 5.95 *(978-1-57874-037-6(1))* Kaeden Corp.

—There Goes Peanut Butter! Ketch, Ann. 2006. (ENG.). 12p. (gr. k-1). pap. 5.95 *(978-1-57874-036-9(3)*, 74-036-3) Kaeden Corp.

Touliatou, Sophia. Flippy Floppy Farm Animals. Poitier, Anton. 2014. 10p. (J). 12.99 *(978-1-61067-310-5(7))* Kane Miller.

—Flippy Floppy Jungle Animals. Poitier, Anton. 2013. 18p. (J). 12.99 *(978-1-61067-169-9(4))* Kane Miller.

—I Wonder Who? Poitier, Anton. 2014. (J). 12.99 *(978-1-61067-242-9(9))* Kane Miller.

—My Busy Farm. Poitier, Anton. 2013. 10p. (J). 9.99 *(978-1-61067-146-0(5))* Kane Miller.

—My Busy Town. Poitier, Anton. 2013. 10p. (J). 9.99 *(978-1-61067-147-7(3))* Kane Miller.

Toulmin-Rothe, Ann. Elizabeth Blackwell, the First Woman Doctor. Sabin, Francene & Macken, JoAnn Early. 2007. 53p. (J). *(978-0-439-66044-0(0))* Scholastic, Inc.

Toume, Kei. Lament of the Lamb, 7 vols., Vol. 7. Toume, Kei, creator. rev. ed. 2005. (Lament of the Lamb Ser.). (JPN & ENG.). 264p. pap. 9.99 *(978-1-59532-006-3(7))* TOKYOPOP, Inc.

Tourlonias, Joëlle. Elephantastic! Engler, Michael. 2014. (ENG.). 32p. (J). 16.99 *(978-1-4413-0841-2(5)*, 9781441308412) Peter Pauper Pr. Inc.

Tov, Basia. Attack of the Giant Stink Bugs. Bennett, Larry. 2015. (Ru-Lan Ser.: 2). (ENG.). 56p. (J). (gr. -1-3). pap. 10.95 *(978-1-940242-73-6(8))* Heritage Builders, LLC.

Tow, Jack. Who's Afraid of Howie? 2013. (ENG.). 40p. (gr. -1-3). 16.99 *(978-88-97737-22-3(6))* Officina Libraria srl ITA. Dist: National Bk. Network.

Tow, Jack. Up All Night with Howie. Tow, Jack. 2012. (ENG.). 48p. 16.99 *(978-88-89854-93-8(6))* Officina Libraria srl ITA. Dist: National Bk. Network.

Townsend, F. H. A Child's History of England. Dickens, Charles. 2007. (ENG.). 420p. per. *(978-1-4065-5448-9(0))* Dodo Pr.

Townsend, Leah. Tana Ray, & Its No Time to Play. Taptich, J. E. I.t. ed. 2011. (ENG.). 46p. pap. 14.99 *(978-1-4538-7380-9(5))* CreateSpace Independent Publishing Platform.

Townsend, Michael. Mr. Ball Makes a to-Do List. Townsend, Michael. 2014. (Jump-Into-Chapters Ser.). (ENG.). 96p. (J). (gr. k-3). 12.99 *(978-1-60905-365-9(6))* Blue Apple Bks.

Townsend, Peter. Machine Mates. Whiting, Sue. 2003. 12p. (J). (gr. k-3). 22.00 *(978-0-7567-6650-4(8))* DIANE Publishing Co.

—Percival's Party. Turner, Jill. 2003. (J). pap. 12.95 *(978-1-74047-235-7(7))* Book Co. Publishing Pty, Ltd., The AUS. Dist: Penton Overseas, Inc.

Townsend, Shannon. Fire & Snow: A Tale of the Alaskan Gold Rush. Gunderson, J. 2007. (Historical Fiction Ser.). (ENG.). 56p. (gr. 2-3). pap. 6.25 *(978-1-59889-405-9(6)*, Graphic Flash) Stone Arch Bks.

Townshend, Katie. Donkey Oatie's Christmas Pageant. Rath, Tom H. 2013. 24p. pap. *(978-0-9918033-6-1(1))* Wood Islands Prints.

Toy Box Staff. Who Lives Here? Wolfe, Jane. 2013. (ENG.). 8p. bds. 6.99 *(978-1-84322-651-2(0)*, Armadillo) Anness Publishing GBR. Dist: National Bk. Network.

—Who Says Moo? Wolfe, Jane. 2013. (ENG.). 8p. bds. 6.99 *(978-1-84322-679-6(0)*, Armadillo) Anness Publishing GBR. Dist: National Bk. Network.

—Who's Hiding? Wolfe, Jane. 2013. (ENG.). 8p. bds. 6.99 *(978-1-84322-657-4(X)*, Armadillo) Anness Publishing GBR. Dist: National Bk. Network.

Toye, Derek. Are Bowling Balls Bullies? Learning about Forces & Motion with the Garbage Gang. Troupe, Thomas Kingsley. 2015. (Garbage Gang's Super Science Questions Ser.). (ENG.). 24p. (gr. k-2). lib. bdg. 25.99 ***(978-1-4795-7057-7(5))*** Picture Window Bks.

Toye, Derek. Do Ants Get Lost? Learning about Animal Communication with the Garbage Gang, 1 vol. Troupe, Thomas Kingsley. 2014. (Garbage Gang's Super Science Questions Ser.). (ENG.). 24p. (gr. k-2). lib. bdg. 25.99 *(978-1-4795-5478-2(2))* Picture Window Bks.

—Do Bees Poop? Learning about Living & Nonliving Things with the Garbage Gang, 1 vol. Troupe, Thomas Kingsley. 2014. (Garbage Gang's Super Science Questions Ser.). (ENG.). 24p. (gr. k-2). lib. bdg. 25.99 *(978-1-4795-5477-5(4))* Picture Window Bks.

Toye, Derek. Do Plants Have Heads? Learning about Plant Parts with the Garbage Gang. Troupe, Thomas Kingsley. 2015. (Garbage Gang's Super Science Questions Ser.). (ENG.). 24p. (gr. k-2). lib. bdg. 25.99 ***(978-1-4795-7059-1(1))*** Picture Window Bks.

—The Garbage Gang's Super Science Questions, 4 vols. Troupe, Thomas Kingsley. (Garbage Gang's Super Science Questions Ser.). (ENG.). 24p. (gr. k-2). 2015. 103.96 ***(978-1-4795-8023-1(6))***; 2014. 103.96 *(978-1-4795-5562-8(2))* Picture Window Bks.

Toye, Derek. Taj. Siegel, Elizabeth. 2007. 48p. (J). lib. bdg. 23.08 *(978-1-4242-1632-1(X))* Fitzgerald Bks.

Toye, Derek. What's with the Long Naps, Bears? Learning about Hibernation with the Garbage Gang. Troupe, Thomas Kingsley. 2015. (Garbage Gang's Super Science Questions Ser.). (ENG.). 24p. (gr. k-2). lib. bdg. 25.99 ***(978-1-4795-7056-0(7))*** Picture Window Bks.

Toye, Derek. Why Do Dead Fish Float? Learning about Matter with the Garbage Gang, 1 vol. Troupe, Thomas Kingsley. 2014. (Garbage Gang's Super Science Questions Ser.). (ENG.). 24p. (gr. k-2). 25.99 *(978-1-4795-5479-9(0))* Picture Window Bks.

—Why Does My Body Make Bubbles? Learning about the Digestive System with the Garbage Gang. Troupe, Thomas Kingsley. 2014. (Garbage Gang's Super Science Questions Ser.). (ENG.). 24p. (gr. k-2). lib. bdg. 25.99 *(978-1-4795-5480-5(4))* Picture Window Bks.

Toye, Derek. You Call That a Nose? Learning about Human Senses with the Garbage Gang. Troupe, Thomas Kingsley. 2015. (Garbage Gang's Super Science Questions Ser.). (ENG.). 24p. (gr. k-2). lib. bdg. 25.99 ***(978-1-4795-7058-4(3))*** Picture Window Bks.

Trabalka, Peggy. Silent Voice. Rudner, Barry. I.t. ed. 2013. (ENG.). 30p. (J). 14.99 *(978-1-940775-00-5(0))* Nick Of Time Media, Inc.

Trabbold, Andrew. Skraelings: Clashes in the Old Arctic, 1 vol. Qitsualik-Tinsley, Rachel & Qitsualik-Tinsley, Sean. 2014. (Arctic Moon Magick Ser.). (ENG.). 120p. (J). (gr. 7). pap. 10.95 *(978-1-927095-54-6(9))* Inhabit Media Inc. CAN. Dist: Independent Pubs. Group.

Trachock, Cathy. Black Bear Cub. Luther, Jacqueline & Lind, Alan. 2006. (ENG.). 32p. (J). pap. 3.95 *(978-1-59249-587-0(7))* Soundprints.

—Polar Bear Cub. Luther, Jacqueline. 2006. (ENG.). 32p. (J). pap. 3.95 *(978-1-59249-589-4(3))* Soundprints.

Trachok, Cathy. Raccoon at Clear Creek Road. Otto, Carolyn B. 2005. (Smithsonian's Backyard Ser.). 32p. (J). (gr. -1-3). pap. 8.95 incl. audio *(978-1-59249-490-3(0)*, SC5008); (ENG.). per. 6.95 *(978-1-59249-481-1(1)*, S5008) Soundprints.

Trachtman, Joseph. Kosher Tales: Not So Grim Stories for Children. Trachtman, Joseph, narrated by. 2007.Tr. of Kosher Tales. (ENG & YID.). 86p. (J). pap. 25.00 *(978-0-9795170-0-6(1))* Trachtman, Joseph.

Tracy, Libba. This House Is Made of Mud (Esta Casa Esta Hecha de Lodo) Buchanan, Ken. 2004. (Reading Rainbow Bks.). (ENG, SPA & MUL.). 32p. (J). (gr. -1-1). pap. 7.95 *(978-0-87358-580-4(1)*, NP801) Rowman & Littlefield Publishers, Inc.

Traini, Agostino. Chef Foody's Field Trip. 2015. (ENG.). 40p. (J). (gr. -1-2). 14.95 ***(978-0-7892-1241-2(2)***, Abbeville Kids) Abbeville Pr., Inc.

Trammell, Brandon. Kody the Conservation Pup: Helps Tori Cross the Road. Birt, Michael. 2012. 58p. 27.95 *(978-0-578-11315-9(5))*; pap. 19.95 *(978-0-578-11306-7(6))* Birt Hse. Publishing.

Trammell, Jeremiah. The Cabin That Moose Built. Stihler, Cherie B. 2006. (Paws IV Ser.). (ENG.). 32p. (J). (gr. -1-2). pap. 10.99 *(978-1-57061-446-0(6))* Sasquatch Bks.

—The Giant Cabbage: An Alaska Folktale. Stihler, Cherie. 2003. (Paws IV Ser.). (ENG.). 32p. (J). (gr. -1-2). pap. 10.99 *(978-1-57061-357-9(5))* Sasquatch Bks.

—Three Bears of the Pacific Northwest. Vaughan, Richard Lee & Vaughan, Marcia. 2011. (ENG.). 32p. (J). (gr. -1-2). 16.99 *(978-1-57061-684-6(1))* Sasquatch Bks.

—Under Alaska's Midnight Sun. Vanasse, Deb. 2005. (Paws IV Ser.). (ENG.). 32p. (J). (gr. -1-2). pap. 10.99 *(978-1-57061-422-4(9))* Sasquatch Bks.

Tramonte, Katherine H. The Word Burglar. Cander, Chris. 2013. (ENG.). 28p. (J). 19.95 *(978-1-936474-96-7(4),* e4daa439-fc4a-4ff6-893d-b9aee8dc3ac7) Bright Sky Pr.

Trapani, Iza. Gabe & Goon. 2016. (J). lib. bdg. *(978-1-58089-640-5(5))* Charlesbridge Publishing, Inc.

Trapani, Iza. How Much Is That Doggie in the Window? Merrill, Bob. 2004. (ENG.). 32p. (J). (gr. k-k). pap. 7.95 *(978-1-58089-030-4(X))* Charlesbridge Publishing, Inc.

—The Wedding. Bunting, Eve. 2005. (ENG.). 32p. (J). (gr. -1-k). per. 7.95 *(978-1-58089-118-9(7))* Charlesbridge Publishing, Inc.

Trapani, Iza. The Bear Went over the Mountain. Trapani, Iza. 2012. (ENG.). 32p. (J). (gr. k-3). 16.95 *(978-1-61608-510-0(X),* 608510, Sky Pony Pr.) Skyhorse Publishing Co., Inc.

—Froggie Went A-Courtin' Trapani, Iza. 2006. (ENG.). 32p. (J). (gr. 2-k). pap. 7.95 *(978-1-58089-029-8(6))* Charlesbridge Publishing, Inc.

—Haunted Party. Trapani, Iza. (ENG.). 28p. (J). (gr. -1-2). 2010. pap. 7.95 *(978-1-58089-247-6(7));* 2009. 16.95 *(978-1-58089-246-9(9))* Charlesbridge Publishing, Inc.

—Here We Go 'Round the Mulberry Bush. Trapani, Iza. 2006. (ENG.). 32p. (J). (gr. -1-k). pap. 7.95 *(978-1-57091-699-1(3))* Charlesbridge Publishing, Inc.

—Jingle Bells. Trapani, Iza. 2007. (ENG.). 32p. (J). (gr. -1-k). 7.95 *(978-1-58089-096-0(2))* Charlesbridge Publishing, Inc.

—Little Miss Muffet. Trapani, Iza. 2013. (ENG.). 32p. (J). (gr. -1-1). 16.95 *(978-1-62087-986-3(7),* 620986, Sky Pony Pr.) Skyhorse Publishing Co., Inc.

—Mary Had a Little Lamb. Trapani, Iza. 2003. (ENG.). 32p. (J). (gr. -1-k). 7.95 *(978-1-58089-090-8(3))* Charlesbridge Publishing, Inc.

—Oh Where, Oh Where Has My Little Dog Gone? Trapani, Iza. 2008. (ENG.). 32p. (J). (gr. -1-k). pap. 7.95 *(978-1-58089-005-2(9))* Charlesbridge Publishing, Inc.

—Old King Cole. Trapani, Iza. 2015. (ENG.). 32p. (J). (-k). lib. bdg. 15.95 *(978-1-58089-632-0(4))* Charlesbridge Publishing, Inc.

—Rufus & Friends: Rhyme Time. Trapani, Iza. 2008. (ENG.). 40p. (J). (gr. -1-3). pap. 7.95 *(978-1-58089-207-0(8))* Charlesbridge Publishing, Inc.

—Rufus & Friends: School Days. Trapani, Iza. 2010. (ENG.). 36p. (J). (gr. -1-3). 16.95 *(978-1-58089-248-3(5));* pap. 7.95 *(978-1-58089-249-0(3))* Charlesbridge Publishing, Inc.

—Shoo Fly! Trapani, Iza. 2007. (ENG.). 32p. (J). (gr. k-3). per. 7.95 *(978-1-58089-076-2(8))* Charlesbridge Publishing, Inc.

—Sing along with Iza & Friends: Row Row Row Your Boat. Trapani, Iza. 2004. 32p. (J). pap. 11.95 incl. audio compact disk *(978-1-58089-102-8(0))* Charlesbridge Publishing, Inc.

—Sing along with Iza & Friends: The Itsy Bitsy Spider. Trapani, Iza. 2004. 32p. (J). pap. 11.95 incl. audio compact disk *(978-1-58089-100-4(4))* Charlesbridge Publishing, Inc.

—Sing along with Iza & Friends: Twinkle, Twinkle Little Star. Trapani, Iza. 2004. 32p. (J). pap. 11.95 incl. audio compact disk *(978-1-58089-101-1(2))* Charlesbridge Publishing, Inc.

—Twinkle, Twinkle, Little Star. Trapani, Iza. 2008. (ENG.). 26p. (J). (gr. -1 — 1). bds. 7.95 *(978-1-58089-015-1(6))* Charlesbridge Publishing, Inc.

Trapp, Karla. My Feelings Workbook. Wiemeier, Aaron. 2011. 104p. (J). pap. 19.95 *(978-1-59850-095-0(3))* Youthlight, Inc.

Trasler, Janee. Jesus Loves the Little Children, 1 vol. Zondervan Publishing Staff. 2008. (I Can Read! / Song Ser.). (ENG.). 32p. (J). (gr. -1-3). pap. 3.99 *(978-0-310-71620-4(9))* Zondervan.

—A Visit to the Farm. Feldman, Thea. 2006. 3p. (J). (gr. -1-3). bds. 5.99 *(978-1-932915-32-7(X))* Sandvik Publishing.

Trasler, Janee. Bathtime for Chickies. Trasler, Janee. 2015. (Chickies Ser.). (ENG.). 24p. (J). (gr. -1 — 1). bds. 8.99 *(978-0-06-234229-4(0),* HarperFestival) HarperCollins Pubs.

—Bedtime for Chickies. Trasler, Janee. 2014. (Chickies Ser.). (ENG.). 24p. (J). (gr. -1 — 1). bds. 8.99 *(978-0-06-227468-7(6),* HarperFestival) HarperCollins Pubs.

—Benny's Chocolate Bunny. Trasler, Janee. 2011. (ENG.). 28p. (J). (gr. k — 1). bds. 7.99 *(978-0-545-26127-2(9),* Cartwheel Bks.) Scholastic, Inc.

—Dinnertime for Chickies. Trasler, Janee. 2014. (Chickies Ser.). (ENG.). 24p. (J). (gr. -1 — 1). bds. 8.99 *(978-0-06-227470-0(8),* HarperFestival) HarperCollins Pubs.

—Mimi & Bear in the Snow. Trasler, Janee. 2014. (ENG.). 32p. (J). (gr. -1-k). 16.99 *(978-0-374-34971-4(1),* Farrar, Straus & Giroux (BYR)) Farrar, Straus & Giroux.

—A New Chick for Chickies. Trasler, Janee. 2014. (Chickies Ser.). (ENG.). 24p. (J). (gr. -1 — 1). bds. 8.99 *(978-0-06-227471-7(6),* HarperFestival) HarperCollins Pubs.

—Pottytime for Chickies. Trasler, Janee. 2014. (Chickies Ser.). (ENG.). 24p. (J). (gr. -1 — 1). bds. 8.99 *(978-0-06-227469-4(4),* HarperFestival) HarperCollins Pubs.

Travis, Caroline. French Quarter Tori & the Red Owl. Black, Cary & Schott, Gretchen Victoria. 2012. 38p. pap. 14.95 *(978-0-9754279-7-2(0));* pap. 12.95 *(978-0-9754279-8-9(9))* Red Owl Pubns.

Travis, Stephanie. Bobby Beaver Learns a Lesson. Bowman, Andy. 26p. (J). (gr. k-5). pap. 6.95 *(978-1-931650-10-6(1));* lib. bdg. 14.95 *(978-1-931650-11-3(X))* Coastal Publishing Carolina, Inc.

—Indian Slim. Bowman, Andy. 29p. (J). (gr. 1-6). pap. 6.95 *(978-1-931650-06-9(3));* lib. bdg. 14.95 *(978-1-931650-07-6(1))* Coastal Publishing Carolina, Inc.

—Pokey's Garden. Bowman, Andy. 26p. (J). (gr. k-5). pap. 6.95 *(978-1-931650-08-3(X));* lib. bdg. 14.95 *(978-1-931650-09-0(8))* Coastal Publishing Carolina, Inc.

—The Quilt. Bowman, Andy. 25p. (J). (gr. 1-6). pap. 6.95 *(978-1-931650-04-5(7));* lib. bdg. 14.95 *(978-1-931650-05-2(5))* Coastal Publishing Carolina, Inc.

Traylor, Waverley, jt. illus. see Roberts, Curt.

Traynor, Elizabeth. F Is for First State: A Delaware Alphabet. Crane, Carol. 2005. (State Ser.). (ENG.). 40p. (J). (gr. -1-3). 17.95 *(978-1-58536-154-0(2))* Sleeping Bear Pr.

—V Is for Venus Flytrap: A Plant Alphabet. Gagliano, Eugene. 2009. (Science Ser.). (ENG.). 40p. (J). (gr. k-8). 17.95 *(978-1-58536-350-6(2))* Sleeping Bear Pr.

Treatner, Meryl. We Both Read-The New Tribe. Carson, Jana. 2013. 44p. (J). pap. 5.99 *(978-1-60115-264-0(7));* 9.95 *(978-1-60115-263-3(9))* Treasure Bay, Inc.

Treatner, Meryle. The Empty Pot: A Chinese Legend. Goldish, Meish. 2005. 14p. pap. 6.00 *(978-0-15-350582-9(6))* Harcourt Schl. Pubs.

Treffeisen, Brian, photos by. Freddy in the City: Memorable Monday. Bird, Janie. 2nd rev. ed. 2005.Tr. of Freddy en la Ciudad un Lunes Memorble. (SPA., 32p. (J). 10.95 *(978-1-59494-005-7(3))* CPCC Pr.

Treffry, Teresa. Playthings: 101 Used for Everyday Objects. Stagnitti, Karen. (J). (gr. k-3). pap. *(978-1-876367-61-9(X))* Wizard Bks.

Treg, Mccoy, jt. illus. see Thomas, Erika.

Treloar, Debi, photos by. Childrens Spaces: From Zero to Ten. Wilson, Judith. 2005. (ENG., 144p. pap. *(978-1-84172-871-1(3))* Ryland Peters & Small.

Tremaine, Michele. It's MY Future: Should I Be a Nurse Practitioner? Wick, Elaine. 2004. 64p. (J). lib. bdg. 12.95 *(978-0-9749769-0-7(3))* NAPNAP.

Tremblay, Carl, photos by. The Chop Chop: The Kids' Guide to Cooking Real Food with Your Family. Sampson, Sally. 2013. (ENG., 208p. pap. 19.99 *(978-1-4516-8587-9(4))* Simon & Schuster.

Treml, Renee. Colour for Curlews. Treml, Renee. 2013. (ENG.). 32p. (J). (gr. -1). 17.99 *(978-1-74275-921-0(1))* Random Hse. Australia AUS. Dist: Independent Pubs. Group.

—One Very Tired Wombat. Treml, Renee. 2014. (ENG.). 32p. (J). (gr. -1-k). pap. 9.99 *(978-1-74275-579-3(8))* Random Hse. Australia AUS. Dist: Independent Pubs. Group.

Tremlin, Nathan. A Quilt of Wishes. Werner, Teresa O. l.t. ed. 2005. 21p. (J). per. 9.99 *(978-1-59879-037-5(4))* Lifevest Publishing, Inc.

—A Quilt of Wishes. Werner, Teresa Orem. l.t. ed. 2005. 26p. (J). 16.95 *(978-1-59879-147-1(8))* Lifevest Publishing, Inc.

Tremlin, Nathan & Chomiak, Joseph. Mookie: A Girl in Maximsubornia. Tremlin, Nathan & Chomiak, Joseph. Swanson, Matt. 2004. 48p. (J). (gr. 4-8). reprint ed. 18.00 *(978-0-7567-9081-3(6))* DIANE Publishing Co.

Trenard Sayago, Mauricio. Baila, Nana, Baila: Cuban Folktales in English & Spanish. Hayes, Joe. 2008.Tr. of Dance, Nana, Dance. (SPA & ENG.). 96p. (J). (gr. 3-6). 20.95 *(978-1-933693-17-0(7))* Cinco Puntos Pr.

—Dance, Nana, Dance (Baila, Nana, Baila) Hayes, Joe. 2010. (ENG & SPA.). 128p. (J). (gr. 3-6). pap. 12.95 *(978-1-933693-61-3(4))* Cinco Puntos Pr.

Trenc, Milan. Another Night at the Museum. Trenc, Milan. 2013. (ENG.). 32p. (J). (gr. k-4). 16.99 *(978-0-8050-8948-6(9),* Holt, Henry & Co. Bks. For Young Readers) Holt, Henry & Co.

Trent, John. StinkyKids Have a Heart. Menzies, Britt. 2012. (ENG.). 32p. 16.95 *(978-1-62167-073-5(2),* Raven Tree Pr.,Csi) Continental Sales, Inc.

Tresilian, S. Behind the Ranges: Tales of Explorers, Pioneers & Travellers. Reynolds, E. E. 2011. (ENG.). 128p. pap. 15.99 *(978-0-521-13526-9(5))* Cambridge Univ. Pr.

—Unknown Ways: More Tales of Explorers, Pioneers & Travellers. Reynolds, E. E. 2011. (ENG.). 126p. pap. 22.99 *(978-1-107-60027-0(8))* Cambridge Univ. Pr.

Tresilian, Stuart. The Island of Adventure. Blyton, Enid. 70th anniv. unabr. ed. 2014. (Adventure Ser.: 1). (ENG.). 400p. (J). (gr. 4-7). 16.99 *(978-0-230-77070-6(3))* Pan Macmillan GBR. Dist: Independent Pubs. Group.

Tress, Arthur, photos by. Facing Up: Tress: Facing Up. ltd. ed. 2004. (ENG & FRE., 1250.00 *(978-0-9761396-7-6(7),* Tress-LE1) Top Choice Pr., LLC.

Trevas, Chris, jt. illus. see Reiff, Chris.

Trevino, Juan. Dingbat: El Gato Voluntario. Johnson, Sandi. Johnson, Britt, ed. Short, Elizabeth, tr. from ENG. l.t. ed. 2003. Orig. Title: Dingbat the Wayward Cat. (SPA.). 14p. (J). (gr. k-5). spiral bd. 4.99 *(978-1-929063-85-7(7),* 326) Moons & Stars Publishing For Children.

Trevino, Juan & Johnson, Jim. 1 - Dorp the Scottish Dragon: Scotland, 7 vols. Johnson, Sandi. Johnson, Britt & Durant, Sybrina, eds. 2nd rev. ed. 2014. (Lost from Loch Lomond Ser.: 1). 38p. (J). (gr. -1-6). pap. 12.99 *(978-1-929063-00-0(8),* 101) Moons & Stars Publishing For Children.

Trevisan, Marco. Anything Is Possible. Belloni, Giulia. 2013. (ENG.). 32p. (J). (gr. k-2). 16.95 *(978-1-926973-91-3(7),* Owlkids) Owlkids Bks. Inc. CAN. Dist: Perseus-PGW.

Treweek, Cherie. Tales of the Tokoloshe. Scholtz, Pieter. 2005. 143p. (J). per. 12.95 *(978-1-86872-970-8(2))* Struik Pubs. ZAF. Dist: International Publishers Marketing.

Trexler, Jennifer Suther. Zipper Finds a Job. Ritch, Catherine. 2014. (White Squirrel Parables Ser.: Vol. 2). (ENG.). 32p. (J). (gr. -1-3). 13.95 *(978-1-933341-40-8(8))* CRM.

Trezzo-Braren, Loretta. Big Fun Craft Book: Creative Fun for 2 to 6 Year Olds. Trezzo-Braren, Loretta. Press, Judy. 2008. (ENG.). (J). (gr. -1-1). 160p. 16.99 *(978-0-8249-6826-7(3));* 142p. pap. 12.99 *(978-0-8249-6827-4(1))* Ideals Pubns. (Williamson Bks.).

Trier, Walter. Emil & the Detectives. Kästner, Erich. Stahl, J. D., tr. 2014. (ENG.). 224p. (J). (gr. 3). pap. 12.99 *(978-1-4683-0829-7(7))* Overlook Pr., The.

—Emil & the Detectives. Kästner, Erich. Martin, W. & Stahl, J. D., trs. 2007. (ENG.). 220p. (gr. 4-13). 19.95 *(978-1-58567-586-9(5),* 856586) Overlook Pr., The.

Trier, Walter. The Jolly Steamship. Trier, Walter. Rowohlt, Harry. 2013. (ENG.). 32p. (J). (gr. -1-3). 17.95 *(978-0-7358-4127-7(6))* North-South Bks., Inc.

Trimble, Anne M. The Crazy Adventure of Nicholas Mouse. Jeswald, Mary J. 2004. 32p. (J). 14.99 *(978-0-9760651-0-4(X))* OrangeFoot Publishing Co.

Trimmer, Tony. A Bill's Journey into Law, 1 vol. Slade, Suzanne. 2011. (Follow It! Ser.). (ENG.). 24p. (gr. 1-3). pap. 7.49 *(978-1-4048-7027-7(X));* lib. bdg. 25.99 *(978-1-4048-6831-1(3))* Picture Window Bks. (Nonfiction Picture Bks.).

—A Germ's Journey, 1 vol. Rooke, Thom. 2011. (Follow It! Ser.). (ENG.). 24p. (gr. 1-3). lib. bdg. 25.99 *(978-1-4048-6268-5(4));* pap. 7.49 *(978-1-4048-6710-9(4))* Picture Window Bks. (Nonfiction Picture Bks.).

—The Good Artist. Place, John. 2007. (ENG.). 36p. *(978-1-85345-424-0(9))* Crusade for World Revival.

Trimmer, Tony & Chatterton, Martin. A Joke a Day: 365 Guaranteed Giggles. Kingfisher Editors. 2007. (Sidesplitters Ser.). (ENG.). 64p. (J). (gr. 1-5). pap. 6.99 *(978-0-7534-6128-0(5),* Kingfisher) Roaring Brook Pr.

Triplett, Chris Harper. Rocky the Sea Turtle. Kreitz, Tina. 2013. (ENG.). (J). 14.95 *(978-1-62086-132-5(1))* Mascot Bks., Inc.

Triplett, Gina & Call, Greg. The Sixty-Eight Rooms. Malone, Marianne. (Sixty-Eight Rooms Adventures Ser.). (ENG.). 288p. (J). (gr. 3-7). 2011. pap. 6.99 *(978-0-375-85711-9(7));* 2010. 16.99 *(978-0-375-85710-2(9))* Random Hse., Inc.

Triplett, Ginger. Graylinger Grotto. Roark, Algernon Michael. 2011. (ENG.). 94p. (J). pap. 22.95 *(978-1-59299-631-5(0))* Inkwater Pr.

Tripp, Christine. The Cool Coats. Brimner, Larry Dane. 2003. (Rookie Choices Ser.). 31p. (J). (gr. 1-2). 13.60 *(978-0-7569-3259-6(9))* Perfection Learning Corp.

—The Cool Coats. Brimner, Larry Dane. 2003. (Rookie Choices Ser.). (ENG.). 32p. (gr. 1-2). pap. 5.95 *(978-0-516-27834-6(7));* (J). 20.50 *(978-0-516-22545-6(6))* Scholastic Library Publishing. (Children's Pr.).

—Summer Fun. Brimner, Larry Dane. 2003. (Rookie Choices Ser.). (ENG.). 32p. (J). (gr. 1-2). 20.50 *(978-0-516-22548-7(0),* Children's Pr.) Scholastic Library Publishing.

—Trash Trouble. Brimner, Larry Dane. 2003. (Rookie Choices Ser.). (ENG.). 32p. (gr. 1-2). pap. 5.95 *(978-0-516-27837-7(1),* Children's Pr.) Scholastic Library Publishing.

Tripp, Christine. Let's Talk about God. Tripp, Christine, tr. Kripke, Dorothy Karp. 2003. (J). 9.95 *(978-1-881283-34-8(8))* Alef Design Group.

Tripp, Kanila, jt. illus. see Farley, Rick.

Tripp, Wallace. No Flying in the House. Brock, Betty & Brock. 2005. (Harper Trophy Bks.). (ENG.). 144p. (J). (gr. 2-6). pap. 5.99 *(978-0-06-440130-2(8))* HarperCollins Pubs.

Trittin, Paul S. Mark's Story: An Introduction to the Gospel of Mark. Baker, Marvin G. 2nd ed. 2003. 136p. 16.95 *(978-0-9729256-1-7(9));* pap. 9.95 *(978-0-9729256-0-0(0))* Baker Trittin Pr. (Innovative Christian Pubns.).

Trobaugh, Scott, jt. illus. see Bersson, Robert.

Trockstad, Marcy. Rat. Unger-Pengilly, Elaine. 2013. 120p. *(978-1-4602-2262-1(8))* FriesenPress.

Trod, Mariano, et al. The Brilliant Dr. Wogan. 2007. (Choose Your Own Adventure Ser.: No. 17). 112p. (J). (gr. 4-7). per. 6.99 *(978-1-933390-17-8(4),* CHC:17) Chooseco LLC.

Trogdon, Kathryn. Tommy Hare & the Color Purple, 1 vol. DeVogt, Rindia M. 2009. (ENG.). 22p. pap. 24.95 *(978-1-61582-827-2(3))* America Star Bks.

Trolenberg, Karl. Play Day with Daddy. Kula, Cheryl. 2013. 20p. pap. 6.95 *(978-1-4575-2336-6(1))* Dog Ear Publishing, LLC.

Trondheim, Lewis. Mister O. Trondheim, Lewis. 2008. (ENG.). 48p. 13.95 *(978-1-56163-382-1(8))* NBM Publishing Co.

—Monster Dinosaur. Trondheim, Lewis. 2012. (Monster Graphic Novels Ser.). (ENG.). 32p. (J). (gr. 1-6). 9.99 *(978-1-59707-322-6(9))* Papercutz.

—Monster Graphic Novels: Monster Christmas. Trondheim, Lewis. 2011. (Monster Graphic Novels Ser.). (ENG.). 32p. (J). (gr. 1-6). 9.99 *(978-1-59707-288-5(5))* Papercutz.

Trondheim, Lewis & Cartier, Eric. Kaput & Zosky. Trondheim, Lewis. Gauvin, Edward, tr. from FRE. 2008. (ENG.). 80p. (J). (gr. 4-7). pap. 13.95 *(978-1-59643-132-4(6),* First Second Bks.) Roaring Brook Pr.

Trone, Jo. A Bee's Kiss. Glass, Graeme. 2012. 60p. pap. 21.50 *(978-1-61897-383-2(5),* Strategic Bk. Publishing) Strategic Book Publishing & Rights Agency (SBPRA).

Trone, Melody Karns. Christopher James Mcabee & the Wonderful Tree. Davis, Lynda S. & Weisel, Kaitlyn E. 2013. 54p. pap. 6.99 *(978-0-9889907-0-8(9))* Sruvis Publishing.

Trotter, Stuart. All the Ways I Love You. Larkin, Susan. 2012. 16p. (J). *(978-1-4351-3857-5(0))* Barnes & Noble, Inc.

—School Bus Bunny Bus. Williams, Sam. 2006. (ENG.). 10p. (J). (gr. -1-1). 12.95 *(978-1-905417-17-9(9))* Boxer Bks., Ltd. GBR. Dist: Sterling Publishing Co., Inc.

—Spanish. Martin, Jane. 3rd rev. unabr. ed. 2006. (ENG & SPA.). 32p. (J). pap. 6.99 *(978-0-330-32871-5(9),* Pan) Pan Macmillan GBR. Dist: Trafalgar Square Publishing.

—What's under the Sea? Tahta, Sophie. rev. ed. 2006. (Starting Point Science Ser.). 24p. (J). (gr. 4-7). pap. 4.99 *(978-0-7945-1409-9(X),* Usborne) EDC Publishing.

Trotter, Stuart, jt. illus. see Gray, Miranda.

Trotter, Stuart, jt. illus. see Rey, Luis.

Troughton, Guy. Whose Egg? A Lift-The-Flap Book. Evans, Lynette. 2013. (ENG.). 36p. (gr. -1). 16.99 *(978-1-60887-203-9(3))* Insight Editions LP.

—Whose Nest? Evans, Lynette. 2013. (ENG.). 36p. (gr. -1). 16.99 *(978-1-60887-204-6(1))* Insight Editions LP.

Troughton, Joanna. The Tiger Child: A Folk Tale from India. Troughton, Joanna. (ENG.). 32p. (J). pap. 11.95 *(978-0-14-038238-9(0))* Penguin Bks., Ltd. GBR. Dist: Trafalgar Square Publishing.

Trounce, Charlotte. Australia - A 3D Expanding Country Guide. Candlewick Press, Candlewick. 2014. (Panorama Pops Ser.). (ENG.). 30p. (J). (gr. k-4). 8.99 *(978-0-7636-7505-9(9))* Candlewick Pr.

Trounce, Charlotte. San Francisco: A 3D Keepsake Cityscape. Trounce, Charlotte. 2013. (Panorama Pops Ser.). (ENG.). 30p. (J). (gr. k-4). 8.99 *(978-0-7636-6471-8(5))* Candlewick Pr.

Troupe, Thomas Kingsley & Ebbeler, Jeffrey. The Truth about Dragons, 1 vol. Troupe, Thomas Kingsley & Ebbeler, Jeffrey. 2010. (Fairy-Tale Superstars Ser.). (ENG.). 32p. (gr. 1-3). lib. bdg. 26.65 *(978-1-4048-5745-2(1),* Nonfiction Picture Bks.) Picture Window Bks.

Trousdale, Taryn. My Name Is Mae. Pelz, Ramona. 2003. (J). per. 9.95 *(978-1-58597-190-9(1))* Leathers Publishing.

Trout Fishing in America Staff & Jorisch, Stéphane. Chicken Joe Forgets Something Important. 2011. (ENG.). 48p. (J). (gr. k-2). 16.95 *(978-2-923163-74-1(5))* La Montagne Secrete CAN. Dist: Independent Pubs. Group.

Trover, Zachary. The Babysitter, 1 vol. Jones, Christianne C. 2005. (Read-It! Readers Ser.). (ENG.). 24p. (gr. -1-3). lib. bdg. 19.99 *(978-1-4048-1187-4(7),* Easy Readers) Picture Window Bks.

Trover, Zachary, et al. The Baseball Adventure of Jackie Mitchell, Girl Pitcher vs. Babe Ruth. Patrick, Jean L. S. 2011. (History's Kid Heroes Ser.). (ENG.). 32p. (gr. 3-5). 26.60 *(978-0-7613-6180-0(4))* Lerner Publishing Group.

Trover, Zachary. Bulldozers. Tourville, Amanda Doering. 2009. (Mighty Machines Ser.). 32p. (J). (gr. -1-3). 28.50 *(978-1-60270-621-7(2))* Magic Wagon.

—Bunches of Buttons: Counting by Tens, 1 vol. Dahl, Michael. 2006. (Know Your Numbers Ser.). (ENG.). 24p. (gr. -1-2). lib. bdg. 25.99 *(978-1-4048-1315-1(2),* Nonfiction Picture Bks.) Picture Window Bks.

—La Carta de Paula, 1 vol. Jones, Christianne C. Ruiz, Carlos, tr. from ENG. 2006. (Read-It! Readers en Español: Story Collection).Tr. of Paula's Letter. (SPA.). 24p. (gr. -1-3). 19.99 *(978-1-4048-1687-9(9),* Easy Readers) Picture Window Bks.

—¡Córrele, Córrele Ciempiés! Cuenta de Diez en Diez. Dahl, Michael. 2010. (Apréndete Tus Números/Know Your Numbers Ser.).Tr. of Speed, Speed Centipede! - Counting by Tens. (SPA & MUL.). 24p. (gr. -1-2). lib. bdg. 25.99 *(978-1-4048-6299-9(4))* Picture Window Bks.

—Cranes. Tourville, Amanda Doering. 2009. (Mighty Machines Ser.). 32p. (J). (gr. -1-3). 28.50 *(978-1-60270-622-4(0))* Magic Wagon.

—Un Cuarto para Dos, 1 vol. Jones, Christianne C. Ruíz, Carlos, tr. 2006. (Read-It! Readers en Español: Story Collection).Tr. of Room to Share. (SPA.). 24p. (gr. -1-3). 19.99 *(978-1-4048-1694-7(1),* Easy Readers) Picture Window Bks.

—Dump Trucks. Tourville, Amanda Doering. 2009. (Mighty Machines Ser.). 32p. (J). (gr. -1-3). 28.50 *(978-1-60270-623-1(9))* Magic Wagon.

—Falling Freddy the Fainting Goat. Emerson, Carl. 2007. (Animal Underdogs Ser.). 32p. (gr. -1-4). 28.50 *(978-1-60270-015-4(X),* Looking Glass Library) ABDO Publishing Co.

—Fire Trucks. Tourville, Amanda Doering. 2009. (Mighty Machines Ser.). (ENG.). 32p. (J). (gr. -1-3). 28.50 *(978-1-60270-624-8(7))* Magic Wagon.

—Garbage Trucks. Tourville, Amanda Doering. 2009. (Mighty Machines Ser.). (ENG.). 32p. (J). (gr. -1-3). 28.50 *(978-1-60270-625-5(5))* Magic Wagon.

—Guatemala ABCs: A Book about the People & Places of Guatemala, 1 vol. Aboff, Marcie. 2006. (Country ABCs Ser.). (ENG.). 32p. (gr. k-5). 27.32 *(978-1-4048-1570-4(8),* Nonfiction Picture Bks.) Picture Window Bks.

—Guillo el Gusano. Jones, Christianne C. Lozano, Clara, tr. from ENG. 2006. (Read-It! Readers en Español: Story Collection). (SPA.). 32p. (gr. -1-3). lib. bdg. 19.99 *(978-1-4048-2743-1(9),* Easy Readers) Picture Window Bks.

—The Life-Saving Adventure of Sam Deal, Shipwreck Rescuer. Ransom, Candice. 2010. (History's Kid Heroes Ser.). (ENG.). 32p. (gr. 3-5). pap. 8.95 *(978-0-7613-6196-1(0),* Graphic Universe); lib. bdg. 26.60 *(978-0-7613-6177-0(4))* Lerner Publishing Group.

—The Midnight Adventure of Kate Shelley, Train Rescuer. Wetterer, Margaret K. 2010. (History's Kid Heroes Ser.). (ENG.). 32p. (gr. 3-5). 26.60 *(978-0-7613-6173-2(1));* pap. 8.95 *(978-0-7613-6192-3(8),* Graphic Universe) Lerner Publishing Group.

—Nosy Arnie the Anteater. Emerson, Carl. 2007. (Animal Underdogs Ser.). 32p. (gr. -1-4). 28.50 *(978-1-60270-016-1(8),* Looking Glass Library) ABDO Publishing Co.

—Opie the Opossum Wakes Up. Emerson, Carl. 2007. (Animal Underdogs Ser.). 32p. (gr. -1-4). 28.50 *(978-1-60270-017-8(6),* Looking Glass Library) ABDO Publishing Co.

—Out & about at City Hall. Attebury, Nancy Garhan. 2005. (Field Trips Ser.). (ENG.). 24p. (gr. -1-3). lib. bdg. 26.65 *(978-1-4048-1146-1(X),* Nonfiction Picture Bks.) Picture Window Bks.

—Out & about at the Baseball Stadium, 1 vol. Kemper, Bitsy. 2006. (Field Trips Ser.). (ENG.). 24p. (gr. -1-3). lib. bdg. 26.65 *(978-1-4048-2280-1(1),* Nonfiction Picture Bks.) Picture Window Bks.

—Out & about at the Dentist, 1 vol. Kemper, Bitsy. 2006. (Field Trips Ser.). (ENG.). 24p. (gr. -1-3). lib. bdg. 26.65 *(978-1-4048-2278-8(X),* Nonfiction Picture Bks.) Picture Window Bks.

—Out & about at the Greenhouse, 1 vol. Kemper, Bitsy. 2006. (Field Trips Ser.). (ENG.). 24p. (gr. -1-3). lib. bdg. 26.65 *(978-1-4048-2279-5(8),* Nonfiction Picture Bks.) Picture Window Bks.

—Out & about at the Hospital. Attebury, Nancy Garhan. 2005. (Field Trips Ser.). (ENG.). 24p. (gr. -1-3). lib. bdg. 26.65 *(978-1-4048-1148-5(6),* Nonfiction Picture Bks.) Picture Window Bks.

—Out & about at the Newspaper. Shea, Kitty. 2005. (Field Trips Ser.). (ENG.). 24p. (gr. -1-3). lib. bdg. 26.65 *(978-1-4048-1149-2(4),* Nonfiction Picture Bks.) Picture Window Bks.

—Out & about at the Theater, 1 vol. Kemper, Bitsy. 2006. (Field Trips Ser.). (ENG.). 24p. (gr. -1-3). lib. bdg. 26.65

(978-1-4048-2281-8(X), Nonfiction Picture Bks.) Picture Window Bks.

Trover, Zachary, et al. The Rooftop Adventure of Minnie & Tessa, Factory Fire Survivors. Littlefield, Holly. 2011. (History's Kid Heroes Ser.). (ENG.). 32p. (gr. 3-5). 26.60 (978-0-7613-6179-4(0)) Lerner Publishing Group.

Trover, Zachary. The Rough-Riding Adventure of Bronco Charlie, Pony Express Rider. Brill, Marlene Targ. 2010. (History's Kid Heroes Ser.). (ENG.). 32p. (gr. 3-5). pap. 8.95 (978-0-7613-6195-4(2), Graphic Universe); lib. bdg. 26.60 (978-0-7613-6176-3(6)) Lerner Publishing Group.

—Sally the Salamander's Lost Tail. Emerson, Carl. 2007. (Animal Underdogs Ser.). 32p. (gr. -1-4). 28.50 (978-1-60270-018-5(4), Looking Glass Library) ABDO Publishing Co.

—Seven Ate Nine. Slater, David Michael. 2007. (Missy Swiss & More Ser.). 32p. (gr. -1-4). 28.50 (978-1-60270-012-3(5), Looking Glass Library) ABDO Publishing Co.

—The Snowshoeing Adventure of Milton Daub, Blizzard Trekker. Wetterer, Margaret K. & Wetterer, Charles M. 2010. (History's Kid Heroes Ser.). (ENG.). 32p. (gr. 3-5). pap. 8.95 (978-0-7613-6194-7(4), Graphic Universe); lib. bdg. 26.60 (978-0-7613-6175-6(8)) Lerner Publishing Group.

—Speed up, Sammy the Tree Sloth! Emerson, Carl. 2007. (Animal Underdogs Ser.). 32p. (gr. -1-3). 28.50 (978-1-60270-019-2(2), Looking Glass Library) ABDO Publishing Co.

—The Stormy Adventure of Abbie Burgess, Lighthouse Keeper. Roop, Peter & Roop, Connie. 2010. (History's Kid Heroes Ser.). (ENG.). 32p. (gr. 3-5). 26.60 (978-0-7613-6172-5(3)); pap. 8.95 (978-0-7613-6191-6(X), Graphic Universe) Lerner Publishing Group.

—The Top-Secret Adventure of John Darragh, Revolutionary War Spy. Roop, Peter & Roop, Connie. 2010. (History's Kid Heroes Ser.). (ENG.). 32p. (gr. 3-5). pap. 8.95 (978-0-7613-6193-0(6), Graphic Universe); lib. bdg. 26.60 (978-0-7613-6174-9(X)) Lerner Publishing Group.

—Tractors. Tourville, Amanda Doering. 2009. (Mighty Machines Ser.). (ENG.). 32p. (J). (gr. -1-3). 28.50 (978-1-60270-626-2(3)) Magic Wagon.

—What Are You, Patty? A Platypus Tale. Emerson, Carl. 2007. (Animal Underdogs Ser.). 32p. (gr. -1-4). 28.50 (978-1-60270-020-8(6), Looking Glass Library) ABDO Publishing Co.

—What's Bugging Pamela?, 1 vol. Dahl, Michael. 2005. (Read-It! Readers Ser.). (ENG.). 32p. (gr. -1-3). lib. bdg. 19.99 (978-1-4048-1189-8(3), Easy Readers) Picture Window Bks.

Trover, Zachary, jt. illus. see Random House Staff.

Troy, Andy, jt. illus. see Lim, Ron.

Troy, Michael. The Quest for the Tellings. Morris, Elizabeth. 2012. 52p. (-18). pap. (978-1-78222-055-8(0)) Paragon Publishing, Rothersthorpe.

Troy, Tony. Deas & Other Imaginings: Ten Spiritual Folktales for Children. Tarico, Valerie. 2011. (ENG.). 132p. (J). 25.95 (978-0-9773929-4-0(5)) Oracle Institute Pr., LLC, The.

Trudeau, Scott. A Treasure to Share: Adventures in Social Skills. Trudeau, Scott. Holzbauer, David. 2003. 68p. (J). (978-0-9743805-0-6(4)) Intellipop, LLC.

Trudell, Devin. 3 Stories. Trudell, Devin, . 2007. (YA). 10.00 (978-0-9794004-0-7(6)) Art Night Bks.

Trueman, Matthew. Hippos Are Huge! London, Jonathan. 2015. (ENG.). 32p. (J). (gr. k-3). 16.99 (978-0-7636-6592-0(4)) Candlewick Pr.

—One Beetle Too Many: The Extraordinary Adventures of Charles Darwin. Lasky, Kathryn. 2014. (Candlewick Biographies Ser.). (ENG.). 48p. (J). (gr. 2-5). 14.99 (978-0-7636-6842-6(7)) Candlewick Pr.

Trueman, Matthew & Phelan, Matt. Big George: How a Shy Boy Became President Washington. Rockwell, Anne F. 2009. (ENG.). 48p. (J). (gr. 1-4). 17.99 (978-0-15-216583-3(5)) Houghton Mifflin Harcourt Publishing Co.

Truesdell, Sue. Chicken Said, "Cluck!" Grant, Judyann. 2008. (My First I Can Read Bks.). 32p. (J). (gr. -1-3). lib. bdg. 16.89 (978-0-06-028724-5(1)) HarperCollins Pubs.

—Chicken Said, "Cluck!" Grant, Judyann Ackerman. 2010. (My First I Can Read Ser.). (ENG.). 32p. (J). (gr. -1-3). pap. 3.99 (978-0-06-444276-3(4)) HarperCollins Pubs.

—Chicken Said, "Cluck!" Grant, Judyann Ackerman. 2008. (My First I Can Read Ser.). (ENG.). 32p. (J). (gr. -1-3). 16.99 (978-0-06-028723-8(3)) HarperCollins Pubs.

—Golly Sisters Go West. Byars, Betsy. 2003. (I Can Read Book 3 Ser.). (ENG.). 64p. (J). (gr. k-3). pap. 3.99 (978-0-06-444132-2(6)) HarperCollins Pubs.

Truesdell, Sue. Hey World, Here I Am! Little, Jean. 2015. 96p. pap. 6.00 **(978-1-61003-607-8(7))** Center for the Collaborative Classroom.

Truesdell, Sue. I Love Dogs. Stainton, Sue. 2010. (J). lib. bdg. 15.89 (978-0-06-117058-4(5)) HarperCollins Pubs.

—A Moose That Says Moo. Hamburg, Jennifer. 2013. (ENG.). 32p. (J). (gr. -1 — 1). 16.99 (978-0-374-35058-1(2), Farrar, Straus & Giroux (BYR)) Farrar, Straus & Giroux.

Truesdell, Sue & Meisel, Paul. How to Talk to Your Cat. George, Jean Craighead. 2003. (ENG.). 40p. (J). (gr. 1-4). pap. 6.99 (978-0-06-000622-8(6)) HarperCollins Pubs.

—How to Talk to Your Dog. George, Jean Craighead. 2003. (ENG.). 40p. (J). (gr. 1-4). pap. 6.99 (978-0-06-000623-5(4)) HarperCollins Pubs.

Truesdell, Sue & Staake, Bob. I Love Dogs! Stainton, Sue. 2014. (ENG.). 32p. (J). (gr. -1-3). 14.99 (978-0-06-117057-7(7)) HarperCollins Pubs.

Trujillo, Robert. A Bean & Cheese Taco Birthday / Un Cumpleaños con Tacos de Frijoles con Queso. Bertrand, Diane Gonzales & Ventura, Gabriela Baeza. 2015. (SPA & ENG.). 32p. (J). (gr. k-3). 17.95 **(978-1-55885-812-1(1))** Arte Publico Pr.

Trukhan, Ekaterina. Five Little Ducks. 2012. (J). (978-1-58865-854-8(6)) Kidsbooks, LLC.

—Max & Sarah Build a Snowman. Ziefert, Harriet. 2015. (¡Hola, English! Ser.). (ENG & SPA.). 28p. (J). (gr. -1-3). 12.99 (978-1-60905-511-0(X)) Blue Apple Bks.

Truog, Chas. Origin of the Species, Vol. 2. Morrison, Grant. 2nd rev. ed. 2005. (ENG.). 224p. (YA). pap. 19.99 (978-1-56389-890-7(X), Vertigo) DC Comics.

Truong, Marcelino. Descubrir la Biblia. Marchon, Benoit & Rosa, Jean-Pierre. (SPA.). 50p. (J). (gr. 3-5). 7.96 (978-84-263-3188-5(2)) Vives, Luis Editorial (Edelvives) ESP. Dist: Lectorum Pubns., Inc.

Tryon, Leslie. Dear Peter Rabbit. Flor Ada, Alma. 2006. (Stories to Go! Ser.). (J). (gr. k-3). 12.65 (978-0-7569-7322-3(8)) Perfection Learning Corp.

—Extra! Extra! Fairy-Tale News from Hidden Forest. Flor Ada, Alma. 2007. (ENG.). 32p. (J). (gr. k-3). 17.99 (978-0-689-82582-8(X), Atheneum Bks. for Young Readers) Simon & Schuster Children's Publishing.

—Pigs Can Fly! The Adventures of Harriet Pig & Friends. Chocolate, Debbi. 2004. (ENG.). 64p. (J). 15.95 (978-0-8126-2706-0(7)) Cricket Bks.

—With Love, Little Red Hen. Flor Ada, Alma. 2004. (ENG.). 40p. (J). (gr. k-3). 7.99 (978-0-689-87061-3(2), Atheneum Bks. for Young Readers) Simon & Schuster Children's Publishing.

Tsai, Dora. Karma: Reaping What We Sow. Young, Lena. 2005. 26p. (J). pap. (978-1-933554-00-6(2)) Primordia.

—One World Healing. Young, Lena. 2005. 26p. (J). pap. (978-1-933554-01-3(0)) Primordia.

Tsairis, Jeannie Brett, jt. illus. see Monroe, Michael Glenn.

Tse, Glenda. Power Up! A Visual Exploration of Energy. Paleja, S. N. 2015. (ENG.). 56p. (J). (gr. 4-7). pap. 12.95 **(978-1-55451-726-8(5)**, 9781554517268) Annick Pr., Ltd. CAN. Dist: Firefly Bks., Ltd.

Tseng, Jean, jt. illus. see Tseng, Mou-Sien.

Tseng, Mou-Sien & Tseng, Jean. Seesaw Girl. Park, Linda Sue. 2009. (ENG.). 96p. (J). (gr. 2-5). pap. 5.99 (978-0-547-24888-2(1)) Houghton Mifflin Harcourt Publishing Co.

Tsilis, Thanos. The Iliad. Homer. 2013. (Greek Classics Ser.). (ENG.). 64p. pap. 6.95 (978-1-906230-53-1(6)) Real Reads Ltd. GBR. Dist: International Publishers Marketing.

—The Odyssey. Homer. 2013. (Greek Classics Ser.). (ENG.). 64p. pap. 6.95 (978-1-906230-54-8(4)) Real Reads Ltd. GBR. Dist: International Publishers Marketing.

Tsong, Jing Jing. Before We Met. Melmed, Laura Krauss. 2016. (J). **(978-1-4424-4156-9(9)**, Beach Lane Bks.) Beach Lane Bks.

Tsong, Jing Jing. A Bucket of Blessings. Sehgal, Kabir & Sehgal, Surishtha. 2014. (ENG.). 32p. (J). (gr. -1-3). 16.99 (978-1-4424-5870-3(4), Beach Lane Bks.) Beach Lane Bks.

Tsong, Jing Jing. Shanghai Sukkah. Hyde, Heidi Smith. 2015. (ENG.). 32p. (J). (gr. k-4). 17.99 **(978-1-4677-3474-5(8))**; pap. 7.99 **(978-1-4677-3475-2(6))** Lerner Publishing Group. (Kar-Ben Publishing).

Tsosie, Dennison. Floating Around in the Middle. Alexander, Carmen. 2005. 30p. (J). (gr. -1-5). pap. 14.99 (978-1-886383-76-0(6)) Blue Forge Pr.

Tsubaki, Izumi. The Magic Touch. Tsubaki, Izumi. 2009. (Magic Touch Ser.: 1). (ENG.). 208p. (gr. 8-18). pap. 9.99 (978-1-4215-1671-4(3)) Viz Media.

Tsuchiya, Fujio. A Christmas Interview: Reporting Live from Bethlehem! Yoshiike, Yoshitaka. 2005. 32p. (J). (gr. -1-3). per. 7.95 (978-0-8198-1572-9(1)) Pauline Bks. & Media.

Tsuda, Efrain Rodriguez. Murmullos de la Selva. Dubuvoy, Silvia et al. 2004. (Montana Encantada Ser.). (SPA.). 60p. (J). (gr. 3-5). pap. 9.99 (978-84-241-8660-9(5)) Everest Editora ESP. Dist: Lectorum Pubns., Inc.

Tsuda, Masami. Kare Kano, Vol. 14. Kobayashi, Michelle, tr. from JPN. rev. ed. 2005. 200p. pap. 9.99 (978-1-59532-588-4(3)) TOKYOPOP, Inc.

Tsuda, Masami. Kare Kano Vols. 1-3: His & Her Circumstances. Tsuda, Masami. rev. ed. 2004. 192p. pap. 9.99 (978-1-59182-472-5(9)) TOKYOPOP, Inc.

—Kare Kano Vols. 1-3: His & Her Circumstances, 15 vols., Vol. 1. Tsuda, Masami. Niida, Jack, tr. from JPN. 2003. 192p. (gr. 6-13). pap. 9.99 (978-1-931514-79-8(8)) TOKYOPOP, Inc.

—Kare Kano Vols. 1-3: His & Her Circumstances, 13 vols. Tsuda, Masami. rev. ed. Vol. 5. 2003. 192p. pap. 9.99 (978-1-59182-180-9(0)); Vol. 6. 2003. 192p. (YA). pap. 9.99 (978-1-59182-181-6(9)); Vol. 13. 2005. 208p. pap. 9.99 (978-1-59532-587-7(5)) TOKYOPOP, Inc.

Tsuda, Masami. Kare Kano, Vol. 15. Tsuda, Masami, creator. rev. ed. 2005. 200p. pap. 9.99 (978-1-59532-589-1(1)) TOKYOPOP, Inc.

Tuason, Scott. Project Seahorse. Turner, Pamela S. 12th ed. 2010. (Scientists in the Field Ser.). (ENG.). 64p. (YA). (gr. 5-7). 18.99 (978-0-547-20713-1(1)) Houghton Mifflin Harcourt Publishing Co.

Tuason, Scott, photos by. The Dolphins of Shark Bay. Turner, Pamela S. 2013. (Scientists in the Field Ser.). (ENG., 80p. (J). (gr. 5-7). 18.99 (978-0-547-71638-1(9)) Houghton Mifflin Harcourt Publishing Co.

Tucci, Al. The Lonely Train. Kivel, Lee. 2005. 36p. (J). per. 14.95 (978-0-9774999-0-8(1)) Kivel, Lee.

Tuccy, Alycia. Mommy Has Lots to Do. Tuccy, Angel. 2011. (ENG.). 32p. pap. 12.95 (978-1-4538-4675-9(1)) CreateSpace Independent Publishing Platform.

Tuck-Bernstein, Cheryl. Chicken Fingers, Mac & Cheese... Why Do You Always Have to Say Please? Rosen, Wendy & End, Jackie. 2005. 32p. (J). 14.99 (978-0-7666-1986-9(9)) Modern Publishing.

Tuck, Beverly. Little Bianca. Webb, Mack Henry, Jr. 2006. 52p. (J). per. 15.95 (978-0-9779576-0-6(8)) Pilinut Pr., Inc.

Tucker, Amanda. The Cutest Little Duckie. Valentine, Victoria. 2007. 80p. (J). per. 15.00 (978-0-9723493-4-5(0), Water Forest Pr.) Skyline Pubn.

Tucker and Hooper Staff, photos by. Pasta. Croce, Julia Della & Williams-Sonoma Staff. Williams, Chuck, ed. rev. ed. 2006. (Food Made Fast Ser.). (ENG., 112p. (gr. 12-17). 17.95 (978-0-8487-3135-9(2)) Oxmoor Hse., Inc.

Tucker, Barclay. Fat Freddy. Holzer, Angela. 2009. 36p. (J). lib. bdg. 8.99 (978-0-9821563-4-6(0)) Good Sound Publishing.

Tucker, Diane. The Proud Beech: A Long Island Folk Tale. Edelson, Madelyn. 2004. 48p. (J). pap. 14.95 (978-0-9658920-7-0(7)) Edelson, Madelyn.

Tucker, E. Jake's Junction: Henry's Listening Ears. Hazlett, V. 2006. (ENG.). 28p. per. 11.95 (978-1-59800-628-5(2)) Outskirts Pr., Inc.

Tucker, Eric. Finnius: The Tale of a Lost Little Elephant. Wundram, Bill. 2003. (J). (978-1-59152-011-5(8), Sweetgrass Bks.) Farcountry Pr.

Tucker, Ezra. The Dark Realm: Skor the Winged Stallion. Scholastic, Inc. Staff & Blade, Adam. 2010. (Beast Quest Ser.: 14). (ENG.). 80p. (J). (gr. 2-5). pap. 4.99 (978-0-545-20032-5(6), Scholastic Paperbacks) Scholastic, Inc.

—Sting the Scorpion Man. Blade, Adam. 2011. (Beast Quest Ser.: 18). (ENG.). 80p. (J). (gr. 2-5). pap. 4.99 (978-0-545-20036-3(9), Scholastic Paperbacks) Scholastic, Inc.

—Tagus the Night Horse. Blade, Adam. 2007. (Beast Quest Ser.: 4). (ENG.). 80p. (J). (gr. 2-5). pap. 4.99 (978-0-439-02456-3(0), Scholastic Paperbacks) Scholastic, Inc.

Tucker, Julie. Chasing the Spirit of Service. Zajac, Kristen. 2013. 24p. 19.95 (978-1-61633-393-5(6)) Guardian Angel Publishing, Inc.

Tucker, Keith. Alexander Graham Bell & the Telephone, 1 vol. Fandel, Jennifer. 2006. (Inventions & Discovery Ser.). (ENG.). 32p. (gr. 3-4). 29.99 (978-0-7368-6478-7(4), Graphic Library) Capstone Pr., Inc.

—The Apollo 13 Mission, 1 vol. Lemke, Donald & Lemke, Donald B. 2006. (Disasters in History Ser.). (ENG.). 32p. (gr. 3-4). 29.99 (978-0-7368-5476-4(2), Graphic Library) Capstone Pr., Inc.

—George Washington Carver: Ingenious Inventor, 1 vol. Olson, Nathan. 2006. (Graphic Biographies Ser.). (ENG.). 32p. (gr. 3-4). 29.99 (978-0-7368-5484-9(3), Graphic Library) Capstone Pr., Inc.

—Philo Farnsworth & the Television, 1 vol. Niz, Ellen Sturm. 2006. (Inventions & Discovery Ser.). (ENG.). 32p. (gr. 3-4). 29.99 (978-0-7368-6487-9(3), Graphic Library) Capstone Pr., Inc.

Tucker, Lewis R. & Mosher, Scott. The Dragon Who Lived Next Door. Gelber, Peter Frost. l.t. ed. 2003. 64p. (J). (gr. -1-6). pap. 12.00 (978-0-9658920-4-9(2)) Fore Angels Pr.

Tucker, Marianne & Gilbert, Elizabeth T. Watch Me Draw Cinderella's Enchanted World. 2013. (Watch Me Draw Ser.). 24p. (J). (gr. -1-2). 25.65 (978-1-936309-86-3(6)) Quarto Publishing Group USA.

Tucker, Marianne & Phillipson, Andy. Learn to Draw Plus Disney Pixar Cars. 2012. (978-1-936309-70-2(X)) Quarto Publishing Group USA.

Tucker, Marianne, jt. illus. see Mosqueda, Olga T.

Tucker, Sian. Magic World of Learning. Young, Jay. 2003. 32p. (978-1-903174-42-5(2), Pavilion Children's Books) Pavilion Bks.

Tucker, Sian. My Book of First Numbers. Tucker, Sian. 2003. (My Book of. . . Ser.). 48p. (YA). (978-1-85602-482-2(2), Pavilion Children's Books) Pavilion Bks.

—My Book of First Words. Tucker, Sian. 2003. (My Book of. . . Ser.). 48p. (YA). (978-1-85602-439-6(3), Pavilion Children's Books) Pavilion Bks.

Tucker, Tracey. When I'm Big & Grown: When I'm Big & Grown: I Want to Be an Entrepreneur When I Grow Up. Black, Cassandra. 2012. (ENG.). 32p. (J). pap. (978-0-9822503-7-2(1)) Stone Cottage Bks.

Tudor, Andy. Diggers Stencil Book. Stowell, Louie & Pearcey, Alice. Doherty, Gillian, ed. 2007. (Stencil Bks.). 14p. (J). bds. 12.99 (978-0-7945-1576-8(2), Usborne) EDC Publishing.

—Planet Earth (Kawkab Al Ard) Pratt, Leonie. Ibrahim, Nouran, tr. from ARA. 2013. (ENG.). 32p. (J). 6.99 (978-99921-94-34-8(0), 149892) Bloomsbury USA.

—Usborne Tractors & Trucks Stencil Book. Pearcey, Alice. Milbourne, Anna, ed. 2006. 10p. (J). bds. 12.99 (978-0-7945-1139-5(2), Usborne) EDC Publishing.

—Volcanoes. Turnbull, Stephanie. 2006. (Usborne Beginners Ser.). 32p. (J). (gr. 1). lib. bdg. 12.99 (978-1-58086-949-2(1)); 4.99 (978-0-7945-1401-3(4)) EDC Publishing. (Usborne).

—Volcanoes. Turnbull, Stephanie. 2005. 32p. (J). pap. (978-0-439-84610-3(2)) Scholastic, Inc.

—200 Paper Planes. ed. 2013. (200 Paper Planes Ser.). 402p. (J). pap. 13.99 (978-0-7945-3371-7(X), Usborne) EDC Publishing.

Tudor, Andy & Haggerty, Tim. Planet Earth: Level 2. Pratt, Leonie. 2007. (Beginners Nature Ser.). 32p. (J). 4.99 (978-0-7945-1707-6(2), Usborne) EDC Publishing.

Tudor, Tasha. Inside the Secret Garden: A Treasury of Crafts, Recipes, & Activities. Collins, Carolyn Strom & Eriksson, Christina Wyss. 2004. 130p. (J). (gr. 2-8). reprint ed. 25.00 (978-0-7567-7630-5(9)) DIANE Publishing Co.

—The Night Before Christmas. Moore, Clement C. 10th anniv. ed. 2009. 32p. pap. 6.99 (978-0-316-18947-7(2)) Hachette Bk. Group.

—The Secret Garden. Burnett, Frances Hodgson. 100th anniv. ed. 2010. (Trophy Bk.). (ENG.). 384p. (J). (gr. 4-18). reprint ed. pap. 6.99 (978-0-06-440188-3(X)) HarperCollins Pubs.

—The Secret Garden Book & Charm. Burnett, Frances Hodgson. deluxe ed. 2005. (Charming Classics). 368p. (J). 9.99 (978-0-06-075771-7(X), HarperFestival) HarperCollins Pubs.

Tudor, Tasha. A Is for Annabelle: A Doll's Alphabet. Tudor, Tasha. 2004. (ENG.). 64p. (J). (gr. -1-3). reprint ed. 7.99 (978-0-689-86996-9(7), Simon & Schuster/Paula Wiseman Bks.) Simon & Schuster/Paula Wiseman Bks.

—Around the Year. Tudor, Tasha. 2004. (ENG.). 64p. (J). (gr. -1-3). 6.99 (978-0-689-87350-8(6), Simon & Schuster/Paula Wiseman Bks.) Simon & Schuster/Paula Wiseman Bks.

—A Tale for Easter. Tudor, Tasha. 2014. (Classic Board Bks.). (ENG.). 34p. (J). (gr. -1 — 1). bds. 7.99 (978-1-4424-8857-1(3), Little Simon) Little Simon.

—A Tale for Easter. Tudor, Tasha. 2004. (ENG.). 32p. (J). (gr. -1-3). 6.99 (978-0-689-86694-4(1), Simon & Schuster/Paula Wiseman Bks.) Simon & Schuster/Paula Wiseman Bks.

Tuell, Julia E., photos by. Women & Warriors of the Plains: The Pioneer Photography of Julia E. Tuell. Aadland, Dan & Michaelides, Marina. rev. ed. 182p. (J). (gr. 4). reprint ed. pap. (978-0-87842-417-7(2), 660) Mountain Pr. Publishing Co., Inc.

Tufts, N. Jo. Wrinkly Socks Make Me Giggle. Wake, Shelley. 2005. (ENG.). 16p. (gr. k-2). pap. 5.95 (978-1-57874-086-4(X)) Kaeden Corp.

Tugeau, Jeremy. Always an Olivia: A Remarkable Family History. Herron, Carolivia. 2012. (Jewish Identity Ser.). (ENG.). 32p. (J). (gr. 2-4). pap. 9.95 (978-0-7613-9100-5(2), Kar-Ben Publishing) Lerner Publishing Group.

—Animal Tales from Mother Goose. 2011. (Mother Goose Nursery Rhymes Ser.). 32p. (gr. -1-2). 28.50 (978-1-61641-142-8(2), Looking Glass Library) ABDO Publishing Co.

—Bedtime with Mother Goose. Hedlund, Stephanie. 2011. (Mother Goose Nursery Rhymes Ser.). 32p. (gr. k-2). 28.50 (978-1-61641-143-5(0), Looking Glass Library) ABDO Publishing Co.

—The Buddy Files: The Case of the School Ghost. Butler, Dori Hillestad. 2012. (Buddy Files Ser.: 6). (ENG.). 128p. (J). (gr. 1-3). 14.99 (978-0-8075-0915-9(9)) Whitman, Albert & Co.

—The Buddy Files Bk. 3: The Case of the Missing Family. Butler, Dori Hillestad. 2010. (Buddy Files Ser.). (ENG.). 128p. (J). (gr. 1-3). 14.99 (978-0-8075-0912-8(4)) Whitman, Albert & Co.

—The Buddy Files Bk. 4: The Case of the Fire Alarm. Butler, Dori Hillestad. 2011. (Buddy Files Ser.: 4). (ENG.). 144p. (J). (gr. 1-3). pap. 5.99 (978-0-8075-0935-7(3)) Whitman, Albert & Co.

—Cars, Trucks, & Planes. 2010. (My World Ser.). (ENG.). 24p. (J). (gr. -1-1). pap. 8.15 (978-1-61533-031-7(3)); lib. bdg. 22.60 (978-1-60754-949-9(2)) Windmill Bks.

—Cars, Trucks & Planes/Carros, Camiones y Aviones. Rosa-Mendoza, Gladys. 2004. (English-Spanish Foundations Ser.). (SPA & ENG.). 20p. (J). (gr. -1). bds. 6.95 (978-1-931398-14-5(3)) Me+Mi Publishing.

—The Case of the Library Monster. Butler, Dori Hillestad. ed. 2012. (Buddy Files Ser.: 5). lib. bdg. 16.00 (978-0-606-23839-7(5), Turtleback) Turtleback Bks.

—The Case of the Library Monster. Butler, Dori Hillestad. 2012. (Buddy Files Ser.: 5). (ENG.). 128p. (J). (gr. 1-3). pap. 5.99 (978-0-8075-0936-4(1)) Whitman, Albert & Co.

—The Case of the Lost Boy. Butler, Dori Hillestad. 2010. (Buddy Files Ser.: Bk. 1). (ENG.). 128p. (J). (gr. 1-3). 14.99 (978-0-8075-0910-4(8));Bk. 1. pap. 5.99 (978-0-8075-0932-6(9)) Whitman, Albert & Co.

—The Case of the Missing Family, 1 vol., Bk. 3. Butler, Dori Hillestad. 2010. (Buddy Files Ser.: 3). (ENG.). 144p. (J). (gr. 1-3). pap. 5.99 (978-0-8075-0934-0(5)) Whitman, Albert & Co.

—The Case of the Mixed-Up Mutts, Bk. 2. Butler, Dori Hillestad. 2010. (Buddy Files Ser.). (ENG.). 128p. (J). (gr. 1-3). 14.99 (978-0-8075-0911-1(6)) Whitman, Albert & Co.

—The Case of the Mixed-Up Mutts Bk. 2, 1 vol., Bk. 2. Butler, Dori Hillestad. 2010. (The Buddy Files Ser.). (ENG.). 128p. (J). (gr. 1-3). pap. 5.99 (978-0-8075-0933-3(7)) Whitman, Albert & Co.

—The Case of the School Ghost, Bk. 6. Butler, Dori Hillestad. 2013. (Buddy Files Ser.: Book 6). (ENG.). 144p. (J). (gr. 1-3). pap. 5.99 (978-0-8075-0937-1(X)) Whitman, Albert & Co.

—Count along with Mother Goose. 2011. (Mother Goose Nursery Rhymes Ser.). 32p. (gr. -1-2). 28.50 (978-1-61641-144-2(9), Looking Glass Library) ABDO Publishing Co.

—I Will Not Be Afraid. Adams, Michelle M. 2008. 32p. (J). (gr. -1-3). 14.99 (978-0-7586-1335-6(0)) Concordia Publishing Hse.

—Lizzie Newton & the San Francisco Earthquake. Krensky, Stephen. 2010. (History Speaks: Picture Books Plus Reader's Theater Ser.). (ENG.). 48p. (gr. 2-4). pap. 9.95 (978-0-7613-3944-1(2)); lib. bdg. 27.93 (978-0-8225-9031-6(X), Millbrook Pr.) Lerner Publishing Group.

—Making Friends with Mother Goose. 2011. (Mother Goose Nursery Rhymes Ser.). 32p. (gr. -1-2). 28.50 (978-1-61641-145-9(7), Looking Glass Library) ABDO Publishing Co.

—Nathan Blows Out the Hanukkah Candles. Lehman-Wilzig, Tami & Katzman, Nicole. 2011. (Hanukkah Ser.). (ENG.). 32p. (J). (gr. k-3). pap. 7.95 (978-0-7613-6658-4(X), Kar-Ben Publishing) Lerner Publishing Group.

—Seeing Colors with Mother Goose. 2011. (Mother Goose Nursery Rhymes Ser.). 32p. (gr. -1-2). 28.50 (978-1-61641-146-6(5), Looking Glass Library) ABDO Publishing Co.

—Weather Fun with Mother Goose. 2011. (Mother Goose Nursery Rhymes Ser.). 32p. (gr. -1-2). 28.50 (978-1-61641-147-3(3), Looking Glass Library) ABDO Publishing Co.

—Who Were the Beatles? Edgers, Geoff. 2006. (Who Was... ? Ser.). (ENG.). 112p. (J). (gr. 3-7). pap. 5.99 (978-0-448-43906-8(9), Grosset & Dunlap) Penguin Publishing Group.

Tulik, Alice, et al. Fishing Adventures. Tulik, Alice et al. 2006. (Adventure Story Collection Ser.). 36p. (J). (gr. 2-6). pap. 12.00 (978-1-58084-248-8(8)) Lower Kuskokwim Schl. District.

Tulip, Jenny. Baby Jesus. Jeffs, Stephanie. 2004. (My First Find Out about Book Ser.). 24p. (gr. -1-18). pap. 3.95 (978-0-8294-1730-2(3)) Loyola Pr.

—My Big Book of Words. Clark, Isobel. 2009. (ENG.). 48p. (J). (gr. 4-7). 9.99 (978-0-7548-1941-7(8)) Anness Publishing GBR. Dist: National Bk. Network.

T

—My Big Book of Words. Clarke, Isabel. 2014. (ENG.). 40p. (J). (gr. -1-k). 12.99 (978-1-86147-325-7(7), Armadillo) Anness Publishing GBR. Dist: National Bk. Network.
—My First French Word Book. 2004. (ENG & FRE.). 48p. (J). 5.99 (978-1-85854-237-9(5)) Brimax Books Ltd. GBR. Dist: Byeway Bks.
—My First Spanish Words. Vaamonde, Conchita, tr. 2004. (SPA.). 12p. (J). bds. 7.99 (978-1-85854-512-7(9)) Brimax Books Ltd. GBR. Dist: Byeway Bks.
Tulip, Jenny. My First Word Book: Pictures & Words to Start Toddlers Reading & to Help Pre-Schoolers Develop Vocabulary Skills. Wotton, Joy. 2012. (ENG.). 200p. 9.99 (978-1-84322-617-8(0), Armadillo) Anness Publishing GBR. Dist: National Bk. Network.
Tulip, Jenny. People Jesus Met. Jeffs, Stephanie. 2004. (My First Find Out about Book Ser.). 24p. (gr. -1-18). pap. 3.95 (978-0-8294-1731-9(1)) Loyola Pr.
—Preparing for Times Tables. Somerville, Louisa & Smith, David. 2014. (ENG.). 32p. (J). (gr. -1 — 1). 5.99 (978-0-7548-1934-9(5)); 5.99 (978-0-7548-1935-6(3)) Anness Publishing GBR. Dist: National Bk. Network.
—Stories Jesus Told. Jeffs, Stephanie. 2004. (My First Find Out about Book Ser.). 24p. (gr. -1-18). pap. 3.95 (978-0-8294-1733-3(8)) Loyola Pr.
—Things Jesus Did. Jeffs, Stephanie. 2004. 24p. (gr. -1-18). pap. 3.95 (978-0-8294-1734-0(6)) Loyola Pr.
—Who Lives Here? (Slide & Find). 10p. (J). bds. (978-1-57755-714-2(X)) Flying Frog Publishing, Inc.
—Who's Hiding in the Garden? 2008. 10p. (gr. -1-k). bds. 6.99 (978-1-57755-785-2(9)) Gardner Pubns.
—Who's Hiding in the Jungle? A Mystery Touch-and-Feel Flap Book! 2008. 10p. (gr. -1-k). bds. 6.99 (978-1-57755-784-5(0)) Flying Frog Publishing.
Tullet, Hervé. Help! We Need a Title! Tullet, Hervé. 2014. (ENG.). 64p. (J). (gr. -1-3). 16.99 (978-0-7636-7021-4(9)) Candlewick Pr.
Tulloch, Scott. Willy's Dad. Tulloch, Scott. 2007. 32p. (978-1-86950-631-5(6)) HarperCollins Pubs. Australia.
Tuma, Tomas. Space Atlas. Dusek, Jiri & Pisala, Jan. 2014. (ENG.). 34p. (J). (gr. 1-3). 16.95 (978-1-4549-1237-8(5)) Sterling Publishing Co., Inc.
Tumminello, Giovanna, jt. illus. see Santitoro, Theresa.
Tunell, Ken. Comprehension Crosswords Grade 3, 6 vols. Shiotsu, Vicky. 2003. 32p. (J). 4.99 (978-1-56472-187-7(6)) Edupress, Inc.
—Selfus Esteemus Personalitus Low. Goss, Leon. 2005. (J). pap. (978-1-933156-08-8(2), VisionQuest Kids) GSVQ Publishing.
—Selfus Esteemus Personalitus Low. Goss, Leon, 3rd. ed. 2005. 32p. (J). per. 16.99 (978-1-933156-00-2(7), VisionQuest Kids) GSVQ Publishing.
Tung, Kadhima Ren. Grandma Lives with Us. Currim, Nazli. 2010. 46p. (J). 16.95 (978-0-9814629-5-0(2)) Acacia Publishing, Inc.
Tung, King. The King of Fighters 2003, Vol. 1. 2005. 128p. (YA). pap. 13.95 (978-1-58899-030-3(3)) DrMaster Pubns. Inc.
Tunnicliffe, C. F. The Seasons & the Fisherman: A Book for Children. Darling, F. Fraser. 2011. (ENG.). 84p. pap. 22.99 (978-0-521-17594-4(1)) Cambridge Univ. Pr.
Tunstel Jr., Robert L. The Gift That Grandma Gave: Including Bloom's Leveled Questions Study Guide. Griffin, Ramona Rorie. 2011. 44p. pap. 24.95 (978-1-4560-1034-8(4)) America Star Bks.
—My Mind Looks Back & Wonders ... Griffin, Ramona Rorie. 2009. (ENG.). 28p. pap. 24.95 (978-1-60813-917-0(4)) America Star Bks.
Tuohy, Hannah. No Sand in the House! Crawford, Jennifer. 2013. (ENG.). 32p. pap. 11.95 (978-0-615-81199-4(X)) No Sand in the House!.
Turakhia, Smita. Finders Keepers? A True Story. Arnett, Robert. 2003. 32p. (J). 16.95 (978-0-9652900-2-9(6)) Atman Pr.
Turchan, Monique. Courage. Roth, Irene. 2012. 24p. pap. 11.95 (978-1-61244-068-2(1)) Halo Publishing International.
—Leah's Voice. Demonia, Lori. 2012. 28p. pap. 12.95 (978-1-61244-089-7(4)) Halo Publishing International.
—Smarty Pig & the Test Taking Terror. Nero, Molly. 2012. 28p. pap. 12.95 (978-1-61244-055-2(X)) Halo Publishing International.
—What Am I Gonna Do? Wamsley, Jody. 2013. 24p. pap. 11.95 (978-1-61244-070-5(3)) Halo Publishing International.
Turchan, Monique. Mydoit. Turchan, Monique. 2013. 24p. pap. 11.95 (978-1-61244-144-3(0)) Halo Publishing International.
Turchyn, Sandie. The Girls' Guide to Dreams. Collier-Thompson, Kristi. 2006. 128p. (YA). (gr. 8-11). reprint ed. pap. 13.00 (978-0-7567-9899-4(X)) DIANE Publishing Co.
Turco, Laura Lo. The Great Pyramid: The Story of the Farmers, the God-King & the Most Astonding Structure Ever Built. Mann, Elizabeth. 2006. (Wonders of the World Book Ser.). (ENG.). 48p. (J). (gr. 4-8). pap. 9.95 (978-1-931414-11-1(4), 9781931414111) Mikaya Pr.
Turconi, Stefano. The Crown of Venice, No. 7. Stevenson, Steve. 2014. (Agatha: Girl of Mystery Ser.: 7). (ENG.). 144p. (J). (gr. 2-5). 5.99 (978-0-448-46225-7(7), Grosset & Dunlap) Penguin Publishing Group.
—The Curse of the Pharaoh, Vol. 1. Stevenson, Steve. 2013. (Agatha: Girl of Mystery Ser.: 1). (ENG.). 144p. (J). (gr. 2-5). pap. 5.99 (978-0-448-46217-2(6), Grosset & Dunlap) Penguin Publishing Group.
—The Eiffel Tower Incident #5. Stevenson, Steve. 2014. (Agatha: Girl of Mystery Ser.: 5). (ENG.). 144p. (J). (gr. 2-5). 5.99 (978-0-448-46223-3(0), Grosset & Dunlap) Penguin Publishing Group.
—The Heist at Niagara Falls. Stevenson, Steve. 2013. (Agatha: Girl of Mystery Ser.: 4). (ENG.). 144p. (J). (gr. 2-5). 5.99 (978-0-448-46221-9(4), Grosset & Dunlap) Penguin Publishing Group.
—The Kenyan Expedition #8. Stevenson, Steve. 2015. (Agatha: Girl of Mystery Ser.: 8). (ENG.). 144p. (J). (gr. 3-7). 5.99 (978-0-448-48679-6(2), Grosset & Dunlap) Penguin Publishing Group.
—The King of Scotland's Sword. Stevenson, Steve. 2013. (Agatha: Girl of Mystery Ser.: 3). (ENG.). 144p. (J). (gr. 2-5). pap. 5.99 (978-0-448-46220-2(6), Grosset & Dunlap) Penguin Publishing Group.
—The Pearl of Bengal, Vol. 2. Stevenson, Steve. 2013. (Agatha: Girl of Mystery Ser.: 2). (ENG.). 144p. (J). (gr. 2-5). pap. 5.99 (978-0-448-46219-6(2), Grosset & Dunlap) Penguin Publishing Group.
Turconi, Stefano, et al. Race for the Ultrapods, Vol. 2. Secchi, Richard & Salati, Giorgio. 2010. (Disney's Hero Squad Ser.). (ENG.). 128p. (J). (gr. 4-7). pap. 9.99 (978-1-60886-560-4(6)) Boom! Studios.
Turconi, Stefano. The Treasure of the Bermuda Triangle, No. 6. Stevenson, Steve. 2014. (Agatha: Girl of Mystery Ser.: 6). (ENG.). 144p. (J). (gr. 2-5). 5.99 (978-0-448-46224-0(9), Grosset & Dunlap) Penguin Publishing Group.
Turcotte, Derek. Colours Made in Heaven, 1 vol. Turcotte, Michael. 2009. 13p. pap. 24.95 (978-1-60836-316-2(3)) America Star Bks.
Turgeon, Stephane. Noah's Ark. 2007. 16p. (J). (gr. -1-3). (978-2-7641-0340-1(9)) Tormont Pubns.
Turk, Caron. Little Boys Bible Storybook for Fathers & Sons. Larsen, Carolyn. rev. ed. 2014. (ENG.). 288p. (J). 14.99 (978-0-8010-1548-9(0)) Baker Bks.
—Little Girls Bible Storybook for Fathers & Daughters. Larsen, Carolyn. rev. ed. 2014. (ENG.). 288p. (J). 14.99 (978-0-8010-1549-6(9)) Baker Bks.
—My 123 Bible Storybook. Larsen, Carolyn. 2008. (My Bible Storybooks Ser.). 30p. (J). (gr. -1-3). bds. (978-1-86920-925-4(7)) Christian Art Pubs.
—My ABC Bible Storybook. Larsen, Carolyn. 2008. (My Bible Storybooks Ser.). 30p. (J). (gr. -1-3). bds. (978-1-86920-926-1(5)) Christian Art Pubs.
—Prayers for Little Boys. Larsen, Carolyn. 2008. (Prayers For... Ser.). 131p. (J). (gr. -1-3). (978-1-86920-527-0(8)) Christian Art Pubs.
—Prayers for Little Girls. Larsen, Carolyn. 2008. (Prayers For... Ser.). 131p. (J). (gr. -1-3). (978-1-86920-526-3(X)) Christian Art Pubs.
Turk, Caron, jt. illus. see Elwell, Ellen Banks.
Turk, Cheri. The Stone Between Kings. Turk, Cheri. 2012. 36p. pap. 12.99 (978-0-9860024-0-3(2)) Specialty Greetings.
Turk, Evan. Be the Change: A Grandfather Gandhi Story. Gandhi, Arun & Hegedus, Bethany. 2016. (J). (978-1-4814-4265-7(1)) Simon & Schuster Children's Publishing.
Turk, Evan. Grandfather Gandhi. Gandhi, Arun & Hegedus, Bethany. 2014. (ENG.). 48p. (J). (gr. -1-3). 17.99 (978-1-4424-2365-7(X)) Simon & Schuster Children's Publishing.
Turk, Evan. The Storyteller. 2016. (J). (978-1-4814-3518-5(3)) Simon & Schuster Children's Publishing.
Turk, Hanne. The Secret House of Papa Mouse. Landa, Norbert. 2004. (Picture Books/Quality Time Ser.). 32p. (gr. k-3). lib. bdg. 26.00 (978-0-8368-4106-0(9), Gareth Stevens Learning Library) Stevens, Gareth Publishing LLLP.
Turley, Joyce M. It's My Birthday. . . Finally! A Leap Year Story. Winfrey, Michelle Whitaker. 2003. 88p. (J). (gr. 3-7). per. 11.95 (978-0-9727179-0-8(0)) Hobby Hse. Publishing Group.
Turley, Joyce Mihran. Awesome Ospreys: Fishing Birds of the World. Love, Donna. rev. ed. 2005. 62p. (J). (gr. 3-7). pap. 12.00 (978-0-87842-512-9(8), 341) Mountain Pr. Publishing Co., Inc.
—One Night in the Everglades. Larsen, Laurel. 2012. (Long Term Ecological Research Ser.). (ENG.). 32p. (J). (gr. 3-7). 15.95 (978-0-9817700-4-8(5)) Taylor Trade Publishing.
Turley, Joyce Mihran. Loons: Diving Birds of the North, Vol. 1. Turley, Joyce Mihran, tr. Love, Donna. rev. ed. 64p. (J). (gr. 4). pap. 12.00 (978-0-87842-482-5(2), 340) Mountain Pr. Publishing Co., Inc.
Turman, Adam. J. B. 's Christmas Presents. Turman, Evelyn. l.t. ed. 2004. 28p. (J). 15.95 (978-0-9753042-0-4(8)) Turman, E.
Turnbloom, Lucas. Dragon & Captain. Allabach, P. R. 2015. (ENG.). 32p. (J). (gr. k-2). 17.95 (978-1-936261-33-8(2)) Flashlight Pr.
Turnbull, Brian. Death or Victory: Tales of the Clan Maclean. Maclean, Fiona. 2011. 128p. (YA). pap. (978-2-930583-06-8(1)) White & MacLean Publishing BEL. Dist: Gardners Bks. Ltd.
Turnbull, Jesse. Hello Hairy Dawg. Aryal, Aimee. 2004. (J). (gr. -1-3). 19.95 (978-1-932888-04-1(7)) Mascot Bks., Inc.
Turnbull, Susan. The Mystery of the Pheasants. Meierhenry, Mark & Volk, David. 2012. 44p. (J). 14.95 (978-0-9845041-9-0(2)) South Dakota State Historical Society Pr.
Turner, Adam. Mystery of the Ballerina Ghost. Diller, Janelle. 2013. 104p. (J). pap. 5.99 (978-1-936376-00-1(8)) WorldTrek Publishing.
Turner, Aubrey. Pity & the Princess. Crawford, Deborah Kay. 2013. 40p. pap. 24.95 (978-1-62709-695-9(7)) America Star Bks.
Turner, Cecilia. Davis & Pop Go Hiking. Wood, Cary D. 2014. (Morgan James Kids Ser.). (ENG.). (gr. -1-4). 30p. 34.95 (978-1-63047-217-7(4)); 32p. pap. 14.95 (978-1-63047-068-5(6)) Morgan James Publishing.
Turner, Cherie. Hope the Hip Hippo. Jay, Gina & Beattie, Julie. 2012. 48p. pap. (978-1-4602-0062-9(4)) FriesenPress.
Turner, Christina. Hello Santa! Turner, Christina. 2007. 16p. (J). (gr. -1). bds. 7.95 (978-0-9790347-0-1(1)) Mackenzie Smiles, LLC.
Turner-Deckert, Dianne. A Pillar of Pepper & Other Bible Rhymes. John Knapp, li. 2012. 130p. 29.99 (978-0-912290-34-8(X)) Ephemeron Pr.
Turner, Diane, jt. illus. see Tigue, Terry.
Turner, Dona. De Que Esta Hecho el Arco Iris? Schwartz, Betty Ann. 2005. (SPA & ENG.). 14p. (J). (gr. -1). 8.95 (978-1-58117-027-6(0), Intervisual/Piggy Toes) Bendon, Inc.
—What Makes a Rainbow? Schwartz, Betty Ann. 2006. (Magic Ribbon Books). (ENG.). 14p. (J). 4.95 (978-1-58117-220-1(6), Intervisual/Piggy Toes) Bendon, Inc.
—What Makes a Rainbow: (British Version) Schwartz, Betty Ann. 2004. 14p. (J). (978-1-58117-367-3(9), Intervisual/Piggy Toes) Bendon, Inc.
—What Makes Music? A Magic Ribbon Book. Schwartz, Betty Ann. 2005. (Stories to Share Ser.). 16p. (J). (gr. -1-3). act. bk. ed. 11.95 (978-1-58117-139-6(0), Intervisual/Piggy Toes) Bendon, Inc.
—You Are a Gift to the World. Duksta, Laura. 2011. (ENG.). 32p. (J). (gr. k-3). 16.99 (978-1-4022-1954-2(7), Sourcebooks Jabberwocky) Sourcebooks, Inc.
Turner, Dona. Ella Minnow Pea. Turner, Dona. 2008. (ENG.). 32p. (J). (978-1-59692-229-7(X)) MacAdam/Cage Publishing, Inc.
Turner, Dona & Brennan, Tim. Ella Minnow Pea. Turner, Dona & Dunn, Mark. gif. ed. 2009. (ENG.). 225p. (978-1-59692-299-0(0)) MacAdam/Cage Publishing, Inc.
Turner, Gil, jt. illus. see Bradbury, Jack.
Turner, Ginger. Abraham Lincoln: The Civil War President. Tiwari, Saral. 2004. 48p. (J). pap. 17.95 (978-0-9742502-1-2(X)) Gossamer Bks., LLC.
Turner, Helen. Amber's First Clue. Shields, Gillian. 2009. (Mermaid S. O. S. Ser.: No. 7). (ENG.). 96p. (J). (gr. 1-3). pap. 4.50 (978-1-59990-336-1(9), Bloomsbury USA Childrens) Bloomsbury USA.
—Holly Takes a Risk. Shields, Gillian. 2008. (Mermaid S. O. S. Ser.: 4). (ENG.). 96p. (J). (gr. 1-4). pap. 4.50 (978-1-59990-214-2(1), Bloomsbury USA Childrens) Bloomsbury USA.
—Joy's Close Call. Moss, Olivia. 2009. (Butterfly Meadow Ser.: 7). (ENG.). 80p. (J). (gr. 2-5). pap. 4.99 (978-0-545-10713-6(X), Scholastic Paperbacks) Scholastic, Inc.
Turner, Helen. Knock, Knock, It's Easter! 2014. (ENG.). 24p. (J). (gr. -1-k). 8.99 (978-1-74297-864-2(9)) Hardie Grant Egmont Pty, Ltd. AUS. Dist: Independent Pubs. Group.
Turner, Helen. Sophie Makes a Splash. Shields, Gillian. 2008. (Mermaid S. O. S. Ser.: 3). (ENG.). 96p. (J). (gr. 1-4). pap. 4.50 (978-1-59990-212-8(5), Bloomsbury USA Childrens) Bloomsbury USA.
Turner, Michael W. Dear Old Granny's Nursery Rymes for the 21st Century. Goodnight, Rosemary. 2009. 64p. (J). 14.99 (978-0-9816282-7-1(3)) Recipe Pubs.
Turner, Rich, photos by. Delta Skies Fine Art Folio, 2003. (978-0-9762410-4-1(8)) Turner, Rich Photographs.
Turner, Sandy. Tales from Gizzard's Grill. Steig, Jeanne. 2004. 80p. (J). 17.89 (978-0-06-000960-1(8), Cotler, Joanna Books) HarperCollins Pubs.
Turner, Suzette. Halloween Ooga-Ooga Ooum. Semple, Veronique & Semple, J. J. Semple, J. J., ed. 2011. (ENG.). 38p. (J). 9.95 (978-0-9795331-5-0(5), Zardoz Pr.) Life Force Bks.
Turnmyre, Dustin. Go, Bluey Go! McClean, Will. 2003. 32p. (J). 14.95 (978-1-57072-252-3(8)) Overmountain Pr.
Turrill, Tiffany. The Journey of the Marmabill. Errico, Daniel. 2013. (ENG.). 32p. (J). (gr. k-3). 16.95 (978-1-62087-736-4(8), 620736, Sky Pony Pr.) Skyhorse Publishing Co., Inc.
—The Journey of the Noble Gnarble. Errico, Daniel. 2013. (ENG.). 32p. (J). (gr. k-3). 16.95 (978-1-62087-732-6(5), 620732, Sky Pony Pr.) Skyhorse Publishing Co., Inc.
Turvey, Raymond. Space. Morris, Ting & Morris, Neil. 2006. (Sticky Fingers Ser.). 32p. (J). lib. bdg. 27.10 (978-1-59771-032-9(6)) Sea-To-Sea Pubns.
Tusa, Tricia. A Beginning, a Muddle, & an End: The Right Way to Write Writing. Avi. 2008. (ENG.). 176p. (J). (gr. 2-5). 14.95 (978-0-15-205555-4(X)) Houghton Mifflin Harcourt Publishing Co.
—The End of the Beginning: Being the Adventures of a Small Snail (and an Even Smaller Ant) Avi. 2008. (ENG.). 144p. (J). (gr. 2-5). pap. 6.95 (978-0-15-205532-5(0)) Houghton Mifflin Harcourt Publishing Co.
—Fred Stays with Me! Coffelt, Nancy. 2011. (ENG.). 32p. (J). (gr. -1-1). pap. 7.00 (978-0-316-07791-0(7)) Little, Brown Bks. for Young Readers.
—How to Make a Night. Ashman, Linda. Date not set. 32p. (J). (gr. -1-3). pap. 5.99 (978-0-06-443699-1(3)) HarperCollins Pubs.
—In a Blue Room. Averbeck, Jim. 2008. (ENG.). 32p. (J). (gr. -1-3). 16.00 (978-0-15-205992-7(X)) Houghton Mifflin Harcourt Publishing Co.
—It's Monday, Mrs. Jolly Bones! Hanson, Warren. 2013. (ENG.). 32p. (J). (gr. -1-1). 16.99 (978-1-4424-1229-3(1), Beach Lane Bks.) Beach Lane Bks.
—Jan Has a Doll. Earl, Janice. 2005. (Green Light Readers Level 1 Ser.). (ENG.). 24p. (J). (gr. -1-3). pap. 3.95 (978-0-15-205167-9(8)) Houghton Mifflin Harcourt Publishing Co.
—The Magic Hat. Fox, Mem. 2006. (ENG.). 32p. (J). (gr. -1-3). reprint ed. pap. 7.00 (978-0-15-205715-2(3)) Houghton Mifflin Harcourt Publishing Co.
—Marlene, Marlene, Queen of Mean. Lynch, Jane et al. 2014. (ENG.). 32p. (J). (gr. -1-2). lib. bdg. 19.99 (978-0-375-97329-1(X), Random Hse. Bks. for Young Readers) Random Hse. Children's Bks.
—Mrs. Spitzer's Garden. Pattou, Edith. gif. ed. 2007. (ENG.). 32p. (J). (gr. -1-3). 9.95 (978-0-15-205802-9(8)) Houghton Mifflin Harcourt Publishing Co.
—The Problem with the Puddles. Feiffer, Kate. (ENG.). (J). (gr. 3-7). 2011. 208p. pap. 6.99 (978-1-4424-2101-1(0)); 2009. 144p. 16.99 (978-1-4169-4961-9(5)) Simon & Schuster/Paula Wiseman Bks. (Simon & Schuster/Paula Wiseman Bks.).
—The Sandwich Swap. Queen Rania of Jordan Al Abdullah Staff et al. 2010. (ENG.). 32p. (J). (gr. -1-2). 16.99 (978-1-4231-2484-9(7)) Hyperion Pr.
—Starring Prima! The Mouse of the Ballet Jolie. Mitchard, Jacquelyn. 2004. 160p. (J). (gr. 3-18). (ENG.). 15.99 (978-0-06-057356-0(2)); 16.89 (978-0-06-057357-7(0)) HarperCollins Pubs.
—Treasure Map. Murphy, Stuart J. & Murphy. 2004. (MathStart 3 Ser.). (ENG.). 40p. (J). (gr. 2-18). pap. 5.99 (978-0-06-446738-4(4)) HarperCollins Pubs.
—A Violin for Elva. Ray, Mary Lyn. 2015. (ENG.). 32p. (J). (gr. -1-3). 16.99 (978-0-15-225483-4(8), HMH Books For Young Readers) Houghton Mifflin Harcourt Publishing Co.
Tusa, Tricia, jt. illus. see Sullivan, Sarah.
Tusan, Stan. African Giants. Prebeg, Rick, photos by. Knowlton, Laurie Lazzaro. 2005. (J). (978-1-933248-08-0(4)) World Quest Learning.
Tuschman, Richard. Painting the Rainbow. Gordon, Amy. 2014. (ENG.). 176p. (J). (gr. 3-7). 16.95 (978-0-8234-2525-9(8)) Holiday Hse., Inc.
Tuska, George, et al. Essential Iron Man - Volume 5. Friedrich, Mike et al. 2013. (ENG.). 520p. (J). (gr. 4-17). pap. 19.99 (978-0-7851-6733-4(1), Marvel Pr.) Disney Publishing Worldwide.
Tuska, George & Pollard, Keith. Avengers: The Coming of the Beast. 2011. (ENG.). 128p. (J). (gr. -1-17). 19.99 (978-0-7851-4468-7(4)) Marvel Worldwide, Inc.
Tust, Dorothea. Experimentos para Cada Dia del Otono. Van Saan, Anita. Bravo, J. A., tr. 2006. (SPA.). 89p. (J). pap. (978-84-9754-221-0(5)) Ediciones Oniro S.A.
Tuttle, Todd. Spot. Tuttle, Todd. 2007. 20p. (J). 19.95 (978-1-889829-16-6(1)) Window Bks.
Tuya, Jez. Tales of a Fifth-Grade Knight. Gibson, Douglas. 2015. (Middle-Grade Novels Ser.). (ENG.). 160p. (gr. 4-7). lib. bdg. 25.32 (978-1-4965-0488-3(7)) Stone Arch Bks.
Tweed, Sean, jt. illus. see Henkel, Vernon.
Tweed, Sean, jt. illus. see McInturff, Linda.
Twigg, Craig. A Special Bug Indeed, 1 vol. Rogers, Bryar Elizabeth. 2009. 41p. pap. 19.95 (978-1-60749-750-9(6)) PublishAmerica, Inc.
Twinem, Neecy. E Is for Enchantment: A New Mexico Alphabet. James, Helen Foster. 2004. (State Ser.). (ENG.). 40p. (J). 17.95 (978-1-58536-153-3(4), 1235984) Sleeping Bear Pr.
—I Love Mud! Williams, Rozanne Lanczak. 2005. (Reading for Fluency Ser.). 8p. (J). pap. 3.49 (978-1-59198-141-1(7), 4241) Creative Teaching Pr., Inc.
—Three Hungry Spiders & One Fat Fly! Bentley, Dawn. 2010. (Stretchies Book Ser.). 16p. (J). (gr. -1-k). 8.99 (978-0-8249-1460-8(0), Ideals Children's Bks.) Ideals Pubns.
Twinem, Neecy. Noisy Beasties. Twinem, Neecy. 2007. (Little Beasties Ser.). (ENG.). 12p. (J). (gr. -1 — 1). 6.95 (978-1-55971-959-9(1)) Cooper Square Publishing Llc.
Twinney, Dick. Brave Little Owl. Davies, Gill. 2006. (ENG.). 24p. (J). (978-1-55168-279-2(6)) Fenn, H. B. & Co., Ltd.
Twins, Pope. Poke-A-Dot!: Who's in the Ocean? (30 Poke-able Poppin' Dots) 2012. (ENG.). 1p. (J). (gr. -1-1). 14.99 (978-1-60169-270-2(6)) Innovative Kids.
Two Bulls, Marty Grant. The Mystery of the Maize. Meierhenry, Mark V. & Volk, David. 2010. (J). (978-0-9822749-1-0(2), South Dakota State Historical Society Pr.) South Dakota State Historical Society Pr.
Twohy, Mike. Outfoxed. Twohy, Mike. 2013. (ENG.). 40p. (J). (gr. -1-3). 16.99 (978-1-4424-7392-8(4), Simon & Schuster Bks. For Young Readers) Simon & Schuster Bks. For Young Readers.
—Poindexter Makes a Friend. Twohy, Mike. 2011. (ENG.). 32p. (J). (gr. -1-3). 15.99 (978-1-4424-0965-1(7), Simon & Schuster/Paula Wiseman Bks.) Simon & Schuster/Paula Wiseman Bks.
—Wake up, Rupert! Twohy, Mike. 2014. (ENG.). 32p. (J). (gr. -1-3). 16.99 (978-1-4424-5998-4(0), Simon & Schuster/Paula Wiseman Bks.) Simon & Schuster/Paula Wiseman Bks.
Twomey, Emily Golden. Buster's Brilliant Dot to Dot. Twomey, Emily Golden. 2014. (ENG.). 64p. (J). (gr. k-4). pap. 4.99 (978-1-78055-201-9(7)) O'Mara, Michael Bks., Ltd. GBR. Dist: Independent Pubs. Group.
—The Dot to Dot. Twomey, Emily Golden. 2014. (ENG.). 64p. (J). (gr. k-4). pap. 4.99 (978-1-78055-115-9(0)) O'Mara, Michael Bks., Ltd. GBR. Dist: Independent Pubs. Group.
Twomey-Lange, Marianna, photos by. The True Legend of White Crow: Adventures of the Fudge Sisters. Halstead, Jayce N. 2004. 80p. (J). per. 7.95 (978-0-9749046-3-4(5)) Aarow Pr.
Twork, Amanda J. O. & Twork, R. Cody, photos by. Rock! Answers to Questions of Faith. Twork, Carol Camp. 2004. 60p. (YA). 6.99 (978-0-9707979-3-3(1)) Contemplation Corner Pr.
Twork, R. Cody, jt. photos by see Twork, Amanda J. O.
Tyger, Rory. Good Night, Sleep Tight! Freedman, Claire. 2007. 32p. (J). (gr. -1-1). pap. 6.95 (978-1-58925-405-3(8)) Tiger Tales.
—Goodnight, Sleep Tight! Freedman, Claire. 2013. (ENG.). 24p. (gr. -1). pap. 3.99 (978-1-58925-440-4(6)) Tiger Tales.
—Maths Machine: A Fun New Way to Do Maths! Faulkner, Keith. 2004. (J). (978-0-439-72174-5(1)) Scholastic, Inc.
Tyger, Rory, et al. Me & My Mommy: By My Side, Little Panda/Just for You!/Big Bear, Little Bear/the Most Precious Thing/Little Bear's Special Wish/My Mommy & Me. Freedman, Claire et al. 2014. (ENG.). (J). (gr. -1). pap. 11.99 (978-1-58925-449-7(X)) Tiger Tales.
Tyler, Craig. A Fine Kettle of Fish. adapted ed. 2005. 42p. (J). lib. bdg. 16.95 (978-0-9761953-0-6(5)) Stairway Publishing.
Tyler, Gillian. The Bus Is for Us. Rosen, Michael. 2015. (ENG.). 32p. (J). (-k). 16.99 (978-0-7636-6983-6(0)) Candlewick Pr.
—Hurry down to Derry Fair. Chaconas, Dori. 2011. (ENG.). 36p. (J). (gr. -1-2). 16.99 (978-0-7636-3208-3(2)) Candlewick Pr.
Tyler, Tim. Pizza Heart. Mazur, Cathy May. 2007. 20p. per. 24.95 (978-1-4241-8747-8(8)) America Star Bks.
Tym, Kate. Princess Stories from Around the World. Williams, Sophy. 2004. 64p. (J). (978-1-84458-142-9(X), Pavilion Children's Books) Pavilion Bks.

Tyminski, Lori, et al. I Love You, My Bunnies. Driscoll, Laura & Disney Book Group Staff. 2008. (ENG.). 24p. (J). (gr. -1-k). pap. 3.99 *(978-1-4231-2095-7(7))* Disney Pr.
—Thumper Finds an Egg. Driscoll, Laura & Disney Book Group Staff. 2009. (ENG.). 24p. (J). (gr. -1-k). pap. 3.99 *(978-1-4231-1717-9(4))* Disney Pr.
Tyminski, Lori. Thumper Goes A-Thumpin' Driscoll, Laura. 2015. (ENG.). 12p. (J). (gr. -1 — 1). bds. 6.99 *(978-1-4847-0960-3(8))* Disney Pr.
Tyminski, Lori & Gordon, Dean. Goodnight, Thumper! Richards, Kitty & Disney Book Group Staff. 2007. (ENG.). 16p. (J). (gr. -1-k). bds. 5.99 *(978-1-4231-0077-5(8))* Disney Pr.
Tyminski, Lori & Vallorani, Giorgio. Thumper's Fluffy Tail. Driscoll, Laura & Disney Book Group Staff. rev. ed. 2008. (Touch-And-feel Book Ser.). (ENG.). 12p. (J). (gr. -1-k). bds. 6.99 *(978-1-4231-0443-8(9))* Disney Pr.
Tyminski, Lori & Ying, Victoria. Disney Princess Little Golden Book Favorites: Volume 3 (Disney Princess) Redbank, Tennant et al. 2014. (Little Golden Book Favorites Ser.). (ENG.). 80p. (J). (-k). 6.99 *(978-0-7364-3098-2(9))*, Golden/Disney) Random Hse. Children's Bks.
Tyminski, Lori, jt. illus. see RH Disney Staff.
Tyrol, Adelaide. A Child of God: Stories of Jesus & Stewardship Activities for Children. Caduto, Michael J. 2005. 48p. (J). 16.95 *(978-0-8091-6726-5(3)*, 6726-3) Paulist Pr.
Tyrrell, Frances. The Huron Carol. 2004. 32p. 16.00 *(978-0-8028-5263-2(7))* Eerdmans, William B. Publishing Co.
Tyrrell, Kayla. Froggy Kisses. Tyrrell, Kevin. 2008. 22p. pap. 24.95 *(978-1-60672-066-0(X))* America Star Bks.
Tyson, Liz. I Am a Monkey. Hevesi, Rachel. 2008. 44p. pap. *(978-1-906210-75-5(6))* Grosvenor Hse. Publishing Ltd.
Tzekov, Jack. Lily & Kayden's 1969 Woodstock Adventure. Soares, Valérie I. O. 2014. pap. *(978-1-927032-12-1(1))* Petra Bks.

U

U. S. National Geographic Society Staff. Bizarre Dinosaurs: Some Very Strange Creatures & Why We Think They Got That Way. U. S. National Geographic Society Staff. Smith, Josh & Sloan, Christopher. 2008. (ENG.). 32p. (J). (gr. 3-7). 16.95 *(978-1-4263-0330-2(0))*; (gr. 5). lib. bdg. 25.90 *(978-1-4263-0331-9(9))* National Geographic Society. (National Geographic Children's Bks.).
U. S. National Geographic Society Staff, photos by. Deadliest Animals. Stewart, Melissa. 2011. (Readers Ser.). (ENG., 48p. (J). (gr. 1-4). pap. 3.99 *(978-1-4263-0757-7(8)*, National Geographic Children's Bks.) National Geographic Society.
Uderzo, A. Asterix 600 Stickers. Goscinny, René & Livre, Hachette. 2012. (ENG.). 32p. (J). (gr. 4-7). 12.99 *(978-1-4440-0883-8(8)*, Orion) Orion Publishing Group, Ltd. GBR. Dist: Hachette Bk. Group.
—Asterix & the Roman Agent. Goscinny, R. 2004. (ENG.). 48p. 17.99 *(978-0-7528-6632-1(X)*, Orion) Orion Publishing Group, Ltd. GBR. Dist: Hachette Bk. Group.
—Asterix Omnibus Vol. 3: Asterix & the Big Fight - Asterix in Britain - Asterix & the Normans. Goscinny, R. 2012. (ENG.). 152p. (J). (gr. 4-7). pap. 22.99 *(978-1-4440-0475-5(1)*, Orion) Orion Publishing Group, Ltd. GBR. Dist: Hachette Bk. Group.
—Asterix Omnibus 7: Asterix & the Soothsayer - Asterix in Corsica - And Asterix & Caesar's Gift. Goscinny, R. 2013. (ENG.). 240p. (J). (gr. 4-7). 29.99 *(978-1-4440-0835-7(8)*, Orion) Orion Publishing Group, Ltd. GBR. Dist: Hachette Bk. Group.
—Asterix Omnibus 8: Includes Asterix & the Great Crossing #22, Obelix & Co. #23, & Asterix in Belgium #24. Goscinny, R. 2013. (ENG.). 152p. (J). (gr. 4-6). 29.99 *(978-1-4440-0837-1(4)*, Orion) Orion Publishing Group, Ltd. GBR. Dist: Hachette Bk. Group.
—Asterix Omnibus 9. Goscinny, R. 2014. (ENG.). 152p. (J). (gr. 4-6). 29.99 *(978-1-4440-0967-5(2)*, Orion) Orion Publishing Group, Ltd. GBR. Dist: Hachette Bk. Group.
—Where's Asterix? Goscinny, R. 2012. (ENG.). 32p. (J). (gr. 4-6). pap. 9.99 *(978-1-4440-0554-7(5)*, Orion) Orion Publishing Group, Ltd. GBR. Dist: Hachette Bk. Group.
—Where's Dogmatix? Goscinny, R. 2013. (ENG.). 32p. (J). (gr. 4-6). pap. 9.99 *(978-1-4440-0843-2(9)*, Orion) Orion Publishing Group, Ltd. GBR. Dist: Hachette Bk. Group.
Uderzo, A. Asterix & Cleopatra. Uderzo, A. Goscinny, R. 2004. (ENG.). 48p. pap. 12.99 *(978-0-7528-6607-9(9)*, Orion) Orion Publishing Group, Ltd. GBR. Dist: Hachette Bk. Group.
Uderzo, Albert. Asterix Omnibus 5: Asterix & the Cauldron - Asterix in Spain - Asterix & the Roman Agent. Goscinny, R. 2013. (ENG.). 240p. (J). (gr. 4-6). pap. 22.99 *(978-1-4440-0490-8(5)*, Orion) Orion Publishing Group, Ltd. GBR. Dist: Hachette Bk. Group.
Uderzo, Albert. El Adivino. Uderzo, Albert. Goscinny, René. 2009. (SPA.). 48p. 19.95 *(978-84-345-6737-5(7))* Grupo Anaya, S.A. ESP. Dist: Baker & Taylor Bks.
—Asterix & the Banquet. Uderzo, Albert. Goscinny, René. 2004. (ENG.). 48p. pap. 12.99 *(978-0-7528-6609-3(5)*, Orion) Orion Publishing Group, Ltd. GBR. Dist: Hachette Bk. Group.
—Asterix & the Big Fight. Uderzo, Albert. Goscinny, R. 2004. (ENG.). 48p. pap. 12.99 *(978-0-7528-6617-8(6)*, Orion) Orion Publishing Group, Ltd. GBR. Dist: Hachette Bk. Group.
—Asterix & the Cauldron. Uderzo, Albert. Goscinny, R. 2004. (ENG.). 48p. pap. 12.99 *(978-0-7528-6629-1(X)*, Orion) Orion Publishing Group, Ltd. GBR. Dist: Hachette Bk. Group.
—Asterix & the Chieftain's Shield. Uderzo, Albert. Goscinny, R. 2004. (ENG.). 48p. pap. 12.99 *(978-0-7528-6625-3(7)*, Orion) Orion Publishing Group, Ltd. GBR. Dist: Hachette Bk. Group.
—Asterix & the Class Act. Uderzo, Albert. Goscinny, René & Goscinny. Bell, Anthea & Hockridge, Derek, trs. from FRE. 2003. (ENG.). 56p. 17.99 *(978-0-7528-6068-8(2)*, Orion) Orion Publishing Group, Ltd. GBR. Dist: Hachette Bk. Group.
—Asterix & the Falling Sky. Uderzo, Albert. Goscinny, René. Bell, Anthea & Hockridge, Derek, trs. from FRE. 2006. (ENG.). 48p. pap. 12.99 *(978-0-7528-7548-4(5)*, Orion) Orion Publishing Group, Ltd. GBR. Dist: Hachette Bk. Group.
—Asterix & the Falling Sky. Uderzo, Albert. Goscinny, Uderzo & Goscinny, René. Bell, Anthea & Hockridge, Derek, trs. from FRE. 2005. (ENG.). 48p. 17.99 *(978-0-7528-7301-5(6)*, Orion) Orion Publishing Group, Ltd. GBR. Dist: Hachette Bk. Group.
—Asterix & the Goths. Uderzo, Albert. Goscinny, René. 2004. (ENG.). 48p. pap. 12.99 *(978-0-7528-6615-4(X)*, Orion) Orion Publishing Group, Ltd. GBR. Dist: Hachette Bk. Group.
—Asterix & the Laurel Wreath. Uderzo, Albert. Goscinny, René. 2004. (ENG.). 48p. 17.99 *(978-0-7528-6636-9(2)*, Orion) Orion Publishing Group, Ltd. GBR. Dist: Hachette Bk. Group.
—Asterix & the Laurel Wreath. Uderzo, Albert. Goscinny, R. 2004. (ENG.). 48p. pap. 12.99 *(978-0-7528-6637-6(0)*, Orion) Orion Publishing Group, Ltd. GBR. Dist: Hachette Bk. Group.
—Asterix & the Normans. Uderzo, Albert. Goscinny, René. 2004. (ENG.). 48p. 17.99 *(978-0-7528-6622-2(2)*, Orion) Orion Publishing Group, Ltd. GBR. Dist: Hachette Bk. Group.
—Asterix & the Normans. Uderzo, Albert. Goscinny, R. 2004. (ENG.). 48p. pap. 12.99 *(978-0-7528-6623-9(0)*, Orion) Orion Publishing Group, Ltd. GBR. Dist: Hachette Bk. Group.
—Asterix & the Roman Agent. Uderzo, Albert. Goscinny, R. 2004. (ENG.). 48p. pap. 12.99 *(978-0-7528-6633-8(8)*, Orion) Orion Publishing Group, Ltd. GBR. Dist: Hachette Bk. Group.
—Asterix & the Soothsayer. Uderzo, Albert. Goscinny, René. 2004. (ENG.). 48p. 17.99 *(978-0-7528-6641-3(9))*; pap. 12.99 *(978-0-7528-6642-0(7))* Orion Publishing Group, Ltd. GBR. (Orion). Dist: Hachette Bk. Group.
—Asterix at the Olympic Games. Uderzo, Albert. Goscinny, René. 2004. (ENG.). 48p. 17.99 *(978-0-7528-6626-0(5)*, Orion) Orion Publishing Group, Ltd. GBR. Dist: Hachette Bk. Group.
—Asterix at the Olympic Games. Uderzo, Albert. Goscinny, Rene. 2004. (ENG.). 48p. pap. 12.99 *(978-0-7528-6627-7(3)*, Orion) Orion Publishing Group, Ltd. GBR. Dist: Hachette Bk. Group.
—Asterix el Galo. Uderzo, Albert. Goscinny, René. 2009. (SPA.). 54p. 19.95 *(978-84-345-6719-1(9))* Grupo Anaya, S.A. ESP. Dist: Baker & Taylor Bks.
—Astérix en Bélgica. Uderzo, Albert. Goscinny, René. 2009. (SPA.). 48p. 19.95 *(978-84-345-6742-9(3))* Grupo Anaya, S.A. ESP. Dist: Baker & Taylor Bks.
—Astérix en Bretaña. Uderzo, Albert. Goscinny, René. 2009. (SPA.). 48p. 19.95 *(978-84-345-6726-9(1))* Grupo Anaya, S.A. ESP. Dist: Baker & Taylor Bks.
—Astérix en Helvecia. Uderzo, Albert. Goscinny, René. 2009. (SPA.). 48p. 19.95 *(978-84-345-6734-4(2))* Grupo Anaya, S.A. ESP. Dist: Baker & Taylor Bks.
—Asterix en Hispania. Uderzo, Albert. Goscinny, René. 2009. (SPA.). 48p. 19.95 *(978-84-345-6732-0(6))* Grupo Anaya, S.A. ESP. Dist: Baker & Taylor Bks.
—Astérix en la India. Uderzo, Albert. Goscinny, René. 2009. (SPA.). 48p. 19.95 *(978-84-345-6784-9(9))* Grupo Anaya, S.A. ESP. Dist: Baker & Taylor Bks.
—Astérix Gladiador. Uderzo, Albert. Goscinny, René. 2009. (SPA.). 48p. 19.95 *(978-84-345-6722-1(9))* Grupo Anaya, S.A. ESP. Dist: Baker & Taylor Bks.
—Asterix in Britain. Uderzo, Albert. Goscinny, René. 2004. (ENG.). 48p. pap. 12.99 *(978-0-7528-6619-2(2)*, Orion) Orion Publishing Group, Ltd. GBR. Dist: Hachette Bk. Group.
—Asterix in Corsica. Uderzo, Albert. Goscinny, René. 2004. (ENG.). 48p. 17.99 *(978-0-7528-6643-7(5)*, Orion) Orion Publishing Group, Ltd. GBR. Dist: Hachette Bk. Group.
—Asterix in Spain. Uderzo, Albert. Goscinny, René. 2004. (ENG.). 48p. pap. 12.99 *(978-0-7528-6631-4(1)*, Orion) Orion Publishing Group, Ltd. GBR. Dist: Hachette Bk. Group.
—Asterix in Switzerland. Uderzo, Albert. Goscinny, René. 2004. (ENG.). 48p. pap. 12.99 *(978-0-7528-6635-2(4)*, Orion) Orion Publishing Group, Ltd. GBR. Dist: Hachette Bk. Group.
—Astérix Legionario. Uderzo, Albert. Goscinny, René. 2009. (SPA.). 48p. 19.95 *(978-84-345-6728-3(8))* Grupo Anaya, S.A. ESP. Dist: Baker & Taylor Bks.
—Asterix the Gaul. Uderzo, Albert. Goscinny, René. 2004. (ENG.). 48p. pap. 12.99 *(978-0-7528-6605-5(2)*, Orion) Orion Publishing Group, Ltd. GBR. Dist: Hachette Bk. Group.
—Asterix the Gladiator. Uderzo, Albert. Goscinny, René. 2004. (ENG.). 48p. 17.99 *(978-0-7528-6610-9(9))*; pap. 12.99 *(978-0-7528-6611-6(7))* Orion Publishing Group, Ltd. GBR. (Orion). Dist: Hachette Bk. Group.
—Asterix the Legionary. Uderzo, Albert. Goscinny, René. 2004. (ENG.). 48p. pap. 12.99 *(978-0-7528-6621-5(4)*, Orion) Orion Publishing Group, Ltd. GBR. Dist: Hachette Bk. Group.
—Asterix y Cleopatra. Uderzo, Albert. Goscinny, René. 2009. (SPA.). 50p. 19.95 *(978-84-345-6724-5(5))* Grupo Anaya, S.A. ESP. Dist: Baker & Taylor Bks.
—Asterix y el Caldero. Uderzo, Albert. Goscinny, René. 2009. (SPA.). 48p. 19.95 *(978-84-345-6731-3(8))* Grupo Anaya, S.A. ESP. Dist: Baker & Taylor Bks.
—Asterix y los Godos. Uderzo, Albert. Goscinny, René. 2009. (SPA.). 52p. 19.95 *(978-84-345-6721-4(0))* Grupo Anaya, S.A. ESP. Dist: Baker & Taylor Bks.
—La Cizaña. Uderzo, Albert. Goscinny, René. 2009. (SPA.). 48p. 19.95 *(978-84-345-6733-7(4))* Grupo Anaya, S.A. ESP. Dist: Baker & Taylor Bks.
—El Combate de los Jefes. Uderzo, Albert. Goscinny, René. 2009. (SPA.). 48p. 19.95 *(978-84-345-6725-2(3))* Grupo Anaya, S.A. ESP. Dist: Baker & Taylor Bks.
—El Escudo Arverno. Uderzo, Albert. Goscinny, René. 2009. (SPA.). 52p. 19.95 *(978-84-345-6729-0(6))* Grupo Anaya, S.A. ESP. Dist: Baker & Taylor Bks.
—El Hijo de Astérix. Uderzo, Albert. Goscinny, René. 2009. (SPA.). 48p. 19.95 *(978-84-345-6783-2(0))* Grupo Anaya, S.A. ESP. Dist: Baker & Taylor Bks.
—La Hoz de Oro. Uderzo, Albert. Goscinny, René. 2009. (SPA.). 48p. 19.95 *(978-84-345-6720-7(2))* Grupo Anaya, S.A. ESP. Dist: Baker & Taylor Bks.
—Los Laureles Del Cesar. Uderzo, Albert. Goscinny, René. 2009. (SPA.). 50p. 19.95 *(978-84-345-6736-8(9))* Grupo Anaya, S.A. ESP. Dist: Baker & Taylor Bks.
—The Mansions of the Gods. Uderzo, Albert. Goscinny, René. 2004. (ENG.). 48p. 17.99 *(978-0-7528-6638-3(9)*, Orion) Orion Publishing Group, Ltd. GBR. Dist: Hachette Bk. Group.
—The Mansions of the Gods. Uderzo, Albert. Goscinny, R. 2004. (ENG.). 48p. pap. 12.99 *(978-0-7528-6639-0(7)*, Orion) Orion Publishing Group, Ltd. GBR. Dist: Hachette Bk. Group.
—Obélix y Compañía. Uderzo, Albert. Goscinny, René. 2009. (SPA.). 48p. 19.95 *(978-84-345-6741-2(5))* Grupo Anaya, S.A. ESP. Dist: Baker & Taylor Bks.
—El Regalo Del César. Uderzo, Albert. Goscinny, René. 2009. (SPA.). 50p. 19.95 *(978-84-345-6739-9(3))* Grupo Anaya, S.A. ESP. Dist: Baker & Taylor Bks.
—La Vuelta a la Galia. Uderzo, Albert. Goscinny, René. 2009. (SPA.). 48p. 19.95 *(978-84-345-6723-8(7))* Grupo Anaya, S.A. ESP. Dist: Baker & Taylor Bks.
Uderzo, M. The Wright Brothers, Vol. 3. Lefèvre-Garros, J. P. 2012. (ENG.). 48p. (YA). (gr. 6-17). pap. 11.95 *(978-1-84918-100-6(4))* CineBook GBR. Dist: National Bk. Network.
Uderzo, M., jt. illus. see Chauvin, D.
Uderzo, Marcel, jt. illus. see Chauvin, Daniel.
Udon, jt. illus. see Stevens, Chris.
Udon Entertainment Corp Staff. Marvel Heroes Super Origins. Reader's Digest Staff & Teitelbaum, Michael. 2009. (Magnetic Playset Ser.). (ENG.). 32p. (J). (gr. -1-2). bds. 15.99 *(978-0-7944-1939-4(9))* Reader's Digest Assn., Inc., The.
Udovic, David. A Child's Guide to Common Household Monsters. Thach, James Otis. 2007. (ENG.). 32p. (J). (gr. k-2). 16.95 *(978-1-932425-58-1(6)*, Front Street) Boyds Mills Pr.
—Eight Wild Nights: A Family Hanukkah Tale. Cleary, Brian P. 2006. (ENG.). 24p. (J). (gr. k-3). 8.95 *(978-1-58013-229-9(4)*, Kar-Ben Publishing) Lerner Publishing Group.
Ueda, Kumiko. The Magical Forest. Nelson, Brett Alan. 2003. 42p. (J). *(978-0-9655078-7-5(4))* Windsong Publishing Co.
Ueda, Miwa. Peach Girl Vol. 11: Change of Heart. Ueda, Miwa. 2004. (YA). pap. 9.99 *(978-1-59182-500-5(8))* TOKYOPOP, Inc.
Ueda, Rinko. Tail of the Moon, Vol. 4. Ueda, Rinko. 2007. (Tail of the Moon Ser.). (ENG.). 200p. (gr. 11). pap. 8.99 *(978-1-4215-0816-0(8))* Viz Media.
Ueyama, Michiro. Chaotic Century. Ueyama, Michiro. (Zoids Ser.). (ENG.). Vol. 11. 2004. 82p. pap. 5.95 *(978-1-56931-858-4(1))*; Vol. 12. 2003. 72p. pap. 5.95 *(978-1-56931-867-6(0))*; Vol. 13. 2003. 81p. pap. 5.95 *(978-1-56931-813-3(1))*; Vol. 14. 2003. 96p. pap. 5.95 *(978-1-56931-898-0(0))* Viz Media.
Uff, Caroline. Get Happy. Doyle, Malachy & Black, Jeremy. 2011. (ENG.). 32p. (J). (gr. -1-1). 15.99 *(978-0-8027-2271-3(7))* Walker & Co.
—Get Happy. Doyle, Malachy. 2013. (ENG.). 26p. (J). (gr. -1-1). bds. 7.99 *(978-0-8027-3478-5(2))* Walker & Co.
—Pig on a Swing. Nimmo, Jenny. 2003. (J). 16.99 *(978-0-340-85241-5(0))* Hodder & Stoughton GBR. Dist: Trafalgar Square Publishing.
Ugalde Alcantara, Felipe. Mother Fox & Mr. Coyote / Mamá Zorra y Don Coyote. Villaseñor, Victor. Turcios, Guadalupe Vanessa, tr. (ENG & SPA.). 32p. (gr. 2-4). 16.95 *(978-1-55885-428-4(2)*, Piñata Books) Arte Publico Pr.
Ugalde, Felipe. La Hormiga de Sayil. Suarez, Carlos Ruiz. rev. ed. 2005. (Castillo de la Lectura Blanca Ser.). (SPA & ENG.). 68p. (J). (gr. -1-7). pap. 6.95 *(978-970-20-0334-2(2))* Castillo, Ediciones, S. A. de C. V. MEX. Dist: Macmillan.
—Zurdo el Que lo Lea! Gazquez, Juan Pablo Hernandez et al. rev. ed. 2007. (Castillo de la Lectura Roja Ser.). (SPA & ENG.). 206p. (YA). (gr. 7). pap. 8.95 *(978-970-20-0181-2(1))* Castillo, Ediciones, S. A. de C. V. MEX. Dist: Macmillan.
Ugawa, Hiroki. Shrine of the Morning Mist, Vol. 1. Ugawa, Hiroki. 2006. Orig. Title: Asagiri No Miko. 200p. per. 14.99 *(978-1-59816-343-8(4)*, Tokyopop Kids) TOKYOPOP, Inc.
Ugliano, Natascia. Abraham's Search for God. Jules, Jacqueline & Hechtkopf, Jacqueline. 2007. (Bible Ser.). (ENG.). 32p. (J). (gr. k-3). lib. bdg. 17.95 *(978-1-58013-243-5(X)*, Kar-Ben Publishing) Lerner Publishing Group.
—Miriam in the Desert. Jules, Jacqueline & Hechtkopf, Jacqueline. 2010. (Bible Ser.). (ENG.). 32p. (J). (gr. k-3). 17.95 *(978-0-7613-4494-0(2))*; pap. 8.95 *(978-0-7613-4496-4(9))* Lerner Publishing Group. (Kar-Ben Publishing).
—Netta & Her Plant. Gellman, Ellie B. 2014. (Tu B'Shevat Ser.). (ENG.). 32p. (J). (gr. -1-2). 17.95 *(978-1-4677-0422-9(9)*, Kar-Ben Publishing) Lerner Publishing Group.
—Sarah Laughs. Jules, Jacqueline. 2008. (Bible Ser.). (ENG.). 32p. (J). (gr. k-3). per. 9.95 *(978-0-8225-9934-0(1)*, Kar-Ben Publishing) Lerner Publishing Group.
Uher, Brett. Dark Moon Diary, Vol. 1. 2007. (Dark Moon Diary Ser.). 192p. pap. 9.99 *(978-1-59532-844-1(0))* TOKYOPOP, Inc.
Uher, John, photos by. Kosher by Design Kids in the Kitchen. Fishbein, Susie. 2005. 192p. (J). (gr. 4-12). 22.99 *(978-1-57819-071-3(1))* Mesorah Pubns., Ltd.
Uhía, Manuel. Alas de Mosca Para Ángel. Uhía, Manuel, tr. Casalderrey, Fina & Casalderrey Fraga, Xosefa. Farias, Juan, tr. 2010. (SPA.). 144p. (J). pap. 10.99 *(978-84-207-8987-3(9))* Lectorum Pubns., Inc.
Uhles, Mary. Beyond the Grave: An Up2U Mystery Adventure. Enderle, Dotti. 2013. (Up2U Adventures Ser.). 80p. (J). (gr. 2-5). 27.07 *(978-1-61641-964-6(4)*, Calico Chapter Bks) Magic Wagon.
Uhles, Mary. The Little Kid's Table. Riehle, Mary Ann McCabe. 2015. (ENG.). 32p. (J). (gr. k-3). 16.99 ***(978-1-58536-913-3(6)***, 203952) Sleeping Bear Pr.
Uhlig, Elizabeth. Between the Shadows. Laub, Frima. 2007. (J). pap. 12.95 *(978-0-9786745-2-6(9))* Marble Hse. Editions.
—Clara Becomes a Citizen. Rothstein, Evelyn. 2009. (ENG.). (J). pap. 12.95 *(978-0-9786745-7-1(X))* Marble Hse. Editions.
—Clara's Great War. Rothstein, Evelyn. 2011. 88p. (J). pap. 12.95 *(978-0-9815345-9-6(7))* Marble Hse. Editions.
—Evelyn & the Two Evas. Rothstein, Evelyn. 2013. 63p. (YA). pap. 12.95 *(978-0-9834030-5-0(8))* Marble Hse. Editions.
—My Sandwich. Anderson, Lillian. 2012. 32p. (J). pap. 12.95 *(978-0-9834030-3-6(1))* Marble Hse. Editions.
Uhlig, Elizabeth. Children Just Like You. Uhlig, Elizabeth. 2007. (J). pap. 12.95 *(978-0-9786745-6-4(1))* Marble Hse. Editions.
—I See America! Uhlig, Elizabeth. 2009. (J). pap. 12.95 *(978-0-9815345-7-2(0))* Marble Hse. Editions.
—I Want to Be. Uhlig, Elizabeth. 2008. (ENG.). (J). pap. 12.95 *(978-0-9815345-1-0(1))* Marble Hse. Editions.
Uhlig, Elizabeth, jt. illus. see Laub, Frima.
Uhlman, Tom. Eruption! Volcanoes & the Science of Saving Lives. Rusch, Elizabeth. 2013. (Scientists in the Field Ser.). (ENG.). 80p. (J). (gr. 5-7). 18.99 *(978-0-547-50350-9(4))* Houghton Mifflin Harcourt Publishing Co.
Uhlman, Tom, photos by. The Bat Scientists. Carson, Mary Kay. (Scientists in the Field Ser.). (ENG., 80p. (J). (gr. 5-7). 2013. pap. 8.99 *(978-0-544-10493-8(5))*; 2010. 18.99 *(978-0-547-19956-6(2))* Houghton Mifflin Harcourt Publishing Co.
—The Bat Scientists. Carson, Mary Kay. ed. 2013. (Scientists in the Field (Houghton Mifflin Harcourt) Ser.). (ENG., 79p. lib. bdg. 19.65 *(978-0-606-33989-6(2)*, Turtleback) Turtleback Bks.
—Emi & the Rhino Scientist. Carson, Mary Kay. 2010. (Scientists in the Field Ser.). (ENG., 64p. (J). (gr. 5-7). pap. 9.99 *(978-0-547-40850-7(1))* Houghton Mifflin Harcourt Publishing Co.
Uhlman, Tom, photos by. Inside Biosphere 2: Earth Science under Glass. Carson, Mary Kay. 2015. (Scientists in the Field Ser.). (ENG., 80p. (J). (gr. 5-7). 18.99 ***(978-0-544-41664-2(3)***, HMH Books For Young Readers) Houghton Mifflin Harcourt Publishing Co.
Uhouse, Debra. The Gift Within. Moss, Lucille. Lt. ed. 2005. 19p. (J). 14.95 *(978-1-59879-063-4(3))* Lifevest Publishing, Inc.
Uihlein, Mary. Hello Little Owl. Uihlein, Mary. 2012. 24p. 22.95 *(978-1-61493-140-9(2))*; pap. 12.95 *(978-1-61493-139-3(9))* Peppertree Pr., The.
—Hello Little Owl, I Am Hermit Crab! Uihlein, Mary. 2013. 28p. 24.95 *(978-1-61493-159-1(3))*; pap. 12.95 *(978-1-61493-158-4(5))* Peppertree Pr., The.
Uitgeverij, Clavis. Encerrada: Anna's Tight Squeeze. De Smet, Marian & Meijer, Marja. Pacheco, Laura Emilia, tr. 2004. 28p. (J). 14.95 *(978-970-29-0665-0(2))* Santillana USA Publishing Co., Inc.
Ulasowski, Muza. Elle & Buddy. Rausin, K. D. 2015. (ENG.). 32p. (J). pap. 13.95 *(978-1-942155-00-3(X))* Randall, Peter E. Pub.
—Extreme Pets. Poulter, J. R. 2014. 72p. pap. 23.99 *(978-1-62563-914-1(7))* Tate Publishing & Enterprises, LLC.
—The Saga of Haggle Lee Ho. Poulter, J. R. 2014. 32p. pap. 19.99 *(978-1-62563-916-5(3))* Tate Publishing & Enterprises, LLC.
—The Sea Cat Dreams. Poulter, J. R. 2014. 34p. pap. 19.99 *(978-1-62563-912-7(0))* Tate Publishing & Enterprises, LLC.
—The Watchers. Poulter, J. R. 2014. 36p. pap. 19.99 *(978-1-62563-920-2(1))* Tate Publishing & Enterprises, LLC.
Ulene, Nancy, jt. illus. see Guler, Greg.
Ulkutay & Co Ltd. Hey, Diddle, Diddle & Other Best-loved Rhymes. Gerlings, Rebecca, ed. 2009. (Nursery Rhymes Ser.). 32p. (J). (gr. -1-2). pap. 10.55 *(978-1-60754-126-4(2))* Windmill Bks.
—Itsy Bitsy Spider & Other Best-loved Rhymes. Gerlings, Rebecca, ed. 2009. (Nursery Rhymes Ser.). 32p. (J). (gr. -1-2). pap. 10.55 *(978-1-60754-129-5(7))* Windmill Bks.
—Little Miss Muffet & Other Best-loved Rhymes. Gerlings, Rebecca, ed. 2009. (Nursery Rhymes Ser.). 32p. (J). (gr. -1-2). pap. 10.55 *(978-1-60754-132-5(7))* Windmill Bks.
—Mary Had a Little Lamb & Other Best-loved Rhymes. Gerlings, Rebecca, ed. 2009. (Nursery Rhymes Ser.). 32p. (J). (gr. -1-2). pap. 10.55 *(978-1-60754-135-6(1))* Windmill Bks.
—Yankee Doodle & Other Best-loved Rhymes. Gerlings, Rebecca, ed. 2009. (Nursery Rhymes Ser.). 32p. (J). (gr. -1-2). pap. 10.55 *(978-1-60754-123-3(8))* Windmill Bks.
Ulkutay & Co Ltd & Ulkutay & Co Ltd. Wee Willie Winkie & Other Best-loved Rhymes. Gerlings, Rebecca, ed. 2009. (Nursery Rhymes Ser.). 32p. (J). (gr. -1-2). pap. 10.55 *(978-1-60754-138-7(6))* Windmill Bks.
Ulkutay & Co Ltd, jt. illus. see Ulkutay & Co Ltd.
Ulkutay Design Group & Choi, Allan. Thumbelina. Landolf, Diane Wright. ed. 2009. (Barbie Step into Reading Ser.). 29p. lib. bdg. 13.55 *(978-1-4364-5096-6(9)*, Turtleback) Turtleback Bks.

U

Ulkutay Design Group, jt. illus. see Mattel Barbie Staff.

Ulkutay Design Group Staff. Barbie in a Mermaid Tale. Reader's Digest Staff. 2010. (Panorama Sticker Storybook Ser.). (ENG.). 16p. (J). (gr. -1-2). pap. 7.99 *(978-0-7944-1934-9(8))* Reader's Digest Assn., Inc., The.

—Barbie Princess Charm School. 2011. (Panorama Sticker Storybook Ser.). (ENG.). 16p. (J). (gr. -1-1). pap. 7.99 *(978-0-7944-2275-2(6))* Reader's Digest Assn., Inc., The.

—Hey, Diddle, Diddle & Other Best-Loved Rhymes. Gerlings, Rebecca, ed. 2009. (Nursery Rhymes Ser.). 32p. (J). (gr. -1-2). lib. bdg. 22.60 *(978-1-60754-125-7(4))* Windmill Bks.

—Itsy Bitsy Spider & Other Best-Loved Rhymes. Gerlings, Rebecca, ed. 2009. (Nursery Rhymes Ser.). 32p. (J). (gr. -1-2). lib. bdg. 22.60 *(978-1-60754-128-8(9))* Windmill Bks.

—Little Miss Muffet & Other Best-Loved Rhymes. Gerlings, Rebecca, ed. 2009. (Nursery Rhymes Ser.). 32p. (J). (gr. -1-2). lib. bdg. 22.60 *(978-1-60754-131-8(9))* Windmill Bks.

—Mary Had a Little Lamb & Other Best-Loved Rhymes. Gerlings, Rebecca, ed. 2009. (Nursery Rhymes Ser.). 32p. (J). (gr. -1-2). lib. bdg. 22.60 *(978-1-60754-134-9(3))* Windmill Bks.

—Wee Willie Winkie & Other Best-Loved Rhymes. Gerlings, Rebecca, ed. 2009. (Nursery Rhymes Ser.). 32p. (J). (gr. -1-2). lib. bdg. 22.60 *(978-1-60754-137-0(8))* Windmill Bks.

—Yankee Doodle & Other Best-Loved Rhymes. Gerlings, Rebecca, ed. 2009. (Nursery Rhymes Ser.). 32p. (J). (gr. -1-2). lib. bdg. 22.60 *(978-1-60754-122-6(X))* Windmill Bks.

Ulkutay Design Group Staff, jt. illus. see Mattel.

Ulmer, Louise. The Bible That Wouldn't Burn: William Tyndale's New Testament. Ulmer, Louise. 3rd ed. 2005. Orig. Title: The Bible That Wouldn't Burn: How the Tyndale English Version of the New Testament Came About. 34p. (YA). per., act. bk. ed. 8.95 *(978-0-941367-24-0(X))* Peach Blossom Pubns.

Ulrich, George. The Hit-Away Kid. Christopher, Matt. 2009. 64p. (J). lib. bdg. 22.60 *(978-1-59953-318-6(9))* Norwood Hse. Pr.

—Simon Says. Willson, Sarah. 2006. (Step-By-Step Readers Ser.). (J). pap. *(978-1-59939-057-4(4)*, Reader's Digest Young Families, Inc.) Studio Fun International.

—The Spy on Third Base. Christopher, Matt. 2009. 64p. (J). lib. bdg. 22.60 *(978-1-59953-321-6(9))* Norwood Hse. Pr.

—What Do You See? Gikow, Louise. 2005. (My First Reader Ser.). (ENG.). 32p. (J). (gr. k-1). 18.50 *(978-0-516-25177-6(5)*, Children's Pr.) Scholastic Library Publishing.

—Who Was Daniel Boone? Kramer, Sydelle. 2006. (Who Was... ? Ser.). (ENG.). 112p. (J). (gr. 3-7). pap. 5.99 *(978-0-448-43902-0(6)*, Grosset & Dunlap) Penguin Publishing Group.

—Who Was Daniel Boone? Kramer, Sydelle. 2006. (Who Was... ? Ser.). 108p. (gr. 2-6). 15.00 *(978-0-7569-6951-6(4))* Perfection Learning Corp.

Ulrich, George. Mrs. Picasso's Polliwog: A Mystery. Ulrich, George. 2003. 32p. pap. 7.95 *(978-1-891577-84-0(0))*; (J). (gr. -1-7). lib. bdg. 15.95 *(978-1-891577-83-3(2))* Images Pr.

Ulrich, Kelly. Carry Me to Kinshasa Our Adoption Journey. Yriana, Colleen. 2012. 24p. pap. *(978-1-77097-655-9(8))* FriesenPress.

—Rusty Finds a Home: A Christmas Miracle. Griffiths, Allen & Godinez, Mary. 2012. 32p. pap. *(978-1-4602-0937-0(0))* FriesenPress.

Uman, Jennifer, jt. illus. see Vidali, Valerio.

Umana, Maria Gomez. Collie Rescue. Archer, Colleen Rutherford. 2004. 112p. (J). pap. *(978-1-894131-67-4(3)*, Virago Press) Penumbra Pr.

Umansky, Kaye & Currey, Anna. Sophie & Abigail. 2004. (Sophie Rabbit Books). (ENG.). 30p. (J). pap. 3.95 *(978-1-56148-444-7(X)*, Good Bks.) Skyhorse Publishing Co., Inc.

Umezu, Kazuo. The Drifting Classroom. Umezu, Kazuo. Roman, Annette, ed. 2007. (Drifting Classroom Ser.: 9). (ENG.). 192p. pap. 9.99 *(978-1-4215-0961-7(X))*; pap. 9.99 *(978-1-4215-0960-0(1))* Viz Media.

—The Drifting Classroom, Vol. 1. Umezu, Kazuo. 2006. (Drifting Classroom Ser.). (ENG.). 208p. pap. 9.99 *(978-1-4215-0722-4(6))* Viz Media.

Umpierre, Migdalia. Sapo Sapito Sapote. Iturrondo, Angeles Molina. 2004. (Green Ser.). 24p. (J). *(978-1-57581-440-7(4))* Ediciones Santillana, Inc.

Umscheid, Kit. Pirate's Alphabet. Wigington, Patti. 2007. (ENG.). 32p. (J). (gr. -1-3). lib. bdg. 15.95 *(978-0-9766805-8-1(0))* Keene Publishing.

Unalp, Janet & Perry, Matt. Jacob's Promise: A Story about Faith. Banks, Celia. 2006. 32p. 14.99 *(978-0-9764460-6-4(5))* HonorNet.

Uncle Henry. Biode, Uncle Henry. 100th ed. 2004. 216p. pap. 7.99 *(978-1-932568-02-8(6)*, UHB003) Uncle Henry Bks.

—How the Tooth Fairy, of All People, Saved the Day, Uncle Henry. 100th ed. 2004. 64p. pap. 5.99 *(978-1-932568-00-4(X)*, UHB001) Uncle Henry Bks.

—The Vlieburgers: With Friends Like This Who Needs Halloween? Uncle Henry. 100th ed. 2004. 88p. pap. 6.99 *(978-1-932568-01-1(8)*, UHB002) Uncle Henry Bks.

Undercuffler, Gary. The Boy Who Cried Wolf: A Tale about Telling the Truth. 2006. (Famous Fables Ser.). (J). 6.99 *(978-1-59939-026-0(4))* Cornerstone Pr.

Undercuffler, Gary. Francisco's Kites. Klepeis, Alicia & Ventura, Gabriela Baeza. 2015. (SPA & ENG.). (J). 17.95 *(978-1-55885-804-6(0)*, Piñata Books) Arte Publico Pr.

Undercuffler, Gary. Happy Birthday: The Story of the World's Most Popular Song, 1 vol. Allen, Nancy Kelly. 2010. (ENG.). 32p. (J). (gr. k-3). 16.99 *(978-1-58980-675-7(1))* Pelican Publishing Co., Inc.

—On the Wings of the Swan. Gulla, Rosemarie. 2008. (Treasury of the Lost Scrolls Ser.). (ENG.). 32p. (J). (gr. 1-4). 17.99 *(978-0-9793000-0-4(2)*, Alazar Pr.) Royal Swan Enterprises, Inc.

Underhill, Alecia. For Horse-Crazy Girls Only: Everything You Want to Know about Horses. Wilsdon, Christina. 2010. (ENG.). 160p. (J). (gr. 3-6). 15.99 *(978-0-312-60323-6(1))* Feiwel & Friends.

Underwood, Kay Povelite. Ferocious Fangs. Fleming, Sally. 2004. (It's Nature! Ser.). 32p. (J). (gr. 3-6). pap. 7.95 *(978-1-55971-587-4(1)*, NorthWord Bks. for Young Readers) T&N Children's Publishing.

—Rapid Runners. Fleming, Sally. 2004. (It's Nature! Ser.). 32p. (J). (gr. 3-6). pap. 7.95 *(978-1-55971-789-2(0)*, NorthWord Bks. for Young Readers) T&N Children's Publishing.

—Sharp Shooters. Feeney, Kathy. 2004. (It's Nature! Ser.). 32p. (J). (gr. 3-6). pap. 7.95 *(978-1-55971-794-6(7)*, NorthWord Bks. for Young Readers) T&N Children's Publishing.

Unger, Erin. Memphis Learns the Hard Way. Gragg, Karla. 2013. 28p. pap. 6.95 *(978-0-9818396-7-7(3))* True Horizon Publishing.

Ungerer, Tomi. El Hombre de la Luna. Ungerer, Tomi. 2003. (Picture Books Collection). (SPA.). 40p. (J). (gr. k-3). pap. 10.95 *(978-968-19-0661-0(6))* Santillana USA Publishing Co., Inc.

—Rufus. Ungerer, Tomi. 2003. (SPA.). 36p. (J). (gr. k-3). pap. 7.95 *(978-968-19-0746-4(9))* Aguilar, Altea, Taurus, Alfaguara, S.A. de C.V MEX. Dist: Santillana USA Publishing Co., Inc.

Ungermann Marshall, Yana. Gilda Gets Wise. Ungermann Marshall, Yana. 2008. 34p. (J). pap. *(978-0-9670982-6-5(2))* Yana's Kitchen.

Ungureanu, Dan Paul. A Tall Southern Tale. DeLong, Lucianne. I.t. ed. 2013. (Possum Squat Ser.). (ENG.). 40p. (J). 15.95 *(978-0-9833237-1-6(2))* Krullstone Publishing, LLC.

—Whiskers Takes a Walk: A Possum Squat Tale. DeLong, Lucianne. 2013. (Possum Squat Ser.). (ENG.). 40p. (J). 15.95 *(978-0-9833237-3-0(9))* Krullstone Publishing, LLC.

Unten, Eren. Bubble Pirates! (Bubble Guppies) Golden Books. 2013. (Little Golden Book Ser.). (ENG.). 24p. (J). (-k). 3.99 *(978-0-449-81769-8(5)*, Golden Bks.) Random Hse. Children's Bks.

Unten, Eren. Chihuahua Power! (Julius Jr.) Posner-Sanchez, Andrea. 2015. (Little Golden Book Ser.). (ENG.). 24p. (J). (-k). 4.99 ***(978-0-553-52388-1(0)**, Golden Bks.)* Random Hse. Children's Bks.

Unten, Eren. The Doctor Is In! Golden Books. 2012. (Little Golden Book Ser.). (ENG.). 24p. (J). (gr. k-k). 3.99 *(978-0-307-97588-1(6)*, Golden Bks.) Random Hse. Children's Bks.

Unten, Eren. Meet Bubble Kitty! Man-Kong, Mary. 2015. (Big Golden Book Ser.). (ENG.). 48p. (J). (gr. -1-2). 9.99 ***(978-0-553-52114-6(4)**,* Golden Bks.) Random Hse. Children's Bks.

Unten, Eren. Triple-Track Train Race! (Bubble Guppies) Tillworth, Mary. 2015. (Little Golden Book Ser.). (ENG.). 24p. (J). (-k). 3.99 *(978-0-553-49769-4(3)*, Golden Bks.) Random Hse. Children's Bks.

Unten, Eren, jt. illus. see Golden Books Staff.

Unten, Eren Blanquet. It's Time for Bubble Puppy! Golden Books Staff. 2012. (Little Golden Book Ser.). (ENG.). 24p. (J). (gr. -1-2). 3.99 *(978-0-307-93028-6(9)*, Golden Bks.) Random Hse., Inc.

Unwin, Mike. World of Animals: Internet-Linked. Davidson, Susanna. 2009. (Nature Encyclopedias Ser.). 144p. (YA). (gr. 3-18). pap. 16.99 *(978-0-7945-2033-5(2)*, Usborne) EDC Publishing.

Unzner, Christa. Leonardo Da Vinci. Dickins, Rosie & Ball, Karen. 2007. (Famous Lives Gift Bks). 63p. (J). (gr. 4-7). 8.99 *(978-0-7945-1594-2(0)*, Usborne) EDC Publishing.

—Princess Me. Wilson, Karma. 2007. (ENG.). 32p. (J). (gr. -1-3). 16.99 *(978-1-4169-4098-2(7)*, McElderry, Margaret K. Bks.) McElderry, Margaret K. Bks.

—The Tiptoe Guide to Tracking Fairies. Paquette, Ammi-Joan. 2009. (ENG.). 32p. (J). (gr. -1-3). 15.95 *(978-1-933718-20-0(X))* Tanglewood Pr.

Uon, Taraku & Gohda, Hiroaki. Mizuho & Kei's Diary. Zappa, Go. Hosaka, Toshi, tr. from JPN. 2005. 245p. pap. 7.95 *(978-1-58899-297-0(7))* ComicsOne Corp./Dr. Masters.

Upadhye, Nitin, photos by. Going to School in India. Heydlauff, Lisa. 2005. (ENG.). 98p. (J). (gr. 4-7). 24.95 *(978-1-57091-666-3(7))* Charlesbridge Publishing, Inc.

Updike, John & Hyman, Trina Schart. A Child's Calendar. Updike, John. 2004. (J). (gr. k-4). 28.95 incl. audio compact disk *(978-1-59112-932-5(X))* Live Oak Media.

Upitis, Alvis, photos by. Amazing Grazing. Peterson, Cris. 2011. (ENG., 32p. (J). (gr. k-2). pap. 10.95 *(978-1-59078-868-4(0))* Boyds Mills Pr.

—Century Farm: One Hundred Years on a Family Farm. Peterson, Cris. 2009. (ENG., 32p. (J). (gr. 2-4). pap. 12.95 *(978-1-59078-773-1(0))* Boyds Mills Pr.

—Extra Cheese, Please! Mozzarella's Journey from Cow to Pizza. Peterson, Cris. 2003. (ENG., 32p. (J). (gr. -1-3). pap. 10.95 *(978-1-59078-246-0(1))* Boyds Mills Pr.

—Harvest Year. Peterson, Cris. 2009. (ENG., 32p. (J). pap. 10.95 *(978-1-59078-783-0(8))* Boyds Mills Pr.

—Wild Horses: Black Hills Sanctuary. Peterson, Cris. 2009. (ENG., 32p. (J). (gr. 4-6). pap. 11.95 *(978-1-59078-799-1(4))* Boyds Mills Pr.

Urasawa, Naoki. Herr Dr Tenma. Urasawa, Naoki. 2006. (Naoki Urasawa's Monster Ser.: Vol. 1). (ENG.). 224p. (gr. 11). pap. 9.99 *(978-1-59116-641-2(1))* Viz Media.

—Urasawa X Tezuka. Urasawa, Naoki. 2010. (Pluto Ser.: 8). (ENG.). 256p. pap. 12.99 *(978-1-4215-3343-8(X))* Viz Media.

—20th Century Boys. Urasawa, Naoki. 2010. (20th Century Boys Ser.: 12). (ENG.). 232p. pap. 12.99 *(978-1-4215-2365-1(5))*; pap. 12.99 *(978-1-4215-2346-0(9))* Viz Media.

Urbain, Christophe, photos by. Emma in Paris. 2013. (ENG., 56p. (J). (gr. k). 17.95 *(978-1-59270-139-1(6))* Enchanted Lion Bks., LLC.

Urban, Chieu Anh. Away We Go! A Shape & Seek Book. Urban, Chieu Anh. 2013. (ENG.). 20p. (J). (— 1). bds. 6.99 *(978-0-545-46179-5(0)*, Cartwheel Bks.) Scholastic, Inc.

Urban, Helle. Little California. James, Helen Foster & Wilbur, Helen L. 2011. (My Little State Ser.). (ENG.). 22p. (J). 9.95 *(978-1-58536-538-6(8))* Sleeping Bear Pr.

—Little Colorado. Brennan-Nelson, Denise. 2011. (My Little State Ser.). (ENG.). 22p. (J). 9.95 *(978-1-58536-530-2(0))* Sleeping Bear Pr.

—Little Halloween. Brennan-Nelson, Denise. 2013. (Little Ser.). (ENG.). 20p. (J). (gr. -1-k). 8.99 *(978-1-58536-885-3(7)*, 202891) Sleeping Bear Pr.

—Little Minnesota. Wargin, Kathy-jo. 2011. (My Little State Ser.). (ENG.). 22p. (J). 9.95 *(978-1-58536-174-8(7))* Sleeping Bear Pr.

—Little Missouri. Young, Judy & Wargin, Kathy-jo. 2012. (My Little State Ser.). (ENG.). 20p. (J). bds. 9.95 *(978-1-58536-206-6(9))* Sleeping Bear Pr.

—Little Wyoming. Gagliano, Eugene M. 2010. (My Little State Ser.). (ENG.). 22p. (J). 9.95 *(978-1-58536-544-9(0))* Sleeping Bear Pr.

—P Is for Pilgrim: A Thanksgiving Alphabet. Crane, Carol. rev. ed. 2007. (ENG.). 40p. (J). (gr. k-6). 7.95 *(978-1-58536-353-7(7))* Sleeping Bear Pr.

—Sonrieta. Brooks, Robert. 2008. 40p. (YA). 17.95 *(978-0-9792294-0-4(5))* Mystic Jaguar Publishing.

Urban, Keith. Teeny Tiny Tulula. Urban, Joyce. 2008. (ENG.). 38p. (J). pap. 9.95 *(978-0-9815370-0-9(6))* Urban, Keith Studios.

Urban, Suzanne. The Sounds of My Jewish Year. Gold-Vukson, Marji. 2003. (Very First Board Bks.). (ENG.). 12p. (J). (gr. -1 — 1). bds. 5.95 *(978-1-58013-047-9(X)*, Kar-Ben Publishing) Lerner Publishing Group.

Urbano, Emilio, et al. Disney Fairies Graphic Novel #4: Tinker Bell to the Rescue. Mulazzi, Paola et al. 2010. (Disney Fairies Ser.: 4). (ENG.). 80p. (J). (gr. 1-6). 12.99 *(978-1-59707-230-4(3))*; pap. 7.99 *(978-1-59707-200-7(1))* Papercutz.

—Disney Fairies Graphic Novel #6: A Present for Tinker Bell. Machetto, Augusto et al. 2011. (Disney Fairies Ser.: 6). (ENG.). 64p. (J). (gr. 1-6). pap. 7.99 *(978-1-59707-256-4(7))* Papercutz.

—Tinker Bell & the Pirate Adventure, No. 5. Mulazzi, Paola et al. 2011. (Disney Fairies Ser.: 5). (ENG.). 64p. (J). (gr. 1-6). 10.99 *(978-1-59707-241-0(9))*; pap. 7.99 *(978-1-59707-240-3(0))* Papercutz.

—Tinker Bell the Perfect Fairy. Mulazzi, Paola et al. 2012. (Disney Fairies Ser.: 7). (ENG.). 64p. (J). (gr. 1-6). 11.99 *(978-1-59707-282-3(6))*; pap. 7.99 *(978-1-59707-281-6(8))* Papercutz.

Urbano, Emilio, jt. illus. see Melaranci, Elisabetta.

Urbanovic, Jackie. The Bully Blockers Club. Bateman, Teresa. 2004. (ENG.). 32p. (J). (gr. 1-4). 6.99 *(978-0-8075-0919-7(1))* Whitman, Albert & Co.

—Don't Squeal Unless It's a Big Deal: A Tale of Tattletales. Ransom, Jeanie Franz. 2005. (J). 32p. 14.95 *(978-1-59147-239-1(3))*; 28p. (gr. -1-3). pap. 9.95 *(978-1-59147-240-7(7))* American Psychological Assn. (Magination Pr.).

—Grandma Lena's Big Ol' Turnip. Hester, Denia Lewis. 2005. (ENG.). 32p. (J). (gr. -1-3). 6.95 *(978-0-8075-3023-8(9))* Whitman, Albert & Co.

—Grandma Lena's Big Ol'turnip. Hester, Denia Lewis. 2014. (AV2 Fiction Readalong Ser.: Vol. 138). (ENG.). 32p. (J). (gr. -1-3). lib. bdg. 34.28 *(978-1-4896-2329-4(9)*, AV2 by Weigl) Weigl Pubs., Inc.

—Horace the Horrible: A Knight Meets His Match, 1 vol. Koller, Jackie French & Koller. 2003. (ENG.). 32p. (J). 16.95 *(978-0-7614-5150-1(1))* Marshall Cavendish Corp.

—If You're Hoppy. Sayre, April Pulley. 2011. (ENG.). 40p. (J). (gr. -1-k). 16.99 *(978-0-06-156634-9(9)*, Greenwillow Bks.) HarperCollins Pubs.

—I've Lost My Hippopotamus. Prelutsky, Jack. 2012. 144p. (J). (gr. k-5). (ENG.). 18.99 *(978-0-06-201457-3(9))*; lib. bdg. 19.89 *(978-0-06-201458-0(7))* HarperCollins Pubs. (Greenwillow Bks.).

—King of the Zoo. Perl, Erica S. 2013. (ENG.). 40p. (J). (gr. -1-k). 16.99 *(978-0-545-46182-5(0)*, Orchard Bks.) Scholastic, Inc.

—No Sleep for the Sheep! Beaumont, Karen. 2011. (ENG.). 32p. (J). (gr. -1-3). 16.99 *(978-0-15-204969-0(X))* Houghton Mifflin Harcourt Publishing Co.

Urbanovic, Jackie. Duck & Cover. Urbanovic, Jackie. 2009. (Max the Duck Ser.: 3). 32p. (J). (gr. -1-2). (ENG.). 17.99 *(978-0-06-121444-8(2))*; lib. bdg. 18.89 *(978-0-06-121445-5(0))* HarperCollins Pubs.

—Duck at the Door. Urbanovic, Jackie. (Max the Duck Ser.: 1). (ENG.). 32p. (J). (gr. -1-2). 2011. pap. 6.99 *(978-0-06-121440-0(X))*; 2007. 17.99 *(978-0-06-121438-7(8))* HarperCollins Pubs.

—Duck Soup. Urbanovic, Jackie. 2008. (Max the Duck Ser.: 2). 32p. (J). (gr. -1-2). (ENG.). 17.99 *(978-0-06-121441-7(8))*; lib. bdg. 18.89 *(978-0-06-121442-4(6))* HarperCollins Pubs.

—Sitting Duck. Urbanovic, Jackie. 2010. 40p. (J). (gr. -1-2). (ENG.). 17.99 *(978-0-06-176583-4(X))*; lib. bdg. 18.89 *(978-0-06-176584-1(8))* HarperCollins Pubs.

Urbanovic, Jackie & Mathieu, Joe. Ducks in a Row. Urbanovic, Jackie. 2011. (I Can Read Book 1 Ser.). (ENG.). 32p. (J). (gr. k-3). 16.99 *(978-0-06-186438-4(2))*; pap. 3.99 *(978-0-06-186437-7(4))* HarperCollins Pubs.

—Happy Go Ducky. Urbanovic, Jackie. 2012. (I Can Read Book 1 Ser.). (ENG.). 32p. (J). (gr. k-3). 16.99 *(978-0-06-186440-7(4))*; pap. 3.99 *(978-0-06-186439-1(0))* HarperCollins Pubs.

Urberuaga, Emilio. El Arbol de los Suenos. Alonso, Fernando. 2005. (Alfaguara Juvenil Ser.).Tr. of Dream Trees. (SPA.). 124p. (J). (gr. 5-8). pap. 10.95 *(978-968-19-0978-9(X))* Santillana USA Publishing Co., Inc.

—Cooper, Flying Dog. Ganges, Montse. 2009. (Cooper Ser.). 24p. (J). (gr. -1-3). 22.60 *(978-1-60754-239-1(0))*; pap. 8.15 *(978-1-60754-240-7(4))* Windmill Bks.

—Cooper, King of Cushion Island. Ganges, Montse. 2009. (Cooper Ser.). 24p. (J). (gr. -1-3). pap. 8.15 *(978-1-60754-243-8(9))* Windmill Bks.

—Fly Hunter. Ganges, Montse. 2009. (Cooper Ser.). 24p. (J). (gr. -1-3). pap. 8.15 *(978-1-60754-237-7(4))*; lib. bdg. 22.60 *(978-1-60754-236-0(6))* Windmill Bks.

—King of Cushion Island. Ganges, Montse. 2009. (Cooper Ser.). 24p. (J). (gr. -1-3). lib. bdg. 22.60 *(978-1-60754-242-1(0))* Windmill Bks.

—Manolito Four-Eyes: the 2nd Volume of the Great Encyclopedia of My Life: The 2nd Volume of the Great Encyclopedia of My Life, 0 vols. Lindo, Elvira. unabr. ed. 2013. (Manolito Four-Eyes Ser.: 2). (ENG.). 148p. (J). (gr. 3-7). pap. 9.99 *(978-1-4778-1700-1(X)*, 9781477817001, Amazon Children's Publishing) Amazon Publishing.

—Manolito Gafotas, 0 vols. Lindo, Elvira. 2010. (SPA & ENG.). 192p. (J). (gr. 3-7). pap. 9.99 *(978-0-7614-5730-5(5)*, 9780761457305, Amazon Children's Publishing) Amazon Publishing.

—Meet Cooper. Ganges, Montse. 2009. (Cooper Ser.). 24p. (J). (gr. -1-3). pap. 8.15 *(978-1-60754-234-6(X))* Windmill Bks.

—Mi Laberinto. Guerrero, Pablo. 2004.Tr. of My Labyrinth. (SPA.). (J). 21.99 *(978-84-88342-42-3(X))* S.A. Kokinos ESP. Dist: Lectorum Pubns., Inc.

—El Misterio Del Dragón de Ojos de Fuego. Liébana, Luisa Villar. 2010. (Librosaurio Ser.). (SPA.). 104p. (J). (gr. 4-7). 12.95 *(978-84-7942-392-6(7))* Heinemann Iberia, S.A. ESP. Dist: Independent Pubs. Group.

—El Niño Gol. Garcia Dominguez, Ramon. 2010. (SPA.). (J). (gr. 2-4). pap. *(978-84-263-7368-7(2))* Vives, Luis Editorial (Edelvives).

Urberuaga, Emilio, jt. illus. see Emilio, Urberuaga.

Urbigkit, Cat, photos by. The Guardian Team: On the Job with Rena & Roo. Urbigkit, Cat. 2011. (ENG., 32p. (J). (gr. 2-5). 16.95 *(978-1-59078-770-0(6))* Boyds Mills Pr.

—A Young Shepherd. Urbigkit, Cat. 2006. (ENG., 32p. (J). (gr. 1-7). 15.95 *(978-1-59078-364-1(6))* Boyds Mills Pr.

U'Ren, Andrea. The Bravest Woman in America. Moss, Marissa. 2011. (ENG.). 32p. (J). (gr. k-3). 16.99 *(978-1-58246-369-8(7)*, Tricycle Pr.) Ten Speed Pr.

—Feeding the Sheep. Schubert, Leda. 2010. (ENG.). 32p. (J). (gr. -1-1). 16.99 *(978-0-374-32296-0(1)*, Farrar, Straus & Giroux (BYR)) Farrar, Straus & Giroux.

—One Potato, Two Potato. DeFelice, Cynthia C. 2006. (ENG.). 32p. (J). (gr. -1-3). 17.99 *(978-0-374-35640-8(8)*, Farrar, Straus & Giroux (BYR)) Farrar, Straus & Giroux.

Urru, Franco. Raphael. Lynch, Brian. 2015. (J). ***(978-1-61479-341-0(7))*** Spotlight.

Ursell, Martin. Astonishing Art. Martineau, Susan. 2011. (Awesome Activities Ser.). (ENG.). 24p. (J). (gr. 3-6). pap. 10.60 *(978-1-61533-406-3(8))*; lib. bdg. 25.25 *(978-1-61533-369-1(X))* Windmill Bks.

—Chariot Race/La Carrera de Carrozas. Benton, Lynne. 2009. (Let's Read! Bks.). (FRE & ENG.). 32p. (J). (gr. 3-7). pap. 4.99 *(978-0-7641-4363-2(8))* Barron's Educational Series, Inc.

—Cool Circuits & Wicked Wires. Bushell, Nick & Martineau, Susan. 2005. (Gruesome Ser.). (ENG.). 24p. (J). (gr. 1-4). pap. 8.99 *(978-1-902915-33-3(X))* B Small Publishing GBR. Dist: Independent Pubs. Group.

—Crazy Contraptions. Martineau, Susan. 2011. (Awesome Activities Ser.). (ENG.). 24p. (J). (gr. 3-6). pap. 10.60 *(978-1-61533-405-6(X))*; lib. bdg. 25.25 *(978-1-61533-367-7(3))* Windmill Bks.

—Danny's Blog/Le Blog de Danny. Rabley, Stephen. Bougard, Marie-Therese, tr. 2008. (Let's Read! Bks.).Tr. of El Blog de Daniel. (ENG & FRE.). 32p. (J). (gr. 3-7). pap. 4.99 *(978-0-7641-4046-4(9))* Barron's Educational Series, Inc.

—Dinosaur Dishes & Fossil Food. Martineau, Susan. 2004. (Gruesome Ser.). (ENG.). 24p. (J). (gr. 1-4). pap. 8.99 *(978-1-902915-06-7(2))* B Small Publishing GBR. Dist: Independent Pubs. Group.

—Dragon Boy. Goodhart, Pippa. 2005. (Red Bananas Ser.). (ENG.). 48p. (J). lib. bdg. *(978-0-7787-1071-4(8))* Crabtree Publishing Co.

—Dragon Boy. Goodhart, Pippa. 2003. (Red Bananas Ser.). (ENG.). 48p. (J). (gr. k-2). pap. 5.99 *(978-1-4052-0593-1(8))* Egmont Bks., Ltd. GBR. Dist: Independent Pubs. Group.

—The Ice Age Tracker's Guide. Lister, Adrian. 2010. (ENG.). 32p. (J). (gr. 1-4). 17.95 *(978-1-84507-718-1(0)*, Frances Lincoln) Quarto Publishing Group UK GBR. Dist: Hachette Bk. Group.

—Marvelous Magic. Martineau, Susan. 2011. (Awesome Activities Ser.). (ENG.). 24p. (J). (gr. 3-6). pap. 10.60 *(978-1-61533-407-0(6))*; lib. bdg. 25.25 *(978-1-61533-368-4(1))* Windmill Bks.

—Where's Toto?/Ou est Toto? Vincent, Jenny & Laird, Elizabeth. Bougard, Marie-Terese, tr. 2009. (Let's Read! Bks.). (FRE.). 32p. (J). pap. 4.99 *(978-0-7641-4219-2(4))* Barron's Educational Series, Inc.

Ursell, Martin. Mad Machines & Dotty Devices. Ursell, Martin, tr. Martineau, Susan. 2003. (Gruesome Ser.). (ENG.). 24p. (J). (gr. 1-4). pap. 8.99 *(978-1-902915-91-3(7))* B Small Publishing GBR. Dist: Independent Pubs. Group.

Ursell, Martin & Pichon, Liz. Swallows & Spiders. Donaldson, Julia. 2013. (ENG.). 88p. (J). (gr. k-2). pap. 6.99 *(978-1-4052-6209-5(5))* Egmont Bks., Ltd. GBR. Dist: Independent Pubs. Group.

Ursell, Martin, jt. illus. see Price, David.

Ursell, Martin, jt. illus. see Rabley, Stephen.

Ury, Laura. Arty's Long Day. Redmond, Mark L. 2003. 102p. pap. *(978-0-87398-042-5(5))* Sword of the Lord Pubs.

Usher, Sam. A Dozen Cousins. Houran, Lori Haskins. 2015. (ENG.). 32p. (J). (gr. k-1). 14.95 *(978-1-4549-1062-6(3))* Sterling Publishing Co., Inc.

Ushler, John. Roy Rogers' Favorite Western Stories. Snow, Dorothea J. 2011. 250p. 46.95 *(978-1-258-04169-4(3))* Literary Licensing, LLC.

Usui, Kanako. My Friend, Fred. Cleary, Daniel. 2013. (ENG.). 40p. (J). (gr. 1-4). 11.99 *(978-1-60905-295-9(1))* Blue Apple Bks.

Usui, Kanako. Fantastic Mr Wani. Usui, Kanako. 2006. 32p. (J). 15.95 *(978-1-58925-054-3(0))* Tiger Tales.

Uting, Justin. Sea Creature Creations: A Hand Print Discovery Book. Kidpressionsl. 2008. 32p. pap. 24.95 *(978-1-60610-853-6(0))* America Star Bks.

Utley, David. Artic Skits. Ross, Kathryn & Pruitt, Kimberly. 2006. 88p. (J). per. 24.95 *(978-0-9725803-9-7(5))* Children's Publishing.

Utley, J. Stacy. What Mommy Does. Harvey Mph, Janera P. 2012. 24p. pap. 24.95 *(978-1-4560-4180-9(0))* America Star Bks.

Uto-Uko, Iniobong. ABC's of People in the Bible. Butler, Darnell. 2006. 56p. (J). (gr. -1-3). per. 28.95 *(978-1-59299-163-1(7))* Inkwater Pr.

Utomo, Gabhor. Blood Island. Windover, Liz. 2014. (ENG.). 144p. (J). mass mkt. 6.99 *(978-1-937133-46-7(X))* Chooseco LLC.

—Eighth Grade Witch. Simpson, C. E. & Smith, C. E. 2014. (ENG.). 144p. (J). mass mkt. 6.99 *(978-1-937133-45-0(1))* Chooseco LLC.

—I Wish I Were a Furry Ferret. Jordan, Christina. 2011. (I Wish I Were ... Ser.). (ENG.). 24p. (J). (gr. k-3). 28.50 *(978-1-61641-656-0(4))* Magic Wagon.

—I Wish I Were a Howler Monkey. Jordan, Christina. 2011. (I Wish I Were ... Ser.). (ENG.). 24p. (J). (gr. k-3). 28.50 *(978-1-61641-657-7(2))* Magic Wagon.

—I Wish I Were a Humpback Whale. Jordan, Christina. 2011. (I Wish I Were ... Ser.). (ENG.). 24p. (J). (gr. k-3). 28.50 *(978-1-61641-658-4(0))* Magic Wagon.

—I Wish I Were a Komodo Dragon. Jordan, Christina. 2011. (I Wish I Were ... Ser.). (ENG.). 24p. (J). (gr. k-3). 28.50 *(978-1-61641-659-1(9))* Magic Wagon.

—I Wish I Were a Speedy Cheetah. Jordan, Christina. 2011. (I Wish I Were ... Ser.). (ENG.). 24p. (J). (gr. k-3). 28.50 *(978-1-61641-660-7(2))* Magic Wagon.

—I Wish I Were an Enormous Elephant. Jordan, Christina. 2011. (I Wish I Were ... Ser.). (ENG.). 24p. (J). (gr. k-3). 28.50 *(978-1-61641-661-4(0))* Magic Wagon.

—Lupita's First Dance / el Primer Baile de Lupita. Ruiz-Flores, Lupe. Baeza Ventura, Gabriela, tr. 2013. (SPA.). 32p. (J). 17.95 *(978-1-55885-772-8(9),* Piñata Books) Arte Publico Pr.

—Sir Wrinkles. Kalomas, Alice & Kerr, Lenora. 2005. (J). 14.95 *(978-0-9766639-0-4(2))* Sir Wrinkles Pr.

—Sir Wrinkles Goes to School. Kalomas, Alice & Kerr, Lenora. 2005. (J). 16.95 *(978-0-9766639-1-1(0))* Sir Wrinkles Pr.

Utopia. My Little Pony. Shears, William. 2005. (Look & Find Ser.). 18p. (J). (gr. -1-3). pap. 24.98 *(978-1-4127-3316-8(2),* 7241700) Publications International, Ltd.

Utt, Mary Ann. The Easter Story. Pingry, Patricia A. (ENG.). (J). 2008. 26p. (gr. -1-3). bds. 12.99 *(978-0-8249-6731-4(3),* Candy Cane Pr.); 2006. 32p. (gr. -1-3). per. 3.95 *(978-0-8249-5531-1(5),* Ideals Children's Bks.); 2003. 26p. bds. 6.95 *(978-0-8249-4231-1(0))* Ideals Pubns.

Utt, Mary Ann, jt. illus. see Rader, Laura.

Utton, Peter. Let's Go on Safari!/Vamos de Safari! Anderson, Jill, ed. 2005. (Word Play/Juegos con Pala Ser.). (ENG & SPA.). 20p. (J). (gr. -1-17). 6.95 *(978-1-58728-522-6(3))* Cooper Square Publishing Llc.

—Shhh! Grindley, Sally. (ENG.). 32p. (J). pap. 13.95 *(978-0-340-74662-2(9))* Hodder & Stoughton GBR. Dist: Independent Pubs. Group.

V

Vaca, Sally. Pete's Angel. Darden, Hunter. 2008. 44p. pap. 12.00 *(978-1-60693-264-3(0),* Strategic Bk. Publishing) Strategic Book Publishing & Rights Agency (SBPRA).

Vachula, Monica. Noah Webster: Weaver of Words. Shea, Pegi Deitz. 2009. (ENG.). 40p. (J). (gr. 4-18). 18.95 *(978-1-59078-441-9(3),* Calkins Creek) Boyds Mills Pr.

—Paul Revere's Ride. Longfello, Henry Wadsworth. 2011. (ENG.). 32p. (J). (gr. 4-6). pap. 11.95 *(978-1-59078-869-1(9))* Boyds Mills Pr.

Vadalia, Hemali. Big Brother Little Brother. Graham, Rita Z. 2013. 42p. pap. 9.95 *(978-0-578-13165-8(X))* Graham, Rita.

Vaganos, Erin. Bonnwit Kabrit. Turnbull, Elizabeth. 2013. 36p. 17.95 *(978-1-61153-075-3(5))* Light Messages Publishing.

Vagharshyan, Lilit. You Are a Really Good Friend of Mine. Liliom, Laura. 2007. 32p. (J). (POL & ENG.). pap. 16.95 *(978-1-60195-107-6(8));* (ARA & ENG.). pap. 16.95 *(978-1-60195-310-0(0))* International Step by Step Assn.

Vagin, Vladimir. The Flying Witch. Yolen, Jane. 2003. 40p. (J). (gr. -1-1). 15.99 *(978-0-06-028536-4(2))* HarperCollins Pubs.

—Here Comes the Cat! Asch, Frank. 25th ed. 2011. (ENG & RUS.). 32p. (J). (gr. -1-3). 12.95 *(978-1-936365-41-8(3))* McSweeney's Publishing.

—Here Comes the Cat! Asch, Frank. 2004. (Bookshelf Ser.). (J). pap. 5.99 *(978-0-439-66942-9(1))* Scholastic, Inc.

—Igual Al Rey. Paterson, Katherine. (Buenas Noches Ser.).Tr. of King's Equal. (SPA.). (J). (gr. 3-5). pap. 7.16 *(978-958-04-4167-0(7))* Norma S.A. COL. Dist: Lectorum Pubns., Inc.

Vagnozzi, Barbara. Jack & the Beanstalk. (Classic Fairy Tales Ser.). (ENG.). 24p. (J). 2011. *(978-1-84643-437-2(8));* 2011. *(978-1-84643-456-3(4));* 2007. (gr. -1-2). *(978-1-84643-086-2(0))* Child's Play International Ltd.

—Jess & the Bean Root. Morgan, Ruth. 2005. (ENG.). 24p. (J). lib. bdg. 23.65 *(978-1-59646-732-3(0))* Dingles & Co.

—The Lion First Book of Nursery Stories. Rock, Lois. 2013. (ENG.). 96p. (J). (gr. -1-k). 16.99 *(978-0-7459-6341-9(2))* Lion Hudson PLC GBR. Dist: Independent Pubs. Group.

—The Lion First Book of Parables. Rock, Lois. 2014. (ENG.). 64p. (J). (gr. k-2). 14.99 *(978-0-7459-6409-6(5))* Lion Hudson PLC GBR. Dist: Independent Pubs. Group.

—Musicians of Bremen: Flip up Fairy Tales. 2008. (Flip-Up Fairy Tales Ser.). (ENG.). 24p. (J). *(978-1-84643-195-1(6))* Child's Play International Ltd.

—Santa's Midnight Sleighride. Pasquali, Elena. 2013. (Finger-Trail Animal Tales Ser.). (ENG.). 10p. (J). (gr. -1-k). bds. 9.99 *(978-0-7459-6242-9(4))* Lion Hudson PLC GBR. Dist: Independent Pubs. Group.

—Sleeping Beauty. 2007. (First Fairy Tales Ser.). 32p. (J). (gr. -1-3). lib. bdg. 28.50 *(978-1-59771-073-2(3))* Sea-To-Sea Pubns.

Vagnozzi, Barbara. Stormy Day & Snowy Day. Cunningham, Anna. 2012. (Talk a Story Ser.). (ENG.). 16p. (J). (-k). pap. 7.99 ***(978-1-4451-0665-6(5))*** Hodder & Stoughton GBR. Dist: Independent Pubs. Group.

—Where Are My Glasses? Adeney, Anne. 2008. (Reading Corner Ser.). (ENG.). 24p. (J). (gr. k-2). pap. 6.99 ***(978-0-7496-7694-0(9))*** Hodder & Stoughton GBR. Dist: Independent Pubs. Group.

Vagreti, Eva. I Can Show the Way: Monte's Rocket Launch. Holloway, Kari. 2013. (Illumination Leadership Series for Children Ser.). (ENG.). 24p. pap. 13.95 *(978-0-615-78492-2(5))* APT Publishing.

Vaing, Jocelang. Trip Through Cambodia. Diep, Bridgette. 32p. (J). (gr. -1-3). 14.95 *(978-0-87592-054-2(3))* Scroll Pr., Inc.

Vainio, Pirkko. Amy. Lukkarinen, Ritva. 2009. (ENG.). 30p. (J). (gr. -1-k). 16.95 *(978-1-60537-058-3(4))* Clavis Publishing.

Vainio, Pirkko. Little Bunny Finds Christmas. Vainio, Pirkko. 2008. (ENG.). 32p. (J). (gr. -1-3). 16.95 *(978-0-7358-2221-4(2))* North-South Bks., Inc.

Vair, Hayley. Flowers by Number. Shapiro, David R. 2013. (Little Naturalist Ser.). (ENG.). 32p. (J). 14.99 *(978-0-9844422-8-7(6))* Craigmore Creations.

Valat, Pierre-Marie. Halloween. Grant, Donald & Vallon, Jacqueline. 2012. (ENG.). 34p. (J). (gr. k-3). pap. 11.99 *(978-1-85103-314-0(9))* Moonlight Publishing, Ltd. GBR. Dist: Independent Pubs. Group.

Valat, Pierre-Marie. Inside the Body. Valat, Pierre-Marie. Houbre, Gilbert. 2012. (ENG.). 36p. (J). (gr. -1-k). 12.99 *(978-1-85103-412-3(9))* Moonlight Publishing, Ltd. GBR. Dist: Independent Pubs. Group.

—Let's Look at Building Sites by Night. Valat, Pierre-Marie. Delafosse, Claude. 2007. (ENG.). 38p. (J). (gr. k-3). pap. 11.99 *(978-1-85103-368-3(8))* Moonlight Publishing, Ltd. GBR. Dist: Independent Pubs. Group.

—Pirates. Valat, Pierre-Marie. 2012. (ENG.). 36p. (J). (gr. k-3). pap. 11.99 *(978-1-85103-343-0(2))* Moonlight Publishing, Ltd. GBR. Dist: Independent Pubs. Group.

—Water. Valat, Pierre-Marie. 2012. (ENG.). 36p. (J). (gr. -1-k). 12.99 *(978-1-85103-403-1(X))* Moonlight Publishing, Ltd. GBR. Dist: Independent Pubs. Group.

Valder, Justin. Henry the Honey Bee. Valder, Margret. 2010. 24p. pap. 11.50 *(978-1-60860-537-8(X),* Eloquent Bks.) Strategic Book Publishing & Rights Agency (SBPRA).

Valderrama, Rosario. Ontario, la Mariposa Viajera. Pettersson, Aline. 2003. (SPA.). 72p. (gr. 3-5). pap. 8.95 *(978-968-19-0276-6(9))* Santillana USA Publishing Co., Inc.

Valdez Y Alanis, Erik. Rumpelstiltskin: La Novela Grafica. Andersen, Hans Christian & Capstone Press Staff. 2010. (Graphic Spin en Español Ser.). (SPA.). 40p. (gr. 1-3). lib. bdg. 23.99 *(978-1-4342-1904-6(6),* Graphic Spin en Español) Stone Arch Bks.

—Rumpelstiltskin: The Graphic Novel. 2008. (Graphic Spin Ser.). (ENG.). 40p. (gr. 1-3). 23.99 *(978-1-4342-0768-5(4),* Graphic Revolve) Stone Arch Bks.

—Snow White. Capstone Press Staff. 2009. (Graphic Spin Ser.). (ENG.). 40p. (gr. 1-3). pap. 5.95 *(978-1-4342-1394-5(3));* lib. bdg. 23.99 *(978-1-4342-1192-7(4))* Stone Arch Bks. (Graphic Revolve).

Valencia, Esau Andrade. Un Tiempo Perfecto para Sonar. Sáenz, Benjamin Alire. 2008. (SPA & ENG.). 40p. (J). (gr. 1-4). 17.95 *(978-1-933693-01-9(0))* Cinco Puntos Pr.

Valente, Christa. A Giraffe fo a Pet, 1 vol. Gray, Elizabeth. 2010. 16p. 24.95 *(978-1-4489-6515-1(2))* PublishAmerica, Inc.

Valentin, Jeannette. The Frog That Went to the Moon. Guardado, Maria. 32p. (J). (gr. 3-18). 16.00 *(978-0-9710860-6-7(0))* Libros, Encouraging Cultural Literacy.

Valentina, Marina. Lost in the Roses. Valentina, Marina. 2007. 24p. (J). (gr. -1-1). 14.95 *(978-1-60108-014-1(X))* Red Cygnet Pr.

Valentine. Dina the Deaf Dinosaur. Addabbo, Carole. 2005. 32p. (J). pap. 19.95 *(978-1-889262-92-5(7))* Hannacroix Creek Bks., Inc.

Valentine, Allison. The Bubble Wrap Queen. Cook, Julia. 2008. (ENG.). 32p. (J). (gr. -1-3). pap. 9.95 *(978-1-931636-83-4(4))* National Ctr. For Youth Issues.

—Melvin the Magnificent Molar. Cook, Julia & Jana, Laura. 2010. (ENG.). 32p. (J). pap. 9.95 *(978-1-931636-74-2(5))* National Ctr. For Youth Issues.

Valentine, M. K. Save the Sleepless Slumbernots! Fantastik, B. 2013. 32p. *(978-1-4602-2777-0(8))* FriesenPress.

Valentine, Madeline. Ava & the Real Lucille, 1 vol. Best, Cari. 2012. (ENG.). 32p. (J). (gr. -1-3). 16.99 *(978-0-374-39903-0(4),* Farrar, Straus & Giroux (BYR)) Farrar, Straus & Giroux.

—Little Red Henry. Urban, Linda. 2015. (ENG.). 40p. (J). (gr. -1-3). 16.99 *(978-0-7636-6176-2(7))* Candlewick Pr.

Valenzuela, Roger. Paulie Pick Finds Studioland. Valenzuela, Roger. Valenzuela, Raquel, tr. from ENG. 2003.Tr. of Paulie Pick encuentra Estudiolandia. (SPA.). 32p. 20.00 *(978-0-944551-69-1(6))* Bk. Pubs. of El Paso.

Valer, Frantisek. The Buffalo & the Boat: Thathánka na Wáta. 2004. (DAK, ENG & SIO.). 18p. (J). 9.95 *(978-0-9761082-3-8(2))* Lakota Language Consortium, Inc.

—Pispiza WAN Wayawa Iyaye/Prairie Dog Goes to School. 2006. (DAK, ENG & SIO.). 24p. (J). (gr. -1-3). pap. 9.95 *(978-0-9761082-4-5(0))* Lakota Language Consortium, Inc.

Valeri, Jim. Eureka! Golden Books. 2014. (Color Plus Crayons & Sticker Ser.). (ENG.). 48p. (J). (gr. -1-2). pap. 4.99 *(978-0-553-49861-5(4),* Golden Bks.) Random Hse. Children's Bks.

Valeri, Jim, jt. illus. see Golden Books Staff.

Valerio, Geraldo. All Aboard for Dreamland! Harby, Melanie. 2012. (ENG.). 32p. (J). (gr. -1-k). 16.99 *(978-1-4424-3091-4(5),* Simon & Schuster Bks. For Young Readers) Simon & Schuster Bks. For Young Readers.

Valério, Geraldo. Do You Have a Cat? Spinelli, Eileen. 2010. 32p. (J). (gr. -1-3). 15.99 *(978-0-8028-5351-6(X),* Eerdmans Bks For Young Readers) Eerdmans, William B. Publishing Co.

—Do You Have a Dog? Spinelli, Eileen. 2011. 26p. (J). 16.00 *(978-0-8028-5387-5(0),* Eerdmans Bks For Young Readers) Eerdmans, William B. Publishing Co.

—Do You Have a Hat? Spinelli, Eileen. 2004. (ENG.). 40p. (J). (gr. -1-3). 17.99 *(978-0-689-86253-3(9),* Simon & Schuster Bks. For Young Readers) Simon & Schuster Bks. For Young Readers.

—Go to Sleep, Gecko! A Balinese Folktale. 2006. (ENG.). 32p. (J). (gr. -1-3). 16.95 *(978-0-87483-780-3(4))* August Hse. Pubs., Inc.

Valerio, Geraldo. Go to Sleep, Gecko! A Balinese Folktale. 2015. (ENG.). 32p. (J). (gr. -1-3). pap. 8.95 ***(978-1-939160-92-8(8))*** August Hse. Pubs., Inc.

Valerio, Geraldo. It's Moving Day! Hickman, Pamela. (ENG.). 32p. (J). 2012. pap. 8.95 *(978-1-55453-929-1(3));* 2008. (gr. -1-2). 17.95 *(978-1-55453-074-8(1))* Kids Can Pr., Ltd. CAN. Dist: Univ. of Toronto Pr.

Valério, Geraldo. Nannycatch Chronicles, 1 vol. Heneghan, James & McBay, Bruce. 2005. (ENG.). 88p. (J). (gr. 3-5). 16.95 *(978-1-896580-56-2(4))* Tradewind Bks. CAN. Dist: Orca Bk. Pubs. USA.

—Surf War! A Folktale from the Marshall Islands. MacDonald, Margaret Read. 2009. (ENG.). 32p. (J). (gr. -1-3). 16.95 *(978-0-87483-889-3(4))* August Hse. Pubs., Inc.

—When You Are Happy. Spinelli, Eileen. 2006. (ENG.). 40p. (J). (gr. -1-3). 18.99 *(978-0-689-86251-9(2),* Simon & Schuster Bks. For Young Readers) Simon & Schuster Bks. For Young Readers.

Vales, Chrissie. Sophie's Tales: Overcoming Obstacles. Paticoff, Melanie. 2012. 42p. 25.95 *(978-0-9851575-6-2(9))* Sophie's Tales, LLC.

Valiant, Kristi. Cora Cooks Pancit. Lazo Gilmore, Dorina K. 2014. (ENG.). 32p. (J). pap. 9.95 *(978-1-885008-48-0(1));* (gr. -1-3). 17.95 *(978-1-885008-35-0(X))* Lee & Low Bks., Inc. (Shen's Bks.).

—Dancing Dreams. Ohrt, Kate. 2014. (ENG.). 18p. (J). bds. 8.99 *(978-1-4494-3554-7(8))* Andrews McMeel Publishing.

—The Goodbye Cancer Garden, 1 vol. Matthies, Jana. 2011. (ENG.). 32p. (J). (gr. 1-5). 16.99 *(978-0-8075-2994-2(X))* Whitman, Albert & Co.

—Little Wings #2: Be Brave, Willa Bean! Galante, Cecilia. 2011. (Stepping Stone Book(TM) Ser.). (ENG.). 112p. (J). (gr. 1-4). 4.99 *(978-0-375-86948-8(4),* Random Hse. Bks. for Young Readers) Random Hse. Children's Bks.

—Little Wings #5: Willa Bean to the Rescue! Galante, Cecilia. 2013. (Stepping Stone Book(TM) Ser.). (ENG.). 112p. (J). (gr. 1-4). 4.99 *(978-0-449-81003-3(8),* Random Hse. Bks. for Young Readers) Random Hse. Children's Bks.

—Oliver's First Christmas. Accord Publishing Staff. 2012. (ENG.). 14p. (J). (-k). bds. 5.99 *(978-1-4494-2245-5(4))* Andrews McMeel Publishing.

—Oliver's First Christmas: A Mini AniMotion Book. Accord Publishing Staff & Hannigan, Paula. 2010. (ENG.). 12p. (J). (gr. -1). 9.99 *(978-0-7407-9798-9(0))* Andrews McMeel Publishing.

—The One & Only Willa Bean. Galante, Cecilia. 2012. (Stepping Stone Book Ser.). (ENG.). 112p. (J). (gr. 1-4). pap. 4.99 *(978-0-375-86950-1(6))* Random Hse., Inc.

—Pretty Minnie in Paris. Steel, Danielle. 2014. (ENG.). 32p. (J). (gr. -1-2). 17.99 *(978-0-385-37000-4(8));* lib. bdg. 20.99 *(978-0-375-97182-2(3))* Random Hse. Children's Bks. (Doubleday Bks. for Young Readers).

Valientes, Corazones. Tortillas & Lullabies. Reiser, Lynn. Hart, Rebecca, tr. 2008.Tr. of Tortillas y Cancioncitas. (SPA.). 48p. (J). (gr. -1-3). pap. 6.99 *(978-0-06-089185-5(8),* Greenwillow Bks.) HarperCollins Pubs.

Valko, Diane, et al. Biology: Overhead Transparencies - Student Reproducibles - Assessment Tools. Kupperstein, Joel. Hults, Alaska, ed. 2003. (Upper-Grade Science Transparency Ser.). 32p. (J). (gr. 5-8). pap. 9.99 *(978-1-57471-977-2(7),* 2799) Creative Teaching Pr., Inc.

Valko, Diane & Corbin, Hillam. Science Fair Projects & Activities: Creative Ideas Using Easy-to-Find Materials. McFarren, Kathleen & Graf, Mike. 2005. 144p. (J). pap. 18.99 *(978-0-88160-376-7(7),* LW407, Learning Works, The) Creative Teaching Pr., Inc.

Valko, Diane & Willardson, David. Leap into Literacy Winter. Geiser, Traci Ferguson & Boylan, Maureen McCourt. Cernek, Kim, ed. 2003. 160p. (J). (gr. k-2). pap. 17.99 *(978-1-57471-958-1(0),* 3374) Creative Teaching Pr., Inc.

Valkov, Julian. The Fork & the Spoon. Valkov, Julian. 2011. (ENG.). 26p. pap. 9.59 *(978-1-4610-1001-2(2))* CreateSpace Independent Publishing Platform.

Valle, Jo Anne, photos by. Sweet Dreams: El Yunque Dreams. Valle, Jo Anne. 2011. (ENG., 46p. pap. 10.95 *(978-1-4611-2852-6(8))* CreateSpace Independent Publishing Platform.

—Taina Wants to Salsa. Valle, Jo Anne. 2010. (ENG., 132p. pap. 9.95 *(978-1-4528-6911-7(1))* CreateSpace Independent Publishing Platform.

Valleau, Gailon. Batchawana Silly Stuff. Hearn, Emily. 2011. *(978-1-897475-70-6(5))* Hidden Brook Pr.

Vallecchi, Alessandro, et al, photos by. Maddy's Amazing African Birthday, 1 vol. Williams, Megan K. 2009. (ENG., 32p. (J). (gr. 1-4). 12.95 *(978-1-897187-47-0(5))* Second Story Pr. CAN. Dist: Orca Bk. Pubs. USA.

Vallejo, Esperanza. Cuentos de la Selva. Quiroga, Horacio. 2004.Tr. of Jungle Stories. (SPA.). 186p. (YA). (gr. -1-7). pap. *(978-958-30-0458-2(8))* Panamericana Editorial.

—Mambro Se Fue a la Guerra. Arciniegas, Triunfo. 2004. (Primer Acto: Teatro Infantil y Juvenil Ser.). (SPA.). 66p. (J). (gr. -1-7). pap. *(978-958-30-0434-6(0))* Panamericana Editorial.

—Memorias de Angola: Cuentos Africanos. Gomez, Luis Marcelino. 2004. (Letras Latinoamericanas Ser.). (SPA.). 131p. (YA). (gr. -1-7). per. *(978-958-30-1257-0(2))* Panamericana Editorial.

—La Ventana y la Bruja. Arciniega, Triunfo. 2003. (Primer Acto: Teatro Infantil y Juvenil Ser.). (SPA.). 61p. (J). (gr. -1-7). pap. *(978-958-30-0995-2(4))* Panamericana Editorial.

Valliant, Kristi. Ethan, a Soccer Player for Jesus. Cunningham, Elaine. 2010. 32p. (J). *(978-0-8341-2486-8(6))* Beacon Hill Pr. of Kansas City.

Valliant, Regina & Lunzer, Lee. Judy Garland Cut-Out Dolls. Valliant, Regina. 2007. (ENG.). 16p. pap. 12.00 *(978-0-9790668-9-4(1))* Paper Studio Pr.

Vallorani, Giorgio, jt. illus. see Tyminski, Lori.

Valverde, Mikel. The Adventures of Shola. Atxaga, Bernardo & Costa, Margaret Jull. 2014. (ENG.). 220p. (YA). (gr. 4-7). 20.00 *(978-1-78269-009-2(3),* Pushkin Children's Bks.) Pushkin Pr., Ltd. GBR. Dist: Random Hse., Inc.

—El Juego del Cambia-Cambia. MacHado, Ana Maria & Machado, Ana María. 2004.Tr. of Change-Change Game. (SPA.). (J). 6.50 *(978-84-348-8716-9(9))* SM Ediciones ESP. Dist: Lectorum Pubns., Inc.

—Mi Hermana Aixa. Torras, Meri. (SPA.). 120p. (J). (gr. 3-5). *(978-84-246-5915-8(5),* GL6491) La Galera, S.A. Editorial ESP. Dist: Lectorum Pubns., Inc.

Vamos, Lesley. My Dad Is a Superhero. Brown, Ruby. 2014. (J). ***(978-1-4351-5488-9(6))*** Barnes & Noble, Inc.

—My Mum Is a Superhero. Brown, Ruby. 2014. 24p. (J). 8.99 *(978-1-74297-784-3(7))* Hardie Grant Egmont Pty. Ltd. AUS. Dist: Independent Pubs. Group.

Van Allsburg, Chris. The Chronicles of Harris Burdick: Fourteen Amazing Authors Tell the Tales. Van Allsburg, Chris. 2011. (ENG.). 208p. (J). (gr. 5-7). 24.99 *(978-0-547-54810-4(9))* Houghton Mifflin Harcourt Publishing Co.

—Just a Dream. Van Allsburg, Chris. 2014. 48p. pap. 9.00 *(978-1-61003-182-0(2))* Center for the Collaborative Classroom.

—The Polar Express Movie Shadowbook: An Interactive Shadow-Casting Bedtime Story. Van Allsburg, Chris. Zemeckis, Robert & Broyles, William, Jr. 2006. 12p. (J). (gr. 4-18). reprint ed. 13.00 *(978-1-4223-5172-7(6))* DIANE Publishing Co.

Van Allsburg, Chris, jt. illus. see Baynes, Pauline.

van Amelsfort, Barbara. Yoga Exercises for Teens: Developing a Calmer Mind & a Stronger Body. Purperhart, Helen. Evans, Amina Marix, tr. from DUT. 2008. (SmartFun Activity Bks.). (ENG.). 160p. (gr. 4). spiral bd. 19.95 *(978-0-89793-504-3(7));* pap. 14.95 *(978-0-89793-503-6(9))* Turner Publishing Co. (Hunter Hse.).

—The Yoga Zoo Adventure: Animal Poses & Games for Little Kids. Purperhart, Helen. 2008. (SmartFun Activity Bks.). (ENG.). 160p. (gr. k-2). pap. 14.95 *(978-0-89793-505-0(5),* Hunter Hse.) Turner Publishing Co.

Van Biesen, Koen. Roger Is Reading a Book. Watkinson, Laura. 2015. 42p. (J). 16.00 *(978-0-8028-5442-1(7),* Eerdmans Bks For Young Readers) Eerdmans, William B. Publishing Co.

Van Buskirk, Steve. Dinosaurs. Van Buskirk, Steve. 2007. (Dinosaurs Pop-up Bks.). (J). (gr. -1-3). 4.99 *(978-1-59340-379-9(8))* Grandreams Bks., Inc.

Van Cleve, Barbara, photos by. Holding the Reins: A Ride Through Cowgirl Life. Talbert, Marc. 2003. 112p. (J). (gr. 3-7). 16.99 *(978-0-06-029255-3(5))* HarperCollins Pubs.

van Dam, M. Nicole. This Little Puppy. van Dam, M. Nicole. Topping, Jay. 2013. (ENG.). 24p. pap. 9.99 *(978-0-615-78978-1(1))* Once Upon a Time Creations.

van de Liejgraaf, Deborah. Anik & Yukon. Wehrmeijer, Annelien. 2015. (My Best Friend & Me Ser.). (ENG.). 10p. (J). (gr. -1-k). bds. 6.99 *(978-0-7641-6763-8(4))* Barron's Educational Series, Inc.

—Dan & Max. Wejrmeijer, Annelien. 2013. (My Best Friend & Me Ser.). (ENG.). 10p. (J). (gr. -1 — 1). bds. 6.99 *(978-0-7641-6634-1(4))* Barron's Educational Series, Inc.

—Emma & Bo. Wejrmeijer, Annelien. 2013. (My Best Friend & Me Ser.). (ENG.). 10p. (J). (gr. -1 — 1). bds. 6.99 *(978-0-7641-6635-8(2))* Barron's Educational Series, Inc.

—Jacob & Rex. Wehrmeijer, Annelien. 2014. (My Best Friend & Me Ser.). (ENG.). 10p. (J). (gr. -1 — 1). bds. 6.99 *(978-0-7641-6663-1(8))* Barron's Educational Series, Inc.

—Kato & Simba. Wehrmeijer, Annelien. 2015. (My Best Friend & Me Ser.). (ENG.). 10p. (J). (gr. -1-k). bds. 6.99 *(978-0-7641-6762-1(6))* Barron's Educational Series, Inc.

—Lily & Dolly. Wejrmeijer, Annelien. 2013. (My Best Friend & Me Ser.). (ENG.). 10p. (J). (gr. -1 — 1). bds. 6.99 *(978-0-7641-6636-5(0))* Barron's Educational Series, Inc.

—Mason & Buddy. Wejrmeijer, Annelien. 2013. (My Best Friend & Me Ser.). (ENG.). 10p. (J). (gr. -1 — 1). bds. 6.99 *(978-0-7641-6637-2(9))* Barron's Educational Series, Inc.

—Mimi & Ling. Wehrmeijer, Annelien. 2015. (My Best Friend & Me Ser.). (ENG.). 10p. (J). (gr. -1-k). bds. 6.99 *(978-0-7641-6765-2(0))* Barron's Educational Series, Inc.

—Noah & Dexter. Wehrmeijer, Annelien. 2014. (My Best Friend & Me Ser.). (ENG.). 10p. (J). (gr. -1 — 1). bds. 6.99 *(978-0-7641-6662-4(X))* Barron's Educational Series, Inc.

—Ruby & Molly. Wehrmeijer, Annelien. 2014. (My Best Friend & Me Ser.). (ENG.). 10p. (J). (gr. -1 — 1). bds. 6.99 *(978-0-7641-6661-7(1))* Barron's Educational Series, Inc.

—Sophie & Daisy. Wehrmeijer, Annelien. 2014. (My Best Friend & Me Ser.). (ENG.). 10p. (J). (gr. -1 — 1). bds. 6.99 *(978-0-7641-6664-8(6))* Barron's Educational Series, Inc.

—Tariq & Mika. Wehrmeijer, Annelien. 2015. (My Best Friend & Me Ser.). (ENG.). 10p. (J). (gr. -1-k). bds. 6.99 *(978-0-7641-6764-5(2))* Barron's Educational Series, Inc.

van Deelen, Fred. Fools' Gold. Gregory, Philippa. 2014. (Order of Darkness Ser.: 3). (ENG.). 384p. (YA). (gr. 9). pap. 9.99 *(978-1-4424-7691-2(5));* 19.99 *(978-1-4424-7690-5(7))* Simon Pulse. (Simon Pulse).

V

—Stormbringers. Gregory, Philippa. 2013. (Order of Darkness Ser.: 2). (ENG.). 336p. (YA). (gr. 9). pap. 9.99 *(978-1-4424-7688-2(5))*; 17.99 *(978-1-4424-7687-5(7))* Simon Pulse. (Simon Pulse).

van Deelen, Fred & Taylor, Sally. Changeling. Gregory, Philippa. 2013. (Order of Darkness Ser.: 1). (ENG.). 352p. (YA). (gr. 9). pap. 9.99 *(978-1-4424-5345-6(1)*, Simon Pulse) Simon Pulse.

van Deelen, Fred, jt. illus. see Taylor, Sally.

Van Den Berg, Helen. Quake! Six Point Five: The Cat Survived. Veldkamp, Debby. 2004. (J). lib. bdg. 16.95 *(978-1-930401-25-9(6))* Central Coast Pr.

Van Der Linden, Gerdien. Monstersong. Stein, Mathilde. 2007. (ENG.). 32p. (J). 15.95 *(978-1-932425-90-1(X)*, Lemniscaat) Boyds Mills Pr.

Van Der Linden, Martijn. Hush Little Turtle. Rinck, Maranke. 2011. (ENG.). 24p. (J). (gr. -1). bds. 8.95 *(978-1-935954-06-4(7)*, 9781935954064) Lemniscaat USA.

Van Der Merwe, Stefan. ABC of All the Questions We Never Dare to Ask. 2010. (ENG.). 144p. per. *(978-0-7957-0154-2(3))* NB Pubs. Ltd.

Van der Paardt, Melissa. Simon's New Bed. Jin, Chris & Trimmer, Christian. 2015. (ENG.). 32p. (J). (gr. -1-3). 17.99 *(978-1-4814-3019-7(X))* Simon & Schuster Children's Publishing.

van der Put, Klaartje. Little Bee. Chronicle Books Staff & ImageBooks Staff. 2006. (Little Finger Puppet Board Bks.: FING). (ENG.). 12p. (J). (gr. -1-7). 6.99 *(978-0-8118-5236-4(9))* Chronicle Bks. LLC.

—Little Bunny. Image Books Staff & Chronicle Books Staff. 2006. (Little Finger Puppet Board Bks.: FING). (ENG.). 12p. (J). (gr. -1 — 1). bds. 6.99 *(978-0-8118-5644-7(5))* Chronicle Bks. LLC.

—Little Butterfly. Image Books Staff & Chronicle Books Staff. 2006. (Little Finger Puppet Board Bks.: FING). (ENG.). 12p. (J). (gr. -1 — 1). 6.99 *(978-0-8118-5645-4(3))* Chronicle Bks. LLC.

—Little Kitten. ImageBooks Staff & Chronicle Books Staff. 2007. (Little Finger Puppet Board Bks.: FING). (ENG.). 12p. (J). (gr. -1 — 1). 6.99 *(978-0-8118-5770-3(0))* Chronicle Bks. LLC.

—Little Spider Finger Puppet Book. ImageBooks Staff & Chronicle Books Staff. 2007. (Little Finger Puppet Board Bks.: FING). (ENG.). 12p. (J). (gr. -1 — 1). bds. 6.95 *(978-0-8118-6104-5(X))* Chronicle Bks. LLC.

Van Der Put, Klaatje. Little Puppy. ImageBooks Staff & Chronicle Books Staff. 2007. (Little Finger Puppet Board Bks.: FING). (ENG.). 12p. (J). (gr. -1 — 1). 6.99 *(978-0-8118-5771-0(9))* Chronicle Bks. LLC.

van der Sterre, Johanna. Feivel's Flying Horses. Hyde, Heidi Smith. 2010. (ENG.). 32p. (J). (gr. k-3). pap. 7.95 *(978-0-7613-3959-5(0)*, Kar-Ben Publishing) Lerner Publishing Group.

—The First Christmas Present. Summerer, Marilyn. 2009. 32p. (J). (gr. -1). 14.99 *(978-0-7586-1663-0(5))* Concordia Publishing Hse.

—Furniture Refinishing in A Class by Yourself. Van Slyke, Marge. Lambert, Barbara, ed. 2004. 91p. per. 9.95 *(978-0-9755548-0-7(8))* Log Cabin Bks.

—Mendel's Accordion. Hyde, Heidi Smith. 2007. (ENG.). 32p. (J). (gr. k-4). pap. 9.95 *(978-1-58013-214-5(6)*, Kar-Ben Publishing) Lerner Publishing Group.

—The Parable of the Lost Sheep. Miller, Claire. 2008. (Arch Bks.). 16p. (J). (gr. k-4). pap. 1.99 *(978-0-7586-1455-1(1))* Concordia Publishing Hse.

—Star of Wonder. Hinkle, Cynthia. 2005. (Arch Bks.). (ENG.). 16p. (J). 1.99 *(978-0-7586-0724-9(5))* Concordia Publishing Hse.

van der Sterre, Johnanna. Why Do I Have to Make My Bed? Bradford, Wade. 2011. (ENG.). 32p. (J). (gr. -1-2). 16.99 *(978-1-58246-327-8(1)*, Tricycle Pr.) Ten Speed Pr.

Van Dijk, Jerianne. Emma Lea's First Tea Party. Donaldson, Babette. 2007. (ENG.). 32p. (J). 16.95 *(978-0-9792612-0-6(1))* Blue Gate Bks.

—Emma Lea's Magic Teapot. Donaldson, Babette. 2007. 32p. (J). lib. bdg. 16.95 *(978-0-9792612-1-3(X))* Blue Gate Bks.

—Jack - Family Ties. Danforth, Suzanne. l.t. ed. 2011. (ENG.). 28p. pap. 9.50 *(978-1-4664-0390-1(X))* CreateSpace Independent Publishing Platform.

—My Personal Story in ABCs. Alt, Susan. 2004. 32p. (J). pap. 15.95 *(978-1-891846-27-4(2)*, TBPERSONAL, Twins Bks.) Sterling Investments I, LLC DBA Twins Magazine.

Van Doninck, Sebastiaan. Foreman Farley Has a Backhoe. Goebel, Jenny. 2014. (Penguin Core Concepts Ser.). (ENG.). 32p. (J). (gr. -1-k). 3.99 *(978-0-448-46398-8(9)*, Grosset & Dunlap) Penguin Publishing Group.

Van Draanen, Wendelin. Sammy Keyes & the Art of Deception. Van Draanen, Wendelin. 2004. (Sammy Keyes Ser.: Bk. 8). pap. 36.95 incl. audio *(978-1-59519-001-7(5))*; pap. 54.95 incl. audio compact disk *(978-1-59519-003-1(1))* Live Oak Media.

—Sammy Keyes & the Search for Snake Eyes. Van Draanen, Wendelin. 2003. (Sammy Keyes Ser.: Bk. 7). pap. 36.95 incl. audio *(978-1-59112-273-9(2))*; pap. 54.95 incl. audio compact disk *(978-1-59112-281-4(3))* Live Oak Media.

Van Dusen, Chris. Francine Poulet Meets the Ghost Raccoon: Tales from Deckawoo Drive, Volume Two. DiCamillo, Kate. 2015. (ENG.). 112p. (J). (gr. 1-4). 12.99 ***(978-0-7636-6886-0(9))*** Candlewick Pr.

—Leroy Ninker Saddles Up. DiCamillo, Kate. (Tales from Deckawoo Drive Ser.: Vol. 1). (ENG.). 96p. (J). (gr. 1-4). 2015. pap. 5.99 ***(978-0-7636-8012-1(5))***; 2014. 12.99 *(978-0-7636-6339-1(5))* Candlewick Pr.

Van Dusen, Chris. Mercy Watson Fights Crime. DiCamillo, Kate. 2010. (Mercy Watson Ser.: 3). (ENG.). 80p. (J). (gr. 1-4). pap. 5.99 *(978-0-7636-4952-4(X))* Candlewick Pr.

—Mercy Watson Goes for a Ride. DiCamillo, Kate. 2006. (Mercy Watson Ser.: 2). (ENG.). 80p. (J). (gr. k-4). 12.99 *(978-0-7636-2332-6(6))* Candlewick Pr.

—Mercy Watson Goes for a Ride. DiCamillo, Kate. 2009. (Mercy Watson Ser.: 2). (ENG.). 80p. (J). (gr. 1-4). pap. 5.99 *(978-0-7636-4505-2(2))* Candlewick Pr.

—Mercy Watson Thinks Like a Pig. DiCamillo, Kate. (Mercy Watson Ser.: 5). (ENG.). 80p. (J). (gr. 1-4). 2011. pap. 5.99 *(978-0-7636-5231-9(8))*; 2008. 12.99 *(978-0-7636-3265-6(1))* Candlewick Pr.

—Mercy Watson to the Rescue. DiCamillo, Kate. 2005. (Mercy Watson Ser.: 1). (ENG.). 80p. (J). (gr. k-4). 12.99 *(978-0-7636-2270-1(2))* Candlewick Pr.

—Princess in Disguise. DiCamillo, Kate. 2010. (Mercy Watson Ser.: 4). (ENG.). 80p. (J). (gr. 1-4). pap. 5.99 *(978-0-7636-4951-7(1))* Candlewick Pr.

—Something Wonky This Way Comes. DiCamillo, Kate. (Mercy Watson Ser.: 6). (ENG.). 96p. (J). (gr. 1-4). 2011. pap. 5.99 *(978-0-7636-5232-6(6))*; 2009. 12.99 *(978-0-7636-3644-9(4))* Candlewick Pr.

Van Dusen, Chris. The Circus Ship. Van Dusen, Chris. (ENG.). 40p. (J). (gr. -1-3). 2015. 6.99 *(978-0-7636-5592-1(9))*; 2009. 16.99 *(978-0-7636-3090-4(X))* Candlewick Pr.

—If I Built a Car. Van Dusen, Chris. (ENG.). (J). 2007. 40p. (gr. k-k). pap. 6.99 *(978-0-14-240825-4(5)*, Puffin); 2005. 32p. (gr. -1-k). 16.99 *(978-0-525-47400-5(5)*, Dutton Juvenile) Penguin Publishing Group.

—If I Built a Car. Van Dusen, Chris. 2007. (gr. -1-3). lib. bdg. 17.00 *(978-0-7569-8149-5(2))* Perfection Learning Corp.

—Princess in Disguise. Van Dusen, Chris. DiCamillo, Kate. 2007. (Mercy Watson Ser.: 4). (ENG.). 80p. (J). (gr. 1-4). 12.99 *(978-0-7636-3014-0(4))* Candlewick Pr.

—Randy Riley's Really Big Hit. Van Dusen, Chris. 2012. (ENG.). 32p. (J). (gr. -1-3). 15.99 *(978-0-7636-4946-3(5))* Candlewick Pr.

Van Dusen, Chris, jt. illus. see DiCamillo, Kate.

Van Dusen, Ross. Crocka Dog in the Evil Forest. 2015. (J). ***(978-1-936744-54-1(6)***, Rio Grande Bks.) LPD Pr.

—How Crocka Dog Came to Be. 2015. (J). ***(978-1-936744-39-8(2))*** LPD Pr.

—What Makes a Rainbow? 2015. (J). ***(978-1-936744-32-9(5)***, Rio Grande Bks.) LPD Pr.

—What Makes a Snowflake? 2015. (J). ***(978-1-936744-48-0(1)***, Rio Grande Bks.) LPD Pr.

Van Fleet, Mara. Little Color Fairies. Van Fleet, Mara. 2012. (ENG.). 16p. (J). (gr. -1-1). 14.99 *(978-1-4424-3434-9(1)*, Simon & Schuster/Paula Wiseman Bks.) Simon & Schuster/Paula Wiseman Bks.

—Night-Night, Princess. Van Fleet, Mara. 2014. (ENG.). 16p. (J). (gr. -1-1). 14.99 *(978-1-4424-8646-1(5)*, Simon & Schuster/Paula Wiseman Bks.) Simon & Schuster/Paula Wiseman Bks.

—Three Little Mermaids. Van Fleet, Mara. 2011. (ENG.). 16p. (J). (gr. -1-k). 14.99 *(978-1-4424-1286-6(0)*, Simon & Schuster/Paula Wiseman Bks.) Simon & Schuster/Paula Wiseman Bks.

Van Fleet, Matthew. Alphabet. Van Fleet, Matthew. Skwarek, Skip, ed. 2008. (ENG.). 20p. (J). (gr. -1-1). 19.99 *(978-1-4169-5565-8(8)*, Simon & Schuster/Paula Wiseman Bks.) Simon & Schuster/Paula Wiseman Bks.

—Heads. Van Fleet, Matthew. 2010. (ENG.). 18p. (J). (gr. -1-1). 19.99 *(978-1-4424-0379-6(9)*, Simon & Schuster/Paula Wiseman Bks.) Simon & Schuster/Paula Wiseman Bks.

—Lick! Van Fleet, Matthew. 2013. (ENG.). 14p. (J). (gr. -1-1). 9.99 *(978-1-4424-6049-2(0)*, Simon & Schuster/Paula Wiseman Bks.) Simon & Schuster/Paula Wiseman Bks.

—Monday the Bullfrog. Van Fleet, Matthew. 2010. (ENG.). 20p. (J). (gr. -1). 24.99 *(978-1-4424-0958-3(4)*, Simon & Schuster/Paula Wiseman Bks.) Simon & Schuster/Paula Wiseman Bks.

—Munch! Van Fleet, Matthew. 2013. (ENG.). 14p. (J). (gr. -1-1). 9.99 *(978-1-4424-9425-1(5)*, Simon & Schuster/Paula Wiseman Bks.) Simon & Schuster/Paula Wiseman Bks.

—Sniff! Van Fleet, Matthew. 2012. (ENG.). 14p. (J). (gr. -1-1). 9.99 *(978-1-4424-6050-8(4)*, Simon & Schuster/Paula Wiseman Bks.) Simon & Schuster/Paula Wiseman Bks.

—Tails. Van Fleet, Matthew. 2003. (ENG.). 20p. (J). (gr. -1 — 1). 13.95 *(978-0-15-216773-8(0))* Houghton Mifflin Harcourt Publishing Co.

—Van Fleet Alphabet Heads: Alphabet; Heads. Van Fleet, Matthew. ed. 2013. (ENG.). 38p. (J). (gr. -1-2). 39.99 *(978-1-4424-8448-1(9)*, Simon & Schuster/Paula Wiseman Bks.) Simon & Schuster/Paula Wiseman Bks.

—Van Fleet Sniff! Lick! Munch! Van Fleet, Matthew. ed. 2013. (ENG.). 42p. (J). (gr. -1-1). 29.99 *(978-1-4424-9509-8(X)*, Simon & Schuster/Paula Wiseman Bks.) Simon & Schuster/Paula Wiseman Bks.

van Frankenhuyzen, Gijsbert. Bambi's First Day. Salten, Felix. 2008. (ENG.). 32p. (J). (gr. k-6). 15.95 *(978-1-58536-422-0(3))* Sleeping Bear Pr.

—The Edmund Fitzgerald: The Song of the Bell. Wargin, Kathy-jo. 2003. (ENG.). 48p. (J). (gr. k-6). 17.95 *(978-1-58536-126-7(7))* Sleeping Bear Pr.

—Friend on Freedom River. Whelan, Gloria. 2004. (Tales of Young Americans Ser.). (ENG.). 32p. (J). 16.95 *(978-1-58536-222-6(0))* Sleeping Bear Pr.

—Itsy Bitsy & Teeny Weeny. Van Frankenhuyzen, Robbyn Smith. 2009. (Hazel Ridge Farm Stories Ser.). (ENG.). 48p. (J). (gr. 1-4). 16.95 *(978-1-58536-417-6(7)*, 202152) Sleeping Bear Pr.

—Kelly of Hazel Ridge. Van Frankenhuyzen, Robbyn Smith. 3rd rev. ed. 2006. (Hazel Ridge Farm Stories Ser.). (ENG.). 32p. (J). (gr. k-5). 17.95 *(978-1-58536-268-4(9))* Sleeping Bear Pr.

—L Is for Lincoln: An Illinois Alphabet. Wargin, Kathy-jo. 2004. (Discover America State by State Ser.). (ENG.). 40p. (J). (gr. 1-3). pap. 7.95 *(978-1-58536-250-9(6)*, 202283) Sleeping Bear Pr.

—The Legend of Leelanau. Wargin, Kathy-jo. 2003. (Great Lakes Legend Ser.). (ENG.). 40p. (J). 17.95 *(978-1-58536-150-2(X))* Sleeping Bear Pr.

Van Frankenhuyzen, Gijsbert. The Legend of Michigan. Noble, Trinka Hakes. 2006. (Legend (Sleeping Bear) Ser.). (ENG.). 40p. (J). (gr. -1-3). 17.95 *(978-1-58536-278-3(6))* Sleeping Bear Pr.

van Frankenhuyzen, Gijsbert. The Legend of the Petoskey Stone. Wargin, Kathy-jo. 2004. (Great Lakes Legend Ser.). (ENG.). 40p. (J). 17.95 *(978-1-58536-217-2(4))* Sleeping Bear Pr.

—Mackinac Bridge: The Story of the Five-Mile Poem. Whelan, Gloria. 2006. (Tales of Young Americans Ser.). (ENG.). 32p. (J). 17.95 *(978-1-58536-283-7(2))* Sleeping Bear Pr.

—Saving Samantha: A True Story. Smith van Frankenhuyzen, Robbyn. 2004. (Hazel Ridge Farm Stories Ser.). (ENG.). 32p. (J). 17.95 *(978-1-58536-220-2(4))* Sleeping Bear Pr.

—T Is for Titanic: A Titanic Alphabet. Shoulders, Debbie & Shoulders, Michael. 2011. (ENG.). 32p. (gr. k-5). 17.95 *(978-1-58536-176-2(3))* Sleeping Bear Pr.

—W Is for Woof: A Dog Alphabet. Strother, Ruth. 2008. (ENG.). 40p. (J). (gr. k-6). 17.95 *(978-1-58536-343-8(X))* Sleeping Bear Pr.

Van Frankenhuyzen, Gijsbert, jt. illus. see Geister, David.

van Garderen, Ilse. A Beautiful Day. Pearce, Margaret. 2012. 24p. pap. 10.95 *(978-1-61633-251-8(4))* Guardian Angel Publishing, Inc.

van Genechten, Guido. Floppy's Friends. van Genechten, Guido. 2004. (ENG & POL.). 28p. (J). bds. *(978-1-84444-659-9(X))* Mantra Lingua.

—Guess Who? van Genechten, Guido. 2010. (ENG.). 28p. (J). (gr. k — 1). 8.95 *(978-1-60537-061-3(4))* Clavis Publishing.

—Kai-Mook. van Genechten, Guido. Frippiat, Stéphanie. 2011. (Kai-Mook Ser.). (ENG.). 32p. (J). (gr. -1-k). 16.95 *(978-1-60537-096-5(7))* Clavis Publishing.

—Knight Ricky. van Genechten, Guido. 2010. (Ricky Ser.). (ENG.). 30p. (J). (gr. -1-k). 16.95 *(978-1-60537-059-0(2))* Clavis Publishing.

—Ricky & Annie. van Genechten, Guido. 2010. (Ricky Ser.). (ENG.). 30p. (J). (gr. -1-k). 16.95 *(978-1-60537-062-0(2))* Clavis Publishing.

—Ricky & the Squirrel. van Genechten, Guido. 2010. (Ricky Ser.). (ENG.). 30p. (J). (gr. -1-k). 16.95 *(978-1-60537-078-1(9))* Clavis Publishing.

—Ricky Is Brave. van Genechten, Guido. 2011. (Ricky Ser.). (ENG.). 32p. (J). (gr. -1-k). 16.95 *(978-1-60537-097-2(5))* Clavis Publishing.

van Gurp, Peggy. Lucky's Little Feather. van Gurp, Peggy. 2011. (ENG.). 30p. (J). (gr. -1-k). 15.95 *(978-1-60537-086-6(X))* Clavis Publishing.

Van Haeringen, Annemarie. 1 2 3 Little Donkey. Kromhout, Rindert. Nagelkerke, Bill, tr. from DUT. 2013. 24p. (J). (gr. -1-1). 14.95 *(978-1-877579-34-9(3))* Gecko Pr. NZL. Dist: Lerner Publishing Group.

van Hamersveld, Madeleine. Good Luck, Tiny Chuck: A Book for Big Brothers & Sisters of Very Small Babies. van Hamersveld, Madeleine. 2011. (ENG.). 40p. pap. 12.99 *(978-1-4637-2644-1(1))* CreateSpace Independent Publishing Platform.

van Heerden, Marjorie. Little Library Literacy: Does your Father Snore? Afrikaans. Luckett, Kathy. 2007. pap. *(978-0-521-70298-0(4))* Cambridge Univ. Pr.

—Little Library Literacy: Does your Father Snore? Sesotho. Luckett, Kathy. 2007. pap. *(978-0-521-70296-6(8))* Cambridge Univ. Pr.

—Little Library Literacy: Does your Father Snore? Setswana. Luckett, Kathy. 2007. pap. *(978-0-521-70295-9(X))* Cambridge Univ. Pr.

—Little Library Literacy: Does your Father Snore? Siswati. Luckett, Kathy. 2007. pap. *(978-0-521-70294-2(1))* Cambridge Univ. Pr.

—Little Library Literacy: Does your Father Snore? Tsonga. Luckett, Kathy. 2007. pap. *(978-0-521-70292-8(5))* Cambridge Univ. Pr.

—Little Library Literacy: Does your Father Snore? Venda. Luckett, Kathy. 2007. pap. *(978-0-521-70293-5(3))* Cambridge Univ. Pr.

—Little Library Literacy: Does your Father Snore? Xhosa. Luckett, Kathy. 2007. pap. *(978-0-521-70289-8(5))* Cambridge Univ. Pr.

Van Hemeldonck, Tineke. Dragon Fire. De Kockere, Geert & Dom, An. 2015. (ENG.). 32p. (J). (gr. -1-k). 16.99 *(978-1-63220-599-5(8)*, Sky Pony Pr.) Skyhorse Publishing Co., Inc.

—Piglet Bo Can Do Anything! De Kockere, Geert. 2015. (ENG.). 32p. (J). (gr. -1-k). 16.99 *(978-1-63220-600-8(5)*, Sky Pony Pr.) Skyhorse Publishing Co., Inc.

Van Hertbruggen, Anton. The Dog That Nino Didn't Have. Van de Vendel, Edward. 2015. 34p. (J). ***(978-0-8028-5451-3(6)***, Eerdmans Bks For Young Readers) Eerdmans, William B. Publishing Co.

Van Hoorn, Aurea. An Open & Loving Heart: Gentle Words of Self-Endearment. Hirabayashi, Suzanne. 2003. 51p. 12.95 *(978-0-87516-701-5(2)*, Devorss Pubns.) DeVorss & Co.

Van Hout, Mies. Brave Ben. Stein, Mathilde. 2006. (ENG.). 32p. (J). (gr. 2-6). 15.95 *(978-1-932425-64-2(0)*, Lemniscaat) Boyds Mills Pr.

—The Child Cruncher. Stein, Mathilde. 2008. (ENG.). 32p. (J). (gr. -1-1). 16.95 *(978-1-59078-635-2(1)*, Lemniscaat) Boyds Mills Pr.

—Lovey & Dovey. Van Lieshout, Elle & Van Os, Erik. 2009. (ENG.). 32p. (J). (gr. k-2). 16.95 *(978-1-59078-660-4(2)*, Lemniscaat) Boyds Mills Pr.

—Mine! Stein, Mathilde. 2007. (ENG.). 26p. (J). (gr. -1-3). 16.95 *(978-1-59078-506-5(1))* Boyds Mills Pr.

Van Kampen, Megan. Dedicated Dads: Stepfathers of Famous People. Hancock, Rusty. 2004. 138p. *(978-0-934981-12-5(4))* Lawells Publishing.

—Warm & Wonderful Stepmothers of Famous People. Wells, Sherry A. 2004. 131p. 20.00 *(978-0-934981-10-1(8))* Lawells Publishing.

van Kampen, Vlasta. The Bears We Know. Silsbe, Brenda. 2009. (ENG.). 32p. (Orig.). (J). (gr. -1-2). 19.95 *(978-1-55451-167-9(4)*, 9781554511679) Annick Pr., Ltd. CAN. Dist: Firefly Bks., Ltd.

—Hoshmakaka. Thury, Fredrick H. 2003.Tr. of Last Straw. (SPA.). (J). (gr. 2-4). 13.56 *(978-84-8418-046-3(8))* Zendrera Zariquiey, Editorial ESP. Dist: Lectorum Pubns., Inc.

van Lieshout, Maria. Catching Kisses. Gibson, Amy. 2013. (ENG.). 32p. (J). (gr. -1-1). 16.99 *(978-0-312-37647-5(2))* Feiwel & Friends.

—Sleep, Baby, Sleep. Love, Maryann Cusimano. 2013. (ENG.). 30p. (J). (gr. -1-k). bds. 6.99 *(978-0-399-16144-5(9)*, Philomel) Penguin Publishing Group.

van Lieshout, Maria. Flight 1-2-3. van Lieshout, Maria. 2013. (ENG.). 40p. (J). (gr. -1 — 1). 14.99 *(978-1-4521-1662-4(8))* Chronicle Bks. LLC.

—Hopper & Wilson. van Lieshout, Maria. (ENG.). (J). (gr. -1-k). 2013. 32p. bds. 6.99 *(978-0-399-16331-9(X))*; 2011. 36p. 16.99 *(978-0-399-25184-9(7))* Penguin Publishing Group. (Philomel).

van Lindehuizen, Eline. Laurie. Nijssen, Elfi. 2010. (ENG & DUT.). 24p. (J). (gr. -1-k). 16.95 *(978-1-60537-072-9(X))* Clavis Publishing.

van Lindenhuizen, Eline. Good-Bye, Fish. Koppens, Judith. 2013. (Animal Square Ser.). (ENG.). 32p. (J). (gr. -1-k). 13.95 *(978-1-60537-153-5(X))* Clavis Publishing.

—The Seesaw. Koppens, Judith. 2013. (Animal Square Ser.). (ENG.). 32p. (J). (gr. -1-k). 13.95 *(978-1-60537-152-8(1))* Clavis Publishing.

Van Loon, Hendrik & Price, Christine. Here & Now Story Book. Mitchell, Lucy Sprague. 2015. (ENG.). 256p. (J). (gr. -1-5). pap. 7.99 ***(978-0-486-79196-8(3))*** Dover Pubns., Inc.

Van Norstrand, Kain. Dominic & the Secret Ingredient. Bonasia, Steve. 2012. (ENG.). 39p. (J). pap. 24.95 *(978-1-4327-9805-5(7))* Outskirts Pr., Inc.

Van Nutt, Robert. The Emperor & the Nightingale. Andersen, Hans Christian. 2007. (Rabbit Ears: A Classic Tale Ser.).Tr. of Nattergalen. 44p. (gr. -1-3). 25.65 *(978-1-59961-307-9(7))* Spotlight.

—The Emperor's New Clothes. Andersen, Hans Christian. 2005. (Rabbit Ears-A Classic Tale Set 2 Ser.). 28p. (gr. k-5). 25.65 *(978-1-59197-746-9(0))* Spotlight.

—The Firebird. Kessler, Brad. 2005. (Rabbit Ears Ser.). 36p. (gr. k-5). 25.65 *(978-1-59679-224-1(8))* Spotlight.

—The Legend of Sleepy Hollow. Irving, Washington. 2005. (Rabbit Ears Ser.). 36p. (J). (gr. k-5). 25.65 *(978-1-59679-225-8(6))* Spotlight.

—The Ugly Duckling. Andersen, Hans Christian. 2005. (Rabbit Ears: A Classic Tale Ser.). 42p. (gr. -1-3). 25.65 *(978-1-59679-348-4(1))* Spotlight.

Van Nutt, Robert & Bogdanovic, Toma. The Ugly Duckling. Van Nutt, Robert. 32p. (J). (gr. -1-3). 16.95 *(978-0-87592-055-9(1))* Scroll Pr., Inc.

Van Ommen, Sylvia. Sheep & Goat. Westera, Marleen. Forest-Flier, Nancy, tr. from DUT. 2006. (ENG.). 99p. (J). 16.95 *(978-1-932425-81-9(0)*, Lemniscaat) Boyds Mills Pr.

Van Order, Laura & VonSeggen, Jon. Living Like a King's Kid. Van Dyke, Jan. rev. ed. 2003. 77p. (J). spiral bd. 30.00 *(978-1-58302-249-8(X))* One Way St., Inc.

Van Patten, Bruce. Tales of Persia: Missionary Stories from Islamic Iran. Miller, William. 2005. 163p. per. 9.99 *(978-0-87552-615-7(2))* P & R Publishing.

Van Patter, Bruce. Grandpa's Box: Retelling the Biblical Story of Redemption. Meade, Starr. 2005. 286p. (J). (gr. 3-7). per. 13.99 *(978-0-87552-866-3(X))* P & R Publishing.

—Heidi. Spyri, Johanna. Hunsicker, Ranelda Mack, ed. 2006. (Classics for Young Readers Ser.). 287p. (J). (gr. 4-7). per. 11.99 *(978-0-87552-739-0(6))* P & R Publishing.

van Rheenen, Barbara. Dinosaurs. Douglas, Jozua. 2012. (Want to Know Ser.). (ENG.). 30p. (J). (gr. -1-2). 16.95 *(978-1-60537-136-8(X))* Clavis Publishing.

Van Severen, Joe. The Fall into Sin: Genesis 2-3 for Children. Sanders, Nancy I. 2004. (Arch Bks.). (ENG.). 16p. (J). 1.99 *(978-0-7586-0618-1(4))* Concordia Publishing Hse.

Van Slyke, Rebecca, jt. illus. see Davis, Katheryn.

Van Stockum, Hilda. A Day on Skates: The Story of a Dutch Picnic. Van Stockum, Hilda. 2007. 40p. (J). (gr. 1). 19.95 *(978-1-932350-18-0(7))* Bethlehem Bks.

Van Stralen, Dirk. Ben's Big Dig, 1 vol. Wakeman, Daniel. 2005. (ENG.). 32p. (J). (gr. -1-3). 17.95 *(978-1-55143-384-4(2))* Orca Bk. Pubs. USA.

—Ben's Bunny Trouble, 1 vol. Wakeman, Daniel. 2007. (ENG.). 32p. (J). (gr. -1-3). 18.95 *(978-1-55143-611-1(6))* Orca Bk. Pubs. USA.

Van Tine, Laura. Captain Tristan Am I. Sharp, Michael. 2009. 20p. (J). pap. *(978-1-897455-10-4(0))* Avatar Pubns., Inc.

—Vayda Jane Bean - Chocolate. Sharp, Michael. 2007. 20p. pap. *(978-1-897455-70-8(4))* Avatar Pubns., Inc.

—Vayda Jayne Bean - Vanilla. Sharp, Michael. 2007. 20p. (J). (gr. -1-3). pap. *(978-0-9780969-5-3(9))* Avatar Pubns., Inc.

Van Veldhoven, Marijke. Jack & the Hungry Bear, 1 vol. Blackford, Andy. 2013. (Start Reading Ser.). (ENG.). 24p. (gr. k-1). pap. 6.99 *(978-1-4765-4107-5(8))* Capstone Pr., Inc.

Van Vynckt, Virginia & Giblin, Sheri, photos by. Wok Every Day: From Fish & Chips to Chocolate Cake, Recipes & Techniques for Steaming, Poaching, Grilling, Deep Frying, Smoking, Braising, & Stir-frying in the World's Most Versatile Pan. Grunes, Barbara. 2003. (ENG., 224p. (gr. 8-17). pap. 24.95 *(978-0-8118-3195-6(7))* Chronicle Bks. LLC.

Van Wagoner, Traci. Candy Canes in Bethlehem. Van Scott, Miriam. 2012. (J). 7.95 *(978-0-8198-1606-1(X))* Pauline Bks. & Media.

Van Wright, Cornelius. The Great Eggscape, 1 vol. Glass, Susan. 2011. 32p. (J). (gr. k-5). (ENG.). 16.95 *(978-1-59572-261-4(0))*; pap. 6.95 *(978-1-59572-253-9(X))* Star Bright Bks., Inc.

—How Do You Get a Mouse to Smile?, 1 vol. Grubman, Bonnie. 2009. (ENG.). 32p. (J). (gr. -1-3). pap. 6.50 *(978-1-59572-167-9(3))* Star Bright Bks., Inc.

—In the Promised Land: Lives of Jewish Americans. Rappaport, Doreen. 2005. 32p. (J). (gr. k-4). lib. bdg. 16.89 *(978-0-06-059395-7(4))* HarperCollins Pubs.

—Nobody Asked the Pea. Stewig, John Warren. 2013. (ENG.). 32p. (J). 16.95 *(978-0-8234-2224-1(0))* Holiday Hse., Inc.

—Sam y el Dinero de la Suerte. Chinn, Karen. 2003.Tr. of Sam & the Lucky Money. (SPA.). (J). *(978-1-58430-167-7(8))* Lee & Low Bks., Inc.

—Zachary's Dinnertime, 1 vol. Levinson, Lara. 2012. (ENG.). 32p. (J). 16.95 *(978-1-59572-329-1(3))*; pap. 6.95 *(978-1-59572-330-7(7))* Star Bright Bks., Inc.

Van Wright, Cornelius & Ha, Ying-Hwa. Willie Covan Loved to Dance. Shahan, Sherry. Van Wright, Cornelius & Ha, Ying-Hwa, trs. 2004. (J). 15.95 *(978-1-59034-445-3(6))*; pap. *(978-1-59034-580-1(0))* Mondo Publishing.

Van Wright, Cornelius & Hu, Ying-Hwa. Alicia's Happy Day, 1 vol. Starr, Meg. 2003. (ENG.). 32p. (J). pap. 5.95 *(978-1-932065-06-0(7))* Star Bright Bks., Inc.

—Alicia's Happy Day (Spanish/English), 1 vol. Starr, Meg. Fiol, Maria, tr. from ENG. 2007. (SPA & ENG.). 32p. (J). (gr. k-3). pap. 6.95 *(978-1-59572-116-7(9))* Star Bright Bks., Inc.

—Alicia's Happy Day (Spanish/English), 1 vol. Starr, Meg. Fiol, Maria, tr. from ENG. 2007. (ENG.). 32p. (J). (gr. -1-3). 15.95 *(978-1-59572-115-0(0))* Star Bright Bks., Inc.

—American Slave, American Hero: York of the Lewis & Clark Expedition. Pringle, Laurence. 2006. (ENG.). 40p. (J). (gr. 3-3). 19.95 *(978-1-59078-282-8(8))* Boyds Mills Pr.

—Baby Flo: Florence Mills Lights up the Stage. Schroeder, Alan. 2012. (ENG.). 40p. (J). 18.95 *(978-1-60060-410-2(2))* Lee & Low Bks., Inc.

—El día más feliz de Alicia, 1 vol. Starr, Meg. Fiol, Maria A., tr. from ENG. 2003.Tr. of Alicia's Happy Day. (SPA.). 32p. (J). pap. 5.95 *(978-1-932065-03-9(2))* Star Bright Bks., Inc.

—I Told You I Can Play! 2006. (ENM.). 32p. (J). 16.95 *(978-1-933491-06-6(X))* Just Us Bks., Inc.

—Jumping the Broom. Black, Sonia W. 2004. 32p. (J). lib. bdg. 15.00 *(978-1-4242-0234-8(5))* Fitzgerald Bks.

—Let's Read About — Ruby Bridges. Bridges, Ruby & Maccarone, Grace. 2003. (Scholastic First Biographies Ser.). (J). *(978-0-439-51362-3(6))* Scholastic, Inc.

—Princess Grace. Hoffman, Mary. 2008. (ENG.). 32p. (J). (gr. -1-3). 18.99 *(978-0-8037-3260-5(0)*, Dial) Penguin Publishing Group.

—Sam y el Dinero de la Suerte. Chinn, Karen. 2003.Tr. of Sam & the Lucky Money. (SPA.). 32p. (J). pap. 9.95 *(978-1-58430-168-4(6))* Lee & Low Bks., Inc.

—Singing for Dr. King. Scholastic, Inc. Staff & Medearis, Angela Shelf. 2004. (Just for You Ser.). (ENG.). 32p. (gr. k-3). pap. 3.99 *(978-0-439-56855-5(2)*, Teaching Resources) Scholastic, Inc.

Van Wright, Cornelius, jt. illus. see Hu, Ying-Hwa.

Van Wyk, Hanri. First Picture Animals. Brooks, Felicity & Litchfield, Jo. 2008. (First Picture Board Bks.). 12p. (J). (gr. -1). bds. 11.99 *(978-0-7945-1831-8(1)*, Usborne) EDC Publishing.

—First Picture Dinosaurs. Taplin, Sam. 2007. (First Picture Board Bks). 12p. (J). bds. 11.99 *(978-0-7945-1752-6(8)*, Usborne) EDC Publishing.

—Usborne Lift & Look Emergency Vehicles. Brooks, Felicity. 2007. (Lift & Look Board Bks.). 10p. (J). (gr. -1-k). bds. 9.99 *(978-0-7945-1596-6(7)*, Usborne) EDC Publishing.

—Usborne Lift & Look Tractors. Brooks, Felicity. 2007. (Lift & Look Board Bks.). 10p. (J). (gr. -1-k). bds. 9.99 *(978-0-7945-1597-3(5)*, Usborne) EDC Publishing.

Van Wyk, Hanri & Newell, Keith. First Picture Trucks. MMStudios, photos by. Helbrough, Emma & Brooks, Felicity. 2007. (First Picture Board Bks.). 16p. (J). (gr. -1-k). bds. 11.99 *(978-0-7945-1454-9(5)*, Usborne) EDC Publishing.

Van Wyk, Rupert. The Pirate Pie Ship. Guillain, Adam & Guillain, Charlotte. 2014. (ENG.). 32p. (J). *(978-0-7787-1309-8(1))*; pap. *(978-0-7787-1368-5(7))* Crabtree Publishing Co.

—The Pirates on Holiday. Guillain, Adam & Guillain, Charlotte. 2014. (ENG.). 32p. (J). *(978-0-7787-1311-1(3))* Crabtree Publishing Co.

van Wyk, Rupert. The Vanishing Rainforest. Platt, Richard. 2007. (ENG.). 32p. (J). pap. *(978-0-7112-2170-3(7)*, Frances Lincoln) Quarto Publishing Group UK.

—The Vanishing Rainforest. Platt, Richard. 2003. 32p. (YA). 14.99 *(978-0-7112-1960-1(5)*, Frances Lincoln) Quarto Publishing Group UK GBR. Dist: Perseus-PGW.

Van Zeyl, Marjan. Little Red Riding-Hood: A Grimm's Fairy Tale. Grimm, Wilhelm K. & Grimm, Jacob. Lawson, Polly, tr. from GER. 2008. (ENG.). 20p. (J). (gr. -1-3). *(978-0-86315-622-9(3))* Floris Bks.

Van Zyle, Daniel. Flight of the Golden Plover: The Amazing Migration Between Hawaii & Alaska. Miller, Debbie S. 2011. (ENG.). 32p. pap. 11.95 *(978-1-60223-151-1(6))* Univ. of Alaska Pr.

Van Zyle, Jon. Arctic Lights, Arctic Nights. Miller, Debbie S. 2003. (ENG.). 32p. (J). (gr. 1-4). 17.95 *(978-0-8027-8856-6(4))* Walker & Co.

—Arctic Lights, Arctic Nights. Miller, Debbie S. 2007. (ENG.). 32p. (J). (gr. k-4). pap. 7.99 *(978-0-8027-9636-3(2))* Walker & Co.

—Big Alaska: Journey Across America's Most Amazing State. Miller, Debbie S. 2006. (ENG.). 40p. (J). (gr. 1-5). 17.95 *(978-0-8027-8069-0(5))* Walker & Co.

—Douggie: The Playful Pup Who Became a Sled Dog Hero. Flowers, Pam. 2008. (ENG.). 32p. (J). (gr. k-5). pap. 10.99 *(978-0-88240-655-8(8)*, Alaska Northwest Bks.) Graphic Arts Ctr. Publishing Co.

—Gone Again Ptarmigan. London, Jonathan. 2013. 32p. (J). pap. 12.95 *(978-1-60223-204-4(0))* Univ. of Alaska Pr.

—The Great Serum Race: Blazing the Iditarod Trail. Miller, Debbie S. 2006. (ENG.). 40p. (J). (gr. 2-7). pap. 9.99 *(978-0-8027-7723-2(6))* Walker & Co.

—Honey Paw & Lightfoot. London, Jonathan. 2014. (ENG.). 32p. (J). 16.99 *(978-1-941821-10-7(3)*, Alaska Northwest Bks.) Graphic Arts Ctr. Publishing Co.

—Kayuktuk: An Arctic Quest. Heinz, Brian J. 2004. (J). pap. 6.95 *(978-0-936335-09-4(2))*; 14.95 *(978-0-936335-08-7(4))* Ballyhoo BookWorks, Inc.

—A King Salmon Journey. Miller, Debbie S. & Eiler, John H. 2014. 44p. 15.95 *(978-1-60223-230-3(X))*; 32p. pap. 12.95 *(978-1-60223-231-0(8))* Univ. of Alaska Pr.

—Mardy Murie Did! Grandmother of Conservation. McDaniel, Jequita Potts. 2011. (J). *(978-1-58979-525-9(3))* Taylor Trade Publishing.

—Ollie's First Year. London, Jonathan. 2014. 32p. (J). 15.95 *(978-1-60223-228-0(8))* Univ. of Alaska Pr.

—A Polar Bear Journey. Miller, Debbie S. 2005. (ENG.). 32p. (J). (gr. 1-4). pap. 7.95 *(978-0-8027-7715-7(5))* Walker & Co.

—Raven & River. Carlstrom, Nancy White. 2011. (ENG.). 32p. pap. 11.95 *(978-1-60223-150-4(8))* Univ. of Alaska Pr.

—Seababy: A Little Otter Returns Home. Levine, Ellen & Megarry, Tim. 2012. (ENG.). 40p. (J). (gr. -1-3). 16.99 *(978-0-8027-9808-4(X)*, 231362); lib. bdg. 17.89 *(978-0-8027-9809-1(8))* Walker & Co.

—The Seasons of Little Wolf. London, Jonathan. ed. 2014. (ENG.). 32p. (J). 16.99 *(978-1-941821-06-0(5)*, West Winds Pr.) Graphic Arts Ctr. Publishing Co.

—Survival at 120 Above. Miller, Debbie S. 2012. (ENG.). 40p. (J). (gr. 2-10). 17.99 *(978-0-8027-9813-8(6))*; lib. bdg. 18.89 *(978-0-8027-9814-5(4))* Walker & Co.

—Survival at 40 Below. Miller, Debbie S. 2010. (ENG.). 40p. (J). (gr. 2-5). 17.99 *(978-0-8027-9815-2(2))*; lib. bdg. 18.89 *(978-0-8027-9816-9(0))* Walker & Co.

—What's a Shrew to You? Shields, Mary & Grace, Susan. 2008. (J). *(978-0-9618348-7-6(0))* Pyrola Publishing.

—A Woolly Mammoth Journey. Miller, Debbie S. 2010. (ENG.). 32p. (J). pap. 9.95 *(978-1-60223-098-9(6))* Univ. of Alaska Pr.

VanArsdale, Anthony. The Mystery of the Grinning Gargoyle. Warner, Gertrude Chandler. 2014. (Boxcar Children Mysteries Ser.: 137). (ENG.). 128p. (J). (gr. 2-5). pap. 5.99 *(978-0-8075-0893-0(4))* Whitman, Albert & Co.

—The Mystery of the Soccer Snitch. Warner, Gertrude Chandler. 2014. (Boxcar Children Mysteries Ser.: 136). (ENG.). 128p. (J). (gr. 2-5). pap. 5.99 *(978-0-8075-0896-1(9))* Whitman, Albert & Co.

Vanarsdale, Anthony. Sacajawea. Norwich, Grace. 2012. (I Am Ser.). (ENG.). 128p. (J). (gr. 3-7). pap. 5.99 *(978-0-545-40574-4(2)*, Scholastic Paperbacks) Scholastic, Inc.

VanBibber, Jodi. Bible Story Concepts for Fours & Fives: A Unique Blend of Bible Concepts & Preschool Skills. VanBibber, Jodi. 2004. 265p. (J). cd-rom 69.95 *(978-0-9755818-1-0(3)*, BSC-4s-5s) Sunny Hollow Pr.

—Bible Story Concepts for Twos & Threes: A Unique Blend of Bible Concepts & Preschool Skills. VanBibber, Jodi. 2004. 255p. (J). cd-rom 69.95 *(978-0-9755818-0-3(5)*, BSC-2s-3s) Sunny Hollow Pr.

VanBuskirk, Alan. Scott & Jake. VanBuskirk, Gary. 2011. (ENG.). 26p. pap. 9.25 *(978-1-4565-7451-2(5))* CreateSpace Independent Publishing Platform.

Vancata, Brad, jt. illus. see Smith, Andy.

Vance, Elsbet. Mistletoe Madness: A Short Story Collection. Vance, Elsbet. ed. 2004. (ENG.). 384p. (J). (gr. 1-5). pap. 8.95 *(978-0-9718348-2-8(2))* Blooming Tree Pr.

Vanden Berg, Myra. Sparkle's Journey. Kreder Sr., Edward G. & Kreder, Mary Ellen DeLuca. 2013. 32p. pap. 5.99 *(978-0-9913232-0-3(3))* Kreder, Mary Ellen DeLuca.

Vanden Broeck, Fabricio. Thirsty, Thirsty Elephants. Markle, Sandra. 2016. (J). lib. bdg. ***(978-1-58089-634-4(0))*** Charlesbridge Publishing, Inc.

Vandenberg, Michael, photos by. My Train Book. Jacob, Ellen et al. 2007. (ENG.). 16p. (J). (gr. -1-k). bds. 6.99 *(978-0-06-089970-7(0)*, Collins) HarperCollins Pubs.

VandenBroeck, Fabricio. Uncle Rain Cloud. Johnston, Tony. 2003. (ENG.). 32p. (J). (gr. k-3). pap. 7.95 *(978-0-88106-372-1(X))* Charlesbridge Publishing, Inc.

—Under the Mambo Moon. Durango, Julia. 2011. (ENG.). 48p. (J). (gr. 3-7). 12.95 *(978-1-57091-723-3(X))* Charlesbridge Publishing, Inc.

VandenBroeck, Fabricio, jt. illus. see Sanchez Vigil, Luis Gerardo.

Vander Pol, Matt. Super Ace & the Space Traffic Jam, 1 vol. Crouch, Cheryl. 2009. (I Can Read! / Superhero Ser.). (ENG.). 32p. (J). pap. 3.99 *(978-0-310-71698-3(5))* Zonderkidz.

Vanderbeek, Don. Stormalong. Metaxas, Eric. 2004. (Rabbit Ears-A Classic Tale Ser.). 36p. (gr. k-5). 25.65 *(978-1-59197-772-8(X))* Spotlight.

Vanderbilt, Amy. Negative Nine: Book 1 of the Early Math Series. Vanderbilt, Amy. Vanderbilt, Sabrina. 2008. 28p. (J). 14.99 *(978-0-7639-0719-8(7))* Trend Factor Pr.

Vanderhoop, Jannette. The Legend of Katama: The Creation Story of Dolphins, A Wampanoag Legend of Martha's Vineyard. 2004. 80p. (J). lib. bdg. 18.95 *(978-0-9755605-0-1(6))* Island Moon Pr.

VanDerTuuk-Perkins, Jennifer E. & Perkins, Rodney R. Life with Gabriel. VanDerTuuk-Perkins, Jennifer E. I.t. ed. 2004. 22p. (J). per. 9.95 *(978-0-9749862-0-3(8))* Theragogy.com.

Vandewater, Rena. The Nine Most Famous Reindeer of All. Sharp, Rhonda Winchell. 2004. 40p. (J). pap. 15.99 *(978-0-9748047-8-1(9))* Hickory Bark Productions.

VanDeWeghe, Lindsay & Bohnet, Christopher. Bur Bur & Friends 3 volume Set. Pastel, JoAnne & Fitzsimmons, Kakie. 2007. (J). lib. bdg. 39.95 *(978-0-9777121-5-1(X))* IGI Pr.

—Bur Bur Throws Out the First Pitch: An Exciting Baseball Experience. Fitzsimmons, Kakie. 2007. (Bur Bur & Friends Ser.). (ENG.). 30p. (J). (gr. -1-3). lib. bdg. *(978-0-9777121-4-4(1))* IGI Pr.

—Bur Bur's Fishing Adventure: An Exciting Fishing Adventure. Fitzsimmons, Kakie. 2007. (Bur Bur & Friends Ser.). 32p. (J). (gr. -1-3). lib. bdg. *(978-0-9777121-3-7(3))* IGI Pr.

Vane, Mitch. A Box Full of Phaeries, Phreddes & Fruit, 3 Vols. French, Jackie. 2003. (ENG.). 100p. *(978-0-207-19849-6(7))* HarperCollins Pubs. Australia.

—Crawfish Hunt. Arena, Felice & Kettle, Phil. 2004. (J). pap. *(978-1-59336-358-1(3))* Mondo Publishing.

—Hit the Beach. Arena, Felice & Kettle, Phil. 2004. (J). pap. *(978-1-59336-361-1(3))* Mondo Publishing.

—Little Lunch Four. Katz, Danny. 2005. (Little Lunch Ser.). 64p. (J). pap. *(978-1-876372-84-2(2)*, Black Dog Books) Walker Bks. Australia Pty, Ltd.

—A Mountain of Mittens. Plourde, Lynn. 2009. (ENG.). 32p. (J). (gr. -1-3). pap. 7.95 *(978-1-57091-466-9(4))* Charlesbridge Publishing, Inc.

—The Patch. Headley, Justina Chen. 2007. (ENG.). 32p. (J). (gr. k-3). pap. 7.95 *(978-1-58089-170-7(5))* Charlesbridge Publishing, Inc.

—A Phaery Named Phredde & Other Stories to Eat with a Banana. French, Jackie. 2004. 128p. (Orig.). *(978-0-207-20000-7(9))* HarperCollins Pubs. Australia.

—Phredde & a Frog Named Bruce & Other Stories to Eat with a Watermelon. French, Jackie. 2004. 128p. (Orig.). *(978-0-207-20001-4(7))* HarperCollins Pubs. Australia.

—Phredde & the Purple Pyramid: A Story to Eat with a Passionfruit. French, Jackie. 2003. (ENG.). 160p. (Orig.). *(978-0-207-19934-9(5))* HarperCollins Pubs. Australia.

—Phredde & the Zombie Librarian: And Other Stories to Eat with a BloodPlum. French, Jackie. 2004. 128p. (Orig.). *(978-0-207-20002-1(5))* HarperCollins Pubs. Australia.

—Poodle & Hound. Lasky, Kathryn. 2011. (ENG.). 48p. (J). (gr. k-3). pap. 6.95 *(978-1-58089-323-7(6))* Charlesbridge Publishing, Inc.

Vane, Mitch. The Princess & the Pea. 2015. (Once upon a Timeless Tale Ser.). (ENG.). 24p. (J). (gr. k-2). 9.99 ***(978-1-921894-93-0(8))*** Little Hare Bks. AUS. Dist: Independent Pubs. Group.

Vane, Mitch. Rotten School Day. Arena, Felice & Kettle, Phil. 2004. (J). pap. *(978-1-59336-364-2(8))* Mondo Publishing.

—Scratch Kitten & the Ghost Ship. Green, Jessica. 2010. (Scratch Kitten Ser.). (ENG.). 92p. (J). (gr. k-2). 6.99 *(978-1-921541-07-0(5))* Little Hare Bks. AUS. Dist: Independent Pubs. Group.

—Scratch Kitten & the Terrible Beasties. Green, Jessica. 2010. (Scratch Kitten Ser.: 4). (ENG.). 96p. (J). (gr. 1-4). 6.99 *(978-1-921272-95-0(3))* Little Hare Bks. AUS. Dist: Independent Pubs. Group.

—Secret Agent Heroes. Arena, Felice & Kettle, Phil. 2004. (J). pap. *(978-1-59336-355-0(9))* Mondo Publishing.

—This Book Is Bugged. Bursztynski, Sue. 2007. (It's True! Ser.). (ENG.). 96p. (J). (gr. 5-8). pap. 5.95 *(978-1-55451-079-5(1)*, 9781554510795) Annick Pr., Ltd. CAN. Dist: Firefly Bks., Ltd.

—The Tree House. Arena, Felice & Kettle, Phil. 2004. (J). pap. *(978-1-59336-357-4(5))* Mondo Publishing.

—Wet World. Arena, Felice & Kettle, Phil. 2004. (J). pap. *(978-1-59336-356-7(7))* Mondo Publishing.

Vane, Mitch, jt. illus. see Gordon, Gus.

vanFrankenhuyze, Gijsbert. H Is for Horse: An Equestrian Alphabet. Ulmer, Michael. rev. ed. 2004. (Sports Ser.). (ENG.). 40p. (J). (gr. -1-5). 17.95 *(978-1-58536-213-4(1))* Sleeping Bear Pr.

Vang Nyman, Ingrid. Pippi Moves In. Lindgren, Astrid. Nunnally, Tiina, tr. from SWE. 2012. (ENG.). 56p. (J). (gr. -1-3). 14.95 *(978-1-77046-099-7(3))* Drawn & Quarterly Pubns. CAN. Dist: Macmillan.

Vang, Richard. My Dad Is a Freemason. Vang, Richard. 2006. (Masonic Family Ser.). (ENG.). 31p. per. 16.95 *(978-0-9789066-0-3(8))* Square Circle Pr. LLC.

Vangsgard, Amy. Look Closer. Williams, Rozanne Lanczak. 2005. (Reading for Fluency Ser.). 8p. (J). pap. 3.49 *(978-1-59198-147-3(6)*, 4247) Creative Teaching Pr., Inc.

Vangsgard, Amy, jt. illus. see Hillam, Corbin.

Vangsgard, Amy, jt. illus. see Hilliam, Corbin.

Vangsgard, Amy, jt. illus. see Rojas, Mary.

Vania, Tatio. City on the Hill. Hall, Mark & West, Matthew. 2014. (ENG.). 32p. (J). (gr. -1-3). 16.99 *(978-1-4336-8231-5(1)*, B&H Kids) B&H Publishing Group.

Vansant, Wayne. The Battle of the Bulge: A Graphic History of Allied Victory in the Ardennes 1944-1945. Vansant, Wayne. 2015. (Graphic Histories Ser.). (ENG.). 104p. (YA). (gr. 8-12). 34.65 ***(978-1-939581-75-4(3))*** Quarto Publishing Group USA.

—Grant vs. Lee: The Graphic History of the Civil War's Greatest Rivals During the Last Year of the War. Vansant, Wayne. 2015. (Graphic Histories Ser.). (ENG.). 104p. (YA). (gr. 8-12). 34.65 ***(978-1-939581-78-5(8))*** Quarto Publishing Group USA.

—The Red Baron: The Graphic History of Richthofen's Flying Circus & the Air War in WWI. Vansant, Wayne. 2015. (Graphic Histories Ser.). (ENG.). 104p. (YA). (gr. 8-12). 34.65 ***(978-1-939581-80-8(X))*** Quarto Publishing Group USA.

Vansant, Wayne, jt. illus. see Golden, Mike.

Vanslette, Roxy. Poe the Crow. Devereux, Jan. Devereux, Jan, ed. 2004. 139p. (J). per. *(978-0-9749677-0-7(X))* Lakeview Pr.

Vant, Tim. The Witch's Cat. Vant, Jeanie. 2010. 24p. pap. 11.50 *(978-1-60976-051-9(4)*, Eloquent Bks.) Strategic Book Publishing & Rights Agency (SBPRA).

VanTuyle, David. The Cake Monster. Liberts, Jennifer. 2015. (Step into Reading Ser.). (ENG.). 24p. (J). (gr. -1-1). 4.99 ***(978-0-553-52314-0(7)*****, Random Hse. Bks. for Young Readers) Random Hse. Children's Bks.

VanTuyle, David. Welcome to Wally's World! Golden Books Staff. 2015. (Pictureback Ser.). (ENG.). 16p. (J). (gr. -1-2). 3.99 *(978-0-385-38764-4(4)*, Golden Bks.) Random Hse. Children's Bks.

VanTuyle, David, jt. illus. see Random House Editors.

Vanzet, Gaston. Bugs, 1 vol. Giulieri, Anne. 2012. (Engage Literacy Red Ser.). (ENG.). 32p. (gr. k-2). pap. 5.99 *(978-1-4296-8934-2(X)*, Engage Literacy) Capstone Pr., Inc.

—Dinosaurs, 1 vol. Dale, Jay. 2012. (Engage Literacy Blue Ser.). (ENG.). 32p. (gr. k-2). pap. 5.99 *(978-1-4296-8974-8(9)*, Engage Literacy) Capstone Pr., Inc.

Vareberg, Gladys. Ryleigh's Little Bug Book, 1 vol. Burns, Helen Marie. 2009. 24p. pap. 24.95 *(978-1-60813-701-5(5))* America Star Bks.

Varekamp, Marjolein. A Wonderful Week. Varekamp, Marjolein. 2009. (ENG.). 32p. (J). (gr. -1-k). 16.95 *(978-0-9802338-3-4(6))* Bees Knees Bks.

Varela, Cecilia. Listen to the Birds: An Introduction to Classical Music. Gerhard, Ana. 2013. (ENG.). 48p. (J). (gr. 2-4). 16.95 *(978-2-923163-89-5(3))* La Montagne Secrete CAN. Dist: Independent Pubs. Group.

Varela, Juan D. Do Fish Kiss? Gummelt, Donna & Melchiorre, Dondino. Wall, Randy Hugh, ed. I.t. ed. 2006.Tr. of Los peces Besan. (SPA.). 32p. (J). 14.95 *(978-0-9764798-0-2(X))* Story Store Collection Publishing.

—Your Name Is Mud. Gummelt, Donna & Melchiorre, Dondino. Wall, Randy Hugh, ed. Varela, Carmen, tr. I.t. ed. 2006.Tr. of Tu nombre es Mud. 34p. (J). 14.95 *(978-0-9764798-3-3(4))* Story Store Collection Publishing.

Varela, Juan D. The Cookie Story. Varela, Juan D., tr. Sinclair, Nicholas et al. Wall, Randy Hugh, ed. I.t. ed. 2005.Tr. of Cuent de Galletas. (SPA.). 33p. (J). 14.95 *(978-0-9764798-1-9(8))* Story Store Collection Publishing.

—Cow Puppies. Varela, Juan D., tr. Gummelt, Donna & Melchiorre, Dondino. Wall, Randy Hugh, ed. 2006.Tr. of Cachorros Vaqueros. (SPA.). 32p. (J). 14.95 *(978-0-9764798-7-1(7))* Story Store Collection Publishing.

—Don't Get My Honey.... HONEY. Varela, Juan D., tr. Gummelt, Donna & Melchiorre, Dondino. Wall, Randy Hugh, ed. 2006. (SPA.). 34p. (J). 14.95 *(978-0-9764798-5-7(0))* Story Store Collection Publishing.

—I'm All Blown Up. Varela, Juan D., tr. Gummelt, Donna & Melchiorre, Dondino. Wall, Randy Hugh, ed. 2006.Tr. of Ya Creci. (SPA.). 34p. (J). 14.95 *(978-0-9764798-4-0(2))* Story Store Collection Publishing.

—Michelina the Magical Musical Good Witch of the Forest. Varela, Juan D., tr. Gummelt, Donna & Melchiorre, Dondino. Wall, Randy Hugh, ed. 2006. (SPA.). 34p. (J). 14.95 *(978-0-9764798-6-4(9))* Story Store Collection Publishing.

—My Sunshine Friend. Varela, Juan D., tr. Gummelt, Donna & Melchiorre, Dondino. Wall, Randy Hugh, ed. ed. 2006. (SPA.). 32p. (J). 14.95 *(978-0-9764798-2-6(6))* Story Store Collection Publishing.

Vargas, Robert. Lottie Bright & the Starmaker's Universe. Grannis, Greg. 2006. (ENG.). 280p. (J). per. *(978-0-9778205-9-7(9))* Helm Publishing.

Vargo, Joseph. Born of the Night: The Gothic Fantasy Artwork of Joseph Vargo. 2005. 182p. per. 24.99 *(978-0-9675756-6-7(4))* Monolith Graphics.

Vargo, Joseph, jt. illus. see Filipak, Christine.

Vargo, Kurt. The Tiger & the Brahmin. Gleeson, Brian. 2005. (Rabbit Ears: A Classic Tale Ser.). 36p. (gr. 2-7). 25.65 *(978-1-59679-347-7(3))* Spotlight.

Vargo, Sharon. Sugar & Shadow. 2012. 8p. (J). *(978-0-7367-2726-6(4))* Zaner-Bloser, Inc.

—A Wild & Woolly Night. Geiger, Lorraine Lynch. 2007. (J). (gr. -1-3). 15.95 *(978-1-891795-25-1(2))* RGU Group, The.

Varian, George & Clinedinst, B. West. Buccaneers & Pirates. Stockton, Frank R. 2007. (Dover Maritime Ser.). (ENG.). 368p. per. 12.95 *(978-0-486-45425-2(8))* Dover Pubns., Inc.

—Buccaneers & Pirates of Our Coasts. Stockton, Frank Richard. 2008. 364p. (gr. 4-7). 46.95 *(978-1-4369-8234-4(0))*; pap. 31.95 *(978-1-4367-9391-9(2))* Kessinger Publishing, LLC.

Various. The Awesome Book of Duckbills & Boneheads. Paiva, Johannah Gilman, ed. 2014. (ENG.). 32p. (J). (gr. 3-7). 7.99 ***(978-1-4867-0343-2(7))*** Flowerpot Children's Pr. Inc. CAN. Dist: Cardinal Pubs. Group.

—The Awesome Book of Flesh-Eaters. Paiva, Johannah Gilman, ed. 2014. (ENG.). 32p. (J). (gr. 3-7). 7.99 ***(978-1-4867-0341-8(0))*** Flowerpot Children's Pr. Inc. CAN. Dist: Cardinal Pubs. Group.

Various. The Awesome Book of Monsters of the Deep. Paiva, Johannah Gilman, ed. 2013. (World of Wonder: the Awesome Book Of Ser.). (ENG.). 32p. (J). (gr. 3-7). 7.99 *(978-1-77093-777-2(3))* Flowerpot Pr.

Various. The Awesome Book of Planets & Their Moons. Paiva, Johannah Gilman, ed. 2014. (ENG.). 32p. (J). (gr. 3-7). 7.99 ***(978-1-4867-0342-5(9))*** Flowerpot Children's Pr. Inc. CAN. Dist: Cardinal Pubs. Group.

Various. The Awesome Book of Prehistoric Animals. Paiva, Johannah Gilman, ed. 2013. (World of Wonder (Library) Ser.). (ENG.). 32p. (J). (gr. 3-7). 7.99 *(978-1-77093-780-2(3))* Flowerpot Pr.

—The Awesome Book of the Universe. Paiva, Johannah Gilman, ed. 2013. (ENG.). 32p. (J). (gr. 3-7). 7.99 *(978-1-77093-779-6(X))* Flowerpot Pr.

Various. The Awesome Book of Tornadoes & Other Storms. Paiva, Johannah Gilman, ed. 2014. (ENG.). 32p. (J). (gr. 3-7). 7.99 ***(978-1-4867-0261-9(9))*** Flowerpot Children's Pr. Inc. CAN. Dist: Cardinal Pubs. Group.

Various. The Awesome Book of Volcanoes. Paiva, Johannah Gilman, ed. 2013. (World of Wonder: the Awesome Book Of Ser.). (ENG.). 32p. (J). (gr. 3-7). 7.99 *(978-1-77093-778-9(1))* Flowerpot Pr.

—Childhood of Famous Americans Ready-To-Read Value Pack: Abe Lincoln & the Muddy Pig; Albert Einstein; John Adams Speaks for Freedom; George Washington's First Victory; Ben Franklin & His First Kite; Thomas Jefferson & the Ghostriders. 2013. (Ready-To-read COFA Ser.). (ENG.). 208p. (J). (gr. k-2). pap. 15.96 *(978-1-4424-9440-4(9)*, Simon Spotlight) Simon Spotlight.

—Dora's 10 Best Adventures. 2010. (Dora the Explorer Ser.). (ENG.). 248p. (J). 15.99 *(978-1-4424-0967-5(3)*, Simon Spotlight/Nickelodeon) Simon Spotlight/Nickelodeon.

Various. HarperCollins Treasury of Picture Book Classics: A Child's First Collection. 2015. (ENG.). 464p. (J). (gr. -1-3). 35.00 ***(978-0-06-242725-0(3))*** HarperCollins Pubs.

Various. Let's Read with Dora! 2010. (Dora the Explorer Ser.). (ENG.). 144p. (J). (gr. -1-1). pap. 7.99 *(978-1-4169-9742-9(3)*, Simon Spotlight/Nickelodeon) Simon Spotlight/Nickelodeon.

—OLIVIA Loves to Read: Olivia Trains Her Cat; Olivia & Her Ducklings; Olivia Takes a Trip; Olivia & the Snow Day; Olivia Plants a Garden; Olivia Goes Camping. 2012. (Olivia TV Tie-In Ser.). (ENG.). 144p. (J). (gr. -1-1). pap. 15.99 *(978-1-4424-5879-6(8)*, Simon Spotlight) Simon Spotlight.

—Olivia Ready-To-Read Value Pack #2: Olivia & the Kite Party; Olivia & the Rain Dance; Olivia Becomes a Vet;

V

Olivia Builds a House; Olivia Measures up; Olivia Trains Her Cat. 2013. (Olivia TV Tie-In Ser.). (ENG.). 144p. (J). (gr. -1-k). pap. 15.96 (978-1-4424-9438-1(7), Simon Spotlight) Simon Spotlight.

Various. The Really Big Awesome Book: Monsters of the Deep, the Universe, Volcanoes, Prehistoric Animals, & Tornadoes. Aladdin Books. Paiva, Johannah Gilman, ed. 2014. (ENG.). 160p. (J). (gr. 3-7). 24.95 (978-1-77093-928-8(8)) Flowerpot Children's Pr. Inc. CAN. Dist: Cardinal Pubs. Group.

—The Really Big I Didn't Know That Book: Bugs, Sharks, Dinosaurs, Cars, & Trains. Aladdin Books. Paiva, Johannah Gilman, ed. 2014. (ENG.). 160p. (J). (gr. 2). 24.95 (978-1-77093-927-1(X)) Flowerpot Children's Pr. Inc. CAN. Dist: Cardinal Pubs. Group.

Various. Story Time with Princess OLIVIA: Olivia the Princess; Olivia & the Puppy Wedding; Olivia Sells Cookies; Olivia & the Best Teacher Ever; Olivia Meets Olivia; Olivia & Grandma's Visit. ed. 2013. (Olivia TV Tie-In Ser.). (ENG.). 144p. (J). (gr. -1-2). pap. 15.99 (978-1-4424-9370-4(4), Simon Spotlight) Simon Spotlight.

Various. 5-Minute Batman Stories. 2015. (ENG.). 192p. (J). (gr. -1-3). 12.99 (978-0-06-235798-4(0), HarperFestival) HarperCollins Pubs.

Various Artists. Colour It! Modern Painters Staff & Quarto Generic Staff. 2004. (First Art Book Ser.). (ENG.). 36p. (J). (gr. -1-17). pap. 7.95 (978-1-84507-275-9(8), Frances Lincoln) Quarto Publishing Group UK GBR. Dist: Hachette Bk. Group.

—Under the Moons of Mars: New Adventures on Barsoom. Adams, John Joseph, ed. 2012. (ENG.). 368p. (YA). (gr. 7). 16.99 (978-1-4424-2029-8(4), Simon & Schuster Bks. For Young Readers) Simon & Schuster Bks. For Young Readers.

Various Authors. Dora's Bedtime Adventures. 2005. (Dora the Explorer Ser.). (ENG.). 36p. (J). bds. 10.99 (978-1-4169-0628-5(2), Simon Spotlight/Nickelodeon) Simon Spotlight/Nickelodeon.

Varkarotas, Heather. Surprise in Auntie's Garden! Morris, Ann. 2013. (ENG.). (J). (gr. -1-3). 14.95 (978-1-62086-224-7(7)) Mascot Bks., Inc.

Varley, Susan. Captain Small Pig, 1 vol. Waddell, Martin. 2010. (ENG.). 32p. (J). (gr. -1-3). 15.95 (978-1-56145-519-5(9)) Peachtree Pubs.

—Jack y el Monstruo. Graham, Richard. (Cotton Cloud Ser.). (SPA.). 32p. (J). (gr. 1-3). (978-84-7722-680-2(6)) Timun Mas, Editorial S.A. ESP. Dist: Lectorum Pubns., Inc.

Varley, Susan. Lovely Old Lion. Jarman, Julia. 2015. (ENG.). 32p. (J). (gr. -1-3). 17.99 (978-1-4677-9310-0(8)) Andersen Pr. GBR. Dist: Lerner Publishing Group.

Varley, Susan. The Monster Bed. Willis, Jeanne. 2007. (ENG.). 32p. (J). (gr. k-2). 13.99 (978-1-84270-222-2(X)) Andersen Pr. GBR. Dist: Independent Pubs. Group.

—The Spring Rabbit. Dunbar, Joyce. 2015. (ENG.). 32p. (J). (gr. -1-k). pap. 13.99 (978-1-78344-078-8(3)) Andersen Pr. GBR. Dist: Independent Pubs. Group.

—Two Shy Pandas. Jarman, Julia. 2013. 32p. (J). (gr. -1-3). 16.95 (978-1-4677-1141-8(1)) Andersen Pr. GBR. Dist: Lerner Publishing Group.

Varma, Ishan. The Quinceañera. Stamper, Judith Bauer. 2010. (J). (978-1-60617-121-9(6)) Teaching Strategies, Inc.

Varnedoe, Catharine E. Whoa, Wiggle-Worm: A Little Lemon Book about an Overly Active Child, 1 bk. Lee, Betsy B. l.t. ed. 2003. 24p. (J). pap. 7.95 (978-0-9720267-3-4(8)) Learning Abilities Bks.

Varner, Kristin. Pink Cupcake Magic. Tegen, Katherine. 2014. (ENG.). 32p. (J). (gr. -1-3). 16.99 (978-0-8050-9611-8(6), Holt, Henry & Co. Bks. For Young Readers) Holt, Henry & Co.

Varon, Sara. Bake Sale. Varon, Sara. 2011. (ENG.). 160p. (J). (gr. 3-7). 19.99 (978-1-59643-740-1(5)); pap. 16.99 (978-1-59643-419-6(8)) Roaring Brook Pr. (First Second Bks.).

—Robot Dreams. Varon, Sara. 2007. (ENG.). 208p. (J). (gr. 3-7). pap. 17.99 (978-1-59643-108-9(3), First Second Bks.) Roaring Brook Pr.

Vasconcellos, Daniel. All Keyed Up. Christopher, Matt. 7th ed. 2003. (ENG.). 64p. (J). (gr. 1-4). pap. 10.99 (978-0-316-73821-7(2)) Little, Brown Bks. for Young Readers.

Vasconcellos, Daniel, et al. The Dog That Stole Football Plays. Christopher, Matt. 2013. (Passport to Reading Level 3 Ser.). (ENG.). 32p. (J). (gr. 1-4). pap. 3.99 (978-0-316-21849-8(9)) Little, Brown Bks. for Young Readers.

Vasconcellos, Daniel. Firsts. Cohn, Arlen. gif. ed. 2004. (ENG.). 28p. (J). bds. 9.99 (978-1-57939-168-3(0)) Andrews McMeel Publishing.

—Frog in the Kitchen Sink. Post, Jim. 2015. (ENG.). 26p. (J). bds. 9.99 (978-1-4494-6709-8(1)) Andrews McMeel Publishing.

—Heads Up. Christopher, Matt. 2003. (Soccer Cats Ser.: Bk. 6). 54p. (J). (gr. 1-4). 12.65 (978-0-7569-3904-5(6)) Perfection Learning Corp.

—Heads Up! Christopher, Matt. 6th ed. 2003. (ENG.). 64p. (J). (gr. 1-4). pap. 10.99 (978-0-316-16497-9(6)) Little, Brown Bks. for Young Readers.

—Kick It! Christopher, Matt. 2003. (ENG.). 64p. (J). (gr. 1-4). pap. 10.99 (978-0-316-73808-8(5)) Little, Brown Bks. for Young Readers.

—Making the Save. Christopher, Matt. 11th ed. 2004. (ENG.). 64p. (J). (gr. 1-4). pap. 10.99 (978-0-316-73745-6(3)) Little, Brown Bks. for Young Readers.

—Master of Disaster. Christopher, Matt. 2003. (ENG.). 64p. (J). (gr. 1-4). pap. 10.99 (978-0-316-16498-6(4)) Little, Brown Bks. for Young Readers.

—Switch Play! Christopher, Matt. 9th ed. 2003. (ENG.). 64p. (J). (gr. 1-4). pap. 10.99 (978-0-316-73807-1(7)) Little, Brown Bks. for Young Readers.

—You Lucky Dog. Christopher, Matt. 8th ed. 2003. (ENG.). 64p. (J). (gr. 1-4). pap. 10.99 (978-0-316-73805-7(0)) Little, Brown Bks. for Young Readers.

—You Lucky Dog. Christopher, Matt. 2003. (Soccer Cats Ser.: Bk. 8). 49p. (J). (gr. 2-4). 12.65 (978-0-7569-3907-6(0)) Perfection Learning Corp.

Vasilevsky, Marina. A Trixi, a Shmoop & a Monster. Dube, Tory. 2013. 32p. 19.99 (978-0-9886193-1-9(8)) Dube, Tory.

Vasilovich, Guy. The 13 Nights of Halloween. Vasilovich, Guy. 2011. (ENG.). 40p. (J). (gr. -1-3). 16.99 (978-0-06-180445-8(2)) HarperCollins Pubs.

Vasquez, Ivan & Redondo, Jesus. Spider-Man 2: Everyday Hero. Figueroa, Acton. movie tie-in ed. 2004. (Festival Reader Ser.). 32p. (J). (gr. -1-2). pap. 3.99 (978-0-06-057363-8(5), HarperFestival) HarperCollins Pubs.

Vásquez, Juan José. Times to Remember, the Fun & Easy Way to Memorize the Multiplication Tables. Warren, Sandra Jane. 2012. 86p. 24.95 (978-0-9836580-0-9(5)) Joyful Learning Publications, LLC.

Vasquez, Juan Jose. Times to Remember, the Fun & Easy Way to Memorize the Multiplication Tables: Home & Classroom Resources. Warren, Sandra J. 2012. 246p. pap. 19.95 (978-0-9836580-1-6(3)) Joyful Learning Publications, LLC.

Vasquez, Natalia. Margo & Marky's Adventures in Reading, 1 vol. Troupe, Thomas Kingsley. 2011. (In the Library). (ENG.). 24p. (gr. k-4). lib. bdg. 25.99 (978-1-4048-6291-3(9), Nonfiction Picture Bks.) Picture Window Bks.

—No Baths at Camp. Fox, Tamar. 2013. (ENG.). 32p. (J). (gr. -1-3). pap. 7.95 (978-0-7613-8121-1(X)); lib. bdg. 17.95 (978-0-7613-8120-4(1)) Lerner Publishing Group. (Kar-Ben Publishing).

—The Pied Piper of Hamelin. 2012. (Flip-Up Fairy Tales Ser.). (ENG.). 24p. (J). (978-1-84643-480-8(7)) Child's Play International Ltd.

Vasquez, Natalie. The Pied Piper of Hamelin. 2012. (Flip-Up Fairy Tales Ser.). (ENG.). 24p. (J). (978-1-84643-519-5(6)) Child's Play International Ltd.

Vasudevan, Vidya. Lizzy Anne's Adventures, Vol. 1. Lizzy Anne's Adventures Staff & Zarrella, Sharon. 2011. 52p. (J). (gr. k-4). pap. 5.99 (978-0-9845887-2-5(8)) Lizzy Anne's Adventures.

—Mbutu's Mangos. Free, Zaccai. 2006. 24p. (J). per. 12.95 (978-0-9785326-0-4(0)) Solar Publishing LLC.

—My Mom Hugs Trees. Ringgold, Robyn. 2006. 24p. (J). per. 15.95 (978-0-9785326-1-1(9)) Solar Publishing LLC.

Vasylenko, Veronica. The Best Snowman Ever! Stahl, Stephanie. 2013. (ENG.). 16p. (gr. -1-k). bds. 8.95 (978-1-58925-605-7(0)) Tiger Tales.

—Deck Halls. Tiger Tales Staff, ed. 2011. 20p. 8.95 (978-1-58925-868-6(1)) Tiger Tales.

—God Is Always Good: Comfort for Kids Facing Grief, Fear, or Change, 1 vol. Fortner, Tama. 2014. (ENG.). 32p. (J). 12.99 (978-0-7180-1145-1(7)) Nelson, Thomas Inc.

—Jingle Bells. 2007. (Padded Board Bks.). 18p. (J). (gr. -1-k). bds. 7.95 (978-1-58925-821-1(5)) Tiger Tales.

—Jingle Bells. Tiger Tales Staff, ed. 2011. 20p. 8.95 (978-1-58925-869-3(X)) Tiger Tales.

—Panda-Monium! Platt, Cynthia. 2011. 32p. (J). (gr. -1-2). (978-1-58925-093-2(1)); pap. 7.95 (978-1-58925-425-1(2)) Tiger Tales.

Vaugelade, Anaïs. The War. Vaugelade, Anaïs. 2007. (Carolrhoda Picture Bks.). (ENG.). 32p. (J). (gr. k-4). per. 6.95 (978-1-57505-918-1(5), First Avenue Editions) Lerner Publishing Group.

Vaughan, Brenna. All about Poop. Hayes, Kate. Garnsworthy, Marlo, ed. 2012. (ENG.). 38p. (J). pap. 14.95 (978-0-9854248-0-0(X)) Pinwheel Bks.

Vaughan, Jack. Basic Concepts in Motion Fun Deck: Fd58. Parks, Amy. 2003. (J). (978-1-58650-286-7(7)) Super Duper Pubns.

Vaughan, Jack, jt. illus. see Golliher, Bill.

Vaughan, Jeremy. Sandwich: Short Stories & Screenplays by Steven Coy. Coy, Steven. Saia, Karla, ed. 2003. 229p. (YA). per. 10.00 (978-0-9743235-0-3(0)) Better Non Sequitur.

Vaughn, Jen. Bridges & Tunnels: Investigate Feats of Engineering with 25 Projects. Latham, Donna. 2012. (Build It Yourself Ser.). (ENG.). 128p. (J). (gr. 3-7). 21.95 (978-1-936749-52-2(1)) Nomad Pr.

Vaughn, Jenn. The Industrial Revolution: Investigate How Science & Technology Changed the World with 25 Projects. Mooney, Carla. 2011. (Build It Yourself Ser.). (ENG.). 128p. (J). (gr. 3-7). 21.95 (978-1-936313-81-5(2)); pap. 15.95 (978-1-936313-80-8(4)) Nomad Pr.

Vaughn, Royce. Seymour Bluffs & Robert Wadlow, the Tallest Man in the World: A Story about Diversity & Tolerance. 2007. 28p. (J). 12.95 (978-0-9728538-4-2(7)) Amica Publishing.

—Seymour Bluffs & the Legend of the Piasa Bird. 2006. 24p. (J). pap. 9.95 (978-0-9728538-2-8(0)) Amica Publishing.

Vaughns, Byron. Come Together! Tanguay, Dave. 2015. (Billy Batson & the Magic of Shazam! Ser.). (ENG.). 32p. (gr. 2-3). lib. bdg. 21.27 (978-1-4342-9744-0(6)) Stone Arch Bks.

—Deception Reception! Tanguay, Dave. 2015. (Billy Batson & the Magic of Shazam! Ser.). (ENG.). 32p. (gr. 2-3). lib. bdg. 21.27 (978-1-4342-9742-6(X)) Stone Arch Bks.

—Fire Fire Everywhere! Tanguay, Dave. 2015. (Billy Batson & the Magic of Shazam! Ser.). (ENG.). 32p. (gr. 2-3). lib. bdg. 21.27 (978-1-4342-9745-7(4)) Stone Arch Bks.

—The Legacy of Mr. Banjo! Tanguay, Dave. 2015. (Billy Batson & the Magic of Shazam! Ser.). (ENG.). 32p. (gr. 2-3). lib. bdg. 21.27 (978-1-4342-9746-4(2)) Stone Arch Bks.

Vaux, Patricia. Five Minutes until Bed. Andrews McMeel Publishing Staff & Wang, Dorthea Deprisco. 2009. (ENG.). 14p. (J). (gr. 4-7). 14.99 (978-0-7407-8428-6(5)) Andrews McMeel Publishing.

—Five Minutes until Bed. Wang, Dorthea Deprisco. 2012. (ENG.). 14p. (J). (-k). bds. 5.99 (978-1-4494-2244-8(6)) Andrews McMeel Publishing.

Vavak, S. Dean. Calie's Gift. Arroyo, Madeline. 2003. 32p. (gr. 2-5). 16.95 (978-0-9740061-0-9(6), 1234106) Stairway Pubns.

—What Matthias Found. Arroyo, Madeline. 2005. 32p. (J). (gr. -1-3). 16.95 (978-0-9740061-1-6(4)) Stairway Pubns.

Vawter, Will. Riley Child-Rhymes with Hoosier Pictures. Riley, James Whitcomb. 4th ed. 2010. (Library of Indiana Classics Ser.). (ENG.). 192p. 17.95 (978-0-253-35569-0(9), 0253355699) Indiana Univ. Pr.

Vayssiere, Frederique. Katie: The Revolting Bridesmaid. Hooper, Mary. 2007. (Katie Ser.). (ENG.). 80p. (J). (gr. 2-4). per. 8.95 (978-0-7475-8611-1(X)) Bloomsbury Publishing Plc GBR. Dist: Independent Pubs. Group.

—The Revolting Baby. Hooper, Mary. 2008. (Katie Ser.). (ENG.). 96p. (J). (gr. 2-4). pap. 8.95 (978-0-7475-8613-5(6)) Bloomsbury Publishing Plc GBR. Dist: Independent Pubs. Group.

—The Revolting Holiday. Hooper, Mary. 2008. (Katie Ser.). (ENG.). 96p. (J). (gr. 2-4). pap. 8.95 (978-0-7475-8614-2(4)) Bloomsbury Publishing Plc GBR. Dist: Independent Pubs. Group.

—The Revolting Wedding. Hooper, Mary. 2007. (Katie Ser.). (ENG.). 96p. (J). (gr. 2-4). per. 8.95 (978-0-7475-8612-8(8)) Bloomsbury Publishing Plc GBR. Dist: Independent Pubs. Group.

Vaz de Carvalho, Joao. There Once Was a Dog. Carvalho, Adelia. 2014. (ENG.). 32p. (J). 15.95 (978-0-7358-4176-5(4)) North-South Bks., Inc.

Veasey, Michele. Listening to the Mukies: And Their Character Building Adventures. Bohlken, Robert L. 2003. (J). pap. 14.95 (978-0-930643-15-7(1)) Images Unlimited.

—Listening to the Mukies & Their Character Building Adventures. Bohlken, Robert L. 2003. (J). 24.95 (978-0-930643-17-1(8)) Images Unlimited.

Vecchio, Luciano. Attack of the Man-Bat! Black, Jake. 2015. (Batman: Comic Chapter Bks.). (ENG.). 88p. (gr. 3-7). lib. bdg. 19.99 (978-1-4965-0513-2(1)) Stone Arch Bks.

Vecchio, Luciano. Batman & the Flock of Fear. Manning, Matthew K. 2013. (Dark Knight Ser.). (ENG.). 88p. (gr. 2-3). pap. 5.95 (978-1-4342-4217-4(X)) Stone Arch Bks.

—Batman & the Villainous Voyage. Sonneborn, Scott. 2013. (Dark Knight Ser.). (ENG.). 88p. (gr. 2-3). pap. 5.95 (978-1-4342-4216-7(1)) Stone Arch Bks.

—Batman: Comic Chapter Books, 1 vol. Stone Arch Books Staff et al. 2014. (Batman: Comic Chapter Bks.). (ENG.). 32p. (gr. k-2). 39.98 (978-1-4342-9377-0(7), DC Super Heroes) Stone Arch Bks.

—Batman vs. the Penguin. Sutton, Laurie S. 2013. (Dark Knight Ser.). (ENG.). 88p. (gr. 2-3). pap. 5.95 (978-1-4342-4825-1(9)) Stone Arch Bks.

—Beware the Batman, Vol. 1. Cohen, Ivan. 2015. (ENG.). 128p. (J). (gr. 2-5). pap. 12.99 (978-1-4012-4936-6(1)) DC Comics.

—Black Manta & the Octopus Army, 1 vol. Mason, Jane B. 2012. (DC Super-Villains Ser.). (ENG.). 56p. (gr. 2-3). pap. 5.95 (978-1-4342-3898-6(9)); lib. bdg. 25.32 (978-1-4342-3797-2(4)) Stone Arch Bks. (DC Super-villains).

—The Black Masquerade. Tulien, Sean. 2013. (Dark Knight Ser.). (ENG.). 88p. (gr. 2-3). pap. 5.95 (978-1-4342-4824-4(0)); lib. bdg. 25.32 (978-1-4342-4486-4(5)) Stone Arch Bks.

—Cat Commander. Hult, Gene & Bright, J. E. (Dark Knight Ser.). (ENG.). 88p. (gr. 2-3). 2013. pap. 5.95 (978-1-4342-4214-3(5)); 2012. 25.32 (978-1-4342-4088-0(6)) Stone Arch Bks.

—Catwoman's Nine Lives, 1 vol. Manning, Matthew K. 2014. (Batman: Comic Chapter Bks.). (ENG.). 88p. (gr. 3-7). 19.99 (978-1-4342-9132-5(4)) Stone Arch Bks.

—Cheetah & the Purrfect Crime, 1 vol. Sutton, Laurie S. 2012. (DC Super-Villains Ser.). (ENG.). 56p. (gr. 2-3). pap. 5.95 (978-1-4342-3900-6(4)); lib. bdg. 25.32 (978-1-4342-3799-6(0)) Stone Arch Bks. (DC Super-villains).

—The Dark Knight: the Penguin's Crime Wave. Sutton, Laurie S. 2013. (ENG.). (J). (gr. 4-7). pap. 35.70 (978-1-4342-4872-5(0)) Stone Arch Bks.

Vecchio, Luciano. The Dark Side of the Apokolips. Sutton, Laurie S. 2015. (Superman: Comic Chapter Bks.). (ENG.). 88p. (gr. 3-7). lib. bdg. 19.99 (978-1-4965-0509-5(3)) Stone Arch Bks.

—DC Super Hero Origins. Manning, Matthew K. & Sazaklis, John. 2015. (DC Super Heroes Origins Ser.). (ENG.). 48p. (gr. k-2). lib. bdg. 90.60 (978-1-4965-0042-7(3), DC Super Heroes) Stone Arch Bks.

Vecchio, Luciano. Demons of Deep Space. Sutton, Laurie S. 2012. (Man of Steel Ser.). (ENG.). 88p. (gr. 2-3). lib. bdg. 25.32 (978-1-4342-4098-9(3)); pap. 5.95 (978-1-4342-4220-4(X)) Stone Arch Bks.

—In the Mouth of the Whale. Beatty, Scott et al. 2015. (Beware the Batman Ser.). (ENG.). 32p. (gr. 2-3). lib. bdg. 21.27 (978-1-4342-9740-2(3)) Stone Arch Bks.

—Killer Croc of Doom! Sutton, Laurie S. (Dark Knight Ser.). (ENG.). 88p. (gr. 2-3). 2013. pap. 5.95 (978-1-4342-4215-0(3)); 2012. 25.32 (978-1-4342-4097-2(5)) Stone Arch Bks.

—Law & Disorder. Cohen, Ivan et al. 2015. (Beware the Batman Ser.). (ENG.). 32p. (gr. 2-3). lib. bdg. 21.27 (978-1-4342-9738-9(1)) Stone Arch Bks.

—Lex Luthor & the Kryptonite Caverns, 1 vol. Bright, J. E. 2012. (DC Super-Villains Ser.). (ENG.). 56p. (gr. 2-3). pap. 5.95 (978-1-4342-3896-2(2)); lib. bdg. 25.32 (978-1-4342-3795-8(8)) Stone Arch Bks. (DC Super-villains).

Vecchio, Luciano. Lex Luthor's Power Grab! Simonson, Louise. 2015. (Superman: Comic Chapter Bks.). (ENG.). 88p. (gr. 3-7). lib. bdg. 19.99 (978-1-4965-0508-8(5)) Stone Arch Bks.

Vecchio, Luciano. Night of a Thousand Doomsdays, 1 vol. Sutton, Laurie S. 2013. (Man of Steel Ser.). (ENG.). 88p. (gr. 2-3). 25.32 (978-1-4342-4487-1(3)) Stone Arch Bks.

—Night of a Thousand Doomsdays. Sutton, Laurie S. 2013. (Man of Steel Ser.). (ENG.). 88p. (gr. 2-3). pap. 5.95 (978-1-4342-4827-5(5)) Stone Arch Bks.

—The Penguin's Crime Wave, 1 vol. Sutton, Laurie S. 2013. (Dark Knight Ser.). (ENG.). 88p. (gr. 2-3). lib. bdg. 25.32 (978-1-4342-4485-7(7)) Stone Arch Bks.

—The Planet Collector, 1 vol. Sutton, Laurie S. 2014. (Superman: Comic Chapter Bks.). (ENG.). 88p. (gr. 3-7). 19.99 (978-1-4342-9133-2(2)) Stone Arch Bks.

—The Poisoned Planet, 1 vol. Manning, Matthew K. 2012. (Man of Steel Ser.). (ENG.). 88p. (gr. 2-3). lib. bdg. 25.32 (978-1-4342-4091-0(6)) Stone Arch Bks.

—Prisoner of the Penguin!, 1 vol. Sonneborn, Scott. 2014. (Batman: Comic Chapter Bks.). (ENG.). 88p. (gr. 3-7). 19.99 (978-1-4342-9131-8(6)) Stone Arch Bks.

—The Real Man of Steel, 1 vol. Sutton, Laurie S. 2014. (Superman: Comic Chapter Bks.). (ENG.). 88p. (gr. 3-7). 19.99 (978-1-4342-9134-9(0)) Stone Arch Bks.

—Scarecrow's Flock of Fear, 1 vol. Manning, Matthew K. 2012. (Dark Knight Ser.). (ENG.). 88p. (gr. 2-3). lib. bdg. 25.32 (978-1-4342-4090-3(8)) Stone Arch Bks.

Vecchio, Luciano. Scarecrow's Panic Plot. Beatty, Scott. 2015. (Batman: Comic Chapter Bks.). (ENG.). 88p. (gr. 3-7). lib. bdg. 19.99 (978-1-4965-0512-5(3)) Stone Arch Bks.

Vecchio, Luciano. The Son of the Man-Bat. Cohen, Ivan et al. 2015. (Beware the Batman Ser.). (ENG.). 32p. (gr. 2-3). lib. bdg. 21.27 (978-1-4342-9741-9(1)) Stone Arch Bks.

—Supergirl vs. Brainiac, 1 vol. Sonneborn, Scott. 2013. (DC Super Heroes Ser.). (ENG.). 56p. (gr. 2-3). lib. bdg. 25.32 (978-1-4342-6015-4(1)) Stone Arch Bks.

—Superman & the Poisoned Planet. Manning, Matthew K. 2012. (Man of Steel Ser.). (ENG.). 88p. (gr. 2-3). pap. 5.95 (978-1-4342-4224-2(2)) Stone Arch Bks.

—Superman: Comic Chapter Books, 1 vol. Stone Arch Books Staff & Sutton, Laurie S. 2014. (Superman: Comic Chapter Bks.). (ENG.). 88p. (gr. 3-7). 39.98 (978-1-4342-9378-7(5), DC Super Heroes) Stone Arch Bks.

Vecchio, Luciano. Superman: Comic Chapter Books, 2 vols. Simonson, Louise & Sutton, Laurie S. 2015. (Superman: Comic Chapter Bks.). (ENG.). 88p. (gr. 3-7). 39.98 (978-1-4965-1999-3(X)) Stone Arch Bks.

Vecchio, Luciano. Superman vs. Bizarro, 1 vol. Sazaklis, John. 2013. (DC Super Heroes Ser.). (ENG.). 56p. (gr. 2-3). lib. bdg. 25.32 (978-1-4342-6012-3(7)) Stone Arch Bks.

—Tattooed Man Trouble!, 1 vol. Cohen, Ivan & Eltaeb, Gabe. 2014. (Green Lantern: the Animated Ser.). (ENG.). 32p. (gr. 2-3). 21.27 (978-1-4342-6480-0(7)) Stone Arch Bks.

—Wonder Woman vs. Circe, 1 vol. Bright, J. E. & Sutton, Laurie S. 2013. (DC Super Heroes Ser.). (ENG.). 56p. (gr. 2-3). lib. bdg. 25.32 (978-1-4342-6014-7(3)) Stone Arch Bks.

Vecchio, Luciano & Brizuela, Dario. Beware the Batman. Cohen, Ivan et al. 2015. (Beware the Batman Ser.). (ENG.). 32p. (gr. 2-3). 85.08 (978-1-4965-0302-2(3)) Stone Arch Bks.

Vecchio, Luciano & DC Comics Staff. Danger on Deck!, 1 vol. Sonneborn, Scott. 2013. (Dark Knight Ser.). (ENG.). 88p. (gr. 2-3). 25.32 (978-1-4342-4092-7(4)) Stone Arch Bks.

Vecchio, Luciano, jt. illus. see Baltazar, Art.

Vedder, Erik. Mad Mod Is in Vogue!, 1 vol. Beechen, Adam & Age, Heroic. 2014. (Teen Titans GO! Ser.). (ENG.). 32p. (gr. 2-3). 21.27 (978-1-4342-9216-2(9)) Stone Arch Bks.

Vega, Alison. Moon Tricks. Foster, Marilyn. 2012. 48p. pap. (978-1-77097-960-4(3)) FriesenPress.

Veinshtein, Debbie. Is God Sad? Daleski, Gil. Kaufman, Shirley, tr. from HEB. 2006. 40p. 14.95 (978-965-229-372-5(5)) Gefen Publishing Hse., Ltd ISR. Dist: Gefen Bks.

Velarde, Chase. When I Fall Asleep. Etherly, L. D. 2013. 36p. pap. 11.95 (978-0-9833877-6-3(1)) Inkspil Publishing.

—Yes, Santa Claus, There Is a Virginia: The True Story of Santa's First Computerized Christmas. Frantz, Kevin. 2011. (ENG.). 68p. pap. 20.00 (978-1-4664-1003-9(5)) CreateSpace Independent Publishing Platform.

Velasco, Francisco Ruiz. The Language of Chaos. Kennedy, Mike. 2003. (Lone Wolf 2100 Ser.: Vol. 2). (ENG.). 104p. (gr. 11-18). pap. 12.95 (978-1-56971-997-8(7)) Dark Horse Comics.

—Lone Wolf 2100 Volume 1: Shadows on Saplings: Shadows on Saplings. Kennedy, Mike. 2003. (Lone Wolf 2100 Ser.: Vol. 1). (ENG.). 104p. pap. 12.95 (978-1-56971-893-3(8)) Dark Horse Comics.

Velasquez, Eric. As Fast As Words Could Fly, 1 vol. Tuck, Pamela M. 2013. (ENG.). 40p. (J). 18.95 (978-1-60060-348-8(3)) Lee & Low Bks., Inc.

—Beautiful Moon: A Child's Prayer. Bolden, Tonya. 2014. (ENG.). 32p. (J). (gr. -1-3). 16.95 (978-1-4197-0792-6(2), Abrams Bks. for Young Readers) Abrams.

—Emma's Escape: A Story of America's Underground Railroad. Gayle, Sharon Shavers. 3rd ed. 2003. (Soundprints' Read-and-Discover Ser.). (ENG.). 48p. (J). (gr. -1-3). pap. 3.95 (978-1-59249-021-9(2), S2009) Soundprints.

—Houdini: World's Greatest Mystery Man & Escape King. Krull, Kathleen. 2007. (ENG.). 32p. (J). (gr. 1-5). pap. 9.99 (978-0-8027-9646-2(X)) Walker & Co.

—I, Matthew Henson: Polar Explorer. Weatherford, Carole Boston. 2007. (ENG.). 32p. (J). (gr. 1-6). 17.99 (978-0-8027-9688-2(5)) Walker & Co.

—Jesse Owens: Fastest Man Alive. Weatherford, Carole Boston. 2006. (ENG.). 32p. (J). (gr. 2-6). 16.95 (978-0-8027-9550-2(1)) Walker & Co.

—My Friend Maya Loves to Dance. Hudson, Cheryl Willis. 2010. (ENG.). 32p. (J). (gr. -1-3). 16.95 (978-0-8109-8328-1(1), Abrams Bks. for Young Readers) Abrams.

—My Uncle Martin's Big Heart. Watkins, Angela Farris. 2010. (ENG.). 32p. (J). (gr. -1-3). 19.95 (978-0-8109-8975-7(1), Abrams Bks. for Young Readers) Abrams.

Velasquez, Eric. My Uncle Martin's Words for America: Martin Luther King Jr. 's Niece Tells How He Made a Difference. Watkins, Angela Farris. (ENG.). 40p. (J). (gr. k-4). 2015. 9.95 (978-1-4197-1836-6(3)); 2011. 21.95 (978-1-4197-0022-4(7)) Abrams. (Abrams Bks. for Young Readers).

Velasquez, Eric. New Shoes. Meyer, Susan Lynn. 2015. (ENG.). 32p. (J). (gr. 1-4). 16.95 *(978-0-8234-2528-0(2))* Holiday Hse., Inc.

—Ol' Clip-Clop: A Ghost Story. McKissack, Patricia C. (ENG.). 32p. (J). 2014. (gr. 1-4). 6.99 *(978-0-8234-3186-1(X))*; 2013. 16.95 *(978-0-8234-2265-4(8))* Holiday Hse., Inc.

—The Price of Freedom: How One Town Stood up to Slavery. Fradin, Dennis Brindell & Fradin, Judith Bloom. 2013. (ENG.). 48p. (J). (gr. k-4). 17.99 *(978-0-8027-2166-2(4)*, 161449); (gr. 2-4). 17.89 *(978-0-8027-2167-9(2))* Walker & Co.

—The Rain Stomper, 0 vols. Boswell, Addie & Addie, Boswell. 2008. (ENG.). 32p. (J). (gr. -1-3). 16.99 *(978-0-7614-5393-2(8)*, 9780761453932, Amazon Children's Publishing) Amazon Publishing.

—Rosetta, Rosetta, Sit by Me!, 0 vols. Walvoord, Linda & Walvoord. 2004. (ENG.). 80p. (J). (gr. 3-6). 14.95 *(978-0-7614-5171-6(4)*, 9780761451716, Amazon Children's Publishing) Amazon Publishing.

—The Sound That Jazz Makes, 0 vols. Weatherford, Carole Boston. 2010. (ENG.). 32p. (J). (gr. k-4). pap. 7.99 *(978-0-7614-5732-9(1)*, 9780761457329, Amazon Children's Publishing) Amazon Publishing.

—A Sweet Smell of Roses. Johnson, Angela. (ENG.). 32p. (J). 2007. (gr. k-3). 7.99 *(978-1-4169-5361-6(2))*; 2005. (gr. -1-3). 17.99 *(978-0-689-83252-9(4))* Simon & Schuster Bks. For Young Readers. (Simon & Schuster Bks. For Young Readers).

—Swim!, 0 vols. Brigham, Marilyn. 2012. (ENG.). 24p. (J). (gr. -1-k). 7.99 *(978-0-7614-6253-8(8)*, 9780761462538, Amazon Children's Publishing) Amazon Publishing.

—A Thirst for Home: A Story of Water Across the World. Ieronimo, Christine. 2014. (ENG.). 32p. (J). (gr. 1-4). 17.99 *(978-0-8027-2307-9(1))* Walker & Co.

—Touch the Sky: Alice Coachman, Olympic High Jumper. Malaspina, Ann. 2012. (ENG.). 32p. (J). (gr. 1-4). 16.99 *(978-0-8075-8035-6(X))* Whitman, Albert & Co.

—Voices of Christmas, 1 vol. Grimes, Nikki. 2009. (ENG.). 32p. (J). (gr. -1-2). 16.99 *(978-0-310-71192-6(4))* Zonderkidz.

Velasquez, Eric. Grandma's Gift. Velasquez, Eric. (ENG.). (J). 2013. 32p. (gr. k-1). pap. 9.99 *(978-0-8027-3536-2(3)*, 244262); 2010. 40p. (gr. -1-3). 17.89 *(978-0-8027-2083-2(8))*; 2010. 32p. (gr. k-3). 16.99 *(978-0-8027-2082-5(X))* Walker & Co.

—Grandma's Records. Velasquez, Eric. 2004. (ENG.). 32p. (J). (gr. k-3). pap. 9.99 *(978-0-8027-7660-0(4))* Walker & Co.

Velasquez, Nicole. It's Okay to Be Different! (Esta Bien Ser Diferente!) Winner, Ramona Moreno. Date not set. (ENG & SPA.). 40p. (J). (gr. k-3). 9.95 *(978-0-9651174-0-1(5))* BrainStorm 3000.

Velazquez, Jose Luis Reye, jt. illus. see Velazquez, Jose Luis Reyes.

Velazquez, Jose Luis Reyes & Velazquez, Jose Luis Reye. La Dulceria de Don Tono. Cohen, Milly. rev. ed. 2006. (Castillo de la Lectura Verde Ser.). (SPA & ENG.). 112p. (J). (gr. 2-4). pap. 7.95 *(978-970-20-0198-0(6))* Castillo, Ediciones, S. A. de C. V. MEX. Dist: Macmillan.

Veldhoven, Marijke, jt. illus. see Geeson, Andrew.

Velert, Miriam. El Libro del Abuelo: Un Mundo de Aventuras Entre la Realidad y la Fantasma. Garrido, Pedro Gelabert. 2003. (Ficcion Interactiva Ser.). (SPA.). 160p. pap. 14.95 *(978-84-89984-11-0(5))* Recursos, Ediciones ESP. Dist: Independent Pubs. Group.

Vélez, Gabriel J., jt. illus. see Barajas, Sal.

Velez, Jill Ondercin. In Your Seat, Mr. Pete! Goss, Leon. 2005. (J). pap. *(978-1-933156-11-8(2))*; per. 16.99 *(978-1-933156-04-0(X))* GSVQ Publishing. (VisionQuest Kids).

Velez, Walter. Black as a Bat. Dingles, Molly. 2005. (Community of Color Ser.). 32p. (J). pap. 10.95 *(978-1-59646-334-9(1))*; per. 10.95 *(978-1-59646-335-6(X))* Dingles & Co.

—Black as a Bat/Negro como un Murcielago. Dingles, Molly. (Community of Color Ser.). 32p. (J). 2005. (ENG & SPA.). pap. 10.95 *(978-1-59646-100-0(4))*; 2005. (ENG & SPA.). per. 10.95 *(978-1-59646-106-2(3))*; 2003. (SPA.). lib. bdg. 21.65 *(978-1-891997-33-4(5))* Dingles & Co.

—Blue as a Blueberry. Dingles, Molly. 2005. (Community of Color Ser.). 32p. (J). (ACE.). pap. 10.95 *(978-1-59646-328-8(7))*; per. 10.95 *(978-1-59646-329-5(5))* Dingles & Co.

—Blue as a Blueberry/Azul como un Arandano. Dingles, Molly. (Community of Color Ser.). 32p. (J). 2005. (ENG & SPA.). pap. 10.95 *(978-1-59646-097-3(0))*; 2005. (ENG & SPA.). per. 10.95 *(978-1-59646-103-1(9))*; 2003. (SPA.). lib. bdg. 21.65 *(978-1-891997-28-0(9))* Dingles & Co.

—Blue as a Blueberry/Bleu comme un Bleuet. Dingles, Molly. 2004. (Community of Color Ser.).Tr. of Bleu comme un Bleuet. (ENG & FRE.). 32p. (J). lib. bdg. 21.65 *(978-1-891997-72-3(6))* Dingles & Co.

—Brown as an Acorn. Dingles, Molly. (Community of Color Ser.). 32p. (J). 2005. per. 10.95 *(978-1-59646-347-9(3))*; 2004. pap. 10.95 *(978-1-59646-346-2(5))* Dingles & Co.

—Brown as an Acorn/Marrón como una Bellota. Dingles, Molly. (Community of Color Ser.).Tr. of Marrón como una Bellota. (ENG & SPA.). 32p. (J). 2005. per. 10.95 *(978-1-59646-109-3(8))*; 2004. lib. bdg. 21.65 *(978-1-891997-37-2(8))* Dingles & Co.

—Gray as a Dolphin. Dingles, Molly. (Community of Color Ser.). 32p. (J). 2005. per. 10.95 *(978-1-59646-343-1(0))*; 2004. pap. 10.95 *(978-1-59646-342-4(2))* Dingles & Co.

—Gray as a Dolphin/Gris como un Delfin. Dingles, Molly. 2004. (Community of Color Ser.).Tr. of Gris como un Delfin. (ENG & SPA.). 32p. (J). pap. 10.95 *(978-1-59646-092-8(X))*; lib. bdg. 21.65 *(978-1-891997-58-7(0))* Dingles & Co.

—Gray as a Dolphin/Gris como un Delfin. Dingles, Molly. 2005. (Community of Color Ser.). (ENG & SPA.). 32p. (J). per. 10.95 *(978-1-59646-110-9(1))* Dingles & Co.

—Green as a Frog. Dingles, Molly. 2005. (Community of Color Ser.). 32p. (J). pap. 10.95 *(978-1-59646-330-1(9))*; per. 10.95 *(978-1-59646-331-8(7))* Dingles & Co.

—Green as a Frog/Verde como una Rana. Dingles, Molly. (Community of Color Ser.). 32p. (J). 2005. (ENG & SPA.). pap. 10.95 *(978-1-59646-098-0(9))*; 2005. (ENG & SPA.). per. 10.95 *(978-1-59646-104-8(7))*; 2003. (SPA.). lib. bdg. 21.65 *(978-1-891997-29-7(7))* Dingles & Co.

—Green as a Frog/Vert comme une Grenouille. Dingles, Molly. 2004. (Community of Color Ser.).Tr. of Vert comme une Grenouille. (ENG & FRE.). 32p. (J). lib. bdg. 21.65 *(978-1-891997-71-6(8))* Dingles & Co.

—Little Red Riding Hood: A Tale about Staying Safe. 2006. (J). 6.99 *(978-1-59939-021-5(3))* Cornerstone Pr.

—Orange as a Pumpkin. Dingles, Molly. 2005. (Community of Color Ser.). 32p. (J). pap. 10.95 *(978-1-59646-332-5(5))*; per. 10.95 *(978-1-59646-333-2(3))* Dingles & Co.

—Orange as a Pumpkin/Anaranjado como una Calabaza. Dingles, Molly. (Community of Color Ser.).Tr. of Anaranjado como una Calabaza. 32p. (J). 2005. (ENG & SPA.). pap. 10.95 *(978-1-59646-099-7(7))*; 2005. (ENG & SPA.). per. 10.95 *(978-1-59646-105-5(5))*; 2003. lib. bdg. 21.65 *(978-1-891997-31-0(9))* Dingles & Co.

—Orange as a Pumpkin/Orange comme une Citrouille. Dingles, Molly. 2004. (Community of Color Ser.).Tr. of Orange comme une Citrouille. (ENG & FRE.). 32p. (J). lib. bdg. 21.65 *(978-1-891997-69-3(6))* Dingles & Co.

—Pink as a Piglet. Dingles, Molly. (Community of Color Ser.). 32p. (J). 2005. pap. 10.95 *(978-1-59646-336-3(8))*; 2005. per. 10.95 *(978-1-59646-337-0(6))*; 2004. lib. bdg. 21.65 *(978-1-891997-25-9(4))* Dingles & Co.

—Pink as a Piglet/Rosa como un Cerdito. Dingles, Molly. (Community of Color Ser.).Tr. of Rosa como un Cerdito. 32p. (J). 2005. (ENG & SPA.). pap. 10.95 *(978-1-59646-348-6(1))*; 2005. (ENG & SPA.). per. 10.95 *(978-1-59646-349-3(X))*; 2004. (SPA & ENG.). lib. bdg. 21.65 *(978-1-891997-34-1(3))* Dingles & Co.

—Purple as a Plum. Dingles, Molly. (Community of Color Ser.). 32p. (J). 2005. pap. 10.95 *(978-1-59646-338-7(4))*; 2005. per. 10.95 *(978-1-59646-339-4(2))*; 2004. lib. bdg. 21.65 *(978-1-891997-24-2(6))* Dingles & Co.

—Purple as a Plum/Morado como una Ciruela. Dingles, Molly. (Community of Color Ser.). 32p. (J). 2005. (ENG & SPA.). pap. 10.95 *(978-1-59646-350-9(3))*; 2005. (ENG & SPA.). per. 10.95 *(978-1-59646-351-6(1))*; 2004. lib. bdg. 21.65 *(978-1-891997-32-7(7))* Dingles & Co.

—Purple as a Plum/Violet comme une Prune. Dingles, Molly. 2004. (Community of Color Ser.).Tr. of Violet comme une Prune. (ENG & FRE.). 32p. (J). lib. bdg. 21.65 *(978-1-891997-68-6(8))* Dingles & Co.

—Red as a Fire Truck. Dingles, Molly. 2005. (Community of Color Ser.). 32p. (J). pap. 10.95 *(978-1-59646-324-0(4))*; per. 10.95 *(978-1-59646-325-7(2))* Dingles & Co.

—Red as a Fire Truck/Rojo como un camion de Bomberos. Dingles, Molly. (Community of Color Ser.).Tr. of Rojo Como un Camion de Bomberos. 32p. (J). 2005. (ENG & SPA.). pap. 10.95 *(978-1-59646-095-9(4))*; 2005. (ENG & SPA.). per. 10.95 *(978-1-59646-101-7(2))*; 2003. (SPA.). lib. bdg. 21.65 *(978-1-891997-27-3(0))* Dingles & Co.

—Red as a Firetruck/Rouge comme un camion de Pompiers. Dingles, Molly. 2004. (Community of Color Ser.).Tr. of Rouge comme un camion de Pompiers. (ENG & FRE.). 32p. (J). lib. bdg. 21.65 *(978-1-891997-73-0(4))* Dingles & Co.

—Turquoise as a Parakeet. Dingles, Molly. 2005. (Community of Color Ser.). (J). 32p. pap. 10.95 *(978-1-59646-344-8(9))*; 2005p. per. 10.95 *(978-1-59646-345-5(7))* Dingles & Co.

—Turquoise as a Parakeet/Turquesa como un Periquito. Dingles, Molly. (Community of Color Ser.).Tr. of Turquesa como un Periquito. (ENG & SPA.). 32p. (J). 2005. per. 10.95 *(978-1-59646-107-9(1))*; 2004. pap. 10.95 *(978-1-59646-094-2(6))*; 2004. lib. bdg. 21.65 *(978-1-891997-60-0(2))* Dingles & Co.

—Where Is Pig? Albee, Sarah. 2006. (Step-By-Step Readers Ser.). (J). pap. *(978-1-59939-056-7(6)*, Reader's Digest Young Families, Inc.) Studio Fun International.

—White as a Seashell. Dingles, Molly. 2005. (Community of Color Ser.). 32p. (J). pap. 10.95 *(978-1-59646-340-0(6))*; per. 10.95 *(978-1-59646-341-7(4))* Dingles & Co.

—White as a Seashell/Blanco como una concha Marina. Dingles, Molly. (Community of Color Ser.).Tr. of Blanco como una concha Marina. (ENG & SPA.). (J). 2005. 2005p. per. 10.95 *(978-1-59646-108-6(X))*; 2004. 32p. pap. 10.95 *(978-1-59646-091-1(1))*; 2004. 32p. lib. bdg. 21.65 *(978-1-891997-38-9(6))* Dingles & Co.

—Yellow as a Lemon. Dingles, Molly. 2005. (Community of Color Ser.). 32p. (J). pap. 10.95 *(978-1-59646-326-4(0))*; per. 10.95 *(978-1-59646-327-1(9))* Dingles & Co.

—Yellow as a Lemon/Amarillo como un Limon. Dingles, Molly. (Community of Color Ser.). 32p. (J). 2005. (ENG & SPA.). pap. 10.95 *(978-1-59646-096-6(2))*; 2005. (ENG & SPA.). per. 10.95 *(978-1-59646-102-4(0))*; 2003. (SPA.). lib. bdg. 21.65 *(978-1-891997-30-3(0))* Dingles & Co.

—Yellow as a Lemon/Jaune comme un Citron. Dingles, Molly. 2004. (Community of Color Ser.).Tr. of Jaune comme un Citron. (ENG & FRE.). 32p. (J). lib. bdg. 21.65 *(978-1-891997-70-9(X))* Dingles & Co.

Velica, Teodora. Carolee Sings in the Christmas Choir: A Christmas Story for Children of All Ages. Myers, Janice Limb. 2013. 48p. pap. 13.77 *(978-0-9897175-1-9(8))* LJM Publishing.

Velikan, Phil. Saint Theodora & Her Promise to God. Doyle, Mary K. 2013. 34p. 16.99 *(978-0-9897397-0-2(8))* Sisters of Providence.

Velitchenko, Olga. Beautiful Queen. Holman, Nedra. 2008. 40p. (J). *(978-1-4363-5461-5(7))* Xlibris Corp.

Venable, James. A Salute to Black Inventors Vol. 1: Coloring Learning Activities. Chandler, Ann, Chapman, Loring F., ed. 96p. (Orig.). (J). (gr. 3-8). pap. 6.95 *(978-1-877804-18-2(5))* Chandler/White Publishing Co.

Venables, Julie. Larry the Llama. Pearson, Georgene. 2005. 44p. (J). (gr. -1). per. 12.95 *(978-1-933148-35-9(7))* Tate Publishing & Enterprises, LLC.

Vene, Alessandro. The Black Suitcase. Cervone, Shannon. 2013. (ENG.). 32p. (J). 15.99 *(978-1-938501-08-1(X))* Turn the Page Publishing.

—Gabi Babaroni on Broadway. Spergel, Heather. 2013. (ENG.). 32p. (J). 18.99 *(978-1-938501-29-6(2))* Turn the Page Publishing.

—The Misphits: Story of Snake. Schleuning, Todd & Schleuning, Cheryl. 2013. (ENG.). (J). (gr. -1-3). 15.95 *(978-1-62086-302-2(2))* Mascot Bks., Inc.

Venema, Lisa J. & Garland, Lynn Rockwell. Periwinkle Island. Coppage, Merry Ann. 2006. 86p. (J). (gr. -1-3). per. 36.99 *(978-1-4259-1931-3(6))* AuthorHouse.

Venezia, Mike. Eat Your Peas, Louise! Snow, Pegeen. 2011. (Rookie Ready to Learn Ser.). 40p. (J). pap. 5.95 *(978-0-531-26709-7(1))*; (gr. -1-k). lib. bdg. 23.00 *(978-0-531-26527-7(7))* Scholastic Library Publishing. (Children's Pr.).

Venezia, Mike. Albert Einstein: Universal Genius. Venezia, Mike. (Getting to Know the World's Greatest Inventors & Scientists Ser.). (ENG.). 32p. (J). 2009. (gr. 3-4). pap. 6.95 *(978-0-531-22206-5(3)*, Children's Pr.); 2008. (gr. 2-5). 28.00 *(978-0-531-14975-1(7))* Scholastic Library Publishing.

—Alexander Graham Bell: Setting the Tone for Communication. Venezia, Mike. (Getting to Know the World's Greatest Inventors & Scientists Ser.). (ENG.). 32p. (J). 2009. (gr. 3-4). pap. 6.95 *(978-0-531-22207-2(1)*, Children's Pr.); 2008. (gr. 2-5). 28.00 *(978-0-531-14976-8(5))* Scholastic Library Publishing.

—Andrew Jackson. Venezia, Mike. 2005. (Getting to Know the U. S. Presidents Ser.). (ENG.). 32p. (J). (gr. 3-4). 28.00 *(978-0-516-22612-5(6)*, Children's Pr.) Scholastic Library Publishing.

—Andrew Jackson: Seventh President, 1829-1837. Venezia, Mike. 2005. (Getting to Know the U. S. Presidents Ser.). (ENG.). 32p. (J). (gr. 3-4). per. 7.95 *(978-0-516-27481-2(3)*, Children's Pr.) Scholastic Library Publishing.

—Andrew Johnson: Seventeenth President. Venezia, Mike. 2005. (Getting to Know the U. S. Presidents Ser.). (ENG.). 32p. (J). (gr. 3-7). lib. bdg. 28.00 *(978-0-516-22622-4(3)*, Children's Pr.) Scholastic Library Publishing.

—Benjamin Franklin: Electrified the World with New Ideas. Venezia, Mike. 2009. (Getting to Know the World's Greatest Inventors & Scientists Ser.). (ENG.). 32p. (J). (gr. 2-5). 28.00 *(978-0-531-23701-4(X))* Scholastic Library Publishing.

—Benjamin Harrison. Venezia, Mike. 2006. (Getting to Know the U. S. Presidents Ser.). (ENG.). 32p. (J). (gr. 3-7). lib. bdg. 28.00 *(978-0-516-22628-6(2)*, Children's Pr.) Scholastic Library Publishing.

—Bill Clinton: Forty-Second President, 1993-2001. Venezia, Mike. 2007. (Getting to Know the U. S. Presidents Ser.). (ENG.). 32p. (J). (gr. 3-4). 28.00 *(978-0-516-22646-0(0)*, Children's Pr.) Scholastic Library Publishing.

—Camille Pissarro. Venezia, Mike. 2004. (Getting. . Know Artists Ser.). (ENG.). 32p. (J). (gr. 3-4). pap. 6.95 *(978-0-516-26977-1(1)*, Children's Pr.) Scholastic Library Publishing.

—Charles Drew: Doctor Who Got the World Pumped up to Donate Blood. Venezia, Mike. 2009. (Getting to Know the World's Greatest Inventors & Scientists Ser.). (ENG.). 32p. (J). (gr. 3-4). pap. 6.95 *(978-0-531-21334-6(X)*, Children's Pr.); (gr. 2-5). 28.00 *(978-0-531-23725-0(7))* Scholastic Library Publishing.

—Chester A. Arthur. Venezia, Mike. 2006. (Getting to Know the U. S. Presidents Ser.). (ENG.). 32p. (J). (gr. 3-7). lib. bdg. 28.00 *(978-0-516-22626-2(6)*, Children's Pr.) Scholastic Library Publishing.

—Chester A. Arthur: Twenty-First President, 1881-1885. Venezia, Mike. 2006. (Getting to Know the U. S. Presidents Ser.). (ENG.). 32p. (J). (gr. 3-7). pap. 7.95 *(978-0-516-25401-2(4)*, Children's Pr.) Scholastic Library Publishing.

—Claude Monet. Venezia, Mike. rev. ed. 2014. (Getting to Know the World's Greatest Artists Ser.). (ENG.). 40p. (J). lib. bdg. 29.00 *(978-0-531-21979-9(8))* Scholastic Library Publishing.

Venezia, Mike. Diego Rivera. Venezia, Mike. 2015. (Getting to Know the World's Greatest Artists Ser.). (ENG.). 40p. (J). lib. bdg. 29.00 ***(978-0-531-21261-5(0)***, Children's Pr.) Scholastic Library Publishing.

Venezia, Mike. Diego Velázquez. Venezia, Mike. 2004. (Getting to Know the World's Greatest Artists Ser.). (ENG.). 32p. (J). (gr. 3-4). pap. 6.95 *(978-0-516-26980-1(1)*, Children's Pr.) Scholastic Library Publishing.

—Dwight D. Eisenhower: Thirty-Fourth President 1953-1961. Venezia, Mike. 2007. (Getting to Know the U. S. Presidents Ser.). 32p. (J). (gr. 3-4). 28.00 *(978-0-516-22638-5(X)*, Children's Pr.) Scholastic Library Publishing.

—Eugene Delacroix. Venezia, Mike. 2003. (Getting to Know World Artists Ser.). (ENG.). 32p. (J). 28.00 *(978-0-516-22576-0(6)*, Children's Pr.) Scholastic Library Publishing.

—Eugène Delacroix. Venezia, Mike. 2003. (Getting to Know the World's Greatest Artists Ser.). (ENG.). 32p. (J). pap. 6.95 *(978-0-516-26976-4(3)*, Children's Pr.) Scholastic Library Publishing.

—Faith Ringgold. Venezia, Mike. (Getting to Know the World's Greatest Artists Ser.). (ENG.). 32p. (J). (gr. 3-4). 2008. pap. 6.95 *(978-0-531-14757-3(6))*; 2007. 28.00 *(978-0-531-18526-1(5))* Scholastic Library Publishing. (Children's Pr.).

—Franklin Pierce: Fourteenth President. Venezia, Mike. 2005. (Getting to Know the U. S. Presidents Ser.). (ENG.). 32p. (J). (gr. 3-7). lib. bdg. 28.00 *(978-0-516-22619-4(3)*, Children's Pr.) Scholastic Library Publishing.

—Frederic Remington. Venezia, Mike. 2003. (Getting to Know the World's Greatest Artists Ser.). (ENG.). 32p. (J). (gr. 3-4). pap. 6.95 *(978-0-516-27812-4(6)*, Children's Pr.) Scholastic Library Publishing.

Venezia, Mike. Frida Kahlo. Venezia, Mike. 2015. (Getting to Know the World's Greatest Artists Ser.). (ENG.). 40p. (J). lib. bdg. 29.00 ***(978-0-531-21259-2(9)***, Children's Pr.) Scholastic Library Publishing.

Venezia, Mike. George Bush. Venezia, Mike. 2008. (Getting to Know the U. S. Presidents Ser.). (ENG.). 32p. (J). (gr. 3-4). pap. 7.95 *(978-0-516-25536-1(3)*, Children's Pr.) Scholastic Library Publishing.

—George Washington. Venezia, Mike. 2005. (Getting to Know the U. S. Presidents Ser.). (ENG.). 32p. (J). (gr. 3-4). pap. 7.95 *(978-0-516-27475-1(9)*, Children's Pr.) Scholastic Library Publishing.

—Georges Seurat. Venezia, Mike. Seurat, Georges. 2003. (Getting. . Know Artists Ser.). (ENG.). 32p. (J). (gr. 3-4). pap. 6.95 *(978-0-516-27813-1(4)*, Children's Pr.) Scholastic Library Publishing.

—Georgia O'Keefe. Venezia, Mike. 2015. (Getting to Know the World's Greatest Artists Ser.). (ENG.). 40p. (J). pap. 7.95 *(978-0-531-21291-2(2))* Scholastic Library Publishing.

—Gerald R. Ford: Thirty-Eighth President, 1974-1977. Venezia, Mike. (Getting to Know the U. S. Presidents Ser.). (ENG.). 32p. (J). (gr. 3-4). 2008. pap. 7.95 *(978-0-516-25597-2(5))*; 2007. 28.00 *(978-0-516-22642-2(8))* Scholastic Library Publishing. (Children's Pr.).

—Getting to Know the World's Greatest Artists - Titian. Venezia, Mike. 2003. (Getting to Know the World's Greatest Artists Ser.). (ENG.). 32p. (J). (gr. 3-4). pap. 6.95 *(978-0-516-26975-7(5)*, Children's Pr.) Scholastic Library Publishing.

—Grandma Moses. Venezia, Mike. 2004. (Getting to Know the World's Greatest Artists Ser.). (ENG.). 32p. (J). (gr. 3-4). pap. 6.95 *(978-0-516-27913-8(0)*, Children's Pr.) Scholastic Library Publishing.

—Grover Cleveland: Twenty-Second & Twenty-Fourth President, 1885-1889, 1893-1897. Venezia, Mike. 2006. (Getting to Know the U. S. Presidents Ser.). (ENG.). 32p. (J). (gr. 3-7). pap. 7.95 *(978-0-516-25402-9(2))*; lib. bdg. 28.00 *(978-0-516-22627-9(4))* Scholastic Library Publishing. (Children's Pr.).

—Harry S. Truman: Thirty-Third President. Venezia, Mike. 2007. (Getting to Know the U. S. Presidents Ser.). 32p. (J). (gr. 3-4). 28.00 *(978-0-516-22637-8(1)*, Children's Pr.) Scholastic Library Publishing.

—Henry Ford: Big Wheel in the Auto Industry. Venezia, Mike. 2009. (Getting to Know the World's Greatest Inventors & Scientists Ser.). (ENG.). 32p. (J). (gr. 3-4). pap. 6.95 *(978-0-531-21335-3(8)*, Children's Pr.); (gr. 2-5). 28.00 *(978-0-531-23726-7(5))* Scholastic Library Publishing.

—Horace Pippin. Venezia, Mike. (Getting to Know the World's Greatest Artists Ser.). (ENG.). 32p. (J). (gr. 3-4). 2008. pap. 6.95 *(978-0-531-14758-0(4))*; 2007. 28.00 *(978-0-531-18527-8(3))* Scholastic Library Publishing. (Children's Pr.).

—James A. Garfield. Venezia, Mike. 2006. (Getting to Know the U. S. Presidents Ser.). (ENG.). 32p. (J). (gr. 3-7). lib. bdg. 28.00 *(978-0-516-22625-5(8)*, Children's Pr.) Scholastic Library Publishing.

—James Buchanan: Fifteenth President. Venezia, Mike. 2005. (Getting to Know the U. S. Presidents Ser.). (ENG.). 32p. (J). (gr. 3-7). lib. bdg. 28.00 *(978-0-516-22620-0(7)*, Children's Pr.) Scholastic Library Publishing.

—James K. Polk: Eleventh President, 1845-1849. Venezia, Mike. 2005. (Getting to Know the U. S. Presidents Ser.). (ENG.). 32p. (J). (gr. 3-4). 28.00 *(978-0-516-22616-3(9)*, Children's Pr.) Scholastic Library Publishing.

—James McNeill Whistler. Venezia, Mike. 2003. (Getting to Know World Artists Ser.). (ENG.). 32p. (J). 28.00 *(978-0-516-22578-4(2)*, Children's Pr.) Scholastic Library Publishing.

—James Monroe. Venezia, Mike. 2005. (Getting to Know the U. S. Presidents Ser.). (ENG.). 32p. (J). (gr. 3-4). pap. 7.95 *(978-0-516-27479-9(1)*, Children's Pr.) Scholastic Library Publishing.

—Jane Goodall: Researcher Who Champions Chimps. Venezia, Mike. 2010. (Getting to Know the World's Greatest Inventors & Scientists Ser.). (ENG.). 32p. (J). (gr. 3-4). 28.00 *(978-0-531-23731-1(1))* Scholastic Library Publishing.

—Jimmy Carter: Thirty-Ninth President 1977-1981. Venezia, Mike. 2007. (Getting to Know the U. S. Presidents Ser.). (ENG.). 32p. (J). (gr. 3-4). 28.00 *(978-0-516-22643-9(6)*, Children's Pr.) Scholastic Library Publishing.

—John Quincy Adams: Sixth President, 1825-1829. Venezia, Mike. 2005. (Getting to Know the U. S. Presidents Ser.). (ENG.). 32p. (J). (gr. 3-4). pap. 7.95 *(978-0-516-27480-5(5)*, Children's Pr.) Scholastic Library Publishing.

—John Tyler: Tenth President, 1841-1845. Venezia, Mike. 2005. (Getting to Know the U. S. Presidents Ser.). (ENG.). 32p. (J). (gr. 3-4). per. 7.95 *(978-0-516-27484-3(8))*; 28.00 *(978-0-516-22615-6(0))* Scholastic Library Publishing. (Children's Pr.).

—Leonardo Davinci. Venezia, Mike. rev. ed. 2015. (Getting to Know the World's Greatest Artists Ser.). (ENG.). 40p. (J). pap. 7.95 *(978-0-531-21289-9(0))* Scholastic Library Publishing.

—Lise Meitner: Had the Right Vision about Nuclear Fission. Venezia, Mike. (Getting to Know the World's Greatest Inventors & Scientists Ser.). (ENG.). 32p. (J). 2010. (gr. 3-4). pap. 6.95 *(978-0-531-20776-5(5)*, Children's Pr.); 2009. (gr. 2-5). 28.00 *(978-0-531-23702-1(8))* Scholastic Library Publishing.

—Luis Alvarez: Wild Idea Man. Venezia, Mike. (Getting to Know the World's Greatest Inventors & Scientists Ser.). (ENG.). 32p. (J). 2010. (gr. 3-4). pap. 6.95 *(978-0-531-20777-2(3)*, Children's Pr.); 2009. (gr. 2-5). 28.00 *(978-0-531-23703-8(6))* Scholastic Library Publishing.

—Lyndon B. Johnson: Thirty-Sixth President, 1963-1969. Venezia, Mike. 2007. (Getting to Know the U. S. Presidents Ser.). 32p. (J). (gr. 3-4). 28.00 *(978-0-516-22640-8(1)*, Children's Pr.) Scholastic Library Publishing.

—Marie Curie: Scientist Who Made Glowing Discoveries. Venezia, Mike. (Getting to Know the World's Greatest Inventors & Scientists Ser.). (ENG.). 32p. (J). 2009. (gr. 3-4). pap. 6.95 *(978-0-531-22208-9(X)*, Children's Pr.);

V

2008. (gr. 2-5). 28.00 *(978-0-531-14977-5(3))* Scholastic Library Publishing.

—Martin Van Buren. Venezia, Mike. 2005. (Getting to Know the U. S. Presidents Ser.). (ENG.). 32p. (J). (gr. 3-4). 28.00 *(978-0-516-22613-2(4)*, Children's Pr.) Scholastic Library Publishing.

—Mary Cassatt. Venezia, Mike. rev. ed. 2015. (Getting to Know the World's Greatest Artists Ser.). (ENG.). 40p. (J). pap. 7.95 *(978-0-531-21292-9(0))* Scholastic Library Publishing.

—Mary Leakey - Archaeologist Who Really Dug Her Work. Venezia, Mike. 2009. (Getting to Know the World's Greatest Inventors & Scientists Ser.). (ENG.). 32p. (J). (gr. 2-5). 28.00 *(978-0-531-23727-4(3))* Scholastic Library Publishing.

—Michelangelo. Venezia, Mike. rev. ed. 2014. (Getting to Know the World's Greatest Artists Ser.). (ENG.). 40p. (J). lib. bdg. 29.00 *(978-0-531-21977-5(1))* Scholastic Library Publishing.

—Millard Fillmore: Thirteenth President. Venezia, Mike. 2005. (Getting to Know the U. S. Presidents Ser.). (ENG.). 32p. (J). (gr. 3-7). lib. bdg. 28.00 *(978-0-516-22618-7(5)*, Children's Pr.) Scholastic Library Publishing.

—Millard Fillmore: Thirteenth President, 1850-1853. Venezia, Mike. 2006. (Getting to Know the U. S. Presidents Ser.). (ENG.). 32p. (J). (gr. 3-7). per. 7.95 *(978-0-516-25487-6(1)*, Children's Pr.) Scholastic Library Publishing.

—Pablo Picasso. Venezia, Mike. 2014. (Getting to Know the World's Greatest Artists Ser.). (ENG.). 40p. (J). pap. 7.95 *(978-0-531-22537-0(2))*; lib. bdg. 29.00 *(978-0-531-21976-8(3))* Scholastic Library Publishing.

—Rachel Carson: Clearing the Way for Environmental Protection. Venezia, Mike. (Getting to Know the World's Greatest Inventors & Scientists Ser.). (ENG.). 32p. (J). 2010. (gr. 3-4). pap. 6.95 *(978-0-531-20778-9(1)*, Children's Pr.); 2009. (gr. 2-5). 28.00 *(978-0-531-23704-5(4))* Scholastic Library Publishing.

—Rembrandt. Venezia, Mike. rev. ed. 2015. (Getting to Know the World's Greatest Artists Ser.). (ENG.). 40p. (J). pap. 7.95 *(978-0-531-21290-5(4))* Scholastic Library Publishing.

—René Magritte. Venezia, Mike. Magritte, Rene. 2003. (Getting to Know the World's Greatest Artists Ser.). (ENG.). 32p. (J). (gr. 3-4). pap. 6.95 *(978-0-516-27814-8(2)*, Children's Pr.) Scholastic Library Publishing.

—Richard M. Nixon: Thirty-Seventh President, 1969-1974. Venezia, Mike. 2007. (Getting to Know the U. S. Presidents Ser.). 32p. (J). (gr. 3-4). (ENG.). pap. 7.95 *(978-0-531-17949-9(4))*; 28.00 *(978-0-516-22641-5(X))* Scholastic Library Publishing. (Children's Pr.).

—Ronald Reagan: Fortieth President, 1981-1989. Venezia, Mike. 2007. (Getting to Know the U. S. Presidents Ser.). (ENG.). 32p. (J). (gr. 3-4). 28.00 *(978-0-516-22644-6(4)*, Children's Pr.) Scholastic Library Publishing.

—Rutherford B. Hayes: Nineteenth President, 1877-1881. Venezia, Mike. 2006. (Getting to Know the U. S. Presidents Ser.). 32p. (J). (gr. 3-7). pap. 7.95 *(978-0-516-25404-3(9))*; (ENG.). lib. bdg. 28.00 *(978-0-516-22624-8(X))* Scholastic Library Publishing. (Children's Pr.).

Venezia, Mike. Salvador Dalí. Venezia, Mike. 2015. (Getting to Know the World's Greatest Artists Ser.). (ENG.). 40p. (J). lib. bdg. 29.00 ***(978-0-531-21262-2(9)***, Children's Pr.) Scholastic Library Publishing.

Venezia, Mike. Stephen Hawking: Cosmologist Who Gets a Big Bang Out of the Universe. Venezia, Mike. 2009. (Getting to Know the World's Greatest Inventors & Scientists Ser.). (ENG.). 32p. (J). (gr. 3-4). pap. 6.95 *(978-0-531-21337-7(4)*, Children's Pr.); (gr. 2-5). 28.00 *(978-0-531-23728-1(1))* Scholastic Library Publishing.

—Thomas Edison: Inventor with a Lot of Bright Ideas. Venezia, Mike. (Getting to Know the World's Greatest Inventors & Scientists Ser.). (ENG.). 32p. (J). 2009. (gr. 3-4). pap. 6.95 *(978-0-531-22209-6(8)*, Children's Pr.); 2008. (gr. 2-5). 28.00 *(978-0-531-14978-2(1))* Scholastic Library Publishing.

—Thomas Jefferson: Third President, 1801-1809. Venezia, Mike. (Getting to Know the U. S. Presidents Ser.). (ENG.). (J). 2005. 32p. (gr. 3-4). pap. 7.95 *(978-0-516-27477-5(5))*; 2004. 28.00 *(978-0-516-22608-8(8))* Scholastic Library Publishing. (Children's Pr.).

—Titian. Venezia, Mike. 2003. (Getting to Know World Artists Ser.). (ENG.). 32p. (J). 28.00 *(978-0-516-22575-3(8)*, Children's Pr.) Scholastic Library Publishing.

—Ulysses S. Grant. Venezia, Mike. 2005. (Getting to Know the U. S. Presidents Ser.). (ENG.). 32p. (J). (gr. 3-7). lib. bdg. 28.00 *(978-0-516-22623-1(1)*, Children's Pr.) Scholastic Library Publishing.

—Vincent Van Gogh. Venezia, Mike. rev. ed. 2014. (Getting to Know the World's Greatest Artists Ser.). (ENG.). 40p. (J). lib. bdg. 29.00 *(978-0-531-21978-2(X))* Scholastic Library Publishing.

—Warren G. Harding: Twenty-Ninth President, 1921-1923. Venezia, Mike. 2006. (Getting to Know the U. S. Presidents Ser.). (ENG.). 32p. (J). (gr. 3-7). lib. bdg. 28.00 *(978-0-516-22633-0(9))* Scholastic Library Publishing.

—William Henry Harrison. Venezia, Mike. 2005. (Getting to Know the U. S. Presidents Ser.). (ENG.). 32p. (J). (gr. 3-4). 28.00 *(978-0-516-22614-9(2)*, Children's Pr.) Scholastic Library Publishing.

—William Henry Harrison: Ninth President 1841. Venezia, Mike. 2005. (Getting to Know the U. S. Presidents Ser.). (ENG.). 32p. (J). (gr. 3-4). per. 7.95 *(978-0-516-27483-6(X)*, Children's Pr.) Scholastic Library Publishing.

—William Howard Taft: Twenty-Seventh President. Venezia, Mike. 2007. (Getting to Know the U. S. Presidents Ser.). 32p. (J). (gr. 3-7). pap. 7.95 *(978-0-516-25239-1(9)*, Children's Pr.) Scholastic Library Publishing.

—William McKinley. Venezia, Mike. 2006. (Getting to Know the U. S. Presidents Ser.). (ENG.). 32p. (J). (gr. 3-7). lib. bdg. 28.00 *(978-0-516-22629-3(0)*, Children's Pr.) Scholastic Library Publishing.

—Winslow Homer. Venezia, Mike. 2004. (Getting . Know Artists Ser.). (ENG.). 32p. (J). (gr. 3-4). pap. 6.95 *(978-0-516-26979-5(8)*, Children's Pr.) Scholastic Library Publishing.

—Woodrow Wilson: Twenty-Eighth President. Venezia, Mike. 2007. (Getting to Know the U. S. Presidents Ser.). 32p. (J). (gr. 3-7). pap. 7.95 *(978-0-516-25462-3(6)*, Children's Pr.) Scholastic Library Publishing.

—The Wright Brothers: Inventors Whose Ideas Really Took Flight. Venezia, Mike. 2010. (Getting to Know the World's Greatest Inventors & Scientists Ser.). (ENG.). 32p. (J). (gr. 3-4). 28.00 *(978-0-531-23732-8(X))* Scholastic Library Publishing.

—Zachary Taylor: Twelfth President, 1849-1850. Venezia, Mike. 2005. (Getting to Know the U. S. Presidents Ser.). (ENG.). 32p. (J). (gr. 3-4). 28.00 *(978-0-516-22617-0(7)*, Children's Pr.) Scholastic Library Publishing.

Venkatakrishnan, Rames. Roadside Geology of Virginia. Frye, Keith. Alt, David & Hyndman, Donald W., eds. rev. ed. (Roadside Geology Ser.). 256p. (J). (gr. 4). pap. *(978-0-87842-199-2(8)*, 211) Mountain Pr. Publishing Co., Inc.

Veno, Joe. Count to Sleep Florida. Gamble, Adam & Jasper, Mark. 2014. (ENG.). 20p. (J). (-k). bds. 7.95 *(978-1-60219-202-7(2))* Our World of Books.

—Count to Sleep Michigan. Gamble, Adam & Jasper, Mark. 2014. (ENG.). 20p. (J). (-k). bds. 7.95 *(978-1-60219-327-7(4))* Our World of Books.

—Count to Sleep Wisconsin. Gamble, Adam & Jasper, Mark. 2014. (ENG.). 20p. (J). (-k). bds. 7.95 *(978-1-60219-328-4(2))* Our World of Books.

—Good Night Alabama. Gamble, Adam & Jasper, Mark. 2015. (ENG.). 20p. (J). (— 1). bds. 9.95 *(978-1-60219-220-1(0))* Our World of Books.

—Good Night Atlanta. Gamble, Adam. 2007. (Good Night Our World Ser.). (ENG.). 22p. (J). (gr. k — 1). bds. 9.95 *(978-1-60219-001-6(1))* Our World of Books.

—Good Night Boston. Gamble, Adam. 2005. (J). bds. 9.95 *(978-0-9758502-4-4(5))* On Cape Pubns.

—Good Night Boston. Gamble, Adam. 2007. (Good Night Our World Ser.). (ENG.). 20p. (J). (gr. k — 1). bds. 9.95 *(978-1-60219-003-0(8))* Our World of Books.

—Good Night Chicago. Gamble, Adam. 2006. (Good Night Our World Ser.). (ENG.). 20p. (J). (gr. k — 1). bds. 9.95 *(978-0-9777979-2-9(9))* Our World of Books.

—Good Night Denver. Bouse, Susan & Gamble, Adam. 2007. (Good Night Our World Ser.). (ENG.). 20p. (J). (gr. k — 1). bds. 9.95 *(978-1-60219-006-1(2))* Our World of Books.

—Good Night Hawaii. Gamble, Adam. 2007. (Good Night Our World Ser.). (ENG.). 20p. (J). (gr. k — 1). bds. 9.95 *(978-1-60219-007-8(0))* Our World of Books.

Veno, Joe, et al. Good Night Maryland. Gamble, Adam & Jasper, Mark. 2011. (Good Night Our World Ser.). (ENG.). 20p. (J). (gr. k — 1). bds. 9.95 *(978-1-60219-046-7(1))* Our World of Books.

Veno, Joe. Good Night Minnesota. Gamble, Adam. 2009. (Good Night Our World Ser.). (ENG.). 20p. (J). (gr. k — 1). bds. 9.95 *(978-1-60219-034-4(8))* Our World of Books.

—Good Night Mississippi. Gamble, Adam & Jasper, Mark. 2015. (ENG.). 20p. (J). (— 1). bds. 9.95 *(978-1-60219-221-8(9))* Our World of Books.

—Good Night Missouri. Gamble, Adam & Jasper, Mark. 2013. (Good Night Our World Ser.). (ENG.). 20p. (J). (— 1). bds. 9.95 *(978-1-60219-077-1(1))* Our World of Books.

—Good Night New Jersey. Gamble, Adam & Clark, Dennis. 2008. (Good Night Our World Ser.). (ENG.). 20p. (J). (gr. k — 1). bds. 9.95 *(978-1-60219-025-2(9))* Our World of Books.

—Good Night New York City. Gamble, Adam. 2006. (Good Night Our World Ser.). (ENG.). 24p. (J). (gr. k — 1). bds. 9.95 *(978-0-9777979-3-6(7))* Our World of Books.

—Good Night Oregon. McCarthy, Dan & Rosen, Anne. 2010. (Good Night Our World Ser.). (ENG.). 20p. (J). (gr. k — 1). bds. 9.95 *(978-1-60219-041-2(0))* Our World of Books.

Veno, Joe. Good Night Race Cars. Gamble, Adam & Jasper, Mark. 2015. (ENG.). 20p. (J). (— 1). bds. 9.95 ***(978-1-60219-228-7(6))*** Our World of Books.

Veno, Joe. Good Night Seattle. Steere, Jay & Gamble, Adam. 2007. (Good Night Our World Ser.). (ENG.). 20p. (J). (gr. k — 1). bds. 9.95 *(978-1-60219-014-6(3))* Our World of Books.

—Good Night Tennessee. Gamble, Adam. 2007. (Good Night Our World Ser.). (ENG.). 20p. (J). (gr. k — 1). bds. 9.95 *(978-1-60219-019-1(4))* Our World of Books.

—Good Night Virginia. Gamble, Adam. 2008. (Good Night Our World Ser.). (ENG.). 20p. (J). (gr. k — 1). bds. 9.95 *(978-1-60219-026-9(7))* Our World of Books.

—Good Night Washington, DC. Gamble, Adam. 2006. (Good Night Our World Ser.). (ENG.). 20p. (J). (gr. k — 1). bds. 9.95 *(978-0-9777979-1-2(0))* Our World of Books.

—What's Eating You, Girls 'n Boysenberries? Hirschfield, Beth. 2009. 32p. (J). 16.95 *(978-0-9818126-3-2(5)*, Ampersand) Ampersand, Inc.

Veno, Joe & Hansen, Red. Good Night Arizona. Gamble, Adam. 2008. (Good Night Our World Ser.). (ENG.). 20p. (J). (gr. k — 1). bds. 9.95 *(978-1-60219-000-9(3))* Our World of Books.

—Good Night Florida. Gamble, Adam & Jasper, Mark. 2nd ed. 2010. (Good Night Our World Ser.). (ENG.). 20p. (J). (gr. k — 1). bds. 9.95 *(978-1-60219-045-0(3))* Our World of Books.

Veno, Joe & Jasper, Mark. Buenas Noches, Nueva York. Gamble, Adam. 2013. (Good Night Our World Ser.). (SPA & ENG.). 24p. (J). (— 1). bds. 9.95 *(978-1-60219-091-7(7))* Our World of Books.

Veno, Joe & Kelly, Cooper. Good Night Ocean. Jasper, Mark & Kelly, Cooper. 2009. (Good Night Our World Ser.). (ENG.). 28p. (J). (gr. k — 1). bds. 9.95 *(978-1-60219-036-8(4))* Our World of Books.

—Good Night Texas. Gamble, Adam. 2nd ed. 2011. (Good Night Our World Ser.). (ENG.). 20p. (J). (gr. k — 1). bds. 9.95 *(978-1-60219-053-5(4))* Our World of Books.

—Good Night Toronto. Gamble, Adam & Jasper, Mark. 2011. (Good Night Our World Ser.). (ENG.). 20p. (J). (gr. k — 1). bds. 9.95 *(978-1-60219-048-1(8))* Our World of Books.

—Good Night Washington State. Gamble, Adam & Jasper, Mark. 2012. (Good Night Our World Ser.). (ENG.). 20p. (J). (gr. k — 1). bds. 9.95 *(978-1-60219-072-6(0))* Our World of Books.

Veno, Joe & Rosen, Anne. Good Night Vancouver. Adams, David J. 2010. (Good Night Our World Ser.). (ENG.). 28p. (J). (gr. k — 1). bds. 9.95 *(978-1-60219-039-9(9))* Our World of Books.

Veno, Joe, jt. illus. see Rosen, Anne.

Vent des Hove, Yaël. Mama, Me Cuentas un Cuento? Vent des Hove, Yaël. Vent des Hove, Yaël. 2006. (SPA.). 32p. (J). (gr. -1-k). 20.99 *(978-84-261-3527-8(7))* Lectorum Pubns., Inc.

Ventling, Elisabeth. Scoop. Cook, Julia. 2007. 32p. (J). 15.95 *(978-1-934073-07-0(5))* National Ctr. For Youth Issues.

Ventura, Marco. C Is for Ciao: An Italy Alphabet. Grodin, Elissa D. et al. 2008. (Discover the World Ser.). (ENG.). 40p. (J). (gr. 1-5). 17.95 *(978-1-58536-361-2(8))* Sleeping Bear Pr.

Ventura, Piero. Historia Ilustrada de la Humanidad: La Comunicación. Ventura, Piero. Piero, Ventura. (SPA.). 64p. (YA). (gr. 5-8). *(978-84-241-5902-3(0))* Everest Editora ESP. Dist: Lectorum Pubns., Inc.

Venturi-Pickett, Stacy. Jonah & the Fish: Based on Jonah 1-3:3. Pingry, Patricia A. 2005. (Stories from the Bible Ser.). (ENG.). 26p. (J). (gr. -1-k). bds. 6.95 *(978-0-8249-6626-3(0))* Ideals Pubns.

—The Story of Loaves & Fishes. Pingry, Patricia A. 2003. 26p. (J). bds. 6.95 *(978-0-8249-6518-1(3))* Ideals Pubns.

—The Story of Mary. Pingry, Patricia A. 2006. (ENG.). 32p. (J). (gr. -1-3). pap. 3.95 *(978-0-8249-5546-5(3))* Ideals Pubns.

—The Story of Noah. Pingry, Patricia A. 2007. (ENG.). 32p. (J). (gr. -1-3). per. 3.99 *(978-0-8249-5569-4(2)*, Ideals Children's Bks.) Ideals Pubns.

—The Story of Thanksgiving. Skarmeas, Nancy J. 2012. 22p. (J). bds. 6.99 *(978-0-8249-1883-5(5)*, Candy Cane Pr.) Ideals Pubns.

—The Story of the Ten Commandments. Pingry, Patricia A. (ENG.). (J). 2008. 32p. (gr. k-3). pap. 3.99 *(978-0-8249-5554-0(4)*, Ideals Children's Bks.); 2006. 26p. (gr. -1-3). bds. 10.95 *(978-0-8249-6656-0(2)*, Candy Cane Pr.) Ideals Pubns.

Venturi-Pickett, Stacy. The Story of Creation. Venturi-Pickett, Stacy, tr. Pingry, Patricia A., tr. 2003. 26p. (J). bds. 7.95 *(978-0-8249-6504-4(3))* Ideals Pubns.

Venturini, Claudia. Ali Baba & the Forty Thieves. 2009. (Flip-Up Fairy Tales Ser.). (ENG.). 24p. (J). (gr. -1-2). pap. *(978-1-84643-251-4(0))* Child's Play International Ltd.

Venturini, Claudia. The Elves & the Trendy Shoes. Foster, Evelyn. 2015. (ENG.). 32p. (J). ***(978-0-7787-1932-8(4))*** Crabtree Publishing Co.

Venturini, Claudia. Tom Thumb. 2007. (Flip-Up Fairy Tales Ser.). (ENG.). 24p. (J). (gr. -1-2). *(978-1-84643-157-9(3))*; *(978-1-84643-116-6(6))* Child's Play International Ltd.

—Tom Thumb: Flip up Fairy Tales. 2008. (Flip-Up Fairy Tales Ser.). (ENG.). 24p. (J). *(978-1-84643-196-8(4))* Child's Play International Ltd.

Venus, Joanna. Starting Fishing - Internet Linked. Patchett, Fiona. rev. ed. 2004. (First Skills Ser.). 32p. (J). pap. 4.95 *(978-0-7945-0672-8(0)*, Usborne) EDC Publishing.

Vera, Andrew. Roy G. Biv Is Mad at Me Because I Love Pink! Guettier, Nancy. 2013. (Morgan James Kids Ser.). (ENG.). 36p. (gr. -1-2). pap. 9.95 *(978-1-61448-671-8(9)*, 9781614486718) Morgan James Publishing.

Vera, Luisa. Ali Baba & the Forty Thieves. 2004. (J). *(978-1-84444-536-3(4))* Mantra Lingua.

Verano, Vladimir. Graveyard of a Queen. Xu, Lei. Mok, Kathy, tr. 2014. (Grave Robbers' Chronicles Ser.: 6). (ENG.). pap. 9.95 *(978-1-934159-36-1(0))* ThingsAsian Pr.

—The Prince, the Demon King, & the Monkey Warrior. 2011. (ENG.). 96p. (J). (gr. 3-6). pap. 9.95 *(978-1-934159-30-9(1))* ThingsAsian Pr.

Verbeck, Frank. Donegal Fairy Stories. MacManus, Seumas. 2012. (Dover Children's Classics Ser.). (ENG.). 288p. (J). (gr. 3-8). pap. 8.95 *(978-0-486-21971-4(2))* Dover Pubns., Inc.

Vercesi, Anthony. Plays to Play with in Class. Milgrim, Sally-Anne. 2003. (Plays & Play Collections). 216p. (YA). (gr. 8-12). pap. 11.00 *(978-0-89390-060-1(5))* Resource Pubns., Inc.

Verdoux, Aurélia. Theo at the Beach. Crupi, Jaclyn. 2013. (J). *(978-1-4351-4722-5(7))* Barnes & Noble, Inc.

Verdu, Jeanyves, jt. illus. see Niepold, Mil.

Vere, Ed. Too Noisy! DOYLE, Malachy. 2012. (ENG.). 32p. (J). (gr. -1-2). 15.99 *(978-0-7636-6226-4(7))* Candlewick Pr.

Vere, Ed. Banana! Vere, Ed. 2010. (ENG.). 32p. (J). (gr. -1 — 1). 12.99 *(978-0-8050-9214-1(5)*, Holt, Henry & Co. Bks. For Young Readers) Holt, Henry & Co.

—Bedtime for Monsters. Vere, Ed. 2012. (ENG.). 32p. (J). (gr. -1-k). 14.99 *(978-0-8050-9509-8(8)*, Holt, Henry & Co. Bks. For Young Readers) Holt, Henry & Co.

Verelst, Suana. Next Week When I'm Big. Guggenheim, Jaenet. l.t. ed. 2005. 32p. (J). (gr. -1-2). 19.95l *(978-1-929115-13-6(X))* Azro Pr., Inc.

—Razia's Ray of Hope: One Girl's Dream of an Education. Suneby, Elizabeth. 2013. (CitizenKid Ser.). (ENG.). 32p. (J). 18.95 *(978-1-55453-816-4(5))* Kids Can Pr., Ltd. CAN. Dist: Univ. of Toronto Pr.

Veres, Laszlo. 3-D Explorer: Bugs. Green, Jen. 2013. (3D Explorers Ser.). (ENG.). 32p. (J). (gr. 1). 17.95 *(978-1-60710-536-7(5)*, Silver Dolphin Bks.) Baker & Taylor Publishing Group.

—3-D Explorer: Predators. Taylor, Barbara. 2014. (3D Explorers Ser.). (ENG.). 32p. (J). (gr. 1). 19.95 *(978-1-60710-882-5(8)*, Silver Dolphin Bks.) Baker & Taylor Publishing Group.

Veres, Laszlo, jt. illus. see Keylock, Andy.

Verheijen, Jan. Mary's Little Donkey: And the Flight to Egypt. 1 vol. Sehlin, Gunhild. Latham, Hugh & Maclean, Donald, trs. from SWE. 2nd rev. ed. 2004. (ENG.). 160p. (J). (gr. 3-6). pap. 12.00 *(978-0-86315-064-7(0))* Floris Bks. GBR. Dist: SteinerBooks, Inc.

Verhoef, Sharon & Pinkham, Pamela. Something Wicked in the Land of Picatrix. Roland-James, Patricia & James, Robert L. Chidgey, Scarlett, ed. 2007. 281p. (J). pap. 12.95 *(978-0-9760789-9-9(6))* Aquila Ink Publishing.

Verhoosky, Michele. Big Green Gorilla. Fonte, Mary Roessler & Hoppe, Jessica. 2013. 34p. 17.99 *(978-1-937260-92-7(5))* Sleepytown Pr.

Verhoosky, Michele. Molly Marie & the Amazing Jimmy. Verhoosky, Michele. 2012. 34p. pap. 10.95 *(978-1-937260-22-4(4))* Sleepytown Pr.

Verhoye, Annabelle. The Book of the Sword. Asai, Carrie. 2003. (Samurai Girl Ser.: 1). (ENG.). 224p. (YA). (gr. 11). pap. 11.99 *(978-0-689-85948-9(1)*, Simon Pulse) Simon Pulse.

Verhoye, Annabelle & Alarcão, Renato. The Book of the Flame. Asai, Carrie. 2004. (Samurai Girl Ser.: 5). (ENG.). 224p. (YA). (gr. 11). pap. 6.99 *(978-0-689-86713-2(1)*, Simon Pulse) Simon Pulse.

Verhoye, Annabelle & Alarcao, Renato. The Book of the Pearl. Asai, Carrie. 2003. (Samurai Girl Ser.: 3). (ENG.). 240p. (YA). (gr. 11). pap. 6.99 *(978-0-689-86432-2(9)*, Simon Pulse) Simon Pulse.

Verhoye, Annabelle & Alarcão, Renato. The Book of the Wind. Asai, Carrie & Gray, Mitchel. 2003. (Samurai Girl Ser.: 4). (ENG.). 224p. (YA). (gr. 11). pap. 6.99 *(978-0-689-86433-9(7)*, Simon Pulse) Simon Pulse.

Verkruysse, Toni. A Gift from Grandma. Gould, Susan Lynn. 2013. 56p. pap. 20.50 *(978-1-61897-230-9(8)*, Strategic Bk. Publishing) Strategic Book Publishing & Rights Agency (SBPRA).

Verma, Dheeraj. The Battle of Gettysburg: Spilled Blood on Sacred Ground. Abnett, Dan. 2007. (Graphic Battles of the Civil War Ser.). (ENG.). 48p. (YA). (gr. 4-7). lib. bdg. 31.95 *(978-1-4042-0777-6(5))* Rosen Publishing Group, Inc., The.

—The Battle of the Wilderness: Deadly Inferno. Abnett, Dan. 2007. (Graphic Battles of the Civil War Ser.). (ENG.). 48p. (YA). (gr. 4-7). lib. bdg. 31.95 *(978-1-4042-0780-6(5))* Rosen Publishing Group, Inc., The.

—Goblins. Jeffrey, Gary. 2012. (Graphic Mythical Creatures Ser.). (ENG.). 24p. (J). (gr. 3-5). pap. 8.15 *(978-1-4339-6761-0(8))*; lib. bdg. 23.95 *(978-1-4339-6759-7(6))* Stevens, Gareth Publishing LLLP. (Gareth Stevens Learning Library).

—The Monitor Versus the Merrimac: Ironclads at War. Abnett, Dan. 2007. (Graphic Battles of the Civil War Ser.). (ENG.). 48p. (YA). (gr. 4-7). lib. bdg. 31.95 *(978-1-4042-0778-3(3))* Rosen Publishing Group, Inc., The.

—Unicorns. Jeffrey, Gary. 2012. (Graphic Mythical Creatures Ser.). (ENG.). 24p. (J). (gr. 3-5). pap. 8.15 *(978-1-4339-6769-6(3))*; lib. bdg. 23.95 *(978-1-4339-6767-2(7))* Stevens, Gareth Publishing LLLP. (Gareth Stevens Learning Library).

—Vampires. Jeffrey, Gary. 2012. (Graphic Mythical Creatures Ser.). (ENG.). 24p. (J). (gr. 3-5). pap. 8.15 *(978-1-4339-6773-3(1))*; lib. bdg. 23.95 *(978-1-4339-6771-9(5))* Stevens, Gareth Publishing LLLP. (Gareth Stevens Learning Library).

Vermeer, Jan. Elske: A Novel of the Kingdom. Voigt, Cynthia. 2003. (ENG.). 320p. (YA). (gr. 7). mass mkt. 6.99 *(978-0-689-86438-4(8)*, Simon Pulse) Simon Pulse.

Vermillion, Danny. Ducky Bill's Great Race. McGhee, Patti Gray. 2013. 46p. 24.95 *(978-1-63000-424-8(3))*; 48p. pap. 24.95 *(978-1-62709-522-8(5))* America Star Bks.

Verne, Jules. Viaje al Centro de la Tierra. Orig. Title: Journey to the Center of the Earth. (SPA.). 160p. (YA). 11.95 *(978-84-7281-084-6(4)*, AF1084) Auriga, Ediciones S.A. ESP. Dist: Continental Bk. Co., Inc.

—Viaje al Centro de la Tierra. 2003. (Advanced Reading Ser.). Orig. Title: Journey to the Center of the Earth. (SPA.). 246p. (J). pap. 11.95 *(978-84-239-9063-4(X))* Espasa Calpe, S.A. ESP. Dist: Planeta Publishing Corp.

Vernick, Audrey & Tate, Don. She Loved Baseball: The Effa Manley Story. Vernick, Audrey. 2010. (ENG.). 32p. (J). (gr. k-5). 16.99 *(978-0-06-134920-1(8)*, Collins) HarperCollins Pubs.

Vernon, Jeff. What Is Dreaming? Boritzer, Etan. 2007. 40p. (J). (gr. -1-3). 14.95 *(978-0-9762743-7-7(X))*; pap. 6.95 *(978-0-9762743-6-0(1))* Lane, Veronica Bks.

—What Is True? Boritzer, Etan. 2010. (J). *(978-0-9637597-0-2(1))* Lane, Veronica Bks.

Vernon, Rion. Sofa Boy. Langteau, Scott. 2008. (ENG.). 40p. 14.95 *(978-0-615-25125-7(0))* Shake the Moon Bks.

Vernon, Ursula. Dragonbreath. Vernon, Ursula. (Dragonbreath Ser.: 1). (ENG.). 160p. (J). (gr. 3-7). 2012. pap. 6.99 *(978-0-14-242095-9(6)*, Puffin); 2009. 12.99 *(978-0-8037-3363-3(1)*, Dial) Penguin Publishing Group.

Verona Publishing. Lazy Robert. DeRosa, Nancy. 2006. (J). 5.95 *(978-0-9769031-0-9(5))* Verona (Bk.) Publishing, Inc.

Verrall, Lisa. One, Two, Baa, Moo: A Pop-Up Book of Counting. Litton, Jonathan. 2015. (My Little World Ser.). bds. 8.99 ***(978-1-68010-507-0(8))*** Tiger Tales.

Verrept, Paul. El Pequeno Soldado. Verrept, Paul. Bourgeois, Elodie, tr. 2004. (SPA.). 26p. (J). (gr. -1-3). 17.99 *(978-84-261-3306-9(1))* Juventud, Editorial ESP. Dist: Lectorum Pubns., Inc.

Verrett, Michael. LSU Night Before Christmas. Wilson, Janet. 2013. (ENG.). (J). 14.95 *(978-1-62086-484-5(3))* Mascot Bks., Inc.

Verrill, William. A Hero Named Mark. Puppel, Douglas. 2012. (J). lib. bdg. 25.00 *(978-0-9788980-6-9(0))* Public Education Foundation, The.

Verroken, Sarah. Pigeon & Pigeonette. Derom, Dirk. 2009. (ENG.). 32p. (J). (gr. -1-2). 16.95 *(978-1-59270-087-5(X))* Enchanted Lion Bks., LLC.

Verstegen, Jeska. The Gift for the Child. Wilkeshuis, Cornelius. (ENG.). 28p. (J). 16.95 *(978-0-86315-349-5(6))* Floris Bks. GBR. Dist: SteinerBooks, Inc.

Verstraete, Elaine. Germ Hunter: A Story about Louis Pasteur. Alphin, Elaine Marie. 2003. (Creative Minds Biographies Ser.). (ENG.). 64p. (gr. 4-8). per. 8.95 *(978-0-87614-929-4(8)*, Carolrhoda Bks.) Lerner Publishing Group.
—Many Ways to Be a Soldier. Pfeffer, Wendy. 2008. (On My Own History Ser.). (ENG.). 48p. (gr. 2-4). lib. bdg. 25.26 *(978-0-8225-7279-4(6)*, Millbrook Pr.) Lerner Publishing Group.
—Shipwreck Search: Discovery of the H. L. Hunley. Walker, Sally M. (On My Own Science Ser.). (ENG.). 48p. (gr. 2-4). 2007. per. 6.95 *(978-0-8225-6449-2(1)*, First Avenue Editions); 2006. lib. bdg. 25.26 *(978-1-57505-878-8(2)*, Millbrook Pr.) Lerner Publishing Group.
Verstraete, Elaine S. The Star of Christmas. DiVencenzo, Maria T. 2009. (ENG.). 36p. (J). (gr. k-2). 16.99 *(978-0-9816003-0-7(1))* Winterlake Pr.
Vervoort, Sarah. It;s More Than A Game! Collar, Bill. 2007. (J). per. 6.95 *(978-1-933556-81-9(1))* Publishers' Graphics, L.L.C.
Verwey, Amanda. Girl at the Bottom of the Sea. Tea, Michelle. 2015. (ENG.). 240p. (gr. 6). 19.95 *(978-1-940450-00-1(4))* McSweeney's Publishing.
Vess, Charles. Blueberry Girl. Gaiman, Neil. (ENG.). 32p. (J). (gr. -1-3). 2011. pap. 6.99 *(978-0-06-083810-2(8))*; 2009. 17.99 *(978-0-06-083808-9(6))* HarperCollins Pubs.
—The Cats of Tanglewood Forest. de Lint, Charles. 2013. (ENG.). 304p. (J). (gr. 3-7). 18.00 *(978-0-316-05357-0(0))* Little, Brown Bks. for Young Readers.
—The Cats of Tanglewood Forest. de Lint, Charles. 2014. (ENG.). 320p. (J). (gr. 3-7). pap. 8.99 *(978-0-316-05359-4(7))* Little, Brown Bks. for Young Readers.
—Firebirds: An Anthology of Original Fantasy & Science Fiction. Alexander, Lloyd et al. Sharyn, November, ed. 2005. (ENG.). 432p. (YA). (gr. 7-11). 9.99 *(978-0-14-240320-4(2)*, Puffin) Penguin Publishing Group.
—Instructions. Gaiman, Neil. 2010. 40p. (J). (gr. -1-3). (ENG.). 14.99 *(978-0-06-196030-7(6))*; lib. bdg. 15.89 *(978-0-06-196031-4(4))* HarperCollins Pubs.
—Instructions. Gaiman, Neil. 2015. (ENG.). 40p. (J). (gr. -1-3). 8.99 *(978-0-06-196032-1(2))* HarperCollins Pubs.
—Rose. Smith, Jeff. 2009. (Bone Ser.). (ENG.). 144p. (J). (gr. 4-8). 26.99 *(978-0-545-13542-9(7))*; pap. 12.99 *(978-0-545-13543-6(5))* Scholastic, Inc. (Graphix).
Vess, Charles. Seven Wild Sisters: A Modern Fairy Tale. de Lint, Charles. (ENG.). 272p. (J). (gr. 3-7). 2015. pap. 8.00 ***(978-0-316-05352-5(X))***; 2014. 18.00 *(978-0-316-05356-3(2))* Little, Brown Bks. for Young Readers.
Vess, Charles. Tumbleweed Baby. Myers, Anna. 2014. (ENG.). 32p. (J). (gr. -1-1). 16.95 *(978-1-4197-1232-6(2)*, Abrams Bks. for Young Readers) Abrams.
Vest, Dianne. Miss Henn & Family. Lewis, Orane. l.t. ed. 2006. 27p. (J). per. 10.99 *(978-1-59879-141-9(9))* Lifevest Publishing, Inc.
Vetro, Daniela, et al. Tinker Bell & the Wings of Rani. Radice, Teresa et al. 2010. (Disney Fairies Ser.: 2). (ENG.). 80p. (J). (gr. 1-6). pap. 7.99 *(978-1-59707-226-7(5))* Papercutz.
Viall, Pauline. My Maize & Blue Day. Richards, Sonja. 2008. 32p. (J). 19.95 *(978-0-9794935-1-5(X))* Olde Towne Publishing.
Vianney, M. John. Little Nellie of Holy God 1903-1908. Dominic, Sister M. 2009. (ENG.). 32p. (J). (-2). pap. 8.00 *(978-0-89555-834-3(3)*, 2120) TAN Bks.
Viano, Hannah. S Is for Salmon: A Pacific Northwest Alphabet. Viano, Hannah. 2014. (ENG.). 32p. (J). (-k). 16.99 *(978-1-57061-873-4(9))* Sasquatch Bks.
Viard, Michel. 1000 Photos of Minerals & Fossils. Eid, Alain. 2003. (One Thousand Photos Ser.). 128p. (YA). (gr. 5-18). pap. 24.95 *(978-0-7641-5218-4(1))* Barron's Educational Series, Inc.
Vicario, Evelyn. Mathematics for Life - Moses Meets the Triangles. Vicario, Evelyn. 2013. 48p. (J). pap. 6.99 *(978-0-9826276-6-2(1)*, Bibia Publishing) Bibia, LLC.
Vicente, Fernando. Peter Pan. Barrie, J. M. Bustelo, Gabriela, tr. 2006. (Alfaguara Infantil y Juvenil Ser.). 229p. (J). (gr. 4-7). pap. *(978-970-770-677-4(5))* Ediciones Alfaguara.
Vicente, Luise San. Lucila Se Llama Gabriela. Aguirre, Sonia Montecino. rev. ed. 2006. (Otra Escalera Ser.). (ENG.). 60p. (J). (gr. -1-k). pap. 12.95 *(978-970-20-0828-6(X))* Castillo, Ediciones, S. A. de C. V. MEX. Dist: Macmillan.
Vickers, Roy Henry. The Elders Are Watching. Bouchard, David. 5th rev. deluxe ed. 2003. (ENG.). 56p. (J). 18.95 *(978-1-55192-641-4(5))* Raincoast Bk. Distribution CAN. Dist: Perseus-PGW.
Vickers, Stormi. My Beautiful Alone. Vickers, Stormi. 2004. (YA). per. 10.95 *(978-1-888141-41-2(7))* Southeast Media.
Victoria, Kirton. Emma & the African Wishing Bead. Redmond, Valerie. 2013. 28p. pap. 13.95 *(978-1-61244-115-3(7))* Halo Publishing International.
Victoria, Lisa. Clara's Gift from the Heart. 2006. (J). 17.95 *(978-0-9674602-9-1(8))* Blue Marlin Pubns.
—A Simple Brown Leaf. Davis, L. J. 2006. 32p. (J). (gr. -1-3). 17.95 *(978-0-9762007-8-9(3))* Abovo Publishing.
Vidal, Beatriz Martin. Bird. 2015. (ENG.). 36p. (J). 16.95 *(978-1-927018-64-4(1))* Simply Read Bks. CAN. Dist: Ingram Pub. Services.
Vidal, Oriol. Bear Says Thank You. Dahl, Michael. (Hello Genius Ser.). (ENG.). 20p. (gr. 1-2). 2013. bds. 4.95 *(978-1-4048-7622-4(7))*; 2011. bds. 7.99 *(978-1-4048-6786-4(4))* Picture Window Bks.
—Bear Says Thank You Kit. Dahl, Michael. 2013. (Hello Genius Ser.). (ENG.). 20p. (gr. 1-2). bds. 29.70 *(978-1-4795-2011-4(X))* Picture Window Bks.
—Big Bed for Giraffe. Dahl, Michael. 2015. (Hello Genius Ser.). (ENG.). 20p. (gr. 1-2). bds. 7.99 *(978-1-4795-5791-2(9))* Picture Window Bks.
—Build a Picture Monsters Sticker Book. 2013. (Build a Picture Sticker Bks.). (ENG.). (J). 6.99 *(978-0-7945-2947-5(X)*, Usborne) EDC Publishing.
—Bunny Eats Lunch, 1 vol. Dahl, Michael. 2010. (Hello Genius Ser.). (ENG.). 20p. (gr. 1-2). bds. 7.99 *(978-1-4048-5728-5(1))* Picture Window Bks.
—Bye-Bye Bottles, Zebra. Dahl, Michael. 2015. (Hello Genius Ser.). (ENG.). 20p. (gr. 1-2). bds. 7.99 *(978-1-4795-5792-9(7))* Picture Window Bks.
—Duck Goes Potty, 1 vol. Dahl, Michael. (Hello Genius Ser.). (ENG.). 20p. (gr. 1-2). 2013. bds. 4.95 *(978-1-4048-7119-9(5))*; 2010. bds. 7.99 *(978-1-4048-5726-1(5))* Picture Window Bks.
Vidal, Oriol. Hello Genius. Dahl, Michael. 2015. (Hello Genius Ser.). (ENG.). 20p. (gr. 1-2). bds. 31.96 ***(978-1-4795-8062-0(7))*** Picture Window Bks.
Vidal, Oriol. Hippo Says "Excuse Me" Dahl, Michael. 2011. (Hello Genius Ser.). (ENG.). 20p. (gr. 1-2). bds. 7.99 *(978-1-4048-6787-1(2))* Picture Window Bks.
—Little Elephant Listens, 1 vol. Dahl, Michael. 2014. (Hello Genius Ser.). (ENG.). 20p. (gr. 1-2). bds. 7.99 *(978-1-4795-2289-7(9))* Picture Window Bks.
—Little Lion Shares, 1 vol. Dahl, Michael. 2014. (Hello Genius Ser.). (ENG.). 20p. (gr. 1-2). bds. 7.99 *(978-1-4795-2287-3(2))* Picture Window Bks.
—Little Monkey Calms Down, 1 vol. Dahl, Michael. 2014. (Hello Genius Ser.). (ENG.). 20p. (gr. 1-2). bds. 7.99 *(978-1-4795-2286-6(4))* Picture Window Bks.
—Little Tiger Picks Up, 1 vol. Dahl, Michael. 2014. (Hello Genius Ser.). (ENG.). 20p. (gr. 1-2). bds. 7.99 *(978-1-4795-2288-0(0))* Picture Window Bks.
Vidal, Oriol. Mind Your Monsters. Bailey, Catherine. 2015. (ENG.). 32p. (J). (gr. -1-2). 14.95 ***(978-1-4549-1103-6(4))*** Sterling Publishing Co., Inc.
Vidal, Oriol. Mouse Says Sorry, 1 vol. Dahl, Michael. 2011. (Hello Genius Ser.). (ENG.). 20p. (gr. 1-2). bds. 7.99 *(978-1-4048-6789-5(9))* Picture Window Bks.
—Nap Time for Kitty, 1 vol. Dahl, Michael. 2011. (Hello Genius Ser.). (ENG.). 20p. (gr. 1-2). bds. 7.99 *(978-1-4048-5216-7(6))* Picture Window Bks.
—No More Pacifier, Duck. Dahl, Michael. 2015. (Hello Genius Ser.). (ENG.). 20p. (gr. 1-2). bds. 7.99 *(978-1-4795-5793-6(5))* Picture Window Bks.
—Penguin Says Please. Dahl, Michael. (Hello Genius Ser.). (ENG.). 20p. (gr. 1-2). 2013. bds. 4.95 *(978-1-4048-7625-5(1))*; 2011. bds. 7.99 *(978-1-4048-6788-8(0))* Picture Window Bks.
—Pig Takes a Bath, 1 vol. Dahl, Michael. 2010. (Hello Genius Ser.). (ENG.). 20p. (gr. 1-2). bds. 7.99 *(978-1-4048-5729-2(X))* Picture Window Bks.
—Play Time for Puppy, 1 vol. Dahl, Michael. 2011. (Hello Genius Ser.). (ENG.). 20p. (gr. 1-2). bds. 7.99 *(978-1-4048-6497-9(0))* Picture Window Bks.
—Pony Brushes His Teeth, 1 vol. Dahl, Michael. (Hello Genius Ser.). (ENG.). 20p. (gr. 1-2). 2013. bds. 4.95 *(978-1-4048-7124-3(1))*; 2010. bds. 7.99 *(978-1-4048-5727-8(3))* Picture Window Bks.
—Snack Time for Cow, 1 vol. Dahl, Michael. 2011. (Hello Genius Ser.). (ENG.). 20p. (gr. 1-2). bds. 7.99 *(978-1-4048-6496-2(2))* Picture Window Bks.
—Story Time for Lamb, 1 vol. Dahl, Michael. 2011. (Hello Genius Ser.). (ENG.). 20p. (gr. 1-2). bds. 7.99 *(978-1-4048-6495-5(4))* Picture Window Bks.
—Thumbs up, Brown Bear. Dahl, Michael. 2015. (Hello Genius Ser.). (ENG.). 20p. (gr. 1-2). bds. 7.99 *(978-1-4795-5794-3(3))* Picture Window Bks.
Vidali, Valerio & Uman, Jennifer. Jemmy Button. Vidali, Valerio & Uman, Jennifer. 2013. (ENG.). 48p. (J). (gr. k-12). 16.99 *(978-0-7636-6487-9(1)*, Templar) Candlewick Pr.
Vidro, Kenn. Square Pears Two: The Equal Sequel. Vidro, Kenn. 2004. (ENG.). 100p. (J). spiral bd. 9.95 *(978-0-9745308-1-9(6))* Gilbert Square Bks.
Vieceli, Emma. Frostbite. Mead, Richelle. 2012. (Vampire Academy Ser.: 2). (ENG.). 144p. (YA). (gr. 7-18). pap. 12.99 *(978-1-59514-430-0(7)*, Razorbill) Penguin Publishing Group.
—Hamlet. Shakespeare, William & Appignanesi, Richard. 2007. (ENG.). 204p. (J). (gr. 2-8). pap. 12.95 *(978-0-8109-9324-2(4)*, Abrams Bks. for Young Readers) Abrams.
—Much Ado about Nothing. Shakespeare, William. 2009. (Manga Shakespeare Ser.). (ENG.). 208p. (YA). (gr. 7-11). pap. 12.95 *(978-0-8109-4323-0(9)*, Amulet Bks.) Abrams.
—Shadow Kiss. Mead, Richelle. 2013. (Vampire Academy Ser.: 3). (ENG.). 160p. (YA). (gr. 7). pap. 12.99 *(978-1-59514-431-7(5)*, Razorbill) Penguin Publishing Group.
—Vampire Academy. Mead, Richelle. 2011. (Vampire Academy Ser.: 1). (ENG.). 144p. (YA). (gr. 7-18). pap. 12.99 *(978-1-59514-429-4(3)*, Razorbill) Penguin Publishing Group.
Vieira, Andrei. Rahab's Promise. Gibbs, Noni & Kahrs, Christina. 2007. 32p. (J). (gr. -1-2). pap. 9.99 *(978-0-8127-0432-7(0))* Autumn Hse. Publishing Co.
Vieira, Sueli. Amusement Trains: The Story of Freddy & Flash. Dahlgren, Leta. 2011. (ENG.). 52p. pap. 16.00 *(978-1-4664-8299-9(0))* CreateSpace Independent Publishing Platform.
Vigil, Cristina. When Winston Wins. Fairchild-Lenyo, Mary. 2007. 36p. per. 14.95 *(978-1-59858-405-9(7))* Dog Ear Publishing, LLC.
Vigil, Luis Gerardo Sanchez & Broeck, Fabricio Vanden. The Flamingo's Legs. Romeu, Emma. 2004. (Colección Animales de América / Animals of the Americas Ser.). (SPA.). 32p. (gr. 3-5). pap. 11.95 *(978-1-59437-846-1(0))* Santillana USA Publishing Co., Inc.
—A Forest for the Monarch Butterfly. Romeu, Emma. 2005. (Colección Animales de América / Animals of the Americas Ser.). (SPA.). 48p. (gr. 3-5). pap. 11.95 *(978-1-59437-844-7(4))* Santillana USA Publishing Co., Inc.
—Here Comes the Grey Wolf. Romeu, Emma. 2004. (Colección Animales de América / Animals of the Americas Ser.). (SPA.). 32p. (gr. 3-5). pap. 11.95 *(978-1-59437-843-0(6))* Santillana USA Publishing Co., Inc.
—My Manatee Friend. Romeu, Emma. 2004. (Colección Animales de América / Animals of the Americas Ser.). (SPA.). 24p. (gr. 3-5). pap. 11.95 *(978-1-59437-845-4(2))* Santillana USA Publishing Co., Inc.
Vigla, Vincent. Being Me. Broski, Julie. 2011. (Rookie Ready to Learn Ser.). 40p. (J). pap. 5.95 *(978-0-531-26653-3(2))*; (gr. -1-k). lib. bdg. 23.00 *(978-0-531-26428-7(9))* Scholastic Library Publishing. (Children's Pr.).
—Blackest Hole in Space. Little, Penny. 2009. (ENG.). 24p. (J). (gr. k-3). pap. 8.99 *(978-0-340-94467-7(6))* Hodder & Stoughton GBR. Dist: Independent Pubs. Group.
—My Magnetic Word Puzzles: Let's Make Words. 2006. (Magnix Learning Fun Ser.). 12p. (J). (gr. -1-3). 9.95 *(978-1-932915-19-8(2))* Sandvik Innovations, LLC.
Vignaga, Francesca Dafne. The Legend of UFOs, 1 vol. Troupe, Thomas Kingsley. 2012. (Legend Has It Ser.). (ENG.). 32p. (gr. 2-4). lib. bdg. 26.65 *(978-1-4048-6657-7(4)*, Nonfiction Picture Bks.) Picture Window Bks.
—The 10 Marys & the Little Gabriel. Magni, Aurora. 2011. (J). *(978-0-8091-6764-7(6))* Paulist Pr.
Vignazia, Franco. An Illustrated Catechism: The Apostles' Creed, the Sacraments, the Ten Commandments, Prayer. Biffi, Inos. 2007. 141p. (J). (gr. 3). per. 19.95 *(978-1-56854-612-4(2))* Liturgy Training Pubns.
—The Life of Mary. Biffi, Inos, ed. 2007. 28p. (J). (gr. -1-3). 12.95 *(978-1-56854-653-7(X))* Liturgy Training Pubns.
Vignoli, Daniella. Wolf on a Leash. Visconti, Guido. 2006. (Wolf on a Leash Ser.). 24p. (gr. k-3). lib. bdg. 24.00 *(978-0-8368-6261-4(9)*, Gareth Stevens Learning Library) Stevens, Gareth Publishing LLLP.
Vignolo, Enrique. Catch of the Day! McMillan, Dawn. 2013. 24p. (gr. 3-8). pap. *(978-1-927197-70-7(8)*, Red Rocket Readers) Flying Start Bks.
—Hopeless to Hopeful. Sommer, Carl. 2009. (Quest for Success Ser.). (ENG.). 56p. (YA). pap. 4.95 *(978-1-57537-278-5(9))*; lib. bdg. 12.95 *(978-1-57537-253-2(3))* Advance Publishing, Inc.
Vignolo, Enrique. Miserable Millie. Sommer, Carl. (J). 2014. pap. ***(978-1-57537-960-9(0))***; 2007. (ENG.). 48p. 16.95 incl. audio compact disk *(978-1-57537-521-2(4))*; 2007. (ENG.). 48p. (gr. -1-3). 9.95 *(978-1-57537-022-4(0))*; 2007. (ENG.). 48p. (gr. -1-3). lib. bdg. 16.95 *(978-1-57537-071-2(9))* Advance Publishing, Inc.
Vignolo, Enrique. Miserable Millie(La Pobrecita Mili) Sommer, Carl. ed. 2009. (Another Sommer-Time Story Bilingual Ser.). (SPA & ENG.). 48p. (J). lib. bdg. 16.95 *(978-1-57537-160-3(X))* Advance Publishing, Inc.
—The Rebel. Sommer, Carl. 2009. (Quest for Success Ser.). (ENG.). 56p. (YA). pap. 4.95 *(978-1-57537-282-2(7))*; lib. bdg. 12.95 *(978-1-57537-257-0(6))* Advance Publishing, Inc.
—The Rebel(El Rebelde) Sommer, Carl. ed. 2009. (Quest for Success Bilingual Ser.). (ENG & SPA.). 104p. (YA). lib. bdg. 14.95 *(978-1-57537-231-0(2))* Advance Publishing, Inc.
—The Runaway(La Escapada) Sommer, Carl. ed. 2009. (Quest for Success Bilingual Ser.). (SPA & ENG.). 104p. (YA). lib. bdg. 14.95 *(978-1-57537-234-1(7))* Advance Publishing, Inc.
Vignolo, Enrique. Spike the Rebel! Sommer, Carl. (J). 2014. pap. ***(978-1-57537-967-8(8))***; 2007. (ENG.). 48p. (gr. -1-3). lib. bdg. 16.95 *(978-1-57537-072-9(7))*; 2007. (ENG.). 48p. 16.95 incl. audio compact disk *(978-1-57537-522-9(2))*; 2007. (ENG.). 48p. 23.95 incl. audio compact disk *(978-1-57537-722-3(5))*; 2007. (ENG.). 48p. (gr. -1-3). lib. bdg. 9.95 *(978-1-57537-023-1(9))* Advance Publishing, Inc.
Vignolo, Enrique. Spike the Rebel!(pua, el Rebelde!) Sommer, Carl. ed. 2009. (Another Sommer-Time Story Bilingual Ser.). (SPA & ENG.). 48p. (J). lib. bdg. 16.95 *(978-1-57537-167-2(7))* Advance Publishing, Inc.
—The Tortoise & the Hare. Sommer, Carl. 2014. (Sommer-Time Story Classics Ser.). (ENG.). 32p. (J). (gr. k-4). 16.95 *(978-1-57537-086-6(7))* Advance Publishing, Inc.
Vignolo, Enrique, jt. illus. see Budwine, Greg.
Vila, Alvaro F. Flood, 1 vol. Capstone Press Staff. 2013. (Fiction Picture Bks.). (ENG.). 32p. (gr. 1-3). 20.99 *(978-1-4048-8006-1(2))* Picture Window Bks.
Vila Delclòs, Jordi. La Bella Durmiente. Bailer, Darice & Domínguez, Madelca. 2007. (SPA & ENG.). 28p. (J). *(978-0-545-03030-4(7))* Scholastic, Inc.
—El Flautista de Hamelín. Bailer, Darice & Domínguez, Madelca. 2007. (SPA & ENG.). 28p. (J). *(978-0-545-02961-2(9))* Scholastic, Inc.
Vilela, Caio, photos by. Goal! Taylor, Sean. 2014. (ENG., 40p. (J). (gr. -1-3). 17.99 *(978-1-62779-123-6(X)*, Holt, Henry & Co. Bks. For Young Readers) Holt, Henry & Co.
Vilela, Fernando. Arroz Con Leche: Un Poema para Cocinar. Argueta, Jorge. ed. 2010. (Bilingual Cooking Poems Ser.).Tr. of Rice Pudding - A Cooking Poem. (SPA & ENG.). 32p. (J). (gr. -1-2). 18.95 *(978-0-88899-981-8(X))* Groundwood Bks. CAN. Dist: Perseus-PGW.
Vilela, Luiz. Pat the Bunny: at the Apple Orchard. Golden Books. 2015. (ENG.). 24p. (J). (— 1). bds. 6.99 ***(978-0-553-51205-2(6)***, Golden Bks.) Random Hse. Children's Bks.
Vilela, Luiz. Pat the Pet (Pat the Bunny) Golden Books. 2014. (Lift-The-Flap Ser.). (ENG.). 16p. (J). (— 1). 14.99 *(978-0-385-37673-0(1)*, Golden Bks.) Random Hse. Children's Bks.
Vilela, Luiz, jt. illus. see Murdocca, Sal.
Villa, Alvaro F. Flood, 1 vol. 2013. (ENG.). 32p. (gr. 1-3). 15.95 *(978-1-62370-001-0(9))* Capstone Pr., Inc.
—Flood. 2013. (Fiction Picture Bks.). (ENG.). 32p. (gr. 1-3). 8.95 *(978-1-4795-2256-9(2))* Picture Window Bks.
Villa, Victor Rivas. Just Jake, No. 1. Marcionette, Jake. 2014. (ENG.). 160p. (J). (gr. 3-7). 11.99 *(978-0-448-46692-7(9)*, Grosset & Dunlap) Penguin Publishing Group.
—Just Jake - Dog Eat Dog, No. 2. Marcionette, Jake. 2015. (Just Jake Ser.: 2). (ENG.). 196p. (J). (gr. 3-7). 11.99 *(978-0-448-46693-4(7)*, Grosset & Dunlap) Penguin Publishing Group.
Villagomez, Raul, jt. illus. see Gomez, Patricio.
Villagran, Ricardo. The Call of the Wild No. 15. London, Jack. 2012. (Classics Illustrated Graphic Novels Ser.: 15). (ENG.). 56p. (J). (gr. 3-9). 9.99 *(978-1-59707-291-5(5))* Papercutz.
Villalobos, Ethel M. Volcanoes A to Z Coloring Book. Pierce, Terry. 2003. 24p. pap. 4.95 *(978-1-57306-123-0(9))* Bess Pr., Inc.
Villaloz, ChiChi & Etheridge, Katy. Do Dogs Dream? Villaloz, ChiChi & Etheridge, Katy. 2003. 32p. (J). lib. bdg. 16.95 *(978-0-9722180-5-4(X))* Malamute Pr.
—Do Dogs Vote? Villaloz, ChiChi & Etheridge, Katy. 2008. 32p. (J). lib. bdg. 24.95 *(978-0-9722180-0-9(9))* Malamute Pr.
Villalta, Ingrid. Mandy & Pandy Play Let's Count. Lin, Chris. 2008. 18p. (J). (gr. -1-3). bds. 9.99 *(978-0-9800156-5-2(0))* Mandy & Pandy Bks., LLC.
—Mandy & Pandy Play Sports. Lin, Chris. 2008. 20p. (J). (gr. -1-3). bds. 9.99 *(978-0-9800156-7-6(7))* Mandy & Pandy Bks., LLC.
—Mandy & Pandy Say Ni Hao Ma? Lin, Chris. 2007. 18p. (J). (gr. -1-3). bds. 9.95 *(978-0-9800156-4-5(2))* Mandy & Pandy Bks., LLC.
—Mandy & Pandy Visit China. Lin, Chris. 2008. 20p. (J). (gr. -1-3). bds. 9.99 *(978-0-9800156-6-9(9))* Mandy & Pandy Bks., LLC.
Villamuza, Noemí. Marc Just Couldn't Sleep. Keselman, Gabriela. (ENG.). 32p. (J). 2007. (gr. -1-k). pap. 5.99 *(978-1-929132-91-1(3))*; 2004. 10.99 *(978-1-929132-68-3(9))* Kane Miller.
—Oscar y el Leon de Correos. Puelles, Vicente Munoz & Muñoz Puelles, Vicente. (SPA.). 60p. (J). *(978-84-207-8986-6(0))* Grupo Anaya, S.A. ESP. Dist: Lectorum Pubns., Inc.
—Pajaruli: Poemas para Sequir Andando. Plaza, José María & María, Plaza José. (SPA.). (J). *(978-84-392-8120-7(X)*, EV0782) Gaviota Ediciones ESP. Dist: Lectorum Pubns., Inc.
Villamuza, Noemí. Me Gusta. Villamuza, Noemí, tr. Sobrino, Javier. (SPA.). 28p. 20.99 *(978-84-88342-35-5(7))* S.A. Kokinos ESP. Dist: Lectorum Pubns., Inc.
Villan, Oscar. Camilla the Zebra. Nunez, Marisa. 2003. 32p. (J). 14.95 *(978-84-95730-39-8(1))* Kalandraka Catalunya, Edicions, S.L. ESP. Dist: Independent Pubs. Group.
—La Cebra Camila. Nunez, Marisa. 2005. (SPA.). 216p. (J). (gr. k-2). 16.95 *(978-84-95123-60-2(6)*, KA8243) Kalandraka Editora, S.L. ESP. Dist: Iaconi, Mariuccia Bk. Imports, Lectorum Pubns., Inc.
Villanueva, Leonard. Kaipo & the Mighty Ahi. Villanueva, Leonard. 2004. (J). 14.95 *(978-0-9729905-6-1(9))* Beachhouse Publishing, LLC.
Villarreal, Tanya E. Izzie's First Christmas, 1 vol. Villarreal, Tanya E. 2009. 28p. pap. 24.95 *(978-1-61546-093-9(4))* America Star Bks.
Villarrubia, Jose, jt. illus. see Futaki, Attila.
Villarrubia, Jose, jt. illus. see Pennington, Mark.
Villavert, Armand, Jr. & Petersen, David. Muppet Robin Hood. Beedle, Tim. 2009. (Muppet Show Ser.). (ENG.). 112p. (J). (gr. 4-7). pap. 9.99 *(978-1-934506-79-0(6))* Boom! Studios.
Villegas, Teresa. Golemito. Stavans, Ilan. 2013. (ENG.). 32p. (J). 16.95 *(978-1-58838-292-4(3)*, NewSouth Bks.) NewSouth, Inc.
Villella, Jessica. Myself, I & Me. Branda, Barnabus. 2013. 28p. pap. 24.95 *(978-1-63004-064-2(9))* America Star Bks.
Villeneuve, Anne. Loula Is Leaving for Africa. Villeneuve, Anne. 2013. (Loula Ser.). (ENG.). 32p. (J). 16.95 *(978-1-55453-941-3(2))* Kids Can Pr., Ltd. CAN. Dist: Univ. of Toronto Pr.
Villet, Olivia. Monster Mess. Pym, Tasha. 2007. (Collins Big Cat Ser.). (ENG.). 16p. (J). pap. 5.99 *(978-0-00-718650-1(9))* HarperCollins Pubs. Ltd. GBR. Dist: Independent Pubs. Group.
—My Day, My Way. McLaren, Thando. 2005. (ENG.). 14p. (J). (gr. -1-k). 16.99 *(978-1-85707-633-2(8))* Tango Bks. GBR. Dist: Independent Pubs. Group.
Villim, Jim. I Love You Just Because. Heitritter, Laura. Date not set. 16p. (Orig.). (J). (gr. -1-18). pap. 6.95 *(978-1-885964-01-4(3))* P2 Educational Services, Inc.
Villines, Leo. Clean Your Room. Villines, Carol. 2008. 20p. pap. 24.95 *(978-1-60441-166-9(X))* America Star Bks.
Villnave, Erica. Sophie's Lovely Locks, 0 vols. Villnave, Erica. 2011. (ENG.). 32p. (J). (gr. k-3). 16.99 *(978-0-7614-5820-3(4)*, 9780761458203, Amazon Children's Publishing) Amazon Publishing.
Villnave, Erica Pelton. A Day at the Lake. Wallingford, Stephanie & Rynders, Dawn. 2013. (ENG.). 32p. (-k). pap. 10.95 *(978-1-938063-03-9(1)*, Mighty Media Kids) Mighty Media Pr.
—Nobody's Perfect: A Story for Children about Perfectionism. Burns, Ellen Flanagan. 2008. 48p. (J). (gr. 3-7). 14.95 *(978-1-4338-0379-6(8))*; pap. 9.95 *(978-1-4338-0380-2(1))* American Psychological Assn. (Magination Pr.).
—Oh Where, Oh Where Has My Little Dog Gone? Galvin, Laura. 2008. (ENG.). 32p. (J). (gr. -1-2). 9.95 *(978-1-59249-860-4(4))* Soundprints.
—Oh Where, Oh Where Has My Little Dog Gone? Galvin, Laura Gates. 2008. (ENG.). 32p. (J). (gr. -1-2). 17.95 *(978-1-59249-859-8(0))* Soundprints.
Vimislik, Matthew. Benji Franklin: Kid Zillionaire. Bean, Raymond. 2014. (Benji Franklin: Kid Zillionaire Ser.). (ENG.). 160p. (gr. 2-3). 9.95 *(978-1-4342-6419-0(X))* Stone Arch Bks.
Vimislik, Matthew. Benji Franklin: Kid Zillionaire, 2 vols. Bean, Raymond. 2015. (Benji Franklin: Kid Zillionaire Ser.). (ENG.). 88p. (gr. 2-3). 42.64 ***(978-1-4965-1992-4(2))*** Stone Arch Bks.
Vimislik, Matthew. Benji Franklin: Kid Zillionare, 1 vol. Bean, Raymond. 2014. (Benji Franklin: Kid Zillionaire Ser.). (ENG.). 88p. (gr. 2-3). 42.64 *(978-1-4342-8927-8(3))* Stone Arch Bks.
—Building Wealth (and Superpowered Rockets!), 1 vol. Bean, Raymond. 2014. (Benji Franklin: Kid Zillionaire Ser.).

(ENG.). 88p. (gr. 2-3). 21.32 *(978-1-4342-6418-3(1))* Stone Arch Bks.

Vimislik, Matthew. Buying Stocks (and Solid Gold Submarines!) Bean, Raymond. 2015. (Benji Franklin: Kid Zillionaire Ser.). (ENG.). 88p. (gr. 2-3). lib. bdg. 21.32 ***(978-1-4965-0367-1(8))*** Stone Arch Bks.

—Investing Well (in Supersonic Spaceships!) Bean, Raymond. 2015. (Benji Franklin: Kid Zillionaire Ser.). (ENG.). 88p. (gr. 2-3). lib. bdg. 21.32 ***(978-1-4965-0368-8(6))*** Stone Arch Bks.

—Money Troubles. Bean, Raymond. 2015. (Benji Franklin: Kid Zillionaire Ser.). (ENG.). 160p. (gr. 2-3). 9.95 ***(978-1-4965-0369-5(4))*** Stone Arch Bks.

Vimislik, Matthew. Saving Money (and the World from Killer Dinos!), 1 vol. Bean, Raymond. 2014. (Benji Franklin: Kid Zillionaire Ser.). (ENG.). 88p. (gr. 2-3). 21.32 *(978-1-4342-6417-6(3))* Stone Arch Bks.

Vin, Lee. Crazy Love Story, Vol. 3. rev. ed. 2005. 208p. pap. 9.99 *(978-1-59182-949-2(6))* TOKYOPOP, Inc.

Vin, Lee. One, 11 vols. Vin, Lee. 192p. 9th rev. ed. 2006. (One Ser.: Vol. 9). per. 9.99 *(978-1-59532-013-1(X))*; 9th rev. ed. 2005. (One Ser.: Vol. 8). per. 9.99 *(978-1-59532-012-4(1))*; Vol. 6. 7th rev. ed. 2005. pap. 9.99 *(978-1-59532-010-0(5))* TOKYOPOP, Inc.

Vin, Lee. One, Vol. 7. Vin, Lee, creator. rev. ed. 2005. 192p. pap. 9.99 *(978-1-59532-011-7(3))* TOKYOPOP, Inc.

Viñals, Noemi. The Kid Silverhair. Alkonada, Jesus Muñoz. I.t. ed. 2011. (ENG.). 32p. pap. 10.00 *(978-1-4637-4831-9(0))* CreateSpace Independent Publishing Platform.

Vince, Dawn. Emily & the Lamb. McAllister, Margaret. 2005. (ENG.). 24p. (J). lib. bdg. 23.65 *(978-1-59646-756-9(8))* Dingles & Co.

—Hero. Langford, Jane. 2005. (ENG.). 24p. (J). lib. bdg. 23.65 *(978-1-59646-720-0(7))* Dingles & Co.

Vincent, Allison, jt. illus. see Cuthbert, R M.

Vincent, Andrew M. & Higgie, Will K. Washington D C , the Nation's Capital: Romance, Adventure, Achievement. Fox, Frances Margaret. 2012. 394p. 53.95 *(978-1-258-23323-5(1))*; pap. 38.95 *(978-1-258-24983-0(9))* Literary Licensing, LLC.

Vincent, Benjamin. Bluebonnet at the Alamo, 1 vol. Casad, Mary Brooke. 2013. (ENG.). 32p. (J). (gr. k-3). 16.99 *(978-1-4556-1806-4(3))* Pelican Publishing Co., Inc.

—Bluebonnet at the East Texas Oil Museum, 1 vol. Casad, Mary Brooke & Brooke Casad, Mary. 2005. (Bluebonnet Ser.). (ENG.). 32p. (J). (gr. k-3). 16.99 *(978-1-58980-358-9(2))* Pelican Publishing Co., Inc.

—Bluebonnet at the Ocean Star Museum, 1 vol. Casad, Mary Brooke. 2012. (ENG.). 32p. (J). (gr. k-3). 16.99 *(978-1-4556-1721-0(0))* Pelican Publishing Co., Inc.

—Charlie the Horse. Abercrombie, Josephine. 2004. (J). 15.99 *(978-0-9769648-0-3(5))* J A Interests, Inc.

—Friends & Foes of Harry Potter: Names Decoded. Agarwal, Nikita & Agarwal, Chitra. 2006. 160p. (YA). pap. 15.95 *(978-1-59800-221-8(X))* Outskirts Pr., Inc.

Vincent, Benjamin & DePew, Robert. Snow Day! Speregen, Devra Newberger & Running Press Staff. 2005. (ENG.). 12p. (J). (gr. -1-1). pap. 12.95 *(978-0-7624-2371-2(4))*, Running Pr. Kids) Running Pr. Bk. Pubs.

Vincent, Eric. The Island of Doctor Moreau, No. 12. Vincent, Eric. Wells, H. G. & Grant, Steven. 2011. (Classics Illustrated Graphic Novels Ser.: 12). (ENG.). 56p. (J). (gr. 3-9). 9.99 *(978-1-59707-235-9(4))* Papercutz.

Vincenti, Antonio. The Creed Explained. Vecchini, Silvia & Daughters of St. Paul Staff. 2015. (J). 6.95 *(978-0-8198-7519-8(8))* Pauline Bks. & Media.

—The 10 Commandments Explained. Vecchini, Silvia. 2015. (J). 6.95 *(978-0-8198-7523-5(6))* Pauline Bks. & Media.

Vincenti, Catherine. Pet Pals Grades 3-4: A Spanish-English Workbook. Vincenti, Catherine, ed. 2003.Tr. of Mascotas Companeros. (SPA.). 34p. wbk. ed. 3.00 *(978-0-941246-21-7(3)*, Humane Society Pr.) National Assn. for Humane & Environmental Education.

—Pet Pals Grades 5-6: A Spanish-English Workbook. Vincenti, Catherine, ed. 2003.Tr. of Mascotas Companeros. (SPA.). 34p. wbk. ed. 3.00 *(978-0-941246-22-4(1)*, Humane Society Pr.) National Assn. for Humane & Environmental Education.

—Pet Pals Grades K-2: A Spanish-English Workbook. Vincenti, Catherine, ed. 2003.Tr. of Mascotas Companeros. (SPA.). 34p. (J). wbk. ed. 3.00 *(978-0-941246-20-0(5)*, Humane Society Pr.) National Assn. for Humane & Environmental Education.

Vincer, Carole. Beds & Bedding. Watson, Mary Gordon. 2nd ed. 2006. (Threshold Picture Guides: 9). (ENG.). 24p. (Orig.). (gr. 3-18). pap. 12.95 *(978-1-872082-69-1(6)*, Allen, J. A. & Company, Limited) Hale, Robert Ltd. GBR. Dist: Perseus-PGW.

—Mounted Games. Webber, Toni. 2006. (Threshold Picture Guides: 30). (ENG.). 24p. pap. 12.95 *(978-1-872082-60-8(2))* Kenilworth Pr., Ltd. GBR. Dist: Perseus-PGW.

Vine, Rachel Shana. Shekhinah. Sherman, Paulette Kouffman. 2013. 26p. pap. 10.95 *(978-0-9852469-5-2(2))* Parachute Jump Publishing.

Viner, Callie Lee, photos by. Pebbles Loves Counting. Viner, Callie Lee. 2013. 24p. pap. 12.95 *(978-1-61493-213-0(1))* Peppertree Pr., The.

Vining, Alex. The Tale of Peter Rabbit. Potter, Beatrix. 2004. (Peter Rabbit Ser.). (ENG.). 32p. (J). (gr. -1-k). mass mkt. 3.99 *(978-0-448-43521-3(7)*, Grosset & Dunlap) Penguin Publishing Group.

Violi, Daniela. Todo Sobre una Wafle. Horvath, Polly. Holguin, Magdalena, tr. 2006. (Coleccion Torre de Papel: Amarilla Ser.). (SPA.). 187p. (J). (gr. 4-7). per. 8.95 *(978-958-04-6495-2(2))* Norma S.A. COL. Dist: Distribuidora Norma, Inc.

—La Vaca de Octavio/la Arana Sube al Monte. Arciniegas, Triunfo. 2003. (Primer Acto: Teatro Infantil y Juvenil Ser.). (SPA.). 51p. (J). (gr. -1-7). pap. *(978-958-30-0312-7(3))* Panamericana Editorial.

Vipah Interactive. Margret & H. A. Rey's Curious George Goes Camping. Rey, Margret. 2015. 24p. pap. 4.00 ***(978-1-61003-550-7(X))*** Center for the Collaborative Classroom.

Vipah Interactive Staff. Curious George's First Day of School, 1 vol. Rey, Margret & Rey, H. A. 2005. (Read along Book & CD Ser.). (ENG.). 24p. (J). (gr. -1-3). 10.99 *(978-0-618-60565-1(7))* Houghton Mifflin Harcourt Publishing Co.

—Feeds the Animals, 1 vol. Rey, Margret & Rey, H. A. 2005. (Read along Book & CD Ser.). (ENG.). 24p. (J). (gr. -1-3). 10.99 *(978-0-618-60387-9(5))* Houghton Mifflin Harcourt Publishing Co.

—Goes to a Movie. Rey, Margret & Rey, H. A. 2005. (Curious George Ser.). (ENG.). 24p. (J). (gr. -1-3). 10.99 *(978-0-618-60386-2(7))* Houghton Mifflin Harcourt Publishing Co.

—The New Adventures of Curious George. Rey, Margret & Rey, H. A. 2006. (Curious George Ser.). (ENG.). 208p. (J). (gr. -1-3). 10.99 *(978-0-618-66373-6(8))* Houghton Mifflin Harcourt Publishing Co.

Viray, Sherwin, jt. illus. see Huey, Debbie.

Virján, Emma J. What This Story Needs Is a Pig in a Wig. Virján, Emma J. 2015. (Pig in a Wig Book Ser.). (ENG.). 40p. (J). (gr. -1-3). 9.99 *(978-0-06-232724-6(0))* HarperCollins Pubs.

Visaya, Artemio. Paulina's Teddy Bear Journey. Schliewen, Richard. 2012. 104p. 24.95 *(978-1-62709-055-1(X))*; pap. 19.95 *(978-1-4626-9597-3(3))* America Star Bks.

Vischer, Frans. Fuddles. Vischer, Frans. 2011. (ENG.). 32p. (J). (gr. -1-2). 17.99 *(978-1-4169-9155-7(7)*, Simon & Schuster/Paula Wiseman Bks.) Simon & Schuster/Paula Wiseman Bks.

—A Very Fuddles Christmas. Vischer, Frans. 2013. (ENG.). 32p. (J). (gr. -1-2). 15.99 *(978-1-4169-9156-4(5)*, Simon & Schuster/Paula Wiseman Bks.) Simon & Schuster/Paula Wiseman Bks.

Visco, Tamara. Let's Play Games in Chinese. Yao, Tao-chung & McGinnis, Scott. rev. ed. 2005. (CHI & ENG.). 164p. (gr. k-18). pap. 25.95 *(978-0-88727-360-5(2))* Cheng & Tsui Co.

Vision, Mutiya Sahar. Daddy Loves His Baby Girl. Vision, Mutiya Sahar. Vision, David. 2009. 32p. 16.00 *(978-0-9659538-7-0(4))* Vision Works Publishing.

Visser, Rino. David & Goliath. van Rijswijk, Cor. 2003. 43p. (J). *(978-1-894666-23-7(2))* Inheritance Pubns.

—Gideon Blows the Trumpet. van Rijswijk, Cor. 2003. 43p. (J). *(978-1-894666-22-0(4))* Inheritance Pubns.

Vita, Ariela. The Donut Yogi. Kay, Sjoukje & Kay, Sjoukje. 2007. (ENG.). 32p. (J). 2.50 *(978-0-9789698-1-3(2))* Kay, Sjoukje.

Vitale, Raoul. The Cat Who Went to Heaven. Coatsworth, Elizabeth. 2008. (ENG.). 96p. (J). (gr. 3-7). pap. 5.99 *(978-1-4169-4973-2(9)*, Simon & Schuster/Paula Wiseman Bks.) Simon & Schuster/Paula Wiseman Bks.

—The Charm Bracelet. Rodda, Emily. 2003. (Fairy Realm Ser.). 128p. (J). (gr. 2-5). 8.99 *(978-0-06-009583-3(0))* HarperCollins Pubs.

—The Charm Bracelet Bk. 1. Rodda, Emily. 2009. (Fairy Realm Ser.: No. 1). (ENG.). 128p. (J). (gr. 2-5). pap. 4.99 *(978-0-06-009585-7(7))* HarperCollins Pubs.

—The Flower Fairies. Rodda, Emily. (Fairy Realm Ser.: No. 2). 128p. (J). 2009. (ENG.). (gr. 2-5). pap. 4.99 *(978-0-06-009588-8(1))*; 2003. 8.99 *(978-0-06-009586-4(5))* HarperCollins Pubs.

—The Last Fairy-Apple Tree. Rodda, Emily. 2007. (Fairy Realm Ser.). 109p. (gr. 3-7). 25.65 *(978-1-59961-326-2(3))* Spotlight.

—The Rainbow Wand. Rodda, Emily. 2007. (Fairy Realm Ser.). 116p. (gr. 3-7). 25.65 *(978-1-59961-332-1(8))* Spotlight.

—The Star Cloak. Rodda, Emily. 2005. (Fairy Realm Ser.: No. 7). (ENG.). 128p. (J). (gr. 2-5). 8.99 *(978-0-06-077758-6(3))* HarperCollins Pubs.

—The Star Cloak. Rodda, Emily. 2007. (Fairy Realm Ser.). (ENG.). 112p. (gr. 3-7). 25.65 *(978-1-59961-329-1(8))* Spotlight.

—The Third Wish. Rodda, Emily. 2007. (Fairy Realm Ser.). 113p. (gr. 3-7). 25.65 *(978-1-59961-325-3(5))* Spotlight.

—The Unicorn. Rodda, Emily. 2007. (Fairy Realm Ser.). 106p. (gr. 3-7). 25.65 *(978-1-59961-328-4(X))* Spotlight.

—The Water Sprites. Rodda, Emily. 2007. (Fairy Realm Ser.). 104p. (gr. 3-7). 25.65 *(978-1-59961-330-7(1))* Spotlight.

Vitale, Raoul & Tank, Daniel. Adam & Eve. 2005. (Family Bible Story Ser.). 93p. (J). pap. *(978-0-8280-1851-7(0))* Review & Herald Publishing Assn.

—Adam & Eve. Brand, Ruth R. 2005. (Family Bible Story Ser.). 95p. (J). (gr. -1-7). per. 19.99 *(978-0-8280-1850-0(2))* Review & Herald Publishing Assn.

Vitale, Stefano. Pond Circle. Franco, Betsy. 2009. (ENG.). 32p. (J). (gr. -1-3). 17.99 *(978-1-4169-4021-0(9)*, McElderry, Margaret K. Bks.) McElderry, Margaret K. Bks.

—There Is a Flower at the Tip of My Nose Smelling Me. Walker, Alice. 2006. (ENG.). 32p. (J). (gr. -1-3). 17.99 *(978-0-06-057080-4(6))* HarperCollins Pubs.

—There Was an Old Man Who Painted the Sky. Sloat, Teri. 2009. (ENG.). 32p. (J). (gr. -1-2). 16.95 *(978-0-8050-6751-4(5)*, Holt, Henry & Co. Bks. For Young Readers) Holt, Henry & Co.

—Why War Is Never a Good Idea. Walker, Alice. 2007. 32p. (J). (gr. -1-3). lib. bdg. 17.89 *(978-0-06-075386-3(2))* HarperCollins Pubs.

Vitali, Daniela. Play with My Animals ABCs. 2003. 16p. (J). bds. 5.99 *(978-1-931722-34-6(X)*, Sixth Avenue Bks.) Grand Central Publishing.

Vitsky, Sally. Alphabet of Earth. Schwaeber, Barbie. 2009. (ENG.). 40p. 17.95 *(978-1-59249-996-0(1))* Soundprints.

—Alphabet of Earth. Schwaeber, Barbie Heit. 2009. (ENG.). 40p. (J). 9.95 *(978-1-59249-997-7(X))* Soundprints.

Vitt, Karren. Mike & a Lynx Named Kitty. Kerr, Mike. 2nd rev. ed. 2006. 112p. per. 13.50 *(978-1-931195-36-2(6))* KiwE Publishing, Ltd.

Vitti, Alessandro. Secret Warriors: Wheels Within Wheels. 2011. (ENG.). 112p. (YA). (gr. 8-17). 19.99 *(978-0-7851-5814-1(6))* Marvel Worldwide, Inc.

Vivanco, Kelly. Snow White & Rose Red. Brothers Grimm. 2014. (ENG.). 40p. (J). (gr. -1-4). 17.95 *(978-1-927018-34-7(X))* Simply Read Bks. CAN. Dist: Ingram Pub. Services.

Vivanco, Kelly. Thumbelina. Andersen, Hans Christian. 2015.Tr. of Tommelise. (ENG.). 48p. (J). (gr. k-4). 17.95 ***(978-1-927018-73-6(0))*** Simply Read Bks. CAN. Dist: Ingram Pub. Services.

Vivas, Julie. I Went Walking. Williams, Sue. 2014. 32p. pap. 27.00 *(978-1-61003-230-8(6))* Center for the Collaborative Classroom.

—I Went Walking. Williams, Sue. 2004. (J). (gr. -1-2). audio compact disk 28.95 *(978-1-59112-720-8(3))*; 2003. pap. 39.95 incl. audio compact disk *(978-1-59112-721-5(1))* Live Oak Media.

—I Went Walking: Lap-Sized Board Book. Williams, Sue. 2005. (ENG.). 30p. (J). (gr. k — 1). bds. 10.95 *(978-0-15-205626-1(2))* Houghton Mifflin Harcourt Publishing Co.

—Let the Celebrations Begin. Wild, Margaret. 2014. (ENG.). 40p. (J). (gr. 2-5). 16.99 *(978-0-7636-7013-9(8))* Candlewick Pr.

—Let's Go Visiting. Williams, Sue. 2003. (ENG.). 32p. (J). (gr. k — 1). bds. 6.95 *(978-0-15-204638-5(0))* Houghton Mifflin Harcourt Publishing Co.

—Noam Mechapes Zichronot. Fox, Mem. Dash Greenspan, Shari, tr. from ENG. 2005. Orig. Title: Wilfrid Gordon McDonald Partridge. (HEB.). 32p. 14.00 *(978-965-7108-43-7(8))* Urim Pubns. ISR. Dist: Coronet Bks.

—Samsara Dog. Manos, Helen. 2007. (ENG.). 40p. (J). (gr. 3-6). 10.99 *(978-1-933605-51-7(0))* Kane Miller.

Vivian, Bart. Imagine. Vivian, Bart. 2013. (ENG.). 32p. (J). (gr. -1-3). 14.99 *(978-1-58270-329-9(9))* Aladdin/Beyond Words.

Vivian, Siobhan, jt. illus. see Seibold, J. Otto.

Vo-Dinh, Mai. Tet: The New Year. Tran, Kim-Lan & Millar, Louise. 2005. (Multicultural Celebrations Ser.). 32p. (J). 4.95 *(978-1-59373-012-3(8))* Bunker Hill Publishing, Inc.

Voake, Charlotte. Antonio Vivaldi, 1 vol. Baumont, Olivier. 2012. (ENG.). 28p. (J). (gr. 2-6). 19.99 *(978-1-85103-323-2(8))* Moonlight Publishing, Ltd. GBR. Dist: Independent Pubs. Group.

—Bach. Khoury, Marielle D. & du Bouchet, Paule. 2012. (ENG.). 28p. (J). (gr. 2-6). 19.99 *(978-1-85103-319-5(X))* Moonlight Publishing, Ltd. GBR. Dist: Independent Pubs. Group.

—Caterpillar, Caterpillar. French, Vivian. 2010. (Read, Listen, & Wonder Ser.). (ENG.). 32p. (J). (gr. -1-3). pap. 8.99 *(978-0-7636-4002-6(6))* Candlewick Pr.

—Caterpillar Caterpillar: Read & Wonder. French, Vivian. 2009. (Read & Wonder Ser.). (ENG.). 32p. (J). (gr. -1-3). pap. 6.99 *(978-0-7636-4263-1(0))* Candlewick Pr.

—Debussy. Babin, Pierre. 2012. (ENG.). 28p. (J). (gr. 2-6). 19.99 *(978-1-85103-321-8(1))* Moonlight Publishing, Ltd. GBR. Dist: Independent Pubs. Group.

—Franz Schubert, 1 vol. Du Bouchet, Paule. 2013. (ENG.). 28p. (J). (gr. 2-6). 19.99 *(978-1-85103-312-6(2))* Moonlight Publishing, Ltd. GBR. Dist: Independent Pubs. Group.

—Frédéric Chopin. Weill, Catherine. 2010. (Descubrimos a Los Músicos Ser.). (SPA.). 24p. (J). (gr. 2-4). 15.95 *(978-84-9825-414-3(0))* Combel Editorial, S.A. ESP. Dist: Independent Pubs. Group.

—Fryderyk Choppin. Weill, Catherine. 2012. (ENG.). 28p. (J). (gr. 2-6). 19.99 *(978-1-85103-308-9(4))* Moonlight Publishing, Ltd. GBR. Dist: Independent Pubs. Group.

—Henry Purcell, 1 vol. Du Bouchet, Paule & Khoury, Marielle D. 2012. (ENG.). 28p. (J). (gr. 2-6). 19.99 *(978-1-85103-309-6(2))* Moonlight Publishing, Ltd. GBR. Dist: Independent Pubs. Group.

—Insect Detective. Voake, Steve. (Read & Wonder Ser.). (J). 2012. (ENG.). 32p. (gr. -1-3). pap. 6.99 *(978-0-7636-5816-8(2))*; 2010. 28p. *(978-1-4063-1051-1(4))* Candlewick Pr.

Voake, Charlotte. Insect Detective. Voake, Steve. 2015. 32p. pap. 7.00 ***(978-1-61003-407-4(4))*** Center for the Collaborative Classroom.

Voake, Charlotte. Johann Sebastian Bach. 2007. (Descubrimos a Los Músicos Ser.). (ENG.). 24p. (J). (gr. 2-4). 14.95 *(978-84-9825-162-3(1))* Combel Editorial, S.A. ESP. Dist: Independent Pubs. Group.

—Ludwig Van Beethoven, 1 vol. Walcker, Yann. 2012. (ENG.). 28p. (J). (gr. 2-6). 19.99 *(978-1-85103-310-2(6))* Moonlight Publishing, Ltd. GBR. Dist: Independent Pubs. Group.

—Piotr Ilyich Tchaikovski. Ollivier, Stephane. 2010. (Descubrimos a Los Músicos Ser.). (SPA.). 24p. (J). (gr. 2-4). 15.95 *(978-84-9825-416-7(7))* Combel Editorial, S.A. ESP. Dist: Independent Pubs. Group.

Voake, Charlotte. Say It! Zolotow, Charlotte. 2015. (ENG.). 32p. (J). (-k). 15.99 ***(978-0-7636-8115-9(6))*** Candlewick Pr.

Voake, Charlotte. Wolfgang Amadeus Mozart, 1 vol. Walcker, Yann. 2012. (ENG.). 28p. (J). (gr. 2-6). 19.99 *(978-1-85103-311-9(4))* Moonlight Publishing, Ltd. GBR. Dist: Independent Pubs. Group.

Voake, Charlotte. Melissa's Octopus & Other Unsuitable Pets. Voake, Charlotte. 2015. (ENG.). 32p. (J). (gr. -1-2). 16.99 *(978-0-7636-7481-6(8))* Candlewick Pr.

—Tweedle Dee Dee. Voake, Charlotte. 2008. (ENG.). 32p. (J). (gr. -1-2). 16.99 *(978-0-7636-3797-2(1))* Candlewick Pr.

Voerg, Kathy. Harry the Happy Caterpillar Grows: Helping Children Adjust to Change. Jett, Cindy. 2010. (Let's Talk Ser.). (ENG.). 48p. (J). (gr. -1-4). pap. 8.95 *(978-0-88282-316-4(7))* New Horizon Pr. Pubs., Inc.

—I Don't Want to Go to School: Helping Children Cope with Separation Anxiety. Pando, Nancy J. 2005. (Let's Talk Ser.). (ENG.). 48p. (J). (gr. -1-1). per. 9.95 *(978-0-88282-254-9(3))* New Horizon Pr. Pubs., Inc.

—The Smith Family's New Puppy: Helping Children Cope with a New Family Member. Smith-Mansell, Dana. 2008. (Let's Talk Ser.). (ENG.). 48p. (J). (gr. -1-4). pap. 8.95 *(978-0-88282-327-0(2))* New Horizon Pr. Pubs., Inc.

—They Call Me Fat Zoe: Helping Children & Families Overcome Obesity. Martin, Don et al. 2012. (Let's Talk Ser.). (ENG.). 48p. (J). (gr. -1-2). pap. 9.95 *(978-0-88282-377-5(9))* New Horizon Pr. Pubs., Inc.

Vogel, Vin. Maddi's Fridge. Brandt, Lois. 2014. (ENG.). 32p. (J). (gr. k-3). 17.95 *(978-1-936261-29-1(4))* Flashlight Pr.

Vogel, Vin. Music Class Today! Weinstone, David. 2015. (ENG.). 40p. (J). (gr. -1 — 1). 17.99 ***(978-0-374-35131-1(7)***, Farrar, Straus & Giroux (BYR)) Farrar, Straus & Giroux.

Vohra, Sibi. The Three Billy Goats Gruff. Asbjørnsen, Peter Christen. 2010. (J). *(978-1-60617-149-3(6))* Teaching Strategies, Inc.

Vohra, Subhash. The Little Red Hen. 2010. (J). *(978-1-60617-129-5(1))* Teaching Strategies, Inc.

Vohwinkel, Astrid. Nanuk Flies Home. Holtei, Christa. 2008. 26p. (J). (gr. 4-7). 16.00 *(978-0-8028-5342-4(0))* Eerdmans, William B. Publishing Co.

Voight, Lisa. Goodnight Cowtown. Drez, Jennifer & Bumstead, Robin. 2012. 40p. (J). 17.95 *(978-0-615-54492-2(4))* Petit Chou Chou, LLC.

Vojtech, Anna. All Things Bright & Beautiful. Alexander, Cecil Frances. ed. 2006. (ENG.). 24p. (J). (gr. -1-2). pap. 6.95 *(978-0-7358-2045-6(7))* North-South Bks., Inc.

—Friendly Beasts: An Old English Christmas Carol, 1 vol. St. James, Rebecca. 2012. (ENG.). 32p. (J). 16.99 *(978-0-310-72012-6(5))* Zonderkidz.

—Over in the Meadow: A Counting Rhyme. Wadsworth, Olive A. 2003. (Cheshire Studio Book Ser.). (ENG.). 32p. (J). pap. 7.95 *(978-0-7358-1871-2(1))* North-South Bks., Inc.

—The Story of the Easter Robin, 1 vol. Mackall, Dandi Daley. 2010. (ENG.). 32p. (J). (gr. -1-2). 15.99 *(978-0-310-71331-9(5))* Zonderkidz.

Vojtech, Anna. Look What I Can Do! Vojtech, Anna. Viau, Nancy. 2013. (ENG.). 32p. (J). (gr. -1-1). 17.95 *(978-1-4197-0529-8(6))*, Abrams Bks. for Young Readers) Abrams.

Vokes, Neil, et al. From the Marvel Vault. 2011. (ENG.). 120p. (YA). (gr. 8-17). pap. 14.99 *(978-0-7851-5784-7(0))* Marvel Worldwide, Inc.

Volinski, Jessica, jt. illus. see DePrince, Erik.

Volke, Gordon, et al. Panda Patrol Big Activity Book. 2004. 24p. 6.00 *(978-1-84161-111-2(5))* Ravette Publishing, Ltd. GBR. Dist: Parkwest Pubns., Inc.

—Panda Patrol Sticker, Story & Activity Book, Vol. 2. 2004. 16p. pap., act. bk. ed. 6.00 *(978-1-84161-112-9(3))* Ravette Publishing, Ltd. GBR. Dist: Parkwest Pubns., Inc.

—Panda Patrol Sticker, Story & Activity Book. 2004. 16p. pap., act. bk. ed. 6.00 *(978-1-84161-072-6(0))* Ravette Publishing, Ltd. GBR. Dist: Parkwest Pubns., Inc.

—Panda Patrol Travel Games with Stickers. 2004. 16p. pap., act. bk. ed. 6.00 *(978-1-84161-110-5(7))* Ravette Publishing, Ltd. GBR. Dist: Parkwest Pubns., Inc.

Volley, Will, et al. Romeo & Juliet. Shakespeare, William. Bryant, Clive, ed. Sanders, Joe Sutliff, tr. 2009. (ENG.). 176p. (gr. 4-18). pap. 16.95 *(978-1-906332-63-1(0)*, Classical Comics, Ltd.) Classical Comics GBR. Dist: Perseus-PGW.

Vollmer, Chuck, jt. illus. see Corley, Rob.

Volpari, Daniela. Oliver Twist. Dickens, Charles. 2014. (Big Picture Book Ser.). (ENG.). 48p. (J). (gr. 1). 16.95 *(978-2-7338-2529-7(1))* Auzou, Philippe Editions FRA. Dist: Consortium Bk. Sales & Distribution.

Voltaggio, Nicholas. Hippocrene Hindi Children's Picture Dictionary. Hippocrene Books Staff. Martin, Robert Stanly, ed. 2006. (ENG.). 112p. (J). pap. 14.95 *(978-0-7818-1129-3(5))* Hippocrene Bks., Inc.

—Vietnamese Children's Picture Dictionary: English-Vietnamese/Vietnamese-English. Martin, Robert, Jr. 2006. (ENG & VIE.). 112p. (J). (gr. 3-7). pap. 14.95 *(978-0-7818-1133-0(3))* Hippocrene Bks., Inc.

Voltz, Ralph. Bible for Me: 12 Favorite Stories, 1 vol. Holmes, Andy. 2003. (ENG.). 48p. 9.99 *(978-1-4003-0234-5(X))* Nelson, Thomas Inc.

—Jackson & Julie the Twelve-Month Chefs: A Holiday Cookbook for Families & Children. Perrenot, Christine. 2011. 32p. (J). 16.95 *(978-1-61254-028-3(7))* Brown Bks. Publishing Group.

Volz, Katie. Tiggy Finds a Home. Volz, Carole A. 2013. 44p. (J). 18.95 *(978-1-62287-445-3(5))* First Edition Design eBook Publishing.

von Allmen, Tania. Ponders, Proverbs & Principles. Weckworth, Rodney R. 2005. 344p. pap. 14.95 *(978-1-929170-16-6(5)*, PDG) Publishers Design Group, Inc.

Von Amelsfort, Barbra. The Yoga Adventure for Children: Playing, Dancing, Moving, Breathing, Relaxing. Purperhart, Helen. Evans, Amina Marix, tr. from DUT. 2007. (ENG.). 144p. (gr. -1-6). per. 14.95 *(978-0-89793-470-1(9)*, Hunter Hse.) Turner Publishing Co.

von Buhler, Cynthia. Tell Us a Tale, Hans! The Life of Hans Christian Andersen. Fradin, Dennis Brindell. 2006. (J). *(978-1-59336-681-0(7))*; pap. *(978-1-59336-682-7(5))* Mondo Publishing.

—They Called Her Molly Pitcher. Rockwell, Anne F. 2006. (ENG.). 40p. (J). (gr. -1-2). 7.99 *(978-0-553-11253-5(8)*, Dragonfly Bks.) Random Hse. Children's Bks.

Von Buhler, Cynthia. But Who Will Bell the Cats? Von Buhler, Cynthia. 2009. (ENG.). 32p. (J). (gr. -1-3). 17.00 *(978-0-618-99718-3(0))* Houghton Mifflin Harcourt Publishing Co.

von Buhler, Cynthia. Nicolaus Copernicus: The Earth Is a Planet. von Buhler, Cynthia, tr. Fradin, Dennis Brindell. 2003. 32p. (J). (gr. 2-6). 15.95 *(978-1-59336-006-1(1))*; pap. *(978-1-59336-007-8(X))* Mondo Publishing.

von der Sterre, Johanna. Moses & the Long Walk. Bader, Joanne. 2006. 16p. (J). 1.99 *(978-0-7586-0874-1(8))* Concordia Publishing Hse.

von Königslöw, Andrea Wayne. Emily's Eighteen Aunts, 1 vol. Parkinson, Curtis. 2003. (ENG.). 30p. (J). *(978-0-7737-3336-7(1))* Fitzhenry & Whiteside, Ltd.

—Emily's Eighteen Aunts, 1 vol. Parkinson, Curtis. 2005. (ENG.). 32p. (J). pap. 5.95 *(978-1-55005-122-3(9)*, 1550051229) Fitzhenry & Whiteside, Ltd. CAN. Dist: Midpoint Trade Bks., Inc.

von Königslöw, Andrea Wayne. How Do You Read to a Rabbit? von Königslöw, Andrea Wayne. 2010. (ENG.). 32p. (J). (gr. -1-k). pap. 7.95 *(978-1-55451-231-7(X)*, 9781554512317) Annick Pr., Ltd. CAN. Dist: Firefly Bks., Ltd.

—Toilet Tales. von Königslöw, Andrea Wayne. 20th rev. ed. 2008. (ENG.). 32p. (J). (gr. -1 — 1). 19.95 *(978-1-55451-132-7(1)*, 9781554511327); pap. 7.95 *(978-1-55451-131-0(3)*, 9781554511310) Annick Pr., Ltd. CAN. Dist: Firefly Bks., Ltd.

VonBokel, Jan. An Extra Ordinary Day. Fonner, Deborah K. 2012. 24p. 19.95 *(978-1-4327-8342-6(4))* Outskirts Pr., Inc.

vonderLuft, Lydia. Mrs. Gowing's Kindergarten. Gowing, Pattie. 2010. (ENG.). 52p. pap. 11.95 *(978-1-4505-8150-9(1))* CreateSpace Independent Publishing Platform.

Vongprapachanh, Somchith. Explore Titanic: Breathtaking New Pictures, Recreated with Digital Technology, 2 vols. Chrisp, Peter. 2011. (ENG.). 40p. (J). (gr. 4-9). 17.99 *(978-1-4380-7159-6(0))* Barron's Educational Series, Inc.

VonRecht. Raspus. Kay, Susan. 2009. 16p. pap. 8.99 *(978-1-4389-8380-6(8))* AuthorHouse.

VonSeggen, Jon, jt. illus. see Van Order, Laura.

Vonthron-Laver, Sarah. Harriet Can Carry It, 1 vol. Mueller, Kirk Jay. 2014. (ENG.). 32p. (J). 16.99 *(978-1-59572-675-9(6))* Star Bright Bks., Inc.

Voorheis, Tracy. Nibbles... a strawberry Tale. Voorheis, Tracy. 2007. 60p. (J). per. 19.00 *(978-0-9787113-0-6(0)*, Ithaca Pr.) Authors & Artists Publishers of New York, Inc.

Vorella2000. Laugh a Little. Tate, Singleton M. 2012. 24p. pap. 24.95 *(978-1-4560-9117-0(4))* America Star Bks.

Vorhees, D. Lawrey. Doorways of New Mexico. 2003. 154p. spiral bd. 29.95 *(978-0-9635589-7-8(8))* Elysian Hills.

Voronina, Natasha. How the Russian Snow Maiden Helped Santa Claus. Buyske, Gail. 2005. 32p. (J). 16.95 *(978-0-9725027-4-0(2))* Vernissage Pr., LLC.

Vosailagi, Jo. Pentapus. 2006. 120p. per. 12.56 *(978-1-4120-9272-2(8))* Trafford Publishing.

Vosburg, L. The Fighting Quaker: The Southern Campaigns of General Nathaniel Greene. Latham, Frank Brown. 2011. 194p. 42.95 *(978-1-258-00848-2(3))* Literary Licensing, LLC.

Vosburg, M. RIP, M. D. Schauer, M. 2010. (ENG.). 88p. pap. 12.99 *(978-1-60699-369-9(0)*, 699369) Fantagraphics Bks.

Vosburgh, Leonard. Davy Crockett. Ford, Anne. 2011. 48p. 35.95 *(978-1-258-06913-1(X))* Literary Licensing, LLC.

Vosburgh, Leonard. Fear in the Forest. De Leeuw, Cateau. 2014. (ENG.). 123p. (J). pap. 14.95 ***(978-1-932350-43-2(8))*** Bethlehem Bks.

Vosburgh, Leonard. A Flag for Lafitte: Story of the Battle of New Orleans. Lane, Frederick A. 2011. 192p. 42.95 *(978-1-258-06624-6(6))* Literary Licensing, LLC.

—The How & Why Wonder Book of Florence Nightingale. Webb, Robert N. 2011. 50p. 35.95 *(978-1-258-09107-1(0))* Literary Licensing, LLC.

—We Were There at the Battle of Gettysburg. Malkus, Alida Sims. 2013. (ENG.). 192p. (J). (gr. 3-8). pap. 6.99 *(978-0-486-49261-2(3))* Dover Pubns., Inc.

Voss, Jonathan D. Winnie: The True Story of the Bear Who Inspired Winnie-the-Pooh. Walker, Sally M. 2015. (ENG.). 40p. (J). (gr. -1-3). 17.99 *(978-0-8050-9715-3(5)*, Holt, Henry & Co. Bks. For Young Readers) Holt, Henry & Co.

Vote, Steven, photos by. Autism & Me: Sibling Stories, 1 vol. Shapiro, Ouisie. 2009. (ENG., 32p. (J). (gr. 2-7). 16.99 *(978-0-8075-0487-1(4))* Whitman, Albert & Co.

—Bullying & Me: Schoolyard Stories, 1 vol. Shapiro, Ouisie. 2010. (ENG., 32p. (J). (gr. 3-8). 16.99 *(978-0-8075-0921-0(3))* Whitman, Albert & Co.

Voute, Kathleen. The Magic Ball from Mars & Starboy. Biemiller, Carl L. 2003. 302p. (J). pap. 19.95 *(978-0-918736-09-3(9)*, Sense of Wonder Pr.) Rock, James A. & Co. Pubs.

—Magic Ball from Mars & Starboy. Biemiller, Carl L. 2003. 256p. (J). reprint ed. 26.95 *(978-0-918736-10-9(2)*, Sense of Wonder Pr.) Rock, James A. & Co. Pubs.

Voutila, Ritva. Outside. Hathorn, Libby. 2014. (ENG.). 32p. (J). (— 1). 18.99 ***(978-1-921894-68-8(7))*** Little Hare Bks. AUS. Dist: Independent Pubs. Group.

—The Stone Lion. Wild, Margaret. 2015. (ENG.). 32p. (J). (gr. k-4). 17.99 ***(978-1-921894-85-5(7))*** Little Hare Bks. AUS. Dist: Independent Pubs. Group.

Vroman, Dave. Jesse & His New Friends. Irwin, Esther. Puett, Gayle, ed. 2006. (J). spiral bd. 10.00 *(978-0-9778462-1-4(0))* Irwin, Esther L.

Vrombaut, An. Henrietta the Hairy Hippo. Vrombaut, An. 2014. (64 Zoo Lane Ser.). (ENG.). 32p. (J). (gr. -1-k). pap. 9.99 *(978-1-4449-1299-9(2))* Hodder & Stoughton GBR. Dist: Independent Pubs. Group.

—Zed the Zebra. Vrombaut, An. 2013. (64 Zoo Lane Ser.). (ENG.). 32p. (J). (gr. -1-k). pap. 10.99 *(978-1-4449-1303-3(4))* Hodder & Stoughton GBR. Dist: Independent Pubs. Group.

Vu, Thi. Red Hot Dot's Fire Safety Book: Fire Safety. Johnson, Sandi. Durant, Sybrina, ed. l.t. ed. 2014. 44p. (J). (gr. k-5). pap. 12.99 *(978-1-929063-86-4(5)*, 279) Moons & Stars Publishing For Children.

—3 - Dorp the Scottish Dragon Bk. 3: Book 3 - Hollywood - the Movie, 7 vols. Johnson, Sandi. Johnson, Britt & Durant, Sybrina, eds. 2004. (Little Choo-Choo Bks.). 28p. (J). (gr. -1-6). pap. 16.99 *(978-1-929063-02-4(4)*, 103) Moons & Stars Publishing For Children.

Vue, Tou. Burning Secrets, 1 vol. Brezenoff, Steve. (Vortex Bks.). (ENG.). 112p. (gr. 2-3). 2008. pap. 7.19 *(978-1-59889-920-7(1))*; 2007. 25.32 *(978-1-59889-854-5(X))* Stone Arch Bks. (Vortex Bks.).

—Claws in the Snow, 1 vol. Dahl, Michael. 2010. (Dragonblood Ser.). (ENG.). 40p. (gr. 1-3). pap. 6.25 *(978-1-4342-2308-1(6)*, Zone Bks.) Stone Arch Bks.

—Dragon in the Desert, 1 vol. Dahl, Michael. (Dragonblood Ser.). (ENG.). 40p. (gr. 1-3). 2010. pap. 6.25 *(978-1-4342-2309-8(4))*; 2009. 22.65 *(978-1-4342-1260-3(2))* Stone Arch Bks. (Zone Bks.).

Vue, Tou, jt. illus. see Evans, Mark.

Vuillamy, Clara. The Bear with Sticky Paws Won't Go to Bed. Vuillamy, Clara. 2010. 32p. (J). (gr. -1-2). 15.95 *(978-1-58925-087-1(7))* Tiger Tales.

Vulliamy, Claire. The Bear with Sticky Paws. 2008. (Tiger Tales Ser.). 24p. (J). (gr. -1-2). 15.95 *(978-1-58925-070-3(2))* Tiger Tales.

Vulliamy, Clara. Bubble & Squeak. Mayhew, James. 2013. (J). *(978-1-4351-4770-6(7))* Barnes & Noble, Inc.

Vulliamy, Clara. Digby o'Day & the Great Diamond Robbery. Hughes, Shirley. 2015. (ENG.). 136p. (J). (gr. k-3). 12.99 ***(978-0-7636-7445-8(1))*** Candlewick Pr.

Vulliamy, Clara. Digby O'Day in the Fast Lane. Hughes, Shirley. 2014. (ENG.). 128p. (J). (gr. k-3). 12.99 *(978-0-7636-7369-7(2))* Candlewick Pr.

—Keep Love in Your Heart, Little One. Andreae, Giles. 2007. 32p. (J). (gr. -1-3). 15.95 *(978-1-58925-066-6(4))* Tiger Tales.

Vulliamy, Clara. The Bear with Sticky Paws Goes to School. Vulliamy, Clara. 2009. 32p. (J). (gr. -1-2). 15.95 *(978-1-58925-081-9(8))* Tiger Tales.

—Bear with Sticky Paws Goes to School. Vulliamy, Clara. 2010. 32p. pap. 7.95 *(978-1-58925-424-4(4))* Tiger Tales.

—Martha Bunny Loves School. Vulliamy, Clara. 2013. (ENG.). 32p. (J). (gr. -1-2). 16.99 *(978-0-8075-4976-6(2))* Whitman, Albert & Co.

—Muffin & the Expedition. Vulliamy, Clara. 2012. (Muffin Ser.). (ENG.). 32p. (J). (gr. -1-k). pap. 9.99 *(978-1-4083-1243-8(3))* Hodder & Stoughton GBR. Dist: Independent Pubs. Group.

Vyas, Bhavana. The Forbidden Temple: Stories from the Past. Padma, T. V. 2004. 95p. (J). *(978-81-8146-041-7(3))* Tulika Pubs.

Vyner, Tim. In the Dark of the Night. Stewart, Paul. 2009. (ENG.). 40p. (J). (gr. -1-2). 17.95 *(978-1-84507-764-8(4)*, Frances Lincoln) Quarto Publishing Group UK GBR. Dist: Perseus-PGW.

W

W., E., jt. illus. see Morgin, W. J.

W, Farnsworth, jt. illus. see Farnsworth, Bill.

W, J. The Three Monsters. Ward, J. 2011. (ENG.). 38p. pap. 12.00 *(978-1-4536-2687-0(5))* CreateSpace Independent Publishing Platform.

Waananen, Lisa. Life Science Through Infographics. Higgins, Nadia. 2013. (Super Science Infographics Ser.). (ENG.). 32p. (gr. 3-5). pap. 8.95 *(978-1-4677-1592-8(1))*; lib. bdg. 26.60 *(978-1-4677-1288-0(4)*, Lerner Pubns.) Lerner Publishing Group.

—The Solar System Through Infographics. Higgins, Nadia. 2013. (Super Science Infographics Ser.). (ENG.). 32p. (gr. 3-5). pap. 8.95 *(978-1-4677-1594-2(8))*; lib. bdg. 26.60 *(978-1-4677-1289-7(2)*, Lerner Pubns.) Lerner Publishing Group.

Waas, Uli. Christmas for the Snowmen. Hanel, Wolfram & Hänel, Wolfram. 2006. (ENG.). 32p. (J). (gr. -1-3). 6.95 *(978-0-7358-2094-4(5))* North-South Bks., Inc.

Waber, Paulis. Lyle Walks the Dogs. Waber, Bernard. 2010. (Lyle the Crocodile Ser.). (ENG.). 24p. (J). (gr. -1-3). 12.99 *(978-0-547-22323-0(4))* Houghton Mifflin Harcourt Publishing Co.

Wach, Delia Bowman. Teddy Bear's Favorite Pictures: A Quiet Time Sharing Book. Wach, Delia Bowman. Cloyd, Nancy J. 2007. 32p. (J). (gr. -1). 15.95 *(978-0-929915-75-3(5))* Headline Bks., Inc.

Wachter, Dave. Breath of Bones: a Tale of the Golem: A Tale of the Golem. Niles, Steve & Santoro, Matt. Allie, Scott, ed. 2014. (ENG.). 80p. 14.99 *(978-1-61655-344-9(8))* Dark Horse Comics.

Wacker, Ranae. God Made My Hands. Comley, Kathryn. 2004. (J). bds. 9.99 *(978-1-4183-0005-0(5))* Christ Inspired, Inc.

Waddington, Nicole. It's Good Sunday. Moore, Shahari. 2003. (J). *(978-0-9743394-0-5(7))* More Pr.

Waddy, F. Grammar-Land. Nesbitt, M. L. 2009. 124p. pap. 8.95 *(978-1-59915-332-2(7))* Yesterday's Classics.

Wade, Gini. The Book of Dragon Myths. Tango Books Staff. 2011. (Pop-Up Board Games Ser.). (ENG.). 10p. (J). (gr. -1-2). 24.99 *(978-1-85707-720-9(2))* Tango Bks. GBR. Dist: Independent Pubs. Group.

—Dic Penderyn. Edwards, Meinir Wyn. 2008. (ENG.). 24p. (J). pap. 4.95 *(978-1-84771-022-2(0))* Y Lolfa GBR. Dist: Dufour Editions, Inc.

—Dragon & Mousie. Peters, Andrew Fusek. 2006. (ENG.). 32p. (J). pap. 7.95 *(978-0-86243-650-6(8))* Y Lolfa GBR. Dist: Dufour Editions, Inc.

—Dragon & Mousie & the Snow Factory. Peters, Andrew Fusek. 2007. (ENG.). 32p. (J). pap. 7.95 *(978-0-86243-945-3(0))* Y Lolfa GBR. Dist: Dufour Editions, Inc.

—Maelgwn, King of Gwynedd. Edwards, Meinir Wyn. 2008. (ENG.). 24p. (J). pap. 4.95 *(978-1-84771-024-6(7))* Y Lolfa GBR. Dist: Dufour Editions, Inc.

—Red Bandits of Mawddwy. Edwards, Meinir Wyn. 2008. (ENG.). 24p. (J). pap. 4.95 *(978-1-84771-023-9(9))* Y Lolfa GBR. Dist: Dufour Editions, Inc.

—Rhys & Meinir. Edwards, Meinir Wyn. 2007. (ENG.). 24p. (J). pap. 4.95 *(978-1-84771-020-8(4))* Y Lolfa GBR. Dist: Dufour Editions, Inc.

—Welsh Tales in a Flash: Cantre'r Gwaelod. Edwards, Meinir Wyn. 2007. (ENG.). 24p. (J). pap. 4.95 *(978-1-84771-021-5(2))* Y Lolfa GBR. Dist: Dufour Editions, Inc.

Wade, Jerry. Fortitude: The Adventures of the Esteem Team. Sargent, Alan E. 2013. 84p. pap. 10.95 *(978-1-62516-984-6(1)*, Strategic Bk. Publishing) Strategic Book Publishing & Rights Agency (SBPRA).

Wade, Mervin, photos by. Prime Time Dimes in the Feds. Wade, Mervin. Wade, Mervin, ed. 2003. 80p. (YA). pap. *(978-0-9722738-0-0(8))* Melzee's Production.

Wademan, Spike. True Life Survival. Vale, Janice. 2007. (Collins Big Cat Ser.). (ENG.). 32p. (J). pap. 7.99 *(978-0-00-723078-5(8))* HarperCollins Pubs. Ltd. GBR. Dist: Independent Pubs. Group.

Wadham, Anna. The Ant & the Big Bad Bully Goat. Peters, Andrew Fusek. 2007. (Traditional Tales with a Twist Ser.). (ENG.). 32p. (J). (gr. -1-3). pap. *(978-1-84643-079-4(8))* Child's Play International Ltd.

—The Ant & the Big Bad Bully Goat. Peters, Andrew. 2010. (Traditional Tales with a Twist Ser.). (ENG.). 32p. (J). (gr. -1-2). *(978-1-84643-348-1(7))* Child's Play International Ltd.

—Dingo Dog & the Billabong Storm. Peters, Andrew Fusek. 2009. (Traditional Tales with a Twist Ser.). (ENG.). 32p. (J). (gr. -1-2). *(978-1-84643-247-7(2))* Child's Play International Ltd.

—Dingo Dog & the Billabong Storm. Peters, Andrew. 2010. (Traditional Tales with a Twist Ser.). (ENG.). 32p. (J). (gr. -1-2). *(978-1-84643-350-4(9))* Child's Play International Ltd.

Wadham, Anna. Summer in Antarctica. Latham, Irene. 2015. (J). ***(978-1-4677-5216-9(9))*** Lerner Publishing Group.

Wadkins, Fran. Resurrection Eggs Activity Book. Bradford, Amy L. & Larmoyeux, Mary. 2006. 58p. (J). (gr. 4-7). pap. 6.99 *(978-1-57229-790-6(5))* FamilyLife.

Waechter, Philip. Bravo! Port, Moni. 2011. (Gecko Press Titles Ser.). 36p. 17.95 *(978-1-877467-71-4(5))* Gecko Pr. NZL. Dist: Lerner Publishing Group.

Waerea, James & Waerea, Mitch. Pukunui. Waerea, James. FireHydrant Creative Studios, ed. 2010. (ENG & MAO.). 26p. (J). pap. 14.95 *(978-0-9826066-0-5(5))* FireHydrant Creative Studios, Inc.

Waerea, Mitch, jt. illus. see Waerea, James.

Wagele, Elizabeth. Finding the Birthday Cake: Helping Children Raise Their Self-Esteem. Wagele, Elizabeth. 2007. (ENG.). 48p. (J). (gr. k-4). per. 8.95 *(978-0-88282-277-8(2))* New Horizon Pr. Pubs., Inc.

Wagner, Andy. When Mama Mirabelle Comes Home. Wood, Douglas. 2007. (ENG.). 32p. (J). (gr. -1-2). 16.95 *(978-1-4263-0194-0(4))*; 24.90 *(978-1-4263-0195-7(2))* National Geographic Society. (National Geographic Children's Bks.).

Wagner, Connie. The Evil Mailbox & the Super Burrito, 1 vol. Wagner-Robertson, Garry. 2011. (ENG.). 96p. (J). 16.99 *(978-0-7643-3856-4(0)*, Schiffer Publishing Ltd) Schiffer Publishing, Ltd.

Wagner, Gavin. The Mobile Monk: A Zen Tale. Cerpok, M. L. 2008. 73p. pap. 19.95 *(978-1-60610-138-4(2))* America Star Bks.

Wagner, Gerard. Three Grimms' Fairy Tales. Steiner, Rudolf. 2010. 88p. (J). 25.00 *(978-0-88010-716-7(2))* SteinerBooks, Inc.

Wagner, Sandra Glahn. The Ants Have Dyed. Wagner, Sandra Glahn. 2013. 20p. pap. 12.95 *(978-1-61493-171-3(2))* Peppertree Pr., The.

Wagner, Steve. Socky, the Soft-Hearted Soccer Ball. Voigt, David & Voigt, Grady. 2011. pap. 12.00 *(978-0-9833310-6-3(5))* Aperture Pr., LLC.

Wagoner, Kim. The Mommy Mole. Medler, John, Jr. 2004. (J). pap. 15.00 *(978-0-8059-6664-0(1))* Dorrance Publishing Co., Inc.

Wahl, Valerie. Kindness: A Treasury of Buddhist Tales & Wisdom. Conover, Sarah. 2010. (ENG.). 184p. (YA). pap. 19.95 *(978-1-55896-568-3(8)*, Skinner Hse. Bks.) Unitarian Universalist Assn.

Wahman, Wendy. Snowboy 1, 2, 3. Wahman, Joe. 2012. (ENG.). 32p. (J). (gr. -1-1). 14.99 *(978-0-8050-8732-1(X)*, Holt, Henry & Co. Bks. For Young Readers) Holt, Henry & Co.

Wahman, Wendy. A Cat Like That. Wahman, Wendy. 2011. (ENG.). 32p. (J). (gr. -1-2). 16.99 *(978-0-8050-8942-4(X)*, Holt, Henry & Co. Bks. For Young Readers) Holt, Henry & Co.

—Don't Lick the Dog: Making Friends with Dogs. Wahman, Wendy. 2009. (ENG.). 32p. (J). (gr. -1-2). 17.99 *(978-0-8050-8733-8(8)*, Holt, Henry & Co. Bks. For Young Readers) Holt, Henry & Co.

Wald, Antoinette M., jt. illus. see Wald, Sara Joyce.

Wald, Antoinette M., jt. illus. see Wald, Sara J.

Wald, Sara J. & Wald, Antoinette M. The Fairy Seekers - the Sand Fairy. 1. Murphy, Breena. l.t. ed. 2006. 284p. (J). per. 14.95 *(978-0-9788010-0-7(8))* Edes Publishing Co.

Wald, Sara Joyce & Wald, Antoinette M. The Fairy Seekers - the Sand Fairy. Murphy, Breena. l.t. ed. 2006. 284p. (J). 24.95 *(978-0-9788010-1-4(6))* Edes Publishing Co.

Waites, Joan. Monsieur Durand's Grosse Affaire, 1 vol. St. Romain, Rose Anne. 2011. (ENG.). 32p. (J). (gr. k-3). 16.99 *(978-1-58980-808-9(8))* Pelican Publishing Co., Inc.

—P Is for Police, 1 vol. Butler, Dori Hillestad. 2009. (ENG.). 32p. (J). (gr. k-3). 16.99 *(978-1-58980-652-8(2))* Pelican Publishing Co., Inc.

—Saint Faustina Kowalska: Messenger of Mercy. Wallace, Susan Helen. 2007. (Encounter the Saints Ser.: 23). (J). pap. 7.95 *(978-0-8198-7101-5(X))* Pauline Bks. & Media.

—What's the Difference? An Endangered Animal Subtraction Story, 1 vol. Slade, Suzanne. 2010. (ENG.). 32p. (J). (gr. -1-3). 16.95 *(978-1-60718-070-8(7))*; pap. 8.95 *(978-1-60718-081-4(2))* Arbordale Publishing.

Waites, Joan C. Daniel Boone: Trailblazer, 1 vol. Allen, Nancy Kelly. 2005. (ENG.). 32p. (J). (gr. k-3). 16.99 *(978-1-58980-212-4(8))* Pelican Publishing Co., Inc.

—F Is for Firefighting, 1 vol. Butler, Dori Hillestad. 2007. (ENG.). 32p. (J). (gr. k-3). 16.99 *(978-1-58980-420-3(1))* Pelican Publishing Co., Inc.

—How-to Cowboy: 22 Secret, Magic How-to Fun Tricks. 2003. 96p. (J). pap. 5.95 *(978-0-9716911-1-7(8))* IM Pr.

—Moon's Cloud Blanket. St. Romain, Rose Anne. 2003. 32p. (J). 15.95 *(978-1-56554-922-7(8))* Pelican Publishing Co., Inc.

—The Waving Girl, 1 vol. Nicholas, J. B. 2004. (ENG.). 32p. (J). (gr. k-3). pap. 8.99 *(978-1-58980-185-1(7))* Pelican Publishing Co., Inc.

Wakageryu, et al. Ryu-Ki System: Sunserra. 2005. 234p. per. 29.95 *(978-0-9770121-0-7(7))* Dragon Dog Pr., Inc.

Wake, Katherine. The Raven's Tale: & other Stories. Steven, Kenneth. 2007. (ENG.). 64p. pap. 13.99 *(978-0-7152-0846-5(2))* Saint Andrew Pr., Ltd. GBR. Dist: Westminster John Knox Pr.

Wake, Rich. The Tricks & Treats of Halloween! Murphy, Angela. 2014. (History of Fun Stuff Ser.). (ENG.). 48p. (J). (gr. 1-3). pap. 3.99 *(978-1-4814-0978-0(6)*, Simon Spotlight) Simon Spotlight.

Wakefield, Scott. The Lion & the Mouse. Olmstead, Kathleen. 2014. (Silver Penny Stories Ser.). (ENG.). 40p. (J). (gr. -1-1). 4.95 *(978-1-4027-8347-0(7))* Sterling Publishing Co., Inc.

—The Three Little Pigs. Namm, Diane. 2012. (Silver Penny Stories Ser.). (ENG.). 40p. (J). (gr. -1-1). 4.95 *(978-1-4027-8434-7(1))* Sterling Publishing Co., Inc.

Wakefield, Scott J. The Gingerbread Boy. Namm, Diane. 2013. (J). *(978-1-4027-8431-6(7))* Sterling Publishing Co., Inc.

—Little Red Riding Hood. McFadden, Deanna. 2013. (Silver Penny Stories Ser.). (ENG.). 40p. (J). (gr. -1-1). 4.95 *(978-1-4027-8337-1(X))* Sterling Publishing Co., Inc.

Wakelin, Bob. Busy Days in Deerfield Valley. Running Press Staff & Speregen, Devra Newberger. 2005. (ENG.). 12p. (J). pap. 11.95 *(978-0-7624-2343-9(9)*, Running Pr.) Running Pr. Bk. Pubs.

Wakelin, Kirsti Anne. Catching Time, 1 vol. Gilmore, Rachna. 2010. (ENG.). 32p. (J). (gr. -1-3). *(978-1-55455-162-0(5))* Fitzhenry & Whiteside, Ltd.

—Dream Boats. Bar-el, Dan. 2013. (ENG.). 44p. (J). (gr. -1-3). 17.95 *(978-1-897476-87-1(6))* Simply Read Bks. CAN. Dist: Ingram Pub. Services.

—A Pod of Orcas, 1 vol. McFarlane, Sheryl. 2006. (ENG.). 28p. (J). (gr. -1-3). per. 9.95 *(978-1-55041-722-7(3)*, 1550417223) Fitzhenry & Whiteside, Ltd. CAN. Dist: Midpoint Trade Bks., Inc.

—When They Are Up..., 1 vol. Thompson, Richard & Spicer, Maggee. 2007. (ENG.). 36p. (J). (gr. -1-k). per. *(978-1-55041-709-8(6))* Fitzhenry & Whiteside, Ltd.

—When They Are Up..., 1 vol. Thompson, Richard & Spicer, Maggee. 2003. (ENG.). 36p. (J). 9.95 *(978-1-55041-707-4(X)*, 155041707X) Fitzhenry & Whiteside, Ltd. CAN. Dist: Midpoint Trade Bks., Inc.

Wakeman, Bill & Langley, Bill. Winnie the Pooh's A to ZZZZ. Ferguson, Don. 2009. 32p. (J). (gr. -1-2). pap. 4.99 *(978-0-7868-4094-6(3))* Disney Pr.

Wakeman, Peter, photos by. Simply Ball: With Pilates Principles. Pohlman, Jennifer & Searle, Rodney. 2005. 64p. (YA). reprint ed. 10.00 *(978-0-7567-9368-5(8))* DIANE Publishing Co.

Wakiyama, Hanako. The Best Pet of All. LaRochelle, David. (ENG.). 32p. (J). (gr. -1-k). 2009. pap. 6.99 *(978-0-14-241272-5(4)*, Puffin); 2004. 16.99 *(978-0-525-47129-5(4)*, Dutton Juvenile) Penguin Publishing Group.

—Cat's Not-So-Perfect Sandcastle. Novesky, Amy. 2012. (ENG.). 28p. (J). (gr. -1-3). 14.95 *(978-0-9837668-2-7(7))* Plushy Feely Corp.

—From Dawn to Dreams: Poems for Busy Babies. Archer, Peggy. 2007. (ENG.). 32p. (J). (gr. k-k). 15.99 *(978-0-7636-2467-5(5))* Candlewick Pr.

—Goldie Locks Has Chicken Pox. Dealey, Erin. 2005. (ENG.). 40p. (J). (gr. -1-2). reprint ed. 7.99 *(978-0-689-87610-3(6)*, Simon & Schuster/Paula Wiseman Bks.) Simon & Schuster/Paula Wiseman Bks.

—Little Bo Peep Can't Get to Sleep. Dealey, Erin. 2010. (ENG.). 40p. (J). (gr. -1-2). 13.99 *(978-1-4424-0935-4(5)*, Atheneum Bks. for Young Readers) Simon & Schuster Children's Publishing.

Wald, Christina. Animal Atlas. Claybourne, Anna. Gwinn, Saskia, ed. 2014. (ENG.). 64p. (J). (gr. -1-3). 17.99 *(978-1-4088-4218-8(1)*, 231931, Bloomsbury USA Childrens) Bloomsbury USA.

—Anna Sewell's Black Beauty. East, Cathy. 2009. (Penguin Young Readers, Level 4 Ser.: No. 3). (ENG.). 48p. (J). (gr. 3-4). pap. 3.99 *(978-0-448-45190-9(5)*, Warne, Frederick Pubs.) Penguin Bks., Ltd. GBR. Dist: Penguin Random Hse., LLC.

—Annie Jump Cannon, Astronomer, 1 vol. Gerber, Carole. 2011. (ENG.). 32p. (J). (gr. 1-5). 16.99 *(978-1-58980-911-6(4))* Pelican Publishing Co., Inc.

—The Barnyard. 2006. (ENG.). 12p. pap. 7.95 *(978-1-58017-640-8(2)*, 67640) Storey Publishing, LLC.

—Big Cats. Bowman, Donna H. 2008. (ENG.). 24p. (J). (gr. 3-18). 19.95 *(978-1-58117-781-7(X)*, Intervisual/Piggy Toes) Bendon, Inc.

—A Cool Summer Tail, 1 vol. Pearson, Carrie. 2014. (ENG.). 32p. (J). (gr. -1-3). 17.95 *(978-1-62855-205-8(0))* Arbordale Publishing.

—A Cool Summer Tail, 1 vol. Pearson, Carrie A. 2014. (ENG.). 32p. (J). (gr. -1-3). pap. 9.95 *(978-1-62855-214-0(X))* Arbordale Publishing.

—Do Dolphins Really Smile? Driscoll, Laura. 2006. (Penguin Young Readers, Level 3 Ser.). (ENG.). 48p. (J). (gr. 1-3). mass mkt. 3.99 *(978-0-448-44341-6(4)*, Grosset & Dunlap) Penguin Publishing Group.

—Extreme Senses: Animals with Unusual Senses for Hunting Prey. Lay, Kathryn. 2012. pap. 28.50 *(978-1-61478-860-7(X))* ABDO Publishing Co.

—Extreme Senses: Animals with Unusual Senses for Hunting Prey. Lay, Kathryn. 2012. (Sensing Their Prey Ser.). 32p. (J). (gr. -1-4). lib. bdg. 28.50 *(978-1-61641-865-6(6)*, Looking Glass Library) Magic Wagon.

Wald, Christina. Fibonacci Zoo, 1 vol. Robinson, Tom. 2015. (ENG.). 32p. (J). (gr. k-3). 17.95 ***(978-1-62855-553-0(X))*** Arbordale Publishing.

W

Wald, Christina. The Fort on Fourth Street, 1 vol. Spangler, Lois. 2013. (ENG.). 32p. (J). (gr. -1-4). 17.95 *(978-1-60718-620-5(9))*; pap. 9.95 *(978-1-60718-632-8(2))* Arbordale Publishing.
—Habitat Spy, 1 vol. Kieber-King, Cynthia. 2011. (ENG.). 32p. (J). (gr. -1-3). 16.95 *(978-1-60718-122-4(3))*; pap. 8.95 *(978-1-60718-132-3(0))* Arbordale Publishing.
—Hearing Their Prey: Animals with an Amazing Sense of Hearing. Lay, Kathryn. 2012. (Sensing Their Prey Ser.). 32p. (J). (gr. -1-4). lib. bdg. 28.50 *(978-1-61641-866-3(4),* Looking Glass Library) Magic Wagon.
—Henry the Impatient Heron, 1 vol. Love, Donna. 2009. (ENG.). 32p. (J). (gr. -1-3). 16.95 *(978-1-934359-90-7(4))*; pap. 8.95 *(978-1-60718-035-7(9))* Arbordale Publishing.
Wald, Christina. I Want to Be a Crocodile. Troupe, Thomas Kingsley. 2015. (I Want to Be... Ser.). (ENG.). 24p. (gr. k-3). lib. bdg. 25.99 ***(978-1-4795-6857-4(0))*** Capstone Pr., Inc.
Wald, Christina. Un Invierno Muy Abrigador, 1 vol. Pearson, Carrie A. 2012. (SPA & ENG.). 32p. (J). (gr. -1-3). 17.95 *(978-1-60718-680-9(2))* Arbordale Publishing.
—Little Red Bat, 1 vol. Gerber, Carole. 2010. 32p. (J). (gr. -1-3). (ENG.). 16.95 *(978-1-60718-069-2(3))*; pap. 8.95 *(978-1-60718-080-7(4))* Arbordale Publishing.
—Macarooned on a Dessert Island, 1 vol. Downing, Johnette. 2014. (ENG.). 32p. (J). (gr. k-3). 16.99 *(978-1-4556-1936-8(1))* Pelican Publishing Co., Inc.
—Seeing Their Prey: Animals with an Amazing Sense of Sight. Lay, Kathryn. 2012. (Sensing Their Prey Ser.). 32p. (J). (gr. -1-4). lib. bdg. 28.50 *(978-1-61641-867-0(2),* Looking Glass Library) Magic Wagon.
—Smelling Their Prey: Animals with an Amazing Sense of Smell. Lay, Kathryn. 2012. (Sensing Their Prey Ser.). 32p. (J). (gr. -1-4). lib. bdg. 28.50 *(978-1-61641-868-7(0),* Looking Glass Library) Magic Wagon.
—Tasting Their Prey: Animals with an Amazing Sense of Taste. Lay, Kathryn. 2012. (Sensing Their Prey Ser.). 32p. (J). (gr. -1-4). lib. bdg. 28.50 *(978-1-61641-869-4(9),* Looking Glass Library) Magic Wagon.
—Touching Their Prey: Animals with an Amazing Sense of Touch. Lay, Kathryn. 2012. (Sensing Their Prey Ser.). 32p. (J). (gr. -1-4). lib. bdg. 28.50 *(978-1-61641-870-0(2),* Looking Glass Library) Magic Wagon.
—A Warm Winter Tail, 1 vol. Pearson, Carrie A. 2012. (SPA & ENG.). 32p. (J). (gr. -1-3). 17.95 *(978-1-60718-529-1(6))*; pap. 9.95 *(978-1-60718-538-3(5))* Arbordale Publishing.
—When Crabs Cross the Sand: The Christmas Island Crab Migration. Cooper, Sharon Katz. 2015. (Extraordinary Migrations Ser.). (ENG.). 24p. (gr. 2-3). lib. bdg. 25.99 *(978-1-4795-6077-6(4))* Picture Window Bks.
—Why the Possum Has a Large Grin, 1 vol. Downing, Johnette. 2012. (ENG.). 32p. (J). (gr. k-3). 16.99 *(978-1-4556-1639-8(7))* Pelican Publishing Co., Inc.
—The Wild Life of Elk. Love, Donna. 2011. (J). pap. *(978-0-87842-579-2(9))* Mountain Pr. Publishing Co., Inc.
Wald, Christina. Un Fresco Cuento de Verano, 1 vol. Wald, Christina. Pearson, Carrie A. 2014.Tr. of Cool Summer Tail. (SPA & ENG.). 32p. (J). (gr. -1-3). pap. 9.95 *(978-1-62855-223-2(9))* Arbordale Publishing.
Waldek, Kelly. The Big Purple Wonderbook. Richemont, Enid. 2009. (Go! Readers Ser.). 48p. (J). (gr. 2-5). pap. 12.85 *(978-1-60754-279-7(X))*; lib. bdg. 29.25 *(978-1-60754-278-0(1))* Windmill Bks.
Waldherr, Kris. Bless the Beasts: Children's Prayers & Poems about Animals. Cotner, June, ed. 2006. 63p. (J). (gr. 4-8). reprint ed. 13.00 *(978-0-7567-9952-6(X))* DIANE Publishing Co.
Waldman, Bruce. Vampires, Werewolves, Zombies: From the papers of Herr Doktor Max Sturm & Baron Ludwig Von Drang. Peter Pauper Press Staff et al. 2010. 168p. 9.95 *(978-1-59359-647-7(2))* Peter Pauper Pr. Inc.
Waldman, Maya. To-Do List. 2007. (ENG.). 48p. (J). (gr. k). 12.95 *(978-0-9741319-5-5(4))* 4N Publishing LLC.
Waldman, Neil. Subway: The Story of Tunnels, Tubes, & Tracks. Brimner, Larry Dane. 2004. (ENG.). 32p. (J). (gr. 2-4). 15.95 *(978-1-59078-176-0(7))* Boyds Mills Pr.
—The Wind That Wanted to Rest. Oberman, Sheldon. 2012. (ENG.). 32p. (J). (gr. k-2). 17.95 *(978-1-59078-858-5(3))* Boyds Mills Pr.
Waldman, Neil. A Land of Big Dreamers: Voices of Courage in America. Waldman, Neil. 2011. (Single Titles Ser.). (ENG.). 32p. (gr. 3-5). lib. bdg. 16.95 *(978-0-8225-6810-0(1))* Lerner Publishing Group.
—Say-Hey & the Babe: Two Mostly True Baseball Stories. Waldman, Neil. 2006. (ENG.). 40p. (J). (gr. 4-7). 16.95 *(978-0-8234-1857-2(X))* Holiday Hse., Inc.
—The Snowflake: A Water Cycle Story. Waldman, Neil. 2003. (ENG.). 32p. (J). (gr. k-3). 17.95 *(978-0-7613-2347-1(3),* Millbrook Pr.) Lerner Publishing Group.
Waldock, Sarah. Tabitha Tabs the Farm Kitten. Waldock, Sarah. 2011. (ENG.). 88p. pap. 6.99 *(978-1-4679-5682-6(1))* CreateSpace Independent Publishing Platform.
Waldrod, Amy. Horace & Morris, but Mostly Dolores. Howe, James. 2003. pap. 39.95 incl. audio compact disk *(978-1-59112-538-9(3))*; 25.95 incl. audio *(978-1-59112-242-5(2))*; pap. 37.95 incl. audio *(978-1-59112-243-2(0))* Live Oak Media.
Waldron, Hannah. Pirate Adventure Dice. 2014. (ENG.). 16p. (J). (gr. 1-4). 14.95 *(978-1-85669-938-9(2))* King, Laurence Publishing GBR. Dist: Hachette Bk. Group.
Waldron, Kevin. Tiny Little Fly. Rosen, Michael. 2010. (ENG.). 32p. (J). (gr. 5-k). 16.99 *(978-0-7636-4681-3(4))* Candlewick Pr.
Waldron, Kevin. Mr. Peek & the Misunderstanding at the Zoo. Waldron, Kevin. 2010. (ENG.). 48p. (J). (gr. k-12). 15.99 *(978-0-7636-4549-6(4))* Candlewick Pr.
—Panda-Monium at Peek Zoo. Waldron, Kevin. 2014. (ENG.). 40p. (J). (gr. -1-2). 16.99 *(978-0-7636-6658-3(0),* Templar) Candlewick Pr.
Walke, Ted. Boating Safety Sidekicks Color a Fish: Freshwater Fish Coloring Book. Walke, Ted, compiled by. 2008. 28p. (J). *(978-0-9718864-4-5(X))* Within Reach, Inc.

Walker, Anna. Collecting Seashells. Mitchell, Ainslie. 2005. (Science (Harcourt) Ser.). 14p. pap. 6.00 *(978-0-15-349999-9(0))* Harcourt Schl. Pubs.
Walker, Anna. Goldilocks & the Three Bears. 2015. (Once upon a Timeless Tale Ser.). (ENG.). 24p. (J). (gr. k-3). 9.99 ***(978-1-921894-92-3(X))*** Little Hare Bks. AUS. Dist: Independent Pubs. Group.
Walker, Anna. Good Night, Sleep Tight: A Book about Bedtime. Quay, Emma. 2011. (ENG.). 24p. (J). (gr. -1 — 1). bds. 5.99 *(978-0-8037-3581-1(2),* Dial) Penguin Publishing Group.
Walker, Anna. The Twelve Dancing Princesses. 2015. (Once upon a Timeless Tale Ser.). (ENG.). 24p. (J). (gr. -1-k). 9.99 ***(978-1-74297-401-9(5))*** Little Hare Bks. AUS. Dist: Independent Pubs. Group.
Walker, Anna. Yummy Ice Cream: A Book about Sharing. Quay, Emma. 2011. (ENG.). 24p. (J). (gr. k — 1). bds. 5.99 *(978-0-8037-3568-2(5),* Dial) Penguin Publishing Group.
Walker, Anna. I Love Birthdays. Walker, Anna. 2010. (ENG.). 32p. (J). (gr. -1-1). 9.99 *(978-1-4169-8320-0(1),* Simon & Schuster Bks. For Young Readers) Simon & Schuster Bks. For Young Readers.
—I Love Christmas. Walker, Anna. 2009. (ENG.). 32p. (J). (gr. -1-1). 9.99 *(978-1-4169-8317-0(1),* Simon & Schuster Bks. For Young Readers) Simon & Schuster Bks. For Young Readers.
—I Love My Dad. Walker, Anna. 2010. (ENG.). 32p. (J). (gr. -1-1). 9.99 *(978-1-4169-8319-4(8),* Simon & Schuster Bks. For Young Readers) Simon & Schuster Bks. For Young Readers.
—I Love My Mom. Walker, Anna. 2010. (ENG.). 32p. (J). (gr. -1-1). 9.99 *(978-1-4169-8318-7(X),* Simon & Schuster Bks. For Young Readers) Simon & Schuster Bks. For Young Readers.
—I Love to Dance. Walker, Anna. 2011. (ENG.). 32p. (J). (gr. -1-1). 9.99 *(978-1-4169-8323-1(6),* Simon & Schuster Bks. For Young Readers) Simon & Schuster Bks. For Young Readers.
—I Love to Sing. Walker, Anna. 2011. (ENG.). 32p. (J). (gr. -1-1). 9.99 *(978-1-4169-8322-4(8),* Simon & Schuster Bks. For Young Readers) Simon & Schuster Bks. For Young Readers.
—I Love Vacations. Walker, Anna. 2011. (ENG.). 32p. (J). (gr. -1-1). 9.99 *(978-1-4169-8321-7(X),* Simon & Schuster Bks. For Young Readers) Simon & Schuster Bks. For Young Readers.
Walker, Bobbie H. Abraham Lincoln. Pace, Betty. 2008. 32p. pap. 12.99 *(978-1-4343-7969-6(8))* AuthorHouse.
Walker, Brad. The Thanos Imperative. 2011. (ENG.). 200p. (YA). (gr. 8-17). pap. 19.99 *(978-0-7851-4902-6(3))* Marvel Worldwide, Inc.
Walker, Bradley. The Adventures of Little Autumn. Schuette, Leslie Elaine. 2013. 24p. pap. 24.95 *(978-1-4626-9778-6(X))* America Star Bks.
Walker, Bradley. The Adventures of Little Autumn. Schuette, Leslie Elaine. 2013. 24p. 24.95 *(978-1-63004-507-4(1))* America Star Bks.
Walker, Christine. Wooleycat's Musical Theater. Walker, Christine. Hysom, Dennis Joe. 2003. (Wooleycat's Favorite Nursery Rhymes Ser.). 32p. (J). (gr. -1-2). 18.95 incl. audio compact disk *(978-1-889910-25-3(2))* Tortuga Pr.
Walker, Cindy. Serenade of the Cricket. 2nd ed. 2004. (J). 12.95 *(978-1-59655-000-1(7))* Cooper Publishing.
Walker, Cory, jt. illus. see Neves, Diogenes.
Walker, David. Baby Says Moo! Macken, JoAnn Early. 2015. (ENG.). 30p. (J). (gr. -1 — 1). bds. 8.99 ***(978-1-4847-2098-1(9))*** Hyperion Bks. for Children.
Walker, David. Bears in Beds. Parenteau, Shirley. 2012. (ENG.). 32p. (J). (gr. k-k). 15.99 *(978-0-7636-5338-5(1))* Candlewick Pr.
—Bears in the Bath. Parenteau, Shirley. 2014. (ENG.). 32p. (J). (-k). 15.99 *(978-0-7636-6418-3(9))* Candlewick Pr.
—Bears on Chairs. Parenteau, Shirley. 2009. (ENG.). 32p. (J). (gr. -1-k). 15.99 *(978-0-7636-3588-6(X))* Candlewick Pr.
—Bears on Chairs. Parenteau, Shirley. 2011. (ENG.). 32p. (J). (gr. -1 — 1). bds. 6.99 *(978-0-7636-5092-6(7))* Candlewick Pr.
—Before You Were Mine. Boelts, Maribeth. 2007. (ENG.). 32p. (J). (gr. -1-3). 15.99 *(978-0-399-24526-8(X),* Putnam Juvenile) Penguin Publishing Group.
—Before You Were Mine. Boelts, Maribeth. 2008. (J). (gr. -1-3). 27.95 incl. audio *(978-0-8045-6961-3(4))*; 29.95 incl. audio compact disk *(978-0-8045-4184-8(1))* Spoken Arts, Inc.
—Boom! Boom! Boom! Swenson, Jamie A. 2013. (ENG.). 32p. (J). (gr. -1-1). 16.99 *(978-0-374-30868-1(3),* Farrar, Straus & Giroux (BYR)) Farrar, Straus & Giroux.
—Flip, Flap, Fly! A Book for Babies Everywhere. Root, Phyllis. (ENG.). 32p. (J). 2011. (gr. -1 — 1). bds. 6.99 *(978-0-7636-5325-5(X))*; 2009. (-k). 14.99 *(978-0-7636-3109-3(4))* Candlewick Pr.
—The Great Easter Egg Scramble. Knapman, Timothy. 2013. (J). *(978-1-4351-4594-8(1))* Barnes & Noble, Inc.
—Hello, Florida! Tomasello, Heather. 2010. (Hello, America! Ser.). (ENG.). 22p. (J). (gr. k-k). bds. 6.95 *(978-1-4027-6670-1(X))* Sterling Publishing Co., Inc.
—Hello, New York City! 2010. (Hello, America! Ser.). (ENG.). 22p. (J). (gr. k-k). bds. 6.95 *(978-1-4027-6768-5(4))* Sterling Publishing Co., Inc.
—Hello, Texas! Jennings, Christopher S. 2010. (Hello, America! Ser.). (ENG.). 22p. (J). (gr. k-k). bds. 6.95 *(978-1-4027-6769-2(2))* Sterling Publishing Co., Inc.
—How Do Lions Say I Love You? Muldrow, Diane. (Little Golden Book Ser.). (ENG.). (J). (-k). 2013. 24p. 3.99 *(978-0-449-81256-3(1))*; 2009. 14p. bds. 7.99 *(978-0-375-85551-1(3))* Random Hse. Children's Bks. (Golden Bks.).
—How Do Penguins Play? Dombey, Elizabeth & Muldrow, Diane. 2011. (Little Golden Book Ser.). (ENG.). 24p. (J). (gr. -1-k). 4.99 *(978-0-375-86501-5(2),* Golden Bks.) Random Hse. Children's Bks.

—If Animals Kissed Good Night. Paul, Ann Whitford. 2014. (ENG.). 32p. (J). (gr. -1-1). 7.99 *(978-0-374-30021-0(6),* Farrar, Straus & Giroux (BYR)) Farrar, Straus & Giroux.
—The Night Parade. Roscoe, Lily. 2014. (ENG.). 32p. (J). (— 1). 16.99 *(978-0-545-39623-3(9),* Orchard Bks.) Scholastic, Inc.
—Nighty-Night, Sleep Tight. Berne, Jennifer. (ENG.). 24p. (J). (gr. -1-k). 2015. bds. 6.95 *(978-1-4549-1390-0(8))*; 2013. 9.95 *(978-1-4027-8088-2(5))* Sterling Publishing Co., Inc.
—Peep & Ducky. Martin, David. (ENG.). (J). (— 1). 2015. 24p. bds. 6.99 *(978-0-7636-7243-0(2))*; 2013. 32p. 14.99 *(978-0-7636-5039-1(0))* Candlewick Pr.
—Peep & Ducky Rainy Day. Martin, David. 2015. (ENG.). 32p. (J). (— 1). 14.99 *(978-0-7636-6884-6(2))* Candlewick Pr.
—Time for a Hug. Gershator, Phillis & Green, Mim. 2013. (Snuggle Time Stories Ser.). (ENG.). 22p. (J). (gr. -1-k). bds. 6.95 *(978-1-4549-0856-2(4))* Sterling Publishing Co., Inc.
—Tiny Rabbit's Big Wish. Engle, Margarita. 2014. (ENG.). 32p. (J). (gr. -1-3). 16.99 *(978-0-547-85286-7(X),* HMH Books For Young Readers) Houghton Mifflin Harcourt Publishing Co.
—You Mean the World to Me. Gibby, Bayne. 2013. (ENG.). 16p. (J). (gr. -1-k). bds. 8.99 *(978-0-545-40570-6(X),* Cartwheel Bks.) Scholastic, Inc.
—Your Daddy Was Just Like You. Bennett, Kelly. 2010. (ENG.). 32p. (J). (gr. -1-k). 16.99 *(978-0-399-25258-7(4),* Putnam Juvenile) Penguin Publishing Group.
—Your Mommy Was Just Like You. Bennett, Kelly. 2011. (ENG.). 32p. (J). (gr. -1-k). 16.99 *(978-0-399-24798-9(X),* Putnam Juvenile) Penguin Publishing Group.
Walker, David, jt. illus. see Sweet, Melissa.
Walker, George. Clueless in the Kitchen: A Cookbook for Teens. Raab, Evelyn. 2nd rev. ed. 2011. (Clueless Ser.). (ENG.). 216p. pap. 14.95 *(978-1-55407-824-0(5),* 9781554078240) Firefly Bks., Ltd.
Walker, Jack. Tamla Bear & the Magic Goblin. Kelly, Diana. 2013. 30p. pap. *(978-1-78148-182-0(2))* Grosvenor Hse. Publishing Ltd.
Walker, John. Gulliver's Travels. Swift, Jonathan. 2010. (Stepping Stone Book(TM) Ser.). (ENG.). 112p. (J). (gr. 1-4). 4.99 *(978-0-375-86569-5(1),* Random Hse. Bks. for Young Readers) Random Hse. Children's Bks.
—The Story of Christmas: The Birth of Jesus. 2008. (ENG.). 24p. (J). (gr. 2). 19.95 *(978-1-58117-793-0(3),* Intervisual/Piggy Toes) Bendon, Inc.
—Thank You for Thanksgiving. Mackall, Dandi Daley. 2008. 32p. (J). (gr. -1). 13.49 *(978-0-7586-1500-8(0))* Concordia Publishing Hse.
—What God Wants for Christmas. Rainey, Barbara. 2011. (J). (gr. 4-7). 29.99 incl. audio compact disk *(978-1-60200-428-3(5))* FamilyLife.
Walker, John, photos by. Ray Conka & the Sortian Jewell. van Gosen, Ryan O'Dell, IV. Maximilian Staff, ed. unabr. ed. 2004. 128p. (YA). lib. bdg. 12.50 *(978-1-930211-55-1(4))* Maximilian Pr. Pubs.
Walker, John & Laiug, Naucie. Blake. Ashley, Jane, IV. Maximilian Press staff, ed. 2004. 32p. (gr. 1-5). pap. 10.00 *(978-1-930211-57-5(0))* Maximilian Pr. Pubs.
Walker, Joni. Jesus Hears Me. 2008. 20p. (J). (gr. -1). bds. 6.49 *(978-0-7586-1508-4(6))* Concordia Publishing Hse.
Walker, Joni. Apostles Creed. Walker, Joni. 2005. (Follow & Do Ser.). 32p. (J). 7.49 *(978-0-7586-0802-4(0))* Concordia Publishing Hse.
—Follow & Do Books: The Lord's Prayer. Walker, Joni. 2004. (Follow & Do Ser.). 32p. (J). 7.49 *(978-0-7586-0678-5(8))* Concordia Publishing Hse.
—Holy Baptism. Walker, Joni. 2005. (Follow & Do Ser.). 32p. (J). 7.49 *(978-0-7586-0800-0(4))* Concordia Publishing Hse.
—Jesus Is with Me. Walker, Joni. 2004. 20p. (J). bds. 5.49 *(978-0-7586-0628-0(1))* Concordia Publishing Hse.
—Jesus Knows Me. Walker, Joni. 2003. 14p. (J). (gr. -1-k). bds. 5.49 *(978-0-7586-0507-8(2))* Concordia Publishing Hse.
—Lords Supper. Walker, Joni. 2005. (Follow & Do Ser.). 23p. (J). (gr. -1-3). 7.49 *(978-0-7586-0801-7(2))* Concordia Publishing Hse.
—Tell Me the Christmas Story. Walker, Joni. 2003. 14p. (J). (gr. -1-k). bds. 5.49 *(978-0-7586-0508-5(0))* Concordia Publishing Hse.
—Tell Me What God Made. Walker, Joni. 2007. 20p. (J). (gr. -1-3). bds. 6.49 *(978-0-7586-1247-2(8))* Concordia Publishing Hse.
Walker, Joni. Tell Me the Easter Story. Walker, Joni, contrib. by. 2004. 14p. (J). bds. 5.49 *(978-0-7586-0629-7(X))* Concordia Publishing Hse.
Walker, Karen. White Fang: With a Discussion of Resilience. London, Jack. 2003. (Values in Action Illustrated Classics Ser.). 191p. (J). *(978-1-59203-038-5(6))* Learning Challenge, Inc.
Walker, Katherine. Hot Dog. Cottringer, Anne. 2005. (ENG.). 24p. (J). lib. bdg. 23.65 *(978-1-59646-738-5(X))* Dingles & Co.
Walker, Kev. Marvel Zombies, Vol. 4. Lente, Fred Van. 2010. (ENG.). 128p. (gr. 10-17). pap. 16.99 *(978-0-7851-3918-8(4))* Marvel Worldwide, Inc.
Walker, Kev & Shalvey, Declan. Thunderbolts: Violent Rejection. 2011. (ENG.). 280p. (YA). (gr. 8-17). pap. 15.99 *(978-0-7851-5221-7(0))* Marvel Worldwide, Inc.
Walker, Kev, jt. illus. see Shalvey, Declan.
Walker, Mark Evan. Clovis Escapes! Bks. 3: Runt Farm. Lorenzo, Amanda. 2009. 136p. 12.95 *(978-0-9800952-2-7(0))* BookitMookti Pr.
Walker, Patricia M. Andromed: Dream Believe Achieve Series. Goguen, Martha M. 2011. 36p. pap. *(978-1-897435-35-9(5))* Agio Publishing Hse.
Walker, Peggy. My First Book of Buddhist Treasures. 2003. 38p. (J). 8.95 *(978-0-915678-81-5(0))* World Tribune Pr.
Walker, Rory. Electricity! Graham, Ian. 2014. (You Wouldn't Want to Live Without... Ser.). (ENG.). 32p. (J). lib. bdg. 29.00 *(978-0-531-21216-5(5),* Watts, Franklin) Scholastic Library Publishing.
—You Wouldn't Want to Live Without Cell Phones! Pipe, Jim. 2014. (You Wouldn't Want to Live Without... Ser.). (ENG.). 32p. (J). lib. bdg. 29.00 *(978-0-531-21217-2(3),* Watts, Franklin) Scholastic Library Publishing.
Walker, Sholto. Louis the Tiger Who Came from the Sea. Kozlowski, Michal. 2011. (ENG.). 32p. (J). (gr. -1-2). 19.95 *(978-1-55451-257-7(3),* 9781554512577); pap. 8.95 *(978-1-55451-256-0(5),* 9781554512560) Annick Pr., Ltd. CAN. Dist: Firefly Bks., Ltd.
—Run, Three Blind Mice! Fuerst, Jeffrey B. 2009. (Reader's Theater Nursery Rhymes & Songs Set B Ser.). 48p. (J). pap. *(978-1-60859-168-8(9))* Benchmark Education Co.
—Three Blind Mice. Fuerst, Jeffrey B. 2010. (Rising Readers Ser.). (J). 3.49 *(978-1-60719-707-2(3))* Newmark Learning LLC.
Walker, Steve. Opposites with Eddie & Ellie, 1 vol. Nunn, Daniel. 2014. (Eddie & Ellie's Opposites Ser.). (ENG.). 20p. (gr. -1-k). bds. 6.99 *(978-1-4109-5355-1(6),* NA-r) Heinemann-Raintree.
Walker, Steve & Kramek, Oren. The Sons of Liberty: Death & Taxes. Lagos, Joseph & Lagos, Alexander. 2011. (Sons of Liberty Ser.). (ENG.). 176p. (J). (gr. 3-7). pap. 12.99 *(978-0-375-85668-6(4),* Random Hse. Bks. for Young Readers) Random Hse. Children's Bks.
Walker, Steve, jt. illus. see Kramek, Oren.
Walker, Steven. Meet Rosa Parks. Pingry, Patricia A. 2008. (ENG.). 32p. (J). (gr. k). per. 7.99 *(978-0-8249-5578-6(1),* Ideals Children's Bks.) Ideals Pubns.
—Rosa's Bus: The Ride to Civil Rights. Kittinger, Jo S. 2010. (ENG.). 40p. (J). (gr. 2-4). 17.95 *(978-1-59078-722-9(6))* Boyds Mills Pr.
—The Story of Coretta Scott King. Pingry, Patricia A. 2007. (ENG.). 26p. (J). (gr. 3-7). bds. 7.69 *(978-0-8249-6717-8(8),* Candy Cane Pr.) Ideals Pubns.
—The Story of Rosa Parks. Pingry, Patricia A. 2008. (ENG.). 24p. (J). (gr. 3-7). bds. 7.69 *(978-0-8249-6687-4(2),* Candy Cane Pr.) Ideals Pubns.
—The Stourbridge Lion: America's First Locomotive. Zimmermann, Karl. 2012. (ENG.). 32p. (J). (gr. k). 16.95 *(978-1-59078-859-2(1))* Boyds Mills Pr.
Walker, Sylvia. I Am a Leader! Parker, David. 2005. (J). *(978-0-439-73585-8(8))* Scholastic, Inc.
—I'm in Charge of Me! Parker, David. 2004. (Best Me I Can Be Ser.). *(978-0-439-62810-5(5))* Scholastic, Inc.
—Three's a Crowd. Scholastic, Inc. Staff & Hooks, Gwendolyn. 2004. (Just for You Ser.). (ENG.). 32p. (gr. k-3). pap. 3.99 *(978-0-439-56865-4(X),* Teaching Resources) Scholastic, Inc.
—Three's a Crowd. Hooks, Gwendolyn. 2004. 32p. (J). lib. bdg. 15.00 *(978-1-4242-0240-9(X))* Fitzgerald Bks.
—What Do You Know? Snow! Scholastic, Inc. Staff & Hudson, Cheryl Willis. 2004. (Just for You Ser.). (ENG.). 32p. pap. 3.99 *(978-0-439-56851-7(X),* Teaching Resources) Scholastic, Inc.
Walker, Tom, photos by. Wild Critters. Jones, Tim. 2nd ed. 2007. (ENG., 48p. (gr. -1-6). 9.95 *(978-0-9790470-2-2(1))* Epicenter Pr., Inc.
Wall Darby, Colleen. My Dog Harpo: The Biggest Kid I Know. Exelby, Kathy. 2007. (J). per. 20.00 *(978-1-932583-39-7(4))* digital@batesjackson llc.
Wall, Karen. ABC & Do. Singh, Lee. 2013. (ENG.). 24p. (J). (gr. -1-k). 19.99 *(978-1-4052-6532-4(9))* Egmont Bks., Ltd. GBR. Dist: Independent Pubs. Group.
—My Little Library, 4 vols. Helmore, Jim. 2014. (Stripy Horse Ser.). (ENG.). 32p. (J). (gr. -1 — 1). 8.99 *(978-1-4052-6437-2(3))* Egmont Bks., Ltd. GBR. Dist: Independent Pubs. Group.
—Oh No, Monster Tomato! Helmore Wall Staff & Helmore, Jim. 2009. (ENG.). 32p. (J). (gr. -1). 16.99 *(978-1-4052-4740-5(1))* Egmont Bks., Ltd. GBR. Dist: Independent Pubs. Group.
—Oh No, Monster Tomato! Helmore, Jim. 2011. (ENG.). 32p. (J). (gr. -1-2). pap. 8.99 *(978-1-4052-4741-2(X))* Egmont Bks., Ltd. GBR. Dist: Independent Pubs. Group.
Wall, Laura. Goose Goes to School. Wall, Laura. 2015. (ENG.). 48p. (J). (gr. -1-3). 12.99 *(978-0-06-232437-5(3))* HarperCollins Pubs.
Wall, Laura. Goose Goes to the Zoo. Wall, Laura. 2016. 48p. (J). (gr. -1-3). 12.99 ***(978-0-06-232441-2(1))*** HarperCollins Pubs.
Wall, Mike. Doc Is the Best Medicine! (Disney Junior: Doc Mcstuffins) Posner-Sanchez, Andrea. 2014. (Big Golden Book Ser.). (ENG.). 64p. (J). (gr. -1-2). 9.99 *(978-0-7364-3264-1(7),* Golden/Disney) Random Hse. Children's Bks.
Wallace, Adam. Rhymes with Art: Learn Cartooning the Fun Way! Wallace, Adam. 2014. (ENG.). 166p. pap. *(978-0-9808282-6-9(0))* Krueger Wallace Pr.
Wallace, Andrea. Captain Benjamin Dale. Fox, Nita. 2008. 32p. (J). (gr. -1-3). pap. 5.99 *(978-0-9816107-0-2(6))* Fox's Den Publishing.
Wallace, Carol. That Doggone Calf. Wallace, Bill. 2010. (ENG.). 160p. (J). (gr. 3-7). pap. 6.95 *(978-0-8234-2303-3(4))* Holiday Hse., Inc.
Wallace, Chad. Earth: Feeling the Heat. Guiberson, Brenda Z. 2010. (ENG.). 32p. (J). (gr. -1-3). 16.99 *(978-0-8050-7719-3(7),* Holt, Henry & Co. Bks. For Young Readers) Holt, Henry & Co.
—Earth Day Birthday. Schnetzler, Pattie. 2004. (Sharing Nature with Children Book Ser.). 32p. (J). 16.95 *(978-1-58469-053-5(4))*; 8.95 *(978-1-58469-054-2(2))* Dawn Pubns.
—Little Panda. Bowen, Sherry. 2003. (Books for Young Learners). (ENG.). 12p. (J). 5.75 net. *(978-1-57274-673-2(4),* 2459, Bks. for Young Learners) Owen, Richard C. Pubs., Inc.
Wallace, Chad. Mighty Mole & Super Soil. Quattlebaum, Mary. 2015. (ENG.). 32p. (J). (gr. k-4). 16.95 ***(978-1-58469-538-7(2))*** Dawn Pubns.
Wallace, Chad. Pass the Energy, Please! McKinney, Barbara Shaw. 2004. (Sharing Nature with Children Book Ser.). 32p. (YA). (gr. 1-8). pap. 16.95 *(978-1-58469-001-6(1))* Dawn Pubns.
—Poetry for Young People: Henry Wadsworth Longfellow. Schoonmaker, Frances, ed. 2010. (Poetry for Young

People Ser.). (ENG.). 48p. (J). (gr. 3). pap. 6.95 *(978-1-4027-7292-4(0))* Sterling Publishing Co., Inc.
—Seahorses. Curtis, Jennifer Keats. 2012. (ENG.). 32p. (J). (gr. -1-3). 16.99 *(978-0-8050-9239-4(0),* Holt, Henry & Co. Bks. For Young Readers) Holt, Henry & Co.
—Wake up, Bertha Bear! Mason, Chad. ed. 2006. (ENG.). 32p. (J). (gr. -1-3). 15.95 *(978-0-89272-655-4(5))* Down East Bks.
Wallace, Chad. The Mouse & the Meadow. Wallace, Chad. 2014. (ENG.). 32p. (J). (gr. k-4). 16.95 *(978-1-58469-481-6(5))* Dawn Pubns.
Wallace, Daggi. Katherine Stinson Otero: High Flyer, 1 vol. Petrick, Neila S. 2006. (ENG.). 32p. (J). (gr. k-3). 16.99 *(978-1-58980-368-8(X))* Pelican Publishing Co., Inc.
Wallace, Ian. Canadian Railroad Trilogy, 1 vol. Lightfoot, Gordon. 2010. (ENG.). 56p. (gr. -1). 24.95 *(978-0-88899-953-5(4))* Groundwood Bks. CAN. Dist: Perseus-PGW.
—Just So Stories, Vol. 1. Kipling, Rudyard. 2013. (ENG.). 64p. (J). (gr. k). 19.95 *(978-1-55498-212-7(X))* Groundwood Bks. CAN. Dist: Perseus-PGW.
—The Mummer's Song, 1 vol. Davidge, Bud. 2009. (ENG.). 32p. (J). (gr. k). pap. 14.95 *(978-0-88899-960-3(7))* Groundwood Bks. CAN. Dist: Perseus-PGW.
—Very Last First Time, 1 vol. Andrews, Jan. 2003. (ENG.). 32p. (J). 18.95 *(978-0-88899-043-3(X))* Groundwood Bks. CAN. Dist: Perseus-PGW.
Wallace, Ian. Mr. Kneebone's New Digs. Wallace, Ian. (J). 16.95 *(978-0-88899-143-0(6))* Groundwood Bks. CAN. Dist: Perseus-PGW.
Wallace, John. The Best Easter Prize. Evans, Kristina. 2010. (ENG.). 32p. (J). (gr. -1-3). pap. 3.99 *(978-0-545-05112-5(6),* Cartwheel Bks.) Scholastic, Inc.
—A Book Is Just Like You! All about the Parts of a Book. Fox, Kathleen. 2012. 32p. (J). 17.95 *(978-1-60213-060-9(4),* Upstart Bks.) Highsmith Inc.
—Clouds. Bauer, Marion Dane. 2004. (Ready-To-Reads Ser.). (ENG.). 32p. (J). (gr. -1-1). pap. 3.99 *(978-0-689-85441-5(2),* Simon Spotlight) Simon Spotlight.
—Earthquake! Bauer, Marion Dane. 2009. (Natural Disasters Ser.). (ENG.). 32p. (J). (gr. -1-1). pap. 3.99 *(978-1-4169-2551-4(1),* Simon & Schuster/Paula Wiseman Bks.) Simon & Schuster/Paula Wiseman Bks.
—Flood! Bauer, Marion Dane. 2008. (Natural Disasters Ser.). (ENG.). 32p. (J). (gr. -1-1). pap. 3.99 *(978-1-4169-2553-8(8),* Simon & Schuster/Paula Wiseman Bks.) Simon & Schuster/Paula Wiseman Bks.
—The Grand Canyon. Bauer, Marion Dane. 2006. (Wonders of America Ser.). (ENG.). 32p. (J). (gr. -1-1). pap. 3.99 *(978-0-689-86946-4(0),* Simon Spotlight) Simon Spotlight.
—The Mighty Mississippi. Bauer, Marion Dane. 2007. (Wonders of America Ser.). (ENG.). 32p. (J). (gr. -1-1). pap. 3.99 *(978-0-689-86950-1(9),* Simon Spotlight) Simon Spotlight.
—Mother's Day Ribbons. Knudsen, Michelle. 2005. (ENG.). 12p. (J). bds. 6.99 *(978-0-689-86381-3(0),* Little Simon) Little Simon.
—Mount Rushmore. Bauer, Marion Dane. 2007. (Wonders of America Ser.). (ENG.). 32p. (J). (gr. -1-1). pap. 3.99 *(978-1-4169-3477-6(4),* Simon Spotlight) Simon Spotlight.
—Niagara Falls. Bauer, Marion Dane. 2006. (Wonders of America Ser.). (ENG.). 32p. (J). (gr. -1-1). pap. 3.99 *(978-0-689-86944-0(4),* Simon Spotlight) Simon Spotlight.
—The Rocky Mountains. Bauer, Marion Dane. 2006. (Wonders of America Ser.). (ENG.). 32p. (J). (gr. -1-1). pap. 3.99 *(978-0-689-86948-8(7),* Simon Spotlight) Simon Spotlight.
—Snow. Bauer, Marion Dane. 2003. (Ready-To-Reads Ser.). (ENG.). 32p. (J). (gr. -1-1). pap. 3.99 *(978-0-689-85437-8(4),* Simon Spotlight) Simon Spotlight.
—Snow. Bauer, Dane. ed. 2005. 32p. (J). lib. bdg. 15.00 *(978-1-59054-934-6(1))* Fitzgerald Bks.
—The Statue of Liberty. Bauer, Marion Dane. 2007. (Wonders of America Ser.). (ENG.). 32p. (J). (gr. -1-1). pap. 3.99 *(978-1-4169-3479-0(0),* Simon Spotlight) Simon Spotlight.
—Volcano! Bauer, Marion Dane. 2008. (Natural Disasters Ser.). (ENG.). 32p. (J). (gr. -1-1). pap. 3.99 *(978-1-4169-2549-1(X),* Simon Spotlight) Simon Spotlight.
—Wind. Bauer, Marion Dane. 2005. (Ready-to-Read Ser.). 32p. (gr. -1-1). 14.00 *(978-0-7569-5622-6(6))* Perfection Learning Corp.
—Wind. Bauer, Marion Dane. 2003. (Ready-To-Reads Ser.). (ENG.). 32p. (J). (gr. -1-1). pap. 3.99 *(978-0-689-85443-9(9),* Simon Spotlight) Simon Spotlight.
—Wonders of America Ready-To-Read Value Pack: The Grand Canyon; Niagara Falls; the Rocky Mountains; Mount Rushmore; the Statue of Liberty; Yellowstone. Bauer, Marion Dane. 2014. (Wonders of America Ser.). (ENG.). 192p. (J). (gr. -1-1). pap. 15.96 *(978-1-4814-2724-1(5),* Simon Spotlight) Simon Spotlight.
—Yellowstone. Bauer, Marion Dane. 2008. (Wonders of America Ser.). (ENG.). 32p. (J). (gr. -1-1). pap. 3.99 *(978-1-4169-5404-0(X),* Simon Spotlight) Simon Spotlight.
Wallace, John. Rain. Wallace, John. Bauer, Marion Dane. 2004. (Ready-To-Reads Ser.). (ENG.). 32p. (J). (gr. -1-1). pap. 3.99 *(978-0-689-85439-2(0),* Simon Spotlight) Simon Spotlight.
Wallace, Joshua. The Life of Babe Didrikson: "Greatness Is Never Forgotten" Riley, Lehman & Austin, Megan. 2005. 47p. (J). pap. *(978-0-9760523-2-6(6))* Matter of Africa America Time.
Wallace, Leslie. Old Neb & the Lighthouse Treasure. Swoboda, Lois. 2015. (Old Neb Ser.). (ENG.). 125p. (J). pap. 10.95 *(978-1-56164-787-3(X))* Pineapple Pr., Inc.
Wallace, Loston, et al. DC Super Friends: Flying High. Eliopulos, Nick & Random House Staff. 2008. (Step into Reading Ser.). (ENG.). 32p. (J). (gr. -1-1). pap. 3.99 *(978-0-375-85208-4(5))*; lib. bdg. 11.99 *(978-0-375-95208-1(X))* Random Hse. Children's Bks. (Random Hse. Bks. for Young Readers).
Wallace, Loston. Race Against Crime. Black, Jake & Meredith Books Staff. 2008. 24p. (J). pap. 3.99 *(978-0-696-23958-8(2))* Meredith Bks.
Wallace, Marianne D. Earthsteps: A Rock's Journey Through Time. Spickert, Diane Nelson. 2010. (ENG.). 32p. (J). (gr. -1-3). pap. 9.95 *(978-1-55591-730-2(5))* Fulcrum Publishing.
Wallace, Mary & Owlkids Books Inc. Staff. The Inuksuk Book. Wallace, Mary. 2004. (Wow Canada! Ser.). (ENG.). 64p. (J). (gr. 3-6). pap. 13.95 *(978-1-897066-13-3(9),* Maple Tree Pr.) Owlkids Bks. Inc. CAN. Dist: Perseus-PGW.
Wallace, Nancy Elizabeth. Look! Look! Look!, 0 vols. Wallace, Nancy Elizabeth. 2006. (ENG.). 40p. (J). (gr. k-3). 16.95 *(978-0-7614-5282-9(6),* 9780761452829, Amazon Children's Publishing) Amazon Publishing.
—Pumpkin Day, 0 vols. Wallace, Nancy Elizabeth. unabr. ed. 2006. (ENG.). 32p. (J). (gr. -1-2). per. 5.99 *(978-0-7614-5327-7(X),* 9780761453277, Amazon Children's Publishing) Amazon Publishing.
—Recycle Every Day!, 0 vols. Wallace, Nancy Elizabeth. 2006. (ENG.). 41p. (J). (gr. -1-3). pap. 9.99 *(978-0-7614-5290-4(7),* 9780761452904, Amazon Children's Publishing) Amazon Publishing.
—Seeds! Seeds! Seeds!, 0 vols. Wallace, Nancy Elizabeth. 2007. (ENG.). 40p. (J). (gr. -1-3). 5.99 *(978-0-7614-5366-6(0),* 9780761453666, Amazon Children's Publishing) Amazon Publishing.
—Stars! Stars! Stars!, 0 vols. Wallace, Nancy Elizabeth. 2009. (ENG.). 40p. (J). (gr. -1-3). 17.99 *(978-0-7614-5612-4(0),* 9780761456124, Amazon Children's Publishing) Amazon Publishing.
—Tell-A-Bunny, 0 vols. Wallace, Nancy Elizabeth. 2007. (ENG.). 36p. (J). (gr. -1-1). 7.99 *(978-0-7614-5369-7(5),* 9780761453697, Amazon Children's Publishing) Amazon Publishing.
Wallace, Robert E., photos by. The Adventures of Ichi, the Baby Deer Bk. 1: The Rescue. Wallace, Robert E. 2004. (Adventures of Ichi the Baby Deer Ser.: Bk. 1). (J). lib. bdg. 16.95 *(978-0-9755678-0-7(2))* Cirrus Publishing, LLC.
Wallace, Sam Amber. ABCs of Character. Miller, Dennis. 2003. 52p. (J). lib. bdg. 15.95 *(978-0-9722259-1-5(9))* Twin Peaks Publishing, Inc.
Waller, Diane Hardy, photos by. Does God Forgive Me? Gold, August. 2006. (ENG.). 32p. (J). pap. 8.99 *(978-1-59473-142-6(X),* Skylight Paths Publishing) LongHill Partners, Inc.
—Does God Hear My Prayer? Gold, August. 2005. (ENG.). 32p. (J). pap. 8.99 *(978-1-59473-102-0(0),* Skylight Paths Publishing) LongHill Partners, Inc.
Waller, Joyce. The Lizard's Secret Door. Nelson, Connie. 2014. 32p. (J). 19.95 ***(978-1-59298-933-1(0))*** Beaver's Pond Pr., Inc.
Walles, Dwight. How, Why, When, Where: A Treasure Chest of Wonderful Bible Facts, Stories, Games! Coleman, William L. 2011. (J). pap. *(978-0-89191-717-5(9))* Cook, David C.
—The 5 Languages of Appreciation in the Workplace: Empowering Organizations by Encouraging People, 4 bks. Nystrom, Carolyn et al. ed. 2012. (ENG.). 224p. (gr. -1-2). pap. 16.99 *(978-0-8024-6176-6(X))* Northfield Publishing.
Walling, Sandy Seeley. Helga, the Hippopotamouse. Shimberg, Elaine Fantle. 2008. (ENG.). 36p. (J). 7.95 *(978-0-9741940-4-2(2))* Abernathy Hse. Publishing.
—Herman, the Hermit Crab. Shimberg, Elaine Fantle. l.t. ed. 2007. 28p. (J). 7.95 *(978-0-9741940-2-8(6))* Abernathy Hse. Publishing.
Walling, Sandy Seeley. A Day at the Beach: A Seaside Counting Book from One to Ten. Walling, Sandy Seeley. 2003. 28p. (J). 6.95 *(978-0-9741940-0-4(X))* Abernathy Hse. Publishing.
Walling, Sandy Seeley. ABC's at the Zoo! The Fun Way to Teach Your Child the Relationship between Upper Case & Lower Case Letters. Walling, Sandy Seeley, text. l.t. ed. 2004. 36p. (J). per. 7.95 *(978-0-9741940-1-1(8))* Abernathy Hse. Publishing.
Wallis, Angie. Ka-Lunk! Gallardo-Walker, Gloria. 2013. (ENG.). 21p. pap. *(978-0-9875296-5-7(X))* Aly's Bks.
Wallis, Becky. Three Stretchy Frogs. Bentley, Dawn. 2010. (Stretchies Book Ser.). 16p. (J). 8.99 *(978-0-8249-1459-2(7))* Hinkler Bks. Pty. Ltd. AUS. Dist: Ideals Pubns.
Wallis, Diz. Charles Darwin & the Beagle Adventure. Twist, Clint & Wood, A. J. 2009. (Historical Notebooks Ser.). (ENG.). 30p. (J). (gr. 3-7). 19.99 *(978-0-7636-4538-0(9))* Candlewick Pr.
Wallis, Diz & Hardcastle, Nick. The Story of an Aviator. Calhoun, Marmaduke Randolph. Twist, Clint, ed. 2008. (Amazing Wonders Collection: 2). (ENG.). 16p. (J). (gr. 1-4). 19.99 *(978-0-7636-3906-8(0))* Candlewick Pr.
Wallis, Diz & Nicholls, Emma. Tyrannosaur. Twist, Clint & Fitzgibbon, Monty. 2008. (Amazing Wonders Collection: 1). (ENG.). 16p. (J). (gr. 1-4). 19.99 *(978-0-7636-3550-3(2))* Candlewick Pr.
Wallis, Rebbeca. On Thanksgiving Day. Zocchi, Judy. 2005. (Holiday Happenings Ser.). 32p. (J). pap. 10.95 *(978-1-59646-212-0(4))* Dingles & Co.
Wallis, Rebecca. Islamic Stories, 1 vol. Ganeri, Anita. 2006. (Traditional Religious Tales Ser.). (ENG.). 32p. (gr. 4-6). 27.32 *(978-1-4048-1313-7(6),* Nonfiction Picture Bks.) Picture Window Bks.
—Number 1 What Grows in the Sun? Zocchi, Judy. 2005. (Holiday Happenings Ser.). 32p. (J). per. 10.95 *(978-1-59646-273-1(6))* Dingles & Co.
—Number 1 What Grows in the Sun? 2005. (Community of Counting Ser.). 32p. (J). pap. 10.95 *(978-1-59646-272-4(8))* Dingles & Co.
—Number 1 What Grows in the Sun?/Número 1 Qué crece en el Sol? Dingles, Molly. 2005. (Community of Counting Ser.).Tr. of Número 1 Qué crece en el Sol?. (ENG & SPA.). 32p. (J). per. 10.95 *(978-1-59646-275-5(2))* Dingles & Co.
—Number 1 What Grows in the Sun?/Número 1 Qué crece en el Sol? 2005. (Community of Counting Ser.). (ENG & SPA.). 32p. (J). pap. 10.95 *(978-1-59646-274-8(4))*; lib. bdg. 21.65 *(978-1-891997-89-1(0))* Dingles & Co.
—Number 10 Where Is the Hen? Dingles, Molly. 2005. (Community of Counting Ser.). 32p. (J). (ENG.). lib. bdg. 21.65 *(978-1-891997-90-7(4))*; per. 10.95 *(978-1-59646-309-7(0))* Dingles & Co.
—Number 10 Where Is the Hen? 2005. (Community of Counting Ser.). 32p. (J). pap. 10.95 *(978-1-59646-308-0(2))* Dingles & Co.
—Number 10 Where Is the Hen?/Número 10 en dónde está la Gallina? Dingles, Molly. 2005. (Community of Counting Ser.). (ENG & SPA.). 32p. (J). per. 10.95 *(978-1-59646-311-0(2))* Dingles & Co.
—Number 10 Where Is the Hen?/Número 10 en dónde está la Gallina? 2005. (Community of Counting Ser.).Tr. of Número 10 en dónde está la Gallina?. (ENG & SPA.). 32p. (J). pap. 10.95 *(978-1-59646-310-3(4))*; lib. bdg. 21.65 *(978-1-891997-80-8(7))* Dingles & Co.
—Number 2 Let's Go to the Zoo! Dingles, Molly. 2005. (Community of Counting Ser.). 32p. (J). 10.95 *(978-1-59646-277-9(9))*; pap. 10.95 *(978-1-59646-276-2(0))* Dingles & Co.
—Number 2 Let's Go to the Zoo!/Número 2 Vamos al Zoologico! Dingles, Molly. 2005. (Community of Counting Ser.).Tr. of Número 2 Vamos al Zoologico!. (ENG & SPA.). 32p. (J). pap. 10.95 *(978-1-59646-278-6(7))*; lib. bdg. 21.65 *(978-1-891997-88-4(2))*; per. 10.95 *(978-1-59646-279-3(5))* Dingles & Co.
—Number 3 What's in the Sea? Dingles, Molly. 2005. (Community of Counting Ser.). 32p. (J). pap. 10.95 *(978-1-59646-280-9(9))*; per. 10.95 *(978-1-59646-281-6(7))* Dingles & Co.
—Number 3 What's in the Sea?/Número 3 Qué hay en el Mar? Dingles, Molly. 2005. (Community of Counting Ser.).Tr. of Número 3 Qué hay en el Mar?. (ENG & SPA.). 32p. (J). pap. 10.95 *(978-1-59646-282-3(5))*; lib. bdg. 21.65 *(978-1-891997-87-7(4))*; per. 10.95 *(978-1-59646-283-0(3))* Dingles & Co.
—Number 4 Shop at the Store! Dingles, Molly. (Community of Counting Ser.). 32p. (J). 2005. pap. 10.95 *(978-1-59646-284-7(1))*; 2005. per. 10.95 *(978-1-59646-285-4(X))*; 2004. (ENG.). lib. bdg. 21.65 *(978-1-891997-96-9(3))* Dingles & Co.
—Number 4 Shop at the Store!/Número 4 Vamos de compras a la Tienda! Dingles, Molly. 2005. (Community of Counting Ser.).Tr. of Número 4 Vamos de compras a la Tienda!. (ENG & SPA.). 32p. (J). pap. 10.95 *(978-1-59646-286-1(8))*; lib. bdg. 21.65 *(978-1-891997-86-0(6))*; per. 10.95 *(978-1-59646-287-8(6))* Dingles & Co.
—Number 5 Let's Go for a Drive! Dingles, Molly. 2005. (Community of Counting Ser.). 32p. (J). pap. 10.95 *(978-1-59646-288-5(4))*; (ENG.). lib. bdg. 21.65 *(978-1-891997-95-2(5))*; per. 10.95 *(978-1-59646-289-2(2))* Dingles & Co.
—Number 5 Let's Go for a Drive!/Número 5 Vamos a viajar en Coche! Dingles, Molly. 2005. (Community of Counting Ser.).Tr. of Número 5 Vamos a viajar en Coche!. (ENG & SPA.). 32p. (J). pap. 10.95 *(978-1-59646-290-8(6))*; lib. bdg. 21.65 *(978-1-891997-85-3(8))*; per. 10.95 *(978-1-59646-291-5(4))* Dingles & Co.
—Number 6 What Can We Mix? Dingles, Molly. 2005. (Community of Counting Ser.). 32p. (J). pap. 10.95 *(978-1-59646-292-2(2))*; per. 10.95 *(978-1-59646-293-9(0))* Dingles & Co.
—Number 6 What Can We Mix ? Dingles, Molly. 2005. (Community of Counting Ser.). 32p. (J). lib. bdg. 21.65 *(978-1-891997-94-5(7))* Dingles & Co.
—Number 6 What Can We Mix?/Número 6 Qué podemos Mezclar? Dingles, Molly. 2005. (Community of Counting Ser.).Tr. of Número 6 Qué podemos Mezclar?. (ENG & SPA.). 32p. (J). pap. 10.95 *(978-1-59646-294-6(9))*; lib. bdg. 21.65 *(978-1-891997-84-6(X))*; per. 10.95 *(978-1-59646-295-3(7))* Dingles & Co.
—Number 7 Stars in the Heaven. Dingles, Molly. (Community of Counting Ser.). 32p. (J). 2005. pap. 10.95 *(978-1-59646-296-0(5))*; 2005. per. 10.95 *(978-1-59646-297-7(3))*; 2004. lib. bdg. 21.65 *(978-1-891997-93-8(9))* Dingles & Co.
—Number 7 Stars in the Heaven/Número 7 Estrellas en el Cielo. Dingles, Molly. (Community of Counting Ser.).Tr. of Número 7 Estrellas en el Cielo. (ENG & SPA.). 32p. (J). 2005. pap. 10.95 *(978-1-59646-298-4(1))*; 2005. per. 10.95 *(978-1-59646-299-1(X))*; 2004. lib. bdg. 21.65 *(978-1-891997-83-9(1))* Dingles & Co.
—Number 8 Let's Stay up Late! Dingles, Molly. 2005. (Community of Counting Ser.). 32p. (J). pap. 10.95 *(978-1-59646-300-4(7))*; per. 10.95 *(978-1-59646-301-1(5))* Dingles & Co.
—Number 8 Let's Stay up Late!/Número 8 Vamos a quedarnos en vela hasta muy Noche! Dingles, Molly. (Community of Counting Ser.).Tr. of Número 8 Vamos a quedarnos en vela hasta muy Noche!. (ENG & SPA.). 32p. (J). 2005. pap. 10.95 *(978-1-59646-302-8(3))*; 2005. per. 10.95 *(978-1-59646-303-5(1))*; 2004. lib. bdg. 21.65 *(978-1-891997-82-2(3))* Dingles & Co.
—Number 9 Dress up to Dine! Dingles, Molly. (Community of Counting Ser.). 32p. (J). 2005. pap. 10.95 *(978-1-59646-304-2(X))*; 2005. per. 10.95 *(978-1-59646-305-9(8))*; 2004. lib. bdg. 21.65 *(978-1-891997-91-4(2))* Dingles & Co.
—Number 9 Dress up to Dine!/Número 9 Vestirse con elegancia para Cenar! Dingles, Molly. 2005. (Community of Counting Ser.).Tr. of Número 9 Vestirse con elegancia para Cenar!. (ENG & SPA.). 32p. (J). pap. 10.95 *(978-1-59646-306-6(6))*; lib. bdg. 21.65 *(978-1-891997-81-5(5))*; per. 10.95 *(978-1-59646-307-3(4))* Dingles & Co.
—On Chinese New Year. Zocchi, Judy. 2005. (Holiday Happenings Ser.). 32p. (J). pap. 10.95 *(978-1-59646-188-8(8))*; lib. bdg. 21.65 *(978-1-891997-55-6(6))*; per. 10.95 *(978-1-59646-189-5(6))* Dingles & Co.
—On Chinese New Year/el Año Nuevo Chino. Zocchi, Judy. 2005. (Holiday Happenings Ser.).Tr. of Año Nuevo Chino. (ENG & SPA.). 32p. (J). pap. 10.95 *(978-1-59646-190-1(X))*; lib. bdg. 21.65 *(978-1-891997-56-3(4))*; per. 10.95 *(978-1-59646-191-8(8))* Dingles & Co.
—On Christmas Eve. Zocchi, Judy. 2005. (Holiday Happenings Ser.). 32p. (J). pap. 10.95 *(978-1-59646-224-3(8))*; lib. bdg. 21.65 *(978-1-891997-47-1(5))* Dingles & Co.
—On Christmas Eve. Dingles, Molly. 2005. (Holiday Happenings Ser.). 32p. (J). per. 10.95 *(978-1-59646-225-0(6))* Dingles & Co.
—On Christmas Eve/la Nochebuena. Zocchi, Judy. 2005. (Holiday Happenings Ser.).Tr. of Nochebuena. 32p. (J). pap. 10.95 *(978-1-59646-226-7(4))*; (ENG & SPA.). lib. bdg. 21.65 *(978-1-891997-48-8(3))*; (ENG & SPA.). per. 10.95 *(978-1-59646-227-4(2))* Dingles & Co.
—On Easter Morning. Zocchi, Judy. 2005. (Holiday Happenings Ser.). 32p. (J). pap. 10.95 *(978-1-59646-192-5(6))*; (ENM.). lib. bdg. 21.65 *(978-1-891997-41-9(6))* Dingles & Co.
—On Easter Morning. Dingles, Molly. 2005. (Holiday Happenings Ser.). 32p. (J). per. 10.95 *(978-1-59646-193-2(4))* Dingles & Co.
—On Easter Morning/la mañana de Pascua. Zocchi, Judy. 2005. (Holiday Happenings Ser.).Tr. of mañana de Pascua. (ENG & SPA.). 32p. (J). pap. 10.95 *(978-1-59646-194-9(2))*; lib. bdg. 21.65 *(978-1-891997-42-6(4))*; per. 10.95 *(978-1-59646-195-6(0))* Dingles & Co.
—On Halloween Night. Zocchi, Judy. 2005. (Holiday Happenings Ser.). (J). 32p. pap. 10.95 *(978-1-59646-220-5(5))*; (ENG.). 32p. lib. bdg. 21.65 *(978-1-891997-77-8(7))*; per. 10.95 *(978-1-59646-221-2(3))* Dingles & Co.
—On Halloween Night/la noche de Halloween. Zocchi, Judy. 2005. (Holiday Happenings Ser.).Tr. of noche de Halloween. 32p. (J). pap. 10.95 *(978-1-59646-222-9(1))*; (ENG & SPA.). per. 10.95 *(978-1-59646-223-6(X))* Dingles & Co.
—On Halloween Night/la Noche de Halloween. Zocchi, Judy. 2005. (Holiday Happenings Ser.). (ENG & SPA.). 32p. (J). lib. bdg. 21.65 *(978-1-891997-76-1(9))* Dingles & Co.
—On Hanukkah. Zocchi, Judy. 2005. (Holiday Happenings Ser.). 32p. (J). pap. 10.95 *(978-1-59646-196-3(9))*; lib. bdg. 21.65 *(978-1-891997-45-7(9))*; per. 10.95 *(978-1-59646-197-0(7))* Dingles & Co.
—On Hanukkah/la Hanukkah. Zocchi, Judy. 2005. (Holiday Happenings Ser.).Tr. of Hanukkah. (ENG & SPA.). 32p. (J). pap. 10.95 *(978-1-59646-198-7(5))*; lib. bdg. 21.65 *(978-1-891997-46-4(7))*; per. 10.95 *(978-1-59646-199-4(3))* Dingles & Co.
—On Independence Day. Zocchi, Judy. 2005. (Holiday Happenings Ser.). 32p. (J). pap. 10.95 *(978-1-59646-208-3(6))*; lib. bdg. 21.65 *(978-1-891997-43-3(2))*; per. 10.95 *(978-1-59646-209-0(4))* Dingles & Co.
—On Independence Day/el día de la Independencia. Zocchi, Judy. 2005. (Holiday Happenings Ser.).Tr. of día de la Independencia. (ENG & SPA.). 32p. (J). pap. 10.95 *(978-1-59646-210-6(8))*; lib. bdg. 21.65 *(978-1-891997-44-0(0))*; per. 10.95 *(978-1-59646-211-3(6))* Dingles & Co.
—On Kwanzaa. Zocchi, Judy. 2006. (Global Adventures I Ser.). (J). pap. 10.95 *(978-1-59646-200-7(0))*; 32p. lib. bdg. 21.65 *(978-1-891997-49-5(1))*; 32p. per. 10.95 *(978-1-59646-201-4(9))* Dingles & Co.
—On Kwanzaa/la Kwanzaa. Zocchi, Judy. 2006. (Global Adventures I Ser.).Tr. of Kwanzaa. (ENG & SPA.). 32p. (J). pap. 10.95 *(978-1-59646-202-1(7))*; lib. bdg. 21.65 *(978-1-891997-50-1(5))*; per. 10.95 *(978-1-59646-203-8(5))* Dingles & Co.
—On New Year's Eve. Zocchi, Judy. 2005. (Holiday Happenings Ser.). 32p. (J). pap. 10.95 *(978-1-59646-216-8(7))*; lib. bdg. 21.65 *(978-1-891997-51-8(3))*; per. 10.95 *(978-1-59646-217-5(5))* Dingles & Co.
—On New Year's Eve/la Nochevieja. Zocchi, Judy. 2005. (Holiday Happenings Ser.).Tr. of Nochevieja. (ENG & SPA.). 32p. (J). pap. 10.95 *(978-1-59646-218-2(3))*; lib. bdg. 21.65 *(978-1-891997-52-5(1))*; per. 10.95 *(978-1-59646-219-9(1))* Dingles & Co.
—On Saint Patrick's Day. Zocchi, Judy. 2005. (Holiday Happenings Ser.). 32p. (J). pap. 10.95 *(978-1-59646-232-8(9))*; (ENG.). lib. bdg. 21.65 *(978-1-891997-39-6(4))*; per. 10.95 *(978-1-59646-233-5(7))* Dingles & Co.
—On Saint Patrick's Day/el día de San Patricio. Zocchi, Judy. 2005. (Holiday Happenings Ser.).Tr. of día de San Patricio. (ENG & SPA.). 32p. (J). pap. 10.95 *(978-1-59646-234-2(5))*; lib. bdg. 21.65 *(978-1-891997-40-2(8))*; per. 10.95 *(978-1-59646-235-9(3))* Dingles & Co.
—On Thanksgiving Day. Zocchi, Judy. (Holiday Happenings Ser.). 32p. (J). 2005. per. 10.95 *(978-1-59646-213-7(2))*; 2004. (ENM.). lib. bdg. 21.65 *(978-1-891997-74-7(2))* Dingles & Co.
—On Thanksgiving Day/el Día de Acción de Gracias. Zocchi, Judy. 2005. (Holiday Happenings Ser.).Tr. of Día de Acción de Gracias. (ENG & SPA.). 32p. (J). pap. 10.95 *(978-1-59646-214-4(0))*; lib. bdg. 21.65 *(978-1-891997-75-4(0))*; per. 10.95 *(978-1-59646-215-1(9))* Dingles & Co.
—On Three Kings Day. Zocchi, Judy. 2005. (Holiday Happenings Ser.). 32p. (J). pap. 10.95 *(978-1-59646-204-5(3))*; lib. bdg. 21.65 *(978-1-891997-53-2(X))*; per. 10.95 *(978-1-59646-205-2(1))* Dingles & Co.
—On Three Kings Day/el día de los tres Reyes Magos. Zocchi, Judy. 2005. (Holiday Happenings Ser.).Tr. of día de los tres Reyes Magos. (ENG & SPA.). 32p. (J). pap. 10.95 *(978-1-59646-206-9(X))*; lib. bdg. 21.65 *(978-1-891997-54-9(8))*; per. 10.95 *(978-1-59646-207-6(8))* Dingles & Co.
—On Valentine's Day. Zocchi, Judy. 2005. (Holiday Happenings Ser.). 32p. (J). lib. bdg. 21.65 *(978-1-891997-79-2(3))*; per. 10.95 *(978-1-59646-229-8(9))* Dingles & Co.

W

—On Valentine's Day/el día de San Valentín. Zocchi, Judy. 2005. (Holiday Happenings Ser.).Tr. of Día de San Valentín. (ENG & SPA.). 32p. (J). pap. 10.95 (978-1-59646-230-4(2)); lib. bdg. 21.65 (978-1-891997-78-5(5)); per. 10.95 (978-1-59646-231-1(0)) Dingles & Co.

Wallner, Alexandra. Write on, Mercy! The Secret Life of Mercy Otis Warren. Woelfle, Gretchen. 2012. (ENG.). 40p. (J). (gr. 3). 16.95 (978-1-59078-822-6(2), Calkins Creek) Boyds Mills Pr.

Wallner, Alexandra. Lucy Maud Montgomery. Wallner, Alexandra. 2006. (ENG.). 32p. (J). (gr. -1-3). 16.95 (978-0-8234-1549-6(X)) Holiday Hse., Inc.

Wallner, Alexandra. Grandma Moses. Wallner, Alexandra, tr. 2004. (ENG.). 32p. (J). (gr. k-3). tchr. ed. 16.95 (978-0-8234-1538-0(4)) Holiday Hse., Inc.

Wallner, Alexandra, jt. illus. see Wallner, John.

Wallner, John. Helen Keller. Adler, David A. 2006. (ENG.). 32p. (J). (gr. -1-3). 4.95 (978-0-8234-2042-1(6)) Holiday Hse., Inc.

Wallner, John, et al. A Picture Book of Patrick Henry. Adler, David A. 2005. (ENG.). 32p. (J). (gr. k-3). pap. 6.95 (978-0-8234-1678-3(X)) Holiday Hse., Inc.

Wallner, John & Wallner, Alexandra. A Picture Book of Benjamin Franklin. Adler, David A. 2008. (Picture Book Biography Ser.). (J). (gr. k-3). 28.95 incl. audio compact disk (978-1-4301-0340-0(X));Set. pap. 37.95 incl. audio (978-1-4301-0338-7(8)) Live Oak Media.

Wallner, John, jt. illus. see Wallner, John C.

Wallner, John C. Honest Abe Lincoln: Easy-to-Read Stories about Abraham Lincoln. Adler, David A. 2009. (ENG.). 32p. (J). (gr. k-3). 15.95 (978-0-8234-2057-5(4)) Holiday Hse., Inc.

Wallner, John C. & Wallner, John. Helen Keller. Adler, David A. 2003. (ENG.). 32p. (J). (gr. k-3). tchr. ed. 14.95 (978-0-8234-1606-6(2)) Holiday Hse., Inc.

—President George Washington. Adler, David A. 2005. (ENG.). 32p. (J). 14.95 (978-0-8234-1604-2(6)) Holiday Hse., Inc.

Walls, Ty. Rocket & the Magical Cosmic Candies. Sawler, Kimberly. 2006. 32p. (J). (gr. 4-7). 18.95 (978-1-933285-51-1(6)) Brown Bks. Publishing Group.

Walluk, Wilbur. The Alaskan Ten-Footed Bear & Other Legends. 2013. 44p. pap. 9.95 (978-1-61646-201-7(9)) Coachwhip Pubns.

Walmsley, Jane. The BFG: A Set of Plays. Dahl, Roald. 2007. (ENG.). 128p. (J). (gr. 3-7). 5.99 (978-0-14-240792-9(5), Puffin) Penguin Publishing Group.

—The BFG: A Set of Plays. Dahl, Roald. 2008. 119p. 16.00 (978-0-7569-8346-8(0)) Perfection Learning Corp.

Walrod, Amy. Horace & Morris but Mostly Dolores. Howe, James. 2003. (J). (gr. -1-3). 15.65 (978-0-7569-2936-7(9)) Perfection Learning Corp.

—Horace & Morris Join the Chorus (but What about Dolores?) Howe, James. 2006. (J). pap. 44.95 incl. audio compact disk (978-1-59112-909-7(5)); pap. incl. audio (978-1-59112-449-8(2)) Live Oak Media.

—Horace & Morris Join the Chorus (but What about Dolores?) Howe, James. 2005. (ENG.). 32p. (J). (gr. -1-3). 7.99 (978-1-4169-0616-2(9), Atheneum Bks. for Young Readers) Simon & Schuster Children's Publishing.

—Horace & Morris Say Cheese (Which Makes Dolores Sneeze!) Howe, James. (ENG.). 32p. (J). (gr. -1-3). 2010. 7.99 (978-0-689-87177-1(5)); 2009. 16.99 (978-0-689-83940-5(5)) Simon & Schuster Children's Publishing. (Atheneum Bks. for Young Readers).

Walrod, Amy. Horace & Morris but Mostly Dolores. Walrod, Amy. Howe, James. 2003. (ENG.). 32p. (J). (gr. -1-3). 7.99 (978-0-689-85675-4(X), Atheneum Bks. for Young Readers) Simon & Schuster Children's Publishing.

Walsh Bellville, Cheryl, photos by. Powwow Summer: A Family Celebrates the Circle of Life. Rendon, Marcie R. 2013. (ENG., 48p. (J). (gr. 3-6). pap. 7.95 (978-0-87351-910-6(8)) Minnesota Historical Society Pr.

Walsh, D. T. Counting with Mike the Tiger. Smith, Sherri. 2013. (ENG.). (J). (gr. -1-k). 14.95 (978-1-62086-349-7(9)) Mascot Bks., Inc.

—Mike the Tiger Teaches the Alphabet. Smith, Sherri. 2013. (ENG.). (J). (gr. -1-k). 14.95 (978-1-62086-348-0(0)) Mascot Bks., Inc.

—UGA Teaches the Alphabet. Smith, Sherri Graves. 2013. (ENG.). 28p. (J). (gr. -1-3). 14.95 (978-1-62086-450-0(9)) Mascot Bks., Inc.

Walsh, Ellen Stoll. Balancing Act. Walsh, Ellen Stoll. 2010. (ENG.). 32p. (J). (gr. -1-1). 16.99 (978-1-4424-0757-2(3), Beach Lane Bks.) Beach Lane Bks.

Walsh, Jennifer. Krickle Forest Adventures, Wizbet's Notebook. Yager, Karen & Williams, Kiersten. 2012. 60p. pap. 7.95 (978-0-9855997-0-6(7)) Krickle Forest Adventures.

—Playing It Safe with Mr. See-More Safety Vol. 2: Let's Learn about Bicycle Safety. Rafael, Janis. Date not set. 24p. (J). (gr. -1-8). (978-0-9655604-1-2(4)) Safeworld Publishing Co.

Walsh, Marilyn. My Mum Says Blah Blah Blah. Walsh, Aly. 2012. 26p. pap. 15.97 (978-1-61204-854-3(4), Strategic Bk. Publishing) Strategic Book Publishing & Rights Agency (SBPRA).

Walsh, Melanie. Living with Mom & Living with Dad. Walsh, Melanie. 2012. (ENG.). 40p. (J). (gr. -1-2). 15.99 (978-0-7636-5869-4(3)) Candlewick Pr.

—Trick or Treat? Walsh, Melanie. 2009. (ENG.). 16p. (J). (gr. -1-2). bds. 6.99 (978-0-7636-4295-2(9)) Candlewick Pr.

—10 Things I Can Do to Help My World. Walsh, Melanie. (ENG.). 40p. (J). (gr. -1-2). 2012. pap. 8.99 (978-0-7636-5919-6(3)); 2008. 16.99 (978-0-7636-4144-3(8)) Candlewick Pr.

Walsh, Mike. ABC Kaleidoscope Book. Jackaman, Philippa. 16p. (J). bds. (978-1-84322-126-5(8)) Alligator Bks. Ltd.

Walsh, Rebecca. The Girl Who Wanted to Dance. Ehrlich, Amy. 2009. (ENG.). 40p. (J). (gr. 1-4). 17.99 (978-0-7636-1345-7(2)) Candlewick Pr.

Walsh, T. B. R. Cat in the Clouds. Pinder, Eric. 2009. (ENG.). 32p. 16.99 (978-1-59629-680-0(1), History Pr., The) Arcadia Publishing.

Walsh, Tina. Jude's Moon. Guettier, Nancy. 2014. (Morgan James Kids Ser.). (ENG.). 32p. (gr. -1-4). pap. 9.95 (978-1-61448-964-1(5)) Morgan James Publishing.

Walsh, William. Grimsel: The Story of A Valiant Saint Bernard & Three Boys in the Swiss Alps. Zahn, Muriel. 2011. 178p. 42.95 (978-1-258-07805-8(8)) Literary Licensing, LLC.

Walshe, Dermot. The Fossil Hunters, 1 vol. Helmer, Marilyn. 2009. (Orca Echoes Ser.). (ENG.). 64p. (J). (gr. 2-3). pap. 6.95 (978-1-55469-191-3(5)) Orca Bk. Pubs. USA.

Walstead, Curt. DJ's Allergies. Ormond, Jennifer. 2011. 16p. (gr. -1-k). bds. 8.95 (978-0-9792010-1-1(2)) Ormond, Jennifer.

—Welcome to Merriweather Farm. Knopf, Susan. 2005. (ENG.). 12p. (J). pap. 12.95 (978-0-7624-2342-2(0)) Running Pr. Bk. Pubs.

Walston, Dave. Twirly Whirly Flowers. Golden Books Staff. 2009. (Paint Box Book Ser.). (ENG.). 48p. (J). (gr. -1-2). pap. 3.99 (978-0-375-85129-2(1), Golden Bks.) Random Hse. Children's Bks.

Walt Disney Animation Studios (Firm) Staff. Tangled. Trimble, Irene. 2010. (Junior Novel Ser.). (ENG.). 128p. (J). (gr. 3-7). 4.99 (978-0-7364-2679-4(5), RH/Disney) Random Hse. Children's Bks.

Walt Disney Company Staff. Three Little Pigs. Golden Books Staff. 2004. (Little Golden Book Ser.). (ENG.). 24p. (J). (gr. -1-2). 3.99 (978-0-7364-2312-0(5), Golden/Disney) Random Hse. Children's Bks.

Walt Disney Company Staff & Golden Books Staff. Scamp. Bedford, Annie North & Golden Books Staff. 2004. (Little Golden Book Ser.). (ENG.). 24p. (J). (gr. -1-2). 3.99 (978-0-7364-2311-3(7), Golden/Disney) Random Hse. Children's Bks.

Walt Disney Company Staff & RH Disney Staff. Mother Goose. RH Disney Staff. 2004. (Little Golden Book Ser.). (ENG.). 24p. (J). (gr. -1-2). 3.99 (978-0-7364-2310-6(9), Golden/Disney) Random Hse. Children's Bks.

Walt Disney Studios Staff. Grandpa Bunny. Werner, Janet & Golden Books Staff. 2007. (Little Golden Book Ser.). (ENG.). 24p. (J). (gr. -1-2). 3.99 (978-0-375-83930-6(5), Golden/Disney) Random Hse. Children's Bks.

Walt Disney Studios Staff & Dempster, Al. Peter Pan. Barrie, J. M. & RH Disney Staff. 2007. (Little Golden Book Ser.). (ENG.). 24p. (J). (gr. -1-2). 3.99 (978-0-7364-0238-5(1), Golden/Disney) Random Hse. Children's Bks.

Walt Disney Studios Staff, jt. illus. see RH Disney Staff.

Walter, Debbie. Introducing Russell. Walter, Debbie. 2007. 68p. (J). per. 6.95 (978-0-9766315-2-1(0)) Moose Run Productions.

Walter, Deborah. Teach a Child to READ in... 3 Simple Steps. Rigg, Diana. 2012. (J). (gr. -1-2). (978-1-921560-88-0(6)) PLD Organisation Pty. Ltd.

Walter, J. Miss Callie Lallie's Mouse Tales. Frederick, Susan. 2006. 48p. pap. 16.95 (978-1-4241-1431-3(4)) PublishAmerica, Inc.

Walter, Lorin. Adding & Subtracting at the Lake. Rauen, Amy. 2008. (Getting Started with Math Ser.). 16p. (gr. -1-2). lib. bdg. 19.00 (978-0-8368-8983-3(5), Weekly Reader Leveled Readers) Stevens, Gareth Publishing LLLP.

—Contando Por la Ciudad. Sharp, Jean. 2007. (Matemáticas en Nuestro Mundo (Math in Our World) Ser.). (SPA.). 24p. (gr. 1-2). lib. bdg. 22.00 (978-0-8368-8486-9(8), Weekly Reader Leveled Readers) Stevens, Gareth Publishing LLLP.

—Counting in the City. Sharp, Jean. 2007. (Math in Our World Ser.). 24p. (gr. 1-2). pap. 8.15 (978-0-8368-8477-7(9)); lib. bdg. 22.00 (978-0-8368-8468-5(X)) Stevens, Gareth Publishing LLLP. (Weekly Reader Leveled Readers).

—Midiendo en la Exposcion de Perros. Rauen, Amy & Ayers, Amy. 2007. (Matemáticas en Nuestro Mundo (Math in Our World) Ser.). (SPA.). 24p. (gr. 1-2). lib. bdg. 22.00 (978-0-8368-8492-0(2), Weekly Reader Leveled Readers) Stevens, Gareth Publishing LLLP.

—Using Math Outdoors. Rauen, Amy. 2008. (Getting Started with Math Ser.). 16p. (gr. -1-2). pap. 5.30 (978-0-8368-8989-5(4)); lib. bdg. 19.00 (978-0-8368-8984-0(3)) Stevens, Gareth Publishing LLLP. (Weekly Reader Leveled Readers).

—Vamos a Sumar y Restar en el Lago. Rauen, Amy. 2008. (Matemáticas para Empezar (Getting Started with Math) Ser.). (SPA.). 16p. (gr. -1-2). lib. bdg. 19.00 (978-0-8368-8993-2(2), Weekly Reader Leveled Readers) Stevens, Gareth Publishing LLLP.

—Vamos a Usar las Matematicas al Aire Libre. Rauen, Amy. 2008. (Matemáticas para Empezar (Getting Started with Math) Ser.). (SPA.). 16p. (gr. -1-2). lib. bdg. 19.00 (978-0-8368-8994-9(0), Weekly Reader Leveled Readers) Stevens, Gareth Publishing LLLP.

Walter, Lorin, photos by. Measuring at the Dog Show. Rauen, Amy & Ayers, Amy. 2007. (Math in Our World Ser.). 24p. (gr. 1-2). lib. bdg. 22.00 (978-0-8368-8474-6(4), Weekly Reader Leveled Readers) Stevens, Gareth Publishing LLLP.

Walter, Wendy D. Return of the Dullaith: Ambril's Tale. Walter, Wendy D. 2012. 318p. (J). pap. 15.99 (978-0-9857147-1-0(9), Angry Bicycle) Walter, Wendy D.

Walters, Bob, jt. illus. see Fields, Laura.

Walters, Kurt K. C. Chief Justice. Wetterer, Charles M. & Wetterer, Margaret K. 2005. 32p. (J). (978-1-59336-306-2(0)); pap. (978-1-59336-307-9(9)) Mondo Publishing.

Walters, Robert. Jurassic World Dinosaur Field Guide (Jurassic World) Brett-Surman, Michael K. & Holtz, Thomas R. 2015. (ENG.). 160p. (J). (gr. 3-7). pap. 12.99 (978-0-553-53685-0(0), Random Hse. Bks. for Young Readers) Random Hse. Children's Bks.

Walters, Robert. We Both Read-about Dinosaurs. McKay, Sindy. 2004. (We Both Read Ser.). 44p. (J). (gr. 1-2). 9.95 (978-1-891327-53-7(4)) Treasure Bay, Inc.

—We Both Read-About Dinosaurs. McKay, Sindy. 2004. (We Both Read Ser.). 44p. (J). (gr. 1-2). pap. 5.99 (978-1-891327-54-4(2)) Treasure Bay, Inc.

—We Both Read Bilingual Edition-About Dinosaurs/Acerca de Los Dinosaurios. McKay, Sindy. ed. 2011. (SPA.). 44p. (J). pap. 5.99 (978-1-60115-050-9(4)) Treasure Bay, Inc.

Walthers, Don. The Fish Smuggler. Walthers, Joanie. 2013. (ENG.). 24p. (J). 19.95 (978-1-4787-1167-4(1)) Outskirts Pr., Inc.

Walton, Alex. Billy Had to Move. Fraser, Theresa. 2009. (J). pap. 14.95 (978-1-932690-87-3(5)) Loving Healing Pr., Inc.

—Billy Had to Move: A Foster Care Story. Fraser, Theresa. 2011. 32p. (gr. 3-7). 32.95 (978-1-61599-118-1(2)) Loving Healing Pr., Inc.

—Eliza's Forever Trees. Tara, Stephanie Lisa. 2012. 290p. (J). pap. 9.99 net. (978-1-61254-067-2(8)) Brown Bks. Publishing Group.

—Little Library Mouse. Tara, Stephanie Lisa. 2006. 32p. (J). (gr. k). lib. bdg. 16.95 (978-1-933285-39-9(7)) Brown Bks. Publishing Group.

—Snowy White World to Save. Tara, Stephanie Lisa. 2007. 32p. (J). (gr. -1-3). 16.95 (978-1-933285-89-4(3)) Brown Bks. Publishing Group.

Walton, J. Ambrose. A Master of Mysteries. Eustace, Robert & Meade, L. T. 2013. 106p. pap. 8.00 (978-1-927558-41-6(7)) Birch Tree Publishing.

Walton, Tony. Dumpy & the Firefighters. Andrews, Julie & Hamilton, Emma Walton. 2003. (Julie Andrews Collection). (ENG.). 32p. (J). (gr. -1-2). 15.99 (978-0-06-052681-8(5), Julie Andrews Collection) HarperCollins Pubs.

—Dumpy to the Rescue! Andrews, Julie & Hamilton, Emma Walton. 2004. 24p. (J). lib. bdg. 13.85 (978-1-4242-0707-7(X)) Fitzgerald Bks.

—Dumpy's Apple Shop. Andrews, Julie. 2004. (My First I Can Read Bks.). 32p. (J). (gr. -1-18). lib. bdg. 15.89 (978-0-06-052693-1(9)) HarperCollins Pubs.

—Dumpy's Happy Holiday. Andrews, Julie. 2005. (Julie Andrews Collection). 32p. (J). lib. bdg. 16.89 (978-0-06-052685-6(8), Julie Andrews Collection) HarperCollins Pubs.

—The Great American Mousical. Andrews, Julie & Hamilton, Emma Walton. 2006. (Julie Andrews Collection). (J). (gr. k-4). 160p. 15.99 (978-0-06-057918-0(8), Julie Andrews Collection); 147p. lib. bdg. 16.89 (978-0-06-057919-7(6)) HarperCollins Pubs.

Walton, William J. Polly. Walton, William J. 2013. 88p. 20.00 (978-0-615-79808-0(X)) Awkward Labs.

Waltrip, Mildred, jt. illus. see Fisher, Leonard Everett.

Walty, Margaret T. Rock-a-Bye Baby: Lullabies for Bedtime. 2005. 40p. (J). (gr. k-4). reprint ed. 15.00 (978-0-7567-8555-0(3)) DIANE Publishing Co.

Waltz, Dan. Angelina Katrina: Bugs in My Backyard. Loper, Kathleen. l.t. ed. 2004. 24p. (J). 17.95 (978-0-9741774-4-1(X)) D. W. Publishing.

—Angelina Katrina: Builds Troy Snowman. Loper, Kathleen. l.t. ed. 2004. 36p. (J). 17.95 (978-0-9741774-5-8(8)) D. W. Publishing.

Waltz, Dan. Dragon Fly: A Gnome's Great Adventure. Waltz, Dan. 2007. 360p. (YA). per. 12.49 (978-0-9741774-7-2(4)) D. W. Publishing.

—Kornstalkers: Corn Maze Massacre. Waltz, Dan. l.t. ed. 2005. (Chilled to the Bone! Ser.: No. 1). 120p. (J). per. 6.99 (978-0-9741774-3-4(1)) D. W. Publishing.

Waltz, Dan Hall. Freckles the Frog: A Read-a-Long/Sing-a-Long Story Book. Waltz, Dan Hall. l.t. ed. 2003. 24p. (J). 19.95 (978-0-9741774-0-3(7)) D. W. Publishing.

Walz, Richard. Babe Ruth Saves Baseball! Murphy, Frank. 2005. (Step into Reading Ser.: Vol. 3). (ENG.). 48p. (J). (gr. k-3). pap. 3.99 (978-0-375-83048-8(0), Random Hse. Bks. for Young Readers) Random Hse. Children's Bks.

—Babe Ruth Saves Baseball. Murphy, Frank. 2005. (Step into Reading Ser.). 46p. (gr. 1-3). 14.00 (978-0-7569-5161-0(5)) Perfection Learning Corp.

—Eat My Dust! Henry Ford's First Race. Kulling, Monica. 2004. (Step into Reading Ser.). 48p. (J). (gr. 1-3). 11.65 (978-0-7569-3231-2(9)) Perfection Learning Corp.

—Eat My Dust! Henry Ford's First Race. Kulling, Monica. 2004. (Step into Reading Ser.). (ENG.). 48p. (J). (gr. k-3). pap. 3.99 (978-0-375-81510-2(4), Random Hse. Bks. for Young Readers) Random Hse. Children's Bks.

—Francis Scott Key's Star-Spangled Banner. Kulling, Monica. 2012. (Step into Reading Ser.). (ENG.). 48p. (J). (gr. k-3). pap. 3.99 (978-0-375-86725-5(2), Random Hse. Bks. for Young Readers) Random Hse. Children's Bks.

Walz, Richard. George Washington & the General's Dog. Murphy, Frank. 2015. 48p. pap. 5.00 (978-1-61003-605-4(0)) Center for the Collaborative Classroom.

Walz, Richard. Just Fine the Way They Are: From Dirt Roads to Rail Roads to Interstates. Wooldridge, Connie Nordhielm. 2011. (ENG.). 32p. (J). (gr. 3-18). 17.95 (978-1-59078-710-6(2), Calkins Creek) Boyds Mills Pr.

—Listen Up! Alexander Graham Bell's Talking Machine. Kulling, Monica. 2007. (Step into Reading Ser.). (ENG.). 48p. (J). (gr. k-3). per. 3.99 (978-0-375-83115-7(0), Random Hse. Bks. for Young Readers) Random Hse. Children's Bks.

—Thomas Jefferson's Feast. Murphy, Frank. 2004. (Step into Reading Ser.). 48p. 14.00 (978-0-7569-3235-0(1)) Perfection Learning Corp.

—Thomas Jefferson's Feast. Murphy, Frank. 2003. (Step into Reading Ser.). (ENG.). 48p. (J). (gr. 2-4). pap. 3.99 (978-0-375-82289-6(5), Random Hse. Bks. for Young Readers) Random Hse. Children's Bks.

Walz, Richard & Cook, Donald. George, Thomas, & Abe! Murphy, Frank & Brenner, Martha. 2012. (Step into Reading Ser.). (ENG.). 160p. (J). (gr. k-3). pap. 7.99 (978-0-449-81288-4(X), Random Hse. Bks. for Young Readers) Random Hse. Children's Bks.

Wan, Joyce. Sleepyheads. Howatt, Sandra J. 2014. (ENG.). 32p. (J). (gr. -1-3). 16.99 (978-1-4424-2266-7(1), Beach Lane Bks.) Beach Lane Bks.

Wan, Joyce. Frog & Friends. Wan, Joyce. 2013. (ENG.). 14p. (J). (gr. -1-k). bds. 6.99 (978-0-8431-7277-5(0), Price Stern Sloan) Penguin Publishing Group.

—Hug You, Kiss You, Love You. Wan, Joyce. 2013. (ENG.). 14p. (J). (— 1). bds. 6.99 (978-0-545-54045-2(3), Cartwheel Bks.) Scholastic, Inc.

—My Lucky Little Dragon. Wan, Joyce. 2014. (ENG.). 14p. (J). (— 1). bds. 6.99 (978-0-545-54046-9(1), Cartwheel Bks.) Scholastic, Inc.

—Owl & Friends. Wan, Joyce. 2013. (ENG.). 14p. (J). (gr. -1-k). bds. 6.99 (978-0-8431-7275-1(4), Price Stern Sloan) Penguin Publishing Group.

—We Belong Together. Wan, Joyce. 2011. (ENG.). 14p. (J). (gr. k — 1). bds. 6.99 (978-0-545-30740-6(6), Cartwheel Bks.) Scholastic, Inc.

—You Are My Cupcake. Wan, Joyce. 2011. (ENG.). 14p. (J). (gr. k — 1). bds. 6.99 (978-0-545-30741-3(4)) Scholastic, Inc.

Wanardi, Jennifer. Romina's Rangoli. Iyengar, Malathi Michelle. 2007. (Romina's Rangoli Ser.). 32p. (J). (gr. -1-3). 16.95 (978-1-885008-32-9(5), Shen's Bks.) Lee & Low Bks., Inc.

Wanaselja, Patricia. Sparky the Super Pig. Steel, Joleen. 2011. (ENG.). 24p. pap. 10.00 (978-1-4664-8413-9(6)) CreateSpace Independent Publishing Platform.

Wandelmaier, Michael. Case Closed? Nine Mysteries Unlocked by Modern Science. Hughes, Susan. 2010. (ENG.). 88p. (J). (gr. 3-7). 17.95 (978-1-55453-362-6(7)) Kids Can Pr., Ltd. CAN. Dist: Univ. of Toronto Pr.

Wandelmaier, Michael. Case Closed? Nine Mysteries Unlocked by Modern Science. Wandelmaier, Michael. Hughes, Susan. 2013. (ENG.). 88p. (J). pap. 12.95 (978-1-55453-363-3(5)) Kids Can Pr., Ltd. CAN. Dist: Univ. of Toronto Pr.

Wanecski, Erica Joan. Young Canaller. Stafford, Gerry. 2012. 60p. (J). pap. (978-0-9667989-7-5(X)) Carlisle Pr.- Walnut Creek.

Wanert, Amandine. Stories of Dolls. Davidson, Susanna. 2006. 48p. (J). (gr. 2-5). 8.99 (978-0-7945-1327-6(1), Usborne) EDC Publishing.

—Usborne Stories of Dolls & Fairies. Davidson, Susanna. 2007. (Usborne Ser.). 96p. (J). 9.99 (978-0-7945-1779-3(X), Usborne) EDC Publishing.

Wang, Eva. Auntie Tigress & Other Favorite Chinese Folk Tales. Kung, Annie, tr. 2006. (ENG.). 48p. (J). (gr. -1). lib. bdg. 16.50 (978-1-933327-29-7(4)) Purple Bear Bks., Inc.

—Auntie Tigress & Other Favorite Chinese Folk Tales. 2006. (ENG.). 48p. (J). 15.95 (978-1-933327-28-0(6)) Purple Bear Bks., Inc.

Wang, Jacqueline. The Rescue of Nanoose, 1 vol. O'Loughlin, Chloe & Borrowman, Mary. 2004. (ENG.). 32p. (J). pap. (978-1-894898-20-1(6)) TouchWood Editions.

Wang, Jen. In Real Life. Doctorow, Cory. 2014. (ENG.). 192p. (YA). (gr. 7). pap. 17.99 (978-1-59643-658-9(1), First Second Bks.) Roaring Brook Pr.

Wang, Jue, jt. illus. see Yu, Chao.

Wang, Lin. All about China: Stories, Songs, Crafts & Games for Kids. Branscombe, Allison. 2014. (ENG.). 64p. (J). (gr. 3-6). 16.95 (978-0-8048-4121-4(7)) Tuttle Publishing.

—Just Like You: Beautiful Babies Around the World, 1 vol. Konrad, Marla Stewart. 2010. (ENG.). 32p. (J). (gr. -1-2). 15.99 (978-0-310-71478-1(8)) Zondervan.

—Little Sima & the Giant Bowl. Qu, Zhi. (On My Own Folklore Ser.). (ENG.). 48p. (gr. 2-4). 2009. pap. 6.95 (978-1-58013-850-5(0), First Avenue Editions); 2008. lib. bdg. 25.26 (978-0-8225-7620-4(1), Millbrook Pr.) Lerner Publishing Group.

Wang, Qi. Grand Old Flag. Schwaeber, Barbie H. Nussbaum, Ben, ed. 2006. (Smithsonian American Favorites Ser.). (ENG.). 32p. (J). (gr. 3-7). 14.95 (978-1-59249-649-5(0)) Soundprints.

Wang, Qi, jt. illus. see Pamintuan, Macky.

Wang, Qi Z. Beyond Little Women: A Story about Louisa May Alcott. Aller, Susan Bivin. 2004. (Creative Minds Biographies Ser.). (ENG.). 64p. (gr. 4-8). pap. 8.95 (978-1-57505-636-4(4)); lib. bdg. 22.60 (978-1-57505-602-9(X)) Lerner Publishing Group.

—El Día de los Veteranos. Brill, Marlene Targ. Fitzpatrick, Julia, tr. from ENG. 2005. (Yo Solo: Festividades (on My Own Holidays) Ser.). (SPA.). 48p. (gr. 2-4). lib. bdg. 25.26 (978-0-8225-3120-3(8), Ediciones Lerner) Lerner Publishing Group.

—Freedom's Fire. Falk, Elizabeth Sullivan. 2004. (J). (978-1-59336-321-5(4)); pap. (978-1-59336-322-2(2)) Mondo Publishing.

—Veterans Day. Brill, Marlene Targ. 2005. (On My Own Holidays Ser.). (ENG.). 48p. (gr. 2-4). pap. 6.95 (978-1-57505-766-8(2)) Lerner Publishing Group.

Wang, Qijun. The Kids Book of Black Canadian History. Sadlier, Rosemary. 2010. (Kids Book Of Ser.). (ENG.). 56p. (J). 14.95 (978-1-55453-587-3(5)) Kids Can Pr., Ltd. CAN. Dist: Univ. of Toronto Pr.

Wang, Sean. Catch That Crook! Steele, Michael Anthony. 2012. 23p. (J). (978-1-4242-5333-3(0)) Scholastic, Inc.

—Halloween Rescue! King, Trey. 2013. (Lego City Ser.). (ENG.). 24p. (J). (gr. -1-3). 4.99 (978-0-545-51572-6(6)) Scholastic, Inc.

—LEGO City: Follow That Easter Egg! King, Trey. 2015. (Lego City Ser.). (ENG.). 24p. (J). (gr. -1-k). pap. 3.99 (978-0-545-64146-3(2)) Scholastic, Inc.

—LEGO DC Comics Super Heroes - Friends & Foes! King, Trey. 2015. (LEGO DC Superheroes Ser.). (ENG.). 24p. (J). (gr. -1-3). pap. 3.99 (978-0-545-78504-4(9)) Scholastic, Inc.

—Mystery on the Lego Express. King, Trey. 2014. (Lego City Ser.). (ENG.). 24p. (J). (gr. -1-3). 3.99 (978-0-545-60366-9(8)) Scholastic, Inc.

Wang, Shaoli. Chinese Fairy Tale Feasts: A Literary Cookbook. 2014. 160p. (J). 25.00 (978-1-56656-993-4(1), Crocodile Bks.) Interlink Publishing Group, Inc.

—Shu-Li & Diego, 1 vol. Yee, Paul. 2009. (ENG.). 32p. (J). (gr. 1-4). pap. 7.95 (978-1-896580-53-1(X)) Tradewind Bks. CAN. Dist: Orca Bk. Pubs. USA.

—Shu-Li & Tamara, 1 vol. Yee, Paul. 2008. (ENG.). 64p. (J). (gr. 1-4). per. 7.95 *(978-1-896580-93-7(9))* Tradewind Bks. CAN. Dist: Orca Bk. Pubs. USA.

Wang, Suling. The Blue Ghost. Bauer, Marion Dane. 2006. (Stepping Stone Book Ser.). (ENG.). 96p. (J). (gr. 1-4). 3.99 *(978-0-375-83339-7(0),* Random Hse. Bks. for Young Readers) Random Hse. Children's Bks.

—The Magic Paintbrush. Yep, Laurence. 2003. (ENG.). 96p. (J). (gr. 3-7). pap. 5.99 *(978-0-06-440852-3(3))* HarperCollins Pubs.

—The Magic Paintbrush. Yep, Laurence. 2003. 89p. (J). (gr. 3-7). 12.65 *(978-0-7569-1444-8(2))* Perfection Learning Corp.

—When the Circus Came to Town. Yep, Laurence. 2004. 112p. (J). (gr. 3-5). 13.65 *(978-0-7569-2969-5(5))* Perfection Learning Corp.

Wang, Zong. D Is for Dancing Dragon: A China Alphabet. Crane, Carol. 2009. (Alphabet-Country Ser.). (ENG.). 48p. (gr. k-6). pap. 7.95 *(978-1-58536-473-2(8))* Sleeping Bear Pr.

Wang, Zong-Zhou. D Is for Dancing Dragon: A China Alphabet. Crane, Carol. rev. ed. 2006. (Discover the World Ser.). (ENG.). 48p. (J). (gr. -1-3). 17.95 *(978-1-58536-273-8(5))* Sleeping Bear Pr.

Wanha Ildih. Purple Butterflies. Menase Debora. 2005. (ENG.). 24p. (J). (gr. -1-12). 13.50 *(978-975-6663-74-5(X))* Citlembik/Nettleberry Pubns. TUR. Dist: National Bk. Network.

Wannamaker, Joni Gruelle. Honest-to-Goodness Story of Raggedy Andy, 1 vol. Hall, Patricia. 2005. (ENG.). 32p. (J). (gr. k-3). 16.99 *(978-1-58980-251-3(9))* Pelican Publishing Co., Inc.

Wapahi, Robert. Dancing Hands: Signs of Learning. Hay, John & Harwich, Mary Belle. 2013. 78p. pap. 16.95 *(978-0-9888972-0-5(2))* Scotland Gate, Inc.

Warabe, Kimika. Joy to the World! Ebina, Hiro. 2006. (JPN.). 12p. (J). (gr. -1-k). bds. 9.95 *(978-0-8198-3985-5(X))* Pauline Bks. & Media.

Warburton, Sarah. After Happily Ever After, 1 vol. Bradman, Tony. 2014. (After Happily Ever After Ser.). (ENG.). 56p. (gr. 2-3). lib. bdg. 143.94 *(978-1-4342-8929-2(X),* After Happily Ever After) Stone Arch Bks.

—Cinderella & the Mean Queen. Bradman, Tony. (After Happily Ever After Ser.). (ENG.). 56p. (gr. 2-3). 2014. pap. 5.05 *(978-1-4342-7960-6(X));* 2009. lib. bdg. 23.99 *(978-1-4342-1301-3(3))* Stone Arch Bks. (After Happily Ever After).

—Fairy Godmother Takes a Break. Bradman, Tony. 2014. (After Happily Ever After Ser.). (ENG.). 56p. (gr. 2-3). pap. 5.05 *(978-1-4342-7961-3(8),* After Happily Ever After) Stone Arch Bks.

—The Fairy Godmother Takes a Break. Bradman, Tony. 2009. (After Happily Ever After Ser.). (ENG.). 56p. (gr. 2-3). 23.99 *(978-1-4342-1302-0(1),* After Happily Ever After) Stone Arch Bks.

—The Frog Prince Hops to It, 1 vol. Bradman, Tony. (After Happily Ever After Ser.). (ENG.). 56p. (gr. 2-3). 2014. pap. 5.05 *(978-1-4342-7962-0(6));* 2009. 23.99 *(978-1-4342-1303-7(X))* Stone Arch Bks. (After Happily Ever After).

—Goldilocks & the Just Right Club. Bradman, Tony. (After Happily Ever After Ser.). (ENG.). 56p. (gr. 2-3). 2014. pap. 5.05 *(978-1-4342-7963-7(4));* 2009. 23.99 *(978-1-4342-1304-4(8))* Stone Arch Bks. (After Happily Ever After).

—Jack & the Bean Snacks, 1 vol. Bradman, Tony. (After Happily Ever After Ser.). (ENG.). 56p. (gr. 2-3). 2014. pap. 5.05 *(978-1-4342-7964-4(2));* 2009. 23.99 *(978-1-4342-1305-1(6))* Stone Arch Bks. (After Happily Ever After).

—Little Dragon. Magee, Wes. 2004. (ENG.). 24p. (J). lib. bdg. 23.65 *(978-1-59646-690-6(1))* Dingles & Co.

—Mabel & Me - Best of Friends. Sperring, Mark. 2015. (ENG.). 32p. (J). 17.99 *(978-0-00-758593-9(4),* HarperCollins Children's Bks.) HarperCollins Pubs. Ltd. GBR. Dist: HarperCollins Pubs.

—Max & the Won't Go to Bed Show. Sperring, Mark. 2014. (ENG.). 32p. (J). (gr. -1-k). 16.99 *(978-0-545-70822-7(2),* Scholastic Pr.) Scholastic, Inc.

—Mr. Bear Gets Alarmed, 1 vol. Bradman, Tony. 2014. (After Happily Ever After Ser.). (ENG.). 56p. (gr. 2-3). lib. bdg. 23.99 *(978-1-4342-7948-4(0),* After Happily Ever After) Stone Arch Bks.

—Mr. Giant & the Beastly Baron, 1 vol. Bradman, Tony. 2014. (After Happily Ever After Ser.). (ENG.). 56p. (gr. 2-3). lib. bdg. 23.99 *(978-1-4342-7949-1(9),* After Happily Ever After) Stone Arch Bks.

—Mr. Wolf Bounces Back, 1 vol. Bradman, Tony. (After Happily Ever After Ser.). (ENG.). 56p. (gr. 2-3). 2013. pap. 5.05 *(978-1-4342-6414-5(9));* 2009. 23.99 *(978-1-4342-1306-8(4))* Stone Arch Bks. (After Happily Ever After).

—Mr. Wolf Bounces Back [Scholastic]. Bradman, Tony. 2009. (After Happily Ever After Ser.). (ENG.). 56p. (gr. 2-3). pap. 4.99 *(978-1-4342-1676-2(4),* After Happily Ever After) Stone Arch Bks.

—My Unwilling Witch Gets a Makeover. Oram, Hiawyn. 2010. (Rumblewick's Diary Ser.: 4). (ENG.). 112p. (J). (gr. 1-4). 7.99 *(978-0-316-03462-3(2))* Little, Brown Bks. for Young Readers.

—My Unwilling Witch Goes to Ballet School. Oram, Hiawyn. 2009. (Rumblewick's Diary Ser.: 1). (ENG.). 112p. (J). (gr. 1-4). 7.99 *(978-0-316-03472-2(X))* Little, Brown Bks. for Young Readers.

—My Unwilling Witch Sleeps Over. Oram, Hiawyn. 2009. (Rumblewick's Diary Ser.: 2). (ENG.). 112p. (J). (gr. 1-4). 7.99 *(978-0-316-03453-1(3))* Little, Brown Bks. for Young Readers.

—My Unwilling Witch Starts a Girl Band. Oram, Hiawyn. 2009. (Rumblewick's Diary Ser.: 3). (ENG.). 112p. (J). (gr. 1-4). 7.99 *(978-0-316-03471-5(1))* Little, Brown Bks. for Young Readers.

—The Princess & the Peas. Hart, Caryl. 2013. (ENG.). 32p. (J). (gr. -1-2). 16.99 *(978-0-7636-6532-6(0),* Nosy Crow) Candlewick Pr.

—The Princess & the Presents. Hart, Caryl. 2014. (ENG.). 32p. (J). (gr. -1-2). 16.99 *(978-0-7636-7398-7(6),* Nosy Crow) Candlewick Pr.

—Rapunzel Lets Her Hair Down, 1 vol. Bradman, Tony. (After Happily Ever After Ser.). (ENG.). 56p. (gr. 2-3). 2014. pap. 5.05 *(978-1-4342-7965-1(0));* 2009. lib. bdg. 23.99 *(978-1-4342-1307-5(2))* Stone Arch Bks. (After Happily Ever After).

—Red Riding Hood Takes Charge, 1 vol. Bradman, Tony. (After Happily Ever After Ser.). (ENG.). 56p. (gr. 2-3). 2013. pap. 5.05 *(978-1-4342-6413-8(0));* 2009. 23.99 *(978-1-4342-1308-2(0))* Stone Arch Bks. (After Happily Ever After).

—Snow White & the Magic Mirror. Bradman, Tony. 2014. (After Happily Ever After Ser.). (ENG.). 56p. (gr. 2-3). pap. 5.05 *(978-1-4342-7956-9(1));* lib. bdg. 23.99 *(978-1-4342-7950-7(2))* Stone Arch Bks. (After Happily Ever After).

—The Three Little Pigs Go Camping, 1 vol. Bradman, Tony. 2014. (After Happily Ever After Ser.). (ENG.). 56p. (gr. 2-3). lib. bdg. 23.99 *(978-1-4342-7952-1(9),* After Happily Ever After) Stone Arch Bks.

Warburton, Sarah. Twinkle. Holabird, Katherine. 2014. (J). *(978-1-4351-5628-9(5))* Barnes & Noble, Inc.

Warburton, Sarah. The Ugly Duckling Returns, 1 vol. Bradman, Tony. 2014. (After Happily Ever After Ser.). (ENG.). 56p. (gr. 2-3). lib. bdg. 23.99 *(978-1-4342-7953-8(7),* After Happily Ever After) Stone Arch Bks.

—The Wicked Stepmother Helps Out, 1 vol. Bradman, Tony. 2014. (After Happily Ever After Ser.). (ENG.). 56p. (gr. 2-3). lib. bdg. 23.99 *(978-1-4342-7951-4(0),* After Happily Ever After) Stone Arch Bks.

Warburton, Tom. 1000 Times No. Warburton, Tom. 2009. (ENG.). 40p. (J). (gr. -1-3). 17.99 *(978-0-06-154263-3(6))* HarperCollins Pubs.

Warchocki, Tim. Have Your Cake & Eat It Too: The Family Plan for Lifelong Health & Fitness. 2004. *(978-0-9747008-0-9(0))* First Class Fitness Systems, Inc.

—My Fit Family. . . a Quick Start. 2004. cd-rom 9.95 *(978-0-9747008-2-3(7))* First Class Fitness Systems, Inc.

Ward, April. Adventure in the Park. Feldman, Thea. 2006. 20p. (J). *(978-0-696-23234-3(0))* Meredith Bks.

—Butterflies on Carmen Street/Mariposas en la Calle Carmen. Brown, Monica. 2007. (SPA & ENG.). 32p. (J). (gr. -1-2). 16.95 *(978-1-55885-484-0(3),* Piñata Books) Arte Publico Pr.

—Growing up with Tamales: Los Tamales de Ana. Zepeda, Gwendolyn & Ventura, Gabriela Baeza. 2008. (SPA & ENG.). 32p. (J). (gr. -1-2). 16.95 *(978-1-55885-493-2(2),* Piñata Books) Arte Publico Pr.

—Juan & the Chupacabras/Juan y el Chupacabras. Garza, Xavier. 2006. (ENG & SPA.). 32p. (J). (gr. -1-2). 16.95 *(978-1-55885-454-3(1),* Piñata Books) Arte Publico Pr.

Ward, Cherise. Another Day. Mitchell, Carol. 2013. 206p. pap. 8.99 *(978-0-9899305-0-5(5))* CaribbeanReads.

—The Shark & the Parrotfish & Other Caribbean Fables. Picayo, Mario et al. 2014. (J). pap. *(978-1-934370-36-0(3))* Editorial Campana.

Ward, Damian. Alphabet of Dance. Schwaeber, Barbie Heit. 2009. (Smithsonian Alphabet Books). (ENG.). 40p. (J). (gr. -1-k). 17.95 *(978-1-60727-110-9(9))* Soundprints.

—Everyone Feels Angry Sometimes, 1 vol. Meister, Cari. 2010. (Everyone Has Feelings Ser.). (ENG.). 24p. (gr. k-2). lib. bdg. 25.32 *(978-1-4048-5753-7(2));* pap. 7.49 *(978-1-4048-6112-1(2))* Picture Window Bks. (Nonfiction Picture Bks.).

—Everyone Feels Happy Sometimes, 1 vol. Meister, Cari. 2010. (Everyone Has Feelings Ser.). (ENG.). 24p. (gr. k-2). lib. bdg. 25.32 *(978-1-4048-5754-4(0));* pap. 7.49 *(978-1-4048-6113-8(0))* Picture Window Bks. (Nonfiction Picture Bks.).

—Everyone Feels Sad Sometimes, 1 vol. Aboff, Marcie. 2010. (Everyone Has Feelings Ser.). (ENG.). 24p. (gr. k-2). lib. bdg. 25.32 *(978-1-4048-5755-1(9));* pap. 7.49 *(978-1-4048-6114-5(9))* Picture Window Bks. (Nonfiction Picture Bks.).

—Everyone Feels Scared Sometimes, 1 vol. Aboff, Marcie. 2010. (Everyone Has Feelings Ser.). (ENG.). 24p. (gr. k-2). lib. bdg. 25.32 *(978-1-4048-5756-8(7));* pap. 7.49 *(978-1-4048-6115-2(7))* Picture Window Bks. (Nonfiction Picture Bks.).

—It's a Thunderstorm! Higgins, Nadia. 2010. (Weather Watchers Ser.). 32p. (J). (gr. k-3). 28.50 *(978-1-60270-729-0(4))* Magic Wagon.

—It's a Tornado! Higgins, Nadia. 2010. (Weather Watchers Ser.). 32p. (J). (gr. k-3). 28.50 *(978-1-60270-730-6(8))* Magic Wagon.

—It's a Tsunami! Higgins, Nadia. 2010. (Weather Watchers Ser.). 32p. (J). (gr. k-3). 28.50 *(978-1-60270-731-3(6))* Magic Wagon.

—It's Hailing! Higgins, Nadia. 2010. (Weather Watchers Ser.). 32p. (J). (gr. k-3). 28.50 *(978-1-60270-732-0(4))* Magic Wagon.

—It's Raining! Higgins, Nadia. 2010. (Weather Watchers Ser.). 32p. (J). (gr. k-3). 28.50 *(978-1-60270-733-7(2))* Magic Wagon.

—It's Snowing! Higgins, Nadia. 2010. (Weather Watchers Ser.). 32p. (J). (gr. k-3). 28.50 *(978-1-60270-734-4(0))* Magic Wagon.

—A Slave's Education in Courage: The Life of Frederick Douglass. Coleman, Wim & Perrin, Pat. 2014. (Setting the Stage for Fluency Ser.). 40p. (gr. 3-5). pap. 8.95 *(978-1-939656-38-4(9))* Red Chair Pr.

Ward, E. F. We Were There at the Boston Tea Party. Webb, Robert N. 2013. (ENG.). 192p. (J). (gr. 3-8). pap. 6.99 *(978-0-486-49260-5(5))* Dover Pubns., Inc.

Ward, Fred, photos by. Gem Care. Ward, Charlotte, ed. 2nd ed. 2003. (Fred Ward Gem Book Ser.). 32p. pap. 9.95 *(978-1-887651-07-3(1))* Gem Bk. Pubs.

Ward, Geoff. Reducing Pollution & Waste, 1 vol. Green, Jen. 2011. (Environment Challenge Ser.). (ENG.). 48p. (gr. 3-3). pap. 9.49 *(978-1-4109-4327-9(5));* 33.99 *(978-1-4109-4320-0(8))* Heinemann-Raintree. (Raintree Freestyle Express).

Ward, Helen. Spots in a Box. Ward, Helen. 2015. (ENG.). 40p. (J). (gr. -1-2). 16.99 *(978-0-7636-7597-4(0),* Templar) Candlewick Pr.

—The Town Mouse & the Country Mouse. Ward, Helen. 2012. (ENG.). 48p. (J). (gr. -1-3). 16.99 *(978-0-7636-6098-7(1),* Templar) Candlewick Pr.

Ward, Jay Bryant. The Secret of the King. Nunes, Rachel Ann. 2005. 32p. (J). (gr. -1-3). 17.95 *(978-1-59038-241-7(2),* Shadow Mountain) Shadow Mountain Publishing.

Ward, John. The Bus Ride. Miller, William. 2013. (ENG.). 30p. (J). (gr. -1-18). reprint ed. pap. 9.95 *(978-1-58430-026-7(4))* Lee & Low Bks., Inc.

Ward, Juliana. Blackie's Day Out. Ward, Teresa. 2011. 32p. pap. *(978-1-77067-933-7(2))* FriesenPress.

Ward, Keith. The Black Stallion. Farley, Walter. 2008. (Black Stallion Ser.). (ENG.). 288p. (J). (gr. 3-7). 15.99 *(978-0-375-85582-5(3),* Random Hse. Bks. for Young Readers) Random Hse. Children's Bks.

Ward, Kelly. The Fox & the Young Rooster. Kelly, Thomas E. 2011. 44p. pap. 24.95 *(978-1-4626-0343-5(2))* America Star Bks.

Ward, Lindsay. Rosco vs. the Baby. 2015. (J). *(978-1-4814-3657-1(0),* Simon & Schuster Bks. For Young Readers) Simon & Schuster Bks. For Young Readers.

Ward, Lindsay. The Yellow Butterfly. Gill, Mehmaz S. 2010. (ENG.). 24p. (J). (gr. k-2). 17.95 *(978-1-933979-71-7(2),* 45f00f36-ed1a-4633-929a-2bb04d2073f4) Bright Sky Pr.

Ward, Lindsay. Pelly & Mr. Harrison Visit the Moon. Ward, Lindsay. ed. 2011. (ENG.). 36p. (J). (gr. -1-3). 11.99 *(978-1-935279-77-8(7))* Kane Miller.

Ward, Lindsay M. A Garden for Pig. Thurman, Kathryn. 2010. (ENG.). 40p. (J). (gr. -1-3). 10.99 *(978-1-935279-24-2(6))* Kane Miller.

Ward, Lynd. Bright Island. Robinson, Mabel L. 75th ed. 2012. (ENG.). 288p. (J). (gr. 5). 6.99 *(978-0-375-97136-5(X),* Yearling) Random Hse. Children's Bks.

—Gaudenzia, Pride of the Palio. Henry, Marguerite. 2014. (ENG.). 304p. (J). (gr. 3-7). pap. 5.99 *(978-1-4814-0397-9(4),* Simon & Schuster/Paula Wiseman Bks.) Simon & Schuster/Paula Wiseman Bks.

—The Little Red Lighthouse & the Great Gray Bridge: Restored Edition. Swift, Hildegarde H. 2003. (ENG.). 64p. (J). (gr. -1-3). pap. 8.00 *(978-0-15-204573-9(2))* Houghton Mifflin Harcourt Publishing Co.

—Spice & the Devil's Cave. Hewes, Agnes Danforth. 2014. (ENG.). 352p. (J). (gr. 4). pap. 5.99 *(978-0-486-49287-2(7))* Dover Pubns., Inc.

Ward, Matt. Dinosaur Rock. Harvey, Damien. 2005. (Collins Big Cat Ser.). (ENG.). 56p. (J). pap. 5.99 *(978-0-00-718540-5(5))* HarperCollins Pubs. Ltd. GBR. Dist: Independent Pubs. Group.

—Dinosaur Rock. Collins Educational Staff & Harvey, Damian. 2012. (Collins Big Cat Ser.). (ENG.). 104p. (J). pap., wbk. ed. 4.99 *(978-0-00-747490-5(3))* HarperCollins Pubs. Ltd. GBR. Dist: Independent Pubs. Group.

Ward, Matthew, photos by. Learn Squash in a Weekend. Khan, Jahangir & Pratt, Kevin. 2005. 95p. (YA). reprint ed. pap. 15.00 *(978-0-7567-9415-6(3))* DIANE Publishing Co.

Ward, Megan. Emily Finds a Dog. Ward, Carla. 2007. (J). 15.95 *(978-0-9793124-0-3(X))* Tinkertown Museum.

Ward, Nick. Deck the Walls: A Wacky Christmas Carol. Dealey, Erin. 2013. (ENG.). (J). *(978-1-58536-857-0(1))* Sleeping Bear Pr.

—Hans Christian Andersen. Fischel, Emma. 2010. (Famous People, Famous Lives Ser.). 38p. (J). *(978-89-491-8824-9(4))* Biryongso Publishing Co.

Ward, Nick. I Wish ... Ward, Nick. 2011. (ENG.). 32p. (J). (gr. -1-k). pap. 7.99 *(978-1-84365-191-8(2),* Pavilion Children's Books) Pavilion Bks. GBR. Dist: Independent Pubs. Group.

Ward, Patricia R. & Pigford, Grady A. Maria Montessori. Sharpe, Paula A. 2010. 51p. (J). *(978-1-892142-47-4(3))* Cedar Tree Bks.

Ward, Sarah. Bouncy, Pouncy Puppy. Macmillan, Sue. 2014. (Cheery Chasers Ser.). (ENG.). 8p. (J). (gr. -1 — 1). bds. 4.99 *(978-0-7641-6698-3(0))* Barron's Educational Series, Inc.

—Happy, Hoppy Bunny. Macmillan, Sue. 2014. (Cheery Chasers Ser.). (ENG.). 8p. (J). (gr. -1 — 1). bds. 4.99 *(978-0-7641-6699-0(9))* Barron's Educational Series, Inc.

—Hoppy Frog's Fly Spy. Macmillan, Sue. 2014. (Cheery Chasers Ser.). (ENG.). 8p. (J). (gr. -1 — 1). bds. 4.99 *(978-0-7641-6700-3(6))* Barron's Educational Series, Inc.

—Racing, Chasing Kitten. Macmillan, Sue. 2014. (Cheery Chasers Ser.). (ENG.). 8p. (J). (gr. -1 — 1). bds. 4.99 *(978-0-7641-6701-0(4))* Barron's Educational Series, Inc.

Ward, Sarah G. Carry & Learn Colors. Scholastic, Inc. Staff. 2015. (ENG.). 10p. (J). (gr. -1 — 1). 7.99 *(978-0-545-78385-9(2),* Cartwheel Bks.) Scholastic, Inc.

Ward, Sarah G. Carry & Learn Numbers. Scholastic, Inc. Staff. 2015. (ENG.). 10p. (J). (— 1). bds. 7.99 *(978-0-545-79790-0(X),* Cartwheel Bks.) Scholastic, Inc.

Ward, Scott. Moon Beam Walking: Dream Space Books, 1 vol. Reynolds, D. G. 2009. 14p. pap. 19.95 *(978-1-61546-726-6(2))* PublishAmerica, Inc.

Ward, Sue Marshall. Sugar Lump's Night Before Christmas, 1 vol. Simmons, Lynn Sheffield. 2007. (Night Before Christmas Ser.). (ENG.). 48p. (J). (gr. k-5). 12.95 *(978-1-58980-439-5(2))* Pelican Publishing Co., Inc.

—Ten Redneck Babies: A Southern Counting Book, 1 vol. Davis, David. 2004. (ENG.). 32p. (J). (gr. k-k). 16.99 *(978-1-58980-232-2(2))* Pelican Publishing Co., Inc.

—Texas Aesop's Fables, 1 vol. Davis, David. 2008. (ENG.). 32p. (J). (gr. k-3). 16.99 *(978-1-58980-569-9(0))* Pelican Publishing Co., Inc.

—Texas Mother Goose, 1 vol. Davis, David. 2006. (ENG.). 40p. (J). (gr. k-3). 17.99 *(978-1-58980-369-5(8))* Pelican Publishing Co., Inc.

Ward, Sylvia. Lift the Flap Noah, 1 vol. David, Juliet. 2009. 12p. (J). 6.99 *(978-0-8254-7387-6(X),* Candle Bks.) Lion Hudson PLC GBR. Dist: Kregel Pubns.

Ward, Sylvia, jt. illus. see Denham, Gemma.

Warden, Gillian. The Cat on the Island. Crew, Gary. 2008. 32p. *(978-0-207-20070-0(X))* HarperCollins Pubs. Australia.

Warder, Aaron. Outside Kitty. Moore, J. S. I.t. ed. 2011. (ENG.). 34p. pap. 10.95 *(978-1-4679-6061-8(6))* CreateSpace Independent Publishing Platform.

Ware, Quinton. Joey & the Magic Dream Pillow. Vana, Dan. 2013. 20p. pap. 24.95 *(978-1-4626-7872-3(6))* America Star Bks.

Warf, Gracie. No Peanuts for Me! Pangan, Catherine Hagerman. 2013. (ENG.). 30p. (J). (gr. -1-3). 14.95 *(978-1-62086-433-3(9))* Mascot Bks., Inc.

Warfield, D. L. Can't Hold Me Down. LeFlore, Lyah B. 2010. (Come Up Ser.). (ENG.). 272p. (J). (gr. 9-18). pap. 8.99 *(978-1-4169-7964-7(6),* Simon Pulse) Simon Pulse.

—The World Is Mine. LeFlore, Lyah B. 2009. (Come Up Ser.). (ENG.). 256p. (YA). (gr. 9-18). pap. 8.99 *(978-1-4169-7963-0(8),* Simon Pulse) Simon Pulse.

Wargin, Ed, photos by. I Spy with My Little Eye: Minnesota. Wargin, Kathy-jo. 2008. (ENG.). 32p. (J). (gr. k-6). 13.95 *(978-1-58536-359-9(6))* Sleeping Bear Pr.

Wargin, Kathy-jo & Bendall-Brunello, John. Scare a Bear. 2010. (ENG.). 32p. (J). (gr. -1-3). 15.95 *(978-1-58536-430-5(4))* Sleeping Bear Pr.

Warhola, James. If You're Happy & You Know It. Warhola, James. Scholastic, Inc. Staff. Geist, Ken, ed. 2007. (ENG.). 32p. (J). (gr. -1-k). 15.99 *(978-0-439-72766-2(9),* Orchard Bks.) Scholastic, Inc.

—Uncle Andy's. Warhola, James. 2005. (ENG.). 32p. (J). (gr. k-3). reprint ed. pap. 5.99 *(978-0-14-240347-1(4),* Puffin) Penguin Publishing Group.

—Uncle Andy's: A Faabbbulous Visit with Andy Warhol. Warhola, James. 2003. (ENG.). 32p. (J). (gr. k-3). 17.99 *(978-0-399-23869-7(7),* Putnam Juvenile) Penguin Publishing Group.

—Uncle Andy's Cats. Warhola, James. 2009. (ENG.). 32p. (J). (gr. k-3). 16.99 *(978-0-399-25180-1(4),* Putnam Juvenile) Penguin Publishing Group.

Warick, Bob. Forestry A-Z, 1 vol. Walsh, Ann & Waldron, Kathleen Cook. 2008. (ENG.). 32p. (J). (gr. 2-7). 19.95 *(978-1-55143-504-6(7))* Orca Bk. Pubs. USA.

Waring, Geoff. Black Meets White. Fontes, Justine. 2005. (ENG.). 24p. (J). (— 1). 12.99 *(978-0-7636-1933-6(7))* Candlewick Pr.

Waring, Geoff. Oscar & the Bat: A Book about Sound. Waring, Geoff. 2009. (Start with Science Ser.). (ENG.). 32p. (J). (gr. -1-3). pap. 6.99 *(978-0-7636-4513-7(3))* Candlewick Pr.

—Oscar & the Bird: A Book about Electricity. Waring, Geoff. 2011. (Start with Science Ser.). (ENG.). 32p. (J). (gr. -1-3). pap. 6.99 *(978-0-7636-5302-6(0))* Candlewick Pr.

—Oscar & the Cricket: A Book about Moving & Rolling. Waring, Geoff. 2009. (Start with Science Ser.). (ENG.). 32p. (J). (gr. -1-3). pap. 6.99 *(978-0-7636-4512-0(5))* Candlewick Pr.

—Oscar & the Frog: A Book about Growing. Waring, Geoff. (Start with Science Ser.). (ENG.). 32p. (J). (gr. -1-3). 2008. pap. 6.99 *(978-0-7636-4030-9(1));* 2007. 11.99 *(978-0-7636-3558-9(8))* Candlewick Pr.

—Oscar & the Moth: A Book about Light & Dark. Waring, Geoff. 2008. (Start with Science Ser.). (ENG.). 32p. (J). (gr. -1-3). pap. 6.99 *(978-0-7636-4031-6(X))* Candlewick Pr.

—Oscar & the Snail: A Book about Things That We Use. Waring, Geoff. (Start with Science Ser.). (ENG.). 32p. (J). (gr. -1-3). 2011. pap. 6.99 *(978-0-7636-5303-3(9));* 2009. 14.99 *(978-0-7636-4039-2(5))* Candlewick Pr.

Warm Day, Jonathan. Kiki's Journey. Orona-Ramirez, Kristy. 2013. (ENG.). 32p. (J). (gr. k-3). 16.95 *(978-0-89239-214-8(2))* Lee & Low Bks., Inc.

Warner, Danielle. Hidden Mickeys: A Mouse in the Land. Warner, Jeremy. 2012. 68p. pap. 5.95 *(978-0-9853555-2-4(2))* Portrait Health Publishing.

Warner, Darrell. Wuthering Heights. Brontë, Emily. 2004. (Paperback Classics Ser.). 158p. (J). (gr. 5). lib. bdg. 12.95 *(978-1-58086-604-0(2))* EDC Publishing.

Warner, Linda. Lighthouse Seeds. Love, Pamela. ed. 2004. (ENG.). 32p. (J). (gr. k-17). 15.95 *(978-0-89272-541-0(9))* Down East Bks.

Warner, Michael. Byron Carmichael Book One: The Human Corpse Trade. King, J. Eric & Graham, Greg. Mizer, Lindsay, ed. 2008. (ENG.). 408p. (gr. 8-12). 18.95 *(978-0-615-15770-2(X))* G & K Publishing.

Warner, Robert. Tales to Make You Scream for Your Momma. Warner, Michael N. 2015. 198p. (J). pap. 11.95 *(978-0-9963756-1-0(9))* All About Kids Publishing.

Warnes, Tim. Bless You, Santa! Sykes, Julie. 2004. 32p. (J). tchr. ed. 15.95 *(978-1-58925-041-3(9))* Tiger Tales.

—Bumbletum. Smallman, Steve. 2006. 24p. (J). (gr. -1-3). 15.95 *(978-1-58925-060-4(5))* Tiger Tales.

—Counting Leopard's Spots & other Stories. Oram, Hiawyn. 2005. 96p. (J). (gr. k-4). reprint ed. 17.00 *(978-0-7567-9252-7(5))* DIANE Publishing Co.

—Do You Have My Purr? West, Judy. 2014. (My First Storybook Ser.). (ENG.). 32p. (J). (gr. -1-1). 6.99 *(978-1-58925-511-1(9))* Tiger Tales.

—Don't Be So Nosy, Posy! Grant, Nicola. 2004. 32p. (J). tchr. ed. 15.95 *(978-1-58925-036-9(2))* Tiger Tales.

—Hands off My Honey! Chapman, Jane. 2013. (ENG.). 32p. (J). (gr. -1-1). 12.95 *(978-1-58925-142-7(3))* Tiger Tales.

Warnes, Tim. I Don't Want to Go to Bed! Sykes, Julie. 2013. (J). *(978-1-58925-148-9(2))* Tiger Tales.

—I Love You As Big As the World. Van Buren, David. 2013. (J). *(978-1-58925-603-3(4))* Tiger Tales.

Warnes, Tim. I've Seen Santa! Bedford, David. 32p. 2008. pap. 6.95 *(978-1-58925-411-4(2));* 2006. (J). (gr. -1-3). 15.95 *(978-1-58925-058-1(3))* Tiger Tales.

—Little Honey Bear & the Smiley Moon, 1 vol. Lobel, Gillian. 2006. (ENG.). 28p. (J). (gr. -1-2). pap. 16.00 *(978-1-56148-533-8(0),* Good Bks.) Skyhorse Publishing Co., Inc.

—Rise & Shine! Public Domain Staff. 2010. (ENG.). 26p. (J). (gr. -1-k). bds. 7.99 *(978-1-4424-0189-1(3),* Little Simon) Little Simon.

W

—Say Boo to the Animals! Whybrow, Ian. ed. 2014. (Say Hello Ser.). (ENG.). 24p. (J). (-k). pap. 9.99 *(978-0-330-54404-7(7))* Pan Macmillan GBR. Dist: Independent Pubs. Group.

—Scaredy Mouse. MacDonald, Alan. 2007. (Storytime Board Bks.). 16p. (J). (gr. -1-k). bds. 6.95 *(978-1-58925-827-3(4))* Tiger Tales.

—Shhh! Sykes, Julie. 2006. (Storytime Board Bks.). 18p. (J). (gr. -1-1). bds. 6.95 *(978-1-58925-796-2(0))* Tiger Tales.

—Sweet Dreams, Little Bear. 2013. (ENG.). 18p. (gr. -1). bds. 8.95 *(978-1-58925-604-0(2))* Tiger Tales.

—A Very Special Hug. Smallman, Steve. 2008. 32p. pap. 6.95 *(978-1-58925-410-7(4))* Tiger Tales.

Warnes, Tim. Bathtime, Little Tiger! Warnes, Tim. Sykes, Julie. 2003. (Little Tiger Lift-the-Flap Ser.). 12p. (J). 5.95 *(978-1-58925-693-4(X))* Tiger Tales.

—Can't You Sleep, Dotty? Warnes, Tim. 2003. 32p. (J). pap. 5.95 *(978-1-58925-376-6(0))* Tiger Tales.

—Can't You Sleep, Little Puppy? Warnes, Tim. 2014. (My First Storybook Ser.). (ENG.). 24p. (gr. -1). 6.99 *(978-1-58925-508-1(9))* Tiger Tales.

—Chalk & Cheese. Warnes, Tim. 2008. (ENG.). 32p. (J). (gr. -1-3). 16.99 *(978-1-4169-1378-8(5)*, Simon & Schuster Bks. For Young Readers) Simon & Schuster Bks. For Young Readers.

—Happy Birthday, Dotty. Warnes, Tim. 2003. 32p. (J). tchr. ed. 15.95 *(978-1-58925-026-0(5))* Tiger Tales.

—Hide & Seek, Little Tiger. Warnes, Tim. Sykes, Julie. 2003. (Little Tiger Lift-the-Flap Ser.). 14p. (J). 5.95 *(978-1-58925-694-1(8))* Tiger Tales.

—Jesus Loves Me! Warnes, Tim. 2006. (ENG.). 32p. (J). (gr. -1-3). 14.99 *(978-1-4169-0065-8(9)*, Simon & Schuster Bks. For Young Readers) Simon & Schuster Bks. For Young Readers.

—No! Warnes, Tim. 2013. 32p. (J). 14.99 *(978-1-58925-150-2(4))* Tiger Tales Pubns.

Warnes, Tim. Tom's Tail. Warnes, Tim, tr. Jennings, Linda. 2003. 32p. (J). pap. 6.95 *(978-1-58925-383-4(3))* Tiger Tales.

Warnes, Tim, jt. illus. see Mendez, Simon.

Warnick, Elsa. Song for the Whooping Crane. Spinelli, Eileen. 2004. 32p. (J). (gr. 3-6). 16.00 *(978-0-8028-5172-7(X))* Eerdmans, William B. Publishing Co.

Warren, Beverly. Little Visits with Jesus. Simon, Mary Manz. 4th ed. 2006. (Little Visits Ser.). 266p. (J). (gr. -1-3). per. 13.49 *(978-0-7586-0846-8(2))* Concordia Publishing Hse.

—My Child, My Princess: A Parable about the King. Moore, Beth. 2014. (ENG.). 32p. (J). (gr. -1-3). 9.99 *(978-1-4336-8468-5(3)*, B&H Kids) B&H Publishing Group.

Warren, Celia. We See a Cloud. Crebbin, June et al. 2015. (Collins Big Cat Ser.). (ENG.). 32p. pap. 7.95 *(978-0-00-759125-1(X))* HarperCollins Pubs. Ltd. GBR. Dist: Independent Pubs. Group.

Warren, Emily. A Christmas-Tastic Carol. Brallier, Max. 2014. (Adventure Time Ser.). (ENG.). 32p. (J). (gr. 3-7). 16.99 *(978-0-8431-8068-8(4)*, Price Stern Sloan) Penguin Publishing Group.

Warren, F. Don Winslow: Face to Face with the Scorpion. Martinek, Frank Victor. 2011. 224p. 44.95 *(978-1-258-07493-7(1))* Literary Licensing, LLC.

—Don Winslow Breaks the Spy Net. Martinek, Frank V. 2011. 226p. 44.95 *(978-1-258-07858-4(9))* Literary Licensing, LLC.

—Don Winslow Saves the Secret Formul. Martinek, Frank V. 2011. 226p. 44.95 *(978-1-258-07446-3(X))* Literary Licensing, LLC.

Warren, Joyce. Benny's Very Special Trip. Broughton, Theresa. 2008. 20p. pap. 24.95 *(978-1-60813-165-5(3))* America Star Bks.

Warren, Leonard. Penny Penguin: A Baby Penguin's Adventures on the Ice & Snow. Colby, Carolyn. 2011. 50p. 35.95 *(978-1-258-09986-2(1))* Literary Licensing, LLC.

Warren, Mnetha. Saving the Tooth Fairy. Riley, Christine. 2005. (J). per. 16.00 *(978-0-9754298-4-6(1)*, Ithaca Pr.) Authors & Artists Publishers of New York, Inc.

Warren Photographic Staff, photos by. Trucks. Calver, Paul & Gunzi, Christiane. 2012. (Little Noisy Bks.). (ENG.). 12p. (J). bds. 5.99 *(978-0-7641-6504-7(6))* Barron's Educational Series, Inc.

Warren, Shari, et al. The Beach Box: Going to the Beach/Sand/Shells. Miller, Pam et al. 2008. (Rookie Reader Ser.). (ENG.). 88p. (J). (gr. k-3). 9.95 *(978-0-516-29687-6(6)*, Children's Pr.) Scholastic Library Publishing.

Warren, Shari. Benny the Big Shot Goes to Camp. Bader, Bonnie. 2003. (Penguin Young Readers, Level 3 Ser.: No. 2). (ENG.). 48p. (J). (gr. 1-3). mass mkt. 3.99 *(978-0-448-42894-9(6)*, Warne, Frederick Pubs.) Penguin Bks., Ltd. GBR. Dist: Penguin Random Hse., LLC.

—Going to the Beach. Kittinger, Jo S. 2011. (Rookie Ready to Learn Ser.). 32p. (J). (ENG.). pap. 5.95 *(978-0-531-26801-8(2))*; (gr. -1-k). lib. bdg. 23.00 *(978-0-531-25641-1(3))* Scholastic Library Publishing. (Children's Pr.).

—I Talk to God about How I Feel: Learning to Pray, Knowing He Cares. Omartian, Stormie. 2010. 32p. (J). 14.99 *(978-0-7369-2685-0(2))* Harvest Hse. Pubs.

Warren, Shari. Little Prayers for Little Kids. Omartian, Stormie. 2015. 32p. (J). 14.99 ***(978-0-7369-6345-9(6))*** Harvest Hse. Pubs.

Warren, Shari. The Prayer That Makes God Smile. Omartian, Stormie. 2009. 32p. (J). 14.99 *(978-0-7369-2314-9(4))* Harvest Hse. Pubs.

—What Happens When I Talk to God? The Power of Prayer for Boys & Girls. Omartian, Stormie. 2007. 32p. (J). 14.99 *(978-0-7369-1676-9(8))* Harvest Hse. Pubs.

Warren, Steven Mathew. All about Charlie Horse: Charlie Horse & His Adventures. Warren, Tania Catherine. 2012. 26p. 24.95 *(978-1-4626-5442-0(8))* America Star Bks.

Warrick, Jessica. Bedtime for Sarah Sullivan. Paniagua, Kelly. 2012. 36p. (J). 13.95 *(978-1-60131-119-1(2))*; pap. 10.95 *(978-1-60131-120-7(6))* Big Tent Bks. (Castlebridge Bks.).

Warrick, Jessica. The Flarg Ate My Homework. Houran, Lori Haskins. 2016. (J). ***(978-1-57565-821-6(6))*** Kane Pr., Inc.

Warrick, Jessica. The Lucky Tale of Two Dogs. Rosenthal, Cathy M. 2012. 40p. (J). pap. 12.95 *(978-0-9853752-0-1(5))* Pet Pundit Publishing.

—Monsters Monsters Go Away. Landgraf, James, Jr. 2008. 40p. (J). 8.99 *(978-0-9819283-0-2(7))* Makdan Publishing.

—Running to the Sun: Another Collection of Rhymes Without Reason. McMahon, Jeff. 2015. (ENG.). 192p. (J). 19.98 *(978-0-9890270-1-4(5))* Leisure Time Pr.

Warrick, Jessica. Spork Out of Orbit. Walker, Nan. 2016. (J). ***(978-1-57565-818-6(6))*** Kane Pr., Inc.

Warrick, Jessica. Swimming to the Moon: A Collection of Rhymes Without Reason. McMahon, Jeff. 2013. (ENG.). 192p. (J). 19.98 *(978-0-9890270-0-7(7))* Leisure Time Pr.

Warstler, Pasqua Cekola. Bunyan & Banjoes: Michigan Songs & Stories. Warstler, Pasqua Cekola. Donohoe, Kitty. 2004. 48p. (J). pap. 19.95 incl. audio compact disk *(978-1-882376-58-2(7))* Thunder Bay Pr.

Warter, Fred. Annie Oakley. Kunstler, James Howard. 2004. (Rabbit Ears-A Classic Tale Ser.). 36p. (gr. k-5). 25.65 *(978-1-59197-759-9(2))* Spotlight.

Warwick, Carrie. The Star-Spangled Banner. Welch, Catherine A. 2004. (On My Own History Ser.). (ENG.). 48p. (gr. 2-4). 25.26 *(978-1-57505-590-9(2))* Lerner Publishing Group.

Warwick, Carrie H. La Bandera de Estrellas Centelleantes: El Himno Nacional. Welch, Catherine A. Translations.com Staff, tr. from ENG. 2005. (Yo Solo: Historia (on My Own History) Ser.).Tr. of Star-Spangled Banner. (SPA.). 48p. (gr. 2-4). lib. bdg. 25.26 *(978-0-8225-3114-2(3)*, Ediciones Lerner) Lerner Publishing Group.

Warwick, Richard. Media Muscle: Body Image & the Media for Guys. Cox, Lisa. 2012. 40p. (gr. 8-12). pap. *(978-1-921633-62-1(X))* Wombat Bks.

Waryanto, Ian. Spotlight Soccer, 1 vol. Sanchez, Ricardo. 2014. (Sports Illustrated Kids Graphic Novels Ser.). (ENG.). 72p. (gr. 2-5). 25.32 *(978-1-4342-4165-8(3))* Stone Arch Bks.

Wasco, Cindy. Charlie's Be Kind Day. Mahany, Patricia Shely. 2014. (Happy Day Ser.). (ENG.). 16p. (J). pap. 2.49 *(978-1-4143-9513-5(2))* Tyndale Hse. Pubs.

Wasden, Kevin. Hazzardous Universe. Wright, Julie. 2011. 242p. (J). pap. *(978-1-60861-206-2(6))* Covenant Communications.

Washam, Christie. Keystones of the Stone Arch Bridge. Ruff, Carolyn. 2014. (ENG.). 64p. (J). (gr. 2-3). pap. 7.95 *(978-0-87351-923-6(X))* Minnesota Historical Society Pr.

Washburn, Cecilia. Grateful Gracie: A Story about Gratitude. Tissot Lcsw, Jennifer. 2013. 34p. pap. 14.95 *(978-0-9882804-1-0(8))* Grateful Day Pr.

Washburn, Lucia. A Baby Panda Is Born. Ostby, Kristin. 2008. (Penguin Young Readers, Level 3 Ser.). (ENG.). 48p. (J). (gr. 1-3). mass mkt. 3.99 *(978-0-448-44720-9(7)*, Grosset & Dunlap) Penguin Publishing Group.

—Cheetah Cubs. Clarke, Ginjer L. 2007. (All Aboard Science Reader Ser.). 48p. (gr. 1-3). 14.00 *(978-0-7569-8169-3(7))* Perfection Learning Corp.

—Cheetah Cubs, Level 3. Clarke, Ginjer L. 2007. (Penguin Young Readers, Level 3 Ser.). (ENG.). 48p. (J). (gr. 1-3). mass mkt. 3.99 *(978-0-448-44361-4(9)*, Warne, Frederick Pubs.) Penguin Bks., Ltd. GBR. Dist: Penguin Random Hse., LLC.

—Did Dinosaurs Have Feathers? Zoehfeld, Kathleen Weidner. (Let's-Read-and-Find-Out Science Ser.). 40p. (J). (gr. k-4). 2004. (ENG.). 15.99 *(978-0-06-029026-9(9))*; 2004. lib. bdg. 16.89 *(978-0-06-029027-6(7))*; 2003. (ENG.). pap. 5.99 *(978-0-06-445218-2(2)*, Collins) HarperCollins Pubs.

—Dinosaur Tracks. Zoehfeld, Kathleen Weidner. 2007. (Let's-Read-And-Find-Out Science 2 Ser.). (ENG.). 40p. (J). (gr. k-4). pap. 6.99 *(978-0-06-445217-5(4)*, Collins) HarperCollins Pubs.

—Pouch Babies. Clarke, Ginjer L. 2011. (Penguin Young Readers, Level 3 Ser.). (ENG.). 48p. (J). (gr. 1-3). pap. 3.99 *(978-0-448-45107-7(7)*, Warne, Frederick Pubs.) Penguin Bks., Ltd. GBR. Dist: Penguin Random Hse., LLC.

—Where Did Dinosaurs Come From? Zoehfeld, Kathleen Weidner. 2010. (Let's-Read-And-Find-Out Science 2 Ser.). (ENG.). 40p. (J). (gr. k-4). 16.99 *(978-0-06-029022-1(6))*; pap. 5.99 *(978-0-06-445216-8(6))* HarperCollins Pubs. (Collins).

Washington, C. E., jt. illus. see Smoak, I. W.

Washington, Joi. Penguin Baby. Lynch, Michelle. 2012. (1G Science Ser.). (ENG.). 28p. (J). pap. 8.50 *(978-1-61406-167-0(X))* American Reading Co.

—These Are Wolves. Fleischer, Jayson. 2011. (2G Predator Animals Ser.). (ENG.). 28p. (J). (gr. k-2). pap. 8.50 *(978-1-61541-508-3(4))* American Reading Co.

Washington, Joi. How the Tiger Takes Care of Her Babies. Washington, Joi. Brown, Penny. 2012. (1B Animal Behaviors Ser.). (ENG.). 24p. (J). pap. 8.50 *(978-1-61406-172-4(6))* American Reading Co.

—The Pink Book. Washington, Joi. 2010. (1-3Y Color My World Ser.). (ENG.). 20p. (J). (gr. k-2). pap. 6.50 *(978-1-61541-161-0(5))* American Reading Co.

—This Is a Savannah. Washington, Joi. Taylor, Trace & Zorzi, Gina. 2011. (1-3Y Ecosystems Ser.). (ENG.). 20p. (J). (gr. k-2). pap. 6.50 *(978-1-61541-226-6(3))* American Reading Co.

—This Is an Ocean. Washington, Joi. Taylor, Trace et al. 2010. (Ecosystems Ser.). (SPA & ENG.). 28p. (J). (gr. k-2). pap. 8.50 *(978-1-61541-224-2(7))* American Reading Co.

—Wolves. Washington, Joi. Dibble, Traci. 2010. (1-3Y Wild Animals Ser.). (ENG.). 16p. (J). (gr. k-2). pap. 6.50 *(978-1-61541-363-8(4))* American Reading Co.

Wasielewski, Margaret. Mariam's Easter Parade. Markarian, Marianne. 2015. 32p. (J). 16.00 ***(978-0-9767377-1-1(X))*** Pomegranate Publishing.

Wasielewski, Margaret M. The Pesky Bird. Markarian, Marianne. l.t. ed. 2005. 32p. (J). 16.00 *(978-0-9767377-0-4(1))* Pomegranate Publishing.

Wasikhongo, Odalo Magruder. My First Book of Numbers. Wasikhongo, Odalo Magruder. 2012. 24p. pap. 5.00 *(978-0-9845203-2-9(5))* WasiWorks Studio LLC.

Wass, Chip. Monster Knows Math. Capote, Lori. 2013. (Monster Knows Math Ser.). (ENG.). (gr. 3-4). 24p. lib. bdg. 95.96 *(978-1-4048-7950-8(1))*; 20p. bds. 31.80 *(978-1-4048-8065-8(8))* Picture Window Bks. (Nonfiction Picture Bks.).

—Monster Knows Math [6 X 6]. Capote, Lori. 2014. (Monster Knows Math Ser.). (ENG.). 20p. (gr. 3-4). bds. 23.96 *(978-1-4795-6064-6(2))* Picture Window Bks.

—Monster Knows More Than, Less Than, 1 vol. Capote, Lori. 2013. (Monster Knows Math Ser.). (ENG.). (gr. 3-4). 20p. bds. 7.95 *(978-1-4048-8039-9(9))*; 24p. lib. bdg. 23.99 *(978-1-4048-7947-8(1))* Picture Window Bks. (Nonfiction Picture Bks.).

—Monster Knows Numbers, 1 vol. Capote, Lori. 2013. (Monster Knows Math Ser.). (ENG.). (gr. 3-4). 20p. bds. 7.95 *(978-1-4048-8038-2(0))*; 24p. lib. bdg. 23.99 *(978-1-4048-7946-1(3))* Picture Window Bks. (Nonfiction Picture Bks.).

—Monster Knows Patterns, 1 vol. Capote, Lori. 2013. (Monster Knows Math Ser.). (ENG.). (gr. 3-4). 20p. bds. 7.95 *(978-1-4048-8040-5(2))*; 24p. lib. bdg. 23.99 *(978-1-4048-7949-2(8))* Picture Window Bks. (Nonfiction Picture Bks.).

—Monster Knows Shapes, 1 vol. Capote, Lori. 2013. (Monster Knows Math Ser.). (ENG.). (gr. 3-4). 20p. bds. 7.95 *(978-1-4048-8041-2(0))*; 24p. lib. bdg. 23.99 *(978-1-4048-7948-5(X))* Picture Window Bks. (Nonfiction Picture Bks.).

Wasserman, Curt, et al. The Adventures of Ruff-N-Rescue: Adventures with the Heroes of New Barker Island. Wasserman, Shannon & Wasserman, Curt. 2006. 40p. (J). (gr. -1-3). 16.95 *(978-1-931643-87-0(3))* Seven Locks Pr.

Wassillie, Eliza, et al. Four Legged Adventures. Wassillie, Eliza et al. 2006. (Adventure Story Collection Ser.). 28p. (J). (gr. 2-6). pap. 10.00 *(978-1-58084-250-1(X))* Lower Kuskokwim Schl. District.

Wassman, Paul A., jt. illus. see Wassmann, Marilyn B.

Wassmann, Marilyn B. & Wassman, Paul A. What the Wind Blew In: 6 Stories to Read with Children. 2010. 29p. (J). *(978-1-4535-6303-8(2))* Xlibris Corp.

Wasson, Dave. The Big Ideas of Buster Bickles. Wasson, Dave. 2015. (ENG.). 40p. (J). (gr. -1-3). 17.99 *(978-0-06-229178-3(5))* HarperCollins Pubs.

Wasvary, Marcia. Mr G Clef & Friends. George, Francis. 2012. 32p. 24.95 *(978-1-4560-9642-7(7))* America Star Bks.

Watanabe, Etsuko. My Japan. Watanabe, Etsuko. 2009. (ENG.). 40p. (J). (gr. k-4). 10.99 *(978-1-933605-99-9(5))* Kane Miller.

Watanabe, Kaori. Fairy Goodnight Kisses. Michalak, Jamie. 2008. 24p. (J). (gr. 4-7). bds. 7.95 *(978-1-58925-841-9(X))* Tiger Tales.

—Fairy Tea Party. Michalak, Jamie. 2008. 24p. (J). (gr. -1-3). bds. 7.95 *(978-1-58925-840-2(1))* Tiger Tales.

—I Love You. Hudson, Sue. 2004. (My First Taggies Book Ser.). (ENG.). 3p. (J). (gr. k — 1). 12.99 *(978-0-439-64947-6(1)*, Cartwheel Bks.) Scholastic, Inc.

—Sweet Dreams. 2003. (My First Taggies Book Ser.). (ENG.). 6p. (J). (gr. -1-k). 12.99 *(978-0-439-53771-1(1)*, Cartwheel Bks.) Scholastic, Inc.

—Thank You Prayer. Grace, Will. Geist, Ken, ed. 2006. (My First Taggies Book Ser.). (ENG.). 10p. (J). (gr. k — 1). 12.99 *(978-0-439-87564-6(1)*, Cartwheel Bks.) Scholastic, Inc.

Watase, Yû. Bandit, 4. Watase, Yû. 2nd ed. 2004. (Fushigi Yugi Ser.). (ENG.). 200p. (YA). pap. 9.95 *(978-1-56931-993-2(6))* Viz Media.

—Ceres - Celestial Legend, 14 vols. Watase, Yû. Olsen, Lillian, tr. from JPN. 2nd ed. 2004. (Ceres Celestial Legend Ser.). (ENG.). 200p. pap. 9.95 *(978-1-56931-982-6(0))* Viz Media.

—Ceres - Celestial Legend, 14 vols., Vol. 9. Watase, Yû. 2004. (Ceres Celestial Legend Ser.). (ENG.). 208p. pap. 9.95 *(978-1-59116-261-2(0))* Viz Media.

—Enemy: Vol. 10, Vol. 10. Watase, Yû. 2004. (Fushigi Yugi; the Mysterious Play Ser.). 200p. lib. bdg. 20.85 *(978-1-4176-5241-9(1)*, Turtleback) Turtleback Bks.

—Fushigi Yûgi, Vol. 11. Watase, Yû. 2004. (Fushigi Yugi Ser.). (ENG.). 200p. pap. 9.95 *(978-1-59116-107-3(X))* Viz Media.

—Fushigi Yugi Vol. 3: Genbu Kaiden. Watase, Yû. Watase, Yuu. 2006. (Fushigi Yugi Genbu Kaiden Ser.). (ENG.). 208p. pap. 8.99 *(978-1-4215-0288-5(7))* Viz Media.

—Girlfriend. Watase, Yû. 2004. (Fushigi Yugi Ser.: No. 12). (ENG.). 200p. pap. 9.95 *(978-1-59116-201-8(7))* Viz Media.

—Imadoki Vol. 4: Nowadays, 5 vols. Watase, Yû. 2004. (Imadoki Ser.). (ENG.). 200p. pap. 9.95 *(978-1-59116-618-4(7))* Viz Media.

—Maya. Watase, Yû. 2004. (Ceres, Celestial Legend Ser.). 200p. lib. bdg. 20.85 *(978-1-4176-5874-9(6)*, Turtleback) Turtleback Bks.

—Mikage, 14 vols. Watase, Yû. 2003. (Ceres Celestial Legend Ser.). (ENG.). 192p. pap. 9.95 *(978-1-56931-979-6(0))* Viz Media.

—Oracle: Vol. 2. Watase, Yû. 2004. (Fushigi Yugi; the Mysterious Play Ser.). 200p. lib. bdg. 20.85 *(978-1-4176-5230-3(6)*, Turtleback) Turtleback Bks.

Watase, Yû & Watase, Yuu. Toya, 14 vols. Watase, Yû & Watase, Yuu. 2005. (Ceres Celestial Legend Ser.: Vol. 12). (ENG.). 200p. pap. 9.95 *(978-1-59116-264-3(5))* Viz Media.

Watase, Yû, jt. illus. see Watase, Yuu.

Watase, Yuu. Absolute Boyfriend, 6 vols., Vol. 2. Watase, Yuu. 2006. (Absolute Boyfriend Ser.). (ENG.). 208p. pap. 9.99 *(978-1-4215-0568-8(1))* Viz Media.

—Alice 19th Vol. 6: Blindness, 7 vols. Watase, Yuu. 2004. (Alice 19th Ser.). (ENG.). 200p. pap. 9.99 *(978-1-59116-243-8(2))* Viz Media.

—Alice 19th - Chained Vol. 3, 7 vols. Watase, Yuu. Caselman, Lance. 2004. (Alice 19th Ser.). (ENG.). 200p. pap. 9.95 *(978-1-59116-230-8(0))* Viz Media.

—Arata: The Legend. Watase, Yuu. 2014. (Arata: the Legend Ser.: 17). (ENG.). 192p. pap. 9.99 *(978-1-4215-5876-9(9))* Viz Media.

—Arata Vol. 5: The Legend. Watase, Yuu. 2011. (Arata Ser.: 5). (ENG.). 200p. pap. 9.99 *(978-1-4215-3846-4(6))* Viz Media.

—Arata Vol. 6: The Legend. Watase, Yuu. 2011. (Arata Ser.: 6). (ENG.). 192p. pap. 9.99 *(978-1-4215-3847-1(4))* Viz Media.

—Aya, 14 vols. Watase, Yuu. Watase, Yû. 2nd ed. 2003. (Ceres Celestial Legend Ser.: Vol. 1). (ENG.). 208p. pap. 9.95 *(978-1-56931-980-2(4))* Viz Media.

—Castaway, Vol. 7. Watase, Yuu. 2nd ed. 2005. (Fushigi Yugi Ser.). (ENG.). 200p. pap. 9.95 *(978-1-59116-139-4(8))* Viz Media.

—Ceres, 14 vols. Watase, Yuu. Olsen, Lillian, tr. from JPN. 2004. (Ceres Celestial Legend Ser.). (ENG.). 200p. pap. 9.95 *(978-1-59116-259-9(9))* Viz Media.

—Ceres Vol. 10: Celestial Legend, 14 vols. Watase, Yuu. 2005. (Ceres Celestial Legend Ser.). (ENG.). 200p. pap. 9.95 *(978-1-59116-262-9(9))* Viz Media.

—Ceres - Celestial Legend. Watase, Yuu. 2005. (Ceres Celestial Legend Ser.: Vol. 13). (ENG.). 200p. pap. 9.95 *(978-1-59116-265-0(3))* Viz Media.

—Ceres, Celestial Legend, 14 vols. Watase, Yuu. 2004. (Ceres Celestial Legend Ser.). (ENG.). 208p. pap. 9.95 *(978-1-56931-981-9(2))* Viz Media.

—Chidori, Vol. 4. Watase, Yuu. 2nd ed. 2004. (Ceres Celestial Legend Ser.: Vol. 4). (ENG.). 192p. pap. 9.95 *(978-1-59116-609-2(8))* Viz Media.

—Dandelion Vol. 1, 5 vols. Watase, Yuu. 2004. (Imadoki Ser.). (ENG.). 208p. pap. 9.95 *(978-1-59116-330-5(7))* Viz Media.

—Fushigi Ygi, Vol. 18. Watase, Yuu. 2006. (Fushigi Yugi Ser.). (ENG.). 200p. pap. 9.95 *(978-1-4215-0393-6(X))* Viz Media.

—Fushigi Yûgi - Assassin, Vol. 16. Watase, Yuu. 2005. (Fushigi Yugi Ser.). (ENG.). 200p. pap. 9.95 *(978-1-4215-0023-2(X))* Viz Media.

—Fushigi Yûgi - Genbu Kaiden. Watase, Yuu. 2014. (Fushigi yûgi: Genbu Kaiden Ser.: 12). (ENG.). 200p. pap. 9.99 *(978-1-4215-6434-0(3))* Viz Media.

—Fushigi Yugi Genbu Kaiden, Vol. 1. Watase, Yuu. 2005. (Fushigi Yugi Genbu Kaiden Ser.). (ENG.). 200p. pap. 8.99 *(978-1-59116-896-6(1))* Viz Media.

—Genbu Kaiden. Watase, Yuu. (Fushigi Yugi Genbu Kaiden Ser.: Vol. 2). (ENG.). 200p. 2005. (gr. 11). pap. 8.99 *(978-1-59116-911-6(9))*; Vol. 4. 2006. pap. 8.99 *(978-1-4215-0579-4(7))* Viz Media.

—Goddess. Watase, Yuu. 2004. (Fushigi Yugi Ser.). (ENG.). 200p. pap. 9.95 *(978-1-59116-086-1(3))* Viz Media.

—Inner Heart Vol. 2, 7 vols. Watase, Yuu. Caselman, Lance. JN Productions Staff, tr. from JPN. 2003. (Alice 19th Ser.). (ENG.). 200p. pap. 9.95 *(978-1-59116-229-2(7))* Viz Media.

—The Legend. Watase, Yuu. 2010. (Arata Ser.: 1). (ENG.). 208p. pap. 9.99 *(978-1-4215-3420-6(7))* Viz Media.

—The Legend Vol. 2, Vol. 2. Watase, Yuu. 2010. (Arata Ser.: 2). (ENG.). 208p. pap. 9.99 *(978-1-4215-3421-3(5))* Viz Media.

—The Lost Word, 7 vols. Watase, Yuu. Caselman, Lance. 2004. (Alice 19th Ser.). (ENG.). 200p. pap. 9.99 *(978-1-59116-244-5(0))* Viz Media.

—Lotis Master Vol. 1, 7 vols. Watase, Yuu. Caselman, Lance. 2003. (Alice 19th Ser.). (ENG.). 192p. pap. 9.95 *(978-1-59116-215-5(7))* Viz Media.

—Maiden, 14 vols., Vol. 11. Watase, Yuu. 2005. (Ceres Celestial Legend Ser.). (ENG.). 200p. pap. 9.95 *(978-1-59116-263-6(7))* Viz Media.

—Miori, 14 vols. Watase, Yuu. 2004. (Ceres Celestial Legend Ser.). (ENG.). 200p. pap. 9.95 *(978-1-59116-260-5(2))* Viz Media.

—The Mysterious Play. Watase, Yuu. (Fushigi Yugi Ser.). (ENG.). Vol. 8. 2nd ed. 2005. 200p. pap. 9.95 *(978-1-59116-087-8(1))*; Vol. 10. 2004. 192p. pap. 9.95 *(978-1-59116-138-7(X))* Viz Media.

—The Mysterious Play - Guardian, Vol. 15. Watase, Yuu. 2005. (Fushigi Yugi Ser.). (ENG.). 200p. pap. 9.95 *(978-1-59116-843-0(0))* Viz Media.

—Nowadays, 5 vols. Watase, Yuu. (Imadoki Ser.: No. 5). (ENG.). 2005. 200p. pap. 9.95 *(978-1-59116-619-1(5))*; Vol. 2. 2004. 192p. pap. 9.95 *(978-1-59116-469-2(9))*; Vol. 3. 2004. 200p. pap. 9.95 *(978-1-59116-504-0(0))* Viz Media.

—Priestess, Vol. 1. Watase, Yuu. 2nd ed. 2003. (Fushigi Yugi Ser.: Vol. 1). (ENG.). 208p. pap. 9.95 *(978-1-56931-957-4(X))* Viz Media.

—The Mysterious Play, Vol. 17. Watase, Yuu. 2006. (Fushigi Yugi Ser.). (ENG.). 200p. pap. 9.95 *(978-1-4215-0180-2(5))* Viz Media.

Watase, Yuu & Watase, Yû. Fushigi Yugi, Vol. 14. Watase, Yuu & Watase, Yû. 2005. (Fushigi Yugi Ser.). (ENG.). 200p. pap. 9.95 *(978-1-59116-737-2(X))* Viz Media.

—The Mysterious Play, Vol. 6. Watase, Yuu & Watase, Yû. 2nd ed. 2005. (Fushigi Yugi Ser.). (ENG.). 200p. pap. 9.95 *(978-1-59116-098-4(7))* Viz Media.

Watase, Yuu, jt. illus. see Watase, Yû.

Watcher, Jill. Anne & Henry. Ius, Dawn. 2015. (ENG.). 304p. (YA). (gr. 9). 17.99 ***(978-1-4814-3941-1(3)***, Simon Pulse) Simon Pulse.

Waterhouse, Stephen. The Lion Book of Five-Minute Bedtime Stories. Goodwin, John. 2010. (ENG.). 48p. (J). (gr. k-2). 16.99 *(978-0-7459-6143-9(6))* Lion Hudson PLC GBR. Dist: Independent Pubs. Group.

—My Pop-Up World Atlas. Ganeri, Anita. 2012. (ENG.). 16p. (J). (gr. k-3). 19.99 *(978-0-7636-6094-9(9)*, Templar) Candlewick Pr.

—Raju's Ride. Mitchell, Pratima. 2005. (ENG.). 24p. (J). lib. bdg. 23.65 *(978-1-59646-726-2(6))* Dingles & Co.

Waters, Erica-Jane. Beach Bummer. Jakubowski, Michele. 2014. (Perfectly Poppy Ser.). (ENG.). 32p. (gr. k-2). lib. bdg. 21.32 *(978-1-4795-2284-2(8))* Picture Window Bks.

The check digit for ISBN-10 appears in parentheses after the full ISBN-13

Waters, Erica-Jane. The Best Kiss. Jarman, Julia. 2014. (ENG.). 32p. (J). (gr. -1-k). pap. 11.99 *(978-1-4449-2091-8(X))* Hodder & Stoughton GBR. Dist: Independent Pubs. Group.

Waters, Erica-Jane. The Big Bike. Jakubowski, Michele. 2015. (Perfectly Poppy Ser.). (ENG.). 32p. (gr. k-2). 21.32 *(978-1-4795-5801-8(X))* Picture Window Bks.

—Bubble Gum Rescue. Perelman, Helen. (Candy Fairies Ser.: 8). (ENG.). 128p. (J). (gr. 2-5). 2014. 15.99 *(978-1-4424-6496-4(8))*; 2012. pap. 5.99 *(978-1-4424-2217-9(3))* Simon & Schuster/Paula Wiseman Bks. (Simon & Schuster/Paula Wiseman Bks.).

—A Candy Fairies Sweet Collection: Chocolate Dreams; Rainbow Swirl; Caramel Moon; Cool Mint. Perelman, Helen. ed. 2013. (Candy Fairies Ser.). (ENG.). 512p. (J). (gr. 2-5). pap. 23.99 *(978-1-4424-9390-2(9))*, Simon & Schuster/Paula Wiseman Bks.) Simon & Schuster/Paula Wiseman Bks.

—Caramel Moon. Perelman, Helen. (Candy Fairies Ser.: 3). (ENG.). 128p. (J). (gr. 2-5). 2013. 15.99 *(978-1-4424-5922-9(0))*; 2010. pap. 5.99 *(978-1-4169-9456-5(4))* Simon & Schuster/Paula Wiseman Bks. (Simon & Schuster/Paula Wiseman Bks.).

—Chocolate Dreams. Perelman, Helen. (Candy Fairies Ser.: 1). (ENG.). (J). (gr. 2-5). 2012. 128p. 15.99 *(978-1-4424-5775-1(9))*; 2010. 96p. pap. 5.99 *(978-1-4169-9454-1(8))* Simon & Schuster/Paula Wiseman Bks. (Simon & Schuster/Paula Wiseman Bks.).

—The Chocolate Rose. Perelman, Helen. 2013. (Candy Fairies Ser.: 11). (ENG.). 128p. (J). (gr. 2-5). 15.99 *(978-1-4424-6499-5(2))*; pap. 5.99 *(978-1-4424-5299-2(4))* Simon & Schuster/Paula Wiseman Bks. (Simon & Schuster/Paula Wiseman Bks.).

—Coconut Jack. Lewis, Jill & Blue Bananas. 2009. (Blue Bananas Ser.). (ENG.). 48p. (J). (gr. k-2). pap. 5.99 *(978-1-4052-4132-8(2))* Egmont Bks., Ltd. GBR. Dist: Independent Pubs. Group.

—Cool Mint. Perelman, Helen. (Candy Fairies Ser.: 4). (ENG.). 128p. (J). (gr. 2-5). 2013. 15.99 *(978-1-4424-5923-6(9))*; 2010. pap. 5.99 *(978-1-4169-9457-2(2))* Simon & Schuster/Paula Wiseman Bks. (Simon & Schuster/Paula Wiseman Bks.).

—Double Dip. Perelman, Helen. 2012. (Candy Fairies Ser.: 9). (ENG.). 128p. (J). (gr. 2-5). 15.99 *(978-1-4424-5972-4(7))*; pap. 5.99 *(978-1-4424-2219-3(X))* Simon & Schuster/Paula Wiseman Bks. (Simon & Schuster/Paula Wiseman Bks.).

—Frozen Treats. Perelman, Helen. 2014. (Candy Fairies Ser.: 13). (ENG.). 128p. (J). (gr. 2-5). pap. 5.99 *(978-1-4424-5303-6(6))*, Simon & Schuster/Paula Wiseman Bks.) Simon & Schuster/Paula Wiseman Bks.

—Gooey Goblins: Halloween Special. Perelman, Helen. (Candy Fairies Ser.). (ENG.). 176p. (J). (gr. 2-5). 2013. 15.99 *(978-1-4424-6495-7(X))*; 2011. pap. 5.99 *(978-1-4424-2213-1(0))* Simon & Schuster/Paula Wiseman Bks. (Simon & Schuster/Paula Wiseman Bks.).

—Jelly Bean Jumble. Perelman, Helen. 2013. (Candy Fairies Ser.: 10). (ENG.). 128p. (J). (gr. 2-5). 15.99 *(978-1-4424-6000-3(8))*; pap. 5.99 *(978-1-4424-5297-8(8))* Simon & Schuster/Paula Wiseman Bks. (Simon & Schuster/Paula Wiseman Bks.).

—Magic Hearts. Perelman, Helen. (Candy Fairies Ser.: 5). (ENG.). 128p. (J). (gr. 2-5). 2013. 15.99 *(978-1-4424-6494-0(1))*; 2011. pap. 5.99 *(978-1-4424-0823-4(5))* Simon & Schuster/Paula Wiseman Bks. (Simon & Schuster/Paula Wiseman Bks.).

—Marshmallow Mystery. Perelman, Helen. 2014. (Candy Fairies Ser.: 12). (ENG.). 128p. (J). (gr. 2-5). 15.99 *(978-1-4424-6500-8(X))*; pap. 5.99 *(978-1-4424-5301-2(X))* Simon & Schuster/Paula Wiseman Bks. (Simon & Schuster/Paula Wiseman Bks.).

—On the Seashore. Milbourne, Anna. 2006. 24p. (J). (gr. -1-3). 9.99 *(978-0-7945-1069-5(8))*, Usborne) EDC Publishing.

—Outside Surprise. Jakubowski, Michele. 2015. (Perfectly Poppy Ser.). (ENG.). 32p. (gr. k-2). 21.32 *(978-1-4795-5802-5(8))* Picture Window Bks.

—Party Pooper. Jakubowski, Michele. 2014. (Perfectly Poppy Ser.). (ENG.). 32p. (gr. k-2). lib. bdg. 21.32 *(978-1-4795-2282-8(1))* Picture Window Bks.

—Poppy's Puppy. Jakubowski, Michele. 2015. (Perfectly Poppy Ser.). (ENG.). 32p. (gr. k-2). 21.32 *(978-1-4795-5799-8(4))* Picture Window Bks.

—Pretty Princess: A Vanity Table Book. Karr, Lily. 2011. (Pretty Princess Ser.). (ENG.). 12p. (J). (gr. -1-k). bds. 9.99 *(978-0-545-34651-1(7))*, Cartwheel Bks.) Scholastic, Inc.

—Rainbow Swirl. Perelman, Helen. (Candy Fairies Ser.: 2). (ENG.). (J). (gr. 2-5). 2012. 128p. 15.99 *(978-1-4424-5776-8(7))*, cvvc); 2010. 96p. pap. 5.99 *(978-1-4169-9455-8(6))* Simon & Schuster/Paula Wiseman Bks. (Simon & Schuster/Paula Wiseman Bks.).

—A Royal Wedding: Super Special. Perelman, Helen. 2013. (Candy Fairies Ser.). (ENG.). 208p. (J). (gr. 2-5). 15.99 *(978-1-4424-8899-1(9))*; pap. 5.99 *(978-1-4424-8898-4(0))* Simon & Schuster/Paula Wiseman Bks. (Simon & Schuster/Paula Wiseman Bks.).

—Scholastic Reader Level 2: Flash Forward Fairy Tales: Cinderella in the City. Meister, Cari. 2014. (Scholastic Reader Level 2 Ser.). (ENG.). 32p. (J). (gr. 1-2). pap. 3.99 *(978-0-545-56568-4(5))* Scholastic, Inc.

—Scholastic Reader Level 2: Flash Forward Fairy Tales: Snow White & the Seven Dogs. Meister, Cari. 2014. (Scholastic Reader Level 2 Ser.). (ENG.). 32p. (J). (gr. 1-2). pap. 3.99 *(978-0-545-56569-1(3))* Scholastic, Inc.

—Snowy Blast. Jakubowski, Michele. 2014. (Perfectly Poppy Ser.). (ENG.). 32p. (gr. k-2). lib. bdg. 21.32 *(978-1-4795-2283-5(X))* Picture Window Bks.

—Soccer Star. Jakubowski, Michele. 2015. (Perfectly Poppy Ser.). (ENG.). 32p. (gr. k-2). 21.32 *(978-1-4795-5800-1(1))* Picture Window Bks.

—The Sugar Ball. Perelman, Helen. (Candy Fairies Ser.: 6). (ENG.). 128p. (J). (gr. 2-5). 2013. 15.99 *(978-1-4424-6498-8(4))*; 2011. pap. 5.99 *(978-1-4424-0825-8(1))* Simon & Schuster/Paula Wiseman Bks. (Simon & Schuster/Paula Wiseman Bks.).

—Sweet Secrets. Perelman, Helen. 2015. (Candy Fairies Ser.: 15). (ENG.). 128p. (J). (gr. 2-5). pap. 5.99 *(978-1-4814-0610-9(8))*, Simon & Schuster/Paula Wiseman Bks.) Simon & Schuster/Paula Wiseman Bks.

—Talent Trouble. Jakubowski, Michele. 2014. (Perfectly Poppy Ser.). (ENG.). 32p. (gr. k-2). lib. bdg. 21.32 *(978-1-4795-2281-1(3))* Picture Window Bks.

—A Valentine's Surprise. Perelman, Helen. (Candy Fairies Ser.: 7). (ENG.). 128p. (J). (gr. 2-5). 2013. 15.99 *(978-1-4424-6497-1(6))*; 2011. pap. 5.99 *(978-1-4424-2215-5(7))* Simon & Schuster/Paula Wiseman Bks. (Simon & Schuster/Paula Wiseman Bks.).

Waters, Fiona. Giant Tales from Around the World. Hall, Amanda. 2004. 96p. (J). 17.95 *(978-1-84458-143-6(8))* Avalon Publishing Group.

—The Princess & the Rainbow Coat. Negrin, Fabian. 2005. 32p. (J). *(978-1-84458-411-6(9))*, Pavilion Children's Books) Pavilion Bks.

Waters, Galadriel. New Clues to Harry Potter: Hints from the Ultimate Unofficial Guide to the Mysteries of Harry Potter, Vol. 5. Waters, Galadriel. Mithrandir, Astre. 2003. 134p. (gr. 3-6). 10.95 *(978-0-9723936-2-1(5)*, 1230146) Wizarding World Pr.

Waters, Kim, photos by. Buddha Altar. Mandala Publishing Staff. 2003. (ENG., 1p. 14.95 *(978-1-886069-34-3(4))* Mandala Publishing.

Waters, Susy Pilgrim. Grandma & the Great Gourd: A Bengali Folktale. Divakaruni, Chitra Banerjee. 2013. (ENG.). 32p. (J). (gr. 1-3). 17.99 *(978-1-59643-378-6(7))* Roaring Brook Pr.

—Mission: Sisterhood. Vander Pluym, Andrea. 2010. 80p. (YA). *(978-0-88441-753-8(0))* Girl Scouts of the USA.

Waters, Tony. Sal & Amanda Take Morgan's Victory March to the Battle of Cowpens. Solesbee, Mary Ann. 2014. Orig. Title: Sal & Amanda Take Morgan's Victory March to the Battle of Cowpens. (ENG.). 128p. pap. 12.99 *(978-1-62619-279-9(0)*, History Pr., The) Arcadia Publishing.

Waters, Tony. Cinnamon's Busy Year. Waters, Tony. Guevara, Linda L. & Merrill, Libby, eds. 2003. 32p. (J). (gr. -1-3). pap. 5.95 *(978-0-9710278-2-4(X))* All About Kids Publishing.

Waterton, Betty & Blades, Ann. Pettranella. Waterton, Betty. 2003. (J). pap. 5.95 *(978-0-88899-108-9(8))* Groundwood Bks. CAN. Dist: Perseus-PGW.

Watjen, Laureen. Stowaways to Smith Island: Hayden & Chloe's Enchanted Journey with the Nurses to Maryland's Mysterious Smith Island. Davidson, Michele R. 2004. 128p. (J). pap. 8.95 *(978-0-9754170-1-0(0))* Smith Island Foundation.

Watkins, Abbey. The Blessed. Hurley, Tonya. 2012. (Blessed Ser.). (ENG.). 416p. (YA). (gr. 9). 17.99 *(978-1-4424-2951-2(8))*, Simon & Schuster Bks. For Young Readers) Simon & Schuster Bks. For Young Readers.

—Precious Blood. Hurley, Tonya. 2013. (Blessed Ser.). (ENG.). 432p. (YA). (gr. 9). pap. 9.99 *(978-1-4424-2952-9(6))*, Simon & Schuster Bks. For Young Readers) Simon & Schuster Bks. For Young Readers.

Watkins, Adam. Stubborn as a Mule & Other Silly Similes. Loewen, Nancy. 2011. (Ways to Say It Ser.). (ENG.). 24p. (gr. 3-5). lib. bdg. 27.32 *(978-1-4048-6271-5(4))*; pap. 7.49 *(978-1-4048-6715-4(5))* Picture Window Bks. (Nonfiction Picture Bks.).

—Talking Turkey & Other Clichés We Say, 1 vol. Loewen, Nancy. 2011. (Ways to Say It Ser.). (ENG.). 24p. (gr. 3-5). lib. bdg. 27.32 *(978-1-4048-6272-2(2))*; pap. 7.49 *(978-1-4048-6716-1(3))* Picture Window Bks. (Nonfiction Picture Bks.).

Watkins, Adam F. Literally Disturbed: More Tales to Keep You up at Night. Winters, Ben H. 2015. (ENG.). 64p. (J). (gr. 3-7). 9.99 *(978-0-8431-7312-3(2)*, Price Stern Sloan) Penguin Publishing Group.

—Literally Disturbed No. 1: Tales to Keep You up at Night. Winters, Ben H. 2013. (ENG.). 64p. (J). (gr. 3-7). 9.99 *(978-0-8431-7194-5(4)*, Price Stern Sloan) Penguin Publishing Group.

Watkins, Adam F. R Is for Robot: A Noisy Alphabet. Watkins, Adam F. 2014. (ENG.). 32p. (J). (gr. -1-k). 16.99 *(978-0-8431-7237-9(1)*, Price Stern Sloan) Penguin Publishing Group.

Watkins, Christopher. Boyd-Friend: His Yippie-Skippie Journey to a Forever Home. Watkins, Patricia. l.t. ed. 2004. 44p. 10.95 *(978-0-9753397-0-1(2))* Frayed Pages Publishing.

Watkins, Courtney. Backyard Wonders. MacCoon, Nancy. l.t. ed. 2003. 38p. (J). pap. 14.95 *(978-0-9742495-0-6(5))* Vibatorium LLC.

Watkins, Greg. A Big Beaked, Big Bellied Bird Named Bill. Watkins, Greg. 2005. 30p. 13.95 *(978-0-9761318-1-6(1)*, 1239651) Cute & Cuddly Productions, Inc.

—A Big Beaked, Big Bellied Bird Named Bill, 1 vol. Watkins, Greg. 2006. (Big Bill & Buddies Ser.). (ENG.). 32p. (J). (gr. k-3). 16.99 *(978-1-58980-441-8(4))* Pelican Publishing Co., Inc.

—Brendon Mouse's Big Idea to Save the Bad Bird Bunch, 1 vol. Watkins, Greg. 2007. (Big Bill & Buddies Ser.). (ENG.). 32p. (J). (gr. k-3). 16.99 *(978-1-58980-449-4(X))* Pelican Publishing Co., Inc.

Watkins, Laura. Bedtime in the Meadow. Shaw, Stephanie. 2013. (ENG.). 18p. (gr. -1). bds. 8.95 *(978-1-58925-626-6(X))* Tiger Tales.

Watkins, Liselotte. Life. Fredericks, Mariah. 2009. (In the Cards Ser.: No. 3). (ENG.). 272p. (J). pap. 5.99 *(978-0-689-87659-2(9))*, Simon & Schuster/Paula Wiseman Bks.) Simon & Schuster/Paula Wiseman Bks.

—Love. Fredericks, Mariah. 2007. (In the Cards Ser.: No. 1). (ENG.). 288p. (YA). (gr. 4-8). pap. 5.99 *(978-0-689-87655-4(6))*, Simon & Schuster/Paula Wiseman Bks.) Simon & Schuster/Paula Wiseman Bks.

Watkins, Michelle, jt. illus. see Peterson, Stacy.

Watkins-Pitchford, Denys. The Little Grey Men: A Story for the Young in Heart. Andrews, Julie. 2004. 304p. (J). 17.89 *(978-0-06-055449-1(5)*, Julie Andrews Collection) HarperCollins Pubs.

Watkins, Richard, photos by. Slavery: Bondage throughout History. Watkins, Richard. 2006. 136p. (J). (gr. 4-8). reprint ed. 18.00 *(978-1-4223-5333-2(8))* DIANE Publishing Co.

Watkins, Tammy. The Magical Ballet Shoes: A Pinta & Polly Story, 1 vol. Franklin, Cathy. 2009. 25p. pap. 24.95 *(978-1-4489-2007-5(8))* America Star Bks.

Watkinson, Laura. Hidden Like Anne Frank: 14 True Stories of Survival. Prins, Marcel & Steenhuis, Peter Henk. 2014. (ENG.). 240p. (J). (gr. 7). 16.99 *(978-0-545-54362-0(2)*, Levine, Arthur A. Bks.) Scholastic, Inc.

Watley, Mitchell. I Would Tuck You In. Asper-Smith, Sarah. (ENG.). (J). 2014. 11p. (— 1). bds. 9.99 *(978-1-57061-944-1(1))*; 2012. 32p. (gr. -1-2). 16.99 *(978-1-57061-844-4(5))* Sasquatch Bks.

Watling, James. Jehoshaphat: 2 Chronicles 20:1-30. 2005. (Little Learner Bible Story Books). 16p. (J). pap. 2.29 *(978-0-7586-0945-8(0))* Concordia Publishing Hse.

—The Key to the Indian. Banks, Lynne Reid. 2004. (Indian in the Cupboard Ser.: No. 5). (ENG.). 288p. (J). (gr. 4-18). pap. 6.99 *(978-0-380-80373-6(9))* HarperCollins Pubs.

—Samuel's Choice. Berleth, Richard. 2012. (ENG.). 40p. (J). (gr. 2-5). pap. 6.99 *(978-0-8075-7219-1(5))* Whitman, Albert & Co.

—SeaMan: The Dog Who Explored the West with Lewis & Clark, 1 vol. Karwoski, Gail Langer. 2003. (Peachtree Junior Publication Ser.). (ENG.). 192p. (J). (gr. 3-7). 16.95 *(978-1-56145-276-7(9)*, Q20194) Peachtree Pubs.

Watson, Ben. The Caterbury Tails. Bush, Randall. 2013. 60p. pap. 13.99 *(978-1-936670-75-8(5))* BorderStone Pr., LLC.

Watson, Chris. Eye of the Cyclaw, Bk. 2. Price, Robin. 2015. (Olympuss Games Ser.: 2). (ENG.). 96p. (J). (gr. 1-3). pap. 11.99 ***(978-1-906132-83-5(6))*** Mogzilla GBR. Dist: Independent Pubs. Group.

Watson, Chris. Son of Spartapuss, Bk. 1. Price, Robin. 2015. (Olympuss Games Ser.: 1). (ENG.). 96p. (J). (gr. 1-3). pap. 11.99 *(978-1-906132-81-1(X))* Mogzilla GBR. Dist: Independent Pubs. Group.

Watson-Dubisch, Carolyn. Night of the Armadillos, 1. Watson-Dubisch, Carolyn. l.t. ed. 2006. 32p. (J). per. 9.95 *(978-0-9779295-2-8(3))* Medusa Road Pr.

Watson, Esther Pearl. An ABC of What Art Can Be. McArthur, Meher. 2010. (ENG.). 32p. (J). (gr. -1-3). 17.95 *(978-0-89236-999-7(X)*, J. Paul Getty Museum) Getty Pubns.

Watson, Jesse Joshua. The Backyard Animal Show. Draper, Sharon M. 2012. (Clubhouse Mysteries Ser.: 5). (ENG.). 128p. (J). (gr. 3-7). 15.99 *(978-1-4424-5023-3(1))*; pap. 5.99 *(978-1-4424-5022-6(3))* Simon & Schuster/Paula Wiseman Bks. (Simon & Schuster/Paula Wiseman Bks.).

—Barfing in the Backseat: How I Survived My Family Road Trip, 12 vols. Winkler, Henry & Oliver, Lin. 2007. (Hank Zipzer Ser.: 12). (ENG.). 160p. (J). (gr. 3-7). 13.99 *(978-0-448-44329-4(5))*; pap. 5.99 *(978-0-448-44328-7(7))* Penguin Publishing Group. (Grosset & Dunlap).

—Barfing in the Backseat: How I Survived My Family Road Trip. Winkler, Henry & Oliver, Lin. 2007. (Hank Zipzer Ser.: No. 12). 152p. (gr. 4-7). 15.00 *(978-0-7569-8162-4(X))* Perfection Learning Corp.

—A Brand-New Me! Winkler, Henry & Oliver, Lin. 2010. (Hank Zipzer Ser.: 17). (ENG.). 160p. (J). (gr. 3-7). 14.99 *(978-0-448-45211-1(1)*, Grosset & Dunlap) Penguin Publishing Group.

—The Buried Bones Mystery. Draper, Sharon M. 2011. (Clubhouse Mysteries Ser.: 1). (ENG.). 112p. (J). (gr. 3-7). pap. 5.99 *(978-1-4424-2709-9(4))*; lib. bdg. 15.99 *(978-1-4424-2710-5(8))* Simon & Schuster/Paula Wiseman Bks. (Simon & Schuster/Paula Wiseman Bks.).

—Chess Rumble. Neri, G. 2007. (ENG.). 64p. (J). (gr. 3-7). 18.95 *(978-1-58430-279-7(8))* Lee & Low Bks., Inc.

—The Curtain Went Up, My Pants Fell Down, 11 vols. Winkler, Henry & Oliver, Lin. 2007. (Hank Zipzer Ser.: 11). (ENG.). 160p. (J). (gr. 3-7). 13.99 *(978-0-448-44268-6(X))*; pap. 4.99 *(978-0-448-44267-9(1))* Penguin Publishing Group. (Grosset & Dunlap).

—Dump Trucks & Dogsleds, 16 vols. Winkler, Henry & Oliver, Lin. 2009. (Hank Zipzer Ser.: 16). (ENG.). 160p. (J). (gr. 3-7). 14.99 *(978-0-448-44381-2(3)*, Grosset & Dunlap) Penguin Publishing Group.

—Dump Trucks & Dogsleds - I'm on My Way, Mom!, 16 vols. Winkler, Henry & Oliver, Lin. 2009. (Hank Zipzer Ser.: 16). (ENG.). 160p. (J). (gr. 3-7). pap. 5.99 *(978-0-448-44380-5(5)*, Grosset & Dunlap) Penguin Publishing Group.

—Ghetto Cowboy. Neri, G. 2013. (ENG.). 224p. (J). (gr. 5). pap. 6.99 *(978-0-7636-6453-4(7))* Candlewick Pr.

—I & I: Bob Marley. Medina, Tony. 2009. (ENG.). 48p. (J). (gr. 3-6). 19.95 *(978-1-60060-257-3(6))* Lee & Low Bks., Inc.

Watson, Jesse Joshua, et al. I Got a D in Salami, 2 vols. Winkler, Henry & Oliver, Lin. 2004. (Hank Zipzer Ser.: 6). (ENG.). 176p. (J). (gr. 3-7). mass mkt. 5.99 *(978-0-448-43163-5(7)*, Grosset & Dunlap) Penguin Publishing Group.

Watson, Jesse Joshua. The Life of Me: Enter at Your Own Risk. Winkler, Henry & Oliver, Lin. 2008. (Hank Zipzer Ser.: 14). (ENG.). 256p. (J). (gr. 3-7). 14.99 *(978-0-448-44377-5(5)*, Grosset & Dunlap) Penguin Publishing Group.

—Life of Me: Enter at Your Own Risk. Winkler, Henry & Oliver, Lin. 2008. (Hank Zipzer Ser.: 14). (ENG.). 256p. (J). (gr. 3-7). pap. 6.99 *(978-0-448-44376-8(7)*, Grosset & Dunlap) Penguin Publishing Group.

—Lost in the Tunnel of Time. Draper, Sharon M. 2011. (Clubhouse Mysteries Ser.: 2). (ENG.). 112p. (J). (gr. 3-7). pap. 5.99 *(978-1-4424-2704-4(3))*; lib. bdg. 15.99 *(978-1-4424-2703-7(5))* Simon & Schuster/Paula Wiseman Bks. (Simon & Schuster/Paula Wiseman Bks.).

—My Dog's a Scaredy-Cat, 10 vols. Winkler, Henry & Oliver, Lin. 2006. (Hank Zipzer Ser.: 10). (ENG.). 160p. (J). (gr. 3-7). pap. 5.99 *(978-0-448-43878-8(X))*;No. 10. 14.99 *(978-0-448-43879-5(8))* Penguin Publishing Group. (Grosset & Dunlap).

Watson, Jesse Joshua, et al. Niagara Falls, or Does It? Winkler, Henry & Oliver, Lin. 2004. (Hank Zipzer Ser.: 1). (ENG.). 144p. (J). (gr. 3-7). pap. 5.99 *(978-0-448-43162-8(9)*, Grosset & Dunlap) Penguin Publishing Group.

Watson, Jesse Joshua. Shadows of Caesar's Creek. Draper, Sharon M. 2011. (Clubhouse Mysteries Ser.: 3). (ENG.). 128p. (J). (gr. 3-7). 15.99 *(978-1-4424-2712-9(4))*; pap. 5.99 *(978-1-4424-2711-2(6))* Simon & Schuster/Paula Wiseman Bks. (Simon & Schuster/Paula Wiseman Bks.).

—The Soccer Fence: A Story of Friendship, Hope, & Apartheid in South Africa. Bildner, Phil. 2014. (ENG.). 40p. (J). (gr. 1-3). 16.99 *(978-0-399-24790-3(4))*, Putnam Juvenile) Penguin Publishing Group.

—The Space Mission Adventure. Draper, Sharon M. 2012. (Clubhouse Mysteries Ser.: 4). (ENG.). 112p. (J). (gr. 3-7). 15.99 *(978-1-4424-4225-2(5))*; pap. 4.99 *(978-1-4424-4226-9(3))* Simon & Schuster/Paula Wiseman Bks. (Simon & Schuster/Paula Wiseman Bks.).

—Stars & Sparks on Stage. Draper, Sharon M. (Clubhouse Mysteries Ser.: 6). (ENG.). (J). 2012. 144p. (gr. 3-7). 15.99 *(978-1-4424-5459-0(8))*; 2012. 144p. (gr. 3-7). pap. 4.99 *(978-1-4424-5457-6(1))*; 2007. 160p. pap. 4.99 *(978-1-4169-0001-6(2))* Simon & Schuster/Paula Wiseman Bks. (Simon & Schuster/Paula Wiseman Bks.).

—A Tale of Two Tails, 15 vols. Winkler, Henry & Oliver, Lin. 2008. (Hank Zipzer Ser.: 15). (ENG.). 160p. (J). (gr. 3-7). pap. 5.99 *(978-0-448-44378-2(3)*, Grosset & Dunlap) Penguin Publishing Group.

Watson, Jesse Joshua & Heitz, Tim. A Brand-New Me!, No. 17. Winkler, Henry & Oliver, Lin. 2010. (Hank Zipzer Ser.: 17). (ENG.). 160p. (J). (gr. 3-7). pap. 5.99 *(978-0-448-45210-4(3)*, Grosset & Dunlap) Penguin Publishing Group.

—Help! Somebody Get Me Out of Fourth Grade!, 7 vols. Winkler, Henry & Oliver, Lin. 2004. (Hank Zipzer Ser.: 7). (ENG.). 160p. (J). (gr. 3-7). mass mkt. 5.99 *(978-0-448-43619-7(1)*, Grosset & Dunlap) Penguin Publishing Group.

—Who Ordered This Baby? Definitely Not Me!, 13 vols. Winkler, Henry & Oliver, Lin. 2007. (Hank Zipzer Ser.: 13). (ENG.). 160p. (J). (gr. 3-7). pap. 5.99 *(978-0-448-44374-4(0)*, Grosset & Dunlap) Penguin Publishing Group.

Watson, Jesse Joshua, jt. illus. see Heyer, Carol.

Watson, Judy. Extraordinary Ernie & Marvelous Maud. Watts, Frances. 2010. 80p. (J). (gr. 2-5). pap. 5.99 *(978-0-8028-5363-9(3)*, Eerdmans Bks For Young Readers) Eerdmans, William B. Publishing Co.

—Heroes of the Year. Watts, Frances. 2012. (J). 6.00 *(978-0-8028-5412-4(5)*, Eerdmans Bks For Young Readers) Eerdmans, William B. Publishing Co.

—The Middle Sheep. Watts, Frances. 2010. 80p. (J). (gr. 2-5). pap. 5.99 *(978-0-8028-5368-4(4))* Eerdmans, William B. Publishing Co.

—Tipper, Tipper! Bedford, David. 2008. 9p. bds. *(978-1-921272-26-4(0))* Little Hare Bks. AUS. Dist: HarperCollins Pubs. Australia.

Watson, Kit. The Day the Birds Sang. Watson, Kit. 2007. 32p. (J). per. 13.99 *(978-1-59886-875-3(6))* Tate Publishing & Enterprises, LLC.

Watson, Laura. Hail to Spring! Ghigna, Charles. 2015. (Springtime Weather Wonders Ser.). (ENG.). (gr. -1-2). 20p. bds. 7.99 ***(978-1-4795-6041-7(3))***; 24p. lib. bdg. 21.32 *(978-1-4795-6029-5(4))* Picture Window Bks.

Watson, Laura. A Love Letter from God. Hallinan, P. K. 2014. 24p. (J). 12.99 *(978-0-8249-5662-2(1))*, Ideals Children's Bks.) Ideals Pubns.

—Peek-a-Little Boo, 1 vol. Fitch, Sheree. 2005. (ENG.). 32p. (J). (gr. -1-3). 17.95 *(978-1-55143-342-4(7))* Orca Bk. Pubs. USA.

Watson, Laura. Rain, Rain, Stay Today: Southwestern Nursery Rhymes. Profiri, Charline. 2014. (J). ***(978-1-933855-85-1(1))*** Rio Nuevo Pubs.

—Raindrops Fall All Around. Ghigna, Charles. 2015. (Springtime Weather Wonders Ser.). (ENG.). (gr. -1-2). 20p. bds. 7.99 ***(978-1-4795-6042-4(1))***; 24p. lib. bdg. 21.32 *(978-1-4795-6030-1(8))* Picture Window Bks.

—So Many Babies, 1 vol. Crozier, Lorna. 2015. (ENG.). 24p. (J). (gr. -1-k). bds. 9.95 ***(978-1-4598-0831-7(2))*** Orca Bk. Pubs. USA.

—Springtime Weather Wonders. Ghigna, Charles. 2015. (Springtime Weather Wonders Ser.). (ENG.). 24p. (gr. -1-2). lib. bdg. 85.28 ***(978-1-4795-6045-5(6))*** Picture Window Bks.

—Sunshine Brightens Springtime. Ghigna, Charles. 2015. (Springtime Weather Wonders Ser.). (ENG.). (gr. -1-2). 20p. bds. 7.99 ***(978-1-4795-6043-1(X))***; 24p. lib. bdg. 21.32 *(978-1-4795-6031-8(6))* Picture Window Bks.

Watson, Laura. A Windy Day in Spring. Ghigna, Charles. 2015. (Springtime Weather Wonders Ser.). (ENG.). (gr. -1-2). 20p. bds. 7.99 ***(978-1-4795-6044-8(8))***; 24p. lib. bdg. 21.32 *(978-1-4795-6032-5(4))* Picture Window Bks.

Watson, Mary. The Heart of the Lion. Watson, Peter. 2005. (ENG.). 32p. (J). (gr. 4-7). 15.95 *(978-0-9726614-1-6(7))* Shenanigan Bks.

Watson, Mary. The Paper Dragonfly. Watson, Mary. 2007. (ENG.). 32p. (J). (gr. k-3). 15.95 *(978-0-9726614-3-0(3))* Shenanigan Bks.

Watson, Nathan. Return of Buzz Lightyear, Vol. 2. Snider, Jesse Blaze. 2010. (Toy Story Ser.). (ENG.). 112p. (J). pap. 9.99 *(978-1-60886-557-4(6))* Boom! Studios.

—Return of Buzz Lightyear Vol. 2. Snider, Jesse Blaze. 2010. (Toy Story Ser.). (ENG.). 112p. (J). 24.99 *(978-1-60886-558-1(4))* Boom! Studios.

—Toy Story: Some Assembly Required. Snider, Jesse Blaze. 2010. (Toy Story Ser.). 112p. (J). pap. 9.99 *(978-1-60886-570-3(3))* Boom! Studios.

—Toy Story: Toy Overboard. Snider, Jesse Blaze. 2011. 128p. (J). pap. 9.99 *(978-1-60886-605-2(X))* Boom! Studios.

W

Watson, Richard. Crabby Pants, 1 vol. Gassman, Julie A. 2010. (Little Boost Ser.). (ENG.). 32p. (gr. k-3). lib. bdg. 22.65 *(978-1-4048-6165-7(3),* Little Boost) Picture Window Bks.
—Crabby Pants, 1 vol. Gassman, Julie. 2012. (Little Boost Ser.). (ENG.). 32p. (gr. k-3). 7.95 *(978-1-4048-7416-9(X))* Picture Window Bks.
—In One End & Out the Other. Goldsmith, Mike. 2014. (Flip Flap Journeys Ser.). (ENG.). 14p. (J). (gr. k-2). 12.99 *(978-1-4052-6830-1(1))* Egmont Bks., Ltd. GBR. Dist: Independent Pubs. Group.
—In One End & Out the Other: What Happens to Poo When It Leaves You? Goldsmith, Mike. 2015. (Flip Flap Journeys Ser.). (ENG.). 14p. (J). (gr. k-2). 12.99 *(978-1-4052-7563-7(4))* Egmont Bks., Ltd. GBR. Dist: Independent Pubs. Group.
—King Donal's Secret. Doyle, Malachy. 2005. (ENG.). 24p. (J). lib. bdg. 23.65 *(978-1-59646-740-8(1))* Dingles & Co.
—Lacey Walker, Nonstop Talker, 1 vol. Jones, Christianne C. (Little Boost Ser.). (ENG.). 32p. (gr. k-3). 2013. 14.95 *(978-1-4795-2156-2(6));* 2012. lib. bdg. 22.65 *(978-1-4048-6796-3(1))* Picture Window Bks. (Little Boost).
—Terrible, Awful, Horrible Manners!, 1 vol. Bracken, Beth. 2011. (Little Boost Ser.). (ENG.). 32p. (gr. k-3). lib. bdg. 22.65 *(978-1-4048-6653-9(1),* Little Boost) Picture Window Bks.
—Terrible, Awful, Horrible Manners, 1 vol. Bracken, Beth. 2012. (Little Boost Ser.). (ENG.). 32p. (gr. k-3). 7.95 *(978-1-4048-7419-0(4))* Picture Window Bks.
Watson, Richard, jt. illus. see Cooper, Jenny.
Watson, Richard J. The Legend of Saint Christopher. Hodges, Margaret. 2004. 32p. (J). (gr. 2-6). 18.00 *(978-0-8028-5077-5(4))* Eerdmans, William B. Publishing Co.
Watson, Richard Jesse. The Legend of Saint Christopher. Hodges, Margaret. 2009. 32p. (YA). (gr. k-5). pap. 8.50 *(978-0-8028-5360-8(9),* Eerdmans Bks For Young Readers) Eerdmans, William B. Publishing Co.
—The Lord's Prayer, 1 vol. Zondervan Publishing Staff & Warren, Rick. 2011. (Illustrated Scripture Ser.). (ENG.). 40p. (J). (gr. -1-2). 16.99 *(978-0-310-71086-8(3))* Zonderkidz.
—The Night Before Christmas. Moore, Clement C. 2008. (ENG.). 40p. (J). (gr. -1-3). pap. 6.99 *(978-0-06-075744-1(2))* HarperCollins Pubs.
—The Night Before Christmas. Moore, Clement C. 2006. (ENG.). 40p. (J). (gr. -1-3). 16.99 *(978-0-06-075741-0(8))* HarperCollins Pubs.
—The Waterfall's Gift. Ryder, Joanne. 2004. (ENG.). 40p. pap. 7.95 *(978-1-57805-113-7(4))* Gibbs Smith, Publisher.
Watson, Richard Jesse. The Magic Rabbit. Watson, Richard Jesse. 2005. (ENG.). 40p. (J). (gr. -1-3). 16.99 *(978-0-590-47964-6(4),* Blue Sky Pr., The) Scholastic, Inc.
Watson, Travis & Lohr, Tyrel. Wars of the Boltians & Kuissians. Waschak, Jay et al. 2004. per. 25.00 *(978-0-9764048-1-1(8))* Victory by Any Means Games.
Watson, Wendy. The Cats in Krasinski Square. Hesse, Karen. 2004. (ENG.). 32p. (J). (gr. 2-5). 17.99 *(978-0-439-43540-6(4),* Scholastic Pr.) Scholastic, Inc.
—Spuds. Hesse, Karen. 2008. (ENG.). 32p. (J). (gr. -1-3). 16.99 *(978-0-439-87993-4(0),* Scholastic Pr.) Scholastic, Inc.
Watsuki, Nobuhiro. Buso Renkin, 10 vols. Watsuki, Nobuhiro. Wall, Frances. 2007. (Buso Renkin Ser.: 8). (ENG.). 200p. pap. 7.99 *(978-1-4215-1046-0(4))* Viz Media.
—Overture to Destruction, Vol. 11. Watsuki, Nobuhiro. 2005. (Rurouni Kenshin Ser.). (ENG.). 192p. pap. 7.95 *(978-1-59116-709-9(4))* Viz Media.
—Rurouni Kenshin. Watsuki, Nobuhiro. (Rurouni Kenshin Ser.: 3). (ENG.). 2008. 584p. pap. 19.99 *(978-1-4215-2075-9(3));* 2006. 208p. pap. 9.99 *(978-1-4215-0338-7(7));* 2006. 208p. pap. 7.95 *(978-1-4215-0196-3(1))* Viz Media.
—Rurouni Kenshin. Watsuki, Nobuhiro. Yagi, Kenichiro, tr. from JPN. 2003. (Rurouni Kenshin Ser.). (ENG.). 208p. pap. 9.99 *(978-1-59116-220-9(3))* Viz Media.
—Rurouni Kenshin. Watsuki, Nobuhiro. (Rurouni Kenshin Ser.). (ENG.). Vol. 3. 2004. 200p. pap. 9.99 *(978-1-59116-250-6(5));* Vol. 5. 2004. 208p. pap. 7.95 *(978-1-59116-320-6(X));* Vol. 13. 2005. 192p. pap. 7.95 *(978-1-59116-713-6(2));* Vol. 14. 2005. 192p. pap. 7.95 *(978-1-59116-767-9(1));* Vol. 20. 2005. 200p. pap. 7.95 *(978-1-4215-0064-5(7));* Vol. 25. 2006. 208p. pap. 9.99 *(978-1-4215-0407-0(3));* Vol. 26. 2006. 192p. pap. 7.95 *(978-1-4215-0673-9(4))* Viz Media.
—Rurouni Kenshin Vol. 8: On the East Sea Road. Watsuki, Nobuhiro. 2004. (Rurouni Kenshin Ser.). (ENG.). 200p. pap. 9.99 *(978-1-59116-563-7(6))* Viz Media.
Watsuki, Nobuhiro, jt. illus. see Miyazaki, Hayao.
Watt, Coulter. Professor Angelicus Visits the Big Blue Ball. Ward, L. B. B. 2005. (J). lib. bdg. 19.95 *(978-0-9759649-0-3(9))* Mumblefish Bks.
Watt, Fiona. Go to Sleep Little Baby. Watt, Fiona. 2009. (Baby Board Books w/CD Ser.). 12p. (J). (gr. -1). bds. 15.99 *(978-0-7945-1936-0(9),* Usborne) EDC Publishing.
Watt, Mélanie. Bearcub & Mama. Jennings, Sharon. 2007. (ENG.). 32p. (J). (gr. k-2). 6.95 *(978-1-55453-162-2(4))* Kids Can Pr., Ltd. CAN. Dist: Univ. of Toronto Pr.
Watt, Mélanie. The Alphabet. Watt, Mélanie. 2005. (Learning with Animals Ser.). (ENG.). 30p. (J). (gr. k-18). bds. 5.95 *(978-1-55337-829-7(6))* Kids Can Pr., Ltd. CAN. Dist: Univ. of Toronto Pr.
—Augustine. Watt, Mélanie. (ENG.). 32p. (J). (gr. -1-2). 2008. pap. 7.95 *(978-1-55453-268-1(X));* 2006. 16.95 *(978-1-55337-885-3(7))* Kids Can Pr., Ltd. CAN. Dist: Univ. of Toronto Pr.
—Chester. Watt, Mélanie. (Chester Ser.). (ENG.). 32p. (J). (gr. -1-3). 2009. pap. 8.95 *(978-1-55453-460-9(7));* 2007. 18.95 *(978-1-55453-140-0(3))* Kids Can Pr., Ltd. CAN. Dist: Univ. of Toronto Pr.
—Chester's Back! Watt, Mélanie. (Chester Ser.). (ENG.). 32p. (J). 2013. 8.95 *(978-1-55453-461-6(5));* 2008. (gr. -1-3). 18.95 *(978-1-55453-287-2(6))* Kids Can Pr., Ltd. CAN. Dist: Univ. of Toronto Pr.
—Chester's Masterpiece. Watt, Mélanie. 2010. (Chester Ser.). (ENG.). 32p. (J). (gr. -1-3). 18.95 *(978-1-55453-566-8(2))* Kids Can Pr., Ltd. CAN. Dist: Univ. of Toronto Pr.
—Colors. Watt, Mélanie. 2005. (Learning with Animals Ser.). (ENG.). 24p. (J). (gr. k-18). bds. 5.95 *(978-1-55337-830-3(X))* Kids Can Pr., Ltd. CAN. Dist: Univ. of Toronto Pr.
—Have I Got a Book for You! Watt, Mélanie. (ENG.). 32p. (J). 2013. pap. 7.95 *(978-1-55453-483-8(6));* 2009. 16.95 *(978-1-55453-289-6(2))* Kids Can Pr., Ltd. CAN. Dist: Univ. of Toronto Pr.
—Leon the Chameleon. Watt, Mélanie. 2003. (ENG.). 32p. (J). (gr. -1-k). pap. 7.95 *(978-1-55337-527-2(0))* Kids Can Pr., Ltd. CAN. Dist: Univ. of Toronto Pr.
—Numbers. Watt, Mélanie. 2005. (Learning with Animals Ser.). (ENG.). 24p. (J). (gr. k-18). bds. 5.95 *(978-1-55337-831-0(8))* Kids Can Pr., Ltd. CAN. Dist: Univ. of Toronto Pr.
—Opposites. Watt, Mélanie. 2005. (Learning with Animals Ser.). (ENG.). 24p. (J). (gr. k-18). bds. 5.95 *(978-1-55337-832-7(6))* Kids Can Pr., Ltd. CAN. Dist: Univ. of Toronto Pr.
—Scaredy Squirrel. Watt, Mélanie. (ENG.). 40p. (J). (gr. -1-3). 2008. pap. 7.95 *(978-1-55453-023-6(7));* 2006. 15.95 *(978-1-55337-959-1(4))* Kids Can Pr., Ltd. CAN. Dist: Univ. of Toronto Pr.
—Scaredy Squirrel at Night. Watt, Mélanie. 2009. (ENG.). 32p. (J). (gr. -1-3). 16.95 *(978-1-55453-288-9(4))* Kids Can Pr., Ltd. CAN. Dist: Univ. of Toronto Pr.
—Scaredy Squirrel Goes Camping. Watt, Mélanie. 2013. (ENG.). 32p. (J). 16.95 *(978-1-894786-86-7(6))* Kids Can Pr., Ltd. CAN. Dist: Univ. of Toronto Pr.
—Scaredy Squirrel Has a Birthday Party, 0 vols. Watt, Mélanie. (ENG.). 32p. (J). 2014. pap. 7.95 *(978-1-55453-716-7(9));* 2011. (gr. -1-3). 16.95 *(978-1-55453-468-5(2))* Kids Can Pr., Ltd. CAN. Dist: Univ. of Toronto Pr.
—Scaredy Squirrel Makes a Friend. Watt, Mélanie. 2007. (ENG.). 32p. (J). (gr. -1-3). 16.95 *(978-1-55453-181-3(0))* Kids Can Pr., Ltd. CAN. Dist: Univ. of Toronto Pr.
—Scaredy Squirrel Prepares for Christmas. Watt, Mélanie. 2012. (ENG.). 80p. (J). 17.95 *(978-1-55453-469-2(0))* Kids Can Pr., Ltd. CAN. Dist: Univ. of Toronto Pr.
—Shapes. Watt, Mélanie. 2005. (Learning with Animals Ser.). (ENG.). 24p. (J). (gr. k-18). bds. 5.95 *(978-1-55337-833-4(4))* Kids Can Pr., Ltd. CAN. Dist: Univ. of Toronto Pr.
—You're Finally Here! Watt, Mélanie. 2011. 40p. (gr. -1-1). 15.99 *(978-1-4231-3486-2(9))* Hyperion Pr.
Wattenberg, Jane. The Duck & the Kangaroo. Lear, Edward. 2009. (ENG.). 40p. (J). (gr. -1-k). 17.99 *(978-0-06-136683-3(8),* Greenwillow Bks.) HarperCollins Pubs.
Watton, Ross. Roman Myths. West, David. 2006. (Graphic Mythology Ser.). (ENG.). 48p. (J). (gr. 4-7). lib. bdg. 31.95 *(978-1-4042-0803-2(8))* Rosen Publishing Group, Inc., The.
Watton, Ross & Moore, Jo. The Encyclopedia of Awesome Machines. Petty, Kate. 2003. 112p. (J). (gr. 4-8). reprint ed. 15.00 *(978-0-7567-6963-5(9))* DIANE Publishing Co.
Watts, Bernadette. The Bernadette Watts Collection: Stories & Fairy Tales. 2015. (ENG.). 300p. (J). 34.95 *(978-0-7358-4212-0(4))* North-South Bks., Inc.
—Caperucita Roja. Grimm, Jacob et al. 2009. (SPA & ENG.). 32p. (J). (gr. -1-3). 7.95 *(978-0-7358-2263-4(8))* North-South Bks., Inc.
—The Lion & the Mouse. Aesop Enterprise Inc. Staff. 2007. (ENG.). 32p. (J). (gr. -1-3). pap. 8.95 *(978-0-7358-2129-3(1))* North-South Bks., Inc.
—Rumpelstiltskin. Grimm, Jacob & Grimm, Wilhelm K. 2010. (ENG.). 32p. (J). (gr. k-4). 16.95 *(978-0-7358-2279-5(4))* North-South Bks., Inc.
—Ugly Duckling. Andersen, Hans Christian & Kurt, Robert. 2008. (ENG.). 32p. (J). (gr. -1-3). pap. 7.95 *(978-0-7358-2146-0(1))* North-South Bks., Inc.
Watts, Bernadette. The Smallest Snowflake. Watts, Bernadette. 2009. (ENG.). 32p. (J). (gr. -1-3). 16.95 *(978-0-7358-2258-0(1))* North-South Bks., Inc.
Watts, Bernadette, jt. illus. see Watts, Edith.
Watts, Edith & Watts, Bernadette. The Star Child. Grimm, Jacob & Grimm, Wilhelm K. 2010. (ENG.). 32p. (J). (gr. -1-3). 16.95 *(978-0-7358-2330-3(8))* North-South Bks., Inc.
Watts, Edith M B. Little Red Riding Hood. Watts, Bernadette et al. 2011. (ENG.). 32p. (J). pap. 7.95 *(978-0-7358-4008-9(3))* North-South Bks., Inc.
Watts, Edith M B. B., Bernadette. The Three Little Pigs. Grimm, J. & W. 2012. (ENG.). 32p. (J). 16.95 *(978-0-7358-4058-4(X))* North-South Bks., Inc.
Watts, James. Hold up the Sky: And Other Native American Tales from Texas & The. Curry, Jane Louise. 2010. (ENG.). 176p. (J). (gr. 3-7). pap. 9.99 *(978-1-4424-2155-4(X),* McElderry, Margaret K. Bks.) McElderry, Margaret K. Bks.
—Zack's Alligator & the First Snow. Mozelle, Shirley. 2011. (I Can Read Book 2 Ser.). (ENG.). 32p. (J). (gr. k-3). 16.99 *(978-0-06-147370-8(7));* pap. 3.99 *(978-0-06-147372-2(3))* HarperCollins Pubs.
Watts, John. When Sea & Sky Are Blue. Parr, Letitia. 32p. (J). (gr. -1-3). 13.95 *(978-0-87592-059-7(4))* Scroll Pr., Inc.
Watts, Juliette. Why Would Anyone Cut a Tree Down? Burzynski, Roberta. Forest Service (U.S.), Northeastern Area State and Private Forestry, ed. 2013. (ENG.). 40p. (J). pap. 10.00 *(978-0-16-091626-7(7),* Forest Service) United States Government Printing Office.
Watts, Leslie Elizabeth. Making Grizzle Grow, 1 vol. Gilmore, Rachna. 2007. (ENG.). 32p. (J). (gr. -1-3). 14.95 *(978-1-55041-885-9(8),* 1550418858) Fitzhenry & Whiteside, Ltd. CAN. Dist: Midpoint Trade Bks., Inc.
—The Most Beautiful Kite in the World, 1 vol. Spalding, Andrea. 2005. (ENG.). 32p. (J). pap. 8.95 *(978-1-55041-805-7(X),* 155041805X) Fitzhenry & Whiteside, Ltd. CAN. Dist: Midpoint Trade Bks., Inc.
Watts, Leslie Elizabeth. The Baabaasheep Quartet, 1 vol. Watts, Leslie Elizabeth. 2005. (ENG.). 32p. (J). 9.95 *(978-1-55041-890-3(4),* 1550418904) Fitzhenry & Whiteside, Ltd. CAN. Dist: Midpoint Trade Bks., Inc.
Watts, Sarah. The Cavendish Home for Boys & Girls. Legrand, Claire. (ENG.). (J). (gr. 5). 2013. 368p. pap. 7.99 *(978-1-4424-4292-4(1));* 2012. 352p. 16.99 *(978-1-4424-4291-7(3))* Simon & Schuster Bks. For Young Readers. (Simon & Schuster Bks. For Young Readers).
—How Gator Says Good-Bye! Samoun, Abigail. 2014. (Little Traveler Ser.). (ENG.). 22p. (J). (gr. -1-k). bds. 6.95 *(978-1-4549-0821-0(1))* Sterling Publishing Co., Inc.
—How Hippo Says Hello! Samoun, Abigail. 2014. (Little Traveler Ser.). (ENG.). 22p. (J). (gr. -1-k). bds. 6.95 *(978-1-4549-0820-3(3))* Sterling Publishing Co., Inc.
—How Penguin Says Please! Samoun, Abigail. 2015. (Little Traveler Ser.). (ENG.). 24p. (J). (gr. -1-k). bds. 6.95 *(978-1-4549-1496-9(3))* Sterling Publishing Co., Inc.
—How Tiger Says Thank You! Samoun, Abigail. 2015. (Little Traveler Ser.). (ENG.). 22p. (J). (gr. -1-k). bds. 6.95 *(978-1-4549-1497-6(1))* Sterling Publishing Co., Inc.
—How to Catch a Bogle. Jinks, Catherine. (ENG.). 320p. (gr. 5-7). 2014. (YA). pap. 6.99 *(978-0-544-33627-8(5),* HMH Books For Young Readers); 2013. 16.99 *(978-0-544-08708-8(9))* Houghton Mifflin Harcourt Publishing Co.
Watts, Sharon. Emily Goes Wild. Phillips, Betty Lou. 2nd ed. 2003. (ENG.). 32p. (J). (gr. -1-3). reprint ed. 16.95 *(978-1-58685-268-9(X))* Gibbs Smith, Publisher.
—Teen Manners: From Malls to Meals to Messaging & Beyond. Post, Peggy & Senning, Cindy Post. 2007. (ENG.). 144p. (YA). (gr. 8-12). 17.99 *(978-0-06-088198-6(4),* HarperTeen) HarperCollins Pubs.
Watts, Suzanne. Bear Hugs: Romantically Ridiculous Animal Rhymes. Wilson, Karma. (ENG.). (J). (gr. -1-1). 2009. 64p. 9.99 *(978-1-4169-9427-5(0));* 2007. 32p. 7.99 *(978-1-4169-4958-9(5))* McElderry, Margaret K. Bks. (McElderry, Margaret K. Bks.).
—Hilda Must Be Dancing. Wilson, Karma. (ENG.). 32p. (J). (gr. -1-3). 2008. 7.99 *(978-1-4169-5083-7(4));* 2004. 17.99 *(978-0-689-84788-2(2))* McElderry, Margaret K. Bks. (McElderry, Margaret K. Bks.).
—Ten Naughty Little Monkeys. Williams, Suzanne. 2007. 32p. (J). (gr. -1-3). lib. bdg. 17.89 *(978-0-06-059905-8(7))* HarperCollins Pubs.
Wauters, Julia. One Night, Far from Here. 2013. (ENG.). 36p. (J). (gr. -1). 20.95 *(978-1-909263-02-4(8))* Flying Eye Bks. GBR. Dist: Consortium Bk. Sales & Distribution.
Way, MaryFaye. Ina the Octopus & Her Shipwreck Adventure. Anton, Amy Way. 2008. 28p. pap. 13.99 *(978-1-4389-2177-8(2))* AuthorHouse.
Waytula, Brian. Missions of Big Zach. Zachary, Ken. 2005. 36p. (J). (gr. -1-3). per. 9.95 *(978-1-59876-061-0(7))* Lifevest Publishing, Inc.
Waywell, Valerie J. Cookie Paws. Jorden, Edwin W. 2nd ed. 2007. (ENG.). 32p. (J). (gr. -1-3). 9.95 *(978-0-9793483-0-3(7))* Gilded Dog Enterprises LLC.
—Cookie Paws/Spreadin' the Sweetness. Jorden, Edwin W. 2008. 32p. (J). 12.95 *(978-0-9793483-1-0(5))* Gilded Dog Enterprises LLC.
Wazem, Pierre. Like a River. Wazem, Pierre. 2003. (Metal Hurlant Presents- Ser.: Vol. 1). 108p. pap. 9.95 *(978-1-930652-97-2(6))* Humanoids, Inc.
Weale, Andrew. Magical Animals at Bedtime: Tales of Guidance & Inspiration for You to Read with Your Child - To Comfort & Enlighten. Kuenzler, Lou. 2013. (ENG.). 144p. (J). (gr. -1-3). pap. 16.95 *(978-1-78028-513-9(2),* Watkins Publishing) Watkins Media Limited GBR. Dist: Penguin Random Hse., LLC.
Weatherford, Carole Boston & Weatherford, Jeffery Boston. You Can Fly: The Tuskegee Airmen. 2016. (J). pap. ***(978-1-4814-4939-7(7))*** Simon & Schuster Children's Publishing.
Weatherford, Jeffery Boston, jt. illus. see Weatherford, Carole Boston.
Weatherford, Robert. Desert Dog, 1 vol. Johnston, Tony. 2008. (ENG.). 32p. (gr. 4). pap. 7.95 *(978-1-57805-133-5(9))* Sierra Club Bks. for Children.
Weatherill, Steve. Treasury of Prayers. Frances Lincoln Staff, ed. 2011. (ENG.). 96p. 14.95 *(978-0-7112-1081-3(0),* Frances Lincoln) Quarto Publishing Group UK GBR. Dist: Hachette Bk. Group.
Weatherwax, Barbara. Gaited Games: Activities for the Young Gaited Horse Fancier. Weatherwax, Barbara. 2004. 50p. (J). (gr. 1-8). 10.00 *(978-0-9740793-2-5(4))* Markwin Pr.
Weaver, Brandon, jt. illus. see Brandon, Dan.
Weaver, Brian M. Do Not Build a Frankenstein! Numberman, Neil. 2009. (ENG.). 40p. (J). (gr. -1-3). 16.99 *(978-0-06-156816-9(3),* Greenwillow Bks.) HarperCollins Pubs.
Weaver, Brian M. & Numberman, Neil. Creepy Crawly Crime. Reynolds, Aaron. 2009. (Joey Fly, Private Eye Ser.: 1). (ENG.). 96p. (J). (gr. 2-4). pap. 12.99 *(978-0-8050-8786-4(9))* Square Fish.
Weaver, Lisa, jt. illus. see Yoder, Laura.
Weaver, Steve. Those Amazing Alligators. Feeney, Kathy. 2006. (Those Amazing Animals Ser.). (ENG.). 55p. (J). (gr. 3-7). 14.95 *(978-1-56164-359-2(9));* per. 9.95 *(978-1-56164-356-1(4))* Pineapple Pr., Inc.
—Those Beautiful Butterflies. Cussen, Sarah. 2008. (Those Amazing Animals Ser.). (ENG.). 55p. (J). (gr. k-4). lib. bdg. 14.95 *(978-1-56164-414-8(5));* (gr. 1-5). pap. 9.95 *(978-1-56164-415-5(3))* Pineapple Pr., Inc.
—Those Colossal Cats. Magellan, Marta. 2009. (Those Amazing Animals Ser.). (ENG.). 55p. (J). (gr. k-4). 14.95 *(978-1-56164-457-5(9));* pap. 8.95 *(978-1-56164-458-2(7))* Pineapple Pr., Inc.
—Those Delightful Dolphins. Wicker, Jan Lee. 2007. (Those Amazing Animals Ser.). (ENG.). 55p. (J). (gr. k). lib. bdg. 14.95 *(978-1-56164-380-6(7));* per. 9.95 *(978-1-56164-381-3(5))* Pineapple Pr., Inc.
—Those Enormous Elephants. Cussen, Sarah. 2012. (Those Amazing Animals Ser.). (ENG.). 56p. (J). 14.95 *(978-1-56164-515-2(X));* pap. 9.95 *(978-1-56164-516-9(8))* Pineapple Pr., Inc.
—Those Excellent Eagles. Moore, H G, III, photos by. Wicker, Jan Lee. 2006. (Those Amazing Animals Ser.). (ENG.). 55p. (J). (gr. -1-3). pap. 9.95 *(978-1-56164-355-4(6))* Pineapple Pr., Inc.
—Those Excellent Eagles. Moore, H G, III, photos by. Wicker, Jan L. 2006. (Those Amazing Animals Ser.). (ENG.). 55p. (J). (gr. 5-9). lib. bdg. 14.95 *(978-1-56164-360-8(2))* Pineapple Pr., Inc.
—Those Funny Flamingos. Wicker, Jan Lee. 2004. (Those Amazing Animals Ser.). (ENG.). 55p. (J). pap. 9.95 *(978-1-56164-295-3(9))* Pineapple Pr., Inc.
—Those Funny Flamingos. Wicker, Jan L. 2006. (Those Amazing Animals Ser.). (ENG.). 55p. (J). (gr. 5-9). lib. bdg. 14.95 *(978-1-56164-357-8(2))* Pineapple Pr., Inc.
—Those Giant Giraffes. Wicker, Jan Lee. 2015. (Those Amazing Animals Ser.). (ENG.). 56p. (J). pap. 9.95 *(978-1-56164-788-0(8))* Pineapple Pr., Inc.
—Those Magical Manatees. Wicker, Jan Lee. 2008. (Those Amazing Animals Ser.). (ENG.). 55p. (J). (gr. k-4). lib. bdg. 14.95 *(978-1-56164-382-0(3))* Pineapple Pr., Inc.
—Those Magical Manatees. Wicker, Jan L. 2008. (Those Amazing Animals Ser.). (ENG.). 55p. (J). (gr. k-4). pap. 9.95 *(978-1-56164-383-7(1))* Pineapple Pr., Inc.
—Those Mischievous Monkeys. Nickel, Bonnie. 2012. (Those Amazing Animals Ser.). (ENG.). 56p. (J). pap. 9.95 *(978-1-56164-509-1(5))* Pineapple Pr., Inc.
—Those Outrageous Owls. Moore, H G, III, photos by. Wyatt, Laura. 2006. (Those Amazing Animals Ser.). (ENG.). 55p. (J). (gr. 3-7). 14.95 *(978-1-56164-365-3(3));* per. 9.95 *(978-1-56164-366-0(1))* Pineapple Pr., Inc.
—Those Peculiar Pelicans. Hammond, Roger, photos by. Cussen, Sarah. 2005. (Those Amazing Animals Ser.). (ENG.). 55p. (J). (gr. 3-7). per. 8.95 *(978-1-56164-340-0(8))* Pineapple Pr., Inc.
—Those Peculiar Pelicans. Hammond, Roger, photos by. Cussen, Sarah R. 2006. (Those Amazing Animals Ser.). (ENG.). 55p. (J). (gr. 5-9). lib. bdg. 14.95 *(978-1-56164-358-5(0))* Pineapple Pr., Inc.
—Those Terrific Turtles. Dennis, David M., photos by. Cussen, Sarah. 2006. (Those Amazing Animals Ser.). (ENG.). 55p. (J). (gr. k-4). 14.95 *(978-1-56164-363-9(7));* per. 9.95 *(978-1-56164-364-6(5))* Pineapple Pr., Inc.
Weaver, Steve, et al. Those Voracious Vultures. Gersing, James & Magill, Ron, photos by. Magellan, Marta. 2008. (Those Amazing Animals Ser.). (ENG.). 55p. (J). (gr. k-4). 14.95 *(978-1-56164-424-7(2));* pap. 8.95 *(978-1-56164-425-4(0))* Pineapple Pr., Inc.
Weaver, Steve, jt. illus. see Gersing, James.
Webb, Arch. With Joffre at Verdun: A Story of the Western Front. Brereton, F. S. 2012. 240p. *(978-1-78139-196-9(3))* Benediction Classics.
Webb, Celia. Webb's Wondrous Tales Book 1. Webb, Mack Henry, Jr. 2006. 184p. (YA). per. 14.95 *(978-0-9779576-1-3(6))* Pilinut Pr., Inc.
—Webb's Wondrous Tales Book 2. Webb, Mack H., Jr. 2007. 156p. (J). per. 14.95 *(978-0-9779576-3-7(2))* Pilinut Pr., Inc.
Webb, Melissa. Fearsome Creatures. Farrer, Vashti. 2004. iv, 36p. (J). pap. *(978-0-7608-6744-0(5))* Sundance/Newbridge Educational Publishing.
Webb, Philip. Bee Alarm! Burslem, Diana & Freeman, Diana. 2013. 24p. (gr. 3-8). pap. *(978-1-77654-020-4(4),* Red Rocket Readers) Flying Start Bks.
—Bubble Trouble: 3-in-1 Package. Eggleton, Jill. (Sails Literacy Ser.). 24p. (gr. k-18). 57.00 *(978-0-7578-8614-0(0))* Rigby Education.
—Bubble Trouble: 6 Small Books. Eggleton, Jill. (Sails Literacy Ser.). 24p. (gr. k-18). 25.00 *(978-0-7578-7726-1(5))* Rigby Education.
—Bubble Trouble: Big Book Only. Eggleton, Jill. (Sails Literacy Ser.). 24p. (gr. k-18). 27.00 *(978-0-7578-6197-0(0))* Rigby Education.
—Lazy Duck. Windsor, Jo. (Sails Literacy Ser.). 24p. (gr. k-18). 27.00 *(978-0-7635-6989-1(5))* Rigby Education.
—Lazy Duck: 3-in-1 Package. Windsor, Jo. (Sails Literacy Ser.). 24p. (gr. k-18). 57.00 *(978-0-7578-3199-7(0))* Rigby Education.
—Let's Play Ball, 6 pack. Holden, Pam. 2009. (Red Rocket Readers Ser.). 16p. (gr. -1-2). pap. *(978-1-877363-17-7(0),* Red Rocket Readers) Flying Start Bks.
—Message from Camp, 6 pack. Holden, Pam. 2009. (Red Rocket Readers Ser.). 16p. (gr. 2-4). pap. *(978-1-877363-64-1(2),* Red Rocket Readers) Flying Start Bks.
—Mrs. Mcfee. Eggleton, Jill. 2009. 39.95 *(978-0-7664-3147-8(9))* Abrams & Co. Pubs., Inc.
—So Fast, 6 pack. Holden, Pam. 2009. (Red Rocket Readers Ser.). 16p. (gr. -1-2). pap. *(978-1-877363-20-7(0),* Red Rocket Readers) Flying Start Bks.
—Stories of Santa. Punter, Russell. 2006. (Young Reading Series 1 Gift Bks.). 48p. (J). 8.99 *(978-0-7945-1476-1(6),* Usborne) EDC Publishing.
—Who Is under There?, 1 vol. Dale, Jay. 2012. (Wonder Words Ser.). (ENG.). 32p. (gr. k-2). pap. 5.99 *(978-1-4296-8924-3(2),* Engage Literacy) Capstone Pr., Inc.
Webb, Sarah. You're Too Small, 1 vol. Claus, Fred J. 2009. 20p. pap. 24.95 *(978-1-60703-757-6(2))* America Star Bks.
Webb, Shamore. Mr Henry's Grass. Nicholson, Wanda. 2008. 76p. pap. 20.95 *(978-1-59800-665-0(7))* Outskirts Pr., Inc.
Webb, Terris. Tee & Tye Learn to Fly. Webb, Ramona. 2008. 20p. pap. 24.95 *(978-1-60703-729-3(7))* America Star Bks.
Webber, Carol. Minnesota Moon. Polinski, Jo. 2007. 20p. per. 12.95 *(978-1-933482-60-6(5))* White Turtle Bks.
Webber, Helen. No One Can Ever Steal Your Rainbow. Meislin, Barbara. 2005. 28p. 19.75 incl. audio compact disk *(978-0-9714506-0-8(9))* Purple Lady Productions.
Webber, John, et al. The Childhood of Jesus / la niñez de Jesús. 2007. Tr. of niñez de Jesús. (ENG & SPA.). 24p. (J). pap. 3.50 *(978-0-9801121-5-3(X))* Holy Heroes LLC.

Webber, John & Cohee, Ron. From an Angel in a Dream, the Story of Saint Joseph, Marys Husband: De un Angel en un Sueño, la Historia de San José, Esposo de María. Drake, Tim. Alvarado, Tomas, tr. 2nd ed. 2003. (SPA.). (J). 5.00 *(978-0-9747571-0-0(1))* Catholic World Mission.

Webber, Mike. Stranded in a Snowstorm! Wozniak, Paul. 2014. (Morgan James Kids Ser.). (ENG.). 82p. pap. 11.95 *(978-1-63047-173-6(9))* Morgan James Publishing.

Webber, Penny. Wow, What a Mama!! Njenga, Wamoro P. 2012. 58p. pap. 13.70 *(978-0-9827461-2-7(1))* Prop-Abilities Inc.

Weber, Andra. Red Rose & Blue Butterfly. Sirotzky, Sara. 2012. (ENG.). 32p. (J). (gr. -1-3). 17.95 *(978-1-4507-9594-4(3))* Ampersand, Inc.

Weber, Caressa. The Purple with Pink Polka Dot Ponies. Carithers, Rochelle. 2010. 102p. pap. 7.95 *(978-1-936107-31-5(7),* Mill City Press, Inc) Hillcrest Publishing Group, Inc.

Weber, Dennis. The Secret of Your Name, 1 vol. Bouchard, David. 2010. (CRP & ENG.). 32p. (gr. 4-7). 23.95 *(978-0-88995-439-7(9))* Red Deer Pr. CAN. Dist: Ingram Pub. Services.

Weber Feeney, Siri. La Llorona: Retelling a Mexican Legend. Coleman, Wim & Perrin, Pat. 2014. (Setting the Stage for Fluency Ser.). 40p. (gr. 3-5). pap. 8.95 *(978-1-939656-13-1(3))* Red Chair Pr.

—Sequoyah & His Talking Leaves: A Play about the Cherokee Syllabary. Coleman, Wim & Perrin, Pat. 2014. (Setting the Stage for Fluency Ser.). 40p. (gr. 3-5). pap. 8.95 *(978-1-939656-35-3(4))* Red Chair Pr.

Weber, Jill. Angel Bites the Bullet. Delton, Judy. 2003. (ENG.). 144p. (J). (gr. 2-5). pap. 10.95 *(978-0-618-36920-1(1))* Houghton Mifflin Harcourt Publishing Co.

—Angel's Mother's Baby. Judy Delton Family Trust Staff & Delton, Judy. 2003. (ENG.). 144p. (J). (gr. 2-5). pap. 10.95 *(978-0-618-36919-5(8))* Houghton Mifflin Harcourt Publishing Co.

—Cat in the City. Salamon, Julie. 2014. (ENG.). 208p. (J). (gr. 3-7). 16.99 *(978-0-8037-4056-3(5),* Dial) Penguin Publishing Group.

—Christmas Tree Farm. Purmell, Ann. 2006. (ENG.). 32p. (J). (gr. -1-3). 16.95 *(978-0-8234-1886-2(3))* Holiday Hse., Inc.

—Even Higher! A Rosh Hashanah Story. Peretz, I. L. 2009. (ENG.). 32p. (J). (gr. -1-3). 16.95 *(978-0-8234-2020-9(5))* Holiday Hse., Inc.

—Even Higher! A Rosh Hashanah Story by I. L. Peretz. Kimmel, Eric A. 2010. (ENG.). 32p. (J). (gr. -1-3). pap. 6.95 *(978-0-8234-2298-2(4))* Holiday Hse., Inc.

—George Washington Carver: The Peanut Wizard. Driscoll, Laura. 2003. (Smart about History Ser.). (ENG.). 32p. (J). (gr. k-4). mass mkt. 5.99 *(978-0-448-43243-4(9),* Grosset & Dunlap) Penguin Publishing Group.

—Maple Syrup Season. Purmell, Ann. 2008. (ENG.). 32p. (J). (gr. -1-k). 16.95 *(978-0-8234-1891-6(X))* Holiday Hse., Inc.

—The Story of Esther. Kimmel, Eric A. 2011. (ENG.). 32p. (J). (gr. -1-3). 16.95 *(978-0-8234-2223-4(2))* Holiday Hse., Inc.

—Story of Hanukkah. Adler, David A. 2011. (ENG.). 32p. (J). 14.95 *(978-0-8234-2295-1(X))* Holiday Hse., Inc.

—The Story of Hanukkah. Adler, David A. 2012. (ENG.). 32p. (J). pap. 6.99 *(978-0-8234-2547-1(9))* Holiday Hse., Inc.

—The Story of Passover. Adler, David A. (ENG.). 32p. (J). (gr. -1-3). 2015. 6.99 *(978-0-8234-3304-9(8));* 2014. 15.95 *(978-0-8234-2902-8(4))* Holiday Hse., Inc.

Weber, Jill & Harrison, Nancy. Who Was John F. Kennedy? McDonough, Yona Zeldis. 2004. (Who Was...? Ser.). (ENG.). 112p. (J). (gr. 3-7). pap. 4.99 *(978-0-448-43743-9(0),* Grosset & Dunlap) Penguin Publishing Group.

Weber, Lisa K. Annie's Adventures. Baratz-Logsted, Lauren. 2008. (Sisters Eight Ser.: 1). (ENG.). 144p. (J). (gr. 1-4). pap. 5.99 *(978-0-547-05338-7(X))* Houghton Mifflin Harcourt Publishing Co.

—The Assistant Vanishes!, 1 vol. Dahl, Michael. 2013. (Hocus Pocus Hotel Ser.). (ENG.). 112p. (gr. 2-3). lib. bdg. 23.99 *(978-1-4342-4101-6(7))* Stone Arch Bks.

—The Bremen Town Musicians: A Grimm Graphic Novel, 1 vol. Grimm, Jacob et al. 2011. (Graphic Spin Ser.). (ENG.). 40p. (gr. 1-3). lib. bdg. 23.99 *(978-1-4342-2518-4(6),* Graphic Revolve) Stone Arch Bks.

—The Case of the Haunted History Museum. Brezenoff, Steven. 2015. (Museum Mysteries Ser.). (ENG.). 128p. (gr. 2-3). lib. bdg. 25.32 *(978-1-4342-9687-0(3))* Stone Arch Bks.

—The Case of the Missing Museum Archives. Brezenoff, Steven. 2015. (Museum Mysteries Ser.). (ENG.). 128p. (gr. 2-3). lib. bdg. 25.32 *(978-1-4342-9688-7(1))* Stone Arch Bks.

—The Case of the Portrait Vandal. Brezenoff, Steven. 2015. (Museum Mysteries Ser.). (ENG.). 128p. (gr. 2-3). lib. bdg. 25.32 *(978-1-4342-9685-6(7))* Stone Arch Bks.

—The Case of the Stolen Sculpture. Brezenoff, Steven. 2015. (Museum Mysteries Ser.). (ENG.). 128p. (gr. 2-3). lib. bdg. 25.32 *(978-1-4342-9686-3(5))* Stone Arch Bks.

—Durinda's Dangers. Baratz-Logsted, Lauren. 2008. (Sisters Eight Ser.: 2). (ENG.). 128p. (J). (gr. 1-4). pap. 5.99 *(978-0-547-05339-4(8))* Houghton Mifflin Harcourt Publishing Co.

—Hocus Pocus Hotel, 1 vol. Dahl, Michael. (Hocus Pocus Hotel Ser.). (ENG.). 2014. 128p. (gr. 2-3). 47.98 *(978-1-4342-8937-7(0));* 2012. 216p. (gr. 4-6). 10.95 *(978-1-4342-4253-2(6))* Stone Arch Bks.

—Marcia's Madness. Baratz-Logsted, Lauren et al. 2010. (Sisters Eight Ser.: 5). (ENG.). 128p. (J). (gr. 1-4). pap. 5.99 *(978-0-547-32864-5(8))* Houghton Mifflin Harcourt Publishing Co.

Weber, Lisa K. Museum Mysteries. Brezenoff, Steve. 2015. (Museum Mysteries Ser.). (ENG.). 128p. (gr. 2-3). 101.28 ***(978-1-4965-0262-9(0),*** Museum Mysteries) Stone Arch Bks.

Weber, Lisa K. Out the Rear Window, 1 vol. Dahl, Michael. 2012. (Hocus Pocus Hotel Ser.). (ENG.). 112p. (gr. 2-3). lib. bdg. 23.99 *(978-1-4342-4038-5(X))* Stone Arch Bks.

—Pecos Bill: Colossal Cowboy. Stone Arch Books Staff. 2010. (Graphic Spin Ser.). (ENG.). 40p. (gr. 1-3). pap. 5.95 *(978-1-4342-2267-1(5),* Graphic Revolve) Stone Arch Bks.

—Pecos Bill, Colossal Cowboy. Capstone Press Staff. 2010. (Graphic Spin Ser.). (ENG.). 40p. (gr. 1-3). lib. bdg. 23.99 *(978-1-4342-1896-4(1),* Graphic Revolve) Stone Arch Bks.

—Pecos Bill Tames a Colossal Cyclone, 1 vol. Braun, Eric & Bowman, James Cloyd. 2014. (American Folk Legends Ser.). (ENG.). 32p. (gr. k-2). lib. bdg. 26.65 *(978-1-4795-5429-4(4))* Picture Window Bks.

—The Prisoners of the Thirteenth Floor, 1 vol. Dahl, Michael. 2014. (Hocus Pocus Hotel Ser.). (ENG.). 128p. (gr. 2-3). 23.99 *(978-1-4342-6508-1(0))* Stone Arch Bks.

Weber, Lisa K. The Return of Abracadabra. Dahl, Michael. (Hocus Pocus Hotel Ser.). (ENG.). 208p. (gr. 4-6). 2015. pap. 7.95 ***(978-1-4965-2486-7(1));*** 2013. 10.95 *(978-1-4342-4721-6(X))* Stone Arch Bks.

Weber, Lisa K. The Thirteenth Mystery, 1 vol. Dahl, Michael. 2014. (Hocus Pocus Hotel Ser.). (ENG.). 224p. (gr. 4-6). 10.95 *(978-1-4342-6509-8(9))* Stone Arch Bks.

—To Catch a Ghost, 1 vol. Dahl, Michael. 2012. (Hocus Pocus Hotel Ser.). (ENG.). 112p. (gr. 2-3). lib. bdg. 23.99 *(978-1-4342-4100-9(9))* Stone Arch Bks.

—The Trouble with Abracadabra, 1 vol. Dahl, Michael. 2013. (Hocus Pocus Hotel Ser.). (ENG.). 112p. (gr. 2-3). lib. bdg. 23.99 *(978-1-4342-4102-3(5))* Stone Arch Bks.

—The Wizard & the Wormhole, 1 vol. Dahl, Michael. 2014. (Hocus Pocus Hotel Ser.). (ENG.). 128p. (gr. 2-3). 23.99 *(978-1-4342-6507-4(2))* Stone Arch Bks.

Weber, Lisa K. You Decide, Ben Franklin! Hirschfeld, Leila & Hirschfeld, Tom. 2016. (J). pap. ***(978-0-553-50952-6(7),*** Salamander Bks.) Pavilion Bks.

Weber, M. S. Harry Goes to the Hospital: A Story for Children about What It's Like to Be in the Hospital. Bennett, Howard J. 2008. 32p. (J). (gr. -1-3). 14.95 *(978-1-4338-0319-2(4));* pap. 9.95 *(978-1-4338-0320-8(8))* American Psychological Assn. (Magination Pr.).

—It Hurts When I Poop! A Story for Children Who Are Scared to Use the Potty. Bennett, Howard J. 2007. 32p. (J). (gr. -1-1). 14.95 *(978-1-4338-0130-3(2),* 4418001); pap. 9.95 *(978-1-4338-0131-0(0),* 4418002) American Psychological Assn. (Magination Pr.).

—Lions Aren't Scared of Shots: A Story for Children about Visiting the Doctor. Bennett, Howard J. 2006. 32p. (J). (gr. -1-3). 14.95 *(978-1-59147-473-9(6),* 441A473); per. 9.95 *(978-1-59147-474-6(4),* 441A474) American Psychological Assn. (Magination Pr.).

Weber, Mark M. The Pirate Princess & Other Fairy Tales. Philip, Neil & Naohman. 2005. 88p. (J). 6.99 *(978-0-590-10856-0(5),* Levine, Arthur A. Bks.) Scholastic, Inc.

Weber, Penny. Always Mom, Forever Dad. Rowland, Joanna. 2014. (ENG.). 32p. (J). 16.95 *(978-0-88448-367-0(3))* Tilbury Hse. Pubs.

—Amazingly Wonderful Things. Hohmeier, Marla. 2011. (ENG & SPA.). 32p. (gr. -1-3). lib. bdg. 16.95 *(978-1-936299-10-2(0),* Raven Tree Pr.,Csi) Continental Sales, Inc.

—Ava's Adventure, 1 vol. 2014. (ENG.). 32p. (J). 16.95 *(978-0-88448-388-5(6))* Tilbury Hse. Pubs.

Weber, Penny. God's Love in Action: The Amazing Gift of Jesus. Kline, Tom. 2015. (ENG.). 62p. pap. 8.99 ***(978-0-9863364-0-9(8))*** Kline, Tom.

—Growing up with a Bucket Full of Happiness: Three Rules for a Happier Life. McCloud, Carol. 2011. (ENG.). 88p. (J). pap. ***(978-1-933916-57-6(5))*** Nelson Publishing & Marketing.

Weber, Penny. On My Way to School. 2009. (J). pap. 13.95 *(978-0-9842146-0-0(7))* Concinnity Initiatives.

—One of Us, 1 vol. Moss, Peggy. 2010. (ENG.). 32p. (J). (gr. 3-7). 16.95 *(978-0-88448-322-9(3),* Harpswell Pr.) Tilbury Hse. Pubs.

—Unplugged: Ella Gets Her Family Back, 1 vol. Pedersen, Laura. 2012. (ENG.). 32p. (J). bds. 16.95 *(978-0-88448-337-3(1))* Tilbury Hse. Pubs.

—Will You Fill My Bucket? Daily Acts of Love Around the World. McCloud, Carol & Wells, Karen. 2012. (ENG.). 32p. (J). pap. 9.95 *(978-1-933916-97-2(4),* Ferne Pr.) Nelson Publishing & Marketing.

Weber, Philip A., Jr. Mark & Dan Go West: Read Well Level K Unit 17 Storybook. Gunn, Barbara et al. 2003. (Read Well Level K Ser.). 20p. (J). *(978-1-57035-688-9(2),* 55571) Cambium Education, Inc.

—Traveling by Train: Read Well Level K Unit 19 Storybook. Gerald, Tom. 2003. (Read Well Level K Ser.). 20p. (J). *(978-1-57035-690-2(4),* 55597) Cambium Education, Inc.

Weber, Phillip A., Jr. Amazing Insects: Read Well Level K Unit 4 Storybook. Sprick, Marilyn et al. 2003. (Read Well Level K Ser.). 20p. (J). *(978-1-57035-676-6(9))* Cambium Education, Inc.

Weber, Rich, jt. illus. see Lenehan, Mary.

Weber, Seth. It Is I. Weber, Seth. 2005. 32p. 10.00 *(978-0-9772447-0-6(9))* Ben Franklin Pr.

Webster, Carroll. Pebbles in the Wind. Baldner, Jean V. 52p. (Orig.). (YA). (gr. 7-18). pap. 5.95 *(978-0-9615317-0-6(3))* Baldner, Jean V.

Webster, Jean. Daddy-Long-Legs. Webster, Jean. 2011. (Looking Glass Library). (ENG.). 208p. (J). (gr. 3-7). 10.99 *(978-0-375-86828-3(3),* Random Hse. Bks. for Young Readers) Random Hse. Children's Bks.

Webster, Kyle T. Jack & Louisa - Act 1. Keenan-Bolger, Andrew & Wetherhead, Kate. 2015. (Jack & Louisa Ser.: 1). (ENG.). 240p. (J). (gr. 3-7). 16.99 *(978-0-448-47839-5(0),* Grosset & Dunlap) Penguin Publishing Group.

Webster, Rob, photos by. 101 More Dance Games for Children: New Fun & Creativity with Movement. Rooyackers, Paul. Marix Evans, Amina, tr. from DUT. 2003. (SmartFun Activity Bks.). (ENG., 176p. (J). spiral bd. 19.95 *(978-0-89793-384-1(2),* Hunter Hse.) Turner Publishing Co.

Webster, Sarah. Un Fantasma con Asma. Gil, Carmen. 2004. (Libros para Sonar Ser.). (SPA.). 40p. (J). 15.99 *(978-84-8464-186-5(4))* Kalandraka Editora, S.L. ESP. Dist: Lectorum Pubns., Inc.

Wechsler, Nathalie. Once upon A Fly: The Adventures of Lamouche. Wechsler, Nathalie. 2005. 24p. (J). per. 7.99 *(978-0-9766998-1-1(8))* Finlay Prints, Inc.

—Once upon A Fly - Hardcover: The Adventures of Lamouche. Wechsler, Nathalie. 2005. 24p. (J). 10.95 *(978-0-9766998-0-4(X))* Finlay Prints, Inc.

Weck, Claudia de. Lisa y el Gato Sin Nombre. Weck, Claudia de, tr. Recheis, Kèathe et al. Jiménez, Alberto, tr. 5th ed. 2009. (SPA.). 88p. (J). pap. 9.99 *(978-84-207-7767-2(6))* Lectorum Pubns., Inc.

Weckmann, Anke. Roar, Bull, Roar! Peters, Polly & Fusek Peters, Andrew. 2007. (ENG.). 155p. (J). (gr. 2-7). per. 8.95 *(978-1-84507-520-0(X),* Frances Lincoln) Quarto Publishing Group UK GBR. Dist: Hachette Bk. Group.

Wedekind, Annie. Wild Blue: The Story of a Mustang Appaloosa. Wedekind, Annie. Haas, Jessie. 2009. (Breyer Horse Collection: 1). (ENG.). 128p. (J). (gr. 4-7). pap. 5.99 *(978-0-312-59917-1(X))* Feiwel & Friends.

Wedge, Chris. Bunny: A Picture Book Adapted from the Animated Film. Wedge, Chris. 2004. 30p. (J). (gr. k-4). reprint ed. 19.00 *(978-0-7567-7460-8(8))* DIANE Publishing Co.

Wedman, Belgin K. The Elephant Prince: The Story of Ganesh. Novesky, Amy. 2004. (ENG.). 32p. (J). 16.95 *(978-1-886069-16-9(6),* BK2304HB) Mandala Publishing.

Wedzin, James. How the Fox Got His Crossed Legs. Football, Virginia & Mantla, Rosa. Siemens, Mary, tr. ed. 2009. (Fox Ser.). (ENG & DGR.). 32p. (gr. 2-3). 20.95 *(978-1-894778-74-9(X))* Theytus Bks., Ltd. CAN. Dist: Univ. of Toronto Pr.

—How the Fox Saved the People. Football, Virginia. ed. 2009. (Fox Ser.). (ENG & DGR.). 56p. (gr. k-6). 26.95 *(978-1-894778-75-6(8))* Theytus Bks., Ltd. CAN. Dist: Univ. of Toronto Pr.

Weedn, Flavia. Angels. York Lumbard, Alexis. 2013. (ENG.). 28p. (J). (gr. -1-1). 14.95 *(978-1-937786-15-1(3),* Wisdom Tales) World Wisdom, Inc.

Week, Jason. The Barftastic Life of Louie Burger. Meyerhoff, Jenny. 2013. (Barftastic Life of Louie Burger Ser.: 1). (ENG.). 240p. (J). (gr. 3-6). 13.99 *(978-0-374-30518-5(8),* Farrar, Straus & Giroux (BYR)) Farrar, Straus & Giroux.

—Class B. U. R. P. Meyerhoff, Jenny. 2014. (Barftastic Life of Louie Burger Ser.: 2). (ENG.). 288p. (J). (gr. 3-6). 13.99 *(978-0-374-30521-5(8),* Farrar, Straus & Giroux (BYR)) Farrar, Straus & Giroux.

Weeks, Jeanne G., jt. illus. see Weeks, Timothy A.

Weeks, Lee, et al. The Amazing Spider-Man: The One & Only. Casey, Joe & Reed, Brian. 2014. (ENG.). 168p. (J). (gr. 4-17). pap. 16.99 *(978-0-7851-9010-3(4))* Marvel Worldwide, Inc.

Weeks, Mary. But Not Quite. Schneider, Judy. 2004. (J). 19.95 *(978-1-59404-005-4(2))* Peanut Butter Publishing.

Weeks, Timothy A. & Weeks, Jeanne G. Goldie's Search for Silver: The Wise Mullet Finale! Weeks, Timothy A. 2009. (ENG.). 48p. (J). pap. 14.99 *(978-0-9779928-2-9(9))* Foolosophy Media.

Wegener, Bill. The Bible Game - New Testament: The Bible Game - New Testament. Wegener, Bill, des. 2004. (YA). bds. 34.95 *(978-0-9753620-1-3(1))* IMAGINEX, LLC.

—The Bible Game - Old Testament: The Bible Game - Old Testament. Wegener, Bill, des. 2004. (YA). bds. 34.95 *(978-0-9753620-0-6(3),* Bible Game) IMAGINEX, LLC.

Wegener, Scott. Avengers, Vol. 1. Marvel Comics Staff. 2012. (ENG.). 32p. (J). (gr. -1-17). pap. 3.99 *(978-0-7851-5363-4(2))* Marvel Worldwide, Inc.

Wegener, Scott & Scherberger, Patrick. Avengers: Earth's Mightiest Heroes. 2011. (ENG.). 112p. (J). (gr. -1-17). pap. 14.99 *(978-0-7851-5619-2(4))* Marvel Worldwide, Inc.

Wegener, Scott, jt. illus. see Scherberger, Patrick.

Wegman, Marcia. Lula Belle. Wegman, Marcia. 2012. 30p. pap. 16.00 *(978-1-932043-82-2(9))* Penfield Bks.

Wegman, William. Dress up Batty. Wegman, William. 2004. (ENG.). 18p. (gr. -1-17). 19.99 *(978-0-7868-1849-5(2))* Hyperion Bks. for Children.

—Farm Days. Wegman, William. 2014. (Penguin Young Readers, Level 2 Ser.). (ENG.). 32p. (J). (gr. 1-3). pap. 3.99 *(978-0-448-48230-9(4),* Warne, Frederick Pubs.) Penguin Bks., Ltd. GBR. Dist: Penguin Random Hse., LLC.

Wegner, Fritz. Star Girl. Winterfeld, Henry. Schabert, Kyrill, tr. from GER. 2015. (ENG.). 192p. (J). (gr. 3-8). pap. 7.99 ***(978-0-486-79468-6(7))*** Dover Pubns., Inc.

Wehr, Julian. The Animated Bunny's Tail. Wehr, Paul. 2005. 20p. (J). 18.95 *(978-0-9748093-1-1(4))* Wehr Animations.

Wehrman, Richard. The Banyan Deer: A Parable of Courage & Compassion. Martin, Rafe. 2010. (ENG.). 48p. (J). (gr. 4). 15.00 *(978-0-86171-625-8(6))* Wisdom Pubns.

Wehrman, Vicki. Hanukkah Around the World. Lehman-Wilzig, Tami. 2009. (Hanukkah Ser.). (ENG.). 48p. (J). (gr. 3-5). pap. 7.95 *(978-0-8225-8762-0(9),* Kar-Ben Publishing) Lerner Publishing Group.

—Night Catch. Ehrmantraut, Brenda. 2005. 32p. (J). lib. bdg. 15.95 *(978-0-9729833-9-6(2))* Bubble Gum Pr.

—Night Catch. Ehrmantraut, Brenda. 2014. (J). pap. *(978-1-934617-28-1(8))* Elva Resa Publishing, LLC.

Wei, Miao & Xianoqing, Pan. Chinese Fables & Folktales (II) Ma, Zheng & Li, Zheng. 2010. (ENG.). 48p. (J). (gr. -1-2). 16.95 *(978-1-60220-963-3(4))* BetterLink Pr., Inc.

Weidemann, Linda. This Fleeting World: An Overview of Human History. Christian, David. 2004. (YA). pap. 8.00 *(978-0-9743091-4-9(1))* Berkshire Publishing Group.

Weidman, James. The Little Boy in a Dog Suit, 1 vol. Schombs, James. 2010. 28p. pap. 24.95 *(978-1-61582-053-5(1))* PublishAmerica, Inc.

Weidner, Teri. Chicken Little. York, J. 2012. (Favorite Children's Stories Ser.). (ENG.). 24p. (J). (gr. k-3). 27.07 *(978-1-61473-213-6(2),* 204907) Child's World, Inc., The.

—Christmas Eve with Mrs. Claus. Hueston, M. P. 2013. (ENG.). 16p. (J). 12.95 *(978-1-4027-7736-3(1))* Sterling Publishing Co., Inc.

—Five Little Ducks. 2010. (Favorite Children's Songs Ser.). (ENG.). 16p. (J). (gr. -1-2). 25.64 *(978-1-60253-528-2(0),* 200111) Child's World, Inc., The.

—Give Yourself to the Rain: Poems for the Very Young. Brown, Margaret Wise. 2012. (ENG.). 32p. (J). (gr. -1-3). pap. 16.99 *(978-1-4424-6063-8(6),* McElderry, Margaret K. Bks.) McElderry, Margaret K. Bks.

—Goodnight Baby Bear. Shoulders, Michael. 2010. (ENG.). 32p. (J). (gr. -1-k). 15.95 *(978-1-58536-471-8(1))* Sleeping Bear Pr.

—Halloween. Heinrichs, Ann. 2013. (Holidays & Celebrations Ser.). (ENG.). 32p. (J). (gr. k-3). 27.07 *(978-1-62323-507-9(3),* 206280) Child's World, Inc., The.

—Read Me a Story. Zimmerman, Brooke. 2003. (My First Treasury Ser.). 40p. (J). bds. 7.98 *(978-0-7853-8247-8(X),* 7181900) Publications International, Ltd.

—Say Daddy! Shoulders, Michael. (ENG.). (J). 2013. 26p. (gr. -1-k). 8.99 *(978-1-58536-863-1(6),* 202383); 2008. 32p. (gr. k-6). 15.95 *(978-1-58536-354-4(5))* Sleeping Bear Pr.

—Sleep, Baby, Sleep. 2009. 20p. (J). (gr. -1-k). 8.95 *(978-1-58925-843-3(6))* Tiger Tales.

—Your Body Belongs to You, 1 vol. Spelman, Cornelia Maude. 2003. (ENG.). 24p. (J). (gr. -1-1). pap. 6.99 *(978-0-8075-9473-5(3))* Whitman, Albert & Co.

Weidner, Teri. Always Twins. Weidner, Teri. 2015. (ENG.). 32p. (J). (gr. -1-k). 16.95 *(978-0-8234-3159-5(2))* Holiday Hse., Inc.

—Three Little Kittens. Weidner, Teri. 2011. (Favorite Mother Goose Rhymes Ser.). (ENG.). 16p. (J). (gr. -1-2). lib. bdg. 25.64 *(978-1-60954-285-6(1),* 200237) Child's World, Inc., The.

Weigand, John, photos by. Beaching It! a Kid's Guide to la Jolla, California. Dyan, Penelope. 2013. 34p. pap. 11.95 *(978-1-61477-092-3(1))* Bellissima Publishing, LLC.

—The Comeback Kids — Book 10 — The American Bison. Dyan, Penelope. 2012. 34p. pap. 14.95 *(978-1-61477-063-3(8))* Bellissima Publishing, LLC.

—Cruisin' 4 Fun! a Kid's Guide to Santa Cruz, Californ. Dyan, Penelope. 2013. 34p. pap. 11.95 *(978-1-61477-082-4(4))* Bellissima Publishing, LLC.

—The Discovery in the Old Mine. Hillan, Pamela & Dyan, Penelope. 2013. 116p. pap. 8.95 *(978-1-61477-095-4(6))* Bellissima Publishing, LLC.

—The Jewels of the Crown. Hillan, Pamela & Dyan, Penelope. 2013. 128p. pap. 8.95 *(978-1-61477-111-1(1))* Bellissima Publishing, LLC.

—The Mummy's Secret. Hillan, Pamela & Dyan, Penelope. 2013. 112p. pap. 8.95 *(978-1-61477-099-2(9))* Bellissima Publishing, LLC.

—The Place of Tales — - a Kid's Guide to Canterbury, Kent, England. Dyan, Penelope. 2011. 40p. pap. 12.95 *(978-1-935630-66-1(0))* Bellissima Publishing, LLC.

—VanCouver's Song — - a Kid's Guide to Vancouver, Bc, Canada. Dyan, Penelope. 2013. 34p. pap. 11.95 *(978-1-61477-104-3(9))* Bellissima Publishing, LLC.

—When in Rome, a Kid's Guide to Rome. Dyan, Penelope. 2010. 50p. pap. 11.95 *(978-1-935630-00-5(8))* Bellissima Publishing, LLC.

Weigand, John D. It's Hot, Hot, Hot! a Kid's Guide to Hawaiian Volcanoes National Park. Dyan, Penelope. 2013. 34p. pap. 11.95 *(978-1-61477-118-0(9))* Bellissima Publishing, LLC.

—The Road to Hilo! a Kid's Guide to Hilo, Hawaii. Dyan, Penelope. 2013. 34p. pap. 11.95 *(978-1-61477-117-3(0))* Bellissima Publishing, LLC.

Weigand, John D., photos by. Abraham Lincoln Was Here! a Kid's Guide to Washington D C. Dyan, Penelope. 2009. 44p. pap. 11.95 *(978-1-935118-82-4(X))* Bellissima Publishing, LLC.

—Animal Rescue, Book 1, Seals, Sea Lions & Elephant Seals, Oh My! Dyan, Penelope. 2008. 60p. pap. 15.95 *(978-1-935118-21-3(8))* Bellissima Publishing, LLC.

—Animal Rescue, Book 2, Hanauma Bay, Hawaii. Dyan, Penelope. 2008. 56p. pap. 15.95 *(978-1-935118-43-5(9))* Bellissima Publishing, LLC.

—An Apple a Day! a Kid's Guide to Julian, Californ. Dyan, Penelope. 2010. 48p. pap. 11.95 *(978-1-935630-12-8(1))* Bellissima Publishing, LLC.

—Around Corners — -A Kid's Guide to Malaga, Spain. Dyan, Penelope. 2012. 34p. pap. 11.95 *(978-1-61477-032-9(8))* Bellissima Publishing, LLC.

—Beyond the Trees! a Kid's Guide to Lake Tahoe, Us. Dyan, Penelope. 2012. 34p. pap. 11.95 *(978-1-61477-027-5(1))* Bellissima Publishing, LLC.

—The Big Clock! a Kid's Guide to Munich, Germany. Dyan, Penelope. 2013. 34p. pap. 11.95 *(978-1-61477-080-0(8))* Bellissima Publishing, LLC.

—By the Bay! a Kid's Guide to San Diego, California. Dyan, Penelope. 2013. 34p. pap. 11.95 *(978-1-61477-087-9(5))* Bellissima Publishing, LLC.

—By the Sea — -A Kid's Guide to Valletta, Malt. Dyan, Penelope. 2011. 36p. pap. 11.95 *(978-1-935630-55-5(5))* Bellissima Publishing, LLC.

—Cabbages & Kings — A Kid's Guide to Tallinn, Estoni. Dyan, Penelope. 2011. 36p. pap. 11.95 *(978-1-61477-002-2(6))* Bellissima Publishing, LLC.

—The Cat Named Blake. Dyan, Penelope. 2013. 76p. pap. 8.95 *(978-1-61477-110-4(3))* Bellissima Publishing, LLC.

—Color Your Life! a Kid's Guide to Lisbon, Portugal. Dyan, Penelope. 2012. 34p. pap. 11.95 *(978-1-61477-030-5(1))* Bellissima Publishing, LLC.

—The Comeback Kids — Book 9 — the Barbary Macaques of Gibraltar. Dyan, Penelope. 2012. 36p. pap. 14.95 *(978-1-61477-036-7(0))* Bellissima Publishing, LLC.

—The Comeback Kids — Book 11 — The Wild Mustangs. Dyan, Penelope. 2013. 34p. pap. 14.95 *(978-1-61477-078-7(6))* Bellissima Publishing, LLC.

—The Comeback Kids, Book 12, the Redwood Forest. Dyan, Penelope. 2013. 34p. pap. 14.95 *(978-1-61477-081-7(6))* Bellissima Publishing, LLC.

—The Comeback Kids, Book 8, the Antioch Burrowing Owl. Dyan, Penelope. 2009. 60p. pap. 22.00 *(978-1-935118-86-2(2))* Bellissima Publishing, LLC.

W

—Do You Know Juneau? a Kid's Guide to Juneau, Alaska. Dyan, Penelope. 2013. 34p. pap. 11.95 *(978-1-61477-105-0(7))* Bellissima Publishing, LLC.
—Endangered — the Peninsular Bighorn Sheep. Dyan, Penelope. 2010. 44p. pap. 11.95 *(978-1-935630-10-4(5))* Bellissima Publishing, LLC.
—Flying High in the Sky — -for Boys Only. Dyan, Penelope. 2009. 42p. pap. 13.95 *(978-1-935118-66-4(8))* Bellissima Publishing, LLC.
—For the Matterhorn's Face, Zermatt Is the Place, a Kid's Guide to Zermatt, Switzerland. Dyan, Penelope. 2010. 50p. pap. 11.95 *(978-1-935630-04-3(0))* Bellissima Publishing, LLC.
—Fun in the Sun! a Kids' Guide to Santa Barbara, Californi. Dyan, Penelope. 2012. 34p. pap. 11.95 *(978-1-61477-051-0(4))* Bellissima Publishing, LLC.
—Gold Rush! a Kid's Guide to Techatticup Gold Mine, Eldorado Canyon, Nevad. Dyan, Penelope. 2010. 48p. pap. 11.95 *(978-1-935630-11-1(3))* Bellissima Publishing, LLC.
—Halfway to the Stars! a Kid's Guide to San Francisco. Dyan, Penelope. 2009. 44p. pap. 11.95 *(978-1-935118-88-6(9))* Bellissima Publishing, LLC.
—Hangin' Loose! a Kid's Guide to Oahu, Hawaii. Dyan, Penelope. 2009. 44p. pap. 11.95 *(978-1-935118-78-7(1))* Bellissima Publishing, LLC.
—High on a Hill! a Kid's Guide to Innsbruck, Austri. Dyan, Penelope. 2011. 40p. pap. 12.95 *(978-1-935630-76-0(8))* Bellissima Publishing, LLC.
—¡Hola Córdoba! a Kid's Guide to Córdoba, Spain. Dyan, Penelope. 2012. 34p. pap. 11.95 *(978-1-61477-035-0(2))* Bellissima Publishing, LLC.
—¡Hola Madrid! a Kid's Guide to Madrid, Spain. Dyan, Penelope. 2012. 34p. pap. 11.95 *(978-1-61477-031-2(X))* Bellissima Publishing, LLC.
—I Remember Still, a Kid's Guide to Seville, Spain. Dyan, Penelope. 2012. 34p. pap. 11.95 *(978-1-61477-034-3(4))* Bellissima Publishing, LLC.
—Island Style! a Kid's Guide to Coronado, California. Dyan, Penelope. 2013. 34p. pap. 11.95 *(978-1-61477-090-9(5))* Bellissima Publishing, LLC.
—It's Magic! a Kid's Guide to Monterey, California. Dyan, Penelope. 2013. 34p. pap. 11.95 *(978-1-61477-119-7(7))* Bellissima Publishing, LLC.
—It's Medieval! a Kid's Guide to Nuremberg, Germany. Dyan, Penelope. 2013. 34p. pap. 11.95 *(978-1-61477-079-4(4))* Bellissima Publishing, LLC.
—It's Nice to Be Gone When You're in Milan, a Kid's Guide to Milan, Italy. Dyan, Penelope. 2010. 50p. pap. 11.95 *(978-1-935630-03-6(2))* Bellissima Publishing, LLC.
—The Kingdom of York, a Kid's Guide to York, Uk. Dyan, Penelope. 2011. 34p. pap. 11.95 *(978-1-61477-004-6(2))* Bellissima Publishing, LLC.
—Kona Forevermore — A Kid's Guide to Kona Hawaii. Dyan, Penelope. 2013. 36p. pap. 11.95 *(978-1-61477-116-6(2))* Bellissima Publishing, LLC.
—Let It Snow! a Kid's Guide to Regensburg, Germany. Dyan, Penelope. 2013. 34p. pap. 11.95 *(978-1-61477-076-3(X))* Bellissima Publishing, LLC.
—A Lot o' Granada, a Kid's Guide to Granada, Spain. Dyan, Penelope. 2012. 34p. pap. 11.95 *(978-1-61477-033-6(6))* Bellissima Publishing, LLC.
—Marco Polo Was Here! a Kid's Guide to Venice, Italy. Dyan, Penelope. 2009. 42p. pap. 11.95 *(978-1-935118-69-5(2))* Bellissima Publishing, LLC.
—Movin' on! a Kid's Guide to Skagway, Alaska. Dyan, Penelope. 2013. 34p. pap. 11.95 *(978-1-61477-106-7(5))* Bellissima Publishing, LLC.
—New York! New York! a Kid's Guide to New York City. Dyan, Penelope. 2009. 44p. pap. 11.95 *(978-1-935118-79-4(X))* Bellissima Publishing, LLC.
—Oh Victoria! a Kid's Guide to Victoria, Bc. Canada. Dyan, Penelope. 2013. 34p. pap. 11.95 *(978-1-61477-108-1(1))* Bellissima Publishing, LLC.
—Oh Vienna! a Kid's Guide to Vienna, Austri. Dyan, Penelope. 2013. 34p. pap. 11.95 *(978-1-61477-073-2(5))* Bellissima Publishing, LLC.
—On the Hill! a Kid's Guide to Melk, Austri. Dyan, Penelope. 2013. 34p. pap. 11.95 *(978-1-61477-074-9(3))* Bellissima Publishing, LLC.
—On the Way to Rome — - a Kid's Guide to Civitavecchia, Italy. Dyan, Penelope. 2011. 34p. pap. 11.95 *(978-1-935630-59-3(8))* Bellissima Publishing, LLC.
—One Big Hole in the Ground, a Kid's Guide to Grand Canyon, Us. Dyan, Penelope. 2010. 50p. pap. 11.95 *(978-1-935630-02-9(4))* Bellissima Publishing, LLC.
—Over a Bridge! a Kid's Guide to Budapest, Hungary. Dyan, Penelope. 2013. 38p. pap. 11.95 *(978-1-61477-071-8(9))* Bellissima Publishing, LLC.
—Over Dover — -A Kid's Guide to Dover, Uk. Dyan, Penelope. 2011. 38p. pap. 11.95 *(978-1-61477-005-3(0))* Bellissima Publishing, LLC.
—Over the Edge, a Kid's Guide to Niagara Falls, Ontario, Canad. Dyan, Penelope. 2010. 48p. pap. 11.95 *(978-1-935630-07-4(5))* Bellissima Publishing, LLC.
—The Rain in Spain — -A Kid's Guide to Barcelona, Spain. Dyan, Penelope. 2011. 38p. pap. 12.95 *(978-1-935630-56-2(3))* Bellissima Publishing, LLC.
—Reindeer & Mermaids, a Kid's Guide to Helsinki Finland. Dyan, Penelope. 2011. 34p. pap. 11.95 *(978-1-61477-000-8(X))* Bellissima Publishing, LLC.
—The Ring of Evil. Hillan, Pamela & Dyan, Penelope. 2013. 124p. pap. 8.95 *(978-1-61477-114-2(6))* Bellissima Publishing, LLC.
—Rockin' the Rock, a Kid's Guide to the Rock of Gibraltar. Dyan, Penelope. 2012. 34p. pap. 11.95 *(978-1-61477-037-4(9))* Bellissima Publishing, LLC.
—A Royal Residence — A Kid's Guide to Windsor Castle. Dyan, Penelope. 2011. 40p. pap. 12.95 *(978-1-935630-65-4(2))* Bellissima Publishing, LLC.
—See You 2-Maui — -A Kid's Guide to Maui, Hawaii. Dyan, Penelope. 2012. 34p. pap. 11.95 *(978-1-61477-038-1(7))* Bellissima Publishing, LLC.
—Shoes & Ships & Sealing Wax — -A Kids's Guide to Wamemünde, Germany. Dyan, Penelope. 2011. 34p. pap. 11.95 *(978-1-935630-99-9(7))* Bellissima Publishing, LLC.
—Smile Seattle! a Kid's Guide to Seattle, Washington. Dyan, Penelope. 2013. 34p. pap. 11.95 *(978-1-61477-109-8(X))* Bellissima Publishing, LLC.
—Spend a Day in Old Pompeii, a Kid's Travel Guide to Ancient Pompeii, Italy. Dyan, Penelope. 2010. 50p. pap. 11.95 *(978-1-935630-01-2(6))* Bellissima Publishing, LLC.
—The Squeaky Wheel Gets to Greece — -A Kid's Guide to Athens, Greece. Dyan, Penelope. 2011. 36p. pap. 11.95 *(978-1-935630-58-6(X))* Bellissima Publishing, LLC.
—Steam Train! All the Way to Canterbury, England. Dyan, Penelope. 2011. 40p. pap. 11.95 *(978-1-935630-75-3(X))* Bellissima Publishing, LLC.
—A Step in Time — A Kid's Guide to Ephesus, Turkey. Dyan, Penelope. 2011. 40p. pap. 12.95 *(978-1-935630-57-9(1))* Bellissima Publishing, LLC.
—Take a Dam Tour! a Kid's Guide to Hoover Dam, Nevad. Dyan, Penelope. 2010. 50p. pap. 11.95 *(978-1-935630-05-0(9))* Bellissima Publishing, LLC.
—This Is Sweden — -A Kid's Guide to Stockholm, Swedem. Dyan, Penelope. 2011. 34p. pap. 11.95 *(978-1-61477-003-9(4))* Bellissima Publishing, LLC.
—This Is the House George Built! a Kid's Guide to Mount Vernon. Dyan, Penelope. 2009. 44p. pap. 11.95 *(978-1-935118-83-1(8))* Bellissima Publishing, LLC.
—Totems & More! a Kid's Guide to Ketchikan, Alaska. Dyan, Penelope. 2013. 34p. pap. 11.95 *(978-1-61477-107-4(3))* Bellissima Publishing, LLC.
—Turkish Delight — A Kid's Guide to Istanbul, Turkey. Dyan, Penelope. 2011. 44p. pap. 12.95 *(978-1-935630-54-8(7))* Bellissima Publishing, LLC.
—Walk the Renaissance Walk — -A Kid's Guide to Florence, Italy. Dyan, Penelope. 2009. 42p. pap. 11.95 *(978-1-935118-70-1(6))* Bellissima Publishing, LLC.
—Water & Blood — A Kid's Guide to St Petersburg, Russi. Dyan, Penelope. 2011. 34p. pap. 11.95 *(978-1-61477-001-5(8))* Bellissima Publishing, LLC.
—What Happens in Vegas a Kid's Guide to Las Vegas, Nevad. Dyan, Penelope. 2010. 48p. pap. 11.95 *(978-1-935630-06-7(7))* Bellissima Publishing, LLC.
—Where Is London Bridge? a Kid's Guide to London. Dyan, Penelope. 2009. 44p. pap. 11.95 *(978-1-935118-80-0(3))* Bellissima Publishing, LLC.
—Yesterday's Rain — - a Kid's Guide to Kauai, Hawaii. Dyan, Penelope. 2013. 34p. pap. 11.95 *(978-1-61477-100-5(6))* Bellissima Publishing, LLC.
—Yummy Solvang! a Kid's Guide to Solvang, Californi. Dyan, Penelope. 2012. 34p. pap. 11.95 *(978-1-61477-052-7(2))* Bellissima Publishing, LLC.
Weigel, Jeff. Jack & Jill Went up to Kill: A Book of Zombie Nursery Rhymes. Spradlin, Michael P. 2011. (ENG.). 96p. pap. 9.99 *(978-0-06-208359-3(7),* William Morrow Paperbacks) HarperCollins Pubs.
Weigel, Jeff. Atomic Ace & the Robot Rampage. Weigel, Jeff. 2006. (ENG.). 32p. (J). (gr. 2-5). 6.95 *(978-0-8075-0485-7(8))*; 15.95 *(978-0-8075-0484-0(X))* Whitman, Albert & Co.
Weigelt, Udo & Henn, Astrid. Becky the Borrower. Weigelt, Udo. 2008. (ENG.). 32p. (J). (gr. -1-3). 16.95 *(978-0-7358-2205-4(0))* North-South Bks., Inc.
Weihs, Erika. Bar Mitzvah: A Jewish Boy's Coming of Age. Kimmel, Eric A. 2004. 143p. (J). (gr. 6-9). reprint ed. pap. 15.00 *(978-0-7567-7261-1(3))* DIANE Publishing Co.
—Menorahs, Mezuzas, & Other Jewish Symbols. Chaikin, Miriam. 2003. 102p. (J). (gr. 5-6). lib. bdg. 14.10 *(978-0-613-73018-1(6),* Turtleback) Turtleback Bks.
Weikert, Dana, jt. illus. see O'Kane, George.
Weiman, Jon. Beluga Passage. Lingemann, Linda. 2011. (Smithsonian Oceanic Collection Ser.). (ENG.). 32p. (J). (gr. -1-3). 19.95 *(978-1-60727-645-6(3))* Soundprints.
—Lobster's Secret. Hollenbeck, Kathleen M. 2011. (Smithsonian Oceanic Collection Ser.). (ENG.). 32p. (J). (gr. -1-3). 19.95 *(978-1-60727-653-1(4))*; 8.95 *(978-1-60727-654-8(2))* Soundprints.
Weinberg, Devorah. Gedalia the Goldfish Who Wanted Be Just Like the King. Yerushalmi, Miriam. 2007. 26p. (J). (gr. -1-3). 16.50 *(978-0-911643-36-7(2))* Aura Printing, Inc.
Weinberg, James. Straw House, Wood House, Brick House, Blow: Four Novellas by Daniel Nayeri. Nayeri, Daniel. 2011. (ENG.). 432p. (YA). (gr. 9). 19.99 *(978-0-7636-5526-6(0))* Candlewick Pr.
Weinberg, Steven. Great Ancient China Projects: You Can Build Yourself. Kramer, Lance. 2008. (Build It Yourself Ser.). (ENG.). 128p. (J). (gr. 3-7). 21.95 *(978-1-934670-03-3(0))*; pap. 21.95 *(978-1-934670-02-6(2))* Nomad Pr.
—To Timbuktu: Nine Countries, Two People, One True Story. Scieszka, Casey. 2011. (ENG.). 496p. (YA). (gr. 9-12). pap. 19.99 *(978-1-59643-527-8(5))* Roaring Brook Pr.
Weinberg, Steven. Rex Finds an Egg! Egg! Egg! Weinberg, Steven. 2015. (ENG.). 40p. (J). (gr. -1-3). 17.99 *(978-1-4814-0308-5(7),* McElderry, Margaret K. Bks.) McElderry, Margaret K. Bks.
Weinbrenner, Jacquelyn. My Silly Willy Loose Tooth. Weinbrenner, Darlene. 2012. 24p. 24.95 *(978-1-4626-5180-1(1))* America Star Bks.
Weiner, Jonathan. Nadia's Hands. English, Karen. 2009. (ENG.). 32p. (J). pap. 9.95 *(978-1-59078-784-7(6))* Boyds Mills Pr.
Weingast, Susana. Percepcion simbolica en el Arte. Weingast, Susana. 2004. 142p. (YA). pap. 19.00 *(978-1-931481-24-3(5))* LiArt-Literature & Art.
Weinheimer, Kim. The Bear Song. Weinheimer, Kim, as told by. 2012. 24p. pap. 9.95 *(978-1-935752-30-1(8))* Bryce Cullen Publishing.
Weinman, Brad. Mythmaker: The Life of J. R. R. Tolkien, Creator of the Hobbit & the Lord of the Rings. Neimark, Anne E. (ENG.). 144p. (YA). (gr. 5-7). 2014. pap. 6.99 *(978-0-544-02324-6(2),* HMH Books For Young Readers); 2012. 12.99 *(978-0-547-99734-6(5))* Houghton Mifflin Harcourt Publishing Co.
—The Postman Always Brings Mice. Holm, Jennifer L. & Hamel, Jonathan. 2005. (Stink Files Ser.: No. 1). 129p. (J). 12.65 *(978-0-7569-6529-7(2))* Perfection Learning Corp.
—Tales from the Brothers Grimm & the Sisters Weird. Vande Velde, Vivian. 2005. (Magic Carpet Bks.). (ENG.). 144p. (J). (gr. 5-7). reprint ed. pap. 6.99 *(978-0-15-205572-1(X))* Houghton Mifflin Harcourt Publishing Co.
—To Scratch a Thief. Holm, Jennifer L. & Hamel, Jonathan. (Stink Files Ser.: No. 2). 144p. 2005. pap. 4.99 *(978-0-06-052984-0(9),* Harper Trophy); 2004. (J). 14.99 *(978-0-06-052982-6(2))*; 2004. (J). lib. bdg. 15.89 *(978-0-06-052983-3(0))* HarperCollins Pubs.
Weinreb, Matthew, photos by. The Synagogue. Meek, H. A. rev. ed. 2004. (ENG., 240p. (gr. 8-17). pap. 35.00 *(978-0-7148-4329-2(6))* Phaidon Pr. Ltd. GBR. Dist: Hachette Bk. Group.
Weinstein, Holly. The Foodie Club. Shear, Dani. 2013. (ENG.). 50p. (J). 16.99 *(978-1-61053-027-9(6))* Blackbird Bks.
Weinstock, Tony. Star of the Show. Ferreri, Della Ross. 2009. (ENG.). 36p. (J). (gr. -1-3). 15.95 *(978-1-934860-03-8(4))* Shenanigan Bks.
Weir, Carrie & Weir, Nolet. What Season Is It? Frigon, Kerry, photos by. Ferguson, Gloria. 2011. 28p. pap. 24.95 *(978-1-4626-4136-9(9))* America Star Bks.
Weir, Doffy. The Jealous Giant. Umansky, Kaye. 2005. 32p. (J). (gr. -1 — 1). pap. 6.95 *(978-1-903015-41-4(3))* Barn Owl Bks, London GBR. Dist: Independent Pubs. Group.
—The Romantic Giant. Umansky, Kaye & Umansky, Kaye. 2006. 29p. (J). (gr. k-2). pap. 6.95 *(978-1-903015-25-4(1))* Barn Owl Bks, London GBR. Dist: Independent Pubs. Group.
Weir, Nolet, jt. illus. see Weir, Carrie.
Weir, Susan, jt. illus. see Students, Shelton Intermediate School Art.
Weisgard, Leonard. The Golden Bunny. Brown, Margaret Wise. 2015. (ENG.). 32p. (J). (-k). 16.99 *(978-0-385-39274-7(5),* Golden Bks.) Random Hse. Children's Bks.
—The Golden Christmas Tree. Wahl, Jan. 2010. (Big Little Golden Book Ser.). (ENG.). 32p. (J). (gr. -1-2). 8.99 *(978-0-375-82747-1(1),* Golden Bks.) Random Hse. Children's Bks.
—The Golden Egg Book. Brown, Margaret Wise. 2004. (Big Little Golden Book Ser.). (ENG.). 32p. (J). (gr. -1-2). 8.99 *(978-0-375-82717-4(X),* Golden Bks.) Random Hse. Children's Bks.
—The Golden Egg Book. Brown, Margaret Wise. 2015. (Little Golden Book Ser.). (ENG.). 24p. (J). (-k). 3.99 *(978-0-385-38476-6(9),* Golden Bks.) Random Hse. Children's Bks.
—The Little Island. Brown, Margaret Wise. 2003. (ENG.). 48p. (gr. -1-2). 15.99 *(978-0-385-74640-3(7),* Doubleday Bks. for Young Readers) Random Hse. Children's Bks.
—Margaret Wise Brown's the Golden Bunny. Brown, Margaret Wise. 2015. (ENG.). 32p. (J). (-k). lib. bdg. 19.99 *(978-0-375-97372-7(9),* Golden Bks.) Random Hse. Children's Bks.
—The Noisy Book Treasury. Brown, Margaret Wise. 2014. (ENG.). 128p. (J). (gr. k-5). pap. 14.99 *(978-0-486-78028-3(7))* Dover Pubns., Inc.
Weishampel, Winifred Ann. Sparky the Firehouse Dog. 1 vol. Gibson, Steve. 2009. 20p. pap. 24.95 *(978-1-60836-254-7(X))* America Star Bks.
Weiskal, N. J. The Skittery Kitten & the Scaredy Cat. Weiskal, N. J. Weiskal, N. J. 2009. 36p. pap. 8.00 *(978-1-935125-59-4(1))* Robertson Publishing.
Weisner, David. Mr. Wuffles! Weisner, David. 2013. 14.99 *(978-0-9777098-8-5(4))*; 49.99 *(978-0-9777098-7-8(6))* Dreamscape Media, LLC.
Weiss, Ellen & Nelson, Marybeth. Dinosaur Rescue. Weiss, Ellen & Nelson, Marybeth. 2009. (J). *(978-1-59292-359-5(3))* SoftPlay, Inc.
—Elmo's Beautiful Day. Weiss, Ellen & Nelson, Marybeth. 2009. (J). *(978-1-59292-358-8(5))* SoftPlay, Inc.
Weiss, Harvey. Every Friday Night. Simon, Norma. (Festival Series of Picture Storybooks). (J). (gr. -1). spiral bd. 4.50 *(978-0-8381-0708-9(7))* United Synagogue of America Bk. Service.
Weiss, Monica. Celebrate Martin Luther King, Jr. Day with Mrs. Park's Class. Flor Ada, Alma. 2006. (Stories to Celebrate Ser.). 30p. (gr. k-6). per. 11.95 *(978-1-59820-125-3(5),* Alfaguara) Santillana USA Publishing Co., Inc.
Weiss, Mónica. Celebra el Día de Martin Luther King, Jr. con la Clase de la Sra. Park. Weiss, Mónica. Flor Ada, Alma. 2006. (Cuentos para Celebrar / Stories to Celebrate Ser.). (SPA.). 30p. (gr. k-6). pap. 11.95 *(978-1-59820-113-0(1),* Alfaguara) Santillana USA Publishing Co., Inc.
Weiss, Tracy. L D the Littlest Dragster. Mors, Peter D. & Mors, Terry M. 2009. 36p. pap. 16.99 *(978-1-4389-7445-3(2))* AuthorHouse.
Weissman, Bari. Celebrate: A Book of Jewish Holidays. Gross, Judith et al. 2005. (Reading Railroad Ser.). (ENG.). 32p. (J). (gr. -1-3). mass mkt. 3.99 *(978-0-448-44300-3(7),* Grosset & Dunlap) Penguin Publishing Group.
Weissman, Bari. From Caterpillar to Butterfly. Heiligman, Deborah. 2015. (Let's-Read-And-Find-Out Science 1 Ser.). (ENG.). 32p. (J). (gr. -1-3). pap. 6.99 ***(978-0-06-238183-5(0))*** HarperCollins Pubs.
Weissman, Bari. From Caterpillar to Butterfly Big Book. Heiligman, Deborah. 2008. (Let's-Read-And-Find-Out Science 1 Ser.). (ENG.). 32p. (J). (gr. -1-3). pap. 24.99 *(978-0-06-111975-0(X),* Collins) HarperCollins Pubs.
Weissmann, Joe. Can Hens Give Milk?, 1 vol. Stuchner, Joan Betty. 2013. (ENG.). 32p. (J). (gr. -1-3). 9.95 *(978-1-4598-0427-2(9))* Orca Bk. Pubs. USA.
—Can I Catch It Like a Cold? Coping with a Parent's Depression. Centre for Addiction and Mental Health Staff. 2009. (Coping Ser.). (ENG.). 32p. (J). (gr. k-3). 17.95 *(978-0-88776-956-6(X),* Tundra Bks.) Tundra Bks. CAN. Dist: Penguin Random Hse., LLC.
—The Gingerbread Man. 2005. (J). 7.95 *(978-0-9770473-0-7(X))* Heersink, Roland.
—My Achy Body. Fromer, Liza & Gerstein, Francine. 2011. (Body Works). (ENG.). 24p. (J). (gr. 1-4). 12.95 *(978-1-77049-204-2(6))* Tundra Bks. CAN. Dist: Random Hse., Inc.
—My Healthy Body. Fromer, Liza & Gerstein, Francine. 2012. (Body Works). (ENG.). 24p. (J). (gr. 1-4). 12.95 *(978-1-77049-312-4(3),* Tundra Bks.) Tundra Bks. CAN. Dist: Penguin Random Hse., LLC.
—My Itchy Body. Fromer, Liza & Gerstein, Francine. 2012. (Body Works). (ENG.). 24p. (J). (gr. 1-4). 12.95 *(978-1-77049-311-7(5),* Tundra Bks.) Tundra Bks. CAN. Dist: Penguin Random Hse., LLC.
—My Messy Body. Fromer, Liza & Gerstein, Francine. 2011. (Body Works). (ENG.). 24p. (J). (gr. 1-4). 12.95 *(978-1-77049-202-8(X))* Tundra Bks. CAN. Dist: Random Hse., Inc.
—My Noisy Body. Fromer, Liza & Francine, Gerstein. 2011. (Body Works). (ENG.). 24p. (J). (gr. 1-4). 12.95 *(978-1-77049-201-1(1))* Tundra Bks. CAN. Dist: Random Hse., Inc.
—My Stretchy Body. Fromer, Liza & Gerstein, Francine. 2011. (Body Works). (ENG.). 24p. (J). (gr. 1-4). 12.95 *(978-1-77049-203-5(8))* Tundra Bks. CAN. Dist: Random Hse., Inc.
Weitzel, Erica. Ben Dhere! Don Dhat! Tall Tales from the Island of Gullah. LaFer, Jenni. 2007. 96p. (YA). per. 18.95 *(978-0-9800816-0-2(2))* Bread & Butter Bks.
Weitzman, David. Jenny: The Airplane That Taught America to Fly. Weitzman, David. 2006. 27p. (J). (gr. k-4). reprint ed. 19.00 *(978-1-4223-5582-4(9))* DIANE Publishing Co.
—Pharaoh's Boat. Weitzman, David. 2009. (ENG.). 32p. (J). (gr. 2-5). 18.00 *(978-0-547-05341-7(X))* Houghton Mifflin Harcourt Publishing Co.
Welch, Chad. Adventures of the Elements Vol. 3: Dangerous Games. James, Richard E., III. Lyle, Maryann, ed. 2004. 169p. (YA). (gr. 3-12). pap. 5.95 *(978-0-9675901-2-7(4))* Alchemy Creative, Inc.
Welch, Gracie. The Deer from Ponchatoula, 1 vol. Wolfe, Susan Markle. 2009. 24p. pap. 24.95 *(978-1-60813-519-6(5))* America Star Bks.
Welch, Holly. Inside All. Mason, Margaret. 2008. 32p. (J). (gr. -1-2). 16.95 *(978-1-58469-111-2(5))*; pap. 8.95 *(978-1-58469-112-9(3))* Dawn Pubns.
Welch, Holly Felsen. Fever Heat. Felsen, Henry Gregor. 2013. 230p. pap. 15.00 *(978-1-62272-002-6(4))* Felsen Ink.
—Henry Gregor Felsen Street Rod Collection. Felsen, Henry Gregor. 2013. 75.00 *(978-1-62272-005-7(9))* Felsen Ink.
Welch, Jaime. Runes from the Woodpile: Runic Knowledge Revealed. 2004. 126p. 20.00 *(978-0-9749416-3-9(8))* Himminbjorg Publishing, Inc.
Welch, Kelly. Ishi: The Last of His People. Collins, David R. et al. 2004. (Notable Americans Ser.). 96p. (YA). (gr. 6-12). 23.95 *(978-1-883846-54-1(4),* First Biographies) Reynolds, Morgan Inc.
Welch, Mark. Counting with the Fairies of Willow Garden. Welch, Lance. 2012. 16p. pap. 24.95 *(978-1-62709-544-0(6))* America Star Bks.
Welch, Sheila Kelly. Sean's Quest. Anderson, Leone Castell. 2003. 162p. (J). 16.95 *(978-0-9638819-6-0(5))*; pap. 10.95 *(978-0-9638819-7-7(3))* ShadowPlay Pr.
—Something in the Air. Jones, Molly. 2005. (J). *(978-1-893516-03-8(2))* Our Child Pr.
Weldin, Frauke. Benito y Melosa (Wally & Mae) Kempter, Christa. 2010. (SPA.). 32p. (J). (gr. -1-3). pap. 7.95 *(978-0-7358-2289-4(1))* North-South Bks., Inc.
—Ernest's First Easter. Stalder, Päivi. 2010. (ENG.). 32p. (J). (gr. -1-3). 16.95 *(978-0-7358-2241-2(7))* North-South Bks., Inc.
—Uncle Rabbit's Busy Visit. Kempter, Christa. 2010. (ENG.). 32p. (gr. -1-3). 16.95 *(978-0-7358-2320-4(0))* North-South Bks., Inc.
—Wake up, It's Easter! Kruss, James. Wilson, David Henry, tr. from GER. 2012. (ENG.). 32p. (J). (gr. -1-3). 16.95 *(978-0-7358-4070-6(9))* North-South Bks., Inc.
—Wally & Mae. Kempter, Christa. 2008. (ENG.). 32p. (J). (gr. -1-3). 16.95 *(978-0-7358-2208-5(5))* North-South Bks., Inc.
Weldon, Andrew. Don't Look Now 3: Haircut & Just a Nibble. Jennings, Paul. 2015. 275p. (J). (gr. 2-6). pap. 9.99 ***(978-1-74331-141-7(9))*** Allen & Unwin AUS. Dist: Independent Pubs. Group.
Weldon, Andrew. Written in Blood: A Brief History of Civilisation (With All the Gory Bits Left In) MacDonald, Beverley. 2004. (ENG.). 216p. (J). (gr. 8-8). pap. 11.95 *(978-1-86508-792-4(0))* Allen & Unwin AUS. Dist: Independent Pubs. Group.
Weldon, Andrew. Lazy Daisy, Cranky Frankie: Bedtime on the Farm. Weldon, Andrew. Jordan, Mary Ellen. 2013. (ENG.). 24p. (J). (gr. -1-2). 15.99 *(978-0-8075-4400-6(0))* Whitman, Albert & Co.
Welin, Raquel. Cuentos Golosos. Ortega, Ingrid. 2006. (SPA.). 64p. (J). mass mkt. 12.50 *(978-1-59835-012-8(9))* Cambridge BrickHouse, Inc.
Welker, Matthew S. Grand Poppa's Favorite Chair: No One Is As Special As You. Buckner, Andrew. 2011. 48p. pap. 24.95 *(978-1-4560-8294-9(9))* America Star Bks.
Weller, Linda. Hands-on Math, Grades K-1: Manipulative Activities for the Classroom. Johnson, Virginia. Hamaguchi, Carla, ed. 2nd ed. 2006. 144p. (J). (gr. k-1). per. 19.99 *(978-1-59198-232-6(4),* 2568) Creative Teaching Pr., Inc.
—Jumping into Journals: Guided Journaling for Beginning Readers & Writers. Jordano, Kimberly & Adsit, Kim. Cernek, Kim, ed. 2006. 112p. pap. 15.99 *(978-1-59198-227-2(8),* 2229) Creative Teaching Pr., Inc.
—Writing Makeovers 5-6: Improving Skills - Adding Style. Jennett, Pamela. Rous, Sheri, ed. 2003. 96p. (YA). (gr. 6-8). pap. 11.99 *(978-1-57471-957-4(2),* 2262) Creative Teaching Pr., Inc.
Weller, Ursula. Que? Como? Por Que?: Autos y Camiones. Caballero, D., tr. 2007. (Junior (Silver Dolphin) Ser.). 16p. (J). (gr. -1). *(978-970-718-490-9(6),* Silver Dolphin en Español) Advanced Marketing, S. de R. L. de C. V.

W

Wellesley, Rosie. The Very Hopeless Sheepdog. Grylls, Pinny. 2014. (ENG.). 32p. (J). (gr. -1-1). pap. 8.99 *(978-1-84365-219-6(6),* Pavilion) Pavilion Bks. GBR. Dist: Independent Pubs. Group.

Wellesley, Rosie. Moonlight Bear. Wellesley, Rosie. 2015. (ENG.). 32p. (J). (gr. -1-3). pap. 9.99 ***(978-1-84365-292-2(7),*** Pavilion) Pavilion Bks. GBR. Dist: Independent Pubs. Group.

Wellesley, Rosie. The Very Helpful Hedgehog. Wellesley, Rosie. 2012. (ENG.). 32p. (J). (gr. -1-k). pap. 8.99 *(978-1-84365-198-7(X),* Pavilion Children's Books) Pavilion Bks. GBR. Dist: Independent Pubs. Group.

Welling, Peter. Back to School, Picky Little Witch!, 1 vol. Brokamp, Elizabeth. 2014. (ENG.). 32p. (J). (gr. k-3). 16.99 *(978-1-4556-1887-3(X))* Pelican Publishing Co., Inc.

—The Kvetch Who Stole Hanukkah, 1 vol. Berlin, Bill & Berlin, Susan. 2010. (ENG.). 32p. (J). (gr. k-3). 16.99 *(978-1-58980-798-3(7))* Pelican Publishing Co., Inc.

Welling, Peter. What's up with This Chicken?, 1 vol. Sutton, Jane. 2015. (ENG.). 32p. (J). (gr. k-3). 16.99 ***(978-1-4556-2085-2(8))*** Pelican Publishing Co., Inc.

Welling, Peter. Joe Van der Katt & the Great Picket Fence, 1 vol. Welling, Peter. 2005. (ENG.). 32p. (J). (gr. k-3). 16.99 *(978-1-58980-281-0(0))* Pelican Publishing Co., Inc.

Welling, Peter J. Darlene Halloween & the Great Chicago Fire, 1 vol. Welling, Peter J. 2007. (ENG.). 32p. (J). (gr. k-3). 16.99 *(978-1-58980-479-1(1))* Pelican Publishing Co., Inc.

—Justin Potemkin & the 500-Mile Race, 1 vol. Welling, Peter J. 2004. (ENG.). 32p. (J). (gr. k-3). 16.99 *(978-1-58980-149-3(0))* Pelican Publishing Co., Inc.

—Michael le Soufflé & the April Fool, 1 vol. Welling, Peter J. 2003. (ENG.). 32p. (J). (gr. k-3). 16.99 *(978-1-58980-105-9(9))* Pelican Publishing Co., Inc.

Wellington, George. People, the World & I. Wellington, George, photos by. Date not set. viii, 94p. (YA). (gr. 7-18). mass mkt. 10.95 *(978-0-9670539-0-5(0))* Thomas, Sheldon Wade.

Wellington, Monica. The Little Snowflake. Metzger, Steve. 2003. (J). *(978-0-439-55656-9(2))* Scholastic, Inc.

Wellington, Monica. Apple Farmer Annie. Wellington, Monica. 2004. (ENG.). 32p. (J). (gr. -1-k). pap. 5.99 *(978-0-14-240124-8(2),* Puffin) Penguin Publishing Group.

—Apple Farmer Annie/ Anna Cultiva Manzanas. Wellington, Monica. Del Risco, Eida & del Risco, Eida, trs. from ENG. 2004. (ENG & SPA.). 32p. (J). (gr. -1-18). 16.99 *(978-0-525-47252-0(5),* Dutton Juvenile) Penguin Publishing Group.

—Apple Farmer Annie Board Book. Wellington, Monica. 2012. (ENG.). 24p. (J). (gr. -1 — 1). bds. 5.99 *(978-0-8037-3888-1(9),* Dial) Penguin Publishing Group.

—Mr. Cookie Baker. Wellington, Monica. 2006. (ENG.). 32p. (J). (gr. -1-k). 16.99 *(978-0-525-47763-1(2),* Dutton Juvenile) Penguin Publishing Group.

—Pizza at Sally's. Wellington, Monica. 2006. (ENG.). 32p. (J). (gr. -1-2). 15.99 *(978-0-525-47715-0(2),* Dutton Juvenile) Penguin Publishing Group.

—Riki's Birdhouse. Wellington, Monica. 2009. (ENG.). 32p. (J). (gr. -1-k). 16.99 *(978-0-525-42079-8(7),* Dutton Juvenile) Penguin Publishing Group.

—Zinnia's Flower Garden. Wellington, Monica. 2007. (ENG.). 32p. (J). (gr. -1-2). pap. 5.99 *(978-0-14-240787-5(9),* Puffin) Penguin Publishing Group.

Wellman, Megan. Being Bella. Zuzo, Cheryl. 2008. (ENG.). 32p. pap. 9.95 *(978-1-933916-27-9(3))* Nelson Publishing & Marketing.

Wellman, Megan D. And That Is Why We Teach: A Celebration of Teachers. Graham, Patti. 2008. (ENG.). 32p. (J). (gr. 4-7). 17.95 *(978-1-933916-23-1(0))* Nelson Publishing & Marketing.

Wells, Aja. Jake & Miller's Big Adventure: A Prepper's Book for Kids. Carr, Bernie. 2014. (ENG.). 32p. (gr. -1). 15.95 *(978-1-61243-271-7(9))* Ulysses Pr.

—That's Not Your Mommy Anymore: A Zombie Tale. Mogk, Matt. 2011. (ENG.). 32p. pap. 10.00 *(978-1-56975-926-4(X))* Ulysses Pr.

Wells, Daryl. Two Mrs. Gibsons. Igus, Toyomi. 2013. (ENG.). 32p. (J). (gr. 1-18). pap. 8.95 *(978-0-89239-170-7(7),* Children's Book Press) Lee & Low Bks., Inc.

Wells, Jack J. If Baby Bucking Bulls Could Talk. Shaw, Bill. 2010. 20p. 14.95 *(978-1-4269-3227-4(8))* Trafford Publishing.

Wells, Joe. Touch & Go Joe: An Adolescent's Experience of OCD. Wells, Joe. 2006. (ENG.). 128p. per. *(978-1-84310-391-2(5))* Kingsley, Jessica Ltd.

Wells, Lorraine. The Story of Easter. Pingry, Patricia A. (ENG.). (gr. -1-3). 2008. 22p. (J). pap. 3.99 *(978-0-8249-5560-1(9),* Ideals Children's Bks.); 2006. 26p. 12.95 *(978-0-8249-6649-2(X),* Candy Cane Pr.) Ideals Pubns.

Wells, Mark. Tommy's Lost Tooth. Wells, Mark. Wells, Meagan. 2011. 28p. pap. 11.99 *(978-1-61170-020-6(5))* Robertson Publishing.

Wells, Quierra LaQuelle. Trinny Bear & Dallas. Wells-Sanders, Glenora. 2012. 24p. pap. 11.50 *(978-1-61897-763-2(6),* Strategic Bk. Publishing) Strategic Book Publishing & Rights Agency (SBPRA).

Wells, Rachel. Animales de la Granja. Watt, Fiona. 2004. (SPA.). 14p. (J). 9.95 *(978-0-7460-6113-8(7),* Usborne) EDC Publishing.

—Animals. Watt, Fiona. 2006. 10p. (J). (gr. -1-k). bds. 9.99 *(978-0-7945-1227-9(5),* Usborne) EDC Publishing.

—Baby Dinosaur Cloth Bk. Watt, Fiona. 2006. 10p. (J). 10.99 *(978-0-7945-1429-7(4),* Usborne) EDC Publishing.

—Baby Monster Cloth Book. Watt, Fiona. 2007. (Usborne Cloth Bks.). 10p. (J). (gr. -1-k). 10.99 *(978-0-7945-1428-0(6),* Usborne) EDC Publishing.

—Baby's Christmas. Brooks, Felicity & Allen, Francesca. 2005. (Baby's World (Usborne Board Books) Ser.). 10p. (J). (gr. -1-k). per., bds. 8.95 *(978-0-7945-1175-3(9),* Usborne) EDC Publishing.

—Baby's Potty. Brooks, Felicity & Allen, Francesca. 2006. (Baby's Day Board Book Ser.). 10p. (J). (gr. -1). bds. 8.99 *(978-0-7945-1362-7(X),* Usborne) EDC Publishing.

—Big Book of Sticker Math. Watt, Fiona. 2008. (Usborne Sticker Math Ser.). 151p. (J). (gr. -1-3). pap. 12.99 *(978-0-7945-1825-7(7),* Usborne) EDC Publishing.

—Christmas Baby Jigsaw Book. Watt, Fiona. 2004. (Jigsaw Books Ser.). 14p. (J). 10.95 *(978-0-7945-0809-8(X),* Usborne) EDC Publishing.

—Christmas Eve. Watt, Fiona. 2007. (Luxury Touchy-Feely Board Bks). 10p. (J). (gr. -1-k). bds. 11.99 *(978-0-7945-1478-5(2),* Usborne) EDC Publishing.

—Esta No Es Mi Muneca. Watt, Fiona. 2005. (Titles in Spanish Ser.). (SPA.). 10p. (J). 7.95 *(978-0-7460-6102-2(1),* Usborne) EDC Publishing.

—Farm. Watt, Fiona. 2008. (Usborne Touchy-Feely Board Bks.). 8p. (J). (gr. -1-k). bds. 15.99 *(978-0-7945-1959-9(8),* Usborne) EDC Publishing.

—Mascotas. Watt, Fiona. 2004. (Titles in Spanish Ser.). (SPA.). 14p. (J). 9.95 *(978-0-7460-6112-1(9),* Usborne) EDC Publishing.

—Muddy Hippo. Durber, Matt & Brooks, Felicity. 2007. (Play Bks). 10p. (J). (gr. -1-k). bds. 10.99 *(978-0-7945-1688-8(2),* Usborne) EDC Publishing.

—The Nativity. Watt, Fiona. 2005. (Usborne Touchy-Feely Board Bks). 10p. (J). (gr. -1-k). bds. 15.95 *(978-0-7945-1172-2(4),* Usborne) EDC Publishing.

—Splish, Splash, Splosh Bath Bk. Cartwright, Mary. 2007. 8p. (J). 14.99 *(978-0-7945-1619-2(X),* Usborne) EDC Publishing.

—That's Not My Bunny. Watt, Fiona. 2004. (Touchy-Feely Board Bks.). (SPA & ENG.). 1p. (J). (gr. -1-18). bds. 7.99 *(978-0-7460-4179-6(9))* EDC Publishing.

—That's Not My Car. Watt, Fiona. 2004. (Touchy-Feely Board Books Ser.). 10p. (J). 7.95 *(978-0-7945-0636-0(4),* Usborne) EDC Publishing.

—That's Not My Donkey. Watt, Fiona. ed. 2011. (Touchy-Feely Board Books Ser.). 10p. (J). ring bd. 8.99 *(978-0-7945-3012-9(5),* Usborne) EDC Publishing.

—That's Not My Dragon... Watt, Fiona. 2006. (Usborne Touchy-Feely Bks.). 10p. (J). (gr. -1-k). bds. 7.99 *(978-0-7945-1285-9(2),* Usborne) EDC Publishing.

—That's Not My Duck... Watt, Fiona. 2014. (ENG.). (gr. -1). bds. 9.99 *(978-0-7945-3193-5(8),* Usborne) EDC Publishing.

—That's Not My Elephant. Watt, Fiona. ed. 2012. (Touchy-Feely Board Bks). 10p. (J). ring bd. 8.99 *(978-0-7945-3167-6(9),* Usborne) EDC Publishing.

—That's Not My Fairy. Watt, Fiona. 2004. 10p. (J). 9.99 *(978-0-7945-0793-0(X),* Usborne) EDC Publishing.

—That's Not My Frog. Watt, Fiona. 2009. (Touchy-Feely Board Bks). 10p. (J). bds. 8.99 *(978-0-7945-2505-7(9),* Usborne) EDC Publishing.

—That's Not My Kitten. Watt, Fiona. rev. ed. 2006. (Touchy-Feely Board Bks.). 10p. (J). (gr. -1-k). bds. 7.99 *(978-0-7945-1266-8(6),* Usborne) EDC Publishing.

—That's Not My Mermaid: Her Hair Is Too Fluffy. Watt, Fiona. 2006. (Usborne Touchy-Feely Board Bks.). 10p. (J). (gr. -1-k). bds. 9.99 *(978-0-7945-1083-1(3),* Usborne) EDC Publishing.

—That's Not My Monster. Watt, Fiona. (Usborne Touchy-Feely Bks.). 10p. (J). 2010. bds. 8.99 *(978-0-7945-2878-2(3));* 2004. 7.99 *(978-0-7945-0818-0(9))* EDC Publishing. (Usborne).

—That's Not My Penguin. Watt, Fiona. 2007. (Usborne Touchy-Feely Board Bks.). 8p. (gr. -1-k). bds. 7.99 *(978-0-7945-1810-3(9),* Usborne) EDC Publishing.

—That's Not My Pig... Its Nose Is Too Fuzzy. Watt, Fiona. 2014. (Usborne Touchy-Feely Board Bks.). (ENG.). 10p. (gr. -1). bds. 9.99 *(978-0-7945-2666-5(7),* Usborne) EDC Publishing.

—That's Not My Pirate. Watt, Fiona. 2007. (Touchy-Feely Board Bks). 10p. (J). (gr. -1-k). bds. 8.99 *(978-0-7945-1702-1(1),* Usborne) EDC Publishing.

—That's Not My Pony... Its Mane Is Too Fluffy. Watt, Fiona. 2007. (Usborne Touchy-Feely Board Bks.). 10p. (J). (gr. -1-k). bds. 7.99 *(978-0-7945-1630-7(0),* Usborne) EDC Publishing.

—That's Not My Prince. Watt, Fiona. 2013. (Usborne Touchy-Feely Board Bks.). (ENG.). 10p. (J). 9.99 *(978-0-7945-2838-6(4),* Usborne) EDC Publishing.

—That's Not My Princess. Watt, Fiona. 2006. (Usborne Touchy-Feely Board Bks.). 10p. (J). (gr. -1). bds. 9.99 *(978-0-7945-1325-2(5),* Usborne) EDC Publishing.

—That's Not My Reindeer... Watt, Fiona. 2014. (Usborne Touchy-Feely Bks.). (ENG.). 10p. (gr. -1). bds. 9.99 *(978-0-7945-3390-8(6),* Usborne) EDC Publishing.

—That's Not My Reindeer: Its Body Is Too Furry. Watt, Fiona. 2008. (Usborne Touchy-Feely Board Bks.). 10p. (J). (gr. -1-k). bds. 9.99 *(978-0-7945-1890-5(7),* Usborne) EDC Publishing.

—That's Not My Robot... Watt, Fiona. 2005. (Usborne Touchy-Feely Board Bks.). 10p. (J). (gr. -1-k). bds. 7.95 *(978-0-7945-1169-2(4),* Usborne) EDC Publishing.

—That's Not My Snowman. Watt, Fiona. 2006. (Usborne Touchy-Feely Board Bks.). 10p. (J). (gr. -1). bds. 9.99 *(978-0-7945-1414-3(6),* Usborne) EDC Publishing.

—That's Not My Sticker Book Christmas. rev. ed. 2012. (That's Not My . . Sticker Bks). 28p. (J). pap. 4.99 *(978-0-7945-3318-2(3),* Usborne) EDC Publishing.

—That's Not My Sticker Book Farm. 2012. (That's Not My Sticker Book Ser.). (ENG.). 24p. (J). (gr. -1-3). 4.99 *(978-0-7945-3204-8(7),* Usborne) EDC Publishing.

—That's Not My Teddy... Watt, Fiona. 2008. (Usborne Touchy-Feely Board Bks.). 8p. (J). (gr. -1). bds. 7.99 *(978-0-7945-2026-7(X),* Usborne) EDC Publishing.

—That's Not My Tiger. Watt, Fiona. 2010. (Touchy-Feely Board Bks.). 10p. (J). bds. 8.99 *(978-0-7945-2820-1(1))* EDC Publishing.

Wells, Robert E. Can We Share the World with Tigers? Wells, Robert E. 2012. (Wells of Knowledge Science Ser.). (ENG.). 32p. (J). (gr. 1-4). 16.99 *(978-0-8075-1055-1(6))* Whitman, Albert & Co.

—Did a Dinosaur Drink This Water? Wells, Robert E. 2006. (Wells of Knowledge Science Ser.). (ENG.). 32p. (J). (gr. 2-5). 7.99 *(978-0-8075-8840-6(7))* Whitman, Albert & Co.

—Polar Bear, Why Is Your World Melting? Wells, Robert E. 2008. (Wells of Knowledge Science Ser.). (ENG.). 32p. (J). (gr. 2-4). 16.99 *(978-0-8075-6598-8(9));* pap. 7.99 *(978-0-8075-6599-5(7))* Whitman, Albert & Co.

—What's Older Than a Giant Tortoise? Wells, Robert E. 2004. (Wells of Knowledge Science Ser.). (ENG.). 32p. (J). (gr. 2-5). 7.99 *(978-0-8075-8832-1(6))* Whitman, Albert & Co.

—What's So Special about Planet Earth? Wells, Robert E. (Wells of Knowledge Science Ser.). (ENG.). 32p. (J). (gr. 2-4). 2010. pap. 6.99 *(978-0-8075-8816-1(4));* 2009. 16.99 *(978-0-8075-8815-4(6))* Whitman, Albert & Co.

—Why Do Elephants Need the Sun? Wells, Robert E. (Wells of Knowledge Science Ser.). (ENG.). 32p. (J). (gr. 2-4). 2012. pap. 7.99 *(978-0-8075-9082-9(7));* 2010. 16.99 *(978-0-8075-9081-2(9))* Whitman, Albert & Co.

Wells, Rosemary. The Christmas Mystery. Gaarder, Jostein. Rokkan, Elizabeth, tr. 2010. (ENG.). 232p. pap. 12.95 *(978-1-55921-395-0(7))* Moyer Bell.

—I Love You! A Bushel & a Peck. Loesser, Frank. 2007. (ENG.). 32p. (J). (gr. -1-1). 6.99 *(978-0-06-443602-1(0))* HarperCollins Pubs.

—I Love You! A Bushel & A Peck. Loesser, Frank. 2004. 32p. (J). (gr. -1-1). lib. bdg. 16.89 *(978-0-06-028550-0(8))* HarperCollins Pubs.

—Mother Goose's Little Treasures. Opie, Iona. 2007. (My Very First Mother Goose Ser.). (ENG.). 56p. (J). (gr. -1-2). 17.99 *(978-0-7636-3655-5(X))* Candlewick Pr.

—My Very First Mother Goose. Opie, Ian, ed. 2004. 107p. (J). reprint ed. 17.00 *(978-0-7567-8384-6(4))* DIANE Publishing Co.

Wells, Rosemary. Snuggle up with Mother Goose. Opie, Iona, ed. 2015. (My Very First Mother Goose Ser.). (ENG.). 26p. (J). (— 1). bds. 8.99 ***(978-0-7636-7867-8(8))*** Candlewick Pr.

Wells, Rosemary. The Very Best Mother Goose Book Tower. Opie, Iona. 2010. (My Very First Mother Goose Ser.). (ENG.). 80p. (J). (gr. -1-k). pap. 9.99 *(978-0-7636-4983-8(X))* Candlewick Pr.

Wells, Rosemary. Bunny Cakes. Wells, Rosemary. 2014. (Max & Ruby Ser.). (ENG.). 32p. (J). (gr. -1-k). 7.99 *(978-0-14-751586-5(6),* Puffin) Penguin Publishing Group.

—Bunny Mail. Wells, Rosemary. 2004. (Max & Ruby Ser.). (ENG.). 32p. (J). (gr. -1-k). 15.99 *(978-0-670-03630-1(7),* Viking Juvenile) Penguin Publishing Group.

—Emily's First 100 Days of School. Wells, Rosemary. 2005. (ENG.). 64p. (J). (gr. -1-1). pap. 9.99 *(978-0-7868-1354-4(7))* Hyperion Pr.

Wells, Rosemary. Felix Stands Tall. Wells, Rosemary. 2015. (ENG.). 32p. (J). (gr. k-3). 14.99 ***(978-0-7636-6111-3(2))*** Candlewick Pr.

Wells, Rosemary. Hands Off, Harry! Wells, Rosemary. 2011. (ENG.). 40p. (J). (gr. -1-1). 14.99 *(978-0-06-192112-4(2),* Tegen, Katherine Bks) HarperCollins Pubs.

—Julieta, Estate Quieta! Wells, Rosemary. 2003. (SPA.). 38p. (J). (gr. k-3). 5.95 *(978-0-88272-433-1(9))* Santillana USA Publishing Co., Inc.

—Love Waves. Wells, Rosemary. 2011. (ENG.). 32p. (J). (gr. -1-2). 15.99 *(978-0-7636-4989-0(9))* Candlewick Pr.

—Love Waves: Midi Edition. Wells, Rosemary. 2012. (ENG.). 32p. (J). (gr. k — 1). 8.99 *(978-0-7636-6224-0(0))* Candlewick Pr.

—Max & Ruby at the Warthogs' Wedding. Wells, Rosemary. 2014. (Max & Ruby Ser.). (ENG.). 40p. (J). (gr. -1-k). 17.99 *(978-0-670-78461-5(3),* Viking Juvenile) Penguin Publishing Group.

—Max & Ruby Play School. Wells, Rosemary. 2003. (Max & Ruby Ser.). (ENG.). 32p. (J). (gr. -1-k). pap. 3.99 *(978-0-448-43182-6(3),* Grosset & Dunlap) Penguin Publishing Group.

—Max's Halloween. Wells, Rosemary. 2004. (Max & Ruby Ser.). (ENG.). 16p. (J). (gr. -1 — 1). bds. 5.99 *(978-0-670-05899-0(8),* Viking Juvenile) Penguin Publishing Group.

—Miracle Melts Down. Wells, Rosemary. 2012. (ENG.). 40p. (J). (gr. -1-3). 14.99 *(978-0-06-192115-5(7),* Tegen, Katherine Bks) HarperCollins Pubs.

—Noisy Nora. Wells, Rosemary. 2007. 28p. (gr. -1-2). 17.00 *(978-0-7569-7870-9(X))* Perfection Learning Corp.

—Otto Runs for President. Wells, Rosemary. 2011. (J). (gr. -1-4). 29.95 *(978-0-545-10690-0(7))* Weston Woods Studios, Inc.

—Read to Your Bunny. Wells, Rosemary. 2003. (ENG.). 6p. (J). bds. 7.99 *(978-0-439-54337-8(1),* Cartwheel Bks.) Scholastic, Inc.

—Ruby's Beauty Shop. Wells, Rosemary. 2004. (Max & Ruby Ser.). (ENG.). 32p. (J). (gr. -1-k). pap. 6.99 *(978-0-14-240194-1(3),* Puffin) Penguin Publishing Group.

—Ruby's Rainy Day. Wells, Rosemary. 2004. (Max & Ruby Ser.). (ENG.). 12p. (J). (gr. -1 — 1). bds. 6.99 *(978-0-448-43184-0(X),* Grosset & Dunlap) Penguin Publishing Group.

—Sophie's Terrible Twos. Wells, Rosemary. 2014. (ENG.). 32p. (J). (gr. -1-k). 16.99 *(978-0-670-78512-4(1),* Viking Juvenile) Penguin Publishing Group.

—Stella's Starliner. Wells, Rosemary. 2014. (ENG.). 32p. (J). (gr. -1-3). 15.99 *(978-0-7636-1495-9(5))* Candlewick Pr.

—Time-Out for Sophie. Wells, Rosemary. 2013. (ENG.). 32p. (J). (gr. -1-k). 15.99 *(978-0-670-78511-7(3),* Viking Juvenile) Penguin Publishing Group.

—A Visit to Dr. Duck. Wells, Rosemary. 2014. (ENG.). 30p. (J). (-k). bds. 7.99 *(978-0-7636-7229-4(7))* Candlewick Pr.

—Yoko. Wells, Rosemary. Rosemary, Wells. Varela, Sandra Lopez, tr. 2003. (SPA.). 34p. (J). (gr. k-2). pap. 8.50 *(978-84-241-8034-8(8))* Everest Editora ESP. Dist: Lectorum Pubns., Inc.

—Yoko. Wells, Rosemary. 2009. (ENG.). 32p. (J). (gr. -1-1). pap. 6.99 *(978-1-4231-1983-8(5))* Hyperion Pr.

Wells, Rosemary, jt. illus. see Williams, Garth.

Wells, Shan. And Dance with the Orange Cow. Mills, Nancy Libbey. 2003. 32p. (J). pap. 7.95 *(978-1-893815-10-0(2));* per. 12.95 *(978-1-893815-09-4(9))* Pie in the Sky Publishing, LLC.

—Never Eat Cabbage on Thursday. Mills, Nancy Libbey. ltd. ed. 2005. 32p. (J). 12.95 *(978-1-893815-08-7(0))* Pie in the Sky Publishing, LLC.

Wells-Smith, Abby. The Big Camping Adventure: Little Tommy Learns Lessons from the Great Outdoors. Toombs, Tom. 2013. 32p. pap. 12.95 *(978-1-61314-035-2(5))* Innovo Publishing, LLC.

Wells Smith, Abby. The Way to Be a Winner: Little Tommy Learns a Lesson in Working Together. Toombs, Tom. 2012. 32p. pap. 12.95 *(978-1-61314-034-5(7))* Innovo Publishing, LLC.

Wells, Steve. Crazy Classrooms. Cookson, Paul. 2015. (ENG.). 96p. (J). (gr. 2-6). pap. 7.99 ***(978-1-84780-505-8(1),*** Frances Lincoln) Quarto Publishing Group UK GBR. Dist: Littlehampton Bk Services, Ltd.

Welply, Michael. The Random House Book of Bible Stories. Osborne, Mary Pope & Boyce, Natalie Pope. 2015. (Random House Book Of ... Ser.). (ENG.). 176p. (J). (gr. k-3). lib. bdg. 27.99 *(978-0-375-97425-0(3),* Random Hse. Bks. for Young Readers) Random Hse. Children's Bks.

Welsh, Hayley. Gingerbread Aliens. Bennett, Sandra. 2012. (ENG.). 56p. (J). pap. *(978-0-9872356-4-0(8))* Australian Self Publishing Group/ Inspiring Pubs.

Welsh, Joey. The Gekkleberry Tree: A Humorous Tail about the Gekkards & One Legendary Tree. Welsh, Joey. 2005. (J). (gr. -1-3). 17.95 *(978-1-59247-244-4(3))* Scholargy Publishing, Inc.

Welsh, Mary Reddick. Sammy, the Little Green Snake Who Wanted to Fly. Welsh, Mary Reddick. 2011. 26p. pap. 11.95 *(978-1-936411-09-2(1))* YBK Pubs., Inc.

Weltevrede, Pieter. How Ganesh Got His Elephant Head. Johari, Harish & Sperling, Vatsala. 2003. (ENG.). 32p. (J). (gr. -1-6). 15.95 *(978-1-59143-021-6(6))* Bear & Co.

—How Parvati Won the Heart of Shiva. Johari, Harish & Sperling, Vatsala. 2004. (ENG.). 32p. (J). (gr. -1-6). 15.95 *(978-1-59143-042-1(9),* Bear Cub Bks.) Bear & Co.

—The Magical Adventures of Krishna: How a Mischief Maker Saved the World. Sperling, Vatsala. 2nd ed. 2009. (ENG.). 32p. (J). (gr. -1-6). 15.95 *(978-1-59143-110-7(7),* Bear Cub Bks.) Bear & Co.

—Ram the Demon Slayer. Sperling, Vatsala. 2006. (ENG.). 32p. (J). (gr. -1-6). 15.95 *(978-1-59143-057-5(7),* Bear Cub Bks.) Bear & Co.

Weltevrede, Pieter, jt. illus. see Johari, Harish.

Weltner, Dave. Canneh, the Reluctant Christmas Camel. Hanna, Margaret Leis. l.t. ed. 2003. 26p. (J). 7.95 *(978-0-9706654-7-8(4))* Sprite Pr.

—Quonby & the Tree Den. Chamberlain, Lyn. l.t. ed. 2004. 12p. (J). 7.95 *(978-0-9706654-8-5(2))* Sprite Pr.

—Summer Day. DuVall, Nell. l.t. ed. 2003. 13p. 7.95 *(978-0-9706654-6-1(6))* Sprite Pr.

Wenckebach, L. W. R., jt. illus. see Scheiner, A.

Wendel, Carie. Rock-A-Bye Baby. Everett, Melissa. 2013. (ENG.). 20p. (J). (gr. -1-3). 8.99 *(978-1-77093-668-3(8))* Flowerpot Children's Pr. Inc. CAN. Dist: Cardinal Pubs. Group.

Wendel, Carrie. Rain, Rain, Go Away. Everett, Melissa. 2013. (ENG.). 20p. (J). (gr. -1-1). 8.99 *(978-1-77093-524-2(X))* Flowerpot Children's Pr. Inc. CAN. Dist: Cardinal Pubs. Group.

—Rock-A-Bye Baby. Everett, Melissa. 2013. (Record-A-Story Ser.). (ENG.). 18p. (J). (gr. -1). bds. *(978-1-77093-464-1(2))* Flowerpot Children's Pr. Inc.

Wendell, Jeremy. Archibald's Swiss Cheese Mountain. Lieberman, Sylvia. 2007. 44p. (J). (gr. k-2). 17.95 *(978-0-9795852-5-8(2))* Seven Locks Pr.

Wendell, Ulises. El Hombrecito Vestido de Gris. Alonso, Fernando. 2003. (SPA.). 94p. (J). (gr. 3-5). pap. 8.95 *(978-968-19-0439-5(7))* Santillana USA Publishing Co., Inc.

WendellDowling. Colorful Men & Women of the Mother Lode. Atkinson, Janet I. Atkinson, Janet I., ed. 2004. 253p. (YA). reprint ed. pap. 16.95 *(978-0-9653428-2-7(4))* Irene, Jan Pubns.

Wendland, Paula. Guinea Fowl & Rabbit Get Justice: An African Folktale. Malaspina, Ann. 2013. (Folktales from Around the World Ser.). (ENG.). 24p. (J). (gr. k-3). 28.50 *(978-1-62323-614-4(2),* 206381) Child's World, Inc., The.

Wendland, Zachary & Miller, Kris Taft. Tic Talk: Living with Tourette Syndrome - A 9-Year-Old Boy's Story in His Own Words. Peters, Dylan. 2nd ed. 2009. (ENG.). 50p. pap. 16.96 *(978-1-58985-162-7(5))* Five Star Pubns., Inc.

Wendt, Matt. Agent Mongoose & the Attack of the Giant Insects. Croall, Marie P. & Jolley, Dan. 2010. (Twisted Journeys (r) Ser.: 15). (ENG.). 112p. (J). (gr. 4-7). lib. bdg. 27.93 *(978-0-8225-9251-8(7))* Lerner Publishing Group.

—Agent Mongoose & the Attack of the Giant Insects. Jolley, Dan & Croall, Marie P. 2010. (Twisted Journeys (r) Ser.: 15). (ENG.). 112p. (J). (gr. 4-7). pap. 7.95 *(978-0-8225-9257-0(6),* Graphic Universe) Lerner Publishing Group.

—Agent Mongoose & the Hypno-Beam Scheme. Jolley, Dan. 2009. (Twisted Journeys (r) Ser.: 9). (ENG.). 112p. (J). (gr. 4-7). 27.93 *(978-0-8225-6203-0(0));* pap. 7.95 *(978-0-8225-6204-7(9))* Lerner Publishing Group.

—Alien Adventure on Planet J. Jolley, Dan. 2008. (Twisted Journeys (r) Ser.: 8). (ENG.). 112p. (J). (gr. 4-7). 27.93 *(978-0-8225-6998-5(1),* Graphic Universe) Lerner Publishing Group.

—Alien Incident on Planet J. Jolley, Dan. 2008. (Twisted Journeys (r) Ser.: 8). (ENG.). 112p. (J). (gr. 4-7). pap. 7.95 *(978-0-8225-8876-4(5))* Lerner Publishing Group.

—Escape from Pyramid X. Jolley, Dan. 2007. (Twisted Journeys (r) Ser.: 2). (ENG.). (J). (gr. 4-7). pap. 45.32 *(978-0-8225-9466-6(8));* 112p. lib. bdg. 27.93 *(978-0-8225-6777-6(6),* Graphic Universe); 112p. per. 7.95 *(978-0-8225-6779-0(2))* Lerner Publishing Group.

—The Time Travel Trap. Jolley, Dan. 2008. (Twisted Journeys (r) Ser.: 6). (ENG.). (J). (gr. 4-7). pap. 45.32

W

(978-0-8225-9470-3(6)); 112p. per. 7.95 *(978-0-8225-8874-0(9))* Lerner Publishing Group.

Wendt, Yohanna. The Bride's Price. Saint, Mimi. 2013. 16p. pap. 24.95 *(978-1-4241-4249-1(0))* America Star Bks.

Wendy, Watson, jt. illus. see Jodie, Dias.

Wenisch, Tanja. Friends Always. 2014. (J). *(978-1-4338-1639-0(3)*, Magination Pr.) American Psychological Assn.

Wennekes, Ron. If I Could Breathe Like Fishes Do, 11 vols. Stanley, Jan. 2006. 25p. (J). bds. 12.99 *(978-0-9776893-0-9(1))* Midwest Graphics, Inc.

Wensell, Ulises. The Best Family in the World. Lopez, Susana. 2010. (ENG.). 28p. (J). (gr. -1-3). 10.99 *(978-1-935279-47-1(5))* Kane Miller.

—The Christmas Star. Wensell, Paloma. Maloney, Linda M., tr. from GER. 2006. (ENG.). 16p. (gr. -1-3). 7.95 *(978-0-8146-3155-3(X)*, Liturgical Pr. Bks.) Liturgical Pr.

—Matías y los Imposibles. Roncagliolo, Santiago. 2006. (SPA.). 111p. (J). *(978-84-7844-988-0(4))* Siruela, Ediciones S.A.

—Platero y Juan Ramon. Reviejo Hernandez, Carlos. 2006. (SPA.). 29p. (J). (gr. 6-8). 12.99 *(978-1-933032-10-8(3))* Lectorum Pubns., Inc.

—Ten Little Puppies/Diez Perritos. Flor Ada, Alma & Campoy, F. Isabel. 2011. (SPA & ENG.). 32p. (J). (gr. -1-3). 16.99 *(978-0-06-147043-1(0))*; lib. bdg. 17.89 *(978-0-06-147044-8(9))* HarperCollins Pubs. (Rayo).

—Where in the World Is God? Kunzler-Behncke, Rosemarie. Maloney, Linda M., tr. from GER. 2006. (ENG.). 26p. (gr. -1-3). 8.95 *(978-0-8146-3156-0(8)*, Liturgical Pr. Bks.) Liturgical Pr.

Wensell, Ulises, jt. illus. see Boldt, Fabienne.

Wenz-Vietor, Else. The Christmas Rose. Bauer, Sepp. 2008. 48p. (J). (gr. -1-3). 12.95 *(978-1-58089-232-2(9))* Charlesbridge Publishing, Inc.

Wenzel, Brendan. Beastly Babies. Jackson, Ellen. 2015. (ENG.). 32p. (J). (gr. -1-3). 17.99 *(978-1-4424-0834-0(0)*, Beach Lane Bks.) Beach Lane Bks.

—Some Bugs. DiTerlizzi, Angela. 2014. (ENG.). 32p. (J). (gr. -1-3). 17.99 *(978-1-4424-5880-2(1)*, Beach Lane Bks.) Beach Lane Bks.

Wenzel, David. Baby Loves You So Much! Spinelli, Eileen. 2008. (ENG.). 40p. (J). (gr. -1-3). 16.99 *(978-0-8249-5550-2(1)*, Ideals Children's Bks.) Ideals Pubns.

—Bell's Breakthrough. Deutsch, Stacia & Cohon, Rhody. (Blast to the Past Ser.: 3). (ENG.). (J). (gr. 2-5). 2013. 128p. pap. 5.99 *(978-1-4424-9536-4(7))*; 2005. 112p. pap. 6.99 *(978-0-689-87026-2(4))* Simon & Schuster/Paula Wiseman Bks. (Simon & Schuster/Paula Wiseman Bks.).

—Disney's Dream. Deutsch, Stacia & Cohon, Rhody. 2013. (Blast to the Past Ser.: 2). (ENG.). 128p. (J). (gr. 2-5). pap. 5.99 *(978-1-4424-9535-7(9)*, Simon & Schuster/Paula Wiseman Bks.) Simon & Schuster/Paula Wiseman Bks.

—Disney's Dream. Deutsch/Cohon. 2005. 108p. (J). lib. bdg. 16.92 *(978-1-4242-1714-4(8))* Fitzgerald Bks.

—Favorite Mother Goose Rhymes. Cricket Books Staff. 2007. (ENG.). 20p. (J). (gr. k-k). bds. 7.95 *(978-0-8126-7935-9(0))* Cricket Bks.

—Frog Went A-Traveling: A Russian Folktale. StJohn, Amanda. 2011. (Folktales from Around the World Ser.). (ENG.). 24p. (J). (gr. k-3). 28.50 *(978-1-60973-136-6(0)*, 201142) Child's World, Inc., The.

—A Hat for Ivan. Lucado, Max. 2004. 32p. (J). 15.99 *(978-1-58134-414-1(7))* Crossway.

—King's Courage. Deutsch, Stacia & Cohon, Rhody. (Blast to the Past Ser.: 4). (ENG.). (J). (gr. 2-5). 2013. 128p. pap. 5.99 *(978-1-4424-9537-1(5))*; 2006. 112p. pap. 6.99 *(978-1-4169-1269-9(X))* Simon & Schuster/Paula Wiseman Bks. (Simon & Schuster/Paula Wiseman Bks.).

—Lincoln's Legacy. Deutsch, Stacia & Cohon, Rhody. 2005. (Blast to the Past Ser.: 1). (ENG.). 112p. (J). (gr. 2-5). pap. 5.99 *(978-0-689-87024-8(8)*, Simon & Schuster/Paula Wiseman Bks.) Simon & Schuster/Paula Wiseman Bks.

—Lincoln's Legacy. Deutsch/Cohon. 2005. 104p. (J). lib. bdg. 16.92 *(978-1-4242-1716-8(4))* Fitzgerald Bks.

—Lincoln's Legacy. Deutsch, Stacia & Cohon, Rhody. 2013. (Blast to the Past Ser.: 1). (ENG.). 128p. (J). (gr. 2-5). pap. 5.99 *(978-1-4424-9534-0(0)*, Simon & Schuster/Paula Wiseman Bks.) Simon & Schuster/Paula Wiseman Bks.

—We Both Read-Soccer! Ross, Dev. 2010. 44p. (J). 9.95 *(978-1-60115-239-8(6))*; pap. 4.99 *(978-1-60115-240-4(X))* Treasure Bay, Inc.

Wenzel, David, jt. illus. see Wenzel, David T.

Wenzel, David T. Easter in the Garden. Kennedy, Pamela. 2008. (ENG.). 32p. (J). (gr. -1-3). 12.99 *(978-0-8249-5577-9(3)*, Ideals Children's Bks.) Ideals Pubns.

—I Like to Eat Treats. Rothenberg, Annye. 2010. 48p. (J). pap. 9.95 *(978-0-9790420-2-7(X))* Perfecting Parenting Pr.

—The King of Little Things, 1 vol. Lepp, Bil. 2013. (ENG.). 32p. (J). (gr. -1-3). 16.95 *(978-1-56145-708-3(6))* Peachtree Pubs.

—More or Less. Murphy, Stuart J. 2005. (MathStart 2 Ser.). (ENG.). 40p. (J). (gr. 1-18). pap. 5.99 *(978-0-06-053167-6(3))* HarperCollins Pubs.

—More or Less. Murphy, Stuart J. 2005. (Mathstart Ser.). 33p. (gr. 1-4). 16.00 *(978-0-7569-5225-9(5))* Perfection Learning Corp.

—Rodeo Time. Murphy, Stuart J. 2006. (MathStart 3 Ser.). (ENG.). 40p. (J). (gr. 2-5). pap. 5.99 *(978-0-06-055779-9(6))* HarperCollins Pubs.

—Why Do I Have To? Rothenberg, Annye. 2009. 40p. (J). pap. 9.95 *(978-0-9790420-1-0(1))* Perfecting Parenting Pr.

Wenzel, David T. & Schories, Pat. Biscuit's ABC Adventure. Capucilli, Alyssa Satin. 2008. (Biscuit Ser.). 32p. (J). (gr. -1-2). pap. 3.99 *(978-0-06-112841-7(4)*, HarperFestival) HarperCollins Pubs.

—Biscuit's Earth Day Celebration. Capucilli, Alyssa Satin. 2010. (Biscuit Ser.). (ENG.). 24p. (J). (gr. -1-1). pap. 3.99 *(978-0-06-162514-5(0)*, HarperFestival) HarperCollins Pubs.

Wenzel, David T. & Wenzel, David. Sacagawea's Strength. Deutsch, Stacia & Cohon, Rhody. 2006. (Blast to the Past Ser.: 5). (ENG.). 128p. (J). (gr. 2-5). pap. 9.99 *(978-1-4169-1270-5(3)*, Simon & Schuster/Paula Wiseman Bks.) Simon & Schuster/Paula Wiseman Bks.

—Your Special Gift. Lucado, Max et al. 2006. (Max Lucado's Wemmicks Ser.: 6). 32p. (J). (gr. -1-3). 16.99 *(978-1-58134-698-5(0))* Crossway.

Wenzel, Gregory. The Deep-Sea Floor. Collard, Sneed B., III. 2003. (ENG.). 32p. (J). (gr. 1-4). pap. 7.95 *(978-1-57091-403-4(6))* Charlesbridge Publishing, Inc.

—Loli the Leopard. Nussbaum, Ben. (ENG.). (J). (gr. -1-2). 2006. 32p. 9.95 *(978-1-59249-516-0(8)*, PS6556); 2006. 36p. 8.95 *(978-1-59249-514-6(1)*, SD6506); 2005. 36p. 14.95 *(978-1-59249-512-2(5)*, H6506); 2005. 36p. pap. 6.95 *(978-1-59249-513-9(3)*, S6506) Soundprints.

—Toko the Hippo. Nussbaum, Ben. 2006. (ENG.). 36p. (J). 14.99 *(978-1-59249-577-1(X))*; 8.95 *(978-1-59249-580-1(X))*; pap. 6.95 *(978-1-59249-578-8(8))*; pap. 2.95 *(978-1-59249-579-5(6))* Soundprints.

Wenzel, Gregory. The Feathered Dinosaurs of China. Wenzel, Gregory. 2004. (ENG.). 32p. (J). (gr. 1-4). pap. 7.95 *(978-1-57091-562-8(8))* Charlesbridge Publishing, Inc.

Werden's class. Nunamiut ABC: A Child's View of Life in an Alaska Village. Written & Illustrated by the 4th & 5th Graders of Anaktuvuk Pass, Alaska. Werden's class. 2003. 28p. (J). 3.95 *(978-0-930931-54-4(8))* Alaska Geographic Assn.

Wernicke, Maria. Candelaria. Galmez, Griselda. 2003. (SPA.). 38p. (J). (gr. k-3). pap. 9.95 *(978-968-19-0666-5(7))* Santillana USA Publishing Co., Inc.

—Sol de los Amigos. Baranda, Maria. 2010. (SPA.). 56p. (J). (gr. 2-5). pap. *(978-607-7661-13-9(9))* Ediciones El Naranjo Sa De Cv.

—Te Presento a Jacobo. White, Amy. Kratky, Lada J., tr. 2009. (Colección Fácil de Leer Ser.). (SPA.). 16p. (gr. k-2). pap. 5.99 *(978-1-60396-415-9(0))* Ediciones Alfaguara ESP. Dist: Santillana USA Publishing Co., Inc.

Werrun, Anna. Ethan Is Caught Blue Faced! Pulchinski, Erin. 2013. 32p. pap. *(978-1-4602-2416-8(7))* FriesenPress.

Werth, Kurt. Alaska Harvest. Pedersen, Elsa. 2012. 194p. 42.95 *(978-1-258-23211-5(1))*; pap. 27.95 *(978-1-258-23973-2(6))* Literary Licensing, LLC.

—Tales Merry & Wise. Mincieli, Rose Laura & Ross, Rose Laura. 2011. 130p. 40.95 *(978-1-258-09714-1(1))* Literary Licensing, LLC.

Wertheim, Anne. Bottlenose Dolphin. Sherrow, Victoria. 2012. (ENG.). 24p. (J). pap. 3.95 *(978-1-60727-724-8(7))* Soundprints.

—Galapagos Fur Seal: At Home in the Tropics. Sherrow, Victoria. 2011. (ENG.). 32p. (J). pap. 8.95 *(978-1-60727-613-5(5))* Soundprints.

—Garter Snake at Willow Creek Lane. Halfmann, Janet. 2011. (ENG.). 32p. (J). (gr. k-4). 19.95 *(978-1-60727-206-9(7))*; pap. 8.95 *(978-1-60727-208-3(3))* Soundprints.

—What Eats What in a Desert Food Chain, 1 vol. Slade, Suzanne. 2012. (Food Chains Ser.). (ENG.). 24p. (gr. 2-3). 25.32 *(978-1-4048-7386-5(4))*; pap. 7.95 *(978-1-4048-7690-3(1))* Picture Window Bks.

—What Eats What in a Rain Forest Food Chain, 1 vol. Amstutz, Lisa J. 2012. (Food Chains Ser.). (ENG.). 24p. (gr. 2-3). 25.32 *(978-1-4048-7387-2(2))*; pap. 7.95 *(978-1-4048-7694-1(4))* Picture Window Bks.

Wertz, Michael. A Curious Collection of Cats. Franco, Betsy. 2009. (ENG.). 40p. (J). (gr. -1-2). 16.99 *(978-1-58246-248-6(8)*, Tricycle Pr.) Ten Speed Pr.

Wertz, Michael. A Spectacular Selection of Sea Critters: Concrete Poems. Franco, Betsy. 2015. (ENG.). 32p. (J). (gr. 2-5). 19.99 ***(978-1-4677-2152-3(2)***, Millbrook Pr.) Lerner Publishing Group.

Wertz, Michael. Where's My Stuff? The Ultimate Teen Organizing Guide. Moss, Samantha. 2007. (ENG.). 96p. (YA). (gr. 8-12). pap. 16.95 *(978-0-9772660-5-0(2))* Zest Bks.

Wertz, Michael, jt. illus. see Starmer, Anika.

Wesley, Omarr. Gusts & Gales: A Book about Wind, 1 vol. Sherman, Josepha. 2003. (Amazing Science: Weather Ser.). (ENG.). 24p. (gr. -1-3). per. 7.95 *(978-1-4048-0338-1(6)*, Nonfiction Picture Bks.) Picture Window Bks.

—Gusts & Gales: A Book about Wind. Sherman, Josepha. 2003. (Amazing Science: Weather Ser.). (ENG.). 24p. (gr. -1-3). 25.99 *(978-1-4048-0094-6(8)*, Nonfiction Picture Bks.) Picture Window Bks.

—Shapes in the Sky: A Book about Clouds. Sherman, Josepha. 2003. (Amazing Science: Weather Ser.). (ENG.). 24p. (gr. -1-3). 25.99 *(978-1-4048-0097-7(2))*; per. 7.95 *(978-1-4048-0341-1(6))* Picture Window Bks. (Nonfiction Picture Bks.).

—Sopla y Silba: Un Libro Sobre el Viento, 1 vol. Sherman, Josepha & Picture Window Books Staff. Robledo, Sol, tr. from ENG. 2007. (Ciencia Asombrosa: el Tiempo Ser.). (SPA.). 24p. (gr. -1-3). 25.99 *(978-1-4048-3217-6(3))* Picture Window Bks.

Wess, Robert. Friends at Work & Play. Wess, Robert, photos by. Bunnett, Rochelle, photos by. 2003. 32p. (J). 14.95 *(978-0-9660884-2-7(5))*; pap. *(978-0-9660884-1-0(7))* Our Kids Pr.

Wesson, Andrea. Argus. Knudsen, Michelle. 2011. (ENG.). 32p. (J). (gr. -1-3). 15.99 *(978-0-7636-3790-3(4))* Candlewick Pr.

—Evangeline Mudd & the Golden-Haired Apes of the Ikkinasti Jungle. Elliott, David. 2004. 208p. pap. *(978-0-7445-8379-3(9))* Walker Bks., Ltd.

—Jack Quack, 1 vol. Nolan, Lucy & Nolan. 2003. (ENG.). 32p. (J). (gr. k-3). pap. 5.95 *(978-0-7614-5153-2(6))* Marshall Cavendish Corp.

—A Pet for Miss Wright. Young, Judy. 2011. (ENG.). 32p. (J). (gr. k-6). lib. bdg. 15.95 *(978-1-58536-509-8(2))* Sleeping Bear Pr.

Wesson, Andrea & Kath, Katie. 101 Ways to Be a Good Granny. Ziefert, Harriet. 2015. (ENG.). 56p. (J). 14.99 *(978-1-60905-514-1(4))* Blue Apple Bks.

Wesson, Tim. Spies vs. Giant Slugs in the Jungle. Catlow, Nikalas. 2012. (Mega Mash-Up Ser.). (ENG.). 96p. (J). (gr. 2-5). pap. 6.99 *(978-0-7636-5902-8(9)*, Nosy Crow) Candlewick Pr.

—Trolls vs. Cowboys in the Arctic. Catlow, Nikalas. 2012. (Mega Mash-Up Ser.). (ENG.). 96p. (J). (gr. 2-5). pap. 6.99 *(978-0-7636-6271-4(2)*, Nosy Crow) Candlewick Pr.

Wesson, Tim, jt. illus. see Catlow, Nikalas.

West, Colin. Grandpa's Boneshaker Bicycle. West, Colin. 2006. (Read-It! Chapter Bks.). (ENG.). 52p. (gr. 2-4). lib. bdg. 21.32 *(978-1-4048-2732-5(3)*, Chapter Readers) Picture Window Bks.

—Have You Seen the Crocodile? Read & Share. West, Colin. 2003. (Reading & Math Together Ser.). (ENG.). 32p. (J). (gr. -1-3). pap. 3.99 *(978-0-7636-0862-0(9))* Candlewick Pr.

—Uncle Pat & Auntie Pat. West, Colin. 2006. (Read-It! Chapter Bks.). (ENG.). 52p. (gr. 2-4). lib. bdg. 21.32 *(978-1-4048-2734-9(X)*, Chapter Readers) Picture Window Bks.

West, D. E. Ferdinand Uses the Potty. Tucker, Jason. 2009. (J). pap. 13.95 *(978-1-932690-82-8(4))* Loving Healing Pr., Inc.

West, David. Demons & Ghouls. Ganeri, Anita. 2010. (Dark Side Ser.). 32p. (J). pap. 10.50 *(978-1-4488-1564-7(9))*; lib. bdg. 26.50 *(978-1-61531-896-4(8))* Rosen Publishing Group, Inc., The. (PowerKids Pr.).

—Ghosts & Other Specters. Ganeri, Anita. 2010. (Dark Side Ser.). 32p. (J). pap. 10.50 *(978-1-4488-1566-1(5))*; (ENG.). lib. bdg. 26.50 *(978-1-61531-897-1(6))* Rosen Publishing Group, Inc., The. (PowerKids Pr.).

—The Illustrated Guide to Mythical Creatures. 2009. 48p. (J). (gr. 5-18). pap. 15.99 *(978-0-8437-1669-6(X))* Hammond World Atlas Corp.

West, David. Coelophysis & Other Dinosaurs & Reptiles from the Upper Triassic. West, David. 2012. (Dinosaurs! Ser.). (ENG.). 32p. (J). (gr. 3-6). pap. 10.50 *(978-1-4339-6713-9(8))*; lib. bdg. 26.60 *(978-1-4339-6711-5(1))* Stevens, Gareth Publishing LLLP. (Gareth Stevens Learning Library).

—Lesothosaurus & Other Dinosaurs & Reptiles from the Lower Jurassic. West, David. 2012. (Dinosaurs! Ser.). (ENG.). 32p. (J). (gr. 3-6). pap. 10.50 *(978-1-4339-6717-7(0))*; lib. bdg. 26.60 *(978-1-4339-6715-3(4))* Stevens, Gareth Publishing LLLP. (Gareth Stevens Learning Library).

—Pets in the Home. West, David. 2014. (Nora the Naturalist's Animals Ser.). 24p. (J). (gr. k-3). pap. 8.95 *(978-1-62588-052-9(9))* Black Rabbit Bks.

West, David & Ganeri, Anita. Giants & Ogres. West, David & Ganeri, Anita. 2010. (Dark Side Ser.). 32p. (J). (ENG.). pap. 10.50 *(978-1-4488-1568-5(1))*; lib. bdg. 26.50 *(978-1-61531-898-8(4))* Rosen Publishing Group, Inc., The. (PowerKids Pr.).

—Vampires & the Undead. West, David & Ganeri, Anita. 2010. (Dark Side Ser.). 32p. (J). (ENG.). pap. 10.50 *(978-1-4488-1570-8(3))*; lib. bdg. 26.50 *(978-1-61531-899-5(2))* Rosen Publishing Group, Inc., The.

—Werewolves & Other Shape-Shifters. West, David & Ganeri, Anita. 2010. (Dark Side Ser.). (ENG.). 32p. (J). pap. 10.50 *(978-1-4488-1572-2(X))*; lib. bdg. 26.50 *(978-1-61531-900-8(X))* Rosen Publishing Group, Inc., The. (PowerKids Pr.).

—Witches & Warlocks. West, David & Ganeri, Anita. 2010. (Dark Side Ser.). 32p. (J). pap. 10.50 *(978-1-4488-1574-6(6))*; (ENG.). lib. bdg. 26.50 *(978-1-61531-901-5(8))* Rosen Publishing Group, Inc., The. (PowerKids Pr.).

West, David & Spender, Nik. Ankylosaurus: The Armored Dinosaur. West, David. 2009. (Graphic Dinosaurs Ser.). (ENG.). 32p. (J). pap. 12.30 *(978-1-4358-8596-7(1))*; (gr. 2-5). 26.50 *(978-1-4358-8590-5(2))* Rosen Publishing Group, Inc., The. (PowerKids Pr.).

West, Jeff. Ancient Times: From the Earliest Nomads to the Last Roman Emperor. Crandell, Joyce & Bauer, Susan Wise. 3rd ed. 2006. (Story of the World Ser.). (ENG.). 319p. pap., act. bk. ed. 34.95 *(978-1-933339-05-4(5)*, 333905) Peace Hill Pr.

—Ancient Times Vol. 1: From the Earliest Nomads to the Last Roman Emperor. Bauer, Susan Wise. 2nd rev. ed. 2006. (Story of the World Ser.). (ENG.). 338p. 21.95 *(978-1-933339-01-6(2)*, 333901) Peace Hill Pr.

—Who in the World Was the Acrobatic Empress ? The Story of Theodora. Phillips, Robin. 2006. (Who in the World Ser.). (ENG.). 56p. (gr. 2-4). per. 9.50 *(978-0-9728603-9-0(8)*, 86039) Peace Hill Pr.

West, Jennifer. What Is Money? Boritzer, Etan. 2006. 40p. (J). pap. 6.95 *(978-0-9762743-3-9(7))* Lane, Veronica Bks.

West, Jeremy. Omni Presents the Universe. Conquistadore, H. I.t. ed. 2003. 51p. per. 8.99 *(978-1-932338-14-0(4))* Lifevest Publishing, Inc.

West, Joyce. The Drovers Road Collection: Three New Zealand Adventures, 3 vols. West, Joyce. 2003. (Bethlehem Budget Bks.). 416p. (YA). pap. 16.95 *(978-1-883937-69-0(8))* Bethlehem Bks.

West, June & Wright, Shannon. A Trip to the Cellar. West, Lily June Wolford. 2007. (J). (gr. -1-3). 16.99 *(978-1-59879-347-5(0))* Lifevest Publishing, Inc.

West, Linzi. Cat. Kemp, Jane & Walters, Clare. 2008. (ENG.). 12p. (J). (gr. -1 — 1). bds. 4.95 *(978-1-84507-121-9(2)*, Frances Lincoln) Quarto Publishing Group UK GBR. Dist: Hachette Bk. Group.

—Mummy, Mummy, What's in Your Tummy? Simpson-Enock, Sarah & Quarto Generic Staff. 2014. (ENG.). 24p. (J). (gr. -1-k). pap. 8.99 *(978-1-84780-535-5(3)*, Frances Lincoln) Quarto Publishing Group UK GBR. Dist: Hachette Bk. Group.

West, Lorraine. I Like You but I Love Me. 2006. 36p. (J). pap. 12.95 *(978-0-9768674-1-8(9))* Hip Hop Schl. Hse.

—The Mirror & Me. 2005. 40p. (J). per. 12.95 *(978-0-9768674-0-1(0))* Hip Hop Schl. Hse.

Westbeld, Kristine. Everyone Called Her Sister Sarah. Bert, Ruth J. 2004. (ENG.). 32p. (J). (gr. -1-3). pap. 4.99 *(978-1-928915-62-1(0))* Evangel Publishing Hse.

Westberg, Jan. Bees to Trees: Reading, Writing, & Reciting Poems about Nature. Freese, Susan M. 2008. (Poetry Power Ser.). 32p. (J). (gr. 1-4). 27.07 *(978-1-60453-001-8(4))* ABDO Publishing Co.

—Buses to Books: Reading, Writing, & Reciting Poems about School. Freese, Susan M. 2008. (Poetry Power Ser.). 32p. (J). (gr. 1-4). 27.07 *(978-1-60453-002-5(2))* ABDO Publishing Co.

—Carrots to Cupcakes: Reading, Writing, & Reciting Poems about Food. Freese, Susan M. 2008. (Poetry Power Ser.). 32p. (J). (gr. 1-4). 27.07 *(978-1-60453-003-2(0))* ABDO Publishing Co.

—Fireworks to Fruitcake: Reading, Writing, & Reciting Poems about Holidays. Freese, Susan M. 2008. (Poetry Power Ser.). 32p. (J). (gr. 1-4). 27.07 *(978-1-60453-004-9(9))* ABDO Publishing Co.

—Guppies to Puppies: Reading, Writing, & Reciting Poems about Pets. Freese, Susan M. 2008. (Poetry Power Ser.). 32p. (J). (gr. 1-4). 27.07 *(978-1-60453-005-6(7))* ABDO Publishing Co.

—Nicknames to Nightmares: Reading, Writing, & Reciting Poems about Me. Freese, Susan M. 2008. (Poetry Power Ser.). 32p. (J). (gr. 1-4). 27.07 *(978-1-60453-006-3(5))* ABDO Publishing Co.

Westbrook, Dick. The Great Royal Race. Sommer, Carl. (J). 2014. pap. ***(978-1-57537-952-4(X))***; 2003. 48p. (gr. k-4). lib. bdg. 23.95 incl. audio compact disk *(978-1-57537-708-7(X))*; 2003. 48p. (gr. 1-4). 16.95 incl. audio compact disk *(978-1-57537-508-3(7))* Advance Publishing, Inc.

Westbrook, Dick. The Great Royal Race(La Gran Carrera Real) Sommer, Carl. ed. 2009. (Another Sommer-Time Story Bilingual Ser.). (SPA & ENG.). 48p. (J). lib. bdg. 16.95 *(978-1-57537-152-8(9))* Advance Publishing, Inc.

Westbrook, Dick. Mayor for a Day. Sommer, Carl. (J). 2014. pap. ***(978-1-57537-959-3(7))***; 2003. (ENG.). 48p. (gr. k-4). lib. bdg. 23.95 incl. audio compact disk *(978-1-57537-713-1(6))*; 2003. (ENG.). 48p. (gr. 1-4). 16.95 incl. audio compact disk *(978-1-57537-513-7(3))* Advance Publishing, Inc.

Westbrook, Dick. Mayor for a Day: Alcalde Por un Dia. Sommer, Carl. ed. 2009. (Another Sommer-Time Story Bilingual Ser.). (SPA & ENG.). 48p. (J). lib. bdg. 16.95 *(978-1-57537-159-7(6))* Advance Publishing, Inc.

—No One Will Ever Know. Sommer, Carl. 2003. (Another Sommer-Time Story Ser.). (ENG.). 48p. (J). (gr. 1-4). 16.95 incl. audio compact disk *(978-1-57537-506-9(0))* Advance Publishing, Inc.

—No One Will Ever Know Read-Along, 1 bk. Sommer, Carl. 2003. (Another Sommer-Time Story Ser.). (ENG.). 48p. (J). lib. bdg. 23.95 incl. audio compact disk *(978-1-57537-706-3(3))* Advance Publishing, Inc.

—No One Will Ever Know(Nadie Se Va a Enterar) Sommer, Carl. ed. 2009. (Another Sommer-Time Story Bilingual Ser.). (SPA & ENG.). 48p. (J). lib. bdg. 16.95 *(978-1-57537-163-4(4))* Advance Publishing, Inc.

Westcott, Nadine Bernard. April Foolishness. Bateman, Teresa. 2004. (ENG.). 32p. (J). (gr. k-2). 6.99 *(978-0-8075-0405-5(X))* Whitman, Albert & Co.

—April Foolishness Book & DVD Set, 1 vol. Bateman, Teresa. 2010. (Book & DVD Packages with Nutmeg Media Ser.). (ENG.). 4p. (J). (gr. -1-3). 49.95 *(978-0-8075-9980-8(8))* Whitman, Albert & Co.

—Don't Forget Your Etiquette! The Essential Guide to Misbehavior. Greenberg, David. 2006. (ENG.). 40p. (J). (gr. 1-4). 17.99 *(978-0-374-34990-5(8)*, Farrar, Straus & Giroux (BYR)) Farrar, Straus & Giroux.

—The Eensy-Weensy Spider. Hoberman, Mary Ann. 2004. (ENG.). 32p. (J). (gr. -1-1). pap. 7.00 *(978-0-316-73412-7(8))* Little, Brown Bks. for Young Readers.

—Even Little Kids Get Diabetes. Pirner, Connie White. 2012. (J). *(978-1-61913-145-3(5))* Weigl Pubs., Inc.

—The Library Doors. Buzzeo, Toni. 2008. (J). (gr. -1-3). 17.95 *(978-1-60213-037-1(X))*; *(978-1-60213-027-2(2))* Highsmith Inc. (Upstart Bks.).

—The Lion Who Had Asthma. London, Jonathan. 2012. (J). *(978-1-61913-119-4(6))* Weigl Pubs., Inc.

—Silly Milly. Lewison, Wendy Cheyette. 2010. (Scholastic Reader Level 1 Ser.). (ENG.). 32p. (J). (gr. -1-3). pap. 3.99 *(978-0-545-06859-8(2))* Scholastic, Inc.

—Todd's Box. Moran, Alex & Sullivan, Paula. 2004. (Green Light Readers Level 1 Ser.). (ENG.). 24p. (J). (gr. -1-3). pap. 3.95 *(978-0-15-205094-8(9))* Houghton Mifflin Harcourt Publishing Co.

—Todd's Box. Sullivan, Paula. 2004. (J). (gr. -1-1). 11.60 *(978-0-7569-5629-5(3))* Perfection Learning Corp.

—Up, down, & Around. Ayres, Katherine. 2008. (Big Bks.). (ENG.). 32p. (J). (-k). pap. 24.99 *(978-0-7636-4018-7(2))*; 6.99 *(978-0-7636-4017-0(4))* Candlewick Pr.

—What's So Yummy? All about Eating Well & Feeling Good. Harris, Robie H. 2014. (Let's Talk about You & Me Ser.). (ENG.). 40p. (J). (-k). 15.99 *(978-0-7636-3632-6(0))* Candlewick Pr.

—Who Has What? All about Girls' Bodies & Boys' Bodies. Harris, Robie H. 2011. (Let's Talk about You & Me Ser.). (ENG.). 32p. (J). (gr. -1-2). 15.99 *(978-0-7636-2931-1(6))* Candlewick Pr.

—Who's in My Family? All about Our Families. Harris, Robie H. 2012. (Let's Talk about You & Me Ser.). (ENG.). 40p. (J). (gr. -1-2). 15.99 *(978-0-7636-3631-9(2))* Candlewick Pr.

Westcott, Nadine Bernard, jt. illus. see Bernard Westcott, Nadine.

Westcott, Nadine Bernard, jt. illus. see Emberley, Michael.

Westenbroek, Ken, jt. illus. see Krueger, Diane.

Westerfield, David. Sea Creatures. Peterson, Tiffany. 2003. (Draw It! Ser.). 32p. (J). (gr. 4-7). lib. bdg. 15.25 *(978-0-613-60983-8(2)*, Turtleback) Turtleback Bks.

Westerfield, William Stephen. Saint Nick & the Space Nicks. Mears, Richard Chase. l.t. ed. 2004. 32p. 16.95 *(978-0-9754056-0-4(8))* Tuxedo Blue, LLC.
Westergard, Jim. The Old Woman & the Hen. Page, P. K. 2008. (ENG.). 32p. (J). pap. 10.95 *(978-0-88984-309-7(0))* Porcupine's Quill, Inc. CAN. Dist: Univ. of Toronto Pr.
Westerman, Johanna. The Christmas Snowman. Cuyler, Margery. 2011. (ENG.). 32p. (J). (gr. k-2). 12.95 *(978-1-61608-483-7(9),* 608483, Sky Pony Pr.) Skyhorse Publishing Co., Inc.
—Mandy. Edwards, Julie Andrews. 2nd ed. 2006. (Julie Andrews Collection). (ENG.). 320p. (J). (gr. 3-7). 17.99 *(978-0-06-113162-2(8));* pap. 6.99 *(978-0-06-120707-5(1))* HarperCollins Pubs.
—We Both Read-The Boy Who Carried the Flag. Carson, Jana. 2010. (We Both Read Ser.). 44p. (J). (gr. 2-5). 9.95 *(978-1-60115-247-3(7));* pap. 5.99 *(978-1-60115-248-0(5))* Treasure Bay, Inc.
Westerskov, Kim, photos by. Albatrosses. 2004. 32p. (J). pap. *(978-0-7685-2117-7(3))* Dominie Pr., Inc.
—Diving in Antarctica. 2004. 32p. (J). *(978-0-7685-2384-3(2))* Dominie Pr., Inc.
—Dolphins. 2004. 32p. (J). pap. *(978-0-7685-2110-8(6))* Dominie Pr., Inc.
—Forests in the Sea. 2004. 32p. (J). *(978-0-7685-2387-4(7));* pap. *(978-0-7685-2116-0(5))* Dominie Pr., Inc.
—Friends in the Sea. 2004. 32p. (J). *(978-0-7685-2112-2(2))* Dominie Pr., Inc.
—Life in a Frozen Sea. 2004. 32p. (J). pap. *(978-0-7685-2114-6(9))* Dominie Pr., Inc.
—Ocean Travelers. 2004. 32p. (J). pap. *(978-0-7685-2118-4(1))* Dominie Pr., Inc.
—Penguins. 2004. 32p. (J). pap. *(978-0-7685-2111-5(4))* Dominie Pr., Inc.
—Whales. 2004. 32p. (J). *(978-0-7685-2109-2(2))* Dominie Pr., Inc.
Westlund, Laura. US History Through Infographics. Kenney, Karen Latchana. 2014. (Super Social Studies Infographics Ser.). (ENG.). 32p. (J). (gr. 3-5). lib. bdg. 26.60 *(978-1-4677-3459-2(4),* Lerner Pubns.) Lerner Publishing Group.
—US History Through Infographics. Kenney, Karen. 2014. (Super Social Studies Infographics Ser.). 32p. (gr. 3-5). pap. 8.95 *(978-1-4677-4568-0(5))* Lerner Publishing Group.
Weston, Chris. Counting to None, No. 5. Morrison, Grant. rev. ed. 2005. (Invisibles Ser.). (ENG.). 240p. (YA). pap. 19.99 *(978-1-56389-489-3(0))* DC Comics.
—Kissing Mister Quimper. Morrison, Grant. rev. ed. 2006. (Invisibles Ser.). (ENG.). 224p. (YA). pap. 19.99 *(978-1-56389-600-2(1),* Vertigo) DC Comics.
Weston, Martha. Curious George & the Birthday Surprise. Rey, H. A. & Rey, Margret. 2003. (Curious George Ser.). (ENG.). 24p. (J). (gr. -1-3). pap. 3.95 *(978-0-618-34687-5(2))* Houghton Mifflin Harcourt Publishing Co.
—Curious George's Neighborhood. Rey, H. A. & Rey, Margret. 2004. (Curious George Ser.). (ENG.). 10p. (J). (gr. -1 — 1). bds. 11.95 *(978-0-618-41203-7(4))* Houghton Mifflin Harcourt Publishing Co.
Weston, Martha. Did You See What I Saw? Winters, Kay. 2015. 32p. pap. 7.00 ***(978-1-61003-529-3(1))*** Center for the Collaborative Classroom.
Weston, Martha. Do You Wanna Bet? Your Chance to Find Out about Probability. Cushman, Jean. 2007. (ENG.). 112p. (J). (gr. 5-7). pap. 6.95 *(978-0-618-82999-6(7))* Houghton Mifflin Harcourt Publishing Co.
—Nate the Great & the Big Sniff. Sharmat, Marjorie Weinman & Sharmat, Mitchell. 2003. (Nate the Great Ser.: No. 23). (ENG.). 80p. (J). (gr. 1-4). pap. 5.99 *(978-0-440-41502-2(0,* Yearling) Random Hse. Children's Bks.
—Nate the Great & the Big Sniff. Sharmat, Marjorie Weinman & Sharmat, Mitchell. ed. 2003. (Nate the Great Ser.). 47p. (gr. -1-3). lib. bdg. 16.00 *(978-0-613-63966-8(9),* Turtleback) Turtleback Bks.
—Owen Foote, Money Man. Greene, Stephanie. 2003. (ENG.). 96p. (J). (gr. -1-3). pap. 5.99 *(978-0-618-37837-1(5))* Houghton Mifflin Harcourt Publishing Co.
—Owen Foote, Money Man. Greene, Stephanie. 2003. 88p. (gr. 2-4). 14.95 *(978-0-7569-1559-9(7))* Perfection Learning Corp.
—Owen Foote, Super Spy. Greene, Stephanie. 2005. (ENG.). 96p. (J). (gr. 1-4). pap. 8.95 *(978-0-618-55159-0(X))* Houghton Mifflin Harcourt Publishing Co.
—Takes a Train. 2010. (Curious George Ser.). (ENG.). 24p. (J). (gr. -1-3). pap. 4.99 *(978-0-547-50424-7(1))* Houghton Mifflin Harcourt Publishing Co.
Weston, Martha. Cats Are Like That. Weston, Martha. (Holiday House Reader Ser.). (ENG.). 32p. (J). (gr. k-3). tchr. ed. 15.95 *(978-0-8234-1419-2(1))* Holiday Hse., Inc.
Weston, Martha, jt. illus. see Sharmat, Mitchell.
Weston, Paul. Storms & Hurricanes. Bone, Emily. ed. 2013. (Beginner's Science Ser.). 32p. (J). ring bd. 4.99 *(978-0-7945-3350-2(7),* Usborne) EDC Publishing.
Weston, Steve. Dinosaur Canyon. Graf, Mike & Kaske, Anne. 2005. 40p. pap. 8.53 *(978-0-7578-9858-7(0))* Houghton Mifflin Harcourt Supplemental Pubs.
Weston, Steve & Field, James. Agustinia & Other Dinosaurs of Central & South America, 1 vol. Dixon, Dougal. 2007. (Dinosaur Find Ser.). (ENG.). 24p. (gr. k-3). lib. bdg. 25.99 *(978-1-4048-2263-4(1),* 1265746, Nonfiction Picture Bks.) Picture Window Bks.
—Aletopelta & Other Dinosaurs of the West Coast, 1 vol. Dixon, Dougal. 2006. (Dinosaur Find Ser.). (ENG.). 24p. (gr. k-3). lib. bdg. 25.99 *(978-1-4048-2744-8(7),* Nonfiction Picture Bks.) Picture Window Bks.
—Diceratops & Other Horned Dinosaurs, 1 vol. Dixon, Dougal. 2008. (Dinosaur Find Ser.). (ENG.). 24p. (gr. k-3). lib. bdg. 25.99 *(978-1-4048-4016-4(8),* Nonfiction Picture Bks.) Picture Window Bks.
—Dromaeosaurus & Other Dinosaurs of the North, 1 vol. Dixon, Dougal. 2006. (Dinosaur Find Ser.). (ENG.). 24p. (gr. k-3). lib. bdg. 25.99 *(978-1-4048-2745-5(5),* Nonfiction Picture Bks.) Picture Window Bks.
—Mahakala & Other Insect-Eating Dinosaurs, 1 vol. 2009. (Dinosaur Find Ser.). (ENG.). 24p. (gr. k-3). lib. bdg. 25.99 *(978-1-4048-5177-1(1),* Nonfiction Picture Bks.) Picture Window Bks.
—Maiasaura & Other Dinosaurs of the Midwest, 1 vol. Dixon, Dougal. 2006. (Dinosaur Find Ser.). (ENG.). 24p. (gr. k-3). lib. bdg. 25.99 *(978-1-4048-2749-3(8),* Nonfiction Picture Bks.) Picture Window Bks.
—Masiakasaurus & Other Fish-Eating Dinosaurs, 1 vol. 2009. (Dinosaur Find Ser.). (ENG.). 24p. (gr. k-3). 25.99 *(978-1-4048-5171-9(2),* Nonfiction Picture Bks.) Picture Window Bks.
—Neovenator & Other Dinosaurs of Europe, 1 vol. Dixon, Dougal. 2007. (Dinosaur Find Ser.). (ENG.). 24p. (gr. k-3). lib. bdg. 25.99 *(978-1-4048-2264-1(X),* Nonfiction Picture Bks.) Picture Window Bks.
—Ornithomimus & Other Fast Dinosaurs, 1 vol. Dixon, Dougal. 2006. (Dinosaur Find Ser.). (ENG.). 24p. (gr. k-3). lib. bdg. 25.99 *(978-1-4048-1326-7(8),* Nonfiction Picture Bks.) Picture Window Bks.
—Saltopus & Other First Dinosaurs, 1 vol. Dixon, Dougal. 2006. (Dinosaur Find Ser.). (ENG.). 24p. (gr. k-3). lib. bdg. 25.99 *(978-1-4048-1328-1(4),* Nonfiction Picture Bks.) Picture Window Bks.
—Saurophaganax & Other Meat-Eating Dinosaurs, 1 vol. 2009. (Dinosaur Find Ser.). (ENG.). 24p. (gr. k-3). lib. bdg. 25.99 *(978-1-4048-5180-1(1),* Nonfiction Picture Bks.) Picture Window Bks.
—Scutellosaurus & Other Small Dinosaurs, 1 vol. Dixon, Dougal. 2006. (Dinosaur Find Ser.). (ENG.). 24p. (gr. k-3). lib. bdg. 25.99 *(978-1-4048-1330-4(6),* Nonfiction Picture Bks.) Picture Window Bks.
—Tsintaosaurus & Other Duck-Billed Dinosaurs. Dixon, Dougal. 2008. (Dinosaur Find Ser.). (ENG.). 24p. (gr. k-3). lib. bdg. 25.99 *(978-1-4048-4018-8(4),* Nonfiction Picture Bks.) Picture Window Bks.
—Tyrannosaurus & Other Dinosaurs of North America, 1 vol. Dixon, Dougal & Picture Window Books Staff. 2007. (Dinosaur Find Ser.). (ENG.). 24p. (gr. k-3). lib. bdg. 25.99 *(978-1-4048-2265-8(8),* Nonfiction Picture Bks.) Picture Window Bks.
Weston, Steve, jt. illus. see Field, James.
Wethington, Julie & Wethington, Lang. Yes I Can! Have My Cake & Food Allergies Too. Wethington, Julie & Wethington, Lang. 2012. (J). *(978-0-9761444-1-0(7))* DragonWing Bks.
Wethington, Lang, jt. illus. see Wethington, Julie.
Wetmore, Barry. The Answer Is NO: Saying It & Sticking to It. Whitham, Cynthia. 2003. 224p. (J). pap. *(978-0-9622036-4-0(5))* Perspective Publishing, Inc.
—Good Friends Are Hard to Find: Help Your Child Find, Make, & Keep Friends. Frankel, Fred. 2003. 242p. (J). pap. 13.95 *(978-0-9622036-7-1(X))* Perspective Publishing, Inc.
—Win the Whining War & Other Skirmishes: A Family Peace Plan. Whitham, Cynthia. 2003. 198p. (J). pap. 13.95 *(978-0-9622036-3-3(7))* Perspective Publishing, Inc.
WFM Services. The Derby: A Timmy Wallings Story. Walsh, Patrick M., Jr. McGriff, Aaron C., ed. 2012. 188p. (J). *(978-0-9842929-4-3(2))* Daddy Bean Bks.
—Who Says Timmy Can't Play: The Derby: A Timmy Wallings Story. Walsh, Patrick M., Jr. McGriff, Aaron, ed. 2011. 135p. (J). *(978-0-9842929-3-6(4))* Daddy Bean Bks.
WGBH. FETCH! with Ruff Ruffman: Show's Over. Candlewick Press, Candlewick. 2014. (Fetch! with Ruff Ruffman Ser.). (ENG.). 48p. (J). (gr. 1-4). pap. 4.99 *(978-0-7636-6809-9(5))* Candlewick Pr.
—Ruff Ruffman's 44 Favorite Science Activities. Candlewick Press, Candlewick. 2015. (Fetch! with Ruff Ruffman Ser.). (ENG.). 132p. (J). (gr. 3-7). pap. 12.99 *(978-0-7636-7432-8(X))* Candlewick Pr.
WGBH Educational Foundation Staff. FETCH! with Ruff Ruffman: Doggie Duties. Candlewick Press Staff. 2014. (Fetch! with Ruff Ruffman Ser.). (ENG.). 48p. (J). (gr. 1-4). pap. 4.99 *(978-0-7636-6815-0(X))* Candlewick Pr.
Whallett, Liz. Why Do You Do That? A Book about Tourette Syndrome for Children & Young People. Chowdhury, Uttom & Robertson, Mary. 2006. (ENG.). 96p. (J). (gr. 3-11). per. *(978-1-84310-395-0(8))* Kingsley, Jessica Ltd.
Whamond, Dave. AlphaBest: The Zany, Zanier, Zaniest Book about Comparatives & Superlatives. Becker, Helaine. 2012. (ENG.). 32p. (J). 16.95 *(978-1-55453-715-0(0))* Kids Can Pr., Ltd. CAN. Dist: Univ. of Toronto Pr.
—And the Surprisingly Slobbery Attack of the Dog-Wash Doggies. Rovetch, L. Bob. 2007. (Hot Dog & Bob Ser.: HOTD). (ENG.). 96p. (J). (gr. 1-5). per. 4.95 *(978-0-8118-5746-8(8))* Chronicle Bks. LLC.
—Bagels Come Home, 1 vol. Stuchner, Joan Betty. 2014. (Orca Echoes Ser.). (ENG.). 64p. (J). (gr. 2-3). pap. 6.95 *(978-1-4598-0346-6(9))* Orca Bk. Pubs. USA.
Whamond, Dave. Bagels the Brave, 1 vol. Stuchner, Joan Betty. 2015. (Orca Echoes Ser.). (ENG.). 64p. (J). (gr. 2-3). pap. 6.95 ***(978-1-4598-0493-7(7))*** Orca Bk. Pubs. USA.
Whamond, Dave. Boy Meets Dog: A Word Game Adventure. Wyatt, Valerie. 2013. (ENG.). 32p. (J). 16.95 *(978-1-55453-824-9(6))* Kids Can Pr., Ltd. CAN. Dist: Univ. of Toronto Pr.
—Hot Dog & Bob: And the Dangerously Dizzy Attack of the Hypno Hamsters. Rovetch, L. Bob. 2007. (Hot Dog & Bob Ser.: HOTD). (ENG.). 96p. (J). (gr. 1-5). per. 4.95 *(978-0-8118-5602-7(X))* Chronicle Bks. LLC.
—Hot Dog & Bob: And the Particularly Pesky Attack of the Pencil People. Rovetch, L. Bob. 2006. (Hot Dog & Bob Ser.: HOTD). (ENG.). 96p. (J). (gr. 1-5). pap. 4.95 *(978-0-8118-5322-4(5))* Chronicle Bks. LLC.
—Justine Mckeen & the Bird Nerd, 1 vol. Brouwer, Sigmund. 2013. (Orca Echoes Ser.). (ENG.). 64p. (J). (gr. 2-3). pap. 6.95 *(978-1-4598-0394-7(9))* Orca Bk. Pubs. USA.
—Justine Mckeen, Eat Your Beets, 1 vol. Brouwer, Sigmund. 2013. (Orca Echoes Ser.). (ENG.). 64p. (J). (gr. 2-3). pap. 6.95 *(978-1-55469-933-9(9))* Orca Bk. Pubs. USA.
—Justine Mckeen, Pooper Scooper, 1 vol. Brouwer, Sigmund. 2012. (Orca Echoes Ser.). (ENG.). 64p. (J). (gr. 2-3). pap. 6.95 *(978-1-55469-931-5(2))* Orca Bk. Pubs. USA.
—Justine Mckeen, Queen of Green, 1 vol. Brouwer, Sigmund. 2011. (Orca Echoes Ser.). (ENG.). 64p. (J). (gr. 2-3). pap. 6.95 *(978-1-55469-927-8(4))* Orca Bk. Pubs. USA.
—Justine McKeen vs. the Queen of Mean, 1 vol. Brouwer, Sigmund. 2014. (Orca Echoes Ser.). (ENG.). 64p. (J). (gr. 2-3). pap. 6.95 *(978-1-4598-0397-8(3))* Orca Bk. Pubs. USA.
—Justine McKeen, Walk the Talk, 1 vol. Brouwer, Sigmund. 2012. (Orca Echoes Ser.). (ENG.). 64p. (J). (gr. 2-3). pap. 6.95 *(978-1-55469-929-2(0))* Orca Bk. Pubs. USA.
—Messy Miranda, 1 vol. Szpirglas, Jeff & Saint-Onge, Danielle. 2013. (Orca Echoes Ser.). (ENG.). 64p. (J). (gr. 2-3). pap. 6.95 *(978-1-4598-0117-2(2))* Orca Bk. Pubs. USA.
Whamond, Dave. Superbrain: The Insider's Guide to Getting Smart. 2015. (ENG.). 72p. (J). (gr. 4-6). pap. 9.95 ***(978-1-55451-734-3(6),*** 9781554517343) Annick Pr., Ltd. CAN. Dist: Firefly Bks., Ltd.
Whamond, Dave & Owlkids Books Inc. Staff. My Think-a-Ma-Jink. Whamond, Dave. 2009. (ENG.). 32p. (J). (gr. -1-4). 16.95 *(978-1-897349-66-3(1))* Owlkids Bks. Inc. CAN. Dist: Perseus-PGW.
Wharton, Jennifer Heyd. Like Me. Martelli, Dawn. 2004. (J). *(978-1-893516-01-4(6))* Our Child Pr.
Whatley, Ben Smith. Tin Toys. Whatley, Bruce. 2012. (ENG.). 32p. (J). (gr. k-2). pap. 13.99 *(978-1-86471-993-2(1))* Random Hse. Australia AUS. Dist: Independent Pubs. Group.
Whatley, Bruce. Christmas Wombat. French, Jackie. 2012. (ENG.). 32p. (J). (gr. -1-3). 16.99 *(978-0-547-86872-1(3))* Houghton Mifflin Harcourt Publishing Co.
—Diary of a Baby Wombat. French, Jackie. 2010. (ENG.). 32p. (J). (gr. -1-3). 16.99 *(978-0-547-43005-8(1))* Houghton Mifflin Harcourt Publishing Co.
—Diary of a Wombat. French, Jackie. 2007. 16p. (J). bds. *(978-0-7322-8662-0(X))* HarperCollins Pubs. Australia.
—Diary of a Wombat. French, Jackie. (ENG.). 32p. (J). (gr. -1-3). 2009. pap. 6.99 *(978-0-547-07669-0(X));* 2003. 16.99 *(978-0-618-38136-4(8))* Houghton Mifflin Harcourt Publishing Co.
—Emily & the Big Bad Bunyip. French, Jackie. 2008. 32p. *(978-0-7322-8692-7(1))* HarperCollins Pubs. Australia.
—The Great Texas Hamster Drive, 0 vols. Kimmel, Eric A. & Korelitz, Jean Hanff. 2007. (ENG.). 40p. (J). (gr. k-3). 16.99 *(978-0-7614-5357-4(1),* 9780761453574, Amazon Children's Publishing) Amazon Publishing.
—Here Comes Santa Claus. Autry, Gene & Haldeman, Oakley. 2004. 24p. (J). (gr. k-4). reprint ed. 17.00 *(978-0-7567-9048-6(4))* DIANE Publishing Co.
—How High Can a Kangaroo Hop? French, Jackie. 2008. 256p. pap. *(978-0-7322-8544-9(5))* HarperCollins Pubs. Australia.
—I Want a Hippopotamus for Christmas. Rox, John. 2005. 32p. (J). (gr. -1-3). 17.99 *(978-0-06-052942-0(3))* HarperCollins Pubs.
—Josephine Wants to Dance. French, Jackie. 2007. (ENG.). 32p. (J). (gr. -1-1). 17.95 *(978-0-8109-9431-7(3),* Abrams Bks. for Young Readers) Abrams.
—Josephine Wants to Dance. French, Jackie. 32p. 2008. (J). pap. *(978-0-207-20080-9(7));* 2006. *(978-0-207-20075-5(0))* HarperCollins Pubs. Australia.
—Martha Doesn't Say Sorry! Berger, Samantha. 2009. (ENG.). 40p. (J). (gr. -1-1). 15.99 *(978-0-316-06682-2(6))* Little Brown & Co.
—My Mom's the Best. Smith, Rosie. 2013. (J). *(978-0-545-60361-4(7))* Scholastic, Inc.
—The Night Before Christmas. Moore, Clement C. 2004. (ENG.). 32p. (J). (gr. -1 — 1). bds. 6.99 *(978-0-06-073917-1(7),* HarperFestival) HarperCollins Pubs.
—On the First Day of Grade School. Brenner, Emily. 2004. 32p. (J). (gr. -1-1). lib. bdg. 16.89 *(978-0-06-051041-1(2))* HarperCollins Pubs.
—The Perfect Pet. Palatini, Margie. 2003. 32p. (J). (gr. -1-2). 16.99 *(978-0-06-000108-7(9))* HarperCollins Pubs.
—Pete the Sheep. French, Jackie. 2008. 30p. (J). bds. *(978-0-7322-8794-8(4))* HarperCollins Pubs. Australia.
—Pig on the Titanic: A True Story. Crew, Gary. 2005. 32p. (J). 15.99 *(978-0-06-052305-3(0))* HarperCollins Pubs.
—The Queen with the Wobbly Bottom. Gwynne, Phillip. 2013. (ENG.). 32p. (J). (gr. -1-2). 17.99 *(978-1-921714-59-7(X))* Little Hare Bks. AUS. Dist: Independent Pubs. Group.
—The Secret World of Wombats. French, Jackie. 2005. 176p. *(978-0-207-20031-1(9))* HarperCollins Pubs. Australia.
—Too Many Pears!, 1 vol. French, Jackie. (ENG.). 32p. (J). 2004. pap. 6.95 *(978-1-932065-48-0(2),* 718-784-9112); 2003. 16.95 *(978-1-932065-47-3(4),* 718-784-9112) Star Bright Bks., Inc.
—Too Many Pears! (Japanese/English), 1 vol. French, Jackie. 2007. (JPN & ENG.). 32p. (J). (gr. -1). pap. 5.95 *(978-1-59572-112-9(6))* Star Bright Bks., Inc.
—Too Many Pears! (Spanish/English), 1 vol. French, Jackie. 2005. 32p. (J). (ABK, SPA & ENG.). 16.95 *(978-1-59572-012-2(X));* (SPA & ENG.). pap. 6.95 *(978-1-59572-013-9(8))* Star Bright Bks., Inc.
Whatley, Bruce. The Little Drummer Boy. Whatley, Bruce. 2011. (ENG.). 32p. (J). (gr. -1-k). pap. 10.99 *(978-1-86471-992-5(3))* Random Hse. Australia AUS. Dist: Independent Pubs. Group.
—The Little Drummer Boy. Whatley, Bruce. 2010. (ENG.). 32p. (J). (gr. -1-k). 14.99 *(978-1-86471-990-1(7))* Random Hse. Australia AUS. Dist: Independent Pubs. Group.
—Wait! No Paint! Whatley, Bruce. Whatley. 2005. (ENG.). 32p. (J). (gr. -1-3). pap. 7.99 *(978-0-06-443546-8(6))* HarperCollins Pubs.
Whatley, Bruce & Beatrice, Chris. Aesop's Fables: A Pop-Up Book of Classic Tales. 2011. (ENG.). 14p. (J). (gr. -1-3). 27.99 *(978-1-4169-7146-7(7),* Little Simon) Little Simon.
Whatmore, Candice. Easy Piano Classics. Marks, Anthony. Rogers, Kirsteen, ed. 2007. (Easy Piano Classics Ser.). 64p. (J). 18.99 *(978-0-7945-1273-6(9),* Usborne) EDC Publishing.
—First Illustrated Science Dictionary. Khan, Sarah. Robson, Kirsteen, ed. 2013. (ENG.). 104p. (J). (gr. -1-3). 9.99 *(978-0-7945-3383-0(3),* Usborne) EDC Publishing.
Whatmore, Candice & Barrance, Reuben. Mysteries & Marvels of Nature. Dalby, Elizabeth. Tatchell, Judy, ed. 2008. (Nature Encyclopedias Ser.). 128p. (J). (gr. 4-7). pap. 16.99 *(978-0-7945-1738-0(2),* Usborne) EDC Publishing.
Whatmore, Candice, jt. illus. see Barrance, Reuben.
Wheatley, Maria. How Do Your Senses Work? Tatchell, Judy. rev. ed. 2004. (Flip Flaps Ser.). 16p. (J). (gr. 2-18). pap. 7.95 *(978-0-7945-0642-1(9),* Usborne) EDC Publishing.
—What Happens to Your Food. Smith, Alastair. 2003. 16p. (J). (gr. 2-18). pap. 7.95 *(978-0-7945-0643-8(7),* Usborne) EDC Publishing.
Whedon, Zack. Dr. Horrible. Rugg, Jim. 2010. (ENG.). 80p. pap. 9.99 *(978-1-59582-577-3(0))* Dark Horse Comics.
Wheeler, David Cole. Scratch & Sketch Trace-Along Robots: An Art Activity Book for Artistic Inventors of All Ages. Nemmers, Lee. 2015. (ENG.). 64p. (J). 14.99 ***(978-1-4413-1812-1(7),*** 9781441318121) Peter Pauper Pr. Inc.
Wheeler, Eliza. Cody & the Fountain of Happiness. Springstubb, Tricia. 2015. (ENG.). 160p. (J). (gr. 2-5). 14.99 *(978-0-7636-5857-1(X))* Candlewick Pr.
—Doll Bones. Black, Holly. 2013. (ENG.). 256p. (J). (gr. 5-9). 17.99 *(978-1-4169-6398-1(7),* McElderry, Margaret K. Bks.) McElderry, Margaret K. Bks.
—The Grudge Keeper, 1 vol. Rockliff, Mara. 2014. (ENG.). 32p. (J). (gr. -1-3). 16.95 *(978-1-56145-729-8(9))* Peachtree Pubs.
—The Incorrigible Children of Ashton Place Bk. IV: The Interrupted Tale. Wood, Maryrose. 2013. (Incorrigible Children of Ashton Place Ser.: 4). (ENG.). 400p. (J). (gr. 3-7). 16.99 *(978-0-06-179122-2(9))* HarperCollins Pubs.
—The Incorrigible Children of Ashton Place Bk. 4: The Interrupted Tale. Wood, Maryrose. 2015. (Incorrigible Children of Ashton Place Ser.: 4). (ENG.). 400p. (J). (gr. 3-7). pap. 6.99 *(978-0-06-179123-9(7))* HarperCollins Pubs.
—The Incorrigible Children of Ashton Place Bk. 5: The Unmapped Sea. Wood, Maryrose. 2015. (Incorrigible Children of Ashton Place Ser.: 5). (ENG.). 416p. (J). (gr. 3-7). 15.99 *(978-0-06-211041-1(1))* HarperCollins Pubs.
Wheeler, Eliza. Miss Maple's Seeds. Wheeler, Eliza. 2013. (ENG.). 32p. (J). (gr. -1-k). 16.99 *(978-0-399-25792-6(6))* Penguin Publishing Group.
Wheeler, Irvin. Justina's Dream. 2005. 30p. (J). *(978-1-887302-12-8(3))* Western Images Pubns., Inc.
Wheeler, Jenny Lee. Heart-Shaped Pickles: Gentle Grief Support for Kids & Grownups. Wheeler, Karla. l.t. ed. 2003. (ENG.). 36p. (J). 4.95 *(978-0-9675532-2-1(9))* Quality of Life Publishing Co.
Wheeler, Jody. A Cat's Tale, One Cat's Search for the Meaning of Life. Lindemann, Lindy. 2007. 28p. per. 12.95 *(978-1-934246-03-0(4))* Peppertree Pr., The.
—Corduroy Lost & Found. Freeman, Don & Hennessy, B. G. 2006. (Corduroy Ser.). (ENG.). 32p. (J). (gr. -1-k). 15.99 *(978-0-670-06100-6(X),* Viking Juvenile) Penguin Publishing Group.
—County Fair. Wilder, Laura Ingalls. 2003. (My First Little House Bks.). 17.00 *(978-0-7569-1727-2(1))* Perfection Learning Corp.
—Nate the Great & the Hungry Book Club. Sharmat, Marjorie Weinman & Sharmat, Mitchell. 2011. (Nate the Great Ser.: No. 26). (ENG.). 80p. (J). (gr. 1-4). 5.99 *(978-0-375-84548-2(8),* Yearling) Random Hse. Children's Bks.
—Nate the Great Talks Turkey. Sharmat, Marjorie Weinman & Sharmat, Mitchell. 2007. (Nate the Great Ser.: No. 25). (ENG.). 96p. (J). (gr. 1-4). per. 5.99 *(978-0-440-42126-9(8),* Yearling) Random Hse. Children's Bks.
—Nate the Great Talks Turkey: With Help from Olivia Sharp. Sharmat, Marjorie Weinman & Sharmat, Mitchell. ed. 2007. (Nate the Great Ser.). (gr. -1-3). lib. bdg. 16.00 *(978-1-4177-9248-1(5),* Turtleback) Turtleback Bks.
—Nate the Great, Where Are You? Sharmat, Marjorie Weinman & Sharmat, Mitchell. 2015. (Nate the Great Ser.). (ENG.). 80p. (J). (gr. 1-4). 5.99 *(978-0-449-81078-1(X),* Yearling) Random Hse. Children's Bks.
—Nate the Great, Where Are You? Sharmat, Mitchell. 2014. (Nate the Great Ser.). (ENG.). 48p. (J). (gr. 1-4). 12.99 *(978-0-385-74336-5(X),* Delacorte Bks. for Young Readers) Random Hse. Children's Bks.
—An Old-Fashioned Thanksgiving. Alcott, Louisa May. 2010. 40p. (J). (gr. -1-3). 14.99 *(978-0-8249-5620-2(6),* Ideals Children's Bks.) Ideals Pubns.
Wheeler, Ron. Exodus: Fun Bible Studies Using Puzzles & Stories. Woodman, Ros. 2005. (Activity Ser.). (ENG.). 64p. (J). (gr. 4-7). pap., act. bk. ed. 7.99 *(978-1-84550-067-2(9))* Christian Focus Pubns. GBR. Dist: Send The Light Distribution LLC.
—Four Square: A Companion to the Four Square Writing Method: Writing in the Content Areas for Grades 5-9. Gould, Judith S. & Gould, Evan Jay. Mitchell, Judy, ed. 2004. 112p. (J). pap. 11.95 *(978-1-57310-422-7(1))* Teaching & Learning Co.
—Four Square: The Personal Writing Coach, Grades 7-9. Gould, Judith S. & Burke, Mary F. 2005. 112p. (J). pap. 12.95 *(978-1-57310-448-7(5))* Teaching & Learning Co.
—Fun Bible Studies Using Puzzles & Stories. Woodman, Ros. 2007. (Bible Detectives Ser.). (ENG.). 64p. pap. 7.99 *(978-1-84550-223-2(X))* Christian Focus Pubns. GBR. Dist: Send The Light Distribution LLC.
—Genesis: Fun Bible Studies Using Puzzles & Stories. Woodman, Ros. 2005. (Activity Ser.). (ENG.). 64p. (J). (gr. 4-7). pap., act. bk. ed. 7.99 *(978-1-84550-066-5(0))* Christian Focus Pubns. GBR. Dist: Send The Light Distribution LLC.

W

—Great Scientists in Action. Shevick, Ed. 2004. (Science Action Labs Ser.). 64p. (J). pap. 9.95 (978-1-57310-436-4(1), 1238118) Teaching & Learning Co.

—Math Phonics Pre-Algebra. Hein, Marilyn B. 2004. 96p. (J). pap. 10.65 (978-1-57310-438-8(8)) Teaching & Learning Co.

—Matthew & Goliath. Davis, Brian. 2003. (Book of Matt Ser.: 3). 80p. (J). pap. 4.99 (978-1-59269-058-9(0)) Mcruffy Pr.

—Matt's Birthday Blessing. Davis, Brian. 2003. (Book of Matt Ser.: Vol. 1). 80p. (J). pap. 4.99 (978-1-59269-056-5(4)) Mcruffy Pr.

—My Shoes Got the Blues. Davis, Brian. 2003. (Book of Matt Ser.: 2). 80p. (J). pap. 4.99 (978-1-59269-057-2(2)) Mcruffy Pr.

Wheelhouse, M. V. A Flat Iron for a Farthing. Ewing, Juliana Horatia. 2007. 212p. per. (978-1-4065-2524-3(3)) Dodo Pr.

Whelan, Kat. One Little Blueberry. Salzano, Tammi. 2011. 24p. (J). (gr. -1-k). 12.95 (978-1-58925-859-4(2)) Tiger Tales.

—'Twas the Night Before Christmas. Moore, Clement C. 2010. 24p. (J). (gr. -1-2). 12.95 (978-1-58925-858-7(4)) Tiger Tales.

Whelan, Kevin. You Wouldn't Want to Sail on the Mayflower! A Trip That Took Entirely Too Long. Cook, Peter. rev. ed. 2013. (ENG.). 40p. (J). (gr. 3-12). pap. 9.95 (978-0-531-23858-5(X)) Scholastic Library Publishing.

Whelan, Michael. The Gunslinger. King, Stephen. rev. exp. ed. 2003. (Dark Tower Ser.: Bk. 1). (ENG.). 272p. (gr. 12-18). pap. 20.00 (978-0-452-28469-2(4), Plume) Penguin Publishing Group.

Whelan, Olwyn. The Barefoot Book of Blessings: From Many Faiths & Cultures. Dearborn, Sabrina. 2007. (ENG.). 40p. (J). (gr. -1-3). 18.99 (978-1-84686-069-0(5)) Barefoot Bks., Inc.

—The Barefoot Book of Pirates. Walker, Richard. (Barefoot Bks.). (ENG.). 64p. (J). 2008. 19.99 (978-1-84686-237-3(X)); 2004. pap. 15.99 (978-1-84148-131-9(9)) Barefoot Bks., Inc.

—The Barefoot Book of Princesses. Matthews, Caitlín. 2004. (ENG.). 64p. (J). pap. 15.99 (978-1-84148-172-2(6)) Barefoot Bks., Inc.

—Celtic Memories. Matthews, Caitlín. 2003. 80p. (J). 19.99 (978-1-84148-097-8(5)) Barefoot Bks., Inc.

—Little Elephant. House, Catherine. 2007. 32p. pap. 11.95 (978-1-59325-093-5(2)) Word Among Us Pr.

—Little Zebra. House, Catherine. 2007. 39p. (J). 11.95 (978-1-59325-094-2(0)) Word Among Us Pr.

—Pirates Artist Card Portfolio. (J). 12.99 (978-1-84148-485-3(7)) Barefoot Bks., Inc.

—Pirates Invitations. (J). 7.99 (978-1-84148-486-0(5)) Barefoot Bks., Inc.

—Princesses Artist Card Portfolio. (J). 12.99 (978-1-84148-484-6(9)) Barefoot Bks., Inc.

—Princesses Invitations. (J). 7.99 (978-1-84148-470-9(9)) Barefoot Bks., Inc.

—Spellbound: Tales of Enchantment from Ancient Ireland. Parkinson, Siobhan. (ENG.). 64p. (J). (gr. 1-4). 2014. pap. 12.99 (978-1-84780-459-4(4)); 2013. 19.99 (978-1-84780-140-1(4)) Quarto Publishing Group UK GBR. (Frances Lincoln). Dist: Hachette Bk. Group.

Whelan, Olwyn. The Barefoot Book of Princesses. Whelan, Olwyn. Matthews, Caitlín & Wolfson, Margaret. 2008. (Barefoot Bks.). (ENG.). 64p. (J). 19.99 (978-1-84686-239-7(6)) Barefoot Bks., Inc.

—Tales from Celtic Lands. Whelan, Olwyn. Matthews, Caitlín & Cusack, Niamh. 2008. (ENG.). 80p. (J). (gr. -1-3). 21.99 (978-1-84686-213-7(2)) Barefoot Bks., Inc.

Whelan, Olwyn. The Star Child. Whelan, Olwyn, tr. Maidment, Stella & Wilde, Oscar. gif. ed. 2003. 40p. (YA). (978-1-84365-012-6(6), Pavilion Children's Books) Pavilion Bks.

Whicheloe, Paul, photos by. Katie Brown's Outdoor Entertaining: Taking the Party Outside. Brown, Katie. 2007. (ENG., 192p. 30.00 (978-0-316-11306-9(9)) Bulfinch.

Whigham, Rod, et al. Amelia Earhart: Legendary Aviator, 1 vol. Anderson, Jameson. 2006. (Graphic Biographies Ser.). (ENG.). 32p. (gr. 3-4). 29.99 (978-0-7368-6496-1(2), Graphic Library) Capstone Pr., Inc.

Whigham, Rod. How to Draw Crazy Fighter Planes, 1 vol. Sautter, Aaron. 2008. (Drawing Cool Stuff Ser.). (ENG.). 32p. (gr. 3-4). 27.32 (978-1-4296-1298-2(3), Edge Bks.) Capstone Pr., Inc.

—How to Draw Indestructible Tanks, 1 vol. Sautter, Aaron. 2008. (Drawing Cool Stuff Ser.). (ENG.). 32p. (gr. 3-4). 27.32 (978-1-4296-1301-9(7), Edge Bks.) Capstone Pr., Inc.

—How to Draw Monster Trucks, 1 vol. Sautter, Aaron. 2007. (Drawing Cool Stuff Ser.). (ENG.). 32p. (gr. 3-4). 27.32 (978-1-4296-0079-8(9), Edge Bks.) Capstone Pr., Inc.

—Jim Thorpe: Greatest Athlete in the World, 1 vol. Fandel, Jennifer. (Graphic Biographies Ser.). (ENG.). 32p. (gr. 3-4). 2008. per. 8.10 (978-1-4296-1773-4(X)); 2007. 29.99 (978-1-4296-0152-8(3)) Capstone Pr., Inc. (Graphic Library).

—Samuel Morse & the Telegraph, 1 vol. Seidman, David et al. 2007. (Inventions & Discovery Ser.). (ENG.). 32p. (gr. 3-4). 29.99 (978-0-7368-6846-4(1), Graphic Library) Capstone Pr., Inc.

Whigham, Rod & Barnett, Charles, III. Christopher Columbus: Famous Explorer, 1 vol. Wade, Mary Dodson & Capstone Press Staff. 2007. (Graphic Biographies Ser.). (ENG.). 32p. (gr. 3-4). 29.99 (978-0-7368-6853-2(4), 1264941, Graphic Library) Capstone Pr., Inc.

—Christopher Columbus: Famous Explorer, 1 vol. Wade, Mary Dodson. 2007. (Graphic Biographies Ser.). (ENG.). 32p. (gr. 3-4). per. 8.10 (978-0-7368-7905-7(6), 1264941, Graphic Library) Capstone Pr., Inc.

—Samuel Morse & the Telegraph, 1 vol. Seidman, David & Williams, Keith. 2007. (Inventions & Discovery Ser.). (ENG.). 32p. (gr. 3-4). pap. 8.10 (978-0-7368-7898-2(X), Graphic Library) Capstone Pr., Inc.

Whild, Katharine. Marlowe the Great Detective. Whild, Katharine. l.t. ed. 2005. 36p. (J). 16.95 (978-0-9712488-4-7(2)) Deerbrook Editions.

Whimp, Pauline. Greedy Gus the Pirate, 6 pack. Holden, Pam. 2009. (Red Rocket Readers Ser.). 16p. (gr. 2-5). pap. (978-1-877363-74-0(X)) Flying Start Bks.

—Hunting for Treasure, 6 pack. Holden, Pam. 2009. (Red Rocket Readers Ser.). 16p. (gr. 2-4). pap. (978-1-877363-65-8(0), Red Rocket Readers) Flying Start Bks.

—Paulo the Pilot, 6 pack. Holden, Pam. 2009. (Red Rocket Readers Ser.). 16p. (gr. 2-4). pap. (978-1-877363-67-2(7), Red Rocket Readers) Flying Start Bks.

—The Rainbow Party, 6 pack. Holden, Pam. 2009. (Red Rocket Readers Ser.). 16p. (gr. 2-4). pap. (978-1-877363-82-5(0)) Flying Start Bks.

—Surprise from the Sky, 6 pack. Holden, Pam. 2009. (Red Rocket Readers Ser.). 16p. (gr. 2-4). pap. (978-1-877363-68-9(5)) Flying Start Bks.

—Two Pirates, 6 pack. Holden, Pam. 2009. (Red Rocket Readers Ser.). 16p. (gr. 2-4). pap. (978-1-877363-71-9(5)) Flying Start Bks.

—Watch the Ball, 6 pack. Holden, Pam. 2009. (Red Rocket Readers Ser.). 16p. (gr. 2-5). pap. (978-1-877363-80-1(4)) Flying Start Bks.

Whipp, Katie. Otis & Baby Jean. Whipp, Jo. 2012. 26p. 24.95 (978-1-4626-5049-1(X)) America Star Bks.

Whipple, Rick, jt. illus. see Cowdrey, Richard.

Whipple, Rick, jt. illus. see deGroat, Diane.

Whitaker, Margaret. Stacie's Geese at Goose Lake. Whitaker, Margaret. 2005. 36p. (J). pap. 12.00 (978-0-9768051-0-6(3)) RoseFountain Pr., LLC.

Whitaker, Suzanne. Lilly & Zander: A Children's Story about Equine-Assisted Activities. Stamm, Linda J. 2014. (J). pap. (978-1-938313-03-5(8)) Graphite Pr.

Whitby, Charlotte. Dog in Danger! Black, Jess. 2013. (Animal Tales Ser.: 5). (ENG.). 92p. (J). (gr. 2-4). 7.99 (978-1-74275-336-2(1)) Random Hse. Australia AUS. Dist: Independent Pubs. Group.

—Double Trouble. Kelly, Helen. 2012. (Animal Tales Ser.: 3). (ENG.). 96p. (J). (gr. 2-4). 7.99 (978-1-74275-330-0(2)) Random Hse. Australia AUS. Dist: Independent Pubs. Group.

—Fright Night! Black, Jess. 2013. (Animal Tales Ser.: 6). (ENG.). 92p. (J). (gr. 2-4). 7.99 (978-1-74275-338-6(8)) Random Hse. Australia AUS. Dist: Independent Pubs. Group.

—Lost in Translation. Kelly, Helen. 2013. (Animal Tales Ser.: 7). (ENG.). 92p. (J). (gr. 2-4). 7.99 (978-1-74275-340-9(X)) Random Hse. Australia AUS. Dist: Independent Pubs. Group.

—The Million Paws Puppy. Kunz, Chris. 2012. (Animal Tales Ser.: 1). (ENG.). 96p. (J). (gr. 2-4). 7.99 (978-1-74275-326-3(4)) Random Hse. Australia AUS. Dist: Independent Pubs. Group.

—Race to the Finish. Harding, David. 2013. (Animal Tales Ser.: 8). (ENG.). 92p. (J). (gr. 2-4). 7.99 (978-1-74275-342-3(6)) Random Hse. Australia AUS. Dist: Independent Pubs. Group.

—Ruby's Misadventure. Kelly, Helen. 2012. (Animal Tales Ser.: 2). (ENG.). 96p. (J). (gr. 2-4). 7.99 (978-1-74275-328-7(0)) Random Hse. Australia AUS. Dist: Independent Pubs. Group.

—An Unexpected Arrival. Black, Jess. 2012. (Animal Tales Ser.: 4). (ENG.). 96p. (J). (gr. 2-4). 7.99 (978-1-74275-332-4(9)) Random Hse. Australia AUS. Dist: Independent Pubs. Group.

White, Annie. Who Am I? Yoga for Children of All Ages. Weisner, Jane Lee. 2006. 32p. (Orig.). (J). pap. 13.95 (978-0-85572-341-5(6)) Warwick Publishing CAN. Dist: Perseus Distribution.

White, Charlotte. My Bed Is a Spaceship: The Globbus. Krasner, Nick. 2013. 122p. pap. (978-1-909593-34-3(6)) Legend Pr.

White, Charlotte L., jt. illus. see Heyer, Carol.

White, Daniel, photos by. Your Safari: In Search of the Real Komodo Dragon. Truscott, Julia. 2005. 48p. (J). 11.95 (978-1-59594-014-8(6), Wingspan Pr.) WingSpan Publishing.

White, Dave. Arctic Blast. Landers, Ace. 2012. 32p. (J). (978-0-545-33455-6(1)) Scholastic, Inc.

—Cave Race! Landers, Ace. 2010. 32p. (J). (978-0-545-20871-0(8)) Scholastic, Inc.

—Hot Wheels: Wild Rides. Landers, Ace. 2009. 32p. (J). (978-0-545-15347-8(6)) Scholastic, Inc.

—Race for Treasure. Landers, Ace. 2011. 32p. (J). pap. (978-0-545-33454-9(3)) Scholastic, Inc.

—Start Your Engines. Landers, Ace. 2007. (Scholastic Reader Ser.). 32p. (J). pap. (978-0-545-02017-6(4)) Scholastic, Inc.

White, Dave, jt. illus. see Wisinski, Ed.

White, David. Body Bones. Rotner, Shelley, photos by. Rotner, Shelley. 2014. (ENG.). 32p. (J). (gr. 1-5). 16.95 (978-0-8234-3162-5(2)) Holiday Hse., Inc.

—The Daughter of Dreams, a Fable of Destiny. Barna, Beverly. 2009. 28p. pap. 14.95 (978-1-936051-09-0(5)) Peppertree Pr., The.

—Destiny's Wild Ride, a Tall Tale of the Legendary Hub Hubbell. Leipold, Judith. 2013. 32p. 24.95 (978-1-61493-168-3(2)); pap. 14.95 (978-1-61493-167-6(4)) Peppertree Pr., The.

—Kicklighter Shadow & the Beeples. Lindemann, Lindy. 2009. 24p. pap. 12.95 (978-0-9822540-9-7(1)) Peppertree Pr., The.

—No Bones about It, Skeleton Jokes. Guess, Alison. 2008. 88p. pap. 9.95 (978-0-9817572-4-7(3)) Peppertree Pr., The.

White, David A. Anakin: Space Pilot. Landers, Ace. 2011. (Lego Star Wars Ser.). (ENG.). 16p. (J). (gr. -1-3). 12.99 (978-0-545-30440-5(7)) Scholastic, Inc.

—Anakin to the Rescue! Landers, Ace. 2012. (Lego Star Wars Ser.). (ENG.). 24p. (J). (gr. -1-3). pap. 3.99 (978-0-545-47066-7(8)) Scholastic, Inc.

—Darth Maul's Mission. Landers, Ace. 2011. (Lego Star Wars Ser.). (ENG.). 24p. (J). (gr. -1-3). pap. 3.99 (978-0-545-30441-2(5)) Scholastic, Inc.

—Heroes! Cohen, Alana. 2011. (Lego City Ser.). (ENG.). 10p. (J). (gr. -1-k). bds. 9.99 (978-0-545-27439-5(7)) Scholastic, Inc.

—My Race Car. Landers, Ace. 2012. (ENG.). 12p. (J). (gr. -1 — 1). bds. 4.99 (978-0-545-43646-5(X)) Scholastic, Inc.

White, David A., jt. illus. see Rotner, Shelley.

White, Deborah. Little Visits with God. Jahsmann, Allan Hart & Simon, Martin P. 4th ed. 2006. (Little Visits Ser.). 413p. (J). (gr. 5-7). per. 13.49 (978-0-7586-0847-5(0)) Concordia Publishing Hse.

—My Name Is Erica Montoya de la Cruz. Zirin, David. 2005. (ENG.). 16p. (J). 5.75 (978-1-57274-732-6(3), 2779, Bks. for Young Learners) Owen, Richard C. Pubs., Inc.

White, Deborah J. Martin Luther. Grube, Edward C. 2012. (Hero of Faith Ser.). (ENG.). 58p. (J). pap. 7.99 (978-0-7586-3075-9(1)) Concordia Publishing Hse.

White, Frances. Mary Jane: Her Visit. Judson, Clara Ingram. 2007. 108p. per. (978-1-4065-4676-7(3)) Dodo Pr.

—Mary Jane - Her Book. Judson, Clara Ingram. 2007. 212p. 22.95 (978-1-934671-13-9(4)); per. 12.95 (978-1-934671-14-6(2)) Salem Ridge Press LLC.

—Mary Jane - Her Visit. Judson, Clara Ingram. 2008. 220p. 22.95 (978-1-934671-15-3(0)); per. 12.95 (978-1-934671-16-0(9)) Salem Ridge Press LLC.

White, Ian. Flash, Bang, Wheee! Clark, Karen. 2004. 24p. (J). (978-1-85269-280-3(4)); (978-1-85269-350-3(9)); (978-1-85269-353-4(3)); (978-1-85269-355-8(X)); (978-1-85269-356-5(8)); (978-1-85269-374-9(6)); (978-1-85269-430-2(0)); (978-1-85269-432-6(7)); (978-1-85269-433-3(5)); (978-1-85269-434-0(3)); (978-1-85269-435-7(1)); (978-1-85269-437-1(8)); (978-1-85269-438-8(6)) Mantra Lingua.

—Flash Bang Wheee! Clark, Karen. 2004. (J). (978-1-85269-678-8(8)) Mantra Lingua.

—Flash Bang Wheee! Clark, Karen. 2004. (ENG & VIE.). (J). pap. 12.95 (978-1-85269-808-9(X)) Mantra Lingua GBR. Dist: Chinasprout, Inc.

White, Ian, jt. illus. see Clark, Karen.

White, Iris Weddell. Rose Colored Glasses. Radford, Ruby Lorraine. 2011. 46p. 35.95 (978-1-258-03586-0(3)) Literary Licensing, LLC.

White, John, Jr. & Tank, Daniel. Abraham. Brand, Ruth Redding. 2004. (Family Bible Story Ser.). 109p. (J). 19.99 (978-0-8280-1856-2(1), 010-570) Review & Herald Publishing Assn.

—Abraham. 2004. (Family Bible Story Ser.). 109p. (J). pap. (978-0-8280-1857-9(X)) Review & Herald Publishing Assn.

White, Kathy. Mommy will always come Home. Summer, Laura LeClair. 2006. 35p. (J). per. 24.95 (978-1-4276-0158-2(5)) Aardvark Global Publishing.

White, Lee. Brewster the Rooster. Scillian, Devin. rev. ed. 2007. (ENG.). 32p. (J). (gr. 3-7). 16.95 (978-1-58536-311-7(1)) Sleeping Bear Pr.

—A Crazy Day at the Critter Café. Odanaka, Barbara. 2009. (ENG.). 32p. (J). (gr. -1-3). 17.99 (978-1-4169-3914-6(8), McElderry, Margaret K. Bks.) McElderry, Margaret K. Bks.

—Druscilla's Halloween. Walker, Sally M. 2009. (Carolrhoda Picture Bks). (ENG.). 32p. (J). (gr. k-3). 16.95 (978-0-8225-8941-9(9), Carolrhoda Bks.) Lerner Publishing Group.

—I Lived on Butterfly Hill. Agosín, Marjorie. 2014. (ENG.). 464p. (J). (gr. 5-9). 17.99 (978-1-4169-5344-9(2), Atheneum Bks. for Young Readers) Simon & Schuster Children's Publishing.

—I'll Do It Later. Ribke, Simone T. (Rookie Ready to Learn Ser.). (J). 2011. 40p. (gr. -1-k). pap. 5.95 (978-0-531-26710-3(5)); 2011. 40p. (gr. -1-k). lib. bdg. 23.00 (978-0-531-26528-4(5)); 2005. (ENG.). 32p. (gr. k-2). lib. bdg. 19.50 (978-0-516-24861-5(8)) Scholastic Library Publishing. (Children's Pr.).

—The Library Ghost. Weatherford, Carole Boston. 2008. 22p. (J). (gr. -1-3). 17.95 (978-1-60213-017-3(5), Upstart Bks.) Highsmith Inc.

—The Lost Track of Time. Britt, Paige. 2015. (ENG.). 320p. (J). (gr. 3-7). 17.99 (978-0-545-53812-1(2), Scholastic Pr.) Scholastic, Inc.

—The Maine Coon's Haiku: And Other Poems for Cat Lovers. Rosen, Michael J. 2015. (ENG.). 56p. (J). (gr. 1-4). 17.99 (978-0-7636-6492-3(8)) Candlewick Pr.

—Sophie's Fish. Cannon, A. E. 2012. (ENG.). 32p. (J). (gr. -1-k). 15.99 (978-0-670-01291-6(2), Viking Juvenile) Penguin Publishing Group.

—Stop That Nose!, 1 vol. Levine, Martha Peaslee. 2006. (ENG.). 32p. (J). (gr. -1-3). 14.95 (978-0-7614-5280-5(X)) Marshall Cavendish Corp.

White, Lee, et al. Tales of Leafy Lane. White, Janet. 2007. 88p. per. (978-1-84748-196-2(5)) Athena Pr.

White, Leslie. Disbelief 101: A Young Person's Guide to Atheism. Hitchcock, S. C. & Flynn, Tom. 2009. (ENG.). 112p. (gr. 9-18). pap. 9.95 (978-1-884365-47-8(7)) See Sharp Pr.

White, Mack. Texas Tales Illustrated: The Revolution. Kearby, Mike. 2011. (Texas Tales Illustrated Ser.: 1). (ENG.). 32p. (J). (gr. k-7). pap. 6.95 (978-0-87565-429-4(0)) Texas Christian Univ. Pr.

—Texas Tales Illustrated — 1A: The Revolution. Kearby, Mike. ed. 2011. (Texas Tales Illustrated Ser.: 1). (ENG.). 32p. (J). (gr. k-7). pap. 6.95 (978-0-87565-439-3(8)) Texas Christian Univ. Pr.

White, Mack. The Trail Drives, No. 2. Kearby, Mike. 2015. (Texas Tales Illustrated Ser.). (ENG.). 24p. pap. 5.95 (978-0-87565-608-3(0)) Texas Christian Univ. Pr.

White, Marsha. Bear's New Classes. White, Marsha. 16p. (J). 10.95 (978-1-58117-294-2(X), Intervisual/Piggy Toes) Bendon, Inc.

White, Mia. Careful- Not to HURT MY BABY, LOVE. White, Mia. 2007. per. 35.00 (978-1-60361-714-7(0)) Belle Media International, Inc.

—CAREFUL, YOU Could HURT the DOLPHINS - Zoe's World Dr. Mia White. White, Mia. 2007. per. 24.00 (978-1-60361-710-9(8)) Belle Media International, Inc.

—Femme FATALE - When Good Girls Are Caught in BAD Situations they become Femme Fatales: Vamp. White, Mia. 2009. pap. 40.00 incl. DVD (978-1-60361-203-6(3)) Belle Media International, Inc.

—VAMP -Chronicles - Pin up Heros don't become BaD: Vamp Series 2 the Golden Vessel. White, Mia. 2009. (978-1-60361-201-2(7)) Belle Media International, Inc.

—VAMP Courtesan - Beauties in Tough Spots an Historic Graphic Novel: Vamp's Adventures Time Travel Chronicles. White, Mia. 2009. pap. 35.00 (978-1-60361-202-9(5), Holmes Bookshop) Belle Lumiere True News.

White, Michael. Sandy Claws & Chris Mouse. Shope, Ray & Shope, Lois. 2003. 32p. (J). 13.95 (978-0-9714734-0-9(4)) Flutter-By Productions.

White, Michael P. The Library Dragon, 1 vol. Deedy, Carmen Agra. 2012. (ENG.). 32p. (J). 19.95 (978-1-56145-639-0(X)) Peachtree Pubs.

—Return of the Library Dragon, 1 vol. Deedy, Carmen Agra. 2012. (ENG.). 32p. (J). 16.95 (978-1-56145-621-5(7)) Peachtree Pubs.

White, Michelle. Twinkle the Tooth Fairy. Ellsworth, Nick. 32p. (J). 5.98 (978-0-7525-7628-2(3)) Parragon, Inc.

White, Nonie H. D. The Woodpecker Who Suffered from Headaches. White, Nonie H. D. 2006. (J). pap. 14.95 (978-0-9786147-0-6(4)) Westside Studio.

White, Rachel. The Perfect Gift. Huppert, Susan. 2007. 24p. (J). per. (978-0-9799635-0-6(8)) Homegrown Pubns.,LLC.

White, Siobhán. Chaya & the Spider Gem. Rankin, H. L. 2011. 152p. (YA). pap. 9.95 (978-2-930583-10-5(X)) White & MacLean Publishing BEL. Dist: Gardners Bks. Ltd.

White, Tara B. A Wish for Little Tommy Turtle. Hughes, John P. 2011. 48p. pap. 24.95 (978-1-4626-0011-3(5)) America Star Bks.

White, Teagan. Bunny Roo, I Love You. Marr, Melissa. 2015. (ENG.). 32p. (J). (gr. -1 — 1). 16.99 (978-0-399-16742-3(0)) Penguin Publishing Group.

—Immortal Lycanthropes. Johnson, Hal. 2012. (ENG.). 304p. (J). (gr. 7). 16.99 (978-0-547-75196-2(6)) Houghton Mifflin Harcourt Publishing Co.

—Perfect Ruin. DeStefano, Lauren. 2013. (Internment Chronicles Ser.: 1). (ENG.). 368p. (YA). (gr. 7). 18.99 (978-1-4424-8061-2(0), Simon & Schuster Bks. For Young Readers) Simon & Schuster Bks. For Young Readers.

—Perfect Ruin. DeStefano, Lauren. 2013. (Internment Chronicles Ser.: 1). (ENG.). 368p. (YA). (gr. 7). pap. 10.99 (978-1-4814-1538-5(7)) Simon & Schuster Children's Publishing.

White, Timothy. A Kayak Full of Ghosts. Millman, Lawrence. 2004. (International Folk Tales Ser.). (ENG.). 208p. pap. 13.95 (978-1-56656-525-7(1)) Interlink Publishing Group, Inc.

White, Tina Jorgenson. Turtle's Journey, 1 vol. Briceno, Carole. 2009. 28p. pap. 24.95 (978-1-60813-934-7(4)) America Star Bks.

White, Tracy. How I Made It to Eighteen: A Mostly True Story. White, Tracy. 2010. (ENG.). 160p. (YA). (gr. 9-13). 21.99 (978-1-59643-454-7(6)) Roaring Brook Pr.

White, Trudy. Could You? Would You? White, Trudy. 2007. (ENG.). 96p. (Orig.). (J). (gr. k-6). pap. 9.99 (978-1-933605-45-6(6)) Kane Miller.

White, Vicky. Ape. Jenkins, Martin. (ENG.). 48p. (J). (gr. -1-2). 2010. pap. 7.99 (978-0-7636-4974-6(0)); 2007. 16.99 (978-0-7636-3471-1(9)) Candlewick Pr.

—Can We Save the Tiger? Jenkins, Martin. (ENG.). 56p. (J). (gr. k-3). 2014. 9.99 (978-0-7636-7378-9(1)); 2011. 16.99 (978-0-7636-4909-8(0)) Candlewick Pr.

Whitehead, Jenny. Punctuation Celebration. Bruno, Elsa Knight. 2012. (ENG.). 32p. (J). (gr. 1-4). pap. 6.99 (978-1-250-00335-5(0)) Square Fish.

Whitehead, Jenny. You're a Crab! A Moody Day Book. Whitehead, Jenny. 2015. (ENG.). 32p. (J). (gr. -1-2). 16.99 (978-0-8050-9361-2(3), Holt, Henry & Co. Bks. For Young Readers) Holt, Henry & Co.

Whitehead, Jerry. Pomiuk, Prince of the North. Walsh, Alice. 2006. (ENG.). 64p. (J). (gr. 3). pap., tchr. ed. 6.95 (978-0-88878-447-6(3)) Dundurn CAN. Dist: Ingram Pub. Services.

Whitehead, Paul. Where's the Chick? Counting Book. Auerbach, Annie. 2005. (J). bds. 14.99 (978-0-9767325-5-6(6)) Toy Quest.

Whitehead, Pete. The Adventures of a Plastic Bottle: A Story about Recycling. Inches, Alison. 2009. (Little Green Bks.). (ENG.). 24p. (J). (gr. -1-1). pap. 3.99 (978-1-4169-6788-0(5), Little Simon) Little Simon.

—Mostly Ink & Wink. 2008. (I'm Going to Read#174; Ser.). (ENG.). 32p. (J). (gr. 1-2). pap. 3.95 (978-1-4027-5544-6(9)) Sterling Publishing Co., Inc.

—Must Be Santa. Moore, Tim. 2011. (Big Little Golden Book Ser.). (ENG.). 32p. (J). (gr. -1-2). 8.99 (978-0-375-86853-5(4), Golden Bks.) Random Hse. Children's Bks.

—Scooters. 2006. (I'm Going to Read(r) Ser.). (ENG.). 32p. (J). (gr. k-1). pap. 3.95 (978-1-4027-3077-1(2)) Sterling Publishing Co., Inc.

Whitehead, Pete & Chambers, Mark L. The Adventures of an Aluminum Can: A Story about Recycling. Inches, Alison. 2009. (Little Green Bks.). (ENG.). 24p. (J). (gr. -1-1). pap. 3.99 (978-1-4169-7221-1(8), Little Simon) Little Simon.

Whitehead, S. B. If Roast Beef Could Fly. Leno, Jay. 2005. 30p. (J). (gr. k-4). 18.00 (978-0-7567-9365-4(3)) DIANE Publishing Co.

Whitehouse, Ben. Sasha Sings: Understanding Parts of a Sentence. Meister, Cari. 2015. (Language on the Loose Ser.). (ENG.). 24p. (gr. 2-4). pap. 7.95 (978-1-4795-6968-7(2)) Picture Window Bks.

Whitehurst, John, et al. Bells Goes to the Fair. Knapp, Susan. l.t. ed. 2003. 40p. (J). (gr. -1-3). 12.95 (978-1-888223-34-7(0)) McMillen Publishing.

Whiteside, Randy. Travis & the Courageous Path: [Black & White Edition]. Whiteside, Randy. 2010. (ENG.). 78p. pap. 9.95 *(978-1-4564-0554-0(3))* CreateSpace Independent Publishing Platform.

Whitethorne, Bahe, Jr. Keepers of the WindClaw Chronicles: The Day of Storms, 3 vols., Vol. 2. Muller, Seth. Dubay, Tayloe, ed. 2nd ed. 2010. 224p. (J). pap. 12.95 *(978-1-893354-10-4(5))* Salina Bookshelf Inc.

—Keepers of the WindClaw Chronicles: The Mockingbird's Manual. Muller, Seth. Tayloe, McConnell Dubay, ed. 2009. (ENG.). 128p. (J). (gr. 4-7). pap. 12.95 *(978-1-893354-04-3(0))* Salina Bookshelf Inc.

—Learn along with Ashkii: First Grade Level 1. Ruffenach, Jessie E. et al. 2003. (NAV & ENG.). 16p. (J). (gr. -1-3). pap. 7.95 *(978-1-893354-41-8(5))* Salina Bookshelf Inc.

—Learn along with Ashkii: First Grade Level 2. Ruffenach, Jessie E. et al. 2003. (NAV & ENG.). 16p. (J). (gr. -1-3). pap. 7.95 *(978-1-893354-42-5(3))* Salina Bookshelf Inc.

—Learn along with Ashkii: Second Grade Level 1. Ruffenach, Jessie E. et al. 2003. (ENG & NAV.). 16p. (J). (gr. -1-3). pap. 7.95 *(978-1-893354-43-2(1))* Salina Bookshelf Inc.

—Learn along with Ashkii: Second Grade Level 2. Ruffenach, Jessie E. et al. 2003. (NAV & ENG.). 16p. (J). (gr. -1-3). pap. 7.95 *(978-1-893354-44-9(X))* Salina Bookshelf Inc.

—Learn along with Ashkii: Third Grade Level 1. Ruffenach, Jessie E. et al. 2003. (NAV & ENG.). 16p. (J). (gr. 4-7). pap. 7.95 *(978-1-893354-45-6(8))* Salina Bookshelf Inc.

—Learn along with Ashkii: Third Grade Level 2. Ruffenach, Jessie E. et al. 2003. (NAV & ENG.). 16p. (J). (gr. 4-7). pap. 7.95 *(978-1-893354-46-3(6))* Salina Bookshelf Inc.

Whitethorne, Bahe, Jr., jt. illus. see Whitethorne, Billy.

Whitethorne, Baje, Sr. Beauty Beside Me: Stories of My Grandmother's Skirts. Yazzie, Seraphine G. Ruffenach, Jessie Eve, ed. 2011. (NAV & ENG.). 32p. (J). (gr. -1-3). 17.95 *(978-1-893354-77-7(6))* Salina Bookshelf Inc.

Whitethorne, Baje. Little Black, a Pony: Lilshzhiin Yazhi. Farley, Walter. Carr, Elsie, tr. 2006. (ENG & NAV.). 64p. (J). (gr. 4-7). 21.95 *(978-1-893354-90-6(3))* Salina Bookshelf Inc.

Whitethorne, Billy. The Navajo Year, Walk Through Many Seasons. Flood, Nancy Bo. 2006. (ENG.). 32p. (J). (gr. 4-7). 17.95 *(978-1-893354-06-7(7))* Salina Bookshelf Inc.

Whitethorne, Billy & Whitethorne, Bahe, Jr. The Navajo Year, Walk Through Many Seasons: Activities for Learning & Exploring. Flood, Nancy Bo. Ruffenach, Jessie E., ed. 2006. (ENG.). 48p. (J). (gr. 4-7). pap. 7.95 *(978-1-893354-98-2(9))* Salina Bookshelf Inc.

Whitfield, Eric. Sometimes, MS Is Yucky. Harrold, Kimberly. 2005. (ENG.). 40p. (J). pap. 12.95 *(978-1-59630-006-4(X)*, 1-59630-006-X) Science & Humanities Pr.

Whitfield, Eric T. Aunt Katie's Visit: A Child's First Book on Disabilities. Banister, Katie Rodriguez & Banister, Steve. 2003. (J). 16.99 *(978-0-9744906-0-9(6))* Access-4-All, Inc.

Whitfirld, Eric. Peggy: And Other Enchanting Character-Building Stories for Smar Boys Who Want to Grow up to Be Strong Men. Showstack, Richard. 2004. 200p. (YA). per. 14.95 *(978-1-888725-66-7(4)*, BeachHouse Bks.) Science & Humanities Pr.

Whiting, Sandra. Sir Waltie of Shoe. Shoemaker, Sharon. 2004. (J). per. 12.95 *(978-0-9759499-0-0(X))* Water Shoe Pr.

Whitlatch, Jessica A. A New Day - a New Beginning: All about a Day on the Farm. Dalton, Sherry A. 2011. 40p. pap. 24.95 *(978-1-4560-7462-3(8))* America Star Bks.

Whitlock, Matt. Cranky Pants. Sanzo, Stephen. 2008. (ENG.). 32p. (J). 16.95 *(978-0-9759627-0-1(1))* Cranky Pants Publishing, LLC.

—Snoopy's Happy Day: A Finger Puppet Book. Cider Mill Press, Cider Mill & Abramson, Andra. 2015. (ENG.). 16p. (J). (gr. -1). bds. 9.99 *(978-1-60433-545-3(9)*, Applesauce Pr.) Cider Mill Pr. Bk. Pubs., LLC.

Whitlock, Matt. Punk 'n Patch. Whitlock, Matt. 2005. 32p. (J). (gr. -1-3). 16.95 *(978-0-9769057-0-7(1))* Little Hero.

—Punk's Christmas Carol: A Punk 'n Patch Book. Whitlock, Matt. 2006. 32p. (J). (gr. -1-3). 16.95 *(978-0-9769057-1-4(X))* Little Hero.

Whitlow, Steve. God Bless My Boo Boo, 1 vol. Hall, Hannah C. 2015. (ENG.). 20p. (J). pap. 9.99 *(978-0-7180-3051-3(6))* Nelson, Thomas Inc.

Whitlow, Steve. God Bless Our Fall, 1 vol. Hall, Hannah C. 2015. (ENG.). 20p. (J). bds. 9.99 ***(978-0-529-12333-6(9))*** Nelson, Thomas Inc.

Whitlow, Steve. The Story of Easter, 1 vol. Dowley, Tim & David, Juliet. 2010. (ENG.). 24p. (J). (gr. -1). bds. 7.99 *(978-1-85985-174-6(6)*, Candle Bks.) Lion Hudson PLC GBR. Dist: Kregel Pubns.

Whitman, Candace. Red, Yellow, Blue & You. Vance, Cynthia. 2008. (My First Colors Ser.). (ENG.). 30p. (J). (gr. -1-k). 8.95 *(978-0-7892-0969-6(1))* Abbeville Pr., Inc.

Whitman, Diana McManus. Finding Kyle Some Style, 1 vol. Guilmette, Patty. 2009. 32p. pap. 24.95 *(978-1-60703-962-4(1))* America Star Bks.

Whitman, Jennifer. Never Enough Frogs, 1 vol. Tessin, Kit Elaine. 2009. 19p. pap. 24.95 *(978-1-60836-185-4(3))* America Star Bks.

Whitmire, Anna. Snowflake. Taylor, Clif. 2010. (J). *(978-1-886769-97-7(4))* Gold Leaf Pr.

Whitmore, Yvette. Dare to Be... Martin Luther King Jr. Alexander, Florence. 2003. (ENG & SPA.). 17p. (J). 3.99 *(978-0-915960-65-1(6))* Ebon Research Systems Publishing, LLC.

Whitney, Caffy. Small Talks on Big Questions Vol. 1: A Historical Companion to the Children's Catechism, 2 vols. Helms, Selah et al. 2003. 216p. 26.99 *(978-1-894400-02-2(X))* Joshua Pr., Inc. CAN. Dist: Gabriel Resources.

—Small Talks on Big Questions Vol. 2: A Historical Companion to the Children's Catechism, 2 vols. Helms, Selah & Thompson, Susan. 2003. 192p. 26.99 *(978-1-894400-05-3(4))* Joshua Pr., Inc. CAN. Dist: Gabriel Resources.

Whitsett, Darron. Princess Joy. Warren, Johnette. 2013. (Princess Joy Ser.). 34p. pap. 16.00 *(978-0-615-74323-3(4))* Princess Joy.

Whitt, Carlynn. Camp Wonderful Wild, 0 vols. Snyder, Laurel. 2013. (ENG.). (J). (gr. -1-3). 17.99 *(978-1-4778-1652-3(6)*, 9781477816523, Amazon Children's Publishing) Amazon Publishing.

—There's a Baby in There!, 0 vols. Mackall, Dandi Daley. 2012. (ENG.). 32p. (J). (gr. -1-3). 16.99 *(978-0-7614-6191-3(4)*, 9780761461913, Amazon Children's Publishing) Amazon Publishing.

Whitt, Shannon. Shakespeare's Seasons. Weiner, Miriam. 2012. (ENG.). 32p. (J). (gr. -1). 16.99 *(978-1-935703-57-0(9))* Downtown Bookworks.

Whittaker, Kay. The Imagineer (Fire Eye Edition) A Book of Miracles. Ashe, Gregory. 3rd ed. 2005. 198p. pap. *(978-1-905532-01-8(6))* Humdrumming, Ltd.

—The Imagineer (Snow Scene Edition) A Book of Miracles. Ashe, Gregory. 2nd ed. 2005. 198p. (YA). pap. *(978-1-905532-00-1(8))* Humdrumming, Ltd.

Whittaker, Stephen. The Crones. Blevins, James. 2008. 36p. pap. 24.95 *(978-1-60610-259-6(1))* America Star Bks.

Whittemore, Constance. The Lonesome Gnome. Hudson, Arthur K. 2011. 28p. pap. 35.95 *(978-1-258-09570-3(X))* Literary Licensing, LLC.

Whitten, Samantha & Lee, Jeannie. How to Draw Manga Chibis & Cute Critters. 2013. (Walter Foster Studio Ser.). 128p. (J). (gr. 3-8). 35.65 *(978-1-936309-93-1(9))* Quarto Publishing Group USA.

Whittingham, Kim. Six-Minute Nature Experiments. Brynie, Faith Hickman. 2006. 80p. (J). (gr. 4-8). reprint ed. pap. 11.00 *(978-1-4223-5105-5(X))* DIANE Publishing Co.

Whittingham, Wendy. Miss Wondergem's Dreadfully Dreadful Pie, 1 vol. Sherrard, Valerie. 2011. (ENG.). 32p. (J). (gr. k-5). pap. 9.95 *(978-1-897174-81-4(0)*, Tuckamore Bks) Creative Bk. Publishing CAN. Dist: Orca Bk. Pubs. USA.

Whittington, Vi. When Grandpa Was a Kid: A Typical Farm Boy Growing up in the 40's & 50's. Brand, Joe. 2011. (ENG.). 156p. pap. 8.95 *(978-1-4565-9863-1(5))* CreateSpace Independent Publishing Platform.

Whitty, Hannah. Little Bit of Love. Platt, Cynthia. 2011. 32p. (J). (gr. -1-2). 15.95 *(978-1-58925-095-6(8))*; pap. 7.95 *(978-1-58925-426-8(0))* Tiger Tales.

—A Woodland Christmas Tale: Lift the Flap for Every Day of Advent. 2012. (ENG.). 8p. (J). (gr. -1-k). bds. 8.99 *(978-0-7641-6539-9(9))* Barron's Educational Series, Inc.

Whitworth, Christy. Come Back, o Tiger! A Jataka Tale. 2012. *(978-1-60103-015-3(0))* Buddhist Text Translation Society.

Who, Carrie Lou. Sean Michael K. Whistles the Wrong Way! Klitzner, Irene. 2011. 48p. (J). 18.95 *(978-0-692-01275-8(3))* Attitude Pie Publishing.

Whyte, Alice. A Tree in the Garden: A New Vision. Oren, Miriam & Schram, Peninnah. 2004. vii, 55p. pap. *(978-0-9752958-0-9(2))* Nora Hse.

Whyte, Hugh. Rock Steady: A Story of Noah's Ark. 2006. 28p. (J). (gr. k-4). reprint ed. 17.00 *(978-1-4223-5556-5(X))* DIANE Publishing Co.

Whyte, Mary. Chestnut, 1 vol. McGeorge, Constance W. 2004. (ENG.). 32p. (J). 16.95 *(978-1-56145-321-4(8))* Peachtree Pubs.

Whytock, Cherry. My Cup Runneth Over: The Life of Angelica Cookson Potts. Whytock, Cherry. 2012. (ENG.). 192p. (YA). (gr. 7). pap. 9.99 *(978-1-4424-6055-3(5)*, Simon Pulse) Simon Pulse.

—My Scrumptious Scottish Dumplings: The Life of Angelica Cookson Potts. Whytock, Cherry. 2006. (ENG.). 192p. (YA). mass mkt. 5.99 *(978-0-689-86552-7(X)*, Simon Pulse) Simon Pulse.

Wiacek, Bob, et al. The Boston Massacre. Burgan, Michael & Hoena, Blake A. 2005. (Graphic History Ser.). (ENG.). 32p. (gr. 3-4). 29.99 *(978-0-7368-4368-3(X)*, Graphic Library) Capstone Pr., Inc.

Wiacek, Bob. More Simple Science Fair Projects: Grades 3-5. Tocci, Salvatore. 2006. (Scientific American Science Fair Projects Ser.). 48p. (gr. 3-5). lib. bdg. 27.00 *(978-0-7910-9055-8(8))* Facts On File, Inc.

Wiacek, Bob, et al. Nat Turner's Slave Rebellion, 1 vol. Burgan, Michael & Hoena, Blake A. 2006. (Graphic History Ser.). (ENG.). 32p. (gr. 3-4). 29.99 *(978-0-7368-5490-0(8)*, Graphic Library) Capstone Pr., Inc.

Wick, Walter. A Christmas Tree. Marzollo, Jean. 2010. (I Spy Ser.). (ENG.). 24p. (J). (gr. -1-3). 9.99 *(978-0-545-22092-7(0)*, Cartwheel Bks.) Scholastic, Inc.

—Four Picture Riddle Books. Marzollo, Jean. 2005. (Scholastic Reader Level 1 Ser.). (ENG.). 128p. (J). (gr. -1-3). 6.99 *(978-0-439-76309-7(6)*, Cartwheel Bks.) Scholastic, Inc.

—I Spy a Balloon. Marzollo, Jean. 2006. (Scholastic Reader Level 1 Ser.). (ENG.). 32p. (J). (gr. -1-3). mass mkt. 3.99 *(978-0-439-73864-4(4)*, Cartwheel Bks.) Scholastic, Inc.

—I Spy a Butterfly. Marzollo, Jean. 2007. (Scholastic Reader Level 1 Ser.). (ENG.). 32p. (J). (gr. -1-3). pap. 3.99 *(978-0-439-73865-1(2)*, Cartwheel Bks.) Scholastic, Inc.

—I Spy a Dinosaur's Eye. Marzollo, Jean. 2003. (Scholastic Reader Level 1 Ser.). (ENG.). 32p. (J). (gr. -1-3). pap. 3.99 *(978-0-439-52471-1(7)*, Cartwheel Bks.) Scholastic, Inc.

—I Spy a Funny Frog. Marzollo, Jean. 2012. (I Spy Ser.). (ENG.). 32p. (J). (gr. -1-k). pap. 3.99 *(978-0-545-41581-1(0))* Scholastic, Inc.

—I Spy a Penguin. Marzollo, Jean. 2005. (Scholastic Reader Level 1 Ser.). (ENG.). 32p. (J). (gr. -1-3). pap. 3.99 *(978-0-439-73862-0(8)*, Cartwheel Bks.) Scholastic, Inc.

—I Spy a Skeleton. Marzollo, Jean. 2010. (Scholastic Reader Level 1 Ser.). (ENG.). 32p. (J). (gr. -1-1). 3.99 *(978-0-545-17539-5(9))* Scholastic, Inc.

—I Spy an Apple. Marzollo, Jean. 2011. (Scholastic Reader Level 1 Ser.). (ENG.). 32p. (J). (gr. -1-2). pap. 3.99 *(978-0-545-22095-8(5)*, Cartwheel Bks.) Scholastic, Inc.

—I Spy Animals. Marzollo, Jean. 2012. (I Spy Ser.). (ENG.). 32p. (J). (gr. -1-k). pap. 3.99 *(978-0-545-41583-5(7))* Scholastic, Inc.

—I Spy Imagine That! Marzollo, Jean & Scholastic / LeapFrog. 2008. (J). 13.99 *(978-1-59319-933-3(3))* LeapFrog Enterprises, Inc.

—I Spy Letters. Marzollo, Jean. 2012. (I Spy Ser.). (ENG.). 32p. (J). (gr. -1-k). pap. 3.99 *(978-0-545-41584-2(5))* Scholastic, Inc.

—I Spy Lightning in the Sky. Marzollo, Jean. 2005. (Scholastic Reader Level 1 Ser.). (ENG.). 32p. (J). (gr. -1-3). pap. 3.99 *(978-0-439-68052-3(2)*, Cartwheel Bks.) Scholastic, Inc.

—I Spy Little Hearts. Marzollo, Jean. 2009. (I Spy Ser.). (ENG.). 26p. (J). (gr. -1-k). bds. 6.99 *(978-0-545-08917-3(4)*, Cartwheel Bks.) Scholastic, Inc.

—I Spy Merry Christmas. Marzollo, Jean. 2007. (Scholastic Reader Level 1 Ser.). (ENG.). 64p. (J). (gr. -1-3). pap. 5.99 *(978-0-545-03945-1(2)*, Cartwheel Bks.) Scholastic, Inc.

—I Spy Numbers. Marzollo, Jean. 2012. (I Spy Ser.). (ENG.). 32p. (J). (gr. -1-k). pap. 3.99 *(978-0-545-41585-9(3))* Scholastic, Inc.

—I Spy Santa Claus. Marzollo, Jean. 2006. (Scholastic Reader Level 1 Ser.). (ENG.). 32p. (J). (gr. -1-3). per. 3.99 *(978-0-439-78414-6(X))* Scholastic, Inc.

—I Spy Spectacular: A Book of Picture Riddles. Marzollo, Jean. 2011. (I Spy Ser.). (ENG.). 40p. (J). 13.99 *(978-0-545-22278-5(8)*, Cartwheel Bks.) Scholastic, Inc.

—I Spy Thanksgiving. Marzollo, Jean. 2011. (Scholastic Reader Level 1 Ser.). (ENG.). 32p. (J). (gr. -1-2). pap. 3.99 *(978-0-545-22094-1(7)*, Cartwheel Bks.) Scholastic, Inc.

—Little Bunnies. Marzollo, Jean. 2006. (I Spy Ser.). (ENG.). 24p. (J). (gr. k — 1). bds. 6.99 *(978-0-439-78535-8(9)*, Cartwheel Bks.) Scholastic, Inc.

—A Pumpkin. Marzollo, Jean. 2006. (Scholastic Reader Level 1 Ser.). (ENG.). 32p. (J). (gr. -1-3). pap. 3.99 *(978-0-439-73863-7(6)*, Cartwheel Bks.) Scholastic, Inc.

—Scholastic Reader Level 1: I Spy School. Marzollo, Jean. 2012. (Scholastic Reader Level 1 Ser.). (ENG.). 32p. (J). (gr. -1-3). pap. 3.99 *(978-0-545-40281-1(6)*, Cartwheel Bks.) Scholastic, Inc.

—School Bus. Marzollo, Jean. 2003. (Scholastic Reader Level 1 Ser.). (ENG.). 32p. (J). (gr. -1-3). pap. 3.99 *(978-0-439-52473-5(3)*, Cartwheel Bks.) Scholastic, Inc.

—Sticker Book & Picture Riddles. Marzollo, Jean. 2012. (I Spy Ser.). (ENG.). 400p. (J). (gr. -1-3). pap. 10.99 *(978-0-545-39074-3(5)*, Cartwheel Bks.) Scholastic, Inc.

—A to Z: A Book of Picture Riddles. Marzollo, Jean. 2009. (I Spy Ser.). (ENG.). 56p. (J). (gr. -1-3). 13.99 *(978-0-545-10782-2(2)*, Cartwheel Bks.) Scholastic, Inc.

—Ultimate Challenger! A Book of Picture Riddles. Marzollo, Jean. 2003. (I Spy Ser.). (ENG.). 40p. (J). (gr. -1-3). pap. 13.99 *(978-0-439-45401-8(8)*, Cartwheel Bks.) Scholastic, Inc.

Wick, Walter. Can You See What I See? Animals. Wick, Walter. 2007. (Scholastic Reader Level 1 Ser.). (ENG.). 32p. (J). (gr. -1-3). pap. 3.99 *(978-0-439-86227-1(2))* Scholastic, Inc.

—Can You See What I See? Dream Machine. Wick, Walter. 2003. (Can You See What I See? Ser.). (ENG.). 40p. (J). (gr. -1-3). 13.99 *(978-0-439-39950-0(5)*, Cartwheel Bks.) Scholastic, Inc.

—Can You See What I See? - Christmas Read-and-Seek. Wick, Walter. 2008. (Scholastic Reader Level 1 Ser.). (ENG.). 32p. (J). (gr. -1-3). pap. 3.99 *(978-0-545-07887-0(3))* Scholastic, Inc.

—On a Scary Scary Night: Picture Puzzles to Search & Solve. Wick, Walter. 2008. (Can You See What I See? Ser.). (ENG.). 40p. (J). (gr. -1-3). 13.99 *(978-0-439-70870-8(2))* Scholastic, Inc.

—Optical Tricks. Wick, Walter. 10th anniv. ed. 2008. (ENG.). 48p. (J). (gr. -1-3). 14.99 *(978-0-439-85520-4(9)*, Cartwheel Bks.) Scholastic, Inc.

—Picture Puzzles to Search & Solve. Wick, Walter. 2004. (Can You See What I See? Ser.). (ENG.). 40p. (J). (gr. -1-18). 13.99 *(978-0-439-61772-7(3)*, Cartwheel Bks.) Scholastic, Inc.

—Seymour & the Juice Box Boat. Wick, Walter. 2004. (Can You See What I See? Ser.). (ENG.). 32p. (J). (gr. -1-k). 8.99 *(978-0-439-61778-9(2)*, Scholastic Paperbacks) Scholastic, Inc.

—Seymour Makes New Friends. Wick, Walter. 2006. (Can You See What I See? Ser.). (ENG.). 32p. (J). (gr. -1-k). 8.99 *(978-0-439-61780-2(4))* Scholastic, Inc.

—Treasure Ship: Picture Puzzles to Search & Solve. Wick, Walter. 2010. (Can You See What I See? Ser.). (ENG.). 40p. (J). 13.99 *(978-0-439-02643-7(1)*, Cartwheel Bks.) Scholastic, Inc.

Wick, Walter. I Spy: A Scary Monster. Wick, Walter, photos by. Marzollo, Jean. 2005. (Scholastic Reader Level 1 Ser.). (ENG.). 32p. (J). (gr. -1-3). pap. 3.99 *(978-0-439-68054-7(9)*, Cartwheel Bks.) Scholastic, Inc.

—I Spy a Candy Can. Wick, Walter, photos by. Marzollo, Jean. 2004. (Scholastic Reader Level 1 Ser.). (ENG.). 32p. (J). (gr. -1-3). pap. 3.99 *(978-0-439-52474-2(1)*, Cartwheel Bks.) Scholastic, Inc.

Wick, Walter. I Spy Adventure: 4 Picture Riddle Books. Wick, Walter, photos by. Marzollo, Jean. 2012. (J). ***(978-1-4351-3984-8(4))*** Scholastic, Inc.

Wick, Walter. I Spy an Egg in a Nest. Wick, Walter, photos by. Marzollo, Jean. 2011. (Scholastic Reader Level 1 Ser.). (ENG.). 32p. (J). (gr. -1-2). pap. 3.99 *(978-0-545-22093-4(9)*, Cartwheel Bks.) Scholastic, Inc.

—I Spy Little Toys. Wick, Walter, photos by. Marzollo, Jean. 2011. (I Spy Ser.). (ENG.). 26p. (J). (gr. -1-k). bds. 6.99 *(978-0-545-22096-5(3))* Scholastic, Inc.

Wick, Walter, photos by. C'est Moi l'Espion: Défis Suprêmes! Marzollo, Jean. Duchesne, Lucie, tr. (I Spy Bks.).Tr. of I Spy Fantasy. (FRE., 37p. (J). (gr. -1-3). pap. 16.99 *(978-0-590-24340-7(3))* Scholastic, Inc.

—C'est Moi l'Espion: Du Monde du Mystère. Marzollo, Jean. (I Spy Bks.).Tr. of I Spy Mystery: A Book of Picture Riddles. (FRE., 37p. (J). (gr. -1-3). pap. 16.99 *(978-0-590-24317-9(9))* Scholastic, Inc.

—I Spy: Interactive Sound Book of Picture Riddles. 2003. 30p. (J). 15.98 *(978-0-7853-8424-3(3))* Publications International, Ltd.

—I Spy Nature: A Book of Picture Riddles. Marzollo, Jean. 2006. (J). *(978-0-439-80732-6(8))* Scholastic, Inc.

Wick, Walter, photos by. Can You See What I See? Night Before Christmas. Wick, Walter. 2005. (Can You See What I See? Ser.). (ENG., 40p. (J). (gr. -1-3). 13.99 *(978-0-439-76927-3(2)*, Cartwheel Bks.) Scholastic, Inc.

—Can You See What I See? - 100 Fun Finds Read-and-Seek. Wick, Walter. 2009. (Scholastic Reader Level 1 Ser.). (ENG., 32p. (J). (gr. -1-3). pap. 3.99 *(978-0-545-07888-7(1)*, Cartwheel Bks.) Scholastic, Inc.

—Can You See What I See? Games. Wick, Walter. 2007. (Scholastic Reader Level 1 Ser.). (ENG., 32p. (J). (gr. -1-3). pap. 3.99 *(978-0-439-86229-5(9))* Scholastic, Inc.

—Dinosaurs. Wick, Walter. 2006. (Can You See What I See? Ser.). (ENG., 16p. (J). (gr. k — 1). bds. 5.99 *(978-0-439-83297-7(7)*, Cartwheel Bks.) Scholastic, Inc.

—Once upon a Time: Picture Puzzles to Search & Solve. Wick, Walter. 2006. (Can You See What I See? Ser.). (ENG., 40p. (J). (gr. -1-3). 13.99 *(978-0-439-61777-2(4)*, Cartwheel Bks.) Scholastic, Inc.

—Out of This World: Picture Puzzles to Search & Solve. Wick, Walter. 2013. (Can You See What I See? Ser.). (ENG., 40p. (J). (gr. -1-3). 13.99 *(978-0-545-24468-8(4)*, Cartwheel Bks.) Scholastic, Inc.

—Toyland Express: Picture Puzzles to Search & Solve. Wick, Walter. 2011. (Can You See What I See? Ser.). (ENG., 40p. (J). 13.99 *(978-0-545-24483-1(8))* Scholastic, Inc.

—Toys - Read-and-Seek. Wick, Walter. 2008. (Can You See What I See? Ser.). (ENG., 32p. (J). (gr. -1-3). pap. 3.99 *(978-0-439-86228-8(0)*, Cartwheel Bks.) Scholastic, Inc.

—Trucks & Cars. Wick, Walter. 2007. (Can You See What I See? Ser.). (ENG., 16p. (J). (gr. k — 1). bds. 5.99 *(978-0-439-86230-1(2)*, Cartwheel Bks.) Scholastic, Inc.

Wickenden, Nadine. The Lion Book of Five-Minute Parables. Ryton, Charlotte. 2009. (ENG.). 48p. (J). (gr. k-2). 16.99 *(978-0-7459-6012-8(X))* Lion Hudson PLC GBR. Dist: Independent Pubs. Group.

—A Plastic Bottle's Journey, 1 vol. Slade, Suzanne. 2011. (Follow It! Ser.). (ENG.). 24p. (gr. 1-3). pap. 7.49 *(978-1-4048-6711-6(2)*, Nonfiction Picture Bks.) Picture Window Bks.

—The Story of Jonah. 2006. 10p. (J). (gr. k-4). reprint ed. 8.00 *(978-0-7567-9923-6(6))* DIANE Publishing Co.

Wickham, Kimberly. Angels & Horses. 2007. 128p. per. 12.85 *(978-1-4251-0215-9(8))* Trafford Publishing.

—Summer of Magic Horses. 2007. 134p. 12.85 *(978-1-4251-3012-1(7))* Trafford Publishing.

Wicks, Maris. Primates: The Fearless Science of Jane Goodall, Dian Fossey, & Biruté Galdikas. Ottaviani, Jim. 2013. (ENG.). 144p. (YA). (gr. 7). 19.99 *(978-1-59643-865-1(7)*, First Second Bks.) Roaring Brook Pr.

—Primates: The Fearless Science of Jane Goodall, Dian Fossey, & Biruté Galdikas. Ottaviani, Jim. 2015. (ENG.). 144p. (YA). (gr. 7). pap. 12.99 *(978-1-250-06293-2(4))* Square Fish.

—Yes, Let's. Longstreth, Galen Goodwin. 2013. (ENG.). 32p. (J). (gr. -1-3). 15.95 *(978-1-933718-87-3(0))* Tanglewood Pr.

Wickstrom, Sylvie, jt. illus. see Kantorovitz, Sylvie.

Wickstrom, Sylvie K. Little Witch Learns to Read. Hautzig, Deborah. 2003. (Step into Reading Ser.). (ENG.). 48p. (J). (gr. k-3). pap. 3.99 *(978-0-375-82179-0(1)*, Random Hse. Bks. for Young Readers) Random Hse. Children's Bks.

Wickstrom, Sylvie K. Loose Tooth. Wickstrom, Sylvie K., tr. Schaefer, Lola M. 2004. (My First I Can Read Bks.). 32p. (J). (gr. -1-18). 14.99 *(978-0-06-052776-1(5))* HarperCollins Pubs.

Wickstrom, Sylvie Kantorovitz. Loose Tooth. Schaefer, Lola M. 2005. (My First I Can Read Ser.). (ENG.). 32p. (J). (gr. -1-3). pap. 3.99 *(978-0-06-052778-5(1))* HarperCollins Pubs.

Wickstrom, Thor. Book Fair Day. Plourde, Lynn. 2006. (J). *(978-1-4156-8095-7(7)*, Dutton Juvenile) Penguin Publishing Group.

Widdowson, Kay. Getting Dressed. Brooks, Felicity. 2010. (Sticker Bks). 16p. (J). pap. 6.99 *(978-0-7945-2668-9(3)*, Usborne) EDC Publishing.

—Getting Dressed Magnet Book. Brooks, Felicity. 2009. (Magnet Bks). 10p. (J). bds. 19.99 *(978-0-7945-2356-5(0)*, Usborne) EDC Publishing.

—God Bless. Rock, Lois. 2010. (Prayers for Little Hands Ser.). (ENG.). 8p. (J). (gr. k — 1). bds. 8.99 *(978-0-7459-6163-7(0))* Lion Hudson PLC GBR. Dist: Independent Pubs. Group.

—God Bless. Piper, Sophie & Rock, Lois. 2nd ed. 2013. (Prayers for Little Hands Ser.). (ENG.). 8p. (J). (— 1). 8.99 *(978-0-7459-6375-4(7))* Lion Hudson PLC GBR. Dist: Independent Pubs. Group.

—Here I Am. Rock, Lois. 2nd ed. 2013. (Prayers for Little Hands Ser.). (ENG.). 8p. (J). (— 1). 8.99 *(978-0-7459-6374-7(9))* Lion Hudson PLC GBR. Dist: Independent Pubs. Group.

—I Can Go to School: An I-Can-Do-It Book. Segal, Douglas. 2007. (ENG.). 10p. (J). (gr. -1-k). bds. 10.95 *(978-1-58117-594-3(9)*, Intervisual/Piggy Toes) Bendon, Inc.

—Panda Kisses. Capucilli, Alyssa Satin. 2008. (Step into Reading Ser.). (ENG.). 32p. (J). (gr. -1-1). pap. 3.99 *(978-0-375-84562-8(3)*, Random Hse. Bks. for Young Readers) Random Hse. Children's Bks.

—Please, Mr. Crocodile. 2006. (Lift-the-Flap Books (Child's Play) Ser.). (ENG.). 24p. (J). (gr. -1-1). *(978-1-84643-025-1(9))* Child's Play International Ltd.

—Thank You, God. Rock, Lois. 2nd ed. 2013. (Prayers for Little Hands Ser.). (ENG.). 8p. (J). (— 1). 8.99 *(978-0-7459-6377-8(3))* Lion Hudson PLC GBR. Dist: Independent Pubs. Group.

—Tiny Tots Bible. Rock, Lois. 2014. (Tiny Tots Ser.). (ENG.). 128p. (J). (gr. -1-k). 12.99 *(978-0-7459-6383-9(8))* Lion Hudson PLC GBR. Dist: Independent Pubs. Group.

Widener, Leslie Stall. Chukfi Rabbit's Big, Bad Bellyache: A Trickster Tale. 2014. (ENG.). 40p. (J). (gr. k-5). 16.95 *(978-1-935955-26-9(8))* Cinco Puntos Pr.

W

Widener, Terry. America's Champion Swimmer: Gertrude Ederle. Adler, David A. 2005. (ENG.). 32p. (J). (gr. -1-3). reprint ed. pap. 7.00 *(978-0-15-205251-5(8))* Houghton Mifflin Harcourt Publishing Co.

—The Babe & I. Adler, David A. 2006. 28p. (gr. 1-4). 18.00 *(978-0-7569-6560-0(8))* Perfection Learning Corp.

—The Babe & I. Adler, David A. 2004. (ENG.). 32p. (J). (gr. -1-3). reprint ed. pap. 7.99 *(978-0-15-205026-9(4))* Houghton Mifflin Harcourt Publishing Co.

—Favorite Folk Songs. Yarrow, Peter. 2008. (ENG.). 48p. (J). (gr. k). 16.95 *(978-1-4027-5961-1(4))* Sterling Publishing Co., Inc.

Widener, Terry. Girl Wonder. Hopkinson, Deborah. 2015. 40p. pap. 8.00 ***(978-1-61003-606-1(9))*** Center for the Collaborative Classroom.

Widener, Terry. Girl Wonder: A Baseball Story in Nine Innings. Hopkinson, Deborah. 2006. (ENG.). 40p. (J). (gr. k-3). reprint ed. 7.99 *(978-1-4169-1393-1(9))*, Simon & Schuster/Paula Wiseman Bks.) Simon & Schuster/Paula Wiseman Bks.

—Let's Sing Together! Yarrow, Peter. 2009. (ENG.). 48p. (J). (gr. k). 16.95 *(978-1-4027-5963-5(0))* Sterling Publishing Co., Inc.

—The Peter Yarrow Songbook: Songs for Little Folks. Yarrow, Peter. 2010. (ENG.). 48p. (J). (gr. k-2). 16.95 *(978-1-4027-5964-2(9))* Sterling Publishing Co., Inc.

—Roy Makes a Car. Lyons, Mary E. 2014. (ENG.). 32p. (J). (gr. -1-3). 17.99 *(978-1-4814-4488-0(3)*, Atheneum Bks. for Young Readers) Simon & Schuster Children's Publishing.

—Sleepytime Songs. Yarrow, Peter. 2008. (Peter Yarrow Songbook Ser.). (ENG.). 48p. (J). (gr. k). 16.95 *(978-1-4027-5962-8(2))* Sterling Publishing Co., Inc.

—Steel Town. Winter, Jonah. 2008. (ENG.). 40p. (J). (gr. -1-3). 19.99 *(978-1-4169-4081-4(2)*, Atheneum Bks. for Young Readers) Simon & Schuster Children's Publishing.

—The Streak: How Joe DiMaggio Became America's Hero. Rosenstock, Barb. 2014. (ENG.). 32p. (J). (gr. 3). 16.95 *(978-1-59078-992-6(X)*, Calkins Creek) Boyds Mills Pr.

—The Twins & the Bird of Darkness: A Hero Tale from the Caribbean. San Souci, Robert D. ed. 2004. (J). (gr. k-3). spiral bd. *(978-0-616-14625-5(6))* Canadian National Institute for the Blind/Institut National Canadien pour les Aveugles.

—You Never Heard of Willie Mays?! Winter, Jonah. 2013. (ENG.). 40p. (J). (gr. -1-3). 17.99 *(978-0-375-86844-3(5))*; 20.99 *(978-0-375-96844-0(X))* Random Hse. Children's Bks. (Schwartz & Wade Bks.).

Widermann, Eva. Arctic Giants, 1 vol. Christopher, Neil. 2010. (ENG.). 128p. (J). (gr. 3). 24.95 *(978-1-926569-09-3(1))* Inhabit Media Inc. CAN. Dist: Independent Pubs. Group.

—The Orphan & the Polar Bear, 1 vol. Qaunaq, Sakiasi. 2011. (ENG.). 40p. (J). (gr. 1-3). 13.95 *(978-1-926569-44-4(X))* Inhabit Media Inc. CAN. Dist: Independent Pubs. Group.

Widowati, Marini. Just a Swim? Norman, Donna Marie. 2008. 29p. pap. 24.95 *(978-1-60672-182-7(8))* America Star Bks.

Wiede, Matt. Star, Circle, Baylor: A Little Bear Shapes Book, 5460 vols. 2013. (Big Bear Bks.). (ENG.). 18p. (gr. 17). bds. 9.95 *(978-1-60258-979-7(8))* Baylor Univ. Pr.

—1, 2, 3 Baylor: A Little Bear Counting Book. Big Bear Books Staff. 2012. (Big Bear Bks.). (ENG.). 18p. (gr. 17). bds. 9.95 *(978-1-60258-660-4(8))* Baylor Univ. Pr.

Wiedemer, Leah. Adventures with Pawpaw: China. Scimone, Diana. 2003. 32p. (J). 8.95 *(978-0-9729507-0-1(2))* Peapod Publishing, Inc.

—Adventures with Pawpaw: Costa Rica. Scimone, Diana. 2003. 32p. (J). 8.95 *(978-0-9729507-2-5(9))* Peapod Publishing, Inc.

—Adventures with Pawpaw: France. Scimone, Diana. 2003. (Adventures with PawPaw Ser.). 32p. (J). 8.85 *(978-0-9729507-1-8(0))* Peapod Publishing, Inc.

Wiegle, Matt. Romeo & Juliet. SparkNotes Staff. 2008. (No Fear Shakespeare Illustrated Ser.). (ENG.). 216p. (gr. 5-7). per. 9.95 *(978-1-4114-9874-7(7)*, Spark Notes) Sterling Publishing Co., Inc.

Wieringo, Mike. Fantastic Four, Vol. 1. Waid, Mark. 2004. (Fantastic Four Ser.). 368p. (YA). 29.99 *(978-0-7851-1486-4(6))* Marvel Worldwide, Inc.

—Imaginauts. Waid, Mark. 2003. (Fantastic Four Ser.: Vol. 1). 144p. (YA). pap. 12.99 *(978-0-7851-1063-7(1))* Marvel Worldwide, Inc.

—Unthinkable, 3 vols., Vol. 2. Waid, Mark. 2003. (Fantastic Four Ser.). 192p. (YA). pap. 17.99 *(978-0-7851-1111-5(5))* Marvel Worldwide, Inc.

Wieringo, Mike & Buckingham, Mike. Fantastic Four by Waid & Wieringo Ultimate Collection Book 1. 2011. (ENG.). 216p. (YA). (gr. 8-17). pap., pap. 24.99 *(978-0-7851-5655-0(0))* Marvel Worldwide, Inc.

Wieringo, Mike & Jones, Casey. Fantastic Four by Waid & Wieringo Ultimate Collection Book 2. Waid, Mark. 2011. (ENG.). 160p. (YA). (gr. 8-17). pap. 24.99 *(978-0-7851-5658-1(5))* Marvel Worldwide, Inc.

Wieringo, Mike & Smith, Paul. Fantastic Four by Waid & Wieringo Ultimate Collection Book 3. Waid, Mark & Porter, Howard. 2011. (ENG.). 272p. (YA). (gr. 8-17). pap. 24.99 *(978-0-7851-5657-4(7))* Marvel Worldwide, Inc.

Wiese, Kurt. The Blue Mittens. Reely, Mary Katharine. 2011. 164p. 41.95 *(978-1-258-10114-5(9))* Literary Licensing, LLC.

—The Clockwork Twin: A Freddy the Pig Book on Everything. Brooks, Walter R. 2013. (Freddy the Pig Ser.). (ENG.). 256p. (gr. 4-13). pap. 10.99 *(978-1-4683-0349-0(X)*, 460349) Overlook Pr., The.

—Freddy & Mr. Camphor. Brooks, Walter R. 2013. (Freddy the Pig Ser.). (ENG.). 256p. (gr. 4-13). pap. 10.99 *(978-1-4683-0666-8(9)*, 460666) Overlook Pr., The.

—Freddy & Simon the Dictator. Brooks, Walter R. (Freddy the Pig Ser.). (ENG.). (gr. 4-13). 2014. 256p. pap. 10.99 *(978-1-4683-0976-8(5)*, 460976); 2003. 220p. (J). 23.95 *(978-1-58567-359-9(5))* Overlook Pr., The.

—Freddy & the Baseball Team from Mars. Brooks, Walter R. 2011. (Freddy the Pig Ser.). (ENG.). 256p. 10.99 *(978-1-59020-696-6(7)*, 902696) Overlook Pr., The.

—Freddy & the Dragon. Brooks, Walter R. 2012. (Freddy the Pig Ser.). (ENG.). 240p. (gr. 4-13). pap. 10.99 *(978-1-59020-866-3(8)*, 902866) Overlook Pr., The.

—Freddy & the Flying Saucer Plans. Brooks, Walter R. 2013. (Freddy the Pig Ser.). (ENG.). 256p. (gr. 4-13). pap. 10.99 *(978-1-4683-0319-3(8)*, 460319) Overlook Pr., The.

—Freddy & the Ignormus. Brooks, Walter R. 2011. (Freddy the Pig Ser.). (ENG.). 288p. (gr. 4-13). pap. 10.99 *(978-1-59020-467-2(0)*, 902467) Overlook Pr., The.

—Freddy & the Men from Mars. Brooks, Walter R. 2011. (Freddy the Pig Ser.). (ENG.). 256p. 10.99 *(978-1-59020-695-9(9)*, 902695) Overlook Pr., The.

—Freddy & the North Pole. Brooks, Walter R. 2013. (Freddy the Pig Ser.). (ENG.). 322p. (gr. 4-13). pap. 10.99 *(978-1-4683-0320-9(1)*, 460320) Overlook Pr., The.

—Freddy & the Perilous Adventure. Brooks, Walter R. 2012. (Freddy the Pig Ser.). (ENG.). 256p. 10.99 *(978-1-59020-742-0(4)*, 902742) Overlook Pr., The.

—Freddy & the Popinjay. Brooks, Walter R. 2011. (ENG.). 256p. (gr. 2-18). 10.99 *(978-1-59020-468-9(9))* Overlook Pr., The.

—Freddy & the Space Ship. Brooks, Walter R. 2011. (ENG.). 272p. (gr. 2-18). 10.99 *(978-1-59020-469-6(7))* Overlook Pr., The.

—Freddy Goes Camping. Brooks, Walter R. 2014. (Freddy the Pig Ser.). (ENG.). 272p. (gr. 4-13). pap. 10.99 *(978-1-4683-0831-0(9)*, 460831) Overlook Pr., The.

—Freddy Goes Camping. Brooks, Walter R. 2003. (ENG.). 272p. (J). (gr. 3-7). pap. 8.99 *(978-0-14-230249-1(X)*, Puffin) Penguin Publishing Group.

—Freddy Goes to Florida. Brooks, Walter R. 2012. (Freddy the Pig Ser.). (ENG.). 224p. (gr. 4-13). 10.99 *(978-1-59020-741-3(6)*, 902741) Overlook Pr., The.

—Freddy Plays Football. Brooks, Walter R. 2013. (Freddy the Pig Ser.). (ENG.). 288p. (gr. 4-13). pap. 10.99 *(978-1-4683-0667-5(7)*, 460667) Overlook Pr., The.

—Freddy Rides Again. Brooks, Walter R. 2013. (Freddy the Pig Ser.). (ENG.). 240p. (gr. 4-13). pap. 10.99 *(978-1-4683-0724-5(X)*, 460724) Overlook Pr., The.

—Freddy the Cowboy. Brooks, Walter R. 2014. (Freddy the Pig Ser.). (ENG.). 240p. (gr. 4-13). pap. 10.99 *(978-1-4683-0830-3(0)*, 460830) Overlook Pr., The.

—Freddy the Detective. Brooks, Walter R. 2010. (Freddy the Pig Ser.). (ENG.). 272p. (gr. 4-13). 11.99 *(978-1-59020-418-4(2)*, 902418) Overlook Pr., The.

—Freddy the Magician. Brooks, Walter R. 2011. (Freddy the Pig Ser.). (ENG.). 224p. (gr. 4-13). pap. 10.99 *(978-1-59020-481-8(6)*, 902481) Overlook Pr., The.

—Freddy the Pied Piper. Brooks, Walter R. 2014. (Freddy the Pig Ser.). (ENG.). 272p. (gr. 4-13). pap. 10.99 *(978-1-4683-0915-7(3)*, 460915) Overlook Pr., The.

—Freddy the Pilot. Brooks, Walter R. 2012. (Freddy the Pig Ser.). (ENG.). 256p. (gr. 4-13). pap. 10.99 *(978-1-59020-867-0(6)*, 902867) Overlook Pr., The.

—Freddy's Cousin Weedly. Brooks, Walter R. 2014. (Freddy the Pig Ser.). (ENG.). 240p. (gr. 4-13). pap. 10.99 *(978-1-4683-0914-0(5)*, 460914) Overlook Pr., The.

—Silver Chief's Revenge. O'Brien, Jack. 2011. 222p. 44.95 *(978-1-258-09709-7(5))* Literary Licensing, LLC.

—Stories of Jesus. Smither, Ethel L. 2012. 82p. 37.95 *(978-1-258-23282-5(0))*; pap. 22.95 *(978-1-258-24854-3(9))* Literary Licensing, LLC.

—The Story of Freginald. Brooks, Walter R. (Freddy the Pig Ser.). (ENG.). 2014. 256p. pap. 10.99 *(978-1-4683-0975-1(7)*, 460975); 2003. 220p. (gr. 4-13). 23.95 *(978-1-58567-360-5(9)*, 856360) Overlook Pr., The.

Wiese, Kurt & Borns, Steven. Knuckleboom Loaders Load Logs: A Trip to the Sawmill. Brooks, Walter R. & Slayton-Mitchell, Joyce. 2003. (ENG.). 40p. (gr. 4-13). 16.95 *(978-1-58567-368-1(4)*, 856368) Overlook Pr., The.

Wiesner, Al. The Bubble Flight. Stoltz, Donald R. 2008. 26p. pap. 24.95 *(978-1-60672-994-6(2))* America Star Bks.

Wiesner, David. Gonna Roll the Bones. Leiber, Fritz. 2004. 32p. (J). 16.95 *(978-0-689-03591-3(8))*; *(978-0-689-03637-8(X))* ibooks, Inc. (Milk & Cookies).

—Night of the Gargoyles. Bunting, Eve. 2014. 32p. pap. 8.00 *(978-1-61003-176-9(8))* Center for the Collaborative Classroom.

Wiesner, David. Free Fall. Wiesner, David. 2008. (ENG.). 32p. (J). (gr. -1-3). 17.99 *(978-0-06-156741-4(8))* HarperCollins Pubs.

—Hurricane, 1 vol. Wiesner, David. 2008. (Read along Book & CD Ser.). (ENG.). 32p. (J). (gr. -1-3). 10.99 *(978-0-547-06433-8(0))* Houghton Mifflin Harcourt Publishing Co.

Wigal, Mike. Green Anole Meets Brown Anole, a Love Story. Escott, Maria. 2010. 28p. pap. 12.95 *(978-1-936051-82-3(6))* Peppertree Pr., The.

Wiggan, Desmond, jt. illus. see Bates, Lindsey E.

Wiggins, Margaret W. My Neighbor Is Gone. Wiggins, Leah Holder. 2006. 28p. (J). per. 17.99 *(978-0-9768579-5-2(2))* eVision, LLC.

—What was Grandma Doing? Hopkins, Nicolia. 2007. (J). per. 9.99 *(978-0-9768579-8-3(7))* eVision, LLC.

Wiggins, Mick. Boats Float! Lyon, George Ella & Lyon, Benn. 2015. (ENG.). 40p. (J). (gr. -1-3). 17.99 ***(978-1-4814-0380-1(X))*** Simon & Schuster Children's Publishing.

Wiggins, Mick. Planes Fly! Lyon, George Ella. 2013. (ENG.). 40p. (J). (gr. -1-2). 17.99 *(978-1-4424-5025-7(8))* Simon & Schuster Children's Publishing.

Wiggs, Sue. Wee-Dolph, the Tiniest Reindeer. Lester, Vivian. 22p. (J). (gr. -1-3). pap. 4.00 *(978-1-929785-01-8(1))* Connexions Unlimited.

Wight, Eric. The Disappearing Magician. Egan, Kate & Lane, Mike. 2015. (Magic Shop Ser.: 4). (ENG.). 160p. (J). (gr. 2-4). 15.99 *(978-1-250-02917-1(1))* Feiwel & Friends.

—Everyone Loves Bacon. DiPucchio, Kelly. 2015. (ENG.). 40p. (J). (gr. -1-1). 17.99 *(978-0-374-30052-4(6)*, Farrar, Straus & Giroux (BYR)) Farrar, Straus & Giroux.

—The Great Escape. Egan, Kate & Lane, Mike. 2014. (Magic Shop Ser.: 3). (ENG.). 176p. (J). (gr. 2-4). 14.99 *(978-1-250-02916-4(3))* Feiwel & Friends.

—The Incredible Twisting Arm, Bk. 2. Egan, Kate & Lane, Mike. 2014. (Magic Shop Ser.: 2). (ENG.). 160p. (J). (gr. 2-4). pap. 5.99 *(978-1-250-04044-2(2))* Feiwel & Friends.

—Jinxed! Scaletta, Kurtis. 2012. (Topps Ser.). (ENG.). 112p. (J). (gr. 2-4). pap. 5.95 *(978-1-4197-0261-7(0))*;Bk. 1. 15.95 *(978-1-4197-0226-6(9))* Abrams. (Amulet Bks.).

—Steal That Base! Scaletta, Kurtis. 2012. (Topps Ser.). (ENG.). 112p. (J). (gr. 2-4). 15.95 *(978-1-4197-0287-7(4))*; pap. 5.95 *(978-1-4197-0262-4(9))* Abrams. (Amulet Bks.).

—A Topps League Story: Book Three: Zip It! Scaletta, Kurtis. 2012. (Topps Ser.). (ENG.). 112p. (J). (gr. 2-4). pap. 5.95 *(978-1-4197-0437-6(0)*, Amulet Bks.) Abrams.

—The Vanishing Coin. Egan, Kate & Lane, Mike. 2014. (Magic Shop Ser.: 1). (ENG.). 160p. (J). (gr. 2-4). pap. 5.99 *(978-1-250-04043-5(4))* Feiwel & Friends.

—The 823rd Hit Bk. 4. Scaletta, Kurtis. 2012. (Topps Ser.). (ENG.). 112p. (J). (gr. 2-4). pap. 5.95 *(978-1-4197-0445-1(1)*, Amulet Bks.) Abrams.

Wight, Eric. Frankie Pickle & the Closet of Doom. Wight, Eric. (Frankie Pickle Ser.). (ENG.). (J). (gr. 2-5). 2010. 96p. pap. 5.99 *(978-1-4424-1304-7(2))*; 2009. 80p. 9.99 *(978-1-4169-6484-1(3))* Simon & Schuster Bks. For Young Readers. (Simon & Schuster Bks. For Young Readers).

—Frankie Pickle & the Mathematical Menace. Wight, Eric. 2011. (Frankie Pickle Ser.). (ENG.). 80p. (J). (gr. 2-5). bds. 9.99 *(978-1-4169-8972-1(2)*, Simon & Schuster Bks. For Young Readers) Simon & Schuster Bks. For Young Readers.

—Frankie Pickle & the Pine Run 3000. Wight, Eric. 2010. (Frankie Pickle Ser.). (ENG.). 96p. (J). (gr. 2-5). bds. 9.99 *(978-1-4169-6485-8(1)*, Simon & Schuster Bks. For Young Readers) Simon & Schuster Bks. For Young Readers.

Wight, Joseph & Espinosa, Rod. The Bombing of Pearl Harbor. Dunn, Joe. 2007. (Graphic History Ser.). 32p. (gr. 3-6). 28.50 *(978-1-60270-074-1(5)*, Graphic Planet-Nonfiction) ABDO Publishing Co.

Wigley, Audrey Watson. The Boy & Girl Who Hated History. Igneri, David S. 2009. 44p. pap. 24.95 *(978-1-61546-828-7(5))* America Star Bks.

Wigsby, Nick. The Truth (and Myths) about Thanksgiving. Peacock, L. A. 2013. 89p. (J). pap. *(978-0-545-56846-3(3))* Scholastic, Inc.

Wigsby, Nick. The Truth (and Myths) about the Presidents. Peacock, L. A. 2014. 94p. (J). pap. ***(978-0-545-56848-7(X))*** Scholastic, Inc.

Wijngaard, Jan. Haywire, Vol. 3. Pinchuk, Tom. 2014. (Max Steel Ser.: 3). (ENG.). 64p. (J). pap. 7.99 *(978-1-4215-5727-4(4))* Viz Media.

—The Parasites. Viz Media Staff & Smith, Brian. 2013. (Max Steel Ser.: 1). (ENG.). 64p. (J). pap. 7.99 *(978-1-4215-5523-2(9))* Viz Media.

Wijngaard, Juan. Cloud Tea Monkeys. Peet, Mal & Graham, Elspeth. 2010. (ENG.). 56p. (J). (gr. -1-3). 15.99 *(978-0-7636-4453-6(6))* Candlewick Pr.

Wik, Jenny. Ellis Goes to the Doctor. Reuterstrand, Siri. 2012. (ENG.). 24p. (J). (gr. -1-1). 12.95 *(978-1-61608-662-6(9)*, 608662, Sky Pony Pr.) Skyhorse Publishing Co., Inc.

—Ellis Is Scared of the Dark. Reuterstrand, Siri. 2012. (ENG.). 24p. (J). (gr. -1-1). 12.95 *(978-1-61608-667-1(X)*, 608667, Sky Pony Pr.) Skyhorse Publishing Co., Inc.

Wikland, Ilon. The Brothers Lionheart. Lindgren, Astrid. Morgan, Jill, tr. from SWE. 2004. 231p. (J). 17.95 *(978-1-930900-24-0(4))* Purple Hse. Pr.

—Happy Times in Noisy Village. Lindgren, Astrid. 2003. Orig. Title: Bullerby Boken. 119p. (J). pap. 10.95 *(978-1-883937-66-9(3))* Bethlehem Bks.

—The Holy Night. Lagerlöf, Selma. 2004. 40p. (J). 17.00 *(978-0-86315-467-6(0))* Floris Bks. GBR. Dist: SteinerBooks, Inc.

—Mio, My Son. Lindgren, Astrid. 2015.Tr. of Mio, Min Mio. (ENG.). 184p. (J). (gr. 3-7). 16.95 *(978-1-59017-870-6(X)*, NYR Children's Collection) New York Review of Bks., Inc., The.

—Mio, My Son. Lindgren, Astrid. 2003.Tr. of Mio, Min Mio. 179p. (J). 17.95 *(978-1-930900-23-3(6))* Purple Hse. Pr.

Wilburn, Kathy. Bunny, Bunny. Hall, Kirsten. 2003. (My First Reader Ser.). (ENG.). 32p. (J). 18.50 *(978-0-516-22923-2(0)*, Children's Pr.) Scholastic Library Publishing.

Wilcox, Brian. Full Moon. Wilcox, Brian. David, Lawrence. 2004. 30p. (J). (gr. k-4). reprint ed. 16.00 *(978-0-7567-7762-3(3))* DIANE Publishing Co.

Wilcox, Cathy. Always Jack. Gervay, Susanne. 2013. 148p. (J). *(978-1-61067-226-9(7))* Kane Miller.

—Super Jack. Gervay, Susanne. 2003. 192p. *(978-0-207-19918-9(3))* HarperCollins Pubs. Australia.

—SuperJack. Gervay, Susanne. 2013. (ENG.). 192p. (J). pap. 5.99 *(978-1-61067-129-3(5))* Kane Miller.

Wild, Gill. Reading Your Bible: A Starter's Guide. Childress, Gavin & Dooley, Audrey. 2005. 101p. (J). (gr. -1-7). per. 9.00 *(978-1-903087-41-1(4))* DayOne Pubns. GBR. Dist: Send The Light Distribution LLC.

Wilde, Carol. The Bells of Freedom. Butters, Dorothy Gilman. 2008. (J). (gr. 4-6). 21.00 *(978-0-8446-6162-9(7))* Smith, Peter Pub., Inc.

Wilde, Cindy. Beautiful Copycat Coloring Book: Pretty Pictures to Copy & Complete. 2015. (ENG.). 48p. (J). (gr. 1-4). pap. 6.99 *(978-1-4380-0636-9(5))* Barron's Educational Series, Inc.

Wilde, George. Mr. Wishing Went Fishing. Wilde, Irma. 2015. (G&d Vintage Ser.). (ENG.). 32p. (J). (gr. -1-k). 7.99 ***(978-0-448-48762-5(4)***, Grosset & Dunlap) Penguin Publishing Group.

Wilde, George. Silver Heels: A Story of Blackfeet Indians at Glacier National Park. Christie, Caroline. 2011. 162p. 41.95 *(978-1-258-00441-5(0))* Literary Licensing, LLC.

Wilde, Irma. The Three Bears. Hillert, Margaret. rev. ed. 2006. (Beginning to Read Ser.). 30p. (J). (gr. -1-2). lib. bdg. 19.93 *(978-1-59953-026-0(0))* Norwood Hse. Pr.

—The Three Little Pigs. Hillert, Margaret. rev. exp. ed. 2006. (Beginning to Read Ser.). 30p. (J). (gr. -1-2). lib. bdg. 14.95 *(978-1-59953-050-5(3))* Norwood Hse. Pr.

Wildish, Lee. All Better: A Touch-and-Heal Book. Wilcox, Leigh Attaway. 2007. (ENG.). 12p. (gr. -1). 12.95 *(978-1-58117-591-2(4)*, Intervisual/Piggy Toes) Bendon, Inc.

—Bears, Bears, Bears! Waddell, Martin. 2013. (J). *(978-1-4351-4999-1(8))* Barnes & Noble, Inc.

—The Boy Who Cried Wolf. 2008. (I'm Going to Read(r) Ser.). (ENG.). 32p. (J). (gr. 1-2). pap. 3.95 *(978-1-4027-5546-0(5))* Sterling Publishing Co., Inc.

—Dancing with the Dinosaurs. Clarke, Jane. 2012. (ENG.). 32p. (J). (gr. -1-2). 12.95 *(978-1-936140-67-1(5)*, Imagine Publishing) Charlesbridge Publishing, Inc.

Wildish, Lee. Dave's Breakfast Blast-Off! Hendra, Sue. 2015. (ENG.). 32p. (J). (-k). 10.99 ***(978-1-4449-1968-4(7))*** Hodder & Stoughton GBR. Dist: Independent Pubs. Group.

Wildish, Lee. Doughnuts for a Dragon. Guillain, Adam & Guillain, Charlotte. 2015. (ENG.). 32p. (J). (gr. -1-k). pap. 10.99 *(978-1-4052-7054-0(3))* Egmont Bks., Ltd. GBR. Dist: Independent Pubs. Group.

Wildish, Lee. How to Amaze a Teacher. Reagan, Jean. 2016. (J). ***(978-0-553-53825-0(X))*** Knopf, Alfred A. Inc.

Wildish, Lee. How to Babysit a Grandpa. Reagan, Jean. 2012. (ENG.). 32p. (J). (gr. k-3). 16.99 *(978-0-375-86713-2(9)*, Knopf Bks. for Young Readers); lib. bdg. 19.99 *(978-0-375-96713-9(3))* Knopf, Alfred A. Inc.

—The KnitWits Make a Move! Frost, Michael, photos by. Tabby, Abigail. 2013. (ENG.). 32p. (J). (gr. -1-1). 14.99 *(978-1-4424-5342-5(7)*, Little Simon) Little Simon.

—Leave Me Alone: A Tale of What Happens When You Stand up to a Bully. Gray, Kes. 2011. 32p. (J). (gr. -1-2). pap. 8.99 *(978-0-7641-4736-4(6))* Barron's Educational Series, Inc.

—Noisy Monsters. Greenwell, Jessica. 2010. (Busy Sounds Board Bks). 10p. (J). bds. 18.99 *(978-0-7945-2769-3(8)*, Usborne) EDC Publishing.

—Noisy Zoo. Taplin, Sam. 2009. (Busy Sounds Board Book Ser.). 10p. (J). (gr. -1). bds. 18.99 *(978-0-7945-2517-0(2)*, Usborne) EDC Publishing.

—Snuggly Bunny. Scholastic, Inc. Staff & Ackerman, Jill. 2009. (Little Scholastic Ser.). (ENG.). 6p. (J). (gr. k — 1). bds. 9.99 *(978-0-545-01378-9(X)*, Cartwheel Bks.) Scholastic, Inc.

—Spaghetti with the Yeti. Guillain, Charlotte & Guillain, Adam. 2014. (ENG.). 32p. (J). (gr. -1-k). pap. 10.99 *(978-1-4052-6351-1(2))* Egmont Bks., Ltd. GBR. Dist: Independent Pubs. Group.

—Thomas & the Dragon Queen. Crum, Shutta. 2011. (ENG.). 272p. (J). (gr. 3-7). 6.99 *(978-0-375-84634-2(4)*, Yearling) Random Hse. Children's Bks.

—Twosomes: Love Poems from the Animal Kingdom. Singer, Marilyn. 2010. (ENG.). 24p. (J). (gr. k-12). 7.99 *(978-0-375-86710-1(4))* Knopf, Alfred A. Inc.

Wildish, Lee, jt. illus. see Guillain, Charlotte.

Wildlife Conservation Society, photos by. Amazing Dolphins! Thomson, Sarah L. 2008. (I Can Read Book 2 Ser.). (ENG., 32p. (J). (gr. k-3). pap. 3.99 *(978-0-06-054455-3(4))* HarperCollins Pubs.

—Amazing Gorillas! Thomson, Sarah L. 2006. (I Can Read Book 2 Ser.). (ENG., 32p. (J). (gr. k-3). pap. 3.99 *(978-0-06-054461-4(9))* HarperCollins Pubs.

—Amazing Sharks! Thomson, Sarah L. 2006. (I Can Read Book 2 Ser.). (ENG., 32p. (J). (gr. k-3). pap. 3.99 *(978-0-06-054456-0(2))* HarperCollins Pubs.

—Amazing Sharks! Thomson, Sarah L. 2006. (I Can Read Bks.). 31p. (gr. -1-3). 14.00 *(978-0-7569-6957-8(3))* Perfection Learning Corp.

—Amazing Snakes! Thomson, Sarah L. 2006. (I Can Read Book 2 Ser.). (ENG., 32p. (J). (gr. k-3). pap. 3.99 *(978-0-06-054464-5(3))* HarperCollins Pubs.

—Amazing Whales! Thomson, Sarah L. 2006. (I Can Read Book 2 Ser.). (ENG., 32p. (J). (gr. k-3). pap. 3.99 *(978-0-06-054467-6(8))* HarperCollins Pubs.

—Amazing Whales! Thomson, Sarah L. 2006. (I Can Read Bks.). (gr. -1-3). 14.00 *(978-0-7569-6665-2(5))* Perfection Learning Corp.

Wilds, Kazumi. The Peace Tree from Hiroshima: A Little Japanese Bonsai with a Big Story. Moore, Sandra. 2015. (ENG.). 32p. (J). (gr. 2-6). 14.95 ***(978-4-8053-1347-3(1))*** Tuttle Publishing.

Wilds, Kazumi. The Wakame Gatherers. Thompson, Holly. 2007. (Wakame Gatherers Ser.). 32p. (J). (gr. -1-3). 16.95 *(978-1-885008-33-6(3)*, Shen's Bks.) Lee & Low Bks., Inc.

Wildsmith, Brian. Les Animaux de la Ferme. 2005. (FRE & ENG.). 16p. (J). (gr. -1 — 1). per., bds. 5.95 *(978-1-59572-032-0(4))* Star Bright Bks., Inc.

—Brian Wildsmith's Amazing Animal Alphabet Book, 1 vol. 2008. (ENG.). 32p. (J). 17.95 *(978-1-59572-104-4(5))* Star Bright Bks., Inc.

—Brian Wildsmith's Animal Colors (Arabic) 2004. (ARA.). 16p. (J). bds. 4.95 *(978-1-932065-44-2(X)*; 718-784-9112) Star Bright Bks., Inc.

—Brian Wildsmith's Animal Colors (Portugese) 2003. (POR.). 16p. (J). bds. 4.95 *(978-1-932065-27-5(X)*, 1-718-784-9112) Star Bright Bks., Inc.

—Brian Wildsmith's Animal Colors (Vietnamese) 2004. (VIE.). 16p. (J). bds. 4.95 *(978-1-932065-51-0(2))* Star Bright Bks., Inc.

—Brian Wildsmith's Animals to Count (Arabic) 2004. (ARA.). 16p. (J). bds. 4.95 *(978-1-932065-45-9(8)*, 718-784-9112) Star Bright Bks., Inc.

—Brian Wildsmith's Animals to Count (Vietnamese) 2003. (VIE.). 16p. (J). bds. 4.95 *(978-1-932065-16-9(4)*, 17187849112) Star Bright Bks., Inc.

—Brian Wildsmith's Farm Animals (Portugese) 2003. (POR.). 16p. (J). bds. 4.95 *(978-1-932065-20-6(2)*, 1-718-784-9112) Star Bright Bks., Inc.

—Brian Wildsmith's Farm Animals (Vietnamese) 2003. (VIE.). 16p. (J). bds. 4.95 *(978-1-932065-21-3(0))* Star Bright Bks., Inc.

—The Cherry Tree. Ikeda, Daisaku. McCraughrean, Geraldine, tr. from JPN. 2013. 6.95 *(978-1-935523-57-4(0))* World Tribune Pr.

—A Child's Garden of Verses: A Collection of Scriptures, Prayers & Poems, 1 vol. Stevenson, Robert Louis. 2008. (ENG.). 32p. (J). 19.95 *(978-1-59572-057-3(X))* Star Bright Bks., Inc.
—Les Couleurs des Animaux. 2005. (FRE & ENG.). 16p. (J). (gr. -1). per., bds. 5.95 *(978-1-59572-031-3(6))* Star Bright Bks., Inc.
—Over the Deep Blue Sea. Ikeda, Daisaku. McCraughrean, Geraldine, tr. from JPN. 2013. 6.95 *(978-1-935523-59-8(7))* World Tribune Pr.
—The Princess & the Moon. Ikeda, Daisaku. McCraughrean, Geraldine, tr. from JPN. 2013. 6.95 *(978-1-935523-58-1(9))* World Tribune Pr.
—The Snow Country Prince. Ikeda, Daisaku. McCraughrean, Geraldine, tr. from JPN. 2013. 6.95 *(978-1-935523-60-4(0))* World Tribune Pr.
Wildsmith, Brian. Brian Wildsmith's Animals to Count (Traditional Cantonese), 1 vol. Wildsmith, Brian. . 2003. (CHI & ENG.). 16p. (J). 4.99 *(978-1-932065-18-3(0)*, 1-718-784-9112) Star Bright Bks., Inc.
Wildsmith, Brian. Animal Colors (Farsi) Wildsmith, Brian. 2004. (PER.). 16p. (J). bds. 4.99 *(978-1-932065-42-8(3))* Star Bright Bks., Inc.
—Animals to Count (Farsi) Wildsmith, Brian. 2004. (PER.). 16p. (J). bds. 4.99 *(978-1-932065-43-5(1))* Star Bright Bks., Inc.
—Animals to Count (Simplified Mandarin) Wildsmith, Brian. 2003. (CHI.). 16p. (J). bds. 4.99 *(978-1-932065-17-6(2)*, 1718-784-9112) Star Bright Bks., Inc.
—Brian Wildsmith's Amazing Animal Alphabet Book. Wildsmith, Brian. 2007. 32p. (J). pap. 8.95 *(978-1-59572-111-2(8))* Star Bright Bks., Inc.
—Brian Wildsmith's Animal Colors (Korean), 1 vol. Wildsmith, Brian. 2003. (KOR & ENG.). 16p. (J). 4.99 *(978-1-932065-28-2(8)*, 1-718-784-9112) Star Bright Bks., Inc.
—Brian Wildsmith's Animal Colors (Navajo), 1 vol. Wildsmith, Brian. 2004. (NAV & ENG.). 16p. (J). 4.99 *(978-1-932065-34-3(2)*, 718-784-9112) Star Bright Bks., Inc.
—Brian Wildsmith's Animal Colors (Simplified Mandarin) Wildsmith, Brian. 2004. (CHI.). 16p. (J). bds. 4.95 *(978-1-932065-52-7(0)*, 7187849112) Star Bright Bks., Inc.
—Brian Wildsmith's Animal Colors (Tagalog), 1 vol. Wildsmith, Brian. 2003. (TAG & ENG.). 16p. (J). 4.99 *(978-1-932065-30-5(X)*, 1-718-784-9112) Star Bright Bks., Inc.
—Brian Wildsmith's Animal Colors (Traditional Cantonese) Wildsmith, Brian. 2004. (CHI.). 16p. (J). bds. 4.99 *(978-1-932065-53-4(9))* Star Bright Bks., Inc.
—Brian Wildsmith's Animals to Count, 1 vol. Wildsmith, Brian. 2009. (ENG.). 32p. (J). bds. 4.99 *(978-1-59572-128-0(2))* Star Bright Bks., Inc.
—Brian Wildsmith's Animals to Count (Korean), 1 vol. Wildsmith, Brian. 2003. (KOR & ENG.). 16p. (J). 4.99 *(978-1-932065-13-8(X)*, 1718-784-9112) Star Bright Bks., Inc.
—Brian Wildsmith's Animals to Count (Portugese) Wildsmith, Brian. 2003. (POR.). 16p. (J). bds. 4.95 *(978-1-932065-15-2(6)*, 17187849112) Star Bright Bks., Inc.
—Brian Wildsmith's Animals to Count (Tagalog), 1 vol. Wildsmith, Brian. 2003. (TAG & ENG.). 16p. (J). 4.99 *(978-1-932065-31-2(8)*, 1-718-784-9112) Star Bright Bks., Inc.
—Brian Wildsmith's Farm Animals (Korean), 1 vol. Wildsmith, Brian. 2003. (KOR & ENG.). 16p. (J). 4.99 *(978-1-932065-19-0(9)*, 1-718-784-9112) Star Bright Bks., Inc.
—Brian Wildsmith's Farm Animals (Tagalog), 1 vol. Wildsmith, Brian. 2003. (TAG & ENG.). 16p. (J). 4.99 *(978-1-932065-29-9(6)*, 1-718-784-9112) Star Bright Bks., Inc.
—The Easter Story. Wildsmith, Brian. 2004. 24p. (gr. -1-7). 18.00 *(978-0-8028-5189-5(4))* Eerdmans, William B. Publishing Co.
—Farm Animals (Simplified Mandarin), 1 vol. Wildsmith, Brian. 2003. (CHI & ENG.). 16p. (J). 4.99 *(978-1-932065-22-0(9)*, 1-718-784-9112) Star Bright Bks., Inc.
—Farm Animals (Traditional Cantonese) Wildsmith, Brian. 2003. (CHI.). 16p. (J). bds. 4.99 *(978-1-932065-23-7(7)*, 1-718-784-9112) Star Bright Bks., Inc.
—Hunter & His Dog, 1 vol. Wildsmith, Brian. 2008. (ENG.). 32p. (J). 16.95 *(978-1-59572-123-5(1))* Star Bright Bks., Inc.
—Jesus. Wildsmith, Brian. 2004. 24p. (gr. 3-7). 20.00 *(978-0-8028-5212-0(2))* Eerdmans, William B. Publishing Co.
—Jungle Party, 1 vol. Wildsmith, Brian. 2006. (ENG.). 32p. (J). pap. 6.95 *(978-1-59572-053-5(7))* Star Bright Bks., Inc.
—The Little Wood Duck, 1 vol. Wildsmith, Brian. 2006. (ENG.). 32p. (J). pap. 6.95 *(978-1-59572-049-8(9))* Star Bright Bks., Inc.
—The Owl & the Woodpecker, 1 vol. Wildsmith, Brian. 2006. (ENG.). 32p. (J). (gr. -1-3). 16.95 *(978-1-59572-043-6(X))*; pap. 6.95 *(978-1-59572-050-4(2))* Star Bright Bks., Inc.
—Professor Noah's Spaceship, 1 vol. Wildsmith, Brian. 2008. (ENG.). 32p. (J). 16.95 *(978-1-59572-124-2(X))* Star Bright Bks., Inc.
Wiles, Frank. The First Fifth Form. Smith, Evelyn. 2013. 176p. pap. *(978-1-909423-05-3(X))* Bks. to Treasure.
—The Small Sixth Form. Smith, Evelyn. 2013. 200p. pap. *(978-1-909423-08-4(4))* Bks. to Treasure.
Wiles, Pat. Isabelle Lives a Dream. Sundberg, Peggy. I.t. ed. 2003. (ENG.). 32p. (J). 11.95 *(978-0-9721057-1-2(9))* Cowgirl Peg Enterprises.
—Jazmine's Incredible Story. Sundberg, Peggy. 2006. 32p. (J). 16.95 *(978-0-9721057-5-0(1)*, Cowgirl Peg Bks.) Cowgirl Peg Enterprises.
—Okey-Dokey Oakie. Sundberg, Peggy. 2008. (ENG.). 32p. (J). 17.95 *(978-0-9721057-9-8(4))*; pap. 11.95 *(978-0-9721057-7-4(8))* Cowgirl Peg Enterprises. (Cowgirl Peg Bks.).
—Stepping Stones to the Sun. Nawashani. 2013. 68p. pap. 11.95 *(978-1-4787-0445-4(4))* Outskirts Pr., Inc.
Wiley, Bee. El Pequeno Dragon. Aiken, Joan. 2004.Tr. of Wooden Dragon. (SPA.). (J). 18.99 *(978-84-88342-52-2(7))* S.A. Kokinos ESP. Dist: Lectorum Pubns., Inc.
Wiley, Judeanne Winter. The Tree of Life: The Wonders of Evolution. Jackson, Ellen B. 2004. (ENG.). 41p. (J). (gr. -1-3). pap. 14.99 *(978-1-59102-240-4(1)*, Pyr Bks.) Prometheus Bks., Pubs.
Wiley, Nancy. Alice's Adventures in Wonderland. Carroll, Lewis. 2009. 88p. 35.00 *(978-0-615-29492-6(8))* OBrien, Wiley Workspace.
Wilharm, Sabine. The Story of the Little Pig Who Couldn't Say No. Ludwig, Sabine. 2013. (ENG.). 32p. (J). (gr. -1-1). 16.95 *(978-1-62087-684-8(1)*, 620684, Sky Pony Pr.) Skyhorse Publishing Co., Inc.
Wilhelm, Doris L. It Is Me. Rogers, Leslie E. 2011. 24p. pap. 24.95 *(978-1-4626-4596-1(8))* America Star Bks.
Wilhelm, Hans. A Hole in the Wall. 2016. (J). ***(978-0-8234-3535-7(0))*** Holiday Hse., Inc.
Wilhelm, Hans. A Monster Is Coming! Harrison, David L. 2011. (Step into Reading Ser.). (ENG.). 32p. (J). (gr. -1-1). pap. 3.99 *(978-0-375-86677-7(9)*, Random Hse. Bks. for Young Readers) Random Hse. Children's Bks.
Wilhelm, Hans. I Love Rainy Days! Wilhelm, Hans. 2011. (Scholastic Reader Level 1 Ser.). (ENG.). 32p. (J). (gr. -1-2). pap. 3.99 *(978-0-545-24503-6(6)*, Cartwheel Bks.) Scholastic, Inc.
—I Love School! Wilhelm, Hans. 2010. (Scholastic Reader Level 1 Ser.). (ENG.). 32p. (J). (gr. -1-k). pap. 3.99 *(978-0-545-13474-3(9)*, Cartwheel Bks.) Scholastic, Inc.
—I Won't Share! Wilhelm, Hans. 2010. (Scholastic Reader Level 1 Ser.). (ENG.). 32p. (J). (gr. -1-2). pap. 3.99 *(978-0-439-77353-9(9))* Scholastic, Inc.
Wilhelm, Lauren. Love Has Many Faces. Merker, Patricia D. 2011. (Grand Master/Little Master Ser.: Bk. 3). (J). pap. *(978-1-921883-09-5(X))* Pick-a-Woo Woo Pubs.
—Sink or Swim. Merker, Patricia D. 2011. (Grand Master/Little Master Ser.: Bk. 2). 28p. pap. *(978-0-9806520-7-9(3))* Pick-a-Woo Woo Pubs.
Wilkerson, Teresa. Piddle Diddle's Lost Hat: Adventures of Piddle Diddle, the Widdle Penguin. Major, Wayne A. & Major, Ralphine. 2015. (ENG.). (J). pap. 9.95 ***(978-1-939289-63-6(7)***, Little Creek Bks.) Jan-Carol Publishing, INC.
Wilkie, E. m. The Garden of Eden Adventure. Wilkie, E. m. 2012. 42p. (J). pap. 9.99 *(978-0-9846685-7-1(8)*, Indie Christian Book Group) IndieGo Publishing LLC.
Wilkin, Eloise. Baby Listens. Wilkin, Esther. 2012. (Little Golden Book Ser.). (ENG.). 24p. (J). (gr. k-k). 3.99 *(978-0-307-93012-5(2)*, Golden Bks.) Random Hse. Children's Bks.
—Baby's Christmas. Wilkin, Esther. 2012. (Golden Baby Ser.). (ENG.). 26p. (J). (gr. k — 1). bds. 6.99 *(978-0-375-87058-3(X)*, Golden Bks.) Random Hse. Children's Bks.
—The Christmas ABC. Johnson, Florence. 2013. (Little Golden Book Ser.). (ENG.). 24p. (J). (-k). 4.99 *(978-0-307-97891-2(5)*, Golden Bks.) Random Hse. Children's Bks.
—Eloise Wilkin Stories. Golden Books Staff. 2005. (Little Golden Book Treasury Ser.). (ENG.). 224p. (J). (gr. -1-2). 10.95 *(978-0-375-82928-4(8)*, Golden Bks.) Random Hse. Children's Bks.
—Prayers for Children. Golden Books Staff. 2007. (Little Golden Treasures Ser.). (ENG.). 26p. (J). (— 1). bds. 4.99 *(978-0-375-83927-6(5)*, Golden Inspirational) Random Hse. Children's Bks.
—Wonders of Nature. Watson, Jane Werner. 2010. (Little Golden Book Ser.). (ENG.). 24p. (J). (gr. -1-2). 3.99 *(978-0-375-85486-6(X)*, Golden Bks.) Random Hse. Children's Bks.
Wilkin, Eloise & Meisel, Paul. Little Golden Book Mommy Stories. Cushman, Jean et al. 2015. (ENG.). 80p. (J). (-k). 6.99 *(978-0-385-39273-0(7)*, Golden Bks.) Random Hse. Children's Bks.
Wilkin, Eloise, jt. illus. see Catusanu, Mircea.
Wilkins, Sarah. A Book Is a Book. Bornholdt, Jenny. 2014. 40p. (J). (gr. k-12). 14.95 *(978-1-877579-92-9(0))* Gecko Pr. NZL. Dist: Lerner Publishing Group.
Wilkins, Wendy H. Timber Howligan Secret Agent Cat. Frederick, H. J. 2015. (J). pap. 8.99 ***(978-0-9964246-9-1(5))*** Lionheart Pr.
Wilkinson, Annie. My Valentine. Cooke, Brandy. 2010. (ENG.). 12p. (J). (gr. -1 — 1). 4.99 *(978-1-4424-0779-4(4)*, Little Simon) Little Simon.
Wilkinson, Richard. Welcome to the Museum: Historium. Nelson, Jo. 2015. (ENG.). 112p. (J). (gr. 3-7). 35.00 ***(978-0-7636-7984-2(4)***, Big Picture Press) Candlewick Pr.
Wilkon, Jozef. Bonko. Schnell, Robert W. 28p. (J). (gr. -1-3). 12.95 *(978-0-87592-008-5(X))* Scroll Pr., Inc.
—Tim, the Peacemaker. Friesel, Uwe. 32p. (J). (gr. -1-3). 13.95 *(978-0-87592-052-8(7))* Scroll Pr., Inc.
Wilks, Peter. It's Your Turn Now: Politeness. Wilks, Peter, tr. Leaney, Cindy. 2003. 31p. (J). 28.50 *(978-1-58952-735-5(6))* Rourke Educational Media.
Will, Clark Moor. Aurora, Daughter of the Dawn: A Story of New Beginnings. Kopp, J. J. 2012. (ENG.). 72p. (gr. 6-12). pap. 12.95 *(978-0-87071-671-3(9))* Oregon State Univ. Pr.
Will, Heidi. The Ghillie Girls: Irish Dance Pals. Will, Heidi. 2008. 24p. (J). pap. 9.99 *(978-0-9821065-0-1(5))* Cinealta Pr.
Will, Sandra. Lacrosse for Fun!, 1 vol. Will, Sandra. 2006. (For Fun!: Sports Ser.). (ENG.). 48p. (gr. 3-6). lib. bdg. 26.65 *(978-0-7565-1685-7(4)*, For Fun!) Compass Point Bks.
Willard, Mary. Hugs Are for Every One... Willard, Baron And Mary. 2013. 54p. pap. 19.99 *(978-0-9896257-0-8(2))* Blue Botte.
Willardson, David, jt. illus. see Mason, Mark.
Willardson, David, jt. illus. see Rojas, Mary.
Willardson, David, jt. illus. see Valko, Diane.
Willemin, Veronique. Te Tumu o Rapa Nui: El Arbolito de Rapa Nui. the Little Tree of Rapa Nui. le Petit Arbre de Rapa Nui. Orliac, Catherine. Haoa Cardinali, Viki et al, trs. 2005. (FRE, SPA & ENG.). 40p. (J). spiral bd. 12.00 *(978-1-880636-02-2(6))* Easter Island Foundation.
Willems, Mo. Don't Let the Pigeon Drive the Bus! 2005. 40p. (J). 19.95 *(978-1-84428-013-1(6))* Walker Bks. Australia Pty. Ltd.
Willems, Mo. Are You Ready to Play Outside? Willems, Mo. 2008. (Elephant & Piggie Book Ser.). (ENG.). 64p. (J). (gr. -1-k). 9.99 *(978-1-4231-1347-8(0))* Hyperion Pr.
—A Big Guy Took My Ball! Willems, Mo. 2013. (Elephant & Piggie Ser.). (ENG.). 64p. (J). (gr. 1-3). 8.99 *(978-1-4231-7491-2(7))* Hyperion Bks. for Children.
—Can I Play Too? Willems, Mo. 2010. (Elephant & Piggie Ser.). (ENG.). 64p. (J). (gr. -1-k). 9.99 *(978-1-4231-1991-3(6))* Hyperion Pr.
—Cat the Cat Who Is That? Willems, Mo. 2010. 32p. (J). (gr. -1-3). (ENG.). 10.99 *(978-0-06-172840-2(3))*; lib. bdg. 14.89 *(978-0-06-172841-9(1))* HarperCollins Pubs.
—A Cautionary Tale. Willems, Mo. ed. 2011. 40p. (J). (gr. -1-1). 19.99 *(978-1-4231-4449-6(X))* Hyperion Pr.
—El Conejito Knuffle: Un Cuento Aleccionador. Willems, Mo. rev. ed. 2007. (Knuffle Bunny Ser.). (ENG & SPA.). 40p. (J). (gr. -1-k). pap. 7.99 *(978-1-4231-0567-1(2))* Hyperion Pr.
—¿Debo Compartir Mi Helado? Willems, Mo. Campoy, F. Isabel. 2015. (Elephant & Piggie Book Ser.). (SPA.). 64p. (J). (gr. -1-k). 9.99 *(978-1-4847-2291-6(4))* Disney Publishing Worldwide.
—Don't Let the Pigeon Drive the Bus! Willems, Mo. 2003. (Pigeon Ser.). (ENG.). 40p. (J). (gr. -1-k). 16.99 *(978-0-7868-1988-1(X))* Hyperion Pr.
—Don't Let the Pigeon Finish This Activity Book! Willems, Mo. 2012. (Pigeon Ser.). (ENG.). 272p. (YA). (gr. 7-12). pap. 19.99 *(978-1-4231-3310-0(2))* Hyperion Pr.
—Don't Let the Pigeon Stay Up Late! Willems, Mo. 2006. (Pigeon Ser.). (ENG.). 40p. (J). (gr. -1-k). 16.99 *(978-0-7868-3746-5(2))* Hyperion Pr.
—The Duckling Gets a Cookie!? Willems, Mo. 2012. (ENG.). 40p. (J). (gr. -1-k). 16.99 *(978-1-4231-5128-9(3))* Hyperion Pr.
—Edwina, the Dinosaur Who Didn't Know She Was Extinct. Willems, Mo. 2006. (ENG.). 40p. (J). (gr. -1-k). 16.99 *(978-0-7868-3748-9(9))* Hyperion Pr.
—Elephants Cannot Dance! Willems, Mo. 2009. (Elephant & Piggie Ser.). (ENG.). 64p. (J). (gr. -1-k). 9.99 *(978-1-4231-1410-9(8))* Hyperion Pr.
—!Estamos en un Libro! Willems, Mo. Campoy, F. Isabel. 2015. (Elephant & Piggie Ser.). (SPA.). 64p. (J). (gr. 1-3). 9.99 *(978-1-4847-2288-6(4))* Hyperion Bks. for Children.
—Goldilocks & the Three Dinosaurs. Willems, Mo. 2012. (ENG.). 40p. (J). (gr. -1-2). 17.99 *(978-0-06-210418-2(7))* HarperCollins Pubs.
—Happy Pig Day! Willems, Mo. 2011. (Elephant & Piggie Book Ser.). (ENG.). 64p. (J). (gr. -1-k). 9.99 *(978-1-4231-4342-0(6))* Hyperion Pr.
—Hooray for Amanda & Her Alligator! Willems, Mo. 2011. (ENG.). 72p. (J). (gr. -1-3). 17.99 *(978-0-06-200400-0(X))* HarperCollins Pubs.
—I Am Going! Willems, Mo. 2010. (Elephant & Piggie Book Ser.). (ENG.). 64p. (J). (gr. -1-k). 8.99 *(978-1-4231-1990-6(8))* Hyperion Pr.
—I Am Invited to a Party! Willems, Mo. rev. ed. 2007. (Elephant & Piggie Ser.). (ENG.). 64p. (J). (gr. -1-k). 9.99 *(978-1-4231-0687-6(3))* Hyperion Pr.
—I Broke My Trunk! Willems, Mo. 2011. (Elephant & Piggie Ser.). (ENG.). 64p. (J). (gr. -1-k). 8.99 *(978-1-4231-3309-4(9))* Hyperion Pr.
—I Love My New Toy! Willems, Mo. 2008. (Elephant & Piggie Ser.). (ENG.). 64p. (J). (gr. -1-k). 8.99 *(978-1-4231-0961-7(9))* Hyperion Pr.
—I Will Surprise My Friend! Willems, Mo. 2008. (Elephant & Piggie Ser.). (ENG.). 64p. (J). (gr. -1-k). 8.99 *(978-1-4231-0962-4(7))* Hyperion Pr.
Willems, Mo. I Will Take a Nap! Willems, Mo. 2015. (Elephant & Piggie Ser.). (ENG.). 64p. (J). (gr. 1-3). 9.99 ***(978-1-4847-1630-4(2))*** Hyperion Bks. for Children.
Willems, Mo. I'm a Frog! Willems, Mo. 2013. (Elephant & Piggie Ser.). (ENG.). 64p. (J). (gr. 1-3). 8.99 *(978-1-4231-8305-1(3))* Hyperion Pr.
—It's a Busload of Pigeon Books! Willems, Mo. 2013. (Pigeon Ser.). (ENG.). 120p. (J). (gr. -1-k). 24.99 *(978-1-4231-7589-6(1))* Hyperion Pr.
—Knuffle Bunny: A Cautionary Tale. Willems, Mo. 2004. (Knuffle Bunny Ser.). (ENG.). 40p. (J). (gr. -1-k). 17.99 *(978-0-7868-1870-9(0))* Hyperion Pr.
—Knuffle Bunny: A Cautionary Tale. Willems, Mo. unabr. ed. 2006. (J). (gr. -1-1). 29.95 *(978-0-439-90583-1(4))* Weston Woods Studios, Inc.
—Knuffle Bunny Free: An Unexpected Diversion. Willems, Mo. 2010. 52p. (J). (gr. -1-3). (ENG.). 17.99 *(978-0-06-192957-1(3))*; lib. bdg. 18.89 *(978-0-06-192958-8(1))* HarperCollins Pubs.
—Knuffle Bunny Too: A Case of Mistaken Identity. Willems, Mo. rev. ed. 2007. (Knuffle Bunny Ser.). (ENG.). 48p. (J). (gr. -1-k). 17.99 *(978-1-4231-0299-1(1))* Hyperion Pr.
—Leonardo, the Terrible Monster. Willems, Mo. 2005. (ENG.). 48p. (J). (gr. -1-k). 17.99 *(978-0-7868-5294-9(1))* Hyperion Pr.
—Let's Go for a Drive! Willems, Mo. 2012. (Elephant & Piggie Ser.). (ENG.). 64p. (J). (gr. -1-k). 8.99 *(978-1-4231-6482-1(2))* Hyperion Pr.
—Let's Say Hi to Friends Who Fly! Willems, Mo. 2010. 32p. (J). (gr. -1-3). (ENG.). 10.99 *(978-0-06-172842-6(X))*; lib. bdg. 14.89 *(978-0-06-172846-4(2))* HarperCollins Pubs.
—Listen to My Trumpet! Willems, Mo. 2012. (Elephant & Piggie Ser.). (ENG.). 64p. (J). (gr. -1-k). 9.99 *(978-1-4231-5404-4(5))* Hyperion Pr.
—My Friend Is Sad. Willems, Mo. 2007. (Elephant & Piggie Ser.). (ENG.). 64p. (J). (gr. -1-k). 9.99 *(978-1-4231-0297-7(5))* Hyperion Pr.
—My New Friend Is So Fun! Willems, Mo. 2014. (Elephant & Piggie Ser.). (ENG.). 64p. (J). (gr. 1-3). 9.99 *(978-1-4231-7958-0(7))* Hyperion Bks. for Children.
—Naked Mole Rat Gets Dressed. Willems, Mo. 2009. (ENG.). 40p. (J). (gr. -1 — 1). 16.99 *(978-1-4231-1437-6(X))* Hyperion Pr.
—¡No Dejes Que la Paloma Conduzca el Autobús! Willems, Mo. 2011.Tr. of Don't Let the Pigeon Drive the Bus. (SPA & ENG.). 40p. (J). (gr. -1-k). pap. 7.99 *(978-1-4231-4052-8(4))* Hyperion Pr.
—¡La Paloma Encuentra un Perro Caliente! Willems, Mo. Campoy, F. Isabel. 2011. (SPA & ENG.). 40p. (J). (gr. -1-1). pap. 9.99 *(978-1-4231-4051-1(6))* Hyperion Pr.
—The Pigeon Finds a Hot Dog! Willems, Mo. 2004. (Pigeon Ser.). (ENG.). 40p. (J). (gr. -1-k). 16.99 *(978-0-7868-1869-3(7))* Hyperion Pr.
—The Pigeon Has Feelings, Too! Willems, Mo. 2005. (Pigeon Ser.). (ENG.). 12p. (J). (gr. -1-k). 6.99 *(978-0-7868-3650-5(4))* Hyperion Pr.
—The Pigeon Loves Things That Go! Willems, Mo. 2005. (Pigeon Ser.). (ENG.). 12p. (J). (gr. -1-k). 6.99 *(978-0-7868-3651-2(2))* Hyperion Pr.
—The Pigeon Needs a Bath! Willems, Mo. 2014. (Pigeon Ser.). (ENG.). 40p. (J). (gr. -1-k). 16.99 *(978-1-4231-9087-5(4))* Hyperion Bks. for Children.
—The Pigeon Wants a Puppy! Willems, Mo. 2008. (Pigeon Ser.). (ENG.). 40p. (J). (gr. -1-k). 16.99 *(978-1-4231-0960-0(0))* Hyperion Pr.
—Pigs Make Me Sneeze! Willems, Mo. 2009. (Elephant & Piggie Book Ser.). (ENG.). 64p. (J). (gr. -1-k). 9.99 *(978-1-4231-1411-6(6))* Hyperion Pr.
—Should I Share My Ice Cream? Willems, Mo. 2011. (Elephant & Piggie Ser.). (ENG.). 64p. (J). (gr. -1-k). 8.99 *(978-1-4231-4343-7(4))* Hyperion Pr.
—That Is Not a Good Idea! Willems, Mo. 2013. (ENG.). 48p. (J). (gr. k-3). 17.99 *(978-0-06-220309-0(6))* HarperCollins Pubs.
—There Is a Bird on Your Head! Willems, Mo. rev. ed. 2007. (Elephant & Piggie Book Ser.). (ENG.). 64p. (J). (gr. -1-k). 9.99 *(978-1-4231-0686-9(5))* Hyperion Pr.
—Time to Pee! Willems, Mo. 2003. (ENG.). 40p. (J). (gr. -1-k). 14.99 *(978-0-7868-1868-6(9))* Hyperion Pr.
—Time to Say Please! Willems, Mo. 2005. (ENG.). 40p. (J). (gr. -1-k). 15.99 *(978-0-7868-5293-2(3))* Hyperion Pr.
—Time to Sleep, Sheep the Sheep! Willems, Mo. 2010. 32p. (J). (gr. -1-3). (ENG.). 10.99 *(978-0-06-172847-1(0))*; lib. bdg. 14.89 *(978-0-06-172848-8(9))* HarperCollins Pubs.
—Today I Will Fly! Willems, Mo. 2007. (Elephant & Piggie Ser.). (ENG.). 64p. (J). (gr. -1-k). 8.99 *(978-1-4231-0295-3(9))* Hyperion Pr.
—Waiting Is Not Easy! (an Elephant & Piggie Book) Willems, Mo. 2014. (Elephant & Piggie Ser.). (ENG.). 64p. (J). (gr. 1-3). 9.99 *(978-1-4231-9957-1(X))* Hyperion Bks. for Children.
—Watch Me Throw the Ball! Willems, Mo. 2009. (Elephant & Piggie Ser.). (ENG.). 64p. (J). (gr. -1-k). 8.99 *(978-1-4231-1348-5(9))* Hyperion Pr.
—We Are in a Book! Willems, Mo. 2010. (Elephant & Piggie Book Ser.). (ENG.). 64p. (J). (gr. -1-k). 9.99 *(978-1-4231-3308-7(0))* Hyperion Pr.
—What's Your Sound, Hound the Hound? Willems, Mo. 2010. 32p. (J). (gr. -1-3). lib. bdg. 14.89 *(978-0-06-172845-7(4))* HarperCollins Pubs.
—What's Your Sound Hound the Hound? Willems, Mo. 2010. (ENG.). 32p. (J). (gr. -1-3). 10.99 *(978-0-06-172844-0(6))* HarperCollins Pubs.
—Who Flies, Cat the Cat? Willems, Mo. 2014. (ENG.). 22p. (J). (gr. -1 — 1). bds. 6.99 *(978-0-06-230652-4(9))* HarperCollins Pubs.
—Who Is That, Cat the Cat? Willems, Mo. 2014. (ENG.). 22p. (J). (gr. -1 — 1). bds. 6.99 *(978-0-06-230653-1(7))* HarperCollins Pubs.
—Who Says That, Cat the Cat? Willems, Mo. 2014. (ENG.). 22p. (J). (gr. -1 — 1). bds. 6.99 *(978-0-06-230654-8(5))* HarperCollins Pubs.
—Who Sleeps, Cat the Cat? Willems, Mo. 2014. (ENG.). 22p. (J). (gr. -1 — 1). bds. 6.99 *(978-0-06-230655-5(3))* HarperCollins Pubs.
—You Can Never Find a Rickshaw When It Monsoons: The World on One Cartoon a Day. Willems, Mo. 2006. (ENG.). 408p. (gr. 8-17). pap. 12.99 *(978-0-7868-3747-2(0))* Hyperion Pr.
Willey, Bee. How to Be a Princess. Matthews, Caitlin. 2009. (ENG.). 32p. (J). (gr. 2-3). 21.95 *(978-1-84732-164-0(X))* Carlton Bks., Ltd. GBR. Dist: Sterling Publishing Co., Inc.
—How to Be the Perfect Princess. Matthews, Caitlin. 2011. (ENG.). 32p. (J). (gr. 2). pap. 9.95 *(978-1-84732-326-2(X))* Carlton Bks., Ltd. GBR. Dist: Sterling Publishing Co., Inc.
—Indian Myths. Husain, Shahrukh. 2007. (Stories from Ancient Civilisations Ser.). (ENG.). 32p. (J). pap. 10.99 *(978-0-237-53376-2(6))* Evans Brothers, Ltd. GBR. Dist: Independent Pubs. Group.
—The Jesse Tree. McCaughrean, Geraldine. 2005. 93p. (J). (gr. k). 20.00 *(978-0-8028-5288-5(2)*, Eerdmans Bks For Young Readers) Eerdmans, William B. Publishing Co.
—El Ladron y la Bailarina. Matthews, Andrew. Rubio, Esther, tr. 2004. (SPA.). 30p. (J). 19.99 *(978-84-88342-39-3(X))* S.A. Kokinos ESP. Dist: Lectorum Pubns., Inc.
—The Mouse Who Saved Egypt. Alrawi, Karim. 2011. 32p. (J). (gr. -1-3). 16.95 *(978-1-56656-856-2(0)*, Crocodile Bks.) Interlink Publishing Group, Inc.
—Read with Me Snow White: Sticker Activity Book. Page, Nick & Page, Claire. 2006. (Read with Me (Make Believe Ideas) Ser.). 12p. (J). (gr. k-2). pap. *(978-1-84610-179-3(4))* Make Believe Ideas.
—River Story. Hooper, Meredith. 2015. (ENG.). 32p. (J). (gr. k-3). 6.99 *(978-0-7636-7646-9(2))* Candlewick Pr.
—School for Princes: Stories from the Panchatantra. Gavin, Jamila & Quarto Generic Staff. 2012. (ENG.). 64p. (J). (gr. 2-5). 19.99 *(978-1-84507-990-1(6)*, Frances Lincoln) Quarto Publishing Group UK GBR. Dist: Hachette Bk. Group.
William, Graf. Max Gets It!, 4 vols. Sparks, Candi. ed. 2008. (Can I Have Some Money? Ser.; Vol. 3). (ENG.). 32p. (J). pap. *(978-0-9789445-1-3(8))* Sparks Fly.

W

William, Harper. Racer Buddies-Opening Day at Daytona. Elliott, Craig. 2004. 40p. (J). per. 12.95 *(978-0-9746445-0-9(1),* 1234022) Powerband, LLC.

William, Iceberg Dunbar. The Wacky Winter Witch. Williams, Guana Dunbar. 2003. (J). per. *(978-0-9740673-1-5(8))* Graphix Network.

Williams, Alexandra & Williams, David. Fairy Nyumbani. 2005. 24p. *(978-9966-956-41-5(7))* Jacaranda Designs Ltd.

Williams, Angela. Kwanzaa: The Seven Principles. Terry, Rod. 2005. 64p. (J). (gr. 4-8). reprint ed. 8.00 *(978-0-7567-8635-9(5))* DIANE Publishing Co.

Williams, Angie, photos by. Daniel Keep Dreaming. Martin, Paige. Price, Ronnalda, ed. 2011. 48p. (J). pap. 15.00 *(978-0-578-08272-1(1))* Paige Martin Bks.

Williams, Ann Marie. I Dream for You a World: A Covenant for Our Children. Carney-Nunes, Charisse. 2007. (ENG.). 32p. (J). (gr. k-2). 16.95 *(978-0-9748142-3-0(7),* Brand Nu Words) Nunes Productions, LLC.

—Nappy. Carney-Nunes Charisse. 2006. (ENG.). 24p. (J). (gr. k-2). 14.99 *(978-0-9748142-1-6(0),* Brand Nu Words) Nunes Productions, LLC.

Williams, Anthony. The Battle of Iwo Jima: Guerilla Warfare in the Pacific. Hama, Larry. 2007. (Graphic Battles of World War II Ser.). (ENG.). 48p. (YA). (gr. 4-7). lib. bdg. 31.95 *(978-1-4042-0781-3(3))* Rosen Publishing Group, Inc., The.

—Dracula. Stoker, Bram. 2014. (ENG.). 32p. 8.95 *(978-1-78404-355-1(9))* Arcturus Publishing GBR. Dist: AtlasBooks Distribution.

—Dracula: A Classic Pop-Up Tale. 2009. (ENG.). 16p. 29.95 *(978-0-7893-2050-6(9))* Universe Publishing.

—Frankenstein. Shelley, Mary. 2014. (ENG.). 32p. pap. 8.95 *(978-1-78404-356-8(7))* Arcturus Publishing GBR. Dist: AtlasBooks Distribution.

—The Hound of the Baskervilles. 2014. (ENG.). 32p. pap. 8.95 *(978-1-78404-357-5(5))* Arcturus Publishing GBR. Dist: AtlasBooks Distribution.

—This Ghost Is Toast! Abnett, Dan. 2007. (Real Ghostbusters Ser.). (ENG.). 96p. per. 8.95 *(978-1-84576-143-1(X))* Titan Bks. Ltd. GBR. Dist: Random Hse., Inc.

Williams, Anthony, jt. illus. see Erskine, Gary.

Williams, Bill. Pirate Party. Lytle, Robert A. 2006. (Mackinac Passage Ser.). 258p. (J). (gr. 4-7). pap. 9.95 *(978-0-9749412-5-7(5))* EDCO Publishing, Inc.

Williams, Brian. Herkimer's Big Day: Herkimer the Police Horse Meets a Young Girl Named Sammy. Tyler, Sandy. 2012. (ENG.). 22p. (J). pap. 20.95 *(978-1-4327-9005-9(6))* Outskirts Pr., Inc.

—The Pursuit of the Ivory Poachers - Kenya, Bk. 6. Hunt, Elizabeth Singer. 2008. (ENG.). 144p. (J). (gr. 1-4). pap. 5.99 *(978-1-60286-021-6(1),* Weinstein Bks.) Perseus Bks. Group.

Williams, Brian. Tunnels, Bk. 1. Williams, Brian. Gordon, Roderick. 2008. (Tunnels Ser.: 1). (ENG.). 480p. (J). (gr. 3-7). 17.99 *(978-0-439-87177-8(8),* Chicken Hse., The) Scholastic, Inc.

Williams, Brittney. Well My Teacher Said. Bodden, Michelle. 2007. 32p. (J). 14.95 *(978-0-9753089-2-9(0))* Water Daughter Publishing.

Williams, C. G. The Incredibly Helpful Helper. 2008. (ENG.). 32p. (J). (gr. -1-1). 14.95 *(978-0-7892-1001-2(0),* Abbeville Kids) Abbeville Pr., Inc.

Williams, Carlene H. Santa's Stray. Basore, Polly M. 2004. 32p. (J). per. *(978-0-9771749-2-8(1))* AngelBooks.

—Santa's Stray in A Piano for Christmas. Basore, Polly M. 2005. 32p. (J). per. *(978-0-9771749-1-1(3))* AngelBooks.

Williams, Caroline. Blessings for a Baby Boy. Piper, Sophie. 2010. (ENG.). 44p. (J). (gr. k-k). 8.99 *(978-0-7459-6184-2(3))* Lion Hudson PLC GBR. Dist: Independent Pubs. Group.

—Blessings for a Baby Girl. Piper, Sophie. 11th ed. 2010. (ENG.). 48p. (J). (gr. k-k). 8.99 *(978-0-7459-6185-9(1))* Lion Hudson PLC GBR. Dist: Independent Pubs. Group.

—Everyone Needs a Friend. Piper, Sophie. 2010. (Everyone Needs Ser.). (ENG.). 6p. (J). (gr. k — 1). bds. 5.99 *(978-0-7459-6225-2(4))* Lion Hudson PLC GBR. Dist: Independent Pubs. Group.

Williams, Caspar. Pick Your Brains about Greece. Sanderson, Caroline. 2005. (Pick Your Brains Ser.). 128p. pap. 9.95 *(978-1-86011-220-1(X))* Cadogan Guides GBR. Dist: Globe Pequot Pr., The.

—Pick Your Brains about Ireland. O'Neill, Mary. 2005. (Pick Your Brains - Cadogan Ser.). (ENG.). 128p. pap. 9.95 *(978-1-86011-221-8(8))* Cadogan Guides GBR. Dist: Globe Pequot Pr., The.

—Pick Your Brains about Scotland. Kirkby, Mandy. 2005. (Pick Your Brains Ser.). 128p. pap. 9.95 *(978-1-86011-223-2(4))* Cadogan Guides GBR. Dist: Globe Pequot Pr., The.

—Pick Your Brains about the USA. Egginton, Jane. 2005. (Pick Your Brains - Cadogan Ser.). (ENG.). 128p. pap. 9.95 *(978-1-86011-222-5(6))* Cadogan Guides GBR. Dist: Globe Pequot Pr., The.

Williams, Christopher. Malcolm & the Money Tree. Esdaille-Richardson, Eudora. 2014. (J). pap. *(978-1-934370-49-0(5))* Editorial Campana.

Williams, David, jt. illus. see Williams, Alexandra.

Williams, Denny. Kelsie's Potty Adventure. Prater, Cindy. 2006. 40p. per. 19.95 *(978-1-59858-271-0(2))* Dog Ear Publishing, LLC.

Williams, Deshantren. The Adventures of Kyree & Kyere: The Basement. Sherry, Raymond. 2008. 24p. pap. 24.95 *(978-1-60703-288-5(0))* America Star Bks.

Williams, Don, et al. Disney Princess Little Golden Book Favorites, Vol. 2. Teitelbaum, Michael. 2010. (Little Golden Book Favorites Ser.). (ENG.). 80p. (J). (gr. -1-2). 6.99 *(978-0-7364-2656-5(6),* Golden/Disney) Random Hse. Children's Bks.

Williams, Don, jt. illus. see Cardona, Jose.

Williams, E. Colin. The Battle for Camillo, 1 vol. Tate, Nikki. 2003. (Estorian Chronicles Ser.). (ENG.). 322p. (J). (gr. 4-8). pap. 8.95 *(978-1-55039-127-5(5))* Sono Nis Pr. CAN. Dist: Orca Bk. Pubs. USA.

Williams-El, Belinda Irene. The King's Mascot. Singh, Rajinder. 2011. (ENG & ACE.). 28p. (J). (gr. -1-3). 10.00 *(978-0-918224-85-9(3))* Radiance Pubs.

williams, Emma Louise. What's That Smell Monkey? Williams, Emma Louise. 2012. 12p. pap. 7.99 *(978-1-939076-07-6(2))* Wiggies, Piggy.

Williams, Emma Louise. 30 Sheep & One Cow. Williams, Emma Louise. 2012. 24p. pap. 8.99 *(978-1-939076-05-2(6))* Wiggies, Piggy.

Williams, Emmy. Prestina Quacks: Emmy Williams. Williams, Emmy. 2011. (ENG.). 24p. pap. 10.20 *(978-1-4565-6367-7(X))* CreateSpace Independent Publishing Platform.

Williams, Eric. Magickeepers Bk. 2: The Pyramid of Souls. Kirov, Erica. 2010. (ENG.). 208p. (J). (gr. 4-7). 14.99 *(978-1-4022-1502-5(9),* Sourcebooks Jabberwocky) Sourcebooks, Inc.

Williams, Eric L. Queen of the Dead. Drago, Ty. 2012. (ENG.). 432p. (J). (gr. 5-8). pap. 7.99 *(978-1-4022-7557-9(9),* Sourcebooks Jabberwocky) Sourcebooks, Inc.

Williams, Frederick C. Happiness Colouring Book. Williams, Frederick C. Chappell, Billie-Jean. 2012. 36p. pap. *(978-0-9566564-2-1(0))* Dreamality Bks.

Williams, G. L. The No Thank You Bite, 1 vol. Evans, Carol Wolfe. 2010. 16p. 24.95 *(978-1-4512-2132-9(0))* PublishAmerica, Inc.

Williams, Gail. The Abominog. Thomas, Amy A. 2013. 120p. pap. 6.99 *(978-0-9898579-0-1(5))* Passionate Purpose.

Williams, Gareth. The Adventures of Medical Man: Kids' Illnesses & Injuries Explained. Evans, Michael & Wichman, David. 2010. (ENG.). 72p. (J). (gr. 3-5). 21.95 *(978-1-55451-263-8(8),* 9781554512638); pap. 12.95 *(978-1-55451-262-1(X),* 9781554512621) Annick Pr., Ltd. CAN. Dist: Firefly Bks., Ltd.

—Outlaws, Spies, & Gangsters: Chasing Notorious Criminals. Scandiffio, Laura. 2014. (ENG.). 144p. (J). (gr. 4-7). 24.95 *(978-1-55451-621-6(8),* 9781554516216); pap. 14.95 *(978-1-55451-620-9(X),* 9781554516209) Annick Pr., Ltd. CAN. Dist: Firefly Bks., Ltd.

Williams, Gareth Glyn. Brotherhoods, Death Squads, & the FBI: The Dramatic History of Policing. Butts, Edward. 2014. (ENG.). 168p. (J). (gr. 5-8). pap. 14.95 *(978-1-55451-674-2(9),* 9781554516742) Annick Pr., Ltd. CAN. Dist: Firefly Bks., Ltd.

Williams, Garth. Aquellos Anos Dorado. Wilder, Laura Ingalls & Ingalls, Laura. 2003. (SPA.). 222p. (J). (gr. 5-8). pap. 11.50 *(978-84-279-3255-5(3))* Noguer y Caralt Editores, S. A. ESP. Dist: Lectorum Pubns., Inc.

—Baby Farm Animals. Golden Books Staff. 2006. (Little Golden Treasures Ser.). (ENG.). 26p. (J). (gr. k-k). bds. 4.99 *(978-0-375-83686-2(1),* Golden Bks.) Random Hse. Children's Bks.

—Bunnies' ABC. Golden Books. 2015. (Little Golden Book Ser.). (ENG.). 24p. (J). (-k). 3.99 *(978-0-385-39128-3(5),* Golden Bks.) Random Hse. Children's Bks.

—By the Shores of Silver Lake. Wilder, Laura Ingalls. (Little House Ser.). (ENG.). 304p. (J). (gr. 3-7). 2008. pap. 6.99 *(978-0-06-440005-3(0));* 2004. pap. 8.99 *(978-0-06-058184-8(0))* HarperCollins Pubs.

—Charlotte's Web. White, E. B. & DiCamillo, Kate. (ENG.). 192p. (J). (gr. 3-7). 2012. 16.99 *(978-0-06-026385-0(7));* 2012. 8.99 *(978-0-06-112495-2(8));* 2012. pap. 7.99 *(978-0-06-440055-8(7));* 2006. 16.99 *(978-0-06-088261-7(1))* HarperCollins Pubs.

—Charlotte's Web. White, E. B. (Charming Classics). (J). 2005. 192p. pap. 7.99 *(978-0-06-084594-0(5),* HarperFestival); 2006. 192p. mass mkt. 7.99 *(978-0-06-122874-2(5),* Harper Trophy); Set. 2006. pap. 19.99 *(978-0-06-121502-5(3))* HarperCollins Pubs.

—Charlotte's Web. White, E. B. 2004. (CHI.). 158p. (YA). pap. *(978-957-08-2568-8(5))* Linking Publishing Co., Ltd.

—Charlotte's Web. White, E. B. 184p. (J). pap. 5.95 *(978-0-8072-8305-9(3),* Listening Library) Random Hse. Audio Publishing Group.

—The Cricket in Times Square. Selden, George. (Chester Cricket Ser.). 151p. (J). (gr. 3-6). pap. 5.50 *(978-0-8072-8311-0(8),* Listening Library) Random Hse. Audio Publishing Group.

—The Cricket in Times Square. Selden, George. 2008. (Chester Cricket & His Friends Ser.). (ENG.). 144p. (J). (gr. 1-4). pap. 6.99 *(978-0-312-38003-8(8))* Square Fish.

—Los Cuatro Primeros Anos. Wilder, Laura Ingalls & Ingalls, Laura. 2006. (Little House Bks.). (SPA.). 126p. (YA). (gr. 3-5). pap. 11.50 *(978-84-279-3259-3(6))* Lectorum Pubns., Inc.

—Farmer Boy. Wilder, Laura Ingalls. (Little House Ser.). (ENG.). 384p. (J). (gr. 3-7). 2008. pap. 6.99 *(978-0-06-440003-9(4));* 2004. pap. 8.99 *(978-0-06-058182-4(4))* HarperCollins Pubs.

—The First Four Years. Wilder, Laura Ingalls. (Little House Ser.). (ENG.). 160p. (J). (gr. 3-7). 2008. pap. 6.99 *(978-0-06-440031-2(X));* 2004. pap. 8.99 *(978-0-06-058188-6(3))* HarperCollins Pubs.

—The Friendly Book. Brown, Margaret Wise. 2012. (Little Golden Book Ser.). (ENG.). 24p. (J). (-k). 3.99 *(978-0-307-92962-4(0),* Golden Bks.) Random Hse., Inc.

—The Giant Golden Book of Elves & Fairies. Werner, Janet. 2008. (Golden Classic Ser.). (ENG.). 80p. (J). (gr. -1-2). 16.99 *(978-0-375-84426-3(0),* Golden Bks.) Random Hse. Children's Bks.

—The Gingerbread Rabbit. Jarrell, Randall. 2003. (ENG.). 64p. (J). (gr. -1-3). 17.95 *(978-0-06-052768-6(4))* HarperCollins Pubs.

—Harry Kitten & Tucker Mouse; Chester Cricket's Pigeon Ride. Selden, George. 2009. (Chester Cricket & His Friends Ser.). (ENG.). 144p. (J). (gr. 1-4). pap. 7.99 *(978-0-312-58248-7(X))* Square Fish.

—Home for a Bunny. Brown, Margaret Wise. (Little Golden Board Book Ser.). (ENG.). (J). 2015. 26p. (-k). bds. 7.99 *(978-0-385-39093-4(9));* 2011. 24p. (gr. k-k). bds. 7.99 *(978-0-375-86128-4(9));* 2003. 32p. (gr. -1-k). reprint ed. 8.99 *(978-0-307-10546-2(6))* Random Hse. Children's Bks. (Golden Bks.).

—Home for a Bunny. Brown, Margaret Wise. 2012. (Little Golden Book Ser.). (ENG.). 24p. (J). (gr. k-k). 3.99 *(978-0-307-93009-5(2),* Golden Bks.) Random Hse., Inc.

—The Kitten Who Thought He Was a Mouse. Norton, Miriam. 2008. (Little Golden Book Ser.). (ENG.). 24p. (J). (gr. -1-2). 3.99 *(978-0-375-84822-3(3),* Golden Bks.) Random Hse. Children's Bks.

—Little Fur Family. Brown, Margaret Wise. (ENG.). 32p. (J). (gr. -1-1). 2005. bds. 7.99 *(978-0-06-075960-5(7));* 2003. pap. 17.99 *(978-0-06-051898-1(7))* HarperCollins Pubs. (HarperFestival).

—A Little House Christmas Treasury: Festive Holiday Stories. Wilder, Laura Ingalls. 2005. (Little House Ser.). (ENG.). 144p. (J). (gr. 3-7). 14.99 *(978-0-06-076918-5(1))* HarperCollins Pubs.

—The Little House Collection, Set. Wilder, Laura Ingalls. 2004. (Little House Ser.). (J). (gr. 3-7). pap. 44.99 *(978-0-06-075428-0(1))* HarperCollins Pubs.

—Little House in the Big Woods. Wilder, Laura Ingalls. (Little House Ser.). (ENG.). 256p. (J). (gr. 3-7). 2008. pap. 6.99 *(978-0-06-440001-5(8));* 2004. pap. 8.99 *(978-0-06-058180-0(8))* HarperCollins Pubs.

—Little House on the Prairie. Wilder, Laura Ingalls. (Little House Ser.). (ENG.). (J). (gr. 3-7). 2008. 352p. pap. 6.99 *(978-0-06-440002-2(6));* 2004. 352p. pap. 8.99 *(978-0-06-058181-7(6));* 75th anniv. ed. 2010. 368p. 16.99 *(978-0-06-195827-4(1))* HarperCollins Pubs.

—Little Silver House. Lindquist, Jennie D. 2008. (J). (gr. 2-6). 21.00 *(978-0-8446-6190-2(2))* Smith, Peter Pub., Inc.

—Little Town on the Prairie. Wilder, Laura Ingalls. (Little House Ser.). 320p. (J). 2008. (ENG.). (gr. 3-7). pap. 6.99 *(978-0-06-440007-7(7));* 2004. (ENG.). (gr. 3-7). pap. 8.99 *(978-0-06-058186-2(7));* 2003. pap. 5.99 *(978-0-06-052242-1(9))* HarperCollins Pubs.

—The Long Winter. Wilder, Laura Ingalls. (Little House Ser.). (ENG.). 352p. (J). (gr. 3-7). 2008. pap. 6.99 *(978-0-06-440006-0(9));* 2004. pap. 8.99 *(978-0-06-058185-5(9))* HarperCollins Pubs.

—Mister Dog. Brown, Margaret Wise. 2003. (Little Golden Book Ser.). (ENG.). 24p. (J). (gr. -1-2). 3.99 *(978-0-307-10336-9(6),* Golden Bks.) Random Hse. Children's Bks.

Williams, Garth. My First Counting Book. Moore, Lilian. 2015. (Little Golden Board Book Ser.). (ENG.). 26p. (J). (-k). bds. 7.99 ***(978-0-553-52223-5(X),*** Golden Bks.) Random Hse. Children's Bks.

Williams, Garth. On the Banks of Plum Creek. Wilder, Laura Ingalls. (Little House Ser.). (ENG.). 352p. (J). (gr. 3-7). 2008. pap. 6.99 *(978-0-06-440004-6(2));* 2004. pap. 8.99 *(978-0-06-058183-1(2))* HarperCollins Pubs.

—The Rescuers. Sharp, Margery. 2011. (ENG.). 160p. (J). (gr. 4-7). 14.95 *(978-1-59017-460-9(7),* NYR Children's Collection) New York Review of Bks., Inc., The.

—Stuart Little. White, E. B. 60th anniv. ed. 2005. (Trophy Bk.). (ENG.). 144p. (J). (gr. 3-7). pap. 6.99 *(978-0-06-440056-5(5));* 16.99 *(978-0-06-026395-9(4))* HarperCollins Pubs.

—Stuart Little. White, E. B. 2004. (SPA.). 144p. (J). (gr. 3-5). pap. 10.95 *(978-1-59437-554-5(2))* Santillana USA Publishing Co., Inc.

—Stuart Little Book & Charm. White, E. B. 2006. (Charming Classics). 144p. (J). (gr. 3-7). 6.99 *(978-0-06-082334-4(8),* HarperFestival) HarperCollins Pubs.

—La Telarana de Carlota. White, E. B. 2005. (SPA.). 224p. (J). (gr. 3-7). pap. 7.99 *(978-0-06-075740-3(X),* Rayo) HarperCollins Pubs.

—The Telarana of Carlota (La Telarana de Carlota) White, E. B. 2005. (Charlotte's Web Ser.). (SPA.). 224p. (J). 16.99 *(978-0-06-075739-7(6),* Rayo) HarperCollins Pubs.

—The Telarana of Carlota (LaTelarana de Carlota) White, E. B. movie tie-in ed. 2006. (Charlotte's Web Ser.). (SPA.). 224p. (J). pap. 7.99 *(978-0-06-112522-5(9),* Rayo) HarperCollins Pubs.

—These Happy Golden Years. Wilder, Laura Ingalls. (Little House Ser.: 8). (ENG.). 304p. (J). (gr. 3-7). 2004. pap. 8.99 *(978-0-06-058187-9(5));* 2008. pap. 6.99 *(978-0-06-440008-4(5))* HarperCollins Pubs.

—Tucker's Countryside. Selden, George. 2012. (ENG.). 192p. (J). (gr. 3-7). pap. 6.99 *(978-1-250-00256-3(7))* Square Fish.

Williams, Garth. Baby Animals. Williams, Garth. 2004. (Little Golden Book Ser.). (ENG.). 24p. (J). (gr. -1-2). 3.99 *(978-0-375-82933-8(4),* Golden Bks.) Random Hse. Children's Bks.

—Baby Farm Animals. Williams, Garth. 2011. (Golden Baby Ser.). (ENG.). 24p. (J). (-k). bds. 6.99 *(978-0-375-86127-7(0),* Golden Bks.) Random Hse. Children's Bks.

—Baby's First Book. Williams, Garth. (Golden Baby Ser.). (ENG.). 24p. (J). 2011. (— 1). bds. 6.99 *(978-0-375-85905-2(5));* 2007. (gr. -1-2). 3.99 *(978-0-375-83916-0(X))* Random Hse. Children's Bks. (Golden Bks.).

Williams, Garth & Maze, Deborah. The World of Little House. Collins, Carolyn Strom & Eriksson, Christina Wyss. 2015. (Little House Ser.). (ENG.). 160p. (J). (gr. 3). 29.99 ***(978-0-06-243049-6(1))*** HarperCollins Pubs.

Williams, Garth & Wells, Rosemary. Stuart Little. White, E. B. 60th anniv. ed. 2005. (Stuart-Little Ser.). (ENG.). 144p. (J). (gr. 3-7). pap. 8.99 *(978-0-06-441092-2(7))* HarperCollins Pubs.

Williams, George Alfred. Ten Girls from Dickens. Sweetser, Kate Dickinson. 2004. reprint ed. pap. 27.95 *(978-1-4179-3165-1(5))* Kessinger Publishing, LLC.

Williams, Glenn. Learning about Cows. Williams, Glenn, photos by. Lapsley, Sarah. 2008. 20p. (J). pap. *(978-1-935289-10-4(1))* Spalding Education International.

Williams, Harland. The Kid with Too Many Nightmares. 2004. (J). *(978-0-8431-1582-6(3),* Price Stern Sloan) Penguin Publishing Group.

Williams, J. H., III & Bianchi, Simone. The Seven Soldiers of Victory, Vol. 1. Morrison, Grant. rev. ed. 2006. (Seven Soldiers of Victory Archives Ser.). (ENG.). 224p. (YA). pap. 14.99 *(978-1-4012-0925-4(4))* DC Comics.

Williams, Jared T. Catie Copley. Kovacs, Deborah. 2007. (ENG.). 32p. (J). (gr. -1-3). 17.95 *(978-1-56792-332-2(1))* Godine, David R. Pub.

—Catie Copley's Great Escape. Kovacs, Deborah. 2009. (J). 17.95 *(978-1-56792-382-7(8));* (ENG.). 32p. (gr. -1-3). 17.95 *(978-1-56792-379-7(8))* Godine, David R. Pub.

Williams, Jayne. Molly's Magic Smile. Cutrer, Elisabeth. Sexton, Jessa R., ed. 2013. 38p. 17.00 *(978-0-9860244-3-6(0))* O'More Publishing.

Williams, Jean. The Stork & the Birthday Stocking. Payne, Jackson. 2009. 24p. pap. 12.00 *(978-1-4389-8146-8(5))* AuthorHouse.

Williams, Jenny. The Princess & the Wise Woman. Riley, Kana. 2012. (Ready Readers: Stage 5 Ser.). (ENG.). 24p. (J). (gr. k-2). pap. 6.97 *(978-0-8136-2371-9(5))* Modern Curriculum Pr.

—A Storyteller Book - Red Riding Hood. Young, Lesley. 2013. (ENG.). 48p. (J). (gr. -1-12). pap. 7.99 *(978-1-84322-909-4(9),* Armadillo) Anness Publishing GBR. Dist: National Bk. Network.

—Twelfth Night. Birch, Beverley & Shakespeare, William. 2007. (Shakespeare's Tales Ser.). (ENG.). 80p. (J). (gr. 4-7). 13.95 *(978-0-7502-4964-5(1),* Wayland) Hachette Children's Group GBR. Dist: Independent Pubs. Group.

—The Week That Led to Easter. Larrison, Joanne. 2004. (Arch Bks.). (ENG.). 16p. (J). (gr. k-4). 1.99 *(978-0-570-07572-1(6))* Concordia Publishing Hse.

—25 Things to Do When Grandpa Passes Away, Mom & Dad Get Divorced, or the Dog Dies: Activities to Help Children Suffering Loss or Change. Kanyer, Laurie A. 2004. (ENG.). 80p. pap. 13.95 *(978-1-884734-53-3(7))* Parenting Pr., Inc.

Williams, John. Runaways. Layburn, Joe. 2014. (ENG.). 144p. (J). (gr. 4-7). pap. 8.95 *(978-1-84780-080-0(7),* Frances Lincoln) Quarto Publishing Group UK GBR. Dist: Hachette Bk. Group.

Williams Jr., Anthony. Granny Says. Williams-Ashe, Marcella Norton. 2012. 46p. pap. 12.00 *(978-0-9764198-4-6(X))* Allecram Publishing.

Williams, Keith, et al. The 1918 Flu Pandemic, 1 vol. Krohn, Katherine. 2007. (Disasters in History Ser.). (ENG.). 32p. (gr. 3-4). 29.99 *(978-1-4296-0158-0(2),* Graphic Library) Capstone Pr., Inc.

Williams, Larry. The League of Clique. Williams, Larry. 2007. (ENG.). 80p. per. 19.95 *(978-1-4241-5976-5(8))* America Star Bks.

Williams, Lisa. Bad Luck, Lucy! Graves, Sue. 2008. (Tadpoles Ser.). (ENG.). 24p. (J). (gr. -1-3). pap. *(978-0-7787-3862-4(5));* lib. bdg. *(978-0-7787-3851-0(5))* Crabtree Publishing Co.

—The Big Turnip. Hughes, Mónica. Moon, Cliff, ed. 2006. (Collins Big Cat Ser.). (ENG.). 16p. (J). pap. 5.99 *(978-0-00-718644-0(4))* HarperCollins Pubs. Ltd. GBR. Dist: Independent Pubs. Group.

—Cave-Baby & the Mammoth. French, Vivian. 2010. 32p. pap. *(978-1-84089-635-0(3))* Zero to Ten, Ltd.

—If I Were an Alien. French, Vivian. 2009. (Get Set Readers Ser.). 32p. (J). (gr. -1-2). lib. bdg. 22.60 *(978-1-60754-267-4(6))* Windmill Bks.

Williams, Lorraine. Wave Goodbye, 1 vol. Reid, Rob. 2013. (ENG.). 24p. (J). pap. 9.95 *(978-1-60060-341-9(6))* Lee & Low Bks., Inc.

Williams, Mandi. Mortimer's Book of What-Ifs (A Children's Rhyming Picture Book of Poetry) Williams, Mandi. 2012. (ENG.). 24p. pap. 10.89 *(978-1-4664-9743-6(2))* CreateSpace Independent Publishing Platform.

Williams, Marcia. Archie's War: My Scrapbook of the First World War. Williams, Marcia. Yang, Belle. 2007. (ENG.). 48p. (J). (gr. 3-7). 18.99 *(978-0-7636-3532-9(4))* Candlewick Pr.

—The Elephant's Friend & Other Tales from Ancient India. Williams, Marcia. (ENG.). 40p. (J). 2014. (gr. 1-4). 6.99 *(978-0-7636-7055-9(3));* 2012. (gr. 3-7). 16.99 *(978-0-7636-5916-5(9))* Candlewick Pr.

—Greek Myths. Williams, Marcia. 2011. (ENG.). 40p. (J). (gr. k-4). pap. 8.99 *(978-0-7636-5384-2(5))* Candlewick Pr.

—Hooray for Inventors! Williams, Marcia. 2013. (ENG.). 40p. (J). (gr. 3-7). pap. 7.99 *(978-0-7636-6749-8(8))* Candlewick Pr.

—Lizzy Bennet's Diary: Inspired by Jane Austen's Pride & Prejudice. Williams, Marcia. 2014. (ENG.). 112p. (J). (gr. 3-7). 16.99 *(978-0-7636-7030-6(8))* Candlewick Pr.

—More Tales from Shakespeare. Williams, Marcia. 2005. (ENG.). 40p. (J). (gr. 3-7). pap. 8.99 *(978-0-7636-2693-8(7))* Candlewick Pr.

—Tales from Shakespeare. Williams, Marcia. Shakespeare, William. 2004. (ENG.). 40p. (J). (gr. 3-7). reprint ed. pap. 7.99 *(978-0-7636-2323-4(7))* Candlewick Pr.

Williams, Matthew. Are You My Bird? Mataya, Marybeth. 2008. (Are You My Pet? Ser.). 32p. (J). (gr. 1-4). 28.50 *(978-1-60270-241-7(1))* Magic Wagon.

—Are You My Cat? Mataya, Marybeth. 2008. (Are You My Pet? Ser.). 32p. (J). (gr. 1-4). 28.50 *(978-1-60270-242-4(X))* Magic Wagon.

—Are You My Dog? Mataya, Marybeth. 2008. (Are You My Pet? Ser.). 32p. (J). (gr. 1-4). 28.50 *(978-1-60270-243-1(8))* Magic Wagon.

—Are You My Fish? Vogel, Julia. 2008. (Are You My Pet? Ser.). 32p. (J). (gr. 1-4). 28.50 *(978-1-60270-244-8(6))* Magic Wagon.

—Are You My Rabbit? Vogel, Julia. 2008. (Are You My Pet? Ser.). 32p. (J). (gr. 1-4). 28.50 *(978-1-60270-245-5(4))* Magic Wagon.

—Are You My Rodent? Mataya, Marybeth. 2008. (Are You My Pet? Ser.). 32p. (J). (gr. 1-4). 28.50 *(978-1-60270-246-2(2))* Magic Wagon.

Williams, Nate. Giving a Presentation. Bodden, Valerie. 2015. (Classroom How-To Ser.). (ENG.). 48p. (J). (gr. 5-8). pap. 12.00 *(978-0-89812-986-1(9),* Creative Paperbacks) Creative Co., The.

—How Fast Can You Go? Riggs, Kate. 2014. (ENG.). 14p. (J). (gr. -1-k). bds. 7.99 *(978-1-56846-253-0(0),* Creative Editions) Creative Co., The.

—Writing a Research Paper. Bodden, Valerie. 2015. (Classroom How-To Ser.). (ENG.). 48p. (J). (gr. 5-8). pap.

12.00 *(978-0-89812-989-2(3)*, Creative Paperbacks) Creative Co., The.

Williams, Nate. Hank & Snoliver in Put down the Phone!, 1 vol. Williams, Nate. Gibbs Smith. 2015. (ENG.). 32p. (J). (gr. 2-3). 16.99 ***(978-1-4236-3925-1(1))*** Gibbs Smith, Publisher.

Williams, Nate. Hank & Snoliver in What Can I Be?, 1 vol. Williams, Nate. Smith, Gibbs. 2015. (ENG.). 32p. (J). (gr. 2-3). 19.99 *(978-1-4236-3928-2(6))* Gibbs Smith, Publisher.

Williams, Raymond. The Unusual Pet Shop. Williams, Brenda May. 2012. 24p. pap. 11.50 *(978-1-61897-798-4(9)*, Strategic Bk. Publishing) Strategic Book Publishing & Rights Agency (SBPRA).

Williams, Rhonda, photos by. Mommy, Daddy, Where Do Babies Come From? Activity Book. Date not set. (Wonderful World of True Love Ser.). 16p. (J). (gr. k-4). pap. 3.95 *(978-0-9675068-0-7(8))* Media For Life.

Williams, Rob, et al. The Amazing Spider-Man: The Fantastic Spider-Man. 2011. (ENG.). 160p. (J). (gr. 4-17). 24.99 *(978-0-7851-5106-7(0))* Marvel Worldwide, Inc.

Williams, Rob. Forever Fingerprints: An Amazing Discovery for Adopted Children. Eldridge, Sherrie. 2014. (ENG.). 32p. (J). *(978-1-84905-778-3(8))* Kingsley, Jessica Ltd.

—I Don't Have Your Eyes. Kitze, Carrie A. 2007. 32p. (J). (gr. -1-3). 16.95 *(978-0-9726244-2-8(2))* EMK Pr.

Williams, Robert. Kwanzaa: African American Celebration of Culture, 1 vol. Doering, Amanda. 2006. (Holidays & Culture Ser.). (ENG.). 24p. (gr. 1-2). 24.65 *(978-0-7368-5390-3(1)*, First Facts) Capstone Pr., Inc.

Williams, Ron. Dad's Falling Apart: Keeping It Together When a Family Member Has Multiple Sclerosis. Smith, Jennifer Crown. 2003. 32p. (J). per. 14.95 *(978-0-929173-36-8(8))* Health Press NA Incorporated.

Williams, Sam. Baby Cakes. Wilson, Karma. 2006. (ENG.). 32p. (J). (gr. -1 — 1). 7.99 *(978-1-4169-0289-8(9)*, Little Simon) Little Simon.

—Baby, I Love You. Wilson, Karma. 2009. (ENG.). 30p. (J). (gr. -1 — 1). bds., bds. 7.99 *(978-1-4169-1910-0(4)*, Little Simon) Little Simon.

—Ballet Kitty: Christmas Recital. Ford, Bernette. 2012. (ENG.). 32p. (J). (gr. -1-1). 16.95 *(978-1-907152-12-2(1))* Boxer Bks., Ltd. GBR. Dist: Sterling Publishing Co., Inc.

—Bathtime for Twins. Weiss, Ellen. 2012. (ENG.). 30p. (J). (gr. -1 — 1). bds. 7.99 *(978-1-4424-3026-6(5)*, Little Simon) Little Simon.

—First Signing ABC. Hyperion Staff. 2007. (ENG.). 64p. (J). (gr. -1-3). 16.99 *(978-1-4231-0248-9(7))* Hyperion Pr.

—Frosty the Snowman. Rollins, Walter & Nelson, Steve. 2013. (ENG.). 16p. (J). (gr. -1-k). bds. 9.99 *(978-0-545-45005-8(5)*, Cartwheel Bks.) Scholastic, Inc.

—Little Red's Autumn Adventure. Ferguson, Sarah & Duchess of York Staff. 2009. (ENG.). 40p. (J). (gr. -1-1). 16.99 *(978-0-689-84341-9(0)*, Simon & Schuster/Paula Wiseman Bks.) Simon & Schuster/Paula Wiseman Bks.

—Little Red's Christmas Story. Ferguson, Sarah & Duchess of York Staff. 2011. (ENG.). 40p. (J). (gr. -1-2). pap. 19.99 *(978-1-4424-3076-1(1)*, Simon & Schuster/Paula Wiseman Bks.) Simon & Schuster/Paula Wiseman Bks.

—Little Red's Summer Adventure. Ferguson, Sarah & Duchess of York Staff. 2006. (ENG.). 40p. (J). (gr. -1-3). 17.99 *(978-0-689-85562-7(1)*, Simon & Schuster/Paula Wiseman Bks.) Simon & Schuster/Paula Wiseman Bks.

—No More Biting for Billy Goat! Ford, Bernette. 2013. (Ducky & Piggy Ser.). (ENG.). 32p. (J). (gr. -1-k). 14.95 *(978-1-907967-31-3(1))* Boxer Bks., Ltd. GBR. Dist: Sterling Publishing Co., Inc.

—No More Blanket for Lambkin! Ford, Bernette. 2010. (Ducky & Piggy Ser.). (ENG.). 26p. (J). (gr. k — 1). bds. 6.95 *(978-1-906250-47-8(2))* Boxer Bks., Ltd. GBR. Dist: Sterling Publishing Co., Inc.

—No More Bottles for Bunny! Ford, Bernette. 2008. (Ducky & Piggy Ser.). (ENG.). 26p. (J). (gr. -1 — 1). bds. 6.95 *(978-1-906250-22-5(7))* Boxer Bks., Ltd. GBR. Dist: Sterling Publishing Co., Inc.

—No More Diapers for Ducky! Ford, Bernette. 2007. (Ducky & Piggy Ser.). (ENG.). 26p. (J). (gr. -1 — 1). bds. 6.95 *(978-1-905417-38-4(1))* Boxer Bks., Ltd. GBR. Dist: Sterling Publishing Co., Inc.

—No More Pacifier for Piggy! Ford, Bernette. 2012. (Ducky & Piggy Ser.). (ENG.). 26p. (J). (gr. k — 1). bds. 6.95 *(978-1-907152-96-2(2))* Boxer Bks., Ltd. GBR. Dist: Sterling Publishing Co., Inc.

—Playtime for Twins. Weiss, Ellen. 2012. (ENG.). 30p. (J). (gr. -1 — 1). bds. 7.99 *(978-1-4424-3027-3(3)*, Little Simon) Little Simon.

—Pretty Princess Pig. Yolen, Jane & Stemple, Heidi E. Y. 2011. (ENG.). 24p. (J). (gr. -1-1). 9.99 *(978-1-4424-0833-3(2)*, Little Simon) Little Simon.

—Princess Puppy. Ford, Bernette G. 2013. (J). *(978-0-545-53967-8(6))*; (ENG.). 32p. (gr. -1-k). pap. 6.99 *(978-0-545-45006-5(3))* Scholastic, Inc. (Cartwheel Bks.).

—Twins in the Park. Weiss, Ellen. 2003. (Ready-To-Reads Ser.). (ENG.). 24p. (J). (gr. -1-k). pap. 3.99 *(978-0-689-85742-3(X)*, Simon Spotlight) Simon Spotlight.

—Whatever You Do, I Love You. Weiss, Ellen. 2010. (ENG.). 16p. (J). (gr. -1 — 1). 7.99 *(978-1-4424-0809-8(X)*, Little Simon) Little Simon.

—You're Getting a Baby Brother! Higginson, Sheila Sweeny. 2012. (ENG.). 24p. (J). (gr. -1-k). bds. 7.99 *(978-1-4424-2021-2(9)*, Little Simon) Little Simon.

—You're Getting a Baby Sister! Higginson, Sheila Sweeny. 2012. (ENG.). 24p. (J). (gr. -1-k). bds. 7.99 *(978-1-4424-2050-2(2)*, Little Simon) Little Simon.

Williams, Sandra. God Knows Me: Pslam 139 for Little Hearts. Williams, Sandra. 2007. 24p. (J). 8.95 *(978-0-9789310-2-5(5))* Hardnett Publishing.

Williams, Scott & Sinclair, Alex. For Tomorrow. Azzarello, Brian & Loeb, Jeph. rev. ed. 2006. (Superman (DC Comics) Ser.). (ENG.). 160p. (YA). pap. 14.99 *(978-1-4012-0352-8(3))* DC Comics.

Williams, Shan. Quacker Meets His Dad the Squirrel: Tales from a Duck Named Quacker. Shelton, Ricky V. Date not set. (J). (gr. -1-1). pap. 17.00 *(978-0-9634257-3-7(0))* RVS Bks., Inc.

Williams, Sophy. Easter Angels. Hartman, Bob. 2010. (ENG.). 32p. (J). (gr. 2-4). 14.99 *(978-0-7459-6922-0(4))* Lion Hudson PLC GBR. Dist: Independent Pubs. Group.

—Grandpa's Boat. Catchpool, Michael. 2008. (ENG.). 32p. (J). (gr. k-k). 21.95 *(978-1-84270-690-9(X))* Andersen Pr. GBR. Dist: Independent Pubs. Group.

—Lost in the Snow. Webb, Holly. 2008. 96p. (J). (gr. 1-5). 3.99 *(978-1-56148-650-2(7)*, Good Bks.) Skyhorse Publishing Co., Inc.

—The Nativity Story. McCaughrean, Geraldine & Dubravka, Kolanovic. 2009. (ENG.). 48p. (J). (gr. 2-4). 14.95 *(978-0-7459-6092-0(8))* Lion Hudson PLC GBR. Dist: Independent Pubs. Group.

Williams, Steve. The Matt & the Monster Do to Mexico - la Mutt y la Monster Van a Mexi. Krakow, Amy. Knaus, Jill, tr. 2003.Tr. of La Mutt Y La Monster Van A Mexico. 32p. (J). (gr. 2-6). 15.00 *(978-0-9715224-1-1(3))* Wagging Tales Publishing.

—The Matt & the Monster 60 Sking & Snowboarding. Krakow, Amy. 2005. 32p. (J). (gr. k-6). 15.00 *(978-0-9715224-2-8(1))* Wagging Tales Publishing.

Williams, Sue. Fun in the Sun. Albee, Sarah. 2006. (Step-By-Step Readers Ser.). (J). pap. *(978-1-59939-058-1(2)*, Reader's Digest Young Families, Inc.) Studio Fun International.

—Under the Ramadan Moon. Whitman, Sylvia. 2012. (J). 32.71 *(978-1-61913-151-4(X))* Weigl Pubs., Inc.

—Under the Ramadan Moon, 1 vol. Whitman, Sylvia. (ENG.). 24p. (J). (gr. -1-2). 2011. 6.99 *(978-0-8075-8305-0(7))*; 2008. 15.99 *(978-0-8075-8304-3(9))* Whitman, Albert & Co.

Williams, Ted. Allie Gator's Halloween Hayride. Alexander, Heather. Running Press Staff, ed. 2006. (ENG.). 24p. (J). (gr. 3-7). pap. 4.95 *(978-0-7624-2658-4(6))* Running Pr. Bk. Pubs.

—Curly Hare Gets It Straight. Douglas, Babette. 2006. (Kiss a Me Teacher Creature Stories Ser.). (J). (gr. -1-3). *(978-1-890343-35-4(8))* Kiss A Me Productions, Inc.

—Making Water Clean, 1 vol. Olien, Rebecca. 2005. (Water All Around Ser.). (ENG.). 24p. (gr. 1-2). 24.65 *(978-0-7368-3703-3(5)*, First Facts) Capstone Pr., Inc.

—My First Dictionary. Miller, Susan A. 2005. (My First Ser.). 160p. (J). 7.98 *(978-0-7853-8369-7(7)*, 7183800) Phoenix International Publications, Inc.

—Squirt: The Magic Cuddlefish. Douglas, Babette. 2006. (Kiss a Me Teacher Creature Stories Ser.). (J). (gr. -1-3). 9.99 *(978-1-890343-47-7(1))* Kiss A Me Productions, Inc.

—The Water Cycle, 1 vol. Olien, Rebecca. 2005. (Water All Around Ser.). (ENG.). 24p. (gr. 1-2). 24.65 *(978-0-7368-3701-9(9)*, First Facts) Capstone Pr., Inc.

—Wind, 1 vol. Sievert, Terri & Dougherty, Terri. 2005. (Weather Update Ser.). (ENG.). 24p. (gr. 2-3). 23.32 *(978-0-7368-3740-8(X)*, Bridgestone Bks.) Capstone Pr., Inc.

Williams, Ted & Kaminski, Karol. My First English-Spanish Picture Dictionary. 2005. (ENG & SPA.). 96p. (gr. -1-3). 6.98 *(978-1-4127-1086-2(3)*, 7242100) Phoenix International Publications, Inc.

Williams, Ted, jt. illus. see McMullen, Anne.

Williams, Tim. Gapper's Grand Tour: A Voyage Through Great American Ball Park. Altman, Joel. 2013. (ENG.). (J). (gr. -1-3). 14.95 *(978-1-62086-213-1(1))* Mascot Bks., Inc.

—Hello, Knightro! Callahan, Lauren & Callahan, Michael T. 2013. (ENG.). (J). (gr. 4-7). 14.95 *(978-1-62086-169-1(0))* Mascot Bks., Inc.

—A Is for Alabama: Roll Tide Roll. Zangas, Sherri. 2009. (J). lib. bdg. 17.95 *(978-0-692-00093-9(3))* Mascot Bks., Inc.

Williams, Toby. I Have a Question, Vol. 4. Martin, Tyler. l.t. ed. 2005. (Sadlier Phonics Reading Program). 8p. (gr. -1-1). 23.00 net. *(978-0-8215-7356-3(X))* Sadlier, William H. Inc.

Williams, Vera B. Amber Was Brave, Essie Was Smart. Williams, Vera B. 2004. (ENG.). 72p. (J). (gr. 2-7). reprint ed. pap. 7.99 *(978-0-06-057182-5(5)*, Greenwillow Bks.) HarperCollins Pubs.

—Amber Was Brave, Essie Was Smart. Williams, Vera B. 2003. (J). (gr. k-3). 25.95 incl. audio *(978-1-59112-186-2(8))* Live Oak Media.

—Amber Was Brave, Essie Was Smart. Williams, Vera B. 2004. 17.00 *(978-0-7569-3181-0(9))* Perfection Learning Corp.

—A Chair for Always. Williams, Vera B. 2009. 40p. (J). (gr. -1-3). (SPA & ENG.). 16.99 *(978-0-06-172279-0(0))*; (SPA.). pap. 6.99 *(978-0-06-172643-9(5))*; lib. bdg. 17.89 *(978-0-06-172280-6(4))* HarperCollins Pubs. (Greenwillow Bks.).

—A Chair for My Mother. Williams, Vera B. 25th anniv. ed. 2007. (Reading Rainbow Bks.). (ENG.). 32p. (J). (gr. -1-3). pap. 6.99 *(978-0-688-04074-1(8)*, Greenwillow Bks.) HarperCollins Pubs.

—Un Sillón para Mi Mamá. Williams, Vera B. Marcuse, Aida E., tr. from ENG. 25th anniv. ed. 2007. (un/Libro Mulberry en Espanol Ser.). (SPA.). 32p. (J). (gr. -1-3). reprint ed. pap. 6.99 *(978-0-688-13200-2(6)*, MR5678, Greenwillow Bks.) HarperCollins Pubs.

—Un Sillón para Siempre. Williams, Vera B. 2009.Tr. of Chair for Always. (SPA & ENG.). 40p. (J). (gr. -1-3). 17.99 *(978-0-06-172283-7(9)*, Greenwillow Bks.) HarperCollins Pubs.

Williams, Walter. A Monster for Tea. Williams, Walter. 2013. (ENG.). 32p. (J). (gr. -1-2). 17.99 *(978-0-9890698-3-0(4))* Fernwood & Hedges Bks.

Williams, Wish. Good Night, Little Sea Otter, 1 vol. Halfmann, Janet. (ENG.). (J). 2012. 24p. 15.95 *(978-1-59572-277-5(7))*; 2010. 32p. (gr. -1-3). pap. 5.95 *(978-1-59572-254-6(8))* Star Bright Bks., Inc.

—Good Night, Little Sea Otter (Burmese Karen/English), 1 vol. Halfmann, Janet. 2012. (KAR & ENG.). 24p. (J). 5.95 *(978-1-59572-371-0(4))* Star Bright Bks., Inc.

—Good Night, Little Sea Otter (Burmese/English), 1 vol. Halfmann, Janet. 2012. (ENG.). 24p. (J). pap. 5.95 *(978-1-59572-370-3(6))* Star Bright Bks., Inc.

—Good Night, Little Sea Otter (Hmong/English), 1 vol. Halfmann, Janet. 2012. (ENG.). 24p. (J). pap. 5.95 *(978-1-59572-365-9(X))* Star Bright Bks., Inc.

—Good Night, Little Sea Otter (Portuguese/English), 1 vol. Halfmann, Janet. 2012. (ENG.). 24p. (J). pap. 5.95 *(978-1-59572-359-8(5))* Star Bright Bks., Inc.

—Good Night, Little Sea Otter (Spanish/English), 1 vol. Halfmann, Janet. 2012. (ENG.). 32p. (J). pap. 5.95 *(978-1-59572-347-5(1))* Star Bright Bks., Inc.

—Witches, 1 vol. Christian, Cheryl. 2011. (ENG.). 32p. (J). pap. 5.95 *(978-1-59572-283-6(1))* Star Bright Bks., Inc.

Williams, Zac, photos by. Barbara Beery's Pink Princess Party Cookbook. Beery, Barbara. 2011. (ENG.). 64p. (J). (gr. 2-7). spiral bd. 15.99 *(978-1-4424-1231-6(3)*, Simon & Schuster Bks. For Young Readers) Simon & Schuster Bks. For Young Readers.

—Cupcake Cakes, 1 vol. Anderson, Lisa Turner & Barlow, Melissa. 2011. (ENG.). 64p. (gr. 3). spiral bd. 14.99 *(978-1-4236-1748-8(7))* Gibbs Smith, Publisher.

Williamson, Ada C. Understood Betsy - Illustrated. Fisher, Dorothy Canfield. 2013. 112p. pap. 3.97 *(978-1-60386-582-1(9)*, Merchant Bks.) Rough Draft Printing.

Williamson, Ada Clendenin. The Sandman: More Farm Stories (Yesterday's Classics) Hopkins, William J. 2009. 150p. pap. 8.95 *(978-1-59915-301-8(7))* Yesterday's Classics.

Williamson, Al, jt. illus. see Davis, Jack.

Williamson, Alan, 8th. Timmy the Tow Truck, 6 vols. Williamson, Jennifer. 2005. 28p. (J). pap. *(978-0-9771678-1-4(X))* Theee Hole Punch Publishing.

Williamson, Brian. The Fight for the Frozen Land, Bk.12. Hunt, Elizabeth Singer. 2009. (ENG.). 128p. (J). (gr. 1-4). pap. 5.99 *(978-1-60286-099-5(8))* Perseus Bks. Group.

—The Mystery of the Mona Lisa, Bk. 3. Hunt, Elizabeth Singer. 2007. (ENG.). 128p. (J). (gr. 1-4). per. 5.99 *(978-1-60286-001-8(7))* Perseus Bks. Group.

—The Puzzle of the Missing Panda, Bk. 7. Hunt, Elizabeth Singer. 2008. (ENG.). 128p. (J). (gr. 1-4). pap. 5.99 *(978-1-60286-020-9(3))* Perseus Bks. Group.

—The Search for the Sunken Treasure. Hunt, Elizabeth Singer. 2007. (ENG.). 128p. (J). (gr. 1-4). per. 5.99 *(978-1-60286-002-5(5))* Perseus Bks. Group.

—Secret Agent Jack Stalwart: The Secret of the Sacred Temple - Cambodia. Hunt, Elizabeth Singer. 2008. (ENG.). 128p. (J). (gr. 1). per. 5.99 *(978-1-60286-003-2(3)*, Weinstein Bks.) Perseus Bks. Group.

—Secret Agent Jack Stalwart Bk. 1: The Escape of the Deadly Dinosaur - USA. Hunt, Elizabeth Singer. 2007. (ENG.). 128p. (J). (gr. 1-4). per. 5.99 *(978-1-60286-004-9(1))* Perseus Bks. Group.

—The Theft of the Samurai Sword - Japan. Hunt, Elizabeth Singer & Weinstein Books Staff. 2009. (ENG.). 128p. (J). (gr. 1-4). pap. 5.99 *(978-1-60286-098-8(X))* Perseus Bks. Group.

Williamson, Brian, jt. illus. see Hansen, Jimmy.

Williamson, Froser. My Clothes: Individual Title Six-Packs. (Sails Literacy Ser.). 16p. (gr. k-18). 27.00 *(978-0-7635-4392-1(6))* Rigby Education.

Williamson, James. ELEMENOPEE, the Day I, M, N, O & P Left the Abc's Hall, Pamela. 2005. 16p. (J). 12.95 *(978-1-58117-209-6(5)*, Intervisual/Piggy Toes) Bendon, Inc.

Williamson, Linda K. Veneti: Lake Michigan's Treasure. Birkholz, Gay Lyn. 2010. 52p. pap. 17.00 *(978-1-60860-129-5(3)*, Strategic Bk. Publishing) Strategic Book Publishing & Rights Agency (SBPRA).

Williamson, Melanie. Drift upon a Dream: Poems for Sleepy Babies. 2004. 32p. (J). 16.95 *(978-1-57091-577-2(6))* Charlesbridge Publishing, Inc.

—The Great Fairy Tale Disaster. Conway, David. 2012. (J). *(978-1-58925-111-3(3))* Tiger Tales.

—The Great Nursery Rhyme Disaster. Conway, David. 2009. 32p. (J). (gr. -1-2). 15.95 *(978-1-58925-080-2(X))* Tiger Tales.

—Hound Dog. Bedford, David. 2006. (J). pap. 6.95 *(978-1-58925-397-1(3))* Tiger Tales.

—The Hungry Wolf: A Story from North America. Don, Lari. 2013. (ENG.). 48p. (J). pap. 7.99 *(978-1-84686-872-6(6))* Barefoot Bks., Inc.

—Masha & the Bear: A Story from Russia. Don, Lari. 2013. (ENG.). 48p. (J). pap. 7.99 *(978-1-84686-874-0(2))* Barefoot Bks., Inc.

—Never Trust a Tiger: A Story from Korea. Don, Lari. 2012. (ENG.). 48p. (J). pap. 7.99 *(978-1-84686-776-7(2))* Barefoot Bks., Inc.

—Sparrow, the Crow & the Pearl. Kerven, Rosalind. 2005. (ENG.). 24p. (J). lib. bdg. 23.65 *(978-1-59646-754-5(1))* Dingles & Co.

—That Pesky Dragon. Sykes, Julie. 2007. 32p. (J). (gr. -1-3). 15.95 *(978-1-58925-069-7(9))* Tiger Tales.

—The Tortoise's Gift: A Story from Zambia. Don, Lari. 2012. (ENG.). 48p. (J). pap. 7.99 *(978-1-84686-774-3(6))* Barefoot Bks., Inc.

—The Wheels on the Bus. Amador Family Staff & Barefoot Books Staff. 24p. 16.99 *(978-1-84686-787-3(8))* Barefoot Bks., Inc.

—The Wheels on the Bus. Barefoot Books Staff & Amador Family Staff. 24p. pap. 9.99 *(978-1-84686-788-0(6))* Barefoot Bks., Inc.

Williamson, Melanie. Cactus Annie. Williamson, Melanie. 2012. (ENG.). 32p. (J). (gr. -1-k). pap. 8.99 *(978-0-340-98142-9(3))* Hodder & Stoughton GBR. Dist: Independent Pubs. Group.

—El magnifico plan de Lobo/ Wolf's Magnificent Plan. Williamson, Melanie. 2008. (SPA.). 29p. 20.95 *(978-84-263-6837-9(9))* Vives, Luis Editorial (Edelvives) ESP. Dist: Baker & Taylor Bks.

Williamson, Pete. Dinkin Dings & the Double from Dimension 9. Bass, Guy. 2011. (Dinkin Dings Ser.). (ENG.). 128p. (J). (gr. 1-3). pap. 7.99 *(978-0-448-45433-7(5)*, Grosset & Dunlap) Penguin Publishing Group.

—Dinkin Dings & the Frightening Things. Bass, Guy. 2011. (Dinkin Dings Ser.). (ENG.). 128p. (J). (gr. 1-4). pap. 7.99 *(978-0-448-45431-3(9)*, Grosset & Dunlap) Penguin Publishing Group.

—The Ghost of Grotteskew, 1 vol. Bass, Guy. 2014. (Stitch Head Ser.). (ENG.). 208p. (gr. 3-4). 10.95 *(978-1-62370-030-0(2))* Capstone Young Readers.

—The Pirate's Eye, 1 vol. Bass, Guy. 2013. (Stitch Head Ser.). (ENG.). 208p. (gr. 3-4). 10.95 *(978-1-62370-008-9(6))* Capstone Young Readers.

—The Spider's Lair. Bass, Guy. 2015. (Stitch Head Ser.). (ENG.). 208p. (gr. 3-4). 10.95 *(978-1-62370-192-5(9))* Capstone Young Readers.

—Stitch Head, 1 vol. Bass, Guy. 2013. (Stitch Head Ser.). (ENG.). 192p. (gr. 3-4). 10.95 *(978-1-62370-007-2(8))*; pap. 262.80 *(978-1-62370-161-1(9))* Capstone Young Readers.

Willingham, Ellie. Wildwood. Willingham, Ellie. 2007. (ENG.). 136p. (J). (gr. -1-3). per. 10.00 *(978-0-9792371-0-2(6))* Keene Publishing.

Willingham, Fred. Busy Fingers. Bowie, C. W. 2004. (ENG.). 28p. (J). (gr. -1 — 1). bds. 7.95 *(978-1-58089-048-9(2))* Charlesbridge Publishing, Inc.

—Laboriosos deditos de las Manos. Bowie, C. W. Canetti, Yanitzia, tr. 2004.Tr. of Busy Fingers. (SPA & ENG.). 32p. (J). (— 1). pap. 7.95 *(978-1-58089-043-4(1))* Charlesbridge Publishing, Inc.

Willis, Caleb. Pajama Knights. Thayer, Kristi. 2010. 24p. pap. 11.50 *(978-1-60860-669-6(4)*, Strategic Bk. Publishing) Strategic Book Publishing & Rights Agency (SBPRA).

Willis-Crowley, Kate. Mommy's Little Monster. McNiff, Dawn. 2013. (ENG.). 32p. (J). (gr. -1-k). 16.99 *(978-0-545-48057-4(4)*, Chicken Hse., The) Scholastic, Inc.

Willis, Drew. Crown of Earth. Bell, Hilari. (Shield, Sword, & Crown Ser.: 3). (ENG.). (J). (gr. 3-7). 2010. 272p. pap. 5.99 *(978-1-4169-0599-8(5))*; 2009. 352p. 16.99 *(978-1-4169-0598-1(7))* Simon & Schuster/Paula Wiseman Bks. (Simon & Schuster/Paula Wiseman Bks.).

—The Forbidden Castle. Packard, Edward. 2013. (U-Ventures Ser.). (ENG.). 192p. (J). (gr. 3-7). pap. 5.99 *(978-1-4424-3428-8(7)*, Simon & Schuster Bks. For Young Readers) Simon & Schuster Bks. For Young Readers.

—Hatchet. Paulsen, Gary. 20th anniv. ed. 2007. (ENG.). 192p. (J). (gr. 5-9). 19.99 *(978-1-4169-2508-8(2)*, Simon & Schuster Bks. For Young Readers) Simon & Schuster Bks. For Young Readers.

—Heroes of Olympus. Freeman, Philip. 2012. (ENG.). 352p. (J). (gr. 3-7). 17.99 *(978-1-4424-1729-8(3)*, Simon & Schuster Bks. For Young Readers) Simon & Schuster Bks. For Young Readers.

—Heroes of Olympus. Freeman, Philip. 2013. (ENG.). 352p. (J). (gr. 3-7). pap. 10.99 *(978-1-4424-1730-4(7)*, Simon & Schuster Bks. For Young Readers) Simon & Schuster Bks. For Young Readers.

—Nerd Camp 2. 0. Weissman, Elissa Brent. 2014. (ENG.). 288p. (J). (gr. 3-7). 16.99 *(978-1-4424-5294-7(3)*, Atheneum Bks. for Young Readers) Simon & Schuster Children's Publishing.

—Nerd Camp 2.0. Weissman, Elissa Brent. 2015. (ENG.). 304p. (J). (gr. 3-7). pap. 7.99 *(978-1-4424-5295-4(1))* Simon & Schuster Children's Publishing.

—Return to the Cave of Time. Packard, Edward. 2012. (U-Ventures Ser.). (ENG.). 160p. (Orig.). (J). (gr. 3-7). pap. 5.99 *(978-1-4424-3427-1(9)*, Simon & Schuster Bks. For Young Readers) Simon & Schuster Bks. For Young Readers.

—Sword of Waters. Bell, Hilari. (Shield, Sword, & Crown Ser.: 2). (ENG.). (J). (gr. 3-7). 2009. 368p. pap. 6.99 *(978-1-4169-0597-4(9))*; No. 2. 2008. 352p. 16.99 *(978-1-4169-0596-7(0))* Simon & Schuster/Paula Wiseman Bks. (Simon & Schuster/Paula Wiseman Bks.).

—Through the Black Hole. Packard, Edward. 2012. (U-Ventures Ser.). (ENG.). 160p. (J). (gr. 3-7). pap. 5.99 *(978-1-4424-3426-4(0)*, Simon & Schuster Bks. For Young Readers) Simon & Schuster Bks. For Young Readers.

Willis, Helena. The Cafe Mystery. Widmark, Martin. 2015. (Whodunit Detective Agency Ser.: 4). (ENG.). 80p. (J). (gr. 2-4). Bk. 4. 5.99 *(978-0-448-48072-5(7))*; No. 4. 13.99 *(978-0-448-48073-2(5))* Penguin Publishing Group. (Grosset & Dunlap).

—The Circus Mystery, No. 3. Widmark, Martin. 3rd ed. 2015. (Whodunit Detective Agency Ser.: 3). (ENG.). 80p. (J). (gr. 2-4). 5.99 *(978-0-448-48070-1(0)*, Grosset & Dunlap) Penguin Publishing Group.

—The Diamond Mystery, No. 1. Widmark, Martin. 2014. (Whodunit Detective Agency Ser.: 1). (ENG.). 80p. (J). (gr. 2-4). 5.99 *(978-0-448-48066-4(2)*, Grosset & Dunlap) Penguin Publishing Group.

—The Hotel Mystery, No. 2. Widmark, Martin. 2014. (Whodunit Detective Agency Ser.: 2). (ENG.). 80p. (J). (gr. 2-4). 5.99 *(978-0-448-48068-8(9)*, Grosset & Dunlap) Penguin Publishing Group.

—The Mummy Mystery. Widmark, Martin. 2015. (Whodunit Detective Agency Ser.: 5). (ENG.). 80p. (J). (gr. 2-4). 5.99 *(978-0-448-48074-9(3)*, Grosset & Dunlap) Penguin Publishing Group.

—The Mummy Mystery #5. Widmark, Martin. 2015. (Whodunit Detective Agency Ser.: 5). (ENG.). 80p. (J). (gr. 2-4). 13.99 *(978-0-448-48075-6(1)*, Grosset & Dunlap) Penguin Publishing Group.

Willis, Janet. A Dad's Delight. 2006. *(978-0-9785077-0-1(3))*; pap. *(978-0-9785077-1-8(1))* Khesed Foundation.

Willis, Michelle "Osawazhinkwaa-Ikwe. Kwezenhs Bimose. Willis, Michelle "Osawazhinkwaa-Ikwe. 2004. (OJI.). 8p. (J). per. *(978-0-9758801-1-1(X))* Bay Mills Indian Community.

W

Willis, Nancy Carol. The Animals' Winter Sleep. Graham-Barber, Lynda. 2008. (ENG.). 24p. (J). (gr. -1-k). pap. 7.95 *(978-0-9662761-6-9(7))* Birdsong Bks.

Willis, Tania. Kidsgo Hong Kong: Tell Your Parents. Debram, Mio. 2011. (ENG.). 80p. pap. 10.00 *(978-988-18967-5-9(4))* Haven Bks.

—Kidsgo London: Tell Your Parents. Debram, Mio. 2011. (ENG.). 64p. pap. 10.00 *(978-988-18967-4-2(6))* Haven Bks.

Willoughby, Yuko. Believers in Christ Volume 29: New Testament Volume 29 Ephesians: God's Workamanship. Lyster, R. Iona. 2010. 34p. (J). pap. *(978-1-932381-26-9(0),* 1029) Bible Visuals International, Inc.

—The Tabernacle, Part 1 A Picture of the Lord Jesus Vol. 09, Pt. 1: Old Testament Volume 9 Exodus Part 4. Piepgrass, Arlene & Hershey, Katherine. 2010. (ENG.). 36p. (J). pap. *(978-1-932381-72-6(4),* 2009) Bible Visuals International, Inc.

Willoughby, Yuko. The Tabernacle, Part 2 A Picture of the Lord Jesus Vol. 10, Pt. 2: Old Testament Volume 10 Exodus Part 5. Hershey, Katherine. 2010. (ENG.). 32p. (J). pap. *(978-1-932381-73-3(2),* 2010) Bible Visuals International, Inc.

Willoughby, Yuko, jt. illus. see Ober, Jonathan.

Willoughby, Yuko, jt. illus. see Olson, Ed.

WillowRaven, Aidana. Katie Bear: Fun Days at School. Sansone, V. K. 2007. 84p. pap. 16.95 *(978-0-9798154-7-8(9))* Living Waters Publishing Co.

—Strangers in the Stable. Laughter, Jim. 2011. 24p. pap. 13.99 *(978-0-9832740-3-2(7))* 4RV Publishing, LLC.

Willy, April. Have You Ever Seen a Moose Brushing His Teeth? McClaine, Jamie. 2003. 30p. (J). 18.95 *(978-0-9709533-2-2(1))* J A F S, Inc.

—Have You Ever Seen a Moose Taking a Bath? McClaine, Jamie. 2003. 28p. (J). per. 18.95 *(978-0-9709533-1-5(3))* J A F S, Inc.

—Three Cups: Teaching Children How to Save, Spend & Be Charitable with Money Is As Easy As 1, 2, 3. St. Germain, Mark. 2007. (ENG.). 28p. (J). pap. 10.00 *(978-0-9794563-0-5(4))* Three Cups, LLC.

—Tres Tazas. St. Germain, Mark. 2010.Tr. of Three Cups. (SPA.). 24p. (J). *(978-0-9794563-1-2(2))* Three Cups, LLC.

Willy, Romont. En Tiempos Difíciles. Canetti, Yanitzia. 2010. (SPA & ENG.). 32p. (J). (gr. k-2). pap. 8.99 *(978-1-59835-102-6(8),* BrickHouse Education) Cambridge BrickHouse, Inc.

—When Times Are Tough. Canetti, Yanitzia. Keating, Alison, tr. 2009. 32p. (J). (gr. k-2). 8.99 *(978-1-59835-103-3(6))* Cambridge BrickHouse, Inc.

Wilmot, Anita. Bulkington. Neyer, Daniel. 2004. 136p. (YA). pap. 9.95 *(978-0-9666701-1-0(6))* One Faithful Harp Publishing Co.

Wilsdorf, Anne. The Best Story. Spinelli, Eileen. 2008. (ENG.). 32p. (J). (gr. 1-3). 16.99 *(978-0-8037-3055-7(1),* Dial) Penguin Publishing Group.

—Dogs on the Bed. Bluemle, Elizabeth. 2013. (ENG.). 32p. (J). (gr. -1-2). pap. 6.99 *(978-0-7636-6736-8(6))* Candlewick Pr.

—Five Funny Bunnies: Three Bouncing Tales, 0 vols. Van Leeuwen, Jean. 2012. (ENG.). 40p. (J). (gr. -1-3). 17.99 *(978-0-7614-6114-2(0),* 9780761461142, Amazon Children's Publishing) Amazon Publishing.

—Homer: The Library Cat. Lindbergh, Reeve. 2011. (ENG.). 32p. (J). (gr. -1-3). 16.99 *(978-0-7636-3448-3(4))* Candlewick Pr.

—Ruby Lu, Brave & True. Look, Lenore. 2006. (Ruby Lu Ser.). 105p. (J). (gr. 1-5). 11.65 *(978-0-7569-6553-2(5))* Perfection Learning Corp.

—Ruby Lu, Brave & True. Look, Lenore. 2006. (ENG.). 112p. (J). (gr. 1-5). pap. 5.99 *(978-1-4169-1389-4(0),* Atheneum Bks. for Young Readers) Simon & Schuster Children's Publishing.

—Ruby Lu, Empress of Everything. Look, Lenore. 2007. 164p. (gr. 1-5). 16.00 *(978-0-7569-8113-6(1))* Perfection Learning Corp.

—Ruby Lu, Empress of Everything. Look, Lenore. (ENG.). (J). (gr. 1-5). 2007. 176p. pap. 5.99 *(978-1-4169-5003-5(6))*; 2006. 160p. 16.99 *(978-0-689-86460-5(4))* Simon & Schuster Children's Publishing. (Atheneum Bks. for Young Readers).

—Sophie's Squash. Miller, Pat Zietlow. 2013. (ENG.). 40p. (J). (gr. -1-2). 16.99 *(978-0-307-97896-7(6),* Schwartz & Wade Bks.) Random Hse. Children's Bks.

—Thelonious Mouse. Protopopescu, Orel Odinov. 2011. (ENG.). 32p. (J). (gr. -1-1). 17.99 *(978-0-374-37447-1(3),* Farrar, Straus & Giroux (BYR)) Farrar, Straus & Giroux.

Wilsdorf, Anne. Ruby Lu, Brave & True. Wilsdorf, Anne. Look, Lenore. 2004. (ENG.). 112p. (J). (gr. 1-5). 16.99 *(978-0-689-84907-7(9),* Atheneum Bks. for Young Readers) Simon & Schuster Children's Publishing.

Wilson, Agy. From Heaven to Earth - Angel on My Shoulder. Wilson, Agy. 2004. (From Heaven to Earth Ser.). 150p. (J). (gr. 2-7). pap. 5.95 *(978-0-9718348-1-1(4))* Blooming Tree Pr.

Wilson, Alex. Brujas y Magos. Hill, Douglas. 2003. (SPA.). 64p. (J). 14.95 *(978-84-372-2321-6(0))* Altea, Ediciones, S.A. - Grupo Santillana ESP. Dist: Santillana USA Publishing Co., Inc.

Wilson, Alisha. Booklet Goes to the Doctor. Edman Lamote, Lisa. 2006. (Bookmann Family Presents Ser.). 32p. (J). (gr. k-3). 15.99 *(978-1-933673-02-8(8),* BookMann Pr.) Mann Publishing Group.

—A Day Out for Opus. Edman Lamote, Lisa. 2006. (Bookmann Family Presents Ser.). 32p. (J). (gr. k-3). 15.99 *(978-1-933673-03-5(6),* BookMann Pr.) Mann Publishing Group.

—Don't Judge a Book by Its Cover. Edman Lamote, Lisa. 2006. (Bookmann Family Presents Ser.). 32p. (J). (gr. k-3). 15.99 *(978-1-933673-01-1(X),* BookMann Pr.) Mann Publishing Group.

Wilson, Alonza S. The Living Ice Cream Guys. Renfroe, Ann. 2012. 34p. pap. 13.95 *(978-0-9858398-9-5(9))* Mindstir Media.

Wilson, Ann. The Barefoot Book of Earth Tales. Casey, Dawn. 2013. (ENG.). 96p. (J). (gr. 2-6). pap. 14.99 *(978-1-84686-941-9(2))* Barefoot Bks., Inc.

Wilson, Anne. The Barefoot Book of Earth Tales. Casey, Dawn. 2009. (ENG.). 96p. (J). (gr. 1-5). 19.99 *(978-1-84686-224-3(8))* Barefoot Bks., Inc.

—A Gift for the Christ Child: A Christmas Folktale. Schlafer, Linda. 2004. 26p. (gr. -1-3). 15.95 *(978-0-8294-1606-0(4))* Loyola Pr.

—The Great Race: The Story of the Chinese Zodiac. Casey, Dawn. (ENG.). 32p. (J). (gr. -1-3). 2008. pap. 7.99 *(978-1-84686-202-1(7))*; 2006. 16.99 *(978-1-905236-77-0(8))* Barefoot Bks., Inc.

—Masha & the Firebird. Bateson Hill, Margaret. 2005. (Folk Tales Ser.: 1). (RUS & ENG.). 32p. (J). pap. *(978-1-84089-201-7(3))* Zero to Ten, Ltd.

—Prayers for Each & Every Day. Piper, Sophie. 2008. (ENG.). 64p. (J). (gr. -1-2). 14.95 *(978-1-55725-622-5(5))* Paraclete Pr., Inc.

—Snakes & Ladders. Morpurgo, Michael. 2006. (Yellow Bananas Ser.). (ENG.). 48p. (J). (gr. -1-3). *(978-0-7787-0998-5(1))*; lib. bdg. *(978-0-7787-0952-7(3))* Crabtree Publishing Co.

—Storytime: First Tales for Sharing. Blackstone, Stella & Broadbent, Jim. 2008. (ENG.). 96p. (J). pap. 12.99 *(978-1-84686-165-9(9))* Barefoot Bks., Inc.

—Storytime: First Tales for Sharing. Blackstone, Stella. 2005. (ENG.). 96p. (J). (gr. -1-3). 19.99 *(978-1-84148-345-0(1))* Barefoot Bks., Inc.

—We're Roaming in the Rainforest. Krebs, Laurie. 40p. (J). 2011. (SPA.). (gr. 1-6). 7.99 *(978-1-84686-551-0(4))*; 2011. (ENG.). (gr. 1-6). pap. 7.99 *(978-1-84686-545-9(X))*; 2010. (ENG.). (gr. -1-5). 16.99 *(978-1-84686-331-8(7))* Barefoot Bks., Inc.

—We're Sailing down the Nile: A Journey Through Egypt. Krebs, Laurie. 2007. (ENG.). 40p. (J). (gr. -1-3). 16.99 *(978-1-84686-040-9(7))* Barefoot Bks., Inc.

Wilson, Anne. The Lord Is My Shepherd. Wilson, Anne. 2004. 32p. 16.00 *(978-0-8028-5250-2(5))* Eerdmans, William B. Publishing Co.

Wilson, Anne & Guay, Rebecca. The Barefoot Book of Ballet Stories. Casey, Dawn et al. 2009. (ENG.). 96p. (J). 21.99 *(978-1-84686-262-5(0))* Barefoot Bks., Inc.

Wilson, Bill. Dorf's Art Lesson. Wilson, Bill. 2008. (ENG.). 16p. (J). spiral bd. 6.95 net. *(978-0-9818747-0-8(3))* Pippin & Maxx Arts & Entertain, LLC.

Wilson, Bob. Football Fred, Vol. 4. 2003. (ENG.). 80p. (J). pap. *(978-0-330-37091-2(X),* Pan) Pan Macmillan.

Wilson, Bonnita. A Tale of Two Cookies: A Message of Kindness & Acceptance. Patterson, Trina Dawkins. 2011. (ENG.). 32p. (J). (gr. -1-3). pap. 10.99 *(978-0-9819860-9-8(9))* Amber Skye Publishing LLC.

Wilson, Charles Banks. The Story of Geronimo. Kjelgaard, Jim. Meadowcroft, Enid Lamonte, ed. 2011. 192p. 42.95 *(978-1-258-05298-0(9))* Literary Licensing, LLC.

—Whispering Wind: A Story of the Massacre at Sand Creek. Reeder, Red. 2011. 216p. 44.95 *(978-1-258-05996-5(7))* Literary Licensing, LLC.

Wilson, Cristi. Just Because. Wilson, Cristi. I.t. ed. 2006. 24p. (J). (gr. -1-3). per. 10.99 *(978-1-59879-251-5(2))* Lifevest Publishing, Inc.

Wilson, Danny. Lots & Lots of Orange: A Trip to Neyland Stadium. Wilson, Danny. 2003. 24p. (J). 8.95 *(978-0-9743968-0-4(X))* Satellite Studio.

Wilson, Donna. Creative Creatures: A Step-by-Step Guide to Making Your Own Creations. Wilson, Donna. 2013. (ENG.). 48p. (J). (gr. 3-9). 15.99 *(978-0-7534-6947-7(2),* Kingfisher) Roaring Brook Pr.

Wilson, Gahan. Brains for Lunch: A Zombie Novel in Haiku?! Roy, Keri Anne & Holt, K. A. 2010. (ENG.). 96p. (J). (gr. 4-9). 15.99 *(978-1-59643-629-9(8))* Roaring Brook Pr.

—The Devil's Dictionary & Other Works, No. 11. Bierce, Ambrose. 2010. (Classics Illustrated Graphic Novels Ser.: 11). (ENG.). 56p. (J). (gr. 3-9). 9.99 *(978-1-59707-223-6(0))* Papercutz.

—The Raven & Other Poems. Poe, Edgar Allen. 4th ed. 2009. (Classics Illustrated Graphic Novels Ser.: 4). (ENG.). 56p. (J). (gr. 3-9). 9.95 *(978-1-59707-140-6(4))* Papercutz.

Wilson, Helen Hughes. The Valiant Seven. Phelps, Netta Sheldon. 2004. (Classic Ser.). 222p. (gr. 4-7). pap. 15.95 *(978-0-87004-410-6(9))* Caxton Pr.

Wilson, Henrike. Brave Charlotte. Stohner, Anu. 2014. 32p. pap. 8.00 *(978-1-61003-341-1(8))* Center for the Collaborative Classroom.

—Brave Charlotte & the Wolves. Stohner, Anu. 2009. (ENG.). 32p. (J). (gr. k-3). 16.99 *(978-1-59990-424-5(1),* Bloomsbury USA Childrens) Bloomsbury USA.

Wilson, Henrike. Brave Charlotte. Wilson, Henrike. Stohner, Anu. 2005. (ENG.). 32p. (J). (gr. -1-3). 17.99 *(978-1-58234-690-8(9),* Bloomsbury USA Childrens) Bloomsbury USA.

Wilson, Janet. Jasper's Day. Parker, Marjorie Blain. 2004. (ENG.). 32p. (J). (gr. k-3). 8.95 *(978-1-55337-764-1(8))* Kids Can Pr., Ltd. CAN. Dist: Univ. of Toronto Pr.

—One Peace: True Stories of Young Activists, 1 vol. 2008. (ENG.). 52p. (J). (gr. 2-7). 19.95 *(978-1-55143-892-4(5))* Orca Bk. Pubs. USA.

—Out of Slavery: The Journey to Amazing Grace. Granfield, Linda. 2009. (ENG.). 40p. (J). (gr. k-12). 15.95 *(978-0-88776-915-3(2),* Tundra Bks.) Tundra Bks. CAN. Dist: Penguin Random Hse., LLC.

—Solomon's Tree, 1 vol. Spalding, Andrea. 2005. (ENG.). 32p. (J). (gr. -1-3). 9.95 *(978-1-55143-380-6(X))* Orca Bk. Pubs. USA.

—Tiger Flowers, 1 vol. Quinlan, Patricia. 2005. (ENG.). 32p. (J). (gr. -1-3). per. 6.95 *(978-1-55005-139-1(3),* 1550051393) Fitzhenry & Whiteside, Ltd. CAN. Dist: Midpoint Trade Bks., Inc.

Wilson, Jef. Hiking for Fun!, 1 vol. Wilson, Jef. 2006. (For Fun!: Sports Ser.). (ENG.). 48p. (gr. 3-6). lib. bdg. 26.65 *(978-0-7565-1686-4(2),* For Fun!) Compass Point Bks.

Wilson, John, jt. illus. see Wilson, Whitleigh.

Wilson, Karma, photos by. Beautiful Babies. Wilson, Karma. 2009. (ENG.). 14p. (J). (gr. -1 — 1). 6.99 *(978-1-4169-1908-7(2),* Little Simon) Little Simon.

Wilson, Katherine. The Velveteen Rabbit. Williams, Margery. 2006. (ENG.). 32p. (J). (gr. -1-1). per. 3.95 *(978-0-8249-5530-4(7),* Ideals Children's Bks.) Ideals Pubns.

Wilson, Kay. Penny's Big Day. Mika, Sharon Ann. 2003. (J). 8.95 *(978-0-9747836-0-4(9))* Button Flower Pr.

Wilson, Keith, et al. Louis Pasteur & Pasteurization, 1 vol. Fandel, Jennifer et al. 2007. (Inventions & Discovery Ser.). (ENG.). 32p. (gr. 3-4). 29.99 *(978-0-7368-6844-0(5),* Graphic Library) Capstone Pr., Inc.

Wilson, Keith. Louis Pasteur & Pasteurization, 1 vol. Fandel, Jennifer et al. 2007. (Inventions & Discovery Ser.). (ENG.). 32p. (gr. 3-4). pap. 8.10 *(978-0-7368-7896-8(3),* Graphic Library) Capstone Pr., Inc.

Wilson, Lorna. Mr Tilly & the Christmas Lights. Leighton, Noreen. 2013. 38p. pap. *(978-0-9573315-7-0(6))* Tatterdemalion Blue.

—Mr Tilly & the Halloween Mystery. Leighton, Noreen. 2013. 42p. pap. *(978-0-9573315-6-3(8))* Tatterdemalion Blue.

Wilson, Lynda Farrington. B Is for Boys & Bees. Velikanje, Kathryn. 2013. 34p. pap. 9.13 *(978-1-939896-05-6(3))* Levity Pr.

—C Is for Crazy Cats. Velikanje, Kathryn. 2013. (ENG.). 40p. pap. 9.13 *(978-1-939896-06-3(1))* Levity Pr.

—D Is for Dragon. Velikanje, Kathryn. 2013. 34p. pap. 9.13 *(978-1-939896-07-0(X))* Levity Pr.

—E Is for Elephant. Velikanje, Kathryn. 2013. 36p. pap. 9.13 *(978-1-939896-08-7(8))* Levity Pr.

—E Is for Elephant. Shan Shan, Kathryn Velikanje. 2013. 36p. pap. 9.87 *(978-1-939896-17-9(7))* Levity Pr.

—Everyday Circus. Shan Shan, Kathryn. 2013. 48p. pap. 10.97 *(978-1-939896-01-8(0))* Levity Pr.

—F Is for Face. Velikanje, Kathryn. 2013. 40p. pap. 9.13 *(978-1-939896-09-4(6))* Levity Pr.

—G Is for Girly Girls. Velikanje, Kathryn. 2013. 36p. pap. 9.13 *(978-1-939896-10-0(X))* Levity Pr.

—H Is for Horse. Velikanje, Kathryn. 2013. 38p. pap. 9.13 *(978-1-939896-11-7(8))* Levity Pr.

—I Is for Ice Cream. Velikanje, Kathryn. 2013. (ENG.). 36p. pap. 9.13 *(978-1-939896-12-4(6))* Levity Pr.

—A Is for Alligator. Velikanje, Kathryn. 2013. (ENG.). 34p. pap. 9.13 *(978-1-939896-04-9(5))* Levity Pr.

—A Is for Alligator. Shan Shan, Kathryn Velikanje. 2013. 34p. pap. 9.97 *(978-1-939896-13-1(4))* Levity Pr.

Wilson, Mark. Carpet of Dreams. Duder, Tessa. 2008. 32p. pap. *(978-0-207-19991-2(4))* HarperCollins Pubs. Australia.

—The Skunk with the Stinky Attitude. McLaughlin, Richard. 2013. 44p. (YA). pap. 13.75 *(978-1-939625-49-6(1))* Inkwell Productions, LLC.

Wilson, Mary Ann. Bucky: The Adventures of the Dinosaur Cowboy. Cunningham, Kay. 2004. 32p. (J). 18.99 *(978-1-57860-173-8(8))* Clerisy Pr.

Wilson-Max, Ken. The Baby Goes Beep. O'Connell, Rebecca. 2010. (ENG.). 16p. (J). (gr. -1-k). bds. 7.99 *(978-0-8075-0508-3(0))* Whitman, Albert & Co.

—Baby Ruby Bawled. Stanley, Malaika Rose. 2010. (ENG.). 32p. (J). (gr. k-2). pap. 9.99 *(978-1-84853-017-1(X))* Transworld Publishers Ltd. GBR. Dist: Independent Pubs. Group.

—I Can Do It Too! Baicker, Karen & Chronicle Books Staff. 2010. (ENG.). (J). (gr. -1 — 1). bds. 9.99 *(978-0-8118-7560-8(1))* Chronicle Bks. LLC.

—I Hate to Be Sick! Scholastic, Inc. Staff & Bermiss, Aamir Lee. 2004. (Just for You Ser.). (ENG.). 32p. (gr. k-3). pap. 3.99 *(978-0-439-56877-7(3),* Teaching Resources) Scholastic, Inc.

—The Little Plant Doctor: The Story of George Washington Carver. Marzollo, Jean. 2011. (ENG.). 32p. (J). (gr. -1-3). 16.95 *(978-0-8234-2325-5(5))* Holiday Hse., Inc.

—You Can Do It Too! Baicker, Karen & Chronicle Books Staff. 2010. (ENG.). (J). (gr. -1 — 1). bds. 9.99 *(978-0-8118-7561-5(X))* Chronicle Bks. LLC.

Wilson, Phil. After the Dinosaurs: Mammoths & Fossil Mammals. Brown, Charlotte Lewis & Brown, Charlotte L. 2007. (I Can Read Book 2 Ser.). (ENG.). 32p. (J). (gr. -1-3). pap. 3.99 *(978-0-06-053055-6(3))* HarperCollins Pubs.

—After the Dinosaurs: Mammoths & Fossil Mammals. Brown, Charlotte Lewis. 2006. (I Can Read Bks.). 32p. (J). (gr. -1-3). lib. bdg. 17.89 *(978-0-06-053054-9(5))* HarperCollins Pubs.

—Baby Santa's Worldwide Christmas Adventure. DeLand, M. Maitland. 2010. 32p. 14.95 *(978-1-60832-062-2(6))* Greenleaf Book Group.

—Beyond the Dinosaurs: Monsters of the Air & Sea. Brown, Charlotte Lewis & Brown, Charlotte L. (I Can Read Book 2 Ser.). (ENG.). 32p. (J). (gr. -1-3). 2008. pap. 3.99 *(978-0-06-053058-7(8))*; 2007. 15.99 *(978-0-06-053056-3(1))* HarperCollins Pubs.

—Beyond the Dinosaurs: Monsters of the Air & Sea. Brown, Charlotte Lewis. 2007. (I Can Read Book 2 Ser.). 32p. (J). (gr. -1-3). lib. bdg. 16.89 *(978-0-06-053057-0(X))* HarperCollins Pubs.

—The Day the Dinosaurs Died. Brown, Charlotte Lewis & Brown, Charlotte L. 2007. (I Can Read Book 2 Ser.). (ENG.). 48p. (J). (gr. -1-3). pap. 3.99 *(978-0-06-000530-6(0))* HarperCollins Pubs.

—The Day the Dinosaurs Died. Brown, Charlotte Lewis. 2006. (I Can Read Bks.). 48p. (J). (gr. k-3). lib. bdg. 16.89 *(978-0-06-000529-0(7))* HarperCollins Pubs.

—Medieval Castle: A Three Dimensional. 2004. (ENG.). (J). 22.00 *(978-1-58117-365-9(2),* Intervisual/Piggy Toes) Bendon, Inc.

—Seven Little Brothers. Livshits, Larisa. 2012. 40p. pap. *(978-1-77097-322-0(2))* FriesenPress.

Wilson, Phil, jt. illus. see Rath, Robert.

Wilson, Raylene Jenee & Gibbons, Deanna. The Three Madelines. Whitmore, Hugh. 2012. 124p. pap. 15.95 *(978-0-9848314-4-9(4))* SignificantFaith.com.

Wilson, Roberta. The Quest: Adventure Story & Songs. Jacobson, John. 2005. (ENG.). 48p. pap. 12.95 incl. audio compact disk *(978-1-4234-0019-6(4),* 1423400194) Leonard, Hal Corp.

Wilson, Ron, et al. Captain America: Scourge of the Underworld. 2011. (ENG.). 296p. (J). (gr. 4-17). pap. 34.99 *(978-0-7851-4962-0(7))* Marvel Worldwide, Inc.

Wilson Sanger, Amy. A Little Bit of Soul Food. Wilson Sanger, Amy. Sanger, Amy Wilson. 2004. (World Snacks Ser.). (ENG.). 20p. (J). (— 1). bds. 6.99 *(978-1-58246-109-0(0),* Tricycle Pr.) Ten Speed Pr.

Wilson, Steve. Lines That Wiggle. Whitman, Candace. 2009. (ENG.). 36p. (J). (gr. -1-3). 14.99 *(978-1-934706-54-1(X))* Blue Apple Bks.

—Shapes That Roll. Nagel, Karen. 2009. (ENG.). 40p. (J). (gr. -1-1). 14.99 *(978-1-934706-81-7(7))* Blue Apple Bks.

Wilson, Susie. A Kid's Herb Book: For Children of All Ages. Tierra, Lesley. 2010. (ENG.). 264p. (gr. -1-18). pap. 19.95 *(978-1-885003-36-2(6))* Reed, Robert D. Pubs.

Wilson, Teddy. Don't Cry but Smile & Remember. Brown, Ivorine. 2009. 20p. pap. 24.95 *(978-1-60836-808-2(4))* America Star Bks.

Wilson, Whitleigh & Wilson, John. Frog Makes a Friend. Wilson, Angela. 2013. 28p. pap. 24.95 *(978-1-63004-048-2(7))* America Star Bks.

Wiltse, Kris, jt. illus. see Blackmore, Katherine.

Wimmer, Michael. A Taste of Blackberries. Smith, Doris Buchanan & Smith. 2004. (Trophy Bk.). (ENG.). 96p. (J). (gr. 3-7). reprint ed. pap. 5.99 *(978-0-06-440238-5(X))* HarperCollins Pubs.

Wimmer, Mike. George: George Washington, Our Founding Father. Keating, Frank. 2012. (Mount Rushmore Presidential Ser.). (ENG.). 32p. (J). (gr. 1-4). 17.99 *(978-1-4169-5482-8(1),* Simon & Schuster/Paula Wiseman Bks.) Simon & Schuster/Paula Wiseman Bks.

—Home Run: The Story of Babe Ruth. Burleigh, Robert. Plimpton, George, ed. 2003. (ENG.). 32p. (J). (gr. -1-3). pap. 7.00 *(978-0-15-204599-9(6))* Houghton Mifflin Harcourt Publishing Co.

—My Teacher Is an Alien. Coville, Bruce. (My Teacher Bks.: 1). (ENG.). 160p. (J). (gr. 3-7). 2014. 16.99 *(978-1-4814-0430-3(X))*; 2005. pap. 6.99 *(978-1-4169-0334-5(8))* Simon & Schuster/Paula Wiseman Bks. (Simon & Schuster/Paula Wiseman Bks.).

—One Giant Leap. Burleigh, Robert. (ENG.). 40p. (J). (gr. 1-3). 2014. 8.99 *(978-0-14-751165-2(8),* Puffin); 2009. 16.99 *(978-0-399-23883-3(2),* Philomel) Penguin Publishing Group.

—Un Sabor a Moras. Smith, Doris Buchanan. Rioja, Alberto Jiménez, tr. (SPA.). (YA). (gr. 3-18). 14.95 *(978-0-930332-25-6(4),* LC31160) Lectorum Pubns., Inc.

—Stealing Home: Jackie Robinson: Against the Odds. Burleigh, Robert. 2007. (ENG.). 32p. (J). (gr. 1-4). 17.99 *(978-0-689-86276-2(8),* Simon & Schuster/Paula Wiseman Bks.) Simon & Schuster/Paula Wiseman Bks.

—Theodore. Keating, Frank. 2006. (Mount Rushmore Presidential Ser.). (ENG.). 32p. (J). (gr. 1-4). 17.99 *(978-0-689-86532-9(5),* Simon & Schuster/Paula Wiseman Bks.) Simon & Schuster/Paula Wiseman Bks.

Wimperis, Sarah. All Quiet on the Western Front. Remarque, Erich Maria. 2014. (World War I Ser.). (ENG.). 64p. pap. 6.95 *(978-1-906230-66-1(8))* Real Reads Ltd. GBR. Dist: International Publishers Marketing.

Winborn, Marsha. America's Promise. Powell, Alma. 2003. 32p. (J). (gr. -1-2). 16.89 *(978-0-06-052173-8(2))* HarperCollins Pubs.

—Digby & Kate & the Beautiful Day. Baker, Barbara. 2004. (Puffin Easy-to-Read Ser.). 48p. (J). (gr. 1-4). 11.65 *(978-0-7569-2959-6(8))* Perfection Learning Corp.

—Emma's Turtle. Bunting, Eve. (ENG.). 32p. (J). 2014. (gr. -1-2). pap. 6.95 *(978-1-62091-735-0(1))*; 2007. (gr. 2-4). 15.95 *(978-1-59078-350-4(6))* Boyds Mills Pr.

—Porky & Bess. Weiss, Ellen & Friedman, Mel. 2011. (Step into Reading Ser.). (ENG.). 48p. (J). (gr. 2-4). pap. 3.99 *(978-0-375-86113-0(0))* Random Hse., Inc.

—Promesa de America. Powell, Alma. 2003.Tr. of America's Promise. (SPA.). 32p. (J). (gr. -1-2). 15.99 *(978-0-06-052175-2(9),* Rayo) HarperCollins Pubs.

—A Winning Attitude. Daniel, Claire. 2007. 14p. pap. 4.75 *(978-0-15-377381-5(2))* Harcourt Schl. Pubs.

Winburn, William B. Knees & Toes. 2009. (Rookie Toddler: Sing along Toddler Ser.). (ENG.). 12p. (J). (gr. -1). bds. 6.95 *(978-0-531-24546-0(2))* Scholastic Library Publishing.

Winch, John. Brother Wolf, Sister Sparrow: Stories about Saints & Animals. Kimmel, Eric A. 2003. (ENG.). 64p. (J). (gr. 4-6). tchr. ed. 18.95 *(978-0-8234-1724-7(7))* Holiday Hse., Inc.

Winchel, Heidi. The Magic Potato - la Papa Magica: Story & coloring book in English & Spanish, 1. Romano, Elaine. Nielsen, Emily, tr. 2nd ed. 2004. (SPA.). 20p. (J). 3.00 *(978-0-9728225-3-4(4))* Mill Park Publishing.

Windett, Dave. Demons & Elementals, No. 2. Gatehouse, John. 2014. (Monster Hunters Unlimited Ser.: 2). (ENG.). 128p. (J). (gr. 3-7). 7.99 *(978-0-8431-6901-0(X),* Price Stern Sloan) Penguin Publishing Group.

—Flying Fiends & Gruesome Creatures, No. 4. Gatehouse, John. 2015. (Monster Hunters Unlimited Ser.: 4). (ENG.). 128p. (J). (gr. 3-7). 7.99 *(978-0-8431-7028-3(X),* Price Stern Sloan) Penguin Publishing Group.

—Man-Monsters & Animal Horrors. Gatehouse, John. 2014. (Monster Hunters Unlimited Ser.: 3). (ENG.). 128p. (J). (gr. 3-7). 7.99 *(978-0-8431-6994-2(X),* Price Stern Sloan) Penguin Publishing Group.

—The Undead & Water Beasts, No. 1. Gatehouse, John. 2014. (Monster Hunters Unlimited Ser.: 1). (ENG.). 128p. (J). (gr. 3-7). 7.99 *(978-0-8431-6980-5(X),* Price Stern Sloan) Penguin Publishing Group.

Windham, Sophie. Henny Penny. French, Vivian. 2006. (ENG.). 32p. (J). (gr. -1-3). 16.95 *(978-1-58234-706-6(9),* Bloomsbury USA Childrens) Bloomsbury USA.

Windsor-Smith, Barry, et al. Avengers, Vol. 5. 2010. (ENG.). 552p. (J). (gr. -1-17). pap. 19.99 *(978-0-7851-2087-2(4))* Marvel Worldwide, Inc.

Windsor-Smith, Barry. Tower of the Elephant & Other Stories. Thomas, Roy & Howard, Robert E. 2003. (Conan Ser.: Vol. 1). (ENG.). 168p. pap. 15.99 *(978-1-59307-016-8(0))* Dark Horse Comics.

—X-Men - Lifedeath. 2011. (ENG.). 152p. (J). (gr. 4-17). 24.99 *(978-0-7851-5524-9(4))* Marvel Worldwide, Inc.
Windsor-Smith, Barry, jt. illus. see Romita, John.
Winfield, Alison. Old Friends, New Friends. Hall, Patricia. ed. 2005. (Ready-to-Read Ser.). 32p. (J). lib. bdg. 15.00 *(978-1-59054-930-8(9))* Fitzgerald Bks.
Winfield, Amy. Peppermint Pixie. Harvey, Natalie. 2013. 44p. pap. *(978-1-909202-10-8(X))* Little Acorns Publishing.
—The Plot Bunny. Jackson, Kristina. 2013. 24p. pap. *(978-1-909202-15-3(0))* Little Acorns Publishing.
Wingerter, Linda. Magic Hoofbeats: Horse Tales from Many Lands. Sherman, Josepha. 2004. (ENG.). 80p. (J). 19.99 *(978-1-84148-091-6(6))* Barefoot Bks., Inc.
—One Grain of Sand: A Lullaby. Seeger, Pete. 2005. 30p. (J). (gr. -1-4). reprint ed. 16.00 *(978-0-7567-8586-4(3))* DIANE Publishing Co.
Winget, Susan. Everyday Angels. Moulton, Mark Kimball. 2003. (ENG.). 32p. (J). 14.95 *(978-0-8249-5479-6(3))* Ideals Pubns.
—The Visit. Moulton, Mark K. 2003. 56p. (J). 14.95 *(978-0-8249-5475-8(0))* Ideals Pubns.
—The Visit: The Origin of the Night Before Christmas, 1 vol. Moulton, Mark Kimball. 2013. (ENG.). 56p. 16.99 *(978-0-7643-4575-3(3))* Schiffer Publishing, Ltd.
Winget, Susan. Tucker's Apple-Dandy Day. Winget, Susan. 2006. 40p. (J). (gr. -1-k). 13.89 *(978-0-06-054647-2(6))* HarperCollins Pubs.
—Tucker's Four-Carrot School Day. Winget, Susan. 2005. (ENG.). 40p. (J). (gr. -1-k). 12.99 *(978-0-06-054642-7(5))* HarperCollins Pubs.
Winget, Susan. The Visit. Winget, Susan, tr. Moulton, Mark Kimball. 2003. (ENG.). 56p. (J). 14.95 *(978-0-8249-5859-6(4))* Ideals Pubns.
Winget, Susan, jt. illus. see Moore, Clement C.
Wingham, Peter. Pyramid Plot. Somper, Justin. 2004. (Puzzle Adventures Ser.). 48p. (J). pap. 4.95 *(978-0-7945-0139-6(7), Usborne)* EDC Publishing.
Winkowski, Jackie, photos by. Miki's Challenge: One sled dog's Story. Winkowski, Jackie. 2006. 44p. (J). 10.95 *(978-0-9791367-1-9(7))* Snowy Plains.
Winn, Chris, jt. illus. see Galey, Chuck.
Winn, Christine M. Clover's Secret. Winn, Christine M. Walsh, David. 2004. 28p. (J). (gr. k-4). reprint ed. 15.00 *(978-0-7567-7653-4(8))* DIANE Publishing Co.
Winn, Christopher. The Sprite Sisters: Magic at Drysdale's School (Vol 7) Winn, Sheridan. 2013. 256p. pap. *(978-0-9574231-2-1(8))* Winn, Sheridan.
Winn, L. B. Butterpod Jerome & the Planet of Gabool. Winn, L. B. 2007. (J). pap. 18.95 *(978-0-9791884-0-4(7))* Winn, Lynnette.
Winship, Daniel. The Tortoise & the Hare: The Tortoise & the Hare. 2012. (SGN, ARA, BOS, CHI & FRE.). 32p. (J). pap. 19.95 incl. DVD *(978-0-9818139-2-9(5))* ASL Tales.
Winslow, Justin. El Perro y el Gato. Hines, Chrissie & Ferreras, Alberto. 2010.Tr. of Perro y el Gato: la Nieve. (SPA.). 28p. 3.99 *(978-0-9828167-1-4(5))* Home Box Office, Inc.
Winslow, Justin. El Perro y el Gato. Winslow, Justin, . 2010.Tr. of Perro y el Gato: la Nieve. (SPA.). 28p. 3.99 *(978-0-9828167-3-8(1))* Home Box Office, Inc.
Winslow, Tim. The Kingdom of Avalon. 2005. 48p. (J). *(978-0-9748505-0-4(0))* Winslow's Art.
Winstead, Leo. Weaver of Song: The Birth of Silent Night. Jackson, Mary Helene. l.t. ed. 2009. 40p. (J). 16.95 *(978-0-9825713-0-9(5))* Clifton Carriage House Pr.
Winstead, Rosie. Someday. Spinelli, Eileen. 2007. (ENG.). 32p. (J). (gr. -1-3). 16.99 *(978-0-8037-2941-4(3), Dial)* Penguin Publishing Group.
Winston, David Lorenz. Life on a Chicken Farm. Winston, David Lorenz, photos by. Wolfman, Judy. 2004. (Life on a Farm Ser.). (ENG.). 48p. (gr. 2-5). lib. bdg. 23.93 *(978-1-57505-191-8(5))* Lerner Publishing Group.
—Life on a Dairy Farm. Winston, David Lorenz, photos by. Wolfman, Judy. 2004. (Life on a Farm Ser.). (ENG.). 48p. (gr. 2-5). lib. bdg. 23.93 *(978-1-57505-190-1(7))* Lerner Publishing Group.
—Life on a Sheep Farm. Winston, David Lorenz, photos by. Wolfman, Judy. 2004. (Life on a Farm Ser.). (ENG.). 48p. (gr. 2-5). lib. bdg. 23.93 *(978-1-57505-192-5(3))* Lerner Publishing Group.
—Life on an Apple Orchard. Winston, David Lorenz, photos by. Wolfman, Judy. 2004. (Life on a Farm Ser.). (ENG.). 48p. (gr. 2-5). lib. bdg. 23.93 *(978-1-57505-193-2(1))* Lerner Publishing Group.
Winston, Dennis. Four-Hundred Meter Champion. Wooden, Thomas James, Jr. 2003. 103p. (J). mass mkt. 12.00 *(978-0-9740195-0-5(X))* New Castle Publishing Co.
Winston, Jeannie. Head, Shoulders, Knees, & Toes. ed. 2005. (Ready-to-Read Ser.). 24p. (J). lib. bdg. 15.00 *(978-1-59054-962-9(7))* Fitzgerald Bks.
—Trick or Treat! A Halloween Shapes Book. Imperato, Teresa. 2005. 12p. (J). 7.95 *(978-1-58117-325-3(3), Intervisual/Piggy Toes)* Bendon, Inc.
—Whooo's That? Winters, Kay. 2009. (ENG.). 14p. (J). (gr. -1 — 1). 9.99 *(978-0-15-206480-8(X))* Houghton Mifflin Harcourt Publishing Co.
Wint, Florence. Cowboy Ed. Grossman, Bill. 2004. 28p. (J). (gr. -1-3). reprint ed. *(978-0-7567-7851-4(4))* DIANE Publishing Co.
Winter, Dave. Super Silly Riddles. Keller, Charles. 2010. (ENG.). 96p. (J). pap. 4.95 *(978-1-4027-7857-5(0))* Sterling Publishing Co., Inc.
Winter, Janet. Cinderbear: Board Book & Puppet Theater. Brandon, Wendy. 2004. (J). *(978-1-883043-47-6(6))* Straight Edge Pr., The.
—Cinderbear: (Imagination in a Box) Brandon, Wendy. 2004. 10p. (J). bds. 17.99 *(978-1-883043-50-6(6), 6020)* Straight Edge Pr., The.
—Little Red Riding Hood Story in a Box. O'Brien, Kristen. 2003. (Story in a Box Ser.). 12p. (J). (gr. -1-1). bds. 8.99 *(978-1-883043-41-4(7))* Straight Edge Pr., The.
Winter, Jeanette. The Secret World of Hildegard. Winter, Jonah. 2007. (J). *(978-0-439-50738-7(3), Levine, Arthur A. Bks.)* Scholastic, Inc.
Winter, Jeanette. Biblioburro: A True Story from Colombia. Winter, Jeanette. 2010. (ENG.). 32p. (J). (gr. 1-4). 16.99 *(978-1-4169-9778-8(4), Beach Lane Bks.)* Beach Lane Bks.
—Follow the Drinking Gourd. Winter, Jeanette. 2008. (ENG.). 48p. (J). (gr. -1-2). 17.99 *(978-0-394-89694-6(7), Knopf Bks. for Young Readers)* Random Hse. Children's Bks.
—Henri's Scissors. Winter, Jeanette. 2013. (ENG.). 40p. (J). (gr. k-3). 16.99 *(978-1-4424-6484-1(4), Beach Lane Bks.)* Beach Lane Bks.
—Kali's Song. Winter, Jeanette. 2012. (ENG.). 40p. (J). (gr. -1-3). 16.99 *(978-0-375-87022-4(9), Schwartz & Wade Bks.)* Random Hse. Children's Bks.
—The Librarian of Basra: A True Story from Iraq. Winter, Jeanette. 2005. (ENG.). 32p. (J). (gr. -1-3). 16.99 *(978-0-15-205445-8(6))* Houghton Mifflin Harcourt Publishing Co.
—Mr. Cornell's Dream Boxes. Winter, Jeanette. 2014. (ENG.). 40p. (J). (gr. -1-3). 17.99 *(978-1-4424-9900-3(1), Beach Lane Bks.)* Beach Lane Bks.
—Nasreen's Secret School: A True Story from Afghanistan. Winter, Jeanette. 2009. (ENG.). 40p. (J). (gr. 1-4). 17.99 *(978-1-4169-9437-4(8), Beach Lane Bks.)* Beach Lane Bks.
—Wangari's Trees of Peace: A True Story from Africa. Winter, Jeanette. 2008. (ENG.). 32p. (J). (gr. -1-3). 17.00 *(978-0-15-206545-4(8))* Houghton Mifflin Harcourt Publishing Co.
—The Watcher: Jane Goodall's Life with the Chimps. Winter, Jeanette. 2011. (ENG.). 48p. (J). (gr. -1-3). 17.99 *(978-0-375-86774-3(0))*; lib. bdg. 20.99 *(978-0-375-96774-0(5))* Random Hse. Children's Bks. (Schwartz & Wade Bks.).
Winter, Milo. The Aesop for Children. Aesop. 2013. 236p. pap. 9.97 *(978-1-60386-613-2(2))* Rough Draft Printing.
—Aesop's Fables. Aesop. 2008. (J). *(978-1-934941-08-9(5))* Red & Black Pubs.
—Aesop's Fables. 2013. (ENG.). 112p. (J). (gr. -1-2). 16.95 *(978-1-4549-0981-1(1), Fall River)* Sterling Publishing Co., Inc.
—Aesops Fables for Children. 2012. 294p. pap. *(978-1-907256-72-1(5))* Abela Publishing.
—The Illustrated Bible Story Book: New Testament. Loveland, Seymour. 2008. (Dover Read & Listen Ser.). (ENG.). 144p. (J). (gr. -1-2). pap. 12.99 *(978-0-486-46835-8(6))* Dover Pubns., Inc.
—The Illustrated Bible Story Book - Old Testament. Loveland, Seymour. 2008. (Dover Read & Listen Ser.). (ENG.). 128p. (J). (gr. -1-2). pap. 12.99 *(978-0-486-46844-0(5))* Dover Pubns., Inc.
—The Three Little Kittens. Mother Goose. 2009. (Shape Bks.). (ENG.). 16p. (J). (gr. -1-1). pap. 9.95 *(978-1-59583-374-7(9)*, 9781595833747, Green Tiger Pr.) Laughing Elephant.
—The Three Little Pigs. 2008. (Shape Bks.). (ENG.). 16p. (J). (gr. -1-3). per. 9.95 *(978-1-59583-265-8(3)*, 9781595832658, Green Tiger Pr.) Laughing Elephant.
Winter, Milo & Becker, Charlotte. The Gingerbread Boy: Fairy Tales from the World Over. Faulkner, Georgene. 2011. 98p. 38.95 *(978-1-258-09946-6(2))* Literary Licensing, LLC.
—The Little Red Hen & the Fox: Fairy Tales from the World Over. Faulkner, Georgene. 2011. 98p. 38.95 *(978-1-258-10173-2(4))* Literary Licensing, LLC.
Winter, Nilo. Aesop's Fables. Handford, S. A. l.t. ed. Date not set. (J). (gr. 1-12). lib. bdg. 22.95 *(978-0-88411-991-3(2))* Amereon LTD.
Winter, P. K. Back at Eagle Lake: More Eagle Lake Giant Stories. Winter, P. K. 2009. 182p. pap. 18.50 *(978-1-4251-8831-3(1))* Trafford Publishing.
Winter, Susan. Little Otter's Big Journey, 1 vol. Bedford, David. 2006. (ENG.). 28p. (J). (gr. -1-k). pap. 16.00 *(978-1-56148-548-2(9), Good Bks.)* Skyhorse Publishing Co., Inc.
—Mommy's Best Kisses. Anastas, Margaret. (ENG.). (J). (gr. -1-k). 2008. 34p. bds. 6.99 *(978-0-06-124130-7(X), HarperFestival)*; 2003. 32p. 17.99 *(978-0-06-623601-8(0))* HarperCollins Pubs.
—Sailing off to Sleep. Ashman, Linda. 2010. (ENG.). 32p. (J). (gr. -1-1). pap. 9.99 *(978-1-4424-1435-8(9), Simon & Schuster Bks. For Young Readers)* Simon & Schuster Bks. For Young Readers.
Winter, Susan, photos by. A Hug for You. Anastas, Margaret. 2005. (ENG., 32p. (J). (gr. -1-1). 15.99 *(978-0-06-623613-1(4))* HarperCollins Pubs.
Winterhalt, Tara. Burton & Isabelle Pipistrelle: Out of the Bat Cave. Dias, Denise. 2010. (ENG.). 32p. 19.99 *(978-0-88854-485-8(5))* Royal Ontario Museum CAN. Dist: Univ. of Toronto Pr.
Winthrop, Elizabeth. Franklin Delano Roosevelt: Letters from a Mill Town Girl. Winthrop, Elizabeth. unabr. ed. 2003. (J). (gr. 4-7). 25.95 incl. audio *(978-1-59112-213-5(9))* Live Oak Media.
Winton, Andrea Evans. Popoki, the Hawaiian Cat: An Amazing Adventure with the Whale. Gleasner, Diana C. 2004. (J). *(978-0-9651185-7-6(6))* Gleasner, Bill & Diana Inc.
Winton, Byron. The Stalker. Droney, Susan K. 2005. (ENG.). 272p. (YA). pap. 14.99 *(978-1-58124-277-5(8))* Fiction Works, The.
Winward, Makenzie. The Sheep & the Chicken. Meyer, Lisa O. 2011. 16p. pap. 24.95 *(978-1-4626-0478-4(1))* America Star Bks.
Wire, Patrick. Kaliya, Serpent King. Greene, Joshua M. rev. ed. 2012. (ENG.). 24p. (J). (gr. -1). 14.99 *(978-1-60887-148-3(7))* Mandala Publishing.
Wireman, Katharine R. The Birds' Christmas Carol. Wiggin, Kate Douglas. 2008. 76p. pap. 9.95 *(978-1-59915-239-4(8))* Yesterday's Classics.
Wirrenga, Shannon. Where Do Deacons Come From? Ficocelli, Elizabeth. 2011. 20p. (J). pap. 7.99 *(978-1-936453-03-0(7))* Bezalel Bks.
—Where Do Priests Come From? Ficocelli, Elizabeth. 2010. (J). pap. 7.99 *(978-0-9844864-0-3(2))* Bezalel Bks.
Wisa, Louis. Adventures of Uncle Wiggily. Garis, Howard. 2008. (Dover Children's Classics Ser.). (ENG.). 96p. (J). (gr. 1-3). 12.95 *(978-0-486-46028-4(2))* Dover Pubns., Inc.
—Bed Time Stories: Uncle Wiggily in the Woods. Garis, Howard R. 2007. 160p. per. *(978-1-4065-2772-8(6))* Dodo Pr.
—Bed Time Stories: Uncle Wiggily's Adventures. Garis, Howard R. 2007. 140p. per. *(978-1-4065-2773-5(4))* Dodo Pr.
—Bed Time Stories: Uncle Wiggily's Travels. Garis, Howard R. 2007. 160p. per. *(978-1-4065-2774-2(2))* Dodo Pr.
—Sammie & Susie Littletail. Garis, Howard R. 2007. 120p. per. *(978-1-4065-2770-4(X))* Dodo Pr.
Wisbauer, Cortney. Rodney, the Ice Dragon. Wisbauer, Cortney. 2006. 48p. (J). 22.95 *(978-1-59879-215-7(6))* Lifevest Publishing, Inc.
Wise, Catlin. Ricky the Picky Koala. Tabernik, John. 2005. (J). 14.95 *(978-0-9773936-0-2(7))* Little Munchkin Bks.
Wise, Jesse D. Myrtle's True Friend. Wise, Alicia. 2008. 15p. pap. 24.95 *(978-1-60610-626-6(0))* America Star Bks.
Wisenfeld, Alison. Saint Francis: The Good Man of Assisi. Joslin, Mary. 2015. (ENG.). 32p. (J). (gr. k-4). 9.99 *(978-0-7459-6492-8(3))* Lion Hudson PLC GBR. Dist: Independent Pubs. Group.
Wish, Katia. Is There an App for That? Smith, Bryan. 2015. 32p. (J). pap. 10.95 ***(978-1-934490-74-7(1))*** Boys Town Pr.
Wish, Katia. Sophie's Animal Parade. Dixon, Amy. 2015. (ENG.). 32p. (J). (gr. -1-k). 16.99 *(978-1-63220-403-5(7), Sky Pony Pr.)* Skyhorse Publishing Co., Inc.
Wisinski, Ed & White, Dave. Hot Wheels: To the Extreme. Harper, Benjamin. 2007. (Scholastic Reader Ser.). 30p. (J). pap. *(978-0-545-02019-0(0))* Scholastic, Inc.
Wisner, Luke. Say Cheese, God! Burciaga, David. l.t. ed. 2006. 24p. (J). (gr. -1-3). per. 11.99 *(978-1-59879-235-5(0))* Lifevest Publishing, Inc.
Wisnewski, Andrea. The Book of Virtues for Boys & Girls: A Treasury of Great Moral Stories. Bennett, William J., ed. 2008. (ENG.). 208p. (J). (gr. 5-9). 24.99 *(978-1-4169-7125-2(4), Simon & Schuster/Paula Wiseman Bks.)* Simon & Schuster/Paula Wiseman Bks.
—The Ink Garden of Brother Theophane. Millen, C. M. 2010. (ENG.). 32p. (J). (gr. k-3). 17.95 *(978-1-58089-179-0(9))* Charlesbridge Publishing, Inc.
Wisniewski, David. Ducky. Bunting, Eve. 2004. (ENG.). 32p. (J). (gr. k — 1). 6.99 *(978-0-618-43240-0(X))* Houghton Mifflin Harcourt Publishing Co.
Wisniewski, David. Golem. Wisniewski, David. 2007. (ENG.). 32p. (J). (gr. 5-7). 7.99 *(978-0-618-89424-6(1))* Houghton Mifflin Harcourt Publishing Co.
Witmer, Ruth. Talking with Hands. Martin, Mabel. 2007. (Little Jewel Book Ser.). 24p. (J). (gr. 2). pap. 2.70 *(978-0-7399-2394-8(3))* Rod & Staff Pubs., Inc.
Witnes, Vitus. Barau Barau. Baia, Edward. 2013. 24p. pap. *(978-9980-86-491-8(5))* University of Papua New Guinea Press.
Witschen, Kay. Clinker's Christmas Star. Witschen, Kay. 2004. 24p. (J). 6.95 *(978-0-9741352-1-2(6))* Dwitt Publishing.
Witschonke, Alan. The Brooklyn Bridge: The Story of the World's Most Famous Bridge & the Remarkable Family That Built It. Mann, Elizabeth. 2006. (Wonders of the World Book Ser.). (ENG.). 48p. (J). (gr. 4-8). pap. 12.95 *(978-1-931414-16-6(5)*, 9781931414166) Mikaya Pr.
—Empire State Building: When New York Reached for the Skies. Hine, Lewis, photos by. Mann, Elizabeth. (Wonders of the World Book Ser.). (ENG.). 48p. (J). (gr. 4-8). 2006. pap. 12.95 *(978-1-931414-08-1(4)*, 9781931414081); 2003. 19.95 *(978-1-931414-06-7(8)*, 9781931414067) Mikaya Pr.
—The Great Wall: The Story of Thousands of Miles of Earth & Stone That Turned a Nation into a Fortress. Mann, Elizabeth. 2006. (Wonders of the World Book Ser.). (ENG.). 48p. (J). (gr. 4-8). pap. 12.95 *(978-1-931414-12-8(2)*, 9781931414128) Mikaya Pr.
—Hail to the Chief: The American Presidency. Robb, Don. rev. ed. 2010. (ENG.). 32p. (J). (gr. 1-4). 17.95 *(978-1-58089-285-8(X))*; pap. 7.95 *(978-1-58089-286-5(8))* Charlesbridge Publishing, Inc.
—The Hoover Dam: The Story of Hard Times, Tough People & the Taming of a Wild River. Mann, Elizabeth. 2006. (Wonders of the World Book Ser.). (ENG.). 48p. (J). (gr. 4-8). pap. 9.95 *(978-1-931414-13-5(0)*, 9781931414135) Mikaya Pr.
—Statue of Liberty: A Tale of Two Countries. Mann, Elizabeth. 2011. (Wonders of the World Ser.). (ENG.). 48p. (J). (gr. 3-18). 22.95 *(978-1-931414-43-2(2)*, 9781931414432) Mikaya Pr.
Witt, David. Attack of the Mutant Meteors. Jolley, Dan. 2010. (Twisted Journeys (r) Ser.: 14). (ENG.). 112p. (J). (gr. 4-7). pap. 7.95 *(978-0-8225-9255-6(X), Graphic Universe)*; lib. bdg. 27.93 *(978-0-8225-9249-5(5))* Lerner Publishing Group.
—Captured by Pirates. Fontes, Ron & Fontes, Justine. 2007. (Twisted Journeys (r) Ser.: 1). (ENG.). 112p. (J). (gr. 4-7). lib. bdg. 27.93 *(978-0-8225-6201-6(4), Graphic Universe)*; per. 7.95 *(978-0-8225-6202-3(2))* Lerner Publishing Group.
—The Hero Twins: Against the Lords of Death [A Mayan Myth]. Jolley, Dan. 2009. (Graphic Myths & Legends Ser.). (ENG.). 48p. (gr. 4-8). pap. 8.95 *(978-1-58013-892-5(6))* Lerner Publishing Group.
—Isis & Osiris: To the Ends of the Earth. Limke, Jeff. 2007. (Graphic Myths & Legends Ser.). (ENG.). 48p. (gr. 4-8). per. 8.95 *(978-0-8225-6482-9(3))* Lerner Publishing Group.
—Isis & Osiris: To the Ends of the Earth - An Egyptian Myth. Limke, Jeff. 2006. (Graphic Myths & Legends Ser.). (ENG.). 48p. (J). 27.93 *(978-0-8225-3086-2(4))* Lerner Publishing Group.
—Nightmare on Zombie Island. Storrie, Paul D. 2008. (Twisted Journeys (r) Ser.: 5). (ENG.). (J). (gr. 4-7). pap. 45.32 *(978-0-8225-9469-7(2))*; 112p. per. 7.95 *(978-0-8225-6200-9(6))* Lerner Publishing Group.
—The Smoking Mountain: The Story of Popocatépetl & Iztaccíhuatl [an Aztec Legend]. Jolley, Dan. 2009. (Graphic Myths & Legends Ser.). (ENG.). 48p. (gr. 4-8). pap. 8.95 *(978-1-58013-826-0(8))* Lerner Publishing Group.
—Tricky Raven Tales. Schweizer, Chris. 2011. (Tricky Journeys Ser.: 4). (ENG.). (J). (gr. 2-4). pap. 39.62 *(978-0-7613-8628-5(9))*; No. 4. 64p. pap. 6.95 *(978-0-7613-7863-1(4))*; No. 4. 64p. lib. bdg. 27.93 *(978-0-7613-6603-4(2))* Lerner Publishing Group. (Graphic Universe).
Witt, Eddie. Arvid & Hornschwatz Go Skunk Scoffing. Vil, Steve. 2011. 32p. pap. 24.95 *(978-1-4560-6043-5(0))* America Star Bks.
Witt, Rici. There's a Bear in my House. Rose, Alea. 2009. (ENG.). 24p. (J). reprint ed. 10.59 *(978-0-9803367-1-9(6))* Buttermoth Pr. AUS. Dist: Lulu Enterprises Inc.
Witte, Anna. El Loro Tico Tango. Witte, Anna. (SPA.). (J). 2011. 36p. pap. 9.99 *(978-1-84686-670-8(7))*; 2005. 24p. pap. 6.99 *(978-1-84148-971-1(9))* Barefoot Bks., Inc.
—The Parrot Tico Tango. Witte, Anna. Amador, Brian. 2011. (ENG.). 36p. (J). pap. 9.99 *(978-1-84686-669-2(3))* Barefoot Bks., Inc.
—The Parrot Tico Tango. Witte, Anna. 2005. 24p. (J). (gr. k-3). 15.99 *(978-1-84148-243-9(9))* Barefoot Bks., Inc.
Wittebrood, Menno. Where Is My Bear? Coxall, Darcy. 2015. (ENG.). 32p. (J). (gr. -1-1). pap. 8.99 ***(978-1-907432-09-5(4))*** Hogs Back Bks. GBR. Dist: Independent Pubs. Group.
Wittenberg, Stella. Norberto Nucagorda, Level 5.5. Ende, Michael. 2003. (SPA.). 32p. (J). (gr. 3-5). pap. 8.95 *(978-84-204-3719-4(0), AF1328)* Santillana USA Publishing Co., Inc.
Witter, Rahad, jt. illus. see Thomas, Tina.
Wittkamp, Frantz. Konrad. Wittkamp, Frantz, tr. Nöstlinger, Christine. Ampudia, María Jesús, tr. 2nd ed. (SPA.). 148p. (J). 9.95 *(978-84-204-4781-0(1))* Ediciones Alfaguara ESP. Dist: Santillana USA Publishing Co., Inc.
Wittlinger, Laurie A., photos by. Crossing Paths: Living & Learning in China. Jin, Hong Gang et al. 2006. (CHI & ENG., 288p. (C). (gr. k-18). pap. 45.95 *(978-0-88727-370-4(X))* Cheng & Tsui Co.
—Shifting Tides: Culture in Contemporary China. Jin, Hong Gang et al. 2006. (Intermediate Chinese Course Ser.). (CHI & ENG., 272p. (C). (gr. k-18). pap. 45.95 *(978-0-88727-372-8(6))* Cheng & Tsui Co.
Wittman, Patricia. Don't Wake up the Bear!, 0 vols. Murray, Marjorie Dennis. unabr. ed. 2006. (ENG.). 34p. (J). (gr. -1-2). per. 9.99 *(978-0-7614-5330-7(X)*, 9780761453307, Amazon Children's Publishing) Amazon Publishing.
Wittwer, Hala. Dragon Egg. Loehr, Mallory. 2007. (Step into Reading Ser.). (ENG.). 32p. (J). (gr. -1-1). pap. 3.99 *(978-0-375-84350-1(7), Random Hse. Bks. for Young Readers)* Random Hse. Children's Bks.
Wittwer, Hala Swearingen. Spring Surprises. Hays, Anna Jane. 2010. (Step into Reading Ser.). (ENG.). 24p. (J). (gr. -1-1). pap. 3.99 *(978-0-375-85840-6(7))* Random Hse., Inc.
Wodin. Just Imagine. Thompson, John M. & Schultz, George M. 2006. 32p. (J). (gr. -1-3). 16.95 *(978-0-9740190-6-2(2))* Illumination Arts Publishing Co., Inc.
Woell, J. Fred. Gloucester: College Life Between Classes. Woell, J. Fred. 144p. (Orig.). (YA). pap. 15.00 *(978-0-9626935-2-6(9))* Turtle Gallery Editions.
Wohnoutka, Mike. Can't Sleep Without Sheep. Hill, Susanna Leonard. 2010. (ENG.). 40p. (J). (gr. -1-1). 16.99 *(978-0-8027-2066-5(8))* Walker & Co.
—Hanukkah Bear. Kimmel, Eric A. (ENG.). 32p. (J). 2014. (gr. -1-3). 6.99 *(978-0-8234-3169-4(X))*; 2013. 17.95 *(978-0-8234-2855-7(9))* Holiday Hse., Inc.
—Head, Shoulders, Knees, & Toes. 2009. (J). *(978-0-545-15604-2(1))* Scholastic, Inc.
—Jack's House. Beil, Karen Magnuson. (ENG.). 32p. (J). (gr. -1-3). 2009. pap. 7.99 *(978-0-8234-2242-5(9))*; 2008. 16.95 *(978-0-8234-1913-5(4))* Holiday Hse., Inc.
—Just Like My Papa. Buzzeo, Toni. 2013. (ENG.). 32p. (J). (gr. -1-k). 16.99 *(978-1-4231-4263-8(2))* Disney Pr.
—Moo! LaRochelle, David. (ENG.). (J). (gr. -1-3). 2014. 32p. 7.99 *(978-0-8027-3802-8(8))*; 2013. 40p. 16.99 *(978-0-8027-3409-9(X))* Bloomsbury USA. (Bloomsbury USA Childrens).
—Moo! LaRochelle, David. 2013. (ENG.). 40p. (J). (gr. -1-1). lib. bdg. 17.89 *(978-0-8027-3410-5(3))* Walker & Co.
—My Bibi Always Remembers. Buzzeo, Toni. 2014. (ENG.). 32p. (J). (gr. -1-k). 16.99 *(978-1-4231-8385-3(1))* Hyperion Bks. for Children.
—Stay Close to Mama. Buzzeo, Toni. 2012. (ENG.). 32p. (J). (gr. -1-k). 15.99 *(978-1-4231-3482-4(6))* Hyperion Pr.
—A Teacher for Bear. Pace, Anne Marie. 2011. (J). *(978-0-545-37776-8(5))* Scholastic, Inc.
—This Little Piggy. 2005. (J). *(978-1-58987-106-9(5))* Kindermusik International.
—The Twelve Days of Christmas in Minnesota. Van Hoven, Constance. 2009. (Twelve Days of Christmas in America Ser.). (ENG.). 32p. (J). (gr. k). 12.95 *(978-1-4027-6395-3(6))* Sterling Publishing Co., Inc.
—When the Wizzy Foot Goes Walking. Schotter, Roni. 2007. (J). *(978-0-525-47791-9(2), Dutton Juvenile)* Penguin Publishing Group.
Wohnoutka, Mike. Little Puppy & the Big Green Monster. Wohnoutka, Mike. 2014. (ENG.). 32p. (J). (gr. -1-k). 16.95 *(978-0-8234-3064-2(2))* Holiday Hse., Inc.
Wohnoutka, Mike, jt. illus. see Francis, Guy.
Wojtko, Kimberlee. C Is for Carbon. Summers, Marilee. 2004. 61p. (J). per. 24.95 *(978-0-9753078-0-9(0))* MackStorm Productions, Inc.
Wojtowycz, David. ABC Animal Jamboree. Andreae, Giles. 2010. 32p. (J). (gr. -1-2). 16.95 *(978-1-58925-092-5(3))* Tiger Tales.
—Bustle in the Bushes. Andreae, Giles. 2012. (J). *(978-1-58925-109-0(1))* Tiger Tales.
—Cock-a-Doodle-Doo! Barnyard Hullabaloo. Andreae, Giles. 2004. 32p. (J). reprint ed. pap. 7.95 *(978-1-58925-387-2(6))* Tiger Tales.

W

—Commotion in Ocean. Andreae, Giles. 2011. 24p. bds. 9.95 *(978-1-58925-863-1(0))* Tiger Tales.
—Dinosaurs Galore! Andreae, Giles. 32p. (J). 2006. (gr. -1-3). pap. 7.95 *(978-1-58925-399-5(X))*; 2005. 16.95 *(978-1-58925-044-4(3))* Tiger Tales.
—Elephant Joe, Brave Firefighter! 2015. (Step into Reading Ser.). (ENG.). 32p. (J). (gr. -1-1). 12.99 *(978-0-375-97203-4(X))* Random Hse., Inc.
—Nursery. ed. 2014. (Puzzle Bunnies Ser.). (ENG.). 12p. (J). bds. 9.99 *(978-1-4472-6101-8(1))* Pan Macmillan GBR. Dist: Independent Pubs. Group.
—Playday. ed. 2014. (Puzzle Bunnies Ser.). (ENG.). 12p. (J). bds. 9.99 *(978-1-4472-6100-1(3))* Pan Macmillan GBR. Dist: Independent Pubs. Group.
—The Pop-Up Dinosaurs Galore! Andreae, Giles. 2008. 14p. (J). (gr. 4-7). 15.95 *(978-1-58925-837-2(1))* Tiger Tales.
—What Will You Wear, Claude? 2004. 10p. (J). (gr. -1-3). reprint ed. 8.00 *(978-0-7567-8259-7(7))* DIANE Publishing Co.
—Whatever the Weather, Clavde! 2004. 10p. (J). (gr. -1-2). reprint ed. 8.00 *(978-0-7567-8257-3(0))* DIANE Publishing Co.
Wolcott, Karen. Barbie. Gordh, Bill & Pugliano-Martin, Carol. 2006. (Step into Reading Ser.). (ENG.). 192p. (J). (gr. -1-1). pap. 8.99 *(978-0-375-84124-8(5)*, Random Hse. Bks. for Young Readers) Random Hse. Children's Bks.
—Barbie: On Your Toes. Jordan, Apple & RH Disney Staff. 2005. (Step into Reading Ser.: No. 1). (ENG.). 32p. (J). (gr. -1-1). pap. 3.99 *(978-0-375-83142-3(8)*, Random Hse. Bks. for Young Readers) Random Hse. Children's Bks.
—Barbie - Horse Show Champ. Kilgras, Heidi & Parker, Jessie. 2009. (Step into Reading Ser.). (ENG.). 32p. (J). (gr. -1-1). pap. 3.99 *(978-0-375-84701-1(4))* Random Hse., Inc.
—Barbie Loves Ballet. Man-Kong, Mary & Roberts, Angela. 2005. (Pictureback Ser.). (ENG.). 24p. (J). (gr. -1-2). pap. 3.99 *(978-0-375-82756-3(0)*, Golden Bks.) Random Hse. Children's Bks.
—Barbie Loves Ballet. Dias, Joe et al, photos by. Roberts, Angela. 2010. (Barbie Ser.). (J). 14.10 *(978-0-7569-7778-8(9))* Perfection Learning Corp.
—Hooray for Halloween! Landolf, Diane Wright. 2004. (Look-Look Ser.). (ENG.). 24p. (J). (gr. -1-2). 3.99 *(978-0-375-82757-0(9)*, Golden Bks.) Random Hse. Children's Bks.
Wolek, Guy. A Brave New Mouse: Ellis Island Approved Immigrant. Horender, Philip M. 2013. (Maximilian P. Mouse, Time Traveler Ser.). 112p. (J). (gr. 3-6). lib. bdg. 27.07 *(978-1-61641-961-5(X)*, Calico Chapter Bks) Magic Wagon.
—Dinner with OLIVIA. 2009. (Olivia TV Tie-In Ser.). (ENG.). 24p. (J). (gr. -1-2). pap. 3.99 *(978-1-4169-7187-0(4)*, Simon Spotlight) Simon Spotlight.
—Eleanor Roosevelt. Donnelly, Shannon. 2005. (Heroes of America Ser.). 236p. (gr. 3-8). 27.07 *(978-1-59679-260-9(4)*, Abdo & Daughters) ABDO Publishing Co.
—Head West, Young Mouse: Transcontinental Railroad Traveler. Horender, Philip M. 2013. (Maximilian P. Mouse, Time Traveler Ser.). 112p. (J). (gr. 3-6). lib. bdg. 27.07 *(978-1-61641-959-2(8)*, Calico Chapter Bks) Magic Wagon.
—Homeward Bound: Civil Rights Mouse Leader. Horender, Philip M. 2013. (Maximilian P. Mouse, Time Traveler Ser.). 112p. (J). (gr. 3-6). lib. bdg. 27.07 *(978-1-61641-962-2(8)*, Calico Chapter Bks) Magic Wagon.
—The Mighty Maximilian: Samuel Clemens's Traveling Companion. Horender, Philip M. 2013. (Maximilian P. Mouse, Time Traveler Ser.). 112p. (J). (gr. 3-6). lib. bdg. 27.07 *(978-1-61641-960-8(1)*, Calico Chapter Bks) Magic Wagon.
—A Monster at School. Huneke, Amanda. 2013. (Monster on the Loose Ser.). 32p. (J). (gr. -1-4). 28.50 *(978-1-61641-931-8(8))* Magic Wagon.
—A Monster in the Park. Huneke, Amanda. 2013. (Monster on the Loose Ser.). 32p. (J). (gr. -1-4). 28.50 *(978-1-61641-932-5(6))* Magic Wagon.
—A Monster on the Bus. Huneke, Amanda. 2013. (Monster on the Loose Ser.). 32p. (J). (gr. -1-4). 28.50 *(978-1-61641-933-2(4))* Magic Wagon.
—A Monster on the Loose. Huneke, Amanda. 2013. (Monster on the Loose Ser.). 32p. (J). (gr. -1-4). 28.50 *(978-1-61641-934-9(2))* Magic Wagon.
—OLIVIA & the Rain Dance. 2012. (Olivia TV Tie-In Ser.). (ENG.). 24p. (J). (gr. -1-1). 15.99 *(978-1-4424-3543-8(7))*; pap. 3.99 *(978-1-4424-3542-1(9))* Simon Spotlight. (Simon Spotlight).
—OLIVIA & the School Carnival. 2010. (Olivia TV Tie-In Ser.). (ENG.). 24p. (J). (gr. -1-2). pap. 3.99 *(978-1-4424-0870-8(7)*, Simon Spotlight) Simon Spotlight.
—OLIVIA Blasts Off! Silverhardt, Lauryn. 2010. (Olivia TV Tie-In Ser.). (ENG.). 12p. (J). (gr. -1-1). 6.99 *(978-1-4169-9538-8(2)*, Simon Spotlight) Simon Spotlight.
—OLIVIA Builds a Snowlady. 2011. (Olivia TV Tie-In Ser.). (ENG.). 24p. (J). (gr. -1-2). pap. 4.99 *(978-1-4424-3286-4(1)*, Simon Spotlight) Simon Spotlight.
—Patriotic Mouse: Boston Tea Party Participant. Horender, Philip M. 2013. (Maximilian P. Mouse, Time Traveler Ser.). 112p. (J). (gr. 3-6). lib. bdg. 27.07 *(978-1-61641-957-8(1)*, Calico Chapter Bks) Magic Wagon.
—Yankee Mouse: Gettysburg Address Observer. Horender, Philip M. 2013. (Maximilian P. Mouse, Time Traveler Ser.). 112p. (J). (gr. 3-6). lib. bdg. 27.07 *(978-1-61641-958-5(X)*, Calico Chapter Bks) Magic Wagon.
Wolf, Bruce. Now I Eat My ABC's. Abrams, Pam. 2004. (ENG.). 8p. (J). (gr. k — 1). bds. 7.99 *(978-0-439-64942-1(0)*, Cartwheel Bks.) Scholastic, Inc.
Wolf, Bruce, photos by. The House That Mouse Built. Rudy, Maggie & Abrams, Pam. 2011. (ENG., 32p. (J). (gr. -1). 14.99 *(978-1-935703-25-9(0))* Downtown Bookworks.
Wolf, Claudia. Blanca Nieves. Blair, Eric. Abello, Patricia, tr. 2006. (Read-It! Readers en Español: Cuentos de Hadas Ser.). (SPA.). 32p. (gr. k-3). 19.99 *(978-1-4048-1640-4(2)*, Easy Readers) Picture Window Bks.
—Bob's Great Escape, 1 vol. Mackall, Dandi Daley. 2011. (I Can Read! / a Horse Named Bob Ser.). (ENG.). 32p. (J). pap. 3.99 *(978-0-310-71784-3(1))* Zonderkidz.
—Double Trouble, 1 vol. Mackall, Dandi Daley. 2011. (I Can Read! / a Horse Named Bob Ser.). (ENG.). 32p. (J). pap. 3.99 *(978-0-310-71785-0(X))* Zonderkidz.
—Fighter Joe: The Fish of Which Dreams Are Made. Nicola, Robbin. 2006. 24p. (J). per. 2.99 *(978-1-59958-001-2(2))* Journey Stone Creations, LLC.
—Hansel y Gretel. Blair, Eric. Abello, Patricia, tr. 2005. (Read-It! Readers en Español: Cuentos de Hadas Ser.). (SPA.). 32p. (gr. k-3). 19.99 *(978-1-4048-1632-9(1)*, Easy Readers) Picture Window Bks.
—A Horse Named Bob, 1 vol. Mackall, Dandi Daley. 2011. (I Can Read! / a Horse Named Bob Ser.). (ENG.). 32p. (J). pap. 3.99 *(978-0-310-71782-9(5))* Zonderkidz.
—Indigo's Gift: Does Indigo Have a Secret Gift? Van Oss, Laura. 2006. 24p. (J). per. 2.99 *(978-1-59958-003-6(9))* Journey Stone Creations, LLC.
—Israel ABCs: A Book about the People & Places of Israel. Schroeder, Holly. 2004. (Country ABCs Ser.). (ENG.). 32p. (gr. k-5). 27.32 *(978-1-4048-0179-0(0)*, Nonfiction Picture Bks.) Picture Window Bks.
—New Zealand ABCs: A Book about the People & Places of New Zealand. Schroeder, Holly. 2004. (Country ABCs Ser.). (ENG.). 32p. (gr. k-5). 27.32 *(978-1-4048-0178-3(2)*, 1229507, Nonfiction Picture Bks.) Picture Window Bks.
—A Perfect Pony, 1 vol. Mackall, Dandi Daley. 2011. (I Can Read! / a Horse Named Bob Ser.). (ENG.). 32p. (J). pap. 3.99 *(978-0-310-71783-6(3))* Zonderkidz.
—100 Years Old with Baby Teeth: Will Caroline Ever Lose Her Tooth? Thompson, Deanna. 2006. 24p. (J). per. 2.99 *(978-1-59958-000-5(4))* Journey Stone Creations, LLC.
Wolf, Claudia. Grandma & Me. Wolf, Claudia. 2006. 24p. (J). per. 2.99 *(978-1-59958-024-1(1))* Journey Stone Creations, LLC.
Wolf, Elizabeth. Lettie's North Star. Falk, Elizabeth Sullivan. 2006. (J). *(978-1-59336-694-0(9))* Mondo Publishing.
—Passover Around the World. Lehman-Wilzig, Tami. 2007. (Passover Ser.). (ENG.). 48p. (J). (gr. 3-5). lib. bdg. 15.95 *(978-1-58013-213-8(8))*; per. 7.95 *(978-1-58013-215-2(4))* Lerner Publishing Group. (Kar-Ben Publishing).
—¿Quién Fue Fernando de Magallanes? (Who Was Ferdinand Magellan?) Kramer, Sydelle. 2009. (¿Quién Fue... ? / Who Was... ? Ser.). (SPA.). 112p. (gr. 3-5). pap. 9.99 *(978-1-60396-426-5(6))* Santillana USA Publishing Co., Inc.
—Who Was Eleanor Roosevelt? Thompson, Gare. 2004. (Who Was... ? Ser.). 106p. (gr. 3-7). 15.00 *(978-0-7569-2829-2(X))* Perfection Learning Corp.
—Who Was Ferdinand Magellan? Kramer, Sydelle. 2004. (Who Was... ? Ser.). 105p. (J). (gr. 3-7). 12.65 *(978-0-7569-4615-9(8))* Perfection Learning Corp.
—Who Was Martin Luther King, Jr. ? Bader, Bonnie. 2008. (Who Was... ? Ser.). 105p. (J). (gr. 2-5). 12.65 *(978-0-7569-8935-4(3))* Perfection Learning Corp.
Wolf, Elizabeth & Harrison, Nancy. Who Was Eleanor Roosevelt? Thompson, Gare. Wolf, Elizabeth, tr. 2004. (Who Was... ? Ser.). (ENG.). 112p. (J). (gr. 3-7). pap. 5.99 *(978-0-448-43509-1(8)*, Grosset & Dunlap) Penguin Publishing Group.
—Who Was Ferdinand Magellan? Kramer, Sydelle. 2004. (Who Was... ? Ser.). (ENG.). 112p. (J). (gr. 3-7). pap. 5.99 *(978-0-448-43105-5(X)*, Grosset & Dunlap) Penguin Publishing Group.
—Who Was Martin Luther King, Jr. ? Bader, Bonnie. 2007. (Who Was... ? Ser.). (ENG.). 112p. (J). (gr. 3-7). pap. 4.99 *(978-0-448-44723-0(1)*, Grosset & Dunlap) Penguin Publishing Group.
—Who Was Ronald Reagan? Milton, Joyce. 2004. (Who Was... ? Ser.). (ENG.). 112p. (J). (gr. 3-7). pap. 4.99 *(978-0-448-43344-8(3)*, Grosset & Dunlap) Penguin Publishing Group.
Wolf, Helmut, photos by. Flowers of India. 2010. (ENG., 24p. (J). (gr. k — 1). bds. 7.95 *(978-81-907546-7-5(X))* Tara Publishing IND. Dist: Perseus-PGW.
Wolf, Matt. All Because of a Cup of Coffee. Stilton, Geronimo. 2004. (Geronimo Stilton Ser.: 10). (ENG.). 128p. (J). (gr. 2-5). pap. 6.99 *(978-0-439-55972-0(3)*, Scholastic Paperbacks) Scholastic, Inc.
—Attack of the Bandit Cats. Stilton, Geronimo. 2004. (Geronimo Stilton Ser.: 8). (ENG.). 128p. (J). (gr. 2-5). pap. 6.99 *(978-0-439-55970-6(7)*, Scholastic Paperbacks) Scholastic, Inc.
—Geronimo Stilton 12-Copy Solid Self-Shipper. Stilton, Geronimo. 2004. (ENG.) (J). pap. 71.88 *(978-0-439-64099-2(7)*, Scholastic Paperbacks) Scholastic, Inc.
—Un granizado de moscas para el Conde. Stilton, Geronimo. (SPA.). 128p. (J). (gr. 3-5). pap. 7.95 *(978-1-59437-452-4(X))* Santillana USA Publishing Co., Inc.
—I'm Too Fond of My Fur! Stilton, Geronimo. 2004. (Geronimo Stilton Ser.: No. 4). 116p. (J). lib. bdg. 10.00 *(978-1-4242-0698-8(7))* Fitzgerald Bks.
—It's Halloween, You 'Fraidy Mouse! Stilton, Geronimo. 2004. 113p. (J). lib. bdg. 10.00 *(978-1-4242-0280-5(9))* Fitzgerald Bks.
—It's Halloween, You 'Fraidy Mouse! Stilton, Geronimo. 2004. (Geronimo Stilton Ser.: 11). (ENG.). 128p. (J). (gr. 2-5). pap. 6.99 *(978-0-439-55973-7(1)*, Scholastic Paperbacks) Scholastic, Inc.
—Lost Treasure of the Emerald Eye. Stilton, Geronimo. 2004. (Geronimo Stilton Ser.: No. 1). 116p. (J). lib. bdg. 10.00 *(978-1-4242-0695-7(2))* Fitzgerald Bks.
—Merry Christmas, Geronimo! Stilton, Geronimo. 2004. (Geronimo Stilton Ser.: No. 12). 113p. (J). lib. bdg. 10.00 *(978-1-4242-0281-2(7))* Fitzgerald Bks.
—Merry Christmas, Geronimo! Stilton, Geronimo. 2004. (Geronimo Stilton Ser.: 12). (ENG.). 128p. (J). (gr. 2-5). pap. 6.99 *(978-0-439-55974-4(X)*, Scholastic Paperbacks) Scholastic, Inc.
—The Mona Mousa Code. Stilton, Geronimo. 2005. (Geronimo Stilton Ser.: No. 15). 113p. (J). lib. bdg. 10.00 *(978-1-4242-0284-3(1))* Fitzgerald Bks.
—The Mona Mousa Code. Stilton, Geronimo. 15th ed. 2005. (Geronimo Stilton Ser.: 15). (ENG.). 128p. (J). (gr. 2-5). pap. 6.99 *(978-0-439-66164-5(1)*, Scholastic Paperbacks) Scholastic, Inc.
—The Phantom of the Subway. Stilton, Geronimo. 2004. (Geronimo Stilton Ser.: No. 13). 112p. (J). lib. bdg. 10.00 *(978-1-4242-0282-9(5))* Fitzgerald Bks.
—The Search for Sunken Treasure. Stilton, Geronimo. 2006. (Geronimo Stilton Ser.: No. 25). 111p. (J). lib. bdg. 10.00 *(978-1-4242-1519-5(6))* Fitzgerald Bks.
—The Temple of the Ruby of Fire. Stilton, Geronimo. 2004. (Geronimo Stilton Ser.: No. 14). 109p. (J). lib. bdg. 10.00 *(978-1-4242-0283-6(3))* Fitzgerald Bks.
Wolf, Matt & Keys, Larry. Cat & Mouse in a Haunted House. Stilton, Geronimo. 2004. (Geronimo Stilton Ser.: 3). (ENG.). 128p. (J). (gr. -1-3). pap. 6.99 *(978-0-439-55965-2(0)*, Scholastic Paperbacks) Scholastic, Inc.
—The Curse of the Cheese Pyramid. Stilton, Geronimo. 2004. (Geronimo Stilton Ser.: 2). (ENG.). 128p. (J). (gr. 2-5). pap. 6.99 *(978-0-439-55964-5(2))* Scholastic, Inc.
—Four Mice Deep in the Jungle. Stilton, Geronimo. 2004. (Geronimo Stilton Ser.: 5). (ENG.). 128p. (J). (gr. 2-5). pap. 6.99 *(978-0-439-55967-6(7)*, Scholastic Paperbacks) Scholastic, Inc.
—I'm Too Fond of My Fur! Stilton, Geronimo. 2004. (Geronimo Stilton Ser.: 4). (ENG.). 128p. (J). (gr. 2-5). pap. 6.99 *(978-0-439-55966-9(9)*, Scholastic Paperbacks) Scholastic, Inc.
—Lost Treasure of the Emerald Eye. Stilton, Geronimo. 2004. (Geronimo Stilton Ser.: 1). (ENG.). 128p. (J). (gr. 2-5). pap. 6.99 *(978-0-439-55963-8(4)*, Scholastic Paperbacks) Scholastic, Inc.
—Paws Off, Cheddarface! Stilton, Geronimo. 2004. (Geronimo Stilton Ser.: 6). (ENG.). 128p. (J). (gr. 2-5). pap. 6.99 *(978-0-439-55968-3(5))* Scholastic, Inc.
—Red Pizzas for a Blue Count. Stilton, Geronimo. 2004. (Geronimo Stilton Ser.: 7). (ENG.). 128p. (J). (gr. 2-5). pap. 6.99 *(978-0-439-55969-0(3))* Scholastic, Inc.
Wolf, Myron, photos by. Orange Fizz. Wolf, Clarissa. 2009. 32p. pap. 9.99 *(978-1-935105-39-8(6))* Avid Readers Publishing Group.
Wolfe, Art, photos by. Northwest Animal Babies. Helman, Andrea. 2006. (ENG., 32p. (J). (gr. -1-2). pap. 10.99 *(978-1-57061-462-0(8))* Sasquatch Bks.
—O Is for Orca: An Alphabet Book. Helman, Andrea. 2003. (ENG., 32p. (J). (gr. -1-2). pap. 10.99 *(978-1-57061-392-0(3))* Sasquatch Bks.
Wolfe, Bob & Wolfe, Diane, photos by. How It Happens at the ATV Plant. Anderson, Jenna. 2004. (How It Happens Ser.). 32p. (J). (gr. 2-5). lib. bdg. 19.95 *(978-1-881508-94-6(3))* Oliver Pr., Inc.
—How It Happens at the Building Site. Anderson, Jenna. 2004. (How It Happens Ser.). 32p. (J). (gr. 2-5). lib. bdg. 19.95 *(978-1-881508-95-3(1))* Oliver Pr., Inc.
—How It Happens at the Cereal Company. Rocker, Megan. 2004. (How It Happens Ser.). 32p. (J). (gr. 2-5). lib. bdg. 19.95 *(978-1-881508-96-0(X))* Oliver Pr., Inc.
—How It Happens at the Fireworks Factory. Rocker, Megan. 2004. (How It Happens Ser.). 32p. (J). (gr. 2-5). lib. bdg. 19.95 *(978-1-881508-97-7(8))* Oliver Pr., Inc.
—How It Happens at the Motorcycle Plant. Shofner, Shawndra. 2006. (How It Happens Ser.). 32p. (J). (gr. 2-5). lib. bdg. 19.95 *(978-1-881508-99-1(4))* Oliver Pr., Inc.
—How It Happens at the Pizza Company. Shofner, Shawndra. 2006. (How It Happens Ser.). 32p. (J). (gr. 2-5). lib. bdg. 19.95 *(978-1-881508-98-4(6))* Oliver Pr., Inc.
Wolfe, Diane, jt. photos by see Wolfe, Bob.
Wolfe, Frances. The Little Toy Shop. Wolfe, Frances. 2008. (ENG.). 32p. (J). (gr. -1-2). 19.95 *(978-0-88776-865-1(2)*, Tundra Bks.) Tundra Bks. CAN. Dist: Penguin Random Hse., LLC.
Wolfe, Linda. Across the Road. 2008. 32p. (J). 10.00 *(978-0-937179-16-1(7))* Blue Scarab Pr.
Wolfe, Lynn. Viku & the Elephant: A story from the Forests of India. 2011. 54p. (J). pap. 12.99 *(978-0-9832227-0-5(3))* Bo-Tree Hse.
Wolferman, Iris. I Am Who I Am. Hachler, Bruno. 2010. (ENG.). 16p. (J). (gr. -1 — 1). bds. 8.95 *(978-0-7358-2299-3(9))* North-South Bks., Inc.
—My Wish Tonight. Stalder, Päivi. 2010. (ENG.). 32p. (J). (gr. -1-3). 12.95 *(978-0-7358-2331-0(6))* North-South Bks., Inc.
Wolfermann, Iris. Call Me Jacob! Hubner, Marie. 2014. (ENG.). 32p. (J). (gr. k-3). 17.95 *(978-0-7358-4134-5(9))* North-South Bks., Inc.
Wolff, Ashley. Compost Stew: An A to Z Recipe for the Earth. Siddals, Mary McKenna. 2010. (ENG.). 40p. (J). (gr. -1-2). 15.99 *(978-1-58246-316-2(6)*, Tricycle Pr.) Ten Speed Pr.
—Compost Stew: An a to Z Recipe for the Earth. Siddals, Mary McKenna. 2014. (ENG.). 40p. (J). (gr. -1-2). 7.99 *(978-0-385-75538-2(4)*, Dragonfly Bks.) Random Hse. Children's Bks.
—I Love My Daddy Because... Porter-Gaylord, Laurel. 2004. (ENG.). 20p. (J). (gr. -1 — 1). bds. 6.99 *(978-0-525-47250-6(9)*, Dutton Juvenile) Penguin Publishing Group.
—I Love My Daddy Because... (Quiero a Mi Papa Porque...) Porter-Gaylord, Laurel. 2004. (ENG & SPA.). 22p. (J). (gr. -1 — 1). bds. 6.99 *(978-0-525-47251-3(7)*, Dutton Juvenile) Penguin Publishing Group.
—I Love My Mommy Because... Porter-Gaylord, Laurel. 2004. (ENG.). 22p. (J). (gr. -1 — 1). bds. 6.99 *(978-0-525-47247-6(9)*, Dutton Juvenile) Penguin Publishing Group.
—In the Canyon. Scanlon, Liz Garton. 2015. (ENG.). 40p. (J). (gr. -1-3). 17.99 *(978-1-4814-0348-1(6)*, Beach Lane Bks.) Beach Lane Bks.
—Mama Me Alimenta. Ross, Michael Elsohn. 2008.Tr. of Mama's Milk. (ENG & SPA.). 32p. (J). (gr. -1-2). pap. 6.99 *(978-1-58246-245-5(3)*, Tricycle Pr.) Ten Speed Pr.
—Mama's Milk. Elsohn Ross, Michael. 2007. (ENG.). 32p. (J). (gr. -1-2). 12.95 *(978-1-58246-181-6(3)*, Tricycle Pr.) Ten Speed Pr.
—Miss Bindergarten & the Best Friends. Slate, Joseph. 2014. (Penguin Young Readers, Level 2 Ser.). (ENG.). 32p. (J). (gr. 1-2). pap. 3.99 *(978-0-448-48132-6(4)*, Warne, Frederick Pubs.) Penguin Bks., Ltd. GBR. Dist: Penguin Random Hse., LLC.
—Miss Bindergarten & the Secret Bag. Slate, Joseph. 2013. (Penguin Young Readers, Level 2 Ser.). (ENG.). 32p. (J). (gr. 1-2). pap. 3.99 *(978-0-448-46803-7(4))*; 14.99 *(978-0-8037-3988-8(5))* Penguin Bks., Ltd. GBR. (Warne, Frederick Pubs.). Dist: Penguin Random Hse., LLC.
—Miss Bindergarten Celebrates the Last Day of Kindergarten. Slate, Joseph. 2008. (ENG.). 40p. (J). (gr. -1-k). pap. 6.99 *(978-0-14-241060-8(8)*, Puffin) Penguin Publishing Group.
—Miss Bindergarten Has a Wild Day in Kindergarten. Slate, Joseph. 2006. (ENG.). 40p. (J). (gr. -1-k). reprint ed. pap. 6.99 *(978-0-14-240709-7(7)*, Puffin) Penguin Publishing Group.
—Miss Bindergarten Plans a Circus with Kindergarten. Slate, Joseph. 2005. (ENG.). 40p. (J). (gr. -1-k). pap. 6.99 *(978-0-14-240273-3(7)*, Puffin) Penguin Publishing Group.
—Miss Bindergarten Stays Home from Kindergarten. Slate, Joseph. 2004. (ENG.). 48p. (J). (gr. -1-k). reprint ed. pap. 6.99 *(978-0-14-230127-2(2)*, Puffin) Penguin Publishing Group.
—Miss Bindergarten Takes a Field Trip with Kindergarten. Slate, Joseph. 2004. (ENG.). 40p. (J). (gr. -1-k). pap. 6.99 *(978-0-14-240139-2(0)*, Puffin) Penguin Publishing Group.
—Old MacDonald Had a Woodshop. Shulman, Lisa. 2004. (ENG.). 32p. (J). (gr. -1-k). reprint ed. pap. 6.99 *(978-0-14-240186-6(2)*, Puffin) Penguin Publishing Group.
—Quiero a Mi Mama Porque. Gaylord, Laurel Porter. 2004.Tr. of I Love My Mommy Because. (SPA & ENG.). 20p. (J). (gr. -1 — 1). bds. 6.99 *(978-0-525-47248-3(7)*, Dutton Juvenile) Penguin Publishing Group.
Wolff, Ashley. Baby Bear Counts One. Wolff, Ashley. 2013. (ENG.). 40p. (J). (gr. -1-1). 16.99 *(978-1-4424-4158-3(5)*, Beach Lane Bks.) Beach Lane Bks.
—Baby Bear Sees Blue. Wolff, Ashley. 2012. (ENG.). 40p. (J). (gr. -1-1). 16.99 *(978-1-4424-1306-1(9)*, Beach Lane Bks.) Beach Lane Bks.
—The Baby Chicks Are Singing: Sing along in English & Spanish! Wolff, Ashley. 2005. (ENG.). 22p. (J). (gr. -1 — 1). bds. 7.99 *(978-0-316-06732-4(6))* Little, Brown Bks. for Young Readers.
—I Call My Grandpa Papa. Wolff, Ashley. 2009. (ENG.). 30p. (J). (gr. -1-2). 15.99 *(978-1-58246-252-3(6)*, Tricycle Pr.) Ten Speed Pr.
—When Lucy Goes Out Walking: A Puppy's First Year. Wolff, Ashley. 2009. (ENG.). 32p. (J). (gr. -1-2). 16.99 *(978-0-8050-8168-8(2)*, Holt, Henry & Co. Bks. For Young Readers) Holt, Henry & Co.
Wolff, Jason. Animals at the Farm/Animales de la Granja. Rosa-Mendoza, Gladys. 2004. (English-Spanish Foundations Ser.). (SPA & ENG.). 20p. (J). (gr. -1). bds. 6.95 *(978-1-931398-13-8(5))* Me+Mi Publishing.
—The Ball of Clay That Rolled Away, 0 vols. Lenhard, Elizabeth. 2012. (Shofar Ser.: 0). (ENG.). 24p. (J). (gr. k-3). 16.99 *(978-0-7614-6142-5(6)*, 9780761461425, Amazon Children's Publishing) Amazon Publishing.
—The Bird Who Ate Too Much. Gonzalez-Jensen, Margarita. 2003. (Rigby on Our Way to English Ser.). (ENG.). 24p. (gr. 3-3). pap. 50.70 *(978-0-7578-4208-5(9))* Rigby Education.
—Dinosaur Goes to Israel. Rauchwerger, Diane Levin. 2012. (Israel Ser.). (ENG.). 24p. (J). (gr. -1-1). pap. 7.95 *(978-0-7613-5134-4(5))*; lib. bdg. 16.95 *(978-0-7613-5133-7(7))* Lerner Publishing Group. (Kar-Ben Publishing).
—Dinosaur on Hanukkah. Rauchwerger, Diane Levin. 2005. (ENG.). 24p. (J). (gr. -1-1). 15.95 *(978-1-58013-145-2(X))*; per. 7.95 *(978-1-58013-143-8(3))* Lerner Publishing Group. (Kar-Ben Publishing).
—Dinosaur on Passover. Rauchwerger, Diane Levin. 2006. (ENG.). 24p. (J). (gr. -1-1). 15.95 *(978-1-58013-156-8(5))*; pap. 7.95 *(978-1-58013-161-2(1))* Lerner Publishing Group. (Kar-Ben Publishing).
—Dinosaur on Shabbat. Rauchwerger, Diane Levin. 2006. (ENG.). 24p. (J). (gr. -1-1). lib. bdg. 15.95 *(978-1-58013-159-9(X))*; per. 7.95 *(978-1-58013-163-6(8))* Lerner Publishing Group. (Kar-Ben Publishing).
—The Hog Prince. Bardhan-Quallen, Sudipta. 2009. (ENG.). 32p. (J). (gr. -1-k). 17.99 *(978-0-525-47900-0(7)*, Dutton Juvenile) Penguin Publishing Group.
Wolfhard, Steve. Sludgment Day. Kloepfer, John. 2012. (Zombie Chasers Ser.: 3). (ENG.). 224p. (J). (gr. 3-7). pap. 5.99 *(978-0-06-185311-1(9))*; 15.99 *(978-0-06-185310-4(0))* HarperCollins Pubs.
—Undead Ahead. Kloepfer, John. 2011. (Zombie Chasers Ser.: 2). (ENG.). 224p. (J). (gr. 3-7). pap. 6.99 *(978-0-06-185308-1(9))*; 16.99 *(978-0-06-185307-4(0))* HarperCollins Pubs.
—The Zombie Chasers. Kloepfer, John. (Zombie Chasers Ser.: 1). (ENG.). 224p. (J). (gr. 3-7). 2011. pap. 6.99 *(978-0-06-185306-7(2))*; 2010. 15.99 *(978-0-06-185304-3(6))* HarperCollins Pubs.
Wolfsgruber, Linda. The Camel in the Sun, 1 vol. Ondaatje, Griffin. 2013. (ENG.). 40p. (J). (gr. k). 17.95 *(978-1-55498-381-0(9))* Groundwood Bks. CAN. Dist: Perseus-PGW.
—I Am Not Little Red Riding Hood. Lecis, Alessandro & Shirtliffe, Leanne. 2013. (ENG.). 32p. (J). (gr. -1-1). 16.95 *(978-1-62087-985-6(9)*, 620985, Sky Pony Pr.) Skyhorse Publishing Co., Inc.
—Stories from the Life of Jesus, 1 vol. Lottridge, Celia Barker. 2004. (ENG.). 148p. (J). 24.95 *(978-0-88899-497-4(4))* Groundwood Bks. CAN. Dist: Perseus-PGW.
Wolk-Stanley, Jessica. Return to Earth. Geiger, Beth & Fuerst, Jeffrey B. ed. 2004. (Reader's Theater Ser.). (J). pap. *(978-1-4108-2306-9(7)*, A23067) Benchmark Education Co.

Wolos-Fonteno, Mary, et al. Tales with Tails: Animal Stories for Young People. Wolos-Fonteno, Mary et al. Salaam, Kiini Ibura, ed. 2006. 168p. (YA). pap. 15.95 *(978-0-940938-43-4(X)*, Pen & Rose Pr.) Harlin Jacque Pubns.

Wolski, Bobbi, jt. illus. see Fisher, Bonnie.

Womble, Louis. Elmo's Daddy. Kleinberg, Naomi. 2013. (ENG.). 12p. (J). (-k). bds. 4.99 *(978-0-307-98122-6(3)*, Random Hse. Bks. for Young Readers) Random Hse. Children's Bks.

—Elmo's Mommy. Kleinberg, Naomi. 2012. (ENG.). 12p. (J). (gr. k-k). bds. 4.99 *(978-0-307-92967-9(1)*, Random Hse. Bks. for Young Readers) Random Hse. Children's Bks.

—Have Yourself a Furry Little Christmas. Kleinberg, Naomi. 2007. (ENG.). 12p. (J). (gr. k — 1). bds. 4.99 *(978-0-375-84133-0(4)*, Random Hse. Bks. for Young Readers) Random Hse. Children's Bks.

—Monsters Munch Lunch! (Sesame Street) Tabby, Abigail. 2013. (Step into Reading Ser.). (ENG.). 32p. (J). (gr. -1-1). pap. 3.99 *(978-0-307-98057-1(X)*, Random Hse. Bks. for Young Readers) Random Hse. Children's Bks.

—My Fuzzy Valentine. Kleinberg, Naomi. 2005. (Board Books). (ENG.). 12p. (J). (gr. k — 1). bds. 4.99 *(978-0-375-83392-2(7)*, Random Hse. Bks. for Young Readers) Random Hse. Children's Bks.

Won, Brian. How to Tell a Story: Read the Book, Roll the Blocks, Build Adventures! Nayeri, Daniel. 2015. (ENG.). 144p. (J). (gr. 3-7). pap. 19.95 ***(978-0-7611-8457-7(0))*** Workman Publishing Co., Inc.

Won, Brian. Outer Space Bedtime Race. Sanders, Robert L. 2015. (ENG.). 40p. (J). (gr. -1-2). lib. bdg. 19.99 *(978-0-375-97354-3(0)*, Random Hse. Bks. for Young Readers) Random Hse. Children's Bks.

Won, Kim Kang. The Queen's Knight, Vol. 2. Won, Kim Kang. rev. ed. 2005. 192p. pap. 9.99 *(978-1-59532-258-6(2))* TOKYOPOP, Inc.

Won, Soo Yon. Full House 3: Discord, Vol. 3. Won, Soo Yon. 2004. (Full House (CPM Media) Ser.). 208p. pap. 9.99 *(978-1-58664-972-2(8)*, CPM Manhwa) Central Park Media Corp.

Wong, Angi Ma. Meet President Obama: America's 44th President. 2009. 32p. (J). *(978-1-928753-28-5(0))* Pacific Heritage Bks.

—My Story: Reggie: The L.A. Gator. 2007. 25p. *(978-1-928753-12-4(4))* Pacific Heritage Bks.

Wong, Benedict Norbert. Lo & Behold. Wong, Benedict Norbert. l.t. ed. 2003. 38p. (gr. 1-18). 16.95 *(978-0-9728192-0-6(7)*, LOBE) Taiji Arts Publishing.

—Lo & Behold: Good Enough to Eat. Wong, Benedict Norbert. l.t. ed. 2003. 40p. (J). (gr. 1-12). 16.95 *(978-0-9728192-1-3(5)*, 1002LB) Taiji Arts Publishing.

Wong, Gabriel. Patches the Beaver: Welcome to Harmony Woods. 2008. 36p. *(978-0-9783398-0-7(0))* Gauthier, Shane.

Wong, Liz. Camp Secret. Mahle, Melissa & Dennis, Kathryn. 2013. (Junior Spies Ser.: 1). (ENG.). 268p. (J). pap. 8.99 *(978-0-9852273-4-0(6))* SpyGirls Pr.

Wong, Melissa Olaivar. Double Rainbow Island: The Mauka Adventure. Ito, Jerilyn. 2013. 36p. pap. 10.95 *(978-1-937260-99-6(2))* Sleepytown Pr.

Wong, Nichole. Ambrosia. Manalang, Dan. 2006. (ENG.). 32p. (J). (gr. k-2). 14.99 *(978-0-9769342-0-2(5))* Flip Publishing.

Wong, Nicole. Always My Grandpa: A Story for Children about Alzheimer's Disease. Scacco, Linda. 2005. 48p. (J). (gr. -1-3). 14.95 *(978-1-59147-311-4(X))*; per. 9.95 *(978-1-59147-312-1(8))* American Psychological Assn. (Magination Pr.).

—Baby in a Manger. Stiegemeyer, Julie. 2004. 32p. (J). (gr. k-4). 9.99 *(978-0-7586-0726-3(1))* Concordia Publishing Hse.

—Brushing Mom's Hair. Cheng, Andrea. 2009. (ENG.). 64p. (J). (gr. 5-8). 17.95 *(978-1-59078-599-7(1)*, Front Street) Boyds Mills Pr.

—Candy Shop. Wahl, Jan. 2005. (ENG.). 32p. (J). (gr. -1-3). pap. 7.95 *(978-1-57091-668-7(3))* Charlesbridge Publishing, Inc.

—Ferry Tail. Kenah, Katharine. 2014. (ENG.). 32p. (J). (gr. k-3). 16.99 *(978-1-58536-829-7(6)*, 203011) Sleeping Bear Pr.

Wong, Nicole. The Hugging Tree: A Story about Resilience. Neimark, Jill. 2015. (J). ***(978-1-4338-1907-0(4)***, Magination Pr.) American Psychological Assn.

Wong, Nicole. L Is for Library. Terry, Sonya. 2006. 32p. (J). (gr. -1-3). lib. bdg. 16.95 *(978-1-932146-44-8(X)*, Upstart Bks.) Highsmith Inc.

—My Grandpa Had a Stroke. Butler, Dori Hillestad. 2007. 31p. (J). (gr. 3-7). 14.95 *(978-1-59147-806-5(5))*; per. 9.95 *(978-1-59147-807-2(3))* American Psychological Assn. (Magination Pr.).

—No Monkeys, No Chocolate. Stewart, Melissa & Young, Allen M. 2013. (ENG.). 32p. (J). (gr. k-3). 16.95 *(978-1-58089-287-2(6))* Charlesbridge Publishing, Inc.

—Only One Year, 1 vol. Cheng, Andrea. 2013. (ENG.). 97p. (J). (gr. 2-5). 16.95 *(978-1-60060-252-8(5))* Lee & Low Bks., Inc.

—R Is for Research. Buzzeo, Toni. 2008. 17.95 *(978-1-60213-032-6(9))*; (J). (gr. 2-4). 17.95 *(978-1-60213-030-2(2))* Highsmith Inc. (Upstart Bks.).

—Wild Rose's Weaving. Churchill, Ginger. 2011. (ENG.). 32p. (J). (gr. -1-3). 15.95 *(978-1-933718-56-9(0))* Tanglewood Pr.

Wong, Nicole E. Candy Shop. Wahl, Jan. 2004. (ENG.). 32p. (J). (gr. -1-3). 15.95 *(978-1-57091-508-6(3))* Charlesbridge Publishing, Inc.

Wong, Priscilla. My Hometown. Griesmer, Russell. 2015. (ENG.). 40p. (gr. 1-4). 15.95 ***(978-1-62370-174-1(0))*** Capstone Young Readers.

Wong, Scott. Power Play, 1 vol. Rogers, Buddy & Avery, Ben. 2008. (Z Graphic Novels / TimeFlyz Ser.). (ENG.). 160p. (J). pap. 6.99 *(978-0-310-71365-4(X))* Zondervan.

—Time Trap, 1 vol. Avery, Ben & Zondervan Publishing Staff. 2009. (Z Graphic Novels / TimeFlyz Ser.). (ENG.). 160p. (J). pap. 6.99 *(978-0-310-71366-1(8))* Zonderkidz.

Wong, Scott & Merced, Eric. Battle Between, 1 vol. Rogers, Bud & Avery, Ben. 2012. (Z Graphic Novels / TimeFlyz Ser.). (ENG.). 160p. (J). pap. 6.99 *(978-0-310-71367-8(6))* Zondervan.

Wong, Stanley. The River. Hathorn, Libby. 2003. 40p. 28.95 *(978-1-86366-516-2(1))* Education Services Australia Ltd. AUS. Dist: Cheng & Tsui Co.

Wong, Tony. The Legendary Couple, Vol. 4. Cha, Louis. 2003. 120p. (YA). (gr. 8-18). pap. 13.95 *(978-1-58899-233-8(0))* ComicsOne Corp./Dr. Masters.

Wong, Walden, jt. illus. see Barberi, Carlo.

Wong, Walden, jt. illus. see Ng, Leandro.

Woo. Rebirth, 11 vols., Vol. 4. Lee, Kang-Woo. Ryu, Youngju, tr. from JPN. rev. ed. 2003. 176p. pap. 9.99 *(978-1-59182-219-6(X))* TOKYOPOP, Inc.

WOO. Rebirth, Vol. 13. Yi, Kang-u. rev. ed. 2005. 200p. pap. 9.99 *(978-1-59532-028-5(8))* TOKYOPOP, Inc.

Woo. Rebirth, 11 vols. Woo. rev. ed. 192p. Vol. 6. 2004. pap. 9.99 *(978-1-59182-524-1(5))*; Vol. 12. 2005. pap. 9.99 *(978-1-59532-027-8(X))* TOKYOPOP, Inc.

—RebirthTM, Vol. 10. Woo. Hahn, Jennifer, tr. from KOR. rev. ed. 2004. 192p. (YA). pap. 9.99 *(978-1-59182-528-9(8))* TOKYOPOP, Inc.

Woo, Howie. Hoaxed! Fakes & Mistakes in the World of Science. Yes Magazine Editors. 2009. (ENG.). 48p. (J). (gr. 3-7). 16.95 *(978-1-55453-206-3(X))* Kids Can Pr., Ltd. CAN. Dist: Univ. of Toronto Pr.

—Hoaxed! Fakes & Mistakes in the World of Science. Yes Magazine Editors. Yes Magazine Editors, ed. 2009. (ENG.). 48p. (J). (gr. 3-7). pap. 8.95 *(978-1-55453-207-0(8))* Kids Can Pr., Ltd. CAN. Dist: Univ. of Toronto Pr.

—Robots: From Everyday to Out of This World. Yes Magazine Editors, ed. 2008. (ENG.). 48p. (J). (gr. 3-7). pap. 8.95 *(978-1-55453-204-9(3))* Kids Can Pr., Ltd. CAN. Dist: Univ. of Toronto Pr.

—Who Discovered America? Wyatt, Valerie. 2008. (ENG.). 40p. (J). (gr. 3-7). 17.95 *(978-1-55453-128-8(4))*; pap. 8.95 *(978-1-55453-129-5(2))* Kids Can Pr., Ltd. CAN. Dist: Univ. of Toronto Pr.

Woo Kim, Jin. Snow White & the Seven Dwarfs. McFadden, Deanna. 2012. (Silver Penny Stories Ser.). (ENG.). 40p. (J). (gr. -1-1). 4.95 *(978-1-4027-8342-5(6))* Sterling Publishing Co., Inc.

Wood, Alix. Body Snatching. 2013. (Why'd They Do That? Strange Customs of the Past Ser.). 32p. (J). (gr. 4-6). pap. 63.00 *(978-1-4339-9574-3(3))* Stevens, Gareth Publishing LLLP.

Wood, Alix. Body Snatching. Wood, Alix. 2013. (Why'd They Do That? Strange Customs of the Past Ser.). 32p. (J). (gr. 4-6). pap. 10.50 *(978-1-4339-9573-6(5))* Stevens, Gareth Publishing LLLP.

—Dueling. Wood, Alix. 2013. (Why'd They Do That? Strange Customs of the Past Ser.). 32p. (J). (gr. 4-6). pap. 10.50 *(978-1-4339-9577-4(8))*; pap. 63.00 *(978-1-4339-9578-1(6))* Stevens, Gareth Publishing LLLP.

—Gladiators: Fighting to the Death. Wood, Alix. 2013. 32p. (J). (gr. 4-6). 26.60 *(978-1-4339-9580-4(8))*; pap. 10.50 *(978-1-4339-9581-1(6))*; pap. 63.00 *(978-1-4339-9582-8(4))* Stevens, Gareth Publishing LLLP.

—Human Sacrifice. Wood, Alix. 2013. (Why'd They Do That? Strange Customs of the Past Ser.). 32p. (J). (gr. 4-6). pap. 63.00 *(978-1-4339-9586-6(7))*; pap. 10.50 *(978-1-4339-9585-9(9))* Stevens, Gareth Publishing LLLP.

—Mummification. Wood, Alix. 2013. 32p. (J). (gr. 4-6). 26.60 *(978-1-4339-9588-0(3))*; pap. 10.50 *(978-1-4339-9589-7(1))*; pap. 63.00 *(978-1-4339-9590-3(5))* Stevens, Gareth Publishing LLLP.

—Witch Trials. Wood, Alix. 2013. 32p. (J). (gr. 4-6). 26.60 *(978-1-4339-9592-7(1))*; pap. 10.50 *(978-1-4339-9593-4(X))*; pap. 63.00 *(978-1-4339-9594-1(8))* Stevens, Gareth Publishing LLLP.

Wood, Audrey. Balloonia. Wood, Audrey. 2005. (Child's Play Library). (ENG.). 32p. (J). pap. *(978-1-904550-49-5(5))* Child's Play International Ltd.

—Magic Shoelaces. Wood, Audrey. 2005. (Child's Play Library). (ENG.). 32p. (J). pap. *(978-1-904550-51-8(7))* Child's Play International Ltd.

—Presto Change-O. Wood, Audrey. 2005. (Child's Play Library). (ENG.). 32p. (J). pap. *(978-1-904550-52-5(5))* Child's Play International Ltd.

—Scaredy Cats. Wood, Audrey. 2005. (Child's Play Library). (ENG.). 32p. (J). pap. *(978-1-904550-48-8(7))* Child's Play International Ltd.

Wood, Audrey & Wood, Bruce Robert. Alphabet Rescue. 2006. (J). *(978-0-439-88927-8(8))* Scholastic, Inc.

Wood, Audrey & Wood, Don. The Napping House. Wood, Audrey. 25th ed. 2009. (ENG.). 32p. (J). (gr. -1-3). 17.99 *(978-0-15-256708-8(9))* Houghton Mifflin Harcourt Publishing Co.

Wood, Bruce. Alphabet Mystery. Wood, Audrey. 2003. (ENG.). 40p. (J). (gr. -1-k). 17.99 *(978-0-439-44337-1(7)*, Blue Sky Pr., The) Scholastic, Inc.

—Alphabet Rescue. Wood, Audrey. 2006. (ENG.). 40p. (J). (gr. -1-k). 17.99 *(978-0-439-85316-3(8)*, Blue Sky Pr., The) Scholastic, Inc.

—Ten Little Fish. Wood, Audrey. 2004. (ENG.). 40p. (J). (gr. -1-k). 17.99 *(978-0-439-63569-1(1)*, Blue Sky Pr., The) Scholastic, Inc.

Wood, Bruce Robert, jt. illus. see Wood, Audrey.

Wood, Chaz. A Hare's Tale 2 - the Golden Hare. Auty, Rob. 2013. 102p. pap. *(978-1-908098-90-0(2))* 2QT Publishing.

Wood, Colleen. Lessons from Mother Earth, 1 vol. McLeod, Elaine. 2010. (ENG.). 24p. (J). (gr. k-k). pap. 7.95 *(978-0-88899-832-3(5))* Groundwood Bks. CAN. Dist: Perseus-PGW.

Wood, Damian. Alphabet of Dance. Schwaeber, Barbie Heit. 2009. (Smithsonian Alphabet Books). (ENG.). 40p. (J). (gr. -1-k). 9.95 *(978-1-60727-111-6(7))* Soundprints.

—If Cookie Had a Cookie. Galvin, Laura Gates. 2009. (Sesame Street Read, Play & Go Ser.). 20p. (J). (gr. -1). 9.99 incl. audio compact disk *(978-1-59069-867-9(3))* Studio Mouse LLC.

Wood, Don. The Birthday Queen. Wood, Audrey. 2013. (ENG.). 32p. (J). (gr. -1-3). 17.99 *(978-0-545-41474-6(1)*, Blue Sky Pr., The) Scholastic, Inc.

Wood, Don. The Full Moon at the Napping House. Wood, Audrey. 2015. (ENG.). 32p. (J). (gr. -1-3). 17.99 ***(978-0-544-30832-9(8)***, HMH Books For Young Readers) Houghton Mifflin Harcourt Publishing Co.

Wood, Don. King Bidgood's in the Bathtub. Wood, Audrey. 2010. (ENG.). 32p. (J). (gr. -1-3). pap. 7.99 *(978-0-15-205435-9(9))* Houghton Mifflin Harcourt Publishing Co.

—The Little Mouse, the Red Ripe Strawberry & the Big Hungry Bear. Wood, Audrey. 2007. (Child's Play Library). (ENG.). 32p. (J). *(978-1-84643-050-3(X))* Child's Play International Ltd.

—The Napping House. Wood, Audrey. (ENG.). (J). (gr. k — 1). 2010. 34p. bds. 8.99 *(978-0-547-48147-0(0))*; 2005. 32p. bds. 11.99 *(978-0-15-205620-9(3))* Houghton Mifflin Harcourt Publishing Co.

—Napping House / La Casa Adormecida. Wood, Audrey. 2012. (ENG & SPA.). 32p. (J). (gr. -1 — 1). bds. 6.99 *(978-0-547-71920-7(5))* Houghton Mifflin Harcourt Publishing Co.

—Piggy Pie Po. Wood, Audrey. 2010. (ENG.). 32p. (J). (gr. -1-3). 16.99 *(978-0-15-202494-9(8))* Houghton Mifflin Harcourt Publishing Co.

Wood, Don. Into the Volcano. Wood, Don. (ENG.). 176p. (J). 2012. pap. 12.99 *(978-0-439-72674-0(3))*; 2008. (gr. 5-8). 18.99 *(978-0-439-72671-9(9))* Scholastic, Inc. (Blue Sky Pr., The).

Wood, Don, jt. illus. see Wood, Audrey.

Wood, Dorreya. Pick-a-WooWoo - Bliss: A breathtaking story of transformation that reveals 'we are never Alone', 16 vols., Vol. 5. Wood, Dorreya. 2009. 32p. pap. *(978-0-9803669-4-5(1))* Pick-a-Woo Woo Pubs.

Wood, Douglas. Wally the Warthog. Tinsley, Jillian. 2012. 24p. (J). pap. 10.99 *(978-1-61254-782-4(6))* Small Pr., The.

Wood, Gerald. Music Theory for Beginners. Danes, Emma. 2006. (Music Theory Ser.). 48p. (J). (gr. 4). lib. bdg. 16.95 *(978-1-58086-562-3(3))* EDC Publishing.

—Viking World. Wingate, Philippa & Millard, Anne. 2004. (Illustrated World History Ser.). 64p. (J). (gr. 6). lib. bdg. 19.95 *(978-1-58086-628-6(X)*, Usborne) EDC Publishing.

—Who Were the First People? Cox, Phil Roxbee & Reid, Struan. rev. ed. 2006. (Starting Point History Ser.). 32p. (J). (gr. 1). lib. bdg. 12.95 *(978-1-58086-499-2(6))* EDC Publishing.

Wood, Gerald, jt. illus. see Jackson, Ian.

Wood, Hannah. Arctic Wonders. Hopgood, Sally & Graham, Oakley. 2012. (Sparkling Slide Bks.). (ENG.). 12p. (J). *(978-1-84956-675-9(5))* Top That! Publishing PLC.

—Café Cosmos. Scott, Janine. 2009. (Treasure Chest Readers Ser.). 24p. (J). (gr. -1-2). pap. 8.15 *(978-1-60754-674-0(4))*; lib. bdg. 22.60 *(978-1-60754-673-3(6))* Windmill Bks.

—Dino Pop-up Faces: A Let's Pretend Pop-up Book. 2007. (ENG.). 12p. (J). (gr. -1-3). 14.95 *(978-1-58117-596-7(5)*, Intervisual/Piggy Toes) Bendon, Inc.

—Dino-School - Alphabet. Junor, Amy. 2014. (Dino-School Ser.). (ENG.). 22p. (J). (— 1). bds. 7.99 *(978-1-74297-657-0(3))* Hardie Grant Egmont Pty, Ltd. AUS. Dist: Independent Pubs. Group.

—Dino-School: Colours. Junor, Amy. 2013. (Dino-School Ser.). (ENG.). 22p. (J). bds. 8.99 *(978-1-74297-656-3(5))* Hardie Grant Egmont Pty, Ltd. AUS. Dist: Independent Pubs. Group.

—Hey, Diddle, Diddle & More Favorite Nursery Rhymes. 2012. (J). *(978-1-58925-870-9(3))* Tiger Tales.

—The Innkeeper, 1 vol. David, Juliet. 2009. (Christmas Trio Ser.). 18p. (J). bds. 4.99 *(978-0-8254-7405-7(1)*, Candle Bks.) Lion Hudson PLC GBR. Dist: Kregel Pubns.

—Mars Mouse. Scott, Janine. 2009. (Treasure Chest Readers Ser.). 24p. (J). (gr. -1-2). pap. 8.15 *(978-1-60754-677-1(9))*; lib. bdg. 22.60 *(978-1-60754-676-4(0))* Windmill Bks.

—Monsters Dance. Hodgman, Ann. 2013. (ENG.). 12p. (gr. -1). bds. 8.95 *(978-1-58925-627-9(1))* Tiger Tales.

—Old MacDonald Had a Farm: And Other Favorite Songs. 2012. (J). *(978-1-58925-874-7(6))* Tiger Tales.

—One Rainy Day. Salzano, Tammi. 2011. 24p. (J). (gr. -1-k). bds. 8.95 *(978-1-58925-860-0(6))* Tiger Tales.

—One Snowy Day. Salzano, Tammi. 2010. 24p. (J). (gr. -1-k). bds. 8.95 *(978-1-58925-857-0(6))* Tiger Tales.

—One Sunny Day. Salzano, Tammi J. 2012. (J). *(978-1-58925-871-6(1))* Tiger Tales.

—One Windy Day. Salzano, Tammi J. 2012. (J). *(978-1-58925-875-4(4))* Tiger Tales.

—Safari Wonders. Hopgood, Sally & Graham, Oakley. 2012. (Sparkling Slide Bks.). (ENG.). 12p. (J). *(978-1-84956-676-6(3))* Top That! Publishing PLC.

—The Shepherds, 1 vol. David, Juliet. 2009. (Christmas Trio Ser.). 18p. (J). bds. 4.99 *(978-0-8254-7406-4(X)*, Candle Bks.) Lion Hudson PLC GBR. Dist: Kregel Pubns.

—Truck Party. Salzano, Tammi. 2011. 20p. 7.95 *(978-1-58925-865-5(7))* Tiger Tales.

—The Wise Men, 1 vol. David, Juliet. 2009. (Christmas Trio Ser.). 18p. (J). bds. 4.99 *(978-0-8254-7407-1(8)*, Candle Bks.) Lion Hudson PLC GBR. Dist: Kregel Pubns.

Wood, Hannah & Mahoney, Daniel J. Rainforest Wonders. Ranson, Erin. 2007. (Sparkling Slide Book Ser.). (ENG.). 12p. (J). (gr. k). *(978-1-84666-356-7(3)*, Tide Mill Pr.) Top That! Publishing PLC.

Wood, Hannah, jt. illus. see Mahoney, Daniel.

Wood, Jakki. A Hole in the Road. 2008. (ENG.). 24p. (J). (gr. -1-1). 15.95 *(978-1-84507-286-5(3)*, Frances Lincoln) Quarto Publishing Group UK GBR. Dist: Hachette Bk. Group.

Wood, Jennifer. The Year of the Horse: Tales from the Chinese Zodiac. Chin, Oliver. 2013. (Tales from the Chinese Zodiac Ser.: 8). (ENG.). 36p. (J). (gr. -1-3). 15.95 *(978-1-59702-080-0(X))* Immedium.

—The Year of the Snake: Tales from the Chinese Zodiac. Chin, Oliver, ed. 2012. (Tales from the Chinese Zodiac Ser.: 8). (ENG.). 36p. (J). (gr. -1-3). 15.95 *(978-1-59702-038-1(9))* Immedium.

Wood, Joe. Everybody Has a Daddy. Williams, Vicki & Williams, Kathy. 2003. 16p. (J). 7.95 *(978-0-9747597-0-8(8))* Self-Esteem Adventures Pr.

Wood, Katie. Cheer Choice, 1 vol. Maddox, Jake. 2014. (Jake Maddox Girl Sports Stories Ser.). (ENG.). 72p. (gr. 2-3). 23.99 *(978-1-4342-4143-6(2))* Stone Arch Bks.

—Cora's Decision. Gurtler, Janet. 2015. (Mermaid Kingdom Ser.). (ENG.). 96p. (gr. 3-5). 22.65 *(978-1-4342-9695-5(4))* Stone Arch Bks.

—Dance Team Dilemma, 1 vol. Maddox, Jake. 2013. (Jake Maddox Girl Sports Stories Ser.). (ENG.). 72p. (gr. 2-3). pap. 5.95 *(978-1-4342-4201-3(3))*; lib. bdg. 23.99 *(978-1-4342-4014-9(2))* Stone Arch Bks.

—Dancing Solo, 1 vol. Maddox, Jake. 2014. (Jake Maddox Girl Sports Stories Ser.). (ENG.). 72p. (gr. 2-3). 23.99 *(978-1-4342-4142-9(4))* Stone Arch Bks.

—Gymnastics Jitters, 1 vol. Maddox, Jake. 2012. (Jake Maddox Girl Sports Stories Ser.). (ENG.). 72p. (gr. 2-3). pap. 5.95 *(978-1-4342-3908-2(X))*; lib. bdg. 23.99 *(978-1-4342-3293-9(X))* Stone Arch Bks.

—Horseback Hurdles, 1 vol. Maddox, Jake & Berne, Emma Carlson. 2012. (Jake Maddox Girl Sports Stories Ser.). (ENG.). 72p. (gr. 2-3). pap. 5.95 *(978-1-4342-3905-1(5))*; lib. bdg. 23.99 *(978-1-4342-3294-6(8))* Stone Arch Bks.

—Jake Maddox Girl Sport Stories. Maddox, Jake. (Jake Maddox Girl Sports Stories Ser.). (ENG.). 72p. (gr. 2-3). 2014. pap. 23.08 *(978-1-4342-8947-6(8))*; 2013. 95.96 *(978-1-4342-4134-4(3))* Stone Arch Bks.

—Jake Maddox Girl Sports Stories, 1 vol. Maddox, Jake. (Jake Maddox Girl Sports Stories Ser.). (ENG.). 72p. (gr. 2-3). 2014. 95.96 *(978-1-4342-6402-2(5))*; 2013. 671.72 *(978-1-4342-4847-3(X))*; 2013. pap. 23.80 *(978-1-4342-4358-4(3))*; 2013. pap. 71.40 *(978-1-4342-4359-1(1))* Stone Arch Bks.

—Jake Maddox Girls Sport Stories. Maddox, Jake. 2014. (Jake Maddox Girl Sports Stories Ser.). (ENG.). 72p. (gr. 2-3). pap. 95.20 *(978-1-4342-8948-3(6))* Stone Arch Bks.

—Rachel's Secret. Gurtler, Janet. 2015. (Mermaid Kingdom Ser.). (ENG.). 96p. (gr. 3-5). 22.65 *(978-1-4342-9694-8(6))* Stone Arch Bks.

—Rebound Time, 1 vol. Maddox, Jake & Berne, Emma Carlson. 2013. (Jake Maddox Girl Sports Stories Ser.). (ENG.). 72p. (gr. 2-3). pap. 5.95 *(978-1-4342-4202-0(1))*; lib. bdg. 23.99 *(978-1-4342-4013-2(4))* Stone Arch Bks.

—Running Scared, 1 vol. Maddox, Jake & Berne, Emma Carlson. 2013. (Jake Maddox Girl Sports Stories Ser.). (ENG.). 72p. (gr. 2-3). pap. 5.95 *(978-1-4342-4203-7(X))*; lib. bdg. 23.99 *(978-1-4342-4015-6(0))* Stone Arch Bks.

—Secrets Beneath the Sea. Gurtler, Janet. 2015. (Mermaid Kingdom Ser.). (ENG.). 288p. (gr. 3-5). 12.95 *(978-1-62370-187-1(2))* Capstone Young Readers.

—Shyanna's Song. Gurtler, Janet. 2015. (Mermaid Kingdom Ser.). (ENG.). 96p. (gr. 3-5). lib. bdg. 22.65 *(978-1-4342-9693-1(8))* Stone Arch Bks.

—Shyanna's Wish. Gurtler, Janet. 2015. (Mermaid Kingdom Ser.). (ENG.). 96p. (gr. 3-5). 22.65 *(978-1-4342-9696-2(2))* Stone Arch Bks.

—Skating Showdown, 1 vol. Maddox, Jake. 2013. (Jake Maddox Girl Sports Stories Ser.). (ENG.). 72p. (gr. 2-3). pap. 5.95 *(978-1-4342-4204-4(8))*; lib. bdg. 23.99 *(978-1-4342-4012-5(6))* Stone Arch Bks.

—Soccer Show-Off, 1 vol. Maddox, Jake. 2014. (Jake Maddox Girl Sports Stories Ser.). (ENG.). 72p. (gr. 2-3). 23.99 *(978-1-4342-4144-3(0))* Stone Arch Bks.

—Soccer Surprise, 1 vol. Maddox, Jake & Berne, Emma Carlson. 2012. (Jake Maddox Girl Sports Stories Ser.). (ENG.). 72p. (gr. 2-3). pap. 5.95 *(978-1-4342-3906-8(3))*; lib. bdg. 23.99 *(978-1-4342-3291-5(3))* Stone Arch Bks.

—Softball Surprise, 1 vol. Maddox, Jake. 2014. (Jake Maddox Girl Sports Stories Ser.). (ENG.). 72p. (gr. 2-3). 23.99 *(978-1-4342-4141-2(6))* Stone Arch Bks.

—Volleyball Dreams, 1 vol. Maddox, Jake. 2012. (Jake Maddox Girl Sports Stories Ser.). (ENG.). 72p. (gr. 2-3). pap. 5.95 *(978-1-4342-3907-5(1))*; lib. bdg. 23.99 *(978-1-4342-3292-2(1))* Stone Arch Bks.

Wood, Laura. If an Armadillo Went to a Restaurant. Fischer, Ellen. 2014. (ENG.). 32p. (J). (-2). 14.95 *(978-1-938063-39-8(2)*, Mighty Media Kids) Mighty Media Pr.

—Lucy in the City: A Story about Spatial Thinking. Dillemuth, Julie. 2015. (J). pap. *(978-1-4338-1928-5(7)*, Magination Pr.) American Psychological Assn.

Wood, Leslie. The Little Red Engine & the Rocket. Ross, Diana. 2005. (Little Red Engine Ser.: 1). (ENG.). 32p. (J). (gr. k-2). pap. 8.99 *(978-0-233-00146-3(8))* Andre Deutsch GBR. Dist: Independent Pubs. Group.

—The Little Red Engine Goes to Town. Ross, Diana. 2005. (Little Red Engine Ser.: 1). (ENG.). 32p. (J). (gr. k-2). pap. 8.99 *(978-0-233-00151-7(4))* Andre Deutsch GBR. Dist: Independent Pubs. Group.

Wood, Madeline. It Happened in Maine. Schmidt, Mollie. 2013. (ENG.). 56p. (J). pap. 10.95 *(978-1-59713-137-7(7))* Goose River Pr.

Wood, Michele. Chasing Freedom: The Life Journeys of Harriet Tubman & Susan B. Anthony, Inspired by Historical Facts. Grimes, Nikki. 2015. (ENG.). 56p. (J). (gr. 2-5). 18.99 *(978-0-439-79338-4(6)*, Orchard Bks.) Scholastic, Inc.

—Going Back Home: An Artist Returns to the South. Igus, Toyomi. 2013. (ENG.). 32p. (J). (gr. 1-18). pap. 9.95 *(978-0-89239-197-4(9)*, Children's Book Press) Lee & Low Bks., Inc.

—I Lay My Stitches Down. Grady, Cynthia. 2012. 17.00 *(978-0-8028-5386-8(2)*, Eerdmans Bks For Young Readers) Eerdmans, William B. Publishing Co.

—I See the Rhythm. Igus, Toyomi. 2013. (ENG.). 32p. (J). (gr. 1). pap. 10.95 *(978-0-89239-212-4(6))* Lee & Low Bks., Inc.

—I See the Rhythm of Gospel, 1 vol. Igus, Toyomi. 2010. (ENG.). 40p. (J). (gr. 4-7). 16.99 *(978-0-310-71819-2(8))* Zonderkidz.

W

Wood, Morgan. Adventures in the Forest. Sackanay, Kathleen. 2007. 24p. (J). pap. 8.45 *(978-0-9791276-2-5(9))* Suzeteo Enterprises.
Wood, Muriel. Aram's Choice, 1 vol. Skrypuch, Marsha Forchuk. 2006. (ENG.). 72p. (J). (gr. 3-6). per. *(978-1-55041-354-0(6))* Fitzhenry & Whiteside, Ltd.
—Call Me Aram, 1 vol. Skrypuch, Marsha. 2008. (ENG.). 86p. (J). (gr. -1-3). *(978-1-55455-000-5(9));* pap. *(978-1-55455-001-2(7))* Fitzhenry & Whiteside, Ltd.
—Light & Color: I Wonder Why. Lowery, Lawrence F. 2014. (ENG.). 36p. (J). pap. 11.95 *(978-1-938946-51-6(0))* National Science Teachers Assn.
—Lizzie's Storm, 1 vol. Fitz-Gibbon, Sally. 2004. (New Beginnings Ser.). (ENG.). 64p. (J). pap. *(978-1-55041-795-1(9))* Fitzhenry & Whiteside, Ltd.
—Old Bird, 1 vol. Morck, Irene. 2005. (ENG.). 32p. (J). pap. 7.95 *(978-1-55041-697-8(9),* 1550416979) Fitzhenry & Whiteside, Ltd. CAN. Dist: Midpoint Trade Bks., Inc.
—The Olden Days Coat. Laurence, Margaret. 2004. (ENG.). 32p. (J). (gr. 2-5). pap. 8.95 *(978-0-88776-704-3(4),* Tundra Bks.) Tundra Bks. CAN. Dist: Penguin Random Hse., LLC.
Wood, Ruth. The Bingity-Bangity School Bus. Conkling, Fleur. 2015. (G&d Vintage Ser.). (ENG.). 24p. (J). (gr. -1-k). 7.99 ***(978-0-448-48763-2(2),*** Grosset & Dunlap) Penguin Publishing Group.
Wood, Ryan. The Worst Twelve Days of Christmas. Bardhan-Quallen, Sudipta. 2011. (ENG.). 32p. (J). (gr. -1-3). 15.95 *(978-1-4197-0033-0(2),* Abrams Bks. for Young Readers) Abrams.
Wood, Steve. Butterfly Magic. Hillyer, Rhonda. 2013. 84p. pap. 12.00 *(978-1-62212-306-3(9),* Strategic Bk. Publishing) Strategic Book Publishing & Rights Agency (SBPRA).
Wood, Steven. Build My Own Main Street: Build My Own Books with Building Bricks. Shaw, Gina. 2015. (Build My Own Ser.: 5). (ENG.). 24p. (J). (gr. -1-1). pap. 12.99 *(978-0-7944-3336-9(7))* Studio Fun International.
Wood, Tracey. See What You Can Be: Explore Careers That Could Be for You! Heiman, Diane & Suneby, Liz. 2009. (ENG.). 108p. (gr. 4-7). spiral bd. 9.95 *(978-1-59369-277-3(3))* American Girl Publishing, Inc.
—What a Girl Loves Puzzle Book. Magruder, Trula. Magruder, Trula, ed. 2004. (ENG.). 128p. spiral bd. 7.95 *(978-1-58485-909-3(1))* American Girl Publishing, Inc.
Woodard, Dana. The Little Pig That Was Afraid of the Mud. Galloway, Shannon. 2007. (J). (gr. -1-3). per. 12.99 *(978-1-59879-244-7(X))* Lifevest Publishing, Inc.
Woodard, Sarah Junkin. Come on Down. Murdock, Bob E. unabr. ed. 2003. 97p. (J). spiral bd. *(978-0-9754363-0-1(9))* Murdock, Bob E.
Woodbury et al, Charles H., jt. illus. see Fuert, L. A.
Woodcock, John. Color & Doodle Your Way Across the USA. 2013. 108p. *(978-1-78157-023-4(X),* Ilex Pr.) Octopus Publishing Group.
—Ride by Moonlight. Bates, Michelle. Leigh, Susannah, ed. rev. ed. 2004. (Sandy Lane Stables Ser.). (ENG.). 118p. (J). pap. 4.95 *(978-0-7945-0547-9(3),* Usborne) EDC Publishing.
—True Desert Adventures. Harvey, Gill. 2004. (True Adventure Stories Ser.). 144p. (J). pap. 4.95 *(978-0-7945-0381-9(0),* Usborne) EDC Publishing.
—True Everest Adventures. Dowswell, Paul. 2004. (True Adventure Stories Ser.). 144p. (J). pap. 4.95 *(978-0-7945-0373-4(X),* Usborne) EDC Publishing.
—True Polar Adventures. Dowswell, Paul. 2004. (True Adventure Stories Ser.). 144p. (J). pap. 4.95 *(978-0-7945-0404-5(3),* Usborne) EDC Publishing.
—Whales & Dolphins. Davidson, Susannah et al. 2003. (Usborne Discovery Ser.). 48p. (J). pap. *(978-0-439-56060-3(8));* pap. *(978-0-439-57780-9(2))* Scholastic, Inc.
Woodcock, John, jt. illus. see Hancock, David.
Woodcock, Marcy. A Grateful Heart under My Bed. Bloom, Janice Stitziel. 2007. 36p. (J). per. 15.99 *(978-1-934643-06-8(8))* Villager Bk. Publishing.
—Wonderfully Made under My Bed. Bloom, Janice Stitziel. 2007. 36p. (J). per. 15.99 *(978-1-934643-00-6(9))* Villager Bk. Publishing.
Wooden, Lenny. Sojourner Truth: Voice for Freedom. Kudlinski, Kathleen. 2003. (Childhood of Famous Americans Ser.). (ENG.). 192p. (Orig.). (J). (gr. 3-7). mass mkt. 5.99 *(978-0-689-85274-9(6),* Simon & Schuster/Paula Wiseman Bks.) Simon & Schuster/Paula Wiseman Bks.
Woodland, Bette. A Walk in Pirate's Cove. Hochman, Marisa. 2012. (ENG.). 32p. (J). *(978-0-9865679-0-2(6))* Fitzhenry & Whiteside, Ltd.
Woodman, Nancy. Dirt. Tomecek, Steve. 2007. (Jump into Science Ser.). (ENG.). 32p. (J). (gr. -1-3). pap. 6.95 *(978-1-4263-0089-9(1),* National Geographic Children's Bks.) National Geographic Society.
—Sand. Prager, Ellen J. 2006. (Jump into Science Ser.). (ENG.). 32p. (J). (gr. -1-3). per. 6.95 *(978-0-7922-5583-3(6))* National Geographic Society.
—Volcano! Prager, Ellen J. 2007. (Jump into Science Ser.). (ENG.). 32p. (J). (gr. -1-3). per. 6.95 *(978-1-4263-0091-2(3),* National Geographic Children's Bks.) National Geographic Society.
Woodman, Ned. Mission 1: Game On. Zucker, Jonny. 2013. (Max Flash Ser.: 1). (ENG.). 144p. (gr. 2-5). pap. 7.95 *(978-1-4677-1465-5(8));* lib. bdg. 27.93 *(978-1-4677-1207-1(8))* Lerner Publishing Group. (Darby Creek).
—Mission 2: Supersonic. Zucker, Jonny. 2013. (Max Flash Ser.: 2). (ENG.). 144p. (gr. 2-5). pap. 7.95 *(978-1-4677-1482-2(8));* lib. bdg. 27.93 *(978-1-4677-1208-8(6))* Lerner Publishing Group. (Darby Creek).
—Mission 3: In Deep. Zucker, Jonny. 2013. (Max Flash Ser.: 3). (ENG.). 144p. (gr. 2-5). pap. 7.95 *(978-1-4677-1473-0(9));* lib. bdg. 27.93 *(978-1-4677-1209-5(4))* Lerner Publishing Group. (Darby Creek).
—Mission 4: Grave Danger. Zucker, Jonny. 2013. (Max Flash Ser.: 4). (ENG.). 144p. (gr. 2-5). pap. 7.95 *(978-1-4677-1466-2(6));* lib. bdg. 27.93 *(978-1-4677-1210-1(8))* Lerner Publishing Group. (Darby Creek).
—Mission 5: Subzero. Zucker, Jonny. 2013. (Max Flash Ser.: 5). (ENG.). 144p. (gr. 2-5). pap. 7.95 *(978-1-4677-1481-5(X));* lib. bdg. 27.93 *(978-1-4677-1212-5(4))* Lerner Publishing Group. (Darby Creek).
—Mission 6: Short Circuit. Zucker, Jonny. 2013. (Max Flash Ser.: 6). (ENG.). 144p. (gr. 2-5). pap. 7.95 *(978-1-4677-1480-8(1));* lib. bdg. 27.93 *(978-1-4677-1211-8(6))* Lerner Publishing Group. (Darby Creek).
Woodman, Ned, jt. illus. see Ruiz, Jose Alfonso Ocampo.
Woodroffe, David. The Grandmas' Book: For the Grandma Who's Best at Everything. Maloney, Alison. 2010. (Best at Everything Ser.). (ENG.). 144p. (J). (gr. 3-7). 9.99 *(978-0-545-13398-2(X))* Scholastic, Inc.
—The Grandpas' Book: For the Grandpa Who's Best at Everything. Gribble, John. 2010. (Best at Everything Ser.). (ENG.). 144p. (J). (gr. 3-7). 9.99 *(978-0-545-13396-8(3),* Scholastic Nonfiction) Scholastic, Inc.
Woodruff, Liza. The Big Scoop, 1 vol. Cirrone, Dorian. 2006. (Marshall Cavendish Chapter Book Ser.). (ENG.). 74p. (J). (gr. 2-5). 14.99 *(978-0-7614-5323-9(7))* Marshall Cavendish Corp.
—The Biggest Pumpkin Ever! Harrod-Eagles, Cynthia. 2007. (J). pap. *(978-0-545-00232-5(X))* Scholastic, Inc.
—If It's Snowy & You Know It, Clap Your Paws! Norman, Kimberly. 2013. (ENG.). 26p. (J). (gr. -1). 14.95 *(978-1-4549-0384-0(8))* Sterling Publishing Co., Inc.
—The Missing Silver Dollar, 1 vol. Cirrone, Dorian & Cirrone. 2006. (Lindy Blues Ser.). (ENG.). 32p. (J). (gr. -1-3). 14.95 *(978-0-7614-5284-3(2))* Marshall Cavendish Corp.
—Montones de Problemas. Brenner, Martha F. 2007. (Math Matters en Espanol Ser.). (SPA.). 32p. (J). (gr. 1-3). pap. 5.95 *(978-1-57565-252-8(8))* Kane Pr., Inc.
—Super Silly School Poems. Greenberg, David. 2014. (ENG.). 32p. (J). (gr. 1-3). 6.99 *(978-0-545-47981-3(9),* Orchard Bks.) Scholastic, Inc.
—Ten on the Sled. Norman, Kimberly. 2010. (ENG.). 26p. (J). (gr. -1). 14.95 *(978-1-4027-7076-0(6))* Sterling Publishing Co., Inc.
—Ten on the Sled. Norman, Kim. 2014. (ENG.). 24p. (J). (— 1). bds. 6.95 *(978-1-4549-1191-3(3))* Sterling Publishing Co., Inc.
—Too-Tall Tina. Pitino, Donna Marie. 2005. (Math Matters Ser.). (ENG.). 32p. (J). (gr. -1-3). pap. 5.95 *(978-1-57565-150-7(5))* Kane Pr., Inc.
—What Time Is It? 2005. (My First Reader Ser.). (ENG.). 32p. (J). (gr. k-4). per. 3.95 *(978-0-516-25279-7(8),* Children's Pr.) Scholastic Library Publishing.
Woodruff, Liza. Mary Had a Little Lamb. Woodruff, Liza. 2011. (Favorite Mother Goose Rhymes Ser.). (ENG.). 16p. (J). (gr. -1-2). lib. bdg. 25.64 *(978-1-60954-281-8(9),* 200233) Child's World, Inc., The.
—What Time Is It? Woodruff, Liza. Demar, Regier. 2005. (My First Reader Ser.). (ENG.). 32p. (J). (gr. k-1). 18.50 *(978-0-516-25180-6(5),* Children's Pr.) Scholastic Library Publishing.
Woodruff, Paul M. Monsters, Myths, & Mysteries: A Tangled Tour Maze Book. Woodruff, Paul. M. 2005. 52p. (J). 8.95 *(978-0-9764327-0-8(6))* Woodruff, Paul.
Woodrum, Larry. The Christmas Tree Fort. Woodrum, Margaret. 2010. 32p. pap. 13.00 *(978-1-60911-329-2(2),* Eloquent Bks.) Strategic Book Publishing & Rights Agency (SBPRA).
Woods, Brenda. The Red Rose Box. Woods, Brenda. 2003. (ENG.). 144p. (J). (gr. 3-7). 5.99 *(978-0-14-250151-1(4),* Puffin) Penguin Publishing Group.
Woods, Christopher & McClintic, Ben. Where's Hanuman? 2009. (ENG.). 32p. (gr. 3-18). pap. 9.95 *(978-0-9779785-8-8(3))* Torchlight Publishing.
Woods, Michael. Butterfly. Johnson, Jinny. 2010. (J). 28.50 *(978-1-59920-352-2(9))* Black Rabbit Bks.
—Duck. Johnson, Jinny. 2010. (J). 28.50 *(978-1-59920-353-9(7))* Black Rabbit Bks.
—Parrot. Johnson, Jinny. 2007. (Zoo Animals in the Wild Ser.). 32p. (J). (gr. -1-3). lib. bdg. 28.50 *(978-1-58340-904-6(1))* Black Rabbit Bks.
Woods, Michele. The Hungry Little Cat. Fotso, Serge. 2011. 32p. pap. 24.95 *(978-1-4626-1805-7(7))* America Star Bks.
—The Little Girl & the Lost Bag. Fotso, Serge. 2011. 20p. pap. 24.95 *(978-1-4626-1741-8(7))* America Star Bks.
Woods, Muriel. Tooga: The Story of a Polar Bear, 1 vol. Woods, Shirley E. 2004. (ENG.). 32p. (J). pap. 7.95 *(978-1-55041-900-9(5),* 1550419005) Fitzhenry & Whiteside, Ltd. CAN. Dist: Midpoint Trade Bks., Inc.
Woods, Pete, photos by. Superman - Back in Action. Busiek, Kurt et al. rev. ed. 2007. (ENG., 144p. (YA). pap. 14.99 *(978-1-4012-1263-6(8))* DC Comics.
Woods, Pete & Camuncoli, Giuseppe. War Crimes. Grayson, Devin et al. rev. ed. 2006. (Batman Ser.). (ENG.). 128p. (YA). per. 12.99 *(978-1-4012-0903-2(3))* DC Comics.
Woods, Rosemary. One Well: The Story of Water on Earth. Strauss, Rochelle. 2007. (ENG.). 32p. (J). (gr. 3-18). 18.95 *(978-1-55337-954-6(3))* Kids Can Pr., Ltd. CAN. Dist: Univ. of Toronto Pr.
Woods, Vanessa. The Breakaway Kid. Atkins, Ben. 2nd rev. ed. 2005. (ENG.). 32p. (J). per. 8.00 *(978-0-9768653-0-8(0))* Summer Day Publishing, LLC.
Woodward, Alice B. The Peter Pan Picture Book. O'Connor, Daniel & Barrie, J. M. 2015. (ENG.). 112p. (J). (gr. -1-5). pap. 12.99 ***(978-0-486-79430-3(X))*** Dover Pubns., Inc.
Woodward, Alice B. The Story of Peter Pan. Barrie, J. M. unabr. ed. 2011. (Dover Children's Thrift Classics Ser.). (ENG.). 96p. (J). (gr. 3-8). reprint ed. pap. 3.50 *(978-0-486-27294-8(X))* Dover Pubns., Inc.
Woodward, Elaine. Young Billy: A New Beginning!, Vol. 2. Sargent, Dave & Sargent, Pat. 2003. (Young Animal Pride Ser.: 2). 24p. (J). pap. 10.95 *(978-1-56763-866-0(X));* lib. bdg. 20.95 *(978-1-56763-865-3(1))* Ozark Publishing.
—Young Dike: Teamwork! Sargent, Dave & Sargent, Pat. 2003. (Young Animal Pride Ser.). (J). 5. pap. 6.95 *(978-1-56763-872-1(4));* Vol. 5. lib. bdg. 20.95 *(978-1-56763-871-4(6))* Ozark Publishing.
—Young Redi: Friendship!, Vol. 3. Sargent, Dave & Sargent, Pat. 2003. (Young Animal Pride Ser.: 3). 24p. (J). pap. 10.95 *(978-1-56763-868-4(6));* lib. bdg. 20.95 *(978-1-56763-867-7(8))* Ozark Publishing.
Woodward II, Ed. The Ferry Boat. Francis, JennaKay. 2013. 12p. pap. 8.95 *(978-1-61633-426-0(6))* Guardian Angel Publishing, Inc.
Woodward, Joanie. Seven Little Monkeys. Woodward, Joanie. 2005. 40p. (J). per. *(978-0-9754676-4-0(6))* Yeoman Hse.
Woodward, Jonathan. Animals Everywhere: A Pop-Up Adventure. Deutch, Yvonne. 2013. (ENG.). 22p. (J). (gr. 1-3). 14.95 *(978-1-4549-0812-8(2))* Sterling Publishing Co., Inc.
Woodward, Sarah. Planet Splooch. Thiveos, Maria, tr. 2003.Tr. of Planeta Splooch. (ENG & SPA.). 59p. (J). pap. 12.99 *(978-0-9728041-0-3(2))* Garcia, Cezanne.
Woodword, Elaine. Young Dawn: Friends Care! Sargent, Dave & Sargent, Pat. 2005. (Young Animal Pride Ser.: 8). 24p. (J). 8. pap. 6.95 *(978-1-56763-878-3(3));* Vol. 8. lib. bdg. 20.95 *(978-1-56763-877-6(5))* Ozark Publishing.
—Young Sammy: I'm a Little Stinker!, Vol. 9. Sargent, Dave & Sargent, Pat. 2005. (Young Animal Pride Ser.). 24p. (J). pap. 10.95 *(978-1-56763-880-6(5))* Ozark Publishing.
—Young White Thunder: I'm a Leader!, Vol. 6. Sargent, Dave & Sargent, Pat. 2005. (Young Animal Pride Ser.). 24p. (J). pap. 10.95 *(978-1-56763-874-5(0))* Ozark Publishing.
Woodworth, Viki. Daisy the Dancing Cow. Woodworth, Viki. 2003. (ENG.). 32p. (J). (gr. -1-2). 15.95 *(978-1-59078-059-6(0))* Boyds Mills Pr.
Woody. Tortoise & the Baboon. Howell, Gill. 2004. (ENG.). 16p. (J). lib. bdg. 23.65 *(978-1-59646-686-9(3))* Dingles & Co.
Woodyard, Sandy Lilly. Cathy, the Castaway Cat. Young, Norene. 2012. 34p. 24.95 *(978-1-4626-6111-4(4))* America Star Bks.
Woolf, Catherine Maria. My First Hike. Woolf, Catherine Maria. 2008. 22p. (J). (gr. -1). bds. 7.95 *(978-1-58469-113-6(1))* Dawn Pubns.
Woolf, Julia. All Gone. North, Merry. 2005. (J). *(978-1-57151-753-1(7))* Playhouse Publishing.
—Black. Stockland, Patricia M. 2008. (Colors Ser.). 24p. (gr. -1-2). 27.07 *(978-1-60270-255-4(1),* 1285037, Looking Glass Library- Nonfiction) Magic Wagon.
—Blue. Stockland, Patricia M. 2008. (Colors Ser.). 24p. (gr. -1-2). 27.07 *(978-1-60270-256-1(X),* 1285038, Looking Glass Library- Nonfiction) Magic Wagon.
—Brown. Stockland, Patricia M. 2011. (Colors Set 2 Ser.). 24p. (gr. -1-2). 27.07 *(978-1-61641-135-0(X),* Looking Glass Library- Nonfiction) Magic Wagon.
—Five Black Cats. Hegarty, Patricia. 2013. (ENG.). 22p. (gr. -1). bds. 8.95 *(978-1-58925-611-8(5))* Tiger Tales.
—Five Busy Elves. Hegarty, Patricia. 2014. 22p. (J). (gr. -1-k). bds. 8.99 *(978-1-58925-561-6(5))* Tiger Tales.
—Five Little Ghosts. Hegarty, Patricia. 2014. 22p. (J). (gr. -1-k). bds. 8.99 *(978-1-58925-587-6(9))* Tiger Tales.
—Gingerbread Joy. 2008. (ENG.). 10p. (J). bds. 4.95 *(978-1-58117-814-2(X),* Intervisual/Piggy Toes) Bendon, Inc.
—Gray. Stockland, Patricia M. 2011. (Colors Set 2 Ser.). 24p. (gr. -1-2). 27.07 *(978-1-61641-136-7(8),* Looking Glass Library- Nonfiction) Magic Wagon.
—Green. Stockland, Patricia M. 2008. (Colors Ser.). 24p. (gr. -1-2). 27.07 *(978-1-60270-257-8(8),* 1285039, Looking Glass Library- Nonfiction) Magic Wagon.
Woolf, Julia. Halloween ABC. Albee, Sarah. (Little Golden Board Book Ser.). (ENG.). (J). 2015. 26p. (-k). bds. 7.99 ***(978-0-553-52422-2(4),*** Random Hse. Bks. for Young Readers); 2009. 24p. (gr. -1-k). 4.99 *(978-0-375-84823-0(1),* Golden Bks.) Random Hse. Children's Bks.
Woolf, Julia. Orange. Stockland, Patricia M. 2011. (Colors Set 2 Ser.). 24p. (gr. -1-2). 27.07 *(978-1-61641-137-4(6),* Looking Glass Library- Nonfiction) Magic Wagon.
—Pink. Stockland, Patricia M. 2011. (Colors Set 2 Ser.). 24p. (gr. -1-2). 27.07 *(978-1-61641-138-1(4),* Looking Glass Library- Nonfiction) Magic Wagon.
—Purple. Stockland, Patricia M. 2011. (Colors Set 2 Ser.). 24p. (gr. -1-2). 27.07 *(978-1-61641-139-8(2),* Looking Glass Library- Nonfiction) Magic Wagon.
—Red. Stockland, Patricia M. 2008. (Colors Ser.). 24p. (gr. -1-2). 27.07 *(978-1-60270-258-5(6),* 1285040, Looking Glass Library- Nonfiction) Magic Wagon.
—Reindeer Run. 2008. (ENG.). 10p. (J). bds. 4.95 *(978-1-58117-813-5(1),* Intervisual/Piggy Toes) Bendon, Inc.
—Snow Wonder. Ghigna, Charles. 2008. (Step into Reading Ser.: Vol. 2). (ENG.). 24p. (J). (gr. -1-1). 3.99 *(978-0-375-85586-3(6),* Random Hse. Bks. for Young Readers) Random Hse. Children's Bks.
—Snowman Surprise. 2008. (ENG.). 10p. (J). bds. 4.95 *(978-1-58117-812-8(3),* Intervisual/Piggy Toes) Bendon, Inc.
—Special Star. 2008. (ENG.). 10p. (J). bds. 4.95 *(978-1-58117-815-9(8),* Intervisual/Piggy Toes) Bendon, Inc.
—Storytime Stickers: the First Christmas. Plourde, Lynn. 2011. (Storytime Stickers Ser.). (ENG.). 16p. (J). (gr. k). pap. 5.95 *(978-1-4027-8187-2(3))* Sterling Publishing Co., Inc.
—Tan. Stockland, Patricia M. 2011. (Colors Set 2 Ser.). 24p. (gr. -1-2). 27.07 *(978-1-61641-140-4(6),* Looking Glass Library- Nonfiction) Magic Wagon.
—White. Stockland, Patricia M. 2008. (Colors Ser.). 24p. (gr. -1-2). 27.07 *(978-1-60270-259-2(4),* 1285041, Looking Glass Library- Nonfiction) Magic Wagon.
—Yellow. Stockland, Patricia M. 2008. (Colors Ser.). 24p. (gr. -1-2). 27.07 *(978-1-60270-260-8(8),* 1285042, Looking Glass Library- Nonfiction) Magic Wagon.
Woollatt, Sue. A Cool Kid's Field Guide to Global Warming. Farrington, Karen. 2009. (Cool Kid's Field Guide Ser.). 26p. (J). (gr. 1-3). spiral bd. 6.99 *(978-0-8416-7146-1(X))* Hammond World Atlas Corp.
Woolley, Kim. Getting to Know Italy & Italian. Sansone, Emma. 2005. 33p. (J). reprint ed. pap. 13.00 *(978-0-7567-9579-5(6))* DIANE Publishing Co.
Woolley, Patricia. The Thrift Store Bears. Evans, Olive. 2004. (ENG.). 41p. (J). 18.97 *(978-0-9748954-0-6(7))* Teddy Traveler Co.
Woolley, Sara. Charlotte & the Quiet Place. Sosin, Deborah. 2015. (ENG.). 40p. (J). (gr. -1-3). 16.95 ***(978-1-941529-02-7(X),*** Plum Blossom Bks.) Parallax Pr.
Woolmer, Nancy. A Christmas Surprise. Gregory, Larry. 2004. 24p. pap. 24.95 *(978-1-4137-3014-2(0))* PublishAmerica, Inc.
Wooten, Neal. Benny the Brave. McKelvey, Lonnie. 2008. 28p. (J). pap. 7.99 *(978-0-9817521-3-6(6))* Mirror Publishing.
—Freddy Freckles: Friends, Flags, Facts & Fun. Skerwarski, N. D. 2007. 52p. (J). pap. 16.99 *(978-0-9800675-3-8(7))* Mirror Publishing.
Wooten, Neal, jt. illus. see Austin, Antoinette.
Wooten, Neal, jt. illus. see Schandy, Rosita.
Wooten, Vernon Lee. Mattie & Percy: The Story of a Chicken & a Duck. Briggs-Anderson, Naomi. 2011. 32p. pap. 24.95 *(978-1-4560-5319-2(1))* America Star Bks.
Wordwindow. Shakespeare for Children Picture Book. 2007. 32p. (J). 14.95 *(978-0-9774484-8-7(7))* Wordwindow LLC.
Workman, Dan. Gossip: Before Word Gets Around, 1 vol. Rondina, Catherine. 2010. (Lorimer Deal with It Ser.). (ENG.). 32p. (J). (gr. 4-6). 24.95 *(978-1-55277-499-1(6))* Lorimer, James & Co., Ltd., Pubs. CAN. Dist: Casemate Pubs. & Bk. Distributors, LLC.
—Gossip: Deal with It Before Word Gets Around, 1 vol. Rondina, Catherine. 2004. (Lorimer Deal with It Ser.). (ENG.). 32p. (J). (gr. 4-6). pap. 12.95 *(978-1-55028-821-6(0))* Lorimer, James & Co., Ltd., Pubs. CAN. Dist: Casemate Pubs. & Bk. Distributors, LLC.
—Lying: Deal with It Straight Up, 1 vol. Rondina, Catherine. 2006. (Lorimer Deal with It Ser.). (ENG.). 32p. (J). (gr. 4-6). pap. 12.95 *(978-1-55028-906-0(3))* Lorimer, James & Co., Ltd., Pubs. CAN. Dist: Casemate Pubs. & Bk. Distributors, LLC.
—Rudeness: Deal with It If You Please, 1 vol. Rondina, Catherine. 2005. (Lorimer Deal with It Ser.). (ENG.). 32p. (J). (gr. 4-6). 12.95 *(978-1-55028-870-4(9))* Lorimer, James & Co., Ltd., Pubs. CAN. Dist: Casemate Pubs. & Bk. Distributors, LLC.
Workman, Lisa. Ballet School. Harimann, Sierra. 2010. (Strawberry Shortcake Ser.). (ENG.). 32p. (J). (gr. 1-2). pap. 3.99 *(978-0-448-45378-1(9),* Grosset & Dunlap) Penguin Publishing Group.
Workman, Lisa, jt. illus. see Workman, Terry.
Workman, Paula J. Our Gang & the Shrinking Machine. Stamps, Sarah. 2008. 33p. pap. 24.95 *(978-1-60610-953-3(7))* PublishAmerica, Inc.
Workman, Terry. Miss Mary Mack & the Jumping Elephants. Fuerst, Jeffrey B. 2009. (Reader's Theater Nursery Rhymes & Songs Set B Ser.). 48p. (J). pap. *(978-1-60859-161-9(1))* Benchmark Education Co.
—My First Sleepover. Cecil, Lauren. 2010. (Strawberry Shortcake Ser.). (ENG.). 24p. (J). (gr. -1-k). pap. 4.99 *(978-0-448-45379-8(7),* Grosset & Dunlap) Penguin Publishing Group.
Workman, Terry & Workman, Lisa. Cartoon How-To. Bellen-Berthézène, Cyndie. 2005. 48p. (J). *(978-0-439-81332-7(8))* Scholastic, Inc.
World-Famous San Diego Zoo Staff, photos by. Little Panda: The World Welcomes Hua Mei at the San Diego Zoo. Ryder, Joanne. 2004. (ENG., 32p. (J). (gr. k-3). 7.99 *(978-0-689-86616-6(X),* Simon & Schuster Bks. For Young Readers) Simon & Schuster Bks. For Young Readers.
Wormell, Chris. Swan Song. Lewis, J. Patrick. 2005. 32p. (J). reprint ed. 17.00 *(978-0-7567-8662-5(2))* DIANE Publishing Co.
Wormell, Chris. Eric!... the Hero? Wormell, Chris. 2013. (ENG.). 32p. (J). (gr. -1-k). pap. 15.99 *(978-1-84941-284-1(7),* Red Fox) Random House Children's Books GBR. Dist: Independent Pubs. Group.
—Molly & the Night Monster. Wormell, Chris. 2011. (ENG.). 32p. (J). (gr. -1-k). pap. 9.99 *(978-1-86230-185-6(9),* Red Fox) Random House Children's Books GBR. Dist: Independent Pubs. Group.
—The Sea Monster. Wormell, Chris. 2005. (ENG.). 32p. (J). (gr. k-2). pap. 12.99 *(978-0-09-945147-1(6),* Red Fox) Random House Children's Books GBR. Dist: Independent Pubs. Group.
—The Wild Girl. Wormell, Chris. 2006. 32p. (J). (gr. -1). 17.00 *(978-0-8028-5311-0(0),* Eerdmans Bks For Young Readers) Eerdmans, William B. Publishing Co.
Wormell, Christopher. A Number of Animals. Green, Kate. 2012. (ENG.). 32p. (J). (gr. -1-k). 15.99 *(978-1-56846-222-6(0),* Creative Editions) Creative Co., The.
—A Number of Animals Nesting Blocks. Green, Kate. 2013. (ENG.). (J). (gr. -1-k). 24.99 *(978-1-56846-248-6(4),* Creative Editions) Creative Co., The.
—Swan Song. Lewis, J. Patrick. 2003. (ENG.). 32p. (J). (gr. 3-17). 18.95 *(978-1-56846-175-5(5),* Creative Editions) Creative Co., The.
—'Twas the Night Before Christmas. Moore, Clement C. 2010. (ENG.). 40p. (J). (gr. -1-3). 16.95 *(978-0-7624-2717-8(5))* Running Pr. Bk. Pubs.
Wormell, Christopher. The Night Before Christmas. Wormell, Christopher. Reasoner, Charles. 2008. (ENG.). 12p. bds. 8.95 *(978-0-7624-3312-4(4))* Perseus Bks. Group.
Worrall, Linda. Snow White & the Seven Dwarfs: A Story about Vanity. 2006. (J). 6.99 *(978-1-59939-025-3(6))* Cornerstone Pr.

Worrell, Nicole. One Day I Will Grow Up. Fraley, Patty. 2013. 18p. pap. 7.75 *(978-1-4575-2142-3(3))* Dog Ear Publishing, LLC.

Worsley, Belinda. Harry's Hat. Graves, Sue. 2008. (Reading Corner Ser.). (ENG.). 24p. (J). (gr. k-2). pap. 6.99 ***(978-0-7496-7692-6(2))*** Hodder & Stoughton GBR. Dist: Independent Pubs. Group.

Worsley, Belinda. Henry & the Hand-Me-Downs. Powell, Jillian. 2005. 32p. (J). lib. bdg. 9.00 *(978-1-4242-0886-9(6))* Fitzgerald Bks.

—Sally Sets Sail. Gurney, Stella. 2009. (Get Ready (Windmill Books) Ser.). 32p. (J). (gr. k-2). lib. bdg. 22.60 *(978-1-60754-261-2(7))* Windmill Bks.

—Yummy in My Tummy! Harrison, Paul. 2009. (Get Ready (Windmill Books) Ser.). 32p. (J). (gr. k-2). lib. bdg. 22.60 *(978-1-60754-263-6(3))* Windmill Bks.

Worsley, John, III. Painkillers: Book One. Worsley, John, III, text. 2004. 48p. (YA). per. 5.00 *(978-0-9764033-0-2(7))* Openvein.

Worthington, Jennifer & Shoals, Melinda. The Gift That Saved Christmas. 2008. 40p. (J). 17.00 *(978-0-9773460-1-1(3))* Spritelee Enterprises.

Worthington, Leonie. Bath Time. Bedford, David. 2010. (Lift-The-Flap Book Ser.). (ENG.). 16p. (gr. -1-k). 9.99 *(978-1-921541-13-1(X))* Little Hare Bks. AUS. Dist: Independent Pubs. Group.

—Billy & Bella. Bowring, Jane. 2009. (ENG.). 32p. (J). (gr. -1-k). 12.99 *(978-1-921272-81-3(3))* Little Hare Bks. AUS. Dist: Independent Pubs. Group.

—Bums. Bedford, David. ed. 2008. (ENG.). 16p. (J). (gr. -1-k). 8.99 *(978-1-921272-34-9(1))* Little Hare Bks. AUS. Dist: Independent Pubs. Group.

—Follow an Elf. McLean, Wendy & Book Company Staff. 2003. (Sparkle Bks.). 10p. (J). bds. 8.95 *(978-1-74047-314-9(0))* Book Co. Publishing Pty, Ltd., The AUS. Dist: Penton Overseas, Inc.

—Mums. Bedford, David. ed. 2010. (ENG.). 16p. (J). (gr. -1 — 1). 5.99 *(978-1-921541-54-4(7))* Little Hare Bks. AUS. Dist: Independent Pubs. Group.

—Tails. Bedford, David. ed. 2008. (ENG.). 16p. (J). (gr. k-k). 5.95 *(978-1-921272-37-0(6))* Little Hare Bks. AUS. Dist: Independent Pubs. Group.

—Who's Yawning? Bedford, David. 2009. (Lift-The-Flap Book Ser.). (ENG.). 16p. (J). (gr. -1-k). 9.95 *(978-1-921272-48-6(1))* Little Hare Bks. AUS. Dist: Independent Pubs. Group.

—Whose Knickers? Munro, Maisie. 2008. *(978-1-921272-20-2(1))* Little Hare Bks. AUS. Dist: HarperCollins Pubs. Australia.

—Whose Pyjamas? A Flip the Flap Book. Munro, Maisie. 2008. *(978-1-921272-21-9(X))* Little Hare Bks. AUS. Dist: HarperCollins Pubs. Australia.

Wotton, Jon. Rosie & Her Formidable Bark, Indomitable Nose & Rambunctioustail. Williams, Vivienne. 2013. 46p. pap. *(978-0-9576680-4-1(X))* Williams, Vivienne.

Woupio, Amy. Making Faces. Woupio, Isaac Jay. 2008. 20p. per. 24.95 *(978-1-4241-9865-8(8))* America Star Bks.

Wozniak, Patricia A. McGooster & Mcgyman Begin Their Adventures. Rochkind, Pat. 2008. 144p. (J). (gr. 4-7). per. 12.95 *(978-0-9792430-1-1(7))* Wing Lane Pr.

Wragg, Nate. Goldi Rocks & the Three Bears. Schwartz, Corey Rosen & Coulton, Beth. 2014. (ENG.). 32p. (J). (gr. k-3). 16.99 *(978-0-399-25685-1(7)*, Putnam Juvenile) Penguin Publishing Group.

Wray, Zoe & Fox, Christyan. Living in Space. Daynes, Katie. 2006. (Beginners Nature: Level 2 Ser.). 32p. (J). (gr. 1-3). 4.99 *(978-0-7945-1339-9(5)*, Usborne) EDC Publishing.

Wray, Zoe & Kushii, Tetsuo. Dinosaurs. Turnbull, Stephanie. 2006. (Beginners Nature: Level 2 Ser.). 32p. (J). (gr. 1-3). 4.99 *(978-0-7945-1334-4(4)*, Usborne) EDC Publishing.

Wray, Zoe, jt. illus. see Donaera, Patrizia.

Wray, Zoe, jt. illus. see Kushii, Tetsuo.

Wreford, Polly, photos by. Baking with Kids. Collister, Linda. 2006. (ENG., 128p. (J). (gr. 3-7). *(978-1-84597-220-2(1))* Ryland Peters & Small.

—Christmas Crafting with Kids. Woram, Catherine. 2011. (ENG., 128p. pap. *(978-1-84975-141-4(2))* Ryland Peters & Small.

—Gardening with Kids. Cox, Martyn & Woram, Catherine. 2008. (ENG., 128p. *(978-1-84597-590-6(1))* CICO Bks.

Wrenn, Charles. The Guns of Europe. Altsheler, Joseph A. (World War I Ser.: Vol. 1). (J). reprint ed. 2010. 338p. (gr. 4-7). 36.76 *(978-1-164-35775-9(1))*; 2010. 338p. (gr. 4-7). pap. 24.76 *(978-1-163-97980-8(5))*; 2008. 336p. 45.95 *(978-0-548-98692-9(4))*; 2007. 340p. per. 30.95 *(978-0-548-66038-6(7))* Kessinger Publishing, LLC.

—The Hosts of the Air: The Story of a Quest in the Great War. Altsheler, Joseph A. (World War I Ser.: Vol. 2). (J). reprint ed. 2010. 346p. (gr. 4-7). 37.56 *(978-1-164-36346-0(8))*; 2010. 346p. (gr. 4-7). pap. 25.56 *(978-1-163-98051-4(X))*; 2008. 344p. 46.95 *(978-0-548-98763-6(7))*; 2007. 348p. per. 31.95 *(978-0-548-65961-8(3))* Kessinger Publishing, LLC.

Wrenn, Charles L. The Great Sioux Trail: A Story of Mountain & Plain. Altsheler, Joseph A. 2009. 258p. (YA). pap. *(978-1-4099-7085-9(X))* Dodo Pr.

—The Sun of Quebec: A Story of a Great Crisis. Altsheler, Joseph A. (French & Indian War Ser.: Vol. 6). 356p. (J). reprint ed. 2010. (gr. 4-7). pap. 25.56 *(978-1-163-19471-3(9))*; 2008. 46.95 *(978-1-4366-7287-0(2))*; 2007. per. 31.95 *(978-1-4325-9779-5(5))* Kessinger Publishing, LLC.

—The Tree of Appomattox: A Story of the Civil War's Close. Altsheler, Joseph A. (Civil War Ser.: Vol. 8). 332p. (J). reprint ed. 2011. (gr. 4-7). 45.95 *(978-1-169-88135-8(1))*; 2010. (gr. 4-7). 36.76 *(978-1-163-21361-2(6))*; 2010. (gr. 4-7). pap. 24.76 *(978-1-162-78752-7(X))*; 2005. 45.95 *(978-1-4326-1333-4(2))* Kessinger Publishing, LLC.

Wrenn, Tom. The Clever Monkey Rides Again. 2007. (Story Cove Ser.). (ENG.). 32p. (J). (gr. -1-3). pap. 3.95 *(978-0-87483-828-2(2))* August Hse. Pubs., Inc.

—The Drum: A Folktale from India. Cleveland, Rob. 2006. (Story Cove Ser.). (ENG.). 32p. (J). (gr. -1-3). pap. 4.95 *(978-0-87483-802-2(9))* August Hse. Pubs., Inc.

—Juan Bobo Sends the Pig to Mass. Acevedo, Ari. 2008. (Story Cove Ser.). (SPA & ENG.). 24p. (J). (gr. -1-3). pap. 4.95 *(978-0-87483-883-1(5))* August Hse. Pubs., Inc.

—The Magic Pot: Story Cove. DeSpain, Pleasant. 2007. (Story Cove Ser.). (ENG.). 32p. (J). (gr. -1-3). pap. 3.95 *(978-0-87483-827-5(4))* August Hse. Pubs., Inc.

—The Stolen Smell. Hamilton, Martha & Weiss, Mitch. 2007. (Story Cove Ser.). (ENG.). 32p. (J). (gr. -1-3). 3.95 *(978-0-87483-838-1(X))* August Hse. Pubs., Inc.

—A Tale of Two Frogs. Hamilton, Martha & Weiss, Mitch. 2006. (Story Cove Ser.). (ENG.). 32p. (J). (gr. -1-3). pap. 4.95 *(978-0-87483-812-1(6))* August Hse. Pubs., Inc.

—The Well of Truth: A Folktale from Egypt. Hamilton, Martha & Weiss, Mitch. 2008. (Story Cove Ser.). (ENG.). 32p. (J). (gr. -1-3). pap. 3.95 *(978-0-87483-880-0(0))* August Hse. Pubs., Inc.

—Why Koala Has a Stumpy Tail. Hamilton, Martha & Weiss, Mitch. 2007. (Story Cove Ser.). (ENG.). 24p. (J). (gr. -1-3). pap. 4.95 *(978-0-87483-879-4(7))* August Hse. Pubs., Inc.

Wright, Alex. Birnbaum's Walt Disney World. Lefkon, Wendy et al, eds. rev. ed. 2007. (ENG.). 272p. (J). (gr. -1-17). pap. 16.95 *(978-1-4231-0392-9(0)*, Disney Editions) Disney Pr.

—Disney Cruise Line 2008. Safro, Jill, ed. rev. ed. 2007. (ENG.). 224p. (gr. -1-17). pap. 13.95 *(978-1-4231-0389-9(0)*, Disney Editions) Disney Pr.

Wright, Alson. God Made Us Special. Wells, Sharon D. 2004. 20p. pap. 19.99 *(978-1-4120-3166-0(4))* Trafford Publishing.

Wright, Annabel. The Lion Who Stole My Arm. Davies, Nicola. 2014. (ENG.). 96p. (J). (gr. 2-5). 14.99 *(978-0-7636-6620-0(3))* Candlewick Pr.

Wright, Bill. Walt Disney's Comics & Stories, No. 689. De Maris, Merrill et al. Clark, John, ed. 2008. (Walt Disney's Comics & Stories Ser.). 64p. pap. 7.99 *(978-1-60360-024-8(8))* Gemstone Publishing, Inc.

Wright, Blanche Fisher. The Real Mother Goose. Scholastic, Inc. Staff. Maccarone, Grace, ed. anniv. ed. 2006. (ENG.). 144p. (J). (gr. 3-7). 10.99 *(978-0-439-85875-5(5)*, Cartwheel Bks.) Scholastic, Inc.

—Real Mother Goose Clock Book. 22p. (J). (gr. -1-2). 6.95 *(978-1-56288-095-8(0))* Checkerboard Pr., Inc.

—The Real Mother Goose Coloring Book. Gache, Stephen Vance. 2009. (Dover Classic Stories Coloring Book Ser.). (ENG.). 32p. (J). (gr. k-5). pap. 3.99 *(978-0-486-46991-1(3))* Dover Pubns., Inc.

Wright, Brent A. Hank the Honking Goose Learns to Listen. Keith, Patty J., photos by. Keith, Patty J. 2013. 36p. pap. 12.95 *(978-0-9893303-1-2(1))* Patty's Blooming Words.

Wright, Carol. It Came from Outer Space. Bradman, Tony. 2004. 25p. (J). *(978-1-85269-336-7(3))*; *(978-1-85269-393-0(2))* Mantra Lingua.

Wright, Chris. Nature Boy Nature Strikes Back. Patterson, Eric. 2008. 108p. pap. 6.95 *(978-1-935105-15-2(9))* Avid Readers Publishing Group.

Wright, Christopher. Carl Nose the Truth. Patterson, Eric. 2007. 104p. (J). pap. 6.95 *(978-0-9797106-6-7(9))* Avid Readers Publishing Group.

—Have You Seen My Pencil? Poems & Musings. Brock, Justin. 2007. (J). pap. *(978-0-9796210-0-0(3))* OPUS II Bks.

—Nature Boy. Patterson, Eric. 2007. 112p. (J). pap. 6.95 *(978-0-9797106-0-5(X))* Avid Readers Publishing Group.

Wright, David, jt. illus. see Kushii, Tetsuo.

Wright, Diane Beem. An Earth Child's Book of the Year. Camden, Marian Louise. 2011. 32p. pap. *(978-1-77067-742-5(9))* FriesenPress.

—An Earth Child's Book of Verse. Camden, Marian Louise. 2011. 32p. pap. *(978-1-77067-695-4(3))* FriesenPress.

Wright, Douglas. La Funcion de Teatro. Lopez, Horacio. 2003. (SPA.). 38p. (J). (gr. k-3). pap. 8.95 *(978-950-511-622-5(5))* Santillana USA Publishing Co., Inc.

Wright, Hawley. I Miss You! A Military Kid's Book about Deployment. Andrews, Beth. 2007. (ENG.). 56p. (J). (-k). per. 12.99 *(978-1-59102-534-4(6))* Prometheus Bks., Pubs.

Wright, Jay. Anorak Vol. 3: The Happy Mag for Kids. Anorak Press Staff. 2013. (ENG.). 68p. (J). pap. 9.99 *(978-1-4236-3389-1(X)*, Anorak Pr.) Gibbs Smith, Publisher.

Wright, Johanna. Clover Twig & the Perilous Path. Umansky, Kaye. 2013. (ENG.). 272p. (J). (gr. 3-7). pap. 7.99 *(978-1-250-02727-6(6))* Square Fish.

—Friendship Over. Sternberg, Julie. 2014. (Top-Secret Diary of Celie Valentine Ser.). (ENG.). 160p. (J). (gr. 3-6). 15.95 *(978-1-59078-993-3(8))* Boyds Mills Pr.

Wright, Johanna. Bunnies on Ice. Wright, Johanna. 2013. (ENG.). 32p. (J). (gr. -1-1). 16.99 *(978-1-59643-404-2(X))* Roaring Brook Pr.

—The Orchestra Pit. Wright, Johanna. 2014. (ENG.). 32p. (J). (gr. -1-1). 16.99 *(978-1-59643-769-2(3))* Roaring Brook Pr.

Wright, John R. Steps to Liberty. Marsh, Laura F. 2007. 32p. (J). 17.95 *(978-0-615-16563-9(X))* Junior League of Central Westchester.

Wright, Kathryn. The Hold-Up Heroes. Bates, Dianne. 2006. (Making Tracks Ser.). (ENG.). 64p. (J). (gr. 2-4). pap. 9.95 *(978-1-876944-38-4(2))* National Museum of Australia AUS. Dist: Independent Pubs. Group.

Wright, Lisa. The Adventures of Sam & Doodle: Escape from Robot Island. Wright, Lisa. Versace, Matthew. 2011. (ENG.). 24p. pap. 12.95 *(978-1-4528-0905-2(4))* CreateSpace Independent Publishing Platform.

Wright, Lucy. Alices Journey Beyond Moon, 1 vol. Carter, R. J. 2004. (ENG.). 98p. *(978-1-903889-76-3(6))* Telos Publishing, Ltd. GBR. Dist: Fitzhenry & Whiteside, Ltd.

—Alice's Journey Beyond the Moon, 1 vol. Carter, R J. ltd. num. ed. (ENG.). 98p. 59.95 *(978-1-903889-77-0(4))* Telos Publishing, Ltd. GBR. Dist: Fitzhenry & Whiteside, Ltd.

Wright, Michael. Jake Goes Peanuts. Wright, Michael. 2010. (ENG.). 48p. (J). (gr. -1-2). 16.99 *(978-0-312-54967-1(9))* Feiwel & Friends.

—Jake Starts School. Wright, Michael. 2008. (ENG.). 48p. (J). (gr. -1-2). 16.95 *(978-0-312-36798-5(8))* Feiwel & Friends.

—Jake Starts School. Wright, Michael. 2010. (ENG.). 48p. (J). (gr. -1-2). pap. 6.99 *(978-0-312-60884-2(5))* Square Fish.

Wright, Mike. Li'l Book O' Big Laughs. 2004. 96p. (J). pap. *(978-0-439-68983-0(X))* Scholastic, Inc.

Wright, Patricia. West African Folk Tales. Vernon-Jackson, Hugh. 2003. (African American Ser.). (ENG.). 160p. pap. 7.95 *(978-0-486-42764-5(1))* Dover Pubns., Inc.

Wright, Petrina. A Lizard Got into the Paint Pots. Pickering, Jill. 2003. (ENG.). 220p. (J). (gr. -1-3). 14.95 *(978-0-333-98858-9(2))* Macmillan Caribbean GBR. Dist: Interlink Publishing Group, Inc.

Wright, Richard. Doggie Doodles: A Picture & Coloring Book of Dog Breeds. George, Erin. l.t. ed. 2011. (ENG.). 40p. pap. 5.89 *(978-1-4564-5760-0(8))* CreateSpace Independent Publishing Platform.

Wright, Sara Ann. Max Makes a Visit. Morimoto, Diana. 2011. 28p. pap. 24.95 *(978-1-4512-4545-5(9))* America Star Bks.

Wright, Sarah Jane. A Christmas Goodnight. Godwin, Laura & Buck, Nola. 2011. (ENG.). 24p. (J). (gr. -1-k). 12.99 *(978-0-06-166491-5(X)*, Tegen, Katherine Bks) HarperCollins Pubs.

—The Secrets of Eastcliff-by-the-Sea: The Story of Annaliese Easterling & Throckmorton, Her Simply Remarkable Sock Monkey. Beha, Eileen. 2015. (ENG.). 288p. (J). (gr. 3-7). pap. 7.99 *(978-1-4424-9841-9(2)*, Beach Lane Bks.) Beach Lane Bks.

Wright, Shannon, jt. illus. see West, June.

Wright Sisters Staff. I Love You This Much. Warburton, Olivia. 2004. (ENG.). 32p. 7.99 *(978-0-7459-5148-5(1)*, Lion Books) Lion Hudson PLC GBR. Dist: Independent Pubs. Group.

—Thank You. Warburton, Olivia. 2004. (ENG.). 32p. 7.99 *(978-0-7459-5149-2(X)*, Lion Books) Lion Hudson PLC GBR. Dist: Independent Pubs. Group.

Wright, Spencer. Little Ant A, 1 vol. Sanborn, Perry F. 2010. 20p. pap. 24.95 *(978-1-4489-6159-7(9))* PublishAmerica, Inc.

Wright, Wendy L. The Adventures of Giggles & Owen: Adventure Two - Pawsistance Pays Off. Terrill Holdman, Shirley. 2011. 46p. pap. 17.95 *(978-1-4575-0568-3(1))* Dog Ear Publishing, LLC.

Wrightson, Berni. Secret of the Swamp Thing. Wein, Len. 2005. 232p. (YA). (gr. 7-18). pap. 9.99 *(978-1-4012-0798-4(7))* DC Comics.

Written by Elli Matthews; Illustrated by. Surprising Katie on Halloween. Matthews, Elli. 2011. 24p. pap. 24.95 *(978-1-4560-7486-9(5))* America Star Bks.

Written by Shelia West; Illustrated by D. Porky Porcupine Tackles Football. West, Shelia. 2011. 20p. pap. 24.95 *(978-1-4560-5528-8(3))* America Star Bks.

Wroth, Dean. Charles & David. Chamberlin, Kate. 2010. 32p. (J). pap. 9.95 *(978-0-944727-37-9(9))*; lib. bdg. 15.95 *(978-0-944727-36-2(0))* Jason & Nordic Pubs. (Turtle Bks.).

—Chef Philip Has Autism. Feuerbach, Jennifer. 2014. 32p. (J). pap. 10.49 *(978-0-944727-61-4(1)*, Turtle Bks.) Jason & Nordic Pubs.

—Two Hands to Hold. Castro, Anita. 2013. 32p. (J). pap. 10.49 *(978-0-944727-57-7(3))*; lib. bdg. 16.95 *(978-0-944727-58-4(1))* Jason & Nordic Pubs. (Turtle Bks.).

Wu, Donald. Dogerella. Boelts, Maribeth. 2008. (Step into Reading Ser.). (ENG.). 48p. (J). (gr. k-3). pap. 3.99 *(978-0-375-83393-9(5))* Random Hse., Inc.

—A Dog's Life, 0 vols. Sherman, Caroline. 2012. (ENG.). 24p. (J). (gr. -1-2). 12.99 *(978-0-7614-6200-2(7)*, 9780761462002, Amazon Children's Publishing) Amazon Publishing.

—J Is for Jack-O'-Lantern: A Halloween Alphabet. Brennan-Nelson, Denise. 2009. (Holiday Ser.). (ENG.). 40p. (J). (gr. -1-3). 14.95 *(978-1-58536-443-5(6))* Sleeping Bear Pr.

—Principal Fred Won't Go to Bed, 0 vols. Crimi, Carolyn. 2010. (ENG.). 32p. (J). (gr. -1-2). 16.99 *(978-0-7614-5709-1(7)*, 9780761457091, Amazon Children's Publishing) Amazon Publishing.

—Shaggy Dogs, Waggy Dogs, 0 vols. Hubbell, Patricia. 2011. (ENG.). 32p. (J). (gr. -1-3). 17.99 *(978-0-7614-5957-6(X)*, 9780761459576, Amazon Children's Publishing) Amazon Publishing.

—She Sells Seashells & Other Tricky Tongue Twisters, 1 vol. Loewen, Nancy. 2011. (Ways to Say It Ser.). (ENG.). 24p. (gr. 3-5). lib. bdg. 27.32 *(978-1-4048-6273-9(0))*; pap. 7.49 *(978-1-4048-6714-7(7))* Picture Window Bks. (Nonfiction Picture Bks.).

—You're Toast & Other Metaphors We Adore, 1 vol. Loewen, Nancy. 2011. (Ways to Say It Ser.). (ENG.). 24p. (gr. 3-5). lib. bdg. 27.32 *(978-1-4048-6270-8(6))*; pap. 7.49 *(978-1-4048-6717-8(1))* Picture Window Bks. (Nonfiction Picture Bks.).

Wu, Julie. Go to Sleep, Hide & Seek. Crowe, Ellie. 2009. 10p. (J). bds. 11.95 *(978-1-59700-759-7(5))* Island Heritage Publishing.

Wu, Leslie. Butterfly Tree, 1 vol. Markle, Sandra. 2011. (ENG.). 32p. (J). (gr. -1-3). 16.95 *(978-1-56145-539-3(3))* Peachtree Pubs.

—The Very Best Daddy of All. Bauer, Marion Dane. 2011. (Classic Board Bks.). (ENG.). 34p. (J). (gr. -1 — 1). bds. 7.99 *(978-1-4169-8517-4(4)*, Little Simon) Little Simon.

—The Very Best Daddy of All. Bauer, Marion Dane. 2007. (ENG.). 40p. (J). (gr. -1-k). 6.99 *(978-1-4169-2736-5(0)*, Simon & Schuster Bks. For Young Readers) Simon & Schuster Bks. For Young Readers.

Wu, Mike. Ellie. Wu, Mike. 2015. (ENG.). 40p. (J). (gr. -1-k). 16.99 *(978-1-4847-1239-9(0))* Disney Publishing Worldwide.

WU, Stacie, jt. illus. see Lee, Hanlim.

Wu, Stacie, jt. illus. see Lee, Han.

Wu, Yoken. Talking Flower Garden: A Series of Ricky's Secret Friends, 6, vol. 5. Yu, Jennifer. 2012. (Ricky's Secret Friends Picturebook Ser.). (ENG.). (gr. -1-5). pap. 9.95 *(978-0-9787591-1-7(7))* Direct World Publishing.

Wulfing, Amy J. A Train Ride to Grandma's (with NO Chocolate Donut!) Shortle, Stacy & Mooney, Dean J. M. 2009. 48p. (J). 18.95 *(978-0-9759850-5-2(1))* Maple Leaf Ctr.

—You Would Be Surprised. Baretz, Susie. 2010. (ENG.). 32p. (J). 16.95 *(978-0-9759850-9-0(4))* Maple Leaf Ctr.

Wulfing, Sulamith. Fairy Tales. 2004. 58p. (gr. -1-3). 9.95 *(978-1-885394-40-8(3))* Amber Lotus Publishing.

Wummer, Amy. Adventure Annie Goes to Kindergarten. Buzzeo, Toni. (ENG.). 32p. (J). (gr. -1-k). 2013. mass mkt. 6.99 *(978-0-14-242695-1(4)*, Puffin); 2010. 16.99 *(978-0-8037-3358-9(5)*, Dial) Penguin Publishing Group.

—The Bay School Blogger. Walker, Nan. 2008. (Social Studies Connects Ser.). 32p. (J). (gr. -1-3). pap. 5.95 *(978-1-57565-258-0(7))* Kane Pr., Inc.

—The Case of the Amazing Zelda. Montgomery, Lewis B. 2009. (Milo & Jazz Mysteries Ser.). 96p. (J). (gr. -1-2). pap. 6.95 *(978-1-57565-296-2(X))*; Vol. 4. (gr. k-3). 22.60 *(978-1-57565-298-6(6))* Kane Pr., Inc.

—The Case of the Amazing Zelda. Montgomery, Lewis B. 2012. (Milo & Jazz Mysteries Ser.: Vol. 4). (ENG.). (J). (gr. 2-4). pap. 20.95 incl. audio compact disk *(978-1-4301-1209-9(3))* Live Oak Media.

—The Case of the Buried Bones. Montgomery, Lewis B. 2014. (Milo & Jazz Mysteries (r) Ser.: 12). 112p. (J). (gr. 2-5). lib. bdg. 22.60 *(978-1-57565-640-3(X))* Kane Pr., Inc.

—The Case of the Crooked Campaign. Montgomery, Lewis B. 2012. (Milo & Jazz Mysteries (r) Ser.: 9). (ENG.). (J). (gr. 2-5). 56p. pap. 6.95 *(978-1-57565-436-2(9))*; 112p. lib. bdg. 22.60 *(978-1-57565-435-5(0))* Kane Pr., Inc.

—The Case of the Diamonds in the Desk. Montgomery, Lewis B. 2012. (Milo & Jazz Mysteries Ser.). 96p. (J). (gr. 2-5). pap. 6.95 *(978-1-57565-391-4(5))*; pap. 39.62 *(978-0-7613-9207-1(6))*; lib. bdg. 22.60 *(978-1-57565-392-1(3))* Kane Pr., Inc.

—The Case of the Haunted Haunted House, Vol. 3. Montgomery, Lewis B. 2009. (Milo & Jazz Mysteries Ser.). 96p. (J). (gr. k-3). 22.60 *(978-1-57565-297-9(8))*; (gr. 3-7). pap. 6.95 *(978-1-57565-295-5(1))* Kane Pr., Inc.

—The Case of the Haunted Haunted House. Montgomery, Lewis B. 2012. (Milo & Jazz Mysteries Ser.: Vol. 3). (ENG.). (J). (gr. 2-4). pap. 20.95 incl. audio compact disk *(978-1-4301-1206-8(9))* Live Oak Media.

—The Case of the July 4th Jinx. Montgomery, Lewis B. 2010. (Milo & Jazz Mysteries Ser.). 96p. (J). (gr. 2-6). pap. 6.95 *(978-1-57565-308-2(7))*; lib. bdg. 22.60 *(978-1-57565-315-0(X))* Kane Pr., Inc.

—The Case of the Locked Box. Montgomery, Lewis B. 2013. (ENG.). 106p. (J). (gr. 2-4). (Milo & Jazz Mysteries (r) Ser.: 11). pap. 6.95 *(978-1-57565-626-7(4))*; (Milo & Jazz Mysteries Ser.: Vol. 11). lib. bdg. 22.60 *(978-1-57565-625-0(6))* Kane Pr., Inc.

—The Case of the Missing Moose. Montgomery, Lewis B. 2011. (Milo & Jazz Mysteries Ser.). 96p. (J). 22.60 *(978-1-57565-331-0(1))*; pap. 39.62 *(978-0-7613-7607-1(0))*; (gr. 2-6). pap. 6.95 *(978-1-57565-322-8(2))* Kane Pr., Inc.

—The Case of the Poisoned Pig. Montgomery, Lewis B. 2009. (Milo & Jazz Mysteries Ser.). 96p. (J). (gr. 2-6). pap. 6.95 *(978-1-57565-286-3(2))* Kane Pr., Inc.

—The Case of the Purple Pool. Montgomery, Lewis B. 2011. (Milo & Jazz Mysteries Ser.). 96p. (J). pap. 6.95 *(978-1-57565-342-6(7))*;No. 7. lib. bdg. 22.60 *(978-1-57565-343-3(5))* Kane Pr., Inc.

—The Case of the Stinky Socks. Montgomery, Lewis B. 2009. (Milo & Jazz Mysteries Ser.). (J). (gr. 2-5). 96p. 22.60 *(978-1-57565-288-7(9))*; 94p. pap. 6.95 *(978-1-57565-285-6(4))* Kane Pr., Inc.

—The Case of the Superstar Scam. Montgomery, Lewis B. 2013. (Milo & Jazz Mysteries (r) Ser.). 112p. (J). (gr. 2-5). 22.60 *(978-1-57565-518-5(7))*; pap. 6.95 *(978-1-57565-519-2(5))* Kane Pr., Inc.

—The Case of Vampire Vivian. Knudson, Michelle. 2003. (Science Solves It! Ser.). 32p. (J). pap. 5.95 *(978-1-57565-127-9(0))* Kane Pr., Inc.

—El Caso de Vivian la Vampira. Knudsen, Michelle. 2008. (Science Solves It! en Espanol Ser.). (SPA.). 32p. (J). (gr. -1-3). pap. 5.95 *(978-1-57565-277-1(3))* Kane Pr., Inc.

—El Caso de Vivian la Vampira (the Case of Vampire Vivian) Knudsen, Michelle. 2009. (Science Solves It! (r) en Espanol Ser.). (SPA.). (gr. 1-3). pap. 33.92 *(978-0-7613-4800-9(X))* Lerner Publishing Group.

—Dear God, Let's Talk about YOU. Moore, Karen. 2006. 128p. (J). pap. 8.99 *(978-0-7847-1247-4(6)*, 42174) Standard Publishing.

—Early Birdy Gets the Worm. Lansky, Bruce. 2010. 10p. (J). bds. 6.99 *(978-1-4169-9316-2(9))* Meadowbrook Pr.

—Five-Minute Bible Devotions for Children: Stories from the New Testament. Kennedy, Pamela & Brady, Anne Kennedy. 2012. 48p. (J). spiral bd. 15.99 *(978-0-8249-5644-8(3)*, Ideals Children's Bks.) Ideals Pubns.

—Five-Minute Bible Devotions for Children: Stories from the Old Testament. Kennedy, Pamela & Brady, Anne Kennedy. 2012. 48p. (J). spiral bd. 15.99 *(978-0-8249-5638-7(9)*, Ideals Children's Bks.) Ideals Pubns.

—Five Minute Devotions for Children: Celebrating God's World As a Family. Kennedy, Pamela. 2004. (ENG.). 48p. (J). 15.95 *(978-0-8249-5485-7(8))* Ideals Pubns.

—Granny's Cozy Quilt of Memories: Remembering Grandmother's Love Through Her Lasting Gift. Kennedy, Pamela. 2006. (ENG.). 32p. (J). (gr. k-3). 8.95 *(978-0-8249-5538-0(2)*, Guideposts) Ideals Pubns.

—Hi God, Let's Talk about My Life. Moore, Karen. 2006. 128p. (YA). pap. 8.99 *(978-0-7847-1246-7(8)*, 42173) Standard Publishing.

—Horrible Harry & the Hallway Bully. Kline, Suzy. (Horrible Harry Ser.: 31). (ENG.). 80p. (J). 2015. (gr. 1-3). 4.99 *(978-0-14-750967-3(X)*, Puffin); 2014. (gr. 2-4). 14.99 *(978-0-670-01551-1(2)*, Viking Juvenile) Penguin Publishing Group.

—Horrible Harry & the June Box. Kline, Suzy. (Horrible Harry Ser.). (ENG.). 80p. (J). (gr. 2-4). 2012. pap. 3.99 *(978-0-14-242185-7(5)*, Puffin); 2011. 14.99

(978-0-670-01265-7(3), Viking Juvenile) Penguin Publishing Group.

—Horrible Harry & the Missing Diamond. Kline, Suzy. (Horrible Harry Ser.: 30). (ENG.). 80p. (J). (gr. 2-4). 2014. pap. 4.99 *(978-0-14-242228-1(2)*, Puffin); 2013. 14.99 *(978-0-670-01426-2(5)*, Viking Adult) Penguin Publishing Group.

—Horrible Harry & the Scarlet Scissors. Kline, Suzy. (Horrible Harry Ser.). (ENG.). 80p. (J). (gr. 2-4). 2013. pap. 3.99 *(978-0-14-242671-5(7)*, Puffin); 2012. 14.99 *(978-0-670-01306-7(4)*, Viking Juvenile) Penguin Publishing Group.

—Horrible Harry & the Secret Treasure. Kline, Suzy. (Horrible Harry Ser.). (ENG.). 80p. (J). (gr. 2-4). 2012. 3.99 *(978-0-14-242021-8(2)*, Puffin); 2011. 14.99 *(978-0-670-01181-0(9)*, Viking Juvenile) Penguin Publishing Group.

—Horrible Harry & the Stolen Cookie. Kline, Suzy. 2013. (Horrible Harry Ser.: 29). (ENG.). 80p. (J). (gr. 2-4). 14.99 *(978-0-670-01425-5(7)*, Viking Juvenile) Penguin Publishing Group.

—Horrible Harry & the Wedding Spies. Kline, Suzy. 2015. (Horrible Harry Ser.: 32). (ENG.). 80p. (J). (gr. 2-5). 14.99 *(978-0-670-01552-8(0)*, Viking Juvenile) Penguin Publishing Group.

—Horrible Harry Goes Cuckoo. Kline, Suzy. (Horrible Harry Ser.). (ENG.). 80p. (J). (gr. 2-4). 2011. 3.99 *(978-0-14-241876-5(5)*, Puffin); 2010. 14.99 *(978-0-670-01180-3(0)*, Viking Juvenile) Penguin Publishing Group.

—Horrible Harry on the Ropes, 24 vols. Kline, Suzy. 2009. (Horrible Harry Ser.: 24). (ENG.). 80p. (J). (gr. 2-4). 14.99 *(978-0-670-01097-4(9)*, Viking Juvenile) Penguin Publishing Group.

—If Jesus Lived Inside My Heart. Lord, Jill Roman. (If Jesus... Ser.). (J). 2014. 22p. bds. 6.99 *(978-0-8249-1937-5(8))*; 2007. (ENG.). 26p. (gr. -1-k). bds. 6.99 *(978-0-8249-6686-7(4))* Ideals Pubns. (Candy Cane Pr.).

—If Jesus Walked Beside Me. Lord, Jill Roman. 2014. (If Jesus Ser.). 22p. (J). bds. 6.99 *(978-0-8249-1920-7(3)*, Candy Cane Pr.) Ideals Pubns.

—Jesus Must Be Really Special. Bishop, Jennie. 2006. (Heritage Builders Ser.). 32p. (J). 14.99 *(978-0-7847-1379-2(0)*, 04029) Standard Publishing.

—Keesha's Bright Idea. May, Eleanor. 2008. (Social Studies Connects Ser.). 32p. (J). (gr. -1-3). pap. 5.95 *(978-1-57565-273-3(0))* Kane Pr., Inc.

—Keesha's Bright Idea. May, Eleanor. 2009. (Social Studies Connects (r) Ser.). (ENG.). (gr. 1-3). pap. 33.92 *(978-0-7613-4806-1(9))* Lerner Publishing Group.

—Monkey See, Monkey Do at the Zoo. Lansky, Bruce. 2010. 10p. (J). bds. 6.99 *(978-1-4169-9317-9(7))* Meadowbrook Pr.

—More Five-Minute Devotions for Children: Celebrating God's World As a Family. Kennedy, Pamela & Kennedy, Douglas. 2005. (ENG.). 48p. (J). 14.95 *(978-0-8249-5502-1(1))* Ideals Pubns.

—Movin' on In. Jordan, Taylor. 2005. (Social Studies Connects). 32p. (J). (gr. 1-3). pap. 5.95 *(978-1-57565-159-0(9))* Kane Pr., Inc.

—My Big Book of 5-Minute Devotions: Celebrating God's World. Kennedy, Pamela. 2006. (ENG.). 96p. (J). (gr. 3-7). pap. 12.99 *(978-0-8249-5556-4(0)*, Ideals Children's Bks.) Ideals Pubns.

—The Night Before Father's Day. Wing, Natasha. 2012. (Night Before Ser.). (ENG.). 32p. (J). (gr. -1-k). pap. 3.99 *(978-0-448-45871-7(3)*, Grosset & Dunlap) Penguin Publishing Group.

—The Night Before Hanukkah. Wing, Natasha. 2014. (Night Before Ser.). (ENG.). 32p. (J). (gr. -1-k). 3.99 *(978-0-448-48140-1(5)*, Grosset & Dunlap) Penguin Publishing Group.

—The Night Before Mother's Day. Wing, Natasha. 2010. (Night Before Ser.). (ENG.). 32p. (J). (gr. -1-k). pap. 3.99 *(978-0-448-45213-5(8)*, Grosset & Dunlap) Penguin Publishing Group.

—The Night Before My Birthday. Wing, Natasha. 2014. (Night Before Ser.). (ENG.). 32p. (J). (gr. -1-k). 3.99 *(978-0-448-48000-8(X)*, Grosset & Dunlap) Penguin Publishing Group.

—Night Before My Birthday Gift Set. Wing, Natasha. 2014. (Night Before Ser.). (ENG.). 32p. (J). (gr. -1-k). 16.99 *(978-0-448-46454-1(3)*, Grosset & Dunlap) Penguin Publishing Group.

—The Night Before New Year's. Wing, Natasha. 2009. (Night Before Ser.). (ENG.). 32p. (J). (gr. -1-k). pap. 4.99 *(978-0-448-45212-8(X)*, Grosset & Dunlap) Penguin Publishing Group.

—The Night Before Preschool. Wing, Natasha. (Night Before Ser.). (ENG.). 32p. (J). (gr. -1-k). 2014. 12.99 *(978-0-448-48254-5(1))*; 2011. pap. 3.99 *(978-0-448-45451-1(3))* Penguin Publishing Group. (Grosset & Dunlap).

—The Night Before St. Patrick's Day. Wing, Natasha. 2009. (Night Before Ser.). (ENG.). 32p. (J). (gr. -1-3). pap. 4.99 *(978-0-448-44852-7(1)*, Grosset & Dunlap) Penguin Publishing Group.

—The Night Before the Fourth of July. Wing, Natasha. 2015. (Night Before Ser.). (ENG.). 32p. (J). (gr. -1-k). 4.99 *(978-0-448-48712-0(8)*, Grosset & Dunlap) Penguin Publishing Group.

—Polar BRRR Delivers. Lansky, Bruce. 2010. 10p. (J). bds. 6.99 *(978-1-4169-9318-6(5))* Meadowbrook Pr.

—Real Heroes Don't Wear Capes. Driscoll, Laura. 2007. (Social Studies Connects). 32p. (J). (gr. -1-3). pap. 5.95 *(978-1-57565-245-0(5))* Kane Pr., Inc.

Wummer, Amy. Ruby Makes It Even! Odd/Even Numbers. Harkrader, Lisa. 2015. (ENG.). 32p. (J). (gr. k-2). pap. 5.95 ***(978-1-57565-805-6(4))*** Kane Pr., Inc.

Wummer, Amy. Sally's Big Save. Driscoll, Laura. 2006. (Social Studies Connects). 32p. (J). (gr. -1-3). pap. 5.95 *(978-1-57565-164-4(5))* Kane Pr., Inc.

—Stressbusters. Walker, Nan. 2006. (Social Studies Connects). 32p. (J). (gr. 1-3). pap. 5.95 *(978-1-57565-185-9(8))* Kane Pr., Inc.

—This Is the Challah. Hepker, Sue. 2012. (J). *(978-0-87441-522-3(5))*; *(978-0-87441-922-1(0))* Behrman Hse., Inc.

—Two Homes for Tyler: A Story about Understanding Divorce. Kennedy, Pamela. 2008. (ENG.). 32p. (J). (gr. -1). 8.99 *(978-0-8249-5582-3(X)*, Guideposts) Ideals Pubns.

—Ty's Triple Trouble. May, Eleanor. 2007. (Social Studies Connects). 32p. (J). (gr. -1-3). pap. 5.95 *(978-1-57565-237-5(4))* Kane Pr., Inc.

—Valentines Are for Saying I Love You. Sutherland, Margaret. 2007. (Reading Railroad Ser.). (ENG.). 24p. (J). (gr. -1-k). mass mkt. 4.99 *(978-0-448-44702-5(9)*, Grosset & Dunlap) Penguin Publishing Group.

—What Is Christmas? Adams, Michelle Medlock. 2012. 24p. (J). bds. 6.99 *(978-0-8249-1885-9(1)*, Candy Cane Pr.) Ideals Pubns.

—What Is Easter? Adams, Michelle Medlock. (ENG.). 26p. (J). 2007. bds. 12.99 *(978-0-8249-6691-1(0))*; 2005. (gr. -1-k). bds. 6.95 *(978-0-8249-6639-3(2)*, Candy Cane Pr.) Ideals Pubns.

—What Is Halloween? Adams, Michelle Medlock. 2007. (ENG.). 26p. (J). (gr. -1-3). bds. 6.99 *(978-0-8249-6712-3(7)*, Candy Cane Pr.) Ideals Pubns.

—What Is Thanksgiving? Adams, Michelle Medlock. (What Is... Ser.). (J). 2014. 22p. bds. 6.99 *(978-0-8249-1938-2(6))*; 2009. (ENG.). 20p. (gr. -1-k). bds. 6.99 *(978-0-8249-1826-2(6)*, Candy Cane Pr.) Ideals Pubns.

—Whatcha Got? Dussling, Jennifer. 2004. (Social Studies Connects). 32p. (J). (gr. 1-3). pap. 5.95 *(978-1-57565-143-9(2))* Kane Pr., Inc.

—#7 the Case of the Purple Pool. Montgomery, Lewis B. 2011. (Milo & Jazz Mysteries Ser.). pap. 39.62 *(978-0-7613-8358-1(1))* Kane Pr., Inc.

Wummer, Amy. Hocus Focus. Wummer, Amy, tr. Wilson, Sarah. 2004. (Science Solves It! Ser.). 32p. (J). pap. 5.95 *(978-1-57565-136-1(X))* Kane Pr., Inc.

Wummer, Amy, jt. illus. see Cuddy, Robin.

Wummer, Amy, jt. illus. see Remkiewicz, Frank.

Wurst, Thomas Scott. Pearl's Christmas Present. Wurst, Thomas Scott. 2006. 40p. (J). 20.00 *(978-0-9772441-1-9(3))* Pearl & Dotty.

Wurster, Laurie. Some of Us Want Wrinkles. Roman, Stacey. 2005. (J). per. 16.95 *(978-1-59858-033-4(7))* Dog Ear Publishing, LLC.

Wurzburg, Robert. Where Are the Dogsharks? 2005. (I'm Going to Read(r) Ser.). (ENG.). 28p. (J). (gr. -1-k). pap. 3.95 *(978-1-4027-2616-3(3))* Sterling Publishing Co., Inc.

Wyatt, David. The Black Cauldron. Alexander, Lloyd. 2nd rev. ed. 2006. (Chronicles of Prydain Ser.: 2). (ENG.). 208p. (J). (gr. 3-7). pap. 6.99 *(978-0-8050-8049-0(X))* Square Fish.

—The Book of Three. Alexander, Lloyd. 2006. (Chronicles of Prydain Ser.: 1). (ENG.). 224p. (J). (gr. 3-7). pap. 6.99 *(978-0-8050-8048-3(1))* Square Fish.

—The Castle of Llyr. Alexander, Lloyd. 3rd rev. ed. 2006. (Chronicles of Prydain Ser.: 3). (ENG.). 208p. (J). (gr. 3-7). pap. 6.99 *(978-0-8050-8050-6(3))* Square Fish.

—Death of a Ghost: Birth of a Nightmare. Butler, Charles, Jr. & Butler, Charles. 2006. (ENG.). 208p. (YA). (gr. 7). per. 9.99 *(978-0-00-712858-7(4)*, HarperCollins Children's Bks.) HarperCollins Pubs. Ltd. GBR. Dist: Independent Pubs. Group.

—The Emerald Throne. Baldry, Cherith. 2003. (Eaglesmount Ser.). (J). 144p. 15.95 *(978-1-59034-584-9(3))*; 141p. pap. *(978-1-59034-585-6(1))* Mondo Publishing.

—The Foundling: And Other Tales of Prydain. Alexander, Lloyd. 6th rev. ed. 2006. (Chronicles of Prydain Ser.: 6). (ENG.). 112p. (J). (gr. 3-7). pap. 6.99 *(978-0-8050-8053-7(8))* Square Fish.

—The High King. Alexander, Lloyd. 5th rev. ed. 2006. (Chronicles of Prydain Ser.: 5). (ENG.). 272p. (J). (gr. 3-7). pap. 6.99 *(978-0-8050-8052-0(X))* Square Fish.

—Ice Road. Lennon, Joan. 2009. 134p. (J). lib. bdg. *(978-1-935279-45-7(9))* Kane Miller.

—The Lake of Darkness. Baldry, Cherith. 2004. (Eaglesmount Ser.). 144p. (J). 15.95 *(978-1-59034-586-3(X))*; pap. *(978-1-59034-587-0(8))* Mondo Publishing.

—Larklight: A Rousing Tale of Dauntless Pluck in the Farthest Reaches of Space. Reeve, Philip. 2006. (ENG.). 250p. (YA). (gr. 5-8). 16.95 *(978-1-59990-020-9(3)*, Bloomsbury USA Childrens) Bloomsbury USA.

—Peter Pan de Rojo Escarlata. McCaughrean, Geraldine. Gonzalez-Gallarza, Isabel, tr. 2006. 296p. (J). (gr. 5-8). 17.95 *(978-958-704-467-6(3))* Ediciones Alfaguara ESP. Dist: Santillana USA Publishing Co., Inc.

—Starcross: A Stirring Adventure of Spies, Time Travel & Curious Hats. Reeve, Philip. 2007. (ENG.). 320p. (J). (gr. 5-18). 16.95 *(978-1-59990-121-3(8)*, Bloomsbury USA Childrens) Bloomsbury USA.

—Stealaway. Peyton, K. M. 2004. (ENG.). 96p. (J). 12.95 *(978-0-8126-2722-0(9))* Cricket Bks.

—Taran Wanderer. Alexander, Lloyd. 4th rev. ed. 2006. (Chronicles of Prydain Ser.: 4). (ENG.). 256p. (J). (gr. 3-7). pap. 6.99 *(978-0-8050-8051-3(1))* Square Fish.

Wyatt, David & Pinfold, Levi. Illusionology: The Secret Science of Magic. Schafer, Albert. 2012. (Ologies Ser.). (ENG.). 30p. (J). (gr. 3-7). 21.99 *(978-0-7636-5588-4(0)*, Templar) Candlewick Pr.

Wyatt, David, jt. illus. see Stevens, Tim.

Wyatt, Michael. The Night Wanderer: A Graphic Novel. Taylor, Drew. 2013. (ENG.). 112p. (J). (gr. 7-12). 24.95 *(978-1-55451-573-8(4)*, 9781554515738); pap. 14.95 *(978-1-55451-572-1(6)*, 9781554515721) Annick Pr., Ltd. CAN. Dist: Firefly Bks., Ltd.

Wyatt, Sue. The Legend of the Seven Sisters: A Traditional Aboriginal Story from Western Australia. O'Brien, May L. 2nd ed. 2010. (ENG.). 20p. (J). (gr. k-5). pap. 17.95 *(978-0-85575-699-4(3))* Aboriginal Studies Pr. AUS. Dist: Independent Pubs. Group.

—Wunambi the Water Snake. O'Brien, May L. 2nd ed. 2005. (ENG.). 32p. (J). (gr. k-5). pap. 17.95 *(978-0-85575-500-3(8))* Aboriginal Studies Pr. AUS. Dist: Independent Pubs. Group.

Wyeth, Andrew N. & Kuerner, Karl J. The Land of Truth & Phantasy: Life & Painting at Ring Farm USA. McLellan, Richard A. gif. ed. 2005. (ENG.). 187p. 24.00 *(978-0-9747536-0-7(2))* McLellan Bks.

Wyeth, Jamie. Sammy in the Sky. Walsh, Barbara. 2011. (ENG.). 32p. (J). (gr. -1-3). 16.99 *(978-0-7636-4927-2(9))* Candlewick Pr.

Wyeth, N. C. The Boy's King Arthur. Lanier, Sidney. 2006. (Dover Children's Classics Ser.). (ENG.). 352p. (YA). (gr. 3-8). per. 14.95 *(978-0-486-44800-8(2))* Dover Pubns., Inc.

—The Last of the Mohicans. Cooper, James Fenimore. 2013. (Scribner Classics Ser.). (ENG.). 368p. (J). (gr. 5). 24.99 *(978-1-4424-8130-5(7)*, Atheneum Bks. for Young Readers) Simon & Schuster Children's Publishing.

—The Yearling. Rawlings, Marjorie Kinnan. 2013. (Scribner Classics Ser.). (ENG.). 416p. (J). (gr. 5-9). 29.99 *(978-1-4424-8209-8(5)*, Atheneum Bks. for Young Readers) Simon & Schuster Children's Publishing.

Wyeth, N. C. Kidnapped. Wyeth, N. C. Stevenson, Robert Louis. 2004. (Scribner Storybook Classics Ser.). (ENG.). 64p. (J). (gr. 3-7). 19.99 *(978-0-689-86542-8(2)*, Atheneum Bks. for Young Readers) Simon & Schuster Children's Publishing.

Wyk, Hanri van, jt. illus. see Meredith, Samantha.

Wyland Studios Staff. Wyland's Spouty And Friends. 2004. 37p. 20.95 *(978-1-884840-59-3(0))* Wyland Worldwide, LLC.

Wyles, Betty. Where's the Kitty. Eichler, Darlene. 2013. 52p. pap. 18.95 *(978-0-9893063-1-7(3))* ProsePress.

Wylie, T. J. The Goodenoughs Get in Sync: A Story for Kids about the Tough Day When Filibuster Grabbed Darwin's Rabbit's Foot... Kranowitz, Carol Stock. 2004. 86p. (J). 14.95 *(978-1-931615-17-4(9)*, 978-1-931615-17-4) Sensory Resources.

Wyman, M. C. & Anderson, Bill. Prince, the Future King: A Father's Example, Harris, Kandi. 2005. 32p. (J). bds. 19.95 *(978-0-9770331-0-2(4))* Harris, K Publishing, Inc.

Wynne, Patricia. Brain: A 21st Century Look at a 400 Million Year Old Organ. DeSalle, Rob. 2010. (Wallace & Darwin Ser.: 2). (ENG.). 40p. (gr. 3-7). 18.95 *(978-1-59373-085-7(3))* Bunker Hill Publishing, Inc.

—When Dinosaurs Walked. Chaikin, Andrew. 2004. (Treasure Tree Ser.). 32p. (J). *(978-0-7166-1607-8(6))* World Bk., Inc.

Wynne, Patricia J. Birds: Nature's Magnificent Flying Machines. Arnold, Caroline. 2003. (ENG.). 32p. (J). (gr. 1-4). pap. 7.95 *(978-1-57091-572-7(5))* Charlesbridge Publishing, Inc.

—The Bumblebee Queen. Sayre, April Pulley. 2006. (ENG.). 32p. (J). (gr. -1-3). pap. 7.95 *(978-1-57091-363-1(3))* Charlesbridge Publishing, Inc.

—The Bumblebee Queen. Sayre, April Pulley. 2006. (gr. -1-3). lib. bdg. 17.95 *(978-0-7569-6968-4(9))* Perfection Learning Corp.

—Cecily's Summer. Lincoln, Nan. 2005. (ENG.). 40p. (J). (gr. 1-3). 16.95 *(978-1-59373-047-5(0))* Bunker Hill Publishing, Inc.

—Hello, Baby Beluga. Lunde, Darrin P. & Stock, Catherine. 2011. (ENG.). 32p. (J). (gr. -1-2). pap. 6.95 *(978-1-57091-740-0(X))* Charlesbridge Publishing, Inc.

—Hello, Bumblebee Bat. Lunde, Darrin. 2007. (J). (gr. -1-1). 14.60 *(978-0-7569-8048-1(8))* Perfection Learning Corp.

—Hello, Mama Wallaroo. Lunde, Darrin P. 2013. (ENG.). 28p. (J). (gr. -1-2). pap. 6.95 *(978-1-57091-797-4(3))*; lib. bdg. 15.95 *(978-1-57091-796-7(5))* Charlesbridge Publishing, Inc.

—Meet the Meerkat. Lunde, Darrin. 2007. (ENG.). 32p. (J). (gr. -1-2). pap. 7.95 *(978-1-58089-154-7(3))* Charlesbridge Publishing, Inc.

—Meet the Meerkat. Lunde, Darrin. 2007. (gr. -1-1). 17.95 *(978-0-7569-8047-4(X))* Perfection Learning Corp.

—Monkey Colors. Lunde, Darrin P. 2012. (ENG.). 32p. (J). (gr. -1-2). 15.95 *(978-1-57091-741-7(8))*; pap. 6.95 *(978-1-57091-742-4(6))* Charlesbridge Publishing, Inc.

Wyrick, Monica. A. D. D. Not B. A. D. Penn, Audrey. 2003. (New Child & Family Press Titles Ser.). 32p. pap. 9.95 *(978-0-87868-849-4(8)*, 8498, Child & Family Pr.) Child Welfare League of America, Inc.

—The Brown Mountain Lights: A North Carolina Legend. Crane, Carol. 2012. 36p. (J). pap. 11.99 *(978-1-935711-19-3(9))* Peak City Publishing, LLC.

Wyrick, Monica Dunsky. A. D. D. Not B. A. D. Penn, Audrey. 2006. (ENG.). 32p. (J). (gr. -1-3). 7.99 *(978-0-9749303-7-4(7))* Tanglewood Pr.

—Feathers & Fur. Penn, Audrey. 2006. (ENG.). 32p. (J). (gr. -1-3). pap. 7.99 *(978-0-9749303-8-1(5))* Tanglewood Pr.

Wysong, Ryan. William's in a Wheelchair. Swaney, Kathleen M. 2008. 24p. pap. 24.95 *(978-1-60703-447-6(6))* America Star Bks.

Wysotski, Chrissie. Caring for a Colony: The Story of Jeanne Mance. Emery, Joanna. Thompson, Allister, ed. 2005. (Stories of Canada Ser.: 8). (ENG.). 72p. (J). (gr. 4-7). 18.95 *(978-1-894917-07-0(3)*, Napoleon & Co.) Dundurn CAN. Dist: Ingram Pub. Services.

—Struggling for Perfection: The Story of Glenn Gould. Konieczny, Vladimir. 2009. (Stories of Canada Ser.: 5). (ENG.). 104p. (J). (gr. 4-7). per. 18.99 *(978-1-894917-48-3(0)*, Napoleon & Co.) Dundurn CAN. Dist: Ingram Pub. Services.

—This is the Dog, 1 vol. McFarlane, Sheryl. 2003. (ENG.). 32p. *(978-1-55041-551-3(4))* Fitzhenry & Whiteside, Ltd.

Wyss, Johann David. The Swiss Family Robinson. Kingston, William Henry Giles, tr. 2005. 188p. per. 6.95 *(978-1-4209-2269-1(6))* Digireads.com.

—The Swiss Family Robinson. 2004. reprint ed. pap. 30.95 *(978-1-4191-5012-8(X))*; pap. 1.99 *(978-1-4192-5012-5(4))* Kessinger Publishing, LLC.

Wyss, Manspeter. King for One Day. Brenner, Peter. 36p. (J). (gr. -1-3). 12.95 *(978-0-87592-027-6(6))* Scroll Pr., Inc.

X

Xanthos, Carol. How Does the Holy Ghost Make Me Feel? Carnesecca, Michele. 2010. 44p. *(978-1-60641-245-9(0))* Deseret Bk. Co.

Xian Nu Studio. Graveyard Games, No. 1. Schreiber, Ellen. 2011. (Vampire Kisses: Blood Relatives Ser.). (ENG.). 192p. (YA). (gr. 8). pap. 9.99 *(978-0-06-202672-9(0)*, Tegen, Katherine Bks) HarperCollins Pubs.

—Resolve. Marr, Melissa. 2011. (Wicked Lovely: Desert Tales Ser.: 3). (ENG.). 176p. (YA). (gr. 8-18). pap. 9.99 *(978-0-06-149350-8(3))* HarperCollins Pubs.

Xian Nu Studio Staff. Challenge. Marr, Melissa. 2010. (Wicked Lovely: Desert Tales Ser.: 2). (ENG.). 176p. (YA). (gr. 8-18). pap. 9.99 *(978-0-06-149349-2(X))* HarperCollins Pubs.

—A Match Made in Heaven. Robbins, Trina. 2013. (My Boyfriend Is a Monster Ser.: 8). (ENG.). 128p. (YA). (gr. 7-12). lib. bdg. 29.27 *(978-0-7613-6857-1(4)*, Graphic Universe) Lerner Publishing Group.

Xian Nu Studio Staff, jt. illus. see Diaz, Irene.

Xianoqing, Pan, jt. illus. see Wei, Miao.

Xiaofang, Ding, jt. illus. see Youzhi, He.

Xiaoming, Wang, jt. illus. see Taixi, Su.

Xiaoqing, Pan, jt. illus. see She, Liu.

Xin, Xiao. Earth Day Every Day. Bullard, Lisa. 2011. (Planet Protectors Ser.). pap. 39.62 *(978-0-7613-8652-0(1)*, Millbrook Pr.); (ENG.). 24p. lib. bdg. 23.93 *(978-0-7613-6109-1(X))* Lerner Publishing Group.

—Look Out for Litter. Bullard, Lisa. 2011. (Planet Protectors Ser.). pap. 39.62 *(978-0-7613-8654-4(8)*, Millbrook Pr.) Lerner Publishing Group.

—Mary's Garden: How Does it Grow? Harris, Brooke. 2009. (Reader's Theater Nursery Rhymes & Songs Set B Ser.). 48p. (J). pap. *(978-1-60859-160-2(3))* Benchmark Education Co.

—Watch over Our Water. Bullard, Lisa. 2011. (Planet Protectors Ser.). pap. 39.62 *(978-0-7613-8657-5(2)*, Millbrook Pr.); (ENG.). 24p. pap. 6.95 *(978-0-7613-8517-2(7)*, Millbrook Pr.); (ENG.). 24p. lib. bdg. 23.93 *(978-0-7613-6106-0(5))* Lerner Publishing Group.

Xin, Xiao & Zheng, Xin. Earth Day Every Day. Bullard, Lisa. 2011. (Cloverleaf Books (tm) — Planet Protectors Ser.). (ENG.). 24p. (gr. k-2). pap. 6.95 *(978-0-7613-8512-7(6)*, Millbrook Pr.) Lerner Publishing Group.

—Look Out for Litter. Bullard, Lisa. 2011. (Cloverleaf Books (tm) — Planet Protectors Ser.). (ENG.). 24p. (gr. k-2). pap. 6.95 *(978-0-7613-8514-1(2)*, Millbrook Pr.); lib. bdg. 23.93 *(978-0-7613-6105-3(7))* Lerner Publishing Group.

Xiong, Kim. The Clay General. 2008. (J). 18.95 *(978-1-60603-002-8(7))* Better Chinese LLC.

—The Dragon Tribe. 2008. (ENG & CHI.). 33p. (J). 18.95 *(978-1-60603-000-4(0))* Better Chinese LLC.

—Kitchen God. 2008. 32p. (J). 18.95 *(978-1-60603-001-1(9))* Better Chinese LLC.

—Paper Horse. 2008. (ENG & CHI.). 37p. (J). 18.95 *(978-1-60603-003-5(5))* Better Chinese LLC.

Xiong, Kim. The Little Stone Lion. Xiong, Kim. 2006. (ENG.). 40p. (J). (gr. k-2). 15.95 *(978-0-9762056-1-6(0))* Heryin Publishing Corp.

Xoul. The Monster That Grew Small. Grant, Joan. 2014. (Classic Stories Ser.). (ENG.). 24p. (J). (gr. 3-6). 28.50 *(978-1-62323-620-5(7)*, 206388) Child's World, Inc., The.

Xu, Cui, jt. illus. see Ji, Zhaohua.

Xu, Wei & Zheng, Xiaoyan. To Share One Moon. Wang, Ruowen. 2008. 32p. (J). (gr. 2-4). *(978-0-9738799-5-7(5))* Kevin & Robin Bks., Ltd.

Xuan, YongSheng. D Is for Dragon Dance. Compestine, Ying Chang. (ENG.). 32p. (J). (gr. -1-3). 2006. pap. 6.95 *(978-0-8234-2058-2(2))*; 2005. 17.95 *(978-0-8234-1887-9(1))* Holiday Hse., Inc.

Y

Yabuki, Go. Scrapped Princess, 3 vols., Vol. 1. 2005. (Scrapped Princess Ser.). 184p. pap. 14.99 *(978-1-59532-981-3(1)*, Tokyopop Adult) TOKYOPOP, Inc.

—Scrapped Princess, 3 vols., Vol. 2. Yubuki, Go & Azumi, Yukinobu. 2nd rev. ed. 2006. (Scrapped Princess Ser.). 192p. per. 14.99 *(978-1-59532-982-0(X)*, Tokyopop Adult) TOKYOPOP, Inc.

Yabuki, Kentaro. Black Cat. Yabuki, Kentaro. (Black Cat Ser.: 12). (ENG.). 2008. 216p. pap. 7.99 *(978-1-4215-1470-3(2))*; 2007. 200p. pap. 7.99 *(978-1-4215-1038-5(3))*; 2006. 216p. pap. 7.99 *(978-1-4215-0607-4(6))*; 2006. 208p. pap. 7.99 *(978-1-4215-0606-7(8))*; Vol. 10. 2007. 200p. pap. 7.99 *(978-1-4215-1039-2(1))* Viz Media.

Yaccarino, Dan. Boy & Bot. Dyckman, Ame. 2012. (J). lib. bdg. *(978-0-375-98724-3(X))* Knopf, Alfred A. Inc.

—Boy & Bot. Dyckman, Ame. 2012. (ENG.). 32p. (J). (gr. k-k). 16.99 *(978-0-375-86756-9(2))*; lib. bdg. 19.99 *(978-0-375-96757-3(5))* Random Hse. Children's Bks. (Knopf Bks. for Young Readers).

—Cooking with Henry & Elliebelly. Parkhurst, Carolyn. 2010. (ENG.). 32p. (J). (gr. -1-k). 16.99 *(978-0-312-54848-3(6))* Feiwel & Friends.

—Count on the Subway. Jacobs, Paul DuBois & Swender, Jennifer. 2014. (ENG.). 32p. (J). (-k). lib. bdg. 17.99 *(978-0-307-97924-7(5))* Knopf, Alfred A. Inc.

—Count on the Subway. Jacobs, Paul DuBois & Swender, Jennifer. 2014. (ENG.). 32p. (J). (-k). 14.99 *(978-0-307-97923-0(7)*, Knopf Bks. for Young Readers) Random Hse. Children's Bks.

—Five Little Ducks. Churchill, Jill. 2005. 26p. (J). (gr. -1 — 1). bds. 5.99 *(978-0-06-073465-7(5),* HarperFestival) HarperCollins Pubs.
—Five Little Pumpkins. Public Domain Staff. 2003. (ENG.). 16p. (J). (gr. -1-k). bds. 6.99 *(978-0-694-01177-3(0),* HarperFestival) HarperCollins Pubs.
—I Love Going Through This Book. Burleigh, Robert. Date not set. 40p. (J). (gr. -1-3). pap. 5.99 *(978-0-06-443647-2(0))* HarperCollins Pubs.
—Kate & Nate Are Running Late! Egan, Kate. 2012. (ENG.). 36p. (J). (gr. k-2). 16.99 *(978-1-250-00080-4(7))* Feiwel & Friends.
—No Nap! Yes Nap! Palatini, Margie. 2014. (ENG.). 32p. (J). (gr. -1 — 1). 17.00 *(978-0-316-24821-1(5))* Little, Brown Bks. for Young Readers.
Yaccarino, Dan. Dan Yaccarino's Mother Goose. Yaccarino, Dan. 2003. (Little Golden Book Ser.). (ENG.). 24p. (J). (gr. -1-2). 3.99 *(978-0-375-82571-2(1),* Golden Bks.) Random Hse. Children's Bks.
—Every Friday. Yaccarino, Dan. 2012. (ENG.). 32p. (J). (gr. -1-2). pap. 7.99 *(978-1-250-00473-4(X))* Square Fish.
—New Pet. Yaccarino, Dan. 2003. (ENG.). 40p. (gr. -1-2). pap. 4.99 *(978-0-7868-1429-9(2))* Hyperion Pr.
—Unlovable. Yaccarino, Dan. rev. ed. 2004. (ENG.). 32p. (J). (gr. -1-1). reprint ed. pap. 7.99 *(978-0-8050-7532-8(1))* Square Fish.
—Where the Four Winds Blow. Yaccarino, Dan. 2003. 104p. (J). 17.89 *(978-0-06-623627-8(4),* Cotler, Joanna Books) HarperCollins Pubs.
Yaeger, Mark. Nathaniel's Journey: The King's Armory. Kelby, Tom. 2003. (J). per. *(978-1-930914-04-9(0))* Hands to the Plow, Inc.
Yagi, Norihiro. Claymore. Yagi, Norihiro. Tarbox, Jonathan. 2006. (Claymore Ser.: Vol. 2). (ENG.). 192p. pap. 9.99 *(978-1-4215-0619-7(X));* Vol. 1. 208p. pap. 9.99 *(978-1-4215-0618-0(1))* Viz Media.
—Claymore, Vol. 4. Yagi, Norihiro. 2006. (Claymore Ser.). (ENG.). 200p. pap. 9.99 *(978-1-4215-0621-0(1))* Viz Media.
Yagmin, Daniel, Jr. Norton B. Nice. 2009. (J). *(978-1-60108-018-9(2))* Red Cygnet Pr.
Yagyu, Geniehiro. All about Scabs. Yagyu, Geniehiro. Stinchecum, Amanda Mayer. 2006. (ENG.). 28p. (J). (gr. -1-3). 9.99 *(978-0-916291-82-2(0))* Kane Miller.
Yalata and Oak Valley Communities. Maralinga: The Anangu Story. Yalata and Oak Valley Communities. Mattingley, Christobel. 2009. (ENG.). 72p. (J). (gr. 5-9). 26.99 *(978-1-74175-621-0(9))* Allen & Unwin AUS. Dist: Independent Pubs. Group.
Yalowitz, Paul. Boy, Can He Dance! Spinelli, Eileen. 2012. (ENG.). 32p. (J). (gr. -1-3). 16.99 *(978-1-4424-7441-3(6),* Simon & Schuster Bks. For Young Readers) Simon & Schuster Bks. For Young Readers.
Yamada, Jane. Character Education Resource Guide. Burch, Regina G. Fisch, Teri L., ed. 2003. 80p. (J). (gr. k-4). pap. 13.99 *(978-1-57471-982-6(3),* 3109) Creative Teaching Pr., Inc.
—Developing Reading Fluency, Grade 3: Using Modeled Reading, Phrasing, & Repeated Oral Reading. Callella, Trisha. Fisch, Teri L., ed. 2003. (Developing Reading Fluency Ser.). 96p. (J). (gr. 3-4). pap. 14.99 *(978-1-57471-996-3(3),* 2240) Creative Teaching Pr., Inc.
—Discover Air. Vogel, Julia. 2014. (Science Around Us Ser.). (ENG.). 24p. (J). (gr. -1-2). 25.64 *(978-1-62687-300-1(3),* 207141) Child's World, Inc., The.
—Discover Dirt. Hall, Pamela. 2014. (Science Around Us Ser.). (ENG.). 24p. (J). (gr. -1-2). 25.64 *(978-1-62687-301-8(1),* 207142) Child's World, Inc., The.
—Discover Electricity. Vogel, Julia. 2014. (Science Around Us Ser.). (ENG.). 24p. (J). (gr. -1-2). 25.64 *(978-1-62687-302-5(X),* 207143) Child's World, Inc., The.
—Discover Energy. Vogel, Julia. 2014. (Science Around Us Ser.). (ENG.). 24p. (J). (gr. -1-2). 25.64 *(978-1-62687-303-2(8),* 207144) Child's World, Inc., The.
—Discover Magnets. Vogel, Julia. 2014. (Science Around Us Ser.). (ENG.). 24p. (J). (gr. -1-2). 25.64 *(978-1-62687-304-9(6),* 207145) Child's World, Inc., The.
—Discover Shadows. Hall, Pamela. 2014. (Science Around Us Ser.). (ENG.). 24p. (J). (gr. -1-2). 25.64 *(978-1-62687-305-6(4),* 207146) Child's World, Inc., The.
—Discover Sound. Hall, Pamela. 2014. (Science Around Us Ser.). (ENG.). 24p. (J). (gr. -1-2). 25.64 *(978-1-62687-306-3(2),* 207147) Child's World, Inc., The.
—Discover Water. Higgins, Nadia. 2014. (Science Around Us Ser.). (ENG.). 24p. (J). (gr. -1-2). 25.64 *(978-1-62687-307-0(0),* 207148) Child's World, Inc., The.
—Interactive Projects & Displays: Ideas for a Student-Created Learning Environment. Groeneweg, Nicole. F. Stacey, ed. 2006. (J). pap. 13.99 *(978-1-59198-315-6(0))* Creative Teaching Pr., Inc.
Yamada, Jane & Ember, Kathi. Catch 'Em Being Good!. Burch, Regina G. Hamaguchi, Carla & Fisch, Teri, eds. 2003. 80p. (J). pap. 10.99 *(978-1-57471-992-5(0))* Creative Teaching Pr., Inc.
Yamada, Kana. Feel the Summer. Thomson, Sarah L. 2006. (ENG.). 32p. (J). (gr. -1-3). 14.95 *(978-1-59687-174-8(1))* IBks., Inc.
Yamada, Utako. The Story of Cherry the Pig. Yamada, Utako. 2007. (ENG.). 32p. (J). (gr. -1-1). 11.99 *(978-1-933605-25-8(1),* 05258) Kane Miller.
Yamaguchi, Keika. Puddle Pug. Norman, Kim. 2014. (ENG.). 32p. (J). (gr. -1). 14.95 *(978-1-4549-0436-6(4))* Sterling Publishing Co., Inc.
Yamaguchi, Keika. What about Moose? Schwartz, Corey Rosen & Gomez, Rebecca J. 2015. (ENG.). 40p. (J). (gr. -1-3). 17.99 ***(978-1-4814-0496-9(2),*** Atheneum Bks. for Young Readers) Simon & Schuster Children's Publishing.
Yamamoto, Lani. Albert. Yamamoto, Lani. 2004. (ENG.). 32p. (J). 10.95 *(978-1-58536-251-6(4))* Sleeping Bear Pr.
—Albert 2. Yamamoto, Lani. 2005. (ENG.). 32p. (J). (gr. k-6). 10.95 *(978-1-58536-265-3(4))* Sleeping Bear Pr.
Yamamoto, Matsuko. Ding Dong. Shimizu, Michio. McLaughlin, Sako, tr. 2009. 32p. 14.95 *(978-1-74126-440-1(5))* R.I.C. Pubns. AUS. Dist: SCB Distributors.
Yamamoto, Satoshi. Black & White. Kusaka, Hidenori. (Pokemon Ser.: 1). (ENG.). (J). 2011. 96p. pap. 4.99 *(978-1-4215-4090-0(8));* Vol. 4. 2014. 200p. pap. 9.99 *(978-1-4215-6180-6(8))* Viz Media.
—Diamond & Pearl-Platinum. Kusaka, Hidenori. (Pokemon Ser.: 8). (ENG.). (J). 2013. 192p. pap. 9.99 *(978-1-4215-5404-4(6));* Vol. 10. 2014. 208p. pap. 9.99 *(978-1-4215-5406-8(2))* Viz Media.
—Pokemon, Vols. 9-14, Set. Kusaka, Hidenori. 2014. (Pokemon Ser.). (ENG.). 504p. (J). pap. 25.99 *(978-1-4215-7774-6(7))* Viz Media.
—Pokémon Adventures. Kusaka, Hidenori. (Pokemon Ser.: 22). (ENG.). (J). 2014. 184p. pap. 9.99 *(978-1-4215-3556-2(4));* 2013. 104p. pap. 9.99 *(978-1-4215-5899-8(8))* Viz Media.
—Pokemon Adventures. Kusaka, Hidenori. 2014. (Pokemon Ser.). (ENG.). (J). Set, Vols. 1-11. 2304p. pap. 89.99 *(978-1-4215-7777-7(1));* Set, Vols. 15-22. 1576p. pap. 59.99 *(978-1-4215-7776-0(3))* Viz Media.
—Pokemon Adventures: Diamond & Pearl - Platinum. Kusaka, Hidenori. 2012. (Pokemon Ser.: 5). (ENG.). 208p. (J). pap. 9.99 *(978-1-4215-3913-3(6))* Viz Media.
—Pokémon Adventures Vol. 6: Diamond & Pearl - Platinum. Kusaka, Hidenori. 2012. (Pokemon Ser.: 6). (ENG.). 216p. (J). pap. 9.99 *(978-1-4215-3914-0(4))* Viz Media.
—Pokemon Adventures Vol. 7: Diamond & Pearl - Platinum. Kusaka, Hidenori. 2013. (Pokemon Ser.). (ENG.). 208p. (J). pap. 9.99 *(978-1-4215-4247-8(1))* Viz Media.
—Pokemon Adventures - Black & White, Vol. 1. Kusaka, Hidenori. 2013. (Pokemon Ser.). (ENG.). 104p. (J). pap. 9.99 *(978-1-4215-5898-1(X))* Viz Media.
—Pokémon Adventures - Black & White, Vol. 6. Kusaka, Hidenori. 2015. (Pokemon Ser.: 6). (ENG.). 224p. (J). pap. 9.99 *(978-1-4215-7181-2(1))* Viz Media.
—Pokémon Adventures - Diamond & Pearl/Platinum. Kusaka, Hidenori. 2014. (Pokemon Ser.: 11). (ENG.). 192p. (J). pap. 9.99 *(978-1-4215-6179-0(4))* Viz Media.
Yamamoto, Satoshi. Pokémon Adventures: Black & White, Vol. 7. Kusaka, Hidenori. 2015. (Pokemon Ser.). (ENG.). 216p. (J). pap. 9.99 ***(978-1-4215-7836-1(0))*** Viz Media.
Yamamoto, Satoshi. Pokémon Adventures: Diamond & Pearl/Platinum, Vol. 9. Kusaka, Hidenori. 2013. (Pokemon Ser.). (ENG.). 208p. (J). pap. 9.99 *(978-1-4215-5405-1(4))* Viz Media.
Yamamoto, Satoshi. Pokémon Adventures, Vol. 29. Kusaka, Hidenori. 2015. (Pokemon Ser.: 29). (ENG.). 224p. (J). pap. 9.99 ***(978-1-4215-3563-0(7))*** Viz Media.
Yamamoto, Satoshi. Pokémon Black & White. Kusaka, Hidenori. (Pokemon Ser.). (ENG.). (J). 2014. 80p. pap. 4.99 *(978-1-4215-6767-9(9));* 2013. 96p. pap. 4.99 *(978-1-4215-5897-4(1));* 2012. 80p. pap. 4.99 *(978-1-4215-4282-9(X));* 2012. 80p. pap. 4.99 *(978-1-4215-4281-2(1));* 2012. 80p. pap. 4.99 *(978-1-4215-4280-5(3));* 2011. 80p. pap. 4.99 *(978-1-4215-4091-7(6));* Vol. 8. 2012. 80p. pap. 4.99 *(978-1-4215-4283-6(8));* Vol. 9. 2013. 96p. pap. 4.99 *(978-1-4215-5893-6(9));* Vol. 10. 2013. 96p. pap. 4.99 *(978-1-4215-5894-3(7));* Vol. 11. 2013. 96p. pap. 4.99 *(978-1-4215-5895-0(5));* Vol. 12. 2013. 96p. pap. 4.99 *(978-1-4215-5896-7(3));* Vol. 14. 2014. 88p. pap. 4.99 *(978-1-4215-6766-2(0));* Vol. 18. 2014. 80p. pap. 4.99 *(978-1-4215-7602-2(3));* Vol. 19. 2014. 80p. pap. 4.99 *(978-1-4215-7603-9(1))* Viz Media.
—Pokémon Black & White, Vol. 16. Kusaka, Hidenori. 2014. (Pokemon Ser.). (ENG.). 80p. (J). pap. 4.99 *(978-1-4215-6768-6(7))* Viz Media.
—Pokémon Black & White, Vol. 17. Kusaka, Hidenori. 2014. (Pokemon Ser.). (ENG.). 88p. (J). pap. 4.99 *(978-1-4215-6769-3(5))* Viz Media.
—Pokémon XY, Vol. 1. Kusaka, Hidenori. 2014. (Pokemon Ser.). (ENG.). 82p. (J). pap. 4.99 *(978-1-4215-7980-1(4))* Viz Media.
—Pokmon Adventures. Kusaka, Hidenori. 2014. (Pokemon Ser.: 21). (ENG.). 208p. (J). pap. 9.99 *(978-1-4215-3555-5(6))* Viz Media.
—Pokmon Adventures - Black & White. Kusaka, Hidenori. 2014. (Pokemon Ser.: 3). (ENG.). 208p. (J). pap. 9.99 *(978-1-4215-6178-3(6))* Viz Media.
Yamamoto, Tadayoshi. Jeeper the Fire Engine. Watanabe, Shigeo. 2005. 28p. (J). 11.95 *(978-4-902216-14-1(0))* R.I.C. Publications Asia Co, Inc. JPN. Dist: Continental Enterprises Group, Inc. (CEG).
Yamamura, Hajime. Rebirth of the Demonslayer. Yamamura, Hajime. 192p. (YA). Vol. 1. 2004. pap. 9.99 *(978-1-58655-540-5(5));* Vol. 3. 2005. pap. 9.99 *(978-1-58655-689-1(4),* AWNOV-0554) Media Blasters, Inc.
Yamasaki, James. Boy Dumplings. Compestine, Ying Chang. 2009. (ENG.). 32p. (J). (gr. -1-3). 16.95 *(978-0-8234-1955-5(X))* Holiday Hse., Inc.
—Christmas Chaos: Hidden Picture Puzzles, 1 vol. Kalz, Jill. 2012. (Seek It Out Ser.). (ENG.). 32p. (gr. 1-2). 9.95 *(978-1-4048-7724-5(X));* lib. bdg. 25.99 *(978-1-4048-7494-7(1))* Picture Window Bks.
Yamasaki, Katie. Pockets. Lynch, Joseph. l.t. ed. (J). pap. 16.98 *(978-0-932970-83-1(4))* Prinit Pr.
Yamasaki, Katie. When the Cousins Came. 2016. (J). ***(978-0-8234-3457-2(5))*** Holiday Hse., Inc.
Yamasaki, Katie. Fish for Jimmy. Yamasaki, Katie. 2013. (ENG.). 32p. (J). 16.95 *(978-0-8234-2375-0(1))* Holiday Hse., Inc.
Yamate, Sandra S. & Yao, Carolina. Char Siu Bao Boy. 2004. 32p. (J). (gr. k-3). pap. 15.95 *(978-1-879965-19-5(4))* Polychrome Publishing Corp.
Yamauchi, Karl, jt. illus. see McKim, Brian.
Yamawaki, Yuriko. Dr. Mouse's Mission. Nakagawa, Masafumi. Perry, Mia Lynn, tr. 2007. (R. I. C. Story Chest Ser.). 27p. (J). (gr. -1-1). 14.95 incl. audio compact disk *(978-1-74126-051-9(5))* R.I.C. Pubns. AUS. Dist: SCB Distributors.
Yan, Stan. 1 Block Down. Carew, Kieran. 2004. 24p. (YA). 2.95 *(978-0-9755041-2-3(6))* Squid Works.
Yanagisawa, Kazuaki. The Seven Magi. Kurimoto, Kaoru. (Guin Saga: Vol. 1). (ENG.). 2007. 200p. (J). (gr. 8-12). per. 12.95 *(978-1-932234-80-0(2));* Vol. 2. 2008. 200p. (gr. 11). per. 12.95 *(978-1-934287-07-1(5));* Vol. 3. 2008. 192p. (gr. 11). per. 12.95 *(978-1-934287-08-8(3))* Vertical, Inc.
Yang, A. & Huang, H Y. Where Is Spring? Yang-Huan & Yang-Huan. 2007. (ENG.). 32p. (J). (gr. k-2). 15.95 *(978-0-9762056-8-5(8))* Heryin Publishing Corp.
Yang, Belle. Always Come Home to Me. Yang, Belle. 2007. (ENG.). 32p. (J). (gr. -1-3). 16.99 *(978-0-7636-2899-4(9))* Candlewick Pr.
—Foo, the Flying Frog of Washtub Pond. Yang, Belle. 2009. (ENG.). 32p. (J). (gr. -1-2). 16.99 *(978-0-7636-3615-9(0))* Candlewick Pr.
—Hannah Is My Name. Yang, Belle. 2007. (J). (gr. k-4). 14.65 *(978-0-7569-8124-2(7))* Perfection Learning Corp.
—Hannah Is My Name: A Young Immigrant's Story. Yang, Belle. 2007. (ENG.). 32p. (J). (gr. k-4). pap. 6.99 *(978-0-7636-3521-3(9))* Candlewick Pr.
—A Nest in Springtime: A Bilingual Book of Numbers. Yang, Belle. ed. 2012. (CHI & ENG.). 24p. (J). (gr. k — 1). bds. 6.99 *(978-0-7636-5279-1(2))* Candlewick Pr.
—Summertime Rainbow: A Mandarin Chinese-English Bilingual Book of Colors. Yang, Belle. 2012. (ENG & CHI.). 22p. (J). (gr. k — 1). bds. 6.99 *(978-0-7636-5280-7(6))* Candlewick Pr.
Yang, Gene Luen. The Rosary Comic Book. Pien, Lark. 2003. 56p. (J). mass mkt. 5.95 *(978-0-8198-6479-6(X),* 332-312) Pauline Bks. & Media.
Yang, Gene Luen. American Born Chinese. Yang, Gene Luen. rev. ed. 2006. (ENG.). 240p. (YA). (gr. 7-12). pap. 18.99 *(978-1-59643-152-2(0),* First Second Bks.) Roaring Brook Pr.
—American Born Chinese. Yang, Gene Luen. 2008. (ENG.). 240p. (YA). (gr. 7-12). pap. 9.99 *(978-0-312-38448-7(3))* Square Fish.
—Boxers. Yang, Gene Luen. Pien, Lark. 2013. (Boxers & Saints Ser.: 1). (ENG.). 336p. (YA). (gr. 7-12). pap. 18.99 *(978-1-59643-359-5(0),* First Second Bks.) Roaring Brook Pr.
—Saints. Yang, Gene Luen. Pien, Lark. 2013. (Boxers & Saints Ser.: 2). (ENG.). 176p. (YA). (gr. 7). pap. 15.99 *(978-1-59643-689-3(1),* First Second Bks.) Roaring Brook Pr.
Yang, Gene Luen & Pien, Lark. American Born Chinese. Yang, Gene Luen. 2007. (ENG.). 240p. (YA). (gr. 7-18). 23.99 *(978-1-59643-373-1(6),* First Second Bks.) Roaring Brook Pr.
Yang, Hae-won. Who Eats First? Yoon, Ae-hae. Cruise, ed. 2015. (ENG.). 38p. (J). (gr. -1-k). 16.95 *(978-1-939248-00-8(0))* Tantan Publishing.
Yang, HyeWon. Green River. Lee, WonKyeong. 2015. (MySELF Bookshelf Ser.). (ENG.). 32p. (J). (gr. k-2). pap. 11.94 *(978-1-60357-695-6(9));* lib. bdg. 22.60 *(978-1-59953-660-6(9))* Norwood Hse. Pr.
Yang, James. Joey & Jet: Book 1 of Their Adventures. Yang, James. 2012. (ENG.). 32p. (J). (gr. -1-k). pap. 16.99 *(978-1-4424-5930-4(1),* Atheneum Bks. for Young Readers) Simon & Schuster Children's Publishing.
—Joey & Jet in Space. Yang, James. 2006. (ENG.). 32p. (J). (gr. -1-k). 17.99 *(978-0-689-86927-3(4),* Atheneum/Richard Jackson Bks.) Simon & Schuster Children's Publishing.
Yang, Kyung-Il. Blade of Heaven, Vol. 2. rev. ed. 2005. 288p. pap. 14.99 *(978-1-59532-328-6(7),* Tokyopop Adult) TOKYOPOP, Inc.
—Blade of Heaven, Vol. 3. rev. ed. 2005. 280p. pap. 14.99 *(978-1-59532-329-3(5),* Tokyopop Adult) TOKYOPOP, Inc.
—Blade of Heaven, Vol. 7. 2005. 296p. pap. 14.99 *(978-1-59532-327-9(9),* Tokyopop Adult) TOKYOPOP, Inc.
Yang, Stella. My Family: Individual Title Six-Packs. (Sails Literacy Ser.). 16p. (gr. k-18). 27.00 *(978-0-7635-4393-8(4))* Rigby Education.
—The Snowman, 6 vols., Pack. (Sails Literacy Ser.). 16p. (gr. k-18). 27.00 *(978-0-7635-4439-3(6))* Rigby Education.
Yang, Yi. You Are My Everything: Determined Little Maghara!!! Peterson, M. E. 2008. 43p. pap. 24.95 *(978-1-60610-807-9(7))* America Star Bks.
Yano, Yuriko. Manga Doodles. Yano, Yuriko. 2010. (ENG.). 128p. (J). (gr. 3). pap. 12.99 *(978-1-906082-70-3(7))* O'Mara, Michael Bks., Ltd. GBR. Dist: Independent Pubs. Group.
Yao, Carolina, jt. illus. see Yamate, Sandra S.
Yap, Weda. Rain, Hail, Sleet & Snow. Larrick, Nancy. 2011. 68p. 36.95 *(978-1-258-08878-1(9))* Literary Licensing, LLC.
Yarbrough, Mark. The Legend of Jake, the Salty Dog. Gossett, Robert A. 2007. (J). 12.00 *(978-0-9793560-0-1(8))* Salty Dog, Inc., The.
Yarchi, Jacky. The Gang of Four Kung-Fooey to the Rescue. Peterseil, Yaacov. 2005. 192p. (J). pap. 7.95 *(978-0-943706-51-1(3),* Devora Publishing) Simcha Media Group.
Yardley, Joanna. B Is for Big Sky Country. Collard, Sneed B., III. 2003. (Discover America State by State Ser.). (ENG.). 40p. (J). 17.95 *(978-1-58536-098-7(8))* Sleeping Bear Pr.
—P Is for Peace Garden: A North Dakota Alphabet. Salonen, Roxane B. 2005. (Discover America State by State Ser.). (ENG.). 40p. (J). (gr. -1-7). 17.95 *(978-1-58536-142-7(9))* Sleeping Bear Pr.
—Shep: Our Most Loyal Dog. Collard, Sneed B., III. 2006. (ENG.). 32p. (J). (gr. k-6). 16.95 *(978-1-58536-259-2(X))* Sleeping Bear Pr.
Yardley, Liz. The Firefly Legacy - Book VI. Yardley, Liz. 2013. 336p. pap. *(978-0-9872013-1-7(X))* BlueFlower Bks.
—The Firefly Legacy - Book VII. Yardley, Liz. 2013. 314p. pap. *(978-0-9872013-2-4(8))* BlueFlower Bks.
Yarlett, Emma. Bear's Big Bottom, 1 vol. Smallman, Steve. 2014. (ENG.). 32p. (gr. -1-2). 14.95 *(978-1-62370-118-5(X))* Capstone Young Readers.
Yarlett, Emma. Sidney, Stella, & the Moon. Yarlett, Emma. 2013. (ENG.). 44p. (J). (gr. k-3). 16.99 *(978-0-7636-6623-1(8),* Templar) Candlewick Pr.
Yarnall, Karen Sturdy. Along the Chesapeake & Delaware Canal. Maxson, H. A. & Young, Claudia H. 2005. 64p. (J). per. 9.95 *(978-0-9741713-2-6(8))* Bay Oak Pubs., Ltd.
Yashima, Taro. Crow Boy. Yashima, Taro. 2004. 34p. (J). (gr. k-3). reprint ed. pap. 14.00 *(978-0-7567-7102-7(1))* DIANE Publishing Co.
—Crow Boy. Yashima, Taro. pap. 35.95 incl. audio compact disk *(978-1-59112-803-8(X))* Live Oak Media.
Yasui, Koji. The King Who Saved the Dove. Kato, Etsuo. 2014. (J). 8.95 *(978-1-935523-68-0(6))* World Tribune Pr.
Yasunari, Toda. Scryed, 5 vols., Vol. 1. Kuroda, Yosuke. 2003. 192p. (YA). pap. 9.99 *(978-1-59182-228-8(9))* TOKYOPOP, Inc.
—Scryed, Vol. 3. Yosuke, Kuroda. rev. ed. 2003. 192p. pap. 9.99 *(978-1-59182-230-1(0))* TOKYOPOP, Inc.
Yates, Gene. The Chameleon Colors Book. 2006. (J). *(978-1-58865-361-1(7))* Kidsbooks, LLC.
—The Dragon Opposites Book. 2006. (J). *(978-1-58865-362-8(5))* Kidsbooks, LLC.
—The Elephant Alphabet Book. 2006. (J). *(978-1-58865-363-5(3))* Kidsbooks, LLC.
—The Giraffe Numbers Book. 2006. (J). *(978-1-58865-364-2(1))* Kidsbooks, LLC.
—The Snake Shapes Book. 2006. (J). *(978-1-58865-365-9(X))* Kidsbooks, LLC.
Yates, Gene. What Can Simon Be? Yates, Gene. Frank, Thomas. 2006. (J). *(978-1-58865-366-6(8))* Kidsbooks, LLC.
Yates, Jolyon. Lego Ninjago Special Edition #2: With Rise of the Serpentine & Tomb of the Fangpyre. Farshtey, Greg & Lee, Paul. 2013. (Ninjago Ser.: 2). (ENG.). 112p. (J). (gr. 1-6). pap. 10.99 *(978-1-59707-698-2(8))* Papercutz.
—Stone Cold. Farshtey, Greg. 2013. (Ninjago Ser.: 7). (ENG.). 64p. (J). (gr. 1-6). 10.99 *(978-1-59707-411-7(X));* pap. 6.99 *(978-1-59707-410-0(1))* Papercutz.
—Warriors of Stone. Farshtey, Greg. 2013. (Ninjago Ser.: 6). (ENG.). 64p. (J). (gr. k-6). 10.99 *(978-1-59707-379-0(2));* pap. 6.99 *(978-1-59707-378-3(4))* Papercutz.
Yates, Jolyon, jt. illus. see Henrique, Paulo.
Yates, Jolyon, jt. illus. see Lee, Paul.
Yates, Kelly. Venomous. Krovatin, Christopher. (ENG.). (YA). (gr. 8). 2011. 336p. pap. 8.99 *(978-1-4424-1298-9(4));* 2008. 176p. 16.99 *(978-1-4169-2487-6(6))* Simon & Schuster Children's Publishing. (Atheneum Bks. for Young Readers).
Yates, Louise. Young Fredle. Voigt, Cynthia. (ENG.). 240p. (J). (gr. 3-7). 2012. 6.99 *(978-0-375-85787-4(7),* Yearling); 2011. 16.99 *(978-0-375-86457-5(1),* Knopf Bks. for Young Readers) Random Hse. Children's Bks.
Yaweera, Sasiprapa, jt. illus. see Pornkerd, Vorrarit.
Yayo. The Hug. Simpson, Lesley. 2010. (ENG.). 26p. (J). (gr. -1-k). bds. 6.95 *(978-1-55451-252-2(2),* 9781554512522) Annick Pr., Ltd. CAN. Dist: Firefly Bks., Ltd.
—I Am the Book. Hopkins, Lee Bennett. 2011. (ENG.). 32p. (J). (gr. -1-3). 17.95 *(978-0-8234-2119-0(8))* Holiday Hse., Inc.
—If I Had a Million Onions, 1 vol. Fitch, Sheree. 2005. (ENG.). 64p. (J). (gr. 2-5). 15.95 *(978-1-896580-78-4(5))* Tradewind Bks. CAN. Dist: Orca Bk. Pubs. USA.
—The King Who Barked. Jones, Charlotte Foltz. 2009. (ENG.). 40p. (J). (gr. 1-5). 16.95 *(978-0-8234-1925-8(8))* Holiday Hse., Inc.
—Night Sky Wheel Ride, 1 vol. Fitch, Sheree. 2013. (ENG.). 32p. (J). (gr. k-2). 16.95 *(978-1-896580-67-8(X))* Tradewind Bks. CAN. Dist: Orca Bk. Pubs. USA.
—Sam Swallow & the Riddleworld League, 1 vol. New, William. 2013. (ENG.). 144p. (J). (gr. 3-5). pap. 12.95 *(978-1-896580-98-2(X))* Tradewind Bks. CAN. Dist: Orca Bk. Pubs. USA.
Yayo & Yayo. Keeper of Soles. Bateman, Teresa. 2006. (ENG.). 32p. (J). (gr. -1-3). 17.95 *(978-0-8234-1734-6(4))* Holiday Hse., Inc.
Yayo, jt. illus. see Yayo.
Yazawa, Ai. Nana. Yazawa, Ai. Wolfe, Allison. 2008. (Nana Ser.: 9). (ENG.). 280p. pap. 8.99 *(978-1-4215-1745-2(0))* Viz Media.
—Nana. Yazawa, Ai. Bates, Megan, ed. 2007. (Nana Ser.: 7). (ENG.). 208p. pap. 8.99 *(978-1-4215-1021-7(9))* Viz Media.
—Nana. Yazawa, Ai. 2007. (Nana Ser.: 6). (ENG.). 192p. pap. 8.99 *(978-1-4215-1020-0(0))* Viz Media.
Yazawa, Nao. Wedding Peach. Tomita, Sukehiro. 2004. (Wedding Peach Ser.). (ENG.). Vol. 4. 192p. pap. 9.95 *(978-1-59116-132-5(0));* Vol. 5. 200p. pap. 9.95 *(978-1-59116-257-5(2))* Viz Media.
—Young Love, Vol. 7. Tomita, Sukehiro. 2004. (Wedding Peach Ser.). (ENG.). 200p. pap. 9.95 *(978-1-59116-450-0(8))* Viz Media.
Yazawa, Nao, jt. illus. see Tomita, Sukehiro.
Yazzie, Benton. The Shaman & the Water Serpent. Dewey, Jennifer Owings. 2007. (ENG.). 40p. (J). 16.95 *(978-0-8263-4211-9(6))* Univ. of New Mexico Pr.
Yazzie, Johnson, jt. illus. see Brycelea, Clifford.
Yazzie, Peterson. The Hogan That Great-Grandfather Built. Flood, Nancy Bo. 2012. (ENG & NAV.). 32p. (J). (gr. -1-3). 17.95 *(978-1-893354-97-5(0))* Salina Bookshelf Inc.
Ybáñez, Terry. That's Not Fair! - ¡No es Justo! Emma Tenayuca's Struggle for Justice - La Lucha de Emma Tenayuca Por la Justicia. Tafolla, Carmen & Teneyuca, Sharyll. 2008. (ENG & SPA.). 40p. (J). (gr. k-2). 17.95 *(978-0-916727-33-8(5))* Wings Pr.
Yeagle, Dean. The Cow in Apple Time. Frost, Robert. 2005. 32p. (J). 15.95 *(978-0-9758970-1-0(2))* Beekman & Hathaway.
Yeates, Thomas. Arthur & Lancelot: The Fight for Camelot - An English Legend. Limke, Jeff. 2007. (Graphic Myths & Legends Ser.). (ENG.). 48p. (gr. 4-8). lib. bdg. 27.93 *(978-0-8225-6296-2(0),* Graphic Universe) Lerner Publishing Group.
—Atalanta: The Race Against Destiny. Fontes, Justine & Fontes, Ron. (Graphic Myths & Legends Ser.). (ENG.). 48p. (gr. 4-8). 2008. per. 8.95 *(978-0-8225-6569-7(2));*

Z

2007. lib. bdg. 27.93 *(978-0-8225-5965-8(X))* Lerner Publishing Group.
—King Arthur: Excalibur Unsheathed. Limke, Jeff. 2006. (Graphic Myths & Legends Ser.). (ENG.). 48p. (gr. 4-8). 27.93 *(978-0-8225-3083-1(X))* Lerner Publishing Group.
—King Arthur: Excalibur Unsheathed. Limke, Jeff. 2007. (Graphic Myths & Legends Ser.). (ENG.). 48p. (gr. 4-8). per. 8.95 *(978-0-8225-6483-6(1))* Lerner Publishing Group.
—Odysseus: Escaping Poseidon's Curse. Jolley, Dan. (Graphic Myths & Legends Ser.). (ENG.). 48p. (gr. 4-8). 2008. pap. 8.95 *(978-0-8225-8515-2(4))*; 2007. lib. bdg. 27.93 *(978-0-8225-6208-5(1)*, Graphic Universe) Lerner Publishing Group.
—Perseus: The Hunt for Medusa's Head. Storrie, Paul D. 2008. (Graphic Myths & Legends Ser.). (ENG.). 48p. (gr. 4-8). lib. bdg. 27.93 *(978-0-8225-7528-3(0))* Lerner Publishing Group.
—Perseus: The Hunt for Medusa's Head [A Greek Myth]. Storrie, Paul. 2009. (Graphic Myths & Legends Ser.). (ENG.). 48p. (gr. 4-8). pap. 8.95 *(978-1-58013-888-8(8))* Lerner Publishing Group.
—El Rey Arturo: La Espada Excalibur Desenvainada: Una Leyenda Inglesa. Limke, Jeff. Translations.com Staff, tr. from ENG. 2007. (Mitos y Leyendas en Viñetas (Graphic Myths & Legends) Ser.).Tr. of King Arthur - Excalibur Unsheathed [An English Legend. (SPA.). 48p. (gr. 4-8). per. 8.95 *(978-0-8225-7968-7(5)*, Ediciones Lerner) Lerner Publishing Group.
—Robin Hood: Outlaw of Sherwood Forest. Storrie, Paul D. 2007. (Graphic Myths & Legends Ser.). (ENG.). 48p. (gr. 4-8). lib. bdg. 27.93 *(978-0-8225-5964-1(1))* Lerner Publishing Group.
—William Tell: A Swiss Legend. Storrie, Paul D. 2008. (Graphic Myths & Legends Ser.). (ENG.). 48p. (gr. 4-8). 27.93 *(978-0-8225-7175-9(7)*, Graphic Universe) Lerner Publishing Group.
—William Tell: One against an Empire [A Swiss Legend]. Storrie, Paul D. 2009. (Graphic Myths & Legends Ser.). (ENG.). 48p. (gr. 4-8). pap. 8.95 *(978-1-58013-828-4(4))* Lerner Publishing Group.
Yeates, Tom, et al. Reunion. Moore, Alan et al. rev. ed. 2006. (Swamp Thing Ser.: Bk. 6). (ENG.). 200p. pap. 19.99 *(978-1-56389-975-1(2))* DC Comics.
Yee, Jeanne. The Saga of Simon the Skinny Pig. Simon Saves the Day. Oshiro, Kimberley. 2012. 38p. pap. 12.50 *(978-1-61170-089-3(2))* Robertson Publishing.
Yee, Josie. Drip, Drop! the Rain Won't Stop! Your Turn, My Turn Reader. Higginson, Sheila Sweeny. 2010. (Playskool Ser.). (ENG.). 24p. (J). (gr. -1-k). pap. 3.99 *(978-1-4169-9046-8(1)*, Simon Spotlight) Simon Spotlight.
—Engines & Animals. Awdry, W. 2005. (Baby Fingers Ser.). (ENG.). 12p. (J). (gr. k — 1). bds. 4.99 *(978-0-375-83162-1(2)*, Random Hse. Bks. for Young Readers) Random Hse. Children's Bks.
—A Surprise Party. Silverhardt, Lauryn. 2003. (Dora the Explorer Ser.). (ENG.). 22p. (J). bds. 4.99 *(978-0-689-85483-5(8)*, Simon Spotlight/Nickelodeon) Simon Spotlight/Nickelodeon.
Yee, Patrick. Asian Children's Favorite Stories: A Treasury of Folktales from China, Japan, Korea, India, the Philippines, Thailand, Indonesia & Malaysia. Lyons, Kay et al. 2006. (ENG.). 112p. (J). (gr. k-8). 24.95 *(978-0-8048-3669-2(8))* Tuttle Publishing.
—Treasury of Chinese Folk Tales: Beloved Myths & Legends from the Middle Kingdom. Fu, Shelley. 2008. (ENG.). 128p. (J). (gr. 4-6). 24.95 *(978-0-8048-3807-8(0))* Tuttle Publishing.
Yee, Tammy. A Is for Aloha: A Hawaii Alphabet. Goldsberry, U'ilani. 2005. (Discover America State by State Ser.). (ENG.). 40p. (J). (gr. k-5). 17.95 *(978-1-58536-146-5(1))* Sleeping Bear Pr.
—Swimming with Humuhumu: A Young Snorkeler's First Guide to Hawaiian Sea Life. Hirschi, Ron. 32p. (J). 14.99 *(978-0-931548-67-3(5)*, 25098-000) Island Heritage Publishing.
—The Tsunami Quilt: Grandfather's Story. Fredericks, Anthony D. rev. ed. 2007. (Tales of Young Americans Ser.). (ENG.). 32p. (J). (gr. -1-3). 17.95 *(978-1-58536-313-1(8))* Sleeping Bear Pr.
Yee, Wong Herbert. Eddie the Raccoon: Brand New Readers. Friend, Catherine. 2004. (Brand New Readers Ser.). (ENG.). 32p. (J). (gr. -1-3). pap. 5.99 *(978-0-7636-2334-0(2))* Candlewick Pr.
—Get That Pest! Douglas, Erin. 2003. (Green Light Readers Level 2 Ser.). (ENG.). 24p. (J). (gr. -1-3). pap. 3.95 *(978-0-15-204833-4(2))* Houghton Mifflin Harcourt Publishing Co.
—Get That Pest! / ¡Agarren a Ése! Douglas, Erin. Campoy, F. Isabel & Flor Ada, Alma, trs. ed. 2008. (Green Light Readers Level 2 Ser.). (SPA & ENG.). 28p. (J). (gr. k-2). pap. 3.95 *(978-0-15-206269-9(6))* Houghton Mifflin Harcourt Publishing Co.
—Moving Day. Brandon, Anthony G. 2005. (Green Light Readers Level 2 Ser.). (ENG.). 32p. (J). (gr. -1-3). pap. 3.95 *(978-0-15-205652-0(1))* Houghton Mifflin Harcourt Publishing Co.
Yee, Wong Herbert. Fine Feathered Friends. Yee, Wong Herbert. 2011. (Mouse & Mole Story Ser.). (ENG.). 48p. (J). (gr. 1-4). pap. 3.99 *(978-0-547-51977-7(X))* Houghton Mifflin Harcourt Publishing Co.
—Mouse & Mole, a Winter Wonderland. Yee, Wong Herbert. (Mouse & Mole Story Ser.). (ENG.). 48p. (J). (gr. 1-4). 2011. pap. 3.99 *(978-0-547-57697-8(8))*; 2010. 15.00 *(978-0-547-34152-1(0))* Houghton Mifflin Harcourt Publishing Co.
—Mouse & Mole, Fine Feathered Friends. Yee, Wong Herbert. 2009. (Mouse & Mole Story Ser.). (ENG.). 48p. (J). (gr. 1-4). 15.00 *(978-0-547-15222-6(1))* Houghton Mifflin Harcourt Publishing Co.
—Mouse & Mole, Secret Valentine. Yee, Wong Herbert. 2013. (Mouse & Mole Story Ser.). (ENG.). 48p. (J). (gr. 1-4). 15.99 *(978-0-547-88719-7(1))* Houghton Mifflin Harcourt Publishing Co.
—My Autumn Book. Yee, Wong Herbert. 2015. (ENG.). 32p. (J). (gr. -1-1). 14.99 *(978-0-8050-9922-5(0)*, Holt, Henry & Co. Bks. For Young Readers) Holt, Henry & Co.
—Summer Days & Nights. Yee, Wong Herbert. 2012. (ENG.). 32p. (J). (gr. -1-1). 15.99 *(978-0-8050-9078-9(9)*, Holt, Henry & Co. Bks. For Young Readers) Holt, Henry & Co.
—Tracks in the Snow. Yee, Wong Herbert. 2007. (ENG.). 32p. (J). (gr. -1-1). per. 6.99 *(978-0-312-37134-0(9))* Square Fish.
Yeh, Alicia. Buddha's Wisdom. Hsuan Hua. 2004. (ENG & CHI.). (J). *(978-0-88139-867-0(5))* Buddhist Text Translation Society.
Yeh, Phil. Dinosaurs Across America. Yeh, Phil. 2007. (ENG.). 32p. (gr. 1-5). 12.95 *(978-1-56163-509-2(X))* NBM Publishing Co.
Yelchin, Eugene. Crybaby. Beaumont, Karen. 2015. (ENG.). 40p. (J). (gr. -1-1). 17.99 *(978-0-8050-8974-5(8)*, Holt, Henry & Co. Bks. For Young Readers) Holt, Henry & Co.
—Seeds, Bees, Butterflies, & More! Poems for Two Voices. Gerber, Carole. 2013. (ENG.). 32p. (J). (gr. -1-3). 17.99 *(978-0-8050-9211-0(0)*, Holt, Henry & Co. Bks. For Young Readers) Holt, Henry & Co.
—Seven Hungry Babies. Fleming, Candace. 2010. (ENG.). 40p. (J). (gr. -1-2). 16.99 *(978-1-4169-5402-6(3)*, Atheneum Bks. for Young Readers) Simon & Schuster Children's Publishing.
—Who Ate All the Cookie Dough? Beaumont, Karen. 2008. (ENG.). 32p. (J). (gr. -1-k). 17.99 *(978-0-8050-8267-8(0)*, Holt, Henry & Co. Bks. For Young Readers) Holt, Henry & Co.
—Won Ton: A Cat Tale Told in Haiku. Wardlaw, Lee. 2011. (ENG.). 40p. (J). (gr. -1-3). 16.99 *(978-0-8050-8995-0(0)*, Holt, Henry & Co. Bks. For Young Readers) Holt, Henry & Co.
—Won Ton & Chopstick. Wardlaw, Lee. 2015. (ENG.). 40p. (J). (gr. -1-3). 17.99 *(978-0-8050-9987-4(5)*, Holt, Henry & Co. Bks. For Young Readers) Holt, Henry & Co.
Yelchin, Eugene. Arcady's Goal. Yelchin, Eugene. 2014. (ENG.). 240p. (J). (gr. 4-7). 15.99 *(978-0-8050-9844-0(5)*, Holt, Henry & Co. Bks. For Young Readers) Holt, Henry & Co.
—Breaking Stalin's Nose. Yelchin, Eugene. 2011. (ENG.). 160p. (J). (gr. 4-7). 15.99 *(978-0-8050-9216-5(1)*, Holt, Henry & Co. Bks. For Young Readers) Holt, Henry & Co.
—Breaking Stalin's Nose. Yelchin, Eugene. 2013. (ENG.). 176p. (J). (gr. 4-7). pap. 7.99 *(978-1-250-03410-6(8))* Square Fish.
Yelchin, Eugene & Kuryla, Mary. Heart of a Snowman. Yelchin, Eugene & Kuryla, Mary. 2009. (ENG.). 40p. (J). (gr. -1-3). 16.99 *(978-0-06-125926-5(8))* HarperCollins Pubs.
—The Next Door Bear. Yelchin, Eugene & Kuryla, Mary. 2011. (ENG.). 40p. (J). (gr. -1-3). 16.99 *(978-0-06-125925-8(X))* HarperCollins Pubs.
Yelenak, Andy. Run, Dad, Run! Blackett, Dulcibella. 2004. (ENG.). 32p. (J). 15.00 *(978-1-891369-44-5(X))* Breakaway Bks.
Yerbey, Lindsey Blake. Worms Like to Wiggle. Peters, Elizabeth Anne. 2007. (J). *(978-0-9769737-1-3(5))* Creative Minds Pubns.
Yeretskaya, Yevgeniya. The Snow Queen: A Pop-Up Adaption of a Classic Fairytale. 2013. (ENG.). 7p. 29.95 *(978-1-60580-955-7(1)*, 9781605809557) Jumping Jack Pr.
—Snowflakes - French Edition: A Pop-Up Book. Preston Chushcoff, Jennifer. 2013. (FRE.). 7p. 24.95 *(978-1-62348-062-2(0))* Jumping Jack Pr.
Yerkes, Lane. Goldilocks & the Three Bears: Pop-up Storybook Theater. Slater, Teddy. 2004. 10p. (J). (gr. k-4). reprint ed. 17.00 *(978-0-7567-8224-5(4))* DIANE Publishing Co.
—Let's Discover the Bible, Vol. 1. Rose, Shirley. 64p. (J). (gr. k-2). pap. 4.75 *(978-0-87441-538-4(1))* Behrman Hse., Inc.
—The Sounds of Music. Casterline, L. C. 2004. (Picture Books/Quality Time Ser.). 16p. (gr. k-3). lib. bdg. 20.00 *(978-0-8368-4100-8(X)*, Gareth Stevens Learning Library) Stevens, Gareth Publishing LLLP.
Yerrill, Gail. Christmas Angels, 1 vol. Freedman, Claire. 2008. (ENG.). 32p. (J). (gr. -1-2). pap. 16.95 *(978-1-56148-637-3(X)*, Good Bks.) Skyhorse Publishing Co., Inc.
—A Magical Christmas. Freedman, Claire. 2008. 24p. (J). (gr. 4-7). 12.95 *(978-1-58925-828-0(2))* Tiger Tales.
—Starry Night, Sleep Tight. 2009. 24p. (J). (gr. -1-1). 12.95 *(978-1-58925-844-0(4))* Tiger Tales.
Yerxa, Leo. Last Leaf First Snowflake to Fall. Yerxa, Leo. (J). 16.95 *(978-0-88899-183-6(5))* Groundwood Bks. CAN. Dist: Perseus-PGW.
Yesh, Jeff. Benjamin Franklin: Writer, Inventor, Statesman. Nettleton, Pamela Hill. 2003. (Biographies Ser.). (ENG.). 24p. (gr. k-3). 25.99 *(978-1-4048-0186-8(3))*; per. 7.95 *(978-1-4048-0459-3(5))* Picture Window Bks. (Nonfiction Picture Bks.).
—Brightest in the Sky: The Planet Venus, 1 vol. Loewen, Nancy. 2008. (Amazing Science: Planets Ser.). (ENG.). 24p. (gr. k-4). lib. bdg. 25.99 *(978-1-4048-3958-8(5)*, 1278898, Nonfiction Picture Bks.) Picture Window Bks.
—Copos y Cristales: Un Libro Sobre la Nieve, 1 vol. Sherman, Josepha. Robledo, Sol, tr. from ENG. 2007. (Ciencia Asombrosa: el Tiempo Ser.). (SPA.). 24p. (gr. -1-3). lib. bdg. 25.99 *(978-1-4048-3215-2(7))* Picture Window Bks.
—Coral Reefs: Colorful Underwater Habitats, 1 vol. Salas, Laura Purdie. 2009. (Amazing Science: Ecosystems Ser.). (ENG.). 24p. (gr. k-3). lib. bdg. 25.99 *(978-1-4048-5373-7(1)*, Nonfiction Picture Bks.) Picture Window Bks.
—Deserts: Thirsty Wonderlands, 1 vol. Salas, Laura Purdie. 2007. (Amazing Science: Ecosystems Ser.). (ENG.). 24p. (gr. k-3). lib. bdg. 25.99 *(978-1-4048-3095-0(2)*, 1265689, Nonfiction Picture Bks.) Picture Window Bks.
—Desiertos: Tierras Secas, 1 vol. Salas, Laura Purdie. Abello, Patricia, tr. from ENG. 2008. (Ciencia Asombrosa: Ecosistemas Ser.). (SPA.). 24p. (gr. k-4). lib. bdg. 25.99 *(978-1-4048-3862-8(7))* Picture Window Bks.
—Do Crocodiles Dance? A Book about Animal Habits. Salas, Laura Purdie. 2006. (Animals All Around Ser.). (ENG.). 24p. (gr. -1-2). lib. bdg. 25.99 *(978-1-4048-2230-6(5)*, Nonfiction Picture Bks.) Picture Window Bks.
—Do Turtles Sleep in Treetops? A Book about Animal Homes, 1 vol. Salas, Laura Purdie. 2006. (Animals All Around Ser.). (ENG.). 24p. (gr. -1-2). lib. bdg. 25.99 *(978-1-4048-2232-0(1)*, Nonfiction Picture Bks.) Picture Window Bks.
—Dwarf Planets: Pluto, Charon, Ceres, & Eris, 1 vol. Loewen, Nancy. 2008. (Amazing Science: Planets Ser.). (ENG.). 24p. (gr. k-4). lib. bdg. 25.99 *(978-1-4048-3950-2(X)*, Nonfiction Picture Bks.) Picture Window Bks.
—Evening Meals Around the World, 1 vol. Zurakowski, Michele. 2004. (Meals Around the World Ser.). (ENG.). 24p. (gr. k-4). per. 7.95 *(978-1-4048-1132-4(X)*, Nonfiction Picture Bks.) Picture Window Bks.
—Farthest from the Sun: The Planet Neptune, 1 vol. Loewen, Nancy. 2008. (Amazing Science: Planets Ser.). (ENG.). 24p. (gr. k-4). lib. bdg. 25.99 *(978-1-4048-3955-7(0)*, Nonfiction Picture Bks.) Picture Window Bks.
—Flakes & Flurries: A Book about Snow. Sherman, Josepha. 2003. (Amazing Science: Weather Ser.). (ENG.). 24p. (gr. -1-3). 25.99 *(978-1-4048-0098-4(0))*; per. 7.95 *(978-1-4048-0342-8(4))* Picture Window Bks. (Nonfiction Picture Bks.).
—From Caterpillar to Butterfly: Following the Life Cycle, 1 vol. Slade, Suzanne. 2008. (Amazing Science: Life Cycles Ser.). (ENG.). 24p. (gr. 1-4). 25.99 *(978-1-4048-4916-7(5)*, Nonfiction Picture Bks.) Picture Window Bks.
—From Egg to Snake: Following the Life Cycle, 1 vol. Slade, Suzanne. 2009. (Amazing Science: Life Cycles Ser.). (ENG.). 24p. (gr. 1-4). lib. bdg. 25.99 *(978-1-4048-5153-5(4)*, Nonfiction Picture Bks.) Picture Window Bks.
—From Mealworm to Beetle: Following the Life Cycle, 1 vol. Salas, Laura Purdie. 2008. (Amazing Science: Life Cycles Ser.). (ENG.). 24p. (gr. 1-4). 25.99 *(978-1-4048-4925-9(4)*, Nonfiction Picture Bks.) Picture Window Bks.
—From Pup to Rat: Following the Life Cycle, 1 vol. Slade, Suzanne. 2009. (Amazing Science: Life Cycles Ser.). (ENG.). 24p. (gr. 1-4). lib. bdg. 25.99 *(978-1-4048-5156-6(9)*, Nonfiction Picture Bks.) Picture Window Bks.
—From Puppy to Dog: Following the Life Cycle, 1 vol. Slade, Suzanne. 2008. (Amazing Science: Life Cycles Ser.). (ENG.). 24p. (gr. 1-4). 25.99 *(978-1-4048-4928-0(9)*, Nonfiction Picture Bks.) Picture Window Bks.
—From Seed to Apple Tree: Following the Life Cycle, 1 vol. Slade, Suzanne. 2009. (Amazing Science: Life Cycles Ser.). (ENG.). 24p. (gr. 1-4). lib. bdg. 25.99 *(978-1-4048-5159-7(3)*, Nonfiction Picture Bks.) Picture Window Bks.
—From Seed to Daisy: Following the Life Cycle, 1 vol. Salas, Laura Purdie. 2008. (Amazing Science: Life Cycles Ser.). (ENG.). 24p. (gr. 1-4). 25.99 *(978-1-4048-4919-8(X)*, Nonfiction Picture Bks.) Picture Window Bks.
—From Seed to Maple Tree: Following the Life Cycle, 1 vol. Salas, Laura Purdie. 2008. (Amazing Science: Life Cycles Ser.). (ENG.). 24p. (gr. 1-4). 25.99 *(978-1-4048-4931-0(9)*, Nonfiction Picture Bks.) Picture Window Bks.
—From Seed to Pine Tree: Following the Life Cycle, 1 vol. Slade, Suzanne. 2009. (Amazing Science: Life Cycles Ser.). (ENG.). 24p. (gr. 1-4). 25.99 *(978-1-4048-5162-7(3)*, Nonfiction Picture Bks.) Picture Window Bks.
—From Tadpole to Frog: Following the Life Cycle, 1 vol. Slade, Suzanne. 2008. (Amazing Science: Life Cycles Ser.). (ENG.). 24p. (gr. 1-4). 25.99 *(978-1-4048-4922-8(X)*, Nonfiction Picture Bks.) Picture Window Bks.
—George Washington: Farmer, Soldier, President. Nettleton, Pamela Hill. 2003. (Biographies Ser.). (ENG.). 24p. (gr. k-3). 25.99 *(978-1-4048-0184-4(7)*, Nonfiction Picture Bks.) Picture Window Bks.
—Humedales: Hábitats Húmedos. Salas, Laura Purdie. Abello, Patricia, tr. from ENG. 2008. (Ciencia Asombrosa: Ecosistemas Ser.). (SPA.). 24p. (gr. k-4). lib. bdg. 25.99 *(978-1-4048-3867-3(8))* Picture Window Bks.
—The Largest Planet: Jupiter, 1 vol. Loewen, Nancy. 2008. (Amazing Science: Planets Ser.). (ENG.). 24p. (gr. k-4). lib. bdg. 25.99 *(978-1-4048-3952-6(6)*, Nonfiction Picture Bks.) Picture Window Bks.
—Midday Meals Around the World, 1 vol. Zurakowski, Michele. 2004. (Meals Around the World Ser.). (ENG.). 24p. (gr. k-4). per. 7.95 *(978-1-4048-1131-7(1)*, Nonfiction Picture Bks.) Picture Window Bks.
—Morning Meals Around the World, 1 vol. Gregoire, Maryellen. 2004. (Meals Around the World Ser.). (ENG.). 24p. (gr. k-4). per. 7.95 *(978-1-4048-1130-0(3)*, Nonfiction Picture Bks.) Picture Window Bks.
—Nearest to the Sun: The Planet Mercury, 1 vol. Loewen, Nancy. 2008. (Amazing Science: Planets Ser.). (ENG.). 24p. (gr. k-4). lib. bdg. 25.99 *(978-1-4048-3954-0(2)*, 1278902, Nonfiction Picture Bks.) Picture Window Bks.
—Océanos: Mundos Submarinos. Salas, Laura Purdie. Abello, Patricia, tr. from ENG. 2008. (Ciencia Asombrosa: Ecosistemas Ser.). (SPA.). 24p. (gr. k-4). lib. bdg. 25.99 *(978-1-4048-3864-2(3))* Picture Window Bks.
—Our Home Planet: Earth, 1 vol. Loewen, Nancy. 2008. (Amazing Science: Planets Ser.). (ENG.). 24p. (gr. k-4). lib. bdg. 25.99 *(978-1-4048-3951-9(8)*, Nonfiction Picture Bks.) Picture Window Bks.
—Pastizales: Campos Verdes y Dorados. Salas, Laura Purdie. Abello, Patricia, tr. from ENG. 2008. (Ciencia Asombrosa: Ecosistemas Ser.). (SPA.). 24p. (gr. k-4). lib. bdg. 25.99 *(978-1-4048-3863-5(5))* Picture Window Bks.
—Pocahontas: Peacemaker & Friend to the Colonists. Nettleton, Pamela Hill. 2003. (Biographies Ser.). (ENG.). 24p. (gr. k-3). 25.99 *(978-1-4048-0187-5(1)*, Nonfiction Picture Bks.) Picture Window Bks.
—Rain Forests: Gardens of Green, 1 vol. Salas, Laura Purdie. 2007. (Amazing Science: Ecosystems Ser.). (ENG.). 24p. (gr. k-3). lib. bdg. 25.99 *(978-1-4048-3098-1(7)*, 1265694, Nonfiction Picture Bks.) Picture Window Bks.
—Ringed Giant: The Planet Saturn, 1 vol. Loewen, Nancy. 2008. (Amazing Science: Planets Ser.). (ENG.). 24p. (gr. k-4). lib. bdg. 25.99 *(978-1-4048-3956-4(9)*, 1278904, Nonfiction Picture Bks.) Picture Window Bks.
—Seeing Red: The Planet Mars, 1 vol. Loewen, Nancy. 2008. (Amazing Science: Planets Ser.). (ENG.). 24p. (gr. k-4). lib. bdg. 25.99 *(978-1-4048-3953-3(4)*, 1278905, Nonfiction Picture Bks.) Picture Window Bks.
—Selvas Tropicales: Mundos Verdes, 1 vol. Salas, Laura Purdie. Abello, Patricia, tr. from ENG. 2008. (Ciencia Asombrosa: Ecosistemas Ser.). (SPA.). 24p. (gr. k-4). lib. bdg. 25.99 *(978-1-4048-3865-9(1))* Picture Window Bks.
—The Sideways Planet: Uranus, 1 vol. Loewen, Nancy. 2008. (Amazing Science: Planets Ser.). (ENG.). 24p. (gr. k-4). lib. bdg. 25.99 *(978-1-4048-3957-1(7)*, 1278906, Nonfiction Picture Bks.) Picture Window Bks.
—Splish! Splash! A Book about Rain, 1 vol. Sherman, Josepha. 2003. (Amazing Science: Weather Ser.). (ENG.). 24p. (gr. -1-3). per. 7.95 *(978-1-4048-0339-8(4)*, Nonfiction Picture Bks.) Picture Window Bks.
—Sunshine: A Book about Sunlight. Sherman, Josepha. 2003. (Amazing Science: Weather Ser.). (ENG.). 24p. (gr. -1-3). 25.99 *(978-1-4048-0096-0(4)*, Nonfiction Picture Bks.) Picture Window Bks.
—Swift Thief: The Adventure of Velociraptor. Dahl, Michael. 2003. (Dinosaur World Ser.). (ENG.). 24p. (gr. k-3). 25.99 *(978-1-4048-0138-7(3)*, Nonfiction Picture Bks.) Picture Window Bks.
—Temperate Deciduous Forests: Lands of Falling Leaves, 1 vol. Salas, Laura Purdie. 2007. (Amazing Science: Ecosystems Ser.). (ENG.). 24p. (gr. k-3). lib. bdg. 25.99 *(978-1-4048-3099-8(5)*, Nonfiction Picture Bks.) Picture Window Bks.
—Tundras: Frosty, Treeless Lands, 1 vol. Salas, Laura Purdie. 2009. (Amazing Science: Ecosystems Ser.). (ENG.). 24p. (gr. k-3). lib. bdg. 25.99 *(978-1-4048-5376-8(6)*, Nonfiction Picture Bks.) Picture Window Bks.
—The United States ABCs: A Book about the People & Places of the United States. Schroeder, Holly. 2004. (Country ABCs Ser.). (ENG.). 32p. (gr. k-5). 27.32 *(978-1-4048-0181-3(2)*, 1229509, Nonfiction Picture Bks.) Picture Window Bks.
Yesh, Jeff & Nichols, Garry. Martin Luther King Jr. Preacher, Freedom Fighter, Peacemaker. Nettleton, Pamela Hill. 2003. (Biographies Ser.). (ENG.). 24p. (gr. k-3). 25.99 *(978-1-4048-0188-2(X)*, Nonfiction Picture Bks.) Picture Window Bks.
—Sally Ride: Astronaut, Scientist, Teacher. Nettleton, Pamela Hill. 2003. (Biographies Ser.). (ENG.). 24p. (gr. k-3). 25.99 *(978-1-4048-0189-9(8)*, Nonfiction Picture Bks.) Picture Window Bks.
Yesh, Jeff, jt. illus. see Peterson, Rick.
Yezerski, Thomas F. Mrs. Muddle's Holidays. Nielsen, Laura F. & Nielsen, Laura. 2008. (ENG.). 32p. (J). (gr. k-3). 16.99 *(978-0-374-35094-9(9)*, Farrar, Straus & Giroux (BYR)) Farrar, Straus & Giroux.
—Pinch & Dash & the Terrible Couch. Daley, Michael J. 2013. (ENG.). 48p. (J). (gr. k-3). 12.95 *(978-1-58089-379-4(1))*; pap. 5.95 *(978-1-58089-380-0(5))* Charlesbridge Publishing, Inc.
—Pinch & Dash Make Soup. Daley, Michael J. 2012. (ENG.). 48p. (J). (gr. k-3). 12.95 *(978-1-58089-346-6(5))*; pap. 5.95 *(978-1-58089-347-3(3))* Charlesbridge Publishing, Inc.
Yezerski, Thomas F. Meadowlands: A Wetlands Survival Story. Yezerski, Thomas F. 2011. (ENG.). 40p. (J). (gr. k-3). 17.99 *(978-0-374-34913-4(4)*, Farrar, Straus & Giroux (BYR)) Farrar, Straus & Giroux.
Yi, Hye Won. Pruebalo, 1 vol. Jones, Christianne C. Ruiz, Carlos, tr. 2006. (Read-It! Readers en Español: Story Collection).Tr. of Just Try It. (SPA.). 24p. (gr. -1-3). 19.99 *(978-1-4048-1692-3(5)*, Easy Readers) Picture Window Bks.
Yi, J. Clementine Rose & the Famous Friend. Harvey, Jacqueline. 2015. 7. 160p. (J). (gr. 2-4). 8.99 ***(978-1-74275-755-1(3))*** Random Hse. Australia AUS. Dist: Independent Pubs. Group.
—Clementine Rose & the Farm Fiasco. Harvey, Jacqueline. 2015. (Clementine Rose Ser.: 4). (ENG.). 160p. (J). (gr. 2-4). 8.99 ***(978-1-74275-547-2(X))*** Random Hse. Australia AUS. Dist: Independent Pubs. Group.
Yi, J. Clementine Rose & the Pet Day Disaster. Harvey, Jacqueline. 2015. (Clementine Rose Ser.: 2). (ENG.). 160p. (J). (gr. 2-4). 8.99 *(978-1-74275-543-4(7))* Random Hse. Australia AUS. Dist: Independent Pubs. Group.
—Clementine Rose & the Surprise Visitor. Harvey, Jacqueline. 2015. (Clementine Rose Ser.: 1). (ENG.). 144p. (J). (gr. 2-4). 8.99 *(978-1-74275-541-0(0))* Random Hse. Australia AUS. Dist: Independent Pubs. Group.
Yi, J. The Clementine Rose Busy Day Book. Harvey, Jacqueline. 2015. 96p. (J). (gr. 2-4). pap. 14.99 ***(978-0-85798-411-1(X))*** Random Hse. Australia AUS. Dist: Independent Pubs. Group.
Yi, Liu, jt. illus. see Lida, Xing.
Yilmaz, Necdet. The Christmas Stick: A Children's Story. Myers, Tim J. 2014. (ENG.). 32p. (J). pap. 13.99 *(978-1-61261-571-4(6))* Paraclete Pr., Inc.
—Firefly Summer, 1 vol. Hardy, Lorién Trover. 2006. (Read-It! Readers Ser.). (ENG.). 24p. (gr. -1-3). lib. bdg. 19.99 *(978-1-4048-2397-6(2)*, Easy Readers) Picture Window Bks.
—Robin Hood & the Golden Arrow, 1 vol. Picture Window Books Staff. 2008. (Read-It! Readers: Legends Ser.). (ENG.). 32p. (gr. k-3). 19.99 *(978-1-4048-4843-6(6)*, Easy Readers) Picture Window Bks.
—The Truth about Unicorns, 1 vol. Blaisdell, Molly. 2010. (Fairy-Tale Superstars Ser.). (ENG.). 32p. (gr. 1-3). lib. bdg. 26.65 *(978-1-4048-5748-3(6)*, Nonfiction Picture Bks.) Picture Window Bks.
Yin, Leah. Zona & the Big Buzzzy Secret. Yin, Leah. 2013. 54p. *(978-0-9918396-0-5(9))* Leah Yin Studio.

The check digit for ISBN-10 appears in parentheses after the full ISBN-13

Ying, Victoria. Bella's Birthday Unicorn. Burkhart, Jessica. 2014. (Unicorn Magic Ser.: 1). (ENG.). 144p. (J). (gr. 1-4). 15.99 *(978-1-4814-1105-9(5))*; pap. 5.99 *(978-1-4424-9822-8(6))* Simon & Schuster/Paula Wiseman Bks. (Simon & Schuster/Paula Wiseman Bks.).

—Don't Chicken Out. Stout, Shawn K. 2013. (Not-So-Ordinary Girl Ser.: 3). (ENG.). 176p. (J). (gr. 1-5). 15.99 *(978-1-4169-7929-6(8))*; pap. 5.99 *(978-1-4169-7111-5(4))* Simon & Schuster/Paula Wiseman Bks. (Simon & Schuster/Paula Wiseman Bks.).

—The Hidden Treasure. Burkhart, Jessica. 2015. (Unicorn Magic Ser.: 4). (ENG.). 112p. (J). (gr. 1-4). pap. 5.99 *(978-1-4424-9829-7(3)*, Simon & Schuster/Paula Wiseman Bks.) Simon & Schuster/Paula Wiseman Bks.

—Where's Glimmer? Burkhart, Jessica. 2014. (Unicorn Magic Ser.: 2). (ENG.). 144p. (J). (gr. 1-4). pap. 5.99 *(978-1-4424-9824-2(2)*, Simon & Schuster/Paula Wiseman Bks.) Simon & Schuster/Paula Wiseman Bks.

Ying, Victoria, jt. illus. see Disney Storybook Artists Staff.

Ying, Victoria, jt. illus. see Tyminski, Lori.

Yo, Yuen Wong. Digimon: Digital Monsters, 5 vols., Vol. 5. rev. ed. 2003. 164p. pap. 9.99 *(978-1-59182-160-1(6))* TOKYOPOP, Inc.

Yockteng, Rafael. Blanca Flor: Una Princessa Maya, 1 vol. Montejo, Victor. 2005. (SPA.). 36p. (J). (gr. 1). 16.95 *(978-0-88899-600-8(4))* Groundwood Bks. CAN. Dist: Perseus-PGW.

—Sopa de Frijoles. Argueta, Jorge. 2009. (Bilingual Cooking Poems Ser.). (ENG & SPA.). 32p. (J). (gr. -1-2). 18.95 *(978-0-88899-881-1(3))* Groundwood Bks. CAN. Dist: Perseus-PGW.

Yockteng, Rafael. Gabriel García Márquez: Gabito. Yockteng, Rafael. Lázaro León, Georgina. 2014. (SPA.). (J). 14.99 *(978-1-933032-85-6(5))* Lectorum Pubns., Inc.

Yocum, Sam, 2nd, photos by. Cowpie Corgi: A Dog's Tale. Yocum, Randi. 2007. 32p. (J). lib. bdg. 16.98 *(978-0-9663629-3-0(4))* By Grace Enterprises.

Yoder, Greg. The Swing: A Storybook to Color. 2003. (J). 4.00 *(978-1-930353-88-6(X))* Masthof Pr.

Yoder, Laura & Weaver, Lisa. Joanna's Journey. Martin, Rebecca. 2006. 168p. (YA). pap. 9.99 *(978-1-933753-01-0(3))* Carlisle Pr.- Walnut Creek.

Yoe! Studio Staff. Dancey Dance. Ciminera, Siobhan & Testa, Maggie. 2009. (Yo Gabba Gabba! Ser.). (ENG.). 32p. (J). 4.99 *(978-1-4169-7100-9(9)*, Simon Scribbles) Simon Scribbles.

—Hello, Friends! Ciminera, Siobhan & Rao, Lisa. 2009. (Yo Gabba Gabba! Ser.). (ENG.). 64p. (J). 4.99 *(978-1-4169-7460-4(1)*, Simon Scribbles) Simon Scribbles.

—I Love to Color. Rao, Lisa. 2009. (Yo Gabba Gabba! Ser.). (ENG.). 32p. (J). (gr. -1-1). 3.99 *(978-1-4169-6871-9(7)*, Simon Scribbles) Simon Scribbles.

—So Yummy! So Yummy! Ciminera, Siobhan & Testa, Maggie. 2009. (Yo Gabba Gabba! Ser.). (ENG.). 32p. (J). (gr. -1-2). 4.99 *(978-1-4169-8494-8(1)*, Simon Scribbles) Simon Scribbles.

Yokococo. Matilda & Hans. Yokococo. 2013. (ENG.). 32p. (J). (gr. -1-2). 16.99 *(978-0-7636-6434-3(0)*, Templar) Candlewick Pr.

Yokota, Hiromitsu. The Tale of the Oki Islands: A Tale from Japan. 2013. (Tales of Honor (Red Chair Press) Ser.). (ENG.). 32p. (J). (gr. 1-4). lib. bdg. 26.60 *(978-1-937529-78-9(9))* Red Chair Pr.

—The Tale of the Oki Islands: A Tale from Japan. Barchers, Suzanne I. 2013. (Tales of Honor Ser.). 32p. (gr. 1-3). pap. 8.95 *(978-1-937529-62-8(2))* Red Chair Pr.

Yomtob, Andrea. Dr. Duncan Dog on Duty! Dunn-Dern, Lisa. 2007. (J). (gr. -1-3). per. 16.99 *(978-1-933156-20-0(1)*, Visikid Bks.) GSVQ Publishing.

Yonezu, Yusuke. We Love Each Other. 2013. (Yonezu Board Book Ser.). (ENG.). 28p. (J). (— 1). bds. 9.95 *(978-988-8240-56-2(0))* Neugebauer, Michael (Publishing) Limited HKG. Dist: Independent Pubs. Group.

Yonts, Barbara, photos by. Catering to Children: With Recipes for Memorable Tea Parties. Hawkins, Linda J. 2003. 56p. (J). (gr. k-5). 19.99 *(978-0-9742806-0-8(7))* Heart to Heart Publishing, Inc.

Yoo, Taeeun. Hands Say Love. Shannon, George. 2014. (ENG.). 32p. (J). (gr. -1 — 1). 17.00 *(978-0-316-08479-6(4))* Little, Brown Bks. for Young Readers.

—Here Is the Baby. Kanevsky, Polly. 2014. (ENG.). 40p. (J). (-k). 17.99 *(978-0-375-86731-6(7))*; 20.99 *(978-0-375-96731-3(1))* Random Hse. Children's Bks. (Schwartz & Wade Bks.).

—Only a Witch Can Fly. McGhee, Alison. movie tie-in ed. 2009. (ENG.). 32p. (J). (gr. -1-3). 16.99 *(978-0-312-37503-4(4))* Feiwel & Friends.

—So Many Days. McGhee, Alison. 2010. (ENG.). 40p. (J). (gr. k-2). 15.99 *(978-1-4169-5857-4(6)*, Atheneum Bks. for Young Readers) Simon & Schuster Children's Publishing.

—Tua & the Elephant. Harris, R. P. (ENG.). (J). (gr. 3-7). 2013. 208p. pap. 6.99 *(978-1-4521-2703-3(4))*; 2012. 204p. 16.99 *(978-0-8118-7781-7(7))* Chronicle Bks. LLC.

—The Umbrella Queen. Bridges, Shirin Yim. 2008. 40p. (J). (gr. k-3). (ENG.). 16.99 *(978-0-06-075040-4(5))*; lib. bdg. 17.89 *(978-0-06-075041-1(3))* HarperCollins Pubs. (Greenwillow Bks.).

Yoo, Taeeun. You Are a Lion! & Other Fun Yoga Poses: And Other Fun Yoga Poses. Yoo, Taeeun. 2012. (ENG.). 40p. (J). (gr. -1-k). 17.99 *(978-0-399-25602-8(4)*, Nancy Paulsen Bks.) Penguin Publishing Group.

Yoon, Jae-Ho. In Dream World, Vol. 3. Yoon, Jae-Ho. 3rd rev. ed. 2005. (In Dream World Ser.). 208p. per. 9.99 *(978-1-59532-518-1(2))* TOKYOPOP, Inc.

Yoon, Jae-Ho. In Dream World, Vol. 2. Yoon, Jae-Ho, creator. rev. ed. 2005. 192p. (YA). pap. 9.99 *(978-1-59532-517-4(4))* TOKYOPOP, Inc.

Yoon, JooHee. Beastly Verse. 2015. (ENG.). 48p. (J). (gr. -1-3). 18.95 *(978-1-59270-166-7(3))* Enchanted Lion Bks., LLC.

Yoon, Salina. At the Beach Mad Art. 2009. (Mad Art Ser.). (ENG.). 12p. (J). (gr. -1-k). 6.99 *(978-0-8431-3527-5(1)*, Price Stern Sloan) Penguin Publishing Group.

—My Shimmery Christmas Book. 2005. 10p. (J). bds. 8.95 *(978-1-58117-045-0(9)*, Intervisual/Piggy Toes) Bendon, Inc.

—My Shining Star. 2011. (ENG.). 10p. (J). (gr. -1). 7.95 *(978-0-7624-3978-2(5))* Running Pr. Bk. Pubs.

—Peek-a-Boo Farm Animals. 2005. (Peek-a-Boo Guess Who Book Ser.: Vol. 2). 10p. (J). 7.95 *(978-1-58117-158-7(7)*, Intervisual/Piggy Toes) Bendon, Inc.

—Peek-a-Boo Wild Animals. 2005. (Peek-a-Boo Guess Who Book Ser.: Vol. 1). 10p. (J). (gr. -1-k). 7.95 *(978-1-58117-157-0(9)*, Intervisual/Piggy Toes) Bendon, Inc.

—Pretend & Play: Firefighter. 2013. (Pretend & Play Ser.). (ENG.). 12p. (J). (gr. -1). bds. 12.95 *(978-1-60710-634-0(5)*, Silver Dolphin Bks.) Baker & Taylor Publishing Group.

—Pretend & Play: on the Farm. 2013. (Pretend & Play Ser.). (ENG.). 12p. (J). (gr. -1). bds. 12.95 *(978-1-60710-635-7(3)*, Silver Dolphin Bks.) Baker & Taylor Publishing Group.

—Pretend & Play: Toolbox. 2013. (Pretend & Play Ser.). (ENG.). 12p. (J). (gr. -1). bds. 12.95 *(978-1-60710-636-4(1)*, Silver Dolphin Bks.) Baker & Taylor Publishing Group.

—Read & Play: in the Jungle. 2013. (Read & Play Ser.). (ENG.). 10p. (J). (gr. -1). 12.95 *(978-1-60710-642-5(6)*, Silver Dolphin Bks.) Baker & Taylor Publishing Group.

—Ziggy the Zebra. Ellis, Libby. 2005. 14p. (J). (gr. k-3). 9.95 *(978-1-58117-104-4(8)*, Intervisual/Piggy Toes) Bendon, Inc.

Yoon, Salina. Five Silly Turkeys. Yoon, Salina. 2005. (ENG.). 10p. (J). (gr. -1-k). bds. 6.99 *(978-0-8431-1416-4(9)*, Price Stern Sloan) Penguin Publishing Group.

—Found. Yoon, Salina. 2014. (ENG.). 40p. (J). (gr. -1-1). 14.99 *(978-0-8027-3559-1(2))* Walker & Co.

—Happy Easter! Yoon, Salina. Knudsen, Michelle. 2003. (Sparkle 'n' Shimmer Ser.). (ENG.). 14p. (J). (gr. -1-k). 5.99 *(978-0-689-85311-1(4)*, Little Simon) Little Simon.

—Humpty Dumpty. Yoon, Salina. 2012. (ENG.). 18p. (J). (gr. -1 — 1). bds. 5.99 *(978-1-4424-1411-2(1)*, Little Simon) Little Simon.

—It's Christmas Time! Yoon, Salina. 2010. (ENG.). 8p. (J). (gr. -1-k). bds. 9.99 *(978-0-545-23410-8(7)*, Cartwheel Bks.) Scholastic, Inc.

—Jack & Jill: A Halloween Nursery Rhyme. Yoon, Salina. 2012. (ENG.). 18p. (J). (gr. -1 — 1). bds. 5.99 *(978-1-4424-1410-5(3)*, Little Simon) Little Simon.

—My Chanukah Playbook. Yoon, Salina. 2009. (ENG.). 10p. (J). (gr. -1-k). 10.99 *(978-1-4169-8957-8(9)*, Little Simon) Little Simon.

—My First Menorah. Yoon, Salina. 2005. (ENG.). 20p. (J). (gr. -1-2). 7.99 *(978-0-689-87746-9(3)*, Little Simon) Little Simon.

—Opposnakes: A Lift-the-Flap Book about Opposites. Yoon, Salina. 2009. (ENG.). 16p. (J). (gr. -1-1). 9.99 *(978-1-4169-7875-6(5)*, Little Simon) Little Simon.

—Penguin & Pinecone. Yoon, Salina. 2012. (ENG.). 40p. (J). (gr. -1-6). 14.99 *(978-0-8027-2843-2(X)*, Bloomsbury USA Childrens) Bloomsbury USA.

—Penguin & Pinecone. Yoon, Salina. 2012. (ENG.). 40p. (J). (gr. -1-1). 15.89 *(978-0-8027-2844-9(8))* Walker & Co.

—Penguin Gets Dressed! Yoon, Salina. 2010. 10p. bds. 7.95 *(978-1-60747-750-1(5)*, Pickwick Pr.) Phoenix Bks., Inc.

—Penguin Gets Ready for Bed! Yoon, Salina. 2010. 10p. bds. 7.95 *(978-1-60747-751-8(3)*, Pickwick Pr.) Phoenix Bks., Inc.

—Penguin Goes to the Farm! Yoon, Salina. 2010. 10p. bds. 7.95 *(978-1-60747-752-5(1)*, Pickwick Pr.) Phoenix Bks., Inc.

—Penguin in Love. Yoon, Salina. 2014. (ENG.). 30p. (J). (gr. -1-1). bds. 7.99 *(978-0-8027-3758-8(7)*, Bloomsbury USA Childrens) Bloomsbury USA.

—Penguin on Vacation. Yoon, Salina. 2015. (Penguin Ser.). (ENG.). 34p. (J). (gr. -1-1). bds. 7.99 *(978-0-8027-3837-0(0)*, Bloomsbury USA Childrens) Bloomsbury USA.

—Penguin on Vacation. Yoon, Salina. 2013. (ENG.). 40p. (J). (gr. -1-1). 14.99 *(978-0-8027-3397-9(2))*; 15.89 *(978-0-8027-3396-2(4))* Walker & Co.

—Stacking Shapes. Yoon, Salina. 2010. (Little Scholastic Ser.). (ENG.). 6p. (J). (gr. k — 1). bds. 12.99 *(978-0-545-23516-7(2)*, Cartwheel Bks.) Scholastic, Inc.

—Toys. Yoon, Salina. 2009. (Little Scholastic Ser.). (ENG.). 10p. (J). (gr. k — 1). 8.99 *(978-0-545-14973-0(8)*, Cartwheel Bks.) Scholastic, Inc.

—What Am I? Yoon, Salina. 2010. (Little Scholastic Ser.). (ENG.). 12p. (J). (gr. k — 1). bds. 8.99 *(978-0-545-17853-2(3)*, Cartwheel Bks.) Scholastic, Inc.

—Who Am I? Yoon, Salina. 2011. (Little Scholastic Ser.). (ENG.). 12p. (J). (gr. k — 1). bds. 8.99 *(978-0-545-17852-5(5)*, Cartwheel Bks.) Scholastic, Inc.

—Wings: A Book to Touch & Feel. Yoon, Salina. 2010. (ENG.). 12p. (J). (gr. -1 — 1). bds. 8.99 *(978-1-4169-8958-5(7)*, Little Simon) Little Simon.

—Zoo. Yoon, Salina. 2010. (Little Scholastic Ser.). (ENG.). 10p. (J). (gr. k — 1). 8.99 *(978-0-545-15072-9(8))* Scholastic, Inc.

Yoon, Seok. A Journey into the Human Body, Vol. 2. Han, Kakao. 2005. (Everyday Science Ser.: 2). (ENG.). 160p. (J). (gr. 3-8). per. 12.95 *(978-981-05-2767-9(5))* Youngjin (Singapore) Pte Ltd. SGP. Dist: Independent Pubs. Group.

Yorinks, Adrienne. Hummingbirds: Facts & Folklore from the Americas. Yorinks, Adrienne. Larson, Jeanette. 2011. (ENG.). 64p. (J). (gr. 4-7). pap. 8.95 *(978-1-58089-333-6(3))* Charlesbridge Publishing, Inc.

York, Deborah Ward. Calvin C. Waxwing. Ward, Eva D. l.t. ed. 2006. 34p. (J). per. 14.00 *(978-0-9776514-5-0(2))* Beech River Bks.

York, Shane. Dexter the Duck Gets His Quack. Witte, Jessica Pierce. 2012. 30p. 24.95 *(978-1-4626-6592-1(6))* America Star Bks.

York, Susanne, photos by. Carousel Kids. Kendall, Diane & Marsh, Merle. 2004. (J). *(978-0-9762385-0-8(0))* Houston Zoo, Inc.

Yoshi. Big Al. Clements, Andrew. 2015. 32p. pap. 8.00 ***(978-1-61003-598-9(4))*** Center for the Collaborative Classroom.

Yoshi. The First Story Ever Told. Jendresen, Erik & Villoldo, Alberto. 2008. (ENG.). 36p. (J). (gr. -1-2). 12.99 *(978-1-4169-8961-5(7)*, Simon & Schuster Bks. For Young Readers) Simon & Schuster Bks. For Young Readers.

—Making the World. Wood, Douglas. 2008. (ENG.). 44p. (J). (gr. -1-2). 13.99 *(978-1-4169-8596-9(4)*, Simon & Schuster Bks. For Young Readers) Simon & Schuster Bks. For Young Readers.

Yoshida, Akimi. Banana Fish. Yoshida, Akimi. (Banana Fish Ser.). (ENG.). Vol. 4. 2nd ed. 2004. 200p. pap. 9.95 *(978-1-59116-133-2(9))*; Vol. 5. 2nd ed. 2004. 192p. pap. 9.95 *(978-1-59116-417-3(6))*; Vol. 6. 2nd ed. 2005. 192p. pap. 9.95 *(978-1-59116-418-0(4))*; Vol. 7. 2nd ed. 2005. 192p. pap. 9.95 *(978-1-59116-419-7(2))*; Vol. 12. 2006. 208p. pap. 9.99 *(978-1-4215-0260-1(7))*; Vol. 13. 2006. 208p. (gr. 11). pap. 9.99 *(978-1-4215-0390-5(5))*; Vol. 14. 2006. 208p. pap. 9.99 *(978-1-4215-0524-4(X))*; Vol. 15. 2006. 208p. pap. 9.99 *(978-1-4215-0525-1(8))* Viz Media.

Yoshida, Reiko. Tokyo Mew Mew, 10 vols., Vol. 7. Ikumi, Mia. 7th rev. ed. 2004. 208p. pap. 9.99 *(978-1-59182-550-0(4)*, Tokyopop Kids) TOKYOPOP, Inc.

—Tokyo Mew-Mew: Volume 5, Vol. 5. Ikumi, Mia. 2006. (Tokyo Mew-Mew (Spanish) Ser.). (SPA.). 184p. reprint ed. pap. 10.95 *(978-1-59497-173-0(0))* Public Square Bks.

—Tokyo Mew Mew Volume 2, Vol. 2. Ikumi, Mia. 2006. (SPA.). 176p. reprint ed. pap. 10.95 *(978-1-59497-170-9(6))* Public Square Bks.

—Tokyo Mew Mew Volume 7, Vol. 7. Ikumi, Mia. 2006. (SPA.). 185p. reprint ed. pap. 10.95 *(978-1-59497-198-3(6))* Public Square Bks.

Yoshikawa, Eiji. Vagabond. Yoshikawa, Eiji. (Vagabond Ser.). (ENG.). (YA). 2004. 200p. pap. 9.95 *(978-1-59116-454-8(0))*; Vol. 7. 2003. 200p. pap. 9.95 *(978-1-59116-073-1(1))*; Vol. 17. 2004. 192p. pap. 9.95 *(978-1-59116-455-5(9))* Viz Media.

Yoshikawa, Eiji & Inoue, Takehiko. Vagabond. Yoshikawa, Eiji & Inoue, Takehiko. (Vagabond Ser.). (ENG.). Vol. 5. 2003. 208p. pap. 9.95 *(978-1-56931-893-5(X))*; Vol. 6. 2003. 216p. pap. 9.95 *(978-1-56931-894-2(8))*; Vol. 8. 2003. 216p. pap. 9.95 *(978-1-59116-119-6(3))*; Vol. 9. 2004. 208p. pap. 9.95 *(978-1-59116-256-8(4))*; Vol. 10. 2004. 224p. pap. 9.95 *(978-1-59116-340-4(4))*; Vol. 11. 2004. 224p. pap. 9.95 *(978-1-59116-396-1(X))*; Vol. 12. 2004. 200p. pap. 9.95 *(978-1-59116-434-0(6))*; Vol. 15. 2004. 200p. pap. 9.95 *(978-1-59116-453-1(2))* Viz Media.

Yoshikawa, Sachiko. The Boy from the Dragon Palace. 2011. (ENG.). 32p. (J). (gr. -1-2). 16.99 *(978-0-8075-7513-0(5))* Whitman, Albert & Co.

—The Boy from the Dragon Palace: A Folktale from Japan. 2012. (J). *(978-1-61913-110-1(2))* Weigl Pubs., Inc.

—But I Read It on the Internet! Buzzeo, Toni. 2013. 32p. (J). 17.95 *(978-1-60213-062-3(0)*, Upstart Bks.) Highsmith Inc.

—Fire up with Reading! Buzzeo, Toni. 2007. 32p. 17.95 *(978-1-60213-019-7(1))*; (J). (gr. -1-3). 17.95 *(978-1-932146-91-2(1))* Highsmith Inc. (Upstart Bks.).

—The Great Dewey Hunt. Buzzeo, Toni. 2009. (Mrs. Skorupski Story Ser.). (J). 36p. (gr. -1-3). 17.95 *(978-1-60213-041-8(8))*; *(978-1-60213-029-6(9))* Highsmith Inc. (Upstart Bks.).

—Hamsters, Shells, & Spelling Bees: School Poems. Hopkins, Lee Bennett. 2008. (I Can Read Bks.). 48p. (J). (gr. -1-3). lib. bdg. 17.89 *(978-0-06-074113-6(9))*; (ENG.). (gr. k-3). 17.99 *(978-0-06-074112-9(0))* HarperCollins Pubs.

—Kindness Is Cooler, Mrs. Ruler. Cuyler, Margery. 2007. (ENG.). 48p. (J). (gr. k-5). 17.99 *(978-0-689-87344-7(1)*, Simon & Schuster Bks. For Young Readers) Simon & Schuster Bks. For Young Readers.

—Kitty Up! Wojtusik, Elizabeth. 2008. (J). *(978-0-8037-3045-8(4)*, Dial) Penguin Publishing Group.

—The Last Day of Kindergarten, 0 vols. Loewen, Nancy. 2011. (ENG.). 32p. (J). (gr. -1-1). 16.99 *(978-0-7614-5807-4(7)*, 9780761458074, Amazon Children's Publishing) Amazon Publishing.

—Late for School! Calmenson, Stephanie. 2008. (ENG.). 32p. (J). (gr. -1-2). lib. bdg. 16.95 *(978-1-57505-935-8(5))* Lerner Publishing Group.

—No T. Rex in the Library. Buzzeo, Toni. 2010. (ENG.). 32p. (J). (gr. -1-3). 17.99 *(978-1-4169-3927-6(X)*, McElderry, Margaret K. Bks.) McElderry, Margaret K. Bks.

—Oopsy, Teacher! Calmenson, Stephanie. 2012. (Carolrhoda Picture Bks). (ENG.). 32p. (J). (gr. -1-2). lib. bdg. 16.95 *(978-0-7613-5894-7(3)*, Carolrhoda Bks.) Lerner Publishing Group.

—Our Librarian Won't Tell Us Anything! Buzzeo, Toni. 2006. 32p. (J). (gr. -1-k). lib. bdg. 17.95 *(978-1-932146-73-8(3)*, Upstart Bks.) Highsmith Inc.

—Shout! Little Poems That Roar. Bagert, Brod. 2007. (ENG.). 32p. (J). (gr. -1-3). 17.99 *(978-0-8037-2972-8(3)*, Dial) Penguin Publishing Group.

—Stars. Tomecek, Steve. 2003. (Jump into Science Ser.). (ENG.). 32p. (J). (gr. -1-3). 16.95 *(978-0-7922-6955-7(1))* National Geographic Society.

—What Is Science? Dotlich, Rebecca Kai. rev. ed. 2006. (ENG.). 32p. (J). (gr. -1-2). 18.99 *(978-0-8050-7394-2(9)*, Holt, Henry & Co. Bks. For Young Readers) Holt, Henry & Co.

Yoshikawa, Sachiko. Razzamadaddy, 1 vol. Yoshikawa, Sachiko, tr. Walvoord, Linda. 2004. (ENG.). 32p. (J). 14.95 *(978-0-7614-5158-7(7))* Marshall Cavendish Corp.

Yoshizaki, Mine. Sgt. Frog. Yoshizaki, Mine. 2005. 10th rev. ed. (Sgt. Frog Ser.: Vol. 10). 184p. pap. 9.99 *(978-1-59182-344-5(7))*; Vol. 6. 6th rev. ed. 192p. pap. 9.99 *(978-1-59182-708-5(6))* TOKYOPOP, Inc.

Yoshizaki, Mine. Sgt. Frog. Yoshizaki, Mine, creator. rev. ed. 2005. 192p. Vol. 7. pap. 9.99 *(978-1-59532-448-1(8))*; Vol. 8. pap. 9.99 *(978-1-59532-449-8(6))* TOKYOPOP, Inc.

Yoshizumi, Carol. Girls Love Gymnastics. American Girl Editors. 2007. 64p. (J). (gr. 4-7). pap. 8.95 *(978-1-59369-283-4(8))* American Girl Publishing, Inc.

—Real Beauty: 101 Ways to Feel Great about You. Kauchak, Therese. 2008. (American Girl Library). (ENG.). 120p. (J). pap. 9.95 *(978-1-58485-908-6(3))* American Girl Publishing, Inc.

Yoshizumi, Wataru. Ultra Maniac. Yoshizumi, Wataru. 2005. (Ultra Maniac Ser.). (JPN & ENG.). 184p. Vol. 1. pap. 9.99 *(978-1-59116-917-8(8))*; Vol. 2. pap. 8.99 *(978-1-59116-974-1(7))*; Vol. 3. pap. 8.99 *(978-1-4215-0056-0(6))* Viz Media.

—Ultra Maniac, Vol. 4. Yoshizumi, Wataru. Yoshizuma, Watara. 2006. (Ultra Maniac Ser.). (JPN & ENG.). 184p. pap. 8.99 *(978-1-4215-0204-5(6))* Viz Media.

—Ultra Maniac, Vol. 5. Yoshizumi, Wataru. 2006. (Ultra Maniac Ser.). (JPN & ENG.). 208p. pap. 8.99 *(978-1-4215-0330-1(1))* Viz Media.

YouDae, Kim. Handy Mr. Hippo. InSeon, Chae. rev. ed. 2014. (MySELF Bookshelf: Social & Emotional Learning/Social Awareness Ser.). (ENG.). 32p. (J). (gr. k-2). pap. 11.94 *(978-1-60357-661-1(4))*; lib. bdg. 22.60 *(978-1-59953-652-1(8))* Norwood Hse. Pr.

Young, Amy. The Mud Fairy. Young, Amy. 2010. (ENG.). 40p. (J). (gr. -1-1). 16.99 *(978-1-59990-104-6(8)*, Bloomsbury USA Childrens) Bloomsbury USA.

Young, Aviance. Pinksta & the Polka Dotted-Pinstriped-Pants-Wearing Princess. Alexander, Sy. 2005. (J). per. 9.00 *(978-0-9655726-2-0(5))* Proud 2-B Me Publishing!.

Young, Beverley. How the Weather Works: A Hands-On Guide to Our Changing Climate. Dorion, Christiane. 2011. (ENG.). 20p. (J). (gr. 2-5). 17.99 *(978-0-7636-5262-3(8)*, Templar) Candlewick Pr.

—How the World Works: A Hands-On Guide to Our Amazing Planet. Dorion, Christiane. 2010. (ENG.). 18p. (J). (gr. 2-5). 18.99 *(978-0-7636-4801-5(9))* Candlewick Pr.

Young, Bill. Copters. Paul, John. 2012. 36p. 24.95 *(978-1-4626-9458-7(6))* America Star Bks.

Young, Bill, jt. illus. see Margolis, Al.

Young, Bruce & Young, Jennifer Law, photos by. Rockbridge: A Photographic Essay. Young, Bruce & Young, Jennifer Law. Wolfe, Andrew, ed. 2005. 124p. 34.95 *(978-0-9768238-4-1(5))* Mariner Publishing.

Young, Clint. Return to the Willows. Kelly, Jacqueline & Grahame, Kenneth. 2012. (ENG.). 288p. (J). (gr. 3-7). 19.99 *(978-0-8050-9413-8(X)*, Holt, Henry & Co. Bks. For Young Readers) Holt, Henry & Co.

Young, Craig. The Adventures of Imhotep. Akinje, Wale. 2006. (J). *(978-0-9768485-0-9(3))* Nile Publishing.

Young, Cybèle. Jack Pine, 1 vol. Patton, Christopher. 2007. (ENG.). 32p. (J). (gr. 1-7). 18.95 *(978-0-88899-780-7(9))* Groundwood Bks. CAN. Dist: Perseus-PGW.

Young, Cybèle. Ten Birds. Young, Cybèle. 2011. (Ten Birds Ser.). (ENG.). 32p. (J). (gr. k-3). 16.95 *(978-1-55453-568-2(9))* Kids Can Pr., Ltd. CAN. Dist: Univ. of Toronto Pr.

Young, Dot. Where Are My Christmas Presents? Rives, J. G. 2007. 44p. (J). 17.95 *(978-0-9790014-0-6(4))* Sterli Publishing.

Young, Ed. Bird & Diz. Golio, Gary. 2015. (ENG.). 26p. (J). (gr. -1-3). 19.99 *(978-0-7636-6660-6(2))* Candlewick Pr.

—Desert Song, 1 vol. Johnston, Tony. ed. 2010. (ENG.). 32p. (gr. 3-4). pap. 7.99 *(978-1-57805-171-7(1))* Sierra Club Bks. for Children.

Young, Ed. The Emperor & the Kite. Yolen, Jane. 2015. 32p. pap. 7.00 ***(978-1-61003-535-4(6))*** Center for the Collaborative Classroom.

Young, Ed. I Blis: An Islamic Tale. Oppenheim, Shulamith. 2004. 29p. (J). (gr. k-4). reprint ed. 16.00 *(978-0-7567-7575-9(2))* DIANE Publishing Co.

—Moon Bear. Guiberson, Brenda Z. 2010. 40p. (J). (ENG.). (gr. -1-3). 16.99 *(978-0-8050-8977-6(2)*, Holt, Henry & Co. Bks. For Young Readers); pap. 7.99 *(978-0-8050-9258-5(7))* Holt, Henry & Co.

—Seven Fathers. Ramsden, Ashley. 2011. (ENG.). 32p. (J). (gr. -1-3). 16.99 *(978-1-59643-544-5(5))* Roaring Brook Pr.

—Shanghai Messenger, 1 vol. Cheng, Andrea. 2005. (ENG.). 40p. (J). (gr. 3-7). 17.95 *(978-1-58430-238-4(0))* Lee & Low Bks., Inc.

—A Strange Place to Call Home: The World's Most Dangerous Habitats & the Animals That Call Them Home. Singer, Marilyn. 2012. (ENG.). 44p. (J). (gr. -1-3). 16.99 *(978-1-4521-0120-0(5))* Chronicle Bks. LLC.

—A Strange Place to Call Home: The World's Most Dangerous Habitats & the Animals That Call Them Home. Singer, Marilyn. 2015. (ENG.). 44p. (J). (gr. k-3). 7.99 *(978-1-4521-4125-1(8))* Chronicle Bks. LLC.

—Tai Chi Morning: Snapshots of China. Grimes, Nikki. 2004. (ENG.). 64p. (J). 15.95 *(978-0-8126-2707-7(5))* Cricket Bks.

—Tiger of the Snows: Tenzing Norgay: the Boy Whose Dream Was Everest. Burleigh, Robert. 2010. (ENG.). 40p. (J). (gr. 2-5). 16.99 *(978-1-4424-2192-9(4)*, Atheneum Bks. for Young Readers) Simon & Schuster Children's Publishing.

—Tsunami! Kajikawa, Kimiko. 2009. (ENG.). 32p. (J). (gr. -1-k). 16.99 *(978-0-399-25006-4(9)*, Philomel) Penguin Publishing Group.

—Wabi Sabi. Reibstein, Mark. 2008. (ENG.). 40p. (J). (gr. -1-1). 18.00 *(978-0-316-11825-5(7))* Little Brown & Co.

—The Yellow Boat. Hillert, Margaret. 2008. 32p. (J). lib. bdg. 19.93 *(978-1-59953-157-1(7))* Norwood Hse. Pr.

Young, Ed. Seven Blind Mice. Young, Ed. 2012. (ENG.). 36p. (J). (gr. -1-k). bds. 8.99 *(978-0-399-25742-1(X)*, Philomel) Penguin Publishing Group.

—Seven Blind Mice. Young, Ed. 2007. pap. 14.95 incl. audio *(978-0-439-02784-7(5))*; (J). 24.95 incl. audio *(978-0-439-02782-3(9))* Scholastic, Inc.

—Seven Blind Mice. Young, Ed. 2011. 18.95 *(978-0-439-02785-4(3))*; (J). 29.95 *(978-0-439-02783-0(7))* Weston Woods Studios, Inc.

—The Sons of the Dragon King: A Chinese Legend. Young, Ed. 2004. (ENG.). 32p. (J). (gr. -1-3). 19.99

(978-0-689-85184-1(7), Atheneum Bks. for Young Readers) Simon & Schuster Children's Publishing.

Young, Ellsworth. More Jataka Tales. Babbitt, Ellen C. 2006. pap. *(978-1-4065-0347-0(9))* Dodo Pr.

—More Jataka Tales. Babbitt, Ellen C. 2008. 92p. pap. 7.95 *(978-1-59915-310-0(6))* Yesterday's Classics.

Young, Emma. Arts & Crafts of Ancient China. Morris, Ting. 2006. (Arts & Crafts of Ser.). 32p. (J). lib. bdg. 27.10 *(978-1-58340-914-5(9)*, 1262690) Black Rabbit Bks.

—Arts & Crafts of Ancient Egypt. Morris, Ting. 2006. (Arts & Crafts of the Ancient World Ser.). 32p. (J). lib. bdg. 28.50 *(978-1-58340-911-4(4))* Black Rabbit Bks.

—Arts & Crafts of Ancient Greece. Morris, Ting. 2006. (Arts & Crafts of Ser.). 32p. (J). lib. bdg. 28.50 *(978-1-58340-912-1(2)*, 1262692) Black Rabbit Bks.

—Arts & Crafts of Ancient Rome. Morris, Ting. 2006. (Arts & Crafts of Ser.). 32p. (J). lib. bdg. 28.50 *(978-1-58340-913-8(0)*, 1262693) Black Rabbit Bks.

—Arts & Crafts of the Aztecs & Maya. Morris, Ting. 2006. (Arts & Crafts of the Ancient World Ser.). 32p. (J). lib. bdg. 28.50 *(978-1-58340-915-2(7)*, 1262694) Black Rabbit Bks.

—Arts & Crafts of the Native Americans. Morris, Ting. 2006. (Arts & Crafts of the Ancient World Ser.). 32p. (J). lib. bdg. 28.50 *(978-1-58340-916-9(5))* Black Rabbit Bks.

Young, Eric. Cupid: God of Love. Temple, Teri & Temple, Emily. 2015. (Roman Mythology Ser.). (ENG.). 32p. (J). (gr. 2-5). 29.93 *(978-1-63143-715-1(1)*, 208558) Child's World, Inc., The.

—Diana: Goddess of Hunting & Protector of Animals. Temple, Teri & Temple, Emily. 2015. (Roman Mythology Ser.). (ENG.). 32p. (J). (gr. 2-5). 29.93 *(978-1-63143-716-8(X)*, 208559) Child's World, Inc., The.

—Juno: Queen of the Gods, Goddess of Marriage. Temple, Teri & Temple, Emily. 2015. (Roman Mythology Ser.). (ENG.). 32p. (J). (gr. 2-5). 29.93 *(978-1-63143-717-5(8)*, 208560) Child's World, Inc., The.

—Jupiter: King of the Gods, God of Sky & Storms. Temple, Teri & Temple, Emily. 2015. (Roman Mythology Ser.). (ENG.). 32p. (J). (gr. 2-5). 29.93 *(978-1-63143-718-2(6)*, 208561) Child's World, Inc., The.

—Mars: God of War. Temple, Teri & Temple, Emily. 2015. (Roman Mythology Ser.). (ENG.). 32p. (J). (gr. 2-5). 29.93 *(978-1-63143-719-9(4)*, 208562) Child's World, Inc., The.

—Mercury: God of Travels & Trade. Temple, Teri & Temple, Emily. 2015. (Roman Mythology Ser.). (ENG.). 32p. (J). (gr. 2-5). 29.93 *(978-1-63143-720-5(8)*, 208563) Child's World, Inc., The.

—Minerva: Goddess of Wisdom, War, & Crafts. Temple, Teri & Temple, Emily. 2015. (Roman Mythology Ser.). (ENG.). 32p. (J). (gr. 2-5). 29.93 *(978-1-63143-721-2(6)*, 208564) Child's World, Inc., The.

—Neptune: God of the Sea & Earthquakes. Temple, Teri & Temple, Emily. 2015. (Roman Mythology Ser.). (ENG.). 32p. (J). (gr. 2-5). 29.93 *(978-1-63143-722-9(4)*, 208565) Child's World, Inc., The.

—Pluto: God of the Underworld. Temple, Teri & Temple, Emily. 2015. (Roman Mythology Ser.). (ENG.). 32p. (J). (gr. 2-5). 29.93 *(978-1-63143-723-6(2)*, 208566) Child's World, Inc., The.

—Raymond's Run. Bambara, Toni Cade. 2014. (Classic Stories Ser.). (ENG.). 24p. (J). (gr. 3-6). 28.50 *(978-1-62323-619-9(3)*, 206387) Child's World, Inc., The.

—Saturn: God of Sowing & Seeds. Temple, Teri & Temple, Emily. 2015. (Roman Mythology Ser.). (ENG.). 32p. (J). (gr. 2-5). 29.93 *(978-1-63143-724-3(0)*, 208567) Child's World, Inc., The.

—Venus: Goddess of Love & Beauty. Temple, Teri & Temple, Emily. 2015. (Roman Mythology Ser.). (ENG.). 32p. (J). (gr. 2-5). 29.93 *(978-1-63143-725-0(9)*, 208568) Child's World, Inc., The.

Young, Eugene Randolph. The Food Convention. Young, Eugene Randolph, des. l.t. ed. 2006. 32p. (J). 16.95 *(978-0-9792000-0-7(8))* Les Lum Pubs.

Young, James. Jack & the Giants. Salsi, Lynn. 2012. (ENG.). 32p. (J). 16.95 *(978-0-938467-52-6(2))* Headline Bks., Inc.

Young, Jennifer Law, jt. photos by see Young, Bruce.

Young, Karen Romano. Across the Wide Ocean: The Why, How, & Where of Navigation for Humans & Animals at Sea. Young, Karen Romano. 2007. 80p. (J). (gr. 4-7). 18.99 *(978-0-06-009086-9(3))*; lib. bdg. 19.89 *(978-0-06-009087-6(1)*, Greenwillow Bks.) HarperCollins Pubs.

Young, Mary. Caminando Bajo la Nieve. Wetterer, Margaret K. & Wetterer, Charles M. 2007. (Yo Solo: Historia (on My Own History) Ser.). (SPA.). 48p. (gr. 2-4). lib. bdg. 25.26 *(978-0-8225-7786-7(0)*, Ediciones Lerner) Lerner Publishing Group.

Young, Mary O'Keefe. Feliz Navidad, Jorge el Curioso. Rey, H. A. ed. 2012. (Curious George Ser.).Tr. of Merry Christmas, Curious George. (ENG & SPA.). 32p. (J). (gr. -1-3). 10.99 *(978-0-547-74503-9(6))* Houghton Mifflin Harcourt Publishing Co.

—Hanukkah. Fishman, Cathy Goldberg. 2003. (On My Own Holidays Ser.). (ENG.). 48p. (gr. 2-4). pap. 6.95 *(978-1-57505-583-1(X))* Lerner Publishing Group.

—Happy Easter, Curious George. Anderson, R. P. et al. 2010. (Curious George Ser.). (ENG.). 24p. (J). (gr. -1-3). 9.99 *(978-0-547-04825-3(4))* Houghton Mifflin Harcourt Publishing Co.

—Happy Valentine's Day, Curious George! Rey, H. A. 2011. (Curious George Ser.). (ENG.). 16p. (J). (gr. -1-3). 8.99 *(978-0-547-13107-8(0))* Houghton Mifflin Harcourt Publishing Co.

—Merry Christmas, Curious George. Rey, H. A. et al. 2012. (Curious George Ser.). (ENG.). 32p. (J). (gr. -1-3). 9.99 *(978-0-547-76054-4(X))* Houghton Mifflin Harcourt Publishing Co.

—The Snow Walker. Wetterer, Margaret K. & Wetterer, Charles M. unabr. ed. (Historical Fiction Ser.). (J). (gr. 1-6). 24.95 incl. audio *(978-0-87499-394-3(6))* Live Oak Media.

Young, Mary O'Keefe & Schories, Pat. Biscuit's 100th Day of School. Capucilli, Alyssa Satin. 2006. (Biscuit Ser.). (ENG.). 20p. (J). (gr. -1-1). pap. 6.99 *(978-0-06-079467-5(4)*, HarperFestival) HarperCollins Pubs.

Young, Mary O'Keefe, jt. illus. see Schories, Pat.

Young, Ned. Big Rig. Swenson, Jamie A. 2014. (ENG.). 32p. (J). (gr. -1-k). 16.99 *(978-1-4231-6330-5(3))* Hyperion Bks. for Children.

Young, Ned. Zoomer. Young, Ned. 2010. (ENG.). 32p. (J). (gr. -1-2). 16.99 *(978-0-06-170088-0(6))* HarperCollins Pubs.

—Zoomer's Out-of-This-World Christmas. Young, Ned. 2013. (ENG.). 32p. (J). (gr. -1-3). 17.99 *(978-0-06-199959-8(8))* HarperCollins Pubs.

—Zoomer's Summer Snowstorm. Young, Ned. 2011. (ENG.). 32p. (J). (gr. -1-2). 16.99 *(978-0-06-170092-7(4))* HarperCollins Pubs.

Young Noh, Mi. Threads of Time, Vol. 5. Hong, Jihae, tr. rev. ed. 2005. 192p. pap. 9.99 *(978-1-59532-036-0(9))* TOKYOPOP, Inc.

Young Noh, Mi. Threads of Time, Vol. 4. Young Noh, Mi, creator. rev. ed. 2005. 192p. pap. 9.99 *(978-1-59532-035-3(0))* TOKYOPOP, Inc.

Young, Norman. Bible Stories. Amery, Heather. gif. ed. 2004. (Bible Tales Readers Ser.). (ENG.). 1p. (J). (gr. -1-3). 24.95 *(978-0-7460-4145-1(4))* EDC Publishing.

—The Christmas Story. rev. ed. 2006. (Usborne Bible Tales Ser.). 16p. (J). (gr. -1-3). pap. 4.99 *(978-0-7945-1286-6(0)*, Usborne) EDC Publishing.

—The Incredible Present. Castor, Harriet. 2004. (Usborne Young Reading: Series Two Ser.). 64p. (J). (gr. k-4). 8.99 *(978-0-7945-1785-4(4)*, Usborne) EDC Publishing.

—Starting Soccer. Edom, Helen & Osborne, Mike. 2006. (First Skills Ser.). 32p. (J). (gr. k-3). lib. bdg. 12.99 *(978-1-58086-907-2(6)*, Usborne) EDC Publishing.

—The Story of Jesus for Young Children. 2005. (Usborne Bible Tales Ser.). 98p. (J). (gr. -1-k). 14.99 incl. audio compact disk *(978-0-7945-0831-9(6)*, Usborne) EDC Publishing.

Young, Norman & Ablett, Barry. Horse & Pony Treasury. Dickins, Rosie & Pratt, Leonie. Sims, Lesley, ed. 2006. (Horse & Pony Treasury Ser.). 93p. (J). 19.99 *(978-0-7945-1431-0(6)*, Usborne) EDC Publishing.

Young, Patricia A. The Holy Monks of Mt. Athos. Young, Patricia A. l.t. ed. 2005. 28p. (J). 20.00 *(978-0-913026-24-3(7))*; 10.00 *(978-0-913026-49-6(2))* St. Nectarios Pr.

Young, Paul. Colm's Lambs. McQuinn, Anna. 2014. (ENG.). 32p. (J). pap. 13.95 *(978-1-84717-339-3(X))* O'Brien Pr., Ltd., The IRL. Dist: Dufour Editions, Inc.

—A Rosette for Maeve? McQuinn, Anna. 2014. (ENG.). 32p. (J). pap. 13.95 *(978-1-84717-340-9(3))* O'Brien Pr., Ltd., The IRL. Dist: Dufour Editions, Inc.

Young, Pippa. On the Farm. (Match & Twist Ser.). (J). 11.99 *(978-0-525-47054-0(9)*, Dutton Juvenile) Penguin Publishing Group.

Young, Ross. Show Me the Number: A Missouri Number Book. Young, Judy. rev. ed. 2007. (State Counting Ser.). (ENG.). 40p. (J). (gr. 1-7). 17.95 *(978-1-58536-156-4(9))* Sleeping Bear Pr.

Young, Sarah. Greek Myths. Turnbull, Ann. 2010. (ENG.). 168p. (J). (gr. 5). 18.99 *(978-0-7636-5111-4(7))* Candlewick Pr.

Young, Sarah. Endangered Animals: a 3D Pocket Guide. Young, Sarah. Candlewick Press Staff. 2014. (Panorama Pops Ser.). (ENG.). 30p. (J). (gr. k-4). 8.99 *(978-0-7636-6985-0(7))* Candlewick Pr.

—Ocean Creatures: a 3D Pocket Guide. Young, Sarah. Candlewick Press Staff. 2014. (Panorama Pops Ser.). (ENG.). 30p. (J). (gr. k-4). 8.99 *(978-0-7636-6802-0(8))* Candlewick Pr.

Young, Selina. Down in the Jungle. French, Vivian. 2013. (Early Reader Ser.). (ENG.). 96p. (J). (gr. 1-2). 7.99 *(978-1-4440-0513-4(8)*, Orion Children's Bks.) Hachette Children's Group GBR. Dist: Independent Pubs. Group.

—The Kitten with No Name. French, Vivian. 2013. (Early Reader Ser.). (ENG.). 64p. (J). (gr. 1-2). 7.99 *(978-1-4440-0078-8(0)*, Orion Children's Bks.) Hachette Children's Group GBR. Dist: Independent Pubs. Group.

—The Kitten with No Name. French, Vivian. 2010. (ENG.). 112p. 14.99 *(978-1-4440-0077-1(2))* Orion Publishing Group, Ltd. GBR. Dist: Hachette Bk. Group.

—Ladybird Ladybird. French, Vivian. 2003. 32p. pap. *(978-1-84255-284-1(8)*, Orion Children's Bks.) Hachette Children's Group.

Young, Shane, photos by. Princess Zelda & the Frog. Gardner, Carol. 2011. (ENG., 40p. (J). (gr. -1-3). 16.99 *(978-0-312-60325-0(8))* Feiwel & Friends.

Young, Shelley. Doc Broc's Cave Adventure. Young, Shelley. 2005. 44p. 19.95 *(978-1-58054-406-1(1))* Woodland Publishing, Inc.

Young, Skott. Spider-Man Legend of the Spider-Clan, 3 vols. Andrews, Kaare. 2003. (Mangaverse Ser.: Vol. 3). 128p. (YA). pap. 11.99 *(978-0-7851-1114-6(X))* Marvel Worldwide, Inc.

Young, Skottie. Fortunately, the Milk. Gaiman, Neil. (ENG.). 128p. (J). (gr. 3-7). 2014. pap. 5.99 *(978-0-06-222408-8(5))*; 2013. 14.99 *(978-0-06-222407-1(7))* HarperCollins Pubs.

—Human Torch: Burn. Kesel, Karl. 2004. (Fantastic Four Ser.). 144p. (YA). pap. 14.99 *(978-0-7851-1236-5(7))* Marvel Worldwide, Inc.

Young, Skottie. The Marvelous Land of Oz: Adapted from the Novel by L. Frank Baum. Shanower, Eric & Baum, L. Frank. 2014. (J). ***(978-1-61479-238-3(0))*** Spotlight.

Young, Skottie. Monstrous. Connolly, MarcyKate. 2015. (ENG.). 432p. (J). (gr. 3-7). 16.99 *(978-0-06-227271-3(3))* HarperCollins Pubs.

—Oz: The Marvelous Land of Oz. 2011. (ENG.). 200p. (J). (gr. -1-17). pap. 19.99 *(978-0-7851-4087-0(5))* Marvel Worldwide, Inc.

—Oz: The Wonderful Wizard of Oz. 2011. (ENG.). 216p. (J). (gr. -1-17). pap. 24.99 *(978-0-7851-2922-6(7))* Marvel Worldwide, Inc.

—Ozma of Oz. 2011. (ENG.). 200p. (J). (gr. -1-17). 29.99 *(978-0-7851-4247-8(9))* Marvel Worldwide, Inc.

Young, Skottie. The Wonderful Wizard of Oz. Shanower, Eric & Baum, L. Frank. 2014. 7p. (J). ***(978-1-61479-229-1(1))*** Spotlight.

Young, Steve. Coalition of Malice, Vol. 1. Karwowski, Chris. 2011. (ENG.). 64p. (J). (gr. 1). pap. 7.99 *(978-1-60886-678-6(5))* Boom! Studios.

—The Incredible Shrinking Allowance. Karwowski, Chris. 2011. (ENG.). 64p. (J). (gr. 1). pap. 7.99 *(978-1-60886-679-3(3))* Boom! Studios.

—Word Up Vol. 3. Karwowski, Chris & Serwacki, Anita. 2012. (ENG.). 64p. (J). pap. 7.99 *(978-1-60886-680-9(7))* Boom! Studios.

—WordGirl - Fashion Disaster, Vol. 4. Karwowski, Chris et al. 2012. (ENG.). 64p. (J). (gr. 1). pap. 7.99 *(978-1-60886-256-6(9))* Boom! Studios.

Young, Sue. Tommy Tractor Goes to the City, 1 vol. Ayers, Sanda. 2009. 29p. pap. 19.95 *(978-1-61582-054-2(X))* PublishAmerica, Inc.

Young, Susan. Piper & Pickle: Smile. Barton, Brittney B. 2013. 68p. 18.99 *(978-0-9856336-0-8(3))* P2 Publishing.

Young, Tim. Hellie & the Sensational Magic Carpet. Young, Helen Ann. 2013. 106p. pap. *(978-1-908353-02-3(3))* Young Editions.

Young, Tim Blair. Hello to Hellie's World. Young, Helen Ann. 2013. 46p. pap. *(978-1-908353-00-9(7))* Young Editions.

—Your World Discovery Scrapbook. Young, Helen Ann. 2013. 40p. pap. *(978-1-908353-03-0(1))* Young Editions.

Young-You, Lee. Moon Boy, Vol 1B. Young-You, Lee. Im, HyeYoung, tr. from KOR. 2006. (ENG.). 192p. (gr. 8-17). pap. 13.00 *(978-89-527-4604-7(X)*, Yen Pr.) Orbit.

Youngblood, Carol. Vacation Paws. Payne, Helen. 2006. 50p. per. 10.00 *(978-0-9786276-6-9(0))* Mentzer Printing Ink.

Youngblood, David W. Dr. Jim & the Special Stethoscope. Nicol, Scott Thomas. 2010. (Adventures of Dr. Jim Ser.). 32p. (J). pap. 12.95 *(978-0-9830355-7-2(1)*, Creative Hse. Kids Pr.) Bourgeois Media & Consulting.

Youngbluth, Chris. The South Overlook Oaks. Reardon, John. 2006. 119p. (J). (gr. 4-7). 16.95 *(978-1-931643-91-7(1))* Seven Locks Pr.

Yourell, Pam. Anya's Gift: A Tale of Two Christmases, 1 vol. Jones, Sandy. 2009. 48p. pap. 24.95 *(978-1-61546-129-5(9))* America Star Bks.

Youso, Justin & Kaino, Kim. The Twined Basket. McNutt, Nan. 2011. (Native American Art Activity Book Ser.). (ENG.). 56p. (J). (gr. 5-7). pap. 9.95 *(978-0-88240-760-9(0)*, West Winds Pr.) Graphic Arts Ctr. Publishing Co.

Youth of the Achuar Tribe of Ecuador. Nantu & Auju: How the Moon & the Potoo Bird Came to Be. Mayaprua, Alejandro Taish. 2005. (J). 15.95 *(978-0-9745477-0-1(0))* Arutam Pr.

Youtsey, Scott, jt. illus. see McCorkindale, Bruce.

Youzhi, He & Xiaofang, Ding. Stories Behind Chinese Idioms (II) Ma, Zheng & Li, Zheng. 2010. (ENG.). 48p. (J). (gr. 3-6). 16.95 *(978-1-60220-966-4(9))* BetterLink Pr., Inc.

Yu, Chao & Wang, Jue. Where the Buffalo Jump. Cook, Gerri. 2003. (Dinosaur Soup Ser.). 120p. (YA). (gr. 3-5). pap. 9.95 *(978-1-895836-95-0(6))* River Bks. CAN. Dist: Fitzhenry & Whiteside, Ltd.

Yu, Chao, jt. illus. see Bennett, Lorna.

Yu, Ji. A Dachshund's Wish. Tavano, Joe. 2006. (ENG.). 80p. (J). (gr. 2-4). pap. 16.99 *(978-0-9744287-1-0(X))* Minted Prose, LLC.

Yu, Sue Mi. Animal Paradise, 3 vols., Vol. 3. Yu, Sue Mi. 2007. (Animal Paradise Ser.: Vol. 3). 232p. pap. 9.95 *(978-1-59697-073-1(1))* Infinity Studios LLC.

Yudetamago. The Kinnikuman LegacyTM. Yudetamago. Yamazaki, Joe, tr. 2005. (Ultimate Muscle Ser.: Vol. 5). (ENG.). 232p. (YA). pap. 7.95 *(978-1-59116-426-5(5))* Viz Media.

—Ultimate Muscle. Yudetamago. (Ultimate Muscle Ser.). (ENG.). 3. 2004. 200p. (YA). pap. 7.95 *(978-1-59116-424-1(9))*; Vol. 2. 2004. 232p. pap. 7.95 *(978-1-59116-423-4(0))*; Vol. 10. 2006. 232p. pap. 7.95 *(978-1-4215-0223-6(2))*; Vol. 11. 2006. 208p. (gr. 11). pap. 7.95 *(978-1-4215-0417-9(0))*; Vol. 12. 2006. 208p. pap. 7.95 *(978-1-4215-0680-7(7))* Viz Media.

—Ultimate Muscle Vol. 6: Battle 6. Yudetamago. 2005. (Ultimate Muscle Ser.). (ENG.). 232p. (YA). pap. 7.95 *(978-1-59116-667-2(5))* Viz Media.

Yue, Stephanie. And Then There Were Gnomes. Venable, Colleen A. F. 2010. (Guinea PIG, Pet Shop Private Eye Ser.: 2). (ENG.). 48p. (J). (gr. 2-5). pap. 6.95 *(978-0-7613-5480-2(8)*, Graphic Universe); lib. bdg. 27.93 *(978-0-7613-4599-2(X))* Lerner Publishing Group.

—The Ferret's a Foot, 3 vols. Venable, Colleen A. F. 2011. (Guinea PIG, Pet Shop Private Eye Ser.: 3). (ENG.). 48p. (J). (gr. 2-5). 27.93 *(978-0-7613-5223-5(6))*; pap. 6.95 *(978-0-7613-5629-5(0)*, Graphic Universe) Lerner Publishing Group.

—Fish You Were Here, No. 4. Venable, Colleen A. F. 2011. (Guinea PIG, Pet Shop Private Eye Ser.: 4). (ENG.). 48p. (J). (gr. 2-5). pap. 6.95 *(978-0-7613-5630-1(4)*, Graphic Universe); lib. bdg. 27.93 *(978-0-7613-5224-2(4))* Lerner Publishing Group.

—Going, Going, Dragon! Venable, Colleen A. F. 2013. (Guinea PIG, Pet Shop Private Eye Ser.: 6). (ENG.). 48p. (J). (gr. 2-5). pap. 6.95 *(978-1-4677-0726-8(0))*; lib. bdg. 27.93 *(978-0-7613-6009-4(3))* Lerner Publishing Group. (Graphic Universe).

—Going, Going, Dragon! Venable, Colleen A. F. ed. 2013. (Guinea Pig, Pet Shop Private Eye Ser.: 6). (ENG.). 46p. lib. bdg. 17.15 *(978-0-606-33994-0(9)*, Turtleback) Turtleback Bks.

—Hamster & Cheese. Venable, Colleen A. F. 2010. (Guinea PIG, Pet Shop Private Eye Ser.: 1). (ENG.). 48p. (J). (gr. 2-5). pap. 6.95 *(978-0-7613-5479-6(4)*, Graphic Universe); lib. bdg. 27.93 *(978-0-7613-4598-5(1))* Lerner Publishing Group.

—Raining Cats & Detectives. Venable, Colleen A. F. 2012. (Guinea PIG, Pet Shop Private Eye Ser.: 5). (ENG.). 48p. (J). (gr. 2-5). pap. 6.95 *(978-0-7613-8541-7(X))*; lib. bdg. 27.93 *(978-0-7613-6008-7(5))* Lerner Publishing Group. (Graphic Universe).

—Raining Cats & Detectives. Venable, Colleen A. F. ed. 2012. (Guinea Pig, Pet Shop Private Eye Ser.: 5). lib. bdg. 17.15 *(978-0-606-26631-4(3)*, Turtleback) Turtleback Bks.

—Such a Little Mouse. Schertle, Alice. 2015. (ENG.). 32p. (J). (gr. -1-k). 16.99 *(978-0-545-64929-2(3))* Scholastic, Inc.

Yuen, Charles. Emeril's There's a Chef in My Soup! Recipes for the Kid in Everyone. Lagasse, Emeril. 2005. (ENG.). 256p. (J). 28.99 *(978-0-688-17706-5(9))* HarperCollins Pubs.

Yuen Jr., Sammy, jt. illus. see Yuen, Sammy, Jr.

Yuen, Sammy. Incarceron. Fisher, Catherine. November, S., ed. 2011. (ENG.). 464p. (YA). (gr. 7-18). pap. 10.99 *(978-0-14-241852-9(8)*, Puffin) Penguin Publishing Group.

Yuen, Sammy, Jr. & Yuen Jr., Sammy. Expedition to Pine Hollow. Decter, Ed. 2007. (Outriders Ser.: 3). (ENG.). 240p. (J). (gr. 3-7). pap. 11.99 *(978-1-4169-1307-8(6)*, Simon & Schuster/Paula Wiseman Bks.) Simon & Schuster/Paula Wiseman Bks.

Yuen Wong Yu. Digimon, 5 vols., Vol. 1. Hongo, Akiyoshi. 2003. 164p. (gr. 2-18). pap. 9.99 *(978-1-59182-076-5(6))* TOKYOPOP, Inc.

Yuji, Iwahara. Quest. Watson, Andi. 2004. (Marvel Heroes Ser.). 120p. (YA). pap. 13.99 *(978-0-7851-1298-3(7))* Marvel Worldwide, Inc.

Yuki, Kaori. Angel Sanctuary. Yuki, Kaori. Roman, Annette, ed. 2007. (Angel Sanctuary Ser.: 19). (ENG.). 200p. pap. 9.99 *(978-1-4215-0977-8(6))* Viz Media.

—Angel Sanctuary. Yuki, Kaori. Wolfman, Marv. (Angel Sanctuary Ser.). (ENG.). Vol. 1. 2004. 198p. pap. 9.95 *(978-1-59116-245-2(9))*; Vol. 2. 2004. 192p. pap. 9.95 *(978-1-59116-312-1(9))*; Vol. 3. 2004. 192p. pap. 9.95 *(978-1-59116-392-3(7))*; Vol. 4. 2004. 192p. pap. 9.95 *(978-1-59116-495-1(8))*; Vol. 5. 2004. 192p. pap. 9.99 *(978-1-59116-576-7(8))*; Vol. 6. 2005. 200p. pap. 9.99 *(978-1-59116-627-6(6))*; Vol. 8. 2005. 200p. pap. 9.99 *(978-1-59116-799-0(X))* Viz Media.

—Angel Sanctuary. Yuki, Kaori. 2005. (Angel Sanctuary Ser.). (ENG.). 200p. Vol. 9. pap. 9.99 *(978-1-59116-862-1(7))*; Vol. 10. (gr. 11). pap. 9.99 *(978-1-4215-0058-4(2))* Viz Media.

—Angel Sanctuary. Yuki, Kaori. Wolfman, Marv. (Angel Sanctuary Ser.). (ENG.). 192p. (gr. 11). Vol. 11. 2005. pap. 9.99 *(978-1-4215-0126-0(0))*; Vol. 12. 2006. pap. 9.99 *(978-1-4215-0259-5(3))* Viz Media.

—Angel Sanctuary. Yuki, Kaori. 2006. (Angel Sanctuary Ser.). (ENG.). Vol. 13. 192p. pap. 9.99 *(978-1-4215-0389-9(1))*; Vol. 14. 192p. pap. 9.99 *(978-1-4215-0520-6(7))*; Vol. 15. 208p. pap. 9.99 *(978-1-4215-0521-3(5))* Viz Media.

—Godchild. Yuki, Kaori. 2006. (GodChild Ser.). (ENG.). 208p. Vol. 1. pap. 9.99 *(978-1-4215-0233-5(X))*; Vol. 2. pap. 8.99 *(978-1-4215-0237-3(2))* Viz Media.

—Godchild, Vol. 7. Yuki, Kaori. Bates, Megan, ed. 2007. (GodChild Ser.: 7). (ENG.). 200p. pap. 8.99 *(978-1-4215-1134-4(7))* Viz Media.

—Grand Guignol Orchestra. Yuki, Kaori. 2011. (Grand Guignol Orchestra Ser.: 3). (ENG.). 208p. pap. 9.99 *(978-1-4215-3797-9(4))*; Vol. 2. 192p. pap. 9.99 *(978-1-4215-3637-8(4))* Viz Media.

—The Sound of a Boy Hatching. Yuki, Kaori. 2006. (Cain Saga Ser.: 2). (ENG.). 208p. pap. 8.99 *(978-1-59116-977-2(1))* Viz Media.

Yuki, Kaori & Tamura, Yumi. Angel Sanctuary, Vol. 7. Yuki, Kaori & Tamura, Yumi. Wolfman, Marv. 2005. (Angel Sanctuary Ser.). (ENG.). 200p. (gr. 11-17). pap. 9.99 *(978-1-59116-745-7(0))* Viz Media.

Yulia, Lushnikova. Moush Wants to Get Lost. Baghdasaryan, Rouzanna. 2010. 32p. (J). (POL & ENG.). pap. 16.95 *(978-1-60195-103-8(5))*; (ARA.). pap. 16.95 *(978-1-60195-091-8(8))* International Step by Step Assn.

Yuly, Toni. Early Bird. Yuly, Toni. (ENG.). (J). (— 1). 2015. 16p. bds. 7.99 *(978-1-250-05706-8(X))*; 2014. 40p. 15.99 *(978-1-250-04327-6(1))* Feiwel & Friends.

—Night Owl. Yuly, Toni. 2015. (ENG.). 40p. (J). (— 1). 15.99 *(978-1-250-05457-9(5))* Feiwel & Friends.

Yum, Hyewon. The Fun Book of Scary Stuff. Jenkins, Emily. 2015. (ENG.). 32p. (J). (gr. -1-1). 16.99 *(978-0-374-30000-5(3)*, Farrar, Straus & Giroux (BYR)) Farrar, Straus & Giroux.

Yum, Hyewon. Mom, It's My First Day of Kindergarten!, 1 vol. Yum, Hyewon. 2012. (ENG.). 36p. (J). (gr. -1-2). 16.99 *(978-0-374-35004-8(3)*, Farrar, Straus & Giroux (BYR)) Farrar, Straus & Giroux.

—This Is Our House. Yum, Hyewon. 2013. (ENG.). 36p. (J). (gr. -1-2). 16.99 *(978-0-374-37487-7(2)*, Farrar, Straus & Giroux (BYR)) Farrar, Straus & Giroux.

—The Twins' Blanket. Yum, Hyewon. 2011. (ENG.). 40p. (J). (gr. -1-1). 17.99 *(978-0-374-37972-8(6)*, Farrar, Straus & Giroux (BYR)) Farrar, Straus & Giroux.

—The Twins' Little Sister. Yum, Hyewon. 2014. (ENG.). 40p. (J). (gr. -1-1). 17.99 *(978-0-374-37973-5(4)*, Farrar, Straus & Giroux (BYR)) Farrar, Straus & Giroux.

Yun, Mi-Kyung. Bride of the Water God Volume 13. Yun, Mi-Kyung. Simon, Philip, ed. 2013. (ENG.). 176p. pap. 9.99 *(978-1-61655-072-1(4))* Dark Horse Comics.

—Bride of the Water God Volume 14. Yun, Mi-Kyung. Simon, Philip, ed. 2013. (ENG.). 168p. pap. 9.99 *(978-1-61655-187-2(9))* Dark Horse Comics.

—Bride of the Water God Volume 4. Yun, Mi-Kyung. 2009. (ENG.). 176p. pap. 9.99 *(978-1-59582-378-6(6))* Dark Horse Comics.

Yung Yoo, Sun. The Red Shoes. Andersen, Hans Christian & Fowler, Gloria. 2008. (ENG.). 32p. (J). (gr. -1-3). 16.95 *(978-1-934429-06-8(6))* AMMO Bks., LLC.

Yunger, Joshua. Wobar & the Quest for the Magic Calumet. Homeyer, Henry. 2012. (ENG.). 144p. (YA). (gr. 3-7). 19.95 *(978-1-59373-108-3(6))* Bunker Hill Publishing, Inc.

Yura, Kairi. The Story of Saiunkoku. Yukino, Sai. 2010. (Story of Saiunkoku Ser.: 1). (ENG.). 176p. pap. 9.99 *(978-1-4215-3834-1(2))* Viz Media.

Yuricich, Jillian Grace. What did Grandma See? 2006. (J). lib. bdg. 15.99 *(978-0-9774696-0-4(3))* Gilboy Publishing.

Yurksaitis, Stephanie. Genevieve the Singing Ladybug. Yurksaitis, Anne. 2013. 28p. pap. 24.95 *(978-1-63000-927-4(X))* America Star Bks.
—The Ingle Bingle. Yurksaitis, Anne. 2012. 16p. pap. 24.95 *(978-1-4626-7687-3(1))* America Star Bks.
Yutenji, Ako. Liling Po, Vol. 1. Yutenji, Ako. 2005. 208p. pap. 14.99 *(978-1-59532-519-8(0),* Tokyopop Adult) TOKYOPOP, Inc.
—Liling-Po, Vol. 3. Yutenji, Ako. 3rd rev. ed. 2005. (Liling-Po Ser.). 192p. per. 14.99 *(978-1-59532-521-1(2),* Tokyopop Adult) TOKYOPOP, Inc.
Yutenji, Ako. Liling-PO, Vol. 2. Yutenji, Ako, creator. rev. ed. 2005. 200p. pap. 14.99 *(978-1-59532-520-4(4),* Tokyopop Adult) TOKYOPOP, Inc.
Yuu, Lee Young. Kill Me, Kiss Me, 5 vols., Vol. 5. Yuu, Lee Young. rev. ed. 2005. 184p. pap. 9.99 *(978-1-59532-420-7(8))* TOKYOPOP, Inc.
Yuzuru & Kanako. Point Blank. Horowitz, Anthony & Johnston, Antony. 2007. (Alex Rider Ser.). (ENG.). 144p. (J). (gr. 5-18). 14.99 *(978-0-399-25026-2(3),* Philomel) Penguin Publishing Group.
Yuzuru, jt. illus. see Kanako.
Yvonne, Symank. Chaves Memories los Recuerdos de Chave. Isabel, Delgado Maria. 2008. 32p. *(978-1-55885-244-0(1),* Piñata Books) Arte Publico Pr.

Z

Zabala, Javier. El Gato con Botas. Maestro, Pepe. 2010. (SPA.). (J). (gr. 1-6). *(978-84-263-7385-4(2))* Vives, Luis Editorial (Edelvives).
Zabarylo-Duma, Ewa. Teddy's Christmas Wish. deVet, L. J. 2013. (J). (ENG.). 48p. *(978-0-9873686-0-7(5));* (ENG.). 48p. pap. *(978-0-9873686-1-4(3));* 46p. pap. *(978-0-9873686-5-2(6))* Print-Rite Publishers.
Zabel, Randy & Broesch, Valerie. Al-the-Gator & Freddy Frog. 2007. 48p. (J). per. 18.99 *(978-0-9797513-0-1(6))* 4RV Publishing, LLC.
Zaboski, Dave. You with the Stars in Your Eyes: A Little Girl's Glimpse at Cosmic Consciousness. Chopra, Deepak. 2010. (ENG & ABK.). 35p. 14.95 *(978-1-4019-2711-0(4))* Hay Hse., Inc.
Zaboski, Dave. Gideon's Dream: A Tale of New Beginnings. Zaboski, Dave, Dychtwald, Ken et al. 2008. 40p. (J). (gr. -1-3). lib. bdg. 17.89 *(978-0-06-143498-3(1))* HarperCollins Pubs.
Zabriskie, Judy Mehn. Freckles: The Mystery of the Little White Dog in the Desert. Howey, Paul M. 2003. 72p. (gr. 2-5). lib. bdg. 14.95 *(978-0-9677292-1-3(1))* AZTexts Publishing, Inc.
Zacchi, Lucia. El Himno de las Ranas. Cross, Elsa. 2005. (SPA.). (J). (gr. k-2). pap. 10.95 *(978-968-494-052-9(1),* CI2003) Centro de Informacion y Desarrollo de la Comunicacion y la Literatura MEX. Dist: Iaconi, Mariuccia Bk. Imports, Lectorum Pubns., Inc.
Zacker, Sandi. The Adventures of Saleiah & Emm: Book 1. Alvarado, I. J. 2009. 16p. pap. 11.99 *(978-1-4490-0515-3(2))* AuthorHouse.
Zaffo, George J. The How & Why Wonder Book of MacHines. Gulkin, Sidney & Notkin, Jerome J. 2011. 48p. pap. 35.95 *(978-1-258-10533-4(0))* Literary Licensing, LLC.
Zagarenski, Pamela. ¿Dónde Me Escondo? American Heritage Dictionary Editors, ed. 2005. (Good Beginnings/Un Buen Comienzo Ser.).Tr. of Where Am I Hiding?. (SPA & ENG.). 4p. (J). (gr. -1 — 1). bds. 3.95 *(978-0-618-51176-1(8))* Houghton Mifflin Harcourt Publishing Co.
—My Very Own Big Spanish Dictionary. American Heritage Dictionary Editors, ed. 2005. (ENG & SPA.). 48p. (J). (gr. -1-k). 12.95 *(978-0-618-62126-2(1))* Houghton Mifflin Harcourt Publishing Co.
—Qué Día Es? American Heritage Dictionary Editors. 2005. (Good Beginnings/Un Buen Comienzo Ser.).Tr. of What Day Is It?. (SPA.). 4p. (J). (— 1). bds. 3.95 *(978-0-618-44874-6(8))* Houghton Mifflin Harcourt Publishing Co.
—Qué Juego? American Heritage Dictionary Editors, ed. 2004. (Good Beginnings Ser.).Tr. of What Am I Playing?. (SPA & ENG.). 4p. (J). (gr. k — 1). bds. 3.95 *(978-0-618-44375-8(4))* Houghton Mifflin Harcourt Publishing Co.
—Red Sings from Treetops: A Year in Colors. Sidman, Joyce. 2009. (ENG.). 32p. (J). (gr. -1-3). 17.99 *(978-0-547-01494-4(5))* Houghton Mifflin Harcourt Publishing Co.
—Sleep Like a Tiger. Logue, Mary. 2012. (ENG.). 40p. (J). (gr. -1-3). 17.99 *(978-0-547-64102-7(8))* Houghton Mifflin Harcourt Publishing Co.
—This Is Just to Say: Poems of Apology & Forgiveness. Sidman, Joyce. 2007. (ENG.). 48p. (J). (gr. 5-7). 16.99 *(978-0-618-61680-0(2))* Houghton Mifflin Harcourt Publishing Co.
—What Can I Do When It Rains? American Heritage Dictionary Editors, ed. 2004. (Good Beginnings Ser.). (ENG.). 4p. (J). (gr. -1 — 1). bds. 3.95 *(978-0-618-43170-0(5))* Houghton Mifflin Harcourt Publishing Co.
—What Can I Do When It Rains? (Qué Puedo Hacer Cuando Llueve?) American Heritage Dictionary Editors, ed. ed. 2004. (Good Beginnings Ser.). (SPA & ENG.). 4p. (J). (gr. k — 1). bds. 3.95 *(978-0-618-44376-5(2))* Houghton Mifflin Harcourt Publishing Co.
—What Day Is It? American Heritage Dictionary Editors. 2005. (Good Beginnings Ser.). (ENG.). 4p. (J). (gr. -1 — 1). bds. 3.95 *(978-0-618-45714-4(3))* Houghton Mifflin Harcourt Publishing Co.
—What the Heart Knows: Chants, Charms, & Blessings. Sidman, Joyce. 2013. (ENG.). 80p. (J). (gr. 7). 16.99 *(978-0-544-10616-1(4))* Houghton Mifflin Harcourt Publishing Co.
—Where Am I Hiding? American Heritage Dictionary Editors. 2005. (Good Beginnings Ser.).Tr. of ¿Donde Me Escondo?. (ENG.). 4p. (J). (gr. -1-k). bds. 3.95 *(978-0-618-45715-1(1))* Houghton Mifflin Harcourt Publishing Co.
Zagnoli, Olimpia. Mister Horizontal & Miss Vertical. Révah, Noémie. 2014. (ENG.). 48p. (J). (gr. -1-3). 17.95 *(978-1-59270-161-2(2))* Enchanted Lion Bks., LLC.
—The World Belongs to You. Bozzi, Riccardo. 2013. (ENG.). 40p. (J). (gr. 3-7). 14.99 *(978-0-7636-6488-6(X),* Templar) Candlewick Pr.
Zahares, Wade. Frosty the Snowman. 2013. (ENG.). 28p. (J). (gr. -1-3). 17.95 *(978-1-62354-012-8(7),* Yarrow, Peter Bks.) Charlesbridge Publishing, Inc.
—Liberty Rising: The Story of the Statue of Liberty. Shea, Pegi Deitz. 2013. (ENG.). 40p. (J). (gr. k-4). 7.99 *(978-1-250-02720-7(9))* Square Fish.
—Red Are the Apples. Harshman, Marc & Ryan, Cheryl. 2007. (ENG.). 32p. (J). (gr. -1-3). pap. 6.99 *(978-0-15-206065-7(0))* Houghton Mifflin Harcourt Publishing Co.
Zaharias, Terrilynn. The Duckie Walk. Hoercher, Donald F. 2011. 28p. pap. 12.50 *(978-1-60976-912-3(0),* Eloquent Bks.) Strategic Book Publishing & Rights Agency (SBPRA).
Zahedi, Morteza. Good Night, Commander, 1 vol. Akbarpour, Ahmad. Eskandani, Shadi & Mixter, Helen, trs. from PER. 2010. (ENG.). 24p. (J). (gr. 1). 17.95 *(978-0-88899-989-4(5))* Groundwood Bks. CAN. Dist: Perseus-PGW.
Zahler, Thomas F. Twilight Sparkle. 2015. (J). ***(978-1-61479-336-6(0))*** Spotlight.
Zahn, Ellsworth E. Dudley. Zahn, Ellsworth E. 2012. (ENG.). 44p. (J). (gr. -1-k). 15.95 *(978-0-9637308-1-7(9))* Marion Street Pr., LLC.
Zahnd, Mark. Ridiculous Knock-Knocks. Tait, Chris. 2010. (ENG.). 96p. (J). pap. 4.95 *(978-1-4027-7852-0(X))* Sterling Publishing Co., Inc.
—Ridiculous Riddles. Tait, Chris. 2010. (ENG.). 96p. (J). pap. 4.95 *(978-1-4027-7853-7(8))* Sterling Publishing Co., Inc.
Zahradka, Miroslav. The Un-Terrible Tiger. Zahradka, Miroslav. 32p. (J). (gr. -1-3). 12.95 *(978-0-87592-056-6(X))* Scroll Pr., Inc.
Zaidi, Ishan. Keep Counting. 2010. (J). *(978-1-60617-145-5(3))* Teaching Strategies, Inc.
Zaidi, Nadeem. Agua Por Todas Partes. Del Moral, Susana. 2006. (SPA.). 8p. (J). (gr. -1). *(978-970-718-452-7(3),* Silver Dolphin en Español) Advanced Marketing, S. de R. L. de C. V. MEX. Dist: Perseus-PGW.
—Animales a Tu Alrededor. Singer, Marilyn. 2004. (Baby Einstein Ser.). (SPA.). 16p. (J). bds. *(978-970-718-152-6(4),* Silver Dolphin en Español) Advanced Marketing, S. de R. L. de C. V.
—Asomate y Ve Las Figuras. Aigner-Clark, Julie. 2004. (Baby Einstein Ser.). (SPA.). 16p. (J). bds. *(978-970-718-151-9(6),* Silver Dolphin en Español) Advanced Marketing, S. de R. L. de C. V.
—Asomate Y Ve Los Numeros. Aigner-Clark, Julie. 2004. (Baby Einstein Ser.). (SPA.). 16p. (J). bds. *(978-970-718-150-2(8),* Silver Dolphin en Español) Advanced Marketing, S. de R. L. de C. V.
—Baby Da Vinci, Mi Cuerpo. Del Moral, Susana. 2006. (Baby Einstein Ser.). (SPA.). 6p. (J). (gr. -1-k). bds. *(978-970-718-455-8(8),* Silver Dolphin en Español) Advanced Marketing, S. de R. L. de C. V. MEX. Dist: Perseus-PGW.
—Baby Einstein Colores: Libro con Ventanas. Aigner-Clark, Julie. 2007. (Baby Einstein Ser.). 5p. (J). (gr. -1). *(978-970-718-469-5(8),* Silver Dolphin en Español) Advanced Marketing, S. de R. L. de C. V.
—Baby Einstein: on the Farm. Aigner-Clark, Julie. 2007. (Baby Einstein Ser.). (ENG.). *(978-0-7634-2150-2(2))* Walt Disney Records.
—Baby Einstein Poemas Preciosos: Pretty Poems & Wonderful Words. Aigner-Clark, Julie. 2004. (SPA.). 10p. (J). 9.95 *(978-970-718-210-3(5),* Silver Dolphin Bks.) Baker & Taylor Publishing Group.
—Baby Mozart: Musica Por Todas Partes. 2005. (Baby Einstein: Libros de Carton Ser.). (SPA.). 16p. (J). (gr. -1). bds. *(978-970-718-309-4(8),* Silver Dolphin en Español) Advanced Marketing, S. de R. L. de C. V.
—La Casa de Violet. Del Moral, Susana. 2005. (Baby Einstein: Libros de Carton Ser.). (SPA.). 10p. (J). (gr. -1). bds. *(978-970-718-305-6(5),* Silver Dolphin en Español) Advanced Marketing, S. de R. L. de C. V.
—Como Me Siento. Del Moral, Susana. 2005. (Baby Einstein: Libros de Carton Ser.). (SPA.). 14p. (J). (gr. -1). bds. *(978-970-718-308-7(X),* Silver Dolphin en Español) Advanced Marketing, S. de R. L. de C. V.
—Formas: Libro con Ventanas. 2007. (Baby Einstein Ser.). 5p. (J). (gr. -1). *(978-970-718-468-8(X),* Silver Dolphin en Español) Advanced Marketing, S. de R. L. de C. V.
—Fun with Animals Friendship Box. Singer, Marilyn. 2009. (J). *(978-1-4231-2797-0(8)); (978-1-4231-2798-7(6)); (978-1-4231-2799-4(4))* Disney Pr.
—El Juego de las Formas. Del Moral, Susana. 2005. (Baby Einstein: Libros de Carton Ser.). (SPA.). 6p. (J). (gr. -1). bds. *(978-970-718-303-2(9),* Silver Dolphin en Español) Advanced Marketing, S. de R. L. de C. V.
—Las Rimas de Bard: Un Libro con Ventanas. Del Moral, Susana. 2005. (Baby Einstein: Libros de Carton Ser.). (SPA.). 16p. (J). (gr. -1). bds. *(978-970-718-304-9(7),* Silver Dolphin en Español) Advanced Marketing, S. de R. L. de C. V.
—Master Pieces. Aigner-Clark, Julie. 2004. (SPA.). 10p. (J). 9.95 *(978-970-718-211-0(3),* Silver Dolphin Bks.) Baker & Taylor Publishing Group.
—El Mundo A Mi Alrededor: El Cielo. Del Moral, Susana. 2005. (Baby Einstein: Libros de Carton Ser.). (SPA.). 12p. (J). (gr. -1). bds. *(978-970-718-312-4(8),* Silver Dolphin en Español) Advanced Marketing, S. de R. L. de C. V.
—El Mundo a Mi Alrededor: El Oceano. Silver Dolphin en Espanol Editors. 2007. (Baby Einstein Ser.). (SPA.). 12p. (J). (gr. -1). bds. *(978-970-718-457-2(4),* Silver Dolphin en Español) Advanced Marketing, S. de R. L. de C. V. MEX. Dist: Perseus-PGW.
—Un Paseo Por la Selva. Del Moral, Susana. 2005. (Baby Einstein: Libros de Carton Ser.). (SPA.). 10p. (J). (gr. -1). bds. *(978-970-718-306-3(3),* Silver Dolphin en Español) Advanced Marketing, S. de R. L. de C. V.
—Que Flota? Un Libro para Banarse y Disfrutar. Del Moral, Susana. 2006. (Baby Einstein Ser.). (SPA.). 8p. (J). (gr. -1). *(978-970-718-453-4(1),* Silver Dolphin en Español) Advanced Marketing, S. de R. L. de C. V. MEX. Dist: Perseus-PGW.
—Una Ventana Al Color. Aigner-Clark, Julie. 2007. (Baby Einstein Ser.). 10p. (J). (gr. -1-k). *(978-970-718-454-1(X),* Silver Dolphin en Español) Advanced Marketing, S. de R. L. de C. V.
Zaikina, Maria. The Greedy Sparrow: An Armenian Tale, 0 vols. Kasbarian, Lucine. 2011. (ENG.). 32p. (J). (gr. -1-3). 17.99 *(978-0-7614-5821-0(2),* 9780761458210, Amazon Children's Publishing) Amazon Publishing.
Zak, Drahos. The Pied Piper of Hamelin. Holden, Robert. 2004. 28p. (J). (gr. k-4). reprint ed. 15.00 *(978-0-7567-7686-2(4))* DIANE Publishing Co.
Zakanitch, Robert Rahway. Our Farm: By the Animals of Farm Sanctuary. Gottfried, Maya. 2010. (ENG.). 40p. (J). (gr. k-3). 17.99 *(978-0-375-86118-5(1))* Knopf, Alfred A. Inc.
Zalben, Jane Breskin. Mousterpiece. Zalben, Jane Breskin. 2012. (ENG.). 36p. (J). (gr. -1-2). 16.99 *(978-1-59643-549-0(6))* Roaring Brook Pr.
—Papa's Latkes. Zalben, Jane Breskin. 2013. (ENG.). 32p. (J). (gr. -1-1). 6.99 *(978-1-250-04668-0(8))* Square Fish.
—Pearl's Eight Days of Chanukah. Zalben, Jane Breskin. 2003. 40p. (J). (gr. -1-3). lib. bdg. 15.30 *(978-0-613-88073-2(0),* Turtleback) Turtleback Bks.
—Pearl's Eight Days of Chanukah: With a Story & Activity for Each Night. Zalben, Jane Breskin. 2012. (ENG.). 48p. (J). (gr. -1-3). 22.99 *(978-1-4424-7294-5(4),* Simon & Schuster Bks. For Young Readers) Simon & Schuster Bks. For Young Readers.
—Saturday Night at the Beastro. Zalben, Jane Breskin. 2004. 40p. (J). (gr. 2-4). lib. bdg. 16.89 *(978-0-06-029228-7(8))* HarperCollins Pubs.
Zalevskaya, Anastacia. Real Girls' Guide to Everything: That Makes It Awesome to Be a Girl! Brereton, Erin. 2011. (ENG.). 192p. (J). pap. 12.95 *(978-1-60078-561-0(1))* Triumph Bks.
Zalewski, Todd. Woolly Mammoths. Wadsworth, Ginger. (On My Own Science Ser.). (ENG.). 48p. (gr. 2-4). 2007. per. 6.95 *(978-0-8225-6447-8(5),* First Avenue Editions); 2006. lib. bdg. 25.26 *(978-1-57505-879-5(0),* Millbrook Pr.) Lerner Publishing Group.
Zalme, Ron. Diego's Buzzing Bee Adventure. Inches, Alison. 2008. (Go, Diego, Go! Ser.: 7). (ENG.). 24p. (J). (gr. -1-1). pap. 3.99 *(978-1-4169-4776-9(0),* Simon Spotlight/Nickelodeon) Simon Spotlight/Nickelodeon.
—Hooray for Best Friends! Golden Books Staff. 2006. (Deluxe Coloring Book Ser.). (ENG.). 96p. (J). (gr. -1-2). pap. 3.99 *(978-0-375-83981-8(X),* Golden Bks.) Random Hse. Children's Bks.
—How to Draw Nintendo Greatest Heroes & Villains. 2007. *(978-0-439-91324-9(1))* Scholastic, Inc.
—How to Draw Sinnoh Superstars. 2010. 32p. (J). pap. *(978-0-545-22625-7(2))* Scholastic, Inc.
—A Humpback Whale Tale. 2006. (Go, Diego, Go! Ser.: Vol. 2). (ENG.). 24p. (J). (gr. -1-2). pap. 3.99 *(978-1-4169-1511-9(7),* Simon Spotlight/Nickelodeon) Simon Spotlight/Nickelodeon.
—It's Sharing Day! Larsen, Kirsten. 2007. (SPA & ENG.). (J). pap. *(978-0-439-92237-1(2),* Scholastic) Scholastic, Inc.
—It's Sharing Day! Larsen, Kirsten. 2007. (Dora the Explorer Ser.: 22). (ENG.). 24p. (J). pap. 3.99 *(978-1-4169-1575-1(3),* Simon Spotlight/Nickelodeon) Simon Spotlight/Nickelodeon.
—Pokémon: How to Draw Unova Heroes. 2011. 31p. (J). pap. *(978-0-545-35086-0(7))* Scholastic, Inc.
—Rainy Day Tales. 2009. (J). *(978-1-59078-734-2(X))* Highlights for Children.
—Sunny Day Tales. 2009. (J). *(978-1-59078-735-9(8))* Highlights for Children.
Zaman, Farida. The Magic Braid. Singh, Rina. Date not set. 134p. (J). pap. *(978-0-920813-25-6(9))* Sister Vision Pr.
—Nearly Nonsense: Hoja Tales from Turkey. Singh, Rina. 2011. (ENG.). 48p. (J). (gr. k-3). 17.95 *(978-0-88776-974-0(8))* Tundra Bks. CAN. Dist: Random Hse., Inc.
—Two Shoes, Blue Shoes, New Shoes!, 1 vol. Fitz-Gibbon, Sally. 2005. (ENG.). 32p. (J). (gr. -1-3). pap. 7.95 *(978-1-55041-731-9(2),* 1550417312) Fitzhenry & Whiteside, Ltd. CAN. Dist: Midpoint Trade Bks., Inc.
—The Yoga Game. Beliveau, Kathy. 2012. (ENG.). 42p. (J). (gr. -1-2). pap. 9.95 *(978-1-897476-72-7(8))* Simply Read Bks. CAN. Dist: Ingram Pub. Services.
Zaman, Farida, jt. illus. see Jamana, Pharida.
Zamanian, Marjan. Celebrating Norouz (Persian New Year) Jalali, Yassaman. 2003. 28p. (J). (gr. -1-6). pap. 12.99 *(978-0-9728020-0-0(2))* Saman Publishing.
Zamazing, Cherie. Birthdays Around the World, 1 vol. Dale, Jay. 2012. (Engage Literacy Yellow Ser.). (ENG.). 32p. (gr. k-2). pap. 5.99 *(978-1-4296-8966-3(8),* Engage Literacy) Capstone Pr., Inc.
—Let's Make a Boat, 1 vol. Dale, Jay. 2012. (Wonder Words Ser.). (ENG.). 32p. (gr. k-2). pap. 5.99 *(978-1-4296-8916-8(1),* Engage Literacy) Capstone Pr., Inc.
—Letter to Sam, 1 vol. Dale, Jay. 2012. (Engage Literacy Green Ser.). (ENG.). 32p. (gr. k-2). pap. 5.99 *(978-1-4296-9033-1(X),* Engage Literacy) Capstone Pr., Inc.
—Off You Go!, 1 vol. Dale, Jay. 2012. (Wonder Words Ser.). (ENG.). 32p. (gr. k-2). pap. 5.99 *(978-1-4296-8910-6(2),* Engage Literacy) Capstone Pr., Inc.
Zambarano, Richard. Wilbur & Wilma's Colorful Campus Tour - University of Arizona A-Z. 2004. (J). 9.99 *(978-1-933069-02-9(3))* Odd Duck Ink, Inc.
Zamboni, David. Balloon Blessing. Marie, Jill Jana. 2008. 28p. pap. 12.95 *(978-0-9820479-7-2(5))* Peppertree Pr., The.
—The Enchanted Tree. Heller, Donna & Payne, James. 2007. 44p. per. 14.95 *(978-1-934246-72-6(7))* Peppertree Pr., The.
—Finnigan the Dragon. Howell, Julie Ann. 2009. 24p. pap. 12.95 *(978-1-936051-61-8(3))* Peppertree Pr., The.
—The True Meaning of Christmas, the Greatest Gift of All. Alpert, Barbara. 2009. 24p. pap. 12.95 *(978-1-936051-18-2(4))* Peppertree Pr., The.
—Zoo Rendezvous. Marie, Jill Jana. 2008. 24p. pap. 12.95 *(978-0-9817572-9-2(4))* Peppertree Pr., The.
Zampino, Phil. Brush Beats: Different Brush Beats Rhythms & Sounds on the Drum Set. Zampino, Phil. 2004. 25p. (YA). (gr. 5-18). pap. 11.50 *(978-0-942253-29-0(9))* PAZ Publishing.
Zanier, Christian, et al. Crypt-Keeping It Real. Van Lente, Fred et al. Kaplan, Ari et al. 4th ed. 2008. (Tales from the Crypt Graphic Novels Ser.: 4). (ENG.). 112p. (J). (gr. 5-12). pap. 7.95 *(978-1-59707-104-8(8))* Papercutz.
Zanotta, Roberta, jt. illus. see Storino, Sara.
Zapater Oliva, Carlos & Depew, Robert. Bathtime with Bubbles. Friden, Chris. 2008. (J). *(978-0-9801849-2-1(4))* Haydenburri Lane.
Zapater Oliva, Carlos & Glazier, Garth. Pajamatime with P.J. Friden, Chris. 2008. (J). *(978-0-9758785-9-0(X));* *(978-0-9801849-5-2(9))* Haydenburri Lane.
—Sleepytime with Rory. Friden, Chris. 2008. (J). *(978-0-9801849-1-4(6))* Haydenburri Lane.
Zarate, Jesus, jt. illus. see de Oaxaco, Jesus.
Zarb, Mike. Mr. Da Vinci's Time Machine. Gold, Robin. 2010. (Belmont & the Dragon Ser.: 3). (ENG.). 48p. (J). (gr. 2-4). pap. 6.99 *(978-1-74166-442-3(X))* Random Hse. Australia AUS. Dist: Independent Pubs. Group.
—Pearlie & Opal. Harmer, Wendy. 2014. (Pearlie Ser.: 3). (ENG.). 48p. (Orig.). (J). (gr. 2-4). pap. 7.99 *(978-1-74051-890-1(X))* Random Hse. Australia AUS. Dist: Independent Pubs. Group.
—Pearlie & the Big Doll. Harmer, Wendy. 2014. (Pearlie Ser.: 2). (ENG.). 48p. (Orig.). (J). (gr. 2-4). pap. 7.99 *(978-1-74051-889-5(6))* Random Hse. Australia AUS. Dist: Independent Pubs. Group.
—Pearlie & the Lost Handbag. Harmer, Wendy. 2014. (Pearlie Ser.: 4). (ENG.). 48p. (Orig.). (J). (gr. 2-4). pap. 7.99 *(978-1-74166-102-6(1))* Random Hse. Australia AUS. Dist: Independent Pubs. Group.
—Pearlie in the Park. Harmer, Wendy. 10th anniv. ed. 2014. (Pearlie Ser.: 1). (ENG.). 48p. (Orig.). (J). (gr. 2-4). pap. 7.99 *(978-1-74275-938-6(6))* Random Hse. Australia AUS. Dist: Independent Pubs. Group.
Zarb, Mike & Taylor, Gypsy. Pearlie & Jasper. Harmer, Wendy. 2014. (Pearlie Ser.: 5). (ENG.). 48p. (Orig.). (J). (gr. 2-4). pap. 7.99 *(978-1-74166-011-1(4))* Random Hse. Australia AUS. Dist: Independent Pubs. Group.
Zarb, Mike, jt. illus. see Taylor, Gypsy.
Zareba, Lukasz. Where Do My Prayers Go? Lee, Stephi. 2013. (ENG.). 32p. (J). 14.95 *(978-0-578-11938-0(2))* Stephi /Lee.
Zarraonandia, Thomas. Johnny Jingle. Zarraonandia, Thomas. 2nd ed. 2003. 30p. (J). (gr. -1-7). per. 20.00 *(978-0-9741070-0-4(X))* Zarraonandia, Anne.
Zarvatski, Derek. The Fisherman & His Wife. Boyd, Roland. Wright, Carol, ed. rev. ed. 20p. (J). (gr. 1-2). pap. 6.95 *(978-0-9701573-0-0(4))* Chameleon Designs.
Zavrel, Stepan. Vodnik. Zavrel, Stepan. 32p. (J). (gr. -1-3). 14.95 *(978-0-87592-058-0(6))* Scroll Pr., Inc.
Zdanowicz, Paul. Let's Get Cleany-Clean! McElroy, Jean. 2009. (Yo Gabba Gabba! Ser.). (ENG.). 24p. (J). (gr. -1-2). pap. 3.99 *(978-1-4169-9099-4(2),* Simon Spotlight) Simon Spotlight.
—Play with Plex. Testa, Maggie. 2010. (Yo Gabba Gabba! Ser.). (ENG.). 14p. (J). (gr. -1-1). bds. 8.99 *(978-1-4169-9740-5(7),* Simon Spotlight) Simon Spotlight.
Zecca, Katherine. In My Backyard, 1 vol. Giogas, Valarie. 2007. (ENG.). 32p. (J). (gr. -1-3). 15.95 *(978-0-9777423-1-8(8));* pap. 8.95 *(978-1-934359-17-4(3))* Arbordale Publishing.
—River Song: With the Banana Slug String Band. Van Zandt, Steve. 2007. (Sharing Nature with Children Book Ser.). 32p. (J). (gr. -1-5). pap. 9.95 incl. audio compact disk *(978-1-58469-094-8(1))* Dawn Pubns.
—River Song: With the Banana Slug String Band (Includes Music CD) Van Zandt, Steve. 2007. 32p. (J). (gr. k-4). 17.95 *(978-1-58469-093-1(3))* Dawn Pubns.
—The Tree That Came Home: An IslandWood Story Inspired by the True Story of a 92-Foot Beam That Returned to Bainbridge Island, Washington. Brainerd, Debbi. 2008. 63p. *(978-0-9821633-0-6(4))* IslandWood.
Zeck, Mike, et al. Spider-Man by Roger Stern Omnibus. Stern, Roger et al. 2014. (ENG.). 1296p. (J). (gr. 4-17). 125.00 *(978-0-7851-8827-8(4))* Marvel Worldwide, Inc.
Zekauskas, Felicia, jt. illus. see Maloney, Peter.
Zelenka, Yvonne. Aprendamos con Tito sobre la Epilepsia. Zelenka, Yvonne. 2007. (SPA.). 24p. (J). 6.95 *(978-0-9787727-1-0(7))* Medicus Pr., Inc.
Zelinsky, Paul O. Awful Ogre Running Wild. Prelutsky, Jack. 2008. 40p. (J). (gr. -1-3). lib. bdg. 18.89 *(978-0-06-623867-8(6),* Greenwillow Bks.) HarperCollins Pubs.
—Awful Ogre's Awful Day. Prelutsky, Jack. 2005. (ENG.). 40p. (J). (gr. k-5). reprint ed. pap. 6.99 *(978-0-06-077459-2(2),* Greenwillow Bks.) HarperCollins Pubs.
—Circle, Square, Moose. Bingham, Kelly. 2014. (ENG.). 48p. (J). (gr. -1-3). 17.99 *(978-0-06-229003-8(7),* Greenwillow Bks.) HarperCollins Pubs.
—Dust Devil. Isaacs, Anne. 2010. (ENG.). 48p. (J). (gr. k-4). 17.99 *(978-0-375-86722-4(8),* Schwartz & Wade Bks.) Random Hse. Children's Bks.
—Earwig & the Witch. Jones, Diana Wynne. 2012. 128p. (J). (gr. 3-7). 15.99 *(978-0-06-207511-6(X),* Greenwillow Bks.) HarperCollins Pubs.

Z

Zelinsky, Paul O., et al. Ralph S. Mouse. Cleary, Beverly. 2014. (Mouse & the Motorcycle Ser.). (ENG.). 192p. (J). (gr. 3-7). 16.99 *(978-0-688-01452-0(6))* HarperCollins Pubs.

Zelinsky, Paul O. The Shivers in the Fridge. Manushkin, Fran. 2006. (ENG.). 32p. (J). (gr. -1-3). 17.99 *(978-0-525-46943-8(5),* Dutton Juvenile) Penguin Publishing Group.

—The Story of Mrs. Lovewright & Purrless Her Cat. Segal, Lore. 2005. (ENG.). 40p. (J). (gr. -1-3). reprint ed. 17.99 *(978-0-689-87327-0(1),* Atheneum/Anne Schwartz Bks.) Simon & Schuster Children's Publishing.

—Toy Dance Party. Jenkins, Emily. 2010. (Toys Go Out Ser.). (ENG.). 176p. (J). (gr. 1-4). 6.99 *(978-0-375-85525-2(4),* Yearling) Random Hse. Children's Bks.

—Toy Dance Party: Being the Further Adventures of a Bossyboots Stingray, a Courageous Buffalo, & a Hopeful Round Someone Called Plastic. Jenkins, Emily. 2008. (Toys Go Out Ser.). (ENG.). 176p. (J). (gr. 1-4). 16.99 *(978-0-375-83935-1(6),* Schwartz & Wade Bks.) Random Hse. Children's Bks.

—Toys Come Home: Being the Early Experiences of an Intelligent Stingray, a Brave Buffalo, & a Brand-New Someone Called Plastic. Jenkins, Emily. 2011. (Toys Go Out Ser.). (ENG.). 144p. (J). (gr. 1-4). 16.99 *(978-0-375-86200-7(5));* 19.99 *(978-0-375-96200-4(X))* Random Hse. Children's Bks. (Schwartz & Wade Bks.).

—Toys Go Out: Being the Adventures of a Knowledgeable Stingray, a Toughy Little Buffalo, & Someone Called Plastic. Jenkins, Emily. (Toys Go Out Ser.). (ENG.). (J). (gr. 1-4). 2008. 144p. 6.99 *(978-0-385-73661-9(4),* Yearling); 2006. 128p. 16.95 *(978-0-375-83604-6(7),* Schwartz & Wade Bks.) Random Hse. Children's Bks.

—Toys Meet Snow. Jenkins, Emily. 2015. (ENG.). 40p. (J). (gr. -1-2). 17.99 *(978-0-385-37330-2(9),* Schwartz & Wade Bks.) Random Hse. Children's Bks.

—Z Is for Moose. Bingham, Kelly. 2012. 32p. (J). (gr. -1-2). (ENG.). 16.99 *(978-0-06-079984-7(6));* lib. bdg. 17.89 *(978-0-06-079985-4(4))* HarperCollins Pubs. (Greenwillow Bks.).

Zelinsky, Paul O. & Rogers, Jacqueline. Ralph S. Mouse. Cleary, Beverly. 2014. (Mouse & the Motorcycle Ser.). (ENG.). 192p. (J). (gr. 3-7). pap. 6.99 *(978-0-380-70957-1(0))* HarperCollins Pubs.

Zeltner, Tim. Little Boo. Wunderli, Stephen. 2014. (ENG.). 32p. (J). (gr. -1-2). 16.99 *(978-0-8050-9708-5(2),* Holt, Henry & Co. Bks. For Young Readers) Holt, Henry & Co.

—Power down, Little Robot. Staniszewski, Anna. 2015. (ENG.). 32p. (J). (gr. -1-1). 16.99 *(978-1-62779-125-0(6),* Holt, Henry & Co. Bks. For Young Readers) Holt, Henry & Co.

Zemach, Kaethe, jt. illus. see Zemach, Margot.

Zemach, Margot & Zemach, Kaethe. Eating up Gladys. 2005. (J). *(978-0-439-66491-2(8),* Levine, Arthur A. Bks.) Scholastic, Inc.

Zeman, Ludmila. Gilgamesh. Zeman, Ludmila, narrated by. 2005. (SPA.). (J). 29.95 *(978-968-7381-51-0(5));* pap. 21.95 *(978-968-7381-47-3(7))* Tecolote, Ediciones, S.A. de C.V. MEX. Dist: Iaconi, Mariuccia Bk. Imports.

Zeman, Ludmila. Sindbad: From the Tales of the Thousand & One Nights. Zeman, Ludmila, retold by. 2011. (ENG.). 32p. (J). (gr. 1-4). pap. 9.95 *(978-1-77049-264-6(X),* Tundra Bks.) Tundra Bks. CAN. Dist: Penguin Random Hse., LLC.

—Sindbad in the Land of Giants: From the Tales of the Thousand & One Nights. Zeman, Ludmila, retold by. 2011. (ENG.). 32p. (J). (gr. 1-4). pap. 9.95 *(978-1-77049-266-0(6),* Tundra Bks.) Tundra Bks. CAN. Dist: Penguin Random Hse., LLC.

—Sindbad's Secret. Zeman, Ludmila, retold by. 2003. (ENG.). 32p. (J). (gr. 1-4). 17.95 *(978-0-88776-462-2(2),* Tundra Bks.) Tundra Bks. CAN. Dist: Penguin Random Hse., LLC.

—Sindbad's Secret: From the Tales of the Thousand & One Nights. Zeman, Ludmila, retold by. 2011. (ENG.). 32p. (J). (gr. 1-4). pap. 9.95 *(978-1-77049-265-3(8),* Tundra Bks.) Tundra Bks. CAN. Dist: Penguin Random Hse., LLC.

Zembrowski, Sunni. Why Ducks Waddle & Geese Don't. Wachob, Chuck. ***(978-0-578-15467-1(6))*** Wachob, Chuck.

Zemke, Deborah. Chicken Doodle Soup. Blue Apple Staff. 2010. (ENG.). 36p. (J). (gr. 1-4). pap. 10.99 *(978-1-60905-014-6(2))* Blue Apple Bks.

—Cock-A-Doodle-Oops! Degman, Lori. 2014. (ENG.). 36p. (J). (gr. -1-4). 16.95 *(978-1-939547-07-1(5))* Creston Bks.

—D Is 4 Doodles. 2012. (ENG.). 80p. (J). (gr. 2-4). pap. 12.99 *(978-1-60905-278-2(1))* Blue Apple Bks.

—Doodles at Breakfast. Ziefert, Harriet. 2011. (ENG.). 36p. (J). (gr. 1-4). pap. 10.99 *(978-1-60905-081-8(9))* Blue Apple Bks.

—Doodles at Lunch: 36 Tear-Off Placemats. 2009. (ENG.). 36p. (J). (gr. 1-4). pap. 10.99 *(978-1-934706-60-2(4))* Blue Apple Bks.

—Fairy Doodles - 36 Tear-Off Placemats. 2013. (ENG.). 36p. (J). (gr. 1-4). pap. 10.99 *(978-1-60905-362-8(1))* Blue Apple Bks.

—How to Win Friends & Influence Creatures. 2009. (ENG.). 48p. (J). (gr. -1-3). 9.99 *(978-1-934706-57-2(4))* Blue Apple Bks.

—Jasper. Galloway, Ginger. 2003. (Books for Young Learners). (ENG.). 16p. (J). 5.75 net. *(978-1-57274-539-1(8),* 2457, Bks. for Young Learners) Owen, Richard C. Pubs., Inc.

—The Night Before First Grade. Wing, Natasha. (Night Before Ser.). (ENG.). 32p. (J). 2014. (gr. k-1). 12.99 *(978-0-448-48256-9(8));* 2005. (gr. -1-3). pap. 3.99 *(978-0-448-43747-7(3))* Penguin Publishing Group. (Grosset & Dunlap).

—Please Pass the Doodles. 2012. (ENG.). 36p. (J). (gr. 1-4). pap. 10.99 *(978-1-60905-232-4(3))* Blue Apple Bks.

—Pocket Packs - Alpha-Doodles. 2012. (ENG.). 78p. (J). (gr. 1-4). pap. 9.99 *(978-1-60905-316-1(8))* Blue Apple Bks.

—Pocket Packs - Doodles 2 Do! 2012. (ENG.). 78p. (J). (gr. 1-4). pap. 9.99 *(978-1-60905-315-4(X))* Blue Apple Bks.

—A Wilcox & Griswold Mystery: the Case of the Missing Carrot Cake. Newman, Robin. 2015. (Wilcox & Griswold Mystery Ser.). (ENG.). 40p. (J). (gr. -1-3). 15.95 *(978-1-939547-17-0(2))* Creston Bks.

—Wise Acres. Shannon, George. 2004. (ENG.). 40p. (J). (gr. -1-7). 15.95 *(978-1-59354-041-8(8),* Handprint Bks.) Chronicle Bks. LLC.

Zemke, Deborah. Green Boots, Blue Hair, Polka-Dot Underwear. Zemke, Deborah. 2007. (I'm Going to Read(r) Ser.). (ENG.). 28p. (J). (gr. k-1). pap. 3.95 *(978-1-4027-4245-3(2))* Sterling Publishing Co., Inc.

Zengin-Karaian, Alex & Fach, Gernot. The Last Word in Astronomy. Feigin, Misha. Zengin-Karaian, Victoria & Zengin-Karaian, Alex, eds. 2004. 86p. per. 11.95 *(978-0-9741277-1-2(X),* Fleur Publishing) Fleur Art Productions.

Zenz, Aaron. Five Little Puppies Jumping on the Bed! Karr, Lily. 2012. (ENG.). 10p. (J). (gr. -1-k). bds. 7.99 *(978-0-545-38252-6(1),* Cartwheel Bks.) Scholastic, Inc.

—Howie Finds a Hug, 1 vol. Henderson, Sara. 2008. (I Can Read! / Howie Ser.). (ENG.). 32p. (J). (gr. -1-3). pap. 3.99 *(978-0-310-71607-5(1))* Zondervan.

—Howie's Tea Party, 1 vol. Henderson, Sara. 2008. (I Can Read! / Howie Ser.). (ENG.). 32p. (J). (gr. -1-3). pap. 3.99 *(978-0-310-71605-1(5))* Zonderkidz.

—Nugget on the Flight Deck. Newman, Patricia. 2009. (ENG.). 40p. (J). (gr. -1-3). 16.99 *(978-0-8027-9735-3(0))* Walker & Co.

Zenz, Aaron. The Runaway Mitten. Lewis, Anne Margaret. 2015. (ENG.). 40p. (J). (gr. -1-k). 15.99 ***(978-1-63450-213-9(2),*** Sky Pony Pr.) Skyhorse Publishing Co., Inc.

—The Runaway Pumpkin. Lewis, Anne Margaret. 2015. (ENG.). 40p. (J). (gr. -1-k). 15.99 ***(978-1-63450-214-6(0),*** Sky Pony Pr.) Skyhorse Publishing Co., Inc.

Zenz, Aaron. Scholastic Reader Level 1: Biggety Bat: Hot Diggety, It's Biggety! Ingalls, Ann. 2014. (Scholastic Reader Level 1 Ser.). (ENG.). 32p. (J). (gr. -1-2). pap. 3.99 *(978-0-545-66263-5(X))* Scholastic, Inc.

—Skeleton Meets the Mummy. Metzger, Steve. 2011. (ENG.). 32p. (J). (gr. -1-3). pap. 6.99 *(978-0-545-23032-2(2),* Cartwheel Bks.) Scholastic, Inc.

—The Spaghetti-Slurping Sewer Serpent, 0 vols. Ripes, Laura. 2012. (ENG.). 32p. (J). (gr. k-3). 16.99 *(978-0-7614-6101-2(9),* 9780761461012, Amazon Children's Publishing) Amazon Publishing.

Zenz, Aaron. Chuckling Ducklings & Baby Animal Friends. Zenz, Aaron. (ENG.). (J). (gr. -1-1). 2013. 32p. bds. 7.99 *(978-0-8027-3436-5(7));* 2011. 40p. 15.99 *(978-0-8027-2191-4(5))* Walker & Co.

—Hug a Bull: An Ode to Animal Dads. Zenz, Aaron. 2013. (ENG.). 32p. (J). (gr. -1-1). 12.99 *(978-0-8027-2824-1(3))* Walker & Co.

—I Love Ewe: An Ode to Animal Moms. Zenz, Aaron. 2015. (ENG.). 22p. (J). (gr. -1-1). bds. 7.99 *(978-1-61963-666-8(2),* Bloomsbury USA Childrens) Bloomsbury USA.

—I Love Ewe: An Ode to Animal Moms. Zenz, Aaron. 2013. (ENG.). 32p. (J). (gr. -1-1). lib. bdg. 13.89 *(978-0-8027-2827-2(8));* 12.99 *(978-0-8027-2826-5(X))* Walker & Co.

Zenz, Aaron, jt. illus. see Henderson, Sara.

Zephyr, Jay, jt. illus. see Aronson, Jeff.

Zerbetz, Evon. Aleutian Sparrow. Hesse, Karen. 2005. 156p. (J). (gr. 5-9). 13.65 *(978-0-7569-5589-2(0))* Perfection Learning Corp.

—Lucky Hares & Itchy Bears: And Other Alaskan Animals. Ewing, Susan. Blessing, Marlene, ed. 2012. (ENG.). 32p. (J). 16.95 *(978-0-9858506-0-9(4))* Octopoda Pr.

—Ten Rowdy Ravens. Ewing, Susan. 2005. (ENG.). 32p. (J). (gr. -1-1). per. 9.95 *(978-0-88240-610-7(8),* Alaska Northwest Bks.) Graphic Arts Ctr. Publishing Co.

Zerbetz, Evon, jt. illus. see McGillivray, Kim.

Zerga, Susan A., photos by. Autumn Rescue. Wilson, Karen Collett. 2004. (Deer Tales Ser.). (J). (gr. k-6). 15.95 *(978-0-9722570-1-5(2))* Snowbound Bks.

Zeringue, Dona. I Am I. Zeringue, Dona. 32p. (Orig.). (YA). (gr. 6-12). pap. 7.50 *(978-1-882913-02-2(7))* Thornton Publishing.

Zettler, Andrew. The Teeniest Tiniest Yawn. Zettler, Andrew. l.t. ed. 2014. (ENG.). 36p. (J). 17.99 *(978-0-9912370-0-5(5))* Royal Penny Pr., The.

Zeveren, Michel van. That's Mine! Zeveren, Michel van. 2013.Tr. of C'est a Moi, ca!. 36p. (J). (gr. -1-3). 17.95 *(978-1-877579-27-1(0))* Gecko Pr. NZL. Dist: Lerner Publishing Group.

Zevgolis, Irene. The Dreamer & the Moon: An Inspirational Story with a Ballet Theme. 2008. (J). *(978-0-615-17590-4(2))* E-City Publishing.

Zezelj, Danijel, jt. illus. see Mandrake, Tom.

Zhang, Annie. A Frog Named Waldor. Rankine-Van Wassenhoven, Jacqueline. 2008. 20p. per. 24.95 *(978-1-4241-9926-6(3))* America Star Bks.

Zhang, Christopher Zhong-Yuan. Moon Festival. Russell, Ching Yeung & Boyds Mills Press Staff. 2003. (ENG.). 32p. (J). (gr. 2-4). pap. 9.95 *(978-1-59078-079-4(5))* Boyds Mills Pr.

Zhang, Nancy. Cute As a Button. Taylor, Chloë. 2014. (Sew Zoey Ser.: 5). (ENG.). 176p. (J). (gr. 3-7). pap. 5.99 *(978-1-4814-0248-4(X),* Simon Spotlight) Simon Spotlight.

—Knot Too Shabby! Taylor, Chloë. 2014. (Sew Zoey Ser.: 7). (ENG.). 176p. (J). (gr. 3-7). 16.99 *(978-1-4814-1399-2(6),* Simon Spotlight) Simon Spotlight.

—Knot Too Shabby! Taylor, Chloe. 2014. (Sew Zoey Ser.: 7). (ENG.). 176p. (J). (gr. 3-7). pap. 5.99 *(978-1-4814-1398-5(8),* Simon Spotlight) Simon Spotlight.

—Lights, Camera, Fashion! Taylor, Chloe. 2013. (Sew Zoey Ser.: 3). (ENG.). 176p. (J). (gr. 3-7). 15.99 *(978-1-4424-8980-6(4));* pap. 5.99 *(978-1-4424-8979-0(0))* Simon Spotlight. (Simon Spotlight).

—Stitches & Stones. Taylor, Chloe. 2013. (Sew Zoey Ser.: 4). (ENG.). 176p. (J). (gr. 3-7). 16.99 *(978-1-4424-9803-7(X));*Bk. 4. pap. 5.99 *(978-1-4424-9802-0(1))* Simon Spotlight. (Simon Spotlight).

—Swatch Out! Taylor, Chloë. 2014. (Sew Zoey Ser.: 8). (ENG.). 176p. (J). (gr. 3-7). 16.99 *(978-1-4814-1536-1(0),* Simon Spotlight) Simon Spotlight.

—Swatch Out! Taylor, Chloe. 2014. (Sew Zoey Ser.: 8). (ENG.). 176p. (J). (gr. 3-7). pap. 5.99 *(978-1-4814-1535-4(2),* Simon Spotlight) Simon Spotlight.

—A Tangled Thread. Taylor, Chloë. 2014. (Sew Zoey Ser.: 6). (ENG.). 176p. (J). (gr. 3-7). 16.99 *(978-1-4814-0444-0(X),* Simon Spotlight) Simon Spotlight.

—A Tangled Thread. Taylor, Chloe. 2014. (Sew Zoey Ser.: 6). (ENG.). 176p. (J). (gr. 3-7). pap. 5.99 *(978-1-4814-0443-3(1),* Simon Spotlight) Simon Spotlight.

Zhang, Nancy, jt. illus. see Christy, Jana.

Zhang, Song Nan. Awakening the Dragon: The Dragon Boat Festival. Chan, Arlene. 2007. (ENG.). 24p. (J). (gr. 1-4). pap. 10.95 *(978-0-88776-805-7(9),* Tundra Bks.) Tundra Bks. CAN. Dist: Penguin Random Hse., LLC.

—The Day I Became a Canadian: A Citizenship Scrapbook. Bannatyne-Cugnet, Jo. 2008. (ENG.). 24p. (J). (gr. 2-4). pap. 10.95 *(978-0-88776-892-7(X),* Tundra Bks.) Tundra Bks. CAN. Dist: Penguin Random Hse., LLC.

—Emma's Story. Hodge, Deborah. 2003. (ENG.). 24p. (J). (gr. k-3). 17.95 *(978-0-88776-632-9(3),* Tundra Bks.) Tundra Bks. CAN. Dist: Penguin Random Hse., LLC.

—The Man Who Made Parks: The Story of Parkbuilder Frederick Law Olmsted. Wishinsky, Frieda. 2009. (ENG.). 32p. (J). (gr. k-12). pap. 10.95 *(978-0-88776-902-3(0),* Tundra Bks.) Tundra Bks. CAN. Dist: Penguin Random Hse., LLC.

Zhang, Song Nan. The Great Voyages of Zheng He. Zhang, Song Nan. Zhang, Hao Yu. 2005. 32p. (J). 16.95 *(978-1-57227-088-6(8));* (ENG & CHI.). 16.95 *(978-1-57227-090-9(X))* Pan Asia Pubns. (USA), Inc.

—The Great Voyages of Zheng He: English/Vietnamese. Zhang, Song Nan. Zhang, Hao Yu. Do, Kim-Thu, tr. from ENG. 2005. (ENG & VIE.). 32p. (J). 16.95 *(978-1-57227-091-6(8))* Pan Asia Pubns. (USA), Inc.

—A Time of Golden Dragons. Zhang, Song Nan. Zhang, Hao Yu. 2006. (ENG.). 24p. (J). (gr. 4-7). pap. 11.95 *(978-0-88776-791-3(5),* Tundra Bks.) Tundra Bks. CAN. Dist: Penguin Random Hse., LLC.

Zhao, Amei. Painted Skies, 1 vol. Mallory, Carolyn. 2015. (ENG.). 36p. (J). (gr. k-2). 16.95 ***(978-1-77227-004-4(0))*** Inhabit Media Inc. CAN. Dist: Independent Pubs. Group.

Zheng, Wen. Star & Cloud: Venerable Master Hsing Yun. Wheeler-Gibb, Madelon, tr. from CHI. 2003. (Buddhist Legends of Adventure & Courage Ser.). 148p. (J). pap. 10.00 *(978-0-9715612-4-3(9))* Buddha's Light Publishing.

Zheng, Xiaoyan, jt. illus. see Xu, Wei.

Zheng, Xin, jt. illus. see Xin, Xiao.

Ziborova, Dasha. En Ingles, por Supuesto. Nobisso, Josephine. 2003. Orig. Title: In English, of Course. (SPA & ENG.). 32p. (J). (gr. k-2). 16.95 *(978-0-940112-14-8(0))* Gingerbread Hse.

—En ingles, por Supuesto. Nobisso, Josephine. 2003. Orig. Title: In English, of Course. (SPA & ENG.). 32p. (J). (gr. k-2). pap. 8.95 *(978-0-940112-16-2(7))* Gingerbread Hse.

—In English, of Course. Nobisso, Josephine. 2003.Tr. of En Ingles, Por Supuesto. 32p. (J). (gr. -1). (SPA & ENG.). 16.95 *(978-0-940112-07-0(8));* (ENG.). pap. 8.95 *(978-0-940112-08-7(6))* Gingerbread Hse.

—The Numbers Dance: A Counting Comedy. Nobisso, Josephine. 2005. (ENG.). 32p. (J). (gr. k-2). 16.95 *(978-0-940112-11-7(6));* pap. 8.95 *(978-0-940112-12-4(4))* Gingerbread Hse.

Zick, Bruce. The Bramble. Nordling, Lee. 2013. (ENG.). 32p. (J). (gr. k-3). 16.95 *(978-0-7613-5856-5(0),* Carolrhoda Bks.) Lerner Publishing Group.

Zick, Bruce, et al. Thor: Blood & Thunder. 2011. (ENG.). 336p. (J). (gr. 4-17). pap. 34.99 *(978-0-7851-5094-7(3))* Marvel Worldwide, Inc.

Ziegler, Michael. The Friendship Alphabet. Ziegler, Michael, photos by. Bramwell, Wendie et al. 2003. 32p. (J). pap. *(978-0-9741388-3-1(5))* Committee for Children.

Zielinski, Dave, photos by. The ABC's of Motocross. Louck, Cheryl. 2003. 24p. (J). per. 14.95 *(978-0-9744230-0-5(9))* Louck, Cheryl.

Ziembo, Daniel. The Wiz Kids of Oz. Bresloff, Robert. 2013. (Bound into the Classics Ser.). (ENG.). 170p. pap. 7.95 *(978-0-615-80349-4(0))* Pumpkinhead Productions.

Zieroth, Emily. Journey to Jazzland. De Saulnier, Gia Volterra. 2013. 44p. 14.99 *(978-0-9851492-8-4(0))* Flying Turtle Publishing.

Ziersch, Nahum. Chip & Chase. Loughlin, Patrick. 2015. 4. 144p. (J). (gr. 2-4). 9.99 *(978-0-85798-270-4(2))* Random Hse. Australia AUS. Dist: Independent Pubs. Group.

—Show & Go. 2015. 3. 144p. (J). (gr. 2-4). 9.99 *(978-0-85798-268-1(0))* Random Hse. Australia AUS. Dist: Independent Pubs. Group.

Zilber, Denis. Alexander Graham Bell Master of Sound. Hood, Ann. 2013. (Treasure Chest Ser.: 7). (ENG.). 192p. (J). (gr. 3-7). 6.99 *(978-0-448-45730-7(X),* Grosset & Dunlap) Penguin Publishing Group.

—Amelia Earhart - Lady Lindy, Vol. 8. Hood, Ann. 2014. (Treasure Chest Ser.: 8). (ENG.). 176p. (J). (gr. 3-7). 6.99 *(978-0-448-45731-4(8));* 15.99 *(978-0-448-45741-3(5))* Penguin Publishing Group. (Grosset & Dunlap).

—Anastasia Romanov - The Last Grand Duchess, No. 10. Hood, Ann. 2014. (Treasure Chest Ser.: 10). (ENG.). 240p. (J). (gr. 3-7). 15.99 *(978-0-448-46770-2(4),* Grosset & Dunlap) Penguin Publishing Group.

—Anastasia Romanovs - The Last Grand Duchess, No. 10. Hood, Ann. 2014. (Treasure Chest Ser.: 10). (ENG.). 240p. (J). (gr. 3-7). 6.99 *(978-0-448-46771-9(2),* Grosset & Dunlap) Penguin Publishing Group.

—Get to Work, Hercules!, 1 vol. McMullan, Kate. (Myth-O-Mania Ser.: Bk. 7). (ENG.). 208p. (gr. 4-8). 2011. pap. 5.95 *(978-1-4342-3440-7(1));* 2010. lib. bdg. 23.99 *(978-1-4342-3196-3(8))* Stone Arch Bks. (Myth-O-Mania).

—Go for the Gold, Atalanta!, 1 vol. McMullan, Kate. (Myth-O-Mania Ser.: Bk. 8). (ENG.). 192p. (gr. 4-8). 2011. pap. 5.95 *(978-1-4342-3441-4(X));* 2010. lib. bdg. 23.99 *(978-1-4342-3197-0(6))* Stone Arch Bks. (Myth-O-Mania).

—Have a Hot Time, Hades!, 1 vol. McMullan, Kate. 2011. (Myth-O-Mania Ser.: Bk. 1). (ENG.). 176p. (gr. 4-8). pap. 5.95 *(978-1-4342-3437-7(1));* lib. bdg. 23.99 *(978-1-4342-2136-0(9))* Stone Arch Bks. (Myth-O-Mania).

—Keep a Lid on It, Pandora!, 1 vol. McMullan, Kate. (Myth-O-Mania Ser.: Bk. 6). (ENG.). 192p. (gr. 4-8). 2011. pap. 5.95 *(978-1-4342-3439-1(8));* 2010. lib. bdg. 23.99 *(978-1-4342-3195-6(X))* Stone Arch Bks. (Myth-O-Mania).

—Leonardo Da Vinci No. 9: Renaissance Master. Hood, Ann. 2014. (Treasure Chest Ser.: 9). (ENG.). 224p. (J). (gr. 3-7). 15.99 *(978-0-448-46768-9(2),* Grosset & Dunlap) Penguin Publishing Group.

—Nice Shot, Cupid!, 1 vol. McMullan, Kate. 2011. (Myth-O-Mania Ser.: Bk. 4). (ENG.). 208p. (gr. 4-8). pap. 5.95 *(978-1-4342-3435-3(5));* lib. bdg. 23.99 *(978-1-4342-1985-5(2))* Stone Arch Bks. (Myth-O-Mania).

—Phone Home, Persephone!, 1 vol. McMullan, Kate. 2011. (Myth-O-Mania Ser.: Bk. 2). (ENG.). 176p. (gr. 4-8). pap. 5.95 *(978-1-4342-3436-0(3));* lib. bdg. 23.99 *(978-1-4342-2135-3(0))* Stone Arch Bks. (Myth-O-Mania).

—Puss in Boots. Namm, Diane. 2012. (Silver Penny Stories Ser.). (ENG.). 40p. (J). (gr. -1-1). 4.95 *(978-1-4027-8435-4(X))* Sterling Publishing Co., Inc.

—Say Cheese, Medusa!, 1 vol. McMullan, Kate. 2011. (Myth-O-Mania Ser.: Bk. 3). (ENG.). 208p. (gr. 4-8). pap. 5.95 *(978-1-4342-3442-1(8));* lib. bdg. 23.99 *(978-1-4342-2998-4(X))* Stone Arch Bks. (Myth-O-Mania).

—Stop That Bull, Theseus!, 1 vol. McMullan, Kate. 2011. (Myth-O-Mania Ser.: Bk. 5). (ENG.). 192p. (gr. 4-8). pap. 5.95 *(978-1-4342-3438-4(X),* Myth-O-Mania) Stone Arch Bks.

—Stop That Bull, Theseus!, 1 vol. Maddox, Jake & McMullan, Kate. 2010. (Myth-O-Mania Ser.: Bk. 5). (ENG.). 192p. (gr. 4-8). 23.99 *(978-1-4342-3034-8(1),* Myth-O-Mania) Stone Arch Bks.

Zilber, Denis & Olafsdottir, Linda. The Princess & the Pea. Namm, Diane & Andersen, Hans Christian. 2013. (Silver Penny Stories Ser.). (ENG.). 40p. (J). (gr. -1-1). 4.95 *(978-1-4027-8436-1(8))* Sterling Publishing Co., Inc.

Zilber, Denis, jt. illus. see Altmann, Scott.

Zilber, Denis, jt. illus. see Kwasney, Karl.

Zilis, Tom. Cats: Read Well Level K Unit 12 Storybook. Sprick, Marilyn et al. 2003. (Read Well Level K Ser.). 20p. (J). *(978-1-57035-683-4(1),* 55520) Cambium Education, Inc.

—The Little Red Hen: Read Well Level K Unit 20 Storybook. 2003. (Read Well Level K Ser.). 20p. (J). *(978-1-57035-691-9(2),* 55600) Cambium Education, Inc.

—Man's Best Friend: Read Well Level K Unit 5 Storybook. Sprick, Marilyn et al. 2003. (Read Well Level K Ser.). 20p. (J). *(978-1-57035-677-3(7))* Cambium Education, Inc.

—Rescue Workers: Read Well Level K Unit 11 Storybook. Sprick, Marilyn et al. 2003. (Read Well Level K Ser.). 20p. (J). *(978-1-57035-682-7(3),* 55511) Cambium Education, Inc.

Zima, Gordon & Zima, Paula. Sun Birds & Evergreens: The Nuk-Chuk Stories. 2005. (J). *(978-0-9742894-3-4(4))* Hutton Electronic Publishing.

Zima, Paula, jt. illus. see Zima, Gordon.

Zima, Siegfried, jt. illus. see Benchimol, Brigitte.

Zimmer, Dirk. An I Can Read Halloween Treat, Set. HarperCollins Publishers Ltd. Staff et al. 2004. (I Can Read Bks.). (J). (gr. k-3). pap. 11.99 *(978-0-06-054237-5(3),* Harper Trophy) HarperCollins Pubs.

—Jaap de Tuinman. Aardvark, Esperanza. 2006. (DUT.). 14.95 *(978-0-9766859-9-9(X))* Macaronic Pr.

Zimmer, Eric. The Turtle & the Deep Blue Sky. Zimmer, Elizabeth. 2007. (ENG.). 32p. (J). (gr. -1-3). 12.95 *(978-1-55591-597-1(3))* Fulcrum Publishing.

Zimmer, Glenn. Dollars & Sense. Deutsch, Tehilla. 2012. 36p. (J). 12.95 *(978-1-929628-65-0(X))* Hachai Publishing.

Zimmer, Joan. Daniel's Dinosaurs: A True Story of Discovery. Helm, Charles & Owlkids Books Inc. Staff. 2004. (ENG.). 32p. (J). (gr. 2-5). pap. 6.95 *(978-1-897066-07-2(4),* Maple Tree Pr.) Owlkids Bks. Inc. CAN. Dist: Perseus-PGW.

Zimmer, Kevin. Buster the Little Garbage Truck. Berneger, Marcia. 2015. (ENG.). 32p. (J). (gr. -1-1). 14.99 *(978-1-58536-894-5(6),* 203814) Sleeping Bear Pr.

—Troo Makes a Big Splash, 1 vol. Crouch, Cheryl. 2011. (I Can Read! / Rainforest Friends Ser.). (ENG.). 32p. (J). (gr. -1-2). pap. 3.99 *(978-0-310-71810-9(4))* Zonderkidz.

—Troo's Big Climb, 1 vol. Crouch, Cheryl. 2011. (I Can Read! / Rainforest Friends Ser.). (ENG.). 32p. (J). (gr. -1-2). pap. 3.99 *(978-0-310-71808-6(2))* Zonderkidz.

—Troo's Secret Clubhouse, 1 vol. Crouch, Cheryl. 2011. (I Can Read! / Rainforest Friends Ser.). (ENG.). 32p. (J). (gr. -1-2). pap. 3.99 *(978-0-310-71809-3(0))* Zonderkidz.

Zimmerman, Andrea & Clemesha, David. Digger Man. Zimmerman, Andrea & Clemesha, David. 2007. (ENG.). 32p. (J). (gr. -1-k). pap. 7.99 *(978-0-8050-8203-6(4))* Square Fish.

—Train Man. Zimmerman, Andrea & Clemesha, David. 2012. (ENG.). 32p. (J). (gr. -1-k). 14.99 *(978-0-8050-7991-3(2),* Holt, Henry & Co. Bks. For Young Readers) Holt, Henry & Co.

Zimmerman, Andrea, jt. illus. see Clemesha, David.

Zimmerman, Andrea Griffing & Clemesha, David. Digger Man. Zimmerman, Andrea Griffing & Clemesha, David. rev. ed. 2003. (ENG.). 32p. (J). (gr. -1-k). 17.95 *(978-0-8050-6628-9(4),* Holt, Henry & Co. Bks. For Young Readers) Holt, Henry & Co.

Zimmerman, Brian. The Story of Tweeker the Time Traveler. Zimmerman, Brian. Foraker, Doreen, ed. 2010. (ENG.). 62p. pap. 19.97 *(978-1-4563-2062-1(9))* CreateSpace Independent Publishing Platform.

Zimmerman, Edith Fay Martin & Kanagy, Audrey Ann Zimmerman. Little Bear Builds a Wigwam. Stoltzfus, Sherman Matthew. 2010. 32p. (J). *(978-0-9646590-2-5(6))* J&M Publishing.

Zimmerman, Kadie. Have You Ever Seen a Bear with a Purple Smile? Budds, Laura. 2013. 16p. (J). 16.95 *(978-1-59152-114-3(9))* Farcountry Pr.

Zimmerman, Louis. That's Bingzy! Busy Building Self-Esteem. Richards, Arlene. 2007. 32p. (J). (gr. -1-3). 19.95 incl. audio compact disk *(978-0-9794323-4-7(0))* Bing Note, Inc.

Zimmerman, Robert. Flying Rubberneckers: High-Flying Fun for the Airport & Plane. Lore, Mark & Lore, Matthew. 2007. (Rubberneckers Ser.: RUBB). (ENG.). 70p. (J). (gr. -1-17). 12.95 *(978-0-8118-5506-8(6))* Chronicle Bks. LLC.

Zimmerman, Rusty. Thunder Rolling down the Mountain: The Story of Chief Joseph & the Nez Perce, 1 vol. Biskup, Agnieszka. 2011. (American Graphic Ser.). (ENG.). 32p. (gr. 3-4). lib. bdg. 29.99 *(978-1-4296-5472-2(4))*; pap. 8.10 *(978-1-4296-6270-3(0))*; pap. 47.70 *(978-1-4296-6437-0(1))* Capstone Pr., Inc. (Graphic Library).

Zimmerman, Suzanne. God's Precious Gift. Mast, Dorcas R. 2011. 107p. (J). pap. *(978-0-7399-2429-7(X))* Rod & Staff Pubs., Inc.

Zimmerman, T. W. The Day the Horse Was Free. Dodgson, Y. K. rev. ed. 2005. 24p. (J). 11.95 *(978-0-9748091-1-3(X))* Alaska Avenue Pr.

Zimmermann, Karl, photos by. All Aboard! Passenger Trains Around the World. Zimmermann, Karl. 2006. (ENG., 48p. (J). (gr. 5-7). 19.95 *(978-1-59078-325-2(5))* Boyds Mills Pr.

Zimmermann, Karl, photos by. Steamboats: The Story of Lakers, Ferries, & Majestic Paddle-Wheelers. Zimmermann, Karl. 2007. (ENG., 48p. (J). (gr. 4-9). 19.95 *(978-1-59078-434-1(0))* Boyds Mills Pr.

Ziner, Amie. There Once Was a Sky Full of Stars. Crelin, Bob. 2005. 36p. pap. 12.95 *(978-1-931559-04-1(X))* Sky Publishing.

Zinn, Alarna. Ruby Who? Bartholomew, Andrew & Bartholomew, Hailey. 2012. 40p. pap. *(978-0-9876653-0-0(8))* Pause for Effect Ltd.

Zinsmeister, Elke. Ten Fat Sausages. (Classic Books with Holes Big Book Ser.). (ENG.). (J). 2006. 16p. (gr. -1-3). *(978-1-84643-008-4(9))*; 2005. 14p. (gr. -1-1). bds. *(978-1-904550-59-4(2))*; 2005. 16p. pap. *(978-1-904550-31-0(2))* Child's Play International Ltd.

Zintoll, Gabreyhl. Mister Ego & the Bubble of Love. Hinton, Amber. 2008. (ENG.). 32p. 16.95 *(978-1-897238-36-3(3))* Namaste Publishing, Inc. CAN. Dist: Perseus-PGW.

Ziolkowski, Ania. Goodnight, Boone. Collins, Yozette Yogi & Jennings, Marlis. 2012. 24p. pap. 11.95 *(978-1-937376-18-5(4))* All Star Pr.

Zipperer, Susan Johnson. Esmerelda the Silly Goose. Childress, Mildred Tickfer. 2004. 52p. (J). (gr. -1-3). 11.95 *(978-1-887774-17-8(3)*, Wynden) Canmore Pr.

Zircher, Patrick, et al. Captain America by Ed Brubaker - Volume 3. 2013. (ENG.). 125p. (J). (gr. 4-17). pap. 19.99 *(978-0-7851-6076-2(0)*, Marvel Pr.) Disney Publishing Worldwide.

Zircher, Patrick, jt. illus. see Brooks, Mark.

Ziskie, Adam. What Does the President Look Like? Cook, Jane Hampton. ed. 2011. (ENG.). 36p. (J). (gr. k-4). 10.90 *(978-1-935279-63-1(7))* Kane Miller.

Ziss, Debra. Be Healthy! It's a Girl Thing: Food, Fitness, & Feeling Great. Jukes, Mavis et al. 2003. (It's a Girl Thing Ser.). (ENG.). 128p. (J). (gr. 3-7). pap. 12.99 *(978-0-679-89029-4(7)*, Crown Books For Young Readers) Random Hse. Children's Bks.

—Dolphin's Big Leap. Weinberger, Kimberly. 2003. (Hello Reader! Ser.). 30p. (J). *(978-0-439-44159-9(5))* Scholastic, Inc.

Zitnak, Allison Day. The Happiness of Being Me: An A-Z Owners Manual, 1 vol. DuBois, Juli. 2009. 47p. pap. 24.95 *(978-1-60749-613-7(5))* America Star Bks.

Zittel, Michael. The Philistine: Anthology/Chronology, 1 book. Mongillo, Michael. 2003. 216p. (YA). pap. 24.95 *(978-0-9743086-0-9(9))* United Comics.

Zivoin, Jennifer. Ahoy, Ghost Ship Ahead!, 2 vols., No. 2. James, Brian. 2007. (Pirate School Ser.: 2). (ENG.). 64p. (J). (gr. 1-3). pap. 3.99 *(978-0-448-44625-7(1)*, Grosset & Dunlap) Penguin Publishing Group.

—All My Stripes: A Story for Children with Autism. Rudolph, Shaina & Royer, Danielle. 2014. (J). pap. *(978-1-4338-1917-9(1)*, Magination Pr.) American Psychological Assn.

—Attack on the High Seas! James, Brian. 2007. (Pirate School Ser.). 64p. (J). (gr. 1-3). 12.90 *(978-1-4178-3019-0(0)*, Turtleback) Turtleback Bks.

—Attack on the High Seas!, No. 3. James, Brian. 2007. (Pirate School Ser.: 3). (ENG.). 64p. (J). (gr. 1-3). pap. 3.99 *(978-0-448-44645-5(6)*, Grosset & Dunlap) Penguin Publishing Group.

—The Curse of Snake Island. James, Brian. 2007. (Pirate School Ser.: 1). (ENG.). 64p. (J). (gr. 1-3). pap. 3.99 *(978-0-448-44574-8(3)*, Grosset & Dunlap) Penguin Publishing Group.

—Port of Spies. James, Brian. 2007. (Pirate School Ser.: 4). (ENG.). 64p. (J). (gr. 1-3). pap. 3.99 *(978-0-448-44646-2(4)*, Grosset & Dunlap) Penguin Publishing Group.

—Treasure Trouble. James, Brian. 2008. (Pirate School Ser.: 5). (ENG.). 64p. (J). (gr. 1-3). pap. 3.99 *(978-0-448-44782-7(7)*, Grosset & Dunlap) Penguin Publishing Group.

—We Both Read-Jack & the Toddler. McKay, Sindy. 2011. (ENG.). 44p. (J). 9.95 *(978-1-60115-249-7(3))*; pap. 5.99 *(978-1-60115-250-3(7))* Treasure Bay, Inc.

—Yo-Ho-Ho! James, Brian. 2008. (Pirate School Ser.: 7). (ENG.). 64p. (J). (gr. 1-3). pap. 3.99 *(978-0-448-44887-9(4)*, Grosset & Dunlap) Penguin Publishing Group.

Zlatic, Tomislav. Market Day. Roberts, Victoria. 2010. (ENG.). 14p. (J). (gr. -1-18). 14.99 *(978-1-935279-78-5(5))* Kane Miller.

—Runny Honey. Clarke, Jane. 2008. (Tadpoles Ser.). (ENG.). 24p. (J). (gr. -1-3). pap. *(978-0-7787-3893-0(0))*; lib. bdg. *(978-0-7787-3862-6(0))* Crabtree Publishing Co.

—Runny Honey. Clarke, Jane. 2008. (Tadpoles Ser.). 23p. (J). (gr. -1-3). 17.15 *(978-1-4178-0935-6(3)*, Turtleback) Turtleback Bks.

Zmina, Stephen. Don't Let the Dead Bugs Bite! Zmina, Stephen. 2015. (ENG.). 32p. (J). (gr. -1-3). 16.95 *(978-0-9801468-1-3(X))* All About Kids Publishing.

Zmora, Avram. Shabbos, Shabbos I Love You. Lieberman, Naomi. Rosenfeld, D. L., ed. 2013. (ENG.). 32p. (J). 10.95 *(978-1-929628-70-4(6))* Hachai Publishing.

Zolan, Donald. My Favorite Farm Animal Friends. 2010. 5p. (J). 5.99 *(978-0-7369-2663-8(1))* Harvest Hse. Pubs.

Zollars, Jaime. Cakes & Miracles: A Purim Tale, 0 vols. Goldin, Barbara Diamond. 2010. (ENG.). 32p. (J). (gr. k-3). 17.99 *(978-0-7614-5701-5(1)*, 9780761457015, Amazon Children's Publishing) Amazon Publishing.

—Greenglass House. Milford, Kate. 2014. (ENG.). 176p. (J). (gr. 5-7). 17.99 *(978-0-544-05270-3(6))* Houghton Mifflin Harcourt Publishing Co.

—Not a Buzz to Be Found: Insects in Winter. Glaser, Linda. 2011. (Exceptional Science Titles for Primary Grades Ser.). (ENG.). 32p. (J). (gr. 2-4). lib. bdg. 25.26 *(978-0-7613-5644-8(4))* Lerner Publishing Group.

—Not in Room 204: Breaking the Silence of Abuse. Riggs, Shannon. 2007. (ENG.). 32p. (J). (gr. 1-4). lib. bdg. 16.99 *(978-0-8075-5764-8(1))* Whitman, Albert & Co.

—The Shabbat Puppy, 0 vols. Kimmelman, Leslie. 2012. (Shofar Ser.: 0). (ENG.). 32p. (J). (gr. -1-3). 17.99 *(978-0-7614-6145-6(0)*, 9780761461456, Amazon Children's Publishing) Amazon Publishing.

Zoller, Jayson D. The Best Pet. Seagreaves, Kelly E. l.t. ed. 2004. 29p. (J). lib. bdg. 14.95 *(978-1-932338-56-0(X))*; per. 8.99 *(978-1-932338-53-9(5))* Lifevest Publishing, Inc.

Zomchek, Rebecca. I Grew up to Be President. Calkhoven, Laurie. 2011. (ENG.). 96p. (J). (gr. 2-5). pap. 8.99 *(978-0-545-33152-4(8)*, Scholastic Paperbacks) Scholastic, Inc.

Zommer, Yuval. The Big Blue Thing on the Hill. Zommer, Yuval. 2015. (ENG.). 32p. (J). (gr. -1-2). 16.99 *(978-0-7636-7403-8(6)*, Templar) Candlewick Pr.

Zong, Grace. Goldy Luck & the Three Pandas. Yim, Natasha. 2014. (ENG.). 32p. (J). (gr. -1-3). lib. bdg. 16.95 *(978-1-58089-652-8(9))* Charlesbridge Publishing, Inc.

Zonjic, Tonci. Heralds. 2011. (ENG.). 120p. (J). (gr. 4-17). pap. 15.99 *(978-0-7851-4761-9(6))* Marvel Worldwide, Inc.

Zonneveld, Famke. What Julianna Could See. Margulies, Paul. 2004. 32p. (J). pap. 11.95 *(978-0-88010-515-6(1))* SteinerBooks, Inc.

Zonta, Rose. The Greenhouse Kids: Dan Delion's Secret. Awad, Shelley. 2009. 127p. (J). pap. *(978-0-88887-379-8(4))* Borealis Pr.

Zoo, Keith. Tomb of Brain Ooze, No. 5. Payne, M. D. 2014. (Monster Juice Ser.: 5). (ENG.). 192p. (J). (gr. 3-7). 5.99 *(978-0-448-48200-2(2)*, Grosset & Dunlap) Penguin Publishing Group.

—Zits from Python Pit #6. Payne, M. D. 2015. (Monster Juice Ser.: 6). (ENG.). 192p. (J). (gr. 3-7). 5.99 *(978-0-448-48247-7(9)*, Grosset & Dunlap) Penguin Publishing Group.

Zoo, Keith, jt. illus. see Dockery, Amanda.

Zornow, Jeff. Werewolf. Zornow, Jeff. 2007. (Graphic Horror Ser.). 32p. (gr. 3-7). 28.50 *(978-1-60270-062-8(1)*, Graphic Planet- Fiction) ABDO Publishing Co.

Zourelias, Diana. A First Sudoku Book. Pazzelli, John. 2006. (Dover Children's Activity Bks.). (ENG.). 64p. (J). (gr. 3-8). per. 3.95 *(978-0-486-45074-2(0))* Dover Pubns., Inc.

—Kids' Kakuro. Pazzelli, John. 2006. (Dover Children's Activity Bks.). (ENG.). 80p. (J). (gr. 3). per. 5.95 *(978-0-486-45344-6(8))* Dover Pubns., Inc.

Zourelias-Noro, Diane. The 1, 2, 3 Bees: A Counting Book. Wheldon, Nicole. 2005. 24p. (J). (gr. -1-7). 17.95 *(978-0-9744792-1-7(7))* Acmon Blue Publishing.

Zoutewelle-Morris, Sarah. Angel Colouring Book. Cooper, Diana. 2004. (ENG.). 32p. (J). (gr. -1-3). pap. 5.95 *(978-1-84409-042-6(6))* Findhorn Pr. GBR. Dist: Perseus-PGW, SteinerBooks, Inc.

Zraick, Robert, jt. illus. see Noon, Connie.

Zschock, Martha. Butterflies & Friends: An Art Activity Book for Adventurous Artists of All Ages. Conlon, Mara. 2009. (Scratch & Sketch Ser.). 64p. (J). (gr. 1). spiral bd., act. bk. ed. 12.99 *(978-1-59359-841-9(6))* Peter Pauper Pr. Inc.

—Circus Scratch & Sketch: An Art Activity Book. Paulding, Barbara. 2009. (Scratch & Sketch Ser.). 64p. (J). (gr. -1). spiral bd. 14.99 *(978-1-59359-832-7(7))* Peter Pauper Pr. Inc.

Zschock, Martha & Zschock, Martha Day. Spooky Scratch & Sketch: For Spooky Artists & Trick-or-Treaters of All Ages. 2007. (Scratch & Sketch sER.). 80p. (J). 12.99 *(978-1-59359-881-5(5))* Peter Pauper Pr. Inc.

Zschock, Martha Day. Monsters: An Art Activity Book for Creative Kids of All Ages. Nemmers, Lee. 2013. (Scratch & Sketch Ser.). (ENG.). 64p. (J). (gr. k). spiral bd. 12.99 *(978-1-4413-1154-2(8))* Peter Pauper Pr. Inc.

—The Night Sky: Stories of the Stars (Bedtime Shadow Book) Tunnell, Amber. 2014. (ENG.). 7p. (J). 12.99 *(978-1-4413-1581-6(0)*, 9781441315816) Peter Pauper Pr. Inc.

Zschock, Martha Day. No Monsters Here! A Bedtime Shadow Book. Nemmers, Lee. 2015. (ENG.). 7p. (J). 12.99 ***(978-1-4413-1833-6(X)***, 9781441318336) Peter Pauper Pr. Inc.

Zschock, Martha Day. Pirates Scratch & Sketch: For Adventurous Artists & Explorers of All Ages. Nemmers, Tom. 2007. 64p. (J). 12.99 *(978-1-59359-871-6(8))* Peter Pauper Pr. Inc.

Zschock, Martha Day. Scratch & Sketch Trace-Along Constellations: An Art Activity Book for Artistic Stargazers of All Ages. Nemmers, Lee. 2014. (ENG.). (J). (gr. k). 14.99 ***(978-1-4413-1726-1(0)***, 9781441317261) Peter Pauper Pr. Inc.

—Scratch & Sketch Trace-Along Doodle Mania: An Art Activity Book for Imaginative Artists of All Ages. Levy, Talia. 2014. (ENG.). (J). (gr. k). 14.99 ***(978-1-4413-1727-8(9)***, 9781441317278) Peter Pauper Pr. Inc.

—Scratch & Sketch Vikings: An Art Activity Book for Legendary Artists & Explorers of All Ages. Gandolfi, Claudine. 2015. (ENG.). 64p. (J). 12.99 ***(978-1-4413-1813-8(5)***, 9781441318138) Peter Pauper Pr. Inc.

Zschock, Martha Day. Who's There? A Bedtime Shadow Book. Zschock, Heather. 2005. (Activity Book Ser.). 16p. (J). (gr. -1-4). 12.99 *(978-1-59359-904-1(8))* Peter Pauper Pr. Inc.

Zschock, Martha Day. Journey Around Nantucket from A to Z. Zschock, Martha Day. 2008. (Journeys Ser.). 32p. (J). (gr. 1-6). 17.95 *(978-1-933212-82-1(9)*, Commonwealth Editions) Applewood Bks.

Zschock, Martha Day, jt. illus. see Zschock, Martha.

Zubal, Lynn. Sonoran Desert Frog. Zubal, Lynn. 2011. (ENG.). 22p. (J). pap. 15.95 *(978-1-59299-600-1(0))* Inkwater Pr.

Zubiat, Gabriel. De Mis Poemas Vividos. González Reyes, Amaury. Hernández, René Mario, ed. l.t. ed. 2003. (SPA.). 100p. (YA). pap. *(978-1-931481-20-5(2))* LiArt-Literature & Art.

Zuckerman, Andrew, photos by. Creature ABC. 2009. (ENG., 120p. (J). (gr. -1-17). 19.99 *(978-0-8118-6978-2(4))* Chronicle Bks. LLC.

—Creature ABC Flash Cards. 2014. (ENG., 26p. (J). (gr. -1-17). 14.99 *(978-1-4521-1181-0(2))* Chronicle Bks. LLC.

—Creature Baby Animals. 2014. (ENG., 20p. (J). (gr. -1 — 1). bds. 7.99 *(978-1-4521-1721-8(7))* Chronicle Bks. LLC.

—Creature Colors. 2014. (ENG., 20p. (J). (gr. -1 — 1). bds. 7.99 *(978-1-4521-1668-6(7))* Chronicle Bks. LLC.

—Creature Matching Game. 2014. (ENG., 36p. (J). (gr. -1-k). bds. 14.99 *(978-1-4521-1723-2(3))* Chronicle Bks. LLC.

—Creature Numbers. 2014. (ENG., 20p. (J). (gr. -1 — 1). 7.99 *(978-1-4521-1667-9(9))* Chronicle Bks. LLC.

—Creature Sounds. 2014. (ENG., 20p. (J). (gr. -1 — 1). bds. 7.99 *(978-1-4521-1722-5(5))* Chronicle Bks. LLC.

Zug, Mark. Darke. Sage, Angie. (Septimus Heap Ser.: 6). 656p. (J). (gr. 4). 2012. (ENG.). pap. 7.99 *(978-0-06-124244-1(6))*; 2011. lib. bdg. 18.89 *(978-0-06-124243-4(8))*; Bk. 6. 2011. (ENG.). 17.99 *(978-0-06-124242-7(X))* HarperCollins Pubs. (Tegen, Katherine Bks).

—Darke. Sage, Angie. ed. 2012. (Septimus Heap Ser.: 6). lib. bdg. 18.40 *(978-0-606-26264-4(4)*, Turtleback) Turtleback Bks.

—Flyte. Sage, Angie. (Septimus Heap Ser.: 2). 544p. (J). (gr. 4-7). 2007. (ENG.). pap. 7.99 *(978-0-06-057736-0(3))*; 2006. (ENG.). 17.99 *(978-0-06-057734-6(7))*; 2006. lib. bdg. 18.89 *(978-0-06-057735-3(5))* HarperCollins Pubs. (Tegen, Katherine Bks).

—Flyte. Sage, Angie. ed. 2007. (Septimus Heap Ser.: 2). 532p. (gr. 4-7). lib. bdg. 18.40 *(978-1-4178-1566-1(3)*, Turtleback) Turtleback Bks.

—Fyre. Sage, Angie. 2013. (Septimus Heap Ser.: 7). (ENG.). 720p. (J). (gr. 3-7). 17.99 *(978-0-06-124245-8(4)*, Tegen, Katherine Bks) HarperCollins Pubs.

—Magyk. Sage, Angie. (Septimus Heap Ser.: 1). (J). 2005. (ENG.). 576p. (gr. 4-18). 17.99 *(978-0-06-057731-5(2))*; 2005. 576p. (gr. 4-18). lib. bdg. 18.89 *(978-0-06-057732-2(0))*; 2006. (ENG.). 608p. (gr. 4-7). reprint ed. pap. 7.99 *(978-0-06-057733-9(9))*; Bk. 1. 2013. (ENG.). 704p. (gr. 3-7). pap. 4.99 *(978-0-06-223692-0(X))* HarperCollins Pubs. (Tegen, Katherine Bks).

—Magyk. Sage, Angie. 2007. (Septimus Heap Ser.: Bk. 1). 564p. (gr. 4-7). 18.00 *(978-0-7569-7760-3(6))* Perfection Learning Corp.

—The Magykal Papers. Sage, Angie. 2009. (Septimus Heap Ser.). (ENG.). 176p. (J). (gr. 3-7). 17.99 *(978-0-06-170416-1(4)*, Tegen, Katherine Bks) HarperCollins Pubs.

—Physik. Sage, Angie. (Septimus Heap Ser.: 3). (ENG.). (J). (gr. 4-7). 2007. 560p. 17.99 *(978-0-06-057737-7(1))*; Bk. 3. 2008. 576p. pap. 7.99 *(978-0-06-057739-1(8))* HarperCollins Pubs. (Tegen, Katherine Bks).

—Queste. Sage, Angie. (Septimus Heap Ser.: 4). (ENG.). (J). (gr. 4). 2009. 624p. pap. 7.99 *(978-0-06-088209-9(3))*; 2008. 608p. 17.99 *(978-0-06-088207-5(7))* HarperCollins Pubs. (Tegen, Katherine Bks).

—Queste. Sage, Angie. ed. 2009. (Septimus Heap Ser.: 4). 596p. lib. bdg. 18.40 *(978-0-606-02607-9(X)*, Turtleback) Turtleback Bks.

—Septimus Heap, Set. Sage, Angie. 2007. (Septimus Heap Ser.: Bks. 1-2). (J). (gr. 4). pap. 15.99 *(978-0-06-136195-1(X)*, Tegen, Katherine Bks) HarperCollins Pubs.

—Septimus Heap - Todhunter Moon. Sage, Angie. 2014. (World of Septimus Heap Ser.: 1). (ENG.). 480p. (J). (gr. 3-7). 17.99 *(978-0-06-227245-4(4)*, Tegen, Katherine Bks) HarperCollins Pubs.

—Septimus Heap, Book Seven: Fyre. Sage, Angie. 2013. (Septimus Heap Ser.: 7). 720p. (J). (gr. 3-7). lib. bdg. 18.89 *(978-0-06-124246-5(2)*, Tegen, Katherine Bks) HarperCollins Pubs.

—Swordbird. Fan, Nancy Yi. 2007. (Swordbird Ser.). (J). (gr. 3-7). 219p. 15.99 *(978-0-06-113099-1(0)*, HarperCollins); 217p. lib. bdg. 16.89 *(978-0-06-113100-4(8))* HarperCollins Pubs.

—Syren. Sage, Angie. (Septimus Heap Ser.: 5). (J). (gr. 4). 2011. (ENG.). 656p. pap. 7.99 *(978-0-06-088212-9(3))*; 2009. 640p. lib. bdg. 18.89 *(978-0-06-088211-2(5))*; 2009. (ENG.). 640p. 17.99 *(978-0-06-088210-5(7))* HarperCollins Pubs. (Tegen, Katherine Bks).

—Todhunter Moon. Sage, Angie. 2015. (World of Septimus Heap Ser.: 1). (ENG.). 496p. (J). (gr. 3-7). pap. 7.99 *(978-0-06-227246-1(2)*, Tegen, Katherine Bks) HarperCollins Pubs.

Zug, Mark. Swordbird. Zug, Mark. Fan, Nancy Yi. 2008. (Swordbird Ser.: 1). (ENG.). 256p. (J). (gr. 3-7). pap. 6.99 *(978-0-06-113101-1(6))* HarperCollins Pubs.

Zulewski, Timothy. Four Friends Find Fun. Doyle, V. L. & Rohm, Robert. 2005. 32p. (J). 18.95 *(978-0-9651672-4-6(0))* Eklektika Pr., Inc.

Zulkifi, Azhari. Aisha Goes in Search of Colour. Dhar, Lisa Jane. 2009. (ENG.). 32p. (J). (gr. k-2). 6.95 *(978-0-86037-472-5(5))* Kube Publishing Ltd. GBR. Dist: Consortium Bk. Sales & Distribution.

Zulkifli, Azhar. Islamic Manners. D'Oyen, Fatima. 2012. (ENG.). 64p. (J). (gr. -1-2). pap., act. bk. ed. 5.95 *(978-0-86037-463-3(7))* Kube Publishing Ltd. GBR. Dist: Consortium Bk. Sales & Distribution.

Zulkifli, Azhari. I Can Make Du'a Anywhere! Ibrahim, Yasmin. 2010. (ENG.). 15p. (J). (gr. -1-k). bds. 9.95 *(978-0-86037-324-7(X))* Kube Publishing Ltd. GBR. Dist: Consortium Bk. Sales & Distribution.

—I Can Pray Anywhere! Ghani, Aisha. 2010. (ENG.). 15p. (J). (gr. -1-k). bds. 9.95 *(978-0-86037-339-1(8))* Kube Publishing Ltd. GBR. Dist: Consortium Bk. Sales & Distribution.

—I Can Read the Qur'an Anywhere! Ibrahim, Yasmin. 2010. (ENG.). 15p. (J). (gr. -1-k). bds. 9.95 *(978-0-86037-309-4(6))* Kube Publishing Ltd. GBR. Dist: Consortium Bk. Sales & Distribution.

—I Can Say Bismillah Anywhere! Ibrahim, Yasmin. 2010. (ENG.). 15p. (J). (gr. -1-k). bds. 9.95 *(978-0-86037-314-8(2))* Kube Publishing Ltd. GBR. Dist: Consortium Bk. Sales & Distribution.

—I Can Wear Hijab Anywhere! Ibrahim, Yasmin. 2010. (ENG.). 15p. (J). (gr. -1-k). bds. 9.95 *(978-0-86037-319-3(3))* Kube Publishing Ltd. GBR. Dist: Consortium Bk. Sales & Distribution.

Zunon, Elizabeth. The Boy Who Harnessed the Wind. Kamkwamba, William & Mealer, Bryan. 2012. (ENG.). 32p. (J). (gr. 1-3). 17.99 *(978-0-8037-3511-8(1)*, Dial) Penguin Publishing Group.

—Grandma Nell. Nelson, Vaunda Micheaux. 2016. (J). lib. bdg. *(978-1-4677-4208-5(2)*, Carolrhoda Bks.) Lerner Publishing Group.

—How Many Spots Does a Leopard Have? An African Folktale. York, J. 2012. (Folktales from Around the World Ser.). (ENG.). 24p. (J). (gr. k-3). 28.50 *(978-1-61473-217-4(5)*, 204912) Child's World, Inc., The.

—Lala Salama: A Tanzanian Lullaby. MacLachlan, Patricia. 2011. (ENG.). 32p. (J). (gr. -1-2). 16.99 *(978-0-7636-4747-6(0))* Candlewick Pr.

—My Hands Sing the Blues: Romare Bearden's Childhood Journey, 0 vols. Harvey, Jeanne Walker. 2011. (ENG.). 40p. (J). (gr. k-3). 17.99 *(978-0-7614-5810-4(7)*, 9780761458104, Amazon Children's Publishing) Amazon Publishing.

—One Plastic Bag: Isatou Ceesay & the Recycling Women of the Gambia. Paul, Miranda. 2015. (ENG.). 32p. (J). (gr. k-3). lib. bdg. 19.99 *(978-1-4677-1608-6(1))* Lerner Publishing Group.

—Poems in the Attic. Grimes, Nikki. 2015. (ENG.). 48p. (J). 19.95 *(978-1-62014-027-7(6))* Lee & Low Bks., Inc.

—A President from Hawaii. Carolan, Joanna & Carolan, Terry. 2012. (ENG.). 24p. (J). (gr. 2-5). 15.99 *(978-0-7636-5230-2(X))*; pap. 7.99 *(978-0-7636-6282-0(8))* Candlewick Pr.

Zuppardi, Sam. Nobody's Perfect. Elliott, David. 2015. (ENG.). 32p. (J). (gr. -1-3). 16.99 *(978-0-7636-6699-6(8))* Candlewick Pr.

—Once upon a Midnight Eerie. McAlpine, Gordon. 2015. (Misadventures of Edgar & Allan Poe Ser.: 2). (ENG.). 208p. (J). (gr. 3-7). 6.99 *(978-0-14-242349-3(1)*, Puffin) Penguin Publishing Group.

—Once upon a Midnight Eerie: Book #2. McAlpine, Gordon. 2014. (Misadventures of Edgar & Allan Poe Ser.: 2). (ENG.). 192p. (J). (gr. 3-7). 16.99 *(978-0-670-78493-6(1)*, Viking Juvenile) Penguin Publishing Group.

—The Pet & the Pendulum. McAlpine, Gordon. 2015. (Misadventures of Edgar & Allan Poe Ser.: 3). (ENG.). 208p. (J). (gr. 3-7). 16.99 *(978-0-670-78492-9(3)*, Viking Juvenile) Penguin Publishing Group.

—The Tell-Tale Start. McAlpine, Gordon. 2013. (Misadventures of Edgar & Allan Poe Ser.: 1). (ENG.). (J). (gr. 3-7). 208p. pap. 6.99 *(978-0-14-242346-2(7)*, Puffin); 192p. 15.99 *(978-0-670-78491-2(5)*, Viking Juvenile) Penguin Publishing Group.

Zuppardi, Sam. The Nowhere Box. Zuppardi, Sam. 2013. (ENG.). 40p. (J). (gr. -1-3). 15.99 *(978-0-7636-6367-4(0))* Candlewick Pr.

Zvonarova, Jenny Desneige. Olivia's Birthday. Carruthers, Deborah. 2011. 20p. (gr. 1-2). 14.99 *(978-1-4269-4967-8(7))* Trafford Publishing.

Zwald, John. Mahmoud Meets Moses. Zwald, John. DesRochers, Diane O. 2012. 26p. pap. 14.99 *(978-0-9838832-9-6(7))* WRB Pub.

Zwebner, Janet. God's World. Rouss, Sylvia. 2005. (Tikkun Olam Ser.). 32p. (J). 16.95 *(978-1-932687-00-2(9))*; pap. 9.95 *(978-1-932687-01-9(7))* Simcha Media Group. (Devora Publishing).

—The Little Room. Desnick, Chaim. 2005. 32p. (J). (gr. -1-1). 14.95 *(978-1-930143-81-4(8))*; pap. 9.95 *(978-1-930143-86-9(9))* Simcha Media Group. (Devora Publishing).

—The Storybook Haggadah. Rossel, Seymour. 2006. 72p. (J). pap. 9.95 *(978-1-932687-84-2(X)*, Pitspopany Pr.) Simcha Media Group.

Zweifel, Frances. Simple Nature Experiments with Everyday Materials. Fredericks, Anthony D. 2004. 128p. (J). (gr. 4-8). reprint ed. pap. 6.00 *(978-0-7567-7727-2(5))* DIANE Publishing Co.

Zwerger, Lisbeth. El Famoso Cohete. Wilde, Oscar & Oscar, Wilde. (SPA.). 72p. (J). *(978-84-392-8693-6(7))* Gaviota Ediciones ESP. Dist: Lectorum Pubns., Inc.

—The Gift of the Magi. Henry, O. 2006. (ENG.). 32p. (J). (gr. 1-4). 17.99 *(978-1-4169-3586-5(X)*, Simon & Schuster Bks. For Young Readers) Simon & Schuster Bks. For Young Readers.

—El Gigante Egoista. Wilde, Oscar & Oscar, Wilde. 2nd ed. (SPA.). 48p. (J). *(978-84-392-8674-5(0))* Gaviota Ediciones ESP. Dist: Lectorum Pubns., Inc.

—Hans Christian Andersen's Fairy Tales. Andersen, Hans Christian. Bell, Anthea, tr. from GER. 2006. (ENG.). 104p. (J). (gr. -1-3). 23.99 *(978-0-698-40035-1(6)*, Minedition) Penguin Publishing Group.

—Little Red Cap. Grimm, Wilhelm K. & Grimm, Jacob. 37p. (J). (gr. k-2). pap. 5.95 *(978-0-8072-1285-1(7)*, Listening Library) Random Hse. Audio Publishing Group.

—The Night Before Christmas. Moore, Clement C. 2014. (Minedition Minibooks Ser.). (ENG.). 32p. (J). (gr. -1-k). 9.99 *(978-988-8240-88-3(9))* Neugebauer, Michael (Publishing) Limited HKG. Dist: Independent Pubs. Group.

—Los Salvadores del Pais. Nesbit, E. & Edith, Nesbit. 2nd ed. (SPA.). 60p. (YA). (gr. 5-8). *(978-84-392-8676-9(7)*, EV7286) Gaviota Ediciones ESP. Dist: Lectorum Pubns., Inc.

—Tales from the Brothers Grimm. Brothers Grimm, Becky & Brothers Grimm. 2013. (ENG.). 96p. (J). (gr. k-2). 29.99 *(978-988-8240-53-1(6))* Neugebauer, Michael (Publishing) Limited HKG. Dist: Independent Pubs. Group.

—The Wizard of Oz. Baum, L. Frank. 2004. 103p. (J). (gr. 4-8). reprint ed. 20.00 *(978-0-7567-7708-1(9))* DIANE Publishing Co.

—Wonderment: The Lisbeth Zwerger Collection. 2014. (ENG.). 164p. (J). 29.95 *(978-0-7358-4187-1(X))* North-South Bks., Inc.

Zwerger, Lisbeth & Aesop. Aesop's Fables. ed. 2006. 32p. (J). (gr. -1-3). pap. 6.95 *(978-0-7358-2069-2(4))* North-South Bks., Inc.

Zyle, Jon Van. Douggie: The Playful Pup Who Became a Sled Dog Hero. Flowers, Pam. 2008. (ENG.). 32p. (J). (gr. k-5). 15.95 *(978-0-88240-654-1(X)*, Alaska Northwest Bks.) Graphic Arts Ctr. Publishing Co.

—Little Puffin's First Flight. London, Jonathan. ed. 2015. (ENG.). 32p. (J). (gr. -1-3). 16.99 *(978-1-941821-40-4(5)*, Alaska Northwest Bks.) Graphic Arts Ctr. Publishing Co.

Numeric

14 Outstanding American Artists Staff. America: A Book of Opposites/Un Libro de Contrarios. Nikola-Lisa, W. 2013. (ENG & SPA.). 32p. (J). (gr. -1). bds. 8.95 *(978-1-58430-028-1(0))* Lee & Low Bks., Inc.

PUBLISHER NAME INDEX

10 Finger Pr., *(978-0-9728131; 978-1-933174)* 8435 Belize Pl., Wellington, FL 33414 USA Tel 561-434-9044; Toll Free: 866-7-author
E-mail: mahesh@10fingerspress.com
Web site: http://www.10fingerspress.com
Dist(s): **Midpoint Trade Bks., Inc.**

10 To 2 Children's Bks., *(978-0-9849487; 978-0-615-74608-1; 978-0-615-74627-2; 978-0-615-79610-9; 978-0-615-79632-1; 978-0-615-84753-5; 978-0-615-87923-9)* P.O. Box 5173, Clinton, NJ 08809 USA Tel 610-570-4196
E-mail: darylkcobb@yahoo.com
Web site: http://www.darylcobb.com
Dist(s): **CreateSpace Independent Publishing Platform.**

100 Book Challenge *See* **American Reading Co.**

101 Bk. *Imprint of* **Michaelson Entertainment**

114th Aviation Co. Assn., *(978-0-9742465)* 15151 Berry Trail, Suite 403, Dallas, TX 75248-6319 USA
E-mail: steve@stibbens.com.

11th Hour Productions *See* **Twilight Tales, Inc.**

121 Pubns., *(978-0-9841931)* 13200 Shadow Mountain Dr., Saratoga, CA 95070 USA (SAN 858-690X)
E-mail: mattweber11@yahoo.com
Web site: http://www.121publications.com
Dist(s): **Independent Pubs. Group.**

1212 Pr., *(978-0-9764985)* 1212 Beverley Rd., Brooklyn, NY 11218 USA Tel 718-462-4004
E-mail: rglstudio@earthlink.net.

123 Bk. *Imprint of* **Michaelson Entertainment**

13 Hands Pubns., *(978-0-9767260)* Div. Crooked Roads Productions, LLC, Orders Addr.: 914 Westwood Blvd., #518, Los Angeles, CA 90024 USA Fax: 310-388-6012
E-mail: mnaughton@earthlink.net
Web site: http://www.13handsonline.com; http://www.gildedhearse.com.

153 Fish Publishing, *(978-0-9747918)* 230 SW Railroad St., Sheridan, OR 97378-1745 USA.

16th Avenue Pr., *(978-0-9742854)* P.O. Box 166, Portage, MI 49081 USA Fax: 269-372-6970
E-mail: theawrites@sbcglobal.net
Web site: http://www.fearnoflame.com.

16th Place Publishing, *(978-0-9745152)* 171 S. 16th Pl., Pocatello, ID 83201 USA
E-mail: brobergbook@yahoo.com
Web site: http://www.stoleninnocencebook.com.

1776 Pr., *(978-0-9825243)* 19 Coleman Rd., Wethersfield, CT 06109 USA.

1-800 ProColor, Incorporated *See* **Robertson Publishing**

1st Impression Publishing, *(978-0-9763365)* P.O. Box 10339, Burbank, CA 91510-0339 USA Tel 818-843-1300; Fax: 818-846-5657
E-mail: sahysen@earthlink.net
Web site: http://www.1stimpressionpublishing.com.

1st World Library *See* **Groundbreaking Pr.**

1st World Library - Literary Society *Imprint of* **1st World Publishing, Inc.**

1st World Publishing *Imprint of* **1st World Publishing, Inc.**

1st World Publishing, Inc., *(978-0-9638502; 978-1-887472; 978-1-59540; 978-1-4218)* Orders Addr.: 1100 N. 4th St., Suite 9, Fairfield, IA 52556-2169 USA Toll Free: 877-209-5004; *Imprints*: 1st World Publishing (Frst Wrld Pub); 1st World Library - Literary Society (1st Wrld); Sunstar Publishing (SunstarPub)
E-mail: ed@1stworldpublishing.com; order@1stworldpublishing.com; info@1stworldpublishing.com; rodney@1stworldlibrary.org
Web site: http://www.1stworldpublishing.com.
Dist(s): **Follett School Solutions**
Lightning Source, Inc.
New Leaf Distributing Co., Inc.

1stBooks Library *See* **AuthorHouse**

1stWorld Library, Limited *See* **1st World Publishing, Inc.**

2 Donn Bks., *(978-0-9770893)* 11354 Links Dr., Reston, VA 20190-4807 USA (SAN 256-7407)
Web site: http://www.2donnbooks.com.

20/20 Publishing, *(978-0-9668718)* Orders Addr.: 3941 S. Bristol Suite D520, Santa Ana, CA 92704 USA Tel 800-991-3296
E-mail: dawn@dawnmartin.com
Web site: http://www.dawnmartin.com
Dist(s): **Distributors, The.**

2020 Vision Pr., *(978-0-9710675)* 2744 Crown Point, Las Cruces, NM 88011 USA Tel 505-532-9693; Fax: 505-532-9694
E-mail: josh@joshhunt.com
Web site: http://www.joshhunt.com.

20th Maine, Inc., *(978-0-9704408)* 859 Lawrence Rd., Pownal, ME 04069-6118 USA
E-mail: pat@20thmaine.com
Web site: http://www.20thmaine.com.

21st Century Pr., *(978-0-9660906; 978-0-9700639; 978-0-9717009; 978-0-9725719; 978-0-9728899; 978-0-9749811; 978-0-9766243; 978-0-9771964; 978-0-9779535; 978-0-9817769; 978-0-9824428; 978-0-9827616; 978-0-9838359; 978-0-9894317; 978-0-9911004; 978-0-9863864)* 3308 S. Meadowlark Ave., Springfield, MO 65807 USA Tel 417-889-4803; Fax: 417-889-2210; Toll Free: 800-658-0284; *Imprints*: Sonship Press (Sonship Pr) Do not confuse with 21st Century Press in Southlake, TX
E-mail: lee@21stcenturypress.com
Web site: http://www.21stcenturypress.com
Dist(s): **Anchor Distributors**
CreateSpace Independent Publishing Platform
Perseus Distribution
Send The Light Distribution LLC.

21st Century Pubs., *(978-0-9607298)* 1320 Curt Gowdy Dr., Cheyenne, WY 82009 USA (SAN 239-1740) Tel 307-638-2254
E-mail: chismaturi@prodigy.net
Web site: http://www.triplecrownwinnerearlsande.com
Dist(s): **Emery-Pratt Co.**
Blackwell.

21st Century Publishing, *(978-0-9722624)* 16 W. Pacific Ave. No. 3, Henderson, NV 89015 USA Tel 702-564-1665; Fax: 702-564-4190
E-mail: brouff55@anv.net.

21st Century Publishing Hse. (CHN) *(978-7-5391; 978-7-88861; 978-7-900386) Dist. by* **Chinasprout.**

22 West Bks., *(978-0-9767788)* Orders Addr.: P.O. Box 155, Sheldonville, MA 02070-0155 USA
E-mail: chris@22wb.com
Web site: http://www.22wb.com.

23rd St. Publishing, *(978-0-9800821)* Orders Addr.: P.O. Box 863734, Plano, TX 75086-3734 USA (SAN 855-1421) Tel 214-717-7244
E-mail: stacy@23rdstpublishing.com
Web site: http://23rdStPublishing.com
Dist(s): **Follett School Solutions.**

25 Dreams Educational Media, *(978-0-9768019)* 8622 Bellanca Ave., Suite J, Los Angeles, CA 90045 USA.

2B Pr., *(978-0-9765430)* 206 Clear Springs, Peachtree City, GA 30269 USA Tel 770-487-1348
E-mail: tami@2bpress.com
Web site: http://www.2bpress.com.

2Giggles, *(978-0-9801020)* 25811 Mill Pond Ln., Spring, TX 77373 USA
E-mail: vineandfig@gmail.com.

2Lakes Publishing, *(978-0-9722400)* Orders Addr.: 3661 Natalie Way, Bandon, OR 97411 USA
E-mail: heidi2lakes@2lakespublishing.com
Web site: http://www.2lakespublishing.com
Dist(s): **Independent Pubs. Group.**

2MPower, *(978-0-9767046)* 25231 Grissom Rd., Laguna Hills, CA 92653-5237 USA Tel 949-837-1268; Fax: 949-470-0659
E-mail: arnovigen@yahoo.com
Web site: http://www.2mpwr.com.

3 Pals Media, LLC, *(978-0-9770960)* 424 Greenleaf Ave., Burlington, WA 98233 USA Tel 360-755-2299; Fax: 360-755-8010
Web site: http://www.pumpkinpatchpals.com.

302 Publishing, *(978-0-9790165)* 9139 SW Excalibur Pl., Portland, OR 97219-9721 USA Tel 503-246-2499 (phone/fax).

306090, Inc., *(978-0-615-18202-5; 978-0-692-00088-5; 978-0-615-34909-1; 978-0-615-77951-5)* 350 Canal St., Box 2092, New York, NY 10013 USA
E-mail: info@306090.org; js@306090.org
Web site: http://www.306090.org
Dist(s): **Hachette Bk. Group**
Princeton Architectural Pr.

353rd Regimental History Project, *(978-0-9748916)* 2650 N. 64th, Wavnatusa, WI 53213-1407 USA Tel 414-444-7120
E-mail: suzannb@wyoming.com.

360 Marketing, LLC, *(978-0-9702654)* 6 Trumbull St., Saintnington, CT 06378 USA Tel 860-535-2240; Fax: 860-535-3243 (call first)
E-mail: three60mrk@aol.com; claudia@chasem2.com.

3-C Institute for Social Development, *(978-0-9779290; 978-0-9789871; 978-1-934409)* 1903 N. Harrison Ave., Suite 101, Cary, NC 27513 USA Tel 919-677-0101; Fax: 919-677-0112
E-mail: info@3cisd.com
Web site: http://www.3cisd.com.

3cs Publishing, The, *(978-0-9773341)* P.O. Box 8096, Silver Spring, MD 20907 USA
Web site: http://www.the3cs.com.

3D Alley, Inc., *(978-0-9776845)* 4525 Harding Rd., Suite 317, Nashville, TN 37205 USA.

3G Publishing, Inc., *(978-0-9833544; 978-0-9854968; 978-1-941247)* 3508 Pk. Lake Ln., Norcross, GA 30092 USA Tel 404-553-1566; Fax: 770-676-0626 Do not confuse with 3G Publishing, Inc in New Berlin, WI
E-mail: myrna.gale@gmail.com
Web site: 3gpublishinginc.com.

3H Dowsing International LLC, *(978-0-9656653; 978-1-932229)* W10160 Cty. Rd. C, Wautoma, WI 54982 USA Tel 920-787-4747; Fax: 920-787-2006
E-mail: ilovedowsing@hotmail.com
Web site: http://store.yahoo.com/dowsing.

3N Media Group, *(978-0-9741686)* P.O. Box 705, Morris Plains, NJ 07950 USA Fax: 240-220-0500
E-mail: 3nmediagrp@optonline.net.

3perfections, *(978-0-9759909)* 833 Great Oaks Trail, Eagan, MN 55123 USA Tel 651-905-1098
E-mail: perfections3@aol.com
Web site: http://www.3perfections.com.

4 Childrens Sake Pubns., *(978-0-9752982)* Orders Addr.: P.O. Box 594, Moosup, CT 06354 USA; Edit Addr.: 357 N. Main St., Moosup, CT 06354 USA.

4 Sonkist Angels *See* **Four Sonkist Angels**

4000 Years of Writing History, *(978-0-9748786)* P.O. Box 484, Redondo Beach, CA 90277-0484 USA
Web site: http://www.lmlk.com.

43 Degrees North LLC, *(978-0-9744444)* P.O. Box 781, Wilson, NY 14172 USA Tel 716-751-3604; Fax: 716-751-0105
E-mail: jeff@tailgatetrivia.com
Web site: http://www.tailgatetrivia.com.

44 Enterprises, *(978-0-615-22510-4; 978-0-615-24951-3)* 820A W. 47th St., Savannah, GA 31405 USA.

45th Parallel Concepts Ltd., *(978-0-9747615)* Orders Addr.: 106 Main St. PMB 152, Houlton, ME 04730 USA
E-mail: postmaster@americanschoolhousereader.com
Web site: http://www.americanschoolhousereader.com
Dist(s): **Unique Bks., Inc.**

47North *Imprint of* **Amazon Publishing**

4All Ages LLC, *(978-0-9787986)* 5 Murdock Rd., Suite 100, East Rockaway, NY 11518 USA (SAN 851-643X) Tel 516-561-3146
E-mail: laws123@aol.com
Web site: http://www.colorpets.com.

4Elliott Publishing, Inc., *(978-0-9846963)* 6829 NW 15th Ave., Miami, FL 33142 USA Tel 786-277-2693
E-mail: sxye320@yahoo.comtees.

4mPr., *(978-0-9896681)* 2639 Sherrie Ln., Thompsons Stn, TN 37179 USA Tel 615-815-7447; Fax: 615-790-6119
E-mail: jpmarrs@gmail.com.

4N Publishing LLC, *(978-0-9741319; 978-0-9798841)* Orders Addr.: 44-73 21st St., D-6, Long Island City, NY 11101 USA Tel 718-482-1135
E-mail: brendan@4npublishing.com; erin@4npublishing.com; lj@4npublishing.com
Web site: http://www.4npublishing.com
Dist(s): **Consortium Bk. Sales & Distribution.**

4RV Publishing, LLC, *(978-0-9797513; 978-0-9818685; 978-0-9840708; 978-0-9825886; 978-0-9826423; 978-0-9826594; 978-0-9828346; 978-0-9832740; 978-0-9838018; 978-0-9852661; 978-0-9889617; 978-1-940310)* P.O. Box 6482, Edmond, OK 73083-6482 USA
E-mail: president@4rvpublishingllc.com
Web site: http://www.4rvpublishingllc.com
Dist(s): **Follett School Solutions.**

4th Dimension Enterprises, Inc., *(978-0-9819088)* 40 Memorial Hwy. Apt. 27N, New Rochelle, NY 10801-8340 USA
E-mail: info@4thdimensionpublishing.com
Web site: http://www.4thdimensionpublishing.com.

4th Division Pr. *Imprint of* **Kurdyla, E L Publishing LLC**

5 Continents (ITA) *(978-88-7439) Dist. by* **HachBkGrp.**

5 Fold Media LLC, *(978-0-9825775; 978-0-9827980; 978-1-936578; 978-1-942056)* 5701 East Cir. Dr. No. 338, Cicero, NY 13039 USA
E-mail: cathy@5foldmedia.com
Web site: http://www.5foldmedia-store.com; http://www.5foldmedia.com.

5 Muses Publishing, *(978-0-9786180)* 100 Andover Pk. Ste 150-108, TUKWILA, WA 98188 USA
E-mail: rlpolhill@5musespublishing.com
Web site: http://www.5MusesPublishing.com.

5 Prince Publishing, *(978-0-615-46134-2; 978-0-615-52891-5; 978-0-9848529; 978-0-9853345; 978-0-615-64941-2; 978-0-615-65268-9; 978-0-615-65747-9; 978-0-615-66869-7; 978-0-615-68734-6; 978-0-615-68919-7; 978-1-939217; 978-1-63112)* Orders Addr.: P.O. Box 16507, Denver, CO 80216 USA Tel 303-257-0389
E-mail: books@5princebooks.com
Web site: http://www.5princebooks.com
Dist(s): **CreateSpace Independent Publishing Platform**
Lightning Source, Inc.
Smashwords.

5 Spot *Imprint of* **Grand Central Publishing**

5 Star Pubns., LLC, *(978-0-9843881; 978-0-9832473; 978-0-9854386)* c/o Tlj Bookstore, Llc, 9134 Piscataway Rd. No. 805, Clinton, MD 20735 USA
E-mail: shawn5star@yahoo.com; shawncvalentine@yahoo.com
Web site: http://www.5starpublications.net
Dist(s): **Icon Distribution.**

5 Star Stories, Inc., *(978-0-9659470)* Orders Addr.: 14625 Greenville St., Houston, TX 77015-4711 USA Tel 713-455-1073; Fax: 713-583-7017
E-mail: isellfantasy@hotmail.com
Web site: http://www.TexasSecedes.com.

50/50 Publishing *See* **Soulo Communications**

5,6 Pickup Sticks Publishing, *(978-0-9762145)* 2493 Sunridge Ave., SE, Atlanta, GA 30315 USA Tel 404-627-9132
E-mail: tcmac1@bellsouth.net.

6-mile Roots, *(978-0-9771255)* 1469 260th, Marion, KS 66861 USA Tel 620-924-5254
E-mail: joel@hillsborofreepress.com.

7 Robots, Inc., *(978-0-9778454)* 714 Washington Ave., Suite No. 9, New York, NY 11238 USA
Web site: http://www.7robots.com
Dist(s): **Diamond Comic Distributors, Inc.**

711 Pr. *Imprint of* **Middleton Publishing**
711Press *Imprint of* **Vendera Publishing**
716 Productions, *(978-0-9795529)* 3200 Airport Ave., Suite 16, Santa Monica, CA 90405 USA
Web site: http://learningwhoweare.com.
7th Generation *Imprint of* **Book Publishing Co.**
80 West Publishing, Inc., *(978-0-9763417)* 2222 Ponce de Leon Blvd., 6th Flr., Coral Gables, FL 33134 USA Tel 305-448-8117; Fax: 305-448-8453
E-mail: joellen@adkinsadv.com.
826 Valencia, *(978-0-9768467; 978-0-9770844; 978-0-9779289; 978-0-9790073; 978-1-934750)* 826 Valencia St., San Francisco, CA 94110 USA
E-mail: alvaro@826valencia.com
Web site: http://www.826valencia.org
Dist(s): **Perseus-PGW.**
826michigan, *(978-0-9779289; 978-0-9827293; 978-0-9966315)* 115 E. Liberty St., Ann Arbor, MI 48104-2109 USA
Web site: http://www.826michigan.org
Dist(s): **Perseus-PGW.**
8-Ball Express, Inc., *(978-0-9747273)* 316 California, Suite 529, Reno, NV 89509-1650 USA Tel 415-776-1596 (for wholesale orders); Toll Free: 877-368-2255 (for retail sales only)
E-mail: rgivens@toast.net
Web site: http://www.8-ballbible.com.
A & B Books *See* **A & B Distributors & Pubs. Group**
A & B Distributors & Pubs. Group, *(978-1-881316; 978-1-886433)* Div. of A&B Distributors, 1000 Atlantic Ave., Brooklyn, NY 11238 USA (SAN 630-9216) Tel 718-783-7808; Fax: 718-783-7267; Toll Free: 877-542-6657; 146 Lawrence St., Brooklyn, NY 11201 (SAN 631-385X)
E-mail: maxtay@webspan.net
Dist(s): **D & J Bk. Distributors**
Red Sea Pr.
A & C Black *Imprint of* **Bloomsbury USA**
A & D Bks., *(978-0-9743294)* 3708 E. 45th St., Tulsa, OK 74135 USA Tel 918-748-4348 (phone/fax)
E-mail: a_dbooks@live.com.
A & E Children's Pr., *(978-0-9728134)* 6107 S. Jericho Way, Centennial, CO 80016 USA
E-mail: maked4@aol.com.
A & E Sivells Pubns. *Imprint of* **Word For Word Publishing Co.**
A & L Communications, Inc., *(978-0-9714320)* 1946 Magnolia Crest Ln., Sugar Land, TX 77478 USA
E-mail: allysoncward@yahoo.com
Web site: http://www.algiershistory.com
Dist(s): **Forest Sales & Distributing Co.**
A & M Writing and Publishing,, *(978-0-9764824; 978-0-9861841)* 3127 Allen Way, Santa Clara, CA 95051 USA Tel 408-244-8053; Fax: 408-244-8098
E-mail: ctillson@amwriting.com
Web site: http://www.amwriting.com
Dist(s): **Partners Bk. Distributing, Inc.**
A & W Enterprises, *(978-0-9617696)* P.O. Box 8133, Roanoke, VA 24014 USA (SAN 665-603X) Tel 540-427-1154; Toll Free: 800-484-1492 (ext. 4267)
E-mail: gwalker@interlink.com.
A B C-123 Publishing, *(978-0-9711474; 978-0-578-16435-9)* Orders Addr.: P.O. Box 100145, Staten Island, NY 10310 USA Fax: 718-980-4416; 718-351-4863; Toll Free: 866-339-3936; Edit Addr.: 159 New Dorp Plaza, 2nd Flr., Staten Island, NY 10306 USA; P.O. Box 30096, Staten Island, NY 30096
E-mail: thomas@deweydoes.com; contact@deweydoes.com
Web site: http://www.deweydoes.com.
A B C-Clio Information Services *See* **ABC-CLIO, LLC**
A B Publishing, *(978-1-881545; 978-1-59765)* P.O. Box 83, North Star, MI 48862-0083 USA Toll Free: 800-882-6443
E-mail: abpub@abpub.com
Web site: http://www.abpub.com
Dist(s): **Send The Light Distribution LLC**
Spring Arbor Distributors, Inc.
A+ Bilingue/Bilingual *Imprint of* **Capstone Pr., Inc.**
A Blessed Heritage Educational Resources, *(978-0-9759320; 978-0-9767866)* 10602 Redwood Dr., Baytown, TX 77520 USA
E-mail: belinda.bullard@blessedheritage.com
Web site: http://www.blessedheritage.com.
A. Borough Bks., *(978-0-9640606; 978-1-893597)* Orders Addr.: 3901 Silver Bell Dr., Charlotte, NC 28211 USA Tel 704-364-1788; Fax: 704-366-9079; Toll Free: 800-843-8490
E-mail: humorbooks@aol.com
Dist(s): **Parnassus Bk. Distributors.**
A Cappela Publishing, *(978-0-9656309; 978-0-9724979; 978-0-9779139; 978-0-9818933; 978-0-9846177; 978-0-9850202)* P.O. Box 3691, Sarasota, FL 34230-3691 USA (SAN 253-567X) Tel 941-351-2050; Fax: 941-351-4735; *Imprints:* Advocate House (Advoca Hse) Do not confuse with A Cappella Publishing, Los Angeles, CA
E-mail: acappub@aol.com
Web site: http://www.acappela.com; http://www.lillythelash.com.
A Cappella Bks., *(978-1-55652)* 814 N. Franklin, Chicago, IL 60610 USA Tel 312-337-0747; Fax: 312-640-0542; Toll Free: 800-888-4741
E-mail: publish@ipgbook.com; orders@ipgbook.com
Web site: http://www.ipgbook.com
Dist(s): **Independent Pubs. Group.**
AEVAC, Inc., *(978-0-913356)* 7 Silver Lake Dr., Summit, NJ 07901-3233 USA (SAN 204-5567).
A Furry Mystery. The Story of the Disappearing Ferret, *(978-0-615-76548-8)* 1837 Fallbrook Dr., Alamo, CA 94507 USA Tel 9258769530
Web site: www.kidsbooksbycurtis.com
Dist(s): **CreateSpace Independent Publishing Platform.**
A H W Publishing, *(978-0-9741434)* 1124 W. 19th Ave., Spokane, WA 99203 USA (SAN 255-4070)
E-mail: annifrommainz@dc4pc.net.
A I G A / Art With Heart *See* **Art With Heart Press**
AIMS International Bks., Inc., *(978-0-922852)* 7709 Hamilton Ave., Cincinnati, OH 45231-3103 USA (SAN 630-270X) Tel 513-521-5590; Fax: 513-521-5592; Toll Free: 800-733-2067
E-mail: aimsbooks@fuse.net
Web site: http://www.aimsbooks.com
Dist(s): **Shen's Bks.**
A I T/Planet Lar, *(978-0-9676847; 978-0-9709360; 978-1-932051)* 2034 47th Ave., San Francisco, CA 94116 USA Tel 415-504-7516 (phone/fax)
E-mail: larry@ait-planetlar.com
Web site: http://www.ait-planetlar.com
Dist(s): **Diamond Comic Distributors, Inc.**
Diamond Bk. Distributors
L P C Group.
A JuneOne Production *Imprint of* **JuneOne Publishing Hub**
AK Peters, Ltd., *(978-1-56881)* 5 Commonwealth Rd. Suite 2c, Natick, MA 01760 USA (SAN 299-1810) Tel 508-651-0887 All inquiries; Fax: 508-651-0889; 7625 Empire Dr., Florence, KY 41042
E-mail: service@akpeters.com
Web site: http://www.akpeters.com
Dist(s): **Follett School Solutions**
MyiLibrary
Taylor & Francis Group.
A Kidz World *Imprint of* **ABUAA, Inc.**
ALPI International, Ltd., *(978-1-886647)* 1685 34th St., Oakland, CA 94608 USA Tel 510-655-6456; Fax: 510-655-2093; Toll Free: 800-678-2574
E-mail: becky@alpi.net.
AMG Pubs., *(978-0-89957; 978-1-61715; 978-1-63070)* Subs. of AMG Publishing Inc., Orders Addr.: P.O. Box 22000, Chattanooga, TN 37422 USA Tel 423-894-6060; Fax: 423-894-9511; Toll Free Fax: 800-265-6690; Toll Free: 800-266-4977; Edit Addr.: 6815 Shallowford Rd., Chattanooga, TN 37421 USA (SAN 211-3074) Toll Free Fax: 800-266-4577; 800-265-6690; *Imprints:* Living Ink Books (Liv Ink Bks)
E-mail: trevor@amgpublishers.com; sales@AMGpublishers.com
Web site: http://www.amgpublishers.com; http://www.livinginkbooks.com
Dist(s): **Anchor Distributors**
Spring Arbor Distributors, Inc.
AMICA Publishing Hse., *(978-1-884187)* Div. of AMICA International, 844 Industry Dr., No. 20, Seattle, WA 98188-3410 USA Tel 206-467-1035; Fax: 206-467-1522
E-mail: amica@ix.netcom.com
Web site: http://www.amicaint.com.
AMSC, Adventures in Math & Social Studies for Children, *(978-1-889639)* Orders Addr.: 818 W. Grover St., Lynden, WA 98264 USA Tel 360-354-4412; Toll Free: 800-306-1772
E-mail: math1@earthlink.net.
A N A D E M, Incorporated *See* **Anadem Publishing, Inc.**
A New Day..A New Way!, *(978-0-9749177)* 5525B Via La Mesa, Laguna Woods, CA 92637 USA Tel 949-340-0615; Fax: 949-723-0030
E-mail: kathleenscott@anewday-anewway.com; kathleen_scott@sbcglobal.net
Web site: http://www.anewday-anewway.com
Dist(s): **New Leaf Distributing Co., Inc.**
APTE, Inc., *(978-1-889651; 978-1-931872; 978-1-932736; 978-1-933229)* 820 Church St., Suite 300, Evanston, IL 60201 USA Toll Free: 800-494-1112
E-mail: pierred@apte.com; sally@apte.com
Web site: http://www.apte.com
Dist(s): **Brodart Co.**
Educational Resources
Follett School Solutions
Learning Services.
A PAR Educational, LLC, *(978-0-578-12712-5)* 856 N. Lincoln Ave., No. 2, Pittsburgh, PA 15233 USA.
ARO Publishing Co., *(978-0-89868)* Box 193, 398 S. 1100 W., Provo, UT 84601 USA (SAN 212-6370) Tel 801-377-8218; Fax: 801-818-0616
E-mail: arobook@yahoo.com
Web site: **Forest Hse. Publishing Co., Inc.**
A Road to Discovery Series Guide *Imprint of* **Perry Heights Pr.**
ASDA Publishing, Inc., *(978-0-9632319)* 904 Forest Lake Dr., Lakeland, FL 33809 USA Tel 841-859-2194.
A S Q C Quality Press *See* **ASQ Quality Pr.**
A Story Plus Children Bks., *(978-0-9778477)* Div. of Top Award, Inc., P.O. Box 1174, Pine Lake, GA 30072-1174 USA (SAN 850-3907) Tel 404-667-2619
E-mail: astoryplu@comcast.net
Web site: http://www.astoryplus.com.
A StoryPlus *See* **A Story Plus Children Bks.**
A. V. P., Incorporated *See* **IBE, Inc.**
A. W. Ink, Inc., *(978-0-9820932)* P.O. Box 1184, Kamas, UT 84036-1184 USA
E-mail: lesliesaunders@kw.com.
A4J Publishing, *(978-0-9831372)* P.O. Box 1101, Orlando, FL 32802 USA Tel 678-358-9820; Fax: 407-237-0135
E-mail: vikki@a4jpublishing.com
Web site: www.a4jpublishing.com.
AAA, *(978-0-916748; 978-1-56251; 978-1-59508)* 1000 AAA Dr., Heathrow, FL 32746-5063 USA (SAN 208-5194)
E-mail: lbonerb@national.aaa.com
Web site: http://www.aaa.com
Dist(s): **National Bk. Network**
Simon & Schuster Children's Publishing
Beeler, Thomas T. Pub.
AAA POP, *(978-0-9762282)* 4147 S. Tenmile Lake, Lakeside, OR 97449 USA
Web site: http://www.aaapop.com.
Aaduna, *(978-0-9768626)* 2021 Del Norte Ave., Saint Louis, MO 63117 USA Tel 314-647-3437
E-mail: mroach@thecollegeschool.org
Web site: http://www.senecorps.com.
Açedrex Publishing *See* **Acedrex Publishing**
A&D Xtreme *Imprint of* **ABDO Publishing Co.**
AAO Publishing, *(978-0-9786431)* a/o Melody Farloe, P.O. Box 6208, Beverly Hills, CA 90212 USA
E-mail: puffybuffy1@yahoo.com
Web site: http://www.puffybuffy.com.
Aardvark Global Publishing, *(978-0-9770328; 978-1-933570; 978-1-59971; 978-1-4276)* 9587 S. Grandview Dr., Sandy, UT 84092 USA Do not confuse with Aardvark Global Publishing, Atlanta, GA
E-mail: info@eckohousepublishing.com
Web site: http://eckohousepublishing.com/; http://aardvarkglobalpublishing.com/; http://eckobooks.com
Dist(s): **AK Pr. Distribution**
AtlasBooks Distribution
Follett School Solutions
Lulu Enterprises Inc.
SPD-Small Pr. Distribution.
Aardvark Pubs., *(978-0-615-13532-8; 978-0-615-13673-8; 978-0-615-14219-7; 978-0-615-17808-0)* 1615 Shannon Rd., Girard, OH 44420 USA
E-mail: info@aardvarkpublishers.com
Web site: http://www.aardvarkpublishers.com
Dist(s): **Lulu Enterprises Inc.**
Aardvark's Weedpatch Pr., *(978-0-9755567)* P.O. Box 1841, Rogue River, OR 97537-1841 USA
Web site: http://www.aardvarksweedpatch.com.
AARO Publishing, *(978-1-893563)* Orders Addr.: P.O. Box 1281, Palisade, CO 81526 USA; Edit Addr.: PO Box 1281 Palisade, Co 81526, Palisade, CO 81526 USA (SAN 255-7185) Tel 970-314-7690 (phone/fax)970 985 4018
E-mail: carwe@earthlink.net
Web site: http://www.snowff.com
Dist(s): **Follett School Solutions.**
Aaron Bk. Publishing, *(978-0-9819195)* 1093 Bristol Caverns Hwy., Bristol, TN 37620 USA (SAN 856-924X) Tel 423-212-1208
E-mail: info@aaronbookpublishing.com
Web site: http://www.aaronbookpublishing.com.
Aaron C Ministries, *(978-1-933519)* 1005 Pine Oak Dr., Edmond, OK 73034-5139 USA Tel 405-348-3410
E-mail: bible@jpdawson.com
Web site: http://www.jpdawson.com.
Aaron Levy Pubns., LLC, *(978-1-931463)* 1760 Stumpf Blvd., Gretna, LA 70056 USA Tel 504-258-4332
E-mail: aaronlevy1@aol.com; kelleylevy12@gmail.com
Web site: http://www.goodlifemediallc.com.
Aaron Press *See* **Publishing Assocs., Inc.**
Aaron-Barrada, Inc., *(978-0-9768671; 978-0-615-12767-5)* 79 Valley High, Ruffs Dale, PA 15679 USA Tel 724-696-4332; Fax: 612-545-3210
E-mail: aaronbarradainc@aol.com
Web site: http://www.pottiestickers.com.
Aarow Pr., *(978-0-9749046)* 3215 Buckingham Ave., Lakeland, FL 33803 USA (SAN 255-8653) Tel 863-709-8882 (phone/fax)
E-mail: aarowpress@yahoo.com.
AB Rolle Publications *See* **ABR Pubns.**
A-BA-BA-HA-LA-MA-HA Pubs. *Imprint of* **Windy Press International Publishing Hse., LLC**
Abacus Bks., Inc., *(978-0-9716292)* Div. of Abacus Bks.com, 1420 58th Ave. N, Saint Petersburg, FL 33703 USA Tel 727-742-3889; Fax: 727-522-0606
E-mail: necole@abacusbooks.com; info@abacusbooks.com
Web site: http://www.abacusbooks.com.
Abadaba Reading LLC, *(978-0-9789473)* P.O. Box 80, Charlottesville, VA 22902-5335 USA (SAN 852-0240)
Web site: http://www.adabadaalphabet.com
Dist(s): **AtlasBooks Distribution.**
aBASK Publishing, *(978-0-9843855; 978-0-9962399)* 320 National Pl., Apt 5, Longmont, CO 80501-3326 USA
E-mail: Publisher@AbaskPublishing.com; kathygode@yahoo.com
Web site: http://abaskpublishing.com.
†ABBE Pubs. Assn. of Washington, D.C., *(978-0-7883; 978-0-88164; 978-0-941864; 978-1-55914)* Orders Addr.: 4111 Gallows Rd., Virginia Div., Annandale, VA 22003 USA (SAN 239-1430)
E-mail: abbe.publishers@verizon.net; vze3hcqz@verizon.net; *CIP.*
Abbeville Kids *Imprint of* **Abbeville Pr., Inc.**
†Abbeville Pr., Inc., *(978-0-7892; 978-0-89659; 978-1-55859)* 137 Varick St., 5th Fl., New York, NY 10013 USA (SAN 211-4755) Tel 212-366-5585; Fax: 212-366-6966; Toll Free: 800-278-2665; 1094 Flex Dr., Jackson, TN 38301; *Imprints:* Abbeville Kids (Abbeville Kids)
E-mail: abbeville@abbeville.com
Web site: http://www.abbeville.com
Dist(s): **Follett School Solutions**
MyiLibrary
Perseus Bks. Group
Perseus Distribution
ebrary, Inc.; *CIP.*
Abbey Pr., *(978-0-87029)* 1 Hill Dr., Saint Meinrad, IN 47577-0128 USA (SAN 201-2057) Tel 812-357-8215; Fax: 812-357-8388; Toll Free: 800-325-2511
E-mail: customerservice@abbeypress.com
Web site: http://www.abbeypress.com/
Dist(s): **Open Road Integrated Media, LLC.**
Abbott Avenue Pr., *(978-0-9767514)* 859 Hollywood Way, Suite 258, Burbank, CA 91505 USA
E-mail: info@abbottavenuepress.com
Web site: http://www.abbottavenuepress.com.
Abbott, Cindy L., *(978-0-615-48291-0)* 22 Gazebo, Irvine, CA 92620 USA Tel 949-857-5112
E-mail: cabbott@fullerton.edu
Dist(s): **CreateSpace Independent Publishing Platform.**
Abbott Pr. *Imprint of* **Author Solutions, Inc.**
ABC *Imprint of* **DC Comics**
ABC Bk. *Imprint of* **Michaelson Entertainment**
ABC Bks., *(978-0-9785108)* P.O. Box 2246, Sunnyvale, CA 94087-2246 USA Do not confuse with ABC Books in Plano, TX.
ABC Development, Inc., *(978-0-9767179)* 6869 Stapoint Ct., Suite 107, Winter Park, FL 32792 USA Tel 407-671-6000; Fax: 407-671-6602; Toll Free: 800-222-3053
E-mail: sales@abc-development.com
Web site: http://www.abc-development.com.
ABC Pr., *(978-0-9758622)* 550 Iron Mountain Rd., El Dorado, AR 71730 USA Tel 870-863-5779 Do not confuse with ABC Pr. in Walnut Creek, CA
E-mail: srwood@suddenlink.net
Web site: http://RamonaWoodBooks.com.
ABC Pubs., *(978-0-9772685)* 32 Meadowlark Ln., Willingboro, NJ 08046-2108 USA Tel 609-880-0897
E-mail: fg@abc-advantage.com
Web site: http://www.abc-advantage.com.
ABC Schermerhorn Walters Company *See* **Schermerhorn, Walters Co.**
†ABC-CLIO, LLC, *(978-0-87436; 978-0-903450; 978-1-57607; 978-1-85109; 978-1-59884; 978-1-61069)* 130 Cremona Dr., Santa Barbara, CA 93117 USA (SAN 301-5467) Tel 805-968-1911; Fax: 805-685-9685; Toll Free: 800-368-6868; P.O. Box 93116, Goleta, CA 93116 (SAN 857-7099)
E-mail: customerservice@abc-clio.com; service@abc-clio.com; salesuk@abc-clio.com
Web site: http://www.abc-clio.com
Dist(s): **Bookhouse, The**
Ebsco Publishing
Follett School Solutions
MyiLibrary
ebrary, Inc.; *CIP.*
Abccurate Business Ventures, *(978-0-9755341)* P.O. Box 2236, Smyrna, TN 37167 USA Tel 615-831-7100
E-mail: editor@abccurate.com
Web site: http://www.abccurate.com.
ABCDE Academic Bks. for Children's Development Through Education, *(978-0-9754008)* P.O. Box 374, Shrub Oak, NY 10588 USA.
ABCDMoon *See* **ABCDMoon Publishing**
ABCDMoon Publishing, *(978-0-9729216)* P.O. Box 910732, Lexington, KY 40591-0732 USA Tel 859-873-5031
E-mail: tex@charliethemonkey.com; amy@charliethemonkey.com
Web site: http://www.charliethemonkey.com.
ABCs Connection, Inc., *(978-0-9755475)* 1209 Caribou Crossing, Suite 101, Durham, NC 27713 USA Tel 919-451-4991; Fax: 919-484-1980
E-mail: casey_wallace@yahoo.com
Web site: http://www.abcsconnection.com.
ABC's Unlimited *See* **See abc's LC**
Abdelsalam Corp., *(978-0-9755975)* 2499 Trewigtown Rd., Colmar, PA 18915 USA.
Abdiel Productions, *(978-0-9768088)* 4802 Nassau Ave., NE, No. 31, Tacoma, WA 98422-4632 USA.
Abdo & Daughter *Imprint of* **ABDO Publishing Co.**
Abdo & Daughters *Imprint of* **ABDO Publishing Co.**
Abdo & Daughters Publishing *See* **ABDO Publishing Co.**
Abdo Kids *Imprint of* **ABDO Publishing Co.**
†ABDO Publishing Co., *(978-0-939179; 978-1-56239; 978-1-57765; 978-1-59197; 978-1-59679; 978-1-59928; 978-1-59961; 978-1-60270; 978-1-60453; 978-1-61613; 978-1-61714; 978-1-61758; 978-1-61783; 978-1-61784; 978-1-61785; 978-1-61786; 978-1-61787; 978-1-61478; 978-1-61479; 978-1-61480; 978-1-62401; 978-1-62402; 978-1-62403; 978-1-62968; 978-1-62969; 978-1-62970; 978-1-68076; 978-1-68077; 978-1-68078; 978-1-68079; 978-1-68080) Div. of ABDO Publishing Group, Orders Addr.: 8000 W. 78th St. Suite 310, Edina, MN 55439 USA (SAN 662-9172) Tel 952-831-2120; Fax: 952-831-1632; Toll Free Fax: 800-862-3480; Toll Free: 800-800-1312; Imprints:* Abdo & Daughters (Abdo & Dghtrs); Checkerboard Library (Checkerboard Library); SandCastle (SndCastle); Buddy Books (Buddy Bks); Super SandCastle (SuperSandcastle); Essential Library (EssentialLibrary); A&D Xtreme (A&DXtreme); SportsZone (SportsZone); Big Buddy Books (BigBuddy); Graphic Planet- Nonfiction (GRAPHIC PLANE); Graphic Planet- Fiction (GRAPHIC FICTI); Looking Glass Library (LOOKING LIBRA); Abdo & Daughter (ABDO & DAUGHTE); Spotlight (Spotlight); Core Library (CoreLibrary); Calico Chapter Books (CalicoChapter); Abdo Kids (AbdoKids)
E-mail: info@abdopublishing.com
Web site: http://www.abdopublishing.com
Dist(s): **Capstone Pub.**
Ebsco Publishing
Follett School Solutions
MyiLibrary; *CIP.*
Abecedarian Bks., *(978-0-9763106; 978-0-9791401; 978-0-9822985; 978-0-9915275)* 2817 Forest Glen Dr., Baldwin, MD 21013-9574 USA Tel 410-692-6777; 877-782-2221; Fax: 410-692-9125 Do not confuse with Abecedarian Books in Portland, OR
E-mail: books@abeced.com
Web site: http://www.abeced.com
Dist(s): **Book Clearing Hse.**
Abednego's Free, LLC *See* **Solomon Waterwine, LLC**
Abedus Pr., *(978-0-9763091)* P.O. Box 8018, La Crescenta, CA 91224-0018 USA (SAN 256-2936)
E-mail: jadams@usc.edu.
Abegg Press *See* **Milner Crest Publishing, LLC**
Abelard Bks. (GBR) *(978-0-9558483) Dist. by* **LuluCom.**

Abernathy Hse. Publishing, *(978-0-9741940)* Orders Addr.: P.O. Box 1109, Yarmouth, ME 04096-1109 USA (SAN 255-4380) Tel 207-838-6170
E-mail: info@abernathyhousepub.com; abernathyhp@aol.com
Web site: http://www.abernathyhousepub.com
Dist(s): **Brodart Co.**
Follett School Solutions.

Abidenme Bks., *(978-0-9714515)* P.O. Box 144, Island Heights, NJ 08732-0144 USA (SAN 254-1203) Fax: 732-573-0551; Toll Free: 888-540-8022
E-mail: angela@booksformilitarykids.com
Web site: http://booksformilitarykids.com

Abiding Life Ministries International, *(978-0-9670843; 978-0-9819546)* Orders Addr.: P.O. Box 620998, Littleton, CO 80162-0998 USA (SAN 299-8629) Tel 303-972-0859; 719-485-5558; Fax: 303-973-2682; Edit Addr.: 8191 Southpark Ln. Unit 102, Littleton, CO 80120-4639 USA; 3525 Canyon Heights Rd., Pueblo, CO 81005; *Imprints:* Abiding Life Press (Abiding Life Pr)
E-mail: AbideLife@aol.com
Web site: http://www.abidinglife.com.

Abiding Life Pr. *Imprint of* **Abiding Life Ministries International**

Abiding Life Press *See* **Abiding Life Ministries International**

Abilene Christian Univ. Pr., *(978-0-89112; 978-0-915547)* ACU Box 29138, Abilene, TX 79699-9138 USA (SAN 207-1681) Tel 325-674-2720; Fax: 325-674-6471; Toll Free: 800-444-4228; *Imprints:* Leafwood Publishers (LeafwoodPubs)
E-mail: lettie.morrow@acu.edu
Web site: http://www.acupressbooks.com/; http://www.leafwoodpublishers.com
Dist(s): **Anchor Distributors**
INscribe Digital
Send The Light Distribution LLC
ebrary, Inc.

†Abingdon Pr., *(978-0-687; 978-1-4267; 978-1-63088; 978-1-5018)* Div. of United Methodist Publishing House, Orders Addr.: P.O. Box 801, Nashville, TN 37202-3919 USA (SAN 201-0054) Tel 615-749-6409; Fax: 615-749-6056; Toll Free: 800-627-1789; Edit Addr.: 201 Eighth Ave., S., Nashville, TN 37202 USA (SAN 699-9956) Tel 615-749-6000; Toll Free Fax: 800-445-8189; Toll Free: 800-672-1789; *Imprints:* Cokesbury (Cokesbury)
E-mail: cokes_serv@cokesbury.com
Web site: http://www.abingdonpress.com/; http://www.umph.org
Dist(s): **Church Publishing, Inc.**
Follett School Solutions
Ingram Pub. Services
ebrary, Inc.; *CIP.*

Abique, Incorporated *See* **Abique Pub**

Abique Pub, *(978-1-892298)* Orders Addr.: 50 Haystack Pl., Pagosa Springs, CO 81147 USA Tel 970-731-2513 during spring and summer; 214-466-1074 during winter; Edit Addr.: 1512 Country Ln., Allen, TX 75002 USA Tel 972-359-0136 Fall and winter
E-mail: abique@gmail.com.

Able Journey Pr., *(978-1-934249)* P.O. Box 5517, Trenton, NJ 08638-9998 USA Toll Free Fax: 877-650-3610; Toll Free: 877-650-3610
E-mail: ivanwright@ablejourneypress.com
Web site: http://ablejourneypress.com
Dist(s): **AtlasBooks Distribution.**

AbleNet, Inc., *(978-0-9666667; 978-0-9764246; 978-0-9819934; 978-0-9825180; 978-1-935696; 978-1-62744)* 2625 Patton Rd., Roseville, MN 55113 USA Tel 651-294-2200; Toll Free: 800-322-0956; 1081 Tenth Ave./Southeast, Minneapolis, MN 55414
E-mail: kbrown@ablenetinc.com; customerservice@ablenetinc.com
Web site: http://www.ablenetinc.com
Dist(s): **Follett School Solutions.**

Abligio Bks., *(978-1-934437)* 4226 S. Rock St., Gilbert, AZ 85297-4536 USA (SAN 853-2362) Tel 480-272-6063
E-mail: publisher@abligio.com
Web site: http://abligio.com

ABM Enterprises, Inc., *(978-0-9656688)* Orders Addr.: P.O. Box 123, Amelia Court House, VA 23002-0123 USA Tel 804-561-3655; Fax: 804-561-2065; Edit Addr.: 16311 Goodesbridge Rd., Amelia Court House, VA 23002 USA
E-mail: LarryDavies@SowingSeedsofFaith.com
Web site: http://www.SowingSeedsofFaith.com.

Abolet Publishing, *(978-0-9774555; 978-0-9818984)* 1348 East Capitol St., NE, Washington, DC 20003 USA (SAN 856-8618)
Web site: http://www.ronkoshes.com.

Aboriginal Studies Pr. (AUS) *(978-0-85575; 978-0-908097; 978-0-646-33600-8; 978-1-922059; 978-1-925302)* *Dist. by* **IPG Chicago.**

Abounding Love Ministries, Inc., *(978-0-9678519)* Orders Addr.: P.O. Box 425, Jackson, CA 95642 USA Tel 209-296-7264 (phone/fax); Edit Addr.: 225 Endicott Ave., Jackson, CA 95642-2512 USA
E-mail: alms@aboundinglove.org
Web site: http://www.aboundinglove.org.

About Comics, *(978-0-9716338; 978-0-9753958; 978-0-9790750; 978-0-9819563; 978-1-936404)* 1569 Edgemont Dr., Camarillo, CA 93010-3130 USA
E-mail: rights@aboutcomics.com
Web site: http://www.aboutcomics.com
Dist(s): **Diamond Comic Distributors, Inc.**
Diamond Bk. Distributors.

About Time Publishing, *(978-0-9791550; 978-0-9821214; 978-0-9847928)* 29792 Harper Rd., Junction City, OR 97448 USA Tel 541-954-6724
E-mail: michael@judeco.net; mfaris1950@gmail.com
Web site: http://www.abouttimepublishing.com; http://www.judeco.net.

About Your Time LLC, *(978-0-9744768; 978-0-9799737; 978-0-9844266)* P.O. Box 582, S. Orange, NJ 07079 USA Tel 646-232-3212; Fax: 973-766-1019
E-mail: ayt1@busybodybook.com
Web site: http://www.busybodybook.com
Dist(s): **Publishers Storage & Shipping.**

Above the Clouds Publishing, *(978-1-60227)* P.O. Box 313, Stanhope, NJ 07874 USA (SAN 852-1328) Fax: 973-448-7789; Toll Free: 800-936-2319
E-mail: publisher@abovethecloudspublishing.com
Web site: http://abovethecloudspublishing.com
Dist(s): **Follett School Solutions.**

Abovo Publishing, *(978-0-9762007)* P.O. Box 1231, Bonita, CA 91908 USA
E-mail: abovo@cox.net
Dist(s): **AtlasBooks Distribution**
Quality Bks., Inc.

ABR Pubns., *(978-0-9742367)* Orders Addr.: 1945 Cliff Valley Way, Ste. 250b, Atlanta, GA 30329 USA Tel 404-510-3131; Fax: 404-371-1838
E-mail: roll6128@bellsouth.net
Web site: http://www.drboydpublications.com
Dist(s): **Follett School Solutions.**

Abrams, *(978-0-8109; 978-1-4197; 978-1-61769; 978-1-61312)* Orders Addr.: The Market Building Third Floor, 72-82 Rosebery Ave., London, EC1R 4RW GBR Tel 020 7713 2060; Fax: 020 7713 2061; Edit Addr.: 115 West 18th St., New York, NY 10011 USA (SAN 200-2434) Tel 212-206-7715; Fax: 212-519-1210; *Imprints:* Amulet Books (Amulet Bks); Abrams Books for Young Readers (ABYR); Abrams Image (Abrams Image); Abrams Appleseed (AbramsAppleseed); Abrams Noterie (Abrams Noterie)
E-mail: webmaster@abramsbooks.com
Web site: http://www.hnabooks.com
Dist(s): **Ediciones Universal**
Follett School Solutions
Hachette Bk. Group.

Abrams & Co. Pubs., Inc.,
Dist(s): **Abrams Learning Trends.**

Abrams Appleseed *Imprint of* **Abrams**

Abrams Bks. for Young Readers *Imprint of* **Abrams**

Abrams, Harry N. Incorporated *See* **Abrams**

Abrams Image *Imprint of* **Abrams**

Abrams Noterie *Imprint of* **Abrams**

ABREN (A Bk. to Read Empowers Nicaraguans), *(978-1-937314)* 1310 Mercy St., Mountain View, CA 94041 USA Tel 415-637-4243
E-mail: kmundera@yahoo.com.

Abril BookStore & Publishing, *(978-0-9704131; 978-0-9772265; 978-0-9796842)* 415 E. Broadway, Suite 102, Glendale, CA 91205 USA Tel 818-243-4112; Fax: 818-243-4158
E-mail: noor@abrilbooks.com; abrilbooks@earthlink.net
Web site: http://www.abrilbooks.com
Dist(s): **Follett School Solutions.**

Absalon Pr., *(978-0-9846687)* 34192 Capistrano by the Sea, Dana Point, CA 92629 USA (SAN 920-1335) Tel 949-493-6953 (phone/fax)
E-mail: jody.payne@cox.net
Web site: www.absalonpress.com.

Absecon Lighthouse, *(978-0-9779988)* 31 S. Rhode Island Ave., Atlantic City, NJ 08401 USA Tel 609-441-1360; Fax: 609-449-1919
E-mail: abseconlighthouse@verizon.net
Web site: http://www.abseconlighthouse.org.

Absey & Co., *(978-1-888842)* 23011 Northcrest, Spring, TX 77389 USA Tel 281-257-2340; Fax: 281-251-4676; Toll Free: 888-412-2739
E-mail: Abseyandco@aol.com
Web site: http://www.absey.biz
Dist(s): **AtlasBooks Distribution**
Bibliotech, Inc.
Brodart Co.
Follett School Solutions.

ABUAA, Inc., *(978-0-9760406)* Orders Addr.: P.O. Box 1542, Whitefish, MT 59937 USA Fax: 406-362-3407; Edit Addr.: 7347 Farm to Market Rd., Whitefish, MT 59937 USA; *Imprints:* A Kidz World (Kidz Wrld)
Web site: http://www.akidzworld.com.

Abuzz Bks., *(978-0-9715865)* P.O. Box 15753, Scottsdale, AZ 85267 USA
E-mail: author@20umbrellas.com
Dist(s): **Quality Bks., Inc.**

Abydos Enterprises, *(978-0-9712596; 978-0-615-64642-8; 978-0-615-64643-5; 978-0-615-64644-2; 978-0-615-64645-9; 978-0-615-64854-5; 978-0-615-64856-9)* P.O. Box 648, Kittitas, WA 98934 USA
E-mail: abydosent@hotmail.com; admin@magictails.com
Web site: http://www.magictails.com
Dist(s): **CreateSpace Independent Publishing Platform**
INscribe Digital.

Abysso Bks., *(978-0-9747228)* 817 E. Mackinac Ave., Oak Creek, WI 53154 USA
E-mail: asala@mac.com
Web site: http://www.pottersfield.posthaven.com; pottersfield.posthaven.com.

AC Pubns. Group LLC, *(978-1-933302)* P.O. Box 260543, Lakewood, CO 80226 USA
E-mail: dksimoneau@acpublicationsgroup.com
Web site: http://www.acpublicationsgroup.com.

AC Writings, *(978-0-9796780)* 7585 Kirwin Ln., Cupertino, CA 95014 USA (SAN 854-0896).

Acacia Publishing, Inc., *(978-0-9666572; 978-0-9671187; 978-0-9762224; 978-0-9774306; 978-0-9788283; 978-0-9790626; 978-0-9792531; 978-0-9793273; 978-0-9814629; 978-1-935089)* 770 N. Monterey St. Ste. C, Gilbert, AZ 85233-3821 USA Toll Free: 866-265-4553
E-mail: jason@hiredpen.com; editor@acaiapublishing.com; kgray@acaciapublishing.com
Web site: http://www.acaciapublishing.com
Dist(s): **Book Clearing Hse.**
Follett School Solutions.

Academic Edge, Inc., *(978-0-9754754; 978-0-9814537)* Orders Addr.: P.O. Box 23605, Lexington, KY 40523-3605 USA Tel 859-224-3000; Fax: 812-331-8021; Edit Addr.: 216 E. Allen St., Suite 143, Bloomington, IN 47402 USA
E-mail: george@academicedge.com
Web site: http://www.academicedge.com.

Academic Internet Publishers Incorporated *See* **Cram101 Inc.**

Academic Solutions, Inc., *(978-0-9635364; 978-0-9740200)* Orders Addr.: P.O. Box 102, Harvard, MA 01451 USA Tel 978-456-6829; Fax: 978-456-3053; Toll Free: 877-222-3765 (877-ACADSOL)
E-mail: asibooks@acadsol.com
Web site: http://www.acadsol.com.

Academic Systems Corp., *(978-1-928962)* 2933 Bunker Hill Ln. Ste. 107, Santa Clara, CA 95054-1124 USA Toll Free: 800-694-6830
E-mail: info@academic.com
Web site: http://www.academic.com.

Academic Therapy Pubns., Inc., *(978-0-87879; 978-1-57128; 978-1-63402)* 20 Commercial Blvd., Novato, CA 94949-6191 USA (SAN 201-2111) Tel 415-883-3314; Fax: 415-883-3720; Toll Free: 800-422-7249
E-mail: sales@academictherapy.com; customerservice@academictherapy.com
Web site: http://www.academictherapy.com; http://www.highnoonbooks.com
Dist(s): **Cambium Education, Inc.**
Follett School Solutions
P C I Education
PRO-ED, Inc.

Academy Chicago Pubs., Ltd. *Imprint of* **Chicago Review Pr., Inc.**

†Academy of American Franciscan History, *(978-0-88382)* 1712 Euclid Ave., Berkeley, CA 94709 USA (SAN 201-1964) Tel 510-548-1755; Fax: 510-549-9466
E-mail: acadafh@fst.edu
Web site: http://www.aafh.org
Dist(s): **Univ. Pr. of Florida**; *CIP.*

Academy Park Pr. *Imprint of* **Williamson County Public Library**

Accelarated Christian Education, Inc., *(978-1-56265)* P.O. Box 1438, Lewisville, TX 75067-1438 USA Tel 972-315-1776; Fax: 972-315-8681.

Accelerator Bks., *(978-0-9815245; 978-0-9841399; 978-0-9838940; 978-0-9848966)* P.O. Box 1241, Princeton, NJ 08542 USA Tel 732-642-9721
E-mail: gemma@acceleratorbooks.com
Web site: http://www.acceleratorbooks.com.

Accent On Success, *(978-0-9743700)* 29 Benton Pl., Saint Louis, MO 63104 USA Tel 314-664-6110; Fax: 314-664-6577
E-mail: jbishop@accentonsuccess.com
Web site: http://www.TeachingMoments.com.

Accent Pubns. *Imprint of* **Ajoyin Publishing, Inc.**

Access for Disabled Americans, *(978-1-928616)* 301 Village Sq., Orinda, CA 94563-2505 USA
E-mail: PSmither@aol.com
Web site: http://maxpages.com/disabledaccess; http://www.accessfordisabled.com.

Access-4-All, Inc., *(978-0-9744908)* P.O. Box 220751, Saint Louis, MO 63122-0751 USA Tel 314-821-7011; Fax: 314-909-8086
E-mail: steve@access-4-all.com
Web site: http://www.access-4-all.com.

Accessibilities, *(978-0-9774546)* 1131 E. Spruce St., Sault Ste. Marie, MI 49783 USA
E-mail: geri.taeckens@isahealthfund.org
Web site: http://www.isahealthfund.org

Acclaim Pr., Inc., *(978-0-9773198; 978-0-9790025; 978-0-9798802; 978-1-935001; 978-1-938905; 978-1-942613)* Orders Addr.: P.O. Box 238, Morley, MO 63767 USA Tel 573-472-9800; Fax: 573-472-1608; Toll Free: 877-427-2665; Edit Addr.: 171 Co. Hwy. 430, Oran, MO 63771 USA
Web site: http://www.acclaimpress.com
Dist(s): **Follett School Solutions**
Partners Bk. Distributing, Inc.

Acclimated Spooks, Light, & Power, *(978-0-615-25755-6)* 1106 W. 2nd, Tahlequah, OK 74464 USA
E-mail: gracelandwest@gmail.com
Web site: http://www.acclimatedspooks.com
Dist(s): **Lulu Enterprises Inc.**

Accordian Bks., *(978-0-9754098)* Orders Addr.: P.O. Box 69912, West Hollywood, CA 90069 USA (SAN 256-0046); Edit Addr.: 69912 W. Hollywood, Hollywood, CA 90069 USA
E-mail: crystalilluminations@msn.com.

Ace Academics, Inc., *(978-1-57633; 978-1-881374)* 69 Tulip St., Bergenfield, NJ 07621 USA Tel 201-784-0001; Fax: 201-784-7704; *Imprints:* Exambusters (Exambusters)
E-mail: highself@aol.com; info@exambusters.com; exambusters@gmail.com
Web site: http://www.exambusters.com
Dist(s): **INscribe Digital**
NACSCORP, Inc.
eBookit.com.

Ace Bks. *Imprint of* **Penguin Publishing Group**

Ace Reid Enterprises *See* **Cowpokes Cartoon Bks.**

Ace Trade *Imprint of* **Penguin Publishing Group**

Acedrex Publishing, *(978-1-937291)* 550 N. Harrison Rd. No. 5101, Tucson, AZ 85748 USA Tel 401-743-0052
E-mail: acedrexpublishing@yahoo.com
Web site: acedrex.com.

Acen Press *See* **DNA Pr.**

ACER Pr. (AUS) *(978-0-85563; 978-0-86431; 978-1-74286)* *Dist. by* **Intl Spec Bk.**

Aceybee Publishing, *(978-0-9763958)* 285 W. Kootenai, No. 7, Richfield, ID 23349-5344 USA.

Achiev *See* **Achieve Pubns.**

Achieve Pubns., *(978-0-9727762; 978-0-615-12053-9)* Orders Addr.: 1216 Scobee Dr., Lansdale, PA 19446 USA Fax: 215-368-1431 (fax orders)
E-mail: achievepub@verizon.net
Web site: http://www.achievepublications.com
Dist(s): **Book Clearing Hse.**
Follett School Solutions.

Achieve3000, *(978-1-932166; 978-0-615-12027-0; 978-1-935675; 978-1-938916; 978-1-63256)* 1091 River Ave., Lakewood, NJ 08701 USA Tel 732-367-5505; Fax: 732-367-2313; Toll Free: 877-803-6505
E-mail: kelly.tanko@achieve3000.com
Web site: http://www.achieve3000.com.

Achievers Technology Resource, Inc., *(978-0-9716113)* PMB No. 455, 442 Rte. 202-206 N., Bedminster, NJ 07921-1522 USA (SAN 254-2811)
Web site: http://www.achieversrus.com.

Achieving Corporate Excellence, Inc., *(978-0-9746262)* Orders Addr.: P.O. Box 651119, Vero Beach, FL 32965-1119 USA Toll Free: 877-656-8313; Edit Addr.: 8003 Kenwood Rd., Fort Pierce, FL 34951 USA
Web site: http://www.acespeaks.com.

ACME Pr., *(978-0-9629880)* Orders Addr.: P.O. Box 1702, Westminster, MD 21158 USA Tel 410-848-7577; Edit Addr.: 1116 E. Deep Run Rd., Westminster, MD 21158 USA
Dist(s): **Follett School Solutions.**

Acmon Blue Publishing, *(978-0-9744792)* P.O. Box 475, Tujunga, CA 91043-0475 USA (SAN 255-5638) Tel 818-352-2551 (phone/fax)
E-mail: info@acmonblue.com
Web site: http://www.acmonblue.com.

Acorn *Imprint of* **Heinemann-Raintree**

Acorn *Imprint of* **Oak Tree Publishing**

Acorn Bks., *(978-0-9648957; 978-0-9837299)* P.O. Box 7348, Springfield, IL 62791-7348 USA Tel 217-525-8202; Fax: 217-525-8212 Do not confuse with companies iwth the same or similar name in Kansas, MO, Bloomington, IN, St. Albans, VT
E-mail: amy@afterabortion.org; elliotinstitute@gmail.com
Web site: http://www.afterabortion.org
Dist(s): **Lightning Source, Inc.**
MyiLibrary.

Acorn Bks., *(978-0-9664470; 978-1-930472)* 7337 Terrace, Kansas City, MO 64114-1256 USA Tel 816-523-8321; Fax: 816-333-3843; Toll Free: 888-422-0320 Do not confuse with companies with the same or similar name in Springfield, IL, Bloomington, IN, St. Albans, VT
E-mail: jami.parkison@micro.com
Web site: http://www.acornbks.com.

Acorn Guild Press, LLC *See* **Marion Street Pr., LLC**

Acorn Hill Pr., *(978-0-9788889)* 155 Parkhurst Dr., Jackson, MS 39202 USA Tel 601-668-3533.

Acorn Pr., The (CAN) *(978-0-9698606; 978-1-894838)* *Dist. by* **Orca Bk Pub.**

Acorn Publishing, *(978-0-937921)* Div. of Vitesse Pr., PMB 367, 45 State St., Montpelier, VT 05601 USA (SAN 659-4840) Tel 802-229-4243; Fax: 802-229-6939 Do not confuse with companies with the same or similar name in Midvale, UT, Broomfield, CO, Battle Creek, MI, Sisters, OR, Suffern, NY,Saltlake City, UT, Portland, OR, Sping Lake, MI
E-mail: dick@vitessepress.com
Web site: http://www.vitessepress.com
Dist(s): **Hood, Alan C. & Co., Inc.**

Acorn Publishing, *(978-0-9678801; 978-0-9710988; 978-0-9728969; 978-0-9774449)* Div. of Development Initiatives, 186 N. 23rd St., Battle Creek, MI 49015-1711 USA (SAN 854-6258) Tel 269-962-8184 (phone\fax); Toll Free: 877-700-2219 (phone\fax) Do not confuse with companies with the same or similar name in Broomfield, CO, Midvale, UT, Montpelier, VT, Sisters, OR, Suffern, NY, Salt Lake City, UT, Portland, OR, Sping Lake, MI
E-mail: editor@acornpublishing.com
Web site: http://www.acornpublishing.com.

Acorn Read-Aloud *Imprint of* **Heinemann-Raintree**

Acoustic Learning Inc., *(978-0-9761435; 978-0-9800581; 978-1-936412)* 215 Prospect Ave., Highland Park, IL 60035-3357 USA
E-mail: eartraining@aruffo.com
Web site: http://www.acousticlearning.com.

Acres Publishing, *(978-0-9741081)* 311 Prospect St., Alton, IL 62002 USA.

Acrobatic Cats Publishing *See* **MJ Brooks Co.**

ACS, LLC Arnica Creative Services, *(978-0-9726535; 978-0-9745686; 978-0-9794771; 978-0-9801942; 978-0-9816822; 978-0-9822482; 978-0-9826401)* 13970 SW 72nd Ave., Portland, OR 97223 USA (SAN 255-0091) Tel (503)886-8900; Fax: (503)746-5224
E-mail: ross@ideasbyacs.com
Web site: http://www.ideasbyacs.com
Dist(s): **American West Bks.**

ACTA Pubns., *(978-0-87946; 978-0-914070; 978-0-915388)* 5559 Howard St., Skokie, IL 60077-2621 USA (SAN 204-7489) Toll Free Fax: 800-397-0079; Toll Free: 800-397-2282; 4848 N. Clark St., Chicago, IL 60640
E-mail: actapublications@aol.com
Web site: http://www.actapublications.com
Dist(s): **BookMobile**
INscribe Digital
Spring Arbor Distributors, Inc.

Action Bks., *(978-0-900575; 978-0-9765692; 978-0-9799755; 978-0-9831480; 978-0-9898048)* Dept

Publisher Name Index

Of English, U. Of Notre Dame 356 O'shaughnessy Hall, Notre Dame, IN 46556 USA
Web site: http://www.actionbooks.org
Dist(s): **SPD-Small Pr. Distribution.**

Action Factor, Inc., *(978-0-9720763; 978-0-9754618)* PMB 218, 3195 Dayton-Xenia Rd., Suite 900, Beavercreek, OH 45434-6390 USA Tel 937-426-4364 (phone/fax)
E-mail: cgifford@actionfactor.com
Web site: http://www.actionfactor.com.

Action Lab Entertainment, *(978-0-9854952; 978-0-9859652; 978-1-939352; 978-1-63229)* 306 Bridlewood Ct., Canonsburg, PA 15317 USA Tel 513-313-7612
E-mail: spryor@actionlabcomics.com
Web site: http://www.actionlabcomics.com
Dist(s): **Diamond Comic Distributors, Inc.**
Diamond Bk. Distributors.

Action Organizing, *(978-0-9721964)* Div. of Successful Organizing Solutions, Orders Addr.: 406 Shato Ln., Madison, WI 53716 USA Tel 608-441-6767; Edit Addr.: P.O. Box 202, Milton, WI 53563 USA Tel 608-868-4079; Toll Free: 888-577-6655
E-mail: info@SOSorganize.net; sales@SOSorganize.net
Web site: http://www.actionorganizing.com.

Action Publishing, Inc., *(978-1-882210)* Div. of Action Products International, Inc., 344 Cypress Rd., Ocala, FL 34472-3108 USA Tel 352-687-2202; Fax: 352-687-4961; Toll Free: 800-772-2846 Do not confuse with companies with the same or similar name in Newport Beach, CA, Burlingame, CA, West Los Angeles, CA, Houstin, TX, Chicago, IL, Glendale, CA, Austin, TX.

Actionopolis *Imprint of* **Komikwerks, LLC**

Active Images, *(978-0-9740567; 978-0-9766761)* Orders Addr.: 8910 Rayford Dr., Los Angeles, CA 90045 USA Tel 310-215-0362; Fax: 775-890-5787 do not confuse with Active Images, Incorporated in Sterling, VA
E-mail: richard@comicraft.com
Web site: http://www.activeimages.com
Dist(s): **Lightning Source, Inc.**
Partners Pubs. Group, Inc.

Active Learning Corp., *(978-0-912813)* P.O. Box 254, New Paltz, NY 12561 USA (SAN 282-7794) Tel 845-255-0844; Fax: 845-255-8796
E-mail: panmans@newpaltz.edu; info@activelearning.com
Web site: http://www.activelearningcorp.com.

Active Learning Systems, LLC, *(978-1-57652)* P.O. Box 254, Epping, NH 03042 USA Tel 603-679-3332; Fax: 603-679-2611; Toll Free: 800-644-5059
E-mail: info@iimresearch.com
Web site: http://www.iimresearch.com.

Active Media Publishing, LLC, *(978-0-9745645; 978-0-9848808; 978-1-940367)* Orders Addr.: 614 E. Hwy 50 No. 235, Clermont, FL 34711 USA (SAN 255-6545); 614 E. Hwy 50 No. 235, Clermont, FL 34711 (SAN 255-6545); *Imprints:* Red Giant Entertainment (RedGiant)
E-mail: wizbenny@aol.com
Web site: http://redgiantentertainment.com
Dist(s): **Diamond Comic Distributors, Inc.**
Diamond Bk. Distributors.

Active Parenting Pubs., *(978-0-9618020; 978-1-880283; 978-1-59723)* 1955 Vaughn Rd. NW, Suite 108, Kennesaw, GA 30144-7808 USA (SAN 666-301X) Tel 770-429-0565; Fax: 770-429-0334; Toll Free: 800-825-0060
E-mail: cservice@activeparenting.com; ckeller@activeparenting.com
Web site: http://www.activeparenting.com
Dist(s): **Follett School Solutions**
National Bk. Network.

Active Spud Pr., *(978-0-9845388)* 324 E. 13th St., No. 3, New York, NY 10003 USA Tel 818-518-7381
E-mail: steve@activespudpress.com
Web site: http://www.activespudpress.com.

Active Synapse, *(978-0-9677255)* Orders Addr.: 5336 Park Lane Dr., Columbus, OH 43231-4072 USA
E-mail: Daryn@ActiveSynapse.com
Web site: http://www.activesynapse.com
Dist(s): **Brodart Co.**
Cold Cut Comics Distribution
Diamond Distributors, Inc.
Emery-Pratt Co.
Follett School Solutions
Midwest Library Service.

Activity Resources Co., Inc., *(978-0-918932; 978-1-882293)* Orders Addr.: P.O. Box 4875, Hayward, CA 94540 USA (SAN 209-0201) Tel 510-782-1300; Fax: 510-782-8172; Edit Addr.: 20655 Hathaway Ave., Hayward, CA 94541 USA
E-mail: info@activityresources.com
Web site: http://www.activityresources.com
Dist(s): **Delta Education, LLC**
Follett School Solutions
Seymour, Dale Pubns.

ACTNew Bks., *(978-0-9762326)* 12687 Blue Star Memorial Hwy., South Haven, MI 49090 USA
E-mail: actnewbooks@yahoo.com
Web site: http://www.actnewbooks.com.

Actual Magic Enterprises, LLC, *(978-0-9891807)* 17606 N. 17th Pl., Unit 1106, Phoenix, AZ 85022 USA Tel 602-992-5552
E-mail: deborahmctiernan@cox.net
Web site: www.deborahmctiernan.com.

Ad Center, The *See* **Leathers Publishing**

Ad Stellae Bks., *(978-0-615-31487-7; 978-0-615-31488-4; 978-0-615-34834-6; 978-0-615-62523-2; 978-0-615-64517-9; 978-0-615-80434-7; 978-0-692-29376-8)* 3088 Delta Pines Dr., Eugene, OR 97408 USA Fax: 866-302-3827
Web site: http://www.adstellaebooks.com
Dist(s): **CreateSpace Independent Publishing Platform**
Smashwords.

Adam Enterprises *See* **Amberwood Pr.**

Adam Hill Pubns., *(978-0-9769360)* Orders Addr.: 9001 SW 55 Ct., Fort Lauderdale, FL 33328 USA Tel 954-983-5005
Web site: http://www.adamhilldesign.com
Dist(s): **Follett School Solutions.**

Adams, Anne Marie Rea, *(978-0-9742782)* 9 Terraza Dr., Newport Coast, CA 92657-1510 USA.

Adams, Clint *See* **Credo Italia**

Adam's Creations Publishing, LLC, *(978-0-9785695)* Div. of JAH Innovations, Inc., 550 Fossett Rd., Zebulon, GA 30295 USA (SAN 851-0091) Tel 404-909-1025
E-mail: info@adamscreationspublishing.com
Web site: http://www.adamscreationspublishing.com
Dist(s): **BCH Fulfillment & Distribution.**

Adams, Evelyn, *(978-0-9761102)* 727 Virginia Ave., Midland, PA 15059-1429 USA Tel 724-643-9968; Fax: 724-775-8648
E-mail: rjb@timesnet.net
Web site: http://www.storiesfromvic.com.

Adams, Jeanette *See* **Camelot Tales**

†Adams Media Corp., *(978-0-937860; 978-1-55850; 978-1-58062; 978-1-59337; 978-1-59869; 978-1-60550; 978-1-4405; 978-1-5072)* Div.of F & W Publications, Inc., Orders Addr.: 57 Littlefield St., Avon, MA 02322 USA (SAN 215-2886) Tel 508-427-6733; Fax: 508-427-6790; Toll Free: 800-872-5627; F & W Publications, Inc. 4700 E. Galbraith, Cincinnati, OH 45236 Tel 513-531-2690; Toll Free: 800-289-0963
E-mail: Allison.Omeara@adamsmedia.com; orders@adamsmedia.com; fw_cin_orders@fwpubs.com; judy.bernardi@adamsmedia.com
Web site: http://www.adamsmedia.com; http://www.fwpubs.com
Dist(s): **Cranbury International**
CreateSpace Independent Publishing Platform
Ebsco Publishing
Follett School Solutions
F&W Media, Inc.
Curreri, Michelle Morrow
MyiLibrary
ebrary, Inc.; *CIP.*

Adams Publishing *See* **Adams Media Corp.**

Adams Publishing, *(978-0-9729189)* 320 Lincoln Rd., Branchland, WV 25506 USA Tel 304-824-2504 (phone/fax) Do not confuse with companies with the same or similar name in Topanga, CA, Rainier, WA, Boston, MA
E-mail: Adamspublisher@zoominternet.net
Web site: http://www.geocities.com/daycarebook/index.html.

Adamson, Mac, *(978-0-9779369)* P.O. Box 690, Midway, UT 84049 USA Tel 801-318-8544
E-mail: madamson@kids4fitkids.org
Web site: http://kids4fitkids.org.

Adams-Pomeroy Pr., *(978-0-9661009; 978-0-9967921)* Orders Addr.: P.O. Box 189, Albany, WI 53502 USA Tel 608-862-3645; Fax: 608-862-3647; Toll Free: 877-862-3645; Edit Addr.: 103 N. Jackson St., Albany, WI 53502 USA
E-mail: adamspomeroy@ckhnet.com
Dist(s): **Follett School Solutions.**

Added Upon, Inc., *(978-0-9740319)* Orders Addr.: P.O. Box 65327, Vancouver, WA 98665 USA
E-mail: dunnjessel@msn.com.

Addi-Boo Bks., *(978-0-9911410)* 78 Ryerson St., Brooklyn, NY 11205 USA Tel 347-512-7882
E-mail: stephen.epps@eppsscholars.org.

Addison Wesley, *(978-0-06; 978-0-13; 978-0-201; 978-0-321; 978-0-582; 978-0-673; 978-0-8053)* 75 Arlington St., Suite 300, Boston, MA 02116 USA Tel 617-848-7500
Web site: http://www.aw-bc.com
Dist(s): **Pearson Education**
Pearson Technology Group.

Addison Wesley Schl., Orders Addr.: a/o Order Dept., 200 Old Tappan Rd., Old Tappan, NJ 07675 USA Toll Free Fax: 800-445-6991; Toll Free: 800-922-0579; Edit Addr.: 75 Arlington St., Boston, MA 02116 USA Tel 617-848-7500; *Imprints:* Scott Foresman (S-Foresman)
Web site: http://www.aw-bc.com.

Addison-Wesley Educational Pubs., Inc., *(978-0-321; 978-0-328; 978-0-673)* Div. of Addison Wesley Longman, Inc., 75 Arlington St., Boston, MA 02116 USA Tel 617-848-7500; Toll Free: 800-447-2226; *Imprints:* Scott Foresman (Scott Frsmn); Scott Foresman (S-Foresman)
Web site: http://www.awl.com.

†Addison-Wesley Longman, Inc., *(978-0-201; 978-0-321; 978-0-582; 978-0-673; 978-0-8013; 978-0-8053; 978-0-9654123)* Orders Addr.: 200 Old Tappan Rd., Old Tappan, NJ 07675 USA (SAN 299-4739) Toll Free: 800-922-0579; Edit Addr.: 75 Arlington St., Suite 300, Boston, MA 02116 USA (SAN 200-2000) Tel 617-848-7500; Toll Free: 800-447-2226
E-mail: pearsoned@eds.com; orderdeptnj@pearsoned.com
Web site: http://www.awl.com
Dist(s): **Continental Bk. Co., Inc.**
MyiLibrary
Pearson Education
Trans-Atlantic Pubns., Inc.; *CIP.*

Addison-Wesley Longman, Ltd. (GBR) *(978-0-582) Dist. by* **Trans-Atl Phila.**

Addison-Wesley Publishing Company, Incorporated *See* **Addison-Wesley Longman, Inc.**

Adelante Productions, Inc., *(978-0-9748017)* 600 Columbus Ave., 8G, New York, NY 10024 USA
E-mail: info@adelantepro.com
Web site: http://www.adelantepro.com.

Adhemar Pr. USA, *(978-0-578-06275-4)* 7440 S. Black Hawk, No. 15-102, Englewood, CO 80112 USA
E-mail: jtbeiser@gmail.com.

AdHouse Bks., *(978-0-9721794; 978-0-9770304; 978-1-935233)* 3905 Brook Road., Richmond, VA 23227 USA
Dist(s): **Diamond Comic Distributors, Inc.**
Diamond Bk. Distributors.

Adibooks.com, *(978-0-9728909; 978-0-9743872; 978-0-9748753; 978-0-9758993; 978-0-9760575; 978-0-9763465; 978-0-9764322; 978-0-9767424; 978-0-9772505; 978-0-9776044; 978-0-9778606; 978-0-9779682; 978-0-9787515; 978-0-9789741; 978-0-9791289; 978-0-9794769; 978-0-9797885; 978-0-9801635; 978-0-9815594; 978-0-9817447; 978-0-9821073; 978-0-9823972; 978-0-9841294; 978-0-9843390; 978-0-9845852; 978-0-9846346; 978-0-9852824; 978-0-9887395; 978-0-9899978; 978-0-9914043; 978-0-9960318; 978-0-9904151; 978-0-9908554;)* 181 Industrial Ave., Lowell, MA 01852 USA *Fax: 978-458-3026*
E-mail: tcampbell@kingprinting.com
Web site: http://www.adibooks.com
Dist(s): **Cardinal Pubs. Group.**

Adirondack Kids Pr., *(978-0-9707044; 978-0-9826250)* 39 Second St., Camden, NY 13316 USA Tel 315-245-2437
E-mail: info@adirondackkids.com
Web site: http://www.adirondackkids.com.

†Adirondack Mountain Club, Inc., *(978-0-935272; 978-1-931951; 978-0-9896073; 978-0-9961168)* 814 Goggins Rd., Lake George, NY 12845-4117 USA (SAN 204-7691) Tel 518-668-4447 (customer service); Fax: 518-668-3746; Toll Free: 800-395-8080 (orders only)
E-mail: johnk@adk.org; pubs@adk.org; adkinfo@adk.org
Web site: http://www.adk.org
Dist(s): **Alpenbooks Pr. LLC**
Equinox, Ltd.
North Country Bks., Inc.
Peregrine Outfitters; *CIP.*

Adisoft, Inc., *(978-0-9674897)* Orders Addr.: P.O. Box 2094, San Leandro, CA 94577-2094 USA Tel 510-483-3556; Fax: 510-483-3885; Edit Addr.: 664 Joaquin Ave., San Leandro, CA 94577 USA; *Imprints:* Wawa Press (Wawa)
E-mail: information@adisoft-inc.com
Web site: http://www.adisoft-inc.com.

Adiva, Incorporated *See* **TEG Publishing**

Adjust Communications, *(978-0-9765973)* 905 Hwy. 321 NW, Suite No. 364, Hickory, NC 28601 USA Tel 828-850-3237; Fax: 866-334-4360
Web site: http://www.victoryafterhighschool.com.

Adler, Karen, *(978-0-9679772)* 34738 McDaniel Dr., Northfork, CA 93643 USA Tel 559-877-2033.

Adonoke Inc., *(978-0-9773180)* 8354 Craine Dr., Manlius, NY 13104-9421 USA
E-mail: info@adonokebooks.com
Web site: http://www.adonokebooks.com.

Adoption Tribe Publishing, *(978-0-9747443)* Orders Addr.: P.O. Box 2328, Santa Fe, NM 87504-2328 USA
E-mail: sarahlbr@earthlink.net
Web site: http://www.adoptionmeanslove.com.

ADR BookPrint *See* **ADR Inc.**

ADR Inc., *(978-0-9742743; 978-0-9761513; 978-0-9795033; 978-0-9802452; 978-0-9819864; 978-0-9908488)* 2012 Northern Ave., Wichita, KS 67216 USA Tel 316-522-5599; Fax: 316-522-5445; Toll Free: 800-767-6066
E-mail: bcatron@adr.biz
Web site: http://www.adr.biz.

Adrema Pr., *(978-0-9717290; 978-1-59611)* Orders Addr.: P.O. Box 14592, North Palm Beach, FL 33408 USA; Edit Addr.: P.O. Box 14157, North Palm Beach, FL 33408-2368 USA
E-mail: contact@adremapress.com
Web site: http://adremapress.com; http://inquiringminds.us
Dist(s): **CreateSpace Independent Publishing Platform**
Lightning Source, Inc.

ADV Manga, *(978-1-57813)* Div. of A. D. Vision, Inc., 5750 Bintliff, Suite 200, Houston, TX 77036 USA
Web site: http://www.ADVFilms.com
Dist(s): **Diamond Comic Distributors, Inc.**
Diamond Bk. Distributors.

Advance Cal Tech, Inc., *(978-0-943759)* 210 Clary Ave., San Gabriel, CA 91776-1375 USA (SAN 242-2603).

Advance Materials Ltd. (GBR) *(978-0-9532440) Dist. by* **Cambridge U Pr.**

Advance Publishers, Incorporated *See* **Advance Pubs. LLC**

Advance Pubs. LLC, *(978-0-9619525; 978-1-57973; 978-1-885222)* 1060 Maitland Center Cmns Blvd. Ste. 365, Maitland, FL 32751-7499 USA (SAN 244-9226) Toll Free: 800-777-2041
E-mail: advpublish@aol.com; questions@adv-pub.com
Web site: http://www.advancepublishers.com.

Advance Publishing, Inc., *(978-0-9610810; 978-1-57537; 978-1-62474)* 6950 Fulton St., Houston, TX 77022 USA (SAN 263-9572) Tel 713-695-0600; Fax: 713-695-8585; Toll Free: 800-917-9630 Do not confuse with Advance Publishing, Brownburg, IN
E-mail: info@advancepublishing.com
Web site: http://www.advancepublishing.com
Dist(s): **Follett School Solutions.**

Advanced Marketing, S. de R. L. de C. V. (MEX) *(978-970-718) Dist. by* **Bilingual Pubns.**

Advanced Marketing, S. de R. L. de C. V. (MEX) *(978-970-718) Dist. by* **PerseuPGW.**

Advanced Publishing LLC, *(978-0-9857367; 978-1-63132)* 3200 A Danville Blvd. Suite 204, Alamo, CA 94507 USA Tel 925-837-7303
E-mail: eric@aliveeastbay.com
Web site: www.alivebookpublishing.com.

Advantage Books *See* **Advantage Bks., LLC**

Advantage Bks., *(978-0-9754332; 978-1-59755)* Div. of Advantage Pr., Inc., Orders Addr.: P.O. Box 160847, Altamonte Springs, FL 32716 USA; *Imprints:* Advantage Childrens (Advan Childrens) Do not confuse with companies with the same or similar name in Newport Beach, CA, Silver Spring, MD
E-mail: mike@advbooks.com
Web site: http://advbookstore.com.

Advantage Bks., LLC, *(978-0-9660366; 978-0-9714609; 978-0-9823326)* 3268 Arcadia Pl.NW, Washington, DC 20015-2330 USA (SAN 253-8237) Tel 202-966-4044; Fax: 2002-966-1561; Toll Free: 888-238-8588 Do not confuse with companies with the same or similar name in New Port Beach, CA, Longwood, FL
E-mail: advantagebooksdc@aol.com
Web site: http://www.addvance.com
Dist(s): **National Bk. Network.**

Advantage Childrens *Imprint of* **Advantage Bks.**

Advantage Publishers Group *See* **Baker & Taylor Publishing Group**

Advent Truth Ministries, *(978-0-9749490)* P.O. Box 307, Forsyth, GA 31029 USA Tel 404-322-5683
E-mail: adventtruth@yahoo.com
Web site: www.adventtruth.org; www.thesabbathtruth.org.

Adventure & Discovery Pr., *(978-0-9744672)* P.O. Box 11631, Syracuse, NY 13218 USA Toll Free: 800-682-2662.

Adventure Beyond The Horizon *See* **Omega Pr.**

Adventure Bks. of Seattle, *(978-0-9823271; 978-0-692-32193-5)* 2415 I St. NE, No. D, Auburn, WA 98002 USA (SAN 857-8664) Tel 253-929-6259
Web site: http://www.adventurebooksofseattle.com
Dist(s): **Lightning Source, Inc.**

Adventure Boys Inc., *(978-0-9791922; 978-0-9791952; 978-0-9796392)* 11005 35th Ave. NE, Seattle, WA 98119-6809 USA (SAN 852-727X) 11/20/06: Do not be confused with Madison Park Greetings & Front Porch Classics, Inc.
Web site: http://www.adventureboys.com.

Adventure Hse., *(978-1-886937; 978-1-59798)* 914 Laredo Rd., Silver Spring, MD 20901-1867 USA Tel 301-754-1589; Fax: 978-215-7412
E-mail: sales@adventurehouse.com
Web site: http://www.adventurehouse.com
Dist(s): **Diamond Comic Distributors, Inc.**
Diamond Bk. Distributors.

Adventure in Discovery, *(978-0-9743414)* 18011 N. Hwy. A1A, Jupiter, FL 33477 USA Tel 561-746-8410
E-mail: books4u@adventureindiscovery.com
Web site: http://adventureindiscovery.com/
Dist(s): **Follett School Solutions**
Southern Bk. Service
Sunburst Bks., Inc., Distributor of Florida Bks.

Adventure Pr., *(978-0-9758654)* Orders Addr.: P.O. Box 1778, Canon City, CO 81215 USA Tel 208-880-7899; P.O. Box 1778, Canon City, CO 81215 Tel 208-880-7899
E-mail: antelope85@hotmail.com
Web site: http://www.kingsventures.com.

Adventure Productions, Inc., *(978-0-9614904)* 3404 Terry Lake Rd., Fort Collins, CO 80524 USA (SAN 693-3955) Tel 970-493-8776; Fax: 970-484-5825 Do not confuse with Adventure Productions, Reno, NV.
E-mail: cjansen@wild-west.com.

Adventure Pubns., Inc., *(978-0-934860; 978-1-885061; 978-1-59193)* Orders Addr.: 820 Cleveland St., S., Cambridge, MN 55008 USA (SAN 212-7199) Tel 763-689-9800; Fax: 763-689-9039; Toll Free Fax: 877-374-9016; Toll Free: 800-678-7006
E-mail: orders@adventurepublications.net; custservice@adventurepublications.net
Web site: http://www.adventurepublications.net
Dist(s): **Consortium Bk. Sales & Distribution**
MyiLibrary
Perseus Bks. Group
Perseus Distribution
TNT Media Group, Inc.

Adventures at Hound Hotel *Imprint of* **Picture Window Bks.**

Adventures Galore, *(978-0-9759542)* Orders Addr.: P.O. Box 748, Lake George, CO 80827 USA Tel 719-748-8458; Fax: 719-748-8459; Edit Addr.: 35100 Hwy. 24, Lake George, CO 80827 USA
Web site: http://www.adventuresgalore.com.

Adventures of Everyday Geniuses, The *Imprint of* **Mainstream Connections Publishing**

Adventures of Henry, LLC, *(978-1-936813)* 627 Evans St., Oshkosh, WI 54901 USA Tel 920-252-3578
E-mail: Darrin.Anderson@gmail.com
Web site: Www.adventuresofhenry.com.

Adventures of Hillary, The *Imprint of* **Nelson Publishing, LLC**

Adventures of Lady LLC, The, *(978-0-9789984)* 4907 White Bud Ct., Windermere, FL 34786 USA (SAN 852-1360).

Adventures Unlimited Pr., *(978-0-932813; 978-1-931882; 978-1-935487; 978-1-939149)* Orders Addr.: P.O. Box 74, Kempton, IL 60946 USA (SAN 630-1126) Tel 815-253-6390; Fax: 815-253-6300; Edit Addr.: 303 Main St., Kempton, IL 60946 USA (SAN 250-3484)
E-mail: auphq@frontiernet.net
Web site: http://www.adventuresunlimitedpress.com
Dist(s): **New Leaf Distributing Co., Inc.**
SCB Distributors.

Advocate Hse. *Imprint of* **A Cappela Publishing**

AE Pubns. (GBR) *(978-1-906672; 978-1-907708) Dist. by* **IPG Chicago.**

Aegaeon Publishing, *(978-1-934810)* Div. of Aegaeon Group International, One Penn Plaza 250 W. 34th St., 36th Flr., New York, NY 10119 USA Tel 212-835-1629
Web site: http://www.aegaeonpublishing.com.

Aegean Design, *(978-0-9758803)* 5009 20th Ave., NW, Seattle, WA 98107 USA Tel 206-612-9698
E-mail: bdarling@handofzeus.com
Web site: http://www.aegeandesign.net.

Aegypan, *(978-1-59818; 978-1-60312)* Div. of Alan Rodgers Bks., 4750 Lincoln Blvd., No. 360, Marina del Rey, CA 90292-9303 USA.

Aenor Trust, The, *(978-0-9724251; 978-0-9766401; 978-0-9768128)* Orders Addr.: P.O. Box 1410, Silverton, OR 97381 USA; Edit Addr.: 1286 Pressler Court S., Salem, OR 97306 USA
Web site: http://www.aenortrust.org; http://www.stellarlane.org.

Aeon Publishing Inc., *(978-0-9713099; 978-0-9718509; 978-1-932047; 978-1-932303; 978-1-932560; 978-1-59526; 978-1-933626; 978-1-60594)* Orders Addr.: 7580 NW 5th St. #16535, Fort Lauderdale, FL 33318 USA Tel 954-726-0902; Fax: 954-726-0903; Toll Free: 866-229-9244; *Imprints:* Llumina Christian Books (LluminaChrist); Llumina Press (Llumina Pr); Llumina Kids (Llumina Kids)
E-mail: diane@llumina.com
Web site: http://www.llumina.com.

AequiLibris Publishing LLC, *(978-0-9816446)* Orders Addr.: P.O. Box 1542, New London, NH 03257 USA
Web site: http://www.AequiLibrisPublishing.com.

Aerial Photography Services, Inc., *(978-0-936672; 978-1-880970; 978-0-9789603; 978-0-9815804; 978-0-9836193; 978-0-9916287)* 2511 S. Tryon St., Charlotte, NC 28203 USA (SAN 214-2791) Tel 704-333-5143; Fax: 704-333-4911
E-mail: aps@aps-1.com; gregg@aps-1.com
Web site: http://www.aps-1.com.

Aerospace 1 Pubns., *(978-0-9705150)* 8 Brookstone Ct., Streamwood, IL 60107 USA
E-mail: aerospace1@aol.com.

AFCHRON, *(978-1-892824; 978-1-938976)* Orders Addr.: P.O. Box 11754, Minneapolis, MN 55411 USA Tel 612-588-9504; 701 Givens Ln., Minneapolis, MN 55411 Tel 612-588-9504
E-mail: afchron5@aol.com
Web site: http://www.afchron.com; http://www.afchrononline.com
Dist(s): **Copyright Clearance Ctr., Inc.**
EBSCO Media.

Affirming Faith, *(978-0-9798627; 978-0-9897373)* 1181 Whispering Knoll Ln., Rochester Hills, MI 48306 USA (SAN 854-591X) Tel 248-909-5735; Fax: 248-608-1756
E-mail: loriwagner@affirmingfaith.com
Web site: http://www.affirmingfaith.com
Dist(s): **Pentecostal Publishing Hse.**

Africa World Pr., *(978-0-86543; 978-1-59221)* 541 W. Ingham Ave., Suite B, Trenton, NJ 08638 USA (SAN 692-3925) Tel 609-695-3200; Fax: 609-695-6466
E-mail: customerservice@africaworldpressbooks.com
Web site: http://www.africaworldpressbooks.com.

African American Chronicle Software Publishing Corporation *See* **AFCHRON**

African American Images, *(978-0-913543; 978-0-9749000; 978-1-934155)* P.O. Box 1799, Chicago Hts, IL 60412-1799 USA Toll Free: 800-552-1991
E-mail: aai@africanamericanimages.com; customer@africanamericanimages.com
Web site: http://AfricanAmericanImages.com
Dist(s): **Ebsco Publishing**
Follett School Solutions
Independent Pubs. Group
MyiLibrary
ebrary, Inc.

African Christian Pr. (GHA) *(978-9964-87)* *Dist. by* **Mich St U Pr.**

African Writers Series *Imprint of* **Heinemann**

Africana Homestead Legacy Pubs., Inc., *(978-0-9653308; 978-0-9770904; 978-0-9799537; 978-0-9818939; 978-0-9825842; 978-0-9831151; 978-1-937622)* Orders Addr.: 811 Church Rd., Suite 105, Cherry Hill, NJ 08002 USA (SAN 914-4811) Tel 856-773-0694; Fax: 856-486-1135; Toll Free: 877-575-0012 ext 2 for Sales Dept.; *Imprints:* Nefu Books (Nefu Bks)
E-mail: editors@ahlpub.com; sales@ahlpub.com; customer-service@ahlpub.com
Web site: http://www.ahlpub.com; http://www.ahlpstore.com; http://africana-homestead-legacy-publ.webstorepowered.com/.

Afrolez Productions, LLC, *(978-0-615-16123-5)* P.O. Box 58085, Philadelphia, PA 19102-8085 USA Tel 215-701-6150
E-mail: contact@notherapedocumentary.org
Web site: http://www.notherapedocumentary.org.

After Happily Ever After *Imprint of* **Stone Arch Bks.**

Afton Historical Society Pr., *(978-0-9639338; 978-1-890434)* Orders Addr.: P.O. Box 100, Afton, MN 55001 USA Tel 651-436-8443; Fax: 651-436-7354; Toll Free: 800-436-8443; Edit Addr.: 3321 Saint Croix Trail, S., Afton, MN 55001 USA
E-mail: aftonpress@aftonpress.com
Web site: http://www.aftonpress.com
Dist(s): **Bookmen, Inc.**
Brodart Co.
Coutts Information Services
Eastern Bk. Co.
Follett School Solutions
Galda Library Services, Inc.

Afton Publishing, *(978-0-89359)* Orders Addr.: P.O. Box 1399, Andover, NJ 07821-1399 USA (SAN 692-2570) Tel 973-579-2442; Fax: 973-579-2842; Toll Free: 888-238-6665
E-mail: info3@aftonpublishing.com
Web site: http://www.aftonpublishing.com.

Aga Khan Museum (CAN) *(978-0-9919928)* *Dist. by* **IngramPubServ.**

Agapy LLC, *(978-0-9721328; 978-1-938522)* 13700 Wood Flower Ct., Granger, IN 46530 USA
E-mail: info@agapy.com; president@agapy.com
Web site: http://www.agapy.com
Dist(s): **Lightning Source, Inc.**

Agapy Publishing *See* **Agapy LLC**

A-Gator Publishing,
Dist(s): **AtlasBooks Distribution.**

AGB Publishing, *(978-1-930908)* Div. of Mini Enterprises - M.E., 19425 Bankers House Dr., Katy, TX 77449-0243 USA; *Imprints:* AGB/me (AGB-me)
E-mail: minienterprises@msn.com; minitaylr@msn.com.

AGB/me *Imprint of* **AGB Publishing**

AGC Outreach Ministry, *(978-0-9774115)* 528 Starrett Ln., Ligonier, PA 15658 USA Tel 724-238-0341
E-mail: stevenjsmith79@adelphia.net
Web site: www.agcoutreach.com.

Ageless Treasures, *(978-0-9705726)* Orders Addr.: 3536 Saint Andrews Village Cir., Louisville, KY 40241-2664 USA (SAN 253-794X) Tel 502-412-5940; Fax: 502-327-6233
E-mail: dcw0810@insightbb.com; carlawebb@agelesstreasures.net.

Agent of Danger *Imprint of* **Komikwerks, LLC**

Agents of Change, *(978-1-928992)* Div. of Granite Publishing, LLC, P.O. Box 1429, Columbus, NC 28722-1429 USA Tel 828-894-3088; Fax: 828-894-8454; Toll Free: 800-366-0264
E-mail: brian@5thworld.com
Web site: http://5thworld.com
Dist(s): **New Leaf Distributing Co., Inc.**

Age-Trotters Press *See* **Cameltrotters Publishing**

Agile Pr., *(978-0-9718239)* P.O. Box 1939, Chicago, IL 60690-1939 USA
E-mail: agilepress@agileresearch.com.

AGL Editions, *(978-0-9745629)* 1000 Bay Dr., No. 524, Niceville, FL 32578 USA.

Aglob Publishing, *(978-0-9708560; 978-1-59427)* P.O. Box 4036, Hallandale, FL 33008 USA Tel 954-456-1476; Fax: 954-456-3903
E-mail: info@aglobpublishing.com; info@aglob.com
Web site: http://www.aglobpublishing.com.

Agora Pubns., Inc., *(978-1-887250; 978-0-9904599)* 17 Dean St., Millis, MA 02054 USA (SAN 851-8521) Tel 508-376-1073 (phone/fax)
E-mail: agorapub@verizon.net; info@agorapublication.com
Web site: http://www.agorapublications.com
Dist(s): **Philosophy Documentation Ctr.**

Agreka Bks., LLC, *(978-1-888106; 978-0-9777072; 978-1-934243)* P.O. Box 14405, Scottsdale, AZ 85267-14405 USA Tel 480-767-1774; Toll Free Fax: 888-771-7758; Toll Free: 800-360-5284
E-mail: info@agreka.com
Web site: http://www.agreka.com; http://www.utahbooks.com; http://www.historypreserved.com
Dist(s): **Lightning Source, Inc.**
Quality Bks., Inc.

Agrippina Pr. *Imprint of* **WigWam Publishing Co.**

Agua Caliente Pr., *(978-0-9768275)* 4352 Riley Rd., Gladwin, MI 48624 USA Tel 989-426-8400
E-mail: maryhansen4@hotmail.com.

Aguilar, Altea, Taurus, Alfaguara, S.A. de C.V (MEX) *(978-968-19)* *Dist. by* **Santillana.**

Aguilar, Altea, Taurus, Alfaguara, S.A. de C.V (MEX) *(978-968-19)* *Dist. by* **Perseus Dist.**

Aguilar Chilena de Ediciones, Ltd. (CHL) *(978-956-239; 978-956-347)* *Dist. by* **Ediciones.**

Aguilar Editorial (MEX) *Dist. by* **Santillana.**

Aguirre Cox, Vicki & Ernest, *(978-0-9767994)* 10810 Lake Path Dr., San Antonio, TX 78217 USA Tel 210-364-8590; Fax: 210-653-3089
E-mail: vacemas@aol.com.

Aha! Elora Danan Productions, *(978-0-9786729)* P.O. Box 428, Estero, FL 33928 USA
Dist(s): **Follett School Solutions.**

aha! Process, Inc., *(978-0-9647437; 978-1-929229; 978-1-934583; 978-1-938248)* P.O. Box 727, Highlands, TX 77562-0727 USA Tel 281-426-5300; Fax: 281-426-5600; Toll Free: 800-424-9484
Web site: http://www.ahaprocess.com
Dist(s): **Follett School Solutions**
Greenleaf Book Group.

A-Head Publishing, *(978-0-9816283)* 41 Via Del Sol, Nicasio, CA 94946 USA (SAN 856-0862)
E-mail: aheadpublishing@gmail.com
Web site: http://www.a-headpublishing.com.

Ahlman Publishing, *(978-0-9712906)* Div. of KODIAK Publishing, 9525 W. 230 St., Morristown, MN 55052 USA Tel 507-685-4247; Fax: 507-685-4280
E-mail: larryahlman@hotmail.com
Web site: http://www.ahlmans.com/mittens.html
Dist(s): **Partners Bk. Distributing, Inc.**

Ahzar's Bk. Co. Publishing, *(978-0-9746130)* 3675 So. Rainbow Blvd No. 107, Las Vegas, NV 89103 USA Tel 702-391-1914; Fax: 702-871-8777
E-mail: croesus@joimail.com.

Aidan's Butterfly Pubns., *(978-0-9787341)* 4946 W. Laurie Ln., Glendale, AZ 85302 USA Fax: 623-776-9921
E-mail: eetagt@aol.com.

Ailam Publishing LLC, *(978-0-9837759)* 9449 S. Kedzie Ave. Suite 117, Evergreen Park, IL 60805 USA (SAN 860-2859)
E-mail: ailampublishing@aol.com
Web site: http://www.ailampublishing.com.

A.I.M. Enterprises, *(978-0-9772303)* 507 Grace - Stockham, Aurora, NE 68818-7019 USA
Web site: http://www.aim4theheart.com.

Aim Higher Bks., *(978-0-9713292)* 10556 Combie Rd., Suite 6242, Auburn, CA 95602 USA
E-mail: sales@aimhigherbooks.com
Web site: http://www.AimHigherBooks.com.

Aim Higher Publishing *See* **Aim Higher Bks.**

AIMS Education Foundation, *(978-1-881431; 978-1-932093; 978-1-60519)* Orders Addr.: 1595 S. Chestnut Ave., Fresno, CA 93702-4706 USA Tel 559-255-4094; Fax: 559-255-6396; Toll Free: 888-733-2467
E-mail: aimsed@aimsedu.org
Web site: http://www.aimsedu.org.

AIMS Multimedia, *(978-0-8068)* 1 Discovery Pl., Silver Spring, MD 20910-3354 USA (SAN 687-3464) Toll Free: 800-367-2467
Web site: http://www.aimsmultimedia.com/
Dist(s): **Follett School Solutions**
Weston Woods Studios, Inc.

Air & Nothingness Pr., *(978-0-9679429)* 2224 Delaware Ave., Pittsburgh, PA 15218 USA Tel 412-371-8385
E-mail: info@aanpress.com
Web site: http://www.aanpress.com.

airjam.com, *(978-0-9786478)* 3379 C1/2 Road, Palisade, CO 81526 USA.

Airplane Reader Publishing, *(978-0-9702405; 978-0-9765485)* Div. of Pro Leisure Tour, Inc., 9260 E. Lake Pl., Greenwood Village, CO 80111 USA (SAN 253-6935) Fax: 303-221-2766 24-hour dedicated fax line; Toll Free: 877-611-6222 voice mail, 24 hours
E-mail: theo@12milestoparadise.com; tedsimendinger@comcast.net; ted@funnyted.com
Web site: http://www.proleisuretour.com; http://www.piggychurch.com; http://www.12milestoparadise.com; http://www.richwithoutmoney.org; http://www.jurassictrout.com; http://www.tukibanjo.com.

Airship 27, *(978-0-615-59443-9; 978-0-615-59752-2; 978-0-615-60898-3; 978-0-615-60923-2; 978-0-615-61889-0; 978-0-615-63129-5; 978-0-615-64560-5; 978-0-615-65300-6; 978-0-615-65997-8; 978-0-615-67138-3; 978-0-615-68950-0; 978-0-615-69177-0; 978-0-615-69589-1; 978-0-615-69649-2; 978-0-615-71077-8; 978-0-615-72553-6; 978-0-615-72599-4; 978-0-615-73497-2; 978-0-615-74388-2; 978-0-615-75652-3; 978-0-615-75823-7; 978-0-615-76203-6; 978-0-615-77272-1; 978-0-615-78545-5; 978-0-615-79715-1; 978-0-615-80778-2; 5200 E. Mt. Zion Church Rd., Hallsville, MO 65255 USA Tel 573 696-2630 (phone/fax)*
Web site: http://www.airship27hangar.com
Dist(s): **CreateSpace Independent Publishing Platform.**

Airways International, Inc., *(978-0-9653993)* Orders Addr.: P.O. Box 1109, Sandpoint, ID 83864 USA Tel 208-263-2098; Fax: 208-263-5906; Edit Addr.: P.O. Box 1109, Sandpoint, ID 83864 USA
E-mail: airways@airwaysmag.com
Web site: http://www.airwaysmag.com.

AJL Publishers, *(978-0-9794618)* 25 Auvergne, Newport Coast, CA 92657 USA (SAN 853-5116) Tel 949-887-9073; Fax: 949-640-0339
E-mail: bachas@cox.net
Dist(s): **AtlasBooks Distribution.**

Ajoyin Publishing, Inc., *(978-0-9787472; 978-0-9792739; 978-0-9818488; 978-1-60920)* Orders Addr.: P.O. Box 342, Three Rivers, MI 49093 USA; Edit Addr.: 55919 Buckhorn Rd., Three Rivers, MI 49093 USA (SAN 852-9817) Toll Free: 888-273-4569; *Imprints:* Accent Publications (Accent)
E-mail: pam@ajoyin.com
Web site: http://www.ajoyin.com.

AJS Pubns., Inc., *(978-0-931298; 978-1-892291; 978-0-9904772)* 229 Brier Ct., Island Lake, IL 60042 USA (SAN 223-5846) Tel 847-526-5027; Fax: 847-487-5229 Do not confuse with AJS Publishing, Inc., Los Angeles, CA
Web site: http://www.ajspublications.com.

AK Classics, LLC, *(978-0-9814945)* P.O. Box 77023, Charlotte, NC 28271-7003 USA
E-mail: marcuskimbrough@aol.com
Web site: www.akclassicstories.com.

Akasha Classics *Imprint of* **Akasha Publishing, LLC**

Akasha Publishing, LLC, *(978-1-60512)* Orders Addr.: 2050 Emerald Ln., Fairfield, IA 52556 USA Fax: 866-485-5727; Toll Free: 877-745-7317; *Imprints:* Akasha Classics (Akasha Classics)
E-mail: registrar@akashapublishing.com
Web site: http://www.akashapublishing.com
Dist(s): **Follett School Solutions**
Lightning Source, Inc.

Akashic Bks., *(978-1-888451; 978-0-9719206; 978-1-933354; 978-1-936070; 978-1-61775)* 232 Third St., No. B404, Brooklyn, NY 11215 USA Tel 718-643-9193; Fax: 718-643-9195; *Imprints:* Black Sheep (BlckSheep)
E-mail: akashic7@aol.com
Web site: http://www.akashicbooks.com
Dist(s): **Consortium Bk. Sales & Distribution**
Follett School Solutions
MyiLibrary
Open Road Integrated Media, LLC
SPD-Small Pr. Distribution
ebrary, Inc.

AKA:yoLa, *(978-0-9842288; 978-1-936688; 978-1-942168)* 315 Bernadette Dr. Ste 3, Columbia, MO 65203 USA Tel 573-864-1479; *Imprints:* Compass Flower Press (CompassFlower)
Web site: http://www.akayola.com; www.compassflowerpress.com; www.aka-publishing.com
Dist(s): **eBookit.com.**

AKB Design, *(978-0-9748702)* Orders Addr.: 17640 Corkill Rd., #27, Desert Hot Springs, CA 92241 USA Tel 760-329-3233; 760-895-5646
Web site: www.akbdesign.com.

Akmaeon Publishing, LLC, *(978-0-9850410)* 309 Pirkle Ferry Rd. Suite C200, Cumming, GA 30040 USA Tel 404-402-3793
E-mail: free3055@bellsouth.net.

AKMO Pubs., *(978-0-9745952)* P.O. Box 669, Odessa, FL 33556-9998 USA.

Akom Publishing Hse., *(978-0-9799134)* 244 Madison Ave., No. 745, New York, NY 10016 USA
E-mail: Akom2000@aol.com
Web site: http://www.akompublishinghouse.com.

Alaafia Kids Co., *(978-0-9788737)* 1020 Stonebrook Rd. Unit B, Sykesville, MD 21784-6173 USA.

Alabama Folklife Assn., *(978-0-9672672; 978-0-9772132)* Orders Addr.: c/o Alabama Center for Traditional Culture, 410 N. Hull St, Montgomery, AL 36104 USA Tel 334-242-3601; Fax: 334-269-9098
E-mail: joycecauthen@bellsouth.net
Web site: http://www.alabamafolklife.org.

Alabaster Bk. Pub., *(978-0-9725031; 978-0-9768108; 978-0-9790949; 978-0-9796866; 978-0-9815763; 978-0-9823005; 978-0-9846137; 978-0-9846320; 978-0-9840004; 978-0-9860300; 978-0-9912660; 978-0-9861790)* Orders Addr.: P.O. Box 401, Kernersville, NC 27285 USA Tel 336-295-4322; Fax: 336-996-2011; P.O. Box 401, Kernersville, NC 27285 Fax: 336-996-2011; Edit Addr.: 324 Lakeside Dr., Kernersville, NC 27284 USA
E-mail: pblshralabaster@aol.com; ljdixie@aol.com
Web site: http://www.publisheralabaster.org; http://www.PublisherAlabaster.biz.

Alabaster Books *See* **Alabaster Bk. Pub.**

Aladdin Library *Imprint of* **Simon & Schuster Children's Publishing**

Aladdin Paperbacks *Imprint of* **Simon & Schuster Children's Publishing**

Aladdin/Beyond Words,
Dist(s): **Simon & Schuster, Inc.**

Alaska Avenue Pr., *(978-0-9748091)* 5770 Alaska Ave., Alto, MI 49302-9714 USA Tel 616-868-0308
E-mail: stonehillis47657@aol.com.

Alaska Geographic Assn., *(978-0-930931; 978-0-9602876; 978-0-9825765; 978-1-938494)* 810 E. Ninth Ave., Anchorage, AK 99501 USA (SAN 223-5269) Tel 907-274-8440; Fax: 907-274-8343
E-mail: loakley@alaskageographic.org
Web site: http://www.alaskageographic.org.

Alaska Independent Pubs., *(978-0-9743369; 978-0-9797442; 978-0-9883390)* Orders Addr.: P.O. Box 1125, Homer, AK 99603 USA Toll Free: 877-210-2665
E-mail: wizard@cosmichamlet.net
Dist(s): **Wizard Works.**

Alaska Native Language Ctr., *(978-0-933769; 978-1-55500)* Univ. of Alaska, P.O. Box 757680, Fairbanks, AK 99775-7680 USA (SAN 692-9796) Tel 907-474-7874; Fax: 907-474-6586
E-mail: fntla@uaf.edu
Web site: http://www.uaf.edu/anlc
Dist(s): **Chicago Distribution Ctr.**
Todd Communications
Wizard Works.

Alaska Natural History Association *See* **Alaska Geographic Assn.**

Alaska Northwest Bks. *Imprint of* **Graphic Arts Ctr. Publishing Co.**

Alaska Zoo, The, *(978-0-9673915)* 4731 O'Malley Rd., Anchorage, AK 99516 USA.

Alazar Pr. *Imprint of* **Royal Swan Enterprises, Inc.**

Alba House *See* **St Pauls/Alba Hse. Pubs.**

Albatros (ARG) *(978-950-24)* *Dist. by* **Lectorum Pubns.**

Albee, Michael, *(978-0-9745405)* 1575 W. Mable, Anaheim, CA 92802 USA Tel 714-863-2149
E-mail: malbee@fairmontschools.net.

Albers, Christine, *(978-0-615-19666-4)* 6924 Brookview Dr., Urbandale, IA 50322 USA Tel 515-270-4606
E-mail: albears5@msn.com.

Albin-Michel, Editions (FRA) *(978-2-226)* *Dist. by* **Distribks Inc.**

Album Publishing Company, Incorporated *See* **RJI Publishing**

ALCAPS, LLC, *(978-0-9769769)* 4004 Cibola Village Dr., NE, Albuquerque, NM 87111 USA
Web site: http://www.heartstohearts.net.

Alchemy Bks., *(978-0-931290)* 1029 Solano Ave., No. E, Albany, CA 94706-1680 USA (SAN 111-3119).

Alchemy Creative, Inc., *(978-0-9675901)* 4650 Cardinal Dr., Beaumont, TX 77705 USA Tel 409-842-5240 ext 18
Web site: http://www.ecpadventures.com; http://www.adventuresoftheelements.com/.

Alchemy Ranch Bks., *(978-0-9881814; 978-0-9909461)* Orders Addr.: 655 Orville Rd. E, Eatonville, WA 98328 USA
E-mail: publisher@alchemyranchstudios.com
Web site: alchemyranchstudios.com.

ALCJR Enterprises, *(978-0-9752760)* P.O. Box 4067, Midlothian, VA 23112-0001 USA Tel 804-744-0100; Fax: 804-744-8961
E-mail: arthur@alcjr.com
Web site: http://www.alcjr.com.

Aldelo Systems Inc., *(978-0-9765992)* 4641 Spyres Way Ste. 4, Modesto, CA 95356-9802 USA
E-mail: sales@aldelo.com
Web site: http://www.aldelo.com.

Alderac Entertainment Group, *(978-1-887953; 978-1-59472)* 4045 Guasti Rd., No. 210, Ontario, CA 91761 USA
E-mail: kcarpenter@alderac.com; dlepore@alderac.com
Web site: http://www.alderac.com
Dist(s): **PSI (Publisher Services, Inc.).**

Aldine de Gruyter *See* **Aldine Transaction**

Publisher Name Index

Aldine Transaction, *(978-0-202)* Div. of Transaction Publishers, 390 Campus Dr., Somerset, NJ 08873 USA (SAN 212-4726) Fax: 732 748 9801; Toll Free: 888 999 6778; c/o Rutgers — The State University of New Jersey, 35 Berrue Cir., Piscataway, NJ 08854
E-mail: orders@transactionpub.com
Web site: http://www.transactionpub.com
Dist(s): **MyiLibrary**
Transaction Pubs.
ebrary, Inc.

Alef Design Group, *(978-1-881283)* 4423 Fruitland Ave., Los Angeles, CA 90058 USA Tel 323-582-1200; Fax: 323-585-0327; Toll Free: 800-845-0662
E-mail: jane@torahaura.com
Web site: http://www.torahaura.com
Dist(s): **Follett School Solutions.**

Alegria Hispana Pubns., *(978-0-944356)* Orders Addr.: P.O. Box 3765, Ventura, CA 93003 USA (SAN 243-4695) Tel 805-642-3969; Edit Addr.: 958 Scenic Way Dr., Ventura, CA 93003-1435 USA (SAN 243-4709).

Alethea In Heart, *(978-0-9719805; 978-1-932370)* 10183 N. Aero Dr. Ste. 2, Hayden, ID 83835-5058 USA
E-mail: truthinheart@hotmail.com
Web site: http://www.truthinheart.com.

Alexander Art L.P., *(978-1-883576)* P.O. Box 1417, Beaverton, OR 97075-1417 USA Tel 503-362-7939; Fax: 503-361-7401; Toll Free: 800-896-4630
E-mail: sales@alexanderart.com
Web site: http://www.alexanderart.com.

Alexander, Lorraine *See* **Alexander, Raine**

Alexander Pubns., *(978-0-9623078)* Orders Addr.: P.O. Box 518, Forney, TX 75126 USA Tel 972-552-9519; Edit Addr.: 806 E. Buffalo St., Forney, TX 75126 USA.

Alexander, Raine, *(978-0-9816301)* 2356 Peeler Rd., Dunwoody, GA 30338 USA
E-mail: 2raine@gmail.com
Web site: www.EdoSchool.org.

Alexander-Marcus Publishing, *(978-0-9760944)* 1115 Tunnel Rd., Santa Barbara, CA 93105 USA
E-mail: andreamarcuslaw@cox.net.

Alexie Bks., *(978-0-9679416)* Div. of Alexie Enterprises, Inc., P.O. Box 3843, Carmel, IN 46082 USA Tel 317-844-5638; Fax: 317-846-0788
E-mail: BusJobs@aol.com; alexie8@aol.com; sales@alexiebooks.com
Web site: http://www.alexieenterprises.com
Dist(s): **Distributors, The.**

AlexMax Publishing Inc., *(978-0-9796643)* Orders Addr.: 4919 Flat Shoals Pkwy Suite 107B-137, Decatur, GA 30034 USA Tel 404-981-4442
E-mail: isbninfo@alexmaxpublishing.com
Web site: http://www.alexmaxpublishing.com.

ALEXZUS Bks., *(978-0-9724733)* 244 Fifth Ave., Suite B260, New York, NY 10001 USA
E-mail: jenbvic@aol.com.

Alfaguara *Imprint of* **Santillana USA Publishing Co., Inc.**

Alfaguara Juvenil *Imprint of* **Santillana USA Publishing Co., Inc.**

Alfaguara S.A. de Ediciones (ARG) *(978-950-511; 978-987-04) Dist. by* **Santillana.**

Alfaguara S.A. de Ediciones (ARG) *(978-950-511; 978-987-04) Dist. by* **Perseus Dist.**

Alfranpedoc, *(978-1-930502)* 4100 W. Coyote Ridge Tr., Tucson, AZ 85746 USA Tel 213-926-0762
E-mail: Waylandhi@aol.com
Web site: http://www.books-by-doc.com.

Alfred Publishing Co., Inc., *(978-0-7390; 978-0-87487; 978-0-88284; 978-1-58951; 978-1-4574; 978-1-4706)* Orders Addr.: P.O. Box 10003, Van Nuys, CA 91410-0003 USA; Edit Addr.: 123 Dry Rd., Oriskany, NY 13424 USA Tel 315-736-1572; Fax: 315-736-7281; *Imprints:* Warner Bros. Publications (Warner Bro); Suzuki (Suzuki)
E-mail: customerservice@alfred.com; permissions@alfred.com; submissions@alfred.com
Web site: http://www.alfred.com
Dist(s): **Follett School Solutions**
Leonard, Hal Corp.

†Algonquin Bks. of Chapel Hill, *(978-0-7611; 978-0-912697; 978-0-945575; 978-1-56512; 978-1-61620)* Div. of Workman Publishing Co., Inc., Orders Addr.: 225 Varick St. Flr. 9, New York, NY 10014-4381 USA Toll Free Fax: 800-521-1832 (fax orders, customer service); Toll Free: 800-722-7202 (orders, customer service); Edit Addr.: P.O. Box 2225, Chapel Hill, NC 27515-2225 USA (SAN 282-7506) Tel 919-967-0108 (editorial, publicity, marketing); Fax: 919-933-0272 (editorial, publicity, marketing)
E-mail: dialogue@algonquin.com; inquiring@algonquin.com; brunson@algonquin.com
Web site: http://www.algonquin.com; http://www.booksellerscorner.com
Dist(s): **Workman Publishing Co., Inc.**; *CIP.*

ALHsiccesslines, *(978-0-615-62527-0)* 13737 Dunbar Terr., Germantown, MD 20874 USA Tel 301-540-2928
E-mail: ALHpromo@aol.com.

Alianza Editorial, S. A. (ESP) *(978-84-206) Dist. by* **Distribks Inc.**

Alianza Editorial, S. A. (ESP) *(978-84-206) Dist. by* **Continental Bk.**

Alianza Editorial, S. A. (ESP) *(978-84-206) Dist. by* **AIMS Intl.**

Alianza Editorial, S. A. (ESP) *(978-84-206) Dist. by* **Lectorum Pubns.**

Alianza Editorial, S. A. (ESP) *(978-84-206) Dist. by* **Libros In Spanish, LLC.**

Alias Enterprises LLC *See* **Lamp Post Inc.**

Alien Time Treasure, *(978-0-9727309)* P.O. Box 2665, Newport, RI 02840 USA
E-mail: webmaster@alientimetreasure.com
Web site: http://alientimetreasure.com.

Aliso Street Productions, *(978-0-9840120)* P.O. Box 36422, Albuquerque, NM 87176 USA Tel 505-414-6366
E-mail: AlisoStreet@aol.com.

All About Kids Publishing, *(978-0-9700863; 978-0-9710278; 978-0-9744446; 978-0-9801468; 978-0-615-11427-9; 978-0-9963756)* Orders Addr.: P.O. Box 159, Gilroy, CA 95021 USA (SAN 253-8601) Tel 408-337-1866; Fax: 408-337-5192
E-mail: lguevara@aakp.com
Web site: http://www.aakp.com
Dist(s): **Pathway Bk. Service.**

All Around Our World Publishing Co., Inc., *(978-0-9799050)* 629 Park Ave., Beloit, WI 53511 USA Tel 608-207-9777; Fax: 608-207-9888
E-mail: brendaaaow@charter.net.

All For One Pr., *(978-0-9745951)* 29193 Northwestern Hwy, No. 658, Southfield, MI 48034 USA (SAN 255-6804) Tel 313-617-4012
E-mail: allforonepress@hotmail.com.

All Gold Publishing Co., *(978-0-9701519)* Orders Addr.: P.O. Box 13504, Dayton, OH 45413-0504 USA Tel 937-586-9804; Edit Addr.: 907 Reist, Dayton, OH 45408-1350 USA
E-mail: allgoldceo@netzero.net
Web site: http://www.allgoldpublishing.com.

All Hallows Eve Pr., *(978-0-9853082)* 20 Robert Dr., Hyde Park, NY 12538 USA Tel 914-489-9529
E-mail: ddavies@artisticwitchery.com
Web site: www.artisticwitchery.com.

All Health Chiropractic Ctrs. Inc., *(978-0-9770527)* 567 Church St., Royersford, PA 19468 USA (SAN 256-6443) Tel 610-948-4161
E-mail: susiequsie6@aol.com
Web site: http://www.drsnappy.com.

All Kidding Aside, *(978-0-9794317)* 2829 S. Cypress, Sioux City, IA 51106 USA Tel 712-276-4315
E-mail: bestma34@cableone.net
Web site: http://www.allkiddingaside.biz.

All Nations Pr., *(978-0-9725110; 978-0-9777954; 978-0-9912721)* P.O. Box 601, White Marsh, VA 23183 USA Do not confuse with companies with the same or similar name in Colorado Springs, CO, Southlake, TX
E-mail: editors@allnationspress.com
Web site: http://www.allnationspress.com
Dist(s): **Follett School Solutions.**

All Over Creation, *(978-0-9788950)* P.O. Box 382, Madera, CA 93639 USA
E-mail: astorybytory@yahoo.com.

All Star Pr., *(978-0-9767816; 978-1-937376)* 944 Oakview Rd., Tarpon Springs, FL 34689 USA Tel 502-713-3149
E-mail: allstarpress@verizon.net
Web site: www.allstarpress.com
Dist(s): **Smashwords.**

All That Productions, Inc., *(978-0-9679441; 978-0-9903422)* Orders Addr.: P.O. Box 1594, Humble, TX 77347 USA Tel 281-878-2062
E-mail: allthat3@peoplepc.com.

Allaf, Mashhad Al, *(978-0-9722722)* P.O. Box 2063, Chester, VA 23831-8440 USA.

Allecram Publishing, *(978-0-9764198)* P.O. Box 6003, Dayton, OH 45405 USA Tel 937-278-6630
E-mail: marcellaashe@sbcglobal.net
Web site: http://www.allecrampublishing.com.

Allegheny Pr., *(978-0-910042)* 19323 Elgin Rd., Corry, PA 16407 USA (SAN 201-2456) Tel 814-664-8504
E-mail: hjohn@tbscc.com
Dist(s): **Follett School Solutions.**

Allen & Unwin (AUS) *(978-0-04; 978-0-86861; 978-1-86373; 978-1-86448; 978-1-875680; 978-0-7299; 978-1-86508; 978-1-74114; 978-1-74115; 978-1-74175; 978-1-74176; 978-1-74237; 978-1-74269; 978-1-877505; 978-0-7316-7153-3; 978-0-646-24696-3; 978-1-74331; 978-1-74343;-1-76011; 978-1-925266; 978-1-925267; 978-1-925268; 978-1-76029; 978-1-925393; 978-1-925394; 978-1-925395) Dist. by* **IPG Chicago.**

Allen, Edward Publishing, LLC, *(978-0-9853123; 978-0-9967663)* 73 Terri Sue Ct., Hampton, VA 23666 USA Tel 757-768-5544
E-mail: jprice@edwardallenpublishing.com
Web site: http://www.edwardallenpublishing.com
Dist(s): **BookBaby.**

Allen Publishing, USA *See* **ALEXZUS Bks.**

Allen, Toi Operations, *(978-0-9753787)* 11300 E. 85th Terr., Raytown, MO 64138 USA Tel 816-737-5293; Fax: 816-923-2634
E-mail: itasca2001@aol.com.

Allen-Ayers Bks., *(978-0-9658702)* 4621 S. Atlantic Ave., No. 7603, Ponce Inlet, PA 32127 USA Tel 386-761-3956
E-mail: allen-ayers@cfl.rr.com.

AllensRusk Pr., *(978-0-9672246)* P.O. Box 100213, Nashville, TN 38134 USA Tel 615-365-0993
E-mail: allensrusk@aol.com.

Allergic Child Publishing Group, *(978-1-58628)* 6660 Delmonico Dr., Suite D249, Colorado Springs, CO 80919 USA Tel 719-338-0202; Fax: 719-633-0375
E-mail: nicole@allergicchild.com
Web site: http://www.allergicchild.com
Dist(s): **Follett School Solutions.**

Alli Kat Publishing, *(978-0-9788725)* 2353 Alexandria Dr., Suite 201, Lexington, KY 40504 USA Tel 859-264-7700; Fax: 859-264-7744
E-mail: eyemanjlh@aol.com.

Allied Publishing *See* **Flying Frog Publishing, Inc.**

Alligator Boogaloo, *(978-0-9721416)* P.O. Box 20070, Oakland, CA 94620 USA
E-mail: business@alligatorboogaloo.com
Web site: http://www.alligatorboogaloo.com.

Alligator Pr., *(978-0-9675658; 978-0-9884057; 978-0-9914334)* Orders Addr.: P.O. Box 526368, Salt Lake City, UT 84152 USA Tel 512-762-5427 Do not confuse with Alligator Press, Carson City, NV
E-mail: k.kimball333@gmail.com
Web site: http://www.alligatorpress.com
Dist(s): **BookBaby.**

Allium Pr. of Chicago, *(978-0-9840676; 978-0-9831938; 978-0-9890535; 978-0-9967558)* 1530 Elgin Ave., Forest Park, IL 60130 USA (SAN 858-3331)
Web site: http://www.alliumpress.com/
Dist(s): **Follett School Solutions**
INscribe Digital
Lightning Source, Inc.
Smashwords.

Allocca Biotechnology, LLC, *(978-0-9659987; 978-0-9769213)* 19 Lorraine Ct., Northport, NY 11768 USA Tel 631-757-3919; Fax: 631-757-3918
E-mail: john@allocca.com
Web site: http://www.allocca.com.

Allocca, Christine A., *(978-0-615-21480-1)* 3940 Laurel Canyon Blvd., No. 399, Studio City, CA 91604 USA Tel 818-486-2730
Web site: http://www.little-green-giants.com.

Allocca Technology & Healthcare Research *See* **Allocca Biotechnology, LLC**

Allosaurus Pubs., *(978-0-9620900; 978-1-888325)* Div. of North Carolina Learning Institute for Fitness & Education, Orders Addr.: P.O. Box 10245, Greensboro, NC 27404 USA (SAN 250-0906) Tel 336-292-6999
E-mail: ally@infionline.net
Web site: http://www.allosauruspublishers.com
Dist(s): **Follett School Solutions.**

Allured Business Media, *(978-0-931710; 978-1-932633)* 336 Gundersen Dr. Ste. A, Carol Stream, IL 60188-2403 USA (SAN 222-4933)
Web site: http://www.alluredbooks.com/
Dist(s): **ebrary, Inc.**

Allured Publishing Corporation *See* **Allured Business Media**

Allworth Pr. *Imprint of* **Skyhorse Publishing Co., Inc.**

AllWrite Advertising & Publishing, *(978-0-9744935; 978-0-9844931; 978-0-9887332; 978-1-941716)* Orders Addr.: 241 Pechtree St. Suite 422, Atlanta, GA 30303 USA; Edit Addr.: P.O. Box 1071, Atlanta, GA 30301 USA Tel 404-221-0703
E-mail: info@allwritepublishing.com; annette@allwritepublishing.com
Web site: http://www.allwritepublishing.com; http://www.e-allwrite.com
Dist(s): **Lightning Source, Inc.**

†Allyn & Bacon, Inc., *(978-0-205; 978-0-321)* Div. of Pearson Higher Education & Professional Group, Orders Addr.: c/o Prentice Hall/Allyn & Bacon, 200 Old Tappan Rd., Old Tappan, NJ 07675 USA Toll Free Fax: 800-445-6991; Toll Free: 800-922-0579 (customer service); 800-666-9433 (ordering); 111 Tenth St., Des Moines, IA 50309 Tel 515-284-6751; Fax: 515-284-2607; Toll Free: 800-278-3525; Edit Addr.: 75 Arlington St., Suite 300, Boston, MA 02116 USA (SAN 201-2510)
E-mail: ab_webmaster@abacon.com
Web site: http://www.abacon.com
Dist(s): **MyiLibrary**
Pearson Education
Pearson Technology Group; *CIP.*

Alma Little *Imprint of* **Elva Resa Publishing, LLC**

Alma Pr., *(978-0-9746333)* 1204 Abbot Kinney Blvd., Venice, CA 90291 USA (SAN 255-6723) Fax: 310-314-3883
E-mail: info@almapress.com
Web site: http://www.almapress.com.

Almadraba Infantil y Juvenil (ESP) *(978-84-92702) Dist. by* **Lectorum Pubns.**

Almanac Publishing Co., *(978-1-928720)* Mt. Hope Ave., Lewiston, ME 04240 USA Tel 207-755-2246; Fax: 207-755-2422
Web site: http://www.farmersalmanac.com
Dist(s): **Sterling Publishing Co., Inc.**

Almond Publishing, *(978-0-9777314)* P.O. Box 573, Petaluma, CA 94953 USA (SAN 850-0673)
E-mail: contact@almondpublishing.com
Web site: http://www.almondpublishing.com.

Aloha Publications *See* **catBOX Entertainment, Inc.**

Aloha Wellness Pubs., *(978-0-9727548)* 2333 Kapiolani Blvd., Suite 2108, Honolulu, HI 96826 USA (SAN 255-0539) Tel 808-941-8253; Fax: 808-925-4233; Toll Free: 866-233-6941
E-mail: crites@hawaii.rr.com
Web site: http://www.alohawellnesstravel.com
Dist(s): **Booklines Hawaii, Ltd.**

Alouette Enterprises, Inc., *(978-0-9797577; 978-0-9799922)* 5517 N. 71st St., Scottsdale, AZ 85253 USA Tel 480-460-1597
E-mail: DonnaFridrych@aol.com.

Alpen Bks, 4602 Chennault Beach Rd. Ste. B1, Mukilteo, WA 98275-5016 USA.

Alpenrose Pr., *(978-0-9603624; 978-1-889385)* Orders Addr.: P.O. Box 499, Silverthorne, CO 80498 USA (SAN 222-2612) Tel 970-468-6273; Fax: 970-468-6273
E-mail: orders@alpenrosepress.com; orders@zoebooks.com
Web site: http://www.zoebooks.com; http://www.alpenrosepress.com
Dist(s): **Alpenbooks Pr. LLC.**

Alpha & Omega Publishing, *(978-0-9767778)* 3409 Daniel Place Dr., Charlotte, NC 28213 USA Tel 704-724-1683; Fax: 270-721-6019 Do not confuse iwth companies with the same name in Fremont, NE, Springfield, OR
E-mail: alphaomega@carolina.rr.com.

Alpha Behavior Consultants, *(978-0-9758755)* 12740 NW 11th St., Miami, FL 33172 USA
E-mail: info@alphbehc.com
Web site: http://www.alphabehc.com.

Alpha Bible Pubns., *(978-1-877917)* P.O. Box 155, Hood River, OR 97031 USA; P.O. Box 157, Morton, WA 98356 USA Tel 541-386-6634
Dist(s): **Pentecostal Publishing Hse.**
eBookit.com.

Alpha Bks. *Imprint of* **Penguin Publishing Group**

Alpha Connections, *(978-0-9715779; 978-0-9747610; 978-1-936933)* 530 W. Idaho Blvd., Emmett, ID 83617 USA
E-mail: contact@dragonsfuryseries.com
Web site: http://www.dragonsfuryseries.com
Dist(s): **Lightning Source, Inc.**
Smashwords.

Alpha Heartland Press *See* **Heartland Foundation, Inc.**

Alpha Learning World, Inc., *(978-0-9791680)* 1064 Mohegan Rd., Venice, FL 34293 USA (SAN 852-6362)
E-mail: trisley1@verizon.net
Web site: http://alphalearningworld.com.

Alpha Omega Pubns., Inc., *(978-0-7403; 978-0-86717; 978-1-58095)* 300 N. McKemy Ave., Chandler, AZ 85226-2618 USA Tel 602-438-2717; Fax: 480-785-8034; Toll Free: 800-682-7391; 804 N. 2nd Ave. E., Rock Rapids, IA 51246 (SAN 853-2826) Tel 800-622-3070; Fax: 712-472-4856; *Imprints:* Lifepac (Lifepac); Horizons (Hmzns AZ); Weaver (Weaver)
E-mail: cpatterson@aop.com
Web site: http://www.aop.com
Dist(s): **Follett School Solutions**
Send The Light Distribution LLC
Spring Arbor Distributors, Inc.

Alpha OmeGa Publishing, *(978-0-9658073)* 1217 Cape Coral Pkwy., Cape Coral, FL 33904 USA Tel 941-542-3666; Fax: 941-945-7963; Toll Free: 800-542-3666; 4219 SE First Ct., Cape Coral, FL 33904
E-mail: GPMueller@aol.com
Web site: http://www.Floridawest.com/Liestorm.

Alpha Run Pr., LLC, *(978-0-9761182; 978-1-933289)* Orders Addr.: P.O. Box 15079, Silver Spring, MD 20914-5079 USA Tel 202-508-3392; Edit Addr.: 1717 K St. NW, Suite 600, Washington, DC 20036 USA
E-mail: alpharp@aol.com
Web site: http://www.alpharunpress.com.

Alpha Shade, Inc., *(978-0-9768705)* 11850 85th Pl., N., Maple Grove, MN 55369 USA Tel 763-424-9316
E-mail: alphashade1@aol.com
Web site: http://www.alpha-shade.com.

Alpha Writers Ltd., *(978-0-9772018)* Orders Addr.: P.O. Box 561262, The Colony, TX 75056 USA (SAN 256-9256) Fax: 425-955-0859; Toll Free: 866-751-4340 Outside of Dallas
E-mail: source@alphawritersltd.com
Web site: http://www.alphawritersltd.com.

Alpha-kidZ, *(978-0-9749220; 978-0-9823534)* P.O. Box 1552, West Monroe, LA 71294-1552 USA Tel 318-651-0833; Fax: 318-396-4073
Web site: http://www.alphakidz.com.

AlphaLove Publishing, *(978-0-9764307)* P.O. Box 248, South Orange, NJ 07079 USA Fax: 973-275-3973.

Alpine Archaeological Consultants, Inc., *(978-0-9743137)* P.O. Box 2075, Montrose, CO 81402-2075 USA Tel 970-249-6761; Fax: 970-249-8482
E-mail: susan_chandler@alpinearchaeology.com
Web site: http://www.alpinearchaeology.com.

†Alpine Pubns., Inc., *(978-0-931866; 978-1-57779)* Orders Addr.: 38262 Linman Rd., Crawford, CO 81415 USA (SAN 255-2094) Tel 970-921-5005; Fax: 970-921-5081; Toll Free: 800-777-7257
E-mail: customerservice@alpinepub.com; alpine@paonia.com; alpinepubl@aol.com
Web site: http://www.alpinepub.com
Dist(s): **Follett School Solutions**
Partners/West Book Distributors; *CIP.*

Alpine River Pr., *(978-0-9891471)* 660 Haley LN, Red Bluff, CA 96080 USA Tel 530-200-2745
E-mail: alpineriverpress@gmail.com.

Alta Omnimedia, *(978-0-9726360)* 2 Valley View Ave., Ste. 116, San Jose, CA 95127 USA
Web site: http://www.altaomnimedia.com.

Alta Publishing LLC, *(978-0-9767120)* P.O. Box 108, Bellvue, CO 80512 USA (SAN 256-4874) Do not confuse with companies with the same name in Sandy, UT, Midvale, UT.

Alta Retreat Ctr., *(978-0-9746151)* 20 Alta School Rd., Alta, WY 83414 USA Tel 307-353-8200; Fax: 208-354-4002
E-mail: altacp@ida.net.

Altea, Ediciones, S.A. - Grupo Santillana (ESP) *(978-84-372) Dist. by* **Lectorum Pubns.**

Altea, Ediciones, S.A. - Grupo Santillana (ESP) *(978-84-372) Dist. by* **Santillana.**

Altea, Ediciones, S.A. - Grupo Santillana (ESP) *(978-84-372) Dist. by* **Perseus Dist.**

Alterna Comics, *(978-0-9797874; 978-1-934985)* Div. of Alterna Comics, Inc., Orders Addr.: 23 Trumpet Ln., Levittown, NY 11756 USA Tel 516-304-6733; Fax: 516-644-2386
E-mail: publisher@alternacomics.com
Web site: http://www.alternacomics.com
Dist(s): **Diamond Comic Distributors, Inc.**
Partners Pubs. Group, Inc.

Alternative Comics, *(978-1-891867; 978-1-934460; 978-1-68148)* 21607B Stevens Creek Blvd., Cupertino, CA 95014 USA Do not confuse with companies with the same or similar name in Goleta, GA, Billerica, MA
E-mail: marc@wowcool.com
Web site: http://www.indyworld.com
Dist(s): **Consortium Bk. Sales & Distribution**
Diamond Comic Distributors, Inc.
Diamond Bk. Distributors
Last Gasp of San Francisco.

Alternative Press, Incorporated *See* **Alternative Comics**

AlterNet Bks., *(978-0-9633687; 978-0-9752724)* 77 Federal St., 2nd Flr., San Francisco, CA 94107 USA Tel 415-284-1420; Fax: 415-284-1414
E-mail: valrie@alternet.org
Web site: http://www.alternet.org.

Althos, *(978-0-9728053; 978-0-9742787; 978-0-9746943; 978-1-932813)* 1500 Piney Plains Rd., Suite 201, Cary, NC 27518 USA Tel 919-557-2260; Fax: 919-557-2261
E-mail: info@althos.com
Web site: http://www.althos.com.

For full information on wholesalers and distributors, refer to the Wholesaler and Distributor Name Index

A-Lu Publishing, (*978-0-9817092*) 4257 Holiday Rd., Traverse City, MI 49686 USA
Dist(s): **BookBaby.**

Alvarado, Rudolph *See* **Caballo Pr. of Ann Arbor**

ALVARADOPLUS, (*978-0-9791782*) 315 Luna St., Apt 1B, San Juan, PR 00901-1488 USA (SAN 852-6710)
E-mail: ALVARADOPlus@aol.com.

Alvarez, Jesus, (*978-0-9792507*) 254 San Diego Ave., Brownsville, TX 78526 USA Tel 956-542-2722
E-mail: alvarcorp@msn.com.

A.M. Green Publishing, (*978-1-935479*) P.O. Box 1085, Amston, CT 06231 USA Tel 617-391-7350
E-mail: JSmith@amgreenpublishing.com
Web site: http://www.amgreenpublishing.com.

AMA Verlag GmbH (DEU) (*978-3-89922; 978-3-927190; 978-3-932587*) *Dist. by* **Mel Bay.**

†Amacom, (*978-0-7612; 978-0-8144*) Div. of American Management Association, Orders Addr.: 600 AMA Way, Saranac Lake, NY 12983 USA (SAN 227-3578) Tel 518-891-5510; Fax: 518-891-2372; Toll Free: 800-250-5308 (orders & customer service); Edit Addr.: 1601 Broadway, New York, NY 10019-7420 USA (SAN 201-1670) Tel 212-586-8100; Fax: 212-903-8168; 1 Ingram Blvd., La Vergne, TN 37086
E-mail: pubservice@amanet.org
Web site: http://www.amacombooks.org
Dist(s): **Ebsco Publishing**
Follett School Solutions
MyiLibrary
Productivity Pr.
Wybel Marketing Group
ebrary, Inc.; *CIP.*

Amadeus Press *Imprint of* **Leonard, Hal Corp.**

amana pubns., (*978-0-915957; 978-1-59008*) Div. of amana corp., 10710 Tucker St., Beltsville, MD 20705-2223 USA (SAN 630-9798) Tel 301-595-5999; Fax: 301-595-5888; Toll Free: 800-660-1777
E-mail: amana@igprinting.com
Web site: http://www.amana-publications.com.

Amani Publishing, LLC, (*978-0-9752851; 978-0-9788937; 978-0-9815847; 978-0-9833666*) P.O. Box 12045, Tallahassee, FL 32317 USA Tel 850-264-3341 Do not confuse with Amani Publishing in Pineville, LA
E-mail: amanipublishing@aol.com
Web site: http://www.barbarajoewilliams.com
Dist(s): **Lightning Source, Inc.**

Amaquemecan, Editorial (MEX) (*978-968-7205*) *Dist. by* **Continental Bk.**

Amaquemecan, Editorial (MEX) (*978-968-7205*) *Dist. by* **AIMS Intl.**

AMARA Entertainment, (*978-0-9760745*) 1024 Frans Rd., Westfield, NC 27053 USA Tel 336-351-3437 (phone/fax)
E-mail: rpitt@charlesthechef.com
Web site: http://www.charlesthechef.com.

Amato, G. J., (*978-0-615-38545-7; 978-0-9829962; 978-0-9894561*) 5 Westview Ct., Avon, CT 06001-4540 USA Tel 860-675-6712
E-mail: gaetanoja@aol.com
Web site: getkidsmovingnow.com.

Amazement Square, (*978-0-9815308*) 27 Ninth St., Lynchburg, VA 24504 USA
Web site: http://www.amazementsquare.org.

Amazing Dreams Publishing, (*978-0-9719628*) P.O. Box 1811, Asheville, NC 28802 USA
E-mail: contact@amazingdreamspublishing.com
Web site: http://www.amazingdreamspublishing.com
Dist(s): **ASP Wholesale**
CreateSpace Independent Publishing Platform.

Amazing Factory, The, (*978-0-9776282; 978-0-9788469; 978-0-9790302*) 5527 San Gabriel Way, Orlando, FL 32837 USA
E-mail: theamazingfactory@hotmail.com
Web site: http://www.theamazingfactory.com.

Amazing Herbs Pr., (*978-0-9742962*) 545 8th Ave., Suite 401, New York, NY 10018 USA Tel 770-982-0107; Fax: 770-982-0273; Toll Free: 800-241-9138 (orders)
E-mail: tnc100@bellsouth.net
Web site: http://www.amazingherbspress.com.

AMazing Pubns., (*978-0-9763434*) 337 W. Napa St., Sonoma, CA 95476 USA.

Amazing Publishing Company, A *See* **Rhymeglow.com**

Amazon Children's Publishing *Imprint of* **Amazon Publishing**

Amazon Publishing, (*978-0-8034; 978-1-61109; 978-1-4778; 978-1-5039*) 551 Boren Ave., N., Seattle, WA 98109 USA Tel 206-266-5123; *Imprints:* Amazon Children's Publishing (AmazonChldns); Thomas & Mercer (Thomas&Mercer); Montlake Romance (Montlake); 47North (FortySevN); Two Lions (TwoLions)
E-mail: fullhart@amazon.com; epub-metadata@amazon.com
Web site: http://www.amazon.com/amazoncrossing; http://www.apub.com/; http://www.amazon.com/amazonpublishing
Dist(s): **Brilliance Publishing**
CreateSpace Independent Publishing Platform
MyiLibrary.

AmazonCrossing *See* **Amazon Publishing**

AmazonEncore, (*978-0-9825550; 978-1-935597; 978-1-61218*) 701 5th Ave., Suite 1500, Seattle, WA 98104 USA; *Imprints:* Montlake Romance (MONTLAKE ROMAN)
Dist(s): **Brilliance Publishing.**

Ambassador Bks. *Imprint of* **Paulist Pr.**

Ambassador Bks., Inc., (*978-0-9646439; 978-1-929039*) 446 Main St. Ste. 19, Worcester, MA 01608-2368 USA Toll Free: 800-577-0909
E-mail: info@ambassadorbooks.com
Web site: http://www.ambassadorbooks.com
Dist(s): **Christian Bk. Distributors**
Spring Arbor Distributors, Inc.

Ambassador International *Imprint of* **Emerald Hse. Group, Inc.**

Ambassador Pubns., (*978-1-58572*) 3110 E. Medicine Lake Blvd., Plymouth, MN 55441 USA Tel 763-545-5631; Fax: 763-545-0079
E-mail: parished@aflc.org
Web site: http://www.aflc.org.

Ambassador-Emerald, International *Imprint of* **Emerald Hse. Group, Inc.**

Amber Bks., (*978-0-9655064; 978-0-9702224; 978-0-9727519; 978-0-9749779; 978-0-9767735; 978-0-9790976; 978-0-9824922; 978-1-937269*) Div. of Amber Communications Group, Inc., Orders Addr.: 1334 E. Chandler Blvd., Suite 5-D67, Phoenix, AZ 85048 USA Tel 602-743-7211; 602-743-7426; Fax: 480-283-0991; *Imprints:* Colossus Books (Colossus)
E-mail: amberbks@aol.com
Web site: http://www.amberbooks.com
Dist(s): **A & B Distributors & Pubs. Group**
African World Bks.
Book Wholesalers, Inc.
Brodart Co.
D & J Bk. Distributors
Follett School Solutions
Independent Pubs. Group
Midwest Library Service
Quality Bks., Inc.
Unique Bks., Inc.

Amber Lotus *See* **Amber Lotus Publishing**

Amber Lotus Publishing, (*978-0-945798; 978-1-56937; 978-1-885394; 978-1-60237; 978-1-63136*) P.O. Box 11329, Portland, OR 97211-0329 USA Toll Free: 800-326-2375
E-mail: info@amberlotus.com
Web site: http://www.amberlotus.com
Dist(s): **Banyan Tree Bks.**
Follett School Solutions.

Amber Marie Publishing, (*978-0-9771981*) 10413 Coffee Grinder Ct., Las Vegas, NV 89129 USA (SAN 256-9744) Tel 702-238-3846.

Amber Skye Publishing LLC, (*978-0-9819860; 978-0-9831839; 978-0-9894003; 978-0-692-47081-7*) 1935 Berkshire Dr., Eagan, MN 55122 USA
E-mail: publisher@amberskyepublishing.com
Web site: http://www.amberskyepublishing.com; www.itascabooks.com
Dist(s): **CreateSpace Independent Publishing Platform**
Itasca Bks.

Amber Trust, The *See* **Aenor Trust, The**

Amber Woods Publishing, (*978-0-9743717*) P.O. Box 280, Excelsior, MN 55331 USA Tel 952-476-1670
Web site: http://www.amberwoodspublishing.com.

Amberley Publishing (GBR) (*978-1-84868; 978-1-4456*) *Dist. by* **Casemate Pubs.**

Amberock Pubns., (*978-0-9754636*) P.O. Box 491, Dallas, NC 28034 USA
Web site: http://www.meandmybassguitar.com.

Amberwaves, (*978-0-9708913*) P.O. Box 487, Becket, MA 01223 USA (SAN 256-4254) Tel 413-623-0012; 413-623-6042 (phone/fax); 305 Brooker Hill Rd., Becket, MA 01223 Tel 413-623-0012; Fax: 413-623-6042
E-mail: shenwa@bcn.net
Web site: http://www.amberwaves.org.

Amberwood Pr., (*978-0-9630243; 978-0-9776445; 978-0-615-95885-9*) 509 Albany Post Rd., New Paltz, NY 12561-3629 USA Do not confuse with Amberwood Pr., in Ventura, CA
E-mail: nava@vegkitchen.com
Web site: http://www.vegkitchen.com
Dist(s): **CreateSpace Independent Publishing Platform**
Independent Pubs. Group.

Ambrosia Press LLC, (*978-0-9729346; 978-0-9778656; 978-0-9525344; 978-0-9862590*) 2 Waban Rd., Timberlake, OH 44095 USA Tel 440-951-7780; Fax: 440-951-0565
E-mail: willowhse@yahoo.com; ambrosia03@att.net
Web site: http://www.ruthfawcettbooks.com.

Ameeramac Bks. *Imprint of* **Ameeramac Bks. Inc.**

Ameeramac Bks., Inc., (*978-0-9762911*) Div. of Ameeramac Reporting, Inc., 168 Putnam Ave., Brooklyn, NY 11216-1606 USA Tel 917-353-1644; Fax: 718-636-8210; *Imprints:* Ameeramac Books (AmeeraBks)
E-mail: ameeramac@optonline.com.

Ameeramac Reporting, Incorporated *See* **Ameeramac Bks. Inc.**

Amelia Street Press *See* **Prytania Pr.**

Amereon LTD., (*978-0-8488; 978-0-88411; 978-0-89190*) Orders Addr.: P.O. Box 1200, Mattituck, NY 11952 USA (SAN 201-2413) Tel 631-298-5100; Fax: 631-298-5631; *Imprints:* Rivercity Press (Rivercity Pr); American Reprint Company (Am Repr)
E-mail: amereon@aol.com
Dist(s): **Follett School Solutions.**

America Sports Publishing, (*978-0-9721199*) Orders Addr.: P.O. Box 132, Brookfield, OH 44403 USA Tel 330-448-0866; Toll Free: 866-255-2267; Edit Addr.: 6881 Stewart Rd., Brookfield, OH 44403 USA Fax: 330-448-0936
E-mail: Info@AthleticScholarshipBook.com
Web site: http://www.AthleticScholarshipBook.com
Dist(s): **Cardinal Pubs. Group**
Quality Bks., Inc.
Unique Bks., Inc.

America Star Bks., (*978-1-61102; 978-1-63249; 978-1-63382; 978-1-63448; 978-1-68090; 978-1-68122; 978-1-68176; 978-1-68229; 978-1-63508*) 550 Highland St. Ste 105, Frederick, MD 21701 USA Tel 301-228-2595; Fax: 301-228-2596; P.O. Box 184, Frederick, MD 21705
Web site: www.americastarbooks.pub.

American Animal Hospital Assn. Pr., (*978-0-941451; 978-0-9616498; 978-1-58326*) Orders Addr.: 12575 W. Bayaud Ave., Lakewood, CO 80228 USA (SAN 224-4799) Tel 303-986-2800; Fax: 303-986-1700; Toll Free: 800-252-2242
E-mail: msc@aahanet.org
Web site: http://press.aahanet.org
Dist(s): **Matthews Medical Bk. Co.**

American Antiquarian Society, (*978-0-912296; 978-0-944026; 978-1-929545*) 185 Salisbury St., Worcester, MA 01609 USA (SAN 206-474X) Tel 508-752-5221; Fax: 508-754-9069
E-mail: library@mwa.org
Web site: http://www.americanantiquarian.org
Dist(s): **Oak Knoll Pr.**

American Assn. of Veterinary Parasitologists, (*978-0-9770942*) 3915 S. 48th St. Terr., Saint Joseph, MO 64503 USA
Web site: http://www.aavp.org.

American Atheist Pr., (*978-0-910309; 978-0-911826; 978-1-57884*) Subs. of Charles E. Stevens, P.O. Box 5733, Parsippany, NJ 07054-6733 USA (SAN 206-7188) Tel 908-276-7300; Fax: 908-276-7402
E-mail: editor@atheists.org; info@atheists.org
Web site: http://www.atheists.org.

American Automobile Association *See* **AAA**

American Bar Assn., (*978-0-89707; 978-1-57073; 978-1-59031; 978-1-60442; 978-1-61632; 978-0-615-36849-8; 978-0-615-36850-4; 978-1-61438; 978-1-62722; 978-1-63425*) 321 N Clark St, 20th FL, Chicago, IL 60654 USA (SAN 211-4798) Tel 312-988-6011 Toll Free: 800-285-2221
E-mail: natalie.cirar@americanbar.org
Web site: http://www.americanbar.org
Dist(s): **MyiLibrary**
National Bk. Network.

American Bible Society, (*978-0-8267; 978-1-58516; 978-1-937628; 978-1-941448; 978-1-941449*) Orders Addr.: 6201 E. 43rd St., Tulsa, OK 74135-6562 USA (SAN 662-7129) Toll Free Fax: 866-570-2877; Edit Addr.: 1865 Broadway, New York, NY 10023-9980 USA (SAN 203-5189) Tel 212-408-1200; Fax: 212-408-1305; 700 Plaza Dr., 2nd Flr., Secaucus, NJ 07094
E-mail: info@americanbible.org
Web site: http://www.bibles.org; http://www.americanbible.org
Dist(s): **Anchor Distributors.**

American Bk. Co., (*978-1-932410; 978-1-59807; 978-1-62800*) 103 Executive Dr., Woodstock, GA 30188 USA Tel 770-928-2834 Toll Free: 888-254-5877 Do not confuse with companies with the same name in Chesterfield, VA, Knoxville, TN, Florence, AL
Web site: http://www.americanbookcompany.com.

American Book Publishing *See* **American Bk. Publishing Group**

American Bk. Publishing Group, (*978-1-930586; 978-1-58982; 978-0-615-54716-9*) P.O. Box 65624, Salt Lake City, UT 84165 USA (SAN 254-4725) Fax: 801-382-0881; Toll Free: 888-288-7413; *Imprints:* Bedside Books (Bedside Bks); Millennial Mind Publishing (Millennial Mind)
E-mail: orders@american-book.com; info@american-book.com; operations@american-book.com
Web site: http://www.american-book.com
Dist(s): **Seven Locks Pr.**

American Bookworks Corp., (*978-0-9622813; 978-1-884965*) 309 Florida Hill Rd., Ridgefield, CT 06877 USA Tel 203-438-0345; Fax: 203-438-0379
E-mail: info@abwcorporation.com
Web site: http://www.abwcorporation.com.

†American Camping Assn., (*978-0-87603*) 5000 State Rd. 67, N., Martinsville, IN 46151-7902 USA (SAN 201-2596) Tel 765-342-8456 (General Info.); Fax: 765-349-6357 (orders); Toll Free: 800-428-2267 (orders)
E-mail: bookstore@aca-camps.org
Web site: http://www.acacamps.org
Dist(s): **Independent Pubs. Group**; *CIP.*

American Cancer Society, Inc., (*978-0-944235; 978-1-60443*) 250 Williams St., Atlanta, GA 30303-1002 USA (SAN 227-6941) Tel 404-320-3333; Fax: 404-325-9341; Toll Free: 800-ACS-2345
Web site: http://www.cancer.org
Dist(s): **Independent Pubs. Group**
McGraw-Hill Cos., The
McGraw-Hill Professional Publishing
MyiLibrary
Wiley-Blackwell.

American Carriage Hse. Publishing, (*978-0-9705734; 978-1-935176*) P.O. Box 1778, Penn Valley, CA 95946 USA Tel 530-432-8860; Fax: 530-265-9650 Do not confuse with Carraige House Publishing in Middleton, CA
E-mail: info@americancarriagehousepublishing.com; editor@americancarriagehousepublishing.com; research@americancarriagehousepublishing.com; assistant@americancarriagehousepublishing.com
Web site: http://www.americancarriagehousepublishing.com
Dist(s): **Send The Light Distribution LLC**
Smashwords.

†American Chemical Society, (*978-0-8412*) 1155 16th St., NW, Washington, DC 20036 USA (SAN 201-2626) Tel 202-872-4600; Toll Free: 800-227-5558; 2001 Evans Rd., Cary, NC 27513
E-mail: service@acs.org; help@acs.org
Web site: http://www.acs.org; http://www.ChemCenter.org
Dist(s): **Follett School Solutions**
Oxford Univ. Pr., Inc.; *CIP.*

American Classical League, The, (*978-0-939507*) Orders Addr.: 860 NW Washington Blvd. Suite A, Hamilton, OH 45013 USA (SAN 225-8358) Tel 513-529-7741; Fax: 513-529-7742
E-mail: info@aclclassics.org
Web site: http://www.aclclassics.org.

American Correctional Assn., (*978-0-929310; 978-0-942974; 978-1-56991*) 206 N. Washington St. Ste. 200, Alexandria, VA 22314-2528 USA (SAN 204-8051) Toll Free: 800-222-5646 (ext. 1860)
Web site: http://www.aca.org.

American Dental Assn., (*978-0-910074; 978-1-932305; 978-1-60122; 978-1-935201; 978-0-9860279; 978-1-941807*) 211 E. Chicago Ave., Chicago, IL 60611 USA (SAN 202-4519) Tel 312-440-2568; 312-440-2500; Fax: 312-440-7461
E-mail: survey@ada.org
Web site: http://www.ada.org.

American Diabetes Assn., (*978-0-945448; 978-1-58040*) Orders Addr.: 1701 N. Beauregard St., Alexandria, VA 22311 USA Toll Free Fax: 800-998-3103 (orders); Toll Free: 800-323-4900 (orders)
E-mail: lboswell@diabetes.org
Web site: http://www.diabetes.org
Dist(s): **McGraw-Hill Cos., The**
McGraw-Hill Professional Publishing
McGraw-Hill Trade
MyiLibrary
Perseus-PGW
Perseus Bks. Group.

American Dog *Imprint of* **Ideate Prairie**

American Driving Society, (*978-0-9727292*) P.O. Box 278, Cross Plains, WI 53528-0278 USA Do not confuse with American Driving Society in Lakeville, CT
E-mail: ann@americandrivingsociety.org
Web site: http://www.americandrivingsociety.org.

American Fisheries Society, (*978-0-913235; 978-1-888569; 978-1-934874*) 5410 Grosvenor Ln., Suite 110, Bethesda, MD 20814-2199 USA (SAN 284-964X) Tel 301-897-8616; Fax: 301-897-5080
E-mail: main@fisheries.org; afspubs@pbd.com
Web site: http://www.fisheries.org
Dist(s): **PBD, Inc.**

American French Genealogical Society, (*978-1-929920; 978-1-932749; 978-1-60305*) Orders Addr.: P.O. Box 830, Woonsocket, RI 02895 USA; Edit Addr.: 78 Earle St., Woonsocket, RI 02895 USA
E-mail: RDBeaudry@afgs.org
Web site: http://www.afgs.org.

American Girl *Imprint of* **American Girl Publishing, Inc.**

†American Girl Publishing, Inc., (*978-0-937295; 978-1-56247; 978-1-58485; 978-1-59369; 978-1-60958*) Subs. of Mattel, Inc., Orders Addr.: P.O. Box 620991, Middleton, WI 53562-0991 USA Tel 608-836-4848; Toll Free Fax: 800-257-3865; Toll Free: 800-233-0264; Edit Addr.: 8400 Fairway Pl., Middleton, WI 53562-0998 USA (SAN 298-6337) Tel 608-836-4848; Fax: 608-831-7089; *Imprints:* American Girl (Amer Girl); Pleasant Company (Pleasnt Co)
Web site: http://www.americangirlpublishing.com
Dist(s): **Follett School Solutions**; *CIP.*

American Ground Water Trust, (*978-0-9641186*) Orders Addr.: 16 Centre St., Concord, NH 03301 USA Tel 603-228-5444; Fax: 603-228-6557
E-mail: trustinfo@agwt.org
Web site: http://www.agwt.org.

American Health Publishing, (*978-0-9754443*) Orders Addr.: P.O. Box 282, Clarence, NY 14031 USA Tel 716-741-0177 Do not confuse with Americanhealth Publishing Company in Dallas, TX
E-mail: americahealthpub@aol.com
Web site: http://www.growingahealthyfamily.com.

American Heritage Publishing, (*978-0-9754859; 978-0-578-12953-2*) 5710 Mt. Repose Ln., NW, Norcross, GA 30092-1428 USA Tel 404-495-3720 (phone/fax)
E-mail: trjc@mindspring.com
Web site: http://www.privilegesofwar.com
Dist(s): **BookBaby.**

American Historical Pr., (*978-0-9654754; 978-1-892724*) 10755 Sherman Way, Suite 2, Sun Valley, CA 91352 USA Tel 818-503-0133; Fax: 818-503-9081; Toll Free: 800-550-5750
E-mail: ahp@amhistpress.com
Web site: http://www.amhistpress.com
Dist(s): **Chicago Distribution Ctr.**

American Home-School Publishing, LLC, (*978-0-9667067; 978-0-9779000*) Orders Addr.: 6102 SE. State Rte. C, Cameron, MO 64429 USA (SAN 254-7244) Tel 816-632-1503; Fax: 816-632-1448; Toll Free Fax: 800-557-0234; Toll Free: 800-684-2121
E-mail: booklovers@ahsp.com
Web site: http://www.ahsp.com.

American Humanist Assn., (*978-0-931779*) 1777 T St., NW, Washington, DC 20009-7125 USA (SAN 266-9412) Tel 202-238-9088; Fax: 202-238-9047; Toll Free: 800-837-3792; *Imprints:* Humanist Press (Humanist Press)
E-mail: bmagee@americanhumanist.org; jxiao@americanhumanist.org
Web site: http://www.thehumanist.org; http://www.americanhumanist.org; http://humanistpress.com
Dist(s): **Lightning Source, Inc.**

American Institute For CPCU, (*978-0-89462; 978-0-89463*) 720 Providence Rd., Malvern, PA 19355 USA (SAN 210-1629) Tel 610-644-2100; Fax: 610-640-9576; Toll Free: 800-644-2101
E-mail: cserv@cpcuiia.org
Web site: http://www.aicpcu.org.

American Institute for Property & Liability Underwriters, Incorporated *See* **American Institute For CPCU**

American International Distribution Corp., Orders Addr.: P.O. Box 574, Williston, VT 05495-0020 USA Tel 800-390-3149; Fax: 802-864-7626; Toll Free: 888-822-9942; Edit Addr.: 50 Winter Sport Ln., Williston,

Publisher Name Index

VT 05495 USA (SAN 630-2238) Toll Free: 800-488-2665
E-mail: jmacon@aidcvt.com
Web site: http://www.aidcvt.com/Specialty/Home.asp.

American International Printing & Marketing *See* **Graphix Network**

American LaserTechnic, *(978-0-9741805)* 1300 NE Miami Gardens Dr. Apt. 407, Miami, FL 33179-4731 USA
E-mail: dan-gregory@attbi.com
Web site: http://www.americanlasertechnic.com.

American Law Institute, *(978-0-8318)* 4025 Chestnut St., Philadelphia, PA 19104-3099 USA (SAN 204-756X) Tel 215-243-1679 Director of Books; 215-245-1654 (Library); 215-243-1700 (Customer Service); Fax: 215-243-0319; Toll Free: 800-253-6397
E-mail: jspitzer@ali-aba.org
Web site: http://www.ali-aba.org; http://www.ali.org.

†American Library Assn., *(978-0-8389; 978-1-937589)* 50 E. Huron St., Chicago, IL 60611 USA (SAN 201-0062) Tel 312-280-2425; 312-944-8085; Fax: 770-280-4155 (Orders); Toll Free: 800-545-2433; 866-746-7252 (Orders); P.O. Box 932501, Atlanta, GA 31193-2501; *Imprints:* Huron Street Press (HuronStPr)
E-mail: EditionsMarketing@ala.org
Web site: http://www.ala.org; http://www.alastore.ala.org
Dist(s): **Ebsco Publishing**
Follett School Solutions
Independent Pubs. Group
MyiLibrary
ebrary, Inc.; *CIP.*

American Literary Pr., *(978-1-56167; 978-1-934696)* Orders Addr.: 8019 Belair Rd., Suite 10, Baltimore, MD 21236 USA Tel 410-882-7700; Fax: 410-882-7703; Toll Free: 800-873-2003; *Imprints:* Shooting Star Edition (SSE)
E-mail: americanliterarypress@comcast.net
Web site: http://www.my-new-publisher.com
Dist(s): **AtlasBooks Distribution**
MyiLibrary.

American Literary Publishing *Imprint of* **LifeReloaded Specialty Publishing LLC**

American Map Corp., *(978-0-8416)* Div. of Langenscheidt Pubs., Inc., P.O. Box 780010, Maspeth, NY 11378-0010 USA (SAN 202-4624) Toll Free: 800-432-6277
E-mail: customerservice@americanmap.com
Web site: http://www.americanmap.com
Dist(s): **Fujii Assocs.**
Langenscheidt Publishing Group.

†American Mathematical Society, *(978-0-8218; 978-0-8284; 978-1-4704)* Orders Addr.: 201 Charles St., Providence, RI 02904 USA (SAN 250-3263) Tel 401-455-4000; Fax: 401-331-3842; Toll Free: 800-321-4267; *Imprints:* Chelsea Publishing Company, Incorporated (Chelsea Pub Co)
E-mail: las@ams.org
Web site: http://www.ams.org
Dist(s): **Author Solutions, Inc.**; *CIP.*

American Meteorological Society, *(978-0-933876; 978-1-878220; 978-1-935704; 978-1-940033)* 45 Beacon St, Boston, MA 02108-3693 USA (SAN 225-2139) Tel 617-227-2425; Fax: 617-742-8718
Web site: http://www.ametsoc.org/ams
Dist(s): **Chicago Distribution Ctr.**
MyiLibrary
ebrary, Inc.

American Poets Society *Imprint of* **Gem Printing**

†American Psychological Assn., *(978-0-912704; 978-0-945354; 978-1-55798; 978-1-59147; 978-0-9792125; 978-1-4338)* Orders Addr.: P.O. Box 92984, Washington, DC 20090-2984 USA (SAN 685-3137) Tel 202-336-6123; 202-336-5510 202-336-5502 (orders); Toll Free: 800-374-2721; Edit Addr.: 750 First St., NE, Washington, DC 20002-4242 USA (SAN 255-5921) Tel 202-336-5500; P.O. Box 77318, Washington, DC 20013-8318 Toll Free: 800-374-2721; *Imprints:* Magination Press (Magination Press)
E-mail: ghughes@apa.org; jmacomber@apa.org; books@apa.org
Web site: http://www.apa.org
Dist(s): **Follett School Solutions**
Oxford Univ. Pr., Inc.; *CIP.*

American Quilter's Society *Imprint of* **Collector Bks.**

American Reading Co., *(978-1-59301; 978-1-61541; 978-1-61406; 978-1-63437)* 201 S. Gulph Rd., King Of Prussia, PA 19406 USA Tel 610-992-4150; Toll Free: 866-810-2665
E-mail: robbie.byerly@americanreading.com
Web site: http://www.americanreading.com
Dist(s): **Follett School Solutions.**

American Reprint Co. *Imprint of* **Amereon LTD.**

American Retrospects, LLC, *(978-0-9747666)* Orders Addr.: P.O. Box 352576, Toledo, OH 43635-2576 USA Tel 419-824-4500; Fax: 419-885-4255
E-mail: jkw@americanretro.net; jkw@bex.net; mds@bex.net; mds@americanretro.net
Web site: http://www.americanretro.net.

American Revolution Publishing, *(978-0-9760948)* 12514 Mustang Dr., Poway, CA 92064 USA Tel 858-842-1812 (phone/fax)
E-mail: amrevpub@cox.net
Web site: http://www.gwuh.com; http://www.amrevpub.com; http://www.americanrevolutionpublishing.com
Dist(s): **Book Clearing Hse.**
Quality Bks., Inc.

American Schl. of Classical Studies at Athens, *(978-0-87661; 978-1-62139)* 6-8 Charlton St., Princeton, NJ 08540-5232 USA (SAN 201-1697) Tel 609-683-0800; Fax: 609-924-0578
E-mail: castein@ascsa.org
Web site: http://www.ascsa.edu.gr/publications
Dist(s): **Casemate Academic**
Firebrand Technologies
MyiLibrary
ebrary, Inc.

American Society for Microbiology *See* **ASM Pr.**

American Society of Plant BIOLOGISTS, *(978-0-943088)* 15501 Monona Dr., Rockville, MD 20855-2768 USA (SAN 240-3366) Tel 301-251-0560; Fax: 301-279-2996
E-mail: aspp@aspp.org
Web site: http://aspp.org.

American Society of Plant Physiologists *See* **American Society of Plant BIOLOGISTS**

American Success Institute, Inc., *(978-1-884864)* 31 Central St. #5, Wellesley, MA 02482 USA Tel 781-237-7368
E-mail: info@Success.org
Web site: http://www.success.org
Dist(s): **BookBaby.**

American Swedish Historical Museum, *(978-0-9800761)* 1900 Pattison Ave., Philadelphia, PA 19145-5901 USA Tel 215-389-1776; Fax: 215-389-9901
E-mail: info@americanswedish.org
Web site: http://www.americanswedish.org.

American Technical Pubs., Inc., *(978-0-8269)* 10100 Orland Pkwy., Orland Park, IL 60467-5756 USA (SAN 206-8141) Toll Free: 800-323-3471
E-mail: service@americantech.net
Web site: http://www.americantech.net
Dist(s): **Follett School Solutions.**

American Traveler Pr., *(978-0-914846; 978-0-935810; 978-0-939650; 978-1-55838; 978-1-885590; 978-1-58581)* Orders Addr.: 5738 N. Central Ave., Phoenix, AZ 85012 USA (SAN 220-0864) Tel 602-234-1574; Fax: 602-234-3062; Toll Free: 800-521-9221; *Imprints:* Golden West Publishers (GoldenWest)
E-mail: info@AmericanTravelerPress.com
Web site: http://www.PrimerPublishers.com; http://www.RenaissanceHousePublishers.com; http://www.AmericanTravelerPress.com; http://www.ClayThompsonBooks.com; http://www.GoldenWestPublishers.com; www.GoldenWestCookbooks.com
Dist(s): **Chicago Distribution Ctr.**
Follett School Solutions.

American Trek Bks., *(978-0-9815221; 978-0-9821178)* 1371 Morley Ave., Rochester Hills, MI 48307 USA (SAN 855-7748).

American Trust Pubns., *(978-0-89259)* 745 Mcclintock Dr., Suite 314, Burr Ridge, IL 60527 USA (SAN 664-6158)
Dist(s): **Halalco Bks.**
Meta Co., LLC.

American Univ. in Cairo Pr. (EGY) *(978-977-424; 978-1-936190; 978-977-416; 978-1-936481; 978-1-61797) Dist. by* **OUP.**

American Water Works Assn., *(978-0-89867; 978-1-58321; 978-1-61300; 978-1-62576)* 6666 W. Quincy Ave., Denver, CO 80235-3098 USA (SAN 212-8241) Tel 303-347-6266; Fax: 303-794-7310; Toll Free: 800-926-7337 (customer service/orders)
E-mail: mramey@awwa.org
Web site: http://www.awwa.org
Dist(s): **Follett School Solutions**
ebrary, Inc.

American Wind Power Ctr., *(978-0-9679480)* Div. of National Windmill Project, Inc., 1501 Canyon Lake Dr., Lubbock, TX 79403 USA Tel 806-747-8734; Fax: 806-740-0668
E-mail: charris@windmill.com
Web site: http://www.windmill.com.

American World Publishing, *(978-0-615-16443-4; 978-0-615-16444-1; 978-0-615-16701-5)* P.O. Box 534, Union City, GA 30291 USA
E-mail: andrewhitmore@yahoo.com
Dist(s): **Lulu Enterprises Inc.**

Americana Souvenirs & Gifts, *(978-1-890541)* 206 Hanover St., Gettysburg, PA 17325-1911 USA (SAN 169-7366) Toll Free: 800-692-7436.

America's Great Stories, *(978-0-615-34265-8)* 10100 Yankee Hill Rd., Lincoln, NE 68526 USA Tel 402-486-1776
E-mail: terrificteam@aol.com.

Americas Group, The, *(978-0-935047)* Subs. of Harris/Ragan Management Group, 654 N. Sepulveda Blvd. Ste. 1, Los Angeles, CA 90049-2170 USA (SAN 694-4698) Toll Free: 800-966-7716
E-mail: hrmg@aol.com
Web site: http://www.americasgroup.com
Dist(s): **Penton Overseas, Inc.**

Amerisearch, Inc., *(978-0-9653557; 978-0-9753455; 978-0-9778085; 978-0-9827101; 978-0-9896491)* Orders Addr.: P.O. Box 20163, Saint Louis, MO 63123 USA (SAN 254-6426) Tel 314-487-4395; Fax: 314-487-4489; Toll Free: 888-872-9673 (888-USA-WORD); Edit Addr.: 4346 Southview Way Dr., Saint Louis, MO 63129 USA
E-mail: wjfederer@gmail.com
Web site: http://www.amerisearch.net.

AmeriTales Entertainment, LLC, *(978-0-9798739)* 3525 Del Mar Heights Rd., Suite 623, San Diego, CA 92130 USA Tel 858-449-6900; Fax: 425-795-6026
E-mail: tcarter@ameritales.com
Dist(s): **Follett School Solutions.**

Amerotica *Imprint of* **NBM Publishing Co.**

Amethyst Moon *See* **Amethyst Moon Publishing and Services**

Amethyst Moon Publishing and Services, *(978-0-9792426; 978-1-935354; 978-1-938714)* Orders Addr.: P.O. Box 87885, Tucson, AZ 85754 USA
Web site: http://www.ampubbooks.com.

Amharic Kids, *(978-0-9797481)* 7201 88th Ave., Brooklyn Park, MN 55445 USA Tel 612-636-7878
E-mail: hamish@bellward.com
Web site: http://www.amharickids.com
Dist(s): **Follett School Solutions.**

Amherst Pr., *(978-0-910122; 978-0-942495; 978-1-930596)* Div. of The Guest Cottage, Inc., Orders Addr.: P.O. Box 774, Saint Germain, WI 54558 USA (SAN 213-9820) Tel 715-477-0424; Fax: 715-477-0405; Toll Free: 800-333-8122; Edit Addr.: P.O. Box 774, Saint Germain, WI 54558 USA (SAN 666-6450) Do not confuse with companies with the same name in Amherst, NY, North Hampton, NH
E-mail: sales@theguestcottage.com
Web site: http://www.theguestcottage.com
Dist(s): **Partners Bk. Distributing, Inc.**

Amiaya Entertainment, *(978-0-9745075; 978-0-9777544)* 1154 E. 229 St., Apt. 12C, Bronx, NY 10466 USA.

Amicus, *(978-1-68152)* Div. of Amicus Publishing, P.O. Box 1329, Mankato, MN 56002 USA Tel 507-388-5164
E-mail: dbrown@amicuspublishing.us; info@amicuspublishing.us
Web site: www.amicuspublishing.us
Dist(s): **Chronicle Bks. LLC**
Hachette Bk. Group.

Amicus Educational, *(978-1-60753; 978-1-68151)* Div. of Amicus Publishing, P.O. Box 1329, Mankato, MN 56002 USA Tel 507-388-5164; Fax: 507-388-4797; *Imprints:* Amicus Readers (Readers)
E-mail: info@amicuspublishing.us
Web site: http://www.amicuspublishing.us
Dist(s): **Follett School Solutions**
MyiLibrary.

Amicus Pr., *(978-0-914861)* 4201 Underwood Rd., Baltimore, MD 21218 USA (SAN 289-0518) Tel 301-889-5056.

Amicus Publishing *See* **Amicus Educational**

Amicus Readers *Imprint of* **Amicus Educational**

AMIDEAST, *(978-0-913957)* 1730 M. St. NW, Suite 1100, Washington, DC 20036-4505 USA (SAN 286-7184) Tel 202-776-9600; Fax: 202-776-7000
E-mail: inquiries@amideast.org
Web site: http://www.amideast.org.

Amigo Pubns., Inc., *(978-0-9658533)* Orders Addr.: P.O. Box 666, Los Olivos, CA 93441-0666 USA Tel 805-686-4616; Fax: 805-688-3427; Toll Free: 888-502-6446; Edit Addr.: 3029 W. Hwy. 154, Los Olivos, CA 93441-0666 USA
E-mail: Amigo@Conquistador.com
Web site: http://www.conquistador.com; http://www.equibooks.com.

Amira Rock Publishing, *(978-0-9821075; 978-0-9828007; 978-0-9833354)* 31 High St., Felton, PA 17322 USA (SAN 857-2844).

Amistad *Imprint of* **HarperCollins Pubs.**

AMMO Bks., LLC, *(978-0-9786076; 978-1-934429; 978-1-62326)* 300 S Raymond Ave Suite 3, Pasadena, CA 91105 USA (SAN 851-1128) Tel 323-223-2666; Fax: 323-978-4200; 1 Ingram Blvd., La Vergne, TN 37086
E-mail: contact@ammobooks.com; paul@ammobooks.com
Web site: http://www.ammobooks.com
Dist(s): **Follett School Solutions**
Ingram Pub. Services.

Ammons Communications, Ltd., *(978-0-9651232; 978-0-9753023; 978-0-9815702; 978-0-9824099; 978-0-9827611; 978-0-9837382; 978-0-9853728; 978-0-9892169; 978-0-9895694; 978-0-9913803; 978-0-9908766; 978-0-9965199)* 29 Regal Ave., Sylva, NC 28779 USA (SAN 851-0881) Tel 828-631-4587 (phone/fax); *Imprints:* Catch the Spirit of Appalachia (CSA)
E-mail: amyammons1@frontier.com
Web site: http://www.spiritofappalachia.org; http://www.catchthespiritofappalachia.org; http://www.storiesofmountainfolk.com; http://www.csabooks.com.

AMN Publishing, *(978-0-9728129)* P.O. Box 352, Massapequa, NY 11758 USA
E-mail: AMNPub@aol.com
Web site: http://amnpub.tripod.com.

Amoeba Bks., *(978-0-9786473)* 5260 Rogers Rd., G-6, Hamburg, NY 14075 USA
E-mail: marketing@amoebabooks.com
Web site: http://www.amoebabooks.com
Dist(s): **Follett School Solutions.**

Amped Media, *(978-0-9742287)* 22 Shaw Pl., Walla Walla, WA 99362 USA.

Ampelon Publishing, LLC, *(978-0-9748825; 978-0-9786394; 978-0-9798104; 978-0-9817705; 978-0-9823286; 978-0-9840095; 978-0-9893419)* P.O. Box 140675, Boise, ID 83714 USA
E-mail: info@ampelonpublishing.com
Web site: http://www.ampelonpublishing.com
Dist(s): **Smashwords.**

Ampersand *Imprint of* **Ampersand, Inc.**

Ampersand, Inc., *(978-0-9761235; 978-0-9818126; 978-0-9905603)* Orders Addr.: 1050 N. State St., Chicago, IL 60610 USA Fax: 312-944-1582; *Imprints:* Ampersand (Ampersnd)
Web site: http://www.ampersandworks.com
Dist(s): **Follett School Solutions.**

Amsco Music *Imprint of* **Music Sales Corp.**

AMSCO Schl. Pubns., Inc., *(978-0-87720; 978-1-56765)* 315 Hudson St., Suite 501, New York, NY 10013-1085 USA (SAN 201-1751) Toll Free: 866-902-6726 all orders
Web site: http://www.amscopub.com
Dist(s): **Bolchazy-Carducci Pubs.**

AMSI Venture, Incorporated *See* **Sleep Garden, Inc.**

Amulet Bks. *Imprint of* **Abrams**

Anachel Communications, *(978-0-615-62081-7)* 2008 Waterstone Dr., Franklin, TN 37069 USA Tel 615-370-8450
E-mail: carrie@anachel.com
Web site: www.carriegerlachcecil.com.

Anadem Publishing, Inc., *(978-0-9646891; 978-1-890018)* 3620 N. High St., Suite 201, Columbus, OH 43214 USA Tel 614-262-2539; Fax: 614-262-6630; Toll Free: 800-633-0055
E-mail: anadem@erinet.com
Web site: http://www.anadem.com.

Anaiah, Ruth, *(978-0-9769675)* P.O. Box 2142, Brandon, FL 33509-2142 USA
E-mail: dozministry2001@yahoo.com.

Anamchara Bks. *Imprint of* **Harding Hse. Publishing Sebice Inc.**

Anancy Bks. LLC, *(978-0-9753297; 978-1-941553)* Div. of Anancy Enterprise LLC, P.O. Box 28677, San Jose, CA 95159-8677 USA Tel 408-286-0726 Call Anytime; Fax: 408-947-0668 Fax Anytime
Web site: http://www.Anancybooks.com.

Anancybooks.com *See* **Anancy Bks. LLC**

Ananda Publications *See* **Crystal Clarity Pubs.**

Ananse Pr., *(978-0-9605670; 978-0-9749437)* Orders Addr.: P.O. Box 22565, Seattle, WA 98122-0565 USA (SAN 216-3292) Tel 206-325-8205; Fax: 206-328-4371; 1504 32nd Ave. S., Seattle, WA 98144-3918 (SAN 241-6123)
E-mail: gumbomedia@earthlink.net; gumbomedia@yahoo.com
Web site: http://home.usaa.net/~gumbomedia/ananse/index.htm.

Anar Bks. LLC, *(978-0-9748285)* 10266 Virginia Swan Pl., Cupertino, CA 95014-2025 USA
E-mail: anoopbusiness@yahoo.com
Web site: http://www.anarbooks.com.

Anaya Multimedia, S.A. (ESP) *(978-84-415; 978-84-7614) Dist. by* **Continental Bk.**

Anbeyond Pr., *(978-0-9744014)* 10420 NE 190th St., Bothell, WA 98011 USA (SAN 255-7886) Tel 425-483-9943; 22833 Bothell Everett Hwy. No. 102, PMB 1227, Bothell, WA 98021
E-mail: rm@anbeyond.com
Web site: http://www.anbeyond.com.

Ancestral Light Publishing, *(978-0-9718530)* 1969 S. Alafaya Trail, No. 322, Orlando, FL 32828 USA Tel 407-382-1707; Fax: 509-356-6971
E-mail: gigante@uaia.org.

Ancestral Tracks, *(978-0-9701266; 978-0-9754161)* P.O. Box 1064, Hillsboro, OR 97123-1064 USA
E-mail: books@ancestraltracks.com; cbeattie@ancestraltracks.com; ginger@ancestraltracks.com
Web site: http://www.ancestraltracks.com.

Anchor *Imprint of* **Knopf Doubleday Publishing Group**

Anchor Group, *(978-0-9852663; 978-0-9855385; 978-0-9882707; 978-0-615-71893-4; 978-0-9886334; 978-0-9888476; 978-0-9891753; 978-0-9897073; 978-0-615-91474-9; 978-0-9915174)* 225 Brookside Dr., FLUSHING, MI 48433 USA Tel 810-964-3767 (Tel/Fax)
E-mail: rourkewrites@gmail.com.

Anchorage Foundation Pr., *(978-0-9795266)* 1518 Mohle Dr., Austin, TX 78703 USA
Dist(s): **Greenleaf Book Group.**

Ancient Days Pubs., *(978-0-9741405)* P.O. Box 356, Landisville, PA 17538 USA
E-mail: abrd@ptd.net.

Ancient Golf Publishing *See* **LuckySports**

Ancient Studios, *(978-0-9744216)* 133 Iroquois Ave., Essex Jct, VT 05452-3572 USA
E-mail: ancientstudios@aol.com
Web site: http://www.ancientstudios.com; http://www.groovycomics.com
Dist(s): **Diamond Comic Distributors, Inc.**

Ancient Wisdom Pubns., *(978-0-9753093; 978-0-9792665; 978-0-9815971; 978-0-692-00084-7; 978-0-9824994; 978-1-936690; 978-0-615-58775-2; 978-1-940849)* Div. of Murine Communications, 2796 Garrett Pl., Woodland, CA 95776 USA
E-mail: andras_nagy@sbcglobal.net
Web site: http://www.andras-nagy.com; http://thepublicdomainbible.com/
Dist(s): **CreateSpace Independent Publishing Platform**
Lulu Enterprises Inc.

Andersen Pr. (GBR) *(978-0-86264; 978-0-905478; 978-1-84270; 978-1-84939; 978-1-78344) Dist. by* **IPG Chicago.**

Andersen Pr. (GBR) *(978-0-86264; 978-0-905478; 978-1-84270; 978-1-84939; 978-1-78344) Dist. by* **Trafalgar.**

Andersen Pr. (GBR) *(978-0-86264; 978-0-905478; 978-1-84270; 978-1-84939; 978-1-78344) Dist. by* **Lerner Pub.**

Anderson, George, *(978-0-9743682; 978-0-9819004)* 12301 Wilshire Blvd., Suite 418, Los Angeles, CA 90025 USA Tel 310-207-3591; Fax: 310-207-6234
E-mail: georgeandereson@aol.com
Web site: http://www.andersonservices.com.

Anderson House Foundation *See* **Windy Press International Publishing Hse., LLC**

Anderson Law Group, *(978-0-9728128; 978-0-9797860)* 3225 Mcleod Dr., Las Vegas, NV 89121 USA; 3225 Mcleod Dr., Las Vegas, NV 89121
E-mail: tmathis@bossoffice.com
Web site: http://www.BossOffice.com.

Anderson Pr., *(978-0-942479)* 706 W. Davis, Ann Arbor, MI 48103-4855 USA (SAN 667-3600) Tel 734-994-6182; Fax: 734-994-5207 Do not confuse with Anderson Pr., Laguna Niguel, CA.

Anderson Publishing, *(978-0-9718249)* Orders Addr.: P.O. Box 5544, Douglasville, GA 30154 USA Toll Free: 866-942-0790 (phone/fax); Edit Addr.: 5178 Holly Springs Dr., Douglasville, GA 30135 USA Do not confuse with companies with the same or similar name in Navato, CA, Saginawi, MI, Burley, ID, Cincinnati, MO, Anacortes, WA, Indio, CA
E-mail: canderson@andersonpub.com
Web site: http://www.andersonpub.com
Dist(s): **ACW Pr.**

ANDInternational, *(978-0-9762291)* 74 Woodcleft Ave., Freeport, NY 11520 USA Tel 516-546-2025; Fax: 516-546-6010; Toll Free: 800-229-2634
E-mail: orders@andihq.com; andihq@aol.com
Web site: http://www.andihq.com.

Andre Deutsch (GBR) *(978-0-233) Dist. by* **IPG Chicago.**

Andre Deutsch (GBR) *(978-0-233) Dist. by* **Trafalgar.**

Andre Deutsch (GBR) *(978-0-233) Dist. by* **Trans-Atl Phila.**

Andres & Blanton, *(978-0-9830318; 978-0-9966721)* 42 Corey Ln., Niantic, CT 06357 USA Tel 860-739-4002 E-mail: sscheyder@sbcglobal.net.

†Andrews McMeel Publishing, *(978-0-8362; 978-0-939251; 978-1-57939; 978-0-7407; 978-1-4494)* Orders Addr.: c/o Simon & Schuster, Inc., 100 Front St., Riverside, NJ 08075 USA Toll Free Fax: 800-943-9831; Toll Free: 800-943-9839 (Customer Service); 800-897-7650 (Credit Dept.); Edit Addr.: 1130 Walnut St., Kansas City, MO 64106-2109 USA (SAN 202-540X) Toll Free: 800-851-8923 Web site: http://www.AndrewsMcMeel.com *Dist(s):* **Follett School Solutions Simon & Schuster, Inc.;** *CIP.*

Andromeda Pr., Inc., *(978-0-9820649; 978-1-938503)* 2600 Birdie Thompson Dr., Pocatello, ID 83201 USA Tel 208-406-1220 E-mail: Andromedapress@gmail.com; strialbe@gmail.com.

Andrus, Ashley, *(978-0-9772000)* 104 Kempton Dr., Lafayette, LA 70508-6547 USA E-mail: ala@andrus.com.

Anela Publishing *See* **Abidenme Bks.**

Anemone Publishing, *(978-0-9759264)* 16 Rope Ferry Rd, Hanover, NH 03755 USA Tel 603-643-0922 E-mail: carolynne.krusi.99@alum.dartmouth.org.

AnEx Pubns., *(978-0-9711774)* 9 Bartlet St., Suite 131, Andover, MA 01810 USA Toll Free: 866-616-4400 E-mail: rich_hewett@yahoo.com Web site: http://www.anexx.com.

Angel Applications, *(978-0-615-18904-8)* 1624 Yorktown Dr., Charlottesville, VA 22901 USA Tel 434-293-2819 (phone/fax) E-mail: kgarstang@cstone.net *Dist(s):* **R J Communications, LLC.**

Angel City Pr., *(978-1-883318; 978-1-62640)* 2118 Wilshire Blvd., PMB 880, Santa Monica, CA 90403-5784 USA (SAN 298-3370) Tel 310-395-9982; Fax: 310-395-3353; Toll Free: 800-949-8039 (orders) E-mail: smcauley@angelcitypress.com Web site: http://www.angelcitypress.com.

Angel Eyes Publishing, *(978-0-9755346)* 1914 Hollywood Rd., Atlanta, GA 30318 USA (SAN 256-0542) Tel 404-566-0598 E-mail: dawnettelounds@yahoo.com Web site: http://www.angeleyespublishing.com.

Angel Fingers Foundation *See* **Mullins Pubns. & Apparel, LLC**

Angel Heart Children's Pr., *(978-0-9712124)* Orders Addr.: P.O. Box 63, East Enterprise, IN 47019 USA Tel 812-594-2438; Fax: 812-594-2438 E-mail: dianemccarty@hotmail.com Web site: http://www.geocities.com/hs_mom2000.

Angel Insights Press *See* **Stop N Go Fitness**

Angel Island Assoc., *(978-0-9667352)* P.O. Box 866, Tiburon, CA 94920 USA Tel 415-435-3522; Fax: 415-435-2950 E-mail: valaia@att.net Web site: http://www.angelisland.org *Dist(s):* **Follett School Solutions.**

Angel Mind, *(978-0-9729866)* 5776-D Lindero Canyon Dr. #123, Westlake Village, CA 91362 USA Tel 818-424-2619; Fax: 818-780-8880 E-mail: bill@angelmind.net Web site: http://www.angelmind.net.

Angel Pr., *(978-0-9716590)* Div. of The Angelic Light Research Institute, Orders Addr.: P.O. Box 1375, Sedona, AZ 86339 USA Tel 928-451-1222; 928-853-5753 Do not confuse with companies with the same or similar names in Tiburon, CA, Pell City, AL, Concord, NC, Rancho Santa Margarita, CA, St. Thomas, VI, TraversAFB, CA. Monterey, CA E-mail: angelpress@angelsangelsangels.org; angels@angelsangelsangels.org Web site: http://www.angelsangelsangels.org; http://www.angelsangelsangels.net; http://www.angellightfeather.com.

Angela's Bookshelf *See* **A B Publishing**

AngelBooks, *(978-0-9771749)* 4340 Janesville, Bel Aire, KS 67220 USA Web site: http://www.thesecretofpink.com.

Angel's Boy Enterprises, *(978-0-9755352)* 8306 Wilshire Blvd., No. 3004, Beverly Hills, CA 90211 USA Web site: http://www.angelboi.com.

Angel's Diary, *(978-0-615-31217-0; 978-0-9860041)* 6321 Thunder Blitz Ave., Las Vegas, NV 89131 USA.

Angels Landing, *(978-0-9899141)* 347 Butterfly Ln., Hermitage, PA 16148 USA Tel 724-977-0847 E-mail: trpags@roadrunner.com Web site: https://sites.google.com/site/littlelambs20/.

Angels of Agape, *(978-0-615-25466-1)* 211 Shawnee Valley, East Stroudsburg, PA 18302 USA Tel 973-460-3882 E-mail: angelsofagape@yahoo.com Web site: http://www.angelsofagape.com.

Angelus Pr., *(978-0-935952; 978-1-892331; 978-1-937843)* Div. of Society of Saint Pius X, 2915 Forest Ave., Kansas City, MO 64109 USA (SAN 222-769X) Tel 816-753-3150; Fax: 816-753-3557; Toll Free Fax: 888-855-9022; Toll Free: 800-966-7337 (orders) E-mail: info@angeluspress.org; stownshend@angeluspress.org Web site: http://www.angeluspress.org.

Angelworks Pr., *(978-0-578-00741-0; 978-0-578-12854-2)* 901 Brutscher St., No.D144, Newberg, OR 97132 USA Tel 503-830-0741; 17884 Kelok Rd., Lake Oswego, OR 97034 E-mail: susan@susanmarek.com *Dist(s):* **Lulu Enterprises Inc.**

Angle Blue Bks., LLC, *(978-0-9677547)* 376 County Road 2740., Mico, TX 78056-5353 USA E-mail: info@AngieBlue.com Web site: http://www.AngieBlue.com.

Anglesink, *(978-0-615-17415-0)* P.O. Box 323, Tuskegee Institute, AL 36087 USA E-mail: angiesink@bellsouth.net *Dist(s):* **Lulu Enterprises Inc.**

Angle Press *See* **Angle Valley Pr.**

Angle Valley Pr., *(978-0-9711950)* P.O. Box 4098, Winchester, VA 22604 USA (SAN 255-8629) Tel 540-539-1260 E-mail: anglevalleypress@yahoo.com Web site: http://www.AngleValleyPress.com *Dist(s):* **Lightning Source, Inc.**

Anglican Bk. Ctr. (CAN) *(978-0-919030; 978-0-919891; 978-0-921846; 978-1-55126) Dist. by* **Forward Movement.**

Angry Bicycle *Imprint of* **Walter, Wendy D.**

Animal Band Productions, Inc., The, *(978-0-9752619)* P.O. Box 392, Mount Juliet, TN 37121 USA Tel 615-754-8701 E-mail: info@theanimalband.com Web site: http://www.theanimalband.com.

Animal Crackers Publishing, LLC, *(978-0-9798343)* 1143 Auraria Pkwy. No. A-201, Denver, CO 80204 USA (SAN 854-5170) Web site: www.animalcrackerspublishing.com.

Animal Teachers Enterprises, *(978-0-9788858)* 5902G Queenston St., Springfield, VA 22152 USA E-mail: snork5902g@yahoo.com Web site: http://funkman.org/animal/services/catalog.html.

Animal Tracks Pr., *(978-0-9760342)* P.O. Box 432, Cotah, CA 94931 USA (SAN 256-1808) Tel 707-776-8019; Fax: 707-795-2919 Web site: http://www.animaltrackspress.com.

Animalations, *(978-0-9776628; 978-1-933818)* 4186 Melodia Songo Ct., Las Vegas, NV 89135 USA (SAN 257-9111) Fax: 702-804-4220; Toll Free Fax: 866-670-8337; Toll Free: 866-670-8337 E-mail: info@animalations.com Web site: http://Animalations.com.

AnimeVillage.com *See* **Bandai Entertainment, Inc.**

Ankh Bks. (CAN) *(978-0-9738036) Dist. by* **Mtn Bk Co.**

Ann Arbor Editions LLC, *(978-1-58726)* 2500 S. State St., Ann Arbor, MI 48104 USA Tel 734-913-1302; Fax: 734-913-1249; 1094 Flex Dr., Jackson, TN 38301; *Imprints:* Mitten Press (Mitten Pr) E-mail: ljohnson@aaeditions.com Web site: http://www.annarbormediagroup.com; http://www.mittenpress.com; http://www.aaeditions.com *Dist(s):* **Follett School Solutions Perseus Distribution.**

Ann Arbor Media Group, LLC *See* **Ann Arbor Editions LLC**

Annade Publishing, *(978-0-9761740)* 18964 Lauder, Detroit, MI 48235 USA Web site: www.annade.com.

Annapolis Publishing Co., *(978-1-884878)* Orders Addr.: 3430 2nd St. # 400, Brooklyn, MD 21225-1603 USA (SAN 631-4414) Toll Free: 800-536-1414 E-mail: Katherine@AnnapolisPublishing.com Web site: http://www.AnnapolisPublishing.com; http://www.mewarren.com; http://www.AnnapolisBooks.com.

AnnArt Pr., *(978-0-9769719)* R R 1, Box 621, Richards, MO 64778 USA.

Annedawn Publishing, *(978-0-9632793; 978-0-9755153)* E-mail: annedawn@aol.com.

Anness Publishing (GBR) *(978-1-85967; 978-1-86147; 978-1-901289; 978-1-901688; 978-1-84038; 978-0-7548; 978-1-84090; 978-1-903141; 978-1-84215; 978-1-84309; 978-1-84322; 978-1-84476; 978-1-84477; 978-1-84681; 978-0-85723; 978-1-78019) Dist. by* **Natl Bk Netwk.**

Anness Publishing, Inc., *(978-1-886890)* 39 Sandy Ln., Eatontown, NJ 07724-2445 USA (SAN 299-0563) Toll Free: 800-354-9657 E-mail: AFioravanti@anness.com *Dist(s):* **National Bk. Network.**

Annick Pr., Ltd. (CAN) *(978-0-920236; 978-0-920303; 978-1-55037; 978-1-55451) Dist. by* **Firefly Bks Limited.**

Annie Mouse Bks., *(978-0-9793379; 978-0-9914094)* P.O. Box 142, Harrisville, PA 16038 USA (SAN 853-1676) E-mail: anniemousebooks@gmail.com; anniemousebooks@yahoo.com Web site: http://www.anniemousebooks.com.

Annie's *Imprint of* **Annie's Publishing, LLC**

Annie's Media, LLC *See* **Annie's Publishing, LLC**

Annie's Publishing, LLC, *(978-0-88195; 978-0-9638031; 978-0-9655269; 978-1-57367; 978-1-882138; 978-1-931171; 978-1-59012; 978-1-59217; 978-0-9748217; 978-1-59635; 978-1-933802)* 111 Corporate Dr., Big Sandy, TX 75755 USA Fax: 260-589-8093 (Clothilde); *Imprints:* Annie's (Annies) Web site: http://www.drgnetwork.com *Dist(s):* **Follett School Solutions Independent Pubs. Group MyiLibrary ebrary, Inc.**

Annika Pubns., *(978-0-9670516)* Orders Addr.: P.O. Box 264, Fergus Falls, MN 56537 USA Tel 218-736-7735; Edit Addr.: R.R. 4, Box 50, Fergus Falls, MN 56537 USA.

Anno Domini, *(978-0-9792145; 978-1-939689)* 584 Ironwood Terr., Woodburn, OR 97071 USA (SAN 852-7946) Tel 971-226-4356.

†Annual Reviews, Inc., *(978-0-8243)* 4139 El Camino Way, P.O. Box 10139, Palo Alto, CA 94303-0139 USA (SAN 201-1816) Tel 650-493-4400; Fax: 650-424-0910; Toll Free: 800-523-8635 (including California, Alaska, Hawaii & Canada) E-mail: service@annualreviews.org Web site: http://www.AnnualReviews.org; *CIP.*

Anointed Pubs., *(978-0-9763841)* Orders Addr.: P.O. Box 25215, Durham, NC 27702 USA Tel 919-806-0651; Edit Addr.: P.O. Box 25215, Durham, NC 27702 USA E-mail: jainjie@msn.com Web site: http://www.joanjai.com *Dist(s):* **Brown Enterprises, Inc.**

Anointed Publishing Co., *(978-0-615-19205-5; 978-0-615-25069-4; 978-0-615-36490-2; 978-0-615-37865-7; 978-0-615-78457-1)* 8123 Winter Blue Ct., Springfield, VA 22153 USA Tel 321-947-0706 Web site: http://www.cheniselytrelle.com.

Anointed Word Pubns., *(978-0-9744024)* 611 N. Pennsylvania Ave., Lansing, MI 48912 USA Tel 517-372-3407.

Anomaly Publishing, *(978-0-9800123)* 3700 Ceres Dr., Salt Lake City, UT 84124 USA Tel 801-278-3245 *Dist(s):* **Smashwords.**

Anorak Pr. *Imprint of* **Gibbs Smith, Publisher**

Another Ep Publishing, *(978-0-9740685; 978-0-615-11795-9)* Div. of Episodes By Wroe, P.O. Box 300, Walnut, CA 91788-0300 USA (SAN 253-2530) Tel 909-448-5356.

Another Language Pr., *(978-0-922852)* 7709 Hamilton Ave., Cincinnati, OH 45231-3103 USA Tel 513-521-5590; Fax: 513-521-5592; Toll Free: 800-733-2067 E-mail: aimsbooks@juno.com *Dist(s):* **AIMS International Bks., Inc.**

Answers in Genesis *See* **Answers in Genesis Ministries**

Answers in Genesis Ministries, *(978-1-893345; 978-1-60092; 978-1-62691)* Orders Addr.: P.O. Box 510, Hebron, KY 41048 USA Fax: 859-727-2299; Toll Free: 800-778-3390 E-mail: dzordel@answersingenesis.org Web site: http://www.answersingenesis.org *Dist(s):* **Master Bks. New Leaf Pr., Inc.**

Antarctic Pr., Inc., *(978-0-930655; 978-0-9663588; 978-0-9728978; 978-1-932453; 978-0-9768043; 978-0-9776424; 978-0-9787725; 978-0-9792723; 978-0-9797719; 978-0-9801255; 978-0-9816647; 978-0-9822253; 978-0-9823742; 978-0-9841107; 978-0-9843375; 978-0-9844879; 978-0-9831823; 978-0-9837934; 978-0-9850925; 978-1-939364) Div. of Ben Dunn Corp., 7272 Wurzbach Rd., Suite 204, San Antonio, TX 78240 USA Tel 210-614-0396; Fax: 210-614-5029 Do not confuse with Antarctic Pr., Bellevue, WA* E-mail: apcog1@gmail.com Web site: http://www.antarctic-press.com *Dist(s):* **Diamond Comic Distributors, Inc. Diamond Bk. Distributors.**

Anthem Pr. (GBR) *(978-1-898855; 978-1-84331; 978-0-85728; 978-1-78308) Dist. by* **Bolchazy-Carducci.**

Anthem Pr. (GBR) *(978-1-898855; 978-1-84331; 978-0-85728; 978-1-78308) Dist. by* **Bks Intl VA.**

AntHill Publishing, *(978-0-9718544)* 5315 Clarendon Rd., Brooklyn, NY 11203 USA Tel 718-629-0294 (phone/fax) Do not confuse with Ant Hill Publishing in Gorman, TX E-mail: anthillpublishing@hotmail.com.

Anthology of Poetry, Inc., *(978-1-883931)* Orders Addr.: P.O. Box 698, Asheboro, NC 27204-0698 USA Tel 336-626-7762; Fax: 336-626-2622; Edit Addr.: 307 E. Salisbury St., Asheboro, NC 27203 USA E-mail: poetry@anthologyofpoetry.com Web site: http://www.anthologyofpoetry.com.

Anthro Co., The, *(978-1-878464)* 200 Carroll St., No. 21, Susanville, CA 96130 USA Tel 530-251-5712 E-mail: devajan@earthlink.net Web site: http://www.ishifacts.com *Dist(s):* **Social Studies Schl. Service.**

Anthroposophic Press, Incorporated *See* **SteinerBooks, Inc.**

Anticipation Pr., *(978-0-9754046)* 3563 Sueldo St. Ste. Q, Sn Luis Obisp, CA 93401-7332 USA Do not confuse with Anticipation Press in Cheyenne, WY E-mail: doingbigbiz@aol.com Web site: http://www.anticipationpress.com; http://www.zacacreekdevelopment.com.

Antioch Publishing Co., *(978-0-7824; 978-0-89954; 978-1-4017)* Div. of Trends International, 5188 W. 74th St., Indianapolis, IN 46268 USA Tel 317-388-4060; 317-388-1414; Toll Free: 800-315-2110 Do not confuse with Antioch Publishing Co., Torrance, CA Web site: http://www.antioch.com.

Antipodes Bks. & Beyond, 9707 Fairway Ave., Silver Spring, MD 20901-3001 USA Tel 301-602-9519; Fax: 301-565-0160 E-mail: Antipode@antipodesbooks.com Web site: http://www.antipodesbooks.com.

Antique Collectors' Club (GBR) *(978-0-902028; 978-0-907462; 978-1-85149; 978-1-905377; 978-0-9504269) Dist. by* **Natl Bk Netwk.**

Antique Collectors' Club, *(978-0-902028; 978-0-907462; 978-1-85149)* Orders Addr.: Eastworks, 116 Pleasant St., Easthampton, MA 01027 USA (SAN 630-7787) Tel 413-529-0861; Fax: 413-529-0862; Toll Free: 800-252-5231 (orders) E-mail: info@antiquecc.com; sales@antiquecc.com Web site: http://www.antiquecollectorsclub.com *Dist(s):* **National Bk. Network.**

Antiques, Incorporated *See* **Kovels Antiques, Inc.**

Antiquity Publishing, *(978-0-9793284)* 4127 McLaughlin Ave., No. 15, Los Angeles, CA 90066-5445 USA Tel 310-390-9093 (phone/fax) E-mail: Randwulf@humnet.ucla.edu *Dist(s):* **AtlasBooks Distribution.**

Antlers & Fins LLC, *(978-0-9800643)* P.O. Box 82, Henefer, UT 84033 USA E-mail: info@billygoeshunting.com Web site: http://www.BillyGoesHunting.com.

Anton Berkshire Publishing, *(978-0-9746330)* Orders Addr.: P.O. Box 372, Markle, IN 46770 USA (SAN 255-6618); Edit Addr.: 9374 N. Marzane Rd., Markle, IN 46770 USA Web site: http://www.antonberkshirepublishing.com.

Antoniades, Basil, *(978-0-615-24661-1)* 9 Belden Ct., Timonium, MD 21093 USA Tel 410-560-9911 E-mail: basilantoniades@earthlink.net Web site: http://www.havingfunwithgreekmythology.com *Dist(s):* **Lulu Enterprises Inc.**

Antrim Hse., *(978-0-9662783; 978-0-9762091; 978-0-9770633; 978-0-9792226; 978-0-9798451; 978-0-9817883; 978-0-9823970; 978-0-9843418; 978-1-936482; 978-1-943826)* 21 Goodrich Rd., Simsbury, CT 06070-1804 USA; P.O. Box 111, Tariffville, CT 06081 Web site: http://www.antrimhousebooks.com *Dist(s):* **BookBaby Distributors, The.**

Antroll Publishing Co., *(978-1-877656)* 2616 Elmont St., Wheaton, MD 20902 USA Tel 301-942-0492.

Anvil Bks., Ltd. (IRL) *(978-0-900068; 978-0-947962; 978-1-901737) Dist. by* **Dufour.**

Anyone Can Write bks., *(978-0-9771470)* 2890 N. Hills Dr., NE, Atlanta, GA 30305-3210 USA Tel 404-261-1616 Web site: http://www.anyonecanwrite.com.

Anystar Publishing, *(978-0-9767047)* P.O. Box 182067, Arlington, TX 76096 USA E-mail: anystarpublishing@yahoo.com Web site: http://www.anystarpub.com.

Anythings Possible, Inc., *(978-1-892186)* Orders Addr.: 1863 N. Farwell Ave., Milwaukee, WI 53202 USA Fax: 414-226-4901; Toll Free: 800-543-7153 E-mail: info@special-kids.com Web site: http://www.special-kids.com.

Anza Pr., *(978-0-615-67002-7; 978-0-615-71154-6)* P.O. Box 8676, Newport Beach, CA 92658 USA Tel 949-707-5747 *Dist(s):* **CreateSpace Independent Publishing Platform.**

Anzalone, Frank, *(978-0-9770788)* P.O. Box 110422, Campbell, CA 95011 USA Tel 408-247-7572; Fax: 408-984-1519 E-mail: info@mckyfoto.com Web site: http://www.mckyfoto.com.

AoPS Inc., *(978-0-9773045; 978-1-934124)* Orders Addr.: P.O. Box 2185, Alpine, CA 91903-2185 USA Tel 619-659-1612; Toll Free Fax: 855-430-9531 E-mail: orders@artofproblemsolving.com Web site: http://www.artofproblemsolving.com.

Aoyama Publishing *See* **Marble Hse. Editions**

AP Bks., *(978-0-9841927)* P.O. Box 799, Pennington, NJ 08534 USA Fax: 609-730-1286 *Dist(s):* **Cardinal Pubs. Group.**

AP Publishing, *(978-0-9722906)* Orders Addr.: P.O. Box 160, Merrimac, WI 53561 USA Web site: http://www.wildlife-trails.com *Dist(s):* **Lightning Source, Inc.**

APA Publications Services (SGP) *(978-9971-925; 978-9971-982; 978-981-234; 978-981-4120; 978-981-246; 978-981-4137; 978-981-258; 978-981-268; 978-981-282) Dist. by* **IngramPubServ.**

Apage4You Bk. Publishing, *(978-0-9723616)* 2025 Balla Way, Suite 200, Grand Prairie, TX 75051-3907 USA Tel 972-264-2892; Fax: 214-722-1254; Toll Free: 800-519-7323 E-mail: apage4you@starband.net Web site: http://www.publishfast.com; http://www.apage4youpublishing.com.

Ape Entertainment, *(978-0-9741398; 978-0-9791050; 978-0-9801314; 978-1-934944; 978-1-936340; 978-1-937676; 978-1-62782)* P.O. Box 7100, San Diego, CA 92167 USA *Dist(s):* **Diamond Comic Distributors, Inc. Diamond Bk. Distributors.**

Ape Pen Publishing *See* **Ballard, Donald W.**

Aperturas Foundation, *(978-0-9745220)* P.O. Box 25163, Chicago, IL 60625 USA Tel 773-478-7973 E-mail: aperturas@yahoo.com Web site: http://www.aperturas.info.

Aperture Pr., LLC, *(978-0-615-40395-3; 978-0-615-41313-6; 978-0-615-41888-9; 978-0-9833310; 978-0-9836878; 978-0-9850026; 978-0-9889351; 978-0-9910962; 978-0-9909302)* 201 Washington St. Suite 533, Reading, PA 19601 USA Tel 484-525-0009 E-mail: steve@aperturepress.net Web site: http://www.aperturepress.net *Dist(s):* **Lulu Enterprises Inc.**

Apex Performance Solutions, LLC, *(978-0-9824519)* 467 Springdale Rd., Westfield, MA 01085 USA Tel 413-562-2299; Fax: 413-562-2289; 113 Ne Carleston Oaks Dr., Port St.Lucie, FL 34983 E-mail: jwojcik@apexperformancesolutions.com Web site: http://www.apexperformancesolutions.com *Dist(s):* **Follett School Solutions Partners Pubs. Group, Inc.**

APG Sales & Distribution Services, Div. of Warehousing and Fulfillment Specialists, LLC (WFS, LLC), 7344 Cockrill Bend Blvd., Nashville, TN 37209-1043 USA (SAN 630-818X) Toll Free: 800-327-5113 E-mail: sswift@agpbooks.com Web site: http://www.apgbooks.com.

APG Sales & Fulfillment *See* **APG Sales & Distribution Services**

Aplastic Anemia + MDS International Foundation, *(978-0-9755572)* Orders Addr.: P.O. Box 613, Annapolis, MD 21404-0613 USA Tel 410-867-0242;

Fax: 410-867-0240; Toll Free: 800-747-2820; Edit Addr.: P.O. Box 310, Churchton, MD 20733-0310 USA
E-mail: help@aamds.org
Web site: http://www.aamds.org.

Aplus Bks. *Imprint of* **Capstone Pr., Inc.**

Apocalyptic Tangerine Pr., *(978-0-9821138; 978-0-9897496)* Orders Addr.: 1969 Laurel Ave., No. 5, Saint Paul, MN 55104-5820 USA Tel 304-942-4912.

Apodixis Press *See* **Read Well Publishing Inc.**

Apollo Computer Systems, Inc., *(978-0-9610582)* 616 14th St., Arcata, CA 95521 USA (SAN 264-651X) Tel 707-822-0318.

Apollo Pubs., *(978-0-9718532; 978-0-9721368; 978-1-932832)* P.O. Box 9, Santa Cruz, CA 95063 USA Tel 831 479 9626 (phone/fax); 800-881-0181
E-mail: msc@greatcreations.net
Web site: http://www.apollopub.com
Dist(s): **TNT Media Group, Inc.**

Apollo Science Pubs., LLC, *(978-0-9814551)* P.O. Box 26671, San Diego, CA 92196 USA Tel 858-635-6558
E-mail: zhibo.zhang@ieee.org
Web site: http://www.aspublishers.com.

Apologetics Pr., Inc., *(978-0-932859; 978-1-60063)* 230 Landmark Dr., Montgomery, AL 36117-2752 USA (SAN 688-9190) Tel 334-272-8558; Fax: 334-270-2002; Toll Free: 800-234-8558 (orders only)
E-mail: mail@apologeticspress.org
Web site: http://www.apologeticspress.org
Dist(s): **Send The Light Distribution LLC.**

Apologia Educational Ministries, Inc., *(978-0-9656294; 978-1-932012; 978-1-935495; 978-1-940110)* 1106 Meridian Plaza Ste 220/340, Anderson, IN 46016 USA Tel 765-608-3280; Fax: 765-608-3290; Toll Free: 888-524-4724
E-mail: mailbag@apologia.com; patti@apologia.com
Web site: http://www.apologia.com.

Apologue Entertainment, LLC, *(978-0-9819825)* Orders Addr.: 1075 Meghan Ave., Algonquin, IL 60102 USA
E-mail: gary.mack@apologueentertainment.com
Web site: http://www.apologueentertainment.com.

Appalachian Hse., *(978-0-9662800)* Orders Addr.: P.O. Box 627, Boiling Springs, PA 17007 USA (SAN 299-5328) Tel 717-609-6234
E-mail: apphouse@pa.net.

Appalachian Log Publishing Co., The, *(978-1-885935)* Orders Addr.: P.O. Box 20297, Charleston, WV 25362-1297 USA Tel 304-342-5789; Edit Addr.: 878 Anaconda Ave., Charleston, WV 25302 USA
E-mail: gregory@newwave.net.

†Appalachian Mountain Club Bks., *(978-0-910146; 978-1-878239; 978-1-929173; 978-1-934028; 978-1-62842)* 5 Joy St., Boston, MA 02108 USA (SAN 203-4808) Tel 617-523-0655; Fax: 617-523-0722; Toll Free: 800-262-4455
E-mail: kbreunig@outdoors.org; alakri@outdoors.org
Web site: http://www.outdoors.org
Dist(s): **Globe Pequot Pr., The**
National Bk. Network; *CIP.*

Applause Theatre & Cinema *Imprint of* **Leonard, Hal Corp.**

Apple Corps Pubs., *(978-0-9619484; 978-1-934397)* 1600 Sunset Ln., Oklahoma City, OK 73127 USA (SAN 245-0461) Fax: 888-375-7017; Toll Free: 800-335-9208
E-mail: tom@tomquaid.com
Dist(s): **Univ. of Oklahoma Pr.**

Apple Cover Books *See* **New Monic Bks.**

Apple Pie Pubs., *(978-0-9675123)* 5745 SW 75th St., PMB 325, Gainesville, FL 32608 USA Tel 352-472-2833 (phone/fax); Fax: 352-335-9080
E-mail: applepienow@aol.com
Web site: http://www.applepienow.com.

AppleNobb Books *See* **Happy Apple Bks.**

Applesauce Pr. *Imprint of* **Cider Mill Pr. Bk. Pubs., LLC**

Appleseed Pr. Bk. Pub. LLC, *(978-1-60464)* Orders Addr.: 12 Port Farm Rd., Kennebunkport, ME 04046-0404 USA (SAN 854-5405) Tel 207-641-3489; Fax: 207-967-8233
E-mail: appleseedgiftbooks@mac.com
Web site: http://www.appleseedpress.com.

†Applewood Bks., *(978-0-918222; 978-1-55709; 978-1-889833; 978-1-933212; 978-1-4290; 978-0-9819430; 978-1-60889; 978-0-9844156; 978-0-9836416; 978-1-938700; 978-0-9882885; 978-1-5162)* 1 River Rd., Carlisle, MA 01741-1820 USA (SAN 210-3419) Toll Free: 800-277-5312; 1 Ingram Blvd., La Vergne, TN 37086; *Imprints:* Commonwealth Editions (CommonwealthEd)
E-mail: applewood@awb.com; svec@awb.com
Web site: http://www.awb.com
Dist(s): **Follett School Solutions**
Ingram Pub. Services; *CIP.*

Applied Database Technology, Inc., *(978-0-9742610)* 715 E. Sprague Ave. Suite 125, Spokane, WA 99202 USA
Web site: http://www.applieddatabase.com.

Apprentice Hse., *(978-1-934074; 978-1-62720)* Dept. Communication/Loyola College in MD, 4501 N. Charles St., Baltimore, MD 21210 USA.

Apprentice Shop Bks., LLC, *(978-0-9723410; 978-0-9842549; 978-0-9850144)* P.O. Box 375, Amherst, NH 03031 USA Fax: 603-472-2588
E-mail: apprenticeshpbks@aol.com
Web site: http://www.apprenticeshopbooks.com
Dist(s): **Follett School Solutions.**

Apricot Pr., *(978-1-885027)* P.O. Box 98, Nephi, UT 84648 USA Toll Free: 800-731-6145
E-mail: books@apricotpress.com
Web site: http://www.apricotpress.com.

April Arts Press & Productions, *(978-0-9650918)* P.O. Box 64, Morgan Hill, CA 95038-0064 USA
E-mail: books@aprilartspress.com
Web site: http://www.aprilartspress.com
Dist(s): **Follett School Solutions.**

April Press *See* **April Arts Press & Productions**

AP's Travels *See* **Aunt Patty's Travels-London**

APT Publishing, *(978-0-615-73118-6; 978-0-615-74354-7; 978-0-615-74850-4; 978-0-615-78492-2; 978-0-615-78496-0)* 2350 Saddlesprings Dr., Milton, GA 30004 USA Tel 6789067062
Dist(s): **CreateSpace Independent Publishing Platform.**

Apte, Stu, *(978-0-615-20409-3; 978-0-9821227)* 133 Plantation Dr., Tavernier, FL 33070 USA Tel 305-852-7440 (phone/fax)
E-mail: stuwho@bellsouth.net
Dist(s): **Emerald Bk. Co.**

Aquarian Age Publishing, Inc., *(978-0-9767530)* 250, 56th St., Fort Lauderdale, FL 33334 USA
E-mail: info@aquarianagepublishing.com
Web site: http://www.lawsofhealing.com; http://www.aquarianagepublishing.com.

Aqueduct Pr., *(978-0-9746559; 978-1-933500; 978-1-61976)* P.O. Box 95787, Seattle, WA 98145-2787 USA (SAN 256-131X); 4 White Brook Rd., Gilsum, NH 6448
Web site: http://www.aqueductpress.com
Dist(s): **Follett School Solutions**
Pathway Bk. Service.

Aquila Ink Publishing, *(978-0-9760789)* P.O. Box 160, Rio Nido, CA 95471 USA (SAN 850-9050) Tel 707-799-5981; 707-887-9090; Fax: 707-869-2973
E-mail: aquila@aquilaink.com
Web site: http://www.aquilaink.com.

Aquinas & Krone Publishing, LLC, *(978-0-9800448; 978-0-9843526; 978-0-9849505)* P.O. Box 1304, Merchantville, NJ 08109 USA (SAN 855-0751) Tel 856-665-3999.

A.R. Harding Publishing Co., *(978-0-936622)* 2878 E. Main St., Columbus, OH 43209 USA (SAN 206-4936) Tel 614-231-9585
E-mail: erics@furfishgame.com.

Aradiance Publishing, *(978-0-9715737)* P.O. Box 13855, Mill Creek, WA 98082 USA.

Arango-Duque, J. F. *See* **Arango's Publishing**

Arango's Publishing, *(978-0-9655750)* 1776 Polk St., No. 3K-032, Hollywood, FL 33020 USA (SAN 299-2078)
E-mail: arangoduke@aol.com
Dist(s): **Hispanic Bks. Distributors & Pubs., Inc.**
Lectorum Pubns., Inc.
Libros Sin Fronteras
Quality Bks., Inc.

Aranjo, Karl, *(978-0-9770667)* 16 Greenwood, Irvine, CA 92604 USA Tel 949-786-8765
E-mail: karlaranjo@yahoo.com
Web site: http://guitaru.com.

Arbiter Pr., *(978-0-9621385; 978-0-615-35216-9; 978-0-615-35859-8)* 1732 N. Lakemont Ave., Winter Park, FL 32792 USA (SAN 251-1282); 1732 Arbor Pk. Dr., Winter Park, FL 32789 Tel 407-647-2606
E-mail: chsblackwell@gmail.com
Dist(s): **Bookazine Co., Inc.**

Arbor Bks., *(978-0-9771870; 978-0-9777764; 978-0-9786107; 978-0-9790469; 978-0-9794118; 978-0-9800582; 978-0-9818658; 978-0-9841992)* 244 Madison Ave., No. 254, New York, NY 10016 USA; 19 Apero Rd., Suite 301, Ramsey, NJ 7446 Do not confuse with Arbor Books in Media, PA
Web site: http://www.arborbooks.com
Dist(s): **Follett School Solutions.**

Arbordale Publishing, *(978-0-9764943; 978-0-9768823; 978-0-9777423; 978-1-934359; 978-1-60718; 978-1-62855)* 612 Johnnie Dodds Blvd., Suite A2, Mount Pleasant, SC 29464 USA (SAN 256-6109) Tel 843-971-6722; Fax: 843-216-3804
E-mail: leegerman@arbordalepublishing.com
Web site: http://www.arbordalepublishing.com
Dist(s): **BWI**
Baker & Taylor Bks.
Brodart Co.
Ediciones Enlace de PR, Inc.
Follett School Solutions
Ingram Pub. Services.

Arborville Bks., *(978-0-9886988)* 2115 Nature Cove Ct. No. 203, Ann Arbor, MI 48104 USA Tel 734-663-8175
E-mail: arborvillebooks@gmail.com
Dist(s): **Lulu Enterprises Inc.**

Arbutus Pr., *(978-0-9665316; 978-0-9766104; 978-1-933926)* Orders Addr.: 2364 Pinehurst Trail, Traverse City, MI 49686 USA Tel 231-946-7240
E-mail: editor@arbutuspress.com
Web site: http://www.arbutuspress.com
Dist(s): **Follett School Solutions**
Partners Bk. Distributing, Inc.

Arc Manor, *(978-0-9786536; 978-0-9794154; 978-1-60450; 978-1-61242)* P.O. Box 10339, Rockville, MD 20849 USA Tel 240-645-2214; Fax: 310-388-8449; *Imprints:* TARK Classic Fiction (TARK Classic Fiction); Serenity Publishers (Serentiy Pubs)
E-mail: admin@arcmanor.com
Web site: http://www.ArcManor.com; http://www.PhoenixPick.com; http://www.PhoenixRider.com; http://http://www.ManorWodehouse.com
Dist(s): **Follett School Solutions**
Smashwords.

Arcade Publishing *Imprint of* **Skyhorse Publishing Co., Inc.**

Arcadia Bks. Ltd. (GBR) *(978-1-900850; 978-1-905147; 978-1-906413; 978-1-908129; 978-1-910050) Dist. by* **Dufour.**

Arcadia Publications *See* **Linden Hill Publishing**

Arcadia Publishing, *(978-0-7385; 978-1-58973; 978-1-59629; 978-1-4396; 978-1-60949; 978-1-61423; 978-1-4671; 978-1-62584; 978-1-62585; 978-1-62619; 978-0-9903765)* Orders Addr.: 420 Wando Park Blvd., Mount Pleasant, SC 29464 USA (SAN 255-268X) Tel 843-853-2070; Fax: 843-853-0044; Toll Free: 888-313-2665; *Imprints:* History Press, The (HistoryPress) Do not confuse with Arcadia Publishing in Greenwood Village, CO
E-mail: sales@arcadiapublishing.com
Web site: http://www.arcadiapublishing.com
Dist(s): **INscribe Digital**
MyiLibrary.

Arcadiam Games, *(978-0-9769951)* 3106 NE 83rd Ave., Portland, OR 97220 USA
E-mail: travisbrown@crossroads-rpg.com
Web site: http://www.crossroads-rpg.com.

Arcadian Hse., *(978-0-9766666)* 3040 Rightmire Blvd., Columbus, OH 43221 USA
E-mail: lyn@arcadianhouse.com
Web site: http://www.arcadianhouse.com.

Arcana Studio, Inc., *(978-0-9763095; 978-0-9809204; 978-1-926914; 978-1-927424; 978-1-927421)* 930 Winthrop Ln., Rockford, IL 61107 USA
Web site: http://www.arcanastudio.com
Dist(s): **Diamond Comic Distributors, Inc.**
Diamond Bk. Distributors.

Archaeopress (GBR) *(978-0-9539923; 978-1-905739; 978-1-78491) Dist. by* **CasemateAcad.**

Archaia Entertainment *Imprint of* **Boom! Studios**

Archangel Studios, LLC, *(978-0-9714714)* 507 S. Parish Pl., Burbank, CA 91506-2951 USA
E-mail: thredstar_hq@hotmail.com
Web site: http://www.theredstar.com
Dist(s): **Diamond Comic Distributors, Inc.**
Diamond Bk. Distributors.

ArcheBooks *Imprint of* **ArcheBooks Publishing, Inc.**

ArcheBooks Publishing, Inc., *(978-1-59507)* 6081 Silver King Blvd. Unit 903, Cape Coral, FL 33914 USA Tel 239-542-7595; 9101 W. Sahara Ave., Las Vegas, NV 89117; *Imprints:* ArcheBooks (ArchBks)
E-mail: publisher@archebooks.com
Web site: http://www.archebooks.com
Dist(s): **Follett School Solutions.**

Archeion Press, LLC *See* **Akasha Publishing, LLC**

Archeological Assessments, Inc., *(978-0-9638956; 978-0-9794044)* P.O. Box 1631, Nashville, AR 71852 USA
E-mail: aaimjb@aol.com
Web site: http://www.arkansasstories.com.

Archer Fields, Inc., *(978-0-9627767; 978-1-56466)* 155 Sixth Ave., New York, NY 10013 USA Tel 212-627-1999; Fax: 212-627-9484; Toll Free: 800-338-2665
Dist(s): **D.A.P./Distributed Art Pubs.**

Archer's Pr., *(978-0-615-68449-9; 978-0-615-70040-3; 978-0-615-70731-0; 978-0-9894749; 978-0-692-23029-9; 978-0-692-41131-5; 978-0-692-47473-0)* 2795 Parker Rd., Florissant, MO 63033 USA Tel 3146168101
Web site: www.archerspress.com
Dist(s): **CreateSpace Independent Publishing Platform.**

Archeworks, *(978-0-9753405)* 625 N. Kingsbury St., Chicago, IL 60610 USA Tel 312-867-7254; Fax: 312-867-7260
E-mail: info@archeworks.org
Web site: http://www.archeworks.org.

Archie Comic Pubns., Inc., *(978-1-879794; 978-1-936975; 978-1-61988; 978-1-62738; 978-1-68183; 978-1-68255)* 629 Fifth Ave, Suite 100, Pelham, NY 10803-1242 USA Tel 914-381-5155; Fax: 914-381-2335; *Imprints:* Archie Comics (Archie Comics); Dark Circle Comics (Dark Circle)
E-mail: haroldb@archiecomics.com
Web site: http://www.archiecomics.com
Dist(s): **Diamond Comic Distributors, Inc.**
Diamond Bk. Distributors
Follett School Solutions
Penguin Random Hse., LLC.
Random Hse., Inc.

Archie Comics *Imprint of* **Archie Comic Pubns., Inc.**

Archie Publishing, *(978-0-9779064)* P.O. Box 521732, Salt Lake City, UT 84152-1732 USA (SAN 850-5616) Tel 801-232-3840
E-mail: mcf@archiepublishing.com
Web site: http://www.archiepublishing.com
Dist(s): **American West Bks.**

Archimede Editions (FRA) *(978-2-211) Dist. by* **Distribks Inc.**

Archipelago Pr., *(978-1-893335)* Orders Addr.: P.O. Box 1540, Los Gatos, CA 95031 USA (SAN 299-7541) Tel 408-354-5587 (phone/fax) Do not confuse with companies with the same name in Saint Thomas, VI, Friday Harbor, WA
E-mail: pelago2000@aol.com
Web site: http://www.rosswell.com.

Archival Services, Incorporated *See* **Red River Pr.**

Archives Pr. *Imprint of* **Media Assocs.**

Archives Press, The *See* **Media Assocs.**

Archus Pr., LLC, *(978-0-9648564; 978-1-893047; 978-0-9852248)* 620 Miller St., Rochester, MI 48307 USA Tel 248-218-0356; Toll Free: 888-275-5639
E-mail: leigharrathoon@gmail.com.

Archway Publishing, *(978-1-4808)* Div. of Author Solutions, Inc., 1663 Liberty Drive, Bloomington, IN 47403 USA Fax: 317-454-0544 Toll Free: 888-242-5904
Web site: http://www.archwaypublishing.com
Dist(s): **AtlasBooks Distribution**
Author Solutions, Inc.

Arco *Imprint of* **Peterson's**

Arcoiris Records, Inc., *(978-1-57417)* P.O. Box 7428, Berkeley, CA 94707 USA Tel 510-527-5539
Dist(s): **Follett School Solutions**
Lectorum Pubns., Inc.

Arctos Pr., *(978-0-9657015; 978-0-9725384; 978-0-9897847)* 116 Cloud View Rd., Sausalito, CA 94965 USA Tel 415 331 2503
Web site: http://www.members.aol.com/runes/index.html
Dist(s): **Quality Bks., Inc.**
SPD-Small Pr. Distribution.

Arcturus Pubs., Inc., *(978-0-916877)* P.O. Box 606, Cherry Hill, NJ 08003 USA (SAN 653-9718) Tel 609-428-3863.

Arcturus Publishing (GBR) *(978-1-900032; 978-1-84193; 978-1-84837; 978-1-84858; 978-1-78212; 978-1-78404; 978-1-78428) Dist. by* **Black Rab.**

Arcturus Publishing (GBR) *(978-1-900032; 978-1-84193; 978-1-84837; 978-1-84858; 978-1-78212; 978-1-78404; 978-1-78428) Dist. by* **AtlasBooks.**

Ardden Entertainment (GBR) *(978-0-9561259) Dist. by* **Diamond Book Dists.**

Arden Pr., Inc., *(978-0-912869)* Orders Addr.: P.O. Box 418, Denver, CO 80201 USA (SAN 277-6553) Tel 303-697-6766; Fax: 303-697-3443; Edit Addr.: 20723 Seminole Rd., Indian Hills, CO 80454 USA Do not confuse with Arden Pr., Inc., Cleveland, OH
E-mail: ardenpress@msn.com
Dist(s): **Follett School Solutions.**

Ardent Writer Pr., LLC, The, *(978-1-938667)* 1014 Stone Dr., Brownsboro, AL 35741 USA Tel 256-694-6744
E-mail: gierhartsteve@att.net.

ARDI Research Pr., *(978-0-9640600)* 13571 Millpond Way, San Diego, CA 92129 USA (SAN 298-1866) Fax: 619-484-0377
E-mail: roger@rdooley.com.

Area Fifty One Productions *See* **Media Blasters, Inc.**

Argami Productions, LLC, *(978-0-9798324)* 774 Verona Lake Dr., Weston, FL 33326 USA; 4501 Forbes Blvd, Lanham, MD 20706
E-mail: ellenwv@aol.com
Dist(s): **Follett School Solutions.**

Argee Pubs., *(978-0-917961)* 4453 Manitou, Okemos, MI 48864 USA (SAN 247-7858) Tel 517-349-1254.

Argo Navis, *(978-0-7867)* Div. of Perseus Books Group, 250 West 57th St. 15th Flr., New York, NY 10107 USA
Dist(s): **MyiLibrary**
Perseus Bks. Group.

Argonaut Publishing Co., *(978-0-9635118)* 284 Clearview Rd., Chuluota, FL 32766 USA (SAN 297-8199) Tel 407-977-5207 (phone) Do not confuse with companies with the same or similar name in Los Angeles, CA, Santa Barbara, CA
E-mail: spottedtail@spottedtail.com
Web site: http://www.spottedtail.com.

Argonauts, The, *(978-0-615-23045-0; 978-0-615-33914-6; 978-0-9827842)* Orders Addr.: 929 Canterbury Ln., Waukesha, WI 53188 USA
E-mail: smkstoll@yahoo.com
Web site: http://www.theArgonauts.com.

Argos Gameware *See* **H&M Systems Software, Inc.**

Argus Enterprises International, Inc., *(978-0-9801555; 978-0-9819075; 978-0-9823050; 978-0-9841342; 978-0-9842596; 978-0-9845142; 978-0-9846195; 978-0-9846348; 978-0-9846439; 978-0-615-50768-2; 978-0-615-50816-0; 978-0-615-50820-7; 978-0-615-51728-5; 978-0-615-51733-9; 978-0-615-51734-6; 978-0-615-52229-6; 978-0-615-52387-3; 978-0-615-52392-7; 978-0-615-52688-1; 978-0-615-53228-8; 978-0-615-53320-9; 978-0-615-53503-6; 978-0-615-53629-3; 978-0-615-54552-3; 978-0-615-55032-9; 978-0-615-55098-5; 978-0-615-55127-2; 978-0-615-55238-5) Orders Addr.: P.O. Box 914, Kernersville, NC 27285 USA Tel 336-354-7173; Fax: 336-993-2497; Edit Addr.: 9001 Ridge Hill St., Kernersville, NC 27284 USA*
Web site: http://www.a-argusbooks.com; http://www.abetterbewrite.com; http://abook4you.com
Dist(s): **CreateSpace Independent Publishing Platform**
Follett School Solutions.

Arimax, Inc., *(978-0-9634287)* 2865 S. Eagle Rd., No. 350, Newtown, PA 18940 USA Tel 215-860-4122; Fax: 215-860-4177
Web site: http://www.arimaxbooks.com
Dist(s): **Independent Pubs. Group.**

Arimax Publishing Company *See* **Arimax, Inc.**

Aris & Phillips (GBR) *(978-0-85668) Dist. by* **CasemateAcad.**

Arise Foundation, *(978-1-58614)* P.O. Box 2147, Jupiter, FL 33468-2147 USA (SAN 253-4835) Toll Free: 888-680-6100
E-mail: yisaacs@ariselife-skills.org
Web site: http://www.ariselife-skills.org
Dist(s): **Follett School Solutions.**

Aristata Publishing, *(978-0-9754912)* 16429 Lost Canyon Rd., Santa Clarita, CA 91387 USA (SAN 256-6508) Tel 661-299-9478 (phone/fax)
E-mail: aristata@craigelliottgallery.com; celliott@socal.rr.com
Web site: http://www.craigelliottgallery.com
Dist(s): **APG Sales & Distribution Services.**

ARIVA Publishing, *(978-0-9822952; 978-1-938056)* 244 Madison Ave, Suite 7100, New York, NY 10016-2817 USA Tel 646-706-7129
E-mail: info@arivapublishing.com
Dist(s): **Greenleaf Book Group.**

Arizona Blueberry Studios, *(978-0-9727894)* P.O. Box 5, Pasadena, CA 91102 USA Toll Free: 800-767-7186
E-mail: books@rossanthony.com
Web site: http://www.rossanthony.com/books.

Arizona Elk Society, *(978-0-9825181)* P.O. Box 190, Peoria, AZ 85380 USA.

Arizona Highways, *(978-0-916179; 978-1-893860; 978-1-932082; 978-0-9822788; 978-0-9845709; 978-0-9837132; 978-0-9887875; 978-0-9916228)* Div. of Arizona Dept. of Transportation, 2039 W. Lewis Ave., Phoenix, AZ 85009 USA (SAN 294-8974)
E-mail: mbianchi@azdot.gov; aphares@azdot.gov; kmero@azdot.gov
Web site: http://www.arizonahighways.com.

†Arizona Historical Society, *(978-0-910037)* 949 E. Second St., Tucson, AZ 85719 USA (SAN 201-6982) Tel 520-628-5774; Fax: 520-628-5695
Dist(s): **University of Arizona Pr.**
Univ. of New Mexico Pr.; *CIP.*

For full information on wholesalers and distributors, refer to the Wholesaler and Distributor Name Index

Arizona Sonora Desert Museum Pr., *(978-1-886679)* Arizona Sonora Desert Museum, 2021 N. Kinney Rd., Tucson, AZ 85743 USA Tel 520-883-3061; Fax: 520-883-3048
E-mail: asdmpress@desertmuseum.org; info@desertmuseum.org
Web site: http://www.desertmuseum.org
Dist(s): **Rio Nuevo Pubs.**

Ark Hse. Pr. (AUS) *(978-0-9752044; 978-0-9757986; 978-0-9775671; 978-0-9803458; 978-0-9804523; 978-0-9805414; 978-1-921589; 978-0-9873888; 978-0-9875839; 978-0-9875932; 978-0-9922699; 978-0-9923452; 978-0-9925192; 978-0-9925726; 978-0-9941941; 978-0-9942832; 978-0-9943675; 978-0-9944299)* *Dist. by* **STL Dist.**

Ark Watch Holdings LLC, *(978-0-9765358; 978-0-615-25019-9; 978-0-615-25020-5; 978-0-615-25021-2; 978-0-578-05938-9; 978-0-615-99015-6; 978-0-692-39260-7)* Div. of Serpentauria Media LLC, 4766 E. Eden Dr., Cave Creek, AZ 85331-3870 USA
E-mail: erikauthor@aol.com; arkwatchholdingsllc@hotmail.com
Web site: http://www.arkwatch.com
Dist(s): **CreateSpace Independent Publishing Platform.**

Arlene, Carmen Hibbs, *(978-0-9762567)* 584 Choctaw Dr., Madisonville, KY 42431 USA Tel 270-821-1968
E-mail: arlenehibbs@yahoo.com
Web site: http://www.heavenlyharborbooks.com.

Arlington Pubns., *(978-0-9753611)* 2205 Manera St., Odessa, TX 79763 USA Tel 432-582-0272; Fax: 432-332-2499 Do not confuse with Arlington Publications Incorporated in Arlington, TX
E-mail: tommwhite@cableone.net.

Armadillo Bks., *(978-0-9786132)* 4735 NE 24th Ave., Portland, OR 97211 USA (SAN 851-0865) Do not confuse with Armadillo Books in Houston, TX
E-mail: phtdoyle@yahoo.com
Web site: http://www.edgarfont.com; http://www.nextreststopearth.com
Dist(s): **Follett School Solutions.**

Armchair Pr., LLC, *(978-0-9744627)* P.O. Box 215, Ross, CA 94957-0215 USA Tel 415-460-9750; Fax: 415-460-0850
E-mail: ozzie@armchairpress.com.

Arment Biological Press *See* **Coachwhip Pubns.**

Armour of Light Publishing, *(978-0-9620604; 978-0-9788590; 978-0-9817120; 978-0-9825476; 978-0-9857539)* P.O. Box 778, Chapel Hill, NC 27514 USA (SAN 249-4337)
E-mail: publisher@armouroflight.org
Web site: http://www.armouroflight.org.

Armstrong, Greg, *(978-0-578-11703-4; 978-0-578-12191-8; 978-0-578-12368-4)* 27082 O Neill Dr., Unit 325, Ladera Ranch, CA 92694 USA Tel 949-701-7190.

Armstrong Valley Publishing Co., *(978-1-928798)* Orders Addr.: P.O. Box 1275, Murfreesboro, TN 37133-1275 USA Tel 615-895-5445; Fax: 615-893-2688; Edit Addr.: 2568 Armstrong Valley Rd., Murfreesboro, TN 37128 USA
E-mail: rsanders@raider.net.

Arnica Publishing, *(978-0-9728538)* Orders Addr.: P.O. Box 543, Choteau, MT 59422 USA; Edit Addr.: 3961 Hwy 89 S., Choteau, MT 59422 USA
E-mail: arnica@3rivers.net; pbechtold1@gmail.com
Dist(s): **Big River Distribution.**

Arnica Publishing, Incorporated *See* **ACS, LLC Arnica Creative Services**

Arnold, Patricia *See* **www.margaretmouse.com publishing co.**

Arnstein, Bennett, *(978-0-9620058)* 3049 W. Eighth St., No. 535, Los Angeles, CA 90005 USA (SAN 247-5162) Tel 213-388-3517
E-mail: b_arnstein@hotmail.com.

ARose Books Publishing, LLC, *(978-0-9723970; 978-0-9740636; 978-0-9819298; 978-0-9846081; 978-0-692-37550-1)* 7090 Miller Rd., Girard, PA 16417 USA Fax: 888-889-6945 (phone/fax)
E-mail: arosebooks_support@arosebooks.com
Web site: http://www.arosebooks.com
Dist(s): **CreateSpace Independent Publishing Platform.**

Around H.I.M. Publishing Co., *(978-0-615-48953-7; 978-0-615-50139-0; 978-0-615-53839-6; 978-0-615-54522-6; 978-0-615-55124-1; 978-0-615-55340-5; 978-0-615-57009-9; 978-0-615-59895-6; 978-0-615-60049-9; 978-0-615-60457-2; 978-0-615-62884-4; 978-0-615-65372-3; 978-0-615-66669-3; 978-0-615-66693-8; 978-0-615-67345-5; 978-0-615-68491-8; 978-0-615-69110-7; 978-0-615-69673-7; 978-0-615-70757-0; 978-0-615-70759-4; 978-0-615-70762-4; 978-0-615-71923-8; 978-0-615-73515-3; 978-0-615-81515-2; 978-0-615-84964-5; 978-0-615-85984-2;) P.O. Box 1373, Wake Forest, NC 27588 USA Tel 919-341-9674*
E-mail: info@aroundhim.com
Web site: http://www.aroundhim.com
Dist(s): **CreateSpace Independent Publishing Platform**
Dummy Record Do Not USE!!!!.

Around The Globe Pr., *(978-0-9760573)* 11505 E. Calle Javelina, Tucson, AZ 85748-6339 USA Tel 520-290-8915
E-mail: aroundtheglobepress@earthlink.net
Web site: http://www.aroundtheglobepress.com.

Around the Way Book Publishers *See* **Around the Way Books**

Around the Way Books, *(978-0-9755342)* P.O. Box 1497, Waterbury, CT 06721 USA Toll Free: 888-610-5969
E-mail: htaylor@AroundTheWayBooks.com; info@aroundthewaybooks.com
Web site: http://www.AroundTheWayBooks.com
Dist(s): **Lushena Bks.**

Around The World Pubns., LLC, *(978-0-9772591)* P.O. Box 1024, Franktown, CO 80116-1024 USA Do not confuse with Around The World Publications in Seattle, WA
E-mail: bbrasier@etsgroup.com
Web site: http://www.worldthroughchildseyes.com.

Arrest Me Not Publishing *See* **As Seen on the Internet / Arrest Me Not**

Arrinton Pubns., *(978-0-9754540)* Orders Addr.: P.O. Box 2573, Chesapeake, VA 23327 USA Tel 757-450-6068; Fax: 757-410-4215; Edit Addr.: 1601 Orchard Grove Dr., Chesapeake, VA 23320-1411 USA
E-mail: gobooks@cox.net.

Arrow Pubns., *(978-0-9715514; 978-0-9765849)* Orders Addr.: 16653 E. Kingstree Blvd., Fountain Hills, AZ 85268-5439 USA Do not confuse with companies with the same or similar names in Cedar Rapids, IA, Kensington, MD
E-mail: arrowpublications@cox.net
Web site: http://www.arrowpublications.net.

Arrowhead Publishing, *(978-0-9640056)* 1238 Riva Rose Cir., Castle Rock, CO 80104-9650 USA Tel 303-663-9415 Do not confuse with companies with the same name in Lake Arrowhead, CA, Carlsbad, CA.

Arruzza, Richard *See* **Three Spots Productions**

Arsenal Pulp Pr. (CAN) *(978-0-88978; 978-1-55152)* *Dist. by* **Consort Bk Sales.**

Arseya, LLC, *(978-0-9745185; 978-1-935093)* 10 Pleasantville Rd., New Vernon, NJ 07976 USA (SAN 255-6588) Tel 973-993-1504; Fax: 973-993-9182
Imprints: Arseya Publishing (Arseya Pub)
E-mail: arseya@arseya.com
Web site: http://www.arseya.com.

Arseya Publishing *Imprint of* **Arseya, LLC**

Art & Creativity For Healing, Inc., *(978-0-9748462)* 26079 Getty Dr., Laguna Niguel, CA 92677 USA Tel 949-367-1902; Fax: 949-367-1904
E-mail: laurie@art4healing.org
Web site: http://www.art4healing.org.

Art & Soul Expressions, *(978-0-9729192)* P.O. Box 957, Mount Shasta, CA 96067 USA.

Art as Responsar *See* **Art as Responsa LLC**

Art as Responsa LLC, *(978-0-578-05270-0; 978-0-9845456)* 2550 Southshore Blvd., Lake Oswego, OR 97034 USA (SAN 859-631X) Tel 503-344-6065 (phone/fax); Fax: 503-344-6065; ART AS RESPONSA LLC 2550 Southshore Blvd., Lake Oswego, OR 97034
E-mail: marsha@art-responsa.com
Web site: http://www.artasresponsa.com; http://www.art-responsa.com; www.marshaplafkin.com.

Art Bks. Publishing Ltd, *(978-1-908970)*
Dist(s): **D.A.P./Distributed Art Pubs.**
Perseus Bks. Group.

Art In The Heartland, *(978-0-9725461; 978-0-9752839; 978-0-9762103; 978-0-9766587; 978-0-9778450)* P.O. Box 1785, Columbus, IN 47202-1785 USA
E-mail: sbreeding@artintheheartland.com
Web site: http://www.breedingbooks.com; http://www.artintheheartlandbooks.com.

Art Night Bks., *(978-0-9794004)* 3348 N. Dousman St., Milwaukee, WI 53212 USA Tel 414-213-7443
E-mail: devintrudell@mac.com
Web site: http://artnightbooks.com.

Art Of Essex Fine Art, The, *(978-0-615-31464-8)* 3007 Lakewood Ct., Jefferson City, MO 65109 USA
Web site: www.essexgamer.com.

Art of War Plus Bks. *Imprint of* **Clearbridge Publishing**

Art Official Media LLC, *(978-0-9768061; 978-0-9834874; 978-0-9883825)* Orders Addr.: P.O. Box 39323, Baltimore, MD 21212 USA Tel 443-693-7622; Edit Addr.: 1044 Radnor Ave., Baltimore, MD 21212 USA
Web site: http://www.artofficialmedia.com; http://www.UrbaniaMag.com
Dist(s): **Afrikan World Bk. Distributor.**

Art With Heart Press, *(978-0-9715240; 978-0-9841365)* Div. of Art with Heart, Orders Addr.: P.O. Box 94402, Seattle, WA 98124-6702 USA (SAN 850-2676)
E-mail: info@artwithheart.org
Web site: http://www.artwithheart.org
Dist(s): **Partners/West Book Distributors.**

ArtAnswer, *(978-0-9755413; 978-0-9771520)* P.O. Box 50387, Billings, MT 59105 USA Tel 406-672-8482
E-mail: artanswer@artanswer.com
Web site: http://www.artanswer.com.

†**Arte Publico Pr.**, *(978-0-934770; 978-1-55885; 978-1-61192; 978-1-5185)* Univ. of Houston 4902 Gulf Fwy, Bldg. 19, Rm. 100, Houston, TX 77204-2004 USA (SAN 213-4594) Tel 713-743-2998; 713-743-3080; Fax: 713-743-2847; Toll Free: 800-633-2783; Univ. of Houston 4902 Gulf Freeway, Rm. 100, Houston, TX 77023; *Imprints:* Piñata Books (Pinata Bks)
E-mail: bkorders@uh.edu; appinfo@uh.edu
Web site: http://www.artepublicopress.com
Dist(s): **Book Wholesalers, Inc.**
Booksource, The
Bound to Stay Bound Bks.
Brodart Co.
Children's Plus, Inc.
Follett School Solutions
Keystone Bks. & Media LLC
Lectorum Pubns., Inc.
Mackin Educational Resources
Midwest Library Service
Perfection Learning Corp.
Perma-Bound Bks.
Quality Bks., Inc.
Rainbow Bk. Co.
Unique Bks., Inc.
Yankee Bk. Peddler, Inc.
ebrary, Inc.; *CIP.*

Artemesia Publishing, LLC, *(978-1-932926)* Orders Addr.: 9 Mockingbird Hill Rd., Tijeras, NM 87059 USA Tel 505-286-0892; *Imprints:* Kinkajou Press (Kinkajou Pr)
E-mail: info@artemesiapublishing.com; g.habiger@artemesiapublishing.com
Web site: http://www.apbooks.net; http://www.artemesiapublishing.com; http://www.tangent-games.com; http://www.kinkajoupress.com/
Dist(s): **Bks. West**
Follett School Solutions
Hachette Bk. Group.

Artemisia Enterprises, *(978-0-9755416)* P.O. Box 3106 Mosshall Way, San Jose, CA 95135 USA
E-mail: sales@amazonheart.org
Web site: http://www.amazonheart.org.

Artesian Pr., *(978-1-58659)* 372 South 900 W., Provo, UT 84601 USA (SAN 253-1259) Tel 801-375-0800; Fax: 801-222-9199; Toll Free Fax: 888-326-3125; Toll Free: 888-734-9355; 20 Commercial Blvd., Novato, CA 94949
E-mail: info@artesianpress.com
Web site: http://www.artesianpress.com
Dist(s): **Follett School Solutions.**

Arthritis Foundation, *(978-0-912423)* 1330 W. Peachtree St., Atlanta, GA 30309 USA (SAN 267-677X) Tel 404-965-7622; Fax: 404-872-9559; Toll Free: 800-283-7800 Do not confuse with Arthritis Foundation, Southfield, MI
E-mail: sbernstein@arthritis.org
Web site: http://www.arthritis.org.

Arthur Pr., *(978-0-615-76617-1; 978-0-615-85167-9)* 11328 SE Beckman Ave., Milwaukie, OR 97222 USA Tel 5038192536
Dist(s): **CreateSpace Independent Publishing Platform.**

Article One *See* **Marsh Creek Pr.**

Artisan, *(978-1-57965; 978-1-885183)* Div. of Workman Publishing Co., Inc., 225 Varick St. Flr. 9, New York, NY 10014-4381 USA Toll Free: 800-967-5630 Do not confuse with Artisan, Wheaton, IL
E-mail: artisan@workman.com
Dist(s): **Workman Publishing Co., Inc.**

Artisan House *See* **Artisan**

Artisan Pubs., *(978-0-934666)* P.O. Box 1529, Muskogee, OK 74402 USA (SAN 211-8408) Tel 918-682-8341; Fax: 918-682-1263.

Artisan Sales *See* **Artisan Pubs.**

Artist Designs, *(978-0-9760409)* P.O. Box 548, Webster, WI 54893 USA Tel 715-222-2362.

Artist Studios, Ltd., *(978-1-931037; 978-1-59487; 978-1-61562)* 444 Spear St. Ste. 101, San Francisco, CA 94105-1693 USA.

Artistic Angels Corp., *(978-0-9890410)* 535 Valley View Rd. Apt. D301, Branson, MO 65616 USA Tel 417-544-1766; Fax: 417-544-1766
E-mail: artisticangels4you@yahoo.com.

Artistic Ventures LLC, *(978-0-9771495)* Orders Addr.: 3 Glade Mallow Rd., Malta, NY 12020 USA; Edit Addr.: 3 Glade Mallow Rd., Malta, NY 12020-4326 USA;
Imprints: Artistic Ventures Publishing (Artistic Ventures)
E-mail: dawn@artistic-ventures.com
Web site: http://www.artistic-ventures.com
Dist(s): **Follett School Solutions.**

Artistic Ventures Publishing *Imprint of* **Artistic Ventures LLC**

Artists On Video, LLC / (d/b/a) MN Productions, *(978-0-9799440; 978-1-937106)* 84 Chaumont Sq. NW, Atlanta, GA 30327 USA.

Artists' Orchard, LLC, The, *(978-0-9843166; 978-0-9857014; 978-0-9964592)* P.O. Box 113317, Pittsburgh, PA 15241 USA (SAN 859-0389) Tel 724-255-6408
E-mail: sales@theartistsorchard.com; publish@theartistsorchard.com
Web site: http://theartistsorchard.com.

Artist's Pr., *(978-0-924556)* P.O. Box 16087, Minneapolis, MN 55416-0087 USA Tel 952-486-8353
E-mail: artistspress@aim.com
Web site: http://www.artistspress.com.

ArtMar Productions, *(978-0-9799089)* 60 W. 71st St., No. 1B, New York, NY 10023 USA (SAN 854-7416)
E-mail: mihorowitz@aol.com
Web site: http://www.marlynhorowitz.com
Dist(s): **AtlasBooks Distribution.**

Art-Medium, *(978-0-9817971)* P.O. Box 390739, Mountain View, CA 94039-0739 USA (SAN 856-5848)
E-mail: tangobelly@yahoo.com
Web site: http://www.AKPhotography.net.

Artos Press Enterprises *See* **Creative Cranium Concept, The**

Artpacks, *(978-0-9790247; 978-0-9834637)* 535 22nd St., NE, Rochester, MN 55906 USA (SAN 852-2227) Tel 507-273-2529
E-mail: storymatters@charter.net.

Artrum Media, *(978-0-9840574; 978-0-9841957; 978-0-9845352; 978-0-9837050; 978-1-938107)* 627 Brickle Ridge Rd., Decatur, TN 37322 USA (SAN 858-3080)
E-mail: info@artrummedia.com
Web site: http://www.artrummedia.com
Dist(s): **New Tradition Bks.**

Arts Pubns., *(978-0-9766590)* P.O. Box 3006, Evansdale, IA 50707-0006 USA (SAN 256-4963) Tel 319-287-5901 (phone/fax) Do not confuse with Arts Publications in Corte Madera, CA
E-mail: ceremonypress@mchsi.com; infoartspublications@mchsi.com
Web site: http://www.artspublicationsbooks.com.

Artstreet LLC, *(978-0-9758971)* 10 Crestmont Rd. Apt. 7P, Montclair, NJ 07042-1936 USA Toll Free: 866-543-7878
E-mail: sjimenez@brandstreetllc.com
Web site: http://www.brandstreetllc.com.

Artsy Bee, LLC, *(978-0-615-75521-2; 978-0-692-48443-2)* 133 Naperville Dr., Cary, NC 27519-5409 USA Tel 919-274-6155
E-mail: rtbliss@gmail.com.

Artust Nasus Publishing, *(978-0-9763260)* 500 Rosita Ave., PO Box 1515, Westcliffe, CO 81252 USA
Web site: http://www.naturallybalancedhealth.com.

Artworks International, *(978-1-57938)* Orders Addr.: 3101 Clairmont Rd., Suite C, Atlanta, GA 30329 USA (SAN 255-6456) Tel 404-214-4331; Fax: 404-214-4390
E-mail: derek.adams@andersonpress.com
Web site: http://www.andersonpress.com.

Arundel Press *See* **Arundel Publishing**

Arundel Publishing, *(978-1-933608)* 36 Crystal Farm Rd., Warwick, NY 10990 USA Do not confuse with Arundel Press in Seattle, WA
E-mail: Sharon.Scott@ArundelPublishing.com
Dist(s): **Follett School Solutions**
Ingram Pub. Services.

Arutam Pr., *(978-0-9745477)* 62 Ave Maria, Monterey, CA 93940 USA Tel 831-375-6005
E-mail: emurray@sacredsite.com
Web site: http://www.elizabethmurray.com.

Arzana, Inc., *(978-0-9770475)* Orders Addr.: P.O. Box 60473, Potomac, MD 20859 USA Tel 301-437-0017
E-mail: balance@arzanaworld.com
Web site: http://www.arzanaworld.com.

As Sabr Pubns. *Imprint of* **Imago Pr.**

As Seen on the Internet / Arrest Me Not, *(978-0-9640336)* P.O. Box 608685, Cleveland, OH 44108-0685 USA Tel 440-487-8413; Fax: 425-963-3821
Web site: http://www.asseenontheinternet.tv.

As Simple As That Publishing, *(978-0-9728666)* Orders Addr.: P.O. Box 25 Fern Road, Southampton, NY 11968 USA
Web site: http://www.simpleasthat.com.

As Sparkle Speaks & Informs/ASSI, *(978-0-9706187)* Orders Addr.: P.O. Box 1313, Madison, TN 37116-1313 USA Tel 615-860-9762; Fax: 615-870-0959; Edit Addr.: 1672 Liberty Hill Dr., Madison, TN 37115 USA
E-mail: searlessparkle@aol.com.

ASA Publishing Co., *(978-1-886528; 978-0-615-13671-4; 978-0-615-14056-8; 978-0-615-14611-9; 978-0-615-15185-4; 978-0-615-15682-8; 978-0-615-17383-2; 978-0-615-18613-9; 978-0-615-18894-2; 978-0-615-21769-7; 978-0-615-21856-4; 978-0-615-25705-1; 978-0-615-26064-8; 978-0-615-26127-0; 978-0-615-27139-2; 978-0-615-27323-5; 978-0-9819570; 978-0-9841442; 978-0-9826490; 978-0-9828135; 978-0-615-44821-3; 978-0-615-46081-9; 978-0-615-46083-3; 978-0-615-46622-4; 978-0-615-46780-1; 978-0-615-47496-0; 978-0-615-47775-6; 97) 105 E. Front St. Suite 205, Monroe, MI 48161 USA Tel 734-629-4848; Fax: 734-322-5887*
E-mail: asapublishingcompany@gmail.com; asapublisher@gmail.com
Web site: http://www.asapublishingcompany.com
Dist(s): **CreateSpace Independent Publishing Platform**
Lightning Source, Inc.

ASA-CSSA-SSSA, *(978-0-89118)* 5585 Guilford Rd., Madison, WI 53711 USA (SAN 206-2879) Tel 608-268-4960; Fax: 608-273-2021
E-mail: books@agronomy.org; books@crops.org; books@soils.org
Web site: http://www.soils.org; http://www.crops.org; http://www.agronomy.org.

A.S.A.P., *(978-0-9797642)* 303 Indian Point Rd., Bar Harbor, ME 04609-9751 USA
Dist(s): **D.A.P./Distributed Art Pubs.**

Asbury Heritage Publishing, *(978-0-9859132)* 4601 Abercorne Terr., Louisville, KY 40241 USA Tel 502-897-3241; Fax: 502-897-3241
E-mail: bakerbutterfly@gmail.com.

Ascended Ideas, *(978-0-9795103; 978-0-692-00063-2; 978-0-9823969)* P.O. Box 120, Coldiron, KY 40819-0120 USA
Web site: http://www.ascendedideas.com.

Ascending Realm Publishing, *(978-0-9762135)* P.O. Box 2223, Centennial, CO 80161-2223 USA
E-mail: brandon@ascendingrealm.com
Web site: http://www.ascendingrealm.com.

Ascension Education, *(978-0-9640837)* Orders Addr.: P.O. Box 504, Venice, CA 90294 USA Tel 310-254-4092; Edit Addr.: 1814 Pacific Ave., No. 17, Venice, CA 90291 USA
E-mail: ascension2020@comcast.net
Web site: http://www.ascension-education.com.

Ascension Lutheran Church, *(978-0-9715472)* 314 W. Main St., Danville, VA 24541 USA Tel 434-792-5795; Fax: 434-799-3900
E-mail: chrismon@gamewood.net
Web site: http://www.chrismon.org.

Ascension Pr., *(978-0-9659228; 978-0-9742238; 978-0-9744451; 978-1-932631; 978-1-932645; 978-1-932927; 978-1-934217; 978-1-935940)* Orders Addr.: W5180 Jefferson St., Necedah, WI 54646 USA (SAN 256-0224) Tel 608-565-2024; Fax: 608-565-2025; Toll Free: 800-376-0520; Edit Addr.: P.O. Box 1990, West Chester, PA 19341 USA Tel 610-696-7795; Fax: 610-696-7796; Toll Free: 800-376-0520; 20 Hagerty Blvd., Suite 3, West Chester, PA 19341
E-mail: mflickinger@ascensionpress.com
Web site: http://www.ascensionpress.com
Dist(s): **Follett School Solutions.**

Ascent Pubns., *(978-0-9815302)* P.O. Box 928, Warrenton, MO 63383 USA
E-mail: michael@ascentpublications.com; info@ascentpublications.com
Web site: http://www.ascentpublications.com.

Ascribed *Imprint of* **dg ink**

Publisher Name Index

ASD Publishing, *(978-0-9836049; 978-0-9853441; 978-0-9961029)* 102 Arlington Ave., Hawthorne, NJ 07506 USA Tel 973-280-0145
E-mail: bbscout@hotmail.com
Dist(s): **BookBaby.**

ASE Media, *(978-0-9768890)* 5777 Crowntree Ln. Apt 208, ORLANDO, FL 32829 USA
E-mail: anne@easterlingfamily.com
Web site: http://www.asemedia.com.

Ashay by the Bay, *(978-0-9704048)* Orders Addr.: P.O. Box 2394, Union City, CA 94587 USA Tel 510-477-0967; Edit Addr.: P.O. Box 2394, Union City, CA 94587-7394 USA
E-mail: poetashay@aol.com
Web site: http://www.ashaybythebay.com.

Ashberry Lane, *(978-0-9893967; 978-1-941720)* P.O. Box 665, Gaston, OR 97119 USA Tel 503-860-5069
E-mail: christina@ashberrylane.net
Web site: www.ashberrylane.net.

†Ashgate Publishing Co., *(978-0-566; 978-0-85331; 978-0-906909; 978-1-84822)* Subs. of Ashgate Publishing, Ltd., Orders Addr.: P.O. Box 423, Brookfield, VT 05036-0423 USA Toll Free: 800-535-9544 (Orders - US & Canada); Edit Addr.: 101 Cherry St., Suite 420, Burlington, VT 05401-4405 USA (SAN 213-4446) Tel 802-865-7641; Fax: 802-865-7847
E-mail: info@ashgate.com; ash.orders@aidcvt.com; ash.cs@aidcvt.com
Web site: http://www.ashgate.com
Dist(s): **Follett School Solutions**
MyiLibrary
ebrary, Inc.; *CIP.*

Ashley & Taylor Publishing, Co., *(978-0-9745469)* P.O. Box 2793, Huntsville, AL 35804 USA Tel 256-430-1889
E-mail: AshleyTaylor4God@comcast.net.

AshleyAlan Enterprises, *(978-0-9702171; 978-0-9710145)* Orders Addr.: P.O. Box 1510, Kyle, TX 78640-1510 USA Tel 512-405-3065; Fax: 512-405-3066; Edit Addr.: 115 Hogan, Kyle, TX 78640 USA
E-mail: celestem@kyle-tx.com
Web site: http://www.ashleyanlan.com.

Ashlye V. Enterprises, LLC, *(978-0-9792934)* P.O. Box 3301, Columbia, SC 29230 USA Tel 803-361-1161; Fax: 803-772-2878; Toll Free: 866-382-3558
E-mail: ashlyev@gmail.com
Web site: http://www.ashlyev.com.

Ashmolean Museum (GBR) *(978-0-900090; 978-0-907849; 978-1-85444) Dist. by* **Natl Bk Netwk.**

Ashtabula County Genealogical Society, *(978-1-888851)* 860 Sherman St., Geneva, OH 44041-9101 USA Tel 440-466-4521; Fax: 440-466-0162
E-mail: acgs@ashtabulagen.org
Web site: http://www.ashtabulagen.org.

Ashway Pr., *(978-0-9754575)* Div. of Ashway, 5624 Double Tree Cir., Birmingham, AL 35242 USA Tel 205-995-8482
E-mail: janetpeine@aol.com
Web site: http://www.givingmeaway.com.

ASI, *(978-0-9759271)* 12 Brandywine Dr., Warwick, NY 10990 USA
Web site: www.asipublishing.com.

Asia for Kids *Imprint of* **Infini Pr., LLC**

Asiana Media, *(978-0-9778944)* Orders Addr.: P.O. Box 13693, Tempe, AZ 85284-0062 USA Tel 602-743-7155; *Imprints:* Juice & Berries, The (The Juice & Ber)
E-mail: info@asianamedia.com; info@thejuiceandberries.com
Web site: http://www.asianamedia.com; http://www.thejuiceandberries.com; http://www.faithittomakeit.com.

Asimow, Dyanne, *(978-0-9859522)* 8071 Willow Glen Rd., Los Angeles, CA 90046 USA Tel 323-654-3075
E-mail: dyanne8071@sbcglobal.net.

ASJA Pr. *Imprint of* **iUniverse, Inc.**

ASK Publishing, L.L.C., *(978-0-9742967)* 34046 Jefferson Ave., St Clr Shores, MI 48082-1162 USA (SAN 255-4976)
E-mail: admin@askpublishingllc.net
Web site: http://www.askpublishingllc.net
Dist(s): **Quality Bks., Inc.**

ASL Tales, *(978-0-9818139)* Orders Addr.: P.O. Box 80354, Portland, OR 97210 USA
E-mail: info@asltales.net
Web site: http://www.asltales.net
Dist(s): **Follett School Solutions.**

Aslan Publishing, *(978-0-944031)* Owned by Renaissance Book Services Corp., 2490 Black Rock Tpke., No. 342, Fairfield, CT 06432 USA (SAN 242-6129) Fax: 203-374-4766; Toll Free: 800-786-5427
E-mail: information@AslanPublishing.com; harold@aslanpublishing.com; aslan@sevenlive.net
Web site: http://www.AslanPublishing.com
Dist(s): **APG Sales & Distribution Services.**

ASM Pr., *(978-0-914826; 978-1-55581)* Div. of American Society For Microbiology, 1752 N St., NW, Washington, DC 20036 USA (SAN 202-1153) Tel 202-737-3600; Fax: 202-942-9342; P.O. Box 605, Herndon, VA 20172 USA
E-mail: books@asmusa.org
Web site: http://www.asmpress.org
Dist(s): **Follett School Solutions**
MyiLibrary
Rittenhouse Bk. Distributors
Wiley, John & Sons, Inc.
ebrary, Inc.

ASMedia Publishing, *(978-0-9743407)* 299 Swanville Rd., Frankfort, ME 04438 USA Fax: 207-223-5241
E-mail: asmedia2002@aol.com.

ASP Corp. Entertainment Group, Inc., *(978-0-9754147)* 3695 F Cascade Rd., Suite 229, Atlanta, GA 30331 USA Tel 404-344-7700; Fax: 404-344-7700
Web site: http://www.hannibaltrilogy.com.

Aspect Bk. *Imprint of* **TEACH Services, Inc.**

Aspen Bks., *(978-1-56236)* Div. of Worldwide Pubs., Inc., P.O. Box 1271, Bountiful, UT 84011-1271 USA Toll Free: 800-748-4850
E-mail: jasay@qwest.net; prawlins@aspenbook.com
Dist(s): **Cedar Fort, Inc./CFI Distribution**
Origin Bk. Sales, Inc.

Aspen Light Publishing, *(978-0-9743620; 978-0-9834896; 978-0-9913920)* Orders Addr.: 13506 Summerport Village Pkwy. Suite #155, Windermere, FL 34786 USA Fax: 407-910-2453; Toll Free: 800-437-1695
E-mail: orders@aspenlightpublishing.com
Dist(s): **DeVorss & Co.**

Aspen MLT, Inc., *(978-0-9774821; 978-0-9823628; 978-0-9854473; 978-1-941511)* 5855 Green Valley Cir. Suite 111, Culver City, CA 90230-9023 USA (SAN 257-6260) Fax: 310-348-9731
Web site: www.aspencomics.com
Dist(s): **Diamond Comic Distributors, Inc.**
Diamond Bk. Distributors.

Asphodel Pr. *Imprint of* **Moyer Bell**

Aspirations Media, Inc., *(978-0-9776043; 978-0-9800034)* 7755 Lakeview Ln., Spring Lake Park, MN 55432 USA (SAN 257-7305)
Web site: http://www.aspirationsmediainc.com
Dist(s): **AtlasBooks Distribution.**

Aspire Publishing, *(978-0-9799021)* 30081 Canyon Creek, Trabuco Canyon, CA 92679 USA
Web site: 4aspirebooks.com.

ASQ Quality Pr., *(978-0-87389)* Div. of American Society for Quality, 600 N. Plankinton Ave., P.O. Box 3005, Milwaukee, WI 53203 USA (SAN 683-5244) Tel 414-272-8575; Fax: 414-270-8810; Toll Free: 800-248-1946
E-mail: cs@asq.org
Web site: http://www.qualitypress.asq.org/
Dist(s): **American Technical Pubs., Inc.**
Follett School Solutions.

Associated Arts Pub., *(978-0-9840358)* 536 Tiara Dr., Grand Junction, CO 81507 USA Tel 970-241-8024
E-mail: suehughey@optimum.net
Web site: http://SCStrange.com; HerbysSecretFormula.com
Dist(s): **CreateSpace Independent Publishing Platform**
Follett School Solutions.

Assn. of Asthma Educators, *(978-0-9821228)* 1215 Anthony Ave., Columbia, SC 29201-1701 USA Tel 803-540-7530; Fax: 803-254-3773; Toll Free: 888-988-7747
E-mail: marie.queen@queencommunicationsllc.com
Web site: http://www.asthmaeducators.org.

Assn. of Christian Schls. International, *(978-1-58331)* Orders Addr.: P.O. Box 65130, Colorado Springs, CO 80962-5130 USA; Edit Addr.: 731 Chapel Hills Dr., Colorado Springs, CO 80920 USA (SAN 689-5751) Tel 719-528-6906; Fax: 719-531-0631; Toll Free: 800-367-0798 (orders only)
E-mail: webmaster@acsi.org; info@acsi.org
Web site: http://www.acsi.org.

Association of Jewish Libraries, *(978-0-929262)* P.O. Box 1118, Teaneck, NJ 07666 USA
E-mail: ajlibs@osu.edu; publications@jewishlibraries.org
Web site: http://www.jewishlibraries.org.

Association of Waldorf Schools of North America, The *See* **Waldorf Pubns.**

Assouline (FRA) *(978-2-84323; 978-2-908228; 978-2-7594) Dist. by* **Perseus Dist.**

AS-Sunnah Foundation of America *See* **Islamic Supreme Council of America**

Asta Publications, LLC, *(978-0-9777060; 978-1-934947)* Orders Addr.: P.O. Box 1735, Stockbridge, GA 30281 USA Fax: 678-814-1370; Toll Free: 800-482-4190
E-mail: acollins@astapublications.com; ahoward@astapublications.com
Web site: http://www.astapublications.com; http://www.astapublication.com; http://www.astaskids.com
Dist(s): **A & B Distributors & Pubs. Group**
BookBaby.

Astakos Publishing, *(978-0-9792991)* P.O. Box 227, Roscoe, IL 61073-9330 USA Tel 815-623-6616
E-mail: astakospublishing@charter.net
Web site: http://www.astakospublishing.com
Dist(s): **Follett School Solutions**
Quality Bks., Inc.

Asteroid Publishing, *(978-0-9841187)* 251 Middle Rd., Boxborough, MA 01719 USA Tel 978-549-0464
Dist(s): **Smashwords.**

Astonish Comics, *(978-0-9721259)* 10061 Riverside Dr., Suite No. 785, Toluca Lake, CA 91602 USA
Web site: http://www.theastonishfactory.com
Dist(s): **Diamond Comic Distributors, Inc.**
Diamond Bk. Distributors.

Astor Pr., *(978-0-9764119; 978-0-615-14497-9; 978-0-615-18601-6; 978-0-615-21360-6; 978-0-615-26465-3; 978-0-578-00527-0; 978-0-578-01799-0; 978-0-578-02611-4; 978-0-578-02667-1; 978-0-9899257)* 12 Walcott St., Maynard, MA 01754 USA
E-mail: info@astorpress.com; mail@shanddaramon.com
Web site: http://www.astorpress.com
Dist(s): **Lulu Enterprises Inc.**
Smashwords.

Astor-Honor, Inc., *(978-0-8392)* 16 E. 40th St., Third Flr., New York, NY 10016 USA (SAN 203-5022) Tel 212-840-8800; Fax: 212-840-7246.

Astral Publishing Co., *(978-0-9645867)* Orders Addr.: P.O. Box 3955, Santa Barbara, CA 93130-3955 USA (SAN 298-5705) Tel 805-967-7667; Edit Addr.: 333 Old Mill Rd., No. 324, Santa Barbara, CA 93110 USA
E-mail: wveigele@aol.com
Web site: http://www.astralpublishing.com
Dist(s): **Quality Bks., Inc.**

Astronaut Ink, *(978-0-9772727)* Orders Addr.: 180 Newbury St. 4106, Danvers, MA 01923 USA
E-mail: joe@popartproperties.com
Web site: http://www.popartproperties.com.

ASunnyDay Publishing, *(978-0-9818366)* 17 Hillside Ave., Suite 102, Rockville Centre, NY 11570 USA Tel 516-884-7661
E-mail: dariarosebooks@gmail.com
Web site: http://www.dariarosebooks.com.

At Ease Pr., *(978-0-917921)* Div. of Be at Ease School of Etiquette, 1212 W. Ben White Blvd., #214, Austin, TX 78704-7197 USA (SAN 656-9900)
E-mail: haroldalmon@gmail.com; schoolofetiquette@ateasepress.com
Web site: http://ateasepress.com; http://baeschoolofetiquette.blogspot.com/; http://baesoe.com
Dist(s): **Lulu Enterprises Inc.**

At Peace Media, LLC, *(978-0-9742002)* 1117 E. Putnam Ave., No. 345, Riverside, CT 06878 USA Tel 203-698-2688; Fax: 203-698-3441; Toll Free: 800-575-7715
E-mail: john@atpeacemedia.com
Web site: http://www.atpeacemedia.com.

Atelier Finwhale, *(978-0-9882561)* P.O. Box 60608, Palo Alto, CA 94306-9991 USA Tel 650-787-2198
E-mail: 3marjorie14@gmail.com.

Atelier Mythologie, *(978-0-9899905)* 3815 E Pike, Seattle, WA 98122 USA Tel 206-724-4144
E-mail: publisher@ateliermythologie.com.

Athanata Arts, Ltd., *(978-0-9727993)* P.O. Box 321, Garden City, NY 11530 USA (SAN 255-5018) Tel 516-742-8735
E-mail: info@athanata.com
Web site: http://www.athanata.com.

Athenaeum Music & Arts Library *Imprint of* **Library Assn. of La Jolla**

Atheneum Bks. for Young Readers *Imprint of* **Simon & Schuster Children's Publishing**

Atheneum/Anne Schwartz Bks. *Imprint of* **Simon & Schuster Children's Publishing**

Atheneum/Richard Jackson Bks. *Imprint of* **Simon & Schuster Children's Publishing**

AthertonCustoms, *(978-0-578-00865-3; 978-0-615-33485-1; 978-0-9827167)* 6536 Aldergate Ln., Las Vegas, NV 89110 USA Tel 702-438-6596
E-mail: jim@athertoncustoms.com
Web site: http://www.athertoncustoms.com
Dist(s): **Lulu Enterprises Inc.**

ATInternational Pubs., *(978-0-9773816)* 227 Sunflower Ln., West Windsor, NJ 08550-2439 USA
E-mail: atinetus@yahoo.com.

Atkinson, Janet Irene *See* **Irene, Jan Pubns.**

Atlantic Bks., Ltd. (GBR) *(978-1-903809; 978-1-84354; 978-1-84887; 978-0-85789; 978-0-85740; 978-1-78239) Dist. by* **IPG Chicago.**

Atlantic Bridge Publishing, *(978-0-9700930; 978-0-9706913; 978-1-931761; 978-1-59578; 978-1-62210)* 10509 Sedgegrass Dr., Indianapolis, IN 46235 USA Tel 317-826-8059 Do not confuse with Bridge Works Publishing Company, Inc. in Bridgehampton, NY
E-mail: linda@atlanticbridge.net
Web site: http://www.liquidsilverbooks.com; http://www.atlanticbridge.net
Dist(s): **INscribe Digital.**

Atlantic Publishing Co., *(978-0-910627; 978-1-60138; 978-1-62023)* 1405 SW. 6th Ave., Ocala, FL 34471-0640 USA (SAN 268-1250) Toll Free: 800-814-1132 Do not confuse with companies with the same or similar name in Tabor City, NC , Aurora, IL, Lakeland, FL , Combs, KY , Neosho, MO
E-mail: info@atlantic-pub.com; sales@atlantic-pub.com
Web site: http://www.atlantic-pub.com
Dist(s): **MyiLibrary.**

Atlantida (ARG) *(978-950-08) Dist. by* **AIMS Intl.**

Atlas Games *Imprint of* **Trident, Inc.**

AtlasBooks *See* **AtlasBooks Distribution**

AtlasBooks Distribution, Div. of BookMasters, Inc., Orders Addr.: 30 Amberwood Pkwy., Ashland, OH 44805 USA (SAN 631-936X) Fax: 419-281-6883; Toll Free: 800-247-6553; 800-537-6727; 800-266-5564
E-mail: orders@atlasbooks.com
Web site: http://www.atlasbooksdistribution.com.

Atman Pr., *(978-0-9652900)* Orders Addr.: 2104 Cherokee Ave., Columbus, GA 31906 USA (SAN 299-142X) Tel 706-323-6377; Fax: 706-321-1140
E-mail: robertarnett@mindspring.com; AtmanPress@gmail.com; smitaturakhia@gmail.com
Web site: http://www.atmanpress.com
Dist(s): **Brodart Co.**
Follett School Solutions
Mackin Bk. Co.

Atom Pr., 926 Flemington St., Pittsburgh, PA 15217 USA Tel 951-801-0391
E-mail: atomtitan@hotmail.com.

Atomic Basement, 1222 N. Commonwealth Ave. Apt. No. 4, Los Angeles, CA 90029-2058 USA Tel 386-679-9106
E-mail: oilerhggns@aol.com
Dist(s): **AtlasBooks Distribution.**

Atomic Fruit Pr., *(978-0-9753225)* 404 13th Ave., Huntington, WV 25701 USA
Web site: http://www.apocalyptictangerine.com.

Atria Bks. *Imprint of* **Simon & Schuster**

Atria Bks., Div. of Simon & Schuster, 1230 Avenue of the Americas, New York, NY 10020 USA; *Imprints:* Beyond Words/Atria Books (AtriaBks)
Dist(s): **Follett School Solutions**
MyiLibrary
Simon & Schuster, Inc.

Atria/Emily Bestler Bks. *Imprint of* **Atria/Emily Bestler Bks.**

Atria/Emily Bestler Bks., 1230 Avenue of the Americas, New York, NY 10020 USA; *Imprints:* Atria/Emily Bestler Books (AEBB)
Dist(s): **Simon & Schuster, Inc.**

Atrium Publishing, Incorporated *See* **mTrellis Publishing, Inc.**

Attack The Text / Magedo Publishing *See* **Attack The Text Publishing**

Attack The Text Publishing, *(978-0-9755923; 978-0-9842882)* 905 N. Pacific St., No. C, Oceanside, CA 92831 USA
Web site: http://www.attackthetext.com; http://www.magedo.com.

Attainment Co., Inc., *(978-0-934731; 978-1-57861; 978-1-943148)* Orders Addr.: P.O. Box 930160, Verona, WI 53593 USA (SAN 694-1656) Tel 608-845-7880; Fax: 608-845-8040; Toll Free: 800-327-4269; Edit Addr.: 504 Commerce Pkwy., Verona, WI 53593 USA (SAN 631-6174); *Imprints:* IEP Resources (IEP Res)
E-mail: info@attainmentcompany.com; sue@attainmentcompany.com; ameyer@attainmentcompany.com
Web site: http://www.attainmentcompany.com/
Dist(s): **AtlasBooks Distribution**
Follett School Solutions
Linx Educational Publishing, Inc.
Sunburst Communications, Inc.

Attic Studio Pr. *Imprint of* **Attic Studio Publishing Hse.**

Attic Studio Publishing Hse., *(978-1-883551)* Orders Addr.: P.O. Box 75, Clinton Corners, NY 12514 USA (SAN 298-2838) Tel 845-266-8100; Fax: 845-266-5515; Toll Free: 800-974-5533 (orders); Edit Addr.: P.O. Box 75, Clinton Corners, NY 12514 USA (SAN 298-2846); *Imprints:* Attic Studio Press (Attic Studio); Maple Corners Press (Maple Corners Pr)
E-mail: collegeavepress@aol.com; atticstudiopress@aol.com
Dist(s): **BookBaby**
Emerald Bk. Co.
Spring Arbor Distributors, Inc.

Atticus, C. J., *(978-0-9887780)* 41 Radford Ct. Sw, Marietta, GA 30060 USA Tel 770-805-9422
E-mail: atticus@cjatticus.com.

Attitude Pie Publishing, *(978-0-692-01275-8)* 2100 NE 214th St., North Miami Beach, FL 33179 USA Tel 305-725-0446; 419-281-5100 X1151
E-mail: MPYANOWSKI@BOOKMASTERS.COM
Dist(s): **AtlasBooks Distribution.**

Attitude Pr. Inc.,
Dist(s): **AtlasBooks Distribution.**

Attitudes in Dressing, Inc., *(978-0-9766640)* 1350 Broadway, New York, NY 10018 USA Tel 212-279-3492; Fax: 212-564-3426; Toll Free: 800-899-0503
Web site: http://www.bodywrappers.com.

ATU Golden Pubns., *(978-0-9753119)* 8283 Main St., Bokeelia, FL 33922 USA
E-mail: chrissydl@aol.com
Web site: http://www.pgaa.com.

Auckland Univ. Pr. (NZL) *(978-1-86940) Dist. by* **IPG Chicago.**

Audio Bookshelf, *(978-1-883332; 978-0-9741711; 978-0-9761932; 978-0-9814890; 978-1-935430)* Orders Addr.: 44 Ocean View Dr., Middletown, RI 02842 USA Tel 401-849-2333; Fax: 401-842-0440; Toll Free: 800-234-1713; Edit Addr.: P.O. Box 83, Belfast, ME 04915-0083 USA
E-mail: dd@audiobookshelf.com
Web site: http://www.audiobookshelf.com
Dist(s): **AudioGO**
Follett School Solutions
Landmark Audiobooks
Professional Media Service Corp.

Audio Craft Press *See* **AudioCraft Publishing, Inc.**

Audio Holdings, LLC, *(978-1-60136)* P.O. Box 119, Franklin Park, NJ 08823 USA (SAN 851-0776) Tel 732-940-4286; Fax: 732-940-0534
E-mail: mgladishev@gmail.com
Dist(s): **Ebsco Publishing.**

Audio Partners, Incorporated *See* **Audio Partners Publishing Corp.**

Audio Partners Publishing Corp., *(978-0-88690; 978-0-945353; 978-1-57270)* 42 Whitecap Dr., North Kingstown, RI 02852-7445 USA (SAN 253-4622) Toll Free Fax: 877-492-0873; Toll Free: 800-621-0182
E-mail: info@audiopartners.com
Web site: http://www.audiopartners.com
Dist(s): **Follett School Solutions**
Landmark Audiobooks
Perseus-PGW
Perseus Distribution.

Audio Renaissance *See* **Macmillan Audio**

AudioCraft Publishing, Inc., *(978-1-893699; 978-1-942950)* Orders Addr.: P.O. Box 281, Topinabee, MI 49791 USA Tel 231-238-0338; Fax: 231-238-0339; Toll Free: 888-420-4244; Edit Addr.: P.O. Box 281, Topinabee, MI 49791 USA
E-mail: ck@americanchillers.com; store@americanchillers.com; shawn@americanchillers.com
Web site: http://www.audiocraftpublishing.com; http://www.michiganchillers.com; http://www.americanchillers.com
Dist(s): **Follett School Solutions**
Partners Bk. Distributing, Inc.

†AudioGO, *(978-0-563; 978-0-7540; 978-0-7927; 978-0-89340; 978-1-55504; 978-1-60283; 978-1-60998; 978-1-62064; 978-1-62460; 978-1-4815; 978-1-4821)* Orders Addr.: c/o Perseus, 1094 Flex Dr., Jackson, TN 38301 USA; Edit Addr.: 42 Whitecap Dr., North Kingstown, RI 02852-7445 USA (SAN 858-7701) Toll Free: 800-621-0182; *Imprints:* Sound Library (SoundLib)
E-mail: laura.almeida@audiogo.com
Web site: http://www.audiogo.com/us/
Dist(s): **Ebsco Publishing**
Findaway World, LLC
Follett School Solutions

INscribe Digital
Perseus Distribution; *CIP.*

Audioscope, *(978-1-57375)* Div. of K-tel International (USA), Inc., 2605 Fernbrook Ln., N., No. H-O, Plymouth, MN 55447 USA Tel 612-559-6888; Fax: 612-559-6848; Toll Free: 800-328-6640
Web site: http://www.ktel.com
Dist(s): **Follett School Solutions.**

Auditors of God, The (GBR) *(978-0-9561587; 978-0-9572919) Dist. by* **LuluCom.**

Audrey Pr., *(978-1-936426)* P.O. Box 6113, Maryville, TN 37802 USA Tel 865-254-4463
E-mail: valarie@audreypress.com
Web site: www.audreypress.com
Dist(s): **AtlasBooks Distribution.**

Audrey Productions, *(978-0-9722673)* 7809 Paper Flower Ct., Las Vegas, NV 89128 USA Tel 702-228-4803 (phone/fax)
Dist(s): **Follett School Solutions.**

Audubon Pr. & Christian Bk. Service, *(978-0-9652883; 978-0-9742365; 978-0-9820731)* Orders Addr.: P.O. Box 8055, Laurel, MS 39441 USA Tel 601-649-8572; Fax: 601-649-8571; Toll Free: 800-405-3788; Edit Addr.: 2601 Audubon Dr., Laurel, MS 39440 USA
E-mail: buybooks@audubonpress.com
Web site: http://www.audubonpress.com.

Augsburg Bks. *Imprint of* **Augsburg Fortress, Pubs.**

†Augsburg Fortress, Pubs., *(978-0-8006; 978-0-8066; 978-1-4514; 978-1-5064)* Orders Addr.: P.O. Box 1209, Minneapolis, MN 55440-1209 USA (SAN 169-4081) Toll Free Fax: 800-722-7766; Toll Free: 800-328-4648 (orders only); Edit Addr.: 510 Marquette 8th Fl., Minneapolis, MN 55402 USA Tel 800-328-4648 800-722-7766; *Imprints:* Augsburg Books (Augsburg Bks); Sparkhouse Family (Sparkhse)
E-mail: customerservice@augsburgfortress.org; info@augsburgfortress.org; subscriptions@augsburgfortress.org; copyright@augsburgfortress.org; international@augsburgfortress.org
Web site: http://www.augsburgfortress.org
Dist(s): **ebrary, Inc.**; *CIP.*

Augsburg Fortress Publishers, Publishing House of The Evangelical Lutheran Church in America *See* **Augsburg Fortress, Pubs.**

†August Hse. Pubs., Inc., *(978-0-87483; 978-0-935304; 978-1-939160; 978-1-941459; 978-1-941460)* 3500 Piedmont Rd. NE, Suite 310, Atlanta, GA 30305 USA (SAN 223-7288) Tel 404-442-4425; Fax: 404-442-4435; Toll Free: 800-284-8784; 3500 Piedmont Rd. Suite 310, Atlanta, GA 30305; *Imprints:* August House Story Cove (August Hse Story Cove)
E-mail: ahinfo@augusthouse.com; order@augusthouse.com
Web site: http://www.augusthouse.com
Dist(s): **Findaway World, LLC**
Follett School Solutions
National Bk. Network; *CIP.*

August House Story Cove *Imprint of* **August Hse. Pubs., Inc.**

August Too Publishing, *(978-0-9767103)* 1346 E. Poinsettia St., Long Beach, CA 90805-3128 USA
E-mail: writeme@paulcarhart.com.

Augusta Win Publishing, *(978-0-9766597)* Orders Addr.: P.O. Box 53, Turin, NY 13473 USA; Edit Addr.: 6159 W. Main, Turin, NY 13473 USA
E-mail: augustawinpub@yahoo.com
Web site: http://www.augustawinpublishing.com.

Augustana College Geology Dept. Pr., *(978-0-9797015)* 639 38th St., Rock Island, IL 61201-2296 USA Tel 309-794-7318; Fax: 309-794-7564
Web site: http://www.augustana.edu.

Augustine Pr., *(978-0-9626431)* 900 Old Koenig Ln., No. 135, Austin, TX 78756 USA Tel 512-459-5194; Fax: 512-451-0755
E-mail: morganp@flash.net.

Augustinians of the Assumption *See* **Ambassador Bks., Inc.**

Augustus Publishing, *(978-0-9759453; 978-0-9792816; 978-0-9825415; 978-1-935883)* Div. of Augustus Productions, 600 W. 218 St., Suite 3K, New York, NY 10034 USA Tel 646-526-7998
E-mail: jc@augustuspublishing.com; gfhood1@aol.com; aw@augustuspublishing.com
Web site: http://www.augustuspublishing.com
Dist(s): **A & B Distributors & Pubs. Group**
Follett School Solutions
Independent Pubs. Group
MyiLibrary
Perseus-PGW
Perseus Bks. Group.

Aunt Dee's Attic, Inc., *(978-0-9679437; 978-0-9829416)* 415 Detroit St., Suite 200, Ann Arbor, MI 48104 USA Tel 734-668-6738; Fax: 734-668-0182; Toll Free: 800-352-6797
E-mail: dianne@elansys.com
Web site: http://www.auntdeesattic.com.

Aunt Patty's Travels-London, *(978-0-9659668)* 4811 Wesleyan Woods Dr., Macon, GA 31210 USA.

Aunt Strawberry Bks., *(978-0-9669988)* Orders Addr.: P.O. Box 819, Boulder, CO 80306-0819 USA (SAN 299-9811) Tel 303-449-3574; Fax: 303-444-9221
E-mail: readasbs@hotmail.com
Dist(s): **Brodart Co.**
Follett School Solutions.

Auntie B Publishing *See* **BaHart Pubns. / Eight Legs Publishing**

Aunty Ems Boutique, *(978-0-9742122)* P.O. Box 1963, Havasu Lake Landing, CA 92363 USA.

Aura Printing, Inc., *(978-0-911643)* 88 Parkville Ave., Brooklyn, NY 11230 USA (SAN 237-9317) Tel 718-435-9103; Fax: 718-871-9488
Dist(s): **Bookazine Co., Inc.**

Aura Productions LLC *See* **Simple Ink, LLC**

Aurandt, Paul H II, *(978-0-9887774)* 1035 Pk. Ave., River Forest, IL 60305 USA Tel 708-366-5371; Fax: 708-366-9184
E-mail: paul@paulharvey.com
Web site: http://www.paulharvey.com.

Auricle Ink Pubs., *(978-0-9661826; 978-0-9825785)* P.O. Box 20607, Sedona, AZ 86341 USA Tel 928-284-0860
E-mail: rcarmen27@yahoo.com
Web site: http://www.hearingproblems.com
Dist(s): **Academic Bk. Ctr., Inc.**
Bk. Hse., Inc., The
Brodart Co.
Coutts Information Services
Emery-Pratt Co.
Follett School Solutions
Franklin Bk. Co., Inc.
Majors, J. A. Co.
Matthews Medical Bk. Co.
Midwest Library Service
Yankee Bk. Peddler, Inc.

Auriga, Ediciones S.A. (ESP) *(978-84-7281) Dist. by* **Continental Bk.**

Aurora Books *Imprint of* **Eco-Justice Pr., LLC**

Aurora Bks., *(978-0-9753508)* 512 Willow Branch Rd., Norman, OK 73072 USA
E-mail: aurorabooks@netzero.net.

Aurora Libris Corp., *(978-1-932233)* 40 E. 83rd St., Apt. 35, New York, NY 10028 USA Toll Free: 866-763-8411
E-mail: lavinia@laviniasworld.com
Web site: http://www.laviniasworld.com.

Aurora Metro Pubns. Ltd. (GBR) *(978-0-9515877; 978-0-9536757; 978-0-9542330; 978-0-9546912; 978-0-9551566; 978-1-906582; 978-0-9566329) Dist. by* **Consort Bk Sales.**

Aurora Pubs., Inc., *(978-0-9791758)* Orders Addr.: 5970 S.W. 18th St., No. 117, Boca Raton, FL 33433-7197 USA; Edit Addr.: 814 N. Franklin St., Chicago, IL 60610 USA
E-mail: aurorapublishers@aol.com
Web site: http://www.aurorapublishers.com
Dist(s): **Ebsco Publishing**
Follett School Solutions
Independent Pubs. Group
MyiLibrary.

Aurora Publishing, Incor[porated *See* **Aurora Publishing, Inc.**

Aurora Publishing, Inc., *(978-1-934496)* 3655 Torrance Blvd., Suite 430, Torrance, CA 90503 USA; *Imprints:* Deux (Deux); LuvLuv (LuvLuv) Do not confuse with companies with the same or similar name in Arlijgton, VA, College Grove, TN,, West Palm Beach, FL, Eagle River, AK, West Hartford, CT, Fort Lauderdale, FL
E-mail: info@aurora-publishing.com
Web site: http://www.aurora-publishing.com; http://www.deux-press.com; http://www.luvluv-press.com
Dist(s): **Diamond Comic Distributors, Inc.**
Diamond Bk. Distributors.

Austin & Charlie Adventures *Imprint of* **Paw Print Pubns.**

Austin & Company, Inc., *(978-0-9657153)* 104 S. Union St., Suite 202, Traverse City, MI 49684 USA (SAN 631-1466) Tel 231-933-4649; Fax: 231-933-4659
E-mail: aandn@aol.com
Web site: http://www.austinandcompanyinc.com.

Austin & Nelson Publishing *See* **Austin & Company, Inc.**

Austin Christopher Swift, *(978-0-9764208)* 154 Golden Autumn Pl., Woodlands, TX 77384 USA Tel 956-421-5750; Fax: 956-421-5721
E-mail: john@toppmarketing.com.

Austin Energy Green Building Program, *(978-0-9679069)* Orders Addr.: P.O. Box 1088, Austin, TX 78767 USA Tel 512-322-6172; Fax: 512-505-3711; Edit Addr.: 721 Barton Springs Rd., Austin, TX 78704 USA
E-mail: dick.peterson@austinenergy.com
Web site: http://www.austinenergy.com.

Austin Macauley Pubs. Ltd. (GBR) *(978-1-905609; 978-1-84963; 978-1-78455) Dist. by* **Midpt Trade.**

Austin, Stephen F. State Univ. Pr., *(978-1-936205; 978-1-62288)* Orders Addr.: P.O. Box 13002, Nacogdoches, TX 75962 USA Tel 936-468-1078; Fax: 936-468-2614; Edit Addr.: 1936 North St. Liberal Arts N., 203 English, Nacogdoches, TX 75962 USA
Dist(s): **MyiLibrary**
Texas A&M Univ. Pr.
ebrary, Inc.

Australian Fishing Network (AUS) *(978-0-9587143; 978-1-86513; 978-1-86252-412-5; 978-0-646-00117-3; 978-0-646-15871-6; 978-0-646-19310-6; 978-0-646-20528-1; 978-0-646-20908-1; 978-0-646-21731-4; 978-0-646-24873-8; 978-0-646-25433-3; 978-0-646-25434-0; 978-0-646-30130-3; 978-0-646-31918-6) Dist. by* **Cardinal PubGr.**

Auteur Publishing (GBR) *(978-1-903663; 978-1-906733) Dist. by* **Col U Pr.**

Authentic Media (GBR) *(978-0-8499; 978-0-85009; 978-1-86024; 978-1-78078) Dist. by* **EMI CMG Dist.**

Author at Work *Imprint of* **Owen, Richard C. Pubs., Inc.**

Author Solutions, Inc., Div. of Penguin Group (USA) Inc., 1663 Liberty Dr., Bloomington, IN 47403 USA Tel 812-334-5223; Toll Free: 877-655-1722; *Imprints:* WestBow Press (WestBowPr); Balboa Press (BalboaPr); Inspiring Voices (InspVoices); Abbott Press (AbbottPr); PartridgeIndia (PARTRIDGEINDIA)
E-mail: sfurr@authorsolutions
Web site: http://www.authorsolutions.com
Dist(s): **AtlasBooks Distribution**
CreateSpace Independent Publishing Platform
Xlibris Corp.
Zondervan.

AuthorHouse, *(978-1-58500; 978-0-9675669; 978-1-58721; 978-1-58820; 978-0-7596; 978-1-4033; 978-1-4107; 978-1-4140; 978-1-4184; 978-1-4208; 978-1-4259; 978-1-4343; 978-1-4389; 978-1-4490; 978-1-4520; 978-1-61764; 978-1-4567; 978-1-4582; 978-1-4624; 978-1-4633; 978-1-4634; 978-0-9846457; 978-1-4670; 978-1-4678; 978-1-4685; 978-1-4772; 978-1-4817; 978-1-4918; 978-1-4969; 978-1-5049; 978-1-5065) Div. of Author Solutions, Inc., 1663 Liberty Dr., Suite 200, Bloomington, IN 47403 USA (SAN 253-7605) Fax: 812-336-5449; Toll Free: 888-519-5121*
E-mail: authorsupport@authorhouse.com; emilyguldin@yahoo.com; sfurr@authorsolutions.com; jburns@authorsolutions.com
Web site: http://www.facebook.com/daveywizzletooth1; http://www.authorhouse.com
Dist(s): **AtlasBooks Distribution**
Author Solutions, Inc.
BookBaby
CreateSpace Independent Publishing Platform
Follett School Solutions
Ingram Pub. Services
Lulu Enterprises Inc.
MyiLibrary
Smashwords.

AuthorMike Ink, *(978-0-9845801; 978-0-9852146; 978-0-9884468; 978-0-9910330; 978-1-943201)* 76 Pheasant Dr., Springfield, MA 01119-0111 USA (SAN 859-8142) Tel 413-222-1143
E-mail: Mike@AuthorMike.com
Web site: http://www.AuthorMikeInk.com; http://authormikedarkink.com/Dark_Ink/Welcome.html.

Authors & Artists Publishers of New York, Inc., *(978-0-9708053; 978-0-9724922; 978-0-9740683; 978-0-9754298; 978-0-9763993; 978-0-9766716; 978-0-9771482; 978-0-9786211; 978-0-9787113; 978-0-9819746; 978-0-9825971; 978-0-9839121; 978-0-9850947)* Orders Addr.: 408 E. Marshall St., Ithaca, NY 14850 USA Tel 607-273-2870; *Imprints:* Ithaca Press (IthacaPress)
E-mail: quotes@ithacapress.com
Web site: http://www.ithacapress.com
Dist(s): **Follett School Solutions.**

Authors Choice Pr. *Imprint of* **iUniverse, Inc.**

Author's Connection Pr., *(978-0-927206)* 777 College Pk. Dr., SW No. 60, Albany, OR 97322-8430 USA
Web site: http://www.acpublish.com.

Authors' Discovery Cooperation, Inc., *(978-0-9794443; 978-0-9800854; 978-0-9844730)* 165 Cherry Ln., Robert Lee, TX 76945 USA (SAN 853-4276) Tel 325-453-4595
E-mail: ldudney@nwol.net
Web site: http://www.authorsdiscovery.com.

Authors' Press, The *See* **Quantum Manifestations Publishing**

Autism Asperger Publishing Co., *(978-0-9672514; 978-1-931282; 978-1-934575; 978-1-937473; 978-1-942197)* Orders Addr.: P.O. Box 23173, Overland Park, KS 66283-0173 USA Tel 913-599-3311; Fax: 913-492-2546; 11209 Strang Line Rd, Lenexa, KS 66215 (SAN 920-9220); Edit Addr.: 15490 Qunvira, Overland Park, KS 66221 USA
E-mail: kmcbr41457@aol.com
Web site: http://www.asperger.net
Dist(s): **Follett School Solutions.**

Autism Research Institute, *(978-0-9740360)* 4182 Adams Ave., San Diego, CA 92116 USA Fax: 619-563-6840
E-mail: sait97302@yahoo.com
Web site: http://www.autismresearchinstitute.com.

Automatic Pictures Publishing, *(978-0-9818737; 978-0-9892221; 978-0-9912729)* 5721 Valley Oak Dr., Los Angeles, CA 90068 USA Tel 323-935-1800; Fax: 323-935-8040
E-mail: automaticstudio@gmail.com
Web site: http://www.lookingglasswars.com
Dist(s): **Diamond Comic Distributors, Inc.**
Diamond Bk. Distributors
Perseus-PGW.

Automatic Publishing *See* **Automatic Pictures Publishing**

Automobile Assn. (GBR) *(978-0-7495; 978-0-86145; 978-0-901088; 978-1-872163) Dist. by* **IPG Chicago.**

Automobile Assn. (GBR) *(978-0-7495; 978-0-86145; 978-0-901088; 978-1-872163) Dist. by* **Trafalgar.**

Automobiles-Memory Lane Publishing, *(978-0-9746667)* Orders Addr.: P.O. Box 228, Vicksburg, MI 49097 USA (SAN 255-7118) Tel 269-649-3614 (phone/fax); Edit Addr.: 2294 E. VW Ave., Vicksburg, MI 49097 USA.

Autonomedia, *(978-0-936756; 978-1-57027)* Orders Addr.: P.O. Box 568, Brooklyn, NY 11211-0568 USA; Edit Addr.: 55 S. Eleventh St., #4b, Brooklyn, NY 11211-0568 USA (SAN 221-3869) Tel 718-963-2603
E-mail: info@autonomedia.org
Web site: http://www.autonomedia.org
Dist(s): **AK Pr. Distribution**
Lulu Enterprises Inc.
SPD-Small Pr. Distribution.

Autumn Breeze Publishing, LLC, *(978-0-615-65105-7; 978-0-615-65191-0)* P.O. Box 691, West Chester, OH 45071 USA Tel 513-777-7908
Dist(s): **CreateSpace Independent Publishing Platform.**

Autumn Hill Bks., Inc., *(978-0-9754444; 978-0-9843036; 978-0-9827466)* P.O. Box 22, Iowa City, IA 52244 USA Tel 319-354-2456; 814 N. Franklin St., Chicago, IL 60610
E-mail: info@autumnhillbooks.com
Web site: http://www.autumnhillbooks.com
Dist(s): **Ebsco Publishing**
Follett School Solutions
Independent Pubs. Group
MyiLibrary.

Autumn Hse. Publishing, *(978-0-9637825)* Orders Addr.: P.O. Box 763833, Dallas, TX 75376 USA; Edit Addr.: 1535 Acapulco Dr., Dallas, TX 75232 USA Tel 214-376-8959 Do not confuse with the same or similar name in Lexington, KY, Hagerstown, MD
E-mail: millijp@earthlink.net.

Autumn Hse. Publishing Co., *(978-0-8127; 978-1-878951)* Div. of Review & Herald Publishing Assn., 55 W. Oakridge Dr., Hagerstown, MD 21740 USA Do not confuse with companies with the same name in Lexington, KY, Dallas, TX.

Autumn Publishing Group, LLC, *(978-1-890877)* Orders Addr.: P.O. Box 71604, Madison Heights, MI 48071 USA Tel 248-589-5249; Fax: 248-585-5715; Toll Free: 888-876-4114; Edit Addr.: 30755 Barrington Ave., Madison Heights, MI 48071 USA
Web site: http://www.wiredin.net/childcare
Dist(s): **Unique Bks., Inc.**

Auzou, Philippe Editions (FRA) *(978-2-7338) Dist. by* **Consort Bk Sales.**

AV2 by Weigl *Imprint of* **Weigl Pubs., Inc.**

Avalon Publishing Group, *(978-0-7867; 978-0-88184; 978-0-929654; 978-0-931188; 978-0-938410; 978-0-941423; 978-1-56025; 978-1-56201; 978-1-56858; 978-1-56924; 978-1-58005; 978-1-878067; 978-1-60094)* Div. of Perseus Books Group, 161 William St., 16th Flr., New York, NY 10038 USA Tel 646-375-2570; Fax: 646-375-2571
Web site: http://www.thundersmouth.com; http://www.avalonpub.com; http://www.sealpress.com; http://www.marlowepub.com
Dist(s): **Bilingual Pubns. Co., The**
CreateSpace Independent Publishing Platform
Ebsco Publishing
Follett School Solutions
MyiLibrary
Perseus-PGW
Perseus Bks. Group.

Avant Garde Publishing *See* **The Publishing Place LLC**

Avant-garde Bks., *(978-0-9743676; 978-0-9908992)* Orders Addr.: P.O. Box 566, Mableton, GA 30126 USA Do not confuse with Avant garde Publishing in Norman, OK.

Avant-garde Publishing Company *See* **Avant-garde Bks.**

Avari Pr., *(978-1-933770)* 2198 Old Philadelphia Pk., Lancaster, PA 17602 USA (SAN 257-9413)
E-mail: av42@antham.net.

Avatar Pr., Inc., *(978-0-9706784; 978-1-59291)* 9 Triumph Dr., Urbana, IL 61802 USA Tel 217-384-2211; Fax: 217-384-2216 Do not confuse with companies with the same or similar name in Sunnyside, NY, Atlanta, GA, Brick, NJ
E-mail: william@avatarpress.net
Web site: http://www.avatarpress.com
Dist(s): **Diamond Comic Distributors, Inc.**
Diamond Bk. Distributors
Simon & Schuster
Simon & Schuster, Inc.

Avatar Pubns., Inc. (CAN) *(978-0-9735379; 978-0-9738442; 978-0-9737401; 978-0-9738555; 978-1-897455) Dist. by* **NACSCORP Inc.**

Ave Maria Pr., *(978-0-87061; 978-0-87793; 978-0-88347; 978-0-939516; 978-1-893732; 978-1-932057; 978-1-59471; 978-1-933495)* P.O. Box 428, Notre Dame, IN 46556-0428 USA (SAN 201-1255) Tel 574-287-2831; Fax: 574-239-2904; Toll Free Fax: 800-282-5681; Toll Free: 800-282-1865
E-mail: avemariapress.1@nd.edu
Web site: http://www.forestofpeace.com; http://www.avemariapress.com; http://www.sorinbooks.com
Dist(s): **Fujii Assocs.**
MyiLibrary.

Aventine Pr, *(978-0-9719382; 978-0-9722932; 978-1-59330)* 750 State St. Unit 319, San Diego, CA 92101-6073 USA Toll Free: 866-246-6142
E-mail: info@aventinepress.com
Web site: http://www.aventinepress.com
Dist(s): **Ingram Pub. Services.**

AverHill Pr., *(978-0-9766107)* 2545 SW Terwilliger Blvd., No. 807, Portland, OR 97201 USA.

Avery *Imprint of* **Penguin Publishing Group**

Avery Color Studios, Inc., *(978-0-932212; 978-1-892384)* 511 D Ave., Gwinn, MI 49841 USA (SAN 211-1470) Tel 906-346-3908; Fax: 906-346-3015; Toll Free: 800-722-9925
E-mail: avery@portup.com
Dist(s): **Partners Bk. Distributing, Inc.**
Hale, Robert & Co., Inc.

Avery Goode-Reid Pubs., *(978-0-9766620)* P.O. Box 702, Ormond Beach, FL 32175-0702 USA Tel 386-615-0493
E-mail: marianstomblin@aol.com
Web site: http://www.mariantomblin.com.

Avery's, Tom Totally Tennis, *(978-0-9727444)* 5771 12th Ave., NW, Naples, FL 34119 USA
Web site: http://tomavery.com.

Avian Welfare Coalition, Inc., *(978-0-615-19395-3)* 1923 Ashland Ave., Saint Paul, MN 55104 USA
E-mail: info@avianwelfare.org
Web site: http://www.avianwelfare.org.

Avid Readers Publishing Group, *(978-0-9797106; 978-0-9801438; 978-1-935105; 978-1-61286)* 2802 Belshire Ave., Lakewood, CA 90715 USA Tel 562-243-5918; Toll Free: 888-966-6835
E-mail: arpg@ericpatterson.name
Web site: http://www.avidreaderspg.com.

Avisson Pr., Inc., *(978-1-888105)* Orders Addr.: P.O. Box 38816, Greensboro, NC 27438-8816 USA (SAN 298-8127) Tel 336-288-6989; Fax: 336-288-6989; Edit Addr.: 3007 Taliaferro Rd., Greensboro, NC 27408 USA (SAN 298-8097)
Dist(s): **Follett School Solutions.**

Avista Products, *(978-0-9798741)* 2411 NE Loop 410. Ste. 108, San Antonio, TX 78217-6600 USA
E-mail: cbooker@avistaproducts.com
Web site: http://www.avistaproducts.com.

Avitable Publisher *See* **Avitable Pub.**

Avocus Publishing, Inc., *(978-0-9627671; 978-1-890765)* 4 White Brook Rd., Gilsum, NH 03448 USA (SAN

248-2223) Tel 603-357-0236; Fax: 603-357-2073; Toll Free: 800-345-6665
E-mail: info@avocus.com
Web site: http://www.avocus.com
Dist(s): **Pathway Bk. Service.**

Avon Bks. *Imprint of* **HarperCollins Pubs.**

A.W.A. Gang *Imprint of* **Journey Stone Creations, LLC**

Awa Pr. (NZL) *(978-0-9582509; 978-0-9582538; 978-0-9582629; 978-0-9582750; 978-0-9582916; 978-1-877551; 978-1-927249) Dist. by* **IPG Chicago.**

Awaken Publishing *See* **Now Age Knowledge**

Awaken Specialty Pr., *(978-0-9794713)* P.O. Box 491, Centerton, AR 72719 USA (SAN 853-5248) Tel 479-586-2574
E-mail: celeste@awakenspecialtypress.com
Web site: http://www.awakenspecialtypress.com
Dist(s): **Follett School Solutions.**

Award Pubns. Ltd. (GBR) *(978-0-86163; 978-1-84135; 978-0-9537785; 978-1-904618; 978-1-905503; 978-1-907604; 978-1-906572; 978-1-78270; 978-1-909763) Dist. by* **Parkwest Pubns.**

Awareness Pubns., *(978-0-9744163)* 310-A S. Alu Rd., Wailuku, HI 96793 USA Tel 808-244-3782 Do not confuse with companies with the same name in Greenfield, WI, Santa Maria, CA, Houston, TX, Pocomoke City, MD
E-mail: awarep@mauigateway.com
Web site: http://www.awarenesspublications.org
Dist(s): **New Leaf Distributing Co., Inc.**

Awen Hse. Publishing, *(978-0-9826670)* 8949 Bellcove Cir., Colorado Springs, CO 80920 USA Tel 719-287-7074
E-mail: dunning.rebecca@gmail.com
Web site: http://www.rebeccadunning.com.

Awesome Bk. Publishing, *(978-0-9840538; 978-0-9895194)* P.O. Box 1157, Roseland, FL 32957 USA Tel 321-632-0177.

Awesome Guides, Inc., *(978-0-9703694; 978-0-9723218)* 127 W. Fairbanks Ave., Suite No. 421, Winter Park, FL 32789 USA Fax: 407-678-4337
E-mail: sales@awesomeguides.com; cl@awesomeguides.com
Web site: http://www.awesomeguides.com.

Awe-Struck E-Books, Incorporated *See* **Awe-Struck Publishing**

Awe-Struck Publishing, *(978-1-928670; 978-1-58749)* Div. of Mundania Pr., LLC, 6470a Glenway Ave. #109, Cincinnati, OH 45211 USA (SAN 854-4980); *Imprints*: Byte/Me Teen Book (Byte Me Teen); Earthling Press (Earthling Prss)
E-mail: dan@mundania.com
Web site: http://www.awe-struck.net.

Awkward Labs, *(978-0-615-79808-0)* P.O. Box 398, Felton, DE 19943 USA Tel 302-430-6077
E-mail: wjwalton@yahoo.com.

AWOC.COM, *(978-0-9707507; 978-1-62016)* P.O. Box 2819, Denton, TX 76202 USA
E-mail: editor@awoc.com
Web site: http://www.awoc.com.

A-Works New York, Incorporated *See* **One Peace Bks., Inc.**

Axial Publishing *Imprint of* **Veritas Publishing**

Axiom Hse., *(978-0-9760237)* P.O. Box 2901, Fairfax, VA 22031 USA
E-mail: orders@axiomhouse.com
Web site: http://www.axiomhouse.com/index.htm
Dist(s): **Follett School Solutions.**

Axiom Pr. *Imprint of* **Genesis Communications, Inc.**

Axios Pr., *(978-0-9661908; 978-0-9753662; 978-1-60419)* P.O. Box 118, Mount Jackson, VA 22842 USA Tel 540-984-3829; Fax: 540-984-3843; Toll Free: 888-542-9467 (orders only); 4501 Forbes Blvd., Lanham, MD 20706 Do not confuse with Axios Publishing Corporation, Seattle, WA
E-mail: info@axiosinstitute.org
Web site: http://www.axiosinstitute.org
Dist(s): **Follett School Solutions**
MyiLibrary
National Bk. Network.

Axle Publishing Co., Inc., *(978-0-9755895)* Orders Addr.: P.O. Box 269, Rockdale, TX 76567 USA (SAN 256-3746) Tel 800-866-2685 (Toll-Free); 512-446-0644 (Jody"s Direct Line); Fax: 512-446-2686 Fax Line; Edit Addr.: 1506 O'Kelley Rd., Rockdale, TX 76567 USA Tel 512-446-0644; Toll Free: 800-866-2685
E-mail: jody@axlegalench.com; jody@laid-back.com; roosterrdz@aol.com
Web site: http://www.axlegalench.com; http://www.laid-back.com; http://www.roostermorris.com
Dist(s): **Follett School Solutions.**

Aylen Publishing, *(978-0-9708623; 978-0-9765040; 978-0-9857708; 978-0-9910084; 978-0-9862848)* Subs. of Master Planning Group International, 7830 E. Camelback Re No. 711, Scottsdale, AZ 85251 USA Toll Free: 800-443-1976
Web site: http://www.masterplanninggroup.com; http://www.Aylen.com.

AZ Bks. LLC, *(978-1-61889)* 9330 LBJ Freeway, Dallas, TX 74243 USA Tel 214-438-3922; Fax: 214-561-6795; 245 8Th Ave., #180, New York, NY 10011
E-mail: anastasia.lobynko@az-books.com; support@booksonix.com
Dist(s): **Follett School Solutions.**

AZ Group Publishing House *See* **AZ Bks. LLC**

Azalea Creek Publishing, *(978-0-9677934)* c/o Tom Kendrick, 308 Bloomfield Rd., Sebastopol, CA 95472 USA Tel 707-823-2911 (phone/fax)
E-mail: azalea@sonic.net
Web site: http://www.sonic.net/dragonfly/azaleaforth.html; http://www.sonic.net/dragonfly/adhtml.html; http://southwestdragonflies.net/Order_Form.html; http://southwestdragonflies.net/ColoringBook.html
Dist(s): **American West Bks.**
Bored Feet Pr.
Rio Nuevo Pubs.

Azimuth Pr., *(978-0-9632074; 978-1-886218)* 4041 Bowman Blvd., Suite 211, Macon, GA 31210 USA Tel 770-994-9449; Fax: 770-996-6928 Do not confuse with companies with the same or similar name in Alexander, NC, Arnold, MD.

Azoka Co., The, *(978-0-9745560)* P.O. Box Box 323, Greenland, NH 03885 USA Tel 603-772-0181; Fax: 603-772-0550
Web site: http://www.seacoastcenter.com.

Azreal Publishing Co., *(978-0-9755566)* Orders Addr.: P.O. Box 21139, Tallahassee, FL 32312 USA; Edit Addr.: 1937 Saxon St., Tallahassee, FL 32310 USA
Web site: http://.

Azrec Book Publishing *See* **Aztec Bk. Publishing**

Azro Pr., Inc., *(978-0-9660239; 978-1-929115)* Orders Addr.: 1704 Llano St., Suite B, PMB 342, Sante Fe, NM 87505 USA Tel 505-989-3272; Fax: 505-989-3832
E-mail: books@azropress.com
Web site: http://www.azropress.com
Dist(s): **Follett School Solutions.**

Aztec 5 Publishing, *(978-0-9769478)* Orders Addr.: P.O. Box 11693, Glendale, AZ 85318 USA Tel 623-537-4567 (phone/fax)
E-mail: aztec5publishing@aol.com.

Aztec Bk. Publishing, *(978-0-9787674; 978-0-9801258; 978-0-9838916; 978-0-9905293)* 1606 Delaware Ave., Wilmington, DE 19806 USA Tel 302-575-1993; Fax: 302-575-1977
Web site: http://www.azteccopies.com.

Aztex Corp., *(978-0-89404)* P.O. Box 50046, Tucson, AZ 85703-1046 USA (SAN 210-0371) Tel 520-882-4656; Fax: 520-792-8501
E-mail: ac@aztexcorp.com
Web site: http://www.aztexcorp.com.

AZTexts Publishing, Inc., *(978-0-9677292)* P.O. Box 93487, Phoenix, AZ 85070-3487 USA Tel 480-283-0994 (phone/fax); 1043 E. Amberwood Dr., Phoenix, AZ 85048
E-mail: aztexts@cox.net
Web site: http://FrecklesFriends.org; http://www.aztexts.com
Dist(s): **Quality Bks., Inc.**

Azure Communications, *(978-0-9618741)* Orders Addr.: P.O. Box 23387, New Orleans, LA 70183 USA (SAN 668-7695); Edit Addr.: 37383 Overland Trail, Prairieville, LA 70769 USA (SAN 668-7709) Tel 225-744-4094
E-mail: gszczurek@eatel.net.

Azure Eyes Publishing, *(978-0-9769923; 978-0-9795588)* 7520 E. Second St., Suite 5, Scottsdale, AZ 85251 USA Tel 480-941-8202
E-mail: vickie@mullinscreative.com
Web site: http://www.IWantYouToKnowMe.com
Dist(s): **Follett School Solutions**
eBookIt.com.

Azuria Bks., *(978-0-9796444)* P.O. Box 535, Clyde, NC 28721 USA Tel 828-627-9685
E-mail: timbramlett@charter.net.

B & B Educational Advancement & Pubns., Inc., *(978-1-937065)* 1407 Ford St., Golden, CO 80401 USA (SAN 860-1801) Tel 303-279-8659; Fax: 303-648-5135
E-mail: lmrpc@aol.com.

B&B Publishing, *(978-1-885813)* 63418 Everett Rd., Coos Bay, OR 97420 USA Tel 541-269-9277 Do not confuse with companies with the same or similar name in Fort Collins, CO, Westminster, CO, Walworth, WI, Greenfield, IN
Dist(s): **Partners/West Book Distributors.**

B & R Samizdat Express, *(978-0-915232; 978-0-931968; 978-1-4553; 978-1-4554)* 33 Gould St., West Roxbury, MA 02132 USA (SAN 207-1037) Tel 617-469-2269
E-mail: seltzer@samizdat.com
Web site: http://www.samizdat.com; http://store.yahoo.com/samizdat
Dist(s): **Smashwords.**

BBY Pubns., *(978-1-885775)* Div. of University of West Alabama, Orders Addr.: P.O. Box 726, Shelbyville, KY 40066-0726 USA Tel 502-633-7013; Univ. Of W. Alabama Sta. 45, Livingston, AL 35470 Tel 205-652-5406
E-mail: randy@bbypublications.com; tpartridge@uwa.edu; tnj@uwa.edu
Web site: http://www.bbypublications.com.

BF Publishing, *(978-0-9653327)* 17503 Brushy River Ct., Houston, TX 77095-6905 USA Tel 281-256-1213 Do not confuse with B.F. Publishing, Huntington Beach, CA
E-mail: BFPub1@aol.com
Dist(s): **Origin Bk. Sales, Inc.**

B F Q Press, Incorporated *See* **TotalRecall Pubns.**

B G R Publishing *See* **EMG Networks**

B.R. Publishing Co., *(978-0-9625593; 978-1-884538)* 1725 Pinebrook Dr., Knoxville, TN 37909 USA Tel 423-691-1990.

B Small Publishing (GBR) *(978-1-874735; 978-1-902915; 978-1-905710; 978-1-908164; 978-1-909767) Dist. by* **IPG Chicago.**

B. T. Brooks, *(978-0-9772282)* Orders Addr.: 7015 Crabapple Ln., Kansas City, MO 64129 USA Tel 816-810-1277; 7015 Crabapple Ln., Kansas City, MO 64129 Tel 816-810-1277
E-mail: btbrookspublish@aol.com.

B V Wespat, *(978-0-9713342; 978-0-9788934; 978-0-9819699)* 1641 N. Memorial Dr., Lancaster, OH 43130 USA
Dist(s): **Brodart Co.**
Partners Bk. Distributing, Inc.

B2Z Publishing, Inc., *(978-0-9712070)* Orders Addr.: P.O. Box 307, Severna Park, MD 21146 USA (SAN 254-1068) Tel 410-431-8890; Fax: 410-431-5236
E-mail: towardcure@aol.com
Web site: http://www.mabcie.com.

B3 Publishing, *(978-0-9767849)* Div. of Dream Believer Factory, Inc., Orders Addr.: P.O. Box 360170, Strongsville, OH 44136 USA; Edit Addr.: 19428 Bennington Dr., Strongsville, OH 44136 USA
E-mail: dbfiest@roadrunner.com.

Babbling Bks., *(978-0-9798609)* 3849 Prado Dr., Sarasota, FL 34235-3528 USA
E-mail: babblingbooks@yahoo.com.

Babel Books, Inc *See* **Divincenzo, Yoselem G.**

Baboosic Enterprises, LLC, *(978-0-9787660)* P.O. Box 6102, Bloomington, IN 47408-9990 USA
Web site: http://www.bunnyrabbitonthemoon.com.

Baby Abuelita Productions, Inc., *(978-0-9788379; 978-0-615-19145-4)* 6619 S. Dixie Hwy. No. 139, Miami, FL 33143 USA (SAN 851-7207) Toll Free: 877-722-8352
E-mail: cfenster@babyabuelita.com
Web site: http://www.babyabuelita.com.

Baby Einstein Co., LLC, The, *(978-1-892309; 978-1-931580)* Subs. of Walt Disney Productions, 1233 Flower St., Glendale, CA 91201 USA Tel 818-544-4842
E-mail: ellen.portantino@disney.com
Web site: http://www.babyeinstein.com
Dist(s): **Disney Publishing Worldwide**
Penton Overseas, Inc.
Right Start, Inc.
Rounder Kids Music Distribution.

Baby Faye Bks. *Imprint of* **Northstar Entertainment Group, LLC**

Baby Music Boom, Inc., *(978-0-9647786)* Orders Addr.: P.O. Box 62188, Minneapolis, MN 55426 USA Tel 612-470-1667; Fax: 612-474-1297; Toll Free: 888-470-1667; Edit Addr.: 19000 Maple Ln., Deephaven, MN 55331 USA
E-mail: babyboomms@aol.com
Web site: http://www.babymusicboom.com.

Baby Professor (Education Kids) *Imprint of* **Speedy Publishing LLC**

Baby Shadows, *(978-0-9744928)* 150 W. 56th St., Suite 4410, New York, NY 10019 USA (SAN 255-6367)
Web site: http://www.babyshadows.com.

Baby Shark Productions, *(978-0-9765125)* 15338 Roberts Ave., Jacksonville, FL 32218-1833 USA Tel 904-751-1564
E-mail: jackbradford90@aol.com
Web site: http://www.gregmoutafis.com.

Baby Tattoo Bks., *(978-0-9729388; 978-0-9778949; 978-0-9793307; 978-0-9845210; 978-1-61404)* 6045 Longridge Ave., Van Nuys, CA 91401 USA (SAN 255-2159) Tel 818-416-5314
E-mail: info@babytatto.com
Web site: http://www.babytattoo.com
Dist(s): **SCB Distributors.**

Bacchus Bks., *(978-0-9717952)* Div. of Petmida, Incorporated, P.O. Box 1801, Pacific Palisades, CA 90272 USA Fax: 310-459-4233; Toll Free: 877-604-6522
E-mail: customerservice@domdeluise.com
Web site: http://www.domdeluise.com
Dist(s): **AtlasBooks Distribution.**

Back Bay Bks. *Imprint of* **Little Brown & Co.**

Back Channel Pr., *(978-0-9767590; 978-0-9789546; 978-1-934582)* 170 Mechanic St., Portsmouth, NH 03801 USA Tel 603-436-9485
E-mail: ngstudio@comcast.net
Web site: http://www.nancygrossmanbooks.com
Dist(s): **Lightning Source, Inc.**

Back Home Industries, *(978-1-880045)* Orders Addr.: P.O. Box 22495, Milwaukie, OR 97269 USA Tel 503-654-2300; Fax: 503-659-9351; Edit Addr.: 8431 SE 36th Ave., Portland, OR 97222 USA
E-mail: backhome@integrity.com
Web site: http://webs.integrity.com/backhome.

Back In THE BRONX, *(978-0-9657221)* Orders Addr.: P.O. Box 141H, Scarsdale, NY 10583 USA Tel 914-592-1647; Fax: 914-592-4893; Toll Free: 800-727-6695; Edit Addr.: 40 Herkimer Rd., Scarsdale, NY 10583 USA
E-mail: info@backinthebronx.com
Web site: http://www.backinthebronx.com.

Back River Company, The, LLC, *(978-0-9672882)* 238 Robinson St. # 13, Wakefield, RI 02879-3549 USA.

Back Yard Pub., *(978-0-9707560; 978-1-931934)* Div. of Wensel Enterprises, 7720 N. Moonwind Terr., Dunnellon, FL 34433 USA Tel 352-795-0844; Fax: 352-795-0813
E-mail: wwensel@backyardpublisher.com; wwensel@hughes.net; wensel@hughes.net
Web site: http://www.backyardpublisher.com.

Back2Life, Inc., *(978-0-9760151)* 8608 N. Richmond Ave., 1st Flr., Kansas City, MO 64157 USA Tel 816-835-4477; Fax: 816-891-7789
E-mail: ckehoe@back2life.us
Web site: http://www.back2life.us.

Back2Life Ministries *See* **Back2Life, Inc.**

Backinprint.com *Imprint of* **iUniverse, Inc.**

Backintyme *Imprint of* **Backintyme Publishing**

Backintyme Publishing, *(978-0-939479)* 1341 Grapevine Rd., Crofton, KY 42217 USA (SAN 663-2726) Tel 270-985-8568; *Imprints*: Backintyme (Backintyme FL)
E-mail: backintyme@mehrapublishing.com
Web site: http://www.backintyme.biz.

Backpack Bowie *See* **Educational Expertise, LLC**

Backpack Pubs., *(978-0-9854439)* P.O. Box 1156, Hermitage, PA 16148 USA Tel 724-346-4636; Fax: 724-346-2007
E-mail: rbs@elink123.net
Web site: www.backpackpublishers.com.

Backroads Pr., *(978-0-9642371; 978-0-9724033)* Orders Addr.: P.O. Box 651, Mooresville, IN 46158 USA Tel 317-831-2815 (phone/fax); Edit Addr.: 452 Tulip Dr., Mooresville, IN 46158 USA
E-mail: wend@iquest.net
Web site: http://www.publishershomepages.com/php/Backroads_Press.

Backwaters Pr., The, *(978-0-9677149; 978-0-9726187; 978-0-9765231; 978-0-9785782; 978-0-9793934; 978-0-9816936; 978-1-935218)* 3502 N. 52nd St., Omaha, NE 68104-3506 USA Tel 402-451-4052
E-mail: thebackwaterspress@gmail.com
Web site: http://www.thebackwaterspress.org
Dist(s): **SPD-Small Pr. Distribution.**

Backwoods Publishing Co., *(978-0-9722501)* Rte. 1, Box 270, Boswell, OK 74727 USA Do not confuse with Backwoods Publishing in Logan, OH.

Backyard Ambassador Reader Publishing Co., *(978-0-9793808)* 2 New Grant Ct., Columbia, SC 29209 USA
E-mail: caroline.bennett@att.com
Web site: http://www.bareader.com.

Backyard Scientist, Inc., *(978-0-9618663; 978-1-888427)* P.O. Box 16966, Irvine, CA 92623 USA (SAN 219-1725) Tel 714-551-2392; Fax: 714-552-5351
E-mail: backyrdsci@aol.com.

Bad Frog Art/SMG Bks, *(978-0-9795361)* Orders Addr.: 14931 251st Pl. SE, Issaquah, WA 98027 USA
E-mail: steve@stevegritton.info
Web site: www.stevegritton.info.

Bad Publishing, *(978-0-9765414)* 21522 5th Pl. S., DeMoines, WA 98198 USA Tel 206-824-6106
E-mail: edwardhl@hsd401.org.

Badalamenti, Andrew, *(978-0-615-25180-6)* 206 Franklin Rd., Denville, NJ 07834 USA
Dist(s): **Lulu Enterprises Inc.**

BadCoaches, Incorporated *See* **Tony Franklin Cos., The**

Badgerland Bks. LLC, *(978-0-9765510)* Orders Addr.: 5407 Marsh Woods Dr., McFarland, WI 53558 USA
E-mail: sales@badgerlandbooks.com; joe_martino@uwbucky.com
Web site: http://www.badgerlandbooks.com; http://www.uwbucky.com
Dist(s): **Follett School Solutions.**

Badi Publishing Corporation *See* **Changing-Times.net**

Badiru, Adedeji, *(978-0-9768100)* P.O. Box 341441, Beavercreek, OH 45434 USA
E-mail: deji@badiru.com
Web site: abicspublications.com.

Baen Bks., *(978-0-671; 978-1-55594; 978-0-7434)* Orders Addr.: c/o Simon & Schuster, 200 Old Tappan Rd., Old Tappan, NJ 07675 USA Fax: 800-445-6991; Toll Free: 800-223-2336; Edit Addr.: c/o Simon & Schuster, 1230 Ave. of the Americas, New York, NY 10020 USA (SAN 658-8417) Tel 212-698-7000; Toll Free: 800-223-2348 (customer service)
Web site: http://www.simonsays.com/
Dist(s): **Diamond Comic Distributors, Inc.**
Diamond Bk. Distributors
Simon & Schuster
Simon & Schuster, Inc.

Baha'i Publishing, *(978-1-931847; 978-1-61851)* Orders Addr.: 2427 Bond St., University Park, IL 60466-3101 USA Toll Free Fax: 800-705-4923; Toll Free: 800-705-4925; Edit Addr.: 415 Linden Ave., Wilmete, IL 60091-2886 USA Tel 847-425-7950; Fax: 847-425-7951
Web site: http://www.bahaibooksusa.com/
Dist(s): **Follett School Solutions.**

Baha'i Publishing Trust, U.S., *(978-0-87743)* 415 Linden Ave., Wilmette, IL 60091 USA
Dist(s): **Baha'i Distribution Service.**

BaHar Publishing, L.C., *(978-0-9718939; 978-0-9818219; 978-0-9837742)* 1429 Commercial St., Waterloo, IA 50702 USA Toll Free: 888-600-6033
E-mail: chaveevahdread@yahoo.com
Web site: http://www.baharpublishing.com.

BaHart Pubns. / Eight Legs Publishing, *(978-0-9760348)* PMB 70, PO Box 7000, Rolling Hills Estates, CA 90274 USA
E-mail: octopusrex@earthlink.net
Web site: http://www.octopusrex.com.

Bailey, Martha, *(978-0-9786448)* 6882 S. Peaceful Hills Rd., Morrison, CO 80465 USA Tel 303-697-4591 (phone/fax)
E-mail: nebjr@earthlink.net.

Bailiwick Pr., *(978-1-934649)* 3836 Tradition St., Fort Collins, CO 80526-3107 USA; 250 W. 57Th St. 15Th Flr., New York, NY 10016
Web site: http://bailiwickpress.com
Dist(s): **Follett School Solutions**
Independent Pubs. Group
Legato Pubs. Group
MyiLibrary
Perseus-PGW
ebrary, Inc.

Baker Academic, *(978-0-8010)* Div. of Baker Publishing Group, Orders Addr.: P.O. Box 6287, Grand Rapids, MI 49516-6287 USA Toll Free Fax: 800-398-3111 (orders only); Toll Free: 800-877-2665 (orders only); Edit Addr.: 6030 Fulton Ave., Ada, MI 49301 USA Tel 616-676-9185; Fax: 616-676-9573
Web site: http://www.bakerpublishinggroup.com
Dist(s): **Baker Publishing Group**
ebrary, Inc.

Baker & Taylor Bks., *(978-0-8480; 978-1-222; 978-1-223)* Orders Addr.: Commerce Service Ctr., 251 Mt. Olive Church Rd., Commerce, GA 30599 USA (SAN 169-1503) Tel 404-335-5000; Toll Free: 800-775-1200 (customer service); 800-775-1800 (orders); Reno Service Ctr., 1160 Trademark Dr., Suite 111, Reno, NV 89511 (SAN 169-4464) Tel 775-850-3800; Fax: 775-850-3826 (customer service); Toll Free Fax: 800-775-1700 (orders); Edit Addr.: Bridgewater Service Ctr. 1120 US Hwy. 22, E., Bridgewater, NJ 08807 USA (SAN 169-4901) Toll Free: 800-775-1500 (customer service); Momence Service Ctr., 501W. Gladiolus St.,

Momence, IL 60954-1799 (SAN 169-2100) Tel 815-472-2444 (international customers); Fax: 815-472-9886 (international customers); Toll Free: 800-775-2300 (customer service, academic libraries)
E-mail: btinfo@btol.com
Web site: http://www.btol.com.

Baker & Taylor Publishing Group, *(978-0-934429; 978-1-57145; 978-1-59223; 978-1-60710; 978-1-62686)* Div. of Baker & Taylor Bks., 10350 Barnes Canyon Rd. Suite 100, San Diego, CA 92121 USA (SAN 630-8090) Toll Free: 800-284-3580; *Imprints:* Thunder Bay Press (Thunder Bay); Silver Dolphin Books (Silver Dolph); Portable Press (Portable Pr)
Web site: http://www.silverdolphinbooks.com; http://www.baker-taylorpublishing.com; http://www.thunderbaybooks.com/; http://www.bathroomreader.com; http://www.baker-taylor.com
Dist(s): **Learning Connection, The**
MyiLibrary
Perseus-PGW
Perseus Bks. Group.

Baker Book House, Incorporated *See* **Baker Publishing Group**

Baker Bks., *(978-0-8010; 978-0-913686)* Div. of Baker Publishing Group, Orders Addr.: P.O. Box 6287, Grand Rapids, MI 49516-6287 USA (SAN 299-1500) Toll Free Fax: 800-398-3111 (orders only); Toll Free: 800-877-2665 (orders only); Edit Addr.: 6030 E. Fulton, Ada, MI 49301 USA (SAN 201-4041) Tel 616-676-9185; Fax: 616-676-9573
Web site: http://www.bakerpublishinggroup.com
Dist(s): **Baker Publishing Group**
Follett School Solutions
Twentieth Century Christian Bks.
ebrary, Inc.

Baker College Publishing Co., *(978-1-885545)* Div. of Baker College, 1050 W. Bristol Rd., Flint, MI 48507 USA Toll Free: 800-339-9879
Dist(s): **Follett School Solutions.**

Baker, Helen Interiors, Inc., *(978-0-9743511)* Orders Addr.: P.O. Box 367, West Harwich, MA 02671 USA Tel 508-432-0287; Fax: 508-430-7744; Edit Addr.: 94 Main St., West Harwich, MA 02671 USA
E-mail: hbunce@attbi.com
Web site: http://www.shoppingthecape.com.

Baker Publishing Group, *(978-0-8007; 978-0-8010; 978-1-58743; 978-1-4412; 978-1-4934; 978-1-68196)* Orders Addr.: P.O. Box 6287, Grand Rapids, MI 49516-6287 USA Tel 616-676-9573; Toll Free Fax: 800-398-3111 (orders only); Toll Free: 800-877-2665 (orders only); Edit Addr.: 6030 E. Fulton, Ada, MI 49301 USA Tel 616-676-9185; Fax: 616-676-9573; Toll Free Fax: 800-398-3111; Toll Free: 800-877-2665
E-mail: webmaster@bakerpublishinggroup.com
Web site: http://www.bakerbooks.com; http://www.bakerpublishinggroup.com
Dist(s): **Follett School Solutions**
Twentieth Century Christian Bks.
christianaudio
ebrary, Inc.

Baker Trittin Concepts *See* **Baker Trittin Pr.**

Baker Trittin Pr., *(978-0-9729256; 978-0-9752880; 978-0-9787316; 978-0-9814893)* P.O. Box 277, Winona Lake, IN 46590-0277 USA Fax: 574-269-6100; Toll Free: 1-888-741-4386; *Imprints:* Innovative Christian Publications (Innov Chris Pubns); Tweener Press (Tweener Pr)
E-mail: paul@btconcepts.com
Web site: http://www.bakertrittinpress.com; http://www.gospelstoryteller.com.

Baker, Walter H. Company *See* **Baker's Plays**

Baker's Plays, *(978-0-87440)* Div. of Samuel French, Inc., 45 W. 25th St., New York, NY 10010 USA (SAN 202-3717) Tel 212-255-8085; Fax: 212-627-7754
E-mail: info@bakersplays.com
Web site: http://www.bakersplays.com.

Balaam Books LLC, *(978-0-9785585)* 1825 W. Ave., Unit 11, Miami Beach, FL 33139-1441 USA (SAN 850-9972) Tel 305-531-9351; Fax: 305-531-9348
E-mail: Info@BalaamBooks.com
Web site: http://www.BalaamBooks.com.

Balance Bks., Inc., *(978-0-9743908)* P.O. Box 86, Des Plaines, IL 60016-0086 USA
Web site: http://www.balance-books.com
Dist(s): **Distributors, The.**

Balanced Families, *(978-0-9759468)* 432 N. 750 E., Lindon, UT 84042 USA Tel 801-380-3247; Fax: 801-785-3938
E-mail: info@starsofthesky.com.

Balanced Systems, Inc., *(978-0-9760037)* 995 Artdale, White Lake, MI 48383 USA.

Balboa Pr. *Imprint of* **Author Solutions, Inc.**

Balboa Pr., Div. of Hay House, Inc., 1663 Liberty Dr., Bloomington, IN 47403 USA Tel 877-407-4847
E-mail: customersupport@balboapress.com
Web site: http://www.balboapress.com
Dist(s): **Author Solutions, Inc.**
Zondervan.

Balcony 7 Media and Publishing, *(978-0-9855453; 978-1-939454)* Orders Addr.: 133 E. De La Guerra St., No. 177, Santa Barbara, CA 93101 USA (SAN 920-3877) Tel 805-679-1821; *Imprints:* Salty Splashes Collection (Salty Splashes)
E-mail: balcony7@icloud.com; randy@balcony7.com
Web site: www.balcony7.com; www.balcony7.com
Dist(s): **Follett School Solutions**
Ingram Pub. Services
MyiLibrary.

Baldner, Jean V., *(978-0-9615317)* 1618 Burnett Ave., Ames, IA 50010-5337 USA (SAN 694-6526).

Baldwin, Christopher John, *(978-1-938384)* P.O. Box 1141, Northhampton, MA 01061 USA Tel 360-705-2742
E-mail: chrisjohnbaldwin@gmail.com.

Balhund Entertainment, LLC, *(978-0-9743277)* 3018 Paulcrest Dr., Los Angeles, CA 90046 USA Tel 323-848-8778
Web site: http://www.magusgame.com.

Baliko, Janelle A., *(978-0-9799012)* 45486 Locust Grove Dr., Valley Lee, MD 20692-3217 USA
E-mail: itdoesnthavetobepink@yahoo.com
Web site: http://www.itdoesnthavetobepink.com.

Ball, Michael, *(978-0-9765750)* 2000 Bradley Ln., Russellville, AR 72801-4627 USA.

Ball Publishing, *(978-0-9626796; 978-1-883052)* Orders Addr.: P.O. Box 9, Batavia, IL 60510-0009 USA Tel 630-208-9080; Fax: 630-208-9350; Toll Free Fax: 888-888-0014; Toll Free: 888-888-0013 (U.S. & Canada only); Edit Addr.: P.O. Box 1660, West Chicago, IL 60186-1660 USA
E-mail: info@ballpublishing.com
Web site: http://www.ballbookshelf.com
Dist(s): **Independent Pubs. Group.**

Ball, Rulon Jay *See* **JBall Publishing**

Ballad Productions, *(978-0-9753663)* Orders Addr.: P.O. Box 4, North Miami Beach, FL 33164 USA Tel 786-285-3619; Edit Addr.: 163rd St., Suite No. 4, North Miami Beach, FL 33164 USA
E-mail: drlaz770@aol.com
Web site: http://www.drlaz.com.

Ballantine Bks. *Imprint of* **Random House Publishing Group**

Ballantine, Robert *See* **P.F.B. Publishing**

Ballard & Tighe Pubs., *(978-0-937270; 978-1-55501; 978-1-59989)* Div. of Educational Ideas, Inc., 471 Atlas St., Brea, CA 92821 USA (SAN 200-7991) Tel 714-990-4332; Fax: 714-255-9828; Toll Free: 800-321-4332
Web site: http://www.ballard-tighe.com.

Ballard, Donald W., *(978-0-9768779)* Orders Addr.: 37823 Menard Ct., Fremont, CA 94536 USA Toll Free: 800-506-7401
E-mail: donballard@comcast.net
Web site: http://www.magicalhotel.com.

BalletMet Dance Centre, *(978-0-692-01667-1)* 322 Mount Vernon Ave., Columbus, OH 43235 USA Tel 614-586-8635
E-mail: education@balletmet.org
Web site: http://www.balletmet.org
Dist(s): **BookMasters.**

Ballinger Printing & Graphics, *(978-0-9754957; 978-0-615-20730-8)* 906 Hutchings Ave., Ballinger, TX 76821 USA Tel 325-365-8206; Fax: 325-365-2209; Toll Free: 888-915-8206
E-mail: michael.o.white@att.net; ballingerprinting@verizon.net
Dist(s): **Publishers Services.**

Balloon Bks. *Imprint of* **Sterling Publishing Co., Inc.**

Balloon Magic, *(978-1-931084)* 928 W. 20 N., Orem, UT 84057-1918 USA; *Imprints:* Penny's Publishing (Pennys Pubng)
E-mail: mlh@balloonmagic.com
Web site: http://www.balloonmagic.com.

Ballybunnion Bks., *(978-0-9726340)* Orders Addr.: P.O. Box 6357, Virginia Beach, VA 23456 USA; Edit Addr.: 833 Maitland Dr., Virginia Beach, VA 23454 USA
E-mail: brian@wbrianmurphy.com
Web site: http://www.warrenmurphy.com.

Ballyhoo Books *See* **Ballyhoo BookWorks, Inc.**

Ballyhoo BookWorks, Inc., *(978-0-936335)* Orders Addr.: P.O. Box 534, Shoreham, NY 11786 USA (SAN 697-8487); Edit Addr.: 1 Sylvan Dr., Wading River, NY 11792 USA (SAN 698-2239) Tel 631-929-8148
E-mail: ballyhoo@optonline.net.

Ballyhoo Printing, *(978-0-9742792; 978-0-9800580)* 187 W. Frontage Rd., Lewistown, MT 59457 USA Tel 406-538-7988
E-mail: ballyhoo@ballyhooprinting.com
Web site: http://www.ballyhooprinting.com.

Balona Bks., *(978-0-9765479; 978-1-934376)* P.O. Box 690106, Stockton, CA 95269-0106 USA
E-mail: author@balona.com; jonathan@balona.com
Web site: http://www.balona.com.

Balticbard Publishing *Imprint of* **Leyva, Barbara**

Balue Fox Publishing Company *See* **McWilliams Mediation Group Ltd.**

Balzer & Bray *Imprint of* **HarperCollins Pubs.**

Bamboo River Pr., *(978-0-9798173)* 12565 SE Callahan Rd., Portland, OR 97086-9708 USA (SAN 854-4484) Tel 503-761-4360
Web site: http://www.bambooriverpress.com.

Bamboo Zoo, LLC, *(978-0-9774493)* 1637 Dahlia St., Denver, CO 80220 USA (SAN 257-5965) Tel 720-323-4955
E-mail: kim@bamboo-zoo.com
Web site: http://www.bamboo-zoo.com.

Banana Bunch Publishing, *(978-0-9761763)* 2260 Banana St., Saint James City, FL 33956 USA Tel 239-283-9306.

Banana Oil Bks. *Imprint of* **Cyberwizard Productions**

Banana Patch Pr., *(978-0-9715333; 978-0-9800063)* Orders Addr.: P.O. Box 950, Hanapepe, HI 96716 USA (SAN 254-3087) Tel 808-335-5944; Fax: 808-335-3830; Toll Free: 800-914-5944
E-mail: carolan@aloha.net
Web site: http://www.bananapatchpress.com
Dist(s): **Booklines Hawaii, Ltd.**
Islander Group.

Banana Pr., *(978-0-9799065)* 2935 S. Fish Hatchery Rd., No. 3, Suite 254, Fitchburg, WI 53711 USA Tel 608-658-0023
E-mail: info@bananalady.com
Web site: http://www.bananalady.com.

Bancroft Pr., *(978-0-9631246; 978-0-9635376; 978-1-890862; 978-1-61088)* P.O. Box 65360, Baltimore, MD 21209-9945 USA Tel 410-358-0658; Fax: 410-764-1967; Toll Free: 800-637-7377 Do not confuse with Bancroft Pr., San Rafael, CA
E-mail: bruceb@bancroftpress.com
Web site: http://www.bancroftpress.com
Dist(s): **Academic Bk. Ctr., Inc.**
AtlasBooks Distribution
BookMasters Distribution Services (BDS)
Book Wholesalers, Inc.
Bk. Hse., Inc., The
Brodart Co.
Coutts Information Services
Emery-Pratt Co.
Follett School Solutions
Mackin Library Media
Midwest Library Service
Smashwords
Yankee Bk. Peddler, Inc.

Banda Pr. International, Inc., *(978-0-9773175)* 6050 Stetson Hills Blvd., No. 313, Colorado Springs, CO 80922 USA
Web site: http://www.bandapress.com.

Bandai Entertainment, Inc., *(978-1-58354; 978-1-59409; 978-1-60496)* Div. of Bandai Entertainment, Inc., 5551 Katella Ave., Cypress, CA 90630 USA Tel 714-816-9760; Fax: 714-816-6708; Toll Free: 877-772-6463
Web site: http://www.bandai-ent.com
Dist(s): **Diamond Comic Distributors, Inc.**
Diamond Bk. Distributors
Follett School Solutions.

B&H Bks. *Imprint of* **B&H Publishing Group**

B&H Kids *Imprint of* **B&H Publishing Group**

†B&H Publishing Group, *(978-0-8054; 978-0-87981; 978-1-55819; 978-1-58640; 978-0-8400; 978-1-4336)* Div. of LifeWay Christian Resources of the Southern Baptist Convention, One LifeWay Plaza MSN 114, Nashville, TN 37234-0114 USA (SAN 201-937X) Tel 615-251-2520; Fax: 615-251-5026 (Books Only); 615-251-2036 (Bibles Only); 615-251-2413 (Gifts/Supplies Only); Toll Free: 800-725-5416; 800-251-3225 (retailers); 800-296-4036 (orders/returns); 800-448-8032 (consumers); 800-458-2772 (churches); *Imprints:* Holman Bible Publishers (Holman Bible); B&H Books (B&H Bks.); B&H Kids (B&H Kids)
E-mail: broadmanholman@lifeway.com; heather.counsellor@bhpublishinggroup.com; wes.banks@bhpublishinggroup.com
Web site: http://www.bhpublishinggroup.com
Dist(s): **Follett School Solutions**
christianaudio; *CIP.*

B&J Marketing LLC, *(978-0-9774606)* 17 Robbins Wilks Rd., Bassfield, MS 39421 USA Tel 601-731-2447
E-mail: wastvedt@bellsouth.net.

Bangzoom Pubs., *(978-0-9728646; 978-0-9772927; 978-0-9779099)* Div. of Bangzoom Software, Inc., 14 Storrs Ave., Braintree, MA 02184 USA (SAN 256-6923) Toll Free: 800-589-7333
Web site: http://www.bangzoom.com
Dist(s): **Partners Pubs. Group, Inc.**

Bangzoom Software, Incorporated *See* **Bangzoom Pubs.**

Banis & Associates *See* **Science & Humanities Pr.**

Banks, A J & Associates, Incorporated *See* **BaHar Publishing, L.C.**

Banner of Truth, The, *(978-0-85151)* Orders Addr.: P.O. Box 621, Carlisle, PA 17013 USA Tel 717-249-5747; Fax: 717-249-0604; Toll Free: 800-263-8085; Edit Addr.: 63 E. Louther St., Carlisle, PA 17013 USA (SAN 112-1553)
E-mail: info@banneroftruth.org
Web site: http://www.banneroftruth.co.uk
Dist(s): **Spring Arbor Distributors, Inc.**

Banta, Sandra, *(978-0-9799729)* 16849A Willow Glen Rd., Brownsville, CA 95919 USA Tel 530-675-2010
E-mail: sfbanta@aol.com
Web site: http://www.llionesbooks.com.

Bantam *Imprint of* **Random House Publishing Group**

Bantam Bks. for Young Readers *Imprint of* **Random Hse. Children's Bks.**

Bantam Doubleday Dell Large Print Group, Inc., *(978-0-385)* Orders Addr.: 2451 S. Wolf Rd., Des Plaines, IL 60018 USA Toll Free: 800-323-9872 (orders); 800-258-4233 (EDI ordering); Edit Addr.: 1540 Broadway, New York, NY 10036-4094 USA
Dist(s): **Beeler, Thomas T. Pub.**

Banyan Bks., *(978-0-615-63108-0)* 251 Bethany Farms Dr., Ball Ground, GA 30107 USA Tel 770-315-1244 Do not confuse with Banyan Books in Miami, FL, Santa Barbara, CA
Web site: www.juliekorzenko.com
Dist(s): **CreateSpace Independent Publishing Platform.**

Banyan Hypnosis Center for Training & Services, Inc., *(978-0-9712290)* 1431 Warner Ave. Ste. E, Tustin, CA 92780-6444 USA (SAN 253-9381)
E-mail: Maureen@hypnosiscenter.com.

Banyan Publishing, Incorporated *See* **Banyan Hypnosis Center for Training & Services, Inc.**

Banyon Publishing, Inc., *(978-0-9747960)* 235 W Brandon Blvd., Suite 223, Brandon, FL 33511 USA Fax: 813-243-0701
E-mail: banyonpublishing@aol.com
Web site: http://www.banyonpublishing.com.

Baptist Publishing Hse., *(978-0-89114)* Div. of Baptist Missionary Assn. of America, P.O. Box 7270, Texarkana, TX 75505-7270 USA (SAN 183-6544) Tel 870-772-4550; Fax: 870-772-5451; Toll Free: 800-333-1442
E-mail: info@bph.org; pathway@bph.org
Web site: http://www.bph.org.

Baptist Spanish Publishing Hse./Casa Bautista de Publicaciones: Mundo Hispano, *(978-0-311)* 7000 Alabama St., El Paso, TX 79914 USA (SAN 299-920X) Tel 916-566-9656; Fax: 916-562-6502; Toll Free: 800-755-5958
E-mail: cbpsales1@juno.com
Web site: http://casabautista.org.

Bara Publishing, *(978-0-9842517)* 131 Gilbert Dr., Beaufort, NC 28516 USA Tel 252-838-1803
Dist(s): **AtlasBooks Distribution**
Follett School Solutions
ebrary, Inc.

Barabara Pr., *(978-0-9719097)* 5929 S. Kolmar Ave., Chicago, IL 60629 USA Tel 773-735-1176 (phone/fax)
E-mail: captsma@comcast.net
Web site: http://www.barabarapress.com.

Barach Publishing, *(978-0-9767453)* 900 N. Walnut Creek, Suite 100, No. 280, Mansfield, TX 76063 USA
E-mail: lgonzalez@barachpublishing.com
Web site: http://www.barachpublishing.com.

Baraka Bks. (CAN) *(978-0-9812405; 978-1-926824) Dist. by* **IPG Chicago.**

Barany Publishing, *(978-0-9832960; 978-0-9895004)* 771 Kingston Ave. No. 108, Oakland, CA 94611 USA Tel 510-332-5384
E-mail: BETH@BETHBARANY.COM
Web site: http://www.bethbarany.com
Dist(s): **Smashwords.**

Barbary Coast Books *See* **Gold Street Pr.**

Barbour & Company, Incorporated *See* **Barbour Publishing, Inc.**

Barbour Bks. *Imprint of* **Barbour Publishing, Inc.**

Barbour Publishing, Inc., *(978-0-916441; 978-1-55748; 978-1-57748; 978-1-58660; 978-1-59310; 978-1-59789; 978-1-60260; 978-1-60742; 978-1-61626; 978-1-62029; 978-1-62416; 978-1-62836; 978-1-63058; 978-1-63409)* Orders Addr.: P.O. Box 719, Uhrichsville, OH 44683 USA (SAN 295-7094) Tel 740-922-6045; Fax: 740-922-5948; Toll Free Fax: 800-220-5948; Toll Free: 800-852-8010; *Imprints:* Barbour Books (Barbour Bks); GoTandem (GoTandem)
E-mail: info@barbourbooks.com
Web site: http://www.barbourbooks.com
Dist(s): **Anchor Distributors**
Follett School Solutions
Spring Arbor Distributors, Inc.

Barcelona Pubs., *(978-0-9624080; 978-1-891278; 978-1-937440)* Orders Addr.: C/o Ware-pak 2427 Bond St., University Park, IL 60484 USA (SAN 298-6299) Tel 708-534-2600; Fax: 708-534-7803; Toll Free: 866-620-6943
E-mail: barcelonapublishers@gvtc.com; barcelonapublishers@ware-pak.com
Web site: http://www.barcelonapublishers.com
Dist(s): **MyiLibrary**
Ware-Pak, Inc.
ebrary, Inc.

Barcharts, Inc., *(978-1-57222; 978-1-4232)* 6000 Park of Commerce, Blvd. D, Boca Raton, FL 33487-8230 USA (SAN 299-5026) Tel 561-989-3666 ext.3054; Fax: 561-989-3722; Toll Free: 800-226-7799
E-mail: jmijares@barcharts.com
Web site: http://www.quickstudycharts.com
Dist(s): **Follett School Solutions.**

Bard College Pubns. Office, *(978-0-941276; 978-1-931493; 978-1-936192)* P.O. Box 5000, Annandale-on-Hudson, NY 12504-5000 USA Tel 845-758-7872 (7418); Fax: 845-758-7554; *Imprints:* Center for Curatorial Studies (Ctr Curatorial Studies)
E-mail: admission@bard.edu; info@levy.org
Web site: http://www.levy.org; http://www.bard.edu
Dist(s): **D.A.P./Distributed Art Pubs.**

Bard, Frank, *(978-0-9767098)* Orders Addr.: 3801 Corbett Rd., North Lewisburg, OH 43060-9616 USA Tel 937-869-0235
E-mail: fbard@ctcn.net
Web site: http://www.ctcn.net/~febard.

Bardic Pr., *(978-0-9745667)* P.O. Box 761, Oregon House, CA 95962-0761 USA Tel 539-692-1180
E-mail: info@bardic-press.com; andrew@bardic-press.com
Web site: http://www.bardic-press.com.

Bardin & Marsee Publishing, *(978-0-9770169; 978-0-9792394; 978-0-9840857; 978-1-60969)* 438 Carr Ave Ste 12, Birmingham, AL 35209 USA (SAN 854-6215) Toll Free: 866-846-4338
E-mail: bobby@bardinmarsee.com
Web site: http://www.bardinmarsee.com.

Bare Bones Training & Consulting Company *See* **Straus, Jane**

BareBones Publishing, *(978-0-9779601)* P.O. Box 8, McDonough, NY 13801 USA
Web site: http://www.dustinwarburton.com; http://www.bonfed.com; http://www.BareBonespublishing.com
Dist(s): **BCH Fulfillment & Distribution.**

Barefoot Bks., Inc., *(978-1-84148; 978-1-898000; 978-1-901223; 978-1-902283; 978-1-905236; 978-1-84686)* Orders Addr.: 2067 Mass Ave., 5th Fl., Cambridge, MA 02140 USA Tel 866-417-2369; Fax: 888-346-9138
E-mail: ussales@barefootbooks.com
Web site: http://www.barefootbooks.com
Dist(s): **Banta Packaging & Fulfillment.**

Barefoot Pr., *(978-1-882133)* Orders Addr.: P.O. Box 28514, Raleigh, NC 27611 USA (SAN 248-5656) Tel 919-834-1164; Edit Addr.: 700 W. Morgan St., Raleigh, NC 27603 USA (SAN 248-5664).

Barker, Lesley, *(978-0-9763211)* 1630 Rathford Dr., Saint Louis, MO 63146-3911 USA
E-mail: asklesley@teamlesley.com
Web site: http://www.teamlesley.com.

Barmarie Pubns., *(978-0-9619463)* 735 Nardo Rd., Encinitas, CA 92024 USA (SAN 245-0070) Tel 760-753-6950.

Barn Owl Bks, London (GBR) *(978-1-903015) Dist. by* **IPG Chicago.**

Publisher Name Index

Barnaby & Co., *(978-0-9642836; 978-0-615-74648-7)* 30 W. Chester St., Nantucket, MA 02554 USA Tel 508-901-1793
E-mail: barnaby@nantucket.net.

Barnaby Bks., Inc., *(978-0-940350)* 3290 Pacific Heights Rd., Honolulu, HI 96813 USA (SAN 217-5010) Fax: 808-531-0089
E-mail: barnaby@lava.net; publisher@barnabybooks.com
Web site: http://www.barnabybooks.com
Dist(s): **Bess Pr., Inc.**

Barnes & Noble Bks.-Imports, *(978-0-389)* 4720 Boston Way, Lanham, MD 20706 USA (SAN 206-7803) Tel 301-459-3366; Toll Free: 800-462-6420
Dist(s): **Rowman & Littlefield Publishers, Inc.**

Barnes & Noble, Inc., *(978-0-7607; 978-0-88029; 978-1-4028; 978-1-4114; 978-1-4351; 978-1-61551; 978-1-61552; 978-1-61553; 978-1-61554; 978-1-61555; 978-1-61556; 978-1-61557; 978-1-61558; 978-1-61559; 978-1-61560; 978-1-61679; 978-1-61680; 978-1-61681; 978-1-61682; 978-1-61683; 978-1-61684; 978-1-61685; 978-1-61686; 978-1-61687; 978-1-61688) 76 Ninth Ave., 9th Flr., New York, NY 10011 USA (SAN 141-3651) Tel 212-414-6385; Imprints:* SparkNotes (SparkNotes)
E-mail: smcculloch@bn.com
Dist(s): **Bookazine Co., Inc.**
Sterling Publishing Co., Inc.

Barnes Printing, *(978-0-9658838; 978-0-9863483)* 1076 Klopman Mill Rd., Denton, NC 27239-7305 USA Tel 336-859-1964; Fax: 336-859-4923
E-mail: elizabeth@barnesprinting.com
Web site: www.barnesprinting.com.

Barnesyard Bks., *(978-0-9674681)* P.O. Box 254, Sergeantsville, NJ 08557 USA Tel 609-397-6600; Fax: 609-397-3262
E-mail: info@barnesyardbooks.com
Web site: http://www.barnesyardbooks.com
Dist(s): **Follett School Solutions.**

Barnette, Donald, *(978-0-9747816)* 591 Mira Vista Ave., Oakland, CA 94610-1928 USA.

Barnhardt & Ashe Publishing, Inc., *(978-0-9715402; 978-0-9801744)* 444 Brickell Ave., Suite 51, PMB 432, Miami, FL 33131 USA Toll Free: 800-283-6360
E-mail: barnhardtashe@aol.com
Web site: http://www.barnhardtashepublishing.com.

Barranca Pr., *(978-1-939604)* 1450 Couse St. (No. 10), Taos, NM 87571 USA Tel 575-613-1026
E-mail: lisa@barrancapress.com
Web site: www.barrancapress.com.

Barren Hill Bks., *(978-0-9769896)* 646 Highland Ave., South Portland, ME 04106 USA Tel 207-767-3268
E-mail: info@BarrenHillBooks.com
Web site: http://www.barrenhillbooks.com/.

Barrett's Bookshelf, *(978-0-9728731)* 16165 SW Inverurie Rd., Lake Oswego, OR 97035 USA Tel 503-697-4208.

Barricks, Jeri Ministry, *(978-0-9743512)* P.O. Box 347, Buffalo, NY 14225 USA Fax: 716-685-6839
E-mail: jeribar37@hotmail.com
Web site: http://www.jeribarricks.net.

Barringer Publishing, *(978-0-9825109; 978-0-9828425; 978-0-9831989; 978-0-9833088; 978-0-9839050; 978-0-9851184; 978-0-9882034; 978-0-9891694; 978-0-9896338; 978-0-9903935; 978-0-9908209; 978-0-9961973)* 2317 Harrier Run, Naples, FL 34105 USA
Web site: barringerpublishing.com
Dist(s): **Follett School Solutions.**

†Barron's Educational Series, Inc., *(978-0-7641; 978-0-8120; 978-1-4380)* Orders Addr.: 250 Wireless Blvd., Hauppauge, NY 11788-3917 USA (SAN 201-453X) Fax: 631-434-3723; 631-434-8067 (Sales Dept. Orders); Toll Free: 800-645-3476 (ext. 204 or 214 for Orders); a/o Georgetown Book Warehouse, 34 Armstrong Ave., Georgetown, ON L7G 4R9 (SAN 115-2033) Tel 905-458-5506; Fax: 905-877-5575; Toll Free Fax: 800-887-1594 Do not confuse with BARRONS, Monroe, WA
E-mail: barrons@barronseduc.com; info@barronseduc.com; orders@barronseduc.com; clopez@barronseduc.com
Web site: http://www.barronseduc.com
Dist(s): **Ebsco Publishing**
Follett School Solutions; *CIP.*

Barrow, Shelley *See* **Mlkenzi's Kardz & Bks. Llc.**

†Barrytown/Station Hill Pr., *(978-0-88268; 978-0-930794; 978-1-58177; 978-1-886449)* 120 Station Hill Rd., Barrytown, NY 12507 USA (SAN 214-1485) Tel 845-758-5293; Fax: 845-758-9838
E-mail: publishers@stationhill.org
Web site: http://www.stationhill.org/
Dist(s): **Midpoint Trade Bks., Inc.**
Redwing Bk. Co.
SPD-Small Pr. Distribution; *CIP.*

Barsotti Bks., *(978-0-9642112; 978-0-9818188)* 2239 Hidden Valley Ln., Camino, CA 95709-9722 USA Tel 530-642-8341; Fax: 530-642-9703
E-mail: jb@barsottibooks.com
Web site: http://www.barsottibooks.com.

Bartleby Pr., *(978-0-910155; 978-0-935437)* 8600 Foundry St. Savage Mill Box 2043, Savage, MD 20763 USA (SAN 241-2098) Tel 301-949-2443; Fax: 301-949-2205; Toll Free: 800-953-9929
E-mail: Inquiries@bartlebythepublisher.com
Web site: http://www.BartlebythePublisher.com
Dist(s): **Casemate Pubs. & Bk. Distributors, LLC**
MyiLibrary.

Barton Bks., *(978-0-615-69695-9; 978-0-615-78343-7)* Orders Addr.: 4505 Sentinel Ct., Rocklin, CA 95677 USA Tel 916-787-0962; *Imprints:* Flickerfawn (Flickerfawn)
E-mail: dredsovm@me.com; dredsovm@wavecable.com
Web site: http://www.flickerfawn.com; www.FionaThornBook.com; www.jbartonbooks.com.

Barton, D.C. Publishing, *(978-0-9759426)* P.O. Box 3057, Lakeland, FL 33801-6602 USA Tel 863-665-5986
E-mail: dfcbible@aol.com.

Barton Publications, *(978-0-9778455)* Orders Addr.: 1613 Sunrise Ln., Eau Claire, WI 54703-2574 USA
E-mail: bartonpub@ymail.com
Web site: http://www.westmusic.com/1002410-print-music-books/m1090-music-therapy-books/m1090i-texts/biomedical-foundations-of-music-as-therapy-838708.htm
Dist(s): **West Music Co.**

Bas Relief, LLC, *(978-0-9657472)* Orders Addr.: P.O. Box 645, Union, WV 24983 USA Tel 304-832-6647
E-mail: Barea@basrelief.org
Web site: http://www.basrelief.org
Dist(s): **Follett School Solutions.**

Bas Relief Publishing *See* **Bas Relief, LLC**

Bascom Hill Bks. *Imprint of* **Hillcrest Publishing Group, Inc.**

Bases Loaded Bks. *Imprint of* **ChildrenzBks.**

Basic Black Publishing, *(978-0-9801320)* Orders Addr.: 8584 W. Appleton Ave., Unit X, Milwaukee, WI 53225 USA.

Basic Distribution, Inc., 360 Hurst St., Linden, NJ 07036 USA Tel 908-523-0555; Fax: 908-523-0373
E-mail: ssullivan@basicdistributioninc.com
Web site: http://www.basicdistributioninc.com.

Basic Health Pubns., Inc., *(978-1-59120)* 28812 Top of the World Dr., Laguna Beach, CA 92651 USA (SAN 858-4893) Tel 949-715-7327; Fax: 949-415-7328; Toll Free: 800-575-8890 (orders only)
E-mail: ngoldfind@basicmediagroup.com
Web site: http://www.basichealthpub.com
Dist(s): **Follett School Solutions.**

Basic Knowledge Publishing Co., *(978-1-885501)* 1024 Debbie Ln., Maryville, MO 64468 USA Tel 816-562-2665.

Basic Skills Assessment & Educational Services, *(978-1-888786)* 19146 S. Molalla Ave., Oregon City, OR 97045-8975 USA Tel 503-650-5282; Fax: 503-557-2953
E-mail: basicsk@MSN.COM
Web site: http://www.basicskills.net.

Basketball Fundamentals *See* **SportAmerica**

Bass Cove Bks., *(978-0-9630074)* 57 North St., Kennebunkport, ME 04046 USA Tel 207-967-4152
E-mail: amabee@adelphia.net.

Bass, Sheila, *(978-0-9766366)* 23 Conn. St., Woodsville, NH 03785 USA
E-mail: a_15bass@yahoo.com.

Bassan, Malca, *(978-0-9744039; 978-0-692-25535-3)* 9801 Collins Ave., Apt. 15Q, Bal Harbor, FL 33154 USA Tel 305-868-0365; Fax: 305-865-6992
E-mail: mabassan27@gmail.com.

Bastion Pr., Inc., *(978-0-9714392; 978-1-59263)* Orders Addr.: P.O. Box 46753, Seattle, WA 98146 USA; Edit Addr.: 8405 16th Ave., SW, Seattle, WA 98106-2365 USA Tel 206-763-3368; Fax: 206-763-3370 Do not confuse with Bastion Pr., Los Angeles, CA
E-mail: jim@bastionpress.com
Web site: http://www.bastionpress.com
Dist(s): **Studio 2 Publishing, Inc.**

Bat Wing Pr *Imprint of* **Harbor Hse.**

Bat-El Publishing, *(978-0-9832025)* 3400 Colville Pl., Encino, CA 91436 USA Tel 818-461-9294
E-mail: talyanai7@gmail.com.

Batelier Publishing, *(978-0-9789429)* 3140 Bourbon St. Cir., Rockwall, TX 75032 USA
E-mail: batelierpublishing@yahoo.com
Web site: http://www.batelier.bravehost.com.

Batfish Bks., *(978-0-9728653)* Div. of O'Neill, Michael P. Photography, Inc., P.O. Box 32909, Palm Beach Gardens, FL 33420-2909 USA (SAN 255-1780) Tel 305-333-7166; Fax: 561-840-1939
E-mail: mpo@msn.com
Web site: http://www.batfishbooks.com
Dist(s): **Follett School Solutions**
Southern Bk. Service.

†Bathtub Row Pr., *(978-0-941232)* Orders Addr.: P.O. Box 43, Los Alamos, NM 87544 USA (SAN 276-9603) Tel 505-662-2660; Fax: 505-662-6312; Edit Addr.: 1050 Bathtub Row, Los Alamos, NM 87544 USA (SAN 241-9025)
E-mail: shar5992@gmail.com
Web site: http://losalamoshistory.org; *CIP.*

Battat, Inc., *(978-0-9794542; 978-0-9843722; 978-0-9844904; 978-0-9883165; 978-0-9891839; 978-0-9963272)* 1560 Military Tpke., Plattsburgh, NY 12901-7458 USA (SAN 853-4683).

Battle Creek Area Mathematics & Science Ctr., *(978-1-933281)* 765 Upton Ave., Battle Creek, MI 49015 USA Tel 269-965-9440
Web site: http://bcmsc.k12.mi.us.

Batyah & Assocs. Publishing, *(978-0-9749571)* 2013 Vernier, Grosse Pointe Woods, MI 48236 USA
E-mail: baroberts07@yahoo.com.

Batyah Productions, Inc., *(978-0-9649608)* 6434 Saxet St., Houston, TX 77055-5317 USA.

BAU Publishing Group, *(978-0-9766770)* Orders Addr.: 1808 STRAWBERRY Dr., RIO RANCHO, NM 87144 USA
E-mail: tize@tize.biz; admin@baupublishing.com
Web site: http://www.baupublishing.com.

Bauer, Linda, *(978-0-9798146)* Orders Addr.: P.O. Box 308, Eastford, CT 06242 USA
Dist(s): **CreateSpace Independent Publishing Platform.**

Bauer Media Bks. (AUS) *(978-0-949128; 978-0-949892; 978-1-86396; 978-1-74245; 978-0-646-36336-3) Dist. by* **HachBkGrp.**

Bauer, Walter, *(978-0-615-77010-9)* 720 Rowland Blvd., Novato, CA 94947 USA Tel 415-892-5802
Dist(s): **CreateSpace Independent Publishing Platform.**

Bauhan Publishing LLC, *(978-0-87233)* Orders Addr.: 44 Main St., Peterborough, NH 03458 USA (SAN 204-384X) Tel 603-567-4430; Toll Free Fax: 888-712-7248
E-mail: sales@bauhanpublishing.com; sbauhan@bauhanpublishing.com
Web site: http://www.bauhanpublishing.com
Dist(s): **East-West Export Bks.**
Univ. Pr. of New England.

Bauhan, William L. Incorporated *See* **Bauhan Publishing LLC**

Baum & Baum, LLC, *(978-0-9839373)* 14196 Cranston St., Livonia, MI 48154-4251 USA Tel 734-422-0546
E-mail: lbaum@mi.rr.com
Dist(s): **AtlasBooks Distribution.**

Baumbach, Laura *See* **MLR Pr., LLC**

Baxter Pr., *(978-1-888237; 978-0-9907879)* 700 S. Friendswood Dr., Suite C, Friendswood, TX 77546 USA Tel 281-992-0628; Fax: 815-572-5115
E-mail: baxter2@flash.net
Web site: http://baxterpress.com
Dist(s): **Greenleaf Book Group**
Spirit Rising.

Bay Horse Creations LLC, *(978-0-9749320)* 508 W. Irvine Rd., Phoenix, AZ 85086 USA Tel 602-818-7879
Web site: http://www.bayhorsecreations.com.

Bay Light Publishing, *(978-0-9670280; 978-0-9741817)* P.O. Box 3032, Mooresville, NC 28117 USA (SAN 299-9196) Tel 704-664-7541; Fax: 704-664-2712; Toll Free: 866-541-3895
E-mail: baylightpub@compuserve.com
Web site: http://www.baylightpub.com.

Bay Media, Inc., *(978-0-9665239; 978-0-9717047; 978-0-9823354)* Orders Addr.: 550m Ritchie Hwy., #271 Severna Pk., Severna Park, MD 21146 USA Tel 410-647-8402; Fax: 410-544-4640
Web site: http://www.baymed.com.

Bay Mills Indian Community, *(978-0-9758801)* 12140 W. Lakeshore Dr., Brimley, MI 49715 USA
Web site: http://www.bmic.net.

Bay Oak Pubs., Ltd., *(978-0-9704692; 978-0-9741713; 978-0-9800874)* 34 Wimbledon Dr., Dover, DE 19904 USA
E-mail: bayoakpublishers@aol.com
Web site: http://www.bayoakpublishers.com
Dist(s): **Follett School Solutions**
Washington Bk. Distributors.

Bay Otter Pr., *(978-0-9778961)* Div. of New Spectrum, Inc, P.O. Box 20492, Palo Alto, CA 94309-0492 USA; 814 N. Franklin St., Chicago, IL 60610
Dist(s): **Follett School Solutions**
Independent Pubs. Group
MyiLibrary
ebrary, Inc.

Bay Publishing, *(978-0-9822046)* P.O. Box 4569, Santa Rosa, CA 95402-4569 USA (SAN 857-5401)
E-mail: ron@bayyellow.com.

Bay Villager, The, *(978-0-9769742)* 4923 43rd. St., Dickinson, TX 77539 USA
E-mail: lindalou36@hotmail.com.

Bayard Editions (FRA) *(978-2-227; 978-2-7009; 978-2-7470; 978-2-915480; 978-2-9518356) Dist. by* **Distribks Inc.**

Bayberry Cottage Gallery, *(978-0-615-61021-4; 978-0-615-89363-1)* 9074 Highland St., Mauricetown, NJ 08329 USA Tel 856-785-9927
E-mail: nanptidy@yahoo.com
Web site: http://nancy-patterson.artistwebsites.com.

Bayeux Arts, Inc. (CAN) *(978-1-896209; 978-1-897411) Dist. by* **Chicago Distribution Ctr.**

Bayliss, Erin, *(978-0-9778471)* 320 Roan Dr., Grants Pass, OR 97526 USA
E-mail: rise4him@q.com.

Baylor College of Medicine, *(978-1-888997; 978-1-944035)* Div. of Center for Educational Outreach, Orders Addr.: Center For Educational Outreach Baylor College Of Medicine One Baylor Plaza, Bcm411, Houston, TX 77030 USA Tel 713-798-8200; Fax: 713-798-8201; Toll Free: 800-798-8244; *Imprints:* BioEd (BioEd)
E-mail: edoutreach@bcm.edu; nmoreno@bcm.edu; marthay@bcm.edu; mslopez@bcm.edu
Web site: http://www.bcm.edu/edoutreach; http://www.bioedonline.org; http://www.bcm.edu.

Baylor Univ. Pr., *(978-0-918954; 978-1-878804; 978-1-932792; 978-1-60258; 978-1-4813)* 1920 S. Fourth St., Waco, TX 76706 USA Tel 254-710-3164; Fax: 254-710-3440
E-mail: Diane_Smith@baylor.edu
Web site: http://www.baylorpress.com
Dist(s): **Hopkins Fulfillment Services**
MyiLibrary
ebrary, Inc.

Bayou Publishing, *(978-1-886298)* Div. of Bayou Publishing, LLC, Orders Addr.: 2524 Nottingham, Houston, TX 77005 USA (SAN 859-2810) Tel 713-526-4558; Fax: 713-526-4342; Toll Free: 800-340-2034 Do not confuse with Bayou Publishing, Longboat Key, FL
E-mail: info@bayoupublishing.com; orders@bayoupublishing.com; vloos@bayoupublishing.com
Web site: http://www.bayoupublishing.com
Dist(s): **AtlasBooks Distribution**
Quality Bks., Inc.
Unique Bks., Inc.

Bayport Pr. *Imprint of* **Wellness Pubn.**

Baysmore Bks., *(978-0-9857160)* P.O. Box 21402, Long Beach, CA 90801 USA Tel 562-208-3646
E-mail: baysmorebooks@gmail.com.

bazow, thomas, *(978-0-9777725)* 4845 Romaine Spring Dr., Fenton, MO 63026-5840 USA
Web site: http://www.inhistimepublishing.com.

Bazuji Publishing LLC, *(978-0-9761555)* 3843 53rd St., SE, Tappen, ND 58487 USA (SAN 256-2626) Toll Free: 800-615-7606
Web site: http://www.bazuji.com.

BB International Productions, Inc., *(978-0-9754329)* 1200 W. Ave., Suite 707, Miami Beach, FL 33139-4316 USA
Web site: http://www.bibiadventures.com.

BBC Audiobooks America *See* **AudioGO**

BBI Incorporated *See* **Bush Brothers & Co.**

BBM Bks., *(978-1-938504)* 21 Harbor Pointe Dr., Corona del Mar, CA 92625 USA Tel 949-302-5849
E-mail: inspiredcreationsca@gmail.com
Dist(s): **AtlasBooks Distribution.**

BBR *Imprint of* **BBR: Books for Brilliance & Resilience**

BBR: Books for Brilliance & Resilience, *(978-0-9753245)* P.O. Box 5236, Takoma Park, MD 20913-5236 USA Toll Free: 888-898-2322; *Imprints:* BBR (B B R)
Web site: http://www.letscommunicate.org.

BBRACK Productions, Inc., *(978-0-9728837)* 1345-B Triad Ctr. Dr., No. 181, Saint Peters, MO 63376 USA Tel 636-936-2311
E-mail: 1stB@bbrack.com
Web site: http://www.bbrack.com.

BBS Publishing Corp., *(978-0-88365; 978-0-88394; 978-0-88486; 978-1-57866)* 252 W. 38th St., New York, NY 10018 USA (SAN 853-9529) Tel 212-842-0700; Fax: 212-842-1771; *Imprints:* Galahad Books (Galah Bks)
Dist(s): **Sterling Publishing Co., Inc.**

BC Publishing, *(978-0-9740511)* 633-1 Elk Ct., Fayetteville, NC 28301 USA Tel 910-578-2621; *Imprints:* Kids1st Books (Kids1st Bks) Do not confuse with BC Publishing in Tampa, FL
E-mail: dbradleyclarke@yahoo.com.

BCM International Inc., *(978-0-86508)* 201 Granite Run Dr., Suite 260, Lancaster, PA 17601 USA (SAN 211-7762) Tel 717-560-9601 Main Phone Number; Toll Free: 888-226-4685
E-mail: info@bcmintl.org
Web site: http://www.bcmintl.org
Dist(s): **CLC Pubns.**
Send The Light Distribution LLC.

BCM Publications, Incorporated *See* **BCM International Inc.**

BCP Pubns., *(978-0-615-20692-9; 978-0-615-21056-8; 978-0-578-02129-4)* 3215 E. 17th St., Vancouver, WA 98661 USA
E-mail: bcpwriter2000@yahoo.com
Web site: http://www.authortree.com/bcpwriter2000
Dist(s): **AuthorHouse.**

BDA Publishing, *(978-0-9794716)* P.O. Box 541715, Dallas, TX 75354-1715 USA Tel 972-532-8805; Fax: 214-350-9275; 3163 Citation Dr., Dallas, TX 75229-5840
E-mail: bbd@sbcglobal.net
Web site: http://www.evanbrain.com; http://barrybdoyle.com/
Dist(s): **AtlasBooks Distribution.**

Beach Bks., *(978-0-9763052; 978-0-615-57831-6)* 430 Noe St., San Francisco, CA 94114 USA Tel 415-251-3845
E-mail: gyaltsen@yahoo.com
Web site: http://www.jefferybeach.com
Dist(s): **CreateSpace Independent Publishing Platform.**

Beach Front Bks., *(978-0-9651281)* P.O. Box 545, East Bridgewater, MA 02333 USA Tel 508-378-9319; Fax: 508-378-7621 Do not confuse with Beach Front Books in East Bridgewater, MA
E-mail: beachfrontbooks@aol.com.

Beach Lane Bks. *Imprint of* **Beach Lane Bks.**

Beach Lane Bks., Div. of Simon & Schuster Children's Publishing, 1230 Ave. of the Americas, New York, NY 10020 USA; *Imprints:* Beach Lane Books (BeachLane)
Dist(s): **Follett School Solutions**
Simon & Schuster, Inc.

Beach Lloyd Pubs., LLC, *(978-0-9743158; 978-0-9792778; 978-0-9819417)* Orders Addr.: P.O. Box 2183, Southeastern, PA 19399-2183 USA (SAN 255-4992) Tel 610-407-0130; Fax: 775-254-0633; Toll Free: 866-218-3253; Edit Addr.: 40 Cabot Dr., Wayne, PA 19087-5619 USA
E-mail: beachlloyd@erols.com
Web site: http://www.beachlloyd.com
Dist(s): **MBS Textbook Exchange, Inc.**

Beachcomber Press.com, *(978-0-9800630)* 33021 Adelante St., Temecula, CA 92592 USA Tel 951-699-2932
E-mail: ashleyludwig@verizon.net.

Beachfront Bks., *(978-0-9768816)* Orders Addr.: P.O. Box 16-287, Seattle, WA 98116 USA; Edit Addr.: 5641 Beach Dr. SW, Seattle, WA 98116 USA
Web site: http://www.beachfront books.org
Dist(s): **Follett School Solutions.**

Beachfront Publishing, *(978-1-892339)* Div. of Words, Words, Words, Inc., Orders Addr.: P.O. Box 811922, Boca Raton, FL 33481 USA; 4705 Brook Top Ct., Raleigh, NC 27606
E-mail: info@beachfrontentertainment.com
Web site: http://www.beachfrontentertainment.com
Dist(s): **BookMasters Distribution Services (BDS)**
Follett School Solutions.

BeachHouse Bks. *Imprint of* **Science & Humanities Pr.**

Beachhouse Publishing, LLC, *(978-0-9729905; 978-1-933067)* P.O. Box 2926, Ewa Beach, HI 96706-0926 USA
E-mail: beachhousepub@hawaii.rr.com
Dist(s): **Booklines Hawaii, Ltd.**
Islander Group.

BeachWalk Bks. Inc., *(978-0-9770158)* P.O. Box 446, Glenview, IL 60025 USA Tel 847-729-2222; Fax: 847-729-5215; Toll Free Fax: 866-720-3222; 2136 Fir St., Glenview, IL 60025
E-mail: amcdonald@beachwalkbooks.com
Web site: http://www.beachwalkbooks.com.

Beachwalker Pr., *(978-0-9727639)* 5557 SW Village Pl., Beaverton, OR 97007 USA Tel 503-799-6061; Fax: 503-644-9335
E-mail: beachwalkerpress@aol.com
Web site: http://www.beachwalkerpress.com.

Beacon Hill Pr. of Kansas City, *(978-0-8341)* Div. of Nazarene Publishing Hse., 2923 Troost, Kansas City, MO 64109 USA (SAN 241-6328) Tel 816-931-1900; Fax: 816-753-4071; Toll Free: 800-877-0700 (orders only)
E-mail: nphdirect@nph.com; orders@nph.com; inquiry@bhillkc.com
Web site: http://www.nph.com; http://www.bhillkc.com
Dist(s): **Nazarene Publishing Hse.**

Beacon Pr., *(978-0-8070)* Orders Addr.: 25 Beacon St., Boston, MA 02108-2892 USA (SAN 201-4483) Tel 617-742-2110; Fax: 617-723-3097
E-mail: marketing@beacon.org
Web site: http://www.beacon.org
Dist(s): **Ebsco Publishing**
Houghton Mifflin Harcourt Publishing Co.
Houghton Mifflin Harcourt Trade & Reference Pubs.
MyiLibrary
Penguin Random Hse., LLC.
Random Hse., Inc.

Beacon Publishing, *(978-1-929266; 978-0-9841318; 978-1-937509; 978-1-942611)* 5150 N. Ocean Dr., Singer Island, FL 33404 USA (SAN 858-5024); 2330 Kemper Ln., Cincinnati, OH 45206 Do not confuse with Beacon Publishing in Theodore, AL, Brimfield, MA
E-mail: shawna@dynamiccatholic.com
Web site: http://www.matthewkelly.org
Dist(s): **BookBaby**
Follett School Solutions
Smashwords.

Beacon Street Girls *Imprint of* **B*tween Productions, LLC**

BeActive Publishing Co., *(978-0-9722714)* 29834 N. Cave Creek Rd., S118, PMB 142, Cave Creek, AZ 85331-7831 USA Tel 480-563-0315; Fax: 480-502-0664
Web site: http://www.beactivesportsmarketing.com.

Beagle Bay Bks., *(978-0-9679591; 978-0-9749610)* Div. of Beagle Bay, Inc., 2325 Homestead Pl., Reno, NV 89509-3657 USA
E-mail: info@beaglebay.com
Web site: http://www.beaglebay.com
Dist(s): **Brodart Co.**

Beagle Bks. Publishing, LLC, *(978-0-9841813)* 43 Highridge Rd., Westport, MA 02790 USA (SAN 858-6519).

Bean Bk. Publishing, *(978-0-9761990)* 9246 E. Havasupai Dr., Scottsdale, AZ 85255 USA Tel 480-502-1257 (phone/fax)
E-mail: dawn.crichton@dcranch.com; Juliecrichton@cox.net
Web site: http://www.stringbeansorjellybeans.com; http://www.bean-books.com.

Bean Sprouts *Imprint of* **Standard Publishing**

Beaner Bks., *(978-0-9849293)* 541 Redford Pl. Dr., Rolesville, NC 27571 USA Tel 855-286-9687
E-mail: alphabetownusa@gmail.com
Web site: http://www.alphabetownusa.com.

BeanPole Bks. *Imprint of* **Harren Communications, LLC**

Beans, Ted E, *(978-0-615-77832-7; 978-0-615-83839-7; 978-0-615-85087-0; 978-0-615-90111-4; 978-0-615-90554-9; 978-0-615-92023-8; 978-0-615-92129-7; 978-0-615-92304-8; 978-0-615-92306-2; 978-0-615-92876-0; 978-0-615-93175-3; 978-0-615-96618-2; 978-0-615-97183-4; 978-0-692-20460-3; 978-0-692-23345-0; 978-0-692-24725-9; 978-0-692-26094-4; 978-0-692-26538-3; 978-0-692-35420-9; 978-0-692-39393-2; 978-0-692-52767-2) 9 ponte bianco 0, lake elsinore, AE 92532 USA Tel 9514718184*
E-mail: miklikmows@aol.com
Dist(s): **CreateSpace Independent Publishing Platform.**

Beanstalk Pubns, *(978-0-9785302)* 4762 Camino del Rey, Santa Barbara, CA 93110 USA Tel 805-448-0898
E-mail: mjmckechnie@beanstalkpublications.com
Web site: http://www.beanstalkpublications.com

Bear & Company *See* **Boyds Collection Ltd., The**

†Bear & Co., *(978-0-939680; 978-1-879181; 978-1-59143)* Orders Addr.: P.O. Box 388, Rochester, VT 05767-0388 USA; Edit Addr.: One Park St., Rochester, VT 05767 USA (SAN 216-7174) Tel 802-767-3174; Fax: 802-767-3726; Toll Free: 800-246-8648; *Imprints:* Bear Cub Books (Bear Cub Books)
E-mail: customerservice@innertraditions.com; info@innertraditions.com
Web site: http://www.innertraditions.com
Dist(s): **Book Wholesalers, Inc.**
Bookazine Co., Inc.
Brodart Co.
Inner Traditions International, Ltd.
Integral Yoga Pubns.
MyiLibrary
New Leaf Distributing Co., Inc.
Nutri-Bks. Corp.
Partners Bk. Distributing, Inc.
Partners/West Book Distributors
Phoenix Distributors
Quality Bks., Inc.
Simon & Schuster
Simon & Schuster, Inc.; *CIP.*

Bear Cub Bks. *Imprint of* **Bear & Co.**

Bear Star Pr., *(978-0-9657177; 978-0-9719607; 978-0-9793745; 978-0-9850584)* 185 Hollow Oak Dr., Cohasset, CA 95973 USA Tel 530-891-0360
E-mail: bgumbo@aol.com
Web site: http://www.bearstarpress.com
Dist(s): **BookMobile**
SPD-Small Pr. Distribution.

Bear State Bks., *(978-1-892622)* Orders Addr.: P.O. Box 96, Exeter, CA 93221 USA Tel 559-592-6760; Fax: 559-592-5779; Edit Addr.: 199 E. Pine St., Exeter, CA 93221 USA
E-mail: 1718K@earthlink.net; bearstatebooks@verizon.net
Dist(s): **American West Bks.**

Bearhead Publishing, LLC, *(978-0-9776260; 978-0-9799153; 978-0-9824373; 978-0-9829307; 978-1-937508)* P.O. Box 16539, Louisville, KY 40256 USA (SAN 257-7798); 2217 Mary Catherine Dr., Louisville, KY 40216
E-mail: garyd@sissymarlyn.com; garydbhp@insightbb.com
Web site: http://www.sissymarlyn.com; http://www.bearheadpublishing.com.

Bearing Bks. *Imprint of* **Red Cygnet Pr.**

Bearly Cooking *Imprint of* **Mountain n' Air Bks.**

Bearport Publishing Co., Inc., *(978-1-59716; 978-1-936087; 978-1-936088; 978-1-936089; 978-1-936090; 978-0-9824758; 978-0-9824759; 978-0-9824760; 978-0-9824761; 978-0-9824762; 978-0-9824763; 978-0-9824764; 978-1-61772; 978-1-62724; 978-1-943074; 978-1-943553; 978-1-944102)* 45 W. 21st St. Suite 3b, New York, NY 10010 USA (SAN 256-2103) Tel 212-337-8577; Toll Free: 877-337-8577
E-mail: kenngoin@earthlink.net; info@bearportpublishing.com; vyaw@bearportpublishing.com
Web site: http://www.bearportpublishing.com
Dist(s): **Follett School Solutions**
MyiLibrary.

Bear's Designs Unlimited, *(978-0-9638473)* 7505 320th St., W., Northfield, MN 55057 USA Tel 507-645-9050; Toll Free: 800-497-8757.

Bearwallow Blessings Ministries, *(978-0-9768514)* HC 63 Box 77A-1 Rte. 637, Jewell Ridge, VA 24622 USA
Web site: http://www.bearwallowblessings.com.

Beascoa, Ediciones S.A. (ESP) *(978-84-488; 978-84-7546)* *Dist. by* **Distribks Inc.**

Beascoa, Ediciones S.A. (ESP) *(978-84-488; 978-84-7546)* *Dist. by* **Lectorum Pubns.**

Beatin' Path Pubns., LLC, *(978-0-9795470; 978-0-9797522; 978-0-9825839; 978-0-9832648; 978-0-9882814; 978-0-9894773; 978-0-9861795; 978-0-9963591)* Orders Addr.: 302 E. College St., Bridgewater, VA 22812-1509 USA (SAN 853-7003) Tel 540-478-4833; Fax: 540-828-6903
E-mail: beatinpath@mac.com
Web site: http://www.beatinpathpublications.com
Dist(s): **Music in Motion**
Music is Elementary
Plank Road Publishing
West Music Co.

Beating Windward Pr., *(978-0-9838252; 978-1-940761)* 524 Astria St., Altamonte Springs,, FL 32701 USA Tel 321-356-7676
E-mail: MatthewPeters@cfl.rr.com
Web site: www.BeatingWindwardPress.com
Dist(s): **SPD-Small Pr. Distribution**
Smashwords.

Beau Francis Pr., *(978-0-9792147)* 4100 Newport Pl., Suite 400, Newport Beach, CA 92660 USA Tel 949-499-0679.

Beaufort Bks., Inc., *(978-0-8253; 978-0-9852135)* 27 W. 20th St., Suite 1102, New York, NY 10011 USA (SAN 215-2304) Tel 212-727-0190; Fax: 212-727-0195
E-mail: midpointny@aol.com
Dist(s): **Follett School Solutions**
Midpoint Trade Bks., Inc.

Beautiful America Publishing Co., *(978-0-89802)* Orders Addr.: P.O. Box 244, Woodburn, OR 97071-0244 USA (SAN 251-2548) Tel 503-982-4616; Fax: 503-982-2825; Toll Free: 800-874-1233; Edit Addr.: 2600 Progress Way, Woodburn, OR 97071 USA (SAN 211-4623)
E-mail: bapco@beautifulamericapub.com
Web site: http://www.beautifulamericapub.com
Dist(s): **Follett School Solutions**
Koen Pacific
Partners/West Book Distributors.

Beautiful Feet Bks., *(978-0-9643803; 978-1-893103)* 1306 Mill St., San Luis Obispo, CA 93401-2817 USA Toll Free: 800-889-1978
E-mail: russell@bfbooks.com
Web site: http://www.bfbooks.com
Dist(s): **Follett School Solutions.**

Beautiful Zion Baptist Church *See* **A & L Communications, Inc.**

Beaver Island Arts, *(978-0-9708575)* P.O. Box 40, Bay City, MI 49708-0040 USA (SAN 253-8385) Tel 517-894-5925
E-mail: mblocksma@yahoo.com
Web site: http://beaverislandarts.com
Dist(s): **Follett School Solutions**
Partners Bk. Distributing, Inc.

Beaver Meadow Publishing, *(978-0-9742085)* 11 Clarence Russell Rd., Thurman, NY 12885 USA Tel 518-623-9305; 352-463-3089
E-mail: PerkinFL@aol.com
Web site: http://www.persisgranger.com.

Beaver's Pond Pr., Inc., *(978-1-890676; 978-1-931646; 978-1-59298)* 7104 Ohms Ln., Suite 101, Edina, MN 55439 USA Tel 952-829-8818
E-mail: heather@beaverspondpress.com
Web site: http://www.beaverspondpress.com
Dist(s): **Itasca Bks.**

Because Time Flies, Inc., *(978-0-9652652; 978-0-9754073)* 155 N. Harbor Dr., Concourse Suite 2, Chicago, IL 60601-7364 USA Tel 312-938-0938; Fax: 312-938-0029; Toll Free: 800-694-4786
E-mail: journals@covad.net
Web site: http://www.becausetimeflies.com.

Beck Global Publishing, *(978-0-9816942)* 10600 E. Rte. Y, Ashland, MO 65010 USA
Web site: http://www.beckpillowtalk.com.

Beck Publishing *See* **Beck Global Publishing**

Becker, Christie, *(978-0-9728116)* 7 Whispering Pines Ct., Hilton Head, SC 29926-2542 USA
E-mail: beachbeckers@msn.com
Web site: http://www.cbeckerbooks.com.

Becker Doyle & Associates *See* **BDA Publishing**

Becker, Frank *See* **Greenbush Pr.**

Becker, Savan C., *(978-0-615-23554-7)* 1521 Farlow Ave., Crofton, MD 21114 USA Tel 443-292-8098; Fax: 443-603-2998
E-mail: savan@psinerspace.net
Dist(s): **Lulu Enterprises Inc.**

becker&mayer! books, *(978-0-9700346; 978-0-9748486; 978-1-932855; 978-1-60380)* 11120 NE 33rd Pl. No. 101, Bellevue, WA 98004-1448 USA (SAN 760-7792) Toll Free: 866-319-5900; *Imprints:* SmartLab (SmartLab)
E-mail: cindyd@beckermayer.com; info@beckermayer.com
Web site: http://www.beckermayer.com; http://www.everydaywisdom.net
Dist(s): **Bks. Are Fun, Ltd.**
Brilliance Publishing
Chronicle Bks. LLC
Hachette Bk. Group
INscribe Digital.

Becket, *(978-0-9898785; 978-1-941240)* 104 Romanza Ln, Palm Desert, CA 92211 USA Tel 760-413-0031
E-mail: ibecket7@gmail.com.

Beckham House Publishers, Incorporated *See* **Beckham Pubns. Group, Inc.**

Beckham Pubns. Group, Inc., *(978-0-931761; 978-0-9802380; 978-0-9816505; 978-0-9823876; 978-0-9841991; 978-0-9827943; 978-0-9833402; 978-0-9848243; 978-0-9905904)* Orders Addr.: P.O. Box 4066, Silver Spring, MD 20914-4066 USA (SAN 683-2237) Tel 301-384-7995; Fax: 866-659-3306; Toll Free Fax: 866-659-3306; Edit Addr.: 13619 Cedar Creek Ln., Silver Spring, MD 20904-5308 USA
E-mail: barry@beckhamhouse.com
Web site: http://www.beckhamhouse.com
Dist(s): **AtlasBooks Distribution.**

Becklyns, LLC, *(978-0-9860222)* 23 Bob White Way, Weatogue, CT 06089 USA.

Beckon Bks., *(978-1-935442)* 2451 Atrium Way, Nashville, TN 37214 USA Tel 800-358-0560; Fax: 615-391-2815.

Become a Millionaire *See* **Grampa Jones's Publishing Co.**

Bed Bks., *(978-1-933652)* 101 Westgate Dr., Trinidad, CA 95570 USA
Web site: http://www.readinginbed.com; http://www.bedbooks.NET.

Bedazzled Ink Publishing Co., *(978-0-9759555; 978-1-934452; 978-1-939562; 978-1-943837)* 2137 Pennsylvania Ave., Fairfield, CA 94533 USA; *Imprints:* Dragonfeather Books (Dragonfeather Bks)
E-mail: publisher@bedazzledink.com
Web site: http://www.bedazzledink.com
Dist(s): **Follett School Solutions**
Independent Pubs. Group.

Bedbug Pr., Inc., *(978-0-9771973; 978-0-9822982)* Orders Addr.: P.O. Box 39, Brownsville, OR 97327-0039 USA (SAN 256-9396) Tel 541-466-5913; Edit Addr.: 308 Averill, Brownsville, OR 97327 USA
E-mail: tg@bedbugpress.com
Web site: http://www.bedbugpress.com
Dist(s): **SPD-Small Pr. Distribution.**

Bedell, Barbara F., *(978-0-9743731)* 74 Hidden Bay Dr., S Dartmouth, MA 02748-3089 USA
E-mail: bb280z@yahoo.com.

Bedford Hse. Bks., *(978-0-9960916)* 93 hancock St., brooklyn, NY 11216 USA Tel 917-815-5969
E-mail: dave@bedfordhousebooks.com.

Bedford/Saint Martin's, *(978-0-312; 978-1-4576)* Div. of Holtzbrinck Publishers, Orders Addr.: 16365 James Madison Hwy., Gordonsville, VA 22942 USA Tel 540-672-7600; Toll Free Fax: 800-672-2054; Toll Free: 888-330-8477; Edit Addr.: 33 Irving Pl., New York, NY 10003 USA Tel 212-375-7000; Fax: 212-614-1885; Toll Free: 800-223-1715; 75 Arlington St., Boston, MA 02116 Tel 617-399-4000; Fax: 617-426-8582; Toll Free: 800-779-7440
E-mail: permissionsdept@bedfordstmartins.com; communication@bedfordstmartins.com
Web site: http://www.bfwpub.com
Dist(s): **Follett School Solutions**
Macmillan.

Bednark, Sara, *(978-0-615-18545-3)* 10013 SE Eastmont Dr., Damascus, OR 97089 USA
E-mail: rbednark@gmail.com
Web site: http://www.sara.bednark.com
Dist(s): **Lulu Enterprises Inc.**

Bedrock Books, Incorporated *See* **Dry, Paul Bks., Inc.**

Bedside Bks. *Imprint of* **American Bk. Publishing Group**

Bee at Ease Press *See* **At Ease Pr.**

Bee Creative, LLC, *(978-0-615-75686-8; 978-0-615-94698-6; 978-0-615-98240-3)* 2704 NW 119th, Oklahoma City, OK 73120 USA Tel 405-924-9265
E-mail: callie.belinda@gmail.com
Web site: www.beecreativeinc.com.

Beech, Michael, *(978-0-9817741)* 8603 W. 84th Cir., Arvada, CO 80005 USA Tel 303-456-5350
Web site: http://www.ebookselfpublishing.com; http://www.digital3dstereo.com.

Beech River Bks., *(978-1-930149; 978-0-9776514; 978-0-9793778; 978-0-9825214; 978-0-9839367; 978-0-9905814)* P.O. Box 62, Center Ossipee, NH 03814 USA Tel 603-539-3537; *Imprints:* Writer's Publishing Cooperative (Writ Pub Coop)
E-mail: banddmarion@roadrunner.com
Web site: http://www.beechriverbooks.com
Dist(s): **Enfield Publishing & Distribution Co., Inc.**

Beech Seal Press, Incorporated *See* **Images from the Past, Inc.**

Beecher Scott, *(978-0-9763077)* 1925 Westchester Rd. Apt. 214, Waterloo, IA 50701-4522 USA.

Beekman & Hathaway, *(978-0-9758970)* P.O. Box 2355, Amherst, MA 01004-2355 USA
E-mail: cdc@beekmanandhathaway.com
Web site: http://www.beekmanandhathaway.com
Dist(s): **Independent Pubs. Group.**

Beekman Bks., Inc., *(978-0-8464)* 300 Old All Angels Hill Rd., Wappingers Falls, NY 12590 USA (SAN 170-1622) Tel 845-297-2690; Fax: 845-297-1002
E-mail: manager@beekmanbooks.com
Web site: http://www.beekmanbooks.com
Dist(s): **Follett School Solutions.**

Beeman Jorgensen, Inc., *(978-0-929758)* 7510 Allisonville Rd., Indianapolis, IN 46250 USA (SAN 250-1279) Tel 317-841-7677; Fax: 317-849-2001; Toll Free: 800-553-5319
Dist(s): **Hachette Bk. Group**
MBI Distribution Services/Quayside Distribution
Practice Ring.

BeerBooks.com, *(978-0-9662084; 978-0-9819282; 978-0-9904513)* P.O. Box 771012, Cleveland, OH 44107 USA
E-mail: email@beerbooks.com
Web site: http://www.beerbooks.com.

Bee's Ink Publishing, *(978-0-615-57799-9; 978-0-615-63296-4)* 15800 Hwy. 3 No. 113, Webster, TX 77598 USA Tel 713-876-3222
E-mail: bwilsonent@aol.com.

Bees Knees Bks., *(978-0-9802338)* P.O. Box 756, Half Moon Bay, CA 94019 USA (SAN 855-5613)
E-mail: nancy@beeskneesbooks.com
Web site: http://beeskneesbooks.com
Dist(s): **Independent Pubs. Group.**

Beeson, Jan, *(978-0-9890482)* 232 E. 52nd St., San Bernardino, CA 92404 USA Tel 714-936-1390
E-mail: rotcmpj@charter.net.

Beetle Bug Bks., *(978-0-9658365)* Orders Addr.: P.O. Box 4636, San Clemente, CA 92674 USA (SAN 299-3864) Tel 949-498-0162; Fax: 949-498-2531; Edit Addr.: 1504 Avenida Hacienda, San Clemente, CA 92672 USA (SAN 299-3872)
E-mail: BookOrders@BeetleBugBooks.com
Web site: http://www.BeetleBugBooks.com
Dist(s): **Follett School Solutions**
Unique Bks., Inc.

Beevinwood, Inc., *(978-0-9652902)* Orders Addr.: 5748 Clark Rd., West Manchester, OH 45382 USA Tel 937-678-9910; Fax: 937-678-7715
E-mail: C1C2C3@aol.com.

Beex Art Bks., *(978-0-9724358)* P.O. Box 9143, Fountain Valley, CA 92728-9143 USA.

Before Christmas Pr., *(978-0-9759902)* Orders Addr.: 15170 State Rte. 550, Athens, OH 45701 USA
Web site: http://www.beforechristmaspress.com.

Begin Smart LLC, *(978-1-934618; 978-1-60906)* 515 Valley St., Suite 180, Maplewood, NJ 07040 USA (SAN 854-0497) Tel 973-763-8191; Fax: 973-763-5944
E-mail: info@beginsmartbooks.com
Dist(s): **Sterling Publishing Co., Inc.**

Begoo Bks., LLC, *(978-0-9884922)* 48 N. Clover Dr., Great Neck, NY 11021 USA Tel 516-314-4808
E-mail: cuilly@aol.com.

Behave'n Kids Pr., *(978-0-9714405)* 8922 Cuming St., Omaha, NE 68114 USA Tel 402-926-4373; Fax: 402-926-3898
E-mail: janiep@behavenkids.com
Web site: http://www.behavenkids.com/
Dist(s): **Book Clearing Hse.**

Behavenkids Press *See* **Behave'n Kids Pr.**

Behavioral Health & Human Development Ctr., *(978-0-9777672)* 4517 Lorino St., Suite 1, Metairie, LA 70006 USA Tel 504-454-3015
E-mail: carlos@littleduckyjr.com
Web site: http://littleduckyjr.com.

Behind the Scenes Bks., *(978-0-9770879)* 90 Windsor Dr., Pine Brook, NJ 07058 USA Tel 973-274-9472; Fax: 973-274-9272
E-mail: ma@behindthescenesmarketing.com.

Behrman Hse., Inc., *(978-0-87441; 978-1-68115)* 11 Edison Pl., Springfield, NJ 07081 USA (SAN 201-4459) Tel 973-379-7200; Fax: 973-379-7280; Toll Free: 800-221-2755
E-mail: webmaster@behrmanhouse.com; orders@behrmanhouse.com; customersupport@behrmanhouse.com
Web site: http://www.behrmanhouse.com; http://www.arepublish.com
Dist(s): **Follett School Solutions.**

Beijing Language & Culture Univ. Pr., China (CHN) *(978-7-5619)* *Dist. by* **China Bks.**

Beil, Frederic C. Pub., Inc., *(978-0-913720; 978-1-929490)* Orders Addr.: 609 Whitaker St., Savannah, GA 31401 USA (SAN 240-9909) Tel 912-233-2446
Web site: http://www.beil.com.

Belgrave Hse., *(978-0-9660643; 978-0-9741068; 978-0-9801778; 978-0-9821717; 978-0-9844144; 978-1-61084)* 190 Belgrave Ave., San Francisco, CA 94117-4228 USA Tel 415-661-5025; Fax: 415-661-5703
E-mail: neff@belgravehouse.com
Web site: http://www.belgravehouse.com.

Believers Publishing, *(978-0-9795680)* 2245 N. Green Valley Pkwy., Suite 282, Henderson, NV 89014 USA
E-mail: believerspublishing@gmail.com
Web site: http://believerspublishing.com
Dist(s): **Send The Light Distribution LLC.**

Belisarian Bks., *(978-0-9658481)* Div. of Iconoclast, 6513 NW 30th Terr., Bethany, OK 73008 USA Tel 405-789-1030
E-mail: belisarianbooks@yahoo.com
Web site: http://www.belisarianbooks.tk/.

Belknap Digital Archives, *(978-0-9747471)* Orders Addr.: P.O. Box 1487, Meredith, NH 03253 USA Tel

603-279-8358; Edit Addr.: 20 True Rd., Unit No. 86, Meredith, NH 03253 USA
E-mail: apollock@worldpath.net
Web site: http://www.belknapdigital.com.
Belknap Pr. *Imprint of* **Harvard Univ. Pr.**
Belknap Publishing & Design, *(978-0-9723420; 978-0-9816403)* P.O. Box 22387, Honolulu, HI 96823-2387 USA; *Imprints:* Calabash Books (Calabash Bks)
Web site: http://belknappublishing.com
Dist(s): **Booklines Hawaii, Ltd.**
Follett School Solutions.
Bell Bridge Bks. *Imprint of* **BelleBks., Inc.**
Bell, Megan, *(978-0-9889775)* 5710 Fox Chase Trail, Galena, OH 43021 USA Tel 740-548-6550
E-mail: meganericbell@gmail.com.
Bell Pond Bks. *Imprint of* **SteinerBooks, Inc.**
Bella & Bruno Bks., *(978-0-9894402)* 34-08 30th St. Apt A22, Astoria, NY 11106 USA Tel 585-746-2696
E-mail: aneeck@rochester.rr.com
Web site: bellaandbrunobooks.com.
Bella & Harry, LLC, *(978-0-9837092; 978-1-937616)* 15057 Sweetgum St., Delray Beach, FL 33446 USA (SAN 920-3052) Tel 855-235-5211; Fax: 561-637-3235; 1 Ingram Rd., La Vergne, TN 37086
E-mail: BellaAndHarryGo@aol.com
Web site: www.BellaAndHarry.com
Dist(s): **Follett School Solutions**
Ingram Pub. Services.
Bella Bks., Inc., *(978-0-930044; 978-0-941483; 978-1-56280; 978-0-9677753; 978-1-931513; 978-1-59493)* Orders Addr.: P.O. Box 10543, Tallahassee, FL 32302 USA Tel 850-576-2370; Fax: 850-576-3498; Toll Free: 800-729-4992
E-mail: Linda@BellaBooks.com
Web site: http://www.bellabooks.com
Dist(s): **Bella Distribution**
Perseus Distribution.
Bella Publishing *See* **Bellissima Publishing, LLC**
Bella Rosa Bks., *(978-0-9747685; 978-1-933523; 978-1-62268)* P.O. Box 4251, Rock Hill, SC 29732 USA
E-mail: info@bellarosabooks.com
Web site: http://www.bellarosabooks.com
Dist(s): **Follett School Solutions.**
Bellaboozle Books, Inc., *(978-0-9765398)* 104 Lariat Dr., Canonsburg, PA 15317-3284 USA
E-mail: lkravec@adelphia.net.
Bellastoria Pr., *(978-0-615-40644-2; 978-0-9910861; 978-1-942209)* 100 Hilltop Rd., Longmeadow, MA 01106 USA Tel 413-567-3278
E-mail: lcardilloplatzer@hotmail.com
Web site: http://www.lindacardillo.com/.
Belle Isle Bks. *Imprint of* **Brandylane Pubs., Inc.**
Belle Lumiere - Belle Media *See* **Belle Media International, Inc.**
Belle Lumiere True News, 2525 Squaw Ct., Antioch, CA 94531-8003 USA Toll Free: 888-473-1555; *Imprints:* Holmes Bookshop (Holmes Bkshop).
Belle Media International, Inc., *(978-0-9703419; 978-1-60361)* Div. of Belle Lumiere True News, Orders Addr.: P.O. Box 191024, San Francisco, CA 94119 USA Tel 949-813-5343
E-mail: holmesbookshop@yahoo.com; BelleBusiness@yahoo.com; dr.miawhite@yahoo.com.
BelleAire Pr., *(978-0-9640138; 978-0-9765234)* 5707 NW 50th Pl., Gainesville, FL 32653-4079 USA Tel 352-377-1870
E-mail: belleairepress@earthlink.net
Dist(s): **BookMasters, Inc.**
Follett School Solutions
MyiLibrary.
BelleBks., Inc., *(978-1-893896; 978-0-9673035; 978-0-9759653; 978-1-933417; 978-0-9768760; 978-0-9802453; 978-0-9821756; 978-0-9841258; 978-0-9843256; 978-1-935661; 978-1-61026; 978-1-61194)* 4513 Ernie Dr., Memphis, TN 38116 USA Tel 901-344-9024; Fax: 901-344-9068; *Imprints:* Bell Bridge Books (Bell Bridge); ImaJinn Books (ImaJinnBooks)
E-mail: bellebooks@bellebooks.com; debbsmith@aol.com
Web site: http://www.BelleBooks.com; http://www.BellBridgeBooks.com
Dist(s): **MyiLibrary.**
Bellerophon Bks., *(978-0-88388)* Orders Addr.: P.O. Box 21307, Santa Barbara, CA 93121-1307 USA (SAN 254-7856) Tel 805-965-7034; Fax: 805-965-8286; Toll Free: 800-253-9943
E-mail: bellerophonbooks@bellerophonbooks.com
Web site: http://www.bellerophonbooks.com
Dist(s): **Follett School Solutions.**
Bellissima Publishing, LLC, *(978-0-9768417; 978-0-9771916; 978-0-9776993; 978-0-9790449; 978-0-9793358; 978-0-9794006; 978-0-9794815; 978-1-935118; 978-1-935630; 978-1-61477)* Orders Addr.: P.O. Box 650, Jamul, CA 91935 USA
E-mail: pdweigandjd@aol.com; admin@bellissimapublishing.com
Web site: http://www.bellissimapublishing.com; http://www.surfergirlsummer.com; http://bellissimapublishing.viewwork.com/bellissima_publishing_llc/sellfolio.html.
Bello, Andres (CHL) *(978-956-13) Dist. by* **Continental Bk.**
Bellota *Imprint of* **Heinemann-Raintree**
Bellwether Media, *(978-1-60014; 978-1-61211; 978-1-61891; 978-1-62617; 978-1-68103)* Orders Addr.: 5357 Penn Ave. S., Minneapolis, MN 55347 USA (SAN 920-8135) Tel 612-825-2545; Fax: 612-825-2544; Toll Free Fax: 800-675-6679; Toll Free: 800-679-8068; *Imprints:* Blastoff! Readers (Blastoff Rdrs); Torque Books (Torque Bks); Pilot Books (PilotBks); Epic Books (EpicBks); Express Books (Express Bks); Black Sheep (BlackISheepUSA)
E-mail: laura@bellwethermedia.com; jmartin@bellwethermedia.com; geena@bellwethermedia.com
Web site: http://www.bellwethermedia.com
Dist(s): **Follett Media Distribution**
Follett School Solutions.
Belly Kids (GBR) *(978-0-9574909) Dist. by* **SCB Distributo.**
Belmar Pubns., *(978-0-9746366)* 504 - 17th Ave., South Belmar, NJ 07719 USA Fax: 212-737-5211
E-mail: arthurpaone@aol.com.
Belshe, Judy *See* **Snuggle Up Bks.**
Beluga-Duga Pr., *(978-1-932176)* Orders Addr.: P.O. Box 923, Willits, CA 95490 USA; Edit Addr.: 700 E. Gobbi St., NO. 138, Ukiah, CA 95482 USA.
Ben Franklin Pr., *(978-0-9772447; 978-0-615-64586-5)* 910 S. Hohokam Dr., Suite 104, Tempe, AZ 85281 USA Tel 480-968-7959; Fax: 480-966-3694
E-mail: rickburress@benfranklinpress.net.
BenBella Bks., *(978-1-932100; 978-1-933771; 978-0-9792331; 978-1-935251; 978-1-935618; 978-1-936661; 978-1-937856; 978-1-939529; 978-1-940363; 978-1-941631; 978-1-942952)* 10300 N Central Expy Suite 400, Dallas, TX 75231 USA Tel 214-750-3600; Fax: 214-750-3645; 387 Park Ave. St., New York, NY 10016
E-mail: brittney@benbellabooks.com
Web site: http://www.benbellabooks.com
Dist(s): **Follett School Solutions**
Independent Pubs. Group
MyiLibrary
Perseus Bks. Group
Perseus Distribution
ebrary, Inc.
Bench Press *See* **Gallant Hse. Publishing**
Benchmark Bks. *Imprint of* **Marshall Cavendish Corp.**
Benchmark Book Craft, *(978-0-9744015)* P.O. Box 19583, Colorado City, CO 81019 USA Tel 719-676-3009.
Benchmark Education Co., *(978-1-58344; 978-1-892393; 978-1-59000; 978-1-4108; 978-1-60437; 978-1-60634; 978-1-935440; 978-1-935441; 978-1-60859; 978-1-935469; 978-1-935470; 978-1-935471; 978-1-935472; 978-1-935473; 978-1-61672; 978-1-936254; 978-1-936255; 978-1-936256;-1-936257; 978-1-936258; 978-1-4509; 978-1-4900; 978-1-5021; 978-1-5125)* 145 Huguenot St 8th Flr, New Rochelle, NY 10801 USA Tel 914-637-7200; Fax: 914-637-7263; Toll Free Fax: 877-732-8273; Toll Free: 877-236-2465*
E-mail: bhaggerty@benchmarkeducation.com
Web site: http://www.benchmarkeducation.com.
Bendon, Inc., *(978-1-57759; 978-1-58117; 978-1-888443; 978-1-888567; 978-1-4037; 978-1-932209; 978-1-59394; 978-1-60139; 978-1-61568; 978-1-4530; 978-1-61405; 978-1-62191; 978-1-62615; 978-1-63109; 978-1-63346; 978-1-5050)* 1840 Baney Rd, Ashland, OH 44805 USA; *Imprints:* Spirit Press (SpiritPr); Intervisual/Piggy Toes (IntervisPiggy)
Web site: http://www.bendonpub.com.
Bendon Publishing International *See* **Bendon, Inc.**
Bendt Family Ministries *See* **Valerie Bendt**
Bene Factum Publishing, Ltd. (GBR) *(978-0-9522754; 978-1-903071) Dist. by* **IPG Chicago.**
Benedetti, Jef, *(978-0-9801372)* 4242 Johnstown Rd., Gahanna, OH 43230 USA (SAN 855-2991).
Benefactory, Inc., The, *(978-1-58021; 978-1-882728)* 3 Baneberry Ln., Riverwoods, IL 60015-3534 USA Toll Free: 800-729-7251
E-mail: benefactry@aol.com.
Benjamin Franklin Pr., *(978-0-9789827; 978-0-9795257; 978-0-9799941)* P.O. Box 51936, Pacific Grove, CA 93950 USA Fax: 831-626-3734
E-mail: loye@benjaminfranklinpress.com
Web site: http://www.benjaminfranklinpress.com
Dist(s): **BookBaby.**
Benjamin Pr., *(978-0-9663478; 978-0-9793431; 978-0-9836106)* Div. of Elmwood Inn Fine Teas, P.O. Box 100, Perryville, KY 40468 USA Tel 859-236-6641; Toll Free Fax: 888-879-0467; Toll Free: 800-765-2139 Do not confuse with Benjamin Pr., Northampton, MA
E-mail: BR@benjaminpress.com
Web site: http://www.benjaminpress.com
Dist(s): **Partners Pubs. Group, Inc.**
Benjey Media *See* **Tuxedo Pr.**
Bennett, Robert *See* **Archeological Assessments, Inc.**
Bennett/Novak & Co., Inc., *(978-0-9713454)* 8500 Holloway Dr., Los Angeles, CA 90069 USA Tel 310-657-2975; Fax: 310-657-4006
Dist(s): **National Bk. Network.**
Bennovations Publishing Services, *(978-0-9721066)* P.O. Box 28906, San Diego, CA 92198 USA Tel 858-663-5302; Fax: 858-777-5779
E-mail: info@bennovations.com
Web site: http://www.bennovations.com.
Benoy Publishing, *(978-0-9720809; 978-1-932162)* 735 Bragg Dr., Unit H, Wilmington, NC 28412 USA Tel 910-796-0424 (phone/fax)
E-mail: bbppdodo@aol.com
Web site: http://www.benoypublishing.com.
Benson, Lyn, *(978-0-615-13524-3)* 7063 E. Briarwood Dr., Centennial, CO 80112 USA Fax: 303-736-4075
E-mail: lynbenson@msn.com.
Benson, Queen M., *(978-0-615-12716-3)* 106 James River Dr., Newport News, VA 23601 USA
E-mail: dbbenson@verizon.net
Web site: http://www.lactose-limited.com.
Bent Castle Workshops, *(978-0-9768848)* P.O. Box 10551, Rochester, NY 14610-0551 USA
E-mail: knot@enchantedglyph.com
Web site: http://www.bentcastle.com.
BentDaiSha, LLC, *(978-0-9749465)* 11020 E. Indigo Bush Pl., Tucson, AZ 85748-3558 USA
E-mail: bentdaisha@cox.net.
Bentivegna, Fred, *(978-0-9766228)* 445 W. 27th St., Chicago, IL 60616 USA Tel 312-225-5514 (phone/fax)
E-mail: fbentivegna@sbcglobal.net.
Bentle Bks., *(978-0-9746904)* Orders Addr.: P.O. Box 2274, Oakhurst, CA 93644 USA Fax: 559-683-6206; Edit Addr.: 42564 Buckeye Rd., Oakhurst, CA 93644 USA
E-mail: terrahulse@sierratel.com
Web site: http://www.bentlebooks.com
Dist(s): **Follett School Solutions.**
Bentley, Trish, *(978-0-9774752)* 347 E. 6th St., Apt. 2B, New York, NY 10002 USA.
Benton, John Bks., *(978-0-9635411)* 127 S. El Molino Ave., Pasadena, CA 91101-2510 USA Tel 626-405-0950; Fax: 818-564-0952
Dist(s): **Spring Arbor Distributors, Inc.**
Berbay Publishing (AUS) *(978-0-9806711; 978-0-9942895; 978-0-9943841) Dist. by* **IPG Chicago.**
Beres, Nancy, *(978-0-9752801)* 2025 Willow Glen Ln., Columbus, OH 43229-1550 USA.
Bergner, Bobby, *(978-0-615-21301-9; 978-0-615-22870-9)* 237 Sycamore Ln., Phoenixville, PA 19460 USA
Web site: http://www.moofax.com.
Bergstrom Bks., *(978-0-9787648)* 521 12th Ave. NE., Devils Lake, ND 58301 USA Tel 701-662-3320
E-mail: Candace@lakechevy.com.
Berkeley Major Publishing, *(978-0-9720691)* 8282 Skyline Cir., Oakland, CA 94605-4230 USA Fax: 419-791-7109
E-mail: dailon@progidy.net; BMP@berkeleymp.com
Web site: http://www.berkeleymp.com.
Berkeley Science Bks., *(978-0-9764138)* 529 Bonnie Dr., El Cerrito, CA 94530 USA Tel 510-524-8094
E-mail: wdflannery@aol.com.
Berkley *Imprint of* **Penguin Publishing Group**
Berkley Hardcover *Imprint of* **Penguin Publishing Group**
Berkley Trade *Imprint of* **Penguin Publishing Group**
Berkshire Publishing Group, *(978-0-9743091; 978-0-9770159; 978-1-933782; 978-1-61472)* 120 Castle St., Great Barrington, MA 01230 USA Tel 413-528-0206; Fax: 413-541-0076
E-mail: info@berkshirepublishing.com
Web site: http://www.berkshirepublishing.com
Dist(s): **Follett School Solutions**
MyiLibrary.
Berlin, Stuart, *(978-0-615-22518-0; 978-0-615-48240-8; 978-0-9914128)* 1910 Larch St., Simi Valley, CA 93065 USA
E-mail: westwing1910@yahoo.com.
Berlin, Theodore *See* **Theodore Berlin Publishing**
Berlitz Publishing, 46-35 54th Rd., Maspeth, NY 11378 USA
E-mail: customerservice@langenscheidt.com
Web site: http://www.berlitzbooks.com
Dist(s): **Ingram Pub. Services**
Langenscheidt Publishing Group.
Bernard Design *See* **Elmdale Park Books**
Bernson Pr., *(978-0-9720509)* Orders Addr.: P.O. Box 55563, Sherman Oaks, CA 91413 USA Tel 818-785-5290; Fax: 818-785-0948; Edit Addr.: 5530 Allot Ave., Sherman Oaks, CA 91401 USA
E-mail: bernsonpress@aol.com
Web site: http://www.thehealingartist.com.
Bernstein, Susan, *(978-0-9706596)* 31100 Northwestern Hwy., Farmington Hills, MI 48344-2519 USA Tel 248-737-8400; Fax: 248-737-4392; Toll Free: 800-225-5726
E-mail: les380414744@aol.com
Web site: http://www.epominonousepstein.com.
Berry, Joy Enterprises, *(978-1-60577)* 146 W. 29th St., Suite 11RW, New York, NY 10001 USA Tel 212-868-8282; Fax: 212-868-4110
Web site: http://www.joyberrymedia.com
Dist(s): **Perseus Distribution.**
Bertelsman, Verlagsgruppe C. GmbH (DEU) *(978-3-570) Dist. by* **Distribks Inc.**
Bertrand Brasil Editora SA (BRA) *(978-85-286) Dist. by* **Distribks Inc.**
Berwick Court Publishing, *(978-0-615-34122-4; 978-0-615-35191-9; 978-0-9838846; 978-0-9889540; 978-0-9909515)* Orders Addr.: 1562 Willow Rd., Northfield, IL 60093 USA Tel 312-772-3799
E-mail: matt@berwickcourt.com
Web site: http://berwickcourt.com.
Beshqoy, Nisreen, *(978-0-9759181)* P.O. Box 3846, Costa Mesa, CA 92628-3846 USA
E-mail: nisreenbeshqoy@hotmail.com
Web site: http://www.arabicandislamicbooksbynisreen.com.
Bess Pr., Inc., *(978-0-935848; 978-1-57306; 978-1-880188)* 3565 Harding Ave., Honolulu, HI 96816 USA (SAN 239-4111) Tel 808-734-7159; Fax: 808-732-3627
E-mail: kelly@besspress.com
Web site: http://www.besspress.com
Dist(s): **China Bks. & Periodicals, Inc.**
Follett School Solutions
Univ. of Hawaii Pr.
Best Books *See* **Library Reprints, Inc.**
Best Fairy Bks., *(978-0-9632524; 978-0-9786791)* 1241 Chateau Green Ct., Bel Air, MD 21015 USA (SAN 851-2930) Tel 410-879-7578; P.O. Box 455, Bel Air, MD 21014
E-mail: fairybooklady@aol.com
Dist(s): **AtlasBooks Distribution**
Follett School Solutions
Independent Pubs. Group.
Best Friends Books *See* **Children's Kindness Network**
Best Friends Productions, *(978-0-9765140)* 131 Bank St., New York, NY 10014-2177 USA
Web site: http://www.bestfriendsproductions.com.
Best of East Texas Pubs., *(978-1-878096)* Div. of Bob Bowman & Assocs., 515 S. First, Lufkin, TX 75901 USA Tel 409-634-7444; Fax: 409-634-7750.
†Bethany Hse. Pubs., *(978-0-7642; 978-0-87123; 978-1-55661; 978-1-56179; 978-1-57778; 978-1-880089; 978-1-59066)* Div. of Baker Publishing Group, Orders Addr.: P.O. Box 6287, Grand Rapids, MI 49516-6287 USA Toll Free Fax: 800-398-3111 (orders); Toll Free: 800-877-2665 (orders); Edit Addr.: 11400 Hampshire Ave., S., Bloomington, MN 55438-2455 USA (SAN 201-4416) Tel 952-829-2500; Fax: 952-996-1393
E-mail: orders@bakerbooks.com
Web site: http://www.bethanyhouse.com
Dist(s): **Anchor Distributors**
Appalachian Bible Co.
Baker Publishing Group
Brodart Co.
Cambridge Univ. Pr.
Follett School Solutions
Send The Light Distribution LLC
Spring Arbor Distributors, Inc.
Beeler, Thomas T. Pub.; *CIP.*
Bethlehem Bks., *(978-1-883937; 978-1-932350)* Div. of Bethlehem Community, Orders Addr.: 10194 Garfield St. S., Bathgate, ND 58216-4031 USA Tel 701-265-3725; Fax: 701-265-3716; Toll Free: 800-757-6831 Do not confuse with Bethlehem Books in Richmond, VA
E-mail: contact@bethlehembooks.com
Web site: http://www.bethlehembooks.com
Dist(s): **Follett School Solutions**
Ignatius Pr.
Spring Arbor Distributors, Inc.
Betrock Information Systems, Inc., *(978-0-9629761)* 7770 Davie Rd. Ext., Hollywood, FL 33024 USA Tel 954-981-2821; Fax: 954-981-2823
E-mail: Lori@betrock.com
Web site: http://www.hortworld.com.
Bettenhausen, Jo Anne *See* **CBM Publishing**
Better Be Write Pub., A, *(978-0-9767732; 978-0-9771971; 978-0-9788985)* Orders Addr.: P.O. Box 914, Kernersville, NC 27284 USA Tel 336-354-7173; 9001 Ridge Hill St., Kernersville, NC 27284
E-mail: argusenterprises@hotmail.com
Web site: http://www.abetterbewrite.com
Dist(s): **AtlasBooks Distribution.**
Better Chinese LLC, *(978-1-60603; 978-1-68194)* P.O. Box 695, Palo Alto, CA 94303 USA Tel 650-384-0902; 2479 E Bayshore Rd., Suite 110, Palo Alto, CA 94303 Tel 650-384-0902; Fax: 702-442-7968
E-mail: usa@betterchinese.com
Web site: http://www.BetterChinese.com.
Better Comics, *(978-0-9728070)* P.O. Box 541924, Dallas, TX 75354-1924 USA
E-mail: JESmith@bettercomics.com
Web site: http://www.bettercomics.com.
Better Day Publishing Company *See* **Better Day Publishing LLC**
Better Day Publishing LLC, *(978-0-9767189; 978-0-9796763)* Orders Addr.: 3695f Cascade Rd. #2161, Atlanta, GA 30331 USA Tel 770-885-7072
E-mail: contact@betterdaypublishing.com
Web site: http://www.betterdaypublishing.com
Dist(s): **Follett School Solutions.**
Better Homes & Gardens Books *See* **Meredith Bks.**
Better Karma, LLC, *(978-0-9824329; 978-0-9828426; 978-0-9847753; 978-0-9962897)* 6018 Goldenrod Ct., Alexandria, VA 22310 USA (SAN 858-1495) Tel 703-971-1072
E-mail: publisher@betterkarmapublishing.com
Web site: http://www.BetterKarmaPublishing.com
Dist(s): **AtlasBooks Distribution**
Smashwords.
Better Me Bks., Inc., *(978-0-9770294)* P.O. Box 834, Marlton, NJ 08053 USA Tel 609-206-6318; Fax: 856-489-0234
E-mail: bettermebooks@aol.Com
Web site: http://www.bettermebooks.com.
Better Non Sequitur, *(978-0-9743235)* 11925 Via Zapata, El Cajon, CA 92019 USA Tel 619-246-5190
E-mail: steven@betternonsequitur.com
Web site: http://www.betternonsequitur.com.
Better Than One Publishing, *(978-0-9758958)* 27582 120th St., Staples, MN 56479 USA
Web site: http://www.creatingedumaterials.com.
Better Tomorrow Publishing, A, *(978-0-9795768)* P.O. Box 2975, Upper Marlboro, MD 20773-2975 USA Fax: 301-576-8070
E-mail: andy@abettertomorrowpublishing.net; sandy@abtpub.com
Web site: http://abettertomorrowpublishing.net.
BetterLink Pr., Inc., *(978-1-60220)* 99 Pk. Ave., R.R. Donnelley, New York, NY 10016 USA
Dist(s): **Penguin Publishing Group**
Simon & Schuster, Inc.
Tuttle Publishing
Univ. of Hawaii Pr.
Bettino, Teresa Adele, *(978-0-9742842)* 8403 Cosby Ln., Mechanicsville, VA 23116 USA Tel 804-779-2672
E-mail: tbettino@msn.com.
Betts, Linda, *(978-0-9767802)* Orders Addr.: 6050 Pagenkopf Rd., Maple Plain, MN 55359 USA Tel 763-479-2789; Fax: 763-476-6508
E-mail: lynrae@hotmail.com.
Betty Crocker *Imprint of* **Houghton Mifflin Harcourt Publishing Co.**
Between the Lakes Group, LLC, *(978-0-9727403; 978-0-9766342; 978-0-9791000; 978-0-9826073)* Orders Addr.: P.O. Box 13, Taconic, CT 06079-0013 USA Tel 860-824-0640
E-mail: geoff@betweenthelakes.com
Web site: http://www.betweenthelakes.com.
Beverly Hills Publishing, *(978-0-9758870; 978-0-9777074; 978-0-9791967)* 291 S. La Cienega Blvd., Suites 107/108, Beverly Hills, CA 90211-3325 USA (SAN 850-0029) Tel 310-854-0705; Fax: 310-854-1840; Toll Free: 800-521-5669
E-mail: silvers@bevhillspub.com
Web site: http://www.bevhillspub.com.
Beyond the Stars, Incorporated *See* **Beyond the Stars Pubns.**

Beyond the Stars Pubns., *(978-0-9763635)* 14902 Preston Rd., Suite 404-764, Dallas, TX 75254 USA
E-mail: rjohnson@beyondthestarsbooks.com
Web site: http://www.beyondthestarsbooks.com.

Beyond Words Publishing, Inc., *(978-0-941831; 978-1-58270; 978-1-885223)* 20827 NW Cornell Rd., Suite 500, Hillsboro, OR 97124-9808 USA (SAN 666-4210) Tel 503-531-8700; Fax: 503-531-8773; Toll Free: 800-284-9673
E-mail: info@beyondword.com; sales@beyondword.com
Web site: http://www.beyondword.com
Dist(s): **Follett School Solutions**
Simon & Schuster, Inc.

Beyond Words/Atria Bks. *Imprint of* **Atria Bks.**

Beyond Your Words, *(978-0-9788789)* P.O. Box 5842, Newport Beach, CA 92662-9266 USA
Web site: http://www.beyondyourwords.com.

Bezalel Bks., *(978-0-9792258; 978-0-9794976; 978-0-9800483; 978-0-9818854; 978-0-9821222; 978-0-9823388; 978-0-9844864; 978-1-936453)* P.O. Box 300427, Waterford, MI 48330 USA
E-mail: bezalelbooks@gmail.com
Web site: http://www.bezalelbooks.com.

BFG Pr., LLC, *(978-0-9820307)* Div. of The PIE Group, P.O. Box 2269, Ewa Beach, HI 96706 USA (SAN 857-0590) Tel 808-428-0733
Web site: http://www.bfgpress.com/.

BFI Publishing (GBR) *(978-0-85170; 978-0-900212; 978-1-903786; 978-1-84457) Dist. by* **Macmillan.**

BGA Stories, *(978-0-9724806)* 3414 Forest Hills Cir., Garland, TX 75044-2000 USA (SAN 254-878X) Tel 972-496-0416
E-mail: bga@bgastories.com
Web site: http://www.bgastories.com.

Bhakta Program Institute *See* **Rupanuga Vedic College**

BHB International, Incorporated *See* **Continental Enterprises Group, Inc. (CEG)**

BHF Publishing, *(978-0-9801913; 978-0-615-13143-6)* 7139 Hwy. 85, Suite 274, Riverdale, GA 30274 USA Tel 678-925-4175
E-mail: melissabowan@hotmail.com; stdennis@highly-favored.net
Web site: http://www.highly-favored.net.

Bibia, LLC, *(978-0-9826276; 978-0-615-74924-2; 978-1-940760)* 878 Dancing Vines Ave., Las Vegas, NV 89183 USA Tel 702-896-0967; *Imprints*: Bibia Publishing (Bibia)
E-mail: abessan@cox.net
Web site: www.bibiapublishing.com
Dist(s): **CreateSpace Independent Publishing Platform.**

Bibia Publishing *Imprint of* **Bibia, LLC**

Bible Based Studies, *(978-0-9797786)* 1134 SE 3rd St., Crystal River, FL 34429 USA Tel 352-795-5128
E-mail: info@biblebasedstudies.org
Web site: http://www.biblebasedstudies.org.

Bible Facts Pr., *(978-0-9762892; 978-0-9772942)* 631 Martin Ave. Suite 1, Rohnert Park, CA 94928 USA
Web site: http://www.biblefactspress.com.

Bible Game *Imprint of* **IMAGINEX, LLC**

Bible League, *(978-1-882536; 978-1-61825; 978-1-61870; 978-1-62826)*
E-mail: info@bibleleagueusa.com
Web site: http://www.bibleleagueusa.com.

Bible Pathway Ministries, *(978-1-879595)* Orders Addr.: P.O. Box 20123, Murfreesboro, TN 37133 USA Tel 615-896-4243; Fax: 615-893-1744; Toll Free: 800-598-7884; Edit Addr.: P.O. Box 20123, Murfreesboro, TN 37129-0123 USA
E-mail: mail@biblepathway.org
Web site: http://www.biblepathway.org
Dist(s): **Send The Light Distribution LLC.**

Bible Visuals International, Inc., *(978-1-932381; 978-1-933206)* Orders Addr.: P.O. Box 153, Akron, PA 17501-0153 USA
Web site: http://www.biblevisuals.org.

Bible-4-Life.com *See* **SundaySchoolNetwork.com**

Bibleco, Inc., *(978-0-9746058; 978-0-9754978)* 153 Pinehurst Dr., Easton, PA 18042 USA (SAN 256-0801) Fax: 610-438-3964; *Imprints*: Biblemania (Bibleman)
E-mail: biblemania@aol.com
Web site: http://www.biblemania.com.

Biblemania *Imprint of* **Bibleco, Inc.**

BibleRhymes *Imprint of* **BibleRhymes Publishing, L.L.C.**

BibleRhymes Publishing, L.L.C., *(978-0-9790605)* Orders Addr.: 54211 Horizon Dr., Shelby Township, MI 48316 USA (SAN 852-3207); *Imprints*: BibleRhymes (BibleRhymes USA)
E-mail: CustomerService@BibleRhymes.com
Web site: http://www.BibleRhymes.com.

Biblesoft, Inc., *(978-1-56514)* 22030 Seventh Ave., S., Suite 204, Seattle, WA 98198-6235 USA (SAN 298-7473) Tel 206-824-0547; Fax: 206-824-2729
Web site: http://www.biblesoft.com
Dist(s): **Anchor Distributors**
Spring Arbor Distributors, Inc.

BiblesPlus, *(978-0-9769109)* 13741 Annandale Dr., No. 20D, Seal Beach, CA 90740 USA Toll Free: 866-924-2537
E-mail: biblesplus7@yahoo.com
Web site: http://www.biblesplus.com.

Biblical Counseling Institute *See* **Skinner, Kerry L.**

Biblical Standards Pubns., *(978-0-9678798)* 287 Caldwell Dr., Maggie Valley, NC 28751 USA Tel 828-926-0606
E-mail: waltdot@primeline.com.

Biblio Bks. International, *(978-0-9729545; 978-0-9741190; 978-0-9748524; 978-0-9766681; 978-0-9785565; 978-0-9833352)* Kendall Tamiami Executive Airport 14005 SW 127th St., Miami, FL 33186 USA Tel 786 573 3999; Fax: 786 573 2090
E-mail: info@bibliobooks.com
Web site: http://www.bibliobooks.com.

Biblio Resource Pubns., Inc., *(978-1-934185)* 108 1/2 S. Moore St., Bessemer, MI 49911 USA Tel 906-364-2190
E-mail: info@BiblioResource.com
Web site: http://www.BiblioResource.com
Dist(s): **Follett School Solutions.**

Biblio Services, Inc., *(978-1-59608; 978-1-61887)* 205 Calle Federico Costa Ste 109, San Juan, PR 00918-1305 USA Tel 787-753-1231; Fax: 787-753-1222
E-mail: vale@biblioservices.com; anthony@biblioservices.com
Web site: http://www.biblioservices.com.

Biblioasis (CAN) *(978-0-9735881; 978-0-9735971; 978-1-897231; 978-0-9738184; 978-1-926845) Dist. by* **Consort Bk Sales.**

BiblioBazaar, *(978-1-115; 978-1-4264; 978-1-4346; 978-1-4375; 978-0-554; 978-0-559; 978-0-699; 978-1-103; 978-1-110; 978-1-113; 978-1-116; 978-1-117; 978-1-140; 978-1-141; 978-1-142; 978-1-143; 978-1-144; 978-1-145; 978-1-146; 978-1-147; 978-1-148; 978-1-149; 978-1-170; 978-1-171; 978-1-172; 978-1-173; 978-1-174; 978-1-175; 978-1-176; 978-1-177; 978-1-178; 978-1-179; 978-1-240; 978-1-241; 978-1-242; 978-1-243; 978-1-244; 978-1-245; 978-1-246; 978-1-247; 978-1-248; 978-1-249; 978-1-270; 978-1-271; 978-1-2)* P.O. Box 21206, Charleston, SC 29413 USA Tel 843-696-0416; Fax: 843-853-9251; 33 Cannon St., Charleston, SC 29403 Tel 843-408-2303; *Imprints*: BiblioLife (Bibliolife); Nabu Press (Nabu Pr); British Library, Historical Print Editions (BritLibrary) 11/15/05 Owner also owns Indigo, Inc. of Charleston, SC but the two companies are not connected. LT
E-mail: info@bibliolife.com; info@bibliolabs.com
Web site: http://www.bibliobazaar.com; www.bibliolabs.com
Dist(s): **MyiLibrary.**

Bibliograf, S.A. (ESP) *(978-84-7153; 978-84-8332) Dist. by* **Distribks Inc.**

Bibliograf, S.A. (ESP) *(978-84-7153; 978-84-8332) Dist. by* **Continental Bk.**

Bibliographisches Institut & F. A. Brockhaus AG (DEU) *(978-3-411) Dist. by* **Distribks Inc.**

Bibliographisches Institut & F. A. Brockhaus AG (DEU) *(978-3-411) Dist. by* **Intl Bk Import.**

Bibliographisches Institut & F. A. Brockhaus AG (DEU) *(978-3-411) Dist. by* **Continental Bk.**

Bibliographisches Institut & F. A. Brockhaus AG (DEU) *(978-3-411) Dist. by* **IBD Ltd.**

BiblioLife *Imprint of* **BiblioBazaar**

Bibliotech Pr., *(978-1-61895)* 2502 Canada Blvd. No. 1, Glendale, CA 91208 USA Tel 818-546-1554
E-mail: BibliotechPress@gmail.com.

Biblo & Tannen Booksellers & Pubs., Inc., *(978-0-8196)* P.O. Box 302, Cheshire, CT 06410 USA (SAN 202-4071) Tel 203-250-1647 (phone/fax); Toll Free: 800-272-8778
E-mail: biblo.moser@gte.net.

BIC Alliance, *(978-0-9768310)* Orders Addr.: P.O. Box 40166, Baton Rouge, LA 70835 USA Fax: 225-751-9993; Toll Free: 800-460-4242; Edit Addr.: 6378 Quinn Dr., Baton Rouge, LA 70817 USA
E-mail: brady@bicalliance.com
Web site: http://www.bicpublishing.com.

Bicast, Inc., *(978-0-9638258; 978-0-9701008; 978-0-9766753)* Orders Addr.: P.O. Box 2676, Williamsburg, VA 23187 USA Tel 757-229-3276; Fax: 757-253-2273; Toll Free: 800-767-8273; Edit Addr.: 231 K Parkway Dr., Williamsburg, VA 23185 USA
E-mail: bicastpub@aol.com; jogaertner@hughes.net
Web site: http://www.lighthousesusa.com.

Bick Publishing Hse., *(978-1-884158)* 307 Neck Rd., Madison, CT 06443 USA Tel 203-245-0073; 203 245 0073; Fax: 203-245-5990; 30 Amberwood Pkwy., Ashland, OH 44805
E-mail: bickpubhse@aol.com
Web site: http://www.bickpubhouse.com
Dist(s): **AtlasBooks Distribution**
Follett School Solutions
Quality Bks., Inc.

Bickico Enterprises, Inc., *(978-0-9746508; 978-0-9834081)* 19W042 Ave. Normandy E., Oak Brook, IL 60523 USA
E-mail: bickico@aol.com.

BICs Pr., *(978-0-9764253)* 1866 John F. Kennedy Blvd., No. B1, Jersey City, NJ 07305 USA.

Bienna Bks., *(978-0-9815075)* 21310 Poplar Way, Brier, WA 98036 USA Tel 206-774-3649.

Bier Brothers, Inc., *(978-0-9677238)* 147 Wild Dunes Way, Jackson, NJ 08527-4050 USA (SAN) Fax: 810-815-2979; *Imprints*: Sweet Dreams Press (Sweet Press)
E-mail: Dsb342@aol.com; contactus@nightsprytes.com
Web site: http://www.newbreedcomics.com; http://www.nightsprytes.com
Dist(s): **AtlasBooks Distribution.**

Big Bear Publishing U.S., *(978-0-9801215)* P.O. Box 191, Ronks, PA 17572-9611 USA (SAN 855-2517) Tel 717-768-4644
E-mail: lonniebrinkley@yahoo.com
Web site: http://www.ibelievesanta.com.

Big Belly Bks., *(978-0-9749554; 978-0-692-37003-2; 978-0-9961792)* Orders Addr.: 2778 W. Schuss Mtn. Dr., Bellaire, MI 49615 USA; Edit Addr.: 2778 W. Schuss Mtn. Dr., Bellaire, MI 49615 USA
E-mail: sc@bigbellybooks.com
Web site: http://www.bigbellybooks.com.

Big Bks. for Little People *Imprint of* **Friendly Planet**

Big Book Pr., LLC, *(978-0-9793219; 978-0-9848920)* Orders Addr.: 47774 Scots Borough Sq., Potomac Falls, VA 20165 USA Tel 240-355-3465
E-mail: frankchawkins@gmail.com; books@boysguidebooks.com; books@bigbookpress.com; books@girlsguidebooks.net; books@boysandgirlsguidebooks.com
Web site: http://www.boysguidebooks.blogspot.com; http://www.boysguidebooks.com; http://www.girlsguidebooks.net; http://www.bigbookpress.com; http://www.boysandgirlsguidebooks.com
Dist(s): **Independent Pubs. Group**
MyiLibrary
Small Pr. United.

Big Bk. Pubns., *(978-0-615-17074-9; 978-0-615-21065-0)* P.O. Box 7867, Largo, MD 20792 USA
E-mail: nicole@bigbookpublications.com
Web site: http://www.nigbookpublications.com.

Big Books, by George!, *(978-1-59246)* Orders Addr.: P.O. Box 1018, Keller, TX 76244 USA; Edit Addr.: 901 Briar Ridge Dr., Keller, TX 76244 USA
Dist(s): **Follett School Solutions.**

Big Brown Box, Inc., The, *(978-0-9764647)* 443 Hill Rd., Douglassville, PA 19518-9530 USA Tel 610-385-7587
Web site: http://www.thebigbrownbox.com
Dist(s): **Book Clearing Hse.**

Big Buddy Bks. *Imprint of* **ABDO Publishing Co.**

Big City Publishing, *(978-0-9762071; 978-0-9845873)* 230 Central St., Auburndale, MA 02492 USA Fax: 617-795-1650
E-mail: mellisa@bigcitypublishing.com
Web site: http://www.anglesfromtheattic.com.

Big Company, LLC, The, *(978-0-9800752)* 4790 Irvine Blvd., Suite 105-176, Irvine, CA 92620 USA (SAN 855-1383)
E-mail: info@thebigcompanyllc.com.

Big Country Publishing, LLC, *(978-0-9845088; 978-0-9847831; 978-1-938487)* 7691 Shaffer Pkwy., Suite C, Littleton, CO 80127 USA.

Big Creek Publishing, *(978-0-9742021)* Orders Addr.: P.O. Box 884, Sunberry, OH 43074 USA Tel 740-965-4127; Fax: 740-965-9541; Edit Addr.: 930 Joe Walker Rd., Sunbury, OH 43074 USA (SAN 255-4054) Tel 740-965-4127
E-mail: bigcreekpublishing@msn.com.

Big Dreams Publishing, *(978-0-9771868)* 8180 S. Allison Ct., Littleton, CO 80128 USA.

Big Drum Pr., *(978-1-890349)* P.O. Box 2406, Chapel Hill, NC 27515-2406 USA (SAN 253-9330) Tel 919-933-1805 (phone/fax)
E-mail: bdpnc@aol.com
Dist(s): **SPD-Small Pr. Distribution.**

†**Big Earth Publishing**, *(978-0-915024; 978-1-879483; 978-1-931599; 978-1-934553)* Orders Addr.: 3005 Ctr. Green Dr., Suite 200, Boulder, CO 80301 USA (SAN 209-2425) Fax: 608-259-8370; Toll Free: 800-258-5830; Edit Addr.: 1637 Pearl St. Ste. 201, Boulder, CO 80302-5447 USA; *Imprints*: Trails Books (Trails Bks)
E-mail: books@bigearthpublishing.com
Web site: http://www.bigearthpublishing.com
Dist(s): **BPDI**
CreateSpace Independent Publishing Platform
Partners Bk. Distributing, Inc.; *CIP*.

Big Entertainment, Inc., *(978-0-9645175; 978-1-57780)* 2255 Glades Rd., Suite 237W, Boca Raton, FL 33431-7395 USA Tel 407-998-8000; Fax: 407-998-2974
Dist(s): **Kable Media Services.**

Big Guy Bks., Inc., *(978-1-929945)* 1615 Orchard Wood Rd., Encinitas, CA 92024-5654 USA (SAN 253-0392) Toll Free: 800-536-3030; 814 N. Franklin, Chicago, IL 60610
E-mail: info@bigguybooks.com; bernadette@bigguybooks.com
Web site: http://www.timesoldiers.com; http://www.bigguybooks.com
Dist(s): **Follett School Solutions**
Independent Pubs. Group.

Big H Bks. *Imprint of* **Harvey, Alan**

Big Idea Productions, *(978-0-9788591)* P.O. Box 189, Lombard, IL 60148 USA Tel 630-652-6000; Fax: 630-652-6001
Dist(s): **Vision Video**
Word Entertainment.

Big Ideas Learning, LLC, *(978-1-60840; 978-1-68033)* 1762 Norcross Rd., Erie, PA 16510 USA (SAN 857-751X) Tel 814-824-6365; 814-824-6370; Fax: 814-824-6377; Toll Free Fax: 888-432-9245; Toll Free: 877-552-7766
E-mail: wputnam@larsontexts.com
Web site: http://bigideaslearning.com
Dist(s): **Houghton Mifflin Harcourt Publishing Co.**
Macmillan.

Big Kid Bks., *(978-0-9771990)* 6671 Sunset Blvd., No. 1585-101, Los Angeles, CA 90028 USA.

Big Kid Science, *(978-0-9721819; 978-1-937548; 978-1-944161)* 680 Iris Ave., Boulder, CO 80304 USA; 814 N. Franklin St., Chicago, IL 60610
E-mail: jeff@bigkidscience.com
Web site: http://www.jeffreybennett.com
Dist(s): **Follett School Solutions**
Independent Pubs. Group
MyiLibrary
ebrary, Inc.

Big Kids Productions (Publishing), *(978-0-930249)* 15 Marco Ln., Rochester, NY 14622-3228 USA (SAN 670-8617)
E-mail: pattiup@rochester.rr.com
Web site: http://www.rochesternyeats.com
Dist(s): **North Country Bks., Inc.**

Big Kids Publishing, Incorporated *See* **Big Kids Productions (Publishing)**

Big Lil' Bks., *(978-0-9749041)* Div. of ShadeTree Publishing, 3625 Tallman SE, Grand Rapids, MI 49508 USA
E-mail: janiceintheshade@msn.com.

Big Mouth Hse. *Imprint of* **Small Beer Pr.**

Big Picture Press *Imprint of* **Candlewick Pr.**

Big Picture, The, *(978-0-9794304; 978-0-9882125)* 5976 Leland, Ann Arbor, MI 48105-9309 USA Tel 734-223-4933
E-mail: kmaclean@kjmaclean.com
Web site: http://www.kjmaclean.com/.

Big Ransom Studio, *(978-0-9754728; 978-1-933732)* P.O. Box 489, Georgetown, TX 78627-0489 USA
E-mail: sales@bigransom.com
Web site: http://www.mindtrippress.com
Dist(s): **Mind Trip Pr.**

Big River Distribution, *(978-0-9795944; 978-0-9823575; 978-0-9845519)* Orders Addr.: 8214 Exchange Way, Saint Louis, MO 63144 USA (SAN 631-9114) Tel 314-918-9800; Fax: 314-918-9804
E-mail: info@bigriverdist.com; randy@bigriverdist.com
Web site: http://www.bigriverdist.com
Dist(s): **Follett School Solutions.**

Big Secret, The, *(978-0-9724924)* P.O. Box 1994, Slidell, LA 70459 USA Tel 985-781-8704 (phone/fax)
Web site: http://www.thebigsecret.org.

Big Sky Stories Publishing *See* **Arnica Publishing**

Big Smile, Inc., *(978-0-9761891)* P.O. Box 1042, Stroudsburg, PA 18360 USA Fax: 646-542-5319
E-mail: marcjohnjefferies@yahoo.com
Web site: http://www.marcjohnonline.com.

Big Smile Pr., LLC, *(978-0-9888462)* 180 Hollow Way, Ingleside, IL 60041 USA Tel 847-973-9084
E-mail: kellyp123@comcast.net.

Big Tent Bks., *(978-1-60131)* 115 Bluebill Dr., Savannah, GA 31419 USA (SAN 851-1136); *Imprints*: Parents Publishing Group (Parents Pub); Castlebridge Books (Castlebridge Bks)
E-mail: admin@dragonpencil.com; admin@bigtentbooks.com
Web site: http://www.bigtentbooks.com
Dist(s): **Castlebridge Distribution**
Music, Bks. & Business, Inc.

Big Tent Entertainment, Inc., *(978-1-59226)* 216 W. 18th St., New York, NY 10011 USA Tel 212-604-0064
Dist(s): **Midpoint Trade Bks., Inc.**

Big Tomato Pr., *(978-0-9791233)* Orders Addr.: 1480 Sutterville Rd., Sacramento, CA 95822 USA Tel 916-798-2125
E-mail: jocelyn@bigtomatopress.com
Web site: http://www.bigtomatopress.com
Dist(s): **Follett School Solutions.**

Big Valley Pr., *(978-0-9765372)* 401 E. Holum St, Deforest, WI 53532 USA Tel 608-513-0724
E-mail: stuart@stotts.com
Web site: http://www.bigvalleypress.com
Dist(s): **Follett School Solutions.**

Big Valley Publishing, *(978-0-9726004)* 516 N. Chinowth, Visalia, CA 93291 USA Do not confuse with company with similar name in Northridge, CA
E-mail: erkna@aol.com.

Big Wave Bks., *(978-0-9754979)* P.O. Box 108, Charlestown, RI 02813 USA Tel 401-322-8711
Web site: http://www.bigwavebooks.com.

Biggaloo Bks., *(978-0-9818145)* 660 Fairway Terr., Naples, FL 34103 USA (SAN 856-6267)
Dist(s): **Music, Bks. & Business, Inc.**

Big-head fish, *(978-0-9765007)* 311 W. 95st., Suite 1an, New York, NY 10025 USA Tel 212-316-0860
E-mail: info@bigheadfish.com/
Web site: http://www.bigheadfish.com/.

BigKids Bilingual Bks., *(978-0-9844310)* P.O. Box 537, Glendale, CA 91209 USA (SAN 859-385X) Tel 626-407-8886
E-mail: jalexan@alumni.usc.edu
Web site: http://www.bigkidsbilingualbooks.com.

Bilbo Bks., *(978-0-9800108)* 1384 W. Peachtree St., NW, No. C-4, Atlanta, GA 30309-2913 USA
E-mail: BilboBooks@comcast.net.

Bilingual Dictionaries, Inc., *(978-0-933146)* Orders Addr.: P.O. Box 1154, Murrieta, CA 92564 USA (SAN 221-9697) Tel 951-296-2445; Fax: 951-296-9911
E-mail: support@bilingualdictionaries.com
Web site: http://www.bilingualdictionaries.com
Dist(s): **Follett School Solutions.**

Bilingual Educational Services, Inc., *(978-0-86624; 978-0-89075)* 2514 S. Grand Ave., Los Angeles, CA 90007 USA (SAN 218-4680) Tel 213-749-6213; Fax: 213-749-1820; Toll Free: 800-448-6032
E-mail: sales@besbooks.com
Web site: http://www.besbooks.com
Dist(s): **Follett School Solutions.**

Bilingual Language Materials *See* **MAAT Resources, Inc.**

Bilingual Language Materials *Imprint of* **MAAT Resources, Inc.**

Bilingual Pr./Editorial Bilingue, *(978-0-916950; 978-0-927534; 978-1-931010; 978-1-939743)* Orders Addr.: Hispanic Research Ctr. Arizona State Univ. P.O. Box 875303, Tempe, AZ 85287-5303 USA (SAN 208-5526) Fax: 480-965-8309; Toll Free: 800-965-2280; Edit Addr.: Bilingual Review Pr. Administration Bldg. Rm. B-255 Arizona State Univ., Tempe, AZ 85281 USA
E-mail: brp@asu.edu
Web site: http://www.asu.edu/brp
Dist(s): **Libros Sin Fronteras**
SPD-Small Pr. Distribution.

Bilingual Pubns., *(978-0-9644678)* P.O. Box 12678, Denver, CO 80212 USA Tel 303-433-0979 Do not confuse with Bilingual Pubns. Co., New York, NY.

Bilingual Pubns. Co., The, 270 Lafayette St., New York, NY 10012 USA (SAN 164-8993) Tel 212-431-3500; Fax: 212-431-3567 Do not confuse with Bilingual Pubns., in Denver, CO
E-mail: lindagoodman@juno.com; spanishbks@aol.com.

Bilingual Stone Arch Readers *Imprint of* **Stone Arch Bks.**

Bill of Rights Institute, The, (*978-1-932785; 978-0-692-23022-0*) 200 N. Glebe Rd. Ste. 200, Arlington, VA 22203-3756 USA Toll Free: 800-838-7870
E-mail: sales@billofrightsinstitute.org; mwong@billofrightsinstitute.org; wneal@billofrightsinstitute.org
Web site: http://www.billofrightsinstitute.org
Dist(s): **CLEARVUE/eav, Inc.**
Social Studies Schl. Service
Teacher's Discovery.

Billiard Congress of America, (*978-1-878493*) 5 Piedmont Ctr NE Ste. 435, Atlanta, GA 30305-1509 USA
E-mail: amy@bca-pool.com; marketing@bca-pool.com
Web site: http://www.bca-pool.com.

Billings, David J., (*978-0-9789036*) 12441 SE Lusted Rd., Sandy, OR 97055-7556 USA
E-mail: david@davidjbillings.com; david@roadtripbook.com
Web site: http://www.roadtripbook.com.

Billings Worldwide Brain, (*978-0-9654169*) P.O. Box 701, Addison, TX 75001 USA (SAN 299-2426)
E-mail: dave@hamr.com
Web site: http://www.hamr.com
Dist(s): **Distributors, The.**

Billion $ Baby Pubns., (*978-0-9707945*) 22817 Ventura Blvd., Suite 408, Woodland Hills, CA 91364 USA (SAN 254-3265) Toll Free Fax: 888-232-9022; Toll Free: 800-499-2771
E-mail: Diedra@BabyPublications.com; dottie@babypublications.com
Web site: http://www.BabyPublication.com.

Billiot, Wendy Wilson, (*978-0-9762592*) 2715 Bayou DuLarge Rd., Theriot, LA 70397 USA
E-mail: wwbilliot@gmail.com
Web site: http://www.wetlandbooks.com.

Billy Jo Bks., (*978-0-9765088*) 9111 Oat Ave., Gerber, CA 96035-9723 USA Tel 530-385-1820
E-mail: biljoho@earthlink.net.

Billy the Bear & His Friends, Inc., (*978-0-9641338*) 1909 Munster Ave., Saint Paul, MN 55116 USA Tel 651-699-7636; Fax: 651-690-4815.

Bimini Bks., (*978-0-9753118*) 9553 SW 189 Terr., Suite 200, Miami, FL 33157 USA Tel 305-256-0638
E-mail: biminibooks@aol.com.

Bindu Bks. *Imprint of* **Inner Traditions International, Ltd.**

Binet International, (*978-0-942787*) P.O. Box 1429, Carlsbad, CA 92008 USA (SAN 667-7088) Tel 760-941-7929.

Bing Note, Inc., (*978-0-9794323*) 300 Caldecott Ln., No. 215, Oakland, CA 94618 USA
E-mail: lisa@bingnote.com
Web site: http://www.bingnote.com.

Bingham Putnam Publishing, (*978-0-9760504*) 326 Newport Dr., No. 1710, Naples, FL 34114 USA.

Bingo Bks., Inc., (*978-1-933530*) P.O. Box 3355, Austin, TX 78763-3355 USA Toll Free: 877-246-4644
Web site: http://www.bingobooks.com.

Binney & Smith, Inc., (*978-0-86696*) P.O. Box 431, Easton, PA 18042 USA (SAN 216-5899).

Binx Bks., (*978-0-9801796*) 33 W. Delaware Pl. Apt. 9F, Chicago, IL 60610-7361 USA.

Bio Rx, (*978-0-9772977*) 10828 Kenwood Rd., Cincinnati, OH 45242-2812 USA
E-mail: info@biorx.net
Web site: http://www.biorx.net.

Bio-Dynamic Farming & Gardening Assn., Inc., (*978-0-938250*) 25844 Butler Rd., Junction City, OR 97448 USA (SAN 224-9871) Tel 541-998-0105; Fax: 541-998-0406; Toll Free: 888-516-7797
E-mail: info@biodynamics.com
Web site: http://www.biodynamics.com
Dist(s): **New Leaf Distributing Co., Inc.**
Small Changes, Inc.
SteinerBooks, Inc.

BioEd *Imprint of* **Baylor College of Medicine**

Biographical Publishing Co., (*978-0-9637240; 978-1-929882; 978-0-9913521*) 95 Sycamore Dr., Prospect, CT 06712-1493 USA (SAN 298-2692) Tel 203-758-3661; Fax: 253-793-2618
E-mail: biopub@aol.com
Web site: http://www.biopub.us
Dist(s): **Pathway Bk. Service.**

Bios for Kids *Imprint of* **Panda Publishing, L.L.C.**

Birch Brook Pr., (*978-0-913559; 978-0-9789974; 978-0-9842003; 978-0-9915777*) P.O. Box 81, Delhi, NY 13753 USA (SAN 631-5321) Fax: 607-746-7453 (phone/fax)
E-mail: birchbrook@copper.net
Web site: http://www.birchbrookpress.info.

Birch Island, (*978-0-9772692; 978-0-9818668; 978-0-615-96113-2*) P.O. Box 988 27 Dillingham Rd., Manchester, VT 05254 USA (SAN 257-1625) Tel 802-362-0074; 802-342-7844
E-mail: historicalpages@yahoo,com
Web site: http://www.historicalpages.com
Dist(s): **CreateSpace Independent Publishing Platform**
Independent Pubs. Group.

Birch Tree Publishing, (*978-0-615-60274-5; 978-0-9894487*) 3830 Valley Centre Dr. Suite 705-432, San Diego, CA 92130 USA Tel 858-212-6111 Do not confuse with Birch Tree Publishing in Miami, FL, Southbury, CT
E-mail: nimpentoad@gmail.com
Dist(s): **CreateSpace Independent Publishing Platform.**

Birdcage Books *See* **Birdcage Pr.**

Birdcage Pr., (*978-1-889613; 978-1-59960*) 853 Alma St., Palo Alto, CA 94301 USA Tel 650-462-6300; Fax: 650-462-6305; Toll Free: 800-247-6553
E-mail: info@birdcagepress.com
Web site: http://www.birdcagepress.com.

Birdsall, Bonnie Thomas, (*978-0-9762679*) 3421 Lacewood Rd., Tampa, FL 33618 USA
E-mail: swimtaichibon@juno.com.

Birdseed Bks., (*978-0-9774142*) 520 17th St., Dallas, WI 54733 USA; *Imprints:* Birdseed Books for Kids (Birdseed Books for Kids)
Web site: http://www.birdseedbooksforkids.com
Dist(s): **Independent Pubs. Group.**

Birdseed Books for Kids *Imprint of* **Birdseed Bks.**

Birdsong Bks., (*978-0-9662761; 978-0-9833406*) Orders Addr.: 1322 Bayview Rd., Middletown, DE 19709 USA Tel 302-378-7274; Fax: 302-378-0339; Edit Addr.: 814 N. Franklin St, Chicago, IL 60610 USA
E-mail: birdsongbooks@delaware.net
Web site: http://www.birdsongbooks.com
Dist(s): **Common Ground Distributors, Inc.**
Follett School Solutions
Independent Pubs. Group
MyiLibrary.

Birkhauser Boston, (*978-0-8176*) Div. of Springer-Verlag GmbH & Co. KG, Orders Addr.: P.O. Box 2485, Secaucus, NJ 07094 USA (SAN 241-6344) Tel 201-348-4033; Edit Addr.: 675 Massachusetts Ave., Cambridge, MA 02139 USA (SAN 213-2869) Tel 617-876-2333; Toll Free: 800-777-4643 (customer service)
Web site: http://www.birkhauser.com
Dist(s): **Follett School Solutions**
Metapress
MyiLibrary
Springer
ebrary, Inc.

Birlinn, Ltd. (GBR) (*978-1-874744; 978-1-84158; 978-1-84341; 978-1-84697; 978-0-85790; 978-1-78027*) *Dist. by* **IPG Chicago.**

Birt Hse. Publishing, (*978-0-578-11306-7; 978-0-578-11315-9*) 100 Bluebonnet St., Apt. 108, Stephenville, TX 76401 USA.

Bisham Hill Bks., (*978-0-9744281*) Orders Addr.: 25 Old Kings Hwy. N. Ste. 13, #192, Darien, CT 06820 USA
E-mail: sales@bishamhill.com
Web site: http://www.bishamhill.com.

Bishop Museum Pr., (*978-0-910240; 978-0-930897; 978-1-58178*) Orders Addr.: 1525 Bernice St., Honolulu, HI 96817-2704 USA (SAN 202-408X) Tel 808-847-8260; 808-848-4135; *Imprints:* Kamahoi Press (Kamahoi Pr)
E-mail: press@bishopmuseum.org
Web site: http://www.bishopmuseum.org
Dist(s): **Booklines Hawaii, Ltd.**
Islander Group.

Bishop, Susan Lynn, (*978-0-9772878*) Orders Addr.: P.O. Box 13, Onley, IL 62450 USA Tel 618-392-4011; Edit Addr.: P.O. Box 13, Olney, IL 62450-0013 USA
E-mail: suzyb@wabash.net.

Bisiar Music Publishing, (*978-0-9753091*) Orders Addr.: P.O. Box 424, Evergreen, CO 80437-0424 USA (SAN 256-0356) Tel 303-670-0752 (phone/fax); Edit Addr.: 3661 A Evergreen Pkwy., Evergreen, CO 80437-0424 USA
E-mail: bisiar@earthlink.net
Web site: http://www.eddiespaghettiusa.com.

Bison Bks. *Imprint of* **Univ. of Nebraska Pr.**

Bit of Boston Bks., A, (*978-0-9788637*) Orders Addr.: 208 Commonwealth Ave., Boston, MA 02116 USA; Edit Addr.: P.O. Box 990208, Boston, MA 02116 USA
E-mail: jamesrholland@mindspring.com.

Bitingduck Pr., (*978-1-938463*) 1262 Sunnyoaks Cir., Altadena, CA 91001 USA Tel 626-507-8033
E-mail: jay@bitingduckpress.com
Web site: http://www.bitingduckpress.com
Dist(s): **Follett School Solutions**
SPD-Small Pr. Distribution.

Bitter Oleander Pr., The, (*978-0-9664358; 978-0-9786335; 978-0-9883525; 978-0-9862049*) 4983 Tall Oaks Dr., Fayetteville, NY 13066-9776 USA (SAN 855-9686)
E-mail: info@bitteroleander.com
Web site: http://www.bitteroleander.com
Dist(s): **SPD-Small Pr. Distribution.**

Bitty Book Pr., (*978-1-887270*) 851 Mt. Vernon Ct., Naperville, IL 60563 USA Tel 630-420-1887; Fax: 630-963-0341; Toll Free: 800-750-6649; 2736 Maple Ave., Downers Grove, IL 60515
E-mail: maryannako@aol.com
Web site: http://www.namepower101.com.

Bixie Gate Publishing, (*978-0-9773433*) 22694 SW Lincoln St., Sherwood, OR 97140 USA (SAN 257-3474)
E-mail: shannonk23@comcast.net
Web site: http://www.bixiegatepublishing.com; http://www.shannonkeegan.com.

Bixtu Bks., (*978-0-615-78054-2; 978-0-615-78450-2*) 31 Riverview Dr., Trabuco Canyon, CA 92679 USA Tel 949-370-5912
E-mail: johnandlisbeth@cox.net
Dist(s): **CreateSpace Independent Publishing Platform.**

Biz4Kids *Imprint of* **Round Cow Media Group**

Bjelkier Pr., (*978-0-9828217*) 1620 Louis Ln., Hastings, MN 55033 USA (SAN 859-9025) Tel 651-437-8244
E-mail: toysammy@embarqmail.com.

Bjelopetrovich, Beba Foundation, (*978-0-9745724*) 5555 W. Howard St., Skokie, IL 60077-2621 USA Tel 847-679-6710; Fax: 847-679-6717.

†BJU Pr., (*978-0-89084; 978-1-57924; 978-1-59166; 978-1-60682; 978-1-62856*) 1700 Wade Hampton Blvd., Greenville, SC 29614 USA (SAN 223-7512) Tel 864-242-5731; 864-370-1800 (ext. 4397; Fax: 864-298-0268; Toll Free Fax: 800-525-8398; Toll Free: 800-845-5731; *Imprints:* JourneyForth (JmyForth); Bloomsbury Visual Arts (BloomsVisual)
E-mail: bjup@bjup.com
Web site: http://www.bjupress.com
Dist(s): **Follett School Solutions**; *CIP.*

BKB Group, Inc., The, (*978-0-9747628*) Orders Addr.: 11146 Harbour Springs Cr., Boca Raton, FL 33428 USA Tel 561-218-1215; Fax: 561-218-1214; Toll Free: 888-321-7664; Edit Addr.: 11146 HARBOUR SPRINGS CR., 11146 HARBOUR SPRINGS CR., BOCA RATON, FL 33428 USA
E-mail: rfproductions@adelphia.net
Web site: http://www.billybutterfly.com.

Bks. for Young Learners *Imprint of* **Owen, Richard C. Pubs., Inc.**

Black, Amy Jackson, (*978-0-615-16743-5*) 107 Southglen, Terre Haute, IN 47802 USA
E-mail: godzgrl4evr@msn.com
Dist(s): **Lulu Enterprises Inc.**

Black and White Publishing Ltd. (GBR) (*978-1-873631; 978-0-9515151; 978-1-902927; 978-1-903265; 978-1-84502*) *Dist. by* **Interlink Pub.**

Black Bart Bks., (*978-0-615-20238-9; 978-0-615-23723-7; 978-0-578-01524-8; 978-0-578-02511-7; 978-0-578-08320-9*) 3447 Little Carpenter Creek Rd., Fernwood, ID 83830 USA
Web site: http://www.blackbaradventures.com
Dist(s): **Lulu Enterprises Inc.**

Black Belt Training, (*978-0-9759744*) 9109 Cochran Heights, Dallas, TX 75220 USA Tel 214-351-2234 (phone/fax)
E-mail: drted@wwwin.com
Web site: http://www.wwwin.com.

Black Bird Bks., (*978-0-9763238*) Orders Addr.: P.O. Box 901, Ankeny, IA 50021 USA; Edit Addr.: P.O. Box 901, Ankeny, IA 50021-0901 USA
E-mail: lizzie3blackbird@hotmail.com.

Black Cat *Imprint of* **Grove/Atlantic, Inc.**

Black, Clinton L., (*978-0-9620180*) Orders Addr.: P.O. Box 9096, Fort Lauderdale, FL 33310 USA Tel 954-722-0415; Fax: 954-720-7674
E-mail: thepurposeofhumanlife@yahoo.com
Dist(s): **Southern Bk. Service.**

Black Coat Pr. *Imprint of* **HollywoodComics.com, LLC**

Black Coffee Publishing, (*978-0-9745238*) Orders Addr.: 5543 Edmondson Pike, No. 213, Nashville, TN 37211-5808 USA Tel 615-969-5516
E-mail: bcpubl@aol.com
Web site: http://www.blackcoffeepublishing.com.

Black Creek Publishing Group, (*978-0-9895323; 978-0-9904596; 978-0-9962919*) 2102 Kimberton Rd. No. 266, Kimberton, PA 19460 USA Tel 832-350-3029
E-mail: jchenry@blackcreekpublishinggroup.com
Web site: www.blackcreekpublishinggroup.com.

Black Diamond Publishing, (*978-0-9715139*) 415 E. 32nd St., Indianapolis, IN 46205 USA Do not confuse with Black Diamond Publishing in Brooklyn,NY
E-mail: LWatk82805@aol.com; BDPub@aol.com; Linda@lindawatkins.org
Web site: http://www.lindawatkins.org.

Black Dog & Leventhal Pubs. Inc. *Imprint of* **Hachette Bks.**

Black Dog Books, (*978-1-884449; 978-1-928619*) 1115 Pine Meadows Ct., Normal, IL 61761 USA Tel 309-310-6984
E-mail: info@blackdogbooks.net; blackdogbooks_tomroberts@yahoo.com
Web site: http://www.blackdogbooks.net.

Black Dog Publishing Ltd. (GBR) (*978-0-9521773; 978-1-901033; 978-1-904772; 978-1-906155; 978-1-907317; 978-1-908966; 978-1-910433*) *Dist. by* **Perseus Dist.**

Black Dolphin Diving, (*978-0-9646281*) 5022 Two Harbors, Avalon, CA 90704-5022 USA Tel 310-510-2109
E-mail: bkdolphin@aol.com
Web site: http://www.divecatalina.com.

Black Dot Pubns., (*978-0-9649740*) Orders Addr.: P.O. Box 1068, Ojai, CA 93024 USA Tel 805-640-8825; Edit Addr.: 1208 Gregory St., Ojai, CA 93023 USA
E-mail: blackdotpubs@yahoo.com
Web site: http://www.backdotpubs.com; http://www.chuckhillig.com
Dist(s): **New Leaf Distributing Co., Inc.**

Black Falcon Publications *See* **LMW Works**

Black Forest Pr., (*978-1-58275; 978-1-881116*) Div. of Black Forest Enterprises, Orders Addr.: P.O. Box 6342, Chula Vista, CA 91909-6342 USA Fax: 619-482-8704; Toll Free: 800-451-9404 (General Information, Submission Inquiries and Acquisitions); 888-808-5440 (Book Sales, Marketing and Promotion); Edit Addr.: 1075 Hayuco Plz., Chula Vista, CA 91910-7006 USA (SAN 298-8445); *Imprints:* Sonnenschein Books (Sonnenschein Bks)
E-mail: bfp@blackforestpress.com
Web site: http://www.blackforestpress.com.

Black Garnet Pr., (*978-0-9832383; 978-0-9911790*) 1313 St. Helena Ave., Santa Rosa, CA 95404 USA Tel 707-526-3331
E-mail: sandybaker131@gmail.com
Web site: sandybakerwriter.com.

Black Hat Pr., (*978-0-9614462; 978-1-887649*) Orders Addr.: P.O. Box 12, Goodhue, MN 55027-0012 USA (SAN 689-4259) Tel 651-923-4590; Edit Addr.: 508 Second Ave., Goodhue, MN 55027-0012 USA
E-mail: blackhatpress@yahoo.com.

Black Hawk Pr., Inc., The, (*978-0-9778731; 978-0-9817613*) 803 Charter Pl., Charlotte, NC 28211 USA Tel 704-364-1164
E-mail: info@blackhawkpress.com
Web site: http://www.blackhawkpress.com
Dist(s): **Blu Sky Media Group.**

Black Heron Pr., (*978-0-930773; 978-1-936364*) Orders Addr.: P.O. Box 13396, Mill Creek, WA 98145 USA (SAN 677-623X) Fax: 425-355-4929; Edit Addr.: 27 West 20Th St., New York, NY 10011 USA
E-mail: Jgoldberon@aol.com
Web site: http://www.blackheronpress.com
Dist(s): **Follett School Solutions**
Midpoint Trade Bks., Inc.
ebrary, Inc.

Black Jasmine, (*978-0-9788802*) 46 Pleasant St., Sharon, MA 02067 USA
E-mail: deemajoan@yahoo.com
Web site: http://www.deemasglass.com.

Black, Judith Storyteller, (*978-0-9701073*) 33 Prospect St., Marblehead, MA 01941 USA Tel 781-631-4417
E-mail: jb@storiesalive.com
Web site: http://www.storiesalive.com.

Black Lab Publishing LLC, (*978-0-9742815*) Orders Addr.: P.O. Box 6244, Laconia, NH 03247 USA Tel 603-714-8023; 606-524-1114
E-mail: loni@bearandkatie.com
Web site: http://www.bearandkatie.com; http://www.blacklabpublishing.com.

Black Literary, Inc., (*978-0-615-22609-5; 978-0-615-30323-9; 978-0-615-37753-7*) P.O. Box 492, Catlett, VA 20119 USA Tel 540-788-4992
E-mail: CHancasky@aol.com.

Black Oak Media, Inc., (*978-0-9790401; 978-1-61876*) P.O. Box 122, Cherry Valley, IL 61016 USA Do not confuse with companies with a similar name in Lincoln, NE, Lambertville, NJ, Springfield, MO
E-mail: info@blackoakmedia.org
Web site: http://www.blackoakmedia.org
Dist(s): **Follett School Solutions.**

Black Oak Press, Illinois *See* **Black Oak Media, Inc.**

Black Orb *See* **Angie Blue Bks., LLC**

Black Pearl Bks., (*978-0-9728005; 978-0-9766007; 978-0-9773438*) Orders Addr.: 3653-F Flakes Mill Road, PMB 306, Atlanta, GA 30034 USA Do not
E-mail: hurst@blackpearlbooks.com
Web site: http://www.blackpearlbooks.com
Dist(s): **African World Bks.**
American Wholesale Bk. Co.
Bookazine Co., Inc.
Brodart Co.
Quality Bks., Inc.

Black Plum Bks., (*978-0-9785317*) Orders Addr.: 1302 Abby Ct., Juneau, AK 99801-9599 USA
Web site: http://www.blackplumebooks.com
Dist(s): **Follett School Solutions.**

Black Rabbit Bks., (*978-1-58340; 978-1-887068; 978-1-59920; 978-1-62310; 978-1-62588; 978-1-68071; 978-1-68072*) Orders Addr.: P.O. Box 3263, Mankato, MN 56002 USA (SAN 925-4862); Edit Addr.: 123 S. Broad St., Mankato, MN 56001 USA (SAN 858-902X); *Imprints:* Stargazer Books (StargazerBks)
E-mail: info@blackrabbitbooks.com; production@blackrabbitbooks.com
Web site: http://www.blackrabbitbooks.com
Dist(s): **Creative Co., The**
Follett School Solutions
RiverStream Publishing.

Black River Trading Co., (*978-0-9649083; 978-0-9797492*) P.O. Box 7, Oxford, MI 48371 USA (SAN 854-2724) Tel 248-628-5150; Fax: 248-628-6422
E-mail: jane@whoopforjoy.com
Web site: http://www.whoopforjoy.com
Dist(s): **Bookmen, Inc.**

Black Rose Writing, (*978-0-615-20158-0; 978-0-615-20274-7; 978-0-615-20494-9; 978-0-615-20616-5; 978-0-9821012; 978-0-9819742; 978-0-9825542; 978-0-9825823; 978-1-935605; 978-1-61296*) P.O. Box 1540, Castroville, TX 78009-1540 USA
E-mail: creator@blackrosewriting.com
Web site: http://www.blackrosewritiing.com; http://www.blackrosewriting.com/books
Dist(s): **Lightning Source, Inc.**
Lulu Enterprises Inc.

Black Sheep *Imprint of* **Akashic Bks.**

Black Sheep *Imprint of* **Bellwether Media**

Black Ship Publishing, (*978-0-9851969; 978-0-9914484; 978-0-9905469*) 1767 12th St. Suite 378, Hood River, OR 97031 USA Tel 310-696-9515
E-mail: smartcookie1@mac.com
Dist(s): **BookBaby**
Independent Pubs. Group
Lightning Source, Inc.
Perseus-PGW.

Black Society Pages, Inc., (*978-0-9758611*) 228 S. Washington St., Alexandria, VA 22314 USA.

Black Squirrel Bks. *Imprint of* **Kent State Univ. Pr.**

Black Threads Pr., (*978-0-9824796*) 3037 S. Buchanan St., Arlington, VA 22206-1512 USA
Web site: http://www.BlackThreads.com
Dist(s): **CreateSpace Independent Publishing Platform**
Lightning Source, Inc.

Blackberry Hill Pr., (*978-0-9792947*) Orders Addr.: 2860 Mohawk St., Sauquoit, NY 13456-3322 USA Tel 315-737-5147
Web site: http://www.dorothystacy.com
Dist(s): **North Country Bks., Inc.**

Blackberry Maine, (*978-0-942396; 978-0-615-15951-5; 978-0-9824389*) 617 E. Neck Rd., Nobleboro, ME 04555 USA (SAN 207-7949) Tel 207-729-5083; Fax: 207-729-6783
E-mail: chimfarm@gwi.net
Web site: http://www.blackberrybooksme.com
Dist(s): **SPD-Small Pr. Distribution.**

Blackberry Pubns., (*978-0-9776987*) 3915 11th Street, Ecorse, MI 48229 USA Tel 313-297-7809
E-mail: blackberrybooks@yahoo.com.

Blackberry Pubs., (*978-0-615-12702-6*) 2545 Hwy. 76, Portland, TN 37148 USA Tel 615-325-3970
E-mail: fussellb@comcast.net
Web site: http://www.blackberrypublishers.com
Dist(s): **Sadler, Dale.**

Blackberry: Salted in the Shell *See* **Blackberry Maine**

Blackbirch Pr., Inc. *Imprint of* **Cengage Gale**

Blackbird Bks., (*978-1-61053*) 1012 3rd Street, Suite 301, Santa Monica, CA 90403 USA Tel 310-422-7098
E-mail: editor@bbirdbooks.com
Web site: http://www.bbirdbooks.com.

Blackbird's World Publishing Co., (*978-0-9789798*) Orders Addr.: P.O. Box 475, Clyde, TX 79510 USA Tel

For full information on wholesalers and distributors, refer to the Wholesaler and Distributor Name Index

325-201-2495; Edit Addr.: Box 475 212 Hunt St., Clyde, TX 79510 USA
E-mail: blackbird@blackbirdsworldpublishingcompany.net
Web site: http://blackbirdsworldpublishingcompany.net.

Blackfoot Burkino Cherokee Publishing, *(978-0-9722724)* Orders Addr.: P.O. Box 58074, Houston, TX 77258 USA Tel 832-504-1331; Edit Addr.: 1912 Trentwood Pl., Charlotte, NC 28216 USA
E-mail: bbcpublishin80@gmail.com.

Blackfairs Pr., *(978-0-9745206)* 2319 Branner Dr., Menlo Park, CA 94025 USA.

Blackhawk Publishing, *(978-0-615-31902-5; 978-0-9826378; 978-0-9897554)* 888 W. 6th St., Los Angeles, CA 90017 USA; 814 N. Franklin St., Chicago, IL 60610
Web site: http://www.blackhawkpub.com
Dist(s): **Follett School Solutions**
Independent Pubs. Group
Outskirts Pr., Inc.

Blackington Publishing, *(978-0-615-75922-7)* 183 Cypress Point, Meadowlakes, TX 78654 USA Tel 325-665-1208
Dist(s): **CreateSpace Independent Publishing Platform.**

BlacknBlue Pr. UK *Imprint of* **Blacknblue Pr.**

Blacknblue Pr., *(978-0-9677652; 978-0-9840718)* 108 Benarr Ave., Fort Walton Beach, FL 32548 USA Tel 850-862-2874 (phone/fax); 13 Dellands Overton, Basingstoke, RG25 3LD Tel 1256 770736 (phone/fax); *Imprints:* BlacknBlue Press UK (BlacknBlue Pr UK)
E-mail: edddwicke@hotmail.com
Web site: http://www.blacknbluepress.info
Dist(s): **Lightning Source, Inc.**

Blacksmith Bks. (HKG) *(978-962-86732; 978-988-17742; 978-988-99799; 978-988-19003; 978-988-16139) Dist. by* **Natl Bk Netwk.**

Blacksmith Bks., LLC, *(978-0-9772515)* P.O. Box 4228, Lisle, IL 60532-9228 USA; 6141 Dixon Dr., Lisle, IL 60532-4151
E-mail: mark@blacksmithbks.com; m-boone@sbcglobal.net.

Black-Smith Enterprises, *(978-0-9762720)* 31536 Avondale, Westland, MI 48186 USA
E-mail: janaya_black@yahoo.com
Web site: http://www.black-smithenterprises.com
Dist(s): **Lightning Source, Inc.**

Blackstaff Pr., Ltd. (GBR) *(978-0-85640) Dist. by* **Dufour.**

Blackstone Editions, *(978-0-9725017; 978-0-9816402)* 312-24 Wellesley St. W., Toronto, ON M4Y 2X6 CAN Tel 647-344-2206
Web site: http://www.blackstoneeditions.com.

Blacktastic.net, *(978-0-9834275; 978-0-9961146)* 7945 Fincastle Ct., Sacramento, CA 95829 USA Tel 916-525-1703
E-mail: brotherhypnotic@hotmail.com.

Blacktypewriter Pr. *Imprint of* **Pittsburgh Literary Arts Network LLC**

BlackWords Press *See* **KA Productions, LLC**

Blade Publishing, *(978-1-929409)* 110 W. C St. Ste. 1300, San Diego, CA 92101-3978 USA (SAN 254-7678)
E-mail: bladeinternational@yahoo.com.

BladeRunner Publishing, *(978-0-9785477)* P.O. Box 4298, Greenville, SC 29608 USA Tel 864-313-6182
E-mail: bladerunnerpublishing@charter.net.

Bladestar Publishing, *(978-0-9787931)* Orders Addr.: 1499 N. 950 W., Orem, UT 84057 USA Fax: 484-414-1674
E-mail: Promotion@BladestarPublishing.com
Web site: http://www.bladestarpublishing.com
Dist(s): **Brodart Co.**

Blaft Pubns., , , CA 1 USA
Web site: http://www.blaft.com/
Dist(s): **SPD-Small Pr. Distribution**
Smashwords.

Blair, John F. Pub., *(978-0-89587; 978-0-910244)* Orders Addr.: 1406 Plaza Dr., Winston-Salem, NC 27103 USA (SAN 201-4319) Tel 336-768-1374; Fax: 336-768-9194; Toll Free: 800-222-9796
E-mail: harwood@blairpub.com
Web site: http://www.blairpub.com
Dist(s): **Smashwords.**

Blake, Edna, *(978-0-9668906)* 7 Babble Creek Ct., O Fallon, MO 63368-8321 USA.

Blake, John Publishing, Ltd. (GBR) *(978-0-905846; 978-1-85782; 978-1-903402; 978-1-904034; 978-1-84358; 978-1-84454; 978-1-78219; 978-1-78418) Dist. by* **IPG Chicago.**

Blake, Monica, *(978-0-9764155)* P.O. Box 475233, San Francisco, CA 94147 USA Tel 415-995-2515; Fax: 415-876-1002
E-mail: blakesfo@yahoo.com
Dist(s): **AtlasBooks Distribution.**

Blake-Virostko, Pamela, *(978-0-9801975)* 7546 S. Virostko Rd., Rockville, IN 47872 USA Tel 765-548-2635
E-mail: PVirostko@aol.com.

Blanchard, Graham, *(978-0-9854090; 978-0-9897949)* P.O. Box 300235, Austin, TX 78703 USA Tel 512-647-2099
E-mail: callie@grahamblanchard.com
Web site: http://www.grahamblanchard.com
Dist(s): **Ingram Pub. Services**
Send The Light Distribution LLC.

Blancmange Publishing LLC, *(978-0-9779488)* P.O. Box 17184, Memphis, TN 38187-7184 USA (SAN 850-7023).

Blanket Street Publishing, *(978-0-9760929)* 17278 Summit Hills Dr., Santa Clarita, CA 91387 USA
E-mail: kstrauss@socal.rr.com.

Blastoff! Readers *Imprint of* **Bellwether Media**

Blatant Times, *(978-0-9744376)* 608 Patton Rd., Great Bend, KS 67530 USA
Web site: http://www.cpcis.net.

Blaumond Pr., *(978-0-9789031)* 740 SE. Greenville Blvd., Suite 400, Box 283, Greenville, NC 27858 USA (SAN 851-9021) Tel 252-754-4837; Fax: 252-353-0732
E-mail: info@blaumondpress.com
Web site: http://www.blaumondpress.com.

Blaze, Ronan *See* **Medal Bks.**

Blazers *Imprint of* **Capstone Pr., Inc.**

Blazing Ideas Ltd., *(978-0-9801243; 978-0-9856029)* 11141 Blackforest way, Gaithersburg, MD 20879 USA Tel 301-515-0139
E-mail: lotit2000@yahoo.com
Web site: www.blazing-ideas.com.

BLD Enterprises *See* **Innovo Publishing, LLC**

Blessed and Highly Favored *See* **BHF Publishing**

Blessed Beginnings Publishing, *(978-0-9727201)* P.O. Box 241282, Milwaukee, WI 53223 USA Tel 414-351-6467
E-mail: pinksolitaire97@yahoo.com.

Blessings Unlimited, LLC, *(978-0-9742796)* P.O. Box 186, Highland Springs, VA 23075 USA Tel 804-640-7137 Do not confuse with Blessings Unlimited in Bloomington, MN
Web site: http://www.blessingsunlimited.info.

Blind Ferret Entertainment (CAN) *(978-0-9736946) Dist. by* **Diamond Book Dists.**

Blind Wolf Studios, *(978-0-9749941)* P.O. Box 465, Cross River, NY 10518 USA
Web site: http://www.blindwolfstudios.com.

Blink,
Dist(s): **Zondervan.**

Bliss Group, *(978-0-9885359; 978-1-940021)* 725 River Rd. No. 32-215, Edgewater, NJ 07020 USA Tel 551-333-9409
E-mail: alansrbradshaw@gmail.com
Dist(s): **Lightning Source, Inc.**
MyiLibrary.

Bliss on Tap, *(978-0-9763768; 978-0-9825098; 978-0-9896143)* 28326 Wellfleet Ln., Saugus, CA 91350 USA
E-mail: pephillipson@aol.com
Web site: http://www.godthedyslexicdog.com
Dist(s): **MyiLibrary.**

Bloated Toe Publishing, *(978-0-9795741; 978-0-9836925; 978-1-939216)* P.O. Box 324, Peru, NY 12972 USA Tel 518-563-9469 (phone/fax)
E-mail: sales@bloatedtoe.com
Web site: http://www.bloatedtoe.com.

Bloch Publishing Co., *(978-0-8197)* 5875 Mining Ter. Ste. 104, Jacksonville, FL 32257-3225 USA (SAN 214-204X)
E-mail: BlochPub@worldnet.att.net
Web site: http://www.blochpub.com/
Dist(s): **Follett School Solutions.**

Block Publishing, *(978-0-9761625)* 1120 Forest Ave., No. 306, Pacific Grove, CA 93950 USA Fax: 831-655-4830
E-mail: blockpub@sbcglobal.net
Web site: http://www.blockpublishing.com
Dist(s): **Follett School Solutions.**

Block System, The, *(978-0-9665545; 978-0-9800875)* 4619 Ranch View Rd., Fort Worth, TX 76109 USA Tel 817-732-2633; Fax: 817-732-0836
E-mail: andblock@gmail.com
Web site: http://www.blockcenter.com.

Blood Moon Productions, Ltd., *(978-0-9748118; 978-0-9786465; 978-1-936003)* 75 St. Marks Pl., Staten Island, NY 10301 USA Tel 718-556-9410; Fax: 718-816-4092; 4501 Forbes Blvd., Lanham, MD 20706
E-mail: DanforthPrince@hotmail.com
Web site: http://www.bloodmoonproductions.com
Dist(s): **Alamo Square Distributors**
Bookazine Co., Inc.
Follett School Solutions
MyiLibrary
National Bk. Network
ebrary, Inc.

Blood-Horse, Inc., The, *(978-0-936032; 978-0-939049; 978-1-58150)* Div. of The Blood-Horse, Inc., 3101 Beaumont Centre Cir., Lexington, KY 40513 USA (SAN 203-5294) Tel 859-278-2361 (Retailers); Fax: 859-276-6868; Toll Free: 800-866-2361 (Retailers); *Imprints:* Eclipse Press (Eclip Press)
E-mail: info@eclipsepress.com
Web site: http://www.eclipsepress.com
Dist(s): **AtlasBooks Distribution**
Smashwords
Western International, Inc.

Bloodletting Pr., *(978-0-9720859; 978-0-9768531; 978-1-935006)* P.O. Box 130, Welches, OR 97067 USA Tel 503-298-4811
Web site: http://www.bloodlettingbooks.com.

Bloom & Grow Bks., *(978-1-931969)* Div. of Bloom & Grow, Inc., Orders Addr.: 149 S. Barrington Ave., #363, Los Angeles, CA 90049 USA Tel 310-472-0505
E-mail: stephanie@bloomandgrow.com; info@bloomandgrow.com
Web site: http://www.bloomandgrow.com; http://www.placetogrow.com
Dist(s): **Beyda for Bks., LLC.**

Bloom & Grow, Incorporated *See* **Bloom & Grow Bks.**

Blooming Tree Pr., *(978-0-9718348; 978-0-9769417; 978-1-933831)* Div. of Hees Enterprises, LLC, Orders Addr.: P.O. Box 140934, Austin, TX 78714-0934 USA Tel 512-921-8846; Fax: 512-873-7710; Edit Addr.: 10703 Jonwood Way, Austin, TX 78753 USA Tel 512-921-8846; Fax: 512-873-7710; *Imprints:* Ready Blade (Ready Blade)
E-mail: email@bloomingtreepress.com; bloomingtree@gmail.com
Web site: http://www.bloomingtreepress.com.

Blooming Twig Books LLC, *(978-0-9777736; 978-1-933918; 978-1-61343; 978-1-937753)* Orders Addr.: 320 S. Boston Suite 1026, Tulsa, OK 74103 USA Tel 866-389-1482; Fax: 866-298-7260
Web site: http://www.bloomingtwig.com
Dist(s): **Cardinal Pubs. Group.**

BloomingFields, *(978-0-9645971)* 44 Voyagers Ln., Ashland, MA 01721 USA; *Imprints:* Wisdom Audio-Books (Wisdom Aud-Bks)
E-mail: markpoetry@hotmail.com.

Bloom's Literary Criticism *Imprint of* **Facts On File, Inc.**

Bloomsbury Academic, 175 Fifth Ave., New York, NY 10010 USA; *Imprints:* Continuum (Continu); Fairchild Books (Fairchild Bks)
E-mail: AskAcademic@BloomsburyUSA.com
Web site: http://www.bloomsburyacademicusa.com/html/
Dist(s): **Macmillan**
MyiLibrary
National Bk. Network.

Bloomsbury Academic & Professional *See* **Bloomsbury Academic**

Bloomsbury Pr., *(978-0-9667039)* 4340 Anza St., No. 6, San Francisco, CA 94121 USA Do not confuse with Bloomsberry Pr., New York, NY
Dist(s): **Macmillan.**

Bloomsbury Publishing *See* **Bloomsbury USA**

Bloomsbury Publishing Inc, *(978-0-225; 978-0-264; 978-0-304; 978-0-485; 978-0-567; 978-0-7136; 978-0-7185; 978-0-7201; 978-0-7220; 978-0-8044; 978-0-8264; 978-0-86187; 978-1-56338; 978-1-85567; 978-1-85805; 978-1-84127; 978-0-223; 978-0-86012; 978-1-84371; 978-1-4411; 978-1-84706; 978-1-62356; 978-1-62892; 978-1-5013) Orders Addr.: 1385 Broadway, 5th Flr., New York, NY 10018 USA (SAN 213-8220) Tel 212-419-5300*
E-mail: info@continuumbooks.com
Web site: http://www.continuumbooks.com; http://www.thoemmes.com; http://www.bloomsbury.com
Dist(s): **CreateSpace Independent Publishing Platform**
Ebsco Publishing
Macmillan
MyiLibrary
National Bk. Network
Send The Light Distribution LLC
ebrary, Inc.

Bloomsbury Publishing Plc (GBR) *(978-0-245; 978-0-333; 978-0-485; 978-0-510; 978-0-540; 978-0-7136; 978-0-7156; 978-0-7475; 978-0-7478; 978-0-85045; 978-0-85177; 978-0-85263; 978-0-85314; 978-0-85496; 978-0-86292; 978-0-906515; 978-0-907582; 978-0-948230; 978-1-85399; 978-1-85532; 978-1-85973; 978-1-899791; 978-1-901362; 978-0-212; 978-0-85146; 978-0-85147; 978-0-85317; 978-0-86019; 978-0-946716; 978-0-9507160; 978-1-902579; 978-1-84113; 978-1-85691; 978-1-897737; 978-0-9506785; 978-1-873590; 978-1-86176; 978-1-84176; 978) Dist. by* **Macmillan.**

Bloomsbury Publishing Plc (GBR) *(978-0-245; 978-0-333; 978-0-485; 978-0-510; 978-0-540; 978-0-7136; 978-0-7156; 978-0-7475; 978-0-7478; 978-0-85045; 978-0-85177; 978-0-85263; 978-0-85314; 978-0-85496; 978-0-86292; 978-0-906515; 978-0-907582; 978-0-948230; 978-1-85399; 978-1-85532; 978-1-85973; 978-1-899791; 978-1-901362; 978-0-212; 978-0-85146; 978-0-85147; 978-0-85317; 978-0-86019; 978-0-946716; 978-0-9507160; 978-1-902579; 978-1-84113; 978-1-85691; 978-1-897737; 978-0-9506785; 978-1-873590; 978-1-86176; 978-1-84176; 978) Dist. by* **IPG Chicago.**

Bloomsbury Publishing Plc (GBR) *(978-0-245; 978-0-333; 978-0-485; 978-0-510; 978-0-540; 978-0-7136; 978-0-7156; 978-0-7475; 978-0-7478; 978-0-85045; 978-0-85177; 978-0-85263; 978-0-85314; 978-0-85496; 978-0-86292; 978-0-906515; 978-0-907582; 978-0-948230; 978-1-85399; 978-1-85532; 978-1-85973; 978-1-899791; 978-1-901362; 978-0-212; 978-0-85146; 978-0-85147; 978-0-85317; 978-0-86019; 978-0-946716; 978-0-9507160; 978-1-902579; 978-1-84113; 978-1-85691; 978-1-897737; 978-0-9506785; 978-1-873590; 978-1-86176; 978-1-84176; 978) Dist. by* **Trafalgar.**

Bloomsbury Publishing Plc (GBR) *(978-0-245; 978-0-333; 978-0-485; 978-0-510; 978-0-540; 978-0-7136; 978-0-7156; 978-0-7475; 978-0-7478; 978-0-85045; 978-0-85177; 978-0-85263; 978-0-85314; 978-0-85496; 978-0-86292; 978-0-906515; 978-0-907582; 978-0-948230; 978-1-85399; 978-1-85532; 978-1-85973; 978-1-899791; 978-1-901362; 978-0-212; 978-0-85146; 978-0-85147; 978-0-85317; 978-0-86019; 978-0-946716; 978-0-9507160; 978-1-902579; 978-1-84113; 978-1-85691; 978-1-897737; 978-0-9506785; 978-1-873590; 978-1-86176; 978-1-84176; 978) Dist. by* **Players Pr.**

Bloomsbury Publishing Plc (GBR) *(978-0-245; 978-0-333; 978-0-485; 978-0-510; 978-0-540; 978-0-7136; 978-0-7156; 978-0-7475; 978-0-7478; 978-0-85045; 978-0-85177; 978-0-85263; 978-0-85314; 978-0-85496; 978-0-86292; 978-0-906515; 978-0-907582; 978-0-948230; 978-1-85399; 978-1-85532; 978-1-85973; 978-1-899791; 978-1-901362; 978-0-212; 978-0-85146; 978-0-85147; 978-0-85317; 978-0-86019; 978-0-946716; 978-0-9507160; 978-1-902579; 978-1-84113; 978-1-85691; 978-1-897737; 978-0-9506785; 978-1-873590; 978-1-86176; 978-1-84176; 978) Dist. by* **Consort Bk Sales.**

Bloomsbury Qatar Foundation Publishing (QAT) *(978-99921-42; 978-99921-95) Dist. by* **Macmillan.**

Bloomsbury USA *Imprint of* **Bloomsbury USA**

Bloomsbury USA, *(978-1-58234; 978-1-59691; 978-1-59990; 978-1-60819; 978-1-61963; 978-1-62040; 978-1-63286; 978-1-68119)* Orders Addr.: 16365 James Madison Hwy., Gordonsville, VA 22942-8501 USA Tel 888-330-8477; Toll Free: 888-330-8477; Edit Addr.: 175 Fifth Ave., Suite 300, New York, NY 10010 USA Toll Free: 888-330-8477; 1385 Broadway, New York, NY 10018 Tel 212-419-5300; *Imprints:* Bloomsbury USA Childrens (Bloom Child); A & C Black (A&CBlack); Bloomsbury USA (BloomsburyUSA)
E-mail: bloomsbury.kids@bloomsburyusa.com; nathaniel.knaebel@bloomsbury.com; mike.o'connor@bloomsbury.com
Web site: http://www.bloomsburyusa.com
Dist(s): **INscribe Digital**
Macmillan
MyiLibrary
Penguin Random Hse., LLC.
St. Martin's Pr.

Bloomsbury USA Childrens *Imprint of* **Walker & Co.**

Bloomsbury USA Childrens *Imprint of* **Bloomsbury USA**

Bloomsbury Visual Arts *Imprint of* **BJU Pr.**

Blow's Innovation to Art - (BIA), *(978-0-9820772)* 8090 Atlantic Blvd, E-160, Jacksonville, FL 32211 USA Tel 904-469-1169 business number
E-mail: biabizz@aol.com; blows.art@gmail.com
Web site: http://www.myspace.com/biabizz1
Dist(s): **Lightning Source, Inc.**

BLPH, Inc., *(978-0-9759158; 978-0-9772425; 978-0-9791099)* P.O. Box 764, Springfield, OR 97477-0132 USA
E-mail: printing@bestlittleprinthouse.com
Web site: http://www.bestlittleprinthouse.com.

BLR Bks., *(978-0-9721839)* 94 Circle Dr., Waltham, MA 02452 USA
Dist(s): **Pathway Bk. Service.**

Blu Phi'er Publishing, LLC, *(978-0-9772034; 978-0-9799884; 978-0-9823845; 978-0-9858378)* 2400 W. Grand Ave., Marshall, TX 75670 USA Tel 903-935-4223
E-mail: phierstarter@bluphier.com
Web site: http://www.bluphier.com.

Blue Apple Bks., *(978-1-934706; 978-1-60905)* 515 Valley St., Suite 180, Maplewood, NJ 07040 USA (SAN 854-4727) Fax: 973-763-5944
E-mail: info@blueapplebooks.com
Web site: http://www.blueapplebooks.com
Dist(s): **Chronicle Bks. LLC**
Consortium Bk. Sales & Distribution
Hachette Bk. Group
Learning Connection, The
Penguin Random Hse., LLC.
Random Hse., Inc.

Blue Bark Pr., *(978-0-615-18110-3)* 7 View South Ave., Jamaica Plain, MA 02130 USA Tel 617-840-3418
Dist(s): **AtlasBooks Distribution.**

Blue Bear Publishing *See* **Beach Front Bks.**

Blue Begonia Pr., *(978-0-911287)* 311 Hillcrest Dr, Selah, WA 98942 USA (SAN 268-3652) Tel 509-452-9748
E-mail: adpeters@charter.net
Web site: http://bluebegoniapress.com
Dist(s): **Partners/West Book Distributors.**

Blue Bk. Pubns., Inc., *(978-0-9625943; 978-1-886768; 978-1-936120)* 8009 34th Ave. S., Suite 175, Minneapolis, MN 55425 USA Tel 952-854-5229; Fax: 952-853-1486; Toll Free: 800-877-4867 Do not confuse with Blue Book Pubs., Inc. in La Jolla, CA
E-mail: bluebook@bluebookinc.com; support@bluebookinc.com
Web site: http://www.bluebookinc.com
Dist(s): **Alfred Publishing Co., Inc.**
Follett School Solutions
Music Sales Corp.
Omnibus Pr.

Blue Botte, *(978-0-9896257)* 14907 W. Autumn Ln., Nine Mile Falls, WA 99026 USA Tel 509-465-4534
E-mail: willarda2z@msn.com.

Blue Boy Publishing Co., *(978-0-9742632)* P.O. Box 691, Camillus, NY 13031-0691 USA.

Blue Brush Media, *(978-0-9777382)* 851 Monroe Ave., NE, Renton, WA 98056 USA (SAN 850-0878) Tel 425-818-8850 Do not confuse with Dolphin Media LLC in Huntsville, AL
E-mail: kunle@mamaAfricana.com
Web site: http://www.bluebrushmedia.com
Dist(s): **Follett School Solutions**
NewLife Bk. Distributors.

Blue Cat (GBR) *(978-0-9559851) Dist. by* **LuluCom.**

Blue Cat Bks, *(978-0-9779763)* P.O. Box 2818, Covina, CA 91722 USA Tel 626-339-1223
E-mail: info@bluecatpublishers.com
Web site: http://bluecatpublishers.com.

Blue Chip Publishing, *(978-0-9673970)* Orders Addr.: P.O. Box 26657, Austin, TX 78755 USA Tel 512-345-3021; Fax: 512-345-0181; Edit Addr.: 4119 Circletree Loop, Austin, TX 78731 USA Do not confuse with Blue Chip Publishing Corp., Keizer, OR
E-mail: MAMA19@aol.com.

Blue Crown Pr., *(978-0-615-52468-9; 978-0-9839308; 978-0-9855874)* P.O. Box 871826, Canton, MI 48187 USA Tel 734-905-0068
E-mail: author@emilynchand.com
Web site: www.novelpublicity.com.

Blue Cubicle Pr., LLC, *(978-0-9745900; 978-0-9827136; 978-1-938583)* P.O. Box 250382, Plano, TX 75025-0382 USA Tel 972-824-0646; *Imprints:* Castle Builder Press (Castle Builder)
Web site: http://www.bluecubiclepress.com.

Blue Devil Games, *(978-0-9763795)* P.O. Box 19359, Plantation, FL 33318 USA Tel 954-315-0920
Web site: http://www.bluedevilgames.com.

Blue Dolphin Publishing, Inc., *(978-0-931892; 978-1-57733)* Orders Addr.: P.O. Box 8, Nevada City, CA 95959 USA (SAN 223-2480) Tel 530-477-1503; Fax: 530-477-8342; Toll Free: 800-643-0765; Edit Addr.: 13340-d Grass Valley Ave., Grass Valley, CA 95945 USA (SAN 696-009X); *Imprints:* Papillon Publishing (Papillon Pubng)
E-mail: bdolphin@bluedolphinpublishing.com; clemens@bluedolphinpublishing.com
Web site: http://www.bluedolphinpublishing.com
Dist(s): **Follett School Solutions**
New Leaf Distributing Co., Inc.

Blue Dream Studios, *(978-0-9789168)* 1133 Cedarview Ln., Franklin, TN 37067-4075 USA
Web site: http://www.bluedreamstudios.com
Dist(s): **Diamond Comic Distributors, Inc.**
Diamond Bk. Distributors
Diamond Distributors, Inc.

Blue Eagle Bks., Inc., *(978-0-9794655)* 5773 Woodway, PMB 190, Houston, TX 77057 USA Tel 713-789-1516 (phone/fax)
E-mail: sjones@blueeaglebooks.com
Web site: http://blueeaglebooks.com
Dist(s): **Independent Pubs. Group.**
Blue Earth Bks. *Imprint of* **Capstone Pr., Inc.**
Blue Eyed Mayhem Publishing, *(978-0-9794545)* 6 Hopemont Dr., Mount Laurel, NJ 08054 USA Tel 609-781-0291
Dist(s): **Smashwords.**
Blue Eyes Publishing *See* **Azure Eyes Publishing**
Blue Forge Pr., *(978-1-883573; 978-1-886383; 978-1-59092)* Div. of Blue Forge Group, Orders Addr.: 7419 Ebbert Dr., SE, Port Orchard, WA 98367 USA (SAN 299-1330) Tel 360-769-7174 phone
E-mail: blueforgepress@gmail.com
Web site: http://www.blueforgepress.com.
Blue Fox Pr., *(978-0-9763119)* Pierce Arrow Bldg., 1685 Elmwood Ave., Suite 315, Buffalo, NY 14207-2407 USA Tel 716-447-1590; Fax: 716-837-7066
E-mail: bluefoxpress@yahoo.com
Web site: http://www.bluefoxpress.com.
Blue Gate Bks., *(978-0-9792612)* P.O. Box 2137, Nevada City, CA 95959 USA (SAN 852-923X) Tel 530-263-4501
E-mail: babette@babettedonaldson.com; info@emmaleabooks.com
Web site: http://www.bluegatebooks.com; http://www.sidecarscooter.com; http://www.emmaleabooks.com; http://www.Fun-With-Tea.com.
Blue Horse Books *Imprint of* **Great Lakes Literary, LLC**
Blue Ink Pr., *(978-0-9817234)* 1246 Heart Ave., Amherst, OH 44001 USA Tel 440-823-8320
E-mail: dougk@icehorseadventures.com
Web site: http://www.icehorseadventures.com
Dist(s): **Blu Sky Media Group.**
Blue Jay Bks. *Imprint of* **Crooked River Pr.**
Blue Kitty, The, *(978-0-9796814)* P.O. Box 254, Syracuse, NY 13214 USA
E-mail: info@thebluekitty.com.
Blue Lantern Books *See* **Laughing Elephant**
Blue Lion Productions, Ltd, *(978-0-9761132)* 302 Smith St., Freeport, NY 11520 USA Tel 516-546-4611
E-mail: info@bluelionproductions.com
Web site: http://www.bluelionproductions.com.
Blue Lobster Pr., *(978-0-9709569)* Orders Addr.: 3919 Union St., Levant, ME 04456-4358 USA
E-mail: books@bluelobsterpress.com; poet@robertpottle.com
Web site: http://www.bluelobsterpress.com.
Blue Logic Publishing, *(978-0-9860669)* P.O. Box 797492, Dallas, TX 75379 USA Tel 972-380-1467
E-mail: contact@bluelogicpublishing.com
Web site: www.bluelogicpublishing.com.
Blue Lotus Wave, *(978-0-9789624)* Orders Addr.: 15 Surrey Dr., Riverside, CT 06878-1516 USA (SAN 852-0631) Tel 203-344-1344 Do not confuse with Blue Lotus Press in Palmyra, MA.
blue manatee children's Bookstore *See* **Blue Manatee Press**
Blue Manatee Press, *(978-1-936669)* 3054 Madison Rd., Cincinnati, OH 45209 USA (SAN 920-4601) Tel 513-731-2665
E-mail: press@bluemanateebooks.com; johnsandy@bluemanateebooks.com
Web site: www.bluemanateepress.com
Dist(s): **Independent Pubs. Group.**
Blue Marble Bks. *Imprint of* **Sphinx Publishing**
Blue Marlin Pubns., *(978-0-9674602; 978-0-9792918; 978-0-9885295)* 823 Aberdeen Rd., West Bay Shore, NY 11706 USA Tel 631-666-0353 (phone/fax)
E-mail: jude@bluemarlinpubs.com
Web site: http://www.BlueMarlinPubs.com
Dist(s): **Follett School Solutions.**
Blue Mountain Arts Inc., *(978-0-88396; 978-1-58786; 978-1-59842; 978-1-68088)* Orders Addr.: P.O. Box 4549, Boulder, CO 80306 USA (SAN 299-9609) Tel 303-449-0536; Fax: 303-417-6434; 303-417-6496; Toll Free Fax: 800-943-6666; 800-545-8573; Toll Free: 800-525-0642; *Imprints:* Blue Mountain Press (Blue Mntn Pr); Rabbit's Foot Press (Rabb Ft Pr)
Web site: http://www.sps.com/.
Blue Mountain Arts (R) by SPS Studios, Incorporated *See* **Blue Mountain Arts Inc.**
Blue Mountain Pr. *Imprint of* **Blue Mountain Arts Inc.**
Blue Mustang Pr., *(978-0-9759737; 978-1-935199)* 175B Mansfield Ave., Suite 240, Norton, MA 02766 USA Tel 206-350-2823 (phone/fax)
E-mail: info@bluemustangpress.com
Web site: http://www.bluemustangpress.com.
Blue Note Bks. *Imprint of* **Blue Note Pubns.**
Blue Note Pubns., *(978-1-878398; 978-0-9830758; 978-0-9855562; 978-0-9895563; 978-0-9903068; 978-0-9963066)* Orders Addr.: 721 N. Dr. Ste. D, Melbourne, FL 32934 USA Toll Free: 800-624-0401 (order number); *Imprints:* Blue Note Books (Blue Note Bks)
E-mail: bluenotepress@gmail.com
Web site: http://www.bluenotebooks.com.
Blue Owl Editions, *(978-0-9672793)* 6254 Girvin Dr., Oakland, CA 94611 USA Tel 510-482-3038 (phone/fax)
E-mail: edanti@ispwest.com; enricoanti@yahoo.com
Dist(s): **Smashwords.**
Blue Peach Publishing, *(978-0-615-15922-5)* 2 Wyeth Cir., Southborough, MA 01772 USA
Dist(s): **Lulu Enterprises Inc.**
Blue Pig Productions, *(978-1-932545)* P.O. Box 691779, Orlando, FL 32869-1779 USA (SAN 255-4763) Tel 407-854-5679 (phone/fax)
E-mail: bluepigprod@aol.com
Web site: http://www.repunzal.com.
Blue Planet Press *See* **Ninth Planet Pr.**
Blue River Pr., *(978-0-9718959; 978-0-9763361; 978-0-9799240; 978-0-9819289; 978-1-935628; 978-1-68157; 978-0-9963247)* Orders Addr.: 2402 N. Shadeland Ave., Suite A, Indianapolis, IN 46219 USA Tel 317-352-8200; Fax: 317-352-8202; Toll Free: 800-296-0481 Do not confuse with Blue River Press in Bloomingdale, IL
E-mail: tdoherty@cardinalpub.com
Web site: http://www.cardinalpub.com; www.brpressbooks.com
Dist(s): **Cardinal Pubs. Group**
MyiLibrary.
Blue Scarab Pr., *(978-0-937179)* P.O. Box 4966, Pocatello, ID 83205-4966 USA (SAN 658-4640) Tel 208-775-3216
E-mail: jswhpw@srv.net.
Blue Scribbles Publishing, *(978-0-615-24897-4)* P.O. Box 2054, Centreville, VA 20120 USA
E-mail: bluescribbles@gmail.com
Web site: http://www.bluescribbles.com.
Blue Shoe Publishing, *(978-0-9725552)* c/o Christine Merser, 38 W. 74th St., 3A, New York, NY 10023 USA Tel 212-579-0310
E-mail: inquiry@blueshoestrategy.com; inquiry@blueshoepublishing.com; LLim@BlueShoeStrategy.com
Web site: http://www.blueshoepublishing.com.
Blue Shutter Bks., *(978-0-9729379)* Orders Addr.: 5125 Schultz Bridge Rd., Zionsville, PA 18092-2543 USA Tel 215-541-3362; Fax: 425-491-4282
E-mail: rworthington@blueshutterbooks.com
Web site: http://www.blueshutterbooks.com.
Blue Skies Above Texas Co., *(978-0-9800019)* 14781 Memorial Dr., No. 399, Houston, TX 77079 USA Tel 281-920-0043
E-mail: BlueSkiesAboveTexas@yahoo.com.
Blue Sky at Night Publishing, *(978-0-9768623)* 25679 360th Ave., Hillman, MN 56338-2431 USA
E-mail: Jill@JournalBuddies.com
Web site: http://www.JournalBuddies.com.
Blue Sky Ink, *(978-1-59475)* P.O. Box 1067, Brentwood, TN 37024-1067 USA (SAN 255-7401) Tel 805-677-6815
Dist(s): **Send The Light Distribution LLC.**
Blue Sky Pr., The *Imprint of* **Scholastic, Inc.**
Blue Sky Pr., *(978-0-9746896)* P.O. Box 6192, Malibu, CA 90264-6192 USA Tel 818-706-9814; 557 Broadway., New York, NY 10012 Do not confuse with Blue Sky Press in San Jose CA, Placerville CO, Silver Spring MD, Berkeley CA, Dallas TX
E-mail: laura@lauralarsen.com
Web site: http://www.lauralarsen.com
Dist(s): **Follett School Solutions.**
Blue State Pr., *(978-0-9773674)* 17771 Plumtree Ln., Yorba Linda, CA 92886 USA.
Blue Suit Bks., *(978-0-9748563)* P.O. Box 840057, New Orleans, LA 70184 USA (SAN 255-8998) Tel 504-450-4334
E-mail: bluesuit@imaginationmovers.com
Web site: http://www.imaginationmovers.com.
Blue Thistle Pr., *(978-0-9760505; 978-0-9786302)* 6187 FM 314, Ben Wheeler, TX 75754-4030 USA Tel 903-539-2500
E-mail: lkayers@hotmail.com
Web site: http://www.lindaayersbooks.com.
Blue Thunder Bks., *(978-0-9673000; 978-0-9839454)* 16717 Van Owens St., Lake Balboa, CA 91406 USA //Do not confuse with Blue Thunder Bks in Grand Rapids, MI
E-mail: d@savage1.com
Web site: http://SAVAGE1.com; http://www.CoolCatLovesYou.com.
Blue Thunder One, Inc., *(978-0-9719284)* P.O. Box 2435, Riverview, MI 48192 USA.
Blue Tie Publishing, *(978-0-9777972)* 1 Hale Rd., East Hampton, CT 06424 USA Tel 860-267-0432
E-mail: tanner@sbcglobal.net.
Blue Tiger Publishing, *(978-0-9759903)* P.O. Box 3776, Glendale, CA 91221-0776 USA Tel 310-497-9291
E-mail: travis_english@charter.net.
Blue Tree LLC, *(978-0-9711321; 978-0-9792014; 978-0-9802245; 978-0-9893088)* Orders Addr.: P.O. Box 148, Portsmouth, NH 03802 USA Tel 603-436-0831; Fax: 603-686-5054
E-mail: contact@thebluetree.com
Web site: http://www.thebluetree.com.
Blue Unicorn Edition, LLC, *(978-1-891355; 978-1-58396)* 12300 NW 56th Ave., Gainesville, FL 32653 USA Toll Free Fax: 866-334-1497 (orders)
E-mail: tienda1@instabook.net
Web site: http://www.instabookpublisher.com.
Blue Vase Productions, *(978-0-9770125)* 2455 Otay Ctr. Dr. Apt 118 Ste 252, San Diego, CA 92154 USA (SAN 257-4454) Fax: 619-819-6311
E-mail: legal@eljarronazul.com; ventas@eljarronazul.com
Web site: http://www.eljarronazul.com.
Blue Water Pr., LLC, *(978-0-9796046)* 8814 Sir Barton Ln., Waxhaw, NC 28173 USA Tel 704-551-9051
E-mail: Tonibranner@aol.com; jmacgregor@cadencemarketinggroup.com.
Blue Water Publishing, *(978-0-9796160)* 805 N. Orange Ave., Fallbrook, CA 92028-1525 USA
E-mail: bluewaterpub@sbcglobal.net.
Blue Willow Pr., *(978-0-9767473)* 197 Lamplight Ln., Bozeman, MT 59718 USA Tel 406-388-0272; Fax: 423-318-2329
E-mail: bluewillowpress@yahoo.com; obachs@juno.com
Web site: http://www.bluewillowpress.com.
Blue Wing Pubns., Workshops & Lectures, *(978-0-9795663)* P.O. Box 947, Tualatin, OR 97062 USA Toll Free: 877-591-4156
E-mail: sdk@bluewingworkshops.com
Web site: http://www.bluewingworkshops.com.
Blue Zebra Entertainment, Incorporated *See* **Murphey, Hiromi**
Bluebonnets, Boots & Bks. Pr., *(978-0-9645493; 978-0-9800061)* 11010 Hanning Ln., Houston, TX 77041-5006 USA; P.O. Box 19632, Houston, TX 77224-9632
E-mail: rita@bookconnectiononline.com
Web site: http://www.ABCsPress.com
Dist(s): **Complete Book & Media Supply**
Follett School Solutions
News Group
Partners Pubs. Group, Inc.
Bluechip Publishers *See* **BlueChip Pubs.**
BlueChip Pubs., *(978-0-930251)* Orders Addr.: P.O. Box 4204, Jackson, WY 83001 USA
E-mail: info@bluechippublishers.com
Dist(s): **Lightning Source, Inc.**
BlueCougar Studios, *(978-0-615-16770-1; 978-0-615-17434-1)* 3805 Grandview Ave., NW No. 4, Roanoke, VA 24012 USA
E-mail: info@bluecougarsrufios.com
Dist(s): **Lulu Enterprises Inc.**
Bluedoor, llc, *(978-1-59984; 978-1-68135)* 10949 Bren Rd., E., Minneapolis, MN 55343 USA Tel 952-934-1624; Fax: 952-934-4269; Toll Free: 800-979-1624
E-mail: mary@bluedoorpublishing.com
Web site: http://bluedoorpublishing.com.
Bluefish River Pr., *(978-0-9714701)* P.O. Box 1398, Duxbury, MA 02332 USA
E-mail: dpallai@bluefishriverpress.com
Web site: http://www.bluefishriverspress.com.
BlueLine Book Publishers *See* **Great American Pubs.**
Blueline Publishing, *(978-0-9776906)* P.O. Box 11569, Denver, CO 80211 USA (SAN 856-2539) Tel 303-477-5272; Fax: 866-876-2915
Web site: http://www.bluelinepub.com
Dist(s): **Follett School Solutions.**
BlueSky Publishing, *(978-0-9724386)* Div. of BlueSky Medical Group, Inc., 6965 El Camino Real Suite 105-602, Carlsbad, CA 92009 USA Tel 760-603-8130; 760-603-8331 (phone/fax)
E-mail: publishingdivision@blueskymedical.com
Web site: http://www.boypresident.com.
Bluestocking Pr., *(978-0-942617)* Orders Addr.: P.O. Box 1014, Placerville, CA 95667 USA (SAN 667-2981) Tel 530-622-8586; Fax: 530-642-9222; Toll Free: 800-959-8586 (orders); Edit Addr.: 3333 Gold Country Dr., El Dorado, CA 95623 USA (SAN 667-299X)
E-mail: customerservice@bluestockingpress.com
Web site: http://www.bluestockingpress.com.
Bluestone Bks., *(978-0-9720046)* P.O. Box 761, Edmonds, WA 98020 USA
Web site: http://www.cmc.net/~jiwrig.
Bluewater Productions, Inc., *(978-0-9792751)* 2950 Newmarket Pl., Suite 101, Bellingham, WA 98226 USA Tel 360-778-1033
Web site: http://www.bluewaterprod.com/
Dist(s): **Diamond Comic Distributors, Inc.**
Diamond Bk. Distributors
MyiLibrary
SCB Distributors.
Bluewater Pubns., *(978-0-9719946; 978-1-934610)* 1812 CR 111, Killen, AL 35645 USA Tel 256-349-6087 Do not confuse with Heart Of Dixie Publishing Corporation in Foley, AL
E-mail: malcolm.broyles@gmail.com
Web site: www.bluewaterpublications.com
Dist(s): **Follett School Solutions.**
Bluewood Bks., *(978-0-912517)* Div. of The Siyeh Group, Inc., P.O. Box 689, San Mateo, CA 94010 USA (SAN 265-3214) Tel 650-548-0754; Fax: 650-548-0654
E-mail: Bluewoodb@aol.com
Dist(s): **Follett School Solutions**
L P C Group
SCB Distributors.
Blume (ESP) *(978-84-89396; 978-84-932442; 978-84-95939; 978-84-9801) Dist. by* **IPG Chicago.**
Blumont Company, The, *(978-0-9776024)* 161 Great Rd., Littleton, MA 01460 USA (SAN 257-702X) Tel 781-899-6468
E-mail: slblu@netway.com.
Blurb, Inc., *(978-1-4579; 978-1-320; 978-1-5184; 978-1-364)* Orders Addr.: 580 California St. #300, San Francisco, CA 94104 USA (SAN 860-0813)
E-mail: msiemers@blurb.com
Web site: http://www.blurb.com
Dist(s): **Lulu Enterprises Inc.**
Blushing Rose Publishing, *(978-1-884807)* Orders Addr.: P.O. Box 2238, San Anselmo, CA 94979-2238 USA Tel 415-407-0170 Toll Free: 800-898-2263
E-mail: nancya555@yahoo.com
Web site: http://www.blushingrose.com.
BMC Advertising, Incorporated *See* **BMCFerrell**
BMCFerrell, *(978-0-9764460; 978-0-9788242)* 6450 S. Lewis Ave. Ste. 300, Tulsa, OK 74136-1068 USA
Web site: http://www.bmcferrell.com.
BMG, Incorporated *See* **RPM Publishing**
BMI Educational Services, *(978-0-922443; 978-1-60884; 978-1-60933; 978-1-63071)* Orders Addr.: 26 Haypress Rd., Cranbury, NJ 08512 USA (SAN 760-7032); Edit Addr.: P.O. Box 800, Dayton, NJ 08810-0800 USA (SAN 169-4669) Tel 732-329-6991; Fax: 732-329-6994; Toll Free Fax: 800-986-9393 (orders only); Toll Free: 800-222-8100 (orders only)
E-mail: info@bmionline.com
Web site: http://www.bmionline.com/.
Boathouse Press *See* **BoathouseBooks**
BoathouseBooks, *(978-0-9776469)* P.O. Box 244, Tiburon, CA 94920 USA
Web site: http://boathousebooks.com
Dist(s): **Follett School Solutions.**
Bob Thomas Bks., *(978-0-9717682)* Orders Addr.: P.O. Box 853, Black Mountain, NC 28711 USA; Edit Addr.: P.O. Box 815, Kure Beach, NC 28449 USA Toll Free Fax: 866-615-0417.
Bobcat Publishing, *(978-0-9776419)* 5105 Cascabel Rd., Atascadero, CA 93422 USA (SAN 852-9051)
E-mail: llyn@llynsplace.com; llyntroy@sbcglobal.net
Web site: http://www.llynsplace.com.
Bobrich Publishing *See* **Wollaston Pr.**
Boca Raton Museum of Art, *(978-0-936859)* 501 Plaza Real, Mizner Park, Boca Raton, FL 33432 USA (SAN 278-2251) Tel 561-392-2500; Fax: 561-391-6410
E-mail: jkaminski@bocamuseum.org; iford@bocamuseum.org
Web site: http://www.bocamuseum.org
Dist(s): **Antique Collectors' Club**
RAM Pubns. & Distribution.
BoCook Publishing, *(978-0-9848791)* 12702 SE 222nd Dr., Damascus, OR 97089 USA Tel 503-853-1362
E-mail: janet_l_carlson@yahoo.com
Dist(s): **AtlasBooks Distribution.**
Bodkin Pointe Pr., *(978-0-9752684)* Orders Addr.: P.O. Box 654, Gibson Island, MD 21056 USA Tel 410-360-0838 (phone/fax)
E-mail: books@bodkinpointepress.com
Web site: http://www.bodkinpointepress.com.
Bodleian Library (GBR) *(978-1-85124; 978-0-900177) Dist. by* **Chicago Distribution Ctr.**
Body & Mind Productions, Inc., *(978-0-9742569; 978-0-9752648; 978-0-9771609; 978-0-9792177; 978-0-9820889; 978-0-9828370; 978-0-9830885; 978-0-9855550; 978-0-9904468)* 9429 Cedar Heights Ave., Las Vegas, NV 89134-0194 USA Tel 949-263-4676
E-mail: bodymindheal@aol.com
Web site: http://www.healingreiki.com
Dist(s): **Follett School Solutions**
New Leaf Distributing Co., Inc.
Quality Bks., Inc.
Body Tone Multimedia, *(978-0-9760650)* P.O. Box 580691, Elk Grove, CA 95758-0012 USA
E-mail: body_tone_multimedia@mac.com
Web site: http://www.bodytonemultimedia.com.
Bodycrafting Systems, Inc., *(978-0-9745265)* Orders Addr.: P.O. Box 1512, Nokomis, FL 34274 USA Fax: 941-484-9650
Web site: http://www.kidpowerfitness.com.
BodyLife Publishers *See* **Windblown Media**
Boettcher, Ashley L., *(978-0-9768123)* Orders Addr.: P.O. Box 997, Southwick, MA 01077-0997 USA (SAN 256-5811) Tel 413-569-9492 available from 10am to 5pm m-f and 11am to 4pm sat; Edit Addr.: 45 Powder Mill Rd., Southwick, MA 01077 USA
E-mail: ljabphil413@juno.com
Web site: http://www.ALBbooks.com.
Bohemian Trash Studios, *(978-0-9767540)* 3322 Clearview, San Angelo, TX 76904 USA Tel 325-944-3282; *Imprints:* Star Cross'd Destiny (Star Cross)
Web site: http://www.bohemiantrash.com.
Bohobza Music, *(978-0-9744943)* P.O. Box 745, Teaneck, NJ 07666-0745 USA Tel 201-862-1692 (phone/fax)
E-mail: wetalkjazz@aol.com
Web site: http://www.ronibenhur.com.
Bois Pubns., *(978-0-9727967)* 5411 Colfax Pl., Oklahoma City, OK 73112 USA Tel 405-947-7988 Evening; 405-713-4757 Daytime
E-mail: au444@cox.net; athomas14@cox.net
Web site: http://au4444.blogspot.com/.
†Bolchazy-Carducci Pubs., *(978-0-86516; 978-1-61041)* 1570 Baskin Rd., Mundelein, IL 60060-4474 USA (SAN 219-7685) Toll Free: 800-392-6453
E-mail: jcull@bolchazy.com
Web site: http://www.bolchazy.com
Dist(s): **Follett School Solutions**
MyiLibrary; *CIP.*
Bold Strokes Bks., *(978-1-933110; 978-1-60282; 978-1-62639)* Orders Addr.: 430 Herrington Rd., Johnsonville, NY 12094 USA Tel 518-753-6642; Fax: 518-753-6648
E-mail: bsb@boldstrokesbooks.com; publisher@boldstrokesbooks.com
Web site: http://www.boldstrokesbooks.com
Dist(s): **Abraham Assocs. Inc.**
Bella Distribution
Bookazine Co., Inc.
Perseus-PGW
Perseus Bks. Group
Perseus Distribution.
Bold Venture Pr., *(978-0-9712246)* Orders Addr.: P.O. Box 64, Bordentown, NJ 08505 USA
E-mail: boldventurepress@aol.com
Web site: http://www.boldventurepress.com.
Bollix Bks., *(978-1-932188)* 1609 W. Callender Ave., Peoria, IL 61606 USA
E-mail: staley.krause@insightbb.com
Web site: http://www.bollixbooks.com
Dist(s): **Follett School Solutions**
PSI (Publisher Services, Inc.).
Bolton Publishing LLC, *(978-0-9855312)* Orders Addr.: 7255 N. US Hwy. 377, Rochelle, TX 76872-3019 USA
E-mail: ghbolton51@gmail.com.
Bon Tiki Bks., *(978-0-9747072)* 8100 Thomas Dr., Panama City Beach, FL 32408 USA
E-mail: bontiki@knology.net
Web site: http://www.sparkythorne.com.
Bondcliff Bks., *(978-0-9657475; 978-1-931271)* Orders Addr.: P.O. Box 385, Littleton, NH 03561 USA Toll Free: 800-859-7581; Edit Addr.: 8 Bluejay Ln., Littleton, NH 03561 USA
E-mail: bondclif@ncia.net
Dist(s): **Peregrine Outfitters.**
Bongiorno Bks., *(978-0-9715819)* P.O. Box 83-2345, Richardson, TX 75083 USA Tel 972-671-6117; Fax: 972-671-0601
E-mail: info@bongiornobooks.com
Web site: http://www.tangledhearts.com; http://www.bongiornobooks.com
Dist(s): **Nonetheless Pr.**
Bongo Comics Group *Imprint of* **Bongo Entertainment, Inc.**
Bongo Entertainment, Inc., *(978-0-9642999; 978-1-892849; 978-1-940293)* 1440 S. Sepulveda, 3rd

Flr., Los Angeles, CA 90025 USA Tel 310-966-6168; Fax: 310-966-6181; *Imprints:* Bongo Comics Group (Bongo Comics Grp).

Bonita and Hodge Publishing Group, LLC, (*978-0-9838935*) Orders Addr.: 105 Weaver Fields Ln. No. 104, Memphis, TN 38109 USA; *Imprints:* Seraphina (Seraphina)
E-mail: bandhpublishing@gmail.com; hdelo1980@yahoo.com; director@bonitaandhodgepublishing.com; booknerd436@gmail.com; contracts@bonitaandhodgepublishing.com; submissions@bonitaandhodgepublishing.com; administration@bonitaandhodgepublishing.com; sheliawritesbooks@gmail.com
Web site: www.bandhpublishing.net; www.bonitaandhodgepublishing.com; www.bandhpublishing.com; www.bonitaandhodgepublishing.net.

Bonita & Hodge Publishing Group *See* **Bonita and Hodge Publishing Group, LLC**

Bonne Amie Publishing *See* **Chantilly Books**

Bonner, Larry, (*978-0-9747855*) 305 Chapwith Rd., Garner, NC 27529-4882 USA
Web site: http://www.bigrawhidebutte.com.

Bonneville Bks. *Imprint of* **Cedar Fort, Inc./CFI Distribution**

Bonneville B.V. (NLD) (*978-90-73304*) *Dist. by* **CFI Dist.**

Bonus Bks., Inc., (*978-0-929387; 978-0-931028; 978-0-933893; 978-1-56625*) 875 N. Michigan Ave., Suite 1416, Chicago, IL 60611 USA (SAN 630-0804) Tel 312-467-0580; Fax: 312-467-9271
E-mail: amanda@bonusbooks.com
Web site: http://www.bonusbooks.com
Dist(s): **National Bk. Network**
Send The Light Distribution LLC.

Boo Bks., Inc., (*978-1-887864*) 7628 S. Paulina, Chicago, IL 60620 USA Tel 312-873-1584; Toll Free: 800-205-1140.

Booger Red's Bks., Inc., (*978-0-9650751*) P.O. Drawer G, Clifton, CO 81520 USA Tel 970-434-4140
E-mail: booger-gj@att.net.

Bk. Bench, The, (*978-1-891142*) 617 Herschler Ave., Evanston, WY 82930 USA Tel 307-789-3642
E-mail: atterol@allwest.net.

Bk. Club of America, (*978-1-59384*) 1812 Front St., Scotch Plains, NJ 07076-1103 USA (SAN 255-3279) Do not confuse with Book Club of America in Mechanicsburg, PA
E-mail: dcarey@bookclubusa.com.

Bk. Club of California, The, (*978-0-9819597*) 312 Sutter St., Suite 510, San Francisco, CA 94108 USA.

Book Co. Publishing Pty, Ltd., The (AUS) (*978-1-74047; 978-1-86309; 978-1-74202*) *Dist. by* **Penton Overseas.**

Bk. Ends, (*978-0-9677817*) 2001 N. Halsted St. Ste. 201, Chicago, IL 60614-4365 USA
E-mail: sacredflight@yahoo.com
Web site: http://www.sacredflight.com
Dist(s): **Independent Pubs. Group.**

Bk. Garden Publishing, (*978-0-9818614*) Orders Addr.: 147 Roesch Ave., Oreland, PA 19075 USA
E-mail: JDHoliday51@gmail.com
Web site: http://jdholiday.blogspot.com.

Book Guild, Ltd. (GBR) (*978-1-85776; 978-0-86332; 978-1-84624; 978-1-909716*) *Dist. by* **Trans-Atl Phila.**

Book Her Publications *Imprint of* **Lyrically Korrect Publishing**

Book Hse. (GBR) (*978-1-904194; 978-1-904642; 978-1-905087; 978-1-906714; 978-1-907184; 978-1-910184*) *Dist. by* **Black Rab.**

Book Hse. (GBR) (*978-1-904194; 978-1-904642; 978-1-905087; 978-1-906714; 978-1-907184; 978-1-910184*) *Dist. by* **Sterling.**

Book Jungle *Imprint of* **Standard Pubns., Inc.**

Bk. Nook Productions, (*978-0-9748990*) P.O. Box 101, Richmond, TX 77406 USA Tel 832-721-7655
E-mail: stephiemara@aol.com
Dist(s): **Follett School Solutions.**

Book of Hope International *See* **OneHope**

Bk. of Signs Foundation, (*978-0-9773009*) 444 E. Roosevelt Rd., Suite 173, Lombard, IL 60148 USA Tel 630-914-5015.

Book Peddlers, (*978-0-916773; 978-1-931863*) 2828 Hedberg Dr., Hopkins, MN 55305-3403 USA (SAN 653-9548) Toll Free: 800-255-3379
E-mail: vlansky@bookpeddlers.com
Web site: http://www.practicalparenting.com; http://www.bookpeddlers.com
Dist(s): **Gryphon Hse., Inc.**
MyiLibrary
Perseus-PGW
Perseus Bks. Group
Skandisk, Inc.

Book Pubs. Network, (*978-1-887542; 978-0-9755407; 978-1-935359; 978-1-937454; 978-1-940598*) P.O. Box 2256, Bothell, WA 98041 USA Tel 425-483-3040; Fax: 425-483-3098; 27 W. 20th St., New York, NY 10011
E-mail: sheryn@earthlink.net
Web site: http://www.bookpublishersnetwork.com
Dist(s): **BookBaby**
Danforth Bk. Distribution
Epicenter Pr., Inc.
Follett School Solutions
Greenleaf Book Group
Midpoint Trade Bks., Inc.
MyiLibrary
Partners Bk. Distributing, Inc.
Smashwords.

Bk. Pubs. of El Paso, (*978-0-944551; 978-0-9836455; 978-0-9916296*) a/o Book Publishers of El Paso, 2200 San Jose Ave., El Paso, TX 79930 USA Tel 915-778-6670 (phone/fax) Do not confuse with Sundance Pr., Glen Carbon, IL
E-mail: bpep2@sbcglobal.net
Web site: bookpublishersofelpaso.com.

†**Book Publishing Co.,** (*978-0-913990; 978-1-57067; 978-0-9669317; 978-0-9673108; 978-0-9779183; 978-1-939053*) P.O. Box 99, Summertown, TN 38483 USA (SAN 202-439X) Tel 931-964-3571; Fax: 931-964-3518; Toll Free: 888-260-8458; *Imprints:* Native Voices (Native Voices); 7th Generation (SeventhGen)
E-mail: info@bookpubco.com
Web site: http://www.bookpubco.com
Dist(s): **CreateSpace Independent Publishing Platform**
Follett School Solutions
Four Winds Trading Co.
Integral Yoga Pubns.
New Leaf Distributing Co., Inc.
Nutri-Bks. Corp.
Partners Bk. Distributing, Inc.
Rio Nuevo Pubs.
Smashwords; *CIP.*

Book Sales, Inc., (*978-0-7628; 978-0-7858; 978-0-89009; 978-1-55521; 978-1-57715; 978-1-4161*) Orders Addr.: 400 1st Ave N. Ste. 300, Minneapolis, MN 55401-1721 USA (SAN 169-488X) Toll Free: 800-526-7257; Edit Addr.: 276 Fifth Ave., Suite 206, New York, NY 10001 USA (SAN 299-4062) Tel 212-779-4972; Fax: 212-779-6058; *Imprints:* Castle Books (Castle Bks Inc); Chartwell (Chrtwell)
E-mail: sales@booksalesusa.com
Web site: http://www.booksalesusa.com/
Dist(s): **Continental Bk. Co., Inc.**
Hachette Bk. Group
MyiLibrary.

Bk. Shelf, (*978-0-9714160; 978-0-9913845*) Orders Addr.: P.O. Box 320804, Fairfield, CT 06825 USA Tel 203-257-0158
E-mail: service@bookshelf123.com; michellespraybooks@gmail.com
Web site: http://www.bookshelf123.com; http://www.myabcsbook.com/; http://www.havingscoliosis.com/.

Book Shop, Ltd., The, (*978-1-936199*) 35 E. 9th St., No. 74, New York, NY 10003 USA Tel 917-388-2493; Fax: 917-534-1304
E-mail: nancy@thebookshopltd.com
Web site: http://thebookshopltd.com.

Bk. Stops Here, (*978-0-9631612*) 1108 Rocky Point Ct., NE, Albuquerque, NM 87123 USA Tel 505-296-9047 (phone/fax)
E-mail: gldjvb@home.com
Web site: http://www.bookstopshere.com.

Book Web Publishing, Limited, (*978-0-9716567; 978-0-9795733*) P.O. Box 81, Bellmore, NY 11710 USA
E-mail: jeri@jerifink.com; donna@bookwebpublishing.com
Web site: http://www.bookwebpublishing.com.

Book Wholesalers, Inc., (*978-0-7587; 978-1-4046; 978-1-4131; 978-1-4155; 978-1-4156; 978-1-4287*) 1847 Mercer Rd., Lexington, KY 40511-1001 USA (SAN 135-5449) Toll Free: 800-888-4478
E-mail: jcarrico@bwibooks.com; lison@bwibooks.com
Web site: http://www.bwibooks.com
Dist(s): **Follett School Solutions.**

Bookaroos Publishing, Inc., (*978-0-9678167*) Orders Addr.: P.O. Box 8518, Fayetteville, AR 72703 USA Tel 479-443-0339; Fax: 479-443-0339; Edit Addr.: 484 E. Pharris Dr., Fayetteville, AR 72703 USA
E-mail: books@bookaroos.com; tammybronson@bookaroos.com
Web site: http://www.bookaroos.com; http://www.seahorserun.com; http://www.tammybronson.com; http://www.tinysnail.com
Dist(s): **Follett School Solutions.**

Bookateer Publishing, (*978-0-9819368; 978-1-936476*) 4 Park Ave., Uncasville, CT 06382 USA
E-mail: mj@denicalisdragonchronicles.com; grizlegirl@sbcglobal.net
Web site: www.grizlegirlproductions.com; www.bookateerpublishing.com; www.denicalisdragonchronicles.com
Dist(s): **Smashwords.**

Bk.Baby Print, (*978-1-61927; 978-1-63192; 978-1-943612; 978-1-68222*) 7905 N. Rt. 130, Pennsauken, NJ 08034 USA Toll Free: 877-961-6878
E-mail: jfoley1@discmakers.com; support@print.bookbaby.com
Web site: bookbaby.com; http://www.print.bookbaby.com
Dist(s): **BookBaby**
Independent Pubs. Group.

BookBound Publishing, (*978-1-932367*) Orders Addr.: 26500 W. Agoura Rd., Suite 102-593, Calabasas, CA 91302 USA (SAN 256-3177) Toll Free: 866-985-2665
E-mail: stacyquest@bookbound.net
Web site: http://www.bookbound.net; http://bookboundpublishing.com.

BookChamp LLC., (*978-0-9760111*) c/o Winter & Company P.C, 605 King Georges Post Rd., Fords, NJ 08863 USA
E-mail: info@bookchamp.net
Web site: http://www.bookchamp.net
Dist(s): **Chicago Review Pr., Inc.**
Independent Pubs. Group.

Bookcraft, Inc. *Imprint of* **Deseret Bk. Co.**

BookCrafters, (*978-0-9845194; 978-0-9832819; 978-0-9837470; 978-1-937862; 978-1-943650*) Orders Addr.: 12056 Ridgeview Ln., Parker, CO 80138-7141 USA (SAN 859-6352) Tel 720-851-0397
E-mail: BookCrafters@comcast.net
Web site: http://www.joemcdaniel.org; http://bookcrafters.net
Dist(s): **Advocate Distribution Solutions**
BookPartners, Inc.
Lightning Source, Inc.
Send The Light Distribution LLC
Smashwords.

Bookends Pr., (*978-0-9724926; 978-0-9740922; 978-1-932667; 978-1-938315*) Orders Addr.: 4130 NW 16th Blvd., Gainesville, FL 32604 USA Fax: 352-373-6905; Toll Free: 800-881-3208; P.O. Box 14513, Gainsville, FL 32604
E-mail: copyright@renaissance-printing.com
Web site: http://www.bookendspress.com
Dist(s): **Freeman Family Ministries**
Rosewood Foundation, The
StarCrossed Productions
Truth Pubns.

Booker Lane Press *See* **Punta Gorda Pr.**

BookLight Pr., (*978-0-9841307; 978-0-615-73688-4*) Orders Addr.: 5994 S. Holly St. #118, Greenwood Village, CO 80111 USA (SAN 858-5164) Tel 303-916-8124; Edit Addr.: P.O. Box 380161, Cambridge, MA 02139-0161 USA
E-mail: jmarsh@booklightpress.com
Web site: www.booklightpress.com
Dist(s): **Follett School Solutions.**

Booklines Hawaii, Ltd., (*978-1-929844; 978-1-58849; 978-1-60274*) Div. of Islander Group, 269 Pali'i St., Mililani, HI 96789 USA (SAN 630-6624) Tel 808-676-0116; Fax: 808-676-0634
E-mail: customerservice@booklines.com
Web site: http://www.booklineshawaii.com
Dist(s): **Follett School Solutions**
Islander Group.

Booklocker.com, Inc., (*978-1-929072; 978-1-931391; 978-1-59113; 978-1-60145; 978-1-60910; 978-1-61434; 978-1-62141; 978-1-62646; 978-1-63263; 978-1-63490; 978-1-63491; 978-1-63492*) 5726 Cortez Rd. W., No. 349, Bradenton, FL 34210 USA (SAN 254-363X) Fax: 305-768-0261
E-mail: booklocker@booklocker.com; writersweekly@writersweekly.com
Web site: http://www.booklocker.com; http://www.writersweekly.com.

BookLogix, (*978-0-615-18278-0; 978-0-615-18390-9; 978-0-615-25890-4; 978-1-61005; 978-1-63183*) 1264 Old Alpharetta Rd., Alpharetta, GA 30005 USA (SAN 860-0376) Tel 770-346-9979; Fax: 888-564-7890
E-mail: Angela@booklogix.com; Ahmad@booklogix.com
Web site: http://www.booklogix.com.

Booklogix Publishing Services *See* **BookLogix**

BookMann Pr. *Imprint of* **Mann Publishing Group**

Bookmark Bks., LLC, (*978-0-9764163*) P.O. Box 2996, Chester, VA 23831 USA Tel 804-706-6399 (phone/fax)
E-mail: bookmarkbooks@verizon.net.

Bookmark, The, (*978-0-930227*) Orders Addr.: 29021 Ave. Sherman, Unit 109, Santa Clarita, CA 91355 USA (SAN 694-6410) Tel 661-294-8022; Fax: 661-294-8027; Toll Free: 800-220-7767 Do not confuse with other companies with the same name in Marietta, GA, Knightstown, IN
E-mail: thebookmark@earthlink.net
Web site: http://www.thebookmark.com.

Bookmates *Imprint of* **Penny Laine Papers, Inc.**

BookMobile *See* **Syren Bk. Co.**

BookPartners, LLC, (*978-1-936495*) 725 3rd St. P.O. Box 790, Cedar Key, FL 32625-0790 USA Tel 352-543-9307; Fax: 603-375-5373
E-mail: jpdwyer@dwyerogrady.com
Web site: www.bookpartners.org.

Bookpublisher.com *See* **Wheatmark**

Bks. Are Fun, Ltd., (*978-0-9649777; 978-1-58209; 978-1-890409; 978-1-59795; 978-1-60626*) 1 Readers Digest Rd., Pleasantville, NY 10570-7000 USA
E-mail: msmall@booksarefun.com
Web site: http://www.booksarefun.com
Dist(s): **Sandvik Publishing.**

Books by Bookends *See* **Long Dash Publishing**

Books by Kids LLC, (*978-0-615-19963-4; 978-0-9830954*) 1021 Oak St., Jacksonville, FL 32204 USA Tel 904-376-7029; Fax: 904-355-1832
Web site: http://www.booksbykids.com
Dist(s): **Chicago Distribution Ctr.**

Bks. by Matt, (*978-0-9727660*) 33 Stoddard Way, Berkeley, CA 94708 USA Tel 510-849-2986; Fax: 510-849-1012
E-mail: mylamby@hotmail.com.

Books for Brats *Imprint of* **Little Redhaired Girl Publishing, Inc.**

Bks. for Children of the World, (*978-0-9661186; 978-0-9762078*) 6701 N. Bryant Ave., Oklahoma City, OK 73121 USA Tel 405-721-7417; Fax: 405-478-4352; Toll Free: 888-838-0003.

Bks. for Children Publishing, (*978-0-9830172*) Orders Addr.: P.O. Box 202, Inlet, NY 13360 USA; Edit Addr.: 578 Oyster Rake Rd., Kiawah Island, SC 29455 USA Tel 843-573-7429; 315-357-3422; 843-513-7023
E-mail: wguiffre@frontiernet.net.

Books International, Inc., (*978-1-891078*) Orders Addr.: P.O. Box 605, Herndon, VA 20172-0605 USA (SAN 131-761X) Tel 703-661-1500; Fax: 703-661-1501
E-mail: bimail@presswarehouse.com.

Bks. on Demand, (*978-0-608; 978-0-7837; 978-0-8357; 978-0-598*) Div. of UMI, 300 N. Zeeb Rd., Ann Arbor, MI 48106-1346 USA Tel 734-761-4700; Fax: 734-665-5022; Toll Free: 800-521-0600
E-mail: info@umi.com
Web site: http://www.umi.com.

Bks. on the Path, (*978-0-9743390*) P.O. Box 436, Barker, TX 77413-0436 USA Tel 281-492-6050; Fax: 832-201-7620; Toll Free: 866-875-7284
E-mail: info@patriarchspath.org
Web site: http://www.booksonthepath.com.

Bks. That Will Enhance Your Life, (*978-0-615-20297-6; 978-0-615-38405-4; 978-0-9831419; 978-0-9838457; 978-0-9848980*) Div. of Andrews Leadership International, 6124 Capistrano Ave. New St., Woodland Hills, CA 91367 USA Tel 8182972189; *Imprints:* BTWEYL (BTWEYL)
E-mail: risingtideentertainment@yahoo.com; vision@booksthatwillenhanceyourlife.com
Web site: http://www.booksthatwillenhanceyourlife.com.

Books To Believe In *Imprint of* **Thornton Publishing, Inc.**

Books To Remember *Imprint of* **Flyleaf Publishing**

Bks. Unbound E-Publishing Co., (*978-1-59201*) 1110 Kerwin St., Piscataway, NJ 08854-3323 USA
Web site: http://www.booksunbound.com.

Books2Go, (*978-1-59590*) 780 Reservoir Ave., Suite 243, Cranston, RI 02910 USA Tel 401-537-9175
E-mail: books2go@writerscollective.net
Web site: http://www.mybooks2go.com.

BooksbyDave Inc., (*978-0-9768867*) Orders Addr.: 5010 James loop, Killeen, TX 76542 USA Tel 254-628-1961
E-mail: project17us@yahoo.com
Web site: http://www.geocities.com/oilsbydave.

Booksforboys, (*978-0-9761440*) 8 Marigold Ct., Holtsville, NY 11742 USA
Web site: http://booksforboys.com.

Bookshelf Global Publishing, (*978-0-9755395; 978-0-9766954; 978-0-9779012; 978-0-9800430; 978-0-9850656*) 503 Second Ave., Destin, FL 32541 USA (SAN 850-4652) Tel 770-560-8016
E-mail: office@bookshelfglobal.com
Web site: http://www.bookshelfglobal.com.

Bookshelf, The *See* **Open Door Publishers, Inc.**

Booksmart Pubns., (*978-0-9790896*) Orders Addr.: P.O. Box 4774, Mission Viejo, CA 92690 USA (SAN 852-4211) Tel 949-462-0076; Edit Addr.: 19 Bolero, Mission Viejo, CA 92692 USA
E-mail: b_smart@cox.net
Web site: http://www.booksmartpublications.com.

booksonnet.com, (*978-1-888562; 978-0-9675540*) Div. of Shoestring Productions, P.O. Box 36, Saint Augustine, FL 32085 USA Tel 904-829-3812 Do not confuse with companies with the same name in Prather CA, Santa Barbara CA, Aptos CA, Belvedere CA, Albion CA, Pensacola, FL
E-mail: billbooks@bellsouth.net
Dist(s): **Lightning Source, Inc.**

Booksource, The, (*978-0-7383; 978-0-8335; 978-0-911891; 978-0-9641084; 978-1-886379; 978-1-890760; 978-0-7568; 978-1-4117; 978-1-4178; 978-1-60446; 978-1-4364*) Div. of GL group, Inc., Orders Addr.: 1230 Macklind Ave., Saint Louis, MO 63110-1432 USA (SAN 169-4324) Tel 314-647-0600 Toll Free Fax: 800-647-1923; Toll Free: 800-444-0435
E-mail: shankins@booksource.com
Web site: http://www.booksource.com.

Bookstand Publishing, (*978-1-58909; 978-1-61863; 978-1-63498*) 305 Vineyard Town Ctr., Suite 302, Morgan Hill, CA 95037 USA Tel 408-852-1832; Fax: 408-852-1812
E-mail: orders@bookstandpublishing.com
Web site: http://www.BookstandPublishing.com.

Bookstrand-Siren Publishing, Incorporated *See* **Siren-BookStrand, Inc.**

BooktiMookti Pr., (*978-0-9800952*) P.O. Box 17520, Seattle, WA 98127 USA
E-mail: helen@booktimookti.com
Web site: http://www.BooktiMookti.com; http://www.RuntFarm.com
Dist(s): **Itasca Bks.**

Booktrope, (*978-0-9841786; 978-1-935961; 978-1-62015; 978-1-5137*) Div. of Libertary Co., 1219 Sixteenth Ave East, Seattle, WA 98112 USA (SAN 858-639X) Tel 206-235-3384; *Imprints:* Booktrope Editions (Booktrope Edtns); Vox Dei (VoxDei)
E-mail: publisher@booktrope.com; production@booktrope.com; info@booktrope.com; accounting@booktrope.com
Web site: http://www.booktrope.com.

Booktrope Editions *Imprint of* **Booktrope**

Bookworm Bks., (*978-0-9749423*) P.O. Box 77277, Washington, DC 20013 USA (SAN 255-8874) Fax: 202-387-5127; Toll Free: 877-302-0067
E-mail: info@bookwormbooks.biz
Web site: http://www.bookwormbooks.biz
Dist(s): **Independent Pubs. Group.**

Boom Entertainment, Inc., 5670 Wilshire Blvd., Ste 450, Los Angeles, CA 90036 USA
Dist(s): **Diamond Comic Distributors, Inc.**
Diamond Bk. Distributors
Follett School Solutions
Simon & Schuster, Inc.

Boom! Studios, (*978-1-932386; 978-1-934506; 978-1-60886; 978-1-936393; 978-1-61398; 978-1-939867; 978-1-68159*) 1800 Century Pk. E., Suite 200, Los Angeles, CA 90067 USA Tel 310-895-7746; 5670 Wilshire Blvd., Suite No. 450, Los Angeles, CA 90036; *Imprints:* Archaia Entertainment (ArchaiaEnt)
E-mail: boomstudios@gmail.com
Web site: http://www.boom-studios.com
Dist(s): **MyiLibrary**
Simon & Schuster, Inc.
Simon & Schuster Children's Publishing.

Boone Bks., (*978-0-9765294*) P.O. Box 262147, Plano, TX 75026-2147 USA Toll Free: 800-755-6628
E-mail: cadprof@boonebooks.com
Web site: http://www.boonebooks.com.

Boosey & Hawkes, Inc., 229 W. 28th St. Flr. 11, New York, NY 10001-5915 USA
E-mail: bhsales@ny.boosey.com
Web site: http://www.boosey.com
Dist(s): **Leonard, Hal Corp.**

Boot in the Door Pubns., (*978-0-9788183*) P.O. Box 2435, Anahuac, TX 77514-2435 USA
E-mail: lesaboutin@gmail.com; dlkboutin@windstream.net.

Booth, John Harvey, (*978-0-9754291*) 246 Schilling St., West Lafayette, IN 47906 USA Tel 765-743-8728
E-mail: jhbooth2003@yahoo.com.

Publisher Name Index

Boothroyd & Allnut, *(978-0-578-11204-6; 978-0-9904207)* 5115 68th Ave. NE, Marysville, WA 98270 USA.
Boptism Music Publications *See* **Boptism Music Publishing**
Boptism Music Publishing, *(978-0-9717983; 978-0-9726185; 978-0-9777503)* Orders Addr.: 23 Oakwood Rd., Candler, NC 28715 USA Tel 828-665-1405; Edit Addr.: 916 Union St., Apt. 2-C, Brooklyn, NY 11215 USA Tel 718-638-2767; Fax: 718-638-2613
E-mail: trbnplyr@aol.com; boptism@charter.net
Web site: http://www.boptism.com.
Borah Pr., *(978-0-9657879)* 1100 Rd. M, Redwood Valley, CA 95470 USA Tel 707-485-0922; Fax: 707-485-7071
E-mail: JPack@pacific.net.
Border Pr., *(978-0-9650977; 978-0-9843150; 978-0-9848915; 978-0-9898641; 978-0-9862801; 978-0-9968737)* Orders Addr.: P.O. Box 3124, Sewanee, TN 37375 USA Tel 337-577-1762; Toll Free Fax: 866-669-3207
E-mail: borderpress@gmail.com
Web site: http://borderpressbooks.com.
Borders Group, Inc., *(978-0-681)* 100 Phoenix Dr., Ann Arbor, MI 48108 USA Tel 734-477-1100
Web site: http://www.borders.com.
Borders Personal Publishing, *(978-1-4134)* a/o Pam Durant, 2 International Plaza, Suite 340, Philadelphia, PA 19113 USA Tel 610-915-5214; Fax: 610-915-0294; Toll Free: 888-795-4274
E-mail: dave@xlibris.com
Dist(s): **Xlibris Corp.**
Borders Pr., *(978-0-681)* Div. of Borders Group, Inc., 100 Phoenix Dr., Ann Arbor, MI 48108 USA; *Imprints:* State Street Press (State St Pr)
Web site: http://www.bordersstores.com; http://www.bordersgroupinc.com; http://www.borders.com.
BorderStone Pr., LLC, *(978-0-9842284; 978-1-936670)* Orders Addr.: P.O. Box 1383, Mountain Home, AR 72653 USA Tel 870-405-1146; 436 Olympic Dr., MOUNTAIN HOME, 72654 Tel 870-405-1146
E-mail: borderstonepress@gmail.com
Web site: http://www.borderstonepress.com; http://www.facebook.com/pages/BorderStone-Press-LLC/137970880138?ref=ts.
Bordighera Incorporated, *(978-1-884419; 978-1-59954)* Orders Addr.: P.O. Box 1374, Lafayette, IN 47902-1374 USA; Edit Addr.: John D. Calandra Italian American Institute 25 W. 43rd St., 17th Flr., New York, NY 10036 USA Tel 212-642-2005
E-mail: dstarewich@verizon.net; anthony.tamburri@qc.cuny.edu
Dist(s): **SPD-Small Pr. Distribution.**
Borealis Bk. *Imprint of* **Minnesota Historical Society Pr.**
Borealis Pr., *(978-0-9632651; 978-0-9819950)* P.O. Box 230, Surry, ME 04684 USA Tel 207-667-3700; Fax: 207-667-9649; Toll Free: 800-669-6845.
Borgo Press *See* **Borgo Publishing**
Borgo Publishing, *(978-0-9843979; 978-0-9883893; 978-0-9905431; 978-0-9968783)* 3811 Derby Downs Dr., Tuscaloosa, AL 35405 USA Tel 205-454-4256
E-mail: borgogirl@bellsouth.net.
Born to Blaze Ministries, *(978-0-9762910)* 2131 20th St SE, Buffalo, MN 55313-4813 USA
E-mail: info@borntoblaze.com
Web site: http://www.borntoblaze.com.
borntalking.com, *(978-0-9720892)* 34116 Blue Heron Dr., Solon, OH 44139-5641 USA
E-mail: david@borntalking.com
Web site: http://www.borntalking.com.
Borromeo Bks., *(978-0-9763098)* Orders Addr.: P.O. Box 7273, Saint Paul, MN 55107 USA.
Boshu Pr., *(978-0-9755624)* 3 Dogwood Ct., Greenville, NC 27858 USA
E-mail: boshucelli@earthlink.net.
BOSS Business Services *See* **Anderson Law Group**
Boss Paws Publishing, *(978-0-9769058)* 2536 Ridgewood Ave., Louisville, KY 40217 USA Tel 502-649-6864
E-mail: ag@animalgambill.org.
Bosse, Andre Ctr., *(978-0-9786128)* 302 Hanson St., Hart, MI 49420-1385 USA Tel 231-873-1707; Fax: 231-873-1456
E-mail: maltbie7@charter.net
Web site: http://www.andrebossecenter.org.
BOT Publishing, LLC, *(978-0-9759493)* P.O. Box 62, Mount Pleasant, SC 29465 USA
Web site: http://thebeautyoftruth.com.
Botero de Borrero, Beatriz & Martha Olga Botero de Gomez (COL) *(978-958-33) Dist. by* **Lectorum Pubns.**
Bothwell Pr., *(978-0-9855353)* 664 H St., Salt Lake City, UT 84103 USA (SAN 920-3397) Tel 801-532-2204 Do not confuse with Bothwell Pr. in Athens, GA
E-mail: Bothwellpress@gmail.com.
Bo-Tree Hse., *(978-0-9832227; 978-0-9968516)* 1749 Del Mar Dr., Idaho Falls, ID 83404 USA Tel 208-524-2491
E-mail: Debu.majumdar@botreehouse.com
Web site: http://www. botreehouse.com
Dist(s): **Follett School Solutions**
Smashwords.
Bottom of the Hill Publishing, *(978-1-935785; 978-1-61203; 978-1-4837)* 200 Terry Rd., Somerville, TN 38068 USA Tel 901-465-8497
E-mail: info@bottomofthehillpublishing.com
Web site: bottomofthehillpublishing.com.
Bottom-Up Media, *(978-0-9765337)* 5413 Nueces Bay Dr., Rowlett, TX 75089 USA (SAN 854-7440) Tel 214-550-2563
E-mail: steve@bottomupmedia.com
Web site: http://www.bottomupmedia.com
Dist(s): **AtlasBooks Distribution**
Lightning Source, Inc.
Bouje Publishing, LLC, *(978-0-9779265)* Orders Addr.: 17659 Montebello Rd, Cupertino, CA 95014 USA.
Boulden Publishing, *(978-1-878076; 978-1-892421)* Div. of Turtle Pine, Inc., Orders Addr.: P.O. Box 1186, Weaverville, CA 96093-1186 USA Tel 530-623-5399; Fax: 530-623-5525; Toll Free: 800-238-8433
E-mail: ken@bouldenpublishing.com
Web site: http://www.bouldenpublishing.com
Dist(s): **Follett School Solutions**
MAR*CO Products, Inc.
Social Studies Schl. Service
Sunburst Communications, Inc.
Boulder Street Bks. LLC, *(978-0-578-06778-0)* P.O. Box 380, Green Mountain Falls, CO 80819 USA
E-mail: editor@boulderstreetbooks.com
Web site: http://www.boulderstreetbooks.com
Dist(s): **Outskirts Pr., Inc.**
Bouncing Ball Bks., Inc., *(978-1-934138)* P.O. Box 6509, Spring Hill, FL 34611-6509 USA (SAN 851-6073)
E-mail: bouncingballbooks@yahoo.com
Web site: http://www.bouncingballbooks.com.
Bound & Determined Pubs., *(978-0-9704006)* Orders Addr.: 18116 Woodrow Rd., Brainerd, MN 56401 USA
E-mail: adamrmarcotte@yahoo.com
Web site: http://www.sover.net/~niliacus/a&h/; http://www.adamandheidi.net.
Bound by Grace Pr., LLC, *(978-0-9787087)* Orders Addr.: 924 Campbell Ct., Batavia, IL 60510 USA Tel 630-772-7172
E-mail: denise@boundbygracepress.com
Web site: http://www.boundbygracepress.com
Dist(s): **Theological Bk. Service.**
Bounty Project, The, *(978-0-9665861)* 6310 Georgetown Pike, McLean, VA 22101 USA Tel 703-442-7557
E-mail: kjackson@1771.org.
Bourgeois Media & Consulting, *(978-0-9796288; 978-0-9827877; 978-0-9830355; 978-0-9831971; 978-0-9834868; 978-0-9840281; 978-0-9854244; 978-0-9967348)* 1712 E. Riverside Dr. 124, Austin, TX 78741 USA; *Imprints:* Creative House Kids Press (CreatHseKids)
E-mail: chpress@live.com
Web site: http://bourgeoismedia.com.
Boutin, Lesa *See* **Boot in the Door Pubns.**
Boutique of Quality Books Publishing Co., *(978-1-60808; 978-0-9828689; 978-0-9831699; 978-1-937084; 978-1-939371)* 960 Oaktree Blvd., Christiansburg, VA 24073 USA Tel 678-316-4150; Fax: 678-999-3738; *Imprints:* BQB Publishing (BQBPubng); WriteLife Publishing (WriteLifePub)
E-mail: writelife@boutiqueofqualitybooks.com
Web site: http://www.bqbpublishing.com
Dist(s): **INscribe Digital**
New Leaf Distributing Co., Inc.
Bow Historical Bks.,
Dist(s): **Oxford Univ. Pr., Inc.**
Bowden Music Co., *(978-0-9702219)* 1511 Grand Ave., Fort Worth, TX 76106 USA Tel 817-624-1547 (phone/fax)
E-mail: essieb@mindspring.com.
Bower Bks. *Imprint of* **Storybook Meadow Publishing**
Bowers, Renata *See* **Frieda B.**
Bowman's Pr., LLC, *(978-1-933142)* P.O. Box 3836, Ithaca, NY 14852-3836 USA Tel 607-257-3737 Toll Free: 866-272-8673
E-mail: info@bowmanspress.com
Web site: http://www.bowmanspress.com
Dist(s): **AtlasBooks Distribution.**
Bowmar/Noble Pubs., *(978-0-8107; 978-0-8372)* 220 E. Danieldale Dr., De Soto, TX 75115-2490 USA (SAN 201-4157).
Bowrider Pr., *(978-0-9825663)* 1451 Fairbanks Pl., Los Angeles, CA 90026 USA Tel 310-497-1789
Dist(s): **Follett School Solutions.**
Box Girls, The, *(978-0-9769906)* 149 S. Barrington Ave, No. 126, Los Angeles, CA 90049 USA Fax: 310-440-0145
Web site: http://www.theboxgirls.com.
Boxer Bks., Ltd. (GBR) *(978-0-9547373; 978-1-905417; 978-1-910126) Dist. by* **Sterling.**
Boxes & Arrows, Incorporated *See* **Backintyme Publishing**
Boyars, Marion Pubs., Inc., *(978-0-7145; 978-0-905223)* 237 E. 39th St., No. 1A, New York, NY 10016-2110 USA (SAN 284-981X) Tel 212-697-1599; Fax: 212-808-0664; Toll Free: 800-283-3572 (orders only)
Dist(s): **Consortium Bk. Sales & Distribution**
MyiLibrary.
Boyce, S. M., *(978-1-939997)* Orders Addr.: 4152 Meridian St. Suite 105-395, Bellingham, WA 98226 USA
E-mail: boyce@smboyce.com
Web site: http://smboyce.com.
Boydell & Brewer, Inc., *(978-0-85115; 978-0-85991; 978-0-907239; 978-0-938100; 978-1-57113; 978-1-58046; 978-1-85566; 978-1-870252; 978-1-878822; 978-1-879751; 978-1-900639; 978-1-84384; 978-1-84383)* Div. of Boydell & Brewer Group, Ltd., Orders Addr.: 668 Mount Hope Ave., Rochester, NY 14620-2731 USA (SAN 013-8479) Tel 585-275-0419; Fax: 585-271-8778
E-mail: boydell@boydellusa.net; boydell@boydell.co.uk
Web site: http://www.boydellandbrewer.com
Dist(s): **MyiLibrary**
Perseus Bks. Group
ebrary, Inc.
Boyds Collection Ltd., The, *(978-0-9712840; 978-0-9713174)* 75 Cunningham Rd., Gettysburg, PA 17325-7142 USA
E-mail: alana@boydsstuff.com
Web site: http://www.boydsstuff.com.
Boyds Mills Pr., *(978-1-56397; 978-1-878093; 978-1-886910; 978-1-59078; 978-1-932425; 978-1-62091; 978-1-62979; 978-0-9961172; 978-0-9961173; 978-1-943283; 978-1-68238)* Div. of Highlights For Children, Inc., 815 Church St., Honesdale, PA 18431-1877 USA (SAN 852-3177) Tel 570-251-4513 Toll Free: 800-490-5111 Admin line; 877-512-8366; 800-874-8817 Cust Svc Columbus, OH; *Imprints:* Wordsong (Wordsong); Calkins Creek (Calkins Creek); Front Street (FrtSt); Lemniscaat (Lemnisca); Highlights (Highlights)
E-mail: admin@boydsmillspress.com; honesdale-cs@boydsmillspress.com; marketing@boydsmillspress.com
Web site: http://www.boydsmillspress.com; http://www.wordsongpoetry.com; http://www.calkinscreekbooks.com; http://www.frontstreetbooks.com
Dist(s): **Follett School Solutions**
INscribe Digital
Lectorum Pubns., Inc.
Perfection Learning Corp.
Perseus Distribution.
Boynton, Colin (GBR) *(978-0-9559931) Dist. by* **LuluCom.**
Boys Read Bks., *(978-0-9801224)* 3211 NW 75th St., Seattle, WA 98117 USA Tel 206-321-5500
E-mail: john@boysread.org.
Boys Town, Nebraska Center, Public Service Division *See* **Boys Town Pr.**
Boys Town Pr., *(978-0-938510; 978-1-889322; 978-1-934490; 978-1-936734)* Div. of Father Flanagan's Boys' Home, Orders Addr.: 14100 Crawford St., Omaha, NE 68010 USA (SAN 215-8477) Tel 402-498-1320; Fax: 402-498-1310; Toll Free: 800-282-6657
E-mail: btpress@boystown.org
Web site: http://www.boystownpress.org
Dist(s): **Brodart Co.**
Quality Bks., Inc.
bPlus Bks. *Imprint of* **Bumble Bee Publishing**
BPM Research LLC, *(978-0-9829224)* 939 Bloomfield St., Hoboken, NJ 07030 USA Tel 551-226-9372
E-mail: michael@bpm-research.com
Web site: http://www.bpm-research.com.
BPT Media, *(978-0-9772126)* P.O. Box 28663, Philadelphia, PA 19151-0663 USA
E-mail: vharris52@gmail.com.
BQB Publishing *Imprint of* **Boutique of Quality Books Publishing Co.**
Bradford Pr., Inc., *(978-0-9705618; 978-0-9801563)* Orders Addr.: P.O. Box 6802, South Bend, IN 46660-6802 USA Tel 574-876-3601; Fax: 574-255-9358 Do not confuse with companies with same name in Bradford, MA, Palm Beach, FL, Chicago, IL
E-mail: BradfordPress@comcast.net; Info@Bradford-Press.com
Web site: http://www.Bradford-Press.com.
Bradford-Franklin, *(978-0-9767676)* P.O. Box 495, Hartsville, TN 37074 USA Tel 615-374-3712; Fax: 615-374-4649
E-mail: bradfordfranklin@bellsouth.net
Web site: http://www.jackmccall.com.
Bradley, Judy & Assocs., LLC, *(978-0-615-57032-7)* 230 E. 45th St., Savannah, GA 31405 USA Tel 912-232-7636
E-mail: judybee58@gmail.com.
Brady GAMES, *(978-0-7440)* 800 E. 96th St., Indianapolis, IN 46240 USA Tel 317-428-3333
Web site: http://www.bradygames.com
Dist(s): **Dorling Kindersley Publishing, Inc.**
Pearson Education
Penguin Random Hse., LLC.
Penguin Publishing Group.
BradyBooks *See* **Nature Works Press**
Bradybooks.biz, *(978-0-9754169)* 1888 County Road 72., Bailey, CO 80421-2175 USA
E-mail: readbradybooks@aol.com
Web site: http://bradybooks.biz.
Braided Image, *(978-0-9725170)* 3064 Old New Cut Rd., Springfield, TN 37172 USA
E-mail: masterbraider@mindspring.com
Web site: http://www.braidedimage.com.
Brailleink, *(978-0-9769313)* 1704 Holly St., Austin, TX 78702-5424 USA Toll Free: 800-324-2919
E-mail: info@brailleink.org
Web site: http://www.brailleink.org.
Brainbow Pr., *(978-0-9796715; 978-0-9825867)* 7914 N. Roundstone Dr., Tucson, AZ 85741 USA (SAN 854-0594) Tel 520-481-1919
E-mail: 19@19.org; edipyuksel@gmail.com; brainbowpress@gmail.com
Web site: http://www.brainbowpress.com; http://www.islamicreform.org; http://www.yuksel.org; http://www.19.org
Dist(s): **Lightning Source, Inc.**
BrainBox, Limited *See* **Gray Jay Bks.**
Brainchild Publishing *See* **Mindfull Publishing**
Brainerd Enterprises, *(978-0-9747441)* 419 Old Clyde Pk. Rd., Livingston, MT 59047 USA Tel 406-222-8273; Fax: 406-222-3769
E-mail: sally@heirofkingmeldh.com
Web site: http://www.heirofkingmeldh.com.
BrainFriendly Learning, *(978-0-9759226)* 6801 6th St., NW, Washington, DC 20012-1911 USA Tel 202-723-7337; Fax: 202-726-6117
E-mail: stevecarroll@speakeasy.net
Web site: http://www.kathleencarroll.com.
Brainstorm Co., The, *(978-0-9728354)* Orders Addr.: 11684 Ventura Blvd., No. 970, Studio City, CA 91604 USA (SAN 255-5174) Tel 818-763-2674
E-mail: weddinggames@hotmail.com
Web site: http://www.TheBrainstormCompany.com
Dist(s): **Independent Pubs. Group.**
Brainstorm Pubns., Inc., *(978-0-9723429)* 24 NE 24th Ave., Pompano Beach, FL 33062 USA Tel 954-941-3329; Fax: 954-943-7708 Do not confuse with Brainstorm Publications in Lake Oswego, OR
E-mail: tditocco@brainstormpublications.com
Web site: http://www.brainstormpublications.com.
BrainStorm 3000, *(978-0-9651174)* P.O. Box 80513, Goleta, CA 93118 USA Tel 805-448-7149; 805-448-7149
Dist(s): **Educational Bk. Distributors.**
BrainStream, *(978-0-9785892)* 21307 Park Valley Dr., Katy, TX 77450-4811 USA
E-mail: bvogt@brainstream.com.
Braintext, Inc., *(978-0-9816270)* 3660 Wilshire Blvd. Ste. 400, Los Angeles, CA 90010-2753 USA
E-mail: info@braintext.com
Web site: http://www.braintext.com.
BrainX, Inc., *(978-0-9741604)* 45 Rincon Dr. Unit 1033B, Camarillo, CA 93012-8424 USA
E-mail: info@brainx.com
Web site: http://www.brainx.com
Dist(s): **Majors, J. A. Co.**
Rittenhouse Bk. Distributors.
Braley & Thompson, Inc., *(978-1-883239)* P.O. Box 1396, Saint Albans, WV 25177-1396 USA Tel 304-722-1704; Fax: 304-722-1709; Toll Free: 800-258-5453.
Bran Nue Productions, *(978-0-615-44662-2; 978-0-9851574)* 7878 LaSalle Ave. No. 231, Baton Rouge, LA 70806 USA Tel 225-200-4451
E-mail: brannuepro@gmail.com.
Branch Springs Publishing, *(978-0-9727622)* Orders Addr.: 500 Watts Dr., Huntsville, AL 35801 USA Tel 256 539 1064; Edit Addr.: 500 Watts Dr., Huntsville, AL 35801 USA
E-mail: fchap10220@aol.com.
Branching Plot Bks., *(978-0-9860166; 978-0-9891840)* 5815 Lacey Blvd SE Unit 8027, Lacey, WA 98509-4101 USA
E-mail: arthurmills@branchingplotbooks.com
Web site: http://www.branchingplotbooks.com.
Brand Nu Words *Imprint of* **Nunes Productions, LLC**
Branded Black Publishing, *(978-0-9746913)* P.O. Box 950781, Oklahoma City, OK 73195 USA
Web site: http://www.ebonymarshal.com; http://www.brandedblackpublishing.com; http://www.gospelofthegun.com; http://www.seanchandler.com.
Brandeis Univ., Rose Art Museum, *(978-0-9726641; 978-0-9761593)* 415 South St., Waltham, MA 02254 USA (SAN 278-243X) Tel 781-736-3434; Fax: 781-736-3439
E-mail: tjking@brandeis.edu
Web site: http://www.brandeis.edu/rose
Dist(s): **D.A.P./Distributed Art Pubs.**
Branden Bks., *(978-0-8283)* Div. of Branden Publishing Co., P.O. Box 812094, Wellesley, MA 02482 USA (SAN 201-4106) Tel 781-235-3634; Fax: 781-790-1056
E-mail: branden@brandenbooks.com; danteu@danteuniversity.org
Web site: http://www.brandenbooks.com; http://www.danteuniversity.org; http://www.adolphcaso.com
Dist(s): **Brodart Co.**
Follett School Solutions
eBookit.com.
Branden Publishing Company *See* **Branden Bks.**
Brandylane Pubs., Inc., *(978-0-9627635; 978-1-883911; 978-0-9838264; 978-0-9849588; 978-0-9859358; 978-1-939930)* Orders Addr.: 5 S. 1st St., Richmond, VA 23219-3716 USA; *Imprints:* Belle Isle Books (Belleisle)
E-mail: rhpruett@brandylanepublishers.com
Web site: http://www.brandylanepublishers.com
Dist(s): **Baker & Taylor International**
Follett School Solutions
Lightning Source, Inc.
Smashwords.
Brass, Robin Studio, Inc. (CAN) *(978-1-896941) Dist. by* **Midpt Trade.**
BrassHeart Music, *(978-0-9673762; 978-0-9721478; 978-0-9826278)* 256 S. Robertson Blvd., Suite 2288, Beverly Hills, CA 90211 USA Tel 323-932-0534; Fax: 323-937-6884; 323-933-4209; *Imprints:* Kid's Creative Classics (Kids Creative Classics); Dream A World (Dream A World)
E-mail: bunny@dreamaworld.com; brassheartmusic@aol.com
Web site: http://www.brassheartmusic.com; http://www.dreamaworld.com
Dist(s): **DeVorss & Co.**
Music Design, Inc.
New Leaf Distributing Co., Inc.
Braun Pubns., *(978-0-9774302)* 150 Clinton Ln., Spring Valley, NY 10977 USA.
Brave Ulysses Bks., *(978-0-9700125; 978-0-615-16272-0; 978-0-615-18969-7; 978-0-615-22032-1; 978-0-615-26030-3)* P.O. Box 1877, Asheville, NC 28802 USA
E-mail: cecil@braveulysses.com; info@braveulysses.com
Dist(s): **Lulu Enterprises Inc.**
Parnassus Bk. Distributors.
Braveheart Pr., LLC, *(978-0-9763935)* 23852 Pacific Coast Hwy., Suite 572, Malibu, CA 90265 USA Tel 310-770-7831; Fax: 310-456-5109 do not confuse with BraveHeart Press in Woodland Park, CO
E-mail: showrunnerbrv@aol.com
Web site: http://www.braveheartpressllc.com.
BraveMouse Bks., *(978-0-9819697; 978-1-940947)* 11056 Rodeo Dr., Oak View, CA 93022 USA
E-mail: bravemouse1@gmail.com
Web site: www.bravemousebooks.com
Dist(s): **Independent Pubs. Group**
MyiLibrary
ebrary, Inc.
Braziller, George Inc., *(978-0-8076)* 171 Madison Ave., Suite 1103, New York, NY 10016 USA (SAN 201-9310) Tel 212-889-0909; Fax: 212-689-5405
Dist(s): **Norton, W. W. & Co., Inc.**
Penguin Random Hse., LLC.
Brazos Valley Pr., *(978-0-9726822)* Orders Addr.: P.O. Box 215, Calvert, TX 77837-0215 USA Tel 979-364-2439;

Fax: 800-881-2032; Edit Addr.: 508 E. Texas, Calvert, TX 77837 USA (SAN 858-2947)
E-mail: jkennedy@brazosvalleypress.com
Web site: http://www.brazosvalleypress.com.

Brda, Tracy, *(978-0-9742355)* P.O. Box 510065, Saint Louis, MO 63129 USA Tel 314-293-0015; Fax: 636-343-0564
E-mail: info@power-twins.com.

Bread & Butter Bks., *(978-0-9800816)* 229 E. Ct. St., Cincinnati, OH 45202 USA Tel 513-884-0468
E-mail: jkiddielit@cinci.rr.com.

Break-A-Leg Bks., *(978-0-9668522)* 12332 Laurel Terr., Studio City, CA 91604 USA Tel 818-508-5585; Fax: 818-752-0682.

Breakaway Bks., *(978-1-55821; 978-1-891369; 978-1-62124)* P.O. Box 24, Halcottsville, NY 12438 USA Tel 607-326-4805; Fax: 212-898-0408; Toll Free: 800-548-4348 (voicemail) Do not confuse with Breakaway Bks., Albany, TX
E-mail: breakawaybooks@gmail.com
Web site: http://www.breakawaybooks.com
Dist(s): **Consortium Bk. Sales & Distribution.**

Breaking Cycles Bks., *(978-0-9741202)* Orders Addr.: P.O. Box 402, Severn, MD 21144-0402 USA Tel 410-519-6787
E-mail: BrCyBks@msn.com
Web site: http://www.breaking-cycles-visions-of-hope.com.

Breaking the Barrier, Inc., *(978-0-9712817; 978-0-9728570; 978-0-9758573; 978-0-9777987; 978-0-9817961; 978-0-9846477; 978-0-9846490; 978-0-9903122; 978-0-9963192)* 63 Shirley Rd., Groton, MA 01450 USA Fax: 978-448-1237; Toll Free: 866-862-7325 Do not confuse with Breaking the Barrier Ministry, Inc. in Pennsauken, NJ
E-mail: info@tobreak.com; john@tobreak.com
Web site: http://www.tobreak.com.

Breakneck Bks. *Imprint of* **Variance Publishing, LLC**

Breakneck Books *See* **Breakneck Media**

Breakneck Media, *(978-0-9786551; 978-0-9796929; 978-0-9836017; 978-0-9840423; 978-0-9886725; 978-1-941539)* 20 Sampson Rd., Rochester, NH 03867 USA
E-mail: info@jeremyrobinsononline.com
Web site: http://www.jeremyrobinsononline.com.

Breath & Shadows Productions, *(978-0-9720176; 978-0-9821029)* P.O. Box 10557, Tampa, FL 33679 USA Tel 813-251-8187
Web site: http://www.breathandshadows.com.

Breathless Vintage Enterprises, *(978-0-9842053)* Orders Addr.: PO Box 28168, Portland, OR 97228 USA (SAN 858-7221)
E-mail: morgan@breathlessvintage.com.

Breckling Pr., *(978-0-9721218; 978-1-933308)* 283 Michigan Ave., Elmhurst, IL 60126 USA
Web site: http://www.brecklingpress.com
Dist(s): **Independent Pubs. Group.**

Bree's Gift Publishing, *(978-0-9748512)* 3840 Listerman Rd., Howell, MI 48855 USA Tel 517-552-9184
E-mail: kimmie67@sbcglobal.net.

Breezy Reads, *(978-0-9759784; 978-1-938327)* Orders Addr.: 2800 N Bogus Basin Rd APT C103, Boise, ID 83702 USA (SAN 256-3762)
E-mail: breezyreads@gmail.com
Web site: http://www.breezyreads.com.

Bremer Press *See* **Zachmeyer, Mary L.**

Brenner Publishing, LLC, *(978-0-9777203)* P.O. Box 584, Hicksville, NY 11802-0584 USA Tel 516-433-0804.

Brentwood Christian Pr. *Imprint of* **Brentwood Communications Group**

Brentwood Communications Group, *(978-0-916573; 978-1-55630; 978-1-59581)* 4000 Beallwood Ave., Columbus, GA 31904 USA (SAN 297-1895) Tel 706-576-5787 Toll Free: 800-334-8861; *Imprints:* Brentwood Christian Press (BrtwdChrist Pr) Do not confuse with Brentwood Communications Group in Vista, CA
E-mail: brentwood@knology.net
Web site: http://www.brentwoodbooks.com; http://www.brentwoodreview.com; http://www.newchristianbooks.com
Dist(s): **Ingram Pub. Services.**

Brentwood Home Video, *(978-0-7378; 978-0-924739; 978-1-57119; 978-1-879902)* Div. of Brentwood Communications, Inc., 810 Lawrence Dr., Suite 100, Newbury Park, CA 91320 USA Toll Free: 888-335-0528
E-mail: brentcom@earthlink.net
Web site: http://www.ssetsites.com/e-bci/default.htm
Dist(s): **Follett School Solutions.**

Brentwood Kids Co. *Imprint of* **Brentwood Music, Inc.**

Brentwood Music, Inc., *(978-0-7601; 978-1-55897)* 2555 Meridian Blvd. Ste. 100, Franklin, TN 37067-6364 USA Toll Free: 800-333-9000 (audio & video orders); 800-846-7664 (book orders); *Imprints:* Brentwood Kids Company (Brentwood Kids)
Web site: http://www.providentmusic.com
Dist(s): **Appalachian Bible Co.**
Central South Christian Distribution
Leonard, Hal Corp.
New Day Christian Distributors Gifts, Inc.
Provident Music Distribution
Spring Arbor Distributors, Inc.

Brentwood Publishing Group *See* **Writing for the Lord Ministries**

Brentwood-Benson Music Publishing, *(978-1-59802; 978-0-9830602)* Orders Addr.: 101 Winners Cir., Brentwood, TN 37027 USA (SAN 256-9574) Toll Free: 800-846-7664
E-mail: sales@brentwoodbenson.com; jroher@brentwoodbenson.net
Web site: http://www.brentwoodbenson.com
Dist(s): **Leonard, Hal Corp.**

†Brethren Pr., *(978-0-87178)* Div. of Church of the Brethren, 1451 Dundee Ave., Elgin, IL 60120-1694 USA (SAN 201-9329) Tel 847-742-5100; 800-441-3712; Fax: 847-742-1407; Toll Free: 800-441-3712
E-mail: brethren_press_gb@brethren.org
Web site: http://www.brethrenpress.com
Dist(s): **Follett School Solutions**; *CIP.*

Brethren Revival Fellowship, *(978-0-9745027; 978-0-9777766; 978-0-9828895)* 26 United Zion Cir., Lititz, PA 17543-7956 USA Fax: 717-625-0511
E-mail: harpri@dejazzd.com; brf@brfwitness.org
Web site: http://www.brfwitness.org.

Brewer, Neil, *(978-0-9771807)* 5290 Cedar Way Dr., NE, Corydon, IN 47112 USA Tel 812-952-3482
E-mail: 8oclock@aye.net
Web site: http://www.booksbybrewer.com
Dist(s): **BookBaby.**

Brewer Technologies, *(978-0-9774748)* P.O. Box 141, Cornwall, PA 17016 USA Tel 717-228-1708; Fax: 717-228-1709; Toll Free: 877-449-2556
E-mail: nicholelmoore@comcast.net
Web site: http://www.tonybrewer.com.

Brewer's Historical Publications *See* **Bear State Bks.**

Brewner, J.P., *(978-0-615-81626-5; 978-0-615-99564-9)* 1416 Clybourne St., Batavia, IL 60510 USA Tel 630 244-1526
Dist(s): **CreateSpace Independent Publishing Platform.**

Brewster Moon, *(978-0-9854423)* 13940 Cedar Rd. Suite 386, University Heights, OH 44118 USA Tel 216-408-1616
E-mail: tbrown@brewstermoon.com.

Brewster, Robert, *(978-0-615-37153-5)* 185 NE 4th Ave. Apt 317, Delray Beach, FL 33483 USA Tel 561-400-7799
Dist(s): **Outskirts Pr., Inc.**

Brickey E-Publishing, *(978-0-9758964)* 1029E Salisbury St., Kernersville, NC 27284-3063 USA
E-mail: mainoffice@brickey-epublishing.com
Web site: http://www.brickey-epublishing.com.

BrickHouse Bks., Inc., *(978-0-932616; 978-1-935916; 978-1-938144)* 306 Suffolk Rd., Baltimore, MD 21218 USA (SAN 209-4622) Tel 410-235 7690
E-mail: charriss@towson.edu
Web site: http://www.towsonu.edu
Dist(s): **INscribe Digital**
Itasca Bks.

BrickHouse Education *Imprint of* **Cambridge BrickHouse, Inc.**

Bridge Ink, *(978-0-9641963)* 32580 SW Arbor Lake Dr., Wilsonville, OR 97070-8471 USA
E-mail: bob@bridgeink.com
Web site: http://www.bridgeink.com
Dist(s): **Far West Bk. Service**
Follett School Solutions
Partners/West Book Distributors.

Bridge Pubns., Inc., *(978-0-88404; 978-1-57318; 978-1-4031; 978-1-61177; 978-1-4572)* Orders Addr.: 5600 E. Olympic Blvd., Commerce, CA 90022 USA (SAN 208-3884) Tel 323-888-6200; Fax: 323-888-6210; Toll Free: 800-722-1733; Edit Addr.: 4751_Fountain Ave., Los Angeles, CA 90029 USA
E-mail: annarnow@bridgepub.com; daniellem@bridgepub.com; donarnow@bridgepub.com
Web site: http://www.bridgepub.com; http://www.clearbodyclearmind.com; http://www.scientology.org; http://www.dianetics.org
Dist(s): **Bookazine Co., Inc.**
Brodart Co.
Follett School Solutions
Landmark Audiobooks.

Bridge Publishing Group, *(978-0-9728439)* P.O. Box 1673, Walnut, CA 91788-1673 USA Tel 909-444-9088; Fax: 909-595-9526
E-mail: dafangzeng@yahoo.com.

Bridge the Gap Publishing, *(978-0-9746610)* 336 Bon Air Ctr., Suite 124, Greenbrae, CA 94904 USA Do not confuse with Bridge the gap Publishing in Luverne, MN
E-mail: maryanne@shomi.us
Dist(s): **Independent Pubs. Group.**

Bridge To Life Ministries, Incorporated *See* **Advent Truth Ministries**

Bridge-Logos Foundation, *(978-0-88270; 978-0-912106; 978-0-9841034; 978-1-61036)* Orders Addr.: 17750 NW 115th Ave., Bldg. 200 Suite 220, Alachua, FL 32615 USA (SAN 253-5254) Tel 386-462-2525; Fax: 386-462-2535; Toll Free: 800-935-6467 (orders only); 800-631-5802 (orders only)
E-mail: info@bridgelogos.com; mail@bridgelogos.com; philedbrand@bridgelogos.com; lhildebrand@bridgelogos.com
Web site: http://www.bridgelogos.com
Dist(s): **Anchor Distributors**
Send The Light Distribution LLC
Spring Arbor Distributors, Inc.

Bridge-Logos Publishers *See* **Bridge-Logos Foundation**

Bridgestone Bks. *Imprint of* **Capstone Pr., Inc.**

Bridgeway Bks., *(978-1-933538; 978-1-934454)* Div. of BookPros, LLC, 2100 Kramer Ln., Suite 300, Austin, TX 78758 USA Tel 512-478-2028
Web site: http://www.bridgewaybooks.net.

BR:IEFing Assocs. of New England, *(978-0-9706105)* Orders Addr.: P.O. Box 3159, Kingston, NY 12402-3159 USA Tel 845-339-0998; Edit Addr.: 289 Fair St., Suite 2A, Kingston, NY 12401-3844 USA.

Briendel Publishing, *(978-0-615-59234-3)* 63 Parry Dr., Hainesport, AE 08036 USA Tel 6097027407
E-mail: evnsanna@comcast.net.

Briggs, Sharon, *(978-0-615-13051-4)* 109 Hope Way, Auburn, KY 42206 USA
E-mail: sharondeneice109@yahoo.com.

Brigham Young Univ., *(978-0-8425)* 205 UPB, Provo, UT 84602 USA (SAN 201-9337) Tel 801-422-2809; Fax: 801-422-0591; *Imprints:* BYU Creative Works (BYUCreative)
E-mail: diane_foerster@byu.edu
Web site: http://www.upb.byu.edu
Dist(s): **AtlasBooks Distribution**
Brigham Young Univ. Print Services
Chicago Distribution Ctr.
Follett School Solutions
Indiana Univ. Pr.
Univ. of Chicago Pr.

Bright Cloud Publishing, *(978-0-9770727)*
E-mail: brightcloud@verizon.net
Web site: http://www.brightcloudpublishing.com.

Bright Connections Media, *(978-1-62267)* 233 N. Michigan Ave. Suite 2000, Chicago, IL 60601 USA Tel 312-729-5800
E-mail: orders@innlog.net
Web site: www.brightconnectionsmedia.com
Dist(s): **Continental Sales**
Independent Pubs. Group.

Bright Eyes Pr., *(978-0-9728019)* 862 Congressional Rd., Simi Valley, CA 93065 USA Tel 805-579-0027
E-mail: kassie@kgraves.com
Web site: http://www.brighteyespress.com.

Bright Girl Publishing, *(978-0-615-54005-4)* 1127 S. Mannheim Rd., suite. 213, Westchester, IL 60154 USA
E-mail: Info@www.Notfatbecauseiwannabe.com
Dist(s): **CreateSpace Independent Publishing Platform**
Dummy Record Do Not USE!!!!.

Bright Ideas! Educational Resources, *(978-1-892427)* P.O. Box 333, Cheswold, DE 19936 USA Toll Free: 877-492-8081
E-mail: hogan@inet.net.

Bright of America, *(978-1-930355)* 300 Greenbrier Rd., Summersville, WV 26651 USA Tel 304-872-3000; Fax: 304-872-3033; Toll Free: 800-917-2368.

Bright Ring Publishing, Inc., *(978-0-935607)* P.O. Box 31338, Bellingham, WA 98228-3338 USA (SAN 696-0537) Tel 360-592-9201; Fax: 360-592-4503; Toll Free: 800-480-4278; 250 W. 57th St. 15th Flr., New York, NY 10107
E-mail: maryann@brightring.com
Web site: http://www.brightring.com/books
Dist(s): **Ebsco Publishing**
Follett School Solutions
Gryphon Hse., Inc.
Legato Pubs. Group
MyiLibrary
Perseus-PGW.

Bright Sky Pr., *(978-0-9704729; 978-0-9709987; 978-1-931721; 978-1-933979; 978-1-936474; 978-1-939055; 978-1-942945)* Orders Addr.: 2365 Rice Blvd., Suite 202, Houston, TX 77005 USA Tel 713-533-9300; Fax: 713-528-2432 Do not confuse with Breakaway Bks., Halcottsville, NY
Web site: http://www.brightskypress.com
Dist(s): **AtlasBooks Distribution**
Follett School Solutions
Independent Pubs. Group
MyiLibrary
Sterling Publishing Co., Inc.
ebrary, Inc.

Bright Solutions for Dyslexia, LLC, *(978-0-9744343; 978-0-9755871)* 2059 Camden Ave., Suite 186, San Jose, CA 95124-2024 USA Tel 408-559-3652; Fax: 408-377-0503
E-mail: susan@brightsolutions.us
Web site: http://www.brightsolutions.us.

Bright Sparks *Imprint of* **Parragon, Inc.**

Bright Spots, *(978-0-9769150)* P.O. Box 3868, Rancho Santa Fe, CA 92067 USA Toll Free: 888-301-8880
E-mail: lmarneson@msn.com
Web site: http://www.brightspotsgames.com.

Bright Tyke Creations LLC, *(978-0-615-33119-5; 978-0-615-63721-1)* 217 Sassafras St., New Florence, PA 15944 USA
Web site: http://www.brighttykecreations.info.

BrightBerry Pr., *(978-0-9720924)* 4262 Kennebec Rd., Dixmont, ME 04932 USA Tel 207-234-4225
E-mail: jeanhay@brightberrypress.com; dbright@brightberrypress.com
Web site: http://www.brightberrypress.com
Dist(s): **CreateSpace Independent Publishing Platform.**

Bright-Brights Media Co., The, *(978-0-9752553)* 1059 Briar Ave., Provo, UT 84604 USA Tel 801-375-3455.

Brighter Child *Imprint of* **Carson-Dellosa Publishing, LLC**

Brighter Day Publishing, *(978-0-615-26080-8; 978-0-9841855)* P.O. Box 505, Washington Township, MI 48094 USA
Web site: http://www.publishinganswers.com.

Brighter Horizons Publishing, *(978-1-929662)* P.O. Box 448, Littleton, CO 80160 USA Tel 303-347-2904; Fax: 303-795-5951
E-mail: brighterhorizons@earthlink.net
Web site: http://home.earthlink.net/~brighterhorizons
Dist(s): **Book Wholesalers, Inc.**

Brighter Minds Children's Publishing, *(978-1-57791)* Div. of Brighter Child Interactive, LLC, 600 D Lakeview Plaza Blvd., Worthington, OH 43085 USA Tel 614-430-3021; Fax: 614-430-3152; *Imprints:* Little Melody Press (Little Melody Pr); Penny Candy Press (Penny Candy Pr)
E-mail: ranf@brightermindsmedia.com; books@Brightermindspublishing.com
Web site: http://www.brightermindspublishing.com
Dist(s): **Perseus Distribution.**

Brighton Publishing LLC, *(978-1-936587; 978-1-62183)* 501 W. Ray Rd. Suite No. 4, Chandler, AZ 85225 USA Tel 480-821-7722
E-mail: kathie@brightonpublishing.com
Web site: brightonpublishing.com.

Brightside Co., *(978-0-9743720)* 5040 S. Elmira St., Greenwood Village, CO 80111-3608 USA (SAN 255-5573) Tel 303-694-6065; Fax: 303-694-1009
E-mail: cynthiadormer@msn.com
Dist(s): **Independent Pubs. Group.**

Brightwell Publishing, LLC, *(978-0-9776033)* 7151 Delmar Blvd., Saint Louis, MO 63130-4304 USA (SAN 257-7046) Tel 314-662-2736
E-mail: publisher@brightwellpublishing.net
Web site: http://www.brightwellpublishing.net; http://maryedwardswertsch.net.

Brilliance Audio *See* **Brilliance Publishing**

Brilliance Publishing, *(978-0-930435; 978-1-56100; 978-1-56740; 978-1-58788; 978-1-59086; 978-1-59355; 978-1-59600; 978-1-59710; 978-1-59737; 978-1-4233; 978-1-4418; 978-1-61106; 978-1-4558; 978-1-4692; 978-1-4805; 978-1-4915; 978-1-5012; 978-1-5113)* Orders Addr.: P.O. Box 887, Grand Haven, MI 49417 USA (SAN 690-1395) Tel 616-846-5256; Fax: 616-846-0630; Toll Free: 800-648-2312 (phone/fax, retail & library orders); Edit Addr.: 1704 Eaton Dr., Grand Haven, MI 49417 USA (SAN 858-138X) Toll Free: 800-648-2312 x330
E-mail: sales@brillianceaudio.com; customerservice@brillianceaudio.com; jcraig@brilliancepublishing.com
Web site: http://www.brilliancepublishing.com
Dist(s): **Diamond Comic Distributors, Inc.**
Diamond Bk. Distributors
Findaway World, LLC
Follett School Solutions.

Brimax Books Ltd. (GBR) *(978-0-86112; 978-0-900195; 978-0-904494; 978-1-85854; 978-1-904952; 978-1-905279; 978-1-84656) Dist. by* **Byeway Bks.**

BrimWood Pr., *(978-0-9770704)* 1941 Larsen Dr., Camino, CA 95709 USA Tel 530-644-7538; Fax: 530-647-9208; *Imprints:* Tools For Young Historians (Tools YngHist)
E-mail: marcia@brimwoodpress.com
Web site: http://www.brimwoodpress.com.

Brindle Pr., *(978-0-9749080)* 14121 Cardinal Ln., Houston, TX 77079 USA
Web site: http://www.brindlepress.com.

Brinkley Bks., Inc., *(978-0-9793288)* P.O. Box 1753, Healdsburg, CA 95448 USA
E-mail: laura@brinkleybooks.com
Web site: http://www.brinkleybooks.com
Dist(s): **BCH Fulfillment & Distribution.**

Brinsights, LLC, *(978-0-9799454; 978-0-615-31228-6; 978-0-615-36380-6)* 141 E. 88th St., New York, NY 10128-2248 USA (SAN 854-848X)
E-mail: geri@brinsights.net; linaperi@gmail.com
Web site: http://www.mygreensanta.com
Dist(s): **Independent Pubs. Group.**

BRIO Pr., *(978-0-9817830; 978-0-9819290; 978-0-9826687; 978-1-937061)* 12 S. Sixth St., No.1250, Minneapolis, MN 55402 USA (SAN 856-5376) Tel 612-746-8800; Fax: 612-746-8811; Toll Free: 888-333-7979
E-mail: tmiller@briobooks.com
Web site: http://www.briobooks.com
Dist(s): **Lerner Publishing Group.**

BRIO Publishing *See* **BRIO Pr.**

Briona Glen Publishing, LLC *See* **Grey Gate Media, LLC**

Brisk Pr., *(978-0-9770885; 978-0-9799254; 978-0-9832758; 978-0-9899895; 978-0-9966774)* 13 Chestnut Ct. Unit D, Brielle, NJ 08730-1371 USA
E-mail: brisk.press@gmail.com
Web site: http://www.briskpress.com
Dist(s): **Bella Distribution**
Perseus Bks. Group
Perseus Distribution.

Bristol Hse., Ltd., *(978-0-917851; 978-1-885224)* P.O. Box 4020, Anderson, IN 46013 USA (SAN 225-4638) Tel 765-644-0856; Fax: 765-622-1045; Toll Free: 800-451-7323.

Bristol Publishing Co., *(978-0-9755667)* P.O. Box 3103, San Angelo, TX 76902-3103 USA Do not confuse with Bristal Publishing Company in San Jacinto, CA
E-mail: bristolpublishing@sbcglobal.net
Dist(s): **Alliance Bk. Co.**

Briston Hse. (CAN) *(978-1-894921) Dist. by* **IPG Chicago.**

Britannica Educational Publishing *Imprint of* **Rosen Publishing Group, Inc., The**

Brite Bks., *(978-0-9726363)* Orders Addr.: P.O. Box 801, Ortonville, MI 48462 USA; Edit Addr.: 1580 Duck Creek Ln., Ortonville, MI 48462 USA
E-mail: twebb@britebooks.org; twebb@tawglobal.com
Web site: http://www.britebooks.org; http://www.tawglobal.com; http://www.promises-for-life.com.

Brite International *See* **Brite Music, Inc.**

Brite Music, Inc., *(978-0-944803)* Orders Addr.: P.O. Box 65688-0688, Salt Lake City, UT 84165 USA (SAN 244-948X) Tel 801-263-9191; Fax: 801-263-9198; Edit Addr.: P.O. Box 171076, Salt Lake City, UT 84117-1076 USA (SAN 244-9498)
Web site: http://www.britemusic.com.

Brite Pr., *(978-0-9743185)* 3447 Countyline Rd., Chalfont, PA 18914-3625 USA Tel 215-822-1659; Fax: 305-402-8163
E-mail: tntdns@aol.com.

British Library, Historical Print Editions *Imprint of* **BiblioBazaar**

British Library, The (GBR) *(978-0-7123) Dist. by* **Chicago Distribution Ctr.**

Britt Allcroft Productions, *(978-0-9743690; 978-0-9767139; 978-0-9793343)* 133 Wadsworth Ave., Santa Monica, CA 90405 USA Tel 310-428-4033; Fax: 310 392 9769
E-mail: holly_wright@verizon.net
Web site: http://www.brittallcroftproductions.com.

Brittany's Bks, *(978-0-9778796)* 1736 Crest Pl., Colorado Spgs, CO 80911-1110 USA
E-mail: admin@brittanysbooks.com
Web site: http://www.brittanysbooks.com.

Publisher Name Index

Broad Creek Pr., *(978-0-9837148; 978-0-9904662)* P.O. Box 43, Mount Airy, NC 27030 USA Tel 336-473-7256
Dist(s): **BookBaby.**

Broad View Publishing, *(978-0-9815384)* P.O. Box 2726, Bristol, CT 06011-2726 USA Tel 860-793-7618
E-mail: info@broadviewpublishing.com; publicity@painisnotadisease.com
Web site: http://www.broadviewpublishing.com; http://www.painisnotadisease.com.

Broadcast Quality Productions, Inc., *(978-0-9716136)* 3199 Nottaway Ct., Atlanta, GA 30341 USA Tel 404-292-7777 (phone/fax)
Web site: http://www.bqproductions.com.

Broader Horizon Books *See* **Littletonhouse Publishing**

Broadman & Holman Publishers *See* **B&H Publishing Group**

Broadnax, Cassandra A.L., *(978-0-9771608)* 295 Pannel Rd., Reidsville, NC 27320 USA.

BroadSword Comics/ Jim Balent Studios, *(978-0-9745367)* P.O. Box 596, Brodheadsville, PA 18322 USA
E-mail: tarot@jimbalent.com
Web site: http://www.jimbalent.com.

Broadway Cares, *(978-0-9754840)* 165 W. 46th St., 13th Flr., New York, NY 10036 USA Tel 212-840-0770; Fax: 212-840-0551
E-mail: viola@bcefa.org.

Broccoli Bks. *Imprint of* **Broccoli International USA, Inc.**

Broccoli International USA, Inc., *(978-1-932480; 978-1-59741)* Orders Addr.: P.O. Box 66078, Los Angeles, CA 90066 USA Tel 310-815-0600; Fax: 310-815-0660; Edit Addr.: 11806 Gorham Ave. Apt. 4, Los Angeles, CA 90049-5446 USA; *Imprints:* Broccoli Books (Broccoli Bks)
E-mail: info@broccolibooks.com; ardith@bro-usa.com; wholesale@broccolibooks.com; books@animegamers.com; wholesale@bro-usa.com
Web site: http://www.bro-usa.com; http://www.broccolibooks.com; http://www.synch-point.com; http://www.boysenberrybooks.com
Dist(s): **Diamond Bk. Distributors**
Perseus-PGW
Simon & Schuster, Inc.

Brockhaus, F. A., GmbH (DEU) *(978-3-325; 978-3-7653)*
Dist. by **Intl Bk Import.**

Brodie, Richard *See* **Firebreak Publishing Co.**

Broken Bread Publishing, *(978-0-9769464)* 6417 S. Iris Way, Littleton, CO 80123-3135 USA
E-mail: books@brokenbreadpublishing.com
Web site: http://www.brokenbreadpublishing.com
Dist(s): **Spring Arbor Distributors, Inc.**

Broken Oak Publishing, *(978-0-9795020)* P.O. Box 255, Ridgetop, TN 37152 USA.

Broken Shackle Publishing, International, *(978-0-9759908)* P.O. Box 20312, Piedmont, CA 94620 USA
E-mail: jstickmon@msn.com.

Brolga Publishing (AUS) *(978-0-909608; 978-1-920785; 978-1-921221; 978-1-921596; 978-1-922036; 978-1-922175; 978-1-925367) Dist. by* **Midpt Trade.**

Bromwell Bks., *(978-0-9753345)* 2500 E. Fourth Ave., Denver, CO 80206 USA Tel 303-388-5969; Fax: 303-764-7544
E-mail: steven_replogle@dpsk12.org
Web site: http://bromwell.dpsk12.org.

Bronwen Publishing, *(978-0-9779267)* 4 Colchester Pl., Suite 4A, Newtown, PA 18940 USA (SAN 850-6426) Tel 215-968-2204
Web site: http://www.bronwenpublishing.com
Dist(s): **Follett School Solutions.**

Bronwynn Pr., LLC, *(978-0-9821404; 978-0-9848487)* P.O. Box 297, Troy, NY 12182 USA Tel 518-328-7891
E-mail: bell@bronwynnpress.com
Web site: http://www.bronwynnpress.com; http://www.gappy.tv.

Brook Farm Bks., *(978-0-919761)* 479 U.S. Hwy. 1, P.O. Box 246, Bridgewater, ME 04735 USA (SAN 133-9095) Tel 506-375-4680 (phone/fax); Toll Free: 877-375-4680
E-mail: jean@brookfarmbook.com; jean@brookfarmbooks.com
Dist(s): **Brodart Co.**
Independent Pubs. Group
ebrary, Inc.

Brookehaven Publishing, *(978-0-9844867; 978-1-940905)* P.O. Box 352, Rocklin, CA 95677 USA
E-mail: info@brookehavenpublishing.com
Web site: http://www.brookehavenpublishing.com
Dist(s): **Lulu Enterprises Inc.**
Smashwords.

Brookes, Paul H. Publishing Co. Inc., *(978-0-933716; 978-1-55766; 978-1-59857; 978-1-68125)* Orders Addr.: P.O. Box 10624, Baltimore, MD 21285-0624 USA (SAN 212-730X) Tel 410-337-9580; Fax: 410-337-8539; Toll Free: 800-638-3775 (customer service/ordering/billing/fulfillment); Edit Addr.: 409 Washington Ave., Suite 500, Baltimore, MD 21204 USA (SAN 666-6485)
E-mail: custserv@brookespublishing.com
Web site: http://www.brookespublishing.com
Dist(s): **Follett School Solutions.**

Brookfield Reader, Inc., The, *(978-0-9660172; 978-1-930093)* 137 Peyton Rd., Sterling, VA 20165-5605 USA (SAN 299-4445)
Dist(s): **Book Wholesalers, Inc.**
Brodart Co.
Quality Bks., Inc.

Brooklyn Botanic Garden, *(978-0-945352; 978-1-889538)* 1000 Washington Ave., Brooklyn, NY 11225-1099 USA (SAN 203-1094) Tel 718-623-7200; 718-625-5838; Fax: 718-622-7839; 718-857-2430
E-mail: ripodell@bbg.org
Web site: http://www.bbg.org
Dist(s): **Sterling Publishing Co., Inc.**

Brooklyn Pubs., *(978-1-930961; 978-1-931000; 978-1-931805; 978-1-932404; 978-1-60003)* Orders Addr.: P.O. Box 248, Cedar Rapids, IA 52406 USA
E-mail: orders@brookpub.com; customerservice@brookpub.com; steven@brookpub.com
Web site: http://www.brookpub.com
Dist(s): **Follett School Solutions.**

Brooklyn Publishing Company *See* **Brooklyn Pubs.**

Brooks & Brooks, *(978-0-9682530)* 5510 Owensmouth Ave. Apt. 102, Woodland Hls, CA 91367-7011 USA
E-mail: runningbrooks@hotmail.com.

Brooks, Andree Aelion, *(978-0-9702700)* 15 Hitchcock Rd., Westport, CT 06880 USA Tel 203-226-9834; Fax: 203-226-0814
E-mail: andreebrooks@hotmail.com.

†Brooks/Cole, *(978-0-12; 978-0-15; 978-0-314; 978-0-534; 978-0-8185; 978-1-56527; 978-0-495)* Div. of Thomson Learning, Orders Addr.: 7625 Empire Dr., Florence, KY 41042-2978 USA Tel 606-525-2230; Toll Free: 800-354-9706 (orders); Edit Addr.: 511 Forest Lodge Rd., Pacific Grove, CA 93950 USA (SAN 202-3369) Tel 831-373-0728; Fax: 831-375-6414; 10 Davis Dr., Belmont, CA 94002 Tel 650-595-2350
E-mail: info@brookscole.com
Web site: http://www.brookscole.com; http://www.duxbury.com
Dist(s): **CENGAGE Learning**
Houghton Mifflin Harcourt Trade & Reference Pubs.; *CIP.*

Brooks/Cole Publishing Company *See* **Brooks/Cole**

Brookshire Pubns., Inc., *(978-1-880976)* 200 Hazel St., Lancaster, PA 17603 USA Tel 717-392-1321; Fax: 717-392-2078
E-mail: carla@brookshireprinting.com.

Brookteam Corp., *(978-0-9745864)* P.O. Box 276225, Boca Raton, FL 33427 USA Fax: 561-367-9976; Toll Free: 866-571-7878; *Imprints:* Shirt Tales (Shirt Tales)
E-mail: brookteam@worldnet.att.net
Web site: http://www.brookteam.com.

Brophy, Doris Anne, *(978-0-9745232)* 90 Bingham Ave., Rumson, NJ 07760 USA Tel 732-345-7276
E-mail: dambrophy@yahoo.com.

Broqueville Publishing, Inc., *(978-0-9669024; 978-0-9719413)* 1260 Logan Ave., Suite B3, Costa Mesa, CA 92626 USA (SAN 255-0083) Tel 714-624-6441; Fax: 714-668-9972
E-mail: bookorders@broqueville.com
Web site: http://www.broqueville.com.

Brosen Bks., *(978-0-9830359)* 124 Wave, Laguna Beach, CA 92651 USA Tel 949-374-4127
E-mail: bryan@brosencreative.com
Web site: www.brosenbooks.com
Dist(s): **Follett School Solutions.**

Brosquil Edicions, S.L. (ESP) *(978-84-95620; 978-84-96154; 978-84-9795) Dist. by* **Lectorum Pubns.**

Bross Publishing, *(978-0-9763561)* 168 Island Pond Rd., No. 1, Manchester, NH 03109 USA (SAN 256-355X) Tel 603-623-2503 (phone/fax)
E-mail: brosspublishing@sunnyfla.us.

BrotherBiz Publishing, *(978-0-615-47658-2)* 96 School St., Lexington, MA 02421 USA Tel 781-862-3962
E-mail: BrotherBiz@earthlink.net.

Brothers N Publishing Corp., *(978-0-9886272)* 565 S. Mason Rd. No. 204, Katy, TX 77450 USA Tel 832-472-8200
E-mail: brothersnbooks@gmail.com.

Brotman-Marshfield Curriculums, *(978-0-9762568)* 22 Howard St., Newton, MA 02458 USA Tel 617-332-5616; Fax: 617-332-9679
E-mail: brotmanco@aol.com.

Broviak Publishing, *(978-0-9897522)* 10203 holly berry Cir., fishers, IN 46038 USA Tel 317-776-0421
E-mail: broviak@evilteacher.com.

Brown Barn Bks., *(978-0-9746481; 978-0-9768126; 978-0-9798824)* Div. of Pictures of Record, Inc., Orders Addr.: Editorial@brownbarnbooks.com 119 Kettle Creek Rd., Weston, CT 06883 USA Tel 203-227-3387; Fax: 203-222-9673
E-mail: editorial@brownbarnbooks.com
Web site: http://www.brownbarnbooks.com
Dist(s): **BookBaby**
Follett School Solutions.

Brown Bear Books, *(978-0-9670861)* 325 High St., Santa Cruz, CA 95060 USA Tel 831-457-1135
E-mail: brwnbear@sasquatch.com.

Brown Bear Bks., *(978-1-933834; 978-1-936333)* PMB 20, 6890 E. Sunrise Dr., Suite 120, Tucson, AZ 85750-0739 USA
E-mail: info@brownreference.com
Dist(s): **Black Rabbit Bks.**

Brown Bks. *Imprint of* **Olivo, Andy**

Brown, Bonnie M., *(978-0-9624705)* 548 Saint Johns Pl., Franklin, TN 37064-8901 USA
E-mail: bonnibear@aol.com.

Brown Bks. Publishing Group, *(978-0-9713265; 978-0-9744597; 978-0-9753907; 978-1-933285; 978-1-934812; 978-1-61254)* 16200 N. Dallas Pkwy., No. 170, Dallas, TX 75248 USA Tel 972-381-0009; Fax: 972-248-4336
E-mail: auburn.layman@brownbooks.com
Web site: http://www.brownbooks.com; http://www.thep3press.com
Dist(s): **BookBaby**
Follett School Solutions.

Brown Books Small Press *See* **Small Pr., The**

Brown County Historical Society, *(978-0-9641499)* Orders Addr.: P.O. Box 1411, Green Bay, WI 54305-1411 USA Tel 920-437-1840; Fax: 920-455-4518; Edit Addr.: 1008 S. Monroe Ave., Green Bay, WI 54301-3206 USA Do not confuse with Brown County Historical Society, Nashville, IN, New Ulm, MN
E-mail: bchs@netnet.net
Web site: http://www.browncohistoricalsoc.org.

Brown County Historical Society, *(978-0-9765095; 978-0-9964029)* 2 N. Broadway, New Ulm, MN 56073 USA Fax: 507-354-1068 Do not confuse with Brown County Historical Society in Green Bay, WI
E-mail: officemanager@browncountyhistorymnusa.org.

Brown, David Book Company, The *See* **Casemate Academic**

Brown Dog Bks., *(978-0-9721967)* P.O. Box 2196, Flemington, NJ 08822 USA
E-mail: darhosta@mac.com
Web site: http://www.browndogbooks.com
Dist(s): **Book Wholesalers, Inc.**
Brodart Co.
Follett Media Distribution
Follett School Solutions.

Brown, Harold *See* **Brown&Matthews**

Brown, Kathleen, *(978-0-9796063)* P.O. Box 1920, Clemmons, NC 27012 USA (SAN 853-8719) Tel 336-778-0699
E-mail: rbrown20221@bellsouth.net.

Brown, Nielsen, *(978-0-9725581)* Orders Addr.: P.O. Box 4174 , Estes Park, CO 80517 USA
E-mail: kristinnielsen@msn.com.

Brown, Samuel E., *(978-0-9770372)* P.O. Box 7009, Jackson, MS 39282 USA Tel 601-540-5470
E-mail: pcsandc@hotmail.com.

Brown, Steven Glenn, *(978-0-615-45712-3; 978-0-9835959)* 201 E. Truman Ave., Salt Lake City, UT 84115 USA Tel 408-429-0980
E-mail: llbrown42@yahoo.com
Dist(s): **CreateSpace Independent Publishing Platform**
Dummy Record Do Not USE!!!!.

Brown&Matthews, *(978-0-9759370)* 2923 E. Michigan St., Orlando, FL 32806 USA (SAN 256-2030)
E-mail: jkmatthews@cfl.rr.com
Web site: http://www.cafepress.com/sitm; http://www.janetmatthews.com.

Brownell, F. & Son, Pubs., *(978-0-9767409; 978-0-9789127)* P.O. Box 76, Montezuma, IA 50171 USA
Web site: http://www.brownells.com.

Brownian Bee Pr., *(978-0-9789688)* 37574 Dew Drop Rd., Lanesboro, MN 55949 USA
E-mail: info@brownianbee.com
Web site: http://www.brownianbee.com
Dist(s): **Unique Bks., Inc.**

Brownstone Monkey Productions, Inc., *(978-0-9785773)* 55 W. 84th St., No. 9, New York, NY 10024-1002 USA Tel 212-933-4168; Fax: 212-228-6149
E-mail: nicole@brownstonemonkey.com; kfiore@nyc.rr.com
Web site: http://brownstonemonkey.com; http://lenithepug.com.

BRP Publishing Group, *(978-0-9801506; 978-1-935460; 978-1-941295)* P.O. Box 822674, Vancouver, WA 98682 USA
E-mail: publisher@nitisbooks.com; publisher@barkingrainpress.org
Web site: http://www.nitisbooks.com; http://www.barkingrainpress.org
Dist(s): **CreateSpace Independent Publishing Platform**
Lightning Source, Inc.
Mackin Educational Resources
OverDrive, Inc.

Brujo Film Production *See* **Pascualina Producciones S.A.**

Bruno, Elizabeth *See* **Uitti, Daniel**

Brunson Publishing, *(978-0-9758614)* Orders Addr.: P.O. Box 1133, Alamogordo, NM 88310 USA Tel 706-367-1334
E-mail: oldmaid4jesus@yahoo.com; tim@teenpact.com
Web site: http://www.oldmaidministries.com; http://www.teenpact.com.

Brunswick Publishing Corp., *(978-0-931494; 978-1-55618)* 593 Southlake Blvd., Richmond, VA 23236-3092 USA (SAN 211-6332)
E-mail: brunswickbooks@verizon.net; info@brunswickbooks.com
Web site: http://www.brunswickbooks.com/.

Bruño, Editorial (ESP) *(978-84-216) Dist. by* **Lectorum Pubns.**

Bruño, Editorial (ESP) *(978-84-216) Dist. by* **Dist Plaza Mayor.**

Bryan House Publishers, Incorporated *See* **ECS Learning Systems, Inc.**

Bryan-Kennedy Entertainment, LLC, *(978-0-615-34098-2; 978-0-615-34699-1; 978-0-9885358)* 177 village blvd, Santa Rosa Beach, FL 32459 USA Tel 615-376-9939
E-mail: mackennedy@mac.com
Web site: http://www.Bryan-Kennedy.com.

Bryce Cullen Publishing, *(978-1-935752)* P.O. Box 731, Alpine, NJ 07620 USA Tel 201-888-8570
E-mail: publish@brycecullen.com
Web site: http://www.brycecullen.com
Dist(s): **Lightning Source, Inc.**

Bryson Taylor Press *See* **Bryson Taylor Publishing**

Bryson Taylor Publishing, *(978-0-9773738; 978-0-9841934; 978-0-9882940)* Div. of Bryson Taylor Inc., 199 New County Rd., Saco, ME 04072 USA (SAN 257-4403) Tel 207-838-2146
E-mail: deb@brysontaylor.com
Web site: http://www.brysontaylorpublishing.com.

Brzamo Publishing, *(978-0-9743580)* 887 Richart Ln., Greenwood, IN 46142 USA.

B'Squeak Productions, *(978-0-9746782)* P.O. Box 151, Menlo Park, CA 94026-0151 USA
E-mail: rights@bsqueak.com
Web site: http://www.bsqueak.com.

B*tween Productions, Inc., *(978-0-9746587; 978-0-9758511; 978-1-933566)* 1666 Massachusetts Ave., Suite 17, Lexington, MA 02420 USA Tel 781-863-8228; Fax: 781-863-8338; *Imprints:* Beacon Street Girls (B Street Girls)
E-mail: kblais@btweenproductions.com
Web site: http://www.beaconstreetgirls.com.

BTWEYL *Imprint of* **Bks. That Will Enhance Your Life**

Bubble Gum Pr., *(978-0-9729833; 978-0-9839907)* 1420 N. State St., Aberdeen, SD 57401-2167 USA
E-mail: bmehrmantraut@msn.com
Web site: http://www.bubblegumpress.com
Dist(s): **Follett School Solutions.**

Bubblegum Bks., *(978-0-9754621)* P.O. Box 94106, Cleveland, OH 44101-6106 USA
E-mail: info@bubblegumbooks.com
Web site: http://www.bubblegumbooks.com
Dist(s): **Mariposa Pr.**
SCB Distributors.

Buchbinder, Leonardo, *(978-0-9774044; 978-0-615-34717-2)* 8001 NW 84 Terr., Tamarac, FL 33321 USA Tel 954-261-9488
E-mail: mstenn5031@aol.com.

Buck Engineering Company, Incorporated, Lab-Volt Systems Division *See* **Lab-Volt Systems, Inc.**

Buck Publishing, *(978-0-9725912)* Orders Addr.: P.O. Box 12231, Roanoke, VA 24023-2231 USA Tel 540-985-0618 (phone/fax); Edit Addr.: 710 Ferdinand Ave., No. 9, Roanoke, VA 24016 USA Do not confuse with companies with the same or similar name in Birmingham, AL, Fairbanks, AK.

Buckbeech Studios, *(978-0-9771494)* Orders Addr.: P.O. Box 430, Stanford, IN 47463-0430 USA Tel 812-369-6061; Edit Addr.: 30 Amberwood Pkwy., Ashland, OH 44805 USA
E-mail: publisher@buckbeech.com
Web site: http://www.buckbeech.com
Dist(s): **Follett School Solutions.**

Bucket of Books *See* **Bimini Bks.**

Bucking Horse Bks., *(978-0-9844460)* P.O. Box 8507, Missoula, MT 59807 USA
E-mail: collard@bigsky.net
Web site: http://www.buckinghorsebooks.com
Dist(s): **Mountain Pr. Publishing Co., Inc.**

Bucknell Univ. Pr., *(978-0-8387)* Taylor Hall, Lewisburg, PA 17837 USA
E-mail: naf006@bucknell.edu
Web site: http://www.departments.bucknell.edu/univ_press/
Dist(s): **Associated Univ. Presses**
Baker & Taylor International
MyiLibrary
Rowman & Littlefield Publishers, Inc.
TextStream
ebrary, Inc.

Buddha's Light Publishing, *(978-0-9715612; 978-0-9717495; 978-1-932293; 978-1-939596)* 3456 S. Glenmark Dr., Hacienda Heights, CA 91745 USA Tel 626-923-5144; 84 Margaret St., London, Tel 020-7636-8394; Fax: 020-7580-6220
E-mail: info@blpusa.com; buddhalightpublishing@ibps.org.uk
Web site: http://www.blpusa.com; http://www.ibps.org.uk/buddhaslightpublishing.htm
Dist(s): **Follett School Solutions**
Greenleaf Book Group
New Leaf Distributing Co., Inc.

Buddhi Pubns., *(978-0-9644226)* Orders Addr.: P.O. Box 208, Canyon, CA 94516 USA Tel 510-376-7796; Fax: 510-376-3503; Edit Addr.: 35 Pinehurst Rd., Canyon, CA 94516 USA.

Buddhist Text Translation Society, *(978-0-88139; 978-0-917512; 978-1-60103)* Affil. of Dharma Realm Buddhist Assoc., Orders Addr.: 4951 Bodhi Way, Ukiah, CA 95482 USA Tel 707-462-0939; Fax: 707-462-0949; Edit Addr.: 4951 Bodhi Way,, Ukiah, CA 95482 USA (SAN 281-3556) Tel 707-468-9112 (phone/fax)
E-mail: hchih@netzero.net; hengdzu@drba.org; bttsonline@snetworking.com
Web site: http://www.bttsonline.org
Dist(s): **Follett School Solutions.**

Budding Artists, Inc., *(978-1-888108)* 222 Palisades Ave., Santa Monica, CA 90402-2734 USA.

Budding Biologist, *(978-0-9855481)* 2939 NE 11TH Terr., Gainesville, FL 32609 USA Tel 919-621-5725
E-mail: kcallis@ufl.edu
Dist(s): **Independent Pubs. Group.**

Budding Family Publishing, *(978-0-9741882)* P.O. Box 2078, Manhattan Beach, CA 90267-2078 USA Fax: 310-374-1030
E-mail: renee@buddingfamily.com
Web site: http://www.buddingfamily.com.

Buddy Bks. *Imprint of* **ABDO Publishing Co.**

Buddy Bks. Publishing, *(978-0-9799980; 978-1-934887)* P.O. Box 3354, Pinehurst, NC 28374 USA Tel 910-295-2876
E-mail: admin@buddybookspublishing.com
Web site: http://www.buddybookspublishing.com.

Buehner, Jeremy A., *(978-0-615-80204-6)* 597 Summit View Dr, Fenton, MO 63026 USA Tel 314-640-5846
Web site: www.facebook.com/SurilatanStormshadow
Dist(s): **CreateSpace Independent Publishing Platform.**

Buenaventura Pr., *(978-0-9766848; 978-0-9800039; 978-1-935443)* P.O. Box 23661, Oakland, CA 94623 USA
Web site: http://www.buenaventurapress.com
Dist(s): **D.A.P./Distributed Art Pubs.**

Buffalo Fine Arts Academy *See* **Buffalo Fine Arts/Albright-Knox Art Gallery**

†Buffalo Fine Arts/Albright-Knox Art Gallery, *(978-0-914782; 978-1-887457)* Albright-Knox Art Gallery, 1285 Elmwood Ave., Buffalo, NY 14222 USA (SAN 202-4845) Tel 716-882-8700; Fax: 716-882-1958; *CIP.*

Buford & Junior Bks., *(978-0-615-81508-4)* 16848 Hamilton Sta. Rd., Hamilton, VA 20158 USA Tel 703-447-1988
Dist(s): **CreateSpace Independent Publishing Platform.**

Bug Boy Bks., *(978-0-615-19036-5)* 2085 Kenneth St., Burton, MI 48529 USA
E-mail: nativeamericanandrew@yahoo.com; andrew@bugboyandy.com
Dist(s): **Lulu Enterprises Inc.**

Bug Boy Publishing *See* **Bug Boy Bks.**

BugaBk. llc, *(978-0-9888974)* 7667 Cahill Rd. Suite 100, Edina, MN 55439 USA Tel 952-943-1441
E-mail: dustinh@bugabook.com
Web site: www.bugabook.com.

Bugeye Bks., *(978-0-9722249)* 10645 N. Tatum Blvd., Suite 200-246, Phoenix, AZ 85028 USA Tel 602-980-7101; Fax: 480-483-3460
E-mail: insightstudios@cox.net
Web site: http://www.bugeyebooks.com.

Buggee's Journal. A boy?s Bk. of magic, mystery & monsters!, *(978-0-615-85095-5)* 1837 Fallbrook Dr., Alamo, CA 94507 USA Tel 9258769530
E-mail: Support@kidsbooksbycurtis.com.

Buggs Books *See* **Mogul Comics**

Buhman, Ron, *(978-0-9747961)* P.O. Box 704028, Dallas, TX 75370-4028 USA Tel 972-306-6324; Fax: 972-307-7204
E-mail: rkb919@juno.com
Web site: http://jam-packed-action.com.

Build Your Story, *(978-0-9748416)* Orders Addr.: P.O. Box 6003, Midlothian, VA 23112 USA Fax: 810-592-2479; Toll Free: 866-807-8679; Edit Addr.: 2212 Water Horse Ct., Midlothian, VA 23112 USA
E-mail: oscar@buildyourstory.com
Web site: http://www.buildyourstory.com.

Builders' Stone Publishing, LLC, *(978-0-9791504)* 6932 Sylvan Woods Dr., Sanford, FL 32771 USA (SAN 852-5994) Tel 407-549-5066
E-mail: pschoemann@broadandcassel.com
Web site: http://www.buildersstonepublishing.com.

Building Blocks, LLC, *(978-0-943452)* 38 W. 567 Brindlewood Ln., Elgin, IL 60123 USA (SAN 240-6063) Tel 847-742-1013; Fax: 847-742-1054 (orders); Toll Free: 800-233-2448 Do not confuse with companies with similar and same name in Madison,NJ, Westbury NY
E-mail: dick@bblocksonline.com
Web site: http://www.bblocksonline.com
Dist(s): **Gryphon Hse., Inc.**

†Bulfinch, *(978-0-8212)* Div. of Little Brown & Co., Orders Addr.: 3 Center Plaza, Boston, MA 02108-2084 USA Tel 617-227-0730; Fax: 617-263-2857; Toll Free Fax: 800-286-9471; Toll Free: 800-759-0190; Edit Addr.: Time & Life Bldg. 1271 Ave. of the Americas, New York, NY 10020 USA Toll Free: 800-343-9204 Do not confuse with Bullfinch Pr., Minnetonka, MN
E-mail: cust.service@twbg.com
Web site: http://www.twbookmark.com/arts/index.html
Dist(s): **Follett School Solutions**
Leonard, Hal Corp.
Hachette Bk. Group
MyiLibrary; *CIP.*

Bull, David Publishing, Inc., *(978-0-9649722; 978-1-893618; 978-1-935007)* 4250 E. Camelback Rd., Suite K150, Phoenix, AZ 85018 USA Tel 602-852-9500; Fax: 602-852-9503; Toll Free: 800-831-1758
E-mail: dbull@bullpublishing.com; info@bullpublishing.com; tmoore@bullpublishing.com
Web site: http://www.bullpublishing.com.

†Bull Publishing Co., *(978-0-915950; 978-0-923521; 978-0-945946; 978-1-933503; 978-1-936693)* Orders Addr.: P.O. Box 1377, Boulder, CO 80306-1377 USA Tel 303-545-6350; Fax: 303-545-6354; Toll Free: 800-676-2855; Edit Addr.: 1905 Mapleton Ave., Boulder, CO 80304 USA
E-mail: jim.bullpubco@comcast.net
Web site: http://www.bullpub.com
Dist(s): **Ebsco Publishing**
Follett School Solutions
Independent Pubs. Group
MyiLibrary
ebrary, Inc.; *CIP.*

Bullard, Belinda *See* **A Blessed Heritage Educational Resources**

Bulldog Pr., *(978-0-9672710)* P.O. Box 620358, Woodside, CA 94062-0358 USA Tel 650-851-8218; Fax: 650-851-1753 Do not confuse with companies with the same name in Frankfort, IN, Whittier, CA
E-mail: dputnam555@aol.com
Web site: http://www.americanbulldogger.com.

Bullfrog Bks. *Imprint of* **Jump! Inc.**

Bullock, Jodi, *(978-0-615-47603-2)* 1945 W Pine Creek Dr., Nampa, ID 83686 USA Tel 714 782-8198
Dist(s): **CreateSpace Independent Publishing Platform**
Dummy Record Do Not USE!!!!.

BullsEye, LLC *See* **Hargrave Pr.**

Bumble Bee Bks., *(978-0-9914701)* 1804 Benodot St., Champaign, IL 61822 USA Tel 217-898-7835
E-mail: storytym@comcast.net.

Bumble Bee Publishing, *(978-0-9754342; 978-1-933982)* Div. of Bumble Bee Productions, Inc., Orders Addr.: 725 Watch Island Reach, Chesapeake, VA 23320 USA (SAN 256-1611) Tel 757-410-9409 (phone/fax); Toll Free: 866-782-9533 (phone/fax); Edit Addr.: P.O. Box 1757, Chesapeake, VA 23327-1757 USA (SAN 256-162X) Tel 747-410-9409; 5721 M St., Lincoln, NE 68510 (SAN 256-1638); *Imprints:* bPlus Books (bPlus Bks)
E-mail: buzz707@bbpmail.com
Web site: http://www.yesterdaywehadahurricane.com; http://www.bumblebeepublishing.com; http://www.rubyleethebumblebee.com; http://www.bumblebeeproductions.com; http://www.bplusbooks.com.

Bumples, *(978-0-9700952)* 676 Post Rd., Darien, CT 06820-4717 USA
E-mail: bumples@aol.com; Bumples@aol.com.

Bumpy Pumpkin, *(978-0-9754696)* 3405 Heather Dr., Augusta, GA 30909 USA
Web site: http://www.bumpypumpkin.com.

Bundoran Pr. (CAN) *(978-0-9782052; 978-0-9877352; 978-1-927881; 978-0-9880674)* *Dist. by* **Diamond Book Dists.**

Bunim and Bannigan Ltd., *(978-1-933480)* PMB 157, 111 E. 14th St., New York, NY 10003-4103 USA
Web site: http://www.bunim&bannigan.com; http://www.bunimbannigan.com
Dist(s): **Itasca Bks.**

Bunker Hill Publishing, Inc., *(978-1-59373)* 285 River Rd., Piermont, NH 03779-3009 USA; 27 W. 20th St., New York, NY 10011
E-mail: mail@bunkerhillpublishing.com
Web site: http://www.bunkerhillpublishing.com
Dist(s): **Follett School Solutions**
Midpoint Trade Bks., Inc.
National Bk. Network.

Bunny & The Crocodile Pr., The, *(978-0-938572)* 1821 Glade Ct., Annapolis, MD 21403-1945 USA Tel 410-267-7432 (phone/fax); *Imprints:* Forest Woods Media Productions (Forest Woods Media)
E-mail: gracecav@comcast.net
Web site: http://www.members.aol.com/grace7623/grace.htm.

Burden-Evans, Patricia, *(978-0-615-15120-5)* 1814 Palmyra Dr., Greenville, MS 38701 USA
E-mail: pevan6@aol.com
Dist(s): **Lulu Enterprises Inc.**

BurgYoung Publishing, *(978-0-9716511)* 4105 E. Florida Ave., No. 300, Denver, CO 80222 USA Tel 303-757-5406
E-mail: tmcco@msn.com; infoby@burgyoungpublishing.com
Web site: http://www.burgyoungpublishing.com; http://www.gettingtoknowgod.com.

Buried Treasure Publishing, *(978-0-9800993; 978-0-615-14018-6)* 2813 NW Westbrooke Cir., Blue Springs, MO 64015 USA
E-mail: sales@buriedtreasurepublishing.com; duaneporter@yahoo.com
Web site: http://buriedtreasurepublishing.com
Dist(s): **Lulu Enterprises Inc.**

Burkhardt The Artist, *(978-0-9762996)* P.O. Box 35, Alexandria, KY 41001 USA Tel 859-694-6000
E-mail: rockyburk@hotmail.com
Web site: http://www.rockyburkhardt.com.

Burkhart Bks., *(978-0-9790975)* 4000 N. Meridian St., Suite 17G, Indianapolis, IN 46208 USA (SAN 852-4270)
E-mail: l.burkhart@sbcglobal.net
Web site: http://www.burkhartnetwork.com
Dist(s): **Distributors, The**
Partners Bk. Distributing, Inc.

Burley Creek Studio *See* **White Dog Studio**

Burlington, David, *(978-0-9772136)* 16723 Basin Oak., San Antonio, TX 78247-6220 USA
E-mail: dave@bassfishingaskdave.com
Web site: http://www.bassfishingaskdave.com.

Burlington National, Inc., *(978-1-57706)* Orders Addr.: P.O. Box 841, Mandeville, LA 70470 USA Tel 504-250-7228; Edit Addr.: 6301 Perrier, New Orleans, LA 70118 USA
E-mail: books@burlingtonnational.com.

Burman Books, Inc. (CAN) *(978-0-9736632; 978-0-9737166; 978-0-9739097; 978-1-897404; 978-0-9781380)* *Dist. by* **InnovativeLog.**

Burney Enterprises Unlimited, *(978-0-9745360)* P.O. Box 401402, Redford, MI 48240-9402 USA.

BurnhillWolf, *(978-0-9645655)* 321 Prospect St., NW, Lenoir, NC 28645 USA Tel 704-754-0287
E-mail: Burnwolf@charter.net
Web site: http://www.burnhillwolf.com
Dist(s): **CreateSpace Independent Publishing Platform.**

Burning Bush Creation, *(978-0-9768680; 978-1-60390)* 2114 Queen Ave. N., Minneapolis, MN 55411-2435 USA Tel 612-529-0198; Fax: 612-529-0199
E-mail: ron@mcconico.com
Web site: http://www.burningbushcreation.com.

Burns, Phillys, *(978-0-9620065)* 7450 Olivetas Ave., No. 230, La Jolla, CA 92037 USA (SAN 247-526X).

BurnsBooks, *(978-0-9726099)* 50 Joe's Hill Rd., Danbury, CT 06811 USA Tel 203-744-0232
E-mail: burnsbookspub@aol.com
Web site: http://www.burnsbookspublishing.com.

Burt Creations *See* **Burt, Steven E.**

Burt, Steven E., *(978-0-9649283; 978-0-9741407; 978-0-9856188)* Orders Addr.: 17101 SE. 94th Berrien Ct., The Villages, FL 32162 USA (SAN 253-925X) Tel 352-391-8292
E-mail: passtev@aol.com
Web site: http://www.SteveBurtBooks.com.

Burton, Kenneth Hugh, *(978-0-9747043)* Orders Addr.: P.O. Box 38142, Atlanta, GA 30334 USA Tel 404-799-1908; Edit Addr.: 406 Collier Ridge Dr. NW, Atlanta, GA 30318-7312 USA
E-mail: notrub18@bellsouth.net.

Buscher, Julie W., *(978-0-9786352)* Orders Addr.: P.O. Box 627, Brighton, CO 80601-0627 USA (SAN 851-1802) Tel 303-659-7354
E-mail: julobush2@q.com
Web site: http://www.homerthehelicopter.com.

Bush, Bill *See* **Bush Publishing Inc.**

Bush Brothers & Co., *(978-0-9779308)* 1016 E. Weisgarber Rd., Knoxville, TN 37909-2683 USA.

Bush Publishing Inc., *(978-0-9723102; 978-0-9778728; 978-0-9798113; 978-0-9824391; 978-0-9836109)* 5427 S. 94th E. Ave., Tulsa, OK 74104 USA
Web site: http://www.bushpublishing.com.

Bushweller, Ellie, *(978-0-615-24478-5)* 9 Worth St., South Burlington, VT 05403 USA
Dist(s): **Lulu Enterprises Inc.**

Business Angel Pr., *(978-0-9798909)* 174 W. Foothill Blvd., No. 327, Monrovia, CA 91016 USA (SAN 854-6738) Tel 626-357-1922; Fax: 818-475-1474; Toll Free: 800-705-6545
E-mail: contact@businessangelpress.com
Web site: http://www.businessangelpress.com.

Business Bks. International, *(978-0-916673)* P.O. Box 1587, New Canaan, CT 06840 USA (SAN 297-1860) Tel 203-966-9645; Fax: 203-966-6018
E-mail: lesdv@businessbooksusa.com
Web site: http://www.businessbooksusa.com.

Business Bks., LLC, *(978-0-9723714)* 2709 Washington Ave., 21A, Evansville, IN 47714 USA
E-mail: mbussingbu@aol.com
Web site: http://www.bussinessbooksllc.com.

Business Jobs *See* **Alexie Bks.**

Business Plus *Imprint of* **Grand Central Publishing**

Business Word, The *See* **Sterling Investments I, LLC DBA Twins Magazine**

Buster B.B. Publishing, *(978-0-9726691)* 1530 Indian Springs Rd., Pine Beach, NY 12566 USA
E-mail: mirror38@aol.com
Web site: http://www.reflectionsseminars.com.

Busy Bee Bks., *(978-0-9759281)* 2160 110th St., SE, Delano, MN 55328 USA Tel 952-237-7218
E-mail: debbyanderson@juno.com.

Butler Bk. Publishing, *(978-0-9627459; 978-1-884532; 978-1-935497; 978-1-941953)* 608 Briar Hill Rd., Louisville, KY 40206 USA Tel 502-897-9393; Fax: 502-897-9797
E-mail: ckbutler@aol.com; eric@butlerbooks.com
Web site: http://www.butlerbooks.com
Dist(s): **Follett School Solutions.**

Butler Book Publishing Services, Incorporated *See* **Butler Bk. Publishing**

Butler Ctr. for Arkansas Studies, *(978-0-9708574; 978-0-9800897; 978-1-935106)* c/o Central Arkansas Library System, 100 Rock St., Little Rock, AR 72201 USA
Web site: http://www.cals.org; http://www.butlercenter.org
Dist(s): **Chicago Distribution Ctr.**
MyiLibrary
Univ. of Arkansas Pr.

BuTo, Ltd. Co., *(978-0-9729569)* P.O. Box 9018, Austin, TX 78766 USA (SAN 255-4321) Fax: 512-450-0372
E-mail: butoltdco@aol.com
Web site: http://www.buto.biz.

Butte Pubns., Inc., *(978-1-884362; 978-1-939349)* Orders Addr.: P.O. Box 1328, Hillsboro, OR 97123-1328 USA (SAN 299-8866) Tel 503-648-9791; Fax: 503-693-9526
E-mail: service@buttepublications.com
Web site: http://www.buttepublications.com
Dist(s): **Follett School Solutions.**

Buttercup Media, *(978-0-9768152)* Orders Addr.: P.O. Box 222003, Dallas, TX 75222 USA Tel 214-890-6833
E-mail: michael.p.collins1@gmail.com
Dist(s): **BookBaby.**

Butterfly Bk. Makers, *(978-0-9754117)* 1450 W. 800 N., Orem, UT 84057 USA
E-mail: hatfiron@aol.com.

Butterfly Books *See* **Black Garnet Pr.**

Butterfly Ink Publishing, *(978-0-9745423)* 20637 Skouras Dr., Winnetka, CA 91306 USA
E-mail: butterflyinkpub@aol.com; kim@butterflyinkpublishing.com
Web site: http://www.butterflyinkpublishing.com.

Butterfly Park Educational Materials, Inc., *(978-0-9744575)* 3126 Elmira Ct., Denver, CO 80238-2929 USA
E-mail: butterflypark@comcast.net
Web site: http://www.butterflyparkphonics.com.

Butterfly Pavilion, *(978-0-9729000)* 6252 W. 104th Ave., Westminster, CO 80020 USA Tel 303-469-5441; Fax: 303-657-5944
E-mail: ptennyson@butterflies.org
Web site: http://www.butterflies.org.

Butterfly Press *See* **Butterfly Productions, LLC**

Butterfly Productions, LLC, *(978-0-9752936)* 165 Shadow Rock Dr., Sedona, AZ 86336 USA Tel 928-204-2811; Fax: 928-204-9118 Do not confuse with companies with the same or similar name in New York, NY, Worcester, MA, Houston, TX, Old Town, ME, Dayton, OH, Cochranville, PA, Princeton, NJ , Amherst, MA, Charston, WV, Pheonix, AZ
E-mail: butterfly@sedona.net
Web site: http://www.butterflyproductions.info.

Butterhouse Publishing, *(978-0-9763971)* 12251 N. 32nd St., Suite 4, Phoenix, AZ 85032 USA
E-mail: financialstories@juno.com.

Buttermoth Pr. (AUS) *(978-0-9803367)* *Dist. by* **LuluCom.**

Butters Pr., *(978-0-9754960)* 2047 Gale Rd., Eaton Rapids, MI 48827 USA
Web site: http://www.throughtheears.com.

Butterworth-Heinemann *Imprint of* **Elsevier Science & Technology Bks.**

Button Flower Pr., *(978-0-9747836)* 7422 Westview Dr., Boardman, OH 44512 USA.

Buttonberry Bks., *(978-0-9768227)* 29 Sawmill Rd., Lebanon, NJ 08833 USA
Web site: http://www.buttonberrybooks.com
Dist(s): **Follett School Solutions.**

Buttonweed Pr., L.L.C., *(978-0-9755675)* 204 7th St W. # 125, Northfield, MN 55057-2419 USA (SAN 256-1700)
E-mail: info@buttonweedpress.com
Web site: http://www.buttonweedpress.com
Dist(s): **Follett School Solutions**
Partners Bk. Distributing, Inc.

Buttonwood Pr., *(978-0-9660685; 978-0-9742920; 978-0-9823351; 978-0-9891462; 978-0-9965562)* Orders Addr.: P.O. Box 716, Haslett, MI 48840 USA Tel 517-339-9871; Fax: 517-339-5908; Edit Addr.: 5951 Buttonwood Dr., Haslett, MI 48840 USA Do not confuse with companies with the same name Champaign, IL, Potomac, MD, New York, NY, Solvang, CA
E-mail: rlbald@aol.com
Web site: http://www.buttonwoodpress.com
Dist(s): **Partners Bk. Distributing, Inc.**

Buy Books on the Web.Com *See* **Infinity Publishing**

Buy Rite, *(978-0-9723744; 978-1-60421)* 88 Vanderveer Rd., Freehold, NJ 07728 USA Tel 732-294-9000; Fax: 732-294-9363; Toll Free: 888-777-7952
Web site: http://www.buyriteinc.com.

Buz-Land Presentations, Inc., *(978-0-9766990)* 73 Harding Rd., Wyckoff, NJ 07481 USA Tel 201-848-0595; 73 Harding Rd., Wyckoff, NJ 07481-2730 (SAN 256-5692)
E-mail: buzi.bee@verizon.net
Web site: http://www.buz-land.com; www.WWRT.org
Dist(s): **AtlasBooks Distribution.**

Buzzard Pr. International, *(978-0-9648488)* 506 W. Donna Dr., Merced, CA 95348 USA Tel 209-723-6738; Fax: 209-723-6253
E-mail: buzzard@buzzardpress.com
Dist(s): **Sunbelt Pubns., Inc.**

Buzzy's Bks., *(978-0-9719054)* P.O. Box 566, Grafton, MA 01519 USA Tel 508-839-2442; Fax: 508-839-7396
E-mail: buzzy@buzzysbooks.org
Web site: http://www.buzzysbooks.org.

By Grace Enterprises, *(978-0-9663629; 978-1-940591)* 9515 Twin Oaks Dr., Manvel, TX 77578-5307 USA
E-mail: hulettepl@aol.com; pamlv@aol.com
Web site: http://www.bygraceenterprises.com
Dist(s): **Follett School Solutions.**

by shayne, *(978-0-9725593)* P.O. Box 221474, Santa Clarita, CA 91322 USA
Web site: http://www.byshayne.com.

ByD Pr., *(978-0-9721035)* 1424 33rd St., NW, Washington, DC 20007 USA Tel 202-342-9189 (phone/fax)
E-mail: bydpress@erols.com.

BYE Publishing Services, *(978-0-9656739)* Orders Addr.: 915 L St., Suite 144, Sacramento, CA 95814 USA Tel 916-529-3119 Corporate Hq; Fax: 916-683-1476; Edit Addr.: 5245 College Ave., Suite 333, Oakland, CA 94618 USA Tel 510-272-0101
E-mail: byepublishing@comcast.net
Web site: http://www.byepublishing.com.

Byeway *Imprint of* **Byeway Bks.**

Byeway Bks., *(978-1-85997; 978-1-904586; 978-1-933581; 978-1-934004; 978-1-60176)* 15941 W. 65th St., Shawnee, KS 66217-9342 USA Toll Free Fax: 866-426-3929; Toll Free: 866-429-3929; *Imprints:* Byeway (Byeway)
E-mail: customerservice@byewaybooks.com
Web site: http://www.byewaybooks.com/how_to_order.html.

Byrd, Fay T., *(978-0-9776805)* 9325 Pan Ridge Rd., Baltimore, MD 21234 USA (SAN 257-9898) Tel 410-661-0295
E-mail: faysangelharp@aol.com
Web site: www.faysangelharp.com.

Byte Me! Inc., *(978-0-9798611; 978-0-615-14953-0)* P.O. Box 60705, Reno, NV 89506 USA (SAN 854-5863) Tel 775-772-6378; 775-972-3322; Fax: 775-972-3323 Never after 5p.m. pst
E-mail: saraw1@clearwire.net; alma_corazon12@yahoo.com
Web site: http://www.cdebooksbyteme.org; http://www.stores.lulu.com/georgiahedrick; http://www.stores.lulu.com/georgiahedrick; http://www.stores.lulu.com/georgiahedrick
Dist(s): **Lulu Enterprises Inc.**

Byte/Me Teen Bk. *Imprint of* **Awe-Struck Publishing**

BYU Creative Works *Imprint of* **Brigham Young Univ.**

C A Filius *See* **Charwood Pubns.**

C & C Educational Materials, LLC, *(978-0-9640524; 978-0-9747205; 978-0-9963509)* 12514 Dermott Dr., Houston, TX 77065 USA
E-mail: barbara.cobaugh@att.net
Web site: www.strategiesforstaar.com.

C & C Productions, *(978-0-9753273)* PMB 254, 330 SW 43rd St., No. K, Renton, WA 98055 USA.

C&D Enterprises, *(978-0-9633231; 978-0-9765938)* P.O. Box 7201, Arlington, VA 22207-7201 USA Fax: 703-276-3033
E-mail: harryfp@comcast.net.

C&D International, *(978-0-937347)* 111 Ferguson Ct., Suite 105, Irving, TX 75062-7014 USA (SAN 659-1523) Toll Free: 800-231-0442.

C & H Pubns., *(978-0-9740882)* 31201 S. 596 Ln., Grove, OK 74344 USA.

†C & T Publishing, *(978-0-914881; 978-1-57120; 978-1-60705; 978-1-61745)* Orders Addr.: 1651 Challenge Dr., Concord, CA 94520 USA (SAN 289-0720) Tel 925-677-0377; Fax: 925-617-0374; Toll Free: 800-284-1114; *Imprints:* FunStitch Studio (FunStitch Stu)
E-mail: ctinfo@ctpub.com
Web site: http://www.ctpub.com
Dist(s): **Follett School Solutions**
MyiLibrary
National Bk. Network
ebrary, Inc.; *CIP.*

CBI Pr., *(978-0-9705812)* 6 Jeffrey Cir., Bedford, MA 01730 USA Do not confuse with C B I Press, Arlington, VA
E-mail: nancy_nugent@comcast.net
Web site: http://www.cbipress.com.

C. B. Publishing House, Incorporated *See* **Cubbie Blue Publishing**

C C L S Publishing Hse., *(978-1-928882; 978-0-7428)* 3191 Coral Way, Suite 114, Miami, FL 33145-3209 USA (SAN 254-4695) Tel 305-529-2257; Fax: 305-443-8538; Toll Free: 800-704-8181
E-mail: info@cclscorp.com
Web site: http://www.cclscorp.com
Dist(s): **Continental Bk. Co., Inc.**

CEF Pr., *(978-1-55976)* Div.of Child Evangelism Fellowship, Orders Addr.: P.O. Box 348, Warrenton, MO 63383

USA Tel 636-456-4321; Fax: 636-456-2078; Toll Free: 800-748-7710; Edit Addr.: 2300 E. Hwy. M, Warrenton, MO 63383 USA (SAN 211-7789)
E-mail: custserv@cefonline.com
Web site: http://www.cefonline.com; http://www.cefpress.com.

CES Industries, Inc., *(978-0-86711)* 2023 New Hwy., Farmingdale, NY 11735-1103 USA (SAN 237-9864)
E-mail: m.nesenoff@cesindustries.com
Web site: http://www.cesindustries.com.

CFKR Career Materials, Inc., *(978-0-934783; 978-1-887481)* P.O. Box 99, Meadow Vista, CA 95722-0099 USA (SAN 694-2547) Toll Free Fax: 800-770-0433; Toll Free: 800-525-5626
E-mail: requestinfo@cfkr.com; cfkr@cfkr.com; order@cfkr.com
Web site: http://www.cfkr.com.

C I S Communications, Inc., *(978-0-935063; 978-1-56062)* 180 Park Ave., Lakewood, NJ 08701 USA (SAN 694-5953) Tel 732-905-3000; Fax: 732-367-6666.

CMSP Projects, *(978-0-942851)* School of Engineering, 51 Astor Pl., New York, NY 10003 USA (SAN 667-6731) Tel 212-228-0950.

CPI Pubs., *(978-0-9648363)* Div. of Christopher Productions, Inc., 1115 David Ave., Pacific Grove, CA 93950 USA Tel 818-831-9268; Fax: 818-845-2128
Dist(s): **Austin & Company, Inc.**

CPI Publishing, Inc., 311 E. 51st St., New York, NY 10022 USA (SAN 218-6896) Tel 212-753-3800
Dist(s): **Modern Curriculum Pr.**

CPM Educational Program, *(978-1-885145; 978-1-931287; 978-1-60328)* 1233 Noonan Dr., Sacramento, CA 95822 USA Tel 916-446-9936; Fax: 916-444-5263
E-mail: cpm@cpm.org; bradley@cpm.org
Web site: http://www.cpm.org.

C R C World Literature Ministries *See* **C R C World Literature Ministries/Libros Desafio**

C R C World Literature Ministries/Libros Desafío, *(978-0-939125; 978-1-55883; 978-1-55955)* Subs. of CRC Pubns., 2850 Kalamazoo Ave., SE, Grand Rapids, MI 49560 USA (SAN 251-3269) Tel 616-224-0785 (customer service); Fax: 616-224-0834; Toll Free: 800-333-8300
E-mail: info@worldliterature.org
Web site: http://www.worldliterature.org/.

CRM, *(978-0-9713534; 978-1-933341)* Orders Addr.: P.O. Box 2124, Hendersonville, NC 28793 USA Tel 828-877-3356; Fax: 828-890-1511; Edit Addr.: 1916 Reasonover Rd., Cedar Mountain, NC 28218 USA
E-mail: crm@ciridmus.com
Web site: http://www.ciridmus.com
Dist(s): **Send The Light Distribution LLC.**

C R Pubns., *(978-0-615-15964-5; 978-0-615-15981-2; 978-0-615-16029-0; 978-0-615-16673-5)* 415 E. 15th, Kearny, NE 68847-6959 USA
Web site: http://www.IDealInHope.com/author
Dist(s): **Lulu Enterprises Inc.**

†CSS Publishing Co., *(978-0-7880; 978-0-89536; 978-1-55673; 978-0-615-84860-0)* Orders Addr.: 5450 N. Dixie Hwy., Lima, OH 45807-9559 USA Tel 800-241-4056; 419-227-1818; Fax: 419-228-9184; Toll Free: 800-241-4056 Customer Service; 800-537-1030 Orders; Edit Addr.: P.O. Box 4503, Lima, OH 45802-4503 USA (SAN 207-0707) Tel 419-227-1818; Fax: 419-228-9184; Toll Free: 800-537-1030 (Orders); 800-241-4056 (Customer Service); *Imprints:* Fairway Press (Fairway Pr) Do not confuse with CSS Publishing in Tularosa, NM
E-mail: editor@csspub.com; csr@csspub.com; info@csspub.com; orders@csspub.com
Web site: http://www.csspub.com
Dist(s): **Spring Arbor Distributors, Inc.**; *CIP.*

C T A, Inc., *(978-0-9712618; 978-0-9718985; 978-0-9728816; 978-0-9744640; 978-0-9747923; 978-0-9754499; 978-0-9759330; 978-1-933234; 978-1-935404; 978-1-943216)* P.O. Box 1205, Fenton, MO 63026-1205 USA Tel 636-305-3100; Toll Free: 800-999-1874
Web site: http://www.ctainc.com.

C. W. Historicals, LLC, *(978-0-9637745)* Orders Addr.: P.O. Box 113, Collingswood, NJ 08108 USA Tel 856-854-1290; Fax: 856-854-1290 (*69); Edit Addr.: 901 Lakeshore Dr., Westmont, NJ 08108 USA
E-mail: cwhist@erols.com.

C Z M Press *See* **Touchstones Discussion Project**

C2 (C squared) Publishing, *(978-0-9773115)* P.O. Box 5269, Vienna, WV 26105 USA
E-mail: noelclntn@yahoo.com; princeofwarwood@gmail.com.

Caballito Children's Bks. *Imprint of* **Caballo Pr. of Ann Arbor**

Caballo Pr. of Ann Arbor, *(978-0-615-18757-0; 978-0-9824766; 978-0-615-44366-9; 978-0-9840418; 978-0-692-39908-8; 978-0-692-50604-2)* Orders Addr.: 24 Frank Lloyd Wright Dr. P.O. Box 415, Ann Arbor, MI 48106-0445 USA Tel 734-972-5790; *Imprints:* Caballito Children's Books (Caballito)
E-mail: admin@caballopress.com
Web site: http://www.caballopress.com
Dist(s): **Lightning Source, Inc.**

Cabat Studio Pubns., *(978-0-913521)* 627 N. Fourth Ave., Tucson, AZ 85705 USA (SAN 285-1539) Tel 520-622-6362
E-mail: junecabat@hotmail.com.

Cabbage Patch Pr., *(978-0-9729044)* 841 Washington St., Suite 111, Franklin Square, NY 11010 USA Tel 516-437-8460; Fax: 516-483-7701
E-mail: cabbagepatchpress@hotmail.com
Web site: http://www.cabbagepatchpress.com.

CABI (GBR) *(978-0-85198; 978-0-85199)* *Dist. by* **Stylus Pub VA.**

Cable Publishing, *(978-0-9799494; 978-1-934980)* 14090 E. Keinenen Rd., Brule, WI 54820 USA Tel 715-372-8497; Fax: 715-372-8448
Web site: http://www.cablepublishing.com
Dist(s): **Follett School Solutions.**

Caboandcoral.com, *(978-0-615-17598-0; 978-0-692-00269-8; 978-0-692-01170-6; 978-0-9833841)* 1227 Stratford Ct., Del Mar, CA 92014 USA
E-mail: udo@caboandcoral.com
Web site: http://www.caboandcoral.com.

Cabrilho Press *See* **LinguaText, Ltd.**

Cacoethes Publishing Hse., LLC, *(978-0-9799015; 978-0-9802447; 978-0-9816190; 978-0-9817733; 978-0-9818208; 978-1-60695)* 14715 Pacific Ave. S., Suite 604, Tacoma, WA 98444 USA (SAN 854-7122) Tel 253-536-3747; Fax: 253-537-3117
E-mail: cacoethespublishing@comcast.net
Web site: http://www.cacoethespublishing.com; http://www.loticmagazine.com
Dist(s): **AtlasBooks Distribution**
Lightning Source, Inc.

Cactus Publishing, LLC, *(978-0-9766674)* 1235 S. Gilbert Rd., Suite 3-62, Mesa, AZ 85204 USA Do not confuse with companies iwht the same or similar name in East Perth, WA, Atlanta, GA, Peoria, AZ
E-mail: glsweetaz@msn.com.

Cadcim Technologies, *(978-0-9663537; 978-1-932709; 978-1-936646; 978-1-942689)* 525 St. Andrews Dr., Schererville, IN 46375 USA Tel 219-614-7235; 219-228-4908; Fax: 270-717-0185
E-mail: cadcim@yahoo.com; sales@cadcim.com
Web site: http://www.cadcim.com.

Cadence Group, The *See* **New Shelves Bks.**

Cadmos Verlag GmbH (DEU) *(978-3-86127; 978-3-925760)* *Dist. by* **IPG Chicago.**

Cadogan Guides (GBR) *(978-0-946313; 978-0-947754; 978-1-85744; 978-1-86011)* *Dist. by* **Globe Pequot.**

Cafe Lango *See* **Pavilion Pubs.**

Cahill Publishing, *(978-0-9744027)* 1016-F Brentwood Way, Atlanta, GA 30350 USA
E-mail: e-diane@hotmail.com.

Cahill Publishing Company *See* **Advance Publishing, Inc.**

Cahokia Mounds Museum Society, *(978-1-881563)* 30 Ramey St., Collinsville, IL 62234 USA Tel 618-344-7316; Fax: 618-346-5162
E-mail: cmms@ezl.com; giftshop@ezl.com
Web site: http://www.cahokiamounds.com.

CAI Publishing, *(978-0-9787766)* Orders Addr.: 807 Black Duck Dr., Port Orange, FL 32127-4726 USA (SAN 851-6006) Tel 386-383-5198; Fax: 440-306-0649
E-mail: wacummins@clearwire.net
Web site: http://www.caipublishing.net
Dist(s): **Lightning Source, Inc.**

Caitboo LLC, *(978-0-9818717)* 2474 Walnut St., No. 260, Cary, NC 27518-9212 USA (SAN 856-7948) Tel 919-851-8646
E-mail: caitboo@gmail.com
Web site: http://www.caitboo.com.

Calabash Bks. *Imprint of* **Belknap Publishing & Design**

Calaca Pr., *(978-0-9660773; 978-0-9717035; 978-0-9843359)* Orders Addr.: P.O. Box 2309, National City, CA 91951 USA Tel 619-434-9036 (phone/fax) Edit Addr.: 502 Rose Dr., National City, CA 91950 USA; *Imprints:* Red CalacArts Publications (Red CalacArts)
E-mail: calacapress@cox.net
Web site: http://calacapress.com; http://redcalacartscollective.org; http://www.myspace.com/calacalandia
Dist(s): **BookMobile**
SPD-Small Pr. Distribution.

Calaroga Publishing, *(978-0-9815793)* 619 Madison St., Suite 110, Oregon City, OR 97045 USA
Web site: www.slimsaneandsexy.com.

Caldwell, Judy, *(978-0-9774463)* 11216 Windy Peak Rdg., Sandy, UT 84094 USA Fax: 801-571-1422
E-mail: jlynncaldwell@msn.com.

Caleb's Pr., *(978-0-9729568)* 421 Seminole Ct., High Point, NC 27265-8631 USA Tel 336-887-6846; Fax: 888-726-9304
E-mail: calebspress@aol.com
Web site: http://www.calebspress.com.

Caledonia Pr., LLC, *(978-0-9890975)* P.O. Box 436166, Louisville, KY 40253 USA Tel 502-773-5874
E-mail: gbgodby@insightbb.com
Web site: http://giovannagodby.com.

Cali Publishing, *(978-0-9793004)* 2875 NE 191st St., Suite 511, Aventua, FL 33180 USA Tel 786-200-9374; Fax: 305-937-4161
E-mail: lallouz@glmace.com
Web site: http://www.calipublishing.com.

Caliber Pubns., *(978-0-9673696)* 1295 Lincoln Dr., Marion, IA 52302 USA Tel 319-294-9468; Fax: 319-373-1370; Toll Free: 877-480-5790
E-mail: larson1965@aol.com
Web site: http://www.calpubs.com.

Caliburn Bks. *Imprint of* **MQuills Publishing**

Calico Chapter Bks. *Imprint of* **ABDO Publishing Co.**

Calico Chapter Bks. *Imprint of* **Magic Wagon**

Calico Chapter Bks. *Imprint of* **Magic Wagon**

Calico Connection, Inc., The, *(978-0-9767658)* 300 N. David Ln., Muskogee, OK 74403 USA Tel 918-687-6577 Do not confuse with Calico Publishing in Seabrook, TX
E-mail: calicoasay@cox.net.

Calico Publishing *See* **Calico Connection, Inc., The**

California Foundation for Agriculture in the Classroom, *(978-0-615-26927-6; 978-0-615-34893-3; 978-0-615-44052-1; 978-0-9850855)* 2300 River Plaza Dr., Sacramento, CA 95833 USA.

California Street *Imprint of* **Firefall Editions**

Calkins Creek *Imprint of* **Boyds Mills Pr.**

Callaway Editions, Inc., *(978-0-935112)* Div. of Callaway Arts & Entertainment, 19 Fulton St., 5th Fl., New York, NY 10038-2100 USA (SAN 213-2931) Fax: 212-929-8087
E-mail: info@callaway.com
Web site: http://www.callaway.com
Dist(s): **Holt, Henry & Co.**
National Bk. Network
Penguin Random Hse., LLC.
Penguin Publishing Group
Simon & Schuster Children's Publishing.

Calliope Pubns., *(978-0-9745249)* P.O. Box 251, Arabi, LA 70032 USA Do not confuse with Calliope Publishing in Steamboat Springs, CO
Web site: http://www.soundsdevine.com.

Callirobics, *(978-0-9630478)* Orders Addr.: P.O. Box 6634, Charlottesville, VA 22906 USA Tel 804-293-7055; Fax: 804-293-9008; Toll Free: 800-769-2891; Edit Addr.: 1616 King Mountain Rd., Charlottesville, VA 22901 USA
E-mail: cal-avir@cfw.com
Web site: http://www.callirobics.com.

Callis Editora Ltda (BRA) *(978-85-7416; 978-85-85642)* *Dist. by* **IPG Chicago.**

Cally Pr., *(978-0-9766199)* 3964 Loftlands Dr., Earlysville, VA 22936 USA
E-mail: callypress@aol.com.

Calm Flame Publishing Co., *(978-0-9745263)* 10745 Gilespie St., Las Vegas, NV 89123 USA.

Calm Unity Books *See* **Calm Unity Pr.**

Calm Unity Pr., *(978-1-882260)* 3922 23rd St., San Francisco, CA 94114-3303 USA Fax: 415-821-5389 (Call before faxing); *Imprints:* Pelagia Press (Pelagia Pr)
E-mail: rabar@mindspring.com.

CalTex Pr. (CAN) *(978-0-9781504; 978-0-9784552; 978-0-9782937)* *Dist. by* **AtlasBooks.**

Calvary Chapel Church, Inc., *(978-0-9708600; 978-1-932283)* 2401 W. Cypress Creek Rd., Fort Lauderdale, FL 33309 USA
E-mail: snt@thecalebgroup.com; kirk@calvaryftl.org
Dist(s): **Send The Light Distribution LLC.**

Calvin Partnership, LLC, *(978-1-891533)* 40 Ardmore Rd., Ho-Ho-Kus, NJ 07443-1008 USA Tel 201-670-8412; Fax: 201-670-0464
E-mail: jahelka@attglobal.net.

Calychio Publishing, *(978-0-9649156; 978-0-9964126)* 4138 Kildare St., Eugene, OR 97404 USA Tel 501-653-8990
E-mail: tshionyim@yahoo.com.

Camas Pr., *(978-0-9856698)* 2219 240th Ave. SE, Sammamish, WA 98075 USA Tel 425-922-5064
E-mail: info@camaspress.com.

Camber Pr., *(978-0-9727455)* 807 Central Ave. # 2, Peekskill, NY 10566-2039 USA
Web site: http://www.camberpress.com.

Cambium Education, Inc., *(978-0-944584; 978-1-57035; 978-1-59318; 978-1-932282; 978-1-4168; 978-1-60218; 978-1-60697)* 4093 Specialty Pl., Longmont, CO 80504 USA (SAN 243-945X) Tel 303-651-2829; Fax: 303-907-8694; Toll Free: 800-547-6747 (orders only)
E-mail: publishing@sopriswest.com; customerservice@cambiumlearning.com
Web site: http://www.sopriswest.com.

Cambria Creations, LLC, *(978-0-9770916)* 515 Main St., Johnston, PA 15901 USA Tel 814-535-5571; Fax: 814-535-1079
E-mail: djwlaw@wvdsl.net
Dist(s): **AtlasBooks Distribution.**

Cambridge Bks. *Imprint of* **Write Words, Inc.**

Cambridge Bk. Co., *(978-0-8428)* Div. of Simon & Schuster, Inc., 4350 Equity Dr., Box 249, Columbus, OH 43216 USA (SAN 169-5703) Toll Free: 800-238-5833
Web site: http://www.simonsays.com/.

Cambridge BrickHouse, Inc., *(978-1-58018; 978-1-59835)* 60 Island St. Suite 102 E., Lawrence, MA 01844 USA; *Imprints:* CBH Books (CBH Bks); BrickHouse Education (BrickHse)
E-mail: edelgado@cambridgebh.com; ycanetti@cambridgebh.com; mkamelle@cambridgebh.com
Web site: http://www.cambridgebh.com; http://www.brickhouseeducation.com
Dist(s): **Ediciones Universal**
Follett School Solutions
Lectorum Pubns., Inc.

Cambridge Educational Services, Inc., *(978-1-58894)* 2860 S River Rd, Des Plaines, IL 60018 USA Tel 847-299-2930; Fax: 847-299-2933 Do not confuse with Cambridge Educational in Charleston, WV
Web site: http://www.cambridgeed.com.

Cambridge House Pr. *Imprint of* **Sterling & Ross Pubs.**

Cambridge Hse. Publishing Co., LLC, *(978-0-9711359)* P.O. Box 383, Saddle River, NJ 07458 USA Fax: 973-777-8075
E-mail: cambridgehouse@verizon.net
Web site: http://www.cezanneismissing.com; http://www.cambridgehousepublishing.com
Dist(s): **Independent Pubs. Group.**

Cambridge Scholars Pub. (GBR) *(978-1-904303; 978-1-84718; 978-1-4438)* *Dist. by* **ISD USA.**

†Cambridge Univ. Pr., *(978-0-521; 978-0-511)* Orders Addr.: 100 Brook Hill Dr., West Nyack, NY 10994-2133 USA (SAN 281-3769) Tel 845-353-7500; Fax: 845-353-4141; Toll Free: 800-872-7423 (orders, returns, credit & accounting); 800-937-9600; Edit Addr.: 32 Avenue of the Americas, New York, NY 10013-2473 USA (SAN 200-206X) Tel 212-924-3900; Fax: 212-691-3239
E-mail: customer_service@cup.org; orders@cup.org; information@cup.org
Web site: http://www.cambridge.org/
Dist(s): **Baker Bks.**
Baker Publishing Group
Boydell & Brewer, Inc.
CreateSpace Independent Publishing Platform
Ebsco Publishing
Cengage Gale
ISD
Ingram Pub. Services
Lightning Source, Inc.
Rittenhouse Bk. Distributors
ebrary, Inc.; *CIP.*

Cambridge Way Publishing, *(978-0-9746976)* 149 Cambridge Way, Macon, GA 31220-8736 USA (SAN 255-8041) Tel 478-475-1763
E-mail: whwatson2@cox.net.

Camelot Publishing, *(978-0-9754063)* Orders Addr.: P.O. Box 500057, Lake Los Angeles, CA 93535 USA (SAN 256-0666)
E-mail: camelotpublishing@hotmail.com
Web site: http://www.camelotpublishing.com.

Camelot Tales, *(978-0-9672375)*
E-mail: jeanette.adams@hotmail.com
Web site: http://www.bellowinghills.com.

Cameltrotters Publishing, *(978-0-9666110; 978-0-9764475)* Orders Addr.: P.O. Box 3026, Pinedale, CA 93650-3526 USA Tel 559-447-9393 (phone/fax)
E-mail: ted@atborgeas.com
Web site: http://www.atborgeas.com.

Cameo Pubns., LLC, *(978-0-9715739; 978-0-9744149; 978-0-9744966; 978-0-9774659)* Orders Addr.: 2175 Deer Run Trl., Jacksonville, FL 32246-1068 USA
E-mail: info@cameopublications.com; publisher@cameopublications.com
Web site: http://www.cameopublications.com
Dist(s): **Bookazine Co., Inc.**
CreateSpace Independent Publishing Platform
Distributors, The
New Leaf Pr., Inc.
Shenanigan Bks.

Camino Bks., Inc., *(978-0-940159; 978-1-933822; 978-1-68098)* P.O. Box 59026, Philadelphia, PA 19102 USA (SAN 664-225X) Tel 215-413-1917; Fax: 215-413-3255
E-mail: camino@caminobooks.com
Web site: http://www.caminobooks.com
Dist(s): **Follett School Solutions**
INscribe Digital
Partners Pubs. Group, Inc.

Camino E.E. & Bk. Co., *(978-0-940808; 978-1-55893)* Orders Addr.: a/o Jan Linzy, P.O. Box 6400, Incline Village, NV 89450 USA (SAN 219-841X) Tel 775-831-3078 (phone/fax); Fax: 775-831-3078 (phone/fax)
E-mail: info@camino-books.com
Web site: http://www.camino-books.com.

Camino Real Calendar LLC, *(978-0-9743501)* P.O. Box 17667, Anaheim, CA 92817 USA Toll Free: 800-200-6331
E-mail: support@caminosports.com
Web site: http://www.caminosports.com.

Camino Real Sports Marketing *See* **Camino Real Calendar LLC**

Cammilleri Productions, *(978-0-615-25933-8)* 2565 San Clemente Dr., Unit 206, Corta Mesa, CA 92626 USA (SAN 857-507X) Tel 714-486-1318
E-mail: jcammilleri@ca.rr.com.

Camp Pope Publishing, *(978-0-9628936; 978-1-929919)* Orders Addr.: P.O. Box 2232, Iowa City, IA 52244 USA Tel 319-351-2407; Fax: 319-339-5964; Toll Free: 800-204-2407; Edit Addr.: 1117 E. Davenport, Iowa City, IA 52245 USA
E-mail: mail@camppope.com
Web site: http://www.camppope.com
Dist(s): **Lightning Source, Inc.**

Campanita Bks. *Imprint of* **Editorial Campana**

CampCrest Publishing, *(978-0-9763257)* 385 Hidden Hollow Ln., Chickamauga, GA 30707 USA
E-mail: sallyworland@mindspring.com.

Camping Guideposts *See* **Wordshed**

Campus Crusade for Christ, *(978-1-56399)* Affil. of Campus Crusade for Christ International, Orders Addr.: 375 Hwy. 74 S., Suite A, Peachtree City, GA 30269 USA Tel 770-631-9940; Fax: 770-631-9916; Toll Free: 800-827-2788
E-mail: customerservice@campuscrusade.org
Web site: http://www.campuscrusade.com.

Can Do Duck Publishing, *(978-0-9768384)* P.O. Box 1045, Voorhees, NJ 08043 USA Tel 856-816-5255; Fax: 856-429-0094
E-mail: ducktormorty@thecandoduck.com
Web site: http://www.thecandoduck.com.

Can of Worms Pr. (GBR) *(978-1-904104)* *Dist. by* **IPG Chicago.**

Canadian Scholars' Pr., Inc. (CAN) *(978-0-921627; 978-0-921881; 978-1-55130)* *Dist. by* **Orca Bk Pub.**

Canadian Scholars' Pr., Inc. (CAN) *(978-0-921627; 978-0-921881; 978-1-55130)* *Dist. by* **IngramPubServ.**

Canal History & Technology Pr. *Imprint of* **Moore, Hugh Historical Park & Museums, Inc.**

Canal History & Technology Press *See* **Moore, Hugh Historical Park & Museums, Inc.**

Canary Connect Pubns., *(978-0-9643462)* Div. of SOBOLE, Inc., 605 Holiday Rd., Coralville, IA 52241-1016 USA Tel 319-338-3827; Fax: 612-435-3340; *Imprints:* Just Think Books (Just Think Bks)
E-mail: sondrak@canaryconnect.com
Web site: http://www.canaryconnect.com; http://www.justthinkbooks.com; http://www.simplechoicesforhealthiereating.com; http://www.transitionstobetterliving.com
Dist(s): **Follett School Solutions**
Integral Yoga Pubns.
Nutri-Bks. Corp.

Candalyse Publishing, *(978-0-9798217; 978-0-9802275; 978-0-9817112)* Orders Addr.: P.O. Box 783, Smallwood, NY 12778 USA; Edit Addr.: 57 Karl Ave.,

Smallwood, NY 12778-0783 USA; *Imprints:* Chaklet Coffee Books (ChakletCoffee)
E-mail: candalysepublishing@gmail.com; chakletcoffee@gmail.com
Web site: http://www.candalysepublishing.com; http://www.chakletbooks.com
Dist(s): **Lightning Source, Inc.**

C&C Educational Materials, LLC *See* **C & C Educational Materials, LLC**

C&K Publishing Co., *(978-0-9844342)* Orders Addr.: P.O. Box 291162, Columbia, SC 29229 USA Tel 803-414-0180; Fax: 803-462-1188; Edit Addr.: 320 Whitehurst Way, Columbia, SC 29229 USA
E-mail: candkpub@bellsouth.net.

Candle Light Pr., *(978-0-9743147; 978-0-9766053; 978-0-9895371; 978-0-9966176)* 1470 Walker Way, Coralville, IA 52242 USA Do not confuse with Candle Light Press in Martinez, CA.
E-mail: ding@candlelightpress.com
Web site: http://www.candlelightpress.com
Dist(s): **Follett School Solutions.**

Candlelight Stories, Inc., *(978-0-615-14024-7)* 9909 Topanga Canyon Blvd., Chatsworth, CA 91311 USA
E-mail: orders@candlelightstories.com
Web site: http://www.candlelightstories.com
Dist(s): **Lulu Enterprises Inc.**

Candleshoe Bks., *(978-0-9825089)* 3122 N. California Ave., Suite 3L, Chicago, IL 60618 USA
E-mail: info@candleshoebooks.com
Web site: http://www.candleshoebooks.com
Dist(s): **Music, Bks. & Business, Inc.**

Candleshoe Press, Inc. *See* **Candleshoe Bks.**

Candlewick Entertainment *Imprint of* **Candlewick Pr.**

†Candlewick Pr., *(978-0-7636; 978-1-56402)* Div. of Walker Bks., London, England, 99 Dover St., Somerville, MA 02144 USA Tel 617-661-3330; Fax: 617-661-0565; *Imprints:* Templar (Templar); Nosy Crow (NosyCrow); Big Picture Press (Big Picture Pr); Candlewick Entertainment (Candlewick Entmt) Do not confuse with Candlewick Pr., Crystal Lake, IL
E-mail: bigbear@candlewick.com; salesinfo@candlewick.com
Web site: http://www.candlewick.com/
Dist(s): **Follett School Solutions**
Penguin Random Hse., LLC.
Perfection Learning Corp.
Perseus Bks. Group
Random Hse., Inc.; *CIP.*

Candy Cane Bks. *Imprint of* **Sunlight Publishing**

Candy Cane Pr. *Imprint of* **Ideals Pubns.**

Candy's Creations *See* **Fruitbearer Publishing, LLC**

Cane River Trading Co., Inc., *(978-0-9744189)* 1473 Cty. Rte. 26, Climax, NY 12042-2211 USA Tel 518-731-8598
E-mail: ny5kmagi@aol.com
Web site: http://members.aol.com/CaneR71456/.

Canh Nam Pubs., *(978-0-9749097; 978-0-9772129; 978-0-9799345; 978-0-9883504)* 2607 Military Rd., Arlington, VA 22207 USA
E-mail: canhnam@dc.net.

Canine Publishing, *(978-0-615-59830-7)* 8650 Rio Grande Rd, Richmond, VA 23229 USA Tel 804-305-9777
Dist(s): **CreateSpace Independent Publishing Platform.**

Canis Lupus Productions, *(978-0-9661789)* Orders Addr.: P.O. Box 128262, San Diego, CA 92102-8262 USA; Edit Addr.: 1940 Third Ave., Unit 406, San Diego, CA 92101-2622 USA Tel 310-873-3232 (phone/fax)
E-mail: jlbrooks@email.com.

Canmore Pr., *(978-1-887774)* Orders Addr.: P.O. Box 510794, Melbourne Beach, FL 32951-0794 USA Tel 321-729-0078; Fax: 321-724-1162; *Imprints:* Wynden (Wynden)
E-mail: publish@canmorepress.com
Web site: http://www.canmorepress.com.

Cannady, John, *(978-0-9754345)* 6126 Dunwoody Ct., Montgomery, AL 36117-5012 USA
E-mail: katphishe@starband.net
Web site: http://www.hopetkd.com.

Cannon, K. L., *(978-0-9675594)* 9412 Meadow Vale, Austin, TX 78758 USA Tel 512-837-6281; Fax: 512-837-7205
E-mail: cankl@msn.com.

Canoed Sun Publishing, LLC, *(978-0-9836081)* 902 Franklin Ave., Council Bluffs, IA 51503 USA Tel 402-541-6452.

Canon Pr., *(978-1-885767; 978-1-930443; 978-1-59128; 978-1-935000)* Div. of Credenda Agenda, Orders Addr.: P.O. Box 8729, Moscow, ID 83843 USA (SAN 257-3792); 205 E. 5th St., Moscow, ID 83843 Do not confuse with companies with the same or similar names in Grand Rapids, MI, Centerville, UT
E-mail: sandy@canonpress.org; brian@canonpress.org
Web site: http://www.canonpress.com
Dist(s): **Follett School Solutions.**

Canon Pubs., *(978-0-9889696)* 10 Canon Cir., Greenwood Village, CO 80111 USA Tel 303-721-8266; Fax: 303-721-8266
E-mail: Debra@DebraFine.com
Dist(s): **Midpoint Trade Bks., Inc.**
ebrary, Inc.

Canongate Bks. (GBR) *(978-0-86241; 978-0-903937; 978-1-84195; 978-1-84767; 978-0-85786; 978-1-78211)* *Dist. by* **IPG Chicago.**

Cantab Publishing, *(978-0-9745150)* P.O. Box 381591, Cambridge, MA 02238-1591 USA.

Cantemos-bilingual bks. and music, *(978-0-9623930; 978-1-892306)* Orders Addr.: 15696 Altamira Dr., Chino Hills, CA 91709 USA Tel 909-393-8372; Toll Free: 800-393-1336
E-mail: jarjetb@writeme.com; bakergeorgette@yahoo.com
Web site: http://www.cantemosco.com; http://www.simplespanishsongs.com
Dist(s): **Continental Bk. Co., Inc.**
Follett School Solutions
Midwest Library Service.

Canterbury Hse. Publishing, Ltd., *(978-0-9825396; 978-0-9829054; 978-0-9881897; 978-0-9908416)* 4535 Ottawa Trail, Sarasota, FL 34233 USA Tel 941-312-6912
Web site: www.canterburyhousepublishing.com
Dist(s): **Ingram Content Group Inc.**
Smashwords.

Canterwine Pr., *(978-0-9764184)* 608 Longview Ave., Anacortes, WA 98221 USA Tel 360-941-4692
E-mail: canterwinepress@hotmail.com
Web site: http://www.canterwinepress.com.

Cantu, Ricardo, *(978-0-615-14898-4; 978-0-615-15149-6; 978-0-615-18600-9)* 2389 Tobello Blvd., Indianapolis, IN 46234 USA
E-mail: ricardocantu6908@sbcglobal.net
Dist(s): **Lulu Enterprises Inc.**

Canyon Beach Visual Communications, *(978-0-9754221)* PMB 108, 10 St. Francis Way, Unit 9, Cranberry Township, PA 16066 USA Tel 724-612-5784
E-mail: info@canyonbeach.com
Web site: http://www.canyonbeach.com.

Cap & Compass, LLC, *(978-0-9717366)* 132 Chestnut St., Branford, CT 06405 USA Tel 203-483-7005
E-mail: jesse@capandcompass.com
Web site: http://www.capandcompass.com
Dist(s): **AtlasBooks Distribution.**

Capercaillie Bks., Ltd (GBR) *(978-0-9542905; 978-0-9545206; 978-0-9549625; 978-0-9551246; 978-1-909305)* *Dist. by* **Wlsn Assocs.**

Capital Apple Pr., *(978-0-9830686)* 742 Front St. No. 1, Catasauqua, PA 18032 USA Tel 610-596-0266.

Capital City Bks. LLC, *(978-0-9842881; 978-0-9835788)* c/o Hartwood Publishing, 1 N. 5th St., Suite 511, Richmond, VA 23219 USA Tel 804-836-6870; Fax: 804-644-3092
E-mail: capitalcitybooks@gmail.com
Web site: http://www.capitalcitybooks.com.

Capital Publishing, *(978-0-9773016)* 6311 10th Ave., Brooklyn, NY 11219 USA Tel 718-921-6400; Fax: 718-921-0160
E-mail: pommedia@pommedia.com.

Capitol Advantage Publishing *See* **Congress At Your Fingertips**

Cappella Publishing, A, *(978-0-9760271)* 20505 Yorba Linda Blvd., Suite 505, Yorba Linda, CA 92886 USA Tel 714-336-2350; Fax: 714-685-7773
E-mail: cgriffiths@acappellapublishing.com
Web site: http://www.acappellapublishing.com.

Capri Publishing, *(978-0-9769132; 978-0-9788612)* 4401 NW 39th St., #518, Midwest City, OK 73112 USA Tel 405-623-7619
E-mail: capripub@aol.com
Web site: http://www.capripublishing.net.

Capriccio Publishing, *(978-0-9770076)* 11100 SW 93rd Ct. Rd., Suite 10-405, Ocala, FL 34481 USA Tel 352-873-1403.

Capricorn Hse. Publishing, *(978-0-9791702; 978-1-60466)* 5122 Annesway Dr., Nashville, TN 37205 USA
E-mail: pclif@comcast.net.

Capricorn Publishing, *(978-0-9753970; 978-0-9774757)* 706 E. Brewster St., Appleton, WI 54911 USA Tel 920-475-0674; Fax: 920-954-9533
E-mail: getovd@yahoo.com
Web site: http://www.CapricornPublishing.com.

Capricorn Publishing, Incorporated *See* **Capricorn Publishing**

CAPS, LLC *See* **ALCAPS, LLC**

Capstone *Imprint of* **Wiley, John & Sons, Inc.**

Capstone Academics LLC, *(978-1-933557)* 3815 N. Brookfield Rd., Suite No. 104-122, Brookfield, WI 53045 USA (SAN 256-6761) Tel 262-754-4699; Toll Free: 888-922-7786
E-mail: contact@capstoneacademics.com
Web site: http://www.capstoneacademics.com.

Capstone Bks. *Imprint of* **Capstone Pr., Inc.**

Capstone Bks., *(978-0-9752843)* P.O. Box 7025, Greenwood, IN 46142 USA Tel 317-414-4770; 1710 Roe Crest Drive, N. Mankato, MN 56003
Web site: http://www.capstonebooks.com
Dist(s): **Follett School Solutions.**

Capstone Classroom, *(978-1-62521; 978-1-4966)* Div. of Capstone Publishers, Orders Addr.: 1710 Roe Crest Dr., North Mankato, MN 56003 USA Toll Free Fax: 888-262-0705; Toll Free: 800-747-4992; Edit Addr.: 5050 Lincoln Dr, Edina, MN 55436 USA; *Imprints:* Legends in Their Own Lunchbox (LegendsIn)
E-mail: k.monyhan@coughlancompanies.com; customerservice@capstonepub.com
Web site: http://www.capstoneclassroom.com
Dist(s): **Capstone Pub.**
Follett School Solutions.

Capstone Digital, Div. of Capstone Pubs., Orders Addr.: 151 Good Counsel Dr., Mankato, MN 56002 USA Toll Free Fax: 888-262-0705; Toll Free: 800-747-4992; Edit Addr.: 7825 Telegraph Rd., Bloomington, MN 55438 USA; *Imprints:* Capstone Interactive Library (CapstoneInter)
Web site: http://www.capstonepub.com
Dist(s): **Capstone Pr., Inc.**
Follett School Solutions.

Capstone Interactive Library *Imprint of* **Capstone Digital**

Capstone Pr., Inc., *(978-0-9667204)* 172 Dipper Ln., No. 6, Decatur, IL 62522 USA Tel 217-422-6033 Do not confuse with Capstone Pr., Inc., Mankato, MN
E-mail: jsjcj@fgi.net.

Capstone Pr., Inc., *(978-0-7368; 978-1-56065; 978-1-4296; 978-1-62065; 978-1-4765; 978-1-4914; 978-1-5157)* Div. of Coughlan Publishing, 1905 Lookout Dr., North Mankato, MN 55033 USA Tel 507-385-8215; Fax: 507-388-3752; Orders Addr.: 1710 Roe Crest Dr., North Mankato, MN 56003 USA (SAN 254-1815) Toll Free Fax: 888-262-0705; Toll Free: 800-747-4992; Edit Addr.: 5050 Lincoln Dr Suite 200, Edina, MN 55436 USA Fax: 952-933-2410; Toll Free: 888-517-8977; *Imprints:* Pebble Books (Pebble Bks); Bridgestone Books (Bridgestone Bks); Blue Earth Books (Blue Earth Bks); A+ Books (Aplus Bks); Capstone Books (Capstone Bks); Yellow Umbrella Books (Yell Umbrella); Edge Books (EdgeBks); Fact Finders (FactFind); First Facts (FirsFacts); Blazers (Blazers); A+ Bilingue/Bilingual (ABiling); Graphic Library (GraphLib); Graphic Library en espanol (GraLibespanol); High Five Reading (RBL) (HiFiveRBL); Let Freedom Ring (LetFreeRing); Letter Books (Letter Bks); NA (CAP) (NC CAP); Pebble Plus (PebPlus); Pebble Plus Bilingue/Bilingual (PebbPlusBil); Phonics Readers (PhonicReads); Snap Books (Snap Bks); Social Studies Collections (SSC); Yellow Umbrella en espanol (Yellowen espan); You Choose Books (Yu Choose); Wonder Readers (WONDER READERS); Engage Literacy (ENGAGE LITERAC) Do not confuse with Capstone Pr., Inc. in Decatur, IL
E-mail: customerservice@capstonepub.com
Web site: http://www.capstone-press.com; http://www.capstonepub.com; http://www.capstoneclassroom.com
Dist(s): **Capstone Pub.**
Continental Bk. Co., Inc.
Follett School Solutions
Lectorum Pubns., Inc.
MyiLibrary
SPD-Small Pr. Distribution.

Capstone Publishing Group LLC *See* **OakTara Publishing Group LLC**

Capstone Young Readers, *(978-1-62370)* Div. of Capstone Publishers, Orders Addr.: 1710 Roe Crest Dr., North Mankato, MN 56003 USA; Edit Addr.: 5050 Lincoln Dr, Edina, MN 55436 USA Tel 952-224-0558; *Imprints:* Wear-A-Book (WearaBook)
E-mail: k.monyhan@coughlancompanies.com
Web site: http://capstoneyoungreaders.com
Dist(s): **Capstone Pub.**

Captain & Harry LLC, The, *(978-0-9724777)* 8875 Section Line Rd., Harbor Beach, MI 48441-9616 USA
E-mail: janlangley5@gmail.com
Web site: http://www.michiganghoststories.net; http://www.thecaptainandharry.com.

Captain Caleb Communications, *(978-0-9703021)* 1250 Cynder Ct., Annapolis, MD 21401-7504 USA Tel 410 626 8904; 410-626-8904
E-mail: jcurtis@toad.net
Web site: http://www.oysterbook.com.

Captain Fiddle Pubns., *(978-0-931877)* 4 Elm Ct., Newmarket, NH 03857 USA (SAN 686-0508) Tel 603-659-2658
E-mail: cFiddle@tiac.net
Web site: http://www.captainfiddle.com.

Captain McFinn and Friends LLC, McFinn Pr., *(978-0-9799283; 978-0-9859482)* 2445 Belmont Ave., Youngstown, OH 44504-0186 USA Tel 330-747-2661; Fax: 330-743-2719
E-mail: kbaker@cafarocompany.com
Dist(s): **AtlasBooks Distribution.**

Captain, Tamira R. *See* **Stories From Four Publishing Co.**

Captio Corp., *(978-0-9766614)* 2230 Tioga Dr., Menlo Park, CA 94025-6640 USA
Web site: http://www.captio.com.

Capture Bks., *(978-0-9798664)* 12331 Checkerboard Cir., Norman, OK 73026 USA (SAN 854-6207) Tel 405-485-8131
Web site: http://capturebooks.com.

Captured Light Distribution, LLC, *(978-0-9761074)* PMB 112 1201 Yelm Ave., Yelm, WA 98597 USA Tel 360-400-2537
E-mail: missbfc@msn.com
Web site: http://www.whatthebleep.com.

Capturing Memories, *(978-0-9727759)* 9228 SW 209th St, Vashon, WA 98070 USA Tel 206-463-5652
E-mail: roger@capturingmemories.com; stories@capturingmemories.com
Web site: http://www.capturingmemories.com.

Captus, LLC, *(978-0-9776627)* 32725 Ledge Hill Dr., Solon, OH 44139 USA Tel 440-498-9178; Fax: 440-238-2967
E-mail: cziance@yahoo.com
Web site: http://www.babyalmamater.com.

Capybara Madness, *(978-0-9899847)* 700 Jerrys Ln., Buda, TX 78610 USA Tel 512-751-6667
E-mail: typaldos@gmail.com
Web site: www.capybaramadness.com.

C.A.R. Pr., *(978-0-9661668)* Div. of the National Society of the Children of the American Revolution, Orders Addr.: P.O. Box 7666, Arlington, VA 22207-0666 USA Tel 202-638-3153; Fax: 202-737-3162; Edit Addr.: 1776 D St., NW, Washington, DC 20006 USA
Dist(s): **Penguin Publishing Group**
Vandamere Pr.

Caravan of Dreams Productions, *(978-0-929856)* Div. of Caravan of Dreams, 512 Main St. Ste. 1500, Fort Worth, TX 76102-3922 USA (SAN 250-4855).

Carazona Creations LLC, *(978-0-9753724)* PO Box 635, Clarkdale, AZ 86324 USA Toll Free: 888-328-3300
E-mail: carazona@carazonacreations.com
Web site: http://www.carazonacreations.com.

Carden Jennings Publishing Co., Ltd., *(978-1-891524)* 375 Greenbrier Dr., Suite 100, Charlottesvle, VA 22901-1618 USA
Web site: http://www.cjp.com.

Cardigras.com *See* **airjam.com**

Cardinal Brands, Inc., *(978-1-932435)* 1251 SW Arrowhead Rd. Ste. A, Topeka, KS 66604-4061 USA Toll Free: 800-444-0038
Web site: http://www.witty-one.com; http://www.cardinalbrands.com.

Cardinal Pr., *(978-0-9779518)* 19 W. 76th St. Suite 1be, New York, NY 10023 USA
Web site: http://www.cardinal-press.com.

Cardinal Pubs. Group, 2402 N. Shadeland Ave. Ste. A, Indianapolis, IN 46219-1746 USA (SAN 631-7936)
E-mail: tdoherty@in.net.

Cardlings, *(978-0-9760108)* Orders Addr.: P.O. Box 931, Pueblo, CO 81002 USA; Edit Addr.: 815 W. 14th St., Pueblo, CO 81003 USA
E-mail: gnome@cardlings.com
Web site: http://www.cardlings.com.

Career Pr., Inc., *(978-1-56414; 978-1-60163; 978-1-63265)* Orders Addr.: 12 Parish Dr., Wayne, NJ 07470 USA (SAN 694-3640) Toll Free: 1-800-227-3371 (outside New Jersey); *Imprints:* New Page Books (New Page Bks)
E-mail: sales@careerpress.com
Web site: http://www.careerpress.com; http://www.newpagebooks.com
Dist(s): **Follett School Solutions**
Lightning Source, Inc.
MyiLibrary
Penguin Random Hse., LLC.
ebrary, Inc.

Carefree Publishing *Imprint of* **Milano, Jacque & Assocs.**

Carey III, John, *(978-0-9799876)* 5510 NE. Antioch Suite 133, Gladstone, MO 64118 USA (SAN 854-9222)
E-mail: ecarey1222@yahoo.com.

Carey, Rebecca, *(978-0-9791331)* 1035 S. 43rd St., Wilmington, NC 28403-4369 USA
E-mail: because@aol.com
Web site: http://www.bigarthouse.com.

Carey, William Library Pubs., *(978-0-87808)* Orders Addr.: 129 Mobilization Dr., Waynesboro, GA 30830 USA (SAN 208-2101) Tel 706-554-1594; Fax: 706-554-7444; Toll Free: 866-732-6657; Edit Addr.: P.O. Box 40129, Pasadena, CA 91114 USA
E-mail: inquiry@wclbooks.com
Web site: http://www.wclbooks.com
Dist(s): **Gabriel Resources**
Send The Light Distribution LLC.

Cargill Consulting, Inc., *(978-0-9743780)* 19836 Linda Ln., Harrah, OK 73045-9351 USA
Web site: http://www.cargillconsulting.com.

Caribbean Publishing *See* **Coconut Pr., LLC**

Caribbean Scene, *(978-0-9678030)* 5 Walnut Ave., East Norwich, NY 11732 USA.

CaribbeanReads, *(978-0-615-22865-5; 978-0-9832978; 978-0-9899305; 978-0-9908659; 978-0-9964358)* 10314 Collingham Dr., Fairfax, VA 22032 USA Tel 202-683-0611
E-mail: carol.mitchell@caribbeanreads.com
Web site: www.caribbeanreads.com.

Caritas Communications, *(978-0-9668228; 978-0-9753259; 978-0-9799390; 978-0-615-76666-9; 978-0-615-87196-7)* 216 N. Green Bay Road, No. 208, Thiensville, WI 53092-2010 USA Tel 414-531-0503; Fax: 262-238-9039 Do not confuse with Caritas Communications Incorporated in New York, NY, Rhinebeck, NY
E-mail: dgawlik@wi.rr.com
Dist(s): **CreateSpace Independent Publishing Platform.**

Carleton Bks., *(978-0-9759738)* 335 N. Main Ave., Tucson, AZ 85701 USA.

Carlisle Pr.- Walnut Creek, *(978-0-9642548; 978-1-890050; 978-1-933753)* 2673 Township Rd., No. 421, Sugarcreek, OH 44681 USA Tel 330-852-1900; Fax: 330-852-3285; Toll Free: 800-852-4482 Do not confuse with companies with the same name in Mechanicsburg, PA, Sedona, AZ, Benbrook, TX.

CarLou Interactive Media & Publishing, *(978-0-9759325)* 12439 Magnolia Blvd., No. 170, Valley Village, CA 91607 USA
E-mail: tess@worldtrust.org
Web site: http://www.carloumedia.com.

Carlsbad Caverns Guadalupe Mountains Assn., *(978-0-916907)* P.O. Box 1417, Carlsbad, NM 88221-1417 USA (SAN 268-6627) Tel 505-785-2485.

Carlsbad Caverns Natural History Association *See* **Carlsbad Caverns Guadalupe Mountains Assn.**

Carlsen Verlag (DEU) *(978-3-551)* *Dist. by* **Distribks Inc.**

Carlson, Debra R., *(978-0-9765950)* 1705 N. 160th St., Omaha, NE 68118-2408 USA
Web site: http://www.cozykidspress.com.

Carlton Bks., Ltd. (GBR) *(978-1-85868; 978-1-84222; 978-1-84442; 978-1-84732; 978-1-78097)* *Dist. by* **IPG Chicago.**

Carlton Bks., Ltd. (GBR) *(978-1-85868; 978-1-84222; 978-1-84442; 978-1-84732; 978-1-78097)* *Dist. by* **Sterling.**

Carlton Kids (GBR) *(978-1-78312)* *Dist. by* **Sterling.**

Carmean Productions LLC, *(978-0-9839799)* 1905 NW 37th Blvd., Gainesville, FL 32605 USA Tel 352-514-5625
E-mail: John@johncarmean.com
Web site: www.carmeanproductions.com.

Carmel Concepts, Ltd., *(978-0-9646285)* 50 Mt. Tiburon Rd., Tiburon, CA 94920 USA Tel 415-435-8066; Fax: 415-435-3750.

Caregie Learning Inc., *(978-1-930804; 978-1-932409; 978-1-934239; 978-1-934800; 978-1-935162; 978-1-936152; 978-1-60972)* 437 Grant St., Frick Bldg., 20th Flr., Pittsburgh, PA 15219 USA Tel 412-690-2442 Toll Free: 888-851-7094
Web site: http://carnegielearning.com.

Carney Educational Services, *(978-1-930288)* 1150 Foothill Blvd., Ste B, La Canada, CA 91011 USA Toll Free: 888-511-7737
E-mail: michellecarroll67@gmail.com
Web site: http://www.thebrightmind.com
Dist(s): **Sunbelt Pubns., Inc.**

Carnifex Pr., *(978-0-9759727; 978-0-9789583)* P.O. Box 1686, Ormond Beach, FL 32175 USA Tel 386-677-2980
E-mail: carnifexpress@hotmail.com
Web site: http://www.carnifexpress.net.

Carnivore Games, *(978-0-9749150)* Orders Addr.: P.O. Box 846, Londonderry, NH 03053-0846 USA; Edit Addr.: 12 Emerald Dr., Derry, NH 03038 USA
E-mail: brad@carnivoregames.com
Web site: http://www.carnivoregames.com/.

Publisher Name Index

Carol Kalhagen-Tamanaha, *(978-0-9799493)* 36020 Big Trout Rd., Hebo, OR 97122 USA
E-mail: beartotem@earthlink.net
Web site: http://www.CarolKalhagenWildlifeart.com.

Carolina Academic Pr., *(978-0-89089; 978-1-59460; 978-1-61163)* 700 Kent St., Durham, NC 27701 USA (SAN 210-7848) Tel 919-489-7486; Fax: 919-493-5668
E-mail: tim@cap-press.com; css@cap-press.com
Dist(s): **Follett School Solutions.**

Carolina Biological Supply Co., *(978-0-89278; 978-1-4350)* 2700 York Rd., Burlington, NC 27215-3398 USA (SAN 249-2784) Tel 336-584-0381; Fax: 910-584-3399; Toll Free Fax: 800-222-7112; Toll Free: 800-334-5551
E-mail: carolina@carolina.com
Web site: http://www.carolina.com
Dist(s): **Follett School Solutions.**

Carolina Canines for Service Inc., *(978-0-9800070)* P.O. Box 12643, Wilmington, NC 28405-1823 USA Tel 910-362-8181; Fax: 910-362-8184; Toll Free: 866-910-3647
Web site: http://www.carolinacanines.org.

Carolina Children, *(978-0-9794580)* P.O. Box 862, Mauldin, SC 29662 USA
Web site: http://carolinachildren.net.

†Carolina Wren Pr., *(978-0-932112)* 120 Morris St., Durham, NC 27701 USA (SAN 213-0327) Tel 919-560-2738; Fax: 919-560-2759
E-mail: carolinawrenpress@earthlink.net
Web site: http://www.carolinawrenpress.org
Dist(s): **Follett School Solutions**
MyiLibrary; *CIP.*

Carolrhoda Bks. *Imprint of* **Lerner Publishing Group**

Carolrhoda LAB *Imprint of* **Lerner Publishing Group**

Carolyn & Kristina's Bookshelf, *(978-0-615-18357-2)* 550 Brittany Ct., North Huntingdon, PA 15642 USA
E-mail: prin66@aol.com; cnkbkshelf@aim.com
Dist(s): **Lulu Enterprises Inc.**

Carousel Pubns., Inc., *(978-0-9759382)* P.O. Box 225, Springfield, NJ 07081 USA
Web site: http://www.net2infinity/aplaceinthesky.

Carp Cove Pr., *(978-0-9703752)* Orders Addr.: 9099 Oneida River Pk. Dr., Clay, NY 13041 USA Tel 315-652-4964
E-mail: carpcovepress@holisticanimal.com; Colleen@holisticanimal.com
Web site: http://www.holisticanimal.com/.

Carpe Viam Productions, LLC, *(978-0-9892949)* Orders Addr.: 3217 E. Shea Blvd. No. 305, Phoenix, AZ 85028 USA (SAN 920-8356) Tel 602-762-1473
E-mail: dwight@theLittleRedRacingCar.com
Web site: www.theLittleRedRacingCar.com.

Carpenter's Son Publishing, *(978-0-9832846; 978-0-9835571; 978-0-9839876; 978-0-9849771; 978-0-9849772; 978-0-9851085; 978-0-9883043; 978-0-9883962; 978-0-9885931; 978-0-9889403; 978-0-9893722; 978-1-940262; 978-1-942557; 978-1-942587)* 307 Verde Meadow Dr., Franklin, TN 37067 USA Tel 615-472-1128
E-mail: larry@christianbookservices.com
Dist(s): **MyiLibrary**
Send The Light Distribution LLC
Smashwords.

Carriage House Publishing *See* **American Carriage Hse. Publishing**

Carrier, Therese, *(978-0-9797648)* 2020 Fieldstone Pkwy., Suite 900 PMB 121, Franklin, TN 37069 USA
Web site: http://hwbdproductions.com.

Carrington Bks., *(978-0-9787143; 978-0-9820003; 978-0-9819656)* P.O. Box 451399, Los Angeles, CA 90045 USA Tel 310-628-5557; 12975 Agustin Pl., No. A-109, Playa Vista, CA 90094
Web site: http://www.StudentSafetyTips.com.

Carroll, Sherry, *(978-0-9752994)* P.O. Box 34603, Washington, DC 20774 USA
E-mail: carrollcom01@aol.com.

Carson, Tracy, *(978-0-9767077)* 1998 66th St., SE, Bismarck, ND 58504-3835 USA
Web site: http://www.grandmaisnowabutterfly.com.

Carson-Dellosa Christian *Imprint of* **Carson-Dellosa Publishing, LLC**

Carson-Dellosa Publishing Company, Incorporated *See* **Carson-Dellosa Publishing, LLC**

Carson-Dellosa Publishing, LLC, *(978-0-88724; 978-1-57156; 978-1-57332; 978-1-59441; 978-1-60022; 978-1-60418; 978-1-936022; 978-1-936023; 978-1-936024; 978-0-9823625; 978-0-9823626; 978-0-9823627; 978-0-692-00200-1; 978-1-60996; 978-1-62057; 978-1-62223; 978-1-62399; 978-1-62442; 978-1-62648; 978-1-4838) Orders Addr.: P.O. Box 35665, Greensboro, NC 27425 USA Tel 336-632-0084; Fax: 336-808-3249; Toll Free: 800-321-0943; Imprints:* Carson-Dellosa Christian (CDChristian); DJ Inkers (DJInk); HighReach Learning, Incorporated (HghRchLrn); Brighter Child (BrighterChild); Spectrum (Spectrum Dell); Frank Schaffer Publications (FS Pubns); Instructional Fair (InstFair); Key Education Publishing Company, LLC (KeyEduc)
Web site: http://www.carsondellosa.com
Dist(s): **Follett School Solutions.**

Carsume, *(978-0-9883927)* 16509 Old Forest Rd., Hacienda Heights, CA 91745 USA Tel 626-968-2192
E-mail: sumeta@verizon.net.

Cartoon Connections Pr., *(978-0-9657136)* P.O. Box 10889, White Bear Lake, MN 55110 USA (SAN 299-352X) Tel 651-429-1244; 651-429-7660; 24145 435Th Ave., Aitkin, MN 56431
E-mail: CartoonC@aol.com
Web site: http://www.cartooningbasics.com; http://www.cartoonconnections.com
Dist(s): **Follett School Solutions**
F&W Media, Inc.

Cartoonmario.com, *(978-0-9766755)* 5084 S. 65th St., Greenfield, WI 53220-4504 USA Tel 414-541-9221 (phone/fax)
E-mail: mdm@cartoonmario.com
Web site: http://www.cartoonmario.com.

Cartwheel Bks. *Imprint of* **Scholastic, Inc.**

Caruso, Kevin M. *See* **Aerospace 1 Pubns.**

Caryn Solutions, LLC, *(978-0-9791046)* Orders Addr.: P.O. Box 635, Naples, FL 34106 USA (SAN 852-4726) Tel 239-404-5820
E-mail: caryn@carynsolutions.com
Web site: http://www.carynsolutions.com.

Casa Bautista de Publicaciones, *(978-0-311)* Div. of Southern Baptist Convention, Orders Addr.: P.O. Box 4255, El Paso, TX 79914 USA (SAN 220-0139) Tel 915-566-9656; Fax: 915-562-6502; Toll Free: 800-755-5958; *Imprints:* Editorial Mundo Hispano (Edit Mundo)
E-mail: epena@casabautista.org
Web site: http://www.casabautista.org
Dist(s): **Smashwords.**

Casa Creacion *Imprint of* **Charisma Media**

Casa de Estudios de Literatura y Talleres Artisticos Amaquemecan A.C. (MEX) *(978-968-6465) Dist. by* **Lectorum Pubns.**

Casa de Periodistas Editorial, *(978-0-9743102)* Orders Addr.: P.O. Box 9021787, San Juan, PR 00902-1787 USA; Edit Addr.: Calle de la Luna, Esq. Calle de San José, San Juan, PR 00902-1787 USA
E-mail: multiser@coqui.net
Web site: http://www.asppro.org.

Casa de Snapdragon LLC, *(978-0-9793075; 978-0-9840530; 978-0-9845681; 978-1-937240)* Orders Addr.: 12901 Bryce Ave., NE, Albuquerque, NM 87112 USA Tel 505-508-5513
E-mail: sales@casadesnapdragon.com; managingeditor@casadesnapdragon.com
Web site: http://www.casadesnapdragon.com
Dist(s): **Smashwords.**

Casa Nazarena de Publicacions, *(978-1-56344)* 6401 The Paseo, Kansas City, MO 64131 USA Tel 816-333-7000; Fax: 816-333-1748; Toll Free: 800-462-8711
E-mail: donnie@nph.com
Dist(s): **Nazarene Publishing Hse.**

Cascade Design Publishing *See* **Cascade, Inc.**

Cascade, Inc., *(978-0-9726173)* 1085 Commonwealth Ave., PMB 253, Boston, MA 02215 USA Tel 617-558-1038; *Imprints:* Philograph (Philograph)
E-mail: info@philograph.com
Web site: http://www.philograph.com.

Cascade Pass, Inc., *(978-1-880599; 978-0-615-39461-9; 978-1-935999)* Orders Addr.: 4223 Glencoe Ave., Suite C-105, Marina del Rey, CA 90292 USA Tel 310-305-0210; Fax: 310-305-7850; Toll Free: 888-837-0704
E-mail: jlc@cascadepass.com
Web site: http://www.cascadepass.com
Dist(s): **Follett School Solutions.**

Cascade Writing, *(978-0-9767519)* 1808 Lake Dr., Camano Island, WA 98282 USA Tel 360-387-8023
E-mail: dennisc@whidbey.net.

Cascarano, John *See* **Lock & Mane**

Casemate Academic, *(978-0-9774094; 978-1-935488)* Orders Addr.: P.O. Box 511, Oakville, CT 06779 USA (SAN 630-9461) Tel 860-945-9329; Fax: 860-945-9468; Toll Free: 800-791-9354; Edit Addr.: 20 Main St., Oakville, CT 06779 USA
E-mail: queries@dbbconline.com
Web site: http://www.oxbowbooks.com
Dist(s): **Casemate Pubs. & Bk. Distributors, LLC.**

Casemate Pubs. & Bk. Distributors, LLC, *(978-0-9711709; 978-1-932033; 978-1-935149; 978-1-61200)* Orders Addr.: 908 Darby Rd., Havertown, PA 19083-4608 USA; 22883 Quicksilver Dr., Herndon, VA 20166 (SAN 631-9386) Tel 703-661-1500; Edit Addr.: 180 Varick St. Suite 816, New York, NY 10014 USA
E-mail: casemate@casematepublishing.com
Web site: http://www.casematepublishing.com
Dist(s): **Follett School Solutions**
MBI Distribution Services/Quayside Distribution
MyiLibrary
Open Road Integrated Media, LLC
ebrary, Inc.

Caseys World Bks., *(978-0-9765872)* Orders Addr.: 1998 Skyline Dr., Saintughton, WI 53589 USA Tel 608-335-0401 Please call with any questions. Leave a voice message if no answer.
E-mail: kate@caseysworld.net
Web site: http://www.caseysworld.net.

Caslon Books *See* **Slangman Publishing**

Caslon Pr., *(978-0-9728144)* 315 Richards Ave., Portsmouth, NH 03801-5239 USA Tel 603-431-6823
E-mail: jbf@fergus.com
Web site: http://www.jbf.fergus.com.

Caso, George R., *(978-0-9719290)* 2445 Babylon Tpke., Merrick, NY 11566 USA Tel 516-379-9397.

Cassandra Armstrong *See* **Storm Moon Pr., LLC**

Cassette & Video Learning Systems *See* **Watch & Learn, Inc.**

Castellated Pr., *(978-0-9746416)* P.O. Box 4406, Warren, NJ 07059 USA
E-mail: scottzarnek@castellatedpress.com
Web site: http://www.castellatedpress.com.

Casterman, Editions (FRA) *(978-2-203; 978-2-542) Dist. by* **Distribks Inc.**

Castillo, Ediciones, S. A. de C. V. (MEX) *(978-968-6635; 978-968-7415; 978-970-20) Dist. by* **Macmillan.**

Castillo, Ediciones, S. A. de C. V. (MEX) *(978-968-6635; 978-968-7415; 978-970-20) Dist. by* **Mariuccia Iaconi Bk Imports.**

Castle Books *Imprint of* **Book Sales, Inc.**

Castle Builder Pr. *Imprint of* **Blue Cubicle Pr., LLC**

Castle Keep Pr. *Imprint of* **Rock, James A. & Co. Pubs.**

Castle Pacific Publishing, *(978-0-9653869; 978-0-9749305; 978-0-9774168)* P.O. Box 77089, Seattle, WA 98177 USA Tel 206-839-0984; Toll Free: 888-756-2665 (888-756-BOOK)
Web site: http://www.castlepacific.com.

Castle Pr., *(978-0-9669263; 978-0-9835012)* 1222 N. Fair Oaks Ave., Pasadena, CA 91103 USA Fax: 626-789-7385
E-mail: george@castlepress.com.

Castlebay, Inc., *(978-0-9748145)* P.O. Box 168, Round Pond, ME 04564-0168 USA Tel 207-529-5438
E-mail: castlebay@castlebay.net.

Castleberry Farms Pr., *(978-1-891907)* Orders Addr.: P.O. Box 337, Poplar, WI 54864 USA Tel 715-364-8404
E-mail: cbfarmpr@centurytel.net
Web site: http://www.castleberryfarmspress.com; http://www.cbfarmpr.com.

Castlebridge Bks. *Imprint of* **Big Tent Bks.**

Castlebrook Pubns., *(978-0-9641697; 978-0-9798242; 978-0-615-99230-3; 978-0-692-53831-9)* Orders Addr.: P.O. Box 132, Camp Meeker, CA 95419 USA; 1535 Farmers Ln., Pmb #237, Santa Rosa, CA 95405
E-mail: castlebrookpublications@aol.com
Web site: http://www.youdrawitbooks.com; http://www.printanddraw.com
Dist(s): **CreateSpace Independent Publishing Platform**
Follett School Solutions.

Castleconal Pr., *(978-0-9677348)* 1517 National Ave., Madison, WI 53716 USA Tel 608-222-6051; Fax: 608-221-5264
E-mail: dfleming@madison.k12.wi.us.

Castlegate Pr., *(978-0-9743588)* 457 Terraces Ct., Mesquite, NV 89027 USA Tel 303-550-3360; Fax: 702-346-2058.

Castleton, Julia J, *(978-0-578-06109-2)* P.O. Box 880371, Pukalani, HI 96788 USA
Dist(s): **AtlasBooks Distribution.**

Castro, Shirley, *(978-0-9790307)* 10110 Oldham Ln., Bakersfield, CA 93306 USA Tel 661-374-8436
Web site: http://www.pelicanfamily.com.

Cat Marcs Publishing, *(978-0-9843899; 978-1-943786)* P.O. Box 54, Silverdale, WA 98383 USA Tel 360-271-4448
E-mail: crysmm307@aol.com; info@catmarcs.com
Web site: http://crystalmarcos.com/; http://catmarcs.com/.

Catalpa Pr., *(978-0-9745665; 978-0-9763810; 978-0-615-56579-8)* P.O. Box 27303, Oakland, CA 94602-0303 USA (SAN 256-4068)
E-mail: jack@jackschroder.com; staff@catalpapress.com
Web site: http://www.jackschroder.com; http://www.malpracticebooks.com.

Catalyst Game Labs *Imprint of* **InMediaRes Productions**

Catamount Publishing LLC, *(978-0-9752922)* P.O. Box 30015, Denver, CO 80218 USA Tel 303-839-1687 Do not confuse with Catamount Publishing LLC in Allenstown, NH.

Catapulta Pr., *(978-0-9762986)* 2242 Hemingway Dr., Suite H, Fort Myers, FL 33912 USA.

Catawba Publishing Co., *(978-1-59712)* 5945 Orr Rd. Ste. F, Charlotte, NC 28213-7314 USA
E-mail: info@catawbapublishing.com
Web site: http://www.catawbapublishing.com.

catBOX Entertainment, Inc., *(978-0-9706062)* Orders Addr.: P.O. Box 1077, Oklahoma City, OK 73101 USA Tel 405-232-1400; Edit Addr.: P.O. Box 1077, Oklahoma City, OK 73101 USA
E-mail: alohapublishing@aol.com
Web site: http://www.catdetectives.com; http://www.catboxentertainment.com.

Catch 22 Publishing Inc., *(978-0-9759691)* 1511M Sycamore Ave #198, Hercules, CA 94547 USA Tel 510-691-6695
E-mail: info@catch22publishing.com
Web site: http://www.catch22publishing.com.

Catch the Spirit of Appalachia *Imprint of* **Ammons Communications, Ltd.**

Catch-A-Winner Publishing, *(978-0-9845630)* P.O. Box 160125, San Antonio, TX 78280 USA Tel 210-387-8189
E-mail: jamestaylor22@live.com.

Catechesis of the Good Shepherd *Imprint of* **Liturgy Training Pubns.**

Cathedral of the Holy Spirit, *(978-0-917595)* Div. of Chapel Hill Harvester Church, 4650 Flat Shoals Rd., Decatur, GA 30034 USA (SAN 657-1484) Tel 404-243-5020; Fax: 404-243-5927; Toll Free: 800-241-4702.

Cathedrall Pr./Encycloware, *(978-0-9626554)* 2703 Townes Dr., Greenville, NC 27858 USA Tel 252-341-8906
E-mail: encycloware@suddenlink.net
Web site: http://www.KabalyonKey.com.

Cathie, Kyle Ltd. (GBR) *(978-1-85626) Dist. by* **IPG Chicago.**

Cathier Pr., *(978-0-9720445)* 156 Gates Rd., Lizella, GA 31052 USA.

Catholic Answers, Inc., *(978-1-888992; 978-1-933919; 978-1-938983; 978-1-941663)* 2020 Gillespie Way, El Cajon, CA 92020 USA Tel 619-387-7200; Fax: 619-387-0042; Toll Free: 888-291-8000 (orders)
E-mail: jvercillo@catholic.com; mobrien@catholic.com
Web site: http://www.catholic.com.

Catholic Authors Pr., *(978-0-9776168; 978-0-9789432)* 203 Fairfield Ave., Hartford, CT 06114 USA
E-mail: books@catholicauthors.org
Web site: http://www.catholicauthors.org.

Catholic Bk. Publishing Corp., *(978-0-89942; 978-0-9623410; 978-1-878718; 978-1-933066; 978-1-937913; 978-1-941243)* 77 West End Rd., Totowa, NJ 07512-1405 USA (SAN 204-3432) Tel 973-890-2400; Fax: 973-890-2410; Toll Free: 800-892-6657; *Imprints:* Resurrection Press (Resurrection Pr)
E-mail: resurpress@aol.com
Web site: http://www.catholicbkpub.com
Dist(s): **ACTA Pubns.**
Moshy Brothers, Inc.
Spring Arbor Distributors, Inc.

Catholic Heritage Curricula *See* **Little Way Pr.**

Catholic Heritage Curricula, *(978-0-9788376; 978-0-9824585; 978-0-9836832; 978-0-9851642; 978-0-9858343; 978-0-9883797; 978-0-9913264)* P.O. Box 579090, Modesto, CA 95357 USA
Web site: https://www.chcweb.com.

Catholic World Mission, *(978-0-9747571; 978-0-9765180; 978-1-933643)* 33 Rossotto Dr., Hamden, CT 06514 USA Tel 203-848-3323; Fax: 203-407-4823
E-mail: george.sirois@catholicworldmission.org
Web site: http://www.catholicworldmission.org.

Cats Ink, *(978-0-9763441)* P.O. Box 387, Chagrin Falls, OH 44022 USA Tel 440-247-6486
Web site: http://www.lillieandrose.com.

CatsCurious Pr., *(978-0-9790889)* 5312 Dillon Cir., Haltom City, TX 76137 USA (SAN 852-4084) Tel 210-326-8239; Toll Free Fax: 866-372-2490
E-mail: catscuriouspress@yahoo.com
Web site: http://www.catscratchbooks.com; http://www.catscuriouspress.com
Dist(s): **Follett School Solutions.**

Catskill Ctr. for Conservation & Development, Inc., *(978-0-9616712)* General Delivery, Arkville, NY 12406 USA (SAN 660-9953) Tel 914-586-2611; Fax: 914-586-3044; Rte. 28, Arkville, NY 12406 (SAN 660-9961)
E-mail: cccd@catskill.net
Web site: http://catshillcenter.org.

Catslip Arts, LLC, *(978-0-9729414)* 668 Cook St., Suite 200, Denver, CO 80206 USA Tel 303-322-9483; Fax: 303-758-6388
E-mail: books@catsliparts.com
Web site: http://www.catsliparts.com.

Catterfly Pr., *(978-0-9741074)* 122 Eagle Ridge Rd., Lake Orion, MI 48360-2612 USA Tel 248-789-2227; Fax: 248-393-2535
E-mail: frejen111@aol.com
Web site: http://www.catterflypress.com.

CattLeLogos Brand Management Systems, *(978-0-9745612)* 2522 Lombard St., Suite 300, Philadelphia, PA 19146-1025 USA Fax: 215-827-5578
E-mail: info@cattlelogos.com
Web site: http://www.cattlelogos.com.

Catto Creations, LLC, *(978-0-9702633; 978-1-938078)* 3125 Crusade Ln., Green Bay, WI 54313 USA Tel 920-494-4237; 920 494 4237
E-mail: cattocreations@gmail.com
Web site: http://www.cattocreations.com.

Caution Bks., *(978-0-9754148)* P.O. Box 2235, Newport Beach, CA 92659 USA
Web site: http://www.cautionbooks.com.

Cave Hollow Pr., *(978-0-9713497)* 304 Grover St., Warrensburg, MO 64093-2439 USA
E-mail: rmkinder@sprintmail.com
Web site: http://www.rmkinder.com.

Caveat Press, Incorporated *See* **White Cloud Pr.**

Cavendish Children's Bks. *Imprint of* **Marshall Cavendish Corp.**

Cavendish Square *See* **Cavendish Square Publishing**

Cavendish Square Publishing, *(978-0-7614; 978-1-60870; 978-1-62712; 978-1-5026)* 303 Pk. Ave. S. Suite 1247, New York, NY 10010 USA Tel 646-205-7426; *Imprints:* Exhibit A (Exhibit A)
Web site: http://www.cavendishsq.com
Dist(s): **Follett School Solutions**
MyiLibrary.

Cavizzana Press *See* **21st Century Pubs.**

†Caxton Pr., *(978-0-87004)* Div. of Caxton Printers. Ltd., 312 Main St., Caldwell, ID 83605-3299 USA (SAN 201-9698) Tel 208-459-7421; Fax: 208-459-7450; Toll Free: 800-657-6465
E-mail: publish@caxtonprinters.com; wcornell@caxtonpress.com; sgipson@caxtonpress.com
Web site: http://www.caxtonpress.com
Dist(s): **MyiLibrary**
Univ. of Nebraska Pr.; *CIP.*

Caxton Printers, Limited *See* **Caxton Pr.**

Caxton, Wm Ltd., *(978-0-940473)* P.O. Box 220, Ellison Bay, WI 54210-0220 USA (SAN 135-1303) Tel 920-854-2955.

CB Publishing & Design *Imprint of* **UBUS Communications Systems**

CBAY Bks., 4501 Forbes Blvd., Lanham, MD 20706 USA
Dist(s): **Follett School Solutions**
Independent Pubs. Group
National Bk. Network.

CBH Bks. *Imprint of* **Cambridge BrickHouse, Inc.**

CBM Publishing, *(978-0-9743988)* P.O. Box 6938, Lincoln, NE 68506 USA
E-mail: mvbettenhausen@alltel.net.

CCA & B, LLC, *(978-0-9769907; 978-0-9843651; 978-0-9887032)* Orders Addr.: 1174 Hayes Industrial Dr, Marietta, GA 30062 USA Fax: 678-990-1182; Toll Free: 877-919-4105
E-mail: sales@elfontheshelf.com; sarah@elfontheshelf.com; christa@elfontheshelf.com
Web site: http://elfontheshelf.com; http://www.ccaandb.com; http://alightinthenight.com.

CCC of America, *(978-1-56814)* P.O. Box 166349, Irving, TX 75016-6349 USA (SAN 298-7546) Toll Free: 800-935-2222
E-mail: customerservice@cccofamerica.com
Web site: http://www.cccofamerica.com
Dist(s): **Liguori Pubns.**

CCH Services, Inc., *(978-0-9768383)* 8862 Earhart Ave., Los Angeles, CA 90045 USA Tel 562-895-0682
Web site: http://www.realworldrecovery.com.

CCP Publishing & Entertainment, *(978-0-9677385; 978-0-9800655; 978-0-9801265)* 9602 Glenwood Rd. No. 362, Brooklyn, NY 11236 USA
E-mail: info@cccowan.com
Web site: http://www.cccowan.com; http://www.isaiahbooksworldwide.com; http://www.acuriousmindbooks.com; http://www.ccppublishing.com; http://www.amandaadventures.com.

CCRiddles, *(978-0-9785118; 978-0-9819833; 978-1-941747)* 878 Laramie Ct., Newbury Park, CA 91320 USA Tel 805-338-4170; Fax: 805-498-2901
E-mail: ccriddles@gmail.com
Web site: http://www.ccriddles.com.

CD Publishing, *(978-0-9859042)* 38041 Manzanita St., Newark, CA 94560 USA Tel 510-709-7459
E-mail: caseydevargas@yahoo.com.

CDS Books *See* **Vanguard Pr.**

CE Bilingual Bks. LLC, *(978-0-9801305)* P.O. Box 31848, Philadelphia, PA 19104-1848 USA (SAN 855-2819) Fax: 215-352-0409; 28 Eight St., Hicksville, NY 11801
E-mail: cebilingualbooks@gmail.com
Web site: http://www.cebilingualbooks.com
Dist(s): **Follett School Solutions.**

Cebrano Publishing, *(978-0-9761366)* P.O. Box 27236, Barrigada, GU 96921 USA
E-mail: billyb1937@yahoo.com.

Cedar Bay Pr., L.L.C., *(978-1-57555)* P.O. Box 230084, Portland, OR 97281-0084 USA (SAN 298-6361)
E-mail: cedarbay@hotmail.com.

Cedar Creek Publishing, *(978-0-9790205; 978-0-9842449; 978-0-9839192; 978-0-9891465; 978-1-942882)* P.O. Box 115, Bremo Bluff, VA 23022 USA (SAN 857-1368) Tel 434-842-6203
E-mail: cedarcreekbooks@aol.com
Web site: http://www.cedarcreekauthors.com
Dist(s): **BCH Fulfillment & Distribution.**

Cedar Creek Publishing Service, *(978-0-9659419)* P.O. Box 115, Bremo Bluff, VA 23022 USA Tel 434-842-6203 Do not confuse with companies with same or similar names in Hayward, CA, Anderson, IN, Indianapolis, IN
E-mail: cedarcreekbooks@aol.com.

Cedar Crest Bks., *(978-0-910291)* 17 Lookout Ave., Natick, MA 01760 USA (SAN 241-2837) Tel 508-653-8839
E-mail: davidrottenberg@yahoo.com; publisher@cedarcrestbooks.com
Web site: http://www.cedarcrestbooks.com
Dist(s): **Follett School Solutions.**

Cedar Fort, Inc. *Imprint of* **Cedar Fort, Inc./CFI Distribution**

Cedar Fort, Inc./CFI Distribution, *(978-0-88290; 978-0-934126; 978-1-55517; 978-1-59955; 978-1-4621)* 2373 West 700 South, Springville, UT 84663 USA (SAN 170-2858) Tel 801-489-4084; Fax: 801-489-1097; Toll Free: 800-759-2665; *Imprints*: Bonneville Books (Bonneville Bks); Horizon Publishers (HorPubs); Cedar Fort, Incorporated (Cedar Fort); Sweetwater Books (Sweetwater Bks)
E-mail: skybook@cedarfort.com
Web site: http://www.cedarfort.com
Dist(s): **Follett School Solutions**
Todd Communications.

Cedar Grove Bks., *(978-0-9740212; 978-0-9835077; 978-1-941958)* 2215 High Point Dirve, Carrolton, TX 75007 USA (SAN 255-3732) Tel 415-364-8292; Fax: 415-276-9858; *Imprints*: Sapling Books (SaplingBks)
E-mail: queries@cedargrovebooks.com
Web site: http://www.cedargrovebooks.com.

Cedar Hse. Pubs., *(978-0-9676289)* Orders Addr.: P.O. Box 399, Monroe, VA 24574 USA Tel 434-929-8002 (phone/fax); Fax: 434-929-1059; Edit Addr.: 407 Eastview Dr., Madison Heights, VA 24572 USA
E-mail: info@cedarhousepublishers.com
Web site: http://www.cedarhousepublishers.com
Dist(s): **Send The Light Distribution LLC.**

Cedar Shamrock Publishing, *(978-0-9760680)* P.O. Box 70775, Madison, WI 53707 USA
Web site: http://www.wyattwalker.com
Dist(s): **Partners Bk. Distributing, Inc.**

Cedar Tree Bks., *(978-0-9657328; 978-1-892142)* P.O. Box 4256, Wilmington, DE 19807-0256 USA
E-mail: books@ctpress.com
Web site: http://www.cedartreebooks.com.

Cedar Tree Publishing, *(978-0-9658075)* 201 Matilda St NE Ste. B, Grand Rapids, MI 49503-1593 USA Do not confuse with Cedar Tree Publishing, Cedaredge, CO
E-mail: georan@tapshoe.com
Web site: http://www.cedartreepublishing.com; www.johnnietuitel.com
Dist(s): **Austin & Company, Inc.**

Cedar Valley Publishing, *(978-0-615-12024-9)* P.O. Box 621, Jesup, IA 50648 USA Do not confuse with Cedar Valley Publishing in Cascade, WI.

Cedar Valley Publishing, *(978-1-933476)* N6854 Cedar Valley Rd., Fredonia, WI 53021 USA Tel 920-994-9906; Fax: 262-376-2991 Attn: Tracey Jackson Do not confuse with Cedar Valley Publishing in Cascade, WI, Jesup, IA
E-mail: stacey@cedarvalleypublishing.com
Web site: http://www.cedarvalleypublishing.com
Dist(s): **Follett School Solutions.**

Cedartip Co., The, *(978-0-9771844)* Orders Addr.: P.O. Box 231, Manhattan, KS 66505-0231 USA; Edit Addr.: 3004 Pawnee Cir., Manhattan, KS 66502-1973 USA
E-mail: orders@cedartip.com
Web site: http://www.cedartip.com.

Celebra *Imprint of* **Penguin Publishing Group**

Celebration Pr., Orders Addr.: 135 South Mount Zion Rd. P.O. Box 2500, Lebanon, IN 46052 USA Toll Free Fax: 800-393-3156; Toll Free: 800-526-9907; *Imprints*: Good Year Books (GYB) Do not confuse with Celebration Press in Onalaska WI, Denver CO
Web site: http://www.aw-bc.com; http://www.pearsonlearning.com/rightsPerm.rtf.

Celeste Ediciones, S.A. (ESP) *(978-84-8211; 978-84-87553)* *Dist. by* **Lectorum Pubns.**

Celestial Arts *Imprint of* **Ten Speed Pr.**

Celestine Pr., *(978-0-9749382; 978-0-578-08538-8)* 25 Ashland St., Rochester, NY 14620 USA (SAN 255-9927)
E-mail: hellerest@earthlink.net
Web site: http://www.celestinepress.com
Dist(s): **Lulu Enterprises Inc.**

Cellar Door Publishing, *(978-0-9766831)* 3439 NE Sandy Blvd, Suite 309, Portland, OR 97232 USA
Web site: http://www.cellardoorpublishing.com.

Celltrition, *(978-0-9746378)* 13472 Vidalia Rd., Pass Christian, MS 39571 USA Tel 228-586-2455.

Cellular Publishing, *(978-1-886358)* Div. of Lakeshore Business Services, P.O. Box 119, Sedona, AZ 86339-0119 USA Tel 520-300-7711; Fax: 413-825-8356.

Celo Valley Bks., *(978-0-923687)* 160 Ohle Rd., Burnsville, NC 28714 USA (SAN 251-7973) Tel 828-675-5918
E-mail: diatoday@msn.com.

Celstumo Publishing, *(978-0-9761041)* A Subs. of Celebration Studios of Missouri, Orders Addr.: P.O. Box 201, Glencoe, MO 63038 USA Tel 636-458-1819 (phone/fax)
E-mail: celstumo@celstumo.com
Web site: http://www.celstumo.com.

Celtic Cat Publishing, *(978-0-9658950; 978-0-9819238; 978-0-9847836; 978-0-9891380; 978-0-9905945)* Orders Addr.: 2654 Wild Fern Ln., Knoxville, TN 37931 USA Tel 865-250-9964
E-mail: celtic01@comcast.net
Web site: http://www.celticcatpublishing.net.

Celtic Cross Communications, *(978-0-9740981; 978-0-9887271)* 5114 Canyon Oaks Dr., Brighton, MI 48114 USA
Web site: http://www.celticcrosscommunications.com
Dist(s): **Send The Light Distribution LLC.**

Celtic Marketing Inc., *(978-0-9777135)* 6311 W. Gross Point Rd., Niles, IL 60714-3919 USA (SAN 853-0688)
E-mail: info@projectplaybooks.com
Web site: www.projectplaybooks.com.

Celtic Sunrise, *(978-0-9840893)* P.O. Box 174, New Ringgold, PA 17960 USA (SAN 858-3900) Fax: 570-943-2102
Web site: http://www.celticsunrise.com
Dist(s): **AtlasBooks Distribution.**

CEM Ventures, Ltd., *(978-0-9760072)* P.O. Box 1713, Harwich, MA 02645 USA Tel 508-896-4988; Fax: 508-896-2586; Toll Free: 866-246 — 7800; 112 Griffith's Pond Rd., Brewster, MA 02631
E-mail: cemventures@yahoo.com
Web site: http://www.jaysonthebluejay.com.

†Cengage Gale, *(978-0-13; 978-0-7876; 978-0-8103; 978-0-936474; 978-1-57302; 978-1-878623; 978-1-59413; 978-1-59414; 978-1-59415; 978-1-4144; 978-1-4205; 978-1-59722; 978-1-4328)* Subs. of Cengage Learning, Orders Addr.: P.O. Box 9187, Farmington Hills, MI 48333-9187 USA Toll Free Fax: 800 414 5043; Toll Free: 800 877 4253; Edit Addr.: 27500 Drake Rd., Farmington Hills, MI 48331-3535 USA (SAN 213-4373) Tel 248 699 4253; a/o Wheeler Publishing, 295 Kennedy Memorial Dr., Waterville, ME 04901 Toll Free: 800 223 1244; *Imprints*: UXL (UXL); Macmillan Reference USA (Macmillan Ref); Charles Scribner's Sons (C Scribners Sons); Kidhaven (Kidhaven); Blackbirch Press, Incorporated (Blackbirch Pr); Lucent Books (Lucent Books); Greenhaven Press, Incorporated (Greenhaven Pr); Five Star (Five Star ME); Wheeler Publishing, Incorporated (Wheel); Walker Large Print (Walker Large Pt); Five Star Trade (Five Star Trade); Kennebec Large Print (Kennebec Lrg)
E-mail: gale.salesassistance@thomson.com
Web site: http://www.gale.com
Dist(s): **Follett School Solutions**
Send The Light Distribution LLC
Smashwords
Thorndike Pr.; *CIP.*

†Cengage Heinle, *(978-0-8384; 978-0-88377; 978-0-912066; 978-1-4130)* Div. of Cengage Learning, Orders Addr.: 10650 Toebben Dr., Independence, KY 41051 USA Toll Free Fax: 800 487 8488
E-mail: reply@heinle.com
Web site: http://www.heinle.com
Dist(s): **CENGAGE Learning**; *CIP.*

Cengage Learning (GBR) *(978-0-15; 978-1-86152; 978-1-84480; 978-1-4080)* *Dist. by* **CENGAGE Learn.**

Cengage Learning *Imprint of* **CENGAGE Learning**

CENGAGE Learning, Orders Addr.: 10650 Toebben Dr., Independence, KY 41051 USA (SAN 200-2213) Tel 859-525-6620; Fax: 859-525-0978; Toll Free Fax: 800-487-8488; Toll Free: 800-354-9706; *Imprints*: Cengage Learning (CengLearning)
Web site: http://www.cengage.com/
Dist(s): **Delmar Cengage Learning**
Follett School Solutions
OptumInsight, Inc.

Cengage Learning Australia (AUS) *(978-0-17; 978-0-646-20862-6; 978-0-646-20863-3; 978-0-646-22565-4; 978-0-646-22598-2; 978-0-646-24330-6; 978-0-646-26850-7; 978-0-646-26853-8; 978-0-646-26854-5; 978-0-646-26855-2; 978-0-646-47716-9)* *Dist. by* **Cheng Tsui.**

CENGAGE Learning Custom Publishing, *(978-0-87393; 978-0-931920; 978-0-7593; 978-1-4266; 978-1-4390; 978-1-111; 978-1-133; 978-1-285; 978-1-305; 978-1-337)* 5191 Natrop Blvd., Mason, OH 45040 USA Toll Free: 800-543-0487
E-mail: debbie.stowell@cengage.com
Web site: http://www.thomsoncustom.com
Dist(s): **CENGAGE Learning**
Follett School Solutions.

†Cengage South-Western, *(978-0-03; 978-0-324; 978-0-538)* Div. of Cengage Learning, 5191 Natorp Blvd., Mason, OH 45040 USA (SAN 202-7518) Tel 513 229 1000; Toll Free Fax: 800-437-8488; Toll Free: 800-354-9706 (orders only); 800-543-0487
Web site: http://www.thomsonedu.com/
Dist(s): **CENGAGE Learning**
International Thomson Computer Pr.; *CIP.*

Cenozoic Pr., *(978-0-615-38180-0; 978-0-615-52278-4)* 354 Via La Canada No. 7, Orange, CA 92869 USA Tel 714-928-6648
E-mail: arajic@gmail.com.

Ctr. for American Places, Inc., *(978-1-930066; 978-1-935195)* 600 S. Michigan Ave., Chicago, IL 60605 USA Tel 312-344-6943; Fax: 312-344-8070
E-mail: CAPwest@att.net
Web site: http://www.americanplaces.org
Dist(s): **Chicago Distribution Ctr.**
Univ. of Chicago Pr.
Univ. Pr. of Mississippi
Univ. Pr. of Virginia
Univ. of Georgia Pr.

Ctr. for Appalachian Trail Studies, *(978-0-9636342; 978-0-9707916)* Orders Addr.: 17 S. Meadow Dr., Sudbury, MA 01776 USA Tel 781-752-6100 (phone/fax)
E-mail: orders@trailplace.com
Web site: http://trailplace.com/orders.html.

Center for Applications of Psychological Type, Inc., *(978-0-935652)* 2815 NW 13th St., Suite 401, Gainesville, FL 32609 USA (SAN 213-9162) Tel 352-375-0160; Fax: 352-378-0503; Toll Free: 800-777-2278
E-mail: naima@capt.org
Web site: http://www.capt.org.

Center for Applied Psychology, Incorporated *See* **Childswork/Childsplay**

Ctr. for Basque Studies, *(978-1-877802; 978-1-935709)* 1664 N. Virginia St., MS 2322, Reno, NV 89557-2322 USA Tel 775-784-4854; Fax: 775-784-1355
E-mail: basque@unr.edu
Web site: http://basquebooks.myshopify.com/
Dist(s): **University of Nevada Pr.**

Ctr. For Cultural Leadership, *(978-0-9745948)* P.O. Box 70, La Grange, CA 95239 USA
Web site: http://www.christianculture.com.

Center for Economic Research & Social Change *See* **Haymarket Bks.**

Ctr. for Educational Policy Research, *(978-0-9729538)* 720 E. 13th Ave., Suite 201, Eugene, OR 97401 USA Tel 541-346-6153; Fax: 541-346-6154; Toll Free: 877-766-2279
E-mail: Terri_Heath@s4s.org
Web site: http://www.s4s.org.

Center for Learning, The, *(978-1-56077)* Orders Addr.: 590 E. Western Reserve Rd. Unit 10-h, Youngstown, OH 44514 USA Tel 800-767-9090; Toll Free Fax: 888-767-8080; Toll Free: 800-767-9090 (ordering); Edit Addr.: 29313 Clemens Rd. Ste. 2E, Westlake, OH 44145-1052 USA (SAN 248-2029)
E-mail: ahollis@centerforlearning.org
Web site: http://www.centerforlearning.org.

Center for Loss & Life Transition *See* **Companion Pr.**

Center for Self-Actualization, Incorporated, The, *(978-0-9758799; 978-0-9788389; 978-0-9823847; 978-0-615-38102-2; 978-0-9846266; 978-0-9851608)* P.O. Box 98466, Atlanta, GA 30359-2166 USA Tel 770-623-4133; Fax: 770-623-3853
E-mail: centerforself@yahoo.com
Web site: http://www.selfactualized.org.

Ctr. for the Affirmation of Responsible Education, *(978-0-9740071)* 496 Gold Ct., San Andreas, CA 95249 USA Tel 209-754-9218
E-mail: jnorton2@earthlink.net.

Center for the Collaborative Classroom, *(978-1-57621; 978-1-885603; 978-1-59892; 978-1-61003; 978-1-68246)* 1250 53 rd St., Ste. 3, Emeryville, CA 94608 USA Tel 510-533-0213; Fax: 510-464-3670; Toll Free: 800-666-7270
E-mail: pubs@devstu.org; brandon_holroyd@devstu.org; bholroyd@collaborativeclassroom.org
Web site: http://www.devstu.org; http://www.collaborativeclassroom.org
Dist(s): **Booksource, The.**

Ctr. for Victims of Torture, The, *(978-0-9759789)* 717 E. River Rd., Minneapolis, MN 55455 USA Tel 612-436-4800.

Ctr. for Western Studies, *(978-0-931170)* Div. of Augustana College, Orders Addr.: Augustana College 2001 S. Summit Ave., Sioux Falls, SD 57197 USA (SAN 211-4844) Tel 605-274-4007; Fax: 605-274-4999
E-mail: harry.thompson@augie.edu; cws@augie.edu
Web site: http://augie.edu/cws
Dist(s): **Dakota West Bks.**

Center For Youth Issues, Incorporated *See* **National Ctr. For Youth Issues**

Ctr. of SW Studies, Fort Lewis College, *(978-0-9727664)* 1000 Rim Dr., Durango, CO 81301 USA
E-mail: gulliford_a@fortlewis.edu
Web site: http://www.swcenter.fortlewis.edu.

Ctr. Stage Puppets, *(978-0-9795087)* P.O. Box 8279, Bend, OR 97708 USA Tel 541-420-7943
E-mail: info@centerstagepuppets.com
Web site: http://www.centerstagepuppets.com.

Centering Corp., *(978-1-56123)* P.O. Box 4600, Omaha, NE 68104-0600 USA (SAN 298-1815) Tel 402-553-1200; Fax: 402-553-0507
E-mail: j1200@aol.com
Web site: http://www.centering.org
Dist(s): **Follett School Solutions.**

CenterLine Media, *(978-0-9754212; 978-0-9814896)* 115 Greenwood Ave., Ambler, PA 19002-5709 USA Tel 215-646-4591; Fax: 215-933-6819
E-mail: info@centerlinemedia.com
Web site: http://www.centerlinemedia.com.

Centerpunch Pr., *(978-0-9724882)* P.O. Box 43151, Cincinnati, OH 45243 USA Tel 513-561-3392 (phone/fax)
E-mail: info@centerpunchpress.com
Web site: http://www.centerpunchpress.com.

Centerstream Publishing, *(978-0-931759; 978-1-57424)* Orders Addr.: P.O. Box 17878, Anaheim Hills, CA 92817 USA (SAN 683-8022) Tel 714-779-9390 (phone/fax)
E-mail: centerstrm@aol.com
Web site: http://www.pma-online.org
Dist(s): **Booklines Hawaii, Ltd.**
Leonard, Hal Corp.
MyiLibrary.

Central Ave. Pr, *(978-0-9715344; 978-0-9798452)* 8400 Menaul Blvd. NE, Suite A No. 211, Albuquerque, NM 87112 USA
E-mail: oelfkej@aol.com
Web site: http://www.centralavepress.com
Dist(s): **AtlasBooks Distribution**
Quality Bks., Inc.

Central Coast Books *See* **Central Coast Pr.**

Central Coast Pr., *(978-0-9658776; 978-1-930401)* Orders Addr.: P.O. Box 3654, San Luis Obispo, CA 93403 USA (SAN 631-1547) Tel 805-534-0307 (phone/fax); Edit Addr.: 1181 17th St., Los Osos, CA 94302 USA (SAN 631-1539)
E-mail: ccbooks@surfari.net.

Central Conference of American Rabbis/CCAR Pr., *(978-0-88123; 978-0-916694)* 355 Lexington Ave., 18th Flr., New York, NY 10017-6603 USA (SAN 204-3262) Tel 212-972-3636; Fax: 212-692-0819; Toll Free: 800-935-2227
E-mail: ccarpress@ccarnet.org; info@ccarnet.org
Web site: http://ccarpress.org.

Central Orb Publishing, *(978-0-9818818)* P.O. Box 830, Orem, UT 84059-0830 USA
E-mail: Thesoulalliance@Hotmail.com
Web site: http://www.createspace.com/3347335; http://www.lulu.com/thesoulalliance; http://www.createspace.com/3351702.

Central Park Media Corp., *(978-1-56219; 978-1-57800; 978-1-887692; 978-1-58664)* 250 W. 57th St. Ste. 1723, New York, NY 10107-1708 USA (SAN 631-3191) Toll Free: 800-833-7456; *Imprints*: CPM Manga (CPM Manga); CPM Comics (CPM Comics); Manga 18 (Manga Eighteen); CPM Manhwa (CPM Manhwa)
E-mail: info@teamcpm.com
Web site: http://www.centralparkmedia.com/; http://www.cpmpress.com/
Dist(s): **Hobbies Hawaii Distributors.**

Central Recovery Pr., *(978-0-9799869; 978-0-9818482; 978-1-936290; 978-1-937612; 978-1-942094)* 3321 N. Buffalo Dr. Suite 275, Las Vegas, NV 89129 USA (SAN 854-9532) Tel 702-868-5830; Fax: 702-868-5831; 387 Pk. Ave. S., New York, NY 10016
E-mail: nschenck@centralrecovery.com; vkilleen@centralrecovery.com
Web site: http://www.centralrecoverypress.com
Dist(s): **Consortium Bk. Sales & Distribution**
Follett School Solutions
Health Communications, Inc.
MyiLibrary
Perseus Bks. Group.

Centro Bks., LLC, *(978-1-933572)* 3636 Fieldston Rd. Apt. 6P, Bronx, NY 10463-2041 USA (SAN 256-7229)
Web site: http://www.centrobooks.com.

Centro de Informacion y Desarrollo de la Comunicacion y la Literatura (MEX) *(978-968-494)* *Dist. by* **Continental Bk.**

Centro de Informacion y Desarrollo de la Comunicacion y la Literatura (MEX) *(978-968-494)* *Dist. by* **Mariuccia Iaconi Bk Imports.**

Centro de Informacion y Desarrollo de la Comunicacion y la Literatura (MEX) *(978-968-494)* *Dist. by* **AIMS Intl.**

Centro de Informacion y Desarrollo de la Comunicacion y la Literatura (MEX) *(978-968-494)* *Dist. by* **Lectorum Pubns.**

Centurion Pr., *(978-0-9800805)* 740 Breeze Hill Rd., #171, Vista, CA 92081 USA Fax: 760-631-3607
E-mail: fedthought@gmail.com
Web site: http://www.centurionpress.com.

Cepia LLC., *(978-0-9777241)* 121 Hunter Ave., Suite 103, Saint Louis, MO 63124 USA Tel 314-725-4900; Fax: 314-725-4919
E-mail: support@cepiallc.com
Web site: http://www.cepiallc.com.

Cerebellum Corp., *(978-1-58198; 978-1-886156; 978-1-59626; 978-1-61867)* 1661 Tennessee St., Suite 3D, San Francisco, CA 94107 USA (SAN 299-240X) Tel 415-541-9901; Fax: 805-426-8136; Toll Free: 800-238-9669
E-mail: customerservice@cerebellum.com; cerebell@mindspring.com
Web site: http://www.cerebellum.com; http://www.standarddeviants.com
Dist(s): **Follett School Solutions.**

Cerebral Press International, *(978-0-916309)* HC-71 Box 121-1, Thornfield, MO 65762 USA (SAN 295-9461) Tel 417-679-4748
E-mail: lagunapress@braintypes.com
Web site: http://www.braintypes.com.

Ceres Pr., *(978-0-9606138; 978-1-886101)* P.O. Box 87, Woodstock, NY 12498 USA (SAN 217-0949) Tel 845-679-5573; Toll Free: 888-804-8848 Do not confuse with Ceres Pr., Stamford, CT
E-mail: cem620@aol.com
Web site: http://www.heathyhighways.com
Dist(s): **Integral Yoga Pubns.**
New Leaf Distributing Co., Inc.
Nutri-Bks. Corp.
Partners Bk. Distributing, Inc.

Ceres Software, Incorporated *See* **Inspiration Software, Inc.**

Certified Firearms Instructors, LLC, *(978-0-9741480)* P.O. Box 131254, Saint Paul, MN 55113-1254 USA Tel 952-935-2414; Fax: 952-935-4122
E-mail: jolson@gw.hamline.edu
Web site: http://www.aacfi.com.

CET *Imprint of* **Greater Cincinnati TV Educational Foundation**

C E V Multimedia, Ltd., *(978-1-57078; 978-1-59535; 978-1-60333; 978-1-61459)* Orders Addr.: P.O. Box 65265, Lubbock, TX 79464 USA Tel 806-745-8820; Fax: 806-745-5300; Toll Free Fax: 800-243-6398; Toll Free: 800-922-9965; Edit Addr.: 1020 SE Loop 289, Lubbock, TX 79404 USA
E-mail: cev@cevmultimedia.com
Web site: http://www.cevmultimedia.com
Dist(s): **Follett School Solutions.**

CFM, *(978-0-9728620; 978-0-9769071; 978-0-9908661)* 112 Greene St., New York City, NY 10012 USA Tel 212-966-3864; Fax: 212-226-1041
E-mail: info@cfmgallery.com
Web site: http://www.cfmgallery.com.

CG Star, L.L.C. *See* **C-It Entertainment Group, LLC**

C.G.S. Pr., *(978-0-9660726)* P.O. Box 1394, Mountainside, NJ 07092 USA Tel 908-233-8293 (phone/fax)
E-mail: Gwynnic2000@aol.com.

Chacmool Pr., *(978-0-9789391)* 849 W. University Pkwy., Baltimore, MD 21210 USA
E-mail: publisher@chacmoolpress.com
Web site: http://www.chacmoolpress.com.

Chafie Pr., LLC, *(978-0-9833190; 978-0-9903532)* 7557 Rambler Rd. Suite 626, Dallas, TX 75231 USA Tel 214-628-8600
E-mail: trish.jones@chafiehds.com
Web site: http://www.chafiepress.com
Dist(s): **Follett School Solutions**
Pathway Bk. Service.

Chagrin River Publishing Co., *(978-1-929821; 978-0-615-32246-9)* Orders Addr.: P.O. Box 173, Chagrin Falls, OH 44022 USA Tel 440-893-9250; Edit Addr.: 21 E. Summit St., Chargrin Falls, OH 44022 USA
Dist(s): **Follett School Solutions.**

Chai Yo Maui Pr., *(978-0-615-31840-0; 978-0-9855804)* P.O. Box 331, Kihei, HI 96753 USA.

Chaklet Coffee Bks *Imprint of* **Candalyse Publishing**

Chamberlain Hart Enterprises, Inc., *(978-0-9749756)* P.O. Box 1600, Fairfield, IA 52556 USA Tel 641-469-3717; Fax: 641-469-6647
E-mail: che@iowatelecom.net
Web site: http://www.chamberlainhart.com.

Chambers Kingfisher Graham Publishers, Incorporated *See* **Larousse Kingfisher Chambers, Inc.**

Chameleon Designs, *(978-0-9701573)* P.O. Box 61855, North Charleston, SC 29419 USA Tel 843-761-7426
E-mail: yeleth@aol.com.

Chamike Pubs., *(978-1-884876)* 9000 Doris Dr., Fort Washington, MD 20744 USA Tel 301-248-4034.

Champion Athlete Publishing Company *See* **National Assn. of Speed & Explosion**

Championship Chess, *(978-0-9729456; 978-0-9772489)* Div. of Teachable Tech, Inc., Orders Addr.: 3565 Evans Rd., Atlanta, GA 30340 USA Toll Free: 888-328-7373
E-mail: dj@championshipchess.net
Web site: http://www.championshipchess.net.

Champlain Avenue Bks., Inc., *(978-0-9855008; 978-0-9896347; 978-0-9908256; 978-1-943063)* 2360 Corporate Cir. Suite 400, Henderson, NV 89074-7722 USA Tel 760-684-5861
E-mail: champlainavenuebooks@hotmail.com
Web site: champlainavenuebooks@hotmail.com
Dist(s): **Smashwords.**

Chan, David, *(978-0-9754302)* 12511 Fox Trace Ln., Houston, TX 77066-4029 USA Tel 281-580-7042
E-mail: david@chancomputerhelp.com.

Chanda Hahn, *(978-0-615-81223-6; 978-0-9961048; 978-0-692-31352-7; 978-0-692-43262-4)* 13135 SW Morningstar Dr., Tigard, OR 97223 USA Tel 708-334-2816
Dist(s): **CreateSpace Independent Publishing Platform.**

Chandler Hse. Pr., *(978-0-9636277; 978-1-886284)* P.O. Box 20126, Worcester, MA 01602 USA Fax: 508-753-7419
E-mail: chandlerhousepress@yahoo.com
Web site: http://www.chandlerhousebooks.com
Dist(s): **Follett School Solutions.**

Chandler/White Publishing Co., *(978-1-877804)* 517 W. Midvale Ave., Philadelphia, PA 19144-4617 USA
Dist(s): **Alliance Hse., Inc.**

Change Is Strange, Inc., *(978-0-9755902)* 3630 21st St., Boulder, CO 80304-1608 USA
E-mail: info@changeisstrange.com
Web site: http://www.changeisstrange.com
Dist(s): **Follett School Solutions.**

Change the Universe Pr., *(978-0-615-21144-2)* 9607 Bolton Rd., Los Angeles, CA 90034 USA Tel 310-963-8644
E-mail: yasgur@jclla.org; jlipner@irell.com
Web site: http://www.maxsaidyes.com.

Changing Lives Changing The World, Incorporated *See* **Changing Lives Publishing**

Changing Lives Publishing, *(978-0-9653700; 978-0-9774513; 978-0-9798553)* Div. of Changing Lives Changing The World, Inc., P.O. Box 132, Sharpes, FL 32959 USA Tel 321-637-1128; Toll Free: 866-578-1900
E-mail: print2publish@gmail.com
Web site: http://www.print2publish.com.

Changing-Times.net, *(978-0-9741930)* Orders Addr.: P.O. Box 39651, Phoenix, AZ 85069-9651 USA
Web site: http://www.changing-times.net.

Channel Kids *Imprint of* **Channel Photographics**

Channel Photographics, *(978-0-9744029; 978-0-9766708; 978-0-9773399; 978-0-9819942; 978-0-9826137; 978-0-9832983)* 980 Lincoln Ave Ste 200B, San Rafael, CA 94901 USA; *Imprints:* Channel Kids (ChannKids)
E-mail: adrianne@globalpsd.com; steven@globalpsd.com
Web site: http://www.channelphotographics.com
Dist(s): **Perseus-PGW**
SCB Distributors.

Channel Publishing, Ltd., *(978-0-945501; 978-1-933053)* 4750 Longley Ln., Suite 110, Reno, NV 89502 USA (SAN 247-1256) Tel 775-825-0880; Fax: 775-825-5633; Toll Free: 800-248-2882
E-mail: info@channelpublishing.com
Web site: http://www.channelpublishing.com.

Chantilly Books, *(978-0-9841960)* Div. of Boone Amie Publishing, Orders Addr.: 14240-A Sullyfield Cir., Chantilly, VA 20151 USA (SAN 858-6853) Fax: 703-830-7100
E-mail: sue@a-childs-book.com
Web site: http://www.a-childs-book.com.

Chapel Hill Press, Inc., *(978-1-880849; 978-1-59715)* 1829 E. Franklin St., Bldg. 700a, Chapel Hill, NC 27514-5863 USA Tel 919-942-8389; Fax: 919-869-2066
E-mail: publisher@chapelhillpress.com; dennis.mcgill@chapelhillpress.com; luz@chapelhillpress.com; edwina.woodbury@chapelhillpress.com
Web site: http://www.chapelhillpress.com
Dist(s): **Follett School Solutions.**

Chapelle *Imprint of* **Sterling Publishing Co., Inc.**

Chapin Hse. Bks. *Imprint of* **Florida Historical Society**

Chapman, Chris & Eric P. Hvolboll, *(978-0-9765061)* 2741 Cuerta Rd., Santa Barbara, CA 93105 USA Tel 805-882-9897.

Chapman Pr., LLC, *(978-0-9725420)* 949 S. Josephine St., Denver, CO 80209 USA
E-mail: taylor@babsonfarms.com; taylor@babsonfarms.com
Web site: http://www.chapmanpress.com.

Chapter & Verse Pr., *(978-0-9724549)* 7350 Detrick Jordan Pike, Springfield, OH 45502-9660 USA Tel 937-964-0294
E-mail: nashvila@bright.net.

Chapter Bks. *Imprint of* **Spotlight**

Chapter Readers *Imprint of* **Picture Window Bks.**

Character Arts, *(978-0-9772259)* 37 Pond Rd., Bldg. 2, Wilton, CT 06897 USA Tel 203-834-0323.

Character Development Group, Inc., *(978-0-9653163; 978-1-892056)* Div. of Character Development Group, Inc., Orders Addr.: P.O. Box 35136, Greensboro, NC 27425-5136 USA Tel 336-668-9373; Fax: 336-668-9375; Edit Addr.: 8646 W. Market St. Suite 102, Greensboro, NC 27409 USA
E-mail: info@charactereducation.com
Web site: http://www.charactereducation.com
Dist(s): **Follett School Solutions.**

Character Development Publishing *See* **Character Development Group, Inc**

Character Publishing, *(978-0-9839355; 978-0-9890797; 978-1-940684)* Orders Addr.: P.O. Box 322, Pass Christian, MS 39571 USA (SAN 920-7929) Tel 228-452-2883
E-mail: mssoundpub@gmail.com
Web site: www.characterpublishing.org.

Character-in-Action *Imprint of* **Quiet Impact, Inc.**

CharFaye Publishing, Incorporated *See* **FayeHouse. Pr. International**

Charisma Hse. *Imprint of* **Charisma Media**

Charisma Kids *Imprint of* **Charisma Media**

Charisma Media, *(978-0-88419; 978-0-930525; 978-1-59185; 978-1-59979; 978-1-61638; 978-1-62136; 978-1-62998; 978-1-62999)* Div. of Creation House Pr., 600 Rinehart Rd., Lake Mary, FL 32746 USA (SAN 677-5640) Tel 407-333-0600; Fax: 407-333-7100; Toll Free: 800-283-8494; *Imprints:* Charisma House (Charisma Hse); Casa Creacion (Casa Cre); Creation House (CreatHse); Siloam Press (Siloam Pr); Charisma Kids (Charisma Kids); Realms (Realms); Frontline (Frontline FLA)
Web site: http://www.charismamedia.com/
Dist(s): **Dake Publishing**
Follett School Solutions
INscribe Digital
Lulu Enterprises Inc.
SPD-Small Pr. Distribution
Send The Light Distribution LLC.

Charles Reasoners Little Cuddles *Imprint of* **Picture Window Bks.**

Charles River Media, *(978-1-886801; 978-1-58450)* Orders Addr.: P.O. Box 960, Herndon, VA 20172 USA (SAN 254-1564) Fax: 703-996-1010; Toll Free: 800-382-8505; Edit Addr.: 25 Thomson Pl., Boston, MA 02210-1202 USA
E-mail: info@charlesriver.com
Web site: http://www.charlesriver.com
Dist(s): **CENGAGE Learning**
Delmar Cengage Learning
ebrary, Inc.

Charles River Pr., *(978-0-9754913; 978-0-9791304; 978-0-9793844; 978-0-9820946; 978-1-936185; 978-1-940676)* 37 Evergreen Rd., Norton, MA 02766 USA Fax: 508-297-3628; P.O. Box 1122, Mansfield, MA 02048 (SAN 256-2251); *Imprints:* Gap Tooth Publishing (Gap Tooth Pubng) Do not confuse with Charles River Pr. in Alexandria, VA
E-mail: jwomack@charlesriverpress.com; customerservice@charlesriverpress.com
Web site: http://www.charlesriverpress.com.

Charles Scribner's Sons *Imprint of* **Cengage Gale**

Charlesbridge Publishing, Inc., *(978-0-88106; 978-0-935508; 978-1-57091; 978-1-58089; 978-1-879085; 978-1-60734; 978-0-9822939; 978-0-9823064; 978-1-936140; 978-1-63289)* Orders Addr.: 85 Main St., Watertown, MA 02472 USA (SAN 240-5474) Tel 617-926-0329; Fax: 617-926-5720; Toll Free Fax: 800-926-5775; Toll Free: 800-225-3214; *Imprints:* Yarrow, Peter Books (PeteYarrow); Mackinac Island Press, Incorporated (Mackinac); Imagine Publishing (ImaginePub)
E-mail: orders@charlesbridge.com
Web site: http://www.charlesbridge.com
Dist(s): **BookMasters Distribution Services (BDS)**
Continental Bk. Co., Inc.
Follett School Solutions
Lectorum Pubns., Inc.
MyiLibrary
Penguin Random Hse., LLC.
Random Hse., Inc.

Charlie & Albert, *(978-0-9801329)* 2920 Applewood Ct., Suite 192, Atlanta, GA 30345-1401 USA Tel 770-938-8863.

Charlie's Gift, *(978-0-9786795)* 920 York Rd., Suite 350, Hinsdale, IL 60521 USA Tel 630-399-8164.

Charming Pubns., *(978-0-9773531)* Orders Addr.: P.O. Box 90792, Austin, TX 78709-0792 USA Tel 512-288-4803
E-mail: minia.lopez@gmail.com
Web site: http://www.happychildrenbooks.com.

Chartwell *Imprint of* **Book Sales, Inc.**

Charwood Pubns., *(978-0-615-58076-0; 978-0-615-66672-3; 978-0-9910347)* Orders Addr.: P.O. Box 14881, Long Beach, CA 90853 USA Tel 928-274-2687
E-mail: charlesfilius@gmail.com
Web site: www.charlesfilius.com; www.charwoodpublications.com.

Chaser Media LLC, *(978-0-9747447)* P.O. Box 99, Dorset, VT 05251 USA
Web site: http://www.chasermedia.com.

Chateau Thierry Pr., *(978-0-935046)* Div. of Joan Thiry Enterprises, Ltd., 2100 W. Estes, Chicago, IL 60645 USA (SAN 281-4056) Tel 773-262-2234; Fax: 773-262-2235
E-mail: percival6390@sbcglobal.net.

Chauncey Park Pr., *(978-0-9667808)* Div. of Charles Chauncey Wells, Inc., 735 N. Grove Ave., Oak Park, IL 60302-1551 USA Tel 708-524-0695; Fax: 708-524-0742
E-mail: chauncey@wells1.com
Web site: http://www.wells1.com.

CHB Media, *(978-0-9822819; 978-0-9851507; 978-0-9886315; 978-0-9911189; 978-0-9863842)* Div. of Christian Heartbeat, Inc., 3039 Needle Palm Dr., Edgewater, FL 32141 USA Tel 386-690-9295
E-mail: christianheartbeat@gmail.com
Web site: http://www.chbmediaonline.com.

Checker Book Publishing Group *See* **Devil's Due Digital, Inc. - A Checker Digital Co.**

Checkerboard Library *Imprint of* **ABDO Publishing Co.**

†Checkerboard Pr., Inc., *(978-1-56288)* 1560 Revere Rd., Yardley, PA 19067-4351 USA; *CIP.*

Checkmark Bks. *Imprint of* **Facts On File, Inc.**

Cheerful Cherub, *(978-0-9753417)* Orders Addr.: 10071 S. Maples Ln., Highlands Ranch, CO 80129 USA Tel 303-471-8472; Edit Addr.: 10071 S. Maples Ln., Highlands Ranch, CO 80129 USA
E-mail: coloradodonna@q.com
Web site: http://www.cheerfulcherub.com.

Chelsea Clubhouse *Imprint of* **Facts On File, Inc.**

Chelsea Green Publishing, *(978-0-930031; 978-1-890132; 978-1-931498; 978-1-933392; 978-1-60358)* Orders Addr.: P.O. Box 428, White River Junction, VT 05001 USA (SAN 669-7631) Tel 802-295-6300; Fax: 802-295-6444; Toll Free: 800-639-4099; Edit Addr.: 85 N. Main St., Suite 120, White River Junction, VT 05001 USA
E-mail: info@chelseagreen.com
Web site: http://www.chelseagreen.com
Dist(s): **Follett School Solutions.**

Chelsea Hse. *Imprint of* **Facts On File, Inc.**

Chelsea Media *See* **Chelsea Multimedia**

Chelsea Multimedia, *(978-0-9822348)* P.O. Box 4668 19830, New York, NY 10163-4668 USA Tel 203-853-0540; *Imprints:* Chelsea Press (Chelsea Press)
Web site: http://www.chelseapress.com
Dist(s): **CreateSpace Independent Publishing Platform.**

Chelsea Pr. *Imprint of* **Chelsea Multimedia**

Chelsea Publishing Co., Inc. *Imprint of* **American Mathematical Society**

Chemical Heritage Foundation, *(978-0-941901)* 315 Chestnut St., Philadelphia, PA 19106-2702 USA (SAN 666-0193) Tel 215-925-2222; Fax: 215-925-1954; Toll Free: 888-224-6006
E-mail: booksales@chemheritage.org
Web site: http://www.chemheritage.org.

Cheng & Tsui Co., *(978-0-88727; 978-0-917056; 978-1-62291)* 25 West St., Boston, MA 02111-1213 USA (SAN 169-3387) Tel 617-988-2401; Fax: 617-426-3669
E-mail: service@cheng-tsui.com
Web site: http://www.cheng-tsui.com
Dist(s): **Chinasprout, Inc.**
Follett School Solutions.

Cheng Chung Bk. Co., Ltd. (TWN) *(978-957-09) Dist. by* **Cheng Tsui.**

Cheniere Pr., *(978-0-9725146; 978-0-9786260)* 151 La Jolla Dr., Santa Barbara, CA 93109 USA
E-mail: webmaster@cheniere.org.

Cherakota Books *See* **Cherakota Publishing**

Cherakota Publishing, *(978-0-9795678)* Orders Addr.: P.O. Box 603, Two Harbors, MN 55616 USA
E-mail: info@cherakotapublishing.com
Web site: http://www.cherakotapublishing.com.

Cherish the Children *See* **Chris A. Zeigler Dendy Consulting LLC**

Cherokee Bks., *(978-0-9640458; 978-1-930052)* Orders Addr.: 24 Meadow Ridge Pkwy. Dover, De 19904, Dover, DE 19904-5800 USA Tel 302-734-8782; Fax: 302-734-3198 Do not confuse with Cherokee Bks., Ponca City, OK
E-mail: milthanna@aol.com
Web site: http://www.cherokeebooks.com
Dist(s): **Washington Bk. Distributors.**

Cherokee Publishing Company *See* **Cherokee Bks.**

Cherry Lake Publishing, *(978-1-60279; 978-1-61080; 978-1-62431; 978-1-62753; 978-1-63137; 978-1-63188; 978-1-63362; 978-1-63470; 978-1-63471; 978-1-63472)* 1215 Overidgeview Ct., Ann Arbor, MI 48103 USA Tel 248-705-2045; 1750 Northway Dr., Suite 101, North Mankato, MN 56003 (SAN 858-9275) Tel 866-918-3956; Toll Free Fax: 866-489-6490
E-mail: customerservice@cherrylakepublishing.com; benmondloch@me.com; amy.lennex@sleepingbearpress.com
Web site: http://cherrylakepublishing.com
Dist(s): **Follett School Solutions**
MyiLibrary.

Cherry Lane Books *See* **Cherry Lane Music Co.**

†Cherry Lane Music Co., *(978-0-89524; 978-1-57560; 978-1-60378)* 6 E. 32nd St., 11th Flr., New York, NY 10016 USA (SAN 219-0788) Tel 212-561-3000; Fax: 212-251-0822
E-mail: print@cherrylane.com
Web site: http://www.cherrylane.com
Dist(s): **Leonard, Hal Corp.**
MyiLibrary; *CIP.*

Cherry Street Pr., *(978-0-9764921)* 139A N. 22nd St., Philadelphia, PA 19103 USA Fax: 215-568-4329
Dist(s): **Follett School Solutions.**

Cherry Tree Bks., *(978-0-9666832; 978-0-9774665)* 433 Perkins Rd., Weybridge, VT 05753 USA Tel 802-545-2474
E-mail: idahw@pshift.com; lmwash@together.net
Web site: http://www.cherrytreebooks.net.

Cherry Tree Lane Publishing, *(978-0-9771858)* 125 Cobblestone Ct., Berea, OH 44017-1079 USA
E-mail: sharesom@wowway.com.

Cherry Tree Pr. LLC, *(978-0-9772771)* Orders Addr.: 525 W. 14th St., #185, Traverse City, MI 49684-4968 USA Tel 231-421-1012; Edit Addr.: 526 W. 14th St., No. 185, Traverse City, MI 49684-4968 USA Do not confuse with Cherry Tree Press in Palo Alto, CA
E-mail: info@cherrytreepress.com
Web site: http://www.CherryTreePress.com; http://www.AmlaColorToo.com
Dist(s): **Partners Bk. Distributing, Inc.**

Cherrytree Pubns., Inc., *(978-0-9677757)* 881 Ocean Dr., No. 18B, Biscayne, FL 33149 USA Tel 305-361-1828.

Chesed Avraham Temple, *(978-0-9801799)* Orders Addr.: P.O. Box 35456, Los Angeles, CA 90035 USA (SAN 855-4137) Tel 310-654-0303
E-mail: meissany@ca.rr.com
Web site: http://www.EbrahimNeissany.com.

Cheshire House Bks., *(978-0-9675073)* P.O. Box 2484, New York, NY 10021 USA Tel 212-861-5404 (phone/fax)
E-mail: Chershirehouse@webtv.net
Web site: http://www.samthecat.com
Dist(s): **Brodart Co.**
Follett Higher Education Grp
Follett School Solutions.

Chess Library, The, *(978-0-9661889)* 12615 SW 297th Way, Vashon, WA 98070 USA
E-mail: pkmccready@netscape.net; admin@thechesslibrary.com
Web site: http://www.thechesslibrary.com.

Chester Comix, LLC, *(978-0-9729616; 978-1-933122)* P.O. Box 5653, Williamsburg, VA 23188 USA
E-mail: chestercomix@yahoo.com
Web site: http://www.chestercomix.com
Dist(s): **Follett School Solutions.**

Chester Music (GBR) *(978-0-7119) Dist. by* **H Leonard.**

Chester Music *Imprint of* **Music Sales Corp.**

Cheval International, *(978-0-9640610; 978-1-885351)* P.O. Box 706, Black Hawk, SD 57718-0706 USA
E-mail: cheval@rapidnet.com
Web site: http://www.chevalinternational.com
Dist(s): **Barnes & Noble Bks.-Imports.**

Chi Chi Rodriguez Bks., *(978-0-9797641)* P.O. Box 1155, Avondale, PA 19311 USA Tel 610-806-2013 Alternate #610-806-2013
Web site: http://www.marisadejesus.com.

Chiappini, Lydia , *(978-0-9669355)* 60 Gaisler Rd., Blairstown, NJ 07825 USA Tel 908-362-5604
E-mail: lydiachiappini@yahoo.com.

Chiaramonti, Gregory, *(978-0-615-13848-0)* 825 Cherry St., Trenton, NJ 08638-3322 USA
E-mail: gcmonti@yahoo.com
Web site: http://www.probie-thespaceprobe.com
Dist(s): **Lulu Enterprises Inc.**

Chicago Allergist Pubns., *(978-0-615-66842-0)* 2500 Ridge Ave, Suite 211A, Evanston, IL 60201 USA Tel 847 328 7909
Dist(s): **CreateSpace Independent Publishing Platform.**

Chicago Children's Museum, *(978-0-9759580)* Navy Pier, 700 E. Grand Ave., Chicago, IL 60611 USA Tel 312-527-1000; Fax: 312-527-9082
Web site: http://www.chichildrensmuseum.org
Dist(s): **Follett School Solutions**
Independent Pubs. Group
ebrary, Inc.

Chicago Distribution Ctr., Orders Addr.: 11030 S. Langley Ave., Chicago, IL 60628 USA (SAN 630-6047) Tel 773-702-7000 (International); Fax: 773-702-7212 (International); Toll Free Fax: 800-621-8476 (USA/Canada); Toll Free: 800-621-2736 (USA/Canada); 800-621-8471 (credit & collections)
E-mail: custserv@press.uchicago.edu; orders@press.uchicago.edu
Web site: http://www.press.uchicago.edu; http://www.press.uchicago.edu/presswide/cdc/.

†Chicago Review Pr., Inc., *(978-0-89733; 978-0-912777; 978-0-913705; 978-0-914090; 978-0-914091; 978-0-915864; 978-1-55652; 978-1-56976; 978-1-61373; 978-1-61374)* 814 N. Franklin St., Chicago, IL 60610 USA (SAN 213-5744) Tel 312-337-0747; Toll Free: 800-888-4741 (orders only); *Imprints:* Hill, Lawrence Books (Lawrence Hill); Zephyr Press (ZephPr); Academy Chicago Publishers, Limited (AcadChicagoPubs)
E-mail: frontdesk@chicagoreviewpress.com; orders@ipgbook.com
Web site: http://www.ipgbook.com; http://www.chicagoreviewpress.com
Dist(s): **AK Pr. Distribution**
Cobblestone Publishing Co.
Ebsco Publishing
Follett School Solutions
Gryphon Hse., Inc.
Independent Pubs. Group
Lulu Enterprises Inc.
MyiLibrary
SAGE Pubns., Inc.
ebrary, Inc.; *CIP.*

Chicago Spectrum Pr., *(978-1-58374; 978-1-886094)* Div. of Evanston Publishing Inc., Orders Addr.: 6611 Foxcroft Rd., Prospect, KY 40059 USA Tel 502-899-1919; Toll Free: 800-594-5190; 888-266-5780 (888-BOOKS-80)
E-mail: dorothykavka@twc.com
Web site: www.fineartbykavka.com.

Chicago Unzipped, *(978-0-9771699; 978-0-9817538)* 633 Clark St., No. 2-634, Evanston, IL 60208 USA (SAN 856-4558) Tel 847-491-8757
Web site: http://www.chicagounzipped.com.

Chick Light Publishing, *(978-0-9769198)* 845 Monticello Ct., Cape Coral, FL 33904 USA Tel 239-945-1939 (phone/fax)
E-mail: vince@chicklight.com
Web site: http://chicklight.com.

Chick Pubns., Inc., *(978-0-937958; 978-0-7589)* P.O. Box 3500, Ontario, CA 91761-1019 USA (SAN 211-7770) Tel 909-987-0771; Fax: 909-941-8128; Toll Free: 800-932-3050
E-mail: orderdesk@chick.com
Web site: http://www.chick.com.

Chickaloon Village Publishing, *(978-0-9767217)* Orders Addr.: P.O. Box 1105, Chickaloon, AK 99674 USA Tel 907-745-0707; Fax: 907-745-0709
E-mail: cvadmin@chickaloon.org
Web site: http://www.chickaloon.org.

Chicken Hse., The *Imprint of* **Scholastic, Inc.**

Chicken Socks *Imprint of* **Klutz**

Chicken Soup for the Soul Publishing, LLC, *(978-1-935096; 978-1-61159)* 132 E. Putnam Ave., Cos Cob, CT 06807 USA; 180 Varick St. Suite 816, New York, NY 10014; *Imprints:* CSS Backlist (CSSBacklist)
E-mail: evergreenstables@hotmail.com
Dist(s): **Follett School Solutions**
Leonard, Hal Corp.
MyiLibrary
Open Road Integrated Media, LLC
Simon & Schuster
Simon & Schuster, Inc.

Chickering-Moller Project, *(978-0-9860799)* 414 W. 16th Street, Traverse City, MI 49684 USA.

Chicory Pr., *(978-0-9785886)* 49 Maple Ave., Morgantown, WV 26501 USA Tel 304-292-1115
E-mail: efaulkes@mail.wvu.edu.

Chien, Paris *See* **La Librairie Parisienne**

Chihuly Workshop, Inc., *(978-0-9608382; 978-1-57684)* Orders Addr.: P.O. Box 70856, Seattle, WA 98127 USA (SAN 240-3579) Tel 206-297-1304; Fax: 206-297-6207; Toll Free: 800-574-7272 (trade orders) Do not confuse with Portland Pr., Inc., Chapel Hill, NC
E-mail: jacobb@portlandpress.net
Web site: http://www.chihuly.com; http://www.portlandpress.net; http://www.chihulyworkshop.com
Dist(s): **Follett School Solutions.**

ChikChatr Ink, *(978-0-9766634)* P.O. Box 3302, Brentwood, TN 37024-3302 USA Tel 615-731-7422.

Child Advocates, Inc., *(978-0-9754953)* 2401 Portsmouth, Suite 210, Houston, TX 77098 USA Tel 713-529-1396; Fax: 713-529-1390
Web site: http://www.childadvocates.org
Dist(s): **Follett School Solutions.**

Child & Family Pr. *Imprint of* **Child Welfare League of America, Inc.**

Child Life Bks., LLC, *(978-0-9771143; 978-0-9791687)* 22303 Charlotte Dr., Torrance, CA 90505-2118 USA
E-mail: liana@mannersicare.com.

Child Management, Incorporated *See* **ParentMagic, Inc.**

Child Scope Productions, *(978-0-9678778)* Div. of Moschea Promotions, 5016 N. Lydell Ave., White Fish Bay, WI 53217 USA Tel 414-332-1897; Fax: 414-332-1609
E-mail: mosch@execpc.com.

Child Sensitive Communication, LLC, *(978-0-9743197; 978-1-933803)* P.O. Box 150806, Nashville, TN 37215-0806 USA; *Imprints:* Karyn Henley Resources (Krayn Henley)
Web site: http://www.karynhenley.com; http://throatofthenight.com.

†Child Welfare League of America, Inc., *(978-0-87868; 978-1-58760)* Orders Addr.: P.O. Box 932831, Atlanta, GA 31193-2831 USA Tel 770-280-4164; Toll Free: 800-407-6273; Edit Addr.: 2345 Crystal Dr., Suite 250, Arlington, VA 22202 USA (SAN 201-9876) Tel 703-412-2400; Fax: 703-412-2401 (orders only); PBD 420 Eagleview Blvd., Exton, PA 19341 (SAN 851-2558) Tel 202-638-2952; Fax: 202-638-4004; *Imprints:* C W L A Press (CWLA Pr); Child & Family Press (Child-Family Pr)
E-mail: order@cwla.org
Web site: http://www.cwla.org/pubs
Dist(s): **Lectorum Pubns., Inc.**; *CIP.*

Child1st Pubns., LLC, *(978-0-9844972; 978-0-9829873; 978-1-936981)* Orders Addr.: PO Box 150226, Grand Rapids, MI 49515 USA; Edit Addr.: 3302 S. New Hope Rd., Gastonia, NC 28056 USA
Web site: http://www.child1st.com
Dist(s): **Follett School Solutions.**

Childcraft Education Corp., *(978-1-890275; 978-1-58669)* Div. of School Speciality, 2920 Old Tree Dr., Lancaster, PA 17603 USA Tel 717-391-4027; Fax: 717-397-7436; Toll Free: 800-631-5652
E-mail: kmyers@childcrafteducation.com
Web site: http://www.childcrafteducation.com/.

Childhood Anxiety Network *See* **Selective Mutism Anxiety Research & Treatment Ctr.**

Children *Imprint of* **Star Light Pr.**

Children Concept Publishing, *(978-0-9745219)* Orders Addr.: P.O. Box 1179, Highland, MI 48357 USA; Edit Addr.: 1651 S. Milford Rd., Highland, MI 48357 USA.

Children Learning Awareness, Safety & Self-Defense, *(978-0-9768273)* Orders Addr.: 16815 Gault St., Lake Balboa, CA 91406 USA Tel 818-990-9909 (phone/fax); *Imprints:* CLASS Publications (CLASS Publns)
E-mail: janet@classeducation.org; janet@classpublications.com
Web site: http://www.classeducation.org; http://www.classpublications.com
Dist(s): **Class Pubns., Inc.**

Children of Color/The Indra Collection, *(978-0-9746779)* P.O. Box 992, Great Falls, VA 22066 USA
Web site: http://www.childrenofcolor.com.

Children's Better Health Institute, *(978-1-885453)* Div. of Benjamin Franklin Literary & Medical Society, Inc., 1100 Waterway Blvd., Indianapolis, IN 46202 USA Tel 317-636-8881; Fax: 317-684-8094; Toll Free: 800-558-2376.

Childrens Bible Society, *(978-0-9777446)* Orders Addr.: P.O. Box 96, Hemet, CA 92546 USA Tel 951-652-9456; Edit Addr.: 1123 W. Acacia Ave., Hemet, CA 92543 USA
E-mail: kristy@actstracts.com
Web site: http://www.childrensbiblesociety.org/.

Children's Book Press *Imprint of* **Lee & Low Bks., Inc.**

Children's Bookshoppe Stop, The, *(978-0-9728393)* P.O. Box 62261, Virginia Beach, VA 23466 USA Tel 757-671-7779 (phone/fax)
E-mail: seetcbs@exis.net
Web site: http://www.surftcbs.com.

Children's Classic Book Pubs., *(978-0-9794753)* Orders Addr.: 103 Josh Ln., Poolville, TX 76487 USA (SAN 853-5280)
E-mail: orders@snerfycat.com; misterfish@snerfycat.com; ccbp@snerfycat.com
Web site: www.SnerfyCat.com.

Children's Express Foundation, Inc., *(978-0-9621641)* 1331 H St, NW, Suite 900, Washington, DC 20005 USA (SAN 251-6993) Tel 202-737-7377; Fax: 202-737-0193
E-mail: s1@dc.ce.org
Web site: http://www.ce.org.

Children's Heart Publishing Company *See* **CHPublishing, Inc.**

Children's Insight *Imprint of* **Insight Services, Inc**

Children's Kindness Network, *(978-0-9662268; 978-0-9745184)* Orders Addr.: 1323 Barkleigh Ln., Franklin, TN 37064 USA Tel 970-453-0410; Fax: 970-453-7375; Toll Free: 800-699-4541
E-mail: ted@moozie.com
Dist(s): **Bibliotech, Inc.**

Children's Legacy, *(978-0-9629365)* Orders Addr.: P.O. Box 300305, Denver, CO 80203 USA; Edit Addr.: 2553 Dexter St., Denver, CO 80207 USA Tel 303-830-7595.

Children's Literacy Pubns., *(978-0-9710432)* P.O. Box 5581, Sun City Center, FL 33571 USA Toll Free Fax: 1-866-350-4502; Toll Free: 1-800-585-1893
E-mail: janet@makereadingfirst.com
Web site: http://www.makereadingfirst.com.

Children's Melanoma Education Bk., A, *(978-0-615-79018-3)* 15 Kingsmont Ct., Saint Peters, MO 63376 USA Tel 636.577.1839
Web site: www.milesagainstmelanoma5k.org
Dist(s): **CreateSpace Independent Publishing Platform.**

Children's Pr. *Imprint of* **Scholastic Library Publishing**

Children's Psychological Health Ctr., Inc., The, *(978-0-9790846)* 2105 Divisadero St., San Francisco, CA 94115 USA Tel 415-292-7119; Fax: 415-749-2802
E-mail: gil.kliman@cphc-sf.org
Web site: http://www.cphc-sf.org.

Children's Publishing, *(978-0-9725803; 978-0-9789347)* Orders Addr.: 101 Crepe Myrtle Ln., Georgetown, TX 78633-4724 USA (SAN 254-9328) Toll Free: 877-864-7364
E-mail: carlson@childrenspublishing.com
Web site: http://www.childrenspublishing.com
Dist(s): **Quality Bks., Inc.**
Speech Bin, Inc., The.

Children's Success Unlimited LLC, *(978-0-9829613)* 160 Greentree Dr., Suite 101, Dover, DE 19904 USA Tel 917-208-7785
E-mail: bolbrys@ion-partners.com
Dist(s): **Emerald Bk. Co.**
Greenleaf Book Group.

Children's Village Foundation, Inc., *(978-0-9740481)* 1350 W. Hanley Ave., Coeur d'Alene, ID 83815 USA Tel 208-667-1189; Fax: 208-664-5735
E-mail: tinka@thechildrensvillage.org
Web site: http://www.thechildrensvillage.org.

ChildrenzBks., *(978-0-9748989)* P.O. Box 1431, Tucson, AZ 85702-1431 USA; *Imprints:* Bases Loaded Books (Bases Loaded Bks)
E-mail: sales@childrenzbooks.com
Web site: http://www.childrenzbooks.com.

†Child's World, Inc., The, *(978-0-89565; 978-0-913778; 978-1-56766; 978-1-59296; 978-1-60253; 978-1-60954; 978-1-60973; 978-1-61473; 978-1-62323; 978-1-62687; 978-1-63143; 978-1-63407; 978-1-5038)* 1980 Lookout Dr., Mankato, MN 56003 USA (SAN 858-5385) Tel 507-385-1044; Fax: 888-320-2329; Toll Free Fax: 800-599-7323
E-mail: info@childsworld.com; mary.berendes@childsworld.com; mike.peterson@childsworld.com
Web site: http://www.childsworld.com
Dist(s): **Follett School Solutions**; *CIP.*

Childswork/Childsplay, *(978-1-882732; 978-1-58815; 978-1-931704)* Div. of The Guidance Channel, Orders Addr.: P.O. Box 760, Plainview, NY 11803-0760 USA Tel 516-349-5520; Fax: 516-349-5521; Toll Free Fax: 800-262-1886; Toll Free: 800-962-1141; 45 Executive Dr. Ste. 201, Plainview, NY 11803-1738
E-mail: karens@at-risk.com; info@childswork.com
Web site: http://www.childswork.com.

Chiliric Pubns., *(978-0-9755253)* 1423 6th St., Eureka, CA 95501 USA Tel 707-443-4046
Web site: http://www.geocities.com/harleysgreatadventures/; http://www.Geocities.com/harleys_great_adventures.

Chim Chimney Bks., *(978-0-615-77092-5; 978-0-692-25274-1)* 27613 NE 150th Pl., Duvall, WA 98019 USA Tel 206-972-2072
Dist(s): **CreateSpace Independent Publishing Platform.**

Chimera Publishing, *(978-0-9744612; 978-0-9769523; 978-0-9779749)* 719 Arena Dr., Hamilton, NJ 08610 USA Fax: 609-888-1802; Toll Free: 800-448-0295
E-mail: norm@chimerapublishing.com
Web site: http://www.chimerapublishing.com
Dist(s): **AtlasBooks Distribution.**

Chimera Publishing, LLC *See* **ShaGru Entertainment, LLC**

Chimera Pubns. (GBR) *(978-1-901388; 978-1-903931) Dist. by* **PerseuPGW.**

Chin & A Pr., *(978-0-9746341)* 2809 79th Ave., Brooklyn Park, MN 55444 USA Tel 763-549-8821
E-mail: jlodien@earthlink.net; ChinAndAPress@earthlink.net
Web site: http://www.allbeethere.com.

Chin Music Pr., *(978-0-9741995; 978-0-9844576; 978-0-9850416; 978-0-9887693; 978-1-63405)* 2621 24th Ave. W., Seattle, WA 98199 USA Tel 206-380-1947 (phone/fax)
E-mail: bruce@chinmusicpress.com
Web site: http://www.chinmusicpress.com
Dist(s): **Consortium Bk. Sales & Distribution**
Follett School Solutions
MyiLibrary
Perseus Bks. Group.

†China Bks. & Periodicals, Inc., *(978-0-8351)* 360 Swift Ave., Suite 48, South San Francisco, CA 94080 USA (SAN 145-0557) Tel 800-818-2017; 650-872-7076; Fax: 650-872-7808
E-mail: chris@chinabooks.com
Web site: http://www.chinabooks.com
Dist(s): **Follett School Solutions**
SPD-Small Pr. Distribution; *CIP.*

China House Gallery, China Institute in America *See* **China Institute Gallery, China Institute in America**

China Institute Gallery, China Institute in America, *(978-0-9654270; 978-0-9774054; 978-0-9893776)* Div. of China Institute in America, 125 E. 65th St., New York, NY 10065 USA (SAN 110-8743) Tel 212-744-8181; Fax: 212-628-4159
E-mail: gallery@chinainstitute.org
Web site: http://www.chinainstitute.org
Dist(s): **Art Media Resources, Inc.**
Simon & Schuster, Inc.
Tuttle Publishing.

China Language University Pr. (CHN) *(978-7-88703) Dist. by* **China Bks.**

Chinasoft (AUS) *(978-1-876739; 978-0-646-06656-1; 978-0-646-06657-8; 978-0-646-06658-5; 978-0-646-13326-3; 978-0-646-13327-0; 978-0-646-13328-7; 978-0-646-22328-5; 978-0-646-22329-2; 978-0-646-22330-8; 978-0-646-25096-0; 978-0-646-25097-7) Dist. by* **Cheng Tsui.**

Chinasprout, Inc., *(978-0-9707332; 978-0-9747302; 978-0-9820227)* 110 W. 32nd St., Flr. 6, New York, NY 10001-3205 USA Toll Free: 800-644-2611
E-mail: info@chinasprout.com
Web site: http://www.chinasprout.com
Dist(s): **China Bks. & Periodicals, Inc.**
Follett School Solutions.

Ching Ying Center *See* **Manning, Laurie**

Chipman, Marilyn, *(978-0-9745857)* P.O. Box 441233, Aurora, CO 80044-1233 USA
E-mail: chipman@mscd.edu
Web site: http://www.marilynchipman.com.

Chipotle Publishing, LLC, *(978-0-9823918; 978-0-9965218)* 631 N. Stephanie St., Suite 372, Henderson, NV 89014 USA Tel 702-565-0746; Fax: 702-558-1728
E-mail: office@sadefensejournal.com
Web site: http://www.sadefensejournal.com
Dist(s): **Casemate Pubs. & Bk. Distributors, LLC.**

Chippewa Valley Museum, *(978-0-9636191)* Orders Addr.: P.O. Box 1204, Eau Claire, WI 54702 USA Tel 715-834-7871; Fax: 715-834-6624; Edit Addr.: Carson Park Dr., Eau Claire, WI 54702 USA
E-mail: info@cvmuseum.com
Web site: http://www.cvmuseum.com
Dist(s): **Chicago Distribution Ctr.**
Univ. of Wisconsin Pr.

ChironBooks *Imprint of* **Coleman/Perrin**

Chisholm, Juan Phillip *See* **Green Light Bks. and Publishing, LLC**

ChiZine Pubns. (CAN) *(978-0-9809410; 978-0-9812978; 978-1-926851; 978-0-9813746; 978-1-77148) Dist. by* **Diamond Book Dists.**

Choc Lit Limited (GBR) *(978-1-906931; 978-1-78189) Dist. by* **Casemate Pubs.**

Chock-Lit Pubns., *(978-0-9742344)* 26 Douvaine Ct., The Woodlands, TX 77382 USA
E-mail: publisher@chocklitpublications.com
Web site: http://www.chocklitpublications.com.

Chocolate Sauce, *(978-0-9740268; 978-0-9911314)* 211 E. 60th street, sweet C3, New York, NY 10022 USA
Web site: http://www.chocolatesaucebooks.com
Dist(s): **SPI Bks.**

Choice PH, *(978-0-9841910; 978-0-9887595)* 412 Olive Ave., Suite 305, Huntington Beach, CA 92648 USA (SAN 858-6829)
E-mail: choiceph@aol.com
Dist(s): **eBookIt.com.**

Choice Point Editions, *(978-0-9778774)* 7883 N. Pershing AVE., Stockton, CA 95207 USA Tel 209-952-7108; Fax: 209-951-3216
E-mail: choicepointeditions@inreach.com
Web site: http://www.choicepointeditions.com.

Choice Publishing House *See* **Choice PH**

ChoiceMaker Pty. Ltd., The (AUS) *(978-0-9805673; 978-1-921790; 978-1-925186; 978-1-925233; 978-1-925234; 978-1-925235; 978-1-925246; 978-1-925247; 978-1-925248; 978-1-925249; 978-1-925250; 978-1-925251; 978-1-925252) Dist. by* **Lerner Pub.**

Choices Education Program, Watson Institute, Brown University *See* **Choices Program, Watson Institute, Brown Univ.**

Choices For Tomorrow, *(978-0-9748689)* 43H Meadow Pond Dr., Leominster, MA 01453 USA
E-mail: moniquehoude@yahoo.com.

Choices International, *(978-0-9768530)* Orders Addr.: P.O. Box 408, Berries Springs, MI 49103 USA Tel 269-471-9718 (phone/fax); Edit Addr.: P.O. Box 408, Berrien Sprgs, MI 49103-0408 USA
E-mail: pennyturner@sbcglobal.net; yourchoices@choicesinternational.info.

Choices Program, Watson Institute, Brown Univ., *(978-1-891306; 978-1-60123)* The Choices Program-Brown Univ. Box 1948, Providence, RI 02912 USA Tel 401-863-3155; Fax: 401-863-1247
E-mail: choices@brown.edu
Web site: http://www.choices.edu.

Cholita Prints & Pub. Co., *(978-0-9742956)* Orders Addr.: P.O. Box 8018, Sante Fe, NM 87504 USA; Edit Addr.: 655 W. San Francisco St., Sante Fe, NM 87501 USA
E-mail: cholitaprints@comcast.net
Dist(s): **Follett School Solutions.**

Choo Choo Clan, *(978-0-9788670)* 1616 Brockton Ave., Apt. 104, Los Angeles, CA 90025 USA Tel 626-715-3342
E-mail: joey0724@hotmail.com
Web site: http://www.choochooclan.com.

Chooseco LLC, *(978-0-9745356; 978-1-933390; 978-1-937133)* Orders Addr.: P.O. Box 46, Waitsfield, VT 05673 USA (SAN 852-1131); Edit Addr.: 49 Fiddler's Green, Waitsfield, VT 05673 USA (SAN 852-1158) Tel 802-496-2595
E-mail: mbounty@chooseco.com; liz@chooseco.com
Web site: http://www.cyoa.com; http://www.chooseco.com
Dist(s): **Follett School Solutions.**

Choosing The Best Publishing, *(978-0-9724890; 978-0-9819748; 978-0-9819759)* 2625 Cumberland Pkwy., Suite 200, Atlanta, GA 30339 USA Tel 770-803-3100; Fax: 770-803-3110; Toll Free: 800-774-2378
E-mail: bcook@ctbpublishing.com; book@ctbpublishing.com
Web site: http://www.choosingthebest.org
Dist(s): **Independent Pubs. Group.**

Choristers Guild, *(978-1-929187)* 2834 W. Kingsley Rd., Garland, TX 75041-2498 USA (SAN 689-9188) Tel 972-271-1521; Fax: 972-840-3113
E-mail: choristers@choristersguild.org
Web site: http://www.choristersguild.org
Dist(s): **Lorenz Corp., The.**

Chosen Bks., *(978-0-8007)* Div. of Baker Publishing Group, Orders Addr.: P.O. Box 6287, Grand Rapids, MI 49516-6287 USA Toll Free Fax: 800-398-3111 (orders only); Toll Free: 800-877-2665 (orders only); Edit Addr.: 6030 E. Fulton, Ada, MI 49301 USA Tel 616-676-9185; Fax: 616-676-9573
Web site: http://www.bakerpublishinggroup.com
Dist(s): **Baker Publishing Group.**

Chosen Word Publishing, *(978-0-9707536; 978-0-9748056; 978-0-9754779)* P.O. Box 481886, Charlotte, NC 28269 USA Tel 704-527-2177; Fax: 704-527-1677
E-mail: jeannette@chosenwordpublishing.com
Web site: http://www.chosenwordpublishing.com.

Chou Chou Pr., *(978-0-9606140; 978-0-9716605; 978-0-9789152)* 4 Whimbrel Ct., Okatie, SC 29909 USA (SAN 220-2379) Tel 631-744-5784
E-mail: chouchou@hargray.com; info@bilingualkids.com
Web site: http://www.bilingualkids.com
Dist(s): **Follett School Solutions.**

Chowder Bay Bks., *(978-0-9795364)* P.O. Box 5542, Lake Worth, FL 33466-5542 USA (SAN 853-7119)
Web site: http://www.chowderbaybooks.com.

Publisher Name Index

CHPublishing, Inc., *(978-0-9786681; 978-0-9852789)* Orders Addr.: P.O. Box 691223, Orlando, FL 32869-1223 USA Tel 407-614-5176; Fax: 407-614-5200
E-mail: LHarris@chpublishing.org
Web site: http://www.chpublishing.org; http://www.facebook.com/chpublishing; http://www.twitter.com/ch_publishing; http://lorettafaithharris.com/products/.

Chris A. Zeigler Dendy Consulting LLC, *(978-0-9679911)* P.O. Box 189, Cedar Bluff, AL 35959 USA Fax: 256-779-5203
E-mail: chrisdendy@mindspring.com
Web site: http://www.chrisdendy.com
Dist(s): **Follett School Solutions.**

Chris Six Group, The, *(978-0-9899182)* P.O. Box 1829, New York, NY 10159-1829 USA Tel 718-514-0452
E-mail: thechrissixgroup@msn.com.

Christ Inspired, Inc., *(978-1-4183)* 2263 Dicey Rd., Weatherford, TX 76085-3619 USA
Web site: http://www.christinspired.com.

Christian Aid Ministries, *(978-1-885270)* Orders Addr.: P.O. Box 360, Berlin, OH 44610 USA Tel 330-893-2428; Fax: 330-893-2305; Edit Addr.: 4464 S.R. 39 E., Berlin, OH 44610 USA Tel 216-893-2428.

Christian Bible Studies, *(978-0-9763357)* P.O. Box 11155, Lansing, MI 48911 USA Tel 517-272-9076
E-mail: verseyawilliams@sbcglobal.net
Web site: http://www.christianstudies7.com.

Christian Courier Pubns., *(978-0-9678044; 978-1-932723)* P.O. Box 55265, Stockton, CA 95205 USA Tel 209-472-2475
E-mail: david@christiancourier.com
Web site: http://www.christiancourier.com.

Christian Education Resources, *(978-1-933479)* P.O. Box 320099, Cocoa Beach, FL 32932 USA.

Christian Focus Pubns. (GBR) *(978-0-906731; 978-1-85792; 978-1-871676; 978-1-84550; 978-1-78191)* *Dist. by* **Spring Arbor Dist.**

Christian Focus Pubns. (GBR) *(978-0-906731; 978-1-85792; 978-1-871676; 978-1-84550; 978-1-78191)* *Dist. by* **STL Dist.**

Christian, Harvey Pubs. Inc., *(978-1-932774)* 3107 Hwy. 321, Hampton, TN 37658 USA Tel 423-768-2297
E-mail: books@harveycp.com
Web site: http://www.harveycp.com.

Christian Heartbeat Incorporated *See* **CHB Media**

Christian Liberty Pr., *(978-1-930092; 978-1-930367; 978-1-932971; 978-1-935796; 978-1-62982)* Div. of Church of Christian Liberty, 502 W. Euclid Ave., Arlington Heights, IL 60004 USA
E-mail: e.shewan@christianlibertypress.com; linak@christianlibertypress.com; larsj@christianlibertypress.com
Web site: http://www.christianlibertypress.com.

Christian Life Bks., *(978-0-9646289; 978-1-931393)* Subs. of River Revival Ministries, Inc., Orders Addr.: P.O. Box 36355, Pensacola, FL 32516-6355 USA Tel 850-457-7057; Fax: 850-458-9339
E-mail: mail@drlarrymartin.org
Web site: http://www.rrmi.org.

Christian Life Workshops *See* **Noble Publishing Assocs.**

Christian Light Pubns., Inc., *(978-0-87813)* 1066 Chicago Ave., Harrisonburg, VA 22802 USA (SAN 206-7315) Tel 540-434-0768; Fax: 540-433-8896
E-mail: johnh@clp.org.

Christian Living Books, Inc. *Imprint of* **Pneuma Life Publishing, Inc.**

Christian Logic, *(978-0-9745315)* PMB 168, 429 Lake Park Blvd., Muscatine, IA 52761 USA Tel 309-537-3641
E-mail: hans@christianlogic.com
Web site: http://www.christianlogic.com.

Christian Novel Studies, *(978-0-9707712)* 5208 E. Lake Rd., Saginaw, MN 55779 USA Tel 218-729-9733; Fax: 509-271-8614
E-mail: cnsroe@aol.com; chsroe@aol.com
Web site: http://www.christiannovelstudies.homestead.com.

Christian Science Publishing Society, The *See* **Eddy, The Writings of Mary Baker**

Christian Services Publishing, *(978-1-879854)* Div. of Christian Services Network, 1975 Janich Ranch Ct., El Cajon, CA 92019 USA Tel 619-334-0706; Fax: 619-579-0685; Toll Free: 800-484-6184 Do not confuse with Christian Services, Damascus, MD
E-mail: tim@csnbooks.com
Web site: http://csnbooks.com.

Christian Visionary Communications, *(978-0-9746867)* P.O. Box 63, Sharon Center, OH 44274-0063 USA
E-mail: lorshir3@verizon.net
Web site: http://www.christianary.org.

Christian Visual Arts of California, *(978-0-9766584)* 64969 Pine St., Hume, CA 93628-9619 USA Tel 559-335-2797; Fax: 559-335-2107
E-mail: dajohnson@spiralcomm.net.

Christian Voice Publishing, A, *(978-0-9776747; 978-0-9786580; 978-1-934327)* 2031 W. Superior St. Ste. 1, Duluth, MN 55806-2036 USA.

Christiangela Productions, *(978-0-9720773)* 9 Casey's Way, Ocean View, DE 19970 USA.

Christine, Yates, *(978-0-9741210)* 13165 Oak Farm Dr., Woodbridge, VA 22192 USA
Web site: http://www.freekidcrafts.com.

Christine's Closet, *(978-0-9713405)* 10300 Grand Oak Dr., Austin, TX 78750 USA Tel 512-918-9255; Fax: 512-873-9818; Toll Free: 800-591-1165
E-mail: chrissy@chrissy.com
Web site: http://www.chrissy.com.

Christopher Winkle Products *See* **First Stage Concepts**

†Chronicle Bks. LLC, *(978-0-8118; 978-0-87701; 978-0-938491; 978-1-4521)* Orders Addr.: 680 Second St., San Francisco, CA 94107 USA (SAN 202-165X) Tel 415-537-4200; Fax: 415-537-4460; Toll Free Fax: 800-286-9471; Toll Free: 800-759-0190 (orders only); Edit Addr.: 3 Center Plaza, Boston, MA 2108 USA;
Imprints: SeaStar Books (SeaStar Chronic); Handprint Books (HandprintBks)
E-mail: order.desk@hbgusa.com; customer.service@hbgusa.com
Web site: http://www.chroniclebooks.com
Dist(s): **Diamond Bk. Distributors**
Follett School Solutions
Leonard, Hal Corp.
Hachette Bk. Group
Ingram Pub. Services
Music Sales Corp.; *CIP.*

Chronicle Guidance Pubns., Inc., *(978-0-912578; 978-1-55631)* Orders Addr.: 66 Aurora St., Moravia, NY 13118-3569 USA Tel 315-497-0330; 315-497-3359; Toll Free: 800-622-7284
E-mail: CustomerService@ChronicleGuidance.com
Web site: http://www.chronicleguidance.com
Dist(s): **Follett School Solutions.**

Chronos Press *See* **WingSpan Publishing**

Chrysalis Education, *(978-1-929298; 978-1-930643; 978-1-931983; 978-1-932333; 978-1-59389)* Div. of The Creative Company, 1980 Lookout Dr., North Mankato, MN 56003 USA Tel 507-388-6273; Fax: 507-388-2746; Toll Free: 800-445-6209
E-mail: schlichted@aol.com
Dist(s): **Black Rabbit Bks.**
Creative Co., The.

Chrysalis Pr., *(978-0-9795933)* Orders Addr.: P.O. Box 13129, Newport Beach, CA 92658 USA (SAN 853-8514)
E-mail: amber@chrysalispress.com
Web site: http://www.Chrysalispress.com
Dist(s): **Follett School Solutions.**

Chubasco Publishing Company *See* **Perelandra Publishing Co.**

Chucklebks. Publishing, *(978-0-9702730)* 27 Brown St., Andover, MA 01810 USA Tel 978-749-0674
E-mail: jeff@chucklebooks.com
Web site: http://www.chucklebooks.com; http://www.incredibleassemblies.com
Dist(s): **Partners Bk. Distributing, Inc.**

Chung, Jo Anne *See* **Vision Unlimited Pr.**

Church at Cane Creek *See* **No Greater Joy Ministries, Inc.**

Church Hse. Publishing (GBR) *(978-0-7151)* *Dist. by* **Westminster John Knox.**

Church Hymnal Corporation *See* **Church Publishing, Inc.**

Church Publishing, Inc., *(978-0-89869; 978-1-59627; 978-1-59628)* 445 Fifth Ave., New York, NY 10016-0109 USA (SAN 857-0140) Tel 212-592-1800; Fax: 212-779-3392; Toll Free: 800-242-1918; *Imprints:* Seabury Books (Seabury Bks); Morehouse Publishing (MoreHse Pubng); Living the Good News (LTGN)
E-mail: churchpublishing@cpg.org
Web site: http://www.churchpublishing.org; http://morehousepublishing.org
Dist(s): **Abingdon Pr.**
Bloomsbury Publishing Inc
Macmillan
MyiLibrary.

Church Without Walls Publications, Incorporated *See* **Church Without Walls Pubns., USA**

Church Without Walls Pubns., USA, *(978-0-9755927)* Div. of SEGUN MASHA, INC., Orders Addr.: 1035 Franklin Rd. SE. #c04, Marietta, GA 30067 USA
E-mail: segunmasha@gmail.com
Web site: http://www.faith365.org; www.marketplacemissions.com.

Chuttani, Kabir, *(978-0-9749364)* 8 Nameloc Rd., Plymouth, MA 02360-1418 USA.

CicadaSun, *(978-0-9779808)* P.O. Box 90834, Austin, TX 78709-0834 USA
E-mail: service@cicadasun.com
Web site: http://www.cicadasun.com.

Cideb (ITA) *(978-88-7754; 978-88-530)* *Dist. by* **Distribks Inc.**

Cider Mill Pr. Bk. Pubs., LLC, *(978-1-933662; 978-1-60433; 978-1-941868)* 12 Port Farm Rd., Kennebunkport, ME 04046 USA (SAN 257-1927) Tel 207-967-8232; Fax: 207-967-8233; *Imprints:* Applesauce Press (Applesauce Pr)
E-mail: johnwhalen@cidermillpress.com
Web site: http://www.cidermillpress.com
Dist(s): **Simon & Schuster**
Simon & Schuster, Inc.
Sterling Publishing Co., Inc.

Cidermill Bks., *(978-0-9748483)* P.O. Box 32250, San Jose, CA 95152-2250 USA
E-mail: info@cidermillbooks.com
Web site: http://www.cidermillbooks.com.

Ciletti Publishing Group, Inc., The, *(978-0-917665; 978-0-9788655)* 2421 Redwood Ct., Longmont, CO 80503 USA Tel 720-494-1473; Fax: 720-494-1471
E-mail: barbaraj@odysseybooks.net
Dist(s): **Follett School Solutions.**

Cinco Puntos Pr., *(978-0-938317; 978-1-933693; 978-1-935955; 978-1-941026)* 701 Texas Ave., El Paso, TX 79901 USA (SAN 661-0080) Tel 915-838-1625; Fax: 915-838-1635; Toll Free: 800-566-9072
E-mail: leebyrd@cincopuntos.com
Web site: http://www.cincopuntos.com
Dist(s): **Consortium Bk. Sales & Distribution**
Follett School Solutions
Lectorum Pubns., Inc.
MyiLibrary
Perseus Bks. Group.

Cinealta Pr., *(978-0-9821065)* 2060 W. Mulberry Dr., Chandler, AZ 85286-6771 USA
Web site: http://www.cinealtapress.com.

CineBook (GBR) *(978-1-905460; 978-1-84918)* *Dist. by* **Natl Bk Netwk.**

Cinnamon Bay Entertainment Group, *(978-0-9727116)* P.O.Box 4501, San Clemente, CA 92674-4501 USA
E-mail: rsdan@verizon.net.

Cinnamon Ridge Publishing, *(978-0-9800762)* 7121 W. Craig Rd., Suite 113, No. 284, Las Vegas, NV 89129 USA.

Circelli, Kristina, *(978-0-9763728; 978-0-615-40270-3)* 6410 San Jose Blvd. W., Jacksonville, FL 32217 USA Tel 386-290-7294
E-mail: kristina@circelli.info.

Circle Journey, Ltd., *(978-0-9741104)* 22 East Gay St., Suite 801, Columbus, OH 43215 USA Fax: 614-564-7795; Toll Free: 877-247-2534
E-mail: connections@circlejourney.com
Web site: http://www.circlejourney.com.

Circle Pr., *(978-0-9651601; 978-0-9743661; 978-1-933271)* Div. of Circle Media, Inc., Orders Addr.: 33 Rossotto Dr., Hamden, CT 06514 USA Tel 203-230-3805; Fax: 203-230-3838; Toll Free: 888-881-0729; Edit Addr.: 432 Washington Ave., North Haven, CT 06473 USA Do not confuse with companies with the same name in Huntington Beach, CA, New York, NY, Itasca, IL
E-mail: victor@catholicformation.com.

Circle Studios, *(978-0-9768022)* 200 Medicine Way, Eureka Springs, AR 72632 USA Tel 479-253-5826
Dist(s): **Follett School Solutions.**

Circumpolar Pr., *(978-1-878051)* Subs. of Wizard Works, P.O. Box 1125, Homer, AK 99603 USA Tel 907-235-8757 (phone/fax); Toll Free: 877-210-2665
E-mail: wizard@xyz.net
Web site: http://www.xyz.net/~wizard.

Ciro's Bks., *(978-0-9676643; 978-1-934499)* 4152 Meridian St., No. 6, Bellingham, WA 98226 USA
E-mail: info@cirosbooks.com
Web site: http://www.cirosbooks.com; http://www.howwouldyouvote.us; http://www.onepersononevoteonline.com
Dist(s): **BCH Fulfillment & Distribution**
Smashwords.

Cirrus Publishing, LLC, *(978-0-9755678)* Orders Addr.: P.O. Box 291724, Davie, FL 33329-1724 USA Fax: 954-965-2643
E-mail: cirruspublish@aol.com
Web site: http://www.yessy.com/wildimages.

Cisco Pr., *(978-0-7357; 978-1-57870; 978-1-58705; 978-1-58713)* Div. of Pearson Technology Group, 800 E. 96th St., Indianapolis, IN 46240-3770 USA Toll Free: 800-545-5914 Do not confuse with Cisco Pr., Torrance, CA
E-mail: bulkorders@ciscopress.com
Web site: http://www.ciscopress.com
Dist(s): **Alpha Bks.**
MyiLibrary
Pearson Education
Pearson Technology Group.

C-It Entertainment Group, LLC, *(978-0-9718151)* 230 S. Hamilton Dr. Unit 204, Beverly Hills, CA 90211 USA Tel 213-925-1535; Fax: 213-291-1473
E-mail: dennischristen@hotmail.com
Web site: http://www.booksnflicks.com.

Citified Pubns., *(978-0-9832174)* 1310 Valley Lake Dr., Schaumburg, IL 60195 USA Tel 708-308-2854
E-mail: djsbchi@gmail.com.

Citizen Pr, *(978-0-9779100)* P.O. Box 1369, Glendale, CA 91209-1369 USA Tel 310-497-7419; Fax: 818-450-0518
E-mail: citizen@citizenpress.net
Web site: http://www.citizenpress.net.

Citizens Publishing, *(978-0-9755597)* 17636 W. Neuberry Ridge Dr., Lockport, IL 60441 USA
Web site: http://www.citizenspublishing.com.

Citlembik/Nettleberry Pubns. (TUR) *(978-975-6663; 978-9944-424)* *Dist. by* **Natl Bk Netwk.**

Citrus Roots - Preserving Citrus Heritage Foundation, *(978-0-9669508)* Orders Addr.: P.O. Box 4038, BALBOA, CA 92661 USA Tel 949-673-7877
Web site: http://www.citrusroots.com.

City Castles Publishing, *(978-0-615-22213-4; 978-0-615-26743-2; 978-0-615-56258-2)* 12160 E. Iowa Dr., Aurora, CO 80012 USA
Web site: http://www.citycastles.com.

City Creek Pr., Inc., *(978-1-883841)* P.O. Box 8415, Minneapolis, MN 55408-0415 USA
E-mail: orders@citycreek.com
Web site: http://www.citycreek.com
Dist(s): **Follett School Solutions.**

†City Lights Bks., *(978-0-87286)* 261 Columbus Ave., San Francisco, CA 94133 USA (SAN 202-1684) Tel 415-362-1901; Fax: 415-362-4921
E-mail: staff@citylights.com
Web site: http://www.citylights.com
Dist(s): **Consortium Bk. Sales & Distribution**
MyiLibrary
Perseus Bks. Group
SPD-Small Pr. Distribution; *CIP.*

City of Elmhurst, *(978-0-9708003)* 209 N. York St., Elmhurst, IL 60126 USA Tel 630-530-3000; Fax: 630-530-3014
E-mail: nancy.wilson@elmhurst.org
Web site: http://www.elmhurst.org.

City of God, St. Joseph's Hill of Hope, *(978-1-892957)* Orders Addr.: P.O. Box 1055, Brea, CA 92822 USA Tel 714-528-6962; Fax: 714-528-0707; Edit Addr.: 7351 Carbon Canyon Rd., Brea, CA 92823 USA
E-mail: mail@themiracleofstjoseph.org
Web site: http://www.themiralceofstjoseph.org.

City of Manassas Department of Social Services, *(978-0-9747385)* 9324 West St. Ste. 201, Manassas, VA 20110-5198 USA.

City on a Hill, Inc., *(978-0-9779521)* 4085 Hancock Bridge Pkwy., Suite 111-269, North Fort Myers, FL 33903 USA Tel 614-488-6953
E-mail: info@cityonahillinc.org
Web site: http://www.cityonahillinc.org.

City Salvage Records, *(978-0-9713865)* 195 St. Marks Ave., No. 4, Brooklyn, NY 11238 USA Tel 718-857-6822
E-mail: andy@citysalvagerecords.com
Web site: http://citysalvagerecords.com.

CityLit Pr., *(978-1-936328)* c/o CityLit Project, 120 S. Curley St., Baltimore, MD 21224-2235 USA Tel 410-274-5691
E-mail: info@citylitproject.org
Web site: http://www.citylitprojet.org.

CityWeb Corp., *(978-0-9719803)* P.O. Box 702216, Tulsa, OK 74170-2216 USA Tel 918-369-0544
E-mail: citywebcorporation@acken.com
Web site: http://www.citywebbooks.com.

Civitas:Institute for the Study of Civil Society (GBR) *(978-1-903386)* *Dist. by* **Coronet Bks.**

CJR, *(978-0-9796411; 978-1-941607; 978-1-943764)* 8079 Barcarole Ct., Springfield, VA 22153-2945 USA Tel 571-481-5396
E-mail: books.kiteb@gmail.com
Web site: http://www.go2melik.org/NewBridgesTextbooks.lsp.

CK Bks., *(978-0-9797580)* 395A S. Hwy. 65, No. 324, Lincoln, CA 95648 USA.

CKE Pubns., *(978-0-935133; 978-1-932327)* Div. of Carolyn Kyle Enterprises, Orders Addr.: P.O. Box 12869, Olympia, WA 98508-2869 USA (SAN 695-197X) Toll Free: 800-428-7402; Edit Addr.: P.O. Box 12869, Olympia, WA 98508-2869 USA
E-mail: ckepubs@aol.com
Web site: http://www.ckepublications.com.

CKK Educational, LLC., *(978-0-9743499; 978-0-9963087)* 17 W. 8th St., Ocean City, NJ 08226-3430 USA Tel 609-398-1949; Toll Free: 866-543-5463
Web site: http://www.tannersmanners.com.

cky *See* **Congregation Kehilas Yaakov (CKY)**

CLADACH Publishing, *(978-0-9670386; 978-0-9759619; 978-0-9818929; 978-0-9891014)* P.O. Box 336144, Greeley, CO 80633 USA Tel 970-371-9530
E-mail: office@cladach.com
Web site: http://www.cladach.com.

Claim Stake Productions *See* **Claim Stake Publishing, LLC**

Claim Stake Publishing, LLC, *(978-1-936284)* P.O. Box 1586, Aspen, CO 81612 USA
E-mail: pfioravante@tmwent.com
Web site: http://www.travelswithgannonandwyatt.com.

Claire Pubns. (GBR) *(978-1-871098; 978-1-904572)* *Dist. by* **Parkwest Pubns.**

Clairmont Pr., Inc., *(978-0-9623319; 978-1-56733)* Orders Addr.: P.O. Box 11743, Montgomery, AL 36111 USA Tel 334-874-8638; Edit Addr.: Rte. 2, Box 191, Selma, AL 36701 USA.

Clandestine Pr., The, *(978-0-9766261)* 314 Taylor Pl., Ithaca, NY 14850-3135 USA Tel 607-273-8036
E-mail: dohertyprint@juno.com.

Clapper Publishing Co., *(978-0-930184)* Div. of Clapper Publishing Co., Inc., 2400 E. Devon, Suite 375, Des Plaines, IL 60018 USA (SAN 210-7104) Tel 847-635-5800; Fax: 847-635-6311.

Clara Publishing, *(978-0-9706347; 978-0-692-45828-0)* Orders Addr.: 680 Napa Ct., Claremont, CA 91711-1553 USA (SAN 254-7236)
E-mail: clarapub@ca.rr.com
Web site: http://www.magicunion.com.

Clarence-Henry Bks., *(978-0-615-19572-8; 978-0-578-05235-9; 978-0-615-42297-8; 978-0-9882909)* 4135 Teton Pl., Alexandria, VA 22312 USA
Web site: http://www.c-hbooks.com.

Claretian Pubns., *(978-0-89570)* 205 W. Monroe St., 9th Flr., Chicago, IL 60606 USA (SAN 207-5598) Tel 312-236-7782
E-mail: taylorm@claretians.org.

Clarion Bks. *Imprint of* **Houghton Mifflin Harcourt Trade & Reference Pubs.**

Clarionton Press *See* **Twelve Star Pr.**

Clark Bks., *(978-0-9741677; 978-0-615-11591-7; 978-0-615-11769-0)* 599 Shapleigh Corner Rd., Shapleigh, ME 04076 USA (SAN 630-2017) Tel 207-636-1769 Do not confuse with Clark Books in Baton Rouge, LA
E-mail: clarkbooks@metrocast.net
Web site: http://www.clarkbooksmaine.com.

Clark, I. E. Publications *See* **Family Plays**

Clark, N. Laurie *See* **Clark Pubs.**

Clark Productions Ltd. Inc., *(978-0-9777289)* P.O. Box 583, Little Rock, AR 72203 USA Tel 501-280-9424
E-mail: ouida-clark56@yahoo.com.

Clark Pubs., *(978-0-9641197)* 133 Chestnut St., Amherst, MA 01002 USA Tel 413-549-0575; 941-255-0431
E-mail: ellusmith@aol.com
Dist(s): **Brodart Co.**
North Country Bks., Inc.
Quality Bks., Inc.

Clark Publishing, Inc., *(978-1-883589; 978-0-9822201; 978-0-9825057; 978-0-9827453; 978-0-9832639)* Orders Addr.: P.O. Box 34102, Lexington, KY 40588 USA Toll Free: 800-944-3995; Edit Addr.: 250 E. Short St., Lexington, KY 40507 USA Toll Free: 859-944-3995 Do not confuse with companies with same or similar names in Tacoma, WA, Topeka, KS, Annapolis, MD
E-mail: bclark@theclarkgroupinfo.com
Web site: http://www.theclarkgroupinfo.com; http://www.kyalmanac.com; http://www.clarkpublishing.com; http://www.clarklegacies.com
Dist(s): **Follett School Solutions.**

Class Clown Academy, *(978-0-615-75102-3)* 2121 Dewey St., Santa Monica, CA 90405 USA Tel 9493226152
Dist(s): **CreateSpace Independent Publishing Platform.**

CLASS Publications *Imprint of* **Children Learning Awareness, Safety & Self-Defense**

Classic Bks., *(978-1-58201; 978-0-7426)* Orders Addr.: P.O. Box 130, Murrieta, CA 92564-0130 USA Tel 951-767-1803; Fax: 951-767-0133
Dist(s): **Reprint Services Corp.**

Classic Bookwrights *Imprint of* **Lindaloo Enterprises**

Classic Comic Store, Ltd. (GBR) *(978-1-906814)* *Dist. by* **Casemate Pubs.**

Classic Textbooks, *(978-1-4047)* Div of Classic Books, Orders Addr.: P.O. Box 130, Murrieta, CA 92564-0130 USA
E-mail: newbookorders@gmail.com.

Classical Academic Pr., *(978-1-60051)* 3920 Market St., Camp Hill, PA 17011-4202 USA
Web site: http://www.classicalacademicpress.com.

Classical Comics (GBR) *(978-1-906332; 978-1-907127)* *Dist. by* **PerseuPGW.**

Classical Home Education *See* **Pandia Pr.**

Classical Learning Universe, LLC, *(978-0-9721733; 978-0-9763376; 978-0-9793021)* 305 W. Broadway, Suite 184, New York, NY 10013 USA Tel 718-357-2431; Fax: 718-357-2432; Toll Free: 888-684-5922
E-mail: lindsay@classicallearning.com
Web site: http://www.classicallearning.com.

Classical Magic, Inc., *(978-0-9675997; 978-0-9794947)* P.O. Box 1809, Banner Elk, NC 28604 USA Tel 828-898-7764 (phone/fax); 828-898-9571
E-mail: comapers@skybest.com
Web site: http://www.classicalmagic.net
Dist(s): **Book Clearing Hse.**

Classics International Entertainment, Inc., *(978-1-57209)* 324 Main Ave., Suite 183, Norwalk, CT 06851 USA Tel 203-849-8977; Fax: 203-847-5746.

Classroom Complete Pr. *Imprint of* **Rainbow Horizons Publishing, Inc.**

Claudia & Monica: Freshman Girls *Imprint of* **Stone Arch Bks.**

Claudia Cristina Cortez *Imprint of* **Stone Arch Bks.**

Clavis Publishing, *(978-1-60537)* 814 N. Franklin St., Chicago, IL 60610 USA; 250 West 57Th St. 15Th Flr., New York, NY 10016
E-mail: info@clavis.be
Web site: http://www.clavis.be
Dist(s): **Follett School Solutions**
Independent Pubs. Group
Legato Pubs. Group
Perseus-PGW.

Clawfoot Publishing, *(978-0-9747881)* 1236 S. Pekin Rd., Woodland, WA 98674 USA Tel 360-901-9932; Fax: 360-225-1311
E-mail: bobsbooks@zerfing.com
Web site: http://www.zerfing.com/bobsbooks.

Claybar Publishing, *(978-0-9787918)* 4007 Greenbriar Dr., Suite E, Stafford, TX 77477-3923 USA (SAN 851-5778) Tel 281-491-4009; Fax: 281-491-4024; Toll Free: 888-491-9533
E-mail: cbarclay@qdiinc.com
Web site: http://www.qdiinc.com
Dist(s): **AtlasBooks Distribution.**

Clayro Corp., *(978-0-9709523)* P.O. Box 270605, Oklahoma City, OK 73137-0605 USA Tel 405-373-2347; Fax: 405-373-0923
E-mail: waderoddy@yahoo.com
Web site: http://tcpublishers.com.

Claystone Bks. *Imprint of* **Ingalls Publishing Group, Inc.**

Clayton, Mike, *(978-0-9772622)* 639 Howard Rd., West Point, NY 10996-1510 USA
Web site: http://www.session6wrestling.com.

Clean Teen Publishing, *(978-0-9894701; 978-1-940534; 978-1-63422)* P.O. Box 561326, The Colony, TX 75056 USA Tel 469-583-8737
E-mail: submissions@cleanteenpublishing.com
Web site: http://www.cleanteenpublishing.com; www.crimsontreepublishing.com
Dist(s): **Lightning Source, Inc.**
Midpoint Trade Bks., Inc.

Clear Braces L.L.C., *(978-0-9790682)* 1530 Palisade Ave., Fort Lee, NJ 07024 USA Tel 201-947-6453
E-mail: drjfortlee@aol.com
Web site: http://www.pediatric-dentistry.com.

Clear Creek Pubs., *(978-0-9653543)* Orders Addr.: 115 Clear Creek Ct., Fayetteville, GA 30215 USA Tel 770-461-9460
E-mail: patcruzan@aol.com.

Clear Horizon, *(978-0-9773569; 978-1-936187)* 605 Silverthorn Rd., Gulf Breeze, FL 32561 USA Tel 850-934-0819; Fax: 850-934-9981
E-mail: info@maxpress.com; ginac@maxpress.com
Web site: http://www.maxpress.com.

Clear Light Pubs., *(978-0-940666; 978-1-57416)* 823 Don Diego, Santa Fe, NM 87501 USA (SAN 219-7758) Tel 505-989-9590; Fax: 505-989-9519; Toll Free: 800-253-2747; 823 Don Diego, Sante Fe, CA 87501 Do not confuse with Clear Light Pub., Seattle, WA
E-mail: service@clearlightbooks.com; janet@clearlightbooks.com
Web site: http://www.clearlightbooks.com
Dist(s): **Follett School Solutions.**

Clear Water Pr., *(978-0-9742972; 978-0-9828995)* 1909 S. Stagecoach Dr., Olathe, KS 66062 USA Do not confuse with Clear Water Press in Reno, NV
E-mail: editor@clearwaterpress.com
Web site: http://www.clearwaterpress.com
Dist(s): **Send The Light Distribution LLC.**

Clearbridge Publishing, *(978-1-929194)* Orders Addr.: P.O. Box 33772, Seattle, WA 98133 USA (SAN 857-8524) Tel 206-533-9357; Fax: 206-546-9756; *Imprints:* Art of War Plus Books (Art War Plus)
E-mail: garyg@clearbridge.com
Web site: http://www.clearbridge.com; http://www.booksonstrategy.com.

Clearwater Publishing, *(978-0-9769465)* 4300 NW 23rd Ave. Ate. 233, Gainesville, FL 32605 USA Toll Free: 866-766-5103.

ClearWaters Publishing, *(978-0-9841439)* 7539 Parkview Dr., Columbia, SC 29223 USA Tel 803-404-8893
E-mail: clearwatersllc@yahoo.com; thomashuntersjr@yahoo.com
Web site: http://www.tjhunteronline.com.

Cleis Pr., *(978-0-939416; 978-1-57344; 978-1-936740; 978-1-62778; 978-1-940550; 978-1-63228)* 2246 Sixth St, Berkeley, CA 94710-2219 USA (SAN 284-9976) Tel 510-845-8000; Fax: 510-845-8001; Toll Free: 800-780-2279; 387 Pk. Ave. S., New York, NY 10016
E-mail: kwuest@cleispress.com
Web site: http://www.cleispress.com
Dist(s): **Follett School Solutions**
MyiLibrary
Perseus-PGW
Perseus Bks. Group.

Clem Publishing, *(978-0-9772225)* P.O. Box 246, Danvers, IL 61732 USA Tel 309-530-0710; 116 W. North St., Danvers, IL 61732
E-mail: josephclem@hotmail.com.

Clements, J. S. Corporation *See* **Clements, Jehan**

Clements, Jehan, *(978-0-9622500)* Orders Addr.: P.O. Box 543, Tarrytown, NY 10591 USA Tel 914-293-7884
E-mail: storyteller1@optonline.net
Web site: http://www.flipoverpicturebooks.com.

Clendenin Fine Art Concepts, *(978-0-9897662)* 8160 Manitoba St., No. 104, Playa del Rey, CA 90293 USA Tel 310-821-3941; Fax: 310-821-2282
E-mail: aclendenin@verizon.net
Web site: www.clendeninfineart.com.

Clerisy Pr., *(978-0-9617367; 978-1-57860; 978-1-878208; 978-0-9777651)* Div. of Keen Communications, Orders Addr.: 2204 First Ave. South Suite 102, Birmingham, AL 35233 USA (SAN 255-478X) Tel 513-861-4045; Fax: 512-861-4430; Toll Free: 800-913-9563; Edit Addr.: 387 Pk. Ave. S., New York, NY 10016 USA
E-mail: info@emmisbooks.com; info@guildpress.com
Web site: http://www.clerisypress.com
Dist(s): **Follett School Solutions**
MyiLibrary
Perseus-PGW
Perseus Bks. Group
ebrary, Inc.

Cleveland Clinic Pr., *(978-1-59624)* c/o Lawrence D. Chilnick, 9500 Euclid Ave., NA32, Cleveland, OH 44195 USA Tel 216-444-1158; Fax: 216-444-9385
E-mail: chilnil@ccf.org
Web site: http://www.clevelandclinicpress.org
Dist(s): **Ingram Pub. Services.**

†**Cleveland Museum of Art,** *(978-0-910386; 978-0-940717; 978-1-935294)* 11150 East Blvd., Cleveland, OH 44106-1797 USA (SAN 278-4572) Tel 216-421-7340; Fax: 216-421-9409; Toll Free: 1-877-262-4748
E-mail: bbradley@clevelnadart.org
Web site: http://www.clevelandart.org
Dist(s): **Art Media Resources, Inc.**
Chicago Distribution Ctr.
D.A.P./Distributed Art Pubs.
Hopkins Fulfillment Services
Hudson Hills Pr. LLC
Ohio Univ. Pr.
Univ. of Washington Pr.; *CIP.*

Cleveland Stock Images, *(978-0-9617637)* Two Bratenahl Pl., Suite 9 EF, Cleveland, OH 44108 USA (SAN 664-8533) Tel 216-681-5621; Fax: 216-249-5828
E-mail: jsjidc@aol.com.

Clever Factory, The, *(978-1-59277)* 545 Mainstream Dr., Suite 406, Nashville, TN 37228 USA.

CleverKits,LLC, *(978-0-9778771)* 12 Brinckerhoff Ave, Stamford, CT 06905-3201 USA Fax: 267-821-7523
E-mail: cleverkits@yahoo.com
Web site: http://www.cleverkits.com.

CLF Publishing, *(978-0-9857372; 978-0-9884237; 978-0-9892358; 978-0-9899408; 978-0-9960815; 978-0-9961971)* 10063 Maple Ave., Hesperia, CA 92345 USA Tel 760-669-8149
E-mail: DRCWE@YAHOO.COM
Dist(s): **Lulu Enterprises Inc.**

Client Distribution Services *See* **Perseus-PGW**

Cliff Road Bks., *(978-1-60261)* 3437 Cliff Rd., Birmingham, AL 35222 USA (SAN 857-409X)
E-mail: holly@cliffroadbooks.com.

Clifton Carriage House Pr., *(978-0-9825713)* 12 S. Sixth St., No. 1250, Minneapolis, MN 55402 USA Fax: 612-746-8811
E-mail: wreynolds@briobooks.com
Web site: http://www.briobooks.com.

Clinch, David *See* **Clinch Media**

Clinch Media, *(978-0-9800835)* 1339 Mill Glen Dr., Atlanta, GA 30338 USA (SAN 855-1588) Tel 770-730-1721
E-mail: clinch@bellsouth.net
Web site: http://www.theleprechauntrap.com.

Cline Enterprises, *(978-0-615-76635-5; 978-0-692-26940-4)* 77 Cline Dr., Greenfield twp., ME 04418 USA Tel 207-827-2836
E-mail: acline@umche.maine.edu
Dist(s): **CreateSpace Independent Publishing Platform.**

Clocktower Hill Research & Publishing Group, LLC, *(978-0-9832130)* 23 Oakfield Dr., Rome, GA 30161 USA Tel 706-936-0254; Fax: 973-201-1755; *Imprints:* Lucas Violet (LucasViolet)
E-mail: davidehrler@clocktowerhill.com
Web site: http://www.clocktowerhill.com.

ClockTower Pubns., *(978-0-9704280)* 203 Skyland Dr., Dept. I, Staunton, VA 24401-2358 USA Tel 540-885-6614
E-mail: trgww@ntelos.net.

CLOJ Publishing, *(978-0-9767711)* 544 Rialto Ave., Venice, CA 90291-4248 USA (SAN 256-5129) Tel 310-399-6126
E-mail: publisher@clojpublishing.com
Web site: http://www.clojpublishing.com.

Cloonfad Pr., *(978-0-9744744; 978-0-9769404; 978-0-9797772)* Orders Addr.: P.O. Box 106, Cassville, NJ 08527 USA Tel 732-833-9800 (phone/fax)
E-mail: cloonfad@optonline.net
Web site: http://www.cloonfadpress.com
Dist(s): **Wilson & Assocs.**

Cloquet River Pr., *(978-0-9720050; 978-0-9792175)* 5353 Knudsen Rd, Duluth, MN 55803 USA Tel 218-721-3213; Fax: 218-725-5074
E-mail: cloquetriverpress@yahoo.com
Web site: http://www.cloquetriverpress.com
Dist(s): **Partners Bk. Distributing, Inc.**

Close, Rosa *See* **Misha Foundation**

Closer Looks Bks., *(978-0-9763593)* 864 Horns Corners Rd., Cedarburg, WI 53012 USA
E-mail: sggk@wi.rr.com
Web site: http://home.wi.rr.com/acloserlookbooks.

Clotho Pr., *(978-0-9821271)* 13205 Bluhill Rd., Silver Spring, MD 20910 USA Tel 301-962-8984
E-mail: polka.dot@verizon.net
Web site: http://www.womenmakingamerica.com
Dist(s): **Midpoint Trade Bks., Inc.**

Cloud 9 Ranch, *(978-0-9767690)* 231 Jung Blvd., E, Naples, FL 34120 USA Tel 239-353-6877; Fax: 239-353-7579
E-mail: nsfcloud9@aol.com
Web site: http://www.cloud9ranch.info.

Cloud Lake Publications *See* **Cloud Lake Publishing**

Cloud Lake Publishing, *(978-0-9787054)* Orders Addr.: 1083 Vine St., #185, Healdsburg, CA 95448-9544 USA
E-mail: marylynn@winecountrywriter.com
Web site: http://www.winecountrywriter.com.

Cloud Mountain Publishing *See* **Easter Island Foundation**

Cloudmaker Entertainment, *(978-0-9743989)* 7654 195th Ave. Ct. E., Bonney Lake, WA 98390 USA Tel 253-862-1490 (phone/fax)
E-mail: trox@cloudmakerentertainment.com
Web site: http://www.cloudmakerentertainment.com.

Cloudstone, *(978-1-879846)* 10 Patchin Pl., New York, NY 10011 USA Tel 212-929-6871.

Cloudwalker Publications *See* **Working Title Publishing**

Club Pro Products, *(978-0-9725721)* 153 Raquet Club Dr., Rancho Mirage, CA 92270 USA
E-mail: info@robstanger.com
Web site: http://www.robstanger.com.

Club4Girls *Imprint of* **Club4Girls Publishing Co.**

Club4Girls Publishing Co., *(978-0-9712297)* 4017 Dutch Harbor Ct., Raleigh, NC 27606-8604 USA Tel 919-387-9939; *Imprints:* Club4Girls (ClubFourGirls)
E-mail: bob@sas.com.

ClueSearchPuzzles.com, *(978-0-9753879)* 7645 N. Union Blvd. #175, Colorado Springs, CO 80920-3863 USA Tel 719-659-9034
E-mail: books@cluesearchpuzzles.com
Web site: http://www.cluesearchpuzzles.com.

Cluster Storm Publishing, *(978-1-56998)* Orders Addr.: 507 E. 3750 N., Provo, UT 84604 USA Tel 801-623-9101
E-mail: cjmartell@gmail.com.

CMB Publishing Co., *(978-0-9722969)* 24 Appleton St., Suite 1, Boston, MA 02116 USA Tel 617-306-5581; Fax: 617-451-0168
E-mail: info@cmbpublishing.com
Web site: http://www.cmbpublishing.com/.

CMC Publishing, *(978-0-9787336)* 1 Heritage Pl., Nesconset, NY 11767 USA
E-mail: colleenssite@yahoo.com.

CMS Enterprises, *(978-0-9768170)* Orders Addr.: P.O. Box 8039, Van Nuys, CA 91409 USA (SAN 256-5226); Edit Addr.: 6429 Whitman Ave., Van Nuys, CA 91406 USA
E-mail: cms55@hotmail.com.

CMX *Imprint of* **DC Comics**

CNL Publishing, *(978-0-9766921)* 105 Wedgewood Dr., Fairfield, AL 35064 USA Tel 205-835-5444; Fax: 205-923-3218.

Coach Enterprises, *(978-0-9636706)* 616 Munntown Rd., Finleyville, PA 15332 USA Tel 724-348-4843; Fax: 724-348-5549.

Coach Hse. Bks. (CAN) *(978-1-55245; 978-1-77056)* *Dist. by* **Consort Bk Sales.**

Coachwhip Pubns., *(978-1-930585; 978-1-61646)* 1505 English Brook Dr., Landisville, PA 17538 USA
E-mail: chadarnent@verizon.net
Web site: http://www.coachwhipbooks.com.

Coal City Stories, *(978-0-9849028)* 1101 Cole Dr., Lilburn, GA 30047 USA Tel 678-896-9493 (Tel/Fax)
E-mail: emilie.bush@gmail.com; machineseat@hotmail.com
Web site: CoalCItySteam.com.

Coal Hole Productions, *(978-0-9709630)* 207 Hemlock Ln., Bloomsburg, PA 17815 USA Tel 570-784-4561
E-mail: ceo@coalhole.com
Web site: http://www.coalhole.com
Dist(s): **Partners Bk. Distributing, Inc.**

Coal Under Pressure Pubns., *(978-0-9763400; 978-0-9913704)* Div. of Coal Under Pressure, LLC, Orders Addr.: 42625 Hwy. 27 N. #156, Davenport, FL 33837 USA Tel 347-829-7487
E-mail: coalunderpressurepubs@gmail.com
Web site: http://www.coalunderpressure.com.

Coast View Publishing, *(978-0-9849732)* 638 Camino De Los Mares Suite H130-157, San Clemente, CA 92673 USA Tel 949-388-7996
E-mail: coastviewpublishing@yahoo.com.

Coastal Carolina Pr., *(978-1-928556)* Orders Addr.: P.O. Box 9111, Chapel Hill, NC 27515-9111 USA
E-mail: books@coastalcarolinapress.org
Web site: http://www.coastalcarolinapress.org
Dist(s): **Blair, John F. Pub.**
Parnassus Bk. Distributors.

Coastal Publishing Carolina, Inc., *(978-0-9705727; 978-1-931650)* 504 Amberjack Way, Summerville, SC 29485 USA Tel 843-821-6168; Fax: 843-851-6949
E-mail: coastalpublishing@earthlink.net
Web site: http://coastalpublishing.net/.

Coastal Publishing, LLC, *(978-0-9755573)* No. 226, 1133 Bal Harbor Blvd., Suite 1139, Punta Gorda, FL 33950-6574 USA Tel 941-505-5547.

Cobalt Pr., *(978-0-9747805)* P.O. Box 5393, Hauppauge, NY 11788 USA Do not confuse with Cobalt Pr. in Minneapolis, MN
Web site: http://www.geocities.com/corrinedzwil/index.html.

Cobblestone Publishing Co., *(978-0-382; 978-0-942389; 978-0-9607638)* Div. of Cricket Magazine Group, 30 Grove St., Suite C, Peterborough, NH 03458 USA (SAN 237-9937) Tel 603-924-7209; Fax: 603-924-7380; Toll Free: 800-821-0115; P.O. Box 487, Effingham, IL 62401
E-mail: custsvc@cobblestone.mv.com
Web site: http://www.cobblestonepub.com
Dist(s): **Americana Publishing, Inc.**
Follett School Solutions
Perseus-PGW.

Cochise County Juvenile Detention Ctr., *(978-0-9771011)* P.O. Box 208, Bisbee, AZ 85603 USA Fax: 520-432-7136
Web site: http://www.co.cochise.az.us/schools.

Cochran, Russ Co., The, *(978-0-939947; 978-0-9816923)* P.O. Box 469, West Plains, MO 65775 USA (SAN 663-8236) Fax: 417-256-6666
E-mail: russcochran333@gmail.com
Web site: http://www.russcochran.com.

Cockburn Publishing, *(978-1-887461)* 1504 Mithra St., New Orleans, LA 70122-2018 USA.

Cockey, EJ & Company *See* **ThePaintedWord, Ltd.**

Coconut Info, *(978-1-929317)* Orders Addr.: P.O. Box 75460, Honolulu, HI 96836 USA Tel 808-947-6543; Fax: 808-923-6544
E-mail: sales@coconutinfo.com; info@coconutinfo.com
Web site: http://www.coconutinfo.com
Dist(s): **Booklines Hawaii, Ltd.**

Coconut Pr., LLC, *(978-0-9702168; 978-0-9778913)* Div. of Puerto Rico Postcard Co., Inc, Orders Addr.: P.O. Box 309540, Saint Thomas, VI 00803 USA Tel 787-248-3774; Fax: 787-253-8449; Edit Addr.: P.O. Box 79710, Carolina, PR 00984 USA Do not confuse with companies with same or similar names in Coral Gables, FL, Missouri City, TX
E-mail: Angelaspenceley1@msn.com
Dist(s): **Puerto Rico Postcard.**

Coda Grove Publishing, *(978-0-9889113)* P.O. Box 275, Fairfax, VT 05454 USA Tel 802-849-2777
E-mail: codagrovepub@gmail.com.

Cody's Guide, *(978-0-9755305)* 3855 Humbug Creek Rd., Applegate, OR 97530 USA
Web site: http://www.codysguide.com.

Coffee Hse. Ink, *(978-0-9663176)* 32370 SE Judd Rd., Eagle Creek, OR 97022 USA Tel 503-637-3277; Fax: 503-423-7980
E-mail: donmillllll@aol.com
Web site: http://www.coffeehouseink.com.

Coffee Hse. Pr., *(978-0-918273; 978-1-56689)* 79 13th Ave NE Ste. 110, Minneapolis, MN 55413-1073 USA (SAN 206-3883); 387 Pk. Ave. S., New York, NY 10016
Web site: http://www.coffeehousepress.org
Dist(s): **BookMobile**
Consortium Bk. Sales & Distribution
Follett School Solutions
MyiLibrary
Perseus Bks. Group
SPD-Small Pr. Distribution.

Coffragants (CAN) *(978-2-921997; 978-2-89517; 978-2-89558)* *Dist. by* **Penton Overseas.**

Coghlan Group, The *See* **Phoenix International, Inc.**

Cohen, Deanna Moreau, *(978-0-9747081)* 1626a Garden St., Santa Barbara, CA 93101-1110 USA
E-mail: liftveil2@cs.com.

Cohen Lane Productions *See* **Favonian Bks.**

Cohen, Sonia *See* **Gigi Enterprises**

Cohn, Tricia, *(978-0-9743847)* 16158 Highgate Dr., Riverside, CA 92503-8718 USA Tel 714-272-6972
E-mail: triciacohn@beobi.com
Web site: http://www.beobi.com.

Coho Press *See* **Dot Dot Bks.**

Cokesbury *Imprint of* **Abingdon Pr.**

Cola, Arthur, *(978-0-9789423)* 425 Robins Run, Papa Adventures, Burlington, WI 53105 USA
E-mail: arthurcola@yahoo.com
Dist(s): **Partners Bk. Distributing, Inc.**

Colbert Hse., LLC, The, *(978-1-887399)* Orders Addr.: P.O. Box 786, Mustang, OK 73064-0786 USA Tel 405-204-0043
E-mail: customerservice@colberthouse.com
Web site: http://www.colberthouse.com.

Colbert House, The *See* **Colbert Hse., LLC, The**

Colbyjack.net, *(978-0-615-46679-8)* 2243 Crary, Green Bay, WI 54304 USA Tel 920-544-7024
E-mail: rlferguson@colbyjack.net
Web site: www.colbyjack.net
Dist(s): **CreateSpace Independent Publishing Platform**
Dummy Record Do Not USE!!!!
Smashwords.

Cold River Pubns., *(978-0-9712867; 978-0-692-52577-7)* P.O. Box 606, Long Lake, NY 12847-0606 USA Tel 518-624-3581
E-mail: criver@telenet.net; criver@telenent.net
Web site: http://www.coldriverwoodworks.com
Dist(s): **AtlasBooks Distribution**
Smashwords.

Cole, Lois, *(978-0-615-83990-5; 978-0-692-28806-1)* 23707 Hopewell Dr., Katy, TX 77493 USA Tel 2816394545
Web site: http://www.amazon.com/dp/B00DJE8YC0
Dist(s): **CreateSpace Independent Publishing Platform.**

Cole Publishing, *(978-0-9678779; 978-0-9773973; 978-0-9787317)* 13428 Maxella Ave., Suite 701, Marina Del Rey, CA 90292 USA (SAN 256-856X) Fax: 310-209-2448
E-mail: candace@candacecole.com; ccpprod@aol.com
Web site: http://candacecole.com/.

Cole-Dai, Phyllis, *(978-0-615-24350-4)* 712 6th St., Brookings, SD 57006 USA Tel 605-692-7001
E-mail: phyllis@phylliscoledai.com; coledai@brookings.net
Web site: http://www.phylliscoledai.com.

Coleman, CJ, *(978-0-9773651)* 2191 Craig Springs Rd., Sturgis, MS 39769 USA Tel 662-312-4383
E-mail: cillycreations@hotmail.com
Web site: http://www.cillycreations.com.

Coleman Ranch Pr., *(978-0-9677069)* Orders Addr.: P.O. Box 1496, Sacramento, CA 95812 USA Tel 916-393-9032; Toll Free Fax: 888-532-4190; Toll Free: 877-765-3225
E-mail: colemanranch@comcast.net
Web site: http://www.CRPRESS.com.

Coleman, Wim *See* **Coleman/Perrin**

Coleman/Perrin, *(978-1-935178)* 405 Walnut St., Chapel Hill, NC 27517 USA Tel 919-338-8119; *Imprints:* ChironBooks (ChironBooks)
E-mail: wim-pat@gmail.com; info@chironbooks.com
Web site: http://www.playsonideas.com; http://www.chironbooks.com; http://www.madeirapress.com
Dist(s): **BookBaby**
Pathway Bk. Service.

Colihue (ARG) *(978-950-581) Dist. by* **AIMS Intl.**

Collector Bks., *(978-0-89145; 978-1-57432; 978-1-60460)* Div. of Schroeder Publishing Co., Inc., Orders Addr.: P.O. Box 3009, Paducah, KY 42003 USA (SAN 157-5368) Tel 270-898-6211; 270-898-7903; Fax: 270-898-8890; 270-898-1173; Toll Free: 800-626-5420 (orders only); Edit Addr.: 5801 Kentucky Dam Rd., Paducah, KY 42003 USA (SAN 200-7479); *Imprints:* American Quilter's Society (Am Quilters Soc)
E-mail: Info@collectorbooks.com; info@AQSquilt.com
Web site: http://www.collectorbooks.com; http://www.americanquilter.com/.

Collectors Pr., Inc., *(978-0-9635202; 978-1-888054; 978-1-933112)* Orders Addr.: P.O. Box 230986, Portland, OR 97281 USA Tel 503-684-3030; Fax: 503-684-3777; Toll Free: 800-423-1848; Edit Addr.: P.O. Box 230986, Portland, OR 97281-0986 USA
E-mail: lperry@collectorspress.com; rperry@collectorspress.com
Web site: http://www.collectorspress.com
Dist(s): **Universe Publishing**
Worldwide Media Service, Inc.

College & Career Pr., LLC, *(978-0-9745251; 978-0-9829210)* P.O. Box 300484, Chicago, IL 60630 USA Tel 773-282-4671; Fax: 773-282-4671; P.O. Box 300484, Chicago, IL 60630
E-mail: andymorkes@gmail.com
Web site: http://www.collegeandcareerpress.com; http://www.ccpnewsletters.com
Dist(s): **Brodart Co.**
Follett School Solutions.

College Assistance & Scholarship Help, Incorporated *See* **College Assistance, Inc.**

College Assistance, Inc., *(978-0-9760251)* Orders Addr.: 7235 Promenade Dr. Apt. J401, Boca Raton, FL 33433-6982 USA Toll Free: 866-346-7890
E-mail: librodereecy@aol.com; thecollegebook@aol.com
Web site: http://www.librodelauniversidad.com; http://www.thecollegebook.com; http://www.reecysbook.com.

College Board, The, *(978-0-87447; 978-1-4573)* Orders Addr.: Two College Way, Forrester Center, WV 25438 USA (SAN 203-5685) Toll Free Fax: 800-525-5562; Toll Free: 800-323-7155 (for Visa, Mastercard, American Express, & Discover); Edit Addr.: 45 Columbus Ave., New York, NY 10023-6992 USA (SAN 203-5677) Tel 212-713-8000; Fax: 212-713-8309
Web site: http://www.collegboard.com
Dist(s): **Holt, Henry & Co.**
Macmillan.

College Entance Examination Board *See* **College Board, The**

College Hse. Enterprises, LLC, *(978-0-9655911; 978-0-9700675; 978-0-9723567; 978-0-9762413; 978-0-9792581; 978-1-935673)* 5713 Glen Cove Dr., Knoxville, TN 37919-8611 USA (SAN 253-5831) Tel 865-558-6111 (phone/fax)
Web site: http://www.collegehousebooks.com.

College of DuPage Pr., *(978-1-932514)* Orders Addr.: 425 Fawell Blvd., Glen Ellyn, IL 60137 USA Fax: 630-942-3333; Toll Free: 800-290-4474
E-mail: software@cod.edu
Web site: http://www.dupagepress.com.

College Planning Network, *(978-1-880344)* 914 E. Jefferson, Campion Tower, Seattle, WA 98122 USA Tel 206-323-0624; Fax: 206-323-0623
E-mail: seaspn@collegeplan.org
Web site: http://www.collegeplan.org.

College Prowler, Inc., *(978-1-932215; 978-1-59658; 978-1-4274)* 5001 Baum Blvd. Ste. 750, Pittsburgh, PA 15213-1856 USA Toll Free Fax: 800-772-4972; Toll Free: 800-290-2682; *Imprints:* Off The Record (Off The Rcd)
E-mail: joey@collegeprowler.com; luke@collegeprowler.com
Web site: http://www.collegeprowler.com.

Collegiate Kids Bks., LLC, *(978-0-9836211; 978-0-692-01848-4; 978-0-9886542)* 3956 2nd St. Dr. NW, Hickory, NC 28601 USA Tel 828-773-5398
E-mail: bryan@collegiatekidsbooks.com
Web site: http://www.collegiatekidsbooks.com.

Colleton County Memorial Library, *(978-0-615-80497-2; 978-0-615-80499-6; 978-0-615-83707-9; 978-0-615-83711-6; 978-0-615-88290-1; 978-0-615-88291-8; 978-0-615-92781-7; 978-0-615-92782-4)* 600 Hampton St., Walterboro, SC 29488 USA Tel 843-549-5621
E-mail: skeaise@colletoncounty.org
Dist(s): **CreateSpace Independent Publishing Platform.**

Collins *Imprint of* **HarperCollins Pubs.**

Collins Design *Imprint of* **HarperCollins Pubs.**

Collins Pr., The (IRL) *(978-0-9516306; 978-1-898256; 978-1-903464; 978-1-905172; 978-1-84889) Dist. by* **Dufour.**

Collins, Robert, *(978-0-9766426)* 865 Helke Rd., Vandalia, OH 45377 USA; *Imprints:* Peregrine Communications (Peregrine Comm)
E-mail: adagio@gemair.com
Web site: http://www.ufoconspiracy.com/.

Colonel Davenport Historical Foundation, *(978-0-9755934)* P.O. Box 4703, Rock Island, IL 61204 USA
Web site: http://www.davenporthouse.org.

†Colonial Williamsburg Foundation, *(978-0-87935; 978-0-910412)* P.O. Box 3532, Williamsburg, VA 23187-3532 USA (SAN 128-4630) Fax: 757-565-8999 (orders only); Toll Free: 800-446-9240 (orders only)
Web site: http://www.colonialwilliamsburg.com
Dist(s): **Antique Collectors' Club**
National Bk. Network
Univ. Pr. of Virginia; *CIP.*

Color & Learn, *(978-0-9795190)* P.O. Box 1592, Saint Augustine, FL 32085-1592 USA (SAN 853-6023)
Web site: http://www.colorandlearn.com.

Color & Light Editions, *(978-0-9671527; 978-0-9835239)* 371 Drakes View Dr., Inverness, CA 94937 USA Tel 415-663-1616
E-mail: kathleenpgoodwin@gmail.com
Web site: http://BlairGoodwin.com
Dist(s): **Partners Bk. Distributing, Inc.**

Color Loco *See* **Color Loco, LLC**

Color Loco, LLC, *(978-0-9770652; 978-0-9788778)* 213 Woodland Dr., Downingtown, PA 19335-9335 USA
Web site: http://www.ColorLoco.com.

Colorado Associated University Press *See* **Univ. Pr. of Colorado**

Colorful Bks. Pr., *(978-0-9746152)* 935 Ottawa Ave., Ypsilanti, MI 48198 USA.

Colorful Crayons For Kids Publishing, LLC *See* **Jeb Cool Kids Entertainment, Inc**

Colossus Bks. *Imprint of* **Amber Bks.**

Columba Pr. (IRL) *(978-0-948183; 978-1-85607; 978-1-78218) Dist. by* **Dufour.**

†Columbia Univ. Pr., *(978-0-231)* Orders Addr.: 61 W. 62nd St., New York, NY 10023-7015 USA (SAN 212-2480) Toll Free Fax: 800-944-1844; Toll Free: 800-944-8648 x 6240 (orders); Edit Addr.: 61 W. 62nd St., New York, NY 10023 USA (SAN 212-2472) Tel 212-459-0600; Fax: 212-459-3678; 387 Pk. Ave., S., New York, NY 10016
E-mail: cupbooks@columbia.edu
Web site: http://www.columbia.edu/cu/cup
Dist(s): **CreateSpace Independent Publishing Platform**
Ebsco Publishing
Follett School Solutions
ISD
MyiLibrary
Perseus Bks. Group
Perseus Distribution
Perseus Academic
ebrary, Inc.; *CIP.*

Columbine Pr., *(978-0-9651272; 978-0-9768570; 978-0-9965407)* Orders Addr.: P.O. Box 1950, Cripple Creek, CO 80813 USA Tel 719-689-2141; Edit Addr.: 340 Colorado Ave., Cripple Creek, CO 80813 USA Do not confuse with companies with the same name in Bainbridge Island, WA, East Hampton, NY
E-mail: pkmacv@earthlink.net.

Columbus Zoo & Aquarium, The, *(978-0-9841554)* 4850 W. Powell Rd., P.O. Box 400, Powell, OH 43065 USA (SAN 858-589X) Tel 614-645-3400; Fax: 614-645-3465
E-mail: fran.baby@columbuszoo.org
Web site: http://www.columbuszoo.org
Dist(s): **Lerner Publishing Group.**

Column Hall Concepts, LLC, *(978-0-9786584)* 217 - 82nd St., Brooklyn, NY 11209 USA Tel 718-836-1072
Web site: http://www.heydadthebook.com
Dist(s): **Follett School Solutions.**

Combel Editorial, S.A. (ESP) *(978-84-7864; 978-84-9825) Dist. by* **IPG Chicago.**

Combs-Hulme Publishing, *(978-0-9769854)* 1720 Eldridge Ave. W., Saint Paul, MN 55113 USA Tel 651-631-2173 Do not confuse with Combs Publishing in Winston-Salem, NC
E-mail: lvhulme@aol.com.

Come & Get It Publishing, *(978-0-9653042; 978-0-9753883)* Orders Addr.: P.O. Box 1562, Madison, VA 22727 USA Tel 540-829-0516 Toll Free: 800-825-9008; Edit Addr.: 214 E. Spencer St., No. 1, Culpeper, VA 22701 USA
E-mail: hereme@aol.com
Dist(s): **Perseus-PGW.**

Comfort Publishing, Incorporated *See* **Comfort Publishing Services, LLC**

Comfort Publishing Services, LLC, *(978-0-9802051; 978-0-9821154; 978-1-935361; 978-0-9845598; 978-1-936695; 978-1-938388)* P.O. Box 6265, Concord, NC 28027-1521 USA Tel 704-782-2353; Fax: 704-782-2393
E-mail: khuddle@comfortpublishing.com; ptolen@comfortpublishing.com
Web site: http://www.comfortpublishing.com
Dist(s): **Music, Bks. & Business, Inc.**
Midpoint Trade Bks., Inc.

Comfort Tales, LLC, *(978-0-9741586)* Orders Addr.: 47 Watsons Way, Medford, NJ 08055 USA (SAN 255-464X) Tel 856-988-0884; Fax: 856-988-8499
E-mail: comforttales@aol.com.

Comic Library International, *(978-1-929515)* 2049 Alfred St., Pittsburgh, PA 15212-1426 USA; *Imprints:* Solovisions (Solovisions)
E-mail: gbstudios@comcast.net
Web site: http://www.geocities.com/SoHo/Cafe/9669/clipage.html
Dist(s): **Diamond Comic Distributors, Inc.**

Comics Lit *Imprint of* **NBM Publishing Co.**

ComicsOne Corp./Dr. Masters, *(978-1-58899)* P.O. Box 14232, Fremont, CA 94539-1532 USA
Dist(s): **Diamond Comic Distributors, Inc.**
Diamond Bk. Distributors
L P C Group.

Command Performance Language Institute, *(978-0-929724)* 25 Hopkins Ct., Berkeley, CA 94706 USA (SAN 250-1694) Tel 510-524-1191; Fax: 510-527-9880
E-mail: consee@aol.com
Web site: http://www.hometown.aol.com/commandperform1/myhomepage/business.html
Dist(s): **Alta English Publishers**
Applause Learning Resources
Athelstan Pubns.
Betty Segal, Inc.
BookLink
Calliope Bks.
Carlex
Continental Bk. Co., Inc.
Delta Systems Company, Inc.
Educational Showcase
Edumate-Educational Materials, Inc.
European Bk. Co., Inc.
Follett School Solutions
Gessler Publishing Co., Inc.
International Bk. Ctr., Inc.
Midwest European Pubns.
Miller Educational Materials
Multi-Cultural Bks. & Videos, Inc.
Sky Oaks Productions, Inc.
SpeakWare
Teacher's Discovery
Tempo Bookstore
2Learn-English
World of Reading, Ltd.

Command Publishing, LLC, *(978-0-9778356)* 43311 Joy Rd. Suite 201, Canton, MI 48187-2075 USA (SAN 850-2706).

Commercial Communications Incorporated *See* **Great Lakes Design**

Commission on Culture and Tourism, *(978-0-9759389)* 1 Constitution Plz., Hartford, CT 06103-1803 USA
E-mail: kazkozlowski@snet.net.

Committee for Children, *(978-0-9741388)* 568 First Ave. S., Suite 600, Seattle, WA 98104-2804 USA Toll Free: 800-634-4449
Web site: http://www.cfchildren.org.

Common Courtesy, *(978-0-9746148)* 709 Uwharrie St., Asheboro, NC 27203 USA Tel 336-629-5274
E-mail: jjdortch@earthlink.net.

Commonwealth Books, LLC *See* **Commonwealth Books of Virginia, LLC**

Commonwealth Books of Virginia, LLC, *(978-0-9825922; 978-0-9854863; 978-0-9904018; 978-0-9909592; 978-0-9961368; 978-1-943642)* 59 McFarland Point Dr, No. 12, Boothbay Harbor , ME 04538 USA Tel 703-307-7715; 434-242-4128
E-mail: jct@commonwealthbooks.org; info@commonwealthbooks.org
Web site: http://www.commonwealthbooks.org; http://www.commonwealthbooks.org; www.thomasjeffersonsenlightenment.org; www.bayardtberndt.org
Dist(s): **Casemate Pubs. & Bk. Distributors, LLC**
Independent Pubs. Group
MyiLibrary
Small Pr. United
ebrary, Inc.

Commonwealth Editions *Imprint of* **Applewood Bks.**

Commonwealth Secretariat (GBR) *(978-0-85092; 978-1-84929) Dist. by* **Stylus Pub VA.**

Communication Service Corporation *See* **Gryphon Hse., Inc.**

Community Voice Media, LLC, *(978-0-9776613; 978-0-9885741)* P.O. Box 564, Round Hill, VA 20142-5640 USA Tel 540-751-2214; Fax: 540-751-2215
E-mail: bobbicarducci@communityvoicemedia.com
Web site: http://www.communityvoicemedia.com.

Community Works!, *(978-0-9742213)* 13313 Country Way Cir., Fredericksburg, VA 22404 USA
E-mail: arayu1@comcast.net; carol@carolynnfitzpatrick.com
Web site: http://www.carolynnfitzpatrick.com
Dist(s): **New Leaf Distributing Co., Inc.**

Companhia das Letras (BRA) *(978-85-7164; 978-85-85095; 978-85-85466; 978-85-359) Dist. by* **Distribks Inc.**

Companhia Melhoramentos de Sao Paulo Industrias de Papel (BRA) *(978-85-06) Dist. by* **Lectorum Pubns.**

Compania Editorial Continental (MEX) *(978-968-26) Dist. by* **Fondo CA.**

Companion Pr., *(978-1-879651; 978-1-61722)* Div. of Ctr. for Loss & Life Transition, 3735 Broken Bow Rd., Fort Collins, CO 80526 USA Tel 970-226-6050; Fax: 970-226-6051; Toll Free Fax: 800-922-6051 (orders only) Do not confuse with companies with the same name in Santa Barbara, CA, Aliso Viejo, CA
E-mail: wolfelt@centerforloss.com
Web site: http://www.centerforloss.com
Dist(s): **Ebsco Publishing**
Independent Pubs. Group
MyiLibrary
ebrary, Inc.

Compass *Imprint of* **Raphel Marketing, Inc.**

Compass Books *See* **Lake Street Pubs.**

Compass Flower Pr. *Imprint of* **AKA:yoLa**

Compass Point Bks., *(978-0-7565)* Div. of Coughlan Publishing, Orders Addr.: 1710 Roe Crest Dr., North Mankato, MN 56003 USA (SAN 254-2013) Toll Free Fax: 877-371-1539; Toll Free: 877-371-1536; 1710 Roe Crest Dr., North Mankato, MN 56003; *Imprints:* Compass Point Phonics Readers (CPPP); CPB Grades 4-8 (CPBFour); CPB Grades K-3 (CPBK); Exploring Science (ExplorSci); First Reports (First Rep); For Fun! (For Fun); Global Connections (GlobConnect); Profiles of the Presidents (ProPres); Signature Lives (SigLives); Snapshots in History (SnapHist); We the People (WethePeople); Write Your Own (Write Your Own); Headline Science (HEADLINE SCIEN)
E-mail: custserv@compasspointbooks.com; k.monyhan@coughlancompanies.com
Web site: http://www.compasspointbooks.com; http://www.capstonepub.com
Dist(s): **Capstone Pr., Inc.**
Capstone Pub.
Chinasprout, Inc.
Ebsco Publishing
Follett School Solutions.

Compass Point Phonics Readers *Imprint of* **Compass Point Bks.**

Compass Publishing, *(978-0-9753102)* Orders Addr.: P.O. Box 280188, Lakewood, CO 80228-0188 USA (SAN 256-0186) Tel 818-264-9606 (phone/fax); Fax: 818-433-7445; Edit Addr.: 1912 Rivera Rd., Santa Fe Spring, CA 90670 USA
E-mail: billhowey@actorsmenu.com
Web site: http://www.actorsmenu.com
Dist(s): **Follett School Solutions**
Independent Pubs. Group.

Compassion Outreach Ministry *See* **Stott, Darrel Ministry**

Compassion Pets Publishing, *(978-0-615-13428-4; 978-0-615-30968-2)* 34672 Hardtack Ln., Shingletown, CA 96088 USA (SAN 858-5954) Tel 530-474-1038
E-mail: compassionpet.pub@frontiernet.net
Web site: http://www.compassionpets.com.

Compendium, Inc., Publishing & Communications, *(978-0-9640178; 978-1-888387; 978-1-932319; 978-1-935414; 978-1-938298; 978-1-943200)* Orders Addr.: P.O. Box 5308, Lynnwood, WA 98046-5308 USA (SAN 253-7109) Tel 425-673-2238; Fax: 425-673-6949; Toll Free: 800-914-3327; Edit Addr.: 600 N. 36th St. Ste. 400, Seattle, WA 98103-8699 USA
E-mail: kobi@compendiuminc.com; connie@compendiuminc.com; carolanne@compendiuminc.com
Web site: http://www.compendiuminc.com; http://www.live-inspired.com
Dist(s): **APG Sales & Distribution Services.**

Comprecom, *(978-0-9772809)* 411 Hess Ave., Golden, CO 80401 USA.

Comprehensive Health Education Foundation, *(978-0-935529; 978-1-57021)* 159 S. Jackson St. Ste. 510, Seattle, WA 98104-4416 USA (SAN 696-3668) Toll Free: 800-323-2433
E-mail: chefstaff@chef.org
Web site: http://www.chef.org/.

Compsych Systems, Inc., Pubns. Div., *(978-0-929948)* Div. of Compsych Systems, Inc., P.O. Box 1568, Pacific Palisades, CA 90272 USA (SAN 250-8281) Tel 310-454-6426 (phone/fax)
Web site: http://www.jeanettegriver.com
Dist(s): **Follett School Solutions.**

Computer Age Education *See* **Learning Net, The**

Computer Athlete Media, *(978-0-9820447)* P.O. Box 687, Princeton Junction, NJ 08550 USA
E-mail: support@computerathlete.net
Web site: http://www.computerathlete.net.

Computer Classics (R), *(978-0-9721216; 978-0-9748870; 978-0-9836019; 978-0-9899265)* 5036 Suter Dr., Nashville, TN 37211-5155 USA
E-mail: computerclassics@mindspring.com
Web site: http://www.computer-classics.com.

ComQwest, LLC, *(978-0-9753454)* 1350 E. Flamingo Rd., Suite No. 265, Las Vegas, NV 89119 USA
Web site: http://www.comqwest.com.

ComteQ Publishing, *(978-0-9674074; 978-0-9766889; 978-0-9793771; 978-1-935232; 978-1-941501)* Div. of ComteQ Communications, LLC, Orders Addr.: 101 N. Washington Ave. Suite 1b, Margate, NJ 08402 USA Tel 609-487-9000; Fax: 609-487-9099
E-mail: publisher@comteqpublishing.com
Web site: http://www.comteqpublishing.com
Dist(s): **BookBaby.**

Comunicadora Koine, Inc., *(978-0-9794682; 978-0-9834966)* Orders Addr.: P.O. Box RR3 Box 3801, San Juan, PR 00926 USA Tel 787-642-2053; Fax: 787-753-7077; Edit Addr.: 1118 Calle Padres Capuchinos, Rio Piedras, PR 00925 USA
E-mail: comunicadorakoine@gmail.com
Web site: http://www.comunicadorakoine.com.

ConArtistE Pubng., *(978-0-9755386)* 6084 Churn Creek Rd., Redding, CA 96002 USA Tel 530-209-4338
E-mail: conartiste@msn.com
Web site: www.conartiste.com.

Concepcion, Jorge, *(978-0-9761779)* 9125 SW 56th Ter., Miami, FL 33173-1605 USA
E-mail: jconcepcion1@msn.com.

Concept Media Group, LLC, The, *(978-0-9864191)* P.O. Box 211801, Dallas, TX 75211-1801 USA Tel 214-854-2150
E-mail: sherilyn@theconceptmediagroup.com
Web site: www.TheConceptMediaGroup.com.

Concepts *See* **Developmental Vision Concepts**

Concepts 'N' Publishing, *(978-1-879940)* Orders Addr.: P.O. Box 10413, College Station, TX 77842 USA
Web site: http://www.ethaemm.homestead.com.

Concerned Christians, *(978-0-9768352)* P.O. Box 18, Mesa, AZ 85211 USA Tel 480-833-2537; Fax: 480-833-4116
E-mail: jim@concernedchristians.org
Web site: http://www.concernedchristians.org.

Concerned Communications, *(978-0-936785; 978-1-58938)* Orders Addr.: P.O. Box 1000, Siloam Springs, AR 72761-1000 USA (SAN 699-8623) Tel 501-594-9000; Fax: 501-549-4002; Toll Free: 800-447-4332; Edit Addr.: 700 E. Granite St., Siloam Springs, AR 72761 USA (SAN 699-8631)
E-mail: lustwrt@areasonfor.com
Web site: http://www.areasonfor.com
Dist(s): **Project Patch.**

Conciliar Pr., *(978-0-9622713; 978-1-888212; 978-0-9822770; 978-1-936270)* Orders Addr.: P.O. Box 76, Ben Lomond, CA 95005-0076 USA Tel 831-336-5118; Fax: 831-336-8882; Toll Free: 800-967-7377; Edit Addr.: 10090-A Hwy. 9, Ben Lomond, CA 95005 USA (SAN 175-8624) Tel 831-336-5118; Fax: 831-336-8682; Toll Free: 800-967-7377
Web site: http://www.conciliarpress.com
Dist(s): **Midpoint Trade Bks., Inc.**
Spring Arbor Distributors, Inc.

Concinnity Initiatives, *(978-0-9842146; 978-0-615-49009-0; 978-0-615-53946-1)* 2733 Meade St., Denver, CO 80211-4076 USA
E-mail: kevin.mccaffrey@firstpersonpublishing.com; jeffrey.fugate@navy.mil
Web site: http://www.firstpersonpublishing.com.

Concordia Publishing Hse., *(978-0-570; 978-0-7586)* Subs. of Lutheran Church Missouri Synod, 3558 S. Jefferson Ave., Saint Louis, MO 63118-3968 USA (SAN 202-1781) Tel 314-268-1000; Fax: 314-268-1360; Toll Free Fax: 800-490-9889 (orders only); Toll Free: 800-325-3040 (orders only); 800-325-0191
E-mail: cphorder@cph.org
Web site: http://www.cph.org.

Concourse Pr., *(978-0-911323)* Subs. of East-West Fine Arts Corp., Orders Addr.: 14 Ridgeview Rd., Newtown Sq, PA 19073-3002 USA (SAN 269-249X); Edit Addr.: P.O. Box 8265, Philadelphia, PA 19101 USA
E-mail: site.concoursepress@gmail.com
Web site: http://www.ConcoursePress.com
Dist(s): **Brodart Co.**

Concrete Jungle Pr., *(978-0-9749048)* 47-04 168th St., Flushing, NY 11358 USA
E-mail: dw@dwaynedworsky.com
Web site: http://www.dwaynedworsky.com; www.alphacentauriandbeyond.com
Dist(s): **AtlasBooks Distribution.**

Conerly, Lawrence, *(978-0-9765669)* 85 Mt. Canaan Rd., Tylertown, MS 39667 USA
E-mail: augsept@bellsouth.net.

Conexion Educativa, *(978-0-9702021)* 900 Alameda St., Villa Granada, San Juan, PR 00923 USA Tel 787-766-4448; Fax: 787-250-8709
E-mail: conexion@coqui.net
Web site: http://home.coqui.net/conexion.

Conflict Games, LLC, *(978-0-9824507)* Orders Addr.: 15 Green Hill Ct., Nanuet, NY 10954 USA Tel 845-689-9014
E-mail: mscott@conflictroleplaying.com
Web site: http://www.conflictbooks.com/.

Cong Bais Tziporah, *(978-0-9728849; 978-0-9767166; 978-1-934098)* 3 Harrison Ave., Spring Valley, NY 10977 USA.

Congregation Agudat Achim, *(978-0-9770172)* 2117 Union St., Schenectady, NY 12309 USA
Web site: http://www.divinekosher.com.

Congregation Kehilas Yaakov (CKY), *(978-0-9770352; 978-0-9847019)* 2 Omni Ct., Lakewood, NJ 08701 USA Tel 732-942-8374.

Congress At Your Fingertips, *(978-1-879617)* Div. of Capitol Advantage, LLC, Orders Addr.: P.O. Box 309, Newington, VA 22122 USA Tel 703-550-9500; Fax: 703-550-0406; Toll Free: 877-827-3321; 8382-h Terminal Rd., Lorton, VA 22079
Web site: http://congressatyourfingertips.com.

Congressional Publishing, Inc., *(978-0-9762916)* P.O. Box 1318, Leesburg, VA 20177 USA Tel 703-777-6737; Fax: 703-777-6272
E-mail: congressionalpub@verizon.net
Web site: http://www.congressionalpublishing.com.

Coniston Designs (AUS) *(978-0-86435) Dist. by* **IPG Chicago.**

Conjunctions, *(978-0-941964)* Bard College, Annandale-on-Hudson, New York, NY 12504 USA (SAN 239-5169) Tel 914-758-1539; Fax: 914-758-2660
E-mail: conjunctions@bard.edu
Web site: http://www.conjunctions.com
Dist(s): **D.A.P./Distributed Art Pubs.**
Follett School Solutions
MyiLibrary
SPD-Small Pr. Distribution.

Conley, Connie, *(978-0-9800898)* 4555 SW Willow St., Seattle, WA 98136 USA (SAN 855-1731)
E-mail: puppyluck@comcast.net.

Connect *Imprint of* **Stone Arch Bks.**

Connect With Your Kid Bks., *(978-0-9746094)* 106 Central Park Sq., No.150, Los Alamos, NV 87544 USA Toll Free: 888-388-5437
E-mail: DrSillyScience@comcast.net
Web site: http://www.DrSillyScience.com.

Connected 2 The Father Publishing *See* **Urban Advocacy**

Connecticut Pr., The, *(978-0-9825468)* 135 Church St., Monroe, CT 06468 USA Tel 203-268-6784
E-mail: pjmalia@connecticutpress.com
Web site: http://www.connecticutpress.com
Dist(s): **Lightning Source, Inc.**

Connection, *(978-0-9743687)* 601 Daniel Ct., Nashville, TN 37221-6512 USA.

Connections Bk. Publishing, Ltd. (GBR) *(978-1-85906) Dist. by* **Red Wheel Weiser.**

Connelly Pr., The, *(978-0-9797415)* 243 Abrahams Ln., Villanova, PA 19085 USA
Dist(s): **AtlasBooks Distribution**
eBookIt.com.

Connexions Unlimited, *(978-1-929785)* 1021 Silver Lake Blvd., Frankfort, KY 40601 USA Tel 502-695-5181.

Connors, E. W. Publishing Co., *(978-0-9635587)* P.O. Box 691, Buffalo, NY 14205-0691 USA Tel 716-851-1343.

Conscience Studio, *(978-0-9828492)* 90 W. Univ. St., Alfred, NY 14802-1134 USA (SAN 859-9203) Tel 607-587-9111
E-mail: ConscienceStudio@gmail.com
Web site: http://www.consciencestudio.com.

Conscious Living Pubns., *(978-1-890580)* 15 Linden Ln., York, ME 03909 USA Tel 207-351-3316; Fax: 207-351-3369
E-mail: leosar@aol.com
Dist(s): **New Leaf Distributing Co., Inc.**

Consciousness-Based Education Association, *(978-0-9727877)* 1100 Univ. Manor Dr., B-24, Fairfield, IA 52556 USA Tel 641-472-1663; Fax: 641-472-3116; Toll Free: 888-472-1677
E-mail: info@cbeprograms.org
Web site: http://www.cbeprograms.org.

Consejo Estatal Electoral (MEX) *(978-970-58) Dist. by* **Santillana.**

Consilient Pubns., *(978-0-9746242)* 8176 S. Centaur Dr., Evergreen, CO 80439 USA Tel 303-679-1538
E-mail: stephanie@cost-benefit-jr.com
Web site: http://www.cost-benefit-jr.com.

Consortium Bk. Sales & Distribution, Div. of Perseus Bks. Group, Orders Addr.: 1094 Flex Dr., Jackson, TN 38301-5070 USA; Edit Addr.: 34 13th Ave NE, Suite 100, Minneapolis, MN 55413-1007 USA (SAN 200-6049) Toll Free: 800-283-3572 (orders)
E-mail: info@cbsd.com
Web site: http://www.cbsd.com/
Dist(s): **Follett School Solutions.**

Consortium Publishing Co., *(978-0-9644681; 978-0-9707173; 978-0-9748830)* Div. of Creative Ideas, Inc., Orders Addr.: P.O. Box 998, Jacksonville, IL 62651 USA; Edit Addr.: P.O. Box 1535, Jacksonville, IL 62651-1535 USA Tel 217-243-7628 (phone/fax); Toll Free: 800-419-8698; 888-456-7235; 4 Sunnydale Ave., Jacksonville, IL 62650
E-mail: consortm@aol.com
Web site: http://www.creativeideas.com.

Consortium, The *See* **Consortium Publishing Co.**

Constitutional Rights Foundation, *(978-1-886253)* 601 S. Kingsley Dr., Los Angeles, CA 90005 USA (SAN 225-6401) Tel 213-487-5590; Fax: 213-386-0459; Toll Free: 800-488-4273 Do not confuse with Constitutional Rights Foundation Chicago in Chicago, IL
E-mail: crf@crf.usa
Web site: http://www.crf-usa.org.

Consultant's Unlimited *See* **Schwarz Pauper Pr.**

Consumer Pr., The, *(978-0-9717119)* 6 Berkley Rd., Glenville, NY 12302 USA (SAN 254-5446)
E-mail: richesq@mindspring.com
Web site: http://www.theconsumerpress.com.

†Consumer Reports Bks., *(978-0-89043)* Div. of Consumers Union of U. S., Inc., 101 Truman Ave., Yonkers, NY 10703 USA (SAN 224-1048) Tel 914-378-2000; Fax: 914-378-2925; Toll Free: 800-500-9760 (book dept.)
Web site: http://www.consumerreports.org/
Dist(s): **Ingram Pub. Services**; *CIP.*

Consumers Union of U. S., Inc., *(978-0-89043; 978-0-9755388; 978-1-933524)* Orders Addr.: 540 Barnum Ave., Bridgeport, CT 06608 USA (SAN 661-9800); Edit Addr.: 101 Truman Ave., Yonkers, NY 10703 USA (SAN 269-3518) Tel 914-378-2000; Fax: 914-378-2925
Web site: http://ConsumersReports.org
Dist(s): **Ingram Pub. Services**
Macmillan.

Contemplation Corner Pr., *(978-0-9707979; 978-0-9758748)* 1229 Randy Rd., Ashland City, TN 37015 USA Tel 615-746-8220; Fax: 615-746-3697
E-mail: ccpress1@bellsouth.net
Web site: http://www.contemplationcornerpress.com.

Contemplative Pubns., *(978-0-9777612)* P.O. Box 5435, Manchester, NH 03108-5435 USA (SAN 850-1882)
Dist(s): **AtlasBooks Distribution.**

Contender Entertainment Group (GBR) *(978-1-84357) Dist. by* **IPG Chicago.**

Continental Bk. Co., Inc., *(978-0-9626800)* Eastern Div., 80-00 Cooper Ave., Bldg. No. 29, Glendale, NY 11385 USA (SAN 169-5436) Tel 718-326-0560; Fax: 718-326-4276; Toll Free: 800-364-0350; Western Div., 625 E. 70th Ave., No. 5, Denver, CO 80229 (SAN 630-2882) Tel 303-289-1761; Fax: 303-289-1764
E-mail: hola@continentalbook.com; esl@continentalbook.com; bonjour@continentalbook.com; tag@continentalbook.com
Web site: http://www.continentalbook.com
Dist(s): **Follett School Solutions.**

Continental Enterprises Group, Inc. (CEG), Orders Addr.: 108 Red Row St., Easley, SC 29640-2820 USA (SAN 631-0915)
E-mail: ContactUs@centerprisesgrp.com.

Continental Pr., Inc., *(978-0-8454)* Orders Addr.: 520 E. Bainbridge St., Elizabethtown, PA 17022 USA (SAN 202-182X) Tel 717-367-1836; Fax: 717-367-5660; Toll Free: 800-233-0759; *Imprints:* Seedling Publications (Seedlg Pubns)
E-mail: educationsales@continentalpress.com
Web site: http://www.continentalpress.com.

Continental Sales, Inc.,; *Imprints:* New in Chess (New Chess); Raven Tree Press (Raven Tree Pr); Raven Tree Press,Csi (RAVEN TREE PRE); New In Chess,Csi (NEW IN CHESS,C)
Dist(s): **National Bk. Network.**

Continuum *Imprint of* **Bloomsbury Academic**

Continuum International Publishing Group, Limited *See* **Bloomsbury Publishing Inc**

Contmedia Inc,
Dist(s): **AtlasBooks Distribution.**

CONVERPAGE, *(978-0-9728155; 978-0-9815720; 978-0-9820733; 978-0-9825854; 978-0-9835784; 978-0-9851721; 978-0-9858282; 978-0-615-84393-3; 978-0-9910923)* 23 Acorn St., Scituate, MA 02066-3324 USA
E-mail: pmccallum@comcast.net
Web site: www.converpage.com.

Cook, Cheryl *See* **Heavenly C. Publishing**

Cook Communication, *(978-0-9726996)* Orders Addr.: 6086 Dunes Dr., Sanford, NC 27332 USA Tel 312-859-8090; 919-498-6421; Fax: 866-652-8493
E-mail: cookcomm@gte.net; cookcomm@ameritech.net
Web site: http://www.author-me.com; http://www.reservebooks.com.

Cook, David, *(978-0-9741629)* P.O. Box 657, Albemarle, NC 28001 USA Do not confuse with companies with the same name in Chapel Hill, NC, Boerne, TX
E-mail: info@dac-and.com
Web site: http://www.dac-and.com.

Cook, David C., *(978-0-7814; 978-0-88207; 978-0-89191; 978-0-89693; 978-0-912692; 978-1-55513; 978-1-56476; 978-1-4347)* 4050 Lee Vance View, Colorado Springs, CO 80918 USA (SAN 206-0981) Tel 719-536-0100; Fax: 719-536-3244; Toll Free: 800-708-5550; 800-323-7543 (Customer Service)
E-mail: wendi.lord@davidccook.com
Web site: http://www.davidccook.com
Dist(s): **Follett School Solutions.**

Cook, David C. Publishing Company *See* **Cook, David C.**

Cook, Ken Co., *(978-0-9652491)* 9929 W. Silver Spring Dr., Milwaukee, WI 53225 USA Tel 414-466-6060; Fax: 414-466-0840
E-mail: nics@kencook.com
Web site: http://www.kencook.com.

Cookbook Resources, LLC, *(978-0-9677932; 978-1-931294; 978-1-59769)* 541 Doubletree Dr., Highland Village, TX 75077 USA (SAN 253-5262) Tel 972-317-0245; Fax: 972-317-6404; Toll Free: 866-229-2665
E-mail: lauren@cookbookresources.com
Web site: http://www.cookbookresourses.com
Dist(s): **Bk. Marketing Plus.**

Cookie Bear Pr., Inc., *(978-0-9701155)* Orders Addr.: P.O. Box 5074, Buffalo Grove, IL 60089 USA (SAN 253-6579) Tel 847-955-0001; 847-478-9202; Fax: 847-955-0002; Edit Addr.: 205 Thompson Blvd., Buffalo Grove, IL 60089 USA
E-mail: info@cookiebearpress.com
Web site: http://www.cookiebearpress.com
Dist(s): **Distributors, The**
Independent Pubs. Group.

Cookie Jar, *(978-1-933799; 978-1-60095)* Cookie Jar Entertainment, Inc., P.O. Box 35665, Greensboro, NC 27425 USA Fax: 336-808-3249; Toll Free: 800-321-0903; *Imprints:* Doodlebops (Doodlebops)
Web site: http://www.cinar.com/EN/
Dist(s): **Carson-Dellosa Publishing, LLC.**

Cool Grove Pr., *(978-1-887276; 978-0-615-45974-5)* 512 Argyle Rd., Brooklyn, NY 11218 USA Tel 718-287-7221
E-mail: tej@coolgrove.com
Web site: http://www.coolgrove.com
Dist(s): **New Leaf Distributing Co., Inc.**
SPD-Small Pr. Distribution.

Cool Grove Publishing, Incorporated *See* **Cool Grove Pr.**

Cool Kids Create, *(978-0-9797297)* 48 Beach 217 St., Breezy Point, NY 11697 USA
Web site: http://www.coolkidscreate.com
Dist(s): **BCH Fulfillment & Distribution.**

Cool, Kim @ Historic Venice Pr., *(978-0-9721655)* 312 Shore Rd., Venice, FL 34285 USA
Web site: http://www.historicvenicepress.com
Dist(s): **American Wholesale Bk. Co.**
Bk. Warehouse
Southern Bk. Service.

Cool Things Pr., *(978-0-615-20795-7; 978-0-615-20796-4; 978-0-615-78176-1; 978-0-692-45762-7)* P.O. Box 3852, Concord, NH 03302-3952 USA Tel 6037157852
Dist(s): **CreateSpace Independent Publishing Platform**
Lulu Enterprises Inc.

Coolmath.com, Inc., *(978-0-9791628)* P.O. Box 4386, Costa Mesa, CA 92628-4386 USA
Web site: http://Coolmath.com.

Coon, Kathy, *(978-0-9741300)* P.O. Box 14267, Baton Rouge, LA 70898 USA
Web site: http://www.dogintelligencetest.com.

Cooper, Gene, *(978-0-615-85312-3)* 6 Peter Cooper Rd. Apt. 3C, New York, NY 10010 USA Tel 212-228-5083
E-mail: cooper.gene82@gmail.com.

Cooper Publishing, *(978-1-59655)* Orders Addr.: P.O. Box 1974, Englewood, FL 34295 USA Tel 941-587-0396
E-mail: cooper.publishing@yahoo.com.

Cooper, Robbi, *(978-0-9749643)* 9 Scott Crescent, Austin, TX 78703 USA
Web site: http://www.everythingfromthegarden.com.

Cooper Square Publishing Llc,
Dist(s): **National Bk. Network.**

Cooperative Kids, *(978-0-9821121)* P.O. Box 432, Enfield, CT 06083-0432 USA (SAN 857-2917) Tel 860-265-2272
E-mail: info@cooperativekids.com
Web site: http://www.cooperativekids.com.

Cooperfly Books *See* **Cooperfly Creative Arts**

Cooperfly Creative Arts, *(978-0-9669504)* 3184 Plainfield NE PMB 248, Grand Rapids, MI 49525 USA Tel 616-364-5870; Fax: 616-364-5871; Toll Free: 877-986-6286
E-mail: kevin@tomatocollection.com; tomatocollection@charter.net
Web site: http://www.tomatocollection.com
Dist(s): **Indig, Stanley M. Specialty Pubn.**

Cooper's Pack, *(978-0-9794882)* Div. of Cooper's Pack Publishing, Orders Addr.: 1900 W. Nickerson St., Suite 116-130, Seattle, WA 98119 USA (SAN 853-5825) Tel 206-235-1886 Toll Free: 877-278-3278
E-mail: brandon@cooperspack.com
Web site: http://www.CoopersPack.com.

Copeland, Kenneth Pubns., *(978-0-88114; 978-0-938458; 978-1-57562; 978-1-60463)* Subs. of Eagle Mountain International Church, Kenneth Copeland Ministries, Fort Worth, TX 76192 USA Tel 817-252-2700; Toll Free: 800-600-7395
E-mail: mjohnson@kcm.org
Web site: http://www.kcm.org.contact.html
Dist(s): **Anchor Distributors**
Appalachian Bible Co.
Central South Christian Distribution
Harrison House Pubs.
New Day Christian Distributors Gifts, Inc.
Spring Arbor Distributors, Inc.

Copernicus Pr., *(978-0-9741638)* 933 Dwyer Ave., Saint Louis, MO 63122 USA Tel 314-822-8597 Do not confuse with Copernicus Pr. in Atlanta, GA
E-mail: nikolom@slu.edu
Web site: http://www.Copernicuspress.com
Dist(s): **Unique Bks., Inc.**

Copley Custom Textbooks, *(978-0-87411; 978-1-58152; 978-1-58390)* Div. of XanEdu Publishing Inc., 530 Great Rd., Acton, MA 01720 USA (SAN 687-4959) Tel 978-263-9090; Fax: 978-263-9190; Toll Free: 800-562-2147; *Imprints:* Copley Publishing Group (Copley Pub Grp)
E-mail: textbook@copleypublishing.com; publish@copleycustom.com
Web site: http://www.xanedu.com.

Copley Publishing Group *See* **Copley Custom Textbooks**

Copley Publishing Group *Imprint of* **Copley Custom Textbooks**

Coppenrath, F. Verlag KG (DEU) *(978-3-88547; 978-3-920192; 978-3-8157) Dist. by* **Distribks Inc.**

Copper Moon Press *See* **TangleTown Media Inc.**

Coptic Orthodox Church - Diocese of Los Angeles Saint Paul Brotherhood *See* **Saint Paul Brotherhood**

Coram Deo Pr., *(978-0-9769054)* One Nelson Pkwy., 2400 FM 407, Highland Village, TX 75077 USA Tel 972-318-5222; Fax: 972-692-5140
E-mail: press@coramdeoacademy.org
Web site: http://www.coramdeopress.com.

Corbett Features, *(978-0-9762294)* Div. of Corbett Features, 100 Cummings Ctr. Suite 432-a, Beverly, MA 01915 USA Tel 978-232-1124; Fax: 978-232-1124; *Imprints:* Griffin Comics (Griffin Comics)
E-mail: cdesign.ma.ultranet@rcn.com
Web site: http://www.corbettfeatures.com.

Corbus Systems, *(978-0-9742347)* 20368 Forestwood, Southfield, MI 48076 USA Tel 248-356-9427
E-mail: info@corbus-systems.com
Web site: http://www.corbus-systems.com.

Corby Books, *(978-0-9776458; 978-0-9819605; 978-0-9827846; 978-0-9833586; 978-0-9859377; 978-0-9890731; 978-0-9912451; 978-0-9961362)* 51679 Stoneham Way, Granger, IN 46530 USA
E-mail: prestonward1@aol.com; jimtach@aol.com.

CORD Communications, *(978-1-55502; 978-1-57837)* Subs. of Ctr. for Occupational Research & Development, Orders Addr.: P.O. Box 21206, Waco, TX 76702-1206 USA Tel 254-776-1822; Fax: 254-776-3906; Toll Free: 800-231-3015; Edit Addr.: 324 Kelly Dr., Waco, TX 76710 USA
E-mail: webmaster@cord.org
Web site: http://www.cord.org/index.cfm.

Cordon Pubns., *(978-0-9822083; 978-0-9826984; 978-0-615-39009-3; 978-0-9829049; 978-0-9834908; 978-0-9839858; 978-1-937912)* 731 Erie Ave. Apt. C, Evansville, IN 47715 USA (SAN 857-5460) Tel 812-303-9070
E-mail: coraseaman@hotmail.com
Web site: http://www.Cordon Publications.com.

Cordoves, Barbara & Gladys M., *(978-0-9637252)* 2800 SW 106th Ave., Miami, FL 33165-2748 USA.

Core Knowledge Foundation, *(978-1-890517; 978-1-933486)* Orders Addr.: 801 E. High St., Charlottesville, VA 22902 USA Tel 434-977-7550; Fax: 434-977-0021; Toll Free: 800-238-3233
E-mail: mjones@coreknowledge.org
Web site: http://www.coreknowledge.org.

Core Library *Imprint of* **ABDO Publishing Co.**

Core Publishing & Consulting, Inc., *(978-1-933079)* 13016 Bee St., Suite 208, Dallas, TX 75234 USA (SAN 256-1514) Tel 214-926-4742; Fax: 972-243-5854
E-mail: stan.peterson@sbcglobal.net
Web site: www.core-publishing.com.

Corgi Tales Publishing, *(978-0-615-26492-9)* 57715 Hwy. 58, McKittrick, CA 93251 USA
Dist(s): **Lulu Enterprises Inc.**

Corimbo, Editorial S.L. (ESP) *(978-84-8470; 978-84-95150) Dist. by* **Distribks Inc.**

Corimbo, Editorial S.L. (ESP) *(978-84-8470; 978-84-95150) Dist. by* **Mariuccia Iaconi Bk Imports.**

Corimbo, Editorial S.L. (ESP) *(978-84-8470; 978-84-95150) Dist. by* **Lectorum Pubns.**

Cork Hill Pr., *(978-1-59408)* P.O. Box 117, Carmel, IN 46082-0117 USA
Web site: http://www.corkhillpress.com
Dist(s): **CreateSpace Independent Publishing Platform.**

Corman Productions, *(978-0-9655749)* 6729 Dume Dr., Malibu, CA 90265 USA Tel 310-457-7524; Fax: 310-457-5941
E-mail: Dikkybird@aol.com.

Publisher Name Index

Cormier, Shawn *See* **Pine View Pr.**

Corn Tassel Pr., *(978-0-9752597)* 9655 Corn Tassel Ct., Columbia, MD 21046 USA Fax: 301-776-6538.

Cornell, A.J. Pubns., *(978-0-9727439; 978-0-9850501)* 18-74 Corporal Kennedy St., Bayside, NY 11360 USA Tel 718-423-4082
Dist(s): **AtlasBooks Distribution.**

Cornell Maritime Pr./Tidewater Pubs. *Imprint of* **Schiffer Publishing, Ltd.**

†Cornell Univ. Pr., *(978-0-8014; 978-0-87546; 978-1-5017)* Orders Addr.: P.O. Box 6525, Ithaca, NY 14851 USA (SAN 281-5680) Tel 607-277-2211; Toll Free Fax: 800-688-2877; Toll Free: 800-666-2211; Edit Addr.: Sage House, 512 E. State St., Ithaca, NY 14851 USA (SAN 202-1862) Tel 607-277-2338
E-mail: cupressinfo@cornell.edu; orders@nbninternational.com; cupress-sales@cornell.edu
Web site: http://www.cornellpress.cornell.edu
Dist(s): **CUP Services**
Follett School Solutions
MyiLibrary
ebrary, Inc.; *CIP.*

Cornerstone Bk. Publishers *Imprint of* **Poll, Michael Publishing**

Cornerstone Family Ministries/Lamplighter Publishing, *(978-1-58474)* Orders Addr.: P.O. Box 777, Waverly, PA 18471 USA Tel 717-585-1314; Fax: 717-587-4246; Toll Free: 888-246-7735; Edit Addr.: Waverly Community Ctr., Main St., S. Wing, 2nd Flr., Waverly, PA 18471 USA
E-mail: cfm@epix.net
Web site: http://www.agospel.com
Dist(s): **Follett School Solutions.**

Cornerstone Pr., *(978-0-918476)* 1825 Bender Ln., Arnold, MO 63010-0388 USA (SAN 210-0584) Tel 636-296-9662 Do not confuse with companies with the same name in Edison, NJ, Kents Hill, ME, Pearland, TX, Stevens Point, WI
E-mail: anthsum@sbcglobal.net.

Cornerstone Pr., *(978-0-9668488; 978-0-9774802; 978-0-9846739)* c/o Univ. of Wisconsin, Dept. of English, TLC @ LRC, University of Wisconsin — Stevens Point, Stevens Point, WI 54481-3897 USA Tel 715-346-2849; Fax: 715-346-2849 Do not confuse with companies with the same name in Kents Hill, ME, Arnold, MO
E-mail: dan.dieterich@uwsp.edu.

Cornerstone Pr. Chicago, *(978-0-940895)* 939 W. Willson, Chicago, IL 60640 USA (SAN 664-7200) Tel 773-561-2450; 773-989-4920; Fax: 773-989-2076; Toll Free: 888-407-7377
E-mail: cspress@jpusa.org
Web site: http://www.cornerstonepress.com.

Cornerstone Press, Incorporated *See* **Patria Pr., Inc.**

Cornerstone Publishing, Inc., *(978-1-882185)* Orders Addr.: P.O. Box 23015, Evansville, IN 47715 USA (SAN 298-735X) Tel 812-470-3971 Do not confuse with companies with the same name in Decatur, GA, Altamonte Springs, FL, Wichita, KS
E-mail: cornerstonepublishinghouse@gmail.com
Web site: http://www.cornerstonepublishinghouse.com
Dist(s): **Book Clearing Hse.**
Lightning Source, Inc.

Cornerstonia, *(978-0-9828588)* 9457 Venezia Plantation Dr., Orlando, FL 32829 USA Tel 407-222-4287
E-mail: author@cornerstonia.com
Web site: http://www.cornerstonia.com.

CornerWind Media, L.L.C., *(978-0-9741072)* Orders Addr.: 2635 Whitehall Ct., Rock Hill, SC 29732 USA Tel 803-329-7140; Fax: 803-329-7145
Web site: http://www.twiggyleaf.com; http://www.cornerwind.com.

Corning Museum of Glass, *(978-0-87290)* One Museum Way, Corning, NY 14830 USA (SAN 202-1897) Fax: 607-974-7365; Toll Free: 800-732-6845
E-mail: cmg@cmog.org; pr@cmog.org
Web site: http://www.cmog.org
Dist(s): **Associated Univ. Presses**
Hudson Hills Pr. LLC
National Bk. Network.

Corona Pr., *(978-1-891619)* 4535 Palmer Ct., Niwot, CO 80503 USA Tel 303-247-1455; Fax: 303-417-0355; Toll Free: 888-648-3877 Do not confuse with Corona Pr., Brooklandville, MD
E-mail: coronapress@aol.com.

Coronet Bks., *(978-0-89563)* 311 Bainbridge St., Philadelphia, PA 19147 USA (SAN 210-6043) Tel 215-925-2762; Fax: 215-925-1912 Do not confuse with Coronet Bks. & Pubns., Eagle Point, OR
E-mail: ronsmolin@earthlink.net; order@coronetbooks.com
Web site: http://www.coronetbooks.com
Dist(s): **MyiLibrary.**

Corpus Communications *See* **Caritas Communications**

Corraini (ITA) *(978-88-86250; 978-88-87942; 978-88-7570)* *Dist. by* **Dist Art Pubs.**

Cortright Fellowship Pr., *(978-0-9706684)* P.O. Box 434, Allegan, MI 49010 USA
E-mail: ekklesia@accn.org
Web site: http://www.redbay.com/ekklesia.

Corunda, Ediciones, S.A. de C.V. (MEX) *(978-968-6044; 978-968-7444)* *Dist. by* **AIMS Intl.**

Corwin Pr., *(978-0-7619; 978-0-8039; 978-1-57517; 978-1-879179; 978-1-4129)* Affil. of Sage Pubns., Inc., 2455 Teller Rd., Thousand Oaks, CA 91320-2218 USA Tel 805-499-9734; 805-499-9774 (customer service); Fax: 805-499-0871; 805-499-5323
E-mail: info@sagepub.com
Web site: http://www.corwinpress.com
Dist(s): **Follett School Solutions**
MyiLibrary
SAGE Pubns., Inc.
ebrary, Inc.

Corwin Press, Incorporated *See* **Corwin Pr.**

Coryell, Skip *See* **White Feather Press, LLC**

Cosimo Classics *Imprint of* **Cosimo, Inc.**

Cosimo, Inc., *(978-1-59605; 978-1-60206; 978-1-60520; 978-1-61640)* 191 Seventh Ave., Suite 2F, New York, NY 10011-1818 USA Tel 212-989-3616; Fax: 212-989-3662; *Imprints:* Cosimo Classics (CosClassics)
E-mail: adake@cosimobooks.com; info@cosimobooks.com
Web site: http://www.cosimobooks.com
Dist(s): **Follett School Solutions**
INscribe Digital.

Cosmic Gargoyle Creative Solutions, *(978-0-9835843)* 3883 Turtle Creek Blvd. No. 1202, Dallas, TX 75219 USA Tel 214-679-4725; *Imprints:* Lonely Swan Books (Lonely Swan)
E-mail: cosmicgargoyle@gmail.com
Dist(s): **Smashwords.**

COSMIC VORTEX, *(978-0-9719580)* Div. of TETRA XII Inc., Orders Addr.: P.O. Box 322, Paia, HI 96779 USA
E-mail: atlantis@archaeologist.com; aloha@mauivortex.com
Web site: http://www.atlantistoday.com; http://atlantis-motherland.com.

Cosmographia Pubns., *(978-0-615-60710-8)* 6 1/2 W. 3rd St., Spencer, IA 51301 USA Tel 712-580-3271
E-mail: hnewgard@gmail.com.

Cosmos Books *See* **Prime**

Cosmos Publishing, *(978-0-9660449; 978-1-932455)* 262 River Vale Rd., River Vale, NJ 07675 USA (SAN 631-0486) Tel 201-664-3494; Fax: 201-664-3402 Do not confuse with companies with the same in Bellevue, WA, Saint Louis, MO
E-mail: info@greeceinprint.com
Web site: http://www.greeceinprint.com.

Cosmos Publishing Company, Incorporated *See* **Cosmos Publishing**

Costume & Fashion Pr. *Imprint of* **Quite Specific Media Group, Ltd.**

Cote Literary Group, The, *(978-1-929175)* 483 Old Carolina Ct., Mount Pleasant, SC 29464 USA (SAN 850-4881) Tel 843-881-6080; Fax: 843-278-8456
E-mail: editor@corinthianbooks.com; dickcote@earthlink.net
Web site: http://www.corinthianbooks.com
Dist(s): **Brodart Co.**
Follett School Solutions
Quality Bks., Inc.
eBookIt.com.

Coteau Bks. (CAN) *(978-0-919926; 978-1-55050; 978-0-9780316)* *Dist. by* **Orca Bk Pub.**

Cotler, Joanna Books *Imprint of* **HarperCollins Pubs.**

Cotsen Occasional Pr., *(978-0-9666084; 978-0-9745168)* Div. of Cotsen Family Foundation, 12100 Wilshire Blvd. Suite 905, Los Angeles, CA 90025 USA Tel 310-826-9113
E-mail: jolie@cotsenfamilyoffice.com
Web site: http://www.hesdegraaf.com/hes/.

Cotton Candy Pr. *Imprint of* **Unveiled Media, LLC**

Cottonwood Graphics, Incorporated *See* **Cottonwood Publishing, Inc.**

Cottonwood Pr., Inc., *(978-1-877673; 978-1-936162)* 109-B Cameron Dr., Fort Collins, CO 80525 USA Tel 970-204-0715; Fax: 970-204-0761; Toll Free: 800-864-4297 Do not confuse with companies with same name in Novato, CA, Lawrence, KS, Wilsonville, OR
E-mail: cottonwood@cottonwoodpress.com
Web site: http://www.cottonwoodpress.com
Dist(s): **Independent Pubs. Group**
ebrary, Inc.

CottonWood Publishing Co., *(978-0-9766804)* 840 W. Washington St., Ann Arbor, MI 48103 USA Do not confuse with Cottonwood Publishing Company in Saint George, UT Helena MT.

Cottonwood Publishing, Inc., *(978-0-9626999; 978-1-886370)* 296 Willowbrook Dr., Helena, MT 59602-7764 USA Toll Free: 800-937-6343 Do not confuse with Cottonwood Publishing in Saint George, UT Ann Arbor MI
E-mail: oldmt@mt.net
Web site: http://www.oldmontana.com
Dist(s): **CreateSpace Independent Publishing Platform**
Mountain Pr. Publishing Co., Inc.

Coulee Region Pubns., Inc., *(978-0-9650629)* 307 Twin Oak Dr., Altoona, WI 54720-1383 USA.

Counce, Paula, *(978-0-9762776)* 1628 Bob O Link Dr., Venice, FL 34293 USA
Web site: http://www.ajourneyremembered.com.

†Council for Agricultural Science & Technology (CAST), *(978-1-887383)* 4420 W. Lincoln Way, Ames, IA 50014-3347 USA (SAN 225-7416) Tel 515-292-2125; Fax: 515-292-4512; Toll Free Fax: 800-375-2278; Toll Free: 800-762-4232
E-mail: cast@cast-science.org
Web site: http://www.cast-science.org; *CIP.*

Council for Indian Education, *(978-0-89992)* Orders Addr.: 1240 Burlington Ave., Billings, MT 59102-4224 USA Tel 406-248-3465; Fax: 406-248-1297
E-mail: cie@cie-mt.org
Web site: http://www.cie-mt.org
Dist(s): **Follett School Solutions.**

Council Oak Bks., *(978-0-933031; 978-1-57178)* Orders Addr.: 2822 Van Ness Ave., San Francisco, CA 94109 USA (SAN 689-5522) Tel 415-931-7700; Fax: 415-931-9911; Toll Free: 800-247-8850 (orders only)
E-mail: order@counciloakbooks.com; publicity@counciloakbooks.com
Web site: http://www.counciloakbooks.com
Dist(s): **Independent Pubs. Group**
New Leaf Distributing Co., Inc.
Perseus-PGW
Univ. of Oklahoma Pr.

Count On Learning, *(978-0-9771472)* 1406 Arlington Ave., Baton Rouge, LA 70808 USA
E-mail: admin@countonlearning.com
Web site: http://www.countonlearning.com.

Counterbalance Bks., *(978-0-9774906; 978-0-9799592)* P.O. Box 876, Duvall, WA 98019-0876 USA
E-mail: admin@counterbalancebooks.com; publisher@counterbalancebooks.com
Web site: http://www.counterbalancebooks.com.

Counterpath Pr., *(978-1-933996)* P.O. Box 18351, Denver, CO 80218 USA
E-mail: tr@counterpathpress.org
Web site: http://www.counterpathpress.org
Dist(s): **SPD-Small Pr. Distribution.**

Counterpoint *Imprint of* **Counterpoint LLC**

Counterpoint LLC, *(978-1-59376; 978-1-61902)* 1919 Fifth St., Berkeley, CA 94710-2205 USA Fax: 510-704-0268; *Imprints:* Soft Skull Press (Soft); Counterpoint (Countpt)
E-mail: info@counterpointpress.com
Web site: http://www.counterpointpress.com
Dist(s): **Lulu Enterprises Inc.**
MyiLibrary
Perseus-PGW
Perseus Bks. Group.

Countinghouse Pr., Inc., *(978-0-9664732; 978-0-9786191; 978-0-9911102)* 6632 Telegraph Rd., Suite 311, Bloomfield Hills, MI 48301 USA Tel 248-642-7191; Fax: 248-642-7192
E-mail: lcharla@comcast.net
Web site: http://www.countinghousepress.com.

Country Boy Publishing Co., *(978-0-9795574)* Orders Addr.: 300 Collier Dr., Winter Haven, FL 33884 USA
E-mail: dgreenl2@tampabay.rr.com
Web site: http://www.countryboypublishing.com.

Country Bumpkin Pubns, *(978-0-9677938)* 212 California Ave., Watertown, NY 13601 USA Tel 315-782-0941
E-mail: bsteve3@twcny.rr.com.

Country Girl Publishing, *(978-0-615-26902-3)* 5537 Shallowriver Rd., Clinton, MD 20735 USA.

Country Kid Publishing LLC, *(978-0-9754624; 978-0-9963649)* 1475 NW 700th Rd, Holden, MO 64040 USA
E-mail: michaelwaguespack@gmail.com
Web site: http://www.countrykidpublishing.com
Dist(s): **Angler's Bk. Supply**
Follett School Solutions.

Country Messenger Pr. Publishing Group, LLC, *(978-0-9619407; 978-0-9801554; 978-1-937162)* 27657 Hwy. 97, Okanogan, WA 98840 USA (SAN 244-5638) Tel 253-216-6364
E-mail: kfreel@cmppg.org; edna@cmppg.org
Web site: http://www.cmppg.com.

Country Side Pr., The, *(978-0-9746360)* Orders Addr.: 49850 Miller Rd., North Powder, OR 97867 USA Tel 541-856-3239
E-mail: debbys@rconnects.com
Web site: http://www.thecountrysidepress.com.

Courage Bks. *Imprint of* **Running Pr. Bk. Pubs.**

Courage to Change *See* **CTC Publishing**

Courier Publications *See* **Christian Courier Pubns.**

Course Technology, *(978-0-534; 978-0-619; 978-0-7600; 978-0-7895; 978-0-87709; 978-0-87835; 978-0-89426; 978-0-928763; 978-1-56527; 978-1-878748; 978-1-4188; 978-1-59863; 978-1-4239; 978-1-60334)* Div. of Cengage Learning, Orders Addr.: 20 Channel Ctr St., Boston, MA 02210-3402 USA Toll Free Fax: 800-881-8922
E-mail: Esales@thomsonlearning.com; stacy.hiquet@thomson.com; cheryl.mondillo@thomson.com
Web site: http://www.course.com/
Dist(s): **CENGAGE Learning**
Delmar Cengage Learning
Ebsco Publishing
Leonard, Hal Corp.
ebrary, Inc.

Courtyard Publishing, LLC, *(978-0-9795260)* Div. of Alchemical Courtyard, LLC, 1688 Meridian Ave., 10th Flr., Miami Beach, FL 33139 USA Tel 305-695-9380
E-mail: info@courtyardpublishing.com
Web site: http://www.courtyardpublishing.com.

†Covenant Communications, *(978-0-9649122)* 1009 Jones St., Old Hickory, TN 37138 USA Tel 615-847-2066; Fax: 615-860-3601; Toll Free: 800-979-3882 Do nt oconfuse with Covenant Communications in Old Hickory, TN
Dist(s): **Quality Bks., Inc.;** *CIP.*

Covenant Communications, Inc., *(978-1-55503; 978-1-57734; 978-1-59156; 978-1-59811; 978-1-60861; 978-1-62108; 978-1-68047)* Orders Addr.: 920 E State Rd Ste F, American Fork, UT 84003-0416 USA (SAN 169-8540) Tel 801-756-9966; 801-756-1041; Fax: 801-756-1049; Toll Free: 800-662-9545; Edit Addr.: 920 E. State Rd., Suite F, American Fork, UT 84003 USA Do not confuse with Covenant Communications in American Fork, UT
E-mail: verls@covenant-lds.com
Web site: http://www.covenant-lds.com
Dist(s): **Follett School Solutions.**

Covenant of Light Publishing *See* **Sorcerer's Pr., The**

Covenant Support Network, *(978-0-9772313; 978-0-9817033; 978-0-9848624)* Orders Addr.: 3037 Hebron Rd., Hendersonville, NC 28739 USA; Edit Addr.: P.O. Box 2862, Hendersonville, NC 28793 USA
Web site: http://www.covenantsupportnetwork.com.

Coventry Pool & Garden Houses *See* **Manor Hse. Publishing Co., Inc.**

Covered Bridge Bks., *(978-0-9722027)* 336 Covered Bridge Rd., Cherry Hill, NJ 08034-2949 USA.

Covered Bridge Children's Books *See* **Covered Bridge Bks.**

Covered Wagon Publishing LLC, *(978-0-9723259)* P.O. Box 473038, Aurora, CO 80047 USA (SAN 254-7813) Tel 303-751-0992; Fax: 303-632-6794
E-mail: CoveredWagon@comcast.net
Web site: http://www.RockyMountainMysteries.com.

Cow Heard Records, *(978-0-9763012)* 3622 Altura Ave., La Crescenta, CA 91214 USA
Web site: http://www.thesunflowers.com.

Cowan, Pricilla J., *(978-0-9822542; 978-0-9841194; 978-0-9840083; 978-0-9891159; 978-0-9896988)* 11594 SW 135th Ave., Tigard, OR 97223 USA
Web site: http://www.storiesbypj.com.

Cowboy Collector Pubns., *(978-0-9628078)* Orders Addr.: P.O. Box 7486, Long Beach, CA 90807 USA Tel 714-840-3942; Edit Addr.: 4677 Rio Ave., Long Beach, CA 90805 USA Tel 213-428-6972
Dist(s): **Hervey's Booklink & Cookbook Warehouse.**

Cowboy Magazine, *(978-0-9765969)* Orders Addr.: P.O. Box 126, La Veta, CO 81055 USA Tel 719-742-5250; Fax: 719-742-3034; Edit Addr.: 124 N. Main St., La Veta, CO 81055 USA
E-mail: workincowboy@amigo.net
Web site: http://www.cowboymagazine.com.

Cowgirl Peg Bks. *Imprint of* **Cowgirl Peg Enterprises**

Cowgirl Peg Enterprises, *(978-0-9721057; 978-0-615-59075-2)* Orders Addr.: P.O. Box 293055, Kerrville, TX 78029 USA; *Imprints:* Cowgirl Peg Books (Cowgirl Peg Books)
E-mail: cowgirlpeg2@gmail.com
Web site: http://www.cowgirlpeg.com
Dist(s): **Bks. West**
Follett School Solutions.

†Cowley Pubns., *(978-0-936384; 978-1-56101)* Div. of Society of St. John the Evangelist, 4 Brattle St., Cambridge, MA 02138 USA (SAN 213-9987) Fax: 617-441-0300; Toll Free: 800-225-1534; 4501 Forbes Blvd., Lanham, MD 20706
E-mail: cowley@cowley.org
Web site: http://www.cowley.org
Dist(s): **Follett School Solutions**
Forward Movement Pubns.
Ingram Pub. Services
MyiLibrary
National Bk. Network
Rowman & Littlefield Publishers, Inc.
ebrary, Inc.; *CIP.*

Cowpokes Cartoon Bks., *(978-0-917207)* P.O. Box 290868, Kerrville, TX 78029-0868 USA (SAN 656-089X) Tel 830-257-7446 (phone/fax); Toll Free: 800-257-7441 (phone/fax)
E-mail: cartoons@cowpokes.com
Web site: http://www.cowpokes.com.

Cox, Gene, *(978-0-9669672)* 2309 Limerick Dr., Tallahassee, FL 32308 USA Tel 850-893-1789
E-mail: gccox@mail.istal.com.

Cox, Julie, *(978-0-9742118)* P.O. Box 77966, Fort Worth, TX 76177 USA
E-mail: info@facereadingacademy.com
Web site: http://www.facereadingacademy.com.

Coyote Canyon Pr., *(978-0-9796607; 978-0-9821298; 978-0-9890080)* 693 Black Hills Dr., Claremont, CA 91711-2928 USA Toll Free Fax: 800-319-4707
E-mail: tom@coyotecanyonpress.com
Web site: http://www.coyotecanyonpress.com.

Coyote Cowboy Co., *(978-0-939343)* Orders Addr.: P.O. Box 2190, Benson, AZ 85602 USA (SAN 663-0820) Tel 520-586-1077; Toll Free: 800-654-2550; Edit Addr.: 1251 S. Red Chile Rd., Benson, AZ 85602 USA
E-mail: cindylou@baxterblack.com
Web site: http://www.baxterblack.com
Dist(s): **Follett School Solutions.**

Coyote Moon Publishing *See* **Cowgirl Peg Enterprises**

CoZi Publishing LLC, *(978-0-9749151)* P.O. Box 211, Rutland, VT 05702-0211 USA
E-mail: publish@cozi.com
Web site: http://www.cozi.com.

Cozy Graphics Corp., *(978-1-932002; 978-1-59343)* 61-20 G.C.P., Apt. B1204, Forest Hills, NY 11375 USA Tel 718-592-9782 (phone/fax); *Imprints:* Cozy Publishing House (Cozy Pub Hse)
E-mail: publisher@cozygraphics.com
Web site: http://www.cozygraphics.com.

Cozy Publishing Hse. *Imprint of* **Cozy Graphics Corp.**

CPB Grades 4-8 *Imprint of* **Compass Point Bks.**

CPB Grades K-3 *Imprint of* **Compass Point Bks.**

CPCC Pr., *(978-1-59494)* P.O. Box 35009, Charlotte, NC 28235-5009 USA Tel 704-330-6789
E-mail: cpccpress@cpcc.edu; melissa.wilson@cpcc.edu
Web site: http://www.cpccservicescorp.com.

CPM Comics *Imprint of* **Central Park Media Corp.**

CPM Manga *Imprint of* **Central Park Media Corp.**

CPM Manhwa *Imprint of* **Central Park Media Corp.**

CPR Pubng, *(978-0-9778597)* 740 13th St., Fennimore, WI 53809 USA.

CQ Pr. Library Reference *Imprint of* **CQ Pr.**

†CQ Pr., *(978-0-7401; 978-0-87187; 978-0-9625531; 978-1-56692; 978-1-56802; 978-1-933116; 978-1-60426; 978-0-9823537; 978-1-60871)* Div. of SAGE Pubns., Inc., Orders Addr.: a/o Order Dept., 2300 N. St. NW, Suite 800, Washington, DC 20037 USA (SAN 256-470X) Toll Free: 866-427-7737 (customer service - orders); *Imprints:* C Q Press Library Reference (CQ Pr Lib Ref)
E-mail: customerservice@cqpress.com
Web site: http://www.cqpress.com
Dist(s): **MyiLibrary**
SAGE Pubns., Inc.
ebrary, Inc.; *CIP.*

Cracked Egg Brand Pr., *(978-1-882820)* Orders Addr.: P.O. Box 134, Stowell, TX 77661 USA Tel 409-296-2053; Fax: 409-835-5413; Edit Addr.: Main & Third, Stowell, TX 77661 USA.

Cracker the Crab LLC, *(978-0-9725560)* P.O. Box 80475, Simpsonville, SC 29680-0475 USA Do not confuse with Two Bear Publishing Company in Alpine, CA
E-mail: jillkcogdill@twobearproducts.com; jcogdill@crackerthecrab.com; jkcogdill@msn.com
Web site: http://www.crackerthecrab.com.

Craig, Frankye, *(978-0-9794904)* 1735 Caughlin Creek Rd., Reno, NV 89519 USA Tel 775-747-1138; Fax: 775-747-1138
E-mail: FrankyeEBD@aol.com.

Craigmore Creations, *(978-0-9844422; 978-1-940052)* Orders Addr.: 4110 SE Hawthorne Blvd PMB 114, Portland, OR 97214-5246 USA (SAN 860-2786)
E-mail: info@craigmorecreations.com
Web site: http://www.craigmorecreations.com
Dist(s): **Independent Pubs. Group Partners/West Book Distributors.**

Crain, Suzanne, *(978-0-9763254)* 10423 Brickey Rd., Red Bud, IL 62278-3519 USA
E-mail: slcrain@hcis.net.

Cram101 Inc., *(978-1-4288; 978-1-61654; 978-1-61698; 978-1-61744; 978-1-61461; 978-1-61490; 978-1-61812; 978-1-61830; 978-1-61905; 978-1-61906; 978-1-4672; 978-1-4784; 978-1-4902; 978-1-4970)* 40 W. Easy St., Suite 1, Simi Valley, CA 93021 USA (SAN 851-2175); 6593 Collins Dr., Ste. D18, Moorpark, CA 93021
Web site: http://www.cram101.com.

Cranberry Quill Publishing Co., *(978-0-9741406; 978-0-9884899; 978-0-9914246; 978-0-9965986)* 111 Lamon St. Suite 204, Fayetteville, NC 28301-4901 USA
E-mail: rgibbsquill@gmail.com; info@cranberryquill.com
Web site: http://www.cranberryquill.com.

Crane Bks., *(978-0-9647924)* Div. of Math in Motion, 668 Stony Hill Rd., No. 233, Yardley, PA 19067 USA Tel 215-321-5556; Fax: 215-310-9412
E-mail: info@mathinmotion.com
Web site: http://www.mathinmotion.com.

†Crane Hill Pubs., *(978-0-9621455; 978-1-57587; 978-1-881548)* 3608 Claimont Ave., Birmingham, AL 35222-3508 USA Tel 205-714-3007; Fax: 205-714-3008
E-mail: cranemail@cranehill.com
Web site: http://www.cranehill.com
Dist(s): **Independent Pubs. Group**; *CIP*.

Crane Institute of America, Inc., *(978-0-9744279; 978-0-9855502)* 3880 Saint Johns Pkwy., Sanford, FL 32771 USA Tel 407-322-6800; Fax: 407-330-0660; Toll Free: 800-832-2726
E-mail: annc@craneinstitute.com; info@craneinstitute.com
Web site: http://www.craneinstitute.com.

Crane Publishing, *(978-0-9753608)* 308 Trinity Rd., Venice, FL 34293 USA Do not confuse with companies with the same name in Paramus, New Jersey.
E-mail: jborza@josephborza.com; jborza@cranepublishing.net
Web site: http://www.cranepublishing.net.

Cranky Pants Publishing, LLC, *(978-0-9759627)* 2 Upland Rd., W., Arlington, MA 02474 USA
E-mail: ssanzo@yahoo.com
Dist(s): **AtlasBooks Distribution.**

Crawford, Quinton Douglass, *(978-0-615-14879-3)* 225 Santa Ana Ct., Fairfield, CA 94533 USA
Web site: http://www.knowledgefortomorrow.com
Dist(s): **Lulu Enterprises Inc.**

Crazy Man Press, LLC, *(978-0-9743553)* 33 University Sq., Suite 254, Madison, WI 53715-1042 USA Tel 608-215-0532
E-mail: info@crazymanpress.com
Web site: http://www.crazymanpress.com.

Crazy Pet Pr., The, *(978-0-9744749)* 655 N. Azusa Ave., No. 104, Azusa, CA 91708 USA Tel 831-438-2730; Fax: 831-438-2764; Toll Free: 877-860-2100
E-mail: kpbooks@calcentral.com
Web site: http://www.crazydog.com; http://www.crazypetpress.com; http://www.kidoodlepetpress.com.

Created For You, *(978-0-615-17773-1; 978-0-615-17775-5; 978-0-9819968)* Orders Addr.: P.O. Box 4448, Horseshoe Bay, TX 78657 USA; Edit Addr.: 305 Sunspot, Horseshoe Bay, TX 78657-4448 USA Tel 830-596-2726
Dist(s): **Publishers Services.**

CreateSpace *See* **CreateSpace Independent Publishing Platform**

CreateSpace Independent Publishing Platform, *(978-1-58898; 978-1-59109; 978-1-59456; 978-1-59457; 978-1-4196; 978-1-4348; 978-1-4382; 978-1-4392; 978-1-4404; 978-1-4414; 978-1-4421; 978-1-61550; 978-1-4486; 978-1-4495; 978-1-4499; 978-1-4505; 978-1-4515; 978-1-4528; 978-1-4536; 978-1-4537; 978-1-4538; 978-1-4563; 978-1-4564; 978-1-4565; 978-1-61789; 978-1-4609; 978-1-4610; 978-1-4611; 978-1-61396; 978-1-61397; 978-1-4635; 978-1-4636; 978-1-4637; 978-1-4662; 978-1-4663; 978-1-4664; 978-1-61914; 978-1-61915; 978-1-61916; 978-1-4679; 978) Orders Addr.: 4900 LaCross Rd., North Charleston, SC 29406 USA (SAN 255-2132) Tel 843-225-4700 (Ask for ordering department); Fax: 843-577-7506; Toll Free: 866-308-6235; 4900 LaCross Rd., North Charleston, SC 29406*
E-mail: info@createspace.com
Web site: http://www.createspace.com.

Creation By Design, *(978-0-9828077; 978-1-936532)* 95 Bennett Rd., Teaneck, NJ 07666 USA Tel 914-714-3300
E-mail: CrtnByDsgn@aol.com
Dist(s): **Send The Light Distribution LLC.**

Creation Hse. *Imprint of* **Charisma Media**

Creation Instruction Publishing, *(978-1-928765)* Orders Addr.: P.O. Box 304, Plentywood, MT 59254 USA Tel 406-895-2689; Edit Addr.: 1770 S. Overland, Juniata, NE 68955 USA
E-mail: creation1@juno.com
Web site: http://www.creationinstruction.org/.

Creation Resource Foundation, *(978-0-9672713)* P.O. Box 570, El Dorado, CA 95667 USA Tel 530-626-4447; Fax: 530-626-5215; Toll Free: 800-497-1454
E-mail: info@creationresource.org
Web site: http://www.awesomeworks.com; http://www.creationresource.org/
Dist(s): **Send The Light Distribution LLC.**

Creative 3, LLC, *(978-1-933815)* 2236 E Spring Hill Rd., Springfield, MO 65804 USA Tel 417-882-2145; Fax: 417-882-2145; Toll Free Fax: 800-866-1360; Toll Free: 800-866-1360; *Imprints*: Quirkles, The (The Quirkles)
E-mail: info@quirkles.com; thequirkles@aol.com
Web site: http://www.quirkles.com.

Creative Attic, Inc., The, *(978-0-9653955)* P.O. Box 187, Canterbury, NH 03224 USA Tel 603-783-9103; Fax: 603-783-0118; Toll Free: 888-566-6539
E-mail: the5kids@aol.com.

Creative Bk. Publishing (CAN) *(978-0-920021; 978-0-920884; 978-1-895387; 978-1-894294; 978-1-897174; 978-1-77103) Dist. by* **Orca Bk Pub.**

Creative Bk. Pubs., *(978-0-9754818; 978-0-9763093; 978-0-9765467; 978-0-9779662; 978-0-9795460)* 1912 Falcon Dr., Ridgefield, WA 98642 USA
Web site: http://www.creativebookpublishers.com.

Creative Communication, *(978-1-60050)* Orders Addr.: P.O. Box 303, Smithfield, UT 84335 USA Tel 435-713-4411; Fax: 435-713-4422; Edit Addr.: 1488 200 W., Logan, UT 84341 USA Do not confuse with companies with the same or similar name in Forest Grove, OR, Seattle, WA, Trabuco Canyon, CA, Nixa, MO, Chelan, WA, La Mesa, CA, Kalamazoo, MI
E-mail: drtom@poeticpower.com
Web site: http://www.poeticpower.com.

Creative Co., The, *(978-0-87191; 978-0-88682; 978-0-89812; 978-1-56660; 978-1-56846; 978-1-58341; 978-1-60818; 978-1-62832; 978-1-68277)* 123 S. Broad St., Mankato, MN 56001 USA Tel 507-388-2109; Fax: 507-388-2746; Toll Free: 800-445-6209; *Imprints*: Creative Editions (Creative Eds); Creative Education (Creat Educ); Creative Paperbacks (Creative Paperbks) Do not confuse with The Creative Co., Lawrenceburg, IN
E-mail: info@thecreativecompany.us; lmaker@thecreativecompany.us
Web site: http://www.thecreativecompany.us
Dist(s): **Abraham Assocs. Inc. Hachette Bk. Group RiverStream Publishing.**

Creative Continuum, Inc., *(978-0-9713804; 978-1-932252; 978-1-62192)* 2910 E. La Palma Ave. Ste. C, Anaheim, CA 92806-2618 USA
E-mail: info@creativecontinuum.com
Web site: http://www.creativecontinuum.com.

Creative Conversations, *(978-0-9768235)* 11767 W. Coal Mine Dr., Littleton, CO 80127 USA Tel 303-437-8533.

Creative Cranium Concept, The, *(978-0-9741009)* Orders Addr.: 2560 Reed Ave, Marshalltown, IA 50158 USA Tel 303-875-8742; Edit Addr.: 2560 Reed Ave, Marshalltown, IA 50158 USA Tel 303-875-8742
E-mail: Rhonda@RhondaSpellman.com
Web site: http://www.rhondaspellman.com; http://AutismWithRhonda.com.

Creative Curriculum Initiatives, *(978-0-9786500; 978-1-60409)* 80 Fifth Ave., Suite 1503, New York, NY 10011 USA Tel 212-242-7827; Fax: 212-242-3523.

Creative Dragon Pr., *(978-0-9831996)* 208A Oxhead Rd., Centereach, NY 11720 USA Tel 631-738-9082
E-mail: cheryl_orlassino@hotmail.com.

Creative Dreaming Ltd., *(978-0-615-14010-0; 978-0-615-14725-3; 978-0-615-15431-2; 978-0-615-15487-9; 978-0-615-15521-0; 978-0-615-16439-7; 978-0-615-17664-2; 978-0-615-18006-9; 978-0-615-18260-5; 978-0-615-18340-4; 978-0-615-18424-1; 978-0-615-18654-2; 978-0-615-18886-7; 978-0-615-23631-5) 6433 Topanga Canyon Blvd., No. 120, Woodland Hills, CA 91303 USA*
Dist(s): **Lulu Enterprises Inc.**

Creative Editions *Imprint of* **Creative Co., The**

Creative Education *Imprint of* **Creative Co., The**

Creative Education & Publishing, *(978-0-9824964; 978-0-9825969; 978-0-9835315; 978-0-9859066; 978-0-9903851)* 3339 Ardley Ct., Falls Church, VA 22041 USA Tel 703-856-7005
E-mail: alameddine_kaddoura@yahoo.com; info@creativeeducationandpublishing.com
Web site: http://www.creativeeducationandpublishing.com.

Creative Educational Video *See* **C E V Multimedia, Ltd.**

Creative Energy, LLC, *(978-0-9821062; 978-0-9829825)* 20119 Timberstone Ln., Spring, TX 77379 USA (SAN 857-2771)
E-mail: drkmcleod@yahoo.com.

Creative Enterprises, *(978-1-880675)* 1040 Harvard Blvd., Dayton, OH 45406-5047 USA (SAN 253-5491) Tel 937-278-7159; Toll Free: 888-266-5777 Do not confuse with companies with the same or similar name in Mattapoisett, MA, Cordova, TN, Brooklyn, NY, Kittery, ME, Montgomery Village, MD
E-mail: allen45406@aol.com
Web site: http://creative-enterprises.org.

†Creative Homeowner, *(978-0-932944; 978-1-58011; 978-1-880029)* Div. of Courier Corporation, 24 Park Way, Upper Saddle River, NJ 07458-9960 USA (SAN 213-6627) Tel 201-934-7100; Fax: 201-934-8971; Toll Free: 800-631-7795
E-mail: info@creativehomeowner.com
Web site: http://www.creativehomeowner.com
Dist(s): **Dover Pubns., Inc. Follett School Solutions MyiLibrary**; *CIP*.

Creative House Press *See* **Bourgeois Media & Consulting**

Creative Hse. Kids Pr. *Imprint of* **Bourgeois Media & Consulting**

Creative Image Pubs., *(978-0-9742667)* 102 E. Main, Georgetown, KY 40324 USA
E-mail: Kathy@creativeimagepublishers.com
Web site: http://www.creativeimagepublishers.com.

Creative Learning Books *See* **Aradiance Publishing**

Creative Learning Consultants, Incorporated *See* **Pieces of Learning**

Creative Learning Exchange, *(978-0-9753169; 978-0-9960128)* 27 Central St., Acton, MA 01720-3522 USA (SAN 850-8836) Tel 978-287-0070; Fax: 978-287-0080
E-mail: stuntzin@clexchange.org
Web site: http://www.clexchange.org.

Creative Life Publishing, *(978-0-9779072)* 210 Indian Oak Dr., No. 1163, Waleska, GA 30183 USA Tel 770-720-1975
E-mail: affiliate@caroleoconnell.com
Web site: http://www.caroleoconnell.com.

Creative Marketing Concepts, Inc., *(978-0-9761408)* 2775 Jade St., Mora, MN 55051 USA Tel 320-679-4105; Fax: 320-679-3349; Toll Free: 800-605-4280 Do not confuse with companies with the same name in Saint Louis, MO, Los Angeles, CA
E-mail: cmc@creativemk.com
Web site: http://www.creativemk.com.

Creative Media Publishing, *(978-0-9826435; 978-0-9835393; 978-1-938438)* P.O. Box 6270, Whittier, CA 90609-6270 USA Tel 714-542-1212
E-mail: info@creativemedia.net
Web site: http://www.CreativeMedia.net
Dist(s): **Lulu Enterprises Inc.**

Creative Minds Pubns., *(978-0-9769737)* Orders Addr.: 2325 Crowncrest Dr., Richmond, VA 23233 USA Tel 804-740-6010; Fax: 804-798-1531
E-mail: kcstarke@aol.com
Dist(s): **Follett School Solutions.**

Creative Nutrition & Wellness, *(978-0-615-12437-7)* P.O. Box 7000-233, Redondo Beach, CA 90277 USA Fax: 310-792-0428
Web site: http://www.creativenutrition.com.

Creative Paperbacks *Imprint of* **Creative Co., The**

Creative Publishing, *(978-0-9744833)* 2221 Justin Rd., No. 119-123, Flower Mound, TX 75028 USA Tel 281-251-1751 (phone/fax) Do not confuse with companies with the same or similar name in Roseboro, NC, Greenville, SC, Lawrenceville, GA, Shrevport, LA, College Station, TX, Tustin, CA
E-mail: support@creativekidsonthemove.com
Web site: http://www.creativekidsonthemove.com.

Creative Publishing International *Imprint of* **Quarto Publishing Group USA**

Creative Publishing International *Imprint of* **Quarto Publishing Group USA**

Creative Quill Publishing, Inc., *(978-0-9709906)* Orders Addr.: P.O. Box 4028, Salem, OR 97302 USA; Edit Addr.: 460 Myers S., Salem, OR 97302 USA Tel 503-363-2843
E-mail: mavist@aol.com; Creativequill@aol.com
Web site: http://www.creativequill.us.

Creative Sharp Presentations, Incorporated *See* **SHARP Literacy, Inc.**

Creative Sources, *(978-0-9759613)* 105 N. Harvest Crest Ct., Highland, IL 62249 USA
E-mail: LLS@empowering.com
Web site: http://www.KidsDoRead.com; http://www.creativesourcespublishing.com.

Creative Styles *See* **JFW, Ltd.**

Creative Success Works, *(978-0-9759551)* 752 E. Lake Lndg., Marietta, GA 30062-3876 USA
E-mail: creativesuccess@comcast.net
Web site: http://www.creativesuccessworks.com.

Creative Teaching Assocs., *(978-1-878669; 978-1-930818; 978-1-931474; 978-1-932918)* Orders Addr.: P.O. Box 7766, Fresno, CA 93747 USA (SAN 297-6803) Tel 559-294-2141 Toll Free: 800-767-4282 (800-767-4CTA); Edit Addr.: P.O. Box 7766, Fresno, CA 93747-7766 USA
Web site: http://www.mastercta.com
Dist(s): **Follett School Solutions.**

Creative Teaching Pr., Inc., *(978-0-88160; 978-0-916119; 978-1-57471; 978-1-59198; 978-1-60689; 978-1-61601; 978-1-62186; 978-1-63445)* Orders Addr.: P.O. Box 2723, Huntington Beach, CA 92647-0723 USA Tel 714-895-5047; Fax: 714-895-6547; Toll Free Fax: 800-444-4287; Edit Addr.: 6262 Katella Ave., Cypress, CA 90630-5204 USA (SAN 294-9180) Tel 714-895-5047; Toll Free Fax: 800-229-9929; Toll Free: 800-444-4287; *Imprints*: Learning Works, The (The Lrning Works)
E-mail: webmaster@creativeteaching.com; we.listen@creativeteaching.com
Web site: http://www.creativeteaching.com; http://www.thelearningworks.com; http://www.learntoreadkidsclub.com
Dist(s): **Follett School Solutions Pacific Learning, Inc.**

Creative Thinkers, Incorporated *See* **Let's Think-kids Foundation, Inc.**

Creative Well, The, *(978-0-9700108)* P.O. Box 2121, Ashtabula, OH 44005 USA Tel 440-964-0338.

Creative with Words Pubns., *(978-0-936945)* P.O. Box 223226, Carmel, CA 93922 USA (SAN 658-6961) Fax: 408-655-8627
E-mail: cwwpub@usa.net.

Creative Works, *(978-0-9727499)* 3747 Redwood Cir., Palo Alto, CA 94306 USA Tel 650-493-3747.

Creative Writing & Publishing Co., *(978-1-887636)* P.O. Box 511848, Milwaukee, WI 53203-0311 USA
E-mail: Cbritt1@wi.rr.com.

Creative Writing Pr., Inc., *(978-0-9708382)* 1830 Stephenson Hwy., Troy, MI 48083-2173 USA Toll Free: 800-760-6397
E-mail: rodgers@mich.com
Web site: http://thepoetrylady.com.

CreativeMedia, Incorporated *See* **Creative Media Publishing**

Creatopia Productions - Lamy, New Mexico, *(978-0-9637467; 978-0-9854527)* 31 Cerro Cir. # B, Lamy, NM 87540-9682 USA
E-mail: wrayl@hotmail.com
Web site: http://www.members.tripod.com/~lyne4lyne/
Dist(s): **Adventures Unlimited Pr. Barnes & Noble Bks.-Imports CreateSpace Independent Publishing Platform.**

Creatrix! LLC, *(978-0-9760604)* P.O. Box 366, Cottage Grove, WI 53527 USA
Dist(s): **AtlasBooks Distribution.**

Credo Italia, *(978-0-9768375)* Orders Addr.: 350 Bay St., Suite 100-124, San Francisco, CA 94123 USA
E-mail: info@ClintAdams.com
Web site: http://www.ClintAdams.com.

Creed, Julie, *(978-0-9728181)* 17 Los Abitos, Rancho Santa Margarita, CA 92688 USA
E-mail: julie@qabranding.com
Web site: http://www.qabranding.com.

Creek Sound Bks., *(978-0-9743840)* 120 Misty Way, Cosby, TN 37722 USA Tel 606-523-5324
E-mail: rapowell7@msn.com.

Creepy Little Productions, *(978-0-9704159)* 3726 W. Augusta Ave., Phoenix, AZ 85051 USA Tel 602-625-6596; Fax: 602-242-3046
E-mail: christy@atgproductions.com; madamem@creepylittlestories.com
Web site: http://www.creepylittlestories.com
Dist(s): **PSI (Publisher Services, Inc.).**

Creevy, Anne *See* **ABC Bks.**

Creflo Dollar Ministries Pubns., *(978-1-931172; 978-1-59089)* Orders Addr.: P.O. Box 490124, College Park, GA 30349 USA Tel 770-210-5700; Fax: 770-210-5701; Edit Addr.: 2500 Burdett Rd., College Park, GA 30349 USA
E-mail: mfleming@worldchangers.org; mocarter@worldchangers.org; dfidler@worldchangers.org; tdavis@worldchangers.org
Web site: http://www.creflodollarministries.org
Dist(s): **Send The Light Distribution LLC.**

CreoXimius Publishing Company, *(978-0-9776617)* 970 E. Smith Rd., Medina, OH 44256 USA
Web site: http://www.debrae.com.

Crescent Moon Pr., *(978-0-9816011; 978-0-9818484; 978-0-9823065; 978-0-9841805; 978-0-9828200; 978-0-9846394; 978-1-937254; 978-1-939173; 978-0-9906274; 978-0-9908827; 978-0-9862871)* 1385 Hwy. 35, Box 269, Middletown, NJ 07748 USA
E-mail: publisher@crescentmoonpress.com
Web site: http://www.crescentmoonpress.com.

Crescent Moon Publishing (GBR) *(978-1-86171; 978-1-871846) Dist. by* **NACSCORP Inc.**

Crescent Renewal Resource, *(978-0-615-19983-2; 978-0-615-21952-3; 978-0-578-01626-9; 978-0-9842897)* 1915 Moonlight Rd., Smithfield, VA 23430 USA Tel 757-357-9292
Web site: http://www.tamiracithayne.com
Dist(s): **Lulu Enterprises Inc.**

CREST Pubns., *(978-0-9725546; 978-0-9912995)* P.O. Box 481022, Charlotte, NC 28269 USA Do not confuse with Crest Publications, Richardson, TX
Web site: http://www.crestpub.com.

Creston Bks., *(978-1-939547)* 965 Creston Rd., Berkeley, CA 94708 USA Tel 510-928-1765
E-mail: solsetimo@yahoo.com
Dist(s): **Perseus-PGW Perseus Distribution.**

Crews Pubns., LLC, *(978-0-9795236)* 7483 Garnet Dr., Jonesboro, GA 30236 USA Tel 770-617-9688
E-mail: crewspublications@yahoo.com
Web site: http://www.gscrews.com.

Cribsheet Publishing *See* **Blue Shoe Publishing**

Crichton, Sarah Bks. *Imprint of* **Farrar, Straus & Giroux**

Cricket Bks., *(978-0-8126)* Div. of Carus Publishing Co., 70 E. Lake St. Ste. 300, Chicago, IL 60601-5945 USA
Web site: http://www.cricketmag.com/home.asp
Dist(s): **Cobblestone Publishing Co. Ebsco Publishing Follett School Solutions Perseus-PGW.**

Cricket Productions, Incorporated *See* **Scrumps Entertainment, Inc.**

Cricket XPress of Minnesota, *(978-0-9822534)* 504 Bluebird Ct., Sartell, MN 56377 USA Tel 320-267-8978
E-mail: CricketXPressMN@charter.net.

Crickhollow Bks. *Imprint of* **Great Lakes Literary, LLC**

Crimson Oak Publishing LLC, *(978-0-9822725; 978-0-9829505)* P.O. Box 1389, Pullman, WA 99163 USA
E-mail: info@crimsonoakpublishing.com
Web site: http://www.crimsonoakpublishing.com
Dist(s): **Smashwords.**

Crippen & Landru Pubs., *(978-1-885941; 978-1-932009; 978-1-936363)* Orders Addr.: P.O. Box 9315, Norfolk, VA 23505-9315 USA Tel 757-622-6656 (phone/fax); Toll Free: 877-622-6656 (phone/fax); Edit Addr.: 627 New Hampshire Ave., Norfolk, VA 23508 USA Tel 757-622-6656 (phone/fax)
E-mail: info@crippenlandru.com
Web site: http://www.crippenlandru.com
Dist(s): **Follett School Solutions.**

Criqueville Pr., *(978-0-9705404)* Orders Addr.: P.O. Box 1227, Princeton, NJ 08542-1227 USA Tel 908-359-7834; Edit Addr.: 2 Dogwood Ln., Princeton, NJ 08542-1227 USA (SAN 255-982X)
E-mail: criquevillepress@hotmail.com.

Crises Research Pr., *(978-0-86627)* 301 W. 45th St., New York, NY 10036 USA (SAN 238-9274).

Crispus Medical Pr., *(978-0-9640389)* 7923 Leschi Rd., SW, Lakewood, WA 98498 USA Toll Free: 877-464-6469.

Cristal Publishing Co., *(978-0-9779124)* P.O. Box 14-4828, Coral Gables, FL 33114-4828 USA
E-mail: cristal228@bellsouth.net
Dist(s): **Ediciones Universal**
Follett School Solutions.

Critical Path Publishing, *(978-0-9740605)* P.O. Box 1073, Clayton, CA 94517-9073 USA Do not confuse with Critical Path Publishing Company in Denville, NJ
E-mail: cpp@silicon.com
Dist(s): **Book Publishing Co.**

Critical Thinking Books & Software *See* **Critical Thinking Co., The**

Critical Thinking Co., The, *(978-0-89455; 978-0-910974; 978-1-60144)* Orders Addr.: 1991 Sherman Ave Ste 200, North Bend, OR 97459 USA (SAN 207-0510) Tel 800-458-4849 Toll Free: 800-458-4849
E-mail: GaleO@criticalthinking.com; AbbeyH@criticalthinking.com; service@criticalthinking.com
Web site: http://www.criticalthinking.com
Dist(s): **Follett School Solutions.**

Critter Camp Inc., *(978-0-9772825)* 1190 Scenic Ave., Lummi Island, WA 98262 USA Tel 360-758-4269 (phone/fax)
E-mail: midiana@clearwire.net.

Critter Pubns., *(978-1-928972)* P.O. Box 413, Leicester, MA 01524-0413 USA
E-mail: del@critterp.com
Web site: http://www.critterp.com.

Critter Publishing, *(978-0-9754615)* Orders Addr.: P.O. Box 585, Readfield, ME 04355 USA Tel 207-685-5527 (phone/fax); Edit Addr.: 70 Walker Rd., Readfield, ME 04355 USA
E-mail: soniccomics@gwi.net
Web site: http://www.sonicpublishing.com.

Critters Up Close *Imprint of* **Wildlife Education, Ltd.**

CrittersInc, *(978-0-9745997)* 19611 Longview Terr., Salinas, CA 93908 USA
Web site: http://www.crittersinc.com.

CRM Enterprises, *(978-0-615-13155-9; 978-0-615-13278-5; 978-0-615-33279-6; 978-0-615-96051-7)* 411 Coram Avenue, Shelton, CT 06484 USA.

Croce, Pat & Co., *(978-0-9897533)* P.O. Box 520A, Villanova, PA 19085 USA Tel 610-520-1890; Fax: 610-525-5279
E-mail: sbarbacane@piratesoul.com.

Crockett, Sonja Michelle, *(978-0-578-08438-1; 978-0-615-58662-5; 978-0-615-75539-7)* P.O. Box 2154, Calumet City, IL 60409 USA
E-mail: taisanaa03@yahoo.com
Web site: www.facebook.com/sonjamcrockett.author; www.createspace.com/3666146; www.createspace.com/3712066
Dist(s): **CreateSpace Independent Publishing Platform**
Lulu Enterprises Inc.

Crocodile Bks. *Imprint of* **Interlink Publishing Group, Inc.**

Crocodiles Not Waterlilies Entertainment, *(978-0-9798297)* 58 Maiden Ln., Fifth Flr., San Francisco, CA 94108 USA (SAN 854-4921) Fax: 801-892-2230
E-mail: jodeen@crocpond.com.

Crofton Creek Pr., *(978-0-9700917; 978-0-9767268)* 2303 Gregg Rd., SW, South Boardman, MI 49680 USA Tel 231-369-2325; Fax: 231-369-4382; Toll Free: 877-255-3117
E-mail: publisher@croftoncreek.com
Web site: http://www.croftoncreek.com
Dist(s): **Partners Bk. Distributing, Inc.**
Wayne State Univ. Pr.

Cronies, *(978-1-929566)* Div. of Reproductive Images, 22738 Roscoe Blvd., No. 225, Canoga Park, CA 91304-3350 USA Tel 818-773-4888; Fax: 818-773-8808; Toll Free: 800-232-8099
E-mail: SethJ@CRONIES.com.

Cronus College, *(978-0-9760045; 978-0-9779897)* Div. of e-Pluribus Unum Publishing Co., P.O. Box 941, Lafayette, CA 94549 USA; *Imprints:* Reluctant Reader Books (ReluctRead)
Web site: http://www.cronuscollege.com.

Crooked Creek Publishing, LLC, *(978-0-9786084)* Orders Addr.: P.O. Box 479, Iola, WI 54945 USA Tel 715-445-5359; Edit Addr.: 460 E State St., Iola, WI 54945 USA
E-mail: crookedcreekpublishing@gmail.com
Dist(s): **Stevens International.**

Crooked River Pr., *(978-0-9778586)* P.O. Box 21, Cuyahoga Falls, OH 44221 USA Tel 330-701-3375; *Imprints:* Blue Jay Books (Blue Jay Bks)
E-mail: Books@CrookedRiverPress.com
Web site: http://www.CrookedRiverPress.com.

Crosam Pr., *(978-0-9774822; 978-0-9790337; 978-0-9798351; 978-0-9818903)* Orders Addr.: 681 Beverly Dr., Lake Wales, FL 33853 USA Tel 863-676-5737; Fax: 863-676-2285; Toll Free: 877-676-2285
E-mail: winksampson22@aol.com
Web site: http://www.feathersandfur.com; http://www.crosampress.com.

Cross & Crown Publishing, *(978-0-9785523; 978-0-9817728; 978-0-9886778)* 342 Meadow Green Dr., Ringgold, GA 30736 USA Tel 706-937-3798
E-mail: eddunlop@juno.com
Web site: http://www.dunlopministries.com
Dist(s): **Follett School Solutions.**

Cross Dove Publishing, LLC, *(978-0-9656513)* 1704 Esplanade, Front, Redondo Beach, CA 90277-8710 USA Tel 310-375-8400; Fax: 310-373-5912; 27 West 20Th St., New York, NY 10011
Web site: http://www.marysson.com; http://www.crossdove.com
Dist(s): **Follett School Solutions**
MyiLibrary.

Cross Pointe Printing, *(978-0-9742154)* 14417 N. 42nd St., Phoenix, AZ 85032-5437 USA
E-mail: dan@crosspointeprinting.com.

Cross Product Pubns., *(978-0-9793087; 978-0-9826837)* 3222 Cascade Hills Dr., NW, Cleveland, TN 37312 USA.

Cross Pubns., *(978-0-9771926; 978-0-9850996)* Orders Addr.: 502 E. Liberty Ave., Stillwater, OK 74075 USA Tel 405-564-5641 Do not confuse with Cross Publications in Safford, AZ, Savannah, GA
Web site: www.lulu.com/greenpheon7
Dist(s): **Lulu Enterprises Inc.**

Cross Reference Imprints, *(978-0-9725139)* 3607 Hycliffe Ave., Louisville, KY 40207 USA Tel 502-897-2719
E-mail: Pneuma@eclipsetel.com.

Cross Time *Imprint of* **Crossquarter Publishing Group**

Cross Training Publishing, *(978-1-887002; 978-1-929478; 978-0-9821652; 978-0-9845750; 978-1-938254)* P.O. Box 1874, Keary, NE 68848 USA (SAN 298-7406) Tel 308-293-3891; Fax: 308-338-2058; Toll Free: 800-430-8588
E-mail: gordon@crosstrainingpublishing.com; gthiessen@mac.com
Web site: http://www.crosstrainingpublishing.com
Dist(s): **Follett School Solutions.**

CrossBearers Publishing, *(978-0-9716365)* Div. of Reconciliation Ministries, Inc., Orders Addr.: 3101 Troost Ave., Kansas City, MO 64109 USA Tel 816-931-4751; Fax: 816-931-0142; P.O. Box 45642, Kansas City, MO 64171 Tel 816-449-2825; Fax: 816-449-5231; *Imprints:* St. Nicholas Press (St Nich Pr)
E-mail: frpaisius@hotmail.com; stnicholaspress@gmail.com
Web site: http://www.stmaryofegypt.net/.

CrossGeneration Comics, Inc., *(978-1-931484; 978-1-59314)* 9030 Lake Chase Island Way, Tampa, FL 33626-1942 USA
E-mail: jbreitbeil@crossgen.com
Web site: http://www.crossgen.com
Dist(s): **Diamond Comic Distributors, Inc.**

Crossing Guard Bks. *Imprint of* **Crossing Guard Bks., LLC**

Crossing Guard Bks., LLC, *(978-0-9770141)* Orders Addr.: P.O. Box 1792, Loveland, CO 80538 USA Tel 970-672-8078; *Imprints:* Crossing Guard Books (CrossGrdBks)
E-mail: Sarah@CrossingGuardBooks.com
Web site: http://www.CrossingGuardBooks.com.

Crossing Trails Pubns., *(978-0-9726095)* 4804 Kentwood Ln., Woodbridge, VA 22193 USA Tel 703-590-4449; Fax: 703-878-2119
E-mail: whnesbitt@compuserve.com
Web site: http://www.crossingtrails.com.

Cross-Lengua Productions *See* **KALEXT Productions, LLC**

Cross-Over, *(978-0-9749455; 978-0-9882835)* 190 Vista Linda Ave., Durango, CO 81303 USA Tel 970-385-1809 (phone/fax); Toll Free: 866-385-1809
E-mail: crossover@ellison.net
Web site: http://crossover.ellison.net; http://homeschoolhowtos.com/.

Crossover Comics *See* **Gavila Publishing**

Crossquarter Publishing Group, *(978-1-890109)* Div. of Earth Healers Inc., Orders Addr.: P.O. Box 23749, Santa Fe, NM 87502 USA Tel 505-690-3923 (phone); Fax: 214-975-9715 (fax); Edit Addr.: P.O. Box 23749, Santa Fe, NM 87502-3749 USA; *Imprints:* Cross Time (Crosstime)
E-mail: info@crossquarter.com
Web site: http://www.crossquarter.com
Dist(s): **Follett School Solutions**
New Leaf Distributing Co., Inc.

Crossroad Pr., *(978-0-9834348; 978-1-937530; 978-1-941408)* 141 Brayden Dr., HERTFORD, NC 27944 USA Tel 252-340-3952
E-mail: publisher@crossroadpress.com
Web site: http://store.crossroadpress.com
Dist(s): **Follett School Solutions.**

†Crossroad Publishing Co., The, *(978-0-8245)* 831 Chestnut Ridge Rd., Spring Valley, NY 10977-6356 USA (SAN 287-0118); 814 N. Franklin St., Chicago, IL 60610
E-mail: office@crossroadpublishing.com
Web site: http://www.crossroadpublishing.com
Dist(s): **ACTA Pubns.**
CreateSpace Independent Publishing Platform
Follett School Solutions
Independent Pubs. Group; *CIP.*

CrossStaff Publishing, *(978-0-9743876; 978-0-9800755)* P.O. Box 288, Broken Arrow, OK 74013 USA Tel 918-369-9293; Fax: 413-723-4384; Toll Free: 866-862-2278
E-mail: info@crossstaff.com
Web site: http://www.crossstaff.com.

Crosswalk Bks., *(978-0-9746269)* P.O. Box 176, American Fork, UT 84003 USA (SAN 255-7657)
Web site: http://www.crosswalkbooks.com.

†Crossway, *(978-0-89107; 978-1-58134; 978-1-4335; 978-1-68216)* Div. of Good News Pubs., 1300 Crescent St., Wheaton, IL 60187 USA (SAN 211-7991) Tel 708-682-4300; Fax: 630-682-4785; Toll Free: 800-323-3890 (sales only); *Imprints:* Crossway Bibles (Crossway Bibles)
E-mail: permissions@gnpcb.org
Web site: http://www.crossway.org
Dist(s): **L I M Productions, LLC**
Vision Video; *CIP.*

Crossway Bibles *Imprint of* **Crossway**

Crossway Books *See* **Crossway**

Crossways International, *(978-1-891245)* 7930 Computer Ave., S., Minneapolis, MN 55435-5415 USA Tel 952-832-5454; Fax: 952-832-5553; Toll Free: 800-257-7308
E-mail: info@crossways.org
Web site: http://www.crossways.org.

Crosswinds Bks., *(978-0-9726573)* P.O. Box 143, Keller, TX 76244 USA
E-mail: jroach35@earthlink.net.

Crosswinds Pr., Inc., *(978-0-9825559; 978-0-9838155)* 126 Crosswinds Dr., Groton, CT 06340 USA
Web site: http://www.crosswindspress.com
Dist(s): **Hillcrest Publishing Group, Inc.**

Crouch, Valeria *See* **Zig the Pig**

Crouse, Donna J., *(978-0-9765339)* P.O. Box 250, Jersey, VA 22481 USA Tel 540-775-7787; Fax: 540-775-1682
E-mail: df_crouse@msn.com.

Crow Dog Pr., *(978-0-9727656)* 541 Hunter Ave., Modesto, CA 95350 USA
E-mail: jackrandom@earthlink.net
Web site: http://www.jackrandom.com.

Crow Flies Pr., *(978-0-9814910)* P.O. Box 614, South Egremont, MA 01258 USA (SAN 855-7144)
E-mail: publisher@crowfliespress.com
Web site: http://www.crowfliespress.com
Dist(s): **BookBaby**
Follett School Solutions
SCB Distributors.

Crow, R.L. Pubns., *(978-0-9722958)* P.O. Box 262, Penn Valley, CA 95946 USA
E-mail: rlcrow@oro.net
Dist(s): **SPD-Small Pr. Distribution.**

Crowder, Jack L., *(978-0-9616589)* Orders Addr.: P.O. Box 250, Bernalillo, NM 87004 USA (SAN 659-8064) Tel 505-867-5812 (phone/fax); Edit Addr.: 500 Beehive Ln., Bernalillo, NM 87004 USA (SAN 659-8072)
E-mail: crowdercon@aol.com.

Crowell, Peter T. Pubns., *(978-0-9740290)* 1323 Marlborough St., Philadelphia, PA 19125 USA
E-mail: petertcrowell@gmail.com
Web site: http://www.petertcrowell.com
Dist(s): **Partners Bk. Distributing, Inc.**

Crown *Imprint of* **Crown Publishing Group**

Crown Books For Young Readers *Imprint of* **Random Hse. Children's Bks.**

Crown Peak Publishing, *(978-0-9645663)* Orders Addr.: P.O. Box 317, New Castle, CO 81647 USA Tel 970-618-1748
E-mail: ann@crownpeakpublishing.com
Web site: http://www.methetree.com; http://www.annlouiseramsey.com; http://www.crownpeakpublishing.com; http://www.justbeyoubook.com; http://www.tamingthedragon.net; http://www.icannotsleep.net.

†Crown Publishing Group, Div. of Random Hse., Inc., Orders Addr.: 400 Hahn Rd., Westminster, MD 21157 USA Tel 410-848-1900; Toll Free Fax: 800-659-2436; Toll Free: 800-733-3000; 800-726-0600; Edit Addr.: 1745 Broadway, New York, NY 10019 USA (SAN 200-2639) Tel 212-751-2600; Toll Free Fax: 800-659-2436; *Imprints:* Crown (Crown); Three Rivers Press (Three River Pr); Potter Craft (Pott Craft)
E-mail: customerservice@randomhouse.com; crownpublicity@randomhouse.com
Web site: http://www.randomhouse.com/
Dist(s): **Follett School Solutions**
MyiLibrary
Penguin Random Hse., LLC.
Random Hse., Inc.; *CIP.*

Crowned Warrior Publishing *Imprint of* **Walters, Steve Ministries**

Crowood Pr., Ltd. (GBR) *(978-0-946284; 978-1-85223; 978-1-86126; 978-1-84797) Dist. by* **IPG Chicago.**

Crowood Pr., Ltd. (GBR) *(978-0-946284; 978-1-85223; 978-1-86126; 978-1-84797) Dist. by* **HachBkGrp.**

CrowsNest Publishing, *(978-0-9710225)* 11513 Crows Nest Rd., Clarksville, MD 21029-1601 USA Tel 410-531-3110
E-mail: hannon@erols.com.

Crowther, Debra, *(978-0-9741295)* P.O. Box 1870, Three Rivers, TX 78071 USA Tel 361-786-4703; Fax: 361-786-2579
Web site: http://www.jackthewestie.com.

Crucifiction Games, *(978-0-9778263)* P.O. Box 654, Selah, WA 98942 USA Tel 509-697-7393; 509-952-6270
E-mail: cweedin@crucifictiongames.com
Web site: http://www.crucifictiongames.com
Dist(s): **Lightning Source, Inc.**

Crumb Elbow Publishing, *(978-0-89904)* P.O. Box 294, Rhododendron, OR 97049 USA (SAN 679-128X) Tel 503-622-4798.

CrumbGobbler Pr. *Imprint of* **Downtown Wetmore Pr.**

Crumly, Billie, *(978-0-9760577)* P.O. Box 281, Geraldine, AL 35974 USA.

Crumm, David Media, LLC, *(978-1-934879; 978-1-939880; 978-1-942011)* 42015 Ford Rd., Suite 234, Canton, MI 48187 USA (SAN 855-3637) Tel 734-786-3813
E-mail: admin@DavidCrummMedia.com
Web site: http://www.ReadTheSpirit.com.

Crunchpeep Media, *(978-0-9749469)* a/o Steven Merahn, 1700 Market St., 6th Flr., Philadelphia, PA 19103 USA Tel 215-832-0181
E-mail: smerahn@crunchpeep.com.

Crush Publishing, *(978-0-9798869; 978-0-9853434; 978-0-9910756)* Orders Addr.: 8209 Foothill Blvd No. A124, Sunland, CA 91040 USA Do not confuse with Crush Publishing in Brooklyn, NY
E-mail: wink@crushpublishing.com
Web site: http://www.crushpublishing.com.

Crushing Hearts and Black Butterfly Publishing, *(978-0-615-60362-9; 978-0-615-60460-2; 978-0-615-60592-0; 978-0-615-60593-7; 978-0-615-60597-5; 978-0-615-61380-2; 978-0-615-61435-9; 978-0-615-62403-7; 978-0-615-63475-3; 978-0-615-66682-2; 978-0-615-66683-9; 978-0-615-66684-6; 978-0-615-66760-7; 978-0-615-67525-1; 978-0-615-68166-5; 978-0-615-68247-1; 978-0-615-69025-4; 978-0-615-70249-0; 978-0-615-70607-8; 978-0-615-70608-5; 978-0-615-70656-6; 978-0-615-71144-7; 978-0-615-72063-0; 978-0-615-72064-7; 978-0-615-72065-4; 978-0-615-72906-0;)* 710 Saratoga Cir., Algonquin, IL 60102 USA Tel 224-234-9677
Web site: www.crushingheartsandblackbutterfly.com
Dist(s): **CreateSpace Independent Publishing Platform.**

Crying Cougar Pr., *(978-0-615-31150-0; 978-0-615-33106-5; 978-0-615-34888-9; 978-0-615-40439-4; 978-0-615-53634-7; 978-0-9859802)* 3559 Ruffin Rd. Suite 155, San Diego, CA 92123 USA
Dist(s): **Smashwords.**

Crysalis Publishing, Inc., *(978-0-9745190)* 10 Main St., Suite 4A, PMB 227, Woodbridge, NJ 07095 USA
Web site: http://www.chrysalispublishinc.com.

crysta luna studios, *(978-0-615-43657-9; 978-0-9887006)* 14995 SW Onyx Ct., Beaverton, OR 97007 USA Tel 503-933-1817
E-mail: smirlsmirl@gmail.com.

Crystal Ball Publishing, LLC., *(978-1-932277)* 107 Skiff Ave., Frankfort, NY 13340 USA
E-mail: Nerbo@msn.com; Sales@CrystalBallPublishing.com; Insight@CrystalBallPublishing.com
Web site: http://www.crystalballpublishing.com; http://www.gypsykids.com.

Crystal Clarity Pubs., *(978-0-916124; 978-1-56589; 978-1-878265)* 14618 Tyler-Foote Rd., Nevada City, CA 95959 USA (SAN 201-1778) Tel 530-478-7600 (intl. orders, cust. serv.); Fax: 530-478-7610 (orders); Toll Free: 800-424-1055
E-mail: sales@crystalclarity.com
Web site: http://www.crystalclarity.com
Dist(s): **Instructional Video**
Koen Pacific
MyiLibrary
National Bk. Network
New Leaf Distributing Co., Inc.
Nutri-Bks. Corp.
Princeton Bk. Co. Pubs.
ebrary, Inc.

Crystal Journeys Publishing, *(978-1-880737)* 130 Cochise Dr., Sedona, AZ 86351-7927 USA Tel 520-284-5730
Dist(s): **Light Technology Publishing, LLC.**

Crystal Mosaic Bks., *(978-0-9836303; 978-0-9911061)* PO Box 1276, Hillsboro, OR 97123 USA Tel 971-645-3204
E-mail: liome45@hotmail.com.

Crystal Pr., *(978-0-9632123; 978-0-9670886; 978-0-9746109)* 1750 Orr Ave., Simi Valley, CA 93065 USA Tel 805-527-4369; Fax: 805-582-3949 Do not confuse with Crystal Pr. in Houston, TX
E-mail: crystalpress@aol.com
Web site: http://www.Crystalpress.org.

Crystal Productions, *(978-0-924509; 978-1-56290)* Orders Addr.: 1812 Johns Dr., Glenview, IL 60025 USA (SAN 920-8224); Edit Addr.: 1812 Johns Dr., Glenview, IL 60025 USA (SAN 653-2489) Tel 847-657-8144; Fax: 847-657-8149; Toll Free Fax: 800-657-8149; Toll Free: 800-255-8629
E-mail: custserv@crystalproductions.com
Web site: http://www.crystalproductions.com
Dist(s): **Baker & Taylor Fulfillment, Inc.**
Follett School Solutions.

Crystal Springs Bks. *Imprint of* **Staff Development for Educators**

CS Media Resources, *(978-0-9764992)* Orders Addr.: 12 W. Willow Grove Ave. Suite 121, Philadelphia, PA 19118-3952 USA Toll Free: 877-866-8309
E-mail: csmr@csmediaresources.com
Web site: http://www.csmediaresources.com.

CSE Publishing, *(978-0-9743567)* 706 Radcliffe Ave., Lynn Haven, FL 32444-3039 USA (SAN 255-5581) Fax: 850-271-9874; Toll Free: 866-262-8776
E-mail: tchardy@bellsouth.net.

CSI Publishing *See* **Decere Publishing**

CSIRO Publishing (AUS) *(978-1-922173; 978-1-4863) Dist. by* **Stylus Pub VA.**

CSS Backlist *Imprint of* **Chicken Soup for the Soul Publishing, LLC**

CSS Publishing, *(978-0-9721679)* 108A Gallegos Ln., Tularosa, NM 88352 USA (SAN 254-6477) Fax: 505-585-4908 Do not confuse with C S S Publishing Company in Lima, OH
E-mail: rblanks@netmdc.com; csspublishing@hotmail.com.

CTC Publishing, *(978-0-9747789; 978-1-934073)* 10431 Lawyers Rd., Vienna, VA 22181-2822 USA (SAN 851-7908) Toll Free: 800-942-0962
E-mail: pitts@ndmc.com
Web site: http://www.couragetochange.com/
Dist(s): **Follett School Solutions.**

CTO Bks., *(978-0-9724411)* Div. of CTO Publishing LLC, Orders Addr.: P.O. Box 825, Kokomo, IN 46903 USA
E-mail: ctobooks@gmail.com
Web site: http://www.ctobooks.com
Dist(s): **AtlasBooks Distribution**
MyiLibrary
ebrary, Inc.

Ctr. for Curatorial Studies *Imprint of* **Bard College Pubns. Office**

Ctrl+Alt+Del Prodns., *(978-0-9764678)* P.O. Box 206392, New Haven, CT 06520 USA Tel 508-274-5804
E-mail: absath@ctrlaltdel-online.com
Web site: http://www.ctrlaltdel-online.com.

Cub Bks. *Imprint of* **Global Business Information Strategies, Inc.**

Cubbie Blue Publishing, *(978-0-9706341; 978-1-932824)* 546 Flanders Dr., Saint Louis, MO 63122-1618 USA
E-mail: rahandler@earthlink.net
Web site: ravencrestpublishing.com
Dist(s): **BookBaby.**

Cubby Hole Tales, *(978-0-9754591)* 524 Moores Mill Rd., Pelzer, SC 29669 USA Tel 864-947-6426
E-mail: telvajo@bellsouth.net
Web site: http://www.talesfromtwocousins.com.

Cube Marketing, *(978-0-9893091)* 51 9th Ave., Newark, NJ 07107 USA Tel 973-482-4101
E-mail: deidre.knight@gmail.com.

Cuccia, Louis, *(978-0-9727415)* 603 Winthrop, Smyrna, TN 37167 USA Tel 615-355-6821; Fax: 615-355-0171
E-mail: Lcuccia@aol.com.

Cuddehe Services *See* **Found Link**

Cuento de Luz SL (ESP) *(978-84-937814; 978-84-15241; 978-84-938240; 978-84-15503; 978-84-15619; 978-84-15784; 978-84-16078) Dist. by* **PerseuPGW.**

Culpepper, Felix International, Inc., *(978-0-9740435)* Orders Addr.: P.O. Box 70, Jefferson City, TN 37760-0070 USA (SAN 255-2752) Tel 865-475-4993; Fax: 914-470-1091; Edit Addr.: 2476 Tarr Rd., Talbott, TN 37877 USA
E-mail: gfac@cshore.com; peteculpepper@helpkidswhohavecancer.org; pete@felixculpepper.com
Web site: http://www.bigboxhead.com; http://www.felixculpepper.com
Dist(s): **American Wholesale Bk. Co.**

Cultural Connections, *(978-0-9636629; 978-1-57371)* P.O. Box 1582, Alameda, CA 94501 USA Toll Free: 888-234-5412
E-mail: info@culture-connect.org
Web site: http://www.culture-connect.org.

Culturatti Ink, *(978-0-9712383; 978-0-692-42185-7; 978-0-692-42186-4)* 9465 Counselors Row Suite 200, Indianapolis, IN, IN 46240 USA
E-mail: erika@culturattikids.net
Web site: http://www.culturattiink.com.

Culture Connection, The *See* **Culturatti Ink**

Culture Hse., *(978-0-9676080; 978-0-9819484)* Orders Addr.: P.O. Box 293, Newton, IA 50208 USA Tel 641-792-0920; Edit Addr.: 3830 Harbor Ave., Newton, IA 50208-9040 USA
E-mail: museum@pcpartner.net
Web site: http://www.mike-chapman.com.

Culture of Life, Inc., *(978-0-9761457)* 1054 Windy Knoll Rd., West Chester, PA 19382-7433 USA.

CultureGrams World Edition *Imprint of* **ProQuest LLC**

Culturelink Pr., *(978-0-9759276)* Orders Addr.: P.O. Box 3538, San Diego, CA 92163 USA (SAN 256-1174); Edit Addr.: 1435 Essex St., No.3, San Diego, CA 92103 USA
Web site: http://www.culturelinkpress.com.

Cumberland Hse. *Imprint of* **Sourcebooks, Inc.**

Cummings Pr., *(978-0-9767063)* 1939 Mt. Vernon Pl., Dunwoody, GA 30338-4417 USA Tel 770-512-8115 (phone/fax).

Cummins Associates International *See* **CAI Publishing**

Cummins, Judi, *(978-0-9760377)* Orders Addr.: P.O. Box 10 Chosen Spot Apartments, Canandaigua, NY 14424 USA
E-mail: jcummins1@rochester.rr.com.

Cumquat Publishing Company *See* **Floppinfish Publishing Co., Ltd.**

Cumuli, *(978-0-9709730)* Div. of Cumuli, Inc., P.O. Box 1174, Port Orchard, WA 98366 USA Tel 360-871-9493 (phone/fax)
E-mail: fletcher@cumuli.com; susan@cumuli.com
Web site: http://www.cumuli.com; http://www.cumulipress.com.

Cune *See* **Cune Pr., LLC**

Cune Pr., LLC, *(978-1-885942; 978-1-61457)* Div. of Scott Davis Co., P.O. Box 31024, Seattle, WA 98103 USA (SAN 298-3648) Tel 206-789-7055; Fax: 206-774-0592
E-mail: bowker@cunepress.com
Web site: http://www.cunepress.com; http://www.cunepress.net
Dist(s): **Bolchazy-Carducci Pubs.**
Smashwords.

Cupola Pr., *(978-0-9793345; 978-0-9834046; 978-0-9857932)* 3280 Withers Ave., Lafayette, CA 94549-2128 USA Tel 925-285-7754
E-mail: info@cupolapress.com
Web site: http://www.cupolapress.com
Dist(s): **Independent Pubs. Group**
MyiLibrary.

†Curbstone Pr., *(978-0-915306; 978-1-880684; 978-1-931896)* P.O. Box 45, Willimantic, CT 06226-0045 USA (SAN 209-4282)
E-mail: info@curbstone.org
Web site: http://www.curbstone.org
Dist(s): **Chicago Distribution Ctr.**
Lectorum Pubns., Inc.
SPD-Small Pr. Distribution; *CIP.*

Curcumin Bks. *Imprint of* **Davlaw Press**

Curiosity Quills Pr., *(978-1-62007)* Orders Addr.: P.O. Box 2160, Reston, VA 20195 USA (SAN 920-9700) Tel 800-998-2509
E-mail: editor@curiosityquills.com
Web site: http://curiosityquills.com.

Curiosmith, *(978-0-9817505; 978-1-935626; 978-1-941281)* P.O. Box 390293, Minneapolis, MN 55439-0293 USA (SAN 856-4450)
E-mail: shopkeeper@curiosmith.com
Web site: http://www.curiosmith.com.

Curious Kids Guides, *(978-0-9789140)* 2561 Bunker Hill, Ann Arbor, MI 48105-3432 USA Tel 734-665-0533
E-mail: eisbruchs@aol.com
Web site: http://www.CuriousKidsGuides.com
Dist(s): **Partners Bk. Distributing, Inc.**

Currach Pr. (IRL) *(978-1-85607) Dist. by* **Dufour.**

Curran, M.J., *(978-0-9768984)* 640 Gooseberry Dr., No. 1207, Longmont, CO 80503 USA Tel 720-206-9099
E-mail: mjcurran@hotmail.com.

Currency Pr. (AUS) *(978-0-86819; 978-0-9596937; 978-1-921428; 978-1-921429; 978-1-925004; 978-1-925005; 978-1-925210; 978-1-925359) Dist. by* **Antipodes Bks.**

Current Clinical Strategies Publishing, *(978-0-9626030; 978-1-881528; 978-1-929622; 978-1-934323)* P.O. Box 1753, Blue Jay, CA 92317 USA (SAN 298-4490) Tel 949-348-8404; Fax: 949-348-8405; Toll Free Fax: 800-965-9420; Toll Free: 800-331-8227
E-mail: info@ccspublishing.com
Web site: http://www.ccspublishing.com/ccs
Dist(s): **Majors, J. A. Co.**
Matthews Medical Bk. Co.
Rittenhouse Bk. Distributors.

Current Publishing Corp., *(978-1-878663)* 30151 Tomas St., Rancho Santa Margarita, CA 92688 USA Toll Free: 800-729-7234.

Curriculum Associates, Incorporated *See* **Curriculum Assocs., LLC**

Curriculum Assocs., LLC, *(978-0-7609; 978-0-89187; 978-1-55915; 978-1-4957)* Orders Addr.: P.O. Box 2001, North Billerica, MA 01862-0901 USA (SAN 659-6304) Toll Free: 800-225-0248; Edit Addr.: 153 Rangeway Rd., North Billerica, MA 01862 USA Tel 978-667-8000; Toll Free Fax: 800-366-1158; Toll Free: 800-225-0248
E-mail: DAndreoli@CAinc.com; info@curriculumassociates.com; info@cainc.com
Web site: http://www.curriculumassociates.com.

Curriculum Publishing, Presbyterian Church (U. S. A.), *(978-1-57153)* 100 Witherspoon St., Louisville, KY 40202-1396 USA Tel 502-569-5090; Fax: 502-569-8329; Toll Free: 800-524-2612; *Imprints:* Witherspoon Press (Witherspoon Pr)
Web site: http://www.pcusa.org/pcusa/currpub; http://www.bridgeresources.org
Dist(s): **Westminster John Knox Pr.**

Currie & Smith Publishing *See* **T.Y.M. Publishing**

Currier Davis Publishing *See* **GRAND Media, LLC**

Curry Brothers Publishing Group, *(978-0-9798364; 978-0-9818956)* 608 Sandy Spring Trail, Madison, TN 37115 USA
E-mail: cbmpg@yahoo.com
Web site: http://currybrotherspublishing.com.

Cursack Bks., *(978-1-933439)* 31 Hubbard Rd., Dover, NH 03820 USA
E-mail: info@cursackbooks.com
Web site: http://www.cursackbooks.com
Dist(s): **Ediciones Universal.**

Curtis Elliott Designs, Ltd., *(978-0-9742438)* 5250 Franklin St., Unit C-1, Hilliard, OH 43026 USA Tel 614-771-7978
E-mail: info@creativecoloringbooks.com
Web site: http://www.creativecoloringbooks.com.

Curtis Publishing Company *See* **Cedar Creek Publishing Service**

Customer Centered Consulting Group, Inc., *(978-0-9762493)* 5729 Lebanon Dr., Suite 144-222, Frisco, TX 75034 USA Tel 469-633-9833; Fax: 469-633-9843
E-mail: dreed@cccginc.com
Web site: http://www.cccginc.com.

Cute & Cuddly Productions, Inc., *(978-0-9761318)* 4401 Shallowford Rd., Suite 162-161, Roswell, GA 30075 USA Tel 678-478-6071 (phone/fax)
E-mail: cuteandcuddlyproductions@msn.com
Web site: http://www.bigbillandbuddies.com.

CVD Publishing, *(978-0-9743520)* 1254 Grizzly Flat Ct., Auburn, CA 95603 USA Tel 530-885-4988
E-mail: grizlyflat@jps.net
Web site: http://www.CVDbooks.com.

CWG Pr., *(978-0-9788186; 978-0-9906714)* 1517 NE. 5th Ter Apt 1, Fort Lauderdale, FL 33304 USA Tel 954-524-5953
E-mail: editor@cwgpress.com
Web site: http://www.cwgpress.com.

CWLA Pr. *Imprint of* **Child Welfare League of America, Inc.**

CWS Studios, Inc., *(978-0-9785827; 978-0-615-92291-1)* 5414 W. Barry Ave., Chicago, IL 60641 USA
Web site: http://www.cws-studios.com.

Cyan Communications (GBR) *(978-0-9542829; 978-1-904879; 978-1-905736) Dist. by* **IPG Chicago.**

Cyber Haus, *(978-1-931373)* 159 Delaware Ave., #145, Delmar, NY 12054 USA Tel 518-478-9798
E-mail: cyhaus@msn.com
Web site: http://www.revolutionaryday.com/; http://www.cyhaus.com/.

Cyber Publishing Co., *(978-0-9637419; 978-0-9747870)* 421 Ave. De Teresa, Grants Pass, OR 97526 USA (SAN 255-691X) Tel 541-474-1077; Fax: 541-474-2829
E-mail: intrchild@aol.com.

Cyber Tiger Pr., *(978-0-615-18259-9)* Planetarium Station, New York, NY 10024 USA
E-mail: bill@billweberstudios.com
Dist(s): **Lulu Enterprises Inc.**

Cyberlab Publishing, *(978-0-9746501)* P.O. Box 618, Dimondale, MI 48821-0618 USA Tel 517-974-8068; Fax: 517-887-9029
E-mail: ministerjd@yahoo.com
Web site: http://www.cyberlabpublishing.com.

Cyberosia Publishing, *(978-0-9709474; 978-0-9742713)* 3864 Shelley Dr., Mobile, AL 36693-3933 USA
E-mail: scottobrown@gmail.com
Dist(s): **Diamond Distributors, Inc.**

Cyberwizard Productions, *(978-0-9795788; 978-0-9815669; 978-0-9821352; 978-1-936021)* Orders Addr.: 1029 N. Saginaw Blvd Suite F10-124, Saginaw, TX 76179 USA; *Imprints:* Banana Oil Books (Banana Oil)
Web site: http://cyberwizardproductions.com; http://www.cyberwizardproductions.com/Chaco_Canyon_Books/; http://wildplainspress.webs.com; http://www.cyberwizardproductions.com/Ancient_Tomes_Press; http://www.cyberwizardproductions.com/Altered_Dimensions_Press; http://www.cyberwizardproductions.com/Banana_Oil_Books/; http://www.cyberwizardproductions.com/Diminuendo_Poetry/; http://firesidemysteries.webs.com; http://www.cyberwizardproductions.com/Toy_Box_Books/
Dist(s): **NACSCORP, Inc.**
Send The Light Distribution LLC.

Cyclops Pr., *(978-0-9740269)* 1342 Van Buren Ave., Saint Paul, MN 55104-1926 USA.

Cyclotour Guide Bks., *(978-1-889602)* Orders Addr.: P.O. Box 10585, Rochester, NY 14610-0585 USA; Edit Addr.: 160 Harvard St., Rochester, NY 14607 USA
E-mail: cyclotour@cyclotour.com; cyclotour@frontiernet.net
Web site: http://www.cyclotour.com.

Cygnet Publishing Group, Inc./Coolreading.com (CAN) *(978-1-55305) Dist. by* **Orca Bk Pub.**

Cymbal Technique 101, *(978-0-9762593)* 440 Ross Rd., Fort Walton Beach, FL 32547 USA
E-mail: edward_capps@cymbaltechnique101.com
Web site: http://www.cymbaltechnique101.com.

Cypress Bay Publishing, *(978-0-9746747)* 910 W. Harney Ln., Lodi, CA 95242 USA (SAN 255-6928) Tel 209-365-6114
E-mail: nclaus@clearwire.net.

Cypress Communications, *(978-0-9636412; 978-0-9896043)* 35 E. Rosemont Ave., Alexandria, VA 22301 USA Tel 703-548-0532 (phone/fax) Do not confuse with companies with similar names in Leawood, KS, Saint Paul, MN, Cypress, TX
E-mail: jcclifford@earthlink.net
Web site: http://www.lighthousehistory.info; http://www.CivilWarDrummerBoy.com
Dist(s): **Partners Bk. Distributing, Inc.**

Cypress Knees Publishing, *(978-0-9745863; 978-0-9763757)* Div. of Top Brass Outdoors, Orders Addr.: P.O. Box 209, Starkville, MS 39760 USA Tel 662-323-1559; Fax: 662-323-7466; Edit Addr.: 312 Industrial Pk., Rd., Starkville, MS 39759 USA
E-mail: eric@topbrasstackle.com
Web site: http://www.topbrasstackle.com; http://www.outdooryouthadventures.com.

CyPress Pubns., *(978-0-9672585; 978-0-9776958; 978-1-935083)* P.O. Box 2636, Tallahassee, FL 32316-2636 USA Fax: 850-254-7112
E-mail: lraymond@nettally.com
Web site: http://cypresspublications.com
Dist(s): **Smashwords.**

Cypress Publishing *See* **Cypress Communications**

Cyr Design Publishing, *(978-0-9774543)* P.O. Box 1662, Nashua, NH 03061-1662 USA
Web site: http://cyrdesign.com.

Cyrano Bks., *(978-0-615-55618-5)* 3348 kaunaoa St., Honolulu, HI 96815 USA Tel 808-381-5205
E-mail: cindykm@hawaii.rr.com.

Czechoslovak Genealogical Society International, *(978-0-9651932)* Orders Addr.: P.O. Box 16225, Saint Paul, MN 55116-0225 USA Tel 763-595-7799; Edit Addr.: 8582 Timberwood Rd., Woodbury, MN 55125-7620 USA
E-mail: cgsi@aol.com
Web site: http://www.cgsi.org.

Czerwonka, Larry Co., The, *(978-0-615-59209-1; 978-0-615-61190-7; 978-0-615-62803-5; 978-0-615-65033-3; 978-0-615-65493-5; 978-0-615-65542-0; 978-0-615-65692-2; 978-0-615-66007-3; 978-0-615-66010-3; 978-0-615-66483-5; 978-0-615-67027-0; 978-0-615-68405-5; 978-0-615-69496-2; 978-0-615-69659-1; 978-0-615-70185-1; 978-0-615-70456-2; 978-0-615-70661-0; 978-0-615-71627-5; 978-0-615-72077-7; 978-0-615-72594-9; 978-0-615-73452-1; 978-0-615-73514-6; 978-0-615-73574-0; 978-0-615-73629-7; 978-0-615-73842-0; 978-0-615-74848-1;)* *1102 Apono Pl., Hilo, HI 96720 USA Tel 808-959-6974*
Dist(s): **CreateSpace Independent Publishing Platform.**

D.A.P./Distributed Art Pubs., *(978-1-881616; 978-1-891024; 978-1-933045; 978-1-935202; 978-1-938922; 978-1-942884)* Orders Addr.: 155 Sixth Ave., 2nd Flr., New York, NY 10013-1507 USA (SAN 630-6446) Tel 212-627-1999; Fax: 212-627-9484; Toll Free Fax: 800-478-3128; Toll Free: 800-338-2665
E-mail: dap@dapinc.com
Web site: http://www.artbook.com/
Dist(s): **Perseus-PGW**
Perseus Bks. Group
Perseus Distribution.

D A W Bks., Inc. *Imprint of* **Penguin Publishing Group**

D & S Marketing Systems, Inc., *(978-1-878621; 978-0-9787199; 978-1-934780)* 1205 38th St., Brooklyn, NY 11218-3705 USA Tel 718-633-8383; Fax: 718-633-8385; Toll Free: 800-633-8383
E-mail: dsmarketing@aol.com; info@dsmarketing.com
Web site: http://www.dsmarketing.com.

D B W, Incorporated *See* **Just Like Me, Inc.**

DC Pr. LLC, *(978-0-9708444; 978-1-932021)* Orders Addr.: 750 Powderhorn Cir., Lake Mary, FL 32746 USA (SAN 254-1262) Tel 407-688-1156; Fax: 877-203-1805 (orders)
E-mail: dennis.dcpress@gmail.com
Web site: www.dcpressbooks.com
Dist(s): **Midpoint Trade Bks., Inc.**
MyiLibrary
ebrary, Inc.

DDDD Pubns., *(978-0-9635341; 978-1-885519)* 3407 Brown Rd., Saint Louis, MO 63114-4329 USA (SAN 631-2675).

D H Publishing LLC, *(978-0-9800263)* 515 E. Carefree Hwy., No. 652, Phoenix, AZ 85085-8839 USA
E-mail: deserthillspublishing@hotmail.com.

D K Publishing, Incorporated *See* **Dorling Kindersley Publishing, Inc.**

D. W. Ink, *(978-1-892313)* P.O. Box 5470, Huntsville, AL 35814 USA Fax: 205-721-1269.

D. W. Publishing, *(978-0-9741774)* 226 McFarland St., Grand Blanc, MI 48439 USA Tel 810-695-8985
E-mail: dan@dwpublishing.com
Web site: http://www.dwpublishing.com.

Da Wong Bks., *(978-0-9744360; 978-0-615-73234-3)* 4070 Cactus Rd., Shingle Springs, CA 95682 USA Tel 530-676-6060 (phone/fax)
E-mail: eslhotel@yahoo.com.

DAAB Media Gmbh (DEU) *(978-3-942597) Dist. by* **InnovativeLog.**

Dabel Brothers Production LLC., *(978-0-9764011; 978-0-9779333)* 6070 Autumn View Trail, Acworth, GA 30101 USA
E-mail: ldabel@dabelbrothers.com
Web site: http://www.dabelbrothers.com/
Dist(s): **Diamond Comic Distributors, Inc.**
Diamond Bk. Distributors.

DAC Educational Pubns., *(978-1-930731)* 4325 Carlton Pl., Yorba Linda, CA 92886 USA
E-mail: DACpublis@aol.com.

DaChosen Publishing, *(978-0-9762627)* Orders Addr.: 4278 Babette Ct., Stone Mountain, GA 30083 USA Toll Free: 800-442-7170
E-mail: traewing@gmail.com
Web site: http://www.dachosen.com.

Daddy Bean Bks., *(978-0-9842929)* 42 W. 38th St., Suite 1001, New York, NY 10018 USA Tel 212-840-2326
E-mail: Pwalsh@walshfamilymedia.com
Web site: http://www.walshfamilymedia.com.

Daddy's Heroes, Inc., *(978-0-9792111)* 4799 Baxter St., Santa Barbara, CA 93110 USA
E-mail: karun@daddysheroes.com
Web site: http://www.daddysheroes.com.

Dadielte Production, *(978-0-9799273)* P.O. Box 1266, Moreno Valley, CA 92556-1266 USA (SAN 854-7645)
E-mail: gema118@hotmail.com.

Dahomey Publishing Co., *(978-0-9723570)* Orders Addr.: 50 Hall Rd., Winchendon, MA 01475 USA (SAN 255-4542) Tel 978-297-1820; Fax: 978-297-2519
Web site: http://www.DahomeyPublishing.com.

Dailey International Pubs., *(978-0-9666251)* 500 Laurel Oaks Ln., Alpharetta, GA 30004-4508 USA
E-mail: franklyn@daileyint.com
Web site: http://www.daileyint.com.

Daily Racing Form,
Dist(s): **National Bk. Network.**

Daimon Verlag (CHE) *(978-3-85630) Dist. by* **AtlasBooks.**

Daisy Publishing, *(978-0-9740641)* P.O. Box 681171, Franklin, TN 37068 USA Do not confuse with Daisy Publishing in Massapequa Park, NY, Altoona, PA.

Dakitab, Inc., *(978-0-9791059)* Orders Addr.: 2906 W. Grand Blvd., Detroit, MI 48202 USA (SAN 852-4408) Fax: 248-360-6148
E-mail: aid@awaytoread.com
Web site: http://www.awaytoread.com.

Dakota Assocs., Inc., *(978-0-615-14589-1; 978-0-615-18375-6)* P.O. Box 321, W. Bloomfield, NY 14585 USA
Web site: http://www.dakotaassociates.com
Dist(s): **Lulu Enterprises Inc.**

Dakota Bks., *(978-0-9632861)* Orders Addr.: 2801 Daubenbiss, No. 1, Soquel, CA 95073 USA (SAN 630-9445) Tel 831-477-7174
E-mail: llogan@cruzio.com.

Dakota Rose, *(978-0-9727056)* 23725 260th Ave., Okaton, SD 57562 USA Tel 605-669-2529
E-mail: dakotarose746@goldenwest.net.

Dakota Skies Photography *See* **Johnny Sundby Photography**

Dale, Shelley *See* **Norman Bks.**

Dales Large Print Bks. (GBR) *(978-1-85389; 978-1-84262) Dist. by* **Ulverscroft US.**

Daley, Robert, *(978-0-9800839)* P.O. Box 5518, Keaau, HI 96749-5518 USA Tel 808-982-6688; Fax: 808-982-7824
E-mail: thedaleys@bythebookministries.org.

Dally, James W. Associates *See* **College Hse. Enterprises, LLC**

Dalton Publishing (GBR) *(978-0-9541886) Dist. by* **Midpt Trade.**

Dalton, William, *(978-0-9764395)* 1338 N. Laurel Ave., West Hollywood, CA 90046 USA Tel 310-800-0811
E-mail: urban_mystic@yahoo.com.

Damamli Publishing Co., *(978-0-9753584)* 25A Crescent Dr., No.171, Pleasant Hill, CA 94523-3501 USA (SAN 256-100X) Fax: 923-674-9461
E-mail: tookie@tookie.com; president@damamli.com
Web site: http://www.damamli.com.

Damiano Sara, Janeen, *(978-0-9786404)* 108 W. Village Dr., Saint Augustine, FL 32095 USA
Web site: http://www.whereslily.com.

Damnation Bks., *(978-1-61572; 978-1-62929)* P.O. Box 3931, Santa Rosa, CA 95402-9998 USA
Web site: http://www.damnationbooks.com; http://www.eternalpress.biz.

Dan Dan Fantasy, *(978-0-9834315)* 18483 Five Points, Redford, MI 48240 USA Tel 734-776-5478
E-mail: paintballman@sbcglobal.net.

Dance & Movement Pr. *Imprint of* **Rosen Publishing Group, Inc., The**

Dance Horizons *Imprint of* **Princeton Bk. Co. Pubs.**

Dancer's Publishing, *(978-0-9794848)* 2103 Harrison NW, Suite 2-336, Olympia, WA 98502 USA.

Dances With Horses, Inc., *(978-0-9763489)* P.O. Box 819, Rexburg, ID 83440 USA Tel 800-871-7635; Fax: 208-356-7817; Toll Free: 800-871-7635
E-mail: frankbell@horsewhisperer.com
Web site: http://www.horsewhisperer.com.

Publisher Name Index

Dancing Force, The, *(978-0-9726119)* 2249 Reeves Creek Rd., Suite B, Selma, OR 97538 USA (SAN 255-156X) Tel 541-597-2093 (phone/fax)
E-mail: dancingforce@ureach.com
Dist(s): **DeVorss & Co.**

Dancing Journey Pr., *(978-0-9847662)* 434 Ulman Rd., Thetford Center, VT 05075 USA Tel 802-785-4717
E-mail: Ginger.Wallis@valley.net.

Dancing Magic Heart Bk., *(978-0-9790041)* Div. of Douglas/Steinman Productions, 1841 Broadway, Suite 1103, New York, NY 10023 USA Tel 212-765-9848; Fax: 212-765-9848
E-mail: faithdouglas@earthlink.net
Web site: http://www.douglas-steinman.com
Dist(s): **New Leaf Resources.**

Dancing Moon Pr., *(978-1-892076; 978-1-937493)* P.O. Box 832, Newport, OR 97365-0062 USA Tel 541-574-7708 (work)
E-mail: carla@dancingmoonpress.com
Web site: http://www.dancingmoonpress.com
Dist(s): **Partners/West Book Distributors.**

Dancing Words Pr., Inc., *(978-0-9716346)* Orders Addr.: P.O. Box 1575, Severna Park, MD 21146 USA; Edit Addr.: 12 Sonneborn Ln., Severna Park, MD 21146 USA Tel 410-647-1441 (phone/fax)
E-mail: dwpinc@aol.com
Web site: http://www.dancingwordspress.com
Dist(s): **Quality Bks., Inc.**

Dandelion Publishing, *(978-0-9793930)* 6234 Eliza Ln., North Las Vegas, NV 89031 USA (SAN 853-330X)
E-mail: sand.d@cox.net
Web site: http://DandelionPublishing.com.

Dandy Lion Pubns., *(978-0-931724; 978-1-883055)* P.O. Box 190, Sn Luis Obisp, CA 93406-0190 USA (SAN 211-5565) Toll Free: 800-776-8032
E-mail: dandy@dandylionbooks.come
Web site: http://www.dandylionbooks.com.

Dangberg, Grace Foundation, Incorporated *See* **Sage Hill Pubs., LLC**

DAngelo, Gus, *(978-0-615-45567-9; 978-0-615-70443-2)* 752 Clayton St., San Francisco, CA 94117 USA Tel 415-550-0514
E-mail: gus@sanfranciscoabc.com
Dist(s): **Independent Pubs. Group.**

Daniel & Daniel, Pubs., Inc., *(978-0-931832; 978-0-936784; 978-1-56474; 978-1-880284)* P.O. Box 2790, McKinleyville, CA 95519 USA (SAN 215-1995) Tel 707-839-3495; Fax: 707-839-3242; Toll Free: 800-662-8351; *Imprints:* Fithian Press (Fithian Press)
E-mail: dandd@danielpublishing.com
Web site: http://www.danielpublishing.com
Dist(s): **SCB Distributors.**

Dankworth Publishing, *(978-0-9855676)* 309 Reamer Pl., Oberlin, OH 44074 USA Tel 612-309-5126
E-mail: mindybrueggemann@yahoo.com.

DanMar Publishing, *(978-0-9749407)* 112 E. Pennsylvania Blvd., Feasterville, PA 19053 USA Tel 215-364-1112; Fax: 215-364-3231
E-mail: drlavanga@aol.com
Web site: http://www.drlavanga.com.

Dante's Publishing *See* **Solomon's Bks.**

Danza Pubns., *(978-0-9774552)* P.O. Box 252053, West Bloomfield, MI 48325 USA Toll Free: 800-457-2157
Web site: http://www.elaineserling.com.

Dar Asadeeq Publishing & Distribution, Inc., *(978-0-615-52712-3; 978-0-9853772)* 646 Oaklawn Ave., Chula Vista, CA 91910 USA Tel 619-761-5329
E-mail: alsadeeq.usa@gmail.com
Web site: www.daralsadeeq.com.

Darby Creek *Imprint of* **Lerner Publishing Group**

Dare to Dream Scholarship, Incorporated *See* **Cole Publishing**

Dare Wright Media, *(978-0-615-75722-3; 978-0-615-76436-8; 978-0-615-77738-2; 978-0-615-77739-9; 978-0-615-77740-5; 978-0-615-82784-1; 978-0-615-82786-5; 978-0-615-82788-9; 978-0-615-83495-5; 978-0-615-97776-8; 978-0-9965827)* 136 Cedar Ln., Santa Barbara, CA 93108 USA Tel 8058848488
Web site: www.darewright.com
Dist(s): **CreateSpace Independent Publishing Platform.**

Dargaud Publishing Co. (FRA) *(978-0-917201; 978-2-205) Dist. by* **Distribks Inc.**

Dark Circle Comics *Imprint of* **Archie Comic Pubns., Inc.**

Dark Continents Publishing, *(978-0-9831603; 978-0-9836245; 978-0-9848931; 978-0-615-68082-8; 978-0-615-69182-4; 978-0-615-71013-6; 978-0-615-71015-0; 978-0-615-71017-4; 978-0-615-71018-1; 978-0-615-71019-8; 978-0-615-71840-8; 978-0-615-83145-9; 978-0-615-84491-6; 978-0-615-88140-9; 978-0-615-91582-1; 978-0-615-96489-8; 978-0-615-97495-8; 978-0-692-24951-2) P.O. Box 276, Tiskilwa, IL 61368 USA Tel 815-646-4748*
E-mail: DMYoungquist@darkcontinents.com
Web site: www.darkcontinents.com
Dist(s): **CreateSpace Independent Publishing Platform.**

Dark Forest Pr., *(978-0-9764226)* 1310 N. Oak St., Apt. 408, Arlington, VA 22209 USA Tel 202-368-4341; P.O. Box 9133, Arlington, VA 22210 (SAN 256-4475) Tel 202-368-4341 Do not confuse with Dark Forest Press in Denver, CO.

Dark Horse Comics, *(978-1-56971; 978-1-878574; 978-1-59307; 978-1-59582; 978-1-59617; 978-1-61655; 978-1-61659; 978-1-62115; 978-1-63008; 978-1-5067)* 10956 SE Main St., Milwaukie, OR 97222 USA Tel 503-652-8815; Fax: 503-654-9440
E-mail: dhcomics@darkhorse.com
Web site: http://www.darkhorse.com
Dist(s): **Diamond Comic Distributors, Inc.**
Diamond Bk. Distributors
Penguin Random Hse., LLC.
Perseus-PGW
Random Hse., Inc.

Dark Overlord Media *See* **Empty Set Entertainment**

Dark Passages *Imprint of* **Whorl Bks.**

Dark Skull Studios, *(978-0-9797080)* 17711 Barker Bluff Ln., Cypress, TX 77433 USA (SAN 854-1922) Tel 832-220-6734
E-mail: richardleon@darkskullstudios.com
Web site: http://www.darkskullstudios.com.

Darker Intentions Pr., *(978-0-9769612; 978-0-9827597)* P.O. Box 569, Freehold Twp., NJ 07728-0569 USA Tel 732-299-6212
E-mail: jzdakota@hotmail.com.

Darkerwood Publishing Group, *(978-0-9669788; 978-0-9788975; 978-1-938839)* P.O. Box 2011, Arvada, CO 80001 USA
E-mail: swordarkeereon@gmail.com; ofs.admin@gmail.com; darkerwoodpublishing@gmail.com
Web site: http://www.demonolatry.org/dbpub.htm.

Darling & Co. *Imprint of* **Laughing Elephant**

Darling Pr. LLC, *(978-0-9765761)* Orders Addr.: 19740 SW 49th Ave., Tualatin, OR 97062 USA
Web site: http://www.darlingpress.com
Dist(s): **Bottman Design, Inc.**

Darnell Publishing, *(978-0-9755616)* P.O. Box 341825, Tampa, FL 33694 USA
Web site: http://www.abrink.com.

DASANBOOKS, *(978-0-9819542; 978-0-9828016; 978-0-9839594)* 120 Sylvan Ave., Englewood Cliffs, NJ 07632 USA
Dist(s): **Midpoint Trade Bks., Inc.**

Dash & Doodles Productions, *(978-0-615-22279-0; 978-0-578-08121-2)* 4810 Kellywood Dr., Glen Allen, VA 23060 USA Tel 804-527-1033
E-mail: dashanddoodles@aol.com
Web site: http://www.askdash.com
Dist(s): **Lulu Enterprises Inc.**

Data Trace Legal Publishers, Incorporated *See* **Data Trace Publishing, Co.**

Data Trace Publishing, Co., *(978-0-9637468; 978-1-57400)* Orders Addr.: P.O. Box 1239, Brooklandville, MD 21022 USA Tel 410-494-4994; Fax: 410-494-0515; Toll Free: 800-342-0454; Edit Addr.: 110 West Rd., Suite 227, Towson, MD 21204 USA
E-mail: info@datatrace.com
Web site: http://www.datatrace.com/legal.

Databooks *See* **Chandler Hse. Pr.**

Daughter Culture Pubns., *(978-0-935281)* 1840 41st Ave., Suite 102-301, Capitola, CA 95010 USA (SAN 695-7447) Tel 408-476-0199.

Daughters Arise, LLC, *(978-0-9744178)* 2648 E. Workman Ave., Suite 314, West Covina, CA 91791 USA Tel 770-808-1199; Fax: 770-216-1626
E-mail: fhenley@daughtersarise.com
Web site: http://www.daughtersarise.com.

Daven, Christian Publishing, *(978-0-578-00257-6)* 6504 Mendius Ave., NE, Albuquerque, NM 87109 USA Tel 505-315-2984
Dist(s): **Lulu Enterprises Inc.**

Davenport, May Pubs., *(978-0-943864; 978-0-9603118; 978-0-9794140)* 26313 Purissima Rd., Los Altos Hills, CA 94022-4539 USA (SAN 212-467X) Tel 650-947-1325; Fax: 650-947-1373
E-mail: mdbooks@earthlink.net
Dist(s): **Todd Communications.**

Davenport Pr. (CAN) *(978-0-9736803; 978-0-9782552) Dist. by* **IPG Chicago.**

Davenport, Sheena, *(978-0-9747625)* 3535 Riverview Approach, Ellenwood, GA 30294 USA Tel 404-241-3106
E-mail: szdavenport@yahoo.com.

Daventry Pr., *(978-0-615-76838-0)* 2010 Woodland Ave. #2, Duluth, MN 55803 USA Tel 6519837471
Web site: http://daventrypress.webs.com/
Dist(s): **CreateSpace Independent Publishing Platform.**

David & Charles Pubs. (GBR) *(978-0-7153; 978-1-4463) Dist. by* **FplusW Media.**

David, Elizabeth A., *(978-0-9740170)* P.O. Box 766, Fairhaven, MA 02719-0700 USA Tel 508-979-5593
E-mail: yasny@comcast.net
Web site: http://www.zorena.com.

†David, Jonathan Pubs., Inc., *(978-0-8246)* 68-22 Eliot Ave., Middle Village, NY 11379 USA (SAN 169-5274) Tel 718-456-8611; Fax: 718-894-2818
E-mail: jondavpub@aol.com
Web site: http://www.jdbooks.com; *CIP.*

David Mortimore Baxter *Imprint of* **Stone Arch Bks.**

†Davidson, Harlan Inc., *(978-0-88295)* 773 Glenn Ave., Wheeling, IL 60090-6000 USA (SAN 201-2375) Tel 847-541-9720; Fax: 847-541-9830
E-mail: harlandavidson@harlandavidson.com
Web site: http://www.harlandavidson.com; *CIP.*

Davis, A. S. Media Group, *(978-0-9666352; 978-0-9729150; 978-0-9759022; 978-0-9766013; 978-0-9776245; 978-0-9787719; 978-1-934724)* Orders Addr.: P.O. Box 590780, San Francisco, CA 94159 USA
E-mail: info@greenlinepub.com
Web site: http://www.greenlinepub.com.

Davis Bks. LLC, *(978-0-9770142)* Orders Addr.: P.O. Box 6291, Cincinnati, OH 45206 USA Tel 513-687-1943
E-mail: georgedisselkamp@yahoo.com
Web site: http://www.davisbooks.cjb.net
Dist(s): **Docustar.**

Davis, James (Jim), *(978-0-9760960)* 1700 W. Washington St. Apt. A507, Springfield, IL 62702-6447 USA.

Davis, Paul *See* **Royal Hse. Publishing**

Davis Pubns., Inc., *(978-0-87192; 978-1-61528)* 50 Portland St., Worcester, MA 01608 USA (SAN 201-3002) Tel 508-754-7201; Fax: 508-791-0779; Toll Free: 800-533-2847
E-mail: rfrederics@davisart.com; mnicholson@davisart.com
Web site: http://www.davisart.com
Dist(s): **Sterling Publishing Co., Inc.**

Davis, Tamela, *(978-0-9772923; 978-0-9821196; 978-0-9826608; 978-0-9836089)* P.O. Box 502, Carmel, IN 46082 USA
E-mail: sales@growingwithgrammer.com; tinydee64@sbcglobal.net
Web site: http://www.growingwithgrammer.com.

Davlaw Press, *(978-0-9776917)* Orders Addr.: P.O. Box 4317, Harrisburg, PA 17111 USA (SAN 257-9863) Tel 717-441-5451; Fax: 717-441-4925; *Imprints:* Curcumin Books (Curcumin Bks)
E-mail: larry@davlawpress.com
Web site: http://www.davlawpress.com.

Davus Publishing, *(978-0-915317)* P.O. Box 1101, Buffalo, NY 14213-7101 USA (SAN 289-9787) Tel 519-426-2077
E-mail: davus@kwic.com; davuspub@sympatico.ca
Web site: http://www.kwic.com/~davus; www3.sympatico.ca/drbeasley; www.davuspublishing.com
Dist(s): **Coutts Information Services.**

Daw Enterprises, *(978-0-9628081)* 1338 Parrish St., Philadelphia, PA 19123-1817 USA Tel 215-424-2016.

DAW Hardcover *Imprint of* **Penguin Publishing Group**

DAW Trade *Imprint of* **Penguin Publishing Group**

Dawasoft, *(978-0-9764218)* 150-35 119th Rd., Jamaica, NY 11434 USA Tel 347-954-6479
E-mail: dawasoft@yahoo.com.

Dawn of a New Day Pubns., The *Imprint of* **Konkori International**

Dawn of Day Childrens Publishing Co., Inc., *(978-0-9666857)* 73 Ireland Pl., PMB 201, Amityville, NY 11757 USA (SAN 253-0198) Tel 631-225-5513; Fax: 631-225-5431; Toll Free: 800-575-7040
E-mail: information@dawnofday.com
Web site: http://www.dawnofday.com.

Dawn Pubns., *(978-0-916124; 978-1-878265; 978-1-883220; 978-1-58469)* 12402 Bitney Springs Rd., Nevada City, CA 95959 USA (SAN 856-8294) Tel 530-478-0111; Fax: 530-274-7778; Toll Free: 800-545-7475 Do not confuse with Dawn Pubns. in Pasadena, TX
E-mail: nature@dawnpub.com; info@dawnpub.com
Web site: http://www.dawnpub.com
Dist(s): **Brodart Co.**
Common Ground Distributors, Inc.
Follett School Solutions
Ingram Bk. Co.
Territory Titles.

DawQuin LLC, *(978-0-9842787)* P.O. Box 1800, Troy, MI 48099 USA (SAN 858-9461) Tel 248-765-7276
E-mail: publisher@dawquin.com
Web site: www.dawquin.com.

Dawson, Kathy Bks. *Imprint of* **Penguin Publishing Group**

Day By Day *See* **Day By Day Recovery Resources, LLC**

Day By Day Recovery Resources, LLC, *(978-0-9764915; 978-1-934569)* Orders Addr.: 2186 N. Clack Canyon Rd., Kingman, AZ 86409 USA Tel 887-447-1683
E-mail: business@pocketsponsor.com
Web site: http://www.day-by-day.org
Dist(s): **Mentor Bks.**

Day I Hit a Home Run Enterprise, The, *(978-0-9831950)* 7389 Brookville Rd., Oxford, OH 45056 USA Tel 513-290-2189
E-mail: mullenmike122@yahoo.com
Web site: www.thedayihitahomerun.com
Dist(s): **Independent Pubs. Group.**

Day to Day Enterprises, *(978-1-890905)* Orders Addr.: 8396 Maryland Rd., Pasadena, MD 21122-4655 USA (SAN 299-7118) Tel 443-817-2129; Fax: 443-817-2129; *Imprints:* Eco Fiction Books (Eco Fiction Bks); Writers Collective, The (Writers Coll)
E-mail: books@daytodayenterprises.com
Web site: http://www.daytodayenterprises.com
Dist(s): **Book Clearing Hse.**
Midpoint Trade Bks., Inc.

Day3 Productions, Inc., *(978-0-9777361)* 215 Tower Rd, McKenzie, TN 38201 USA (SAN 850-0770) Tel 731-352-6081
E-mail: jeff@day3productions.com
Web site: http://www.day3productions.com.

Daylight Pubs., *(978-0-9764103; 978-0-9792755)* 8255 S Wright Pl., Broken Arrow, OK 74014 USA Tel 918-357-1266
E-mail: kathy@daylightpublishers.com
Web site: http://www.daylightpublishers.com.

DayOne Pubns. (GBR) *(978-0-902548; 978-1-903087; 978-1-84625) Dist. by* **STL Dist.**

Days of Glory Publishing, *(978-0-9770206)* 28 Branden Way, Tolland, CT 06084 USA.

Dayton International Peace Museum *See* **Peace Power Pr.**

Dazzling Inc., *(978-0-9749170)* P.O. Box 236, Allston, MA 02134 USA
Web site: http://www.rootfriends.com.

DC Comics, *(978-0-930289; 978-1-56389; 978-1-4012)* Div. of Warner Bros.- A Time Warner Entertainment Co., 1700 Broadway, New York, NY 10019 USA Tel 212-636-5400; Fax: 212-636-5979; *Imprints:* Vertigo (Vertigo); Paradox (Paradox); A B C (A B C); Wildstorm (Wildstorm); CMX (CMX); DC Kids (DCKids); Minx (Minx)
E-mail: booksales@dccomics.com
Web site: http://www.dccomics.com
Dist(s): **Eastern News Distributors**
MyiLibrary
Penguin Random Hse., LLC.
Random Hse., Inc.

DC Kids *Imprint of* **DC Comics**

DC Super Heroes *Imprint of* **Stone Arch Bks.**

DC Super-Pets *Imprint of* **Picture Window Bks.**

DC Super-villains *Imprint of* **Stone Arch Bks.**

DCTS Publishing, *(978-0-9653904)* Div. of Hamilton Ministry, P.O. Box 40216, Santa Barbara, CA 93140 USA Tel 805-570-3168; Toll Free: 800-965-8150
E-mail: dennis@dctspub.com
Web site: http://www.dctspub.com.

de Fosseway, Marquis (GBR) *(978-0-9561561) Dist. by* **LuluCom.**

De La Flor (ARG) *(978-950-515) Dist. by* **LD Bks Inc.**

De La Luz Pubns., *(978-0-9748326)* 121 W. Hickory St., Denton, TX 76201 USA Tel 940-367-1651; Fax: 940-323-0488
E-mail: ccarrasco1@chater.net.

De Loach, George P., *(978-0-9768362)* 475 W. Fallen Leaf Cir., Wasilla, AK 99654 USA Tel 907-376-2680
E-mail: gdeloach@juno.com.

Deaf Missions, *(978-1-59799)* Orders Addr.: 21199 Greenview Rd., Council Bluffs, IA 51503-4190 USA
Web site: http://www.deafmissions.com.

Deal, Darlene, *(978-0-9747299)* P.O. Box 521, North Hollywood, CA 91603-0521 USA Tel 818-752-7065 (phone/fax).

DeAngelis, Anthony, *(978-0-9754853)* 101 Cypress Ave., San Bruno, CA 94066-5420 USA
E-mail: a.deangelis@worldnet.att.net.

Dean's Bks., Inc., *(978-0-9728607)* 1426 S. Kansas Ave., Topeka, KS 66612 USA Tel 785-357-4708
E-mail: contact@oilcanbook.com
Web site: http://www.oilcanbook.com.

Dearborn Publishing, *(978-1-891685)* Div. of The Mae Group LLC, Orders Addr.: 7389 N. 150 W., Lake Village, IN 46349 USA Tel 219-689-1286; Fax: 219-992-9356
E-mail: chermytalent@yahoo.com; johngraham@att.net.

Dearborn Real Estate Education *Imprint of* **Kaplan Publishing**

Dearborn Trade, A Kaplan Professional Company *See* **Kaplan Publishing**

Deb on Air Bks., *(978-0-9727615)* Orders Addr.: P.O. Box 580055, Elk Grove, CA 95758 USA Tel 916-684-3551.

Debate, Editorial (ESP) *(978-84-7444; 978-84-8306) Dist. by* **AIMS Intl.**

Debi, Kennedy *See* **nJoy Bks.**

DeCa Communications, LLC, *(978-0-9762262)* 300 Williamsburg Dr., Mandeville, LA 70471 USA
Web site: http://www.decacom.info.

Decent Hill Pubs. LLC,
Dist(s): **AtlasBooks Distribution.**

Decere Publishing, *(978-0-9717013; 978-0-9816572)* 5590 Bunky Way, Atlanta, GA 30338 USA Tel 404-474-2830; Fax: 770-399-5883 Do not confuse with CSI Publishing in Monterey Park, CA
E-mail: mark@decere.com
Web site: http://www.decere.com.

Deep Dish Design, *(978-0-9755033)* 15012 Cherry Ln., Burnsville, MN 55306 USA
E-mail: jb@deepdishdesign.com
Web site: http://www.deepdishdesign.com.

Deep Roots Pubns., *(978-0-9671713; 978-0-9819528)* Orders Addr.: P.O. Box 114, Saratoga, NY 12866 USA Tel 518-583-8920; Fax: 518-584-3919; Edit Addr.: 229 Lake Ave., Saratoga, NY 12866 USA
E-mail: drpalmer2002@yahoo.com
Web site: http://www.deeprootspublications.com
Dist(s): **North Country Bks., Inc.**

Deep South Bks. (ZAF) *(978-0-9584542; 978-0-9584915) Dist. by* **Intl Spec Bk.**

Deep Waters Pr., *(978-0-9748171)* Suite 100, 77 Court St., Laconia, NH 03246 USA (SAN 255-8777) Tel 603-520-1214; P.O. Box 452, Meredith, NH 03253 Tel 603-524-2585
E-mail: halclyon@yahoo.com; deepwaterspress@yahoo.com
Web site: http://www.DeepWaterspress.com.

Deeper Roots Pubns. & Media, *(978-1-930547)* Orders Addr.: 13 W. Lakeshore Dr., Cherokee Village, AR 72529 USA
E-mail: deeperroots@aol.com
Web site: http://www.DeeperRoots.com.

Deeper Waters, *(978-0-615-36602-9; 978-0-615-43255-7; 978-0-615-58840-7)* 11520 Grandview Rd., Kansas City,, MO 64137 USA Tel 816-765-9900
E-mail: blake.cadwell@gmail.com.

Deepercalling Media, Inc., *(978-0-9726135; 978-1-59601)* 1200 Mt. Diablo Blvd., Suite 108, Walnut Creek, CA 94596 USA (SAN 254-9360) Fax: 925-939-4010
E-mail: info@deepercalling.com
Web site: http://www.deepercalling.com
Dist(s): **Whitaker Hse.**

Deer Creek Publishing, *(978-0-9651452)* Orders Addr.: P.O. Box 2594, Nevada City, CA 95959 USA Fax: 530-478-1759 Do not confuse with Deer Creek Publishing, Provo, UT.

Deer Oaks, Inc., *(978-0-9764700)* P.O. Box 429, Barrington, IL 60011-0429 USA.

Deerbrook Editions, *(978-0-9712488; 978-0-9828100; 978-0-9904287)* P.O. Box 542, Cumberland, ME 04021-0542 USA
E-mail: jewilh@gmail.com; info@deerbrookeditions.com
Web site: http://www.deerbrookeditions.com; http://www.idesignbooks.com; http://deerbrookeditions.wordpress.com
Dist(s): **SPD-Small Pr. Distribution.**

Defense Dept. *Imprint of* **United States Government Printing Office**

Defense Research LLC, *(978-0-9749873)* 211 Kirkland Ave. Apt. 216, Kirkland, WA 98033-6578 USA
E-mail: sales@defenseresearch.org
Web site: http://www.defenseresearch.org.

Defiance In Print, *(978-0-9771641)* Orders Addr.: 9412 S Belfort Cr, Tamarac, FL 33321 USA (SAN 256-9663) Tel 561-235-1828
E-mail: miller2554@gmail.com.

Defiant Pr. *Imprint of* **Passkey Pubns.**

Defined Mind, Inc., *(978-0-9763767)* 580 Broadway, Suite 912, New York, NY 10012 USA Tel 212-925-5138 (Hours: M-F 9:30 am-5:30 pm)
E-mail: info@defmind.com
Web site: http://www.defmind.com.

DeForest Pr., *(978-0-9649922; 978-1-930374; 978-0-615-99631-8)* Orders Addr.: P.O. Box 383, Rogers, MN 55374 USA Tel 763-428-2997; Fax: 877-747-3123; Toll Free: 877-747-3123; Edit Addr.: P.O. Box 383, Rogers, MN 55374 USA
E-mail: shane@deforestpress.com
Web site: http://www.deforestpress.com.

DeFranco Entertainment, *(978-1-929845)* P.O. Box 1425, Thousand Oaks, CA 91358-1425 USA Fax: 805-376-2953
E-mail: tdefranco@vcnet.com.

Degenhardt, Scott, *(978-0-9765671)* P.O. Box 11182, Murfreesboro, TN 37129 USA Tel 615-890-9484
E-mail: anything@thedegshop.com
Web site: http://www.thedegshop.com.

DeGraaf Publishing, *(978-0-9678385)* 903 W. Morse St., Plant City, FL 33563 USA Tel 813-752-2348; 813-967-7489 (Cell phone)
E-mail: robdegraaf@verizon.net
Web site: http://www.degraafpublishing.com.

Degree Network, LLC *See* **Marilux Pr.**

Dehghanpisheh, Corine, *(978-0-9851930; 978-0-692-41280-0)* P.O. Box 30302, New York, NY 10011 USA Tel 646-580-8655
E-mail: cmardi2@gmail.com.

Deitch, Jeffrey Inc., *(978-0-9633037; 978-0-9648530; 978-0-9753243; 978-0-9778686; 978-0-9815771)* 76 Grand St., New York, NY 10013 USA Tel 212-343-7300
E-mail: info@deitch.com
Web site: http://www.deitch.com
Dist(s): **D.A.P./Distributed Art Pubs.**

Dejohn Enterprises, *(978-0-9754528)* 1121 Elm St., Peekskill, NY 10566 USA
E-mail: dejohnenterprise@aol.com
Web site: http://www.thereturnofsf.com.

Deka Pr., *(978-0-9645045)* P.O. Box 812, Christmas Valley, OR 97641 USA Tel 541-576-3900; Fax: 541-576-3909
E-mail: katym@teleport.com.

DEKpress *See* **Parent Positive Pr.**

DeKruyff, Ruth, *(978-0-9797549)* Orders Addr.: P.O. Box 380604, San Antonio, TX 78268 USA; Edit Addr.: 5911 Forest Rim, San Antonio, TX 78240 USA.

Del Gatto, Maria, *(978-0-9747509)* 2227 South 3rd St., Philadelphia, PA 19148 USA Tel 215-271-7165
Web site: http://www.shapettes.com.

Del George, Dana, *(978-0-578-00730-4)* 1025 1/2 Magnolia St., South Pasadena, CA 91030 USA
Dist(s): **Lulu Enterprises Inc.**

Del Rey *Imprint of* **Random House Publishing Group**

Del Sol Pubns., *(978-0-9722936)* P.O. Box 1112, Ventura, CA 93002 USA Do not confuse with Del Sol Publications in Two River, WI
E-mail: info@delsolpublications.com
Web site: http://www.delsolpublications.com.

Del Sol Publishing, *(978-1-58186)* 29257 Bassett Rd., Westlake, OH 44145 USA (SAN 299-4178) Tel 440-892-5524; Fax: 440-892-5546; Toll Free: 888-335-7651
E-mail: delsolbooks@telocity.com
Dist(s): **Lectorum Pubns., Inc.**

Delabarre Publishing, *(978-0-9829247; 978-0-9836125; 978-1-61941)* P.O. Box 714, Conway, MA 01341 USA Tel 413-475-0087
E-mail: jeff@jeffrutherford.com.

Delacorte Bks. for Young Readers *Imprint of* **Random Hse. Children's Bks.**

Delacorte Bks. for Young Readers *Imprint of* **Random House Publishing Group**

Delacorte Pr *Imprint of* **Random Hse. Children's Bks.**

Delacorte Pr *Imprint of* **Random House Publishing Group**

DeLaVega, T., *(978-0-9754328)* Orders Addr.: P.O. Box 760, Hanapepe, HI 96716 USA Tel 808-335-2704; Fax: 808-335-5469; Edit Addr.: 3691 Uwao St., Hanapepe, HI 96716 USA
E-mail: tim.delavega@verizon.net
Web site: http://www.napaliphoto.com.

Delittle Storyteller Co., *(978-1-892633)* Orders Addr.: 1562 Pinehurst Dr., Casselberry, FL 32707 USA Tel 407-699-7769
E-mail: delittlestoryteller@yahoo.com
Web site: http://www.delittlestoryteller.com.

Dell Books for Young Readers *Imprint of* **Random Hse. Children's Bks.**

Dell, Jacob J., *(978-0-9744544)* 6518 Chasethorn Dr., San Antonio, TX 78249-4825 USA
E-mail: books@jacobjdell.com
Web site: http://www.jacobjdell.com/books.

Dellas, Melanie, *(978-0-9830163)* 4405 Pescadero Ave., San Diego, CA 92107 USA Tel 858-442-7916
E-mail: mdellas@hotmail.com
Web site: http://www.Mythological-Creatures.com.

Dellinger, Hampton, *(978-0-615-24971-1)* 4306 Peachway Dr., Durham, NC 27705 USA
Dist(s): **Lulu Enterprises Inc.**

Dellwin Publishing Co., Inc., *(978-0-9765267)* P.O. Box 23391, Brooklyn, NY 11202-3391 USA
E-mail: dellwin5@aol.com
Web site: http://www.therockmastersystem.com.

†Delmar Cengage Learning, *(978-0-314; 978-0-7668; 978-0-7693; 978-0-8273; 978-0-87350; 978-0-916032; 978-0-944132; 978-0-9653629; 978-1-56253; 978-1-56593; 978-1-56930; 978-1-4018; 978-1-4180; 978-1-4283; 978-1-4354)* Div. of Cengage Learning, Orders Addr.: c/o Thomson Learning Order Fulfilment, P.O. Box 6904, Florence, KY 41022 USA Toll Free Fax: 800 487 8488; Toll Free: 800 347 7707; c/o Thomson Delmar Learning Clinical Health Care Series, P.O. Box 3419, Scranton, PA 18505-0419 Fax: 570-347-9072; Toll Free: 888-427-5800; Edit Addr.: P.O. Box 15015, Albany, NY 12212-5015 USA (SAN 206-7544) Tel 518-348-2300; Fax: 518-373-6345; Toll Free: 800-998-7498; 5 Maxwell Dr., Clifton Park, NY 12065-(SAN 658-0440) Tel 518-348-2300; Fax: 518-881-1256; Toll Free: 800-998-7498
E-mail: matthew.grover@thomson.com; clinicalmanuals@thomson.com
Web site: http://www.delmarlearning.com; http://www.clinicalmanuals.com/
Dist(s): **CENGAGE Learning**
Follett School Solutions
Gryphon Hse., Inc.
OptumInsight, Inc.
Pearson Education
Rittenhouse Bk. Distributors
ebrary, Inc.; *CIP.*

DeLorme, *(978-0-89933)* P.O. Box 298, Yarmouth, ME 04096 USA (SAN 220-1208) Tel 207-846-7000; Fax: 207-846-7051; Toll Free Fax: 800-575-2244 (orders); Toll Free: 800-335-6763 (orders only)
E-mail: reseller@delorme.com
Web site: http://www.delorme.com
Dist(s): **Benchmark LLC**
Hammond World Atlas Corp.
Langenscheidt Publishing Group
Many Feathers Bks. & Maps
Rand McNally.

DeLorme Mapping Company *See* **DeLorme**

Delphi Bks., *(978-0-9663397; 978-0-9765185; 978-0-9846015)* Orders Addr.: P.O. Box 6435, Lee's Summit, MO 64064 USA Toll Free: 800-431-1579 (orders)
E-mail: DelphiBks@yahoo.com
Web site: http://www.DelphiBooks.us; http://www.FranBaker.com
Dist(s): **Brodart Co.**
Emery-Pratt Co.
Midwest Library Service.

Delphinium Bks., Inc., *(978-1-883285)* 127 W. 24th St., New York, NY 10011 USA Tel 212-255-6098 Do not confuse with Delphinium Pr. in Wellfleet, MA
E-mail: DelphBks@aol.com
Dist(s): **HarperCollins Pubs.**
MyiLibrary.

Delta Education, Incorporated *See* **Delta Education, LLC**

Delta Education, LLC, *(978-0-87504; 978-1-58356; 978-1-59242; 978-1-59821; 978-1-60395; 978-1-60902; 978-1-62571)* 80 Northwest Blvd., Nashua, NH 03063 USA (SAN 630-1711) Toll Free: 800-442-5444
E-mail: ngosselin@delta-edu.com
Web site: http://www.delta-education.com.

Delta Gamma Ctr., *(978-0-9748523)* 1750 S. Big Bend Blvd., Saint Louis, MO 63117-2402 USA Toll Free: 800-341-4310
E-mail: info@dgckids.org
Web site: http://www.dgckids.org.

Delta Stream Media, *(978-0-9776939)* Div. of Natural Math, 309 Silvercliff, Cary, NC 27513 USA (SAN 257-9987) Tel 919-388-1721
E-mail: maria@naturalmath.com
Web site: http://www.naturalmath.com.

Delta Systems Company, Inc., *(978-0-937354; 978-1-887744; 978-1-932748; 978-1-934960; 978-1-936299; 978-1-936402; 978-1-62167)* Orders Addr.: 1400 Miller Pkwy., McHenry, IL 60050-7030 USA (SAN 220-0457) Tel 815-363-3582; Fax: 815-363-2948; Toll Free Fax: 800-909-9901; Toll Free: 800-323-8270; *Imprints:* Raven Tree Press (Raven Tree Pr)
E-mail: d.patchin@DeltaPublishing.com; L.Bruell@DeltaPublishing.com; j.patchin@deltapublishing.com
Web site: http://www.deltapublishing.com; http://www.raventreepress.com
Dist(s): **Follett Media Distribution**
National Bk. Network.

DEMDACO, *(978-1-932139)* Div. of DD Traders, Inc., 5000 W. 134th St., Leawood, KS 66209-7806 USA Toll Free: 888-336-3226
Web site: http://www.demdaco.com.

Demeter Books *See* **Lake Street Pr.**

DeMosi *See* **DeMosi Publishing**

DeMosi Publishing, *(978-0-9708523)* Orders Addr.: P.O. Box 60606, Chicago, IL 60660 USA
E-mail: demosipublishing@gmail.com.

Den Publishing Co., *(978-0-9742195)* P.O. Box 93336, Albuquerque, NM 87199-3336 USA Fax: 505-822-8035.

DeNicest Concepts, *(978-0-9763973)* P.O. Box 1831, Buffalo, NY 14240 USA.

Denim Design Lab LLC, *(978-0-9773012)* P.O. Box 5853, San Clemente, CA 92674-9998 USA Tel 949-366-3307; Fax: 949-366-3304
E-mail: denimdesignlab@aol.com
Web site: http://www.denimdesignlab.com.

Denison, T. S. & Co., Inc., *(978-0-513)* Orders Addr.: P.O. Box 1650, Grand Rapids, MI 49501-5431 USA (SAN 201-3142) Tel 616-802-3000; Fax: 616-802-3009; Toll Free Fax: 800-543-2690; Toll Free: 800-253-5469
Dist(s): **Lectorum Pubns., Inc.**

Denlinger, Dennis, *(978-0-9742567)* Orders Addr.: 46 Purdy St., Harrison, NY 95821 USA; Edit Addr.: P.O. Box 60431, Sacramento, CA 95860-0431 USA Tel 916-488-9643 Phone/fax); Toll Free: 800-431-1579 fulfilment
E-mail: dennis@footarch.com
Web site: http://www.footarch.com
Dist(s): **Book Clearing Hse.**

Denney Literary Services, *(978-0-9654698; 978-0-9707469)* 2907 Noah St., Chattanooga, TN 37406-1928 USA Tel 423-622-0419; *Imprints:* DLS Books (DLS Bks)
E-mail: denney2907@earthlink.net
Dist(s): **AtlasBooks Distribution.**

Dennison, Donna, *(978-0-9760484)* 121 Tuxedo, San Antonio, TX 78209-3712 USA.

Densmore-Reid Pubns., *(978-0-9700827)* 67 S. 24th St., Richmond, IN 47374 USA Tel 765-939-2984 (phone/fax)
E-mail: ddgreens@netscape.net
Web site: http://www.densmorereid.com/.

Dental Wellness Institute, *(978-0-9815630)* 321 S. Main St., No. 503, Sebastopol, CA 95472 USA (SAN 855-8795) Tel 707-829-7220; Toll Free: 800-335-7755
E-mail: dentwell@pacbell.net
Web site: http://www.dentalwellness4u.com
Dist(s): **Cardinal Pubs. Group.**

Denver Broncos, *(978-0-9759579)* INVESCO Field at Mile High, 1701 Bryant St., Suite 900, Denver, CO 80204 USA
Web site: http://www.denverbroncos.com.

DEO Consulting, Inc., *(978-0-9728793)* 16334 Boardwalk Terr., Orland Hills, IL 60477 USA
E-mail: dale@mbd2.com
Web site: http://www.mbd2.com.

DePalma, Vanessa, *(978-0-9728135)* 49 Tropez Point, Rochester, NY 14626 USA Tel 585-723-9699
E-mail: vdepalma@frontiernet.net.

Dept. of Chamorro Affairs, *(978-1-883488)* P.O. Box 2950, Hagatna, GU 96932 USA Tel 671-477-6447
E-mail: lbaguon@yahoo.com
Web site: http://www.dca.guam.gov.

Depot Bks., *(978-0-9717611)* Orders Addr.: 87 Throckmorton Ave., Mill Valley, CA 94941 USA; Edit Addr.: 8 Madrona St., Mill Valley, CA 94941 USA.

Dept. of the Army *Imprint of* **United States Government Printing Office**

Dercum Audio, *(978-1-55656)* 1501 County Hospital Rd., Nashville, TN 37218 USA (SAN 658-7607) Tel 615-254-2408
E-mail: DawsonC@locc.com
Web site: http://www.bookcase.com/Dercum
Dist(s): **APG Sales & Distribution Services.**

Dercum Press/Dercum Audio *See* **Dercum Audio**

Derke, Connie, *(978-0-9747063)* 6418 W. 13100 S., Herriman, UT 84065 USA Tel 801-254-8711
E-mail: derke1904@msn.com.

Derrick, Paul, *(978-0-9744875)* Orders Addr.: 918 N. 30th St., Waco, TX 76707-2502 USA Tel 254-753-6920 (phone/fax)
E-mail: pjderrick@aol.com
Web site: http://stargazerpaul.com.

Derrydale Pr., The, *(978-1-56416; 978-1-58667)* Div. of Rowman & Littlefield Publishing Group, Orders Addr.: 15200 NBN Way, Blue Ridge Summit, PA 17214 USA Tel 717-794-3800 (Sales, Customer Service, MIS, Royalties, Inventory Mgmt., Dist., Credit & Collections); Fax: 717-794-3803 (Customer Service &/or orders only); 717-794-3857 (Sales & MIS); 717-794-3856 (Royalties, Inventory Mgmt., & Dist.); Toll Free Fax: 800-338-4550 (Customer Service &/or orders); Toll Free: 800-462-6420 (Customer Service &/or orders); Edit Addr.: 4501 Forbes Blvd., Lanham, MD 20706 USA Tel 301-459-3366; Fax: 301-459-5748
E-mail: sdriver@derrydalepress.com
Web site: http://www.derrydalepress.com
Dist(s): **MyiLibrary**
National Bk. Network
Rowman & Littlefield Publishers, Inc.
ebrary, Inc.

†Deseret Bk. Co., *(978-0-87579; 978-0-87747; 978-1-57345; 978-1-59038; 978-1-60641; 978-1-60907; 978-1-60908; 978-1-62972; 978-1-62973)* Div. of Deseret Management Corp., P.O. Box 30178, Salt Lake City, UT 84130 USA (SAN 150-763X) Tel 801-517-3165 (Wholesale Dept.); 801-534-1515; Fax: 801-517-3338; Toll Free: 800-453-3876; *Imprints:* Bookcraft, Incorporated (Bkcraft Inc); Shadow Mountain (ShadMtn); Ensign Peak (EnsignPeak)
E-mail: wholesale@deseretbook.com; dbwhsale@deseretbook.com
Web site: http://www.deseretbook.com; http://www.shadowmountain.com; *CIP.*

Desert Badger Pr., *(978-0-9767555)* 4147 E. Megan Dr., Tucson, AZ 85712 USA
Web site: http://www.elderlawtucson.com.

Desert Bear Publishing, *(978-0-9765389)* P.O. Box 72313, Phoenix, AZ 85050 USA Tel 480-538-0842; Fax: 602-926-2429.

Desert Hills Publishing *See* **D H Publishing LLC**

Desert Sage Pr., *(978-0-615-72020-3; 978-0-9897133)* P.O. Box 357, Eagle, ID 83616 USA Tel 208-860-2464; Fax: 208-938-1554
Web site: www.desertsagepress.com
Dist(s): **CreateSpace Independent Publishing Platform.**

Desert Song Productions, *(978-0-9743402)* P.O. Box 35052, Tucson, AZ 85740 USA
E-mail: brian@brianjharris.com
Web site: http://www.brianjharris.com.

Desert West Publishing, *(978-0-578-03542-0)* P.O. Box 35, Fairview, UT 84629 USA
Dist(s): **Lulu Enterprises Inc.**

DesertStar Communications, LLC, *(978-0-9769815)* Orders Addr.: P.O. Box 243988, Boynton Beach, FL 33424-3988 USA
Web site: http://www.desertstarcommunications.com.

Design Media Publishing Ltd. (HKG) *(978-988-19738-4-9; 978-988-12967) Dist. by* **AtlasBooks.**

Design Originals *Imprint of* **Fox Chapel Publishing Co., Inc.**

Design Pr. Bks. *Imprint of* **Savannah College of Art & Design Exhibitions**

Design Studio Pr., *(978-0-9726676; 978-1-933492; 978-1-62465)* 8577 Higuera St., Culver City, CA 90232 USA
Web site: http://www.designstudiopress.com
Dist(s): **Diamond Bk. Distributors**
Ingram Pub. Services.

Design Vault, LLC, *(978-0-9768974; 978-0-615-93708-3)* 12925 N. 124th E. Pl, Collinsville, OK 74021 USA Tel 918.625.1483
Web site: www.designvault.net
Dist(s): **CreateSpace Independent Publishing Platform.**

DesignAbility, *(978-0-9786425)* P.O. Box 9988, Salt Lake City, UT 84109 USA
Web site: http://www.design-ability.com.

Designed World Learning, LLC, *(978-0-9763351)* Suite 105-124, 1933 Hwy. 35, Wall, NJ 07719 USA
Web site: http://www.designedworldlearning.com.

Designs For Progress, Inc., *(978-0-9793902)* 24601 Milfay Rd., No. 5, Depew, OK 74028 USA
E-mail: dmccalment@aol.com.

Desktop Prepress Services, *(978-0-615-15679-8; 978-0-615-15817-4; 978-0-615-19039-6; 978-0-615-19643-5; 978-0-615-19723-4; 978-0-615-25624-5; 978-0-578-00420-4; 978-0-578-01448-7; 978-0-578-02385-4; 978-0-578-02469-1; 978-0-578-03167-5; 978-0-578-04693-8; 978-0-578-08235-6; 978-0-578-15292-9) 808 S. New Bethel Blvd., Ada, OK 74820 USA*
Web site: http://www.desktopprepress.com
Dist(s): **Lulu Enterprises Inc.**

Deste Foundation (GRC) *Dist. by* **Dist Art Pubs.**

Destination Pubs. *Imprint of* **Pulte, Therese Marie**

Destined For Greatness Publisher *See* **Empowering People Pub.**

Destinee Media, *(978-0-9759082; 978-0-9832768; 978-1-938367)* c/o McCall, 301 Iberian Way, Apt. 253, Sandpoint, ID 83864 USA
Web site: http://www.destineemedia.com.

Destiny Image Europe (ITA) *(978-88-900588; 978-88-89127; 978-88-96727) Dist. by* **STL Dist.**

Destiny Image Pubs., *(978-0-7684; 978-0-914903; 978-1-56043; 978-0-9716036)* 167 Walnut Bottom Rd., Shippensburg, PA 17257 USA (SAN 253-4339) Tel 717-532-3040; Fax: 717-532-9291; Toll Free: 800-722-6774
E-mail: dnj@destinyimage.com
Web site: http://www.destinyimage.com
Dist(s): **Anchor Distributors**
Appalachian Bible Co.
Send The Light Distribution LLC
Spring Arbor Distributors, Inc.

Detail Press *See* **Blue Tree LLC**

Determined Productions, Inc., *(978-0-915696)* P.O. Box 2150, San Francisco, CA 94126-2150 USA (SAN 212-7385) Tel 415-433-0660; Fax: 415-421-0929.

Detroit International Pr., *(978-0-9766622)* 900 Wilshire Dr. Ste. 202, Troy, MI 48084-1600 USA
E-mail: vince@detroitip.com.

Dettman Design Services, *(978-0-615-38527-3)* 718 Logan Ave., Elgin, IL 60120 USA Tel 847-888-2178
E-mail: t.dettman@sbcglobal.net.

Deutscher Taschenbuch Verlag GmbH & Co KG (DEU) *(978-3-423) Dist. by* **Distribks Inc.**

Deux *Imprint of* **Aurora Publishing, Inc.**

DeuxRay Productions, *(978-0-615-52915-8)* 2401 Capitan Ave., San Diego, CA 92104 USA Tel 619-987-5505; Fax: 619-291-4404
E-mail: deuxray@cox.net
Web site: www.inmyownbackyard.org.

Developmental Studies Center *See* **Center for the Collaborative Classroom**

Developmental Vision Concepts, *(978-0-9635507; 978-0-9747810)* Orders Addr.: P.O. Box 400, Tehachapi, CA 93581 USA Tel 661-822-3106; Edit Addr.: 316 S. Green, Tehachapi, CA 93581 USA
E-mail: stoebner@lightspeed.net.

Devere Publishing, Inc., *(978-0-9787988)* P.O. Box 970965, Orem, UT 84097-0965 USA (SAN 851-6456) Tel 801-434-7558 (phone/fax)
E-mail: boblamx@gmail.com
Web site: http://winningorlosing.com.

Devil's Due Digital, Inc. - A Checker Digital Co., *(978-0-9710249; 978-0-9741664; 978-0-9753808; 978-1-933160; 978-1-61799)* 217 Byers Rd., Miamisburg, OH 45342 USA
E-mail: info@checkerbpg.com
Web site: http://www.checkerbpg.com
Dist(s): **Brodart Co.**
Haven Distributors
Tales of Wonder.com.

Devil's Due Publishing, Inc., *(978-1-932796; 978-1-934692)* 2217 W. Roscoe St., Chicago, IL 60618-6209 USA
E-mail: swells@devilsdue.net; d.davis@devilsdue.net
Web site: http://www.devilsdue.net
Dist(s): **Diamond Comic Distributors, Inc.**
Diamond Bk. Distributors.

†Devin-Adair Pubs., Inc., *(978-0-8159)* P.O. Box A, Old Greenwich, CT 06870 USA (SAN 112-062X) Tel 203-531-7755; Fax: 718-359-8568; *CIP.*

Devonshire Bks., *(978-0-615-33660-2)* 918 W. Browning St., Appleton, WI 54914 USA Tel 920-954-5733
E-mail: flwrgirl3@hotmail.com.

Devora Publishing *Imprint of* **Simcha Media Group**

DeVore & Sons, Incorporated *See* **Fireside Catholic Bibles**

DeVorss & Co., *(978-0-87516)* Orders Addr.: P.O. Box 1389, Camarillo, CA 93011-1389 USA (SAN 168-9886) Tel 805-322-9010; Fax: 805-322-9011; Toll Free: 800-843-5743; Edit Addr.: 553 Constitution Ave.,

Publisher Name Index

Camarillo, CA 93012-8510 USA; *Imprints:* Devorss Publications (Devorss Pubns)
E-mail: service@devorss.com
Web site: http://www.devorss.com
Dist(s): **Health and Growth Assocs.**
New Leaf Distributing Co., Inc.

Devorss Pubns. *Imprint of* **DeVorss & Co.**

DeWard Publishing Co., Ltd., *(978-0-9798893; 978-0-9819703; 978-1-936341)* P.O. Box 6259, Chillicothe, OH 45601 USA Toll Free: 800-300-9778
E-mail: nathan_ward@hotmail.com
Web site: http://www.dewardpublishing.com.

Dewberry Pr., *(978-0-9854076; 978-0-9910340)* P.O. Box 604, Pflugerville, TX 78660 USA Tel 512-522-0596
E-mail: dewberrypress@yahoo.com
Web site: www.dewberrypress.com
Dist(s): **Lightning Source, Inc.**

Dewey Does *See* **A B C-123 Publishing**

Dewey Pubns., Inc., *(978-0-9615053; 978-1-878810; 978-1-932612; 978-1-934651; 978-1-941825)* 1840 Wilson Blvd Suite 203, Arlington, VA 22201 USA (SAN 694-1451) Tel 703-524-1355
E-mail: deweypublications@gmail.com
Web site: http://www.deweypub.com.

Dewey's Good News Balloons, *(978-1-880215)* 1202 Wildwood Dr., Deer Park, TX 77536 USA Tel 281-479-2759; Fax: 281-476-9997; Toll Free: 888-894-6597
E-mail: balloonz@flash.net.

Dezaim Productions and Management, LLC, *(978-0-9770111)* 1385 Chancellor Cir., Bensalem, PA 19020 USA.

Deziner Media International, *(978-0-9743971; 978-0-615-23060-3; 978-0-615-28400-2; 978-0-9819912)* P.O. Box 239, Marrero, LA 70073 USA Tel 504-292-9101; 1472 Ames Blvd., Marrero, LA 70072
E-mail: dezinermedia@aol.com
Web site: http://www.writeabc123.com
Dist(s): **AtlasBooks Distribution.**

DFC Pubs., *(978-0-9793987)* 31 W. Smith St., Amityville, NY 11701 USA (SAN 853-3695)
E-mail: contactus@urbanclubbooks.com
Web site: http://www.urbanclubbooks.com.

dg ink, *(978-0-9772577)* Orders Addr.: P.O. Box 1182, Daly City, CA 94017-1182 USA Tel 650-994-2662; Fax: 650-991-3050; *Imprints:* Ascribed (Ascribed)
E-mail: dg@dg-ink.net; info@dg-ink.net
Web site: http://www.dg-ink.net
Dist(s): **Follett School Solutions.**

†**Dharma Publishing,** *(978-0-89800; 978-0-913546)* Orders Addr.: 35788 Hauser Bridge Rd., Cazadero, CA 95421 USA (SAN 201-2723) Tel 707-847-3717; Fax: 707-847-3380; Toll Free: 800-873-4276
E-mail: contact@dharmapublishing.com; order@dharmapublishing.com
Web site: http://www.dharmapublishing.com/
Dist(s): **National Bk. Network**
Wisdom Pubns.; *CIP.*

Di Angelo Pubns., *(978-0-9850853; 978-1-942549)* 4265 San Felipe No. 1100, Houston, TX 77027 USA Tel 713-960-6636.

Di Bella, Brenda, *(978-0-615-38253-1)* 6643 Haskell Ave. No. 205, Van Nuys, CA 91406 USA Tel 818-235-3040
E-mail: comiab@yahoo.com
Web site: http://www.imuptobigthings.com.

Di Capua, Michael *Imprint of* **Scholastic, Inc.**

di Capua, Michael Bks. *Imprint of* **Hyperion Bks. for Children**

Di Maggio, Richard *See* **Consumer Pr., The**

Diakonia Publishing, *(978-0-9676528; 978-0-9725609; 978-0-9747278; 978-0-9772483; 978-0-9800877)* P.O. Box 9512, Greensboro, NC 27429-0512 USA Tel 336-707-2610
E-mail: diakoniapublishing@hotmail.com
Web site: http://www.ephesians412.com.

Dial *Imprint of* **Penguin Publishing Group**

Dialogue Systems, Incorporated *See* **Metropolitan Teaching & Learning Co.**

Dialogues in Self Discovery LLC, *(978-1-934450)* P.O. Box 43161, Montclair, NJ 07043 USA (SAN 853-2745) Tel 973-714-2800; Fax: 973-746-2853
E-mail: discoveroption@aol.com.

Diamond Bk. Distributors, Div. of Diamond Comic Distributors, Inc., Orders Addr.: 1966 Greenspring Dr., Suite 300, Timonium, MD 21093 USA (SAN 110-9502) Tel 410-560-7100; Fax: 410-560-2583; Toll Free: 800-452-6642; *Imprints:* William M. Gaines Agent, INC. (WILLIAM M. GAI); Humanoids, Inc. (HUMANOIDS, INC)
E-mail: books@diamondbookdistributors.com
Web site: http://www.diamondcomics.com; http://www.diamondbookdistributors.com/
Dist(s): **MyiLibrary**
SCB Distributors
SPD-Small Pr. Distribution.

Diamond Book Distributors Inc. *See* **Diamond Comic Distributors, Inc.**

Diamond Clear Vision *Imprint of* **Illumination Arts LLC**

Diamond Comic Distributors, Inc., *(978-1-59396; 978-1-60584)* 1966 Greenspring Dr., Suite 300, Timonium, MD 21093 USA Tel 410-560-7100; Fax: 410-560-2583; Toll Free: 800-452-6642
E-mail: books@diamondbookdistributors.com
Web site: http://www.diamondbookdistributors.com/
Dist(s): **Diamond Bk. Distributors.**

Diamond Creek Publishing, *(978-0-9713811)* P.O. Box 2068, Flagstaff, AZ 86003-2068 USA
Web site: http://www.apathways.com.

Diamond Event Planning, Inc., *(978-0-9766901)* 50-44 193rd St., Fresh Meadows, NY 11365 USA Tel 718-357-6144; Fax: 718-357-6685
E-mail: bridepro@aol.com
Web site: http://www.awedwitharedhead.com.

Diamond Farm Bk. Pubs., Div. of Yesteryear Toys & Books, Inc., Orders Addr.: P.O. Box 537, Alexandria Bay, NY 13607 USA (SAN 674-9054) Tel 613-475-1771; Fax: 613-475-3748; Toll Free Fax: 800-305-5138 (Order Line); Toll Free: 800-481-1353 (Order Line)
E-mail: info@diamondfarm.com
Web site: http://www.diamondfarm.com.

Diamond Fly Publishing, Inc., *(978-0-9817938)* 5224 Kings Mills Rd. Suite 264, Mason, OH 45040-2319 USA (SAN 856-566X)
Web site: http://www.diamondflypublishing.com.

Diamond Select Toys & Collectibles, *(978-1-931724)* Div. of Diamond Comics Distributors, 1966 Greenspring Dr., Suite 300, Timonium, MD 21093 USA Tel 410-560-7100; Fax: 410-560-7589; Toll Free: 800-452-6642
E-mail: wjason@diamondcomics.com
Web site: http://www.diamondselectoys.com
Dist(s): **Diamond Comic Distributors, Inc.**
Diamond Bk. Distributors
Simon & Schuster, Inc.

Diamond Spine Publishing, *(978-0-9765119; 978-0-9906238)* 42 Lake Ave., Ext., Suite 188, Danbury, CT 06811 USA Fax: 203-775-3311
E-mail: steeling@sinfulnyms.com.

Diamond Springs Pr., *(978-0-9729940)* 8085 Diamond Springs Dr., Helena, MT 59602 USA Tel 406-458-9220
E-mail: sagewood@qwest.net.

Diamond Star Pr., *(978-0-9774335)* P.O. Box 490817, Los Angeles, CA 90049-0817 USA (SAN 257-6457)
E-mail: info@diamondstarpress.com.

Diamond Triple C Ranch, *(978-0-9790652)* 801 Floral Vale Blvd., Yardley, PA 19067 USA (SAN 852-324X) Tel 215-497-3188; Fax: 215-497-3190
Web site: http://www.diamondtriplecranch.com.

DIANE Publishing Co., *(978-0-7881; 978-0-941375; 978-1-56806; 978-0-7567; 978-1-4223; 978-1-4289; 978-1-4379; 978-1-4578)* Orders Addr.: P.O. Box 617, Darby, PA 19023-0617 USA (SAN 667-1217) Tel 610-461-6200; Fax: 610-461-6130; Toll Free: 800-782-3833; Edit Addr.: 330 Pusey Ave., No. 3 rear, Collingdale, PA 19023 USA Tel 610-461-6200; Fax: 610-461-6130; Toll Free: 800-782-3833
E-mail: cfisher@dianepublishing.net
Web site: http://www.dianepublishing.net.

Diarnuid Inc., *(978-1-59347)* Orders Addr.: P.O. Box 357580, Gainesville, FL 32635 USA Toll Free: 877-475-3277; Edit Addr.: 2630 N.W. 41st St., Suite D-1, Gainesville, FL 32606 USA
E-mail: kuc49@aol.com; dalia@greatleaps.com
Web site: http://www.greatleaps.com.

DiaShah Pr., LLC, *(978-0-9761207)* Orders Addr.: P.O. Box 43804, Nottingham, MD 21236 USA
E-mail: diashahpress@yahoo.com
Web site: http://www.debrasawyer.com; http://www.diashahpress.com.

DIASOT Pubns., *(978-0-9844649)* P.O. Box 705, Pittsburg, KS 66762 USA (SAN 859-4759)
E-mail: DIASOTPublications@gmail.com.

Dibble Institute for Marriage Education, The, *(978-0-9652427; 978-0-9761349; 978-0-9828395; 978-1-940815)* Orders Addr.: P.O. Box 7881, Berkeley, CA 94707-0881 USA Tel 510-528-7975 (Main Office); Fax: 972-226-2824 (Customer Service Fax); Toll Free: 800-695-7975 (Customer Service); Edit Addr.: 728 Coventry Rd., Kensington, CA 94707 USA
E-mail: relationshipskills@DibbleInstitute.org
Web site: http://www.buildingrelationshipskills.org; http://www.DibbleInstitute.org.

Dickow, Gregory Ministries, *(978-1-932833)* Orders Addr.: P.O. Box 7000, Chicago, IL 60680 USA Fax: 847-842-9904; Toll Free: 888-438-5433; Edit Addr.: 180 N. Hawthorne Rd., Barrington Hills, IL 60010 USA
E-mail: gdmpartnerrelations@changinglives.org
Web site: http://www.changinglives.org.

Dickson Keanaghan, LLC, *(978-0-9749146; 978-1-933230)* 265 Jerusalem Ave., Hicksville, Long Island,, NY 11801-4931 USA Tel 516-578-5874 cell phone; Fax: 516-433-5734 office fax
E-mail: jckunzjr@EmpowermentEducation.com
Web site: http://www.EmpowermentEducation.com
Dist(s): **Lightning Source, Inc.**

Dickson-Keanaghan Publishing Group, LLC *See* **Dickson Keanaghan, LLC**

Dictionary Project, Inc., The, *(978-0-9745292; 978-0-9771777; 978-1-934669)* P.O. Box 566, Sullivan's Islanld, SC 29482 USA (SAN 255-5999)
E-mail: wordpower2@aol.com.

Die Gestalten Verlag (DEU) *(978-3-931126; 978-3-89955)* *Dist. by* **Prestel Pub NY.**

Diettribe Enterprises *See* **Steve Diet Goedde**

Dietz Pr., *(978-0-87517)* Orders Addr.: 930 Winfield Rd., Petersburg, VA 23803-4748 USA Tel 804-733-0123; Fax: 804-733-3514; Toll Free: 800-391-6833
E-mail: rbeville@dietzpress.com; customerservice@dietzpress.com
Web site: http://www.dietzpress.com
Dist(s): **American Wholesale Bk. Co.**
Barnes&Noble.com
Emery-Pratt Co.
Follett School Solutions.

Different Friends, *(978-1-892750)* Orders Addr.: P.O. Box 40208, Cincinnati, OH 45240 USA Tel 513-825-1514; Edit Addr.: 703 Yorkhaven Rd., Cincinnati, OH 45246 USA.

Different Worlds Pubns., *(978-0-9753999)* 1600 Portola Dr., San Francisco, CA 94127-1402 USA (SAN 256-0577)
E-mail: info@diffworlds.com
Web site: http://www.diffworlds.com.

DiFrancesco, Joe, *(978-0-9712682)* 35 Meadow Creek Ln., Glenmoore, PA 19343-2017 USA
E-mail: josephdifran@comcast.net.

Digging Clams n Oregon, *(978-0-9767508)* P.O. Box 746, Newport, OR 97365 USA (SAN 850-9700) Tel 541-265-5847
E-mail: williamlackner001@msn.com.

Digibots Corp., *(978-0-9755725)* Orders Addr.: P.O. Box 6803, Katy, TX 77491 USA Tel 281-599-1095; Fax: 281-599-0391; Toll Free: 877-375-8794; Edit Addr.: 3710 Havenmoor Pl., Katy, TX 77449 USA
E-mail: drew3710@msn.com
Web site: http://www.digibots.us.

Digireads.com, *(978-0-9753222; 978-1-59625; 978-1-59674; 978-1-4209)* 3921 Harvard Rd., Lawrence, KS 66049 USA
E-mail: digireads@yahoo.com
Web site: http://www.digireads.com
Dist(s): **Ingram Pub. Services**
Lightning Source, Inc.
Neeland Media, LLC.

Digital Antiquaria, Inc., *(978-1-58057)* 2 Sand Hill Rd., Morristown, NJ 07960-5928 USA
E-mail: info@DigitalAntiquaria.com
Web site: http://digitalantiquaria.com.

Digital Fabulists, *(978-0-615-54838-8; 978-0-615-68883-1; 978-0-615-71535-3; 978-0-615-72300-6; 978-0-615-73097-4; 978-0-615-73330-2; 978-0-615-78913-2; 978-0-615-82496-3; 978-0-615-83220-3; 978-0-615-85024-5; 978-0-615-90055-1; 978-0-615-90823-6; 978-0-615-91649-1; 978-0-615-91753-5; 978-0-615-91754-2; 978-0-615-92525-7; 978-0-692-21897-6) 11684 Ventura Blvd #205, Studio City, CA 91604 USA Tel 310-621-5599; Fax: 818-446-4747*
Web site: http://www.digitalfabulists.com
Dist(s): **CreateSpace Independent Publishing Platform.**

Digital Manga Distribution *See* **Digital Manga Publishing**

Digital Manga Publishing, *(978-1-56970)* Div. of Digital Manga, Inc., 1487 W. 178th St. Ste. 300, Gardena, CA 90248-3253 USA (SAN 111-817X) Toll Free: 866-897-7300
E-mail: contact@emanga.com
Web site: http://www.dmpbooks.com/
Dist(s): **Diamond Comic Distributors, Inc.**
Diamond Bk. Distributors
Random Hse., Inc.

Digital Quest Inc., *(978-1-934873)* 525 Thomastown Ln., Ridgeland, MS 39157 USA Tel 601-856-2237; Fax: 601-856-2576
Web site: http://www.digitalquest.com.

Digital Scanning, Inc., *(978-1-58218)* 344 Gannett Rd., Scituate, MA 02066 USA (SAN 299-8734) Tel 781-545-2100
E-mail: info@digitalscanning.com
Web site: http://www.digitalscanning.com
Dist(s): **Lightning Source, Inc.**
TextStream
ebrary, Inc.

digital@batesjackson llc, *(978-1-932583; 978-0-9831157; 978-0-9885895)* 17-21 Elm St., Buffalo, NY 14203 USA Tel 716-854-3000; Fax: 716-847-1965
E-mail: mybook@batesjackson.com
Web site: http://www.batesjackson.com.

DigitalKu, *(978-0-9763168)* 7913 N. Highview Dr., Milwaukee, WI 53223 USA
Web site: http://www.digitalku.com/.

Digitex-U Pubns., *(978-0-615-15579-1)* 6655 Malyern Ave., Philadelphia, PA 19151 USA Tel 215-738-4678
E-mail: raincloud1@gmail.com
Web site: http://www.myspace.com/raincoud1
Dist(s): **Lulu Enterprises Inc.**

DiGuiseppi, Joseph, *(978-0-9768348)* Orders Addr.: 4 Richmond Rd., Newtown, CT 06470-1214 USA
E-mail: joedigspi@hotmail.com
Web site: http://www.joedigspi.com.

Dillies, Lyn, *(978-0-615-66530-6; 978-0-615-67484-1)* 15 Laurel Ln., Westport, MA 02790 USA Tel 508-636-2484
E-mail: lyn@magicoflyn.com.

Dilligaf Publishing, *(978-0-9639070; 978-0-9701020; 978-1-931207)* Orders Addr.: 98 Main St., Ellsworth, ME 04605 USA Tel 207-667-5351
E-mail: studio3marty@acadia.net; vze277g4@verizon.net.

Dillon, Elena, *(978-0-9886353; 978-0-9908804)* 15035 Live Oak Springs, Canyon Country, CA 91387 USA Tel 661-406-2369
E-mail: info@elenadillon.com.

Dilly Green Bean Games, *(978-0-9744698; 978-0-9801898)* 33 Hillview Rd., Gorham, ME 04038 USA
E-mail: dillygreenbeangames@dillygreenbeangames.com; jay@indirpg.com; jay@dillygreenbeangames.com
Web site: http://www.dillygreenbeangames.com.

Dimensions in Media, Inc., *(978-0-9762273)* 24191 N. Forest Dr., Lake Zurich, IL 60047 USA Tel 847-726-2093
E-mail: debbie@dimensionsinmedia.com
Web site: http://www.be-still.com
Dist(s): **Independent Pubs. Group.**

Dingles & Co., *(978-1-891997; 978-1-59646)* P.O. Box 508, Sea Girt, NJ 08750 USA
E-mail: dinglesco@aol.com
Dist(s): **Central Programs**
Gumdrop Bks.

Dingobi Publishing, *(978-0-9772819)* P.O. Box 4533, Rock Island, IL 61204-4533 USA.

Dings Bks., *(978-0-9748890)* 411 Schoolhouse Ln., Shippensburg, PA 17257 USA
E-mail: dingscenter@yahoo.com.

Dino Entertainment AG (DEU) *(978-3-89748; 978-3-8332)* *Dist. by* **Distribks Inc.**

Dino-Mike! *Imprint of* **Stone Arch Bks.**

DINOSAUR BKS. *Imprint of* **Parkwest Pubns., Inc.**

Dinosaur Fund, *(978-0-9748618)* 711 E. St. SE, No. 104, Washington, DC 20003-2879 USA Tel 202-547-3326
E-mail: dinosaurfund@juno.com; shill@laser-image.com
Web site: http://www.dinosaurfund.org.

Dinoship, Inc., *(978-0-9728585; 978-1-933384)* 105 W. 73rd St., No. 1B, New York, NY 10023 USA Tel 212-721-5056; Fax: 212-595-0247; 299 Broadway, No. 1016, New York, NY 10007
E-mail: bob@dinoship.com
Web site: http://www.dinoship.com.

DinRo, *(978-0-9744412)* 7545 Gladstone Dr., No. 205, Naperville, IL 60565 USA Fax: 630-305-3695.

Diogenes Verlag AG (CHE) *(978-3-257)* *Dist. by* **Distribks Inc.**

Diogenes Verlag AG (CHE) *(978-3-257)* *Dist. by* **Intl Bk Import.**

Diomo Square Bks., *(978-0-9765948)* 4911 SW 43rd Ave., Portland, OR 97206-5011 USA
E-mail: diomo@earthlink.net.

Dion's Pubn., *(978-0-9795739; 978-0-9836893)* 3002 Royston Rd., Charlotte, NC 28208 USA Tel 574-307-2496
E-mail: tokereke@gmail.com.

Direct Access Publishing, *(978-0-9796473)* 1402 Auburn Wy No. No. 232, Auburn, WA 98002 USA (SAN 853-9952) Tel 206-725-3001; Toll Free: 877-725-3009
E-mail: directt_access@yahoo.com.

Direct World Publishing, *(978-0-9787591)* Orders Addr.: 11711 Jefferson Ave STE D, Newport News, VA 23606 USA Tel 757-818-8016; Edit Addr.: 11711 Jefferson Ave STE D, Newport News, VA 23606 USA Tel 757-818-8016
E-mail: jenniferyu28@gmail.com; directworldusa@gmail.com
Web site: http://www.JenniferYu.com; www.directworldapp.com.

Directions in Education, Training & Consultation, *(978-0-9664681)* Orders Addr.: P.O. Box 2478, Gig Harbor, WA 98335 USA Tel 253-858-7261; Edit Addr.: 4720 Birchtree Ln., NW, Gig Harbor, WA 98335 USA
E-mail: lbaker@HarborNet.com
Web site: http://www.pebblesinthepond.com.

DirkDesigns, LLC, *(978-0-9790923)* P.O. Box 3754, West Lafayette, IN 47996 USA.

Dirks Publishing *See* **Dirks Publishing, LLC**

Dirks Publishing, LLC, *(978-0-9823145)* P.O. Box 348, Rantoul, IL 61866-0348 USA Fax: 206-339-8510
E-mail: julie@dirkspublishing.com
Web site: http://www.dirkspublishing.com.

Disciple One Publishing, *(978-0-9791883)* Div. of Disciple Group Production, 10153 1/2 Riverside Dr., No. 467, Toluca Lake, CA 91602 USA Tel 323-654-8579
E-mail: baronjay@yourlittleblackbook.net
Web site: http://www.yourlittleblackbook.net
Dist(s): **Lushena Bks.**

Disciple Publishing Co., *(978-0-615-23763-3)* P.O. Box 554, Beaufort, SC 29901 USA Tel 843-379-9955; Fax: 843-379-9956; Toll Free: 866-245-8182
E-mail: dpc@hargray.com
Web site: http://www.dpchope.com.

Discipleship Pubns. International, *(978-1-57782; 978-1-884553)* 300 5th Ave. Ste. 5, Waltham, MA 02451-8749 USA Toll Free: 888-374-2665
E-mail: spjones@icoc.org; dpibooks@icoc.org
Web site: http://www.dpibooks.org
Dist(s): **Independent Pubs. Group**
ebrary, Inc.

Discipleship Resources *Imprint of* **Upper Room Bks.**

Discover Writing Company *See* **Discover Writing Pr.**

Discover Writing Pr., *(978-0-9656574; 978-1-931492)* Orders Addr.: P.O. Box 264, Shoreham, VT 05770 USA Tel 802-897-7022; Fax: 802-897-2084; Toll Free: 800-613-8055
E-mail: registrar@discoverwriting.com; ann@discoverwriting.com; administrator@discoverwriting.com; barry@discoverwriting.com
Web site: http://www.discoverwriting.com.

Discovery Communications *See* **Discovery Education**

Discovery Education, *(978-1-56331; 978-1-58738; 978-1-59527; 978-1-60288; 978-1-60711; 978-0-9824299; 978-1-61629; 978-1-61708; 978-1-61828; 978-1-68220)* One Discovery Pl., Silver Spring, MD 20910 USA Tel 240-662-2000; Toll Free: 888-892-3484
E-mail: megan.faller@discovery.com; sara_fisher@discovery.com
Web site: http://www.discoveryeducation.com
Dist(s): **Explorations**
Follett School Solutions
Insight Guides
Langenscheidt Publishing Group.

Discovery Enterprises, Limited *See* **History Compass, LLC**

Discovery Hse. Pubs., *(978-0-929239; 978-1-57293; 978-1-62707)* Div. of R B C Ministries, Orders Addr.: P.O. Box 3566, Grand Rapids, MI 49501 USA (SAN 248-8949) Tel 616-942-9218; Fax: 616-957-5741; Toll Free: 800-653-8333; Edit Addr.: 3000 Kraft Ave., SE, Grand Rapids, MI 49512 USA (SAN 248-8957) Tel 616-942-6770; Fax: 616-974-2224
E-mail: dhp@rbc.org; rwatson@dhp.org
Web site: http://www.dhp.org
Dist(s): **CLC Pubns.**

Discovery Pr. Pubns., Inc., *(978-0-9645159)* 400 E. 3rd Ave., No. 901, Denver, CO 80203 USA (SAN 298-5691) Tel 303-355-9689; Fax: 303-733-3474
E-mail: discoverypresspub@comcast.net
Web site: http://www.discoverypresspub.com
Dist(s): **Brodart Co.**
Quality Bks., Inc.

Discovery Pubns. (GBR) *(978-0-9538222; 978-0-9550458)* *Dist. by* **Irish Bks Media.**

For full information on wholesalers and distributors, refer to the Wholesaler and Distributor Name Index

Disenos del Arte, Inc., *(978-0-9820784)* P.O. Box 11441, San Juan, PR 00910 USA Tel 787-722-1060; Fax: 787-728-3092
E-mail: dasant@delartepr.com
Web site: http://www.delartepr.com.

Disinformation Co. Ltd., The, *(978-0-9713942; 978-0-9729529; 978-1-932857; 978-1-934708; 978-1-939517)* 220 E. 23rd St., Suite 500, New York, NY 10010 USA
E-mail: books@disinfo.com
Dist(s): **Consortium Bk. Sales & Distribution**
Follett School Solutions
Perseus Bks. Group
Red Wheel/Weiser
ebrary, Inc.

Disney Editions *Imprint of* **Disney Pr.**

Disney Lucasfilm Press *Imprint of* **Disney Publishing Worldwide**

†Disney Pr., *(978-0-7868; 978-1-56282; 978-1-4231)* Div. of Disney Bk. Publishing, Inc., A Walt Disney Co., 44 S. Broadway. Flr. 16, White Plains, NY 10601-4411 USA Toll Free: 800-759-0190; *Imprints:* Disney Editions (Disney Ed)
Web site:
http://www.disney.com/disneybooks/index.html
Dist(s): **Hachette Bk. Group**
Libros Sin Fronteras
Little Brown & Co.
Perfection Learning Corp.; *CIP*

Disney Publishing Worldwide, *(978-1-892309; 978-1-931580; 978-1-4231; 978-1-4847)* Subs. of Walt Disney Productions, 44 S. Broadway, 10th Flr., White Plains, NY 10601 USA Tel 914-288-4316; *Imprints:* Marvel Press (Marvel Pr); Disney Lucasfilm Press (Lucasfilm Pr)
Web site: http://www.disney.go.com;
http://www.hyperionbooksforchildren.com
Dist(s): **Follett School Solutions**
Hachette Bk. Group.

Disneyland/Vista Records & Tapes *See* **Walt Disney Records**

Disposition Sketch Bks. *Imprint of* **MacBride, E. J. Pubn., Inc.**

Disruptive Publishing, *(978-1-59654; 978-1-60872; 978-1-62657)* 735 Ivy League Ln., Rockville, MD 20850 USA
E-mail: service.blackmask@gmail.com
Web site: http://www.dispub.com
Dist(s): **Diamond Bk. Distributors.**

Distribooks, Inc., Div. of MED, Inc., 8124 N. Ridgeway, Skokie, IL 60076 USA (SAN 630-9763) Tel 847-676-1596; Fax: 847-676-1195
E-mail: info@distribooks.com.

Distribuidora Norma, Inc., *(978-1-881700; 978-1-935164)* Div. of Carvajal International, Orders Addr.: P.O. Box 195040, San Juan, PR 00919-5040 USA Tel 787-788-5050; Fax: 787-788-7161; Edit Addr.: Carretera 869 Km 1.5 Barrio Palmas Royal Industrial, Catano, PR 00962 USA
Web site: http://www.norma.com.

Distribuidora Plaza Mayor, 1500 Ave. Ponce de Leon Local 2 El Cinco, San Juan, PR 1 USA.

Distribution General,
Dist(s): **Abrams.**

Éditions Chouette (CAN) *(978-2-89450; 978-2-921198; 978-2-9800909; 978-2-89718) Dist. by* **Distribks Inc.**

Éditions Chouette (CAN) *(978-2-89450; 978-2-921198; 978-2-9800909; 978-2-89718) Dist. by* **PerseuPGW.**

Diversified A+ Pubns., *(978-0-9773526)* P.O. Box 13, Winchendon, MA 01475 USA
E-mail: Dpipub@aol.com
Web site: http://www.dpublications.com.

Diversion Bks., *(978-0-9845151; 978-0-9829050; 978-0-9833371; 978-0-9838395; 978-0-9839885; 978-1-938120; 978-1-62681; 978-1-68230)* 443 Park Aveue S., Ste. 1008, New York, NY 10016 USA Tel 212-675-5556; 212-961-6390
E-mail: info@diversionbooks.com; charles@efit.com
Web site: http://www.diversionbooks.com
Dist(s): **Ingram Pub. Services**
Perseus Distribution
Smashwords.

Diversion Media *See* **Diversion Bks.**

Diversion Pr., *(978-1-935290)* P.O. Box 30277, Clarksville, TN 37040 USA (SAN 857-0264)
E-mail: diversionpress@yahoo.com
Web site: http://www.diversionpress.com.

Diversity Foundation, The, *(978-0-9797193)* 505 W., 10200 S., South Jordan, UT 84095 USA Tel 801-553-4556; Fax: 801-553-4600; Toll Free: 888-216-2122
Web site: http://www.thediversityfoundation.org
Dist(s): **Partners Pubs. Group, Inc.**

Diversity Ink Publishing, *(978-0-9767258)* P.O. Box 2414, Santa Maria, CA 93457 USA.

Dividion Group, LLC, The, *(978-0-9769366)* Orders Addr.: P.O. Box 2678, North Canton, OH 44720 USA
E-mail: turnekash22@aol.com; bigheds@bigheds.com
Web site: http://www.bigheds.com.

Divincenzo, Yoselem G., *(978-0-9800127; 978-1-61196)* 93-64 204th St., Hollis, NY 11423 USA Tel 646-634-9490
E-mail: yoselem@hotmail.com
Web site: http://www.babelbooksinc.com
Dist(s): **Follett School Solutions.**

Divine House Ministries *See* **Kingdom Sound Pubs.**

Divine Inspiration Publishing, LLC, *(978-0-9820490)* P.O. Box 210414, Auburn Hills, MI 48326 USA (SAN 857-1090) Fax: 248-927-0357
E-mail: stevecogswell@comcast.net;
scogswell@divineinspirationpublishing.com
Web site: http://www.divineinsirationpublishing.com
Dist(s): **AtlasBooks Distribution.**

Divine Intertwine Publishing, *(978-0-9754489)* P.O. Box 4088, Ocean City, MD 21843 USA.

Divine Mercy Pr., *(978-0-9755471)* 3216 Mission Ave. Apt. 138, Oceanside, CA 92058-1348 USA
E-mail: divinemercy@hypersurf.com.

Divine Ministry of North Florida, Inc., *(978-0-9773356)* P.O. Box 5668, Gainesville, FL 32627-5668 USA (SAN 257-3652)
E-mail: ade0201@yahoo.com
Web site: http://www.divineministry.net.

DJ Blues Publishing, *(978-0-9743985)* 403 Dula Cir., Duncanville, TX 75116 USA
E-mail: hipdjblues@earthlink.net
Web site: http://www.djblues.com.

DJ Inkers *Imprint of* **Carson-Dellosa Publishing, LLC**

Dksmo-Press, Izdatel'skaja firma (RUS) *(978-5-04) Dist. by* **Distribks Inc.**

DL Grant, LLC, *(978-0-9853713; 978-0-9882084; 978-0-9889947; 978-0-9914542; 978-1-942017)* 3621 Huntwick Dr., Orange, TX 77632 USA Tel 409-779-6807
E-mail: dgauthor@gmail.com.

DLG, LLC *See* **DL Grant, LLC**

dLife - For Your Diabetes Life, *(978-0-9777463)* Div. of LifeMed Media, 101 Franklin St., Westport, CT 06880-0688 USA (SAN 850-1254) Tel 203-454-6985; Fax: 203-454-6986
E-mail: info@dlife.com
Web site: http://www.dlife.com.

DLS Bks. *Imprint of* **Denney Literary Services**

DM Creative, *(978-0-9798445)* 16032 Samoa Ct., Tega Cay, SC 29708-2970 USA
Web site: http://www.hamstersam.com;
http://davemcdonald.com/.

Dm Productions, *(978-0-615-14860-1; 978-0-615-15990-4)* 10596 N. Washington Blvd., Indianapolis, IN 46280 USA
Web site: http://dmprod.blogspot.com/
Dist(s): **Lulu Enterprises Inc.**

DMCD Productions, Inc. *See* **DMcD Productions, Inc.**

DMcD Productions, Inc., *(978-0-9771521)* Orders Addr.: P.O. Box 40, Grand Rapids, MN 55744-0040 USA (SAN 256-9019)
E-mail: sven@ohforsmart.com
Web site: http://www.ohforsmart.com.

DMH Pr., Inc., *(978-0-9746153)* 10 Beachside Dr., No. 302, Vero Beach, FL 32963 USA (SAN 256-0127) Fax: 631-325-1340
Web site: http://www.dollyadventures.com.

DMT Publishing, *(978-0-9726189; 978-0-9749144; 978-0-9785553; 978-0-9800813; 978-0-9824259; 978-1-935821)* 900 N. 400 W. , Bldg. 12, North Salt Lake, UT 84054 USA
Web site: http://www.dmtpublishing.com.

DNA Pr., *(978-0-9664027; 978-0-9748765; 978-1-933255)* P.O. Box 572, Eagleville, PA 19408-0572 USA (SAN 256-5005) Fax: 501-694-5495
E-mail: editors@dnapress.com
Web site: http://www.dnapress.com
Dist(s): **Independent Pubs. Group.**

DNS Technology Consultants, Inc., *(978-0-615-74879-5)* 1397 Leyton Dr., Youngstown, OH 44509 USA Tel 3305072270
Dist(s): **CreateSpace Independent Publishing Platform.**

do be you, *(978-0-9794262)* 229 Vincent Ave. N., Minneapolis, MN 55405 USA
E-mail: info@i-get-around.com
Web site: http://www.i-get-around.com.

Do it Yourself Florist Enterprises, *(978-0-9794595)* 2425 Olea Ct., Gilroy, CA 95020 USA Tel 408-848-5092; Fax: 408-848-5234
E-mail: flowers@garlic.com
Web site: http://flowersmadesimple.net
Dist(s): **Independent Pubs. Group**
MyiLibrary.

Do Life Right, Inc., *(978-0-9824829; 978-1-937848)* P.O. Box 61, Sahuarita, AZ 85629 USA
E-mail: lisa@wrightontimebooks.com
Web site: http://www.doliferight.com
Dist(s): **CreateSpace Independent Publishing Platform.**

Do The Write Thing, Inc., *(978-1-930357)* 56 T. St. , NW, Washington, DC 20001-1009 USA Tel 202-758-0397; Fax: 202-758-0397
E-mail: chillshil@netscape.net.

Dobie Book Publishing *See* **Mowery, Julia**

Dockter, Toni, *(978-0-9712201)* P.O. Box 1532, Soquel, CA 95073-1532 USA
E-mail: tonette101@aol.com
Web site: http://percyveerance.com.

Doctor Dolittle's Library *Imprint of* **PhotoGraphics Publishing**

Dodi Pr., *(978-0-9767273; 978-0-9851067)* Orders Addr.: 10 Brookstone Dr., Sicklerville, NJ 08081 USA (SAN 860-3200)
E-mail: cherilnc@cherilnclarke.com;
monica.r.bey@gmail.com
Web site: www.myfamilyproducts.net.

Dog Ear Publishing, LLC, *(978-0-9762173; 978-0-9766603; 978-1-59858; 978-1-60844; 978-1-4575)* 4010 W. 86th St., Suite H, Indianapolis, IN 46268 USA Tel 317-228-3656; Fax: 317-489-3506; Toll Free: 866-823-9613
E-mail: rayr@dogearpublishing.net
Web site: http://www.dogearpublishing.net
Dist(s): **Ingram Pub. Services**
Lightning Source, Inc.
Lulu Enterprises Inc.
Smashwords.

Dog Soldier Pr., *(978-0-9718658)* P.O. Box 1782, Ranchos de Taos, NM 87557-1782 USA (SAN 254-4733) Tel 505-751-3781; Fax: 505-758-4071
E-mail: dogsoldier@newmexico.com
Web site: http://www.dogsoldierpress.com.

Dog-Eared Pubns., *(978-0-941042)* Orders Addr.: P.O. Box 620863, Middleton, WI 53562-0863 USA (SAN 281-6059) Tel 608-831-1410 (phone/fax); Toll Free: 888-364-3277; Edit Addr.: 4642 Toepfer Rd., Middleton, WI 53562 USA
E-mail: field@dog-eared.com
Web site: http://www.dog-eared.com
Dist(s): **Common Ground Distributors, Inc.**
Paradise Cay Pubns.
Partners/West Book Distributors.

Doggerel Daze, *(978-0-9722820)* 10144 Riedel Pl., Cupertino, CA 95014 USA.

DogHouse Pr., *(978-0-9761497)* 150 Chestnut St., Park Forest, IL 60466 USA Toll Free: 877-413-8997
E-mail: kimberly@rjsystems.us
Web site: http://www.doghousepress.com.

Doghouse Publishing, Incorporated *See* **Mess Hall Writers**

Doghouse Reilly Studios, *(978-0-615-73281-7; 978-0-615-86213-2)* P.O. Box 70, Southbury, CT 06488 USA Tel (203)313-8544
Dist(s): **CreateSpace Independent Publishing Platform.**

Dogs in Hats Children's Publishing Co., *(978-1-59445)* P.O. Box 182, Grand Haven, MI 49417 USA Tel 616-844-2220; Fax: 616-844-2922
E-mail: customerservice@dogsinhats.com
Web site: http://www.dogsinhats.com
Dist(s): **Follett School Solutions.**

Dogs4dogs, *(978-0-9771265)* P.O. Box 675432, Rancho Santa Fe, CA 92067-5432 USA
Web site: http://www.dogs4dogs.com.

Dogtown Artworks, *(978-0-9777126)* 704 N. Main St. Suite 102, Tuscola, IL 61953 USA Tel 217-689-4575
E-mail: dogtownartworks@mac.com;
dogtownartworks@gmail.com;
pringle.photography@gmail.com
Web site: http://www.dogtownartworks.com
Dist(s): **Independent Pubs. Group.**

Dogwalk Pr., *(978-0-9766846)* Div. of Dan Gersten & Assocs., LLC, 29636 Quail Run Dr., Agoura Hills, CA 91301 USA Tel 818-735-0280; Fax: 818-991-1838
Web site: http://www.askcurtisthedog.com.

Dogwise *See* **Dogwise Publishing**

Dogwise Publishing, *(978-1-929242; 978-1-61781)* Orders Addr.: 403 S. Mission, Wentachee, WA 98801 USA (SAN 631-1415) Tel 509-663-9115; Fax: 509-662-7233; Toll Free: 800-776-2665
E-mail: mail@dogwise.com; charlenew@dogwise.com;
natewoodward@dogwise.com
Web site: http://www.dogwise.com.

Dohate Pr., *(978-0-9767003)* Orders Addr.: 1809 Brookhaven Dr., Austin, TX 78704 USA Tel 512-442-0576
E-mail: donbutlerbooks@earthlink.net.

Doherty, Tom Assocs., LLC, *(978-0-312; 978-0-7653; 978-0-8125)* Div. of Holtzbrinck Publishers, Orders Addr.: 16365 James Madison Hwy., Gordonsville, VA 22942-8501 USA Toll Free Fax: 800-672-2054; Toll Free: 888-330-8477; Edit Addr.: 175 Fifth Ave., New York, NY 10010 USA Tel 212-674-5151; Fax: 540-672-7540 (customer service); *Imprints:* Forge Books (Forge Bks); Orb Books (Orb Bks); Tor Books (Tor Books); Starscape (Starscape); Tor Teen (Tor Teen)
E-mail: inquiries@tor.com
Web site: http://www.tor.com/
Dist(s): **Cambridge Univ. Pr.**
CreateSpace Independent Publishing Platform
Libros Sin Fronteras
Macmillan
MyiLibrary
Perfection Learning Corp.

Doing Good Ministries, *(978-0-9667054)* 217 Bayview Way, Chula Vista, CA 91910 USA Tel 619-476-7230
E-mail: moehlenpah@aol.com
Web site: http://www.doinggood.org.

Dokument forlag, Fotograf Malcolm Jacobsson (SWE) *(978-91-973981; 978-91-85639) Dist. by* **SCB Distributo.**

Dolce Bks., *(978-0-615-68537-7; 978-0-615-78130-3; 978-0-615-90388-0)* 1189 Edgemont Rd., Emmett, ID 83617 USA Tel 208-365-4676
E-mail: debbiedee4@yahoo.com
Dist(s): **CreateSpace Independent Publishing Platform.**

Dollison Road Bks., *(978-0-9855540)* 247 E. 4700 N., Provo, UT 84604 USA Tel 417-883-0601
E-mail: JeanStringam@gmail.com
Web site: jeanstringam.com; DollisonRoadBooks.com.

Dollworks, *(978-0-9760064; 978-1-60304)* 6693 Lake Shore Dr., Newport, MI 48166-9716 USA; P.O. Box 66075, Newport, MI 48166
E-mail: nanciejack@aol.com.

Dolly Dimple Ink Children's Bks., *(978-0-9773506)* 5484 Atlantic View, Saint Augustine, FL 32080 USA Tel 904-460-0997
E-mail: effiemaeshearin@aol.com
Web site: http://www.dollydimpleink.com.

Dolphin Media *See* **Blue Brush Media**

Dolphin Publishing, *(978-1-878400)* P.O. Box 16656, West Palm Beach, FL 33416-6656 USA Tel 561-585-8901; Toll Free: 800-547-7867 Do not confuse with companies with the same name in Richardson, TX, Mattawan, MI
E-mail: nicotinefree@bellsouth.net
Web site: http://www.davidcjones.com.

Dolphins Publishing, *(978-0-9892565)* 1931 SW 17th Pl., Cape Coral, FL 33991 USA
E-mail: coach4u13@yahoo.com.

Dominick Pictures, *(978-0-9726092)* P.O. Box 1925, New York, NY 10013 USA.

Dominie Pr., Inc., *(978-0-7685; 978-1-56270)* Div. of Pearson Learning, 145 S. Mount Zion Rd., Lebanon, IN 46052-8186 USA (SAN 630-947X) Toll Free: 800-232-4570
E-mail: info@dominie.com
Web site: http://www.dominie.com.

DOMINIONHOUSE Publishing & Design, *(978-0-9755234; 978-0-9815463; 978-0-9828366; 978-0-9839869; 978-0-9888718; 978-0-9905031)* Orders Addr.: P.O. Box 681938, Orlando, FL 32868 USA Tel 407-880-5790 (phone/fax)
Web site: http://www.mydominionhouse.com.

Don Cohen-The Mathman, *(978-0-9621674; 978-0-9779493)* Orders Addr.: 809 Stratford Dr., Champaign, IL 61821-4140 USA (SAN 251-866X) Tel 217-356-4555; Fax: 217-356-4593; Toll Free: 800-356-4559
E-mail: mathman@shout.net
Web site: http://www.shout.net/~mathman
Dist(s): **Rainbow Re-Source Ctr.**

Don Paul Publishing, LLC, *(978-0-9655792; 978-0-9816477; 978-1-941818)* P.O. Box 17062, Portland, OR 97217 USA Tel 503-764-9100
E-mail: jenna7jennifer@gmail.com;
jennifer@donpaulpublishing.com
Web site: http://www.donpaulpublishing.com.

Don Quixote Publishing Co. Inc., *(978-0-9749196; 978-0-578-06784-1)* 905 Brickell Bay Dr., Unit 230, Miami, FL 33131 USA (SAN 255-884X) Tel 305-379-6151; Fax: 305-379-5156
E-mail: panza1209@aol.com;
camote@manuelmartinezdreamer.com
Web site: http://www.manuelmartinezdreamer.com.

Don Rand's Classy Collectibles, *(978-0-9773775)* 26585 Fawn., Lake Forest, CA 92630-6728 USA.

DoNascimento.com/Bks., *(978-0-9835120)* 520 Ashford Dr., Coppell, TX 75019 USA Tel 214-810-2443; Fax: 501-423-3868
E-mail: douglas@donascimento.com;
nicoledonascimento@gmail.com
Web site: http://www.donascimento.com/Books.

Donegal Publishing Co., *(978-0-9788128)* Orders Addr.: 1850 Industrial St., #307, Los Angeles, CA 90021 USA (SAN 851-6782) Tel 310-598-6340; Fax: 310-349-3441; Toll Free: 866-964-4919
E-mail: editor@donegalpublishing.com;
richie-d@comcast.net; donegalpublishing@mac.com
Web site: http://www.donegalpublishing.com;
http://www.jerryland.net.

Donkey Publishing, *(978-0-9887454)* 16582 Hutchison Rd., Odessa, FL 33556 USA Tel 813-781-7143
E-mail: TOM@BRAYFIELDS.COM.

Donkey Quest Books *See* **Donkey's Quest Pr.**

Donkey's Quest Pr., *(978-0-9961139)* 40 Sherwood Rd., Medford, MA 02155 USA
E-mail: ccbaha1@gmail.com
Web site: http://donkeysquestpress.com.

Donnellan, Martha *See* **Pine Cone Pr.**

Donovan, Kevin M. *See* **Billy the Bear & His Friends, Inc.**

Don't Eat Any Bugs Prodns., *(978-0-9728177; 978-0-9802314; 978-0-9887329)* P.O. Box 291, Tehachapi, CA 93581 USA
E-mail: Ray@rayfriesen.com
Web site: http://www.donteatanybugs.com
Dist(s): **National Bk. Network.**

Don't Eat Any Bugs Productions,
Dist(s): **National Bk. Network.**

Don't Forget The Magic Publishing, *(978-0-615-73376-0)* 19073, Bend, OR 97702 USA Tel 541 241 0572
Dist(s): **CreateSpace Independent Publishing Platform.**

Don't Look Publishing, *(978-0-9728234)* P.O. Box 486, Moose Lake, MN 55767 USA.

Don't Run With Knives Publications *See* **Academic Solutions, Inc.**

Dontstickdontstuff, *(978-0-9888861)* 5426 E. Via Los Caballos, Paradise Valley, AZ 85253 USA Tel 480-600-4690
E-mail: dontstickdontstuff@gmail.com
Dist(s): **BookBaby**
New Shelves Distribution.

Doodle Publishing, *(978-0-9719518)* 2219 Tam-O-Shanter Ct., Carmel, IN 46032 USA Tel 317-538-6995
E-mail: adam10spro@aol.com.

Doodlebops *Imprint of* **Cookie Jar**

Dooley Bks., Ltd, *(978-0-9786605)* 53 W. Jackson No. 1240, CHICAGO, IL 60604 USA
Web site: http://www.Dooleybooks.com.

Doolittle Edutainment Corp., *(978-0-9793144)* 2445 Fifth Ave., Suite 440, San Diego, CA 92101 USA (SAN 853-0912)
Web site: http://www.doolittleedutainment.com
Dist(s): **AtlasBooks Distribution.**

Doorlight Pubns., *(978-0-9778372; 978-0-9838653)* 4 Central Ave., South Hadley, MA 01075 USA.

Doorposts, *(978-1-891206)* 5905 SW Lookingglass Dr., Gaston, OR 97119-9241 USA Tel 503-357-4749; Fax: 503-357-4909 Do not confuse with Doorposts, Lansdale, PA
E-mail: orders@doorposts.com
Web site: http://www.doorposts.com.

Dorcas Pubns., LLC, *(978-0-9769829)* 890 Woodland Ave., Corydon, IN 47112 USA Tel 812-738-4361; Fax: 812-738-2259
E-mail: wfwilson@aol.com
Web site: http://www.dorcaspublications.com.

Dorcas Publishing, *(978-0-9762375)* Div. of Heavenly Patchwork Charity Bks., Orders Addr.: 12101 N. MacArthur, Suite 137, Oklahoma City, OK 73162-1800 USA Tel 405-751-3885 (phone/fax)
E-mail: buckboardquilts@cox.net
Web site: http://www.heavenlypatchwork.com.

Dorchester Publishing Co., Inc., *(978-0-505; 978-0-8439; 978-1-4285)* Orders Addr.: 200 Madison Ave., Suite 2000, New York, NY 10016 USA (SAN 264-0090); P.O. Box 6640, Wayne, PA 19087 Toll Free: 800-481-9191
Dist(s): **MyiLibrary.**

Publisher Name Index

Dork Storm Pr., *(978-1-930964; 978-1-933288)* P.O. Box 45063, Madison, WI 53744 USA Fax: 608-225-1352
Web site: http://www.dorkstorm.com
Dist(s): **PSI (Publisher Services, Inc.).**

†Dorling Kindersley Publishing, Inc., *(978-0-7894; 978-1-56458; 978-1-879431; 978-0-7566; 978-1-4654)* Div. of Penguin Publishing Group, 375 Hudson St., 2nd Flr., New York, NY 10014 USA (SAN 253-0791) Tel 212-213-4800; Fax: 212-213-5240; Toll Free: 877-342-5357 (orders only); *Imprints:* Kids Play (Kids Play)
E-mail: Annemarie.Cancienne@dk.com; customer.service@dk.com
Web site: http://www.dk.com
Dist(s): **Continental Bk. Co., Inc.**
Ebsco Publishing
Follett School Solutions
Penguin Random Hse., LLC.
Penguin Publishing Group
Hale, Robert & Co., Inc.
Sunburst Communications, Inc.; *CIP.*

Dormouse Productions, Inc., *(978-1-889300)* 25 NE 99th St., Miami, FL 33138-2338 USA Tel 305-379-4990; Fax: 305-379-7990
E-mail: dmouse@juno.com.

Dorn Enterprises *See* **Susy Dorn Productions, LLC**

Dorothy, a publishing project, *(978-0-9844693; 978-0-9897607)* P.O. Box 300433, Saint Louis, MO 63130 USA
E-mail: editors@dorothyproject.com
Web site: http://www.dorothyproject.com
Dist(s): **SPD-Small Pr. Distribution.**

Dorothy Payne & Virginia Letourneau, *(978-0-9747823)* 300 E. 33rd St., Apt. 7C, New York, NY 10016 USA
Web site: http://www.cityislandclamdigger.com.

Dorrance Publishing Co., Inc., *(978-0-8059; 978-1-4349; 978-1-4809)* 701 Smithfield St. Third Flr., Pittsburgh, PA 15222 USA (SAN 201-3363) Tel 412-288-4543; Fax: 412-288-1786; Toll Free: 800-788-7654; 800-695-7599; *Imprints:* RoseDog Books (RoseDog Bks)
E-mail: rpiotrowski@dorrancepublishing.com; dorrordr@dorrancepublishing.com
Web site: http://www.dorrancepublishing.com; www.dorrancebookstore.com.

†Dorset Hse. Publishing, *(978-0-932633)* 3143 Broadway Suite 2b, New York, NY 10027 USA (SAN 687-794X) Tel 212-620-4053; Fax: 212-727-1044; Toll Free: 800-342-6657
E-mail: info@dorsethouse.com; littlewest@dorsethouse.com
Web site: http://www.dorsethouse.com; http://www.littlewestpress.com; *CIP.*

Dory Pr., *(978-0-9633240)* 13396 Wakefield Rd., Sedley, VA 23878 USA Tel 757-220-9206.

Doses of Reality, Inc., *(978-0-9754024)* 634 Ceape Ave, Oshkosh, WI 54901 USA Tel 920-573-9884
E-mail: dosesofreality@yahoo.com.

Dot Dot Bks., *(978-0-9670750)* 420 16th St., Bellingham, WA 98225 USA Tel 360-220-1686
E-mail: dana.rozier@gmail.com
Dist(s): **Independent Pubs. Group**
Small Pr. United.

Dothan Publishing *See* **Moriah Ministries**

Double B Pubns., *(978-0-929526)* 4123 N. Longview, Phoenix, AZ 85014 USA (SAN 249-6615) Tel 602-996-7129; Fax: 602-996-6928
E-mail: bfischerppg@aol.com.

Double Dagger Pr., *(978-0-9729293)* 256 Ridge Ave., Gettysburg, PA 17325-2404 USA (SAN 255-7517) Tel 717-334-5392
E-mail: mplank@doubledaggerpress.com
Web site: http://www.doubledaggerpress.com.

Double Edge Pr., *(978-0-9774452; 978-0-9819514; 978-1-938002)* Orders Addr.: 72 Ellview Rd., Scenery Hill, PA 15360 USA (SAN 257-5019) Tel 724-518-6737; *Imprints:* Hummingbird World Media (HummbirdWrld)
E-mail: cuttingedge@atlanticbb.net
Web site: http://www.doubleedgepress.com
Dist(s): **ebrary, Inc.**

Double R Publishing, LLC, *(978-0-9713381; 978-0-9718696; 978-0-9770534)* 7301 W. Flagler St., Miami, FL 33144 USA Tel 305-262-4240; Fax: 305-262-4115; Toll Free: 877-262-4240
E-mail: abcsbook@abcsbook.com
Web site: http://www.abcsbook.com
Dist(s): **ABC'S Bk. Supply, Inc.**

Double Roads *See* **Karenzo Media**

Doubleday *Imprint of* **Knopf Doubleday Publishing Group**

Doubleday *Imprint of* **Doubleday Religious Publishing Group, The**

Doubleday Bks. for Young Readers *Imprint of* **Random Hse. Children's Bks.**

Doubleday Canada, Ltd. (CAN) *(978-0-385; 978-0-7704)* *Dist. by* **Random.**

Doubleday Publishing *See* **Knopf Doubleday Publishing Group**

Doubleday Religious Publishing Group, The, Div. of Random Hse., Inc., Orders Addr.: 400 Hahn Rd., Westminster, MD 21157 USA Tel 410-848-1900; Toll Free: 800-726-0600 (customer service); 800-733-3000; Edit Addr.: 12265 Oracle Blvd., Suite 200, Colorado Springs, CO 80921 USA (SAN 299-4682) Tel 719-590-4999; Fax: 719-590-8977; Toll Free Fax: 800-294-5686; Toll Free: 800-603-7051; *Imprints:* WaterBrook Press (WaterB Pr); Multnomah (Mltnmah); Multnomah Fiction (Mult Fiction); Multnomah Kidz (Mult Kidz); Doubleday (Doublda) Do not confuse with WaterBrook Pr., Great Falls, VA
Web site: http://www.randomhouse.com/waterbrook
Dist(s): **Anchor Distributors**
MyiLibrary
Penguin Random Hse., LLC.
Random Hse., Inc.

DOUBLE-R BKS. *Imprint of* **Rodrigue & Sons Co./Double R Books Publishing**

DoubleStar, LLC, *(978-0-9742558)* 9672 Litzsinger Rd., Saint Louis, MO 63124-1494 USA
E-mail: doublestarllc@sbcglobal.net
Web site: http://www.cogno.com.

Douglas, Bettye Forum, Inc., The, *(978-0-9703183)* 6608 N. Western Ave., No. 327, Oklahoma City, OK 73116 USA Tel 405-528-1773; Fax: 405-842-7541; Toll Free: 800-354-0680
E-mail: bettye_douglas@excite.com
Web site: http://www.bettyedouglas.com.

Dougy Ctr., *(978-1-890534)* Orders Addr.: P.O. Box 86852, Portland, OR 97286 USA Tel 503-542-4833; Fax: 503-777-3097; Edit Addr.: 3909 SE 52nd Ave., Portland, OR 97206 USA
E-mail: kathleenr@dougy.org
Web site: http://www.dougy.org.

Doulos Christou Pr., *(978-0-9744796; 978-1-934406)* 57 N. Ruial St. Englewood Christian Church, Indianapolis, IN 46201-3330 USA
E-mail: douloschristoupress@yahoo.com
Web site: http://www.douloschristou.com.

Dove Books and Audio *Imprint of* **Phoenix Bks., Inc.**

Dove Publishing, Inc., *(978-0-9766578)* P.O. Box 310326, Atlanta, GA 31131 USA Do not confuse with companies with the same or similar name in Houston, TX, Decatur, GA, Forest heights, MD, Lake Konkonkma, NY
Web site: http://www.dovepub.com.

†Dover Pubns., Inc., *(978-0-486; 978-1-60660)* Div. of Courier Corporation, 31 E. Second St., Mineola, NY 11501 USA (SAN 201-338X) Tel 516-294-7000; Fax: 516-873-1401 (orders only); Toll Free: 800-223-3130 (orders only)
E-mail: rights@doverpublications.com
Web site: http://www.doverdirect.com; http://www.doverpublications.com
Dist(s): **Continental Bk. Co., Inc.**
INscribe Digital
MyiLibrary
Beeler, Thomas T. Pub.; *CIP.*

DoveTail Hse., Inc., *(978-0-9706244; 978-0-9772935; 978-0-9800099; 978-0-9862832; 978-1-943181)* P.O. Box 501995, San Diego, CA 92150 USA Tel 858-581-5954; Fax: 858-668-1771
E-mail: dovepub@san.rr.com.

Dovetail Publishing, *(978-0-9651284)* P.O. Box 19945, Kalamazoo, MI 49019 USA Tel 616-342-2900; Fax: 616-342-1012; Toll Free: 800-222-0070
E-mail: dovetail@mich.com
Web site: http://www.mich.com/~dovetail
Dist(s): **Independent Pubs. Group**
Quality Bks., Inc.

Down East Bks., *(978-0-89272; 978-0-924357)* Div. of Rowman & Littlefield Publishing Group, Inc., P.O. Box 679, Camden, ME 04843 USA (SAN 208-6301) Tel 207-594-9544; Fax: 207-594-0147; Toll Free: 800-766-1670 Wholesale orders; 800-685-7962 Retail orders
E-mail: pblanchard@downeast.com; tbregy@downeast.com
Web site: http://www.countrysportpress.com; http://www.downeastbooks.com
Dist(s): **Follett School Solutions**
MyiLibrary
National Bk. Network
TNT Media Group, Inc.
ebrary, Inc.

Down The Road Publishing, *(978-0-9754427)* 172 White Oak Dr., Batesville, IN 47006 USA (SAN 256-2227)
E-mail: timt@downtheroad.org
Web site: http://www.downtheroad.org.

Down The Shore Publishing Corp., *(978-0-945582; 978-0-9615208; 978-1-59322)* Orders Addr.: P.O. Box 100, West Creek, NJ 08092 USA Tel 609-812-5076; Fax: 609-812-5098; Edit Addr.: P.O. Box 100, West Creek, NJ 08092 USA (SAN 661-082X)
E-mail: info@down-the-shore.com; orders@down-the-shore.com; downshore@comcast.net
Web site: http://www.down-the-shore.com
Dist(s): **Partners Bk. Distributing, Inc.**
Sourcebooks, Inc.

Down-To-Earth-Bks., *(978-1-878115)* P.O. Box 488, Ashfield, MA 01330 USA Tel 413-628-0227
E-mail: maryskole@aol.com
Web site: http://www.spinninglobe.net.

Downtown Bookworks, *(978-1-935703; 978-1-941367)* 285 W. Broadway, Suite 600, New York, NY 10013 USA Tel 646-613-0707
Dist(s): **Simon & Schuster, Inc.**

Downtown Wetmore Pr., *(978-0-9795302)* Orders Addr.: 13451 Wetmore Rd., San Antonio, TX 78247 USA (SAN 853-7070) Tel 210-490-7222; Fax: 210-490-8222; Toll Free Fax: 877-490-8222; Toll Free: 877-490-7222; *Imprints:* CrumbGobbler Press (CrumbGobbler)
E-mail: downtownwetmore@earthlink.net; info@crumbgobbler.com
Web site: http://www.downtownwetmore.com.

Dr. Gazebo Publishing *See* **Snow In Sarasota Publishing**

Dr. Jay, LLC, *(978-0-9860063)* P.O. Box 422, Green Farms, CT 06838 USA
E-mail: yroehler@bookpublishing.com.

Dr. Joyce STARR Publishing, *(978-0-9792333; 978-0-9882394)* Orders Addr.: 20533 Biscayne Blvd., No. 509, Aventura, FL 33180 USA Tel 786-693-4223
E-mail: joyce.starr@gmail.com
Web site: http://drjoycestarr.com; http://starrpublications.com; http://starrpublishing.com.

Dr. Mark Stuart Berlin *See* **Berlin, Stuart**

Dr. Mary's Bks., *(978-0-9765453)* 180 90th Ave. SE, Kensal, ND 58455 USA Tel 701-435-2388
E-mail: dwayneerickson@agristar.net
Web site: http://www.shopnd.com.

Dragon Dog Pr., Inc., *(978-0-9770121)* P.O. Box 5399, Godfrey, IL 62035 USA Tel 618-467-0738
E-mail: ryucope@sbcglobal.net
Web site: http://www.dragondogpress.com.

Dragon Lair Bks., *(978-0-615-43560-2; 978-0-615-47047-4; 978-0-615-48683-3; 978-0-615-57942-9; 978-0-615-58244-3)* 201 Mono Ln., Avenal, CA 93204 USA Tel 559-386-4211
E-mail: TedT1025B@gmail.com
Dist(s): **CreateSpace Independent Publishing Platform**
Dummy Record Do Not USE!!!!.

Dragon Tree Bks., *(978-0-9884024; 978-0-9916200; 978-0-9862641; 978-0-9963081)* 1620 SW 5th Ave., Pompano Beach, FL 33060 USA Tel 954-788-4775
E-mail: editors@editingforauthors.com
Web site: http://editingforauthors.com.

Dragoneagle Pr., *(978-0-9787465)* Orders Addr.: P.O. Box Box 30856, Bethesda, MD 20824 USA Tel 732-861-0449; Fax: 301-897-2786
E-mail: info@dragoneagle.com
Web site: http://www.dragoneagle.com.

Dragonfairy Pr. *Imprint of* **Dragonfairy Pr. LLC**

Dragonfairy Pr. LLC, *(978-0-9850230; 978-1-939452)* 4355 Cobb Pkwy, Ste J116, Atlanta, GA 30339 USA Tel 404-955-8150; *Imprints:* Dragonfairy Press (Dragfairy)
E-mail: info@dragonfairypress.com
Web site: http://www.dragonfairypress.com
Dist(s): **Independent Pubs. Group**
MyiLibrary
Small Pr. United.

Dragonfeather Bks. *Imprint of* **Bedazzled Ink Publishing Co.**

Dragonfly Bks. *Imprint of* **Random Hse. Children's Bks.**

Dragonfly Entertainment, *(978-0-9745213)* 97 Chartwell Ct., Rochester, NY 14618-5376 USA; *Imprints:* Dragonfly Flipz (Dragonfly Flipz)
E-mail: dfly@earthlink.net
Web site: http://www.dragonflyent.net.

Dragonfly Flipz *Imprint of* **Dragonfly Entertainment**

Dragonfly Ministries, *(978-0-9788289)* 295 Noble Cir., Vernon Hills, IL 60061-2927 USA
E-mail: info@dragonflyministries.com
Web site: http://www.dragonflyministries.com.

Dragonfly Publishing, Inc., *(978-0-9710473; 978-0-9755888; 978-0-9765786; 978-0-9778651; 978-0-9787421; 978-0-9794660; 978-0-9797574; 978-0-9801376; 978-0-9817049; 978-0-9819080; 978-0-9840980; 978-1-936381; 978-1-941278)* 2440 Twin Ridge Dr., Edmond, OK 73034-1943 USA Do not confuse with companies with the same or similar name in Mount Enterprise, TX , Whethersfield, CT , San Antonio, TX ,
Web site: http://www.dragonflypubs.com
Dist(s): **Smashwords.**

Dragonflyer Pr., *(978-0-944933)* Div. of American Water Gardens, Inc., 2460 N. Euclid Ave., Upland, CA 91784-1184 USA (SAN 245-7660) Toll Free: 800-558-0676
E-mail: info@dragonflyerpress.com; cuber@uberadv.com
Web site: http://www.vnwg.com; http://www.dragonflyerpress.com
Dist(s): **Midpoint Trade Bks., Inc.**

Dragonhawk Publishing, *(978-1-888767)* Div. of Life Magic Enterprises, Inc., P.O. Box 1316, Jackson, TN 38302 USA Tel 901-987-3334; Fax: 901-987-2484
Dist(s): **Austin & Company, Inc.**
New Leaf Distributing Co., Inc.

Dragonon, Inc., *(978-0-9763398)* 9378 Mason Montgomery Rd., Suite 108, Mason, OH 45040 USA (SAN 256-3398) Tel 513-227-9224
E-mail: dmeyer@dragonon.com.

Dragonseed Pr., *(978-0-9678115)* Orders Addr.: 19020 Brookfield Dr., Chagrin Falls, OH 44023 USA
E-mail: dragonseedpress@aol.com
Web site: http://www.m-c-ryan.com.

DragonWing Bks., *(978-0-9761444)* 9107 Brunners Run Ct., Columbia, MD 21045 USA Tel 301-509-5451
E-mail: liz@dragonwingbooks.com
Web site: http://www.dragonwingbooks.com.

Drake, Edwin, *(978-0-9743405)* R.R. 5, Box 5417, Saylorsburg, PA 18353 USA Tel 570-992-2914
E-mail: edrakee@enter.net.

Drake Feltham Publishing, *(978-0-578-10548-2)* 22113 Palos Verdes Blvd., Torrance, CA 90503 USA
Dist(s): **Outskirts Pr., Inc.**

Drake Univ., Anderson Gallery, *(978-0-9749296)* 25th St. & Carpenter Ave., Des Moines, IA 50311 USA Tel 515-271-1994; Fax: 515-271-2558
E-mail: cira.pascual-marquina@drake.edu
Web site: http://www.drake.edu/andersongallery.

Drama Publishers *See* **Quite Specific Media Group, Ltd.**

Drama Tree Pr., *(978-0-9741670; 978-0-9821852)* 150 Iota Ct., Madison, WI 53706 USA
E-mail: dramatree@mail.com
Web site: http://www.dramatree.com.

Dramaline Pubns., *(978-0-940669; 978-0-9611792)* 36851 Palm View Rd., Rancho Mirage, CA 92270-2417 USA (SAN 285-239X) Tel 760-770-6076; Fax: 760-770-4507
E-mail: drama.line@verizon.net
Web site: http://www.dramaline.com
Dist(s): **Distributors, The.**

DramaQueen, L.L.C., *(978-0-9766045; 978-1-933809; 978-1-60331)* Orders Addr.: P.O. Box 2626, Stafford, TX 77497 USA Fax: 281-498-4723; Toll Free: 800-883-1518 (ext. 2)
E-mail: orders@onedramaqueen.com; info@onedramaqueen.com
Web site: http://www.onedramaqueen.com
Dist(s): **AAA Anime Distribution.**

Dramatic Improvements Publishing, *(978-0-9768251)* 226 Perrine Ave., Auburn, NY 13021-1715 USA
E-mail: twoods@dramaimp.com
Web site: http://www.dramaimp.com.

Dramatic Publishing Co., *(978-0-87129; 978-1-58342; 978-1-61959)* Orders Addr.: 311 Washington St., Woodstock, IL 60098 USA (SAN 201-5676) Tel 815-338-7170; Fax: 815-338-8981; Toll Free Fax: 800-334-5302; Toll Free: 800-448-7469
E-mail: plays@dramaticpublishing.com
Web site: http://www.dramaticpublishing.com.

Dramatists Play Service, Inc., *(978-0-8222)* 440 Park Ave., S., New York, NY 10016 USA (SAN 207-5717) Tel 212-683-8960; Fax: 212-213-1539
E-mail: postmaster@dramatists.com
Web site: http://www.dramatists.com.

Drane, John Wanzer, *(978-0-578-10633-5)* 5 Derry Dr., Horse Shoe, NC 28742 USA.

Draper Publishing, *(978-0-9913342)* 1701 Willow Oak Ln., Dalton, GA 30721 USA Tel 706-260-5496
E-mail: duraniemaria39@yahoo.com
Web site: mariarochelle.com.

Draw Three Lines Publishing, *(978-0-9749418; 978-0-9826202)* P.O. Box 1522, Hillsboro, OR 97123 USA Tel 503-648-9905
E-mail: hastings@draw3lines.com
Web site: http://www.draw3lines.com.

Drawn & Quarterly Pubns. (CAN) *(978-0-9696701; 978-1-896597; 978-1-894937; 978-1-897299; 978-1-77046)* *Dist. by* **Macmillan.**

DrDryland.Com, LLC, *(978-0-9766490)* P.O. Box 1281, Ashland, OR 97520 USA
Web site: http://www.DrDryland.Com.

Dream A World *Imprint of* **BrassHeart Music**

Dream Bee Pubns., *(978-0-9661572)* 3325 C 1/2 Rd., Palisade, CO 81526 USA Tel 970-434-7501
E-mail: bee@dreambee.com
Web site: http://www.dreambee.com
Dist(s): **Bks. West**
Partners/West Book Distributors.

Dream Big Toy Co., *(978-1-940731)* 249 Merton Ave., Alen Ellyn, IL 60137 USA Tel 877-351-1031; *Imprints:* Go! Go! Sports Girls (GoGoSports)
E-mail: jnorgaard@dreambigtoycompany.com
Dist(s): **Independent Pubs. Group**
MyiLibrary.

Dream Character, Inc., *(978-0-9765543; 978-0-9785418)* Orders Addr.: 21143 Hawthorne Blvd. # 453, Torrance, CA 90503 USA; Edit Addr.: 2049 Pacific Coast Hwy. #453, Torrance, CA 90503 USA (SAN 256-4793) Tel 310-530-8015
E-mail: info@dreamcharacter.com
Web site: http://www.dreamcharacter.com
Dist(s): **Independent Pubs. Group.**

Dream Creek Pr., *(978-0-9771515)* 401 Taylor St., Ashland, OR 97520 USA
E-mail: bethart@mind.net
Web site: http://www.bbcreativecards.com.

Dream Dance Pubns., *(978-0-9769192)* P.O. Box 902, Redmond, WA 98073 USA Tel 425-898-9240
E-mail: briggs870@msn.com.

Dream Factory Bks., *(978-0-9701195)* Orders Addr.: P.O. Box 874, Enumclaw, WA 98022 USA (SAN 253-2611) Tel 360-663-0508; Fax: 360-825-7952; Toll Free Fax: 877-377-7030; Edit Addr.: 58402 114th St., E., Enumclaw, WA 98022-7305 USA
E-mail: sensei@earthlink.net
Web site: http://dreamfactorybooks.com
Dist(s): **Independent Pubs. Group.**

Dream, Feral LLC, *(978-0-9835970)* 774 Mays Blvd. Ste 10-473, Incline Village, NV 89451 USA Tel 415-555-1212
E-mail: susan@feraldream.com.

Dream House Pr., *(978-0-9671555)* 2714 Ophelia Ct., San Jose, CA 95122 USA Tel 408-274-4574; Fax: 408-274-0786; Toll Free: 877-274-4574
E-mail: mr_art@prodigy.net; dreamhousepress@yahoo.com
Dist(s): **Brodart Co.**
Midwest Library Service
Milligan News Co., Inc.
Partners/West Book Distributors
Yankee Bk. Peddler, Inc.

Dream Image Pr., LLC, *(978-0-9744812)* P.O. Box 454, Northbrook, IL 60065-0454 USA Tel 847-480-8998
E-mail: drashley@dreamimagepress.com
Dist(s): **Follett School Solutions.**

Dream On Pubns., *(978-0-9761151)* Orders Addr.: P.O. Box 190265, Fort Lauderdale, FL 33319 USA (SAN 256-2057)
E-mail: books@dreamonpublications.com.

Dream Pubns., I, Inc., *(978-0-9763596)* 111 Primrose Ln., Wyomissing, PA 19610 USA
E-mail: sukumar@idreampublications.com
Web site: http://www.idreampublications.com.

Dream Ridge Pr., *(978-0-9792084)* P.O. Box 625, Aurelia, IA 51005 USA Tel 712-660-8409
E-mail: rainbowfarm2006@yahoo.com; tpeiffer67@yahoo.com
Web site: http://www.lulu.com/trishacp; http://www.rainbowfarmbooks.com; http://www.authorsden.com/trishacp
Dist(s): **Lulu Enterprises Inc.**

Dream Scape Publishing, LLC, *(978-0-9795519; 978-0-615-13650-9)* 805 Dunwood Ct., Chesapeake, VA 23322 USA Tel 757-717-2734
E-mail: dreamscape2@cox.net.

Dream Secret Inc., The, *(978-0-615-18103-5)* P.O. Box 2012, Sandy, UT 84091 USA Tel 801-518-7770
E-mail: lscread@yahoo.com.

Dream Ship Publishing Co., *(978-0-9729155)* 1512 River Rock Trace, Woodstock, GA 30188 USA
E-mail: info@dreamshipbooks.com.

Dream Star Productions, *(978-0-9772027)* Orbisson Sq. 4306 S. Peoria Ave., Ste 705, Tulsa, OK 74105-3922 USA Tel 918-630-7580; Fax: 918-749-1717
Web site: http://www.kbaustin.com.

Dream Weaver Ministries, Inc., *(978-0-9800259)* Pmb#123 1631 Rock Springs Rd., Apopka, FL 32712-2229 USA (SAN 855-0239) Toll Free: 888-397-7772.

Dream Workshop Publishing Co., LLC, The, *(978-0-9786940)* Orders Addr.: 4421 Bachelor Creek Rd., Asheboro, NC 27205 USA (SAN 851-3635) Tel 336-879-8108
E-mail: info@dreamworkshoppub.com; publisher@dreamworkshoppub.com
Web site: http://www.dreamworkshoppub.com; http://www.spenceraliens.com.

Dream Yard Pr., *(978-0-615-72969-5)* 1085 Washington Ave., Bronx, NY 10456 USA Tel 718-588-8007; Fax: 718-588-8310
E-mail: neilwald@aol.com
Web site: dreamyard.com; neilwaldman.com.

Dream&Achieve Bks., *(978-0-9859298)* 2609 W. 84th Pl., Merrillville, IN 46410 USA Tel 219-218-5145
Web site: www.weenzcat.com.

Dreamcatcher Bks., *(978-0-9848484)* 892 Jensen Ln., Windsor, CA 95492 USA Tel 707-292-0272 Do not confuse with Dreamcatcher Books in Las Vegas, NM
E-mail: alvarezgang@yahoo.com
Web site: http://thepetwasher.com/.

Dream-Catcher Pubns., *(978-0-9752878)* 22265 Petersburg, Eastpointe, MI 48021 USA.

DreamDog Pr., *(978-0-9666199)* 2308 Mount Vernon Ave., Alexandria, VA 22301-1328 USA
E-mail: rainey@dreamdog.com
Web site: http://www.dreamdog.com.

DreamerLand, *(978-0-9763250)* Orders Addr.: 1018 3rd St., Hermosa Beach, CA 90254 USA Tel 310-406-9371
E-mail: christo@dreamerland.com; info@dreamerland.com
Web site: http://www.Dreamerland.com
Dist(s): **Diamond Bk. Distributors.**

DreamHse. Publishing Inc.,
Dist(s): **AtlasBooks Distribution.**

Dreaming Dragon Publishing LLC, *(978-0-615-47591-2; 978-0-615-47593-6; 978-0-615-55436-5; 978-0-615-56676-4; 978-0-615-56677-1; 978-0-615-72878-0)* 4248 A St SE # 413, Auburn, WA 98002 USA Tel 253-333-6847
E-mail: info@dreamingdragonpublishing.com
Dist(s): **CreateSpace Independent Publishing Platform**
Dummy Record Do Not USE!!!!.

DreamLand Mediaworks LLC, *(978-0-9884657)* 3712 Lake Catherine Dr., Harvey, LA 70058 USA Tel 504-756-5589; Fax: 504-366-2606
E-mail: MavrikLdy@aol.com.

Dreams 2 Wings LLC, *(978-0-9797781)* 100 N. 72nd Ave., Wausau, WI 54401 USA Tel 715-842-1133; Fax: 715-842-1155
E-mail: fred@lanepatents.com.

Dreams Due Media Group, Inc., *(978-0-9789202)* P.O. Box 1018, Firestone, CO 80520 USA Tel 303-241-3155 Toll Free: 877-462-1710
Web site: http://www.dreamsdue.com.

Dreamscape, LLC *See* **Dreamscape Media, LLC**

Dreamscape Media, LLC, *(978-0-9745563; 978-0-9747118; 978-0-9760996; 978-0-9761981; 978-0-9771510; 978-0-9772338; 978-0-9774680; 978-0-9776262; 978-0-9777098; 978-1-933938; 978-1-61120; 978-1-62406; 978-1-62923; 978-1-63379; 978-1-68141; 978-1-68262; 978-1-5200)* Orders Addr.: 6940 Hall St., Holland, OH 43538 USA Tel 419-867-6965
E-mail: molah@dreamscapeab.com
Web site: http://www.dreamscapeab.com
Dist(s): **Findaway World, LLC**
Follett School Solutions
Ingram Pub. Services.

Dreamspinner Pr., *(978-0-9795048; 978-0-9801018; 978-0-9815084; 978-0-9817372; 978-1-935192; 978-1-61581; 978-1-61372; 978-1-62380; 978-1-62798; 978-1-63216; 978-1-63476; 978-1-63477)* 5032 Capital Cir. SW Suite 2, PMB #279, Tallahassee, FL 32305-7886 USA (SAN 915-5562); *Imprints:* Harmony Ink Press (HarmonyInk)
E-mail: contact@dreamspinnerpress.com
Web site: http://www.dreamspinnerpress.com.

Dreamstreet Studios, Inc. (A Div. of DSMV Industries, Inc.), *(978-0-9892295)* 1800 Grand Ave., Nashville, TN 37212 USA Tel 615-321-9029
E-mail: songmerch@aol.com.

Dreamtime Publishing, *(978-0-9741726)* P.O. Box 834, Tahlequah, OK 74465 USA Tel 918-456-8639.

Dreistadt, Jessica R., *(978-0-578-02239-0)* 1700 Sullivan Trail, No. 311, Easton, PA 18040 USA
Dist(s): **Lulu Enterprises Inc.**

Dressler, Avi, *(978-0-9744309)* 35 Old Brick Rd., East Hills, NY 11577-1816 USA.

Dressler, Craig, *(978-0-9778247)* 5341 NE Webster Ct., Portland, OR 97218 USA Tel 503-281-4214.

Driftwood Pr., *(978-0-9638803)* Orders Addr.: P.O. Box 284, Yachats, OR 97498 USA; Edit Addr.: 62 Gender Dr., Yachats, OR 97498 USA Tel 541-547-3484
E-mail: njguni@clubinernet.fr.

Drinian Pr., LLC, *(978-0-9785165; 978-0-9820609; 978-0-9833069; 978-1-941929)* Orders Addr.: P.O. Box 63, Huron, OH 44839 USA
E-mail: drinianpress@frontier.com
Web site: http://drinianpress.com; http://smithwrite.net.

Drinking Gourd Pr., *(978-0-578-13425-3; 978-0-578-13426-0)* 414 Jefferson Ave., Apt. 1, Brooklyn, NY 11221 USA.

Driving Vision, Inc., *(978-0-9766329)* 2117 S. Ventura Dr., Tempe, AZ 85282 USA
Web site: http://www.drivingvision.com.

DrMaster Pubns. Inc., *(978-1-59796)* 48531 Warm Springs Blvd., Suite 408, Fremont, CA 94539 USA Tel 510-687-1388 (phone/fax)
Web site: http://www.drmasterpublications.com
Dist(s): **Diamond Comic Distributors, Inc.**
Diamond Bk. Distributors.

Droemersche Verlagsanstalt Th. Knaur Nachf. - GmbH & Co. (DEU) *(978-3-426)* *Dist. by* **Distribks Inc.**

Drollery Pr., *(978-0-940920)* 1524 Benton St., Alameda, CA 94501-2420 USA (SAN 223-1808) Tel 510-521-4087.

DRT Pr., *(978-1-933084)* Orders Addr.: P.O. Box 427, Pittsboro, NC 27312 USA Tel 919-360-7073; Fax: 866-562-5040; Edit Addr.: 395 Bill Thomas Rd., Moncure, NC 27559 USA
E-mail: editorial@drtpress.com
Web site: http://www.drtpress.com
Dist(s): **BWI**
Bk. Hse., The
Brodart Co.
Follett School Solutions
Quality Bks., Inc.

Drummond Publishing Group, The, *(978-0-9755080; 978-1-59763)* 4 Collins Ave., Plymouth, MA 02360-4809 USA Do not confuse with Rec#s 786442, 791375, 1194043
E-mail: f_allen@drummondpub.com
Web site: http://www.drummondpub.com.

Drumstick Media, *(978-0-9764791)* Div. of Old Goats, Inc., 5805 Hwy. 93 S., Whitefish, MT 59937 USA Tel 406-862-8938; Fax: 406-862-8936; Toll Free: 800-404-8279
E-mail: robert@drumstickmedia.com; james@drumstickmedia.com
Web site: http://www.baxterowengraham.com; http://www.drumstickmedia.com.

Drunk Duck Comics, *(978-0-9748960)* P.O. Box 869, Pittston, PA 18640 USA
E-mail: rubbermallet@verizon.net; arrkelaan@hotmail.com
Web site: http://www.drunkduck.com.

Dry, Paul Bks., Inc., *(978-0-9664913; 978-0-9679675; 978-1-58988)* 1616 Walnut St. Ste. 808, Philadelphia, PA 19103-5308 USA
E-mail: pdb@pauldrybooks.com
Web site: http://www.pauldrybooks.com
Dist(s): **Consortium Bk. Sales & Distribution**
Independent Pubs. Group.

Dryad Pr., *(978-0-931848; 978-1-928755)* P.O. Box 11233, Takoma Park, MD 20913 USA (SAN 206-197X) Tel 301-891-3729
E-mail: dryadpress@yahoo.com
Web site: http://www.dryadpress.com
Dist(s): **SPD-Small Pr. Distribution.**

Dryden Publishing, *(978-0-9644370; 978-1-929204)* P.O. Box 482, Dryden, WA 98821-0482 USA
E-mail: dryden@csiconnect.com.

Dryland, David *See* **DrDryland.Com, LLC**

DSA Publishing & Design, Inc., *(978-0-9774451; 978-0-9818229; 978-0-9848057)* 6900 Edgewater Dr., Mckinney, TX 75070 USA
Web site: http://www.dsapubs.com
Dist(s): **AtlasBooks Distribution**
Chicago Distribution Ctr.

DTaylor Bks., *(978-0-615-36081-2)* 415 Armour Dr., Apt. 12204, Atlanta, GA 30324 USA Tel 404-838-9678.

DTJ, LLC, *(978-0-9765731)* P.O. Box 635, Sequim, WA 98382 USA.

D-Tower Pubns., *(978-0-9770386)* 8028 Pine St., Ethel, LA 70730-3853 USA Tel 225-335-0802
E-mail: swbloopers@yahoo.com.

Dube, Tory, *(978-0-9886193)* 3168 41st St. No. 1f, Astoria, NY 11103 USA Tel 603-781-1440
E-mail: torydube@gmail.com
Web site: www.lovelythankyou.com.

Dubois, Ricardo S., *(978-0-615-15411-4; 978-0-615-15412-1; 978-0-615-15413-8; 978-0-615-16958-3; 978-0-615-17232-3; 978-0-615-18220-9; 978-0-615-19724-1)* 16015 Creekround Dr., Praireville, LA 70769 USA Tel 225-802-6001
E-mail: craftycajun@yahoo.com
Dist(s): **Lulu Enterprises Inc.**

Duckett, Brenda, *(978-0-615-17289-7)* 27 Millswood Dr., Clarkville, TN 37042 USA Tel 931-906-8649
E-mail: bduckett1@bellsouth.net
Dist(s): **Lulu Enterprises Inc.**

Duckpond Publishing, Inc., *(978-0-9720350)* 130 Hillside Ln., Roswell, GA 30076 USA Tel 770-649-9947; Fax: 770-594-8058
E-mail: theducks@duckpondpublishing.com
Web site: http://www.duckpondpublishing.com.

Dude Publishing *Imprint of* **National Professional Resources, Inc.**

Dudek, Mike, *(978-0-9740380; 978-0-9968182)* 505 Duwell St., Johnston, PA 15906 USA Tel 814-536-1500; Fax: 814-536-8952
E-mail: mike@dudekins.com; jetset15906@yahoo.com
Web site: www.rascaljokes.com.

Dudley, Joshua Patrick, *(978-0-615-16396-3; 978-0-615-18871-3)* 4 Heritage Village Dr., Unit 102, Nashua, NH 03062 USA Tel 603-459-9687
E-mail: admin@joshuapatrickdudley.com; lostinozbook@yahoo.com
Web site: http://www.ostinozbook.com; http://www.lostinozbook.com
Dist(s): **Lulu Enterprises Inc.**

DUENDE Bks., *(978-0-9777973; 978-0-615-14984-4; 978-0-615-15099-4)* Div. of DeCo Communications, 13900 Fiji Way, Apt. 306, Marina del Rey, CA 90292 USA Tel 310-486-0983
E-mail: denizr@verizon.net
Web site: http://www.duendebooks.blogspot.com
Dist(s): **Lulu Enterprises Inc.**

†Dufour Editions, Inc., *(978-0-8023)* Orders Addr.: P.O. Box 7, Chester Springs, PA 19425-0007 USA (SAN 201-341X) Tel 610-458-5005; Fax: 610-458-7103; Toll Free: 800-869-5677
E-mail: info@dufoureditions.com
Web site: http://www.dufoureditions.com; *CIP.*

Duke Publishing & Software Corp., *(978-0-9745406)* P.O. Box 3429, Los Altos, CA 94024 USA Tel 408-245-3853; Fax: 408-245-9289
E-mail: info@aboutthekids.org
Web site: http://www.aboutthekids.org.

†Duke Univ. Pr., *(978-0-8223; 978-1-4780)* P.O. Box 90660, Durham, NC 27708-0660 USA (SAN 201-3436) Tel 919-687-3600; Fax: 919-688-4574; 905 W. Main S., Ste.18B, Durham, NC 27701 Tel 919-687-3600; Fax: 919-688-4574; Toll Free: 888-651-0122
E-mail: orders@dukepress.edu; subscriptions@dukepress.edu; hlw@dukeupress.edu
Web site: http://www.dukeupress.edu
Dist(s): **MyiLibrary**
ebrary, Inc.; *CIP.*

Dukes World, Inc., *(978-0-9664506)* P.O. Box 85, Yonkers, NY 10704 USA Tel 917-403-7661
E-mail: dukesworldinc@aol.com
Web site: http://www.chillstreetgang.com.

Dulany, Joseph P., *(978-0-9708830)* 6200 Oregon Ave NW Apt. 236, Washington, DC 20015-1529 USA
E-mail: josephdulany@msn.com
Web site: http://www.onceasoldier.com.

Duling Designs, *(978-0-9743445)* P.O. Box 1996, Marco Island, FL 34146-1996 USA
E-mail: jsduling87@aol.com.

Dume Publishing *See* **Corman Productions**

Dunamis Development, *(978-0-9767066)* 3972-J Barranca Pkwy., Suite 115, Irvine, CA 92606 USA Tel 949-263-0063.

Dundurn (CAN) *(978-0-88762; 978-0-88882; 978-0-88924; 978-0-919028; 978-0-919670; 978-0-9690454; 978-1-55002; 978-1-55488; 978-1-4597; 978-1-77070)* *Dist. by* **IngramPubServ.**

Dunlop, Edward *See* **Cross & Crown Publishing**

Dunn, Hunter, *(978-0-9761732)* 410 Old Spring Rd., Danville, VA 24540-5206 USA.

Dunn, Michael *See* **Big Secret, The**

Dunne, Thomas Bks. *Imprint of* **St. Martin's Pr.**

Dunton Publishing, *(978-0-615-55848-6; 978-0-615-56429-6; 978-0-615-76368-2; 978-0-615-76615-7; 978-0-692-48457-9; 978-0-692-48492-0; 978-0-692-54319-1)* P.O. Box 4, New York, NY 10023 USA Tel 212-799-7402
Web site: duntonpublishing.com
Dist(s): **CreateSpace Independent Publishing Platform.**

Duo Pr. Llc (US) *Imprint of* **Duo Pr. LLC**

Duo Pr. LLC, *(978-0-9796213; 978-0-9825295; 978-0-9838121; 978-1-938093)* 2257 Rogene Dr. T2, Baltimore, MD 21209 USA; *Imprints:* Duo Press Llc (US) (DUO PRESS LLC)
E-mail: info@duopressbooks.com
Web site: http://www.duopressbooks.com
Dist(s): **Legato Pubs. Group**
MyiLibrary
Perseus-PGW
ebrary, Inc.

Duplicates Printing, *(978-0-9749953)* Orders Addr.: P.O. Box 2398, Pawleys Island, SC 29585 USA Tel 843-237-3998; Edit Addr.: 14329 Ocean Hwy. Unit 115, Pawleys Isl, SC 29585-4816 USA
E-mail: slingshot@sc.rr.com.

Dupuis North Publishing, *(978-0-9749199)* 76 N. Church St., Clayton, GA 30525 USA Tel 828-524-9520; Fax: 828-349-1945.

Duracell & the National Ctr. for Missing & Exploited Children (NCMEC), *(978-0-9795307)* 415 Nadison Ave., New York, NY 10018 USA Tel 212-613-4904.

duran, oscar, *(978-0-615-72225-2; 978-0-9886109)* 6204 sw 18th St, Miramar, FL 33023 USA Tel 954-986-4082; Fax: 954-986-4082
Dist(s): **CreateSpace Independent Publishing Platform.**

Durban House Press, Incorporated *See* **Fireside Pr., Inc.**

Durland Alternatives Library, *(978-0-9740184)* 127 Anabel Taylor Hall, Ithaca, NY 14853-1001 USA Tel 607-255-6486; Fax: 607-255-9985
E-mail: alt-lib@cornell.edu
Web site: http://www.alternativeslibrary.org.

Durst, Sanford J., *(978-0-915262; 978-0-942666; 978-1-886720)* 106 Woodcleft Ave., Freeport, NY 11520 USA (SAN 211-6987) Tel 516-867-3333; Fax: 516-867-3397
E-mail: sjdbooks@verizon.net.

Dust Bunny Games LLC, *(978-0-9747833)* Orders Addr.: 3744 Mistflower Ln., Naperville, IL 60564-5921 USA Tel 630-244-0335; Fax: 630-922-6995; Edit Addr.: 3744 Mistflower Ln., Naperville, IL 60564-5921 USA
E-mail: info@dustbunnygames.com
Web site: http://www.dustbunnygames.com.

Duthaluru, Vidhya, *(978-0-9797657)* 247 Levinberg Ln., Wayne, NJ 07470 USA
Dist(s): **AtlasBooks Distribution.**

Dutton Adult *Imprint of* **Penguin Publishing Group**

Dutton Juvenile *Imprint of* **Penguin Publishing Group**

Duval Publishing, *(978-0-9745637)* Orders Addr.: P.O. Box 4255, Key West, FL 33041 USA Toll Free: 800-355-8562; Edit Addr.: 3717 Eagle Ave., Key West, FL 33040 USA
Web site: http://www.southerncoastaldesigns.com.

DVTVFilm, *(978-0-9678094)* 60 N. Main St. Apt. 209, Natick, MA 01760-3455 USA
E-mail: todd@dvtvfilm.com; info@themonkeykingsdaughter.com; todd@themonkeykingsdaughter.com
Web site: http://www.dvtvfilm.com; http://www.themonkeykingsdaughter.com.

Dwitt Publishing, *(978-0-9741352)* 9249 17th St SE, Saint Cloud, MN 56304-9709 USA
E-mail: dickawit@aol.com
Web site: http://www.dwittpublishing.com.

Dykema Engineering, Incorporated *See* **Dykema Publishing Co.**

Dykema, Marjorie *See* **One Coin Publishing, LLC**

Dykema Publishing Co., *(978-0-9660705; 978-0-9701538)* Div. of Dykema Engineering, Inc., 3264 W. Normandy Ave., Roseburg, OR 97470 USA Tel 541-957-0259; Fax: 541-677-7146
E-mail: odykema@mcsi.net
Web site: http://www.oregonwriters.com.

Dykes, William R. III, *(978-0-9740987)* 317 Luchase Rd., Linden, VA 22642 USA.

Dynagraphix *Imprint of* **Elliott, Jane**

Dynamic Forces, Inc., *(978-0-9749638; 978-1-933305; 978-1-60690)* 155 E. 9th Ave. Suite B, Runnemede, NJ 08078-1158 USA; *Imprints:* Dynamite Entertainment (Dyna Enter)
Web site: http://www.dynamicforces.com
Dist(s): **Diamond Comic Distributors, Inc.**
Diamond Bk. Distributors.

Dynamic Publishing Co., Inc., *(978-0-9656808)* Orders Addr.: P.O. Box 120, Calumet City, IL 60409 USA Tel 708-868-0512; Fax: 708-868-0549; Toll Free: 800-884-1840 Do not confuse with Dynamic Publishing, Sugar Land, TX,
E-mail: dpc123@ymail.com
Web site: http://www.DynamicPublishingCompany.com.

Dynamite Entertainment *Imprint of* **Dynamic Forces, Inc.**

DynaStudy, Inc., *(978-0-9776270; 978-0-9777909; 978-1-933854; 978-1-935005)* 1401 Broadway St. Suite 100, Marble Falls, TX 78654 USA
E-mail: info@dynastudy.com
Web site: http://dynanotes.com.

Dynasty Publishing, Inc., *(978-0-9790444; 978-0-9793490)* P.O. Box 11997, Kansas City, MO 64138-0997 USA Do not confuse with Dynasty Publishing in Honolulu, HI
E-mail: info@dynastypublishinginc.com
Web site: http://www.dynastypublishinginc.com.

DZ Publishing, LLC, *(978-0-9753660; 978-0-9889975)* 7360 Lincoln Dr., #2, Scottsdale, AZ 85258 USA Tel 949-644-4433
E-mail: szipp22@gmail.com
Web site: http://www.mycollegesuccess.com.

E & D Bks., Ltd., *(978-0-9794413)* P.O. Box 211, Ruby, NY 12475 USA (SAN 853-4314)
E-mail: info@buddyboobysbirthmark.com
Web site: http://www.buddyboobysbirthmark.com
Dist(s): **Beekman Bks., Inc.**

E & E Publishing, *(978-0-9719898; 978-0-9748933; 978-0-9791606; 978-0-9831499)* P.O. Box 3346, Omaha, NE 68107 USA Tel 415-331-4025 Do not confuse with E & E Publishing, Junction City, OR
E-mail: eandegroup@eandegroup.com; EandEGroup@hotmail.com.

E & H Publishing Co., Inc., *(978-0-9717295)* P.O. Box 4, Burkeville, VA 23922 USA
E-mail: greanes@earthlink.net.

EBP Latin America Group, Inc., *(978-1-56409)* 175 E. Delaware Pl. Apt. 8806, Chicago, IL 60611-7753 USA.

E B S C O Industries, Inc., *(978-0-913956; 978-1-888751)* Orders Addr.: P.O. Box 1943, Birmingham, AL 35201-1943 USA (SAN 201-3584) Tel 205-991-6600; Fax: 205-995-1636; Toll Free: 800-826-3024; Edit Addr.: 5724 Hwy. 280 E., Birmingham, AL 35242 USA
Web site: http://www.ebsco.com.

ECO Herpetological Pub. & Dist., *(978-0-9713197; 978-0-9767334; 978-0-9788979; 978-0-9832789; 978-0-9852936; 978-1-938850)* 4 Rattlesnake Canyon Rd., Rodeo, NM 88056 USA Tel 575-557-5757; Fax: 575-557-7575
E-mail: ecoorders@hotmail.com
Web site: http://www.reptileshirts.com
Dist(s): **BookBaby**
Serpent's Tale Natural History Bk. Distributors, Inc.
T-Rex Products.

EECI, Inc., *(978-0-9649379; 978-0-9722686; 978-1-933193)* 8055 W. Manchester Ave., 1st Flr., Playa Del Rey, CA 90293 USA
E-mail: rwoo@eecinternational.com.

E. F. S. Online Publishing, *(978-0-9701344)* Div. of E. F. S. Enterprises, Inc., 2844 Eighth Ave., Suite 6-E, New York, NY 10039 USA Tel 212-283-8899; Fax: 212-283-6280
E-mail: efsenterprises@hotmail.com
Web site: http://www.efs-enterprises.com.

E Innovative Ideas, *(978-0-9799540)* 800 SE 4th St., Suite 501, Fort Lauderdale, FL 33301 USA Tel 954-527-1070
E-mail: einnovate@aol.com.

E. J. Publishing, *(978-0-9764444; 978-0-9770303)* 4529 Hillcrest Rd., Birmingham, AL 35224-2818 USA Toll Free Fax: 866-864-6087; Toll Free: 866-864-6085
E-mail: elysia@ejpub.com
Web site: http://www.ejpub.com
Dist(s): **Baker & Taylor International**
CreateSpace Independent Publishing Platform.

EKS Publishing Co., *(978-0-939144)* 322 Castro St., Oakland, CA 94607-3028 USA (SAN 216-1281) Tel 510-251-9100; Fax: 510-251-9102; Toll Free: 877-743-2739
E-mail: orders@EKSpublishing.com
Web site: http://www.ekspublishing.com.

E M C Publishing *See* **EMC/Paradigm Publishing**

EMG Networks, *(978-1-56843)* Div. of Educational Management Group, 1 Lake St., No. 3B-47, Upper Saddle River, NJ 07458-1813 USA Tel 602-970-3250; Fax: 602-970-3460; Toll Free: 800-842-6791.

E M Pubns., *(978-0-9749739; 978-0-9794331; 978-0-9893569; 978-0-9905099)* Orders Addr.: P.O. Box 780900, Wichita, KS 67278-0900 USA
Web site: http://www.enloeministries.org.

ERIC Clearinghouse on Rural Education & Small Schls., *(978-1-880785)* Div. of Appalachia Educational Laboratory, Inc., Orders Addr.: P.O. Box 1348, Charleston, WV 25325-1348 USA Tel 304-347-0437; Fax: 304-347-0467; Toll Free: 800-624-9120; Edit

Publisher Name Index

Addr.: 1031 Quarrier St., Suite 610, Charleston, WV 25301 USA
E-mail: ericrc@ael.org
Web site: http://www.ael.org/eric.

ESP, Inc., *(978-0-8209)* Orders Addr.: P.O. Box 839, Tampa, FL 33601-0839 USA; Edit Addr.: 1212 N. 39th St., Suite 444, Tampa, FL 33605-5890 USA (SAN 241-497X) Do not confuse with E S P Inc., Woodlands, TX
E-mail: epublish@tampalay.rr.com
Web site: http://www.espbooks.com.

†ETC Pubns., *(978-0-88280)* 700 E. Vereda del Sur, Palm Springs, CA 92262 USA (SAN 124-8766) Tel 760-325-5352; Fax: 760-325-8841; Toll Free: 800-382-7869
E-mail: etcbooks@earthlink.net; *CIP.*

E T Nedder *Imprint of* **Paulist Pr.**

E3 Concepts LLC, *(978-0-9797375)* 3311 Mulberry Dr., Bloomington, IN 47401 USA Tel 812-360-7488; Fax: 888-876-5152
E-mail: chris.berry@linkedblocks.com
Web site: http://www.linkedblocks.com.

E3 Resources, *(978-1-933383)* 317 Main St., Suite 207, Franklin, TN 37064 USA (SAN 631-9076) Toll Free: 888-354-9411
Web site: http://www.e3resources.org.

Eager Minds Pr. *Imprint of* **Warehousing & Fulfillment Specialists, LLC (WFS, LLC)**

Eagle Bk. Bindery, *(978-0-9772304; 978-1-934333)* 2704 Camelot Ave., NW, Cedar Rapids, IA 52405 USA Tel 319-265-8210
E-mail: sales@eaglebookbindery.com
Web site: http://www.eaglebookbindery.com.

Eagle Creek Pubns., LLC, *(978-0-9769093)* P.O. Box 781166, Indianapolis, IN 46278 USA (SAN 257-3490) Tel 317-870-9902; Fax: 317-870-9904; Toll Free: 866-870-9903 Do not Confuse with Eagle Creek Publications in Prior Lake, MN
E-mail: ben@eaglecreekpubs.com
Web site: http://www.eaglecreekpubs.com.

Eagle Editions, Ltd., *(978-0-914144; 978-0-9660706; 978-0-9721060; 978-0-9761034; 978-0-9794035)* Orders Addr.: P.O. Box 580, Hamilton, MT 59840 USA Tel 406-363-5415; Fax: 406-375-9270; Toll Free: 800-255-1830; Edit Addr.: 752 Bobcat Ln., Hamilton, MT 59840 USA
E-mail: eagle@eagle-editions.com
Web site: http://www.eagle-editions.com
Dist(s): **MBI Distribution Services/Quayside Distribution.**

Eagle Publishing *See* **Majestic Eagle Publishing**

Eagle River Type & Graphics *See* **Northbooks**

Eagle Tree Pr., *(978-0-9792499)* Div. of M. Kay Howell, P.O. Box 1060, Rainier, OR 97048-1060 USA (SAN 852-8950)
Web site: http://fairyempire.biz.

Eaglebrook Press *See* **Oldcastle Publishing**

Eaglehouse, Carolyn, *(978-0-9773263)* 521 E. Uwchlan Ave., Chester Springs, PA 19425 USA
Web site: http://www.chesterspringscreamery.com.

Eaglemont Pr., *(978-0-9662257; 978-0-9748411; 978-1-60040)* 13228 NE 20th St. Ste. 300, Bellevue, WA 98005-2049 USA (SAN 254-2102) Toll Free: 877-590-9744
E-mail: info@eaglemontpress.com
Web site: http://www.eaglemontpress.com.

Eagle's Wings Educational Materials, *(978-1-931292)* P.O. Box 502, Duncan, OK 73534 USA Tel 580-252-1555 (phone/fax)
E-mail: info@EaglesWingsEd.com
Web site: http://www.EaglesWingsEd.com.

Eaglesquest Publishing, *(978-0-9745860)* LTN Enterprises, 11852 Shady Acres Ct., Riverton, UT 84065 USA
E-mail: lestertn@earthlink.net
Web site: http://www.thepaddedgirdle.com; http://www.findingyour new normal.com.

Eakin Pr. *Imprint of* **Eakin Pr.**

†Eakin Pr., *(978-0-89015; 978-1-57168; 978-0-9789150; 978-1-934645; 978-1-935632)* Div. of Sunbelt Media, P.O. Box 90159, Austin, TX 78709-0159 USA (SAN 207-3633) Tel 254-235-6161; Fax: 254-235-6230; Toll Free: 800-880-8642; *Imprints:* Eakin Press (Eakin Pr); Nortex Press (Nortex Pr)
E-mail: sales@eakinpress.com; kris@eakinpress.com
Web site: http://www.eakinpress.com
Dist(s): **Follett School Solutions**
Hervey's Booklink & Cookbook Warehouse
Twentieth Century Christian Bks.
Wolverine Distributing, Inc.; *CIP.*

Eardley Pubns., *(978-0-937630)* Div. of Elizabeth Claire, Inc., Orders Addr.: 2100 Mccomas Way Suite 607, Virginia Beach, VA 23456 USA (SAN 215-6377) Tel 757-430-4308; Fax: 757-430-4309; Toll Free: 888-296-1090
E-mail: eceardley@aol.com
Web site: http://www.elizabethclaire.com
Dist(s): **BookLink, Inc.**
Delta Systems Company, Inc.

Early Foundations Pubs., *(978-0-9670728; 978-0-9742131; 978-1-936215)* P.O. Box 442, Jenison, MI 49429 USA
E-mail: orders@efpublishers.org
Web site: http://www.efpublishers.org.

Early Learning Assessment 2000, *(978-0-9667830; 978-0-9746447)* P.O. Box 21003, Roanoke, VA 24018 USA
E-mail: eanaatwork@aol.com.

Early Learning Foundation, LLC, *(978-0-9755415)* 5184 Milroy, Brighton, MI 48116 USA
E-mail: bob@earlylearningfoundation.com
Web site: http://www.earlylearningfoundation.com.

Early Lighr Pr., LLC, *(978-0-9799179)* P.O. Box 317, Boyds, MD 20841-0317 USA
E-mail: lee@earlylightpress.com
Web site: http://www.earlylightpress.com
Dist(s): **MyiLibrary.**

Early Rise Pubns., *(978-0-9741082)* Orders Addr.: 350 S. Cty. Rd., Suite 102-134, Palm Beach, FL 33480 USA Tel 877-419-3648 (phone/fax)
E-mail: info@earlyrisepublications.com
Web site: http://www.earlyrisepublications.com
Dist(s): **CreateSpace Independent Publishing Platform.**

EarlyLight Bks., Inc., *(978-0-9797455; 978-0-9832014; 978-0-9853037)* P.O. Box 984, Clyde, NC 28721 USA
Web site: http://www.earlylightbooks.com
Dist(s): **BookMasters Distribution Services (BDS)**
Charlesbridge Publishing, Inc.
Random Hse., Inc.

Earnshaw Bks. (HKG) *(978-988-17149) Dist. by* **IPG Chicago.**

Earth Arts NW, *(978-0-9792207)* P.O. Box 25183, Portland, OR 97298-0183 USA
E-mail: tribal@spiritone.com
Web site: http://www.earthandspirit.org.

Earth Star Pubns., *(978-0-944851)* P.O. Box 117, Pagosa Springs, CO 81147-1800 USA (SAN 244-9315) Tel 970-731-0694; Fax: 970-731-0694 call first
E-mail: starbeacon@gmail.com
Web site: http://earthstar.tripod.com.

EarthBound Bks., *(978-0-9771818)* P.O. Box 549, North Egremont, MA 01252 USA (SAN 256-9183) Tel 413-528-9042
E-mail: info@earthboundbooks.com
Web site: www.earthboundbooks.com.

Earthen Vessel Production, Inc., *(978-1-887400)* 3620 Greenwood Dr., Kelseyville, CA 95451 USA Tel 707-279-9621; Fax: 707-279-8769
E-mail: books@earthen.com; request@earthen.com
Web site: http://www.earthen.com.

Earthlight *See* **Light24**

Earthling Pr. *Imprint of* **Awe-Struck Publishing**

Earthshaker Bks., *(978-0-9790357)* 400 Melville Ave., Saint Louis, MO 63130 USA (SAN 852-2545) Tel 314-862-8177
E-mail: albonnie@mindspring.com
Dist(s): **AtlasBooks Distribution**
BookMasters Distribution Services (BDS)
MyiLibrary
ebrary, Inc.

EarthTime Pubns., *(978-0-9663286)* Orders Addr.: 5662 Calle Real, #169, Santa Barbara, CA 93117 USA (SAN 299-5727) Tel 805-898-2263; Fax: 805-898-9460
E-mail: donna@seemamoon.com
Web site: http://www.seemamoon.com.

Earthwalk Pr., *(978-0-915749)* 5432 La Jolla Hermosa Ave., La Jolla, CA 92037-7613 USA (SAN 293-9258)
Dist(s): **Booklines Hawaii, Ltd.**
Langenscheidt Publishing Group.

Earthways *See* **Earthways Guided Canoe Trips and School of Wilderness Living**

Earthways Guided Canoe Trips and School of Wilderness Living, *(978-0-9761714)* 159 Earthways Rd., Canaan, ME 04924 USA Tel 207-426-8138
E-mail: info@earthways.net
Web site: http://www.earthways.net.

Ear Twiggles Productions, Inc., *(978-0-9762573)* 14610 Luna Media, San Diego, CA 92127 USA Tel 858-756-8644; Fax: 858-756-8235
E-mail: contactus@eartwiggles.com
Web site: http://www.eartwiggles.com.

Eas'l Pubns., *(978-1-57377)* Div. of The Idea Shop, Inc., Orders Addr.: P.O. Box 22088, Saint Louis, MO 63126 USA Tel 314-892-9222; Fax: 314-892-9607; Edit Addr.: 11150 Lindbergh Business Ct., Suite 107, Saint Louis, MO 63123 USA
E-mail: easlpub@l1.net
Web site: http://www.easlpublications.com.

East End Hospice, Inc., *(978-0-9754932)* Orders Addr.: P.O. Box 1048, Westhampton Beach, NY 11978 USA Tel 631-288-8400; Fax: 631-288-8492; Edit Addr.: 481 Westhampton River Head Rd., Westhampton Beach, NY 11978 USA
E-mail: info@eeh.org
Web site: http://www.eeh.org.

East River Pr., *(978-0-9791283)* 455 FDR Dr., No. B1205, New York, NY 10002-5915 USA Do not confuse with companies with the same or similar name in Largo, MD, NEw YOrk, NY, Chester, NY.

East Stream Group, LLC, *(978-0-9910342)* 46 Bonnie Brae Dr., Weaverville, NC 28787 USA Tel 828-775-4812
E-mail: robin@eaststreamgroup.com.

East West Discovery Pr., *(978-0-9669437; 978-0-9701654; 978-0-9799339; 978-0-9821675; 978-0-9832278; 978-0-9856237; 978-0-9913454)* P.O. Box 3585, Manhattan Beach, CA 90266 USA Tel 310-545-3730; Fax: 310-545-3731
E-mail: info@eastwestdiscovery.com; icy@eastwestdiscovery.com
Web site: http://www.eastwestdiscovery.com
Dist(s): **Follett School Solutions.**

East West Hse, *(978-0-9778403)* 899 S. Plymouth Ct. Apt 2106, Chicago, IL 60605 USA.

Easter Island Foundation, *(978-1-880636)* Orders Addr.: P.O. Box 6774, Los Osos, CA 93412-6774 USA Tel 805-528-8558; Fax: 805-534-9301
E-mail: eif@att.net
Web site: http://www.islandheritage.org.

Eastern Digital Resources, *(978-0-9815953)* P.O. Box 1451, Clearwater, SC 29822 USA Tel 803-439-2938
E-mail: jrigdon@researchonline.net; sales@researchonline.net
Web site: http://www.researchonline.net.

†Eastern National, *(978-0-915992; 978-1-888213; 978-1-59091)* 470 Maryland Dr., Suite 1, Fort Washington, PA 19034 USA (SAN 630-4044)
E-mail: erich@Easternnational.org
Web site: http://www.easternnational.org; *CIP.*

Eastern National Park & Monument Association *See* **Eastern National**

Eastern Slope Publisher, *(978-0-9746996; 978-0-9839956)* Orders Addr.: P.O. Box 20357, Reno, NV 89515-0357 USA; Edit Addr.: 205 Urban Rd., Reno, NV 89509-3662 USA
E-mail: pdcafferata@sbcglobal.net.

Eastland Pr., *(978-0-939616)* Orders Addr.: 1240 Activity Dr., No. D, Vista, CA 92081 USA (SAN 665-6900) Tel 760-598-9695 sales office; Fax: 760-598-6083 sales office; Toll Free Fax: 800-241-3329 sales office; Toll Free: 800-453-3278 sales office; Edit Addr.: P.O. Box 99749, Seattle, WA 98139 USA (SAN 216-6216) Tel 206-217-0204 editorial office; Fax: 206-217-0205 editorial office
E-mail: orders@eastlandpress.com; info@eastlandpress.com
Web site: http://www.eastlandpress.com
Dist(s): **Blackhawk Hobby Distributors, Incorporated**
Matthews Medical Bk. Co.
Redwing Bk. Co.

Eastland Studios *See* **Eastwind Studios**

Eastlight Pr., *(978-0-9743121)* 1976 Savanna, Fairfield, IA 52556 USA
E-mail: gadef@mac.com.

Easton Studio Pr., LLC, *(978-0-9743806; 978-0-9798248; 978-1-935212; 978-1-63226)* P.O. Box 3131, Westport, CT 06880-3131 USA; *Imprints:* Prospecta Press (PROSPECTA PRES)
Web site: http://www.eastonsp.com/live/
Dist(s): **MyiLibrary**
Perseus Bks. Group
Perseus Distribution
ebrary, Inc.

Eastwaterfront Pr., *(978-0-9769771)* P.O. Box 220-554, Brooklyn, NY 11222 USA
E-mail: pdolack@gis.net.

Eastwind Studios, *(978-0-9755635; 978-0-615-36383-7; 978-0-615-36384-4; 978-0-615-36385-1)* P.O. Box 750, San Bernardino, CA 92402 USA Tel 909-725-7337
E-mail: lindaadams35@yahoo.com; philyeh@mac.com
Web site: http://www.ideaship.com; http://www.wingedtiger.com
Dist(s): **Booklines Hawaii, Ltd.**

Eastword Publications Development, Incorporated *See* **Lincoln Library Pr., Inc., The**

Easy Reach Corp., *(978-0-615-50973-0; 978-0-615-59362-3; 978-0-9883620)* HC 76 Box 121, Daisy, OK 74540 USA Tel 918-569-4803
E-mail: npyle@kiamichiwb.org.

Easy Readers *Imprint of* **Picture Window Bks.**

Easy to Print Publishing, *(978-0-9883020)* 6 Orchard St. 2nd FL, Elmwood Park, NJ 07407 USA Tel 718-926-5799
E-mail: kerenashram@gmail.com.

Eat Your Peas Publishing, *(978-0-9743210)* 330 Conestoga Rd., Wayne, PA 19087 USA Tel 610-995-0495; Fax: 610-995-0496
E-mail: lisa@richeyassociates.com
Web site: http://www.mannerstogo.com.

EB Benjamin, LLC, *(978-0-615-38727-7; 978-0-615-43887-0)* 1248 Loring Run, Charlottesville, VA 22901 USA Tel 219-669-8474
E-mail: solalife@gmail.com
Dist(s): **CreateSpace Independent Publishing Platform.**

Ebed Pr., *(978-0-9741927; 978-1-933484; 978-0-9774825; 978-1-934050)* 3103 Villa Ave., Bronx, NY 11468-1356 USA Tel 718-788-2484; Fax: 718-788-7760; Toll Free: 800-224-7808
E-mail: info@ebedpress.com
Web site: http://www.ebedpress.com.

Ebenezer A.M.E. Church, *(978-0-9748834)* 7707 Allentown Rd., Fort Washington, MD 20744 USA Tel 301-248-8833; Fax: 301-248-6894
Web site: http://www.ebenezerame.org.

Ebks. On The Net *Imprint of* **Write Words, Inc.**

EBL Coaching, *(978-0-9772110; 978-0-9778391)* 167 E. 82nd St., Suite 1A, New York, NY 10023 USA Tel 646-342-9380; Fax: 212-937-2305
E-mail: elevy@eblcoaching.com
Web site: http://www.eblcoaching.com.

Ebon Research Systems *See* **Ebon Research Systems Publishing, LLC**

Ebon Research Systems Publishing, LLC *(978-0-915960; 978-0-9648313)* 812 Sweetwater Club Blvd., Longwood, FL 32779 USA (SAN 254-6698) Tel 407-786-9200; Fax: 407-682-2384
E-mail: femillionaire@embarqmail.com
Web site: http://www.daretobebooks.com; http://www.ebonresearchsystems.com.

EbonyEnergy Publishing, Inc., *(978-0-9722795; 978-0-9755092; 978-1-59825)* Div. of Highest Good Pubns., Orders Addr.: P.O. Box 43476, Chicago, IL 60643 USA (SAN 255-3953) Tel 773-445-4946; Fax: 773-233-5178; Toll Free: 877-447-1266; *Imprints:* Highest Good Publications (Highest Good Pubns)
E-mail: info@ebonyenergypublishing.com; cherylwash@yahoo.com
Web site: http://www.ebonyenergy.com; http://gemliteraryfoundation.org; http://ebonyenergybooks.com; http://ebonyenergykids.com; http://www.ebonyenergypublishing.com; http://highestgoodpublications.com; http://pocketbooksforyoursoul.com
Dist(s): **Biblio Distribution**
ebrary, Inc.

eBookit.com, *(978-1-4566)* Div. of Archieboy Holdings, LLC, 365 Boston Post Rd., No. 311, Sudbury, MA 01776 USA
Web site: http://www.ebookit.com.

E-Booksgen, *(978-1-893767)* 40 Sandy Pond South, East Wakefield, NH 03830 USA Tel 603-522-9951
E-mail: e-booksgen@e-booksgen.com
Web site: http://www.e-booksgen.com; http://www.e-booksgen.com/E-WW2DOC.html.

eBooksOnDisk.com, *(978-0-9719101; 978-1-932157)* Orders Addr.: P.O. Box 30432, Gulf Breeze, FL 32503 USA Tel 850-261-1981
E-mail: thomas@ebooksondisk.com
Web site: http://www.ebooksondisk.com; http://www.confederatemilitaryhistory.com
Dist(s): **CreateSpace Independent Publishing Platform**
Lightning Source, Inc.

ebooksonthe.net *See* **Dilligaf Publishing**

ebooksonthe.net *See* **Write Words, Inc.**

eBookstand Books *See* **Bookstand Publishing**

E-BookTime LLC, *(978-0-9717625; 978-1-932701; 978-1-59824; 978-1-60862)* 6598 Pumpkin Rd., Montgomery, AL 36108 USA Toll Free: 877-613-2665
E-mail: publishing@e-booktime.com
Web site: http://www.e-booktime.com.

Ebury Publishing (GBR) *(978-0-09; 978-0-426; 978-0-7126; 978-0-7535; 978-0-85223; 978-0-86369; 978-1-85227; 978-0-907080; 978-0-903446; 978-1-905042; 978-1-904978; 978-0-427; 978-1-84670; 978-1-905264) Dist. by* **IPG Chicago.**

Ebury Publishing (GBR) *(978-0-09; 978-0-426; 978-0-7126; 978-0-7535; 978-0-85223; 978-0-86369; 978-1-85227; 978-0-907080; 978-0-903446; 978-1-905042; 978-1-904978; 978-0-427; 978-1-84670; 978-1-905264) Dist. by* **Random.**

Ebury Publishing (GBR) *(978-0-09; 978-0-426; 978-0-7126; 978-0-7535; 978-0-85223; 978-0-86369; 978-1-85227; 978-0-907080; 978-0-903446; 978-1-905042; 978-1-904978; 978-0-427; 978-1-84670; 978-1-905264) Dist. by* **PerseuPGW.**

Ecco *Imprint of* **HarperCollins Pubs.**

Echelon Press Publishing, *(978-1-59080)* Orders Addr.: 9055 Thamesmeade Rd. Apt. G, Laurel, MD 20723-5807 USA; *Imprints:* Quake (Quake)
E-mail: admin@echelonpress.com; echelonpress@gmail.com
Web site: http://www.echelonpress.com; http://quakeme.com
Dist(s): **Brodart Co.**
Lightning Source, Inc.
Partners Bk. Distributing, Inc.
Smashwords.

Echo & the Bat Pack *Imprint of* **Stone Arch Bks.**

Echo Valley Pr, *(978-0-9860734)* P.O. Box 449, Glen Arbor, MI 49636 USA.

Echoes Joint Venture, *(978-0-9759995)* Intensive English Program, UD, 1845 E. Northgate Dr., Irving, TX 75062 USA.

ECity Publishing *Imprint of* **ECity Publishing**

E-City Publishing, *(978-0-615-16430-4)* 150 Rustic Ridge Rd., Fredericksburg, VA 22405 USA
Dist(s): **Publishers Services.**

ECity Publishing, *(978-0-9716006; 978-0-9830425)* Orders Addr.: P.O. Box 5033, Everglades City, FL 34139 USA Tel 239-695-2905; 102 E. Broadway, Everglades City, FL 34139; *Imprints:* ECity Publishing (ECity Pubng)
E-mail: ecitypublishing@earthlink.net
Web site: http://www.ecity-publishing.com.

Eckankar, *(978-1-57043)* Orders Addr.: P.O. Box 27300, Minneapolis, MN 55427 USA (SAN 253-7192) Fax: 952-380-2295; Toll Free: 800-568-3463
E-mail: eckbooks@eckankar.org
Web site: http://www.eckankar.org
Dist(s): **BookMobile.**

Eckerd College Leadership Development Institute, *(978-0-9764173)* 4200 54th Ave. S., St. Petersburg, FL 33711 USA Tel 727-864-8213; Fax: 727-864-7575; Toll Free: 800-753-0444
E-mail: ldi@eckerd.edu
Web site: http://www.eckerd.edu/ldi.

Eckl, Joseph J., *(978-0-9746686)* 346 Country Brook Ln., Harvard, IL 60033-7807 USA
E-mail: ecklindpil@aol.com.

Ecky Thump Bks., Inc., *(978-0-9815883)* 1411 N. California St., Burbank, CA 91505-1902 USA
Web site: http://www.achristmasbox.com
Dist(s): **Partners Pubs. Group, Inc.**

Eclectic Dragon Pr., *(978-0-9746016)* P.O. Box 91, Laie, HI 96762-1294 USA.

Eclipse Pr. *Imprint of* **Blood-Horse, Inc., The**

Eclipse Solutions (UK) Ltd. (GBR) *(978-0-9556910) Dist. by* **LuluCom.**

Eco Fiction Bks. *Imprint of* **Day to Day Enterprises**

Eco Images, *(978-0-938423)* Orders Addr.: P.O. Box 61413, Virginia Beach, VA 23466-1413 USA (SAN 661-230X); Edit Addr.: 4132 Blackwater Rd., Virginia Beach, VA 23457 USA (SAN 661-2318) Tel 757-421-3929
E-mail: wildfood@cox.net
Web site: http://www.ecoimages-us.com.

Eco-Busters, *(978-1-885091)* 1198 Old Castleberry Rd, Brewton, AL 36426 USA.

Eco-Justice Pr., LLC, *(978-0-9660370; 978-0-9891296)* P.O. Box 5409, Eugene, OR 97405 USA; *Imprints:* Aurora Books (AuroraBks)
E-mail: info@ecojusticepress.com; orders@ecojusticepress.com
Web site: ecojusticepress.com.

Ecology Comics, *(978-0-9643421)* 465 B. Kawailoa Rd., Kailua, HI 96734 USA Tel 808-261-1018; Fax: 808-531-3177.

EcoSeekers, The, *(978-0-9798800)* P.O. Box 637, Nyack, NY 10960 USA (SAN 854-6339)
E-mail: info@theecoseekers.com
Web site: http://www.theecoseekers.com
Dist(s): **Midpoint Trade Bks., Inc.**

Eco-thumb Publishing Co., *(978-0-9778536)* 1212 S. Naper Blvd., Suite 119-337, Naperville, IL 60540 USA (SAN 850-4113) Tel 630-853-9758
Web site: http://www.ecothumb.com; http://www.sendmethesoap.com.

For full information on wholesalers and distributors, refer to the Wholesaler and Distributor Name Index

Ecotrust, *(978-0-9676364; 978-0-9779332)* 721 NW 9th Ave. Ste. 200, Portland, OR 97209-3448 USA
Web site: http://www.ecotrust.org
Dist(s): **Oregon State Univ. Pr.**
University of Arizona Pr.

ECRH Pr., *(978-0-615-69480-1; 978-0-615-72414-0; 978-0-615-83574-7)* 2600 Pleasant Ave. # 306, Minneapolis, MN 55408 USA Tel 612-670-1040
Dist(s): **CreateSpace Independent Publishing Platform.**

ECS Learning Systems, Inc., *(978-0-944459; 978-1-57022; 978-1-58232; 978-1-60539)* P.O. Box 440, Bulverde, TX 78163 USA (SAN 243-6167) Toll Free Fax: 877-688-3226; Toll Free: 800-688-3224
Web site: http://www.ecslearningsystems.com.

Ecstatic Exchange, The, *(978-0-615-13570-0; 978-0-615-13599-1; 978-0-615-14273-9; 978-0-615-14505-1; 978-0-615-15116-8; 978-0-615-16308-6; 978-0-615-18394-7; 978-0-615-18412-8; 978-0-615-20490-1; 978-0-615-22182-3; 978-0-615-23628-5; 978-0-578-00773-1; 978-0-578-01004-5; 978-0-578-01084-7; 978-0-578-01690-0; 978-0-578-02569-8; 978-0-578-02765-4; 978-0-578-04677-8; 978-0-578-04905-2; 978-0-578-06116-0; 978-0-578-07145-9; 978-0-578-07482-5; 978-0-578-07608-9; 978-0-578-08293-6; 978-0-578-08512-8; 978-0-578-08891-4;) 6470 Morris Pk. Rd., Philadelphia, PA 19151 USA Tel 215-477-8927*
E-mail: abdalhayy@danielmoorepoetry.com
Web site: http://www.danielmoorepoetry.com; www.ecstaticxchange.wordpress.com
Dist(s): **Lulu Enterprises Inc.**

Ectopic Publishing, *(978-0-9759695)* 3638 Lovejoy Ct. NE, Olympia, WA 98506 USA
E-mail: bryanrandall@ectopicpublishing.com
Web site: http://www.ectopicpublishing.com.

ECW Pr. (CAN) *(978-0-920763; 978-0-920802; 978-1-55022; 978-1-77041; 978-1-55490; 978-1-77090) Dist. by* **PerseuPGW.**

Ed. Acespanish S.A.C.- Lima, Peru, *(978-0-9762361)* 4806 Alta Loma Dr., Austin, TX 78749 USA Tel 512-784-6333
Web site: http://www.acespanish.com.

E.D. Insight Bks., *(978-0-9761552)* P.O. Box 514, Beverly Hills, CA 90213-0514 USA
E-mail: brady@edinsight.com
Web site: http://www.edinsight.com.

Edaf, Editorial S.A. (ESP) *(978-84-7640; 978-84-7166; 978-84-414) Dist. by* **Spanish.**

Edamex, Editores Asociados Mexicanos, S. A. de C. V. (MEX) *(978-968-409; 978-970-661) Dist. by* **Giron Bks.**

EDC Publishing, *(978-0-7460; 978-0-86020; 978-0-88110; 978-1-58086; 978-0-7945; 978-1-60130)* Orders Addr.: P.O. Box 470663, Tulsa, OK 74147-0663 USA (SAN 658-0505); Edit Addr.: 10302 E. 55th Pl., Tulsa, OK 74146-6515 USA (SAN 107-5322) Tel 918-622-4522; Fax: 918-665-7919; Toll Free Fax: 800-747-4509; Toll Free: 800-475-4522; *Imprints:* Usborne (UsborneU)
E-mail: edc@edcpub.com
Web site: http://www.edcpub.com
Dist(s): **Continental Bk. Co., Inc.**
Lectorum Pubns., Inc.
Libros Sin Fronteras.

EDCO Publishing, Inc., *(978-0-9712692; 978-0-9749412; 978-0-9798088)* 2648 Lapeer Rd., Auburn Hills, MI 48326 USA (SAN 254-4261) Fax: 248-475-9122; Toll Free: 888-510-3326
E-mail: lynette@edcopublishing.com; martha@edcopublishing.com
Web site: http://www.edcopublishing.com
Dist(s): **Partners Bk. Distributing, Inc.**

EDCON Publishing Group, *(978-0-8481; 978-1-56872)* 30 Montauk Blvd., Oakdale, NY 11769 USA Tel 631-567-7227; Fax: 631-567-8745; Toll Free Fax: 888-518-1564; Toll Free: 888-553-3266
E-mail: dale@edconpublishing.com
Web site: http://www.edconpublishing.com
Dist(s): **Findaway World, LLC**
Follett School Solutions.

Eddie Crabtree Ministries, *(978-0-9765830)* Orders Addr.: P.O. Box 846, Salem, VA 24153 USA Tel 540-562-1500; Fax: 540-562-2695; Edit Addr.: 1928 Loch Haven Dr., Roanoke, VA 24019 USA
E-mail: eddiecrabtreeministries@valleywordministries.org.

Eddy, The Writings of Mary Baker, *(978-0-87510; 978-0-87952)* Orders Addr.: P.O. Box 1875, Boston, MA 02117 USA (SAN 203-6541); Edit Addr.: 175 Huntington Ave., A20-01, Boston, MA 02115 USA Tel 617-450-3537 Administration Queries (Paul Woodsum); Fax: 617-450-2054 Attn: Paul Woodsum, Production Manager; Toll Free Fax: 800-688-2017; Toll Free: 800-515-0160 (Science & Health Direct Orders)
E-mail: woodsump@twmbe.com; broadhurstg@twmbe.com
Web site: http://www.spirituality.com.

Edebé (ESP) *(978-84-236) Dist. by* **Ediciones.**

Edebé (ESP) *(978-84-236) Dist. by* **Lectorum Pubns.**

Edelsa Grupo Didascalia, S.A. (ESP) *(978-84-389; 978-84-7711; 978-84-85786) Dist. by* **Distribks Inc.**

Edelsa Grupo Didascalia, S.A. (ESP) *(978-84-389; 978-84-7711; 978-84-85786) Dist. by* **Continental Bk.**

Edelson, Madelyn, *(978-0-9770131)* 69 Bay Ave., H, Huntington, NY 11743 USA
E-mail: mbedelson@optonline.net
Web site: http://www.beechwindpress.com.

Eden Entertainment Ltd., Inc., *(978-0-9672819; 978-0-9835380)* 1277 1st St. Suite 1, Key West, FL 33040 USA Tel 305-294-7928
E-mail: MarcusVarner@Hotmail.com; DanielJReynen@Hotmail.com
Web site: http://www.truesecretof.com; http://www.dietisdead.com; http://www.webefit.com.

Eden Studios, Inc., *(978-1-891153; 978-1-933105)* 6 Dogwood Ln., Londonville, NY 12211 USA Tel 518-331-2063; Fax: 425-962-2593
E-mail: edenprod@aol.com
Web site: http://www.edenstudios.net
Dist(s): **PSI (Publisher Services, Inc.).**

Edes Publishing Co., *(978-0-9788010; 978-1-943472)* 1224 E. Hadley, Las Cruces, NM 88001 USA (SAN 851-6561)
E-mail: publisher@edes.net
Web site: http://www.edes.net.

Edgar Road Publishing, *(978-0-615-20414-7)* 938 Tuxedo Blvd., Webster Groves, MO 63119 USA Tel 314-541-9235; Fax: 314-961-9044
E-mail: edgarroadpublishing@gmail.com
Dist(s): **R J Communications, LLC.**

Edge Bks. *Imprint of* **Capstone Pr., Inc.**

Edge Science Fiction & Fantasy Publishing (CAN) *(978-1-894063) Dist. by* **IngramPubServ.**

Edgecliff Pr. LLC., *(978-0-9798659; 978-0-9819271; 978-0-9844622; 978-0-9839486)* Mid-century Modern Bldg. 9066 Long Ln., Cincinnati, OH 45231 USA (SAN 854-6150) Tel 513-348-9120 Hours 9 to 5 EST
E-mail: Info@edgecliffpress.com
Web site: http://www.edgecliffpress.com; http://www.edgecliffkids.com.

EDGEucation Publishing, *(978-1-932689)* Orders Addr.: P.O. Box 852013, Yukon, OK 73085-2013 USA; Edit Addr.: 1441 NW 47th St., Oklahoma City, OK 73085-2013 USA
E-mail: edgeucation@sbcglobal.net.

Edgewood Publishing, LLC, *(978-0-9792645)* P.O. Box 153, Adell, WI 53001 USA Tel 920-994-2483.

Ediciones Alas, Inc., *(978-0-9753799)* Orders Addr.: P.O. Box 327495, Fort Lauderdale, FL 33332 USA; Edit Addr.: 6061 SW 195th Ave., Pembroke Pines, FL 33332 USA
E-mail: mm@millymolo.com
Web site: http://www.millymolo.com.

Ediciones Alfaguara (ESP) *(978-84-204) Dist. by* **Lectorum Pubns.**

Ediciones Alfaguara (ESP) *(978-84-204) Dist. by* **Santillana.**

Ediciones Alfaguara (ESP) *(978-84-204) Dist. by* **Perseus Dist.**

Ediciones B (ESP) *(978-84-406; 978-84-7735; 978-84-666; 978-84-9872; 978-84-15420) Dist. by* **IPG Chicago.**

Ediciones B (ESP) *(978-84-406; 978-84-7735; 978-84-666; 978-84-9872; 978-84-15420) Dist. by* **Spanish.**

Ediciones B Mexico (MEX) *(978-84-406; 978-84-7735; 978-607-480) Dist. by* **Spanish.**

Ediciones Cátedra (ESP) *(978-84-376) Dist. by* **Continental Bk.**

Ediciones de la Torre (ESP) *(978-84-7960; 978-84-85277; 978-84-85866; 978-84-86587) Dist. by* **Libros Fronteras.**

Ediciones de la Torre (ESP) *(978-84-7960; 978-84-85277; 978-84-85866; 978-84-86587) Dist. by* **AIMS Intl.**

Ediciones del Bronce (ESP) *(978-84-8453; 978-84-89854) Dist. by* **Planeta.**

Ediciones del Laberinto (ESP) *(978-84-8483; 978-84-87482) Dist. by* **Ediciones.**

Ediciones Destino (ESP) *(978-84-233; 978-84-9710) Dist. by* **Continental Bk.**

Ediciones Destino (ESP) *(978-84-233; 978-84-9710) Dist. by* **AIMS Intl.**

Ediciones Destino (ESP) *(978-84-233; 978-84-9710) Dist. by* **Lectorum Pubns.**

Ediciones Destino (ESP) *(978-84-233; 978-84-9710) Dist. by* **Planeta.**

Ediciones El Salvaje Refinado *See* **Refined Savage Editions / Ediciones El Salvaje Refinado, The**

Ediciones la Gota de Agua, *(978-0-9771987; 978-0-9819303; 978-0-9964627)* 1937 Pemberton St., Philadelphia, PA 19146-1825 USA Tel 215-546-9421
E-mail: info@edicioneslagotadeagua.com
Web site: http://edicioneslagotadeagua.com
Dist(s): **Ediciones Universal**
YBP Library Services.

Ediciones Lerner *Imprint of* **Lerner Publishing Group**

Ediciones Norte, Inc., *(978-1-931928)* P.O. Box 29461, San Juan, PR 00929-0461 USA Tel 787-701-0909; Fax: 787-701-0922
Web site: http://www.edicionesnorte.com
Dist(s): **Independent Pubs. Group.**

Ediciones Nuevo Espacio *See* **Ediciones Nuevo Espacio-AcademicPressENE**

Ediciones Nuevo Espacio-AcademicPressENE, *(978-1-930879)* Orders Addr.: 39 Redfern Rd., Eatontown, NJ 07724 USA
E-mail: AcademicPressENE@aol.com
Web site: http://www.editorial-ene.com; http://www.editorial-ene.com/Experimental.htm
Dist(s): **Book Wholesalers, Inc.**
Brodart Co.

Ediciones Oniro S.A. (ESP) *(978-84-89920; 978-84-922523; 978-84-9754; 978-84-95456) Dist. by* **Bilingual Pubns.**

Ediciones Oniro S.A. (ESP) *(978-84-89920; 978-84-922523; 978-84-9754; 978-84-95456) Dist. by* **Lectorum Pubns.**

Ediciones Santillana, Inc., *(978-1-57581; 978-1-60484; 978-1-61875)* Div. of Santillana-S. A. (SP), P.O. Box 195462, San Juan, PR 00919-5462 USA Tel 787-781-9800; Fax: 787-782-6149; Toll Free: 800-981-9822
E-mail: molivero@santillanapr.net; areynoso@santillanapr.net; cvazquez@santillanapr.net
Web site: http://www.gruposantillana.com
Dist(s): **Santillana USA Publishing Co., Inc.**

Ediciones Situm, Incorporated *See* **Biblio Services, Inc.**

Ediciones SM, *(978-1-933279; 978-1-934801; 978-1-935556; 978-1-936534; 978-1-939075; 978-1-940343; 978-1-63014)* Barrio Palmas, 776 Calle 7 Suite 2, Catano, PR 00962-6335 USA Tel 787-625-9800; Fax: 787-625-9799
Web site: http://www.ediciones-smpr.com.

Ediciones Universal, *(978-0-89729; 978-1-59388)* Orders Addr.: P.O. Box 450353, Miami, FL 33245-0353 USA (SAN 658-0548); Edit Addr.: 3090 SW Eighth St., Miami, FL 33135 USA (SAN 207-2203) Tel 305-642-3355; Fax: 305-642-7978
E-mail: marta@ediciones.com; ediciones@ediciones.com
Web site: http://www.ediciones.com
Dist(s): **Lectorum Pubns., Inc.**

Ediciones Urano S. A. (ESP) *(978-84-7953; 978-84-95618; 978-84-95752; 978-84-86344; 978-84-95787; 978-84-96711; 978-84-96886; 978-84-92916; 978-84-9944) Dist. by* **Spanish.**

Ediciones y Distribuciones Codice, S.A. (ESP) *(978-84-357) Dist. by* **Continental Bk.**

Edifytainment Bks., *(978-0-9753427)* 213 Regent Cir., Inglewood, CA 90301 USA Tel 310-677-9744
E-mail: edifytainmentbooks@prodigy.net
Web site: http://www.bobettejamison-harrison.com/edifytainmentbooks.html.

Edilupa Ediciones, S.L. (ESP) *(978-84-932571; 978-84-932843; 978-84-96252; 978-84-96609) Dist. by* **Lectorum Pubns.**

Edimat Libros, S. A. (ESP) *(978-84-8403; 978-84-923200; 978-84-95002; 978-84-9764; 978-84-9794) Dist. by* **IPG Chicago.**

eDimples, Inc., *(978-0-9787759)* 9249 S. Broadway, 200-161, Highlands Ranch, CO 80129 USA Tel 303-284-1331 (phone/fax)
E-mail: greg@edimples.com
Web site: http://www.edimples.com.

Edinboro Bk. Arts Collective, *(978-0-9747001)* Orders Addr.: P.O. Box 77, Edinboro, PA 16412 USA; Edit Addr.: 103 Tarbell Ln., Edinboro, PA 16412 USA
E-mail: winterberger@edinboro.edu.

Edinborough Pr., *(978-1-889020)* P.O. Box 13790, Roseville, MN 55113-2293 USA (SAN 299-2825) Tel 651-415-1034; Toll Free Fax: 800-566-6145; Toll Free: 888-251-6336 (Orders Only)
E-mail: books@edinborough.com
Web site: http://www.edinborough.com
Dist(s): **Independent Pubs. Group**
ebrary, Inc.

Edinburgh Univ. Pr. (GBR) *(978-0-7486; 978-0-85224) Dist. by* **OUP.**

Edinumen, Editorial (ESP) *(978-84-89756; 978-84-85789; 978-84-95986; 978-84-9848) Dist. by* **Cambridge U Pr.**

Edit et Cetera *See* **Edit et Cetera Ltd.**

Edit et Cetera Ltd., *(978-0-9746122; 978-0-9769989; 978-0-9832270)* P.O. Box 551, Canon City, CO 81215 USA
E-mail: familybookhouse@aol.com
Web site: http://www.familybookhouse.com.

EDITER'S Publishing Hse., *(978-0-9706814; 978-0-9743743)* 654 Schafer Pl., Escondido, CA 92025 USA Tel 619-339-7030; Fax: 760-294-2685
E-mail: books@editers.com
Web site: http://www.editers.com.

EDITER'S Publishing Hse. (MEX) *(978-968-6966; 978-968-5432) Dist. by* **EDITERS Pub Hse.**

Editex, Editorial S.A. (ESP) *(978-84-7131) Dist. by* **Lectorum Pubns.**

Edition Axel Menges GmbH (DEU) *(978-3-930698; 978-3-932565; 978-3-936681) Dist. by* **Natl Bk Netwk.**

Edition Chimaira (DEU) *(978-3-930612; 978-3-89973) Dist. by* **Serpents Tale.**

Edition Q, Inc., *(978-0-86715; 978-1-883695)* 551 N. Kimberly Dr., Carol Stream, IL 60188-1881 USA Tel 630-682-3223; Fax: 630-682-3907; Toll Free: 800-421-0387
E-mail: quintpub@aol.com; service@quintbook.com
Web site: http://www.quintpub.com.

Editions Alexandre Stanke (CAN) *(978-2-89558) Dist. by* **AtlasBooks.**

Editions de la Paix (CAN) *(978-2-921255; 978-2-922565; 978-2-9800785; 978-2-89599) Dist. by* **World of Reading.**

Editions du Petit Music (FRA) *(978-2-84607) Dist. by* **Distribks Inc.**

Editions du Seuil (FRA) *(978-2-02) Dist. by* **Distribks Inc.**

Editions Fleurus (FRA) *(978-2-215; 978-2-250; 978-2-7289) Dist. by* **Distribks Inc.**

Editions Milan (FRA) *(978-2-7459; 978-2-84113; 978-2-86726) Dist. by* **Distribks Inc.**

Editora Campamocha, *(978-1-934802)* 1609 Chicago Av., McAllen, TX 78501 USA.

Editores Mexicanos Unidos (MEX) *(978-968-15) Dist. by* **Ediciones.**

Editorial Betania *See* **Grupo Nelson**

Editorial Brief (ESP) *(978-84-931888) Dist. by* **IPG Chicago.**

Editorial Buenas Letras *Imprint of* **Rosen Publishing Group, Inc., The**

Editorial Busqueda, *(978-0-9744408; 978-0-9760652; 978-0-9798461; 978-0-9843607)* Calle Pinero, No. 113, San Juan, PR 00925-3612 USA.

Editorial Campana, *(978-0-9725611; 978-1-934370)* 19 W. 85th St., New York, NY 10024 USA (SAN 854-2791) Tel 212-721-4062 (phone/fax); *Imprints:* Campanita Books (Campanita Bks)
E-mail: gycultura@aol.com
Web site: http://www.editorialcampana.com
Dist(s): **Downtown Bk. Ctr., Inc.**

Editorial Cultural, Inc., *(978-1-56758; 978-84-399)* Orders Addr.: P.O. Box 21056, San Juan, PR 00928 USA; Edit Addr.: Calle Robles, No. 51, San Juan, PR 00928 USA
E-mail: angiev@editorialculturalpr.com; alamo48@gmail.com
Web site: http://www.editorialculturalpr.com.

Editorial Diana, S.A. (MEX) *(978-968-13) Dist. by* **Continental Bk.**

Editorial Diana, S.A. (MEX) *(978-968-13) Dist. by* **Lectorum Pubns.**

Editorial Diana, S.A. (MEX) *(978-968-13) Dist. by* **Giron Bks.**

Editorial El Antillano, Inc., *(978-0-9755661; 978-0-9793026)* 104 Jefferson St., Suite 5-B, Santurce, PR 00911 USA Tel 787-982-4060
E-mail: olga_otero@mspr.net
Web site: http://www.elantillano.com.

Editorial Everest, S.A (ESP) *(978-84-441) Dist. by* **Lectorum Pubns.**

Editorial Homagno, *(978-0-9727467)* Div. of Homagno Group, Inc., P.O. Box 960227, Miami, FL 33296 USA
Web site: http://www.homagno.com.

Editorial Humanitas, *(978-0-9650104)* Orders Addr.: 2006 23rd Ave., E., Seattle, WA 98112-2936 USA Tel 206-616-9394
E-mail: oberle@mindspring.com
Web site: http://www.mindspring.com/~oberle/PRbirds.htm
Dist(s): **Representaciones Borinquenas, Inc.**

Editorial John Louis von Neumann, Inc., *(978-0-9748297; 978-0-9779982)* Urb. Villa Fontana, 3NS-15 Via Lourdes, Carolina, PR 00983-4650 USA Tel 787-630-6330; Fax: 787-257-4979
E-mail: josejuandiaz@gmail.com
Web site: http://josejuandiaz.com
Dist(s): **Representaciones Borinquenas, Inc.**

Editorial Libros en Red, *(978-1-59754; 978-1-62915)* 5018 57th Ave., Apt. B8, Bladensburg, MD 20710 USA
E-mail: administracion@librosenred.com
Web site: http://www.librosenred.com
Dist(s): **Ediciones Universal.**

Editorial Libsa, S.A. (ESP) *(978-84-7630; 978-84-662) Dist. by* **Continental Bk.**

Editorial Libsa, S.A. (ESP) *(978-84-7630; 978-84-662) Dist. by* **Lectorum Pubns.**

Editorial Lumen (ESP) *(978-84-264) Dist. by* **Distribks Inc.**

Editorial Lumen (ESP) *(978-84-264) Dist. by* **Lectorum Pubns.**

Editorial Miglo Inc., *(978-0-9671705)* 1560 Grand Concourse, Apt. 504, Bronx, NY 10457 USA
E-mail: jcmalone01@aol.com
Web site: http://www.edimiglo.com.

Editorial Mundo Hispano *Imprint of* **Casa Bautista de Publicaciones**

Editorial Panamericana, Inc., *(978-1-881744; 978-1-934139; 978-1-61725)* Orders Addr.: Urb. Puerto Nuevo 1336 F.d. Roosevelt Ave., San Juan, PR 00920 USA Tel 787-277-7988; Fax: 787-277-7240; Edit Addr.: P.O. Box 25189, San Juan, PR 00928-5189 USA Tel 787-277-7988; Fax: 787-277-7240
E-mail: info@editorialpanamericana.com; mlorenzana@editorialpanamericana.com
Web site: http://www.editorialpanamericana.com.

Editorial Pax (MEX) *(978-968-860; 978-968-461) Dist. by* **IPG Chicago.**

Editorial Plaza Mayor, Inc., *(978-1-56328)* Avenida Ponce De Leon 1527, Barrio El Cinco, Rio Piedras, PR 00926 USA Tel 787-764-0455; Fax: 787-764-0465
E-mail: patrigut@prtc.net
Dist(s): **Continental Bk. Co., Inc.**
Ediciones Universal
Lectorum Pubns., Inc.
Libros Sin Fronteras.

Editorial Porrua (MEX) *(978-968-432; 978-968-452; 978-970-07) Dist. by* **Continental Bk.**

Editorial Portavoz *Imprint of* **Kregel Pubns.**

Editorial Resources, Inc., *(978-0-9745923)* 4510 Seneca St., Pasadena, TX 77504-3568 USA
E-mail: anng@editorial-resources.com
Web site: http://www.editorial-resources.com.

Editorial Sendas Antiguas, LLC, *(978-1-932789)* 1730 Leffingwell Ave., Grand Rapids, MI 49525-4532 USA Tel 616-365-9073 (phone/fax); 616-365-0699; Fax: 616-365-1990
E-mail: info@sendasantiguas.com; sales@sendasantiguas.com; greendykbill@aol.com
Web site: http://www.sendasantiguas.com
Dist(s): **Send The Light Distribution LLC.**

Editorial Sudamericana S.A. (ARG) *(978-950-07; 978-950-37) Dist. by* **Distribks Inc.**

Editorial Sudamericana S.A. (ARG) *(978-950-07; 978-950-37) Dist. by* **Lectorum Pubns.**

Editorial Unilit, *(978-0-7899; 978-0-945792; 978-1-56063)* Div. of Spanish Hse., Inc., 1360 NW 88th Ave., Miami, FL 33172-3093 USA (SAN 247-5979) Tel 305-592-6136; Fax: 305-592-0087; Toll Free: 800-767-7726
E-mail: sales1@unidial.com
Web site: http://www.editorialunilit.com/
Dist(s): **Bethany Hse. Pubs.**
Lectorum Pubns., Inc.

Editorial Vida Abundante, *(978-0-9765828)* P.O. Box 1073, Fajardo, PR 00738 USA Tel 787-860-3555
Web site: http://www.vidaabundante.org.

Editorial Voluntad S.A. (COL) *(978-958-02) Dist. by* **Continental Bk.**

Editorial Voluntad S.A. (COL) *(978-958-02) Dist. by* **Distr Norma.**

Editorium, The, *(978-1-60096; 978-1-4341)* 3907 Marsha Dr., West Jordan, UT 84081 USA Tel 801-750-2498 Cell
E-mail: lyon.jack@gmail.com
Web site: http://www.editorium.com; http://www.wakinglionpress.com; http://www.templehillbooks.com.

Edivision Compania Editorial, S.A. de C.V. (MEX) *(978-968-890) Dist. by* **Continental Bk.**

Edizioni PIEMME spa (ITA) *(978-88-384; 978-88-566; 978-88-585) Dist. by* **Distribks Inc.**

EDR, *(978-0-9794615)* P.O. Box 22, Waterport, NY 14571 USA
E-mail: sakina@edrsinc.com
Web site: http://www.edrsinc.com; http://www.omariworld.com.

Edu Designs, *(978-0-9795017)* P.O. Box 660518, Arcadia, CA 91066-0518 USA Tel 626-979-8417
E-mail: silverplume07@earthlink.net.

Educa Vision, *(978-1-881839; 978-1-58432; 978-1-62632)* 7550 NW 47th Ave., Coconut Creek, FL 33073 USA (SAN 760-873X) Tel 954-968-7433; Fax: 954-970-0330
E-mail: educa@aol.com
Web site: http://www.educavision.com; http://www.educabrazil.org; http://www.caribbeanstudiespress.com; www.educalanguage.com
Dist(s): **Follett School Solutions.**

Educare Pr., *(978-0-944638)* P.O. Box 17222, Seattle, WA 98107 USA Tel 206-782-4797; Fax: 206-782-4802 Do not confuse with EduCare, Colorado Springs, CO
E-mail: educarepress@hotmail.com
Web site: http://www.educarepress.com.

Education and More, Inc., *(978-0-9755809)* 1760 Clayton Cir., Cumming, GA 30040-7860 USA Tel 678-455-7667
E-mail: education@educationandmore.com
Web site: http://www.educationandmore.com.

Education Ctr., Inc., *(978-1-56234)* Orders Addr.: P.O. Box 9753, Greensboro, NC 27429 USA Tel 336-854-0309; Fax: 336-547-1590; Toll Free: 800-334-0298; Edit Addr.: 3515 W. Market St., Greensboro, NC 27403 USA (SAN 256-6311) Fax: 336-851-8218; 4224 Tudor Ln. Ste. 101, Greensboro, NC 27410-8145 (SAN 256-632X); *Imprints*: Mailbox Books, The (The Mailbox Bks)
E-mail: jmartin@theeducationcenter.com; mjones@themailbox.com
Web site: http://theeducationcenter.com; http://www.themailbox.com
Dist(s): **Sharpe, M.E. Inc.**

Education Services Australia Ltd. (AUS) *(978-1-86366; 978-0-9758070; 978-1-74200; 978-0-646-19608-4; 978-0-646-21423-8; 978-0-646-24402-0; 978-0-646-24701-4; 978-0-646-25530-9) Dist. by* **Cheng Tsui.**

Educational Activities, Inc., *(978-0-7925; 978-0-89525; 978-0-914296; 978-1-55737)* Orders Addr.: P.O. Box 87, Baldwin, NY 11510 USA; Edit Addr.: 1947 Grand Ave., Baldwin, NY 11510 USA (SAN 207-4400) Tel 516-223-4666; Fax: 516-623-9282; Toll Free: 800-797-3223
E-mail: learn@edact.com
Web site: http://www.edact.com
Dist(s): **Follett School Solutions.**

Educational Adventures *See* **Mighty Kids Media**

Educational Development Corporation *See* **EDC Publishing**

Educational Expertise, LLC, *(978-0-9713450)* 427 E. Belvedere Ave., Baltimore, MD 21212 USA
Web site: http://www.educationalexpertise.com.

Educational Impressions, *(978-0-910857; 978-1-56644)* Orders Addr.: P.O. Box 77, Hawthorne, NJ 07507 USA (SAN 274-4899) Tel 973-423-4666; Fax: 973-423-5569; Toll Free: 800-451-7450; Edit Addr.: 210 Sixth Ave., Hawthorne, NJ 07507 USA
E-mail: awpeller@word.net.att.net
Web site: http://www.awpeller.com
Dist(s): **Continental Bk. Co., Inc.**

Educational Media Corp., *(978-0-932796; 978-1-930572)* Orders Addr.: 1443 Old York Rd., Wartminster, PA 18974 USA Fax: 215-956-9041; Toll Free: 800-448-2197; Edit Addr.: 4256 Central Ave. NE, Minneapolis, MN 55421-2920 USA (SAN 212-4203) Tel 763-781-0088; Fax: 763-781-7753; Toll Free: 800-966-3382
E-mail: emedia@educationalmedia.com
Web site: http://www.educationalmedia.com.

Educators Publishing Concepts, Inc., *(978-1-892354)* P.O. Box 665, Wheaton, IL 60189 USA Tel 630-653-5336; Fax: 630-653-5368 Do not confuse with Educational Publishing Concepts, Inc., Walla Walla, WA
E-mail: Jerryw@newkidsmedia.com
Web site: http://www.newkidsmedia.com.

Educational Publishing LLC, *(978-1-60436)* Orders Addr.: 51 Saw Mill Pond Rd., Edison, NJ 08817-6025 USA Toll Free: 800-554-2296; Edit Addr.: 10 W. 33rd St. Rm. 910, New York, NY 10001-3306 USA (SAN 854-2422)
Web site: http://www.earlystartchild.com.

Educational Research & Applications, LLC, *(978-0-9762724)* P.O. Box 1242, Danville, CA 94526 USA.

Educational Resources, Inc., *(978-1-931574)* 1691 Highland Pkwy., Saint Paul, MN 55116 USA Tel 651-592-3688; Fax: 651-690-2188 Do not confuse with companies with same name in Shawnee Mission, KS, Columbia, SC, Elgin, IL
E-mail: Edres1691@aol.com
Web site: http://www.eduresources.org.

Educational Solutions, Inc., *(978-0-87825)* 99 University Pl., 6th Flr., New York, NY 10003-4555 USA (SAN 205-6186) Tel 212-674-2988 Do not confuse with Educational Solutions, Stafford, TX.

Educational Testing Service, *(978-0-88685)* P.O. Box 6108, Princeton, NJ 08541-6108 USA (SAN 238-034X) Tel 609-771-7243; Fax: 609-771-7385 Do not confuse with Educational Testing Service in Washington, DC
E-mail: lsavadge@ets.org; j.womack@ets.org; cbrodsky@ets.org
Web site: http://www.ets.org
Dist(s): **Independent Pubs. Group.**

Educational Tools, Inc., *(978-0-9766802; 978-0-9774310; 978-1-933797)* 3500 Beachwood Ct., Suite 102, Jacksonville, FL 32224 USA Fax: 904-998-1941; Toll Free: 800-586-9940
E-mail: rpettus@educationaltools.org
Web site: http://www.educationaltools.org.

Educational Video Resources *See* **Summit Interactive**

Educators for the Environment *See* **Energy Education Group**

Educators Publishing Service, Inc., *(978-0-8388; 978-1-4293)* P.O. Box 9031, Cambridge, MA 02139-9031 USA (SAN 201-8225) Toll Free: 800-435-7728; 625 Mount Auburn St., Cambridge, MA 02138
E-mail: epsbooks@epsbooks.com
Web site: http://www.epsbooks.com.

Educ-Easy Bks., *(978-0-9664217; 978-0-9912724; 978-0-9864034; 978-0-9963893; 978-0-9968972)* POB 6366, Greenville, SC 29606 USA Tel 910-798-5042
E-mail: gisela.hausmann@yahoo.com
Web site: http://www.NakedDetermination.com.

EDUKIT, L.L.C., *(978-0-9765917)* P.O. Box 821, Suffern, NY 10901 USA
E-mail: edukitco@aol.com
Web site: http://www.edukit.biz.

Edupress, Inc., *(978-1-56472)* P.O. Box 800, Fort Atkinson, WI 53538-0800 USA Toll Free: 800-835-7978 Do not confuse with EduPress, Pittsburgh, PA
E-mail: info@edupressinc.com
Web site: http://www.edupressinc.com.

Edu-Steps, Inc., *(978-0-9771101; 978-0-9863690)* Orders Addr.: 4644 N. 22nd St. Suite 1161, Phoenix, AZ 85016-4699 USA Tel 480-570-3888; Fax: 602-795-6837
E-mail: patdoran@edu-steps.com
Web site: http://www.edu-steps.com.

Edutech Learning Resource Ctr., *(978-0-9768208)* 1361 NE 158 St., North Miami Beach, FL 33162 USA Tel 305-947-6393
E-mail: edutech_learning@yahoo.com.

Edutunes, *(978-1-930979)* 2067 Rurline Dr., Saint Louis, MO 63146 USA Tel 808-728-8863
E-mail: missjenny@edutunes.com
Web site: http://www.edutunes.com.

Edwards, R. G. Publishing, *(978-0-615-13336-2; 978-0-615-16739-8; 978-0-615-17785-4)* P.O. Box 978, Goodlettsville, TN 37070 USA
Dist(s): **Lulu Enterprises Inc.**

Edwards, R.G. Publishing *See* **Edwards, R. G. Publishing**

ee publishing & productions, inc., *(978-0-9753843; 978-0-9798466)* P.O. Box 7006, Fairfax Station, VA 22039 USA Tel 703-256-1721 (phone/fax)
E-mail: info@eeppinc.com; lsaker@eeppinc.com
Web site: http://www.eeppinc.com
Dist(s): **AtlasBooks Distribution.**

eeBoo Corp., *(978-1-59461; 978-1-68227)* 170 West 74th St., Ste. 102, New York, NY 10023 USA (SAN 860-4371) Fax: 212-678-1922
E-mail: christine@eeboo.com
Web site: http://www.eeboo.com.

Eelman's Pr., *(978-0-9747053)* Orders Addr.: P.O. Box Box 359, South Orleans, MA 02662 USA Tel 607-277-0612; Edit Addr.: Davis Rd., South Orleans, MA 02662 USA.

Eepie Pr., *(978-0-9755606)* 1412 Greenbrier Pkwy., Suite 145-B, Norfolk, VA 23320 USA Tel 757-424-5868; Fax: 757-424-5845
E-mail: info@eepiepress.com
Web site: http://www.eepiepress.com
Dist(s): **Print & Ship.**

Eerdmans Bks For Young Readers *Imprint of* **Eerdmans, William B. Publishing Co.**

†Eerdmans, William B. Publishing Co., *(978-0-8028; 978-1-4674)* 2140 Oak Industrial Dr NE, Grand Rapids, MI 49505 USA (SAN 220-0058) Tel 616-459-4591; Fax: 616-459-6540; Toll Free: 800-253-7521 (orders); *Imprints*: Eerdmans Books For Young Readers (Eerdmans Bks)
E-mail: info@eerdmans.com; customerservice@eerdmans.com
Web site: http://www.eerdmans.com
Dist(s): **David Brown Book Company, The**
Forward Movement Pubns.
Lightning Source, Inc.
Send The Light Distribution LLC; *CIP.*

EFFE Bks., *(978-0-9773583)* P.O. Box 3448, Winter Park, FL 32790-23448 USA (SAN 257-3784) Tel 407-645-2326
E-mail: tfunaro@summittech.us
Web site: http://www.effebooks.com
Dist(s): **Midpoint Trade Bks., Inc.**

Effective Literacy Methods, *(978-0-9706094)* 57 Knollwood Dr., Rochester, NY 14618-3512 USA
E-mail: info@newphonics.com; rkb@newphonics.com
Web site: http://www.newphonics.com.

Efforts Unified, *(978-0-9763523)* 244 Fifth Ave., No. N259, New York, NY 10001 USA.

EG Bks., *(978-0-615-54589-9; 978-0-615-55920-9)* 360 Oak St., Oakfield, WI 53065 USA Tel 920-583-3329
E-mail: e.gamer3@gmail.com.

Egap Gifa Bks. *Imprint of* **Leafcollecting.com Publishing Co.**

Egg Hill Pubns., *(978-0-9652351)* Orders Addr.: 113 Cottontail Ln., Centre Hall, PA 16828-8508 USA Tel 814-360-4401
E-mail: jandhfra2@yahoo.com
Dist(s): **Partners Bk. Distributing, Inc.**

Egger Publishing, Inc., *(978-1-886050; 978-1-934262)* P.O. Box 12248, Scottsdale, AZ 85267 USA Tel 480-596-5100; Fax: 480-951-2276; Toll Free: 888-937-7355
E-mail: regger@sittonspelling.com
Web site: http://www.sittonspelling.com
Dist(s): **Northwest Textbook Depository.**

Egmont Bks., Ltd. (GBR) *(978-0-416; 978-0-603; 978-0-7497; 978-0-7498; 978-1-4052) Dist. by* **IPG Chicago.**

Egmont Bks., Ltd. (GBR) *(978-0-416; 978-0-603; 978-0-7497; 978-0-7498; 978-1-4052) Dist. by* **Trafalgar.**

Eifrig Publishing, *(978-0-9795518; 978-1-936172; 978-1-63233)* P.O. Box 66, Lemont, PA 16851-0066 USA (SAN 858-6462) Fax: 888-340-6543; Toll Free: 888-340-6543
E-mail: contact@eifrigpublishing.com
Web site: http://www.eifrigpublishing.com
Dist(s): **BookBaby**
Follett School Solutions.

Eight Dog Publishing *See* **Studio4264**

Eileen/Morris *See* **Shnoozles, LLC**

EJMP, *(978-0-615-77563-0)* 2421 SW Candletree Dr Apt 6, Topeka, KS 66614 USA Tel 785-338-0625
Dist(s): **CreateSpace Independent Publishing Platform.**

EK Success Ltd., *(978-1-930232)* P.O. Box 1141, Clifton, NJ 07014-1141 USA Tel 973-458-0092; Fax: 973-594-0545; Toll Free: 800-524-1349
E-mail: success@eksuccess.com
Web site: http://www.eksuccess.com.

EKADOO Publishing Group, *(978-0-9747387)* Orders Addr.: P.O. Box 2286, North Redondo Beach, CA 90278 USA Toll Free: 877-252-3404; Edit Addr.: 123 West First St., Suite 675, Casper, WY 82601 USA
E-mail: info@ekadoo.com
Web site: http://www.ekadoo.com.

Ekaré Europa S.L. (ESP) *(978-84-933060; 978-84-934863; 978-84-936504) Dist. by* **Lectorum Pubns.**

Ekare, Ediciones (VEN) *(978-980-257; 978-84-8351; 978-84-937212; 978-84-937767) Dist. by* **Mariuccia Iaconi Bk Imports.**

Ekare, Ediciones (VEN) *(978-980-257; 978-84-8351; 978-84-937212; 978-84-937767) Dist. by* **Lectorum Pubns.**

Ekklesia Pr., *(978-0-9827446)* 1401 So. 64th Ave, Omaha, NE 68106 USA Tel 402-416-4068; *Imprints*: Tamarin Press (Tama Pr)
E-mail: tim@ekklesiapress.com
Web site: http://www.ekklesiapress.com
Dist(s): **Smashwords.**

Eklektika Pr., Inc., *(978-0-9651672; 978-0-9765465; 978-0-9823250)* Orders Addr.: P.O. Box 157, Chelsea, MI 48118 USA Tel 734-730-5161; Edit Addr.: 6401 Conway Rd., Chelsea, MI 48118 USA
Web site: http://www.theseniorsguide.com; http://www.meandmycaregivers.com
Dist(s): **Alliance Bk. Co.**
Distributors, The.

EKR Pubns., *(978-0-9791348)* 257 N. Calderwood St., #356, Alcoa, TN 37701-2111 USA (SAN 852-5293) Tel 727-517-2767 (publisher contact); Toll Free Fax: 866-790-0417 (orders/publisher); Toll Free: 800-266-5564 (orders/AtlasBooks)
Web site: http://www.willigetsahistorylesson.com; http://www.ekrpublications.com.

Ekwike Bks. & Publishing, *(978-0-9661598; 978-0-9789972)* Orders Addr.: P.O. Box 470, New York, NY 10034 USA Tel 718-798-5788 (phone/fax); Edit Addr.: 4417 Edson Ave., Bronx, NY 10466 USA Tel 917-306-7244 (cell)
E-mail: ikebezi@juno.com.

Ekwike Publications *See* **Ekwike Bks. & Publishing**

El Aleph Editores, S.A. (ESP) *(978-84-7669; 978-84-85501) Dist. by* **Ediciones.**

El Assali, Amira, *(978-0-9777650)* 23842 Alicia Pkwy Apt. 248, Mission Viejo, CA 92691 USA Tel 714-478-2114
E-mail: amiraalassaly@hotmail.com.

El Cid Editor Incorporated, *(978-0-9669968; 978-1-4135; 978-1-4492; 978-1-5129)* Div. of E-Libro Corp., 17555 Atlantic Blvd. # 4, Sunny Isl Bch, FL 33160-2996 USA; 16699 Collins Ave., No. 1003, Miami, FL 33160 Tel 305-466-0155
E-mail: editor@e-libro.com
Web site: http://www.e-libro.net; http://www.e-libro.com
Dist(s): **MyiLibrary**
ProQuest LLC
ebrary, Inc.

El Hogar y La Moda, S.A. (ESP) *(978-84-7183) Dist. by* **AIMS Intl.**

El Jefe, *(978-0-9742840)* P.O. Box 7871, Pueblo West, CO 81007 USA
E-mail: rearch145@aol.com.

El Publications *See* **Jesus Estanislado**

El Zarape Pr., *(978-0-9789954)* 1413 Jay Ave., McAllen, TX 78504-3327 USA (SAN 852-1514)
E-mail: wegotwords@hotmail.com
Web site: http://www.elzarapepress.com.

Elan Systems, Incorporated *See* **Aunt Dee's Attic, Inc.**

Elderberry Press, Inc., *(978-0-9658407; 978-1-930859; 978-1-932762; 978-1-934956)* 1393 Old Homestead Rd., Oakland, OR 97462 USA (SAN 254-6604) Tel 541-459-6043 Do not confuse with Elderberry Pr., Encinitas, CA
E-mail: editor@elderberrypress.com
Web site: http://www.elderberrypress.com
Dist(s): **Smashwords.**

Eldergivers, *(978-0-9742262)* 1755 Clay St., San Francisco, CA 94109 USA
E-mail: info@eldergivers.org
Web site: http://www.eldergivers.org.

Eldorado Ink, *(978-1-932904; 978-1-61900)* P.O. Box 100097, Pittsburgh, PA 15233-4842 USA Tel 412-688-0444; Fax: 412-688-8545; Toll Free: 800-783-6767
E-mail: info@eldoradoink.com
Web site: http://www.eldoradoink.com.

Elea Pr., *(978-0-615-34357-0; 978-0-615-67531-2; 978-0-615-75642-4; 978-0-692-21410-7)* Orders Addr.: P.O. Box 2351, Livermore, CA 94551 USA
Web site: http://www.nursiesbook.com; http://www.nightweaning.com
Dist(s): **Lightning Source, Inc.**

Electa Architecture (GBR) *(978-1-904313) Dist. by* **HachBkGrp.**

Electret Scientific Co., *(978-0-917406)* P.O. Box 4132, Star City, WV 26504 USA (SAN 206-4715) Tel 304-594-1639 (phone/fax)
E-mail: U1a00439@wvnet.edu.

Electric Theatre Radio Hour, *(978-0-9848486)* 2200 Market St. Suite 735, Galveston, TX 77550 USA Tel 409-750-8915
E-mail: brendadonalolo@sbcglobal.net.

Elemental Pubs., *(978-0-9765403)* 4404 Whistling Way, Raleigh, NC 27616 USA Tel 919-217-2092.

Elena Marcus Negoita, *(978-0-615-57545-2)* 2240 Blake St. No. 315, Berkeley, CA 94704 USA
Web site: www.doghappiness.net
Dist(s): **CreateSpace Independent Publishing Platform.**

ElephantSide Pr., *(978-0-9716873)* 33 Bedford St., Suite 10, Lexington, MA 02420 USA (SAN 255-4062).

Eleuthera Press *See* **Windsong Publishing Co.**

Elevé Arts Publishing *See* **Eleve Publishing**

Elevator Group, The, *(978-0-9678564; 978-0-9820384; 978-0-9819719; 978-0-9824945; 978-0-9825282)* P.O. Box 207, Paoli, PA 19301 USA (SAN 851-3104) Tel 610-296-4966; Fax: 610-644-4436; P.O. Box 207, Paoli, PA 19301 Tel 610-296-4966; Fax: 610-644-4436
E-mail: TheElevatorGroup@comcast.net
Web site: http://www.TheElevatorGroup.com; http://www.TEGFaith.com
Dist(s): **MyiLibrary**
ebrary, Inc.

Eleve Publishing, *(978-0-9827304)* 3001 S. Jay St., Denver, CO 80227 USA Tel 720-560-2448
E-mail: larryelwood@gmail.com.

Elf Garb, *(978-0-615-64129-4; 978-0-9881822)* 96 Idlewell Bld, Weymouth, MA 02188 USA Tel 781-331-7949
E-mail: kelley@elfgarb.com
Web site: www.elfgarb.com.

Elfa Bks., *(978-0-578-10974-9; 978-0-578-10978-7; 978-0-578-11908-3; 978-0-578-12216-8; 978-0-578-12227-4; 978-0-578-12965-5; 978-0-578-12975-4; 978-0-578-13661-5; 978-0-578-13735-3)* 14967 Merlot Dr., Sterling Heights, MI 48312 USA Tel 586-634-4321
E-mail: elfabooks@yahoo.com
Web site: http://www.elfabooks.com.

Elgar, Edward Publishing, Inc., *(978-1-84064; 978-1-85278; 978-1-85898; 978-1-84376; 978-1-84542; 978-1-84720)* Orders Addr.: P.O. Box 960, Herndon, VA 20172-0960 USA Tel 800-390-3149; Fax: 802-864-7626; Edit Addr.: 9 Dewey Ct., Northampton, MA 01060-3815 USA (SAN 299-4615)
E-mail: elgarinfo@e-elgar.com; kwight@e-elgar.com; asturmer@e-elgar.com
Web site: http://www.e-elgar.com
Dist(s): **Books International, Inc.**
MyiLibrary.

Elias Pubns., LLC, *(978-0-9726247)* P.O. Box 49704, Sarasota, FL 34230 USA Tel 941-556-5656; Fax: 720-920-7262
E-mail: eliaspublications@hotmail.com
Web site: http://www.eliaspublications.com.

Eliassen Creative, *(978-1-937160; 978-0-9892097)* 10328 Horseback Ridge Ave., las Vegas, NV 89144 USA Tel 702-328-2637
E-mail: sunshinenelson@hotmail.com.

eLiberty Pr., *(978-0-9755608)* 2250 N. University Pkwy. No. 4888, Provo, UT 84604 USA Tel 801-427-6630; Fax: 801-373-5999
E-mail: info@elibertypress.com; sales@elibertypress.com
Web site: http://www.elibertypress.com
Dist(s): **Alibris**
Powells.com.

Elim Publishing, *(978-0-9713711; 978-1-59919)* Div. of Elim Gospel Church, 1679 Dalton Rd., Lima, NY 14485 USA Tel 716-624-5560; Fax: 716-624-9677
E-mail: randy@elimpublishing.com
Web site: http://www.elimpublishing.com
Dist(s): **Lightning Source, Inc.**

Elissian Publishing Co., *(978-0-615-47664-3)* 9715 FM 620 N No. 11203, Austin, TX 78726 USA Tel 512-913-5553; Fax: 512-436-9796
E-mail: demiolesen@hotmail.com.

Elizabooks, *(978-0-9762839)* 5515 Catfish Ct., Waunakee, WI 53597 USA Tel 608-849-1984; Fax: 608-849-1985; Toll Free: 888-603-1984
E-mail: liz@elizabookspublishing.com
Web site: http://www.elizabooks.com.

Elk River Pr., *(978-0-9710389)* 1125 Central Ave., Charleston, WV 25302 USA Tel 304-342-1848; Fax: 304-343-0594 Do not confuse with companies with the same or similar name in Altamont, KS, Athens, AL.
E-mail: wvbooks@verizon.net
Web site: http://www.wvbookco.com
Dist(s): **West Virginia Book Co., The.**

Elkarez Publishing Co., *(978-0-9819100)* 327 Sheldon Ave., Staten Island, NY 10312 USA Tel 718-966-5205
E-mail: info@elkarezpublishing.com
Web site: http://www.elkarezpublishing.com.

Eller Books *See* **Brethren Pr.**

Elliott, Jane, *(978-0-9741254)* 707 Country Club Rd., Schofield, WI 54476 USA; *Imprints*: Dynagraphix (Dynagraphix).

Ellis Pr., The, *(978-0-933180; 978-0-944024)* Div. of Spoon River Poetry Pr., P.O. Box 6, Granite Falls, MN 56241 USA (SAN 214-008X) Tel 507-537-6463 Do not confuse with Ellis Pr., in Charlottesville, VA
E-mail: pichaske@southwest.msus.edu
Web site: http://www.southwest.msus.edu/faculty/pichaske/plains.htm.

Ellison, Penny, *(978-0-9771121)* Orders Addr.: P.O. Box 510082, Miami, FL 33151 USA Tel 786-222-1443; Edit Addr.: 4877 Registry Ln NW, Kennesaw, GA 30152-2891 USA.

Elly Blue Publishing *Imprint of* **Microcosm Publishing**

Elma Colletes & Sons, *(978-0-9719337)* 5895 Gardens Reach Cove, Memphis, TN 38120-2523 USA Fax: 901-747-0040
E-mail: mschnap1@midsouth.rr.com.

For full information on wholesalers and distributors, refer to the Wholesaler and Distributor Name Index

Elmdale Park Books, *(978-0-9860593)* 10193 W 96th Ter, Overland Park, KS 66212 USA Tel 913-908-0129; Fax: 913-945-1426
E-mail: tekobernard@yahoo.com
Web site: www.tekobernard.com.

Elohim Bks., *(978-0-9768831)* Orders Addr.: P.O. Box 1027, Howell, MI 48844 USA.

Eloquence Pr., *(978-0-9753300; 978-0-9824954; 978-0-9913283)* Orders Addr.: 51689 Via Bendita, La Quinta, CA 92253 USA (SAN 255-9676) Tel 760-698-8482
E-mail: jeadon@cox.net; jeadon2@gmail.com
Web site: http://www.eadonbooks.com; http://www.theamericandramaseries.com; http://.

Eloquent Bks. *Imprint of* **Strategic Book Publishing & Rights Agency (SBPRA)**

Elora Media, LLC, *(978-0-9786813)* PMB 112, 1201 Yelm Ave., Yelm, WA 98597-9859 USA Tel 360-894-6369
E-mail: betsy@eloramedia.com.

Elora Pr., *(978-0-9786813)* Div. of Elora Media, LLC, PMB 112, 1201 Yelm Ave., Yelm, WA 98597-9859 USA (SAN 851-3228) Toll Free: 888-440-8972
E-mail: betsy@eloramedia.com
Web site: http://www.eloramedia.com.

Elotos Pr., LLC, *(978-0-9821737)* 1220 N. Market St., Suite 808, Wilmington, DE 19808 USA
E-mail: info@elotos.com
Web site: http://www.ELOTOS.com.

ELP Bks., *(978-0-9841650)* P.O. Box 1506, Gardena, CA 90249 USA (SAN 858-6098) Tel 213-928-6724
E-mail: emmja_p@sbcglobal.net
Web site: http://www.elpbooks.net.

Elsevier - Health Sciences Div., *(978-0-323; 978-0-443; 978-0-444; 978-0-7020; 978-0-7216; 978-0-7234; 978-0-7236; 978-0-7506; 978-0-8016; 978-0-8151; 978-0-920513; 978-0-932883; 978-1-55664; 978-1-56053; 978-1-898507; 978-1-932141; 978-1-4160; 978-1-4377; 978-1-4557)* Subs. of Elsevier Science, Orders Addr.: a/o Customer Service, 3251 Riverport Ln., Maryland Heights, MO 63043 USA Tel 314-453-7010; Fax: 314-447-8030; Toll Free Fax: 800-535-9935; Toll Free: 800-545-2522; 800-460-3110 (Customers Outside US); 1799 Highway 50, Linn, MO 65051 (SAN 200-2280); Edit Addr.: 1600 John F. Kennedy Blvd., Suite 1800, Philadelphia, PA 19103-2899 USA Tel 215-239-3900; Fax: 215-239-3990; Toll Free: 800-523-4069; *Imprints:* Mosby (MosElsHlth)
E-mail: usbkinfo@elsevier.com
Web site: http://www.elsevier.com; http://www.us.elsevierhealth.com/
Dist(s): **Elsevier**
MyiLibrary
TNT Media Group, Inc.
ebrary, Inc.

Elsevier Science - Health Sciences Division *See* **Elsevier - Health Sciences Div.**

Elsevier Science & Technology Bks., Orders Addr.: P.O. Box 28430, Saint Louis, MO 63146-0930 USA Toll Free Fax: 800-535-9935; Toll Free: 800-545-2522; 800-460-3110 (Customers Outside US); Edit Addr.: 525 B St., Suite 1900, San Diego, CA 92101 USA Toll Free: 1-800-894-3434; 200 Wheeler Rd., 6th Flr., Burlington, MA 01803 Tel 781-313-4700; *Imprints:* Butterworth-Heinemann (Butter Sci Hein)
E-mail: bookstore.orders@elsevier.com
Web site: http://www.elsevier.com/; http://www.syngress.com
Dist(s): **CreateSpace Independent Publishing Platform**
Ebsco Publishing
Elsevier - Health Sciences Div.
Elsevier
Follett School Solutions
Leonard, Hal Corp.
LEXIS Publishing
MyiLibrary
Oxford Univ. Pr., Inc.
Rittenhouse Bk. Distributors
Vital Source Technologies, Inc.
ebrary, Inc.

Eltanin Publishing, *(978-0-615-48933-9; 978-0-615-54003-0; 978-0-615-54993-4; 978-0-615-60095-6; 978-0-615-60158-8; 978-0-615-72177-4; 978-0-615-85955-2; 978-0-615-96869-8; 978-0-692-23511-9; 978-0-692-34082-0; 978-0-692-42323-3)* 95 Spear St., Charlotte, VT 05445 USA Tel 802-985-3729
Web site: http://eltaninpublishing.com/
Dist(s): **CreateSpace Independent Publishing Platform**
Dummy Record Do Not USE!!!!.

Eltsar Pr., *(978-0-9769275; 978-0-9833990; 978-0-9850892)* 40453 Cherokee Oaks Dr., Three Rivers, CA 93271-9617 USA Tel 559-561-3270
Dist(s): **Lulu Enterprises Inc.**

Elv Enterprises, *(978-0-9829669)* P.O. Box 2225, La Jolla, CA 92038 USA Tel 858-336-6499
E-mail: rainierpage@ymail.com.

Elva Resa *Imprint of* **Elva Resa Publishing, LLC**

Elva Resa Publishing, LLC, *(978-0-9657483; 978-1-934617)* 8362 Tamarack Village, Suite 119-106, Saint Paul, MN 55125 USA Tel 651-357-8770 orders & general info; Fax: 501-641-0777 orders accepted by fax; *Imprints:* Elva Resa (Elva Resa); Alma Little (Alma Little)
E-mail: orders@elvaresa.com
Web site: http://www.elvaresa.com
Dist(s): **Follett School Solutions.**

ELW Pubns., *(978-0-9766233)* 1831 Secretary's Rd., Scottsville, VA 24590 USA Tel 434-295-1678; *Imprints:* His Grace Is Sufficient (HGIS)
E-mail: bridgeministry@aol.com.

Elysian Editions *Imprint of* **Princeton Bk. Co. Pubs.**

Elysian Hills, *(978-0-9635589)* Orders Addr.: P.O. Box 40693, Albuquerque, NM 87196 USA Tel 505-897-2734; Fax: 505-897-4614; Edit Addr.: 919 Western Meadows, Albuquerque, NM 87114 USA
E-mail: EdDziczek@aol.com.

Elytra & Antenna, *(978-0-9719129; 978-0-9802401)* 4663 Ruby Ln., Brunswick Hills, OH 44212 USA Tel 330-273-1918
E-mail: elytraandantenna@lycos.com
Web site: http://www.elytraandantenna.com.

ELZ Publishing, *(978-0-9772717)* 33 Sheridan Rd., Wellesley, MA 02481 USA Tel 781-237-7417; Fax: 781-237-7429
E-mail: elzahniser@mindspring.com
Web site: http://elzpublishing.com.

EM Greenberg Pr., Inc., *(978-0-9634561; 978-0-615-40288-8)* 1245 Sixteenth St., Suite 210, Santa Monica, CA 90402 USA Tel 310-454-0502 (phone/fax)
E-mail: elainergordonphd@gmail.com
Web site: http://elainegordon.com.

Emaculate Publishing, *(978-1-931855)* P.O. Box 1074, Woodbridge, VA 22195-1074 USA (SAN 254-2005)
E-mail: emaculatepublishing@yahoo.com; info@emaculatepublishing.com
Web site: http://www.emaculatepublishing.com.

eMaginationFlow, Inc., *(978-0-9893751)* 81 Prospect St., Acton, MA 01720 USA Tel 978-263-1713; Fax: 978-263-1713
E-mail: books.create@emaginationflow.com
Web site: http://emaginationflow.com/.

Emarketing Of Michigan, LLC, *(978-0-615-38985-1; 978-0-615-88247-5)* Orders Addr.: 11127 Kings Ct., Sterling Heights, MI 48312 USA Tel 586-838-0099; Fax: 586-275-2295
Web site: http://www.readwithmax.com; http://www.emarketingofmichigan.com.

Ember *Imprint of* **Random Hse. Children's Bks.**

Ember *Imprint of* **Random House Publishing Group**

Embrace Communications, *(978-0-9668878)* 6887 Red Mountain Rd., Livermore, CO 80536 USA Tel 970-416-9076; Fax: 970-407-0083
E-mail: suengayReynolds@aol.com
Dist(s): **Spring Arbor Distributors, Inc.**

EMC Publishing, *(978-0-9884707; 978-0-692-36034-7)* 11718 S.E. Federal Hwy. #245, Hobe Sound, FL 33455 USA Tel 504-669-9099.

†EMC/Paradigm Publishing, *(978-0-7638; 978-0-8219; 978-0-88436; 978-0-912022; 978-1-56118)* Div. of EMC Corp., 875 Montreal Way, Saint Paul, MN 55102-4245 USA (SAN 201-3800) Tel 651-290-2800; Fax: 651-290-2828
E-mail: publish@emcp.com; educate@emcp.com
Web site: http://www.emcp.com
Dist(s): **Continental Bk. Co., Inc.**; *CIP.*

Emecé Editores S.A. (ARG) *(978-950-04; 978-950-519) Dist. by* **Lectorum Pubns.**

Emecé Editores S.A. (ARG) *(978-950-04; 978-950-519) Dist. by* **Planeta.**

Emece Editores (ESP) *(978-84-95908) Dist. by* **Ediciones.**

Emece Editores (ESP) *(978-84-95908) Dist. by* **Lectorum Pubns.**

EMedia Corp., *(978-1-891155)* 664 NE Northlake Way, Seattle, WA 98105-6428 USA Toll Free: 888-363-3424
E-mail: custserv@emediamusic.com
Web site: http://www.emediamusic.com.

Emerald Bk. Co., *(978-1-934572; 978-1-937110)* Div. of Greenleaf Bk. Group, 4425 Mo Pac Expy., Suite 600, Austin, TX 78735 USA
Dist(s): **Greenleaf Book Group**
MyiLibrary.

Emerald Bks., *(978-1-883002; 978-1-932096; 978-1-62486)* Orders Addr.: P.O. Box 635, Lynnwood, WA 98046 USA (SAN 298-7538) Tel 425-771-1153; Fax: 425-775-2383; Toll Free: 800-922-2143; Edit Addr.: 7825 230th St. SW, Edmonds, WA 98026 USA Do not confuse with Emerald Bks. in Westfield, NJ
E-mail: wlwalsh@seanet.com
Web site: http://www.ywampublishing.com
Dist(s): **YWAM Publishing.**

Emerald City Publishing, *(978-0-9675082)* Orders Addr.: 13209 35th Ave. NE. #a, Seattle, WA 98125 USA Tel 206-362-2116 (phone/fax, advance notice for fax required) Do not confuse with A Class Act, Sierra Madre, CA
E-mail: chiefhighliner@yahoo.com.

Emerald Hse. Group, Inc., *(978-1-889893; 978-1-932307; 978-1-935507; 978-1-62020)* 427 Wade Hampton Blvd., Greenville, SC 29609 USA Tel 864-235-2434; Fax: 864-235-2491; Toll Free: 800-209-8570; *Imprints:* Ambassador-Emerald, International (Ambassador-Emerald); Ambassador International (Ambassador Intl)
E-mail: info@emeraldhouse.com
Web site: http://www.emeraldhouse.com; www.ambassador-international.com
Dist(s): **Christian Bk. Distributors**
Follett School Solutions
Spring Arbor Distributors, Inc.

Emerald Shamrock Pr. LLC, *(978-0-9841880)* 1031 Parkland Rd., Lake Orion, MI 48360 USA (SAN 858-6675) Tel 248-393-6082
E-mail: bridget.mary@comcast.net
Web site: http://www.onechildoneplanet.com.

Emerald Star Pr., *(978-0-615-29908-2; 978-0-615-36644-9; 978-0-615-39280-6; 978-0-9831993)* P.O. Box 2621, Atlanta, GA 30331 USA.

EMI CMG Distribution,
E-mail: distribution@emicmg.com
Web site: http://www.emicmgdistribution.com.

EMK Pr., *(978-0-9726244; 978-1-942571)* Div. of EMK Group, LLC, 16 Mt. Bethel Rd., No. 219, Warren, NJ 07059 USA (SAN 255-0318) Tel 732-469-7544; Fax: 732-469-7861
E-mail: carriekitze@emkpress.com
Web site: http://www.emkpress.com
Dist(s): **Quality Bks., Inc.**

EMMA Pubns., *(978-0-9800074)* P.O. Box 654, Northville, MI 48168 USA (SAN 854-977X)
E-mail: info@emmapublications.com
Web site: http://www.emmapublications.com
Dist(s): **Partners Bk. Distributing, Inc.**

Emma's Pantry, *(978-0-9648437)* 0373 Sopris Creek Rd., #7, Basalt, CO 81621 USA Tel 970-927-4661
E-mail: eewalling@yahoo.com
Web site: http://www.pages.prodigy.com/legends/.

Emmaus Road, International, *(978-1-880185)* 7150 Tanner Ct., San Diego, CA 92111 USA Tel 619-292-7020
E-mail: emmaus_road@eri.com
Web site: http://www.eri.org.

Emmaus Road Publishing, *(978-0-9663223; 978-1-931018; 978-1-937155; 978-1-940329; 978-1-941447; 978-1-63446)* 827 N. Fourth St., Steubenville, OH 43952 USA Tel 740-283-2484; Fax: 740-283-4011; Toll Free: 800-398-5470
E-mail: shughes@cuf.org
Web site: http://www.emmausroad.org.

Emmis Books *See* **Clerisy Pr.**

Emnes Systems, *(978-0-9661636)* 7212 Antares Dr., Suite 100, Gaithersburg, MD 20879 USA Tel 240-683-8502
E-mail: ecfchang@msn.com
Web site: http://www.emnes.com.

Emotional Content, LLC, *(978-0-9817543)* 1445 S. Carmelina Ave., Los Angeles, CA 90025 USA
E-mail: info@biographicnovel.com; eiji@wadirum.com; latinsamurai@gmail.com
Web site: http://www.biographicnovel.com; http://www.emotionalcontent.net.

Empak Publishing Co., *(978-0-922162; 978-0-9616156)* Subs. of Empak Enterprises, Inc., P.O. Box 8596, Chicago, IL 60680-8596 USA (SAN 699-9182) Tel 312-642-3434; Fax: 312-642-9657; Toll Free: 800-477-4554
E-mail: empak@email.msn.com
Web site: http://www.empakpub.com.

Empire Holdings *Imprint of* **Kodel Group, LLC, The**

Empire Holdins - Literary Division for Young Readers *Imprint of* **Kodel Group, LLC, The**

Empire Publishing, *(978-0-9766246)* 1117 Desert Ln., Suite 1362, Las Vegas, NV 89102 USA Fax: 413-714-5213.

Empire Publishing Service, *(978-1-58690)* P.O. Box 1344, Studio City, CA 91614-0344 USA (SAN 630-5687) Tel 818-784-8918
E-mail: empirepubsvc@att.net.

Empowered Entertainment, *(978-0-9767076)* 5853 Liberty Creek Dr. N., Indianapolis, IN 46254 USA
E-mail: andrew@chameleonchronicles.com
Web site: http://www.chameleonchronicles.com.

Empowered Faith International, *(978-0-9768476)* P.O. Box 156, Marietta, GA 30061 USA Tel 770-218-6215
E-mail: pbbell@ecclive.org
Web site: http://www.empoweredfaith.org.

Empowering People Pub., *(978-0-9762639)* Orders Addr.: P.O. Box 329, Rex, GA 30273 USA Tel 850-328-1698
E-mail: altrell@tinapipkin.com; info@tinapipkin.com; altrellpipkin@yahoo.com
Web site: http://www.tinapipkin.com; http://www.empoweringpeopleinc.com; http://www.altrellpipkin.com.

Emprise Publishing *See* **Emprise Publishing & Media**

Emprise Publishing & Media, *(978-0-9717581; 978-0-9725121)* 3643 South Ave., Springfield, MO 65807 USA
E-mail: martyb@powermarkcomics.com.

Empty Harbor Productions, LLC, *(978-0-9790699)* 4 Sarah Lynn Ln., Suite 127, Conroe, TX 77303 USA Toll Free: 866-419-2921
E-mail: emptyharbor@msn.com
Web site: http://www.sticman.net.

Empty Set Entertainment, *(978-0-615-28744-7; 978-0-615-36542-8; 978-0-9831963; 978-1-939366)* Orders Addr.: 1549 El Prado, Suite One, San Diego, CA 92101 USA (SAN 920-7694)
Dist(s): **BookBaby.**

Empty Sky *Imprint of* **Zeromayo Studios, LLP**

Enchanted Forest Publishing, *(978-0-9910700)* P.O. Box 453, Volcano, HI 96785-0453 USA Tel 808-333-8052
E-mail: enchantedforestpublishing@gmail.com.

Enchanted Lion Bks., LLC, *(978-1-59270)* 201 Richards St. Ste. 4, Brooklyn, NY 11231-1537 USA
E-mail: zoeclaud@earthlink.com; enchantedlionbooks@yahoo.com
Dist(s): **Consortium Bk. Sales & Distribution**
Farrar, Straus & Giroux
Perseus Distribution.

Enchanted Quill Publications *See* **Stuart & Weitz Publishing Group**

Enchanted Self Pr., *(978-0-9798952)* 603 S. Edgemere Dr., West Allenhurst, NJ 07711 USA.

Enclave Publishing *Imprint of* **Marcher Lord Pr.**

Encore Performance Publishing, *(978-1-57514)* Orders Addr.: P.O. Box 692, Orem, UT 84059 USA Tel 801-785-9343; Fax: 801-785-9394
E-mail: encoreplay@aol.com
Web site: http://www.encoreplay.com.

Encore Pubns., *(978-0-9798718)* P.O. Box 117, Stoughton, WI 53589 USA Tel 608-877-9692; Fax: 608-877-9693
E-mail: masonfinancial@charter.net; bonita.mason@peachbandana.com
Web site: http://PeachBandana.com.

Encounter Bks., *(978-1-893554; 978-1-59403)* Div. of Encounter for Culture & Education, Inc., Orders Addr.: 900 Broadway., Suite 600, New York, NY 10003-1237 USA (SAN 253-1585) Toll Free Fax: 877-811-1461 (orders); Toll Free: 800-786-3839 (inquiries, MS proposals)
E-mail: read@encounterbooks.com; judy@encounterbooks.com
Web site: http://www.encounterbooks.com
Dist(s): **Capstone Pub.**
Ebsco Publishing
MyiLibrary
Perseus Bks. Group
Perseus Distribution
ebrary, Inc.

Encyclopaedia Britannica, Inc., *(978-0-7826; 978-0-8347; 978-0-85229; 978-0-87827; 978-1-59339; 978-1-60835; 978-1-61535; 978-0-9823819; 978-0-9823820; 978-0-9823821; 978-0-9823822; 978-0-9823823; 978-0-9823824; 978-1-62513)* 331 N. La Salle St., Chicago, IL 60654 USA (SAN 204-1464) Tel 312-347-7000; Fax: 312-294-2177; Toll Free Fax: 800-344-9624 (fax orders); Toll Free: 800-323-1229; 800-621-3900 (orders); 2nd Flr., Unity Wharf Mill St., London, SE1 2BH Tel 020 7500 7800; Fax: 020 7500 7878
E-mail: enquiries@britannica.co.uk; contact@eb.com
Web site: http://www.eb.com; http://www.britannica.co.uk
Dist(s): **Continental Bk. Co., Inc.**
Ebsco Publishing
Follett School Solutions
MyiLibrary
Pearson Education
Pearson Technology Group
ebrary, Inc.

Endeavor Press *See* **Endeavor Publishing**

Endeavor Pr., *(978-0-9728656)* P.O. Box 4307, Chicago, IL 60680 USA Tel 312-420-6675 Do not confuse with Endeavor Press in Gilbert, AZ
E-mail: rogerrange@endeavorpress.net
Web site: http://www.endeavorpress.com.

Endeavor Publishing, *(978-0-9743843)* 4204 E. Marshall Ave., Gilbert, AZ 85297 USA Tel 480-632-1306 (phone/fax) Do not confuse with Endeavor Press in Annapolis, MD
E-mail: endeavorpublishing@yahoo.com
Web site: http://www.dowkump.com.

Energetic Press, LLC *See* **Four Dolphins Pr., LLC**

Energy Education Group, *(978-0-9744765)* Div. of The California Study, Inc., Orders Addr.: 664 Hilary Dr., Tiburon, CA 94920 USA Tel 415-435-4574; Fax: 415-435-7737
E-mail: energyforkeeps@aol.com
Web site: http://www.energyforkeeps.org
Dist(s): **PixyJack Pr., Inc.**

Engage Literacy *Imprint of* **Capstone Pr., Inc.**

Engine Hse. Bks., *(978-0-615-19130-0; 978-0-615-19495-0; 978-0-615-20663-9; 978-0-615-21565-5; 978-0-578-00775-5; 978-0-578-01960-4; 978-1-936211)* 330 WCR 16½, Longmont, CO 80504 USA
Web site: http://www.enginehousebooks.com
Dist(s): **Lulu Enterprises Inc.**
Smashwords.

Engineering in Elementary, *(978-0-918866; 978-0-9774084; 978-1-933758; 978-1-936789; 978-1-940314)* 1 Science Pk., Boston, MA 02114 USA (SAN 210-4687) Tel 617-589-0230
E-mail: mhiggins@mos.org
Web site: www.mos.org/eie.

Enginuity, LLC, *(978-1-929645)* Orders Addr.: P.O. Box 20607, San Jose, CA 95160 USA Tel 408-268-9740; Toll Free Fax: 888-268-9740; Toll Free: 888-618-4263; Edit Addr.: 3629 Bryant St., Palo Alto, CA 94306-4209 USA
E-mail: sales@enginuity.com; support@enginuity.com
Web site: http://www.enginuity.com.

Englefield & Arnold, Incorporated *See* **Englefield & Assocs., Inc.**

Englefield & Assocs., Inc., *(978-1-884183; 978-1-59230)* Div. of Show What You Know Publishing, Orders Addr.: P.O. Box 341348, Columbus, OH 43234-1348 USA Tel 614-764-1211; Fax: 614-764-1311; Toll Free: 877-727-7464 (877-PASSING); Edit Addr.: 6344 Nicholas Dr., Columbus, OH 43235 USA
E-mail: eapub@eapublishing.com; marketing@eapublishing.com
Web site: http://www.showwhatyouknowpublishing.com/.

English Garden Talk Pr., *(978-0-9763572; 978-0-9779257; 978-0-9858431; 978-0-9915290)* 536 W. Hoptree Ct., Louisville, CO 80027 USA
E-mail: sanddollar5643@aol.com
Dist(s): **Lulu Enterprises Inc.**

Enhancing Health, Inc., *(978-0-9744479)* P.O. Box 1882, Duluth, GA 30096 USA
E-mail: info@thefitgolfer.com.

ENHEART Publishing, *(978-0-9654899; 978-0-9838882)* Orders Addr.: P.O. Box 620086, Charlotte, NC 28262 USA Tel 980-272-1410 (phone/fax)
E-mail: info@enheartpublishing.com
Web site: http://www.enheartpublishing.com
Dist(s): **BookBaby**
Parnassus Bk. Distributors.

Enigma Productions, *(978-0-9794321)* Orders Addr.: 2444 Crooks Rd. Apt. 41, Troy, MI 48084-5335 USA
Web site: http://www.enigmaw.com.

Enisen Publishing, *(978-0-9702908; 978-0-9763070)* 2118 Wilshire Blvd., # 351, Santa Monica, CA 90403-5784 USA (SAN 253-3308) Tel 310-989-4069; Fax: 310-576-7278 Do not confuse with companies with the same name in Clermont, FL, Hollywood, CA, Otis Orchards, WA
E-mail: publishing@enisen.com
Web site: http://www.enisen.com.

Enlighten Learning, *(978-0-9755865)* 269 S. Beverly Dr., No. 139, Beverly Hills, CA 90212 USA Tel 310-358-2995.

Publisher Name Index

Enlighten Pubns., *(978-0-9706226)* Orders Addr.: P.O. Box 525, Vauxhall, NJ 07088 USA Toll Free: 866-862-8626
E-mail: books@enlightenpublications.com
Web site: http://www.authorsden.com/jackiehardrick; www.enlightenpublications.com.

Enlightened Bks., *(978-0-9769541; 978-0-692-02980-0)* Orders Addr.: P.O. Box 7423, NewPort Beach, CA 92658 USA Tel 949-644-1376; Edit Addr.: 1 Belcourt Dr., Newport Beach, CA 92660 USA
E-mail: enlightenedbooks13@gmail.com
Web site: http://www.enlightenedbooks.com.

†Enna, Inc., *(978-0-9737509)* 1602 Carolina St., Unit B3, Bellingham, WA 98229 USA Tel 360-306-5369; Fax: 905-481-0756
E-mail: collin@enna.com; tsepley@enna.com
Web site: http://www.enna.com; *CIP.*

Enricharamics, Inc., *(978-1-889654)* 8416-905 O'Connor Ct., Richmond, VA 23228 USA Tel 804-747-5826.

Ensign Peak *Imprint of* **Deseret Bk. Co.**

Ensign Peak *Imprint of* **Shadow Mountain Publishing**

Enslow Elementary *Imprint of* **Enslow Pubs., Inc.**

†Enslow Pubs., Inc., *(978-0-7660; 978-0-89490; 978-1-59845; 978-1-4644; 978-1-4645; 978-1-4646; 978-1-62285; 978-1-62293; 978-1-62324; 978-1-62400)* Orders Addr.: P.O. Box 398, Berkeley Heights, NJ 07922-0398 USA (SAN 213-7518) Tel 908-771-9400; Fax: 908-771-0925; Toll Free: 800-398-2504; Edit Addr.: 40 Industrial Rd., Berkeley Heights, NJ 07922-0398 USA; *Imprints:* MyReportLinks.com Books (MyRptLnks); Enslow Elementary (Enslow Elmntry)
E-mail: customerservice@enslow.com
Web site: http://www.enslow.com; http://www.chasingroses.com; http://www.jasminehealth.com; http://www.enslowclassroom.com; http://www.myreportlinks.com; www.speedingstar.com; www.bluewaveclassroom.com; www.scarletvoyage.com
Dist(s): **Follett School Solutions**
MyiLibrary; *CIP.*

Entangled Publishing, LLC, *(978-1-937044; 978-1-62061; 978-1-62266; 978-1-63375; 978-1-943113; 978-1-943114; 978-1-943336; 978-1-943892)* 2614 Timberline Rd S No. 109, Fort Collins, CO 80525 USA Tel 724-208-7888; *Imprints:* Entangled Teen (EntangledTeen)
E-mail: publisher@entangledpublishing.com
Web site: http://www.entangledpublishing.com
Dist(s): **Lightning Source, Inc.**
Macmillan
MyiLibrary
Perseus-PGW
Perseus Bks. Group
Perseus Distribution.

Entangled Teen *Imprint of* **Entangled Publishing, LLC**

Enterprise Incorporated *See* **TLK Pubns.**

Enterprize Publishing Co., Inc., *(978-1-893490)* 1036 Parkway Blvd., Brookings, SD 57006 USA Tel 605-692-7778; Fax: 605-997-3194
E-mail: cfcecil@home.com.

Entertaining Diversity Pr., *(978-0-615-80384-5)* P.O. Box 126, Dedham, MA 02027 USA Tel (781) 329-7040
Web site: http://www.entertainingdiversity.com
Dist(s): **CreateSpace Independent Publishing Platform.**

Entertainment Ministry, The, *(978-0-9707798; 978-0-9717316; 978-0-9728003; 978-0-9765142; 978-0-9791259; 978-0-9817549; 978-0-9827891)* 5584 Mountain Rd., Antioch, TN 37013-2311 USA Toll Free: 800-999-0101
Web site: http://www.entmin.com
Dist(s): **Send The Light Distribution LLC.**

Enthusi Adams, Inc., *(978-0-9670245)* 2792 W. Pekin Rd., Spring Boro, OH 45066 USA Tel 937-743-6381; Fax: 513-743-3292
E-mail: enthusiadams@earthlink.net
Web site: http://www.enthusiadams.com.

Entry Way Marketing & Publishing *See* **Entry Way Publishing**

Entry Way Publishing, *(978-0-9785728; 978-0-9793944; 978-0-9802093; 978-0-9840655; 978-0-9828950; 978-0-9913654; 978-0-9863958)* Div. of Digi-Tall Media, 6205 Oregon Ct., Plano, TX 75023 USA Tel 972-517-6513 Digi Tall Media Distributor
E-mail: editorshepherd@gmail.com
Web site: http://www.entrywaypublishing.com; http://www.digi-tall-media.com; http://www.story-e-books.com
Dist(s): **Digi-Tall Media.**

EniCare Consulting, Inc., *(978-0-9710925)* Orders Addr.: 2809 Blairmont Dr., Midland, MI 48642 USA Tel 989-839-9177
E-mail: bstrawter@chartermi.net
Web site: http://www.envicareinc.com.

Environmental Protection Agency *Imprint of* **United States Government Printing Office**

Environmental Systems Research Institute *See* **ESRI, Inc.**

Environments, Inc., *(978-1-59794)* P.O. Box 1348, Beaufort, SC 29901-1348 USA Tel 843-846-8155; Fax: 843-846-2999; Toll Free Fax: 800-343-2987; Toll Free: 800-342-4453
E-mail: environments@eichild.com
Web site: http://www.eichild.com.

Envisage Publishing, *(978-0-9729042)* Orders Addr.: P.O. Box 557, Queens Village, NY 11428 USA; Edit Addr.: 89-52 208th St., Queens Village, NY 11427 USA
E-mail: dmdavoren@hotmail.com
Web site: http://www.envisagepublishing.com
Dist(s): **Lulu Enterprises Inc.**

Envision EMI, Inc., *(978-0-9745760)* 1919 Gallows Rd. Ste. 700, Vienna, VA 22182-4007 USA.

EoH Publishing, *(978-0-9761322)* P.O. Box 120804, Nashville, TN 37212 USA (SAN 256-257X) Tel 615-584-2071; Toll Free: 866-352-9263
E-mail: wanda.scott@live.com.

E-O-L Publishing Corp., *(978-0-9753705)* P.O. Box 110 Keely Circle, New Smyrna Beach, FL 32168 USA
E-mail: jvoss2@cfl.rr.com
Web site: http://www.eolpublishing.com.

Eos *Imprint of* **HarperCollins Pubs.**

EPEI Pr., *(978-0-9729065)* Orders Addr.: 1450 S. New Wilke Rd., Suite 102, Arlington Heights, IL 60005 USA Tel 847-670-6992; Fax: 847-670-7466; Toll Free: 877-670-7444; Edit Addr.: 1749 Golf Rd., No. 204, Mount Prospect, IL 60056 USA
E-mail: sara@getprepared.org
Web site: http://www.getprepared.org.

Ephemeron Pr., *(978-0-912290)* 1510 Perdidio Ct., Melbourne, FL 32940 USA Tel 321-752-0167
E-mail: johnknapp2@gmail.com
Web site: http://www.ephemeronpress.com.

EPI Bks., *(978-0-9726075; 978-0-9796536; 978-0-9843655; 978-0-9826006)* 2364 Roll Dr., San Diego, CA 92154 USA Fax: 619-869-8501; *Imprints:* EPI Kid Books (EPI Kid Bks)
Web site: http://www.EPIBooks.com
Dist(s): **Anderson Merchandisers.**

EPI Kid Bks. *Imprint of* **EPI Bks.**

Epic Bks. *Imprint of* **Bellwether Media**

EPIC Publishing Co., *(978-0-9674025; 978-0-9763870)* 1405 Ten Palms Ct., Las Vegas, NV 89117-1404 USA (SAN 253-2840) Do not confuse with companies with the same or similar name in Erie, PA, Canon City, CO, Greeley, CO
E-mail: rxl@epicpublishing.com
Web site: http://www.epicpublishing.com.

Epicenter Literary Software, *(978-0-9760222; 978-1-938609)* 6514 Seventh St., NW, Washington, DC 20012-2622 USA Tel 202-829-2427
E-mail: carolivia@carolivia.org
Web site: http://www.carolivia.org.

Epicenter Pr., Inc., *(978-0-945397; 978-0-9708493; 978-0-9724944; 978-0-9745014; 978-0-9790470; 978-0-9800825; 978-1-935347)* Orders Addr.: 6524 NE 181st ST No. 2, Kenmore, WA 98028 USA; Edit Addr.: 6524 NE 181st ST No. 2, Kenmore, WA 98028 USA (SAN 246-9405) Do not confuse with companies with similar names in Kanehoe, HI, Long Beach, CA, Oakland, CA
E-mail: slay@epicenterpress.com; phil@epicenterpress.com; aubrey@epicenterpress.com
Web site: http://www.epicenterpress.com
Dist(s): **Smashwords.**

Epigraph Bks. *Imprint of* **Monkfish Bk. Publishing Co.**

Epistelogic, *(978-0-9748319)* 47 White Pl., Bloomington, IL 61701-1859 USA Tel 309-826-4808
Web site: http://www.epistelogic.com; http://www.scholarpress.com
Dist(s): **AtlasBooks Distribution**
Savant Bk. Distribution Co.

e-Pluribus Unum Publishing Company *See* **Cronus College**

Epoca, Editorial, S.A. de C.V. (MEX) *(978-968-6769; 978-970-627) Dist. by* **Giron Bks.**

eProduction Services *See* **Kepler Pr.**

EPS Digital, *(978-0-9772315)* P.O. Box 5185, De Pere, WI 54115-5185 USA.

ePub Bud, *(978-1-61061; 978-1-61979; 978-1-62154; 978-1-62314; 978-1-62590; 978-1-62776; 978-1-62840)* 427 California Ave., Santa Monica, CA 90403 USA Tel 310-980-4668
E-mail: josh@epubbud.com
Web site: http://www.epubbud.com
Dist(s): **BookBaby**
INscribe Digital
Lulu Enterprises Inc.

EQUALS *Imprint of* **Univ. of California, Berkeley, Lawrence Hall of Science**

Equidata Publishing, *(978-0-9714185)* Orders Addr.: P.O. Box 8116, Surprise, AZ 85374 USA Tel 623-476-7503; Edit Addr.: 13781 W. Crocus Dr. Surprise, Az 85379, Surprise, AZ 85379 USA
E-mail: jobrien6@cox.net
Web site: http://www.equidatapublishing.com.

Equimax USA, Inc., *(978-0-9668082)* HC65 Box 271, Alpine, TX 79830 USA Tel 432-371-2610; Fax: 432-371-2612; Toll Free: 800-759-9494
E-mail: employment@equimax.com
Web site: http://www.equixmax.com.

Equine Graphics Publishing Group, *(978-1-887932; 978-0-9855309; 978-0-9962336)* Orders Addr.: 58 Indian Hill Rd., Uncasville, CT 06382 USA Tel 860-892-8891; *Imprints:* SmallHorse Press (SmallHorse Pr)
E-mail: editor@newconcordpress.com; toniweeone@smallhorse.com; info@equinegraphicspublishing.com; sales@romancingthehorse.com
Web site: http://www.smallhorse.com; http://www.newconcordpress.com; http://www.equinegraphicspublishing.com; http://www.tonileland.com
Dist(s): **Smashwords.**

Equitel Publishing Co., *(978-0-9789131)* 53 Mount Ida Rd., Suite.2, Dorchester, MA 02122-1735 USA
Web site: http://www.equitelpublishing.com.

Erazo, Carlos, *(978-0-9759757; 978-0-9796253)* P.O. Box 2111, Bayamon, PR 00960-2111 USA
E-mail: erazo2001@prtc.net
Web site: http://www.erazolabor.com
Dist(s): **Representaciones Borinquenas, Inc.**

E-Reads, *(978-1-58586; 978-0-7592; 978-1-61756)* 171 E. 74th St., New York, NY 10021 USA (SAN 859-7812) Tel 212-772-7363; Fax: 212-772-7393
E-mail: info@ereads.com
Web site: http://www.ereads.com
Dist(s): **EDC Publishing**
Ebsco Publishing
TextStream.

ereads.com *See* **E-Reads**

Erickson Pr., *(978-1-60217)* Orders Addr.: P.O. Box 33, Yankton, SD 57078 USA (SAN 852-0402); Edit Addr.: 329 Broadway, Yankton, SD 57078 USA
Web site: http://www.ericksonpress.com.

Erickson, Rakel L., *(978-0-9744422)* P.O. Box 86, Fertile, MN 56540-0086 USA
E-mail: thomas_robinson@und.nodak.edu.

Erickson, Tim, *(978-1-59492)* 8801 Fremont Ave S., Minneapolis, MN 55420-2642 USA
E-mail: terickson21@mn.rr.com
Web site: http://www.deathswhisper.com.

Erie Harbor Productions, *(978-0-9717828)* Orders Addr.: 223 W. Cornell Ave., Suite B, Pontiac, MI 48340 USA
E-mail: harbormaster@erieharbor.com
Web site: http://www.erieharbor.com.

ErieKIDS, Inc., *(978-0-9779822)* 4544 W. Ridge Rd., Suite One, Erie, PA 16506 USA (SAN 850-668X) Tel 814-835-3430
Web site: http://www.eriekids.com.

Eriginal Bks, LLC, *(978-0-9829213; 978-1-61370)* 13868 SW 151 Ct., Miami, FL 33196 USA Tel 305-763-2706; 10854 SW 88 St Suite 220, Miami, FL 33176
E-mail: marlene.moleon@gmail.com.

Erin Go Bragh Publishing, *(978-0-9882745; 978-1-941345)* 1885 FM 2673 No. 3, Canyon Lake, TX 78133 USA Tel 830-515-8187; Fax: 866-652-5165
E-mail: kjs@hamiltontroll.com; kjs@kathleensbooks.com; kjs@eringobraghpublishing.com
Web site: www.HamiltonTroll.com; www.ErinGoBraghPublishing.com; www.KathleensBooks.com.

Eringer Travel Guides *See* **Writer's Cramp, Inc.**

Erinsillart, *(978-0-9779155)* 739 31 ave, san francisco, CA 94121 USA Tel 415-816-0766
E-mail: erin@erinsillart.com
Web site: http://www.erinsillart.com.

ERPublishing, LLC, *(978-0-9766568)* P.O. Box 152, Old Greenwich, CT 06870 USA
Web site: http://www.erpublishing.com.

Ervin, Imogene *See* **Finer Moments**

Ervin, Randy, *(978-0-578-05732-3; 978-0-578-09147-1; 978-0-578-16686-5)* 1113 Stinson Ave., Mattoon, IL 61938 USA.

Ervin, Robert E., *(978-0-9746189)* 552 Keystone Station Rd., Jackson, OH 45640 USA Tel 740-286-2693; Fax: 740-286-0756
E-mail: multicominc@adelphia.net
Web site: http://johnhuntmorgan.com.

Eryn Lace, *(978-0-615-38779-6)* 223 Pacific St. Unit B, Santa Monica, CA 90405 USA Tel 323-620-7434
E-mail: jwkobernick@hotmail.com.

Escuela de Musica, *(978-1-932637)* 2540 Crooked Trail Rd., Chula Vista, CA 91914-4142 USA
E-mail: escuelademusica@cox.net
Web site: http://escuelademusica.net.

Eslinger Hse. Publishing, *(978-0-9763033)* 17762 Neff Ranch Rd., Yorba Linda, CA 92886-9013 USA
E-mail: gilberstadt@earthlink.net.

Esmaili, Inc., *(978-0-9656185)* P.O. Box 421382, Dallas, TX 75342 USA Tel 214-521-9600; Fax: 214-526-9617.

ESOL Publishing, *(978-0-9793761)* 10305 Colony View Dr., Fairfax, VA 22032 USA (SAN 853-2796) Tel 703-250-7097
E-mail: ESOLPublishing@aol.com; mcpuginrodas@aol.com
Web site: http://www.Createspace.com/3382900
Dist(s): **CreateSpace Independent Publishing Platform**
Reading Matters, Inc.

Espasa Calpe, S.A. (ESP) *(978-84-239; 978-84-339; 978-84-8326; 978-84-670) Dist. by* **Distribks Inc.**

Espasa Calpe, S.A. (ESP) *(978-84-239; 978-84-339; 978-84-8326; 978-84-670) Dist. by* **Continental Bk.**

Espasa Calpe, S.A. (ESP) *(978-84-239; 978-84-339; 978-84-8326; 978-84-670) Dist. by* **Ediciones.**

Espasa Calpe, S.A. (ESP) *(978-84-239; 978-84-339; 978-84-8326; 978-84-670) Dist. by* **Libros Fronteras.**

Espasa Calpe, S.A. (ESP) *(978-84-239; 978-84-339; 978-84-8326; 978-84-670) Dist. by* **Lectorum Pubns.**

Espasa Calpe, S.A. (ESP) *(978-84-239; 978-84-339; 978-84-8326; 978-84-670) Dist. by* **Planeta.**

Esquire Publishing, Inc., *(978-0-9745045; 978-0-9816554)* 5900 Harper Rd., Suite 107, Solon, OH 44139 USA (SAN 856-146X) Tel 440-528-0156; Fax: 440-528-0157
E-mail: esq@pollock-law.com
Web site: http://www.monsterbooks.net
Dist(s): **Partners Pubs. Group, Inc.**

ESRI, Inc., *(978-1-879102; 978-1-58948)* 380 New York St., Redlands, CA 92373-8100 USA Fax: 909-307-3082; Toll Free: 800-447-9778; *Imprints:* ESRI Press (ESRI Pr)
E-mail: esripress@esri.com
Web site: http://www.esri.com/esripress
Dist(s): **Cengage Gale**
Independent Pubs. Group
Ingram Pub. Services
MyiLibrary
Trans-Atlantic Pubns., Inc.

ESRI Pr. *Imprint of* **ESRI, Inc.**

Essemkay Co. Productions, *(978-0-615-43287-8; 978-0-615-44597-7; 978-0-615-61429-8;* *978-0-615-73042-4)* 247 W. Hillside Dr., Nibley, UT 84321-7908 USA Tel 435-753-2692
E-mail: skwenger@aol.com
Dist(s): **CreateSpace Independent Publishing Platform.**

Essential Library *Imprint of* **ABDO Publishing Co.**

Estreno Plays, *(978-0-9631212; 978-1-888463)* 18 Van Hise Dr., Perrineville, NJ 08535 USA Tel 609-443-4787; Fax: 212-346-1435
E-mail: iridelens@aol.com; sberardini@aol.com
Web site: http://www.rci.rutgers.edu/~estrplay/webpage.html.

†ETA hand2mind, *(978-0-7406; 978-0-914040; 978-0-923832; 978-0-938587; 978-1-57162; 978-1-57452; 978-1-63406)* Div. of A. Daigger & Company, 500 Greenview Ct., Vernon Hills, IL 60061 USA (SAN 285-7553) Tel 847-816-5050; Fax: 847-816-5066; Toll Free: 800-445-5985; *Imprints:* SunSprouts (SUNSPROUTS); Super Source The (SUPER SOURCE)
E-mail: info@hand2mind.com
Web site: http://www.hand2mind.com; *CIP.*

ETAhand2mind *See* **ETA hand2mind**

Etcetera Pr. LLC, *(978-0-9785160; 978-0-9826781; 978-1-936824)* 146 Hills W. Way, Richland, WA 99352 USA (SAN 850-864X)
E-mail: ellen@etcpress.info
Web site: http://www.etcpress.net
Dist(s): **CreateSpace Independent Publishing Platform**
Lightning Source, Inc.

Eternal Foundations Curriculum, *(978-1-932505)* P.O. Box 1213, Atascadero, CA 93423 USA Tel 805-466-1910
E-mail: tsgaddis@tcsn.net.

Eternal Studios, *(978-1-887814)* 15235 Rainhollow, Houston, TX 77070 USA Tel 713-370-8384
Dist(s): **Diamond Comic Distributors, Inc.**

Eternity Pr., *(978-0-9758989)* 2828 Brannon Ave., Saint Louis, MO 63139-1438 USA Toll Free: 800-886-7587; 1 Brounger Rd., Constantia, 7806 Tel 447521578414
Web site: http://www.cenveo.com
Dist(s): **Smashwords.**

Ethics Trading (GBR) *(978-0-9556887) Dist. by* **LuluCom.**

Ethos Of Commerce Pubs., Ltd., *(978-0-9741412)* 3535 E. Coast Hwy. No. 216, Corona del Mar, CA 92625 USA Tel 949-862-5826
E-mail: ethosofcommerce@yahoo.com
Web site: http://www.geocities.com/EthosOfCommerce.

Etiquette, Etc., LLC *See* **CKK Educational, LLC.**

ETN, Inc., *(978-0-9759629; 978-0-9855450)* 3540 W. Sahara Ave., No. 25, Las Vegas, NV 89102 USA
E-mail: eworth@etnbooks.com.

Etopia Pr., *(978-1-936751; 978-1-937976; 978-1-939194; 978-1-940223; 978-1-941692; 978-1-944138)* 117 Bellevue Ave. Ste. 202B, Newport, RI 02840 USA Tel 401-846-0010
E-mail: apmelton@gmail.com
Web site: www.etopia-press.net.

eTreasures Publishing, *(978-0-9740537)* Orders Addr.: P.O. Box 71813, Newnan, GA 30271 USA Tel 770-683-8032; Edit Addr.: 4442 Lafayette St., Marianna, FL 32446 USA Tel 850-209-0329
E-mail: publisher@etreasurespublishing.com
Web site: http://www.etreasurespublishing.com
Dist(s): **Smashwords.**

Etruscan Pr., *(978-0-9718228; 978-0-9745995; 978-0-9797450; 978-0-9819687; 978-0-9832944; 978-0-9839346; 978-0-9886922; 978-0-9897532; 978-0-9903221)* 84 West South St., Wilkes-Barre, PA 18766 USA Tel 570-408-4546; Fax: 570-408-3333
E-mail: bill@etruscanpress.org
Web site: http://www.etruscanpress.org
Dist(s): **Consortium Bk. Sales & Distribution**
MyiLibrary
Perseus Bks. Group
SPD-Small Pr. Distribution.

ETS Publishing, *(978-0-9816642)* Orders Addr.: 9341 Clovercroft Rd., Franklin, TN 37067 USA (SAN 856-1583)
E-mail: info@etspublishinghouse.com
Web site: http://www.thisbespromise.com; http://www.etspublishing.com.

Eudon Publishing, *(978-0-9765423)* P.O. Box 9, Goddard, KS 67052 USA Tel 316-210-4649; Fax: 316-233-1075
E-mail: gsmith@EudonPublishing.com
Web site: http://www.EudonPublishing.com
Dist(s): **BWI**
Brodart Co.
Follett School Solutions.

eugenus STUDIOS, *(978-0-578-09572-1)* 445 Lakeview Rd., Craryville, NY 12521 USA
E-mail: victor@eugenus.com
Web site: http://www.captaincrossbones.com; http://www.eugenus.com.

Eupanapue-Auntella's Rooster Pubns., *(978-0-615-32789-1)* P.O. Box 5803, Denver, CO 80217-5803 USA Tel 720-272-5570; *Imprints:* RoosterBugglePue Books (RoosBugglePue)
E-mail: Eupanapue_AuntellasRoosterPub@q.com
Web site: http://www.roosterbugglepue.com.

Euphema Press, *(978-0-9779600)* P.O. Box 2314, Bowie, MD 20718 USA
Web site: http://www.euphema.com.

Eureka Productions, *(978-0-9712464; 978-0-9746648; 978-0-9787919; 978-0-9825630; 978-0-9963888)* 8778 Oak Grove Rd., Mount Horeb, WI 53572 USA
Web site: http://www.graphicclassics.com
Dist(s): **Diamond Comic Distributors, Inc.**
Diamond Bk. Distributors.

Europa Editions, Inc., *(978-1-933372; 978-1-60945; 978-0-9968778)* Div. of Edizioni E/O (Rome, Italy), 214

W. 29th St Suite 1003, New York, NY 10001 USA; Italian Office, Via Gabriela Camozzi 1, Roma, 00195
E-mail: Drew@europaeditions.com
Web site: http://www.europaeditions.com/
Dist(s): **MyiLibrary**
Penguin Random Hse., LLC.
Penguin Publishing Group
Perseus Bks. Group
Random Hse., Inc.

European Language Institute (ITA) *(978-88-8148; 978-88-85148; 978-88-536)* *Dist. by* **Distribks Inc.**

EV Publishing Corp., *(978-0-9727787)* 1628 E. Southern Ave., Suite 9, PMB 237, Tempe, AZ 85282 USA Fax: 480-966-8627
E-mail: info@evpub.com
Web site: http://www.evpub.com.

Eva Publishing, LLC, *(978-0-9786799)* 345 W. Broadway, Shelbyville, IN 46176 USA (SAN 851-321X) Tel 317-398-0231 (phone/fax)
E-mail: jmesser@lightbound.com.

EvangeCube International *See* **E3 Resources**

Evangel Author Services, *(978-1-933858; 978-0-9823957)* Div. of Brethren in Christ Media Ministries, 2000 Evangel Way, P.O. Box 189, Nappanee, IN 46550 USA Tel 574-773-3164; Fax: 574-773-5934; Toll Free: 800-253-9315
E-mail: info@evangelpublishing.com; sales@evangelpublishing.com
Web site: http://www.evangelpress.com; http://www.evangelpublishing.com.

Evangel Press *See* **Evangel Publishing Hse.**

Evangel Publishing Hse., *(978-0-916035; 978-1-928915; 978-1-934233; 978-0-692-00906-2)* Div. of Brethren in Christ Media Ministries, Orders Addr.: P.O. Box 189, Nappanee, IN 46550 USA (SAN 211-7940) Tel 574-773-3164; Fax: 574-773-5934; Toll Free: 800-253-9315 (order); Edit Addr.: 2000 Evangel Way, Nappanee, IN 46550 USA Fax: 574-773-5934; Toll Free: 800-253-9315
E-mail: sales@evangelpublishing.com
Web site: http://www.evangelpublishing.com
Dist(s): **Anchor Distributors**
Partners Bk. Distributing, Inc.
Spring Arbor Distributors, Inc.

Evangelista, Susan, *(978-0-9769602)* 1261 W. Fulton Ave., Grand Rapids,, MI 49504 USA
Web site: http://micart.net.

Evan-Moor Educational Pubs., *(978-1-55799; 978-1-59673; 978-1-4409; 978-1-60792; 978-1-60793; 978-1-935353; 978-1-60823; 978-1-60963; 978-1-61365; 978-1-61366; 978-1-61367; 978-1-61368; 978-1-62938)* Sub. of Evan-Moor Corporation, 18 Lower Ragsdale Dr., Monterey, CA 93940 USA (SAN 242-5394) Tel 800-976-1915; 831-649-5901; Fax: 831-649-6256; Toll Free Fax: 800-777-4332; Toll Free: 800-777-4362
E-mail: customerservice@evan-moor.com; sterling@evan-moor.com
Web site: http://www.evan-moor.com
Dist(s): **Follett School Solutions**
Spring Arbor Distributors, Inc.

Evans Brothers, Ltd. (GBR) *(978-0-237)* *Dist. by* **IPG Chicago.**

†Evans, M. & Co., Inc., *(978-0-87131; 978-1-59077)* 216 E. 49th St., New York, NY 10017 USA (SAN 203-4050) Tel 212-688-2810
E-mail: editorial@mevans.com
Dist(s): **MyiLibrary**
National Bk. Network
Rowman & Littlefield Publishers, Inc.
ebrary, Inc.; *CIP.*

Evans, Robert, *(978-0-9766468; 978-0-9884466)* 1065 Saint Helena Way, Sebastopol, CA 95472 USA
E-mail: rgevans@sonic.net.

Evening Star Enterprise, Inc., *(978-0-9790210; 978-0-9841611)* Orders Addr.: P.O. Box 254, Wilmore, KY 40390-1072 USA (SAN 852-2111) Tel 859-421-0243; Edit Addr.: 408 Kinlaw Dr., Wilmore, KY 40390-1072 USA
E-mail: Rgray@Eveningstarenterprise.com
Web site: http://www.eveningstarenterprise.com/Home.html.

Evening Sun Pr., *(978-0-9726781)* 8332 Melrose Ave., West Hollywood, CA 90069 USA Tel 310-657-9092
E-mail: lc@pictureentertainment.com.

Evenson, Laurel, *(978-0-9666834)* 675 Moon Lake Dr., Cambridge, MN 55008 USA Tel 612-689-4093.

Event-Based Science Institute, Inc., *(978-0-9747576)* 6609 Paxton Rd., Rockville, MD 20852-3659 USA
Web site: http://www.eventbasedscience.com.

Everbind *Imprint of* **Marco Bk. Co.**

Everbind/Marco Book Company *See* **Marco Bk. Co.**

Eveready Letter & Advertising Inc., *(978-0-9758714; 978-0-9777623; 978-0-9814694; 978-0-9820757; 978-0-9826118; 978-0-9837256; 978-0-9858365; 978-0-9897161; 978-0-9963917)* 1817 Broadway, Nashville, TN 37203 USA
Web site: http://eveready-usa.com
Dist(s): **Ingram Pub. Services.**

Everest Bks., *(978-0-9754146)* 16026 N. 54th St., Scottsdale, AZ 85254 USA Tel 602-684-5644; Fax: 602-595-7152
E-mail: grahamhfoster@msn.com
Web site: http://www.pacificseminars.com.

Everest Editora (ESP) *(978-84-241; 978-972-750)* *Dist. by* **Continental Bk.**

Everest Editora (ESP) *(978-84-241; 978-972-750)* *Dist. by* **Lectorum Pubns.**

Everett Pr. *Imprint of* **Rosen Publishing Group, Inc., The**

Everette Publishing (EP), LLC, *(978-0-9672539)* 106 Tillerson Dr., Newport News, VA 23602 USA Tel 757-344-9092; 757-877-6943; Fax: 757-988-0909
E-mail: EverettePublish@cox.net
Web site: http://www.Webunlimted.com.

Evergreen House Publishing LLC *Imprint of* **WaveCloud Corp.**

Evergreen Pr. *Imprint of* **Genesis Communications, Inc.**

Evergreen Press *See* **Genesis Communications, Inc.**

Evergreen Pr. of Brainerd, LLC, *(978-0-9661599; 978-0-9755252; 978-0-9819766)* P.O. Box 465, Brainerd, MN 56401 USA Tel 218-851-4843; 201 W. Laurel St., Brainerd, MN 56401
E-mail: tenlee@evergreenpress.net
Web site: http://www.evergreenpress.net.

Everlasting Publishing, *(978-0-9778083; 978-0-9824844; 978-0-9852739)* P.O. Box 1061, Yakima, WA 98907 USA (SAN 850-2919) Tel 509-225-9829; P.O. Box 1061, Yakima, WA 98907 Tel 509-225-9829
E-mail: dpride42@gmail.com
Web site: http://everlastingpublishing.org.

Everwas Publishing, *(978-0-9777735)* 200 Broken Arrow Way S., Sedona, AZ 86351-8743 USA Tel 928-284-0457; Fax: 928-284-9225
E-mail: kroyce88@esedona.net.

Everybody Run Music, *(978-0-578-04648-8)* 186-A W. Lemon Ave., Monrovia, CA 91016 USA
E-mail: eshouse@hotmail.com.

Everyday Learning Corp., *(978-0-9630009; 978-1-57039; 978-1-877817)* 2 Prudential Plaza, Suite 1200, Chicago, IL 60601 USA Tel 312-233-7820; Fax: 312-540-5848; Toll Free: 800-382-7670
Web site: http://www.everydaylearning.com.

Everyday Mathtools Publishing Company *See* **Everyday Learning Corp.**

Everydaysanctuary Pubns., *(978-0-9761900)* 12514 Maria Cir., Broomfield, CO 80020-5324 USA
Web site: http://www.everydaysanctuary.net.

Everyman Chess (GBR) *(978-1-85744)* *Dist. by* **Natl Bk Netwk.**

Everyman's Library *Imprint of* **Knopf Doubleday Publishing Group**

Everything Goes Media, LLC, *(978-0-9642426; 978-1-893121)* Div. of Everything Goes Media, LLC, Orders Addr.: P.O. Box 1524, Milwaukee, WI 53201 USA Tel 312-226-8400; Fax: 312-226-8420; Edit Addr.: P.O. Box 711, Chicago, IL 60690 USA Tel 312-226-8400; Fax: 312-226-8420; 161 W. Wisconsin Ave. Ste. 2190, Milwaukee, WI 53203 Tel 312-226-8400; Fax: 312-226-8420; *Imprints*: Lake Claremont Press (LakeClaremont)
E-mail: sharon@everythinggoesmedia.com; lcp@lakeclaremont.com
Web site: www.lakeclaremont.com; www.everythinggoesmedia.com; www.swoodhousebooks.com
Dist(s): **Independent Pubs. Group**
MyiLibrary.

Evil Hat Productions LLC, *(978-0-9771534; 978-1-61317)* Orders Addr.: 1905 Blackbriar St, Silver Spring, MD 20903 USA Tel 240-EHP-BLUE (240-347-2583)
E-mail: feedback@evilhat.com
Web site: http://www.evilhat.com/
Dist(s): **Diamond Comic Distributors, Inc.**
Diamond Bk. Distributors.

Evil Twin Pubns., *(978-0-9712972; 978-0-9763355)* P.O. Box 2, Livingston Manor, NY 12758 USA Tel 917-971-2450
E-mail: info@eviltwinpublications.com
Web site: http://www.eviltwinpublications.com
Dist(s): **AK Pr. Distribution**
D.A.P./Distributed Art Pubs.

eVision, LLC, *(978-0-9768579)* Orders Addr.: 334 Sixth Ave. S., Birmingham, AL 35205 USA Tel 205-283-7690; Fax: 205-252-3090
Web site: http://www.eVisionLLC.net
Dist(s): **Parnassus Bk. Distributors.**

Evolved Publishing, *(978-0-615-60885-3; 978-0-615-61939-2; 978-1-62253)* Orders Addr.: 544 Church St., Hartford, WI 53027 USA; Edit Addr.: 3 S. Heathrow Dr. NW, Rome, GA 30165 USA
E-mail: Admin@EvolvedPub.com
Web site: http://www.evolvedpub.com/press/
Dist(s): **CreateSpace Independent Publishing Platform**
Draft2Digital
Lightning Source, Inc.
Smashwords.

Evolved Self Publishing, *(978-0-9779470)* 723 Springtown Rd., Tillson, NY 12486 USA Tel 845-658-8270; Fax: 845-658-3718
E-mail: publisher@evolvedself.com
Web site: http://www.evolvedself.com
Dist(s): **Smashwords.**

EvoraBooks, LLC, *(978-0-9725071)* P.O. Box 397, Canton, CT 06019 USA
E-mail: evorabooks@snet.net
Web site: http://www.booksbyevora.com.

Ewuramma, *(978-0-9849805)* 1850 Lafayette Ave. Apt. 3A, Bronx, NY 10473 USA Tel 646-220-6432
E-mail: ehboah@aol.com.

Exact Change, *(978-1-878972)* 5 Brewster St., Cambridge, MA 02138 USA Tel 617-492-5405; Fax: 617-492-5669
E-mail: info@exactchange.com; mailinglist@exactchange.com
Web site: http://www.exactchange.com
Dist(s): **D.A.P./Distributed Art Pubs.**

Exambusters *Imprint of* **Ace Academics, Inc.**

Exceed, LLC, *(978-0-9771722)* 715 E. 100 N., Lindon, UT 84042 USA (SAN 256-8519) Tel 801-785-7931
E-mail: kcooper@exceed.bz
Web site: http://www.exceed.bz.

Excel Digital Pr., *(978-0-9712249; 978-0-9718254; 978-0-9749202; 978-0-9786376)* Orders Addr.: P.O. Box 703978, Dallas, TX 75370-3978 USA Tel 972-307-3075; Fax: 469-619-2292; Edit Addr.: 2515 Daybreak Dr., Dallas, TX 75287 USA
E-mail: bookeagle@hotmail.com
Web site: http://www.exceldigitalpress.com.

Excellence Enterprises, *(978-0-9627735)* 3040 Aspen Ln., Palmdale, CA 93550-7985 USA Tel 661-267-2220; Fax: 661-267-2946
E-mail: lavonne.taylor@sbcglobal.net
Web site: http://vonnieshealthspot.com.

Excellence Student Incentives, *(978-0-9789612)* 18942 Muirland, Detroit, MI 48221 USA (SAN 852-1107) Tel 313-646-6079; Fax: 313-449-0396
E-mail: beattheneap@yahoo.com
Web site: http://www.beattheneap.com.

Excellent Bks., *(978-0-9628014; 978-1-880780)* P.O. Box 131322, Carlsbad, CA 92013-1322 USA Tel 760-598-5069; Fax: 240-218-7601
E-mail: books@excellentbooks.com
Web site: http://www.excellentbooks.com.

Excite Kids Pr. *Imprint of* **Publishing Services @ Thomson-Shore**

Exclusive Editions *Imprint of* **Parragon, Inc.**

Executive Bks., *(978-0-937539; 978-1-933715; 978-1-936354)* Div. of Life Management Services, Inc., 206 West Allen St., Mechanicsburg, PA 17055-6240 USA (SAN 156-5419) Tel 717-766-9499; Fax: 717-766-6565; Toll Free: 800-233-2665; *Imprints*: Tremendous Life Books (TremLifeBks)
E-mail: JLiller@TremendousLifeBooks.com
Web site: http://www.TremendousLifeBooks.com
Dist(s): **Send The Light Distribution LLC.**

Executive Performances, Inc., *(978-0-9748220)* P.O. Box 93, Palos Park, IL 60464 USA; *Imprints*: Executive Performances Publishing (Exec Perform Pubng)
E-mail: magicriz@aol.com.

Executive Performances Publishing *Imprint of* **Executive Performances, Inc.**

Exeter Pr., *(978-0-9700612; 978-0-9797407)* Orders Addr.: 223 Commonwealth Ave., Boston, MA 02116 USA Tel 617-267-7720; Fax: 617-262-6948; Edit Addr.: 223 Commonwealth Ave., Boston, MA 02116 USA (SAN 854-2554)
E-mail: davidburke@commonwealthfilms.com
Web site: http://www.exeterpress.com.

Exhibit A *Imprint of* **TR Bks.**

Exhibit A *Imprint of* **Cavendish Square Publishing**

Exhibit A Pr., *(978-0-9633954; 978-0-9815519)* 4657 Cajon Way, San Diego, CA 92115 USA Tel 619-286-6350; Fax: 619-286-1591
E-mail: mail@exhibitapress.com
Web site: http://www.exhibitapress.com
Dist(s): **AtlasBooks Distribution.**

Exisle Publishing Ltd. (NZL) *(978-0-908988; 978-1-877437; 978-1-877568; 978-1-921966; 978-1-927147; 978-1-927187; 978-1-77559)* *Dist. by* **HachBkGrp.**

Exit Studio, *(978-0-9640868; 978-0-9831891)* 1466 N. Quinn St., Arlington, VA 22209 USA Tel 703-312-7121; Fax: 703-894-2741
E-mail: efontanez@exitstudio.com
Web site: http://www.exitstudio.com
Dist(s): **Follett School Solutions**
Independent Pubs. Group.

Exley, Helen Giftbooks (GBR) *(978-0-905521; 978-1-85015; 978-1-86187; 978-1-905130; 978-1-84634)* *Dist. by* **Natl Bk Netwk.**

ExpandingBooks.com, *(978-0-9721764; 978-1-934443)* 200 W. 34th, Suite 953, Anchorage, AK 99503 USA Tel 907-278-9800; Fax: 877-552-7200
E-mail: cherylkirk@gmail.com; expandingbooks@gmail.com
Web site: http://www.expandingpress.com; http://www.expandingbooks
Dist(s): **Taku Graphics.**

Expert Systems for Teachers *Imprint of* **Teaching Point, Inc.**

Explorations Early Learning, *(978-0-615-15718-4; 978-0-615-15719-1)* 1524 Summit St., Sioux City, IA 51103 USA Tel 712-202-1627
E-mail: jeffajohnson@cableone.net
Web site: http://www.explorationsearlylearning.com
Dist(s): **Lulu Enterprises Inc.**

Explorer Media *Imprint of* **Simon & Barklee, Inc./ExplorerMedia**

Explorer's Bible Study, *(978-1-889015; 978-0-9787993; 978-1-935424)* 2652 Hwy. 46 S., Dickson, TN 37055 USA Tel 615-446-7316; Fax: 615-446-7951; Toll Free: 800-657-2874; P.O. Box 425, Dickson, TN 37056 Toll Free: 800-657-2874
Web site: http://www.explorerbiblestudy.org.

Exploring California Insects *Imprint of* **Insect Sciences Museum of California**

Exploring Science *Imprint of* **Compass Point Bks.**

Express Bks. *Imprint of* **Bellwether Media**

Expressions Woven, *(978-0-9668179)* P.O. Box 1004, Waterford, CT 06385 USA Tel 860-442-1332; Fax: 860-447-9916
E-mail: dreaminthelight@alum.rpi.edu
Web site: http://www.poetryin.com
Dist(s): **Lightning Source, Inc.**

Expressive Design Group, Inc., *(978-0-9845278; 978-1-936676)* 49 Garfield St., Holyoke, MA 01040 USA (SAN 859-6654) Tel 413-315-6296; Fax: 413-315-6271; Toll Free: 800-848-6685
E-mail: richard.marks@theedg.net
Web site: http://www.theedg.net.

Expressive Ink, *(978-0-9759362)* Orders Addr.: P.O. Box 74, Foreston, MN 56330 USA; Edit Addr.: 305 Pheasant Ln., Foreston, MN 56330-5540 USA Tel 320-294-4022
E-mail: express@bctelco.net
Web site: http://www.natknows.com.

Exquisite Thoughts, Incorporated *See* **CCP Publishing & Entertainment**

Extejt, Gabriele *See* **McGab Publishing**

Exterminating Angel Pr., *(978-1-935259)* 1892 Colestin Rd., Ashland, OR 97520 USA
Dist(s): **Consortium Bk. Sales & Distribution**
MyiLibrary
Perseus Bks. Group.

Eye Bks. (GBR) *(978-1-903070; 978-1-908646; 978-1-78563)* *Dist. by* **IPG Chicago.**

Eye Contact Media, *(978-0-9729187)* 1344 Disc Dr., No. 105, Sparks, NV 89436 USA
Web site: http://www.eyecontactmedia.com
Dist(s): **AtlasBooks Distribution.**

Eye of Newt, The, *(978-0-9762565)* 5203 Cedar Springs Rd, Dallas, TX 75235-8537 USA Tel 214-520-1739
Web site: http://www.theyeofnewt.com.

Eyres, John, *(978-0-9769762)* 12713 Willowyck Dr., Saint Louis, MO 63146 USA.

EZ Comics, *(978-0-9795887)* 12, Pine Top Rd., Barrington, RI 02806-1706 USA
E-mail: vshah.ezcomics@gmail.com; vshah@ezcomics.com
Web site: http://ezcomics.com.

EZ Muzik Publishing, *(978-0-615-24181-4; 978-0-9822805; 978-0-692-01686-2)* P.O. Box 50826, Santa barbara, CA 93108 USA Tel 805-886-0799
E-mail: patrikpiano@aol.com.

Ezra's Earth Publishing, *(978-0-9727855)* P.O. Box 3036, South Pasadena, CA 91031 USA (SAN 255-0555)
E-mail: information@ezrasearth.com
Web site: http://www.ezrasearth.com
Dist(s): **Quality Bks., Inc.**

Ezra's Engine Publishing *See* **Ezra's Earth Publishing**

F & S Music KS Publishing Co., *(978-0-9745630; 978-0-9765787)* Orders Addr.: P.O. Box 11805, Jackson, MS 39283 USA; Edit Addr.: 1902 Queens Road Ave., Jackson, MS 39213 USA
E-mail: lanniespann@yahoo.com
Web site: http://www.lanniespannmcbride.net.

FC&A Publishing, *(978-0-915099; 978-1-890957; 978-1-932470; 978-1-935574)* 103 Clover Green, Peachtree City, GA 30269-1695 USA (SAN 289-7946) Tel 770-487-6307; Fax: 770-631-4357; Toll Free: 800-537-1275
E-mail: charlotte_carpenter@fca.com; anne_kaufmann@fca.com
Web site: http://www.fca.com.

F E A Publishing *See* **FEA Ministries**

F.A. Chekki, *(978-0-615-82414-7)* 1702 California Trail, Plano, TX 75023 USA Tel 972.786.3110
Dist(s): **CreateSpace Independent Publishing Platform.**

Fabbri Editori - RCS Libri (ITA) *(978-88-450; 978-88-451; 978-88-452; 978-88-454)* *Dist. by* **Distribks Inc.**

Faber & Faber, Ltd. (GBR) *(978-0-571; 978-1-78335)* *Dist. by* **Alfred Pub.**

Faber, David *See* **Faber Pr.**

Faber Music, Ltd. (GBR) *(978-0-571)* *Dist. by* **Alfred Pub.**

Faber Piano Adventuresr, *(978-1-61677)* 3042 Creek Dr., Ann Arbor, MI 48108 USA Tel 734-975-1995; Fax: 734-332-7823
Dist(s): **Leonard, Hal Corp.**

Faber Pr., *(978-0-9768763)* Orders Addr.: 5638 Lake Murray Blvd., No.206, La Mesa, CA 91942 USA (SAN 256-8071) Tel 619-517-2662; Fax: 619-255-2354
E-mail: annavennis@yahoo.com
Web site: http://www.becauseofromek.com.

FableVision Pr., *(978-1-891405)* 308 Congress St. # 6, Boston, MA 02210-1027 USA Toll Free: 888-240-3734
E-mail: info@fablevision.com; shoppe@fablevision.com
Web site: http://www.fablevision.com; http://www.fablevision.com/shoppe.

Face 2 Face Games Publishing, *(978-0-9728197; 978-0-9761156)* 36 The Arcade, 65 Weybosset St., Providence, RI 02903 USA Tel 401-351-0362 (phone/fax)
E-mail: lwhalen@face2facegames.com
Web site: http://www.face2facegames.com
Dist(s): **PSI (Publisher Services, Inc.).**

Fact Finders *Imprint of* **Capstone Pr., Inc.**

Factors Pr., *(978-0-9700582)* Orders Addr.: 14718 Ellison Ave., Omaha, NE 68116-4336 USA
E-mail: Info@FactorsPress.com.

†Facts On File, Inc., *(978-0-8160; 978-0-87196; 978-1-60413; 978-1-4381; 978-1-61753)* Orders Addr.: 132 W. 31st St., 17th Flr., New York, NY 10001-2006 USA (SAN 201-4696) Tel 212-967-8800; 212-896-4296 (customer service); Fax: 917-339-0325; 917-339-0323; Toll Free Fax: 800-678-3633; Toll Free: 800-322-8755; *Imprints*: Checkmark Books (Checkmark); Ferguson Publishing Company (Ferg Pub Co); Chelsea House (ChelsHse); Chelsea Clubhouse (ChelseaClub); Bloom's Literary Criticism (Bloom's Lit); World Almanac Books (WrldAlmanac)
E-mail: custserv@factsonfile.com; Sales@ChelseaHouse.com
Web site: http://www.factsonfile.com; http://www.fergpubco.com; http://www.chelseahouse.com
Dist(s): **CreateSpace Independent Publishing Platform**
Ebsco Publishing
Follett School Solutions
MyiLibrary
Simon & Schuster, Inc.
ebrary, Inc.; *CIP.*

Faden, Ellen, *(978-0-9821231)* 145 Plaza Dr., Suite 207-224, Vallejo, CA 94590 USA (SAN 857-3166) Tel 415-342-1552
E-mail: efaden1@gmail.com
Web site: http://www.kabbalah-dating.com.

Faerieground *Imprint of* **Stone Arch Bks.**

Fahnestock Pr., *(978-0-9747981)* 310 Dennytown Rd., Putman Valley, NY 10579-1423 USA (SAN 255-8564) Tel 212-894-1219
E-mail: weigman676@aol.com.

Publisher Name Index

Fair, Barbara A., (978-0-9621174) Orders Addr.: P.O. Box 241155, Detroit, MI 48224 USA (SAN 250-7447); Edit Addr.: P.O. Box 26101, Fraser, MI 48026-6101 USA (SAN 250-7455).

Fair Havens Pubns., (978-0-9664803) P.O. Box 1238, Gainsville, TX 76241 USA Tel 940-668-6044; Fax: 940-668-6984; Toll Free: 800-771-4861
E-mail: fairhavens@fairhavenspub.com
Web site: http://www.fairhavenspub.com; http://www.ageofgrace.com
Dist(s): **Anchor Distributors**
Spring Arbor Distributors, Inc.

Fair Winds Pr. *Imprint of* **Quarto Publishing Group USA**

Fairchild Bks. *Imprint of* **Bloomsbury Academic**

Fairchild Bks., (978-0-87005; 978-1-56367; 978-1-60901) Div. of Bloomsbury Publishing, c/o Sandra Washington, 750 Third Ave., 8th Floor, New York, NY 10017 USA (SAN 201-470X) Tel 212-630-3875; Fax: 212-630-3868; Toll Free: 800-932-4724
Web site: http://www.fairchildbooks.com
Dist(s): **MyiLibrary.**

Fairfax Lectern, Inc., The, (978-0-9701756) 4280-Redwood Hwy., No. 11, San Rafael, CA 94903 USA Tel 415-479-1128; Fax: 415-479-9024
E-mail: scalised@aol.com
Web site: http://www.fairfax-lectern.com; http://www.professordave.com
Dist(s): **NACSCORP, Inc.**

Fairfield Language Technologies *See* **Rosetta Stone Ltd.**

Fairhaven Bk. Pubs., (978-1-929649) Orders Addr.: 35425 Mojave St., Lucerne Vly, CA 92356 USA; Edit Addr.: P.O. Box 105, Lucerne Valley, CA 92356 USA Tel 760-248-6446; Fax: 206-337-5431; Toll Free: 877-342-6657
E-mail: values@charactervalues.com
Web site: http://www.charactervalues.com; http://www.charactervalues.org; http://www.world-peace.org; http://www.charactervalues.net; http://www.charactervalues.com
Dist(s): **Quality Bks., Inc.**

Fairland Bks., (978-0-9818154) P.O. Box 63, West Friendship, MD 21794 USA
Web site: http://fairlandbooks.com
Dist(s): **Emerald Bk. Co.**

†Fairmont Pr., Inc., (978-0-88173; 978-0-915586) 700 Indian Trail, Lilburn, GA 30047 USA (SAN 207-5946) Tel 770-925-9388; Fax: 770-381-9865
Web site: http://www.fairmontpress.com
Dist(s): **Assn. of Energy Engineers**
Ebsco Publishing
Lulu Enterprises Inc.
Taylor & Francis Group; *CIP*.

Fairway Pr. *Imprint of* **CSS Publishing Co.**

Fairwood Pr., (978-0-9668184; 978-0-9746573; 978-1-933846; 978-0-9789078; 978-0-9820730) 21528 104th St. Ct. E., Bonney Lake, WA 98391 USA Tel 253-269-2640; *Imprints*: Media Man! Productions (MeidaMan)
E-mail: patrick@fairwoodpress.com
Web site: http://www.fairwoodpress.com.

Faith & Action Team, (978-1-931984; 978-1-60382) Div. of General Council of the Assemblies of God, 429 Us Hwy. 65, Walnut Shade, MO 65771 USA
E-mail: elizabeth@faithandactionseries.org
Web site: http://www.faithandactionseries.org; http://www.seriefeyaccion.org.

Faith & Action/RD *See* **Faith & Action Team**

Faith & Life Pr., (978-0-87303) Orders Addr.: P.O. Box 347, Newton, KS 67114-0347 USA (SAN 658-0637) Tel 316-283-5100; Fax: 316-283-0454; Toll Free: 800-245-7894 (orders only); Edit Addr.: 718 Main St., Newton, KS 67114-0347 USA (SAN 201-4726)
E-mail: flp@gcmc.org
Web site: http://www.2southwind.net/~gcmc/flp.html
Dist(s): **Herald Pr.**
Spring Arbor Distributors, Inc.

Faith Baptist Church Publications *See* **FBC Pubns. & Printing**

Faith Bks. & MORE, (978-0-9820197; 978-0-9841729; 978-0-9842378; 978-0-9845779; 978-0-9846507; 978-0-9852729; 978-0-9860159; 978-0-9860247; 978-1-939761) 3255 Lawrenceville-Suwanee Rd., Suite P250, Suwanee, GA 30024 USA (SAN 857-0337) Tel 678-232-6156; Fax: 888-479-4540
E-mail: publishing@faithbooksandmore.com
Web site: http://www.faithbooksandmore.com; http://www.facebook.com/corpconnoisseur; http://www.facebook.com/faithbooksandmorepublishing.

Faith Communications *Imprint of* **Health Communications, Inc.**

F.A.I.T.H. Ministries Publishing House *See* **FM Publishing Co.**

Faith Pubns., (978-0-9743167) 5301 Edgewood Rd., College Park, MD 20740 USA Tel 301-982-2061 Do not confuse with companies with the same name in Milton, FL, Haviland, KS
E-mail: faith@alhuda.org.

Faithful Life Pubs., (978-0-9749836; 978-0-9821408; 978-0-9824931; 978-0-9845208; 978-0-9829105; 978-0-9832039; 978-1-937129; 978-1-63073) Div. of With Integrity Ministries, 3335 Galaxy Way, North Fort Myers, FL 33903-1419 USA Tel 239-652-0135; Toll Free: 800-699-2623
E-mail: editor@FLPublishers.com
Web site: http://www.faithfullife.com; http://www.FLPublishers.com.

Faithful Publishing, (978-0-9759941; 978-0-9779889; 978-1-940911) P.O. Box 345, Buford, GA 30515-0345 USA Tel 770-932-7335; Fax: 678-482-4446; *Imprints*: Pixelated Publishing (Pixel Pubng)
E-mail: faithfulpublishing@yahoo.com; alwzapri@bellsouth.net
Web site: http://www.eighttwelvepublishing.com.

FaithWalker Publishing *Imprint of* **Markowitz, Darryl**

Faithwords *Imprint of* **Hachette Nashville**

Falcon Guides *Imprint of* **Globe Pequot Pr., The**

Falcon Pr. International, (978-1-884459) 2150 Almaden Rd., No. 141, San Jose, CA 95125 USA Tel 408-677-4875
E-mail: getty@gettyambau.com.

Falcon Publishing LTD, (978-0-9746959) P.O. Box 6099, Kingwood, TX 77325 USA
E-mail: gwen@falconpublishing.com
Web site: http://www.falconpublishing.com.

Falcor Bks., (978-0-9723530) P.O. Box 1055, Yorktown, VA 23692-1055 USA Tel 757-872-6649; Toll Free: 866-872-6649
E-mail: info@falcorbooks.com
Web site: http://www.falcorbooks.com.

†Falk Art Reference, (978-0-932087) Div. of artprice.com, Orders Addr.: P.O. Box 833, Madison, CT 06443 USA (SAN 686-5240) Tel 203-245-2246; Fax: 203-245-5116; Toll Free: 800-278-4274; Edit Addr.: 61 Beekman Pl., Madison, CT 06443-2400 USA Do not confuse with companies with the same name in Tacoma, WA
E-mail: info@falkart.com
Web site: http://www.falkart.com; http://www.artprice.com; *CIP*.

Fall River *Imprint of* **Sterling Publishing Co., Inc.**

Fall Rose Bks., (978-0-9742185) P.O. Box 39, Kittery Point, ME 03905 USA Tel 207-439-2878
Web site: http://www.fallrosebooks.com.

Falls Media *See* **Seven Footer Pr.**

Falter, Laury, (978-0-615-29498-8; 978-0-615-53342-1; 978-0-615-58386-0; 978-0-9855110; 978-0-9890362) 8245 Cupertino Heights Way, Las Vegas, NV 89178 USA.

Fame's Eternal Bks., LLC, (978-0-9753721) 15740 Rockford Rd. #312, Plymouth, MN 55446 USA Tel 512-468-8873
E-mail: tammymate@aol.com
Web site: http://www.fameseternalbooks.com.

Familius LLC, (978-1-938301; 978-1-939629; 978-1-942672; 978-1-942934) 1254 Commerce Way, Sanger, CA 93657 USA Tel 801-552-7298
E-mail: christopher@familius.com
Web site: www.familius.com
Dist(s): **MyiLibrary.**

Family Bks., (978-0-9728460) Orders Addr.: P.O. Box 730, Petaluma, CA 94953-0730 USA Do not confuse with companies with the same name in Glendale, CA, Dana Point, CA
E-mail: familybooks2003@yahoo.com.

Family Bks. at Home, (978-0-9753127; 978-1-933200) 375 Hudson St., 2nd Flr., New York, NY 10014-3657 USA.

Family Enterprises, (978-0-9773858) 2678 Challis Creek Rd., Box 981, Challis, ID 83226-0981 USA Do not confuse with Family Enterprises in Milwaukee, WI.

Family Guidance & Outreach Ctr. of Lubbock, (978-0-9767215) 5 Briercroft Office Pk., Lubbock, TX 79412-3007 USA Tel 806-747-5577; Fax: 806-747-5119
E-mail: wedwards23@cox.net.

Family Harvest Church, (978-1-889723) 18500 92nd Ave., Tinley Park, IL 60477 USA (SAN 801-4817) Tel 708-614-6000; Fax: 708-614-8288; Toll Free: 800-622-0017
E-mail: winner@winninginlife.org
Web site: http://www.winninginlife.org
Dist(s): **Smashwords.**

Family Learning Assn., Inc., (978-0-9719874) 3925 Hagan St. Ste. 103, Bloomington, IN 47401-8649 USA
Web site: http://www.kidscanlearn.com.

Family Legacy Ministries, (978-0-9797879) Orders Addr.: P.O. Box 811, Rocky Point, NC 28457 USA Tel 910-675-1825
E-mail: publishing@familylegacyministries.org
Web site: http://www.familylegacyministries.org.

Family Life Productions, (978-1-883761) 2460 Hobbit Ln., Fallbrook, CA 92028-3679 USA (SAN 239-1090) Tel 760-728-6437; Fax: 760-728-5309; Toll Free: 800-886-2767.

Family Nutrition Ctr. P.C., (978-0-9770756) 98 Harding Rd., Glen Rock, NJ 07452-1317 USA
E-mail: everyday7foods@earthlink.net.

Family Of Man Pr., The *Imprint of* **Hutchison, G.F. Pr.**

Family Plays, (978-0-87602; 978-0-88680) Div. of Dramatic Publishing, Orders Addr.: 311 Washington St., Woodstock, IL 60098-3308 USA (SAN 282-7433) Tel 815-338-7170
E-mail: msergel@dpcplays.com
Web site: http://www.familyplays.com; http://www.dramaticpublishing.com.

Family Rocks, The, (978-0-9747466) 256 S. Robertson Blvd., Beverly Hills, CA 90211-2898 USA Tel 310-358-5106; Fax: 310-734-1594
E-mail: sales@coupon-directory.com
Web site: http://www.coupon-directory.com.

Family Solutions Publishing, L.L.C. *See* **Tate Publishing & Enterprises, LLC**

Family Value Publishing, (978-0-9645180) R.R. 2, Box 110A, Nevis, MN 56467 USA Tel 218-732-1349.

FamilyLife, (978-1-57229; 978-1-60200) Div. of Campus Crusade for Christ, 5800 Ranch Dr., Little Rock, AR 72223 USA Tel 501-223-8663; Fax: 501-224-2529; Toll Free: 800-404-5052
Web site: http://www.familylife.com.

FancyCrazy Publishing, (978-0-9745386) 254 Harrison St., 1st Fl., Nutley, NJ 07110 USA Tel 917-279-5920
E-mail: fch3000@yahoo.com; baltazarray@gmail.com
Web site: http://www.FancyCrazyHydrants.TV.

F&W Media, Inc., (978-0-89134; 978-0-89879; 978-0-932620; 978-1-55870; 978-1-58180; 978-1-58297; 978-1-884910; 978-1-892127; 978-1-59963; 978-1-60061; 978-1-4402; 978-1-4403; 978-0-578-03300-6; 978-1-940038) Orders Addr.: 10151 Carver Rd., Ste 200, Blue Ash, OH 45242 USA Tel 513-531-2690; Fax: 513-531-1843; Toll Free Fax: 888-590-4082; Toll Free: 800-289-0963; Edit Addr.: Brunel House Forde Close, Newton Abbot, TQ12 4PU GBR Tel 01626 323200; Fax: 01626 323319; *Imprints*: Writer's Digest Books (Wrtrs Digest Bks); North Light Books (North Lght Bks); Impact (Impct); Merit Press Books (MeritPrBks)
E-mail: amber.ziegler@fwmedia.com; mark.griffin@fwmedia.com
Web site: http://www.artistsmagazine.com; http://www.artistsnetwork.com; http://www.davidandcharles.co.uk; http://www.krause.com; http://www.familytreemagazine.com; http://www.howdesign.com; http://www.idonline.com; http://www.memorymakersmagazine.com; http://www.popularwoodworking.com; http://www.writersdigest.com; http://www.writersmarket.com; http://www.writersonlineworkshops.com; http://www.fwpublications.com; http://www.fwmedia.co.uk
Dist(s): **Consortium Bk. Sales & Distribution**
Ebsco Publishing
Follett School Solutions
Leonard, Hal Corp.
MBI Distribution Services/Quayside Distribution
MyiLibrary
ebrary, Inc.

Fantagraphics Bks., (978-0-930193; 978-1-56097; 978-1-60699) 7563 Lake City Way, NE, Seattle, WA 98115 USA (SAN 251-5571) Tel 206-524-1967; Fax: 206-524-2104; Toll Free: 800-657-1100
E-mail: zura@fantagraphics.com; diva@eroscomix.com
Web site: http://www.fantagraphics.com; http://eroscomix.com
Dist(s): **Diamond Comic Distributors, Inc.**
Diamond Bk. Distributors
Norton, W. W. & Co., Inc.

Fantasías Puertorriqueñas, (978-0-9785676) calle Mendez Vigo No. 275, Dorado, PR 00646 USA Tel 787-796-6154
E-mail: drelfrenrios@prtc.net.

Fantasy Flight Games, (978-1-887911; 978-1-58994; 978-1-61661; 978-1-63344) 1975 County Road B2 W. Ste. 1, Saint Paul, MN 55113-2725 USA
Web site: http://www.fantasyflightgames.com
Dist(s): **Diamond Comic Distributors, Inc.**
Diamond Bk. Distributors.

Fantasy Flight Publishing, Incorporated *See* **Fantasy Flight Games**

Fantasy Island Bk. Publishing, (978-0-615-51504-5; 978-0-615-51588-5; 978-0-615-51700-1; 978-0-615-52006-3; 978-0-615-53089-5; 978-0-615-53298-1; 978-0-615-53335-3; 978-0-615-53343-8; 978-0-615-53573-9; 978-0-615-53921-8; 978-0-615-53931-7; 978-0-615-54265-2; 978-0-615-54266-9; 978-0-615-54356-7; 978-0-615-54612-4; 978-0-615-55011-4; 978-0-615-56148-6; 978-0-615-56200-1; 978-0-615-56208-7; 978-0-615-56231-5; 978-0-615-56302-2; 978-0-615-56762-4; 978-0-615-57170-6; 978-0-615-57732-6; 978-0-615-57819-4; 978-0-615-58605-2;) 1244 N. Linwood Ave., Indianapolis, IN 46201 USA Tel 317-966-9814
Web site: htpp://www.fantasyislandbookpublishing.com; htpp://www.fibpub.com
Dist(s): **Lightning Source, Inc.**

Fantasy Island Pr., (978-0-9766628) 320 W. 7th St., Beach Heaven, NJ 08008 USA Tel 609-492-4000; Fax: 609-492-3512
E-mail: webmaster@fantasyislandpark.com
Web site: http://www.fantasyislandpark.com.

Fantasy Prone Comics, (978-0-9762842; 978-0-615-32076-2; 978-0-615-36782-8; 978-0-615-39550-0) 3625 Fredonia Dr., Suite 2, Hollywood, CA 90068 USA (SAN 631-8606) Tel 310-270-6612
E-mail: blakeleibel1@hotmail.com
Web site: http://www.fantasyprone.com
Dist(s): **Diamond Bk. Distributors.**

Far Out Fairy Tales *Imprint of* **Stone Arch Bks.**

Farah, Barbara, (978-0-9769346) P.O. Box 350, Center Harbor, NH 03226 USA Tel 603-253-7142
E-mail: bbfarah@yahoo.com.

Faraway Publishing, (978-0-9710130) Orders Addr.: P.O. Box 765, Highlands, NC 28741-0765 USA Fax: 828-526-5622
E-mail: faraway@nctv.com.

FarBeyond Publishing LLC, (978-1-936872) 8185 SW Birchwood Rd., Portland, OR 97225 USA (SAN 920-5276) Tel 503-683-3013
E-mail: publish@farbeyond.com
Web site: http://farbeyond.com
Dist(s): **CreateSpace Independent Publishing Platform**
Quality Bks., Inc.

Farcountry Pr., (978-0-938314; 978-1-56037; 978-1-59152) Orders Addr.: P.O. Box 5630, Helena, MT 59604 USA (SAN 220-0732) Tel 406-422-1263; Fax: 406-443-5480; Toll Free: 800-821-3874; 2750 Broadwater, Helena, MT 59602; *Imprints*: Sweetgrass Books (SweetgrassBks)
E-mail: books@farcountrypress.com
Web site: http://www.farcountrypress.com
Dist(s): **Partners Bk. Distributing, Inc.**
TNT Media Group, Inc.

Farrar, Straus & Giroux *Imprint of* **Farrar, Straus & Giroux**

†Farrar, Straus & Giroux, (978-0-374) Div. of Holtzbrinck Publishers, Orders Addr.: c/o Holtzbrinck Publishers, 16365 James Madison Hwy., Gordonsville, VA 22942 USA Toll Free Fax: 800-672-2054; Toll Free: 888-330-8477; Edit Addr.: 18 W. 18th St., New York, NY 10011-4607 USA (SAN 206-782X); *Imprints*: Farrar, Straus & Giroux (FarStraGir); Hill & Wang (Hil-Wang); Farrar, Straus & Giroux (BYR) (FSGBYR); Frances Foster Books (FranFosBks); Melanie Kroupa Books (MelKroupa); Sunburst (SunbFSG); Crichton, Sarah Books (S Crichton)
E-mail: sales@fsgee.com; fsg.editorial@fsgee.com
Web site: http://www.fsgbooks.com/
Dist(s): **Continental Bk. Co., Inc.**
Lectorum Pubns., Inc.
Macmillan
Perfection Learning Corp.; *CIP*.

Farrar, Straus & Giroux (BYR) *Imprint of* **Farrar, Straus & Giroux**

F.A.S.T. Learning LLC, (978-1-59792) 2300 S. Brich St., Denver, CO 80222 USA Tel 720-377-0346; Fax: 720-377-0603
E-mail: mcale@fastlearningllc.com
Web site: http://www.fastlearningllc.com.

FastPrncil, Inc., (978-1-60746; 978-1-61933; 978-1-63364; 978-1-4999; 978-1-68133) 307 Orchard City Dr., No. 210, Campbell, CA 95008 USA Tel 408-540-7571; Fax: 408-540-7572; *Imprints*: Premiere (PremierPenc)
E-mail: author_services@fastpencil.com; mfoley@fastpencil.com; mfoley@courier.com
Web site: http://www.fastpencil.com
Dist(s): **AtlasBooks Distribution**
BookMasters Distribution Services (BDS).

FastPublishing.com *See* **ExpandingBooks.com**

Fasttrack Teaching Materials, (978-1-893742) 6215 Lavell Court, Springfield, VA 22152 USA Tel 703-644-4612
E-mail: davburns@fasttrackteaching.com.

Father & Son Publishing, (978-0-942407; 978-1-935802) 4909 N. Monroe St., Tallahassee, FL 32303 USA (SAN 667-0229) Tel 850-562-3927; 850-562-0907; Fax: 850-562-0916; Toll Free: 800-741-2712 (orders only)
E-mail: lance@fatherson.com; jean@fatherson.com
Web site: http://www.fatherson.com
Dist(s): **Dot Gibson Distribution.**

Father's Pr., LLC, (978-0-9779407; 978-0-9795394; 978-0-9824982; 978-0-9825321; 978-0-9833739) 2424 SE 6th. St., Lee's Summit, MO 64063 USA Tel 816-600-6288 (phone/fax)
E-mail: fatherspress@yahoo.com
Web site: http://www.fatherspress.net.

Faux Paw Media Group, (978-0-9777340; 978-0-9779539; 978-0-9825387; 978-1-935824) 718 Cliff Dr., Laguna Beach, CA 92651 USA (SAN 850-637X)
Web site: http://www.fauxpawproductions.com.

FAVA Pr., (978-0-9801396) 1401 Sherman St., Geneva, OH 44041 USA (SAN 855-3173).

Favonian Bks., (978-0-9767048) Div. of Brian Alan Lane & Donna Cohen Lane, 3451 Adina Dr., Los Angeles, CA 90068-1319 USA Tel 323-366-2812 (phonefax)
E-mail: bal@brianalanlane.com; dc@donnacohen.com.

Favorable Impressions, (978-0-7808; 978-0-9674698; 978-1-931360) Div. of Elm Park Pr., Orders Addr.: P.O. Box 69018, Pleasant Ridge, MI 48069 USA Tel 248-544-2421 (phone/fax); Toll Free: 866-246-2341; Edit Addr.: 9 Elm Park Blvd., Pleasant Ridge, MI 48069 USA
E-mail: danoptt@tir.com; danoepp@tir.com.

Favored Publishing, Inc., (978-0-9791374) P.O. Box 734, Jackson, MS 39205-0734 USA Tel 601-316-2193
E-mail: jriley_collins@yahoo.com.

Favorite Uncle Bks., LLC, (978-0-9711665) 23228 Lawrence, Dearborn, MI 48128 USA Tel 313-406-2040
E-mail: john@johntocco.com.

Favortwou Publishing, (978-0-9774107; 978-0-9799006; 978-0-615-12362-2; 978-0-9823883) 6339 Harbin Woods Dr., Morrow, GA 30260-1835 USA
E-mail: favortwou@hotmail.com
Web site: http://www.favortwov.net.

Faye Bks., (978-0-615-16371-0; 978-0-615-16610-0; 978-0-615-16737-4; 978-0-578-02146-1) 305 Halls Ln., Shepherdsville, KY 40165 USA; P.O. Box 387, Shepherdsville, KY 40165
Web site: http://www.fayebooks.zoomshare.com
Dist(s): **Lulu Enterprises Inc.**

FayeHouse. Pr. International, (978-0-9655222) 1568 St. Margaret's Rd., Annapolis, MD 21401 USA Tel 443-822-9144; Fax: 410-349-9413 (Call before faxing)
E-mail: Charletfaye@aol.com.

FayRe Pr., (978-0-9771301) 513 Mount Evans Rd., Golden, CO 80401 USA (SAN 257-9340) Tel 303-526-7726 (phone/fax)
E-mail: theblueumbrella@earthlink.net.

FBC Pubns. & Printing, (978-1-933594; 978-1-60208) 3794 Oleander Ave., Fort Pierce, FL 34982 USA Tel 772-461-6460; Fax: 772-461-6474
E-mail: printing@fbcpublications.com
Web site: http://www.fbcpublications.com.

FBS Publishing Co., (978-0-615-18629-0; 978-0-615-18633-7; 978-0-615-21316-3) 5520 Grandview Ln., Doylestown, PA 18902 USA Tel 877-853-2267
Dist(s): **Publishers Services.**

FEA Ministries, (978-0-9618730; 978-0-9749168; 978-1-933716) Orders Addr.: P.O. Box 1065, Hobe Sound, FL 33475 USA (SAN 668-6877) Tel 772-546-8426; Fax: 772-546-9379; Edit Addr.: 11305 SE Gomez Ave., Hobe Sound, FL 33455 USA
E-mail: orders@gospelpublishingmission.org
Web site: http://www.gospelpublishingmission.org.

Fear2love Pr., (978-1-937861) P.O. Box 1824, Point Roberts, WA 98281 USA Tel 814-409-8083
E-mail: lisa@fear2love.com.

Feather River Publishing, (978-0-615-16630-8) 28 S. Garfield Ave., North Platte, NE 69101 USA Tel 308-532-4025
Dist(s): **Publishers Services.**

Feather Rock Bks., Inc., (978-1-934066) Orders Addr.: 4245 Chippewa Ln., Maple Plain, MN 55359 USA; Edit Addr.: P.O. Box 99, Maple Plain, MN 55359 USA (SAN 851-1829) Tel 952-473-9091
E-mail: jadams@featherrockbooks.com
Web site: http://www.featherrockbooks.com.

Featherproof Bks., (*978-0-9771992; 978-0-9825808; 978-0-9831863*) 2201 W. Crystal St., No. 3, Chicago, IL 60622 USA
E-mail: mail@featherproof.com
Web site: http://www.featherproof.com
Dist(s): **MyiLibrary**
Perseus-PGW
Perseus Bks. Group.

Federal Street Pr., (*978-1-892859; 978-1-59695*) Div. of Merriam Webster, Inc., P.O. Box 281, Springfield, MA 01102 USA (SAN 859-4678) Fax: 413-731-5979; 47 Federal St., Springfield, MA 01105
E-mail: info@federalstreetpress.com; lbrodeur@m-w.com
Web site: http://www.federalstreetpress.com.

Federation Pr. (AUS) (*978-1-86287; 978-1-876067; 978-0-646-17924-7; 978-1-76002*) *Dist. by* **Gaunt.**

Feed My Sheep, (*978-0-9768958*) P.O. Box 16438, Rural Hall, NC 27045 USA Do not confuse with Feed My Sheep in Brunswick, GA, Detroit, MI.

Feed My Sheep Bks., (*978-0-9769152*) P.O. Box 05340, Detroit, MI 48205 USA Do not confuse with companies with the same name in Rural Hall, NC, Brunswick, GA.

Feeley, Lisa & Craig, (*978-0-9743159*) 19229 Lupine Ct., Noblesville, IN 46060 USA.

Fegley, Elizabeth *See* **Healing Hands Pr.**

Feil, (*978-0-9741588*) 15 Fox Meadow Ln., Merrimack, NH 03054 USA
Web site: http://www.theservingart.com/creativewriting.

Fein, Bruce, (*978-0-9745049*) 5400 Lochmor Ave., Las Vegas, NV 89130 USA
Web site: http://www.oxymoronbooks.com.

Feiwel & Friends, (*978-0-312*) 175 Fifth Ave., New York, NY 10010 USA Tel 646-307-5151
Web site: http://www.holtzbrinckus.com
Dist(s): **Macmillan**
Perfection Learning Corp.

Feldheim, Philipp Incorporated *See* **Feldheim Pubs.**

†Feldheim Pubs., (*978-0-87306; 978-1-58330; 978-1-59826; 978-1-68025*) 208 Airport Executive Park., Nanuet, NY 10954-5262 USA (SAN 106-6307) Toll Free: 800-237-7149
E-mail: sales@feldheim.com; eli@feldheim.com
Web site: http://www.feldheim.com
Dist(s): **David, Jonathan Pubs., Inc.**
Libros Sin Fronteras; *CIP.*

Feldick, Les Ministries, (*978-1-885344*) 30706 W. Lona Valley Rd., Kinta, OK 74552 USA Tel 918-768-3218; Fax: 918-768-3219; Toll Free: 800-369-7856
Web site: http://www.lesfeldick.org.

Felix Comics, Inc., (*978-0-615-12660-9*) 123 Rt. 23 S., Hamburg, NJ 07419 USA Toll Free: 800-343-3549 (800-34-FELIX)
Web site: http://www.felixthecat.com.

Fell Pr., The, (*978-0-9759430*) 8926 N. Greenwood, No. 289, Niles, IL 60714 USA
Web site: http://www.thefellpress.com
Dist(s): **SCB Distributors.**

Fellowship Pr., (*978-0-914390; 978-1-943388*) 5820 Overbrook Ave., Philadelphia, PA 19131 USA (SAN 201-6117) Tel 215-879-8929; Fax: 215-879-6307; Toll Free: 888-786-1786
E-mail: info@bmf.org
Web site: http://www.bmf.org
Dist(s): **Ilmhouse Inc.**
New Leaf Distributing Co., Inc.
Omega Pubns., Inc.

Felsen Ink, (*978-1-62272*) 1599 NW 101st St., Clive, IA 50325 USA Tel 515-226-9372
E-mail: holly.welch@gmail.com
Web site: www.felsenink.com.

†Feminist Pr. at The City Univ. of New York, (*978-0-912670; 978-0-935312; 978-1-55861; 978-1-936932*) 365 Fifth Ave., New York, NY 10016 USA (SAN 213-6813) Tel 212-817-7915; Fax: 212-817-2988
E-mail: lglazer@gc.cuny.edu; info@feministpress.org
Web site: http://www.feministpress.org
Dist(s): **Consortium Bk. Sales & Distribution**
Continental Bk. Co., Inc.
CreateSpace Independent Publishing Platform
MyiLibrary
Perseus Bks. Group
SPD-Small Pr. Distribution
Women Ink; *CIP.*

Fencepost Communications Inc., (*978-0-9776487*) Orders Addr.: P.O. Box Fencepost Communications, Inc., P O Box 398, Hinsdale, IL 60522-0398 USA Tel 630-850-9755; Toll Free: 888-648-0008; Edit Addr.: 49 1/2 S. Washington St., Hinsdale, IL 60521 USA.

Feng Liu Productions, (*978-0-9727089*) P.O. Box 248, Mill Valley, CA 94942 USA
Dist(s): **Independent Pubs. Group.**

Fen's Rim, (*978-0-9713603*) Orders Addr.: P.O. Box 885, Elk Rapids, MI 49629 USA Tel 231-264-6800; Edit Addr.: 104 Dexter St., Elk Rapids, MI 49629 USA
E-mail: mail@fensrim.com
Web site: http://www.fensrim.com.

Fenton Publishing Company *See* **Octopus Publishing Co.**

Fenwyn Pr., (*978-0-913062*) Orders Addr.: P.O. Box 245, Rapid City, SD 57709 USA Tel 605-343-6070; Fax: 605-348-2108; Toll Free: 800-821-6343; Edit Addr.: 920 E. Saint Patrick St., Rapid City, SD 57701 USA.

Feral Pr., Inc., (*978-0-9649349; 978-1-930094*) 304 Strawberry Field Rd., Flat Rock, NC 28731 USA Tel 828-694-0438; Fax: 828-694-0438; *Imprints:* Rivet Books (Rivet Bks)
E-mail: gchet@feralpressinc.com
Web site: http://www.feralpressinc.com.

Fergus & Lady Publishing, (*978-0-9786975*) 2310 Del Mar Rd., No. 10, Montrose, CA 91020 USA.

Ferguson, Linda, (*978-0-9755288*) 383 Alewine Dr., Boaz, AL 35957-5034 USA
E-mail: lkinspire@yahoo.com
Web site: http://www.l-n-kinspirationalbooks.com/.

Ferguson Publishing Co. *Imprint of* **Facts On File, Inc.**

Ferguson, Suzanie Pamela, (*978-0-9658745*) 4609 Maplewood Dr., Suffolk, VA 23435 USA Tel 757-483-5721
E-mail: lferg72184@aol.com.

Fern Creek Pr., (*978-0-9625737; 978-1-893651*) P.O. Box 1322, Clayton, GA 30525 USA Tel 706-782-5379; Fax: 706-782-5379
E-mail: brian@ferncreekpress.com
Web site: http://rabun.net/boyd.

Fern Creek Publishing *See* **Fern Creek Pr.**

Fern Rock Falls Pr., (*978-0-9762409*) 22105 Fisk Rd., Noti, OR 97461-9718 USA Tel 541-935-3920
E-mail: dandq@rio.com.

Fernandez USA Publishing, 203 Argonne Ave., Suite B, PMB 151, Long Beach, CA 90803-1777 USA Tel 562-901-2370; Fax: 562-901-2372; Toll Free: 800-814-8080
Web site: http://www.fernandezusa.com
Dist(s): **Continental Bk. Co., Inc.**

Ferne Pr. *Imprint of* **Nelson Publishing & Marketing**

Fernhouse Pr., (*978-0-9759363*) P.O. Box 73, Woodstock, VT 05067 USA
Web site: http://www.fernhouse.com.

Fernwood & Hedges Bks., (*978-0-615-72092-0; 978-0-9890698; 978-0-615-80386-9; 978-0-615-81583-1*) 7612 Fountain Ave., West Hollywood, CA 90046 USA Tel 213-910-2887
Dist(s): **CreateSpace Independent Publishing Platform.**

ferrocement.com, (*978-0-9748016*) P.O. Box 31 S. St., Bernardston, MA 01337-0133 USA Fax: 413-648-9098
E-mail: garrett@ferrocement.com.

Fertig, Howard Incorporated *See* **Fertig, Howard Publisher**

†Fertig, Howard Publisher, (*978-0-86527*) Orders Addr.: 80 E. 11th St., New York, NY 10003 USA (SAN 201-4777) Tel 212-982-7922; Fax: 212-982-1099
E-mail: orders@hfertigbooks.com
Web site: http://www.hfertigbooks.com; *CIP.*

Fetch! Publishing, (*978-0-9746324*) 27881 La Paz Rd., Suite G-124, Laguna Niguel, CA 92677 USA Fax: 877-426-3809; Toll Free Fax: 877-426-3809; Toll Free: 877-899-9454
Web site: http://fetchpublishing.com.

Fey, Sid Designs, Inc., (*978-0-9753530*) Box 184, 335 E. Geneva Rd., Carol Stream, IL 60188 USA Tel 630-668-6607; Fax: 630-668-6282
E-mail: zpdduda@earthlink.net
Web site: http://www.thebeinggame.com.

Fiction Focus *See* **Story Direction**

Fiction Picture Bks. *Imprint of* **Picture Window Bks.**

Fiction Publishing, Inc., (*978-0-9796752; 978-0-9814956; 978-0-9819727; 978-0-9825086; 978-0-9826168; 978-0-9827442; 978-0-9830007; 978-0-9837803*) 5626 Travelers Way, Fort Pierce, FL 34982 USA Tel 772-489-5811
E-mail: fictionpub@bellsouth.net
Web site: http://www.fictionpublishinginc.com.

Fiction Works, The, (*978-1-58124*) Orders Addr.: 3328 SW Cascade Ave., Corvallis, OR 97333 USA Tel 541-730-2044; Fax: 541-738-2648
E-mail: fictionworks@me.com
Web site: http://www.fictionworks.com
Dist(s): **Brodart Co.**
Untreed Reads Publishing, LLC.

FictionSpin, (*978-0-9724007; 978-0-9817897*) P.O. Box 885, Pacific Palisades, CA 90272 USA (SAN 255-0431)
E-mail: FictionSpin@aol.com
Web site: http://www.fictionspin.com.

Fideli Publishing, Inc., (*978-1-60414*) 119 W. Morgan St., Martinsville, IN 46151 USA (SAN 854-0772) Toll Free: 888-343-3542
E-mail: info@fidelipublishing.com
Web site: http://www.fidelipublishing.com
Dist(s): **BookBaby**
MyiLibrary
Smashwords.

Fidelity Heart Publishing, (*978-0-9748522*) Orders Addr.: P.O. Box 1758, Houston, TX 77251 USA; Edit Addr.: 3923 Teal Run Pl., Ct, Fresno, TX 77545-7049 USA
E-mail: slmccraw@fidelityheart.com
Web site: http://www.fidelityheart.com.

Field Mouse Productions, (*978-0-9647586; 978-0-9888021*) Div. of Associated Design Services, Inc., Orders Addr.: P.O. Box 392, Grand Island, NE 68802 USA Tel 308-380-3315; 308-380-3215; Edit Addr.: 454 8th Ave., Palmer, NE 68864 USA
E-mail: skidi@aol.com; rtstron@aol.com; JeanLukesh@aol.com
Web site: http://www.fieldmousebooks.com; http://www.fieldmouseproductions.com
Dist(s): **Lightning Source, Inc.**

Field Stone Pubs., (*978-0-9645272*) 331 Fields Hill Rd., Conway, MA 01341 USA Tel 413-369-4091
E-mail: author@johnrdixonbooks.com
Web site: http://www.JohnRDixonBooks.com.

Fielder Group, (*978-0-9639986; 978-0-9789058*) Orders Addr.: P.O. Box 510, Benton, KY 42025 USA Tel 888-255-9248; Fax: 270-362-7130; Toll Free: 888-255-9248
E-mail: barbara@thefieldergroupusa.com
Web site: http://www.thefieldergroupusa.com.

Fielder, John Publishing, (*978-0-9832769; 978-0-9860004; 978-0-9914990*) P.O. Box 26890, Silverthorne, CO 80497 USA Tel 303-907-2179
E-mail: john@johnfielder.com.

Fields Communications & Publishing *See* **Fields Publishing, Inc.**

Fields of Gold Publishing, Inc., (*978-0-9746296; 978-0-9848034; 978-1-940894*) P.O. Box 128438, Nashville, TN 37212-3304 USA Tel 615-335-2014
E-mail: tneftzger@comcast.net
Web site: http://www.fogink.com
Dist(s): **Brodart Co.**
Lightning Source, Inc.

Fields Publishing, Inc., (*978-1-57843*) 8120 Sawyer Brown Rd. Ste. 108, Nashville, TN 37221-1410 USA
E-mail: Fieldsco@mindspring.com
Web site: http://www.fieldspublishing.com.

Fieldstone Hill Pr., (*978-0-9767762*) 321 Old Saluda Dam Rd., Easley, SC 29640 USA
Web site: http://www.fieldstone-hill.net.

Fiery Studios, (*978-0-9743110*) P.O. Box 51595, Kalamazoo, MI 49005-1595 USA
Web site: http://www.vogelein.com
Dist(s): **Diamond Comic Distributors, Inc.**
Diamond Bk. Distributors.

Fifth Ave Pr., (*978-0-9755390*) 413 Salt Pond Rd., Bethany Beach, DE 19930 USA Tel 302-537-9633; Fax: 302-537-0210; Toll Free: 800-862-6443 Do not confuse with Fifth Avenue Press in Fargo, ND and New York, NY.
E-mail: bethanybil@aol.com
Web site: http://www.e-studio8.com/fifthstreetpress.

Fifth Hse. Pubs. (CAN) (*978-0-920079; 978-1-895618; 978-1-894004; 978-1-894856; 978-1-897252; 978-1-927083*) *Dist. by* **Midpt Trade.**

Fifth Hse. Pubs. (CAN) (*978-0-920079; 978-1-895618; 978-1-894004; 978-1-894856; 978-1-897252; 978-1-927083*) *Dist. by* **IngramPubServ.**

Fifth Paw Pr., (*978-0-9816188*) 40 Adelphi St., No. 3, Brooklyn, NY 11205 USA Tel 718-288-6141
E-mail: demo-dog@earthlink.net; fifthpawpress@earthlink.net
Web site: http://www.fifthpawpress.com
Dist(s): **Ebsco Publishing**
Independent Pubs. Group.

Fifth Planet Pr., (*978-1-880855*) 9604 Southward Cove, Austin, TX 78733 USA
E-mail: nisa@fifthplanetpress.com
Web site: http://www.fifthplanetpress.com
Dist(s): **BookMobile**
SPD-Small Pr. Distribution.

Fig & The Vine, LLC, The, (*978-0-9841087; 978-0-615-49661-0; 978-0-615-62717-5; 978-0-9883370; 978-0-692-48233-9*) Orders Addr.: 753 Winthrop St., Mount Pleasant, SC 29464-2946 USA Fax: 843-881-8425; Toll Free Fax: 843-881-8425
E-mail: figandvine@mail.com; carolinahomeandgarden@gmail.com; publisher@thefigandthevine.com
Web site: http://thefigandthevine.com.

Fighting Words Publishing, (*978-0-9755279*) P.O. Box 7, Highwood, IL 60040 USA Tel 847-266-1965; Fax: 847-266-0840
E-mail: magmem@aol.com; rmk@robertmkatzmanwriter.com
Web site: http://www.fightingwordsbook.com; http://www.robertmkatzmanwriter.com.

Figure 8 Pr., (*978-0-9630376*) Orders Addr.: P.O. Box 248, Rolling Ground, WI 54631 USA
E-mail: figure8press@gmail.com
Web site: http://figure8press.com.

Figures In Motion, (*978-0-9818566*) 6278 Clive Ave., Oakland, CA 94611 USA (SAN 856-7336) Tel 510-482-8500; Fax: 510-482-8500
E-mail: cathy@figuresinmotion.com; info@figuresinmotion.com
Web site: http://www.figuresinmotion.com.

Filaretos, William, (*978-0-9724520*) 220 W. Canton St. # 3, Boston, MA 02116-5814 USA
E-mail: william_filaretos@thepotionoftime.com
Web site: http://www.ThePotionofTime.com.

Filion, Rita-Anneliese, (*978-0-9749142*) 26 Elizabeth Ln., Saratoga Springs, NY 12866-2804 USA
E-mail: sirdino@noblebones.com
Web site: http://www.noblebones.com.

Filiquarian Publishing, LLC, (*978-0-9770505; 978-1-59986*) Orders Addr.: 110 W. Grant St. Unit 2c, Minneapolis, MN 55403 USA Tel 612-207-2335; *Imprints:* FQ Classics (FQ Classics).

Fillet Of Horn Publishing, (*978-0-9753077*) 35000 Muskrat Rd., Barnesville, OH 43713 USA Tel 740-758-5050; Fax: 740-758-5114
Web site: http://www.filletofhorn.com
Dist(s): **ebrary, Inc.**

Film Ideas, Inc., (*978-1-57557; 978-1-60572*) 308 N. Wolf Rd., Wheeling, IL 60090 USA Tel 847-419-0255; Fax: 847-419-8933; Toll Free: 800-475-3456
E-mail: info@filmideas.com
Web site: http://www.filmideas.com
Dist(s): **Follett School Solutions.**

Filsinger & Co., Ltd., (*978-0-916754*) 288 W. 12th St., New York, NY 10014 USA (SAN 208-3574) Tel 212-243-7421.

Filter Pr., LLC, (*978-0-86541; 978-0-910584*) P.O. Box 95, Palmer Lake, CO 80133 USA (SAN 201-484X) Tel 719-481-2420 (phone/fax); Toll Free: 888-570-2663
E-mail: info@filterpressbooks.com; doris@filterpressbooks.com
Web site: http://www.filterpressbooks.com.

Financial Safari Pr., (*978-0-9777993*) 1135 Kildaire Farm Rd., Suite 200, Cary, NC 27512 USA Tel 919-657-4201
E-mail: capitaltax@gmail.com.

Finch Bks. Co., (*978-0-9661457*) Orders Addr.: P.O. Box 545, Tularosa, NM 88352 USA; Edit Addr.: 1418 Apple Ave., Tularosa, NM 88352 USA Tel 505-585-8037; Fax: 505-585-8039
Dist(s): **MBI Distribution Services/Quayside Distribution.**

Find Your Way Publishing, Inc., (*978-0-9824692; 978-0-9849322*) P.O. Box 667, Norway, ME 04268 USA
E-mail: melissa@findyourwaypublishing.com
Web site: http://www.findyourwaypublishing.com.

Findaway World, LLC, (*978-1-59895; 978-1-60252; 978-1-60514; 978-1-60640; 978-1-60775; 978-1-60812; 978-1-60847; 978-1-61545; 978-1-61574; 978-1-61587; 978-1-61637; 978-1-61657; 978-1-61707; 978-1-4676; 978-1-5094*) 31999 Aurora Rd., Solon, OH 44139 USA (SAN 853-8778)
Web site: http://www.findawayworld.com; http://www.playawaydigital.com
Dist(s): **Follett School Solutions**
MyiLibrary.

Findhorn Pr. (GBR) (*978-0-905249; 978-1-899171; 978-0-906191; 978-0-9504268; 978-1-84409*) *Dist. by* **PerseuPGW.**

Finding the Cause, LLC, 39738 Calle Azucar, Murrieta, CA 92562 USA Tel 760-724-8104
E-mail: Dr.king@findingthecause.com
Web site: Www.FindingTheCause.com.

Fine Art Editions *Imprint of* **North American International**

Fine Print Pr., The, (*978-0-9644365; 978-1-888960*) 350 Ward Ave., Suite 106, Honolulu, HI 96814-4091 USA Fax: 425-955-1909
E-mail: info@fineprintpress.com
Web site: http://www.fineprintpress.com
Dist(s): **Partners Pubs. Group, Inc.**

Fine Print Publishing Co., (*978-0-9640713; 978-1-892951*) Orders Addr.: P.O. Box 916401, Longwood, FL 32791-6401 USA Tel 407-814-7777; Fax: 407-814-7677; Edit Addr.: 1350 Sheeler Rd., Apopka, FL 32703 USA
E-mail: books@fprint.net.

Finer Moments, (*978-0-9771549*) P.O. Box 22102, Robbinsdale, MN 55422 USA Tel 612-302-7830
E-mail: finermoments@earthlink.net
Web site: http://www.finermoments.net.

Finest Bks., (*978-1-935679*) 959 W. Jericho Tpke., Smithtown, NY 11787 USA Tel 615-479-0877; Fax: 631-864-1565
E-mail: michaelsheahan@msn.com
Web site: http://www.finestbks.com
Dist(s): **AtlasBooks Distribution.**

Fingerprint Bks., (*978-0-9709861*) P.O. Box 534, Redlands, CA 92373 USA (SAN 253-7923) Tel 909-307-9993 (phone/fax)
E-mail: mglis2t@earthlink.net.

Finial Publishing, (*978-1-933791*) P.O. Box 346, Mercer Island, WA 98040 USA
Web site: http://www.finialpublishing.com.

Finkelstein, Ruth, (*978-0-9628157*) 27 Saddle River Rd., Airmont, NY 10952-3034 USA.

Finlay Prints, Inc., (*978-0-9766998*) Orders Addr.: 74 Fifth Ave., 6D, New York, NY 10011 USA Tel 212-463-7173
E-mail: finlayprints@earthlink.net.

Finley Flowers *Imprint of* **Picture Window Bks.**

Finneran, Lisa, (*978-0-9777744*) 9709 River Rd., Newport News, VA 23601-2360 USA
E-mail: arkangels@cox.net.

Finney Co., Inc., (*978-0-89317; 978-0-912486; 978-0-933855; 978-0-9617677; 978-0-9639705; 978-1-880654; 978-1-893272*) Orders Addr.: 8075 215th St. W., Lakeville, MN 55044 USA (SAN 206-412X) Tel 952-469-6699; Fax: 952-469-1968; Toll Free Fax: 800-330-6232; Toll Free: 800-846-7027; *Imprints:* Windward Publishing (Windward Pubng); Lone Oak Press, Limited (LoneOak)
E-mail: feedback@finneyco.com
Web site: http://www.finneyco.com; http://www.ecopress.com; http://www.pogopress.com; http://www.astragalpress.com
Dist(s): **Book Wholesalers, Inc.**
Brodart Co.
Follett School Solutions
Southern Bk. Service.

Fiore, (*978-0-9661235*) Orders Addr.: P.O. Box 50663, Phoenix, AZ 85076 USA Tel 602-759-0048; Toll Free: 888-443-4677; Edit Addr.: 4030 E. Lavender Ln., Phoenix, AZ 85044 USA.

Fire Flies Entertainment, LLC, (*978-0-9787302*) 1077 North Ave., Suite 114, Elizabeth, NJ 07208 USA Tel 212-561-1654; Fax: 908-351-1888.

Fire Mountain Pr., (*978-1-929374*) Orders Addr.: P.O. Box 3851, Hillsboro, OR 97123 USA Tel 503-846-9057 (phone/fax); 503-219-5643 (phone/fax)
Web site: http://www.firemountainpress.com.

Firebreak Publishing Co., (*978-0-9761448*) Orders Addr.: P.O. Box 995, Pacific Palisades, CA 90272-0995 USA Tel 310-454-3105
E-mail: r.brodie@verizon.net
Web site: http://www.firebreakpublishing.com.

Firebug Fairy Tales, (*978-0-615-58954-1; 978-0-615-58955-8*) P.O. Box 680396, Charlotte, NC 28216 USA Tel 704-398-9923
E-mail: ejkisinger@yahoo.com.

Firefall *See* **Firefall Editions**

Firefall Editions, (*978-0-915090; 978-1-939434*) Div. of Firefallmedia, 4905 Tunlaw St., Alexandria, VA 22312 USA Tel 510-549-2461; *Imprints:* California Street (Calif St)
E-mail: firefallmedia@att.net; literary@att.net
Web site: http://www.firefallmedia.com; http://www.firefallfilms.com; http://www.blotbooks.com; http://www.lostshoerecords.com; http://www.sim-book.com; http://www.lovinglicks.com; http://www.blue-loves.com; http://www.metech.us; http://www.shift-alt-delete.com
Dist(s): **Audible.com**
Brodart Co.
Follett School Solutions.

Firefly Bks., Ltd., (*978-0-920668; 978-1-55209; 978-1-895565; 978-1-896284; 978-1-55297; 978-1-55407*) Orders Addr.: c/o Frontier Distributing, 1000 Young St., Suite 160, Tonawanda, NY 14150 USA

Publisher Name Index

(SAN 630-611X) Tel 203-222-9700; Toll Free Fax: 800-565-6034; Toll Free: 800-387-5085; Edit Addr.: 8514 Long Canyon Dr., Austin, TX 78730-2813 USA
E-mail: service@fireflybooks.com
Web site: http://www.fireflybooks.com/
Dist(s): **Lectorum Pubns., Inc.**

Firefly Games, *(978-0-9747671)* 7525 Garden Gate Dr., Citrus Hts, CA 95621-1909 USA
E-mail: patrick@firefly-games.com
Web site: http://www.firefly-games.com.

FireFly Lights, *(978-0-9856863)* 1403 Delano St. No. 7, Houston, TX 77003 USA Tel 281-536-3915
E-mail: lacycarneywrites@gmail.com.

FireFly Publishings & Entertainment *See* **FireFly Publishings & Entertainment LLC**

FireFly Publishings & Entertainment LLC, *(978-0-9774126; 978-0-9846428)* Orders Addr.: P.O. Box 1346, Snellville, GA 30078 USA; Edit Addr.: 845 Common Oak Pl., Lawrenceville, GA 30045 USA (SAN 257-6597)
E-mail: fireflypublishingent@yahoo.com; dorced58@yahoo.com
Web site: http://www.fireflypublishingent.com
Dist(s): **Follett School Solutions.**

Fireglass Publishing, *(978-0-9857523)* PO Box 10613, Bainbridge Island, WA 98110 USA Tel 206-486-4717
E-mail: info@fireglasspublishing.com.

FireHydrant Creative Studios, Inc., *(978-0-9826066; 978-1-937176)* 52 Huntleigh Woods, Saint Louis, MO 63132 USA Tel 314-822-0833
E-mail: administrator@FireHydrantCS.com
Web site: http://www.FireHydrantCS.com.

Firelight Press, Inc., *(978-0-9786555; 978-1-934517)* 550 Larchmont Dr., Cincinnati, OH 45215 USA (SAN 851-2353); P.O. Box 15758, Cincinnati, OH 45215 Tel 513-646-6803; Fax: 513-821-2830 Do not confuse with companies with the same name in Independence, MO, Solvang, CA
E-mail: books@firelightpress.com
Web site: http://firelightpress.com.

Firelight Publishing, Inc., *(978-0-9707206)* Orders Addr.: P.O. Box 444, Sublimity, OR 97385-0444 USA Toll Free: 866-347-3544; Edit Addr.: 226 Division St., SW, Sublimity, OR 97385-9637 USA Tel 503-767-0444; Fax: 503-769-8980; Toll Free: 866-347-3544
E-mail: info@firelightpublishing.com; editor@firelightpublishing.com; webmaster@firelightpublishing.com; orders@firelightpublishing.com
Web site: http://www.firelightpublishing.com
Dist(s): **Partners/West Book Distributors.**

Firenze Pr., *(978-0-9711236)* Orders Addr.: P.O. Box 6892, Wyomissing, PA 19610-0892 USA (SAN 254-315X); Edit Addr.: 612 Museum Rd., Reading, PA 19610-0892 USA Tel 610-374-7048; Fax: 610-478-7992 Do not confuse with Leonardo Pr., Camden, ME
E-mail: hailejohnjr@msn.com; HaileJohnJr@msn.com; InkPenCJH@msn.com
Web site: http://caroljhaile.com.

Fireproof Ministries, *(978-0-9741849)* P.O. Box 150169, Grand Rapids, MI 49515 USA
E-mail: info@fireproofministries.com
Web site: http://www.fireproofministries.com.

Fireship Pr., *(978-1-934757; 978-1-935585; 978-1-61179)* P.O. Box 68412, Tucson, AZ 85737 USA Tel 520-360-6228
E-mail: tmg@en.com
Web site: http://www.FireshipPress.com.

Fireside Catholic Bibles, *(978-1-55665)* Div. of Fireside Catholic Bibles, Orders Addr.: P.O. Box 780189, Wichita, KS 67278-0189 USA Tel 316-267-3211; Fax: 316-267-1850; Toll Free: 888-676-2040; Edit Addr.: 9020 E. 35th St., N., Wichita, KS 67226 USA (SAN 854-0780)
E-mail: info@firesidebibles.com; llear@devore.cc
Web site: http://www.firesidebibles.com
Dist(s): **Spring Arbor Distributors, Inc.**

Fireside Critters, *(978-0-9753248)* Orders Addr.: P.O. Box 283, Vermilion, OH 44089 USA; Edit Addr.: P.O. Box 283, Vermilion, OH 44089 USA
E-mail: FiresideCritters@AOL.com.

Fireside Pr., Inc., *(978-1-930754; 978-0-9779863; 978-0-9800067; 978-0-9818486; 978-1-935451; 978-0-9825292; 978-1-935764)* 10000 N. Central Exp, Suite 400, Dallas, TX 75231 USA
E-mail: info@durbanhouse.com; john7@durbanhouse.com
Web site: http://www.durbanhouse.com
Dist(s): **BookMasters**
MyiLibrary
National Bk. Network
ebrary, Inc.

Firesidenook, *(978-0-9887214)* 10072 Forestedge Ln, Miamisburg, OH 45342 USA Tel 937-776-0019
E-mail: strangedad1@yahoo.com.

Firestorm Editions, *(978-0-9855541)* 14314 Rockdale Rd., Clear Spring, MD 21722 USA Tel 815-642-0700
E-mail: cashives@gmail.com.

Fireweed Pr., *(978-1-878660)* Orders Addr.: P.O. Box 482, Madison, WI 53701-0482 USA; Edit Addr.: 638 Gately Terr., Madison, WI 53711 USA Tel 608-233-0300 Do not confuse with companies with same name in Falls Church, VA, Fairbanks, AK, Evergreen, CO Seattle, WA
E-mail: tmccormi@wisc.edu.

Fireweed Pr., *(978-0-9772528)* Orders Addr.: P.O. Box 31037, Seattle, WA 98103 USA; Edit Addr.: 1807 N. 36th St., Seattle, WA 98103 USA Do not confuse with Fireweed Press in Falls Church, VA Fairbanks, AK, Madison, WI, Evergreen, CO AJ
E-mail: fireweedpress@comcast.net.

First Assist Pubns., *(978-0-9724865)* P.O. Box 608, Woodland Hills, CA 91365 USA Fax: 818-346-8988
E-mail: e21sherr@aol.com.

First Associates Publishing, *(978-0-9618835)* P.O. Box 1281, Richmond, VA 23218-1281 USA (SAN 242-5289) Tel 804-254-0662; Fax: 804-524-5138; Toll Free: 877-247-8343
E-mail: earl@fapbooks.com.

First Avenue Editions *Imprint of* **Lerner Publishing Group**

First Biographies *Imprint of* **Reynolds, Morgan Inc.**

First Bks., *(978-0-912301; 978-0-9823476; 978-1-61007; 978-1-937090)* 6750 SW Franklin St., Suite A, Portland, OR 97223 USA (SAN 297-9063) Tel 503-968-6777; Fax: 503-968-6779
E-mail: customerservice@firstbooks.com
Web site: http://www.firstbooks.com
Dist(s): **Bookazine Co., Inc.**
Partners Bk. Distributing, Inc.

First Century Publishing, *(978-1-885273)* Div. of First Century Church Ministries, P.O. Box 130, Delmar, NY 12054 USA Tel 518-439-3544; Fax: 518-439-0105; Toll Free: 800-570-6060
E-mail: dnbubar1@nycap.rr.com; 1century@nycap.rr.com
Web site: http://www.firstcenturypublishing.com
Dist(s): **Send The Light Distribution LLC.**

First Choice Entertainment *See* **Papilion Pr.**

First Christmas Project, *(978-0-9769828)* 333 Brooks Bend, Brownsburg, IN 46112 USA
Web site: http://www.firstchristmaspresent.com
Dist(s): **Send The Light Distribution LLC.**

First Class Fitness Systems, Inc., *(978-0-9747008)* 23901 Civic Ctr. Way, Suite 342, Malibu, CA 90265 USA Tel 310-456-3043
E-mail: Mario@myfitfamily.com
Web site: http://myfitfamily.com.

First Edition Design eBook Publishing, *(978-0-9837342; 978-1-937520; 978-1-62287; 978-1-5069)* 5202 Old Ashwood Dr., Sarasota, FL 34233 USA (SAN 860-2719) Tel 941-921-2607; Fax: 617-249-1694; P.O. Box 20217, Sarasota, FL 34276 Tel 941-921-2607; Fax: 941-866-7510
E-mail: dgordon@firsteditiondesign.com
Web site: http://www.firsteditiondesignpublishing.com.

First Facts *Imprint of* **Capstone Pr., Inc.**

First Flight Bks., *(978-0-9763675; 978-0-9836035; 978-0-9860666)* Div. of The Copy Workshop, 2144 N. Hudson, RB, Chicago, IL 60614 USA Tel 773-871-1179; Fax: 773-281-4643
E-mail: firstflightbooks@aol.com
Web site: http://www.firstflightbooks.com.

First Focus Learning Systems, *(978-1-58793)* 1059 El Monte Ave., Mountain View, CA 94040 USA
E-mail: info@firstfocus.com; jconnor@firstfocus.com
Web site: http://www.firstfocus.com.

First Focus Publishing *See* **First Focus Learning Systems**

First Intensity Pr., *(978-1-889960)* P.O. Box 665, Lawrence, KS 66044 USA
Dist(s): **SPD-Small Pr. Distribution.**

First Light Publishing, *(978-0-9754411; 978-0-692-51651-5; 978-0-692-51652-2)* 14402 Twickenham Pl., Chesterfield, VA 23832 USA Do not confuse with First Light Publishing in Chagrin Falls, OH
E-mail: briantherock@cs.com
Dist(s): **Parklane Publishing.**

First Mom's Club, The, *(978-0-9704876; 978-0-9728180; 978-0-9764557; 978-1-935822)* 367 Eric Way, Grants Pass, OR 97526-8820 USA
E-mail: dianne@thefirstmomsclub.com
Web site: http://www.thefirstmomsclub.com
Dist(s): **Alliance Bk. Co.**

First Person Publishing *See* **Concinnity Initiatives**

First Reports *Imprint of* **Compass Point Bks.**

First Second Bks. *Imprint of* **Roaring Brook Pr.**

First Stage Concepts, *(978-0-9667719; 978-1-931430)* Orders Addr.: P.O. Box 3390, Redondo Beach, CA 90277-1390 USA Tel 310-371-6834; Fax: 310-370-3392; Edit Addr.: 5410 W. 190th St., No. 98, Torrance, CA 90503-1045 USA
E-mail: quickstartguitar@msn.com
Web site: http://www.QuickStartGuitar.com.

First Steps Pr., *(978-0-9659944)* Orders Addr.: P.O. Box 380122, Clinton Township, MI 48038-0060 USA Tel 810-463-5670; Edit Addr.: 38453 Gail, Clinton Township, MI 48036 USA.

First Word Publishing, The, *(978-0-9708590)* 305 Lind Ave., SW, No. 9, Renton, WA 98055 USA Tel 425-254-8575
E-mail: dejonfw@ayhoo.com.

Firsthand *Imprint of* **Heinemann**

First-Sight Publishing, *(978-0-9770363)* 9636 Nevada Ave., Chatsworth, CA 91311 USA Tel 818-207-6334
E-mail: sabrinawright1961@yahoo.com.

Fischer, Carl LLC, *(978-0-8258)* Orders Addr.: 588 N. Gulph Rd. Ste. B, Kng Of Prussa, PA 19406-2831 USA Toll Free: 800-762-2328; Edit Addr.: 65 Bleeker St., New York, NY 10012-2420 USA (SAN 107-4245) Tel 212-772-0900; Fax: 212-477-6996; Toll Free: 800-762-2328
E-mail: cf-info@carlfischer.com
Web site: http://www.carlfischer.com
Dist(s): **Follett School Solutions.**

Fish Decoy.com, Ltd., *(978-0-9748721; 978-0-9759386)* Orders Addr.: P.O. Box 321, Cross River, NY 10518 USA (SAN 256-1093) Tel 914-533-5181; Edit Addr.: 71 Conant Valley Rd., Pound Ridge, NY 10576 USA; 218 Honey Hallow Rd., Pound Ridge, NY 10576
Web site: http://www.fishdecoystore.com
Dist(s): **Antique Collectors' Club.**

Fish Head Pubns., LLC, *(978-1-934627)* 5013 W. Buckskin Tr., Glendale, AZ 85310 USA
Web site: http://www.fishheadpublications.com.

Fish Tales Publishing, *(978-0-9795860)* Orders Addr.: 65 Glen Rd., PMB 128, Garner, NC 27529 USA (SAN 853-8344) Tel 919-320-7428
E-mail: Books@fishtales.org
Web site: http://www.fishtales.org.

Fishbowl International, Inc., *(978-0-9745188; 978-0-9765619)* Orders Addr.: P.O. Box 362, Roxie, MS 39661 USA Tel 601-384-0219; Fax: 601-384-1667
E-mail: fishbowlinternational@yahoo.com
Web site: http://www.fishbowlinternational.com.

Fisher & Hale Publishing, *(978-0-9742037)* Div. of Horizon Bks., Orders Addr.: 6525 Gunpark Dr. 370, #250, Boulder, CO 80301 USA; Edit Addr.: 18841 E. Cornell Ave., Aurora, CO 80013 USA
E-mail: slmclean@hotmail.com
Web site: http://www.fisherhale.com.

Fisher Enterprises, *(978-0-9767265)* P.O. Box 1342, Eagle, ID 83616 USA Tel 208-939-6650; Fax: 208-939-7480 Do not confuse with Fisher Enterprises, Inc. In Edmonds, WA
E-mail: ggfisher@earthlink.net.

Fisher Hill, *(978-1-878253)* 5267 Warner Ave., No. 166, Huntington Beach, CA 92649 USA (SAN 254-1289) Tel 714-377-9353; Fax: 714-377-9495; Toll Free: 800-214-8110
E-mail: fisher.k@mac.com
Web site: http://www.Fisher-Hill.com
Dist(s): **Delta Systems Company, Inc.**

Fisher, John Wilfred, *(978-0-9771093)* 25216 Arrow Highline Rd., Juliaetta, ID 83535 USA Tel 208-843-7159
E-mail: jwfisher@starband.net.

Fisher King Pr., *(978-0-9776076; 978-0-9810344; 978-1-926715; 978-1-77169)* Orders Addr.: 109 E 17th St, Ste 80, Cheyenne, WY 82001 USA (SAN 257-7410) Tel 307-222-9575; 831-238-7799; Fax: 831-621-4667
E-mail: orders@fisherkingpress.com; fisherkingpress@gmail.com
Web site: http://www.fisherkingpress.com; http://www.fisherkingbooks.com
Dist(s): **Fisher King Bks.**

Fisher King Publishing *See* **Fisher King Pr.**

Fisher Wilcoxon *See* **Fisher Hill**

Fisher-Paner Publishing, *(978-0-615-19778-4; 978-0-615-23931-6)* 1919 Sorrento Pl., Richmond, VA 23238 USA
Dist(s): **Lulu Enterprises Inc.**

Fishman, Greg *See* **Fishman, Greg Jazz Studios**

Fishman, Greg Jazz Studios, *(978-0-9766153; 978-0-9843492; 978-0-9914078)* 824 Custer Ave., Evanston, IL 60202 USA
E-mail: greg1111@aol.com
Web site: http://www.gregfishmanjazzstudios.com.

Fishnet Pubns./Ministries, *(978-0-9667517)* 8440 Fairwind Ct., Indianapolis, IN 46256 USA
E-mail: canddjohnson@comcast.net.

Fisticuff Publishing, 2529 Whetstone ln, Myrtle Beach, SC 29579 USA Tel 607-759-5075
Dist(s): **CreateSpace Independent Publishing Platform.**

Fit Kids, *(978-0-9709301)* 175 W. 200 S., Suite 2012, Salt Lake City, UT 84101-1459 USA Tel 801-521-0109; Fax: 801-521-8360; Toll Free: 888-234-8543
E-mail: brucebellco@earthlink.net
Web site: http://www.fitkids.org.

Fit Kids Publishing, *(978-0-9895095)* P.O. Box 4149, Auburn, CA 95604 USA Tel 650-339-2727
E-mail: katherine@fitkidspublishing.com
Web site: http://www.fitkidspublishing.com
Dist(s): **Partners Pubs. Group, Inc.**

Fitch, Michele Marko, *(978-0-615-14996-7)* 2103 Wilkerson St., South Boston, MA 24592 USA
E-mail: familyfitch@myembarg.com
Dist(s): **Lulu Enterprises Inc.**

Fithian Pr *Imprint of* **Daniel & Daniel, Pubs., Inc.**

Fitness Information Technology, Inc., *(978-0-9627926; 978-1-885693; 978-1-935412; 978-1-940067)* Orders Addr.: P.O. Box 6116, Morgantown, WV 26506 USA; Edit Addr.: 262 Coliseum, WVU-CPASS, Morgantown, WV 26506-6116 USA Tel 304-293-6888; Fax: 304-293-6658; Toll Free: 800-477-4348
E-mail: ICPE@mail.wvu.edu; matthew.brann@mail.wvu.edu
Web site: http://www.fitinfotech.com
Dist(s): **Cardinal Pubs. Group**
National Bk. Network
Unifacmanu International Trading Co., Inc.
ebrary, Inc.

Fitzgerald Bks., *(978-1-887238; 978-1-59054; 978-1-4242)* Div. of Central Programs, Inc., Orders Addr.: P.O. Box 505, Bethany, MO 64424 USA Tel 660-425-7777; Fax: 660-425-3929; Toll Free: 800-821-7199; Edit Addr.: 802 N. 41st St., Bethany, MO 64424 USA
E-mail: wecare@gumdropbooks.com
Web site: http://www.gumdropbooks.com
Dist(s): **Gumdrop Bks.**

Fitzgerald, Caryn, *(978-0-615-17982-7; 978-0-615-21500-6)* P.O. Box 1343, Mansfield, TX 76063 USA
Web site: http://www.samifitzgerald.com
Dist(s): **Lulu Enterprises Inc.**

Fitzhenry & Whiteside, Ltd. (CAN) *(978-0-88902; 978-1-55005; 978-1-55041; 978-1-55455) Dist. by* **Midpt Trade.**

Fitzroy Dearborn Pubs., Inc., *(978-1-57958; 978-1-884964)* 425 W. Briar Pl. Apt. 1E, Chicago, IL 60657-4767 USA Toll Free: 800-850-8102
E-mail: fitzroy@aol.com
Web site: http://www.fitzroydearborn.com
Dist(s): **Taylor & Francis Group.**

Five Degrees of Frannie, *(978-0-9679115)* P.O. Box 178, North Greece, NY 14515 USA Tel 716-467-9136
E-mail: ohfrannie@aol.com.

Five Oaks Pr., *(978-0-9779325)* P.O. Box 251, Lake Lure, NC 28746-0251 USA
E-mail: davidklett@bellsouth.net
Web site: http://www.lakelurechronicles.com.

Five O'clock Dog, *(978-0-9767887)* Orchid # 1170, Corona del Mar, CA 92625 USA Tel 949-422-5909
Web site: http://www.fiveodog.com.

Five Ponds Pr., *(978-0-9727156; 978-0-9824133; 978-0-9824583; 978-1-935813)* 30 Hidden Spring Dr., Weston, CT 06883-1144 USA
E-mail: lou@fivepondspress.com
Web site: http://www.fivepondspress.com.

Five Star *Imprint of* **Cengage Gale**

Five Star Christian Pubns., *(978-0-9740142; 978-0-9777291)* 312 SE 24th Ave., Cape Coral, FL 33990 USA Tel 239-574-1000
E-mail: info@5scp.com
Web site: http://www.gulfcoastbaptistchurch.com; www.fivestarchristianministries.com.

Five Star Pr., *(978-0-9673102)* Orders Addr.: P.O. Box 8454, Richmond, VA 23226 USA Tel 804-282-6069; Edit Addr.: 1910 Byrd Ave., Suite 12, Richmond, VA 23230 USA.

Five Star Pubns., Inc., *(978-0-9619853; 978-1-877749; 978-1-58985)* Orders Addr.: P.O. Box 6698, Chandler, AZ 85246-6698 USA (SAN 246-7429) Tel 480-940-8182; Fax: 480-940-8787; Edit Addr.: 4696 W. Tyson St., Chandler, AZ 85226-2903 USA; *Imprints:* Little Five Star (LiveStar)
E-mail: info@fivestarpublications.com
Web site: http://www.fivestarpublications.com
Dist(s): **Midpoint Trade Bks., Inc.**
Quality Bks., Inc.
Unique Bks., Inc.
ebrary, Inc.

Five Star Trade *Imprint of* **Cengage Gale**

Five Valleys Publishing (GBR) *(978-0-9566042) Dist. by* **LightSource CS.**

FizzBang Science, *(978-0-9718480)* 807 Murlay Dr., Plain City, OH 43064 USA Tel 614-873-8860 (phone/fax)
E-mail: blrohrig@worldnet.att.net
Web site: http://www.fizzbangscience.com.

Flaghouse, Inc., *(978-0-9713648; 978-1-932032)* 601 Rte. 46 W., Hasbrouck Heights, NJ 07604-3116 USA (SAN 631-3086) Tel 201-288-7600; Fax: 201-288-7887; Toll Free Fax: 800-793-7900
Web site: http://www.flaghouse.com.

Flagship Church Resources *Imprint of* **Group Publishing, Inc.**

Flamburis, Georgia, *(978-0-615-47908-8)* 5 Griggs Pl., Allston, MA 02134 USA Tel 617-783-9425
E-mail: gf_mae@yahoo.com.

Flame Tree Publishing (GBR) *(978-1-874634; 978-1-903817; 978-1-904041; 978-1-84451; 978-1-84786; 978-1-78361) Dist. by* **AtlasBooks.**

Flaming Pen Pr., *(978-0-615-27115-6; 978-0-615-28423-1; 978-0-615-34476-8; 978-0-615-36650-0; 978-0-615-41089-0; 978-0-615-93500-3)* 130 N. Society Rd., Canterbury, CT 06331 USA.

Flammarion et Cie (FRA) *(978-2-08) Dist. by* **Distribks Inc.**

Flammer, Josephine, *(978-0-615-16197-6; 978-0-615-25550-7)* P.O. Box 225, Adirondack, NY 128008 USA
E-mail: joannflammer@aol.com
Web site: http://joannflammer.com
Dist(s): **Lulu Enterprises Inc.**

Flash Blasters, Incorporated *See* **Ace Academics, Inc.**

Flashlight Pr., *(978-0-9729225; 978-0-9799746; 978-1-936261)* 527 Empire Blvd., Brooklyn, NY 11225-3121 USA
E-mail: ed.assist@flashlightpress.com
Web site: http://www.flashlightpress.com
Dist(s): **Independent Pubs. Group**
MyiLibrary
ebrary, Inc.

FlashPaws Productions, *(978-0-9674929)* 7714 Rolling Fork Ln., Houston, TX 77040-3432 USA Tel 713-896-8484 (phone/fax)
E-mail: info@flashpaws.com
Web site: http://www.flashpaws.com
Dist(s): **Greenleaf Book Group.**

Flat Hammock Pr., *(978-0-9718303; 978-0-9758699; 978-0-9773725; 978-0-9795949; 978-0-9818960)* 5 Church St., Mystic, CT 06355 USA Tel 860-572-2722; Fax: 860-572-2755
E-mail: info@flathammockpress.com
Web site: http://www.flathammockpress.com.

Flat Kids *Imprint of* **Smart Smiles Co., The**

Flaxenfluff Pr., LLC, *(978-0-9743890)* P.O. Box 2287, Broken Arrow, OK 74013 USA
Web site: http://www.flaxenfluff.com.

Fleming, G. Faye *See* **Faye Bks.**

Fletcher, C J Publishing LLC, *(978-0-9755255)* Orders Addr.: P.O. Box 784, Independence, KS 67301 USA (SAN 256-1050) Tel 620-331-5182; Fax: 620-331-5183; Toll Free: 800-814-8513; Edit Addr.: 212- 214 E. Myrtle, Independence, KS 67301 USA
E-mail: cjdcpa@cableone.net.

Fletcher, Robert *See* **Iron Mountain Pr.**

Fleur Art Productions, *(978-0-9741277)* 32 N. Goodwin Ave., Elmsford, NY 10523 USA Fax: 914-206-3558; Toll Free: 866-353-8727; *Imprints:* Fleur Publishing (Fleur Pubng)
E-mail: agents@fleur.ws
Web site: http://www.fleur.ws
Dist(s): **E-Pros DG.**

Fleur De Lis Publishing, LLC, *(978-0-9821956)* P.O. Box 2521, South Portland, ME 04116-252121 USA
E-mail: cmunson667@aol.com.

Fleur Publishing *Imprint of* **Fleur Art Productions**

Fleuve Noir (FRA) *(978-2-265) Dist. by* **Distribks Inc.**

Flickerfawn *Imprint of* **Barton Bks.**

Flinders Pr., *(978-0-9843955)* P.O. Box 3975, Burbank, CA 91508-3975 USA (SAN 859-2829) Tel 818-714-0455
E-mail: flinderspress@gmail.com
Web site: http://www.flinderspress.com
Dist(s): **Independent Pubs. Group.**

Flinn Scientific, Inc., *(978-1-877991; 978-1-933709)* Orders Addr.: P.O. Box 219, Batavia, IL 60510 USA (SAN 630-1800) Fax: 866-452-1436; Toll Free: 800-452-1261; Edit Addr.: 770 N. Raddant Rd., Batavia, IL 60510 USA
E-mail: flinn@flinnsci.com.

Flip n Flop Learning, LLC, *(978-0-9801772; 978-0-9853372)* 6752 Castenson Rd., Bryan, TX 77808 USA
E-mail: senoragose@verizon.net
Web site: http://www.flipfloplearning.com.

Flip Publishing, *(978-0-9769342)* P.O. Box 1072, Hawthorne, CA 90251 USA
E-mail: flippublishing@yahoo.com
Web site: www.flippublishing.net
Dist(s): **Independent Pubs. Group.**

Flipp Sports, *(978-0-9744443)* 960 Turnpike St., Canton, MA 02021 USA Tel 781-821-8788; Fax: 781-821-4088
E-mail: jmarnikovic@flippsports.com
Web site: http://www.flippsports.com

Flippin' Bks. LLC, *(978-0-9742500)* 25450 Williams Ridge, Warrenton, MO 63383 USA Tel 636-456-6224
E-mail: thw@flippinbooks.com
Web site: http://www.flippinbooks.com.

FloBound Poems Publications, *(978-0-9705819)* Orders Addr.: P.O. Box 3101, Fredericksburg, VA 22402-3101 USA
E-mail: floboundpoems@aol.com; morningpoemsflog@aol.com
Web site: http://www.floboundpoems.com.

Flood Crest Pr., *(978-1-934130)* 604 E. Spring St., New Albany, IN 47150 USA Tel 812-944-5116; Fax: 812-944-5277
E-mail: ops@destinationsbooksellers.com
Web site: http://www.destinationsbooksellers.com.

Flood, Tim, *(978-0-9797159)* 1349 E. Ellis Dr., Tucson, AZ 85719 USA
Web site: http://www.dreamsofaballinflight.com.

Floodgate Publishing, *(978-0-9761355)* P.O. Box 1475, Castle Rock, WA 98611 USA.

Floppinfish Publishing Co., Ltd., *(978-0-9629124; 978-0-615-70203-2; 978-0-692-34807-9)* P.O. Box 4932, Saint Louis, MO 63108 USA Tel 314-567-8697
E-mail: wm4932@yahoo.com
Web site: http://www.JoeKeylon.com; http://www.pixofpeople.com
Dist(s): **Big River Distribution**
Partners Bk. Distributing, Inc.

Floppy Cat Co., *(978-0-9823818)* 2315 Devon Ave., Tea, SD 57064 USA
E-mail: jenn@greenleafbookgroup.com.

Flora Delaterre Productions, *(978-0-9792302)* P.O. Box 8474, Missoula, MT 59807 USA Tel 406-728-2977
Web site: http://www.floradelaterre.com.

Flores, Travis, *(978-0-9759077)* P.O. Box 143, Newport, OH 45768 USA Tel 740-473-2999 (phone/fax)
E-mail: sparkeythespider@aol.com
Web site: http://www.sparkeythespider.com.

Floricanto Pr., *(978-0-915745; 978-0-9796457)* Div. of Inter American Development, 650 Castro St., Suite 120, No. 331, Mountain View, CA 94041-2055 USA (SAN 293-9169) Tel 415-552-1879; Fax: 702-995-1410
E-mail: info@floricantopress.com; rcabello@floricantopress.com
Web site: http://www.floricantopress.com.

Florida Div. of Historical Resources, *(978-0-9642289; 978-1-889030)* Div. of Florida Dept. of State, c/o Bureau of Historic Preservation, 500 S. Bronough St., Tallahassee, FL 32399-0250 USA Tel 850-487-2333; Fax: 850-922-0496; Toll Free: 800-847-7278
Web site: http://www.flheritage.com.

Florida Historical Society, *(978-1-886104; 978-0-9771079; 978-0-9817337)* 435 Brevard Ave., Cocoa, FL 32922 USA Tel 321-690-1971; *Imprints:* Chapin House Books (Chapin Hse)
E-mail: wynne@metrolink.net
Web site: http://www.fhspress.org; http://www.florida-historical-soc.org.

Florida Kids Pr., Inc., *(978-0-9792304; 978-0-9863325)* 11802 Magnolia Falls Dr., Jacksonville, FL 32258-2587 USA
Web site: http://www.janewoodbooks.com
Dist(s): **Partners Bk. Distributing, Inc.**

Florida Science Source, Inc., *(978-0-944961)* Orders Addr.: P.O. Box 8217, Longboat Key, FL 34228-8217 USA (SAN 245-6974); Edit Addr.: 28 Eagle Ridge Rd., Sapphire, NC 28774-9681 USA (SAN 245-6982)
E-mail: fssource@aol.com
Web site: http://www.ultimacitrus.com/fssource.

Floris Bks. (GBR) *(978-0-86315; 978-0-903540; 978-1-78250)* *Dist. by* **SteinerBooks Inc.**

Floris Bks. (GBR) *(978-0-86315; 978-0-903540; 978-1-78250)* *Dist. by* **Gryphon Hse.**

Flourish Publishing Hse., *(978-0-9851659)* P.O. Box 1661, Frisco, CO 80443 USA Tel 405-760-1118
E-mail: garystallings@yahoo.com.

Flower Press *See* **Flowerfield Enterprises**

Flower Publishing, *(978-0-9852608)* 1003 Deer Creek Church Rd., Forest Hill, MD 21050 USA Tel 443-528-3033
E-mail: gfdbuilders@yahoo.com.

Flower Sprouts, *(978-0-615-21179-4; 978-0-615-21180-0; 978-0-615-21683-6)* P.O. Box 1843, Morro Bay, CA 93443 USA Tel 805-772-5808 (phone/fax); 245 Morro Bay Blvd., Morro Bay, CA 1111
Web site: http://www.seawindgallery.com
Dist(s): **Lulu Enterprises Inc.**

Flowerfield Enterprises, *(978-0-942256)* 10332 Shaver Rd., Kalamazoo, MI 49024-6744 USA (SAN 217-7358) Tel 269-327-0108; Fax: 269-327-7009
E-mail: nancy@wormwoman.com
Web site: http://www.wormwoman.com.

Flowerpot Children's Pr. Inc. (CAN) *(978-1-77093; 978-1-897533; 978-0-9784200; 978-1-926988; 978-1-4867)* *Dist. by* **Cardinal PubGr.**

Flowerpot Pr., Div. of MitSo Media Inc., 142 Second Ave., Franklin, TN 37064 USA
E-mail: anne@flowerpotpress.com
Web site: http://www.flowerpotpress.com.

Fluckiger, Jay D. *See* **Harmony Hse. Publishing Co.**

Fluckiger, Kory, *(978-0-615-15654-5)* 3640 Gramercy Ave., Ogden, UT 84403 USA Tel 801-791-3461
E-mail: kory@koryfluckiger.com
Web site: http://www.koryfluckiger.com
Dist(s): **Lulu Enterprises Inc.**

Flugul Pubng, *(978-0-9779390)* P.O. Box 6090, Cincinnati, OH 45206 USA
E-mail: VLI@flugulpublishing.com
Web site: http://www.Flugulpublishing.com
Dist(s): **Lulu Enterprises Inc.**

Fluharty, Linda Cunningham, *(978-0-9759097)* 833 Camforth Dr., Baton Rouge, LA 70810 USA
E-mail: LCFlu@aol.com
Web site: http://www.lindapages.com.

Flutter-By Productions, *(978-0-9714734)* 1415 Panther Ln. # 214, Naples, FL 34109-7874 USA
Web site: http://www.flutter-byproductions.com
Dist(s): **APG Sales & Distribution Services.**

Flux *Imprint of* **Llewellyn Pubns.**

Flux: Image Theory Group, *(978-0-9790786)* 101 N. 7th St., No. 226, Phoenix, AZ 85034 USA.

Flying Cloud Bks., *(978-0-615-13477-2)* 123 Moore Rd., Sudbury, MA 01776 USA
E-mail: mail@paulgreenspan.com
Web site: http://www.paulgreenspan.com
Dist(s): **Lulu Enterprises Inc.**

Flying Dolphin Pr. *Imprint of* **Knopf Doubleday Publishing Group**

Flying Eye Bks. (GBR) *(978-1-909263)* *Dist. by* **Consort Bk Sales.**

Flying Frog Pubs.,
Dist(s): **Ideals Pubns.**

Flying Frog Publishing, *(978-0-9666647)* 567 Westcove Dr., Wasilla, AK 99654-7161 USA Tel 907-373-6994 (phone/fax); Toll Free: 888-673-6994 Do not confuse with Flying Frog Publishing, Reisterstown, MD
E-mail: jobshlh@corecom.net
Web site: http://www.galaxymall.com/children/alaskariddles
Dist(s): **Todd Communications**
Wizard Works.

Flying Frog Publishing, Inc., *(978-1-57755; 978-1-884628; 978-1-934967; 978-1-60745)* 2219 York Rd., Suite 300, Lutherville, MD 21093 USA Tel 443-901-2100; Fax: 443-901-2104
Web site: http://www.flyingfrogpub.com
Dist(s): **Ideals Pubns.**

Flying Owl Pubns, *(978-0-9820769)* 2268 Brighton, Holland, MI 49424 USA Tel 616-399-3857
E-mail: denuyl@chartermi.net.

Flying Pig Publishing, *(978-0-9746110)* P.O. Box 304, Harvard, MA 01451 USA
E-mail: douglee41@yahoo.com
Web site: http://deelee.net.

Flying Raven Pr., *(978-0-615-43785-9; 978-0-615-48382-5; 978-0-615-52897-7; 978-0-615-57050-1; 978-0-615-60507-4; 978-0-615-62017-6; 978-0-615-64296-3; 978-0-615-83127-5; 978-0-692-23016-9; 978-0-692-24744-0; 978-0-692-41253-4)* 4755 18th Pl. S., Salem, OR 97302 USA Tel 503-931-8317
E-mail: scott@scottwilliamcarter.com
Web site: http://flyingravenpress.com
Dist(s): **CreateSpace Independent Publishing Platform**
Dummy Record Do Not USE!!!!.

Flying Rhino Productions, Incorporated *See* **Flying Rhinoceros, Inc.**

Flying Rhinoceros, Inc., *(978-1-883772; 978-1-59168; 978-0-9822773)* 1440 NW Overton St., Portland, OR 97209 USA (SAN 857-7501) Tel 503-552-8777; Fax: 503-445-8375; Toll Free: 800-537-4466
E-mail: flyingrhino@flyingrhino.com; melson@flyingrhino.com
Web site: http://www.flyingrhino.com.

Flying Scroll Publishing, LLC, *(978-0-9742432; 978-0-9848099)* P.O. Box 246, Fort Atkinson, WI 53538 USA Tel 920-723-3454
E-mail: info@flyingscrollpublishing.com
Web site: http://www.flyingscrollpublishing.com.

Flying Squirrel Press *See* **Heritage Heart Farm**

Flying Turtle Publishing, *(978-0-615-31741-0; 978-0-9851492; 978-0-9911378; 978-0-9907104)* 7216 Birch Ave., Hammond, IN 46324 USA
Web site: http://flyingturtlepublishing.com
Dist(s): **Smashwords.**

Flyleaf Publishing, *(978-0-9658246; 978-1-929262; 978-1-60541)* Orders Addr.: P.O. Box 287, Lyme, NH 03768-0185 USA Tel 800-449-7006; Fax: 888-619-6419; P.O. Box 287, Lyme, NH 03768-0287 Toll Free: 800-449-7006; *Imprints:* Books To Remember (Bks To Remember)
E-mail: laura@flyleafpublishing.com
Web site: http://www.flyleafpublishing.com.

Flywheel Publishing Co., *(978-1-930826)* Orders Addr.: 1375 Sunnyhills Rd., Oakland, CA 94610 USA (SAN 253-2441) Tel 510-407-7577; Fax: 510-373-6060
E-mail: admin@flywheel.us
Web site: http://www.flywheel.us.

FM Publishing Co., *(978-1-931671)* Div. of F.A.I.T.H. Ministries, Inc., Orders Addr.: P.O. Box 215, Cherokee, NC 28719 USA Tel 888-468-5197; Toll Free Fax: 800-518-1219
E-mail: fmpublishing@cox.net; fasthelpministries@cox.net
Web site: http://www.fmpublishingcompany.com
Dist(s): **CreateSpace Independent Publishing Platform**
Lightning Source, Inc.
Lulu Enterprises Inc.

FM Rocks Kids, LLC *See* **Playdate Kids Publishing**

FMA Publishing, *(978-0-9774411)* 1920 Pacific Ave. No. 16152, Long Beach, CA 90806 USA (SAN 257-4977) Tel 310-438-3483; Fax: 310-438-3486
E-mail: info@fmapublishing.com
Web site: http://www.fmapublishing.com.

Fo Guang Shan International Translation Ctr., *(978-1-943211)* 3456 Glenmark Dr., Hacienda Heights, CA 91745 USA Tel 626-330-8361
E-mail: fgsitc@gmail.com
Web site: fgsitc.org.

Focus *Imprint of* **Hackett Publishing Co., Inc.**

Focus Group, Inc., *(978-0-9766968)* 2201 SW 152nd St. Ste. 3, Burien, WA 98166-2080 USA
E-mail: pubs@focusgroupseattle.com.

†Focus on the Family Publishing, *(978-0-929608; 978-1-56179; 978-1-58997; 978-1-60482; 978-1-62405; 978-1-62471)* 8605 Explorer Dr., Colorado Springs, CO 80920-1051 USA (SAN 250-0949) Fax: 719-531-3356; Toll Free: 800-232-6459
E-mail: robert.huntrods@fotf.org
Web site: http://www.family.org
Dist(s): **Follett School Solutions**
Gospel Light Pubns.
Nelson, Tommy
Tyndale Hse. Pubs.
Zondervan; *CIP.*

Focus Publishing, *(978-1-885904; 978-1-936141)* Orders Addr.: P.O. Box 665, Bemidji, MN 56619 USA Tel 218-759-9816 Toll Free: 800-913-6287; Edit Addr.: 502 Third St., NW, Bemidji, MN 56601 USA
E-mail: jan@focuspublishing.com
Web site: http://focuspublishing.com
Dist(s): **Spring Arbor Distributors, Inc.**

Fodor's *Imprint of* **Fodor's Travel Pubns.**

Fodor's Travel Guides *See* **Fodor's Travel Pubns.**

Fodor's Travel Pubns., Div. of Random Hse., Information Group, Orders Addr.: 400 Hahn Rd., Westminster, MD 21157 USA Tel 410-848-1900; Toll Free: 800-726-0600; Edit Addr.: 1745 Broadway, New York, NY 10019 USA Tel 212-782-9000; *Imprints:* Fodor's (Fodor)
Web site: http://www.fodors.com
Dist(s): **Libros Sin Fronteras**
MyiLibrary
Penguin Random Hse., LLC.
Random Hse., Inc.

Fog City Pr., *(978-1-875137; 978-1-887451; 978-1-892374; 978-1-929156; 978-1-74089)* Subs. of Weldon Owen, Inc., 2215-R Market St., No. 123, San Francisco, CA 94114 USA Tel 415-626-9636
E-mail: gilblock@sirius.com
Dist(s): **INscribe Digital**
Ingram Pub. Services.

Foglight Pr., *(978-0-9755848)* Orders Addr.: P.O. Box 160322, Sacramento, CA 95816 USA
E-mail: info@foglightpress.com
Web site: http://www.foglightpress.com
Dist(s): **Bookazine Co., Inc.**

folder leaf *Imprint of* **Story Time Stories That Rhyme**

Foley, Mark, *(978-0-615-19609-1)* 4 3rd Ave., Annville, PA 17003 USA
Dist(s): **Lulu Enterprises Inc.**

Folk Prophet Bks., *(978-0-578-00160-9)* 140 S. 200 E., Lindon, UT 84042 USA
E-mail: books@folkprophet.com
Dist(s): **Lulu Enterprises Inc.**

Follett Library Resources *See* **Follett School Solutions**

Follett School Solutions, *(978-0-329; 978-0-88153; 978-0-924917; 978-1-4898; 978-1-5160; 978-1-5181)* Div. of the Follett Corp., Orders Addr.: a/o McHenry Warehouse, 1340 Ridgeview Dr., McHenry, IL 60050 USA (SAN 169-1902) Toll Free: 888-511-5114; a/o Patti Hall: R & R Bindery Services, 499 Rachel Rd., Girard, IL 62640 (SAN 155-8412) Tel 815-759-1700; *Imprints:* Follettbound (Follettbnd)
Web site: http://www.follett.com
Dist(s): **Baker & Taylor Bks.**

Follettbound *Imprint of* **Follett School Solutions**

Folsom Fallies Pr., *(978-0-9760790)* Orders Addr.: P.O. Box 348, Folsom, NM 88419 USA Tel 505-278-2520
E-mail: kristene@folsomfallies.com
Web site: http://www.folsomfallies.com.

Fond du Lac Head Start, *(978-0-615-69899-1)* 1720 Big Lake Rd., Cloquet, MN 55720 USA Tel 218-878-8130; Fax: 218-878-8115
E-mail: barbaraforcier@fdlrez.com
Web site: fdlrez.com.

Fondo de Cultura Económica,
Dist(s): **Fondo de Cultura Economica USA.**

Fondo de Cultura Economica USA, 2293 Verus St., San Diego, CA 92154 USA (SAN 860-1380) Tel 619-429-0455; Fax: 619-429-0827; Toll Free: 800-532-3872
E-mail: drazo@fceusa.com; fondosales@fceusa.com; dbase@fceusa.com
Web site: http://www.fceusa.com
Dist(s): **Ediciones Universal**
Giron Bks.
Latin American Book Source, Inc.
Lectorum Pubns., Inc.
Libros Sin Fronteras.

Fondo Editorial Grania, Fundacion Hogares Juveniles Campesinos (COL) *(978-958-8233; 978-958-9321)* *Dist. by* **Chelsea Green Pub.**

Fons Vitae *See* **Fons Vitae of Kentucky, Inc.**

Fons Vitae of Kentucky, Inc., *(978-1-887752; 978-1-941610)* 49 Mockingbird Valley Dr., Louisville, KY 40207-1366 USA Tel 502-897-3641
E-mail: fonsvitaeky@aol.com
Web site: http://www.fonsvitae.com
Dist(s): **Independent Pubs. Group.**

Food Allergy & Anaphylaxis Network, *(978-1-882541)* 11781 Lee Jackson Hwy. Suite 160, Fairfax, VA 22033 USA Tel 703-691-3179; Fax: 703-691-2713; Toll Free: 800-929-4040
E-mail: faan@foodallergy.org
Web site: http://www.foodallergy.org.

Food Allergy Network *See* **Food Allergy & Anaphylaxis Network**

Food & Agriculture Organization of the United Nations (ITA) *(978-92-5)* *Dist. by* **Stylus Pub VA.**

Food Enhancement Enterprises, *(978-0-9747247)* Orders Addr.: P.O. Box 60581, Sacramento, CA 95680 USA; Edit Addr.: 2148 Bluebird Ln., Sacramento, CA 95821 USA
E-mail: hsdell@lanset.com
Web site: http://www.pizzareconsidered.com.

Food Marketing Consultants, Inc., *(978-0-9763307; 978-1-59949)* 2805 N. Commerce Pkwy., Miramar, FL 33025 USA Tel 954-322-2668 Toll Free: 877-493-2633
Web site: http://www.colorallabout.com.

Food Network Kitchens *Imprint of* **Meredith Bks.**

FoodPlay Productions, *(978-0-9642858)* 1 Sunset Ave., Hatfield, MA 01038 USA Tel 413-247-5400; Fax: 413-247-5405; Toll Free: 800-366-3752 (Orders)
E-mail: store@foodplay.com
Web site: http://www.foodplay.com
Dist(s): **Partners Pubs. Group, Inc.**

Foolosophy Media, *(978-0-9779928)* 1528 Primrose Ln., Panama City, FL 32404 USA (SAN 850-8186) Tel 850-871-2304; 850-899-1972; Fax: 850-871-2304
E-mail: wisemullet@gmail.com.

Foothill-Hydroponics, *(978-0-9669557)* 10705 Burbank Blvd., N., North Hollywood, CA 91601 USA Tel 818-760-0688; Fax: 818-760-4025
E-mail: mohsen@foothillhydroponics.com
Web site: http://www.foothill-hydroponic.com.

Footprints Pr., *(978-0-9679813)* 71 Hudson St., New York, NY 10013 USA Tel 212-267-9300; Fax: 212-267-9400.

For Children With Love Pubns., *(978-0-578-00980-3; 978-0-9831221)* 99 Peacedale St., Bristol, CT 06010 USA
E-mail: Cathy.forchildren@gmail.com
Web site: http://www.forchildrenwithlove.com.

For Dummies *Imprint of* **Wiley, John & Sons, Inc.**

For Fun! *Imprint of* **Compass Point Bks.**

For Him Pr., *(978-0-9858899)* P.O. Box 2207, Morristown, TN 37816 USA Tel 423-307-8137
E-mail: claudia-scribe@live.com
Web site: claudia-clues.com.

For Little Folks, *(978-0-9771236)* P.O. Box 571, Dresden, OH 43821 USA.

For Such A Time As This Ministries, *(978-0-9725890)* 510 Swank Rd., Hollsopple, PA 15935-8116 USA Tel 814-479-7710; Fax: 814-479-4874; Toll Free: 877-378-4374
E-mail: jpstobaugh@aol.com
Web site: http://www.forsuchatimeasthis.com.

For The Love of Dog Bks., *(978-0-9761124)* 635 NE Buffalo, Portland, OR 97211 USA Tel 503-286-5351
E-mail: stelljes@aol.com
Web site: http://www.silvertonbobbie.com.
Dist(s): **Far West Bk. Service**
Partners/West Book Distributors.

Forbes Literary Ltd. Inc., *(978-0-9776284)* P.O. Box 494, Grover, MO 63040-1621 USA Tel 314-753-6142; Fax: 636-405-1963
E-mail: forbeslit@sbcgobal.net
Web site: http://www.forbesliterary.com.

Fore Angels Pr., *(978-0-9658920; 978-0-9799947)* 267 Woodbury Rd., Huntington, NY 11743 USA Tel 631-385-0336
E-mail: annaarts@verizon.net.

Foreign Policy Assn., *(978-0-87124)* 470 Park Ave. S., 2nd Flr., New York, NY 10016-6819 USA (SAN 212-9426) Tel 212-481-8100; Fax: 212-481-9275; Toll Free: 800-628-5754; 800-477-5836 (orders)
Web site: http://www.fpa.org.

Forelle Graphics, *(978-0-9770918)* 1015 Atlantic Blvd., Suite 89, Atlantic Beach, FL 32233 USA
E-mail: forelle-graphics@yahoo.com.

Forest Hill Publishing, LLC, *(978-0-9759251; 978-0-9771113)* 13200 Forest Hill Ave., East Cleveland, OH 44112 USA Tel 216-761-8316 (phone/fax); Fax: 253-799-8316; *Imprints:* PlayGround (PlayGrnd OH); SpringTree (SpringTree); FortuneChild (FortuneChild) Do not confuse with Forest Hill Publishing in Downers Grove, IL
E-mail: email@foresthillpublishing.com
Web site: http://www.foresthillpublishing.com.

Forest Hse. Publishing Co., Inc., *(978-1-56674; 978-1-878363)* P.O. Box 738, Lake Forest, IL 60045 USA Tel 847-295-8287; Fax: 847-295-8201; Toll Free: 800-394-7323.

Forest Service *Imprint of* **United States Government Printing Office**

Forest Woods Media Productions *Imprint of* **Bunny & The Crocodile Pr., The**

Forever *Imprint of* **Grand Central Publishing**

Forever Young Pubs., *(978-0-9774422)* Orders Addr.: P.O. Box 216, Niles, MI 49120 USA Fax: 269-683-7153
E-mail: cheri@foreveryoungpublishers.com
Web site: http://www.foreveryoungpublishers.com
Dist(s): **Partners Bk. Distributing, Inc.**

Forge Bks. *Imprint of* **Doherty, Tom Assocs., LLC**

Forgotten Bks., *(978-1-60506; 978-1-60620; 978-1-60680; 978-1-4400; 978-1-4510)* 8345 NW 66th St., Miami, FL 33166 USA (SAN 854-9354)
E-mail: director@forgottenbooks.org
Web site: http://www.forgottenbooks.org/
Dist(s): **CreateSpace Independent Publishing Platform.**

Fork in the Road Pubs., *(978-0-9740825)* 1883 145th Pl. SE, Bellevue, WA 98007-6019 USA Tel 425-644-4285
Web site: http://www.raincitycookingschool.com.

Forks Pr., *(978-0-9816641)* 4-02 Summit Ave., Fair Lawn, NJ 07410 USA (SAN 856-1575) Tel 201-310-3297; 646-208-2161
E-mail: info@forkspress.com
Web site: http://www.forkspress.com
Dist(s): **AtlasBooks Distribution.**

Formac Publishing Co., Ltd. (CAN) *(978-0-88780; 978-0-921921; 978-1-55277; 978-1-4595)* *Dist. by* **Orca Bk Pub.**

Formac Publishing Co., Ltd. (CAN) *(978-0-88780; 978-0-921921; 978-1-55277; 978-1-4595)* *Dist. by* **Casemate Pubs.**

Fortitude Graphic Design & Printing, *(978-0-9741611; 978-0-578-06241-9; 978-0-9863173)* 841 Gibson St., Kalamazoo, MI 49001-2540 USA
E-mail: fortitude2@sbcglobal.net
Web site: www.comvoicesonline.com; www.fortitudegdp.com.

Fortner, Ray, *(978-0-9726365)* Orders Addr.: 3501 Baisden Rd., Pensacola, FL 32503-3458 USA.

FortuneChild *Imprint of* **Forest Hill Publishing, LLC**

Forum Gallery, *(978-0-9675826; 978-0-9744129)* 745 Fifth Ave., New York, NY 10051 USA Tel 212-355-4547; 212-355-4545; Fax: 212-355-4547
E-mail: gallery@forumgallery.com
Dist(s): **D.A.P./Distributed Art Pubs.**

Forward Communications *See* **NetNia Publishing Co.**

Forward Movement Pubns., *(978-0-88028)* 300 West Fourth St., Cincinnati, OH 45202 USA (SAN 208-3841) Tel 513-721-6659; Fax: 513-721-0729; Toll Free: 800-543-1813 (orders only)
E-mail: Orders@forwarddaybyday.com
Web site: http://www.forwardmovement.org.

Forword, *(978-0-9623937)* 16526 W. 78th St., Suite 335, Eden Prairie, MN 55346 USA Tel 612-944-7761; Fax: 612-944-8674.

Foster Branch Publishing, 20 Poplar St., No. 2, Jersey City, NJ 07307 USA
E-mail: dolphinupatree@hotmail.com.

Foster, Dennis, *(978-0-9771956)* P.O. Box 363, Millwood, VA 22646 USA.

Foster, Hicks & Assocs., *(978-0-9790709)* Orders Addr.: 4053 Harlan St., loft 201, Emeryville, CA 94608-9460 USA Tel 510-540-1241
E-mail: info@fosterhicks.com
Dist(s): **AtlasBooks Distribution.**

Foster, Walter Publishing, Incorporated *See* **Quarto Publishing Group USA**

Foston Adolescent Workshop, Inc., *(978-0-9641709; 978-1-930362)* P.O. Box 726, Clarksville, TN 37041 USA Tel 931-906-4623; Fax: 931-645-3500; Toll Free: 800-418-0374
E-mail: minfoston@aol.com
Web site: http://www.drfoston.com.

Foulsham, W. Co., Ltd. (GBR) *(978-0-572)* *Dist. by* **APG.**

Found Link, *(978-0-615-43601-2; 978-0-9836659)* 13125 Ladybank Ln., Herndon, VA 20171 USA Tel 703-966-2175
E-mail: jlcuddehe@verizon.net
Web site: www.CuddeheServices.com.

Foundation For Cosmetic Surgery, The, *(978-0-9799438)* 400 Newport Center Dr. Ste. 800, Newport Beach, CA 92660-7607 USA
E-mail: bryan@griffinpublishing.com; ffps2007@yahoo.com
Web site: http://www.beautybybrennan.com
Dist(s): **AtlasBooks Distribution.**

Foundation, Pr. The, *(978-0-9765987)* P.O. Box 182, Westport, CT 06881 USA Do not confuse with companies with the same name in New York, NY, Anaheim, CA
Web site: http://www.thefoundationpress.com.

Foundation Pr., *(978-0-9767272)* 13832 Gimbert Ln., Santa Ana, CA 92705-2849 USA Do not confuse with companies with the same name in New York, NY, Westport, CT.

Foundations for Learning, LLC, *(978-0-9726479; 978-1-933546)* 246 W. Manson Hwy., PMB 144, Chelan, WA 98816 USA Toll Free: 800-553-5950
E-mail: info@gophonics.com
Web site: http://www.gophonics.com.

Foundations in Brass *See* **Cymbal Technique 101**

Foundation, Inc., *(978-0-9797125; 978-0-9859251)* 701 E. Gate Dr. Suite 300, Mt. Laurel, NJ 08054 USA Tel 856-533-1600; Fax: 856-533-1601; Toll Free: 888-977-5437
E-mail: rmclaughlin@foundationsinc.org
Web site: http://www.foundationsinc.org.

Foundry Bks. (GBR) *(978-1-901543)* *Dist. by* **Casemate Pubs.**

Fountain Publishing, *(978-0-9659164; 978-0-9748423; 978-0-9822172; 978-1-936665)* Orders Addr.: P.O. Box 80011, Rochester, MI 48308 USA (SAN 253-8571) Tel 248-651-2934; Toll Free: 877-736-8598; Edit Addr.: 375 Olivewood Ct., Rochester, MI 48306 USA Tel 810-651-1153 Do not confuse with Fountain Publishing in Pittsburgh, PA
E-mail: ftnpublish@aol.com; jk@fountainpublishing.com
Web site: http://www.fountainpublishing.com.

Fountain Square Publishing, *(978-0-9724421)* 786 Old Ludlow, Cincinnati, OH 45220 USA.

Four Blocks, Div. of Carson-Dellosa Publishing Company, Inc., Orders Addr.: P.O. Box 35665, Greensboro, NC 27425 USA Tel 336-632-0084; Fax: 336-808-3249; Toll Free: 800-321-0943
Dist(s): **Carson-Dellosa Publishing, LLC.**

Four Corners Publishing,
Dist(s): **AtlasBooks Distribution.**

Four Dolphins Pr. *Imprint of* **Four Dolphins Pr., LLC**

Four Dolphins Pr., *(978-0-9745746)* Orders Addr.: P.O. Box 93601, Los Angeles, CA 90093 USA (SAN 255-626X) Tel 323-304-2053; Edit Addr.: 2700 N. Cahuenga Blvd., E., Suite 1403, Los Angeles, CA 90068-2139 USA.

Four Dolphins Pr., LLC, *(978-0-9799315)* P.O. Box 833, Scott Depot, WV 25560 USA Tel 304-757-8125; *Imprints:* Four Dolphins Press (Four Dolphin)
Web site: http://www.SadMadGladBooks.com.

Four Dolphins Press/Smart Communications, Incorporated *See* **Four Dolphins Pr.**

Four Elephants Pr., *(978-1-940051)* 11828 La Grange Ave., Los Angeles, CA 90025 USA Tel 310-477-4564
E-mail: annaka.harris@gmail.com
Dist(s): **MyiLibrary**
Perseus-PGW.

Four Foot Pr. LLC, *(978-0-9820817)* 12647 Galveston Ct., Suite 114, Manassas, VA 20112 USA
E-mail: dcgenesis@hotmail.com; fourfootpress@yahoo.com
Web site: http://fourfootpress.com.

Four Menards, The, *(978-0-9887969; 978-0-9891734; 978-0-9903872; 978-0-9904521)* P.O. Box 17265, Asheville, NC 28816 USA Tel 828-335-0284; Fax: 828-484-9873
E-mail: thefourmenards@gmail.com
Web site: N/A.

Four Panel Pr., *(978-0-9674102)* P.O. Box 50032, Eugene, OR 97405 USA Tel 541-343-6436; Fax: 541-684-0787
E-mail: tedlay@comcast.net
Web site: http://www.stonesoupcartoons.com
Dist(s): **AtlasBooks Distribution.**

Four Seasons Bks., Inc., *(978-0-9666858; 978-1-893595)* P.O. Box 395, Ben Wheeler, TX 75754 USA Tel 903-963-1442; Fax: 903-963-1525; Toll Free: 800-852-7484
E-mail: hcmarlow@yahoo.com; editor@fourseasonsbookstore.com
Web site: http://www.herbmarlow.com; http://www.fourseasonsbookstore.com.

Four Seasons Pubs., *(978-0-9656811; 978-1-891929; 978-1-932497)* Orders Addr.: P.O. Box 51, Titusville, FL 32781 USA Tel 321-632-2932; Fax: 321-632-2935; Edit Addr.: 4350 N. U.S. Hwy. 1, Cocoa, FL 32927 USA
E-mail: fseasons@bellsouth.net
Dist(s): **Follett School Solutions.**

Four Seasons Publishing, *(978-0-578-05005-8)* 105 Ansley Pl., Harlem, GA 30814 USA
E-mail: tedhoodjr@arkansas.net
Web site: http://www.thecardinalnest.com.

Four Sonkist Angels, *(978-0-9753117)* 4985 Wiltshire Ln., Suwanee, GA 30024 USA
E-mail: Michelle@FourSonkistAngels.com
Web site: http://www.FourSonkistAngels.com.

Four Star Publishing, *(978-0-9815894)* P.O. Box 871784, Canton, MI 48187 USA
E-mail: fourstarpublishing@comcast.net.

FourFront Media & Music, *(978-0-9743420)* Orders Addr.: 1245 S. 128th St., Seattle, WA 98168 USA Tel 206-282-6116
E-mail: chris@chrisknab.net
Web site: http://www.fourfrontmusic.com.

Foursquare Media, ICFG, *(978-0-9635581; 978-0-9802392)* 1910 W. Sunset Blvd., Suite 200, Los Angeles, CA 90026 USA Tel 213-989-4493; Fax: 213-413-3824
E-mail: rwulfestieg@foursquare.org
Web site: http://www.foursquare.org.

Fourth Generation Pubs., *(978-0-9706186)* PMB 146,14625 Baltimore Ave., Laurel, MD 20707-4902 USA (SAN 253-5513) Tel 301-497-9948.

Fox Chapel Publishing Co., Inc., *(978-0-932944; 978-1-56523; 978-1-57421; 978-1-58011; 978-1-880029; 978-1-85974; 978-0-9777004; 978-1-60765; 978-1-4971; 978-1-4972; 978-1-5048)* Orders Addr.: 1970 Broad St., East Petersburg, PA 17520 USA (SAN 920-8887) Tel 717-560-4703; Fax: 717-560-4702; Toll Free Fax: 888-369-2885; Toll Free: 800-457-9112 (orders); *Imprints:* Design Originals (Design Orig)
E-mail: sales@carvingworld.com; alan@foxchapelpublishing.com; Younger@foxchapelpublishing.com
Web site: http://www.foxchapelpublishing.com/; http://www.scrollsawer.com/; http://www.carvingworld.com; http://www.foxchapelpublishing.com; www.d-originals.com
Dist(s): **Independent Pubs. Group.**

Fox Music Bks. (CAN) *(978-1-894997)* *Dist. by* **SCB Distributo.**

Fox on a cold tin roof, *(978-0-615-46158-8; 978-0-692-35993-8)* 301 Surveyors Ct., Vienna, VA 22180 USA Tel 703-402-3855
E-mail: raymond.lord@hotmail.com
Dist(s): **CreateSpace Independent Publishing Platform**
Dummy Record Do Not USE!!!!.

Fox Print Bks., *(978-0-9729587)* 200 Seashore Ave., Peaks Island, ME 04108 USA Tel 207-899-0781
E-mail: eleanor.morse@gmail.com.

Fox Ridge Pubns., *(978-0-9856215; 978-0-9904281; 978-0-9967683)* 8805 State Rd 144, Kewaskum, WI 53040 USA Tel 715-630-2433
E-mail: lisalickel@gmail.com.

Fox Run Pr., LLC, *(978-0-9819607; 978-0-9825930)* 7840 Bullet Rd., Peyton, CO 80831 USA
Web site: http://www.FoxRunPress.com; http://www.ShadowFoxBook.com.

Fox Song Bks., *(978-0-9744989; 978-0-9837310)* Orders Addr.: P.O. Box 548, Ferndale, WA 98248 USA
E-mail: fox@foxsongbooks.com; orders@foxsongbooks.com; amy.foxsongbooks@gmail.com; foxsongbooks@gmail.com
Web site: http://foxsongbooks.com
Dist(s): **Lightning Source, Inc.**

FoxAcre Pr., *(978-0-9671783; 978-0-9709711; 978-0-9818487; 978-1-936771)* 401 Ethan Allen Ave., Takoma Park, MD 20912 USA Fax: 301-560-2482
E-mail: info@foxacre.com
Web site: http://www.foxacre.com
Dist(s): **Smashwords.**

Foxglove Pr., *(978-1-882959)* P.O. Box 210602, Nashville, TN 37221-0602 USA Fax: 615-646-8188; 2606 Eugenia Ave., Nashville, TN 37211 Do not confuse with companies with the same name in Corte Mandera, CA, Bryn Mawr, PA
Dist(s): **Midpoint Trade Bks., Inc.**

FoxRock, Inc., *(978-0-9643740; 978-0-9714705)* 61 Fourth Ave., No. 4, New York, NY 10003 USA Tel 212-505-6880; Fax: 212-673-1039
E-mail: evergreen@nyc.rr.com
Web site: http://www.evergreenreview.com
Dist(s): **Perseus-PGW.**

Fox's Den Publishing, *(978-0-9816107)* P.O. Box 6156, Sevierville, TN 37864-6156 USA
E-mail: foxsdenpublishing@hotmail.com.

FPI Publishing, *(978-0-9768215)* P.O. Box 247, Havre de Grace, MD 21078 USA Tel 410-459-9087
E-mail: gyleen@colourfulstitches.com
Web site: http://www.colourfulstitches.com
Dist(s): **Independent Pubs. Group.**

FQ Classics *Imprint of* **Filiquarian Publishing, LLC**

Fragile X Assn. of Georgia, *(978-0-9727865)* 3161 W. Somerset Ct., Marietta, GA 30067-5045 USA Tel 770-988-9275; Fax: 770-988-8255; Rood End Hse., 6 Stortford Rd., Great Dunmow, CM6 1DA Tel 01371 875100
E-mail: info@fragilex.k-web.co.uk; frax@bellsouth.net
Web site: www.fragilex.org.uk; http://www.myextraspecialbrother.com.

Frances Foster Bks. *Imprint of* **Farrar, Straus & Giroux**

Frances More International Teaching Systems, *(978-0-9768234)* Div. of Gray Squirrel, Inc., P.O. Box 26659, Collegeville, PA 19426 USA Tel 610-724-6331
E-mail: sales@graysquirrel.org; francesmore.hangingrock@xtra.co.nz
Web site: http://www.qwertyqik.com; http://www.fingerithmatic.com.

Francesca Studios, *(978-0-9741060)* 26 Dole Hill Rd., Holden, ME 04429 USA.

Franciscan Media, *(978-0-86716; 978-0-912228; 978-1-61636; 978-1-63253; 978-1-63254)* Subs. of Franciscan Friars (St. John Baptist Province), 28 W. Liberty St., Cincinnati, OH 45202 USA (SAN 204-6237) Tel 513-241-5615; Fax: 513-241-1197; Toll Free: 800-488-0488
E-mail: caroleD11@AmericanCatholic.org
Web site: http://www.AmericanCatholic.org
Dist(s): **Forward Movement Pubns.**
SPD-Small Pr. Distribution
Spring Arbor Distributors, Inc.

Franckowiak, Jon, *(978-0-9715415)* 4981 Shallow Ridge Rd., NE., Kennesaw, GA 30144 USA
E-mail: psukeljon@aol.com
Dist(s): **Partners Bk. Distributing, Inc.**

Franco, Nick Art, *(978-0-615-24474-7; 978-0-578-03402-7)* 5757 W. Euglie Ave., No. 2050, Glendale, AZ 85304 USA
E-mail: nickfrancoart@yahoo.com
Web site: http://www.nickfrancoart.com
Dist(s): **Lulu Enterprises Inc.**

Frank Schaffer Pubns. *Imprint of* **Carson-Dellosa Publishing, LLC**

Franklin Green Publishing, *(978-0-9826387; 978-1-936487)* 500 Wilson Pike Cir. Suite 100, Brentwood, TN 37027 USA Tel 615-277-5553
E-mail: lgessner@coolspringspress.com
Dist(s): **Hachette Bk. Group**
MBI Distribution Services/Quayside Distribution
MyiLibrary.

Franklin, J.E., *(978-0-9746669)* P.O. Box 517, New York, NY 10031 USA Tel 212-283-8666
E-mail: je413@aol.com
Web site: http://www.geocities.com/haveplaywilltravel/playseries.html.

Franklin Mason Pr., *(978-0-9679227; 978-0-9760469; 978-0-9857218)* Orders Addr.: P.O. Box 3808, Trenton, NJ 08629 USA (SAN 253-1828) Tel 609-291-5030; Fax: 609-291-7807; 415 Route 68, Columbus, NJ 08022
E-mail: lwill0517@aol.com
Web site: http://www.franklinmasonpress.com; http://www.nickyfifth.com
Dist(s): **BMI Educational Services.**

Franklin Publishing, *(978-0-9708129)* 1917 Warrington Rd., SW, Roanoke, VA 24015-3037 USA Tel 540-982-1654 (phone/fax on demand) Do not confuse with Franklin Publishing, Tempe, AZ, Chandler, AZ
E-mail: arnpaw@aol.com.

Franklin, Stephanie Michelle *See* **Heavenly Realm Publishing**

Franklin Street Books *See* **Inkwater Pr.**

Frayed Pages Publishing, *(978-0-9753397)* P.O. Box 1360, Pickens, SC 29671 USA
E-mail: writings@bellsouth.net
Dist(s): **Continental Enterprises Group, Inc. (CEG).**

Frazier, Jeffrey R. *See* **Egg Hill Pubns.**

Frederic, Marc *See* **World of Whimsy Productions, LLC**

Fredonia Bks., *(978-1-58963; 978-1-4101)* 4440 NW 73rd Ave., PTY 362, Miami, FL 33166-6437 USA Tel 407-650-2537 (phone/fax)
E-mail: bip@fredoniabooks.com
Web site: http://www.fredoniabooks.com.

Fredrickson, Anne, *(978-0-615-20146-7)* 6905 290th St. W., Northfield, MN 55057 USA
Dist(s): **Aardvark Global Publishing.**

Free Assn. Bks. Ltd. (GBR) *(978-0-946960; 978-1-85343)* *Dist. by* **Intl Spec Bk.**

Free Focus Publishing, *(978-0-9826747)* P.O. Box 716, Blaine, WA 98231 USA Tel 310-562-8165 (phone/fax)
E-mail: elke@freefocuspublishing.com
Web site: http://www.freefocuspublishing.com.

Free Pr. *Imprint of* **Free Pr.**

†Free Pr., *(978-0-02; 978-0-669; 978-0-671; 978-0-684; 978-0-7432)* Orders Addr.: 100 Front St., Riverside, NJ 08075 USA; Edit Addr.: 1230 Ave. of the Americas, New York, NY 10020 USA; *Imprints:* Free Press (Free Imp)
Dist(s): **CreateSpace Independent Publishing Platform**
Simon & Schuster
Simon & Schuster, Inc.; *CIP.*

Free Pr. Pubs., *(978-0-943751)* Orders Addr.: P.O. Box 4717, Monroe, LA 71211 USA (SAN 242-6242) Tel 318-388-1310; Fax: 318-388-2911
E-mail: RooseveltWright@prodigy.net
Web site: http://www.sermonideas.com.

F.R.E.E. Publishing House, *(978-0-86639; 978-0-9762472)* Div. of Friends of Refugees of Eastern Europe, 1383 President St., Brooklyn, NY 11213 USA Tel 718-467-0860 ext 118; Fax: 718-467-2146
E-mail: publications@russianjewry.org
Web site: http://www.JRBooks.org.

†Free Spirit Publishing, Inc., *(978-0-915793; 978-1-57542; 978-1-63198)* 6325 Sandburg Rd., Ste. 100, Warehouse Docks 42/43, Golden Valley, MN 55427-3629 USA (SAN 293-9584) Tel 612-338-2068; Fax: 612-337-5050; Toll Free: 800-735-7323
E-mail: help4kids@freespirit.com
Web site: http://www.freespirit.com
Dist(s): **Brodart Co.**
Follett School Solutions
Independent Pubs. Group
MyiLibrary; *CIP.*

Free Your Mind Publishing, *(978-0-9760056)* P.O. Box 70, Boston, MA 02131 USA Fax: 202-889-5056; 2724 Knox Terrace, SE, Washington, DC 20020 (SAN 256-1883) Do nopt confuse with Free Your Mind Publishing in Indianapolis, IN
E-mail: omekongo@omekongo.com
Web site: http://www.freeyourmindpublishing.com
Dist(s): **Smashwords.**

Freedom Archives, The, *(978-0-9727422; 978-0-9790789)* 522 Valencia St., San Francisco, CA 94110 USA Tel 415-863-9977
E-mail: info@freedomarchives.org
Web site: http://www.freedomarchives.org
Dist(s): **AK Pr. Distribution**
Consortium Bk. Sales & Distribution
SPD-Small Pr. Distribution.

Freedom of Speech Publishing, Inc., *(978-1-938634)* 4552 W 138 Terr, Leawood, KS 66224 USA Tel 815-290-9605
E-mail: admin@freedomofspeechpublishing.com
Web site: www.freedomofspeechpublishing.com.

Freedom Pr., *(978-0-9664326)* P.O. Box 2228, Wrightwood, CA 92397-2228 USA Tel 505-573-0737 Do not confuse with companies with the same name in Allentown, PA, Scottsdale, AZ, Pawcatuck, CT, Southaven, MS, Liberty Lake, WA, Saint Louis, MO, Nutley, NJ
E-mail: freedompress@hotmail.com
Web site: http://freedompress.4t.com
Dist(s): **Bristlecone Publishing Co.**
New Leaf Distributing Co., Inc.

Freedom Reading Foundation, Incorporated *See* **Edu-Steps, Inc.**

Freedom Voices Pubns., *(978-0-915117; 978-0-9625153)* Div. of Tenderloin Reflection & Education Ctr., P.O. Box 423115, San Francisco, CA 94142 USA
E-mail: jess@freedomvoices.org; spottywest@freedomvoices.org; art@arthazelwood.com
Web site: http://www.freedomvoices.org
Dist(s): **AK Pr. Distribution**
Lightning Source, Inc.
SPD-Small Pr. Distribution.

Freefox Publishing, *(978-0-9801527)* Orders Addr.: 32 Doncaster Cir., Lynnfield, MA 01940 USA
Web site: http://www.freefoxpublishing.com.

Freeman, Kimberly *See* **Keys For Kids Publishing Co.**

Freeman-Smith LLC, *(978-0-9640955; 978-1-58334; 978-1-887655; 978-1-60587)* Div. of Worthy Media, Inc., P.O. Box 50, Nashville, TN 37202 USA
E-mail: walnutgrovepress@yahoo.com
Web site: http://www.quotedoctor.com
Dist(s): **Midpoint Trade Bks., Inc.**
MyiLibrary
Worthy Publishing.

FreeStar Pr., *(978-0-9661315)* P.O. Box 54552, Cincinnati, OH 45254-0552 USA Tel 513-734-0102
E-mail: Freestarpr@aol.com.

Freet Publishing, *(978-0-9676717)* Orders Addr.: P.O. Box 219, Willow Hill, PA 17271-0219 USA Tel 717-349-7873 (phone/fax); Edit Addr.: 18028 Pigeon Hill Rd., Willow Hill, PA 17271-0219 USA
E-mail: freepbl@pa.net.

Freeverse Enterprises Inc., *(978-0-9743789)* 1200 E. River Rd. C-35, Tucson, AZ 85718 USA.

Fremantle Pr. (AUS) *(978-1-86368; 978-0-909144; 978-0-949206; 978-1-920731; 978-1-921064; 978-1-921361; 978-1-921696; 978-1-921888; 978-0-646-39543-2; 978-0-646-50123-9; 978-1-922089; 978-1-925160; 978-1-925161; 978-1-925162; 978-1-925163; 978-1-925164)* *Dist. by* **IPG Chicago.**

French & European Pubns., Inc., *(978-0-320; 978-0-7859; 978-0-8288)* 425 E. 58th St., Suite 27D, New York, NY 10022-2379 USA (SAN 206-8109) Fax: 212-265-1094
E-mail: frenchbookstore@aol.com
Web site: http://www.frencheuropean.com.

French, Samuel Inc., *(978-0-573)* 235 Pk. Ave. S., New York, NY 10003 USA Tel 212-206-8990; Fax: 212-206-1429; 7623 Sunset Blvd., Hollywood, CA

90046 (SAN 200-6855) Tel 323-876-0570; Fax: 323-876-6822; Toll Free: 800-822-8669
E-mail: info@samuelfrench.com
Web site: http://www.samuelfrench.com
Dist(s): **INscribe Digital**
SCB Distributors.

French Workshop, The *See* **Aaron Levy Pubns., LLC**

FREOMM Publishing, *(978-0-9659891)* 77635 Malone Cir., Palm Desert, CA 92211 USA Tel 760-772-6628; Fax: 760-772-0169
E-mail: odyssey@odysseyofthesoul.org
Web site: http://www.odysseyofthesoul.org
Dist(s): **New Leaf Pr., Inc.**

Fresh Baby LLC, *(978-0-9727227; 978-0-9826303; 978-0-9884295; 978-0-9895938)* 202 Grove St., Petoskey, MI 49770-2712 USA
E-mail: info@freshbaby.com
Web site: http://www.freshbaby.com
Dist(s): **Independent Pubs. Group**
MyiLibrary.

Fresh Breeze Publishing, *(978-0-615-82932-6)* 2056 Berry Roberts Dr., Sun City Center, FL 33573 USA Tel 530-845-6488
Dist(s): **CreateSpace Independent Publishing Platform.**

Fresh Ink Group, *(978-1-936442)* 1332 Woodbrook Ln, Southlake, TX 76092 USA Tel 817-481-4790; Fax: 817-329-7165
E-mail: info@freshinkgroup.com
Web site: www.freshinkgroup.com.

Freundship Pr., LLC, *(978-0-9822204; 978-0-9839957)* P.O. Box 9171, Boise, ID 83707 USA Tel 208-407-7457
E-mail: info@freundshippress.com
Web site: http://www.freundshippress.com.

Frick Art & Historical Ctr., The, *(978-0-9703425; 978-0-615-57373-1; 978-0-615-57374-8)* 7227 Reynolds St., Pittsburgh, PA 15208 USA Tel 412-371-0600; Fax: 412-241-5393
E-mail: tsmart@frickart.org; info@frickart.org
Web site: http://www.frickart.org.

Fried, Scott *See* **TALKAIDS, Inc.**

Frieda B., *(978-0-9843862)* 55 Long Hill Dr., Somers, CT 06071 USA (SAN 859-2640)
Web site: http://www.friedab.com.

Friedman, Michael Publishing Group, Inc., *(978-0-9627134; 978-1-56799; 978-1-58663; 978-1-4114)* Div. of Barnes & Noble, Inc., 122 Fifth Ave., Fifth Flr., New York, NY 10011 USA (SAN 248-9732) Tel 212-685-6610; Fax: 212-633-3327
E-mail: rlamarche@bn.com
Web site: http://www.metrobooks.com
Dist(s): **MyiLibrary**
Perseus Bks. Group
Sterling Publishing Co., Inc.
Texas A&M Univ. Pr.

Friedman, Yuda, *(978-0-9677313)* 11 Quickway Rd. Unit 103, Monroe, NY 10950-8804 USA.

Friedrich, Paul, *(978-0-9793676)* 323 W. Martin St., SPC 70, Raleigh, NC 27601 USA
Web site: http://onionheadmonster.com.

Friend Family Ministries, *(978-0-9767524)* 1601 Hamilton Richmond Rd., Hamilton, OH 45013 USA.

Friendly Isles Pr., *(978-0-9678979)* Orders Addr.: 8503 Sun Harbor Dr., Bakersfield, CA 93312 USA Tel 661-587-0645
E-mail: ofalisiate@yahoo.com.

Friendly Planet, *(978-0-9742469)* 101 Third St., Cambridge, MA 02141 USA; *Imprints:* Big Books for Little People (Big Bks)
E-mail: mike@friendlyplanet.org
Web site: http://www.friendlyplanet.org.

Friends of Hildene, Inc., *(978-0-9754917; 978-0-692-31124-0)* 1005 Hildene Rd., PO Box 377, Manchester, VT 05254 USA Tel 802-362-1788; Fax: 802-362-1564
Web site: http://www.hildene.org.

Friends of Lulu, *(978-0-9740960)* P.O. Box 1114, New York, NY 10013-0866 USA
E-mail: info@friends-lulu.org
Web site: http://www.friends-lulu.org/.

Friends Of The Goshen Grange, The, *(978-0-9771473)* P.O. Box 1016, Goshen, NH 03752-1016 USA.

Friends Without a Border, *(978-0-9653574)* 1123 Broadway Ste. 1210, New York, NY 10010-2007 USA
E-mail: fwab@fwab.org
Web site: http://www.fwab.org
Dist(s): **SCB Distributors.**

Friendship Craze, *(978-0-615-80859-8)* 265 Rock Hill Dr., Fayetteville, GA 30215 USA Tel 770-716-6033
Web site: friendshipcraze.com
Dist(s): **CreateSpace Independent Publishing Platform.**

Frog Legs Ink *Imprint of* **Gauthier Pubns. Inc.**

Frog Legs Ink, *(978-0-615-76413-9; 978-0-615-77206-6; 978-0-615-77391-9; 978-0-615-87736-5; 978-0-615-94568-2)* 2057 Lennon, Grosse Pointe Woods, MI 48236 USA Tel 313-458-7141; Fax: 586-279-1515
E-mail: elizabeth@gauthierpublications.com
Dist(s): **CreateSpace Independent Publishing Platform.**

Frog Ltd. *Imprint of* **North Atlantic Bks.**

Frog Pond Enterprises, *(978-0-615-12821-4; 978-0-9915037)* 2821 Sheffield Ct., Trophy Club, TX 76262 USA Tel 862-502-4827
E-mail: joyclassalive2@gmail.com
Web site: www.joyclassalive.com; http://www.joyforchurches.com.

F.R.O.G. the Rock Pubns., *(978-0-9727142)* 3524 Parkview Dr., Marietta, GA 30062 USA Tel 770-587-4902; Fax: 770-993-0394
E-mail: frogtherock@aol.com.

Froglogic Concepts LLC *See* **Leadline Publishing**

From the Asylum Bks. & Pr., *(978-0-9715860)* P.O. Box 1516, Dickinson, TX 77539 USA
Web site: http://www.fromtheasylum.com.

Front Street *Imprint of* **Boyds Mills Pr.**

Front Street/Cricket Books *See* **Cricket Bks.**

Fronte, Kathy, *(978-0-9727725)* 5604 Greenwood Cir., Naples, FL 34112 USA.

Frontier Books *See* **Frontier Pr.**

Frontier Image Pr., *(978-0-9634309; 978-1-888571)* Orders Addr.: P.O. Box 3055, Silver City, NM 88061 USA Tel 505-534-4032; Fax: 505-590-1301
E-mail: frontr@cybermcs.com.

Frontier Pr., *(978-0-9768465)* 180 E. Ocean Blvd., Fl 4, Long Beach, CA 90802-9080 USA Tel 562-491-8331; Fax: 562-491-8791
E-mail: new_frontier@usw.salvationarmy.org.

Frontiera, Deborah *See* **Jade Enterprises**

Frontline *Imprint of* **Charisma Media**

Frontline Communications *See* **YWAM Publishing**

Frontline Pr., *(978-0-930201)* Orders Addr.: P.O. Box 764499, Dallas, TX 75376-4499 USA Tel 972-572-8336; Fax: 972-572-8335 Do not confuse with companies with the same or similar name in Washington, DC, Taylors, SC, Charlston, SC
E-mail: info@youthdirect.org
Web site: http://www.youthdirect.org.

Frost, C. A., *(978-0-9847236)* 8113 Cloverglen Ln., Fort Worth, TX 76123 USA Tel 817-994-2420
E-mail: theewordnerd@yahoo.com.

Frost Hollow Pubs., LLC, *(978-0-9658523; 978-0-9720922; 978-0-9794273; 978-0-9829636; 978-0-9890965)* 411 Barlow Cemetery Rd., Woodstock, CT 06281 USA Tel 860-974-2081; Fax: 860-974-0813; Toll Free: 877-974-2081
E-mail: frosthollow@mindspring.com
Web site: http://www.frosthollowpub.com.

Frugal Bear Communications, *(978-0-9678694)* P.O. Box 5154, Inglewood, CA 90310 USA; *Imprints:* FrugalBear.com (FrugalBear)
E-mail: regresa@hotmail.com; frugalbear@email.com
Web site: http://www.frugalbear.com.

FrugalBear.com *Imprint of* **Frugal Bear Communications**

Fruitbearer Publishing, LLC, *(978-1-886068; 978-1-938796)* Orders Addr.: P.O. Box 777, Georgetown, DE 19947 USA (SAN 920-380X) Tel 302-856-6649; Fax: 302-856-7742; Edit Addr.: 107 Elizabeth St., Georgetown, DE 19947 USA
E-mail: cfa@candyabbott.com; info@fruitbearer.com
Web site: http://www.fruitbearer.com
Dist(s): **AtlasBooks Distribution**
BookBaby
Lightning Source, Inc.

Fruition Online Publishing, *(978-0-9712079)* Div. of Cherokee Ventures, 120 St. Albans Dr., #469, Raleigh, NC 27609 USA Tel 919-743-2500; Fax: 919-743-2501
E-mail: customersupport@fruitiononline.com
Web site: http://www.fruitiononline.com.

Fry, Debbie, *(978-0-9759647)* 301 N. Gleason Ave., Fowler, CA 93625-2162 USA.

FT Richards Publishing, *(978-0-9746561)* 41 Tailwinds Ln., North East, MD 21901 USA
Web site: http://www.fairwindsstables.com.

Ft. Valley Geology Study Ctr. *Imprint of* **InterPress**

FTD, *(978-0-9747637)* 3113 Woodcreek Dr., Downers Grove, IL 60515 USA Toll Free: 800-383-6659.

FTL Pubns., *(978-0-9653575; 978-0-9825232; 978-1-936881)* Orders Addr.: P.O. Box 1363, Minnetonka, MN 55345-0363 USA Tel 952-938-4275; Edit Addr.: 5137 Clear Springs Dr., Minnetonka, MN 55345-4312 USA
E-mail: mail@ftlpublications.com
Web site: http://www.FTLPublications.com
Dist(s): **Diamond Comic Distributors, Inc.**
Smashwords.

Fuel Media Group, Inc., *(978-0-9772047)* 15305 NW 60th Ave. Suite 100, Miami Lakes, FL 33014 USA Tel 305-822-7000
E-mail: bob@calvarywired.com
Web site: http://www.fuelmg.com.

†Fulcrum Publishing, *(978-0-912347; 978-1-55591; 978-1-56373; 978-1-936218; 978-1-938486; 978-1-68275)* Orders Addr.: 4690 Table Mountain Dr. Suite 100, Golden, CO 80403 USA (SAN 200-2825) Toll Free Fax: 800-726-7112; Toll Free: 800-992-2908
E-mail: info@fulcrumbooks.com
Web site: http://www.fulcrumbooks.com
Dist(s): **Abraham Assocs. Inc.**
Alibris
Consortium Bk. Sales & Distribution
Copyright Clearance Ctr., Inc.
Independent Pubs. Group
MyiLibrary
Perseus Bks. Group
ebrary, Inc.; *CIP.*

Full Circle Pr. *Imprint of* **WillowTree Pr., L.L.C.**

Full Court Pr., *(978-0-9709477; 978-0-578-01482-1; 978-0-578-02337-3; 978-0-578-02841-5; 978-0-578-03345-7; 978-0-578-05544-2; 978-0-578-05545-9; 978-0-9846113; 978-0-9833711; 978-0-9837411; 978-0-9849536; 978-1-938812)* 601 Palisade Ave., Englewood Cliffs, NJ 07632 USA Fax: 201-567-7202
Web site: http://writingcenternj.com
Dist(s): **AtlasBooks Distribution**
Follett School Solutions.

Full Effect Gospel Ministries, Inc., *(978-0-9679516; 978-0-615-76085-8; 978-0-692-29621-9)* 900 New Lots Ave, Brooklyn, NY 11208 USA Tel 7189270476
Web site: www.effect900.com
Dist(s): **CreateSpace Independent Publishing Platform.**

Full Gospel Family Pubns., *(978-0-9745599)* 419 E. Taft Ave., Appleton, WI 54915-2079 USA Tel 920-734-6693
E-mail: character@characterbuildingforfamilies.com; pilgrims@juno.com
Web site: http://www.characterbuildingforfamilies.com.

Full House Productions, *(978-0-615-27092-0; 978-0-9832564)* 2466 Center Point Rd., Fredericksburg, TX 78624 USA.

Full Moon Creations, Incorporated *See* **LeLeu, Lisa Studios! Inc.**

Full Moon Publishing LLC, *(978-0-9666021; 978-0-9785402; 978-0-9820352; 978-0-9846357; 978-0-9888683)* Orders Addr.: 433 Mystic Point Dr., Bluffton, SC 29909 USA Tel 219-688-3093 Do not confuse with Full Moon Publishing, Norton, MA
E-mail: fullmoonpub@sc.rr.com
Web site: http://www.fullmoonpub.com
Dist(s): **Smashwords.**

Full Quart Pr. *Imprint of* **Holly Hall Pubns., Inc.**

Full Satchel Pr. (CAN) *(978-0-9731960) Dist. by* **Wlsn Assocs.**

Fullerton Bks., Inc., *(978-0-9652918)* Orders Addr.: P.O. Box 1, Waveland, MS 39576 USA Tel 972-412-3131; 228-457-5323; Fax: 509-278-0766
E-mail: info@vincevance.com
Web site: http://www.vincevance.com.

FullofPep Pubns., *(978-0-9760684)* P.O. Box 367, Columbia, SC 29202 USA
E-mail: fullofpeppublications@yahoo.com.

Fulton, David Pubs. (GBR) *(978-1-85346; 978-1-84312) Dist. by* **Taylor and Fran.**

Fultus *See* **Fultus Corp.**

Fultus Corp., *(978-0-9744339; 978-1-59682)* P.O. Box 50095, Palo Alto, CA 94303 USA Fax: 650-745-0873; *Imprints:* Fultus Publishing (Ful Pubng)
E-mail: production@fultus.com
Web site: http://www.fultus.com; http://elibrary.fultus.com; http://store.fultus.com; http://writers.fultus.com
Dist(s): **Lightning Source, Inc.**

Fultus Publishing *Imprint of* **Fultus Corp.**

Fun Fitness Publishing, *(978-0-9762483; 978-0-615-35686-0)* 16 Paulsboro Rd., Woolwich, NJ 08055 USA Tel 609-410-3717 (phone/fax); Fax: 609-257-4079
E-mail: jeyre2@comcast.net; funfitness@comcast.net
Web site: http://www.janeeyre-art.com; http://www.funfitnesstraining.weebly.com.

Fun Places Publishing, *(978-0-9646737; 978-0-9833832)* 6124 Capetown St., Lakewood, CA 90713 USA Tel 562-867-5223
E-mail: orders@funplaces.com
Web site: http://www.funplaces.com
Dist(s): **American West Bks.**
Sunbelt Pubns., Inc.

Fun Publishing Co., *(978-0-938293)* 2121 Alpine Pl., No. 402, Cincinnati, OH 45206 USA (SAN 661-1761) Tel 513-533-3636; Fax: 513-421-7269 Do not confuse with companies with the same or similar names in Scottsdale, AZ, Fort Lauderdale, FL, Indianapolis, IN
E-mail: funpublish@aol.com
Web site: http://www.funpublishing.com.

Fun Time Flowers *See* **Flower Sprouts**

Fun to Read Bks. with Royally Good Morals *Imprint of* **MKADesigns**

Funcastle Pubns., *(978-0-9645771)* Orders Addr.: P.O. Box 51217, Riverside, CA 92517 USA Tel 951-653-5200; Fax: 951-653-4300; Edit Addr.: 20833 Millbrook St., Riverside, CA 92508 USA.

Fundacion Coleccion Thyssen-Bornemisza (ESP) *(978-84-88474; 978-84-96233; 978-84-15113) Dist. by* **Dist Art Pubs.**

Fundacion Intermon (ESP) *(978-84-604; 978-84-8452; 978-84-89970; 978-84-921977) Dist. by* **Marluccia Iaconi Bk Imports.**

Fundacion Intermon (ESP) *(978-84-604; 978-84-8452; 978-84-89970; 978-84-921977) Dist. by* **Lectorum Pubns.**

Fundamental Christian Endeavors, *(978-1-931787)* 49191 Cherokee Rd., Newberry Springs, CA 92365 USA Tel 760-257-3503; Fax: 760-257-3075
Web site: http://www.ironwood.org.

Fundamental Wesleyan Pubs., *(978-0-9629383; 978-0-9761003; 978-0-9914251)* 2120 Culverson Ave., Evansville, IN 47714 USA Tel 812-476-2996
E-mail: victorpau@aol.com
Web site: http://www.fwponline.cc.

FUNdamentals/Leap In Faith, *(978-0-9834645)* P.O. Box 491, Abingdon, MD 21009 USA Tel 443-484-2512
E-mail: Fundamentals123@aol.com
Web site: Fundamentals123.com
Dist(s): **Partners Pubs. Group, Inc.**

Fundcraft Publishing, *(978-1-931413; 978-1-935397)* Orders Addr.: P.O. Box 340, Collierville, TN 38027 USA Tel 901-853-7070; Fax: 901-853-6196; Edit Addr.: 410 Hwy. 72 W., Collierville, TN 38017 USA Tel 901-853-7070
E-mail: info@fundcraft.com
Web site: http://www.fundcraft.com.

Funnel Cloud 9, Inc., *(978-0-9767297)* 545 Tom Treece Rd., Morristown, TN 37814 USA
Web site: http://www.fc9.net.

Funny Bone Bks., *(978-0-9771836; 978-0-9790240; 978-0-9799121; 978-0-9822288; 978-0-9841507)* 3435 Golden Ave., No. 302, Apt. 302, Cincinnati, OH 45226 USA
E-mail: dpendery@newforms.com
Web site: http://www.bookmasters.com/funnybones
Dist(s): **AtlasBooks Distribution.**

Funny Bones Publishing, *(978-0-615-67275-5; 978-0-615-75349-2)* 19971 Crestknoll Dr. 0, Yorba Linda, AE 92886 USA Tel 714-312-0598
E-mail: caryn@webteaching.com
Dist(s): **CreateSpace Independent Publishing Platform.**

FunnyGuy.Comedy, *(978-0-9747398)* 123 N. Kings Rd., Los Angeles, CA 90048 USA
E-mail: dave@funnyguy.com
Web site: http://www.funnyguy.com.

FunStitch Studio *Imprint of* **C & T Publishing**

Funtext Publishing, *(978-0-615-46185-4; 978-0-615-46186-1; 978-0-615-52909-7; 978-0-615-61275-1; 978-0-615-69932-5; 978-0-615-70114-1)* 9723 Summit Circle, Suite 3D, Largo, MD 20774 USA Tel 202-640-2077
E-mail: srsholdinggroup@gmail.com
Dist(s): **CreateSpace Independent Publishing Platform**
Dummy Record Do Not USE!!!!.

Fur, George, *(978-0-9752985)* 165 Laurel Ave., Menlo Park, CA 94025 USA
E-mail: yfur@msn.com.

Fury Publishing & Distributing, *(978-0-9747049)* 325 Washington Ave. No. 214, Kent, WA 98032 USA Tel 253-520-3111
E-mail: furypublishing@msn.com
Web site: http://www.fury2000.com.

Futech Educational Products, Inc., *(978-0-9627001; 978-1-889192)* 2999 N. 44th St., Suite 225, Phoenix, AZ 85018-7248 USA Tel 602-808-8765; Fax: 602-278-5667; Toll Free: 800-597-6278.

Future Comics, *(978-0-9744225)* 220 W. Brandon Blvd., Brandon, FL 33511 USA Tel 813-655-1900; Fax: 813-662-3250; Toll Free: 877-226-6427
E-mail: info@futurecomicsonline.com
Web site: http://www.futurecomicsonline.com.

Future Education, Incorporated *See* **Future Horizons, Inc.**

Future Horizons, Inc., *(978-1-885477; 978-1-932565; 978-1-935274; 978-1-935567; 978-0-9860673; 978-1-941765)* 721 W. Abram St., Arlington, TX 76013 USA Tel 817-277-0727; Fax: 817-277-2270; Toll Free: 800-489-0727
E-mail: kelly@fhautism.com
Web site: http://www.FHautism.com
Dist(s): **BookBaby**
Follett School Solutions
Ingram Pub. Services.

F+W Media, Incorporated *See* **F&W Media, Inc.**

FWOMP Publishing, *(978-0-9760096)* 935 Lighthouse Ave. No. 21, Pacific Grove, CA 93950 USA
Web site: http://www.fwomp.com
Dist(s): **Sunbelt Pubns., Inc.**

FX Digital Photo, *(978-0-9769009)* 9 Maison Way, Toms River, NJ 08757-6413 USA
Web site: http://www.fxdigitalphoto.com.

G & K Publishing, *(978-0-615-15770-2)* P.O. Box 445, Johnstown, OH 43031 USA
E-mail: eking@byroncarmichael.com
Web site: http://www.byroncarmichael.com; http://GandKPublishing.com.

G & R Publishing, *(978-1-56383)* 507 Industrial St., Waverly, IA 50677 USA Toll Free Fax: 800-866-7496; Toll Free: 800-383-1679; 800-887-4445
E-mail: gandr@gandrpublishing.com; gifts@cqbookstore.com
Web site: http://www.cookbookprinting.com; http://www.cqbookstore.com
Dist(s): **CQ Products.**

G. B. Enterprises *See* **Kent Communications, Ltd.**

G C B Publishing *See* **Holly Hall Pubns., Inc.**

G F W C of South Dakota/Daughters of Dakota *See* **Sky Carrier Pr.**

G I A Pubns., Inc., *(978-0-941050; 978-1-57999; 978-1-62277)* 7404 S. Mason Ave., Chicago, IL 60638 USA (SAN 205-3217) Tel 708-496-3800; Fax: 708-496-3828; Toll Free: 800-442-1358
E-mail: custserv@giamusic.com
Web site: http://www.giamusic.com
Dist(s): **Independent Pubs. Group**
MyiLibrary.

G J & B Publishing, *(978-0-9635006)* 22442 University Ave., N., Cedar, MN 55011 USA Tel 612-434-0786.

G Publishing *See* **G Publishing LLC**

G Publishing LLC, *(978-0-9727582; 978-0-9773267; 978-0-9776780; 978-0-9788536; 978-0-9790691; 978-0-9796978; 978-0-9801297; 978-0-9814650; 978-0-9820002; 978-0-9823533; 978-0-9843426; 978-0-9834307; 978-0-9849360; 978-0-9883374; 978-0-9862379)* P.O. Box 24374, Detroit, MI 48224-2348 USA Toll Free: 866-882-1159; 4826 Harvard Rd., Detroit, MI 48224 Do not confuse with G Publishing in Sebastopol, CA
E-mail: jhun@gpublishingsuccess.com; juthegen@sbcglobal.net
Web site: http://www.gpublishingsuccess.com
Dist(s): **AtlasBooks Distribution.**

G R M Assocs., *(978-0-933813; 978-0-929093)* 290 W. End Ave., 16A, New York, NY 11111 USA Tel 212-874-5964; Fax: 212-874-6425; *Imprints:* Taylor Productions (Taylor Prods)
Dist(s): **Independent Pubs. Group.**

G R Publishing, *(978-0-9668530)* 460 Brookside Way, Felton, CA 95018 USA
E-mail: pub@grandmarose.com
Web site: http://www.grandmarose.com.

G R T Pubns., *(978-0-9678420; 978-0-9716906)* P.O. Box 1845, Provo, UT 84603 USA Tel 801-374-2587 (phone/fax)
E-mail: grtpublications@juno.com
Web site: http://www.rogerpminert.

G Schirmer, Inc. *Imprint of* **Leonard, Hal Corp.**

G T Labs, *(978-0-9660106; 978-0-9788037)* P.O. Box 8145, Ann Arbor, MI 48107 USA Tel 734-994-0474; Fax: 734-764-4487
E-mail: info@gt-labs.com
Web site: http://www.gt-labs.com
Dist(s): **Diamond Comic Distributors, Inc.**
Diamond Bk. Distributors.

Publisher Name Index

G340 Publishing, (978-0-9843837) 7115 N. Division St. Suite B #132, Spokane, WA 99207-2242 USA (SAN 859-2462) Tel 509-850-0340
E-mail: service @g340.com; grealy@gmail.com
Web site: http://g340.com.

Gabriel Pr., (978-0-9721888) 255 Calle San Sebastian, San Juan, PR 00901 USA Do not confuse with companies with the same name in Phoenix, AZ, Ventura, CA, Fort Lauderdale, FL, Saratoga, CA, Sacramento, CA, San Juan, PR, Littleton, CO
E-mail: paolanogueras@gmail.com
Web site: http://www.paolanogueras.net
Dist(s): **Lectorum Pubns., Inc.**

Gabriel Resources, Orders Addr.: P.O. Box 1047, Waynesboro, GA 30830 USA Tel 706-554-1594; Fax: 706-554-7444; Toll Free: 800-732-6657 (8MORE-BOOKS); Edit Addr.: 129 Mobilization Dr., Waynesboro, GA 30830 USA.

Gabriele Capelli Editore Sagl (CHE) (978-88-87469) *Dist. by* **SPD-Small Pr Dist.**

Gaff Pr., (978-0-9619629) Orders Addr.: P.O. Box 1024, Astoria, OR 97103 USA (SAN 245-8403); Edit Addr.: P.O. Box 1024, Astoria, OR 97103-1024 USA (SAN 245-8411)
E-mail: gaffpres@pacifier.com
Web site: http://www.gaffpress.com.

Gaffney, Linda, (978-0-9787501) Orders Addr.: PMB 2682 2103 Harrison Ave., NW, Olympia, WA 98502 USA Tel 360-584-8566
Web site: http://www.HomeplacePress.com.

Gail's Guides, (978-1-881005) Orders Addr.: 134 West Canyonview Dr., Longview, WA 98632 USA
E-mail: guides@oz.net; info@gailsguides.com
Web site: http://www.gailsguides.com
Dist(s): **Anderson News - Tacoma**
Aramark
News Group, The
Partners/West Book Distributors.

Gain Literacy Skills / Lynette Gain Williams, (978-0-9779063) 10659 Rookwood Dr., San Diego, CA 92131-1619 USA (SAN 850-5608)
E-mail: gainliteracy@sbcglobal.net.

Galactic Bks., (978-0-9769400) 9827 Endora Ct., Owings Mills, MD 21117 USA
Web site: http://www.galacticbooks.usafreespace.com.

Galahad Bks. *Imprint of* **BBS Publishing Corp.**

Galahad Publishing, (978-0-918483) 6035 Vantage Ave., Suite 100, North Hollywood, CA 91606-4637 USA (SAN 657-680X) Tel 818-761-5198; Fax: 818-766-8645; Toll Free: 888-349-4878
Web site: http://www.GalahadPublishing.com.

Galaxia Publishing Group, LLC, (978-0-9741657) P.O. Box 61054, Phoenix, AZ 85082-1054 USA Tel 480-279-0836; Fax: 480-279-0863
E-mail: info@galaxiapg.com; LatonyaJordanSmith@yahoo.com
Web site: http://www.galaxiapg.com.

Galaxias Productions, (978-0-9835631; 978-0-9850529) 200 W. 90th St. No. 9B, New York, NY 10024 USA Tel 212-712-1540
E-mail: alwooten411@yahoo.com
Web site: www.arthurwooten.com
Dist(s): **Smashwords.**

Galaxy Pr., LLC, (978-1-59212; 978-1-61986) Orders Addr.: 7051 Hollywood Blvd., Suite 200, Hollywood, CA 90028 USA (SAN 254-6906) Tel 323-466-7815; Fax: 323-466-7817; Edit Addr.: 6121 Malburg Way, vernon, CA 90058 USA
E-mail: jwills@galaxypress.com; kcatalano@galaxypress.com; jgoodwin@galaxypress.com; sarahc@galaxypress.com
Web site: http://www.galaxypress.com/; http://www.battlefieldearth.com; http://www.writersofthefuture.com; http://www.goldenagestories.com
Dist(s): **Follett School Solutions**
Gumdrop Bks.

Galen Pr., Ltd., (978-1-883620) Orders Addr.: P.O. Box 64400, Tucson, AZ 85728-4400 USA (SAN 254-1823) Tel 520-577-8363; Fax: 520-529-6459; Toll Free: 800-442-5369 (orders only) Do not confuse with Galen Pr. in Madison, NJ
E-mail: ml@galenpress.com; sales@galenpress.com
Web site: http://www.galenpress.com
Dist(s): **Majors, J. A. Co.**
Matthews Medical Bk. Co.
Rittenhouse Bk. Distributors.

Gali Girls, Inc., (978-0-9773673) 48 Cranford Pl., Teaneck, NJ 07666 USA Tel 201-862-1989
Web site: http://www.galigirls.com.

Galileo Pr., (978-0-913123; 978-0-9817519) 3637 Blackrock Rd., Upperco, MD 21155-9322 USA (SAN 240-6543) Do not confuse with companies with the same or similar name in Edmonds, WA, Brooklyn, NY
E-mail: jawendell@aol.com
Dist(s): **Pathway Bk. Service.**

Galison, (978-0-7353; 978-0-929648; 978-0-939456; 978-1-56155) 28 W. 44th St., Suite 1411-12, New York, NY 10036 USA Tel 212-354-8840; Fax: 212-944-8682; Toll Free: 800-322-6663
E-mail: sales@galison.com
Web site: http://www.galison.com
Dist(s): **Hachette Bk. Group.**

Gallagher, Carole M., (978-0-9702197) 431 S. Main St., Williamstown, NJ 08094 USA Tel 856-875-1575; Fax: 856-875-1998.

Gallant Hse. Publishing, (978-0-9660373) 1329 Hwy. 395n, Ste 10 Pmb 114, Gardnerville, NV 89410 USA Toll Free: 877-577-2244
E-mail: gallanthouse@hotmail.com.

†Gallaudet Univ. Pr., (978-0-913580; 978-0-930323; 978-1-56368) 800 Florida Ave., NE, Washington, DC 20002-3695 USA (SAN 205-261X) Tel 202-651-5488; Fax: 202-651-5489; Toll Free Fax: 800-621-8476; Toll Free: 888-630-9347 (TTY)
E-mail: valencia.simmons@gallaudet.edu
Web site: http://gupress.gallaudet.edu
Dist(s): **Chicago Distribution Ctr.**
Ebsco Publishing
Follett School Solutions; *CIP.*

Gallery Bks. *Imprint of* **Gallery Bks.**

Gallery Bks., 1230 Ave. of the Americas, New York, NY 10020 USA; *Imprints:* Gallery Books (Gallery Imp)
Dist(s): **Perseus Bks. Group**
Simon & Schuster, Inc.

Gallery Books/Karen Hunter Publishing *Imprint of* **Gallery Books/Karen Hunter Publishing**

Gallery Books/Karen Hunter Publishing, 1230 Ave. of the Americas, New York, NY 10020 USA; *Imprints:* Gallery Books/Karen Hunter Publishing (GBKHP)
Dist(s): **Simon & Schuster, Inc.**

Galletti, Barbara, (978-0-9748737) 2509 Lawnside Rd., Timonium, MD 21093-2605 USA Tel 410-252-6568
E-mail: gallettinotes@hotmail.com.

Gallimard, Editions (FRA) (978-2-07) *Dist. by* **Distribks Inc.**

Gallopade International, (978-0-635; 978-0-7933; 978-0-935326; 978-1-55609) Orders Addr.: 6000 Shakerag Hl. # 314, Peachtree Cty, GA 30269-6523 USA (SAN 213-8441) Toll Free Fax: 800-871-2979; Toll Free: 800-536-2438; *Imprints:* Marsh, Carole Family CD-Rom (C Marsh); Marsh, Carole Books (C Mrsh Bks); Marsh, Carole Mysteries (CarolMarshMyst)
E-mail: michael@gallopade.com
Web site: http://www.gallopade.com
Dist(s): **Follett School Solutions.**

Gallopade: Publishing Group *See* **Gallopade International**

Gallup Pr., (978-1-59562) 1251 Avenue of the Americas, 23rd Fl., New York, NY 10020 USA Tel 212-899-4709; Fax: 212-899-4899; Toll Free: 877-242-5587
Web site: http://www.gallup.com
Dist(s): **MyiLibrary**
Perseus-PGW
Simon & Schuster
Simon & Schuster, Inc.

Gambit Pubns., Ltd. (GBR) (978-1-901983; 978-1-904600; 978-1-906454; 978-1-910093) *Dist. by* **Perseus Dist.**

Game Day Press *See* **Timberwood Pr.**

Game Designers' Workshop, (978-0-943580; 978-1-55878) 1418 N. Clinton Blvd., Bloomington, IL 61701 USA (SAN 240-656X) Tel 309-827-5534
E-mail: farfuture@gmail.com
Dist(s): **PSI (Publisher Services, Inc.).**

Gam-Jam Publishing Company *See* **Pendleton Publishing, Inc.**

Gamlin, Stephen, (978-0-9767993) P.O. Box 5, Goffstown, NH 03045 USA Tel 603-560-3360; Fax: 603-774-8698; Toll Free: 877-560-3360
E-mail: Steve@InspiredBySteve.com
Web site: http://www.InspiredBySteve.com.

Gamoke, John, (978-0-9771290) 6645 Humboldt Ave. S., Richfield, MN 55423 USA.

GanDale Associates Houston *See* **Holocaust Museum Houston**

Gant, Linda G. Gifted Creations *See* **Readers Are Leaders**

Gantt Smith Publishing Hse., (978-0-9847885) 875 Victor Ave. Apt., 235, Inglewood, CA 90302 USA Tel 310-673-5114
E-mail: migs13@sbcglobal.net.

Gaon Bks., (978-0-9820657; 978-0-9825439; 978-1-935604) Div. of Gaon Institute for Tolerance Studies, P.O. Box 23924, Santa Fe, NM 87502-3924 USA Tel 505-920-7771
E-mail: gaonbooks@gmail.com
Web site: http://www.gaonbooks.com.

Gap Tooth Publishing *Imprint of* **Charles River Pr.**

Garcia, Cezanne, (978-0-9728041) 30405 Cupeno Ln., Temecula, CA 92592-2540 USA Tel 951-506-6407 (phone\fax)
E-mail: stgarcia@fda.net.

Garcia, Jeffrey, (978-0-9840942) 3000 Avenida Ciruela, Carlsbad, CA 92009 USA Tel 760-822-0222.

Garden Fleetfoot Pr., (978-0-9762544) Orders Addr.: P.O. Box 1188, Okemos, MI 48805 USA
E-mail: info@gardenfleetfoot.com
Web site: http://gardenfleetfoot.com
Dist(s): **Partners Pubs. Group, Inc.**

Garden, Randa, (978-0-615-12322-6) 3503 Portia Pl., Norfolk, NE 68701 USA Tel 402-371-0544
E-mail: jrgarden@cableone.net
Web site: www.pennythepenguin.com.

Gardner, Colin, (978-0-9720348; 978-0-615-11851-2) 1677 S. 75 E., Bouniful, UT 84010-5218 USA Tel 801-296-2109 (phone/fax)
E-mail: colingardner@juno.com.

Gardner Pubns., (978-0-9659163) 235 E. Main St., No. 119, Hendersonville, TN 37075 USA Tel 615-824-5100; Fax: 615-824-3400; Toll Free: 800-297-8179
E-mail: harveylgardner@bbsco.com
Web site: http://www.bbsco.com.

Gareth Stevens Hi-Lo Must Reads *Imprint of* **Stevens, Gareth Publishing LLLP**

Gareth Stevens Learning Library *Imprint of* **Stevens, Gareth Publishing LLLP**

Gareth Stevens Secondary Library *Imprint of* **Stevens, Gareth Publishing LLLP**

Garfein, Stanley, (978-0-9787422) 1110 Lasswade Dr., Tallahassee, FL 32312-2845 USA Tel 850-385-1538; Fax: 850-531-0276
E-mail: StaGarfein@aol.com.

Garing, Bernard, (978-0-9765809) 6304 Caleigh Dr., Charlestown, IN 47111-7713 USA.

Garland City Bks. of Watertown, (978-0-9890509) P.O. Box 604, Black River, NY 13612 USA Tel 315-783-0728
E-mail: rothensu@yahoo.com.

Garland, Daniel, (978-0-9768414) 6247 Cascade Hwy., NE, Silverton, OR 97381 USA
E-mail: danielggarland@msn.com.

Garlic Pr., (978-0-931993; 978-1-930820) Orders Addr.: 899 S. College Mall, Suite 381, Bloomington, IN 47401 USA (SAN 686-1105) Tel 800-789-0554; Toll Free Fax: 800-789-5576 Do not confuse with companies with the same name in Kirkwood, MO, New London, NH, Abingdon MD, Lenox MA, Kansas City, MO
E-mail: garlic.press@att.net
Web site: http://www.garlicpress.com
Dist(s): **Independent Pubs. Group.**

Garr, Sherry B., (978-0-9759866) 3456 S. Mulberry Dr., Saint George, UT 84790 USA
Web site: http://www.gumfounded.com.

Garrelts, Christopher *See* **Squarey Head, Inc.**

Garrett, Debbie Behan, (978-0-615-24202-6; 978-0-615-42184-1) P.O. Box 210571, Dallas, TX 75211-0571 USA Tel 214-337-5928; Fax: 214-337-8127
E-mail: blackdolls@sbcglobal.net
Web site: http://blackdollcollecting.com.

Garrigues Hse. Pubs., (978-0-9620844; 978-1-931014) 2746 Stein Ln., Lewisburg, PA 17837 USA (SAN 249-969X) Tel 570-204-2906; 2746 Stein Ln., Lewisburg, PA 17837 (SAN 249-9703)
E-mail: jim@garrigueshouse.com
Web site: http://www.garrigueshouse.com.

Garry & Donna, LLC, (978-0-9815617) P.O. Box 30021, Las Vegas, NV 89173 USA.

Gasior, Julie, (978-0-615-18824-9; 978-0-615-18884-3) 6404 Shadow Oaks Ct., Monmouth Jct, NJ 08852-2297 USA
E-mail: juliespotions@gmail.com
Web site: http://juliespotions.com
Dist(s): **Lulu Enterprises Inc.**

Gask Castle Pr., (978-0-9843717) 1725 Starmont Trail, Knoxville, TN 37909 USA Tel 865-310-8947
E-mail: phillip@gaskcastlepress.com.

Gaslight Pubns., (978-0-934468) P.O. Box 1344, Studio City, CA 91614-0344 USA Tel 818-784-8918
Dist(s): **Empire Publishing Service**
Players Pr., Inc.

GASLight Publishing, (978-0-9754796; 978-1-933869) P.O. Box 1025, Leander, TX 78646 USA Tel 512-528-1727; Fax: 512-259-8671
E-mail: ken@gaslightpublishing.com; kenschaefer@totalaccess.net
Web site: http://www.gsalightpublishing.com
Dist(s): **Smashwords.**

GateKeepers International, Incorporated, (978-0-9745483) 15245 Jessie Dr., Colorado Springs, CO 80921 USA
E-mail: Femritegki@gmail.com
Web site: http://www.gatekeepersintl.org.

GateKeepers Ministries International, (978-0-9754535) 3600 Earl Ave., Pennsauken, NJ 08110 USA Toll Free: 866-910-2810
Web site: http://www.gkmi.org.

Gateway Learning Corporation *See* **HOP, LLC**

Gateways Bks. & Tapes, (978-0-89556) Div. of I.D.H.H.B., Inc., P.O. Box 370, Nevada City, CA 95959 USA (SAN 211-3635) Tel 530-477-8101; Fax: 530-272-0184; Toll Free: 800-869-0658
E-mail: orders@gatewaysbooksandtapes.com; info@gatewaysbooksandtapes.com
Web site: http://www.gatewaysbooksandtapes.com
Dist(s): **Independent Pubs. Group**
MyiLibrary
ebrary, Inc.

Gathering Place Pubs., Inc., (978-0-9754622; 978-0-615-38236-4; 978-0-9828311) P.O. Box 341, Kaysville, UT 84037-8403 USA (SAN 256-0658) Fax: 801-451-6008
E-mail: sales@stonesquest.com
Web site: http://www.rebuildshattereddreams.com; http://www.stonesquest.com.

†Gaunt, Inc., (978-0-912004; 978-1-56169; 978-1-60449) 3011 Gulf Dr., Holmes Beach, FL 34217-2199 USA (SAN 202-9413) Tel 941-778-5211; Fax: 941-778-5252
E-mail: info@gaunt.com; sales@gaunt.com
Web site: http://www.gaunt.com; *CIP.*

Gaunt, William W. & Sons, Incorporated *See* **Gaunt, Inc.**

Gauntlet, Inc., (978-0-9629659; 978-1-887368; 978-1-934267) 5307 Arroyo St., Colorado Springs, CO 80922 USA Tel 719-591-5566; Fax: 719-591-6676
E-mail: gauntlet66@aol.com; info@gauntletpress.com
Web site: http://www.gauntletpress.com.

Gauthier Pubns. Inc., (978-0-9820812; 978-0-9833593; 978-0-615-71779-1; 978-1-942314) P.O. Box 806241, Saint Clair Shores, MI 48080 USA (SAN 857-2119) Tel 313-458-7141; Fax: 586-279-1515; *Imprints:* Frog Legs Ink (Frog Legs Ink); Hungry Goat Press (Hungry Goat)
E-mail: info@gauthierpublications.com
Web site: http://www.FrogLegsInk.com; http://www.EATaBOOK.com
Dist(s): **BWI**
Brodart Co.
CreateSpace Independent Publishing Platform
Diamond Bk. Distributors
Follett School Solutions.

Gavila Publishing, (978-0-9748466) 20-23 43 St., Astoria, NY 11105 USA
Web site: http://www.gavila.com.

Gavin, Fred Enterprises, (978-0-935668) 96 Byron St., East Boston, MA 02128 USA (SAN 221-1629).

Gaviota Ediciones (ESP) (978-84-392) *Dist. by* **Lectorum Pubns.**

Gavlak, L.J. Publishing, (978-0-9740357) Orders Addr.: P.O. Box 72, Kylertown, PA 16847 USA Tel 814-345-6391; Edit Addr.: Rollingston Rd., Kylertown, PA 16847 USA
E-mail: largav@juno.com.

Gazarik, Rebecca, (978-0-9802258) 637 Pine Run Rd., Apollo, PA 15613-9313 USA
Web site: http://www.rebeccagazarik.com/.

Gazing In Publishing, (978-0-9839318) P.O. Box 197, Columbia, SC 29147 USA Tel 803-743-8810
E-mail: winmilawe@gmail.com.

Gazoobi Tales, (978-0-9679364) P.O. Box 19614, Seattle, WA 98109-6614 USA
E-mail: info@gazoobitales.com
Web site: http://www.gazoobitales.com.

GDG Publishing, (978-0-9787549; 978-0-9796625; 978-0-9797952; 978-0-9855335) Orders Addr.: 2063 Continental Dr. NE, Atlanta, GA 30345 USA (SAN 851-5182) Tel 404-248-0012; Fax: 404-248-1487 Do not confuse with GDG Publishing in Oxnard, CA
E-mail: glennondesign@comcast.net
Web site: http://www.gdgpublishing.com.

GDL Multimedia, LLC, (978-1-60245) 2513 179th Ave E., Lake Tapps, WA 98391-6453 USA
E-mail: greg@gdlmultimedia.com
Web site: http://www.gdlmultimedia.com
Dist(s): **KSG Distributing.**

GDM Consulting Services LLC, (978-0-9763738) 5 Alluvium Lakes Dr., Voorhees, NJ 08043 USA
Web site: http://www.gdmcs.com.

Gecko Pr. (NZL) (978-0-9582598; 978-0-9582787; 978-0-9582720; 978-1-877467; 978-1-877579; 978-1-927271; 978-1-77657) *Dist. by* **Lerner Pub.**

Gecko Productions, Inc., (978-1-891694) Orders Addr.: P.O. Box 573, Woods Hole, MA 02543 USA Tel 508-548-3313; Fax: 508-548-3317; Edit Addr.: 55 Harbor Hill Rd., Woods Hole, MA 02543 USA
E-mail: nath51@verizon.net.

Geckostufs, Incorporated *See* **Words & Pictures Publishing, Inc.**

Geddes, Anne Publishing (AUS) (978-1-921652; 978-1-922024) *Dist. by* **Perseus Dist.**

Geek Parade Bks., (978-0-615-79901-8) 701 Moss Cliff, McKinney, TX 75071 USA Tel (972) 302-2214
Dist(s): **CreateSpace Independent Publishing Platform.**

Geez Pr., (978-0-9816574) P.O. Box 711, Elmore, OH 43416-0711 USA
Web site: http://home.woh.rr.com/geezpress.

Gefen Bks., (978-0-86343) 11 Edison Pl., Springfield, NJ 07081 USA (SAN 856-8065)
E-mail: gefenny@gefenpublishing.com
Web site: http://www.gefenpublishing.com.

Gefen Publishing Hse., Ltd (ISR) (978-965-229) *Dist. by* **Gefen Bks.**

Gefen Publishing Hse., Ltd (ISR) (978-965-229) *Dist. by* **Strauss Cnslts.**

Gem Bk. Pubs., (978-0-9633723; 978-1-887651) Div. of Fred Ward Productions, Inc., Orders Addr.: 2575 Barrymore Dr., Malibu, CA 90265-2955 USA Tel 310-456-9949; Fax: 310-456-9799
E-mail: fred@fredwardgems.com; charlotte@fredwardgems.com
Web site: http://www.fredwardgems.com/.

Gem Printing, (978-0-9743429) Orders Addr.: 600 Reisterstown Rd., Suite 200G, Baltimore, MD 21208 USA Tel 410-764-1617; Fax: 410-764-7471; *Imprints:* American Poets Society (Amer Poets)
E-mail: poetryamericaorders@yahoo.com
Web site: http://www.poetryamerica.com.

Gem Pubns., (978-0-9742354) 3520 McNally Ave., Altadena, CA 91001 USA
E-mail: gregmiddleton@earthlink.net
Web site: http://www.gempublications.com.

GemmaMedia, (978-1-934848; 978-1-936846) 230 Commercial St., Boston, MA 02109 USA (SAN 855-2037)
E-mail: info@gemmamedia.com; trish@gemmamedia.com
Web site: http://www.gemmamedia.com
Dist(s): **Ingram Pub. Services**
MyiLibrary.

GEMS *Imprint of* **Univ. of California, Berkeley, Lawrence Hall of Science**

Gems International Incorporated *See* **Gems International, LLC**

Gems International, LLC, (978-0-9728626) 640 S. Ave. Apt. I-8 Secane, Pa 19018, Secane, PA 19018 USA
Web site: http://www.nicolegay.com.

Gemstone Publishing, Inc., (978-0-911903; 978-1-888472; 978-1-60360) Div. of Diamond Comic Distributors, Inc., 1966 Greenspring Dr., Suite 405, Timonium, MD 21093 USA Tel 410-427-9432; Fax: 410-252-4582 Do not confuse with companies with same or similar names in Thornville, OH, Lebanon, OR, Lauderdale Lakes, FL, Sugarland, TX
Web site: http://www.gemstonepub.com
Dist(s): **Diamond Comic Distributors, Inc.**
Diamond Bk. Distributors
SPD-Small Pr. Distribution.

Gen Manga Entertainment, Inc., (978-0-9836134; 978-0-9850644; 978-1-939012) 250 Pk. Ave., Suite 7002, New York, NY 10177 USA Tel 646-535-0090
E-mail: editor@genmanga.com
Web site: www.genmanga.com
Dist(s): **Diamond Comic Distributors, Inc.**
Diamond Bk. Distributors.

Genealogical Publishing Company, Incorporated *See* **Genealogical.com**

†Genealogical.com, (978-0-8063) 3600 Clipper Mill Rd. Suite 260, Baltimore, MD 21211-1953 USA (SAN 206-8370) Toll Free: 800-296-6687 (orders & customer service); 3600 Clipper Mill Rd. Suite 260, Baltimore, MD 21211 (SAN 920-8755) Tel 410-837-8271; Fax: 410-752-8492
E-mail: hoffman@genealogical.com
Web site: http://www.Genealogical.com; *CIP.*

General Board of Global Ministries, The United Methodist Church, (978-1-890569; 978-1-933663) 475 Riverside Dr. Rm. 1473, New York, NY 10115 USA Tel

212-870-3731; Fax: 212-870-3654; *Imprints:* WD/GBGM Books (WD GBGM)
E-mail: cscott@gbgm-umc.org; KDonato@gbgm-umc.org
Web site: http://www.gbgm-umc.org
Dist(s): **Cokesbury**
Mission Resource Ctr.

General Bks. LLC, *(978-1-234; 978-1-77045; 978-1-150; 978-1-151; 978-1-152; 978-1-153; 978-1-154; 978-1-155; 978-1-156; 978-1-157; 978-1-158; 978-1-159; 978-1-230; 978-1-231; 978-1-232; 978-1-233; 978-1-235; 978-1-236; 978-1-238; 978-1-239; 978-1-130)* Orders Addr.: Box 29000, NAS485, Miami, FL 33102 USA
E-mail: support@general-books.net
Web site: www.general-books.net.

Genesis Communications, Inc., *(978-0-9637311; 978-1-58169)* P.O. Box 191540, Mobile, AL 36619 USA Tel 251-443-7900; Fax: 251-443-7090; Toll Free: 800-367-8203; *Imprints:* Evergreen Press (Evergrn Pr AL); Axiom Press (Axiom Press)
E-mail: Jeff@evergreen777.com
Web site: http://www.evergreenpress.com
Dist(s): **BookBaby**
Spring Arbor Distributors, Inc.

Genius In A Bottle Technology Corp, *(978-0-9768429)* Orders Addr.: 910 NW 42nd St., Miami, FL 33127-2755 USA
E-mail: geniusinfo@geniusinabottle.net
Web site: http://www.geniusinabottle.net; http://www.cafepress.com/forevergirl; http://www.cafepress.com/geniusbooks; http://www.cafepress.com/gumo; http://www.cafepress.com/gkid; http://www.cafepress.com/cleversunburst; http://www.cafepress.com/tou; http://www.cafepress.com/foreverman; http://www.cafepress.com/forever4; http://www.cafepress.com/whatever; http://www.cafepress.com/robospace; http://www.cafepress.com/battlegirlgear; http://www.cafepress.com/geniusinabottle; http://www.ca

Gentle Giraffe Pr., *(978-0-9747921; 978-0-9777394; 978-0-9801746)* 7405 Barra Dr., Bethesda, MD 20817 USA Tel 202-423-4205; Fax: 334-460-0724; Toll Free: 888-424-4723
E-mail: info@gentlegiraffe.com
Web site: http://www.gentlegiraffe.com.

Gently Spoken Communications, *(978-0-9711794; 978-0-9746491; 978-0-9776096; 978-0-615-11369-2; 978-0-615-11845-1)* P.O. Box 245, Anoka, MN 55303 USA Tel 763-506-9933; Fax: 763-506-9934; Toll Free: 877-224-7886
E-mail: info@gentlyspoken.com
Web site: http://www.gentlyspoken.com.

Genuine Prints, LLC, *(978-0-615-23040-5)* P.O. Box 328, Carpentersville, IL 60110 USA Fax: 847-844-9073; Toll Free: 888-853-0001
E-mail: info@nicoandlola.com
Web site: http://www.nicoandlola.com.

Geography Matters, Inc., *(978-0-9702403; 978-1-931397; 978-1-62863)* P.O. Box 92, Nancy, KY 42544 USA Tel 606-636-4678; Fax: 606-636-4697; Toll Free: 800-426-4650
E-mail: geomatters@geomatters.com
Web site: http://www.geomatters.com.

George, H. Publishing, *(978-0-9728183)* Orders Addr.: 14513 Bayes Ave., Lakewood, OH 44107 USA Tel 216-319-4575
E-mail: ninthohio@sbcglobal.net.

Geoscience Information Services, *(978-0-9777100)* Orders Addr.: P.O. Box 911, West Falmouth, MA 02574-0911 USA Tel 508-540-6490
E-mail: gis@cape.com.

Gequalsa, *(978-0-9792518)* 2710 Walnut St., Orlando, FL 32806 USA.

Gerardian Inkspot & Paint Society, *(978-0-9786675)* St. Gerard's Church, 240 W. Robb Ave., Lima, OH 45801 USA.

Gerber, Judie *See* **Seachild**

Gere Publishing, *(978-0-9743995)* 113 Leonard Rd., Shutesbury, MA 01072-9783 USA (SAN 257-4594) Tel 413-259-1741
E-mail: claudia@claudiagereco.com
Web site: http://www.gerepublishing.com.

Gerhardt, Paul L., *(978-0-615-13556-4; 978-0-615-16208-9; 978-0-615-16270-6; 978-0-615-23707-7; 978-0-615-23721-3)* P.O. Box 111141, Tacoma, WA 98411 USA
Web site: http://www.paulgerhardt.com
Dist(s): **Lulu Enterprises Inc.**

Geringer, Laura Book *Imprint of* **HarperCollins Pubs.**

Gernand, Linda, *(978-0-9755025)* 523 Oyster Creek Dr., Richwood, TX 77531 USA.

Gersten, Dan & Associates LLC *See* **Dogwalk Pr.**

Gerstenblatt, Judith Furedi *See* **Lucky & Me Productions, Inc.**

Gestalt Pubns., *(978-0-9764065)* 3828 Clinton Ave. S., Minneapolis, MN 55409-1314 USA Tel 612-822-4419.

Gestalt Publishing Pty, Ltd. (AUS) *(978-0-9775628; 978-0-9807823; 978-1-922023) Dist. by* **D C D.**

Get Happy Tips, LLC, *(978-0-9860272)* 515 SW 18th Ave. No. 19, Fort Lauderdale, FL 33312 USA Tel 786-314-8199
E-mail: gethappytips@gmail.com
Web site: http://www.gethappytips.com.

Get Life Right Foundation, The *See* **Life Force Bks.**

Get Published, *(978-1-4501; 978-1-4525)* 1663 Liberty Dr., Bloomington, IN 47403 USA Tel 812-650-0913; Fax: 812-339-6554; Toll Free: 877-217-3420 Do not confuse with Get Published in Valparaiso, IN
E-mail: customersupport@dellartepress.com
Dist(s): **Author Solutions, Inc.**
CreateSpace Independent Publishing Platform.

Getting There, *(978-0-9707274)* P.O. Box 1412, Asheville, NC 28802-1412 USA Tel 828-645-5908
E-mail: bmayers@charter.net
Web site: http://www.paddlingasheville.com
Dist(s): **Common Ground Distributors, Inc.**

Getty, J. Paul Trust Publications *See* **Getty Pubns.**

†Getty Pubns., *(978-0-89236; 978-0-941103; 978-1-60606)* Orders Addr.: P.O. Box 49659, Los Angeles, CA 90049-0659 USA Tel 310-440-7333; Fax: 818-779-0051; Edit Addr.: 1200 Getty Ctr. Dr., Suite 500, Los Angeles, CA 90049-1682 USA (SAN 208-2276) Tel 310-440-7365; Fax: 310-440-7758; Toll Free: 800-223-3431; *Imprints:* J. Paul Getty Museum (J P Getty)
E-mail: pubsinfo@getty.edu; pubsinfo@getting.edu
Web site: http://www.getty.edu/publications
Dist(s): **Chicago Distribution Ctr.**
Lectorum Pubns., Inc.
Libros Sin Fronteras
Oxford Univ. Pr., Inc.; *CIP.*

GGMI Incorporated *See* **God's Glory Media**

Ghim, John Yun, *(978-0-9656864)* 1139 Queen Anne Pl. Apt. 106, Los Angeles, CA 90019-7105 USA
E-mail: coolghim@yahoo.com.

GHL Publishing LLC, *(978-0-9726419)* P.O. Box 26462, Collegeville, PA 19426 USA (SAN 254-9875) Tel 610-831-1442; Fax: 610-831-1443
E-mail: c.lagunilla@att.net
Web site: http://www.GHLPublishing.com.

Gholson, C. D., *(978-0-9725974)* 2341 W. Pierce, Harrison, MI 48625 USA Tel 898-539-5312
E-mail: goatlocker@msn.com.

Ghost Hse. Bks. *Imprint of* **Lone Pine Publishing USA**

Ghost Hunter Productions, *(978-0-9717234; 978-1-934307)* P.O. Box 1199, Helena, MT 59624 USA
E-mail: info@ibw-books.com
Web site: http://www.ibw-books.com.

G-Host Publishing, *(978-0-9649088)* Orders Addr.: 8701 Lava Pl., West Hills, CA 91304-2126 USA Tel 818-340-6676 (phone/fax)
E-mail: robanne@ix.netcom.com.

Giant in the Playground, *(978-0-9766580; 978-0-9854139)* 2417 Welsh Rd., Suite 21 No. 328, Philadelphia, PA 19114 USA
E-mail: rich@giantitp.com
Web site: http://www.giantitp.com
Dist(s): **Diamond Comic Distributors, Inc.**
Diamond Bk. Distributors.

Giant in the Playground Games *See* **Giant in the Playground**

Giant Robot Bks., *(978-0-9749492)* P.O. Box 641639, Los Angeles, CA 90064 USA Tel 310-479-7311
E-mail: books@giantrobot.com
Web site: http://www.giantrobot.com
Dist(s): **Trucatriche.**

†Gibbs Smith, Publisher, *(978-0-87905; 978-0-941711; 978-1-58685; 978-1-4236)* Orders Addr.: P.O. Box 667, Layton, UT 84041 USA (SAN 201-9906) Tel 801-544-9800; Fax: 801-544-5582; Toll Free Fax: 800-213-3023 (orders); Toll Free: 800-748-5439 (orders); 800-835-4993 (Customer Service order only); Edit Addr.: 1877 E. Gentile St., Layton, UT 84040 USA Tel 801-544-9800; Fax: 801-546-8853; *Imprints:* Anorak Press (Anorak Pr)
E-mail: info@gibbs-smith.com; tradeorders@gibbs-smith.com
Web site: http://www.gibbs-smith.com
Dist(s): **Perseus-PGW**
Publishers Group International, Inc.; *CIP.*

Gibson Bks. *Imprint of* **Glory Days Group Publishing**

Gibson, C. R. Co., *(978-0-7667; 978-0-8378; 978-0-937970)* 401 BNA Dr., Bldg 200, Suite 600, Nashville, TN 37217 USA Toll Free: 800-243-6004 (ext. 2895)
E-mail: customerservice@crgibson.com
Web site: http://www.andersonpress.com.

Gibson, Cita, *(978-0-9727964)* P.O. Box 411236, Melbourne, FL 32941 USA Tel 316-210-6422; Fax: 321-757-7385
E-mail: maloon57@aol.com
Web site: http://www.citagibson.com.

Gibson Tech Ed, Incorporated *See* **GSS Tech Ed**

Giddy Up, LLC, *(978-1-932125; 978-1-59524)* 3630 Plaza Dr., Ann Arbor, MI 48108 USA (SAN 255-6847)
E-mail: stiehl@giddyup.com
Web site: http://www.giddyup.com.

Gifted Education Pr., *(978-0-910609)* Orders Addr.: P.O. Box 1586, Manassas, VA 20108 USA; Edit Addr.: 10201 Yuma Ct., Manassas, VA 20109 USA (SAN 694-132X) Tel 703-369-5017; Toll Free: 800-484-1406 (code 6857)
E-mail: mfisher345@home.com
Web site: http://GIFTEDEDPRESS.COM.

Gigarjian, Ani & Linda Avedikian, *(978-0-9717799)* 169 S. Main St., Sherborn, MA 01770 USA
E-mail: gigarjian@comcast.net
Web site: http://www.armeniankids.com.

Giggletins *Imprint of* **Le Bk. Moderne, LLC**

Giggling Gorilla Productions, LLC, *(978-0-9770700)* 3444 Laredo Ln., Escondido, CA 92025-7807 USA
E-mail: zoomanmike@earthlink.net
Web site: http://www.gigglinggorillaproductions.com.

GiGi Bks., *(978-0-9740847)* 17480 Old Waterford Rd., Leesburg, VA 20176 USA Tel 703-669-9781; Fax: 703-669-9782
E-mail: ganderson@gigiaudiobooks.com
Web site: http://www.gigiaudiobooks.com.

Gigi Enterprises, *(978-0-615-12926-6)* P.O. Box 133, Irvington, NY 10533-0133 USA Fax: 914-591-9249
E-mail: sonia0904@aol.com.

GIL Pubns., *(978-0-9626035; 978-0-9802185; 978-0-615-75814-5)* P.O. Box 80275, Brooklyn, NY 11208 USA Fax: 718-386-6434
E-mail: kumasi@gilpublications.com
Web site: http://www.gilpublications.com
Dist(s): **A & B Distributors & Pubs. Group**
Bk. Hse., Inc., The.

Gilbert, Drexel Enterprises, Inc., *(978-0-9818464)* Orders Addr.: P.O. Box 364, Daphne, AL 36526 USA
E-mail: drexelgilbert@drexelgilbert.com
Web site: http://www.drexelgilbert.com.

Gilbert Square Bks., *(978-0-9745308)* 2115 Plymouth SE, Grand Rapids, MI 49506 USA Tel 616-245-1050
E-mail: kvidro2003@yahoo.com
Web site: http://www.squarepears.com.

Gilboy Publishing, *(978-0-9774696)* 3521 River Narrows Rd., Hilliard, OH 43026-7833 USA.

Gilchrist & Guy Publishing, *(978-0-9747990)* 2112 Colina Vista Way, Costa Mesa, CA 92627 USA
E-mail: rguy2112@comcast.net.

Gilded Dog Enterprises LLC, *(978-0-9793483)* 106 High Point Dr., Churchville, PA 18966 USA (SAN 853-1943) Tel 215-322-5592; Fax: 215-396-6832
Web site: http://gildeddog.com.

Gilder Lehrman Institute of American History, The, *(978-0-9663843; 978-1-932821)* Orders Addr.: 49 W. 45th St., 6th Flr., New York, NY 10036 USA Tel 646-366-9666; Fax: 646-366-9669
E-mail: ahlstrom@gilderlehrman.org
Web site: http://www.gilderlehrman.org.

Gile, John Communications *See* **JGC/United Publishing Corps**

Giles, D. Ltd. (GBR) *(978-1-904832; 978-1-907804) Dist. by* **Consort Bk Sales.**

Giles, W. Marie *See* **Giles, Willie M.**

Giles, Willie M., *(978-0-9728944)* Orders Addr.: P.O. Box 3757, Pensacola, FL 32516-3757 USA
Web site: http://www.wix.com/booksbywmariegiles
Dist(s): **CreateSpace Independent Publishing Platform.**

Gilgamesh Publishing (GBR) *(978-1-908531) Dist. by* **Consort Bk Sales.**

Gilgit Pr., LLC, *(978-0-9746283)* P.O. Box 4881, Richmond, VA 23220 USA
Web site: http://www.gilgitpress.com.

Gill & MacMillan, Ltd. (IRL) *(978-0-7171) Dist. by* **Dufour.**

Gill, Jim Music, *(978-0-9679038; 978-0-9815721)* Subs. of Jim Gill, Inc., Orders Addr.: P.O. Box 2263, Oak Park, IL 60303 USA Tel 708-763-9864; Fax: 708-763-9888; Edit Addr.: 835 N. Kenilworth Ave., Oak Park, IL 60303-9888 USA
E-mail: jimgill@jimgill.com
Web site: http://www.jimgill.com.

Gillette, Frances A., *(978-0-9636066)* P.O. Box 351, Yacolt, WA 98675 USA
E-mail: copia@copia.com; ward@infinitecolor.com; lithoinusa@centurytel.net
Web site: http://www.copia.com
Dist(s): **Adventure Pubns., Inc.**

Gilliam, T. & Associates, LLC, *(978-0-9762703)* 1696 Georgetown Rd., Unit B, Hudson, OH 44236 USA Tel 330-342-5940; Fax: 330-463-5730; Toll Free: 877-316-5097
E-mail: tgilliam@healthybodyweight.com
Web site: http://www.healthybodyweight.com.

Gilpatrick, Gil, *(978-0-9650507)* Orders Addr.: P.O. Box 461, Skowhegan, ME 04976 USA Tel 207-453-6959; Edit Addr.: 369 Middle Rd., Fairfield, ME 04937 USA
E-mail: gil@gilgilpatrick.com
Web site: http://www.gilgilpatrick.com.

Gimme Gimme Toys & Games, Inc., *(978-0-9762524)* 1418 N. Clinton Blvd., Bloomington, IL 61701 USA
Web site: http://www.gimmegimme.ca
Dist(s): **PSI (Publisher Services, Inc.).**

Gina's Ink, *(978-0-9740454)* P.O. Box 11650, Denver, CO 80211 USA
Web site: http://www.cassandrasangel.com.

Ginebra, Fidel, *(978-0-615-15410-7)* Urb. La Plata, M-19 Calle Rubi, Cayey, PR 00736 USA
E-mail: fbloodguard@gmail.com
Dist(s): **Lulu Enterprises Inc.**

Ginger Pr., The, *(978-0-9785151)* P.O. Box 45753, Omaha, NE 68145-0753 USA
Dist(s): **Greenleaf Book Group**
Independent Pubs. Group.

Gingerbread Hse., *(978-0-940112)* 602 Montauk Hwy., Westhampton Beach, NY 11978 USA (SAN 217-0760) Tel 631-288-5119; Fax: 631-288-5179 Do not confuse with Gingerbread House, The, Savannah GA
Web site: http://www.gingerbreadbooks.com
Dist(s): **Independent Pubs. Group.**

Gingko Pr., Inc., *(978-1-58423; 978-1-934471)* Orders Addr.: 1321 5th St., Berkeley, CA 94710-1307 USA (SAN 630-7418) Tel 510-898-1195; Fax: 510-898-1196 Do not confuse with Gingko Pr. in New York, NY
E-mail: rick@gingkopress.com
Web site: http://www.gingkopress.com
Dist(s): **MyiLibrary**
Perseus-PGW
Perseus Bks. Group.

Ginn, Don & Co., *(978-0-9755438)* 11228 Vista Sorrento Pkwy, Suite I-303, San Diego, CA 92130 USA Tel 859-720-8433; Fax: 858-720-8733; Toll Free: 888-357-7313
E-mail: donginn@sbcglobal.net.

GIP House *See* **Summit Hse. Pubs.**

Girasol Collectables Inc., *(978-0-9797639; 978-0-9820890; 978-0-9820891; 978-0-9854755)* P.O. Box 5289, Mansfield, OH 44901-5289 USA
Web site: http://www.girasolcollectables.com.

Girl Named Pants, Inc., A, *(978-0-9755959)* 8954 Stonebriar Dr., Clarence Ctr., NY 14032-9373 USA
Web site: http://www.agirlnamedpants.com.

Girl Pr., Inc., *(978-0-9659754)* P.O. Box 480389, Los Angeles, CA 90048-1389 USA
E-mail: gp@girlpress.com
Web site: http://www.girlpress.com.

Girl Scouts of the USA, *(978-0-88441)* 420 Fifth Ave., New York, NY 10018 USA (SAN 203-4611) Tel 212-852-8000; Fax: 212-852-6511
E-mail: bnelson@girlscouts.org
Web site: http://www.girlscouts.org/.

Girl Twirl Comics, *(978-0-9742450; 978-0-9766707; 978-0-9794207)* Orders Addr.: P.O. Box 88, Sebastopol, CA 95473 USA Tel 707-546-7121 Do not confuse with Jane's World in Seattle, WA
Web site: http://www.janecomics.com
Dist(s): **Diamond Comic Distributors, Inc.**
Diamond Bk. Distributors.

Girls Explore *Imprint of* **Girls Explore LLC**

Girls Explore LLC, *(978-0-9749456)* Orders Addr.: P.O. Box 54, Basking Ridge, NJ 07920 USA (SAN 256-2677) Fax: 908-842-9166; *Imprints:* Girls Explore (GilExplore)
Web site: http://www.girls-explore.com
Dist(s): **Brodart Co.**

Girls In Da Game Publishing, *(978-0-9674454)* Orders Addr.: 5916 Las Virgenes Rd. No. 596, Calabasas, CA 91302 USA
E-mail: corneliagailgroundup@gmail.com
Web site: http://www.facebookthenewlook.com
Dist(s): **Lightning Source, Inc.**

GIRLS KNOW HOW *Imprint of* **NouSoma Communications, Inc.**

Girls of Faith, *(978-0-9764304)* P.O. Box 535, Rogersville, MO 65742 USA
E-mail: orders@girlsoffaith.com
Web site: http://www.girlsoffaith.com.

Giro Pr., *(978-1-878857)* Orders Addr.: P.O. Box 203, Croton-on-Hudson, NY 10520 USA Tel 914-271-8924; Fax: 914-271-6552; Edit Addr.: 44 Morningside Dr., Croton-on-Hudson, NY 10520 USA
E-mail: info@giropress.com
Web site: http://www.giropress.com.

Giron Bks., *(978-0-9741393; 978-0-9915442)* 2141 W. 21st St., Chicago, IL 60608-2608 USA Tel 773-847-3000; Fax: 773-847-9197; Toll Free: 800-405-4276
E-mail: juanmanuel@gironbooks.com
Web site: http://www.gironbooks.com.

Gish Creative, *(978-0-9728507; 978-0-615-74202-1)* 1940-A Fountainview, PMB 116, Houston, TX 77057 USA Tel 713-532-1173 (phone/fax)
Web site: http://www.gishcreative.com; http://www.thesummerbook.com.

Giunti Gruppo Editoriale (ITA) *(978-88-09; 978-88-507; 978-88-440) Dist. by* **Distribks Inc.**

Giusti-Gambini, J.M. Publishing, LLC, *(978-0-615-36873-3; 978-0-9829496)* 7259 Creeks Bend Ct., West Bloomfield, MI 48322 USA Tel 248-855-0869
E-mail: jogambini@comcast.net
Web site: http://www.poetino.com; http://www.jmgiusti-gambinipublishing.com.

Gival Pr., LLC, *(978-1-928589; 978-1-940724)* P.O. Box PO Box 3812, Arlington, VA 22203 USA (SAN 852-9787) Tel 703-351-0079 (phone)
E-mail: givalpress@yahoo.com
Web site: http://www.givalpress.com; http://www.givalpressstore.com
Dist(s): **CreateSpace Independent Publishing Platform**
Ediciones Universal
Follett School Solutions.

Givens, Florence Rosie *See* **FloBound Poems Publications**

Givinity Pr., *(978-0-9728654; 978-1-943803)* 3374 Maplewood Ct., Fargo, ND 58104-6224 USA (SAN 255-1527) Tel 701-235-4241; Fax: 701-280-2016; Toll Free: 866-221-5860
E-mail: ellen@givinity.com
Web site: http://www.givinity.com
Dist(s): **Brodart Co.**
Follett School Solutions.

Gizicki-Lipson, Coryn *See* **In the Sky Publishing**

Gizmo Enterprises, Inc., *(978-0-9759638)* Orders Addr.: 6511 Nova Driver No. 108, Davie, FL 33317 USA
E-mail: perry@colorcutter.com
Web site: http://www.colorcutter.com; http://www.gizmoLine.com.

Gizmo Pr., *(978-0-9749911)* 6990 Poco Bueno Cir., Sparks, NV 89436 USA Tel 775-626-4533; Fax: 775-425-5290
E-mail: mjarcher@aol.com; greg.nielsen@charter.net.

GL Design, *(978-0-9745882; 978-1-933983)* 1930 Central Ave. Unit E., Boulder, CO 80301 USA
E-mail: distrib@gldesignpub.com
Web site: http://www.gldesignpub.com
Dist(s): **Lightning Source, Inc.**

Gladstone Publishing, *(978-1-928681)* Do not confuse with Gladstone Publishing, Prescott, AZ
E-mail: dmsmart@onesmartladyproductions.com
Web site: http://www.gladstonepublishing.com; http://www.onesmartladyproductions.org
Dist(s): **BookBaby.**

Glass, Michael B. & Assocs., Inc., *(978-0-940429)* 735 Calebs Path/Glaro Bldg., Hauppauge, NY 11788 USA (SAN 664-3574).

†Glastonbury Pr., *(978-0-944963)* Orders Addr.: 454 Las Gallinas Ave., No. 108, San Rafael, CA 94903 USA Tel 415-492-2140; 415-686-4150 Do not confuse with Glastonbury Pr., Whittier, CA
E-mail: starstone@comcast.net; misty@glastonburypress.com
Web site: http://www.glastonburypress.com
Dist(s): **CreateSpace Independent Publishing Platform**; *CIP.*

Glavin, Kevin, *(978-0-9825466)* 23 Vassar Aisle, Irvine, CA 92612 USA
E-mail: admin@kevinglavinpublishing.com
Web site: http://www.rockstarsrainbow.com; http://www.kevinglavinpublishing.com.

Gleasner, Bill & Diana Inc., *(978-0-9651185)* 7994 Holly Ct., Denver, NC 28037 USA Tel 704-483-9301; Fax: 704-483-6309
E-mail: dgleasner@aol.com
Dist(s): **Booklines Hawaii, Ltd.**

Glenbridge Publishing, Ltd., *(978-0-944435)* 19923 E. Long Ave., Centennial, CO 80016 USA (SAN 243-5403) Tel 720-870-8381; Fax: 720-230-1209; Toll Free: 800-986-4135 (orders only)
E-mail: glenbridge@qwestoffice.net
Web site: http://www.glenbridgepublishing.com.

Glencannon Pr., *(978-0-9637586; 978-1-889901)* Orders Addr.: P.O. Box 1428, El Cerrito, CA 94530 USA; *Imprints:* Palo Alto Books (Palo Alto)
E-mail: merships@yahoo.com
Web site: http://www.glencannon.com.

†**Glencoe/McGraw-Hill,** *(978-0-02; 978-0-07)* Div. of The McGraw-Hill Education Group, 8787 Orion Pl., Columbus, OH 43240-4027 USA Toll Free: 800-334-7344
E-mail: customer.service@mcgraw-hill.com
Web site: http://www.glencoe.com
Dist(s): **Follett School Solutions**
Libros Sin Fronteras
McGraw-Hill Cos., The; *CIP.*

Glenhaven Pr., *(978-0-9637265; 978-0-9741279)* 24871 Pylos Way, Mission Viejo, CA 92691 USA Tel 949-770-1486
E-mail: glenhavn@thevision.net; jacki@hydrasystems.com
Dist(s): **J & J Bk. Sales.**

Glenmere Pr., *(978-0-9852948; 978-0-9903139)* Orders Addr.: 26 Kings Ridge Rd., Warwick, NY 10990 USA
E-mail: lois@glenmerepress.com; lois@wingedbooks.com
Web site: http://www.glenmerepress.com; http://www.wingedbooks.com
Dist(s): **CreateSpace Independent Publishing Platform**
INscribe Digital
Lightning Source, Inc.

Glenn, Lauren, *(978-0-9772459)* 2436 Oakdale St., Tallahassee, FL 32308 USA.

Glenn, Peter Pubns., *(978-0-87314)* 824 E. Atlantic Ave. Ste. 7, Delray Beach, FL 33483-5300 USA (SAN 201-9930)
E-mail: gjames@pgdirect.com
Web site: http://www.pgdirect.com.

Glenneyre Pr. LLC, *(978-0-9768040; 978-1-934602)* 20555 Devonshire St., Box 203, Chatsworth, CA 91311-9133 USA
E-mail: myn@wordsushi.com
Web site: http://www.glenneyrepress.com.

Glens Falls Printing LLC, *(978-1-933575)* 51 Hudson Ave., Glens Falls, NY 12801 USA (SAN 256-7148) Tel 518-793-0555; Fax: 518-793-8624; Toll Free: 866-793-0555
E-mail: bob@gfprinting.com
Web site: http://www.gfprinting.com; http://www.spiritoftheadirondacksbook.com; http://www.commonmanbooks.com.

Glitter & Razz Productions LLC, *(978-0-615-77472-5)* P.O. Box 22932, Oakland, CA 94609 USA Tel 510-550-5340
Web site: www.glitterandrazz.com
Dist(s): **CreateSpace Independent Publishing Platform.**

Glitter Creek, Inc., *(978-0-9744520)* 2919 Westridge Ave., Cincinnati, OH 45238 USA Toll Free: 888-982-7335
Web site: http://www.glittercreek.com.

Glitterati, Inc., *(978-0-9721152; 978-0-9765851; 978-0-9777531; 978-0-9793384; 978-0-9801557; 978-0-9822669; 978-0-9823412; 978-0-9823799; 978-0-9832702; 978-0-9851696; 978-0-9881745; 978-0-9891704; 978-0-9913419; 978-0-9903808; 978-0-9905320; 978-0-9862500; 978-0-9962930; 978-1-943876)* 322 W. 57th St. No. 19T, New York, NY 10019 USA Tel 212-362-9119; Fax: 646-607-4433
E-mail: jguerrero@glitteratiincorporated.com
Web site: http://www.glitteratiincorporated.com
Dist(s): **National Bk. Network.**

GLMP Ltd. (GBR) *(978-1-84285)* *Dist. by* **Chicago Distribution Ctr.**

Global Academic Publishing, *(978-0-9633277; 978-1-883058; 978-1-58684)* Global Academic Publishing, Binghamton Univ., Binghamton, NY 13902-6000 USA Tel 607-777-4495; 607-777-2745 (contact Barnes & Noble for orders); Fax: 607-777-6132
E-mail: gporders@binghamton.edu
Web site: http://www.academicpublishing.binghamton.edu
Dist(s): **Hesteria Records & Publishing Co.**
State Univ. of New York Pr.

Global Age Publishing/Global Academy Pr., *(978-1-887176)* 16057 Tampa Palms Blvd., W., No. 219, Tampa, FL 33647 USA Tel 813-991-4982; Fax: 813-973-8166.

Global Alliances, *(978-0-9759126)* 82-09 166th St., Hillcrest, NY 11432 USA.

Global Authors Pubns., *(978-0-9728513; 978-0-9742161; 978-0-9766449; 978-0-9779680; 978-0-9798087; 978-0-9821223; 978-0-9845926; 978-0-9846536; 978-0-9861109)* P.O. Box 954, Green Cove Springs, FL 32043 USA; 730 Donnelly St., Eustis, FL 32726 Tel 904-425-1608
E-mail: gapbook@yahoo.com
Web site: http://www.globalauthorspublications.com.

Global Awareness Publishing Co., *(978-1-885888)* 1102 Hickory St., Madison, WI 53715-1726 USA.

Global Business Information Strategies, Inc., *(978-1-60231)* Orders Addr.: P.O. Box 610135, Newton, MA 02461 USA (SAN 852-1980) Tel 617-795-0519; Fax: 617-795-0211; Edit Addr.: 965 Walnut St., Suite 100, Newton, MA 02461 USA; *Imprints:* Cub Books (Cub Bks)
E-mail: publishing@gbisi.com
Web site: http://gbisi.com
Dist(s): **AtlasBooks Distribution.**

Global Commitment Publishing, *(978-1-884931)* Div. of Alpert & Assocs., 3544 Winfield Ln., NW, Washington, DC 20007 USA Tel 202-338-4975; Fax: 202-835-0668; 5505 Connecticut Ave., Washington, DC 20015.

Global Communications *See* **Inner Light - Global Communications**

Global Connections *Imprint of* **Compass Point Bks.**

Global Content Ventures, *(978-0-9799901)* P.O. Box 6370, Lancaster, PA 17607 USA.

Global Education Advance, *(978-0-9796019; 978-0-9801674; 978-1-935434)* 345 Barton Rd. at Lone Mountain, Dayton, TN 37321-7635 USA Tel 423-775-2949
E-mail: GlobalEdAdvance@aol.com
Web site: http://www.globaledadvance.org.

Global Education Resources, LLC, *(978-1-934046)* 37 Station Rd., Madison, NJ 07940 USA (SAN 851-1012) Tel 973-410-0840; Fax: 973-410-1603
E-mail: myoshida@globaledresources.com
Web site: http://www.globaledresources.com.

Global Institute for Maximizing Potential, Incorporated, *(978-0-9772020; 978-0-9825776; 978-0-9830337)* 92 Mt. Zion Way, Ocean Grove, NJ 07756 USA Tel 732-776-7360
E-mail: richert@globalinst.com
Web site: http://www.globalinst.com.

Global Learning, Inc., *(978-1-59867)* 1001 SE Water Ave., Suite 310, Portland, OR 97214 USA Toll Free: 888-548-2787 Do not confuse with Global Learning Inc. in Brielle, NJ
Web site: http://www.litart.com.

Global Partnership, LLC, *(978-0-9644706)* Orders Addr.: P.O. Box 894, Murray, KY 42071 USA (SAN 255-4186) Tel 562-884-0062; Edit Addr.: 100 N. 6th St., Murray, KY 42071 USA
E-mail: steveneschmitt@cs.com; erin@wakeuplive.com
Web site: http://www.businessolympians.com
Dist(s): **Seven Locks Pr.**

Global Pr., *(978-0-9792151)* 2083 Ridge Point Dr., Los Angeles, CA 90049 USA Tel 310-476-8336.

Global Publications (S S I P S) *See* **Global Academic Publishing**

Global Publishing, *(978-0-911649)* 51 Bell Rock Plaza, Suite A, PMB 511, Sedona, AZ 86351 USA (SAN 299-3627) Tel 928-284-5544; Fax: 928-284-5545 Do not confuse with companies with the same or similar name in Meimingham, MI, Costa Mesa, CA, Las Angeles, CA, Florence, MA, Memphis, TN, Sauk Rapids, MN, Fort Lauderdale, FL, Fort Worth, TX, Salt Lake City, UT
E-mail: minorwood@earthlink.net
Web site: http://www.wealthysoul.com
Dist(s): **New Leaf Distributing Co., Inc.**

Global Truth Publishing, *(978-0-9740465)* Orders Addr.: 1001 Bridgeway, Suite 474, Sausalito, CA 94965 USA Tel 415-331-1102; Fax: 415-331-2265
E-mail: sales@globaltruthpublishing.com
Web site: http://www.globaltruthpublishing.com.

Global Village Kids, LLC, *(978-0-9760472)* 4111 Calavo Dr., La Mesa, CA 91941-7051 USA Tel 619-303-0929; Fax: 925-888-8471
E-mail: seth.burns@globalvillagekids.com
Web site: http://www.globalvillagekids.com
Dist(s): **AV Cafe, Inc., The**
BWI
Iaconi, Mariuccia Bk. Imports
Wayland Audio-Visual.

GlobalVision Travel Resources, Inc., *(978-0-9800147)* 4831 Las Virgenes Rd., No. 115, Calabasas, CA 91302-1911 USA
E-mail: LCohen@getglobalvision.com
Web site: http://getglobalvision.com.

Globe Fearon Educational Publishing, *(978-0-13; 978-0-8224; 978-0-8359; 978-0-87065; 978-0-88102; 978-0-912925; 978-0-915510; 978-1-55555; 978-1-55675)* Div. of Pearson Education Corporate Communications, Orders Addr.: 4350 Equity Dr., P.O. Box 2649, Columbus, OH 43216-2649 USA Toll Free Fax: 800-393-3156; Toll Free: 800-848-9500; 800-321-3106 (customer service); Edit Addr.: One Lake St., Upper Saddle River, NJ 07458 USA
Web site: http://www.pearsonschool.com
Dist(s): **Cambridge Bk. Co.**
Follett School Solutions
IFSTA.

†**Globe Pequot Pr., The,** *(978-0-7627; 978-0-87106; 978-0-88742; 978-0-914788; 978-0-933469; 978-0-934802; 978-0-941130; 978-1-56440; 978-1-57034; 978-1-58574; 978-1-59228; 978-1-59921; 978-1-4779; 978-1-4930)* Orders Addr.: P.O. Box 480, Guilford, CT 06437-0480 USA (SAN 201-9892) Tel 888-249-7586; Toll Free Fax: 800-820-2329 (in Connecticut); Toll Free: 800-243-0495 (24 hours); 800-336-8334; Edit Addr.: 246 Goose Ln., Guilford, CT 06437 USA Tel 203-458-4500; Fax: 203-458-4600; Toll Free Fax: 800-336-8334; *Imprints:* Lyons Press (Lyons); Falcon Guides (Fal-Guides); TwoDot (Two-D)
E-mail: info@globepequot.com
Web site: http://www.globepequot.com
Dist(s): **Chelsea Green Publishing**
MyiLibrary
National Bk. Network
Rowman & Littlefield Publishers, Inc.; *CIP.*

Globe Pubs., *(978-0-9623663; 978-1-882614)* 724 Fair Meadows Dr., Saginaw, TX 76179-1017 USA.

Globe Publishing, *(978-0-9765168)* Orders Addr.: P.O. Box 3040, Pensacola, FL 32516-3040 USA Tel 850-453-3453; Fax: 850-456-6001; Edit Addr.: 8590 Hwy 98 W., Pensacola, FL 32506 USA Do not confuse with Globe Publishing in Salt Lake City, UT
Web site: http://www.gme.org.

Globo, Editora SA (BRA) *(978-85-217; 978-85-250)* *Dist. by* **Distribks Inc.**

Globo Libros, *(978-0-9706953)* Orders Addr.: P.O. Box 4025, Sunnyside, NY 11104 USA; Edit Addr.: 402 E. 64th St. Apt. 6C, New York, NY 10021-7826 USA
E-mail: dstockwell@globolibros.com
Web site: http://www.globolibros.com.

Glolar Multimedia Productions, *(978-0-9707746)* P.O. Box 721452, San Diego, CA 92172-1452 USA
E-mail: info@Glolar.com; info@glolar.com
Web site: http://www.glolar.com.

Glory Be Collectibles, *(978-0-9795127; 978-0-578-06528-1; 978-0-578-07491-7)* 2169 Green Canyon Rd., Fallbrook, CA 92028 USA (SAN 853-6627) Tel 760-723-5222; Fax: 760-723-4433
E-mail: sales@glorybe.com
Web site: http://www.glorybe.com.

Glory Bound Books Las Vegas *See* **Glorybound Publishing**

Glory Days Group Publishing, *(978-0-9755145)* P.O. Box 1869, Glen Burnie, MD 21060-1869 USA Tel 410-766-0005 (phone/fax); *Imprints:* Gibson Books (Gibson Bks)
E-mail: drgibson123@yahoo.com
Web site: http://www.glorydayspublishing2day4u.com.

Glorybound Publishing, *(978-0-9766718; 978-0-9779654; 978-0-9802481; 978-1-60789)* 6401 E. 2nd St. #f, Prescott Valley, AZ 86314 USA (SAN 256-4564) Do not confuse with Glory Bound Books in Marlette, MI
E-mail: sherihauser@yahoo.com; gloryboundpublishing@yahoo.com
Web site: http://www.gloryboundpublishing.com.

Glowacki, Helen, *(978-0-9847211; 978-0-9890214; 978-0-9893807; 978-0-9913916)* 401 Lake Shore Dr. No. 802, Lake Park, FL 33403 USA Tel 561-845-8493
E-mail: wally_helen@yahoo.com
Web site: www.helenglowacki.com.

Glynworks Publishing, *(978-0-9795912)* 2630 International Dr. #929b, Ypsilanti, MI 48197 USA
Web site: http://www.glynworkspublishing.com
Dist(s): **Lightning Source, Inc.**

GMC Distribution (GBR) *(978-0-946819; 978-1-86108)* *Dist. by* **IngramPubServ.**

GMI Bks., *(978-0-9841809)* 7250 Franklin Ave., No.1407, Hollywood, CA 90046 USA
E-mail: richard@thegirlfromatlantis.com; doubleosix@aol.com
Web site: http://www.thegirlfromatlantis.com.

Gnatcatcher Children'S Bks., *(978-0-9778005)* 1451 E. Armando Dr., Long Beach, CA 90807 USA Tel 562-427-1200
E-mail: maryhoch@excite.com.

GND Publishing *See* **Y-IREAD Publishing**

Gnomon Pr., *(978-0-917788)* P.O. Box 475, Frankfort, KY 40602-0475 USA (SAN 209-0104) Tel 502-223-1858 (phone/fax)
E-mail: jgnomon@aol.com
Dist(s): **SPD-Small Pr. Distribution.**

Gnosophia Pubs., *(978-0-9773391)* 3800 New Hampshire Ave. NW Apt 507, Washington, DC 20011-7932 USA (SAN 257-3210) Tel 202-709-7580; Toll Free Fax: 866-525-0247
E-mail: admin@wisdomforthesoul.org; info@wisdomforthesoul.org; admin@gnosophia.com
Web site: http://www.wisdomforthesoul.org; http://www.gnosophia.com.

Go Ask Anyone, Inc., *(978-0-9742866)* 38 Irwin St., No.3, Winthrop, MA 02152 USA
Web site: http://www.goaskanyone.com.

Go Daddy Productions, Inc., *(978-0-9753938)* 2010 Ripley Point Ct., Odenton, MD 21113 USA Tel 443-226-4747
E-mail: mejagan@yahoo.com
Web site: http://www.go-daddyproductions.com.

Go Flag Football, *(978-0-9772203)* 1978 Shiloh Valley Trail, Kennesaw, GA 30144 USA
Web site: http://www.goflagfootball.com.

Go! Go! Sports Girls *Imprint of* **Dream Big Toy Co.**

Go Team, LLC, *(978-0-9797040)* 1427 Heatherwood Rd., Columbia, SC 29205 USA (SAN 854-1566)
E-mail: deliacorrigan@mindspring.com
Web site: http://www.goteambooks.com.

Goals Unlimited Pr., *(978-0-9632562)* Div. of Equestrian Education Systems, P.O. Box 460125, Huson, MT 59846 USA Tel 406-626-5764; Fax: 406-626-5774
E-mail: jhascoop@aol.com
Web site: http://www.equestrianeducation.org
Dist(s): **Mountain Pr. Publishing Co., Inc.**
Western International, Inc.

Goatee Graphics, *(978-0-9657257)* P.O. Box 591840, San Francisco, CA 94159-1840 USA (SAN 256-8985) Tel 415-272-6117
E-mail: goatee848@yahoo.com
Web site: http://www.undertherimbook.com
Dist(s): **AtlasBooks Distribution.**

Goblin Fern Pr. *Imprint of* **HenschelHAUS Publishing**

†**Godine, David R. Pub.,** *(978-0-87923; 978-1-56792; 978-1-57423)* Orders Addr.: P.O. Box 450, Jaffrey, NH 03452 USA Tel 603-532-4100; Fax: 603-532-5940; Toll Free Fax: 800-226-0934; Toll Free: 800-344-4771; Edit Addr.: Fifteen Court Sq., Suite 320, Boston, MA 02108 USA (SAN 213-4381) Tel 617-451-9600; Fax: 617-350-0250
E-mail: info@godine.com; order@godine.com
Web site: http://www.godine.com
Dist(s): **Baker & Taylor International**
INscribe Digital
MyiLibrary
eBookit.com; *CIP.*

Godinez-Hammermaster Design, *(978-0-9773205)* 122 Eugenia Dr., Ventura, CA 93003 USA (SAN 257-7127)
E-mail: artposter@sbcglobal.net.

Godiva Girl Records & Publishing, Incorporated *See* **Girls In Da Game Publishing**

God's Bible School & College *See* **Revivalist Pr., The**

God's Glory Media, *(978-0-9772647)* Div. of God'sGloy Ministries International Inc., P.O. Box 1430, Dacula, GA 30019 USA (SAN 257-1528)
E-mail: office@godsglory.org
Web site: http://www.GodsGlory.org.

God's Greatest Gift, LLC, *(978-0-9796477)* Orders Addr.: P.O. Box 185, Manchester, MI 48158-8513 USA (SAN 853-9855) Tel 734-320-5111; Edit Addr.: 520 City Rd., Manchester, MI 48158-8513 USA Fax: 734-428-0084
E-mail: godsgreatestgift@comcast.net
Web site: http://www.godsgreatestgift.net
Dist(s): **Partners Pubs. Group, Inc.**

God's World Publications *See* **God's World Pubns. Inc.**

God's World Pubns. Inc., *(978-1-882440; 978-0-9844605; 978-0-9855957)* 12 All Souls Crescent, Asheville, NC 28803 USA (SAN 254-1696) Tel 828-253-8063; Fax: 828-253-1556
E-mail: edufeedback@ gwpub.com; pub@gwnews.com
Web site: http://www.learnwithworld.com/writewithworld/.

Godspeed Pr., *(978-0-9798250)* 430 Davis Dr., Suite 270, Morrisville, NC 27560 USA Tel 404-457-4097
E-mail: deanthewriter@gmail.com.

GoGo Pr., *(978-0-9769028)* Orders Addr.: 6007 Hickory Valley Rd., Nashville, TN 37205 USA (SAN 257-1412) Tel 615-356-6571; Fax: 615-356-9609
E-mail: info@gogopress.com; paul@pbuff.com
Web site: http://www.gogopress.com
Dist(s): **AtlasBooks Distribution.**

Goin' Native, Inc., *(978-0-9891323)* P.O. Box 617153, Orlando, FL 32861 USA Tel 407-897-3522; Fax: 407-896-4614
E-mail: info@goinnative.com.

Going Natural, Inc.,
Dist(s): **Independent Pubs. Group.**

GoKnow, Incorporated *See* **GoKnow Learning**

GoKnow Learning, *(978-0-9762083; 978-0-9767504; 978-0-9786499)* 2084 S. State St., Ann Arbor, MI 48104-4608 USA Toll Free: 877-482-3439
Web site: http://www.goknow.com.

Golan, Hanna, *(978-0-9779723)* 17340 Hamlin St., Lake Balboa, CA 91406 USA (SAN 850-7732) Tel 818-342-4969
E-mail: hannagolan2000@yahoo.com
Web site: http://blessthechildren.com.

GO-LA-NV Pr., *(978-0-9741828)* P.O. Box 1897, Huntsville, TX 77342-1897 USA Tel 936-291-2906
E-mail: rhvann@sbcglobal.net.

Gold Angel Press *See* **ONLY1EARTH, LLC**

Gold Boy Music & Pubn., *(978-0-9761992)* 230 Red Oak Trail, Spring Hill, TN 37174 USA (SAN 256-2499) Tel 615-584-2695
E-mail: robwesterman@bellsouth.net
Web site: http://www.stardancermusic.com
Dist(s): **Booklines Hawaii, Ltd.**

Gold Boy Music & Publishing *See* **Gold Boy Music & Pubn.**

Gold Charm Publishing, LLC, *(978-0-9744855)* Orders Addr.: P.O. Box 161, Nottingham, NH 03290 USA Tel 603-942-7925 (phone/fax); Edit Addr.: 82 Priest Rd., Nottingham, NH 03290 USA.

Gold Design, LLC *See* **Toy Rocket Studios, LLC**

Gold Leaf Pr., *(978-1-886769)* Orders Addr.: 2229 Alter Rd., Detroit, MI 48215 USA Tel 313-331-3571; 262-342-0018 Oleand Publications; Fax: 313-308-3063; 262-342-0018 Oleand Publications; Toll Free: 800-838-8854 Do not confuse with companies with the same name in Seattle, WA, Starke FL
E-mail: rebecca@goldleafpress.com; wings@oleand.com
Web site: http://www.goldleafpress.com; http://www.oleand.com
Dist(s): **Oleand Pubns.**

Gold Medallion *Imprint of* **Medallion Pr., Inc.**

Gold Street Pr., *(978-1-934533)* 814 Montgomery St., San Francisco, CA 94133 USA Tel 415-291-0100; Fax: 415-291-8841
E-mail: michelledl@weldonowen.com
Web site: http://www.weldonowen.com; http://www.goldstreetpress.com.

Golden Anchor Pr., *(978-1-886864)* 625 Elrod Rd., Bowling Green, KY 42104 USA Tel 270-780-9334
E-mail: smithdale2@aol.com; goldnanchr@aol.com
Web site: http://www.Everykidawinner.com
Dist(s): **Partners/West Book Distributors**
Quality Bks., Inc.
Unique Bks., Inc.

Golden Bks. *Imprint of* **Random Hse. Children's Bks.**

Golden Bks. *Imprint of* **Random Hse., Inc.**

Golden Bks. Adult Publishing Group *Imprint of* **St. Martin's Pr.**

Golden, Brian *See* **PastWays Inc.**

Golden Eagle Publishing Hse., Inc., *(978-0-9744205; 978-0-9753533; 978-0-9759122; 978-0-9769364)* 9201 Wilshire Blvd., Suite 205, Beverly Hills, CA 90210 USA Tel 310-273-9176; Fax: 310-273-0954
E-mail: info@goldeneaglepublishing.com
Web site: http://www.goldeneaglepublishing.com
Dist(s): **AtlasBooks Distribution**
Greenleaf Book Group.

Golden Gryphon Pr., *(978-0-9655901; 978-1-930846)* 3002 Perkins Rd., Urbana, IL 61802 USA (SAN 299-1829) Tel 217-384-4205 (phone/fax); Fax: 217-352-9748
E-mail: Gryphon@goldengryphon.com
Web site: http://www.goldengryphon.com
Dist(s): **Independent Pubs. Group**
MyiLibrary
ebrary, Inc.

Golden Guides from Saint Martin's Pr. *Imprint of* **St. Martin's Pr.**

Golden Harvest Publishing Co., (*978-0-9747904*) 4849 Valley Rd., Rosedale, VA 24280 USA Tel 276-880-9862; Fax: 276-880-1146
E-mail: adda@mounet.com.

Golden Inspirational *Imprint of* **Random Hse. Children's Bks.**

Golden Mastermind Seminars, Inc., (*978-0-9740924; 978-1-934919; 978-0-692-03130-8*) Orders Addr.: 6507 Pacific Ave., Suite 329, Stockton, CA 95207 USA (SAN 255-2639) Fax: 209-467-3260; Toll Free: 800-595-6632
E-mail: erica@goldenmastermind.com
Web site: http://www.goldenmastermind.com
Dist(s): **AtlasBooks Distribution.**

Golden Monkey Publishing, LLC, (*978-0-9719632*) 24 Meadowood Ln., Old Saybrook, CT 06475 USA (SAN 254-5322)
Web site: http://www.goldenmonkeypublishing.com.

Golden Oak Publishers *See* **Golden Oak Pubs. L.P.**

Golden Oak Pubs. L.P., (*978-1-929248; 978-1-936346*) Orders Addr.: P.O. Box 136967, Fort Worth, TX 76163 USA Tel 800-479-3545; Toll Free Fax: 800-479-3545
E-mail: MattS@goldenoakpublishers.com
Web site: http://www.HaroldBullock.com.

Golden Peach Publishing, (*978-1-930655*) 1223 Wilshire Blvd., #1510, Santa Monica, CA 90403 USA Tel 310-623-0835; 310-272-6809
E-mail: marketing@goldenpeachbooks.com; info@goldenpeachbooks.com; goldenpeachbooks@gmail.com
Web site: http://goldenpeachbooks.com.

Golden Perils Pr., (*978-0-615-15007-9; 978-0-615-19452-3; 978-0-578-00320-7; 978-0-578-00360-3; 978-0-578-00361-0*) 2 McKee Dr., Old Orchard Beach, ME 04064 USA Tel 207-934-3074
E-mail: goldenperils@aol.com
Web site: http://www.howardhopkins.com
Dist(s): **Lulu Enterprises Inc.**

Golden Rain Tree Pr., (*978-0-9744107*) Div. of Leland Foerster Photography, 307 Fowles St., Oceanside, CA 92054 USA Tel 760-433-2554 (phone/fax)
E-mail: lelandfoerster@sbcglobal.net
Web site: http://www.lelandfoerster.com
Dist(s): **Sunbelt Pubns., Inc.**

Golden Valley Pr., (*978-0-9718053*) 24905 Mica Ridge Rd., Custer, SD 57730 USA
E-mail: horsted@dakotaphoto.com
Web site: http://www.goldenvalleypress.com.

Golden Voice Enterprises, (*978-0-9643301*) 8503 Summerdale Rd., No. 371, San Diego, CA 92126 USA.

Golden West Publishers *Imprint of* **American Traveler Pr.**

Golden Wings Enterprises, (*978-0-9700103; 978-0-9749241; 978-0-9794340*) P.O. Box 468, Orem, UT 84059-0468 USA
E-mail: BJ@bjrowley.com
Web site: http://www.bjrowley.com.

Golden/Disney *Imprint of* **Random Hse. Children's Bks.**

Goldenrod Pr., (*978-0-9748333*) Orders Addr.: P.O. Box 71, Algona, IA 50511 USA Tel 515-295-7090; Edit Addr.: 2509 S. State St., Algona, IA 50511-7296 USA
E-mail: slotjm@yahoo.com.

Goldleaf Games, LLC, (*978-0-9748757*) P.O. Box 804, Lawrence, KS 66044 USA
E-mail: gary@goldleafgames.com
Web site: http://www.goldleafgames.com.

Goldmann, Wilhelm Verlag GmbH (DEU) (*978-3-442*) *Dist. by* **Distribks Inc.**

Goldner, Harriet LLC, (*978-0-9779676*) P.O. Box 480003, Delray Beach, FL 33448 USA
E-mail: hgoldnerbooks@bellsouth.net
Web site: http://www.JewishFamilyFun.com.

Goldsberry, Booty, (*978-0-9792875*) 10 Windsor Pl., Poland, ME 04274 USA Tel 207-998-5710
E-mail: elattanzi@bookmasters.com.

Goldwrite Publishing, (*978-0-9767933; 978-0-615-13858-9*) 1224 Gallatin Ct., Hampton, GA 30228 USA Tel 678 510-6941
E-mail: asheagold@yahoo.com
Dist(s): **BookBaby**
Lulu Enterprises Inc.

Gom Foxtail *Imprint of* **Gom Publishing, LLC**

Gom Publishing, LLC, (*978-0-9729197; 978-1-932966*) P.O. Box 211110, Columbus, OH 43221 USA (SAN 255-3988) Tel 614-876-7097; Toll Free Fax: 866-422-8292; Toll Free: 866-466-2608; *Imprints:* Gom Foxtail (Gom Foxtail)
E-mail: sfox@gompublishing.com
Web site: http://www.gompublishing.com
Dist(s): **AtlasBooks Distribution.**

Gomer Pr. (GBR) (*978-0-85088; 978-0-86383; 978-1-85902; 978-1-84323; 978-1-84851*) *Dist. by* **IPG Chicago.**

Gonzalez, David J. Ministries, (*978-0-9741561*) P.O. Box 847, Lake Delton, WI 53940 USA Tel 608-254-5150
E-mail: dgm@mountainfaith.org
Web site: http://www.mountainfaith.org.

Good Bks. *Imprint of* **Skyhorse Publishing Co., Inc.**

Good Catch Publishing, (*978-0-9772383; 978-0-9785152; 978-0-9792475; 978-1-934635; 978-1-938478; 978-1-68085*) Orders Addr.: P.O. Box 6551, Aloha, OR 97007 USA (SAN 257-0289) Tel 503-475-2005; Fax: 503-356-9685; Toll Free: 877-967-3224; Edit Addr.: 4074 NW 169th Ave., Beaverton, OR 97006 USA Fax: 503-356-9685; Toll Free: 877-967-3224
E-mail: nathanlindley@goodcatchpublishing.com; admingcp@gmail.com
Web site: http://www.goodcatchpublishing.com; http://www.testimonybooks.com.

Good Harbor Pr., (*978-0-9799638; 978-0-615-32057-1*) 80 Walsh St., Medford, MA 02155 USA Tel 781-396-1733.

Good News Connections, (*978-0-9728900*) Orders Addr.: P.O. Box 66573, Austin, TX 78766 USA Toll Free: 888-899-3207 Do not confuse with The Good News Connections, Inc. in Orlando, FL
E-mail: stayton@xc.org
Web site: http://www.GoodNewsConnections.com.

Good News Fellowship Ministries, (*978-0-9629559; 978-1-888081*) Div. of Funtasy Pubns., 220 Sleepy Creek Rd., Macon, GA 31210-5720 USA Tel 478-757-8071; Fax: 478-757-0136; Toll Free: 800-300-9630
E-mail: goodnews@reynoldscable.net
Web site: http://www.goodnews.netministries.org; http://kathiewaltersministry.com
Dist(s): **Anchor Distributors.**

Good News Productions, International, (*978-1-59305*) Orders Addr.: P.O. Box 222, Joplin, MO 64802-0222 USA Tel 417-782-0060; Fax: 417-782-3999; Edit Addr.: 2111 N. Main, Joplin, MO 64802-0222 USA
E-mail: gnpi@gnpi.org
Web site: http://www.gnpi.org.

Good Reading Bks., (*978-1-888042*) Div. of Southern Printing, Imaging & Typography, Inc., 153 Shady Oaks Dr., Lafayette, LA 70506 USA.

Good Roots Publishing, (*978-0-9745187*) Orders Addr.: P.O. Box 3493, Homer, AK 99603-3493 USA Tel 907-235-5283; Edit Addr.: 62315 Fireweed Ave., Homer, AK 99603-3493 USA
Dist(s): **Wizard Works.**

Good Sound Publishing, (*978-0-9821563; 978-1-935743*) 295 Olive Ave., Palo Alto, CA 94306 USA Fax: 650-227-2320; Toll Free: 888-686-2669
E-mail: info@goodsoundpublishing.com
Web site: http://www.goodsoundpublishing.com.

Good Thoughts Publishing *See* **Cardinal Pr.**

Good Times at Home LLC, (*978-0-9840338*) 1933 Hwy. 35 Suite 105-335, Belmar, NJ 07719 USA Tel 732-803-1902
E-mail: vinnie@vinniecurto.com.

Good Turn Publishing, (*978-0-9794393*) 1 Bancroft Rd., Wellesley, MA 02481 USA
Web site: http://www.goodturnpublishing.com.

Good vs Evil *Imprint of* **Stone Arch Bks.**

Good Works Pr., (*978-0-9634472; 978-1-888572*) 4121 Whitfield Ave., Fort Worth, TX 76109 USA Tel 817-927-8808.

Good Works Publishing Hse., (*978-0-9744733*) P.O. Box 52217, Houston, TX 77052-2217 USA Tel 713-708-8852
E-mail: wonderlandhudson@yahoo.com.

Good Year Bks. *Imprint of* **Celebration Pr.**

Good Year Bks., (*978-1-59647*) P.O. Box 91858, Tucson, AZ 85752-1858 USA (SAN 854-4050) Toll Free Fax: 888-511-1501; Toll Free: 888-511-1530
E-mail: publisher@goodyearbooks.com; sales@goodyearbooks.com; marketing@goodyearbooks.com; orders@goodyearbooks.com
Web site: http://www.goodyearbooks.com.

Goodall, Barry, (*978-0-9763932*) 218 Tucker Sta. Rd, Louisville, KY 40243 USA Tel 502-817-8530
E-mail: bgoodal1@jefferson.k12.ky.us.

Goode, Ty *See* **Tytam Publishing**

Goodheart-Willcox Pub., (*978-0-87006; 978-1-56637; 978-1-59070; 978-1-60525; 978-1-61960; 978-1-63126*) Orders Addr.: 18604 West Creek Dr., Tinley Park, IL 60477-6243 USA (SAN 203-4387) Tel 708-687-5000; Fax: 708-687-5068; Toll Free Fax: 888-409-3900; Toll Free: 800-323-0440
E-mail: custserv@g-w.com
Web site: http://www.g-w.com.

Goodmedia Communications, LLC, (*978-0-615-60107-6; 978-0-9883237; 978-0-9911148*) 25 Highland Pk. Village, No. 100-810, Dallas, TX 75205 USA Tel 214-240-4503
E-mail: info@GoodMediaCommunications.com
Web site: www.GoodMediaCommunications.com.

Goodtimes Software *See* **GT Interactive Software**

Goodwin, Brian, (*978-0-615-16104-4*) 53-823 Kamehameha Hwy., Hauula, HI 96717-9658 USA
Dist(s): **Lulu Enterprises Inc.**

Goodwin, Evelyn, (*978-0-615-16145-7; 978-0-615-16344-4*) 2345 Ala Wai Blvd. Apt. 917, Honolulu, HI 96815-5017 USA
Dist(s): **Lulu Enterprises Inc.**

goodworksebooks.com, (*978-0-9773192*) 3084 CR 310, Brazoria, TX 77422 USA
Web site: http://goodworksebooks.com.

GoodyGoody Bks., (*978-0-9702546*) P.O. Box 1073, Sun City, AZ 85372-1073 USA
E-mail: charlie-the-cat@cox.net
Web site: http://www.charliethecat.com.

Goofy Guru Publishing, (*978-0-9726130*) 405 Kiowa Pl., Boulder, CO 80303 USA.

Goon Dog Publishing, (*978-0-9791612*) 309 W. 14th, Suite 32, New York, NY 10014-0014 USA (SAN 852-6206) Tel 212-645-2096
E-mail: monk@ispwest.com
Web site: http://owenopolis.com.

Goops Unlimited, (*978-0-9712368; 978-0-9834865*) P.O. Box 1809, Battle Ground, WA 98604-1809 USA Tel 360-687-1891; Fax: 360-687-2097; Toll Free: 800-861-1891
E-mail: barbara@thegoops.com
Web site: http://www.thegoops.com.

Goose Creek Pubs., Inc., (*978-1-59633*) 4227 Vermont Ave., Louisville, KY 40211 USA Tel 502-714-9985
E-mail: wanda@goosecreekpublishers.com
Web site: http://www.goosecreekpublishers.com.

Goose River Pr., (*978-1-930648; 978-1-59713*) 3400 Friendship Rd., Waldoboro, ME 04572 USA Tel 207-832-6665
E-mail: gooseriverpress@roadrunner.com
Web site: http://www.gooseriverpress.com
Dist(s): **Lightning Source, Inc.**

Gooseberry Patch *Imprint of* **Rowman & Littlefield Publishers, Inc.**

Goosebottom Bks. LLC, (*978-0-9845098; 978-0-9834256; 978-1-937463*) 543 Trinidad Ln., Foster City, CA 94404-6061 USA (SAN 859-8029) Tel 650-204-4076
E-mail: info@goosebottombooks.com; shirin.bridges@goosebottombooks.com
Web site: http://www.goosebottombooks.com
Dist(s): **Independent Pubs. Group**
Perseus-PGW.

Gordon Rocket, (*978-1-941037*) P.O. Box 120023, Chula, CA 91912 USA Tel 619-272-8235
E-mail: mxreynoso@gmail.com
Web site: gordonrocket.com.

Goretti Publishing, (*978-0-9778451*) Orders Addr.: 1150 N. Loop 1604 W., Ste. 108-410, San Antonio, TX 78248 USA (SAN 850-3176) Tel 210-274-2769; Fax: 210-493-6080 attn: 410
E-mail: publishedworks@aol.com
Web site: http://www.thetexasmermaid.com
Dist(s): **Bk. Marketing Plus.**

Gorgias Pr., LLC, (*978-0-9713097; 978-0-9715986; 978-1-931956; 978-1-59333; 978-1-60724; 978-1-61719; 978-1-61143; 978-1-4632*) 954 River Rd., Piscataway, NJ 08854-5504 USA (SAN 853-0629)
E-mail: info@gorgiaspress.com; sales@gorgiaspress.com
Web site: http://www.gorgiaspress.com
Dist(s): **ebrary, Inc.**

Gormley Publishing, (*978-0-9794500; 978-0-9827503*) Orders Addr.: 1520 Courtney Dr., Washington Court House, OH 43160-8920 USA
Web site: http://www.gormleypublishing.com.

Gorp Group Pr., The, (*978-0-9724249*) 7450 OLIVETAS Ave. No. 386, LA JOLLA, CA 92037 USA Tel 858-412-4424; 208-720-7980; Toll Free: 888-729-4677
E-mail: gorp2@earthlink.net
Web site: http://www.thegorp.com.

Gospel Light *Imprint of* **Gospel Light Pubns.**

Gospel Light Pubns., (*978-0-8307*) Orders Addr.: 1957 Eastman Ave., Ventura, CA 93003 USA (SAN 299-0873) Tel 805-644-9721; Fax: 805-289-0200; Toll Free: 800-446-7735 (orders only); *Imprints:* Gospel Light (Gospel Light); Regal Books (Regal Bks) Do not confuse with companies with similar names in Brooklyn, NY, Delight, AR
E-mail: info@gospellight.com; kyleloffelmacher@gospellight.com
Web site: http://www.gospellight.com
Dist(s): **Christian Bk. Distributors.**

Gospel Missionary Union, (*978-0-9617490; 978-1-890940*) 10000 N. Oak Trafficway, Kansas City, MO 64155 USA (SAN 664-1830) Tel 816-734-8500; Fax: 816-734-4601
E-mail: info@gmu.org
Web site: http://www.gmu.org.

Gospel Puzzles *See* **Cluster Storm Publishing**

Gossamer Bks., (*978-0-9729016*) 444 Eastwood Dr., Petaluma, CA 94954 USA (SAN 255-2671) Tel 707-765-1992; Fax: 707-765-6507 Do not confuse with Gossamer Books LLC in Belmont, CA
E-mail: dcr530@cs.com.

Gossamer Bks., LLC, (*978-0-9742502*) P.O. Box 455, Belmont, CA 94002 USA Fax: 650-257-4058 Do not confuse with Gossamer Books in Petaluma, CA
E-mail: info@gossamerbooks.com
Web site: http://www.gossamerbooks.com.

GoTandem *Imprint of* **Barbour Publishing, Inc.**

Gotham *Imprint of* **Penguin Publishing Group**

Goulasche Pr., (*978-0-9771466*) 1352 Ithilien, Excelsior, MN 55331 USA.

Gozo Books, LLC *See* **Premio Publishing & Gozo Bks., LLC**

G.P. Hoffman Publishing, (*978-0-9798230*) 2224 Heather Ln., Lincoln, NE 68512 USA.

GPKids *Imprint of* **Ideals Pubns.**

Grace Acres Pr., (*978-1-60265*) P.O. Box 22, Larkspur, CO 80118 USA (SAN 852-5978) Tel 303-681-9995; Fax: 303-681-2716
E-mail: Anne@GraceAcresPress.com
Web site: http://www.graceacrespress.com.

Grace & Mercy Publishing, (*978-0-9672049; 978-0-9764763*) Orders Addr.: P.O. Box 11531, Fort Wayne, IN 46857 USA; Edit Addr.: 7408 Mill Run, Suite B, Fort Wayne, IN 46819 USA.

Grace Communications Publishing *See* **Grace Publishing**

Grace Contrino Abrams Peace Education Foundation *See* **Peace Education Foundation**

Grace Hse. Publishing, (*978-0-9633633*) Div. of R. Allan McCauley Law Office, 6237 N. 15th St., Phoenix, AZ 85014 USA Tel 602-265-9151 Do not confuse with Grace House Publishing in Mahomet, IL.

Grace Publishing, (*978-1-893555*) Div. of Abundant Grace Fellowship, 11118 Robious Rd., Richmond, VA 23235-3724 USA Toll Free: 877-884-7223 Do not confuse with companies with companies with the same name in Seattle, WA, Farmington Hills, MI, Broken Arrow, OK, Waldorf, MD, Elma, NY, Woodinville, WA & New Prague, MN
E-mail: drmhunt@bellsouth.net; carylives@atthi.com; dremlenehunt@earthlink.net
Web site: http://www.abundantgrace.org; http://www.drmarlenehunt.com.

Grace Publishing, (*978-0-9769985*) P.O. Box 17980, Seattle, WA 98123 USA (SAN 256-6257) Tel 206-818-9769 Do not confuse with companies with the same name in Farmington Hills, MI, Broken Arrow, OK, Waldorf, MD, RICHMOND, VA, Elma, NY, Woodinville, WA & New Prague, MN
E-mail: vonukk@comcast.net
Web site: http://www.rcberg.com.

Grace Walk Ministries *See* **Grace Walk Resources, LLC**

Grace Walk Resources, LLC, (*978-0-9664736*) Orders Addr.: P.O. Box 6537, Douglasville, GA 30135 USA Tel 800-472-2311; Toll Free: 800-472-2311
E-mail: info@gracewalk.org
Web site: http://www.gracewalk.org.

GraceWorks Interactive, (*978-0-9760548; 978-1-935915*) P.O. Box 2613, Corvallis, OR 97339-2613 USA Toll Free: 877-785-3496 (phone/fax)
E-mail: tim@graceworksinteractive.com
Web site: http://www.graceworksinteractive.com.

Graffeg Limited (GBR) (*978-0-9544334; 978-1-905582*) *Dist. by* **IPG Chicago.**

grafixCORP, (*978-0-9778374*) Orders Addr.: P.O. Box 1441, Mount Vernon, WA 98273-9827 USA
Web site: http://www.grafixCORP.com.

Grafton and Scratch Pubs. (CAN) (*978-0-9879023; 978-0-9881216; 978-1-927979; 978-1-926495*) *Dist. by* **AtlasBooks.**

Graham Bay, Jeanette, (*978-0-9771210*) 770 Victor Rd., Macedon, NY 14502 USA.

Graham Cracker Kids, (*978-0-9716475; 978-0-615-11409-5*) 1661 Hunt Rd., El Cajon, CA 92019 USA Tel 619-258-7571; Fax: 619-258-5412
E-mail: grmcrkrkds@aol.com
Web site: http://www.grahamcrackerkids.com.

Graham, Rita, (*978-0-578-13165-8*) .

Grampa Jones's Publishing Co., (*978-0-9748266; 978-0-615-11169-8; 978-0-9893868*) P.O. Box 93, Heron, MT 59844-0093 USA (SAN 214-4700)
Web site: http://www.become-a-millionaire.com.

Gran Gran Series, (*978-0-9840237*) 8549 Hartham Pk. Ave., Raleigh, NC 27616 USA Tel 919-295-4750
E-mail: mhopkins25@nc.rr.com.

Grand Bks., Inc., (*978-0-930809*) P.O. Box 212, Crystal, MI 48818 USA (SAN 677-6361) Tel 517-875-4674; 517-235-4427
E-mail: jwrites@yahoo.com.

Grand Canyon Assn., (*978-0-938216; 978-1-934656*) Orders Addr.: P.O. Box 399, Grand Canyon, AZ 86023-0399 USA (SAN 215-7675) Tel 928-638-7141; 928-638-7030; Fax: 928-638-2494; Toll Free: 800-858-2808
E-mail: lsantamaria@grandcanyon.org; clittleboy@grandcanyon.org
Web site: http://www.grandcanyon.org.

Grand Canyon Natural History Association *See* **Grand Canyon Assn.**

Grand Canyon Orphan, (*978-0-9764260*) P.O. Box 438, Mina, NV 89422 USA
E-mail: info@grandcanyonorphan.com
Web site: http://www.grandcanyonorphan.com.

Grand Central Pr., (*978-0-9771696; 978-0-9817987*) 125 N. Broadway, Santa Ana, CA 92701 USA (SAN 256-8284) Tel 714-567-7238
E-mail: tgayer@fullerton.edu
Web site: http://www.grandcentralartcenter.com
Dist(s): **SCB Distributors.**

†**Grand Central Publishing,** (*978-0-445; 978-0-446; 978-0-7595; 978-1-4555*) Orders Addr.: c/o Little Brown & Co., 3 Center Plaza, Boston, MA 02108-2084 USA Toll Free Fax: 800-286-9471; Toll Free: 800-759-0190; Edit Addr.: 237 Park Ave., New York, NY 10017 USA (SAN 281-8892) Fax: 800-331-1664; Toll Free Fax: 800-759-0190; *Imprints:* Vision (VisionC); Business Plus (Busn Plus); Forever (Forever); Sixth Avenue Books (SixthAveBks); 5 Spot (FiveSpot)
E-mail: renee.supriano@twbg.com
Web site: http://www.hbgusa.com
Dist(s): **Findaway World, LLC**
Follett School Solutions
Hachette Bk. Group
Lectorum Pubns., Inc.
Libros Sin Fronteras
Little Brown & Co.
MyiLibrary
Perelandra, Ltd.
Beeler, Thomas T. Pub.
TextStream
Thorndike Pr.
IPublish.com; *CIP.*

Grand Daisy Pr., (*978-0-9848608; 978-0-9962843*) 625 Stetson Rd., Elkins Park, PA 19027-2524 USA Tel 215-380-6710
E-mail: karenptoz@gmail.com
Web site: www.granddaisypress.com; www.karentoz.com.

Grand Hank Productions, Inc., (*978-0-9767236*) P.O. Box 23488, Philadelphia, PA 19143 USA Tel 215-724-5260
Web site: http://www.grandhank.com.

Grand Kidz, The *Imprint of* **Vertical Connect Pr.**

Grand Marais Publishing, (*978-0-615-34796-7*) 1441 Huntington Dr., No. 234, South Pasadena, CA 91030 USA Tel 626-441-1154
E-mail: grandmaraispublishing@gmail.com.

GRAND Media, LLC, (*978-0-930507; 978-0-615-51541-0*) 4791 Baywood Point Dr. S., Gulfport, FL 33711 USA (SAN 670-963X) Tel 727-327-9039; Fax: 727-323-9587
E-mail: jonmicocci@att.net
Web site: http://www.deathfromchildabuse.com.

Grand Productions, (*978-0-9795386*) 1914 Karly Ct., Panama City, FL 32405 USA (SAN 853-7194).

Grandfeather Pr., (*978-0-9832355*) 1221 S. 7th St., Renton, WA 98057 USA Tel 425-902-1852
E-mail: publishing@grandfeather.com
Web site: www.grandfeather.com
Dist(s): **Lightning Source, Inc.**

Grandin Bk. Co., (*978-0-910523*) P.O. Box 2206, Provo, UT 84603-2206 USA (SAN 260-1931) Tel 801-225-2020; Fax: 801-222-0176; Toll Free: 800-292-2003.

Grandkidsandme, Inc., (*978-0-9741710*) 1764 Hampshire Ave., Saint Paul, MN 55116 USA (SAN 255-3902) Tel 651-695-1988; Fax: 651-699-5966
E-mail: don@grandkidsandme.com
Web site: http://www.grandkidsandme.com
Dist(s): **Independent Pubs. Group.**

Grandma Chubby's Bks., (*978-0-9728535*) P.O. Box 902308, Sandy, UT 84090-2308 USA Tel 801-571-6617; Fax: 801-571-2285
E-mail: lsashby@juno.com
Dist(s): **Granite Publishing & Distribution.**

"Grandma's Hope Notes", *(978-0-9677477)* P.O. Box 868, Anchor Point, AK 99556 USA Tel 907-235-0502 (phone/fax).
Grandoc Publishing, *(978-0-9761739)* 3923 Hidden Way NE, Rochester, MN 55906-5590 USA Tel 507-287-9121
E-mail: grandoc@mac.com; drjohngraner@mac.com.
Grandreams Bks., Inc., *(978-1-59340)* Div. of Robert Frederick, 360 Hurst St., Linden, NJ 07036 USA (SAN 254-9832) Fax: 908-523-0373
E-mail: ssullivan@grandreamsbooks.com.
Grandy Pubns., *(978-0-9729237)* 290 E. Verdugo Ave., Stuite 105, Burbank, CA 91502 USA Tel 818-848-1313; Fax: 818-551-0305; Toll Free: 800-326-8953
E-mail: MannersA2Z@aol.com
Web site: http://www.youvegotmanners.com
Dist(s): **Independent Pubs. Group.**
Granite Publishing & Distribution, *(978-1-890558; 978-1-930980; 978-1-932280; 978-1-59936)* 868 N. 1430 W., Orem, UT 84057 USA (SAN 631-0605) Tel 801-229-9023; Fax: 801-229-1924; Toll Free: 800-574-5779 Do not confuse with companies with same or similar names in Madison, WI, Columbus, NC
E-mail: granite@granitepublishing.biz; gregg@granitepublishing.biz
Web site: http://granitepublishing.biz.
Granite Publishing, LLC, *(978-0-926524; 978-0-9632310; 978-1-893183)* P.O. Box 1429, Columbus, NC 28722 USA Tel 828-894-3088; Fax: 828-894-8454; Toll Free: 800-366-0264 Do not confuse with companies with same or similar names in Madison, WI, Orem, UT, Siloam Springs, AR
E-mail: brian@5thworld.com
Web site: http://www.5thworld.com
Dist(s): **New Leaf Distributing Co., Inc.**
Smashwords.
Grannie Annie Family Story Celebration, The, *(978-0-9677685; 978-0-9793296)* P.O. Box 11343, Saint Louis, MO 63105 USA Tel 314-863-0775; Fax: 314-863-0775
E-mail: familystories@thegrannieannie.org
Web site: http://www.TheGrannieAnnie.org.
Granny's Pub Co., *(978-0-9749950)* P.O. Box 1701, Granbury, TX 76048 USA Tel 817-605-9004; Fax: 817-605-1180
E-mail: granny@loralie.com
Web site: http://www.loralie.com.
Granville Island Publishing (CAN) *(978-1-894694; 978-1-926991) Dist. by* **Partners Bk Dist.**
Grape Elephant MarketPr., *(978-0-9760646)* 13025 Ct. Pl., Burnsville, MN 55337 USA Tel 612-281-2566
E-mail: jill@grapeelephant.com
Web site: http://www.grapeelephant.com.
Graphic Arts Ctr. Publishing Co., Orders Addr.: P.O. Box 10306, Portland, OR 97296-0306 USA (SAN 201-6338) Tel 503-226-2402; Fax: 503-223-1410 (executive & editorial); Toll Free Fax: 800-355-9685 (sales office); Toll Free: 800-452-3032; *Imprints*: Alaska Northwest Books (Alaska NW Bks); West Winds Press (West Winds Pr)
E-mail: sales@gacpc.com
Web site: http://www.gacpc.com
Dist(s): **Ingram Pub. Services**
Univ. of Oklahoma Pr.
Graphic Expressions *See* **Graphics North**
Graphic Flash *Imprint of* **Stone Arch Bks.**
Graphic Library *Imprint of* **Capstone Pr., Inc.**
Graphic Library en espanol *Imprint of* **Capstone Pr., Inc.**
Graphic Novels *Imprint of* **Spotlight**
Graphic Planet *Imprint of* **Magic Wagon**
Graphic Planet- Fiction *Imprint of* **ABDO Publishing Co.**
Graphic Planet- Nonfiction *Imprint of* **ABDO Publishing Co.**
Graphic Quest *Imprint of* **Stone Arch Bks.**
Graphic Revolve *Imprint of* **Stone Arch Bks.**
Graphic Revolve en Español *Imprint of* **Stone Arch Bks.**
Graphic Sparks *Imprint of* **Stone Arch Bks.**
Graphic Spin en Español *Imprint of* **Stone Arch Bks.**
Graphic Universe *Imprint of* **Lerner Publishing Group**
Graphically Speaking, Inc., *(978-0-9729975)* 15509 Lloyd St., Omaha, NE 68144 USA Tel 402-330-1144; Fax: 402-334-3311
E-mail: fontstudios@cox.net
Web site: http://www.fontstudios.com.
Graphics North, *(978-0-9643452; 978-0-615-29759-0; 978-0-9829503)* P.O. Box 218, Jay, NY 12941 USA Tel 518-946-7741
E-mail: mvf@charter.net.
Graphic-Sha (JPN) *(978-4-7661) Dist. by* **Diamond Book Dists.**
Graphic International, Inc., *(978-0-916189)* 8780 19th St., No. 199, Alto Loma, CA 91701 USA (SAN 294-9342) Tel 909-987-1921; Fax: 435-514-5975
E-mail: lmartres@phototripusa.com
Web site: http://www.phototripusa.com
Dist(s): **Bks. West**
Canyonlands Pubns.
Mountain n' Air Bks.
Graphis, U.S., Inc., *(978-1-888001; 978-1-931241; 978-1-932026)* Orders Addr.: c/o ABDI, Inc., Buncher Commerce Pk. Ave. A, Bldg. 16, Leetsdale, PA 15056-1304 USA Tel 412-741-3679; Fax: 412-741-0934; Toll Free: 800-209-4234 (for Canada & USA); Edit Addr.: 307 Fifth Ave., 10th Flr., New York, NY 10016 USA Tel 212-532-9387 (ext. 226); Fax: 212-213-3229; Toll Free: 800-209-4234
Web site: http://www.graphis.com
Dist(s): **Innovative Logistics**
Watson-Guptill Pubns., Inc.
Graphite Pr., *(978-0-9755810; 978-1-938313)* 2025 Lexington Parkway, Niskayuna, NY 12309-4205 USA (SAN 256-0712) Tel 206-222-2400; Fax: 206-222-2002
E-mail: publish@graphitepress.com
Web site: http://www.graphitepress.com.
Graphix *Imprint of* **Scholastic, Inc.**
Graphix Network, *(978-0-9740673; 978-0-9752832; 978-0-9762301; 978-0-9777043)* Orders Addr.: P.O. Box 2745, Evans, GA 30809 USA Tel 706-210-1000; Fax: 706-210-1111; Edit Addr.: 4104 Colben Blvd., Suite C, Evans, GA 30809 USA Tel 706-210-1000; Fax: 706-210-1111
E-mail: graphixnetwork@hotmail.com; sales@graphixnetwork.com
Web site: http://www.graphixnetwork.com.
Grappling Arts Pubns., LLC, *(978-0-9721097)* 1282 Watson Ave., Costa Mesa, CA 92626 USA
E-mail: info@grapplingarts.net
Web site: http://www.grapplingarts.net
Dist(s): **BookMasters, Inc.**
Cardinal Pubs. Group.
Grass Root Enterprises, *(978-1-886075)* 16315 Forest Way Dr., Houston, TX 77090-4716 USA Tel 281-444-4103; Fax: 281-444-5804.
Grassdale Publishers, Incorporated *See* **Saxon Pubs., Inc.**
Grasshopper Dream Productions, *(978-0-615-12337-0; 978-0-615-12724-8; 978-0-615-35616-7)* Orders Addr.: P.O. Box 1831, Saint Petersburg, FL 33731-1831 USA Tel 813-382-4230; Edit Addr.: 121 E. Davis Blvd., No. 104, Tampa, FL 33731 USA
E-mail: kokopelli911@hotmail.com
Web site: http://www.kokopelli-butterfly.com.
Grassroots Educational Service *See* **Right On Programs, Inc.**
Grassroots Publishing Group, *(978-0-9794805)* 9404 Southwick Dr., Bakersfield, CA 93312 USA (SAN 853-5493) Tel 661-368-2624; Fax: 661-368-2624
E-mail: nesta@sbcglobal.net.
Grateful Day Pr., *(978-0-9882804)* 24 Dewey Mt Rd., Saranac Lake, NY 12983 USA Tel 518-891-2278; Fax: 518-891-1645
E-mail: gratefuldaypress@gmail.com.
Grateful Steps, *(978-0-9789548; 978-1-935130; 978-0-9962490)* 1091 Hendersonville Rd., Asheville, NC 28801 USA (SAN 856-471X) Tel 828-277-0998; Fax: 828-277-8027
Web site: http://www.gratefulsteps.com.
Gratia et Veritas Press *See* **Papillon Publishing**
Gratitude Works, *(978-0-578-13447-5)* 6255 Whitsett Ave, North Hollywood, CA 91606 USA.
Grau, Ryon, *(978-0-9772559)* 6824 Falstone Dr., Frederick, MD 21702 USA
E-mail: ryon@landmarkletters.com
Web site: http://www.spankledelia.com.
Gravitas Pubns., Inc., *(978-0-9749149; 978-0-9765097; 978-0-9799459; 978-0-9817731; 978-0-9823163; 978-1-936114; 978-1-941181)* PO Box 90338, Albuquerque, NM 97199 USA Tel 505-266-2761; Fax: 505-266-2762; Toll Free: 888-466-2761
E-mail: office@gravitaspublications.com
Web site: http://www.gravitaspublications.com.
Gravley, Debbie Bybee, *(978-0-9771793)* Orders Addr.: P.O. Box 268, Gaston, OR 97119 USA; Edit Addr.: 12320 S.W. Springhill Rd., Gaston, OR 97119 USA.
Graw, Victoria, *(978-0-9787901)* P.O. Box 458, Orange, MA 01364 USA (SAN 851-6138)
E-mail: Vgraw@aol.com.
Gray and Company, Publishers, *(978-0-9631738; 978-1-886228; 978-1-59851; 978-1-938441)* Orders Addr.: 1588 E. 40th St., 3A, Cleveland, OH 44103 USA Tel 216-431-2665; Fax: 216-431-7933; Toll Free: 800-915-3609
E-mail: sales@grayco.com
Web site: http://www.grayco.com.
Gray Jay Bks., *(978-0-9754539)* 3086 Decatur Hwy., Gardendale, AL 35071 USA
E-mail: saril@aol.com
Web site: http://www.grayjaybooks.com.
Gray, Susan *See* **Two's Company**
Grayer Publishing, *(978-0-9785536)* P.O. Box 788, Flossmoor, IL 60422 USA
E-mail: ac@grayerpublishing.com
Web site: http://www.grayerpublishing.com.
Grayson, Kate, *(978-0-9774357)* 2307 58th Ave. E., Bradenton, FL 34203 USA (SAN 257-5000)
E-mail: kgrayson1@aol.com.
Graziano, Claudia *See* **Meerkat's Adventures Bks.**
GRC Bks., *(978-0-578-06866-4; 978-0-578-08611-8; 978-0-578-12011-9)* 704 Robinson Rd., Sebastopol, CA 95472 USA Tel 707-829-9191
E-mail: martyr@sonic.net
Dist(s): **Lulu Enterprises Inc.**
Great AD-Ventures, *(978-0-9665053)* P.O. Box 8011, Boise, ID 83707 USA Fax: 208-336-5797; Toll Free: 800-390-5687
E-mail: theplace@lesbois.com; book@freeread.com
Web site: http://www.freeread.com/.
Great Adventures Publishing, *(978-0-9747972)* 465 Hill St., Laguna Beach, CA 92651 USA Tel 949-494-5797
E-mail: paigeturner5@hotmail.com.
Great American Pr., The, *(978-0-9777996; 978-0-9798776; 978-0-9814627)* 551 League City Pkwy., League City, TX 77573 USA (SAN 850-2773) Tel 281-557-4300 (phone/fax)
Web site: http://www.thegreatamericanpress.com.
Great American Pubs., *(978-0-9779053; 978-1-934817)* 171 Lone Pine Church Rd., Lena, MS 39094 USA Tel 601-854-5954; Fax: 601-854-5958
E-mail: info@gapublishers.com; ssimmons@gapublishers.com
Web site: http://www.greatamericanpublishers.com
Dist(s): **Appalachian Bk. Distributors**
Bk. Marketing Plus
Bks. West
Dot Gibson Distribution
Forest Sales & Distributing Co.
Rumpf, Raymond & Son
Southwest Cookbook Distributors.
Great Authors Online, *(978-0-9773869)* 16440 Monterey St., Lake Elsinore, CA 92530 USA Tel 951-674-3246; Fax: 951-245-3608
E-mail: rodgerolsen@yahoo.com
Web site: http://greatauthorsonline.com.
Great Big Comics *See* **Great Big Comics, Big Tex Films**
Great Big Comics, Big Tex Films, *(978-0-9746784; 978-0-9844728; 978-0-615-49875-1)* Div. of The Big Tex Movin' Picture Company, LLC, 31 E. Bonneymead Cir., The Woodlands, TX 77381 USA
E-mail: bh@wondervista.com; avast@shebucaneer.com
Web site: http://www.wondervista.com; http://www.greatbigcomics.com
Dist(s): **Diamond Distributors, Inc.**
Great Bks. Foundation, *(978-0-945159; 978-1-880323; 978-1-933147; 978-1-939014)* 35 E. Wacker Dr. Ste. 400, Chicago, IL 60601-2105 USA (SAN 205-3292) Toll Free: 800-222-5870
E-mail: hurleyp@greatbooks.org
Web site: http://www.greatbooks.org.
Great Character Development Workbook, The, *(978-0-9728417)* P.O. Box 1852, Kingston, WA 98346 USA
Web site: http://www.thegreatcharacterdevelopmentworkbook.com.
Great Expectations Bk. Co., *(978-1-883934)* P.O. Box 2067, Eugene, OR 07402 USA Tel 541-343-2647; Fax: 541-343-0568
E-mail: fred@pinehillgraphics.com.
Great I-AM Publishing Co., The, *(978-0-9762788)* Orders Addr.: P.O. Box 30412, Wilmington, DE 19805 USA Tel 302-888-2477; Fax: 302-416-5085; Edit Addr.: 25 Roselane Rosegate, New Castle, DE 19720 USA
E-mail: watkinstyree2@aol.com.
Great Ideas for Teaching, Inc., *(978-1-886143)* Orders Addr.: P.O. Box 444, Wrightsville Beach, NC 28480-0444 USA Tel 910-256-4494; Fax: 910-256-4493; Toll Free Fax: 800-839-8498; Toll Free: 800-839-8339; Edit Addr.: 6800 Wrightsville Ave., No. 16, Wilmington, NC 28403 USA
E-mail: gift@wilmington.net
Web site: http://www.gift-inc.com.
Great Ideas Pr., Ltd., *(978-1-884949)* 4130 166th Pl. SW, Lynnwood, WA 98037 USA Tel 425-774-6611
E-mail: JamesRobert@jamesrobertdeal.com
Web site: http://www.whattoserveagoddess.com.
Great Kids Helping Great Kids, Incorporated *See* **America's Great Stories**
Great Lakes Bks. *Imprint of* **Wayne State Univ. Pr.**
Great Lakes Design, *(978-0-9761274)* P.O. Box 511534, Milwaukee, WI 53203 USA
Web site: http://www.vikingadventure.net.
Great Lakes Literary, LLC, *(978-1-883953; 978-1-933987)* 3147 S. Pennsylvania Ave., Milwaukee, WI 53207 USA; *Imprints*: Crickhollow Books (Crickhollow); Blue Horse Books (BlueHorse)
E-mail: info@CrickhollowBooks.com
Web site: http://www.CrickhollowBooks.com; http://www.CrispinBooks.com
Dist(s): **BookBaby**
BookMobile
Itasca Bks.
Great Lakes Literary, LLCorp. *See* **Great Lakes Literary, LLC**
Great Lakes Press, Inc., *(978-0-9614760; 978-1-881018; 978-1-939085)* Orders Addr.: P.O. Box 374, Cottleville, MO 63338 USA Fax: 636-273-6086
E-mail: service@glpbooks.com
Web site: http://www.glpbooks.com; http://www.greatlakespress.com.
Great Mastiff Corp., *(978-0-9759166)* 9945 E. Whitebirch Rd., Port wing, WI 54865 USA Tel 715-774-3247
E-mail: greatmastiff@hotmail.com
Web site: http://www.greatmastiff.com.
Great Nation Publishing, *(978-0-578-05549-7; 978-0-578-06529-8; 978-0-615-44374-4; 978-0-615-60214-1; 978-0-9891056)* Orders Addr.: 3828 Salem Rd., No. 56, Covington, GA 30016 USA
E-mail: brian@authorbrianthompson.com
Web site: http://www.authorbrianthompson.com
Dist(s): **Smashwords.**
Great Ocean Publishers *See* **Great River Bks.**
Great Persuader Publishing, The, *(978-0-9712581)* Orders Addr.: a/o , P.O. Box 1100, New York, NY 10030 USA Tel 646-271-2188
E-mail: greatpersuader@hotmail.com; Info@Poetryisalive.com
Web site: http://www.Poetryisalive.com.
Great Plains Pr., *(978-0-9632459; 978-0-9861616)* 1103 Canyon Rd., Santa Fe, NM 87501 USA
E-mail: dirk@rainbowplace.com
Web site: http://www.greatplainspress.com/.
Great Reads Bks., *(978-0-9718694)* P.O. Box 2112, Bellaire, TX 77402-2112 USA (SAN 254-5462)
E-mail: greatreads@earthlink.net; publish@novelpro.com
Web site: http://www.novelpro.com.
†Great River Bks., *(978-0-915556)* 161 M St., Salt Lake City, UT 84103 USA (SAN 207-527X) Tel 801-532-4833
E-mail: info@greatriverbooks.com
Web site: http://www.greatriverbooks.com
Dist(s): **Midpoint Trade Bks., Inc.**; *CIP.*
Great Smoky Mountains Assn., *(978-0-937207)* 115 Park Headquarters Rd., Gatlinburg, TN 37738 USA (SAN 658-7267) Tel 865-436-7318; Fax: 865-436-6884
E-mail: Curt@gsmassoc.org
Web site: http://www.smokiesinformation.org.
Great Smoky Mountains Natural History Association *See* **Great Smoky Mountains Assn.**
Great Source Education Group, Inc., *(978-0-669; 978-0-9638133; 978-1-57185)* Subs. of Houghton Mifflin Harcourt Supplemental Pubs., 181 Ballardvale St., Wilmington, MA 01887 USA Tel 978-661-1500; Fax: 978-661-1331; Toll Free Fax: 800-289-3994; Toll Free: 800-289-4490
Web site: http://www.greatsource.com
Dist(s): **Houghton Mifflin Harcourt Publishing Co.**
Great Texas Line Pr., *(978-1-892588)* Orders Addr.: P.O. Box 11105, Fort Worth, TX 76110 USA Tel 817-922-8929; Fax: 817-926-0420
E-mail: greattexas@hotmail.com
Web site: http://www.greattexasline.com
Dist(s): **Bk. Marketing Plus**
Bks. West
Forest Sales & Distributing Co.
Partners Bk. Distributing, Inc.
Great Valley Bks. *Imprint of* **Heyday**
Great West Publishing, *(978-0-9796199)* Orders Addr.: P.O. Box 31631, Tucson, AZ 85751-1631 USA (SAN 853-9146); *Imprints*: Sentry Books (Sentry Bks)
Web site: http://www.sentrybooks.com.
Great White Bird Publishing, *(978-0-9792474)* Orders Addr.: P.O. Box 667, Hiram, GA 30141-0667 USA Tel 770-947-6817; *Imprints*: GWB (GWB)
E-mail: davidthackston@bellsouth.net
Web site: http://www.myspace.com/thackston.
Great White Dog Picture Company *See* **Light-Beams Publishing**
Greater Cincinnati TV Educational Foundation, *(978-0-9744419)* 1223 Central Pkwy., Cincinnati, OH 45214-2812 USA Tel 513-381-4033; Fax: 513-381-7520; *Imprints*: CET (Cet)
E-mail: edtech@wcet.pbs.org
Web site: http://www.wcet.org.
Greater Truth Pubs., *(978-0-9653078; 978-1-937151)* P.O. Box 4332, Lafayette, IN 47903 USA Do not confuse with Griffin Publishing, Glendale, CA
E-mail: gtp@ao-soft.com
Web site: http://www.ao-soft.com/gtpub/.
GreatWineFinds.com *See* **GWF Publishing & Henry's Helpers**
GreeHee Publishing, *(978-0-9779590)* Orders Addr.: 125 Susan St., Myrtle Creek, OR 97457-9741 USA Tel 541-863-6631
E-mail: astrologyandmore@gmail.com
Web site: http://www.greehee.com; http://www.talesoftamoor.com
Dist(s): **Quality Bks., Inc.**
Smashwords.
†Green Dragon Bks., *(978-0-89334; 978-1-62386)* Orders Addr.: P.O. Box 7400, Atlanta, GA 30357-0400 USA (SAN 208-3833) Tel 561-533-6231; Fax: 404-874-1976; Toll Free: 888-874-8844; Edit Addr.: 12 S. Dixie Hwy., Suite 203, Lake worth, FL 33460 USA (SAN 658-0882) Tel 561-533-6231; Fax: 561-533-6233; Toll Free Fax: 888-874-8844; Toll Free: 800-874-8844; *Imprints*: Humanics Learning (Humanics Lrng) Do not confuse with Humanics ErgoSystems, Inc., Reseda, CA
E-mail: humanics@mindspring.com
Web site: http://www.humanicspub.com; http://www.humanicslearning.com; http://www.humanicsdealer.com
Dist(s): **Borders, Inc.**
Midpoint Trade Bks., Inc.
New Leaf Distributing Co., Inc.; *CIP.*
Green Ghost Pr., *(978-0-615-24430-3; 978-0-615-24648-2; 978-0-615-33363-2; 978-0-615-38560-0)* P.O. Box 691882, West Hollywood, CA 90069 USA
E-mail: waideriddle@hotmail.com; greenghostpress@hotmail.com
Web site: http://www.waideriddle.com
Dist(s): **Left Bank Bks.**
Tattered Cover Bookstore.
Green Goat Bks., *(978-0-615-15585-2)* P.O. Box 11256, Bainbridge Island, WA 98110 USA Tel 206-842-3412; Fax: 206-842-0570; Toll Free: 866-776-4543
E-mail: contact@greengoatbooks.com
Web site: http://www.greengoatbooks.com
Dist(s): **Greenleaf Book Group.**
Green Igric Pr., *(978-0-9776170)* P.O. Box 82454, Columbus, OH 43202 USA Tel 614-267-9426.
Green Irene, *(978-0-9742280)* P.O. Box 5, Huron, OH 44839 USA
E-mail: chager@buckeye-express.com
Web site: http://www.redandgreenchoices.com.
Green Key Books *See* **Practical Christianity Foundation**
Green Kids Club, Inc., *(978-0-9836602; 978-1-939871)* 1425 Higham St., Idaho Falls, ID 83402 USA Tel 208-528-8718
E-mail: peggy_hinman@yahoo.com.
Green Kids Pr., LLC, *(978-1-939377)* 23 T St. NW, Washington, DC 20001-1008 USA (SAN 920-458X) Tel 202-518-7070; Fax: 202-588-0931
E-mail: jucles@hotmail.com
Web site: www.Green-KidsPress.com
Dist(s): **Partners Pubs. Group, Inc.**
Green Lady Pr., The *Imprint of* **RealityIsBooks.com, Inc.**
Green Light Bks. and Publishing, LLC, *(978-0-9755110)* Orders Addr.: 4509 Lake Lawne Ave., Orlando, FL 32808 USA
E-mail: juan_chisholm@yahoo.com
Web site: http://www.greenlightbooks.org.
Green Mansion Pr. LLC, *(978-0-9714612; 978-0-9746457)* 501 E. 79th St., Suite 16A, New York, NY 10021-0773 USA (SAN 254-2684) Tel 212-396-2667; Fax: 212-937-4685
E-mail: info@greenmansionpress.com
Web site: http://www.greenmansionpress.com.
Green, Mary, *(978-0-9764639)* 737 Buffalo Valley Rd., Cookeville, TN 38501-3862 USA
E-mail: greenmaj@frontiernet.net
Web site: http://www.bigfootlady.net.
Green Nest LLC, *(978-0-9772392)* 18662 Macarthur Blvd. Suite 200, Irvine, CA 92612 USA Fax: 949-387-3806
Web site: http://www.greennest.com
Dist(s): **Pathway Bk. Service.**

Green Owl, Inc., *(978-0-9727273)* 23834 SE 248th St., Maple Valley, WA 98038 USA (SAN 255-0679)
E-mail: owl@greenowl.org
Web site: http://www.greenowl.org.

Green Pastures Pr., *(978-0-9627643; 978-1-884377)* HC 67, Box 91-A, Mifflin, PA 17058 USA Tel 717-436-9115.

Green Pastures Publishing, Inc., *(978-0-9664276; 978-0-9720580)* Orders Addr.: P.O. Box 804, Windsor, CO 80550 USA Tel 970-686-7242
Dist(s): **Independent Pubs. Group.**

Green Pr., *(978-0-615-68596-0; 978-0-615-68647-9; 978-0-615-71928-3; 978-0-615-77410-7; 978-0-615-78494-6; 978-0-615-88283-3; 978-0-9899990; 978-0-9862214)* 20011 Park ranch, San Antonio, TX 78259 USA Tel 1-210-490-2677
Dist(s): **CreateSpace Independent Publishing Platform.**

Green Sheet Inc., The, *(978-0-9670947)* P.O. Box 6008, Petaluma, CA 94955-6008 USA Fax: 707-586-1738; Toll Free: 800-757-4441
E-mail: grnsht@aol.com
Web site: http://www.greensheet.com.

Green Tiger Pr. *Imprint of* **Laughing Elephant**

Greenberg, Carmel *See* **Kicks and Giggles Today**

Greenberg, Scott *See* **Jump Start Performance Programs**

Greenblatt, Kim, *(978-0-9777282; 978-1-60622)* 6600 Melba Ave., West Hills, CA 91307 USA (SAN 850-0649).

Greenbrier/Scentex *See* **Bright of America**

Greenbush Pr., *(978-0-9766720; 978-0-9836460; 978-0-615-95792-0)* Orders Addr.: 21518 Karpathos Ln., Spring, TX 77388-3262 USA (SAN 256-5048) Tel 281-907-0884 Office phone
E-mail: frankbecker@depressionproofchurch.com; frankbecker@frankbecker.com; frank@greenbushpress.com; joy@joybecker.com; info@warsdesolation.com
Web site: http://www.depressionproofchurch.com; http://www.cross-trainer.org; http://www.greenbushpress.com; http://www.frankbecker.com; http://www.warsdesolation.com.

Greene & Sandell, *(978-0-9834681)* 45 Church St. Apt. 1, Boston, MA 02116 USA Tel 617-426-7278
E-mail: greenesandell@gmail.com.

Greene, A.S. & Co., *(978-0-9761723)* 1828 Kings Hwy., Lincoln Park, MI 48146 USA Fax: 313-388-0447
E-mail: collegefundproductions@yahoo.com.

Greene Bark Pr., Inc., *(978-1-880851)* P.O. Box 1108, Bridgeport, CT 06601-1108 USA Tel 203-372-4861; Fax: 203-371-5856
E-mail: Greenebark@aol.com
Web site: http://www.greenebarkpress.com.

Greene, Brenda H. *See* **Three Willows Pr.**

Greene, Marjorie A., *(978-0-9741764)* 124 Caughman Park Dr., Columbia, SC 29209 USA Tel 803-783-5430; Fax: 803-783-5430
E-mail: remaininme@msn.com.

Greenfield Enterprises, Ltd. (HKG) *(978-962-563) Dist. by* **Cheng Tsui.**

Greenhaven Pr., Inc. *Imprint of* **Cengage Gale**

Greenhill Bks./Lionel Leventhal, Ltd. (GBR) *(978-0-947898; 978-1-85367) Dist. by* **HachBkGrp.**

Greenleaf Book Group, *(978-0-9665319; 978-1-929774; 978-0-9790842; 978-1-60832; 978-1-61486; 978-1-62634)* Orders Addr.: 4005-B Banister Ln., Austin, TX 78704 USA Tel 512-891-6100; Fax: 512-891-6150; Toll Free: 800-932-5420; Edit Addr.: P.O. Box 91869, Austin, TX 78709 USA; *Imprints:* Greenleaf Book Group Press (GBGP)
E-mail: tanya@greenleafbookgroup.com
Web site: http://www.greenleafbookgroup.com.

Greenleaf Book Group Pr. *Imprint of* **Greenleaf Book Group**

Greenleaf Pr., *(978-1-882514)* 1570 Old Laguardo Rd E., Lebanon, TN 37087-8958 USA (SAN 297-8555) Toll Free Fax: 866-725-0785 Do not confuse with Greenleaf Pr., Breckenridge, CO
E-mail: info@greenleafpress.com
Web site: http://www.greenleafpress.com.

Greenline Publications *See* **Davis, A. S. Media Group**

GreenPoint Computer Services *See* **GIL Pubns.**

Greenroom Bks., *(978-0-9712163)* 12 N. Juniper St., Hampton, VA 23669-2416 USA (SAN 254-2501) Tel 757-726-2651 (phone/fax)
E-mail: brad@greenroombooks.com; publisher@greenroombooks.com
Web site: http://www.greenroombooks.com
Dist(s): **Brodart Co.**

Greensboro Historical Museum, Inc., *(978-0-9747456)* 130 Summit Ave., Greensboro, NC 27401-3016 USA Tel 336-373-2043; Fax: 336-373-2204
Web site: http://www.greensborohistory.org.

Greentown Glass Co., *(978-0-9723958)* Orders Addr.: P.O. Box 771, Westfield, IN 46074-0771 USA Tel 765-455-0595; Edit Addr.: 3703 Robin Dr., Kokomo, IN 46902 USA
Web site: http://www.greentownglasscompany.com.

Greenville Family Partnership, *(978-0-9759699)* P.O. Box 10203, Greenville, SC 29603-0203 USA Tel 864-467-4099; Fax: 864-467-4102
Web site: http://www.redribbonworks.org.

Greenwich Press, Limited *See* **Greenwich Workshop Pr.**

Greenwich Workshop Pr., *(978-0-86713)* Orders Addr.: P.O. Box 875, Seymour, CT 06483 USA (SAN 216-8170) Tel 203-881-3336; Fax: 203-881-9575; Toll Free: 800-243-4246; Edit Addr.: 151 Main St., Seymour, CT 06483 USA
E-mail: info@greenwichworkshop.com
Web site: http://www.greenwichworkshop.com
Dist(s): **Artisan**
Workman Publishing Co., Inc.

Greenwillow Bks. *Imprint of* **HarperCollins Pubs.**

Greenwood Hill Pr., *(978-0-9797868; 978-0-9836382; 978-0-9846912; 978-0-9881748; 978-0-9915961)* W 7048 Savannah Ln., Delavan, WI 53115 USA; *Imprints:* OddInt Media (OddIntMedia)
E-mail: mjohnson@fullpo.com.

Greenwood, Lori Ministries, Inc., *(978-0-9747956)* Orders Addr.: 17622 32nd Pl W., Lynnwood, WA 98037-7714 USA (SAN 255-8297)
E-mail: lgministries@cs.com
Web site: http://www.thevisionlink.com.

Greenwood Pr. *Imprint of* **Greenwood Publishing Group, Inc.**

Greenwood Press, Incorporated *See* **Greenwood Publishing Group, Inc.**

†**Greenwood Publishing Group, Inc.,** *(978-0-275; 978-0-313; 978-0-8371; 978-0-86569; 978-0-89789; 978-0-89930; 978-1-56720; 978-1-4408)* Orders Addr.: P.O. Box 6926, Portsmouth, NH 03802 USA (SAN 213-2028) Fax: 603-431-2214 (customer service and sales); Toll Free: 800-225-5800 (orders only); Linacre House Jordan Hill Bus Pk, Banbury Rd, Oxford, OX2 8DP Tel 01865 888181; Fax: 01865 314981; *Imprints:* Greenwood Press (Greenwood Pr); Praeger Publishers (Praeger Pubs); Middle School Reference (Mid Schl Ref) Do not confuse with Greenwood Publishing in Glenview, IL
E-mail: customer-service@greenwood.com; celeste.bilyard@greenwood.com; Greenwood.enquiries@harcourteducation.co.uk
Web site: http://www.greenwood.com
Dist(s): **ABC-CLIO, LLC**
Ebsco Publishing
Follett School Solutions
Libraries Unlimited, Inc.
MyiLibrary
ebrary, Inc.; *CIP.*

Greenwood Street Publishing. GSP, *(978-0-9745553)* 1539 W. Townley Ave., Phoenix, AZ 85021 USA Tel 602-997-4444; Fax: 602-997-5959 Do not confuse with Greenwood Publishing in Wixom, MI
E-mail: julie@gg-az.com; info@greenwoodstreet.com
Web site: http://www.greenwoodstreet.com.

Gregory, Charles, *(978-0-9745432)* 17697 Palmer St., Melvindale, MI 48122 USA (SAN 255-7991) Tel 313-389-2836
E-mail: charles_gregory@ameritech.net
Web site: http://www.charles_gregory/index.html
Dist(s): **Lulu Enterprises Inc.**

Gregory, Charles Matthew, *(978-0-9766442)* 5600 Camerata Way, Unit 141, Minneapolis, MN 55416 USA
Web site: www.mikascomic.com.

Grendel Roleplaying, *(978-1-929928)* 1420 S. Ave. F, Portales, NM 88130 USA
E-mail: author@paulbspence.com
Web site: http://www.paulbspence.com.

Grenevitch, Betsy Coffman, *(978-0-9747113)* 1450 Hewatt Rd., Lilburn, GA 30047 USA Tel 678-344-6100 (phone/fax)
E-mail: blindangel@joimail.com.

Grenwood Publishing *See* **Greenwood Street Publishing. GSP**

Gresham, Joel, *(978-0-9708446)* 2201 Morgan Pl., Atlanta, GA 30324 USA Tel 404-512-0445
E-mail: undercolorjg@yahoo.com.

Grey Bear Publishing, *(978-0-615-83310-1)* 592 Shepherds Ranch Rd, Bulverde, TX 78163 USA Tel 830-438-2889
Dist(s): **CreateSpace Independent Publishing Platform.**

Grey Gate Media, LLC, *(978-0-9787318; 978-0-9801004; 978-1-61807)* 20 Fisherville Rd., #173, Concord, NH 03303 USA Tel 603-801-2208; Fax: 603-676-7882; *Imprints:* Little Blue Flower Press (Little Blue Flow).

Grey Gecko Pr., *(978-0-9836185; 978-0-9854400; 978-1-938821)* 565 S. Mason Rd. Suite 154, Katy, TX 77450 USA Tel 713-489-5731
E-mail: bowker@greygeckopress.com
Web site: http://www.greygeckopress.com
Dist(s): **Lightning Source, Inc.**

†**Grey Hse. Publishing,** *(978-0-939300; 978-1-891482; 978-1-930956; 978-1-59237; 978-1-61925; 978-1-68217)* 4919 Rte. 22, Amenia, NY 12501 USA Tel 518-789-8700; Fax: 518-789-0556; Toll Free: 800-562-2139; 4919 Rte. 22, Amenia, NY 12501 Tel 518-789-8700; Fax: 518-789-0556; Toll Free: 800-562-2139; *Imprints:* Universal Reference Publications (Universal Ref Pubns)
E-mail: books@greyhouse.com
Web site: http://www.greyhouse.com
Dist(s): **Ebsco Publishing**
MyiLibrary
ebrary, Inc.; *CIP.*

GreyCore Pr., *(978-0-9671851; 978-0-9742074)* 3833 Hilton Ave NE, Albuquerque, NM 87110-1059 USA
E-mail: joan123@frontiernet.net.

Greyhound Bks., *(978-0-9724136; 978-1-59677)* 2000 Stock Creek Rd., Knoxville, TN 37920 USA Tel 865-405-3002
E-mail: cynmob@aol.com; editor@bushidopress.com
Web site: http://www.dogbooks.org.

Greystone Books Ltd. (CAN) *(978-1-55365; 978-1-77100) Dist. by* **PerseuPGW.**

Grief Watch, *(978-0-9615197; 978-0-9724241; 978-0-9916312; 978-0-692-37070-4)* Div. of Metanoia Peace Community United Methodist Church, 2116 NE 18th Ave., Portland, OR 97212 USA (SAN 694-2911) Tel 503-284-7426; Fax: 503-282-8985
E-mail: webmaster@griefwatch.com
Web site: http://www.griefwatch.com
Dist(s): **ACTA Pubns.**
CreateSpace Independent Publishing Platform.

Griffin Comics *Imprint of* **Corbett Features**

Griffin, Curtis Monroe, *(978-0-9749563)* 3250 Oneal Cir., Boulder, CO 80301-1424 USA.

Griffin Group Publishing LLC, *(978-0-692-01920-7)* 3419 Westminister Suite 320, Dallas, TX 75205 USA.

Griffin Publishing *See* **Greater Truth Pubs.**

Griffin Publishing Group, *(978-1-58000; 978-1-882180)* P.O. Box 28627, Santa Ana, CA 92799-8627 USA Toll Free: 800-472-9741 Do not confuse with Griffin Publishing, Ogden, UT
E-mail: griffinbooks@earthlink.net; mvonarx@griffinpublishing.com
Web site: http://www.griffinpublishing.com
Dist(s): **BHB Fulfillment**
Perseus-PGW
Sundaykool Bulletins.

Griffin, Sandi Zambarano, *(978-1-883838)* 10840 Kimberfyld Ln., Port Saint Lucie, FL 34986 USA Tel 561-461-6830
Dist(s): **Bookazine Co., Inc.**

Griffith, John *See* **Rosetta Stone Communications**

Griggs Music Co., *(978-0-9753385)* 228 Pope Bend Rd., Cedar Creek, TX 78612 USA Tel 512-303-2744
Web site: http://www.griggsmusic.net.

Grigsby, Cynthia, *(978-0-9786840)* 4304 Hillyer St., Fairfax, VA 22032-1418 USA
E-mail: cgrigsby6@yahoo.com.

Griha, *(978-0-9748503)* 23 iron Bark Ln., Aliso Viejo, CA 92656 USA
Web site: http://www.griha.com.

Grijalbo, Editorial (MEX) *(978-968-419; 978-970-05) Dist. by* **Continental Bk.**

Grijalbo, Editorial (MEX) *(978-968-419; 978-970-05) Dist. by* **AIMS Intl.**

Grijalbo Mondadori, S.A.-Junior (ESP) *(978-84-253; 978-84-397; 978-84-7419; 978-84-478; 978-84-7423) Dist. by* **Continental Bk.**

Grijalbo Mondadori, S.A.-Montena (ESP) *(978-84-7515; 978-84-85297; 978-84-8441) Dist. by* **Lectorum Pubns.**

Grijalbo-Dargaud, S.A. Editores (ESP) *(978-84-7510) Dist. by* **Distribks Inc.**

Grimes, Richard, *(978-0-9770594)* 111 Lankford Dr., Georgetown, KY 40324 USA.

Gripper Products, *(978-0-916176)* 787 N. 24th St., Philadelphia, PA 19130-2540 USA (SAN 206-3816) Tel 215-765-9362
E-mail: cormo@iname.com.

Grizlegirl Productions *See* **Bookateer Publishing**

Grizzly Adams Productions, Inc., *(978-0-9667985; 978-1-929296; 978-1-931602; 978-1-933424; 978-1-934646)* Orders Addr.: P.O. Box 298, Baker City, OR 97814 USA; Edit Addr.: 2850 Myrtle St., Baker City, OR 97814 USA
Dist(s): **Send The Light Distribution LLC.**

Grizzly Bks Publishing, *(978-0-9747951; 978-0-9749634)* Orders Addr.: PMB Box 136, Dahlonega, GA 30533 USA Tel 706-864-2349 (phone/fax); Edit Addr.: 240 Wal-Mart Way, Dahlonega, GA 30533 USA
E-mail: ancient12@linkamerica.net
Web site: http://www.grizzlybookz.com.

Grizzly Ridge Publishing, *(978-0-9793963)* P.O. Box 268, West Glacier, MT 59936 USA
Web site: http://www.grizzlyridgepublishing.com.

Grolier *Imprint of* **Scholastic Library Publishing**

Grolier Online *Imprint of* **Scholastic Library Publishing**

Grolier Publishing *See* **Scholastic Library Publishing**

Grolier Publishing, *(978-0-516; 978-0-531)* 90 Old Sherman Tpke., Danbury, CT 06816E USA Tel 203-797-3500; Fax: 203-797-3657
E-mail: agraham@grolier.com
Web site: www.scholasticlibrary.com.

Grosinger, Crain Publishing, *(978-0-9720054)* Orders Addr.: P.O. Box 55, Mandan, ND 58554 USA Tel 701-202-1293; Edit Addr.: 210 Collins Ave., Mandan, ND 58554 USA
Web site: http://www.johnsbook.net; http://www.crainbooks.com
Dist(s): **Partners Bk. Distributing, Inc.**

Gross, H. H., *(978-0-9754699)* P.O. Box 122606, San Diego, CA 92112 USA
E-mail: hhgross@lycos.com
Web site: http://www.hhgross.net.

Gross, Roxanna, *(978-0-615-16398-7)* 3 S. Cedarwood Ct., Alexandria, KY 41001 USA
E-mail: roxie@zoomtown.com
Dist(s): **Lulu Enterprises Inc.**

Grosset & Dunlap *Imprint of* **Penguin Publishing Group**

Grossman, Dina *See* **Tzipora Pubns., Inc.**

Groundbreaking Pr., *(978-0-9718562; 978-0-9745624; 978-0-9765821; 978-0-9773535; 978-0-9777795; 978-0-9793542; 978-0-9831030; 978-0-9850651)* Orders Addr.: 8305 Arboles Cir., Austin, TX 78737 USA Tel 512-657-8780
E-mail: brad@groundbreaking.com
Web site: http://www.groundbreaking.com.

Groundwood Bks. (CAN) *(978-0-88899; 978-1-55498) Dist. by* **PerseuPGW.**

Group Books *See* **Group Publishing, Inc.**

†**Group Publishing, Inc.,** *(978-0-7644; 978-0-931529; 978-0-936664; 978-1-55945; 978-1-4707)* Orders Addr.: 1515 Cascade Ave., Loveland, CO 80538-8681 USA (SAN 214-4689) Tel 970-669-3836; Fax: 970-679-4373; Toll Free: 800-635-0404; 800-447-1070 (consumer orders only); 800-541-5200 (trade orders only); *Imprints:* Flagship Church Resources (Flagship Church)
E-mail: cbuxman@grouppublishing.com
Web site: http://www.grouppublishing.com
Dist(s): **Appalachian Bible Co.**
Spring Arbor Distributors, Inc.
Twentieth Century Christian Bks.; *CIP.*

Grove Creek Publishing, LLC, *(978-1-933963)* 1159 N. 950 E., Pleasant Grove, UT 84062 USA Tel 801-471-5652
E-mail: noonws@yahoo.com
Web site: http://www.grovecreekpublishing.com.

Grove Educational Technologies, *(978-0-936735)* 6435 Yamhill St., SE, Portland, OR 97215-2027 USA (SAN 699-9840); 27 Hy Pl., Lake Grove, NY 11755 (SAN 699-9859)
E-mail: geta@juno.com.

†**Grove/Atlantic, Inc.,** *(978-0-8021; 978-0-87113; 978-1-55584; 978-1-61185)* 841 Broadway, 4th Flr., New York, NY 10003-4793 USA (SAN 201-4890) Tel 212-614-7850; Fax: 212-614-7886; Toll Free: 800-521-0178; *Imprints:* Black Cat (BlackCat)
Web site: http://www.groveatlantic.com/
Dist(s): **MyiLibrary**
Perseus-PGW
Perseus Bks. Group
Perseus Distribution; *CIP.*

Growing & Learning Pr., *(978-0-9795773)* 228 Woodward Ave, Buffalo, NY 14214 USA (SAN 853-8093).

Growing Art Pr., *(978-1-934367)* 419 NW 16th St., Corvallis, OR 97330 USA (SAN 852-9612)
E-mail: stickmaker@comcast.net.

Growing Field Bks., *(978-0-9770391; 978-0-9857057; 978-0-9891881)* 2012 Pacific Ct., Fort Collins, CO 80528 USA (SAN 851-7193) Do not confuse with companies with the same or similar name in Lawrence, KSThomaston, CT, Los Angeles, CA, Huntsville, AL, New YOrk, NY, Glen Head, NY
E-mail: Mhoog@growingfield.com
Web site: http://www.Growingfield.com
Dist(s): **Brodart Co.**
Follett School Solutions
Hertzberg-New Method Inc.

Growing Little Readers, *(978-0-9777150)* 1105 Kyle Ct., Chesapeake, VA 23322 USA
Web site: http://growinglittlereaders.com.

Growing with the Saints, Inc., *(978-0-9798889)* 2812 Longwood Ct., Fort Wayne, IN 46845 USA Tel 260-489-8493
E-mail: melissa@growingwiththesaints.com
Web site: http://www.growingwiththesaints.com.

Growing Years *Imprint of* **Port Town Publishing**

Growth Publishing, *(978-1-893505)* Div. of Growth Central LLC, Orders Addr.: 6545 N. Via Divina, Tucson, AZ 85750-0971 USA Tel 520-299-2550; Fax: 520-577-6998
E-mail: growthcentral@gmail.com
Web site: http://www.growthcentral.com/.

Growth-Ink, *(978-0-9799636)* 4025 State St., No. 9, Santa Barbara, CA 93110 USA (SAN 854-9303)
E-mail: Growthink1@aol.com.

Gruber Enterprises, *(978-0-9770413)* 21521 Finlan, Saint Clair Shores, MI 48080 USA
Web site: http://www.thelegendofthebrog.com.

Grubish, Donald, *(978-0-9771179)* 1326 Goodwin Ave N., Saint Paul, MN 55128-6164 USA.

Grubnedor Pr., *(978-0-9795407)* 8121 Allison Pl., Arvada, CO 80005 USA (SAN 853-7186)
E-mail: dmrodenburg@comcast.net
Web site: grubnedorpress.com.

Grupo Anaya, S.A. (ESP) *(978-84-207; 978-84-667) Dist. by* **Distribks Inc.**

Grupo Anaya, S.A. (ESP) *(978-84-207; 978-84-667) Dist. by* **Continental Bk.**

Grupo Anaya, S.A. (ESP) *(978-84-207; 978-84-667) Dist. by* **AIMS Intl.**

Grupo Anaya, S.A. (ESP) *(978-84-207; 978-84-667) Dist. by* **Lectorum Pubns.**

Grupo Nelson, *(978-0-8499; 978-0-88113; 978-0-89922; 978-1-60255)* Div. of Thomas Nelson, Inc., 501 Nelson Pl., Nashville, TN 37217 USA (SAN 240-6349) Tel 615-889-9000; Fax: 615-883-9376; Toll Free: 800-251-4000
Web site: http://www.editorialcaribe.com
Dist(s): **Ediciones Universal**
Libros Sin Fronteras
Luciano Bks.
Nelson, Thomas Inc.
Pan De Vida Distributors
Peniel Productions
Twentieth Century Christian Bks.
Zondervan.

Gryphon Hse., Inc., *(978-0-87659; 978-0-917505; 978-1-58904)* Orders Addr.: 6848 Leon's Way, Lewisville, NC 27023 USA (SAN 169-3190) Tel 800-638-0928; Fax: 800-638-7576; Toll Free: 800-638-0928; *Imprints:* School Age Notes (School-Age)
E-mail: info@ghbooks.com
Web site: http://www.gryphonhouse.com
Dist(s): **CENGAGE Learning**
Consortium Bk. Sales & Distribution
INscribe Digital
Independent Pubs. Group
MyiLibrary
Perseus Bks. Group
ebrary, Inc.

Gryphon Pr., The, *(978-0-940719)* 6808 Margarets Ln., Edina, MN 55439 USA Tel 952-941-5993; Fax: 952-941-6593
E-mail: eb6@earthlink.net
Dist(s): **Consortium Bk. Sales & Distribution**
Perseus Bks. Group.

G.S. Enterprises of America Inc., *(978-0-9763141)* P.O. Box 776, Frankfort, KY 40602-0776 USA Tel 502-227-8226; Fax: 502-227-8223
E-mail: lstafford173@gmail.com
Web site: http://www.bedtimeboomer.com.

GS Publishers *See* **GSVQ Publishing**

GSP Players, LLC, *(978-0-9792640)* 8033 Sunset Blvd., No. 1024, Los Angeles, CA 90046 USA.

GSR Communications, *(978-0-9717507)* 6090 SW Elm Ave., Beaverton, OR 97005 USA
E-mail: gsr@teleport.com.

GSS Tech Ed, *(978-0-9712340; 978-0-9895576)* 31500 Grape St. Bldg. 3-364, Lake Elsinore, CA 92532 USA

Publisher Name Index

Tel 951-471-4932; Fax: 951-471-4981; Toll Free Fax: 866-367-6180; Toll Free: 800-422-1100
Web site: http://www.GSSTechEd.com
Dist(s): **All Electronics Corp.**
Pitsco Education.

GSVQ Publishing, *(978-1-933156)* 1350 E. Flamingo Rd., Suite 50, Las Vegas, NV 89119-5263 USA Tel 866-347-9244; *Imprints*: VisionQuest Kids (VisionQuest Kids); Visikid Books (Visikid Bks)
E-mail: contactus@gsvisionquest.com
Web site: http://www.gsvisionquest.com; http://www.visikidbooks.com.

GT Bks. LLC, *(978-0-9765845)* 19 Housman Ct., Maplewood, NJ 07040-3006 USA
Web site: http://www.gtbooks.net.

GT Interactive Software, *(978-1-56893; 978-1-58869)* 417 Fifth Ave., New York, NY 10016 USA Tel 212-726-4243; Fax: 212-726-4204
E-mail: efierro@gtinteractive.com
Web site: http://gtinteractive.com.

Guadeloupe, Emmanuel & Augustine 'Gus' Logie *See* **Plain Vision Publishing**

Guardian Angel Publishing, *(978-0-9763990)* 415 Meadow View Dr., Lavon, TX 75166-1245 USA Do not confuse with companies with the same or similar name in Carby, OR, Saint Louis, MO
E-mail: admin@tommytellbooks.com
Web site: http://www.tommytellbooks.com.

Guardian Angel Publishing, Inc., *(978-1-933090; 978-1-935137; 978-1-61633)* 12430 Tesson Ferry Rd., No. 186, Saint Louis, MO 63128 USA (SAN 858-7833) Do not confuse with companies with same name in Canby, OR and Hubbard, OR., The Colony, TX
E-mail: publisher@guardianangelpublishing.com
Web site: http://www.guardianangelpublishing.com.

Guardian of Truth Foundation, *(978-0-9620615; 978-1-58427)* Orders Addr.: P.O. Box 9670, Bowling Green, KY 42102 USA Tel 317-745-4708; Edit Addr.: 420 Old Morgantown Rd., Bowling Green, KY 42102 USA (SAN 249-4221)
E-mail: mikewillis1@compuserve.com.

Guardians of Order (CAN) *(978-0-9682431; 978-1-894525)* *Dist. by* **PSI Ga.**

Guardsman Press *See* **Moondance Publishing**

Guevara, Alexis S., *(978-0-9765663)* 1625 Palo Alto St., No. 208, Los Angeles, CA 90026 USA
E-mail: sa_guevara@msn.com
Web site: http://www.selectaUSA.com; http://www.alexisguevara.com.

Guia, Elizabeth, *(978-0-9764280)* 2956 Bird Ave. # 8, Miami, FL 33133-4542 USA
E-mail: eguiam@msn.com.

Guide to South Florida Off-Road Bicycling *See* **DeGraaf Publishing**

Guideline Pubns. Co., *(978-1-882951)* Div. of Marketing Support Services, Orders Addr.: P.O. Box 801094, Atlanta, GA 30101 USA Fax: 770-424-0778; Toll Free: 800-552-1076
E-mail: sales@guidelinepub.com
Web site: http://www.guidelinepub.com.

Guideposts *Imprint of* **Ideals Pubns.**

GuidepostsBooks *Imprint of* **Ideals Pubns.**

Guiding Horizons, *(978-0-9749763)* 2201 Heritage Crest Dr., Valrico, FL 33594-5120 USA
Web site: http://www.guidinghorizons.com.

Guidry Assocs., Inc., *(978-0-9724667)* P.O. Box 2280, Winchester, VA 22604 USA Tel 540-545-8800; *Imprints*: Who's Who In Sports (Who's Who In Sp)
E-mail: info@whoswhoinsports.com
Web site: http://www.whoswhoinsports.com.

Guilford Pubns., *(978-0-89862; 978-1-57230; 978-1-59385; 978-1-60623; 978-1-60918; 978-1-4625)* Orders Addr.: 370 Seventh Avenue, Suite 1200, New York, NY 10001-1020 USA (SAN 212-9442) Tel 212-431-9800; Fax: 212-966-6708; Toll Free: 800-365-7006
E-mail: info@guilford.com
Web site: http://www.guilford.com
Dist(s): **MyiLibrary**
Rittenhouse Bk. Distributors
ebrary, Inc.

Guilin City Publishing, *(978-0-9818622)* P.O. Box 9621, Pittsburgh, PA 15226 USA
E-mail: info@guilincitypublishing.com
Web site: http://www.guilincitypublishing.com.

Guilty Mom Pr., *(978-0-9708415)* 172 Dolphin Cir., Marina, CA 93933 USA Tel 831-384-8459
E-mail: plumtckrd@aol.com
Dist(s): **One Small Voice Foundation.**

GuitarVoyager Inc., *(978-0-9785992)* 3616 Calvend Ln., Kensington, MD 20895 USA Tel 240-486-3849; Fax: 301-949-1647
E-mail: guitarvoyager@gmail.com
Web site: http://www.guitarvoyager.com.

Gulley, Wayne, *(978-0-9843505; 978-0-9886117)* P.O. Box 8807, Spring Valley Lake (Victorville), CA 92395 USA
E-mail: wagpublishing@me.com
Web site: www.michelangelotangelo.com.

Gulliver Bks. *Imprint of* **Harcourt Children's Bks.**

Gumbo Multimedia Entertainment, *(978-0-9762838; 978-0-9832329)* P.O. Box 371641, Miami, FL 32821 USA
E-mail: srodriguez@lushenabks.com; Jeff@JeffRivera.com
Web site: http://www.JeffRivera.com; http://www.GumboWriters.com
Dist(s): **NetSource Distribution**
Smashwords.

GumShoe Press, *(978-0-9777538)* Orders Addr.: 411 Chartley Pk. Rd., Reisterstown, MD 21136 USA (SAN 850-1769) Tel 410-971-8229
E-mail: tjmysteryauthor@aol.com
Web site: http://www.authorsden.com/tjperkins.

Gunga Peas Bks., *(978-0-615-76907-3; 978-0-615-77768-6; 978-0-692-02337-2; 978-0-692-02338-9)* Orders Addr.: P.O. Box 34512, Reno, NV 89533 USA; Edit Addr.: 7000 Mae Ann Ave 1122, Reno, NV 89523 USA Tel 775-351-5549
Dist(s): **CreateSpace Independent Publishing Platform**
Smashwords.

Guppy Publishing LLC, *(978-0-9788553)* PMB 221, 6749 S. Westnedge, Suite K, Portage, MI 49002 USA Fax: 269-327-3168
E-mail: dkennis@charter.net
Web site: http://www.guppypublishing.com.

Gurevich, Leonid, *(978-0-9753458)* 4 Remington Ln., Plymouth, MA 02360-1424 USA
E-mail: lgurev3007@aol.com.

Guru Graphics, *(978-0-9729759)* 500 Creekside Ct., Golden, CO 80403-1903 USA Tel 303-278-0177
E-mail: levropes@attbi.com.

Gurze Bks., *(978-0-936077)* Orders Addr.: P.O. Box 2238, Carlsbad, CA 92018 USA (SAN 697-0818) Tel 760-434-7533; Fax: 760-434-5476; Toll Free: 800-756-7533; Edit Addr.: 5145-B Avenida Encinas, Carlsbad, CA 92018 USA (SAN 697-0826)
E-mail: gurze@aol.com; qzcati@aol.com
Web site: http://www.gurze.com
Dist(s): **MyiLibrary**
Perseus-PGW
Perseus Bks. Group
Quality Bks., Inc.

Gusabaloo Publications *See* **Quimby & Sneet Pubns.**

Gustav's Library, *(978-0-9758914)* 1011 E. High St., Davenport, IA 52803 USA Tel 563-323-2283
E-mail: gustav@gustavslibrary.com
Web site: http://www.gustavslibrary.com.

Guzman, Maria del C., *(978-0-9855639)* 39 Arenas St., Aguirre, PR 00794 USA Tel 787-853-2542
E-mail: mguzman_aguirre@yahoo.com.

GW Publishing (GBR) *(978-0-9535397; 978-0-9546701; 978-0-9551564; 978-0-9554145; 978-0-9561211; 978-0-9570844)* *Dist. by* **Wlsn Assocs.**

Gwasg Prifysgol Cymru / Univ. of Wales Pr. (GBR) *(978-0-7083; 978-0-900768; 978-1-900477; 978-1-78316)* *Dist. by* **Chicago Distribution Ctr.**

GWB *Imprint of* **Great White Bird Publishing**

GWF Publishing & Henry's Helpers, *(978-0-9768442)*
E-mail: henryshelpers@yahoo.com
Web site: http://www.henryshelpers.com.

Gye Nyame Hse., *(978-1-886098)* Orders Addr.: P.O. Box 42248, Philadelphia, PA 19101 USA (SAN 299-0415) Tel 215 229 1751; Edit Addr.: 6810 Old York Rd., Philadelphia, PA 19126 USA Tel 215-548-2175
E-mail: gyenyamehouse@aol.com.

Gye Nyame Press *See* **Love II Learn Bks.**

Gypsy Heart Pr., *(978-0-9832514)* P.O. Box 11681, College Station, TX 77842 USA Tel 086-069-9398
E-mail: erin@erin-casey.com
Dist(s): **Ingram Pub. Services.**

Gypsy Hill Publishing,
Dist(s): **AtlasBooks Distribution.**

Gypsy Pubns., *(978-0-9842375; 978-1-938768)* 325 Green Oak Dr., Troy, OH 45373-4396 USA
E-mail: fishermh@juno.com; meg.fisher@yahoo.com
Web site: http://www.gypsypublications.com.

H & R Magic Bks., *(978-0-9727938)* 3839 Liles Ln., Humble, TX 77396 USA Tel 281-540-7229
Web site: http://www.magicbookshop.com.

H Bar Pr., *(978-0-9794104; 978-0-9893092)* 729 Westview St., Philadelphia, PA 19119-3533 USA (SAN 853-3644) Tel 215-844-8054; Fax: 215-844-1399
E-mail: kwford@verizon.net; hbar.press@verizon.net
Dist(s): **Smashwords.**

H E C Software, Inc., *(978-0-9728424; 978-1-62382)* 60 N. Cutler Dr., No. 101, North Salt Lake, UT 84054 USA (SAN 669-6201) Tel 801-295-7054; Fax: 801-295-7088; Toll Free: 800-333-0054
E-mail: info@readinghorizons.com
Web site: http://www.readinghorizons.com.

H H Krsna Balaram Swami, *(978-0-9631403)* Orders Addr.: P.O. Box 27127, Baltimore, MD 21230 USA; Edit Addr.: 1613 Webster St., Baltimore, MD 21230 USA Tel 301-752-7531.

H M Bricker, *(978-0-615-42163-6; 978-0-9838738)* Orders Addr.: 2279 Grass Lake Rd., Lindenhurst, IL 60046 USA
E-mail: santanobeard@comcast.net; birdman1211@comcast.net
Web site: http://www.grandpabrickerbooks.com.

H M S Pubns., Inc., *(978-1-888732)* P.O. Box 524, Niantic, CT 06357 USA Tel 860-739-3187; Toll Free: 888-739-3187
E-mail: hmspublications@earthlink.net
Dist(s): **AtlasBooks Distribution**
BookMasters Distribution Services (BDS)
Follett School Solutions
Quality Bks., Inc.
ebrary, Inc.

H. O. M. E. (Holding Onto Memorable Experiences) *See* **Do The Write Thing, Inc.**

H R M Software *See* **Human Relations Media**

Haag Environmental Press *See* **Haag Pr.**

Haag Pr., *(978-0-9665497; 978-0-9710260; 978-0-9797511)* Div. of Haag Environmental Co., Inc., Orders Addr.: 315 E. Market St., Sandusky, OH 44870 USA (SAN 852-6583) Tel 419-621-9329; Fax: 419-621-8669
E-mail: haagpress@aol.com; help@haagpress.com
Web site: http://www.haagpress.com.

Haan Graphic Publishing Services, Limited *See* **Southfarm Pr.**

Haber-Schaim & Associates *See* **Science Curriculum, Inc.**

Hability Solution Services, Inc., *(978-1-932062)* P.O. Box 2595, Kearney, NE 68848 USA Tel 308-338-9238; Fax: 308-338-9208; Toll Free: 888-814-3238
E-mail: info@habsol.com; info@ideamagicbooks.com
Web site: http://www.habsol.com; http://www.ideamagicbooks.com.

Habit House *See* **Roedway Pr.**

Hachai Publications, Incorporated *See* **Hachai Publishing**

Hachai Publishing, *(978-0-922613; 978-1-929628)* 527 Empire Blvd., Brooklyn, NY 11225 USA (SAN 251-3749) Tel 718-633-0100; Fax: 718-633-0103
E-mail: info@hachai.com
Web site: http://www.hachai.com
Dist(s): **Kerem Publishing.**

Hachette Audio, *(978-1-57042; 978-1-58621; 978-1-59483; 978-1-60024; 978-1-60788)* Div. of Hachette Book Group, 237 Park Ave., New York, NY 10017 USA Tel 212-364-1100; Toll Free: 800-452-2707
E-mail: audiobooks.publicity@hbgusa.com
Web site: http://www.hachettebookgroupusa.com/publishing_hachette-audio.aspx
Dist(s): **Findaway World, LLC**
Follett School Solutions
Grand Central Publishing
Hachette Bk. Group
Libros Sin Fronteras
Landmark Audiobooks.

Hachette AudioBooks *See* **Hachette Audio**

Hachette Bks. *Imprint of* **Hachette Bks.**

Hachette Bk. Group, *(978-0-446; 978-1-60941; 978-1-61113; 978-1-61969; 978-1-4789)* Div. of Hachette Group Livre, Orders Addr.: 3 Center Plaza, Boston, MA 02108 USA (SAN 852-5463) Tel 617-263-1828; Toll Free Fax: 800-286-9471; Toll Free: 800-759-0190; Edit Addr.: 237 Park Ave., New York, NY 10017 USA Tel 212-363-1100; P.O. Box 2146, Johannesburg, 2196 Tel 2711 783-7565; Fax: 2711 883-6866; *Imprints*: L,B Kids (LB Kids)
Web site: http://www.hachettebookgroup.com
Dist(s): **Blackstone Audio, Inc.**
Findaway World, LLC
Follett School Solutions
MyiLibrary
Perfection Learning Corp.
Time Inc. Bks.

Hachette Bks., Div. of Hachette Book Group, Orders Addr.: 3 Center Plaza, Boston, MA 02108-2084 USA Tel 617-227-0730; Toll Free Fax: 800-286-9471; Toll Free: 800-759-0730; Edit Addr.: 237 Park Ave., New York, NY 10017 USA Tel 212-364-0600; Fax: 212-364-0952; *Imprints*: Hachette Books (HachetteBks); Black Dog & Leventhal Publishers, Inc. (BlackDog Lev)
Dist(s): **Hachette Bk. Group**
MyiLibrary.

Hachette Children's Group (GBR) *(978-0-7502; 978-1-85881; 978-1-84255; 978-1-4440; 978-1-4449)* *Dist. by* **IPG Chicago.**

Hachette Children's Group (GBR) *(978-0-7502; 978-1-85881; 978-1-84255; 978-1-4440; 978-1-4449)* *Dist. by* **HachBkGrp.**

Hachette Groupe Livre (FRA) *(978-2-01)* *Dist. by* **Distribks Inc.**

Hachette Nashville, *(978-0-446)* Div. of Hachette Book Group, 10 Cadillac Dr., Brentwood, TN 37027 USA Tel 615-221-0996; *Imprints*: Faithwords (Faithwrds)
Dist(s): **Hachette Bk. Group**
MyiLibrary.

†Hackett Publishing Co., Inc., *(978-0-87220; 978-0-915144; 978-0-915145; 978-0-941051; 978-1-58510; 978-1-60384; 978-1-62466)* Orders Addr.: P.O. Box 44937, Indianapolis, IN 46244-0937 USA (SAN 201-6044) Tel 317-635-9250; Fax: 317-635-9292; Toll Free Fax: 800-783-9213; *Imprints*: Focus (FocusUSA)
E-mail: customer@hackettpublishing.com
Web site: http://www.hackettpublishing.com
Dist(s): **ebrary, Inc.**; *CIP.*

Hadrosaur Pr., *(978-1-885093)* P.O. Box 2194, Mesilla Park, NM 88047-2194 USA Tel 505-527-4163; *Imprints*: LBF/Hadrosaur (LBF Hadrs)
E-mail: hadrosaur@zianet.com
Web site: http://www.hadrosaur.com.

Hafabanana Press *See* **KB Bks. & More**

Hagan, Theda *See* **Hagan, Theda Bks.**

Hagan, Theda Bks., *(978-0-9678032; 978-0-9827155)* 47 Comer Dr., Madisonville, KY 42431 USA Tel 270-821-6968
E-mail: thedahagan@yahoo.com
Web site: http://www.heavenlyharborbooks.com/default.htm.

Hager, Robert, *(978-0-9727676)* 101 Crawford, Suite 2C, Houston, TX 77002 USA
Web site: http://www.saurcana.com/pages/about_author.html.

Hahn, Beverly, *(978-0-9722494)* Orders Addr.: P.O. Box 66, Hilmak, CA 95324 USA; Edit Addr.: 9613 Ailanthus Ave., Delhi, CA 95315 USA (SAN 254-7376).

Hairball Pr., *(978-0-9646781)* 2318 2nd Ave., Suite 591, Seattle, WA 98121 USA Tel 206-932-8173.

Hairston Enterprises, LLC, *(978-0-9762958)* 582 Bristol Ln., Birmingham, AL 35226 USA Tel 205-369-4022
E-mail: kchairston@yahoo.com
Web site: http://www.forgottenrules.com; http://www.forgottenrules.org; http://www.theforgottenrules.com; http://www.theforgottenrules.org.

Hairston, Rodney, *(978-0-9760689)* 75 Fern Oak Cir. Apt. 201, Stafford, VA 22554-8459 USA
E-mail: rhairston@jbmanagement.com.

Haislip, Allen, *(978-0-9767640)* Orders Addr.: 32 Marquette Dr., Florissant, MO 63031-3839 USA.

Haiti World, *(978-0-9793039)* P.O. Box 5663, Vernon Hills, IL 60061 USA Tel 847-514-9967
E-mail: haitiworld@yahoo.com.

Halbur Publishing, *(978-0-9603520)* 142 Angela Dr., Santa Rosa, CA 95403-1702 USA (SAN 212-9469)
E-mail: dhalbur@sonic.net.

Halcyon Pr., *(978-0-941970)* 18-05 215 St., Flushing, NY 11360 USA (SAN 238-244X) Tel 212-631-9640 Do not confuse with companies with same or similar name in Hendersonville, NC, Dallas, TX, Houston, TX.

Halcyon Pr., Ltd., *(978-0-9706054; 978-1-931823; 978-0-9830676)* P.O. Box 260, Pearland, TX 77588-0260 USA (SAN 253-9934) Toll Free: 866-774-5786 Do not confuse with companies with same or similar name in Hendersonville, NC, Flushing, NY, Dallas, TX
E-mail: david.raley@gmail.com
Web site: http://www.halcyonpress.com
Dist(s): **Bk. Marketing Plus.**

Haldane Mason, Ltd. (GBR) *(978-1-902463)* *Dist. by* **Trans-Atl Phila.**

Hale Kuamo'o Hawaiian Language Ctr. at UHH, *(978-0-9665331; 978-1-930339; 978-0-9741580)* Div. of Ka Haka 'Ula o Ke'elikolani/College of Hawaiian Language at UH Hilo, 200 W. Kawili St., Hilo, HI 96720-4091 USA Tel 808-974-7339; Fax: 808-974-7686
E-mail: contact@ahapunanaleo.org
Web site: http://www.olelo.hawaii.edu; http://www.ahapunanaleo.org.

Hale Publishing, *(978-0-9636219; 978-0-9729583; 978-0-9772268; 978-0-9815257; 978-0-9823379; 978-0-9845039; 978-0-9833075; 978-0-9847746; 978-0-9858893; 978-1-939847)* 1712 N. Forest St., Amarillo, TX 79106 USA Tel 806-376-9900 Toll Free: 800-378-1317
E-mail: books@ibreastfeeding.com; alicia.ingram@halepublishing.com
Web site: http://www.ibreastfeeding.com.

Hale, Robert Ltd. (GBR) *(978-0-7090; 978-0-7091; 978-0-7198; 978-0-85131; 978-1-910208)* *Dist. by* **PerseuPGW.**

Haley's, *(978-0-9626308; 978-1-884540; 978-0-9897667; 978-0-9916102; 978-0-9967730)* Orders Addr.: 488 S. Main St., Athol, MA 01331 USA Tel 978-249-9400 (phone/fax); Toll Free: 800-215-8805 (phone/fax); Edit Addr.: 488 S. Main St., Athol, MA 01331 USA
E-mail: haley.antique@verizon.net
Web site: http://www.mattawasongcycle.com; http://www.haleysantiques.com
Dist(s): **Follett School Solutions.**

Half-Pint Kids, Inc., *(978-1-59256)* 820 Walnut Dr., Ellwood City, PA 16117 USA
Web site: http://halfpintkids.com.

Hall & Humphries Publishing Hse., *(978-0-9758521)* Orders Addr.: P.O. Box 371021, Decatur, GA 30037-1021 USA; Edit Addr.: 2652 Rainbow Pkwy., Decatur, GA 30034 USA Tel 404-625-4486.

Hall, Annalisa, *(978-0-615-22113-7)* 14271 Anabelle Dr., Poway, CA 92064 USA
Dist(s): **Lulu Enterprises Inc.**

Hall, Kenneth, *(978-0-615-19649-7)* 1857 Morris Ave., Lincoln Park, MI 48146-1328 USA
E-mail: kenhall321@yahoo.com
Dist(s): **Lulu Enterprises Inc.**

Hall, Monique P. Productions, *(978-0-9772634)* 167 Wyatt Earp Loop, Nolanville, TX 76559 USA (SAN 851-6391) Tel 254-698-5965
E-mail: nickiepop777@gmail.com
Web site: nickiepopart.com.

Hall, Nancy Inc., *(978-1-884270)* 7 W. 18th St., 6th Flr., New York, NY 10011 USA Tel 212-674-3408; Fax: 212-353-1521
E-mail: Nhallinc@aol.com.

Hall Press *See* **Hallcienda**

Hall, Stephen & Denise, *(978-0-9753305)* 1237 Prairie Dell Rd., Union, MO 63084-4310 USA
E-mail: wordsofahunter@cs.com.

Hallcienda, *(978-0-932218)* Orders Addr.: P.O. Box 9066, San Bernardino, CA 92427 USA (SAN 211-7061) Tel 909-887-3466; P.O. Box 9066, San Bernardino, CA 92427 (SAN 665-7060) Tel 909-887-3466.

Hallelujah Acres Publishing, *(978-0-929619)* P.O. Box 2388, Shelby, NC 28151 USA (SAN 249-7891) Tel 704-481-1700; Fax: 704-481-0345
E-mail: chet@hacres.com
Web site: http://www.hacres.com
Dist(s): **AtlasBooks Distribution**
Send The Light Distribution LLC.

Haller Company, The, *(978-0-9743961)* Orders Addr.: P.O. Box 207, Burlingame, CA 94010 USA Tel 650-348-3900; Fax: 650-558-9012; Edit Addr.: 1325 Howard Ave., Burlingame, CA 94010 USA
Web site: http://www.hallercompany.com.

Hallmark Card, Inc., *(978-0-87529; 978-1-59530; 978-1-63059)* 2501 McGee, Kansas City, MO 64141-6580 USA (SAN 202-2672) Tel 816-274-5111
Dist(s): **Independent Pubs. Group**
Univ. of New Mexico Pr.

Hallmark Emporium, *(978-0-9665055)* 9201 Russell Ave. S., Bloomington, MN 55431 USA Tel 612-884-2601; Fax: 612-703-0218
E-mail: dead541@aol.com
Web site: http://members.aol.com/dead 541/index.html.

Halo Publishing International, *(978-0-9718350; 978-0-9797429; 978-1-935268; 978-1-61244)* 5549 Canal Rd., Cleveland, OH 44125 USA
Web site: http://www.halopublishing.com.

Hameray Publishing Group, Inc., *(978-1-60559; 978-1-62817)* 11545 Sorrento Valley Rd., Suite 310, San Diego, CA 92121 USA Tel 858-369-5200; Fax: 858-369-5201; Toll Free Fax: 858-369-5209; Toll Free: 866-918-6173
E-mail: christine@hameraypublishing.com
Web site: http://www.hameraypublishing.com.

Hamilton Bks., *(978-0-7618)* Div. of Rowman & Littlefield Publishing Group, Orders Addr.: 15200 NBN Way, Blue Ridge Summit, PA 17214 USA Tel 717-794-3800 (Sales, Customer Service, MIS, Royalties, Inventory Mgmt., Dist., Credit & Collections); Fax: 717-794-3803 (Customer Service &/or orders only); 717-794-3857 (Sales & MIS); 717-794-3856 Royalties, Inventory Mgmt. & Dist.); Toll Free Fax: 800-338-4550 (Customer

Service &/ or orders); Toll Free: 800-462-6420 (Customer Service &/ or orders); Edit Addr.: 4501 Forbes Blvd., Suite 200, Lanham, MD 20706 USA Tel 301-459-3366; Fax: 301-459-5748 Short Discount, please contact rlpgsales@rowman.com
Web site: http://www.rlpgbooks.com
Dist(s): **Follett School Solutions**
MyiLibrary
National Bk. Network
Rowman & Littlefield Publishers, Inc.
ebrary, Inc.

Hamilton Ministries *See* **DCTS Publishing**

Hamline Univ. Pr., *(978-0-9633686; 978-0-9723721; 978-1-934458)* 1536 Hewitt Ave., MS-C1916, Saint Paul, MN 55104-2490 USA
E-mail: bhansonhegg01@hamline.edu
Web site: http://www.hamline.edu.

Hammad, Salma *See* **Lucent Interpretations, LLC**

Hammersmark Books *See* **Kluis Publishing, LLC**

Hammond, Incorporated *See* **Hammond World Atlas Corp.**

Hammond, Roger, *(978-0-9763822)* 4915 Avon Ln., Sarasota, FL 34238 USA
Web site: http://www.pelithepelican.com.

†**Hammond World Atlas Corp.**, *(978-0-7230; 978-0-8437)* Subs. of Langenscheidt Pubs., Inc., 193 Morris Ave., Springfield, NJ 07081-1211 USA (SAN 202-2702)
E-mail: rstrung@americanmap.com
Web site: http://www.Hammondmap.com
Dist(s): **Langenscheidt Publishing Group**; *CIP*.

Hampton Roads Publishing Co., Inc., *(978-0-9624375; 978-1-57174; 978-1-878901)* Orders Addr.: P.O. Box 8107, Charlottesvle, VA 22906-8107 USA (SAN 299-8874) Toll Free Fax: 800-766-9042; Toll Free: 800-766-8009
E-mail: hrpc@hrpub.com
Web site: http://www.hamptonroadspub.com
Dist(s): **Hay Hse., Inc.**
Red Wheel/Weiser.

Hampton-Brown Books *See* **National Geographic School Publishing, Inc.**

Hamster Huey Pr., *(978-0-9749090)* 7627 84th Ave., Ct., NW, Gig Harbor, WA 98335-6237 USA Tel 253-851-7839; Fax: 253-853-3493
E-mail: phs@oz.net
Web site: http://www.hamsterhueypress.com.

Hamster Pr., *(978-0-9645669; 978-0-9724630)* Orders Addr.: P.O. Box 27471, Seattle, WA 98125 USA Fax: 206-363-2878
E-mail: hamstrpres@aol.com
Web site: http://www.billschelly.com
Dist(s): **Diamond Comic Distributors, Inc.**
FM International
Syco Distribution.

†**Hancock Hse. Pubs.**, *(978-0-88839; 978-0-919654; 978-1-55205)* 1431 Harrison Ave., Blaine, WA 98230-5005 USA (SAN 665-7079) Tel 604-538-1114; Fax: 604-538-2262; Toll Free Fax: 800-983-2262; Toll Free: 800-938-1114; 19313 Zero Ave., Surrey, BC V3S 9R9 (SAN 115-3730)
E-mail: sales@hancockhouse.com
Web site: http://www.hancockhouse.com; *CIP*.

Hand Print Pr., *(978-0-9679846; 978-0-615-74893-1; 978-0-9914762)* Orders Addr.: P.O. Box 576, Blodgett, OR 97326 USA Tel 541-438-4300; Edit Addr.: 395 Grant Creek Rd., Eddyville, OR 97343 USA
E-mail: kiko@handprintpress.com; potlatch@cmug.com
Web site: http://www.handprintpress.com
Dist(s): **Chelsea Green Publishing**
CreateSpace Independent Publishing Platform.

Handfinger Pr., *(978-0-9838294)* 833 Eastview Ave., Delray Beach, FL 33483 USA Tel 561-654-8680; Fax: 561-684-1508
E-mail: wendyg52@hotmail.com
Dist(s): **Independent Pubs. Group.**

H&M Systems Software, Inc., *(978-1-885936)* 600 E. Crescent Ave., Suite 203, U Saddle Riv, NJ 07458-1846 USA Toll Free: 800-327-3713; *Imprints*: StudioLine Photo (StudioLine)
E-mail: Info@HM-Software.com
Web site: http://www.Gameware.com; http://www.HM-Software.com; http://www.StudioLine.biz
Dist(s): **Victory Multimedia.**

Handprint Bks. *Imprint of* **Chronicle Bks. LLC**

Handprint Bks., *(978-1-929766; 978-1-59354)* 413 Sixth Ave., Brooklyn, NY 11215-3310 USA
E-mail: publisher@handprintbooks.com
Web site: http://www.handprintbooks.com
Dist(s): **Chronicle Bks. LLC**
Hachette Bk. Group
Learning Connection, The
Penton Overseas, Inc.
Random Hse., Inc.

Hands to the Plow, Inc., *(978-1-930914)* P.O. Box 567, Webster, WI 54893 USA Tel 715-349-7185
E-mail: tomkelby@handstotheplow.org
Web site: http://www.handstotheplow.org.

Handstand Kids, *(978-0-9792107; 978-0-9847476)* 23346 Pk. Colombo, Calabasas, CA 91302 USA (SAN 852-7822) Tel 818-917-7200
E-mail: yvette@handstandkids.com
Web site: http://www.handstandkids.com.

H&W Publishing Inc., *(978-0-9800934)* P.O. Box 53515, Cincinnati, OH 45253 USA Tel 513-687-3968; Fax: 513-761-4221
E-mail: kwatkins1@fuse.net
Web site: http://www.handwpublishing.com.

Handwriting Without Tears, *(978-1-891627; 978-1-934825; 978-1-939814)* Div. of No Tears Learning Inc., 8001 MacArthur Blvd., Cabin John, MD 20818-1607 USA Tel 301-263-2700; Fax: 301-263-2707; Toll Free: 888-983-8409
Web site: http://www.hwtears.com; http://www.getsetforschool.com.

Hanford Mead Pubs., Inc., *(978-0-9643158; 978-1-59275)* P.O. Box 8051, Santa Cruz, CA 95061 USA (SAN 253-9195) Tel 831-459-6855; Fax: 831-426-4474
E-mail: info@hanfordmead.com
Web site: http://www.hanfordmead.com; http://www.soulcollage.com; http://www.ethicsofcaring.com
Dist(s): **New Leaf Distributing Co., Inc.**

†**Hanging Loose Pr.**, *(978-0-914610; 978-1-882413; 978-1-931236; 978-1-934909)* 231 Wyckoff St., Brooklyn, NY 11217 USA (SAN 206-4960) Fax: 212-243-7499
E-mail: print225@aol.com
Web site: http://www.hangingloosepress.com
Dist(s): **Partners/West Book Distributors**
SPD-Small Pr. Distribution; *CIP*.

Hanks, Scott, *(978-0-9794157; 978-0-9799518; 978-0-9815083)* 1781 E. 800th Rd., Lawrence, KS 66049 USA (SAN 853-4098) Tel 785-887-2203; Fax: 785-887-2204
E-mail: mt@heritagebaptistchurch.cc
Web site: http://www.heritagebaptistchurch.cc.

Hannacroix Creek Bks., Inc., *(978-1-889262; 978-1-938998)* 1127 High Ridge Rd., No. 110, Stamford, CT 06905-1203 USA (SAN 299-9560) Tel 203-968-8098; Fax: 203-968-0193
E-mail: Hannacroix@aol.com
Web site: http://www.hannacroixcreekbooks.com
Dist(s): **Brodart Co.**
Emery-Pratt Co.
Follett School Solutions
Midwest Library Service
Quality Bks., Inc.
TextStream
Unique Bks., Inc.

Hannel Educational Consulting, *(978-0-9764776)* 1131 W. Palm Ln., Phoenix, AZ 85007-1536 USA Tel 602-524-7647; Fax: 602-253-2693
Web site: http://www.hannel.com.

Hannibal Bks., *(978-0-929292; 978-1-934749; 978-1-61315)* Div. of KLMK Communications, Inc., Orders Addr.: 313 S. 11th St. Suite A, Garland, TX 75040 USA Tel 800-747-0738; Fax: 888-252-3022; Toll Free Fax: 888-252-3022; Toll Free: 800-747-0738; Edit Addr.: 313 S. 11th St., Garland, TX 75040 USA Fax: 888-252-3022
E-mail: hannibalbooks@earthlink.net; orders@hannibalbooks.com; louismoore@hannibalbooks.com
Web site: http://www.hannibalbooks.com
Dist(s): **Lightning Source, Inc.**
Spring Arbor Distributors, Inc.

Hannover Hse. *Imprint of* **Truman Pr., Inc.**

Hansen, Charles Educational Music & Bks., Inc., *(978-0-8494)* 1820 West Ave., Miami Beach, FL 33139 USA (SAN 205-0609) Tel 305-532-5461; Fax: 305-672-8729
E-mail: khansen507@aol.com
Web site: http://www.hansenpublications.com/
Dist(s): **Hansen Hse.**

Hansen, Diane, *(978-0-9761988)* P.O. Box 1051, Redondo Beach, CA 90278 USA Tel 310-379-8006
Web site: http://thosearemyprivateparts.com.

Hansen House Publishing, Inc., *(978-0-9819709)* 711 W. 17th St., Suite D-2, Costa Mesa, CA 92627 USA Do not confuse with Mark Victor Hansen & Associates in Newport Beach, CA
Dist(s): **Hay Hse., Inc.**

Hansen, Marc Stuffl, *(978-0-9794643)* P.O. Box 621, Greenville, MI 48838 USA
E-mail: marchansenstuff@gmail.com
Web site: http://www.marchansenstuff.com.

Hanson, Tracie, *(978-0-9799185)* Orders Addr.: 94 Pletcher Dr., Yorkville, IL 60560 USA Tel 815-440-5681
E-mail: tracie777@sbcglobal.net
Web site: http://www.newworldbaby.net.

Happy About, *(978-0-9633302; 978-1-60005; 978-1-60773)* 21265 Stevens Creek Blvd., Suite 205, Cupertino, CA 95014 USA Tel 408-257-3000
E-mail: info@happyabout.info
Web site: http://www.happyabout.info
Dist(s): **Ebsco Publishing**
MyiLibrary
OverDrive, Inc.

Happy Apple Bks., *(978-0-9890903)* 852 Riven Oak Dr., Murrells Inlet, SC 29576 USA Tel 843-458-8740
E-mail: wickedisbetter@yahoo.com; mattellerin@yahoo.com
Web site: http://www.happyapplebooks.com.

Happy Bks. Pr., *(978-0-9787826)* 29877 Westhaven Dr., Agoura, CA 91301 USA Tel 818-879-1268
E-mail: ghuyette@charter.net; happybookspress@vrillustration.com
Web site: http://www.vrillustration.com.

Happy Cat Bks. (GBR) *(978-1-899248; 978-1-903285; 978-1-905117) Dist. by* **Star Brght Bks.**

Happy Day *Imprint of* **Tyndale Hse. Pubs.**

Happy Hamster Press, The *See* **Imagination Workshop, The**

Happy Heart Kids Publishing, *(978-0-9763143)* Orders Addr.: 2912 Beane Rd., Lenoir, NC 28645-8653 USA (SAN 256-3029) Tel 828-302-9500; 828-754-4126 (phone/fax); Fax: 828-758-8409
E-mail: mshelen@charter.net
Web site: http://www.happyheartkids.com.

Happy Hearts Family, The, *(978-0-615-34485-0; 978-0-9899470)* 2044 Loggia, Newport Beach, CA 92660 USA Tel 949-701-8296
E-mail: marianal@cox.net
Web site: http://thehappyheartsfamily.com.

Happy Horse Publishing, Ltd., *(978-0-9727849)* Orders Addr.: P.O. Box 15767, Chevy Chase, MD 20825 USA Tel 301-589-8888; Edit Addr.: 5910 Connecticut Ave., Chevy Chase, MD 70875 USA
E-mail: eashe@happyhorse.us
Web site: http://www.happyhorsekids.com.

HAPPY HOUSE PR., *(978-0-615-87080-9; 978-0-615-88154-6)* 1301 Birdsall St., Old Hickory, TN 37138 USA Tel 6155547064 Do not confuse with Happy House Press in Tillamook, OR
Web site: www.happyhousepress.com
Dist(s): **CreateSpace Independent Publishing Platform.**

Happy Kappy Karacters, *(978-0-615-45522-8; 978-0-615-65651-9)* 20 Secora Rd., Suite 312, Monsey, NY 10952 USA
E-mail: georgegeisser@aol.com; marshall@nydesign.com
Web site: www.nydesign.com; www.kappythekangaroo.com.

Happy Viking Crafts, *(978-0-9740175)* Orders Addr.: P.O. Box 35, Mahomet, IL 61853 USA; Edit Addr.: 1001 Sunrise Cir., Mahomet, IL 61853-3536 USA Tel 217-586-2497.

Happy Women Publishing Co., *(978-0-9745627)* 11487 57th St E., Parrish, FL 34219-5818 USA
E-mail: hwp@toerrific.com
Web site: http://toerrific.com
Dist(s): **Continental Enterprises Group, Inc. (CEG).**

Happyland Media, *(978-0-9726418)* Orders Addr.: P.O. Box 20398, Castro Valley, CA 94546 USA; Edit Addr.: 20283 Santa Marie Ave., Castro Valley, CA 94546 USA
E-mail: info@happylandmedia.com
Web site: http://www.happylandmedia.com.

Harambee Pr., *(978-0-9769846)* P.O. Box 353, Macatawa, MI 49434 USA
Web site: http://www.harambeepress.com.

Harbinger Pr., *(978-0-9674736; 978-0-9723998)* 2711 Buford Rd. PMB 383, Richmond, VA 23235-2423 USA (SAN 299-9994) Do not confuse with companies with the same or similar names in Woodland Hills, CA, Corte Madera, CA
E-mail: keith@harbpress.com
Web site: http://www.harbpress.com.

Harbor Hse., *(978-1-891799)* 629 Stevens Xing., Augusta, GA 30907-9566 USA; *Imprints*: Bat Wing Press (Bat Wing Pr)
E-mail: peggycheney@harborhousebooks.com; harborhouse@harborhousebooks.com
Web site: http://www.harborhousebooks.com.

Harbor Hse. Pubs., Inc., *(978-0-937360)* 221 Water St., Boyne City, MI 49712 USA (SAN 200-5751) Tel 616-582-2814; Fax: 616-582-3392; Toll Free: 800-491-1760
E-mail: harbor@harborhouse.com
Web site: http://www.harborhouse.com.

Harbor Island Bks., *(978-0-9741787)* 1214 W. Boston Post Rd., No. 245, Mamaroneck, NY 10543 USA (SAN 255-9137) Tel 914-420-9782; Fax: 914-835-7897
E-mail: publisher@lyingawake.net; hfurbush@earthlink.net
Web site: http://www.lyingawake.net/
Dist(s): **Partners/West Book Distributors.**

Harbor Mountain Pr., *(978-0-9786009; 978-0-9815560; 978-0-9882755)* P.O. Box 519, Brownsville, VT 05037 USA
Web site: http://www.harbormountainpress.org; www.spdbooks.org; petermoney.com
Dist(s): **GenPop Bks.**
SPD-Small Pr. Distribution.

Harbor Pr., Inc., *(978-0-936197)* Orders Addr.: P.O. Box 1656, Gig Harbor, WA 98335 USA (SAN 696-8953) Tel 253-851-5190; Fax: 253-851-5191; Edit Addr.: P.O. Box 1656, Gig Harbor, WA 98335-3656 USA (SAN 696-8961) Do not confuse with companies with the same name in Friday Harbor, WA, Austin, TX, Ardmore, PA
E-mail: young2327@mindspring.com
Web site: http://www.harborpress.com
Dist(s): **National Bk. Network.**

Harborseal Publishing Co., *(978-0-9652963; 978-0-9787308)* Orders Addr.: P.O. Box 126, Seal Cove, ME 04674-0126 USA Tel 207-244-7753; Edit Addr.: Rte. 102, Captain's Quarters Rd., Seal Cove, ME 04674 USA
Dist(s): **Magazines, Inc.**

HarborTown Histories, *(978-0-9710984)* 6 Harbor Way, Santa Barbara, CA 93109 USA
E-mail: baker@sbcc.net.

Harbour Arts, LLC, *(978-0-9778196)* 1790 Philippe Pkwy., Safety Harbor, FL 34695 USA
Web site: http://www.harbourarts.com.

Harbourside Pr., *(978-0-9740552)* 7892 Sailboat Key Blvd., Suite 506, South Pasadena, FL 33707 USA Tel 727-543-5855
E-mail: harbours@harboursidepress.com
Web site: http://www.harboursidepress.com
Dist(s): **Greenleaf Book Group.**

Harcourt Achieve *See* **Houghton Mifflin Harcourt Supplemental Pubs.**

Harcourt Brace & Company *See* **Harcourt Trade Pubs.**

Harcourt Brace School Publishers *See* **Harcourt Schl. Pubs.**

Harcourt Children's Bks *Imprint of* **Harcourt Children's Bks.**

Harcourt Children's Bks., *(978-0-15)* Div. of Houghton Mifflin Harcourt Trade & Reference Pubs., Orders Addr.: 6277 Sea Harbor Dr., Orlando, FL 32887 USA Toll Free Fax: 800-235-0256; Toll Free: 800-543-1918; 465 S. Lincoln Dr., Troy, MO 63379 Toll Free Fax: 800-235-0266; Toll Free: 800-543-1918; Edit Addr.: 15 E. 26th St., 15th Flr., New York, NY 10010 USA Tel 212-592-1000; Fax: 212-592-1011; 525 B St., Suite 1900, San Diego, CA 92101 Tel 619-231-6616; *Imprints*: Gulliver Books (Gulliver Bks); Red Wagon Books (Red Wagon Bks); Harcourt Children's Books (HCB)
E-mail: Andrew.porter@harcourt.com
Web site: http://www.HarcourtBooks.com
Dist(s): **Houghton Mifflin Harcourt Publishing Co.**
Harcourt Trade Pubs.

Harcourt Schl. Pubs., *(978-0-15)* Div. of Houghton Mifflin Harcouty School Publishers, 9205 Southpark Ctr. Loop, Orlando, FL 32819 USA (SAN 299-4585) Tel 407-345-2000; Fax: 407-352-3445; Toll Free Fax: 800-874-6418 (orders); Toll Free: 800-225-5425 (orders)
E-mail: hbspcs@harcourt.com
Web site: http://www.harcourtschool.com/
Dist(s): **Houghton Mifflin Harcourt Trade & Reference Pubs.**
Lectorum Pubns., Inc.

†**Harcourt Trade Pubs.**, *(978-0-15)* Div. of Houghton Mifflin Harcourt Trade & Reference Pubs., Orders Addr.: 6277 Sea Harbor Dr., Orlando, FL 32887 USA (SAN 200-285X) Tel 619-699-6707; Toll Free Fax: 800-235-0256; Toll Free: 800-543-1918 (trade orders, inquiries, claims); Edit Addr.: 15 E. 26th St., New York, NY 10010 USA Tel 212-592-1000; Fax: 212-592-1011; 525 B St., Suite 1900, San Diego, CA 92101-4495 (SAN 200-2736) Tel 619-231-6616; *Imprints*: Silver Whistle (Silver Whistle)
E-mail: andrewporter@harcourt.com
Web site: http://www.HarcourtBooks.com
Dist(s): **MyiLibrary**; *CIP*.

hard girl bk. club, *(978-0-9748712)* 4143 S. Adelle, Mesa, AZ 85212 USA Tel 480-241-1351; Fax: 480-354-4727; Toll Free: 800-307-5261
E-mail: tkempton@cox.net
Web site: http://hardgirlbookclub.com.

Hard Made Books *See* **HM Bks.**

Hard Shell Word Factory, *(978-1-58200; 978-0-7599)* Orders Addr.: 6470a Glenway Ave. #109, Cincinnati, OH 45211 USA (SAN 631-4899) Toll Free Fax: 888-460-4752; Toll Free: 888-232-0808; Edit Addr.: 6470a Glenway Ave. #109, Cincinnati, OH 45211 USA Toll Free: 888-232-0808
E-mail: books@hardshell.com; books@mundania.com
Web site: http://www.hardshell.com
Dist(s): **CreateSpace Independent Publishing Platform**
News Group, The.

Harder, Polly *See* **R. H. Publishing**

Hardie Grant Bks. (AUS) *(978-1-86498; 978-1-876719; 978-1-74066; 978-1-74270; 978-1-74273; 978-0-9807835; 978-0-646-49937-6; 978-1-74358; 978-1-74379) Dist. by* **IPG Chicago.**

Hardie Grant Bks. (AUS) *(978-1-86498; 978-1-876719; 978-1-74066; 978-1-74270; 978-1-74273; 978-0-9807835; 978-0-646-49937-6; 978-1-74358; 978-1-74379) Dist. by* **Random.**

Hardie Grant Egmont Pty, Ltd. (AUS) *(978-1-920878; 978-1-921098; 978-1-921288; 978-1-921417; 978-1-921502; 978-1-921564; 978-1-921690; 978-1-921759; 978-1-921848; 978-1-74297; 978-1-76012) Dist. by* **IPG Chicago.**

Hardin Publishing, LLC, *(978-0-9742704)* 1380 W. Paces Ferry Rd., Suite 180, Atlanta, GA 30327 USA Tel 404-504-6619; Fax: 404-264-3583 Do not confuse with Hardin Publishing Company in Avera, GA
E-mail: proper@piedmont-atl.com; yntema@hardinpublishing.net
Web site: http://www.hardinpublishing.net.

Harding Hse. Publishing Sebice Inc., *(978-1-933630; 978-1-937211; 978-1-62524)* 220 Front St., Vestal, NY 13850-1514 USA; *Imprints*: Anamchara Books (Anamchara Bks); Village Earth Press (Village Earth)
E-mail: lkaras@hardinghousepages.com
Web site: http://www.hardinghousepages.com; http://www.villageearthpress.com; http://www.anamcharabooks.com
Dist(s): **Follett School Solutions**
Smashwords.

Hardnett Publishing, *(978-0-9789310; 978-0-692-21182-3)* 2114 Keithshire Ct., Conyers, GA 30013 USA
E-mail: info@hardnettpublishing.com
Web site: http://www.hardnettpublishing.com.

Hardtke Publishing Co., *(978-0-9718166)* 2217 Second Ave. E., No. 1, Hibbing, MN 55746-1966 USA (SAN 254-4601) Tel 218-262-6510
Web site: http://www.libertyandlove.com/.

Hardway Pr, *(978-0-9717148; 978-0-9840221)* 16 W. Pacific Ave. No.3, Hendersen, NV 89015-7383 USA Tel 702-564-1665; Fax: 702-564-4190
Web site: http://www.brianrouff.com.

Hardy, John M. Publishing Co., *(978-0-9717667; 978-0-9798391; 978-0-9903714)* 14781 Memorial Dr., Ste 559, Houston, TX 77079 USA Tel 281-438-7500; Fax: 281-438-7501
E-mail: publisher@johnhardypublishing.com
Web site: http://www.johnmhardy.com.

Hargrave Pr., *(978-0-9744885; 978-0-9817195)* P.O. Box 524, Nantucket, MA 02554 USA (SAN 856-3519)
E-mail: sales@hargravepress.com
Web site: http://www.hargravepress.com
Dist(s): **BookMasters.**

Hargroves, Ann *See* **Hargroves Publishing Co.**

Hargroves Publishing Co., *(978-0-9742277)* P.O. Box 985, Virginia Beach, VA 23451-0985 USA
Web site: http://www.annhhargroves.com.

Harlan Publishing Company *See* **Diakonia Publishing**

Harlan Rose Publishing, *(978-0-9853466)* 920 Fall Creek, Grapevine, TX 76051 USA Tel 469-951-8499
E-mail: Flyingunicorn99@yahoo.com.

Harlin Jacque Pubns., *(978-0-940938)* Orders Addr.: P.O. Box 336, Garden City, NY 11530 USA (SAN 281-7667) Tel 516-489-0120; Fax: 516-292-9120; Edit Addr.: 89 Surrey Ln., Hempstead, NY 11550-3521 USA (SAN

281-7659) Tel 516-489-8564; *Imprints:* Pen & Rose Press (Pen&Rose Pr)
E-mail: harlinjacquepub@aol.com
Web site: http://www.lindamichellebaron.com.

Harmon Creek Pr., *(978-0-9820852)* 1763 Diamond Head Dr., Tiki Island, TX 77554 USA
E-mail: lnicholson@bookpublishing.com.

Harmony Healing Hse., *(978-0-9787179; 978-0-9854037)* 530 Miramonte Ave., Lakeport, CA 95453 USA (SAN 851-3570).

Harmony Hse. Publishing Co., *(978-0-9725289)* P.O. Box 858, Rexburg, ID 83440 USA Tel 208-359-1595 (phone/fax)
E-mail: jaydef@cableone.net
Web site: http://www.debtfreestepbystep.com.

Harmony Ink Pr. *Imprint of* **Dreamspinner Pr.**

Harmony Pubns., LLC, *(978-0-9787586)* 100 W. Sta. Sq. Dr. Suite 230, Pittsburgh, PA 15219 USA (SAN 851-5468) Tel 412-670-3901; Fax: 724-934-4275
E-mail: harmonypublications@hotmail.com
Web site: http://www.colormyworld.info/.

Harmony Spirit Publishing Co., Inc., *(978-0-9762392)* 148 Westgate Dr., Saint Peters, MO 63376 USA
E-mail: lynowak@mail.win.org.

Harold, Elsie L., *(978-0-9764644)* 1701 Eleni Ct., Virginia Bch, VA 23453-2886 USA
E-mail: turtlelsie@aol.com.

Harper Entertainment *Imprint of* **HarperCollins Pubs.**

Harper, Joel D., *(978-0-9714254)* 310 n. indian hill blvd No. 442, Claremont, CA 91711 USA Tel 909-447-5320
E-mail: info@freedomthree.com
Web site: http://www.freedomthree.com; www.joelharper.net; www.allthewaytotheocean.com.

Harper Kids Hse., *(978-0-9747218)* 10061 Riverside Dr., Suite 438, Toluca Lake, CA 91602 USA Tel 818-955-5301; *Imprints:* Young Women Programming (YWProgram)
E-mail: hannah@hannahsway.com
Web site: http://www.hannasway.com.

Harper Paperbacks *Imprint of* **HarperCollins Pubs.**

Harper Trophy *Imprint of* **HarperCollins Pubs.**

Harper, Vicky *See* **Little Bookstore Who Could, The**

Harper-Arrington Publishing, *(978-0-9764161)* 18701 Grand River Ave., 105, Detroit, MI 48223 USA Tel 313-283-4494; Fax: 248-281-0373; Toll Free: 888-435-9234
E-mail: info@harperarringtonmedia.com
Web site: http://www.hapub.com/.

HarperChildren's Audio *Imprint of* **HarperCollins Pubs.**

HarperCollins *Imprint of* **HarperCollins Pubs.**

HarperCollins *Imprint of* **HarperCollins Pubs.**

†HarperCollins Pubs., *(978-0-00; 978-0-06; 978-0-380; 978-0-688; 978-0-690; 978-0-694; 978-0-87795; 978-1-55710)* Div. of News Corp., Orders Addr.: 1000 Keystone Industrial Pk., Scranton, PA 18512-4621 USA (SAN 215-3742) Tel 570-941-1500; Toll Free: 800-822-4090; Toll Free: 800-242-7737 (orders only); Edit Addr.: 10 E. 53rd St., New York, NY 10022-5299 USA (SAN 200-2086) Tel 212-207-7000; *Imprints:* Julie Andrews Collection (Julie Andrews); Harper Trophy (HarperTrophy); HarperFestival (HarperFestival); Cotler, Joanna Books (JoCotler); Geringer, Laura Book (LauraGeringer); Greenwillow Books (GreenwillowBks); HarperCollins (HarperCollCh); HarperChildren's Audio (HarperChildAud); Tegen, Katherine Books (KTegenBooks); Morrow, William & Company (WmMorrow); Avon Books (AvonBooks); Eos (Eos Harper); Harper Entertainment (HarperEntert); HarperCollins (HarperCollinsT); HarperPerennial (HarperPerenl); Harper Paperbacks (HarperPaper); Amistad (AmistadHarper); Rayo (Rayo Harper); Ecco (Ecco Harper); ReganBooks (ReganBooks); Collins (Collins); Morrow, William Cookbooks (MorrowCookbks); Collins Design (CollinsDesign); HarperTeen (HarperTeen); HarperLuxe (HarperLuxe); HarperOne (HarperOne); William Morrow Paperbacks (WILLIAM MORROW); Balzer & Bray (Balzer & Bray); Walden Pond Press (Walden Pond); Newmarket for It Books (NewmarketforItBks); Witness Impulse (WitnessImp)
Web site: http://www.harpercollins.com; http://www.harpercollinschildrens.com
Dist(s): **Ebsco Publishing**
Findaway World, LLC
Follett School Solutions
F&W Media, Inc.
Lectorum Pubns., Inc.
MyiLibrary
Zondervan; *CIP.*

HarperCollins Pubs. Ltd. (GBR) *(978-0-00; 978-0-01; 978-0-06; 978-0-246; 978-0-261; 978-0-586; 978-0-85152; 978-0-411; 978-1-55468) Dist. by* **IPG Chicago.**

HarperCollins Pubs. Ltd. (GBR) *(978-0-00; 978-0-01; 978-0-06; 978-0-246; 978-0-261; 978-0-586; 978-0-85152; 978-0-411; 978-1-55468) Dist. by* **Trafalgar.**

HarperCollins Pubs. Ltd. (GBR) *(978-0-00; 978-0-01; 978-0-06; 978-0-246; 978-0-261; 978-0-586; 978-0-85152; 978-0-411; 978-1-55468) Dist. by* **HarperCollins Pubs.**

HarperFestival *Imprint of* **HarperCollins Pubs.**

HarperLuxe *Imprint of* **HarperCollins Pubs.**

HarperOne *Imprint of* **HarperCollins Pubs.**

HarperPerennial *Imprint of* **HarperCollins Pubs.**

HarperTeen *Imprint of* **HarperCollins Pubs.**

Harpswell Pr. *Imprint of* **Tilbury Hse. Pubs.**

Harren Communications, LLC, *(978-0-9667359; 978-0-9831032)* Southern Belle Books, P.O. Box 242, Midway, FL 32343 USA Tel 850-294-8923; Fax: 850-539-9731; *Imprints:* BeanPole Books (BeanPole Bks)
E-mail: publisher@beanpolebooks.com
Web site: http://www.beanpolebooks.net
Dist(s): **Perseus-PGW**
Perseus Bks. Group
Perseus Distribution.

Harren Press/Harren Professional Press *See* **Harren Communications, LLC**

Harrington Artwerkes Booksellers, *(978-0-9778042)* P.O. Box 10648, Burke, VA 22009-0648 USA
E-mail: sjph@cox.net
Web site: http://www.amazingartbros.com.

Harrington Park Pr. *Imprint of* **Haworth Pr., Inc., The**

Harris, Candice *See* **Harris, K Publishing, Inc.**

Harris Communications, Inc., *(978-0-9727520)* 15155 Technology Dr., Eden Prairie, MN 55344-2277 USA (SAN 255-0512) Tel 952-906-1180; Fax: 952-906-1099; Toll Free: 800-825-6758
E-mail: mail@harriscomm.com
Web site: http://www.harriscomm.com.

Harris, H. E. & Company *See* **Whitman Publishing LLC**

Harris, K Publishing, Inc., *(978-0-9770331)* P.O. Box 3091, Brandon, FL 33509-3091 USA
Web site: http://www.khpinc.com.

Harris, Monica *See* **Keep Empowering Yourself Successfully**

Harris, Pleshette Communications Inc. Publishing, *(978-0-9754380)* P.O. Box 491282, Lawrenceville, GA 30049 USA Tel 678-910-6128; Fax: 770-237-9358
E-mail: contact@phc1.org
Web site: http://phc1.org.

Harris, Polly, *(978-0-9749375)* 6041 E Akron St., Mesa, AZ 85205 USA Tel 480-654-1213
E-mail: pollyharris@sbcglobal.net.

Harris, Samuel, *(978-0-9759253)* 21660 Boschome Dr., Kildeer, IL 60047-8616 USA
E-mail: sf864@aol.com; eharris864@aol.com
Dist(s): **Partners Bk. Distributing, Inc.**

Harrison, Bobby, *(978-0-9771752)* 444 Shooting Star Tr., Gurley, AL 35748 USA Tel 256-776-2003; Fax: 256-776-2003
E-mail: bnharr@aol.com; ivorybillwp@aol.com
Web site: http://www.bobbyharrison.com
Dist(s): **Impact Photographics.**

Harrison House, Incorporated *See* **Harrison House Pubs.**

†Harrison House Pubs., *(978-0-89274; 978-1-57794; 978-1-60683; 978-1-68031)* Orders Addr.: P.O. Box 35035, Tulsa, OK 74153 USA (SAN 208-676X) Tel 918-523-5700; Toll Free Fax: 800-830-5688; Toll Free: 800-888-4126; Edit Addr.: 7498 E. 46th Pl., Tulsa, OK 74145 USA Tel 918-523-5700; Toll Free Fax: 800-830-5688; Toll Free: 800-888-4126
E-mail: lisad@harrisonhouse.com; juliew@harrisonhouse.com
Web site: http://www.harrisonhouse.com
Dist(s): **Anchor Distributors**
Appalachian Bible Co.
Distributors, The
Spring Arbor Distributors, Inc.; *CIP.*

Harry & Stephanie Bks., *(978-0-9760875)* P.O. Box 172, Bronxville, NY 10708 USA Tel 914-961-6601
E-mail: harryandstephanie@yahoo.com
Web site: http://www.harryandstephanie.com.

Harseal Publications *See* **Harborseal Publishing Co.**

Hart, Chris Bks. *Imprint of* **Sixth&Spring Bks.**

Hart Street Pubs., *(978-0-9793637)* 12157 Antibes St., Jacksonville, FL 32224 USA.

Hart-Burn Pr., *(978-0-9740318)* P.O. Box 99, Newton Junction, NH 03859-0099 USA
E-mail: stevehart7@yahoo.com
Web site: http://www.facebook.com/stevehart7
Dist(s): **Smashwords.**

Hartland Pubns., *(978-0-923309; 978-1-60564)* Div. of Hartland Institute of Health & Education, P.O. Box 1, Rapidan, VA 22733 USA (SAN 252-0834) Tel 540-672-3566; Fax: 540-672-3568; Toll Free: 800-774-3566
E-mail: jcarmouche@hartland.edu
Web site: http://www.hartlandpublications.com; http://www.hartlandbooks.com.

Hartlyn Kids Media, LLC, *(978-0-615-48984-1; 978-0-615-50182-6; 978-0-615-50503-9; 978-0-615-54948-4)* 45 Cowles St., Hartford, CT 06114 USA Tel 866-962-9993
E-mail: info@hartlynkids.com
Web site: http://www.hartlynkids.com.

Hartsuyker, Alice, *(978-0-9770441)* 1258 Fordham Dr. Apt. 204, Glendale Hts, IL 60139-4869 USA
E-mail: info@insidedharma.org; info@alicememoir.com
Web site: http://www.insidedharma.org; http://www.alicememoir.com.

Hart-Whitlow Pubs., *(978-0-9637951)* 1845 Brandywine Dr., Lenoir City, TN 37772 USA Tel 865-986-8553
E-mail: dickins@utk.edu.

†Harvard Common Pr., *(978-0-87645; 978-0-916782; 978-1-55832)* 535 Albany St., Boston, MA 02118 USA (SAN 208-6778) Tel 617-423-5803; Fax: 617-695-9794; Toll Free: 888-657-3755
E-mail: orders@harvardcommonpress.com
Web site: http://www.harvardcommonpress.com
Dist(s): **Houghton Mifflin Harcourt Publishing Co.**
Houghton Mifflin Harcourt Trade & Reference Pubs.
MyiLibrary
ebrary, Inc.; *CIP.*

Harvard Education Publishing Group (HEPG), *(978-0-916690; 978-1-891792; 978-1-934742; 978-1-61250; 978-1-68253)* Orders Addr.: c/o Pssc, Harvard Education Press 46 Development Rd., Fitchburg, MA 01420 USA Fax: 978-348-1233 (book order); Toll Free: 888-437-1437 Book Order Line; Edit Addr.: 8 Story St., First Flr., Cambridge, MA 02138 USA (SAN 913-9753) Tel 617-495-3432 editorial office phone; Fax: 617-496-3584 (orders); *Imprints:* Harvard Educational Review Reprint Series (Harv Ed Review)
E-mail: laura_clos@harvard.edu; sumita_mukherji@gse.harvard.edu; christina_deyoung@gse.harvard.edu
Web site: hepg.org.

Harvard Educational Review Reprint Series *Imprint of* **Harvard Education Publishing Group (HEPG)**

Harvard Perspectives in American Sports *Imprint of* **Harvard Perspectives Pr.**

Harvard Perspectives Pr., *(978-0-9715778)* P.O. Box 400827, Cambridge, MA 02140-0009 USA; *Imprints:* Harvard Perspectives in American Sports (Harvard Pers Amer Sp)
E-mail: harvardperspecpr@aol.com; indieKindle@gmail.com
Web site: http://indieKindle.blogspot.com.

†Harvard Univ. Pr., *(978-0-674; 978-0-916724; 978-0-935617)* Orders Addr.: c/o Triliteral LLC, 100 Maple Ridge Dr., Cumberland, RI 02864 USA Tel 401-531-2800; Fax: 401-531-2801; Toll Free Fax: 800-406-9145; Toll Free: 800-405-1619; 800-448-2242; Edit Addr.: 79 Garden St., Cambridge, MA 02138 USA (SAN 200-2043) Tel 617-495-2600; Fax: 617-495-5898; *Imprints:* Belknap Press (Belknap)
E-mail: contact_hup@harvard.edu
Web site: http://www.hup.harvard.edu
Dist(s): **Ebsco Publishing**
ebrary, Inc.; *CIP.*

Harvest Hse. Pubs., *(978-0-7369; 978-0-89081; 978-1-56507)* 990 Owen Loop, N., Eugene, OR 97402-9173 USA (SAN 207-4745) Tel 541-302-0729; Fax: 541-302-0731; Toll Free: 888-501-6991
E-mail: pat.mathis@harvesthousepublishers.com; onix@harvesthousepublishers.com
Web site: http://www.harvesthousepublishers.com
Dist(s): **INscribe Digital**
Lulu Enterprises Inc.
MyiLibrary
Twentieth Century Christian Bks.

Harvest Pubns., *(978-0-9654272)* 1928 Oxbow Rd., Minneapolis, KS 67467 USA Tel 913-392-2750 Do not confuse with companies with same name in Berkeley, CA, Arlington Heights, IL, Fort Worth, TX, Jacksonville, TX
E-mail: Adharvest@juno.com
Web site: http://www.pma-online.org/list/7345.html.

Harvest Sun Pr., LLC, *(978-0-9743668)* Orders Addr.: P.O. Box 826, Fairacres, NM 88033 USA Tel 479-283-4000; Fax: 505-526-6930; Edit Addr.: 4109 Broken Arrow Cv., Springdale, AR 72764-7503 USA
E-mail: info@harvestsunpress.com
Web site: http://www.harvestsunpress.com.

Harvey, Alan, *(978-0-9766354)* P.O. Box 235, Chapel Hill, NC 27514 USA; *Imprints:* Big H Books (Big H Bks)
Web site: http://www.lomeharvey.com.

Harwell, William, *(978-0-9728274)* HC 63 Box 1, Hanna, UT 84031 USA.

Haskell, Rachael A., *(978-0-615-21356-9; 978-0-615-25625-2)* 6177 Sun Blvd., No. 404, Staint Petersburg, FL 33715 USA Tel 727-698-2543; Fax: 727-865-6507
E-mail: hangingwithib@yahoo.com
Dist(s): **Lulu Enterprises Inc.**

Hassan, Marian, *(978-0-9766616)* 430 Mendota Rd. W., Suite 219, West Saint Paul, MN 55118 USA
E-mail: mhassan1@yahoo.com.

Hat Trick Publishing, *(978-0-9860405)* 8169 Outer Dr., S., Traverse City, MI 49685 USA.

Hatch Ideas, Inc., *(978-0-9792558)* P.O. Box 14, Pine Plains, NY 12567 USA.

Hatherleigh Co., Ltd., The, *(978-1-57826; 978-1-886330)* 5-22 46th Ave., Suite 200, Long Island City, NY 11101-5215 USA (SAN 298-878X) Tel 212-832-1584; Fax: 212-832-1502; Toll Free Fax: 800-621-8892; Toll Free: 800-367-2550; *Imprints:* Hatherleigh Press (Hath Pr)
E-mail: info@hatherleigh.com
Web site: http://www.hatherleigh.com; http://www.getfitnow.com
Dist(s): **MyiLibrary**
Penguin Random Hse., LLC.
Random Hse., Inc.

Hatherleigh Pr. *Imprint of* **Hatherleigh Co., Ltd., The**

Hathi Chiti Bks. for Kids, *(978-0-615-37071-2; 978-0-615-37072-9; 978-0-9829362)* 203 Rivington St. Suite 2L, New York, NY 10002 USA Tel 212-920-1844
Web site: http://www.hathichiti.com
Dist(s): **National Bk. Network.**

Hatpin Press *See* **MusiKinesis**

Hats Off Bks. *Imprint of* **Wheatmark**

Have Hope Publishing, *(978-0-9762044)* Orders Addr.: P.O. Box 20892, Baltimore, MD 21209 USA Tel 410-367-6179 (phone/fax); Edit Addr.: 5033 Yellowwood Ave., Baltimore, MD 21209 USA
E-mail: teachertalk@jhu.edu.

Haven Bks., *(978-0-9659480; 978-1-58436)* 10153 1/2 Riverside Dr., Suite 629, North Hollywood, CA 91602 USA Tel 818-503-2518; Fax: 818-508-0299
E-mail: Havenbks@aol.com; reya@havenbooks.net; info@havenbooks.net
Web site: http://www.havenbooks.net
Dist(s): **National Bk. Network**
ebrary, Inc.

Haven Harbor, *(978-0-9729863)* P.O. Box 2197, Huntington Beach, CA 92647-0197 USA
Web site: http://www.havenharbor.com.

HavenBound Publishing, *(978-0-9761733)* Orders Addr.: 1076 Pinnacle Dr., Waynesville, NC 28786 USA; Edit Addr.: 1305 Old Balsam Rd., Waynesville, NC 28786 USA; *Imprints:* HBHavenBound Publishing (HBHavenBnd)
E-mail: joseph@introductiontojesus.com; carolyn@havenbound.net; havenbound@havenbound.net.

Haver, Nancy, *(978-0-9795696)* 19 Moorland St., Amherst, MA 01002 USA Tel 413-549-1337
E-mail: nhaver@crocker.com.

Hawaii Fine Art Studio, *(978-0-615-21549-5)* 1028 Tirol Ln., Lake Arrowhead, CA 92352 USA.

Hawaii Fishing News, *(978-0-944462; 978-0-9884939)* 6650 Hawaii Kai Dr., No. 201, Honolulu, HI 96825 USA (SAN 243-6612) Tel 808-395-4499; Fax: 808-396-3474
E-mail: fishnews@pixi.com
Web site: http://www.hawaiifishingnews.com/hfn
Dist(s): **Booklines Hawaii, Ltd.**

Hawaiian Service, Inc., *(978-0-930492)* 94-527 Puahi St., Waipahu, HI 96797-4208 USA (SAN 205-0463) Tel 808-676-5026; Fax: 808-676-5156
Dist(s): **Booklines Hawaii, Ltd.**

Hawaya, Inc., *(978-0-9644149)* Orders Addr.: P.O. Box 300, Kailua, HI 96734 USA Tel 808-261-0589; Fax: 808-531-0957; Edit Addr.: 1564 Ulupii St., Kailua, HI 96734 USA
E-mail: ksullivan@pixi.com
Dist(s): **Booklines Hawaii, Ltd.**

Hawk Mountaintop Publishing, *(978-0-9672162)* P.O. Box 88, Piercy, CA 95587 USA Tel 707-247-3409
E-mail: hawk@saber.net.

Hawk Planners, *(978-0-9759702; 978-0-9776843)* 916 Silver Spur Rd. Suite 203, Rolling Hills Estates, CA 90274 USA Toll Free: 888-442-9575
E-mail: matthawkphd@msn.com
Web site: http://www.hawkplanners.com; http://www.satorsports.com
Dist(s): **Cardinal Pubs. Group.**

HAWK Publishing Group, *(978-0-9673131; 978-1-930709)* 7107 S. Yale, No. 345, Tulsa, OK 74136 USA (SAN 299-9293) Tel 918-492-3677; Fax: 918-492-2120
E-mail: wb@hawkpub.com
Web site: http://www.hawkpub.com
Dist(s): **AtlasBooks Distribution.**

Hawkeye Enterprises, *(978-0-9743061)* P.O. Box 252, Seal Rock, OR 97376-0252 USA Tel 541-563-4577
E-mail: hawkeye@oregonfast.net.

Hawkibinkler Pr., *(978-0-9721069)* 7725 N. Fowler, Portland, OR 97217 USA Tel 503-286-0945
E-mail: ruskin@streetfoodsecrets.com
Web site: http://www.streetfoodsecrets.com.

Haworth, Margaret, *(978-0-9740313)* 1625 W. May St. Apt. 3, Wichita, KS 67213-3578 USA.

†Haworth Pr., Inc., The, *(978-0-7890; 978-0-86656; 978-0-917724; 978-1-56022; 978-1-56023; 978-1-56024)* Div. of Taylor & Francis Group, 325 Chestnut St., Philadelphia, PA 19106-2614 USA (SAN 211-0156) Tel 800-895-0582; Toll Free: 800-429-6784; *Imprints:* Harrington Park Press (Harrington Park)
E-mail: orders@haworthpress.com; getinfo@haworthpress.com; barnold@haworthpress.com; docdelivery@haworthpress.com; tbronstein@haworthpress.com
Web site: http://www.haworthpress.com
Dist(s): **Barnes & Noble, Inc.**
Bookazine Co., Inc.
Borders, Inc.
Columbia Univ. Pr.
Distributors, The
Matthews Medical Bk. Co.
New Leaf Distributing Co., Inc.
Quality Bks., Inc.
Rittenhouse Bk. Distributors
SPD-Small Pr. Distribution
Unique Bks., Inc.
Waldenbooks, Inc.; *CIP.*

Hawthorn Pr. (GBR) *(978-0-9507062; 978-1-869890; 978-1-903458; 978-1-907359) Dist. by* **SteinerBooks Inc.**

Hawthorne Bks. & Literary Arts, Inc., *(978-0-9716915; 978-0-9766311; 978-0-9790188; 978-0-9833049; 978-0-9834775; 978-0-9838504; 978-0-9860007; 978-0-9893604; 978-0-9904370)* 2201 NE 23rd Ave. 3rd Flr., Portland, OR 97212 USA
E-mail: rhughes@hawthornebooks.com
Web site: Http://hawthornebooks.com
Dist(s): **Perseus-PGW**
Perseus Bks. Group.

†Hay Hse., Inc., *(978-0-937611; 978-0-945923; 978-1-56170; 978-1-891751; 978-1-58825; 978-1-4019)* Orders Addr.: P.O. Box 5100, Carlsbad, CA 92018-5100 USA (SAN 630-477X) Tel 760-431-7695 ext 112; Fax: 760-431-6948; Toll Free Fax: 800-650-5115 (orders only); Toll Free: 800-654-5126 (orders only); 2776 Loker Ave. W, Carlsbad, CA 92010 (SAN 257-3024) Tel 800-654-5126; Fax: 800-650-5115; *Imprints:* Hay House Lifestyles (Hay Hse Lifestyles)
E-mail: kjohnson@hayhouse.com; pcrowe@hayhouse.com
Web site: http://www.hayhouse.com
Dist(s): **Follett School Solutions**
Lectorum Pubns., Inc.; *CIP.*

Hay Hse. Lifestyles *Imprint of* **Hay Hse., Inc.**

Haydenburri Lane, *(978-0-9758785; 978-0-9801849; 978-0-9822149)* 6114 LaSalle Ave., No. 285, Oakland, CA 94611-2802 USA Toll Free: 888-425-2636
Web site: http://www.haydenburrilane.com.

Haymarket Bks., *(978-1-931859; 978-1-60846)* 4015 N. Rockwell, Chicago, IL 60618 USA Tel 773-583-7884
E-mail: orders@haymarketbooks.org
Web site: http://www.haymarketbooks.org
Dist(s): **Consortium Bk. Sales & Distribution**
MyiLibrary
Perseus Bks. Group
ebrary, Inc.

Haynes Manuals, Inc., *(978-1-56392; 978-1-85010; 978-1-85960; 978-1-62092)* Div. of Haynes Publishing Group, 861 Lawrence Dr., Newbury Park, CA 91320 USA (SAN 200-9838) Tel 805-498-6703; Fax:

805-498-2867; Toll Free: 800-442-9637; 1299 Bridgestone Pkwy., LaVergne, TN 37086 Fax: 615-793-5325; Toll Free: 800-242-4637
Web site: http://www.haynes.com/
Dist(s): **Delmar Cengage Learning**
Hachette Bk. Group
MBI Distribution Services/Quayside Distribution.

Haynes Publications, Incorporated *See* **Haynes Manuals, Inc.**

Haynes Publishing PLC (GBR) *(978-0-85696; 978-0-900550; 978-1-56392; 978-1-85010; 978-1-85260; 978-1-85960; 978-1-84425; 978-0-85733) Dist. by* **HachBkGrp.**

Haynes,Chilton,

HazardousWeather Preparedness Institute, *(978-0-9742794)* 5203 N. Oaks Dr., Greensboro, NC 27455-1229 USA
E-mail: rjackson@weatherpreparedness.com
Web site: http://www.weatherpreparedness.com.

Hazel Street Productions, *(978-0-9786988)* P.O. Box 5936, Sherman Oaks, CA 91413-5936 USA
Web site: http://www.hazelst.com.

†Hazelden, *(978-0-89486; 978-0-89638; 978-0-935908; 978-0-942421; 978-1-56246; 978-1-56838; 978-1-59285; 978-1-61649)* 15251 Pleasant Valley Rd., P.o. Box 176, Center City, MN 55012-0176 USA (SAN 209-4010) Fax: 651-213-4044; Toll Free: 800-328-9000; P.O. Box 176, RW4, Center City, MN 55012 Tel 651-213-4000; Toll Free: 800-328-9000
E-mail: bosterbauer@hazelden.org
Web site: http://www.hazelden.org
Dist(s): **BookMobile**
Follett School Solutions
Health Communications, Inc.
MyiLibrary
Perseus-PGW
Perseus Bks. Group
Perseus Distribution
ebrary, Inc.; *CIP.*

Hazelden Publishing & Educational Services *See* **Hazelden**

HBHavenBound Publishing *Imprint of* **HavenBound Publishing**

H.B.P., Inc., *(978-0-9753285; 978-0-9789617; 978-0-9853898)* 952 Frederick St., Hagerstown, MD 21740 USA
Web site: http://www.hbp.com.

HCI Teens *Imprint of* **Health Communications, Inc.**

Head On Dialogue Publishing, *(978-0-9770550)* Orders Addr.: P.O. Box 11400, Oakland, CA 94611 USA; Edit Addr.: 509 El Dorado No. 309, Piedmont, CA 94611 USA Tel 510-677-3267
E-mail: headondialogue@yahoo.com.

Head Pr. Publishing, *(978-0-9758924; 978-0-9832837)* 3804 Pk. Bend Dr., Flower Mound, TX 75022 USA Tel 817-410-9490
E-mail: headpresspublish@aol.com
Web site: http://www.headpress.info
Dist(s): **Send The Light Distribution LLC.**

Headline Bks., Inc., *(978-0-929915; 978-0-938467; 978-1-882658)* Orders Addr.: P.O. Box 52, Terra Alta, WV 26764 USA (SAN 250-8559) Tel 304-789-3001; Fax: 304-789-6427; Toll Free: 800-570-5951; *Imprints:* Publisher Page (Pub Page); Headline Kids (HeadlineKids)
E-mail: cathy@headlinebooks.com
Web site: http://www.headlinebooks.com; http://www.publisherpage.com; http://www.headlinekids.com
Dist(s): **American Wholesale Bk. Co.**
American West Bks.
Brodart Co.
Coutts Information Services
Follett School Solutions
Midwest Library Service
News Group, The.

Headline Kids *Imprint of* **Headline Bks., Inc.**

Headline Publishing Group (GBR) *(978-0-7472; 978-0-7553; 978-1-4722) Dist. by* **IPG Chicago.**

Headline Publishing Group (GBR) *(978-0-7472; 978-0-7553; 978-1-4722) Dist. by* **Trafalgar.**

Headline Science *Imprint of* **Compass Point Bks.**

Headrick, Gordon, *(978-0-9771385)* M. F. W. High School 1775 W. Lowell Ave., Tracy, CA 95376 USA.

Heads First (1st), *(978-0-9761969)* 4207 Magnolia Ln., Sugar Land, TX 77478 USA Tel 281-844-3719
E-mail: heads1st@aol.com
Web site: http://www.headsfirst.com.

Healing Arts Pr. *Imprint of* **Inner Traditions International, Ltd.**

Healing Flood Bks., Inc., *(978-0-9746497)* Orders Addr.: 3108 N. Longmore St., Chandler, AZ 85224 USA
E-mail: freebook@healingflood.com; prb@healingflood.com; sales@hospitalbooks.net; jerry@hospitalbooks.net; marketing@healingflood.com
Web site: http://www.healingflood.com; http://www.hospitalbooks.net.

Healing Hands Pr., *(978-0-9747686)* Div. of Holistic Home Health Care, 1329 N. Wembley Cir., Port Orange, FL 32128 USA Tel 386-322-4888
Web site: http://www.love-heals.com.

Healing Society, Inc., *(978-0-9720282; 978-1-932843)* Orders Addr.: P.O. Box 4503, Sedona, AZ 86340-9978 USA; Edit Addr.: 6560 Hwy. 179, Suite 114, Sedona, AZ 86351 USA Toll Free: 877-504-1106
E-mail: dcrenshaw@hspub.com; moh@hspub.com
Web site: http://www.healingsociety.com; http://www.bodynbrain.com
Dist(s): **New Leaf Distributing Co., Inc.**

Healing Tree Arts, *(978-0-9779643)* P.O. Box 3398, Laguna Hills, CA 92654 USA (SAN 850-7775)
Web site: http://www.healingtreearts.com.

Health & Beauty Ctr., LLC, *(978-0-9747253)* P.O. Box 363, Oregon City, OR 97045 USA Toll Free: 888-648-7771
E-mail: support@healthnbeauty.com; support@perfect-prescription.com
Web site: http://www.healthnbeauty.com; http://www.perfect-prescription.com.

†Health Communications, Inc., *(978-0-932194; 978-1-55874; 978-0-7573; 978-0-9910732)* Orders Addr.: 3201 SW 15th St., Deerfield Beach, FL 33442-8190 USA (SAN 212-100X) Tel 954-360-0909; Fax: 954-360-0034; Toll Free: 800-441-5569; *Imprints:* HCI Teens (HCi Teens); Faith Communications (Faith Comns) Do not confuse with Health Communications, Inc., Edison, NJ
E-mail: terip@hcibooks.com; lorig@hcibooks.com
Web site: http://www.hcibooks.com
Dist(s): **Bookazine Co., Inc.**
Islander Group
Partners/West Book Distributors
Southern Bk. Service
Western Pubns. Service; *CIP.*

Health 'n' Life Publishing (GBR) *(978-0-9531766; 978-0-9552648) Dist. by* **Midpt Trade.**

Health New England, *(978-0-9777159)* One Monarch Pl., Springfield, MA 01144-1500 USA (SAN 850-0436) Tel 413-787-4000; Toll Free: 800-842-4464
Web site: http://www.hne.com; http://www.hnestore.com; http://www.hnewhizkidz.com.

Health Press *See* **Health Press NA Incorporated**

Health Press NA Incorporated, *(978-0-929173)* P.O. Box 37470, Albuquerque, NM 87176 USA (SAN 248-5036) Tel 505-888-1394; Fax: 505-212-0612
E-mail: goodbooks@healthpress.com
Web site: http://www.healthpress.com.

Health Success Media, LLC, *(978-0-9820121)* P.O. Box 21092, Bradenton, FL 34204 USA (SAN 857-0043)
E-mail: elana.devorah@gmail.com; Elana@ConquerProstateCancer.com
Web site: http://www.ConquerProstateCancer.com.

Healthful Living Bks. *Imprint of* **Unique Executive Pubs.**

HealthMark Multimedia, *(978-0-9717399)* 1828 L St., NW, Suite 250, Washington, DC 20036 USA
E-mail: hm@healthmarkmultimedia.com; amcfarren@healthmarkmultimedia.com
Web site: http://www.HealthMarkMultimedia.com.

Healthnets, *(978-0-615-20972-2)* 2921 Emmorton Rd., Abingdon, MD 21009 USA Tel 410-515-7858
E-mail: milleniumdiet@gmail.com
Web site: http://www.Milleniumdiet.com/.

HealthSprings, LLC, *(978-0-9718120; 978-0-9740697; 978-0-9748263)* 1759 Grandstand, San Antonio, TX 78238 USA Tel 210-521-7650; Fax: 210-521-7141
E-mail: sabra@zoeyzones.com
Web site: http://www.zoeyzones.com.

HealthTeacher, *(978-0-9785578; 978-0-9817969)* 5200 Maryland Way Ste. 100, Brentwood, TN 37027-5072 USA Toll Free: 800-514-1362
E-mail: tod@relegent.com
Web site: http://www.healthteacher.com.

Heard Word Publishing, LLC, *(978-0-9801060)* 3051 W. 105th Ave. No. 350253, Westminster, CO 80031 USA
E-mail: hispublishingllc@yahoo.com; Beatrice@TheGetOverItGal.com
Web site: www.TheGetOverItGal.com.

Heart 4 Clowning Pr., A, *(978-0-9799093)* 905 Hwy 321 NW., No. 215, Hickory, NC 28601 USA Tel 828-326-0662
E-mail: aheart4clowning@gmail.com
Web site: http://www.AHeart4Clowning.com.

Heart & Harp LLC, *(978-0-9742174)* Orders Addr.: P.O. Box 818, Walled Lake, MI 48390-0818 USA Tel 313-938-9847
E-mail: HeartandHarp@comcast.net
Web site: http://www.heartandharp.net.

Heart Arbor Bks., *(978-1-891452)* Orders Addr.: P.O. Box 542, Grand River, OH 44045 USA (SAN 299-6073) Tel 440-257-0722; Toll Free: 877-977-4422.

Heart Bound Pr., *(978-0-615-25721-1)* Orders Addr.: 2141 Via Pacheco, Palos Verdes, CA 90274 USA Tel 310-375-3716; Fax: 310-373-2702
E-mail: heartboundpublishing@yahoo.com.

Heart Communications, *(978-0-9694176; 978-0-9747516)* P.O. Box 710791, Oak Hill, VA 20171 USA (SAN 116-404X) Tel 641-715-3900 (ext. 20889)
E-mail: info@heartcommunications.com
Web site: http://www.HeartCommunications.com.

Heart Flame Publishing, *(978-0-9726618)* P.O. Box 790038, Virgin, UT 84779-0038 USA (SAN 853-2532) Fax: 435-635-2613
Web site: http://www.heartflamepublishing.com
Dist(s): **AtlasBooks Distribution.**

Heart Of Dixie Publishing *See* **Bluewater Pubns.**

Heart Path Publishing, *(978-0-9712305)* P.O. Box 44, Keene, TX 76059 USA Tel 817-681-3877 Do not confuse with Heart Path Publishing, Atlanta, GA
Web site: http://www.guidemagazine.org.

Heart to Heart Publishing, Inc., *(978-0-9742806; 978-0-9802486; 978-1-937008)* Orders Addr.: 528 Mud Creek Rd., Morgantown, KY 42261 USA Tel 270-526-5589; Fax: 270-526-7489; Toll Free: 888-526-5589
E-mail: hawkinslindaj@yahoo.com
Web site: http://www.lindajhawkins.com; http://www.hearttoheartpublishinginc.com
Dist(s): **BookBaby.**

Heartfelt Bks., *(978-0-9763933)* 149 Thunderbird Trail, Carol Stream, IL 60188-1982 USA.

HeartFelt Stories LLC, *(978-0-9778113)* 5767 Kempton Run Ct., Columbus, OH 43235 USA (SAN 850-3036)
E-mail: heartfeltstories@hotmail.com
Web site: http://www.heartfeltstoriesllc.com
Dist(s): **Blu Sky Media Group.**

Heartful Loving Pr., *(978-0-9723639)* Div. of Illui International, 1450 Orange Grove Ave., Santa Barbara, CA 93105 USA Tel 805-687-7442; Fax: 805-687-3042
E-mail: howard@heartfullovingpress.com
Web site: http://www.heartfullovingpress.com; http://www.howtobeafamily.com; http://www.firstloveremembrances.com; http://www.howtobethebestlover.com
Dist(s): **Partners Bk. Distributing, Inc.**

Hearthstone Rose, *(978-0-9836682)* 1156 Valleyview Dr., Lawrence, PA 15055 USA Tel 724-746-0662
E-mail: conniedonaldson@comcast.net.

Heartland Foundation, Inc., *(978-0-943177)* Orders Addr.: P.O. Box 887, Ames, IA 50010 USA Toll Free: 866-385-2027; Edit Addr.: 413 Northwestern Ave., Ames, IA 50010 USA (SAN 668-3010) Tel 515-232-1054
E-mail: lssn@att.net
Web site: http://mcmillenbooks.com
Dist(s): **McMillen Bk. Distributors.**

Heartlight Girls, *(978-0-9787689)* P.O. Box 370546, Denver, CO 80237 USA Tel 303-690-5603
E-mail: debra @heartlightgirls.com; debragano@aol.com
Web site: http://www.heartlightgirls.com.

Heartohopia Pr., *(978-0-9725184)* 2007 NE 59 Pl., Suite 105, Fort Lauderdale, FL 33308 USA
Web site: http://www.heartohopia.com.

HeartQuake Publishing *See* **Hunt Thompson Media**

Heartrock Pr., *(978-0-9817668)* P.O. Box 135, Langley, WA 98260 USA Tel 360-321-5603
Web site: http://NWDragons.com.

Heartsome Press *See* **Heartsome Publishing**

Heartsome Publishing, *(978-0-9726408)* 220 Norfolk St., Walpole, MA 02081 USA Tel 508-553-3858; Fax: 508-668-1998
E-mail: rrhearts@comcast.net
Web site: http://www.nolobsterplease.com/.

Heartstrings Publishing, *(978-0-9760733)* Orders Addr.: P.O. Box 8255, Fernando Beach, FL 32035 USA; Edit Addr.: Marchette Burette Market, Amelia Island Plantation, Fernandina Beach, FL 32034 USA
E-mail: mledlen@aol.com.

Heart-to-Heart Pubns., *(978-0-9744565)* 18237 N. 51st Pl., Scottsdale, AZ 85254 USA Tel 602-485-0793
E-mail: cpruett1@cox.net.

Heath, Jonathan Publishing, *(978-0-9715837)* 10 Willowstream Dr., Vernon, CT 06066 USA Tel 860-875-8373
E-mail: lenpam@snet.net.

Heather & Highlands Publishing, *(978-1-58478)* Div. of Heather & Highlands Publishing, Orders Addr.: 2384 Tokay Ct., Paradise, CA 95969 USA (SAN 254-0932) Tel 530-876-8986; Fax: 530-876-8989; Toll Free: 888-999-2358; *Imprints:* Highland Children's Press (Hghlnd Child)
E-mail: pawprintsorders@pawprintspress.com; pawprints@pawprintspress.com; tew@tewatsononline.com; heatherandhighlands@heatherandhighlandspublishing.com
Web site: http://www.pawprintspress.com; http://www.tewatsononline.com; http://heatherandhighlandspublishing.com
Dist(s): **Book Wholesalers, Inc.**
Brodart Co.

Heavenly C. Publishing, *(978-0-9746361)* P.O. Box 335, West Chester, OH 45071 USA
Web site: http://www.heavenlyCPublishing.com.

Heavenly Realm Publishing, *(978-0-9714874; 978-0-9825589; 978-0-9828802; 978-0-9833418; 978-0-9835202; 978-0-9839969; 978-1-937911)* Orders Addr.: P.O. Box 682532, Houston, TX 77268 USA Tel 866-216-0696; Toll Free: 877-599-3237
E-mail: heavenlyrealm@heavenlyrealmpublishing.com
Web site: http://www.heavenlyrealmpublishing.com
Dist(s): **Lightning Source, Inc.**

Hebler, Dave, *(978-0-9765392)* 5891 S. Military Trail, 5A-PMB, Lake Worth, FL 33463-6920 USA Tel 561-642-6696
E-mail: daveahebler@aol.com
Web site: http://www.protectingwomen.com.

Hebler, Michael, *(978-0-615-39525-8; 978-0-9833884)* 1344 Kingswood Ct., Fort Myers, FL 33919 USA Tel 562-857-1524; *Imprints:* Night After Night Publications, Incorporated (NightAfterNight)
E-mail: michaelhebler@gmail.com
Web site: http://www.michaelhebler.com.

Hedgebury (AUS) *(978-0-9873437) Dist. by* **NewShelves.**

Hedger, Ralph, *(978-0-9753880)* 208 Chaucer Rd., Charlottesville, VA 22901-2215 USA
E-mail: rehedger@aol.com.

Heel Verlag GmbH (DEU) *(978-3-89365; 978-3-922858; 978-3-89880) Dist. by* **Natl Bk Netwk.**

Heersink, Roland, *(978-0-9770473)* 18303 Starboard Dr., Houston, TX 77058-4362 USA
Web site: http://www.fairytunes.com.

Heflin & Thrall Language Pubns., Inc., *(978-0-9723341)* 2109 Stanford, Jacksonville, TX 75766 USA Toll Free: 888-313-3310
E-mail: jheflin@language-publications.com.

Hegemony Pr., *(978-0-9754114)* 5205 Pacific Ave., Tacoma, WA 98405 USA Tel 253-671-2665; Fax: 253-475-2665; Toll Free: 888-671-2665.

Heiderer, Conrad, *(978-0-9746699)* P.O. Box 405, Glen Arbor, MI 49636 USA Tel 231-334-6680 Toll Free: 888-877-0994
E-mail: cehj1200@hotmail.com
Web site: http://www.twigma.com.

Heidhausen, Eric, *(978-0-615-48856-1)* 3100 Spring House Ct., Woodbine, MD 21797 USA Tel 410-707-5771; 410-489-4818; Fax: 301-345-7305
Dist(s): **CreateSpace Independent Publishing Platform**
Dummy Record Do Not USE!!!!.

Heifer Project International, *(978-0-9755996; 978-0-9798439; 978-0-9819788)* Orders Addr.: 1 World Ave., Little Rock, AR 72203-8058 USA Tel 800-422-1311; Fax: 501-907-2802
E-mail: info@heifer.org
Web site: http://www.heifer.org.

†Heinemann, *(978-0-325; 978-0-434; 978-0-435; 978-1-59469)* Orders Addr.: P.O. Box 6926, Portsmouth, NH 03802 USA Toll Free: 800-225-5800; Edit Addr.: 361 Hanover St., Portsmouth, NH 03801 USA (SAN 210-5829) Tel 603-431-7894; Fax: 603-431-7840; *Imprints:* African Writers Series (African Write); Firsthand (Firsthnd)
E-mail: info@heinemann.com
Web site: http://www.heinemann.com
Dist(s): **ABC-CLIO, LLC**
Follett School Solutions
Greenwood Publishing Group, Inc.
Leonard, Hal Corp.
Pearson Education
Trans-Atlantic Pubns., Inc.; *CIP.*

Heinemann Educational Books, Incorporated *See* **Heinemann**

Heinemann First Library *Imprint of* **Heinemann-Raintree**

Heinemann Iberia, S.A. (ESP) *(978-84-7942) Dist. by* **IPG Chicago.**

Heinemann InfoSearch *Imprint of* **Heinemann-Raintree**

Heinemann Know It *Imprint of* **Heinemann-Raintree**

Heinemann Lee y aprende *Imprint of* **Heinemann-Raintree**

Heinemann Read & Learn *Imprint of* **Heinemann-Raintree**

Heinemann State Studies *Imprint of* **Heinemann-Raintree**

.Heinemann-Raintree *See* **Heinemann-Raintree**

Heinemann-Raintree, *(978-0-431; 978-1-57572; 978-1-58810; 978-1-4034; 978-1-4109; 978-1-4329; 978-1-4846)* Div. of Capstone, Orders Addr.: 1710 Roe Crest Dr., North Mankato, MN 56003 USA Toll Free Fax: 888-844-5329; Toll Free: 800-747-4992; Halley Court Freepost PO Box 1125, Oxford, OX2 8YY; *Imprints:* Acorn (AcornHR); Acorn Read-Aloud (Acorn Read); Bellota (Bellota); Heinemann First Library (HeineFirst Lib); Heinemann InfoSearch (HeineInfoSearc); Heinemann Know It (HeinKnow It); Heinemann Lee y aprende (HeinLeeyaprend); Heinemann Read & Learn (HeinReadnLearn); Heinemann State Studies (HeinemanStStud); NA-h (NA-h); NA-r (NA-r); Raintree Atomic (RaintreeAtomic); Raintree Freestyle (RaintrFreestyl); Raintree Freestyle en Espanol (RainFEE); Raintree Freestyle Express (RantFreExp); Raintree Fusion (RaintreeFusion); Raintree Perspectives (RainPerspect); Raintree Sprouts (RainSprouts); Sci-Hi (SciHi); Read Me! (Read Me)
E-mail: k.monyhan@coughlancompanies.com; customerservice@capstonepub.com
Web site: http://www.heinemannlibrary.com/; http://www.capstonepub.com; http://www.capstoneclassroom.com
Dist(s): **Capstone Pub.**
Follett School Solutions
Lectorum Pubns., Inc.

Heinle & Heinle Publishers, Inc. *See* **Cengage Heinle**

Heinrich, Tyson Chul, *(978-0-615-23894-4; 978-0-578-00492-1; 978-0-578-01337-4; 978-0-578-01343-5; 978-0-9962209)* 4295 Hitch Blvd., Moorpark, CA 93021 USA
Web site: http://www.tysonheinrich.com.

Heins Pubns., *(978-0-9671762; 978-0-9748680)* 2016 Leonard Ct., Eau Claire, WI 54703 USA Toll Free: 800-554-3467
E-mail: revheins@wwt.net.

Helen Bolton Ministries *See* **Bolton Publishing LLC**

Helen Darling *See* **My Darling-Tots Pubns.**

Heliand Publishing Corp., *(978-0-9770712)* P.O. Box 477, Pleasant Grove, UT 84062 USA
E-mail: submissions@heliandpublishing.com
Web site: http://www.heliandpublishing.com.

Heliograph, Inc., *(978-0-9668926; 978-1-930658)* 26 Porter St., Somerville, MA 02143-2215 USA
E-mail: info@heliograph.com
Web site: http://www.heliograph.com.

Helm Literary Publishing *See* **Helm Publishing**

Helm Publishing, *(978-0-9723011; 978-0-9760919; 978-0-9769193; 978-0-9778205; 978-0-9792328; 978-0-9801780; 978-0-9820605; 978-0-9841397; 978-0-9830109; 978-0-9850488)* Orders Addr.: P.O. Box 9691, Treasure Island, FL 33740 USA (SAN 254-7562) Tel 815-621-3336; Edit Addr.: P.O. Box 9691, Treasure Island, FL 33740 USA Tel 815-621-3336.
E-mail: dianne@publishersdrive.com
Web site: http://www.publishersdrive.com.

Helms, Jo Publishing, *(978-0-9745319)* 824 S. Schaefer St., Appleton, WI 54915 USA
E-mail: cheesedawg@earthlink.net; ilovegrizz@earthlink.net
Web site: http://www.grizz.20megsfree.com.

HELORO Publishing Group, *(978-0-9785435; 978-0-615-15932-4; 978-0-615-15933-1; 978-0-615-16034-4)* 860 Appletree Ct., Northbrook, IL 60062-3402 USA (SAN 850-9549) Tel 847-207-1087 mobile phone Do not confuse with companies with the same or similar name in Minneapolis, MN, Great Neck, NY
Web site: http://www.HELORO.com
Dist(s): **Lulu Enterprises Inc.**

H.E.L.P. for Self-Education, *(978-0-9766991)* 960 Perth Rd., Troutman, NC 28166 USA Tel 704-528-5866; Fax: 704-585-9397
E-mail: swedship@bellsouth.net
Web site: http://www.home.bellsouth.net/p/pwp-helpeducate.

Helping Hands Children's Bks., *(978-0-9762274)* 421 26th St., Marion, IA 52302 USA Tel 319-373-4169
E-mail: mary@mysak.com.

Helpingwords, *(978-0-615-16066-5; 978-0-615-23505-9; 978-0-578-03620-5; 978-0-578-05059-1;*

Publisher Name Index

978-0-578-06008-8; 978-0-9828529) 66 Prospect St., Manchester, NH 03104 USA Tel 603-668-1975
E-mail: kathy@kathybrodsky.com
Web site: http://www.kathybrodsky.com
Dist(s): **Enfield Publishing & Distribution Co., Inc.**

Helps4Teachers, (*978-0-9778548*) 145 Gardenside Ct., Fallbrook, CA 92028 USA (SAN 850-4180) Tel 760-723-0504
E-mail: rstur@roadrunner.com
Web site: http://www.helps4teachers.com.

Hemed Books, Incorporated *See* **Lambda Pubs., Inc.**

Henderson Publishing, (*978-1-891029*) Orders Addr.: 811 Eva's Walk, Pounding Mill, VA 24637 USA Tel 276-964-2291.

Hendley, Jeff *See* **L'Edge Pr.**

Hendrickson Publishers, Incorporated *See* **Hendrickson Pubs. Marketing, LLC**

†**Hendrickson Pubs. Marketing, LLC**, (*978-0-913573; 978-0-917006; 978-0-943575; 978-1-56563; 978-1-59856; 978-1-61970*) Orders Addr.: P.O. Box 3473, Peabody, MA 01961-3473 USA (SAN 285-2772) Fax: 978-531-8146; Toll Free: 800-358-3111; Edit Addr.: 140 Summit St., Peabody, MA 01960 USA (SAN 663-6594) Fax: 978-573-8414 Do not confuse with Hendrickson Group, Sandy Hook, CT
E-mail: editorial@hendrickson.com
Web site: http://www.hendrickson.com; *CIP.*

Henisz, Jerzy E., (*978-0-615-13851-0*) Orders Addr.: P.O. Box 1089, Sharon, CT 06069 USA; Edit Addr.: 33 Hospital Hill Rd., Sharon, CT 06069 USA
Dist(s): **Lulu Enterprises Inc.**

Henry Helps *Imprint of* **Picture Window Bks.**

Henry, Ian Pubns. (GBR) (*978-0-86025*) *Dist. by* **Empire Pub Srvs.**

Henry, Ian Pubns. (GBR) (*978-0-86025*) *Dist. by* **Players Pr.**

Henry, Patti, (*978-0-9817155*) 9114 Tepee Trail, Houston, TX 77064 USA (SAN 856-3268) Tel 281-894-4131
E-mail: patti@patti-henry.com
Web site: http://www.patti-henry.com.

Henry Quill Pr., (*978-1-883960*) 7340 Lake Dr., Fremont, MI 49412-9146 USA Tel 231-924-3026; Fax: 231-928-2802.

HenschelHAUS Publishing, (*978-0-9647663; 978-0-9722099; 978-1-59598*) 2625 S. Greeley St., Suite 201, Milwaukee, WI 53207 USA Tel 414-486-0653; Fax: 262-565-2058; *Imprints:* Goblin Fern Press (Goblin Fern)
E-mail: kira@henschelHAUSbooks.com
Web site: http://www.goblinfernpress.com; http://www.mavenmarkbooks.com; http://www.henschelHAUSbooks.com; http://www.threetowerspress.com
Dist(s): **Smashwords.**

Hensley, Michael, (*978-0-9747389*) P.O. Box 2952, Ranchos de Taos, NM 87557 USA
Web site: http://www.michaelmhensley.com.

Henzel, Richard, (*978-0-9747237; 978-0-9826688; 978-0-9846715*) 1106 N. Taylor, Oak Park, IL 60302 USA Tel 312-296-8396
E-mail: richard@richardhenzel.com
Web site: http://www.richardhenzel.com; http://www.richardhenzel.com/marktwain
Dist(s): **Audible.com**
Midwest Tape.

†**Herald Pr.**, (*978-0-8361; 978-1-5138*) Div. of MennoMedia, Inc., Orders Addr.: 1251 Virginia Ave., Harrisonburg, VA 22802 USA (SAN 202-2915) Fax: 1-316-283-0454; Toll Free: 1-800-245-7894; 800-631-6535 (Canada only) Do not confuse with Herald Pr., Charlotte, NC
E-mail: info@mennomedia.org
Web site: http://www.mennomedia.org
Dist(s): **Ebsco Publishing**
Send The Light Distribution LLC
Spring Arbor Distributors, Inc.; *CIP.*

†**Herald Publishing Hse.**, (*978-0-8309*) Orders Addr.: P.O. Box 390, Independence, MO 64051-0390 USA Tel 816-521-3015; Fax: 816-521-3066 (customer services); Toll Free: 800-767-8181; Edit Addr.: 1001W. Walnut St., Independence, MO 64051-0390 USA (SAN 111-7556) Tel 816-257-0200
E-mail: sales@HeraldHouse.org
Web site: http://www.heraldhouse.org; *CIP.*

Here & Now Publishing, (*978-0-9763491*) 5662 Calle Real, No. 139, Goleta, CA 93117 USA (SAN 256-3339) Fax: 805-683-8181
E-mail: info@hereandnowmeditation.com
Web site: http://www.hereandnowmeditation.com.

Heritage Bks., (*978-0-7884; 978-0-917890; 978-0-940907; 978-1-55613; 978-1-888265; 978-1-58549*) 100 Railroad Ave., Suite 104, Westminster, MD 21157-5026 USA (SAN 209-3367) Tel 410-876-6101; Fax: 410-871-2674; Toll Free: 800-876-6103
E-mail: Info@HeritageBooks.com
Web site: http://www.HeritageBooks.com; http://www.WillowBendBooks.com
Dist(s): **CreateSpace Independent Publishing Platform.**

Heritage Builders, LLC, (*978-0-615-30423-6; 978-0-615-30734-3; 978-0-615-30735-0; 978-0-615-31024-4; 978-0-692-00827-0; 978-1-939011; 978-1-940242; 978-1-941437; 978-1-942603*) 3105 Locan Ave., Clovis, CA 93619 USA
Dist(s): **MyiLibrary**
Perseus-PGW.

Heritage Heart Farm, (*978-0-9706348*) Orders Addr.: 21387 Rd. 128, Oakwood, OH 45873 USA Tel 419-594-2258
E-mail: heritageheartfarm@roadrunner.com; kohart@tds.net
Web site: http://www.heritageheartfarm.com.

Heritage Music Pr., (*978-0-89328*) Div. of The Lorenz Corp., Orders Addr.: 501 E. Third St., Dayton, OH 45401-0802 USA Tel 937-228-6118; Toll Free: 800-444-1144
E-mail: order@lorenz.com
Web site: http://www.lorenz.com.

Heritage Publishing, (*978-0-9672363*) 23507 E. State Rte. P, Pleasant Hill, MO 64080 USA Tel 816-540-4768; 913-338-3893 Do not confuse with companies with the same or similar names in Dallas, TX, Enumclaw, WA, Chicago, IL, Beverly Hills, CA, Loveland, CO, Valley Center, KS, Peabody, MA, Whitesboro, TX, Pleasant Hill, MO, Springdale, AR, Charlotte, NC, Thomasville, GA, North Little Rock, AR, Baton Rouge, LA, Stockton, CA, carthage, MO
E-mail: peggytucker@juno.com.

Heritage Publishing Co., (*978-0-9787462*) 4393 Mission Inn Ave., Riverside, CA 92501 USA (SAN 851-5247) Tel 951-788-7878; Fax: 951-788-1206
E-mail: rich1rodriguez@sbcglobal.net; isabel@isabelelias.com
Web site: http://IsabelElias.com.

Heritage Youth, Inc., (*978-0-9740753*) 6245 Esplanade Ave., Baton Rouge, LA 70806-6144 USA.

Hermes Pr., (*978-0-9710311; 978-1-932563; 978-1-61345*) 2100 Wilmington Rd., New Castle, PA 16105-1931 USA Tel 724-652-0511; Fax: 724-652-5597 Do not confuse with companies with same or similar names in Brooks, ME, Vista, CA. Ferndale, MI
Web site: http://www.hermespress.com
Dist(s): **Diamond Comic Distributors, Inc.**
Diamond Bk. Distributors.

Hermes Pubs., Inc., (*978-0-9766543*) P.O. Box 186, Roselle Park, NJ 07207 USA (SAN 256-453X) Toll Free: 888-557-5527
E-mail: dollarnet@aol.com.

Hermit Chum Publishing, (*978-0-9760317*) 6901 S. McCliateck, No. 245, Tempe, AZ 89283 USA.

Hermit's Grove, The, (*978-0-9655687; 978-0-9863639*) P.O. Box 0691, Kirkland, WA 98083-0691 USA Tel 425-828-4124; Fax: 425-803-2025
E-mail: paul@thehermitsgrove.org
Web site: http://www.thehermitsgrove.org
Dist(s): **New Leaf Distributing Co., Inc.**

Hermosa Pubs., (*978-0-913478*) P.O. Box 9110, Albuquerque, NM 87119 USA (SAN 203-0012) Tel 505-866-5323 (phone/fax)
E-mail: hermosa@swcp.com
Web site: http://www.hermosa-pub.com/hermosa.

Hern, Nick Bks., Ltd. (GBR) (*978-1-85459; 978-1-84842; 978-1-78001*) *Dist. by* **Consort Bk Sales.**

Hero Builder Comics, (*978-0-615-31157-9*) 1713 Golden Ct., Bellingham, WA 98226 USA.

Hero Dog Pubns., (*978-0-9743659*) 14 Eastview Ave., Pleasantville, NY 10570 USA (SAN 255-545X) Tel 914-525-6483
E-mail: herodogpubl@msn.com
Web site: http://www.herodogpublications.com
Dist(s): **BCH Fulfillment & Distribution.**

Heroes & Leaders, (*978-0-9801408*) 616 Kaufman St., Forney, TX 75126 USA (SAN 855-3165)
Web site: http://www.zertelo.com.

Heroic Publishing, Inc., (*978-0-929729*) 6433 California Ave., Long Beach, CA 90805 USA (SAN 250-0582) Tel 562-428-4124 (phone/fax)
E-mail: heroicpub@aol.com
Web site: http://www.heroicpub.com
Dist(s): **Diamond Comic Distributors, Inc.**

Herrington Teddy Bears, (*978-0-9722343*) 8945 Research Dr., Irvine, CA 92618-4237 USA Toll Free: 866-482-2327
E-mail: chris@herringtonco.com
Web site: http://www.herringtonteddybears.com.

Herrod, Ron L. Evangelism Ministries Association (R.H.E.M.A), (*978-0-9763789*) P.O. Box 6447, Sevierville, TN 37864 USA
E-mail: emily@ronherrod.org; ron@ronherrod.org
Web site: http://ronherrod.org.

Hershberger, Ivan & Fannie, (*978-0-9725806*) 8219 CR 192, Holmesville, OH 44633 USA.

Hershenson, Bruce, (*978-1-887893*) Orders Addr.: P.O. Box 874, West Plains, MO 65775 USA Tel 417-256-9616; Fax: 417-257-6948
E-mail: mail@emovieposter.com
Web site: http://www.emovieposter.com
Dist(s): **Austin & Company, Inc.**
Partners Pubs. Group, Inc.

Hersom Hse. Publishing, (*978-0-615-83541-9; 978-0-615-83633-1; 978-0-615-83663-8; 978-0-615-83720-8; 978-0-615-83853-3; 978-0-615-85918-7; 978-0-615-87526-2; 978-0-615-88547-6; 978-0-615-90226-5; 978-0-615-91492-3; 978-0-615-92976-7; 978-0-615-93940-7*) 3365 NE 45th St, Suite 101, Ocala, FL 34479 USA Tel 352-497-9040
Dist(s): **CreateSpace Independent Publishing Platform.**

Heryin Publishing Corp., (*978-0-9762056; 978-0-9787550; 978-0-9845523*) 1033 E. Main St., No. 202, Alhambra, CA 91801 USA Tel 626-289-2238; Fax: 626-289-3865
E-mail: info@heryin.com
Dist(s): **Independent Pubs. Group.**

Herzog, Joyce, (*978-1-887225*) 900 Airport Rd., #21, Chattanooga, TN 37421 USA Tel 423-553-6387
E-mail: joyceoffice@aol.com
Web site: http://JoyceHerzog.com; http://JoyceHerzog.info; http://ScaredyCatReadingSystem.com.

Hesperus Pr. (GBR) (*978-1-84391; 978-1-78094*) *Dist. by* **IPG Chicago.**

Hester Publishing, (*978-0-9789388*) 219 Blackberry Cir., Colchester, VT 05446 USA
E-mail: sales@hesterpublishing.com
Web site: http://hesterpublishing.com.

Hetherington Hall, (*978-0-9839963*) 888 Logan St. Suite 9A, Denver, CO 80203 USA Tel 720-883-4848
E-mail: lisa@hetheringtonhall.com
Web site: www.hetheringtonhall.com.

Hetman Publishing (GBR) (*978-0-9561592*) *Dist. by* **LuluCom.**

Hewell Publishing, (*978-1-56870*) 2722 N. Josey Ln. Suite 100, Carrollton, TX 75007 USA
E-mail: sally.hewell@alphagraphics.com
Web site: http://www.hewellpublishing.com
Dist(s): **AtlasBooks Distribution.**

Hewett, Katherine J.E., (*978-0-578-03065-4; 978-0-578-09202-7*) 625 Gregory Dr. Apt. 85, Crp Christi, TX 78412-3061 USA
E-mail: kathewett@aol.com
Dist(s): **Lulu Enterprises Inc.**

Hewitt Research Foundation, Inc., (*978-0-913717; 978-1-57896*) Orders Addr.: P.O. Box 9, Washougal, WA 98671 USA (SAN 286-1852) Tel 360-835-8708; Fax: 360-835-8697; Toll Free: 800-348-1750; Edit Addr.: 2103 B St., Washougal, WA 98671 USA
E-mail: hewitths@aol.com
Web site: http://www.homeeducation.org.

Hewitt Research, Incorporated *See* **Hewitt Research Foundation, Inc.**

Hexagon Blue, (*978-0-9729958*) P.O. Box 1790, Issaquah, WA 98027-0073 USA (SAN 255-3406)
E-mail: maryjesse@gmail.com
Web site: http://www.hexagonblue.com
Dist(s): **Quality Bks., Inc.**

Hey U.G.L.Y., Inc., (*978-0-9759004*) 8057 N. 300 E., Rolling Prairie, IN 46371 USA
Web site: http://www.heyugly.org.

Heyday, (*978-0-930588; 978-0-9666691; 978-1-890771; 978-1-59714*) Orders Addr.: P.O. Box 9145, Berkeley, CA 94709 USA (SAN 207-2351) Tel 510-549-3564; Fax: 510-549-1889; 1633 University Ave., Berkeley, CA 94703-1424; *Imprints:* Great Valley Books (Grt Valley Bks)
E-mail: orders@heydaybooks.com; david@heydaybooks.com; christopher@heydaybooks.com
Web site: http://www.heydaybooks.com.

Heyday Books *See* **Heyday**

Hez-N-Tales, (*978-0-9745349*) 11037 Hopewell Rd., Boaz, KY 42027 USA
Web site: http://www.feedinghislambs.org.

Hi Willow Research & Publishing, (*978-0-931510; 978-1-933170*) Orders Addr.: P.O. Box 720400, San Jose, CA 95172-0400 USA (SAN 211-3945) Toll Free: 800-873-3043
E-mail: sales@lmcsource.com
Web site: http://www.lmcsource.com
Dist(s): **Follett School Solutions**
L M C Source.

Hibiscus Publishing, (*978-0-9792963; 978-0-9842831*) 1499 Gormican Ln., Naples, FL 34110 USA Fax: 239-514-0238
E-mail: hibiscus311@comcast.net
Web site: http://www.hibiscuspublishing.com
Dist(s): **AtlasBooks Distribution.**

Hiccup Cottage Pubns., (*978-0-9718724*) 316 10th St., NE, Charlottesville, VA 22902 USA Tel 434-980-5347
E-mail: hiccupcottage@yahoo.com.

Hickle Pickle Publishing, (*978-1-881958*) 4450 Allison Dr., Michigan Center, MI 49254 USA Tel 517-764-1117
E-mail: hicklepickle@modempool.com
Web site: www.hicklepickle.com.

Hickory Bark Productions, (*978-0-9748047*) 3355 N. Five Mile Rd., Suite 332, Boise, ID 83713 USA Tel 208-322-7239.

Hickory Grove Pr., (*978-0-9679915; 978-0-9854725*) Orders Addr.: 3151 Treeco Ln., Bellevue, IA 52031 USA Tel 563-583-4767 (phone/fax) Do not confuse with Hickory Grove Pr., Canton, OH
E-mail: challengemath@aol.com
Web site: http://www.challengemath.com.

Hickory Tales Publishing, (*978-0-9709104; 978-0-9787555*) Orders Addr.: 841 Newberry St., Bowling Green, KY 42103 USA Tel 270-791-3242
E-mail: jadonel@aol.com
Web site: http://www.hickorytales.com.

Hickory Tree Publishing, (*978-0-9893157*) 123 High St., Ashland, OR 97520 USA Tel 541-864-0541
E-mail: finley.ra@gmail.com
Web site: http://www.hickorytreebooks.blogspot.com
Dist(s): **eBookit.com.**

Hidden Curriculum Education, (*978-0-9755103*) Orders Addr.: P.O. Box 222041, Hollywood, FL 33022 USA Tel 954-457-8098; Fax: 954-457-3331
Web site: http://www.collegefaqbook.com.

Hidden Forest Pubs., (*978-0-9755117*) 269 Co. Hwy. 250, Guin, AL 35563-2700 USA.

Hidden Manna Pubns., (*978-0-9891683; 978-0-9915261; 978-0-9864066*) 249 Larch St., Priest River, ID 83856 USA Tel 208-412-3087
E-mail: artnbooks@gmail.com
Web site: www.gentleshepherd.com.

Hidden Path Pubn., Inc., (*978-0-9711534*) 304 Briarwood Rd., Statesville, NC 28677 USA Tel 704-878-0716; 704-224-4832
E-mail: dkellysteele@aol.com.

Hidden Pictures, (*978-0-9678159; 978-0-9843088*) Orders Addr.: P.O. Box 63, Tipp City, OH 45371-9103 USA (SAN 253-6862) Tel 937-667-6288; Fax: 937-669-4178
E-mail: liz@hiddenpictures.com
Web site: http://www.hiddenpicturepuzzle.com.

Hidden Talent Pr., (*978-0-9776114*) Orders Addr.: P.O. Box 9052, Missoula, MT 59807 USA
Web site: http://www.iysofwar.com.

Hidden Valley Farm Pub., (*978-0-615-17173-9*) P.O. Box 172, Perry, NY 14530 USA
E-mail: theotherherald@yahoo.com
Web site: http://www.tfrice.etsy.com
Dist(s): **Lulu Enterprises Inc.**

HiddenSpring *Imprint of* **Paulist Pr.**

Hierophant Publishing Services *See* **Hieropub LLC**

Hierophantasm, (*978-0-9837905*) 190 W. Fifth Ave. P. O. Box 792, Clifton, IL 60927 USA Tel 815-694-0010
E-mail: Andy@hierophantasm.com
Web site: hierophantasm.com.

Hieropub LLC, (*978-0-9727940*) P.O. Box 895, Pottstown, PA 19464 USA Tel 610-705-0282
E-mail: patholl@hieropub.com; pholl@comcast.net
Web site: http://www.hieropub.com; http://www.hatheadbooks.com
Dist(s): **Quality Bks., Inc.**

Higginson Bk. Co., (*978-0-7404; 978-0-8328*) 148 Washington St., Salem, MA 01970 USA (SAN 247-9400) Tel 978-745-7170; Fax: 978-745-8025
E-mail: higginsn@cove.com
Web site: http://higginsonbooks.com.

High Country Publishers *See* **Ingalls Publishing Group, Inc.**

High Desert Productions, (*978-0-9652920*) Orders Addr.: P.O. Box 5506, Bisbee, AZ 85603 USA Tel 520-432-5288; Edit Addr.: 511 Mance St., Bisbee, AZ 85603 USA
Dist(s): **Rio Nuevo Pubs.**

High Five *Imprint of* **Red Brick Learning**

High Five Reading (RBL) *Imprint of* **Capstone Pr., Inc.**

High Ground Productions, Incorporated *See* **High Ground Pubns.**

High Ground Pubns., (*978-0-9720153*) 80 Supai Dr., Sedona, AZ 86351 USA (SAN 254-5748) Tel 360-945-2485
E-mail: Karen@amatteroftime.org
Web site: http://www.amatteroftime.org.

High Hill Pr., (*978-1-60653*) 2731 Cumberland Landing, Saint Charles, MO 63303 USA (SAN 856-2806) Tel 636-928-2212
E-mail: HighHillPress@aol.com
Web site: http://www.highhillpress.com.

High Hopes Publishing, (*978-0-9708417; 978-0-9905129*) Subs. of Communication Arts Multimedia, Inc., 1618 Williams Dr., Suite No. 5, Georgetown, TX 78628 USA Tel 512-868-0548 (phone/fax); Toll Free: 888-742-0074
E-mail: mail@commartsmultimedia.com
Web site: http://www.highhopespublishing.com.

High Mountain Publishing, (*978-0-9718609*) Bookmasters (high Mountain Pub) 30 Amberwood Pkwy. P.o. Box 388, Ashland, OH 44805 USA Tel 818-645-8621
E-mail: uescher@hotmail.com
Web site: http://www.howtotrick.com.

High Noon Bks., (*978-0-87879; 978-1-57128*) Div. of Academic Therapy Pubns., Inc., 20 Leveroni Ct., Novato, CA 94949-5746 USA Tel 415-883-3314; Fax: 415-883-3720; Toll Free: 800-422-7249
E-mail: atpub@aol.com
Web site: http://www.highnoonbooks.com.

High Standards Publishing, Incorporated *See* **True Exposures Publishing, Inc.**

High Tide Pr., (*978-0-9653744; 978-1-892696*) 2081 Calistoga Dr. Ste. 2N, New Lenox, IL 60451-4833 USA Do not confuse with The Trinity Foundation, Hobbs, NM
E-mail: alex@hightidepress.com; mregan@hightidepress.com
Web site: http://www.hightidepress.com.

Higher Balance Institute, (*978-0-9759080; 978-1-939410*) 515 NW Saltzman Rd., No.726, Portland, OR 97229 USA Tel 503-646-4000; Toll Free: 800-935-4007
E-mail: publishing@higherbalance.com
Web site: http://www.higherbalance.com.

Higher Ground Pr., (*978-0-9766062; 978-0-9838321*) Orders Addr.: P.O. Box PO 1381, Allen, TX 75013 USA Tel 214-680-9779
E-mail: info@highergroundpress.com
Web site: http://www.highergroundpress.com
Dist(s): **Brigham Distribution.**

Higher Power Publishing, (*978-0-9787631*) 702 Twilight Dr., Garland, TX 75040 USA Tel 214-298-9563
E-mail: higherpowerpublishing@hotmail.com
Web site: http://www.higherpowerpublishing.biz
Dist(s): **Lightning Source, Inc.**

Highest Good Pubns. *Imprint of* **EbonyEnergy Publishing, Inc.**

Highland Children's Pr. *Imprint of* **Heather & Highlands Publishing**

Highland Press *See* **Highland Pr. Publishing**

Highland Pr., (*978-0-9630273*) Div. of The Alabama Booksmith, 5512 Crestwood Blvd., Birmingham, AL 35212-4131 USA (SAN 297-8628) Do not confuse with companies with the same name in Boerne, TX, Wilsonville, OR, Tonasket, WA, Bryson City, NC, San Rafael, CA, High Springs, FL
E-mail: booksmith@mindspring.com.

Highland Pr., (*978-0-910722*) 10108 Johns Rd., Boerne, TX 78006 USA (SAN 204-0522) Do not confuse with companies of the same name or similar in Birmingham, AL, Wilsonville, OR, Tonasket, WA, Bryson City, NC, San Rafael, CA, High Springs, FL.

Highland Pr. Publishing, (*978-0-9746249; 978-0-9787139; 978-0-9800356; 978-0-9815573; 978-0-9818550; 978-0-9823615; 978-0-9842499; 978-0-9833960; 978-0-9846541; 978-0-9850690; 978-0-9895262; 978-0-9916439; 978-1-942606*) Orders Addr.: P.O. Box 2292, High Springs, FL 32655 USA (SAN 851-4275); *Imprints:* Pandora (Pandora) Do not confuse with companies with the same or similar name in Sacramento, CA, Birmingham, AL, Wilsonville, ORBoerne, TX, San Rafael, CA, Bryson City, NC, Tonasket, WA
E-mail: The.Highland.Press@gmail.com; Mickeytl@aol.com
Web site: http://www.highlandpress.org.

Highlight Publishing, (*978-0-9741734*) P.O. Box 27, Little Falls, MN 56345 USA Tel 320-630-1463; Toll Free: 866-336-6681
E-mail: books@highlightpublishing.com
Web site: http://www.highlightpublishing.com.

Highlights *Imprint of* **Boyds Mills Pr.**

Highlights for Children, (*978-0-87534*) Orders Addr.: P.O. Box 269, Columbus, OH 43216-0269 USA (SAN 281-7810) Tel 614-486-0631; Fax: 614-876-8564; Toll Free: 800-255-9517; Edit Addr.: 803 Church St.,

For full information on wholesalers and distributors, refer to the Wholesaler and Distributor Name Index

Honesdale, PA 18431 USA (SAN 281-7802) Tel 570-253-1080; Fax: 570-253-1179
E-mail: eds@highlights.com
Web site: http://www.highlights.com
Dist(s): **Boyds Mills Pr.**
INscribe Digital.

Highlights of Chicago Pr., *(978-0-9710487; 978-0-9907771)* 4325 N. Central Park Ave., Chicago, IL 60618 USA Tel 773-509-0008 (phone/fax)
E-mail: bturner@highlightsofchicago.com
Web site: http://www.highlightsofchicago.com.

High-Lonesome Bks., *(978-0-944383)* Orders Addr.: P.O. Box 878, Silver City, NM 88062 USA (SAN 243-3079) Tel 505-388-3763; Fax: 505-388-5705; Toll Free: 800-380-7323 (orders only)
E-mail: Cherie@High-LonesomeBooks.com
Web site: http://www.high-lonesomebooks.com
Dist(s): **Univ. of New Mexico Pr.**

High-Pitched Hum Inc., *(978-0-9759818; 978-0-9777290; 978-0-9787995; 978-0-9792780; 978-1-934666; 978-0-9885818; 978-0-9914847)* 321 15th St., N., Jacksonville Beach, FL 32250 USA
E-mail: breynolds@jettyman.com
Web site: http://www.highpitchedhum.net.

HighPoint Publishing, Inc., *(978-1-933190)* Orders Addr.: 3975 E. Highway 290., Dripping Spgs, TX 78620-4287 USA (SAN 256-2952)
E-mail: kenc@highpointpublishing.com; milena@highpointpublishing.com
Web site: http://www.HighPointPublishing.com.

HighReach Learning, Incorporated *Imprint of* **Carson-Dellosa Publishing, LLC**

†High/Scope Pr., *(978-0-929816; 978-0-931114; 978-1-57379)* Div. of High/Scope Educational Research Foundation, 600 N. River St., Ypsilanti, MI 48198-2898 USA (SAN 211-9617) Tel 734-485-2000; Fax: 734-485-0704; Toll Free Fax: 800-442-4329 (orders); Toll Free: 800-407-7377 (orders only)
E-mail: info@highscope.org
Web site: http://www.highscope.org
Dist(s): **CENGAGE Learning**
Delmar Cengage Learning
Follett School Solutions; *CIP.*

Highsmith Inc., *(978-0-913853; 978-0-917846; 978-1-57950; 978-1-932146; 978-1-59847; 978-1-60213)* P.O. Box 5210, Janesville, WI 53547-5210 USA (SAN 159-8740) Toll Free: 800-448-4887; 401 S. Wright Rd., Janesville, WI 53547 (SAN 858-9674) Toll Free Fax: 800-835-2329; Toll Free: 800-554-4661; *Imprints:* Upstart Books (Upstart Bks)
Web site: http://www.highsmith.com
Dist(s): **Mackin Bk. Co.**

Highsmith Press, LLC *See* **Highsmith Inc.**

Hignites, Tom Miracle Studio, *(978-1-934017)* Orders Addr.: 1977 Mayfield Rd., Richfield, WI 53076-5307 USA (SAN 850-9611) Tel 262-628-5577; Fax: 262-628-5580; Edit Addr.: 3070 Hwy. 145, Richfield, WI 53076-5307 USA
E-mail: jbrown@miracle-homes.com
Web site: http://tomhignitesmiraclestudios.com.

Hilarity Waters Pr., *(978-0-615-49668-9)* 1117 SW 126th St., Oklahoma City, OK 73170 USA Tel 405-990-9891
E-mail: andrews.africabound@gmail.com
Web site: www.hilaritywaterspress.com.

Hildebrand, Betty, *(978-0-9753729)* 116 Rosetta Ct., Springdale, OH 45246 USA
E-mail: deona@bethart.com
Web site: http://www.bethart.com.

Hill & Wang *Imprint of* **Farrar, Straus & Giroux**

Hill, Lawrence Bks. *Imprint of* **Chicago Review Pr., Inc.**

Hill, Napoleon Foundation, *(978-1-880369)* Friends of Napoleon Hill, 19458 S. La Grange Rd., Mokena, IL 60448 USA Tel 847-998-0408; Fax: 847-998-6890; Toll Free Fax: 800-957-9124; Toll Free: 800-957-9114
E-mail: 70543.3377@compuserve.com
Web site: http://www.naphill.org.

Hill Publishing *See* **SunHill Pubs.**

Hill, Stephanie & Clarissa, *(978-0-9785539)* P.O. Box 13212, Baltimore, MD 21203-3212 USA (SAN 850-9816) Tel 443-838-9426
E-mail: sachedesignsinc@yahoo.com
Web site: http://www.sachedesigns.com.

Hill Street Pr., LLC, *(978-1-892514; 978-1-58818)* P.O. Box 49468, Athens, GA 30604-9468 USA Toll Free: 800-295-0365
E-mail: info@hillstreetpress.com
Web site: http://www.hillstreetpress.com
Dist(s): **Gibbs Smith, Publisher**
Beeler, Thomas T. Pub.

Hillcrest Publishing Group, Inc., *(978-0-9723806; 978-0-9744668; 978-0-9754803; 978-0-9764981; 978-1-934248; 978-0-9798246; 978-0-9798467; 978-0-9799120; 978-1-934937; 978-1-934938; 978-0-9802455; 978-0-9802456; 978-1-935097; 978-1-935098; 978-1-935204; 978-0-9820938; 978-1-935456; 978-1-936107; 978-1-936183; 978-0-9841965; 978-1-936198; 978-1-936400; 978-1-936401; 978-0-9846204; 978-0-9846205; 978-1-937003; 978-1-936780; 978-1-936782; 978-1-937293; 978-1-937563; 978-1-937600; 978-1-937860; 978-0-9848028; 978-1-937928; 978-) 212 3rd Ave. N., Suite 290, Minneapolis, MN 55401-2420 USA Toll Free: 888-645-2489; Imprints:* Langdon Street Press (LangdonSt); Jabberwocky Books, Incorporated (Jabberwocky Bks); Bascom Hill Books (Bascom Hill); Mill City Press, Inc (Mill City); Two Harbors Press (TwoHarbors)
E-mail: paigen@twoharborspress.com; paigen@jabberwocky-books.com; paigen@seraphinapress.com
Web site: http://www.seraphinapress.com; http://www.jabberwocky-books.com; http://www.langdonstreetpress.com; http://www.bascomhillpublishing.com; http://www.twoharborspress.com; http://www.millcitypress.net/
Dist(s): **BookBaby**
INscribe Digital
Itasca Bks.
PDR Network, LLC
Smashwords
West
ebrary, Inc.

Hillside Education, *(978-0-9766386; 978-0-9798469; 978-0-9831800; 978-0-9885106; 978-0-9906720)* 475 Bidwell Hill Rd., Lake Ariel, PA 18436 USA (SAN 257-4446)
E-mail: info@hillsideeducation.com; sales@hillsideeducation.com
Web site: http://www.hillsideeducation.com

Hillside Pr., *(978-0-9627530)* Affil. of Ridgetop Pr., 280 E. Birch Hill Rd., Fairbanks, AK 99712 USA Tel 907-457-7834; Fax: 907-457-7835; Toll Free: 800-390-8999 Do not confuse with companies with the same name in Los Angeles, CA, Carversville, PA, Vista, CA, Collegeville, PA, Wolcott, CT
E-mail: jhaigh@polarnet.com
Web site: http://www2.polarnet.com/~jhaigh/
Dist(s): **News Group, The**
Partners/West Book Distributors
Todd Communications.

Hillside Pr., *(978-0-9815895)* P.O. Box 241, Midway, FL 32343 USA
E-mail: ljhill@hillsidepress.net
Web site: http://www.hillsidepress.net
Dist(s): **Perseus Bks. Group**
Perseus Distribution.

Hilton Publishing *See* **Hilton Publishing Co.**

Hilton Publishing Co., *(978-0-9654553; 978-0-9675258; 978-0-9716067; 978-0-9743144; 978-0-9764443; 978-0-9773160; 978-0-9777779; 978-0-9800649; 978-0-9815381; 978-0-9841447; 978-0-9847566; 978-0-9904283)* Orders Addr.: 1630 45th Ave. Ste. 103, Munster, IN 46321-3959 USA Toll Free: 866-455-1070
E-mail: info@hiltonpub.com
Web site: http://www.hiltonpub.com
Dist(s): **Independent Pubs. Group**
SCB Distributors.

Himminbjorg Publishing, Inc., *(978-0-9749416)* P.O. Box 6493, Napa, CA 94581 USA Tel 707-251-9526 (phone/fax)
E-mail: himminbjorg@aol.com
Web site: http://www.wyrdsway.com.

Hines, Jerry, *(978-0-615-17723-6)* 2660 Suzanne Cir., White Bear Lake, MN 55110 USA
E-mail: jerryhines@comcast.net
Dist(s): **Lulu Enterprises Inc.**

Hinkler Bks. Pty, Ltd. (AUS) *(978-1-86515; 978-1-74121; 978-1-875980; 978-1-74157; 978-1-74181; 978-1-74182; 978-1-74183; 978-1-74184; 978-1-74185; 978-1-74281; 978-1-74308; 978-1-74352; 978-1-74363; 978-1-74367; 978-1-4889) Dist. by* **Ideals.**

Hinman, Bobbie E. Incorporated *See* **Best Fairy Bks.**

Hinman Publishing, *(978-0-9723525)* 2943 Breakwater Way, Longmont, CO 80503 USA
E-mail: jshinman@earthlink.net.

Hinterland Sky Pr., *(978-0-9818880)* 37 W. Black Oak Dr., Asheville, NC 28804-1809 USA
E-mail: frances.ruiz@gmail.com
Web site: http://www.hinterlandsky.com.

HinterWelt Enterprises, LLC, *(978-0-9740096)* 7504 W. Hickory Creek Dr., Frankfort, IL 60423-9094 USA
E-mail: winna@hinterwelt.com
Web site: http://www.hinterwelt.com.

Hip Hop Schl. Hse., *(978-0-9768674)* 8618 S. Constance, Chicago, IL 60617 USA Tel 793-218-4204
Dist(s): **AtlasBooks Distribution.**

Hippocratic Pr., The, *(978-0-9753516)* 281A Fairhaven Hill Rd., Concord, MA 01742 USA Tel 978-369-0739
E-mail: ccowanmd@hippocraticpress.com
Web site: http://www.hippocraticpress.com.

†Hippocrene Bks., Inc., *(978-0-7818; 978-0-87052; 978-0-88254)* 171 Madison Ave., New York, NY 10016-1002 USA (SAN 213-2060) Tel 718-454-2366 (sales); 212-685-4371 (editorial); Fax: 718-454-1391 (sales/order inquiry); 212-779-9338 (editorial)
E-mail: hippocre@ix.netcom.com
Web site: http://www.hippocrenebooks.com
Dist(s): **Continental Bk. Co., Inc.**; *CIP.*

Hired Pen, Inc., The *See* **Acacia Publishing, Inc.**

His Feast Publishing, *(978-0-9677722)* Div. of Feast of Tabernacles Ministries, P.O. Box 444, Forest Lake, MN 55025 USA
E-mail: Hisfeast@aol.com.

His Grace Is Sufficient *Imprint of* **ELW Pubns.**

His Hands, Inc., *(978-0-9720881)* Orders Addr.: P.O. Box 7063, Oak Ridge, TN 37831 USA Tel 865-482-9562; Edit Addr.: 82 E. Tennesse Ave., Apt. 117, Oak Ridge, TN 37830 USA (SAN 255-2930) Tel 865-482-9562
E-mail: hishandstn@netzero.com
Web site: http://www.hishands.org.

His Kids Publishing, Inc., *(978-0-9720417)* Orders Addr.: P.O. Box 72172, Marietta, GA 30007 USA Tel 770-998-3240; Fax: 770-998-4943; Edit Addr.: 1544 Sandpoint Dr., Roswell, GA 30075 USA
E-mail: management@intrag-publishing.com
Web site: http://www.intrag-publishing.com.

H.I.S. Publishing LLC *See* **Heard Word Publishing, LLC**

His Sonshine, Inc., *(978-0-9758880)* 13214 Barwick Rd., Del Ray Beach, FL 33445 USA.

His Story, *(978-0-9766951)* 1409 Coolhurst, Sherwood, AR 72120 USA
Web site: http://www.hisstory.org.

His Work Christian Publishing, *(978-0-9778328; 978-0-9798290; 978-0-9799189; 978-0-615-43443-8; 978-0-9854469)* Div. of His Work Christian Ministries, Orders Addr.: P.O. Box 563, Ward Cove, AK 99928 USA Tel 206-274-8474; Fax: 614-388-0664
E-mail: hiswork@hisworkpub.com; editor@hisworkpub.com
Web site: http://www.hisworkpub.com
Dist(s): **Lightning Source, Inc.**

Hispanic Institute of Social Issues, *(978-0-9771167; 978-0-9797814; 978-1-936885)* P.O. Box 50553, Mesa, AZ 85208-0028 USA
Web site: http://www.hisi.org.

Historic Mint Co., The, *(978-0-9753767)* 36 Sandwedge Dr., Henderson, NV 89074-1714 USA Toll Free: 877-264-6266
Web site: http://www.historicmint.com.

Historic Philadelphia, Inc., *(978-0-9855319)* 150 S. Independence Mall, W. Suite 550, Philadelphia, PA 19106 USA Tel 215-629-5801
E-mail: debiflora@about-books.com; msdariaf@gmail.com
Web site: http://www.historicphiladelphia.org.

Historic Pr.-South, *(978-0-9645990)* Orders Addr.: P.O. Box 407, Gatlinburg, TN 37738 USA Tel 423-436-4163; Toll Free: 800-279-2603; Edit Addr.: 367 Buckhorn Rd., Gatlinburg, TN 37738 USA.

Historic Tours of America, Inc., *(978-0-9752698)* 201 Front St., Suite 224, Key West, FL 33040 USA Tel 305-292-8920; Fax: 305-295-4999
E-mail: psmith@historictours.com
Web site: http://www.historictours.com.

Historical Pages Company *See* **Birch Island**

Historical Society of Michigan, The, *(978-0-9614344; 978-1-880311)* 1305 Abbott Rd., East Lansing, MI 48823 USA (SAN 687-8008) Tel 517-324-1828; Fax: 517-324-4370
E-mail: hsm@hsmichigan.org
Web site: http://www.hsmichigan.org
Dist(s): **Partners Bk. Distributing, Inc.**

Historical Society of Western Pennsylvania, *(978-0-936340)* 1212 Smallman St., Pittsburgh, PA 15222-4208 USA (SAN 214-0276)
E-mail: babutko@heinzhistorycenter.org
Web site: http://www.einzhistorycenter.org.

History Compass, LLC, *(978-1-57960; 978-1-878668; 978-1-932663)* 25 Leslie Rd., Auburndale, MA 02466 USA (SAN 297-2611) Tel 617-332-2202; Fax: 617-332-2210
E-mail: info@historycompass.com; lisa@historycompass.com
Web site: http://www.historycompass.com
Dist(s): **Follett School Solutions**
Ingram Pub. Services
Social Studies Schl. Service.

History Factory, *(978-1-882771)* 14140 Parke Long Ct., Suite G, Chantilly, VA 20151 USA Tel 703-631-0500; Fax: 703-631-1124
E-mail: jburkitt@historyfactory.com; info@historyfactory.com; mgaffney@historyfactory.com.

History Jukebox, LLC, *(978-0-9791118)* P.O. Box 467, Marshall, MI 49068 USA Tel 269-781-8357; Fax: 269-781-8760; Toll Free: 866-977-7664
E-mail: info@historyjukebox.org
Web site: http://www.historyjukebox.org.

History Pr. Ltd., The (GBR) *(978-0-7509; 978-0-7524; 978-0-86299; 978-0-904387; 978-1-84015) Dist. by* **IPG Chicago.**

History Pr., The *Imprint of* **Arcadia Publishing**

HI-Tech Software, *(978-1-928618; 978-1-936735)* 10 Little Tarn Ct., Hamburg, NJ 07419-1262 USA
E-mail: harry@htsoftware.com
Web site: http://www.htsoftware.com.

Hither Creek Pr., *(978-0-9700555)* 14 Holman St., Laconia, NH 03246-3016 USA Do not confuse with Hither Creek Press in Nantucket, MA
E-mail: hithercreekpress@aol.com.

Hi-Time Pflaum *See* **Pflaum Publishing Group**

Hive Collective, *(978-0-9884774)* 30 Shelburne Rd., Merrimack, NH 03054 USA Tel 603-423-1071
E-mail: stan@findtheaxis.com
Web site: http://hiveauthors.wordpress.com.

HK Comics Ltd. (HKG) *(978-962-85278; 978-988-98437; 978-988-97972) Dist. by* **Diamond Book Dists.**

HM Bks., *(978-0-9796476; 978-0-9820126)* Div. of HM Entertainment Inc., P.O. Box 26411, Columbus, OH 43226-0411 USA
E-mail: hmbooks@hmproductionsinternational.com; mejamwangi@yahoo.com
Web site: http://www.hmproductionsinternational.com.

HMH Books For Young Readers *Imprint of* **Houghton Mifflin Harcourt Publishing Co.**

HMSI, Inc., *(978-0-615-29442-1; 978-0-9842662; 978-0-9826945; 978-0-9851996)* 50768 Van Buren Dr., Plymouth, MI 48170 USA
Web site: http://www.PublishHMSI.com.

HNB Publishing, *(978-0-9664286; 978-0-9728061; 978-0-9828874)* Orders Addr.: 250 W. 78th St., No. 3FF, New York, NY 10024 USA Tel 212-873-5382; 347-260-1376
E-mail: sales@hnbpub.com
Web site: http://www.hnbpub.com.

Hoard, W.D. & Sons Co., *(978-0-932147; 978-0-9960753)* P.O. Box 801, Fort Atkinson, WI 53538-0801 USA (SAN 686-4341) Tel 920-563-5551; Fax: 920-563-7298; *Imprints:* Hoard's Dairyman (Hoards Dairyman)
Web site: http://www.hoards.com.

Hoard's Dairyman *Imprint of* **Hoard, W.D. & Sons Co.**

Hobar Pubns., *(978-0-89317; 978-0-913163; 978-0-933855; 978-0-9616847; 978-1-55797)* Div. of Finney Co., Orders Addr.: 8075 215th St. W., Lakeville, MN 55044 USA (SAN 283-1120) Tel 952-469-6699; Fax: 952-469-1968; Toll Free Fax: 800-330-6232; Toll Free: 800-846-7027
E-mail: feedback@finneyco.com
Web site: http://www.finney-hobar.com
Dist(s): **Book Wholesalers, Inc.**
Brodart Co.
Follett School Solutions
Midpoint Trade Bks., Inc.
Southern Bk. Service.

Hobbes End Publishing, LLC, *(978-0-9763510; 978-0-9859110)* Div. of Hobbes End Entertainment, P.O. Box 193, Aubrey, TX 76227 USA
Web site: http://www.hobbesendpublishing.com
Dist(s): **Smashwords.**

Hobblebush Bks., *(978-0-9636413; 978-0-9760896; 978-0-9801672; 978-0-9845921; 978-1-939449)* 17-a Old Milford Rd., Brookline, NH 03033 USA
E-mail: hobblebush@charter.net; amy.hobblebush@charter.net
Web site: http://www.Hobblebush.com; www.poorrichardslament.com
Dist(s): **Distributors, The**
SPD-Small Pr. Distribution.

Hobbs, Brenda F., *(978-0-9772970)* 14303 Greenview Rd., Detroit, MI 48223 USA
E-mail: bhobbs101@aol.com.

Hobbs, Constance (GBR) *(978-0-9556783) Dist. by* **LuluCom.**

Hobby Horse Publishing, LLC, *(978-0-615-89154-5)* P.O. Box 22, Peterborough, NH 03458 USA Tel 555-555-5555
E-mail: info@hobbyhorsepublishing.com
Web site: www.HobbyHorsePublishing.com.

Hobby Hse. Publishing Group, *(978-0-9727179)* Orders Addr.: 48 Hickory Hill Rd., Box 1527, Jackson, NJ 08527 USA
Web site: http://www.hobbyhousepublishinggroup.com.

Hodder & Stoughton (GBR) *(978-0-245; 978-0-340; 978-0-550; 978-0-7131; 978-0-7195; 978-1-85998; 978-1-84032; 978-1-84456; 978-1-84854; 978-1-4447; 978-1-4736) Dist. by* **IPG Chicago.**

Hodder & Stoughton (GBR) *(978-0-245; 978-0-340; 978-0-550; 978-0-7131; 978-0-7195; 978-1-85998; 978-1-84032; 978-1-84456; 978-1-84854; 978-1-4447; 978-1-4736) Dist. by* **Trafalgar.**

Hodder Arnold Pubs.,
Dist(s): **Oxford Univ. Pr., Inc.**

Hodder Education Group (GBR) *(978-0-340; 978-0-412; 978-0-450; 978-0-7122; 978-0-7131; 978-0-7506; 978-0-85264; 978-0-947054; 978-0-86003; 978-1-874958; 978-1-902984; 978-1-4441; 978-1-905735; 978-1-4718) Dist. by* **Trafalgar.**

Hodder Education Group (GBR) *(978-0-340; 978-0-412; 978-0-450; 978-0-7122; 978-0-7131; 978-0-7506; 978-0-85264; 978-0-947054; 978-0-86003; 978-1-874958; 978-1-902984; 978-1-4441; 978-1-905735; 978-1-4718) Dist. by* **OUP.**

Hodder Education Group (GBR) *(978-0-340; 978-0-412; 978-0-450; 978-0-7122; 978-0-7131; 978-0-7506; 978-0-85264; 978-0-947054; 978-0-86003; 978-1-874958; 978-1-902984; 978-1-4441; 978-1-905735; 978-1-4718) Dist. by* **Trans-Atl Phila.**

Hoffman, Mark *See* **Hramiec Hoffman Publishing**

Hoffmann Partnership, The, *(978-0-9753106)* 349 Martin Ln., Bloomingdale, IL 60108-1326 USA
E-mail: Catherine@WriteHappy.com; info@writehappy.com
Web site: http://www.writehappy.com
Dist(s): **Publishers' Graphics, L.L.C.**

Hogan Publishing LLC, *(978-0-9779504)* 2708 E. Edison, Tucson, AZ 85716 USA
E-mail: benjamin@madseadog.com
Web site: http://www.madseadog.com.

Hogs Back Bks. (GBR) *(978-1-907432) Dist. by* **IPG Chicago.**

Hohm Pr., *(978-0-934252; 978-1-890772; 978-1-935387)* Div. of Hohm, Inc., P.O. Box 2501, Prescott, AZ 86302 USA (SAN 221-0924) Tel 520-778-9189; Fax: 520-717-1779; Toll Free: 800-381-2700 (orders only)
E-mail: staff@hohmpress.com; pinedr@goodnet.com; hpproduction@cableone.net
Web site: http://www.hohmpress.com
Dist(s): **SCB Distributors.**

Holberton, Paul Publishing (GBR) *(978-1-903470; 978-1-907372) Dist. by* **Casemate Pubs.**

Holbrook Studios, *(978-0-9762440)* Orders Addr.: P.O. Box 3064, Beverly Hills, CA 90212 USA; Edit Addr.: 754 E. S. Temple, Salt Lake city, UT 84102 USA.

Holes In My Socks Publishing, *(978-0-9771891)* P.O. Box 266, Paola, KS 66071 USA Tel 913-557-4508
E-mail: stephgun2@aol.com; christydreiling@att.net.

†Holiday Hse., Inc., *(978-0-8234)* Orders Addr.: 425 Madison Ave., New York, NY 10017 USA (SAN 202-3008) Tel 212-688-0085; Fax: 212-688-0395
E-mail: holiday@holidayhouse.com
Web site: http://www.holidayhouse.com
Dist(s): **MyiLibrary**
Open Road Integrated Media, LLC; *CIP.*

Holiness.com, *(978-0-9743831)* 1271 Washington Ave., PMB 165, San Leandro, CA 94577 USA Tel 510-384-8082
E-mail: suppliers@holiness.com
Web site: http://www.holiness.com.

Holism Publishing, *(978-0-9818297)* Orders Addr.: P.O. Box 3385, Palm Beach, FL 33480-1585 USA Tel 561-533-7704 (phone/fax)
E-mail: curecare@bellsouth.net; info@holismpublishing.com
Web site: http://www.HolismPublishing.com; http://www.HolismMovement.com
Dist(s): **New Leaf Distributing Co., Inc.**

Holland Brown, *(978-0-9797006; 978-0-9897544)* 732 E. Market St., Suite 300, Louisville, KY 40202-1008 USA
E-mail: stephanie@thegreenbuilding.com
Web site: http://www.hollandbrownbooks.com.

Holland, Gretchen, *(978-0-9768340)* 4437 Craig Dr., Fort Collins, CO 80526 USA Tel 970-282-1338.

Hollandays Publishing Corp., *(978-0-9708224; 978-0-9728844; 978-0-9753239; 978-0-9769459;*

Publisher Name Index

978-0-9799003) 8459 N. Main St. Ste. 118, Dayton, OH 45415-1324 USA Toll Free: 800-792-3537
E-mail: zhensler@hollandays.net
Web site: http://www.hollandays.net
Dist(s): **Partners Bk. Distributing, Inc.**
Hollar, Cheryl Public Relations, *(978-0-9763826)* Orders Addr.: 218 S. Cheatham St., Franklinton, NC 27525 USA Tel 919-494-2150
E-mail: cherylfhollar@yahoo.com; billythebunnybooks@yahoo.com.
Hollingsworth, Kenneth, *(978-0-9771572)* 2215 Janet Ct., Cedar Hill, TX 75104-1021 USA (SAN 256-8926)
Web site: http://www.hollingsworthtexas.com/plantingtheseeds.
Holly Hall Pubns., Inc., *(978-0-9645396; 978-1-888306)* P.O. Box 254, Elkton, MD 21922-0254 USA Tel 410-392-2300; Fax: 410-620-9877; Toll Free: 800-211-0719; *Imprints:* Full Quart Press (Full Quart Pr)
Dist(s): **Spring Arbor Distributors, Inc.**
HollyBear Pr., *(978-0-9651067)* Orders Addr.: P.O. Box 4257, Prescott, AZ 86302-4257 USA Tel 928-776-4689; Edit Addr.: 910 Stevens Dr., Prescott, AZ 86305 USA
E-mail: monamc2@msn.com.
Hollygrove Publishing, Inc., *(978-0-9777939; 978-0-9840904)* 4100 W. Eldorado Pkwy., Suite 100-182, McKinney, TX 75070 USA (SAN 850-170X) Tel 972-837-6191
E-mail: bsmith@hollygrovepublishing.com
Web site: http://www.hollygrovepublishing.com.
Hollym International Corp., *(978-0-930878; 978-1-56591)* 18 Donald Pl., Elizabeth, NJ 07208 USA (SAN 211-0172) Tel 908-353-1655; Fax: 908-353-0255 Do not confuse with Hollym Corporation Pubs., New York, NY
E-mail: hollym2@optonline.net; contact@hollym.com
Web site: http://www.hollym.com.
Hollywood Jesus Bks., *(978-0-9759577; 978-0-9787554)* P.O. Box 48282, Burien, WA 98166 USA Tel 206-241-6149
E-mail: editor@hjbooks.com
Web site: http://www.hjbooks.com.
Hollywood Operating System, *(978-1-893899)* 3108 W. Magnolia Blvd., Burbank, CA 91505-3045 USA
E-mail: hollywoodos@aol.com
Web site: http://www.HollywoodOS.com
Dist(s): **AtlasBooks Distribution.**
HollywoodComics.com, LLC, *(978-0-9740711; 978-1-932983; 978-1-934543; 978-1-935558; 978-1-61227)* P.O. Box 17270, Encino, CA 91416 USA (SAN 255-366X) Tel 818-995-7733; *Imprints:* Black Coat Press (Black Coat Pr)
E-mail: info@hollywoodcomics.com; info@riviereblanche.com; jean-marc@hollywoodcomics.com; info@blackcoatpress.com
Web site: http://www.hexagoncomics.com; http://www.blackcoatpress.com; http://www.riviereblanche.com.
Holman, Doris Anne, *(978-0-9667192; 978-0-9758630)* 5 Oak Ledge Rd., Harpswell, ME 04079 USA.
Holman Pubs. *Imprint of* **B&H Publishing Group**
Holmes Bookshop *Imprint of* **Belle Lumiere True News**
Holmes Futures Pty, Limited *See* **Winger Publishing**
Holocaust Museum Houston, *(978-0-9659781; 978-0-9773988)* 5401 Caroline St., Houston, TX 77004-6804 USA Tel 713-942-8000; Fax: 713-942-7953
E-mail: info@hmh.org
Web site: http://www.hmh.org
Dist(s): **Hervey's Booklink & Cookbook Warehouse.**
Holocaust Survivors' Memoirs Project, *(978-0-9760739; 978-0-9814686)* c/o World Jewish Congress, 633 Third Ave., Flr. 21, New York, NY 10017 USA Fax: 212-318-6176
E-mail: survivorsmemoirs@aol.com.
Holofcener, Mark, *(978-0-9718626)* 7323 Island Cir., Boulder, CO 80301-3905 USA
E-mail: mark@evansadventure.com
Web site: http://www.evansadventure.com.
Holt Enterprise, LLC, *(978-0-9740016)* Orders Addr.: P.O. Box 414, Riverside, NJ 08075 USA (SAN 255-2760) Tel 856-764-7043; Fax: 856-764-0851; Toll Free: 888-944-4658; Edit Addr.: 147 N. Fairview St., Riverside, NJ 08075 USA
E-mail: HoltEnterprise@comcast.net; holt109@comcast.net
Dist(s): **Quality Bks., Inc.**
Holt, Henry & Co. Bks. For Young Readers *Imprint of* **Holt, Henry & Co.**
†Holt, Henry & Co., *(978-0-03; 978-0-8050)* Div. of Holtzbrinck Publishers, Orders Addr.: 16365 James Madison Hwy., Gordonsville, VA 22942-8501 USA Toll Free Fax: 800-672-2054; Toll Free: 888-330-8477; Edit Addr.: 115 W. 18th St., 5th Flr., New York, NY 10011 USA (SAN 200-6472) Tel 212-886-9200; Fax: 540-672-7540 (customer service); *Imprints:* Owl Books (Owl); Metropolitan Books (Metropol Bks); Times Books (Times Bks); Holt, Henry & Company Books For Young Readers (HH Bks Yng Read); Viking Juvenile (VCB); Holt Paperback (Holt Paperbck); Ottaviano, Christy Books (C Ottaviano)
E-mail: info@hholt.com
Web site: http://www.henryholt.com
Dist(s): **Giron Bks.**
Lectorum Pubns., Inc.
Macmillan
Perfection Learning Corp.
Weston Woods Studios, Inc.; *CIP.*
Holt McDougal, *(978-0-395; 978-0-8123; 978-0-86609; 978-0-88343; 978-0-618)* Subs. of Houghton Mifflin Harcourt Publishing Co., Orders Addr.: 1900 S. Batavia Ave., Geneva, IL 60134 USA Toll Free: 888-872-8380; Edit Addr.: P.O. Box 1667, Evanston, IL 60204 USA (SAN 202-2532) Toll Free: 800-323-5435; 800-462-6595 (customer service); 909 Davis St., Evanston, IL 60201 Tel 847-869-2300; Fax: 847-869-0841
Web site: http://www.mcdougallittell.com.
Holt Paperback *Imprint of* **Holt, Henry & Co.**
Holtz Creative Enterprises, *(978-0-9817247; 978-0-9837617)* 3103 Terry Ln., Eau Claire, WI 54703 USA Tel 715-835-2705
E-mail: holtzenterprises@sbcglobal.net.
Holtzbrinck Publishers *See* **Macmillan**
Holy Heroes LLC, *(978-0-9801121; 978-1-936330)* 728 Hanna Woods, Cramerton, NC 28032 USA (SAN 855-2401)
E-mail: kandkdavison@bellsouth.net
Web site: http://www.holyheroes.com.
Holy Macro! Bks. *Imprint of* **Tickling Keys, Inc.**
Homa & Sekey Bks., *(978-0-9665421; 978-1-931907; 978-1-62246)* 3rd Floor, North Tower Mack-Cali Center III 140 East Ridgewood Ave, Paramus, NJ 07652 USA Tel 800-870-HOMA (4662) (Orders only); 201-261-8810; Fax: 201-261-8890
E-mail: info@homabooks.com
Web site: http://www.homabooks.com.
Homagno Group, Incorporated *See* **Editorial Homagno**
Home Box Office, Inc., *(978-0-910765; 978-0-9828167)* 1100 Sixth Ave., New York, NY 10036 USA (SAN 260-2032) Tel 212-512-1000.
Home Discipleship Pr., *(978-0-9753133; 978-0-9785678)* 6645 W. Steger Rd., Monee, IL 60449 USA Tel 708-235-1901; Fax: 708-235-1904
E-mail: leaders@homediscipleship.orf
Web site: http://www.homediscipleshippress.org.
Home Planet Bks., *(978-0-9743712; 978-0-9887978)* 2300 8th St., Olivenhain, CA 92024-6565 USA Tel 760-634-4947
E-mail: sales@homeplanetbooks.com.
Home Sales Enhancements *See* **Castlebrook Pubns.**
Home Schl. in the Woods, *(978-0-9720265; 978-0-9815523; 978-0-9842041; 978-0-9913678)* 3997 Roosevelt Hwy., Holley, NY 14470 USA Tel 585-964-8188
E-mail: eduardoopak@yahoo.com
Web site: http://www.homeschoolinthewoods.com.
Homegrown Pubns.,LLC, *(978-0-9799635)* P.O. Box 173, Red Wing, MN 55066 USA
Web site: http://www.homegrownpublications.com.
Homelight Pr., *(978-0-9749936)* P.O. Box 1901, Huntersville, NC 28070-1901 USA Toll Free: 877-438-6657
E-mail: homeligh@bellsouth.net.
Homer Historical Society, *(978-0-9770022)* 107 N. Main St., Homer, IL 61849 USA Tel 217-896-2549.
Homes for the Homeless Institute, Inc., *(978-0-9641784; 978-0-9724425; 978-0-9825533)* 50 Cooper Sq. Flr. 4, New York, NY 10003-7144 USA; *Imprints:* White Tiger Press (Wht Tiger Pr)
E-mail: info@icphusa.org
Web site: http://www.icphusa.org; www.whitetigerpress.org.
HomeScholar Bks., *(978-0-9754934)* 2311 Harrison Rd., Nashville, NC 27856 USA Tel 252-459-9279; *Imprints:* Literary Lessons (LitLessons)
Web site: http://www.homescholarbooks.com.
Homeschool Journey, *(978-0-9762918; 978-0-9825006)* 4625 Devon, Lisle, IL 60532 USA Tel 630-277-6200
E-mail: homeschooljourney@gmail.com
Web site: http://www.homeschooljourney.com.
Homespun Video, P.O. Box 340, Woodstock, NY 12498 USA Tel 914-246-2550; Fax: 914-246-5282; Toll Free: 800-338-2737
E-mail: hmspn@aol.com
Web site: http://www.homespuntapes.com
Dist(s): **Follett Media Distribution**
Leonard, Hal Corp.
Homestead Publishing, *(978-0-943972)* 4388 17th St., San Francisco, CA 94114 USA (SAN 241-029X) Tel 415-621-5039
E-mail: info@homesteadpublishing.net
Web site: http://homesteadpublishing.net; http://www.homesteadpublishing.net.
Honey Locust Pr. *Imprint of* **Wolfmont, LLC**
Honeycomb Adventures Pr., LLC, *(978-0-9820886; 978-0-9836808)* P.O. Box 1215, Hemingway, SC 29554 USA Tel 843-558-0133
E-mail: queenbjan@sc.rr.com
Web site: http://honeycombadventures.com
Dist(s): **Lightning Source, Inc.**
Honeycomb Inc., *(978-0-9793799)* 1017 Avon, Flint, MI 48503 USA (SAN 853-3024) Tel 810-397-8025; Fax: 810-234-1794
E-mail: tandtvison@aol.com
Web site: http://www.101waysyoucansave.com
Dist(s): **AtlasBooks Distribution.**
Honno Welsh Women's Pr. (GBR) *(978-1-870206; 978-1-906784; 978-1-909983) Dist. by* **IPG Chicago.**
Honorable Pr., *(978-0-9719727)* 2432 Wilshire Ct., Decatur, GA 30035 USA.
HonorNet, *(978-0-9753036; 978-0-9788726; 978-0-9820590; 978-1-938021)* P.O. Box 910, Sapulpa, OK 74067 USA
E-mail: mail@honornet.net
Web site: http://honornet.net
Dist(s): **Destiny Image Pubs.**
Hood, Alan C. & Co., Inc., *(978-0-911469)* P.O. Box 775, Chambersburg, PA 17201 USA (SAN 270-8221) Tel 717-267-0867; Fax: 717-267-0572; Toll Free Fax: 888-844-9433; 4501 Forbes Blvd., Lanham, MD 20706
E-mail: hoodbooks@pa.net
Web site: http://www.hoodbooks.com
Dist(s): **Follett School Solutions.**
Hood, Ted *See* **Four Seasons Publishing**
Hooker, Lou, *(978-0-9755106)* 6900 Chamberlain, Fremont, MI 49412 USA Tel 231-924-3555
E-mail: lvhook@ncats.net.
Hoopoe Bks. *Imprint of* **I S H K**
Hoot N' Cackle Pr., *(978-0-9659381)* 1928 S. Mayfair, Springfield, MO 65804 USA Tel 417-887-0837; Fax: 417-886-3994
E-mail: rlipe@usipp.net
Web site: http://www.mowrites4kids.drury.edu/authors/lipe/.
HOP, LLC, *(978-1-887942; 978-1-931020; 978-1-933863; 978-1-60143; 978-1-60242; 978-1-60498; 978-1-60499)* Educate, Inc., 1407 Fleet St. Flr. 1, Baltimore, MD 21231-2859 USA
Web site: http://www.hookedonphonics.com
Dist(s): **Simon & Schuster, Inc.**
Hope Chest Legacy, Inc., *(978-1-59565)* P.O. Box 1398, Littlerock, CA 93543 USA Toll Free: 888-554-7292
E-mail: hopechestlegacy@aol.com
Web site: http://hopechestlegacy.com.
Hope Farm Pr. & Bookshop, *(978-0-910746)* 15 Jane St., Saugerties, NY 12477-1511 USA (SAN 204-0697) Toll Free: 800-883-5778 (orders)
E-mail: hopefarm@hopefarm.com
Web site: http://www.hopefarm.com; http://www.hopefarmbooks.com
Dist(s): **North Country Bks., Inc.**
Hope for Families, Inc., *(978-0-9676489)* P.O. Box 238, Hatfield, PA 19440 USA Tel 215-280-5369
E-mail: ibmbam@fast.net.
Hope Harvest Ministries *See* **Hope Harvest Publishing**
Hope Harvest Publishing, *(978-0-9716523; 978-0-9763695; 978-0-9771318; 978-0-9779898)* Div. of H&H Bindery & Distribution Centre, P.O. Box 8353, Kentwood, MI 49518 USA Tel 616-307-3080; Fax: 616-458-8991
E-mail: hopeharvest@comcast.net
Web site: http://www.hopeharvest.com; http://www.blessly.com
Dist(s): **Anchor Distributors**
Anderson Merchandisers
H & H Distribution
Spirit Filled Pr., Inc.
Spring Arbor Distributors, Inc.
Hope International Printshop, *(978-0-9748096)* Orders Addr.: P.O. Box 1182, Hobe Sound, FL 33475 USA; Edit Addr.: 8436 SE Bayberry Terr., Hobe Sound, FL 33475 USA.
Hope of Vision Publishing, *(978-0-9753795; 978-0-9818253; 978-0-9831371; 978-0-9837082; 978-0-9852746; 978-0-9884773; 978-0-9912483; 978-1-942871)* 43 Yale St., Bridgeport, CT 06605 USA (SAN 856-6410) Tel 203-338-1301; Fax: 203-413-1593
Web site: http://www.hopeofvisionpublishing.com.
Hope Pr., *(978-1-878267)* Orders Addr.: P.O. Box 188, Duarte, CA 91009-0188 USA (SAN 200-3244) Tel 626-303-0644; Fax: 626-358-3520; Toll Free: 800-321-4039; Edit Addr.: 1110 Mill Run, Monvaia, CA 91016 USA Tel 626-303-0644 Do not confuse with Hope Pr., Pittsville, WI
E-mail: hoepress@earthink.net; dcomings@earthlink.net
Web site: http://www.hopepress.com; http://www.didmancreategod.com.
Hope Rekindled Pr. *See* **Risen Heart Pr.**
Hopewell Pubns., LLC, *(978-0-9726906; 978-1-933435)* P.O. Box 11, Titusville, NJ 08560-0011 USA Tel 609-818-1049; Fax: 609-964-1718 Do not confuse with companies with the same or similar name in Longmont, CO, Austin, TX, Springdale, AZ
E-mail: publisher@hopepubs.com
Web site: http://www.hopepubs.com
Dist(s): **Univ. Pr. of New England.**
Hopkins, KC, *(978-0-615-23929-3)* 409 Orchid Trail, Franklin, TN 37174 USA Tel 615-618-4997
E-mail: kchopkins1276@yahoo.com
Dist(s): **Lulu Enterprises Inc.**
Hopkins Publishing, *(978-0-9839326; 978-1-62080)* 201 Faircrest Dr. No. 3687, Cleburne, TX 76033 USA Tel 210-595-9313
E-mail: leah@hopkinspublishing.com; justin@hopkinspublishing.com
Web site: http://www.facebook.com/churchofchristbooks; http://hopkinspublishing.com/; http://twitter.com/#!/cofcbooks; https://www.smashwords.com/profile/view/hopkinspublishing
Dist(s): **Lightning Source, Inc.**
Send The Light Distribution LLC.
Hoppenbrouwers, Toke *See* **Monte Nido Pr.**
HOPS Pr., LLC, *(978-1-892784)* Orders Addr.: 12 Quartz St., Pony, MT 59747-0697 USA Tel 406-685-3222
E-mail: orders@hollowtop.com
Web site: http://www.hopspress.com
Dist(s): **Chelsea Green Publishing**
Mountain Pr. Publishing Co., Inc.
Horan Publishing, *(978-0-9769980)* P.O. Box 740485, Orange City, FL 32774-0485 USA
E-mail: horanpublishing@wmconnect.com.
Horizon Bks., *(978-0-9787987)* Orders Addr.: 768 Hardtimes Rd., Farmville, VA 23901 USA (SAN 851-6243) Tel 434-223-3235 (phone/fax)
E-mail: eicherjs@kinex.net
Web site: http://www.readingwithhorizon.com.
Horizon Line Pr., *(978-0-9749426)* 77 N. River Dr., Roseburg, OR 97470 USA
E-mail: dj@knights-of-avalon.com
Web site: http://www.knights-of-avalon.net/.
Horizon Pubs. *Imprint of* **Cedar Fort, Inc./CFI Distribution**
Horizons *Imprint of* **Alpha Omega Pubns., Inc.**
Horowitz Creative Media, Incorporated *See* **ArtMar Productions**
Horse & Dragon Publishing, *(978-0-9759488)* 241 Coast Hill Dr., Suite A, Indian Harbour Beach, FL 32937 USA Tel 321-821-2220; Fax: 321-821-2226; Toll Free: 877-374-6815
E-mail: bob@robertclark.us
Web site: http://www.robertclark.us.
Horse Creek Pubns., *(978-0-9722217)* 945 Mockingbird Ln., Norman, OK 73071-4802 USA
E-mail: sue.schrems@horsecreekpublications.com
Web site: http://www.horsecreekpublications.com.
Horse Hollow Pr., Inc., *(978-0-9638814; 978-0-9795780)* P.O. Box 456, Goshen, NY 10924 USA Tel 845-651-2390; Fax: 845-651-2389; Toll Free: 800-414-6773
E-mail: info@horsehollowpress.com; jevers@warwick.net
Web site: http://www.horsehollowpress.com
Dist(s): **Independent Pubs. Group.**
Horton, David *See* **Negro Publishing, LLC**
Horvath, Janet, *(978-0-9713735)* 122 Virginia St., Saint Paul, MN 55102 USA (SAN 255-5441) Tel 612-870-4200; Fax: 612-454-2554
E-mail: jhorvathcello@hotmail.com
Web site: http://www.playinglesshurt.com.
Ho's, Jane Children Bks., *(978-0-9619126)* 700 Kipling Ct., El Sobrante, CA 94803 USA (SAN 243-4954) Tel 510-222-2621.
Hosannah Pubns., *(978-0-9786031)* 507 W. Manheim St., Bldg.18 , Apt.D, Philadelphia, PA 19144-4859 USA Tel 215-991-6154; Fax: 215-991-0609
E-mail: fourhosannah@verizon.net.
Hospice & Community Care Pubns., *(978-0-9774691)* Orders Addr.: P.O. Box 993, Rock Hill, SC 29731 USA (SAN 257-6309) Tel 803-329-4663; Fax: 803-329-5935; Toll Free: 800-895-2273; Edit Addr.: P.O. Box 993, Rock Hill, SC 29731-6993 USA
Web site: http://www.hospicecommunitycare.org.
Hospice of Saint John, The, *(978-0-9742849)* 1320 Everett Ct., Lakewood, CO 80215 USA.
Hot off the Pr., *(978-0-933491; 978-0-9605904; 978-1-56231; 978-1-59776)* 1250 NW 3rd Ave., Canby, OR 97013 USA (SAN 216-3977) Toll Free: 800-227-9595
E-mail: info@hotp.com
Web site: http://www.craftpizazz.com.
Hot Page Pr. *Imprint of* **Potter Assocs.**
HotComb Pr., *(978-0-9787940)* 6230 Wilshire Blvd., Suite 805, Los Angeles, CA 90048-5104 USA
E-mail: info@hotcombpress.com
Web site: http://hotcombpress.com.
HotDiggetyDog Pr., *(978-0-9741417; 978-0-9844645)* P.O. Box 747, Shepherdsville, KY 40165 USA Tel 502-376-5966; Fax: 208-474-1227
E-mail: leighanne@thewoodybooks.com
Web site: http://www.thewoodybooks.com.
Houghton Mifflin Bks. for Children *Imprint of* **Houghton Mifflin Harcourt Trade & Reference Pubs.**
Houghton Mifflin Company *See* **Houghton Mifflin Harcourt Publishing Co.**
Houghton Mifflin Company (School Division) *See* **Houghton Mifflin Harcourt School Pubs.**
Houghton Mifflin Company Trade & Reference Division *See* **Houghton Mifflin Harcourt Trade & Reference Pubs.**
Houghton Mifflin Harcourt Learning Technology, *(978-0-7630; 978-1-930106)* Div. of Houghton Mifflin Harcourt Publishing Co., 100 Pine St. Ste. 1900, San Francisco, CA 94111-5205 USA Toll Free: 800-223-6925; 125 Cambridgepark Dr., Cambridge, MA 02140-2329
E-mail: info@riverdeep.net; international@riverdeep.net
Web site: http://www.riverdeep.net
Dist(s): **Follett School Solutions**
Perseus-PGW.
†Houghton Mifflin Harcourt Publishing Co., *(978-0-395; 978-0-87466; 978-0-631591; 978-1-57630; 978-1-881527; 978-0-618; 978-0-544; 978-0-547; 978-1-328)* Orders Addr.: 9205 Southpark Ctr. Loop, Orlando, FL 32819 USA Toll Free: 800-225-3362; Edit Addr.: 222 Berkeley St., Boston, MA 02116 USA (SAN 215-3793) Tel 617-351-5000; *Imprints:* Betty Crocker (Betty Crocker); HMH Books For Young Readers (HMH Bks FYR)
Web site: http://www.hmco.com
Dist(s): **CENGAGE Learning**
Cheng & Tsui Co.
Continental Bk. Co., Inc.
ETA hand2mind
Ebsco Publishing
Follett School Solutions
Houghton Mifflin Harcourt Trade & Reference Pubs.
Houghton Mifflin Harcourt Supplemental Pubs.
Larousse Kingfisher Chambers, Inc.
Lectorum Pubns., Inc.
MyiLibrary
Perelandra, Ltd.
TextStream
ebrary, Inc.; *CIP.*
Houghton Mifflin Harcourt School Pubs., *(978-0-395; 978-0-669)* Orders Addr.: 1900 Batavia Ave., Geneva, IL 60134-3399 USA Toll Free Fax: 800-733-2098; Toll Free: 800-733-2828; 1175 N. Stemmons Fwy., Lewisville, TX 75067-2516 Toll Free: 800-733-2828; Edit Addr.: 222 Berkeley St., Boston, MA 02116 USA Tel 617-351-5000; Fax: 617-227-5409
E-mail: eduwebmaster@hmco.com
Web site: http://www.eduplace.com
Dist(s): **Follett School Solutions.**
Houghton Mifflin Harcourt Supplemental Pubs., *(978-1-60032; 978-1-60277)* 10801 N. Mopac Expressway, Bldg. 3, Austin, TX 78759 USA
Web site: www.harcourtachieve.com.
Houghton Mifflin Harcourt Trade & Reference Pubs., *(978-0-395; 978-0-89919; 978-0-618)* Orders Addr.: 9205 Southpark Ctr. Loop, Orlando, FL 32819 USA Tel 978-661-1300; Toll Free: 800-225-3362; Edit Addr.: 222 Berkeley St., Boston, MA 02116 USA (SAN 200-2388) Tel 617-351-5000; Fax: 617-227-5409; 215 Park Ave S., 12th Flr., New York, NY 10003-1621; *Imprints:*

Clarion Books (Clarion Bk); Sandpiper (Sandpiper); Houghton Mifflin Books for Children (HMBC)
E-mail: trade_sub_rights@hmco.com
Web site: http://www.hmco.com/; http://www.houghtonmifflinbooks.com
Dist(s): **CENGAGE Learning**
CreateSpace Independent Publishing Platform
Ebsco Publishing
Follett School Solutions
Houghton Mifflin Harcourt Publishing Co.
Harcourt Trade Pubs.
Lectorum Pubns., Inc.
MyiLibrary.

Houkura (AUS) (978-0-9805090) *Dist. by* **AtlasBooks.**

Ho'ulu Hou Project: Stories Told by Us *Imprint of* **Na Kamalei Koolauloa Early Education Program**

HourGlass Publishing, (978-0-9860205) 2095 Hwy. 211 NW Suite 2F-152, Braselton, GA 30517 USA Tel 678-439-9229; Fax: 866-855-1971
E-mail: info@hourglasspublishing.com
Web site: www.HourGlassPublishing.com.

House, David, (978-0-9777086) 1488 Madelyn Ave SE, Salem, OR 97306-3552 USA
Web site: http://www.space-worthy.com.

House of Anansi Pr. (CAN) (978-0-88784; 978-1-77089) *Dist. by* **PerseuPGW.**

House of David *See* **Key of David Publishing**

House of Prayer Ministries, Inc., (978-1-882825) 2428 Florian Ct., Decatur, IL 62526 USA Tel 217-428-7077 (phone/fax)
E-mail: vikischerer@comcast.net
Web site: www.houseofprayerministries.com.

House of the Guilded Scribe, (978-0-615-28905-2; 978-0-615-55608-6; 978-0-9914351) P.O. Box 432, Mount Pocono, PA 18344 USA
E-mail: sales@prissyandmissy.com; theguildedscribe@gmail.com
Web site: http://www.wonderfulwondersart.com; http://www.prissyandmissy.com; http://www.prissyandmissy.com.

House of The Lord Fellowship, (978-0-9673530) Orders Addr.: P.O. Box 235, Lock Haven, PA 17745 USA Tel 570-748-6455; Fax: 570-748-6858; Edit Addr.: 201 W. Main St., Lock Haven, PA 17745 USA
E-mail: ssnyder@houseofthelordfellowship.org
Web site: http://www.houseofthelordfellowship.org.

House of Usher *See* **Abysso Bks.**

House Upon A Hill Bks., (978-0-9795826) Orders Addr.: P.O. Box 140322, Broken Arrow, OK 74014 USA; Edit Addr.: 19546 E. 42nd St. S., Broken Arrow, OK 74014 USA.

Houston Enterprises, (978-0-9712861; 978-0-9907800; 978-0-9862339; 978-0-9862349) Orders Addr.: 6320 Rucker Rd. Suite E, Indianapolis, IN 46220 USA Tel 317-726-1901; Fax: 317-726-1902; Toll Free: 888-826-8082
E-mail: info@scotthouston.com
Web site: http://www.scotthouston.com.

Houston Zoo, Inc., (978-0-9762385) 1513 N. MAcGregor, Houston, TX 77030 USA Tel 713-533-6500; Fax: 713-533-6755
E-mail: gwarfield@houstonzoo.org
Web site: http://www.houstonzoo.org.

"How Do You Know", (978-0-9675574) Orders Addr.: P.O. Box 831172, Stone Mountain, GA 30083 USA
E-mail: pjgastonbooks@yahoo.com.

How Great Thou ART Pubns., (978-0-9700405; 978-0-9717874; 978-0-9859000) Orders Addr.: P.O. Box 48, Mcfarlan, NC 28102-0048 USA Tel 704-851-3117; Fax: 704-851-3111; Toll Free: 800-982-3729; Edit Addr.: 357 McFarlin Rd, Morven, NC 28119 USA
E-mail: matthew@howgreatthouart.com
Web site: http://www.howgreatthouart.com/.

Howard Bks. *Imprint of* **Howard Books**

Howard Books, Div. of SIMON & SCHUSTER, 1230 Ave. of the Americas, New York, NY 10020 USA; *Imprints*: Howard Books (Howard Imp)
Dist(s): **Simon & Schuster, Inc.**

Howard, Emma Bks., (978-1-886551) P.O. Box 385, New York, NY 10024-0385 USA Tel 212-996-2590 (phone/fax)
E-mail: emmahowardbooks@verizon.net
Web site: http://www.EellGrassGirls.com.

Howard Printing, Inc., (978-0-9793790) 14 Noahs Ln., Brattleboro, VT 05301 USA Tel 802-254-3550; Fax: 802-257-1453
E-mail: info@howardprintinginc.com
Web site: http://www.howardprintinginc.com.

Howe, Tina Field, (978-0-9768585) P.O. Box 581, Waverly, NY 14892 USA (SAN 256-8276) Tel 607-329-2458
Web site: http://www.tinafieldhowe.com.

Howell Bk. Hse. *Imprint of* **Wiley, John & Sons, Inc.**

Howell Canyon Pr., (978-1-931210) 1475 N Bundy Dr., Los Angeles, CA 90049 USA (SAN 255-3015) Toll Free: 888-252-0411 (Orders)
E-mail: info@HowellCanyonPress.com
Web site: http://www.AddisonTheDog.com; http://www.howellcanyonpress.com/; http://www.drdeanhowell.com/; http://www.TrishaHowell.com
Dist(s): **Ingram Pub. Services.**

Howell, M Kay *See* **Eagle Tree Pr.**

Howell, Steven, (978-0-615-15346-9; 978-0-615-19997-9) 697 Superior Ln., Clarksville, TN 37043 USA Tel 931-358-6022
E-mail: mrmrshowell2@yahoo.com
Dist(s): **Lulu Enterprises Inc.**

Howle, C.J. Co., (978-1-885275) 1695 Quigley Rd., Columbus, OH 43227-3433 USA Tel 614-237-5474.

HP Trade *Imprint of* **Penguin Publishing Group**

HPN Publishing, (978-0-9768451) 22902 Sonriente Trail, Trabuco Canyon, CA 92679 USA.

Hramiec Hoffman Publishing, (978-0-9746901) 6911 M-119 Hwy., Harbor Springs, MI 49740 USA Tel 231-526-1011
Dist(s): **Partners Bk. Distributing, Inc.**

Hub City Pr., (978-0-9638731; 978-1-891885; 978-1-938235) Orders Addr.: 186 West Main St., Spartanburg, SC 29306 USA Tel 864-577-9349; Fax: 864-577-0188
E-mail: bteter@bellsouth.net
Web site: http://www.hubcity.org
Dist(s): **Blair, John F. Pub.**

Hub City Writers Project *See* **Hub City Pr.**

Hubbard Scientific, Inc., (978-0-8331) Orders Addr.: P.O. Box 760, Chippewa Falls, WI 54729-1468 USA (SAN 202-3121) Tel 715-723-4427; Fax: 715-723-8021; Toll Free: 800-323-8368; Edit Addr.: P.O. Box 760, Chippewa Fls, WI 54729-0760 USA
Web site: http://www.hubbardscientific.com.

Hubbell, Gerald, (978-0-9762042) 4127 Roanoke Rd., Kansas City, MO 64111 USA Tel 816-531-4427
Web site: http://www.malverack.com.

Huckleberry Pr., (978-0-9653035; 978-1-890570; 978-1-58584) Orders Addr.: P.O. Box 51772, Durham, NC 27707 USA Tel 646-205-8057 (phone/fax) Do not confuse with Huckleberry Pr., Gig Harbor, WA
E-mail: HucksPress@yahoo.com
Web site: http://www.huckleberrypress.com.

Hudson Bks., (978-0-9749860; 978-0-9762502; 978-0-9764459; 978-0-9767789; 978-0-9786296; 978-0-9822553) 244 Madison Ave., No. 254, New York, NY 10016 USA Fax: 718-225-5556; Toll Free: 877-822-2500
Web site: http://www.thefloatinggallery.com.

Hudson Hills Press, Incorporated *See* **Hudson Hills Pr. LLC**

†Hudson Hills Pr. LLC, (978-0-933920; 978-0-9646042; 978-1-55595) Orders Addr.: P.O. Box 205, Manchester, VT 05254 USA; Edit Addr.: 74-2 Union St., Manchester, VT 05254 USA (SAN 213-0815) Tel 802-362-6450; Fax: 802-362-6459
E-mail: artbooks@hudsonhills.com
Web site: http://www.hudsonhills.com/
Dist(s): **Art Institute of Chicago**
National Bk. Network; *CIP.*

Hudson House Publishing & Productions *See* **Whorl Bks.**

Hudson, Jessie, (978-0-9778922) 14814 Forward Pass, San Antonio, TX 78248 USA
Web site: http://www.OLLIEANDFRIENDS.com.

Hudson, Mary C., (978-0-9627745; 978-0-9722937) 1125 Karen Way, Mountainview, CA 94040 USA Tel 650-948-1270.

Hudson Publishing Group, The, (978-1-60349) 356 Glenwood Ave., East Orange, NJ 07017 USA Tel 973-672-7701; Fax: 973-677-7570; *Imprints*: Marimba Books (MarimbaBks)
E-mail: justusbook@aol.com
Dist(s): **Just Us Bks., Inc.**

Hufnagel Software, (978-0-9743881) P.O. Box 747, Clarion, PA 16214-0747 USA Tel 814-226-5600; Fax: 814-226-5551
Web site: http://www.hufsoft.com/books.

Hughes, Betty Barber *See* **Puwaii International, LLC**

Huginn & Muninn, (978-1-937571) 1240 W. Sims Way No. 93, Port Townsend, WA 98368 USA Tel 206-202-0998
E-mail: wyrddesign@unseen.is
Web site: huginnandmuninn.net.

Hula Pubs. (NZL) (978-0-908975; 978-1-877266; 978-1-877241; 978-1-877283; 978-1-86969; 978-0-9582517; 978-1-77550) *Dist. by* **UH Pr.**

Hula Moon Pr., (978-0-9794649) P.O. Box 11173, Honolulu, HI 96828 USA Tel 808-947-6470
Dist(s): **BookBaby.**

Human Factor LLC, (978-0-9816472) P.O. Box 3742, Washington, DC 20027 USA (SAN 856-1109)
E-mail: info@humanfactor.net
Web site: http://www.humanfactor.net.

†Human Kinetics Pubs., (978-0-7360; 978-0-87322; 978-0-88011; 978-0-918438; 978-0-931250; 978-1-4504; 978-1-4925) Orders Addr.: P.O. Box 5076, Champaign, IL 61825-5076 USA (SAN 211-7088) Tel 217-351-5076; Toll Free: 800-747-4457; Edit Addr.: 1607 N. Market St., Champaign, IL 61820 USA (SAN 658-0866) Tel 217-351-5076; Fax: 217-351-2674; Toll Free: 800-747-4457
E-mail: humank@hkusa.com; info@hkusa.com
Web site: http://www.humankinetics.com; http://www.hkusa.com
Dist(s): **Follett School Solutions**
ebrary, Inc.; *CIP.*

Human Relations Media, (978-1-55548; 978-1-62706) 41 Kensico Dr., Mount Kisco, NY 10549 USA (SAN 287-4873) Tel 914-244-0486; Fax: 914-244-0485; Toll Free: 800-431-2050
Web site: http://www.hrmvideo.com
Dist(s): **Follett School Solutions.**

Human Values 4 Kids Foundation, The, (978-0-9798986) Orders Addr.: 11498 Pyrites Way, Gold River, CA 95670-6226 USA; Edit Addr.: 11498 Pyrites Way, Gold River, CA 95670-6226 USA
E-mail: vvnambiar@sbcglobal.net
Web site: http://www.thehumanvalues4kidsfoundation.org.

Humane Society Pr. *Imprint of* **National Assn. for Humane & Environmental Education**

Humanics Learning *Imprint of* **Green Dragon Bks.**

Humanics Publishing Group *See* **Green Dragon Bks.**

Humanist Pr. *Imprint of* **American Humanist Assn.**

Humanoids, Inc. *Imprint of* **Diamond Bk. Distributors**

Humanoids, Inc., (978-0-9672401; 978-1-930652; 978-1-59465) Orders Addr.: 8033 Sunset Blvd. #628, Los Angeles, CA 90046 USA Tel 323-522-5466; Fax: 323-892-2848
E-mail: alex.donoghue@humanoids.com
Web site: http://www.humanoids.com/
Dist(s): **Diamond Comic Distributors, Inc.**
DKE Toys.

Humming Meadow Ranch, (978-0-9766431) 47265 Twin Pines Rd., Banning, CA 92220-9656 USA Tel 951-849-1803; Fax: 951-849-9091
E-mail: elaine@hummingmeadowranch.com
Web site: http://www.hummingmeadowranch.com.

Hummingbird Mountain Pr., (978-0-9746792) P.O. Box 127, Midpines, CA 95345-0127 USA
Web site: http://www.sierratel.com/hummingbirdmountain.

Hummingbird World Media *Imprint of* **Double Edge Pr.**

Humor & Communication, (978-0-9677844; 978-0-9820466) 709 Doe Trail, Edmond, OK 73012 USA
E-mail: hduncan2@cox.net
Web site: http://www.hallduncan.com.

Humphreys, Kevin, (978-0-9745727) P.O. Box 10731, Spokane, WA 99220 USA; 1312 N. Brook Terrace St., Spokane, WA 99224-5678.

Hundred Ways LLC, A, (978-0-9789544) 18034 Ventura Blvd., No. 491, Encino, CA 91316 USA Tel 818-708-0558
E-mail: admin@ahundredways.com
Web site: http://www.whenwordsdream.com.

Hungry Bear Publishing, (978-0-9754007; 978-0-9857607) Orders Addr.: 40 McClelland St., Saranac Lake, NY 12983 USA Tel 518-891-5559
Web site: http://www.hungrybearpublishing.com
Dist(s): **North Country Bks., Inc.**

Hungry Goat Pr. *Imprint of* **Gauthier Pubns. Inc.**

Hungry Tiger Pr., (978-0-9644988; 978-1-929527) 5995 Dandridge Ln., Suite 121, San Diego, CA 92115-6575 USA
E-mail: books@hungrytigerpress.com
Web site: http://www.hungrytigerpress.com.

Hunt, J. L. Publishing, (978-0-9769401) Orders Addr.: 27881 La Paz Rd., Suite G-124, Laguna Niguel, CA 92677 USA Tel 949-751-7511; Fax: 949-363-8559
E-mail: james@chewnomore.com.

Hunt, J.L. Publishing *See* **Hunt, J. L. Publishing**

Hunt, John Publishing Ltd. (GBR) (978-1-85608; 978-1-903019; 978-1-84298; 978-1-903816; 978-1-905047; 978-1-84694; 978-1-78099) *Dist. by* **Natl Bk Netwk.**

Hunt, John Publishing Ltd. (GBR) (978-1-85608; 978-1-903019; 978-1-84298; 978-1-903816; 978-1-905047; 978-1-84694; 978-1-78099) *Dist. by* **STL Dist.**

Hunt Thompson Media, (978-0-9630377) P.O. Box 8927, Santa Fe, NM 87504 USA Tel 415-794-0667 (cell)
E-mail: cjhunt@huntthompsonmedia.com; cjhunt3@gmail.com
Web site: http://www.PerfectHumanDiet.com; http://www.HuntThompsonMedia.com; www.CJHuntReports.com.

Hunter Hse. *Imprint of* **Turner Publishing Co.**

Hunter, J. H. Publishing, (978-0-9718274) 8100 Schmuck Rd., Evansville, IN 47712 USA Tel 812-985-5013.

Hunter, Julius K. *See* **J.K.H. Enterprises**

Hunter, Karen Media, (978-0-9820221; 978-0-9845060) P.O. Box 632, South Orange, NJ 07079 USA (SAN 857-0167)
Web site: http://www.karenhuntermedia.com; http://www.karenhuntermedia.com; www.readourbooks.com.

Hunter Pubns., (978-0-9654185) P.O. Box 433, Vallejo, CA 94589 USA Tel 707-645-8714; Fax: 707-644-7880.

Hunter Publishing, Inc., (978-1-55650; 978-1-58843) Orders Addr.: 222 Clematis St., West Palm Beach, FL 33401 USA Do not confuse with Hunter Publishing, Inc., Hobe Sound, FL
E-mail: comments@hunterpublishing.com
Web site: http://www.hunterpublishing.com
Dist(s): **Ebsco Publishing**
MyiLibrary
ebrary, Inc.

HuntForMo Creations, (978-0-9740182) 3718 Brentford Rd., Randallstown, MD 21133 USA Toll Free: 800-327-9779
E-mail: monique@huntformo.com
Web site: http://www.huntformo.com.

Hunthaven Pr., (978-0-615-82262-4; 978-0-615-82442-0; 978-0-615-82675-2; 978-0-615-82771-1; 978-0-615-82925-8; 978-0-615-83042-1; 978-0-615-83408-5; 978-0-615-83872-4; 978-0-615-84118-2; 978-0-615-84170-0; 978-0-615-84244-8; 978-0-615-84448-0; 978-0-615-84497-8; 978-0-615-84817-4; 978-0-615-85290-4; 978-0-615-87041-0; 978-0-615-87186-8; 978-0-615-87314-5; 978-0-615-88172-0; 978-0-615-88202-4; 978-0-615-88266-6; 978-0-615-88316-8; 978-0-615-88474-5; 978-0-615-88563-6; 978-0-615-88681-7; 978-0-615-89187-3;) *8092 Willow Ct., Seminole, FL 33776 USA Tel 727 319-4929; Fax: 727 319-4828*
Web site: www.angelahuntbooks.com
Dist(s): **CreateSpace Independent Publishing Platform.**

Huntington Library Pr., (978-0-87328) Div. of Huntington Library, Art Collections & Botanical Gardens, 1151 Oxford Rd., San Marino, CA 91108 USA (SAN 202-313X) Tel 626-405-2172; Fax: 626-585-0794
E-mail: booksales@huntington.org
Web site: http://www.Huntington.org/HEHPubs.html
Dist(s): **California Princeton Fulfillment Services**
D.A.P./Distributed Art Pubs.
Univ. of California Pr.

Huntington Library Publications *See* **Huntington Library Pr.**

Huntington Ludlow Media Group, (978-0-9789057) 5320 Maverick Dr., Grand Prairie, TX 75052-2617 USA (SAN 851-9080)
Web site: http://www.huntingtonludlow.com
Dist(s): **AtlasBooks Distribution.**

Huntly Hse., (978-0-9885349; 978-0-615-73405-7) 1965 Murcer Ln., Elgin, IL 60123 USA Tel 847-312-5904
E-mail: cfurtick@huntlyhouse.com
Web site: www.huntlyhouse.com.

Hunton, Carroll & Wenonah, (978-0-9758873) P.O. Box 1048, Albuquerque, NM 87103-1048 USA
E-mail: alan@excelstaff.com.

Huqua Pr., (978-0-615-43791-0; 978-0-9838120; 978-0-9906966; 978-0-692-41669-3) 8730 Sunset Blvd., Los Angeles, CA 90069 USA Tel 818-981-5262
E-mail: judy@magpyemedia.com
Dist(s): **Open Road Integrated Media, LLC.**

Huron River Pr., (978-1-932399) Orders Addr.: P.O. Box 310, Chelsea, MI 48118 USA Tel 734-913-9447; Fax: 734-332-4733; Edit Addr.: 320 N. Main St., Suite 100, Chelsea, MI 48118 USA
E-mail: info@huronriverpress.com
Web site: http://www.huronriverpress.com
Dist(s): **Partners Bk. Distributing, Inc.**

Huron Street Pr. *Imprint of* **American Library Assn.**

Hurst, Carol Consultants, (978-0-9748509) 41 Colony Dr., Westfield, MA 01085 USA Tel 413-562-3412
E-mail: carol@carolhurst.com
Web site: http://www.carolhurst.com
Dist(s): **Follett School Solutions.**

Huseby, Kirby, (978-0-9778494) P.O. Box 8034, Kentwood, MI 49518 USA
E-mail: staytoond@aol.com.

Husky Trail Pr. LLC, (978-0-9722918; 978-1-935258) Orders Addr.: P.O. Box 705, East Lyme, CT 06333-0705 USA Tel 860-739-7644; Fax: 860-739-3702
Web site: http://www.huskytrailpress.com.

Hussl, Gloria, (978-0-9791468) 5818 Trinity Rd., Needville, TX 77461 USA Tel 832-595-5678
E-mail: gloriasunrisefarms@yahoo.com.

Hutchings, John Pubs., (978-1-935014) 621 Dogleg Ln., Bartlett, IL 60103 USA Tel 630-736-6088; *Imprints*: Lessons From The Vine (LFTV)
E-mail: kaththompson@att.net.

Hutchison, G.F. Pr., (978-1-885631; 978-0-9796279) 319 S. Block, Suite 17, Fayetteville, AR 72701-6484 USA Tel 479-587-1726; *Imprints*: Family Of Man Press, The (Family Of Man Pr)
E-mail: drwriterguy@netscape.net
Web site: http://www.thehappinessplace.com.

Hutman Productions, (978-0-9702386; 978-0-9833573; 978-0-9854486) P.O. Box 268, Linthicum, MD 21090 USA Tel 410-789-0930
E-mail: cbladey@mail.bcpl.net
Web site: http://www.bcpl.net/~cbladey/hutmanA.html.

Hutt, Sarah, (978-0-9743417) 1140 Washington St., No. 7, Boston, MA 02118 USA Tel 617-482-4722
Web site: http://www.mymotherslegacy.com.

Hutton Electronic Publishing, (978-0-9742894; 978-0-9785171; 978-0-9888775) 160 N. Compo Rd., Westport, CT 06880 USA
E-mail: huttonbooks@hotmail.com
Web site: http://www.huttonelectronicpublishing.com.

Hydra Pubns., (978-0-615-43242-7; 978-0-615-49378-7; 978-0-615-49820-1; 978-0-615-49950-5; 978-0-615-50445-2; 978-0-615-56017-5; 978-0-615-56345-9; 978-0-615-56584-2; 978-0-615-59650-1; 978-0-615-59651-8; 978-0-615-59822-2; 978-0-615-60737-5; 978-0-615-63328-2; 978-0-615-63783-9; 978-0-615-63858-4; 978-0-615-63863-8; 978-0-615-63882-9; 978-0-615-65016-6; 978-0-615-67766-8; 978-0-615-67970-9; 978-0-615-67972-3; 978-0-615-67974-7; 978-0-615-68018-7; 978-0-615-68422-2; 978-0-615-68969-2; 978-0-615-69010-0;) *337 Clifty Dr., Madison, IN 47250 USA Tel 812-574-4113*
Web site: http://www.hydrapublications.com
Dist(s): **CreateSpace Independent Publishing Platform**
Dummy Record Do Not USE!!!!.

Hydra Publishing *See* **Hylas Publishing**

Hydrangea Pr., (978-0-9768418) 22 Plumer Rd., Epping, NH 03042 USA Tel 603-679-9544
E-mail: mswegles@comcast.net
Web site: http://www.plumercrest.com.

Hylas Publishing, (978-1-59258) 129 Main St., Irvington, NY 10533 USA Fax: 914-591-3220
E-mail: hydrapublishing@mac.com
Dist(s): **St. Martin's Pr.**

Hyles Pubns., (978-0-9709488; 978-0-9745499; 978-0-9764247; 978-0-9778936; 978-0-9800594; 978-0-9819603; 978-1-62289) Div. of Prepare Now Resources, Orders Addr.: 507 State St., Hammond, IN 46320 USA Tel 219-932-0711
E-mail: arrowcomp@sbcglobal.net; stubblefieldl@fbchammond.com; dillon@pulse18.com
Web site: http://www.pulse18.com.

Hymns Ancient & Modern Ltd (GBR) (978-0-334; 978-1-85311; 978-0-907547; 978-1-84825) *Dist. by* **Westminster John Knox.**

†Hyperion Bks. for Children, (978-0-7868; 978-1-56282) Div. of Disney Bk. Publishing, Inc., A Walt Disney Co., Orders Addr.: 3 Center Plaza, Boston, MA 02108 USA Toll Free: 800-759-0190; Edit Addr.: 114 Fifth Ave., New York, NY 10011 USA Tel 212-633-4400; Fax: 212-633-4833; *Imprints*: Jump at the Sun (Jump at the Sun); Volo (Volo); di Capua, Michael Books (diCapua Bks)
Web site: http://www.disney.com; http://www.hyperionbooksforchildren.com
Dist(s): **Disney Publishing Worldwide**
Hachette Bk. Group
Little Brown & Co.; *CIP.*

Publisher Name Index

†Hyperion Paperbacks for Children, (*978-0-7868; 978-1-56282*) Div. of Disney Bk. Publishing, Inc., A Walt Disney Co., 114 Fifth Ave., New York, NY 10011 USA Tel 212-633-4400; Fax: 212-633-4833
Web site: http://www.disney.com
Dist(s): **Hachette Bk. Group**
Little Brown & Co.; *CIP.*

†Hyperion Pr., (*978-0-7868; 978-1-56282; 978-1-4013*) Div. of Disney Bk. Publishing, Inc., A Walt Disney Co., Orders Addr.: c/o HarperCollins Publishers, 1000 Keystone Industrial Park, Scranton, PA 18512-4621 USA Toll Free: 800-242-7737; Edit Addr.: 114 Fifth Ave., New York, NY 110011 USA Tel 917-661-2000
Web site: http://www.hyperionbooks.com
Dist(s): **Follett School Solutions**
Hachette Bk. Group
MyiLibrary; *CIP.*

hyperwerks *See* **Hyperwerks Entertainment**

Hyperwerks Entertainment, (*978-0-9770213*) 1830 Stoner Ave. Apt. 6, Los Angeles, CA 90025-7319 USA
Web site: http://www.hyperwerks.com.

I ZGOOL Media, (*978-0-9885898*) 100 Andover Pk. W Suite 150-237, Tukwila, WA 98188 USA Tel 206-851-1065
E-mail: fredbc11@gmail.com.

I AM Foundation, The, (*978-0-9645224; 978-0-9831780; 978-0-615-70944-4*) 7825 Fay Ave., Suite 200, La Jolla, CA 92037 USA Tel 619-297-7010
E-mail: iam@iamfoundation.org
Web site: http://www.iamfoundation.org
Dist(s): **CreateSpace Independent Publishing Platform**
DeVorss & Co.
New Leaf Distributing Co., Inc.

I Am Your Playground LLC, (*978-0-9769580*) P.O. Box 301, Fanwood, NJ 07023-0301 USA Fax: 908-301-0777; Toll Free: 888-759-4736 (888-PLY-GRND)
E-mail: john@iamyourplayground.com
Web site: http://www.iamyourplayground.com.

I & L Publishing, (*978-0-9661244; 978-1-930002*) 174 Oak Dr. Pkwy., Oroville, CA 95966 USA Tel 530-589-5048; Fax: 530-589-3551; Toll Free: 888-443-4722
E-mail: iolamoore@juno.com
Dist(s): **Morris Publishing.**

I. b. d., Ltd., (*978-0-88431*) 24 Hudson St., Kinderhook, NY 12106 USA (SAN 630-7779) Tel 518-758-1755; Fax: 518-758-6702
E-mail: lankhof@ibdltd.com
Web site: http://www.ibdltd.com.

IBE, Inc., (*978-0-916547; 978-0-9785848*) Div. of Inspiration Bks. East, Inc., Orders Addr.: P.O. Box 352, Jemison, AL 35085 USA (SAN 295-4672) Tel 205-646-2941; Edit Addr.: 170 Cty. Rd. 749, Jemison, AL 35085 USA
E-mail: communications@inbookseast.org
Web site: http://www.inbookseast.org.

I. B. Hoofinit Co., (*978-1-928890*) Orders Addr.: 94 Rte. 130, Forestdale, MA 02644 USA
E-mail: ibhoofinit@yahoo.com
Web site: http://ibhoofinit.com.

I. B. Tauris & Co., Ltd. (GBR) (*978-0-302; 978-0-85667; 978-1-85043; 978-1-86064; 978-1-84511; 978-1-84885; 978-1-78076; 978-0-85773*) *Dist. by* **Macmillan.**

I C A, (*978-0-9747506*) P.O. Box 910, Wayne, MI 48184-9998 USA Fax: 734-595-1869
E-mail: codemanray@aol.com
Web site: http://www.thefemalecode.com.

I Can Do All Things Productions, (*978-0-9745787*) 8 Loveland St., Madison, NJ 07940 USA Tel 973-377-5970; Fax: 973-377-5970
E-mail: seucony@optonline.net
Web site: http://www.perfectpraisebooks.com.

I E E E * Standards *See* **IEEE**

I F V, Inc., (*978-1-931861*) 1045 Coddington Rd., Ithaca, NY 14850 USA
E-mail: ifv@lightlink.com
Web site: http://www.classicalfencing.com.

I Gotta Read It! Publishing, (*978-0-615-54132-7; 978-0-615-77185-4*) 5064 Tatra Ave., Maple Hts., OH 44137 USA Tel 216-581-7208; Fax: 216-587-5950; Toll Free: 800-455-1340
Web site: http://www.igottareaditpublishing.webs.com
Dist(s): **CreateSpace Independent Publishing Platform**
Dummy Record Do Not USE!!!!.

I Have A Voice Enterprises, (*978-0-9746192*) P.O. Box 83, Peshtigo, WI 54157 USA
Web site: http://www.thehidersstory.com.

I Play Math Games *See* **IPMG Publishing**

I S H K, (*978-0-86304; 978-0-900860; 978-1-883536; 978-1-933779; 978-1-942698*) Div. of Institute for the Study of Human Knowledge, Orders Addr.: P.O. Box 381069, Cambridge, MA 02238-1069 USA (SAN 226-4536) Tel 617-497-4124; Fax: 617-500-0268; Toll Free Fax: 800-223-4200; Toll Free: 800-222-4745; Edit Addr.: P.O. Box 176, Los Altos, CA 94023 USA Tel 650-948-9428; *Imprints:* Malor Books (Malor Bks); Hoopoe Books (Hoopoe Books)
E-mail: ishkbooks@aol.com
Web site: http://www.ishkbooks.com
Dist(s): **Borders, Inc.**
New Leaf Distributing Co., Inc.

I S M Teaching Systems, Inc., (*978-1-56775*) 14132 Desert Willow, El Paso, TX 79938 USA Tel 915-856-6365; Fax: 915-856-6367; Toll Free: 800-453-4476
E-mail: Email4ism@aol.com
Web site: http://www16.inetba.com/ismteachingsystemsinc.

I S R P Press *See* **Sound Reading Solutions**

I Save A Tree, (*978-0-9714299; 978-0-9744670; 978-0-9745659; 978-1-61015*) Orders Addr.: P.O. Box 3006, Arcadia, FL 34265 USA
Web site: http://www.garrettbooks.com; http://www.isaveatree.com.

I See *Imprint of* **Picture Window Bks.**

I See Puppy, LLP, (*978-0-9774277*) Orders Addr.: 107 Richard Mine Rd., Wharton, NJ 07801 USA (SAN 257-554X) Tel 973-361-8637; Fax: 973-361-8035
E-mail: info@iseepuppy.com
Web site: http://www.iseepuppy.com.

I wantz Publishing, (*978-0-9727998*) P.O. Box 9305, Grand Rapids, MI 49509-0305 USA
E-mail: elizabeth@iwantz.com
Web site: http://www.iwantz.com.

I-5 Publishing LLC, (*978-0-87714; 978-0-944875; 978-0-9629525; 978-1-882770; 978-1-889540; 978-1-931993; 978-1-59378; 978-0-9745407; 978-1-933342; 978-1-933958; 978-1-935484; 978-1-937049; 978-1-62008; 978-1-62187*) 10 Bridge St., Bldg. C, Metuchen, NJ 08840 USA Tel 949-855-8822 (ext. 1003); Fax: 732-960-3107; *Imprints:* Kennel Club Books (KennelClubBks)
Dist(s): **MyiLibrary**
Perseus Distribution.

IAC Publishing, (*978-0-9748383*) 3432 Denny St., No. 3, Pittsburgh, PA 15201 USA Toll Free: 877-592-0237
Web site: http://www.irishamericancatholic.com.

Iaconi, Mariuccia Bk. Imports, (*978-0-9628720*) P.O. Box 77023, San Francisco, CA 94107-0023 USA (SAN 161-1364) Toll Free: 800-955-9577
E-mail: mibibook@ixnetcom.com
Web site: http://www.mibibook.com
Dist(s): **Lectorum Pubns., Inc.**

Iacovello, Dick, (*978-0-615-45131-2*) P.O. Box 2753, Vineyard Haven, MA 02568 USA Tel 508-693-7792
E-mail: montuse.lives@verizon.net
Dist(s): **CreateSpace Independent Publishing Platform**
Dummy Record Do Not USE!!!!.

IAD Pr. (AUS) (*978-0-949659; 978-1-86465; 978-0-9596206; 978-0-7316-3607-5; 978-0-7316-7458-9; 978-0-7316-7915-7; 978-0-646-04154-4; 978-0-646-20261-7*) *Dist. by* **IPG Chicago.**

IamCoach.com Publishing, (*978-0-9754761*) P.O. Box 60088, King of Prussia, PA 19406 USA
E-mail: publishing@iamcoach.com
Web site: http://www.IamCoach.com/chess/publishing/
Dist(s): **SCB Distributors.**

IAMPress, (*978-0-9768782; 978-0-9794839*) 3053 Dumbarton Rd., Memphis, TN 38128 USA Tel 901-358-2226; Fax: 901-358-8102
E-mail: renford@iam-cor.org
Web site: http://www.iam-cor.org
Dist(s): **Lulu Enterprises Inc.**

Iberian Press *See* **7 Robots, Inc.**

Ibex Pubs., Inc., (*978-0-936347; 978-1-58814*) Orders Addr.: P.O. Box 30087, Bethesda, MD 20824 USA (SAN 696-866X) Tel 301-718-8188; Fax: 301-907-8707; Toll Free: 888-718-8188
E-mail: info@ibexpub.com
Web site: http://www.ibexpublishers.com.

IBJ Custom Publishing, (*978-0-9745673; 978-0-9776675; 978-0-9798830; 978-1-934922; 978-1-939550*) 41 E. Washington St., Suite 200, Indianapolis, IN 46204 USA
Dist(s): **Cardinal Pubs. Group.**

IBJ Media Custom Publishing *See* **IBJ Custom Publishing**

IBks., Inc.,
Dist(s): **National Bk. Network.**

ibooks, Inc., (*978-0-671; 978-0-7434; 978-1-58824; 978-1-59176; 978-1-59687*) 100 Jericho Quadrangle, Ste. 300, Jericho, NY 11753-2702 USA; *Imprints:* Milk & Cookies (Milk-Cookie); ipicturebooks (Ipicbks)
Web site: http://www.ibooksinc.com.

ibooks, Incorporated/ipictures.com *See* **ibooks, Inc.**

I C Creative, Inc., (*978-0-9742714*) 2300 Michigan Ct., Suite B, Arlington, TX 76016 USA Tel 817-459-8079; Fax: 817-460-0430
E-mail: joi@stayintouchmail.com
Web site: http://www.stayintouchmail.com.

ICAN Press *See* **Black Forest Pr.**

ICanPublish, (*978-0-9711480*) Div. of Heckman Bindery, Inc., P.O. Box 89, North Manchester, IN 46962 USA (SAN 253-9500) Tel 260-982-2107; Fax: 260-982-1130; Toll Free: 800-334-3628
E-mail: dave_mcintyre@heckmanbindery.com.

Ice Age Park and Trail Foundation, Inc., (*978-0-9627079*) 2453 Atwood Ave. STOP 4, Madison, WI 53704-5682 USA
E-mail: iat@iceagetrail.org
Web site: http://www.iceagetrail.org.

Ice Cube Pr., LLC, (*978-1-888160*) 205 N. Front St., North Liberty, IA 52317 USA (SAN 298-9085) Tel 319-626-2055; 319-594-6022
E-mail: steve@icecubepress.com; steve@southslope.net
Web site: http://www.icecubepress.com
Dist(s): **Partners Bk. Distributing, Inc.**
Quality Bks., Inc.
Smashwords.

Ice Mountain Publishing, (*978-0-9748814*) P.O. Box 1418, Salida, CO 81201 USA
E-mail: nathanward@amigo.net.

Icecat Bks., (*978-0-9764308; 978-0-9768670*) 1243 Old Canyon Dr., Hacienda Heights, CA 91745 USA Tel 626-333-2430
E-mail: contact@icecatbooks.com
Web site: http://www.icecatbooks.com.

Ichabod Ink, (*978-0-9766641*) 418 Lake George Cir., West Chester, PA 19382 USA.

Icicle Falls Publishing Co., (*978-0-9749360*) Orders Addr.: HC 31, Box 5118A, Wasilla, AK 99654 USA; Edit Addr.: Hc31 B0x 5118a, Wasilla, AK 99654 USA
Web site: www.alaskanstoires.com
Dist(s): **News Group, The.**

Icon Bks., Ltd. (GBR) (*978-1-874166; 978-1-84046; 978-1-906850; 978-1-84831; 978-1-78578*) *Dist. by* **Consort Bk Sales.**

Icon Group International, Inc., (*978-0-7576; 978-0-7418; 978-0-597; 978-0-497; 978-0-546; 978-1-114*) Div. of Icon Group, Ltd., P.O. Box 27740, Las Vegas, NV 89126-7440 USA (SAN 299-8122) Tel 858-635-9410; Fax: 858-635-9414
E-mail: ula@icongroupbooks.com; meta@icongroupbooks.com; orders@icongroupbooks.com
Web site: http://www.icongrouponline.com
Dist(s): **CreateSpace Independent Publishing Platform**
Ebsco Publishing
MyiLibrary.

Idaho State Journal, (*978-0-9749865; 978-0-615-47497-7*) Orders Addr.: P.O. Box 431, Pocatello, ID 83204 USA; Edit Addr.: P.O. Box 431, Pocatello, ID 83204-0431 USA
Web site: http://www.journalnet.com.

Idea & Design Works, LLC, (*978-0-9712282; 978-0-9719775; 978-1-932382; 978-1-933239; 978-1-60010; 978-1-61377; 978-1-62302; 978-1-63140*) 2645 Financial Ct., Suite E, San Diego, CA 92117 USA (SAN 255-1926) Tel 858-270-1315; Fax: 858-270-1308; 5080 Santa Fe St., San Diego, CA 92109-1609; *Imprints:* Worthwhile Books (Worthwhile Bks)
E-mail: chris@idwpublishing.com
Web site: http://www.idwpublishing.com/
Dist(s): **Diamond Comic Distributors, Inc.**
Diamond Bk. Distributors
L P C Group
MyiLibrary
Open Road Integrated Media, LLC.

Idea, Inc., (*978-0-9701566*) 403 5th Pl NW, Austin, MN 55912-3051 USA Toll Free: 800-828-1231 (phone/fax)
E-mail: Idea_inc@smig.net
Web site: http://www.ccjournal.com.

Idea Network LA Inc., (*978-0-9773301*) 201 S. Santa Fe Ave. No. 105, Los Angeles, CA 90012 USA Tel 213-613-1252; Fax: 213-613-1440.

IdeaList Enterprises, Inc., (*978-0-9758794*) P.O. Box 101187, Chicago, IL 60610 USA.

Ideals *Imprint of* **Ideals Pubns.**

Ideals Children's Bks. *Imprint of* **Ideals Pubns.**

Ideals Pr. *Imprint of* **Ideals Pubns.**

Ideals Pubns., (*978-0-8249; 978-0-89542*) Div. of Guideposts, Orders Addr.: 2630 Elm Hill Pike., Suite 100, Nashville, TN 37214 USA; *Imprints:* Ideals (Ideals TN); Candy Cane Press (Candy Cane Pr); Ideals Children's Books (Ideals Chldrns Bks); Ideals Press (Ideals Pr); Williamson Books (Williamson Bks); Guideposts (Guideposts TN); GuidepostsBooks (GuidepostsBks); GPKids (GPKids)
E-mail: hhulse@guideposts.org
Web site: http://www.idealsbooks.com
Dist(s): **Learning Connection, The**
Worthy Publishing
ebrary, Inc.

Ideals Publishing Corporation *See* **Ideals Pubns.**

Ideate Prairie, (*978-0-9762564*) P.O. Box 65, Genoa, IL 60135 USA Tel 815-986-6577; *Imprints:* American Dog (Am Dog)
E-mail: cpierce@ideate-prairie.com
Web site: http://www.americandogtales.com; http://www.ideate-prairie.com.

Identity Pr., (*978-0-9753482*) P.O. Box 46224, Cincinnati, OH 45246-0224 USA Tel 513-313-5907 Do not confuse with companies with the same or similar name in Fountain Valley, CA, Cambridge, MA
E-mail: discovteenesteem@aol.com.

Idlehour Entertainment, (*978-0-9778063*) P.O. Box 12048, Glendale, AZ 85318 USA (SAN 850-3001) Tel 623-780-1434; Fax: 623-780-1438
Web site: http://www.idlehourentertainment.com.

Idyllworks, LLC, (*978-0-9794647*) 2904 Rippling Brook Ln., Dickinson, TX 77539-6199 USA
Web site: http://www.JamboNation.com.

†IEEE, (*978-0-7803; 978-0-87942; 978-1-55937; 978-0-7381; 978-1-4244; 978-1-61284; 978-1-4577; 978-1-4673; 978-1-62195; 978-1-4799; 978-1-5044; 978-1-5090*) Orders Addr.: P.O. Box 1331, Piscataway, NJ 08855-1331 USA (SAN 250-6130) Tel 732-981-0060; Fax: 732-981-0027; Toll Free: 800-701-4333; Edit Addr.: 445 Hoes Ln., Piscataway, NJ 08855-1331 USA Tel 732-981-0060; 732-981-5300; 732-562-3828; 800-678-4333; Fax: 732-981-1769; 732-562-1746; 732-562-1971
E-mail: confpubs@ieee.org; customer-service@ieee.org
Web site: http://www.ieee.org
Dist(s): **Curran Assocs., Inc.**
MyiLibrary
Oxford Univ. Pr., Inc.
Wiley, John & Sons, Inc.; *CIP.*

IEP Resources *Imprint of* **Attainment Co., Inc.**

IFLY Bks., (*978-0-9758888*) P.O. Box 894134, Temecula, CA 92589 USA.

I.Form Ink, Publishing, (*978-0-9763274*) Div. of Insu-Form, Inc., 41921 Beacon Hill, Suite A, Palm Desert, CA 92211 USA Tel 760-779-0657; Fax: 760-779-5143
E-mail: john@hackergroup.org.

IFWG Publishing Inc., (*978-0-9843298; 978-0-615-50936-5; 978-0-615-51846-6; 978-0-615-52105-3; 978-0-615-55249-1; 978-0-615-55424-2; 978-0-615-55642-0; 978-0-615-56093-9; 978-0-615-56121-9*) 302 Horseshoe Ln., Rockaway Beach, MO 65740 USA (SAN 859-0842) Toll Free: 800-337-3038
E-mail: ifwg-publishing@live.com; r.a.knowlton@ifwgpublishing.com
Web site: http://ifwgpublishing.weebly.com/index.html
Dist(s): **CreateSpace Independent Publishing Platform.**

Ig Publishing *See* **Ig Publishing, Inc.**

Ig Publishing, Inc., (*978-0-9703125; 978-0-9752517; 978-0-9771972; 978-0-9788431; 978-0-9815040; 978-1-935439; 978-1-939601; 978-1-63246*) 392 Clinton Ave. Apt. 1S, Brooklyn, NY 11238-1187 USA (SAN 254-0444)
Web site: http://www.igpub.com; www.lizzieskurnickbooks.com
Dist(s): **Consortium Bk. Sales & Distribution**
Perseus Bks. Group
SPD-Small Pr. Distribution
ebrary, Inc.

IGI Pr., (*978-0-9709443; 978-0-9777121; 978-0-9799963; 978-0-9820870; 978-0-9825503; 978-0-9829273*) 241 First Ave. N., Minneapolis, MN 55401 USA (SAN 854-1876) Tel 612-338-8973 Toll Free: 888-805-8973
E-mail: igi@igipublishing.com
Web site: http://www.igipublishing.com
Dist(s): **AtlasBooks Distribution.**

IGMI Publishing, (*978-0-9655933*) Div. of PrissyH, P.O. Box 1735, Las Vegas, NM 87745-9602 USA Tel 505-425-9292
E-mail: favplagget@aol.com.

Ignatius Pr., (*978-0-89870; 978-1-58617; 978-1-62164; 978-1-68149*) Orders Addr.: P.O. Box 1339, Fort Collins, CO 80522-1339 USA (SAN 855-3556) Tel 970-221-3920; Fax: 970-221-3964; Toll Free Fax: 800-278-3566; Toll Free: 877-320-9276 (bookstore orders); 800-651-1531 (credit card orders, no minimum, individual orders); Edit Addr.: 1348 10th Ave., San Francisco, CA 94122 USA (SAN 214-3887) Toll Free: 800-651-1531
E-mail: info@ignatius.com
Web site: http://www.ignatius.com
Dist(s): **Follett School Solutions**
Midpoint Trade Bks., Inc.
Spring Arbor Distributors, Inc.

Ignite! Learning, (*978-0-9791935; 978-0-9798418; 978-1-934763; 978-1-937822*) 2905 San Gabriel Suite 212, Austin, TX 78705 USA Tel 512-697-7000; Fax: 512-697-7001; Toll Free: 866-464-4648
E-mail: support@ignitelearning.com; jbohls@ignitelearning.com
Web site: http://www.ignitelearning.com.

Ignite Reality, (*978-0-9776771; 978-0-9816258*) P.O. Box 1804, Burlingame, CA 94011-1804 USA (SAN 856-0781)
E-mail: drjenniferleigh@gmail.com
Web site: http://www.drjenniferaustinleigh.com
Dist(s): **AtlasBooks Distribution.**

Ignition Pr. *Imprint of* **Publishing Services @ Thomson-Shore**

IGR Limited *See* **EKADOO Publishing Group**

Iguana Adventures Publishing *See* **Publish To Go Pubns.**

I.H.S. Pubs., (*978-0-9847656*) 3920 S. Old Hwy. 94 Suite 33, St. Charles, MO 63304 USA Tel 636-447-6000.

IIEI Pr., (*978-0-9773098; 978-0-9797244; 978-0-615-52608-9*) 11225 N. 28th Dr., Suite B-201, Phoenix, AZ 85029 USA Tel 602-648-5750; Fax: 602-648-5755; Toll Free: 800-474-8013
E-mail: info@expandglobal.com
Web site: http://www.expandglobal.com/iiei-press/.

Ijiwola Pr., Gregory *Imprint of* **Summit Hse. Pubs.**

IJN Publishing, Inc., (*978-1-933894*) 724 NE. 4th St. #9, Hallandale, FL 33009 USA (SAN 850-4474) Fax: 954-457-2277; P.O. Box 630577, Miami, FL 33163
E-mail: gerald@ijnpublishing.com
Web site: http://www.whatliesbeneaththebed.com; http://www.ijnpublishing.com.

IJustWantToSleep, Inc., (*978-0-9744357*) 18 Timothy Ln., Candler, NC 28715 USA
E-mail: store@ijustwanttosleep.com; author@ijustwanttosleep.com
Web site: http://www.ijustwanttosleep.com.

IKIDS *Imprint of* **Innovative Kids**

Ile Orunmila Communications, (*978-0-9644247; 978-0-9714949; 978-0-9825100*) Orders Addr.: P.O. Box 2326, San Bernardino, CA 92405 USA Tel 909-475-5851; Fax: 909-475-5850; Toll Free: 888-678-6645; Edit Addr.: 515 W. 21st St., San Bernardino, CA 92405 USA
E-mail: fsorunmila@aol.com
Web site: http://www.IleOrunmila.com
Dist(s): **Original Pubns.**

Illui International *See* **Heartful Loving Pr.**

Illumina Publishing, (*978-0-9718600; 978-0-9818092*) P.O. Box 2643, Friday Harbor, WA 98250-2643 USA Tel 360-378-6047
E-mail: illumina@rockisland.com
Web site: http://www.illuminapublishing.com; http://www.illuminabookdesign.com.

Illumination Arts *See* **Inspire Every Child dba Illumination Arts**

Illumination Arts LLC, (*978-0-9829225; 978-0-9846874*) 6788 Lakeview Dr, FRAZIER PARK, CA 93225 USA Tel 617-472-1443; 661-289-5007; *Imprints:* Diamond Clear Vision (DiamondClear)
E-mail: thpjr52@aol.com
Web site: http://www.illuminationarts.us; http://www.diamondclearvision.com.

Illumination Arts Publishing Co., Inc., (*978-0-935699; 978-0-9701907; 978-0-9740190*) Orders Addr.: P.O. Box 1865, Bellevue, WA 98009 USA (SAN 696-2599) Tel 425-644-7185; Fax: 425-644-9274; Toll Free: 888-210-8216; Edit Addr.: 808 6th St S. Ste. 200, Kirkland, WA 98033-6768 USA
E-mail: liteinfo@illumin.com
Web site: http://www.illumin.com
Dist(s): **DeVorss & Co.**
Follett School Solutions
Koen Pacific
New Leaf Distributing Co., Inc.
Partners/West Book Distributors
Quality Bks., Inc.

Illumination Pubns., *(978-0-9789511)* 2802 Floore Ct., Louisville, KY 40299-1610 USA (SAN 852-0313) Tel 502-491-5664 Do not confuse with Illumination Publications in West Toluca lake, CA.

Illumination Studios, *(978-0-9741381)* 5924 Woodoak Dr., Dallas, TX 75249 USA
E-mail: contact@illuminationstudios.com
Web site: http://www.illuminationstudios.com.

Illusion Factory, The, *(978-0-9747331; 978-1-932949)* 21800 Burbank Blvd., Suite 225, Woodland Hills, CA 91367 USA (SAN 255-7096) Tel 818-598-8400; Fax: 818-598-8494
E-mail: ewong@illusionfactory.com
Web site: http://www.illusionfactory.com.

Illusionary Magic LLC, *(978-0-9834201)* 104 Donato Cir., Scotch Plains, NJ 07076 USA Tel 877-322-2723; Fax: 908-322-0421
E-mail: info@bradross.com
Web site: http://www.BradRoss.com.

Illustrate to Educate, *(978-0-9892732)* 2313 Quincy St. Apt. No. 2, Durham, NC 27703 USA Tel 919-908-1254
E-mail: everettar@hotmail.com.

ILMHOUSE LLC, *(978-0-9726607)* P.O. Box 535, Unionville, PA 19375-0535 USA
Web site: http://www.thetruemarriage.com.

ILT Publishing, *(978-0-9774409)* Div. of Integrated Learning Technology, Inc., P.O. Box 72420, Thorndale, PA 19372-0420 USA (SAN 257-4950) Tel 610-518-6860 (phone/fax)
E-mail: info@iltpublishing.com
Web site: http://www.iltpublishing.com; http://www.tommilance.com.

I.M. Enterprises, *(978-0-9777882)* P.O. Box 111, Rochester, MA 02770 USA (SAN 850-1645); *Imprints:* Light Works Publishing (Light Works)
E-mail: imenterprises@hotmail.com
Web site: http://www.imenterprises.org.

IM Pr., *(978-0-9654651; 978-0-9716911; 978-0-615-43634-0; 978-0-9857952)* Orders Addr.: P.O. Box 5346, Takoma Park, MD 20913-5346 USA Tel 301-587-1202; Edit Addr.: 7214 Cedar Ave., Takoma Park, MD 20912 USA Do not confuse with companies with the same name in Cincinnati, OH, Fairfax Station, VA
E-mail: efaine@yahoo.com
Web site: http://www.takoma.com/ned/home.htm
Dist(s): **Book Clearing Hse.**

Imaajinn This, *(978-0-9767342)* P.O. Box 294, West Haven, CT 06516 USA (SAN 256-484X) Tel 203-710-4906
Web site: http://www.robleyblake.com.

Image Cascade Publishing, *(978-0-9639607; 978-1-930009; 978-1-59511)* 420 Lexington Ave., Suite 300, New York, NY 10170 USA (SAN 253-2972) Tel 212-297-6240; Toll Free: 800-691-7779
E-mail: jc@imagecascade.com
Web site: http://www.imagecascade.com
Dist(s): **BookMasters, Inc.**

Image Comics, *(978-1-58240; 978-1-887279; 978-1-60706; 978-1-63215)* 1942 University Ave. 3rd Floor, Suite 305, Berkeley, CA 94704 USA Tel 510-644-4980; Fax: 510-644-4988
E-mail: info@imagecomics.com
Web site: http://www.imagecomics.com/
Dist(s): **Diamond Comic Distributors, Inc.**
Diamond Bk. Distributors
L P C Group
Trucatriche.

Image Express Inc., *(978-0-9664634; 978-0-615-50572-5)* P.O. Box 66536, Austin, TX 78766 USA Tel 512-401-4900; Toll Free: 888-794-4300
Web site: http://greatday.com
Dist(s): **CreateSpace Independent Publishing Platform.**

Image Formation, *(978-0-9763440)* 23233 N. Pima, No. 113-102, Scottsdale, AZ 85255 USA
E-mail: lance@themummymountainstory.com
Web site: http://www.themummymountainstory.com.

Image Pr., Inc., *(978-1-891548)* Orders Addr.: P.O. Box 2407, Edmond, OK 73083-2407 USA Tel 405-844-6007; Fax: 405-348-5577; Edit Addr.: 247 N. Broadway, Suite 101, Edmond, OK 73034 USA.

Image Publishing, Ltd., *(978-0-911897)* Subs. of Roger Miller Photo, Ltd., 1411 Hollins St., Baltimore, MD 21223 USA (SAN 264-6781) Tel 410-566-1222; 410-233-1234; Fax: 410-233-1241 Do not confuse with companies with the same or similar names in Encino, CA, Wilton, CT
E-mail: rmpl.ipl@verizon.net
Web site: http://www.rogermillerphoto.com.

IMAGECRAFTERS, *(978-0-9773478)* Orders Addr.: 1644 Masters Ct., Naperville, IL 60563 USA (SAN 257-3709) Tel 630-355-1449
E-mail: imgcft@mc.net.

Imagery Pr., *(978-0-9754287)* P.O. Box 337, Carpinteria, CA 93014-0337 USA
E-mail: books@imagerypress.com.

Images & Pages, *(978-0-9788332)* P.O. Box 118120, Carrollton, TX 75007 USA
E-mail: deguzman@imagesandpages.com
Web site: http://imagesandpages.com.

Images Co., *(978-0-9677017; 978-1-62385)* 109 Woods of Arden Rd., Staten Island, NY 10312 USA
E-mail: j.iovine@verizon.net; imagesco@bellatlantic.net; imagesco@verizon.net
Web site: http://www.imagesco.com.

Images For Presentation, *(978-0-9749531)* 176 Second St., Saint James, NY 11780 USA Tel 631-361-7908
E-mail: imagesforpres@aol.com.

Images from the Past, Inc., *(978-1-884592)* 155 W. Main St., P.O. Box 137, Bennington, VT 05201-0137 USA Tel 802-442-3204 (phone/fax); Toll Free: 888-442-3204
E-mail: info@ImagesfromthePast.com
Web site: http://www.ImagesfromthePast.com
Dist(s): **Ingram Pub. Services.**

Images Pr., *(978-1-891577)* 27920 Roble Alto St., Los Altos Hills, CA 94022 USA (SAN 299-4844) Tel 650-948-9251; 650-948-8251; Fax: 650-941-6114 Do not confuse with companies with the same name in San Leandro, CA, New York, NY
E-mail: bugsmom2@aol.com
Web site: http://www.images-press.com
Dist(s): **Quality Bks., Inc.**

Images Unlimited, *(978-0-930643)* P.O. Box 305, Maryville, MO 64468 USA (SAN 242-0163) Tel 660-582-4279; Toll Free: 800-366-1695
E-mail: images@cebridge.net
Web site: http://www.imagesunlimitedpub.com; http://www.snaptail.com; http://www.snaptailpress.com; http://www.imagesunlimitedpublishing.com; http://www.cookingandkids.com/blog
Dist(s): **Brodart Co.**
Follett School Solutions.

Imaginary Lines, Incorporated *See* **Sally Ride Science**

Imagination Arts Pubns., *(978-0-9746119)* P.O. Box 103, Mahwah, NJ 07430 USA Tel 201-529-5105; Fax: 201-529-5105
E-mail: imaginationarts@optonline.net
Web site: http://www.iapbooks.com.

Imagination Publishing-Orlando, *(978-0-9817123; 978-0-615-38566-2)* P.O. Box 802, Loughman, FL 33858 USA (SAN 856-3152)
E-mail: paul@HubbleRevealsCreation.com
Web site: http://www.TheSecretDoorway.com; http://www.HubbleRevealsCreation.com/
Dist(s): **BookBaby.**

Imagination Stage, Inc., *(978-0-9723729)* 4908 Auburn Ave., Bethesda, MD 20814 USA Tel 301-961-6060; Fax: 301-718-9526
E-mail: lagogliati@aol.com
Web site: http://www.imaginationstage.org.

Imagination Station Pr., *(978-0-9742575)* 4560 N. 25th Rd., Arlington, VA 22207-4147 USA Tel 703-528-5828
E-mail: epyatt1@comcast.net.

Imagination Workshop, The, *(978-0-9744437)* 4150 Abbott Ave., N., Minneapolis, MN 55422 USA
E-mail: imaginationworkshop@yahoo.com.

Imaginative Publishing, Ltd., *(978-0-9743335; 978-0-9767948)* P.O. Box 150008, Fort Worth, TX 76108 USA Tel 817-246-6436 (phone/fax); Toll Free: 877-246-6436 (phone/fax)
E-mail: publisher@imaginativepublishing.com
Web site: http://www.imaginativepublishing.com.

Imaginator Pr., *(978-0-9745603; 978-1-936917)* 6400 Baltimore National Pike Suite 170A-194, Baltimore, MD 21228-3915 USA
E-mail: sruth@ImaginatorPress.com
Web site: http://www.ImaginatorPress.com
Dist(s): **Beagle Bay Bks.**
Lightning Source, Inc.

Imagine Books *See* **Imagine! Studios**

Imagine Publishing *Imprint of* **Charlesbridge Publishing, Inc.**

Imagine Publishing, *(978-0-9758899)* 7620 Dogleg Rd., Dayton, OH 45414 USA Fax: 937-890-7949
E-mail: skyblu40@earthlink.net.

Imagine! Studios, *(978-0-9761317; 978-0-9764353; 978-0-9767913; 978-1-937944)* PO Box 16298, High Point, NC 27261 USA Tel 941-999-1278
E-mail: contact@artsimage.com
Web site: http://www.artsimagine.com
Dist(s): **BookBaby.**

Imagine That Enterprises, *(978-0-9723067)* P.O. Box 29315, Saint Louis, MO 63126 USA
E-mail: underthedove@hotmail.com
Web site: http://www.underthedove.com.

Imagine the Possibilities, LLC *See* **Imagining Possibilities**

Imagineland, Ltd., *(978-0-9765038)* P.O. Box 10134, College Station, TX 77842-0134 USA
Web site: http://www.imagineland.com
Dist(s): **Smashwords.**

IMAGINEX, LLC, *(978-0-9753620)* P.O. Box 1375, Frisco, TX 75034 USA; *Imprints:* Bible Game (BibleGame)
Web site: http://www.imnex.net.

Imagining Possibilities, *(978-0-9747426)* P.O. Box 266, Gwynedd Valley, PA 19437-0266 USA.

Imago, *(978-0-9765179)* 14220 Duckett Rd., Brandywine, MD 20613-9343 USA Tel 856-812-0400; Toll Free Fax: 866-268-9003; Toll Free: 866-413-6864.

Imago Pr., *(978-0-9725303; 978-0-9799341; 978-1-935437)* 3710 E. Edison St., Tucson, AZ 85716-2912 USA; *Imprints:* As Sabr Publications (AsSabr)
Web site: http://www.imagobooks.com; http://www.oasisjournal.org.

ImaJinn Bks. *Imprint of* **BelleBks., Inc.**

Imani Productions, *(978-0-615-14325-5)* 2261 Bernwood Dr., Erie, PA 16510 USA Tel 814-897-0502
E-mail: umemesababu@aol.com
Web site: http://www.imaniproductions.org.

Imani-MCHS, *(978-0-9729586)* 3445 W. 66th Pl., Chicago, IL 60629 USA Tel 773-925-6473
E-mail: imanimchs@aol.com.

I-Mar, *(978-0-9741052)* 5150 Rancho Rd., Huntingtn Bch, CA 92647-2074 USA
Web site: http://www.i-mar.net.

ImaRa Publishing, *(978-0-9843111)* Orders Addr.: 3002 230th Ln., SE, Sammamish, WA 98075 USA
E-mail: vrpearce@msn.com
Web site: http://www.imarapublishing.com.

ImBost Inc., *(978-0-9848626)* 158 E. 100 St. Ste 6R, New York, NY 10029 USA Tel 917-482-5178
E-mail: taekwontales@gmail.com.

Imdalind Pr., *(978-0-9884837; 978-0-9914313; 978-0-9964632)* 7377 W. Jefferson Rd., Magna, UT 84044 USA Tel 801-259-4043
E-mail: me@rebeccaethington.com.

Immediex Publishing, *(978-1-932968)* 540 Evelyn Pl., Beverly Hills, CA 90210 USA Tel 310-273-1585
E-mail: rodney@immediex.com
Web site: www.immediex.com
Dist(s): **Smashwords.**

Immedium, *(978-1-59702)* P.O. Box 31846, San Francisco, CA 94131 USA
Web site: http://www.immedium.com
Dist(s): **Consortium Bk. Sales & Distribution**
MyiLibrary
Perseus Bks. Group.

Immortality Pr., *(978-0-9795753)* 1005 Winthrope Chase Dr., Alpharetta, GA 30004 USA
E-mail: publisher@immortalitypress.com; order@immortalitypress.com
Web site: http://www.immortalitypress.com.

Imogen Rose, *(978-0-615-34507-9; 978-0-615-37681-3; 978-0-9828002; 978-0-9850797; 978-0-9856766; 978-1-940015)* 18 Westwinds Dr., Princeton Junction, NJ 08550 USA
E-mail: portalchronicles@hotmail.com
Dist(s): **Lulu Enterprises Inc.**
Smashwords.

Impact *Imprint of* **F&W Media, Inc.**

Impact Bks. *Imprint of* **Stone Arch Bks.**

Impact Pubns., *(978-0-942710; 978-1-57023)* Div. of Development Concepts, Inc., 9104 Manassas Dr., Suite N, Manassas Park, VA 20111-5211 USA (SAN 240-1142) Tel 703-361-7300; Fax: 703-335-9486 Do not confuse with companies with the same name in Evanston, IL, Mandeville, LA, Southfield, MI
E-mail: krannich@impactpublications.com
Web site: http://www.impactpublications.com
Dist(s): **Follett School Solutions**
MyiLibrary
National Bk. Network
ebrary, Inc.

Impact Publications, Incorporated *See* **Specialty Pr., Inc.**

†**Impact Pubs., Inc.**, *(978-0-915166; 978-0-9621333; 978-1-886230)* Orders Addr.: P.O. Box 6016, Atascadero, CA 93423 USA (SAN 202-6864) Tel 805-466-5917; Fax: 805-466-5919; Toll Free: 800-246-7228; *Imprints:* Rebuilding Books (Rebuilding Bks) Do not confuse with Impact Pubns. in Manassas Park, VA or Plantation, FL.
E-mail: publisher@impactpublishers.com
Web site: http://www.impactpublishers.com
Dist(s): **New Harbinger Pubns.**; *CIP*

Impetus Pr., *(978-0-9776693)* P.O. Box 10025, Iowa City, IA 52240-0001 USA Tel 319-321-6282 Do not confuse with Impetus Press in Atlanta, GA
E-mail: jennifer@impetuspress.com
Web site: http://www.impetuspress.com
Dist(s): **SPD-Small Pr. Distribution.**

Impossible Dreams Publishing Co., *(978-0-9786422)* 4123 Rancho Grande Pl., NW., Albuquerque, NM 87120 USA (SAN 851-139X)
E-mail: Quixote1818@aol.com
Web site: http://www.impossibledreamspub.com.

Impressions Ink, *(978-1-882626)* 3918 Peachtree Ln., Memphis, TN 38135-9115 USA Tel 901-388-5382; Fax: 901-385-0256; Toll Free: 800-388-5382.

Imprexions Publishing Co., *(978-0-9742922)* 4910 Benley Ct., Apt 1, Manitowoc, WI 54220 USA Tel 309-550-1243
E-mail: listinsky@hotmail.com.

Imprint Academic (GBR) *(978-0-907845; 978-1-84540)* *Dist. by* **IngramPubServ.**

Imprint.II, *(978-0-9894891; 978-0-9897418)* 11015 122nd Ave. Kp N., Gig Harbor, WA 98329 USA Tel 253-853-4199
E-mail: carolyn@imprint.ll
Web site: www.imprint.ll.

Imprints, *(978-1-883986)* Div. of Spectrum Bks., Orders Addr.: P.O. Box 4365, Thousand Oaks, CA 91359 USA Tel 808-707-3336; Fax: 808-707-4446; Edit Addr.: 32151 Sailview Ln., Westlake Village, CA 91359 USA
Dist(s): **Continental Bk. Co., Inc.**

Impulse Surf, *(978-0-9744247)* Orders Addr.: 1106 Second St., PMB 823, Encinitas, CA 92024 USA Tel 760-431-6883; Fax: 760-436-7158; Edit Addr.: 7200 Ponto Dr., Carlsbad, CA 92009 USA
E-mail: franklinlives@yahoo.com
Web site: http://www.impulsesurf.com.

In Ardua Tendit Pr., *(978-0-9749673)* 464 Leton Dr., Columbia, SC 29210 USA Tel 803-608-0804
E-mail: mail@jessmaccallum.com
Web site: http://www.jessmaccallum.com
Dist(s): **BookBaby.**

In Audio *Imprint of* **Sound Room Pubs., Inc.**

In Between Bks., *(978-0-935430; 978-0-9802007)* P.O. Box 790, Sausalito, CA 94966 USA (SAN 213-6236) Tel 415-383-8447; Fax: 415-381-1938; 415-381-3513
E-mail: inbetweenbooks@atthebutterflytree.com; karla@inbetweenbooks.com; juno@inbetweenbooks.com
Web site: http://www.atthebutterflytree.com.

In Cahoots, *(978-0-9745990)* 105 Los Padres Way, Unit 6 Buellton, CA 93427 USA Do not confuse with In Cahoots in Marietta, GA
Dist(s): **SPD-Small Pr. Distribution.**

In Cider Pr., *(978-0-9721716)* P.O. Box 228, Barton 05822 USA Tel 802-754-8889.

In Motion Books Incorporated *See* **Dakitab, In**

In the Desert, *(978-0-9744005)* 7990 E. Snyde 5106, Tucson, AZ 85750-9009 USA
Web site: http://www.inthedesert.biz.

In the Hands of a Child, *(978-1-60308)* 32 Rd., Coloma, MI 49038-8913 USA T 866-426-3701
E-mail: niki@handsofachild.com; sales@handsofachild.com; info
Web site: http://www.Handsofa

In The Hse. Publishing Co., *(978-0-9760441)* 1122 N. 84th St., Seattle, WA 98103 USA
E-mail: projectfille@hotmail.com
Web site: http://www.projectgirl.com.

In The Lead Publishing *See* **Lone Cypress Pubs.**

In the Sky Publishing, *(978-0-9740438)* Orders Addr.: 26300 Ford Rd., No. 407, Dearborn Heights, MI 48127 USA Tel 313-792-0694
E-mail: cmlipson@wideopenwest.com
Web site: http://www.intheskypublishing.com.

In the Think of Things *See* **Rainbow Resource Ctr., Inc.**

In the Think of Things *Imprint of* **Rainbow Resource Ctr., Inc.**

In This Together Media, *(978-0-9858956; 978-0-9898166)* 5 Evergreen Ln., Larchmont, NY 10538 USA Tel 914-833-1189
E-mail: calbertine@gmail.com
Web site: www.inthistogethermedia.com
Dist(s): **INscribe Digital.**

In Time Pubns. Inc., *(978-0-9762857)* P.O. Box 190537, Fort Lauderdale, FL 33319 USA
Web site: http://www.intimepublications.com.

Inane Blabbering Bks. (GBR) *(978-0-9559798)* *Dist. by* **LuluCom.**

Incentive Pubns., Inc., *(978-0-86530; 978-0-913916; 978-1-62950)* 233 N. Michigan Ave., Suite 2000, Chicago, IL 60601 USA (SAN 203-8005) Toll Free: 800-421-2830
E-mail: info@incentivepublications.com
Web site: http://www.incentivepublications.com
Dist(s): **Independent Pubs. Group**
MyiLibrary
ebrary, Inc.

Inch By Inch Pubns., LLC, *(978-0-9670941)* P.O. Box 15, Okemos, MI 48805 USA Tel 716-688-1515; Fax: 716-636-4058; Toll Free: 877-462-4967
E-mail: chofher@aol.com
Web site: http://www.inchbyinchbooks.com
Dist(s): **Partners Pubs. Group, Inc.**

Inclement Pr., *(978-0-9819736; 978-0-9886669)* P.O. Box 120, Sidney, IA 51652 USA.

Inclusive Books LLC, *(978-0-9778143)* 3027 New Natchez Trace, Nashville, TN 37215 USA Tel 615-383-1065
E-mail: estelle@estellecondra.com
Web site: http://www.inclusivebooks.com.

Incorporated Trustees of the Gospel Worker Society, The, *(978-0-9617506; 978-1-59843; 978-1-934981; 978-1-935338; 978-1-936272; 978-1-936897; 978-1-936898)* Div. of Union Gospel Pr., 1980 Brookpark Rd., Cleveland, OH 44109 USA (SAN 664-2845) Toll Free: 800-638-9988
Web site: http://www.uniongospelpress.com.

Incredible Kid, LLC, *(978-0-9755836)* 7095 Hollywood Blvd., Suite 461, Hollywood, CA 90028 USA.

Independence Books *See* **America Star Bks.**

Independent Media Institute *See* **AlterNet Bks.**

Independent Pub., (978-1-4243; 978-1-59975; 978-1-60402; 978-1-60461; 978-1-60530; 978-1- 978-1-60643; 978-1-60702; 978-1-60725; 978 978-1-61539; 978-1-61584; 978-1-61623; 978 978-1-4507; 978-1-4675; 978-1-4951; 978- Div. of Bar Code Graphics, 875 N. Michiga 2650, Chicago, IL 60615 USA Fax: 312- Free: 800-662-0701 Do not confuse wit Publishers in Bountiful, UT
E-mail: pubserv@barcode-us.com
Web site: http://www.publisherservi
Dist(s): **AtlasBooks Distribution**
Consortium Bk. Sales
D.A.P./Distributed Ar
Ebsco Publishing
Epicenter Pr., Inc.
Follett School So
Hay Hse., Inc.
Independent P
Lulu Enterpr
Midpoint Tr
Outskirts F
SCB Dist
SPD-Sm
Smash
TNT
Univ
eB
e

Independent
978-1-
104,
E-m
Di

Inde

605; 743; 558; 47) uite Toll ent
r, Suite
6-1233
Orders
o, IL 60611
s. of Chicago
0610 USA
312-337-5985;
5508 W. Bell
3436 USA Tel
rints: INDI Best
3423

India Research Pr. (IND) *(978-81-87943; 978-81-901098)*
Dist. by **IPG Chicago.**

Indian Hill Gallery of Fine Photography, *(978-0-9669079)* 671 River Rd., Wells, VT 05774 USA Tel 802-325-2274; Fax: 802-325-2276
E-mail: info@stephenschaub.com
Web site: http://www.indianhillgallery.com
Dist(s): **RAM Pubns. & Distribution.**

Indian Territory Publishing, *(978-0-9727068)* P.O. Box 43, Bennington, OK 74723-0043 USA
E-mail: wes@wesparker-itp.com; wes.parker@us.army.mil
Web site: http://www.wesparker-itp.com.

†Indiana Historical Society, *(978-0-87195)* 450 W. Ohio St., Indianapolis, IN 46202-3269 USA (SAN 201-5234) Tel 317-233-9557; 317-232-1882; Fax: 317-233-0857; Toll Free: 800-447-1830
E-mail: rvaught@indianahistory.org; cbennett@indianahistory.org
Web site: http://www.indianahistory.org
Dist(s): **Distributors, The**
Indiana Univ. Pr.; *CIP.*

†Indiana Univ. Pr., *(978-0-253; 978-0-86196)* 601 N. Morton St., Bloomington, IN 47404-3797 USA (SAN 202-5647) Fax: 812-855-7931; Toll Free: 800-842-6796; *Imprints:* Quarry Books (Quarry Books)
E-mail: iuporder@indiana.edu
Web site: http://www.iupress.indiana.edu
Dist(s): **Ebsco Publishing**
Ingram Pub. Services
Lightning Source, Inc.
MyiLibrary
Transaction Pubs.
ebrary, Inc.; *CIP.*

Indie Christian Book Group *Imprint of* **IndieGo Publishing LLC**

IndieArtz, Inc., *(978-0-9753252)* 1650 Margaret St., Suite 302-131, Jacksonville, FL 32204-3869 USA
Web site: http://www.indieartz.com.

IndieGo ePublishing LLC *See* **IndieGo Publishing LLC**

IndieGo Publishing LLC, *(978-0-9846685; 978-0-9887048; 978-0-9916307; 978-0-9860953)* Orders Addr.: 2341 Evenglow Ct., Deltona, FL 32725 USA; *Imprints:* Indie Christian Book Group (Indie Christ BG)
E-mail: indiegopublishing@gmail.com
Web site: http://www.indiegopublishing.com/.

Indigo Custom Publishing *See* **Sphinx Publishing**

Indigo Impressions, *(978-0-9788339)* Orders Addr.: P.O. Box 501, Speonk, NY 11972-0501 USA
E-mail: meghanspd@yahoo.com
Dist(s): **BookBaby.**

Indigo, LLC, *(978-0-9758995)* 7486 North Shore Rd., Norfolk, VA 23505 USA Tel 757-622-3319
E-mail: lee@indigoart.net
Web site: http://www.indigoart.net
Dist(s): **Norfolk SPCA.**

Ind... Pubns., *(978-0-9646660)* Orders Addr.: 68-1030 Mauna Lani Point Dr. Kamuela, HI 96743 USA (SAN 298-9921) Tel 808-345-2001; 808-345-0805
...mail: mel@malinowski.com; judy@malinowski.com
... site: http://www.snorkelguides.com.
...a Pr., LLC, *(978-1-935171; 978-1-938101; ...63066)* 931-B S. Main St., Box 145, Kernersville, ...284 USA
...willhodam@yahoo.com;
...apress@gmail.com
... http://secondwindpublishing.com/;
...oseapress.com
...ashwords.
...ducation Systems/Poppy Lane
...*(978-0-938911)* Orders Addr.: P.O. Box
... CA 93755 USA (SAN 661-8405) Tel
... Edit Addr.: 134 Poppy Ln., Clovis, CA
...N 661-8413)
...4@aol.com
...ww.poppylane.com
... West Bks.
...ng.com, *(978-1-60444)* 4215
...7, Studio City, CA 91602 USA
...gmail.com
...uropeanPublishing.com.
...*2191)* 250 N. 3rd Ave. #224,
... USA Tel 612-379-4743
...ulgencepress.com.
...*-0-9860691)* 61-33
...ARK, NY 11374 USA Tel
...chase.com.
... *978-1-4043; 978-1-4142;*
...*-1-4353; 978-1-4378;*
...e 405, Cambridge, MA
...*510; 978-1-931026)*
...92057 USA Tel
... Toll Free:
...P.O. Box 9096,
... Americas,
...*nts:* Asia for

Infinite Adventure, *(978-0-9790720)* 6043 S. Danielson Way, Chandler, AZ 85249 USA
E-mail: amb0457@cox.net
Web site: http://www.members.cox.net/valuevolga.

Infinite Light Publishing, *(978-0-9884537)* 5142 Hollister Ave. No. 115, Santa Barbara, CA 93111 USA Tel 805-350-3239
E-mail: aynsgold@yahoo.com.

Infinite Love Publishing, *(978-0-9794827)* 15127 NE 24th St., No. 341, Redmond, WA 98052 USA (SAN 853-5264) Toll Free: 888-733-7105
E-mail: sales@jackiechristie.com; dotti@dotdesign.net
Web site: http://www.jackiechristie.com.

Infinite Visions Forum, *(978-0-9770405)* Orders Addr.: P.O. Box 938, La Verne, CA 91750 USA Tel 909-593-7332 (phone/fax); Edit Addr.: 4095 Fruit St., SP 938, La Verne, CA 91750 USA
E-mail: ivforum@aol.com.

Infinity Oak Bks., *(978-0-9885066)* Orders Addr.: P.O. Box 195964, Dallas, TX 75219 USA Tel 972-803-4744
E-mail: jillksayre@me.com.

Infinity Publishing *See* **Macro Publishing Group**

Infinity Publishing, *(978-0-9665678; 978-1-892896; 978-0-7414; 978-1-4958)* Div. of Buy Books On The Web.Com, 1094 New Dehaven St., Suite 100, West Conshohocken, PA 19428 USA Tel 610-941-9999; Fax: 610-941-9959; Toll Free: 877-289-2665
E-mail: info@infinitypublishing.com
Web site: http://www.buybooksontheweb.com; http://www.infinitypublishing.com/
Dist(s): **Smashwords.**

Infinity Publishing, *(978-0-9640184)* 8525 Evergreen Ln., Darien, IL 60561 USA Tel 708-985-2300; Fax: 708-985-2339 Do not confuse with companies with same name in Seattle WA, Lansing IL, West Palm Beach, FL.

Infinity Publishing Co., *(978-0-9799487)* 11111 N. Scottsdale Rd., Suite 205, Scottsdale, AZ 85260 USA Tel 480-703-0606
E-mail: pchambers8@cox.net
Web site: http://www.infinitypublishingcompany.com
Dist(s): **AtlasBooks Distribution.**

Infinity Studios LLC, *(978-1-59697)* 2601 Hilltop Dr. Apt. 815, San Pablo, CA 94806-5797 USA Do not confuse with companies with the same or similar name in Austin, TX
E-mail: info@infinitystudios.com
Web site: http://www.infinitystudios.com
Dist(s): **Diamond Comic Distributors, Inc.**
Diamond Bk. Distributors.

Infobus, Inc., *(978-0-9771184)* 19 Yellow Brook Rd., Holmdel, NJ 07733-1967 USA Tel 732-332-0232.

InfoHi Publishing, *(978-0-9678605; 978-0-9717849)* P.O. Box 1688, Fremont, CA 94538 USA Tel 831-685-1063
E-mail: linda@infohi.com
Web site: http://www.infohi.com
Dist(s): **Booklines Hawaii, Ltd.**

Information Age Publishing, Inc., *(978-1-930608; 978-1-931576; 978-1-59311; 978-1-60752; 978-1-61735; 978-1-62396; 978-1-68123)* P.O. Box 79049, Charlotte, NC 28271 USA (SAN 925-9228) Tel 704-752-9125; Fax: 704-752-9113 Do not confuse with Information Age Publishing in Exeter, NH
E-mail: iap@infoagepub.com; info@infoagepub.com
Web site: http://www.infoagepub.com
Dist(s): **ebrary, Inc.**

Infusionmedia Publishing, *(978-0-9704852; 978-0-9718677; 978-0-9796586; 978-0-9843101)* 140 N. 8th St., Suite 205, Lincoln, NE 68508-1358 USA (SAN 253-9136) Tel 402-477-2065 (phone/fax)
E-mail: info@infusionmediapublishing.com
Web site: http://www.infusionmediapublishing.com
Dist(s): **Smashwords.**

Ingalls Publishing Group, Inc., *(978-0-9713045; 978-1-932158)* Orders Addr.: P.O. Box 2500, Banner Elk, NC 28604 USA (SAN 254-3753) Tel 828-297-6884; Fax: 828-297-6880 (sales dept.); *Imprints:* Caystone Books (Claystne Bks) Do not confuse with High Country Pubs., Lakewood, CO
E-mail: bookkeeper@ingallspublishinggroup.com; editor@ingallspublishinggroup.com
Web site: http://www.ingallspublishinggroup.com; http://www.highcountrypublishers.com
Dist(s): **Lightning Source, Inc.**

Ingenuity 31 Inc., *(978-0-578-05331-8)* 109 N. Church St., Waynesboro, PA 17268 USA
E-mail: ingenuity31@yahoo.com.

Ingle, Rosalie, *(978-0-578-09876-0)* P.O. Box 8636, St. Joseph, MO 64508 USA.

Ingleside Pr., *(978-1-929883)* P.O. Box 30029, Baltimore, MD 21270 USA Fax: 320-205-6697
E-mail: inglesidepress@yahoo.com
Web site: http://www.behance.net/inglesidepress.

Ingram Pub. Services, Orders Addr.: Customer Services, Box 512 1 Ingram Blvd., LaVergne, TN 37086 USA Toll Free Fax: 800-838-1149; Edit Addr.: 1 Ingram Blvd., LaVergne, TN 37086 USA (SAN 631-8630) Tel 615-793-5000; Fax: 615-213-5811
E-mail: customer.service@ingrampublisherservices.com; Publisher@ingrampublisherservices.com; Retailer@ingrampublisherservices.com
Web site: http://www.ingrampublisherservices.com.

Ingram's Nutrition Consultations, *(978-0-9769379)* 43889 Bayview Ave. Apt. 40107, Clinton Twp, MI 48038-7073 USA; 7701 Corporate Dr., No.212, Houston, TX 77036 (SAN 850-5179) Tel 281-513-4596; Fax: 713-771-2177
E-mail: admin@ingramsnutritionconsultations.com
Web site: http://www.ingram's nutrition.com.

Inhabit Media Inc. (CAN) *(978-0-9782186; 978-1-926569; 978-1-927095; 978-1-77227) Dist. by* **IPG Chicago.**

Inheritance Pr., Inc., *(978-0-9638086; 978-0-9749501)* Orders Addr.: P.O. Box 580, Trenton, NC 28585-0580 USA; Edit Addr.: 388 Henderson Ln., Trenton, NC 28585 USA.

Inherst, Marie, *(978-0-9749785)* 52670 TH 180, Beallsville, OH 43716-9226 USA.

Ink & Feathers Comics, *(978-0-9664974)* Div. of Ink & Feathers Calligraphy, Orders Addr.: 202 E. Grove St., Streator, IL 61364 USA Tel 815-672-1171
E-mail: nerwonduh@hotmail.com
Web site: http://www.ifcomics.com.

Ink & Scribe, *(978-0-9679817; 978-1-931947)* Div. of Wise River Companies, Inc., 3101 Kintzley Ct. Unit J, Laporte, CO 80535-9393 USA Toll Free: 888-616-7720
E-mail: books@northfortynews.com
Web site: http://www.inkandscribe.com.

Ink Well, *(978-0-9767578)* P.O. Box 786, Winlock, WA 98596 USA; *Imprints:* Ink Well Publishing (I W P) Do not confuse with Ink Well in Hermosa Beach, CA.

Ink Well Publishing *Imprint of* **Ink Well**

Inkberry Pr., *(978-0-9742148)* 15521 Shell Point Blvd., Fort Myers, FL 33908 USA Tel 239-466-2757
E-mail: wallykain@comcast.net.

Inkberry Pr., *(978-0-9838293)* 4110 S. Highland Dr. Suite 340, Salt Lake City, UT 84124 USA Tel 801-949-1083
E-mail: editorial@leatherwoodpress.com.

Inkling Bks., *(978-1-58742)* 6528 Phinney Ave., N., Suite A, Seattle, WA 98103-5260 USA Tel 206-365-1624
E-mail: editor@inklingbooks.com
Web site: http://www.inklingbooks.com/
Dist(s): **Smashwords.**

Inknbeans Pr., *(978-0-615-62429-7; 978-0-615-62896-7; 978-0-615-63408-1; 978-0-615-64400-4; 978-0-615-68085-9; 978-0-615-71952-8; 978-0-615-72837-7; 978-0-615-73222-0; 978-0-9886670; 978-0-615-73861-1; 978-0-615-74204-5; 978-0-615-74488-9; 978-0-615-74719-4; 978-0-615-74944-0; 978-0-615-74958-7; 978-0-615-74961-7; 978-0-615-75145-0; 978-0-615-75791-9; 978-0-615-75854-1; 978-0-615-76442-9; 978-0-615-76749-9; 978-0-615-77178-6; 978-0-615-77534-0; 978-0-615-78970-5; 978-0-615-80657-0; 978-0-615-81135-2; 978-) 25060 Hancock Ave. Bldg 103 Suite 458, Murrieta, CA 92560 USA Tel 951-471-8184*
Web site: inknbeans.com
Dist(s): **CreateSpace Independent Publishing Platform.**

Inkshares, *(978-1-941758; 978-1-942645)* 415 Jackson St Suite B, San Francisco, CA 94111 USA Tel 919-418-0895
E-mail: thad@inkshares.com
Web site: inkshares.com
Dist(s): **Ingram Pub. Services.**

Inkspil Publishing, *(978-0-9833877; 978-0-615-79874-5)* 1676 W. Bryn Mawr, Chicago, IL 60660 USA Tel 708-824-8465
E-mail: inkspillbooks@gmail.com
Web site: www.inkspillbooks.com
Dist(s): **CreateSpace Independent Publishing Platform.**

Inkspill Publishing House *See* **Inkspil Publishing**

Inkwater Pr., *(978-0-9719414; 978-1-59299; 978-1-62901)* Div. of First Books, 6750 SW Franklin St., Suite A, Portland, OR 97223 USA Tel 503-968-6777; Fax: 503-968-6779
E-mail: orders@inkwaterpress.com
Web site: http://www.inkwaterpress.com; http://www.firstbooks.com.

Inkwell Productions, LLC, *(978-0-9658158; 978-0-9718155; 978-0-9728118; 978-0-9749701; 978-0-9766340; 978-0-9786202; 978-0-9814648; 978-0-9829589; 978-0-9833247; 978-0-9848019; 978-0-9852501; 978-0-9883568; 978-1-939625; 978-0-9861743)* Orders Addr.: 10869 N. Scottsdale Rd., #103-128, Scottsdale, AZ 85254-5280 USA Tel 480-315-3781
E-mail: info@inkwellproductions.com
Web site: http://www.inkwellproductions.com.

InMediaRes Productions, *(978-0-9792047; 978-1-934857; 978-1-936876; 978-1-941582; 978-1-942487)* 303 91st Ave., PMB 202 E502, Lake Stevens, WA 98258 USA Fax: 425-948-1301; *Imprints:* Catalyst Game Labs (Catalyst Game)
Web site: http://www.imrpro.com; http://www.catalystgamelabs.com
Dist(s): **PSI (Publisher Services, Inc.).**

Innate Foundation Publishing, *(978-0-9745866)* 9682 Sherwood Dr., Blaine, WA 98230 USA Tel 360-441-9156
E-mail: rca@robertclydeaffolter.com
Web site: http://www.innatefoundation.com.

Inner Circle Publishing, *(978-0-9770682)* 1407 Crane St., Schenectady, NY 12303 USA Tel 518-377-0548.

Inner City Publications *See* **Citified Pubns.**

Inner Learning, *(978-1-930640)* 349 N. Detroit St., Los Angeles, CA 90036 USA Tel 323-549-0279; 923-549-0279; Fax: 323-549-0289
Dist(s): **Feldheim Pubs.**

Inner Light - Global Communications, *(978-0-938294; 978-1-892062; 978-1-60611)* Orders Addr.: P.O. Box 753, New Brunswick, NJ 08903 USA (SAN 662-0191) Tel 646-331-6777; Edit Addr.: 1231 Hamilton St., Somerset, NJ 08873 USA
E-mail: mrufo@hotmail.com
Dist(s): **Distributors, The**
Distributors International
New Leaf Distributing Co., Inc.
Quality Bks., Inc.
Red Wheel/Weiser
Unique Bks., Inc.

†Inner Traditions International, Ltd., *(978-0-89281; 978-1-59477; 978-1-62055)* Orders Addr.: P.O. Box 388, Rochester, VT 05767-0388 USA Tel 802-767-3174; Fax: 802-767-3726; Toll Free Fax: 800-246-8648; Edit Addr.: One Park St., Rochester, VT 05767 USA (SAN 208-6948) Tel 802-767-3174; Fax: 802-767-3726; *Imprints:* Healing Arts Press (Heal Arts VT); Bindu Books (Bindu Bks)
E-mail: customerservice@innertraditions.com; info@innertraditions.com
Web site: http://www.innertraditions.com
Dist(s): **Beekman Bks., Inc.**
Book Wholesalers, Inc.
Bookazine Co., Inc.
Brodart Co.
Integral Yoga Pubns.
Library Sales of N.J.
Lotus Pr.
MyiLibrary
New Leaf Distributing Co., Inc.
Nutri-Bks. Corp.
Partners/West Book Distributors
Quality Bks., Inc.
Simon & Schuster
Simon & Schuster, Inc.
Unique Bks., Inc.; *CIP.*

Inner Wisdom Pubns., *(978-0-9656741; 978-0-9774921)* 22850 Summit Rd., Los Gatos, CA 95033 USA (SAN 299-2450) Tel 408-353-2050; Fax: 408-353-4663; Toll Free: 888-468-4335
E-mail: 15minutemiracle@verizon.net
Web site: http://www.15MinuteMiracle.com.

InnerChamp Bks., *(978-0-9663949)* P.O. Box 11362, Santa Rosa, CA 95406 USA Tel 707-571-8023; Fax: 707-546-3764
E-mail: inrchamp@aol.com
Web site: http://www.innerchamp.com.

Innerchild Publishing, Inc., *(978-0-9768078)* Orders Addr.: P.O. Box 142317, Fayetteville, GA 30214-2317 USA.

Innerchoice Publishing, *(978-0-9625486; 978-1-56499)* 24426 S. Main, Carson, CA 90745 USA Tel 310-816-3085; Fax: 310-816-3092
Dist(s): **Jalmar Pr.**

InnerCircle Publishing, *(978-1-882918; 978-0-9723191; 978-0-9755214; 978-0-9762924)* 522 Sadie St. Apt. 2, Laurens, IA 50554-1553 USA
Web site: http://www.innercirclepublishing.com; http://www.rev-press.com
Dist(s): **AtlasBooks Distribution.**

InnerRESOURCES Pubns., *(978-0-9728389)* 109 E. 73rd St., New York, NY 10021 USA
E-mail: jeff@jeffandau.com; jeffandau@innerresources.org
Web site: http://jeffs.smugmug.com/; http://www.jeffandau.com; http://www.innerresources.org; http://www.flickr.com/photos/8ideas/
Dist(s): **Lightning Source, Inc.**

Innertuber, *(978-0-9742742)* 2124 NE 7th St., Gainesville, FL 32609 USA.

Innov8 Studios, *(978-0-9754544)* 16 Cedarwood Dr., Ballston Lake, NY 12019 USA
E-mail: innov8studios@nycap.rr.com.

Innovation Game, The, *(978-0-9643819)* 8509 Irvington Ave., Bethesda, MD 20817 USA Tel 301-530-4299.

Innovation Pr., The, *(978-1-943147)* 391 SE Crystal Creek Cir, Issaquah, WA 98027 USA Tel 360-870-9988
E-mail: asiacitro@gmail.com
Web site: www.theinnovationpress.com
Dist(s): **Perseus-PGW.**

Innovative Christian Pubns. *Imprint of* **Baker Trittin Pr.**

Innovative Kids, *(978-1-58476; 978-1-60169)* Div. of Innovative USA, Inc., 18 Ann St., Norwalk, CT 06854-2258 USA Tel 203-838-6400; Fax: 203-855-5582; *Imprints:* IKIDS (IKIDS)
E-mail: info@innovativekids.com
Web site: http://www.innovativekids.com
Dist(s): **Hachette Bk. Group.**

Innovative Language, LLC, *(978-0-9765236)* P.O. Box 1593, Eugene, OR 97440-1593 USA.

Innovative Logistics, Orders Addr.: 575 Prospect St., Lakewood, NJ 08701 USA (SAN 760-6532) Tel 732-534-7001; 732-363-5679; Fax: 732-363-0338
E-mail: innlogorders@innlog.net
Web site: http://www.innlog.net.

Innovo Pr. *Imprint of* **Innovo Publishing, LLC**

Innovo Publishing, LLC, *(978-0-9815403; 978-1-936076; 978-1-61314)* 159 College St., Collierville, TN 38017 USA Fax: 901-221-4055; Toll Free: 888-546-2111; *Imprints:* Innovo Press (Innovo Pr)
E-mail: info@innovopublishing.com; terry@innovopublishing.com
Web site: http://www.innovopublishing.com.

Insect Lore, *(978-1-891541)* Orders Addr.: P.O. Box 1535, Shafter, CA 93263 USA Tel 661-746-6047; Fax: 661-746-0334; Toll Free: 800-548-3284; Edit Addr.: 132 S. Beech St., Shafter, CA 93263 USA
E-mail: john@insectlore.com
Web site: http://www.insectlore.com.

Insect Sciences Museum of California, *(978-0-9764454)* 3644 Calafia Ave., Oakland, CA 94605 USA; *Imprints:* Exploring California Insects (Ex CA In)
E-mail: insectnet@aol.com
Web site: http://www.bugpeople.org.

Inside Pocket Publishing *Imprint of* **Lerner Publishing Group**

Inside Pocket Publishing, Ltd. (GBR) *(978-0-9562315; 978-0-9567449; 978-0-9567122; 978-1-908458) Dist. by* **Lerner Pub.**

Insight Editions LP, *(978-1-933784; 978-1-60887; 978-0-615-39977-5; 978-0-615-50360-8; 978-0-615-50366-0)* 800 A St., San Rafael, CA 94901 USA
Web site: http://www.insighteditionscreative.com
Dist(s): **Perseus-PGW**
Perseus Bks. Group.

Insight Publishing Group, *(978-1-930027; 978-1-932503)* Div. of Insight International, Inc., 8801 S. Yale, Suite 410, Tulsa, OK 74137 USA Tel 918-493-1718; Fax: 918-493-2219; Toll Free: 800-924-8264 Do not confuse with companies with similar names in Parker, CO,

Yreka,CA, Jacksonville, FL, Woodbridge, VA, Salt Lake City, UT
E-mail: info@freshword.com
Web site: http://www.freshword.com
Dist(s): **Smashwords.**

Insight Services, Inc, (*978-0-9786034*) 1020 Hummingbird Ct., Springfield, TN 37172-5563 USA (SAN 851-092X); *Imprints:* Children's Insight (Children's Insight)
E-mail: childrensinsight@learnlivebetter.com
Web site: http://www.learnlivebetter.com.

Insight Studios, LLC *See* **Bugeye Bks.**

Insight Technical Education, (*978-0-9722058; 978-0-9755280*) 13410 NE 92nd St., Vancouver, WA 98682 USA Tel 360-852-6152
E-mail: webinfo@sixbranches.com
Web site: http://www.insightteched.com.

Inspirasian Pr. LLC, (*978-0-9743882*) P.O. Box 460256, San Francisco, CA 94146-0256 USA Tel 415-282-7925; Fax: 415-282-6427
Web site: http://www.inspirasian.com
Dist(s): **AtlasBooks Distribution.**

Inspiration Pr. Inc., (*978-0-9798395*) 8598 N. W. St., Coral Springs, FL 33071 USA
Dist(s): **TNT Media Group, Inc.**

Inspiration Software, Inc., (*978-0-928539; 978-1-932463; 978-1-933238; 978-1-934425*) 9400 SW Beaverton Hillsdale Hwy., No. 300, Beaverton, OR 97005 USA (SAN 670-8234) Toll Free: 800-877-4292
E-mail: jbrooks@inspiration.com
Web site: http://www.inspiration.com
Dist(s): **Follett School Solutions.**

Inspirational Hse. of America, (*978-0-9768598*) 93 Jay Ln., Gasburg, VA 23857 USA.

Inspire Every Child dba Illumination Arts, (*978-0-615-50779-8; 978-0-9855417*) 808 6th St. S., Ste 200, Kirkland, WA 98033 USA Tel 425-968-5097; Fax: 425-968-5634
E-mail: jthompson@illumin.com
Web site: www.illumin.com.

Inspire Media, LLC *See* **Motivision Media**

Inspire Press, Inc., (*978-0-9741800*) P.O. Box 33241, Los Gatos, CA 95030 USA Tel 408-395-2003; Fax: 408-904-4662
E-mail: sharper@inspirepress.com
Web site: http://www.inspirepress.com.

Inspire Pubns., (*978-0-9725292*) 13229 Middle Canyon Rd., Carmel Valley, CA 93924 USA (SAN 255-1225) Tel 831-917-6059; Fax: 831-659-8460
E-mail: larryhayes@mynamestartswith.com; lhayes@mynamestartswith.com
Web site: http://www.mynamestartswith.com.

Inspire U., LLC, (*978-0-9792361*) 30520 Rancho California Rd., Suite 107-64, Temecula, CA 92591 USA (SAN 852-8535).

Inspired By Family, (*978-0-9787074*) 1332 Westmore Ct., Srevens Point, WI 54481 USA
Web site: http://www.inspiredbyfamily.com.

Inspired by the Beach Co., (*978-0-9790415*) Orders Addr.: P.O. Box 174, Simpsonville, MD 21150-0174 USA
E-mail: mjareaux@ureach.com
Web site: http://www.26thingstoteach.com.

Inspired By the Beach Publishing *See* **Inspired by the Beach Co.**

InspirEd Educators, (*978-1-933558; 978-1-938275*) 350 Waverly Hall Cir., Roswell, GA 30075 USA Tel 770-649-7571; Fax: 770-642-7568; Toll Free: 866-WE-INSPIRE (866-934-6774)
E-mail: sharon@inspirededucators.com; lainey@inspirededucators.com
Web site: http://www.inspirededucators.com.

Inspired Idea, (*978-1-931203*) 165 Forestbrook Dr. #713, Lewisville, TX 75067 USA
E-mail: Eve@kneelingmedia.org; Eve@Engelbrite.com
Web site: http://www.kneelingmedia.org.

Inspiring Voices *Imprint of* **Author Solutions, Inc.**

Inspirio, (*978-0-310*) 5300 Patterson Ave., SE, Grand Rapids, MI 49530 USA Tel 1-800-727-3480
E-mail: zprod@zondervan.com
Web site: http://www.zondervan.com
Dist(s): **Zondervan.**

Instant Pub., (*978-1-59196; 978-1-59872; 978-1-60458; 978-1-61422*) Orders Addr.: P.O. Box 985, Collierville, TN 38027 USA Tel 901-853-7070; Fax: 901-853-6196; Toll Free: 800-259-2592; Edit Addr.: 410 Hwy, 72 W., Collierville, TN 38017 USA
Web site: http://www.instantpublisher.com
Dist(s): **BookBaby**
Lulu Enterprises Inc.
Smashwords.

Instantpublisher.com *See* **Instant Pub.**

Institute For Behavior Change Incorporated The, (*978-0-9770503*) 9900 W. Sample Rd., Suite 300, Coral Springs, FL 33065 USA Tel 954-755-6639; Fax: 954-755-4100
E-mail: rhall3318@acn.net
Web site: http://www.afterthestormchildrensbook.com.

Institute for Conscious Change, The, (*978-0-9743443*) Div. of BioPlan Associates, Inc., Orders Addr.: 8987 E. Tanque Verde Rd. Ste. 309, Tucson, AZ 85749-9399 USA
E-mail: info@ConsciousChange.org
Web site: http://www.ConsciousChange.org.

Institute for Creation Research, (*978-0-932766; 978-1-935587*) 1806 Royal Ln., Dallas, TX 75229 USA Tel 214-615-8331.

Institute for Disabilities Research & Training, Inc., (*978-0-9667589; 978-0-9752933; 978-0-9760818; 978-0-9789373*) 11323 Amherst Ave., Wheaton, MD 20902 USA Tel 301-942-4326; Fax: 301-942-4439
E-mail: sales@idrt.com
Web site: http://www.idrt.com.

Institute for Economic Democracy Pr., Inc., (*978-0-9624423; 978-0-9753555; 978-1-933567*) 13851 N. 103rd Ave., Sun City, AZ 85351-4520 USA Tel 623-583-2518; Toll Free: 888-533-1020 (credit card orders)
E-mail: cc@ccus.info; ied@ied.info
Web site: http://www.ied.info.

Institute for Food & Development Policy/Food First Bks., (*978-0-935028*) 398 60th St., Oakland, CA 94618-1212 USA (SAN 213-327X) Tel 510-654-4400; Fax: 510-654-4551
E-mail: marthak@foodfirst.org
Web site: http://www.foodfirst.org
Dist(s): **L P C Group**
Perseus-PGW
Perseus Bks. Group
Perseus Distribution.

Institute For Outdoor Awareness, Inc, (*978-0-9835176; 978-0-9915227*) 41 Linden Ave., Rutledge, PA 19070 USA Tel 610-544-8335
E-mail: phil@bartowassoc.com
Web site: phil@bartowassoc.com.

Institute for Preventative Sports Med., (*978-0-9745655*) P.O. Box 7032, Ann Arbor, MI 48107 USA Tel 734-434-3390; Fax: 734-572-4503
E-mail: admin@ipsm.org
Web site: http://www.ipsm.org.

Institute of Cybernetics Research, Inc., (*978-1-893375; 978-1-58578*) Orders Addr.: 15 W. 139th St. Apt. 10G, New York, NY 10037-1516 USA
E-mail: icri@usa.net; journal_of_amateur_computing-subscribe@yahoogroups.com
Web site: http://groups.yahoo.com/groups/journal_of_amateur_computing/join
Dist(s): **American Heritage Magazine**
Analos Magazine
Theme Stream, Inc.
Wiley, John & Sons, Inc.

Institute of Physics Publishing, (*978-0-7503; 978-0-85274; 978-0-85498*) The Public Ledte Bldg., Suite 1035 150 S. Independence Mall, W., Philadelphia, PA 19106 USA (SAN 298-2315) Tel 215-627-0880; Fax: 215-627-0879; Toll Free: 800-632-0880; Dirac House Temple Back, Bristol, BS1 6BE Tel 44 (0) 117 929 7481; Fax: 44 (0) 117 930 1186
E-mail: book.enquiries@iop.org
Web site: http://bookmark.iop.org
Dist(s): **American International Distribution Corp.**
CRC Pr. LLC
National Bk. Network.

Instream Flow Council, (*978-0-9716743*) c/o Wyoming Game & Fish, 5400 Bishop Blvd., Cheyenne, WY 82002 USA Tel 307-777-4600; Fax: 307-777-4611
E-mail: tannea@state.wy.us
Dist(s): **AtlasBooks Distribution.**

Instructional Fair *Imprint of* **Carson-Dellosa Publishing, LLC**

Instructional Resources Co., (*978-1-879478*) P.O. Box 111704, Anchorage, AK 99511-1704 USA Tel 907-345-6689 (phone/fax)
E-mail: susan@susancanthony.com
Web site: http://www.susancanthony.com.

Instrument Society of America *See* **ISA**

Insu-Form, Incorporated *See* **I.Form Ink, Publishing**

Intaglio, Inc., (*978-0-9748034*) P.O. Box 211296, Montgomery, AL 36109 USA Tel 706-593-2749; Fax: 334-260-9373
E-mail: sperez@intaglioinc.com
Web site: http://www.intaglioinc.com.

Intaglio Pr., (*978-0-944091*) Orders Addr.: P.O. Box 9952, College Station, TX 77842 USA (SAN 242-7133) Tel 409-696-7800; Toll Free: 800-768-5565; Edit Addr.: 8709 Bent Tree, College Station, TX 77845 USA (SAN 242-7141)
E-mail: HDETHL9414@aol.com.

†Integral Yoga Pubns., (*978-0-932040; 978-1-938477*) Satchidananda Ashram-Yogaville, 108 Yogaville Way, Buckingham, VA 23921 USA (SAN 285-0338) Tel 434-969-3121 ex 102; Fax: 434-969-1303; Toll Free: 800-262-1008 (orders)
Web site: http://www.yogaville.org
Dist(s): **AtlasBooks Distribution**
BookMasters Distribution Services (BDS)
MyiLibrary
New Leaf Distributing Co., Inc.
ebrary, Inc.; *CIP.*

Intelligent Concepts, Inc., (*978-0-9740612*) 1889 N. Airport Dr., Lehi, UT 84043 USA Tel 801-766-0262
E-mail: joe@intelcon.biz
Web site: http://www.intelcon.biz.

Intellipop, LLC, (*978-0-9743805*) 2701 Troy Center Dr., Suite 275, Troy, MI 48084 USA Tel 248-269-6091; Fax: 248-269-6092
E-mail: info@intellipop.com
Web site: http://www.intellipop.com.

Interaction Point Games, LLC, (*978-1-936326*) 4544 Chowen Ave. N., Robbinsdale, MN 55422 USA
E-mail: brent@interactionpoint.com; info@interactionpoint.com
Web site: http://www.interactionpoint.com.

Interaction Pubs., Inc., (*978-1-57336*) Orders Addr.: P.O. Box 900, Fort Atkinson, WI 53538 USA; Edit Addr.: W5527 State Rd. 106, Fort Atkinson, WI 53538-0800 USA (SAN 631-2950) Tel 920-563-9571; Fax: 920-563-7395; Toll Free: 800-359-0961
E-mail: sales@interact-simulations.com; interact@highsmith.com
Web site: http://www.interact-simulations.com/; http://www.teachinteract.com.

Interactive Eye, L.L.C. *Imprint of* **Interactive Knowledge, Inc.**

Interactive Knowledge, Inc., (*978-0-9759464*) 142 High St., No. 618, Portland, ME 04101 USA Tel 207-775-2278; Fax: 413-778-6861; *Imprints:* Interactive Eye, L.L.C. (InterEye) Do not confuse with Interactive Knowledge, Inc., Charlotte, NC
E-mail: support@iknow.net
Web site: http://www.iknow.net.

Interactive Media Publishing, (*978-0-9744391; 978-1-934332*) Orders Addr.: P.O. Box 1407, Phoenix, OR 97535-1407 USA (SAN 256-095X) Tel 541-535-5552; Fax: 888-900-1598; *Imprints:* Once Upon A Time in a Classroom (OnceUponTime)
E-mail: orders@i-mediapub.com; linda@i-mediapub.com
Web site: http://www.i-mediapub.com; http://www.interactivemediapub.com
Dist(s): **New Leaf Distributing Co., Inc.**

Interactive Pubns. Pty, Ltd. (AUS) (*978-1-876819; 978-1-921479; 978-1-921869; 978-0-646-32685-6; 978-0-646-32746-4; 978-1-922120; 978-1-925231*)
Dist. by **SPD-Small Pr Dist.**

Interactive Pubns. Pty, Ltd. (AUS) (*978-1-876819; 978-1-921479; 978-1-921869; 978-0-646-32685-6; 978-0-646-32746-4; 978-1-922120; 978-1-925231*)
Dist. by **LightSource CS.**

Interactive Pubns. Pty, Ltd. (AUS) (*978-1-876819; 978-1-921479; 978-1-921869; 978-0-646-32685-6; 978-0-646-32746-4; 978-1-922120; 978-1-925231*)
Dist. by **CreateSpace.**

Intercollegiate Studies Institute, Incorporated *See* **ISI Bks.**

Intercultural Communication Services, Inc., (*978-0-9741881; 978-0-9773359*) 2580 SW 76th Ave., Portland, OR 97225-3305 USA Fax: 503-292-6817
E-mail: jolinda@jolindaosborne.com
Web site: http://www.jolindaosborne.com.

†Intercultural Pr., Inc., (*978-0-933662; 978-1-877864; 978-1-931930; 978-0-9842471*) Div. of Nicholas Brealey Publishing, Ltd., 20 Park Plaza, Suite 1115A, Boston, MA 02116 USA (SAN 212-6699) Tel 617-523-3801; Fax: 617-523-3708; Toll Free: 888-273-2539
E-mail: books@interculturalpress.com; cdresner@nicholasbrealey.com
Web site: http://www.interculturalpress.com
Dist(s): **Consortium Bk. Sales & Distribution**
MyiLibrary
National Bk. Network
Perseus Bks. Group; *CIP.*

Interdimensional Pr., (*978-0-9827753; 978-0-9911970*) 480 Lakeview Dr. Suite 107, Brentwood, CA 94513 USA Tel 925-513-1596 (phone/fax)
E-mail: pmcculley@comcast.net
Dist(s): **Lightning Source, Inc.**

Interface Publishing *See* **IGI Pr.**

Interior Dept. *Imprint of* **United States Government Printing Office**

Interlink Bks. *Imprint of* **Interlink Publishing Group, Inc.**

Interlink Publishing Group, Inc., (*978-0-940793; 978-1-56656; 978-1-62371*) 46 Crosby St., Northampton, MA 01060-1804 USA (SAN 664-8908) Tel 413-582-7054; Fax: 413-582-6731; Toll Free: 800-238-5465; *Imprints:* Crocodile Books (Crocodile Bks); Interlink Books (Interlink Bks)
E-mail: info@interlinkbooks.com; editor@interlinkbooks.com
Web site: http://www.interlinkbooks.com
Dist(s): **Constellation Digital Services**
MyiLibrary
Perseus Bks. Group.

Interlink Resources International *See* **CJR**

Intermedia Publishing Group, (*978-0-9820458; 978-0-9819682; 978-1-935529; 978-1-935906; 978-1-937654; 978-0-615-56309-1*) Orders Addr.: P.O. Box 2825, Peoria, AZ 85380 USA Tel 623-337-8710; Fax: 623-867-9469
E-mail: halton@intermediapr.com; ldavis@intermediapr.com
Web site: http://www.intermediapub.com.

Intermedio Editores S.A. (COL) (*978-958-637*) *Dist. by* **Random.**

International Arts & Artists, (*978-0-9662859; 978-0-9767102; 978-0-9883497*) 9 Hillyer Ct., NW, Washington, DC 20008 USA Fax: 202-333-0758
E-mail: design@artsandartists.org; designstudio@artsandartists.org
Web site: http://www.artsandartists.org
Dist(s): **Tuttle Publishing**
Univ. of Washington Pr.

†International Bk. Ctr., Inc., (*978-0-86685; 978-0-917062*) 2007 Laurel Dr., P.O. Box 295, Troy, MI 48099 USA (SAN 169-4014) Tel 248-879-8720; 586-254-7230; Fax: 586-254-7230
E-mail: ibc@ibcbooks.com
Web site: http://www.ibcbooks.com; *CIP.*

International Bk. Import Service, Inc., Orders Addr.: 161 Main St., P.O. Box 8188, Lynchburg, TN 37352-8188 USA (SAN 630-5679) Tel 931-759-7400; Fax: 931-759-7555; Toll Free: 800-277-4247
E-mail: IBIS@IBIService.com
Web site: http://www.IBIService.com.

International Business Pubns., USA, (*978-0-7397; 978-0-9646241; 978-1-57751; 978-1-4330; 978-1-4387; 978-1-5145*) P.O. Box 15343, Washington, DC 20003 USA Tel 202-546-2103; Fax: 202-546-3275; 6301 Stevenson Ave., # 1317, Alexandria, VA 22304 Tel 202-656-2103; Fax: 202-546-3275 Do not confuse with International Business Pubn., Inc. in Cincinnati, OH
E-mail: rusric@erols.com; ibpusa@comcast.net; ibpusa3@gmail.com
Web site: http://www.ibpus.com
Dist(s): **Lulu Enterprises Inc.**

International Church of the Foursquare Gospel *See* **Foursquare Media, ICFG**

International Comics & Entertainment L.L.C., (*978-1-929090; 978-1-932575*) 1005 Mahone St., Fredericksburg, VA 22401 USA Tel 540-899-9186; Fax: 540-899-9196
E-mail: kblue@ic-ent.com
Web site: http://www.ic-ent.com
Dist(s): **Diamond Comic Distributors, Inc.**

International Council for Computers in Education *See* **International Society for Technology in Education**

International Council for Gender Studies, (*978-1-929656*) Orders Addr.: P.O. Box 702, Waxahachie, TX 75168 USA Fax: 972-937-9930; Toll Free: 800-317-6958
E-mail: rivilian@yahoo.com; icgsinfo@yahoo.com
Web site: http://www.fiveaspects.com; www.5aspects.org.

International Debate Education Assn., (*978-0-9702130; 978-0-9720541; 978-1-932716; 978-1-61770*) 224 W. 57th St., New York, NY 10019 USA Tel 212-547-6932; Fax: 646-557-2416; 105 E. 22nd St. Suite 915, New York, NY 10010 Tel 212-300-6076 x9
E-mail: martin.greenwald@opensocietyfoundations.org
Web site: http://www.idebate.org
Dist(s): **Books International, Inc.**

International Development Ctr., (*978-0-9774483; 978-0-9799873*) P.O. Box 25163, Arlington, VA 22202 USA Tel 703-766-0643
E-mail: mi.productions@yahoo.com; ouatiss@yahoo.com.

International Educational Improvement Ctr. Pr., (*978-1-884169*) Orders Addr.: c/o Dr. Archie W. Earl, Sr., Mathematics Dept. School of Science & Technology Norfork State University, Norfolk, VA 23504 USA Tel 757-823-9564
E-mail: awearl@nsu.edu
Web site: http://www.webspawner.com/users/ieicpress/index.html.

International Graphic Group, (*978-0-9821692*) 838 Reedy St., Cincinnati, OH 45202 USA Tel 513-321-7884; Fax: 513-621-1619
E-mail: sales@iggbooks.com.

International Institute for Ecological Agriculture, (*978-0-9790437*) 309 Cedar St. No.127, Santa Cruz, CA 95060 USA (SAN 852-2847) Tel 831-471-9164; Toll Free: 888-737-6228
E-mail: ourstore@permaculture.com
Web site: http://www.permaculture.com.

International Language Centre, 1753 Connecticut Ave., NW, Washington, DC 20009 USA (SAN 209-1615) Tel 202-332-2894; Fax: 202-462-6657
E-mail: richard@newsinform.com; zisa@newsinform.com
Web site: http://www.newsinform.com.

International Learning Systems, Incorporated *See* **International Language Centre**

International Linguistics Corp., (*978-0-939990; 978-1-887371; 978-0-9814540*) 12220 Blue Ridge Blvd., Suite G, Grandview, MO 64030 USA (SAN 220-2573)
E-mail: jennifer@learnables.com
Web site: http://www.learnables.com.

International Localization Network, (*978-1-935018*) 9419 South Hill Rd., Colden, NY 14033 USA Tel 913-773-8323
E-mail: randy2905@gmail.com.

International Marine/Ragged Mountain Pr. *Imprint of* **McGraw-Hill Professional Publishing**

†International Monetary Fund, (*978-0-939934; 978-1-55775; 978-1-58906; 978-1-61635; 978-1-4518; 978-1-4519; 978-1-4527; 978-1-4552; 978-1-4623; 978-1-4639; 978-1-4755; 978-1-4843; 978-1-4983; 978-1-5135*) c/o Publications Department, 700 19th St., NW, Washington, DC 20431 USA (SAN 203-8188) Tel 202-623-7899
E-mail: tdelrosario@imf.org; salavi@imf.org; jbeardow@imf.org
Web site: http://www.imf.org; http://.www.cibrary.imf.org
Dist(s): **Bernan Assocs.**
MyiLibrary
ebrary, Inc.; *CIP.*

International Pacific Halibut Commission, (*978-0-9776931*) P.O. Box 95009, Seattle, WA 98145-2009 USA Tel 206-634-1838
E-mail: lauri@iphc.washington.edu
Web site: http://www.iphc.washington.edu.

International Scientific Ctr., (*978-0-9630594*) 2655 E. 21st St., Brooklyn, NY 11235 USA Tel 718-368-2918.

International Society for Technology in Education, (*978-0-924667; 978-1-56484*) 175 W. Broadway., Suite 300, Eugene, OR 97401-3003 USA (SAN 296-7693) Toll Free: 800-336-5191
E-mail: iste@iste.org
Web site: http://www.iste.org
Dist(s): **Follett School Solutions.**

International Society of Sephardic Leadership Council *See* **ISLC**

International Specialized Bk. Services, 920 NE 58th Ave., Suite 300, Portland, OR 97213-3786 USA (SAN 169-7129) Tel 503-287-3093; Fax: 503-280-8832; Toll Free: 800-944-6190
E-mail: info@isbs.com
Web site: http://www.isbs.com
Dist(s): **ebrary, Inc.**

International Standard Book Numbering (ISBN) Agency (interim numbering procedure) *See* **U. S. ISBN Agency**

International Step by Step Assn., (*978-1-931854; 978-1-60195*) 400 W. 59th St., New York, NY 10019 USA
E-mail: info@issa.nl
Web site: http://www.issa.nl.

International Tamil Language Foundation, (*978-0-9676212; 978-0-9793059*) 8417 Autumn Dr., Woodridge, IL 60517 USA Tel 630-985-3141; Fax: 630-985-3199
E-mail: Thiru@kural.org
Web site: http://www.kural.org.

International Training, Inc., *(978-1-931451; 978-1-61011)* 18 Elm St., Topsham, ME 04086 USA Tel 207-729-4201; Fax: 207-729-4453; Toll Free: 888-778-9073
E-mail: worldhq@tdisdi.com
Web site: http://www.tdisdi.com.

International Univ. Line, *(978-0-9636817; 978-0-9720774)* P.O. Box 2525, La Jolla, CA 92038 USA Tel 858-457-0595; Fax: 858-581-9073
E-mail: info@iul-press.com.

International Vaquero Productions, *(978-0-9761103)* 730 W. 8th St., Claremont, CA 91711 USA
E-mail: ivp1@me.com
Web site: http://www.kurtbeardsley.com.

International Wizard of Oz Club, The, *(978-1-930764)* P.O. Box 26249, San Francisco, CA 94126-6249 USA Fax: 510-642-7589 Do not confuse with International Wizard of OZ Club, Appleton, WI
E-mail: phanff@library.berkeley.edu
Web site: http://ozclub.org.

Interpact Pr., *(978-0-9628700; 978-0-9964019)* Orders Addr.: 545 Westport Dr., Old Hickory, TN 37138-1115 USA Tel 727-393-6600; Fax: 866-374-3470
E-mail: sherra@alwayschaos.com
Web site: http://www.interpactinc.com.

Interplay Productions, *(978-1-57629)* 16815 Von Karman Ave., Irvine, CA 92606-4920 USA Tel 714-553-6655; Fax: 714-252-2820.

InterPress, *(978-0-9744173)* 14056 Fort Valley Rd., Fort Valley, VA 22652 USA; *Imprints*: Fort Valley Geology Study Center (Ft Valley)
E-mail: wjmelson@shentel.net
Web site: http://interpressusa.com.

InterRelations Collaborative, Inc., *(978-0-9761753)* P.O. Box 6280, Hamden, CT 06517-3503 USA.

Interset Pr., *(978-1-57433)* Orders Addr.: 35 Burns Hill Rd., Wilton, NH 03086 USA Tel 603-654-2949
E-mail: artistafloat@earthlink.net; woad@earthlink.net
Dist(s): **Lulu Enterprises Inc.**

Interstellar Publishing Co., *(978-0-9645957; 978-1-889599)* Orders Addr.: P.O. Box 7306, Beverly Hills, CA 90212 USA (SAN 298-5829) Tel 310-247-8154 (orders); Fax: 310-247-0622
E-mail: Interstlr@aol.com
Web site: http://www.interstellarpublishing.com.

Interstellar Trading & Publishing Company *See* **Interstellar Publishing Co.**

†InterVarsity Pr., *(978-0-8308; 978-0-85110; 978-0-85111; 978-0-87784; 978-1-85684; 978-1-84474; 978-1-5140; 978-1-78359)* Div. of InterVarsity Christian Fellowship of the USA, Orders Addr.: P.O. Box 1400, Downers Grove, IL 60515 USA (SAN 202-7089) Tel 630-734-4000; Fax: 630-734-4200; Toll Free: 800-843-7225 (other depts.); 800-843-9487 (orders); 800-843-1019 (customer service); 800-873-0143 (electronic ordering)
E-mail: email@ivpress.com
Web site: http://www.ivpress.com
Dist(s): **Midpoint Trade Bks., Inc.**
christianaudio
ebrary, Inc.; *CIP*.

Intervisual/Piggy Toes *Imprint of* **Bendon, Inc.**

InterWeave Corp., *(978-0-9771936; 978-0-9841041)* Orders Addr.: 5364 Ehrlich Rd. No. 248, Tampa, FL 33624 USA Tel 813-933-4431; Fax: 813-933-4311
E-mail: kimberly@wheredoyoufindgod.com; kking@wheredoyoufindgod.com
Web site: http://www.wheredoyoufindgod.com.

Into Action Publications *Imprint of* **Microcosm Publishing**

IntoPrint Publishing LLC, *(978-1-62352)* 4322 Harding Pike, SUite 417, Nashville, TN 37205 USA Tel 615-210-8593
E-mail: jpcampbell3@mac.com; jonathanperry@comcast.net.

Intralife Systems Publishing, *(978-0-9703102)* P.O. Box 1555, Layton, UT 84041 USA Tel 801-544-2470; Fax: 801-544-2518
E-mail: admin@frogbuster.com
Web site: http://www.frogbuster.com.

Intrepid Films, LLC, *(978-1-929931)* Orders Addr.: P.O. Box 566, Boulder, CO 80306-0566 USA Tel 303-443-2426; Fax: 303-541-9737; Toll Free: 800-279-0802
E-mail: sportinc@msn.com; marya@intrepidfilms.com
Web site: http://www.intrepidfilms.com.

Intrepid Ink, LLC, *(978-0-9843857; 978-1-935774; 978-1-937022; 978-1-943403)* Orders Addr.: P.O. Box 302, McFarland, WI 53558 USA Tel 608-318-3636; *Imprints*: Resurrected Press (ResurrectedPr)
E-mail: publisher@intrepidink.com; irene@intrepidink.com
Web site: http://www.intrepidink.com.

Intrigue Publishing, *(978-0-9762181; 978-0-9794788; 978-0-9893696; 978-1-940758)* 10200 Twisted Stalk Ct., Upper Marlboro, MD 20772 USA
E-mail: dbcamacho@hotmail.com
Web site: http://www.intriguepublishing.com.

Intuitive Arts Pr., *(978-0-9741334)* 15 E. Northwest Hwy., Suite 15 B, Palatine, IL 60067 USA
E-mail: katychance@juno.com
Web site: http://www.peakperformanceliving.info.

invenTEAM, LLC, *(978-0-9729599; 978-0-9833729)* 65064 Cline Falls Rd., Bend, OR 97701 USA (SAN 255-4593) Tel 541-948-0015
E-mail: e.wally@bendcable.com
Web site: http://www.e-wally.org.

Invisible College Pr., LLC, The, *(978-1-931468)* Orders Addr.: P.O. Box 209, Woodbridge, VA 22194 USA Tel 703-590-4005; Edit Addr.: 1206 N. Danville St., Arlington, VA 22201 USA; 3703 Del Mar Dr., Woodbridge, VA 22193
E-mail: manager@invispress.com
Web site: http://www.invispress.com/.

Invision Pubns., *(978-0-9767337)* 1136 Sherman Ave., Suite C4, Bronx, NY 10456 USA Tel 718-538-6102
E-mail: puzzles@puzzlesforus.com
Web site: http://www.puzzlesforus.com.

Invoke A Blessing Inc., *(978-0-9831902)* P.O. Box 163772, Fort Worth, TX 76161-3772 USA
E-mail: yuritereshchenko@hotmail.com; Yuritereshchenko@hotmail.com.

Invoke A Blessing Ministry *See* **Invoke A Blessing Inc.**

Inward Reflections, Inc., *(978-0-9746783)* P.O. Box 1747, Brockton, MA 02303-1747 USA
E-mail: inwardreflections@homestead.com.

Inyati Press, *(978-0-9777440)* P.O. Box 453, fulton, CA 95439 USA
E-mail: milton@webbellis.org
Web site: http://www.webbellis.org.

I.Om.Be Pr., *(978-1-882161)* Orders Addr.: P.O. Box 1387, New York, NY 10159 USA
Web site: http://about.me/josefinaBaezAyombeT.

IOS Pr., Inc., *(978-90-407; 978-90-5199; 978-90-6275; 978-0-9673355; 978-1-58603; 978-90-298; 978-1-60750; 978-1-61499)* 4502 Rachael Manor Dr., Fairfax, VA 22032 USA Tel 703-323-5600; Fax: 703-323-3668; Nieuwe Hemweg 6B, Amsterdam, 1013 BG Tel 31 (0)20 688 33 55; Fax: 31 (0)20 687 00 19
E-mail: iosbooks@iospress.com; orders@iospress.com
Web site: http://www.iospress.com
Dist(s): **Ebsco Publishing**
Metapress
MyiLibrary
ebrary, Inc.

Iowa Greyhound Association *See* **McKinnon, Robert Scott**

ipicturebooks *Imprint of* **ibooks, Inc.**

iPlayMusic, Inc., *(978-0-9760487; 978-0-9797683)* P.O. Box 391775, Mountain View, CA 94039 USA Tel 650-969-3387; Fax: 650-969-3680; Toll Free: 866-594-3344
E-mail: quincy@iplaymusic.com
Web site: http://www.iplaymusic.com
Dist(s): **Leonard, Hal Corp.**
Music Sales Corp.

IPMG Publishing, *(978-1-934218)* 18362 Erin Bay, Eden Prairie, MN 55347 USA (SAN 852-2057)
E-mail: webmaster@iplaymathgames.com
Web site: http://www.iplaymathgames.com.

Ippolito, Eva Marie, *(978-0-9705350; 978-0-615-11326-5)* 10316 W. Oakmont Dr., Sun City, AZ 85351-3528 USA.

Iran Books *See* **Ibex Pubs., Inc.**

Irene, Jan Pubns., *(978-0-9653428)* Orders Addr.: P.O. Box 934, Sonora, CA 95370 USA Tel 209-532-2470; Fax: 209-532-0277; Edit Addr.: 19575 Roselyn Ln., Sonora, CA 95370 USA
E-mail: janirene@mlode.com.

Iris Pallas-Luke E-Writings/E-Literature, *(978-0-9765637)* 12472 Lake Underhill Rd., Suite 267, Orlando, FL 32828 USA
E-mail: irispallasluke@msn.com; noir@noirpallasluke.com
Web site: http://www.irispallas-luke.com; http://www.barbarapallas-luke.com; http://www.vernninapallas-luke.com; http://www.noirpallas-luke.com.

Iris Publishing Group, Inc., The, *(978-0-916078; 978-1-60454)* 969 Oak Ridge Turnpike, No. 328, Oak Ridge, TN 37830-8832 USA Tel 865-483-0837; Fax: 865-481-3793; Toll Free: 800-881-2119
E-mail: rcumming@irisbooks.com
Web site: htt://irisbooks.com.

Irish American Bk. Co., Subs. of Roberts Rinehart Pubs., Inc., P.O. Box 666, Niwot, CO 80544-0666 USA Tel 303-652-2710; Fax: 303-652-2689; Toll Free: 800-452-7115
E-mail: irishbooks@aol.com
Web site: http://www.irishvillage.com.

Irish Bks. & Media, Inc., *(978-0-937702)* Orders Addr.: 2904 41st Ave S., Minneapolis, MN 55406-1814 USA (SAN 111-8870) Toll Free: 800-229-3505 Do not confuse with Irish Bks. in New York, NY
E-mail: Irishbook@aol.com
Web site: http://www.irishbook.com.

Irish Genealogical Foundation, *(978-0-940134)* Div. of O'Laughlin Pr., P.O. Box 7575, Kansas City, MO 64116 USA (SAN 218-4834) Tel 816-454-2410
E-mail: mike@Irishroots.com
Web site: http://www.IrishRoots.com
Dist(s): **Irish Bks. & Media, Inc.**

Irma's Bks., *(978-0-615-79138-8)* 930 W. Gunnison St., Chicago, IL 60640 USA Tel 5044278076
Dist(s): **CreateSpace Independent Publishing Platform.**

Iron Arm International, *(978-0-9746989)* 1 Reid St., Amsterdam, NY 12010-3424 USA Tel 518-842-9299
E-mail: Ironarm1@aol.com
Web site: http://www.uechiryu-karate.com
Dist(s): **Tuttle Publishing.**

Iron Ax Pr., *(978-0-9839469; 978-1-939746; 978-0-615-82878-7)* 4507 Clayhead Rd., Richmond, TX 77406 8118 USA Tel 281-341-5388
E-mail: uphofftx@hotmail.com
Dist(s): **CreateSpace Independent Publishing Platform.**

Iron Mountain Pr., *(978-0-9722961)* Orders Addr.: P.O. Box 7, New Milford, NY 10959 USA (SAN 256-0097)
E-mail: info@ironmountainpress.com
Web site: http://www.ironmountainpress.com.

Ironbound Pr., *(978-0-9763857)* P.O. Box 250, Winter Harbor, ME 04693-0250 USA Tel 207-963-2355; Fax: 320-323-2434 Do not confuse with Ironbound Pr. in Scotch Plains, NJ
E-mail: sales@ironboundpress.com
Web site: http://www.ironboundpress.com.

Ironcreek Pr., *(978-0-9766017)* 530 S. Pk. St., Asheboro, NC 27203 USA Tel 336-629-9533
E-mail: crottymartha@yahoo.com.

Ironcroft Publishing, *(978-0-9771688)* 11093 Alberta Dr., Brighton, MI 48114 USA
Web site: http://www.ironcroft.com
Dist(s): **BookBaby**
Partners Bk. Distributing, Inc.

Irongate Pr., *(978-0-9754746)* Orders Addr.: 1237 W. Seascape Dr., Gilbert, AZ 85233 USA Tel 480-813-2056
E-mail: jpascoe@irongatepress.com; j3pascoe@gmail.com
Web site: http://www.irongatepress.com
Dist(s): **Canyonlands Pubns.**
Forest Sales & Distributing Co.
Rio Nuevo Pubs.

Ironhorse Publishing Co., *(978-0-9747039)* 308 B W. Market St., Gratz, PA 17030 USA Fax: 717-365-7399 do not confuse with Ironhorse Publishing in Hayden Lake, ID
E-mail: pennvalleyprint@epix.net.

†Irvington Pubs., *(978-0-512; 978-0-8290; 978-0-8422; 978-0-89197)* Orders Addr.: P.O. Box 286, New York, NY 10276-0286 USA Fax: 212-861-0998; Toll Free Fax: 800-455-5520; Toll Free: 800-472-6037
Dist(s): **Addicus Bks.**
MyiLibrary; *CIP*.

Irwin, Christine, *(978-0-615-15008-6; 978-0-578-00787-8)* 4N 265 Avard Rd., West Chicago, IL 60185 USA
Dist(s): **Lulu Enterprises Inc.**

Irwin, Esther L., *(978-0-9778462)* 3531 Grove Dr., Cheyenne, WY 82001 USA Tel 307-632-2060
E-mail: Elivroman@bresnan.net.

†ISA, *(978-0-87664; 978-1-55617; 978-0-9791330; 978-0-9792343; 978-1-934394; 978-1-936007; 978-1-937560; 978-1-939660; 978-1-941546)* 67 Alexander Dr., Research Triangle Park, NC 27709 USA (SAN 202-7054) Tel 919-549-8411; Fax: 919-549-8288
E-mail: info@isa.org; ebell@isa.org
Web site: http://www.isa.org
Dist(s): **INscribe Digital**; *CIP*.

Isaac Publishing *See* **Ajoyin Publishing, Inc.**

Isaac Publishing, *(978-0-9787141; 978-0-9825218; 978-0-9853109; 978-0-9885930; 978-0-9892905; 978-0-9916145; 978-0-9967245)* 6731 Curran St., McLean, VA 22101 USA Tel 703-288-1681
E-mail: usa@barnabasaid.org
Web site: http://www.barnabasbooks.org
Dist(s): **BookBaby**
Send The Light Distribution LLC.

Isaacs, John, *(978-0-9779606)* 643 N. Main St., Lawrenceburg, KY 40342 USA (SAN 850-6191) Tel 502-418-1521
E-mail: jisaacs@kheaa.com.

iScribe Pubns. LLC, *(978-0-9883126)* 1006 Westbriar Dr., Henrico, VA 23238 USA Tel 804-441-3400; Fax: 804-741-7741
E-mail: info@iscribepublications.com.

ISD, 70 Enterprise Dr., Bristol, CT 06010 USA Tel 860-584-6546; Fax: 860-540-1001.

Isha Enterprises, Inc., *(978-0-936981)* P.O. Box 25970, Scottsdale, AZ 85255 USA (SAN 658-7895) Tel 480-502-9454; Fax: 480-991-5635; Toll Free: 800-641-6015
E-mail: info@easygrammar.com
Web site: http://www.easygrammar.com.

Ishi Pr. International, *(978-0-923891)* Div. of The Ishi Pr. (Japan), 461 Peachstone Terr., San Rafael, CA 94903-1327 USA (SAN 249-0749) Tel 917-507-7226
E-mail: samhsloan@gmail.com
Web site: http://www.anusha.com/ordering.html.

ISI Bks., *(978-1-882926; 978-1-932236; 978-1-933859; 978-1-935191; 978-1-61017)* 3901 Centerville Rd., Wilmington, DE 19807-1938 USA Toll Free Fax: 800-621-8476 (orders in the US & CAN); Toll Free: 800-526-7022; 800-621-2736 (orders M-F in the US & CAN)
E-mail: bookpub@isi.org
Web site: http://www.isibooks.org
Dist(s): **Chicago Distribution Ctr.**
MyiLibrary
Open Road Integrated Media, LLC
Univ. of Chicago Pr.

ISIS Large Print Bks. (GBR) *(978-0-7531; 978-1-85089; 978-1-85695) Dist. by* **Transaction Pubs.**

ISIS Large Print Bks. (GBR) *(978-0-7531; 978-1-85089; 978-1-85695) Dist. by* **Ulverscroft US.**

Isis Publishing Hse., Inc., *(978-0-9662281)* 4620 Kings Hwy., Brooklyn, NY 11234 USA
E-mail: isispublishingco@aol.com.

Islamic Bk. Service, 1209 Cleburne, Hoston, TX 77004 USA (SAN 169-2453) Tel 713-528-1440; Fax: 713-528-1085.

Islamic Ctr. of Sacramento, The, *(978-0-9769245)* Div. of Sacramento Computers, c/o Sacramento Computers, 2022 4th St. #2, Sacramento, CA 95818 USA
E-mail: shamdani@mindspring.com
Web site: http://www.hineaf.net.

Islamic Supreme Council of America, *(978-1-930409; 978-1-938058)* Orders Addr.: 17195 Silver Pkwy. #401 Fenton, MI 48430, Fenton, MI 48430 USA Tel 810-593-1222; Fax: 810-815-0518; Toll Free: 800-278-6624; Edit Addr.: 17195 Silver Pkwy. #401 Fenton Michigan 48430, Fenton, MI 48430 USA
E-mail: staff@islamicsupremecouncil.org; aliyah@sunnah.org
Web site: http://www.worde.org.

Island Friends LLC, *(978-0-9729987)* 11 Promontory Ct., Hilton Head Island, SC 29928 USA
E-mail: benjo@adelphia.net
Web site: http://www.islandfriends.net
Dist(s): **Sandlapper Publishing Co., Inc.**

Island Heritage Publishing, *(978-0-89610; 978-0-931548; 978-1-59700)* Div. of The Madden Corp., 94-411 Koaki St., Waipahu, HI 96797 USA (SAN 211-1403) Tel 808-564-8800; Fax: 808-564-8888; Toll Free: 800-468-2800
E-mail: ihorders@welcometotheislands.com
Web site: http://www.welcometotheislands.com
Dist(s): **Madden Corp., The.**

Island In The Sky Publishing Co., *(978-0-9760328)* 60 Meadow Lakes, East Windsor, NJ 08520 USA
Web site: http://www.MemoriesOfWWII.com.

Island Ink, *(978-0-9657849)* Orders Addr.: P.O. Box 1818, Indiantown, FL 34956 USA Tel 561-597-3778; Fax: 561-597-4691.

Island Institute, *(978-0-942719; 978-0-9835613)* 386 Main St., Box 648, Rockland, ME 04841-3345 USA (SAN 667-7274) Tel 207-594-9209; Fax: 207-594-9314
E-mail: inquiry@islandinstitute.org; publications@islandinstitute.org
Web site: http://www.islandinstitute.org
Dist(s): **Magazines, Inc.**

Island Media Publishing, LLC, *(978-0-9829908)* 120 N. 15th St., Fernandina Beach, FL 32034 USA Tel 904-556-3002
E-mail: islandmediapublishing@gmail.com.

Island Moon Pr., *(978-0-9755605)* P.O. Box 956, Oaks, PA 19456-0956 USA Tel 610-935-2378; Toll Free: 877-252-8262
E-mail: islandquest@msn.com
Web site: http://www.IslandMoonPress.com.

Island Nation Pr., LLC, *(978-0-9657437; 978-1-892738)* Orders Addr.: 144 Rowayton Woods Dr., Norwalk, CT 06854 USA Tel 203-852-0028; Fax: 203-852-0528; Toll Free: 888-356-1450 [Direct Order Line]
E-mail: cvaleallen@earthlink.net
Web site: http://www.charlottevaleallen.com.

Island Paradise Publishing, *(978-0-9705889; 978-0-9855153)* Orders Addr.: P.O. Box 163, Haleiwa, HI 96712 USA Tel 808-638-9640; Edit Addr.: 59-465 KeWaena Rd., Haleiwa, HI 96712 USA
E-mail: CooperKool@Hawaii.rr.com
Dist(s): **Booklines Hawaii, Ltd.**

Islandport Pr., Inc., *(978-0-9671662; 978-0-9763231; 978-1-934031; 978-1-939017)* Orders Addr.: P.O. Box 10, Yarmouth, ME 04096 USA Tel 207-846-3344; Fax: 207-846-3955; Edit Addr.: 267 US Rte. 1, Suite B, Yarmouth, ME 04096 USA
E-mail: deanlunt@islandportpress.com
Web site: http://www.islandportpress.com
Dist(s): **AtlasBooks Distribution**
Follett School Solutions
INscribe Digital
MyiLibrary
ebrary, Inc.

IslandWood, *(978-0-9821633)* Orders Addr.: 4450 Blakely Ave. NE, Bainbridge Island, WA 98110 USA Tel 206-855-4300; Fax: 206-855-4301
Web site: http://www.IslandWood.org.

ISLC, *(978-0-9763226)* c/o Alfassa, 15 W. 16th St., 6th Flr., New York, NY 10011 USA Tel 917-207-4344
E-mail: shelomo@alfassa.com.

Isle of Dogs Publishing, Co., *(978-0-9741321)* 4008 - 83rd Ave. SE, Snohomish, WA 98290 USA
E-mail: connieraestrain@msn.com; ConnieRaeStrain@IsleofDogsPublishing.com
Web site: http://www.isleofdogspublishing.com.

Isles of the Sea Pubs., *(978-0-9728126)* Orders Addr.: P.O. Box 51352, Provo, UT 84605-1352 USA Tel 801-427-5209; Edit Addr.: 2052 S. California Ave., No. 12, Provo, UT 84044 USA
E-mail: drrlesa@hotmail.com.

Islewest Publishing, *(978-0-9641919; 978-1-888461)* Div. of Carlisle Communications, Ltd., 4242 Chavenelle Dr., Dubuque, IA 52002-2650 USA (SAN 299-5018)
E-mail: mjgraham@carcomm.com
Web site: http://www.islewest.com.

Israel Book Shop *See* **Israel Bookshop Pubns.**

Israel Bookshop Pubns., *(978-0-9670705; 978-1-931681; 978-1-60091)* 501 Prospect St., No. 97, Lakewood, NJ 08701 USA Tel 732-901-3009; Fax: 732-901-4012; Toll Free: 888-536-7427
E-mail: sales@israelbookshoppublications.com
Web site: http://www.israelbookshoppublications.com.

ISS, *(978-1-934942)* 2 Shaker Rd. Ste. D103, Shirley, MA 01464-2535 USA (SAN 855-6164)
E-mail: print@issexpress.com
Web site: http://www.imagesoftware.com.

Istoria Hse., *(978-0-9816538)* Orders Addr.: P.O. Box 6342, Vernon Hills, IL 60061 USA (SAN 856-1370)
E-mail: info@istoriahouse.com
Web site: http://www.istoriahouse.com.

Italica Pr., *(978-0-934977; 978-1-59910)* 595 Main St., Suite 605, New York, NY 10044 USA (SAN 695-1805) Tel 917-371-0563
E-mail: inquiries@italicapress.com
Web site: http://www.italicapress.com.

Itasca Bks., *(978-0-9767054)* Orders Addr.: 5120 Cedar Lake Rd. S., Minneapolis, MN 55416 USA (SAN 855-3823) Tel 952-345-4488; Fax: 952-920-0541; Toll Free: 800-901-3480
E-mail: mjung@itascabooks.com
Web site: http://www.itascabooks.com
Dist(s): **BookMobile.**

ITeenBooks Inc., *(978-0-9798997; 978-0-9852925)* P.O. Box 171, Middletown, NJ 07748-0171 USA.

Ithaca Pr. *Imprint of* **Authors & Artists Publishers of New York, Inc.**

Ithuriel's Spear, *(978-0-9749502; 978-0-9793390; 978-0-9835791; 978-1-943209)* 939 Eddy St., Apt. 102, San Francisco, CA 94109 USA Tel 415-440-3204 plainfeather@gmail.com
E-mail: plainfeather@gmail.com
Web site: http://www.ithuriel.com
Dist(s): **BookMobile**
SPD-Small Pr. Distribution.

Itiya Publishing, Inc., *(978-0-9770312)* 217 Ave. Unvi. Interanericana PMB 161, San German, PR 00683 USA
E-mail: gpita@itiyainc.com
Web site: http://www.itiyainc.com.

ITRON Publishing, *(978-0-9786863)* 6510 LBJ Freeway, Suite 200, Dallas, TX 75240 USA (SAN 851-2817) Tel 972-934-2811; Fax: 972-934-1705.

It's A Habit! Co., The, *(978-0-9713664)* 2238 Harwood St., Los Angeles, CA 90031-1238 USA Tel 323-254-7772
Web site: http://www.itsahabit.com.

It's a Lifestyle Fitness, *(978-0-9890227)* 1 Evergreen Pl., Morristown, NJ 07960 USA (SAN 920-783X) Tel 973-267-2121
E-mail: gregorycrawford@ymail.com.

It's About Time, Herff Jones Education Division *See* **It's About Time, Herff Jones Education Div.**

It's About Time, Herff Jones Education Div., *(978-1-891629; 978-1-58591; 978-1-60720; 978-1-68231)* Orders Addr.: 333 N. Bedford Rd. # 110, Mt. Kisco, NY 10549 USA Tel 914-273-2233; Fax: 914-273-2227; Toll Free: 888-698-8463 Do not confuse with companies with the same name in Los Gatos, CA, Santa Monica, CA
E-mail: gerneralinfo@herffjones.com
Web site: http://www.its-about-time.com.

It's Good 2B Good LLC,
Dist(s): **AtlasBooks Distribution.**

It's Me Briana, LLC, *(978-0-9793904; 978-0-9838492)* P.O. Box 12386, Atlanta, GA 30355 USA
Web site: http://www.briananeighborhood.com.

ITSMEEE Industries, *(978-0-9677231)* 13918 E. Mississippi Ave., No 213, Aurora, CO 80012 USA Tel 303-229-7584
E-mail: itsmeeeindustries@hotmail.com.

Itty Bitty Bks., *(978-0-9760691)* 1682 NW 785 Rd., Bates City, MO 64011 USA Tel 816-697-3617 (phone/fax)
E-mail: waynedyer@gmail.com.

Itty Bitty Kitty *Imprint of* **Singing Moon Pr.**

Itty Bitty Witch Works, *(978-0-9768573)* P.O. Box 532, Kernville, CA 93238 USA Tel 760-376-3973 (phone/fax)
E-mail: ittybittywitch@sierranet.us
Web site: http://ittybittywitch.com.

iUniverse, Inc. *Imprint of* **iUniverse, Inc.**

iUniverse, Inc., *(978-0-9665514; 978-1-58348; 978-0-9668591; 978-1-893652; 978-0-595; 978-0-9795279; 978-1-60528; 978-1-4401; 978-1-936236; 978-1-4502; 978-1-4620; 978-1-4697; 978-1-4759; 978-1-4917)* Orders Addr.: 1663 Liberty Dr., Suite 300, Bloomington, IN 47403 USA (SAN 254-9425) Toll Free: 800-288-4677; *Imprints:* Writers Club Press (Writers Club Pr); Writer's Showcase Press (Writers Showcase); Backinprint.com (Backinprint); ASJA Press (ASJA Pr); Authors Choice Press (Authors Choice Pr); Mystery Writers of America Presents (Myst Write Amer); Mystery & Suspense Press (Mystery & Suspense); Weekly Reader Teacher's Press (Weekly Rd Tch); Writers Advantage Press (Writers Adv Pr); iUniverse, Inc. (iUni Inc); iUniverse Star (iUniverse Star)
E-mail: post.production@iuniverse.com; book.orders@iuniverse.com; bethany.dirks@iuniverse.com
Web site: http://www.iUniverse.com; http://iuniverse.com
Dist(s): **AtlasBooks Distribution**
Author Solutions, Inc.
CreateSpace Independent Publishing Platform
Smashwords
Zondervan.

iUniverse Star *Imprint of* **iUniverse, Inc.**

iUniverse.com, Incorporated *See* **iUniverse, Inc.**

Iverson, Theodore, *(978-0-9747378)* P.O. Box 3671, Grand Canyon, AZ 86023-3671 USA.

Ivoryton Pr., *(978-0-9814663)* P.O. Box 485, Ivoryton, CT 06442 USA Tel 860-581-8133
E-mail: Ivoryton.Press@gmail.com.

Ivy Advising LLC, *(978-0-9771568)* 50 Livingston St., Brooklyn, NY 11201 USA (SAN 256-8934).

Ivy Fund, The, *(978-0-9754003)* 33 Irving St., Waltham, MA 02451-0758 USA
E-mail: courtney@ivysplace.org
Web site: http://ivysplace.org.

Ivy Hill Bunch, LLC, *(978-0-9743619)* P.O. Box 1053, La Quinta, CA 92253 USA Tel 760-771-0834; Fax: 760-771-1910; Toll Free: 866-892-5795
E-mail: lynn@ivyhillbunch.com
Web site: http://www.saddyandgladdy.com.

Ivy House Publishing Group *Imprint of* **Pentland Pr., Inc.**

IvyStone Pr., *(978-0-9755771)* P.O. Box 50, Emmalena, KY 41740 USA
E-mail: hodson@tgtel.com
Web site: http://www.mountainrainbow.com.

Iwishyouicecreamandcake, *(978-0-9792019)* 3871 W. Millers Bridge Rd., Tallahassee, FL 32312 USA Fax: 850-893-9616
E-mail: carolhmoore@yahoo.com
Web site: http://iwishyouicecreamandcake.com.

Iyengar, Malathi, *(978-0-9753912)* 14748 Morrison St., Sherman Oaks, CA 91403 USA
E-mail: msiyengar@yahoo.com
Web site: http://www.rangoli.org.

Iynx publishing (GBR) *(978-0-9535413; 978-0-9540583)* *Dist. by* **Dufour.**

IZA Publishing Co., *(978-0-9674241)* 253 Pvt. Rd. 2410, Uvalde County, TX 78801 USA Tel 361-946-3132; Fax: 361-946-2000
E-mail: smith-ma@swbell.net.

IZS, Inc., *(978-0-9764684)* 34 E. Franklin St., Bellbrook, OH 45305-1746 USA Tel 937-848-8896
E-mail: pantherbay@aol.com
Web site: http://www.pantherbay.com.

J A F S, Inc., *(978-0-9709533)* 8846 Worthington Cir., Indianapolis, IN 46278 USA Tel 317-802-9784; Fax: 317-870-8772
E-mail: jmcclaine3@home.com
Dist(s): **Austin & Company, Inc.**
Partners Pubs. Group, Inc.

J A G Pubns., *(978-0-943327)* 11288 Ventura Blvd., No. 301, Studio City, CA 91604 USA (SAN 668-4157) Tel 818-505-9002 (phone/fax) Do not confuse with Jag Publications in Los Angeles, CA
E-mail: info@jagpublications-esl.com
Web site: http://www.jagpublications-esl.com.

J A Interests, Inc., *(978-0-9769648)* P.O. Box 1472, Versailles, KY 40383 USA.

J A S Pr., Inc., *(978-0-9666920; 978-0-9773316)* Orders Addr.: P.O. Box 1925, Bolingbrook, IL 60440 USA Tel 630-226-1635; Edit Addr.: 155 Ashcroft Dr., Bolingbrook, IL 60490 USA Tel 630-226-1635
E-mail: jaspress@mindspring.com.

J & J Publishing Co., *(978-0-9759831)* Box 305, 9728 US Hwy. 277, Elgin, OK 73538 USA Do not confuse with companies with same or similar name in Los Angeles, CA, Buffalo, NY, Englewood, CO, Darien, IL, Frankfurt, IL MD
E-mail: djw73@aol.com.

J & J Publishing Co., *(978-0-9705008; 978-0-615-73754-6; 978-0-9961018)* P.O. Box 291205, Columbia, SC 29229 USA Tel 803-968-5196
E-mail: jjpublisher@yahoo.com
Web site: http://www.jandjpublishingonline.com.

J & K Publishing, *(978-0-9790487)* 5221 Collins St., Suite 101, Panama City, FL 32404 USA
E-mail: jnbowen@netscape.com.

J&M Publishing, *(978-0-9646590)* 2417 Valley View Rd., Narvon, PA 17555 USA Tel 610-286-5489 Do not confuse with companies with the same name in Lebanon, TN, Fayetteville, NC, Phoenix, AZ.

J B Communications, Inc., *(978-1-55987)* 101 W. 55th St., No. 2D, New York, NY 10019-5346 USA Tel 212-246-0900; *Imprints:* Sunny Books (Sunny Bks).

J. B. J. Enterprises *See* **Morgan, E. A.**

J. Caro & Associates *See* **Cowboy Collector Pubns.**

J J Publishing, *(978-0-9604610)* 1312 Arthur St., Hollywood, FL 33019 USA (SAN 220-0090) Tel 954-929-3559 (phone/fax).

J L Publishing Co., *(978-0-9740774)* 669 Buzzard Roost Cutoff, Mountain Home, AR 72653 USA.

J M D's Business Services, *(978-0-9712641)* 52 Lee Ave., Wallingford, CT 06492-3610 USA
Web site: http://www.jmdsbusinessservices.com; http://www.liquidchariot.com.

J M Pubns., *(978-0-9638007)* Orders Addr.: P.O. Box 753427, Memphis, TN 38115 USA; Edit Addr.: 3830 Scottsdale Ave., Memphis, TN 38115 USA (SAN 255-0598) Tel 901-368-3414; Fax: 901-566-1978; Toll Free: 888-321-4747
E-mail: jmpub1@midsouth.rr.com
Web site: http://www.jmpublications.com.

J. Paul Getty Museum *Imprint of* **Getty Pubns.**

J. Taylor Publishing, *(978-0-9834058; 978-1-937744)* 5448 Apex Peakway No. 198, Apex, NC 27502 USA Tel 919-249-7318
E-mail: production@jtaylorpublishing.com
Web site: http://www.jtaylorpublishing.com.

J2B Publishing LLC, *(978-0-9911994; 978-1-941927)* 4251 Columbia Pk. Rd., Pomfret, MD 20675 USA Tel 202-557-8097
E-mail: GladToDoIt@gmail.com
Web site: www.GladToDoIt.net.

Jabberwocky Bks., Inc. *Imprint of* **Hillcrest Publishing Group, Inc.**

Jacana Media (ZAF) *(978-1-874955; 978-1-919931; 978-1-919777; 978-1-4314)* *Dist. by* **IPG Chicago.**

Jack Hook Publishing, *(978-0-9837863)* 1288 Columbus Ave., No. 279, San Francisco, CA 94133 USA Tel 310-889-4728
E-mail: susan.saville@jackhook.com
Web site: www.jackhook.com.

Jack's Bookshelf, Inc., *(978-1-928907)* 224 Woodland Dr., Vista, CA 92083 USA.

Jackson, Linda *See* **Jackson Publishing**

Jackson Publishing, *(978-0-9716442)* 7661 Forstoria Cove, Southaven, MS 38672 USA Tel 901-413-5748 Do not confuse with companies with the same name in Jackson, MS; Clarkston, MI
E-mail: jackson35015@bellsouth.net.

Jackson, Robert, *(978-0-9761420)* 12807 Prospect Knolls Dr., Bowie, MD 20720 USA
E-mail: trebor_jackson@yahoo.com
Web site: http://www.amazinglibertees.com.

Jacobob Pr., LLC, *(978-0-9705827; 978-0-9772817; 978-0-9820960; 978-0-9838072; 978-0-9852887; 978-0-9857477; 978-0-9860361; 978-0-9911151; 978-0-9914066; 978-0-9916416; 978-0-692-53701-5)* 11035 Ridge Forest Ct., Saint Louis, MO 63126-3429 USA (SAN 257-1862) Tel 314-843-4829
E-mail: jacobobsw@sbcglobal.net
Web site: http://jacobobpress.com
Dist(s): **Follett School Solutions**
Jacobob Pr. Distributing
Unique Bks., Inc.

Jacobs, Karen, *(978-0-9850440)* 40 Indian Carry Rd., Moultonborough, NH 03254 USA Tel 617-838-1872
E-mail: kjacobs@bu.edu.

Jacqueline Beverly Hills, *(978-0-9664783)* 650 The Village, Unit 215, Redondo Beach, CA 90277-2734 USA
E-mail: jacquih3@yahoo.com
Web site: http://jbhbooks.com.

Jacquet-Acea, Russell, *(978-0-9771919)* 3645 Whitman Ave. N., Seattle, WA 98103 USA Tel 206-547-7026; Fax: 810-454-1721
E-mail: rjacquet2@msn.com
Web site: http://rjacquet.tripod.com.

JADA Pr., *(978-0-9747501; 978-0-9761110; 978-0-9764115; 978-0-9771343; 978-0-9788724; 978-0-9800629; 978-0-9843558; 978-0-9848365; 978-0-9907961)* 4375 Confederate Point Rd. #6-H, Jacksonville, FL 32210 USA Tel 904-226-8876 (leave a message)
Web site: http://www.jadapress.com.

JadaStar *See* **Star Publish LLC**

Jade Enterprises, *(978-0-9753410)* 11807 S. Fair Hollow Ln., Suite 106, Houston, TX 77043-1033 USA Tel 713-416-0109
Web site: http://www.authorsden.com/deborahkfrontiera.

Jade Ram Publishing, *(978-1-877721)* 3003 Wendy's Way, No. 9, Anchorage, AK 99517-1466 USA Tel 907-248-0979; Fax: 907-272-8432
E-mail: jaderam@alaska.net
Dist(s): **Publication Consultants**
Todd Communications
Wizard Works.

Jadenaila Publishing, *(978-0-615-12544-2)* 7340 S. Union Creek Way 5G, Salt Lake City, UT 84047 USA Tel 801-916-1037
E-mail: kidsbooksbynaila@hotmail.com
Web site: http://www.kidsbooksbynaila.com.

Jades Publishing, *(978-0-9743352)* Orders Addr.: P.O. Box 485, Fayette, OH 43521 USA Tel 419-237-3128; Edit Addr.: 24022-T, Fayette, OH 43521 USA
E-mail: amadsj@bright.net; amadsj@bright.nett.

Jaffrey, Kamal, *(978-0-9753673)* 400 Technology Sq., Cambridge, MA 02139 USA.

Jahs Publishing Group, *(978-0-9701144; 978-0-9747550; 978-0-615-49893-5; 978-0-615-50005-8)* 6304 Somerset Rd., Riverdale, MD 20737 USA Tel 301-326-6468
Web site: http://www.jahspublishing.com
Dist(s): **CreateSpace Independent Publishing Platform.**

Jalali, Yassaman *See* **Saman Publishing**

JA-M Pubs., LLC, *(978-0-9728975)* 305 Locust St. W. Apt. 2, Three Oaks, MI 49128 USA Tel 269-820-2092 Do not confuse with companies with the same or similar name in Mount Pleasant, SC, Comstock Park, MI
E-mail: joycex4@msn.com; jandrews-mckinne@ccc.edu.

Jama Kids, *(978-0-9772711)* 612 N. St., Beaufort, SC 29902 USA Tel 843-522-1577
E-mail: janspringle@earthlink.net.

Jamaldinian, Yousef, *(978-0-9766657)* 5207 Olley Ln., Burke, VA 22015 USA Tel 571-212-9471
E-mail: joedinian@yahoo.com.

James, JoAnn, *(978-0-9764406)* P.O. Box 11459, Eugene, OR 97440 USA
E-mail: joann_james@comcast.net.

James Stevenson Pub., *(978-1-885852)* 1500 Oliver Rd., Suite K-109, Fairfield, CA 94533 USA Tel 707-469-0237; Fax: 206-350-2954
E-mail: ceo@jspub.com
Web site: http://www.jspub.com
Dist(s): **Marangio, Charles F. Distribution.**

Jamestown, *(978-0-07; 978-0-8092; 978-0-8442; 978-0-89061; 978-0-913327; 978-0-941263; 978-1-56943)* Div. of Glencoe/McGraw-Hill, Orders Addr.: P.O. Box 543, Blacklick, OH 43004-0543 USA Fax: 614-860-1877; Toll Free: 800-334-7344; Edit Addr.: P.O. Box 508, Columbus, OH 43216 USA Toll Free: 800-872-7323
Web site: http://www.jamestowneducation.com
Dist(s): **Libros Sin Fronteras**
McGraw-Hill Cos., The.

Jamiram Publishing, *(978-0-9790434)* 1760 Harbeck Rd., Grants Pass, OR 97527 USA
Web site: http://jamiram.com.

JamSum Limited, *(978-0-9770754)* 621 S. Main St., Bellefontaine, OH 43311-1725 USA Toll Free: 866-857-2061
E-mail: publish@jamsum.com
Web site: http://www.jamsum.com.

Jan & San, *(978-0-9729741)* 273 Roy Huie Rd., Riverdale, GA 30274 USA
E-mail: feedback@providerhouse.com
Web site: http://www.providerhouse.com.

Jan-Carol Publishing, INC., *(978-0-9767793; 978-0-9801504; 978-0-9822337; 978-0-9841870; 978-0-9843192; 978-0-9845470; 978-0-9846398; 978-0-9834885; 978-0-9848050; 978-0-9850272; 978-1-939289)* Orders Addr.: PO Box 701, Johnson City, TN 37605 USA Tel 423-926-9983; *Imprints:* Little Creek Books (LittleCreek)
Web site: www.voicemagazineforwomen.com; www.jancarolpublishing.com.

Jandie Jams Music LLC, *(978-0-9796150)* 1036 Katy Ln., Longmont, CO 80504 USA (SAN 853-8999)
E-mail: jandiejams@comcast.net
Web site: http://www.kidcleveronline.com.

Jane & Street Pubs. Ltd., *(978-0-9745077)* 302-A W. 12th St., No. 197, New York, NY 10014 USA
Web site: http://www.janeandstreet.com.

Janelle Pubns., Inc., *(978-0-9626739; 978-1-890265)* Orders Addr.: P.O. Box 811, De Kalb, IL 60115-0811 USA Tel 815-756-2300; Fax: 815-756-4799; Toll Free: 800-888-8834; Edit Addr.: 1189 Twombley Rd., De Kalb, IL 60115 USA
E-mail: info@janellepublications.com
Web site: http://www.janellepublications.com.

Jane's World *See* **Girl Twirl Comics**

Janik Pr., *(978-0-9883938)* P.O. Box 12034, Fort Wayne, IN 46862 USA Tel 260-804-8044
E-mail: nikbenedict@yahoo.com.

Janis, Tim Ensemble, Inc., *(978-0-9773335)* P.O. Box 315, Kennebunk, ME 04043 USA (SAN 257-280X) Tel 207-985-3463.

Jan's Bks., *(978-0-9797139)* Orders Addr.: 1780 Phillips, Berkley, MI 48072 USA Tel 248-545-5160.

Jan's Looks & Books *See* **Jan's Bks.**

Jansen, Marilyn, *(978-0-9761070)* P.O. Box 278, Makawao, HI 96768 USA Tel 808-572-0699 phone/fax
E-mail: jamarilyn2008@aol.com
Web site: http://amaryllisofhawaii.com
Dist(s): **Booklines Hawaii, Ltd.**

Janze Pubns., *(978-0-9629142; 978-0-9794955)* 930 Bargo St, London, KY 40741-2713 USA
E-mail: janzepub@windstream.net.

Japan Pubns. (U.S.A.), Inc., *(978-0-87040; 978-1-57863)* Subs. of Japan Pubns., Inc. (Tokyo, Japan), 160 Spruce Knob Rd., Middletown Springs, VT 05757-4432 USA (SAN 680-0513) Tel 802-235-2814
Dist(s): **Diamond Comic Distributors, Inc.**
Diamond Bk. Distributors
Oxford Univ. Pr., Inc.

Japan Pubns. Trading Co. (JPN) *(978-4-88996)* *Dist. by* **OUP.**

Japanime Co., Ltd. (JPN) *(978-4-921205)* *Dist. by* **Diamond Book Dists.**

Jappa Pubns., *(978-0-9720694)* 1808 N. 79th St., Kansas City, KS 66112 USA Tel 913-205-2361
E-mail: Ongi.entertainment@gmx.com
Web site: http://www.pandaoki.com.

Jappamation Studios *See* **Jappa Pubns.**

Jarndyce & Jarndyce Pr., *(978-0-9721916; 978-0-9772720; 978-0-9817269; 978-0-9836173; 978-0-9894271; 978-0-9910077; 978-0-9864238)* Div. of PSA Consulting, Inc., 305 Snow Shoe Dr., Southgate, KY 41071 USA (SAN 860-2433) Tel 513-382-4315; 513-304-3633; Fax: 855-361-8591
E-mail: info@cincybooks.com
Web site: http://www.cincybooks.com
Dist(s): **BookBaby.**

Jarrett Publishing Co., *(978-0-9624723; 978-1-882422; 978-0-9795493; 978-1-935022)* P.O. Box 1460, Ronkonkoma, NY 11779-0426 USA Toll Free: 800-859-7679
E-mail: info@jarrettpub.com
Web site: http://www.jarrettpub.com.

Jarvis Printing *See* **Mitchell, Damien Pardow**

Jasmine Pr., *(978-0-930069)* 2224 Ogden Ave., Bensalem, PA 19020 USA (SAN 669-9650) Tel 215-244-0525.

Jasnans Publishing Co., *(978-0-9761759)* P.O. Box 873633, Wasilla, AK 99687-3633 USA
E-mail: hallalfa@mtaonline.net
Web site: http://www.jasnanspublishing.com.

Jason & Nordic Pubs., *(978-0-944727)* P.O. Box 441, Hollidaysburg, PA 16648 USA (SAN 244-9374) Tel 814-696-2920; Fax: 814-696-4250; *Imprints:* Turtle Books (Turtle Books)
E-mail: turtlbks@jasonandnordic.com
Web site: http://www.jasonandnordic.com.

Jason Foundation for Education *See* **JASON Project, The**

Jason Jacques Gallery Pr. The, *(978-0-9788371; 978-0-615-55775-5)* 29 E. 73rd St., No. 1, New York, NY 10021-3501 USA (SAN 851-7568) Tel 212-535-7500; Fax: 212-535-5757
E-mail: jason@jasonjacques.com
Web site: http://www.jasonjacques.com.

JASON Project, The, *(978-0-9763809; 978-0-9787574; 978-1-935211)* Subs. of National Geographic Society, Orders Addr.: 44983 Knoll Sq. Suite 150, Ashburn, VA 20147 USA Tel 703-726-4236; Fax: 703-726-8366; Toll Free: 888-527-6600
E-mail: info@jason.org
Web site: http://www.jason.org.

Jasper State Brand, Inc., *(978-0-9820228; 978-0-9833366)* 311 N. Robertson Blvd., Suite 363, Beverly Hills, CA 90211 USA (SAN 857-0213) Tel 310-801-7737
E-mail: judith@jasperstate.com.

javariBook, *(978-0-9679161)* P.O. Box 230551, New York, NY 10023 USA
E-mail: javaribook@javari.com
Web site: http://www.javaribook.com; http://www.globalwidetrade.com.

Jawbone Publishing Corp., *(978-0-9702959; 978-1-59094)* 1540 Happy Valley Cir., Newnan, GA 30263-4035 USA (SAN 253-5335); *Imprints:* Top Shelf (Top); Jawbreakers for Kids (Jawbreakers)
E-mail: marketing@jawbonepublishing.com
Web site: http://www.jawbonepublishing.com.

Jawbreakers for Kids *Imprint of* **Jawbone Publishing Corp.**

JaxPublishing.net, *(978-0-9798316)* 11727 Invierno Dr., San Diego, CA 92124-2883 USA Tel 619-757-7016; Fax: 858-277-6418
E-mail: atom@atomart.net
Web site: http://www.atomart.net.

Jay Street Pubs., *(978-0-9639999; 978-1-889534)* Div. of G-Communications, P.O. Box 230944, New York, NY 10023-0016 USA
E-mail: jaystpub@i-2000.com.

JayJo Bks., LLC, *(978-0-9639449; 978-1-891383)* Orders Addr.: P.O. Box 760, Plainview, NY 11803-0760 USA (SAN 178-5435) Tel 516-349-5520; Fax: 800-262-1886; Toll Free: 800-999-6884; Edit Addr.: 45 Executive Dr. Ste. 201, Plainview, NY 11803-1738 USA
E-mail: jayjobook@guidancechannel.com
Web site: http://www.jayjo.com
Dist(s): **Follett School Solutions**
Quality Bks., Inc.
Unique Bks., Inc.

Jaylil Publishing Co., *(978-0-9748165)* Orders Addr.: P.O. Box 656551, Flushing, NY 11365 USA
E-mail: jaylilpublishing@aol.com
Web site: http://www.jaylilpublishing.com
Dist(s): **Culture Plus Bk. Distributors**
Seaburn Bks.

Jazwares Distribution, Inc., *(978-0-9724983; 978-0-9765714; 978-1-933752)* 555 Sawgrass Corporate Pkwy., Sunrise, FL 33325-6211 USA
E-mail: julio@jazwares.com
Web site: http://www.projectkitsforkids.com.

Jazz Path Publishing, *(978-0-9760977)* P.O. Box 381810, Cambridge, MA 02238 USA
Web site: http://www.jazzpath.com.

Jazzy Kitty Greetings Marketing & Publishing Co., *(978-0-9768540; 978-0-9843255; 978-0-9830548; 978-0-9851453; 978-0-9892656; 978-0-9916648)* 2 Ashley Dr., New Castle, DE 19720 USA Tel 877-782-5550; Fax: 302-380-3296; Toll Free: 877-782-5550
Web site: http://www.jazzykittypublishing.com.

JazzyKitty Greetings *See* **Jazzy Kitty Greetings Marketing & Publishing Co.**

JB Information Station, *(978-0-934334)* P.O. Box 19333, Saint Louis, MO 63125 USA (SAN 213-4128) Tel 314-638-3404; 3888 Via Miralesta Dr., Saint Louis, MO 63125
E-mail: empoweredparenting@earthlink.net
Web site: http://www.JoanBramsch.com.

JB Max Publishing (CAN) *(978-0-9736330) Dist. by* **IPG Chicago.**

JBall Publishing, *(978-0-9764179)* 393 W. 300 N., Smithfield, UT 84335 USA Tel 435-563-9437
Web site: http://pumpkinglow.com.

JBIRD INK, Ltd., *(978-0-9715253; 978-0-9850732)* 109 Knutson Dr., Madison, WI 53704 USA Tel 608-554-0803
E-mail: info@jbirdink.com
Web site: http://www.jbirdink.com.

JBT Publishing, *(978-0-9792059)* Orders Addr.: 1485 Christina Ln., Lake Forest, IL 60045 USA (SAN 852-7644) Tel 781-760-2357; Fax: 419-735-0603
E-mail: jtedesco@gis.net.

JCCJ Pr., *(978-0-9770207)* 81 River Rd., Norfolk, MA 02056 USA Tel 508-528-4767.

JCTT, LLC, *(978-0-9766926)* 412 Capote Peak Dr., Georgetown, TX 78633 USA
E-mail: linleyw@msn.com
Web site: http://www.mathemagicians.info.

JD Entertainment, *(978-0-9772240)* 1731 Cherry Rd., Memphis, TN 38117 USA
E-mail: directorrsp@yahoo.com
Web site: http://www.jkdenny.com
Dist(s): **Partners Bk. Distributing, Inc.**

JD Publishing, *(978-0-9793972)* Div. of Redpsych Production, P.O. Box 696, Fairfax, CA 94978 USA (SAN 853-3431) Tel 773-793-7622
E-mail: redpsychproductions@yahoo.com
Web site: http://www.redpsych.com; http://www.monkeyandtheengineer.com.

Jeb Cool Kids Entertainment, Inc, *(978-0-9744123; 978-0-9859430)* 8208 Norton Ave., Unit 2, Los Angeles, CA 90046 USA
E-mail: jebcoolkids@gmail.com
Web site: http://www.jebcoolkids.com
Dist(s): **BookBaby.**

JEC Publishing Company *See* **Recipe Pubs.**

Jeffers Pr., *(978-0-9745776; 978-0-9777618)* 2700 Neilson Way, Suite 1428, Santa Monica, CA 90405 USA Tel 310-450-4008; Toll Free: 877-450-4008
E-mail: mark@jefferspress.com
Web site: http://www.jefferspress.com
Dist(s): **Hillcrest Publishing Group, Inc.**
National Bk. Network.

Jefferson Pr., *(978-0-9718974; 978-0-9778086; 978-0-9800164; 978-0-615-27680-9)* P.O. Box 115, Lookout Mountain, TN 37350 USA
E-mail: dmagee@jeffersonpress.com; info@jeffersonpress.com
Web site: http://www.jeffersonpress.com
Dist(s): **Independent Pubs. Group.**

Jefferson, Thomas University Press *See* **Truman State Univ. Pr.**

Jellyroll Productions *See* **Osborne Enterprises Publishing**

JEM Bks., Inc., *(978-0-9754317)* 10466 E. Sheena Dr., Scottsdale, AZ 85255-1742 USA
E-mail: rmahoney@jem-books.com
Web site: http://www.jem-books.com.

Jenkins-Simmons, Glenda, *(978-0-9758586)* 692 Mulberry Dr., Biloxi, MS 39532 USA Tel 228-388-7540
E-mail: res55472@cs.com.

Jennings, J. Publishing Company *See* **Jennings Publishing**

Jennings Publishing, *(978-0-9700038)* 5012 Kahn St., Carmichael, CA 95608 USA Tel 916-863-1638; Fax: 916-863-5807
E-mail: jane@jenningspub.com
Web site: http://www.jenningspub.com
Dist(s): **Omnibus Pr.**

Jenpet Publishing, *(978-0-9726794)* P.O. Box 2542, Alameda, CA 94501 USA Tel 510-521-3582
E-mail: jj@jenpet.com
Web site: http://www.jenpet.com.

JenPrint Pubns., LLC, *(978-0-9653791)* 12195 Hwy. 92 Suite 114-162, Woodstock, GA 30188 USA
E-mail: margarette@jenprint.com
Web site: http://www.jenprint.com
Dist(s): **Book Clearing Hse.**
Follett School Solutions
Quality Bks., Inc.

Jensen, Elizabeth, *(978-0-615-78027-6)* 109 Tammy Dr., Hammond, LA 70403 USA Tel 504-473-4931
Dist(s): **CreateSpace Independent Publishing Platform.**

Jensen, Lissa, *(978-0-9666973)* 958 Summer Holly Ln., Encinitas, CA 92024 USA Tel 760-944-6345.

Jensen, Travis, *(978-0-9754439)* 23 Los Palmos Dr., San Francisco, CA 94127-2309 USA
E-mail: thesfmasher@yahoo.com
Web site: http://www.sfmasher.cjb.net.

Jensonbooks, *(978-0-9794414)* P.O. Box 416, Greenfield, MA 01302-0416 USA (SAN 853-4322).

Jentmedia, *(978-0-578-03676-2)* P.O. Box 1304, Lonbard, IL 60148 USA
Dist(s): **Lulu Enterprises Inc.**

Jeremy's Things, *(978-0-9747878)* 410 Fifth Ave., 2nd Flr., Brooklyn, NY 11215 USA Tel 718-788-3987
E-mail: jeremy@jeremybullis.com
Web site: http://www.jeremybullis.com.

Jeriger Pr., *(978-1-59810)* P.O. Box 1249, Stafford, TX 77477-1249 USA Tel 888-447-5495 (phone/fax)
E-mail: info@jeriger.com
Web site: http://www.jeriger.com.

Jersey Classic Publishing, *(978-0-9765261)* 75 Locust Ave., Wallington, NJ 07057 USA.

Jerusalem Pubns., *(978-0-9707572; 978-0-9743911; 978-0-9761862; 978-0-9773885; 978-0-9792230; 978-0-9815567; 978-0-9844921; 978-0-9888958; 978-0-9863253)* 4917 Ravenswood Dr., Apt. 513, San Antonio, TX 78232 USA Tel 732-901-3009; Fax: 732-901-4012
E-mail: rapaport@netvision.net.il
Web site: http://www.israelbookshop.com/; http://www.feldheim.com/
Dist(s): **Feldheim Pubs.**
Israel Bookshop Pubns.

JESSPress *See* **JESSPress/Susie Yakowicz**

JESSPress/Susie Yakowicz, *(978-0-9652546)* 4231 Wexford Way, Eagan, MN 55122 USA Tel 651-681-9537
E-mail: syakowicz@comcast.net
Web site: http://www.jesspress.com; susieyakowicz.com/blog.

Jester Bks., *(978-0-9723382)* 39 E. 12th St., 506, New York, NY 10003 USA Tel 212-529-9209 Do not confuse with companies with the same or similar names in Woodland Hills, CA, Orinda, CA
E-mail: davidmkorn@earthlink.net.

Jesus Estanislado, *(978-0-9776291)* P.O. Box 6373, Lakewood, CA 90714 USA
E-mail: jesscortez01@gmail.com.

JETM Publishing & Distribution *See* **I Am Your Playground LLC**

Jetpack Publishing, *(978-0-9898533)* 3 Maybrook Dr., Glenville, NY 12302 USA Tel 518-929-1895
E-mail: ethancrownberry@nycap.rr.com.

Jetway Geographer, LLC, *(978-0-9711640)* Orders Addr.: 431 S. Cooke, Helena, MT 59601 USA Tel 406-586-6879
E-mail: jgeographer@bresnan.net
Web site: www.jetwaygeographer.com.

Jew-El Pr. Co., *(978-0-9767618)* 40022 Milkmaid Ln., Murrieta, CA 92562 USA Tel 951-600-7054 (phone/fax)
E-mail: jew-el-press@verizon.net
Web site: http://www.jew-el-press.com.

Jewel Publishing, *(978-0-9629715; 978-1-936499)* Orders Addr.: 6815 W. Floyd Ave., Denver, CO 80227 USA Tel 303-980-1957 Do not confuse with companies with similar names in Cincinnati, OH, New York, NY, Baltimore, MD, Detroit, MI, Chino HIlls, CA
E-mail: jewelpub@aol.com; motivatingothers@aol.com.

Jewel Publishing, *(978-0-9744944)* P.O. Box 38, Chino Hills, CA 91709 USA Fax: 909-606-1092 Do not confuse with companies with the same or similar name in Baltimore, MD, Denver, CO, Detroit, MI, Cincinnati, OH
E-mail: cmckee7721@aol.com.

Jewell Histories, *(978-0-9678413)* 143 Breckenridge St., Gettysburg, PA 17325 USA Tel 717-420-5344
E-mail: jewellhistories@superpa.net.

Jewish Community Federation of Rochester, NY, Inc., *(978-0-9710686)* 441 East Ave., Rochester, NY 14607 USA Tel 585-461-0490; Fax: 585-461-0912
E-mail: bappelbaum@jewishrochester.org
Web site: http://www.jewishrochester.org
Dist(s): **Wayne State Univ. Pr.**

Jewish Educational Media, *(978-1-931607; 978-1-932349; 978-0-9890522)* 784 Eastern Pkwy., Suite 403, Brooklyn, NY 11213 USA Tel 718-774-6000; Fax: 718-774-3402
E-mail: eli@jemedia.org
Web site: http://www.jemedia.org
Dist(s): **Kehot Pubn. Society.**

Jewish Lights Publishing *Imprint of* **LongHill Partners, Inc.**

†Jewish Pubn. Society, *(978-0-8276)* Orders Addr.: 22883 Quicksilver Dr., Dulles, VA 20166 USA (SAN 253-9446) Tel 703-661-1165; 703-661-1529; Fax: 703-661-1501; Toll Free: 800-355-1165; Edit Addr.: 2100 Arch St., 2nd Flr., Philadelphia, PA 19103-1399 USA Tel 215-832-0600
E-mail: marketing@jewishpub.org
Web site: http://www.jewishpub.org
Dist(s): **Ebsco Publishing**
MyiLibrary
Univ. of Nebraska Pr.; *CIP.*

JFA Productions, *(978-0-9723024)* 806 Homestead Ave., Maybrook, NY 12543 USA Tel 845-427-5008
E-mail: carrdero@warwick.net.

JFAR Bks., *(978-0-615-45886-1)* Orders Addr.: P.O. Box 331621, West Hartford, CT 06133 USA Tel 617-388-2489
E-mail: J_Farquharson@yahoo.com
Web site: http://www.PlaytimetoBedtime.com.

JFK Online Studios, LLC, *(978-0-9742249)* 293 2nd Ave., West Haven, CT 06516-5127 USA
Web site: http://www.jfkonlinestudios.com.

JFW, Ltd., *(978-0-9710071)* 400 N. Church St., Unit 602, Charlotte, NC 28202 USA Tel 704-277-8378 (phone/fax)
E-mail: create2000@earthlink.net; jfwbird@earthlink.com.

JG Pr. *Imprint of* **World Pubns. Group, Inc.**

JGC/United Publishing Corps, *(978-0-910941)* 1710 N. Main St., Rockford, IL 61103 USA (SAN 270-5109) Tel 815-968-6601; Fax: 815-968-6600
E-mail: mailbox@jgcunited.com
Web site: http://www.jgcunited.com.

J.G.R. Enterprises, *(978-0-9758746)* 100 Oak St., Patchogue, NY 11772 USA Tel 631-790-0932
E-mail: joannros12@aol.com.

JGracia Publishing, *(978-0-9837403)* 2998 Valley View Cir., Powder Springs, GA 30127 USA Tel 678-668-6286
E-mail: jgraciaenterprises@gmail.com
Dist(s): **Lulu Enterprises Inc.**

JIMAPCO, Inc., *(978-1-56914)* Orders Addr.: P.O. Box 1137, Clifton Park, NY 12065 USA Fax: 518-899-5093; Toll Free: 800-627-7123; Edit Addr.: 2095 Rte. 9, Round Lake, NY 12151 USA Tel 518-899-5091
E-mail: cfisk@jimapco.com
Dist(s): **Benchmark LLC**
Langenscheidt Publishing Group
Rand McNally.

Jimmyland Corp., *(978-0-9760140; 978-0-9792672; 978-0-9820618; 978-0-9837021)* Jimmyland Corp., Orders Addr.: 2804 E. Crosley Dr., Suite H, West Palm Beach, FL 33415 USA Tel 561-602-1400
E-mail: jimmydrobinson@comcast.net
Web site: http://www.jimmydrobinson.com
Dist(s): **AtlasBooks Distribution**
BookBaby.

Jimsam Incorporated *See* **Jimsam Inc. Publishing**

Jimsam Inc. Publishing, *(978-0-9790768; 978-0-9816914; 978-0-9820587; 978-0-9841074; 978-0-615-57183-6; 978-0-615-66583-2; 978-0-615-67879-5)* P.O. Box 3363, Riverview, FL 33569 USA Tel 813-748-9523
E-mail: contact@jimsaminc.com; ms1free@aol.com
Web site: http://www.jimsam-inc.com.

Jinks, Elizabeth Schneider, *(978-0-9666312)* 7624 W. Mauna Loa Ln., Peoria, AZ 85381-4388 USA Tel 602-486-5362
E-mail: ee_jinks@qwest.net.

JINKS Studio Art & Publishing, *(978-0-9749672)* Orders Addr.: 9421 Woodlief Rd., Wake Forest, NC 27587-8993 USA
E-mail: jinksstudio@comcast.net
Web site: http://www.jinksstudio.com.

Jiovanie, *(978-0-578-10152-1)* 503 La Costa, Leander, TX 78641 USA.

JIST Life *Imprint of* **JIST Publishing**

†JIST Publishing, *(978-0-942784; 978-1-56370; 978-1-57112; 978-1-59357; 978-1-63332)* Div. of EMC Publishing, 875 Montreal Way, Saint Paul, MN 55102 USA (SAN 240-2351) Tel 651-290-2800 Toll Free Fax: 800-547-8329; *Imprints:* KIDSRIGHTS (Kidsrts); JIST Works (JIST Works); JIST Life (JIST Lfe)
E-mail: info@jist.com
Web site: http://www.jist.com
Dist(s): **Cardinal Pubs. Group**
Ebsco Publishing
Follett School Solutions
Linx Educational Publishing, Inc.
MyiLibrary; *CIP.*

JIST Works *Imprint of* **JIST Publishing**

JIST Works, Incorporated *See* **JIST Publishing**

Jitterbug Bks., *(978-0-9763031; 978-0-615-49452-4)* 25 Whale Rock Rd., Jamestown, RI 02835 USA Tel 401-423-2823
E-mail: jitterbugbooks@cox.net.

JJ Bks. (GBR) *(978-0-9569212; 978-1-909661) Dist. by* **Casemate Pubs.**

J.K.H. Enterprises, *(978-0-9761422)* MSC 5033, Busch Student Center 20 N. Grand Blvd., Saint Louis, MO 63103 USA
E-mail: juliushunter@slu.edu
Web site: http://juliushunter.tripod.com.

JL Thomas Pub., *(978-0-9786537)* 1287 Hadaway Trl., Lawrenceville, GA 30043-4670 USA
E-mail: jlthomas@jlthomas-author.com
Web site: http://jlthomas-author.com.

JLM CD-ROM Publishing Co., *(978-0-9749905)* 150 Idora Ave., San Francisco, CA 94127-1016 USA (SAN 255-9552)
Web site: http://www.jlmcd-rompublishing.com.

JM2 Publishing Co., *(978-0-9767210)* 6316 Monte Cresta, Richmond, CA 94806 USA Fax: 510-237-4305
E-mail: jeanmock@comcast.net.

JMC Printing, *(978-0-9638586)* Div. of JMC Marketing, Orders Addr.: 6730 W. 84th Cir. Suite 88, Arvada, CO 80003 USA Tel 303-564-1606 mobile
E-mail: jmcpublishing@aol.com.

JMG Studio, *(978-0-9771117)* Div. of John-Marc Grob Studios, 6 Southwind Dr., Flanders, NJ 07836 USA (SAN 256-8691) Tel 973-347-5399
E-mail: johnmarc@jmgstudio.net
Web site: http://www.jmgstudio.net.

JMK Music Publishing, *(978-0-9743218)* 22 Maple Ln., Northborough, MA 01532 USA
Web site: http://www.jmkmusicpub.com.

Jo Fletcher Books *Imprint of* **Quercus NA**

JoAnn Vergona Krapp & Gene Zaner, *(978-0-9722576)* 94 Sunset Ave., Farmingdale, NY 11735 USA
E-mail: jkrapp1940@aol.com.

Joanne Faye Pr., *(978-0-9747375)* c/o Goblin Fern Pr., Inc., 852 Hemlock Dr., Verona, WI 53593 USA Tel 608-835-5523; Fax: 608-442-0212
E-mail: jritland@mac.com
Web site: http://www.loveybooks.com.

Joanne Frances Pr., *(978-0-9777640)* Orders Addr.: 210 Piney Hill Rd., Oakland, MI 48363-1449 USA Toll Free: 800-960-2347
Web site: http://www.JoanneFrancesPress.com.

JoAnne/Horatio Books *See* **Gumbo Multimedia Entertainment**

JoBen Books, LLC *See* **Unveiled Media, LLC**

Jodan Collections, *(978-0-9747181)* Orders Addr.: 2716 N. Univ. Rd., Spokane, WA 99206 USA Tel 509-927-1882; Edit Addr.: 6405 S. Dishman Mica Rd., Spokane, WA 99206 USA
E-mail: joanne@inlandbindery.com
Web site: http://www.inlandbindery.com.

Jodaviste Publishing, *(978-0-9789016)* P.O. Box 473444, Charlotte, NC 28247 USA (SAN 851-920X)
E-mail: jodavistepublishing@earthlink.net
Web site: www.margosmagictrunk.com.

Joe Girl Ink, *(978-0-9766080)* 111S. Morgan, No. 502, Chicago, IL 60607 USA.

Joewolf Pubs., *(978-0-9671344)* Orders Addr.: P.O. Box 80127, Conyer, GA 30013 USA Tel 770-922-6655; Fax: 770-388-0521
E-mail: joewolf@bellsouth.net.

Joey Publishing, *(978-0-9799444)* 300 Atlantic St., Suite 500, Stamford, CT 06902 USA Fax: 203-363-7825
E-mail: jeanne@joeypublishing.com.

Johannesen Printing & Publishing, *(978-1-881084)* Orders Addr.: P.O. Box 24, Whitethorn, CA 95589 USA Tel 707-986-7465; Fax: 707-986-1656
E-mail: books@johannesen.com
Web site: http://www.johannesen.com.

Johnny Sundby Photography, *(978-0-9747152)* 4780 Easy St., Rapid City, SD 57702 USA Tel 605-343-5646; Fax: 605-342-0139
E-mail: dsp@rap.midco.net
Web site: http://www.johnnysundby.com.

Johnson, Anthony, *(978-0-9773760)* P.O. Box 731, Burbank, CA 91503-0731 USA (SAN 257-4187) Fax: 818-558-6771
E-mail: leedobug@hotmail.com.

Johnson, Bonnie, *(978-0-9769756)* Orders Addr.: 6 Son Ct., Valley Center, KS 67147-2659 USA.

Johnson Bks., *(978-0-917895; 978-0-933472; 978-1-55566)* Div. of Big Earth Publishing Co., Orders Addr.: 1637 Pearl St. Ste. 201, Boulder, CO 80302-5447 USA (SAN 201-0313) Toll Free: 800-258-5830
E-mail: books@bigearthpublishing.com
Web site: http://www.johnsonbooks.com
Dist(s): **Big Earth Publishing.**

Johnson, Colleen, *(978-0-9785002)* 2500 63rd St NW, Minot, ND 58703 USA Tel 701-839-5768
E-mail: gchristi@minot.com
Web site: http://icecreamforbreakfastbook.com.

Johnson, Earl Photography, *(978-0-9649645; 978-0-9779024)* Orders Addr.: P.O. Box 870165, Stone Mountain, GA 30087 USA Tel 678-476-3950; Fax: 678-476-3951
E-mail: books@earljohnsontruckbooks.com
Web site: http://earljohnsontruckbooks.com.

Johnson, Gary, *(978-0-9791794)* 938 E. Lois Ln., Phoenix, AZ 85020-1189 USA (SAN 852-6931) Tel 602-944-7517 (phone/fax); Toll Free: 888-665-2762
E-mail: gjohnson@molarman.com
Web site: http://www.molarman.com.

Johnson, James *See* **Strategies Publishing Co.**

Johnson Tribe Publishing, *(978-0-9896733; 978-0-692-30715-1)* 1484 Uncle Ben Dr., Powder Springs, GA 30127 USA Tel 770-815-6477
E-mail: johnsontribepublishing@gmail.com
Web site: johnsontribepublishing@gmail.com.

Johnston, Ann, *(978-0-9656776)* Orders Addr.: P.O. Box 388, Ashland, OH 44805 USA Toll Free: 800-247-6553 (ordering & shipping information); Edit Addr.: P.O. Box 944, Lake Oswego, OR 97034 USA (SAN 852-9043) Tel 503-635-6791; Fax: 503-675-0366
E-mail: order@bookmaster.com
Web site: http://www.annjohnston.net
Dist(s): **CreateSpace Independent Publishing Platform.**

Johnston, Ann, *(978-0-9796010)* 2409 Crest St., Alexandria, VA 22302 USA Tel 703-629-2175
E-mail: growhealthy@gmail.com.

Johnston, Don Inc., *(978-1-893376; 978-1-58702; 978-1-4105)* Orders Addr.: 26799 W. Commerce Dr., Volo, IL 60073 USA Tel 847-740-0749; Fax: 847-740-7326; Toll Free: 800-999-4660
Web site: http://www.donjohnston.com.

Johnston-Brown, Anne Publishing Co. *See* **Retriever Pr.**

Joint Committee on Printing *Imprint of* **United States Government Printing Office**

Joint Heir Multimedia, *(978-0-9796148)* P.O. Box 108, Edgewater, NJ 07020 USA
Web site: http://www.jointheirmultimedia.net.

Joint Publishing Co. (HKG) *(978-962-04) Dist. by* **China Bks.**

Joint Publishing Co. (HKG) *(978-962-04) Dist. by* **Chinasprout.**

Jokar Productions, LLC *See* **Save Our Seas, Ltd.**

Jolly Fish Pr., *(978-0-9848801; 978-0-9886491; 978-1-939967; 978-1-63163)* P.O. Box 1773, Provo, UT 84603-1773 USA Tel 435-512-1683
E-mail: christopher@jollyfishpress.com; kirk@jollyfishpress.com
Web site: http://www.jollyfishpress.com
Dist(s): **Independent Pubs. Group**
MyiLibrary
ebrary, Inc.

Jolly Geranium, Inc., *(978-0-9644524)* 2953 E. Pawnee Dr., Sierra Vista, AZ 85635-8511 USA Tel 520-321-4747.

Jolly Learning, Ltd. (GBR) *(978-1-870946; 978-1-903619; 978-1-84414) Dist. by* **Am Intl Dist.**

Jolt, *(978-0-9831498)* Orders Addr.: P.O. Box 201013, Montgomery, AL 36120 USA Tel 256-390-3722
E-mail: information@jolt-books.com
Web site: http://www.jolt-books.com.

†Jones & Bartlett Learning, LLC, *(978-0-7637; 978-0-86720; 978-1-4496; 978-1-284)* 5 Wall St., Burlington, MA 01803 USA (SAN 285-0893) Toll Free: 800-832-0034
Web site: http://www.jblearning.com
Dist(s): **Ebsco Publishing**
Rittenhouse Bk. Distributors
ebrary, Inc.; *CIP.*

Jones & Bartlett Publishers, Incorporated *See* **Jones & Bartlett Learning, LLC**

Jones, Augustine R., *(978-0-9743223)* 4213 N. Knoll Ridge Rd. Apt. B2, Peoria, IL 61614-7439 USA.

For full information on wholesalers and distributors, refer to the Wholesaler and Distributor Name Index

Jones, Bob University Press *See* **BJU Pr.**

Jones Bks., *(978-0-9721217; 978-0-9763539; 978-0-9790475)* 3 Loon Ln., Madison, WI 53717-1854 USA
E-mail: info@jonesbooks.com
Web site: http://www.jonesbooks.com.

Jones, Kirk, *(978-0-9759688)* P.O. Box 74702, Richmond, VA 23236 USA
E-mail: kirkjonesillustrations@juno.com.

Jones, Linda, *(978-0-9776450)* 2700 Woodland Park Dr. Apt. 705, Houston, TX 77082-6605 USA
E-mail: amiasthefirst@aol.com.

JonesHarvest Publishing, *(978-0-9794455; 978-1-60388)* 5400 E. State Rd. 45, Bloomington, IN 47408 USA Tel 812-323-2330; Fax: 812-323-2339; Toll Free: 877-400-0075
E-mail: jonesharvest@sbcglobal.net
Web site: http://www.jonesharvest.com.

Jonquil Books *See* **Miglior Pr.**

Jon'taar Graphxs, *(978-0-9764385)* 75 Lantern Chase Dr., Delaware, OH 43015 USA Tel 740-972-6321
E-mail: msuplicki@jontaar.com; information@mirthburdz.com
Web site: http://www.jontaar.com; http://www.mirthburdz.com.

Jordan Music Productions, Inc., *(978-1-895523; 978-1-894262; 978-1-55386)* M.P.O. Box 490, Niagara Falls, NY 14302-0490 USA
E-mail: sjordan@sara-jordan.com
Web site: http://www.sara-jordan.com; http://www.SongsThatTeach.com; http://www.edu-mart.com
Dist(s): **Follett Media Distribution iLeon.**

Jordan Publishing Hse., *(978-1-890875)* Orders Addr.: P.O. Box 671, Columbia, CA 95310 USA Fax: 209-532-5503; Edit Addr.: 22620 Parrotts Ferry Rd., Columbia, CA 95310 USA Do not confuse with companies with the same name in Las Vegas, NV, Nappanee, IN, Reston, VA, Phoenix, AZ, Prescott, AZ
E-mail: gpview@erli.net.

Jordan, Sara Publishing, *(978-1-895523; 978-1-894262; 978-1-55386)* Div. of Jordan Music Productions, Inc., Orders Addr.: M.P.O. Box 490, Niagara Falls, NY 14302-0490 USA (SAN 118-959X) Tel 416-760-7664; Fax: 416-762-2770; Toll Free Fax: 800-229-3855; Toll Free: 800-567-7733
E-mail: sjordan@sara-jordan.com
Web site: http://www.edu-mart.com; http://www.sara-jordan.com; http://www.songsthatteach.com
Dist(s): **Follett School Solutions.**

Jordan Valley Heritage Hse., *(978-0-939810)* P.O. Box 99, Stayton, OR 97383-0099 USA (SAN 216-7425) Tel 503-769-4236
E-mail: jvhh5@wvi.com.

Jorge Pinto Bks., *(978-0-9742615; 978-0-9774724; 978-0-9790766; 978-0-9795576; 978-0-9801147; 978-1-934978)* 6216 Vorlich Ln., Bethesda, MD 20816 USA (SAN 853-7526)
Web site: http://www.pintobooks.com; jpintobooks.com
Dist(s): **D.A.P./Distributed Art Pubs.**

Jorlan Publishing *See* **Jorlan Publishing, Inc.**

Jorlan Publishing, Inc., *(978-0-9710696; 978-1-933830)* P.O. Box 2882, Cedar City, UT 84721-2882 USA
Web site: http://www.jorlanpublishing.com.

Joseph Henry Pr. *Imprint of* **National Academies Pr.**

Joseph Pubns., *(978-0-9773243)* P.O. Box 401, Killington, VT 05751 USA Tel 917-502-7328
Web site: http://www.josephpublications.com
Dist(s): **Independent Pubs. Group.**

Joseph's Coat Publishing *See* **Breezy Reads**

Joseph's Heartprint, *(978-0-9787035)* 728 Creek Rd., Carlisle, PA 17013 USA Tel 717-258-8796; Fax: 717-243-4254
E-mail: george@catholicartworks.com
Web site: http://www.catholicartworks.com.

Joseph's Labor, *(978-0-9729800)* P.O. Box 176265, Covington, KY 41017-6265 USA Tel 859-578-8112
E-mail: JosephsLabor@aol.com.

Joshua Pr., Inc. (CAN) *(978-1-894400) Dist. by* **Gabriel Res.**

Joshua Tree Publishing, *(978-0-9710954; 978-0-9768677; 978-0-9778311; 978-0-9823703; 978-0-9845904; 978-0-9829803; 978-0-9886577; 978-1-941049)* 1016 W. Jackson Blvd. Suite 500, Chicago, IL 60607 USA Tel 312-893-7525; 1016 W. Jackson Blvd. Suite 500, Chicago, IL 60607 Tel 312-893-7525 Do not confuse with companies with the same or similar names in Mentor, OH, Lake San Marcos, CA
E-mail: info@joshuatreepublishing.com
Web site: http://joshuatreepublishing.com; http://centaurbooks.com; http://chiralhouse.com.

Jossey-Bass *Imprint of* **Wiley, John & Sons, Inc.**

Jostens Bks., *(978-0-9759530; 978-0-9788398)* 116 Independence Dr., Indian Trail, NC 28079-9452 USA Toll Free: 800-458-0319
E-mail: sherry.clontz@jostens.com
Web site: http://www.jostens.com.

Jots & Tittles Publishing, *(978-0-9894379)* 310 W. 39th St., Vancouver, WA 98660 USA Tel 360-566-2781
E-mail: ghost@writingasaghost.com.

Journals Unlimited, Inc., *(978-1-892033; 978-0-9818414; 978-0-9842578; 978-0-9832414; 978-0-9859025; 978-0-9907307)* P.O. Box 1882, Bay City, MI 48707 USA Tel 989-686-3377; Fax: 989-686-3380; Toll Free Fax: 800-897-8529; Toll Free: 800-897-8528
E-mail: barb@journalsunlimited.com; tech@journalsunlimited.com
Web site: http://www.journalsunlimited.com.

Journalstone, *(978-0-9828119; 978-1-936564; 978-1-940161; 978-1-942712)* 1261 Peachwood Ct., San Bruno, CA 94066 USA Tel 415-235-6734
E-mail: christophercpayne@journalstone.com
Web site: http://journalstone.com.

Journey of a Dream Pr., *(978-0-9749876; 978-0-9818251; 978-0-9839777; 978-0-9897142)* 2888 Winchester Ct., Duluth, GA 30096 USA Tel 770-789-9796
E-mail: journeyofadream@comcast.net
Web site: www.journeyofadream.com.

Journey Pubns., LLC, *(978-0-9728716; 978-0-9748087; 978-0-9772078; 978-0-9798171)* Orders Addr.: P.O. Box 2442, Warminster, PA 18974-2442 USA (SAN 255-1675) Do not confuse with companies with the same or similar names in Woodstock, NY, Savannah, GA, Avon Park, FL, Metairie, LA, Lacey, WA
E-mail: journeypubs@aol.com
Web site: http://www.journeypublications.com.

Journey Stone Creations, LLC, *(978-0-9758709; 978-1-59958)* 3533 Danbury Rd., Fairfield, OH 45014 USA Fax: 513-860-0176; *Imprints:* A.W.A. Gang (AWA Gang)
E-mail: pat@journeystonecreations.com
Web site: http://www.journeystonecreations.com; http://www.myezbookclub.com; http://www.jscbooks.com.

JourneyForth *Imprint of* **BJU Pr.**

Journique Publishing Group, Inc., *(978-0-9795586)* P.O. Box 524, Knightdale, NC 27545 USA Fax: 407-796-6394
E-mail: pjordan@journique.com
Web site: http://www.journique.com
Dist(s): **Lightning Source, Inc.**

Jove *Imprint of* **Penguin Publishing Group**

Joy of my Youth Pubns., The, *(978-0-9774345)* P.O. Box 128702, Cincinnati, OH 45212 USA Tel 513-531-2709
E-mail: thejoyofmyyouth@netzero.net
Web site: http://www.thejoyofmyyouth.com.

J.O.Y. Pubns., *(978-0-9762975)* 186 Gatewood Ave., Rochester, NY 14624-1737 USA Do not confuse with companies with the same or similar name in Santa Maria, CA Gardena, CA, Pittsboro, NC, Woburn, MA
E-mail: rainbowvillagecc@yahoo.com; rainbowvillage@homewithGod.net
Web site: www.our.homewithGod.com/rainbowvillage/.

J.O.Y. Publishing, *(978-0-9755454)* Orders Addr.: P.O. Box 540912, Merritt Island, FL 32594-0912 USA; *Imprints:* Laughing Zebra - Books for Children (Laugh Zebra)
E-mail: jdelgado@laughing-zebra-children-books.com
Web site: http://zooprisepartyfiestazoorpresa.blogspot.com; http://www.laughing-zebra-children-books.com.

JoyceHerzog.com, Incorporated *See* **Herzog, Joyce**

Joyful Learning Publications, LLC, *(978-0-9836580)* 3148 Plainfield Ave NE suite 153, Grand Rapids, ME 49525-3285 USA Tel 207-693-5257
E-mail: sandyjane05@yahoo.com.

Joyful Learning Publishing *See* **Joyful Learning Publications, LLC**

Joyful Noise, *(978-0-9772109)* 312 Stonewall Rd., Concord, VA 24538 USA (SAN 257-0149)
E-mail: j.b.designs@att.net.

JoyRox, LLC, *(978-0-9754972)* 11585 Hooker St., Westminster, CO 80031-7121 USA
E-mail: info@joy-rox.com
Web site: http://www.joy-rox.com.

JoySoul Corp., *(978-0-9727786)* Orders Addr.: 1940 S. Broadway, Minot, ND 58701-6508 USA Tel 701-683-4859 (business line); 701-308-0594 (mobile phone); Fax: 866-518-4760; Toll Free: 866-569-8486 (order line)
E-mail: jscontact@joysoul.com; joysoul@drtel.net
Web site: http://www.joysoul.com.

JPA Assocs., *(978-0-9727125)* 11026 Maple Rd., Lafayette, CO 80026 USA Tel 303-665-6764.

JR Comics (KOR) *(978-89-94208; 978-89-92836; 978-89-98341) Dist. by* **Lerner Pub.**

Jr Imagination, *(978-0-9837404; 978-0-9893189)* 17310 Trosa St., Granada Hills, CA 91344 USA Tel 818-366-4194; Fax: 818-366-2134
E-mail: marty@jrimagination.com
Web site: http://www.jrimagination.com; http://www.samatart.com; http://www.doublemgraphics.com.

JRP Ringier Kunstverlag AG (CHE) *(978-2-940271; 978-3-905701; 978-3-905770; 978-3-03764; 978-3-905829) Dist. by* **Dist Art Pubs.**

JRV Publishing, *(978-0-9771250)* P.O. Box 82, West Simsbury, CT 06092 USA
E-mail: jverney1@jrvpublishing.com.

JSP Bks., *(978-0-9728519)* 6886 Hickory Lake Cove, Memphis, TN 38119 USA Tel 901-757-0694
E-mail: contact@jspbooks.com
Web site: http://www.jspbooks.com.

Juba Bks. *Imprint of* **NetNia Publishing Co.**

Judah Bks., Inc., *(978-0-9767469)* 3535 W. Tierra Buena Ln., Apt. No. A273, Phoenix, AZ 85053 USA.

Judaica Pr., Inc., The, *(978-0-910818; 978-1-880582; 978-1-932443; 978-1-60763)* 123 Ditmas Ave., Brooklyn, NY 11218 USA (SAN 204-9856) Tel 718-972-6200; Fax: 718-972-6204; Toll Free: 800-972-6201; *Imprints:* Shayach Comics (Shayach Comics)
E-mail: info@judaicapress.com
Web site: http://www.judaicapress.com.

JuDe Publishing, *(978-0-9712585)* Orders Addr.: P.O. Box 264 s lacienega blvd #1283, beverly hills, CA 90211 USA Tel 310-600-9729
E-mail: judepublishing@yahoo.com
Dist(s): **Bookazine Co., Inc.**

†Judson Pr., *(978-0-8170)* Div. of American Baptist Churches, U.S.A., P.O. Box 851, Valley Forge, PA 19482-0851 USA (SAN 201-0348) Tel 610-768-2118; Fax: 610-768-2107; Toll Free: 800-458-3766
Web site: http://www.judsonpress.com
Dist(s): **A & B Distributors & Pubs. Group**
Afrikan World Bk. Distributor
Anchor Distributors
Appalachian Bible Co.
Partners Bk. Distributing, Inc.
Send The Light Distribution LLC
Sociedad Biblica de Puerto Rico
Spring Arbor Distributors, Inc.
Wizard Works; *CIP.*

Juice & Berriesr, The *Imprint of* **Asiana Media**

Julenda Enterprises, *(978-0-9747994)* 219 E. El Valle, Green Valley, AZ 85614-2903 USA Tel 520-393-0071
E-mail: judylgarcia@aol.com
Web site: http://www.judylenore.com.

Julie Andrews Collection *Imprint of* **HarperCollins Pubs.**

Julio C. Malone *See* **Editorial Miglo Inc.**

Julson, D. K., *(978-0-9746564; 978-0-615-11699-0)* 28704 County Hwy B., Richland Ctr, WI 53581-6721 USA.

July-Eight Publishing *See* **Three Socks Publishing**

Jump at the Sun *Imprint of* **Hyperion Bks. for Children**

Jump! Inc., *(978-1-62031; 978-1-62496)* 5357 Penn Ave. S., Minneapolis, MN 55419 USA (SAN 920-8143) Tel 888-960-1346; *Imprints:* Bullfrog Books (BullfrogBks)
E-mail: david@jumplibrary.com; casie@jumplibrary.com
Web site: http://www.jumplibrary.com
Dist(s): **Follett School Solutions.**

Jump Start Performance Programs, *(978-1-893962)* P.O. Box 3448, Van Nuys, CA 91407 USA Toll Free Fax: 800-990-9667; Toll Free: 800-450-0432
E-mail: scott@scottgreenberg.com
Web site: http://www.scottgreenberg.com.

Jumping Cow Pr., *(978-0-9801433; 978-0-9980010)* P.O. Box 8982, Scarborough, NY 10510-8982 USA (SAN 855-305X) Tel 914-373-9816
E-mail: jumpingcowpress@gmail.com
Web site: http://www.JumpingCowPress.com.

Jumping Jack Pr., *(978-0-9795441; 978-1-60580; 978-1-62348)* Div. of Up With Paper, LLC, 6049 Hi-Tek Ct., Mason, OH 45040 USA Tel 513-759-7473; Fax: 513-336-3119
E-mail: info@upwithpaper.com; georgew@upwithpaper.com
Web site: http://www.jumpingjackpress.com
Dist(s): **Ingram Pub. Services.**

June Bks., LLC, *(978-0-9835558)* 408 W. Lotta St. Suite No. 1, Sioux Falls, SD 57105 USA Tel 512-630-3380
E-mail: trevor@junebooks.com; hello@junebooks.com
Web site: http://www.junebooks.com.

Junebug Bks. *Imprint of* **NewSouth, Inc.**

JuneOne Publishing Hub, *(978-0-9763082)* 27762 Antonio Pkwy., L1-404, Ladera Ranch, CA 92694 USA Tel 949-364-6179; Fax: 757-299-4407; *Imprints:* A JuneOne Production (A JuneOne Prod)
E-mail: info@juneonehub.com
Web site: http://www.juneonehub.com.

Jungle Communications, Incorporation *See* **Allergic Child Publishing Group**

Jungle Hse. Pubns., *(978-0-9769332)* Orders Addr.: 736 Cardium St., Sanibel, FL 33957-6704 USA Tel 239-395-4518
E-mail: junglehousepub@yahoo.com
Web site: http://junglehousepublications.com.

Jungle Jeep Press *See* **Jungle Wagon Pr.**

Jungle Wagon Pr., *(978-0-9834092; 978-0-9904271)* 5116 Didier Ave., Rockford, IL 61101 USA (SAN 920-6426) Tel 815-988-9048
E-mail: junglewagonpress@gmail.com
Web site: http://www.junglewagonpress.com.

Junior History Pr., *(978-0-9744556)* Orders Addr.: P.O. Box 157, Summerville, SC 29484-0157 USA Tel 843-873-8117; Edit Addr.: 1311 Jahnz Ave., Summerville, SC 29485 USA
E-mail: gteaster@juniorhistory.com
Web site: http://www.juniorhistory.com.

Junior League of Central Westchester, *(978-0-615-16563-9)* 1039 Post Rd., Scarsdale, NY 10583 USA Tel 914-723-6139; Fax: 914-723-6016
E-mail: jlcw@verizon.net
Web site: http://www.jlcentralwestchester.org.

Junior League of Grand Rapids Michigan, Inc., *(978-0-9611316; 978-0-9634927)* 25 Sheldon Blvd., Suite 124, Grand Rapids, MI 49503 USA (SAN 282-9452) Tel 616-451-0452; Fax: 616-451-1936
E-mail: juniorleague@iserv.net
Web site: http://www.junioreagiegr.com.

Junior League of Tyler, Inc., The, *(978-0-9607122)* 1919 S. Donnybrook, Tyler, TX 75701 USA (SAN 238-9975) Tel 903-593-8141; Fax: 903-595-1362.

Juniper Berry Pr., *(978-0-9760076)* 6609 Cornelia Dr., Edina, MN 55435 USA Tel 952-285-4447
E-mail: gjudso@aol.com
Web site: http://www.juniperberrypress.com.

Juniper Grove, *(978-1-60355)* 2129 E. Stearns, Fayetteville, AR 72703 USA (SAN 853-5078)
E-mail: JuniperGrove@gmail.com
Web site: http://www.junipergrove.com
Dist(s): **CreateSpace Independent Publishing Platform.**

Juping Horse Pr., *(978-0-615-55671-0; 978-0-615-75585-4)* 845 N. 27th St., Philadelphia, PA 19130 USA Tel 215-978-0844
E-mail: karin@jumpinghorsepress.com
Web site: http://www.jumpinghorsepress.com.

Jupiter Coins *See* **Adventure in Discovery**

juputer2 bks., *(978-0-9779404)* 309 Claymille Pl., Nashville, TN 37207 USA
Web site: http://www.juputer2books.com.

Just Be Publishing, Inc., *(978-0-9668219)* 746 E. Rosemore Ct., Salt Lake City, UT 84107 USA (SAN 299-7479) Tel 801-265-3435 (phone/fax)
E-mail: bl_ehrler@att.net
Web site: http://www.justbepublishing.com.

Just Chill Pubns., *(978-0-9726548)* P.O. Box 5990, Chicago, IL 60680 USA
E-mail: chill1960@comcast.net; contact@justchill.org; contact@communityaccesstoresources.org
Web site: http://www.justchill.org; http://www.communityaccesstoresources.org.

Just Enjoyable Memorable Story Bks., *(978-0-9724472)* 8258 Balsam Way, Arvada, CO 80005 USA
E-mail: jemsbooks@hotmail.com.

Just For Kids Pr., LLC, *(978-1-934650; 978-1-935498; 978-1-935747; 978-1-936918; 978-1-937962)* 360 Hurst St., Linden, NJ 07036 USA
E-mail: ssullivan@justforkidspress.com.

Just Like Me, Inc., *(978-1-928889)* P.O. Box 4494, Washington, DC 20017 USA Tel 202-526-1725
E-mail: info@justlikemebooks.com
Web site: http://www.justlikemebooks.com.

Just Me Productions, *(978-0-9821118)* 4255 Us 1 S., Suite 18-212, Saint Augustine, FL 32086 USA Tel 904-797-7242
Web site: http://www.justmeproductions.com.

Just Think Bks. *Imprint of* **Canary Connect Pubns.**

Just Us Bks., Inc., *(978-0-940975; 978-1-933491)* 356 Glenwood Ave., 3rd Flr., East Orange, NJ 07017-2108 USA (SAN 664-7413) Tel 973-672-7701; *Imprints:* Sankofa Books (Sankofa Bks)
E-mail: justusbook@aol.com
Web site: http://www.justusbooks.com.

Just Write Bks., *(978-0-9722839; 978-0-9766533; 978-0-9777614; 978-0-9788628; 978-1-934949)* Just Write Communications, 14 Maine St., Suite 105, Box 8, Brunswick, ME 04011 USA (SAN 855-5109) Tel 207-729-3600; Fax: 207-729-4600
E-mail: jstwrite@jstwrite.com
Web site: http://www.jstwrite.com.

Justice Link Publishing, *(978-0-692-00612-2)* P.O. Box 3144, Glendale, CA 91221 USA.

Juvenescent Research Corp., *(978-0-9600148; 978-1-884996)* 807 Riverside Dr., Apt. 1F, New York, NY 10032 USA (SAN 206-7250) Tel 212-795-3749
Dist(s): **Barnes & Noble, Inc.**

Juventud, Editorial (ESP) *(978-84-261) Dist. by* **Distribks Inc.**

Juventud, Editorial (ESP) *(978-84-261) Dist. by* **Continental Bk.**

Juventud, Editorial (ESP) *(978-84-261) Dist. by* **AIMS Intl.**

Juventud, Editorial (ESP) *(978-84-261) Dist. by* **Lectorum Pubns.**

JVED Publishing, *(978-0-9768833)* 18140 Zane St., NW No. 410, Elk River, MN 55330 USA
Web site: http://www.jvedpublishing.org.

JWall Publishing, *(978-0-9760518)* 287 Jones Rd., Statham, GA 30666 USA Tel 770-725-7465.

JWD Publishing, *(978-0-9843365; 978-0-9846315; 978-1-941574)* P.O. Box 32, Sylvania, GA 30467 USA Tel 912-564-2427
E-mail: jwpublishing@gmail.com
Web site: http://www.revolutionarydisciples.com.

JYZ Books, LLC *See* **JYZ Bks., LLC**

K and K Publishing, *(978-0-9828886)* P.O. Box 20517, Carson City, NV 89721 USA Tel 775-885-7986
E-mail: okmarge@charter.net; marge@kankpublishing.com
Web site: http://kankpublishing.com.

K Coil, *(978-0-615-47148-8; 978-0-615-47214-0; 978-0-615-47476-2; 978-0-615-47881-4; 978-0-615-47907-1)* 101 N. Second St. Apt. 7, Princeton, WV 24740 USA Tel 304-888-9484
E-mail: krcoil@yahoo.com
Dist(s): **CreateSpace Independent Publishing Platform**
Dummy Record Do Not USE!!!!.

K. F. Enterprises *See* **Production Assocs., Inc.**

K T Graphics, *(978-0-9755259)* 5300 Standing Rock Pl., Las Vegas, NV 89130 USA Tel 702-808-3773
Web site: http://www.ktgraphicsolutions.com.

K12, *(978-1-931728; 978-1-60153)* 2300 Corporate Park Dr., Herndon, VA 20171 USA Tel 703-483-7000; Fax: 703-483-7330
Web site: http://www.k12.com.

K-Twelve MicroMedia Publishing, Inc., *(978-0-943646; 978-1-56419)* 16 McKee Dr., Mahwah, NJ 07430 USA (SAN 286-990X) Tel 201-529-4500; Fax: 201-529-5282; Toll Free: 800-292-1997
E-mail: sales@k12mmp.com
Web site: http://www.k12mmp.com.

KA Productions, LLC, *(978-1-888018)* Orders Addr.: P.O. Box 21, Alexandria, VA 22313-0021 USA Tel 703-371-4325 (phone/fax); *Imprints:* Word of Mouth Books (Word of Mouth Bks)
E-mail: stephanie@bookinaday.com
Web site: http://www.kwamealexander.com
Dist(s): **SPD-Small Pr. Distribution.**

Kabet Pr. (GBR) *(978-0-948662) Dist. by* **Empire Pub Srvs.**

Kadima Pr., *(978-0-9723229)* 410 Pine St. No., 802 C, Abilene, TX 79601-5163 USA Fax: 501-636-7425
E-mail: KadimaPress@juno.com
Web site: http://www.kadimapress.com; http://www.AuntLaya.com
Dist(s): **Bks. West.**

Kaeden Bks. *Imprint of* **Kaeden Corp.**

Kaeden Corp., *(978-1-57874; 978-1-879835; 978-1-61181)* Orders Addr.: P.O. Box 16190, Rocky River, OH 44116 USA Tel 440-617-1400; Fax: 440-617-1403; Toll Free: 800-890-7323; *Imprints:* Kaeden Books (Kaeden)
E-mail: info@kaeden.com
Web site: http://www.kaeden.com
Dist(s): **Follett School Solutions.**

Kagan Cooperative Learning *See* **Kagan Publishing**

Kagan Publishing, *(978-1-879097; 978-1-933445)* Div. of Resources for Teachers, Orders Addr.: P.O. Box 72008, San Clemente, CA 92673 USA Tel 949-545-6300; Fax: 949-545-6301; Toll Free: 800-933-2667
E-mail: carol@kaganonline.com; parker@kaganonline.com; Hannah@KaganOnline.com
Web site: http://www.kaganonline.com.

Kahley, Glenn, *(978-0-9788914)* 1575 England Dr., Columbus, OH 43240 USA
E-mail: kahley.1@osu.edu.

Kaimanu Prodns., Ltd., *(978-0-9764474)* 135-A Kaimanu Pl., Kihei, HI 96753 USA Tel 808-268-9092; Fax: 808-442-0013
E-mail: customerservice@kaimanu.net
Web site: http://www.kaimanu.net
Dist(s): **Booklines Hawaii, Ltd.**

Kairos Publishing, *(978-0-9665831; 978-0-9818864; 978-0-615-92130-3)* Orders Addr.: P.O. Box 450, Clarence, NY 14031 USA Tel 716-759-1058; Edit Addr.: 10501 Main St., Clarence, NY 14031 USA Do not confuse with Kairos Publishing in Llano de San Juan, NM
E-mail: office@eagleswings.to
Web site: http://www.eagleswings.to
Dist(s): **Destiny Image Pubs.**
Send The Light Distribution LLC.

KAK, *(978-0-615-40229-1)* 776 Highland Hills Dr., Howard, OH 43028 USA Tel 740-294-3202
E-mail: saucie776@yahoo.com.

Kalandraka Catalunya, Edicions, S.L. (ESP) *(978-84-95730)* *Dist. by* **IPG Chicago.**

Kalandraka Editora, S.L. (ESP) *(978-84-8464; 978-84-923553; 978-84-95123)* *Dist. by* **Mariuccia Iaconi Bk Imports.**

Kalandraka Editora, S.L. (ESP) *(978-84-8464; 978-84-923553; 978-84-95123)* *Dist. by* **Lectorum Pubns.**

Kalawantis Computer Services, Incorporated *See* **Kalawantis Publishing Services, Inc**

Kalawantis Publishing Services, Inc, *(978-0-9665909)* Orders Addr.: P.O. Box 25004, Charlotte, NC 28227 USA Tel 704-754-1108
E-mail: publisher@kalawantis.com
Web site: http://www.kalawantis.com.

Kalcom Publishing, *(978-0-9797530)* 84-01 Lefferts Blvd., Kew Gardens, NY 11415 USA Tel 718-805-5555
E-mail: yek@kalcom.com.

Kaleta Publishing, LLC, *(978-0-615-39881-5; 978-0-9830222)* 161 Trail E., Pataskala, OH 43062 USA Tel 614-352-3583
E-mail: mindyjkaleta@gmail.com
Dist(s): **AtlasBooks Distribution**
MyiLibrary.

KALEXT Productions, LLC, *(978-0-9617451; 978-0-9748792)* 12795 75th Lane N., West Palm Beach, FL 33412 USA (SAN 664-0613) Tel 561-310-4338; Fax: 561-790-6294 Call 561-310-4338 first
E-mail: xela319@comcast.net
Web site: http://www.bilingualgames.com; http://www.biznizgames.com.

Kalindi Pr., *(978-1-935826; 978-0-9838455)* 2508 Shadow Valley Ranch Rd., Prescott, AZ 86305 USA Tel 928-636-3759
E-mail: balazuccarello@gmail.com
Web site: http://www.kalindipress.com
Dist(s): **SCB Distributors.**

Kallyan Publishing, *(978-0-9762065)* P.O. Box 473, Stephens City, VA 22655-9998 USA.

†**Kalmbach Publishing Co., Bks. Div.**, *(978-0-8238; 978-0-87116; 978-0-89024; 978-0-89778; 978-0-913135; 978-0-933168; 978-1-62700)* Orders Addr.: P.O. Box 1612, Waukesha, WI 53186 USA (SAN 201-0399) Tel 262-796-8776 Toll Free: 800-533-6644 (customer sales); 800-446-5489 (customer service); 800-558-1544 (trade sales); Edit Addr.: 21027 Crossroads Cir., Waukesha, WI 53186 USA Tel 262-796-8776
E-mail: customerservice@kalmbach.com
Web site: http://corporate.kalmbach.com/; http://kalmbach.com
Dist(s): **Perseus-PGW**
Perseus Bks. Group
Watson-Guptill Pubns., Inc.; *CIP.*

Kalmia Publishing, *(978-0-9676620)* Orders Addr.: 826 Amiford Dr., San Diego, CA 92107 USA Tel 619-222-7074 (phone/fax)
E-mail: pixieh@mymailstation.com; folsom@islc.net
Web site: http://www.islc.net/~folsom/language.

Kalyani Navyug Media Pty. Ltd. (IND) *(978-81-906963; 978-81-907326; 978-81-907829)* *Dist. by* **Random.**

KAM Publishing, *(978-0-9795474)* Orders Addr.: 1716 Worley St., Durant, OK 74701-2468 USA
E-mail: sharonm@llibs.com
Web site: http://www.llibs.com
Dist(s): **Library Integrated Solutions & Assocs.**

Kamahoi Pr. *Imprint of* **Bishop Museum Pr.**

Kamaron Institute Pr., Div. of Kamaron Institute for Rapid Business Results, 104 Strawflower Path, Peachtree City, GA 30269 USA
E-mail: info@kamaron.org; kamaroninstitute@earthlink.net
Web site: http://www.kamaron.org.

†**Kamehameha Publishing**, *(978-0-87336)* 567 S. King St., Suite 118, Honolulu, HI 96813 USA Tel 808-534-8205; Fax: 808-541-5305
E-mail: publishing@ksbe.edu
Web site: http://www.kamehamehapublishing.org
Dist(s): **Bess Pr., Inc.**
Booklines Hawaii, Ltd.
Follett School Solutions
Native Bks.; *CIP.*

Kamehameha Schools Press *See* **Kamehameha Publishing**

Kana'i Records, *(978-0-9754567)* 95-1168 Makaikai St. Apt. 113, Mililani, HI 96789-4307 USA
E-mail: bhelemano@aol.com
Dist(s): **Booklines Hawaii, Ltd.**

K&B Products, *(978-0-9646181; 978-0-9740841; 978-0-9772372; 978-1-935122)* P.O. Box 548, Yellville, AR 72687 USA Toll Free Fax: 888-871-5856; Toll Free: 800-700-5096
E-mail: brmp@aol.com
Web site: http://www.thecompletepet.com; http://www.whitehallpublishing.com
Dist(s): **Western International, Inc.**

Kane, Kimberly Brougham, *(978-0-615-17610-9; 978-0-578-04556-6)* 1406 Campfire Rd., Lake Charles, LA 70611 USA
Web site: http://www.mommysheart.com
Dist(s): **Lulu Enterprises Inc.**

†**Kane Miller**, *(978-0-916291; 978-1-929132; 978-1-933605; 978-1-935279; 978-1-61067)* Div. of EDC Publishing, Orders Addr.: P.O. Box 470663, Tulsa, OK 74146 USA (SAN 295-8945) Tel 858-456-0540; Fax: 858-456-9641; Edit Addr.: P.O. Box 8515, La Jolla, CA 92038 USA Tel 858-456-0540; *Imprints:* Libros del Mundo (Libros del Mundo)
E-mail: info@kanemiller.com
Web site: http://www.kanemiller.com; http://www.edcpub.com
Dist(s): **EDC Publishing;** *CIP.*

Kane Pr., Inc., *(978-1-57565)* 350 5th Ave., Suite 7206, New York, NY 10118-7200 USA Tel 212-268-1435
E-mail: ndmattia@kanepress.com
Web site: http://www.kanepress.com
Dist(s): **Bookmen, Inc.**
Brodart Co.
Follett School Solutions
Lerner Publishing Group
MyiLibrary.

Kane Press, The *See* **Kane Pr., Inc.**

Kane/Miller#Book Publishers, Incorporated *See* **Kane Miller**

Kanlearn, Inc., *(978-0-9772077)* 8950 W. Olympic Blvd., No. 128, Beverly Hills, CA 90211 USA Tel 310-430-6806
E-mail: mattie3rd@yahoo.com
Web site: www.thekanlearnfoundation.com.

Kansas Alumni Assoc., *(978-0-9742918)* 1266 Oread Ave., Lawrence, KS 66044 USA
Web site: http://www.kualumni.org.

Kansas City Guidebooks, *(978-0-9763873)* P.O. Box 14082, Parkville, MO 64152 USA
Web site: http://www.kckidsguide.com.

Kansas City Star Bks., *(978-0-9604884; 978-0-9679519; 978-0-9709131; 978-0-9712920; 978-0-9717080; 978-0-9722739; 978-0-9740009; 978-0-9746012; 978-0-9754804; 978-0-9764021; 978-1-933466; 978-1-935362; 978-1-61169)* Cypress Media L L P, Orders Addr.: 1729 Grand Blvd., Kansas City, MO 64108 USA; Edit Addr.: 1729 Grand Blvd., Kansas City, MO 64108 USA Tel 816-234-4292; *Imprints:* Rockhill Books (Rockhill Bks)
E-mail: weaver@kcstar.com
Web site: www.TheKansasCityStore.com
Dist(s): **National Bk. Network**
Partners Bk. Distributing, Inc.

Kanto Productions, LLC, *(978-1-929956)* P.O. Box 630435, Simi Valley, CA 93063 USA Tel 805-584-9639; Fax: 310-507-0142; Toll Free: 800-335-2686
E-mail: info@atophill.com
Web site: http://www.atophill.com.

†**Kaplan Publishing**, *(978-0-7931; 978-0-88462; 978-0-9617404; 978-0-936894; 978-0-942103; 978-1-57410; 978-1-60714; 978-1-60978; 978-1-61865; 978-1-62523; 978-1-5062)* 395 Hudson St., New York, NY 10014 USA (SAN 211-2280); 395 Hudson St., New City, NY 10014; *Imprints:* Dearborn Real Estate Education (Dearbrn Real Est Ed)
E-mail: deb.darrock@kaplan.com; shayna.webb@kaplan.com; alexander.noya@kaplan.com
Web site: http://www.kaplanpublishing.com
Dist(s): **BookBaby**
Cranbury International
Dearborn Financial Publishing, Inc.
JAGCO & Associates Inc.
LibreDigital
MBI Distribution Services/Quayside Distribution
Simon & Schuster
Simon & Schuster, Inc.; *CIP.*

Kapp Bks. LLC, *(978-1-60346)* 3602 Rocky Meadow Ct., Fairfax, VA 22033 USA Fax: 703-621-7162
E-mail: pravin@kappbooks.com
Web site: http://www.kappbooks.com.

Karadi Tales Co. Pvt. Ltd. (IND) *(978-81-8190)* *Dist. by* **Consort Bk Sales.**

Kar-Ben Publishing *Imprint of* **Lerner Publishing Group**

Kardec, Allan Educational Society, *(978-0-9649907)* 5020 N. Eighth St., Philadelphia, PA 19120 USA Tel 215-329-4010 (phone/fax)
E-mail: akesbooks@cox.net
Web site: http://www.allan-kardec.org.

Karen Pokras Toz *See* **Grand Daisy Pr.**

Karenzo Media, *(978-0-9798164; 978-0-9899318)* 5695 E. Great Marsh Church Rd., Saint Pauls, NC 28384 USA Tel 910-633-9358
E-mail: karenzomedia@gmail.com; khsilvestri@live.com
Web site: http://www.karenzomedia.com; http://www.publishersmarketplace.com/members/kazsilvestri/; http://www.writingyourlifetales.com.

Karina Library Pr., *(978-0-9824491; 978-1-937902)* P.O. Box 35, Ojai, CA 93024-9302 USA Tel 805-500-4535
E-mail: michael@karinalibrary.com; sails@karinalibrary.com
Web site: http://www.karinalibrary.com.

Karma Kollection LLC, *(978-0-9896966; 978-0-692-33207-8; 978-0-692-33208-5)* 549 W. Eugenie St., Chicago, IL 60614 USA Tel 312-952-0776
E-mail: roopaweber@gmail.com
Web site: www.messypenny.com.

Karma Valley Music, *(978-0-9746011)* 505 Lovins Ln., Somerset, KY 42503 USA Tel 606-274-5194
E-mail: flo@floydlovins.com.

Karnak Co., *(978-0-9630951)* Orders Addr.: P.O. Box 497-158, Chicago, IL 60649-7158 USA Tel 773-684-5298; Edit Addr.: 1616 E. 50th Pl., No. 5-C, Chicago, IL 60615 USA
E-mail: tyrone.greer2@verizon.net.

Karosa Publishing, *(978-0-9706312)* 4636 Almond Ln., Boulder, CO 80301 USA Tel 303-484-8856 Do not confuse with companies with same or similar name in Lower Burnell, PA, Paradise Valley, AZ, Sheffield, PA, hailey, ID
E-mail: karpub@comcast.net
Web site: http://www.spadesbook.com.

Karsonkina, Tatiana, *(978-0-9779672)* P.O. Box 191, Brooklyn, NY 11223 USA.

Karuna Press *See* **Utopia Pr.**

Karyn Henley Resources *Imprint of* **Child Sensitive Communication, LLC**

Kaseberg, W. G. Publishing, *(978-0-9761138)* 49 Red Bud Ln., Glen Carbon, IL 62034 USA Tel 618-288-5269; Fax: 618-288-0712
E-mail: wgkasebergpub@empowering.com.

Kasson Publishing, *(978-0-9729435)* 201 E. St., Elmo Rd., Austin, TX 78745-1217 USA Tel 512-447-1988 (phone/fax)
E-mail: publishing@kassonscastings.com
Web site: http://www.kassonscastings.com.

Kasten, Victoria, *(978-0-9788850; 978-1-937363)* 5465 Glencoe Ave., Webster, MN 55088 USA Tel 952-652-6065
E-mail: rkasten@integra.net
Web site: http://www.epicscrolls.com.

Kat Kirst, *(978-0-615-58633-5; 978-0-615-71063-1; 978-0-9898140)* 5005 Bayou Bend Dr., Dickinson, TX 77539 USA Tel 713-446-8865; Fax: 281-337-3362
Dist(s): **CreateSpace Independent Publishing Platform.**

Kat Tales Publishing *See* **EMC Publishing**

Kat Tales Publishing, *(978-0-9744330)* 2515 Clarkson St., Denver, CO 80205 USA Tel 303-394-6380
E-mail: alluptojah@aol.com.

KATastroPHE, *(978-0-9769698)* 6389 Florio St., Oakland, CA 94618 USA Tel 510-601-9631
E-mail: info@katastrophemusic.com
Web site: http://www.katastrophemusic.com.

Kathy's Pen, *(978-0-9777034)* 24 Ridgewood Pkwy, Newport News, VA 23608 USA Tel 757-872-6258
E-mail: regmcc@cox.net
Web site: http://www.kathyspen.com.

Kati Bee & Friends Publishing, *(978-0-9793760)* 8304 Limonite Ave. Suite D-3, Riverside, CA 92509 USA (SAN 853-2818) Tel 951-685-7256; Fax: 951-332-0436
E-mail: ContactKati@katibeeandfriends.com
Web site: http://www.katibeeandfriends.com.

Katie Cook, *(978-0-9883554)* 1201 Kenwood Dr., Nashville, TN 37216 USA Tel 615-430-8128
E-mail: cookontv@comcast.net.

Kat's Kids Kreation, A, *(978-0-9749516)* 413 Fairlawn Ave., Saint Louis, MO 63119-2614 USA Fax: 314-963-0494
E-mail: katbuck123@aol.com.

Katsoris, Nicholas C. *See* **NK Pubns.**

Kattan, Peter I., *(978-0-615-15334-6; 978-0-615-18718-1; 978-0-578-03642-7)* 147-29 182nd St. Box AMM 2232, Springfield Gardens, NY 11413 USA Tel 718-553-8740
E-mail: info@kindergardensudoku.com; info@petrabooks.com
Web site: http://www.kindergardensudoku.com
Dist(s): **Lulu Enterprises Inc.**

Katydid Pubns., *(978-1-879945)* Orders Addr.: P.O. Box 526, Point Lookout, MO 65726 USA; Edit Addr.: Acacia Club Rd., Hollister, MO 65672 USA Tel 417-335-8134
E-mail: mgcameron@aol.com; kay@camerons-crag.com
Web site: http://www.katydid-publications.com.

Katydid Publishing LLC, *(978-0-9724272)* 5845 Eldorado, San Joaquin, CA 93660 USA Tel 559-693-4565 Do not confuse with Latydid Publishing in Mincie, IN.

Kaukini Ranch Pr., *(978-0-9643674)* P.O. Box 2462, Wailuku, HI 96793 USA Tel 808-244-3371; Fax: 808-395-0738.

Kav Books, Incorporated *See* **Royal Fireworks Publishing Co.**

Kawainui Pr., *(978-0-943357)* P.O. Box 163, Captain Cook, HI 96704 USA (SAN 668-6427) Tel 808-328-9126 (phone/fax)
E-mail: herbkane@kona.net
Web site: http://www.hitrade.com
Dist(s): **Booklines Hawaii, Ltd.**

Kay, Janet Consulting, *(978-0-9768786)* 115 Brighton Pk., Battle Creek, MI 49015 USA.

Kay Productions LLC, *(978-0-9707201)* Orders Addr.: 1115 W. Lincoln Ave., Suite 107, Yakima, WA 98902 USA Tel 509-853-0860; Fax: 509-853-0861; Toll Free: 800-619-4345; Edit Addr.: 732 Summitview Ave., Suite 628, Yakima, WA 98902 USA Do not confuse with Kay Productions, San Rafael, CA
E-mail: marketing@kayproductions.com
Web site: http://www.kayproductions.com.

Kay, Sjoukje, *(978-0-9789698)* 4500 Broadway Suite 6i, New York, NY 10040 USA
E-mail: pdolan@fairpoint.net
Web site: http://www.thedonutyogi.com.

KayStar Publishing, *(978-0-9749886)* P.O. Box 571, Saddle River, NJ 07458 USA Fax: 201-825-3912.

Kazi Pubns., Inc., *(978-0-933511; 978-0-935782; 978-1-56744; 978-1-871031; 978-1-930637)* 3023 W. Belmont Ave., Chicago, IL 60618 USA (SAN 162-3397) Tel 773-267-7001; Fax: 773-267-7002
E-mail: info@kazi.org
Web site: http://www.kazi.org.

KB Bks. & More, *(978-0-9761128; 978-1-934486)* Orders Addr.: P.O. Box 56, Channing, TX 79018 USA Tel 806-235-2665; Fax: 866-282-1658; 715 Sante Fe, Channing, TX 79018 Fax: 866-282-1658
E-mail: kbbooks@windstream.net
Dist(s): **Follett School Solutions.**

KB Publishing, *(978-0-9768129)* 11 Running Fox Rd., Columbia, SC 29223 USA.

KBA, LLC, *(978-1-880931)* P.O. Box 3673, Carbondale, IL 62902 USA Tel 618-549-2893
E-mail: thriving@colorado.net
Web site: http://www.benziger.org.

KBR Mutti's Pubns., *(978-0-9762664)* P.O. Box 907431, Santa Barbara, CA 93190 USA
E-mail: kbrmuttis@cox.net
Web site: http://www.matthewsbox.com.

K.C. Fox Publishing, *(978-0-9767078)* Div. of The Kerr Co., P.O. Box 5446, Takoma Park, MD 20913 USA Tel 301-434-9191
E-mail: publisher@kcfoxpublishing.com
Web site: http://www.poutorpurpose.com; http://www.kcfoxpublishing.com.

KCI Sports *See* **KCI Sports Publishing**

KCI Sports Publishing, *(978-0-9758769; 978-0-9798729; 978-0-9843882; 978-0-9831985; 978-0-9837337; 978-0-9885458; 978-1-940056)* 3340 Whiting Ave., Suite 5, Stevens Point, WI 54481 USA Fax: 715-344-2668; Toll Free: 800-697-3756
Web site: http://www.kcisports.com
Dist(s): **Partners Bk. Distributing, Inc.**

K.Co.Kids, LLC, *(978-0-9801423)* 6804 Peter's Path, Colleyville, TX 76034 USA (SAN 855-3092) Tel 817-886-8402
E-mail: kristine@kcokids.com
Web site: http://www.kcokids.com; http://www.katieandthemagicumbrella.com
Dist(s): **Midpoint Trade Bks., Inc.**

Keaster, Diane W. *See* **ZC Horses Series of Children's Bks.**

Keenan Tyler Paine, *(978-0-9740907)* 1715 Brae Burn Rd., Altadena, CA 91001 USA (SAN 255-3414)
E-mail: pmgoddard@earthlink.net.

Keene Publishing, *(978-0-9724853; 978-0-9766805; 978-0-9792371; 978-0-9815972)* P.O. Box 54, Warwick, NY 10990-0054 USA (SAN 254-8631) Tel 845-987-7750; Fax: 845-987-7845; *Imprints:* Moo Press (Moo)
E-mail: dtinney@KeeneBooks.com; info@KeeneBooks.com; mbrowne@KeeneBoooks.com
Web site: http://www.KeeneBooks.com.

Keen's Martial Arts Academy, *(978-0-9702958; 978-1-60243)* Orders Addr.: P.O. Box 144, Tannersville, PA 18372-0144 USA (SAN 852-3002)
E-mail: LOHON6@msn.com
Web site: http://www.kmaa.info.

Keenspot Entertainment, *(978-0-9722350; 978-1-932775)* Orders Addr.: P.O. Box 110, Cresbard, SD 57435 USA Tel 605-324-3332; Toll Free: 888- 533-6776
E-mail: TeriCrosby@gmail.com
Web site: http://www.keenspot.com.

Keep Bks., *(978-1-893986)* Div. of The Ohio State Univ., 1100 Kinnear Rd., Columbus, OH 43212 USA Tel 800-678-6484; Fax: 614-688-3452; Toll Free: 800-678-6484
E-mail: keepbooks@osu.edu
Web site: http://www.keepbooks.org.

Keep Coming Back *See* **Puddledancer Pr.**

Keep Empowering Yourself Successfully, *(978-0-9762009)* 5630 S. Division, Grand Rapids, MI 49548 USA Tel 616-261-3000; Fax: 616-261-3355
E-mail: monicaharris@grar.com
Web site: http://www.successfulkeys.com.

Keep Hope Alive, *(978-1-887831)* P.O. Box 270041, West Allis, WI 53227 USA Tel 414-545-6539; Fax: 414-329-0653
E-mail: khope@access4less.net
Web site: http://www.keephopealive.org
Dist(s): **New Leaf Distributing Co., Inc.**

Keep Me Company Publishing Co., *(978-0-9718632)* 214 Blue Ridge Rd., Plymouth Meeting, PA 19462 USA Tel 610-828-2641.

Keepers of Wisdom and Peace Bks., *(978-0-9844079)* P.O. Box 1314, Woodstock, NY 12498 USA (SAN 859-3159) Tel 845-679-9258
E-mail: KeepersofWisdomandPeace@gmail.com
Web site: http://KeepersofWisdomandPeace.com
Dist(s): **Ingram Pub. Services.**

Keepworthy Creations LLC, *(978-0-9833155)* P.O. Box 3529, Peoria, IL 61612 USA
E-mail: bob@keepworthy.com
Web site: www.keepworthy.com.

Kehot Pubn. Society, *(978-0-8266)* Div. of Merkos L'Inyonei Chinuch, Orders Addr.: 291 Kingston Ave., Brooklyn, NY 11213 USA Tel 718-778-0226; Fax: 718-778-4148; Toll Free: 877-463-7567 (877-4MERKOS); Edit Addr.: 770 Eastern Pkwy., Brooklyn, NY 11213 USA (SAN 220-7060) Tel 718-604-2785
E-mail: orders@kehotonline.com; info@kehot.com
Web site: http://www.kehotonline.com
Dist(s): **Follet Higher Education Grp**
Follett School Solutions.

Keira Pr., *(978-0-9824506)* P.O. Box 815, Joliet, IL 60434 USA Tel 815-726-4200
Web site: http://www.keirapress.com.

Keith Pubns., LLC, *(978-1-936372; 978-1-62882)* Orders Addr.: 1526 W. Sea Haze Dr., Gilbert, AZ 85233 USA
E-mail: KeithPublications@cox.net; mary@keithpublications.com
Web site: http://www.keithpublications.com.

Kelley, James *See* **Lypton Publishing**

KelleyGreenworks Publishing, *(978-0-9791029)* Orders Addr.: 607 Woodsman Way, Crownsville, MD 21032 USA
Web site: http://www.readysetgo-organic.com.

Kelly Bear Pr., Inc., (*978-0-9621054*) 20493 Pine Vista, Bend, OR 97702 USA (SAN 250-5746) Fax: 541-330-6846; Toll Free: 800-431-1934 (orders only)
E-mail: kellybear@bendcable.com
Web site: http://www.kellybear.com
Dist(s): **Sunburst Visual Media.**

Kelly, D Scott, (*978-0-9755442*) 208 W. Lincoln, Charlevoix, MI 49720 USA Tel 231-547-1144; Fax: 231-547-4970
E-mail: info@basesteencenter.org
Web site: http://www.basesteencenter.org.

Kelly, Jason Pr., (*978-0-9664387*) 15 Ken Pratt Blvd. Suite 200, Longmont, CO 80501 USA Tel 303-772-7209
E-mail: jason@jasonkelly.com
Web site: http://www.JasonKelly.com
Dist(s): **BookBaby.**

Kelly, Katherine, (*978-0-9773481*) 4203 Cty. Rd., 3100, Lubbock, TX 79403-7869 USA
E-mail: kellytomkat@sptc.net
Web site: www.informationsleuth.wordpress.com.

Kelly, Kimberly, (*978-0-9747363*) 9801 E. Homestead Rd., Poplar, WI 54864 USA
E-mail: kimkellykimkelly@yahoo.com
Dist(s): **Partners Bk. Distributing, Inc.**

Kelly, Matthew Foundation, The *See* **Beacon Publishing**

Kelsey Enterprises Publishing *See* **Cheval International**

†**Kelsey Street Pr.**, (*978-0-932716*) 2824 Kelsey St., Berkeley, CA 94705-2302 USA (SAN 212-6729)
E-mail: kelseyst@sirius.com
Web site: http://www.kelseyst.com
Dist(s): **BookMobile**
SPD-Small Pr. Distribution; *CIP.*

Kemtec Educational Corp., (*978-1-877960*) 4780 Interstate Dr., Cincinnati, OH 45246-1112 USA Toll Free: 877-536-8321
E-mail: prekem@kemtecscience.com
Web site: http://www.kemtecscience.com.

Ken Pr., (*978-1-928771*) 4001 N. Paseo de los Rancheros, Tucson, AZ 85745 USA (SAN 299-9714) Tel 520-743-3200; Fax: 520-743-3210
E-mail: office@kenpress.com
Web site: http://www.kenpress.com
Dist(s): **Distributors, The.**

Kenamar, Inc., (*978-0-9753207*) P.O. Box 689, West Dundee, IL 60110-0689 USA
E-mail: kenamarpublish@aol.com.

Kendahl Hse. Pr. *Imprint of* **Youngs, Bettie Bks.**

Kendall Hunt Publishing Co., (*978-0-7872; 978-0-8403; 978-0-7575; 978-1-4652*) Orders Addr.: P.O. Box 1840, Dubuque, IA 52004-1840 USA; Edit Addr.: 4050 Westmark Dr., Dubuque, IA 52002 USA (SAN 203-9184) Tel 563-589-1000; Fax: 563-589-1046; Toll Free Fax: 800-772-9165; Toll Free: 800-228-0810
E-mail: orders@kendallhunt.com; kkelly@kendallhunt.com
Web site: http://www.kendallhunt.com
Dist(s): **Smashwords.**

Kendar Publishing Company *See* **Kendar Publishing, Inc.**

Kendar Publishing, Inc., (*978-1-889506*) 310 5th St., Suite 101, Racine, WI 53403 USA Tel 262-632-4070; Fax: 262-632-7089; Toll Free: 866-632-7040.

Kendelle Pr., (*978-0-615-44111-5; 978-0-9859934*) 216 Pk. Pl., Jupiter, FL 33458 USA Tel 561-601-6751
E-mail: traciella@aol.com
Web site: www.traciehall.com
Dist(s): **CreateSpace Independent Publishing Platform**
Dummy Record Do Not USE!!!!
Smashwords.

Kendu Films, (*978-0-615-19233-8; 978-0-9825050*) Orders Addr.: 27068 la paz rd, No. 543, Aliso Viejo, CA 92656 USA
Web site: http://www.kendufilms.com
Dist(s): **Publishers Services.**

Kenilworth Pr., Ltd. (GBR) (*978-0-600; 978-0-901366; 978-1-872082; 978-1-872119; 978-1-905693; 978-1-910016*) *Dist. by* **IPG Chicago.**

Kenilworth Pr., Ltd. (GBR) (*978-0-600; 978-0-901366; 978-1-872082; 978-1-872119; 978-1-905693; 978-1-910016*) *Dist. by* **PerseuPGW.**

Kennebec Large Print *Imprint of* **Cengage Gale**

Kennedy Christian Publishing, (*978-0-9743136*) P.O. Box 5385, Texarkana, TX 75505-5385 USA
E-mail: knndytgr@aol.com.

Kennedy Enterprises, LLC, (*978-0-9836230*) 600 Baver St., Clarksburg, WV 26301 USA Tel 304-685-1239
E-mail: kennedykonnection@yahoo.com
Dist(s): **Lulu Enterprises Inc.**

Kennel Club Bks. *Imprint of* **I-5 Publishing LLC**

Kensington Publishing Corp., (*978-0-7860; 978-0-8065; 978-0-8184; 978-0-8217; 978-1-55817; 978-1-57566; 978-0-7582; 978-1-4201; 978-1-59983; 978-1-60183; 978-0-9817144; 978-0-9818905; 978-0-9824170; 978-0-9841132; 978-1-61650; 978-1-61773; 978-1-4967; 978-1-5161*) 119 W. 40th St., New York, NY 10018 USA Tel 212-407-1500; Fax: 212-935-0699; Toll Free: 800-221-2647; 499 North Canon Dr., Beverly Hills, CA 90210 Tel 310-887-7082; *Imprints:* K-Teen (K-TEEN); K-Teen/Dafina (K-TEEN/DAFINA)
E-mail: jmclean@kensingtonbooks.com; melley@kensingtonbooks.com
Web site: http://www.kensingtonbooks.com
Dist(s): **Ebsco Publishing**
MyiLibrary
Penguin Random Hse., LLC.
Penguin Publishing Group
Random Hse., Inc.
Worldwide Media Service, Inc.

Kent Communications, Ltd., (*978-0-9627106; 978-1-888206; 978-0-9830963*) Orders Addr.: 25 Poplar Plain Rd., Westport, CT 06880 USA Tel 203-454-9646; *Imprints:* Kent Press (Kent Pr)
E-mail: mhoule@gbiplaw.com
Dist(s): **Independent Pubs. Group**
MyiLibrary
National Bk. Network
Small Pr. United.

Kent Fine Art *See* **Kent Gallery**

Kent Gallery, (*978-1-878607*) P.O. Box 684, New York, NY 10012-0013 USA
E-mail: info@kentfineart.net
Web site: http://www.kentfineart.net.

Kent Pr. *Imprint of* **Kent Communications, Ltd.**

†**Kent State Univ. Pr.**, (*978-0-87338; 978-1-60635; 978-1-61277; 978-1-63101*) Orders Addr.: c/o BookMasters, Inc., 30 Amberwood Pkwy., Ashland, OH 44805 USA Tel 419-281-1802; Fax: 419-281-6883; Toll Free: 800-247-6553; Edit Addr.: 1118 Univ. Library Bldg. 1125 Risman Dr., Kent, OH 44242-0001 USA (SAN 201-0437) Tel 330-672-7913; Fax: 330-672-3104; *Imprints:* Black Squirrel Books (Blck Squir)
E-mail: scash@kent.edu
Web site: http://www.kentstateuniversitypress.com
Dist(s): **BookMasters Distribution Services (BDS)**
BookMasters, Inc.
Follett School Solutions
MyiLibrary
Partners Bk. Distributing, Inc.
ebrary, Inc.; *CIP.*

Keogh, Anne, (*978-1-938993*) 132 S. Battery St., Charleston, SC 29401 USA Tel 843-722-7350
E-mail: akeogh98@hotmail.com
Web site: www.annetoddbooks.com.

Kepler Pr., (*978-0-9713770*) Orders Addr.: P.O. Box 400326, Cambridge, MA 02140 USA (SAN 255-6014) Tel 617-413-7204
E-mail: ealex@keplerpress.com
Web site: http://www.keplerpress.com
Dist(s): **Lightning Source, Inc.**

Kerpluggo Bks. LLC, (*978-0-9762429*) 1015 W. Webster Ave., Suite 3, Chicago, IL 60614 USA Tel 773-665-8075
E-mail: mbwillian2@yahoo.com.

Kerr, Alex, (*978-0-9753076*) 145 Lincoln Rd. Apt. 2L, Brooklyn, NY 11225-4017 USA
E-mail: alexkerr@earthlink.net.

Kerr, Charles H. Publishing Co., (*978-0-88286*) 1726 W. Jarvis Ave., Chicago, IL 60626 USA (SAN 207-7043) Tel 773-465-7774 (orders); 847-328-2132 (orders); Fax: 773-472-7857 (orders)
E-mail: arcane@ripco.com
Web site: http://www.charleshkerr.net
Dist(s): **SPD-Small Pr. Distribution.**

Kerr Company, The *See* **K.C. Fox Publishing**

Kerr, Justin & Shelley, (*978-0-9766408*) 10735 Atascadero Ave., Atascadero, CA 93422-5723 USA
Web site: http://www.kirra-rincon.com.

Kersting Publishing, (*978-0-615-70768-6*) 500 Saddle Creek Cir. 0, Roswell, AE 30076 USA Tel 404 597-1075
E-mail: hamilt_e@bellsouth.net
Dist(s): **CreateSpace Independent Publishing Platform.**

Kessinger Publishing Company *See* **Kessinger Publishing, LLC**

Kessinger Publishing, LLC, (*978-0-7661; 978-0-922802; 978-1-56459; 978-1-4179; 978-1-4191; 978-1-4192; 978-1-4253; 978-1-4254; 978-1-4286; 978-1-4304; 978-1-4325; 978-1-4326; 978-0-548; 978-1-4365; 978-1-4366; 978-1-4367; 978-1-4368; 978-1-4369; 978-1-4370; 978-1-4371; 978-1-4372; 978-1-4373; 978-1-4374; 978-1-104; 978-1-120; 978-1-160; 978-1-161; 978-1-162; 978-1-163; 978-1-164; 978-1-165; 978-1-166; 978-1-167; 978-1-168; 978-1-169) Orders Addr.: P.O. Box 1404, Whitefish, MT 59937 USA (SAN 251-4621); Edit Addr.: 186 N. Prairesmoke Cir., Whitefish, MT 59937 USA*
E-mail: bip@kessinger.net
Web site: http://www.kessinger.net
Dist(s): **Lightning Source, Inc.**

Kesterson & Associates *See* **Big Valley Publishing**

Kestrel Pubns., (*978-0-9628472; 978-0-9881925*) 1811 Stonewood Dr., Dayton, OH 45432-4002 USA Tel 937-426-5110; Fax: 937-320-1832; Toll Free: 800-314-4678 (orders only)
E-mail: invisiblei@aol.com.

Keszler, E., (*978-0-615-19548-3; 978-0-615-36360-8*) 6779 Sienna Club Pl., Lauderhill, FL 33319 USA
E-mail: uniqueart613@gmail.com.

Ketabe Gooya Publishing LLC, (*978-1-933429*) Orders Addr.: 6400 Canoga Ave., Suite 355, Woodland Hills, CA 91367 USA Tel 818-346-8338; Toll Free: 800-515-0069
E-mail: nasser@farrokh.us
Web site: http://www.ketabegooya.com.

Ketman Publishing *See* **Wooster Bk. Co., The**

Kew Publishing (GBR) (*978-0-947643; 978-1-900347; 978-0-85521; 978-1-84246*) *Dist. by* **Chicago Distribution Ctr.**

Key Answer Products, Inc., (*978-0-9642823*) 108 S. Third St., Suite 4, Bloomingdale, IL 60108 USA (SAN 255-805X) Tel 630-893-4007; Fax: 630-893-4030; Toll Free: 800-539-1233
E-mail: dcowhey@ci-inc.com
Web site: http://www.ci-inc/what/what.htm.

Key Education Publishing Company, LLC *Imprint of* **Carson-Dellosa Publishing, LLC**

Key of David Publishing, (*978-1-886987*) Subs. of House of David, Orders Addr.: P.O. Box 700217, Saint Cloud, FL 34770 USA Tel 407-344-7700 (phone/fax); Toll Free: 800-829-8777 Do not confuse with Key of David Publishing, Poughquag, NY
E-mail: batya@mim.net
Web site: http://www.keyofdavidpublishing.com.

Key Publishers, Incorporated *See* **City Creek Pr., Inc.**

Key Publishing Hse., Inc., The (CAN) (*978-0-9782526; 978-0-9780431; 978-0-9811606; 978-1-926780*) *Dist. by* **AtlasBooks.**

Keyboarding First, LLC, (*978-0-9768426*) 6919 Prairie Dr., Middleton, WI 53562-5356 USA Tel 608-836-4404 (phone/fax); Fax: 608-836-4405
E-mail: psm.janet@tds.net.

KEYGARD, (*978-0-9767086*) Orders Addr.: 7887 Broadway, Suite 506, San Antonio, TX 78209 USA Tel 210-829-5074; Fax: 210-829-5132
E-mail: bhkeyser@aol.com.

Keys For Kids Publishing Co., (*978-0-9725827*) 1256 Cranwood Square N., Columbus, OH 43229-1341 USA Tel 614-431-5311
E-mail: kfd43229@aol.com
Web site: http://www.keys.decisivenet.com.

Keysquake Music, (*978-0-9760837*) 42 Blackfoot Ct., Guilford, CT 06437 USA
E-mail: bgillie48@yahoo.com
Web site: http://www.briangillie.com.

Keystone Bks. *Imprint of* **Stone Arch Bks.**

Keytochange Publishing, Inc., (*978-0-9729798*) 7484 University Ave. Ste. T, La Mesa, CA 91941-6030 USA
E-mail: sjones@keytochange.com
Web site: http://www.keytochange.com.

Khanna, Rachel, (*978-0-9779568*) 163 John St., Greenwich, CT 06831 USA (SAN 850-7260)
Web site: http://www.liveeatcookhealthy.com
Dist(s): **Partners Pubs. Group, Inc.**

Khesed Foundation, (*978-0-9785077*) Orders Addr.: 633 S. Plymouth Ct, Chicago, IL 60605-6060 USA Tel 615-792-1449; Edit Addr.: 1030 Trouble Ct., No. 1005, Ashland City, TN 37015-6060 USA (SAN 850-7236)
E-mail: hankbo@juno.com.

Khunum Productions, Inc., (*978-0-9797010*) Khunum Productions, Inc. 149 Bainbridge St., Suite 3, Brooklyn, NY 11233 USA Tel 718-924-8779
E-mail: Khunumproductions@gmail.com; Nehpri@msn.com
Web site: http://www.NehpriAmenii.com.

Kiba Kiba Books *See* **Kiba Kiba Bks**

Kick The Ball, (*978-0-9790396; 978-1-934372; 978-1-61320*) Orders Addr.: 8595 Columbus Pike Suite 197, Lewis Center, OH 43035 USA
E-mail: pfwilson@triviagamebooks.com; tprippey@triviagamebooks.com
Web site: http://www.triviagamebooks.com; http://www.bythenumberbook.com
Dist(s): **Partners Bk. Distributing, Inc.**

Kickapoo Farms *See* **Genuine Prints, LLC**

Kicks and Giggles Today, (*978-0-615-20924-1; 978-0-615-54874-6*) P.O. Box 1023, Ross, CA 94957 USA
Web site: http://www.kicksandgigglestoday.com
Dist(s): **AtlasBooks Distribution.**

Kid by Kid, Incorporated, (*978-0-9745496*) 54249 Myrica Dr., Macomb, MI 48042 USA Tel 586-781-2345 (phone/fax)
E-mail: kidbykid@comcast.net
Web site: http://www.crystalkids.net.

Kid Niche Publishing, (*978-0-9852712; 978-0-9904626*) P.O. Box 5845, Traverse City, MI 49686-5845 USA.

Kid Prep, Inc., (*978-1-58312*) 6942 FM 1960 E-132, Humble, TX 77346 USA Tel 281-852-5261; Fax: 281-852-4901; *Imprints:* Little Chameleon Books (Little Chameleon)
E-mail: customerservice@kidprep.com
Web site: http://www.kidprep.com.

KiD Sounds, (*978-0-9767650*) P.O. Box 13888, Las Vegas, NV 89112-1888 USA
Web site: http://www.kid-sounds.com.

KidBiz 3000 *See* **Achieve3000**

KidBookInk Publishing, LLC, (*978-0-9776772*) Orders Addr.: 25809 Nichols Rd., Columbia Station, OH 44028 USA (SAN 257-9103) Tel 440-725-7587; Fax: 440-236-5356; Toll Free: 888-978-1669
E-mail: dbvanhorn@yahoo.com
Web site: http://www.kidbookink.com; http://www.storyboard4kidz.com.

Kidder, Clark, (*978-0-615-15313-1*) 1620 Sienna Crossing, Janesville, WI 53546 USA
E-mail: cokidder@charter.net; ckidder@jvlnet.com.

Kidderature Publishing, (*978-0-9729703*) P.O. Box 612, Hammondsport, NY 14840 USA Tel 607-292-3026
E-mail: bobhicks@citlink.net
Web site: http://www.kidderature.com.

Kiddy Chronicles Publishing (CAN) (*978-0-9699203; 978-0-9733994*) *Dist. by* **Firefly Bks Limited.**

KID-E Bks. *Imprint of* **Word Prodns.**

Kidhaven *Imprint of* **Cengage Gale**

Kidpub Pr., (*978-0-9840807; 978-1-936184; 978-1-61018*) P.O. Box 724, North Attleboro, MA 02761 USA (SAN 858-365X) Tel 401-466-4176; Toll Free: 800-252-5224 (orders/editorial)
E-mail: pd@kidpub.com; orders@kidpub.com
Web site: http://bookstore.kidpub.com; http://www.kidpub.com.

Kidrich Corp., (*978-0-9761051*) 347 5th Ave., Suite 610, New York, NY 10016 USA Tel 718-767-5135; Toll Free: 800-231-7385
Web site: http://www.kidrich.com.

Kids 4 Ever, (*978-0-9764433*) P.O. Box 1784, Holland, MI 49422 USA Tel 616-566-1231
E-mail: kids4ever@charter.net
Web site: http://www.kids4everbooks.com.

Kids Ahead Bks. *Imprint of* **WND Bks, Inc.**

Kids At Heart Publishing & Bks., (*978-0-615-36340-0; 978-0-9828109; 978-0-9836641; 978-0-9855202; 978-0-9886360; 978-0-9899472; 978-0-9905734; 978-0-9964962*) P.O. Box 492, Milton, IN 47357 USA Tel 765-478-5873.

Kids At Our House, Inc., The, (*978-0-9705773; 978-1-942390*) Orders Addr.: 47 Stoneham Pl., Metuchen, NJ 08840 USA Tel 732-548-1779
E-mail: info@dannyandkim.com
Web site: www.dannyandkim.com
Dist(s): **Follett School Solutions**
Indig, Stanley M. Specialty Pubn.

Kids Can *Imprint of* **Proactive Publishing**

Kids Children & Teens World 2000 & Beyond, (*978-0-9747543*) Orders Addr.: P.O. Box 385, Brandywine, MD 20613 USA Fax: 301-372-9979; Edit Addr.: 8300 Belding Ct., Brandywine, MD 20613 USA
E-mail: djospeh301@aol.com.

Kid's Creative Classics *Imprint of* **BrassHeart Music**

Kids, Critters & Country Publishing, (*978-0-9755200*) P.O. Box 866874, Plano, TX 75086-6874 USA
E-mail: jlarsen@chasewest.com
Web site: http://www.kidscrittersandcountry.com.

Kids Donate, Inc., (*978-0-9754131*) 221 Chesley Ln., Chapel Hill, NC 27514 USA Tel 919-967-0882.

Kids For Health, Inc., (*978-0-9759517; 978-1-933847*) P.O. Box 326, Springdale, AR 72763 USA Tel 479-756-9551; Fax: 479-756-0949.

Kid's Fun Pr., (*978-0-9772848*) 2708 Coastal Range Way, Lutz, FL 33559 USA (SAN 257-2168) Tel 813-786-9457
E-mail: kidsfunpress@verizon.net
Web site: http://ijbooks.com
Dist(s): **Independent Pubs. Group.**

Kids Go Europe, Inc., (*978-0-9772699*) P.O. Box 4014, Menlo Park, CA 94026 USA Tel 650-743-7404
E-mail: info@kidsgoeurope.com
Web site: http://www.kidsgoeurope.com.

Kids in Ministry International, (*978-0-9767647; 978-0-9815940*) P.O. Box 549, Mandan, ND 58554-0549 USA
Web site: http://www.kidsinministry.com.

Kids Life Pr., (*978-0-9755348; 978-0-9903172*) P.O. Box 3484, Pismo Beach, CA 93448-3484 USA Fax: 805-888-2838; Toll Free: 800-262-8973
E-mail: tuzee@charter.net.

Kids Play *Imprint of* **Dorling Kindersley Publishing, Inc.**

Kid's Shelf, (*978-0-9729339*) 19600 Baker Rd., Gambier, OH 43022 USA Tel 740-247-2427.

Kids Think Big LLC, (*978-0-9797362*) P.O. Box 11013, Greenwich, CT 06831 USA (SAN 854-2597)
E-mail: info@kidsthinkbig.com
Web site: http://www.kidsthinkbig.com
Dist(s): **Distributors, The**
Follett School Solutions.

Kids Write On, LLC, (*978-0-615-23574-5*) Orders Addr.: P.O. Box 700924, Dallas, TX 75370 USA Tel 972-862-7257; Fax: 972-862-0194; Toll Free: 877-596-7257
Web site: http://www.thestaplercaper.com.

Kids1st Bks. *Imprint of* **BC Publishing**

Kidsafety of America, (*978-1-884413*) 6288 Susana St., Chino, CA 91710 USA
E-mail: peter@kidsafetystore.com
Web site: http://www.kidsafetystore.com
Dist(s): **Follett School Solutions.**

KidsAndParentsPr.Com, (*978-0-615-46844-0; 978-0-615-47486-1; 978-0-615-47487-8; 978-0-615-47488-5*) 509 Saint Andrews Blvd., Lady Lake, FL 32159 USA Tel 414-807-5433
E-mail: gordonpralph@gmail.com
Web site: KidsAndParentsPress.Com
Dist(s): **CreateSpace Independent Publishing Platform**
Dummy Record Do Not USE!!!!.

Kidsbooks, Incorporated *See* **Kidsbooks, LLC**

Kidsbooks, LLC, (*978-0-942025; 978-1-56156; 978-1-58865; 978-1-62885*) 3535 W. Peterson Ave., Chicago, IL 60659 USA (SAN 666-3729)
E-mail: sales@kidsbooks.com
Web site: http://www.kidsbooks.com.

Kidscope, Inc., (*978-0-9647798*) 2045 Peachtree Rd NE Ste. 150, Atlanta, GA 30309-1405 USA.

KidsDiscuss.com, (*978-0-9749244*) PCS, Orders Addr.: P.O. Box 6102, Edmonds, WA 98026 USA
E-mail: JeanTracy@KidsDiscuss.com
Web site: http://www.KidsDiscuss.com.

KidsGive, LLC, (*978-0-9792912; 978-0-9845910*) 5757 W. Century Blvd., Suite 800, Box 8, Los Angeles, CA 90045 USA (SAN 853-0297) Tel 310-665-9777; Fax: 310-665-9494
E-mail: lmuniz@kidsgive.com
Web site: http://www.kidsgive.com.

Kidskills America *Imprint of* **Kidskills International**

Kidskills International, (*978-0-9710641*) Div. of Creekside Creations, 1031 Cahoon Rd., Westlake, OH 44145-1232 USA Tel 440-835-5071 (phone/fax); *Imprints:* Kidskills America (Kidskills Amer)
E-mail: kidskills@wowway.com; diane@kidskills.com
Web site: http://www.kidskills.com.

KIDSRIGHTS *Imprint of* **JIST Publishing**

Kidsrights, 10100 Park Cedar Dr., Charlotte, NC 28210 USA (SAN 299-2809) Tel 704-541-0100; Fax: 704-541-0113; Toll Free: 888-970-5437 Do not confuse with Kidsrights, Mount Dora, FL.

Kidstalk, LLC, (*978-0-9776144*) P.O. Box 520, Sherman, TX 75091 USA (SAN 257-7992) Tel 903-436-0858; Fax: 903-893-1614
E-mail: kidstalk@cableone.net
Web site: http://www.kidstalkmag.com.

Kidstory Pr., (*978-0-9772231*) P.O. Box 75, Brighton, MI 48116-0075 USA Tel 517-204-9030
E-mail: kidstorypress@comcast.net
Web site: http://www.kidstorypress.home.comcast.net.

Kidwick Bks., (*978-0-9703809*) 363 S. Saltair Ave., First Fl., Los Angeles, CA 90049 USA Tel 310-471-2472; Fax: 310-861-8111
E-mail: mail@kidwick.com
Web site: http://www.kidwick.com
Dist(s): **National Bk. Network.**

Kidz & Katz Publishing Co., (*978-1-883371*) 752 Brandon Pl., Wheeling, IL 60090 USA Fax: 708-860-0513.

Kidz By Dezign Pr., Inc., (*978-0-9771030*) 1881 Kingston Way, Lawrenceville, GA 30044 USA (SAN 256-7121) Tel 770-962-2181; Fax: 678-615-2247; Toll Free: 800-719-5439
E-mail: info@slumbergirls.com
Web site: http://www.slumbergirls.com.

Publisher Name Index

Kidz Entertainment, Inc., *(978-0-9795049; 978-0-9891954)* P.O. Box 0301, Baldwin, NY 11510 USA Fax: 516-223-6546
E-mail: dcorrado@optonline.net
Web site: http://www.chanteusemusic.com.

Kidz Krave Inc., *(978-0-9764144)* P.O. Box 88350, Houston, TX 77288 USA
Web site: http://www.prettypainful.com.

Kidzpoetz Publishing, *(978-0-9760220)* P.O. Box 621, New City, NY 10956 USA Tel 845-536-5505; Fax: 845-323-4272
E-mail: robertkurkela@kidzpoetz.com
Web site: http://www.kidzpoetz.com
Dist(s): **Quality Bks., Inc.**

Kidzup Productions, *(978-1-894281; 978-1-894677)* 555 VT Rte. 78, Suite 146, Box 717, Swanton, VT 05488 USA Toll Free: 888-321-5437 (888-321-KIDS)
E-mail: info@kidzup.com
Web site: http://www.kidzup.com
Dist(s): **Penton Overseas, Inc.**

Kieliszewski, Sheila, *(978-0-615-25575-0; 978-0-578-00002-2)* 2192 Willow Springs Dr., Stevens Point, WI 54481 USA
E-mail: sheilabrt@yahoo.com
Dist(s): **Lulu Enterprises Inc.**

Kies Publishing Co., *(978-0-9767437)* Orders Addr.: P.O. Box 923572, Sylmar, CA 91392-3572 USA Tel 818-367-8416
E-mail: kies@kies.org
Web site: http://www.kies.org.

Kila Springs Pr., *(978-0-9716481)* Div. of Kila Springs Group, 4231 Oak Meadow Rd., Placerville, CA 95667 USA Tel 530-621-2297; Fax: 206-202-1309
E-mail: press@kilasprings.net
Web site: http://kilasprings.net/KSPress.html.

Killer Sports Publishing, *(978-1-933135)* Orders Addr.: P.O. Box 862, Berea, OH 44017 USA Tel 440-239-1854; Edit Addr.: 201 S. Rocky River Rd., Berea, OH 44017 USA
Web site: http://www.killersports.com.

Killingbeck, Dale, *(978-0-9762758)* 18300 Tustin Rd., Tustin, MI 49677 USA Tel 231-829-3084.

Kilsby, Raymond *See* **RK Enterprises, Inc.**

Kimber Stories, *(978-0-9767773)* Orders Addr.: P.O. Box 143, Woodlake, CA 93286 USA; Edit Addr.: 37811 Millwood Dr., Woodlake, CA 93286 USA
E-mail: kimberstories@yahoo.com.

Kimberlite Publishing Co., *(978-0-9632675)* 44091 Olive Ave., Hemet, CA 92544-2609 USA Tel 951-927-7726 Do not confuse with Kimberlite Publishing, Ventura, CA
E-mail: frumpypapa@yahoo.com.

Kimberly Pr., LLC, *(978-0-9668611)* 100 Westport Ave., Norwalk, CT 06851 USA (SAN 251-2483) Tel 203-750-6101; Fax: 203-846-3472.

Kimble, George J., *(978-0-9767024)* 4941 Hickory Woods E., Antioch, TN 37013 USA
Web site: http://www.theroadpoet.com.

Kind Critter Junction, *(978-0-9752842)* P.O. Box 30249, Indianapolis, IN 46220 USA Toll Free: 888-366-3525
E-mail: info@kindcritterjunction.com
Web site: http://www.kindcritterjunction.com.

KinderBach L.L.C., *(978-0-9773005)* P.O. Box 336, Hudson, IA 50643 USA (SAN 257-2397) Toll Free: 866-988-9814
E-mail: info@kinderbach.com
Web site: http://www.kinderbach.com.

Kinderhaus Publishing Co., *(978-0-578-05104-8)* 2970 Edgewick Dr., Glendale, CA 91206 USA
E-mail: bettyfritz@kinderhauspublishing.com.

Kindermusik International, *(978-0-945613; 978-1-931127; 978-1-58987)* Orders Addr.: P.O. Box 26575, Greensboro, NC 27415 USA (SAN 247-3747) Tel 336-273-3363; Fax: 336-273-2023; Toll Free: 800-628-5687; Edit Addr.: 6204 Corporate Park Dr., Browns Summit, NC 27214 USA (SAN 247-3755)
E-mail: info@kindermusik.com
Web site: http://www.kindermusik.com.

Kindred Press *See* **Kindred Productions**

Kindred Productions, *(978-0-921788; 978-0-919797)* Orders Addr.: 315 S. Lincoln St., Hillsboro, KS 67063 USA Tel 316-947-3151; Fax: 316-947-3266; Toll Free: 800-545-7322
E-mail: kindred@mbconf.ca
Web site: http://www.mbconf.org/kindred.htm
Dist(s): **Spring Arbor Distributors, Inc.**

Kinfolk Research Pr., *(978-0-9712564)* P.O. Box 6303, Plymouth, MI 48170 USA Tel 734-454-1883
E-mail: KinfolkPress@aol.com
Web site: http://cheekfamilychronicles.homestead.com/CheekFamilyChronicles.html.

King Joe Educational Enterprises, Inc., *(978-0-9728596; 978-0-9773902)* Orders Addr.: P.O. Box 86, Los Alamitos, CA 90720 USA Tel 562-430-8600; Fax: 562-598-5940; Toll Free: 866-818-5464 (866-818-KING); Edit Addr.: 3112 Inverness Dr., Los Alamitos, CA 90720 USA
E-mail: lindarodgers@kingjoe.com
Web site: http://www.kingjoe.com.

King, Joel, *(978-0-9787820)* 547 McLean Ave., Hopkinsville, KY 42240 USA
E-mail: joelk3@bellsouth.net.

King, Julia, *(978-0-615-34585-7; 978-0-615-37032-3; 978-0-9839827)* 13565 Watsonville Rd., Morgan Hill, CA 95037 USA Tel 408-591-6465
E-mail: wyethia3@yahoo.com.

King, Laurence Publishing (GBR) *(978-1-85669; 978-1-898113; 978-1-78067) Dist. by* **HachBkGrp.**

King, Marcy, *(978-0-9850752)* 4107 Sunset Ave., Chester, VA 23831 USA Tel 804-683-0517
E-mail: marcy.king@yahoo.com.

King Production, A, *(978-0-9755811; 978-0-9843325; 978-0-9860045; 978-0-9913890; 978-1-942217)* P.O. Box 912, Collierville, TN 38017 USA Tel 917-279-1363; Fax: 201-624-7225
E-mail: joyking1993@yahoo.com
Web site: www.joydejaking.com.

King St Bks./Stabler-Leadbeater Apothecary Museum, *(978-0-9763945)* 410 S Fairfax St., Alexandria, VA 22314 USA Fax: 703-456-7890
Web site: http://apothecarymuseum.org.

King, Terri Ann *See* **Paulus Publishing**

Kingdom Kaught Publishing LLC, *(978-0-9824550; 978-0-9964040)* 1242 Painted Fern Rd., Denton, MD 21629 USA (SAN 858-2033)
Web site: http://www.kingdomkaughtpublishing.com.

Kingdom Publishers *See* **Cathedral of the Holy Spirit**

Kingdom Publishing Co., *(978-0-9765636)* 17100 Halsted St., Harvey, IL 60426-6131 USA
Dist(s): **AtlasBooks Distribution.**

Kingdom Publishing Group, Inc., *(978-0-9745324; 978-0-9772964; 978-0-9792074; 978-0-9796130; 978-0-9801564; 978-0-9817706; 978-0-9821411; 978-0-9824084; 978-0-9825104; 978-0-9825849; 978-0-9826370; 978-0-9827484; 978-0-9829775; 978-0-9831452; 978-0-9833651; 978-0-9835721; 978-0-9839090; 978-0-9848940; 978-0-9852679; 978-0-9854693; 978-0-9896581; 978-0-9862492; 978-0-9962629) P.O. Box 3273, Henrico, VA 23228-9705 USA*
Web site: http://www.kingdompublishing.org.

Kingdom Sound Pubs., *(978-0-9662666; 978-0-9856206)* Orders Addr.: P.O. Box 371917, Decatur, GA 30037 USA Tel 404-384-3795; Edit Addr.: 3622 Summit Trace, Suite 400, Decatur, GA 30034 USA
E-mail: kvjackson@yahoo.com.

Kingdom Talk Publishing, Incorporated *See* **Rapha Publishing**

Kingfisher *Imprint of* **Roaring Brook Pr.**

Kingfisher Bks., *(978-0-9662218)* Orders Addr.: P.O. Box 4628, Helena, MT 59604 USA Tel 406-442-2168; Toll Free: 800-879-4576; Edit Addr.: 2480 Broadway, No. 18D, Helena, MT 59601 USA
Dist(s): **Houghton Mifflin Harcourt Trade & Reference Pubs.**
Partners/West Book Distributors.

KingMaker Bks. LLC, *(978-0-9744870)* 13315 E. Cindy St., Chandler, AZ 85225 USA
E-mail: mbogumill@juno.com.

King's Kids Trading Cards, Inc., *(978-0-9703880)* P.O. Box 923271, Sylmar, CA 91392-3271 USA Fax: 818-364-2443; Toll Free: 800-910-2690
E-mail: visioninprint@brandx.net
Web site: http://www.kingskidscards.com.

King'S Land Pr. Inc,
Dist(s): **AtlasBooks Distribution.**

King's Treasure Box Ministries, The, *(978-0-9910841)* 7735 Castle Combe Ct., Cumming, GA 30040 USA Tel 678-455-3710
E-mail: roy.nancyj@gmail.com
Web site: www.kingstreasurebox.org.

Kingston Pr. (CAN) *(978-1-894997) Dist. by* **SCB Distributo.**

Kingsway Pubns. (GBR) *(978-0-85476; 978-0-86065; 978-0-902088; 978-1-84291) Dist. by* **STL Dist.**

KiniArt Publishing, *(978-0-578-06335-5)* 658 SE Jerome St., Oak Harbor, WA 98277 USA
E-mail: publishing@kiniart.com
Web site: http://kiniart.com
Dist(s): **Lulu Enterprises Inc.**

KINJIN Global, *(978-0-9759152)* 4960 SW 32nd Ave., Dania Beach, FL 33312 USA Tel 347-826-6272
E-mail: l@dangoldman.net
Web site: http://dangoldman.net; http://redlightproperties.com.

Kinkachoo Pr., The, *(978-0-9729285)*
Web site: http://www.zhibit.org/bolan.

Kinkajou Pr. *Imprint of* **Artemesia Publishing, LLC**

Kip Kids of New York, *(978-0-9789384)* 85 Christopher St., Suite No. 5B, New York, NY 10014 USA
E-mail: KipKids@aol.com
Web site: http://www.KipKids.com.

Kirkham, Sharon Birlson, *(978-0-9767100)* 1530 Michigan Ave., La Porte, IN 46350 USA
Dist(s): **INscribe Digital.**

KIRKLAND, JUSTIN B., *(978-0-615-81456-8)* 906 BENDLETON TRACE, ALPHARETTA, GA 30004 USA Tel 404-434-8035
E-mail: KIRKLANDJUSTIN@YMAIL.COM.

Kiss A Me Productions, Inc., *(978-1-890343)* 90 Garfield Ave., Sayville, NY 11782 USA Tel 516-589-4886; Fax: 516-218-8927; Toll Free: 888-547-7263.

KISSFAQ.COM Publishing, *(978-0-9722253; 978-0-9822537)* P.O. Box 210686, San Francisco, CA 94121-0686 USA
E-mail: kissfaq@sbcglobal.net; webmaster@kissfaq.com
Web site: http://www.kissfaq.com/
Dist(s): **CreateSpace Independent Publishing Platform.**

Kissing Frog Bks., *(978-0-615-61266-9; 978-0-615-61883-8; 978-0-615-66798-0; 978-0-615-70912-3)* P.O. Box 757, Yorkville, IL 60560 USA Tel 630-882-8790
E-mail: kim@KOsbornSullivan.com
Web site: www.KOsbornSullivan.com
Dist(s): **CreateSpace Independent Publishing Platform.**

Kiba Kiba Bks, *(978-0-9821262; 978-0-9841195; 978-1-935734)* P.O. Box 97, Saratoga Springs, NY 12866 USA (SAN 857-3263)
Web site: http://www.kitanie.com.

Kitchen Table Pubs., *(978-0-9707685)* Orders Addr.: 136 Cook-McDonald Rd., Collins, MS 39428 USA Tel 601-765-8329; Edit Addr.: 802 S. Cherry St., Collins, MS 39428 USA Tel 601-765-8329
E-mail: knight3230@bellsouth.net.

Kite Tales Publishing, *(978-1-935332)* 9122 N Tennyson Dr, Milwaukee, WI 53217 USA Tel 414-803-9259
E-mail: cbohlen@wi.rr.com
Web site: http://kitetalespublishing.com.

Kith Bks., *(978-0-615-74201-4; 978-0-9897318)* 9932 E Amanda Paige Dr, Tucson, AZ 85748 USA Tel 520-445-5055
Dist(s): **CreateSpace Independent Publishing Platform.**

KITS Publishing, *(978-0-9643177; 978-0-9778797)* 2359 E. Bryan Ave., Salt Lake City, UT 84108 USA Tel 801-582-2517; Fax: 801-582-2540
Dist(s): **Perseus-PGW**
Todd Communications.

Kitsune Bks., *(978-0-9792700; 978-0-9819495; 978-0-9827409; 978-0-9840058; 978-0-9840059)* P.O. Box 1154, Crawfordville, FL 32326-1154 USA (SAN 852-9760) Tel 850-926-3464
E-mail: anne@kitsunebooks.com; contact@kitsunebooks.com
Web site: http://www.kitsunebooks.com
Dist(s): **Bella Distribution**
Smashwords.

Kittyco Pr., *(978-1-937922)* 6D Auburn Ct., Alexandria, VA 22305 USA Tel 703-684-3699
E-mail: kittyerussell@comcast.net.

Kiva Publishing, Inc., *(978-1-885772)* 21731 E. Buckskin Dr., Walnut, CA 91789 USA Tel 909-595-6833; Fax: 909-860-5424; Toll Free: 800-634-5482
E-mail: kivapub@aol.com
Web site: http://www.kivapub.com
Dist(s): **Canyonlands Pubns.**
New Leaf Distributing Co., Inc.
Quality Bks., Inc.
Rio Nuevo Pubs.

Kivel, Lee, *(978-0-9774999)* 6010 E. Paseo Santa Teresa, Tucson, AZ 85750 USA Tel 520-529-2802
E-mail: ghostriver@gainusa.com.

KiwE Publishing, Ltd., *(978-1-931195; 978-1-933973)* 2980 Glacier St., Anchorage, AK 99508 USA Tel 907-333-5493
E-mail: kiwe@kiwepublishing.com
Web site: http://www.kiwepublishing.com.

Kiwi Media Group, Inc., *(978-0-9743319)* P.O. Box 493, Hopkinton, MA 01748 USA Tel 508-435-4986; Fax: 508-435-0378.

Kiwi Publishing *See* **Kiwi Media Group, Inc.**

KJ Pubns., *(978-0-9792383)* 7069 Middlebury Dr., Boynton Beach, FL 33436 USA
E-mail: contactus@kidshyperspace.com
Web site: http://www.thenutrigang.com.

Kjelberg & Sons, Incorporated *See* **Kjellberg, Inc.**

Kjellberg, Inc., *(978-0-912868)* 805 W. Liberty Dr., Wheaton, IL 60187-4844 USA (SAN 201-5102) Tel 630-653-2244; Fax: 630-653-6233; *Imprints:* Kjellberg Publishers (Kjellberg Pubs)
E-mail: wsc@kjellbergprinting.com
Web site: http://kjellbergprinting.com.

Kjellberg Pubs. *Imprint of* **Kjellberg, Inc.**

Klare & Taylor Publishing Company *See* **Klare Taylor Pubs.**

Klare Taylor Pubs., *(978-0-9764403)* P.O. Box 637, Ashland, OR 97520 USA
Web site: http://www.klaretaylorpublishers.com; http://www.pacificwestcom.com/klare; http://www.pacificwestcom.com/amazon; http://www.pacificwestcom.com/shipsofchildren; http://www.pacificwestcom.com/richardpoem.

K,L.Corgliano, *(978-0-615-56735-8)* 926 Holly hills Ct., Keller, TX 76248 USA Tel 817-914-2344
E-mail: corgliano@verizon.net.

Klemm, Rebecca Charitable Foundation *See* **NumbersAlive! Pr.**

Klett, Ernst, Verlag GmbH (DEU) *(978-3-12) Dist. by* **Intl Bk Import.**

Klett, Ernst, Verlag GmbH (DEU) *(978-3-12) Dist. by* **Continental Bk.**

Kline, Tom, *(978-0-9863364)* 3034 Cullens Dr, Graham, NC 27253 USA Tel 336-270-3757
E-mail: tom@todera.net.

KLITZNER, IRENE *See* **Attitude Pie Publishing**

KLS LifeChange Ministries *Imprint of* **Skinner, Kerry L.**

KLT & Assocs., *(978-0-9799119)* 11829 E. Parkview Ln., Scottsdale, AZ 85255 USA Tel 480-342-9638.

Kluis Publishing, LLC, *(978-0-9776878; 978-0-9830382)* Orders Addr.: 901 Twelve Oaks Ctr. Dr. Suite 907, Wayzata, MN 55391 USA Tel 952-767-5504; Toll Free: 888-345-2855
E-mail: info@kluispublishing.com; kt@alkluis.com
Web site: http://www.alkluis.com.

Klutz, *(978-0-932592; 978-1-57054; 978-1-878257; 978-1-59174)* Div. of Scholastic, Inc., 450 Lambert St., Palo Alto, CA 94306 USA (SAN 212-7539) Tel 650-857-0888; Fax: 650-857-9110; Toll Free: 800-737-4123; *Imprints:* Chicken Socks (Chick Socks); Klutz Certified (Klutz Cert)
E-mail: thefolks@klutz.com
Web site: http://www.klutz.com
Dist(s): **Scholastic, Inc.**

Klutz Certified *Imprint of* **Klutz**

Klutz Latino (MEX) *Dist. by* **IPG Chicago.**

KMR Scripts, *(978-1-932240)* P.O. Box 189, Webster City, IA 50595 USA
Web site: http://www.kmrscripts.com.

KnackPacks, Inc., *(978-0-9726619)* P.O. Box 3716, Oak Park, IL 60303-3716 USA Tel 708-358-1760
E-mail: comments@knackpacks.com
Web site: http://www.knackpacks.com.

KnausWorks, *(978-0-9758742)* 4160-87 Jade St., Capitola, CA 95010 USA
E-mail: ltrsfmspace@aol.com.

Knee-High Adventures, *(978-0-615-16825-8)* 13450 Oak Hollow, Cypress, TX 77429 USA
Web site: http://www.davidsdonkeytales.com
Dist(s): **Lulu Enterprises Inc.**

Knight Publishing, *(978-0-9740535)* P.O. Box 7452, Fremont, CA 94537-7452 USA Tel 209-743-7390; Fax: 510-818-1166
E-mail: knightpublishing@sbcglobal.net; childrenbooks@sbcglobal.net.

Knights of Soul Publishing, *(978-0-615-21482-5; 978-0-615-32994-9)* P.O. Box 715, Las Vegas, NV 89133 USA
E-mail: Paul@Dhunami.com
Web site: http://www.dhunami.com.

KNK Bks., *(978-0-9742010)* P.O. Box 23841, Alexandria, VA 22304 USA Tel 202-321-1425
E-mail: knkrecords@yahoo.com
Web site: http://www.knkrecords.com.

†Knoll, Allen A. Pubs., *(978-0-9627297; 978-1-888310)* 200 W. Victoria St., Santa Barbara, CA 93101 USA (SAN 299-0539) Tel 805-564-3377 (orders); Fax: 805-966-6657 (orders); Toll Free: 800-777-7623 (orders)
E-mail: accounts@knollpublishers.com
Web site: http://www.knollpublishers.com
Dist(s): **Brodart Co.**
Follett School Solutions; *CIP.*

†Knopf, Alfred A. Inc., Div. of The Knopf Publishing Group, Orders Addr.: 400 Hahn Rd., Westminster, MD 21157 USA Tel 410-848-1900; Toll Free: 800-726-0600 (orders); Edit Addr.: 1745 Broadway, New York, NY 10019 USA (SAN 202-5825) Tel 212-782-9000; Toll Free: 800-726-0600; *Imprints:* Knopf Books for Young Readers (Knop)
E-mail: customerservice@randomhouse.com
Web site: http://www.randomhouse.com/knopf
Dist(s): **Libros Sin Fronteras**
MyiLibrary
Penguin Random Hse., LLC.
Random Hse., Inc.; *CIP.*

Knopf Bks. for Young Readers *Imprint of* **Knopf, Alfred A. Inc.**

Knopf Bks. for Young Readers *Imprint of* **Random Hse. Children's Bks.**

†Knopf Doubleday Publishing Group, Div. of Doubleday Broadway Publishing Group, Orders Addr.: 400 Hahn Rd., Westminster, MD 21157 USA (SAN 281-6083) Tel 410-848-1900; Toll Free: 800-726-0600; Edit Addr.: 1745 Broadway, New York, NY 10019 USA (SAN 201-0089) Tel 212-782-9000; 212-572-4961 Bulk orders; Toll Free Fax: 800-659-2436 Orders only; Toll Free: 800-669-1536 Electronic orders; 800-726-0600 Customer service; *Imprints:* Doubleday (Double); Flying Dolphin Press (FDP); Everyman's Library (Everymns Lib); Pantheon (Pantheon); Schocken (Schocken); Vintage (Vin Bks); Anchor (AncKPG)
E-mail: ddaypub@randomhouse.com
Web site: http://www.doubleday.com
Dist(s): **Follett School Solutions**
MyiLibrary
Penguin Random Hse., LLC.
Random Hse., Inc.; *CIP.*

Knosis, LLC *See* **SkyMark Corp.**

Knot Garden Pr., *(978-0-9655018)* 7712 Eagle Creek Dr., Dayton, OH 45459 USA Tel 937-433-2592 (phone/fax)
E-mail: marthaboice@aol.com.

Knott, Joan, *(978-0-9779895)* 132 W. High St., Jackson, MI 49203 USA.

Know Me Pubn. LLC, *(978-0-9790934)* Orders Addr.: 1679 Valdosta Cir., Pontiac, MI 48340 USA Tel 248-212-0204
E-mail: knowmepub@yahoo.com
Web site: http://www.cwren.bravehost.com.

Know Wonder Publishing, LLC, *(978-0-615-18112-7)* 12832 71st Ave., Kirkland, WA 98034 USA
Dist(s): **Publishers Services.**

Knowing Pr., The, *(978-0-936927)* Orders Addr.: 400 Sycamore, McAllen, TX 78501 USA (SAN 658-361X) Tel 956-686-4033
E-mail: janseale@rgv.rr.com.

Knowledge Box Central, *(978-1-61625; 978-1-62472)* 155 Clements Rd., Plain Dealing, LA 71064 USA Tel 318-207-2454
Web site: http://www.knowledgeboxcentral.com.

Knowledge College Planning, *(978-0-9761218)* P.O. Box 321, Stockbridge, GA 30281 USA Tel 770-331-0739
Web site: http://www.kcplan.com.

Knowledge Kids Enterprises, Incorporated *See* **LeapFrog Enterprises, Inc.**

Knowledge Power Communications, *(978-0-9818790; 978-0-9854107; 978-0-9888644; 978-0-9907199; 978-0-9967162)* 25379 Wayne Mills Dr., Suite 131, Valencia, CA 91355 USA (SAN 856-8189) Tel 661-513-0308; Fax: 661-513-0381
Web site: http://www.knowledgepowerinc.com.

Knowledge Quest, *(978-1-932786)* P.O. Box 474, Boring, OR 97009-0474 USA Tel 503-663-1210; Fax: 503-663-0670 Do not confuse with Knowledge Quest, Dieterich, IL
E-mail: orders@knowledgequestmaps.com; terri@knowledgequestmaps.com
Web site: http://www.knowledgequestmaps.com.

Knowledge Wand, LLC, *(978-0-9766680)* 100 Kennewyck Cir., Slingerlands, NY 12159 USA Tel 518-456-3110; Fax: 518-456-6990; Toll Free: 800-376-5669
E-mail: djahnel@gmail.com
Web site: http://www.knowledgewand.com.

KnowledgeGain Inc., *(978-0-9779844)* 3936 Hwy 52 N, Suite 121, Rochester, MN 55901 USA (SAN 850-802X) Tel 507-398-2384; Fax: 928-832-6568
E-mail: Publisher@KnowledgeGain.com
Web site: http://www.KnowledgeGain.com.

Knowtivate, LLC, *(978-0-9787021)* Orders Addr.: 116 Milton St., Lake Mills, WI 53551-5355 USA Tel 920-478-3936; Edit Addr.: N7894 Cty. Rd., O, Waterloo, WI 53594-5355 USA
Web site: http://www.knowtivate.com.

Knox, John Press *See* **Westminster John Knox Pr.**

KO Kids Bks., *(978-0-9723946)* 16 Baytree Rd., San Rafael, CA 94903-3801 USA
Web site: http://www.kokidsbooks.com
Dist(s): **Perseus-PGW.**

Koala Jo Publishing, *(978-0-9764698)* Orders Addr.: 352 N. El Camino Real, San Mateo, CA 94401 USA
Web site: http://www.koalajo.com.

KOBZ, *(978-0-9772222)* 2230 Rockingham Dr., Maryville, TN 37803 USA Tel 865-980-7755.

Koch, Chris, *(978-0-9764338)* 3344 Louisville Rd., Harrodsburg, KY 40330-9190 USA.

Kochevar, Steven, *(978-0-9763546)* 7 Beth Lee Dr., Grafton, MA 01519-1139 USA.

†**Kodansha America, Inc.**, *(978-0-87011; 978-1-56836; 978-1-935429; 978-1-61262; 978-1-63236)* 451 Park Ave S. Flr. 7, New York, NY 10016-7390 USA (SAN 201-0526) Toll Free: 800-451-7556
E-mail: t-sumi@kodansha-usa.com; ka-koide@kodansha.co.jp
Web site: http://kodanshacomics.com/; www.kodanshausa.com
Dist(s): **Oxford Univ. Pr., Inc.**
Penguin Random Hse., LLC.
Random Hse., Inc.; *CIP.*

Kodansha International (JPN) *(978-4-7700) Dist. by* **Cheng Tsui.**

Kodansha International (JPN) *(978-4-7700) Dist. by* **Kodansha.**

Kodansha USA Publishing *See* **Kodansha America, Inc.**

Kodel Group, LLC, The, *(978-0-9844784; 978-0-9850142; 978-1-62485)* Orders Addr.: P.O. Box 38, Grants Pass, OR 97528-0003 USA (SAN 859-4961) Tel 541-471-1234; Edit Addr.: 132 NW 6th St., Grants Pass, OR 97528 USA; *Imprints:* Empire Holdings (Empire Holds); Empire Holdins - Literary Division for Young Readers (EH LDYR)
E-mail: info@kodelgroup.com
Web site: stevietenderheart.com; kodelempire.com.

Koehler Bks. *Imprint of* **Morgan James Publishing**

Koenisha Pubns., *(978-0-9700458; 978-0-9718758; 978-0-9741685; 978-0-9759621; 978-0-9800098)* 3196-53rd St., Hamilton, MI 49419 USA
E-mail: koenisha@macatawa.org
Web site: http://www.koenisha.com.

Kofford, Greg Books, Inc., *(978-1-58958)* P.O. Box 1362, Draper, UT 84020 USA (SAN 253-5882) Tel 801-523-6063; Fax: 801-576-0583
E-mail: gregk@koffordbooks.com
Web site: http://www.koffordbooks.com.

Koho Pono, LLC, *(978-0-9845424; 978-1-938282; 978-1-941379)* 15024 SE Pinegrove Loop, Clackamas, OR 97015-7629 USA (SAN 859-6956) Tel 503-723-7392
E-mail: burrs@kohopono.com
Web site: http://kohopono.com.

Kokopelli Pr., *(978-0-9759270)* 9611 Paseo del Rey NE, Albuquerque, NM 87111-1649 USA Do not confuse with companies with the same name in Las Cruces, NM, Sedona, AZ.

Koldarana Pubns., *(978-1-884993)* Orders Addr.: P.O. Box 973, Dover, AR 72837 USA; Edit Addr.: 958 SR 164 E., Dover, AR 72837 USA
E-mail: ctn47496@yahoo.com.

Kolluri, Alina M., *(978-0-9787319)* 10124 Queens Park Dr., Tampa, FL 33647-3179 USA
E-mail: alinakolluri@yahoo.com.

Komikwerks, LLC, *(978-0-9742803; 978-0-9778809; 978-1-933925)* 1 Ruth St., Worcester, MA 01602 USA; *Imprints:* Actionopolis (Actionopolis); Agent of Danger (AgentofDanger)
E-mail: patrick@komikwerks.com; shannon@komikwerks.com; kristendenton@gmail.com
Web site: http://www.komikwerks.com; http://www.actionopolis.com.

Kommon Cents, Inc., *(978-0-9745982)* Orders Addr.: P.O. Box 313274, Jamaica, NY 11431-3274 USA Tel 917-541-8568; Toll Free: 877-566-2368
E-mail: info@kommoncents.com
Web site: http://www.kommoncents.com.

Kommon Cents Publishing Company *See* **Kommon Cents, Inc.**

Konaa Publishing *See* **Smallbag Bks.**

Konecky & Konecky *Imprint of* **Konecky, William S. Assocs., Inc.**

Konecky, William S. Assocs., Inc., *(978-0-914427; 978-1-56852)* 72 Ayers Point Rd., Old Saybrook, CT 06475-4301 USA (SAN 663-2432) Tel 860-388-0878; Fax: 860-388-0273; *Imprints:* Konecky & Konecky (Konecky & Konecky)
E-mail: seankon@comcast.net.

Konkori International, *(978-0-9647012)* P.O. Box 102441, Denver, CO 80250 USA Tel 303-744-6318; Fax: 303-296-9113; *Imprints:* Dawn of a New Day Publications, The (Dawn of a New Day)
E-mail: dabdulai@yahoo.com
Dist(s): **Emery-Pratt Co.**

Konopka, Ann Marie, *(978-0-615-18598-9)* 20 Palmer Rd., Kendall Pk., NJ 08824 USA Tel 732-821-5415
E-mail: annmkonopka@yahoo.com
Dist(s): **Lulu Enterprises Inc.**

Kookalook Publishing, *(978-0-9706323)* 53 Garden Pl., Brooklyn, NY 11201-4501 USA
E-mail: kookypubs@hotmail.com.

Korean Culture Research, Inc., *(978-0-9762990)* 38 W. 32nd St., Suite 1112, New York, NY 10001 USA Tel 212-563-5763; Fax: 212-563-6707
E-mail: leekle@sprynet.com
Web site: http://www.learnkoreannow.com.

Koroknay, Thomas, *(978-0-9749705)* 3718 Lindsey Rd., Lexington, KY 44904 USA Tel 419-884-0222.

Kosemund Hse., *(978-0-615-48086-2)* 3316 N. Union Ave., Shawnee, OK 74804 USA Tel 405-275-7751
Dist(s): **CreateSpace Independent Publishing Platform**
Dummy Record Do Not USE!!!!.

Kotzig Publishing, Inc., *(978-0-9715411; 978-0-9767163)* 1109 NW 16th St., Delray Beach, FL 33444 USA
E-mail: susan@kotzigpublishing.com
Web site: http://www.kotzigpublishing.com
Dist(s): **Independent Pubs. Group.**

Kountz Marketing Group, *(978-0-9859601)* 700 E Ash Dr No. 13208 C/O Charity Van Vleet, Euless, TX 76060 USA Tel 214-326-4356
E-mail: charitykountz@gmail.com
Web site: http://www.charitykountz.com.

Kovels Antiques, Inc., *(978-0-9646683)* 22000 Shaker Blvd., Shaker Heights, OH 44122 USA Tel 216-752-2252; Fax: 216-752-3115; Toll Free: 800-303-1996
E-mail: kkovel@kovels.com
Web site: www.kovels.com.

KP Bks., *(978-0-9748549)* 354 Sequoia Ct., Antioch, IL 60002-2600 USA
E-mail: pudaitem@sbcglobal.net; bluehorizon1@sbcglobal.net; marylpk625@me.com.

Kramer, H.J. Inc., *(978-0-915811; 978-1-932073)* P.O. Box 1082, Tiburon, CA 94920 USA (SAN 294-0833) Fax: 415-435-5364; Toll Free: 800-972-6657
E-mail: hjkramer@jps.net
Web site: http://www.newworldlibrary.com
Dist(s): **New Leaf Distributing Co., Inc.**
New World Library
Perseus-PGW.

Kraszewski, Terry, *(978-0-9821989)* 2162 Avenida De La Playa, La Jolla, CA 92037 USA (SAN 857-5223) Tel 858-456-9283; Fax: 858-456-9551
E-mail: ricswave@cox.net
Web site: http://www.surfangelbook.com.

Krause, Claudia, *(978-0-9655689)* P.O. Box 7083, Capistrano Beach, CA 92624 USA Tel 714-492-7778.

Kravec & Kravec & Associates *See* **Bellaboozle Books, Inc.**

Krazy Duck Productions, *(978-0-9776739; 978-0-9961622)* Orders Addr.: P.O. Box 105, Danville, KY 40423 USA Tel 606-787-2571; Fax: 606-787-8207; Edit Addr.: 2227 Wood Creek Rd., Liberty, KY 42539 USA
E-mail: KrazyduckProductions@msn.com
Web site: http://www.krazyduck.com.

KRBY Creations, LLC, *(978-0-9745715)* 2 Leeds Ct., Brick, NJ 08724-4011 USA
E-mail: krbyenterprises@comcast.net
Web site: http://www.krbycreations.com.

Kreations, *(978-0-9766621)* 19842 Needles St., Chatsworth, CA 91311 USA
E-mail: kreations@socal.rr.com
Web site: http://www.skelanimals.com.

Kreativ Kaos, *(978-0-9790572)* P.O. Box 27955, Anaheim Hills, CA 92809 USA (SAN 852-310X)
E-mail: admin@kreativkaos.com
Web site: http://www.kreativkaos.com.

Kreative Character Kreations, Inc., *(978-0-9641381)* 9 Endicott Dr., Huntington, NY 11743 USA Tel 516-673-8230; Fax: 516-346-6620.

Kreative X-Pressions Pubns., *(978-0-9798536; 978-0-9800552)* Orders Addr.: 87 Kennedy Dr., Colchester, CT 06415-1315 USA (SAN 854-5561) Tel 860-537-2673
E-mail: novelwriter@comcast.net
Web site: http://www.kreativexpressionsonline.com.

KreativeMindz Prodns. LLC, P.O. Box 2413, New York, NY 10108 USA Tel 212-222-3069
E-mail: KLB@kreativemindzproductions.com
Web site: http://www.kreativemindzproductions.

Kreder, Mary Ellen DeLuca, *(978-0-615-92430-4; 978-0-9913232)* 364 Quaker St., Wallkill, NY 12589 USA Tel 845-853-2803
E-mail: MaryEd4466@verizon.net.

†**Kregel Pubns.**, *(978-0-8254)* Div. of Kregel, Inc., Orders Addr.: P.O. Box 2607, Grand Rapids, MI 49501-2607 USA (SAN 206-9792) Tel 616-451-4775; Fax: 616-451-9330; Toll Free: 800-733-2607; Edit Addr.: 733 Wealthy St., SE., Grand Rapids, MI 49503-5553 USA (SAN 298-9115); *Imprints:* Editorial Portavoz (Edit Portavoz)
E-mail: kregelbooks@kregel.com; acquisitions@kregel.com
Web site: http://www.kregel.com
Dist(s): **Send The Light Distribution LLC**
Spring Arbor Distributors, Inc.; *CIP.*

Kreizel Enterprises, Inc., *(978-0-9729232)* P.O. Box 224, Monsey, NY 10952 USA; 26 Charles Ln., Spring Valley, NY 10977-3330
E-mail: info@kreizelplating.com; books@kreizelplating.com.

Kremer Pubns, Inc., *(978-0-9707591; 978-0-9745631; 978-0-9817272)* 12615 W. Custer Ave., Butler, WI 53007 USA Toll Free: 800-669-0887
E-mail: info@kremerpublications.com
Web site: http://www.kremerpublications.com.

Krickle Forest Adventures, *(978-0-9855997)* 4081 Jeri Rd., Interlochen, MI 49643 USA Tel 231-753-6025
E-mail: customerservice@krickleforest.com
Web site: http://www.krickleforest.com.

Kringle Enterprises Company *See* **North Pole Pr.**

Krisaran Publishing Co., *(978-0-9773146)* 850 NC 55 E., Mount Olive, NC 28365 USA (SAN 257-3903)
E-mail: bjackson@esn.net; brenda@krisaran.com
Web site: http://www.krisaran.com.

KRO Publishing *See* **Preschool Prep Co.**

Kruger, Wolfgang Verlag, GmbH (DEU) *(978-3-8105) Dist. by* **Distribks Inc.**

Kruger, Wolfgang Verlag, GmbH (DEU) *(978-3-8105) Dist. by* **Intl Bk Import.**

Krullstone Publishing, LLC, *(978-0-9833237; 978-0-9882170; 978-0-9889578; 978-1-941851)* 8751 Clayton Cove Rd., Springville, AL 35146 USA (SAN 860-1240) Tel 205-681-9455; Fax: 205-681-3774
E-mail: charlotte@krullstonepublishing.com
Dist(s): **Krullstone Distributing, LLC**
Smashwords.

K's Kids Publishing, *(978-0-9797208)* 12706 SW 94 Ct., Miami, FL 33176 USA (SAN 854-1892) Tel 305-969-5570
E-mail: ks_kids@bellsouth.net.

†**Ktav Publishing Hse., Inc.**, *(978-0-87068; 978-0-88125; 978-1-60280)* Orders Addr.: 930 Newark Ave. 4th Flr., Jersey City, NJ 07306 USA (SAN 201-0038) Tel 201-963-9524; Fax: 201-963-0102; Toll Free Fax: 800-626-7517 (orders)
E-mail: orders@ktav.com; editor@ktav.com; questions@ktav.com
Web site: http://www.ktav.com
Dist(s): **eBookIt.com**; *CIP.*

K-Teen *Imprint of* **Kensington Publishing Corp.**

K-Teen/Dafina *Imprint of* **Kensington Publishing Corp.**

ktf-writers-studio, *(978-0-615-41134-7; 978-0-615-44161-0; 978-3-9523908; 978-0-578-10595-6; 978-0-9913395)* 5712 Ashley Sq. S., Memphis, TN 38120 USA Tel 901-683-4210; 478 W. Racquet Club Pl., Memphis, TN 38117
E-mail: frigonormfr@aol.com; ktf-writers-studio@hotmail.com
Web site: www.ktf-writers-studio.ch
Dist(s): **AtlasBooks Distribution.**

Kube Publishing Ltd. (GBR) *(978-1-84774) Dist. by* **Consort Bk Sales.**

Kudakon Publishing, *(978-0-9793989)* P.O. Box 2461, Cedar City, UT 84721-2461 USA Tel 435-238-0253
E-mail: esz0001@gmail.com
Dist(s): **Brodart Co.**
Follett School Solutions.

Kulupi Pr., *(978-0-9661867; 978-0-9817653)* 5082 Warm Springs Rd., Glen Ellen, CA 95442 USA Tel 707-996-1149
E-mail: kulupi@vom.com
Web site: http://www.kulupi.com
Dist(s): **Partners Bk. Distributing, Inc.**

Kumon Publishing North America, Inc., *(978-1-933241; 978-4-7743; 978-1-934968; 978-1-935800; 978-1-941082; 978-0-692-47466-2)* Glenpointe Ctr. E., Suite 6 300 Frank W. Burr Blvd., Teaneck, NJ 07666 USA Tel 201-836-2105; Fax: 201-836-1559; Toll Free: 800-657-7970; Goban-cho Grand, Bldg. 3F 3-1 Goban-cho Chiyoda-ku, Tokyo, 102-8180 Tel 0081 0332343485; Fax: 0081 0332344018
E-mail: books@kumon.com
Web site: http://www.kumonbooks.com
Dist(s): **Bookazine Co., Inc.**
Ingram Pub. Services
Sterling Publishing Co., Inc.

Kumon U.S.A., Inc., *(978-0-9702092)* 300 Frank W. Burr Blvd., Teaneck, NJ 07666 USA
E-mail: falcbooks@home.com.

Kunce, Craig LLC *See* **Windhill Bks. LLC**

Kunz, C.A., *(978-0-615-43574-9; 978-0-615-56353-4)* 2616 Cobalt Ct., Orlando, FL 32837 USA Tel 386-334-1341
E-mail: tiadcoleman@hotmail.com
Dist(s): **CreateSpace Independent Publishing Platform**
Dummy Record Do Not USE!!!!.

Kuperman, Marina, *(978-0-9801109)* 8 Forge Rd., Hewitt, NJ 07421 USA Tel 973-728-0835
E-mail: marinakuperman@yahoo.com
Web site: http://turtlefeetsurfersbeat.com.

Kupu Kupu Pr., *(978-0-9883448)* 1710 Franklin No. 300, Oakland, CA 94612 USA Tel 510-452-1912
E-mail: inno@designaction.org
Web site: http://aisforactivist.com.

Kurdyla, E L Publishing LLC, *(978-1-61751)* Orders Addr.: P.O. Box 958, Bowie, MD 20718-0958 USA Tel 301-805-2191; Fax: 301-805-2192; Edit Addr.: P.O. Box 958, Bowie, MD 20718-0958 USA Tel 301-805-2191; Fax: 301-805-2192; *Imprints:* 4th Division Press (FourthDiv)
E-mail: publisher@kurdylapublishing.com
Web site: http://www.kurdylapublishing.com.

Kurz, Ron, *(978-0-939829)* P.O. Box 95551, Las Vegas, NV 89193 USA (SAN 663-8333) Tel 702-837-6395 (phone/fax); 3060 Sunrise Heights Dr., Henderson, NV 89052 (SAN 663-8341) Tel 702-870-5968
E-mail: ronkurz@earthlink.net
Web site: http://www.ronkurz.com.

Kush Univ. Pr., *(978-1-893731)* Orders Addr.: 8247 S. Oglesby Ave., Chicago, IL 60617 USA Tel 773-598-5707; *Imprints:* Mandolin House (MandolinHse)
E-mail: esmith334@kushuniversitypress.net
Web site: http://kushuniversitypress.net/opencart/; http://kushuniversitypress.net/KU_press.html.

Kutie Kari Bks., Inc., *(978-1-884149)* 4189 Ethan Dr., Eagan, MN 55123 USA Tel 651-450-7427
E-mail: gharbo@garyharbo.com
Web site: http://www.garyharbo.com.

Kvale Good Natured Games LLC, *(978-0-9793583)* 771 Parkview Ave., Saint Paul, MN 55117-4045 USA Tel 651-204-6781; Fax: 651-204-6966
E-mail: admin@kvalegames.com
Web site: http://www.kvalegames.com.

Kvalvasser, Leonid, *(978-0-9753110)* 1124 Blake Ct. # 1A, Brooklyn, NY 11235-5219 USA.

Kwazy Kitty Publishing Co., *(978-0-9770012)* Orders Addr.: P.O. Box 178, Monkton, MD 21111-0178 USA.

Kwela Bks. (ZAF) *(978-0-7957) Dist. by* **IPG Chicago.**

KWIP, Inc., *(978-0-9790267; 978-0-692-25867-5)* 1400 Broadway Blvd., Polk City, FL 33868 USA
E-mail: stevec@fantasyofflight.com.

Kwist, Karla, *(978-0-9795046)* 2420 Golden Arrow, Las Vegas, NV 89120 USA Tel 702-768-8406
E-mail: karlakk@aol.com
Web site: http://www.karlakwist.com.

Kylie Jean *Imprint of* **Picture Window Bks.**

Kyoodoz, *(978-0-9771172)* Orders Addr.: P.O. Box 5431, Beaverton, OR 97006-0431 USA
E-mail: customerservice@kyoodoz.com; sales@kyoodoz.com
Web site: http://www.kyoodoz.com.

L A 411 Publishing Company *See* **Reed Business Information**

L. A. Eng Bks., *(978-0-9748598)* 231 W. Hillcrest Blvd., Inglewood, CA 90301 USA
E-mail: luis_arevalo@lennox.k12.ca.us.

L. A. Media, LLC *See* **Mardi Gras Publishing, LLC**

L & L Enterprises, *(978-0-9760046)* 6960 W. Peoria Ave. LOT 132, Peoria, AZ 85345-6038 USA
Web site: https://www.latinandlanguage.com.

L. C. D., *(978-0-941414)* 663 Calle Miramar, Redondo Beach, CA 90277 USA (SAN 239-0035) Tel 310-375-6336
E-mail: lenduncan@earthlink.net
Web site: http://www.phonicsplus.com.

LED Publishing, *(978-1-885674)* Div. of Logical Expression In Design, 1730 M St. NW, Suite 407, Washington, DC 20036 USA Tel 703-558-0100; Fax: 703-558-4970.

L G Productions *See* **L G Publishing**

L G Publishing, *(978-0-9768486)* Orders Addr.: 281 Fielding, Ferndale, MI 48220 USA
E-mail: admin@lgproductions.info
Web site: http://www.lgproductions.info.

L L Teach, *(978-0-9676545; 978-1-931104)* 709 Country Club Rd., Bridgewater, NJ 08807-1601 USA Tel 908-575-8830; Fax: 908-704-1730; Toll Free: 800-575-7670
E-mail: ann4480@aol.com; llteach5757670@aol.com
Web site: http://www.LLteach.com.

LMA Publishing, *(978-1-892426)* Div. of Lifestyle Management Assocs., 111 Grove St., Apt. 1, West Roxbury, MA 02132 USA Tel 617-325-6752 (phone/fax)
E-mail: pentz@ix.netcom.com
Web site: http://www.lifestylemanagement.com.

L P D Enterprises *See* **LPD Pr.**

L W S Bks., *(978-0-9704361)* 227 Bayshore Dr., Hendersonville, TN 37075 USA Tel 615-826-3871; Fax: 615-826-3883; Toll Free: 800-643-4718
E-mail: clazzy@mindspring.com
Web site: http://www.janethan.com; http://www.imsonofman.com.

L W S Publishers *See* **L W S Bks.**

La Caille Nous Publishing Co., *(978-0-9647635; 978-0-9718191)* 328 Flatbush Ave, Suite 240, Brooklyn, NY 11238 USA Tel 212-726-1293; Fax: 212-591-6465
E-mail: gcadet@lcnpub.com.

La Di La Dah, *(978-0-9816629)* 5508 Vantage Point Rd., Columbia, MD 21044-2631 USA
E-mail: r.higgins@xs4all.net
Dist(s): **Lulu Enterprises Inc.**

La Frontera Publishing, *(978-0-9785634; 978-0-9857551)* 2710 Thomes Ave., Suite 181, Cheyenne, WY 82001 USA (SAN 851-0180) Tel 307-778-4752 general office number
E-mail: company@lafronterapublishing.com
Web site: http://www.lafronterapublishing.com
Dist(s): **Univ. of New Mexico Pr.**

La Galera, S.A. Editorial (ESP) *(978-84-246; 978-84-7515; 978-84-85297) Dist. by* **AIMS Intl.**

La Galera, S.A. Editorial (ESP) *(978-84-246; 978-84-7515; 978-84-85297) Dist. by* **Lectorum Pubns.**

La Librairie Parisienne, *(978-0-615-54542-4; 978-0-9886058)* 17844 Porto Marina Way, Pacific Palisades, CA 90272 USA Tel 310-392-2143
E-mail: JACKIEMANCUSO@GMAIL.COM; jackie@parischienbook.com
Web site: http://www.jackiemancuso.com/la-librairie-parisienne
Dist(s): **Independent Pubs. Group.**

La Luz Comics, *(978-0-9755193)* 1516 10th Ave. S., No. 6, Minneapolis, MN 55404-1795 USA
E-mail: sam@samhiti.com
Web site: http://www.samhiti.com.

La Mancha Publishing Group, *(978-1-890701)* 14534 Victory Blvd., Van Nuys, CA 91411 USA Tel 818-994-8195.

La Montagne Secrete (CAN) *(978-2-923163) Dist. by* **IPG Chicago.**

La Oferta Publishing Co., *(978-0-9665876; 978-0-9791624)* 1376 N. Fourth St., San Jose, CA 95112 USA Tel 408-436-7850; Fax: 408-436-7861; Toll Free: 800-336-7850
E-mail: sales@laoferta.com; mary@laoferta.com
Web site: http://www.laoferta.com
Dist(s): **Bilingual Pubns. Co., The**
Lectorum Pubns., Inc.
Libros Sin Fronteras
SPD-Small Pr. Distribution.

LA Ruocco, *(978-0-9743454; 978-1-941593)* Orders Addr.: 31 Lake St., Brooklyn, NY 11223 USA
E-mail: laruocco@cs.com.

Laasya Design, *(978-0-9774147)* 400 N. Catalina St., Burbank, CA 91505 USA
E-mail: info@laasyadesign.com
Web site: http://www.laasyadesign.com.

Lab-Aids, Inc., *(978-1-887725; 978-1-933298; 978-1-60301; 978-1-63093)* 17 Colt Ct., Ronkonkoma, NY 11779 USA Tel 631-737-1133; Fax: 631-737-1286; Toll Free Fax: 800-381-8003
E-mail: lab-aids@lab.aids.com.

Labarco, *(978-0-9762439)* P.O. Box 1734, Alief, TX 77411 USA
Web site: http://www.cushcity.com; http://www.Amazon.com.

L'Abeille Publishing Incorporated *See* **Orndee Omnimedia, Inc.**

Label Buster, Incorporated *See* **Block System, The**

Labor, Editorial S. A. (ESP) *(978-84-335) Dist. by* **Continental Bk.**

Labosh Publishing, *(978-0-9744341)* P.O. Box 588, East Petersburg, PA 17520-0588 USA Tel 717-898-3813 (phone/fax)
E-mail: laboshpublishing@msn.com
Web site: http://laboshpublishing.com.

Lab-Volt Systems, Inc., *(978-0-86657; 978-1-60533)* Orders Addr.: P.O. Box 686, Farmingdale, NJ 07727 USA (SAN 238-7050) Tel 732-938-2000 Toll Free: 800-522-8658
E-mail: us@labvolt.com; lvanbrug@labvolt.com
Web site: http://www.labvolt.com.

Lacey Productions, *(978-0-9771076)* 611 Druid Rd., Suite 705, Clearwater, FL 33767 USA
E-mail: sherry@laceyproductions.com
Web site: http://www.laceyproductions.com.

Lacey Publishing Co., *(978-0-9709249)* 29 Bounty Rd W., Benbrook, TX 76132-1003 USA Tel 817-738-3185 (phone/fax)
E-mail: jamesb50@charter.net
Web site: http://www.marfalightsresearch.com
Dist(s): **MyiLibrary**
ebrary, Inc.

LaChrisAnd Productions, *(978-0-9765063)* P.O. Box 969, Desert Hot Springs, CA 92240 USA Tel 760-309-2263
Web site: http://www.lachrisandproductions.com.

Lackner, William *See* **Digging Clams n Oregon**

Ladd, David Pr., *(978-0-9774563)* 56 Coolidge Ave., South Portland, ME 04106 USA Tel 207-767-2836
E-mail: davidladdpress@yahoo.com.

LaDow Publishing, *(978-0-9723623)* 308 Reynolds Ln., West Chester, PA 19380-3300 USA Tel 219-689-4565; Fax: 610-918-9571
E-mail: wmladow@aol.com
Web site: http://www.wmladow.com.

Lady Hawk Pr., *(978-0-9829082)* 3831 Abbey Ct., Newbury Park, CA 91320 USA Tel 310-460-8744
Web site: ladyhawkpress.com
Dist(s): **ebrary, Inc.**

Lady Illyria Pr., *(978-0-9765572)* 30 Lamprey Ln., Lee, NH 03824 USA Tel 603-659-3826
E-mail: patricia.emison@unh.edu.

Laffin Minor Pr., *(978-0-9770516)* P.O. Box 273, Alma, CO 80420 USA Tel 970-409-8857; Fax: 207-967-5492
E-mail: lydia@laffinminorpress.com
Web site: http://www.laffinminorpress.com.

Lagesse Stevens *Imprint of* **Martell Publishing Co**

Laguna Press/BTI *See* **Cerebral Press International**

Lake 7 Creative, LLC, *(978-0-9774122; 978-0-9821187; 978-0-9883662; 978-1-940647)* 3419 Vincent Ave. N., Minneapolis, MN 55412 USA (SAN 257-5167) Tel 612-412-5493
E-mail: ryan@lake7creative.com
Web site: http://www.lake7creative.com
Dist(s): **Adventure Pubns., Inc.**
Consortium Bk. Sales & Distribution
Perseus Bks. Group.

Lake Claremont Pr. *Imprint of* **Everything Goes Media, LLC**

Lake Claremont Press *See* **Everything Goes Media, LLC**

Lake Isle Pr., Inc., *(978-0-9627403; 978-1-891105)* 16 W. 32nd St., Suite 10B, New York, NY 10001 USA Tel 212-273-0796; Fax: 212-273-0198; Toll Free: 800-462-6420 (Orders only)
E-mail: lakeisle@earthlink.net; hiroko@lakeislepress.com
Web site: http://www.lakeislepress.com
Dist(s): **National Bk. Network.**

Lake Limericks, *(978-0-9761711)* P.O. Box 478, Lake Waccamaw, NC 28450 USA Tel 910-646-4998; Fax: 910-371-1133
E-mail: aldrich@weblnk.net.

Lake Street Pr., *(978-1-936181)* 4064 N. Lincoln Ave. #402, Chicago, IL 60618-3038 USA Tel 773-525-8953; Fax: 773-525-1455
Web site: http://www.lakestreetpress.com
Dist(s): **Partners Pubs. Group, Inc.**

Lake Street Pubs., *(978-1-58417)* Orders Addr.: 4537 Chowen Ave S., Minneapolis, MN 55410-1364 USA
E-mail: compass@sd.cybernex.net.

Lake Superior Port Cities, Inc., *(978-0-942235; 978-1-938229)* Orders Addr.: P.O. Box 16417, Duluth, MN 55816-0417 USA Tel 218-722-5002; Fax: 218-722-4096; Toll Free: 888-244-5253; Edit Addr.: 310 E. Superior St. #125, Duluth, MN 55802-3134 USA (SAN 666-9980)
E-mail: reader@lakesuperior.com
Web site: http://www.lakesuperior.com
Dist(s): **Partners Bk. Distributing, Inc.**
TNT Media Group, Inc.

Lakefront Research LLC, *(978-0-9764665)* P.O. Box 667, East Hampstead, NH 03826-0667 USA.

Lakeshore Curriculum Materials Company *See* **Lakeshore Learning Materials**

Lakeshore Learning Materials, *(978-1-929255; 978-1-58970; 978-1-59746; 978-1-60666)* Orders Addr.: 2695 E. Dominguez St., Carson, CA 90895 USA (SAN 630-0251) Toll Free: 800-421-5354; Edit Addr.: 2695 E. Dominguez St., Carson, CA 90895 USA Tel 310-537-8600; Fax: 310-632-8314
E-mail: ubeckham@lakeshorelearning.com
Web site: http://www.lakeshorelearning.com.

Lakeview Pr., *(978-0-9749677)* c/o Jan Devereux, 255 Lakeview Ave., Cambridge, MA 02138 USA Do not confuse with Lake View Press in New Orleans, LA, Mooresville, NC, Lake Oswego, OR.

Lakin, Laqwacia, *(978-0-9891103)* 3290 Osterley Way, Cumming, GA 30041 USA Tel 678-237-8495
E-mail: llakin.consulting@gmail.com.

Lakota Language Consortium, Inc., *(978-0-9761082; 978-0-9821107; 978-0-9834363; 978-1-941461)* 2620 N Walnut St. Suite 1280, Bloomington, IN 47404 USA Tel 812-961-0140; Fax: 812-961-0141; Toll Free: 888-525-6828
E-mail: orders@lakhota.org; sales@lakhota.org
Web site: http://www.lakhota.org; http://www.languagepress.com; http://www.llcbookstore.com.

Lamar, Mel Ministries *See* **Lamar, Melvin Productions**

Lamar, Melvin Productions, *(978-0-9716068)* 900 Downtowner Blvd., Apt. 89, Mobile, AL 36609-5409 USA
E-mail: melvinelamar@att.net; melvinlamar31@gmail.com.

Lamb, Wendy *Imprint of* **Random Hse. Children's Bks.**

Lambda Pubs., Inc., *(978-0-915361; 978-1-55774)* 3709 13th Ave., Brooklyn, NY 11218-3622 USA (SAN 291-0640) Tel 718-972-5449; Fax: 718-972-6307
E-mail: judaica@email.msn.com.

Lambert Bk. Hse., Inc., *(978-0-89315)* 4139 Parkway Dr., Florence, AL 35630-6347 USA (SAN 180-5169) Tel 256-764-4098; 256-764-4090; Fax: 256-766-9200; Toll Free: 800-551-8511
E-mail: Info@lambertbookhouse.com
Web site: http://www.lambertbookhouse.com.

LaMothe, Karin, *(978-0-9728763)* P.O. Box 672, Belleville, MI 48112-0672 USA
Web site: http://www.angelslullaby.com.

Lamp Post Inc., *(978-0-9708587; 978-1-933428; 978-1-60039)* 29348 Ariel St., Murrieta, CA 92563 USA
E-mail: burner@lamppostpubs.com
Web site: http://www.lamppostpubs.com
Dist(s): **Diamond Comic Distributors, Inc.**
Diamond Bk. Distributors.

Lamp Post Publishing, Inc., *(978-1-892135)* 1741 Tallman Hollow Rd., Montoursville, PA 17754 USA (SAN 253-4681) Tel 570-435-2804; Fax: 570-435-2803; Toll Free: 800-326-9273
E-mail: lamppostp@aol.com
Web site: http://www.lamppostpublishing.com; http://www.beyondthegloesmur.com; http://www.heartstringsbio.com.

Lamplight Ministries, Inc., *(978-0-915445)* Orders Addr.: P.O. Box 1307, Dunedin, FL 34697 USA (SAN 291-4719) Fax: 727-733-8467; Toll Free: 800-540-1597
E-mail: judyann@lamplight.net
Web site: http://www.lamplight.net.

Lamplight Publications *See* **Lamplight Ministries, Inc.**

Lampo Group Incorporated, The *See* **Lampo Licensing, LLC**

Lampo Licensing, LLC, *(978-0-9635712; 978-0-9718554; 978-0-9720044; 978-0-9726323; 978-0-9753033; 978-0-9769630; 978-0-9774895; 978-0-9777767; 978-0-9785620; 978-0-9786577; 978-1-934629; 978-0-9800873; 978-0-9816839; 978-0-9829862; 978-1-936948; 978-1-937077; 978-1-938400; 978-1-942121) 1749 Mallory Ln., Brentwood, TN 37027 USA Tel 615-515-3223; 888-227-3223; Fax: 615-371-5007; Toll Free: 888-227-3223*
E-mail: preston.cannon@daveramsey.com; thom.chittom@daveramsey.com
Web site: http://www.daveramsey.com.

Lampstand Pr., Ltd., *(978-1-935301)* Orders Addr.: P.O. Box 5798, Derwood, MD 20855 USA Tel 301-963-0808; Fax: 301-963-1868; Toll Free: 800-705-7487; Edit Addr.: 8073 Snouffer School Rd., Derwood, MD 20855 USA
Web site: http://www.lampstandpress.com.

LaMuth Publishing Company *See* **Fairhaven Bk. Pubs.**

Lamweg Publishing, *(978-0-9801146)* 176 W. 100 S., Kouts, IN 46347 USA Tel 219-766-2174.

Landauer Corporation *See* **Landauer Publishing, LLC**

Landauer Publishing, LLC, *(978-0-9646870; 978-1-890621; 978-0-9770166; 978-0-9793711; 978-0-9800688; 978-0-9818040; 978-0-9825586; 978-1-935726)* Orders Addr.: 3100 101st St., Suite A, Urbandale, IA 50322 USA (SAN 915-2334) Tel 515-287-2144; Fax: 515 276 5102; Toll Free: 800-557-2144
E-mail: info@landauercorp.com; jeramy@landauercorp.com; acounting@landauercorp.com
Web site: http://www.landauerpub.com
Dist(s): **American Wholesale Bk. Co.**
Baker & Taylor Bks.
Bookazine Co., Inc.
Brodart Co.

Landfall Co., The, *(978-0-9747445)* 18640 Mack Ave., P.O. Box 36551, Grosse Pointe Farms, MI 48236 USA Fax: 313-886-6250
E-mail: mhslandfall@landfallcompany.com.

L&L Publishing, *(978-0-615-65534-5; 978-0-615-65553-6; 978-0-615-66008-0; 978-0-615-69126-8; 978-0-615-69127-5; 978-0-615-84017-8)* 4749 S Washington Ave, Titusville, FL 32780 USA Tel 321-593-0905
Dist(s): **CreateSpace Independent Publishing Platform.**

Landmark Editions, Incorporated *See* **landmark Hse., Ltd.**

landmark Hse., Ltd., *(978-0-933849; 978-0-9822874)* 1949 Foxridge Dr., Kansas City, KS 66106 USA
Web site: http://www.landmarkhouse.com.

Landmark Publishing Inc., *(978-0-9726738)* P.O. Box 46403, Minneapolis, MN 55446 USA (SAN 254-9689) Tel 763-694-8907; Fax: 763-694-8909
E-mail: info@brainerdbound.com
Web site: http://www.brainerdbound.com.

Lane, Sondra Corp., *(978-0-9743874)* 2436 N. Federal Hwy., No. 300, Lighthouse Point, FL 33064 USA
Web site: http://www.hallelujahkids.com.

Lane, Veronica Bks., *(978-0-9637597; 978-0-9762743; 978-0-9826513; 978-0-9910083)* Orders Addr.: 2554 Lincoln Blvd., Suite 142, Venice, CA 90291 USA (SAN 298-1157) Tel Free: 800-651-1001 (phone/fax)
E-mail: etan@veronicalanebooks.com
Web site: http://www.veronicalanebooks.com
Dist(s): **Bored Feet Pr.**
DeVorss & Co.
Follett School Solutions
INscribe Digital
Integral Yoga Pubns.
New Leaf Distributing Co., Inc.

Lang Graphics, Ltd., *(978-0-933617; 978-1-55962; 978-1-57832; 978-0-7412)* Div. of Perfect Timing, Inc., Orders Addr.: P.O. Box 1605, Waukesha, WI 53188 USA; Edit Addr.: 514 Wells St., Delafield, WI 53018 USA (SAN 692-4689) Tel 414-646-3399; Fax: 414-646-2224; Toll Free: 800-262-2611
E-mail: support@shop.lang.com
Web site: http://www.lang.com
Dist(s): **TNT Media Group, Inc.**

†Lang, Peter Publishing, Inc., *(978-0-8204; 978-1-4331; 978-1-4539; 978-1-4540; 978-1-4541; 978-1-4542)* Subs. of Verlag Peter Lang AG (SZ), 29 Broadway, New York, NY 10006 USA (SAN 241-5534) Tel 212-647-7700; 212-647-7706 (Outside USA); Fax: 212-647-7707; Toll Free: 800-770-5264
E-mail: customerservice@plang.com
Web site: http://www.peterlangusa.com
Dist(s): **MyiLibrary**
ebrary, Inc.; *CIP.*

Langdon Street Pr. *Imprint of* **Hillcrest Publishing Group, Inc.**

Langenscheidt Publishing Group, *(978-0-88729; 978-1-58573)* Subs. of Langenscheidt KG, Orders Addr.: 15 Tyger River Dr., Duncan, SC 29334 USA Fax: 888-773-7979; Toll Free: 800-432-6277; Edit Addr.: 36-36 33rd St., Long Island City, NY 11106 USA
Web site: http://www.americanmap.com; http://www.langenscheidt.com
Dist(s): **Bilingual Pubns. Co., The**
Ingram Pub. Services.

Lange-Patton, Lorraine, *(978-0-9752874)* P.O. Box 96811, Las Vegas, NV 89193-6811 USA.

Langley, Jan *See* **Captain & Harry LLC, The**

LangMarc Publishing, *(978-1-880292)* Orders Addr.: P.O. Box 90488, Austin, TX 78709 USA (SAN 297-519X) Tel 512-394-0989; Fax: 512-394-0829; Toll Free: 800-864-1648 (orders only); Edit Addr.: 7500 Shadowridge Run, No. 28, Austin, TX 78749 USA
E-mail: langmarc@booksails.com
Web site: http://www.langmarc.com.

Language 911, Inc., *(978-1-933451)* 12924 Calais Cir., Palm Beach Gardens, FL 33410 USA.

Language Adventure Pubns., *(978-0-9671053)* 2311 E. Stadium Blvd., Suite 105 N, Ann Arbor, MI 48104 USA Tel 734-763-8378; Fax: 734-769-8409
E-mail: andrearojo@aol.com.

Language Quest Corp., *(978-0-9744691)* 1 Tartan Lakes, Westmont, IL 60559 USA.

Language Research Educational Series, *(978-0-9609446)* 4309 20th St., NE, Washington, DC 20018 USA (SAN 260-0927) Tel 202-636-9306
E-mail: lresduke@gmail.com.

Language Resource Manual for Schools *Imprint of* **Language Treasures**

Language Transformer Bks. *Imprint of* **Velichko, Vera**

Language Treasures, *(978-0-9765293)* 2141 SE 113th Ave., Portland, OR 97216 USA; *Imprints:* Language Resource Manual for Schools (L R M S)
E-mail: vrisk@comcast.net
Web site: http://www.languagetreasures.com.

Language Workshop for Children, The, *(978-0-9754205; 978-0-9755659; 978-0-9759664; 978-0-9819458)* 888 Lexington Ave., 2nd Flr., New York, NY 10065 USA (SAN 256-0704)
E-mail: info@professortoto.com
Web site: http://www.professortoto.com
Dist(s): **China Bks. & Periodicals, Inc.**

LANIUS Software *See* **PassionQuest Technologies, LLC**

Lanphier Pr., *(978-0-9762151; 978-0-9786039; 978-1-934570)* Div. of Corporate Chaplains of America, 1300 Corporate Chaplain Dr., Wake Forest, NC 27587-6596 USA
E-mail: dwhite@chaplain.org
Dist(s): **Send The Light Distribution LLC.**

Lantern Bks., *(978-1-930051; 978-1-59056)* Div. of Booklight, Inc., 128 2nd Pl., Brooklyn, NY 11231-4102 USA
E-mail: martin@booklightinc.com
Web site: http://www.booklightinc.com
Dist(s): **Smashwords**
SteinerBooks, Inc.

LAPOP (Latin American Public Opinion Project), *(978-0-9777042; 978-0-9792178; 978-0-9817299; 978-0-9821456; 978-0-9846260; 978-0-9846303; 978-1-939186)* 230 Appleton Pl, PMB 505 PSCI Dept at Vanderbilt Univ., Nashville, TN 37203 USA
E-mail: liz.zechmeister@vanderbilt.edu
Web site: http://vanderbilt.edu/lapop.

Laramie, Charles, *(978-0-9769536)* 11 W. St., Fair Haven, VT 05743 USA Tel 802-265-3538
E-mail: chucklaramie@adelphia.net.

†Laredo Publishing Co., Inc., *(978-1-56492)* 465 Westview Ave., Englewood, NJ 07631 USA Tel 201-408-4048; Fax: 201-408-5011
E-mail: info@laredopublishing.com
Web site: http://www.laredopublishing.com; *CIP.*

Large Print Bk. Co., The, *(978-1-59688)* P.O. Box 970, Sanbornville, NH 03872-0970 USA Tel 603-569-4215.

Large Print Pr. *Imprint of* **Thorndike Pr.**

Lariat Pubns., *(978-0-9748459)* P.O. Box 364, Plympton, MA 02364 USA (SAN 255-8521) Tel 781-582-0700; Fax: 781-585-6328; Toll Free: 800-829-0715
E-mail: lisa@usstablingguide.com
Web site: http://www.usstablingguide.com
Dist(s): **Independent Pubs. Group.**

Lark Bks., *(978-0-937274; 978-1-57990; 978-1-887374; 978-1-60059; 978-1-4547)* Div. of Sterling Publishing Co., Inc., 67 Broadway St., Asheville, NC 28801-2919 USA (SAN 219-9947)
E-mail: info@larkbooks.com
Web site: http://www.larkbooks.com
Dist(s): **Hearst Bks.**
Sterling Publishing Co., Inc.

†Larksdale, *(978-0-89896)* P.O. Box 801222, Houston, TX 77280 USA (SAN 220-0643) Tel 713-461-7200; Fax: 713-467-4770 (purchase orders); Toll Free: 877-461-7200; *CIP.*

Larousse, Ediciones, S. A. de C. V. (MEX) *(978-968-6042; 978-968-6147; 978-968-6347; 978-970-607; 978-970-22) Dist. by* **Continental Bk.**

Larousse, Ediciones, S. A. de C. V. (MEX) *(978-968-6042; 978-968-6147; 978-968-6347; 978-970-607; 978-970-22) Dist. by* **HM.**

Larousse, Ediciones, S. A. de C. V. (MEX) *(978-968-6042; 978-968-6147; 978-968-6347; 978-970-607; 978-970-22) Dist. by* **Giron Bks.**

Larousse, Editions (FRA) *(978-2-03) Dist. by* **HM.**

Larousse Kingfisher Chambers, Inc., *(978-0-7534; 978-1-85697)* 215 Park Ave., S., New York, NY 10003 USA (SAN 297-7540); 181 Ballardvale St., Wilmington, MA 01887
Dist(s): **Macmillan.**

Larry Huch Ministries, *(978-0-9745301)* Orders Addr.: P.O. Box 2197, Mansfield, TX 76063-0039 USA
E-mail: cory@larryhuchministries.com
Web site: http://www.larryhuchministries.com
Dist(s): **Anchor Distributors.**

Lars Muller Pubs. (CHE) *(978-3-907044; 978-3-906700; 978-3-907078; 978-3-03778) Dist. by* **Prestel Pub NY.**

Larson Learning, Inc., *(978-0-9639121; 978-1-58123; 978-1-887050)* Div. of Larson Texts, Inc., 1762 Norcross Rd., Erie, PA 16510-3838 USA Tel 814-824-6365; Fax: 814-824-6377; Toll Free: 800-530-2355
Web site: http://www.larsonlearning.com.

Larson Pubns., *(978-0-943914; 978-1-936012)* 4936 Rte. 414, Burdett, NY 14818 USA (SAN 241-130X) Tel 607-546-9342; Fax: 607-546-9344; Toll Free: 800-828-2197 Do not confuse with Larson Pubns., Joliet, IL
E-mail: larson@lightlink.com
Web site: http://www.larsonpublications.org
Dist(s): **National Bk. Network**
New Leaf Distributing Co., Inc.
Red Wheel/Weiser
ebrary, Inc.

Larstan Publishing, Inc., *(978-0-9764266; 978-0-9776895; 978-0-9789182)* 209 Canterbury Ct., Blue Bell, PA 19422 USA (SAN 256-3460) Fax: 707-922-7280
E-mail: sgenkin@larstan.net
Web site: http://www.theblackbooks.com.

Laser Productions *See* **Global Publishing**

Lash & Assocs. Publishing/Training, Inc., *(978-1-931117)* Orders Addr.: 100 Boardwalk Dr. Suite 150, Youngsville, NC 27596 USA Tel 919-556-0300 phone; Fax: 919-556-0900 fax
E-mail: mlyn@lapublishing.com
Web site: http://www.lapublishing.com.

Last Gasp Eco-Funnies, Incorporated *See* **Last Gasp of San Francisco**

Last Gasp of San Francisco, *(978-0-86719)* Orders Addr.: 777 Florida St., San Francisco, CA 94110 USA (SAN 216-8308); Edit Addr.: 777 Florida St., San Francisco, CA 94110-2025 USA (SAN 170-3242) Tel 415-824-6636; Fax: 415-824-1836; Toll Free: 800-366-5121
E-mail: colin@lastgasp.com
Web site: http://www.lastgasp.com
Dist(s): **SCB Distributors.**

Last Knight Publishing *See* **Last Knight Publishing Co.**

Last Knight Publishing Co., *(978-0-9720442)* P.O. Box 270006, Fort Collins, CO 80527 USA Tel 970-391-6857
Web site: http://www.lastknightpublishing.com
Dist(s): **Bks. West.**

Last Play Publishing, *(978-0-9760181)* 17931 Inverness Ave., Baton Rouge, LA 70810 USA Tel 225-751-6419
E-mail: djones@dow.com.

Lasting Bks. Publishing Co., *(978-0-9767511)* 8433 Briggs Dr., Roseville, CA 95747-5951 USA
E-mail: director@lastingbooks.com
Web site: http://www.lastingbooks.com.

Latinarte *See* **I.Om.Be Pr.**

Latino, Frank Publishing Co., *(978-0-9640474)* 6806 Newport Lake Cir., Boca Raton, FL 33496 USA Tel 561-241-3880; Fax: 561-995-6975; Toll Free: 800-922-8565
E-mail: frank@hollyboy.com
Web site: http://www.hollyboy.com.

Latino Literacy Press *See* **Lectura Bks.**

Latitude 20 Bks. *Imprint of* **Univ. of Hawaii Pr.**

Laudati, Joe, *(978-0-615-20324-9; 978-0-578-06902-9)* 425 E. 76th St., No. 9B, New York, NY 10021-2516 USA Tel 212-737-3515
E-mail: joelaudati33@earthlink.net
Web site: http://www.joelaudati.com
Dist(s): **Lulu Enterprises Inc.**

Laugh-A-Lot Bks., *(978-0-615-28469-9)* 25 W. Broadway, Apt. 310, Long Beach, NY 11561 USA
Web site: http://www.laughalotpoetry.com; http://www.laughalotbooks.com.

Laughing Baby Pubns., *(978-0-615-18948-2)* 3662 Big Spring Rd., Lake Almanor, CA 96137 USA Tel 530-596-4397
E-mail: jennifer@babyinspirations.net
Web site: http://www.laughingbabypublications.com.

Laughing Buddha Pubns., *(978-0-615-80930-4)* 6308 Boardman Rd NW, Olympia, WA 98502 USA Tel 360-359-1522; Fax: 360-867-0151
Web site: www.loveisacircle.com
Dist(s): **CreateSpace Independent Publishing Platform.**

Laughing Elephant, *(978-0-9621131; 978-1-883211; 978-1-59583; 978-1-5149)* Orders Addr.: 3645 Interlake Ave., N., Seattle, WA 98103 USA Tel 206-447-9229; Fax: 206-447-9189; Toll Free: 800-354-0400 (orders only); Edit Addr.: 4649 Sunnyside Ave., N., Seattle, WA 98103 USA (SAN 250-7722) Tel 206-632-7075; Fax: 206-632-0466; *Imprints:* Darling & Company (Darling & Comp); Green Tiger Press (Gm Tiger Pr)
E-mail: laughingelephant@laughingelephant.com
Web site: http://www.laughingelephant.com
Dist(s): **Ingram Pub. Services.**

Laughing Gull Pr., *(978-0-9726699)* P.O. Box 23272, Brooklyn, NY 11202-3272 USA
E-mail: laughinggullpress@earthlink.net.

Laughing Rhino Bks., *(978-0-9859603)* 23830 25th Dr. SE, Bothell, WA 98021 USA Tel 425-420-8144
E-mail: gordon.glessner@gmail.com
Web site: www.laughinrhinobooks.com.

Laughing Zebra - Bks. for Children *Imprint of* **J.O.Y. Publishing**

Laurel *Imprint of* **Random House Publishing Group**

Laurel & Herbert, Inc., *(978-0-9619155)* P.O. Box 440266, Sugarloaf Shores, FL 33044 USA (SAN 243-4687) Tel 305-745-3506; Fax: 305-745-9070.

Laurel Fork Pr., *(978-0-615-76119-0; 978-0-615-76134-3; 978-0-615-94974-1; 978-0-692-34634-1)*
Dist(s): **CreateSpace Independent Publishing Platform**
Smashwords.

Laurel Leaf *Imprint of* **Random Hse. Children's Bks.**

Laurel Press *See* **Laurel & Herbert, Inc.**

Laurel Street Pr., *(978-0-615-79201-9)* 112 W 34th St. 17th Flr., New York, NY 10120 USA Tel 8009618820; Fax: 8886847665
Dist(s): **CreateSpace Independent Publishing Platform.**

Laurel Valley Graphics, Inc., *(978-0-9717475; 978-0-9853454)* 1511 Monastery Dr., Latrobe, PA 15650 USA Fax: 724-532-1957
Web site: http://www.lvgraphics.net.

Lauren Elizabeth Design, *(978-0-9779594)* 2002 Duboin Rd, New Iberia, LA 70560 USA
E-mail: chad@turnkeybid.com.

Laurob Pr., *(978-0-9787376)* 4204 Anjou Ct., Chico, CA 95973 USA.

Laurus Bks., *(978-0-9841680; 978-0-9826957; 978-0-9847683; 978-1-938526; 978-1-943523)* Orders Addr.: 133 S. Charles Richard Beall Blvd., DeBary, FL 32753-0173 USA Tel 386-259-5188; Fax: 386-259-5144; Edit Addr.: P.O. Box 530173, DeBary, FL 32753-0173 USA Tel 386-259-5144; Fax: 386-259-5144; Toll Free: 800-596-7370
E-mail: info@thelauruscompany.com; bookstore@thelauruscompany.com; nancywilliams@thelauruscompany.com
Web site: http://www.TheLaurusCompany.com; http://www.LaurusBooks.com; www.BookShelfDepot.com
Dist(s): **Laurus Co., The.**

Laurus Company, The *See* **Laurus Bks.**

Laurus Co., The, Orders Addr.: 524 Guinevere Court, McDonough, GA 30252 USA (SAN 858-608X) Tel 678-814-4047; Fax: 678-272-7255; Toll Free: 800-596-7370
E-mail: thelaurusco@charter.net
Web site: http://www.thelauruscompany.com.

LaVa Pubns., *(978-0-9638838; 978-0-9714261; 978-0-9761449; 978-0-9792400)* Div. of Field O Dreams Farm, Orders Addr.: P.O. Box 9372, Dothan, AL 36303 USA (SAN 255-2027)
E-mail: spharr@centurytel.net.

Lavender Bks., *(978-0-9742739)* Orders Addr.: P.O. Box 3555, Culver City, CA 90231-3555 USA; Edit Addr.: 11111 Jefferson Blvd., Culver City, CA 90230 USA
E-mail: lavender_books33@aol.com; kc_kang@yahoo.com; lavenderbooks33@aol.com.

Lavoie, Louis, *(978-0-9791018)* 1300 W. Medicine Lake Dr., No. 211, Plymouth, MN 55441 USA
E-mail: lavoielouis6@hotmail.com.

Law Offices of Harry Glick, *(978-0-9717419)* 100 Quentin Rossevelt Blvd. No. 511, Garden City, NY 11530 USA Tel 516-456-1088; Fax: 805-473-9025
Web site: http://www.harryglick.com
Dist(s): **BookMasters, Inc.**

Lawe Street Bks., *(978-0-9713179)* 1818 S. Lawe St., Appleton, WI 54915 USA Tel 920-739-4577
E-mail: stedjee@aol.com.

Lawells Publishing, *(978-0-934981)* P.O. Box 1338, Royal Oak, MI 48068-1338 USA (SAN 694-602X) Tel 248-543-5297
E-mail: lawells@tm.net
Web site: http://www.lawells.net.

Lawrence Educational Services, Inc., *(978-1-932959; 978-1-59699)* Orders Addr.: P.O. Box 6256, Bridgewater, NJ 08807 USA Tel 908-575-8830; Fax: 908-704-1730; Toll Free: 800-575-7670; Edit Addr.: 674 Rte. 202-206 N, Suite 4, Bridgewater, NJ 08807 USA
E-mail: llteach5757670@aol.com
Web site: http://www.llteach.com.

Lawrence Publishing, *(978-0-9716039)* Div. of Educational Services & Publications, 2935 E. Rose Ln., Phoenix, AZ 85016 USA Tel 602-912-9553 Do not confuse with companies with the same or similar names in Flower Mound, TX, Van Nuys, CA, Los Angeles, CA, Wichita, KS, Baton Rouge, LA
E-mail: llawre2222@aol.com; walton90@alltel.net.

Lawson, Archie B., *(978-0-9762660)* 1168 Shashas Way, Riverton, UT 84065-4111 USA Tel 801-302-0440
E-mail: archiebl@msn.com.

Layne Morgan Media, Inc., *(978-0-9762904; 978-0-9772007; 978-0-9774803; 978-1-4265)* 2101 W. Chesterfield Blvd. Ste. A102, Springfield, MO 65807-8672 USA
E-mail: kimberlym@laynemorgan.com
Web site: http://www.laynemorgan.com.

L,B Kids *Imprint of* **Hachette Bk. Group**

LBF Bks., LLC, *(978-0-9754533; 978-0-9773082)* Orders Addr.: P.O. Box 7989, Pittsburgh, PA 15216 USA; Edit Addr.: 1537 Dormont Ave., Pittsburgh, PA 15216 USA
E-mail: lbf@lbfbooks.com.

LBF/Hadrosaur *Imprint of* **Hadrosaur Pr.**

L'Chaim Pubns., *(978-0-9766946)* 521 Fifth Ave., Suite 1740, New York, NY 10175 USA
E-mail: lchaim@att.biz
Web site: http://lchaimpublications.com/.

LD Bks., Inc., *(978-0-9772669; 978-0-9785897; 978-1-939048; 978-1-940281; 978-1-943387)* 8313 NW 68th St., Miami, FL 33166 USA (SAN 631-8088) Tel 305-406-2292; Fax: 305-406-2293
E-mail: vilmac@ldbooks.com; sales@ldbooks.com
Web site: http://www.sinlimites.net; http://www.ldbooks.com.

LD Coach, LLC, *(978-0-9745938; 978-0-9764112)* 1401 Johnson Ferry Rd., Suite 328-C13, Marietta, GA 30062-5241 USA Toll Free: 888-848-6224
E-mail: bill.allen@ldcoach.com
Web site: http://www.ldcoach.com.

LDS & Assocs., LLC, *(978-1-883574)* Orders Addr.: No. 354, 13681 Newport Ave., Suite 8, Tustin, CA 92780 USA Tel 800-331-3610; Fax: 714-573-0314; Toll Free: 800-331-3610
E-mail: trainers@ldsassoc.com
Web site: http://www.ldsassoc.com.

Le Bk. Moderne, LLC, *(978-0-9768450)* 2849 W. 23rd Ave., Denver, CO 80211 USA Tel 303-523-6401; *Imprints:* Giggletins (Gigglet)
E-mail: michael@lebookmoderne.com
Web site: http://www.lebookmoderne.com.

Le Petit Chien, *(978-0-9717019)* 2415 Daybreaker Dr., Park City, UT 84098 USA.

Le Robert (FRA) *(978-2-85036; 978-2-84902) Dist. by* **Distribks Inc.**

Le Robert (FRA) *(978-2-85036; 978-2-84902) Dist. by* **Continental Bk.**

Lead Life Pr., LLC, *(978-0-9762408)* The Lead Life Institute, 2111 Deerfield Dr., New Hope, PA 18938 USA Tel 215 794 8516; Fax: 215 794 8532
E-mail: mdec@leadlifeinstitute.com.

Leaderbrook, *(978-0-9719079)* P.O. Box 864, Amherst, OH 44001-0864 USA Tel 440-985-5844
E-mail: timothy@clevelandceo.com
Web site: http://www.leaderbrook.com.

Leadership Horizons, LLC, *(978-0-9668868)* 959 Keystone Way, Carmel, IN 46032-2823 USA Tel 317-844-5587; Fax: 317-581-9226; Toll Free: 888-262-2477
E-mail: ron@leadershiphorizons.com.

Leadership Loft, The *See* **Green Owl, Inc.**

LeaderTreks NFP, *(978-1-934577; 978-1-939031)* 25w560 Geneva Rd. #30, Carol Stream, IL 60188 USA Tel 630-668-0936; Fax: 630-668-0980; Toll Free: 800-502-0699
E-mail: danc@leadertreks.com; angie@leadertreks.com
Web site: http://www.leadertreks.com; http://www.leadertreks.org.

Leading Lady Pubns., *(978-0-9776746; 978-0-9798084; 978-0-9802468; 978-0-9818753)* Orders Addr.: P.O. Box 35, Worton, MD 21678 USA Toll Free: 800-597-9428; Edit Addr.: 306 Sunrise Ave., Ridgely, MD 21660 USA
Web site: http://www.publishyourchristianbook.com
Dist(s): **CreateSpace Independent Publishing Platform**
Lushena Bks.

Leadline Publishing, *(978-0-9801464)* Orders Addr.: 2101 NW Corporate Blvd Ste 206, Boca Raton, FL 33431 USA
Web site: http://www.teamfroglogic.com.

Leaf & Vine Bks, *(978-0-9786087; 978-0-615-18762-4)* 387 Ivy St., San Francisco, CA 94102 USA
E-mail: editor@leafvinebooks.com
Dist(s): **Lulu Enterprises Inc.**

Leafcollecting.com Publishing Co., *(978-0-9747654)* 189 N. Jefferson Ave., Bradley, IL 60915-1829 USA Tel 815-932-0850; *Imprints:* Egap Gifa Books (Egap Gifa Bks)
E-mail: Darlene@leafcollecting.com; Thegreatlakes189@yahoo.com
Web site: http://www.leafcollecting.com.

Leafwood Pubs. *Imprint of* **Abilene Christian Univ. Pr.**

Lean Pr., *(978-1-932475)* Div. of Hopefuls, Inc., Orders Addr.: P.O. Box 80334, Portland, OR 97280-1334 USA (SAN 255-6286) Tel 503-708-4415; Fax: 503-626-9098
E-mail: sean@leanpress.com; mike@leanpress.com
Web site: http://www.leanpress.com.

Leap Bks., *(978-1-61603)* P.O. Box 112, Reidsville, NC 27320-0112 USA (SAN 858-5431)
E-mail: leapbks@gmail.com
Web site: http://www.leapbks.com.

Leap Forward Pubns., *(978-0-9743664)* 12108 Scribe Dr., Austin, TX 78759-3133 USA
E-mail: mjanthony@sbcglobal.net.

L.E.A.P. (Learning through an Expanded Arts Program, Inc), *(978-0-9713649)* 441 W. End Ave., Suite 2G, New York, NY 10024 USA Tel 212-769-4160; Fax: 212-724-4479
E-mail: leap@leapnyc.org
Web site: http://www.leapnyc.org.

LeapFrog Enterprises, Inc., *(978-1-58605; 978-1-932256; 978-1-59319; 978-1-60685)* 6401 Hollis St., Suite 125, Emeryville, CA 94608 USA Tel 510-420-5000; Fax: 510-596-6821; *Imprints:* LeapFrog School House (LeapSchHse)
E-mail: crymer@leapfrog.com
Web site: http://www.leapfrog.com.

Leapfrog Pr., *(978-0-9654578; 978-0-9679520; 978-0-9728984; 978-0-9796415; 978-0-9815148; 978-1-935248)* Orders Addr.: P.O. Box 2110, Teaticket, MA 02536 USA; Edit Addr.: 59 Tanglewood Dr., Teaticket, MA 02536 USA Do not confuse with Leapfrog Pr., Wyandotte, MI
E-mail: books@leapfrogpress.com; lisa@leapfrogpress.com
Web site: http://www.leapfrogpress.com
Dist(s): **Consortium Bk. Sales & Distribution**
Perseus Bks. Group
SPD-Small Pr. Distribution.

Leapfrog Press, Incorporated, The *See* **Leapfrog Pr.**

LeapFrog Schl. Hse. *Imprint of* **LeapFrog Enterprises, Inc.**

Leaping Antelope Productions, *(978-0-9659222; 978-0-9762059)* Div. of Armadillo Pr., Orders Addr.: 101 Industrial Way Ste. 10, Belmont, CA 94002-8207 USA (SAN 253-7974) Toll Free: 888-909-5327
E-mail: print123@leapingantelope.com
Web site: http://www.leapingantelope.com
Dist(s): **Distributors, The**
Quality Bks., Inc.

Learn & Sign Funtime *See* **Learn & Sign Funtime Bks.**

Learn & Sign Funtime Bks., *(978-0-9753717)* Orders Addr.: 0255 E. Yellowstone Trail, Hamlet, IN 46532 USA Tel 219-775-7080; Fax: 888-308-2606; 0255 E. Yellowstone Trail Hamlet, In 46532, Hamlet, IN 46532
E-mail: learnandsign@aol.com; jujub121@aol.com.

Learn As You Grow, L.L.C., *(978-0-9824652)* P.O. Box 103, Mount Horeb, WI 53572 USA
E-mail: chad.lindley@learnasyougrow.com.

Learn2study, *(978-0-9729557)* 1935 Columbia Pike No. 24, Arlington, VA 22204 USA
Web site: http://www.learn2study.org.

Learning Abilities Bks., *(978-0-9658853; 978-0-9720267)* 166 Glyndale Cir., Brunswick, GA 31520 USA (SAN 850-3087) Tel 912-264-5308; Fax: 775-305-0063; Toll Free: 800-779-5088
E-mail: contactlab@gate.net
Web site: http://www.gate.net/~labooks.

Learning All About Me, LLC, *(978-0-9763961)* Orders Addr.: P.O. Box 161923, Boiling Springs, SC 29316 USA; Edit Addr.: 8 Montford Ave., Boiling Springs, SC 29316 USA.

Learning Challenge, Inc., *(978-1-59203)* 36 Washington St., Wellesley, MA 02481 USA Tel 781-239-9900; Fax: 781-239-3273
Web site: http://www.learningchallenge.com.

Learning Co. Bks., *(978-0-7630)* 100 Pine St. Ste. 1900, San Francisco, CA 94111-5205 USA
E-mail: lstarr@riverdeep.net
Web site: http://www.riverdeep.net
Dist(s): **Perseus-PGW.**

Learning Connection, The, *(978-1-56831)* Orders Addr.: 4100 Silver Star Rd. Ste. D, Orlando, FL 32808-4618 USA Toll Free: 800-218-8489
Web site: http://www.tlconnection.com.

Learning Curve Brands, Incorporated *See* **TOMY International, Inc.**

Learning Fasten-Ations, Inc., *(978-0-9673268; 978-0-9729476)* 5014-16th Ave., Suite 195, Brooklyn, NY 11204 USA Tel 718-854-3808; Fax: 718-854-9436; Toll Free: 800-252-8152
Web site: http://www.velcroboards.com.

Learning in Motion, *(978-1-889775)* 113 Cooper St., Santa Cruz, CA 95060-4526 USA Toll Free: 800-560-5670 Do not confuse with Learning in Motion, Mount Laurel, NJ
Web site: http://www.learn.motion.com.

Learning Links Inc., *(978-0-7675; 978-0-88122; 978-0-934048; 978-1-56982)* Orders Addr.: 26 Haypress Road, Cranbury, NJ 08512 USA (SAN 241-3302) Tel 516-437-9071; Fax: 516-437-5392; Toll Free: 800-724-2616
E-mail: info@learninglinks.com
Web site: http://www.learninglinks.com; http://www.novel-ties.com/estore/search/.

Learning Management Systems *See* **Active Learning Corp.**

Learning Net, The, *(978-1-887946)* 567 Catnip Rd., Cullowhee, NC 28723 USA Tel 828-293-2542.

Learning Parent, The, *(978-0-9708770; 978-0-9777685; 978-0-9785859; 978-0-9860433)* 2430 Sunnymeade Rd., Rustburg, VA 24588 USA Tel 434-845-8345; Fax: 434-845-3020
E-mail: learningparent@aol.com
Web site: http://www.thelearningparent.com.

Learning Props, *(978-0-9741549; 978-0-9768706; 978-1-935292)* P.O. Box 774, Racine, WI 53401 USA Toll Free: 877-776-7750
E-mail: bev@learningprops.com
Web site: http://www.learningprops.com
Dist(s): **Follett School Solutions.**

Learning Research Associates, Incorporated *See* **National Reading Styles Institute, Inc.**

Learning Resources, Inc., *(978-1-56911)* 380 N. Fairway Dr., Vernon Hills, IL 60061 USA (SAN 630-057X) Tel 847-573-8400; Fax: 847-573-8425
E-mail: info@learningresources.com
Web site: http://www.learningresources.com.

Learning Series Pr., *(978-0-9769701)* P.O. Box 590812, Fort Lauderdale, FL 33359 USA (SAN 256-6060) Tel 954-552-4855
E-mail: mdgeddes@comcast.net
Web site: http://www.learningtodream.com.

Learning to Give, *(978-0-9774155)* 16924 Buchanan St., Grand Haven, MI 49417-8625 USA
Web site: http://www.learningtogive.org.

Learning Together, *(978-1-931840)* 5509b W. Friendly Ave. Ste. 201, Greensboro, NC 27410-4279 USA
E-mail: wtled@aol.com.

Learning Tools Co., *(978-0-938017)* Orders Addr.: P.O. Box 657, Berkeley Springs, WV 25411 USA (SAN 692-7297) Tel 304-258-1304; Edit Addr.: 714 Rockwell St., Berkeley Springs, WV 25422 USA.

Learning Wood, LLC, *(978-1-933577)* 3535 W. Peterson Ave., Chicago, IL 60659 USA Tel 773-509-0707; Fax: 773-509-0404.

Learning Works, The *Imprint of* **Creative Teaching Pr., Inc.**

Learning Wrap-Ups, Inc., *(978-0-943343; 978-1-59204)* 1660 West Gordon Ave., No. 4, Layton, UT 84041 USA (SAN 668-3975) Tel 801-497-0050; Fax: 801-497-0063; Toll Free: 800-992-4966
E-mail: info@learningwrapups.com
Web site: http://www.learningwrapups.com.

Learning ZoneXpress, *(978-1-57175)* Orders Addr.: P.O. Box 1022, Owatonna, MN 55060 USA Tel 507-455-9076; Fax: 507-455-3380; Toll Free: 888-455-7003
E-mail: customerservice@learningzonexpress.com
Web site: http://www.learningzonexpress.com
Dist(s): **Follett School Solutions.**

LearningExpress, LLC, *(978-1-57685; 978-1-61103)* 2 Rector St., Flr. 26, New York, NY 10006-3754 USA Tel 646-274-6453; 800-295-9556
E-mail: info@learnatest.com; customerservice@learnatest.com
Web site: http://www.learnatest.com
Dist(s): **MyiLibrary**
National Bk. Network
ebrary, Inc.

LearningSuccess Pr., *(978-0-9772350)* 353 Sanjon Rd., Ventura, CA 93001 USA (SAN 257-0726) Tel 805-648-1739
Web site: http://www.learningsuccessinstitute.com.

Learnovation, LLC, *(978-0-9705790; 978-0-9796434)* Orders Addr.: P.O. Box 502150, Indianapolis, IN 46250 USA (SAN 255-4577); Edit Addr.: 10831 Thistle Ridge, Fishers, IN 46038 USA Tel 317-577-1190; Fax: 317-598-0816; Toll Free: 888-577-1190
E-mail: anna@learnovation.com; karen@learnovation.com
Web site: http://learnovation.com.

Leatherbound Bestsellers, *(978-1-62715)* Orders Addr.: 20325 N. 51st. Ave. Suite 134, Glendale, AZ 85308 USA Tel 602-616-4334
E-mail: leatherboundbestsellers@gmail.com
Web site: www.leatherboundbestsellers.com.

Leatherbound Booksellers *See* **Leatherbound Bestsellers**

Leatherman, Diane *See* **Bounty Project, The**

Leatherman, Gregory, *(978-0-578-09100-6)* 956 S. 1100 E., Salt Lake City, UT 84105 USA.

Leathers Publishing, *(978-0-9646898; 978-1-890622; 978-1-58597)* Div. of Ad Ctr., 4500 College Blvd., Overland Park, KS 66211-1760 USA Tel 913-498-2625; Fax: 913-498-1561; Toll Free: 888-888-7696
E-mail: barbara@leatherspublishing.com
Web site: http://www.leatherspublishing.com.

Leatherwood Press *See* **Walnut Springs Bks.**

Leatherwood Publishing, *(978-0-9741725)* 20395 Cty. 86, Long Prairie, MN 56347 USA Tel 320-732-2879
E-mail: tann0042@umn.edu
Web site: http://www.alexweb.net/whimsy/index.htm.

Leave No Sister Behind Pubns., *(978-0-9787004)* Orders Addr.: 13 Pecan Ln., Long Beach, MS 39560 USA (SAN 851-3759)
E-mail: info@leavenosisterbehind.net
Web site: http://www.leavenosisterbehind.net
Dist(s): **Lightning Source, Inc.**

LeBlanc, Terry Leonard, *(978-0-9755913)* Orders Addr.: P.O. Box 387, Loyalton, CA 96118 USA; Edit Addr.: 805 Mill St., Loyalton, CA 96118 USA
E-mail: terrythetrashman@cwo.com.

Lectorum Pubns., Inc., *(978-0-9625162; 978-1-880507; 978-1-930332; 978-1-933032; 978-1-941802; 978-1-63245)* 205 Chubb Ave., Lyndhurst, NJ 07071 USA (SAN 860-0597) Tel 201-559-2200; Fax: 201-559-2201; Toll Free Fax: 877-532-8676; Toll Free: 800-345-5946
E-mail: acorrea@lectorum.com
Web site: http://www.lectorum.com; http://www.librerialectorum.com
Dist(s): **Libros Sin Fronteras**
MyiLibrary
Perfection Learning Corp.

Lectorum, S.A. de C.V. (MEX) *(978-968-7748; 978-968-5270; 978-970-732) Dist. by* **LD Bks Inc.**

Lectura Bks., *(978-0-9716580; 978-0-9772852; 978-1-60448)* 1107 Fair Oaks Ave., Suite 225, South Pasadena, CA 91030 USA
E-mail: info@lecturabooks.com
Web site: http://www.lecturabooks.com.

L'Edge Pr., *(978-0-9762014; 978-1-935256)* P.O. Box 2567, Boone, NC 28607 USA
E-mail: jeffhendley@charter.net
Web site: http://www.upsidedownministries.com.

LeDor Publishing, *(978-0-9747382)* 4885 McKnight Rd., No. 350, Pittsburgh, PA 15237 USA Tel 888-624-9094; Fax: 412-421-1628; Toll Free: 888-624-9094
E-mail: drichman@ledorgroup.com
Web site: http://www.ledorgroup.com.

Lee & Low Bks., Inc., *(978-0-89239; 978-1-880000; 978-1-885008; 978-1-58430; 978-1-60060; 978-1-62014)* 95 Madison Ave., New York, NY 10016 USA (SAN 920-7546) Tel 212-779-4400 (General info./Editorial); Fax: 212-683-1894 (orders); Toll Free: 888-320-3190 (ext. 28, orders); *Imprints:* Tu Books (Tu Books); Children's Book Press (ChilBkPr); Shen's Books (ShensBks)
E-mail: clow@leeandlow.com
Web site: http://www.leeandlow.com
Dist(s): **Follett School Solutions**
Lectorum Pubns., Inc.
Perfection Learning Corp.
Perseus-PGW.

Lee Bks., *(978-0-9660653)* Orders Addr.: 514 Jamacha Rd., No. 16J, El Cajon, CA 92019 USA Tel 619-447-8789 Do not confuse with other companies with the same or similar names in San Anselmo, CA, Columbia, SC
E-mail: leebooks@juno.com
Web site: http://www.readatleebooks.com.

Publisher Name Index

Lee, Deborah I, *(978-0-9858839)* 3800 Bexley Sq., Reno, NV 89503 USA Tel 775-848-7797
E-mail: debbaleereno@yahoo.com.

Lee, Howard, *(978-0-9766137)* 191 Lorraine Dr., Berkeley Heights, NJ 07922 USA.

Lee Instruments, *(978-0-9704913)* Orders Addr.: P.O. Box 460-999, Leeds, UT 84746 USA; Edit Addr.: 555 E. 900 N., Leeds, UT 84746 USA; 1050 N. Main, Leeds, UT 84746 Tel 435-879-6907
E-mail: leeinst@infowest.com; violguy@infowest.com
Web site: http://kevinleeluthier.com.

Lee, J. & L. Co., *(978-0-934904)* P.O. Box 5575, Lincoln, NE 68505 USA (SAN 213-8557) Tel 402-488-4416; Fax: 402-489-2770; Toll Free: 888-665-0999
E-mail: leebooks@radiks.net
Web site: http://www.leebooksellers.com
Dist(s): **Big River Distribution.**

Lee, James V. *See* **Salado Pr., LLC**

Lee, Keith Russel Publishing *See* **Lee, Keith Russel Publishing Hse.**

Lee, Keith Russel Publishing Hse., *(978-0-9768684)* Orders Addr.: P.O. Box 630, Hazel Crest, IL 60429 USA
E-mail: keith@keithrlee.com
Web site: http://www.keithrlee.com.

Lee, Michael, *(978-0-9766830)* 5503 Harvard, Detroit, MI 48224 USA.

Lee, Quentin Daschel, *(978-0-9789007)* 4949 Harris Ave., Las Vegas, NV 89110 USA (SAN 851-867X) Tel 702-463-9692.

Lee, Shelley, *(978-0-9786757)* Orders Addr.: 441 Frazee Ave., Suite A, Bowling Green, OH 43402-1834 USA Tel 419-354-4673
E-mail: bgpc@wcnet.org
Web site: http://BeforeIKnewYou.com.

Leeth, Dawna, *(978-0-9799184)* Orders Addr.: 400 W. Bay Dr., Largo, FL 33770 USA Fax: 727-536-6863.

Leeway Pubs., *(978-0-9744929)* Div. of Leeway Artisans, Orders Addr.: P.O. Box 1577, Laurel, MD 20707 USA Tel 301-404-3355
E-mail: info@LeewayArtisans.com
Web site: http://www.LeewayArtisans.com.

Lefall & Co., Inc., *(978-0-9761778)* 2020 Edmondson Ave., Baltimore, MD 21223 USA (SAN 256-2596)
E-mail: lefallandco@aol.com
Web site: http://www.jockobook.com.

Lefkowits,, John Ph.D., *(978-0-615-76239-5)* 13135 Hutchinson Way, Silver Spring, MD 20906 USA Tel 4432851885
Web site: www.suburbanpsychology.com
Dist(s): **CreateSpace Independent Publishing Platform.**

Left Field,Angel Gate,

Left Hand Publishing Co., *(978-0-9744799)* P.O. Box 253, Moose Lake, MN 55767 USA
E-mail: nemadji@computerpro.com
Web site: http://computerpro.com/~nemadji.

Left Paw Pr., *(978-0-9818360; 978-0-615-17884-4; 978-0-9829132; 978-0-9838044; 978-1-943356)* Orders Addr.: P.O. Box 133, Greens Fork, IN 47345 USA; Edit Addr.: 17 Washington Blvd., Greens Fork, IN 47345 USA
E-mail: lauren@laurenoriginals.com
Web site: http://www.leftpawpress.com
Dist(s): **Lulu Enterprises Inc.**

Legacy *Imprint of* **WordWright.biz, Inc.**

Legacy Book Publishing, Incorporated *See* **Legacy Family History, Inc.**

Legacy Family History, Inc., *(978-0-9655835; 978-0-9716705)* 5902 Woodshire Ln., Highland, UT 84003 USA Tel 801-763-1686 (phone/fax)
E-mail: tristantolman@comcast.net
Dist(s): **Send The Light Distribution LLC.**

Legacy Group Productions, LLC, *(978-0-9740585)* 3980 Greenmount Rd., Harrisonburg, VA 22802-0504 USA Toll Free: 877-227-6027
E-mail: cheryl@legacymatters.org
Web site: http://www.legacymatters.org.

Legacy Planning Partners, LLC, *(978-0-9719177; 978-0-9823220)* 254 Plaza Dr., Suite B, Oviedo, FL 32765 USA Tel 407-977-8080; Fax: 407-977-8078
E-mail: peggy@hoytbryan.com.

Legacy Pr. *Imprint of* **Rainbow Pubs. & Legacy Pr.**

Legacy Pr., *(978-0-9653198; 978-0-9777897)* 11381 Mallard Dr., Rochester, IL 62563 USA Tel 217-498-8159; Fax: 217-498-7178 Do not confuse with companies with the same or similar name in Pensacola, FL, Fort Lauderdale, FL, Columbus, GA, Thinelander, WI, Sacremento, CA, Hollywood, FL, Fairfax, VA, Argle, TX
E-mail: legacypressbooks@aol.com
Web site: http://legacypress.homestead.com.

Legacy Pubns., *(978-0-933101)* Subs. of Pace Communications, Inc., Orders Addr.: 1301 Carolina St., Greensboro, NC 27401 USA (SAN 662-2852) Tel 336-378-6065; Fax: 336-378-8265 ATTN: Dena Caulder Do not confuse with companies with the same or similar name in Tumon GU, Overland KS, Brentwood TN, Canyon TX, Irving TX, Lilburn GA, Midlothian, VA
E-mail: dena.caulder@paceco.com.

Legacy Pubs., *(978-1-932957)* 1866 Oak Harbor Dr., Ocean Isle Beach, NC 28469 USA Tel 910-755-6873; Toll Free: 800-290-8055 Do not confuse with Legacy Publishers in Natural Bridge, VA, Austin, TX
E-mail: mroofer@amadeusbooks.com
Web site: http://www.amadeusbooks.com; http://www.amadeus.bz.

Legacy Pubs., *(978-0-9754685)* 12126 Trotwood Dr., Austin, TX 78753 USA Tel 512-837-5366 Do not confuse with Legacy Publishers in Snellville GA, Natural Bridge VA
E-mail: legacypublishers@austin.rr.com.

Legacy Pubs. International, *(978-1-880809)* P.O. Box 9690, Rcho Santa Fe, CA 92067-4690 USA (SAN 257-0718)
E-mail: Michele@LegacyPublishersInternational.com; dmiller@hccweb.org
Web site: http://www.LegacyPublishersInternational.com
Dist(s): **Destiny Image Pubs.**

Legacy Publishing Services, Inc., *(978-0-9628733; 978-0-9708395; 978-0-9764982; 978-0-9776777; 978-1-934449; 978-1-937952)* 1883 Lee Rd. Ste. B, Winter Park, FL 32789-2108 USA Tel 407-647-3787 Do not confuse with companies with the same or similar name in Ojai, CA, Berkeley, CA, Atlanta, GA, West Chester, OH, Birmingham, AL, Daty, TX, Fort Meyers, Fl, Baton Rouge, LA
E-mail: legacybookpublishing@yahoo.com; legacypublishing@earthlink.net
Web site: http://www.legacybookpublishing.com
Dist(s): **AtlasBooks Distribution**
BookBaby.

Legend eXpress Publishing, *(978-0-9773648; 978-0-9846324)* 3831 E. Clovis Ave., Mesa, AZ 85206-8520 USA Tel 480-664-1047; Fax: 480-641-6043; 480-641-6043
E-mail: jana@legendexpress.biz
Web site: http://www.legendexpress.biz.

Legend Publishing Co., *(978-0-615-22552-4; 978-0-615-22553-1; 978-0-615-22554-8; 978-0-9821687; 978-0-9909373)* Orders Addr.: P.O. Box 429, Garden City, MI 48136 USA Tel 734-595-0663; Edit Addr.: 33807 Calumet Ct., Westland, MI 48186 USA
E-mail: bobwilly81897@Yahoo.com.

Legenderry.com, *(978-0-9776967)* 6154 Meadowbrook Dr., Morrison, CO 80465 USA Fax: 720-222-0490
Web site: http://www.legenderry.com.

LegendMaker Scriptoria, *(978-0-9759355)* 9400 Wade Blvd. #817, Frisco, TX 75035 USA Tel 413-313-9127
E-mail: scriptoria@legendmaker.com
Web site: http://legendmaker.com.

Legends in Their Own Lunchbox *Imprint of* **Capstone Classroom**

Legends of the West Publishing Co., *(978-0-9786904)* 174 Santa Rosa Ave., Sausalito, CA 94965-2060 USA (SAN 851-2825) Do not Copnfuse with Know DeFeet Publishing Company 2 Different companies. LD
E-mail: knowdefeet@aol.com.

Leger, Jarett, *(978-0-615-46654-5)* 1212 La Rue De Chene, New Iberia, LA 70560 USA Tel 512-949-9686
E-mail: leger.jarett@yahoo.com
Dist(s): **CreateSpace Independent Publishing Platform**
Dummy Record Do Not USE!!!!.

Legler, Caroline, *(978-0-9771233)* Orders Addr.: 1930 Bonanza Ct., Winter Park, FL 32792 USA
E-mail: glegler@cfl.rr.com.

Legwork Team Publishing, *(978-0-578-00665-9; 978-0-578-00666-6; 978-0-578-01705-1; 978-0-578-01865-2; 978-0-578-01866-9; 978-0-578-01999-4; 978-0-578-02016-7; 978-0-578-02310-6; 978-0-578-02407-3; 978-0-578-02845-3; 978-0-9841535; 978-0-9843539; 978-0-9827337; 978-1-935905) 4 Peacock Ln., Commack, NY 11725 USA*
E-mail: info@legworkteam.com
Web site: http://www.legworkteam.com
Dist(s): **Follett School Solutions.**

leharperwilliamsdesign group, *(978-0-615-37424-6)* 3819 Wake Forest Rd., Decatur, GA 30034 USA Tel 770-593-4687; Fax: 770-593-5466
E-mail: lhwdesign@me.com
Web site: http://leharperwilliamsdesign.com.

Lehman Publishing, *(978-0-9792686)* 15997 Hough, Allenton, MI 48002 USA
E-mail: dlehman@iwarp.net; dana@lehmanpublishing.com
Web site: http://www.lehmanpublishing.com
Dist(s): **Partners Bk. Distributing, Inc.**

Lehmann, Peter Publishing, *(978-0-9788399)* P.O. Box 11284, Eugene, OR 97440-3484 USA Tel 541-345-9106; Fax: 541-345-3737; Toll Free: 877-623-7743
E-mail: info@peter-lehmann-publishing.com
Web site: http://www.peter-lehmann-publishing.com.

Lehua, Inc., *(978-0-9647491)* P.o. Box 25548, Honolulu, HI 96825-0548 USA
E-mail: lehua@ohia.com
Web site: http://www.lehuainc.com
Dist(s): **Booklines Hawaii, Ltd.**

Leigh, Kimbra, *(978-0-9718851)* P.O. Box 20255, Rochester, NY 14602 USA
Web site: http://www.kimbraleigh.com.

Leisure Arts, Inc., *(978-0-942237; 978-1-57486; 978-1-60140; 978-1-60900; 978-1-4647)* Orders Addr.: 5701 Ranch Dr., Little Rock, AR 72223 USA (SAN 666-9565) Tel 501-868-8800; Fax: 501-868-1001; Toll Free Fax: 877-710-5603; Toll Free: 800-643-8030 (customer service); 800-526-5111
E-mail: hermine_linz@leisurearts.com
Web site: http://www.leisurearts.com
Dist(s): **Checker Distributors**
Midpoint Trade Bks., Inc.
Notions Marketing.

Leisure Time Pr., *(978-0-9890270)* 27259 Prescott Way, Temecula, CA 92591 USA Tel 951-219-3168
E-mail: j13m@aol.com
Web site: www.leisuretimepress.com.

Lekha Pubs., LLC, *(978-0-9725901; 978-1-937675)* 4204 Latimer Ave., San Jose, CA 95130 USA
Web site: http://www.lekhapublishers.com.

LeLeu, Lisa Puppet Show Bks. *Imprint of* **LeLeu, Lisa Studios! Inc.**

LeLeu, Lisa Studios! Inc., *(978-0-9710537; 978-0-9770299)* 100 Mechanics St., Doylestown, PA 18901 USA Tel 215-345-1233; Fax: 215-348-5378; *Imprints:* LeLeu, Lisa Puppet Show Books (Li LeLeu Puppet)
E-mail: lisa.leleu@lisaleleustudios.com; Frederic.Leleu@LisaLeLeuStudios.com
Web site: http://www.LisaLeLeuStudios.com.

Lemniscaat *Imprint of* **Boyds Mills Pr.**

Lemniscaat USA, *(978-1-935954)* 413 Sixth Ave., New York, NY 11215 USA Tel 718-768-3696; Fax: 718-369-0844
E-mail: janetta@lemniscaat.nl
Web site: http://www.lemniscaatusa.com/
Dist(s): **Ingram Pub. Services.**

Lemon Grove Pr., *(978-0-9815240)* 1158 26th St. #502, Santa Monica,, CA 90403 USA Tel 310-471-1740; Fax: 310-476-7627
E-mail: info@lemongrovepress.com
Web site: http://www.lemongrovepress.com
Dist(s): **AtlasBooks Distribution**
Brodart Co.
MyiLibrary
ebrary, Inc.

Lemon Pr. LLC, *(978-0-9844183; 978-1-936617)* Orders Addr.: P.O. Box 459, Emerson, GA 30137 USA (SAN 859-3477) Tel 404-791-7742
E-mail: lemonpresspublishing@gmail.com
Web site: http://www.lemonpresspublishing.com
Dist(s): **Smashwords.**

Lemon Shark Pr., *(978-0-9741067)* 1604 Marbella Dr., Vista, CA 92081-5463 USA Tel 760-727-2850 [phone after 9AM PCT]
E-mail: lemonsharkpress@yahoo.com
Web site: http://www.lemonsharkpress.com
Dist(s): **Coutts Information Services**
Eastern Bk. Co.
Yankee Bk. Peddler, Inc.

Lemon Sherbet Pr., *(978-0-9897411)* 87 Guernsey St., Roslindale, MA 02131 USA Tel 781-799-5412
E-mail: lemonsherbetpress@gmail.com.

Lemon Vision Productions, *(978-1-934789)* 27475 Ynez Rd., No. 642, Temecula, CA 92591 USA (SAN 854-9346) Tel 951-526-2942 Toll Free: 866-580-1675
E-mail: info@lemonvision.com
Web site: http://www.lemonvision.com.

Lemondrop Pr., *(978-0-9704718)* 19210 Ambiance Way, Franklin, TN 37067 USA Tel 615-599-6765
E-mail: dplj@bellsouth.net
Web site: http://www.mistertubby.com.

Lemonflavor Productions, *(978-0-9740169)* 100 Pk. Ave., 18th Flr. (Dept. MSM), New York, NY 10017 USA Tel 212-316-4278; Fax: 212-937-2211
E-mail: info@lemonflavor.com
Web site: http://www.lemonflavor.com.

Lemur Conservation Foundation, *(978-0-9766009; 978-0-9856728; 978-0-615-97588-7)* P.O. Box 249, Myakka City, FL 34251 USA Tel 941-322-8494; Fax: 941-322-9264
Web site: http://www.lemurreserve.org.

Leni Bks., *(978-0-9828173)* 11036 S. Tripp, Oak Lawn, IL 60453 USA Tel 708-712-4021; Fax: 708-398-1546
E-mail: ntalty@me.com
Web site: http://clie-yack-is-under-attack.com.

Leo Publishing, *(978-0-9834735; 978-1-941157)* 303 Augusta Cir., Saint Augustine, FL 32086 USA Tel 310-598-8943
E-mail: lp10leo@gmail.com.

Leo Publishing Works, Inc., *(978-0-615-35488-0)* 3 Monroe Pkwy., Suite P455, Lake Oswego, OR 97035 USA Tel 800-675-7564; Fax: 888-362-5891
E-mail: bethany@leopublishingworks.com
Web site: http://www.LeoPublishingWorks.com.

Leonard, Dennis Publications *See* **Legacy Pubs. International**

†Leonard, Hal Corp., *(978-0-634; 978-0-7935; 978-0-87910; 978-0-87930; 978-0-88188; 978-0-931340; 978-0-9607350; 978-1-56516; 978-1-57467; 978-1-4234; 978-1-61713; 978-1-61774; 978-1-61780; 978-1-4584; 978-1-4768; 978-1-4803; 978-1-4950)* Orders Addr.: P.O. Box 13819, Milwaukee, WI 53213-0819 USA Tel 414-774-3630; Fax: 414-774-3259; Toll Free: 800-524-4425; Edit Addr.: 7777 W. Bluemound Rd., Milwaukee, WI 53213 USA (SAN 239-250X); *Imprints:* G Schirmer, Incorporated (G Schirmer); Limelight Editions (LimelightEd); Amadeus Press (AmadeusPress); Applause Theatre & Cinema (ApplauseTheatr)
E-mail: halinfo@halleonard.com
Web site: http://www.halleonard.com
Dist(s): **Follett School Solutions**
Giron Bks.
Hachette Bk. Group
MyiLibrary
Penguin Random Hse., LLC.
Penguin Publishing Group
Perseus-PGW; *CIP.*

Leonard Pr., *(978-0-9769114; 978-1-934223)* P.O. Box 752, Bolivar, MO 65613-0752 USA Tel 417-326-5001
Web site: http://www.leonardpress.com.

Leonardo Press *See* **Firenze Pr.**

Leonard's, Stew Holdings, LLC *See* **Kimberly Pr., LLC**

Lerner Publishing *Imprint of* **Lerner Publishing Group**

†Lerner Publishing Group, *(978-0-7613; 978-0-8225; 978-0-87406; 978-0-87614; 978-0-929371; 978-0-930494; 978-1-57505; 978-1-58013; 978-1-58196; 978-1-4677; 978-1-5124)* Orders Addr.: 1251 Washington Ave. N., Minneapolis, MN 55401 USA (SAN 256-0283) Tel 612-332-3344; Fax: 612-204-9208; Edit Addr.: 241 First Ave., N., Minneapolis, MN 55401 USA (SAN 201-0828) Tel 612-332-3344; Fax: 612-215-6230; Toll Free Fax: 800-332-1132; Toll Free: 800-328-4929; *Imprints:* First Avenue Editions (First Ave Edns); Lerner Publications (Lerner Publictns); Carolrhoda Books (Carolrho Bks); Ediciones Lerner (EdiciLerner); Millbrook Press (Millbrok Pr); Twenty-First Century Books (TwentFrstCent); Graphic Universe (Graphic Univ); Kar-Ben Publishing (Kar-Ben); Carolrhoda LAB (CarolrhodaLAB); Darby Creek (DarbyCreek); Lerner Publishing (LERNER PUBLISH); Inside Pocket Publishing (INSIDE POCKET) ; Stoke Books (Stoke Books)
E-mail: info@lernerbooks.com; custserve@lernerbooks.com
Web site: http://www.lernerbooks.com; http://www.karben.com
Dist(s): **Chinasprout, Inc.**
Ebsco Publishing
Follett School Solutions
MyiLibrary
Open Road Integrated Media, LLC
Perfection Learning Corp.; *CIP.*

Lerner Pubns. *Imprint of* **Lerner Publishing Group**

LERN-LEARN, *(978-0-9763195)* 340 Vallejo Dr., Suite 82, Millbrae, CA 94030 USA.

Lerue Pr., LLC, *(978-0-9797460; 978-1-938814)* Orders Addr.: 280 Greg St., #10, Reno, NV 89502 USA Tel 775-849-3814
E-mail: janiceh@lerurpress.com; custserv@leruepress.com
Web site: http://www.leruepress.com; http://www.lrpnv.com.

Les Lurn Pubs., *(978-0-9792000)* 5451 Bancroft Ave., Oakland, CA 94601 USA (SAN 852-7512).

Les Penseurs, *(978-0-9764999; 978-0-9820676)* 309 Weatherstone Ln., Marietta, GA 30068 USA Tel 678-575-7052; Fax: 678-560-1580
E-mail: jsands@lespenseurs.com
Web site: http://www.lespenseurs.com.

Lesen Pub., *(978-0-9767200)* 2207 Shermont Pl., Brandon, FL 33511 USA Tel 813-857-6629; Fax: 813-684-7876
E-mail: jem2207@aol.com.

Leslie, Beverly J., *(978-0-9769722)* 1911 Patton Pl., Lithonia, GA 30058 USA Tel 770-987-8769; Fax: 770-987-8018
E-mail: bjleslie1@comcast.net; Beverly@lesliegraphicdesigns.com
Web site: http://LeslieGraphicDesigns.com.

Less is More Publishing, LLC, *(978-0-9769618)* 405 N. Woodlawn Ave., Kirkwood, MO 63122 USA
Web site: http://www.aboutheaven.net
Dist(s): **Big River Distribution.**

Less Pr., *(978-0-9657367)* 100 Hannah Niles Way, Braintree, MA 02184-7261 USA Tel 781-848-0555.

Lesson Ladder, *(978-0-9848657; 978-0-9884499; 978-0-9964067)* 21 Orient Ave, Melrose, MA 02176 USA Tel 800-301-4647; Fax: 617-583-5552
E-mail: accounting@xamonline.com
Dist(s): **Ingram Pub. Services.**

Lessons From The Vine *Imprint of* **Hutchings, John Pubs.**

Let Freedom Ring *Imprint of* **Capstone Pr., Inc.**

LeTay Publishing, *(978-0-9753434; 978-0-9830731)* Div. of LeTay Corp., Orders Addr.: P.O. Box 170233, Atlanta, GA 30317 USA Tel 404-667-2810
E-mail: booksales@letaypublishing.com; publisher@letaypublishing.com
Web site: http://www.letaypublishing.com
Dist(s): **Lightning Source, Inc.**

Letona, Oscar, *(978-0-615-24938-4)* 51 Cedar Pl., Yonkers, NY 10705 USA
E-mail: mrletona@thetrojancurse.com; mrletona@hotmail.com
Web site: http://www.thetrojancurse.com.

Let's Learn Library of Knowledge Series, *(978-0-9771015)* P.O. Box 9910, Canoga Park, CA 91309-9910 USA (SAN 256-7849)
E-mail: letslearn@letslearnlibrary.net
Web site: http://www.letslearnlibrary.net.

Let's Think-kids Foundation, Inc., *(978-1-58237)* 3925 Blackburn Ln., Burtonsville, MD 20866 USA Toll Free: 800-841-2883
E-mail: thinkkids@aol.com; sftierno@aol.com
Web site: http://www.LTKF.org.

Letter Bks. *Imprint of* **Capstone Pr., Inc.**

Level 4 Press, Inc., *(978-0-9768001; 978-1-933769)* 13518 Jamul Dr., Jamul, CA 91935 USA Tel 619-669-3100; Fax: 619-374-7311
E-mail: sales@level4press.com
Web site: http://www.level4press.com
Dist(s): **Follett School Solutions**
Midpoint Trade Bks., Inc.
MyiLibrary.

Level Green Bks., *(978-0-9788771)* 11 Level Green Rd., Brooktondale, NY 14817 USA (SAN 851-8319).

Level Ground Pr., *(978-0-9773461)* 2810 San Paula Ave., Dallas, TX 75228 USA Tel 214-796-2135
Web site: http://www.levelgroundfilms.com.

Levenger Pr., *(978-1-929154)* 420 S. Congress Ave., Delray Beach, FL 33445 USA Tel 561-276-2436; Fax: 561-276-3584
E-mail: mvogel@levenger.com
Web site: http://www.levenger.com.

Leverage Factory, *(978-0-9773000)* 38 Rogerson Dr., Chapel Hill, NC 27517-4037 USA (SAN 257-2710)
E-mail: info@leveragefactory.com
Web site: http://www.beawriter.us; http://www.leveragefactory.com
Dist(s): **Independent Pubs. Group.**

Levi Bass Publishing, *(978-0-9835651)* PO Box 608355, Orlando, FL 32860 USA Tel 407-709-0578; Fax: 407-271-8552
E-mail: carolyndenisekemp@msn.com
Web site: www.carolyndenise.com.

Levin, Hugh Lauter Assocs., *(978-0-88363)* 140 Sherman St. Ste. 2D, Fairfield, CT 06824-5849 USA (SAN 201-6109)
E-mail: inquiries@hlla.com
Web site: http://www.hlla.com
Dist(s): **Random Hse., Inc.**

Levine, Arthur A. Bks. *Imprint of* **Scholastic, Inc.**

Levine, Bette M., *(978-0-9721094)* 4605 Regiment Way, Manlius, NY 13104 USA
E-mail: rampa505@aol.com.

Levity Pr., *(978-0-615-64986-3; 978-0-615-68151-1; 978-0-615-70890-4; 978-0-615-70893-5; 978-1-939896)* 10170 Palm Glen Dr. No. 46, Santee, CA 92071 USA
Web site: www.englishcorner.me
Dist(s): **CreateSpace Independent Publishing Platform.**

Lewis & Clark Bicentennial Corps of Discovery Arch, *(978-0-9763970)* 1907 NE 75th Ave., Portland, OR 97213 USA Tel 503-201-2494
E-mail: faith.ruffing@bicencorpsarchive.com
Web site: http://www.bicencorpsarchive.com.

Lewis International, Inc., *(978-0-9666771; 978-1-930983)* 2201 NW 102nd Pl., No. 1, Miami, FL 33172 USA Tel 305-436-7984; Fax: 305-436-7985; Toll Free: 800-259-5962.

Lewis Lynn Bks., *(978-0-9745544)* 1143 N. Carey Ave., Clovis, CA 93611-7371 USA Fax: 559-322-9038
E-mail: cconn@cwnet.com
Web site: http://www.borainiansector.com.

Lewis-Thornton, Rae, *(978-0-9747983)* 1507 E. 53rd St., Suite 315, Chicago, IL 60615 USA Tel 773-643-4316; Fax: 773-643-4356
E-mail: rae_lewis_thornton@hotmail.com
Web site: http://www.raelewisthornton.org.

Lexicon Marketing Corporation *See* **Lexicon Marketing, LLC**

Lexicon Marketing, LLC, *(978-1-59172)* 6380 Wilshire Blvd. Ste. 1400, Los Angeles, CA 90048-5018 USA
E-mail: Jbelletti@lexiconmarketing.com; icruz@lexiconmarketing.com.

Lexingford Publishing, *(978-0-9844938; 978-0-9859480; 978-0-9863343; 978-0-9963948)* 165 Backwoods Rd., Colton, NY 13625 USA (SAN 859-5674) Tel 415-328-5465
E-mail: abell@clarkson.edu.

Lexington Bks., *(978-0-7391; 978-1-4985)* Div. of Rowman & Littlefield Publishing Group, Orders Addr.: 15200 NBN Way, Blue Ridge Summit, PA 17214 USA Tel 717-794-3800 (Sales, Customer Service, MIS, Royalties, Inventory Mgmt., Dist., Credit & Collections); Fax: 717-794-3803 (Customer Service &/or orders only); 717-794-3857 (Sales & MIS); 717-794-3856 (Royalties, Inventory Mgmt., & Dist.); Toll Free Fax: 800-338-4550 (Customer Service &/or orders); Toll Free: 800-462-6420 (Customer Service &/or orders); 67 Mowat Ave., Suite 241, Toronto, ON M6K 3E3 Tel 416-534-1660; Fax: 416-534-3699; Edit Addr.: 4501 Forbes Blvd., Blvd., Ste. 200, Lanham, MD 20706 USA Tel 301-459-3366; Fax: 301-429-5749; Toll Free: 1-800-462-6420 Short Discount, contact rlpgsales@rowman.com
E-mail: custserv@rowman.com; edebusk@rowman.com; lexingtonbooks@rowman.com
Web site: http://www.lexingtonbooks.com; http://www.rlpgbooks.com; http://www.rowman.com
Dist(s): **CreateSpace Independent Publishing Platform**
Ebsco Publishing
Follett School Solutions
MyiLibrary
National Bk. Network
Rowman & Littlefield Publishers, Inc.
Send The Light Distribution LLC
Transaction Pubs.
ebrary, Inc.

Lexington Pubs., *(978-1-933361)* P.O. Box 750018, Arlington Heights, MA 02475 USA
E-mail: lexingtonpublishers@gmail.com.

Leyva, Barbara, *(978-0-9729056)* P.O. Box 3295, Clewiston, FL 33440-3295 USA; *Imprints:* Balticbard Publishing (Balticbard Pub)
E-mail: balticbard@yahoo.com
Web site: http://www.geocities.com/balticbard/index.html.

L.G. Publishing, *(978-0-615-16242-3)* P.O. Box 5098, Sarasota, FL 34277 USA Tel 941-312-4725
E-mail: glickmanfamily@aol.com.

LGE Performance Systems, Inc., *(978-0-9778776)* 9757 Lake Nona Rd., Orlando, FL 32827 USA (SAN 850-5055) Tel 407-438-9911; Fax: 407-438-6667.

LGR Productions *See* **LGR Publishing, Inc.**

LGR Publishing, Inc., *(978-0-9657610)* 3219 NW C St., Richmond, IN 47374 USA Tel 765-939-8924 (phone/fax)
E-mail: jwilde@indiana.edu; mcphd@infocom.com
Web site: http://www.angerchillout.com.

Lóguez Ediciones (ESP) *(978-84-85334; 978-84-89804; 978-84-96646)* *Dist. by* **Lectorum Pubns.**

LH Pubns. & Productions, *(978-0-9749013)* Orders Addr.: P.O. Box 914, Center Harbor, NH 03226 USA
E-mail: mcat_lh@yahoo.com
Web site: http://www.laurahickey.com.

Li, Richard T., *(978-0-9675988)* 4554 Rose Tree Ct., Fort Worth, TX 76137 USA Tel 817-656-5178; Fax: 817-656-4138.

LiArt-Literature & Art, *(978-1-931481)* P.O. Box 245686, Pembroke Pines, FL 33024-5686 USA Tel 954-986-6886 (phone/fax)
E-mail: liartpe@aol.com.

Libertary Company *See* **Booktrope**

Liberty Artists Management, *(978-0-9785427)* Orders Addr.: 31 Liberty St., Catskill, NY 12414-1442 USA
E-mail: admin@libertyartists.com
Web site: http://www.beckyblume.com; http://www.libertyartists.com.

Liberty Communications House *See* **JB Information Station**

Liberty Fund, Inc., *(978-0-86597; 978-0-913966; 978-1-61487)* Orders Addr.: c/o Total Response, Inc., 5804 Churchman By-Pass, Indianapolis, IN 46203 USA; Edit Addr.: 8335 Allison Pointe Trail, No. 300, Indianapolis, IN 46250-1684 USA (SAN 202-6740) Tel 317-842-0880; Fax: 317-579-6060; Toll Free: 800-866-3520; 800-955-8335 (customer service)
E-mail: webmaster@libertyfund.org
Web site: http://www.libertyfund.org
Dist(s): **Chicago Distribution Ctr.**
MyiLibrary
ebrary, Inc.

Liberty Manuals Co., *(978-0-9710748; 978-0-9820955; 978-1-940069)* Orders Addr.: P.O. Box 453, Rumson, NJ 07760 USA Tel 732-842-3000; Fax: 732-741-5820.

Liberty Publishing Group, *(978-1-893095)* Div. of The Holton Consulting Group, Inc., Orders Addr.: 1405 Autumn Ridge Dr., Durham, NC 27712-2680 USA Tel 919-767-9620; Toll Free Fax: 866-500-7697; Toll Free: 877-819-7489
E-mail: bil@holtonconsulting.com; cher@holtonconsulting.com
Web site: http://www.holtonconsulting.com; http://www.prosperityPublishing.com; http://www.themetaphysicalwebsite.com
Dist(s): **Prosperity Publishing Hse.**
Smashwords.

Liberty St. *Imprint of* **Time Inc. Bks.**

Liberty University Press, *(978-0-9819357; 978-1-935986)* 1971 University Blvd., Lynchburg, VA 24502 USA Tel 434-592-3100
E-mail: libertyuniversitypress@liberty.edu.

Librado Pr., *(978-1-879571)* 11223 Leatherwood Dr., Reston, VA 22091 USA Tel 703-476-0516 Do not confuse with Librad Press in San Francisco, CA.

Librairie du Liban Pubns. (FRA) *Dist. by* **Intl Bk Ctr.**

Librairie Larousse (FRA) *(978-2-03)* *Dist. by* **Distribks Inc.**

†Libraries Unlimited, Inc., *(978-0-313; 978-0-87287; 978-1-56308; 978-1-59158)* Div. of Greenwood Publishing Group, Orders Addr.: a/o Customer Service Group, Dept. 2229, P.O. Box 5007, Westport, CT 06881 USA Fax: 603-431-2214; Toll Free: 800-225-5800; Edit Addr.: 88 Post Rd W., Westport, CT 06880-4208 USA; *Imprints:* Teacher Ideas Press (TIP)
E-mail: lubooks@lu.com
Web site: http://www.lu.com
Dist(s): **ABC-CLIO, LLC**
CreateSpace Independent Publishing Platform
Ebsco Publishing
Greenwood Publishing Group, Inc.
MyiLibrary; *CIP.*

Library Assn. of La Jolla, *(978-0-9744804; 978-0-9828289)* 1008 Wall St., La Jolla, CA 92037-4418 USA Tel 858-454-5872; Fax: 858-454-5835; *Imprints:* Athenaeum Music & Arts Library (Athenaeum Music)
E-mail: Athlibrary@pacbell.net; kpeterson@ljathenaeum.org.

Library of America, The, *(978-0-940450; 978-1-883011; 978-1-931082; 978-1-59853)* Div. of Literary Classics of the U. S., Inc., 14 E. 60th St., New York, NY 10022 USA (SAN 286-9918) Tel 212-308-3360; Fax: 212-750-8352
E-mail: info@loa.org
Web site: http://www.loa.org
Dist(s): **Penguin Random Hse., LLC.**
Penguin Publishing Group
Random Hse., Inc.

Library Reprints, Inc., *(978-0-7222)* Orders Addr.: P.O. Box 890820, Temecula, CA 92589-0820 USA (SAN 254-0258) Fax: 951-767-1803; 951-767-0133
E-mail: newbookorders@gmail.com.

Library Sales of N.J., *(978-1-888032)* Orders Addr.: P.O. Box 335, Garwood, NJ 07027-0335 USA Tel 908-232-1446; Edit Addr.: 607 S. Chestnut St., Westfield, NJ 07090-1369 USA
E-mail: Librarysalesofnj@aol.com.

LIBRI Bks., Division of Seasons & A Muse, Incorporated *See* **LIBRI Pubs.**

LIBRI Pubs., *(978-0-9763952)* P.O. Box 5849, Playa Del Rey, CA 90296-5849 USA Tel 310-827-6495; Fax: 310-827-8166
E-mail: libri@seasonsandamuse.com
Web site: http://www.seasonsandamuse.com.

Libris Draconis Pr., *(978-0-9728124)* PMB 279 1296 E. Gibson Rd., Suite A, Woodland, CA 95776 USA (SAN 255-1179)
Dist(s): **BookMasters, Inc.**

Libros del Mundo *Imprint of* **Kane Miller**

Libros Desafio, *(978-0-939125; 978-1-55883; 978-1-55955)* Subs. of CRC Pubns., 2850 Kalamazoo Ave., SE, Grand Rapids, MI 49560 USA (SAN 248-9775) Tel 616-224-0785; Fax: 616-224-0834; Toll Free: 800-333-8300
E-mail: info@librosdesafio.org
Web site: http://www.librosdesafio.org.

Libros, Encouraging Cultural Literacy, *(978-0-9675413; 978-0-9710860)* Orders Addr.: P.O. Box 453, Long Beach, NY 11561 USA Tel 516-889-6077; Fax: 516-889-6365; Toll Free: 800-260-9915; Edit Addr.: 160 LaFayette Blvd., Long Beach, NY 11561 USA (SAN 253-374X)
E-mail: librospress@msn.com
Web site: http://www.librospress.com.

Libros in Spanish, LLC, 1941 NE 147th Terr., North Miami, FL 33181 USA Tel 786-274-1556; Fax: 305-948-0333
E-mail: admin@librosinspanish.com.

Libros Liguori *Imprint of* **Liguori Pubns.**

Libros Para Ninos *Imprint of* **Libros Para Ninos**

Libros Para Ninos, Div. of Simon & Schuster Children's Publishing, 1230 Ave. of the Americas, New York, NY 10020 USA; *Imprints:* Libros Para Ninos (LibPara)
Dist(s): **Simon & Schuster**
Simon & Schuster, Inc.

Librosa Publishing, *(978-0-9837458; 978-0-9851769; 978-0-9906713)* 24040 Camino Del Avion No. A225, Monarch Beach, CA 92629 USA Tel 949-201-9477; Fax: 949-661-9098
E-mail: librospublishing@cox.net
Dist(s): **AtlasBooks Distribution**
BookMasters Distribution Services (BDS)
Follett School Solutions
ebrary, Inc.

Libros Sin Fronteras, P.O. Box 2085, Olympia, WA 98507 USA Tel 360-357-4332; Fax: 360-357-4964
E-mail: info@librossinfronteras.com
Web site: http://www.librossinfronteras.com.

Libros-Latin American Treasures For Kids *See* **Libros, Encouraging Cultural Literacy**

Librujas, *(978-0-9771566)* 4335 Van Nuys Blvd., Suite 117, Sherman Oaks, CA 91403 USA (SAN 256-887X) Tel 818-905-7221
E-mail: jamie@librujas.com; patricia@librujas.com
Web site: http://www.librujas.com
Dist(s): **Quality Bks., Inc.**

Liburdi, Mariana *See* **Happy Hearts Family, The**

Lickel, Lisa Publishing, also operating as Five Loaves *See* **Fox Ridge Pubns.**

Life Action Publishing, *(978-0-940110; 978-0-9667124; 978-1-934718)* Orders Addr.: P.O. Box 31, Buchanan, MI 49107 USA Tel 269-697-8600; Fax: 269-695-2974; Toll Free: 800-321-1538; Edit Addr.: 2727 Niles Buchanan Rd., Buchanan, MI 49107 USA (SAN 220-2859)
Web site: http://www.lifeaction.org; http://www.ReviveOurHearts.com.

LIFE Bks. *Imprint of* **Time Inc. Bks.**

Life by Design Youth Leadership Resources *See* **Youthleadership.com**

Life Changers International Church *See* **Dickow, Gregory Ministries**

Life Force Bks., *(978-0-9795331; 978-0-9896540; 978-0-9962386)* P.O. Box 302, Bayside, CA 95524 USA; *Imprints:* Zardoz Press (ZardozPr)
E-mail: jjsemple@suddenlink.net; jjsemple@lifeforcebooks.com
Web site: http://www.lifeforcebooks.com; http://www.goldenflowermeditation.com; http://www.commonsensekundalini.com; http://www.kundaliniconsortium.org/
Dist(s): **Smashwords.**

Life Letters Publishing, *(978-0-9746022)* P.O. Box 360111, Strongsville, OH 44136 USA
E-mail: lifeletter@aol.com
Web site: http://www.lifeletter.net.

Life Line, Inc., *(978-0-9647089)* P.O. Box 7990, New York, NY 10116-8715 USA Tel 212-947-0661; Fax: 212-947-0681 Do not confuse with Life Lines, Rimrock, AZ
E-mail: lifel@aol.com.

Life Line Publishing, *(978-0-9761604)* P.O. Box 1482, Bridgeport, CT 06601-1482 USA Do not confuse with Life Line Publishing in Franklin, VA.

Life Link Worldwide Pubs., *(978-1-880608)* 175 Raymond Ct., Fayetteville, GA 30214 USA Tel 770-994-1683.

Life Pubs. International, *(978-0-7361; 978-0-943258; 978-1-890219)* 1625 N. Robberson Ave., Springfield, MO 65803 USA (SAN 213-5817) Tel 417-831-7766; Fax: 417-831-6445; Toll Free: 888-776-2425
E-mail: info@lifepublishers.org
Dist(s): **AtlasBooks Distribution.**

Life Story Publishing, LLC *See* **Wizard Academies, LLC**

LifeApplicationBible.com *See* **Livingstone Corp.**

Lifeforce Enterprises, Inc., *(978-0-9709796)* 250 Pacific Ave., Suite 326, Long Beach, CA 90802 USA Tel 562-366-2617; Toll Free: 866-543-3367
E-mail: ajyager@entertheforce.com
Web site: http://www.entertheforce.com
Dist(s): **Midpoint Trade Bks., Inc.**

Lifelight Bks., *(978-0-9743801)* 2629 262nd Pl SE, Sammamish, WA 98075-7900 USA (SAN 850-8070)
E-mail: lynne@lifelightbooks.com
Web site: http://www.lifelightbooks.com.

LifeLine Studios, Inc., *(978-0-9714753)* 1390 W. Main St., Lancaster, TX 75146 USA Tel 972-275-0468; Fax: 972-275-0469
E-mail: afoutsjr@lifelinestudios.com
Web site: http://www.lifelinestudio.com.

Lifepac *Imprint of* **Alpha Omega Pubns., Inc.**

Liferays Publishing, *(978-0-9795397)* 5390 Elliott Rd., Powder Springs, GA 30127-3803 USA Tel 770-943-6123
E-mail: liferays@bellsouth.net
Web site: http://liferays02.googlepages.com/home.

LifeReloaded *See* **LifeReloaded Specialty Publishing LLC**

LifeReloaded Specialty Publishing LLC, *(978-0-9776414; 978-1-60800)* 2256 Huber Dr., Manheim, PA 17545 USA; *Imprints:* American Literary Publishing (Amer Literary)
E-mail: admin@lifereloaded.com; Editor@LifeReloaded.com; Sales@LifeReloaded.com; Publisher@LifeReloaded.com
Web site: http://www.LifeReloaded.com; http://www.GhostTrainToFreedom.com; http://www.MooKittyFindsAHome.Com; http://www.JMPMysterySeries.com.

Life's Journey of Hope Pubns., *(978-0-9747815)* Orders Addr.: P.O. Box 1277, Groton, MA 01450 USA (SAN 255-7789) Tel 978-448-1252; Edit Addr.: 90 Martins Pond Rd., Groton, MA 01450 USA
E-mail: LLeonard@lifesjourneyofhope.com; lifesjourneyofhope@hotmail.com
Web site: http://www.lifesjourneyofhope.com.

Lifeskills Press *See* **Uplift Pr.**

LifeSong Pubs., *(978-0-9718306; 978-0-9799116)* Orders Addr.: P.O. Box 183, Somis, CA 93066-0183 USA Tel 805-504-3916; Toll Free: 866-266-6917
Web site: http://www.lifesongpublishers.com
Dist(s): **Send The Light Distribution LLC.**

Lifestage, Inc., *(978-0-9799905)* 496 Smithtown ByPass, Suite 202, Smithtown, NY 11787 USA (SAN 854-9192) Tel 631-366-4265
E-mail: lifestage_2000@yahoo.com
Web site: http://www.lifestage.org.

LifeStory Publishing, *(978-0-9758988)* 5328 Runnymede Rd., Jackson, MS 39211 USA Tel 601-978-3478
E-mail: maxwell@thewellpublishing.org.

LifeTime Media, Inc., *(978-0-9675967; 978-0-9816368; 978-0-9822171; 978-0-9823975)* 352 Seventh Ave., 7th Flr., New York, NY 10001 USA (SAN 856-0978) Tel 212-631-7524; Fax: 212-631-7529
E-mail: sales@lifetimemedia.com; jgrace@lifetimemedia.com
Web site: http://www.lifetimemedia.com
Dist(s): **Perseus Bks. Group**
Perseus Distribution.

Lifetime Relationship Center *See* **Intralife Systems Publishing**

Lifetrack Resources, *(978-0-9743826)* 709 Univ. Ave. W., Saint Paul, MN 55104-4804 USA Tel 651-227-8471; Fax: 651-227-0621
E-mail: familiestogether@lifetrackresources.org
Web site: http://www.lifetrackresources.org.

Lifevest *Imprint of* **Lifevest Publishing, Inc.**

Lifevest Publishing, Inc., *(978-0-9724680; 978-1-932338; 978-1-59879)* 4910 E. Dry Creek Rd., Suite 170, Centennial, CO 80122 USA Tel 303-221-1007; Fax: 303-771-1166; Toll Free Fax: 877-843-1007; *Imprints:* Lifevest (Livevst)
E-mail: ric.simmons@lifevestpublishing.com; publisher@lifevestpublishing.com
Web site: http://www.lifevestpublishing.com.

LifeWay Christian Resources, *(978-0-7673; 978-0-633; 978-1-4158; 978-1-4300)* Div. of The Southern Baptist Convention, One Lifeway Plaza, Nashville, TN 37234 USA Fax: 615-277-8221 (product info., ordering, order tracking); 615-251-2626 (shipping/transportation); Toll Free: 888-227-9493 (product info., ordering); *Imprints:* Serendipity House (Serendip Hse)
E-mail: customerservice@lifeway.com
Web site: http://www.lifewaystores.com; http://www.lifeway.com
Dist(s): **Spring Arbor Distributors, Inc.**

Liffey Pr., The (IRL) *(978-1-904148; 978-1-905785; 978-1-908308)* *Dist. by* **Dufour.**

Lift Every Voice *Imprint of* **Moody Pubs.**

Light & Life Publishing Co., *(978-0-937032; 978-1-880971; 978-1-933654)* Orders Addr.: 4808 Park Glen Rd., Minneapolis, MN 55416 USA (SAN 213-8565) Tel 952-925-3888; Fax: 888-925-3918; Toll Free Fax: 888-925-3918
E-mail: ivy@light-n-life.com
Web site: http://www.light-n-life.com.

Light Bugs Publishing, *(978-0-9765514)* 1400 Champions Green Dr., Gulf Breeze, FL 32563 USA Tel 850-932-9325
E-mail: allen911@bellsouth.net; russ@lightbugspublishing.com; jan@lightbugspublishing.com
Web site: http://www.lightbugspublishing.com.

Light Energy Bks., *(978-0-9740480)* 731 Mandana Blvd., Oakland, CA 94610 USA Tel 510-268-9999.

Light Incorporated, The *See* **Tughra Bks.**

Light Internal Publishing, *(978-0-9823732)* Orders Addr.: 6130 E. Fair Ave., Centennial, CO 80111 USA (SAN 857-9822)
E-mail: marnie@lightinternal.com
Web site: http://www.lightinternal.com.

Light Line, *(978-0-9773244)* 353 E. Pittsfield St., Pennsville, NJ 08070 USA (SAN 257-2540) Toll Free: 877-427-8271
E-mail: jildadf@comcast.net.

Light Messages *Imprint of* **Light Messages Publishing**

Light Messages Publishing, *(978-0-9679937; 978-0-9800756; 978-1-61153)* 5216 Tahoe Dr., Durham, NC 27713 USA (SAN 920-9298) Tel 919-361-5041; Toll Free Fax: 866-585-4635; *Imprints:* Light Messages (LightMess)
E-mail: books@lightmessages.com
Web site: http://www.lightmessages.com
Dist(s): **INscribe Digital**
New Leaf Distributing Co., Inc.

Light Pubns., *(978-0-9702642; 978-0-9824707; 978-1-940060)* Orders Addr.: P.O. Box 2462, Providence, RI 02906 USA Tel 401-272-8707; Edit Addr.: 393 Morris Ave., Providence, RI 02906 USA (SAN 852-7407) Tel 401-272-8707
E-mail: info@lightpublications.com
Web site: http://www.lightpublications.com.

Light Sword Publishing, LLC *See* **LSP Digital, LLC**

Light Works Publishing *Imprint of* **I.M. Enterprises**

Light24, *(978-0-9700002)* Orders Addr.: 85-42 160th St., Jamaica Queens, NY 11432 USA Tel 718-526-7021 Do not confuse with companies with the same name in Worthington, OH, Kirkland, WA.

Light-Beams Publishing, *(978-0-9708104; 978-0-9766289; 978-1-941506)* Orders Addr.: 10 Toon Ln., Lee, NH 03861 USA Tel 603-659-1300
E-mail: mforman@light-beams.com; info@light-beams.com
Web site: http://www.light-beams.com
Dist(s): **Independent Pubs. Group**
Library Video Co.
Midwest Tape
MyiLibrary
NewSound, LLC.

Lighted Lamp Pr., *(978-1-888350)* Orders Addr.: P.O. Box 1234, Wheat Ridge, CO 80034 USA; Edit Addr.: 4945 Gray St., Denver, CO 80212 USA (SAN 298-8348)
E-mail: robertjinye@msn.com.

Lighthearted Pr., Inc., *(978-0-9659225)* Orders Addr.: P.O. Box 90125, Portland, OR 97290 USA Tel

Publisher Name Index

503-786-3085; Fax: 503-786-0315; Edit Addr.: 10585 SE Fairway Dr., Portland, OR 97266 USA
E-mail: davis@lightheartedpress.com
Web site: http://www.lightheartedpress.com.

Lighthouse Bk. Publishing, *(978-0-9791168)* Orders Addr.: P.O. Box 310534, Houston, TX 77231 USA Toll Free: 800-247-9100
E-mail: book@journeytoseetheking.com
Web site: http://www.journeytoseetheking.com.

Lighthouse Christian Products Co., *(978-0-9712894)* 1050 Remington Rd., Schaumburg, IL 60173-4518 USA
Web site: http://lcpgifts.com.

Lighthouse eBooks *See* **Lighthouse Publishing**

Lighthouse for Leaders, *(978-0-9820576)* P.O. Box 1990, San Benito, TX 78586 USA Tel 956-412-1131; *Imprints:* Lighthouse for Leaders, A (LighthseforLea)
Web site: http://www.LighthouseforLeaders.com.

Lighthouse for Leaders, A *Imprint of* **Lighthouse for Leaders**

Lighthouse Point Pr., *(978-0-9637966; 978-0-9792998)* Div. of Yearick-Millea, Inc., 7412 Lighthouse Point, Pittsburgh, PA 15221 USA Tel 412-242-9382; Fax: 412-242-9382
Web site: http://lighthousepointpress.com.

LightHouse Pr., *(978-0-9703823; 978-0-9724442; 978-0-9747189; 978-0-9762898; 978-0-9791372; 978-0-9823218)* 2053 Williams Valley Dr., Madison, TN 37115-7610 USA Do not confuse with companies with the same or similar names in Culver City, CA, Millersburg, OH, York, ME, Marblehead, MA, Deerfield Beach, FL, La Junta, CO, Rochester, NY, San Mateo, CA.

Lighthouse Pr., Inc., *(978-0-9677347; 978-0-9795392)* 5448 Apex Peakway #230, Apex, NC 27502-3924 USA (SAN 253-0961) Do not confuse with companies with the same or similar names in York, ME, Marblehead, MA, La Junta, CO, Deerfield Beach, FL, San Mateo, CA, Sanford, MI, Minneapolis, MN, Millersburg, OH
E-mail: swagner@lighthouse-press.com
Web site: http://www.lighthouse-press.com
Dist(s): **Midpoint Trade Bks., Inc.**

Lighthouse Publications *See* **I AM Foundation, The**

Lighthouse Publishing, *(978-0-9773766; 978-0-9797863; 978-1-935079)* 251 Overlook Park Ln., Lawrenceville, GA 30043-7355 USA (SAN 257-4330)
E-mail: andyoverett@lighthousechristianpublishing.com
Web site: http://www.lighthouseebooks.com; http://www.lighthousechristianpublishing.com; http://www.loneoakpublishing.com
Dist(s): **CreateSpace Independent Publishing Platform.**

Lighthouse Publishing of the Carolinas, *(978-0-9822065; 978-0-9833196; 978-0-9847655; 978-1-938499; 978-0-615-89890-2; 978-1-941103)* Div. of Christian Devotions Ministries, Orders Addr.: 2333 Barton Oaks Dr., Raleigh, NC 27614 USA
E-mail: aground@mindspring.com
Web site: lighthousepublishingofthecarolinas.com
Dist(s): **CreateSpace Independent Publishing Platform**
Send The Light Distribution LLC
Smashwords
Spring Arbor Distributors, Inc.

Lightly Pr., *(978-0-9794452)* 26 Quay Ct., No. 65, sacramento, CA 95831-1540 USA Tel 916-427-7840
E-mail: regdown@hotmail.com.

Lightning Bug Flix, *(978-1-933262)* 1126 S. 70th St., Suite N601, Milwaukee, WI 53214 USA Tel 414-475-4445; Fax: 414-475-3621
E-mail: vicky@lightningbugflix.com
Web site: http://www.lightningbugflix.com.

Lightning Bug Learning Corporation *See* **Lightning Bug Learning Pr.**

Lightning Bug Learning Pr., *(978-0-9817826; 978-0-9832098)* Reviewer Relations Dept. 316 Mid Valley Ctr., #130, Carmel, CA 93923 USA (SAN 856-5449) Tel 831-250-1866; Fax: 971-250-2582; Toll Free: 877-695-7312
E-mail: mail@lightningbuglearning.com
Web site: http://www.lightningbuglearning.com; http://www.lightningbuglearningpress.com
Dist(s): **Book Clearing Hse.**

Lightning Creek *See* **Perceval Pr.**

Lightning Source, Inc., Orders Addr.: 150 Fieldcrest Ave. Lightning Source, Edison, NJ 08837 USA (SAN 920-4288); 4260 Port Union Rd. No. 100 Lightning Source, Fairfield, OH 45011 (SAN 920-4296); Edit Addr.: 1246 Heil Quaker Blvd., LaVergne, TN 37086 USA (SAN 179-6976) Tel 615-213-4595; Fax: 615-213-4426.

LightningBolt Pr., *(978-0-9746398)* 1481 Applegate Dr. Suite 101, Naperville, IL 60565-1225 USA Tel 630-778-7310; Fax: 630-778-7890
E-mail: info@mygreatdebate.net
Web site: http://www.greatdebate.net.

Lightwatcher Publishing *See* **Illumina Publishing**

Liguori Pubns., *(978-0-7648; 978-0-89243)* One Liguori Dr., Liguori, MO 63057-9999 USA (SAN 202-6783) Tel 636-464-2500; Fax: 636-464-8449; Toll Free Fax: 800-325-9526; Toll Free: 800-325-9521 (orders); *Imprints:* Libros Liguori (Libros Liguori)
E-mail: liguori@liguori.org
Web site: http://www.liguori.org
Dist(s): **ACTA Pubns.**
Follett School Solutions
MyiLibrary.

LikeMinds Pr., *(978-0-9764724; 978-0-9915853)* Orders Addr.: 3151 Airway Ave. Suite K-205 Suite K-205, Costa Mesa, CA 92626 USA Fax: 714-556-2354
E-mail: shendl@cox.net
Web site: http://www.likemindspress.com.

Lilac Pr., *(978-0-9662568)* Orders Addr.: P.O. Box 1356, Scottsdale, AZ 85252-1356 USA Fax: 480-368-5551; Edit Addr.: 6268 N. 85th St., Scottsdale, AZ 85250 USA
E-mail: lilacp@cholesterolnodiet.com; lilacp@frontiernet.net
Web site: http://www.cholesterolnodiet.com.

Lillenas Publishing Co., *(978-0-8341)* Div. of Nazarene Publishing Hse., P.O. Box 419527, Kansas City, MO 64141 USA (SAN 298-7619) Tel 816-931-1900; Fax: 816-753-4071; Toll Free Fax: 800-849-9827; Toll Free: 800-877-0700 (Orders Only)
E-mail: music@lillenas.com
Web site: http://www.lillenas.com
Dist(s): **Leonard, Hal Corp.**
Nazarene Publishing Hse.
Spring Arbor Distributors, Inc.

Lillian Press *See* **Smith & Assocs.**

Lillis, Holly, *(978-0-9762733)* P.O. Box 1082, Aptos, CA 95001-0000 USA.

Lill-Till Pr., *(978-0-9742808)* 15305 Walvern Blvd., Maple Heights, OH 44137 USA.

Lily & Co. Publishing, *(978-1-929265)* Orders Addr.: 15 Willow Rd., Greenville, RI 02828 USA
E-mail: erinesquedesign@mac.com
Web site: http://www.lilycopublishing.com.

Lily Wish Factory, *(978-0-9792472)* 44 W. Main St., Mystic, CT 06355 USA (SAN 852-8861) Tel 860-245-0629
E-mail: shipandshimmer@aol.com
Web site: http://shipandshimmer.com.

Lima Bear Pr LLC, The, *(978-1-933872)* 2305 MacDonough Rd., Wilmington, DE 19805 USA
E-mail: lbp.books@yahoo.com
Web site: http://www.limabearpress.com
Dist(s): **Independent Pubs. Group.**

Limelight Editions *Imprint of* **Leonard, Hal Corp.**

Limerock Bks., *(978-0-9746589)* 15 Mechanic St., Thomaston, ME 04861 USA Tel 207-354-8191 Do not confuse with Limerock Books, Inc., New Canaan, CT
E-mail: limebks@midcoast.com
Web site: http://www.ChristopherFahy.com
Dist(s): **Brodart Co.**

Lincoln Bks., *(978-0-9910560)* 406 Diana Ct., Highland Heights, OH 44124 USA Tel 440-813-0274
E-mail: robthomas@hotmail.com
Web site: Rob Thomas.

Lincoln, Emma *See* **Awesome Bk. Publishing**

Lincoln Library Pr., Inc., The, *(978-0-912168)* Orders Addr.: 812 Huron Rd., SE, Suite 401, Cleveland, OH 44115-1126 USA (SAN 205-5953) Fax: 216-781-9559 (phone/fax); Toll Free: 800-516-2656
E-mail: tgall@thelincolnlibrary.com
Web site: http://www.thelincolnlibrary.com
Dist(s): **Follett School Solutions**
INscribe Digital.

Lincoln Public Schls., *(978-0-9671920)* P.O. Box 82889, Lincoln, NE 68501 USA (SAN 508-9964) Tel 401-436-1628; Fax: 401-436-1638
E-email: dpeters@lps.org
Web site: http://www.lps.org.

Linda Cardillo, Author *See* **Bellastoria Pr.**

Linda Hall Library, *(978-0-9763590)* 5109 Cherry St., Kansas City, MO 64110-2498 USA Tel 816-363-4600; Fax: 816-926-8790
E-mail: bradleyb@lindahall.org
Web site: http://www.lindahall.org.

Linda Kaye's Birthdaybakers, Partymakers, *(978-0-9759161)* 195 East 76th St., New York, NY 10021 USA Tel 212-288-7112; Fax: 212-879-6785
E-mail: lindak@partymakers.com
Web site: http://www.partymakers.com.

Lindaloo Enterprises, *(978-0-9800923; 978-1-937564)* P.O. Box 90135, Santa Barbara, CA 93190 USA; *Imprints:* Classic Bookwrights (ClassicBook)
E-mail: sales@lindaloo.com
Web site: http://www.lindaloo.com; http://www.tporigami.com
Dist(s): **Lightning Source, Inc.**

Linden Hill Publishing, *(978-0-9704754; 978-0-9820153)* Subs. of Arcadia Productions, 11923 Somerset Ave., Princess Anne, MD 21853 USA Tel 410-651-0757 (phone/fax)
E-mail: lindenhill2@comcast.net
Web site: http://www.lindenhill.net.

Linden Publishing Co., Inc., *(978-0-941936; 978-1-933502; 978-1-61035)* 2006 S. Mary, Fresno, CA 93721 USA (SAN 238-6089) Tel 559-233-6633 (phone/fax); Toll Free: 800-345-4447 (orders only) Do not confuse with Linden Publishing in Avon, NY
E-mail: richard@lindenpub.com
Web site: http://www.lindenpub.com
Dist(s): **CreateSpace Independent Publishing Platform**
Independent Pubs. Group
Ingram Pub. Services
Quality Bks., Inc.
Smashwords.

Linderoth, Joel, *(978-0-615-77239-4)* 335 Pierce St., San Francisco, CA 94117 USA Tel 415.215.1303
Dist(s): **CreateSpace Independent Publishing Platform.**

Lindisfarne Bks. *Imprint of* **SteinerBooks, Inc.**

Lindsay Pubns., Inc., *(978-0-917914; 978-1-55918)* Orders Addr.: P.O. Box 12, Bradley, IL 60915 USA (SAN 209-9462) Tel 815-935-5353; Fax: 815-935-5477.

Lindsey, Elanna, *(978-0-615-83876-2; 978-0-615-86070-1; 978-0-615-94879-9; 978-0-692-29457-4)* 30364 Highland Pk. Ln., Lithonia, GA 30038 USA Tel 678-418-7383
Dist(s): **CreateSpace Independent Publishing Platform.**

Lindsley, David Studio, *(978-0-9796008)* P.O. Box 431, Springville, UT 84663 USA.

Linear Wave Publishing, *(978-0-9767196)* P.O. Box 177, Liberty, KY 42539-0177 USA Tel 606-787-8189
E-mail: blaine.staat@linearwavepublishing.com
Web site: http://www.linearwavepublishing.com.

Lingenfelser, Lynda L., *(978-0-615-13290-7; 978-0-615-14072-8)* 3284 Spruce Creek Glen, Daytona Beach, FL 32198 USA; P.O. Box 290714, Port Orange, FL 32129
Dist(s): **Lulu Enterprises Inc.**

Linger Longer Books *See* **Artists' Orchard, LLC, The**

Lingo Pr. LLC, *(978-0-9777419)* 1020 Janet Dr., Lakeland, FL 33805 USA (SAN 850-119X) Tel 863-868-5996 (phone/fax)
E-mail: customerservice@lingopress.com
Web site: http://www.lingopress.com.

Linguatechnics Publishing, *(978-0-9767837)* 2114 Pauline Blvd., Ann Arbor, MI 48103 USA Tel 734-662-0434; Fax: 734-662-0248
E-mail: info@linguatechnics.com
Web site: http://www.linguatechnics.com.

LinguaText, Ltd., *(978-0-936388; 978-0-942566; 978-1-58871; 978-1-58977)* Orders Addr.: 103 Walker Way, Newark, DE 19711-6119 USA (SAN 238-0307) Tel 302-453-8695; Fax: 302-453-8601
E-mail: linguatext@juno.com
Web site: http://www.LinguatextLtd.com; http://www.EuropeanMasterpieces.com; http://www.JuandelaCuesta.com.

LinguiSystems, Inc., *(978-0-7606; 978-1-55999)* 3100 Fourth Ave., East Moline, IL 61244-9700 USA Tel 309-755-2300; Fax: 309-755-2377; Toll Free: 800-776-4332; 800-577-4555
E-mail: kmicka@linguisystems.com
Web site: http://www.linguisystems.com.

Linive Kreyol Publishing, *(978-0-9720954)* 339 Howell Dr. SE, Suite 3-F, Atlanta, GA 30316 USA.

Link & Rosie Pr., *(978-0-9762434)* Orders Addr.: c/o Goblin Fern Press, Inc., 1118 Sequoia Trail, Madison, WI 53713 USA Tel 608-335-0542; Fax: 608-210-7235
E-mail: ssharron@sbcglobal.net
Web site: http://www.linkandrosie.com.

Linky & Dinky Enterprises, *(978-0-9768588)* P.O. Box 418, Oldsmar, FL 34677 USA
E-mail: uncle-url@linkydinky.com
Web site: http://www.linkydinky.com.

Linmore Publishing, Inc., *(978-0-916591; 978-1-934472)* Orders Addr.: P.O. Box 1545, Palatine, IL 60078 USA (SAN 662-2291) Fax: 612-729-9125; Toll Free: 800-336-3656
E-mail: linmore@linmore.com
Web site: http://www.linmore.com.

Linwood Hse. Publishing, *(978-0-9753098)* 843 Cypress Pkwy., No. 338, Kissimmee, FL 34759 USA Tel 407-595-6220
E-mail: zippityzem@comcast.net.

Linworth Publishing, Inc., *(978-0-938865; 978-1-58683)* 3650 Olentangy River Rd., Suite 250, Columbus, OH 43214 USA (SAN 662-5800) Tel 614-884-9995; Fax: 614-884-9993; Toll Free: 800-786-5017
E-mail: linworth@linworthpublishing.com
Web site: http://www.linworth.com
Dist(s): **ABC-CLIO, LLC**
Follett School Solutions
Cengage Gale
MyiLibrary.

Linx Educational Publishing, Inc., *(978-1-891818; 978-0-9797510)* P.O. Box 50009, Jacksonville Beach, FL 32240 USA Tel 904-241-1861; Fax: 904-241-3279; Toll Free Fax: 888-546-9338; Toll Free: 800-717-5469
E-mail: mimi@lixedu.com; info@linxedu.com
Web site: http://www.linxedu.com
Dist(s): **American Assn. for Vocational Instructional Materials**
Films Media Group
Follett School Solutions
JIST Publishing
S V E & Churchill Media.

†Lion Bks., *(978-0-87460)* 235 Garth Rd. Apt. D5A, Scarsdale, NY 10583-3994 USA (SAN 241-7529)
Dist(s): **AtlasBooks Distribution**
BookMasters, Inc.; *CIP.*

Lion Hudson PLC (GBR) *(978-0-7459; 978-0-85648; 978-0-85721) Dist. by* **IPG Chicago.**

Lion Hudson PLC (GBR) *(978-0-7459; 978-0-85648; 978-0-85721) Dist. by* **Trafalgar.**

Lion Hudson PLC (GBR) *(978-0-7459; 978-0-85648; 978-0-85721) Dist. by* **Kregel.**

Lion Prints Publishing, *(978-0-9797699)* Rhodes Ln., Suite 480, West Hempstead, NY 11552-1155 USA Tel 646-240-1633
E-mail: lesleynu@mac.com
Dist(s): **Lulu Enterprises Inc.**

Lion Stone Bks., *(978-0-9658486; 978-0-9859618)* Orders Addr.: 4921 Aurora Dr., Kensington, MD 20895 USA Tel 301-949-3204; Fax: 301-949-3860
E-mail: lionstone@juno.com
Dist(s): **Book Wholesalers, Inc.**
Brodart Co.
Follett School Solutions.

Lionheart Foundation, The, *(978-0-9644933; 978-0-9799338)* P.O. Box 194, Boston, MA 02117 USA Tel 781-444-6667; Fax: 781-444-6855
E-mail: judith@lionheart.org
Web site: http://www.lionheart.org.

Lionheart Pr., *(978-0-9964246)* 3711 Fews Ford Ln., Durham, NC 27712 USA Tel 919-812-6204
E-mail: hejafred@gmail.com
Web site: www.timberhowligan.com.

Lion's Crest Pr., *(978-0-9763798)* 1900 S. Rock Rd., Suite 5205, Wichita, KS 67207 USA Tel 316-305-5813.

Lions Den Publishing, LLC, *(978-0-9786786)* P.O. Box 91254, Washington, DC 20090-1254 USA (SAN 851-2477) Tel 202-256-0508
Dist(s): **Independent Pubs. Group.**

Lion's Tale Pr., LLC, *(978-0-9748478)* 4895 Kings Valley Dr., Suite 200, Roswell, GA 30075 USA Tel 770-998-3302; Fax: 770-998-3874
E-mail: ebbenator@mindspring.com.

LionX Publishing, *(978-0-9716085)* 24988 Blue Ravine Rd., #108-113, Folsom, CA 95630 USA (SAN 254-2021) Tel 916-939-9422; Fax: 916-939-9424
E-mail: info@lionxpublishing.com
Web site: http://www.lionxpublishing.com.

LIP Publishing LLC, *(978-0-9771114)* 903 Oakridge Dr, Suite 100, Round Rock, TX 78681 USA
E-mail: thelifeip@yahoo.com
Web site: http://www.thelifeip.com.

Liquid Space Publishing, *(978-0-9710366)* 37 Endicott St., Salem, MA 01970 USA Tel 978-745-5529
E-mail: donniedives@earthlink.net
Web site: http://www.home.earthlink.net/~donniedives.

Lire Bks., *(978-0-9849323; 978-1-939652)* 7 Debaun Pl., Spring Valley, NY 10977 USA Tel 845-659-2018
E-mail: raedanbocs@gmail.com
Web site: lirebooks.com; http://simplylire.com/.

Lisa The Weather Wonder Inc., *(978-0-9740997)* 187 Summer Lake Dr., Marietta, GA 30060 USA
Web site: http://www.lisamozer.com.

Lisboa, David, *(978-0-9752740)* 9060 Palisade Ave., Apt. 307, North Bergen, NJ 07047 USA Tel 201-869-3494.

Listen & Live Audio, Inc., *(978-1-885408; 978-1-931953; 978-1-59316)* Orders Addr.: P.O. Box 817, Roseland, NJ 07068 USA Tel 201-558-9000; Fax: 201-558-9800; Toll Free: 800-653-9400; Edit Addr.: 1700 Manhattan Ave., Union City, NJ 07087-5473 USA
E-mail: Alfred@Listenandlive.com
Web site: http://www.listenandlive.com
Dist(s): **Audible.com**
Ebsco Publishing
Findaway World, LLC
Follett School Solutions
OverDrive, Inc.
Smashwords.

Listening Chamber, *(978-0-9639321)* 1341 Seventh St., Berkeley, CA 94710 USA Tel 510-524-1668; Fax: 510-524-0852; Toll Free: 800-869-7553; *Imprints:* Parrhesia Press (Parrhesia Pr)
Dist(s): **SPD-Small Pr. Distribution.**

Listening Library *Imprint of* **Random Hse. Audio Publishing Group**

Listening Library *Imprint of* **Penguin Random House Audio Publishing Group**

Lister, Tresina, *(978-0-9791171)* 541 S. Staunton Dr., Tucson, AZ 85710 USA Tel 520-751-8630.

Lit Torch Publishing, *(978-1-887357)* 4204 Danmire Dr., Richardson, TX 75082 USA Tel 312-239-8633 (phone/fax)
E-mail: littorch@gmail.com
Web site: http://www.littorch.com.

Lit Verlag (DEU) *(978-3-8258; 978-3-89473; 978-3-88660; 978-3-643) Dist. by* **Intl Spec Bk.**

LiteBooks.net LLC *See* **Stress Free Kids**

Literacy Resources, Inc., *(978-0-9759575)* 143 Franklin Ave., River Forest, IL 60305-2113 USA Tel 708-366-5947; Fax: 708-366-9149
E-mail: tcorless@literacyresourcesinc.com
Web site: http://www.literacyresourcesinc.com.

Literal Publishing Inc., *(978-0-9770287; 978-0-9897957; 978-1-942307)* 5425 Renwick Dr., Houston, TX 77081 USA Tel 713-626-1433.

Literally Speaking Publishing Hse., *(978-1-929642)* 2020 Pennsylvania Ave., NW, No. 406, Washington, DC 20006 USA (SAN 852-8896) Tel 202-491-5774; Fax: 202-403-3535
E-mail: Distribution@LiterallySpeaking.com; bookinfo@literallyspeaking.com
Web site: http://www.literallyspeaking.com.

Literary Architects, LLC, *(978-1-933669)* 1427 W. 86th St., Suite 324, Indianapolis, IN 46260 USA Tel 317-462-6329
E-mail: info@literaryarchitects.com
Web site: http://www.literaryarchitects.com.

Literary Lessons *Imprint of* **HomeScholar Bks.**

Literary Licensing, LLC, *(978-1-258; 978-1-4940; 978-1-4941; 978-1-4978; 978-1-4979; 978-1-4980; 978-1-4981)* P.O. Box 1404, Whitefish, MT 59937 USA
E-mail: literarylicensing@gmail.com
Web site: http://www.literarylicensing.com.

Literary Works Specialist, *(978-0-9746687)* P.O. Box 58908, New Orleans, LA 70158-8908 USA
E-mail: rdomio@aol.com
Web site: http://www.lwspublishing.net.

Literate Chigger Pr., Ink, Inc., The, *(978-0-9759042; 978-0-615-56517-0)* 1175 Queen Anne Rd., Teaneck, NJ 07666 USA Tel 201-741-6529
E-mail: emily@hipbo.org.

Literations, *(978-0-943514)* Div. of Dan Valenti Communications, P.O. Box 1845, Pittsfield, MA 01202 USA (SAN 240-706X) Tel 413-499-1459; *Imprints:* Raven Books (Raven Bks)
Dist(s): **Orca Bk. Pubs. USA.**

Literature Dramatization Pr., *(978-0-9644186)* 1089 Sunset Cliffs Blvd., San Diego, CA 92107-4037 USA Tel 619-222-2462
Dist(s): **Educational Bk. Distributors**
Empire Publishing Service
Lectorum Pubns., Inc.

LITHBTH Educational Services, *(978-0-9744920)* P.O. Box 55495, Hayward, CA 94545-5495 USA
E-mail: teachingkids@mindspring.com
Web site: http://www.home.mindspring.com/~teachingkids.

Litho Tech, LLC, *(978-0-9742791)* 3045 Highland Ave., Grants Pass, OR 97526 USA Tel 541-479-8905; Fax: 541-474-6937
E-mail: gpprint@charterinternet.com; lithotech541@charter.net.

Litkus Pr., *(978-1-932629)* P.O. Box 34785, Los Angeles, CA 90034 USA Tel 310-391-5629
E-mail: litkuspress@earthlink.net.

Little Acorn Assocs., Inc., *(978-0-9741579; 978-0-9844010; 978-1-937257)* P.O. Box 8787, Greensboro, NC 27419-8787 USA
E-mail: lilacorn@bellsouth.net.

Little Acorn LLC, *(978-0-9766703; 978-0-9964448)* Orders Addr.: 112 W. Calista Dr., Tahlequah, OK 74464-7446 USA
E-mail: info@littleacornkids.net
Web site: http://www.littleacornkids.net.

Little Band Man Co., LLC, The, *(978-0-615-12596-1)* 1415 Easy St., New Iberia, LA 70560 USA Tel 337-365-4136; Fax: 337-365-4137
E-mail: jady@littlebandman.com
Web site: http://www.littlebandman.com.

Little Bay Pr., *(978-0-9745192)* 40 Salmon Beach, Tacoma, WA 98407 USA Tel 253-756-0987
E-mail: kcampbell@littlebaypress.com
Web site: http://www.littlebaypress.com.

Little Beach Bks., *(978-0-615-37246-4; 978-0-9891340)* P.O. Box 6148, Falmouth, ME 04105 USA Tel 207-878-8804
Dist(s): **Independent Pubs. Group.**

Little Bee Books Inc., *(978-1-4998)* 401 Park Ave South, 10th Floor, New York, NY 10016 USA Tel 917-280-6600
E-mail: info@littlebeebooks.com
Web site: http://www.littlebeebooks.com
Dist(s): **Simon & Schuster, Inc.**

Little Big Tomes, 1275 Trail Ridge Dr., Canyon Lake, TX 78133 USA Tel 830-899-6888
E-mail: cottage@gvtc.com.

Little Bigfoot *Imprint of* **Sasquatch Bks.**

Little Bird Publishing, *(978-0-9728838)* 285 W. 8th St., Ship Bottom, NJ 08008 USA Tel 609-494-7485; Fax: 609-494-9569
E-mail: gwennhotaling@aol.com
Web site: http://www.gwennhotaling.com.

Little Blue Flower Pr. *Imprint of* **Grey Gate Media, LLC**

Little Blue Pr., *(978-0-9725584)* 14403 Little Blue Rd., Kansan City, MO 64136 USA Tel 816-455-1110
E-mail: littlebluepress@softhome.net.

Little Bookroom, *(978-0-9641262; 978-1-892145; 978-1-936941)* Orders Addr.: P.O. Box 260, Jackson, MS 39205 USA Tel 601-354-5306; Fax: 601-353-0176; Edit Addr.: 1755 Broadway, Fifth Flr., New York, NY 10019-3780 USA Tel 212-293-1643; Fax: 212-333-5374
E-mail: editorial@littlebookroom.com
Web site: http://www.littlebookroom.com
Dist(s): **Granta**
MyiLibrary
New York Review of Bks., Inc., The
Penguin Random Hse., LLC.
Random Hse., Inc.

Little Bookstore Who Could, The, *(978-0-9746997)* 1303 Windsong Way, Augusta, GA 30907 USA Tel 706-868-0075
E-mail: vickyharperselah@yahoo.com; vicky@thelittlebookstorethatcould.com
Web site: http://www.thelittlebookstorethatcould.com.

Little Boost *Imprint of* **Picture Window Bks.**

Little Boots Publishing, *(978-0-9767230)* P.O. Box 3110, Pawtucket, RI 02861 USA Tel 401-475-5852 (phone/fax)
E-mail: Info@littlebootspublishing.com
Web site: http://www.littlebootspublishing.com.

Little Britches Childrens Bks., *(978-0-9798189)* P.O. Box 1188, Willow, AK 99688-1188 USA.

†Little Brown & Co., *(978-0-316; 978-0-8212; 978-0-7595)* Div. of Hachette Bk. Group, Orders Addr.: 3 Center Plaza, Boston, MA 02108-2084 USA (SAN 630-7248) Tel 617-227-0730; Toll Free Fax: 800-286-9471; Toll Free: 800-759-0190; Edit Addr.: 237 Park Ave., New York, NY 10017 USA (SAN 200-2205) Tel 212-364-0600; Fax: 212-364-0952; *Imprints*: Back Bay Books (Back Bay); Mulholland Books (Mulholland Bk)
E-mail: customer.service@hbgusa.com
Web site: http://www.hachettebookgroup.com
Dist(s): **Continental Bk. Co., Inc.**
Follett School Solutions
Grand Central Publishing
Hachette Bk. Group
Hastings Bks.
Lectorum Pubns., Inc.
MyiLibrary
Rounder Kids Music Distribution
Beeler, Thomas T. Pub.
TextStream
Thorndike Pr.; *CIP*.

Little, Brown Book Group Ltd. (GBR) *(978-0-09; 978-0-316; 978-0-7088; 978-0-7499; 978-0-7515; 978-0-8212; 978-0-86188; 978-0-948164; 978-1-85004; 978-1-85487; 978-1-85703; 978-1-85018; 978-1-84119; 978-0-86007; 978-0-9536151; 978-1-903608; 978-1-84529; 978-1-84528; 978-1-84901; 978-1-4087; 978-1-908974) Dist. by* **IPG Chicago.**

Little, Brown Book Group Ltd. (GBR) *(978-0-09; 978-0-316; 978-0-7088; 978-0-7499; 978-0-7515; 978-0-8212; 978-0-86188; 978-0-948164; 978-1-85004; 978-1-85487; 978-1-85703; 978-1-85018; 978-1-84119; 978-0-86007; 978-0-9536151; 978-1-903608; 978-1-84529; 978-1-84528; 978-1-84901; 978-1-4087; 978-1-908974) Dist. by* **Trafalgar.**

Little, Brown Bks. for Young Readers, *(978-0-316; 978-0-8212; 978-0-7595; 978-0-7596)* Div. of Hachette Bk. Group, 1271 Ave. of the Americas, New York, NY 10020 USA Tel 212-522-8700; Fax: 212-522-2067; Toll Free: 800-343-9204; 3 Center Plaza, Boston, MA 02108-2084 USA Tel 617-227-0730; Toll Free Fax: 800-286-9471; Toll Free: 800-759-0190; *Imprints*: Tingley, Megan Books (Megan Tingley Bks); Poppy (Poppy)
Dist(s): **Follett School Solutions**
Grand Central Publishing
Hachette Bk. Group
Lectorum Pubns., Inc.
Little Brown & Co.
MyiLibrary.

Little Brown Children's Books *See* **Little, Brown Bks. for Young Readers**

Little Bunny Bks., *(978-0-615-46734-4; 978-0-615-58595-6; 978-0-615-66757-7; 978-0-692-48194-3)* P.O. Box 151, Cabin John, MD 20818 USA Tel 978-712-8669
E-mail: littlebunnybooks@gmail.com
Dist(s): **CreateSpace Independent Publishing Platform.**

Little Chameleon Bks. *Imprint of* **Kid Prep, Inc.**

Little Clive Pr., *(978-0-615-58866-7; 978-0-615-69435-1; 978-0-615-79920-9; 978-0-9911479)* 306 N. 19th Ave., Kelso, WA 98626 USA Tel 503-381-3923
E-mail: bendertzu@yahoo.com; joey.wardell@gmail.com
Web site: http://www.littleclivepress.com.

Little Cottonwood River Bks., *(978-0-9884268)* 2918 71st St., Dundee, MN 56131 USA Tel 507-274-5316
E-mail: paplowp@gmail.com.

Little Creek Bks. *Imprint of* **Jan-Carol Publishing, INC.**

Little Creek Press, *(978-0-9828023; 978-0-9849245; 978-0-9896431; 978-0-9899780; 978-0-9899784; 978-1-942586)* Div. of Kristin Mitchell Design, LLC, 5341 Sunny Ridge Rd., Mineral Point, WI 53565 USA (SAN 920-2862) Tel 608-987-3370
E-mail: info@littlecreekpress.com
Web site: www.littlecreekpress.com.

Little Cubans, LLC, *(978-1-934113)* P.O. Box 260944, Pembroke Pines, FL 33026-7944 USA
E-mail: littlecubans@bellsouth.net
Web site: http://www.littlecubans.com.

Little, Cynthia M. *See* **Sleepless Warrior Publishing**

Little Deer Pr., *(978-1-891360)* P.O. Box 1220, Rainier, WA 98576 USA Tel 360-894-3459
E-mail: mollypiper@hotmail.com
Web site: http://www.focusbloom.com.

Little Devil Bks., *(978-0-9858280; 978-0-9911534)* 5139 Maxon Terr., Sanford, FL 32771 USA Tel 407-443-6494
E-mail: dave@littledevilbooks.com
Web site: http://www.littledevilbooks.com
Dist(s): **Lightning Source, Inc.**
Smashwords.

Little Dixie Publishing Co., *(978-0-9628099)* Orders Addr.: P.O. Box 215, Wynnewood, OK 73098 USA Tel 405-665-4811 Do not confuse with Rebel Pr., Chino, CA
E-mail: LittleDixie@itinet.net
Web site: www.michaelandrewgrissom.com.

Little Dog Pubns., *(978-0-9774143)* P.O. Box 8680, Kansas City Missouri, MO 64114-0680 USA (SAN 257-5051)
E-mail: jeffr@littledogpress.net
Web site: http://littledogpress.net.

Little Fiddle Co., Inc., The, *(978-0-9700489; 978-0-9798643)* 700 Kinderkamack Rd., Oradell, NJ 07649 USA Fax: 201-265-6499; Toll Free: 888-678-5636
E-mail: info@minimaestro.com; jeofficemgr@osen.us
Web site: http://www.minimaestro.com
Dist(s): **Penton Overseas, Inc.**

Little Five Star *Imprint of* **Five Star Pubns., Inc.**

Little Germ That Could..Creations, Inc., The, *(978-0-9763233; 978-0-9960186)* 6815 Edgewater Dr., No.108, Coral Gables, FL 33133 USA Tel 305-775-0281
Web site: www.littlegerm.com.

Little Guardians, Inc., *(978-0-9660879)* 111 Melody Dr., Metairie, LA 70001 USA Tel 504-837-3328; Fax: 504-835-9993; Toll Free: 800-582-4923.

Little Hands Bk. Co., LLC, *(978-0-9814878)* 32094 Vintage Way, Afton, OK 74331-5600 USA
Web site: http://www.littlehandsbook.com.

Little Hare Bks. (AUS) *(978-1-877003; 978-1-921049; 978-1-921272; 978-1-921541; 978-1-921714; 978-1-921894) Dist. by* **IPG Chicago.**

Little Hero, *(978-0-9769057)* P.O. Box 771371, Orlando, FL 32877 USA
E-mail: whitlockmatt@hotmail.com
Web site: http://www.littlehero.net.

Little Hill Pubs., *(978-0-9835048)* Orders Addr.: P.O. Box 282, Ashland, MA 01721 USA; Edit Addr.: 18 Pennock Rd., Ashland, MA 01721 USA Tel 508-881-0011
E-mail: contact@littlehillpublishers.com.

Little Hse. Pr., *(978-0-9773812)* 3618 Bayshore Rd., Sarasota, FL 34234 USA
Dist(s): **Independent Pubs. Group**
MyiLibrary.

Little Hse. Site Tours LLC, *(978-0-9765951)* 2430 Marlette Rd., Applegate, MI 48401 USA Tel 810-633-9973; Fax: 810-633-9027
E-mail: lhsitetours@email.com
Web site: http://www.lhsitetours.homestead.com.

Little Island (IRL) *(978-1-84840; 978-1-908195) Dist. by* **IPG Chicago.**

Little Laura Music, LLC, *(978-0-9845226)* 1171 Cottage Ln., Hercules, CA 94547 USA
Dist(s): **Independent Pubs. Group.**

Little League Pr., *(978-0-9747883)* P.O. Box 249, Stanleytown, VA 24168 USA
E-mail: hooneybgood@adelphia.net
Dist(s): **Bassett Printing Corp.**

Little Light Pr., *(978-0-9755374)* Orders Addr.: 549 Broadway, Bethpage, NY 11714 USA Tel 516-938-3343 Do not confuse with Little Light Press in Oklahoma City, OK
E-mail: littlelightpress@yahoo.com
Web site: http://www.littlelightpress.biz.

Little Linguists Press, *(978-0-9777085)* P.O. Box 169, Owings Mills, MD 21117 USA.

Little Lion Pr., *(978-0-9796393)* 4911 Cumberland Ave., Chevy Chase, MD 20815 USA Tel 301-980-4344; Fax: 301-656-0086.

Little Lyrics Pubns., *(978-1-893429)* 12310 Old Barn Rd., Elbert, CO 80106 USA Tel 719-495-4941
E-mail: littlelyrics@prodigy.com
Web site: http://www.littlelyrics.com.

little m Bks., *(978-0-9830487)* 756 Pompton Ave., Cedar Grove, NJ 07009 USA Tel 201-704-7886
E-mail: wmadsen@me.com.

Little Mai Pr., *(978-1-893237)* 102 River Dr., Lake Hiawatha, NJ 07034 USA Tel 973-331-9648; Fax: 973-331-1856; Toll Free: 800-438-2719
E-mail: lmaipress@aol.com; f1promo@aol.com
Web site: http://www.littlemaipress.com.

Little Melody Pr. *Imprint of* **Brighter Minds Children's Publishing**

Little Moose Pr., *(978-0-9720227; 978-0-9786049; 978-0-9841021; 978-0-9841441; 978-0-9831161; 978-0-9838386; 978-0-9893988)* Orders Addr.: 269 S. Beverly Dr. #1065, Beverly Hills, CA 90212 USA (SAN 254-9778) Tel 310-862-2574; Fax: 310-862-2575; Toll Free: 866-234-0626
E-mail: ellen@littlemoosepresspub.com; bookshep@mac.com
Web site: http://www.littlemoosepresspub.com; www.louisegaylordauthor.com; www.pippinpb.com
Dist(s): **Book Clearing Hse.**
Pathway Bks.
Smashwords.

Little Munchkin Bks., *(978-0-9773936)* 2893 Rockefeller Rd., Willoughby Hills, OH 44092-1423 USA (SAN 257-411X) Tel 440-585-4950
E-mail: tara_tabernik@yahoo.com
Web site: http://www.littlemunchkinbooks.com.

Little Noggin LLC, *(978-0-9743760)* 1350 Grand Summit Dr., Suite 288, Reno, NV 89523 USA Tel 916-435-9737; Fax: 530-673-9680
E-mail: info@akidatart.com
Web site: http://www.akidatart.com.

Little Ones *Imprint of* **Port Town Publishing**

Little P Pr. Co., *(978-0-9853430)* 6387 Camp Bowie Blvd Ste B PMB No. 292, Fort Worth, TX 76116 USA Tel 817-501-8229
E-mail: pitch129@aol.com
Web site: ChazzKids.com.

Little Patriot Pr. *Imprint of* **Regnery Publishing, Inc., An Eagle Publishing Co.**

Little Pear Pr., *(978-0-9746911)* P.O. Box 343, Seekonk, MA 02771-1409 USA
Web site: http://www.littlepearpress.com.

Little Pemberley Pr., *(978-0-9763359)* Orders Addr.: 1528 Tulane St., Suite F, Houston, TX 77008-4146 USA Tel 713-862-8542; Fax: 713-862-6399
E-mail: littlepemberleypress@hotmail.com
Web site: http://www.giraffeofmontana.com; http://www.littlepemberleypress.com.

Little People Bks., *(978-0-9764114)* 2 Victor Ave., Worcester, MA 01603 USA Tel 508-963-2004.

Little Petals *Imprint of* **Roses Are READ Productions**

Little Pickle Press LLC, *(978-0-9840806; 978-0-9829938; 978-1-939775)* 3701 Sacramento St. #494, San Francisco, CA 94118 USA (SAN 858-3641) Fax: 415-366-1520; Toll Free: 877-415-4488
E-mail: info@littlepicklepress.com
Web site: http://www.littlepicklepress.com
Dist(s): **Ingram Pub. Services**
MyiLibrary.

Little Pigeon Bks., *(978-0-9818976)* 5354 Washington St., Downers Grove, IL 60515 USA Tel 630-541-3700
Dist(s): **AtlasBooks Distribution**
ebrary, Inc.

Little Prince Publishing, *(978-0-615-46053-6; 978-0-615-46977-5; 978-0-615-47049-8; 978-0-9835220; 978-0-615-58516-1; 978-0-615-59301-2; 978-0-615-59908-3; 978-0-615-59909-0; 978-1-939947)* 7942 Indica Ct., North Charleston, SC 29418 USA
E-mail: sybilnelson@hotmail.com
Web site: www.sybilnelson.com; www.littleprincepublishing.com
Dist(s): **CreateSpace Independent Publishing Platform**
Dummy Record Do Not USE!!!!
Smashwords.

Little Red Acorns *Imprint of* **Little Red Tree Publishing LLC**

Little Red Cat Publishing, *(978-0-9726375)* 939A Terra Bella Ave., Mountainview, CA 94043 USA (SAN 254-9549) Tel 650-960-4040; Fax: 650-960-1040
E-mail: email@comprintingco.com; e-mail@comprintingco.com.

Little Red Tree Publishing LLC, *(978-0-9789446; 978-1-935656)* 635 Ocean Ave., New London, CT 06320 USA (SAN 852-0143) Tel 860-287-1660; *Imprints*: Little Red Acorns (LR Acorns)
E-mail: mikelinnard@yahoo.co.uk
Web site: http://www.littleredtree.com.

Little Redhaired Girl Publishing, Inc., *(978-0-9729264)* 120 Riverside Blvd., #2e, New York, NY 10069 USA (SAN 857-6041) Fax: 225-410-6739; *Imprints*: Books for Brats (Books for Brats)
E-mail: booksforbrats@aol.com
Web site: http://www.booksforbrats.com.

Little River Bookshelf, *(978-0-9769856)* 2707 Silver Leaf Ct., Grapevine, TX 76051 USA Tel 817-308-2510
E-mail: mark.storer@usa.net.

Little Santa Bks., Inc., *(978-0-615-17411-2)* P.O. Box 806, Buffalo, NY 14220 USA Tel 716-316-1545
E-mail: sergioroguez@gmail.com
Web site: http://www.littlesantaclaus.com.

Little Scribblers Bks., LLC, *(978-0-9747689)* 2545 NW 55th Pl., Oklahoma City, OK 73112-7101 USA Tel 405-615-8662
E-mail: littlescribblers@cox.net
Web site: http://www.littlescribblers.com.

Little Shepherd *Imprint of* **Scholastic, Inc.**

Little Simon *Imprint of* **Little Simon**

Little Simon, *(978-0-671; 978-0-689; 978-1-4169)* Div. of Simon & Schuster Children's Publishing, 1230 Ave. of the Americas, New York, NY 10020 USA; *Imprints*: Little Simon (LSimon)
Dist(s): **Simon & Schuster**
Simon & Schuster, Inc.

Little Simon Inspirations *Imprint of* **Little Simon Inspirations**

Little Simon Inspirations, Div. of Simon & Schuster Children's Publishing, 1230 Ave. of the Americas, New York, NY 10020 USA; *Imprints*: Little Simon Inspirations (LSimonInsp)
Dist(s): **Simon & Schuster, Inc.**

Little Soundprints *Imprint of* **Soundprints**

Little Sprout Publishing Hse., *(978-0-9779194)* Orders Addr.: 520 Berry Way, La Habra, CA 90631 USA; *Imprints*: Psalms for Kidz (Psalms for Kidz)
Web site: http://psalmsforkidz.com.

Little Thoughts For Little Ones Publishing, Inc., *(978-0-9748884; 978-0-9861870)* Orders Addr.: P.O. Box 665, Tavernier, FL 33070 USA Fax: 305-852-4274
E-mail: vhandelsman@att.net
Web site: http://www.littlethoughtspublishing.net.

Little Tiger Pr., *(978-1-888444; 978-1-58431)* Div. of Futech Interactive Products, 39 S. La Salle St. Ste. 1410, Chicago, IL 60603-1706 USA Toll Free: 800-541-2205 Do not confuse Little Tiger Press in San Francisco, CA
E-mail: jody@futechsales.com
Dist(s): **Futech Educational Products, Inc.**
Lectorum Pubns., Inc.
MyiLibrary.

Little Treasure Bks., *(978-0-9639838; 978-0-9814571)* P.O. Box 362, Bensalem, PA 19020-0362 USA
Web site: http://www.littletreasurebooks.com.

Little Treasure Publications, Incorporated *See* **Little Treasure Bks.**

Little T's Corner, *(978-0-9842397; 978-1-938037)* Orders Addr.: 17344 S. Parker Rd., Homer Glen, IL 60491 USA (SAN 858-821X) Tel 815-717-6212; Fax: 815-717-8236
E-mail: donna@littletscorner.com; 72allshookup@gmail.com
Web site: http://www.littletscorner.com; http://www.donnazadunajskymalacina.blogspot.com
Dist(s): **AtlasBooks Distribution**
BookBaby
MyiLibrary
ebrary, Inc.

Little Tule Bks., *(978-0-9773133)* P.O. Box 549, Carmel Valley, CA 93924-0549 USA (SAN 257-2311) Tel 831-659-0107; Fax: 831-659-0106
E-mail: bill@littletulebooks.com
Web site: http://www.littletulebooks.com.

Little Vegan Monsters Publishing, *(978-0-9787590)* P.O. Box 9258, New Haven, CT 06533 USA
E-mail: Lourdes@littleveganmonsters.com
Web site: http://www.littleveganmonsters.com.

Little Way Pr., *(978-0-9764691)* 18252 Little Fuller Rd., Twain Harte, CA 95383 USA
Web site: http://www.littlewaypress.com
Dist(s): **Catholic Heritage Curricula.**

Little Willow Tree Bks., *(978-0-9743795)* 4900 Dodd St., Lynchburg, VA 24502 USA Do not confuse with Willow Tree Press in Monsey, NY
E-mail: willowtreebooks@yahoo.com.

Little Wooden Bks., *(978-0-929949)* 11001 S. Degray Ln., Spokane, WA 99224 USA (SAN 250-7943) Tel 509-932-4729.

Little Worm Publishing, *(978-0-9911382)* 920 Litchfield Pl., Roswell, GA 30076 USA Tel 706-258-8925
E-mail: hetheringtonlin@gmail.com
Web site: www.littlewormpub.com.

Littletonhouse Publishing, *(978-0-9746849)* Orders Addr.: P.O. Box 2954, Littleton, CO 80161-2954 USA (SAN 256-3371) Tel 303-740-2003; Fax: 303-771-0305
E-mail: info@thesecretcovebook.com; treis@littletonhousepublishing.com
Web site: http://www.thesecretcovebook.com; http://www.virobacter.com.

Liturgical Pr. Bks. *Imprint of* **Liturgical Pr.**

†Liturgical Pr., *(978-0-8146; 978-0-916134)* Div. of Order of St. Benedict, Inc., Orders Addr.: a/o St. Johns Abbey, P.O. Box 7500, Collegeville, MN 56321-7500 USA (SAN 202-2494) Tel 320-363-2213; 612 363 2326; Fax: 320-363-3299; Toll Free Fax: 800-445-5899; Toll Free: 800-858-5450; *Imprints*: Liturgical Press Books (Liturg Pr Bks)
E-mail: sales@litpress.org; bwoods@csbsju.edu
Web site: http://www.litpress.org; http://sjbible.org; http://cistercianpublications.com
Dist(s): **BookMobile**
Metapress; *CIP*.

Liturgy Training Pubns., *(978-0-929650; 978-0-930467; 978-1-56854; 978-1-61671; 978-1-61833)* Div. of Archdiocese of Chicago, 3949 S. Racine Ave., Chicago, IL 60609-2523 USA (SAN 670-9052) Toll Free Fax: 800-933-7094 (orders); Toll Free: 800-933-1800 (orders); *Imprints*: Catechesis of the Good Shepherd (Catechesis Good Shepherd)
E-mail: lguzman@ltp.org
Web site: http://www.ltp.org.

Live Oak Games, *(978-0-9764394)* P.O. Box 780932, Orlando, FL 32878 USA Toll Free Fax: 800-214-4632 (phone/fax)
E-mail: sales@liveoakgames.com
Web site: http://www.liveoakgames.com.

Live Oak Media, *(978-0-87499; 978-0-941078; 978-1-59112; 978-1-59519; 978-1-4301)* Orders Addr.: P.O. Box 652, Pine Plains, NY 12567-0652 USA (SAN

Publisher Name Index

217-3921) Tel 518-398-1010; Fax: 518-398-1070; Toll Free: 800-788-1121
E-mail: info@liveoakmedia.com
Web site: http://www.liveoakmedia.com
Dist(s): **AudioGO**
Ebsco Publishing
Findaway World, LLC
Follett School Solutions
Greathall Productions, Inc.
Lectorum Pubns., Inc.
Lerner Publishing Group.

†Liveright Publishing Corp., *(978-0-87140; 978-1-63149)* Subs. of W. W. Norton Co., Inc., 500 Fifth Ave., New York, NY 10110 USA (SAN 201-0976) Tel 212-354-5500; Fax: 212-869-0856; Toll Free Fax: 800-458-6515; Toll Free: 800-233-4830
Web site: http://www.wwnorton.com
Dist(s): **Norton, W. W. & Co., Inc.**
Penguin Random Hse., LLC.; *CIP.*

Living Bks. Pr., *(978-0-9790876; 978-0-9818093; 978-1-938192)* 5497 S. Gilmore Rd., Mount Pleasant, MI 48858 USA (SAN 852-4114) Toll Free: 888-331-3481
E-mail: lbcinfo@livingbookscurriculum.com
Web site: http://www.livingbookscurriculum.com.

Living Dead Pr., *(978-1-935458; 978-1-61199)* 58 Dedham St., Revere, MA 02151 USA
Dist(s): **Smashwords.**

Living History Pr., *(978-0-9664925)* 7426 Elmwood Ave., Middleton, WI 53562 USA Tel 608-836-7426; Fax: 608-836-0176 Do not confuse with Living History Pr., Bellevue, WA
E-mail: pferd@tds.com
Web site: http://www.inwave.com/Milton/MiltonHouse/.

Living in Grace, *(978-0-9659319)* 10051 Siegen Ln., Baton Rouge, LA 70810 USA Tel 504-769-8844; Fax: 504-767-5655; Toll Free: 800-484-2046 ext. 9506
E-mail: QRBC@aol.com.

Living Ink Bks. *Imprint of* **AMG Pubs.**

Living Language *Imprint of* **Random Hse. Information Group**

Living Life Publishing Co., *(978-0-9768773; 978-0-9769166; 978-0-9774499; 978-1-934796)* Div. of Bianca Productions, LLC, 24165 IH-10, W., Suite 217-474, San Antonio, TX 78257 USA (SAN 256-5684) Tel 210-698-6392; Fax: 210-698-1754
E-mail: livinglifepublishing@msn.com
Web site: http://www.livinglifepublishing.com; http://www.biancaproductions.com.

Living Ministry, Inc., *(978-0-9763167)* 800 Prospect Blvd., Pasadena, CA 91103 USA Tel 626-356-9491; Fax: 626-584-0290
Web site: http://www.livingministry.com.

Living Stone Arts, *(978-0-9763901)* 3806 Owl Dr., Rolling Meadows, IL 60008 USA
Web site: http://www.livingstonearts.com.

Living Stream Ministry, *(978-0-7363; 978-0-87083; 978-1-57593)* 2431 W. La Palma Ave., Anaheim, CA 92801 USA (SAN 253-4266) Tel 714-236-6001; 714-991-4681; Fax: 714-991-4685
E-mail: books@lsm.org
Web site: http://www.lsm.org
Dist(s): **Anchor Distributors**
Spring Arbor Distributors, Inc.

Living the Good News *Imprint of* **Church Publishing, Inc.**

Living Water Pubns., *(978-1-59521)* P.O. Box 4653, Rockford, IL 61110-4653 USA Fax: 815-394-0140 Do not confuse with Living Water Publications in Edwardsville, KS
E-mail: lwministry@aol.com
Web site: http://www.livingwaterpublications.org.

Living Waters Publishing Co., *(978-0-9798154; 978-0-9814532; 978-0-9821153)* P.O. Box 1361, Marion, AR 72364-1361 USA
E-mail: administration@livingwaterspc.com
Web site: http://www.livingwaterspc.com
Dist(s): **Lightning Source, Inc.**

Livingston Pr., *(978-0-930501; 978-0-942979; 978-1-931982; 978-1-60489)* Div. of Univ. Of West Alabama, Univ. of West Alabama, Sta. 22, Livingston, AL 35470 USA (SAN 851-917X) Tel 205-652-3470; Fax: 205-652-3717; Toll Free: 800-959-3245 Do not confuse with Livingston Pr., Anaheim, CA
E-mail: jwt@uwa.edu
Web site: http://www.livingstonpress.uwa.edu
Dist(s): **SPD-Small Pr. Distribution.**

Livingstone Corp., *(978-0-9724616)* 351 S. Main Pl. Suite 110, Carol Stream, IL 60188 USA Tel 630-871-1212; Fax: 630-871-1651
E-mail: accounting@livingstonecorp.com
Web site: http://www.livingstonecorp.com
Dist(s): **BookBaby.**

Livraria Martins Editora (BRA) *(978-85-336) Dist. by* **Distribks Inc.**

Liwayway Piano, *(978-0-615-75896-1)* 937 Del Negro Ct, South Plainfield, NJ 07080 USA Tel 732-306-6321
Dist(s): **CreateSpace Independent Publishing Platform.**

Lizard Library, *(978-0-615-58336-5)* 105 Brodhead Rd., West Shokan, NY 12494 USA Tel 845-657-6476; 914-678-9088
Dist(s): **CreateSpace Independent Publishing Platform.**

LizStar Bks, *(978-0-9779753)* 2648 Jolly Acres Rd., White Hall, MD 21161 USA Tel 410-557-9388
E-mail: tracy@lizstarbooks.com
Web site: http://www.lizstarbooks.com.

Lizzy Anne's Adventures, *(978-0-9845887; 978-0-9835168)* P.O. Box 97, Monrovia, MD 21770-0097 USA (SAN 859-8320)
Web site: http://www.lizzyannesadventures.com.

LJK Publishing LLC, *(978-0-9771476)* P.O. Box 993, Springer, NM 87747 USA Tel 505-483-2451 (fax as well - phone to turn on)
E-mail: chieftalkjaw@aol.com.

LJM Publishing, *(978-0-615-46906-5; 978-0-615-48518-8; 978-0-9897175; 978-0-615-92333-8; 978-0-9861946)* 2597 CR 2101, Palestine, TX 75801 USA Tel 214-956-5656; 817-703-1844
Web site: www.RachelsLittleQuoteBook.org
Dist(s): **CreateSpace Independent Publishing Platform**
Dummy Record Do Not USE!!!!.

Llama Pr., *(978-0-9857816)* 10128 Briargrove Way, Highlands Ranch, CO 80126 USA Tel 720-347-0771
E-mail: lbirchall@comcast.net.

†Llewellyn Pubns., *(978-0-7387; 978-0-87542; 978-1-56718)* Div. of Llewellyn Worldwide, Ltd., Orders Addr.: 2143 Wooddale Dr., Woodbury, MN 55125-2989 USA Tel 651-291-1970; Fax: 651-291-1908; Toll Free: 800-843-6666; *Imprints*: Midnight Ink (MidnightInk); Flux (Flux Llew)
E-mail: sales@llewellyn.com
Web site: http://www.llewellyn.com; http://www.midnightinkbooks.com
Dist(s): **Follett School Solutions**
Lectorum Pubns., Inc.
Libros Sin Fronteras
Llewellyn Worldwide Ltd.
New Leaf Distributing Co., Inc.
Partners/West Book Distributors
Perrone; *CIP.*

Llumina Christian Bks. *Imprint of* **Aeon Publishing Inc.**

Llumina Kids *Imprint of* **Aeon Publishing Inc.**

Llumina Pr. *Imprint of* **Aeon Publishing Inc.**

LM Digital, *(978-0-9760770)* 4501 Mirador Dr., Pleasanton, CA 94566-7435 USA
E-mail: luke@lm-digital.com
Web site: http://www.lm-digital.com.

LMS Bks., *(978-0-9764185)* 1007 Manor Dr., Ripon, CA 95366 USA Tel 209-599-4685.

LMW Works, *(978-1-889584)* 85 St. Michael Way NE., Hanceville, AL 35077 USA Tel 716-946-1060
E-mail: lynne@lmwworks.com; pviverito@yahoo.com
Web site: http://www.lmwworks.com.

LOA Quantum Growth LLC, *(978-0-9786158)* 7805 Tylerton Dr., Raleigh, NC 27613-1554 USA Tel 919-368-8041; Fax: 919-571-8769
E-mail: publisher@loaquantumgrowth.com
Web site: http://www.loaquantumgrowth.com
Dist(s): **AtlasBooks Distribution.**

Lobster Pr. (CAN) *(978-1-894222; 978-1-897073) Dist. by* **Orca Bk Pub.**

Local History Co., The, *(978-0-9711835; 978-0-9744715; 978-0-9770429)* Orders Addr.: 112 N. Woodland Rd., Pittsburgh, PA 15232 USA (SAN 257-5264); *Imprints*: Towers Maguire Publishing (Towers Mag)
E-mail: Sales@TheLocalHistoryCompany.com; Sales@TowersMaguire.com
Web site: http://www.TheLocalHistoryCompany.com; http://www.TowersMaguire.com
Dist(s): **AtlasBooks Distribution.**

Lock & Mane, *(978-0-615-20562-5; 978-0-615-30969-9; 978-0-615-62282-8)* 2012 Spring Garden St., No. 3, Philadelphia, PA 19130 USA.

Lockman, James Consulting, *(978-0-9759988)* P.O. Box 278, Gorham, ME 04038-0278 USA
E-mail: james@jameslockman.com
Web site: http://www.jameslockman.com.

Lockman, Vic, *(978-0-936175)* 233 Rogue River Hwy No. 360, Grants Pass, OR 97527 USA (SAN 697-2063) Fax: 541-472-1083
E-mail: vlockman@budget.net.

Lodestone Pr., *(978-0-9678922)* 17 Appleby Rd., Suite B-2, Wellesley, MA 02482 USA
E-mail: books@lodestone.nu
Web site: http://www.lodestone.nu.

Loew-Cornell, Inc., *(978-0-9776925; 978-0-9794445)* Div. of Jarden Corporation, 2834 Schoeneck Rd., Macungie, PA 18062-9679 USA
E-mail: joleary@loew-cornell.com
Web site: http://www.loew-cornell.com
Dist(s): **Watson-Guptill Pubns., Inc.**

Loewe Verlag GmbH (DEU) *(978-3-7855; 978-3-8390) Dist. by* **Distribks Inc.**

LOF Publishing, *(978-0-9764441)* Orders Addr.: 7500 Bellerive, Suite 412, Houston, TX 77036 USA Tel 832-251-6867
E-mail: pslam144ym@aol.com; info@lofpublishing.com
Web site: http://www.lofpublishing.com; http://www.mbridges05.com
Dist(s): **AtlasBooks Distribution.**

Log Cabin Bks., *(978-0-9755548; 978-0-9848911)* 6607 Craine Lake Rd., Hamilton, NY 13346 USA Tel 315-750-9157
Web site: http://www.logcabinbooks.us/; http://www.logcabinbooks.com/.

Logan Bks., *(978-0-9728691)* P.O. Box 21451, Columbia Heights, MN 55421 USA
Web site: http://www.loganbooks.com.

Logan Hse., *(978-0-9674123; 978-0-9769935)* Orders Addr.: Rte. 1, Box 154, Winside, NE 68790 USA Tel 402-286-4891; Edit Addr.: Rte. 1 Box 154, Winside, NE 68790 USA
E-mail: jim@loganhousepress.com
Web site: http://www.loganhousepress.com.

Logos Productions, Inc., *(978-0-9618891; 978-1-885361)* 6160 Carmen Ave., E., Inver Grove Heights, MN 55076-4422 USA Tel 612-451-9945; Fax: 612-457-4617; Toll Free: 800-328-0200 Do not confuse with Logos Productions, Carmel, CA
E-mail: lpstaff@mn.uswest.net
Web site: http://www.1logos.com.

LOGOS System Assocs., *(978-0-9727146; 978-0-9752605; 978-0-9768168)* 1405 Frey Rd., Pittsburgh, PA 15235 USA Tel 412-372-1341; Fax: 412-372-8447; Toll Free: 877-937-2572
E-mail: patjanssen@logos-system.org
Web site: http://www.logos-system.org.

Logos-Rhema Publishing *See* **Triumph Publishing**

Lollipop Media Productions, LP, *(978-0-9815111; 978-0-9824926; 978-0-9909073)* 3600 S. Harbor Blvd. Apt No. 81 Apt. No. 81, Channel Islands Harbor, CA 93035 USA
E-mail: Suzy@keopu.com.

Lollipop Publishing, LLC, *(978-0-9709793; 978-1-931737)* P.O. Box 6354, Chesterfield, MO 63006-6354 USA Tel 314-434-6011; Fax: 314-434-6040; Toll Free: 800-383-7767
E-mail: jbenigas@aol.com
Web site: http://www.lollipoppublishing.com.

Lollipop Publishing, LLC, *(978-0-615-30165-5)* 10710 Moore Cir., Westminster, CO 80021 USA.

Loma, LLC, *(978-0-9769460)* 6 Bryan Valley Ct., O'Fallon, MO 63366-3465 USA
E-mail: dudleytg@aol.com.

London Town Pr., *(978-0-9666490; 978-0-9766134; 978-0-9799759)* 2026 Hilldale Dr., La Canada, CA 91011 USA
E-mail: martin@londontownpress.com
Web site: http://www.londontownpress.com
Dist(s): **Perseus-PGW.**

Lone Butte Pr., *(978-0-9666860; 978-0-9893518)* 32 S. Fork Extended, Santa Fe, NM 87508 USA Tel 505-424-3574; Fax: 505-473-1227
E-mail: wilddogbooks@cnsp.com
Dist(s): **Wild Dog Bks.**

Lone Cypress Pubs., *(978-0-9741413)* 3588 Hwy. 138 S.E., No. 193, Stockbridge, GA 30281 USA Tel 404-421-7445
E-mail: graysenwalles@yahoo.com
Web site: http://www.lonecypresspublishers.com.

Lone Loon Pr., *(978-0-615-78952-1; 978-0-692-44528-0)* 145 E. Shore Dr., Adirondack, NY 12808 USA Tel 518-494-5792
Web site: www.joannflammer.com
Dist(s): **CreateSpace Independent Publishing Platform.**

Lone Oak Pr., Ltd. *Imprint of* **Finney Co., Inc.**

Lone Pine Publishing USA, *(978-0-919433; 978-1-55105)* Orders Addr.: 1808 B St., NW Suite 140, Auburn, WA 98001 USA (SAN 859-0427) Tel 253-394-0400; Fax: 253-394-0405; Toll Free Fax: 800-548-1169; Toll Free: 800-518-3541; *Imprints*: Ghost House Books (Ghost Hse Bks)
E-mail: mikec@lonepinepublishing.com
Web site: http://www.lonepinepublishing.com; http://www.companyscoming.com/; http://overtimebooks.com; http://www.folklorepublishing.com/.

Lone Star Pubns., *(978-0-9766157)* P.O. Box 810872, Dallas, TX 75381 USA Do not confuse with Lone Star Publication in Dallas, TX
E-mail: info@lonestarpublications.com
Web site: http://www.lonestarpublications.com.

Lone Star Publishing Co., *(978-0-9777274)* 906 SW St., Lucie W. Blvd., Port Saint Lucie, FL 34986 USA Tel 772-486-3214; Fax: 772-785-8496 do not confuse with companies with the same name in Paradise, TX, Amarillo, TX, Bryan, TX.

Lone Wolf Productions *See* **Canis Lupus Productions**

Lonejack Mountain Pr., *(978-0-9729101)* P.O. Box 28424, Bellingham, WA 98228-0424 USA.

Lonely Planet Pubns., *(978-1-55992)* Orders Addr.: 150 Linden St., Oakland, CA 94607 USA (SAN 659-6541) Tel 510-893-8555; Fax: 510-893-8572; Toll Free: 800-275-8555 (orders, 9am - 5pm Pacific Time)
E-mail: orders@lonelyplanet.com; customerservice@lonelyplanet.com
Web site: http://www.lonelyplanet.com.

Lonely Swan Bks. *Imprint of* **Cosmic Gargoyle Creative Solutions**

Lonestar Abilene Publishing *Imprint of* **LoneStar Abilene Publishing, LLC**

LoneStar Abilene Publishing, LLC, *(978-0-9749725)* 402 Cedar St., Suite 208, Abilene, TX 79601 USA Tel 325-676-9800; Fax: 325-676-2790; *Imprints*: Lonestar Abilene Publishing (LoneStarAbil)
E-mail: michael@yrbks.com
Web site: http://www.yrbks.com/LoneStar.html.

Long Beach City Schl. District, *(978-0-9677925)* 235 Lido Blvd., Lido Beach, NY 11561 USA Tel 516-897-2104; Fax: 516-897-2107
E-mail: RLF@li.net.

Long Dash Publishing, *(978-1-59899)* 49 Orchard St., Hackensack, NJ 07601-4806 USA
E-mail: longdash@gmail.com
Web site: http://www.longdash.com.

Long Life Publishing Co., *(978-0-9725836)* P.O. Box 1564, Escondido, CA 92033 USA.

Long Riders' Guild Pr., The, *(978-1-59048)* 2201 Coyle Ln., Walla Walla, WA 99362-8873 USA
E-mail: longriders@thelongridersguild.com
Web site: http://www.thelongridersguild.com.

Long Stories LLC, *(978-0-615-15295-0; 978-0-615-18961-1)* N3865 County Rd. H, Lake Geneva, WI 53147 USA
E-mail: chad@lycanjournal.com
Web site: http://www.lycanjournal.com.

Long Stride Books, *(978-0-615-56178-3; 978-0-9857836)* 1471 James Rd., Weybridge, VT 05753 USA
Dist(s): **CreateSpace Independent Publishing Platform**
Independent Pubs. Group
MyiLibrary.

Longevity Publishing, LLC, *(978-0-9777323)* Orders Addr.: 10179 E. Pinewood Ave., Englewood, CO 80111 USA Tel 720-489-7243
E-mail: info@longevitypublishing.com
Web site: http://www.longevitypublishing.com
Dist(s): **Partners Bk. Distributing, Inc.**

LongHill Partners, Inc., *(978-0-943763; 978-1-58023; 978-1-879045; 978-1-893361; 978-1-59473; 978-0-9904152)* P.O. Box 237, Woodstock, VT 05091 USA; *Imprints*: Jewish Lights Publishing (JewishLights); Skylight Paths Publishing (SkylightPaths)
E-mail: production@longhillpartners.com
Dist(s): **Ingram Pub. Services.**

Longhorn Creek Pr., *(978-0-9714358; 978-0-9764026; 978-0-615-99574-8)* 3780 County Road 4317., De Kalb, TX 75559-5681 USA
E-mail: editor@longhorncreekpress.com; Ron@longhorncreekpress.com
Web site: http://www.longhorncreekpress.com
Dist(s): **Wilson & Assocs.**

Longman Publishing, *(978-0-02; 978-0-06; 978-0-13; 978-0-201; 978-0-205; 978-0-321; 978-0-582; 978-0-673; 978-0-7248; 978-0-8013; 978-1-57322; 978-0-7339)* 75 Arlington St., Boston, MA 02116 USA Tel 617-848-7500
Web site: http://www.aw-bc.com
Dist(s): **Giron Bks.**
Libros Sin Fronteras
Pearson Education.

†Longman Publishing Group, *(978-0-13; 978-0-201; 978-0-321; 978-0-582; 978-0-8013)* Div. of Addison Wesley Longman, Inc., The Longman Bldg.; 10 Bank St., White Plains, NY 10606-1951 USA (SAN 202-6856) Tel 914-993-5000; Fax: 914-997-8115 800-922-0579 (college, bkstores, customer service only)
Web site: http://www.pearsonlongman.com
Dist(s): **Coronet Bks.**
Giron Bks.
MyiLibrary
Pearson Education
Pearson Technology Group
Sourcebooks, Inc.
Trans-Atlantic Pubns., Inc.; *CIP.*

Longoria, Eugene R., *(978-0-9796818)* 2222 W. Central Ave., Coolidge, AZ 85228 USA (SAN 854-1116)
E-mail: ElJunior@ElJunior.com
Web site: http://eljunior.com; http://eugenelongoria.com.

Longs Peak Publishing, Incorporated *See* **Crossing Guard Bks., LLC**

Longseller S.A. (ARG) *(978-987-550; 978-987-9481; 978-987-98516) Dist. by* **Bilingual Pubns.**

Longseller S.A. (ARG) *(978-987-550; 978-987-9481; 978-987-98516) Dist. by* **Libros Fronteras.**

LongTale Publishing, LLC, *(978-0-9818054; 978-0-9854705; 978-1-941515)* P.O. Box 266597, Houston, TX 77207-6597 USA Fax: 713-896-9701
Web site: http://www.iggytheiguana.com.

Look Again Pr., LLC, *(978-0-9801113)* 2461 Mountain Vista Dr., Birmingham, AL 35243 USA (SAN 855-2266) Tel 205-823-8556
Web site: www.lookagainpress.com
Dist(s): **CreateSpace Independent Publishing Platform.**

Look, Learn & Do Pubns., *(978-1-893327)* 24 Highland Blvd., Kensington, CA 94707 USA Fax: 510-524-7577
E-mail: professor@lldkids.com
Web site: http://www.looklearnanddo.com
Dist(s): **Ten Speed Pr.**

Look-About Bks., *(978-0-9800208)* P.O. Box 1907, Nampa, ID 83653 USA (SAN 854-9869) Tel 208-466-6260
E-mail: lpowersraptor@msn.com
Web site: http://www.look-aboutbooks.com.

Looking Glass Library *Imprint of* **ABDO Publishing Co.**

Looking Glass Library *Imprint of* **Magic Wagon**

Looking Glass Library- Nonfiction *Imprint of* **Magic Wagon**

Loonfeather Pr., *(978-0-926147)* Orders Addr.: P.O. Box 1212, Bemidji, MN 56619 USA
E-mail: books@loonfeatherpress.com
Web site: http://www.loonfeatherpress.com.

Loose Change, *(978-0-9744707)* 936 Sixth St., Los Banos, CA 93635 USA (SAN 244-9692) Tel 209-826-3797; Fax: 209-826-1514
E-mail: nco4242@sbcglobal.net.

Loose In The Lab, *(978-0-9660965; 978-1-931801)* 9462 S. 560 W., Sandy, UT 84070 USA Tel 801-568-9596; Fax: 801-568-9586; Toll Free: 888-403-1189
E-mail: mail@looseinthelab.com
Web site: http://www.looseinthelab.com.

Loose Leaves Publishing, *(978-1-62432)* 4218 E. Allison Rd, Tucson, AZ 85712 USA Tel 520-310-7528
E-mail: Talminia@gmail.com.

Looseleaf Law Pubns., Inc., *(978-0-930137; 978-1-889031; 978-1-932777; 978-1-60885)* Orders Addr.: P.O. Box 650042, Fresh Meadows, NY 11365-0042 USA Tel 718-359-5559; Fax: 718-539-0941; Toll Free: 800-647-5547
E-mail: info@looseleaflaw.com; lynette@looseleaflaw.com
Web site: http://www.looseleaflaw.com.

Loosey Goosey Pr., *(978-0-9820991)* 120 Daven Dr., Hopkinsville, KY 42240 USA (SAN 857-2623)
Web site: http://www.ganderpress.com.

Lopez, David, *(978-0-9744097)* 3441 Twinberry Ct., Bonita Springs, FL 34134 USA Tel 239-947-2532 (phone/fax)
E-mail: jazzpop@aol.com
Web site: http://www.maddiesmagicmarkers.com.

Loquacious Publishing Co., *(978-0-9763811)* 2115 Wintermere Pointe Dr., Winter Garden, FL 34787-5439 USA.

Lorenz Corp., The, *(978-0-7877; 978-0-88335; 978-0-89328; 978-1-55863; 978-1-57310; 978-1-885564; 978-1-4291)* 501 E. Third St., Dayton, OH 45401-0802 USA (SAN 208-7413) Tel 937-228-6118; Fax: 937-223-2042; Toll Free: 800-444-1144
E-mail: service@lorenz.com
Web site: http://www.lorenz.com.

Lorian Assn., The, *(978-0-936878)* P.O. Box 1368, Issaquah, WA 98027 USA (SAN 666-6663) Tel 425-427-9071
E-mail: info@lorian.org
Web site: http://www.lorian.org.

Lorian Press *See* **Lorian Assn., The**

Lorimer, James & Co., Ltd., Pubs. (CAN) *(978-0-88862; 978-1-55028; 978-1-65277; 978-1-4594)* *Dist. by* **Casemate Pubs.**

Lorito Bks., Inc., *(978-0-9815686; 978-0-9842981; 978-0-9835197; 978-0-9883561; 978-0-9904930)* 10395 W. 74th Pl., Arvada, CO 80005 USA (SAN 855-8876) Fax: 303-425-3277; Toll Free: 800-420-6936
Web site: http://www.loritobooks.com
Dist(s): **Follett School Solutions.**

Lormax Communications, *(978-0-9641239)* P.O. Box 40304, Raleigh, NC 27629 USA Tel 919-878-9108.

Los Alamos Historical Society Publications *See* **Bathtub Row Pr.**

Los Andes Publishing Co., *(978-0-9637065; 978-1-57159)* P.O. Box 190, Chino Hills, CA 91709 USA Tel 562-789-1540; Toll Free: 800-532-8872
E-mail: losandes@losandes.com
Web site: http://www.losandes.com
Dist(s): **Lectorum Pubns., Inc.**

Los Perros Publishing Co., *(978-0-9764685)* 3565 Parches Cove, Union Grove, AL 35175-8422 USA
E-mail: jr@losperros.com; mrgsd@hiwaay.net
Web site: http://www.mrgsd.com.

Losantiville Pr., Inc., *(978-0-9794946)* Orders Addr.: P.O. Box 42604, Cincinnati, OH 45242-6040 USA; Edit Addr.: 7012 Beech Hollow Dr., Cincinnati, OH 45236 USA
E-mail: losantivillepress@fuse.net.

Lost Candy Bar Pr., LLC, *(978-0-9786794)* P.O. Box 5193, Madison, WI 53705-0193 USA Tel 608-233-5690; Fax: 608-231-2312
Web site: http://www.lostcandybarpress.com.

Lost Classic Bks.,
Dist(s): **National Bk. Network.**

Lost Classics Bk. Co., *(978-0-9652735; 978-1-890623)* Orders Addr.: P.O. Box 1756, Fort Collins, CO 80522 USA Tel 970-493-3793 (Distribution Center); Toll Free Fax: 888-211-2665 (Libraries & Schools); Toll Free: 888-611-2665 (credit card orders only); Edit Addr.: P.O. Box 3429, Lake Wales, FL 33859-3429 USA Tel 863-678-3149; Fax: 863-678-0802
E-mail: mgeditor@lostclassicsbooks.com
Web site: http://lcbcbooks.com; http://www.lcbcbooks.com/homeright.htm
Dist(s): **National Bk. Network.**

Lost Coast Pr., *(978-1-882897; 978-1-935448)* 155 Cypress St., Fort Bragg, CA 95437 USA Tel 707-964-9520; Fax: 707-964-7531; Toll Free: 800-773-7782
E-mail: forms@cypresshouse.com
Web site: http://www.cypresshouse.com
Dist(s): **Continental Bk. Co., Inc.**
Cypress Hse.
New Leaf Distributing Co., Inc.
Partners/West Book Distributors.

Lost Hills Bks., *(978-0-9798535)* P.O. Box 3054, Duluth, MN 55803 USA (SAN 854-5553)
Web site: http://www.losthillsbks.com.

Lost Lake Pr., *(978-0-9906450)* N7130 N. Lost Lake Rd., Randolph, WI 53956 USA Tel 920-326-5554
E-mail: LostLakePress@gmail.com
Web site: http://www.LostLakePress.com.

Lost Scout Pr., *(978-0-9741310)* P.O. Box 86, Loveland, OH 45140-0086 USA (SAN 255-7193) Fax: 719-457-5952; 1283 Sand Trap Ct., Loveland, OH 45140-6060
E-mail: hq@lostscout.com
Web site: http://www.lostscout.com.

Lotti, Marc, *(978-1-932341)* P.O. Box 5841, Carefree, AZ 85377-5841 USA
E-mail: mlotti@mandragore.com

Lotus Art Works Inc., *(978-0-9800637)* 11833 Mississippi Ave., Suite 200, Los Angeles, CA 90025 USA Tel 310-442-3335.

Lotus Blossom Bks., *(978-0-9801414)* 1220 Rosecrans St., No. 325, San Diego, CA 92106 USA (SAN 855-3181) Tel 619-224-7771
E-mail: publisher@lotusblossombooks.com
Web site: http://www.lotusblossombooks.com
Dist(s): **BookBaby.**

Lotus Lights Publications *See* **Lotus Pr.**

Lotus Petal Publishing, *(978-0-9787672; 978-0-9820949)* Div. of Lotus Petal, P.O. Box 1394, Nashville, IN 47448-1394 USA Tel 812-988-1250; Toll Free Fax: 800-867-4851
E-mail: info@lotuspetalpublishing.com
Web site: http://www.lotuspetalpublishing.com.

Lotus Pond Media, *(978-0-9791021)* 176 Broadway, Suite 9C, New York, NY 10038 USA Tel 212-608-3329
E-mail: scgrant@goatkids.net; scgrant@customerresearchcenter.com
Web site: http://www.goatkids.net; http://www.highimpactquality.com.

Lotus Pr., *(978-0-910261; 978-0-914955; 978-0-940676; 978-0-940985; 978-0-941524; 978-1-60869)* Div. of Lotus Brands, Inc., P.O. Box 325, Twin Lakes, WI 53181 USA (SAN 239-1120) Tel 262-889-2461; Fax: 262-889-8591; Toll Free: 800-824-6396 Do not confuse with companies with the same or similar name in Lotus, CA, Westerville, OH, Bokeelia, FL, Brattleboro, VT, Detroit, MI, Tobyhanna, PA
E-mail: lotuspress@lotuspress.com
Web site: http://www.lotuspress.com
Dist(s): **National Bk. Network.**

Lotus Publications *See* **Johnson, Earl Photography**

Louck, Cheryl, *(978-0-9744230)* 2708 Avalon Ln., Montgomery, IL 60538 USA Tel 630-853-0653
Web site: http://www.cheryllouck.com.

Loucks-Christenson Publishing, *(978-1-59819; 978-0-9771365)* 4125 E. Frontage Rd NW, Rochester, MN 55901 USA Tel 866-562-5125; Toll Free: 866-562-5125; *Imprints:* Waiting Room to Heaven (Wait Room Hvn)
E-mail: lisawatts@gmail.com
Web site: http://www.catalog.louckschristenson.com
Dist(s): **Ecompass Business Ctr.**

Loughton Bks., *(978-0-9704974)* 101 W. 23rd St., New York, KS 37215 USA Do not confuse with companies with similar names in Newport, RI, San Diego, CA, Mary Esther, FL,
E-mail: mbraden@loghtonbooks.com
Web site: http://www.loughtonbooks.com.

Louisiana Ladybug Pr., *(978-0-9753435)* 210 Pinecrest Rd., Arcadia, LA 71001 USA
Web site: http://www.LouisianaPotpourriFromAtoZ.com.

†Louisiana State Univ. Pr., *(978-0-8071)* 3990 W. Lakeshore Dr., Baton Rouge, LA 70808 USA Tel 225-578-6294; Fax: 225-578-6461; Toll Free Fax: 800-272-6817; Toll Free: 800-848-6224
E-mail: lsupress@lsu.edu
Web site: http://lsupress.org/
Dist(s): **Ebsco Publishing**
ebrary, Inc.; *CIP.*

Love & Blessings, *(978-0-9644765)* P.O. Box 55116, Valencia, CA 91385 USA Tel 661-288-1711; Toll Free: 800-906-3629
E-mail: vloveland@babybonding.com; vloveland@earthlink.net
Web site: http://www.babybonding.com
Dist(s): **New Leaf Distributing Co., Inc.**

Love Bug Bks., *(978-0-9787174)* 1117 Ariana Rd., Suite 102, San Marcos, CA 92069-8122 USA Tel 760-798-9415; Fax: 760-798-9415
E-mail: rolwink@cox.net
Web site: http://www.lovebugbooks.com.

Love Cultivating Editions, *(978-0-9744999)* 2665 Reed Rd., Hood River, OR 97031-9609 USA
Web site: http://www.lovecultivatingeditions.com.

Love II Learn Bks., *(978-0-9796679)* 860 Johnson Ferry Rd., Suite 140-345, Atlanta, GA 30342 USA (SAN 854-0535) Tel 404-808-0458
Web site: http://www.booksbykobie.com; http://www.loveiilearbooks.com
Dist(s): **BookMasters, Inc.**

Love Ink LLC, *(978-1-940426)* Orders Addr.: 4625 Hinsdale Way No. 399, Colorado Springs, CO 80917 USA Tel 913-575-3572
E-mail: Love_Ink_LLC@yahoo.com.

Love Language Pubns., *(978-0-9749924)* 2111 E. Santa Fe, No. 268, Olathe, KS 66062 USA
E-mail: anne@lovelanguageforbabies.com
Web site: http://www.lovelanguageforbabies.com.

Love Your Life, *(978-0-9664806; 978-0-9798554; 978-0-9820477)* Orders Addr.: P.O. Box 2, Red Lion, PA 17356 USA (SAN 256-1387) Tel 717-200-2852; Fax: 310-496-0716; Edit Addr.: 755 Conndly Dr., Red Lion, PA 17356 USA Tel 717-200-2852; Fax: 310-496-0716
E-mail: publish@loveyourlife.com
Web site: http://www.loveyourlife.com
Dist(s): **Ingram Pub. Services.**

Loveland Pr., LLC, *(978-0-9662696; 978-0-9744851)* P.O. Box 7001, Loveland, CO 80537-0001 USA Tel 970-593-9557 Toll Free: 800-593-9557
E-mail: info@lovelandpress.com
Web site: http://www.lovelandpress.com.

LoveLight Media, *(978-0-9893181)* 216 Regina Dr., Fort Collins, CO 80525 USA Tel 970-218-2592
E-mail: Deidre@lovelightmedia.com
Web site: None yet.

Love's Creative Resources, *(978-1-929548)* Orders Addr.: P.O. Box 44306, Charlotte, NC 28215 USA Tel 704-563-7469
E-mail: mjet64@aol.com; ml9734@yahoo.com.

Loving Guidance, Inc., *(978-1-889609)* P.O. Box 622407, Oviedo, FL 32762 USA Tel 407-366-0233; 407-977-8862; Fax: 407-366-4293; Toll Free: 800-842-2846; 50 Smith St., Oviedo, FL 32765-9608
E-mail: bryan@lovingguidance.com; kate@lovingguidance.com; becky.bailey@consciousdiscipline.com
Web site: http://www.beckybailey.com; http://www.consciousdiscipline.com
Dist(s): **Gryphon Hse., Inc.**

Loving Healing Pr., Inc., *(978-1-932690; 978-1-61599)* 5145 Pontiac Trail, Ann Arbor, MI 48105-9279 USA (SAN 255-7770) Tel 734-662-6864; Fax: 734-663-6861; Toll Free: 888-761-6268; *Imprints:* Marvelous Spirit Press (MarvelousSpir)
E-mail: info@lovinghealing.com
Web site: http://www.beyondtrauma.com/; http://www.TurtleDolphinDreams.com; http://www.TIRbook.com; http://www.LifeSkillsBook.com; http://www.VictorianHeritage.com; http://www.PhysicalLoss.com; http://www.gotparts.org; http://www.lovinghealing.com/
Dist(s): **New Leaf Distributing Co., Inc.**
Quality Bks., Inc.
ebrary, Inc.

Lovstad, Joel Publishing, *(978-0-9749058)* 701 Henry St., No. 203, Waunakee, WI 53597 USA
E-mail: jlfred@chorus.net
Web site: http://www.joellovstad-books.com.

Low Fat Express, Incorporated *See* **Learning ZoneXpress**

†Lowell Hse., *(978-0-7373; 978-0-8092; 978-0-929923; 978-1-56565)* 2020 Avenue of the Stars, Suite 300, Los Angeles, CA 90067-4704 USA (SAN 250-863X) Tel 310-552-7555; Fax: 310-552-7573
Dist(s): **Independent Pubs. Group**
McGraw-Hill Trade; *CIP.*

Lowell Hse. Juvenile, *(978-0-7373; 978-0-929923; 978-1-56565)* 2020 Avenue of the Stars, No. 300, Los Angeles, CA 90067 USA Tel 310-552-7555; Fax: 310-552-7573; *Imprints:* Roxbury Park Juvenile (Roxbury Pk Juvenile)
Dist(s): **McGraw-Hill Trade.**

†Lowell Pr., The, Gallion Communications, *(978-0-913504; 978-0-932845)* Orders Addr.: P.O. Box 411877, Kansas City, MO 64141-1877 USA (SAN 207-0774) Tel 816-753-4545; Fax: 816-753-4057; Toll Free: 800-736-7660 Do not confuse with Lowell Pr. in Eugene, OR
E-mail: plowell@accessus.net; sales@thelowellpress.com
Web site: http://www.thelowellpress.com; *CIP.*

Lowell, Shelley, *(978-0-9765344)* Orders Addr.: c/o Montage Gallery, 925 South Charles St., Baltimore, MD 21230 USA.

Lower Kuskokwim Schl. District, *(978-1-58084)* Orders Addr.: P.O. Box 305, Bethel, AK 99559 USA Tel 907-543-4928; Fax: 907-543-4935
E-mail: catalog@fc.lksd-do.org
Web site: http://www.lksd.org/catalog.

Lower Lane Publishing LLC, *(978-0-9797790)* 2105 Carehill Rd., Vienna, VA 22181 USA.

†Loyola Pr., *(978-0-8294)* 3441 N. Ashland Ave., Chicago, IL 60657 USA (SAN 211-6537) Tel 773-281-1818; Fax: 773-281-0555; Toll Free: 800-621-1008
E-mail: customerservice@loyolapress.com
Web site: http://www.loyolabooks.org
Dist(s): **Spring Arbor Distributors, Inc.**; *CIP.*

L.Patrick Publishing, *(978-0-9774418)* 2710 W. 76th St., Inglewood, CA 90305 USA.

LPD Pr., *(978-0-9641542; 978-1-890689; 978-1-936744; 978-1-943681)* 925 Salamanca, NW, Los Ranchos, NM 87107-5647 USA Tel 505-344-9382; Fax: 505-345-5129; *Imprints:* Rio Grande Books (Rio Grande Bks)
E-mail: info@nmsantos.com
Web site: http://www.nmsantos.com
Dist(s): **Smashwords.**

LRS, *(978-1-58118)* 14214 S. Figueroa St., Los Angeles, CA 90061-1034 USA Tel 310-354-2610; Fax: 310-354-2601; Toll Free: 800-255-5002
E-mail: lrsprint@aol.com
Web site: http://www.lrs-largeprint.com
Dist(s): **Beeler, Thomas T. Pub.**

LSG Pubns., *(978-1-933532)* 29165 Clover Ln., Big Pine Key, FL 33043-6046 USA
E-mail: lisagaljanic@optonline.net
Web site: http://www.lsgpublications.com.

LSP *Imprint of* **LSP Digital, LLC**

LSP Digital, LLC, *(978-0-9792030; 978-0-9800733; 978-0-9817654)* P.O. Box 851556, Westland, MI 48185 USA Tel 734-355-3733; Fax: 734-261-0155; *Imprints:* LSP (LSP USA)
E-mail: admin@lspdigital.com
Web site: http://www.lspdigital.com.

LTI Publishing, *(978-0-9743048)* Div. of Let's Talk Interactive, Inc., P.O. Box 371, Huntersville, NC 28070 USA
E-mail: art@LTIPublishing.net
Web site: http://www.letstalkinterctive.com; http://www.FathersTouch.com; http://www.SexualAbuse.ws; http://www.ChildHoodItShouldNotHurt.com; http://www.ChildHoodShouldNotHurt.com; http://www.AgainstSexualAbuse.org; http://www.LetsTalkCounseling.com.

LTL Media LLC, *(978-0-9785744)* P.O. Box 12766, Tempe, AZ 85284 USA
Web site: http://www.mylittlethinkers.com.

Lu, Melissa Productions, *(978-0-9726832)* 5356 Rose Ridge Ln., Colorado Springs, CO 80917 USA Fax: 719-594-6993
E-mail: patsy@melissalu.com
Web site: http://www.melissalu.com.

Lua Publishing, *(978-0-9746304)* P.O. Box 3250, Fairfield, CA 94533 USA Tel 707-426-9480
E-mail: info@luapublishing.com
Web site: http://www.luapublishing.com
Dist(s): **New Leaf Distributing Co., Inc.**

Luath Pr. Ltd. (GBR) *(978-0-946487; 978-1-84282; 978-1-905222; 978-1-906307; 978-1-906817; 978-1-908373; 978-1-910021)* *Dist. by* **Midpt Trade.**

Luath Pr. Ltd. (GBR) *(978-0-946487; 978-1-84282; 978-1-905222; 978-1-906307; 978-1-906817; 978-1-908373; 978-1-910021)* *Dist. by* **IngramPubServ.**

Lubbers, Theresa *See* **Mr. Emmett Publishing**

Lucas Co., *(978-0-9715916)* P.O. Box 9245, Moscow, ID 83843 USA
Web site: http://www.lucasco.com.

Lucas Enterprises, *(978-0-9770611)* P.O. Box 9201, Chico, CA 95927 USA
E-mail: lucasent1@earthlink.net.

Lucas, Mattie, *(978-0-9762456)* P.O. Box 47070, Windsor Mills, MD 21244 USA Fax: 410-944-2597
E-mail: bishop@digc.org.

Lucas Violet *Imprint of* **Clocktower Hill Research & Publishing Group, LLC**

†Luce, Robert B. Pubs., *(978-0-88331)* Owned by Renaisance Book Services Corp., 2490 Black Rock Tpke., Fairfield, CT 06432 USA Tel 203-372-0300; Fax: 203-374-4766; Toll Free: 800-786-5427
E-mail: info@aslanpublishing.com
Web site: http://www.aslanpublishing.com
Dist(s): **APG Sales & Distribution Services**; *CIP.*

Lucent Bks. *Imprint of* **Cengage Gale**

Lucent Interpretations, LLC, *(978-0-9787849; 978-1-935146)* P.O. Box 3931, Lisle, IL 60532-8831 USA (SAN 856-6364)
E-mail: salmahammad@hotmail.com.

Lucia Pubs., *(978-0-9762297)* Orders Addr.: P.O. Box 3, Churubusco, IN 46723-0003 USA Tel 260-693-0852; Fax: 260-693-0082; Edit Addr.: 209C S. Main St., Churubusco, IN 46723 USA
E-mail: diannegg@peoplepc.com; giannakeff@iquest.net
Web site: http://www.luciapublishers.com.

Lucky & Me Productions, Inc., *(978-0-9721256; 978-0-615-71754-8)* Orders Addr.: 410 East 74th St., 6H, New York, NY 10021-3918 USA (SAN 255-0873) Tel 212-288-7203; Fax: 401-783-7815 call before faxing/not always on
E-mail: writermyst@aol.com
Web site: http://www.dearjohnlennon.com.

Lucky Bamboo Crafts, *(978-0-9884648)* P.O. Box 1022, Yarmouth, ME 04096 USA Tel 207-310-8101
E-mail: info@luckybamboocrafts.com
Web site: http://www.luckybamboocrafts.com
Dist(s): **Independent Pubs. Group.**

Lucky Duck Designs, *(978-0-9790632)* P.O. Box 2192, Petaluma, CA 94953-2192 USA
E-mail: stuart@lucky-duck.com
Web site: http://www.lucky-duck.com.

Lucky Publications *See* **Covered Wagon Publishing LLC**

Lucky Red Pr., LLC, *(978-0-9790690)* 10061 Riverside Dr., Suite 812, Toluca Lake, CA 91602 USA Tel 818-795-2388; Fax: 818-566-4995
E-mail: Susan@frankiespals.com
Web site: http://www.frankiespals.com.

Lucky 3 Ranch, Inc., *(978-1-928624)* 2457 S. County Rd. 19, Loveland, CO 80537-9044 USA Tel 970-663-0066; Fax: 970-663-0676; Toll Free: 800-816-7566
E-mail: meredith@luckythreeranch.com
Web site: http://www.luckythreeranch.com/
Dist(s): **MediaTech Productions.**

LuckySports, *(978-0-935938)* 39844 Somerset Ave., Palm Desert, CA 92211 USA (SAN 213-7453) Tel 760-861-2174 (cell)
E-mail: chuck@LuckySports.net
Web site: http://www.bogiegolf.com; http://www.sportcartoonbooks.com; http://www.LuckySports.net
Dist(s): **AtlasBooks Distribution.**

Lucy Rose Publishing LLC, *(978-0-9789386; 978-0-9821936)* P.O. Box 3034, Fort Polk, LA 71459 USA
E-mail: admin@lucyrosepublishing.com
Web site: http://www.lucyrosepublishing.com.

Lueck Studios, *(978-0-9774547)* 8353 11th Ave. NW, Seattle, WA 98117 USA (SAN 257-6023)
E-mail: jenny@lueckstudios.com
Web site: http://www.chicabee.com
Dist(s): **BookMasters, Inc.**

Luke & Lori Bks., *(978-0-9747792)* Orders Addr.: 5908 90th St., Lubbock, TX 79424 USA Tel 806-783-9941; Fax: 806-783-3099
E-mail: Melissa@lukeandlori.com
Web site: http://www.LukeAndLori.com.

Lulilite Productions, *(978-0-9759631)* P.O. Box 20847, Sedona, AZ 86341-0847 USA Tel 928-284-5442 (phone/fax)
E-mail: ariamagi@npgcable.com
Web site: http://www.lulilites.com.

Lulu Enterprises Inc., *(978-1-4116; 978-1-84728; 978-1-4303; 978-1-4357; 978-1-60552; 978-0-557; 978-1-4583; 978-1-257; 978-1-105; 978-1-300; 978-1-4834; 978-1-304; 978-1-312; 978-1-329)* 3101 Hillsborough St., Raleigh, NC 27607 USA; 26-28 Hammersmith Grove, London, W6 7BA Tel 0208 834 1020
E-mail: sparker@lulu.com
Dist(s): **Booklines Hawaii, Ltd.**
Copyright Clearance Ctr., Inc.
CreateSpace Independent Publishing Platform
Lightning Source, Inc.
Smashwords
Valjean Pr.

Lulu.com *See* **Lulu Enterprises Inc.**

Lulu.com (GBR) *(978-1-84753; 978-1-4092; 978-1-4461; 978-1-4457; 978-1-4452; 978-1-84799; 978-1-4476; 978-1-4466; 978-1-4467; 978-1-4475; 978-1-4477; 978-1-4478; 978-1-4709; 978-1-4710; 978-1-291; 978-1-4717; 978-1-4716; 978-1-326)* *Dist. by* **LuluCom.**

Lumen (ARG) *(978-950-724; 978-950-9017; 978-987-00)* *Dist. by* **Lectorum Pubns.**

LUMEN-US Pubns., *(978-0-9703611; 978-0-9787788; 978-0-9794862; 978-0-9815359; 978-0-9819935; 978-1-936405)* 234 Main St., Park Forest, IL 60466-2098 USA Toll Free: 866-219-9637
E-mail: Lumenuspubl@aol.com
Web site: http://www.lumen-us.com
Dist(s): **BookBaby.**

Lumina Pr. LLC, *(978-0-9708442)* P.O. Box 1106, Wrightsville Beach, NC 28480-1106 USA Do not confuse with Lumina Press in Springfield, MO
E-mail: david@luminapress.com.

Luminary Media Group *Imprint of* **Pine Orchard, Inc.**

Luminations Media Group, Inc., *(978-0-9821199; 978-1-61222)* P.O. Box 538, Monterey Park, CA 91754 USA Tel 626-571-0115
E-mail: office@luminationsmedia.com
Web site: http://www.LuminationsMedia.com.

Luminis Bks., Inc., *(978-1-935462; 978-1-941311)* 13245 Blacktern Way, Carmel, IN 46033 USA (SAN 857-8125) Tel 317-250-9539
E-mail: publisher@luminisbooks.com
Web site: http://www.luminisbooks.com
Dist(s): **Independent Pubs. Group**
MyiLibrary
ebrary, Inc.

Lumpkin, Carol *See* **Peace Rug Company, Inc., The**

Luna Publishing, *(978-0-9791785)* Orders Addr.: 5815 82nd St., No. 145, PMB 137, Lubbock, TX 79424 USA Tel 806-687-3479; Fax: 806-687-3401 Do not confuse with Luna PUblishing Company in Los Angeles, CA
E-mail: ccrmgr2@nts-online.net
Web site: http://www.lunapublish.com.

Luna, Rachel Nickerson *See* **Howard, Emma Bks.**

Luna Rising *Imprint of* **Northland Publishing**

Lunar Donut Pr., *(978-0-9725638)* P.O. Box 692625, Orlando, FL 32869 USA Tel 407-298-7779; Fax: 407-298-7779
E-mail: caricatureconnection@cfl.rr.com
Web site: http://www.caricatureconnection.com.

Publisher Name Index

Lunasea Studios, *(978-0-9799290)* 9450 Mira Mesa Blvd., Suite B-107, San Diego, CA 92126 USA
Web site: http://www.lunasea-studios.com/.

Lunatic Pr., *(978-0-9772590)* P.O. Box 4571, West Hills, CA 91308 USA
Web site: http://www.lunaticpress.com
Dist(s): **Independent Pubs. Group.**

Lunchbox Lessons, *(978-1-60507)* 970 E. Broadway, Suite 406, Jackson, WY 83001 USA (SAN 854-9540) Tel 307-462-4173
E-mail: info@lunchboxlessons.com
Web site: http://www.lunchboxlessons.com.

Lunchbox Stories Inc., *(978-0-9798059)* 20425 NW Quail Hollow Dr., Portland, OR 97229 USA
Web site: http://www.lunchboxstories.com.

Luquer St. Pr., *(978-0-9729735)* 199 Luquer St., Brooklyn, NY 11231-4518 USA Tel 718-237-4456; Fax: 718-488-7574
E-mail: editors@luquerstreet.org; events@luquerstree.org
Web site: http://www.luquerstreet.org
Dist(s): **SPD-Small Pr. Distribution.**

Luse, Sandra I., *(978-0-615-22394-0)* P.O. Box 431, Wilber, NE 68465 USA Tel 402-821-2641.

Lutherworth Pr., The (GBR) *(978-0-7188) Dist. by* **CasemateAcad.**

Lutz, William G., *(978-0-615-15622-4; 978-0-615-18287-2; 978-0-615-21273-9)* 10248 Ramm Rd., Whitehouse, OH 43571 USA
Dist(s): **Lulu Enterprises Inc.**

Luv U Bks., *(978-0-9715322)* P.O. Box 42037, Cincinnati, OH 45242-0037 USA
E-mail: luvubooks@fuse.net
Web site: http://www.luvubooks.com.

Luvlife Publishing, *(978-0-9764316)* Orders Addr.: 69 Shore Dr., Old Lyme, CT 06371 USA Tel 860-434-0723
E-mail: mistlove@earthlink.net
Web site: http://www.snakesofnewengland.com.

LuvLuv *Imprint of* **Aurora Publishing, Inc.**

L.W. Communications, *(978-0-9723378)* 16815 Victory Blvd. #226, Van Nuys, CA 91406-5550 USA Tel 818-787-9550 (phone, fax - call first)
E-mail: lancecoach@aol.com
Web site: http://www.lancecoach.com.

Lyceum Bks., Inc., *(978-0-925065; 978-1-933478; 978-1-935871; 978-1-943137)* 5758 S. Blackstone Ave., Chicago, IL 60637 USA Tel 773-643-1902; Fax: 773-643-1903
E-mail: lyceum@lyceumbooks.com
Web site: http://www.lyceumbooks.com.

Lynch, Marietta & Patricia Perry, *(978-0-9610962)* 240 Atlantic Rd., Gloucester, MA 01930 USA (SAN 265-2722) Tel 508-283-6322.

Lynn Tyner Mitchum & James Rogers, *(978-0-9745191)* P.O. Box 5799, Sevierville, TN 37864 USA
Web site: http://jamesrogersonline.com.

Lynne Ellen, Inc., *(978-0-9748889)* 670 N. Stiles Dr., Charleston, SC 29412 USA Tel 843-817-2530
E-mail: lynne@metoommy.com.

Lynn's Bookshelf, *(978-0-9618608)* Orders Addr.: P.O. Box 2224, Boise, ID 83701 USA (SAN 667-1314) Tel 208-331-1987 (phone/fax); Edit Addr.: 3423 Scenic Dr., Boise, ID 83703 USA
E-mail: lynnsbooks@cableone.net.

†Lynx Hse. Pr., *(978-0-89924)* 420 W. 24th Ave., Spokane, WA 99203-1922 USA (SAN 250-3344) Tel 309-624-4594; Fax: 309-623-4238
E-mail: cnhowell@mail.ewu.edu
Dist(s): **SPD-Small Pr. Distribution**
Univ. of Washington Pr.; *CIP.*

Lyon, Ernest Media Productions, *(978-0-9741328)* P.O. Box 26101, San Francisco, CA 94126-6101 USA (SAN 255-7460) Tel 415-387-5569 (phone/fax)
E-mail: davidlyon@mindspring.com.

Lyons Pr. *Imprint of* **Globe Pequot Pr., The**

Lypton Publishing, *(978-0-9752780)* 35409 S. Fairbank Point, Drummond Island, MI 49726 USA (SAN 256-0143).

Lyrical Learning, *(978-0-9646367; 978-0-9741635; 978-0-692-37347-7; 978-0-692-38790-0; 978-0-9964731)* 8008 Cardwell Hill, Corvallis, OR 97330 USA Tel 541-754-3579 (phone/fax); Toll Free: 800-761-0906
Web site: http://www.lyricallearning.com.

Lyrically Korrect Publishing, *(978-0-9727776)* 5402 Belle Vista Ave., Baltimore, MD 21206 USA; *Imprints:* Book Her Publications (Bk Hr Pubns)
Web site: http://www.lyricallykorrect.com.

M A Joines, *(978-0-615-47069-6; 978-0-615-54738-1)* 1901 Kodiak Ave. SW, Albany , OR 97321 USA Tel 541-926-6979
E-mail: d.joines@comcast.net
Dist(s): **CreateSpace Independent Publishing Platform**
Dummy Record Do Not USE!!!!.

M & B Publishing, *(978-0-9758580)* 930 Edgecliffs Dr., Langley, WA 98260 USA
E-mail: wistful@whidbey.com.

M & D Publishing, Inc., *(978-0-9768667)* '2980 SE Fairway W., Stuart, FL 34997 USA Tel 772-286-9781; Fax: 772-286-5169 Do not confuse with M & D Publishing in Phoenix, AZ
E-mail: manddpublishing@bellsouth.net.

M D C T Publishing, *(978-0-9674491)* 31990 SW Village Crest Ln., Wilsonville, OR 97070-8427 USA
E-mail: mdundy@teleport.com
Dist(s): **Partners/West Book Distributors.**

M G L S, Inc., *(978-0-9601682; 978-1-888833)* 700 S. First St., Marshall, MN 56258 USA (SAN 212-2170) Tel 507-532-4311; Fax: 507-532-4313
E-mail: carberry@mgls.com.

M J Stadtler Productions, *(978-0-615-61857-9; 978-0-615-62042-8)* 9050 Blue Jay Ln., Mentor, OH 44060 USA Tel 440-669-5482
E-mail: mjs@theothersideofinsanity.com
Web site: www.theothersideofinsanity.com
Dist(s): **CreateSpace Independent Publishing Platform.**

M K L Publishing, *(978-0-9746204)* Orders Addr.: P.O. Box 407, Ballston Spa, NY 12020 USA; Edit Addr.: 5019 Fairground Ave., Ballston Spa, NY 12020 USA
E-mail: mklpublishing@aol.com.

MM Co., *(978-1-883473)* 15007 Avon St., Independence, MO 64055 USA Tel 816-246-6365.

M Q Pubns. (GBR) *(978-1-84072; 978-1-897954; 978-1-84601; 978-0-9797400) Dist. by* **Wybel Market.**

M Q Pubns. (GBR) *(978-1-84072; 978-1-897954; 978-1-84601; 978-0-9797400) Dist. by* **IngramPubServ.**

M R L, Inc., *(978-1-892860)* 1445 Cannon St., Louisville, CO 80027-1453 USA Tel 303-666-8164
E-mail: moyazena@aol.com.

M T E, Ltd., *(978-1-888679)* 3095 S. Trenton St., Denver, CO 80231-4164 USA Tel 303-696-0839.

M2M Partners, *(978-0-9768884)* P.O. Box 60923, Phoenix, AZ 85082-0923 USA Toll Free: 800-658-8790
Web site: http://www.mamaroses.com; http://www.printserve.net; http://www.nonnieskitchen.com
Dist(s): **Partners/West Book Distributors.**

MAAT Resources, Inc., *(978-0-9624096; 978-1-893447)* 130 East Grand Ave., South San Francisco, CA 94080 USA Tel 650-871-4449; 650-871-4111; Fax: 650-871-4551; *Imprints:* Bilingual Language Materials (Biling Lang)
E-mail: info@blmteachaids.com
Web site: http://www.blmteachaids.com/; http://www.transparentpower.com/.

Mabbul Publishing Co., *(978-0-9762860)* 915 Hunting Horn Way, Evans, GA 30809 USA
Web site: http://www.mabbul.com.

MAC Productions, *(978-1-878591)* P.O. Box 84, Duvall, WA 98019 USA Tel 425-256-2652; Fax: 425-749-7065
E-mail: macproductions1@verizon.net
Web site: http://www.macsgolfguides.com
Dist(s): **Partners/West Book Distributors.**

MacAdam/Cage Publishing, Inc., *(978-1-878448; 978-0-9673701; 978-1-931561; 978-1-59692)* 155 Sansome St., Suite 550, San Francisco, CA 94104 USA (SAN 299-9730) Tel 415-986-7503; Fax: 415-986-7414
E-mail: david@macadamcage.com
Web site: http://www.macadamcage.com.

Macalester Park Publishing Co., Inc., *(978-0-910924; 978-0-930286; 978-1-886158)* 24558 546th Ave., Austin, MN 55912 USA (SAN 110-8077) Tel 507-396-0135; Toll Free: 800-407-9078
E-mail: macalesterpark@macalesterpark.com
Web site: http://www.macalesterpark.com
Dist(s): **Bookmen, Inc.**
Spring Arbor Distributors, Inc.

Macaronic Pr., *(978-0-9766859; 978-1-59864)* P.O. Box 1542, Sebastopol, CA 95473-1542 USA Tel 707-813-7047; Toll Free: 888-364-8253
E-mail: vivienka@msn.com
Web site: http://www.macaronicpress.com.

Macaulay, David Studio *Imprint of* **Roaring Brook Pr.**

Macauley, Myron Christian, *(978-0-578-05300-4)* 106 Monroe St., No. 2, Brooklyn, NY 11216 USA
E-mail: danae@kgn6.com.

Macaw Books LLC *See* **Kapp Bks. LLC**

MacBride, E. J. Pubn., Inc., *(978-1-892511)* 129 W. 147th St., No. 20B, New York, NY 10039 USA; *Imprints:* Disposition Sketch Books (Disposition Sketch).

MacGill, William V. & Company, *(978-0-9744720)* 1000 N. Lombard Rd., Lombard, IL 60148-1232 USA Tel 800-323-2841; Toll Free Fax: 800-727-3433
E-mail: macgill@macgill.com; nickh@macgill.com
Web site: http://www.macgill.com.

MacGregor, Doug, *(978-0-9654843)* 1578 Rosada Way, Fort Myers, FL 33901 USA Tel 941-337-3980
E-mail: dmacgregor@news-press.com.

MacHillock Publishing, *(978-0-9744996)* 2537 Pine Cove Dr., Tucker, GA 30084 USA
E-mail: sdh@mindspring.com
Dist(s): **Independent Pubs. Group**
MyiLibrary.

MacIntyre & Purcell Publishing (CAN) *(978-0-9738063; 978-0-9784784; 978-0-9810941; 978-1-926916; 978-1-927097) Dist. by* **IPG Chicago.**

Mackenzie Smiles, LLC, *(978-0-9790347; 978-0-9815761)* P.O. Box 1373, Sausalito, CA 94965 USA Toll Free: 888-800-5978; P.O. Box 1373, Sausalito, CA 94965
Web site: http://www.mackenziesmiles.com.

Mackin, Dan, *(978-0-615-12303-5)* 8395 SE Palm St., Hobe Sound, FL 33455 USA Tel 772-546-3008; Fax: 772-546-5374
E-mail: danmackinartist@aol.com
Web site: http://www.danmackin.com.

Mackinac Island Press, Inc. *Imprint of* **Charlesbridge Publishing, Inc.**

Mackinac Island State Park Commission *See* **Mackinac State Historic Parks**

Mackinac State Historic Parks, *(978-0-911872)* Orders Addr.: P.O. Box 873, Mackinaw City, MI 49701 USA; Edit Addr.: 207 W. Sinclair, Mackinaw City, MI 49701 USA (SAN 202-5981) Tel 231-436-5564; Fax: 231-436-4210.

MackStorm Productions, Inc., *(978-0-9753078)* 1410 Prairie Crossing Dr., West Chicago, IL 60185 USA Tel 630-231-3998
E-mail: marilee@americanslidechart.com.

MacMenamin Pr., *(978-0-9761414)* P.O. Box 133, Zionsville, PA 18092 USA Tel 610-739-9527
E-mail: sales@macmenaminpress.com
Web site: http://www.macmenaminpress.com.

Macmillan, *(978-0-374; 978-1-4668; 978-1-68274)* Div. of Holtzbrinck Publishing, Orders Addr.: 16365 James Madison Hwy., Gordonsville, VA 22942 USA (SAN 631-5011) Tel 540-672-7600; Fax: 540-672-7664; 540-672-7540 (Customer Service); Toll Free Fax: 800-672-2054 (Order Dept.); Toll Free: 888-330-8477; Edit Addr.: 175 Fifth Ave., 20th Flr., New York, NY 10010 USA Tel 212-674-5151; Fax: 212-677-6487; Toll Free Fax: 800-258-2769; Toll Free: 800-488-5233
E-mail: customerservice@mpsvirginia.com
Web site: http://www.macmillan.com
Dist(s): **Child's World, Inc., The**
Follett School Solutions
ebrary, Inc.

Macmillan Audio, *(978-0-940687; 978-1-55927; 978-1-893564; 978-1-59397; 978-1-59768; 978-1-4272)* Div. of Macmillan, Orders Addr.: 16365 James Madison Hwy., Gordonsville, VA 22942-8501 USA Toll Free Fax: 800-672-2054; Toll Free: 888-330-8477; Edit Addr.: 175 Fifth Ave., Suite 315, New York, NY 10010 USA (SAN 665-1275) Tel 646-307-5000; Fax: 917-534-0980; Toll Free: 800-221-7945
E-mail: audio@hbpub.com
Web site: http://www.macmillanaudio.com
Dist(s): **AudioGO**
Findaway World, LLC
Follett School Solutions
Landmark Audiobooks
MPS
Macmillan.

Macmillan Caribbean (GBR) *(978-0-333; 978-1-4050) Dist. by* **Interlink Pub.**

Macmillan Education, Ltd. (GBR) *(978-0-333; 978-1-4050) Dist. by* **Players Pr.**

Macmillan Pubs., Ltd. (GBR) *(978-0-330; 978-0-333; 978-1-4050) Dist. by* **IPG Chicago.**

Macmillan Pubs., Ltd. (GBR) *(978-0-330; 978-0-333; 978-1-4050) Dist. by* **Trafalgar.**

Macmillan Pubs., Ltd. (GBR) *(978-0-330; 978-0-333; 978-1-4050) Dist. by* **Trans-Atl Phila.**

Macmillan Reference USA *Imprint of* **Cengage Gale**

Macmillan/McGraw-Hill Schl. Div., *(978-0-02)* Div. of The McGraw-Hill Education Group, Orders Addr.: 220 E. Daniel Dale Rd., DeSoto, TX 75115 USA Fax: 972-228-1982; Toll Free: 800-442-9685
Dist(s): **McGraw-Hill Cos., The.**

Macro Publishing Group, *(978-0-9702699; 978-0-9754130; 978-0-9826829)* 6700 Oglesby, Suite 1101, Chicago, IL 60649 USA Toll Free: 888-854-8823 (phone/fax)
E-mail: lissawoodson@aol.com
Dist(s): **INscribe Digital.**

Macromedia Education *Imprint of* **Macromedia, Inc.**

Macromedia, Inc., *(978-0-9742273; 978-1-932719)* 600 Townsend St., San Francisco, CA 94103 USA Tel 415-252-2000; Fax: 415-832-5555; Toll Free: 800-457-1774; *Imprints:* Macromedia Education (Macromedia Educ) Do not confuse with Macromedia, Inc. in Lake Placid, NY
Web site: http://www.macromedia.com/education.

Mad Island Communications LLC, *(978-0-9677458; 978-0-9910109)* P.O. Box 153, La Pointe, WI 54850-0153 USA Tel 715-209-5471
E-mail: barbwith@gmail.com
Web site: http://www.barbarawith.com; http://partyof12.wordpress.com/
Dist(s): **Lightning Source, Inc.**

Mad Island Publishing *See* **Mad Island Communications LLC**

Mad Yak Pr., *(978-0-9717995)* 8232 Styers Ct., Laurel, MD 20723-2100 USA Tel 301-317-8817
Dist(s): **Diamond Comic Distributors, Inc.**
Diamond Bk. Distributors.

Madame Fifi Pubns., *(978-0-9667418; 978-0-9762900; 978-0-9821707)* P.O. Box 310967, Newington, CT 06131-0967 USA
Web site: http://www.madamefifi3.com.

Madd Mindz Publishing, Inc., *(978-0-9802262)* P.O. Box 20437, Brooklyn, NY 11202-0437 USA Tel 347-661-4030; Fax: 718-425-9919
E-mail: C.Brandon@MaddMindzPublishing.com
Web site: http://www.maddmindzpublishing.com.

Maddness, Inc., *(978-0-9761619)* P.O. Box 76551, Oklahoma City, OK 73147-2551 USA
E-mail: osheashamir@aol.com
Web site: http://www.osheashamir.com.

Mader, Lothar, *(978-0-615-24577-5; 978-0-578-05621-0)* 2130 Professional Dr., Suite 240, Roseville, CA 95661 USA
Dist(s): **Lulu Enterprises Inc.**

Madison, Dr. Ron *See* **Ned's Head Productions**

Madison Pr. Bks. (CAN) *(978-1-895892; 978-1-897330) Dist. by* **IPG Chicago.**

Maerkle Pr., *(978-0-9721966; 978-0-9819479)* 66 E. Shore Blvd., Timberlake, OH 44095 USA Tel 440-269-8653; Fax: 440-269-8035
Web site: http://www.maerklepress.com.

Maerov, Jeffrey, *(978-0-578-11402-6; 978-0-578-11504-7)* 24 Fecamp, Newport Coast, CA 92657 USA.

Maestro Classics, *(978-1-932684)* Div. of Simon & Simon, LLC, Orders Addr.: 1745 Broadway 17th Fl, New York, NY 10019 USA Tel 212-519-9847
E-mail: bsimon@maestroclassics.com
Web site: http://www.MaestroClassics.com
Dist(s): **CD Baby**
Follett School Solutions.

Maestro Learning, *(978-0-9740533)* 24 Chilton St., Cambridge, MA 02138-6802 USA
E-mail: peter@maestrolearning.com
Web site: http://www.maestrolearning.com.

MaestroMedia Pr., *(978-0-9773731)* 408 Pearl St., Richmond, IN 47374 USA Tel 765-962-8380
E-mail: rosecitysp@msn.com.

Maeva, Ediciones, S.A. (ESP) *(978-84-86478; 978-84-95354; 978-84-92695; 978-84-96231; 978-84-96748; 978-84-15120; 978-84-15532; 978-84-15893) Dist. by* **Lectorum Pubns.**

Magabala Bks. (AUS) *(978-0-9588101; 978-1-875641; 978-1-921248; 978-0-7316-0335-0; 978-0-7316-1622-0; 978-0-7316-1623-7; 978-0-7316-1736-4; 978-0-7316-3328-9; 978-0-646-22120-5; 978-0-646-26784-5; 978-1-922142; 978-1-925360) Dist. by* **IPG Chicago.**

Mage Pubs., Inc., *(978-0-934211; 978-1-933823)* 1408 35th St., NW, Washington, DC 20007 USA (SAN 693-0476) Tel 202-342-1642; Fax: 202-342-9269; Toll Free: 800-962-0922 (orders only)
E-mail: as@mage.com
Web site: http://www.mage.com.

Magee, Burke & Glenna, *(978-0-9748424)* Orders Addr.: P.O. Box 581, Carnation, WA 98014 USA; Edit Addr.: 2015 290th Ave., NE, Carnation, WA 98014 USA
E-mail: rtg@returntogod.com
Web site: http://www.returntogod.com.

MaggieMooseTracks, *(978-0-9895205)* 1766 Sand Hill Rd., No. 102, Palo Alto, CA 94304 USA Tel 650-322-8860
E-mail: girlfins@aol.com.

Magic Factory, LLC, The, *(978-1-938155)* Orders Addr.: 3818 Somerset Dr., Durham, NC 27707 USA Tel 310-943-6972; Edit Addr.: 3818 Somerset Dr., Durham, NC 27707 USA Tel 310-943-6972 (Tel/Fax)
E-mail: orders@magicfactory.com; orders@magicfactory.com; info@magicfactory.com; books@magicfactory.com
Web site: http://magicfactory.com; http://signofthesandman.com; http://rangerbaldy.com.

Magic Lamp Pr., *(978-1-56891; 978-1-882629)* Div. of Magic Lamp Productions, 1838 Washington Way, Venice, CA 90291-4704 USA (SAN 256-1670) Tel 310-822-2985; Fax: 310-827-9123; Toll Free: 800-367-9661
E-mail: videopage@earthlink.net
Web site: http://www.magiclamppress.com
Dist(s): **Smashwords.**

Magic Lamp Productions *See* **Magic Lamp Pr.**

Magic of African Rhythm (TMOAR), The, *(978-0-9820926)* Orders Addr.: P.O. Box 14724, Raleigh, NC 27620-4724 USA Tel 919-828-1906; Fax: 419-781-8209
E-mail: shabutaso@gmail.com.

Magic Penny Reading, *(978-0-9761987; 978-0-9899114)* 61 Wehrle Dr., Amherst, NY 14225 USA Tel 800-873-0396; Fax: 888-728-0754
E-mail: sandyschneider@magicpennyreading.org
Web site: http://magicpennyreading.org.

Magic Picture Frame Studio, LLC, *(978-0-9749269)* Orders Addr.: P.O. Box 2603, Issaquah, WA 98027 USA Tel 425-222-7562
E-mail: publisher@magicpictureframe.com; mvm@magicpictureframe.com; class@magicpictureframe.com
Web site: http://www.magicpictureframe.com
Dist(s): **BookMasters, Inc.**

Magic Propaganda Mill, *(978-0-9760117)* Please Send All Correspondence To: Info@mpmill.com, Brooklyn, NY 11238 USA
E-mail: info@mpmill.com
Web site: http://www.magicpropagandamill.com.

Magic Tails Press *See* **Abydos Enterprises**

Magic Valley Pubs., *(978-0-9716681; 978-0-9774833; 978-0-9785509; 978-0-9800879; 978-0-9821496; 978-0-9845275)* 6390 E. Willow St., Long Beach, CA 90815 USA Tel 562-795-0289; Fax: 562-795-0490 Do not confuse with Magic Valley Publishers in Burly, ID
Web site: http://www.magicvalleypub.com.

Magic Wagon, *(978-1-60270; 978-1-61641)* Div. of ADBO Publishing Group, Orders Addr.: P.O. Box 398166, Minneapolis, MN 55439-8166 USA Fax: 952-831-1632; Toll Free: 800-458-8399; Edit Addr.: 8000 W. 78th St., Suite 310, Edina, MN 55439 USA Toll Free: 800-458-8399; *Imprints:* Looking Glass Library (LookngGlassLib); Graphic Planet (Graphic Planet); Short Tales (Short Tales); Calico Chapter Books (CalicoChap Bks); Looking Glass Library- Nonfiction (LOOKING GLASS) ; Calico Chapter Books (CalicoChapter)
E-mail: info@abdopublishing.com
Web site: http://www.abdopublishing.com
Dist(s): **ABDO Publishing Co.**
Follett School Solutions
MyiLibrary.

Magic Woman Pubns., *(978-0-9760062)* 1527 Veteran Ave., Suite 7, Los Angeles, CA 90024-5566 USA Tel 310-478-7743; Fax: 310-478-9892
E-mail: artdivin@yahoo.com
Web site: http://www.magicwomanpublications.com.

Magic Wordweaver Pr., *(978-0-9754116; 978-0-615-12456-8)* Orders Addr.: P.O. Box 1315, Conifer, CO 80433 USA (SAN 255-8459) Tel 303-838-7515 (phone/fax); Edit Addr.: 29580 S. Sunset Trail, Conifer, CO 80433 USA
E-mail: premalee108@yahoo.com.

Magic Works Publishing & Production, *(978-0-9799545)* 27 Greenmoor, Irvine, CA 92614 USA Tel 714-309-4824; Fax: 949-651-8895
E-mail: selina@superachievement.net
Web site: http://SuperAchievement.net.

Magical Child Bks. *Imprint of* **Shades of White**

Magical Creations, *(978-0-9744879)* P.O. Box 324, Chicago Park, CA 95712 USA Tel 530-477-7429
E-mail: doris_rainville@hotmail.com.

Magical Mischief Maker, *(978-0-9754004)* P.O. Box 1075, Douglasville, GA 30133 USA
Web site: http://www.magicalmischiefmaker.com.

MagicStar Inc., *(978-0-9821387)* 2021 Midwest Rd., Suite 200, Oak Brook, IL 60523 USA (SAN 857-3336) Tel 510-740-4045
E-mail: publisher@magicstarpub.com
Web site: http://www.magicstarpub.com.

Magill's Choice *Imprint of* **Salem Pr., Inc.**

Magination, *(978-1-881597)* 3579 E. Foothill Blvd., No. 330, Pasadena, CA 91107 USA Tel 626-306-1190; Fax: 626-306-1193.

Magination Pr. *Imprint of* **American Psychological Assn.**

Magiscule Publishing Group, L.L.C., *(978-0-9772232)* 12 Armstrong Ave., Suite 3 W., Providence, RI 02903 USA Fax: 401-861-7030
E-mail: Krystalstream@excite.com.

Magna Large Print Bks. (GBR) *(978-0-7505; 978-0-86009; 978-1-84137; 978-1-85057; 978-1-78502) Dist. by* **Ulverscroft US.**

Magnatic Music, *(978-0-9719897)* 13806 Delaney Rd., Dale City, VA 22193 USA
E-mail: alstonsongs@aol.com.

Magner Publishing *See* **Magner Publishing & American Binding & Publishing**

Magner Publishing & American Binding & Publishing, *(978-1-929416; 978-1-60080)* P.O. Box 60049, Corpus Christi, TX 78466 USA Tel 361-658-4221; Toll Free: 800-863-3708
E-mail: rmmagner@pyramid3.net
Web site: http://www.americanbindingpublishing.com.

Magness, Robert Pubns., LLC, *(978-0-9774577)* 1412 Kent St., Sturgis, MI 49091-2334 USA Tel 269-651-7473
E-mail: sengam@netzero.com.

Magnetar Venture Group, LLC, *(978-0-692-37543-3; 978-0-9861212)* P.O. Box 540324, Houston, TX 77254 USA Tel 5127632652
E-mail: itjk100@hotmail.com; itjk100@hotmail.com; itjk100@hotmail.com
Dist(s): **CreateSpace Independent Publishing Platform.**

Magnetic Image, Inc., *(978-0-9678542)* 900 SW 13th St., Boca Raton, FL 33486 USA
E-mail: info@magneticimageinc.com
Web site: http://www.magneticimageinc.com.

Magni, *(978-1-882330; 978-1-937026)* 7106 Wellington Point Rd., McKinney, TX 75070 USA Tel 972-540-2050; Fax: 972-540-1057
E-mail: sales@magnico.com
Web site: http://www.magnico.com
Dist(s): **Book Publishing Co.**

Magpie Press *See* **Magpie Pr., Pine Mountain Club, CA**

Magpie Pr., Pine Mountain Club, CA, Orders Addr.: P.O. Box 6434, Pine Mountain Club, CA 93222-6434 USA Tel 661-242-1265 (phone/fax) Do not confuse with Magpie Pr. in Wallington, NJ
E-mail: MagSmith1265@msn.com
Web site: www.magpiepress.com.

Magrane, Etna International, *(978-0-9741167)* 8 Hill Point Ave., San Francisco, CA 94117 USA Tel 415-681-5157; Fax: 415-681-5820
E-mail: emagrane@aol.com.

Magsimba Pr., *(978-1-932956)* 1821 Bruce Rd., NE, Atlanta, GA 30329-2508 USA Tel 404-633-9153
E-mail: info@magsimba.org
Web site: http://www.magsimba.org; http://www.tagalog1.com/Ordinary/Learn_Filipino.jsp
Dist(s): **Quality Bks., Inc.**

MAHVL Publishing, *(978-0-9790072)* P.O. Box 134, Deerfield, IL 60015-0134 USA
Web site: http://michaelslewismd.com
Dist(s): **Chicago Distribution Ctr.**
Independent Pubs. Group
Ingram Pub. Services.

Maia Press Ltd., The (GBR) *(978-1-904559) Dist. by* **Dufour.**

Mailbox Bks., The *Imprint of* **Education Ctr., Inc.**

Main Asset Pubns., *(978-0-9667617)* P.O. Box 1153, Teaneck, NJ 07666 USA Tel 201-837-6400; Fax: 201-837-8842
E-mail: mathispublishing@aol.com
Web site: http://www.whyarentumarried.com.

Main Event Pr., *(978-0-9774129)* 1714 Boxwood Cir., Saint Cloud, MN 56303-0148 USA.

Main Street Pubns., *(978-0-9745033)* 11810 Dice Rd., Freeland, MI 48623 USA.

Main Street Publishing, Inc. *See* **Main St Publishing, Inc.**

Main St Publishing, Inc., *(978-0-9666676; 978-0-9710470; 978-0-9741294; 978-0-9748591; 978-0-9760414; 978-0-9765369; 978-0-9776480; 978-0-9785934; 978-0-9791154; 978-1-934615; 978-1-939999)* 206 E. Main, Suite 207, Jackson, TN 38301 USA Fax: 731-427-7380; Toll Free: 866-457-7379; *Imprints:* MSP (MSP) Do not confuse with companies with same or similar names in Kingston, NJ, Shorewood, WI, Osage Beach MO,
E-mail: editor@mainstreetpublishing.com
Web site: http://www.mainstreetpublishing.com.

Mainstay, LLC, *(978-0-9798854)* 4134 W. View Pointe Dr., Highland, UT 84003 USA
Web site: http://www.MainstayEducation.com.

Mainstream Ctr., Schl. for the Deaf, The, *(978-0-9797287)* 48 Round Hill Rd., Northampton, MA 01060-2124 USA Tel 413-582-1121; Fax: 413-586-6654
E-mail: akot@clarkeschool.org
Web site: http://www.clarkeschool.org.

Mainstream Connections Publishing, *(978-1-60336)* 10103 Queens Cir., Ocean City, MD 21842 USA Tel 410-213-7861 fax or email requests; *Imprints:* Adventures of Everyday Geniuses, The (Adv Evryday)
E-mail: barb.esham@mainstreamconnections.org; lisa.spielman@mainstreamconnections.org
Web site: http://www.mainstreamconnections.org
Dist(s): **Brodart Co.**
Emery-Pratt Co.
Follett School Solutions
Quality Bks., Inc.
Yankee Bk. Peddler, Inc.

Mainstreet Systems & Software Inc., *(978-0-9726871)* P.O. Box 577, Harleysville, PA 19438-0577 USA (SAN 255-335X) Toll Free: 800-257-4535
E-mail: epwhelan@netcarrier.com
Web site: http://www.promotecopyrights.com.

Maire, Lucy Bedoya, *(978-0-9768436)* Orders Addr.: P.O. Box 2632, Westport, CT 06880 USA Tel 203-454-5204; Fax: 203-454-5204; Edit Addr.: 19 River Oak Rd., Westport, CT 06880 USA
E-mail: twelvetreasures@yahoo.com
Dist(s): **Raimond Graphics Inc.**

Majestic Eagle Publishing, *(978-0-9797495)* Div. of James J. Brown & Assoc., Inc., 6649 Navajo, Lincolnwood, IL 60712 USA Tel 847-679-3447; Fax: 847-679-6191
E-mail: jola1@aol.com.

Majestic Publishing, LLC, *(978-0-9755314; 978-1-942156)* Orders Addr.: P.O. Box 1560, Lithonia, GA 30058 USA Tel 770-482-9129 Do not confuse with Majestic Publishing, LLC in Santa Barbara, CA
E-mail: majpublish@bellsouth.net
Web site: http://www.majesticpublishing.net.

Majesty Publishing, *(978-0-9754839)* 12 Paddock Ln., Hampton, VA 23669 USA
E-mail: customerservice@faithfrontier.com
Web site: http://www.faithfrontier.com.

Major, Christina, *(978-0-692-02524-6; 978-0-692-46530-1)* 1910 Yosemite Ave. No. 205, Simi Valley, CA 93063 USA Tel 818-517-1076
E-mail: delphina2k@gmail.com
Web site: http://www.horizonscape.com.

Majority Press, Incorporated, The *See* **Majority Pr., The**

Majority Pr., The, *(978-0-912469)* Orders Addr.: 46 Development Rd., Fitchburg, MA 01420 USA (SAN 249-3012) Tel 978-342-9676; Fax: 978-348-1233; Edit Addr.: P.O. Box 538, Dover, MA 02030 USA (SAN 265-2757) Tel 508-744-6097 (phone/fax)
E-mail: tmpress@earthlink.net
Web site: http://www.themajoritypress.com
Dist(s): **A & B Distributors & Pubs. Group**
Lexicon Pubns., Inc.

Majzik, Bill *See* **Mill Creek Metro Publishing**

Makai Concepts, LLC, *(978-0-9744035)* Orders Addr.: 3 King William Ct., Hilton Head Island, SC 29926 USA (SAN 255-6219)
E-mail: betsys@hargray.com.

Makdan Publishing, *(978-0-9819283)* P.O. Box 7560, Bonney Lake, WA 98391 USA Tel 253-720-1059
E-mail: jimlandgraf@hotmail.com.

Make Believe Ideas (GBR) *(978-1-905051; 978-1-84610; 978-1-84879; 978-1-78065; 978-1-78235; 978-1-78393) Dist. by* **Nelson.**

Make Me A Story Pr., *(978-1-878847)* 1737 N. 2580 E. Rd., Sheldon, IL 60966 USA Tel 815-429-3501 (phone/fax)
E-mail: info@earthesquirrel.com
Web site: http://www.earthesquirrel.com.

Maker Media, Inc,
Dist(s): **Ingram Pub. Services**
O'Reilly Media, Inc.

Malachite Quills Publishing *See* **MQuills Publishing**

Malamih Publishing Hse., *(978-0-9820804)* 4311 Jamboree Rd., No. 170, Newport Beach, CA 92660 USA.

Malamute Pr., *(978-0-9722180)* Orders Addr.: P.O. Box W, Aspen, CO 81612 USA; Edit Addr.: P.O. Box W, Aspen, CO 81612-7424 USA
E-mail: info@dodogsvote.com; sales@malamutepress.com
Web site: http://www.malamutepress.com.

Malbrough, Michael, *(978-0-9758883)* 163-167 N. Pk. St., Apt. 5, East Orange, NJ 07019 USA.

Malibu Bks. for Children, *(978-1-929084)* Div. of Malibu Films, Inc., 48 Broad St., No. 134, Red Bank, NJ 07701 USA Tel 732-933-0446 (phone/fax); Toll Free: 888-629-9947 (phone/fax)
E-mail: malibuinc@aol.com
Web site: http://www.malibubooks.com.

Malik, Sakinah A. *See* **EDR**

Malone-Ballard Book Publishers, *(978-0-9729484)* 160 S. Third St., Lansing, IA 52151 USA Tel 319-389-7174 (phone/fax)
Web site: http://www.malone-ballard.com
Dist(s): **Partners Bk. Distributing, Inc.**

Malor Bks. *Imprint of* **I S H K**

Mama Incense Publishing, *(978-0-9761523)* P.O. Box 4635, Long Beach, CA 90804-9998 USA Tel 310-490-9097
E-mail: mama@mamaincense.com
Web site: http://www.mamaincense.com.

Mama Specific Productions, *(978-0-9749480)* P.O. Box 110393, Cleveland, OH 44111-0393 USA Tel 440-396-1963; Fax: 801-640-2494; *Imprints:* MSPpress (MSPpr)
E-mail: info@msppress.com; trula@MSPpress.com
Web site: http://www.msppress.com.

Mama's Boyz, Inc., *(978-0-9796132)* 304 Main Ave. #114, Norwalk, CT 06851 USA (SAN 854-1914)
E-mail: jerrycraft@aol.com
Web site: http://www.jerrycraft.net
Dist(s): **Follett School Solutions.**

MaMbabooks.com, *(978-0-9817448; 978-0-9887867)* Div. of Mamba Books & Publishing, 355 Liberty St., Dendron, VA 23839 USA
E-mail: mambabooks@gmail.com
Web site: http://www.mambabooks.com; http://www.mambabooks.biz.

Mamoo Hse., *(978-1-933014)* 17 W. Browning Rd., Collingswood, NJ 08108 USA Tel 856-858-6616
E-mail: melisma@earthlink.net
Web site: http://www.mamoohouse.com.

MAMP Creations, *(978-0-9772210)* P.O. Box 4253, Hopkins, MN 55343 USA Tel 952-938-9320 (phone/fax); *Imprints:* Phil the Pill & Friends (Phil PillFrnds)
E-mail: mampcreations@aol.com
Web site: http://www.cafepress.com/mampcreations.

Management Pocketbooks (GBR) *(978-1-870471; 978-1-903776; 978-1-906610) Dist. by* **Ware-Pak Inc.**

Management Services, *(978-0-9747418)* 302 S. 2nd St. Apt. 711, Champaign, IL 61820-4141 USA Do not confuse with Managment Services Incorporated in Atlanta, GA
E-mail: aepelbaum@yahoo.com
Web site: http://moscowtechchicago.com.

Manassas Museum, The, *(978-1-886826)* Orders Addr.: P.O. Box 560, Manassas, VA 20108 USA Tel 703-368-1873; Edit Addr.: 9101 Prince William St., Manassas, VA 201110-5615 USA
Web site: http://www.manassasmuseum.org.

Manchester Univ. Pr. (GBR) *(978-0-7190; 978-1-84779) Dist. by* **OUP.**

Mandala Publishing, *(978-0-945475; 978-1-886069; 978-1-932771; 978-1-60109)* 3160 Kerner Blvd. Ste. 108, San Rafael, CA 94901-5454 USA Toll Free: 800-688-2218 (orders only)
E-mail: info@mandala.org
Web site: http://www.mandala.org; http://earthawareeditions.com/catalog/
Dist(s): **MyiLibrary**
Perseus-PGW
Perseus Bks. Group.

Mandala Publishing Group *See* **Mandala Publishing**

Mandell, Ted, *(978-0-9749156)* 2232 Pine Creek Ct., South Bend, IN 46628 USA Tel 574-631-6953
E-mail: tmandell@nd.edu.

Mandeville, Terry M., *(978-0-9762475)* 7933 NE 124th St., Kirkland, WA 98034 USA
E-mail: terrymand@aol.com.

M&J Southwest, Inc., *(978-0-9744534)* 4402 E. Desert Willow Rd., Phoenix, AZ 85044 USA Tel 480-940-4046
E-mail: michaelc@gotwords.com
Web site: http://www.gotwords.com.

Mandolin House *See* **Kush Univ. Pr.**

Mandolin Hse. *Imprint of* **Kush Univ. Pr.**

Mandracchia Bks. *Imprint of* **Mandracchia, Charles**

Mandracchia, Charles, *(978-0-9721957)* 7914 Rockaway Beach Blvd. Apt. 6L, Rockaway Beac, NY 11693-2081 USA; *Imprints:* Mandracchia Books (Mandracchia Bks)
E-mail: charlesmandracchia@yahoo.com
Web site: http://www.kungfoogrannys.com; http://www.showtoonz.com.

Mandragora (ITA) *(978-88-7461; 978-88-85957) Dist. by* **Natl Bk Netwk.**

Mandy & Andy Bks., Inc., *(978-0-9772757)* 124 Meridian Ave., Poinciana, FL 34759-3241 USA (SAN 257-1765) Tel 407-319-3880; 863-427-4643
E-mail: wadams23@cfl.rr.com
Web site: http://mandyandandybooks.com.

Mandy & Pandy Bks., LLC, *(978-0-9800156; 978-0-9834411)* 2590 Cook Creek Ct., Ann Arbor, MI 48103 USA Tel 734-904-1916
E-mail: tsinkule@heulegordon.com
Dist(s): **China Bks. & Periodicals, Inc.**
Perseus-PGW.

Manga 18 *Imprint of* **Central Park Media Corp.**

Manga Punk, *(978-0-9748966)* P.O. Box 966, Meadows of Dan, VA 24120 USA
Web site: http://www.mangapunk.com.

MANGACANDY, LLC, *(978-0-9785891)* 13937 W. 73rd St., Shawnee, KS 66216 USA Tel 913-638-9940
E-mail: nami.bunny@gmail.com
Web site: http://www.mangacandy.com.

Mango (FRA) *(978-2-7404; 978-2-84270; 978-2-910635) Dist. by* **Distribks Inc.**

Mango Tree Pr., *(978-0-9708571)* Orders Addr.: P.O. Box 853, Mackinaw City, MI 49701 USA Tel 231-627-7322 (phone/fax); Edit Addr.: 2562 Pinewood Cir., Cheboygan, MI 49721 USA
E-mail: ids@mangotreepress.com; lds@mangotreepress.com
Web site: http://www.mangotreepress.com
Dist(s): **Partners Bk. Distributing, Inc.**

Mangrove Seed Expressions *Imprint of* **Mangrove Seed, Inc.**

Mangrove Seed, Inc., *(978-0-9797158)* Orders Addr.: P.O. Box 2, Sarasota, FL 34230-0002 USA Toll Free: 866-549-1549 to contact publisher; P.O. Box 02, Sarasota, FL 34230; *Imprints:* Mangrove Seed Expressions (Mangve Seed)
E-mail: dan@mangroveseed.org
Web site: http://www.mangroveseed.org; http://www.mangroveseedchronicles.com.

Mangrum, Kaylea J., *(978-0-9883009)* 1521 Carrick Dr., Murfreesboro, TN 37128 USA Tel 615-579-3663
E-mail: donmangrum@yahoo.com; phillipmangrum@mac.com.

Mangrum-Strichart Learning Resources, *(978-0-9745999; 978-0-9797723)* 2634 Glendale Dr., Loveland, CO 80538 USA Tel 970-593-1586; Fax: 970-962-0057; Toll Free: 866-409-0585
E-mail: study@mangrum-strichart.com
Web site: http://www.mangrum-strichart.com.

Manhattan Academia, *(978-0-615-16120-4; 978-0-615-18454-8; 978-0-615-18503-3; 978-1-936581)* 26 Norwood Terr., Millburn, NJ 07041 USA
Web site: http://www.manhattanacademia.com
Dist(s): **Lulu Enterprises Inc.**

Manic D Pr., *(978-0-916397; 978-1-933149)* Orders Addr.: P.O. Box 410804, San Francisco, CA 94141 USA (SAN 670-6932) Tel 415-648-8288 (phone/fax); Edit Addr.: 250 Banks St., San Francisco, CA 94110 USA
E-mail: info@manicdpress.com
Web site: http://www.manicdpress.com
Dist(s): **Consortium Bk. Sales & Distribution**
Last Gasp of San Francisco
MyiLibrary
Perseus Bks. Group
SPD-Small Pr. Distribution.

Manifest Pubns., *(978-0-9627896; 978-1-929354)* Orders Addr.: P.O. Box 429, Carpinteria, CA 93014 USA Tel 805-684-4905; Fax: 805-684-3100; Edit Addr.: P.O. Box 429, Carpinteria, CA 93014-0429 USA
E-mail: editor@manifestpub.com; publisher@manifestpub.com
Web site: http://www.manifestpub.com
Dist(s): **Sunbelt Pubns., Inc.**

Maninge Mali, *(978-0-9729698)* 204 Garden Pl., Radnor, PA 19087 USA (SAN 255-4623) Tel 610-254-0846
E-mail: maningemali@aol.com.

Manis, Shirley, *(978-0-9839286)* 2205 Francesco Cr., Capitola, CA 95010 USA Tel 831-462-4126
E-mail: smanis@cruzio.com.

Manitowish River Pr., *(978-0-9656763)* 4245 Hwy. 47, Mercer, WI 54547 USA Tel 715-476-2828; Fax: 715-476-2818
E-mail: manitowish@centuryinter.net
Dist(s): **Adventure Pubns., Inc.**

Mankamyer, Laura, *(978-0-9728431)* 343 Stonebrook Dr., Canonsburg, PA 15317-3409 USA.

Mann Publishing Group, *(978-0-9726888; 978-1-932577; 978-1-933673)* 710 Main St., 6th Flr., Rollinsford, NH 03869 USA (SAN 255-5409) Tel 603-601-0325; Fax: 603-601-0334; Toll Free: 877-877-6266; *Imprints:* BookMann Press (BkMann Pr)
E-mail: tmann@mannpublishing.com
Web site: http://www.askopus.com; http://www.rationalpress.com; http://www.agilitypress.com; http://www.incpress.com; http://www.mannpublishing.com.

Mann Publishing Inc. *See* **Mann Publishing Group**

Manners Toy Co., LLC, *(978-0-615-17967-4)* Orders Addr.: 2546 Lochness Rd, Richmond, VA 23235 USA Tel 804-307-5154
E-mail: mmadore@mannerstoycompany.com.

Mannheim Steamroller, LLC, *(978-0-9754149)* 9130 Mormon Bridge Rd., Omaha, NE 68152 USA Tel 402-457-4341; Fax: 402-457-4332
E-mail: jcarr@americangramaphone.com
Web site: http://www.mannheimsteamroller.com.

Manning, Laurie, *(978-1-892686)* Orders Addr.: 2640 Violet, Glenview, IL 60025 USA
E-mail: chinaqi888@aol.com.

Manning Pubns. Co., *(978-1-884777; 978-1-930110; 978-1-932394; 978-1-933988; 978-1-935182; 978-1-61729; 978-1-63343)* 180 Broad St. Apt. #1323, Saintmpford, CT 06901 USA; 178 S. Hill Dr., Westamptomn, NJ 08060 Tel 609-835-2793
E-mail: kidi@manning.com
Web site: http://www.manning.com
Dist(s): **Ebsco Publishing**
Independent Pubs. Group
Ingram Pub. Services
O'Reilly Media, Inc.

Manoa Pr., *(978-1-891839)* 2702 Menoa Rd., Honolulu, HI 96822 USA Tel 808-988-4904
Dist(s): **Native Bks.**

Manor Hse. Publishing Co., Inc., *(978-0-9645844; 978-0-9796239; 978-0-9836634; 978-0-9858774)* 880 Louis Dr., Warminster, PA 18974-2819 USA Tel 215-259-1700 Toll Free: 800-768-3222
E-mail: rdean@mgadvertising.com
Web site: http://www.poolspaliving.com.

Mansfield, J. Hse. Publishing Co., *(978-0-9707428)* P.O. Box 191575, Los Angeles, CA 90019 USA Fax: 323-935-6169
E-mail: jlmansfield@usa.net.

Mansion Publishing, Ltd., *(978-0-9675941)* c/o The Maggiore Companies, 60 Myopia Rd., Winchester, MA 01890 USA Tel 781-729-7210; 781-718-2003; Fax: 781-729-6444
E-mail: mansionpub@aol.com
Web site: http://wdressingthewholeperson.com.

Mantra Lingua (GBR) *(978-1-85269; 978-0-947679; 978-1-84444; 978-1-84611) Dist. by* **Chinasprout.**

Manual In Truth, A, *(978-0-9763252)* P.O. Box 541486, Miami, FL 33054 USA
E-mail: customersupport@amanualintruth.com
Web site: http://www.amanualintruth.com.

Manufacturers Alliance/MAPI, *(978-0-9745674)* 1600 Wilson Blvd. Ste. 1100, Arlington, VA 22209-2594 USA
E-mail: ssumler@mapi.net
Web site: http://www.mapi.net.

Manufacturing Application Konsulting Engineering (MAKE)in, *(978-1-62495)* 705 W. Azure Ln., Litchfield PArk, AZ 85340 USA Tel 469-265-8212
E-mail: trythaiketco@gmail.com
Web site: www.trythaiketco.com
Dist(s): **Lulu Enterprises Inc.**

Many Kites Pr., *(978-0-9618469; 978-0-9729002)* Orders Addr.: P.O. Box 711, Cass Lake, MN 56633 USA Tel 605-341-4232 (phone/fax); Toll Free: 800-486-8940; Edit Addr.: 6511 160th St. NW, Cass Lake, MN 56633 USA
E-mail: info@manykites.com; jamie@manykites.com
Web site: http://www.manykites.com; http://www.manykites.org
Dist(s): **Independent Pubs. Group**
Smashwords.

Many Voice Pr., *(978-0-9795185; 978-0-9833679)* Flathead Valley Community College 777 Grandview Dr., Kalispell, MT 59901 USA (SAN 853-6686) Tel 406-756-3907; Fax: 406-756-3815 Do not confuse with companies with the same name in Long Islanf City, NY, Cincinnati, OH
E-mail: ljaegermontana@hotmail.com
Dist(s): **SPD-Small Pr. Distribution.**

Manzanita Falls Pubs., *(978-0-9763916)* P.O. Box 991920, Redding, CA 96099-1920 USA (SAN 256-3347)
Web site: http://www.manzanitafallspublishers.com.

Mapin Publishing Pvt. Ltd (IND) *(978-81-85822; 978-81-88204) Dist. by* **Natl Bk Netwk.**

Maple Bend Farms Pr., *(978-0-9740799)* 4804 Laurel Canyon Blvd., Suite 224, Valley Village, CA 91607 USA
E-mail: ocsage@aol.com
Web site: http://www.maplebend.com.

Maple Canyon Co., (978-0-9669760; 978-0-9787164) P.O. Box 565, Mapleton, UT 84663 USA Tel 801-489-8948
E-mail: chuckclifton@maplecanyon.com; customerservice@maplecanyon.com
Web site: http://www.maplecanyon.com.

Maple Corners Press *Imprint of* **Attic Studio Publishing Hse.**

Maple Lane Writing & Desktop Publishing, (978-0-9667527) 16821 W. County Hill Rd., Hayward, WI 54843 USA Tel 715-634-9600; Fax: 715-634-1871
E-mail: mapleln@win.bright.net.

Maple Leaf Ctr., (978-0-9759850; 978-0-9827210) 167 N. Main St., Wallingford, VT 05773 USA Tel 802-446-3601; Fax: 802-446-3801
E-mail: mapleleaf@vermontel.net
Web site: http://www.mapleleafcenter.com.

Maple Leaf Publishing *See* **Spreeda Publishing**

Maple Road Publishing, Inc., (978-0-9844453) Orders Addr.: P.O. Box 10143, McLean, VA 22102 USA
Web site: http://www.mapleroadpublishing.com.

Maps For Kids Inc., (978-0-9759433) 1550 Poly Dr., Billings, MT 59102 USA Tel 406-238-7131; Fax: 406-259-4021; Toll Free: 877-897-7131
E-mail: banjo@floberg.com
Web site: http://www.mapsforkids.com.

Maps.com, (978-1-930194) 120 Cremona Dr. Ste. H, Goleta, CA 93117-5564 USA (SAN 254-4180) Toll Free: 800-929-4627
E-mail: info@maps.com
Web site: http://www.maps.com
Dist(s): **Cram, George F. Co., Inc.**

Marable, Justin, (978-0-9831104) 136 SW Kendall Ave., Topeka, KS 66606 USA Tel 785-286-7944
E-mail: justinmarableks@gmail.com.

Marak, Michael, (978-0-9795866) 6205 Daffan Ln., Austin, TX 78724-1501 USA
E-mail: sue@rezulting.com.

Marandu, Thobias L., (978-0-9767605) 2913 Columbiana Rd. Apt. B, Birmingham, AL 35216-3537 USA
E-mail: tiekundayo@yahoo.com.

Marble Hse. Editions, (978-0-9677047; 978-0-9786745; 978-0-9815345; 978-0-9834030; 978-0-9966224) 96-09 66th Ave., Suite 1d, Rego Park, NY 11374 USA (SAN 253-6536); 96-09 66th Ave., Suite 1d, Rego Park, NY 11374 (SAN 253-6536)
E-mail: elizabeth.uhlig@yahoo.com
Web site: http://www.marble-house-editions.com/.

Marble Mountain Pr., (978-0-9748552) PMB 214, 2019 Aero Way, Suite 103, Medford, OR 97504 USA Tel 530-926-2473
E-mail: marblemountain@snowcrest.net
Web site: http://www.rvinnz.com.

Marcabru Publishing, (978-0-615-61495-3) 108 E. 38th St., New York, NY 10016 USA Tel 917-596-0650
Web site: www.glennberger.net
Dist(s): **CreateSpace Independent Publishing Platform.**

Marcasa Bks., (978-0-9763015) Paloma del Lago No. 67, Campolago, Cidra, PR 00739-9361 USA Tel 787-739-0815 (phone/fax)
E-mail: MarcasaBooks@ElPoderDeLaPalabra.net
Web site: http://www.ElPoderDeLaPalabra.net.

March Media, Inc., (978-0-9634824) 1114 Oman Dr., Brentwood, TN 37027 USA Tel 615-377-1146; Fax: 615-373-1705
E-mail: etta.wilson@comcast.net.

March Street Pr., (978-0-9624453; 978-1-882983; 978-0-9745909; 978-1-59661) 3413 Wilshire Dr., Greensboro, NC 27408-2923 USA Fax: 336-282-9754 prefer orders by email (rbixby@earthlink.net)
E-mail: rbixby@earthlink.net
Web site: http://www.marchstreetpress.com
Dist(s): **Bottom Dog Pr.**

Marcher Lord Pr., (978-0-9821049; 978-0-9825987; 978-1-935929; 978-1-940163) 5025 N. Central Ave., No. 635, Phoenix, AZ 85012 USA; *Imprints*: Enclave Publishing (EnclavePub)
E-mail: steve@marcherlordpress.com
Web site: http://www.enclavepublishing.com.

Marcia's Menagerie, (978-0-9777359) 2960 W. Stuart St., A-203, Fort Collins, CO 80526 USA Tel 970-493-6373
E-mail: tangome27@hotmail.com.

Marco Bk. Co., (978-0-9710756; 978-0-9729765) 60 Industrail Rd., Lodi, NJ 07644 USA Tel 973-458-0485; Fax: 973-458-5289; Toll Free: 800-842-4234; *Imprints*: Everbind (Everbind)
E-mail: everbind5@aol.com
Dist(s): **Bks. & Media, Inc.**

MAR*CO Products, Inc., (978-1-57543; 978-1-884063) Orders Addr.: 1443 Old York Rd., Warminster, PA 18974 USA Tel 215-956-0313; Fax: 215-956-9041; Toll Free: 800-448-2197
E-mail: csfunk@marcoproducts.com; marcoproducts@comcast.net
Web site: http://www.store.yahoo.com/marcoproducts; http://www.marcoproducts.com.

Marcoux, Tom Media, LLC, (978-0-9624660; 978-0-9800511; 978-0-615-78342-0; 978-0-615-78657-5; 978-0-615-80157-5; 978-0-615-80934-2; 978-0-615-81302-8; 978-0-615-83582-2; 978-0-615-91576-0; 978-0-615-92869-2; 978-0-615-97539-9; 978-0-615-99188-7; 978-0-692-21096-3; 978-0-692-22704-6; 978-0-692-22972-9; 978-0-692-23525-6; 978-0-692-33069-2; 978-0-692-35850-4; 978-0-692-38436-7; 978-0-692-45951-5; 978-0-692-52718-4) 674 Morse Ave. Unit F, Sunnyvale, CA 94085 USA Tel 415-572-6609
Dist(s): **CreateSpace Independent Publishing Platform.**

Mardi Gras Publishing, LLC, (978-0-9787262; 978-0-9789024; 978-0-9789986; 978-0-9790649; 978-0-9791570; 978-1-934329) 6845 Hwy. 90 E. Suite 255, Daphne, AL 36526 USA
E-mail: contactlamedia@gmail.com
Web site: http://lamediaonline.com.

Marduk Publishing Inc., (978-1-893138) Orders Addr.: a/o Marduk Publishing Inc., P.O. Box 480608, Delray Beach, FL 33448 USA (SAN 256-3053) Tel 561-638-6070; 516 695-8077; Toll Free: 888-462-7385 (phone/fax)
E-mail: docbloc@marduk1.com; docbloc@marpub.com; docbloc@hotmail.com
Web site: http://www.marpub.com; http://www.marduk1.com; http://www.all-a.us; http://www.all-ace.com.

Marn Green Publishing, Inc., (978-1-934277) 5630 Memorial Ave N. # 3, Stillwater, MN 55082-1087 USA (SAN 852-4920) Toll Free: 800-287-1512
E-mail: toddsnow@marengreen.com
Web site: http://www.marengreen.com
Dist(s): **Crabtree Publishing**
Follett School Solutions.

Maresca, Wendi, (978-0-9772897) 6130 Murfield Dr., Gurnee, IL 60031-5357 USA.

Margaret Weis Productions, Ltd., (978-1-931567; 978-1-936685) P.O. Box 1131, Williams Bay, WI 53191 USA Fax: 866-668-5730 Do not confuse with Sovereign Pr. in Rochester, WA
E-mail: margaret@margaretweis.com; christi@margaretweis.com
Web site: http://www.margaretweis.com
Dist(s): **Diamond Comic Distributors, Inc.**
Diamond Bk. Distributors
PSI (Publisher Services, Inc.).

Margolis, Amy Publishing, (978-0-9776692) Orders Addr.: 31 Saddle Ln., Old Brookville, NY 11545 USA (SAN 257-9294)
E-mail: Amy@ButterfliesandMagicalWings.com
Web site: http://www.ButterfliesandMagicalWings.com.

Margolis, Marion, (978-0-9753184) 1 W. 72nd St., Apt. No. 95, New York, NY 10023 USA Tel 212-595-7555
E-mail: chasmargolis@aol.com
Dist(s): **Xlibris Corp.**

Marhouse, Inc., (978-0-9752703) Orders Addr.: a/o Marhouse Inc., P.O. Box 150605, Altamonte Springs, FL 32715 USA Tel 407-499-5307 (phone/fax)
E-mail: marhouse12@yahoo.com
Web site: http://www.adventurefox.com.

Marian Pr., (978-0-944203; 978-1-932773; 978-1-59614) Marian Helpers Ctr., Eden Hill, Stockbridge, MA 01263-0004 USA (SAN 243-1548) Tel 413-298-3691; Fax: 413-298-1356; Toll Free: 800-462-7426
E-mail: mromaniak@marian.org
Web site: http://www.marian.org
Dist(s): **Send The Light Distribution LLC.**

Marianist Pr., (978-0-9628309) Orders Addr.: 1116 Imperial Blvd., Kettering, OH 45419-2434 USA Tel 937-298-8509; Edit Addr.: 233 E. Helena St., Dayton, OH 45404-1003 USA.

Marianne Richmond Studios, Inc. *Imprint of* **Sourcebooks, Inc.**

Marilux Pr., (978-0-9710281) 4100 Corporate Sq., Suite 161, Naples, FL 34104 USA Tel 239-398-7018; Fax: 917-591-0387
E-mail: sales@mariluxpress.com
Web site: http://www.MariluxPress.com.

Marimba Bks. *Imprint of* **Hudson Publishing Group, The**

Marinaro, Stacy, (978-0-615-20684-4; 978-0-615-20807-7; 978-0-615-20883-1; 978-0-615-21988-2; 978-0-578-02365-6) 420 Matthews St., Bristol, CT 06010 USA
E-mail: stacymarinaro@yahoo.com
Dist(s): **Lulu Enterprises Inc.**

Mariner Publishing, (978-0-9768238; 978-0-9776841; 978-0-9800077; 978-0-9820172; 978-0-9841128; 978-0-9833478; 978-0-9835565; 978-0-9849214; 978-0-9909653) Div. of Mariner Media, Inc., 131 W. 21st St., Buena Vista, VA 24416 USA Tel 540-264-0021; Fax: 540-261-1881 Do not confuse with Mariner Publishing in Tampa, FL Oklahoma City, OK
E-mail: andy@marinermedia.com
Web site: http://www.marinermedia.com
Dist(s): **Perseus Bks. Group**
Virginia Pubns.

Marion Street Pr., LLC, (978-0-9665176; 978-0-9710050; 978-0-9729937; 978-1-933338; 978-1-936863) 4207 SE. Woodstock Blvd. #168, Portland, OR 97206 USA Tel 503-888-4624; Toll Free Fax: 866-571-8359
E-mail: info@acornguild.com; acornguild@yahoo.com
Web site: http://www.acornguild.com; http://www.marionstreetpress.com
Dist(s): **Independent Pubs. Group.**

Maritime Kids Quest Pr., (978-0-9761178) P.O. Box 700, Manteo, NC 27954 USA Tel 252-473-6933
E-mail: maritimekidsquest@earthlink.net.

Maritime Museum Assn. of San Diego, (978-0-944580) 1492 N. Harbor Dr., San Diego, CA 92101 USA (SAN 279-5027) Tel 619-234-9153; Fax: 619-234-8345
E-mail: museumstore@sdmaritime.com
Web site: http://www.sdmaritime.com/mains'lhaul
Dist(s): **Sunbelt Pubns., Inc.**

Marker, Margaret Penfield, (978-0-9716721) 64 Colonial Dr., Rancho Mirage, CA 92270-1600 USA
E-mail: tmlrmarker@aol.com.

Market 1 Group Inc., (978-0-9748109) 118 Worthington Business Ctr. 1550 Douglas Ave., Charleston, IL 61920 USA Tel 217-345-8281
E-mail: bmcelwee@consolidated.net
Web site: http://www.familyjourneys.net.

Markins Enterprises, (978-0-937729) 2039 SE 45th Ave., Portland, OR 97215 USA (SAN 659-3224) Tel 503-235-1036.

Markowitz, Darryl, (978-0-9818469) 354 Park Blvd., Worthington, OH 43085 USA Tel 412-613-1733; *Imprints*: FaithWalker Publishing (FaithWalker)
Web site: http://www.thefaithwalkerseries.com.

Marks, William *See* **MPC Pr. International**

Markwin Pr., (978-0-9740793) Orders Addr.: P.O. Box 1143, Silver Springs, NV 89429 USA Tel 775-577-0676; Edit Addr.: 3220 E. 9th St., Silver Springs, NV 89429 USA
E-mail: softgaits@wildblue.com
Web site: www.TheFabulousFloatingHorses.com.

Marlor Pr., Inc., (978-0-943400; 978-1-892147) 4304 Brigadoon Dr., Saint Paul, MN 55126 USA (SAN 240-7140) Tel 651-484-4600; Fax: 651-490-1182; Toll Free: 800-669-4908
E-mail: marlor@minn.net
Dist(s): **Independent Pubs. Group**
MyiLibrary.

MarMooWorks,LLC, (978-0-9853579; 978-0-9853580) 318 Beverly Dr., Erie, PA 16505 USA Tel 814-454-1888
E-mail: marymoodey@gmail.com
Web site: jason@conveyorarts.org.

MarniPosa Services and Productions, (978-0-9727687) P.O. Box 812, Middletown, DE 19709 USA
E-mail: niamaebrown@gmail.com
Web site: http://www.marniwilliams.com; http://www.nia22.zumba.com; http://www.nia22.com.

Maroma Bks., (978-0-9796465) 5615 Kirby Dr., Suite 820, Houston, TX 77005 USA Toll Free Fax: 800-525-0910; Toll Free: 888-627-6628
E-mail: molly@maromabooks.com
Web site: http://www.maromabooks.com
Dist(s): **Lightning Source, Inc.**

Marquette Bks., LLC, (978-0-922993; 978-0-9816018; 978-0-9826597; 978-0-9833476) Orders Addr.: 16421 N. 31 Ave., Phoenix, AZ 85053 USA (SAN 251-5261) Tel 509-290-9240; Fax: 602-464-9675
E-mail: books@marquettebooks.com
Web site: http://www.marquettebooks.com
Dist(s): **Ambassador Bks. & Media**
Bk. Hse., The
Brodart Co.
Coutts Information Services
Eastern Bk. Co.
Emery-Pratt Co.
Levant USA, Inc.
Midwest Library Service
Blackwell.

Marquise Publishing, (978-0-9745264) Orders Addr.: 11470 Euclid Ave Suite 338, Cleveland, OH 44106 USA
E-mail: marquisepublishing@gmail.com
Web site: http://www.marquisepublishing.com.

Marrero, Rafael, (978-0-9747569) 2121 Red Rd., Ave., Coral Gables, FL 33155-2232 USA Tel 305-267-0163
E-mail: rafelitomarrero@hotmail.com.

Marriwell Publishing, (978-0-9742891) P.O. Box 116, Center Valley, PA 18034 USA Tel 610-282-6807; Fax: 610-282-0909
Web site: http://www.marriwell.com.

Mars Media Publishers *See* **Audio Holdings, LLC**

Marsh, Carole Bks. *Imprint of* **Gallopade International**

Marsh, Carole Family CD-Rom *Imprint of* **Gallopade International**

Marsh, Carole Mysteries *Imprint of* **Gallopade International**

Marsh Creek Pr., (978-0-937750) Div. of Don Aslett, Inc., Orders Addr.: P.O. Box 700, Pocatello, ID 83204 USA (SAN 216-1028) Tel 208-232-3535; Fax: 208-235-5481; Edit Addr.: 311 S. Fifth Ave., Pocatello, ID 83201 USA
E-mail: Tobih@aol.com
Web site: http://www.aslett.com.

Marsh Media *See* **Witcher Productions**

Marsh, Thomas E. Inc., (978-0-9633682) 914 Franklin Ave., Youngstown, OH 44502 USA Tel 216-743-8600; Toll Free: 800-845-7930.

Marshall Cavendish (GBR) (978-0-7614; 978-0-86307; 978-1-85435; 978-0-9533784; 978-1-902741; 978-0-462; 978-0-85080; 978-1-905992) *Dist. by* **Marshall C.**

†Marshall Cavendish Corp., (978-0-7614; 978-0-85685; 978-0-86307; 978-1-85435; 978-1-60870) Member of Times Publishing Group, 99 White Plains Rd., Tarrytown, NY 10591-9001 USA (SAN 238-437X) Tel 914-332-8888; Fax: 914-332-8882; Toll Free: 800-821-9881; *Imprints*: Benchmark Books (Benchmark NY); Marshall Cavendish Reference Books (M C Ref Bks); Cavendish Children's Books (Cav Child Bks)
E-mail: npalazzo@marshallcavendish.com
Web site: www.MCEducation.us
Dist(s): **BookBaby**
Ebsco Publishing
Follett School Solutions
Fujii Assocs.
Lectorum Pubns., Inc.
MyiLibrary; *CIP.*

Marshall Cavendish International (Asia) Private Ltd. (SGP) (978-981-204; 978-981-232; 978-2-85700; 978-981-261; 978-981-4302; 978-981-4312; 978-981-4328; 978-981-4346; 978-981-4351; 978-981-4361; 978-981-4382; 978-981-4398; 978-981-4408; 978-981-4426; 978-981-4430; 978-981-4433; 978-981-4435; 978-981-4484; 978-981-4516; 978-981-4561) *Dist. by* **Natl Bk Netwk.**

Marshall Cavendish Reference Bks. *Imprint of* **Marshall Cavendish Corp.**

Marshall, George Publishing, (978-0-9729403) P.O. Box 375, Bedford, VA 24523 USA.

Marshall, John High Schl. Alumni Assn., (978-0-9759618) 347 Pineview Cir., Berea, OH 44017 USA
E-mail: jmhalumni@ameritech.com
Web site: http://www.jmhalumni.com.

Martell Publishing Co, (978-1-893181; 978-1-930200) P.O. Box 83554, San Diego, CA 92138-3554 USA Toll Free Fax: 800-805-3329; *Imprints*: Lagesse Stevens (LagesseS)
E-mail: martell@martellpublishing.com.

Martella, Liz, (978-0-615-14941-7; 978-0-615-25506-4) 393 Lathrop Rd., Lathrop, CA 95330 USA
E-mail: lizmartella@yahoo.com
Web site: http://www.lulu.com/lizmartella
Dist(s): **Lulu Enterprises Inc.**

Marti Bks., (978-0-9766006) Orders Addr.: P.O. Box 603, West Tisbury, MA 02575 USA Tel 508-696-7496 (phone/fax); Edit Addr.: 635 State Rd., West Tisbury, MA 02575 USA
E-mail: ffen2@aol.com
Web site: http://www.martibooks.com.

Martin, Amy, (978-0-9882051) 2733 Braden Way, Lexington, KY 40509 USA Tel 859-797-0156
E-mail: amart71@rocketmail.com.

Martin & Brothers, (978-0-9719842; 978-0-9767500) Orders Addr.: P.O. Box 122, Abbott, TX 76621 USA Tel 254-235-8588; Edit Addr.: 101 Bordon, Abbott, TX 76621 USA
E-mail: martinbrothers@aol.com.

Martin, Carolyn, (978-0-9746808) 1890 N. 36th St., Galesburg, MI 49053-9528 USA Tel 269-665-9953 Do not confuse with Carolyn Martin in Philadelphia, PA
E-mail: carmartin@earthlink.net
Web site: http://www.finefrets.com/metalhorses.

Martin, Elizabeth B., (978-0-578-12912-9; 978-0-578-12913-6; 978-0-9910543; 978-0-9904213)
E-mail: elizabeth@elizabethbmartin.com
Dist(s): **Lulu Enterprises Inc.**

Martin, Jack & Assocs., (978-0-9649530) Orders Addr.: 9422 S. Saginaw, Grand Blanc, MI 48439 USA Tel 810-694-5698; Fax: 810-694-7851
E-mail: jdmart@tir.com
Web site: http://www.Pre-Apprenticetraining.com.

Martin, James Jr., (978-0-9799465) P.O. Box 4207, Greenwitch, CT 06831 USA Fax: 516-060-1177
E-mail: JMJ723@optonline.com
Web site: http://williamthegarbagetruck.com.

Martin, Kevin, (978-0-578-10705-9) 7450 Globe Rd., Lenoir, NC 28645 USA.

Martin Publishing, (978-0-9753992) 1600 S. 30th, Lot 36, Escanaba, MI 49829 USA Do not confuse with companies with the same or similar name in Fort Morgan, CO; Tampico, IL; La Mesa, CA; Perry, OK; Cowpens, SC; Lincoln, ME.

Martinez, Leroy F., (978-0-9748002) 4045 E. 3rd St. Unit 111, Long Beach, CA 90814-2883 USA Tel 562-443-7727
Web site: http://leroymartinez.com.

†Martingale & Co., (978-0-943574; 978-1-56477; 978-1-60468) Orders Addr.: 19021 120th Ave. NE. Suite 102, Bothell, WA 98011 USA (SAN 665-7923) Fax: 425-486-7596; Toll Free: 800-426-3126; *Imprints*: That Patchwork Place (That Patchwrk Pl)
E-mail: ssanta@martingale-pub.com; mburns@martingale-pub.com; info@martingale-pub.com
Web site: http://www.martingale-pub.com
Dist(s): **Bookazine Co., Inc.**; *CIP.*

Martino Publishing, (978-1-57898; 978-1-888262; 978-1-61427) P.O. Box 373, Mansfield Centre, CT 06250 USA Tel 860-974-2277; Fax: 860-974-3665
E-mail: martino@martinopublishing.com
Web site: http://www.martinopublishing.com.

Martin's *See* **Green Pastures Pr.**

Marvel Enterprises, Incorporated *See* **Marvel Worldwide, Inc.**

Marvel Pr. *Imprint of* **Disney Publishing Worldwide**

Marvel Worldwide, Inc., (978-0-7851; 978-0-87135; 978-0-939766; 978-0-9604146; 978-1-4695; 978-1-302) Subs. of The Walt Disney Co, 135 W. 50th St., New York, NY 10020 USA (SAN 216-9088); c/o Marvel Enterprises Japan, Inc., Hill House B, 9-10 Hachiyama-cho Sibuya, Tokyo, 150-0034
E-mail: mail@marvel.com; amorales@marvel.com
Web site: http://www.marvel.com
Dist(s): **Hachette Bk. Group.**

Marvelous Dream, (978-0-9771016) Div. of Marvelous World LLC, P.O. Box 252, Bloomfield, NJ 07003-9998 USA (SAN 256-7857).

Marvelous Spirit Pr. *Imprint of* **Loving Healing Pr., Inc.**

MarWel Enterprises, Inc., (978-0-9759582) P.O. Box 31227, Washington, DC 20030 USA
E-mail: marwel@earthlink.net.

Marx Group, The, (978-0-9773962; 978-1-935309) 2111 Jefferson Davis Hwy. 303N., Arlington, VA 22202 USA Tel 703-418-1956; Fax: 703-418-0224
E-mail: don@themarxgroup.com
Web site: http://www.the marxgroup.com.

Marx, Jeff, (978-0-9667824; 978-0-9793134) 3160 N. 35th St., Hollywood, FL 33021-2630 USA (SAN 853-1021)
E-mail: JeffMarx@schoolelection.com
Web site: http://www.schoolelection.com
Dist(s): **Independent Pubs. Group.**

Mary B./French, (978-0-9852821) 1355 Pine St. # 5, San Francisco, CA 94109 USA Tel 415-931-8691.

Maryknoll Fathers & Brothers *See* **Maryknoll Missioners**

Maryknoll Missioners, (978-0-941395) P.O. Box 308, Maryknoll, NY 15054-0308 USA (SAN 219-3752) Tel 914-941-7590; Toll Free: 800-227-8523
E-mail: jgoldbeck@maryknoll.org.

†Maryland Historical Society, (978-0-938420; 978-0-9842135; 978-0-9965944) 201 W. Monument St., Baltimore, MD 21201 USA (SAN 203-9788) Tel 410-685-3750; Fax: 410-385-2105
E-mail: panderson@mdhs.org
Web site: http://www.mdhs.org
Dist(s): **Hood, Alan C. & Co., Inc.**
Johns Hopkins Univ. Pr.; *CIP.*

Maryruth Bks., Inc., (978-0-9713518; 978-0-9720295; 978-0-9746475; 978-1-933624; 978-1-62544) 18660 Ravenna Rd. Bldg. 2, Chagrin Falls, OH 44023 USA Tel 440-834-1105; Toll Free Fax: 800-951-4077
E-mail: admin@maryruthbooks.com
Web site: http://www.maryruthbooks.com.

For full information on wholesalers and distributors, refer to the Wholesaler and Distributor Name Index

Marzetta Bks., *(978-0-9657033)* P.O. Box 274, Lombard, IL 60148 USA Tel 630-424-1403
E-mail: marzetta@concentric.net.

Masalai Pr., *(978-0-9714127)* 368 Capricorn Ave., Oakland, CA 94611-2058 USA
E-mail: THSlone@yahoo.com
Web site: http://THSlone.tripod.com/masalaipress.html.

Mascot Bks., Inc., *(978-0-9743442; 978-1-932888; 978-1-934878; 978-1-936319; 978-1-937406; 978-1-62086; 978-1-63177)* Orders Addr.: 560 Herndon Pkwy. Suite 120, Herndon, VA 20170 USA Tel 703-437-3584; Fax: 703-437-3554; Toll Free: 877-862-7568
E-mail: info@mascotbooks.com; josh@mascotbooks.com; naren@mascotbooks.com; laura@mascotbooks.com
Web site: http://www.mascotbooks.com
Dist(s): **Partners Bk. Distributing, Inc.**

Mason Crest, *(978-1-59084; 978-1-59482; 978-1-4222)* Div. of Highlights Inc., Orders Addr.: 450 Parkway Dr., Suite D, Broomall, PA 19008-0914 USA Tel 610-543-6200; Fax: 610-543-3878; Toll Free: 866-627-2665 (866-MCP-Book)
E-mail: gbaffa@masoncrest.com
Web site: http://www.masoncrest.com
Dist(s): **Follett School Solutions**
Smashwords.

Mason Crest Publishers *See* **Mason Crest**

Massachusetts Continuing Legal Education, Inc., *(978-0-944490; 978-1-57589)* 10 Winter Pl., Boston, MA 02108-4751 USA (SAN 226-3033) Tel 617-350-7006; Fax: 617-482-9498; Toll Free: 800-966-6253
Web site: http://www.mcle.org.

Massey Publishing, *(978-0-9640883)* P.O. Box 8945, Atlanta, GA 31106-0945 USA Tel 404-406-5034 (phone/fax)
E-mail: galemassey7@aol.com
Dist(s): **New Leaf Distributing Co., Inc.**

Master Bks., *(978-0-89051; 978-1-61458)* P.O. Box 726, Green Forest, AR 72638-0726 USA (SAN 205-6119) Tel 870-438-5288; Fax: 870-438-5120; Toll Free: 800-999-3777
E-mail: nlp@newleafpress.net
Web site: http://www.masterbooks.net; NLPG.com
Dist(s): **MyiLibrary**
Spring Arbor Distributors, Inc.

Master Communications, Inc., *(978-1-888194; 978-1-60480)* 2692 Madison Rd., Suite N1-307 N1-307, Cincinnati, OH 45208 USA (SAN 299-2140) Tel 513-563-3100; Fax: 513-563-3105; Toll Free: 800-765-5885
E-mail: sales@master-comm.com
Web site: http://www.worldculturemedia.com; http://www.master-comm.com
Dist(s): **Follett School Solutions.**

Master Publishing, Inc., *(978-0-945053)* 6019 W. Howard St., Niles, IL 60714-4801 USA (SAN 245-8829)
E-mail: pete@w5yi.com
Web site: http://www.MasterPublishing.com; http://www.ForrestMims.com; http://www.w5yi.org
Dist(s): **WFiveYI Group, Inc., The.**

Master Strategies Publishing, *(978-0-9766485)* 5806 Chatsworth Ct., Arlington, TX 76018 USA Toll Free: 888-792-5105.

Masterpiece Creations Graphics & Publishing, *(978-0-615-23057-3; 978-0-9842171)* 305 Friendship Ln., Suite 100, Gettysburg, PA 17325 USA (SAN 858-7507) Tel 717-337-1829
E-mail: dj@masterpiececreations.biz
Web site: http://www.masterpiececreations.biz.

MasterVision, *(978-1-55919)* 969 Park Ave., New York, NY 10028 USA Tel 212-879-0448
E-mail: stadin1@aol.com
Web site: http://www.mastervision.com/.

Mastery Education Corporation *See* **Charlesbridge Publishing, Inc.**

Mastery For Strings Pubns., *(978-0-9753919)* 1005 Meriden Ln., Austin, TX 78703 USA Tel 512-474-8196
E-mail: musipro@aol.com.

Mastery Learning Systems, *(978-1-888976)* 532 N. School St., Ukiah, CA 95482 USA Fax: 707-462-9307; Toll Free: 800-433-4181 (phone/fax)
E-mail: mastery@pacific.net
Web site: http://www.masterylearningsystems.com.

Masthof Pr., *(978-1-883294; 978-1-930353; 978-1-932864; 978-1-60126)* 219 Mill Rd., Morgantown, PA 19543-9701 USA Tel 610-286-0258; Fax: 610-286-6860
E-mail: mast@masthof.com
Web site: http://www.masthof.com.

Mateboer, Johannes Aart, *(978-0-9759487)* Div. of Captain's Publishing, 6514 Wakehurst Rd., Charlotte, NC 28226 USA Tel 704-540-7617 (phone/fax)
E-mail: hlmateboer@hotmail.com
Web site: http://www.captainspublishing.com
Dist(s): **eBookIt.com.**

Math Essentials, *(978-0-9666211; 978-0-9821901; 978-0-9843629)* P.O. Box 1723, Los Gatos, CA 95031 USA Fax: 408-358-3738; Toll Free: 866-444-6284; 265 Carlton Ct., Los Gatos, CA 95032
E-mail: rickwfisher@yahoo.com
Web site: http://www.mathessentials.com.

Math In Motion *See* **Crane Bks.**

Math Solutions, *(978-0-941355; 978-1-935099)* Div. of Marilyn Burns Education Assocs., Orders Addr.: 150 Gate 5 Rd., Sausalito, CA 94965 USA (SAN 665-5424) Tel 415-332-4181; Fax: 415-331-1931; Toll Free Fax: 877-942-8837; Toll Free: 800-868-9092
E-mail: info@mathsolutions.com; jcross@mathsolutions.com; jwayland@mathsolutions.com
Web site: http://www.mathsolutions.com
Dist(s): **MyiLibrary**
Scholastic, Inc.

Math Solutions Publications *See* **Math Solutions**

Math Studio, The, *(978-1-929362)* 271 Lafayette St., Salem, MA 01970-5404 USA
E-mail: cdraper@mathstudio.com
Web site: http://www.mathstudio.com.

Mathematical Assn. of America, *(978-0-88385; 978-0-9835005; 978-1-61444; 978-1-939512)* Orders Addr.: P.O. Box 91112, Washington, DC 20090-1112 USA; Edit Addr.: 1529 18th St., NW, Washington, DC 20036 USA (SAN 203-9737) Tel 301-617-7800; Fax: 301-206-9789; Toll Free: 800-331-1622
E-mail: cbaxter@maa.org; swebb@maa.org
Web site: http://www.maa.org
Dist(s): **Cambridge Univ. Pr.**
ebrary, Inc.

Mathematical Sciences Research Institute, *(978-0-9639003; 978-0-9824800)* 17 Gauss Way, Berkeley, CA 94720-5070 USA Tel 510-642-0143; Fax: 510-642-8609
E-mail: librarian@msri.org
Web site: http://www.msri.org/.

Mathematical Solutions Publishing Co., *(978-0-9718019; 978-0-9815629)* P.O. Box 36365, Grosse Pointe Farms, MI 48236-0365 USA (SAN 855-8787) Fax: 313-881-4277.

MathisJones Communications, LLC, *(978-0-9799482; 978-0-9840117; 978-0-9850542; 978-0-9853093; 978-0-9889643; 978-0-9964948)* Orders Addr.: P.O. Box 569, Chesterfield, MO 63006-0569 USA (SAN 854-8102) Tel 636-938-1100; Fax: 636-349-1100; Edit Addr.: 1 Putt Ln., Eureka, MO 63025-2828 USA
E-mail: info@mathisjones.com
Web site: monographpublishing.com
Dist(s): **eBookIt.com.**

Mathis-Njie, Joan J. *See* **Anointed Pubs.**

MATHSTORY.COM, *(978-0-9702641)* Div. of Rak Productions, P.O. Box 20226, New York, NY 10025-1511 USA Tel 212-864-5462
E-mail: mathstory2000@aol.com
Web site: http://mathstory.com.

MathWord Pr., LLC, *(978-0-9840425; 978-1-939431)* 97 Fennbrook Dr., Hamden, CT 06517 USA Tel 203-288-8114
E-mail: mathwordpress@aol.com
Web site: mwpenn.com.

Matinicus Pr., *(978-0-9765689)* 734 Cleveland Ave., Brackenridge, PA 15014-1501 USA.

Matter of Africa America Time, *(978-0-9760523)* 2114 Vincent Ave. N., Minneapolis, MN 55411 USA.

Matting Leah Publishing Co., *(978-0-9761528; 978-0-9905764)* P.O. Box 265, Warwick, NY 10990-0265 USA
Web site: http://www.mattingleahpublishing.com.

Matzah Ball Bks., *(978-0-9753629)* 1830 Walgrove Ave., Los Angeles, CA 90066-2233 USA
E-mail: asneram@gmail.com
Web site: http://www.matzahballbooks.com.

Mau, C. Publishing Co., *(978-0-9778843)* Orders Addr.: P.O. Box 30084, Edmond, OK 73003-0002 USA
E-mail: cmaupublishing@cox.net.

Maui Arthoughts Co., *(978-0-945045)* P.O. Box 967, Wailuku, HI 96793-0967 USA (SAN 245-8799) Tel 808-244-0156; Toll Free: 800-403-3472
E-mail: books@maui.net
Web site: http://www.booksmaui.com
Dist(s): **Quality Bks., Inc.**

Maupin Hse. Publishing, *(978-0-929895; 978-1-934338; 978-1-936700; 978-1-937412)* Div. of Capstone Press, Incorporated, Orders Addr.: 1710 Roe Crest Dr., North Mankato, MN 56003 USA (SAN 250-7676) Toll Free Fax: 888-262-0705; Toll Free: 800-747-4992 (orders)
E-mail: k.monyhan@coughlancompanies.com
Web site: http://www.maupinhouse.com; http://www.capstoneclassroom.com.

Maval Medical Education *See* **Maval Publishing, Inc.**

Maval Publishing, Inc., *(978-1-884083; 978-1-59134)* Div. of Maval Printing Co., 5335 Victoria Cir., Firestone, CO 80504 USA Tel 303-682-9424
E-mail: info@jejerre.com
Web site: http://www.jejerre.com
Dist(s): **Majors Scientific Bks., Inc.**
Matthews Medical Bk. Co.

Maven Of Memory Publishing, *(978-0-9768042; 978-0-9833277; 978-0-9864412)* P.O. Box 398, Hurst, TX 76053-0398 USA Fax: 817-282-0000
Web site: http://www.mavenofmemory.com.

MavenMark Books, LLC *See* **HenschelHAUS Publishing**

Maverick Bks. *Imprint of* **Trinity Univ. Pr.**

Maverick Bks., *(978-0-9672355)* P.O. Box 897, Woodstock, NY 12498 USA (SAN 253-9284) Toll Free: 866-478-9266 (phone/fax) Do not confuse with Maverick Books, Perryton, TX
E-mail: maverickbooks@aol.com; hank1@ptsi.net
Dist(s): **Perseus-PGW.**

Maverick Bks., Inc., *(978-0-916941; 978-0-9608612; 978-1-59188)* Orders Addr.: P.O. Box 549, Perryton, TX 79070 USA (SAN 240-7183) Tel 806-435-7611; Fax: 806-435-2410; Edit Addr.: 14492 N.W. Loop 143, Perryton, TX 78070 USA Do not confuse with Maverick Books, Woodstock, NY
E-mail: hank1@ptsi.net
Web site: http://www.hankthecowdog.com
Dist(s): **Follett School Solutions**
Ingram Pub. Services.

Maverick Press *See* **Maverick Bks.**

Mawco, Inc., *(978-0-9853523)* 22172 Bakers Mill Rd., Dacula, GA 30019 USA Tel 404-202-7615
E-mail: a1missy@aol.com.

Mawi, Inc., *(978-0-9743901)* P.O. Box 471666, Chicago, IL 60647-6525 USA
E-mail: info@mawibooks.com
Web site: http://www.mawibooks.com.

Max & Zoe *Imprint of* **Picture Window Bks.**

Max Publication, Inc., *(978-0-9633577; 978-0-9799882)* Div. of DL Services, Inc., Orders Addr.: 825 Malvern Hill, Alpharetta, GA 30022 USA Tel 770-851-0935; Fax: 770-740-0188
E-mail: info@maxpubguides.com
Web site: http://www.italyluxuryfamilyhotels.com; http://www.italyluxhotels.com.

Maxim Pr., *(978-0-9767096)* 6947 Coal Creek Pkwy. SE, No. 137, Newcastle, WA 98059-3159 USA
E-mail: lg@maximpress.com
Web site: http://www.maximpress.com/.

Maximilian Pr. Pubs., *(978-0-9668650; 978-1-930211; 978-0-9827717)* Orders Addr.: P.O. Box 64841, Virginia Beach, VA 23467-4841 USA Tel 757-482-2273; Fax: 757-482-0325; Edit Addr.: 920 S. Battlefield Blvd., No. 100, Chesapeake, VA 23322 USA
E-mail: mp-publishing@inter-source.org
Web site: http://www.maximilianpressbookpublishers.com/.

Maximus Publishing, *(978-0-9792439)* P.O. Box 4455, Whitefish, MT 59937-4455 USA (SAN 852-8829)
E-mail: MaximusPublishing@bresnan.net
Web site: http://www.maximuspublishing.com.

Maxwell, Andre, *(978-0-578-10115-6; 978-0-578-10116-3; 978-0-9881811)* 722 Sawyer St. SE, Olympia, WA 98501 USA Tel 253-509-4022
E-mail: aleighmaxwell@gmail.com
Dist(s): **Follett School Solutions.**

Maxwell, Joseph *See* **LifeStory Publishing**

May, Cynthia D., *(978-0-615-12578-7)* 7720 W. 14 Rd., Mesick, MI 49668-9792 USA.

May, L. B. & Assocs., 3517 Neal Dr., Knoxville, TN 37918 USA Tel 865-922-7490; Fax: 865-922-7492
E-mail: lbmay@aol.com.

Mayhaven Publishing, Inc., *(978-1-878044; 978-1-932278; 978-1-939695)* P.O. Box PO Box 557, Mahomet, IL 618530557 USA Tel 217-586-4493; *Imprints:* Wild Rose (Wild Rose)
E-mail: mayhavenpublishing@mchsi.com
Web site: http://www.mayhavenpublishing.com
Dist(s): **Brodart Co.**
Deseret Bk. Co.
Distributors, The
Follett School Solutions
Mumford Library Bks., Inc.
Quality Bks., Inc.

Mayhem Bks., *(978-0-9770055)* P.O. Box 313, Bon Secour, AL 36511 USA
E-mail: sweetzer@gulftel.com.

Maylin, Grace, *(978-0-9792384)* 204 S. Roycroft Blvd., Cheektowaga, NY 14225 USA
E-mail: gmds@adelphia.net.

Maynestream Pr., *(978-0-9715183)* 3189 Cocoplum Cir., Coconut Creek, FL 33063 USA
E-mail: contact@maynestream.com
Web site: http://www.weirdthings.com.

Mayo, Johnny, *(978-0-9765918)* P.O. Box 5484, Columbia, SC 29250 USA Tel 803-767-6756
E-mail: k9heroes@att.net
Web site: http://www.bucksheroes.com.

Mayreni *Imprint of* **Mayreni Publishing**

Mayreni Publishing, *(978-0-9653718; 978-1-931834)* P.O. Box 5881, Monterey, CA 93944-5881 USA Tel 831-655-4377 (phone/fax); *Imprints:* Mayreni (Mayreni)
E-mail: mayrenipublishing@comcast.net; vatcheg@gmail.com
Web site: http://www.mayreni.com
Dist(s): **Perseus-PGW.**

Maytag Messerschmitt Media Concern, *(978-0-9768470)* 931 W. 19th St., Santa Ana, CA 92706 USA.

Mazaa, LLC, *(978-0-9849624)* 1555 Botelho Dr., No. 433, Walnut Creek, CA 94596 USA Tel 925-954-7182
E-mail: jofarrell@mazaallc.com.

Maze Creek Studio, *(978-0-9742285)* Orders Addr.: 1495 E. Thirteenth St., Carthage, MO 64836-9507 USA Tel 417-359-8787
E-mail: studio@andythomas.com
Web site: http://www.andythomas.com.

Mazeology, *(978-0-9793043)* 284 W. 12th St., No. 2, New York, NY 10014-6000 USA Tel 212-929-0734
E-mail: mazeology@yahoo.com
Web site: http://www.mazeology.net.

Mazie, Bernard *See* **Pangus Publishing**

Mazo Pubs., *(978-965-90462; 978-965-7344; 978-1-936778)* P.O. Box 10474, Jacksonville, FL 32247 USA Tel 815-301-3559 (phone/fax)
E-mail: mazopublishers@gmail.com; cm@mazopublishers.com
Web site: http://http://www.mazopublishers.com
Dist(s): **Smashwords.**

Mazur, Kathy *See* **Spring Ducks Bks., LLC**

MB Publishing, LLC, *(978-0-9624166; 978-0-9850814; 978-0-9913646; 978-0-9908430)* 7831 Woodmont Ave., Pmb 312, Bethesda, MD 20814 USA Toll Free: 866-530-4732
Web site: http://www.mbpublishing.com
Dist(s): **AtlasBooks Distribution**
BWI
BookBaby
Quality Bks., Inc.

MBT, *(978-0-9768419)* P.O. Box 215, Guilford, CT 06437 USA.

MC Basset, LLC, *(978-0-9774800)* P.O. Box 241, Asbury, NJ 08802 USA Tel 908-537-6410 (phone/fax)
E-mail: mkuderka@mcbasset.com.

MC Math Comics, *(978-0-9728453)* 720 Sutton Dr., Carlisle, PA 17013 USA Tel 717-243-4470
E-mail: clarkcherry@aol.com
Web site: http://plusman.org.

MC123 *See* **Taven Hill Studio**

McArdle, Donald, *(978-0-615-14212-8)* 11556 110th Ter., Largo, FL 33778-3716 USA
Web site: http://www.santaandbugsy.com
Dist(s): **Lulu Enterprises Inc.**

McArthur & Co. (CAN) *(978-1-55278; 978-1-77087) Dist. by* **Natl Bk Netwk.**

McBook Pubs., LLC, *(978-0-9705777)* Orders Addr.: P.O. Box 35513, Tulsa, OK 74005 USA Tel 918-671-6656
E-mail: jdokla@cableone.net.

McBride, Heddrick, *(978-0-615-70075-5; 978-0-615-70923-9; 978-0-615-71693-0; 978-0-615-72059-3; 978-0-615-72339-6; 978-0-615-78846-3; 978-0-615-86353-5; 978-0-615-91076-5; 978-0-615-95937-5)* 70-02 parsons blvd. apt 7c, Flushing, NY 11365 USA Tel 917-771-4463
Web site: www.mcbride-collection-of-stories.com
Dist(s): **CreateSpace Independent Publishing Platform.**

McCall, Philip Lee II, *(978-0-9822656; 978-0-615-77486-2; 978-0-615-77543-2)* 11381 SW 17th CT, Miramar, FL 33025 USA Tel 305-206-3699; *Imprints:* Mythix Studios (Mythix Stud)
E-mail: phil.mccallii@gmail.com
Web site: plmii.com
Dist(s): **CreateSpace Independent Publishing Platform.**

McCarthy, Maria Skantzaris, *(978-0-9755844)* P.O. Box 1308, Westford, MA 01886 USA
E-mail: msmccarthy@mindspring.com.

McCarthy, Sally Studios, *(978-0-9898968)* 7 Patriot Ln., Whitman, MA 02382 USA Tel 781-771-3394
E-mail: sallyjm@comcast.net.

McClain Printing Co., *(978-0-87012)* Orders Addr.: P.O. Box 403, Parsons, WV 26287-0403 USA (SAN 203-9478) Tel 304-478-2881; Fax: 304-478-4658; Toll Free: 800-654-7179
E-mail: mcclain@mcclainprinting.com; mmckinnie@mcclainprinting.com
Web site: http://www.McClainPrinting.com.

McClanahan Publishing Hse., Inc., *(978-0-913383; 978-1-934898; 978-0-9829785; 978-0-615-40157-7; 978-0-9836687; 978-0-9847933; 978-0-9895424; 978-0-9897078)* P.O. Box 100, Kuttawa, KY 42055 USA (SAN 285-8371) Tel 270-388-9388; Fax: 270-388-6186; Toll Free: 800-544-6959
E-mail: books@kybooks.com
Web site: http://www.kybooks.com
Dist(s): **Partners Bk. Distributing, Inc.**

McClelland & Stewart (CAN) *(978-0-396; 978-0-7710) Dist. by* **Random.**

McClenney Publishing *See* **First Associates Publishing**

McCourtie, Anne, *(978-0-9744448)* 15700 154th Rd., Mayetta, KS 66509 USA.

McCowan, Linda, *(978-0-9814596)* 1739 S. Hwy., 89 A, Kanab, UT 84741 USA.

McCray, Kathy *See* **Kathy's Pen**

McDaniel, Megan Faux *See* **25 Dreams Educational Media**

McDonald & Woodward Publishing Co., The, *(978-0-939923; 978-1-935778)* Orders Addr.: 431-B E. College St., Granville, OH 43023-1319 USA (SAN 663-6977) Tel 740-321-1140; Fax: 740-321-1141; Toll Free: 800-233-8787
E-mail: mwpubco@mwpubco.com
Web site: http://www.mwpubco.com.

McDonald Publishing Co., *(978-1-55708; 978-1-934256; 978-1-937664; 978-1-943600)* 567 Hanley Industrial Ct., Saint Louis, MO 63144 USA (SAN 249-5813) Tel 314-781-7400; Toll Free: 800-722-8080
E-mail: janet@mcdonaldpublishing.com.

McDougal Littell Incorporated *See* **Holt McDougal**

McDougal Publishing Co., *(978-1-58158; 978-1-884369)* Orders Addr.: P.O. Box 3595, Hagerstown, MD 21742-3595 USA (SAN 856-8286) Tel 301-797-6637; Fax: 301-733-2767; Toll Free: 800-962-3684
E-mail: publishing@mcdougal.org
Web site: http://www.mcdougalpublishing.com
Dist(s): **Anchor Distributors**
Spring Arbor Distributors, Inc.

McDowell Health-Science Bks., LLC, *(978-0-9741238)* P.O. Box 81, Lafayette, CO 80026 USA Tel 303-570-7231; Fax: 303-604-0773
E-mail: McDPubCo@mcdowellpublishing.com; McDPubCo@aol.com; healthscience@mcdowellpublishing.com
Web site: http://www.mcdowellpublishing.com.

McElderry, Margaret K. Bks. *Imprint of* **McElderry, Margaret K. Bks.**

McElderry, Margaret K. Bks., Div. of Simon & Schuster Children's Publishing, 1230 Ave. of the Americas, New York, NY 10020 USA; *Imprints:* McElderry, Margaret K. Books (MMcElderry)
Dist(s): **Simon & Schuster, Inc.**

McElreath, K.M., *(978-0-9769271)* 10420 Rivertown Rd., Fairburn, GA 30213 USA Tel 770-969-1718; Fax: 770-969-0183
E-mail: tmcelreath@bellsouth.net.

McElroy & Assocs., *(978-0-9673917)* 6651 Avignon Blvd., Falls Church, VA 22043-1724 USA Tel 703-237-5993; Fax: 703-237-5994
E-mail: roland@mcelroyassoc.com
Web site: http://www.mcelroyassoc.com.

McEwen, Judith A., *(978-0-9780693)* 22342 Chimayo Bend, San Antonio, TX 78258 USA Tel 210-630-9226; Fax: 210-595-7490
E-mail: chickensonthego@hotmail.com
Web site: http://www.chickensonthego.com.

McFadden, Tara, *(978-0-615-79631-4)* 1074 SW Maggie Glen Apt. # 103, Lake City, FL 32025 USA Tel (386) 984-2751
Dist(s): **CreateSpace Independent Publishing Platform.**

†**McFarland & Co., Inc. Pubs.**, *(978-0-7864; 978-0-89950; 978-1-4766)* Orders Addr.: P.O. Box 611, Jefferson, NC 28640 USA (SAN 215-093X) Tel 336-246-4460; Fax: 336-246-5018; 336-246-4403; Toll Free: 800-253-2187

Publisher Name Index

(orders only); Edit Addr.: 960 Hwy., 88 W., Jefferson, NC 28640 USA
E-mail: info@mcfarlandpub.com
Web site: http://www.mcfarlandpub.com
Dist(s): **Ebsco Publishing**
Follett School Solutions
Metapress
MyiLibrary
ebrary, Inc.; *CIP.*

McFinn Press *See* **Captain McFinn and Friends LLC, McFinn Pr.**

McGab Publishing, *(978-0-9788092)* 12438 Prather Ave., Pt Charlotte, FL 33981-1352 USA
Web site: http://weirdobook.com.

McGovern, Matthew /700acres Communications, *(978-0-9749445)* 27 McGovern Dr., Buxton, ME 04093 USA
E-mail: matt@mattmcgovern.com
Web site: http://www.mattmcgovern.com.

McGraw, Jason A., *(978-0-615-13681-3)* 254 Westminster Rd., Rochester, NY 14607 USA Tel 585-771-7777
E-mail: jaymcgraw18@aol.com
Dist(s): **Lulu Enterprises Inc.**

†**McGraw-Hill Cos., The**, *(978-0-07)* 6480 Jimmy Carter Blvd., Norcross, GA 30071-1701 USA (SAN 254-881X) Tel 614-755-5637; Fax: 614-755-5611; Orders Addr.: 860 Taylor Station Rd., Blacklick, OH 43004-0545 USA (SAN 200-254X) Fax: 614-755-5645; Toll Free: 800-722-4726 (orders & customer service); 800-338-3987 (college); 800-525-5003 (subscriptions); 800-352-3566 (books - US/Canada orders); P.O. Box 545, Blacklick, OH 43004-0545 Fax: 614-759-3759; Toll Free: 877-833-5524
E-mail: customer.service@mcgraw-hill.com
Web site: http://www.mcgraw-hill.com; http://www.ebooks.mcgraw-hill.com/
Dist(s): **Cambridge Univ. Pr.**
Ebsco Publishing
Libros Sin Fronteras
McGraw-Hill Osborne
McGraw-Hill Create (TM)
MyiLibrary
Sams Technical Publishing, LLC
ebrary, Inc.; *CIP.*

McGraw-Hill Education (GBR) *(978-0-07)* *Dist. by* **McGraw.**

McGraw-Hill Higher Education, *(978-0-07; 978-1-121)* Orders Addr.: P.O. Box 545, Blacklick, OH 43004-0545 USA Toll Free: 800-338-3987; Edit Addr.: 1333 Burr Ridge Pkwy., 3rd Flr., Burr Ridge, IL 60527 USA; *Imprints*: McGraw-Hill/Dushkin (Dshkn McG-Hill); McGraw-Hill Science, Engineering & Mathematics (McG-H Sci Eng)
E-mail: customer.service@mcgraw-hill.com
Web site: http://www.mhhe.com
Dist(s): **Follett School Solutions**
McGraw-Hill Cos., The
MyiLibrary
Oxford Univ. Pr., Inc.
ebrary, Inc.

McGraw-Hill Osborne, *(978-0-07; 978-0-88134; 978-0-931988)* Div. of The McGraw-Hill Professional, 160 Spear St. Flr. 7, San Francisco, CA 94105-1544 USA (SAN 274-3450) Toll Free: 800-227-0900
E-mail: customer.service@mcgraw-hill.com
Web site: http://www.osborne.com
Dist(s): **Ebsco Publishing**
McGraw-Hill Cos., The
MyiLibrary
ebrary, Inc.

McGraw-Hill Professional Book Group *See* **McGraw-Hill Schl. Education Group**

McGraw-Hill Professional Publishing, *(978-0-07)* Div. of McGraw-Hill Higher Education, Orders Addr.: P.O. Box 545, Blacklick, OH 43004-0545 USA Fax: 614-755-5645; Toll Free: 800-722-4726; Edit Addr.: 2 Penn Plaza, New York, NY 10121-2298 USA Tel 212-904-2000; *Imprints*: International Marine/Ragged Mountain Press (Inter Mar/Rag)
Dist(s): **Amacom**
American Pharmacists Assn.
Berrett-Koehler Pubs., Inc.
Ebsco Publishing
Entrepreneur Media Inc/Entrepreneur Pr.
Harvard Business Review Pr.
McGraw-Hill Cos., The
McGraw-Hill Medical Publishing Div.
McGraw-Hill Trade
MyiLibrary
ebrary, Inc.

McGraw-Hill Schl. Education Group, *(978-0-07; 978-0-7602; 978-0-8306; 978-0-911314; 978-0-917253; 978-1-55738; 978-1-307)* Div. of The McGraw-Hill Companies, Orders Addr.: P.O. Box 545, Blacklick, OH 43004-0545 USA Fax: 614-755-5645; Toll Free: 800-442-9685 (customer service); 800-722-4726; Edit Addr.: 8787 Orion Pl., Columbus, OH 43240 USA Tel 614-430-4000; Toll Free: 800-344-7344; c/o Grand Rapids Distribution Center, 3195 Wilson NW, Grand Rapids, MI 49544 (SAN 253-6420) Fax: 614-755-5611
E-mail: customer.service@mcgraw-hill.com
Web site: http://www.accessmedbooks.com; http://www.MHEducation.com
Dist(s): **Ebsco Publishing**
McGraw-Hill Cos., The
Urban Land Institute
ebrary, Inc.

McGraw-Hill Science, Engineering & Mathematics *Imprint of* **McGraw-Hill Higher Education**

McGraw-Hill Trade, *(978-0-07; 978-0-658; 978-0-8442)* Div. of McGraw-Hill Professional, Orders Addr.: P.O. Box 545, Blacklick, OH 43004-0545 USA Tel 800-722-4726; Fax: 614-755-5645; Edit Addr.: 2 Penn Plaza, New York, NY 10121 USA Tel 212-904-2000; *Imprints*: Passport Books (Passport Bks)
E-mail: Jeffrey_Krames@mcgraw-hill.com
Web site: http://www.books.mcgraw-hill.com
Dist(s): **Ebsco Publishing**
McGraw-Hill Cos., The
MyiLibrary
ebrary, Inc.

McGraw-Hill/Contemporary, *(978-0-658; 978-0-8092; 978-0-8325; 978-0-8442; 978-0-88499; 978-0-89061; 978-0-913327; 978-0-940279; 978-0-941263; 978-0-9630646; 978-1-56626; 978-1-56943; 978-1-57028)* Div. of McGraw-Hill Higher Education, Orders Addr.: P.O. Box 545, Blacklick, OH 43004-0545 USA Toll Free Fax: 800-998-3103; Toll Free: 800-621-1918; Edit Addr.: 4255 W. Touhy Ave., Lincolnwood, IL 60712 USA (SAN 169-2208) Tel 847-679-5500; Fax: 847-679-2494; Toll Free Fax: 800-998-3103; Toll Free: 800-323-4900; *Imprints*: National Textbook Company (Natl Textbk Co)
E-mail: ntcpub@tribune.com
Web site: http://www.ntc-cb.com
Dist(s): **Continental Bk. Co., Inc.**
Ebsco Publishing
Giron Bks.
Libros Sin Fronteras
McGraw-Hill Cos., The
ebrary, Inc.

McGraw-Hill/Dushkin *Imprint of* **McGraw-Hill Higher Education**

McHay, Micki, *(978-0-9786826)* 8212 Dolphin Bay Ct., Las Vegas, NV 89128 USA (SAN 854-655X).

McIntyre, Connie *See* **Grannie Annie Family Story Celebration, The**

McKatlib Pr., *(978-0-9745440)* P.O. Box 76693, Atlanta, GA 30358-1693 USA
Web site: http://www.bethanyadventures.com.

†**McKay, David Co., Inc.**, *(978-0-679; 978-0-88326; 978-0-89440)* Subs. of Random Hse., Inc., Orders Addr.: 400 Hahn Rd., Westminster, MD 21157 USA Tel 410-848-1900; Toll Free: 800-733-3000 (orders only); Edit Addr.: 201 E. 50th St., MD 4-6, New York, NY 10022 USA (SAN 200-240X) Tel 212-751-2600; Fax: 212-872-8026
Dist(s): **Libros Sin Fronteras**; *CIP.*

McKellen-Caffey, *(978-0-9794191)* 15543 Sprig St., Chino Hills, CA 91709-2853 USA (SAN 853-4144) Tel 909-393-0894
E-mail: mckellencaffey@yahoo.com
Web site: http://chiselhedgehog.com.

McKenna, Mark, *(978-0-9727681)* P.O. Box 633, Florida, NY 10921 USA.

McKenna Publishing Group, *(978-0-9713659; 978-1-932172)* 425 Poa Pl., San Luis Obispo, CA 93405 USA Tel 805-550-1667; Fax: 805-783-2317
E-mail: ric@mckennapubgrp.com
Web site: http://www.mckennapubgrp.com
Dist(s): **Booklines Hawaii, Ltd.**

McKenny, Stephanie L. *See* **J & J Publishing Co.**

McKenzie's Expressions, *(978-0-578-11179-7; 978-0-615-73173-5)* P.O. Box 1121, New Paltz, NY 12561 USA Tel 845-417-5271
Dist(s): **CreateSpace Independent Publishing Platform.**

McKinnon, Robert Scott, *(978-0-9651943)* 1608 Seventh St., S., Great Falls, MT 59405 USA Tel 406-452-3500
E-mail: maddog526@bresnan.net
Web site: http://home.bresnan.net/~maddog526/.

McLellan Bks., *(978-0-9747536)* Orders Addr.: P.O. Box 341, Claymont, DE 19703-0341 USA Tel 302-798-4006; Fax: 302-798-2567
E-mail: richardmclellan@dca.net; richard@mclellanbooks.com
Web site: http://www.mclellanbooks.com.

MCM Prime, Inc., *(978-0-9742351)* 6355 E. Duke Ranch Rd., Pearce, AZ 85625-6113 USA Tel 520-824-4051; Fax: 775-249-9133
E-mail: paulmc@vtc.net
Web site: http://www.mcmprime.pair.com/mcmpindx.htm.

McMillen Publishing, *(978-0-9635812; 978-1-888223)* Orders Addr.: 304 Main St., Ames, IA 50010 USA (SAN 254-9085) Tel 515-232-0208; Fax: 515-232-0402 (orders); Toll Free: 800-750-6997 (In Iowa); 800-453-3960 (Outside Iowa)
E-mail: denise.sunvold@sigler.com
Web site: http://www.mcmillenbooks.com.

McMurtrey, Martin A., *(978-0-9623961)* 808 Camden, San Antonio, TX 78215 USA Tel 210-223-9680.

McNatmar Ventures LLC, *(978-0-9787540)* P.O. Box 1324, Clover, SC 29710-7533 USA Tel 803-222-4043
E-mail: rhcisjdm@comporium.net
Web site: http://www.mcnatmar.com.

McNeil & Richards, *(978-0-9825602)* 2715 N. Wisconsin Ave., Peoria, IL 61603 USA.

McPugh, Kathleen, *(978-0-9742062)* Orders Addr.: P.O. Box 8372, Fresno, CA 93747 USA; Edit Addr.: P.O. Box 2552, Fallbrook, CA 92088-2552 USA
Web site: http://home.att.net/~kathfreeman/book.html; http://home.att.net/~kathfreeman
Dist(s): **Lightning Source, Inc.**

McQueen Publishing Co., *(978-0-917186)* 1211 S. Osceola Ave., Orlando, FL 32806-2223 USA (SAN 203-9516).

McRae Bks. Srl (ITA) *(978-88-89272; 978-88-6098; 978-88-88166; 978-88-900466; 978-88-900126)* *Dist. by* **IPG Chicago.**

McRitchie, Mike, *(978-0-578-03644-1)* 109 Falcon Creek Dr., McKinney, TX 75070 USA Tel 972-540-6800
E-mail: mmcritchie@tx.rr.com
Dist(s): **Lulu Enterprises Inc.**

Mcruffy Pr., *(978-1-59269)* P.O. Box 212, Raymore, MO 64083 USA Tel 816-331-2500; Fax: 816-331-3868; Toll Free Fax: 888-967-1300; Toll Free: 888-967-1200
E-mail: brian@mcruffy.com
Web site: http://www.mcruffy.com.

McSweeney's Books *See* **McSweeney's Publishing**

McSweeney's Publishing, *(978-0-9703355; 978-0-9719047; 978-1-932416; 978-1-934781; 978-1-936365; 978-1-938073; 978-1-940450; 978-1-944211)* Orders Addr.: 849 Valencia St., San Francisco, CA 94110-1736 USA (SAN 254-3184)
E-mail: custservice@mcsweeneys.net; adam@mcsweeneys.net
Web site: http://www.mcsweeneys.net
Dist(s): **MyiLibrary**
Perseus-PGW
Perseus Bks. Group.

MCW Publishing, *(978-0-9753773)* 50 Brookdale Ave., Rochester, NY 14621 USA Tel 585-317-5780
E-mail: itm2000@hotmail.com.

McWilliams Mediation Group Ltd., *(978-0-9768663)* P.O. Box 6216, Denver, CO 80206 USA (SAN 257-5442) Tel 303-830-0171
E-mail: joan@peacefinder.com
Web site: http://www.peacefinder.com
Dist(s): **ebrary, Inc.**

McWitty Pr., Inc., *(978-0-9755618; 978-0-9852227)* 110 Riverside Dr., No. 1A, New York, NY 10024 USA Tel 212-595-4161
E-mail: elliemcgra@aol.com
Web site: http://www.mcwittypress.com
Dist(s): **MyiLibrary**
Perseus-PGW
Perseus Bks. Group.

MCWong Ink, *(978-0-9820881)* 440 Kent Ave., Apt. PH1B, Brooklyn, NY 11211 USA
Web site: http://www.gordonandlili.com
Dist(s): **Emerald Bk. Co.**

m.d. hughes, *(978-0-9788541)* 9 Pasadena Rd., Branford, CT 06405 USA
Web site: http://www.cryofthefalcon.com.

Avitable Pub., *(978-0-9769794; 978-0-578-09899-9)* P.O. Box 38, East Meadow, NY 11554 USA Fax: 516-826-6843
E-mail: milliemsrd@aol.com
Web site: http://www.CaloriestheBottomLine.com.

ME Media LLC *See* **Tiger Tales**

Mead, Brian Publishing, *(978-0-9717509)* 203 E. Grove Rd., Long Grove, IA 52756 USA (SAN 255-2329)
E-mail: meadpub@juno.com; mattedeye@aol.com.

Mead Lommen Publishing *See* **Calaroga Publishing**

†**Meadowbrook Pr.**, *(978-0-88166; 978-0-915658)* 5451 Smetana Dr., Minnetonka, MN 55343 USA (SAN 207-3404) Tel 612-930-1100; Fax: 612-930-1940; Toll Free: 800-338-2232
E-mail: mballard@meadowbrookpress.com
Web site: http://www.meadowbrookpress.com
Dist(s): **Simon & Schuster**
Simon & Schuster, Inc.
Simon & Schuster Children's Publishing; *CIP.*

Meadowview Pubs., *(978-0-9741218)* Orders Addr.: P.O. Box 444, Portland, CT 06480 USA Tel 860-342-2646; Edit Addr.: 221 E. Cotton Hill Rd., Portland, CT 06480 USA
E-mail: marketbase@peoplepc.com.

MEAR LLC, *(978-0-9787628)* 636 Twp. Rd., 2724, Loudonville, OH 44842 USA Tel 419-994-3462 (phone/fax)
E-mail: mearllc@gmail.com
Web site: www.twralphabetbook.com.

MEC Publishing, *(978-0-9746865)* 1923 W. 17th St., Santa Ana, CA 92706 USA (SAN 256-405X)
E-mail: mecpublishing@aol.com
Web site: http://www.mecpublishing.com.

Mechanech Pubns., *(978-0-9702861; 978-0-9856497)* 4 Kaser Terr., Monsey, NY 10952 USA Tel 914-352-1926.

Mechling Bookbindery, *(978-0-9703825; 978-0-9744657; 978-0-9760563; 978-0-9793772; 978-0-9841400; 978-1-938184)* Div. of Mechling Associates, Inc., 1124 Oneida Valley Rd., Route 38, Chicora, PA 16025-3820 USA Tel 724-287-2120; Fax: 724-285-9231; Toll Free: 800-941-3735
E-mail: sales@mechlingbooks.com
Web site: http://www.mechlingbooks.com
Dist(s): **Partners Bk. Distributing, Inc.**

Medal Bks., *(978-0-9764300; 978-0-9785667)* P.O. Box 7231, Clearwater, FL 33758-7231 USA
E-mail: ronan@ronanblaze.com
Web site: http://www.ronanblaze.com.

Medallion Pr., Inc., *(978-0-9743639; 978-1-932815; 978-1-933836; 978-1-934755; 978-1-60542; 978-1-942546)* Orders Addr.: 4222 Meridian Pkwy. Ste 110, Aurora, IL 60504 USA (SAN 255-5360) Tel 630-513-8316; Fax: 630-513-8362; *Imprints*: Gold Medallion (Gold Medallion)
E-mail: jeanne@medallinmediagroup.com
Web site: http://www.medallionmediagroup.com
Dist(s): **Legato Pubs. Group**
Perseus-PGW.

Medernach, T.K. *See* **ThunderBolt Pubns.**

Media Alert!, *(978-0-9676616)* P.O. Box 735, Littleton, CO 80160-0735 USA Toll Free: 800-986-5560 (code 02)
E-mail: CNFsueLS@aol.com.

Media Angels, Inc. *See* **Knowledge Box Central**

Media Angels, Inc., *(978-0-9700385; 978-1-931941)* Orders Addr.: 15720 S. Pebble Ln., Fort Myers, FL 33912-2341 USA
E-mail: felice@mediaangels.com
Web site: http://www.mediaangels.com
Dist(s): **Send The Light Distribution LLC.**

Media Assocs., *(978-0-918501)* P.O. Box 46, Wilton, CA 95693 USA (SAN 657-3207) Toll Free: 800-373-1897; *Imprints*: Archives Pr. (Archives Pr) Do not confuse with Media Assocs., Marina Del Rey, CA
E-mail: arkivz10@aol.com
Dist(s): **Lulu Enterprises Inc.**

Media Blasters, Inc., *(978-1-890228; 978-1-58655; 978-1-59883)* 132 W. 36th St. Rm. 401, New York, NY 10018-8837 USA (SAN 859-5712)
E-mail: info@media-blasters.com
Web site: http://www.media-blasters.com; http://www.kittymedia.com
Dist(s): **Diamond Comic Distributors, Inc.**
Diamond Bk. Distributors
Follett School Solutions.

Media Creations, Incorporated *See* **Aeon Publishing Inc.**

Media For Life, *(978-0-9675068)* P.O. Box 1214, Little Falls, NJ 07424 USA Fax: 603-250-8553
E-mail: EduFun@aol.com.

Media Magic New York, *(978-0-9744211)* 15 W. 39th St., 13th Flr., New York, NY 10018 USA Tel 212-926-5575
E-mail: mediamagicny@aol.com; info@mediamagic-ny.com.

Media Man! Productions *Imprint of* **Fairwood Pr.**

Media Rodzina (POL) *(978-83-7278; 978-83-85594)* *Dist. by* **Distribks Inc.**

Medical Alternative Pr., *(978-0-9660882)* 4173 Fieldbrook Rd., West Bloomfield, MI 48323 USA Tel 248-851-3372; Fax: 248-851-0421; Toll Free: 888-647-5616 Do not confuse with Medical Alternative Pr., Colleyville, TX
E-mail: alselko@hotmail.com
Web site: http://www.drbrownstein.com.

Medical Manor Bks., *(978-0-934232)* Subs. of Manor Hse. Pubns., Inc., 3501 Newberry Rd., Philadelphia, PA 19154 USA (SAN 217-2526) Tel 800-343-8464; Fax: 215-440-9255; Toll Free: 800-343-8464
E-mail: info@diet-step.com; sales@diet-step.com; sales@medicalmanorbooks.com; marketing@diet-step.com; DrWalk@diet-step.com; info@medicalmanorbooks.com
Web site: http://www.medicalmanorbooks.com/; http://www.peace-healingbooks.com; http://www.manorhousepublications.com
Dist(s): **AtlasBooks Distribution**
BookMasters Distribution Services (BDS)
Distributors, The
Follett School Solutions
Quality Bks., Inc.
Unique Bks., Inc.
ebrary, Inc.

Medici Publishing, Inc., *(978-0-9743791; 978-0-9823853)* P.O. Box 282, Beulah, CO 81023 USA Tel 719-485-1167
E-mail: marcprat@juno.com
Web site: http://www.medicibooks.org.

Medicine Woman Inc., The, *(978-0-9771906)* Orders Addr.: P.O. Box 613, Cascade, ID 83611 USA Tel 208-382-6653; Edit Addr.: 843 S. Main Hwy. 55, Cascade, ID 83611 USA
E-mail: tmw@ctcweb.net
Web site: http://www.themedicinewoman.com.

Medicus Pr., Inc., *(978-0-9787727)* P.O. Box 284, Leonia, NJ 07605-0284 USA (SAN 851-5905) Tel 201-816-7363; Fax: 201-266-0537
E-mail: medicuspress@yahoo.com.

Medina Publishing, Ltd. (GBR) *(978-0-9570233; 978-1-909339; 978-0-9564170; 978-0-9567081)* *Dist. by* **CasemateAcad.**

Medio Media *See* **Medio Media Publishing**

Medio Media Publishing, *(978-0-9666941; 978-0-9725627; 978-1-933182)* 627 N. 6th Ave., Tucson, AZ 85705-8330 USA Toll Free: 800-324-8305
E-mail: JoeD846136@aol.com; meditate@mediomedia.org
Web site: http://www.mediomedia.org
Dist(s): **Bloomsbury Publishing Inc**
Continuum International Publishing Group, Inc.
Macmillan
National Bk. Network.

Medley, *(978-1-890034)* 1620 Los Alamos, SW, Albuquerque, NM 87104 USA Tel 505-247-3921; *Imprints*: Medley Publications (Medley Pubns)
E-mail: litchman@unm.edu.

Medley Pubns. *Imprint of* **Medley**

MedPress & Quality Publishers *See* **Quality Pubs.**

Medusa Road Pr., *(978-0-9779295)* 6 Rte. 75, Norton Hill, NY 12083 USA Tel 518-966-5281
E-mail: MedusaRoadStudio@aol.com
Web site: http://CarolynsWebsite.net.

Medwag Publishing, *(978-0-9654963)* P.O. Box 36037, Richmond, VA 23235 USA Tel 804-794-8186
E-mail: alrx1@juno.com.

Meehl Foundation Pr., *(978-0-9767049)* P.O. Box 2089, Brazoria, TX 77422-2089 USA Tel 979-798-7972
E-mail: meehlfou@meehlfoundation.org
Web site: http://www.meehlfoundation.org.

MeeraMasi, Inc., *(978-0-9773645; 978-0-9797191)* 449 London Pk. Ct., San Jose, CA 95136 USA Tel 408-365-8044; Fax: 408-225-8586
E-mail: info@meeramasi.com; sonali@meeramasi.com
Web site: http://www.meeramasi.com.

Meerkat's Adventures Bks., *(978-0-9778072)* 510 Diamond St, Suite A, San Francisco, CA 94114 USA (SAN 850-2862)
Web site: http://www.meerkatsadventures.com.

Meet Bks., LLC, *(978-0-615-31579-9; 978-0-615-38973-8)* 806 Seale Ave., Palo Alto, CA 94303 USA.

Meet the Author *Imprint of* **Owen, Richard C. Pubs., Inc.**

Mefford, David, *(978-0-9762143)* 274 W. 700 N., American Fork, UT 84003 USA
E-mail: david@mefford.org.

Meg and Lucy Bks. (GBR) *Dist. by* **IPG Chicago.**

Megami Pr. LLC, *(978-0-615-39156-4; 978-0-615-40446-2; 978-0-9853471)* P.O. Box 128557, Nashville, TN 37212 USA
E-mail: Megamipress@gmail.com
Web site: http://www.megamipress.com.

Megyeri, Graham Bks., *(978-0-9711971; 978-0-9791994)* 439 Lakeview Blvd., Albert Lea, MN 56007 USA Tel 507-377-1255; Toll Free: 866-755-5942
E-mail: minnmemory@aol.com
Web site: http://www.minnesotamemories.com
Dist(s): **Partners Bk. Distributing, Inc.**

Mehr Iran Publishing Co. *See* **Mehriran Publishing Co.**

Mehriran Publishing Co., *(978-0-9633129)* 14900 Talking Rock Ct., Suite B, N. Potomac, MD 20878 USA Tel 301-279-6778; Fax: 301-738-2174
E-mail: pirnia@pirnia.com
Web site: http://www.pirnia.com.

MEIER Enterprises Inc., *(978-0-9726808)* 8697 Gage Blvd., Kennewick, WA 99336 USA Tel 509-735-1589; Fax: 509-783-5075; Toll Free: 800-239-7589
E-mail: sranderson@meierinc.com; info@learningtowrite.com
Web site: http://www.meierinc.com; http://www.learningtowrite.comw.

Meirovich, Igal, *(978-0-9820556; 978-1-60796)* 6408 Elray Dr., Apt. E, Baltimore, MD 21209 USA Tel 410-764-6423
E-mail: lightoncds@gmail.com
Dist(s): **BookBaby**
Lulu Enterprises Inc.

Meister-Home, Inc., *(978-0-9702497)* P.O. Box 471250, Charlotte, NC 28247-1250 USA (SAN 256-1794) Tel 704-968-6741; Fax: 704-544-2034; *Imprints*: Meister-Home Press (Meister-Home Pr)
E-mail: ragilmartin@hotmail.com; rgilmartin@meister-home.com
Web site: http://www.meister-home.com.

Meister-Home Pr. *Imprint of* **Meister-Home, Inc.**

Mel Bay Pubns., Inc., *(978-0-7866; 978-0-87166; 978-1-56222; 978-1-60974; 978-1-61065; 978-1-61911; 978-1-5134)* 4 Industrial Dr., Pacific, MO 63069-0066 USA (SAN 657-3630) Tel 636-257-3970; Fax: 636-257-5062; Toll Free: 800-863-5229
E-mail: email@melbay.com; sharon@melbay.com
Web site: http://www.melbay.com; www.melbaydealers.com
Dist(s): **Alfred Publishing Co., Inc.**

Melanie Kroupa Bks. *Imprint of* **Farrar, Straus & Giroux**

Melissa Productions, Inc., *(978-0-9842394; 978-0-9834751; 978-0-9898293)* 2003 Arundale Ln., Matthews, NC 28104 USA (SAN 858-8252) Tel 704-246-7304
E-mail: melissa@melissaproductions.com
Web site: http://www.melissaproductions.com.

MELJAMES, Inc., *(978-0-9755195; 978-1-933419)* 107 Suncreek Dr., Suite 300, Allen, TX 75013 USA
Web site: http://www.meljamesinc.com.

†Mellen, Edwin Pr., The, *(978-0-7734; 978-0-88946; 978-0-935106; 978-0-7799; 978-1-4955)* Orders Addr.: P.O. Box 67, Queenston, ON LOS 1L0 CAN; Edit Addr.: P.O. Box 450, Lewiston, NY 14092-0450 USA (SAN 207-110X) Tel 716-754-2266; 716-754-2788; Fax: 716-754-1860
E-mail: sales@mellenpress.com
Web site: http://www.mellenpress.com; *CIP*.

Melton Hill Media, *(978-0-9816793)* 9119 Solway Ferry Rd., Oak Ridge, TN 37830 USA (SAN 856-2288)
E-mail: wendy@meltonhillmedia.com
Web site: http://www.meltonhillmedia.com.

Melzee's Production, *(978-0-9722738)* P.O. Box 394, Hawthorne, CA 90251-0394 USA Tel 310-263-7804
E-mail: melzee3@juno.com.

Me+Mi Publishing, *(978-0-9679748; 978-1-931398)* 400 Knoll St. Ste. B, Wheaton, IL 60187-4557 USA Toll Free: 888-251-1444
E-mail: m3@memima.com
Web site: http://www.memima.com
Dist(s): **Lectorum Pubns., Inc.**
Quality Bks., Inc.

Memoir Bks., *(978-0-9793387; 978-1-937748)* Div. of Heidelberg Graphics, Orders Addr.: 2 Stansbury Ct., Chico, CA 95928 USA Tel 530-342-6582
Web site: http://www.heidelberggraphics.com.

Memoria Pr., *(978-1-930953; 978-1-61538)* Orders Addr.: 4603 Poplar Level Rd., Louisville, KY 40213-2337 USA Toll Free: 877-862-1097
E-mail: magister@memoriapress.com
Web site: http://www.memoriapress.com
Dist(s): **Chicago Distribution Ctr.**

Memories Publishing, *(978-0-9748984)* P.O. Box 82516, Austin, TX 78708 USA Tel 512-907-1821
E-mail: mindyred@aol.com.

Mennonite Board of Missions *See* **Mennonite Mission Network**

Mennonite Mission Network, *(978-1-877736; 978-1-933845)* 500 S. Main St., P.O. Box 370, Elkhart, IN 46515-0370 USA Tel 219-294-7523; Fax: 574-294-8669; Toll Free: 866-866-2872
Web site: http://www.mennonitemission.net
Dist(s): **Follett School Solutions**
Herald Pr.

Mennonite Pr. Inc., *(978-0-9772745)* Orders Addr.: P.O. Box 867, Newton, KS 67114 USA Tel 316-283-4680; Fax: 316-283-2068; Toll Free: 800-536-4686; Edit Addr.: 532 N. Oliver Rd., Newton, KS 67114 USA
E-mail: reliability@mennonitepress.com
Web site: http://www.mennonitepress.com.

Mental Health Historic Preservation Society Of Central Illinois, *(978-0-9748742)* 209 Arnold Ave., East Peoria, IL 61611 USA Tel 309-699-3051
E-mail: aparr12345@aol.com
Dist(s): **Partners Bk. Distributing, Inc.**

Mental Wellness Publishing House *See* **Wellness pH**

Mentoring Minds, LP, *(978-0-9763559; 978-0-9767940; 978-1-935123; 978-1-938935; 978-1-62763)* P.O. Box 8843, Tyler, TX 75711 USA Fax: 800-838-8186; Toll Free: 800-585-5258
E-mail: gavin@mentoringminds.com
Web site: http://www.mentoring-minds.com.

MentorSource, LLC, *(978-0-9773324)* P.O. Box 24436, Minneapolis, MN 55424 USA Tel 612-269-8242
E-mail: gianna_bl@msn.com
Web site: http://www.rosyproses.com.

Mentzer Printing Ink, *(978-0-9746705; 978-0-9786276; 978-0-9797502; 978-0-9894927)* 1054 Virginia Ave., Indianapolis, IN 46203-1754 USA Toll Free: 800-514-6017
E-mail: info@m2print.com
Web site: http://www.m2print.com.

Menucha Pubs. Inc., *(978-1-61465)* 250 44th St. Suite No. B2, Brooklyn, NY 11232 USA (SAN 860-2115) Tel 718-232-0856; Fax: 718-232-0856
E-mail: hirshmt@hotmail.com.

Mercer, Christina, *(978-0-615-77637-8; 978-0-615-96978-7; 978-0-692-22484-7)* PO Box 1845, Shingle Springs, CA 95682 USA Tel 5303635664; Fax: 5306761876
Web site: http://christinamercer.com/
Dist(s): **CreateSpace Independent Publishing Platform.**

†Mercer Univ. Pr., *(978-0-86554; 978-0-88146)* 1501 Mercer Univ. Dr., Macon, GA 31207 USA (SAN 220-0716) Tel 478-301-2880; Fax: 478-301-2585; Toll Free: 866-895-1472
E-mail: mupressorders@mercer.edu
Web site: http://www.mupress.org; *CIP*.

Merchant Bks. *Imprint of* **Rough Draft Printing**

Mercier Pr., Ltd., The (IRL) *(978-0-85342; 978-1-85635; 978-1-86023; 978-1-78117)* *Dist. by* **Dufour.**

Mercury Publishing, Inc., *(978-0-9778793)* Orders Addr.: 35 Fieldstone Way, Alpharetta, GA 30005 USA (SAN 850-5020)
E-mail: goga7n@gmail.com
Dist(s): **BCH Fulfillment & Distribution.**

Mercy Place, Inc., *(978-0-9677402; 978-0-9707919)* P.O. Box 134, Shippensburg, PA 17257 USA Tel 717-532-6899; Fax: 717-532-8646; Toll Free: 800-722-6774
E-mail: mpm@reapernet.com
Web site: http://mercyplace.com
Dist(s): **Destiny Image Pubs.**

†Meredith Bks., *(978-0-696; 978-0-89721; 978-0-917102)* Div. of Meredith Corp., Orders Addr.: 1716 Locust St., LN-110, Des Moines, IA 50309-3023 USA (SAN 202-4055) Tel 515-284-2363; 515-284-2126 (sales); Fax: 515-284-3371; Toll Free: 800-678-8091; *Imprints*: Food Network Kitchens (Food Net) Do not confuse with Meredith Pr. in Skaneateles, NY
E-mail: John.OBannon@meredith.com
Web site: http://www.bhgstore.com
Dist(s): **Follett School Solutions**
MyiLibrary
Sterling Publishing Co., Inc.; *CIP*.

Meredith Group Ltd., The, *(978-0-9765341)* Orders Addr.: 24 N. Bryn Mawr Ave., Box117, Bryn Mawr, PA 19010 USA (SAN 256-4920) Tel 610-642-0199; Edit Addr.: 71 Eden View Rd. # 6, Elizabethtown, PA 17022-3124 USA
E-mail: mmbellamy1@verizon.net
Web site: http://www.goldiesbook.com.

Meridia Pubs. LLC, *(978-0-615-40498-1; 978-0-9832330; 978-0-9904031)* 29439 Sayle Dr., Willoughby Hills, OH 44092 USA Tel 440-944-8047
E-mail: al.ruksenas@gmail.com
Dist(s): **BookBaby**
Smashwords.

Meridian Creative Group *See* **Larson Learning, Inc.**

Merit Pr. Bks. *Imprint of* **F&W Media, Inc.**

Meritage Publishing, *(978-0-9769866)* Orders Addr.: 12339 Meritage Ct., Rancho Cucamonga, CA 91739 USA
E-mail: meritagepub@charter.net
Dist(s): **Quality Bks., Inc.**

Meriwether Publishing, Ltd., *(978-0-916260; 978-1-56608)* Orders Addr.: P.O. Box 7710, Colorado Springs, CO 80933 USA (SAN 208-4716) Tel 719-594-4422; Fax: 719-594-9916; P.O. Box 4267, Englewood, CO 80155 Tel 303-779-4035; Fax: 303-779-4315; Edit Addr.: 885 Elkton Dr., Colorado Springs, CO 80907 USA Tel 719-594-4422; 9707 E. Easter Ln. Suite A, Englewood, CO 80112 Tel 303-779-4035
E-mail: mzapel@aol.com; editor@meriwether.com; wholesale@pioneerdrama.com
Web site: http://www.contemporarydrama.com; http://www.meriwetherpublishing.com; http://www.pioneerdrama.com; http://https://www.Christianplaysandmusicals.com
Dist(s): **Follett School Solutions.**

Merkos L'Inyonei Chinuch, *(978-0-8266)* 291 Kingston Ave., Brooklyn, NY 11213 USA Tel 718-778-0226; Fax: 718-778-4148
E-mail: yonason@kehot.net
Web site: http://www.kehotonline.com.

Merlin, Debbi, *(978-0-9793568)* 12339 Scarcella Ln., Stafford, TX 77477-1609 USA (SAN 853-232X)
E-mail: merlin@merlinmagic.cc
Web site: http://www.merlinmagic.cc.

Merlin Enterprises, *(978-0-9761017)* Orders Addr.: 11881 S. Fortuna Rd., No. 451, Yuma, AZ 85367 USA
E-mail: napuff@gmail.com
Web site: http://cafepress.com/npuff.

Merlot Group, LLC, The, *(978-0-9816123; 978-0-9887117)* P.O. Box 302, Covington, KY 41012-0302 USA Tel 859-743-1003
Web site: http://www.merlotgroup.com
Dist(s): **Lulu Enterprises Inc.**

Meroe Publishing, *(978-0-9768306)* P.O. Box 664, Cusseta, GA 31805 USA
E-mail: tonieshort@meroepublishing.com
Web site: http://www.meroepublishing.com.

Merriam-Webster *Imprint of* **Merriam-Webster, Inc.**

Merriam-Webster, Inc., *(978-0-87779; 978-1-68150)* Subs. of Encyclopaedia Britannica, Inc., Orders Addr.: 47 Federal St., Springfield, MA 01102 USA (SAN 202-6244) Tel 413-734-3134; Fax: 413-731-5979; 413-734-2014; Toll Free: 800-828-1880; *Imprints*: Merriam-Webster (Merriam-Webstr)
E-mail: sales@Merriam-Webster.com; orders@Merriam-Webster.com; jsantoro@Merriam-Webster.com
Web site: http://www.WordCentral.com; http://www.Merriam-Webster.com
Dist(s): **CENGAGE Learning**
Delmar Cengage Learning
Perfection Learning Corp.

Merril Pr., *(978-0-936783)* 12500 NE Tenth Pl., Bellevue, WA 98005 USA (SAN 699-9387) Tel 425-454-7009; Fax: 425-451-3959
E-mail: editor@merrilpress.com
Web site: http://www.merrilpress.com
Dist(s): **Midpoint Trade Bks., Inc.**

Merrimack Bk. Works, *(978-0-9799090)* 23 Pleasant St., No. 508, Newburyport, MA 01950-2632 USA (SAN 854-7424) Tel 978-417-9277
E-mail: mary@maryleemattison.com
Web site: http://www.maryleemattison.com.

Merritt Publishing *See* **Silver Lake Publishing**

Merriwell, Frank Inc., *(978-0-8373)* Subs. of National Learning Corp., 212 Michael Dr., Syosset, NY 11791 USA (SAN 209-259X) Tel 516-921-8888; Toll Free: 800-645-6337.

Merry Lane Pr., *(978-0-9744307)* 18 E. 16th St., 7th Flr., New York, NY 10003 USA Tel 212-633-6505; Fax: 212-242-6077
E-mail: alan@merrylanepress.com
Web site: http://www.merrylanepress.com.

Merryant Pubs., *(978-1-877599)* P.O. Box 1921, Vashon, WA 98070-1921 USA Toll Free: 800-228-8958
E-mail: jmboule@aol.com.

Merrybooks & More, *(978-0-9615407; 978-1-882607)* 1214 Rugby Rd., Charlottesville, VA 22903 USA (SAN 695-5053) Tel 804-979-3658; Fax: 804-296-8446; Toll Free: 800-959-2665.

Mesorah Pubns., Ltd., *(978-0-89906; 978-1-57819; 978-1-4226)* 4401 Second Ave., Brooklyn, NY 11232 USA (SAN 213-1269) Tel 718-921-9000 Toll Free: 800-637-6724; *Imprints*: Shaar Press (Shaar Pr)
E-mail: info@ArtScroll.com
Web site: http://www.artscroll.com.

Mesquite Tress Pr., LLC, *(978-0-9729835)* Orders Addr.: P.O. Box 17513, Louisville, KY 40217 USA; Edit Addr.: 212 W. Ormsby Ave, Louisville, KY 40203 USA
Web site: http://www.onetinytwig.com; http://www.mesquitetreepress.com; http://bluegrassbreeze.com.

Mess Hall Writers, *(978-1-885531)* P.O. Box 1551, Jeffersonville, IN 47130 USA Tel 812-288-9888; Fax: 812-288-9695
E-mail: fooddudes2@aol.com.

Message in a Bottle Translators *See* **Pangloss Publishing**

Messiah Publishing - Pearables, *(978-0-9792446)* P.O. Box 272000, Fort Collins, CO 80527 USA (SAN 852-8837) Tel 719-549-0662
Web site: http://www.pearables.com.

Messianic Perspectives, *(978-0-9674319; 978-0-9882120; 978-0-9898240)* Orders Addr.: P.O. Box 345, San Antonio, TX 78292-0345 USA Tel 210-226-0421; Fax: 210-226-2140; Toll Free: 800-926-5397; Edit Addr.: 611 Broadway St., San Antonio, TX 78215 USA
E-mail: info@cjfm.org
Web site: http://www.cjfm.org.

Meta Adventures *See* **Meta Adventures Publishing & DIA Publishing**

Meta Adventures Publishing & DIA Publishing, *(978-0-9721202)* Orders Addr.: P.O. Box 1894, Sedona, AZ 86339 USA (SAN 254-6183) Tel 928-204-1560
E-mail: info@dreamsinaction.us; publishing@dreamsinaction.us; orderinfo@dreamsinaction.us
Web site: http://www.dreamsinaction.us; http://www.MrSedona.com
Dist(s): **Dreams In Action Distribution.**

Metacognition Pr., *(978-0-9859707)* 48 Michael Ln., Orinda, CA 94563 USA Tel 925-360-9159
E-mail: Metacognitionblog@yahoo.com.

Metal Lunchbox Publishing, *(978-0-9843437)* P.O. Box 252, Keedysville, MD 21756 USA (SAN 859-1202) Tel 412-916-0211
E-mail: info@metallunchboxpublishing.com
Web site: http://www.metallunchboxpublishing.com.

Metalmark Pr., *(978-0-9767239)* 7116 New Sharon Church Rd., Rougemont, NC 27572 USA
E-mail: birdcr@concentric.net
Web site: http://www.rlephoto.com.

Metamedix, Incorporated *See* **Science2Discover, Inc.**

Metaphors 4 Life, *(978-0-9817291)* P.O. Box 270812, West Hartford, CT 06127 USA (SAN 856-3772)
E-mail: writeme@danarondel.com
Web site: http://www.danarondel.com; http://www.metaphors4life.org.

Metapublishing, *(978-0-9654522)* 500 Center Ave. Apt. 211, Westwood, NJ 07675-1677 USA Do not confuse with Metapublishing, North Miami Beach, FL
Dist(s): **New Leaf Distributing Co., Inc.**

Metchnikoff, Elie Memorial Library, *(978-0-9634067)* 230 Orange St., No. 6, Oakland, CA 94610-4139 USA Tel 510-444-3435; Fax: 510-642-7175
E-mail: jbibel@arg.org.

Metric Moon Press *See* **Graphite Pr.**

Metro Bks., *(978-0-9752732)* 1706 W. Jarvis, 1W, Chicago, IL 60626 USA.

Metropolitan Bks. *Imprint of* **Holt, Henry & Co.**

Metropolitan Museum of Art, The, *(978-0-87099; 978-1-58839)* 1000 Fifth Ave., New York, NY 10028 USA (SAN 202-6279) Tel 212-879-5500; Fax: 212-396-5062
Web site: http://www.metmuseum.org
Dist(s): **Chicago Distribution Ctr.**
Continental Bk. Co., Inc.
Yale Univ. Pr.

Metropolitan Teaching & Learning Co., *(978-0-928415; 978-1-58120; 978-1-58830)* 317 Madison Ave., New York, NY 10017 USA Tel 212-475-8826; Fax: 212-475-8311; Toll Free: 800-235-6931
Web site: http://metrotlc.com.

Meyer & Meyer Sport, Ltd. (GBR) *(978-1-84126; 978-1-78255)* *Dist. by* **Lewis Intl Inc.**

Meyer & Meyer Sport, Ltd. (GBR) *(978-1-84126; 978-1-78255)* *Dist. by* **Cardinal PubGr.**

Meyer Enterprises *See* **Western New York Wares, Inc.**

Meyer, Tjaden, *(978-0-9744536)* Orders Addr.: P.O. Box 230015, Saint Louis, MO 63123 USA Tel 314-352-2253; Edit Addr.: 7045 Parkwood St., Saint Louis, MO 63116 USA
E-mail: klmeyer@worldnet.att.net.

Meza, Marti, *(978-0-615-16571-4)* 1515 W. 7th St., Apt. 4-D, Brooklyn, NY 11204 USA
Dist(s): **Lulu Enterprises Inc.**

MF Unlimited, *(978-0-9712278)* P.O. Box 55346, Atlanta, GA 30308 USA
Web site: http://www.mfunews.com
Dist(s): **Lightning Source, Inc.**

Mfg Application Konsulting Engineering, *(978-0-9762208)* 1071 E. 425 N., Ogden, UT 84404 USA.

M-Graphics *Imprint of* **M-Graphics Publishing**

M-Graphics Publishing, *(978-0-9753075; 978-0-9777003; 978-0-9792808; 978-1-934881; 978-1-940220)* One Dead Eye Run, Swampscott, MA 01907 USA Tel 781-990-8778 Weekdays 9AM - 4 PM; *Imprints*: M-Graphics (M-Grap)
E-mail: mgraphics.books@gmail.com
Web site: http://www.mgraphics-publishing.com.

MHC Ministries, *(978-0-9895422)* 1170 NE 133rd St., North Miami, FL 33161 USA Tel 786-286-5210
E-mail: mmuc31@gmail.com
Web site: www.mhcministries.com.

Mia Sharon, Inc., *(978-0-9759098)* 600 Academy Dr., No. 130, Northbrook, IL 60062 USA Tel 847-826-8196
Web site: http://www.miasharon.com.

†Micah Pubns., *(978-0-916288)* 255 Humphrey St., Marblehead, MA 01945 USA (SAN 209-1577) Tel 781-631-7601; Fax: 781-639-0772; Toll Free: 877-268-9963
E-mail: micah@micahbooks.com
Web site: http://www.micahbooks.com
Dist(s): **Book Publishing Co.**
David, Jonathan Pubs., Inc.; *CIP*.

Miceli, Mary Anne, *(978-0-578-08747-4; 978-0-578-10145-3; 978-0-578-10979-4)* 10 Daniels Rd., Wenham, MA 01984 USA; P.O. Box 2027, Danvers, MA 01923
E-mail: mary_miceli@comcast.net
Web site: bostonnorthshorestoriesandpoems.com.

Micelle Pr., Inc., *(978-0-9608752; 978-1-870228)* Orders Addr.: P.O. Box 1519, Port Washington, NY 11050-0306 USA Tel 516-767-7171; Fax: 516-944-9824
E-mail: micellepress@googlemail.com
Web site: http://www.scholium.com
Dist(s): **Schollum International, Inc.**

MiceWorks, *(978-0-9764719)* 544 13th Ave., W., Kirkland, WA 98033 USA.

Michael Dahl - Super Funny Joke Bks. *Imprint of* **Picture Window Bks.**

Michael Neugebauer Bks. *Imprint of* **North-South Bks., Inc.**

Michael-Christopher Bks., *(978-0-9710398)* Orders Addr.: P.O. Box 75313, Washington, DC 20013-0313 USA Tel 301-927-3179
E-mail: mc@michael-christopher.com
Web site: http://www.michael-christopher.com
Dist(s): **BookBaby.**

MichaelsMind LLC *See* **Right Stuff Kids Bks.**

Michaelson Entertainment, *(978-0-9727702; 978-1-932530; 978-1-60730)* 36 Cabrillo Terr., Aliso Viejo, CA 92656 USA Tel 949-916-0575 phone; Fax: 949-916-0574 fax; *Imprints*: 101 Book (101 Bk); 123 Book (123 Bk); ABC Book (ABCBk)
E-mail: brad@michaelsonentertainment.com
Web site: http://www.michaelsonentertainment.com
Dist(s): **Partners Bk. Distributing, Inc.**

Michalek, Curtis, *(978-0-9786177)* P.O. Box 403, Montezuma, IA 50171 USA Tel 641-623-3368
E-mail: c.a.michalek@hotmail.com
Web site: www.aluris.com.

Michele, Mary, *(978-0-615-25486-9)* 27638 N. 45th Way, Cave Creek, AZ 85331 USA Tel 602-952-8604
E-mail: scriptsrelief@cox.net
Dist(s): **Lulu Enterprises Inc.**

Michelle's A & E (KOR) *(978-89-954869)* *Dist. by* **APG.**

Michelle's Bks. & More, Ltd. Co., *(978-0-9763080)* 800 Fabric X-Press Way, Dallas, TX 75234 USA Tel 972-625-1444; Fax: 972-406-1321
E-mail: michelle@michellesbooks.com
Web site: http://www.michellesbooks.com.

Michelle's Designs, *(978-0-9789694; 978-0-9817663; 978-0-9842520)* 3702 Sandpoint Ct, Carlsbad, CA 92010 USA Tel 760-720-4335; Fax: 802-609-2629
E-mail: patterns@michelles-designs.com; jen@condormedia.com
Web site: http://www.michelles-designs.com.

Michigan Publishing, *(978-0-9745109; 978-1-4181; 978-1-4255; 978-1-60785)* Div. of University of Michigan Library, 1210 Buhr Bldg. 839 Greene St., Ann Arbor, MI 48109 USA (SAN 255-9889)
E-mail: spo.pod@umich.edu; lib.pod@umich.edu
Web site: http://www.lib.umich.edu/michigan-publishing.

Michigan State Univ., Julian Samora Research Institute, *(978-0-9650557)* 301 Nisbet Bldg., 1407 S. Harrison,

Publisher Name Index

East Lansing, MI 48823-586 USA Tel 517-432-1317; Fax: 517-432-2221
E-mail: info@jsri.msu.edu
Web site: http://jsri.msu.edu.

†**Michigan State Univ. Pr.**, *(978-0-87013; 978-0-937191; 978-1-60917; 978-1-61186; 978-1-938065; 978-1-62895; 978-1-62896; 978-1-941258; 978-0-9967252)* Orders Addr.: 1405 S. Harrison Rd. Suite 25, East Lansing, MI 48823 USA (SAN 202-6295) Tel 517-355-9543; Fax: 517-432-2611; Toll Free: 800-678-2120
E-mail: msupress@msu.edu
Web site: http://www.msupress.msu.edu
Dist(s): **Chicago Distribution Ctr.**; *CIP.*

Micro Publishing Media, Inc., *(978-0-9827716; 978-1-936517; 978-1-944068)* 29 Pk. St., Stockbridge, MA 01262 USA; *Imprints:* Pop Pop Press (Pop Pop Pr)
E-mail: Deborah@micropublishingmedia.com
Web site: http://www.micropublishingmedia.com.

Microcosm Publishing, *(978-0-9726967; 978-0-9770557; 978-0-9788665; 978-1-934620; 978-1-62106)* 636 SE. 11th Ave., Portland, OR 97214 USA Tel 503-232-3666 joe@microcosmpublishing.com; Toll Free Fax: 888-503-0599; *Imprints:* Elly Blue Publishing (Elly Blue); Into Action Publications (Into Action)
E-mail: joe@microcosmpublishing.com
Web site: http://www.microcosmpublishing.com
Dist(s): **AK Pr. Distribution**
Follett School Solutions
Independent Pubs. Group
Legato Pubs. Group
MyiLibrary
Perseus-PGW.

Microsoft Pr. *Imprint of* **Pearson Education**

†**Microsoft Pr.**, *(978-0-7356; 978-0-914845; 978-0-925550; 978-1-55615; 978-1-57231; 978-1-879021)* Orders Addr.: 3 Center Plaza, Boston, MA 02108-2084 USA Toll Free: 800-677-7377; Edit Addr.: One Microsoft Way, Redmond, WA 98052-6399 USA (SAN 264-9969) Tel 425-882-8080; 206-882-8080; 425-703-0942; Fax: 425-936-7329 Do not confuse with Microsoft Pr., Dunmore, PA
E-mail: msporder@msn.com; duanedr@microsoft.com; chriscai@microsoft.com
Web site: http://www.microsoft.com/mspress/
Dist(s): **Follett School Solutions**
Pearson Education; *CIP.*

Mid-Atlantic Highlands Publishing *Imprint of* **Publishers Place, Inc.**

Middelhauve Verlags GmbH (DEU) *(978-3-7876) Dist. by* **Distribks Inc.**

†**Middle Atlantic Pr.**, *(978-0-912608; 978-0-9705804; 978-0-9754419)* 400 Pond View Dr., Moorestown, NJ 08057 USA Tel 856-273-9062; Fax: 856-273-7526
E-mail: blake@middleatlanticpress.com; info@middleatlanticpress.com
Web site: http://www.middleatlanticpress.com
Dist(s): **Partners Bk. Distributing, Inc.**; *CIP.*

Middle River Pr., *(978-0-9785656; 978-0-9817036; 978-0-9846071; 978-0-9838203; 978-0-9857295; 978-0-9896724; 978-0-9964086)* 1498 NE 30th Ct., Oakland Park, FL 33334-4414 USA Tel 954-630-8192
E-mail: info@middleriverpress.com
Web site: http://www.middleriverpress.com.

Middle School Reference *Imprint of* **Greenwood Publishing Group, Inc.**

Middleburry Hse. Publishing, *(978-0-9792067)* 3225 Middleburry Ln., Charleston, SC 29414 USA
Web site: http://www.rwridley.com; http://www.choytcaldwell.com.

Middleton Classics *See* **Middleton Publishing**

Middleton Publishing, *(978-0-9787871; 978-1-935702; 978-1-63104)* P.O. Box 226, Williamstown, NY 13493 USA (SAN 851-6308); *Imprints:* 711 Press (SevEleven)
Web site: http://www.middletonpublishing.com.

Midnight Hologram, LLC, *(978-1-938516)* 1180 Beacon Hill Crossing, Alpharetta, GA 30005 USA Tel 678-393-0420
E-mail: yvet77@comcast.net
Web site: www.midnighthologram.com.

Midnight Ink *Imprint of* **Llewellyn Pubns.**

Midpoint Trade Bks., Inc., *(978-1-940416)* Orders Addr.: 1263 Southwest Blvd., Kansas City, KS 66103 USA (SAN 631-3736) Tel 913-831-2233; Fax: 913-362-7401; Toll Free: 800-742-6139 (consumer orders); Edit Addr.: 27 W. 20th St., No. 1102, New York, NY 10011 USA (SAN 631-1075) Tel 212-727-0190; Fax: 212-727-0195
E-mail: info@midpointtrade.com
Web site: http://www.midpointtrade.com; http://www.midpointtradebooks.com/
Dist(s): **Ingram Bk. Co.**
ebrary, Inc.

MidRun Pr., *(978-0-9664095; 978-0-9824397)* 90 Larch Row, Wenham, MA 01984-1624 USA Tel 978-468-9953 (phone/fax)
E-mail: midrunpress@aol.com
Web site: http://www.midrunpress.com.

Midwest Christian Center *See* **Family Harvest Church**

Midwest Cylinder Management, Inc., *(978-0-9729026)* 1203 Paramount Pkwy., Batavia, IL 60510-1458 USA Tel 630-673-9770; Fax: 630-406-9922
E-mail: prminalt@yahoo.com
Web site: http://www.kidsmenus.com.

Midwest Graphics, Inc., *(978-0-9776893)* 180 N. Wacker Dr., Suite 104, Chicago, IL 60606 USA Tel 312-641-2236; Fax: 312-641-2256
E-mail: mark@mwgchicago.com
Web site: http://www.mwgchicago.com.

Midwest Screen and Media Production, *(978-0-9719665)* P.O. Box 133, Greeley, KS 66033 USA (SAN 254-5527)
Web site: http://www.msmediaproduction.com.

Midwest Writng, *(978-0-9778290; 978-0-9818089; 978-0-9834116; 978-0-9906190)* 225 E.2nd St., Suite 303, Davenport, IA 52801 USA Tel 563-324-1410; Fax: 563-324-1410
Web site: http://www.midwestwritingcenter.org.

Mielcarek, David, *(978-0-9785480)* 3387 Ocean Beach Hwy, Longview, WA 98632 USA
E-mail: thebook@timeforyourmind.com
Web site: http://timeforyourmind.com.

Mighty Kids Media, *(978-0-9765953; 978-0-9770455; 978-1-933934; 978-0-9884241)* 4201 Congress St, Suite 451, Charlotte, NC 28209 USA Toll Free Fax: 877-723-3388 Do not confuse with companies with the same name in Dobbs Ferry, NY, Medofrd, OR, Lanett, AL
Web site: http://www.dangerrangers.com.

Mighty Lion Ventures, *(978-0-615-30860-9; 978-0-9831449)* P.O. Box 2950, Cypress, TX 77410 USA.

Mighty Media Junior Readers *Imprint of* **Mighty Media Pr.**

Mighty Media Kids *Imprint of* **Mighty Media Pr.**

Mighty Media Pr., *(978-0-9765201; 978-0-9798249; 978-0-9824584; 978-0-9830219; 978-1-938063)* Div. of Mighty Media, 1201 Currie Ave., Minneapolis, MN 55403 USA Tel 612-455-0252; Fax: 612-338-4817; *Imprints:* Mighty Media Junior Readers (MMJrRead); Mighty Media Kids (MMKids)
E-mail: info@scarlettapress.com; josh@scarlettapress.com
Web site: http://www.mightymediapress.com
Dist(s): **Continental Enterprises Group, Inc. (CEG)**
MyiLibrary
Perseus-PGW
Perseus Bks. Group.

Miglior Pr., *(978-0-9827614; 978-0-9836484)* P.O. Box 7487, Athens, GA 30604 USA Tel 706-338-0017
E-mail: info@migliorpress.com
Web site: http://migliorpress.com
Dist(s): **AtlasBooks Distribution.**

Mijade Editions (BEL) *(978-2-87142) Dist. by* **Distribks Inc.**

Mikaya Pr., *(978-0-9650493; 978-1-931414)* 12 Bedford St., New York, NY 10014 USA Tel 212-647-1831; Fax: 212-727-0236
E-mail: Waldman@Mikaya.com
Web site: http://www.mikaya.com
Dist(s): **Firefly Bks., Ltd.**

Mikazuki Jujitsu *See* **Mikazuki Publishing Hse.**

Mikazuki Publishing Hse., *(978-0-615-47311-6; 978-0-615-48054-1; 978-0-9835946; 978-1-937981; 978-0-9910285; 978-1-942825)* 530 E. 8th St. Suite 400, Los Angeles, CA 90014 USA Tel 010-982-2379
E-mail: kambizmostofizadeh1@gmail.com
Web site: http://www.MikazukiPublishingHouse.com
Dist(s): **BookBaby**
Lightning Source, Inc.

Mike-Auri Bks., *(978-0-9747587)* P.O. Box 420966, Del Rio, TX 78842 USA Tel 830-774-2789
E-mail: dfitzgibbon@stx.rr.com
Web site: http://www.texasredhen.com; http://www.mikeauri.com.

Mike-Mike Distribution, *(978-0-9741043)* 1003 N., Fifth St., Champaign, IL 61820 USA Tel 217-352-4215.

Mikenzi's Kardz & Bks. Llc., *(978-0-9792647)* 1115 S. Alhambra Cir., Coral Gables, FL 33146-3711 USA
E-mail: sgbarrow@hotmail.com.

Milano, Jacque & Assocs., *(978-0-9728432)* 700 N. Dobson Rd., No. 15, Chandler, AZ 85224 USA; *Imprints:* Carefree Publishing (Carefree Pubng)
Web site: http://www.carefreepublishing.com.

Mile Oak Publishing, Inc. (CAN) *(978-1-896819) Dist. by* **Austin and Co.**

Miles & Assocs., *(978-0-9778623)* P.O. Box 15566, Phoenix, AZ 85060 USA Tel 386-446-9291
E-mail: drlinda03@aol.com
Web site: http://www.thenewmarriage.com.

Miles, Linda *See* **Miles & Assocs.**

Miles Music, *(978-0-9710446)* Div. of Miles Enterprises, 3060 Larson Rd., Weippe, ID 83553 USA Tel 208-435-4600; Fax: 208-435-1116
E-mail: milesmusic@idamail.com
Web site: http://www.idamail.com.

Milestone Pr., Inc., *(978-0-9631861; 978-1-889596)* Orders Addr.: P.O. Box 158, Almond, NC 28702 USA Tel 828-488-6601 (phone/fax)
E-mail: maryellenhammond@milestonepress.com
Web site: http://www.milestonepress.com
Dist(s): **America's Cycling Pubns.**
Common Ground Distributors, Inc.

Milestones Publishing, *(978-0-9786154)* P.O. Box 1556, Wylie, TX 75098 USA Tel 214-403-9852; Fax: 972-442-1613
E-mail: kaylasadams@hotmail.com
Web site: http://www.kaylaadams.net.

Milet Publishing, *(978-1-84059)* P.O. Box 2459, Chicago, IL 60690-2459 USA
E-mail: info@milet.com
Web site: http://www.milet.com
Dist(s): **Chinasprout, Inc.**
Independent Pubs. Group
Tuttle Publishing.

Milk & Cookies *Imprint of* **ibooks, Inc.**

Milk Mug Publishing, *(978-0-9721882)* 9190 W. Olympic Blvd., Suite 253, Beverly Hills, CA 90212 USA Tel 310-278-1153 (phone/fax)
E-mail: orders@thehoopsterbook.com
Web site: http://www.thehoopsterbook.com
Dist(s): **SCB Distributors.**

Milken Family Foundation, *(978-0-9646425)* 1250 Fourth St., 4th Flr., Santa Monica, CA 90404-1353 USA Tel 310-998-2825; Fax: 310-998-2899
E-mail: jboone@mff.org
Web site: http://www.milkenexchange.org.

Milkweed Editions, *(978-0-915943; 978-1-57131)* 1011 Washington Ave. S., Suite 300, Minneapolis, MN 55415-1246 USA (SAN 294-0671) Tel 612-332-3192; Fax: 612-215-2550; Toll Free: 800-520-6455
E-mail: market@milkweed.org
Web site: http://www.milkweed.org; http://www.worldashome.org
Dist(s): **MyiLibrary**
Perseus-PGW
Perseus Bks. Group.

Mill City Press, Inc *Imprint of* **Hillcrest Publishing Group, Inc.**

Mill City Press, Incorporated *See* **Hillcrest Publishing Group, Inc.**

Mill Creek Metro Publishing, *(978-0-9741989)* P.O. Box 90134, Youngstown, OH 44509 USA Tel 330-797-0024
E-mail: ianjcue@ianjcue.com
Web site: http://www.ianjcue.com
Dist(s): **Book Clearing Hse.**

Mill Park Publishing, *(978-0-9728225; 978-0-9883980)* E & M Group, LLC, Orders Addr.: 981 W. Cherry Bello Dr., Eagle, ID 83616 USA Tel 208-890-8122
E-mail: elaine@elaineambrose.com; elaine@millparkpublishing.com
Web site: http://www.Elaineambrose.com; www.millparkpublishing.com
Dist(s): **Lulu Enterprises Inc.**

Mill Street Forward, The, *(978-0-9654628)* 15 1/2 Van Houten St., Apt. 117, Paterson, NJ 07505 USA Tel 973-345-9539.

Millbrook Pr. *Imprint of* **Lerner Publishing Group**

Millennial Mind Publishing *Imprint of* **American Bk. Publishing Group**

Millennium Marketing & Publishing, *(978-1-886161)* 2455 Glen Hill Dr., Indianapolis, IN 46240-3460 USA Tel 317-815-9828; Fax: 317-815-9829
E-mail: MMPbooks@comcast.net
Web site: http://www.chicksguidetofootball.com
Dist(s): **Cardinal Pubs. Group**
Independent Pubs. Group
Journey Pubns., LLC
Quality Bks., Inc.

Millennium Workshop Production, *(978-0-9725344)* 11501 Maple Ridge Rd., Reston, VA 20190-3604 USA (SAN 255-1624) Tel 703-925-0610 (phone/fax)
E-mail: victor@millenniumworkshop.com
Web site: http://www.millenniumworkshop.com.

Miller, Ann *See* **Jaylil Publishing Co.**

Miller, Bruce, *(978-0-9765598)* 10011 Bridgeport Way SW., Suite 1500 PMB128, Lakewood, WA 98499 USA Tel 253-227-2292
E-mail: warofpowers@comcast.net.

Miller, Deanna, *(978-0-9725424)* 12215 Fuller St., Silver Spring, MD 20902 USA
E-mail: info@deannamiller.com
Web site: http://www.deannamiller.com.

Miller, Debra Juanita, *(978-0-9706782; 978-0-9776014)* P.O. Box 20593, Chicago, IL 60620 USA
E-mail: monogrambooklets@yahoo.com; djpmspinsstories@yahoo.com.

Miller, Don G., *(978-0-615-12836-8)* 5051 S. 172nd. St., Omaha, NE 68135 USA.

Miller, J. Cris & Assocs., *(978-0-9725308)* 10555 W. 74th St., Countryside, IL 60525 USA Tel 708-579-1707 (phone/fax)
E-mail: jcmtales@hotmail.com.

Miller, J. Garnet Ltd. (GBR) *(978-0-85343) Dist. by* **Empire Pub Srvs.**

Miller, Michael, *(978-0-9723474; 978-0-9743522; 978-0-9825155; 978-0-9839356)* 2418 Hagerman St., Colorado Springs, CO 80904 USA Tel 719-635-0017; Fax: 501-421-1495
E-mail: michael@mail.sabineundmichael.com
Web site: http://www.sabineundmichael.com.

Miller, Peter Mitchell *See* **Silver Print Pr., Inc.**

Miller, Randy, *(978-0-9770530)* 17 N. Rd., Alstead, NH 03602 USA Tel 603-835-7889
E-mail: jrmiller@sover.net
Web site: http://www.randymillerprints.com.

Miller, Smit Enterprises, *(978-0-9769433)* 112 Misty Creek Dr., Colorado Springs, CO 80132-6032 USA
E-mail: dawn@dawnsmit.com.

Miller, Walton, *(978-0-615-77997-3)* 13506 Summerport Village Pkwy, #246, Windermere, FL 34786 USA Tel 3215276905
Dist(s): **CreateSpace Independent Publishing Platform.**

MillerWrite, Inc., *(978-0-9723948)* 2875-F Northtowne Ln., No. 302, Reno, NV 89512-2062 USA Tel 775-673-2152
E-mail: chrisshelton78@msn.com; jmiller@millerwrite.com
Web site: http://www.millerwrite.com.

Millfree Mursaps Media, *(978-0-9904093)* 2850 Annunciation St., New Orleans, LA 70115 USA Tel 504-233-3369
E-mail: ryan@nouveausouth.org
Web site: millfreemursaps.com
Dist(s): **Independent Pubs. Group.**

Milligan Books *See* **Professional Publishing Hse. LLC**

Millman, Selena, *(978-0-9793058; 978-0-9794584; 978-0-9795756; 978-0-9798417; 978-0-9798603; 978-0-9802400; 978-0-615-15137-3; 978-0-615-23804-3; 978-0-578-00466-2; 978-0-578-00564-5)* 4984 Ridgebury, Lyndhurst, OH 44124 USA
Web site: http://www.freewebs.com/heal4michael
Dist(s): **Lulu Enterprises Inc.**

Millmark Education, *(978-1-4334; 978-1-61618)* Orders Addr.: 7272 Wisconsin Ave, Suite 300, Bethesda, MD 20814-2081 USA (SAN 852-4912) Tel 301-941-1974; Fax: 301-656-0183; Edit Addr.: 7272 Wisconsin Ave. Suite 300, Suite 300, Bethesda, MD 20814-2081 USA
E-mail: rachel.moir@millmarkeducation.com; info@millmarkeducation.com
Web site: http://www.millmarkeducation.com/.

Mills & Morris Publishing Corporation *See* **Bluebonnets, Boots & Bks. Pr.**

Milner Crest Publishing, LLC, *(978-0-9820651)* P.O. Box 10754, Portland, OR 97296-0754 USA (SAN 857-1376)
E-mail: danielbruton@gmail.com
Web site: http://www.milnercrestpublishing.com
Dist(s): **BookBaby.**

Milo Educational Bks. & Resources, *(978-1-933668; 978-1-60698)* P.O. Box 41353, Houston, TX 77241-1353 USA Tel 713-466-6456; Fax: 713-896-6456
E-mail: milo_books@yahoo.com
Web site: http://www.miloeducationalbooks.com.

Milstein & Hauptman Publishing *See* **Wonderful Publishing**

Miltenberg, Robert Allen, *(978-0-615-63925-3; 978-0-615-66467-5; 978-0-615-77522-7; 978-0-9893031)* 210 LIME KEY Ln., NAPLES, FL 34114 USA Tel 310-994-2407
E-mail: Rmiltenberg@yahoo.com
Web site: www.blurb.com; www.artworq.com.

MiMar Publishing, *(978-0-9754241; 978-0-615-16688-9; 978-0-615-16689-6)* 714 Enchanted Rock Trail, Georgetown, TX 78633 USA
Web site: http://www.bakerstreetbunch.com
Dist(s): **Lulu Enterprises Inc.**

Mimi Bee Pubns., *(978-0-9745944)* Orders Addr.: P.O. Box 188, Accord, NY 12404 USA
E-mail: mimibee@att.com
Web site: http://mrallergyhead.com.

Mimi's Funhouse, LLC, *(978-0-9841589)* 10611A Crystal Cove Dr., Magnolia, TX 77354 USA
Web site: http://www.mimisfunhouse.com
Dist(s): **AtlasBooks Distribution.**

Minardi Photography, *(978-1-878444)* 5501 Harvest Scene Ct., Columbia, MD 21044 USA Tel 410-964-5403; Fax: 410-964-5643.

Minch, John & Assocs., Inc., *(978-0-9631090)* P.O. Box 4244, Mission Viejo, CA 92690-4244 USA Tel 949-367-1000; Fax: 949-367-0117; Toll Free: 800-367-2995
E-mail: jmainc@earthlink.net.

Mind - Stretch, *(978-0-9676409)* 3124 Landrum Rd., Columbus, NC 28722 USA Tel 828-863-4235; Fax: 828-863-2584; Toll Free: 888-538-8911
E-mail: marklevin@alltel.net
Web site: http://www.mindstretch.com.

Mind Candy, LLC, *(978-0-9786929)* P.O. Box 2185, Garden City, NY 11531-2185 USA (SAN 851-3392) Tel 516-318-4433
Web site: http://mindcandymedia.com.

Mind Touch Communications LLC, *(978-0-615-74472-8; 978-0-615-74793-4)* P.O. Box 54, S. Rockwood, MI 48179 USA Tel 7343654866
Web site: http://MindTouchCommunications.com
Dist(s): **CreateSpace Independent Publishing Platform.**

Mind Trip Press *See* **Big Ransom Studio**

Mindanao Publishing Co., *(978-0-9710841)* 1222 Hazel St., N., Saint. Paul, MN 55119-4500 USA Tel 651-274-6602; Fax: 651-771-9772
E-mail: jararick@worldnet.att.net
Web site: http://www.sanpedrocollege.org; http://www.eslseminarschina.org; http://www.eslseminars.org; http://www.ielts4nurses.org.

Mind/Body Workshops, *(978-0-9748548)* 131 S. Euclid, Westfield, NJ 07090 USA Tel 718-273-3682
Web site: http://www.kickoutstress.com.

Mindcastle Bks., Inc., *(978-0-9677204)* Orders Addr.: P.O. Box 3005, Woodinville, WA 98072 USA Tel 425-424-8860; Fax: 425-398-1354
E-mail: vanessa@mindcastle.com
Web site: http://www.mindcastle.com.

MindCatcher Pr., *(978-0-9724113)* 284 Mattison Dr., Concord, MA 01742 USA Tel 978-369-7868
E-mail: marian@mindcatcherpress.com
Web site: http://www.mindcatcherpress.com; http://www.readylady.com.

Mindfull Publishing, *(978-0-9669551)* 177 W. Norwalk Rd., Norwalk, CT 06850 USA Tel 203-831-0855
E-mail: mindfullpub@hotmail.com
Web site: http://www.homestead.com/mindfullpublishing/.

Mindfull Publishing Co., *(978-0-9720308)* Orders Addr.: P.O. Box 34, Clairton, PA 15025 USA Toll Free: 888-946-0816; Edit Addr.: 329 Mitchell Ave., Clairton, PA 15025 USA
E-mail: gbberryauthor@yahoo.com.

MindMaze Publishing Co., *(978-0-9747668)* P.O. Box 251278, Woodbury, MN 55125 USA
E-mail: mindmaze@comcast.net
Dist(s): **AtlasBooks Distribution.**

Mindo Pr., *(978-0-9747971)* P.O. Box 34, Danielsville, PA 18038-9754 USA
E-mail: rshade@fast.net.

MindOH! Foundation, The, *(978-0-9773689)* 2525 Robinhood St., Houston, TX 77005 USA (SAN 257-3741) Tel 713-533-1138 Toll Free: 866-646-3641
Web site: http://www.mindohfoundation.org.

Mindsong Math, *(978-0-9758592)* 1111 NE 322nd Ave., Washougal, WA 98671 USA Tel 360-335-1373
E-mail: info@breachingbooks.com
Web site: http://www.thewhaleslibrary.com.

MindsOrb, Inc., *(978-0-9741877)* P.O. Box 162706, Austin, TX 78716 USA
Web site: http://www.mindsorb.com.

Mindstir Media, *(978-0-9819648; 978-0-9836771; 978-0-9853650; 978-0-9858398; 978-0-9883162; 978-0-9885180; 978-0-9886409; 978-0-9889595; 978-0-9890288; 978-0-9892711; 978-0-9894748; 978-0-9897168; 978-0-9898820; 978-0-9910324; 978-0-9911512; 978-0-9913190; 978-0-9914884; 978-0-9916230; 978-0-9903626; 978-0-9906106; 978-0-9908137; 978-0-9862149; 978-0-9863057; 978-0-9961434; 978-0-9962872; 978-0-9964615;*

For full information on wholesalers and distributors, refer to the Wholesaler and Distributor Name Index

978-0-9967294) 1931 Woodbury Ave. No. 182, *Portsmouth, NH 03801 USA*
Dist(s): **Smashwords.**

MindWare Holdings, Inc., *(978-0-9648481; 978-1-892069; 978-1-933054; 978-1-936300)* 2100 County Rd. C W., Roseville, MN 55113 USA (SAN 859-9157) Fax: 651-582-0556; Toll Free: 800-999-0398
Web site: http://mindware.com.

Mindwing Concepts, Inc., *(978-0-9761393; 978-0-9769527; 978-0-9791307; 978-0-9792917; 978-0-9793185; 978-0-9816818)* 1 Federal St. Bldg. 103-1, Springfield, MA 01105 USA Toll Free: 888-228-9746
Web site: http://www.mindwingconcepts.com.

MindWorks Pr., *(978-1-886554)* 4019 Westerly Pl., Suite 108, Newport Beach, CA 92660 USA (SAN 850-4873) Tel 949.266.3714; Fax: 949.266.3770; Toll Free: 800-626-2720
E-mail: mindworkspress@aol.com; sposs@amenclinic.com
Web site: http://www.mindworkspress.com
Dist(s): **Lulu Enterprises Inc.**

Minedition *Imprint of* **Penguin Publishing Group**

Minerva Bks., *(978-0-9620125)* Div. of Hulbert Performance Rating, Inc., 316 Commerce St., Alexandria, VA 22314 USA (SAN 247-493X) Tel 703-683-5905 Do not confuse with companies with the same or similar name in Palo Alto, CA, New York, NY, Louisville, KY.

Minerva Bks., Ltd., *(978-0-8056)* 30 W. 26th St., New York, NY 10010 USA (SAN 205-8367) Tel 212-675-0465; Fax: 212-675-0573 Do not confuse with companies with the same or similar name in Alexandria, VA, Palo Alto, CA, Louisville, KY
Dist(s): **Continental Bk. Co., Inc.**
Lectorum Pubns., Inc.

Mini Enterprises - M.E. *See* **AGB Publishing**

Minikin Pr., *(978-0-9772320)* P.O. Box 528, Barrington, RI 02806-0280 USA (SAN 257-0076) Tel 401-245-7960
E-mail: jill@minikinpress.com
Web site: http://www.minikinpress.com
Dist(s): **Independent Pubs. Group.**

Minimal Pr., The, *(978-0-9742516; 978-0-615-25627-6; 978-0-615-25629-0; 978-0-9824665)* 406 Colchester Ave., Burlington, VT 05401 USA
Dist(s): **Lulu Enterprises Inc.**

Minna Pr., *(978-0-9829630)* 8015 Stoneham Ct., Matthews, NC 28105 USA Tel 704-817-0343
E-mail: lj1838@gmail.com
Dist(s): **BookBaby.**

Minnesota Assn. for Children's Mental Health, *(978-0-9820482)* 165 Western Ave., Suite 2, Saint Paul, MN 55102 USA Tel 651-644-7333; Fax: 651-644-7391; Toll Free: 800-528-4511
E-mail: info@macmh.org
Web site: http://www.macmh.org.

Minnesota Department of Economic Security *See* **Minnesota Dept. Employment & Economic Development**

Minnesota Dept. Employment & Economic Development, *(978-0-9670505; 978-0-9845780; 978-0-615-50484-1)* 332 Minnesota St. Ste. E200, Saint Paul, MN 55101-1349 USA Toll Free: 888-234-1114
E-mail: Amy.yerkes@state.mn.us
Web site: http://www.positivelyminnesota.com.

†Minnesota Historical Society Pr., *(978-0-87351; 978-1-68134)* Orders Addr.: 11030 S. Langley Ave., Chicago, IL 60628 USA Toll Free Fax: 800-621-8476; Toll Free: 800-621-2736; Edit Addr.: 345 Kellogg Blvd., W., Saint Paul, MN 55102-1906 USA (SAN 202-6384) Tel 651-297-2221; 651-259-3202; Fax: 651-297-1345; Toll Free: 800-647-7827; *Imprints:* Borealis Book (Borealis Book)
E-mail: greg.britton@mnhs.org
Web site: http://www.mnhs.org/mhspress; mnhspress.org
Dist(s): **BookMobile**
Chicago Distribution Ctr.; *CIP.*

Minnesota Humanities Ctr., *(978-0-9629298; 978-1-931016; 978-0-578-03464-5; 978-0-9884539)* 987 E. Ivy Ave., Saint Paul, MN 55106-2046 USA Tel 651-774-0105 Toll Free: 866-268-7293
E-mail: info@minnesotahumanities.org
Web site: http://www.minnesotahumanities.org.

Minnesota Humanities Commission *See* **Minnesota Humanities Ctr.**

Minnesota's Bookstore, *(978-0-9647451; 978-0-9754338)* 660 Olive St., Saint Paul, MN 55155 USA Tel 651-297-3000; Fax: 651-215-5733; Toll Free: 800-657-3757
E-mail: mnbookstore@state.mn.us
Web site: http://www.minnesotasbookstore.com
Dist(s): **Univ. of Texas Pr.**

Minnewaska Pr., *(978-0-9799410)* 24535 165th St., Glenwood, MN 56334 USA
E-mail: minnewaskapress@yahoo.com
Web site: http://www.debmercier.com.

Minnie Troy Pubs., *(978-0-9727480)* Div. of Historically Speaking, 309 Union St., Murfreesboro, NC 27855 USA Tel 252-398-5098; Fax: 252-398-5098 ext 51
E-mail: lion5098@aol.com.

Minon, S.A. (ESP) *(978-84-355) Dist. by* **Lectorum Pubns.**

Minotaur Bks. *Imprint of* **St. Martin's Pr.**

Minotauro Ediciones (ESP) *(978-84-450) Dist. by* **Distribks Inc.**

Minotauro Ediciones (ESP) *(978-84-450) Dist. by* **Lectorum Pubns.**

Minotauro Ediciones (ESP) *(978-84-450) Dist. by* **Planeta.**

Minted Prose, LLC, *(978-0-9744287; 978-0-9905721; 978-0-9965454)* 176 Broadway, Suite 11A, New York, NY 10038 USA (SAN 255-6138) Tel 646-789-7368; Fax: 347-493-3545
E-mail: linda@mintedprose.com
Web site: http://www.mintedprose.com; http://www.traitordachshund.com
Dist(s): **CreateSpace Independent Publishing Platform**
Independent Pubs. Group
MyiLibrary.

Minton, Art, *(978-0-615-15948-5)* Orders Addr.: P.O. Box 16294, Jackson, MS 39236-6294 USA Tel 601-966-6699; Fax: 206-202-3329; Edit Addr.: 1939 Cherokee Dr., jackson, MS 39211 USA
E-mail: rentjackson@gmail.com
Web site: http://birdingforchildren.com.

Minuteman Press of Green Bay *See* **EPS Digital**

Minx *Imprint of* **DC Comics**

Mira Pr., The, *(978-0-9762947)* P.O. Box 590207, Newton Centre, MA 02459 USA.

Miracle Mountain Images, *(978-0-615-68766-7)* 692 Yearly Way, Grants Pass, OR 97527 USA Tel 541 474.4650
Web site: www.miraclemountainimages.com
Dist(s): **CreateSpace Independent Publishing Platform.**

Miracle Pr., *(978-0-929889)* 2808 W. Lexington Way, Edmond, OK 73003-4224 USA (SAN 250-975X) Tel 405-359-0369; Fax: 703-883-1861
E-mail: miraclepress@cox.net.

Miraculous Fingerprints Pubs., *(978-1-886134)* 74565 Dillon Rd., MH 15, Desert Hot Springs, CA 92241 USA Tel 760-251-3037.

Miramax Bks., *(978-0-7868; 978-1-4013)* Div. of Walt Disney Productions, 11 Beach St., 5th Flr., New York, NY 10013 USA Fax: 212-625-5075
Web site: http://www.miramax.com
Dist(s): **Disney Publishing Worldwide**
Hachette Bk. Group
Hyperion Pr.

MiraQuest, *(978-0-9748329; 978-0-615-26973-3; 978-0-9819958)* Orders Addr.: P.O. Box 29722, Los Angeles, CA 90029-0722 USA
Web site: http://www.islandlili.com
Dist(s): **Lightning Source, Inc.**

Mirhady, Farhad, *(978-0-9760323)* 2055 Beverly Beach Dr NW, Olympia, WA 98502-3427 USA
E-mail: fmirhady@comcast.net
Web site: http://www.poeticliterature.com.

MIROGLYPHICS, *(978-0-9773064; 978-0-9801073)* Orders Addr.: 5734 N. 4th St., Philadelphia, PA 19120 USA (SAN 257-2451) Tel 215-224-2486; *Imprints:* Romoulous (Romoulous)
E-mail: germic2008@gmail.com; mnik1972@aol.com
Web site: http://www.miroglyphics.biz
Dist(s): **Lightning Source, Inc.**

Mirror Pond Publishing, *(978-0-9777683)* 63090 Casey Pl., Bend, OR 97701 USA Tel 541-385-6927
E-mail: speedyread@hotmail.com.

Mirror Publishing, *(978-0-9796519; 978-0-9800675; 978-0-9815904; 978-0-9817521; 978-0-9821171; 978-0-9822560; 978-1-936046; 978-1-936352; 978-1-61225)* 6434 W. Dixon St., Milwaukee, WI 53214-1750 USA Tel 414-763-1034
E-mail: info@pagesofwonder.com
Web site: http://www.pagesofwonder.com
Dist(s): **Lightning Source, Inc.**

Mirrorstone *Imprint of* **Wizards of the Coast**

MirthMarks Publishing, *(978-0-9789591)* 675 Deis Dr., STE 123, Fairfield, OH 45014 USA
E-mail: flymaster@coppershoo.com.

Misakonis, Amy, *(978-0-615-74795-8; 978-0-615-79881-3)* 23 Spindrift Way, Annapolis, MD 21403 USA Tel 3862354363
Web site: www.amymisakonis.com
Dist(s): **CreateSpace Independent Publishing Platform.**

Misfit Mous *See* **Misfit Mouse**

Misfit Mouse, *(978-0-578-11067-7; 978-0-578-12084-3; 978-0-578-15002-4; 978-0-692-42251-9; 978-0-692-48383-1)* 3382 Habersham Rd. NW, Atlanta, GA 30305 USA
Web site: www.misfitmouse.com.

Misha Foundation, *(978-0-615-66676-1; 978-0-615-68421-5; 978-0-9885003)* 206 Erskine Dr. E., Greensboro, NC 27410 USA
E-mail: mishafoundation@msn.com
Web site: http://www.littlefoxbook.com; http://www.mishafoundation.org
Dist(s): **CreateSpace Independent Publishing Platform**
Lightning Source, Inc.

Missing Piece Pr., *(978-0-9703729)* 37042 S. Hollygreen Dr., Tucson, AZ 857398 USA Tel 520-338-2582
E-mail: Questions@MissingPiecePress.com
Web site: http://www.missingpiecepress.com
Dist(s): **Reveal Entertainment, Inc.**

Mission City Pr., Inc., *(978-1-928749; 978-1-934306)* 8122 Datapoint Dr. Ste. 1000, San Antonio, TX 78229-3273 USA Toll Free: 800-840-2641
E-mail: busaffair@missioncitypress.com
Web site: http://www.alifeoffaith.com
Dist(s): **Zondervan.**

Mission Creek Studios, *(978-0-929702)* 1040 Mission Canyon Rd., Santa Barbara, CA 93105-2122 USA (SAN 249-9630) Tel 805-682-6724; Fax: 805-682-6761
E-mail: dave@missioncreek.com
Web site: http://www.missioncreek.com.

Mission Manuscripts, Inc., *(978-0-9768880)* 1000 Jorie Blvd., Suite 206, Oak Brook, IL 60523 USA Tel 630-990-0220; Fax: 630-990-2556
E-mail: kathy.hill@arends-inc.com.

Mission Mill Museum, *(978-0-9753484)* 1313 Mill St., SE, Salem, OR 97301 USA Tel 503-585-7012; Fax: 503-588-9902
E-mail: info@missionmill.org
Web site: http://www.missionmill.org.

Mision Ridge Pr., *(978-0-9763956)* 4660 Eastus Dr., San Jose, CA 95129 USA.

†Mississippi Museum of Art, *(978-1-887422)* 380 S. Lamar St., Jackson, MS 39201-4007 USA (SAN 279-6198)
E-mail: rpb@netdoor.com
Web site: http://www.msmuseumart.org
Dist(s): **Pennsylvania State Univ. Pr.**
Univ. Pr. of Mississippi
Univ. of Washington Pr.; *CIP.*

Missouri Historical Society Pr., *(978-1-883982)* Orders Addr.: P.O. Box 11940, Saint Louis, MO 63112-0040 USA Fax: 314-746-4548
E-mail: jstevens@mohistory.org
Web site: http://www.mohistory.org
Dist(s): **Chicago Distribution Ctr.**
SPD-Small Pr. Distribution
Univ. of Missouri Pr.
Univ. of New Mexico Pr.
Wayne State Univ. Pr.

Mister C Music, *(978-0-9755333)* P.O. Box 28, Rochester, PA 15074 USA Toll Free: 877-687-4258
E-mail: misterc437@aol.com
Web site: http://www.mistercmusic.com.

†MIT Pr., *(978-0-262; 978-0-89706)* Orders Addr.: c/o Triliteral LLC, 100 Maple Ridge Dr., Cumberland, RI 02864 USA Tel 401-531-2800; Fax: 401-531-2801; Toll Free Fax: 800-406-9145; Toll Free: 800-405-1619; Edit Addr.: 55 Hayward St., Cambridge, MA 02142-1315 USA (SAN 202-6414) Tel 617-253-5646; Fax: 617-253-6779
E-mail: orders@triliteral.org
Web site: http://mitpress.mit.edu
Dist(s): **Ebsco Publishing**
MyiLibrary
ebrary, Inc.; *CIP.*

Mitchell, Carol *See* **CaribbeanReads**

Mitchell, Damien Pardow, *(978-0-615-18469-2)* 13834 Doolittle Dr., San Leandro, CA 94577 USA
Web site: http://jarvisprinting.com
Dist(s): **Publishers Services.**

Mitchell, Karan, *(978-0-9763793)* 79 Baruch Dr., Apt.5E, New York, NY 10002-3659 USA Tel 212-982-7977
E-mail: mtchllkm@aol.com.

Mitchell Lane Pubs., Inc., *(978-1-883845; 978-1-58415; 978-1-61228; 978-1-68020)* Orders Addr.: P.O. Box 196, Hockessin, DE 19707 USA (SAN 858-3749) Tel 302-234-9426; Fax: 302-234-4742; Toll Free: 800-814-5484
E-mail: orders@mitchellane.com; barbaramitchell@mitchellane.com
Web site: http://www.mitchelllane.com.

Mitchell, P. S., *(978-0-615-80354-8)* 3682 King St. Unit 16831, Alexandria, VA 22302 USA Tel 571-214-4805
E-mail: psmitchellbook@gmail.com.

Mitchell Publishing, Incorporated *See* **Teaching & Learning Co.**

Mitchell Publishing, Inc., *(978-0-938188)* 160 Spear St. Ste. 700, San Francisco, CA 94105-1562 USA (SAN 215-7896) Toll Free: 800-435-2665 Do not confuse with companies with the same or similar names in Spokane, WA, Medina, NY, Medicine Lodge, KS.

Mitre's Touch Gallery, The, *(978-0-9764384)* 1414 Adams Ave., La Grande, OR 97850 USA Tel 541-963-3477
E-mail: weframe@eoni.com.

Mitten Pr. *Imprint of* **Ann Arbor Editions LLC**

Mixta Publishing Co., *(978-0-9675951)* 3179 San Francisco Ave., Long Beach, CA 90806 USA Tel 562-427-4270
E-mail: michael.archuleta@gte.net; michael@mixtapublishing.com
Web site: http://www.mixtapublishing.com; http://www.mixtapublishing.net
Dist(s): **Leonard, Hal Corp.**

Mizzou Media - University BookStores *See* **Mizzou Publishing - The Mizzou Store**

Mizzou Publishing - The Mizzou Store, *(978-1-61600)* Div. of University of Missouri, Mu Student Ctr. 911 E. Rollins St., Columbia, MO 65211 USA Tel 573-882-8567; Fax: 573-884-8050
E-mail: mizzoupublishing@missouri.edu
Web site: http://www.themizzoustore.com/t-Espresso-About.aspx.

MJ Brooks Co., *(978-0-9787864)* 325 Liliwahi Loop, Kailua, HI 96734 USA Tel 808-254-4691.

MJS Music & Entertainment, LLC, *(978-0-9762917; 978-0-9817451)* 9699 W. Fort Island Trail, Crystal River, FL 34429 USA Tel 352-257-3261; Fax: 352-795-1658 Do not confuse with comapnies with the same or similar name in Boyertown, PA, Searsport, ME
E-mail: msternal@mjspublications.com; wriverroad@aol.com
Web site: http://www.mjspublications.com
Dist(s): **Dumont, Charles Son, Inc.**
Omnibus Pr.
TNT Media Group, Inc.

MJS Music Publications *See* **MJS Music & Entertainment, LLC**

MJS Publishing Group LLC, *(978-0-9764336)* P.O. Box 6582, Evanston, IL 60204-6582 USA Tel 847-869-5901; Fax: 847-745-0219
E-mail: mjspg@ameritech.net
Web site: http://www.mjspub.com
Dist(s): **AtlasBooks Distribution.**

MK Publishing, *(978-0-9720484; 978-0-9747147; 978-0-9760534; 978-0-9763271; 978-0-9770933; 978-0-9785081)* 25123 22nd Ave. S., Saint Cloud, MN 56301 USA; P.O. Box 945, St Cloud, MN 56302 (SAN 256-4092) Tel 320-252-1023; Fax: 320-252-4574
Web site: http://www.yourbookpublisher.net
Dist(s): **Closet Case Bks.**
J & N Creations, LLC
JMS Distribution
Main Trail Productions
Ozark Bk. Distributors
Perfume River Pubns.
Puzzle Piece Pubns.

MKADesigns, *(978-0-9745839)* 131 Frankie Ln., Madison, AL 35757-6922 USA Tel 256-721-0200; *Imprints:* Fun to Read Books with Royally Good Morals (Fun to Read Bk)
E-mail: mike.dozier@mkadesigns.com
Web site: http://www.mkadesigns.com.

ML Publishing, *(978-0-9768347)* Div. of MIHP, 31500 Dequindre Rd., Warren, MI 48092-1057 USA Tel 586-268-6942
E-mail: smclaughlin@mihp.net
Web site: http://mlpublishing.com.

MLM Ranch Publishing, *(978-0-9743098)* P.O. Box 910251, St. George, UT 84791 USA.

MLR Pr., LLC, *(978-0-9793110; 978-1-934531; 978-0-615-13459-8; 978-1-60820)* 3052 Gaines Waterport Rd., Albion, NY 14411 USA (SAN 853-1013) Tel 585-589-7831
E-mail: mlrpress@gmail.com
Web site: http://www.mlrpress.com
Dist(s): **Lulu Enterprises Inc.**

MMG Technology Corp., *(978-0-9754886)* 379 Amherst St., Suite 204, Nashua, NH 03063 USA
Web site: http://www.the-common.com.

M-m-mauleg Publishing, *(978-0-9790111)* Orders Addr.: P.O. Box 5258, Mangilao, GU 96923 USA; Edit Addr.: 303 University Dr., Mangila, GU 96923-5258 USA
E-mail: millhoff@uog.edu.

MMP *See* **Millennium Marketing & Publishing**

MMP Publishing, *(978-0-615-76258-6; 978-0-615-77083-3; 978-0-615-77333-9; 978-0-615-77334-6; 978-0-615-77663-7; 978-0-615-79398-6; 978-0-615-80885-7; 978-1-941488)* 124 Janice St. 0, Martinsburg, AE 25404 USA Tel 304-263-2772
E-mail: JanetMcNulty84@gmail.com
Dist(s): **CreateSpace Independent Publishing Platform**
Lulu Enterprises Inc.

MNMC, *(978-0-9728518; 978-0-9763532)* 17 Old Shelter Rock Rd., Danbury, CT 06810 USA Tel 203-798-6936; Toll Free: 866-210-0004
E-mail: order@muslimplanet.com
Web site: http://www.muslimpublisher.com.

Mobius Communications, Ltd., *(978-1-891304; 978-1-928583)* Div. of Publication Services, Inc., 1802 S. Duncan Rd., Champaign, IL 61822-5222 USA Fax: 217-398-3923; Toll Free: 800-662-4875
Web site: http://www.8-mobius.com.

Mocha Enterprises, *(978-0-9707163)* 6322 Chesapeake Cir., Stockton, CA 95219 USA (SAN 253-620X) Tel 209-478-0635 (phone/fax); 209-946-3064
E-mail: mochaenterprises@aol.com
Web site: http://www.welcometotheprofessionalwork.com.

Mockingbird Lane Pr., *(978-0-9856906; 978-0-9889542; 978-0-9893105)* 2441 Washington Rd., Maynard, AR 72444 USA Tel 870-647-2137
E-mail: mockingbirdlanepress@gmail.com.

Mockingbird Publishing, *(978-0-9828528)* Orders Addr.: P.O. Box 442, Fairhope, AL 36533 USA Tel 334-546-0710
E-mail: ashley@mockingbirdpublishing.com
Web site: http://www.mockingbirdpublishing.com.

†Modern Curriculum Pr., *(978-0-7652; 978-0-8136; 978-0-87895)* Div. of Pearson Education, Orders Addr.: P.O. Box 2500, Lebanon, IN 46052-3009 USA (SAN 206-6572) Toll Free: 800-526-9907 (Customer Service)
Web site: http://www.pearsonlearning.com
Dist(s): **Follett School Solutions**
Lectorum Pubns., Inc.
Pearson Learning; *CIP.*

Modern Evil Pr., *(978-1-934516)* 913 S 2nd Ave, Phoenix, AZ 85003-2511 USA Tel 602-999-6449
E-mail: teel@modernevil.com
Web site: http://modernevil.com/
Dist(s): **Smashwords.**

Modern Learning Pr., *(978-0-935493; 978-1-56762)* P.O. Box 167, Rosemont, NJ 08556 USA Tel 609-397-2214; Fax: 845-277-3548; Toll Free Fax: 888-558-7350; Toll Free: 800-627-5867
E-mail: Rlow@tasa.com.

Modern Library *Imprint of* **Random House Publishing Group**

Modern Living Media *See* **Pirouz, Raymond**

Modern Publishing, *(978-0-7666; 978-0-87449; 978-1-56144)* Div. of Unisystems, Inc., 155 E. 55th St., New York, NY 10022 USA (SAN 253-2921) Tel 212-826-0850; Fax: 212-759-9096
E-mail: info@modernpublishing.com
Web site: http://www.modernpublishing.com.

MoGho Bks., LLC, *(978-0-9712559; 978-0-615-11888-8)* Box 200, 9801 Hartley Rd., Hallsville, MO 65255 USA Tel 573-696-3537 (phone/fax)
E-mail: moghobks@tranquility.net
Dist(s): **Cowley Distributing, Inc.**
Univ. of Missouri Pr.

Mogul Comics, *(978-0-9657723)* 102 6th Ave. 2nd Flr., WaterVliet, NY 12189 USA.

Mogzilla (GBR) *(978-0-9546576; 978-1-906132) Dist. by* **IPG Chicago.**

Mohr Siebeck GmbH & Co. KG (DEU) *(978-3-16) Dist. by* **ISD USA.**

Mohsena Memorial Foundation, Inc., *(978-0-9617273)* P.O. Box 2309, Princeton, NJ 08543 USA (SAN 663-5075) Tel 609-799-6545; Fax: 609-799-7311.

Mohsena Memorial Trust *See* **Mohsena Memorial Foundation, Inc.**

MoJo InkWorks, *(978-0-9820381)* 16 Foxglove Row, Riverhead, NY 11901 USA Tel 516-695-6690
E-mail: maureensullivan@gmail.com
Web site: http://www.maureensullivancommunications.com.

Molino, Editorial (ESP) *(978-84-272) Dist. by* **Distribks Inc.**

Molino, Editorial (ESP) *(978-84-272) Dist. by* **Continental Bk.**

Molino, Editorial (ESP) *(978-84-272) Dist. by* **AIMS Intl.**

Publisher Name Index

Molino, Editorial (ESP) *(978-84-272) Dist. by* **Lectorum Pubns.**
Molino, Editorial (ESP) *(978-84-272) Dist. by* **Santillana.**
Molly Brave, *(978-1-61245)* 3682 Quiet Pond Ln., Sarasota, FL 34235 USA Tel 941-955-0091
E-mail: mollybrave@gmail.com
Web site: http://www.mollybrave.com.
Momentpoint Media, *(978-0-9710448)* 2385 Friesian Rd., York, PA 17406 USA Tel 717-848-4528 (phone/fax) Do not confuse with Moment Point Press Inc. of NH/ME.
E-mail: momentpoint@suscom.net
Web site: http://www.momentpointmedia.com.
Momentum Books, Limited *See* **Momentum Bks., LLC**
Momentum Bks., LLC, *(978-0-9618726; 978-1-879094; 978-1-938018)* Div. of Hour Media, LLC, 117 W. Third St., Royal Oak, MI 48067 USA (SAN 668-7067) Tel 248-691-1800; Fax: 248-691-4531
E-mail: info@momentumbooks.com
Web site: http://www.momentumbooks.com
Dist(s): **Partners Bk. Distributing, Inc.**
TNT Media Group, Inc.
MomGeek.com *Imprint of* **Wood Designs, Inc.**
Mommy Has Tattoos, *(978-0-9770232)* P.O. Box 231059, New York, NY 10023-0023 USA
E-mail: info@mommyhastattoos.com
Web site: http://www.mommyhastattoos.com.
Mommy Workshop Bks., *(978-0-9817565)* P.O. Box 265, Doylestown, PA 18901 USA (SAN 856-4655) Tel 215-489-8649; Fax: 480-393-5692
E-mail: kristie@mommyworkshop.com
Web site: http://www.mommyworkshop.com/.
Momotombo Pr., *(978-0-9710465; 978-0-9797446)* Institute for Latino/University of Notre Dame, Notre Dame, IN 46556 USA; Inst. for Latino Studies Univ. of Notre Dame 230 McKenna Hall, Notre Dame, IN 46556
E-mail: faragon@nd.edu
Web site: http://www.momotombopress.com
Dist(s): **SPD-Small Pr. Distribution.**
Mom's Pride Enterprises, *(978-0-9720549)* 16521 N. 69th Dr., Peoria, AZ 85382 USA Tel 623-487-7589; Fax: 623-487-1504
E-mail: mrsb4kids@yahoo.com
Web site: http://www.mrsbstorytime.com.
Monacelli Pr., Inc., *(978-1-58093; 978-1-885254)* 1745 Broadway., New York, NY 10019-4305 USA Tel 212-782-9000
E-mail: info@monadcellipress.com
Web site: http://www.monacellipress.com
Dist(s): **MyiLibrary**
Penguin Random Hse., LLC.
Penguin Publishing Group
Random Hse., Inc.
Monarch Baby Publishing, *(978-0-9749499)* Orders Addr.: P.O. Box 22, Salem, VA 24153 USA Tel 504-669-1044
E-mail: monarchbaby@blackbutterflyrecords.com
Web site: http://blackbutterflyrecords.com\monarch_baby_publishing.thml.
Monarch Pubs., *(978-0-9774038; 978-0-615-12659-3)* Orders Addr.: 305 Holly Tree Ln., Simpsonville, SC 29681 USA
E-mail: joconnor@uscupstate.edu
Web site: http://www.monarchpublishers.com
Dist(s): **Follett School Solutions**
Parnassus Bk. Distributors
Bryan, R. L.
Monarch Publishing Hse., *(978-0-9797861)* 2573 Lake Cir., Jackson, MS 39211-6630 USA (SAN 859-4627) Tel 601-982-1233
Dist(s): **AtlasBooks Distribution.**
Monarchs in the Classroom, *(978-0-9800653)* 1980 Folwell Ave., 200 Hodson Hall, Saint Paul, MN 55108 USA Tel 612-624-8706; Fax: 612-625-5299
E-mail: oberh001@umn.edu
Web site: http://www.monarchlab.org.
Mondadori (ITA) *(978-88-04; 978-88-356; 978-88-86372; 978-88-520; 978-88-521) Dist. by* **Distribks Inc.**
Mondial, *(978-1-59569)* 203 W 107th St., No. 6C, New York, NY 10025 USA
E-mail: contact@mondialbooks.com
Web site: http://www.mondialbooks.com
Dist(s): **Smashwords.**
Mondo Fax Publishing, *(978-0-9710095)* 26235 Ravenhill Rd., Suite M, Santa Clarita, CA 91350-4754 USA Tel 661-250-0990; Fax: 661-251-4452
E-mail: argapc@socal.rr.com
Web site: http://mondofax.com.
Mondo Publishing, *(978-1-57255; 978-1-879531; 978-1-58653; 978-1-59034; 978-1-59336; 978-1-60201; 978-1-60715; 978-1-61736; 978-1-62889; 978-1-63060; 978-1-63061; 978-1-68156)* Div. of Music Plus, Inc., 980 6th Ave., New York, NY 10018 USA Toll Free: 888-268-3560
E-mail: ckracuna@mondopub.com
Web site: http://www.mondopub.com.
Money Management Books *See* **Prism Hse. Media**
Mongoose Pr., *(978-0-9791482; 978-1-936277)* 1005 Boylston St., Suite 324, Newton Highlands, MA 02461 USA Tel 617-875-6298
E-mail: info@mongoosepress.com
Web site: http://www.MongoosePress.com
Dist(s): **MyiLibrary**
National Bk. Network
ebrary, Inc.
Mongoose Publishing (GBR) *(978-1-903980; 978-1-904577; 978-1-904854; 978-1-905176; 978-1-905476; 978-1-905471; 978-1-905850; 978-1-906103; 978-1-906508; 978-1-907218) Dist. by* **Diamond Book Dists.**
Monique Patrice Hall *See* **Hall, Monique P. Productions**
Monkey Barrel Pr., *(978-0-9802000)* 4738 Andrea Way, Union City, CA 94587 USA
Web site: http://www.monkeybarrelpress.com.
Monkey Business *See* **Monkeying Around**
Monkeyfeather *Imprint of* **Summer Fit Learning, Inc.**
MonkeyGod Enterprises, *(978-0-9708094; 978-0-9717729; 978-0-9728197)* Div. of Face 2 Face Games Publishing, 36 The Arcade, 65 Weybosset St., Providence, RI 02903 USA Tel 401-351-0362 (phone/fax)
E-mail: fmf@pipeline.com
Web site: http://www.monkeygodenterprses.com.
Monkeying Around, *(978-0-9700437; 978-0-9799753)* P.O. Box 10131, Rochester, NY 14610 USA Tel 585-256-2660; Fax: 585-442-2965
E-mail: info@monkeyingaround.com
Web site: http://www.monkeyingaround.com.
Monkeyshines Publishers *See* **Allosaurus Pubs.**
Monkeytoes Pr., *(978-0-615-12555-8)* 125 Sycamore Rd., Braintree, MA 02184-7318 USA
E-mail: jvgandkdlarson@comcast.net
Web site: http://www.monkeytoespress.com.
Monkfish Bk. Publishing Co., *(978-0-9726357; 978-0-9749359; 978-0-9766843; 978-0-9789427; 978-0-9798828; 978-0-9823246; 978-0-9824530; 978-0-9825255; 978-0-9826441; 978-0-9830517; 978-0-9833589; 978-1-936940; 978-1-939681; 978-1-944037)* Orders Addr.: 22 E. Market St. Suite 304, Rhinebeck, NY 12572 USA; *Imprints:* Epigraph Books (Epigraph Bks)
E-mail: paul@monkfishpublishing.com
Web site: http://www.monkfishpublishing.com; http://www.epigraphps.com
Dist(s): **Consortium Bk. Sales & Distribution**
Lightning Source, Inc.
MyiLibrary
Perseus Bks. Group
SPD-Small Pr. Distribution.
Monogram Booklets *See* **Miller, Debra Juanita**
Monolith Graphics, *(978-0-9675756; 978-0-9788857; 978-0-9824899)* Orders Addr.: P.O. Box 360801, Strongsville, OH 44136 USA
E-mail: goth@monolithgraphics.com; nox@noxarcana.com
Web site: http://www.monolithgraphics.com; http://www.noxarcana.com.
Monroe Educational Media, *(978-0-9721146)* 2965 Taylor Rd., Reynoldsburg, OH 43068 USA Tel 614-866-4289; Fax: 740-927-9131
E-mail: jon@gooddebt.com
Web site: http://www.monroemedia.com.
Monroe, Guy, *(978-0-9742443)* P.O. Box 2325, Newport, OR 97365-0171 USA Toll Free: 877-562-3866
Web site: http://www.pinerystreet.com.
Monroe Media *See* **Monroe Educational Media**
Monsoon Bks. Pte. Ltd. (SGP) *(978-981-05; 978-981-4358; 978-981-4423; 978-981-4625) Dist. by* **Tuttle Pubng.**
Monsoon Bks. Pte. Ltd. (SGP) *(978-981-05; 978-981-4358; 978-981-4423; 978-981-4625) Dist. by* **Natl Bk Netwk.**
Monster Street *Imprint of* **Picture Window Bks.**
MonsterHaven, *(978-0-615-38690-4)* 385 Camino dos Palos, Thousand Oaks, CA 91360 USA Tel 805-208-8383
E-mail: marmaxdesigns@hotmail.com
Web site: http://www.monsterhaven.com.
Monsters in My Head, LLC, The, *(978-0-9792860; 978-0-9914952)* 344 Grove St. #119, Jersey City, NJ 07302 USA (SAN 853-0254) Tel 917-881-8326
E-mail: info@worrywoos.com
Web site: http://www.worrywoos.com.
Monstrosities Inc., *(978-0-9825796)* 5 Winifred Dr., Merrick, NY 11566 USA Tel 516-378-1338 (phone/fax); 516-754-1405; 516-635-2661
E-mail: monstrositiesinfo@gmail.com; sophia829@gmail.com
Web site: www.rexriders.com
Dist(s): **Independent Pubs. Group**
MyiLibrary.
Montag Pr., *(978-0-9822809; 978-1-940233)* 1066 47th Ave., Unit #9, Oakland, CA 94601 USA Tel 916-806-8341
E-mail: c.lanfranco@gmail.com
Dist(s): **SPD-Small Pr. Distribution.**
Montana Historical Society Pr., *(978-0-917298; 978-0-9721522; 978-0-9759196; 978-0-9801292; 978-1-940527)* P.O. Box 201201, Helena, MT 59620 USA (SAN 208-7693) Toll Free: 800-243-9900
E-mail: mholz@mt.gov
Web site: http://www.montanahistoricalsociety.org
Dist(s): **Globe Pequot Pr., The**
National Bk. Network
Univ. of Nebraska Pr.
Montana Publishing Group *See* **Loughton Bks.**
Montanha Pr., *(978-0-9743380)* 1547 Palos Verdes Mall , Suite 139, Walnut Creek, CA 94597 USA.
Monte Nido Pr., *(978-0-9742663)* Rm 9L19, 1240 Mission Rd., Los Angeles,, CA 90033 USA Tel 323-226-3406; Fax: 323-226-3440
E-mail: hoppenbrou@earthlink.net
Web site: http://www.toke.hoppenbrouwers.net.
Montemayor Pr., *(978-0-9674477; 978-1-932727)* P.O. Box 526, Millburn, NJ 07041 USA Tel 973-761-1341
E-mail: mail@montemayorpress.com
Web site: http://www.montemayorpress.com.
†Monterey Bay Aquarium, *(978-1-878244)* 886 Cannery Row, Monterey, CA 93940 USA Tel 831-648-4942; 408-648-4800; 831-648-4847; Fax: 831-644-7568; Toll Free: 877-665-2665
E-mail: mmckenzie@mbayaq.org
Web site: http://www.montereybayaquarium.org; *CIP.*
Monterey Bay Sanctuary Foundation, *(978-0-9742810)* 299 Foam St., Monterey, CA 93940 USA
E-mail: info@mbnmsf.org
Web site: http://www.mbnmsf.org
Dist(s): **Sunbelt Pubns., Inc.**
Montessori Advantage, *(978-0-9766453)* Orders Addr.: P.O. Box 272, Wickatunk, NJ 07765 USA Toll Free: 888-946-2114; Edit Addr.: 257 Rt. 79N, Wickatunk, NJ 07765 USA.
Montevallo Historical Pr., Inc., *(978-0-9658624)* 1727 West 17th St., Davenport, OH 52804 USA Tel 563-823-5749
E-mail: dean@mhpress.com
Web site: http://www.mhpress.com.
Montgomery County Historical Society, *(978-0-9720965)* 1000 Carillon Blvd., Dayton, OH 45409-2023 USA Do not confuse with Montgomery County Historical Society in Rockville MD, Fort Johnson NY
Web site: http://www.daytonhistory.org.
Month 9 Bks., *(978-0-9850294; 978-0-9853278; 978-0-9882513; 978-0-9883409; 978-1-939765; 978-0-692-24201-8; 978-0-9907812; 978-0-9862793; 978-0-692-33728-8; 978-0-692-33730-1; 978-0-692-33732-5; 978-0-692-33733-2; 978-0-692-33734-9; 978-0-692-33737-0; 978-0-692-33738-7; 978-1-942664; 978-0-9968904) Orders Addr.: P.O. Box 1892, Fuquay Varina, NC 27526 USA*
E-mail: georgia@month9books.com
Web site: http://month9books.com; http://month9booksblog.com
Dist(s): **CreateSpace Independent Publishing Platform**
Independent Pubs. Group
MyiLibrary
Small Pr. United.
Montlake Romance *Imprint of* **AmazonEncore**
Montlake Romance *Imprint of* **Amazon Publishing**
Montville Pr., *(978-0-9706527)* P.O. Box 4304, Greensboro, NC 27410-4304 USA Tel 336-292-8268; Fax: 336-218-0410
E-mail: bas236@aol.com.
Moo Pr. *Imprint of* **Keene Publishing**
Moo Press, Incorporated *See* **Keene Publishing**
†Moody Pubs., *(978-0-8024)* Div. of Moody Bible Institute, Orders Addr.: 210 W. Chestnut, Chicago, IL 60610 USA; Edit Addr.: 820 N. LaSalle, Chicago, IL 60610 USA (SAN 202-5604) Tel 312-329-2101; Fax: 312-329-2144; Toll Free: 800-678-8812; *Imprints:* Lift Every Voice (LEV)
E-mail: mpcustomerservice@moody.edu
Web site: http://www.moodypublishers.com
Dist(s): **BJU Pr.**
Follett School Solutions; *CIP.*
Moody Valley, *(978-1-59513)* 475 Church Hollow Rd., Boone, NC 28607 USA Tel 828-963-5331; Fax: 828-963-4101
E-mail: moodyvalley@skybest.com
Web site: http://www.moodyvalley.com
Dist(s): **Partners Bk. Distributing, Inc.**
Moody, William, *(978-0-9762556)* 301 Willard Hall, Univ. of Delaware, Newark, DE 19711 USA Tel 302-831-1658; Fax: 302-831-0591
E-mail: wmoody@udel.edu
Web site: http://www.udel.edu/educ/solveit.htm.
Mookind Pr., *(978-0-9792761)* 1600 S. Eads St., Suite 822N, Arlington, VA 22202 USA Tel 703-920-1884
E-mail: cnadel999@yahoo.com.
Moombaya Bks., *(978-0-9766799)* 2118 Wilshire Blvd., Suite 528, Santa Monica, CA 90403-9040 USA
E-mail: diponzagroup@aol.com.
Moon, Alice *See* **PeachMoon Publishing**
Moon Bear Pr., *(978-0-944164)* P.O. Box 468, Velarde, NM 87582 USA (SAN 242-9144) Tel 505-852-4897
E-mail: orders@moonbearpress.com
Web site: http://www.moonbearpress.com
Dist(s): **New Leaf Distributing Co., Inc.**
Moon Mountain Publishing, Inc., *(978-0-9677929; 978-1-931659)* P.O. Box 188, West Rockport, ME 04865 USA Tel 207-236-0958; Fax: 978-719-6290; Toll Free: 800-353-5877
E-mail: hello@moonmountainpub.com
Web site: http://www.moonmountainpub.com.
Moon Over Mountains Publishing (M.O.M.), *(978-1-891665)* Div. of Gallery of Diamonds Jewelers, 1000 Bristol St. N. # 8, Newport Beach, CA 92660 USA (SAN 299-5492) Tel 949-476-2000; Fax: 949-222-2277; Toll Free: 800-667-4440
E-mail: info@galleryofdiamonds.com
Web site: http://www.whymomdeservesadiamond.com.
Moon Pie Pr., *(978-0-9761744)* 53 Faye Dr., Smithfield, VA 23430 USA Tel 757-356-1690
E-mail: cathyk@visi.net
Web site: http://www.moonpiepress.net.
Moon Trail Bks., *(978-0-9773140)* 24 W. 4th St., Bethlehem, PA 18015-1604 USA (SAN 850-6922) Tel 610-866-6482
E-mail: pnmca21@aol.com.
Moon Valley Productions, *(978-0-934290)* P.O. Box 1342, Healdsburg, CA 95448 USA (SAN 221-2900) Tel 707-823-9340; 707-523-8525
E-mail: zaksartandsoul@yahoo.com
Web site: http://www.zakzaikine.com.
Moonbow Pr., LLc, *(978-0-9789092)* P.O. Box 95, Bethel, OH 45106 USA (SAN 851-9110).
Moondance Publishing, *(978-0-9671865; 978-1-931524)* Orders Addr.: P.O. Box 16, Upper Black Eddy, PA 18972 USA Tel 610-442-1951; Fax: 610-982-5331; Edit Addr.: 1525 Oak Ln., Upper Black Eddy, PA 18972 USA (SAN 254-5101) Tel 610-442-1951
E-mail: caravan@moondancepublishing.com
Web site: http://www.moondancepublishing.com.
Moonjar, LLC, *(978-0-9724282; 978-0-9764231)* 612 19th Ave., E., Seattle, WA 98112 USA Fax: 206-726-0769; Toll Free: 888-323-0001
E-mail: contact@moonjar.com
Web site: http://www.moonjar.com
Dist(s): **Ten Speed Pr.**
Moonlight Publishing, Ltd. (GBR) *(978-0-907144; 978-1-85103) Dist. by* **IPG Chicago.**
MoonRattles, *(978-0-9790920)* P.O. Box 939, Carmel, CA 93921 USA; 70 Dapplegray Rd., Bell Canyon, CA 91307 (SAN 854-2201) Fax: 818-932-9631; Toll Free: 800-961-6073
E-mail: info@moonrattles.com
Web site: http://www.moonrattles.com.
Moons & Stars Publishing For Children, *(978-1-929063)* Div. of Moon Star Unlimited, Inc., P.O. Box 1763, Pasadena, TX 77505 USA Tel 713-473-7120; Fax: 713-473-1105
E-mail: services@dorpexpress.com
Web site: http://www.dorpexpress.com.
Moonshell Bks., Inc. *Imprint of* **Shelley Adina**
MoonStar Pr., *(978-0-9672107)* 4360 E. Main St., Suite 408, Ventura, CA 93003 USA Tel 805-648-7753
E-mail: toutzhag@earthlink.net
Dist(s): **New Leaf Distributing Co., Inc.**
Moonstone, *(978-0-9710129; 978-0-9712937; 978-0-9721668; 978-0-9726443; 978-0-9748501; 978-1-933076; 978-1-936814; 978-1-944017)* Div. of Amazing Fantasy Comic Shop Ltd., 582 Torrence Ave., Calumet City, IL 60409 USA Fax: 708-891-0644
E-mail: afbooks_frankfort@sbcglobal.net
Web site: http://www.moonstonebooks.com
Dist(s): **Diamond Comic Distributors, Inc.**
Diamond Bk. Distributors.
Moonstone Pr., LLC, *(978-0-9707768; 978-0-9727697; 978-0-9769542; 978-0-9834983)* 4816 Carrington Cir., Sarasota, FL 34243 USA (SAN 852-5625) Tel 301-765-1081; Fax: 301-765-0510
E-mail: mazeprod@erols.com
Web site: http://www.moonstonepress.net
Dist(s): **Independent Pubs. Group**
Lectorum Pubns., Inc.
PSI (Publisher Services, Inc.).
Moonview Pr., *(978-0-9828987)* 5460 Linda Ln., Santa Rosa, CA 95404 USA Tel 707-578-2269
E-mail: ctmarkee@gmail.com
Web site: http://www.charlesmarkee.comzbandit
Dist(s): **Smashwords.**
Moonwater Products, *(978-0-9769033)* 63 Roycroft Dr., Rochester, NY 14621 USA
E-mail: djed_ra_maat@yahoo.com.
Moore, Ammanuel, *(978-0-9744060)* P.O. Box 3295, Baltimore, MD 21228 USA Tel 410-788-7271
E-mail: info@acmoorebooks.com
Web site: http://www.acmoorebooks.com.
Moore, Evans, *(978-0-9709762)* P.O. Box 30311, Washington, DC 20030 USA Tel 202-889-3648
E-mail: evansmoore@hotmail.com.
Moore, Greg Publishing, *(978-0-9639495)* Orders Addr.: 6202 Wallina Ct., SE, Salem, OR 97309 USA Tel 503-749-1393; Fax: 503-588-7707
E-mail: yoyo@tdn.com.
†Moore, Hugh Historical Park & Museums, Inc., *(978-0-930973)* 30 Centre Sq., Easton, PA 18042-7743 USA (SAN 678-8831) Tel 610-559-6617; 610-559-6613; Fax: 610-559-6690; *Imprints:* Canal History & Technology Press (Canal Hist Tech)
E-mail: ncm@canals.org
Web site: http://www.canals.org; *CIP.*
Moore, Hullihen, *(978-0-9785775)* P.O. Box 116, Oldhams, VA 22529 USA (SAN 850-9468).
Moore, Lonnie W. *See* **I & L Publishing**
Moore Publishing, *(978-0-9800791)* 646 Beautiful Run Rd., Madison, VA 22727 USA.
Moose Hill Bks., Inc., *(978-0-9728627)* P.O. Box 222271, Anchorage, AK 99522 USA (SAN 255-1616)
E-mail: publisher@moosehillbooks.com
Web site: http://www.moosehillbooks.com
Dist(s): **AtlasBooks Distribution.**
Moose Run Productions, *(978-0-9766315)* 22010 Highview, Clinton Township, MI 48036 USA Tel 586-718-7700
Web site: http://www.moose-run.com.
Morals & Values Pr., *(978-0-9754191; 978-0-9842140; 978-0-9898501)* P.O. Box 23804, Baltimore, MD 21203 USA
Web site: http://www.greatnessnow.org.
Morari Specialties Inc., *(978-0-9770618)* 13901 SW 22nd St., Miami, FL 33175-7006 USA
Web site: http://www.moraríspecialties.com.
Morcan, Dorina, *(978-0-9763663)* P.O. Box 1564, Malvern, AR 72104 USA Fax: 501-262-4127
E-mail: dmorcan@ix.netcom.com.
More Books Press *See* **SCOJO ENTERTAINMENT**
More, Frances International Teaching Systems *See* **Frances More International Teaching Systems**
More, Francisco J., *(978-0-9747851)* 221 Majorca Ave., No. 207, Coral Gables, FL 33134-4429 USA Tel 305-448-5081.
More Heart Than Talent Pub Inc,
Dist(s): **AtlasBooks Distribution.**
More Heart Than Talent Publishing, Incorporated *See* **Golden Mastermind Seminars, Inc.**
More Pr., *(978-0-9743394)* Div. of More Consulting Co., 1634 E. 53rd St., Chicago, IL 60615-4389 USA
E-mail: shaharimoore@aol.com.
M.O.R.E. Pubs., *(978-0-9719984; 978-0-9758549; 978-0-9801647; 978-0-9820354; 978-0-9830325; 978-0-692-27449-1)* Orders Addr.: P.O. Box 621, Collierville, TN 38027-0621 USA; Edit Addr.: 4466 Elvis Presley Blvd. 1st Memphis Plaza - Suite 103, Memphis, TN 38116 USA (SAN 255-1055)
E-mail: stlouiswpguild@aol.com; MOREPublishersCO@AOL.com
Web site: http://www.MOREPublishers.biz; http://www.TheScaleMagazine.MagCloud.com.
Morehouse Publishing *Imprint of* **Church Publishing, Inc.**
Morelmasters LLC, *(978-0-615-12829-0)* Orders Addr.: 6294 Reynolds Ridge Rd., Potosi, WI 53820 USA Tel 608-732-2175; Fax: 608-763-2799
E-mail: morelmasters@tds.net
Web site: http://www.morelmasters.com.
Morgan, E. A., *(978-0-9631975)* Orders Addr.: P.O. Box 7452, Naples, FL 34101 USA Fax: 941-598-9809
E-mail: rhymetime@mailstation.com.

Morgan Foundation Pubs.: International Published Innovations, *(978-1-885679)* Orders Addr.: 182 Fourth St., Ashland, OR 97520 USA Fax: 815-550-4456
E-mail: morganfoundation@earthlink.net
Web site: http://www.morganfoundationpublishers.com.

Morgan James Publishing, *(978-0-9746133; 978-0-9758570; 978-0-9760901; 978-0-9768491; 978-1-933596; 978-1-60037; 978-0-9815058; 978-0-9817906; 978-0-9820750; 978-0-9823793; 978-0-9846170; 978-0-9828590; 978-0-9833715; 978-0-9835013; 978-1-61448; 978-0-9837125; 978-0-9840316; 978-1-938467; 978-1-63047; 978-1-63195) Div. of Morgan James, LLC, 23rd Flr. 5 Penn Plaza, New York, NY 10001 USA; Imprints:* Koehler Books (KoehlerBks)
Web site: http://www.morganjamespublishing.com
Dist(s): **Ingram Pub. Services**
Lightning Source, Inc.
Lulu Enterprises Inc.
MyiLibrary.

Morgan Publishing Co., *(978-0-9639940)* Orders Addr.: P.O. Box 28718, San Jose, CA 95159 USA (SAN 298-1432) Fax: 408-637-1674; Edit Addr.: 338 Fifth St., Hollister, CA 95023 USA Tel 408-637-7031.

Morgan Publishing, Incorporated *See* **Augustine Pr.**

Morgan Rice Bks., Div. of Lukeman Literary Management Ltd., 157 Bedford Ave., Brooklyn, NY 11211 USA Tel 718-599-8988; Fax: 718-264-2189
Dist(s): **Lukeman Literary Management, Ltd.**
MyiLibrary.

Moriah Ministries, *(978-0-9728454; 978-0-9774836)* P.O. Box 23823, Chagrin Falls, OH 44023 USA Tel 440-543-9304 (phone/fax)
E-mail: info@davidicdance.com; info@moriahministries.org
Web site: http://www.davidicdance.com; http://www.moriahministries.org.

Mormon Comics, *(978-0-9764965)* 435 N. 150 W., Blackfoot, ID 83221 USA Tel 208-785-4558 (phone/fax)
E-mail: info@mormoncomics.com
Web site: http://www.mormoncomics.com.

Mornin' Light Media, *(978-0-9763534)* Orders Addr.: 31203 N. Course View, Franklin, TN 37067 USA; *Imprints:* Mornin'Light Media (MorninLight)
E-mail: shawnsurber@comcast.net; hopebook@bellsouth.net
Web site: http://www.thehopebook.com.

†Morning Glory Pr., Inc., *(978-0-930934; 978-1-885356; 978-1-932538; 978-0-9844283)* 6595 San Haroldo Way, Buena Park, CA 90620 USA (SAN 211-2558) 888-327-4362; Toll Free: 888-612-8254 Do not confuse with Morning Glory Press in Nashua, NH
E-mail: jwl@morningglorypress.com; info@morningglorypress.com
Web site: http://www.morningglorypress.com
Dist(s): **Independent Pubs. Group**
MyiLibrary; *CIP.*

Morning Glory Pubns., *(978-0-9762929)* Orders Addr.: 1104 Blue ridge Dr., Clarkston, MI 48348 USA
E-mail: klinejane@hotmail.com.

Morning Joy Media, *(978-0-9826102; 978-1-937107)* 359 Bridge St., Spring City, PA 19475 USA Tel 610-256-2906
E-mail: debbie@morningjoymedia.com
Web site: http://www.morningjoymedia.com
Dist(s): **BookBaby.**

Morning Star Music Pubs., *(978-0-944529)* 1727 Larkin Williams Rd., Fenton, MO 63026 USA (SAN 243-8496)
E-mail: morningstar@morningstarmusic.com
Web site: http://www.morningstarmusic.com
Dist(s): **BookBaby.**

Morning Sun Bks., Inc., *(978-0-9619058; 978-1-58248; 978-1-878887)* 9 Pheasant Ln., Scotch Plains, NJ 07076 USA (SAN 243-1157) Tel 908-755-5454; Fax: 908-755-5455
E-mail: morningsunbooks@comcast.net
Web site: http://www.morningsunbooks.com
Dist(s): **Walthers, William K. Inc.**

MorningGlory Publishing, *(978-0-9705090)* Orders Addr.: P.O. Box 15523, Plantation, FL 33318-5523 USA Tel 954-370-7205; Fax: 954-370-6817; Edit Addr.: 9951 NW Sixth Ct., Plantation, FL 33324 USA
E-mail: tandtsm@aol.com.

Morningside Publishing, LLC, *(978-1-936210)* 2380 Garrison St., Lakewood, CO 80215-1636 USA (SAN 858-835X)
Web site: http://www.morningsidepublishing.com
Dist(s): **Smashwords.**

Morningstar Christian Chapel, *(978-0-9715733; 978-0-9729477; 978-0-9842943; 978-1-940198; 978-0-9964131)* 16241 Leffingwell Rd., Whittier, CA 90603 USA Tel 562-943-0297; Fax: 562-943-3608
E-mail: jacobeelen@morningstarcc.org
Web site: http://www.morningstarcc.org.

MorningStar Pubns., Inc., *(978-1-878327; 978-1-929371; 978-1-59933; 978-1-60708)* Div. of MorningStar Fellowship Church, Orders Addr.: 375 Star Light Dr., Fort Mill, SC 29715 USA Fax: 704-285-7251; Toll Free: 800-542-0278 (orders only); Edit Addr.: 1605 Industrial Dr., Wilkesboro, NC 28697 USA Do not confuse with Morningstar Pubns., Boulder, CO
E-mail: info@morningstarministries.org
Web site: http://www.morningstarministries.org
Dist(s): **Anchor Distributors**
Destiny Image Pubs.
Whitaker Hse.

Morningtide Pr., *(978-0-9790395)* P.O. Box 312, St. Augustine, FL 32085-0312 USA
Web site: http://www.morningtidepress.com
Dist(s): **Quality Bks., Inc.**

Mornin'Light Media *Imprint of* **Mornin' Light Media**

Morris Publishing, *(978-0-7392; 978-0-9631249; 978-1-57502; 978-1-885591; 978-0-9863567)* Orders Addr.: P.O. Box 2110, Kearney, NE 68848 USA Fax: 308-237-0263; Toll Free: 800-650-7888 Do not confuse with companies with the same Wesley Chapel, FL, Elkhart, IN
Web site: http://www.morrispublishing.com.

Morris, Tami *See* **2B Pr.**

Morrow, William Cookbooks *Imprint of* **HarperCollins Pubs.**

Morrow, William & Co. *Imprint of* **HarperCollins Pubs.**

Morten Moore Publishing, *(978-0-9672576)* Div. of K & M Marketing, 415 E. Mohawk, Flagstaff, AZ 86001 USA Tel 520-779-2209; Fax: 520-779-0126
Dist(s): **Canyonlands Pubs.**

Morton Arts Media, *(978-0-9796868)* P.O. Box 291, Summerfield, NC 27358 USA.

Morton Bks., *(978-1-929188)* 47 Stewart Ave., Irvington, NJ 07111 USA Tel 973-374-8327; Fax: 973-374-1125
E-mail: rmo1033555@aol.com
Web site: http://www.mortonbooks.com.

MOS, Inc., *(978-0-9778570)* 5271 E MANN RD, Pekin, IN 47165-8807 USA Tel 812-967-2531; Fax: 812-967-2980; Toll Free: 800-451-3993
E-mail: info@joyfulcatholic.com
Web site: http://www.traditionalcatholicpublishing.com/.

Mo's Nose, LLC, *(978-0-9816255)* 222 Palisades Ave., Santa Monica, CA 90402-2734 USA (SAN 856-0811) Tel 310-451-8125
Web site: http://www.mosnose.com
Dist(s): **Independent Pubs. Group**
Midpoint Trade Bks., Inc.

Mosaic Paradigm Group, LLC, *(978-0-578-07392-7; 978-0-9852542)* 3 Pasco Ct., Pikesville, MD 21208 USA (SAN 920-2889) Tel 877-733-7308
E-mail: info@mpg-publishing.com
Web site: http://www.mpg-publishing.com.

Mosaic Pr. (CAN) *(978-0-88962; 978-1-77161) Dist. by* **AtlasBooks.**

Mosaic Publishing *See* **Branded Black Publishing**

Mosby *Imprint of* **Elsevier - Health Sciences Div.**

Moscow Ballet *Imprint of* **Sports Marketing International, Inc.**

Mosdos Pr., *(978-0-9671009; 978-0-9742160; 978-0-9801670; 978-0-9858078; 978-0-9888286)* Div. of Mosdos Ohr Hatorah, 1508 Warrensville Ctr. Rd., Cleveland, OH 44121 USA Tel 216-291-4158; Fax: 216-291-4169
E-mail: mosdospress@moh1.org; jfactor@moh1.org
Web site: http://www.mosdospress.com.

Moselle Productions, Inc., *(978-0-9701289)* P.O. Box 1304, League City, TX 77574 USA Tel 732-623-9908; Toll Free: 800-598-2519
Web site: http://www.mangoeandmarlie.com.

Mosely, Winifred, *(978-0-9769610)* 6600 E. River Rd., Tucson, AZ 85750 USA Tel 520-327-3681
E-mail: njmosely@comcast.net.

Moshire Pr., *(978-0-615-39082-6)* 2355 Carlysle Cove, Lawrenceville, GA 30044 USA Tel 404-784-5987
Web site: http://www.moshirepress.com.

Mosley, Kim, *(978-0-9663215)* 1312 W. 40th St., Austin, TX 78756-3615 USA Tel 512-762-6790
E-mail: mrkimmosley@gmail.com
Web site: http://kimmosley.com/workbook.

Moss, Michael, *(978-0-9763003)* 610 Prestwick Dr., Frankfort, IL 60423 USA Tel 312-437-7827 (312-437-STAR)
Web site: http://www.5starpc.com.

Moss Press Publishing, *(978-0-578-12603-6)* 616 Corporate Way Suite 2-4348, Valley Cottage, NY 10989 USA.

Mosscovered Gumbo Barn, *(978-0-9725853)* 15960 Highland Rd., Baton Rouge, LA 70810 USA
Dist(s): **Greenleaf Book Group.**

Mostats, Marie C., *(978-0-9742848)* Orders Addr.: P.O. Box 230053, Las Vegas, NV 89123-0001 USA; Edit Addr.: 608 NW 29th St., Wilton Manors, FL 33311-2443 USA.

Mother Goose Programs, *(978-0-9753985; 978-0-9841366; 978-1-935784)* P.O. Box 423, Chester, VT 05143-0423 USA
E-mail: debbi@mothergooseprograms.org
Web site: http://www.mothergooseprograms.org
Dist(s): **National Bk. Network.**

Mother Moose Pr., *(978-0-9724570)* Orders Addr.: 21010 Southbank St., PMB No. 435, Potomac Falls, VA 20165 USA Tel 571-223-6472
E-mail: books@mothermoosepress.com
Web site: http://www.mothermoosepress.com.

Mother Necessity Inc., *(978-0-9796579)* P.O. Box 2135, Bonita Springs, FL 34133 USA
E-mail: cfergus@mothernecessity.com
Web site: http://www.mothernecessity.com.

M.O.T.H.E.R. Publishing Co., Inc., The, *(978-0-9718431)* Orders Addr.: P.O. Box 477, Rock Springs, WY 82902 USA Tel 307-382-5027; Fax: 307-382-6492; Edit Addr.: 616 Elias Ave., Rock Springs, WY 82901 USA
E-mail: motherpublishing@wyoming.com
Web site: http://www.motherpublishing.com.

Motherboard Bks., *(978-0-9749653; 978-0-692-42438-4; 978-0-692-42562-6; 978-0-692-43162-7)* P.O. Box 430041, Saint Louis, MO 63143 USA
E-mail: info@motherboardbooks.com
Web site: http://motherboardbooks.com
Dist(s): **CreateSpace Independent Publishing Platform.**

Motherhood Printing & Etc., *(978-1-60225)* Orders Addr.: 45973 Rd. 795, Ansley, NE 68814-5126 USA (SAN 852-1212) Tel 308-880-1021; Fax: 308-732-3280
E-mail: motherhoodprinting@nctc.net; mary@motherhoodprinting.com
Web site: http://motherhoodprinting.com.

Motherly Way Enterprises, *(978-0-9671428)* P.O. Box 11, Marylhurst, OR 97036-0011 USA Tel 503-723-2879; Toll Free: 877-666-7929
E-mail: julie@motherlyway.com
Web site: http://www.motherlyway.com.

Mother's Hse. Publishing, *(978-0-9743869; 978-0-9773990; 978-0-9792704; 978-0-9797144; 978-0-9816245; 978-1-935086; 978-0-9827525; 978-1-61888)* Orders Addr.: 6180 Lehman Suite 104, Colorado Springs, CO 80918 USA Tel 719-266-0437; Fax: 719-266-9978; Toll Free: 800-266-0999; 2814 E. Woodmen Rd., Colorado Springs, CO 80920 (SAN 920-5632) Tel 719-266-0437; Fax: 719-266-9978; *Imprints:* Private Label Publishing (PrivLabel)
E-mail: jackie@mothershousepublishing.com; info@mothershousepublishing.com
Web site: http://www.mothershousepublishing.com; http://wholesale.mothershousepublishing.com; http://www.privatelabelpublishing.org; http://www.godcallsyoubyname.org
Dist(s): **Bks. West.**

Mother's Love Publishing, A, *(978-0-9777022)* 4962 Bristol Rock Rd, Florissant, MO 63033 USA (SAN 257-9707)
Dist(s): **Lushena Bks.**

Mothwing Pr. *Imprint of* **Mothwing.com**

Mothwing.com, *(978-0-9724528)* 80 Sheffield Rd., Waltham, MA 02451-2374 USA Tel 781-899-8153; *Imprints:* Mothwing Press (Mothwng Pr)
E-mail: mothwingpress@mothwing.com; andylevesque@rcn.com
Web site: http://www.mothwing.com/mothwingpress.

Motion Fitness LLC, *(978-0-9744568)* P.O. Box 2179, Palatine, IL 60078-2179 USA
E-mail: sales@motionfitness.com
Web site: http://www.motionfitness.com.

Motivision Media, *(978-0-9722332)* 9528 Blossom Valley Rd., El Cajon, CA 92021 USA
E-mail: dehaven@motivisionmedia.com; dehaven1@cox.net
Web site: http://www.motivisionmedia.com; http://www.MyFootballMentor.com.

Motorbooks *Imprint of* **Quarto Publishing Group USA**

†Mott Media, *(978-0-88062; 978-0-915134; 978-0-940319)* 1130 Fenway Cir., Fenton, MI 48430 USA (SAN 207-1460) Tel 810-714-4280; Fax: 810-714-2077 Do not confuse with Mott Media in Stamford, CT
E-mail: sales@mottmedia.com; bill@mottmedia.com
Web site: http://www.mottmedia.com
Dist(s): **Spring Arbor Distributors, Inc.**; *CIP.*

Mottley, William, *(978-0-9769216)* 428 N. Genito Rd., Burkeville, VA 23922 USA Tel 434-767-5594
E-mail: emottley@ceva.net
Web site: http://www.narrowstrip.com.

Moulton, Kathy Verner, *(978-0-615-43516-9; 978-0-615-44147-4; 978-0-615-45397-2; 978-0-615-45917-2; 978-0-9839279)* 111 W Center College St., Yellow Springs, OH 45387 USA Tel 937-767-9166
Dist(s): **CreateSpace Independent Publishing Platform.**

Mount Baldy Pr., Inc., *(978-0-9715863)* P.O. Box 469, Boulder, CO 80306-0469 USA (SAN 254-2625) Tel 303-440-7393; Fax: 303-532-1007
E-mail: simeon5@att.net
Web site: http://www.mountbaldy.com
Dist(s): **New Leaf Distributing Co., Inc.**
Quality Bks., Inc.

Mount Helicon Pr. *Imprint of* **Rock, James A. & Co. Pubs.**

Mount Olive College Pr., *(978-0-9627087; 978-1-880994; 978-1-59761)* Mount Olive College, Administration Bldg. 634 Henderson St., Mount Olive, NC 28365 USA (SAN 297-7729) Tel 919-658-2502; Toll Free Fax: 800-653-0854.

Mount Rushmore Bookstores, *(978-0-9646798; 978-0-9752617; 978-0-9798823)* Div. of Mount Rushmore National Memorial Society, 13030 Hwy. 244, Keystone, SD 57751 USA Tel 605-341-8883; Fax: 605-341-0433; Toll Free: 800-699-3142
E-mail: debbie_ketel@mtrushmore.org
Web site: http://www.mountrushmoresociety.com
Dist(s): **Partners Distributing.**

Mount Rushmore History Association *See* **Mount Rushmore Bookstores**

†Mount Vernon Ladies' Assn. of the Union, *(978-0-931917)* Orders Addr.: P.O. Box 110, Mount Vernon, VA 22121 USA (SAN 225-3976); Edit Addr.: 3200 Mount Vernon Memorial Hwy., Mount Vernon, VA 22121 USA
E-mail: ajohnson@mountvernon.org
Web site: http://www.mountvernon.org
Dist(s): **Univ. Pr. of Virginia**
Wimmer Cookbooks; *CIP.*

Mountain Air Bks., *(978-0-615-24940-7; 978-0-615-24941-4; 978-0-615-26703-6; 978-0-615-29319-6; 978-0-615-29829-0; 978-0-615-41620-5; 978-0-615-56237-7; 978-0-615-64830-9)* 1045 University Ave. Apt. 2, Rochester, NY 14607-1624 USA
E-mail: scottkny@yahoo.com; mairbooks123@yahoo.com.

Mountain Bk. Co., P.O. Box 778, Broomfield, CO 80038-0778 USA Tel 303-436-1982; Fax: 917-386-2769
E-mail: wordguise@aol.com
Web site: http://www.mountainbook.org.

Mountain Girl Press *See* **Jan-Carol Publishing, INC.**

Mountain Maid *See* **Light Messages Publishing**

Mountain Memories Bks. *Imprint of* **Quarrier Pr.**

Mountain Ministries, *(978-0-9787761)* 18055 100th St., Lindsay, OK 73052-3308 USA Do not confuse with Mountain Ministries Sitka, Alaska.

Mountain n' Air Bks., *(978-1-879415)* Div. of Mountain n' Air Sports, Inc., Orders Addr.: P.O. Box 12540, La Crescenta, CA 91224 USA (SAN 630-5598) Tel 818-248-9345; Toll Free Fax: 800-303-5578; Toll Free: 800-446-9696; Edit Addr.: 2947-A Hololulu Ave., La Crescenta, CA 91214 USA (SAN 631-4198); *Imprints:* Bearly Cooking (Bearly Cooking)
E-mail: books@mountain-n-air.com
Web site: http://mountain-n-air.com
Dist(s): **Alpenbooks Pr. LLC**
CreateSpace Independent Publishing Platform
Partners/West Book Distributors.

Mountain Path Pr., *(978-0-9653149)* 111 Bank St., Ste 152, Grass Valley, CA 95945 USA Toll Free: 888-224-9997
E-mail: Info@MountainPathPress.com
Web site: http://www.mountainpathpress.com
Dist(s): **Bks. West**
Integral Yoga Pubns.
New Leaf Distributing Co., Inc.
Partners Bk. Distributing, Inc.

Mountain Path Publications *See* **Mountain Path Pr.**

†Mountain Pr. Publishing Co., Inc., *(978-0-87842)* Orders Addr.: P.O. Box 2399, Missoula, MT 59806-2399 USA (SAN 202-8832) Tel 406-728-1900; Fax: 406-728-1635; Toll Free: 800-234-5308; Edit Addr.: 1301 S. Third West, Missoula, MT 59801 USA (SAN 662-0868)
E-mail: jrimel@mtnpress.com; info@mtnpress.com; anne@mtnpress.com
Web site: http://www.mountain-press.com
Dist(s): **Bks. West**
Partners Bk. Distributing, Inc.; *CIP.*

Mountain States Specialties, *(978-0-9726022)* 1671 Valtec Ln., Boulder, CO 80301 USA Tel 303-444-6186 Toll Free: 800-353-2147.

Mountain Thunder Publishing, *(978-0-615-69738-3; 978-0-9887625)* P.O. Box 6264, Snowmass Village, CO 81615 USA Tel 6462836884
Dist(s): **CreateSpace Independent Publishing Platform.**

Mountain Trail Pr., *(978-0-9676938; 978-0-9770808; 978-0-9777933; 978-0-9799171; 978-0-9821162; 978-0-9844218; 978-0-9892870)* Orders Addr.: 1818 Presswood Rd., Johnson City, TN 37604 USA Tel 423-335-8245
E-mail: Greerphoto@gmail.com
Web site: http://www.mountaintrailpress.com
Dist(s): **Chicago Distribution Ctr.**
Independent Pubs. Group
TNT Media Group, Inc.

Mountain Valley Publishing, LLC, *(978-1-59453; 978-1-60002; 978-1-934940)* Orders Addr.: 1420 Maple Ct., Martinsville, IN 46151 USA Tel 765-349-8908; Fax: 765-349-8908
E-mail: bdenton308@comcast.net
Web site: http://www.mountainvalleypublishing.com.

Mountain Voices Pubs., *(978-0-9671908)* Orders Addr.: 2 Junaluska Rd., Andrews, NC 28901 USA Tel 828-321-5553; Fax: 828-321-2446
E-mail: MountainTeller@mountainvoice.com
Web site: http://www.mountainvoice.com.

Mountain World Media LLC, *(978-0-9763309)* Orders Addr.: P.O. Box 687, Telluride, CO 81435 USA Tel 970-729-0289; Edit Addr.: 135 Hillside Ln., Telluride, CO 81435 USA
E-mail: damon@mountainworldmedia.com
Web site: http://www.mountainworldmedia.com
Dist(s): **Alpenbooks Pr. LLC**
Bks. West.

Mountaintop Pr., *(978-0-9711106)* Orders Addr.: P.O. Box 550, Cary, NC 27512-0550 USA Tel 919-567-9550; Fax: 919-567-9694; Edit Addr.: 201-D Foliage Cir., Cary, NC 27511 USA
Dist(s): **Send The Light Distribution LLC.**

MountainView *Imprint of* **Treble Heart Bks.**

Mountan Creek Pubns., *(978-0-615-52752-9; 978-0-615-55170-8; 978-0-9853574)* 80 Post Ave., Rochester, NY 14619 USA Tel 585-966-9669
E-mail: nailahbaniti@gmail.com
Web site: Mountaincreekpublications.com.

Mousel Publishing, *(978-0-9643512)* Orders Addr.: P.O. Box 1674, Honolulu, HI 96806 USA Tel 808-625-7522; Fax: 808-284-5516; Edit Addr.: 419 South St., Suite 133, Honolulu, HI 96813 USA
Dist(s): **Booklines Hawaii, Ltd.**

Mouse Works, *(978-0-7364; 978-1-57082)* Div. of Disney Bk. Publishing, Inc., A Walt Disney Co., 114 Fifth Ave., New York, NY 10011 USA (SAN 298-0797) Tel 212-633-4400; Fax: 212-633-4811
Web site: http://www.disneybooks.com
Dist(s): **Random Hse., Inc.**

Mousetime Bks. *Imprint of* **Mousetime Media LLC**

Mousetime Media LLC, *(978-0-9723213)* 7960-B Soquel Dr., No. 297, Aptos, CA 95003 USA; *Imprints:* Mousetime Books (Msetime Bks)
E-mail: books@mousetime.com
Web site: http://www.mousetime.com.

Move Bks., LLC, *(978-0-9854810)* 10 N. Main St., Beacon Falls, CT 06403 USA Tel 203-709-0490
Web site: http://www.move-books.com
Dist(s): **Independent Pubs. Group**
MyiLibrary
Small Pr. United.

Movement Makers International, *(978-0-9766930)* P.O. Box 3940, Broken Arrow, OK 74013-3940 USA
Web site: http://www.j12.com.

Movies for the Ear, LLC, *(978-1-935793)* 8362 Tamarack Village No. 119-327, St. Paul, MN 55125 USA Tel 612-209-3864
E-mail: moviesfortheear@comcast.net
Web site: www.CreepersMysteries.com
Dist(s): **Lightning Source, Inc.**

Mowery, Julia, *(978-0-9710529)* 6308 Starfish Ave, North Port, FL 34291 USA
E-mail: storyteller2000@msn.com; storytellerjm@aol.com
Web site: http://dobiebookpublishing.com.

†Moyer Bell, *(978-0-918825; 978-1-55921)* 549 Old North Rd., Kingston, RI 02881-1220 USA (SAN 630-1762) Tel 401-783-5480; Fax: 401-284-0959; Toll Free: 888-789-1945; *Imprints:* Asphodel Press (Asphodel Pr); Papier-Mache Press (Papier-Mache)
Web site: http://www.moyerbellbooks.com/
Dist(s): **Acorn Alliance**
Midpoint Trade Bks., Inc.
MyiLibrary

Publisher Name Index

Perseus-PGW
ebrary, Inc.; *CIP.*
Moznaim Publishing Corp., *(978-0-940118; 978-1-885220)* 4304 12th Ave., Brooklyn, NY 11219 USA (SAN 214-4123) Tel 718-438-7680; Fax: 718-438-1305; Toll Free: 800-364-5118.
MP Publishing Ltd. (GBR) *(978-0-9555792; 978-1-84982)* *Dist. by* **Midpt Trade.**
MP2ME Enterprise, *(978-0-9717947; 978-0-9776679; 978-0-9841360)* 16754 SE 45th St., Issaquah, WA 98027 USA Tel 425-957-9459
E-mail: mpighin1@comcast.net
Dist(s): **Lightning Source, Inc.**
MPC Pr. International, *(978-0-9628453; 978-0-9715541)* P.O. Box 26142, San Fransisco, CA 94126-6142 USA
E-mail: info@laughingcookiejar.com
Web site: http://www.laughingcookiejar.com.
MPR Publishing, *(978-0-9831857)* 3550 N. Daisy Dr., Rialto, CA 92377 USA Tel 323-259-2884
E-mail: sales@mprpublishing.com.
MPublishing *See* **Michigan Publishing**
MQuills Publishing, *(978-0-615-55835-6; 978-0-615-56307-7; 978-0-615-63989-5; 978-1-62375)* 4179 Choteau Cir., Rancho Cordova, CA 95742 USA Tel 916-205-6999; *Imprints:* Caliburn Books (Caliburn Bks); Paramance (Paramance)
E-mail: mquills@mquills.com
Web site: www.mquills.com
Dist(s): **CreateSpace Independent Publishing Platform**
Lightning Source, Inc.
Mr Do It All, Inc., *(978-0-9722038)* 2212 S. Chickasaw Trail, No. 220, Orlando, FL 32825 USA Toll Free: 800-425-9206
E-mail: info@planet-heller.com
Web site: http://www.planet-heller.com.
Mr. Emmett Publishing, *(978-0-9759346)* 37 Harleston Pl., Charleston, SC 29401 USA Tel 843-853-5728
E-mail: talubbers@comcast.net.
Mracek, Ann, *(978-0-9766488)* 22 Morwood Ln., Creve Coeur, MO 63141 USA (SAN 257-0009) Tel 314-432-5713; Fax: 314-569-2202
E-mail: anmracek@springmail.com.
MrDuz.com, *(978-0-9796226)* 1325 W. Sunshine No. 515, Springfield, MO 65807 USA (SAN 853-9332) Tel 417-831-9898; Fax: 417-863-6655 (please include To: MrDuz.com on cover pg.); Toll Free: 866-966-7389
E-mail: patrick@patrickwellman.com; patrick@mrduz.com
Web site: http://www.mrduz.com; http://www.patrickwellman.com.
MrExcel.com Publishing *See* **Tickling Keys, Inc.**
MRG Professional Services, *(978-0-9760310)* 6255 Cherry Ln. Farm Dr., West Chester, OH 45069 USA
E-mail: kgillis85@gmail.com.
MRN Pubns., *(978-0-9630495)* 1417 Noble St., Longwood, FL 32750 USA Tel 407-831-2947 (phone/fax)
E-mail: marjorie@partnersinlearning.com
Web site: http://www.partnersinglelearning.com.
Mroczka Media, *(978-0-9846800; 978-1-938397; 978-0-692-54800-4)* 2531 Southwick St., Houston, TX 77080 USA Fax: 832-365-7982; *Imprints:* Pagan Writers Press (PaganWriters)
E-mail: angie@paganwriters.com
Web site: http://www.paganwriterspress.com.
Mrs. L's Reading Room, *(978-0-9767278)* Orders Addr.: 110 Wedgefield Dr., Hilton Head Island, SC 29926 USA Tel 843-682-2820 (telephone/fax)
Web site: http://www.readroom.com.
M.S.C. Bks. *Imprint of* **Mustard Seed Comics**
MSJ Music Publishing, *(978-0-9764521)* P.O. Box 3185, Rancho Santa Fe, CA 92067-3185 USA.
MSP *Imprint of* **Main St Publishing, Inc.**
MSPpress *Imprint of* **Mama Specific Productions**
MsRevenda.com, *(978-0-9768538)* P.O. Box 370109, Decatur, GA 30037 USA
Web site: http://www.msrevenda.com.
M.T. Publishing Co., Inc., *(978-1-932439; 978-1-934729; 978-1-938730)* Orders Addr.: P.O. Box 6802, Evansville, IN 47719-6802 USA Toll Free: 888-263-4702; Edit Addr.: 2425 U.S. Hwy., 41 N. Suite 139, Evansville, IN 47711 USA
Web site: http://www.mtpublishing.com.
mTrellis Publishing, Inc., *(978-0-9663281; 978-1-930650)* Orders Addr.: P.O. Box 280, New York Mills, MN 56567 USA (SAN 299-6669) Fax: 218-385-3708; Toll Free: 800-513-0115
E-mail: trellis2@aol.com; mary@trellispublishing.com
Web site: http://www.trellispublishing.com
Dist(s): **Independent Pubs. Group**
MyiLibrary
Small Pr. United.
MTV Bks. *Imprint of* **MTV Books**
MTV Books, 1230 Ave. of the Americas, New York, NY 10020 USA; *Imprints:* MTV Books (MTV Imp)
Dist(s): **Simon & Schuster, Inc.**
Mu Alpha Theta, National High Schl. Mathematics Club, *(978-0-940790)* 601 Elm Ave., Rm. 423, Norman, OK 73019 USA (SAN 204-0077) Tel 405-325-4489; Fax: 405-325-7184
E-mail: matheta@ou.edu
Web site: http://www.mualphatheta.org.
Mud Pie Pr., *(978-0-9714941)* 4201 Morrow Ave., Waco, TX 76710 USA Tel 254-716-3193
E-mail: bjelmore@msn.com; belmore1@hot.rr.com
Web site: http://www.mudpiepress.com
Dist(s): **Quality Bks., Inc.**
Mud Puddle, Inc., *(978-1-59412; 978-1-60311)* 54 W. 21st St., Suite 601, New York, NY 10010 USA Tel 212-647-9168.
Mugsy and Sugar Pressed, *(978-0-9798886)* 1117 Nobb Hill Dr., West Chester, PA 19380 USA
E-mail: tlaurento@comcast.net.
Mukund Pubns., *(978-0-9663831)* 3033 Arbor Bnd., Birmingham, AL 35244-1573 USA
E-mail: pratibhakhare@hotmail.com
Web site: http://www.learnhindi.com.
Mulholland Books *Imprint of* **Little Brown & Co.**
Mulholland Teacher Resources *See* **Sonic Sword Productions**
Mullings Media, *(978-0-9767657)* P.O. Box 934, Woodbridge, NJ 07095 USA.
Mullins Pubns. & Apparel, LLC, *(978-0-9760160)* 6600 Plaza Dr., No.2000, New Orleans, LA 70127 USA.
Multables, Inc., *(978-0-9645004)* 6398 S. Louthan St., Littleton, CO 80120 USA Tel 303-794-0786; Toll Free: 800-320-6857.
Multicultural Pubns., *(978-0-9634932; 978-1-884242)* 936 Slosson St., Akron, OH 44320 USA Tel 330-865-9578; Fax: 330-734-0737; Toll Free: 800-238-0297
E-mail: multiculturalpub@prodigy.net
Web site: http://www.multiculturalpub.net
Dist(s): **Brodart Co.**
Follett School Solutions.
Multi-Language Pubns., *(978-0-9703210; 978-1-931891)* 2500 George Dieter, El Paso, TX 79936 USA Tel 915-857-5852; Fax: 915-857-7644; Toll Free: 800-876-1388
E-mail: paul.hartman@wels.net; jan.gamble@wels.net.
Multi-Language Publications Program *See* **Multi-Language Pubns.**
Multnomah *Imprint of* **Doubleday Religious Publishing Group, The**
Multnomah Fiction *Imprint of* **Doubleday Religious Publishing Group, The**
Multnomah Kidz *Imprint of* **Doubleday Religious Publishing Group, The**
Mumblefish Bks., *(978-0-9759649)* Orders Addr.: P.O. Box 139, Point Pleasant, PA 18950-0139 USA Tel 215-297-5002; Fax: 215-297-5299
E-mail: info@mumblefishbooks.com
Web site: http://mumblefishboooks.com.
Mumford Institute, *(978-0-615-25457-9; 978-0-692-00349-7)* 330 Shore Dr., Unit C5, Highlands, NJ 07732 USA Tel 732-291-8243.
Mundania Pr. *Imprint of* **Mundania Pr.**
Mundania Pr., *(978-0-9723670; 978-1-59426; 978-1-60659)* 6470A Glenway Ave., No. 109, Cincinnati, OH 45211 USA (SAN 255-013X) Tel 513-490-2822; Fax: 513-598-9220; *Imprints:* Mundania Press (MundPr)
E-mail: bob@mundania.com; books@mundania.com
Web site: http://www.mundania.com; http://www.phaze.com
Dist(s): **Lightning Source, Inc.**
Munson, Craig *See* **Fleur De Lis Publishing, LLC**
Murdoch Bks. Pty Ltd. (AUS) *(978-0-86411; 978-1-74045; 978-1-921259; 978-1-921208; 978-1-74196; 978-1-74266; 978-0-7316-4258-8; 978-0-646-32800-3; 978-1-74325; 978-1-74336)* *Dist. by* **IPG Chicago.**
Murdock, Bob E., *(978-0-9754363)* 352 Carly Ln., Rock Hill, SC 29732-7750 USA Tel 803-366-2666 (phone/fax)
E-mail: pbmurdock@comporium.net
Web site: http://www.sermonsforchildren.com.
Murdock Publishing Co., *(978-0-9743359; 978-1-934102)* Orders Addr.: 127 Belk Ct., Clayton, NC 27520 USA Tel 919-934-2393; Fax: 919-938-2394
Web site: http://www.murdockmedia.com.
Murine Press *See* **Ancient Wisdom Pubns.**
Murphey, Hiromi, *(978-0-9761350)* 4049 Madison Ave. Apt. 102, Culver City, CA 90232-3246 USA
Web site: http://www.nabiland.com.
Murphy, Indera *See* **Tolana Publishing**
Murphy's Bone Publishing, *(978-0-9748226)* P.O. Box 56835, Sherman Oaks, CA 91413-6835 USA Toll Free: 877-811-2663
E-mail: murphysbone@aol.com
Web site: http://www.murphysbone.com.
Murray, David M., *(978-0-9729807)* Orders Addr.: ., Seekonk, MA 02916 USA; Edit Addr.: 30 Wnterberry Ln., Seekink, MA 02771-4816 USA.
Murray Hill Bks., LLC, *(978-0-9719697; 978-1-935139)* 7 Evergreen Ln., Woodstock, NY 12498 USA (SAN 256-3622) Tel 845-679-6749
E-mail: robinsegal@earthlink.net; info@murrayhillbooks.com
Web site: http://www.murrayhillbooks.com
Dist(s): **Independent Pubs. Group**
Learning Connection, The.
Murray, Regina Waldron, *(978-0-9636918; 978-0-9664042)* 300 Hollinshead Spring Rd. Apt. AL137, Skillman, NJ 08558-2049 USA
E-mail: reginawmurray@yahoo.com.
Musa Publishing, *(978-1-61937; 978-1-68009)* 4815 Iron Horse Trail, Colorado Springs, CO 80917 USA Tel 719-393-2398
E-mail: kerry@musapublishing.com
Web site: www.musapublishing.com.
Muscatello Publishing, *(978-0-9722774)* P.O. Box 620011, Orlando, FL 32862-0011 USA Tel 407-888-3060; Fax: 407-650-3222; Toll Free: 877-888-3060
E-mail: info@muscatellopublishing.com
Web site: http://www.muscatellopublishing.com.
Museum Mysteries *Imprint of* **Stone Arch Bks.**
†**Museum of Fine Arts, Boston**, *(978-0-87846)* 465 Huntington Ave., Boston, MA 02115-4401 USA (SAN 202-2230) Tel 617-369-3438; Fax: 617-369-3459
E-mail: kmullins-mitchell@mfa.org
Web site: http://www.mfa.org
Dist(s): **Casemate Academic**
Brown, David Bk. Co.
D.A.P./Distributed Art Pubs.
MyiLibrary
Perseus Bks. Group
Perseus Distribution; *CIP.*
Museum of Fine Arts, Houston, *(978-0-89090)* P.O. Box 6826, Houston, TX 77265-6826 USA (SAN 202-2559) Tel 713-639-7300
Dist(s): **D.A.P./Distributed Art Pubs.**
Perseus Distribution
Texas A&M Univ. Pr.
Univ. of Texas Pr.
Yale Univ. Pr.
Museum of Glass, *(978-0-9726649; 978-0-692-46250-8)* 1801 Dock St., Tacoma, WA 98402 USA Toll Free: 866-468-7386 (866-4-MUSEUM)
Web site: http://www.museumofglass.org
Dist(s): **Univ. of Washington Pr.**
Museum of Glass: International Center for Contemporary Art *See* **Museum of Glass**
Museum of Modern Art, *(978-0-87070; 978-1-63345)* 11 W. 53 St., New York, NY 10019-5497 USA (SAN 202-5809) Tel 212-708-9700; Fax: 212-333-1127; Toll Free: 800-447-6662 (orders)
E-mail: MoMA_Publications@moma.org
Web site: http://www.moma.org/publications
Dist(s): **Abrams**
D.A.P./Distributed Art Pubs.
Hachette Bk. Group.
Museum of New Mexico Pr., *(978-0-89013)* Div. of New Mexico Department of Cultural Affairs, Orders Addr.: 1312 Basehart Rd. SE, Albuquerque, NM 87106-4363 USA (SAN 202-2575) 505-272-7778; Toll Free: 800-249-7737; Edit Addr.: P.O. Box 2087, Santa Fe, NM 87504-2087 USA
E-mail: custserv@upress.unm.edu
Web site: http://www.mnmpress.org
Dist(s): **Univ. of New Mexico Pr.**
Museum of Science *See* **Engineering in Elementary**
Museum of Texas Tech Univ., *(978-0-9640188; 978-1-929330)* Div. of Texas Tech Univ., 3301 4th St., Box 43191, Lubbock, TX 79409-3191 USA Tel 806-742-2442; Fax: 806-742-1136
E-mail: museum.texastech@ttu.edu
Web site: http://www.museum.ttu.edu.
Mushgush Pr., *(978-0-9795818)* 335 Cantlegate Close, Johns Creek, GA 30022 USA
Web site: http://tidalpress.com.
Mushroom Cloud Pr. of Orlando, *(978-0-9679552)* 278 Leslie Ln., Lake Mary, FL 32746 USA Tel 407-328-7311
E-mail: mushroomcloudpress@hotmail.com.
Music Awareness, *(978-0-9753599)* P.O. Box 188, Amherst, MA 01004 USA Tel 413-253-4216; Fax: 413-253-1397
E-mail: pwb@valinet.com
Web site: http://www.musicawareness.com.
Music Bks. & Games, *(978-0-9744427)* P.O. Box 97, McNeil, TX 78651 USA
E-mail: info@musicbooksandgames.com
Web site: http://www.musicbooksandgames.com/.
Music City Publishing, *(978-1-933215)* P.O. Box 41696, Nashville, TN 37204-1696 USA (SAN 256-288X)
E-mail: manager@musiccitypublishing.com
Web site: http://www.musiccitypublishing.com.
Music for Little People, Inc., *(978-1-56628; 978-1-877737)* 390 Lake Benbow Dr., No. C, Garberville, CA 95542 USA Tel 707-923-3991; Fax: 707-923-3241; Toll Free: 800-346-4445
Web site: http://www.musicforlittlepeople.com
Dist(s): **Educational Record Ctr., Inc.**
Follett School Solutions
Goldenrod Music, Inc.
Linden Tree Children's Records & Bks.
Music Design, Inc.
New Leaf Distributing Co., Inc.
Rounder Kids Music Distribution
Western Record Sales.
Music Institute of California, *(978-0-9624062; 978-1-883993)* Orders Addr.: P.O. Box 3535, Vista, CA 92085-3535 USA (SAN 297-5955) Tel 760-891-0226
Dist(s): **BookBaby**
Brodart Co.
Music, Movement & Magination Bks., *(978-0-9818635; 978-1-935572)* 3165 S. Alma School Rd., Suite 29-195, Chandler, AZ 85248 USA (SAN 856-7662) Tel 480-247-3129; Fax: 480-634-7148; Toll Free: 888-637-1313
E-mail: info@MMMKids.com
Web site: http://www.MMMKids.com.
Music Resources International *See* **Kindermusik International**
Music Sales Corp., *(978-0-7119; 978-0-8256; 978-1-84609)* Orders Addr.: 445 Bellvale Rd., P.O. Box 572, Chester, NY 10918 USA (SAN 662-0876) Tel 845-469-2271; Fax: 845-469-7544; Toll Free Fax: 800-345-6842; Toll Free: 800-431-7187; Edit Addr.: 257 Park Ave., S., 20th Flr., New York, NY 10010 USA (SAN 282-0277) Tel 212-254-2100; Fax: 212-254-2103; *Imprints:* Amsco Music (Amsco Music); Chester Music (Chester Music); Schirmer Trade Books (Schirmer Trade Bks)
E-mail: info@musicsales.com
Web site: http://www.musicroom.com; http://www.musicsales.com
Dist(s): **Beekman Bks., Inc.**
Dumont, Charles Son, Inc.
Chesbro Music Co.
Leonard, Hal Corp.
Ingram Pub. Services
Quality Bks., Inc.
Musical Linguist, The, *(978-0-9706829)* Orders Addr.: 14419 Greenwood Ave. N., Suite A, No. 354, Seattle, WA 98133 USA Fax: 509-693-4160; Toll Free: 866-297-2128
E-mail: mlinguist@aol.com
Web site: http://www.musicalspanish.com.
Musictech College Pr., *(978-0-9729879)* 19 Exchange St., E., Saint Paul, MN 55101 USA Tel 651-291-0177; Fax: 651-291-0366; Toll Free: 800-594-9500
E-mail: dsmith@musictech.com
Web site: http://www.musictech.com.
MusicWorks, *(978-0-9763194; 978-0-9820900)* Orders Addr.: P.O. Box 1971, Maryland Heights, MO 63043 USA; Edit Addr.: 13233 Amiot Dr., Saint Louis, MO 63146 USA; P.O. Box 1971, Saint Louis, MO 63043 (SAN 857-2291) Tel 314-439-5334 Do not confuse with MusicWorks in Marietta, GA
Web site: http://www.the-music-works.com; http://www.the-music-works.net.
MusiKinesis, *(978-0-9701416)* 3734 Cross Bow Ct., Ellicott City, MD 21042 USA Fax: 410-465-8472
E-mail: monicadale@musikinesis.com
Web site: http://www.musikinesis.com.
Muslim Writers Publishing, *(978-0-9767861; 978-0-9793577; 978-0-9819770; 978-0-9854638)* 2821-B O'Kelly St., Raleigh, NC 27607 USA Tel 919-817-8656
E-mail: debmcnichol@gmail.com
Web site: http://www.muslimwriterspublishing.com
Dist(s): **Smashwords.**
Mustang BKS, *(978-0-9766270)* P.O. Box 1193, Crooked River Ranch, OR 97760 USA Tel 541-504-9620.
Mustard Seed Comics, *(978-0-9769819; 978-0-9826975; 978-0-9964631)* 1609 Stoney Grove Church Rd., Warrenton, GA 30828 USA Tel 706-466-1633; *Imprints:* M.S.C. Books (MSCBks)
E-mail: mail@mustardseedcomics.com; benitomsc@yahoo.com
Web site: http://www.mustardseedcomics.com.
Mustard Seed Pr., *(978-0-9797703)* 263 Northampton Rd., Amherst, MA 01002 USA
Web site: http://www.bagelsbuddyandme.com.
Muszynski, James A., *(978-0-9766461)* 1446 Yoder Rd., Manister, MI 49660 USA Tel 231-723-6500 (phone/fax)
E-mail: lsmuszyk@hotmail.com
Web site: http://www.jaminjimbooks.com.
Mutual Publishing LLC, *(978-0-935180; 978-1-56647; 978-1-939487)* 1215 Center St., Suite 210, Honolulu, HI 96816 USA (SAN 222-6359) Tel 808-732-1709; Fax: 808-734-4094
E-mail: info@mutualpublishing.com
Web site: http://www.mutualpublishing.com
Dist(s): **Booklines Hawaii, Ltd.**
Islander Group
Mel Bay Pubns., Inc.
MVCD, Inc., *(978-0-9753617)* 4711 E. Falcon Dr., Suite 251, Mesa, AZ 85215 USA.
MVmedia, *(978-0-9800842; 978-0-9960167)* 145 Ridgewood Dr., Fayetteville, GA 30215 USA.
MX No Fear, *(978-0-9766918)* 2251 Faraday Ave., Suite A, Carlsbad, CA 92008 USA Toll Free: 866-787-3691
Web site: http://www.mxnofear.com.
My Ancestors, My Heroes *Imprint of* **Parker-Wallace Publishing Co., LLC**
My Campus Adventure, Inc., *(978-1-935159)* Orders Addr.: 7705 Orly Ct., Plano, TX 75025 USA (SAN 856-6690)
E-mail: kim@mycampusadventure.com
Web site: http://www.mycampusadventure.com.
My Children Publishing Inc., *(978-0-9799376)* 17410 Vinwood Ln., Yorba Linda, CA 92886 USA (SAN 854-7890)
Web site: http://www.mychildrenpublishing.com.
My Darling-Tots Pubns., *(978-0-9797674)* 8593 Pantherburn Trace, Cordova, TN 38018 USA
E-mail: hdarling30@yahoo.com
Web site: http://www.helendarling.com.
My First Classic Story *Imprint of* **Picture Window Bks.**
My First Graphic Novel *Imprint of* **Stone Arch Bks.**
My Grandma & Me Pubs., *(978-0-9742732)* 1275 E. Parks Rd., Saint Johns, MI 48879 USA
E-mail: info@mygrandmaandme.com; janemarysinke@gmail.com
Web site: http://www.mygrandmaandme.com
Dist(s): **Partners Pubs. Group, Inc.**
My Heart Yours Publishing, *(978-1-932721)* P.O. Box 4975, Wheaton, IL 60187 USA (SAN 255-6774)
E-mail: tanya@myheartyours.com; jeannine@myheartyours.com
Web site: http://www.myheartyours.com.
My Journey Bks., *(978-0-9766295)* P.O. Box 1169, Olney, MD 20830-1169 USA Toll Free: 877-965-2665
E-mail: KGF@billiesworld.com; KGF@myjourneybooks.com
Web site: http://www.billiesworld.com; http://www.myjourneybooks.com.
My Little Jessie Pr., *(978-0-9740743)* Orders Addr.: P.O. Box 529, Bethel, VT 05032 USA (SAN 255-321X) Tel 802-234-9725; Edit Addr.: One Cushing Ave., Bethel, VT 05032 USA
E-mail: jhaywardburnham@aol.com.
My Little Planet *Imprint of* **Picture Window Bks.**
My Lyric's Hse., *(978-0-9761446)* 593 Vanderbilt Ave., No. 135, Brooklyn, NY 11238 USA Tel 347-408-7786
E-mail: itsmeisha@yahoo.com.
My Purple Toes, LLC, *(978-0-9844556; 978-0-9834778)* P.O. Box 826, Mt. Pleasant, SC 29465 USA
E-mail: blair@blairhahnbooks.com
Web site: http://www.blairhahnbooks.com; http://www.mypurpletoes.com
Dist(s): **Emerald Bk. Co.**
My Second Language Publishing, USA, *(978-0-615-23709-1; 978-0-615-24460-0; 978-0-615-26150-8; 978-0-615-26238-3; 978-0-615-26239-0; 978-0-615-26240-6; 978-0-578-00208-8; 978-0-578-00209-5; 978-0-578-02214-7)* 165 River Hills Dr., Clayton, NC 27527 USA
E-mail: publisher@mysecondlanguagepublishingusa.com
Web site: http://www.mysecondlanguagepublishingusa.com
Dist(s): **Lulu Enterprises Inc.**
My Special Thoughts, *(978-0-9743019)* P.O. Box 150747, Nashville, TN 37215 USA Fax: 615-297-3138
Web site: http://www.myspecialthoughts.com.

My Student-Athlete, Inc., *(978-0-9767250)* P.O. Box 15, Redan, GA 30074 USA Tel 770-981-3000
Web site: http://www.morethanvictories.com.

My Sunshine Bks., *(978-0-9749561)* 1370 Little Brier Creek Rd., Warrenton, GA 30828 USA Toll Free: 800-765-4663.

My Three Sisters Publishing, *(978-0-615-73283-1; 978-0-615-73697-6; 978-0-615-73769-0; 978-0-615-74341-7; 978-0-615-74542-8; 978-0-615-74664-7; 978-0-615-74890-0; 978-0-615-74922-8; 978-0-615-75048-4; 978-0-615-75245-7; 978-0-615-75261-7; 978-0-615-75276-1; 978-0-615-75367-6; 978-0-615-75421-5; 978-0-615-75460-4; 978-0-615-75518-2; 978-0-615-75534-2; 978-0-615-75556-4; 978-0-615-75716-2; 978-0-615-75752-0; 978-0-615-75770-4; 978-0-615-75825-1; 978-0-615-75897-8; 978-0-615-75904-3; 978-0-615-75910-4; 978-0-615-75938-8;) 13817 W. Rovey Ave., Litchfield Park, AZ 85340 USA Tel 847-769-9824*
E-mail: Jenniseco@aol.com
Dist(s): **CreateSpace Independent Publishing Platform.**

My Time Pubns., *(978-0-9820530; 978-0-9843257; 978-0-9830518)* 2984 Spring Falls Dr., West Carrollton, OH 45449 USA Tel 937-344-4805
E-mail: leila@mytimepublications.com; ljeff25@yahoo.com
Web site: http://www.mytimepublications.com.

MyBoys3 Pr., *(978-0-9893414; 978-0-9861473)* 14400 Roberts Mill Ct., Midlothian, VA 23113 USA Tel 804-379-6964
E-mail: steve@myboys3.com
Web site: www.myboys3.com.

Myers, Connie Ellis *See* **Say Out Loud, LLC**

Myers, Jack Ministries, Inc., *(978-0-9720928)* P.O. Box 158, Orland Park, IL 60462-0158 USA
E-mail: jmm.revival@juno.com
Web site: http://www.jackmyersministries.com.

Myers Publishing Co., *(978-0-9745210; 978-0-9745929)* Orders Addr.: 207 Shelley Ct., Roseville, CA 95747 USA Tel 916-987-7668 (phone/fax) Do not confuse with Myers Publishing Company in Tarpon Springs, FL
E-mail: myerspubco@myerspublishing.com
Web site: http://www.myerspublishing.com.

MyHandiwork, *(978-0-9742555)* 7520 Walker St., Saint Louis Park, MN 55426-4042 USA Fax: 952-935-2840
E-mail: myhandiwork@earthlink.net
Web site: http://www.myhandiwork.com.

MYHRECO, *(978-0-9753704)* 9033 1/2 Hubbard St., Culver City, CA 90232-2508 USA.

Myrddin Publishing Group, *(978-0-9883828; 978-1-939296; 978-1-68063)* 54 Mill Pond Rd., Jackson, NJ 08527 USA Tel 732-822-8920
E-mail: alisondeluca@hotmail.com; cjjasp@gmail.com
Dist(s): **Lulu Enterprises Inc.**

MyReportLinks.com Bks. *Imprint of* **Enslow Pubs., Inc.**

Myrin Institute, Incorporated *See* **Orion Society, The**

Myrtle Learns, *(978-1-930694)* Orders Addr.: P.O. Box 3645, Rancho Cucamonga, CA 91729 USA Fax: 909-428-2401 (phone/fax); Edit Addr.: 14034 Fort Ross Ct., Fontana, CA 92336 USA Tel 909-428-2401
E-mail: jaajdeem@aol.com
Web site: http://myrtlelearns.com.

MySheri Enterprises, LLC, *(978-0-9766782)* P.O. Box 141111, Detroit, MI 48214 USA.

Myst of the Oracle Corp., *(978-0-9786812)* P.O. Box 133, Piney Creek, NC 28663 USA
E-mail: administrator@mystoftheoracle.com
Web site: http://www.mystoftheoracle.com.

Mysteries by Vincent, LLC, *(978-1-932169)* Orders Addr.: 2707 Mountain Green Trail, Kingwood, TX 77345 USA Tel 281-312-0120; Toll Free: 866-946-3864 1-866-WHODUNIT
E-mail: robert@mysteriesbyvincent.com; cindy@mysteriesbyvincent.com
Web site: http://www.mysteriesbyvincent.com; http://www.buckleyandbogey.com; http://www.whodunitpress.com.

Mystery & Suspense Pr. *Imprint of* **iUniverse, Inc.**

Mystery Writers of America Presents *Imprint of* **iUniverse, Inc.**

Mystic Arts, LLC, *(978-0-9771700)* P.O. Box 1110, Riverton, UT 84065 USA (SAN 256-8217)
Web site: http://www.reading-with-kids.com.

Mystic Hippo Media Publishing, *(978-0-9848694)* 5 Bald Hill Ct., Saint Peters, MO 63304 USA Tel 636-922-3593
E-mail: 88fingerslouie@att.net.

Mystic Jaguar Publishing, *(978-0-9792294)* 10821 Margate Rd., Suite A, Silver Spring, MD 20901-1615 USA (SAN 852-8365)
E-mail: Mysticjaguar@verizon.net.

Mystic Night Bks. *Imprint of* **Pink Stucco Pr.**

Mystic Publishing, *(978-0-9747454)* 16613 195th Ave., Mystic, IA 52574-8678 USA Do not confuse with Mystic Publishing in North, VA
E-mail: sharon@freddiethefrog.com; sharon@freddiethefrogbooks.com
Dist(s): **Leonard, Hal Corp.**

Mystic Ridge Bks., *(978-0-9672182; 978-0-9742845)* Div. of Mystic Ridge Productions, Inc., 222 Main St., Sutie 142, Farmington, CT 06032 USA (SAN 853-9898)
E-mail: mysticridge@att.net
Web site: http://www.mysticridgebooks.com; http://www.blackjacktoday.com; http://www.helixeye.com.

Mystic River Ink, *(978-0-9724752)* P.O. Box 441357, Somerville, MA 02144 USA
Web site: http://www.mysticriverink.com.

Mystic Seaport Museum, Inc., *(978-0-913372; 978-0-939510)* 75 Greenmanville Ave., Mystic, CT 06355-0990 USA (SAN 213-7550) Tel 860-572-5347; Fax: 860-572-5348; Toll Free: 800-248-1066
E-mail: publications@mysticseaport.org; wholesale@mysticseaport.org
Web site: http://www.mysticseaport.org
Dist(s): **Peabody Essex Museum Univ. Pr. of New England.**

Mystic World Pr., *(978-0-9854289)* 115 San Jose Ave. No. 2, San Francisco, CA 94110 USA Tel 415-373-8533
E-mail: william@mysticworldpress.com.

Mystical Willow Productions, *(978-0-9763205)* P.O. Box 95, Wheaton, IL 60189 USA
E-mail: mysticalwillow@comcast.net.

Mystique International, Ltd., *(978-0-9745333)* 2533 N. Carson St., Suite 593, Carson City, NV 89706-0147 USA
E-mail: metamind@eznet.net.

Myth Breakers *See* **Happy About**

Mythix Studios *Imprint of* **McCall, Philip Lee II**

Myth-O-Mania *Imprint of* **Stone Arch Bks.**

MythSeries, *(978-0-9776472)* P.O. Box 211, Millville, MN 55957 USA (SAN 257-8743) Tel 507-798-2450
E-mail: lisa@mythseries.com
Web site: http://mythseries.com.

Mz. Rosa Notions, *(978-0-9740267)* P.O. Box 114, Turlock, CA 95380 USA
E-mail: ninarule62@aol.com.

N A L Hardcover *Imprint of* **Penguin Publishing Group**

N A L Trade *Imprint of* **Penguin Publishing Group**

NAPSAC Reproductions, *(978-0-934426; 978-1-932747; 978-0-615-45573-0)* Rte. 4, Box 646, Marble Hill, MO 63764 USA (SAN 222-4607) Tel 573-238-4846; Fax: 573-238-2010
E-mail: napsac@clas.net
Dist(s): **Send The Light Distribution LLC.**

N&N Publishing Co., Inc., *(978-0-9606036; 978-0-935487)* 18 Montgomery St., Middletown, NY 10940 USA (SAN 216-4221) Tel 845-342-1677; Fax: 845-342-6910; Toll Free: 800-664-8398; *Imprints:* STAReviews (STAReviews); X-treme Reviews (X-treme Reviews)
E-mail: info@nandnpublishing.com; sales@nandnpublishing.com
Web site: http://www.nandnpublishing.com; http://www.nn4text.com; http://www.starreview.com; http://www.big8review.com.

N Gallerie Pr. LLC, *(978-0-9818347; 978-0-9962748)* Div. of N Gallerie Studios, LLC, Orders Addr.: 1213 Culbreth Dr. Suite 233, Wilmington, NC 28405 USA Tel 910-398-6411
E-mail: sales@ngallerie.com
Web site: http://www.ngallerie.com.

N2Print *Imprint of* **New Age World Publishing**

N8TIVE, *(978-0-9769575)* 620 S. 19th St., Philadelphia, PA 19146 USA
Web site: http://www.n8tve.com.

NA (CAP) *Imprint of* **Capstone Pr., Inc.**

Na Kamalei Koolauloa Early Education Program, *(978-0-9773495; 978-0-9760892; 978-1-935111)* P.O. Box 900, Hauula, HI 96717 USA Tel 808-237-8500; Fax: 808-237-8501; *Imprints:* Ho'ulu Hou Project: Stories Told by Us (Houlu Hou)
E-mail: nkpublishing@nakamalei.org
Web site: http://www.nakamalei.org.

Nabors, Murray W., *(978-0-615-38301-9; 978-0-615-40572-8; 978-0-615-49157-8; 978-0-615-85999-6)* 3051 NE State Rte. W., Saint Joseph, MO 64507 USA Tel 816-244-0354
E-mail: mnabors@missouriwestern.edu.

Nabu Pr. *Imprint of* **BiblioBazaar**

NACSCORP, Inc., Orders Addr.: 528 E. Lorain St., Oberlin, OH 44074-1298 USA (SAN 134-2118) Tel 440-775-7777; Toll Free Fax: 800-344-5059; Toll Free: 800-321-3883 (orders only); 800-458-9303 (backorder status only); 800-334-9882 (support programs/technical support)
E-mail: service@nacscorp.com; orders@nacscorp.com
Web site: http://www.nacscorp.com.

Nadores Publishing & Research, *(978-0-9797847)* Orders Addr.: P.O. Box 1202, Gilroy, CA 95021-1202 USA
E-mail: regulo-zapata@Verizon.net
Web site: http://www.nadorespublishing.com.

Nags Head Art, Inc., *(978-0-9616344; 978-1-878405)* Orders Addr.: P.O. Box 2149, Manteo, NC 27954 USA (SAN 200-9145) Tel 252-441-7480; Fax: 252-475-9893; Toll Free Fax: 800-246-7014; Toll Free: 800-541-2722; Edit Addr.: 7728 Virginia Dare Trail, Manteo, NC 27954 USA (SAN 658-8107)
E-mail: suzannetate@yahoo.com
Web site: http://www.suzannetate.com
Dist(s): **Florida Classics Library Mistco, Inc.**

NA-h *Imprint of* **Heinemann-Raintree**

NAHSH M'ISTAH Pub., *(978-0-9665427)* 8614 E. Dahlia Dr., Scottsdale, AZ 85260 USA Tel 480-998-8189
E-mail: nashmista@aol.com.

Naim, Deborah, *(978-0-9762828)* 20801 Biscayne Blvd., Suite 403, Aventura, FL 33180 USA
E-mail: dnaim@mercadeoecologico.com.

Namaste Publishing, Inc. (CAN) *(978-0-9682364; 978-0-9736512; 978-0-9738436; 978-1-897238) Dist. by* **PerseuPGW.**

Nambennett Publishing, *(978-0-9742208)* 11748 Fremont Ave. N., Seattle, WA 98133 USA
E-mail: kelly@nambennett.com
Web site: http://www.nambennett.com.

namelos llc, *(978-1-60898)* 133 Main Ave., South Hampton, NH 03827 USA Tel 828-221-
E-mail: roxburgh@namelos.com
Web site: http://www.namelos.com.

Nana's Stories, *(978-0-9857362)* 22 St. Nicholas Ave., Worcester, MA 01606 USA Tel 508-560-5888
E-mail: kfinneron@yahoo.com.

Nancy Paulsen Bks. *Imprint of* **Penguin Publishing Group**

Nancy's Artworks, *(978-0-9748074)* Orders Addr.: 6185 Faxon Ct., Colorado Spgs, CO 80922-1839 USA
E-mail: sales@nancyweb.com
Web site: http://www.multcamp.com; http://www.nancyweb.com; http://www.seanotes.net.

NANUQ Publishing, *(978-0-9795400)* 111 Linwood Ave., Williamsville, NY 14221 USA Tel 716-634-4379
E-mail: cralt37@yahoo.com.

NAO Pubns., *(978-0-9760838)* 35895 Conroy Rd., Suite 1015, Orlando, FL 32839 USA
E-mail: bbgwyn12@netzero.net; briangwyn@bellsouth.net
Web site: http://www.notanotheroverdraft.com; http://notanotheroverdraft.blogspot.com.

NAPNAP, *(978-0-9749769)* 20 Brace Rd., Suite 200, Cherry Hill, NJ 08034-2634 USA Tel 856-857-9700; Fax: 856-857-1600
E-mail: info@napnap.org
Web site: http://www.napnap.org.

Napue & Tucker Publishing, L.L.C. *See* **NT Publishing, L.L.C.**

NA-r *Imprint of* **Heinemann-Raintree**

Narragansett Graphics, *(978-0-615-12390-5)* P.O. Box 1492, Coventry, RI 02816-0029 USA
E-mail: lsousa@narragansettgraphics.com
Web site: http://www.narragansettgraphics.com.

Nastari, Nadine, *(978-0-9798387)* 8408 Salerno Rd., Fort Pierce, FL 34951-4506 USA
Web site: http://www.three-leggedcat.com.

NASW Pr. *Imprint of* **National Assn. of Social Workers/NASW Pr.**

Natasha S Brown, *(978-0-615-59173-5; 978-0-615-73124-7)* 11708 W. Aqueduct Dr, Littleton, CO 80127 USA Tel 303-972-4106
Web site: www.natashasbrown.com
Dist(s): **CreateSpace Independent Publishing Platform.**

Natavi Guides, *(978-0-9719392; 978-1-932204)* 44 Pine St., West Newton, MA 02465-1425 USA
E-mail: info@nataviguides.com
Web site: http://www.nataviguides.com.

Nathan, Fernand (FRA) *(978-2-09) Dist. by* **Distribks Inc.**

Nathaniel Max Rock, *(978-0-9749392; 978-1-59980)* 1418 S. Orange Ave., Monterey Park, CA 91755 USA
Web site: http://rockmath.com.

†National Academies Pr., *(978-0-309)* Orders Addr.: 8700 Spectrum Dr., Landover, MD 20785 USA; Edit Addr.: 500 Fifth St., NW Lockbox 285, Washington, DC 20001 USA (SAN 202-8891) Tel 202-334-3313; Fax: 202-334-2451; Toll Free: 888-624-7654; *Imprints:* Joseph Henry Press (Joseph Henry Pr)
E-mail: zjones@nas.edu
Web site: http://www.nap.edu
Dist(s): **Ebsco Publishing MyiLibrary ebrary, Inc.**; *CIP.*

National Academy Press *See* **National Academies Pr.**

National Assn. for Humane & Environmental Education, *(978-0-941246)* Div. of Humane Society of the U.S., P.O. Box 362, East Haddam, CT 06423 USA (SAN 285-0680) Tel 860-434-8666; Fax: 860-434-9579; *Imprints:* Humane Society Press (Humane Soc Pr)
E-mail: nahee@nahee.org
Web site: http://www.nahee.org.

National Assn. for Visually Handicapped, *(978-0-89064)* 3201 Balboa St., San Francisco, CA 94121 USA (SAN 202-0971) Tel 415-221-3201; Fax: 415-221-8754; 111 E. 59th St. # 6, New York, NY 10022-1202 (SAN 669-1870)
E-mail: staff@navh.org
Web site: http://www.navh.org.

†National Assn. of Social Workers/NASW Pr., *(978-0-87101)* Orders Addr.: P.O. Box 431, Annapolis Junction, MD 20701 USA Fax: 301-206-7989; Toll Free: 800-227-3590; Edit Addr.: 750 First St., NE, Suite 700, Washington, DC 20002-4241 USA (SAN 202-893X) Tel 202-408-8600; Fax: 202-336-8312; Toll Free: 800-638-8799; *Imprints:* N A S W Press (NASW Pr)
E-mail: press@naswdc.org
Web site: http://www.naswpress.org; *CIP.*

National Assn. of Speed & Explosion, *(978-0-938074)* P.O. Box 1784, Kill Devil Hills, NC 27948 USA (SAN 215-6148) Tel 252-441-1185; Fax: 252-449-4125
E-mail: naseinc@aol.com.

National Bk. Network, Div. of Rowman & Littlefield Pubs., Inc., Orders Addr.: 15200 NBN Way, Blue Ridge Summit, PA 17214 USA (SAN 630-0065) Tel 717-794-3800; Fax: 717-794-3828; Toll Free Fax: 800-338-4550 (Customer Service); Toll Free: 800-462-6420 (Customer Service); a/o Les Petriw, 67 Mowat Ave., Suite 241, Toronto, ON M6P 3K3 Tel 416-534-1660; Fax: 416-534-3699
E-mail: custserv@nbnbooks.com
Web site: http://www.nbnbooks.com.

National Braille Pr., *(978-0-939173)* Orders Addr.: 88 St. Stephen St., Boston, MA 02115 USA (SAN 273-0952) Tel 617-266-6160; Fax: 617-437-0456; Toll Free: 800-548-7323
E-mail: orders@nbp.org
Web site: http://www.nbp.org.

National Ctr. For Youth Issues, *(978-1-931636; 978-1-937870)* Orders Addr.: P.O. Box 22185, Chattanooga, TN 37422-2185 USA Tel 423-899-5714; Fax: 423-899-4547; Toll Free: 800-477-8277; Edit Addr.: 6101 Preservation Dr., Chattanooga, TN 37416 USA
E-mail: info@ncyi.org
Web site: http://www.ncyi.org
Dist(s): **Follett School Solutions MAR*CO Products, Inc. Youthlight, Inc.**

National Children's Book Project *See* **Public Square Bks.**

National Conference of State Legislatures, *(978-0-941336; 978-1-55516; 978-1-58024)* 7700 E. First Pl., Denver, CO 80230-7143 USA (SAN 225-1000) Tel 303-364-7700; Fax: 303-364-7800
E-mail: rita.morris@ncsl.org
Web site: http://www.ncsl.org.

†National Council of Teachers of English, *(978-0-8141)* Orders Addr.: 1111 W. Kenyon Rd., Urbana, IL 61801-1096 USA (SAN 202-9049) Tel 217-328-3870 Main Switchboard; Fax: 217-328-0977 Editorial Fax; 217-328-9645 Customer Service Fax; Toll Free: 800-369-6283 Main Switchboard Toll Free Tel; 877-369-6283 Customer Service Toll Free Tel
E-mail: kaustin@ncte.org; orders@ncte.org
Web site: http://www.ncte.org
Dist(s): **APG Sales & Distribution Services**; *CIP.*

†National Council of Teachers of Mathematics, *(978-0-87353; 978-1-68054)* 1906 Association Dr., Reston, VA 20191-1502 USA (SAN 202-9057) Tel 703-620-9840; Fax: 703-476-2970; 703-715-9536; Toll Free Fax: 800-220-8483; Toll Free: 800-235-7566 (orders only)
E-mail: info@nctm.org; cnoddin@nctm.org
Web site: http://www.nctm.org; *CIP.*

National Crime Prevention Council, *(978-0-934513; 978-1-929888; 978-1-59686)* 2345 Crystal Dr. Suite 500, Arlington, VA 22202 USA (SAN 693-8574) Tel 202-466-6272; Fax: 202-296-1356; Toll Free: 800-627-2911 (orders only) Do not confuse with The National Crime Prevention Assn., also in Washington, D.C.
E-mail: kirby@ncpc.org; demenno@ncpc.org
Web site: http://www.ncpc.org; http://www.mcgruff.org.

National Dance Education Organization, *(978-1-930798)* 8609 2nd Ave. Ste. 203B, Silver Spring, MD 20910-6359 USA
E-mail: ndeo@erols.com
Web site: http://www.ndeo.org
Dist(s): **Chicago Distribution Ctr.**

National Deacons Association *See* **Tommy Bks. Pubng.**

†National Education Assn., *(978-0-8106)* Orders Addr.: P.O. Box 404846, Atlanta, GA 30384-4846 USA (SAN 203-7262) Tel 202-822-7208; Fax: 202-822-7377; Toll Free: 800-229-4200; Edit Addr.: 1201 16th St., NW. Suite 514, Washington, DC 20036 USA Tel 770-280-4080; Fax: 770-280-4134
E-mail: nea-orders@pbd.com
Web site: http://www.nea.org/books; *CIP.*

National Educational Systems, Inc., *(978-1-893493)* P.O. Box 691450, San Antonio, TX 78269-1450 USA Toll Free: 800-442-2604.

National Film Network LLC, *(978-0-8026)* Orders Addr.: 4501 Forbes Blvd., Lanham, MD 20706 USA (SAN 630-1878) Tel 301-459-8020 ext 2066
E-mail: info@nationalfilmnetwork.com
Web site: http://www.nationalfilmnetwork.com.

National Foundation for Teaching Entrepreneurship, The, *(978-1-890859)* Orders Addr.: 120 Wall St., 29th Flr., New York, NY 10005 USA Tel 212-232-3333; Fax: 212-232-2244; Toll Free: 800-367-6383
E-mail: nfte@nfte.com
Web site: http://www.nfte.com.

National Gallery of Australia (AUS) *(978-0-646-30472-4) Dist. by* **U of Wash Pr.**

National Gallery of Victoria (AUS) *(978-0-7241) Dist. by* **Antique Collect.**

National Gallery of Victoria (AUS) *(978-0-7241) Dist. by* **Natl Bk Netwk.**

National Geographic *Imprint of* **National Geographic Society**

National Geographic Children's Bks. *Imprint of* **National Geographic Society**

National Geographic School Publishing, Inc., *(978-0-7362; 978-0-917837; 978-1-56334)* Div. of CENGAGE Learning, Orders Addr.: 10650 Toebben Dr., Independence, KY 41051 USA Tel 859-282-5700; Toll Free Fax: 800-487-8488; Toll Free: 800-354-9706; 888-915-3276; Edit Addr.: 1 Lower Ragsdale Dr., Bldg. 1, Suite 200, Monterey, CA 93940 USA
Web site: http://www.hampton-brown.com
Dist(s): **CENGAGE Learning.**

†National Geographic Society, *(978-0-7922; 978-0-87044; 978-1-4262; 978-1-4263)* 1145 17th St., NW, Washington, DC 20036 USA (SAN 202-8956) Tel 202-857-7000; Fax: 301-921-1575; Toll Free: 800-647-5463; 800-548-9797 (TTD users only); *Imprints:* National Geographic Children's Books (NGCB); National Geographic (NatlGeo)
E-mail: askngs@nationalgeographic.com
Web site: http://nationalgeographic.com
Dist(s): **Benchmark LLC Follett Media Distribution Follett School Solutions Lectorum Pubns., Inc. MyiLibrary Penguin Random Hse., LLC. Rand McNally Random Hse., Inc.**; *CIP.*

National Honor Roll, LLC, *(978-0-9714201; 978-0-9721652; 978-0-9729406; 978-1-932654)* 777 Sunrise Hwy. Ste. 300, Lynbrook, NY 11563-2950 USA Toll Free: 800-416-2185
Web site: http://www.nationalhonorroll.org.

National Horseman Publishing Inc., The, *(978-0-9762854)* 16101 N. 82nd St., Suite 10, Scottsdale, AZ 85260-1830 USA Tel 480-922-5202
Web site: http://www.tnh1865.com.

National Institute for Trauma & Loss in Children (TLC), The, *(978-1-931310)* 900 Cook Rd., Grosse Pointe Woods, MI 48236 USA Tel 313-885-0390; Fax: 313-885-1861; Toll Free: 877-306-5256
E-mail: steele@hcinst.org
Web site: http://www.hcinst.org.

Publisher Name Index

National Marfan Foundation, The, *(978-0-918335)* 22 Manhasset Ave., Prt Washingtn, NY 11050-2023 USA (SAN 657-2855) Toll Free: 800-862-7326
E-mail: staff@marfan.org
Web site: http://www.marfan.org.

National Marine Fisheries Service *Imprint of* **United States Government Printing Office**

National Maritime Museum (GBR) *(978-0-905555; 978-0-948065; 978-0-9501764; 978-1-906367) Dist. by* **IPG Chicago.**

National Maritime Museum (GBR) *(978-0-905555; 978-0-948065; 978-0-9501764; 978-1-906367) Dist. by* **Casemate Pubs.**

National Museum of Australia (AUS) *(978-1-876944; 978-1-921953) Dist. by* **IPG Chicago.**

National Network of Digital Schls., *(978-0-9816745; 978-1-935193; 978-1-936318; 978-1-938165; 978-1-943303; 978-1-944075)* 294 Massachusetts Ave., Rochester, PA 15074 USA
Web site: http://www.nndsonline.org.

†National Park Service Div. of Pubns., *(978-0-912627)* Harpers Ferry Ctr., Harpers Ferry, WV 25425 USA (SAN 282-7980) Tel 304-535-6018; Fax: 304-535-6144
Dist(s): **United States Government Printing Office;** *CIP.*

National Professional Resources, Inc., *(978-1-887943; 978-1-934032; 978-0-9819919; 978-1-935609; 978-1-938539)* 25 S. Regent St., Port Chester, NY 10573 USA Tel 914-937-8879; Fax: 914-937-9327; Toll Free: 800-453-7461; *Imprints:* Dude Publishing (Dude Pubng)
E-mail: lhanson@NPRinc.com; ncassone@nprinc.com
Web site: http://www.NPRinc.com
Dist(s): **Rowman & Littlefield Publishers, Inc.**

National Reading Styles Institute, Inc., *(978-0-929192; 978-1-883186; 978-1-933533)* Orders Addr.: P.O. Box 737, Syosset, NY 11791 USA (SAN 248-8191) Tel 516-921-5500; Fax: 516-921-5591; Toll Free: 800-331-3117; Edit Addr.: 179 Lafayette Dr., Syosset, NY 11791 USA (SAN 248-8205)
E-mail: readingstyle@nrsi.com
Web site: http://www.literacy.org; http://www.nrsi.com.

National Rehabilitation Services *See* **Northern Speech Services**

National Review, Inc., *(978-0-9627841; 978-0-9758998; 978-0-9847650)* 215 Lexington Ave., 4th Flr., New York, NY 10016 USA (SAN 226-1685) Tel 212-679-7330; Fax: 212-696-0340
E-mail: jfowler@nationalreview.com
Web site: http://www.nationalreview.com
Dist(s): **Chicago Distribution Ctr.**

National Science Resources Center (NSRC) *See* **Smithsonian Science Education Ctr. (SSEC)**

†National Science Teachers Assn., *(978-0-87355; 978-1-933531; 978-1-935155; 978-1-936137; 978-1-936959; 978-1-938946; 978-1-941316; 978-1-68140)* 1840 Wilson Blvd., Arlington, VA 22201 USA (SAN 203-7173) 703-243-7177; Toll Free: 888-433-0526 (orders); Toll Free: 800-277-5300 (orders); 800-722-6782
E-mail: pubsales@nsta.org; dyudkin@nsta.org
Web site: http://www.nsta.org/store
Dist(s): **Ebsco Publishing**
Independent Pubs. Group
MyiLibrary
ebrary, Inc.; *CIP.*

National Self-Esteem Resources & Development Ctr., *(978-0-9632276)* 851 Irwin St., Suite 205, San Rafael, CA 94901-3343 USA Tel 415-457-4411; Fax: 415-457-0356.

National Society of Professional Engineers, *(978-0-915409)* 1420 King St., Alexandria, VA 22314-2715 USA (SAN 225-168X) Tel 703-684-2800; Fax: 703-836-4875; Toll Free: 888-285-6773
E-mail: customer.service@nspe.org
Web site: http://www.nspe.org.

National Textbook Co. *Imprint of* **McGraw-Hill/Contemporary**

National Training Network, Inc., *(978-1-57290)* Orders Addr.: P.O. Box 36, Summerfield, NC 27358 USA
Web site: http://www.algebraicthinking.com.

National Writers Pr., The, *(978-0-88100)* Div. of National Writers Assn., 17011 Lincoln Ave., No. 421, Parker, CO 80134 USA (SAN 240-320X) Tel 720-851-1944; Fax: 303-841-2607
E-mail: natlwritersassn@hotmail.com
Web site: http://www.nationalwriters.com.

National Writing Institute, *(978-1-888344)* PMB 248, 624 W. University Dr., Denton, TX 76201-1889 USA Tel 940-382-0044; Fax: 940-383-4414; Toll Free Fax: 888-663-7855; Toll Free: 800-688-5375
E-mail: info@writingstrands.com
Web site: http://www.writingstrands.com.

Nations Hope, Inc., The, *(978-0-9761415)* P.O. Box 691446, Orlando, FL 32869-1446 USA
Web site: http://www.nationshope.org.

Native American Pubns., *(978-0-9745867)* Orders Addr.: P.O. Box 9, Dulac, LA 70353-0009 USA Tel 985-223-3857; Edit Addr.: 443 Ashland Dr., Houma, LA 70363-7283 USA
E-mail: ccbilliot@aol.com.

Native Nature *See* **Niche Publishing & Marketing**

Native Sun Pr., *(978-0-9746848)* Orders Addr.: P.O. Box 1139, Summerland, CA 93067 USA (SAN 255-6839) Tel 805-969-2234 (phone/fax); Edit Addr.: 2240 Banner Ave., Summerland, CA 93067 USA.

Native Voices *Imprint of* **Book Publishing Co.**

Natl Bk. Network,
Dist(s): **Perfection Learning Corp.**

Natural Child Project Society, The (CAN) *(978-0-9685754) Dist. by* **Consort Bk Sales.**

Natural Genius Bks., *(978-0-9765070)* P.O. Box 191088, Sacramento, CA 95819 USA Toll Free: 800-917-9321
E-mail: mjsee3@earthlink.net
Web site: http://www.naturalgeniusbooks.com.

Natural Heritage/Natural History, Inc. (CAN) *(978-0-920474; 978-1-896219; 978-1-897045) Dist. by* **IngramPubServ.**

Natural History Museum Pubns. (GBR) *(978-0-565) Dist. by* **IPG Chicago.**

Natural Learning Concepts, Inc., *(978-0-9778866; 978-0-9800300)* 21 Gallatin Dr., Suite B, Dix Hills, NY 11746 USA Tel 631-858-0188 (phone/fax); Toll Free: 800-823-3430
E-mail: sales@nlconcepts.com
Web site: http://www.nlconcepts.com.

Natural Math *See* **Delta Stream Media**

Naturally You Can Sing, *(978-0-9708397)* 3026 South St., East Troy, WI 53120 USA (SAN 255-4712)
E-mail: mary@flowformsamerica.com
Web site: http://www.maturallyyoucansing.com
Dist(s): **SteinerBooks, Inc.**

Nature Study Guild, *(978-0-912550; 978-0-9963531)* Orders Addr.: 54 QUEENS ST, Rochester, NY 14609 USA (SAN 203-722X) Toll Free: 800-954-2984 can fax to this no. also
E-mail: blackwalnutbooks@gmail.com
Web site: http://www.blackwanutbooks.com
Dist(s): **Common Ground Distributors, Inc.**
Perseus-PGW
Wilderness Pr.

Nature Works Press, *(978-0-915965)* Orders Addr.: P.O. Box 469, Talent, OR 97540 USA (SAN 293-9738) Tel 541-535-3189; Toll Free Fax: 866-749-3077
E-mail: irene@natureworkspress.com; natureworks1@gmail.com
Web site: http://www.natureworkspress.com
Dist(s): **Bks. West**
Partners/West Book Distributors.

Naturegraph Pubs., Inc., *(978-0-87961; 978-0-911010)* Box 1047, 3543 Indian Creek Rd., Happy Camp, CA 96039 USA (SAN 202-8999) Tel 530-493-5353; Fax: 530-493-5240; Toll Free: 800-390-5353
E-mail: nature@sisqtel.net
Web site: http://www.naturegraph.com
Dist(s): **American West Bks.**
Gem Guides Bk. Co.
New Leaf Distributing Co., Inc.
Sunbelt Pubns., Inc.

NaturEncyclopedia *Imprint of* **Stemmer Hse. Pubs.**

Natures Beauty Publishing, *(978-0-9754701)* P.O. Box 107, Oxford, MI 48371-0107 USA Tel 248-236-9314; Fax: 248-236-9315
E-mail: Ron@Naturesbeautyphotography.com
Web site: http://www.naturesbeautyphotography.com.

Nature's Hopes & Heroes, *(978-0-9822942)* 265 Kings Hwy., Boulder Creek, CA 95006 USA Tel 831-423-8973
E-mail: jimcruz@cruzers.com
Dist(s): **AtlasBooks Distribution.**

Nature's Pr., *(978-0-9741883)* Orders Addr.: P.O. Box 371, Mercer, WI 54547 USA
Web site: http://www.naturespressbooks.com.

Naumann, Jennifer, *(978-0-9883902)* 2777 420th Ave, Elmore, MN 56027 USA Tel 507-943-3673
E-mail: jen.naumann@yahoo.com.

†Naval Institute Pr., *(978-0-87021; 978-1-55750; 978-1-59114; 978-1-61251; 978-1-68247; 978-1-68269)* Orders Addr.: 291 Wood Rd, Annapolis, MD 21402-5034 USA (SAN 662-0930) Tel 410-268-6110; Fax: 410-295-1084; Toll Free: 800-233-8764; Edit Addr.: 291 Wood Rd., Beach Hall, Annapolis, MD 21402-5034 USA (SAN 202-9006)
E-mail: tskord@usni.org; books@usni.org
Web site: http://www.usni.org
Dist(s): **Fujii Assocs.**
MyiLibrary
Perseus-PGW
Perseus Bks. Group; *CIP.*

NavPress Publishing Group, *(978-0-89109; 978-1-57683; 978-1-60006; 978-1-61521; 978-1-61747; 978-1-61291; 978-1-63146)* 3820 N. 30th St., Colorado Springs, CO 80904 USA Fax: 719-260-7223; Toll Free Fax: 800-343-3902; Toll Free: 800-366-7788; *Imprints:* Th1nk Books (Th1nk Bks)
Web site: http://www.navpress.com
Dist(s): **Follett School Solutions**
Tyndale Hse. Pubs.

Naynay Bks *See* **Naynay Bks.**

Naynay Bks., *(978-0-9769589)* 122 Arbor Rd., NW, Minerva, OH 44657 USA
E-mail: naynaybooks@aol.com
Web site: http://www.naynaybooks.com.

Naypree Enterprises, LLC, *(978-0-9786565)* P.O. Box 31602, Aurora, CO 80041 USA (SAN 851-237X) Tel 303-856-3354
E-mail: dana@naypree-enterprises.com
Web site: http://www.naypree-enterprises.com.

Nazarene Publishing Hse., *(978-0-8341)* Orders Addr.: 2923 Troost Ave., Kansas City, MO 64109 USA (SAN 253-0902); Edit Addr.: P.O. Box 419527, Kansas City, MO 64141 USA (SAN 202-9022) Tel 816-931-1900; Fax: 816-531-0923; Toll Free Fax: 800-849-9827; Toll Free: 800-877-0700
E-mail: heather@nph.com
Web site: http://www.bhillkc.com; http://www.nph.com
Dist(s): **Leonard, Hal Corp.**
Spring Arbor Distributors, Inc.

NBM Publishing Co., *(978-0-918348; 978-1-56163; 978-1-68112)* Orders Addr.: 40 Exchange Pl., Suite 1308, New York, NY 10005 USA (SAN 210-0835) Tel 212-643-5407; Fax: 212-643-1545; Toll Free: 800-886-1223; Edit Addr.: 160 Broadway, Suite. 700, E. Wing, New York, NY 10038 USA Tel 646-559-4681; Fax: 212-643-1545; Toll Free: 800-886-1223; *Imprints:* Comics Lit (Comics Lit); Amerotica (Amerotica)
E-mail: catalog@nbmpublishing.com
Web site: http://www.nbmpub.com
Dist(s): **Independent Pubs. Group**
MyiLibrary.

N'Deeo Beauty *See* **N'Deeo, LLC**

N'Deeo, LLC, *(978-0-9724203; 978-0-9753811)* Orders Addr.: P.O. Box 460574, Aurora, CO 80046 USA Tel 770-896-6606; P.O. Box 1425, Mableton, GA 30126; Edit Addr.: 20511 E. Union Ave., Aurora, CO 80015 USA
E-mail: cservice@ndeeo.com
Web site: http://www.ndeeo.com.

Ndegwa, Catherine W., *(978-0-9742688)* Orders Addr.: P.O. Box 220411, Saint Louis, MO 63122-0411 USA; Edit Addr.: 119 Oakside Ln., Saint Louis, MO 63122-0411 USA
E-mail: catherine@varietystl.com.

NdueCzon Publishing Group, *(978-0-9755679)* P.O. Box 341825, Tampa, FL 33694 USA Tel 813-269-9351; Fax: 813-968-1941
E-mail: ndueczon@aol.com
Dist(s): **Culture Plus Bk. Distributors.**

Neal, Ann-Marie F, *(978-0-9747734; 978-0-9862096)* 903 Dale St., Edgewater, MD 21037 USA Tel 401-662-2411
E-mail: sunflower683@reagan.com
Web site: http://www.clarencethefrog.com.

Neal Morgan Publishing, *(978-0-9786117)* 51 Arrowgate Dr., Randolph, NJ 07869 USA Tel 973-598-9601; Fax: 973-927-8727
E-mail: Daleb6@aol.com.

†Neal-Schuman Pubs., Inc., *(978-0-918212; 978-1-55570)* Div. of American Library Assn., 100 William St., Suite 2004, New York, NY 10038 USA (SAN 210-2455) Tel 212-925-8650; Fax: 212-219-8916; Toll Free Fax: 800-584-2414
E-mail: info@neal-schuman.com
Web site: http://www.neal-schuman.com
Dist(s): **ebrary, Inc.;** *CIP.*

Nebador Archives, *(978-1-936253)* P.O. Box 592, Kelso, WA 98626 USA
E-mail: jzc23@nebador.com
Web site: http://www.nebador.com.

Nebbadoon Pr., *(978-1-891331)* Div. of Nebbadoon, Inc., Orders Addr.: 371 Hubbard St., Glastonbury, CT 06033 USA Toll Free: 800-500-9086
E-mail: george@4554.com
Web site: http://www.nebbadoonpress.com.

Nebe, Charles, *(978-0-9773091)* Orders Addr.: P.O. Box 631143, Irving, TX 75063-1143 USA
Web site: http://www.boonefiles.com.

Nebraska Wealth.com, *(978-0-9746206)* 1803 Stagecoach Rd., Grand Island, NE 68801 USA
Web site: http://www.nebraskawealth.com.

Necessary Evil Pr., *(978-0-9753635)* P.O. Box 178, Escanaba, MI 49829 USA
E-mail: info@necessaryevilpress.com
Web site: http://www.necessaryevilpress.com.

Nectar Pubns., *(978-0-9859986)* P.O. Box 6552, Savannah, GA 31404 USA Tel 912-631-9214
E-mail: contact@nectarpublications.com
Web site: www.nectarpublications.com.

Ned's Head Productions, *(978-1-887206)* 307 State St., Apt. B3, Johnstown, PA 15905 USA (SAN 253-8059) Tel 814-255-6646 (phone/fax)
E-mail: drron@charter.net
Web site: http://nedsheadbooks.com
Dist(s): **APG Sales & Distribution Services.**

Need To Know Publishing, *(978-1-940705)* 11019 N. 73rd St., Scottsdale, AZ 85260 USA Tel 888-377-3158; Fax: 888-377-3158
E-mail: brad@needtoknowpublishing.com
Dist(s): **MyiLibrary**
Perseus-PGW.

Neely, Judy, *(978-1-893968)* 54505 NW Scofield Rd., Buxton, OR 97109 USA Tel 503-324-8222; Fax: 503-324-8252
E-mail: jneely@neelyranch.com
Web site: http://www.neelyranch.com.

Neema's Children Literature Assn., Inc., *(978-0-9740653)* Orders Addr.: P.O. Box 440073, Chicago, IL 60644-1937 USA Tel 773-378-0607; Fax: 773-378-0042; Edit Addr.: 5345 W. Ferdinand St., Chicago, IL 60644-1937 USA Tel 773-575-4639
E-mail: nclapub@gmail.com.

Nefu Bks. *Imprint of* **Africana Homestead Legacy Pubs., Inc.**

Negro Publishing LLC *Imprint of* **Negro Publishing, LLC**

Negro Publishing, LLC, *(978-0-9763583)* Orders Addr.: P.O. Box 78, Mableton, GA 30126 USA Tel 770-265-0822; Fax: 770-948-2460; *Imprints:* Negro Publishing LLC (Negro Pub)
E-mail: supadave@negropublishing.com; dhhorton_2000@yahoo.com
Web site: http://www.negropublishing.com
Dist(s): **Culture Plus Bk. Distributors.**

NEHA Training LLC, *(978-0-944111)* 720 S. Colorado Blvd. Ste. 1000N, Denver, CO 80246-1926 USA
E-mail: support@nehatraining.com
Web site: http://www.nehatraining.com.

Neighborhood Pubs., *(978-0-615-75249-5)* 3317 Manor Rd., Austin, TX 78723 USA Tel 512-291-2314
E-mail: johnatpbp@yahoo.com.

Nelsbok Publishing, *(978-0-9763072)* 3312 Cedar Ave S., Minneapolis, MN 55407-2335 USA
Web site: http://www.nelsbok.com.

Nelsen, Margie, *(978-0-615-22008-6; 978-0-615-25480-7)* 804 Spruce Pl., Saint Peter, MN 56082 USA
E-mail: margienelsen@mchsi.com
Web site: http://www.snuggiebooks.com.

Nelson Publishing & Marketing, *(978-1-933916; 978-0-9785075; 978-1-938326)* 366 Welch Rd., Northville, MI 48167-1160 USA Tel 248-735-0418; *Imprints:* Ferne Press (Ferne Press)
E-mail: marian@nelsonpublishingandmarketing.com; kris@nelsonpublishingandmarketing.com
Web site: http://nelsonpublishingandmarketing.com
Dist(s): **Partners Pubs. Group, Inc.**

Nelson Publishing, LLC, *(978-0-9794171)* 15480 Annapolis Road, Suite No. 202-216, Bowie, MD 20715 USA; *Imprints:* Adventures of Hillary, The (AdventuresHillary)
E-mail: info@nelson-publishing.com
Web site: http://www.nelson-publishing.com.

Nelson, R. E. & Assoc., *(978-0-9749636)* 1535 SW Plass Ave., Topeka, KS 66604 USA Tel 785-235-3041
Web site: http://www.renelson.com.

Nelson, Roy *See* **Nelson, R. E. & Assoc.**

†Nelson, Thomas Inc., *(978-0-529; 978-0-7852; 978-0-8407; 978-0-8499; 978-0-86605; 978-0-88113; 978-0-89840; 978-0-89922; 978-0-918956; 978-0-7180; 978-1-4002; 978-1-4003; 978-1-4016; 978-1-59145; 978-1-4041; 978-1-59554; 978-1-59555; 978-1-4185; 978-1-59951; 978-1-4261; 978-1-60255; 978-1-4845; 978-1-5000) Orders Addr.: P.O. Box 141000, Nashville, TN 37214-1000 USA (SAN 209-3820) Fax: 615-902-1866; Toll Free: 800-251-4000; Edit Addr.: 501 Nelson Pl., Nashville, TN 37214 USA*
Web site: http://www.thomasnelson.com
Dist(s): **Christian Bk. Distributors**
CreateSpace Independent Publishing Platform
Follett School Solutions
Twentieth Century Christian Bks.; *CIP.*

Nelson Thornes Ltd. (GBR) *(978-0-17; 978-0-7487; 978-0-85950; 978-1-871402; 978-1-873732; 978-1-4085) Dist. by* **OUP.**

Nelson Thornes Ltd. (GBR) *(978-0-17; 978-0-7487; 978-0-85950; 978-1-871402; 978-1-873732; 978-1-4085) Dist. by* **Trans-Atl Phila.**

NEMESIS Enterprises, L.P., *(978-0-9713230)* Orders Addr.: 1048 S. Wardsboro Rd., Wardsboro, VT 05355 USA
E-mail: nemesis@myfairpoint.net
Web site: http://www.gophergo.com.

Nemo Publishing, LLC, *(978-0-9817132)* 86 Newbury St., Portland, ME 04101 USA (SAN 856-3381) Tel 207-761-0807; Fax: 207-775-5567
E-mail: tami@maine.rr.com
Web site: http://www.captneli.com
Dist(s): **Diamond Comic Distributors, Inc.**
Diamond Bk. Distributors.

Nemsi Bks., *(978-0-9718164; 978-0-9766400; 978-0-9794855; 978-0-9815313; 978-0-9821427; 978-0-9825011)* Div. of Morphtek.com, Inc., P.O. Box 191, Pierpont, SD 57468-0191 USA Fax: 605-325-3393
E-mail: psiccusa@dailypost.com
Web site: http://www.nemsi-books.net.

Neo-Tech Publishing Co., *(978-0-911752)* P.O. Box PO Box 531330, Henderson, NV 89053-1330 USA (SAN 202-3156)
E-mail: rapper@neo-tech.com
Web site: http://www.neo-tech.com; http://www.neo-tech.com/front/cservice.html.

Nerdel Co., The, *(978-0-9823357)* 1000 West McNab Road, Pompano Beach, FL 33069 USA (SAN 858-7205)
Web site: http://www.nerdel.com.

NERO International Holding Co., Inc, *(978-0-9700563)* Orders Addr.: P.O. Box 2763 nc highway 731 west, MOUNT GILEAD, NC 27306 USA Tel 914-628-9497; Edit Addr.: 2763 NC Hwy. 731 W., MOUNT GILEAD, NC 27306 USA
E-mail: jvalenti@nerolarp.com
Web site: http://www.nerolarp.com; http://nerolarponline.com.

NESFA Pr. *Imprint of* **New England Science Fiction Assn., Inc.**

Neshee Pubn., *(978-0-9747017; 978-0-9770907; 978-0-9785794; 978-0-9823053)* P.O. Box 48028, Philadelphia, PA 19144 USA
E-mail: info@nesheepublicaiton.com
Web site: http://www.nesheepublication.com.

Neshui Publishing, Inc., *(978-0-9652528; 978-1-931190)* 6310 Rosebury Ave. #2, Saint Louis, MO 63105 USA
E-mail: info@neshuipress.com
Web site: http://www.neshuipress.com
Dist(s): **Raven West Coast Distribution.**

NetClinger, *(978-0-9760308)* P.O. Box 38144, Houston, TX 77238-8144 USA
Web site: http://www.netclinger.com.

Netcomics, *(978-1-60009)* P.O. Box 16484, Jersey City, NJ 07306 USA
Dist(s): **Diamond Comic Distributors, Inc.**
Diamond Bk. Distributors.

NetNia Publishing Co., *(978-1-884163)* 9218 Rockbrook Dr., Dallas, TX 75220 USA; *Imprints:* Juba Books (Juba Bks)
E-mail: jeffery.bradley@outlook.com
Web site: http://www.howtogrowdreadlocks.com; http://www.netnia.com; http://www.africanamericanchildrenplays.com
Dist(s): **Lightning Source, Inc.**

NETroplex Books *See* **Yankee Cowboy**

Network CPU Learning Technologies, *(978-1-932257)* 172 Fifth Ave., Suite 37, Brooklyn, NY 11217-3504 USA (SAN 254-9298)
E-mail: roxceyluv@yahoo.com.

NETWORK Inc., The, *(978-1-878234)* Div. of NETWORK, Inc., 136 Fenno Dr., Rowley, MA 01969-1004 USA Tel 978-948-7764; Fax: 978-948-7836; Toll Free: 800-877-5400
E-mail: info@thenetworkinc.org
Web site: http://www.thenetworkinc.org.

Neuburger Publishing, *(978-0-9762419)* Orders Addr.: P.O. Box 3928, Taulatin, OR 97062-3928 USA Tel 503-925-0400; Edit Addr.: 24386 SW Baker Rd., Sherwood, OR 97140 USA
Web site: http://www.takethefearoutofmath.com.

Neugebauer, Michael (Publishing) Limited (HKG) *(978-988-8240) Dist. by* **IPG Chicago.**

Neumann Pr. *Imprint of* **TAN Bks.**

Nevaeh Publishing, LLC, *(978-0-9787899; 978-0-9839187)* P.O. Box 962, Redan, GA 30074-0962 USA (SAN 851-6111) Tel 770-363-5669
E-mail: dwanabrams1@aol.com
Web site: http://www.dwanabrams.com; http://www.nevaehpublishing.com
Dist(s): **Smashwords.**

Never Quit Productions, Inc., *(978-0-615-26231-4)* 4832 Wind Hill Ct. W., Fort Worth, TX 76179 USA
Dist(s): **Lulu Enterprises Inc.**

Never Stop Reading Never Stop Learning, *(978-0-9741750)* 3221 S. Indiana St., Lakewood, CO 80228 USA Tel 303-829-8699
E-mail: neverstopreading@aol.com
Web site: http://www.jdmcdoil.com.

New Academia Publishing, LLC, *(978-0-9744934; 978-0-9767042; 978-0-9777908; 978-0-9787713; 978-0-9794488; 978-0-9800814; 978-0-9818654; 978-0-9823867; 978-0-9844062; 978-0-9828061; 978-0-615-43269-4; 978-0-9832451; 978-0-9836899; 978-0-9845832; 978-0-9855698; 978-0-9860216;-0-9886376; 978-0-9899169; 978-0-9915047; 978-0-9904471; 978-0-9906939; 978-0-9864353; 978-0-9966484) P.O. Box 27420, Washington, DC 20038-7420 USA; Imprints:* Vellum (Vellum)
Web site: http://www.newacademia.com
Dist(s): **Lightning Source, Inc.**
eBookit.com.

New Age Dimensions, Incorporated *See* **Adrema Pr.**

New Age World Publishing, *(978-1-59405)* 4071 San Pablo Dam Rd. # 141, El Sobrante, CA 94803-2903 USA Toll Free Fax: 888-739-6129; Toll Free: 877-411-8744; *Imprints:* N2Print (N2Print)
E-mail: NAWP@comcast.net
Web site: http://www.nawpublishing.com.

New & Living Way Publishing Co., *(978-0-910003)* P.O. Box 830384, Tuskegee, AL 36083-0384 USA (SAN 241-2314) Tel 334-727-5372
E-mail: nlwpc@bellsouth.net; clgpgt@bellsouth.net
Web site: http://www.clgpgt.org/NLW/nlw1.html.

New & Living Way Publishing House *See* **New & Living Way Publishing Co.**

New Art & Vision, LLC, *(978-0-9742322)* 1360 E. 300 N., Layton, UT 84040 USA Tel 801-543-3383
E-mail: bnybo@elmojackson.com
Web site: http://www.elmojackson.com.

New Baby Productions, *(978-0-9818530)* Orders Addr.: 4143 Tanglewood Ct., Bloomfield Township, MI 48301 USA (SAN 856-7298)
E-mail: eric@elementalfources.com
Web site: http://www.ElementalFources.com
Dist(s): **Haven Distributors**
Lightning Source, Inc.

New Birth Publishing, *(978-0-9755489)* 1900 Preston Rd., No. 267, PMB 264, Plano, TX 75093 USA
Web site: http://www.newbirthpublishing.com.

New Buds Publishing Hse. (CHN) *(978-7-5307) Dist. by* **Chinasprout.**

New Canaan Publishing Co. LLC, *(978-1-889658)* 2384 N. Hwy. 341, Rossville, GA 30741 USA Tel 423-285-8672
E-mail: djm@newcanaanpublishing.com
Web site: http://www.newcanaanpublishing.com
Dist(s): **Send The Light Distribution LLC.**

New Castle Publishing Co., *(978-0-9740195)* 512 Wadsworth Dr., Richmond, VA 23236 USA
E-mail: newcastlepubl@aol.com.

New Century Pr., *(978-1-890035)* Orders Addr.: 1055 Bay Blvd., Suite C, Chula Vista, CA 91911-1628 USA (SAN 859-3760) Tel 619-476-7400; Fax: 619-476-7474; Toll Free: 800-519-2465 (orders) Do not confuse with companies with the same or similar name in Bermuda Dunes CA, New York NY
E-mail: sales@newcenturypress.com
Web site: http://www.newcenturypress.com.

New Century Pr., *(978-0-9748013)* P.O. Box 73381, Richmond, VA 23235-8040 USA Tel 804-897-2824 Do not confuse with companies with the same or similar name in Bermuda Dunes CA, Chula Vista CA, New York NY
E-mail: newcenturypress@aol.com.

New Century Publishing, LLC, *(978-0-9768052; 978-0-9820729; 978-0-9822344; 978-0-9824711; 978-0-9841819; 978-0-9843666; 978-0-9844661)* 1040 E. 86th St., Suite 42A, Indianapolis, IN 46240 USA Tel 317-663-8741; Fax: 317-663-8745
E-mail: dwcaswell@newcentrypublishing.orrg
Web site: http://www.newcenturypublishing.org.

New Chapter Pub., *(978-0-9792012; 978-0-9841745; 978-0-9827918; 978-0-9836184; 978-1-938842)* 1765 Ringling Blvd. Suite 300, Sarasota, FL 34236-6873 USA Fax: 941-954-0111
E-mail: info@newchapterpublisher.com
Web site: http://www.newchapterpublisher.com
Dist(s): **Midpoint Trade Bks., Inc.**
MyiLibrary.

New City Community Pr., *(978-0-9712996; 978-0-9819560; 978-0-9840429; 978-0-9887635)* 7715 Crittenden St., #222, Philadelphia, PA 191182 USA Tel 315-443-1912 Do not confuse with New City Press in Hyde Park, NY
E-mail: sjparks@syr.edu
Web site: http://www.newcitypress.org
Dist(s): **Chicago Distribution Ctr.**
SPD-Small Pr. Distribution.

New City Press *See* **New City Press of the Focolare**

New City Press *See* **New City Community Pr.**

†New City Press of the Focolare, *(978-0-911782; 978-1-56548)* 202 Comforter Blvd., Hyde Park, NY 12538 USA (SAN 203-7335) Tel 845-229-0335; Fax: 845-229-0351; Toll Free: 800-462-5980 (orders only)
E-mail: info@newcitypress.com
Web site: http://www.newcitypress.com; *CIP.*

New Classics Pr., *(978-0-9755704)* 2400 Ridgecroft SE, Grand Rapids, MI 49546 USA.

New Concepts Publishing, *(978-1-891020; 978-1-58608; 978-1-60394)* 5202 Humphreys Rd., Lake Park, GA 31636 USA Tel 229-257-0367; Fax: 229-219-1097
E-mail: newconcepts@newconceptspublishing.com; service@newconceptspublishing.com
Web site: http://www.newconceptspublishing.com
Dist(s): **Smashwords.**

New Dawn Pr., Inc., *(978-0-9729607; 978-1-932705; 978-1-904910)* 244 S. Randall Rd., No. 90, Elgin, IL 60123 USA
E-mail: maildrop@newdawnpress.com
Web site: http://www.newdawnpress.com
Dist(s): **Independent Pubs. Group.**

New Dawn Publishing, *(978-0-9721948)* P.O. Box 11151, Portland, ME 04104 USA Tel 207-839-8809 Do not confuse with companies with the same or similar name in Elk Mills, MD, Dexter, NY
Web site: http://www.mynewdawn.com.

New Day Pr., *(978-0-913678)* c/o Karamu Hse., 2355 E. 89th St., Cleveland, OH 44106 USA (SAN 279-2664) Tel 216-795-7070 ext 228; Fax: 216-795-7073 Do not confuse wtih New Day Press in Las Vegas, NV
E-mail: editor@newdaypress.com.

New Day Publishing, Inc., *(978-0-9789056; 978-0-9798247)* 26 Bluff Ridge Ct., Greensboro, NC 27455 USA Tel 336-545-1545; Fax: 336-545-1640; Toll Free: 866-763-2977 Do not confuse with companies with the same or similar name in Winston-Salem, NC, Phoenix, AZ, North Miami, FL
E-mail: ateich@newdaypublishing.net
Web site: http://www.newdaypublishing.net.

†New Directions Publishing Corp., *(978-0-8112)* 80 Eighth Ave., New York, NY 10011 USA (SAN 202-9081) Tel 212-255-0230; Fax: 212-255-0231; Toll Free: 800-233-4830
E-mail: nd@ndbooks.com
Web site: http://www.ndpublishing.com
Dist(s): **Continental Bk. Co., Inc.**
Norton, W. W. & Co., Inc.
Penguin Random Hse., LLC.
SPD-Small Pr. Distribution; *CIP.*

New Eden Publishing, *(978-0-9882368; 978-0-692-32667-1)* 50513 W Esch Trail, Maricopa, AZ 85139 USA Tel 480-217-0776
E-mail: anitasmail3@gmail.com
Dist(s): **Lulu Enterprises Inc.**

New England Science Fiction Assn., Inc., *(978-0-915368; 978-1-886778; 978-1-61037)* P.O. Box 809, Framingham, MA 01701-0809 USA (SAN 223-8187) Tel 508-653-7397; Fax: 617-776-3243; *Imprints:* N E S F A Press (NESFA Pr)
E-mail: press@nesfa.org
Web site: http://www.nesfa.org/press/.

New Europe Bks., *(978-0-9825781; 978-0-9850623; 978-0-9900043)* 54 Arnold St., Williamstown, MA 01267 USA Tel 203-779-9660
E-mail: paul@neweuropebooks.com; info@neweuropebooks.com
Web site: http://www.NewEuropeBooks.com; http://www.NewEuropeBooks.com
Dist(s): **MyiLibrary**
Penguin Random Hse., LLC.
Random Hse., Inc.

New Family Pr., *(978-0-9742008)* 389 Belmont St., Suite 105, Oakland, CA 94610 USA Tel 510-866-3984
E-mail: newfamilypress@yahoo.com
Dist(s): **Book Wholesalers, Inc.**

New Forums Pr., *(978-0-913507; 978-1-58107)* Orders Addr.: P.O. Box 876, Stillwater, OK 74076 USA (SAN 285-8673) Tel 405-372-6158; Fax: 405-377-2237; Toll Free: 800-606-3766; Edit Addr.: 1018 S. Lewis, Stillwater, OK 74074 USA
E-mail: dougdollar@provalue.net; design@newforums.com
Web site: http://www.newforums.com
Dist(s): **BookBaby.**

New Global Publishing, *(978-0-9762292; 978-0-9770043; 978-0-9785609; 978-0-9791748; 978-0-9830940; 978-0-9896334)* Orders Addr.: 2310 SE. Bordeaux Ct., Port Saint Lucie, FL 34952 USA
Web site: http://www.newglobalpublishing.com.

New Growth Pr., *(978-0-9762308; 978-0-9770807; 978-0-9785567; 978-1-934885; 978-1-935273; 978-1-936768; 978-1-938267; 978-1-939946; 978-1-942572)* Orders Addr.: P.O. Box 4485, Greensboro, NC 27404 USA Tel 3363787775; Toll Free: 877-647-2233; Edit Addr.: 533 Woodland Dr., Greensboro, NC 27408 USA Tel 336-378-7775; Fax: 336-464-2722
Web site: http://www.newgrowthpress.com
Dist(s): **Cook, David C.**

New Harbinger Pubns., *(978-0-934986; 978-1-57224; 978-1-879237; 978-1-60882; 978-1-62625)* Orders Addr.: 5674 Shattuck Ave., Oakland, CA 94609 USA (SAN 205-0587) Tel 510-652-2002; 510-652-0215; Fax: 510-652-5472; Toll Free: 800-652-1613
E-mail: customerservice@newharbinger.com
Web site: http://www.newharbinger.com
Dist(s): **MyiLibrary**
ebrary, Inc.

New Holland Pubs., Ltd. (GBR) *(978-1-85368; 978-1-85974; 978-1-84330; 978-1-84636; 978-1-84537; 978-1-84773; 978-1-78009) Dist. by* **Sterling.**

New Holland Pubs. Pty, Ltd. (AUS) *(978-1-86436; 978-1-875580; 978-1-876334; 978-1-877069; 978-1-74110; 978-1-921024; 978-1-921073; 978-1-921072; 978-1-921517; 978-1-921580; 978-1-921655; 978-1-74257; 978-1-74268; 978-1-921740; 978-1-921836; 978-0-7316-1991-7; 978-0-646-15496-1;-1-74337) Dist. by* **Tuttle Pubng.**

New Holland Pubs. Pty, Ltd. (AUS) *(978-1-86436; 978-1-875580; 978-1-876334; 978-1-877069; 978-1-74110; 978-1-921024; 978-1-921073; 978-1-921072; 978-1-921517; 978-1-921580; 978-1-921655; 978-1-74257; 978-1-74268; 978-1-921740; 978-1-921836; 978-0-7316-1991-7; 978-0-646-15496-1;-1-74337) Dist. by* **Midpt Trade.**

New Hope *See* **Woman's Missionary Union**

New Hope Pubs., *(978-1-56309)* Orders Addr.: P.O. Box 830010, Birmingham, AL 35283 USA Tel 205-991-8100; Fax: 205-995-4825; Toll Free: 800-968-7301 Do not confuse with New Hope Publishers in New Hope, MN
E-mail: info@newhopepublishers.com
Web site: http://www.newhopepublishers.com
Dist(s): **B&H Publishing Group**
MyiLibrary
Send The Light Distribution LLC.

New Horizon Pr. Pubs., Inc., *(978-0-88282)* Orders Addr.: P.O. Box 669, Far Hills, NJ 07931 USA (SAN 677-119X) Tel 908-604-6311; Fax: 908-604-6330; Toll Free: 800-533-7978 (orders only); *Imprints:* Small Horizons (Small Horizons)
E-mail: nhp@newhorizonpressbooks.com
Web site: http://www.newhorizonpressbooks.com
Dist(s): **Kensington Publishing Corp.**
MyiLibrary
Penguin Publishing Group
Perseus-PGW
Perseus Bks. Group.

New Horizons Christian Ctr., *(978-0-9728532)* 16 Foxbriar Rd., Hilton Head, SC 29926 USA.

New Horizons Pr., *(978-0-9647933)* Orders Addr.: 26 Nottingham Dr., Cartersville, GA 30121 USA; Edit Addr.: 2815 New South Dr., Marietta, GA 30066 USA Do not confuse with companies with the same name in, Lake Mary, FL, Ferrisburgh, VT, Leesburg, VA, Orlando, FL.

New in Chess *Imprint of* **Continental Sales, Inc.**

New In Chess,Csi *Imprint of* **Continental Sales, Inc.**

New Internationalist Pubns., Ltd. (GBR) *(978-1-869847; 978-0-9540499; 978-1-904456; 978-1-906523; 978-1-78026) Dist. by* **Consort Bk Sales.**

New Island Books (IRL) *(978-1-85186; 978-1-874597; 978-1-902602; 978-1-904301; 978-1-905494) Dist. by* **Dufour.**

New Issues Poetry & Prose, Western Michigan Univ., *(978-0-932826; 978-1-930974; 978-1-936970)* 1903 West Michigan Ave. Western Michigan University, Kalamazoo, MI 49008 USA (SAN 276-6299) Tel 269-387-8185; Fax: 269-387-2562
E-mail: new-issues@wmich.edu
Web site: http://www.wmich.edu/newissues
Dist(s): **SPD-Small Pr. Distribution.**

New Leaf Bks. *Imprint of* **WigWam Publishing Co.**

New Leaf Education, Inc. *See* **New Leaf Educ., Inc.**

New Leaf Educ., Inc., *(978-0-9722452; 978-0-9764217; 978-1-933655)* Orders Addr.: P.O. Box 16230, Baltimore, MD 21210 USA Tel 410-467-7835; Fax: 410-951-0419; Edit Addr.: 2050 Rockrose Ave., Baltimore, MD 21211 USA
E-mail: contactus@newleafeducation.com
Web site: http://www.newleafeducation.com.

New Leaf Pr., Inc., *(978-0-89221)* P.O. Box 726, Green Forest, AR 72638 USA (SAN 207-9518) Tel 870-438-5288; Fax: 870-438-5120 Toll Free: 800-643-9535 Do not confuse with companies with the same or similar name in Los Angeles, CAStone Mountain, GA
E-mail: nlp@newleafpress.net
Web site: http://www.newleafpress.net
Dist(s): **MyiLibrary**
Spring Arbor Distributors, Inc.
ebrary, Inc.

New Learning Publishing, *(978-0-9793576)* 123 Wolcott Ave., Rochester, NY 14606 USA (SAN 853-2273) Tel 585-426-9454
E-mail: callen10@rochester.rr.com.

New Library Press LLC, *(978-0-7950)* Orders Addr.: 3419 Chapman Ave. #133, Orange, CA 92869 USA; Edit Addr.: P.O. Box 130, Murrieta, CA 92564 USA
E-mail: newbookorders@gmail.com.

New Life Publishing Hse., *(978-0-9785573)* Orders Addr.: 2835 Cedar Ln., Vienna, VA 22180 USA (SAN 850-8844) Tel 703-942-8440 (phone/fax)
E-mail: garrygenser@me.com
Dist(s): **AtlasBooks Distribution.**

New Line Bks., *(978-1-57717; 978-1-880908; 978-1-59764)* 245 Eighth Ave., No. 180, New York, NY 10011-1607 USA Toll Free Fax: 888-719-7723; Toll Free: 888-719-7722
E-mail: info@newlinebooks.com
Web site: http://www.newlinebooks.com.

New Millenium Pr., The, *(978-0-9706728)* 311 E. Seventh St., Tama, IA 52339 USA Tel 515-484-2313 Do not confuse with New Millennium Press in Augusta, GA.

New Millennium Bks., *(978-0-9672333)* c/o Gail Mathabane, 901 SW King St. Suite 1006, Portland, OR 97205 USA Tel 503-758-2628 Do not confuse with New Millennium Bks., Petersburg, VA
E-mail: gem@mathabane.com
Web site: http://www.mathabane.com.

New Monic Bks., *(978-0-9652422; 978-0-9840966)* P.O. Box 511314, Punta Gorda, FL 33951-1314 USA Toll Free: 800-741-1295
E-mail: bburchers@earthlink.net
Web site: www.vocabularycartoons.com.

New Orleans Stories, *(978-0-9758996)* 7401 Slaughter Ln., PMB 5015, Austin, TX 78739 USA Tel 512-923-5015
E-mail: sean@neworleansstories.com
Web site: http://neworleansstories.com
Dist(s): **Forest Sales & Distributing Co.**

New Page Bks. *Imprint of* **Career Pr., Inc.**

New Paradigm Bks., *(978-1-892138)* 22491 Vistawood Way, Boca Raton, FL 33428 USA Tel 561-482-5971; Fax: 561-852-8322; Toll Free: 800-808-5179
E-mail: darbyc@earthlink.net
Web site: http://www.newpara.com
Dist(s): **New Leaf Distributing Co., Inc.**

New Paradigm Pubns., *(978-0-615-35944-1; 978-0-9827673)* 12 Cherokee St., Dover, NH 03820 USA (SAN 860-2255) Tel 603-742-4162
E-mail: jim@mastromedia.com; info@newparadigmpublications.com
Web site: http://www.newparadigmpublications.com.

New Poets Series, Incorporated/Chestnut Hills Press/Stonewall *See* **BrickHouse Bks., Inc.**

New Pr., The, *(978-1-56584; 978-1-59558; 978-1-62097)* 38 Greene St., 4th Flr., New York, NY 10013 USA Tel 212 629 8802; Fax: 212 629 8617; Toll Free Fax: 800 458 6515; Toll Free: 800 233 4830
E-mail: newpress@thenewpress.com
Web site: http://www.thenewpress.com
Dist(s): **China Bks. & Periodicals, Inc.**
MyiLibrary
Perseus Bks. Group
Perseus Distribution
ebrary, Inc.

New Shelves Bks., *(978-1-935355)* Orders Addr.: 614 Fifth Ave, Troy, NY 12182 USA (SAN 857-3700) Tel 518-261-1300; Fax: 518-633-1211
Web site: http://www.newshelves.com.

New Shelves Distribution, 103 Remsen St., Cohoes, NY 12047 USA Tel 518-391-2300; Fax: 518-391-2365
Web site: http://www.newshelvesdistribution.com.

New Song Publishing Co., *(978-0-942925)* Div. of Al Menconi Ministries, Orders Addr.: P.O. Box 131147, Carlsbad, CA 92013 USA (SAN 667-8475) Tel 760-591-4696; Toll Free: 800-786-8742; Edit Addr.: 1635 S. Rancho Santa Fe Rd., Suite 105, San Marcos, CA 92069 USA (SAN 667-8483)
E-mail: patty@almenconi.com; al@almenconi.com
Web site: http://www.AlMenconi.com.

New Spectrum Incorporated *See* **Bay Otter Pr.**

New Star Bks., Ltd. (CAN) *(978-0-919573; 978-0-919888; 978-0-921586; 978-1-55420) Dist. by* **SPD-Small Pr Dist.**

New Strategist Pr., LLC, *(978-0-9628092; 978-1-885070; 978-1-933588; 978-1-935114; 978-1-935775; 978-1-937737; 978-1-940308)* Orders Addr.: P.O. Box 635, Amityville, NY 11701 USA Tel 631-608-8795; Edit Addr.: 26 Austin Ave., Amityville, NY 11701 USA (SAN 860-4002) Tel 800-848-0842; 631-608-8795; Fax: 631-691-1770
E-mail: accounting@newstrategist.com
Web site: http://www.newstrategist.com
Dist(s): **MyiLibrary.**

New Sweden Pr., *(978-0-9702646)* 10509 Schmidt Ln., Manor, TX 78653 USA Fax: 512-278-1251 Do not confuse with New Sweden Pr., South Saint Paul, MN
E-mail: shrout@mail.utexas.edu.

New Tribes Mission, Inc., *(978-1-890040; 978-1-61565)* 1000 E. First St., Sanford, FL 32771-1487 USA Tel 407-323-3430; Fax: 407-330-0376; 407-547-2450; Toll Free: 800-321-5375
E-mail: ntm@ntm.org; doug_lotz@ntm.org
Web site: http://www.ntm.org.

New Virginia Pubns., *(978-0-9755030)* 9185 Matthew Dr., Manassas Park, VA 20111 USA (SAN 256-0453) Tel 703-928-8316; Fax: 703-331-0577
E-mail: lab49@att.net.

New Vision Entertainment, LLC, *(978-0-9778310)* Orders Addr.: 30 Estuary Trail, Clearwater, FL 33759 USA
E-mail: jim@newvisionentertainment.us.

New Voices Publishing Co., *(978-1-931642)* Div. of KidsTerrain, Inc., P.O. Box 560, Wilmington, MA 01887 USA (SAN 253-9047) Tel 978-658-2131; Fax: 978-988-8833 Do not confuse with companies with the same or similar names in Sarasota, FL, Flushing, NY
E-mail: egilmartin@kidsterrain.com
Web site: http://www.newvoicespublishing.com; http://www.kidsterrain.com.

New Wave Bks. & CD, *(978-0-9727753; 978-0-9741493)* Orders Addr.: 7850 S. Normandie Ave., Apt. 69, Los Angeles, CA 90044 USA; Edit Addr.: 11050 Bryant St., No. 292, Yucaipa, CA 92399 USA.

New Wave Pubns., *(978-0-9749674; 978-0-9786660; 978-0-9800452)* 1419 New York Ave., Rm 3A, New York, NY 11210-1221 USA Do not confuse with New Wave Publications in Lincoln, NE.

†New Win Publishing, *(978-0-8329; 978-0-87691)* 9682 Telstar Ave., Suite 110, El Monte, CA 91731 USA (SAN 217-1201) Tel 626-448-4422; *Imprints:* Z Health Books (Z Hlth Bks)
E-mail: info@AcademicLearningCompany.com
Web site: http://www.newwinpublishing.com; *CIP.*

†New World Library, *(978-0-931432; 978-0-945934; 978-1-57731; 978-1-880032; 978-1-60868)* 14 Pamaron Way, Novato, CA 94949 USA (SAN 211-8777) Tel 415-884-2100; Fax: 415-884-2199; Toll Free: 800-972-6657 (retail orders only) Do not confuse with New World Library Publishing Co., Los Altos, CA
E-mail: escort@nwlib.com
Web site: http://www.newworldlibrary.com
Dist(s): **Brilliance Publishing**
Ebsco Publishing
Islander Group
Landmark Audiobooks
New Leaf Distributing Co., Inc.
Perseus-PGW; *CIP.*

New World Publishing, *(978-0-9771939; 978-0-9776818; 978-0-9787112; 978-0-9796815; 978-0-9821528)* 4540 State Rd., Cleveland, OH 44109 USA Tel 216-635-1671 Do not confuse with New World Publishing in Riverdale, GA, Scottsdale, AZ and Auburn, CA
E-mail: rkisner5@sbcglobal.net
Web site: http://www.silverquillpoetry.net.

New World Revelation Pr., *(978-0-9762105)* Orders Addr.: P.O. Box 839, Ellijay, GA 30540 USA Tel 706-635-7720; Fax: 706-635-8170
E-mail: fess1944@etcmail.com; office@awakeandlive.org
Web site: http://www.awakeandlive.org
Dist(s): **Lightning Source, Inc.**

New Worlds Press *See* **Institute for Economic Democracy Pr., Inc.**

New Year Publishing, *(978-0-9671565; 978-0-9760095; 978-0-9799885; 978-1-935547; 978-1-61431)* 144 Diablo Ranch Ct., Danville, CA 94506 USA Tel 925-348-0481; Fax: 425-984-7256 Do not confuse with New Year Publishing in Oceanside, CA
E-mail: dmorris@newyearpublishing.com
Web site: http://www.newyearpublishing.com
Dist(s): **Distributors, The**
Innovative Logistics.

New York Review of Bks., Inc., The, *(978-0-940322; 978-1-59017; 978-1-68137)* 435 Hudson St., 3rd Flr. Suite 300, New York, NY 10014 USA (SAN 220-3448) Tel 212-757-8070; Fax: 212-333-5374; *Imprints:* NYR Children's Collection (NY Rev Child); NYRB Classics (NYRB Class)
E-mail: mail@nybooks.com; nyrb@nybooks.com
Web site: http://www.nyrb.com
Dist(s): **MyiLibrary**
Penguin Random Hse., LLC.
Random Hse., Inc.

†New York Univ. Pr., *(978-0-8147; 978-1-4798)* Div. of New York Univ., Orders Addr.: 838 Broadway, 3rd Flr., New York, NY 10003-4812 USA (SAN 658-1293) Tel 212-998-2575; Fax: 212-995-3833; Toll Free: 800-996-6987 (ordering)
E-mail: orders@nyupress.org
Web site: http://www.nyupress.org
Dist(s): **CreateSpace Independent Publishing Platform**
Ebsco Publishing
ebrary, Inc.; *CIP.*

Newburyport Pr., *(978-1-882266)* Orders Addr.: P.O. Box 389, Newburyport, MA 01950 USA Tel 978-465-5751; Fax: 978-462-2043; Toll Free: 800-491-4700 (in Massachusetts only); Edit Addr.: 477 Commerce Blvd., Oldsmar, FL 34677-2809 USA
E-mail: mail@newburyportpress.com
Dist(s): **D.A.P./Distributed Art Pubs.**

Newburyport Press, Incorporated *See* **Newburyport Pr.**

NeWest Pubs., Ltd. (CAN) *(978-0-920316; 978-0-920897; 978-1-896300; 978-1-897126; 978-1-927063) Dist. by* **Strauss Cnslts.**

NewLife Publications *See* **Campus Crusade for Christ**

Newman Educational Publishers *See* **Newman Educational Publishing Co.**

Newman Educational Publishing Co., *(978-0-938990)* P.O. Box 461, Glen Ellyn, IL 60138 USA (SAN 239-8273) Tel 630-668-7027
E-mail: bizfootstep@aol.com
Web site: http://www.ugrr.illinois.com.

Newmark Learning LLC, *(978-1-60719; 978-1-61269; 978-1-4788)* 629 Fifth Ave., Pelham, NY 10803 USA Tel 1-877-279-8388; 1-877-280-0375
E-mail: bhaggerty@benchmarkeducation.com
Dist(s): **Follett School Solutions.**

Newmarket for It Bks. *Imprint of* **HarperCollins Pubs.**

†Newmarket Pr., *(978-0-937858; 978-1-55704)* Div. of Newmarket Publishing & Communications Corp., 18 E. 48th St., New York, NY 10017 USA (SAN 217-2585) Tel 212-832-3575; Fax: 212-832-3629; Toll Free Fax: 800-458-6515 (trade orders); Toll Free: 800-233-4830 (trade orders)
E-mail: mailbox@newmarketpress.com
Web site: http://www.newmarketpress.com
Dist(s): **MyiLibrary**
Perseus Bks. Group
Perseus Distribution
Worldwide Media Service, Inc.
ebrary, Inc.; *CIP.*

Newport Valley Pr, *(978-0-9778602)* P.O. Box 32, Solon, IA 52333-0032 USA Tel 319-351-8854.

NewSage Pr., LLC, *(978-0-939165)* Orders Addr.: P.O. Box 607, Troutdale, OR 97060-0607 USA (SAN 662-8370) Tel 503-695-2211
E-mail: info@newsagepress.com
Web site: http://www.newsagepress.com
Dist(s): **MyiLibrary**
Perseus-PGW
Perseus Bks. Group.

NewsChannelChurch *See* **Asiana Media**

NewSound, LLC, 81 Demeritt Pl., Waterbury, VT 05676 USA Tel 802-244-7858; Fax: 802-244-1808; Toll Free: 800-342-0295 (wholesale orders)
E-mail: sales@newsoundmusic.com.

NewSouth Bks. *Imprint of* **NewSouth, Inc.**

NewSouth, Inc., *(978-1-58838; 978-1-60306)* P.O. Box 1588, Montgomery, AL 36102-1588 USA Tel 334-834-3556; Fax: 334-834-3557; Toll Free: 866-639-7688; *Imprints:* NewSouth Books (NewSouth AL); Junebug Books (Junebug Bks)
E-mail: info@newsouthbooks.com
Web site: http://www.newsouthbooks.com
Dist(s): **Blair, John F. Pub.**
ebrary, Inc.

NewSouth Publishing (AUS) *(978-0-86840; 978-0-909465; 978-0-908237; 978-1-921410; 978-1-74223; 978-1-74224; 978-0-646-09872-2; 978-0-646-27463-8) Dist. by* **IPG Chicago.**

Newton, J. Britt *See* **Twelve Stones Publishing LLC**

Newtonian Golf & Particle Physics, Inc., *(978-0-9725355)* 107 Bordeaux Ln., Cary, NC 27511 USA Tel 919-469-0180
E-mail: sales@saintmulligan.com
Web site: http://www.stmulligan.com.

New-York Historical Society, *(978-0-916141)* Two W. 77th St., New York, NY 10024 USA (SAN 294-975X) Tel 212-873-3400
Dist(s): **Ingram Pub. Services.**

Next Century Publishing, *(978-0-9791957; 978-0-9824967; 978-0-9826665; 978-1-936417; 978-1-939268; 978-1-62903)* 317 Appaloosa Trl., Woodway, TX 76712-8816 USA.

Next Chapter Pr., *(978-0-9816265)* P.O. Box 1937, Boca Grande, FL 33921 USA.

Next Generation Pr., *(978-0-9762706; 978-0-9815595)* P.O. Box 603252, Providence, RI 02906 USA Tel 401-247-7665; Fax: 401-245-6428
E-mail: info@nextgenerationpress.org
Web site: http://www.nextgenerationpress.org.

Next Step Magazine, Inc., The, *(978-0-9752926)* 86 W. Main St., Victor, NY 14564 USA Tel 585-742-1260; Fax: 585-742-1263; Toll Free: 800-771-3117
Web site: http://www.nextstepmagazine.com.

Next Step Pr., *(978-1-892876)* Sub. of New Wisdom, Inc., 1201 Delta Glen Ct., Vienna, VA 22182-1320 USA Tel 703-757-7945; Fax: 703-757-7946
E-mail: Wyattwooodsmall@compuserve.com
Web site: http://www.peoplepatterns.com; http://www.mindcoach.org.

Nextpos Corporation *See* **Aldelo Systems Inc.**

NF Publishing *See* **SouthWest Pubns.**

Nia Publishing Company, Incorporated *See* **Urban Spirit!**

Nicco Boss, LLC, *(978-0-9891635)* 524 Cala Morlanda St., Las Vegas, NV 89138 USA Tel 702-595-4884
E-mail: niccoboss@yahoo.com.

Nicewood Imagined, *(978-0-9720334)* 6823 NW 52nd Ln., Gainesville, FL 32653 USA Tel 352-271-3306 (phone/fax)
E-mail: nicewoodimagined@yahoo.com
Web site: http://www.macecora.com.

Niche Publishing & Marketing, *(978-0-9726628)* 3310 Bexley Park Rd., Columbus, OH 43213 USA Tel 614-338-0783
E-mail: sairapriest@me.com; svpmba@aol.com
Web site: http://www.nativenature.us.

NicheMarket.com *See* **Passion Profit Co., The/NicheMarket**

Nicho The Tiger LLC, *(978-0-9820801)* 43-31 223 St., Bayside, NY 11361 USA Tel 347-853-2694.

Nick Of Time Media, Inc., *(978-1-940775)* 8661 NW 16th St., Pembroke Pines, FL 33024 USA Tel 888-540-7593
E-mail: Bsamarel33414@yahoo.com
Web site: http://www.nickoftime.us.

Nick The Cat, LLC, *(978-1-936193)* 26541 Dundee Rd., Huntington Woods, MI 48070 USA Tel 313-570-7996
Dist(s): **AtlasBooks Distribution.**

Nickel Pr., *(978-1-57122; 978-1-879424)* Div. of S.R. Jacobs & Assocs., 107 Knob Hill Pk. Dr., Reisterstown, MD 21136 USA Do not confuse with Nickel Press, Inc., Enterprise, AL.

Nicolin Fields Publishing, Inc., *(978-0-9637077; 978-1-892066)* 861 Lafayette Rd., Unit 2A, Hampton, NH 03842-1232 USA Toll Free: 800-431-1579 (orders only)
E-mail: nfp@nh.ultranet.com
Web site: http://www.nicolinfields.com
Dist(s): **Alpenbooks Pr. LLC**
Peregrine Outfitters
Quality Bks., Inc.
Univ. Pr. of New England.

Nicoll Creations, *(978-0-9747527)* 5608 Evergreen, Midland, MI 48642 USA Tel 989-839-8293
E-mail: hgnicoll@sbcglobal.net.

Nicolo Whimsey Pr., *(978-1-935550)* 14411 Baden Westwood Rd., Brandywine, MD 20613 USA
Dist(s): **Consortium Bk. Sales & Distribution**
MyiLibrary
Perseus Bks. Group.

Nicolosi, Gaetano, *(978-0-9763828)* 74 W. Fountain Ave., Delaware, OH 43015-1629 USA
E-mail: ciaogaetano@yahoo.com.

Nielsen, Lester *See* **Eaglesquest Publishing**

Nieves (CHE) *(978-3-905714) Dist. by* **Dist Art Pubs.**

Night After Night Pubns., Inc. *Imprint of* **Hebler, Michael**

Night Howl Productions, *(978-0-9702176)* P.O. Box 1, Clay Center, NE 68933 USA Tel 402-984-2566
E-mail: dirtytricksforchicks@yahoo.com
Dist(s): **AK Pr. Distribution.**

Night Light Pubns., LLC, *(978-0-9740418; 978-0-9743785)* 6101 E. Wethersfield Rd., Scottsdale, AZ 85254 USA Tel 480-948-2607; Fax: 480-948-9921
E-mail: reg@nightlightpublications.com
Web site: http://www.nightlightpublications.com.

Night Sky Bks., *(978-1-59014)* Div. of North-South Books, Inc., 11 E. 26th St., 17th Fr., New York, NY 10010 USA Tel 212-706-4545; Fax: 212-706-4546; Toll Free: 800-282-8257 Do not confuse with companies with the same name in Santa Fe, NM
E-mail: nightsky@northsouth.com
Web site: http://www.northsouth.com
Dist(s): **Ingram Pub. Services**
Lectorum Pubns., Inc.

Night Sky, LLC, *(978-0-9888901)* 4 Buckskin Heights Dr., Danbury, CT 06811 USA Tel 203-826-9690
E-mail: jrivot@yahoo.com.

Nightengale Pr., *(978-0-9743348; 978-0-9761289; 978-1-933449; 978-1-935993)* Div. of Nightengale Media LLC, 370 S. Lowe Ave. Suite A-122, Cookeville, TN 38501 USA Tel 931-854-1390; Fax: 866-830-2624
E-mail: publisher@nightengalepress.com
Web site: http://www.nightengalepress.com; http://www.nightengalepublishing.com.

Nightwood Editions (CAN) *(978-0-88971) Dist. by* **IngramPubServ.**

NIIS Publishing, *(978-0-9745013; 978-0-615-11294-7)* 7349 Milliken, No. 140164, Rancho Cucamonga, CA 91730 USA.

Nile Publishing, *(978-0-9768485)* 213 Hancock St., Brooklyn, NY 11216 USA Tel 718-810-1148 Do not confuse with Nile PUblishing in Cincinnati, OH
E-mail: wale1@hotmail.com.

Nilsson Media, *(978-0-9724771)* Box 1371, Brentwood, TN 37024-1371 USA Tel 615-776-2593; Fax: 615-776-3193; Toll Free: 888-801-5190; *Imprints:* Nilsson, Troy (Troy Nilsson)
E-mail: books@nilssonmedia.org
Web site: http://www.nilssonmedia.com.

Nilsson, Troy *Imprint of* **Nilsson Media**

Nimble Bks. LLC, *(978-0-9754479; 978-0-9765406; 978-0-9777424; 978-0-9788138; 978-0-9799205; 978-1-934840; 978-1-60888)* 1521 Martha Ave., Ann Arbor, MI 48103 USA
E-mail: wfz@nimblebooks.com
Web site: http://www.nimblebooks.com
Dist(s): **Smashwords.**

Nimbus Publishing, Ltd. (CAN) *(978-0-919380; 978-0-920852; 978-0-921054; 978-1-55109; 978-1-77108) Dist. by* **Orca Bk Pub.**

Ninety & Nine Records *See* **Blooming Twig Books LLC**

Ninos Aprenden Ingles Corp., *(978-1-934665)* 15476 NW 77 Ct., No. 360, Miami Lakes, FL 33016 USA (SAN 854-249X)
E-mail: ar@childrenlearninglanguages.com
Web site: http://www.ChildrenLearningLanguages.com.

Ninth Planet Pr., *(978-0-615-41386-0; 978-0-615-54486-1; 978-0-615-60901-0; 978-0-692-26010-4; 978-0-692-41572-6)* 402 Buckeye Trail, Austin, TX 78746 USA Tel 512-330-1726; Fax: 512-289-0595; 909 Live Oak Ridge Rd., Austin, TX 78746
E-mail: bmccandless@austin.rr.com.

Nistraman Consulting, *(978-0-9706387)* P.O. Box 1314, Brookline, MA 02446 USA
E-mail: alex_belenky@lycos.com.

Nithyananda Univ., *(978-0-9790806; 978-1-934364; 978-1-60607)* 9720 Central Ave., Montclair, CA 91763 USA Tel 909-625-1400
E-mail: galleriaorders@yahoo.com
Web site: http://www.lifeblissfoundation.org.

Nithyananda Yoga & Meditation University *See* **Nithyananda Univ.**

NJL College Preparation, *(978-0-9753913)* 880 Willis Ave., Albertson, NY 11507 USA Tel 516-741-3550
E-mail: njlcp@aol.com
Dist(s): **Topical Review Bk Co., Inc.**

NJM *See* **Allen-Ayers Bks.**

nJoy Bks., *(978-0-9769959)* Orders Addr.: 18 S. 2nd St., Madison, WI 53704 USA
E-mail: office@njoybooks.com
Web site: http://www.njoybooks.com.

NK nPrint *See* **nVision Publishing**

NK Pubns., *(978-0-9705100; 978-0-9841610)* P.O. Box 1735, New York, NY 10101-1735 USA
E-mail: nkatsoris@aol.com
Dist(s): **Michigan State Univ. Pr.**
Midpoint Trade Bks., Inc.

NLAlex Publishing *See* **Joe Girl Ink**

NMS Enterprises Ltd. - Publishing (GBR) *(978-0-948636; 978-0-900733; 978-1-901663; 978-1-905267) Dist. by* **Natl Bk Netwk.**

No Dream Too Big LLC, *(978-0-9745717; 978-0-9838415)* Div. of AsAMan Thinketh.net LLC, P.O. Box 1220, Melrose, FL 32666 USA
E-mail: ebooks@asamanthinketh.net
Web site: http://www.asamanthinketh.net
Dist(s): **CreateSpace Independent Publishing Platform.**

No Frills Buffalo, *(978-0-578-04711-9; 978-0-578-08224-0; 978-0-615-48945-2; 978-0-615-51315-7; 978-0-615-54031-3; 978-0-615-56207-0; 978-0-615-58847-6; 978-0-615-59426-2; 978-0-615-61034-4; 978-0-615-62237-8; 978-0-615-62696-3; 978-0-615-66171-1; 978-0-615-66520-7; 978-0-615-66821-5; 978-0-615-70800-3; 978-0-615-70801-0; 978-0-615-72411-9; 978-0-615-72567-3; 978-0-615-75542-7; 978-0-615-75973-9; 978-0-615-78493-9; 978-0-615-78813-5; 978-0-615-81005-8; 978-0-615-81239-7; 978-0-615-82396-6; 978-0-615-83012-4)* 119 Dorchester, Buffalo, NY 14213 USA
E-mail: contact@nofrillsbuffalo.com
Web site: http://nofrillsbuffalo.com
Dist(s): **CreateSpace Independent Publishing Platform**
Lightning Source, Inc.

No Frills Press Buffalo *See* **No Frills Buffalo**

No Greater Joy Ministries, Inc., *(978-1-892112; 978-0-9786372; 978-1-934794; 978-1-935370; 978-1-61644)* 1000 Pearl Rd., Pleasantville, TN 37033 USA (SAN 914-5958) Toll Free: 866-292-9936
E-mail: ngj@nogreaterjoy.org; cjoyner@nogreaterjoy.org
Web site: http://www.nogreaterjoy.org
Dist(s): **AtlasBooks Distribution**
Follett School Solutions
MyiLibrary
Send The Light Distribution LLC
ebrary, Inc.

No Limits Communications, *(978-0-9712842)* P.O. Box 220, Horsham, PA 19044 USA Tel 215-675-9133; Fax: 215-675-9376.

No Limitz Productions, Inc., *(978-0-9766942)* 3257 Primera Ave., Los Angeles, CA 90068 USA Tel 323-876-7149
E-mail: nolimitz@aol.com
Web site: http://www.suzannelopez.com.

No Sand in the House!, *(978-0-615-81199-4)* 2695 Powell Creek Dr., Charlottesville, VA 22911 USA Tel 434-906-8680
Web site: www.nosandinthehouse.com
Dist(s): **CreateSpace Independent Publishing Platform.**

No Starch Pr., Inc., *(978-1-886411; 978-1-59327)* 555 De Haro St., Suite 250, San Francisco, CA 94107 USA Tel 415-863-9900; Fax: 415-863-9950; Toll Free: 800-420-7240 Do not confuse with No Starch Pr., in Berkeley, CA
E-mail: info@nostarch.com
Dist(s): **Ebsco Publishing**
Follett School Solutions
Ingram Pub. Services
O'Reilly Media, Inc.

No Voice Left Behind Publishing, *(978-0-9773513)* P.O. Box 1109, Ceres, CA 95307 USA Tel 209-968-3425
E-mail: fernando_pena@sbcglobal.net
Web site: http://www.nvlb.net.

N.O.A.H Bks., *(978-0-615-59068-4; 978-0-9859770)* 16022 Beechnut St., Houston, TX 77083 USA Tel 713-582-9153; Fax: 281-277-4298
E-mail: cheryl_hil@msn.com
Web site: http://www.empoweringchildrentoread.blogspot.com/.

Noah Educational Projects *See* **N.O.A.H Bks.**

Noble Hero Pr., *(978-0-9768410)* 3754 Salem Walk, No. A1, Northbrook, IL 60062 USA
E-mail: mike@nobleheropress.com
Web site: http://www.nobleheropress.com.

Noble, John A. Collection *See* **Noble Maritime Collection, The**

†Noble Maritime Collection, The, *(978-0-9623017)* 1000 Richmond Terr., Staten Island, NY 10301-1114 USA Tel 718-447-6490
E-mail: erinurban@earthlink.net; *CIP.*

Noble Publishing *See* **20/20 Publishing**

Noble Publishing Assocs., *(978-0-923463; 978-1-56857)* 1300 NE 131st Cir., Vancouver, WA 98685 USA (SAN 251-656X) Tel 360-258-3119; Fax: 360-258-3122; Toll Free: 800-225-5259; 1300 NE 131st St., Vancouver, WA 98685-3164
E-mail: noblebooks@noblepublishing.com
Web site: http://www.noblepublishing.com.

Nobrow Ltd. (GBR) *(978-1-907704; 978-0-9562135) Dist. by* **Consort Bk Sales.**

Nodin Pr., *(978-0-931714; 978-1-932472; 978-1-935666)* c/o The Bookmen, Inc., 530 N. Third St., Suite 120, Minneapolis, MN 55401 USA (SAN 204-398X) Tel 612-333-6300; Fax: 612-333-6303
Dist(s): **Adventure Pubns., Inc.**
Itasca Bks.

Noesis, Inc., *(978-0-9742091)* 10530 Linden Lake Plaza, Manassas, VA 20109 USA Tel 703-369-2924; Fax: 703-392-7978
E-mail: fstilley@noesis-inc.com
Web site: http://www.noesis-inc.com/drydockhistory.

Noesis Publishing, *(978-0-9794328)* Div. of Noesis Communications International, Orders Addr.: 4425 S., Mo Pac Expway Suite 600, Austin, TX 78735 USA Tel 512-891-6100 Greenleaf Book Group; Edit Addr.: 5777 W. Century Blvd., Suite 200, Los Angeles, CA 90045 USA Tel 310-645-5604 Noesis Publishing; 512-891-6100 Greenleaf Book Group; Fax: 310-215-3018 Noesis Publishing
E-mail: diana@cmsbiz.com; candice@greenleafbookgroup.com
Web site: http://noesispublishing.com; http://www.greenleafbookgroup.com; http://www.kandide.com
Dist(s): **Greenleaf Book Group.**

Noguer y Caralt Editores, S. A. (ESP) *(978-84-217; 978-84-279) Dist. by* **Lectorum Pubns.**

Noixia's Reading Circle, *(978-0-9749122)* 8002 Avenida Navidad, San Diego, CA 92122 USA Tel 858-550-9519
E-mail: contact@noixia.com
Web site: http://www.noixia.com.

Noller, Gail, *(978-0-9744877)* 1416 Oakwood Dr., Anoka, MN 55303 USA Tel 763-427-6897
E-mail: nolle005@tc.umn.edu.

Nomad Pr., *(978-0-9659258; 978-0-9722026; 978-0-9749344; 978-0-9771294; 978-0-9785037; 978-0-9792268; 978-1-934670; 978-1-936313; 978-1-936749; 978-1-61930)* Div. of Nomad Communications, Inc., 2456 Christian St., White River Junction, VT 05001 USA Tel 802-649-1995; Fax: 802-649-2667 Do not confuse with Nomad Pr., Clewiston, FL, Fort Collins, CO
E-mail: rachel@nomadcom.com; rachel@nomadpress.net
Web site: http://www.nomadpress.net
Dist(s): **Ebsco Publishing**
Follett School Solutions
Legato Pubs. Group
MyiLibrary
Perseus-PGW.

Nonetheless Pr., *(978-1-932053)* 20332 W. 98th St., Lenexa, KS 66220-2650 USA Tel 913-254-7266; Fax: 913-393-3245
E-mail: mschutte@nonethelesspress.com
Web site: http://www.nonethelesspress.com; http://www.lookingglasspress.com
Dist(s): **Bookazine Co., Inc.**
Brodart Co.
Greenleaf Book Group
Midwest Library Service.

Nonfiction Picture Bks. *Imprint of* **Picture Window Bks.**

Non-ISBN Publisher, 630 Central Ave., New Providence, NJ 07974 USA.

Noodle Holdings LLC, *(978-0-615-41968-8)* Rood Hill Farm 53 Rood Hill Rd., Sandisfield, MA 01255 USA
E-mail: hoover205@gmail.com
Web site: http://www.stevehooverauthor.com.

Noodle Pr., *(978-0-9601022)* Orders Addr.: P.O. Box 42542, Washington, DC 20015 USA; Edit Addr.: P.O. Box 42542, Washington, DC 20015 USA (SAN 208-7871) Tel 202-363-5078; Fax: 202-364-0090
E-mail: Noodlepress@aol.com.

Nooni Publishing, *(978-0-9796832)* 1211 Garden Lake Dr., Riverdale, GA 30296 USA
E-mail: Nooni-pub@hotmail.com.

Noor Foundation-International, *(978-0-9632067; 978-0-9766972; 978-1-942043)* P.O. Box 758, Hockessin, DE 19707 USA (SAN 854-3712) Tel 302-234-8860; Fax: 208-279-5341; Toll Free: 888-937-2665; 249 Peoples Way, Hockessin, DE 19707
E-mail: cyrusomar@hotmail.com; alnoorfoundation@hotmail.com
Web site: http://www.islamusa.org.

NooVoo Publishing LLC, *(978-0-9767513)* 28257 Thornybrae, Farmington Hills, MI 48331 USA Tel 248-762-4858
E-mail: glennrader@noovoo.com.

Nora Hse., *(978-0-9752958)* 9122 White Eagle Ct., Raleigh, NC 27617 USA
E-mail: oren2a@yahoo.com.

Norcor Enterprises, *(978-0-9622469)* 6147 N. Sheridan Rd., Chicago, IL 60660 USA Tel 773-743-6792
E-mail: norcorent@juno.com.

Nordic Studies Pr., *(978-0-9772714)* 5226 N. Sawyer, Chicago, IL 60625-4716 USA (SAN 257-1498) Tel 773-610-4283
E-mail: cpeterson@igc.org
Web site: http://www.nordicstudiespress.com.

Nordskog Publishing, Inc., *(978-0-9796736; 978-0-9824929; 978-0-9827074; 978-0-9831957; 978-0-9882976; 978-0-9903774)* Orders Addr.: 4562 Westinghouse St., Suite E, Ventura, CA 93003-5797 USA; Edit Addr.: 2716 Sailor Ave., Ventura, CA 93001 USA
E-mail: Jerry@NordskogPublishing.com; books@sendmethatbook.com
Web site: http://www.NordskogPublishing.com; http://www.SendMeThatBook.com
Dist(s): **Anchor Distributors**
Send The Light Distribution LLC.

Norfleet Pr., Inc., *(978-0-9649934)* 1 Gracie Ter. Apt. 4C, New York, NY 10028-7956 USA
Dist(s): **Continental Enterprises Group, Inc. (CEG)**
North Country Bks., Inc.

Noriiana Bks., *(978-1-934169; 978-1-934648; 978-1-60762)* Orders Addr.: P.O. Box 224, Highgate Center, VT 05459-0224 USA (SAN 851-8556); Edit Addr.: 145 Dubois Dr., Highgate Center, VT 05459-0224 USA; *Imprints*: YA Angst (YA Angst)
E-mail: service@noriiana.com; vnazarian@gmail.com
Web site: http://www.noriiana.com/
Dist(s): **Smashwords.**

NORKY AMERICA, *(978-0-9769209)* Orders Addr.: 4712 Admiralty Way, No. 614, Marina Del Rey, CA 90292 USA Tel 310-985-3039
Web site: http://www.norky.com.

Norma S.A. (COL) *(978-958-04; 978-958-45) Dist. by* **Continental Bk.**

Norma S.A. (COL) *(978-958-04; 978-958-45) Dist. by* **Distr Norma.**

Norma S.A. (COL) *(978-958-04; 978-958-45) Dist. by* **AIMS Intl.**

Norma S.A. (COL) *(978-958-04; 978-958-45) Dist. by* **Lectorum Pubns.**

Norman & Globus, Inc., *(978-1-886978)* Orders Addr.: P.O. Box 20533, El Sobrante, CA 94803 USA; Edit Addr.: 4130 Lakeside Dr., San Pablo, CA 94806-1941 USA
E-mail: info@electrowiz.com; drpenny@sciencewiz.com
Web site: http://www.electrowiz.com; http://www.sciencewiz.com.

Norman Bks., *(978-0-9708617)* 900 Euclid St., Suite 302, Santa Monica, CA 90403 USA Tel 310-899-9310; Fax: 503-961-9523
E-mail: normanbooks@adelphia.net
Web site: http://www.normanbooks.com
Dist(s): **Book Wholesalers, Inc.**
Follett School Solutions
Lectorum Pubns., Inc.
Iaconi, Mariuccia Bk. Imports
Quality Bks., Inc.
Rio Nuevo Pubs.
Sunbelt Pubns., Inc.

Nortex Pr. *Imprint of* **Eakin Pr.**

North American International, *(978-0-88265)* P.O. Box 251, Penn Laird, VA 22846 USA (SAN 202-9200) Tel 540-435-6454; *Imprints*: Fine Art Editions (Fine Art Edtns)
E-mail: naibooks@yahoo.com; naibooks@gmail.com
Web site: http://erniehippo.ecrater.com; http://finekidsbooks.webs.com; http://kidsbook.zoomshare.com.

North American Mission Board, SBC, *(978-1-59312)* 4200 North Point Pkwy, Alpharetta, GA 30022-4176 USA Tel 770-410-6100; Fax: 770-410-6051; Toll Free: 866-407-6262
E-mail: marketing@namb.net
Web site: http://www.namb.net.

North American Vexillological Assoc. (NAVA), *(978-0-9747728)* 101 Belair Dr., New Milford, CT 06776 USA
E-mail: tmealf@aol.com
Web site: http://www.nava.org.

†North Atlantic Bks., *(978-0-913028; 978-0-938190; 978-0-942941; 978-1-55643; 978-1-883319; 978-1-58394)* Div. of The Society of the Study of Native Art & Science, Orders Addr.: P.O. Box 12327, Berkeley, CA 94712 USA (SAN 203-1655) Fax: 510-559-8277; Toll Free: 800-337-2665 (orders only); Edit Addr.: 1435 4th St. # A, Berkeley, CA 94710-1335 USA; *Imprints*: Frog Limited (Frog Ltd)
E-mail: orders@northatlanticbooks.com
Web site: http://www.northatlanticbooks.com
Dist(s): **China Bks. & Periodicals, Inc.**
MyiLibrary
Nutri-Bks. Corp.
Penguin Random Hse., LLC.
Random Hse., Inc.
SPD-Small Pr. Distribution; *CIP.*

North Bay Bks., *(978-0-9725200; 978-0-9749098)* Orders Addr.: P.O. Box 21234, El Sobrante, CA 94820-1234 USA Tel 510-758-4276; Fax: 510-758-4659; Toll Free: 800-870-3194; Edit Addr.: 3110 Whitecliff Ct., Richmond, CA 94803 USA Do not confuse with companies with the same name in El Sobrante, CA, Richmond, CA
Web site: www.northbaybooks.com.

North Bks., *(978-0-939495; 978-1-58287)* P.O. Box 1277, Wickford, RI 02852 USA (SAN 663-4052) Tel 401-294-3682; Fax: 401-294-9491
E-mail: north@ids.net.

North Cape Pubns., Inc., *(978-1-882391)* P.O. Box 1027, Tustin, CA 92781 USA Tel 714-832-3621; Fax: 714-832-5302; Toll Free: 800-745-9714
E-mail: ncape@ix.netcom.com
Web site: http://www.northcapepubs.com.

North Carolina Division of Archives & History *See* **North Carolina Office of Archives & History**

North Carolina Office of Archives & History, *(978-0-86526)* Orders Addr.: Historical Publications Section 4622 Mail Service Ctr., Raleigh, NC 27699-4622 USA (SAN 203-7246) Tel 919-733-7442 ext. 223; Fax: 919-733-1439
Web site: http://www.ncpublications.com.

North Carolina State Univ. Humanities Extension Pubns./Program, *(978-1-881507; 978-1-885647)* North Carolina State Univ., Box 8101 026 Winston Hall, Raleigh, NC 27695 USA Tel 919-515-1334; Fax: 919-515-8738
Web site: http://www.ncsu.edu/chass/extension.

North Carolina Symphony Society, Inc., The, *(978-0-9618952)* 4361 Lassiter At North Hills A. Ste. 105, Raleigh, NC 27609-5781 USA (SAN 242-5378).

†North Country Bks., Inc., *(978-0-925168; 978-0-932052; 978-0-9601158; 978-1-59531)* 220 Lafayette Street, Utica, NY 13502 USA (SAN 110-828X) Tel 315-735-4877; Fax: (315) 738-4342
E-mail: ncbooks@verizon.net
Web site: http://www.northcountrybooks.com; *CIP.*

North Dakota Center for Distance Education *See* **State Historical Society of North Dakota**

North Dakota Institute for Regional Studies *See* **North Dakota State Univ., Institute for Regional Studies**

North Dakota State Univ., Institute for Regional Studies, *(978-0-911042)* Orders Addr.: P.O. Box 6050, Fargo, ND 58108-6050 USA (SAN 203-1574) Tel 701-231-8338; Fax: 701-231-1047
E-mail: cathy.heiraas@ndsu.edu; nancy.nelson@ndsu.edu
Web site: http://www.ndsu.edu/ahss/ndirs/publications
Dist(s): **Big River Distribution**
Partners Bk. Distributing, Inc.
Partners/West Book Distributors.

North Dakota State Univ. Libraries, *(978-0-9629777; 978-1-891193)* Orders Addr.: NDSU Dept 2080, Fargo, ND 58105-6050 USA Tel 701-231-8416; Fax: 701-231-7138; Edit Addr.: 1201 Albrecht Blvd., Fargo, ND 58105 USA
E-mail: michael.miller@ndsu.edu; jeremy.kopp@ndsu.edu
Web site: http://library.ndsu.edu/grhc/.

North Gap Publishing, *(978-0-9677379)* 636 Golden Hill St., Cheyenne, WY 82009 USA Tel 307-778-8761
E-mail: twalkwyo@hotmail.com.

North Light Bks. *Imprint of* **F&W Media, Inc.**

North Pole Chronicles, *(978-0-9636442)* 7306 Park Ln., Dallas, TX 75225-2462 USA Tel 214-696-1717; Fax: 214-696-5288.

North Pole Pr., *(978-0-9787129)* 537 Belle Ave., Sevierville, TN 37862 USA Tel 865-360-5565
E-mail: santa@santaclausunplugged.com; mrsclaus@santaclausunplugged.com
Web site: http://santaclausunplugged.com; http://santaclausstories.com.

North River Press, Incorporated *See* **North River Pr. Publishing Corp., The**

†North River Pr. Publishing Corp., The, *(978-0-88427)* P.O. Box 567, Great Barrington, MA 01230 USA (SAN 202-1048) Tel 413-528-0034 (phone/fax); Toll Free Fax: 800-266-5329; Toll Free: 800-486-2665
E-mail: agallagher@northriverpress.com
Web site: http://www.northriverpress.com; *CIP.*

North Shore Records, Inc., *(978-0-9746229)* Orders Addr.: P.O. Box 1035, Los Alamos, CA 93440 USA (SAN 257-3733) Tel 800-771-7531
E-mail: info@jacirae.com
Web site: http://www.winningromance.com; http://www.christmaswithlove.com; http://www.theindieguide.com; http://www.winningpoints.net; http://www.jacirae.com; http://www.thequeenofgreen.com; http://www.pennymeals.com.

North Star Press of Saint Cloud *See* **North Star Pr. of St. Cloud**

†North Star Pr. of St. Cloud, *(978-0-87839; 978-1-68201)* P.O. Box 451, Saint Cloud, MN 56302-0451 USA (SAN 203-7491) Tel 320-558-9062; Toll Free: 888-820-1636
E-mail: info@northstarpress.com
Web site: http://www.northstarpress.com
Dist(s): **Partners Bk. Distributing, Inc.**; *CIP.*

Northbooks, *(978-0-9653074; 978-0-9720604; 978-0-9789766; 978-0-9815193; 978-0-9830764; 978-0-9888954)* Orders Addr.: P.O. Box 671832, Chugiak, AK 99567 USA Tel 907-696-8973
E-mail: tg@northbooks.com
Web site: http://www.northbooks.com.

Northcote Hse. Publishers, Ltd. (GBR) *(978-0-7463) Dist. by* **CasemateAcad.**

†Northern Illinois Univ. Pr., *(978-0-87580; 978-1-60909)* 2280 Bethany Rd., DeKalb, IL 60115-2854 USA (SAN 202-8875) Tel 815-753-1826; Fax: 815-753-1845
E-mail: bberg@niu.edu
Web site: http://www.niu.edu/univ_press/
Dist(s): **Chicago Distribution Ctr.**; *CIP.*

Northern Publications, Incorporated *See* **Northern Publishing**

Northern Publishing, *(978-0-9639869; 978-0-9741684)* P.O. Box 871803, Wasilla, AK 99687 USA Tel 907-376-6474
E-mail: tony@tonyruss.com
Web site: http://www.tonyruss.com
Dist(s): **News Group, The**
Partners Bk. Distributing, Inc.
Partners/West Book Distributors.

Northern Speech Services, *(978-0-9708947; 978-0-9761967; 978-0-9765497; 978-0-9785581; 978-0-9799245; 978-0-9823449; 978-1-935578)* 325 Meecher Rd., Gaylord, MI 49735 USA Toll Free Fax: 888-696-9655; Toll Free: 888-337-3866; P.O. Box 1247, Gaylord, MI 49734
E-mail: tslominski@nss-nrs.com
Web site: http://www.nss-nrs.com
Dist(s): **BookBaby.**

Northern State Univ. Pr., *(978-1-883120)* Div. of NSU Foundation, Orders Addr.: Northern State Univ. 1200 S Jay St, Aberdeen, SD 57401 USA.

Northern Virginia Writing Project, *(978-0-9759524)* GMU, MSN3E4, 4400 University Dr., Fairfax, VA 22030 USA Tel 703-993-1168; Fax: 703-993-1184
E-mail: sbaker@gmu.edu; contact@nvwp.org
Web site: http://www.nvwp.org.

Northfield Publishing, *(978-1-881273)* Div. of Moody Pr., 215 W. Locust, Chicago, IL 60610 USA (SAN 297-6404) Tel 312-329-2110; Fax: 312-329-8062; Toll Free: 800-678-8001
E-mail: michele.forrider@moody.edu
Web site: http://www.moodypublishers.com
Dist(s): **Moody Pubs.**

Northland Press *See* **Northland Publishing**

†Northland Publishing, *(978-0-87358)* Div. of Rowman & Littlefield Publishing Group, Orders Addr.: P.O. Box 15200 NBN Way, Blue Ridge Summit, PA 17214 USA Tel 301-459-3366; Fax: 301-429-5745; Toll Free Fax: 800-338-4550; Toll Free: 800-462-6420; *Imprints*: Rising Moon Books for Young Readers (Rising Moon Bks); Luna Rising (Luna Rising) Do not confuse with companies with the same or similar name in Menomonie, WI, Cleveland, OH
E-mail: dbreier@nbnbooks.com
Dist(s): **Fujii Assocs.**
Lectorum Pubns., Inc.
Libros Sin Fronteras
Learning Connection, The
National Bk. Network; *CIP.*

Northlight Communications, Inc. *See* **Sign2Me Early Learning / Northlight Communications, Inc.**

Northopolis, *(978-0-615-69125-1; 978-0-9898090)* 1105 Jasmine, Weslaco, TX 78596 USA Tel 956-373-1134
E-mail: rbanda@gmail.com
Web site: www.northopolis.com.

Northshire Pr., *(978-1-60571)* Orders Addr.: P.O. Box 2200, Manchester Center, VT 05255 USA; Edit Addr.: 4869 Main St., Manchester Center, VT 05255 USA Tel 802-362-3565; Fax: 802-362-1233; *Imprints*: Shires Press (Shires Pr)
Web site: http://www.northshire.com/printondemand.

†North-South Bks., Inc., *(978-0-7358; 978-1-55858; 978-1-58717)* 350 7th Ave. Rm. 1400, New York, NY 10001-5013 USA; *Imprints*: Michael Neugebauer Books (M Neugebauer Bks)
E-mail: mnavarro@northsouth.com
Web site: http://www.northsouth.com
Dist(s): **Continental Bk. Co., Inc.**
Ingram Pub. Services
Lectorum Pubns., Inc.
Libros Sin Fronteras; *CIP.*

Northstar Entertainment Group, LLC, *(978-0-9741544)* 9009 Danwood Manor Ter., Richmond, VA 23227-1269 USA; *Imprints*: Baby Faye Books (Baby Faye)
E-mail: northstarent2003@yahoo.com
Web site: http://www.northstarent.net.

Northwestern Publishing Hse., *(978-0-8100)* 2949 N. Mayfair Rd., Suite 200, Milwaukee, WI 53222 USA (SAN 206-7943) Tel 414-454-2100; Fax: 414-454-2170
E-mail: kuehlt@nph.wels.net; johnsonr@nph.wels.net
Web site: http://www.nph.net.

Northwestern Univ. Pr., *(978-0-8101)* Orders Addr.: c/o Univ. of Chicago Pr. Distribution Ctr., 11030 S. Langley Ave., Chicago, IL 60628 USA Tel 773-568-1550; Fax: 773-660-2235; Toll Free Fax: 800-621-8476; Toll Free: 800-621-2736; Edit Addr.: 629 Noyes St., Evanston, IL 60208-4210 USA (SAN 202-5787) Tel 847-491-5313; 847-491.2046; Fax: 847-491-8150
E-mail: nupress@northwestern.edu
Web site: http://www.nupress.northwestern.edu
Dist(s): **Chicago Distribution Ctr.**
MyiLibrary
Random Hse., Inc.
Univ. of Chicago Pr.
ebrary, Inc.

Northwind Sailing, Inc., *(978-0-9752700)* P.O. Box 973, Grand Marais, MN 55604-0973 USA.

NorthWord Bks. for Young Readers *Imprint of* **T&N Children's Publishing**

Norton, Frances M., *(978-0-9632938)* 1012 N. Wheaton Ave., Wheaton, IL 60187 USA Tel 630-665-0249.

†Norton, W. W. & Co., Inc., *(978-0-393; 978-1-324)* Orders Addr.: c/o National Book Company, 800 Keystone Industrial Pk., Scranton, PA 18512 USA (SAN 157-1869) Tel 570-346-2020; Fax: 570-346-1442; Toll Free: 800-233-4830; Edit Addr.: 500 Fifth Ave., New York, NY 10110-0017 USA (SAN 202-5795) Tel 212-354-5500; Fax: 212-869-0856; Toll Free: 800-223-2584
Web site: http://www.wwnorton.com
Dist(s): **Penguin Random Hse., LLC.**
US PubRep, Inc.; *CIP.*

Norvik Pr. (GBR) *(978-1-870041) Dist. by* **Dufour.**

Norwen Pubns., *(978-0-9852869)* 820 West Shore Dr., Culver, IN 46511 USA.

Norwood Hse. Pr., *(978-1-59953; 978-1-60357)* Orders Addr.: P.O. Box 316598, Chicago, IL 60631 USA (SAN 257-1552) Tel 773-467-0837; Fax: 773-467-9686
E-mail: customerservice@norwoodhousepress.com
Web site: http://www.norwoodhousepress.com
Dist(s): **Follett School Solutions.**

Nosy Crow *Imprint of* **Candlewick Pr.**

Not Available Books *Imprint of* **Not Available Comics**

Not Available Comics, *(978-0-9744767)* Orders Addr.: 2627 Pulaski St., Hamtramck, MI 48212 USA; *Imprints*: Not Available Books (NotAvailBks)
E-mail: feazell038@comcast.net
Web site: http://www.cynicalman.com.

Not Home Yet Publishing, *(978-0-615-20928-9; 978-0-615-21258-6)* 8 Catamount Ln., Littleton, CO 80127 USA Tel 303-972-0895
E-mail: nothomeyetmin@msn.com.

Note.Well.Pubs., *(978-0-9744793)* Orders Addr.: 1001 N. Ave., Highland Park, IL 60035 USA Tel 847-432-3736; Fax: 847-432-3272
E-mail: alias9@sbcglobal.net; alias36@gmail.com
Web site: http://www.charliesbooks.com.

Notgrass Co., *(978-1-933410; 978-1-60999)* Orders Addr.: 370 S Lowe Ave., Suite A PMB 211, Cookeville, TN 38501 USA Tel 800-211-8793; Fax: 800-891-8335; Toll Free: 800-211-8793
E-mail: books@notgrass.com
Web site: http://www.notgrass.com
Dist(s): **BookBaby.**

NouSoma Communications, Inc., *(978-0-9743604)* 35 Founders Way, Downingtown, PA 19335-4520 USA Tel 610-458-1580; Fax: 610-458-1556; *Imprints*: GIRLS KNOW HOW (Girls Know How)
Web site: http://www.nousoma.com
Dist(s): **Book Wholesalers, Inc.**
Brodart Co.

Nova Blue, Inc., *(978-0-9725584)* 14403 Little Blue Rd., Kansas City, MO 64136 USA Tel 816-737-8895
E-mail: novablueco@aol.com.

Nova Media, Inc., *(978-0-9618567; 978-1-884239)* 1724 N. State St., Big Rapids, MI 49307-9073 USA (SAN 668-0372) Tel 231-796-4637 (phone/fax)
E-mail: trund@netonecom.net
Web site: http://www.novamediainc.com.

Nova Pr., *(978-0-9637371; 978-1-889057; 978-0-692-38359-9)* Orders Addr.: 9058 Lloyd Pl., West Hollywood, CA 90069 USA (SAN 858-8317) Tel 310-275-3513; Fax: 310-281-5629; Toll Free: 800-949-6175
E-mail: novapress@aol.com
Web site: http://www.novapress.net
Dist(s): **CreateSpace Independent Publishing Platform**
Ebsco Publishing
ebrary, Inc.

†Nova Science Pubs., Inc., *(978-0-941743; 978-1-56072; 978-1-59033; 978-1-59454; 978-1-60021; 978-1-60456; 978-1-60692; 978-1-60741; 978-1-60876; 978-1-61668; 978-1-61728; 978-1-61761; 978-1-61122; 978-1-61209; 978-1-61324; 978-1-61470; 978-1-62100; 978-1-61942; 978-1-62081; 978-1-62257; 978-1-62417; 978-1-62618; 978-1-62808; 978-1-62948; 978-1-63117; 978-1-63321; 978-1-63463; 978-1-63482; 978-1-63483; 978-1-63484; 978-1-63485)* *400 Oser Ave., Suite 1600, Hauppauge, NY 11788-3619 USA (SAN 666-0266)*
E-mail: novascience@earthlink.net; novapublishers@earthlink.net; suzy@novapublishers.com; nova.main@novapublishers.com; cathy@novapublishers.com
Web site: http://www.novapublishers.com
Dist(s): **Ebsco Publishing**
ebrary, Inc.; *CIP.*

Novanglus Publishing, LLC, *(978-0-9837186)* Orders Addr.: 15 E. Putnam Avenue, No. 232, Greenwich, CT 06830 USA (SAN 920-4504) Tel 203-885-7476; 15 E. Putnam Ave., #232, Greenwich, CT 06830 Tel 203-885-7476; Fax: 203-724-1867
E-mail: mpeacockphd@gmail.com; michelle@novanglusphublishing.com
Web site: http://www.novanglusphublishing.com; http://fairandsquarebook.com.

Novel Units, Inc., *(978-1-56137; 978-1-58130; 978-1-60878)* Orders Addr.: 2709 Bulverde Rd., Bulverde, TX 78163 USA (SAN 253-9276) Tel 830-438-4262; Fax: 830-438-4263; Toll Free Fax: 877-688-3226; Toll Free: 800-688-3224; P.O. Box 97, Bulverde, TX 78163-0097
E-mail: editors@educyberstor.com
Web site: http://www.educyberstor.com
Dist(s): **Lectorum Pubns., Inc.**
Perma-Bound Bks.

Novello & Co., Ltd. (GBR) *(978-0-85360) Dist. by* **H Leonard.**

Novello Festival Pr., *(978-0-9708972; 978-0-9760963; 978-0-9815192; 978-0-615-15969-0; 978-0-615-16624-7)* Div. of Public Library of Charlotte & Mecklenburg County, 310 N. Tryon St., Charlotte, NC 28202 USA (SAN 254-3206) Tel 704-416-0706
Dist(s): **Blair, John F. Pub.**

Novosel, Scott, *(978-0-9768353)* P.O. Box 541, Lawrence, KS 66044 USA.

Now Age Knowledge, *(978-0-9729259)* Orders Addr.: 8315 Lake City Way, NE, Seattle, WA 98115 USA; Edit Addr.: 16626 6th Ave. W. #m301, Lynnwood, WA 98037 USA (SAN 255-2876) Do not confuse with Awaken Publishing in Houston, TX
E-mail: nowageknowledge@gmail.com
Web site: http://nowageknowledge.com.

Nowata Press Publishing Consultants, *(978-0-615-21595-2; 978-0-692-00130-1; 978-0-692-01778-4; 978-0-615-81419-3;*

Publisher Name Index

978-0-9907950) 1338 Old Coach Road, SW, Marietta, GA 30008 USA
E-mail: dmyles3784@yahoo.com
Web site: http://nowatapress.wordpress.com/.

NPG Newspapers, Inc., *(978-0-9724933)* Orders Addr.: P.O. Box 29, St Joseph, MO 64502-0029 USA Tel 816-271-8500; Fax: 816-271-8631; Toll Free: 800-779-6397; Edit Addr.: 825 Edmond St., St Joseph, MO 64502-0029 USA
E-mail: brucek@npgco.com.

NQSBks., *(978-0-9793168)* 477 Brentview Hills Dr., Nashville, TN 37220 USA Tel 615-832-1125
E-mail: nqsbooks@comcast.net
Web site: http://www.nqsbooks.com.

NRG Pubns., *(978-0-9741647)* 3510 Plum Brook, Missouri City, TX 77459 USA
E-mail: info@nrgpublications.com
Web site: http://www.nrgpublications.com.

NRS Enterprises, *(978-0-615-27983-1)* 2237 NW. Terr. Pines Dr., Bend, OR 97701 USA.

NSR Pubns., *(978-0-9761724)* 1482 51st Rd., Douglass, KS 67039 USA Tel 620-986-5472; Toll Free: 866-677-2624
E-mail: gumm@wheatstate.com
Web site: http://www.nsrpublications.com.

NT Publishing, L.L.C., *(978-0-9741864; 978-0-9787123)* P.O. Box 461540, Aurora, CO 80047 USA Tel 303-484-1071; Fax: 303-484-1072
E-mail: questions@ntpublishing.net
Web site: http://www.ntpublishing.net.

NTC/Contemporary Publishing Company *See* **McGraw-Hill/Contemporary**

Nu Energy Horizons *See* **SonoMagnetics**

NUA Multimedia, *(978-0-9777573)* Orders Addr.: 15480 Annapolis Rd., Suite 202, No. 422, Bowie, MD 20715 USA Tel 410-710-2700
E-mail: pr@nuamultimedia.com; orders@nuamultimedia.com
Web site: http://www.soniahayes.com
Dist(s): **Brodart Co.**
Follett School Solutions.

NuAngel, Inc., *(978-0-9626614)* 14717 Friend Rd., Athens, AL 35611 USA Tel 256-729-5000; Fax: 256-729-5111
E-mail: sales@nuangel.com
Web site: www.nuangel.com.

NuBaby, Incorporated *See* **NuAngel, Inc.**

Nubiangodess Publishing, *(978-0-9744291)* P.O. Box 12224, Columbus, GA 31917-2224 USA
E-mail: ngpublishing@cs.com; admin@nubiangodesspublishing.com
Web site: http://www.nubiangodesspublishing.com.

Nubiano Project, Inc., The, *(978-0-9762837)* P.O. Box 371, Chapel Hill, NC 27514 USA
E-mail: info@thenubianoproject.com.

Nude Son Publishing *See* **Canoed Sun Publishing, LLC**

Nuevo Bks., *(978-1-936745)* 925 Salamanca NW, Los Ranchos, NM 87107 USA Tel 505-344-9382; Fax: 505-345-5129
E-mail: paul@nmsantos.com
Web site: www.NuevoBooks.com.

Nuf-Love Publishing, *(978-0-9636109)* P.O. Box 120976, Clermont, FL 34712 USA
E-mail: ashersbooks@earthlink.net
Web site: http://www.ashersbooks.com.

Nui Media & Entertainment, LLC, *(978-0-9817388)* P.O. Box 364, Santa Monica, CA 90406 USA
E-mail: publishing@nui.com.

NumbersAlive! Pr., *(978-0-9853667)* 975 F St., NW., Washington, DC 20004-1454 USA Tel 202-652-1820; Fax: 202-667-5793
E-mail: rebecca@numbersalive.org
Web site: http://www.numbersalive.org.

Nu-Nature, *(978-0-9759008)* 858 Heritage Valley Rd., Norcross, GA 30093 USA Tel 404-376-8917
E-mail: nunatureinfo@aol.com
Web site: http://www.nu-nature.com.

Nunes, H. William, *(978-0-9646934; 978-0-9787994)* 3029 Mark Trail, Glen Carbon, IL 62034 USA Tel 618-288-5185; Fax: 618-205-3053
E-mail: bnunesbook@aol.com
Dist(s): **Big River Distribution**
Partners Bk. Distributing, Inc.

Nunes Productions, LLC, *(978-0-9748142)* 1314 Fairmont St., NW, Washington, DC 20009 USA Tel 202-387-1314; *Imprints:* Brand Nu Words (Brand Nu)
E-mail: charisse@nunesproductions.com
Web site: http://www.nunesproductions.com; http://www.brandnuwords.com
Dist(s): **Independent Pubs. Group.**

Nur Pubns., *(978-0-9764947)* Orders Addr.: 562 Sawmill River Rd., Millwood, NY 10546 USA
E-mail: s_nadimi@yahoo.com
Web site: http://www.nurpublications.com.

Nurse, Lesley *See* **Lion Prints Publishing**

Nursery Bks., *(978-0-9894505)* 119 Old Chester Rd., Haddam, CT 06438 USA Tel 860-308-4303
E-mail: sophie.helenek@gmail.com
Web site: www.nurserybooks.net.

Nurturing Your Children Pr., *(978-0-9767198)* P.O. Box 5066, Larkspur, CA 94977-5066 USA Tel 415-927-4839 (phone/fax)
E-mail: nurturingpress@aol.com
Web site: http://nurturingyourchildren.com
Dist(s): **Independent Pubs. Group.**

Nutrishare Publishing, *(978-0-9746116)* 10519 E. Stockton Blvd., Suite 110, Elk Grove, CA 95624 USA.

Nutshell Publishing *See* **Enisen Publishing**

NuVision Pubns., LLC, *(978-1-932681; 978-1-59547; 978-1-61536)* 1504 E. 70th St N., Sioux Falls, SD 57104-9429 USA
E-mail: sales@nuvisionpublications.com
Web site: http://www.nuvisionpublications.com
Dist(s): **CreateSpace Independent Publishing Platform**
Lightning Source, Inc.

Nvision Publishing *Imprint of* **Power Play Media**

nVision Publishing, *(978-0-9766086)* Div. of Written by Nicole Kearney Enterprises, P.O. Box 88731, Indianapolis, IN 46208 USA Tel 317-724-8926
E-mail: nicoleckearney@yahoo.com
Web site: http://www.nicolekearney.com.

NY Media Works, LLC, *(978-0-9890914)* 112 Franklin St. First Flr., New York, NY 10013 USA (SAN 920-5187) Tel 646-369-5681
E-mail: jgribble@nymediaworks.com
Web site: http://www.nymediaworks.com
Dist(s): **Brodart Co.**
Quality Bks., Inc.

Nye Products, *(978-0-9746665)* P.O. Box 177, Wexford, PA 15090-0177 USA Tel 724-935-8710
E-mail: nyeproducts@stargate.net
Web site: http://nyeproducts.com; http://www.beverlynye.com/.

NYR Children's Collection *Imprint of* **New York Review of Bks., Inc., The**

NYRB Classics *Imprint of* **New York Review of Bks., Inc., The**

NyreePr. Literary Group, *(978-0-615-76536-5; 978-0-9890039; 978-0-615-83176-3; 978-0-9910489; 978-0-9915412; 978-0-9903486; 978-0-9906662; 978-0-9909652; 978-0-9860866)* 4809 Pemberton Ln., The Colony, TX 75056 USA Tel 972-793-3736
E-mail: info@nyreepress.com
Web site: www.nyreepress.com.

OSS Publishing Co., *(978-0-9660286)* Orders Addr.: P.O. Box 610, White Plains, NY 10603 USA Tel 914-946-6521; Fax: 914-949-5380; Toll Free: 888-677-6521
E-mail: OSSpublishing@att.net
Web site: http://www.osspublishing.com.

Oak Court Pr., *(978-0-9767696)* 34612 Oak Ct., Elizabeth, CO 80107 USA Tel 303-703-6633
E-mail: oakcourtpress@msn.com.

†Oak Knoll Pr., *(978-0-938768; 978-1-884718; 978-1-58456; 978-1-872116)* 310 Delaware St., New Castle, DE 19720 USA (SAN 216-2776) Tel 302-328-7232; Fax: 302-328-7274; Toll Free: 800-996-2556 Do not confuse with Oak Knoll Press in Hardy, VA
E-mail: oakknoll@oakknoll.com
Web site: http://www.oakknoll.com; *CIP.*

Oak Lake Pr., *(978-0-9744115)* Orders Addr.: 1432 Higuera, San Luis Obispo, CA 93406 USA Tel 916-791-2309; Edit Addr.: P.O. Box 529, Loomis, CA 95650 USA
E-mail: abowler@surewest.net
Web site: http://www.annmartinbowler.net.

Oak Leaf Systems, *(978-0-9659546; 978-0-9848809)* 2710 John Tyler Hwy., Williamsburg, VA 23185 USA Tel 757-208-0200 Landline; 757-634-1441 Mobile
E-mail: carolfeltman@gmail.com
Web site: ATruckNamedTravis.com.

Oak Manor Publishing, Inc., *(978-0-9747361; 978-0-9791757)* 161 Boutwell St., Manchester, NH 03102-2933 USA Tel 603-860-5551
E-mail: customerservice@aokmanorpublishing.com
Web site: http://www.oakmanorpublishing.com.

Oak Ridge Publishing, *(978-0-9814735; 978-0-9843270; 978-0-9851416)* P.O. Box 682, Lady Lake, FL 32158 USA Tel 352-259-7450
E-mail: ldridgley@comcast.net.

Oak Tree Publishing, *(978-1-892343; 978-1-61009)* Orders Addr.: 1820 W. Lacey Blvd. #220, Hanford, CA 93230 USA; *Imprints:* Acorn (AcornIL) Do not confuse with companies with the same or similar name in Virginia Beach, VA, Seminole, FL
E-mail: oaktreepub@aol.com; Publisher@oaktreebooks.com; info@oaktreebooks.com
Web site: http://www.oaktreebooks.com; http://www.otpblog.blogspot.com.

Oakana Hse., *(978-0-9762197)* Orders Addr.: P.O. Box 1680, Ramona, CA 92065 USA (SAN 257-5418)
Web site: http://OakanaHouse.com.

Oakdale Pr., *(978-0-9656364)* Orders Addr.: P.O. Box 555, Caulfield, MO 65626 USA Tel 417-284-3512; Fax: 417-284-3623 Do not confuse with companies with the same name in Lincoln., MA, Tallahassee, FL
E-mail: oakdale@webound.com
Web site: http://www.oakdalepress.com.

Oaklawn Marketing, Inc., *(978-0-9764628)* P.O. Box 190615, Dallas, TX 75219 USA Tel 713-542-7642; Fax: 832-550-2079
E-mail: admin@bookofcontext.com.

OakTara Publishing Group LLC, *(978-1-60290)* 2206 N. Main St., Suite 343, Wheaton, IL 60187 USA
E-mail: rtucker@oaktara.com
Web site: http://www.oaktara.com
Dist(s): **Follett School Solutions.**

Oakwood Solutions, LLC, *(978-1-893806; 978-1-933093)* 4 Brookwood Ct., Appleton, WI 54914-8618 USA
E-mail: bschmitz@conovercompany.com; conover@execpc.com
Web site: http://www.conovercompany.com.

Oasis, Producciones Generales de Comunicacion, S.L. (ESP) *(978-84-7871; 978-84-7901; 978-84-85351) Dist. by* **Lectorum Pubns.**

Oasis Pubns., *(978-0-9652736; 978-0-9837859)* 2344 Cambridge Dr., Sarasota, FL 34232 USA Tel 941-371-2223; Fax: 941-342-1228
E-mail: oasis.dianne@juno.com
Web site: http://www.nutrikid2.com
Dist(s): **Nelson's Bks.**
New Leaf Distributing Co., Inc.
Teva Nature.

Oasis Studios Inc, *(978-0-9785605)* Orders Addr.: 7701 Witherspoon Dr., Baltimore, OH 43105 USA Tel 740-862-8620
E-mail: ekayzer@hotmail.com
Web site: http://www.championoasisstudios.com
Dist(s): **Send The Light Distribution LLC.**

Obelisco, Ediciones S.A. (ESP) *(978-84-7720; 978-84-86000; 978-84-9777) Dist. by* **Spanish.**

†Oberlin College Pr., *(978-0-932440)* 50 N. Professor St., Oberlin, OH 44074 USA (SAN 212-1883) Tel 440-775-8408; Fax: 440-775-8124
E-mail: oc.press@oberlin.edu
Web site: http://www.oberlin.edu/ocpress
Dist(s): **CUP Services**
Univ. Pr. of New England; *CIP.*

Oberon Bks., Ltd. (GBR) *(978-0-948230; 978-1-84002; 978-1-870259; 978-1-84943; 978-1-78319) Dist. by* **Consort Bk Sales.**

O'Brien, Gerard, *(978-0-9743850)* 115 Essex St., Indian Orchard, MA 01151-1409 USA Tel 413-543-5939
E-mail: gob@ifriendly.com.

O'Brien, Lara Publishing, *(978-0-9896752)* 47 Davis st, Vineyard Haven, MA 02568 USA Tel 774-563-0292
E-mail: laraeobrien@yahoo.com.

O'Brien Pr., Ltd., The (IRL) *(978-0-86278; 978-0-86322; 978-0-905140; 978-0-9502046; 978-1-902011; 978-1-84717) Dist. by* **Dufour.**

OBrien, Wiley Workspace, *(978-0-615-29492-6; 978-0-615-97038-7)* 125 Washington St., Canandaigua, NY 14424 USA
Web site: http://www.WonderlandBook.com.

Ocean Front Bk. Publishing, Inc., *(978-1-934190)* Orders Addr.: 9101 W. Sahara Ave. Suite 105-130, Las Vegas,, NV 89117 USA (SAN 852-0046) Tel 702-499-0608; 9101 W. Sahara Ave. Suite 105-130, Las Vegas,, NV 89117 (SAN 852-0046) Tel 702-499-0608
E-mail: jhorowitz@oceanfrontbooks.com
Web site: http://www.oceanfrontbooks.com.

Ocean World Photography, *(978-0-9766749)* 6461 Running Brook Rd., Manassas, VA 20112 USA
E-mail: wgregorybrown@comcast.net
Web site: http://www.wgregorybrown.com.

OceanAir Publishing *See* **Mayreni Publishing**

Oceano Grupo Editoria, S.A. (ESP) *(978-84-494; 978-84-7069; 978-84-7505; 978-84-7555; 978-84-7764; 978-84-85531; 978-84-9719) Dist. by* **Gale.**

Oceanus Bks. *Imprint of* **Warrington Pubns.**

Ocher Moon Pr., *(978-0-9765303)* 391 Joppa Mountain Rd., Rutledge, TN 37861 USA Tel 865-828-8280
E-mail: jeri@hopalonggreetings.com
Web site: http://www.hopalonggreetings.com.

OCRS, Incorporated *See* **River Pr.**

Octagon Pr., Ltd. (GBR) *(978-0-86304; 978-0-900860) Dist. by* **ISHK.**

Octagon Pr/ISHK Bk. Service *See* **I S H K**

OctiRam Publishing Co., *(978-0-9830423)* Orders Addr.: P.O. Box 5859, Vancouver, WA 98668 USA Tel 360-464-7670
E-mail: raski@comcast.net.

Octopoda Pr., *(978-0-9858506; 978-0-9908818)* P.O. Box 8943, Ketchikan, AK 99901 USA Tel 907-225-8212
E-mail: evon@evonzerbetz.com
Web site: octopodapress.com.

Octopus Publishing Co., *(978-0-9824433)* Div. of Octopus Enterprises LLC, 100 S. River Bend, Jackson, GA 30233-3204 USA
E-mail: rogerfen@bellsouth.net; geletaf@bellsouth.net.

Octopus Publishing Group (GBR) *(978-0-600; 978-0-905879; 978-1-84091; 978-1-86007; 978-1-84202; 978-1-84430; 978-1-904705; 978-1-84403; 978-1-84696; 978-1-905814; 978-1-84898; 978-1-908150; 978-1-907579; 978-1-78157; 978-1-78325) Dist. by* **HachBkGrp.**

Odd Duck Ink, Inc., *(978-1-933069)* P.O. Box 533, Norwell, MA 02061-0533 USA
E-mail: jennifer@oddduckink.com
Web site: http://www.oddduckink.com.

Oddint Media *Imprint of* **Greenwood Hill Pr.**

Oddo Publishing, Inc., *(978-0-87783)* Storybook Acres, Box 68, Fayetteville, GA 30214 USA (SAN 282-0757) Tel 770-461-7627.

Odds Bodkin Storytelling Library, The *Imprint of* **Rivertree Productions, Inc.**

Oden, Rachel, *(978-0-9729914)* 133 E. Graham Ave., Council Bluffs, IA 51503 USA Tel 712-323-7222 (phone/fax)
E-mail: cbmarketadmin@juno.com.

Odenwald Pr., *(978-0-9623216; 978-1-884363)* 6609 Brooks Dr., Temple, TX 76502 USA Tel 254-773-4884; Fax: 254-773-4884
E-mail: CSho777@aol.com
Dist(s): **SMMA Distributors.**

Odyssey Bks. (AUS) *(978-0-9806909; 978-0-9872325; 978-1-922200) Dist. by* **LightSource CS.**

Off The Record *Imprint of* **College Prowler, Inc.**

Officer Byrd Publishing Co., *(978-0-9787322)* 15730 Williams Cir., Lake Mathews, CA 92570 USA (SAN 851-4712) Tel 951-334-6111
E-mail: officerbyrd@aol.com.

Officina Libraria srl (ITA) *(978-88-89854; 978-88-97737) Dist. by* **Natl Bk Netwk.**

OffTheBookshelf.com *See* **Micro Publishing Media, Inc.**

Oglethorpe Pr., Inc., *(978-1-891495)* 326 Bull St., Savannah, GA 31401 USA Tel 912-231-9900; Fax: 912-234-7258
E-mail: sjackel@comcast.net
Dist(s): **Parnassus Bk. Distributors.**

Ogma Pr., *(978-0-9785853)* 4717 Broad Rd., Syracuse, NY 13215 USA Tel 315-491-9339
E-mail: bernie@ogmapress.com
Web site: http://www.ogmapress.com.

Oh My Stars Publishing, *(978-0-615-20153-5)* 222 3rd St., Suite 4, Lemoyne, PA 17043 USA
Dist(s): **APG Sales & Distribution Services**
Lulu Enterprises Inc.

OHC Group LLC, *(978-0-9763213)* P.O. Box 7839, Westlake Village, CA 91359 USA Tel 805-384-4800
Web site: http://www.onlyheartsclub.com.

Ohio Distinctive Publishing, Inc., *(978-0-9647934; 978-1-936757)* 6500 Fiesta Dr., Columbus, OH 43235 USA Tel 614-459-0453; Fax: 614-457-2488
E-mail: tim@ohio-distinctive.com
Web site: http://www.ohio-distinctive.com.

†Ohio Univ. Pr., *(978-0-8214)* Orders Addr.: 11030 S. Langley Ave., Chicago, IL 60628 USA Tel 773-702-7000; Fax: 773-702-7212; Toll Free Fax: 800-621-8476; Toll Free: 800-621-2736; Edit Addr.: 19 Circle Dr. The Ridges, Athens, OH 45701 USA (SAN 282-0773) Tel 740-593-1154; Fax: 740-593-4536
Web site: http://www.ohiou.edu/oupress/
Dist(s): **Chicago Distribution Ctr.**
Ebsco Publishing
Trajectory, Inc.
Univ. of Chicago Pr.
Univ. of Hawaii Pr.
ebrary, Inc.; *CIP.*

Ohnick Enterprises, *(978-0-9746222)* Orders Addr.: P.O. Box 969, Meade, KS 67864-0969 USA Tel 620-873-2900; Fax: 620-873-2603; Toll Free: 800-794-2356; Edit Addr.: 102 N. Fowler, Meade, KS 67864-0969 USA
E-mail: nancy@prairiebooks.com
Web site: http://backroomprinting.com.

Oka, Joseph *See* **Joseph's Labor**

Okasan & Me, *(978-0-9743613)* 829 N. Sixth St., San Jose, CA 95112 USA
Web site: http://www.okasanandme.com.

Oki, Blessed, *(978-0-9721336)* 2465 Heaton Dri., Suite A, East Point, GA 30344 USA
E-mail: blessiebeke@yahoo.com.

Oklahoma Energy Resources Board, *(978-0-615-19844-6; 978-0-615-39316-2)* 3555 NW 58th St., Suite 430, Oklahoma City, OK 73112 USA Tel 405-942-5323; Fax: 405-942-3435; Toll Free: 800-664-1301
Web site: http://www.oerb.com.

Olandar Pr. Ltd., *(978-0-9729502)* Orders Addr.: 2222 Parview Rd., Middleton, WI 53562 USA Tel 608-831-1222; Fax: 608-831-1647
Web site: http://www.leighmccloskey.com.

Ola's Hanalei LTD, *(978-0-9763907)* P.O. Box 488, Hanalei, HI 96714 USA
E-mail: olashanalei@hawaiiantel.net.

Old Bay Publishing, *(978-0-9745854)* 19 Meeting St., Huntsville, AL 35806-5230 USA
E-mail: msikes@hiwaay.net
Dist(s): **Partners Bk. Distributing, Inc.**

Old Bess Publishing Co., *(978-0-9631912; 978-0-9762132)* Orders Addr.: P.O. Box 277, Brunswick, ME 04011 USA Tel 207-725-8575; P.O. Box P.O. Box 277, Brunswick, ME 04011
E-mail: sbutcherr@mcn.net.

Old Bow Publishing, *(978-0-615-54029-0; 978-0-9853219)* 1816 Morgan Horse Farm Rd., Weybridge, VT 05753 USA Tel 410-456-7151
E-mail: achambleton@earthlink.net
Web site: www.oldbowpublishing.com
Dist(s): **Independent Pubs. Group.**

Old Farm Pr., *(978-0-9788227)* P.O. Box 20894, Oklahoma City, OK 73156-0894 USA (SAN 851-6995) Tel 405-748-7072; Fax: 405-748-7073
E-mail: spi@mbo.net
Web site: http://www.BobbyBrightBooks.com.

Old Hogan Publishing Co., *(978-0-9638851)* Orders Addr.: P.O. Box 91978, Tucson, AZ 85752 USA Tel 520-579-9321; Fax: 520-579-0502; Toll Free: 800-867-1506; Edit Addr.: 3600 W. Mesa Ridge Trail, Tucson, AZ 85742 USA
E-mail: mgaraway@juno.com
Web site: http://www.oldhogan.com
Dist(s): **Hispanic Bks. Distributors & Pubs., Inc.**
Rio Nuevo Pubs.

O.L.D. Inc., *(978-0-9830470)* 118 N Ross St N. 6, Auburn, AL 36830 USA Tel 334-787-1713
E-mail: cwjones@oldinc.net.

Old Line Publishing, LLC, *(978-0-9786948; 978-0-9841065; 978-0-9844768; 978-0-9845704; 978-0-9846143; 978-1-937004; 978-1-939928)* 1194 N. Carroll St., Hampstead, MD 21074 USA
E-mail: maplecreekmedia@comcast.net
Web site: http://www.oldlinepublishing.com.

Old Maps, *(978-0-911653; 978-0-9747639)* P.O. Box 54, West Chesterfield, NH 03466 USA (SAN 264-2689)
E-mail: daven@sover.net
Web site: http://www.old-maps.com.

Old Silver Pr., *(978-0-9800975)* 224 Coonamessett Cir., East Falmouth, MA 02536 USA
E-mail: OldSilverPress@yahoo.com.

Old Soldier Publishing, *(978-0-9764167)* Orders Addr.: P.O. Box 1113, Richmond, TX 77469 USA Tel 281-341-0781 (phone/fax); Edit Addr.: 1110 Pioneer Dr., Richmond, TX 77469 USA
Dist(s): **ebrary, Inc.**

Old St. Augustine Pubns., *(978-0-9833684; 978-0-692-38918-8)* P.O. Box 162056, Altamonte Springs, FL 32716 USA Tel 407-774-8799
E-mail: doug@oldstaugustinepublications.com
Web site: http://www.oldstaugustinepublications.com
Dist(s): **Lightning Source, Inc.**

Old Stone Pr., *(978-1-938462)* 520 Old Stone Ln., Louisville, KY 40207 USA Tel 502-693-1506
E-mail: john@JHClarkandAssociates.com
Web site: OldStonePress.com
Dist(s): **AtlasBooks Distribution.**

Old Time Stories, *(978-0-9792770)* 116 Beasley Rd., Cusseta, GA 31805-3206 USA.

Old Vine Oublishing Co., *(978-0-9794291)* P.O. Box 6774, Pine Mountain Club, CA 93222-6774 USA.

Old West Co., The, *(978-0-9654341; 978-0-9801743; 978-0-9898004)* Orders Addr.: 5118 Village Trail Dr., San Antonio, TX 78218-3831 USA; *Imprints:* Sweetwater Stagelines (Sweetwtr Stage)
E-mail: kirkwest@sbcglobal.net
Web site: http://lulu.com/sweetwater.

Oldcastle Bks., Ltd. (GBR) *(978-0-948353; 978-1-874061; 978-1-84243; 978-1-84344; 978-1-904915)* *Dist. by* **IPG Chicago.**

Oldcastle Publishing, *(978-0-932529)* Orders Addr.: P.O. Box 1193, Escondido, CA 92033 USA (SAN 297-9039) Tel 760-489-0336; Fax: 760-747-1198; Edit Addr.: 3415 Laredo Ln., Escondido, CA 92025 USA (SAN 297-9047)
E-mail: abcurtiss@cox.net
Web site: http://www.abcurtiss.com; http://www.depressionisachoice.com
Dist(s): **National Bk. Network.**

Olde Springfield Shoppe *See* **Masthof Pr.**

Olde Town Publishing, *(978-0-9755906)* 703 W. Main, Jonesborough, TN 37659 USA
Web site: http://www.drisbell.com.

Olde Towne Publishing, *(978-0-9794935)* P.O. Box 98, Old Mission, MI 49673 USA Do noty confuse with Olde Towne Publishing Company in Fredericksburg, VA
Web site: http://www.strolltraversecity.com
Dist(s): **Partners Bk. Distributing, Inc.**

Oleson, Susan, *(978-0-9779251)* 511 E Iowa St, Monona, IA 52159 USA
E-mail: sammytails@netins.net.

Olinville Pr., *(978-0-615-66946-5)* 533 2nd St., Brooklyn, NY 11215 USA Tel 718-499-4030
Dist(s): **CreateSpace Independent Publishing Platform.**

Olive Branch Publishing, LLC *See* **OlivesAngels Publishing, LLC**

Olive Grove Pubs., *(978-0-9752508)* 1420 King Rd., Hinckley, OH 44233 USA Tel 330-278-4028
E-mail: RSpirko@Roadrunner.com
Web site: http://www.atlasbooks.com
Dist(s): **AtlasBooks Distribution**
BookMasters, Inc.
New Leaf Distributing Co., Inc.
ebrary, Inc.

Olive Leaf Pubns., *(978-0-9761583)* 782 San Gabriel Loop, New Braunfels, TX 78132 USA (SAN 256-6206) Tel 830-626-7671
E-mail: sharon@oliveleafpublications.com
Web site: http://www.oliveleafpublications.com
Dist(s): **Lightning Source, Inc.**

Olive Pr., The, *(978-0-9769298)* Orders Addr.: P.O. Box 2056, Saintilwater, MN 55082 USA Tel 651-251-3063 Do not confuse with Olive Press i Ann Arbor, MI West Orange, NJ Estes Park, CO
E-mail: olivepressinc@yahoo.com
Web site: http://jumpstartfuture.com.

Olive Tree of Life, *(978-0-9768182)* P.O. Box 344, Tijeras, NM 87059 USA
Web site: http://www.olivetreeoflife.com.

Oliver Pr., Inc., *(978-1-881508; 978-1-934545)* Orders Addr.: 5707 W. 36th St., Minneapolis, MN 55416-2510 USA Tel 952-926-8981; Fax: 952-926-8965; Toll Free: 800-865-4837
E-mail: orders@oliverpress.com
Web site: http://www.oliverpress.com.

Oliver, Sarah (GBR) *(978-0-9559820)* *Dist. by* **LuluCom.**

Oliver, Wade, *(978-0-9768030)* P.O. Box 1605, Logan, UT 84322-1605 USA
E-mail: wademan@cache.net
Web site: http://www.dovepage.com.

OlivesAngels Publishing, LLC, *(978-0-9793147)* P.O. Box 940725, Plano, TX 75094-0725 USA (SAN 853-0955) Tel 972-977-4881
E-mail: olivesangels@tx.rr.com.

Olivo, Andy, *(978-0-9743376)* 1807 Glengarry St., Carrollton, TX 75006 USA Tel 972-242-0924; Fax: 972-242-1754; *Imprints*: Brown Books (Brown BksTX).

OLLY Publishing Co., *(978-0-9720427)* 4335 Lake Michigan Dr., NW Suite H, Grand Rapids, MI 49544 USA (SAN 254-587X) Tel 616-735-0553
E-mail: diane@ollypublishing.com
Web site: http://www.ollypublishing.com.

Olms, Georg Verlag AG (DEU) *(978-3-487)* *Dist. by* **IPG Chicago.**

Olmstead LLC *See* **Olmstead Publishing LLC**

Olmstead Publishing LLC, *(978-0-9667696; 978-1-934194)* Orders Addr.: 2629 Grassmoor Lp, Apopka, FL 32712-5005 USA Tel 954-559-0192 (phone); Fax: 650-479-8273
E-mail: olmsteadpublishing@usa.com
Web site: http://www.olmsteadpublishing.com; http://https://squareup.com/market/olmstead-publishing-llc; http://www.facebook.com/olmsteadpublishing.

Olsen, Mary Bks., *(978-0-9715374)* P.O. Box 882, Eastsound, WA 98245-0882 USA
E-mail: mary@maryolsenbooks.com.

Olson, Robin, *(978-0-9818695)* P.O. Box 5294, Laytonsville, MD 20882 USA (SAN 856-7719)
E-mail: robin@robinsweb.com
Web site: http://www.robinsweb.com.

Oma Publishing Co., *(978-0-9747175)* 325 River Springs Dr., Seguin, TX 78155-0179 USA.

Omaha Bks., *(978-0-9745410; 978-0-9788429; 978-0-9908000)* Div. of Eventive Marketing, 9312 Leavenworth St., Omaha, NE 68114 USA (SAN 857-1295) Tel 402-614-0056
E-mail: kristine.gerber@cox.net; eventive.marketing@cox.net
Dist(s): **Partners Bk. Distributing, Inc.**

O'Mara, Michael Bks., Ltd. (GBR) *(978-1-85479; 978-0-946429; 978-0-948397; 978-1-84317; 978-1-903840; 978-1-904613; 978-1-907151; 978-1-78243)* *Dist. by* **IPG Chicago.**

O'Mara, Michael Bks., Ltd. (GBR) *(978-1-85479; 978-0-946429; 978-0-948397; 978-1-84317; 978-1-903840; 978-1-904613; 978-1-907151; 978-1-78243)* *Dist. by* **Trans-Atl Phila.**

O'Mara, Michael Bks., Ltd. (GBR) *(978-1-85479; 978-0-946429; 978-0-948397; 978-1-84317; 978-1-903840; 978-1-904613; 978-1-907151; 978-1-78243)* *Dist. by* **IngramPubServ.**

Omega Hse. Publishing, *(978-0-9672519)* Div. of Spectrum Group, Inc., Orders Addr.: P.O. Box 68, Three Rivers, MI 49093 USA Tel 269-273-7070; Fax: 269-273-7026; Edit Addr.: 58690 US 131, Three Rivers, MI 49093 USA
E-mail: zendra@omega777.com.

Omega Pr., *(978-0-9626087; 978-0-9754923; 978-1-933951)* 5823 N. Mesa, No. 823, El Paso, TX 79912-3340 USA Tel 915-584-6844; Toll Free: 888-560-1243 Do not confuse with companies with the same name in Tustin, CA
E-mail: ken@kenhudnall.com
Web site: http://www.omegapress.us; http://www.kenhudnall.com; http://shop.kenhudnall.com.

Omega Prime, LLC, *(978-0-9897588)* 3521 Hartzdale Dr., Camp Hill, PA 17011-7231 USA Tel 717-579-0038
E-mail: SusanRShutt@OmegaPrime.net
Web site: http://www.loveoffizz.com; http://www.fortheloveoffizz.com; http://www.omegaprime.net.

Omega Publishing, *(978-0-9748494)* P.O. Box 53626, Lubbock, TX 79453 USA (SAN 255-8815) Tel 806-748-9880; Fax: 806-748-9870; Toll Free: 877-842-9880 do not confuse with companies iwth the same or similar name in Madisonville, KY, Stockton, GA, Snohomish, WA, Norcross, GA
E-mail: jpartin@omega-pub.com
Web site: http://www.omega-pub.com.

Omega Publishing Hse., *(978-1-886297)* Subs. of B. C. & G. Graphics, Orders Addr.: 2935 Glenwood Ave., Youngstown, OH 44511 USA Tel 330-881-1344; Fax: 330-782-7599
E-mail: omegapublishing@ymail.com; craiga2356@msn.com
Web site: http://omegapublishinghouse.com.

Omen Sky Pubns., *(978-0-9744192)* 3600 Brookewind Way, No. 1201, Lexington, KY 40515 USA Tel 859-543-2026 (phone/fax)
E-mail: omensky@qx.net.

Omni Arts Publishing *Imprint of* **Read Street Publishing, Inc.**

Omni Arts Publishing, Incorporated *See* **Read Street Publishing, Inc.**

Omnibus Pr., *(978-0-7119; 978-0-8256; 978-0-86001; 978-1-84449)* Div. of Music Sales Corp., Orders Addr.: 445 Bellvale Rd., Chester, NY 10918-0572 USA Tel 845-469-4699; Fax: 845-469-7544; Toll Free Fax: 800-345-6842; Toll Free: 800-431-7187; Edit Addr.: 257 Park Ave., S., 20th Flr., New York, NY 10010 USA Tel 212-254-2100; Fax: 212-254-2013 Do not confuse with Omnibus Pr., Menasha, WI
E-mail: info@musicsales.com
Web site: http://www.musicsales.com
Dist(s): **Leonard, Hal Corp.**
Ingram Pub. Services
Music Sales Corp.

Omnibus Publishing, *(978-0-9740599)* 3402 Beresford Ave., Belmont, CA 94002 USA Tel 650-622-9702; Fax: 650-240-3586
E-mail: yuhogan@omnibuspublishing.com
Web site: http://www.omnibuspublishing.com.

†Omnigraphics, Inc., *(978-0-7808; 978-1-55888)* Orders Addr.: P.O. Box 8002, Aston, PA 19014-8002 USA Tel 800-234-1340; Fax: 800-875-1340; Toll Free Fax: 800-875-1340 (orders & customer service); Toll Free: 800-234-1340 (orders & customer service); Edit Addr.: 155 W. Congress, Suite 200, Detroit, MI 48226 USA (SAN 249-2520)
E-mail: info@omnigraphics.com; customerservice@omnigraphics.com
Web site: http://www.omnigraphics.com
Dist(s): **Ebsco Publishing**
Gale Virtual Reference Library
Independent Pubs. Group
Mackin Educational Resources
MyiLibrary
Rittenhouse Bk. Distributors
Visible Ink Pr.
ebrary, Inc.; *CIP.*

O'More Publishing, *(978-0-9717444; 978-0-9800285; 978-0-9822618; 978-0-9846244; 978-0-9860150; 978-0-9860244)* 423 S. Margin St., Franklin, TN 37064 USA Fax: 615-790-1662; 615-790-1666
E-mail: mhilliard@omorecollege.edu; jsexton@omorecollege.edu
Web site: http://www.omorepublishing.com.

On Cape Pubns., *(978-0-9653283; 978-0-9719547; 978-0-9758502; 978-0-9785766; 978-0-9913401)* Orders Addr.: 87 Barley Neck Rd., Orleans, MA 02638 USA Tel 508-385-2108 Toll Free: 877-662-5839
Web site: http://www.oncapepublications.com
Dist(s): **Independent Pubs. Group**
Legato Pubs. Group
Perseus-PGW.

On The Ball Publishing, *(978-0-615-21079-7; 978-0-615-25047-2; 978-0-615-45284-5; 978-0-615-45296-8; 978-0-9834341)* 12821 Stratford Dr. Suite 114, Oklahoma City, OK 73120 USA Tel 405-549-1174
E-mail: admin@ontheballpublishing.com
Web site: http://www.ontheballpublishing.com
Dist(s): **Lulu Enterprises Inc.**

On The Edge Pubns., *(978-0-9762360)* P.O. Box 690007, Stockton, CA 95269 USA Tel 209-473-8553
E-mail: ontheedgepublications@msn.com
Web site: http://www.ontheedgepublications.com.

On the Spot! Bks., *(978-0-9652998)* 1492 Tipperary St., Boulder, CO 80303 USA Tel 303-666-0550
E-mail: onthespotbooks@msn.com
Web site: www.kerryleemaclean.com
Dist(s): **Bks. West**
New Leaf Distributing Co., Inc.

On Tour Publishing, *(978-0-9767234)* Orders Addr.: 512 Northampton St., 151, 303, Edwardsville, PA 18704 USA
E-mail: otp@ontourpublishing.com.

ON Words Publishing, LLC, *(978-0-9787589)* 8720 Ferguson Ave., Savannah, GA 31406 USA.

ONA Healthy Life, L.L.C., *(978-0-9716585)* Div. of ONA New Body - New Life, Inc., Orders Addr.: 639 4th Ave, Apt. 6B, Brooklyn, NY 11232 USA Toll Free: 800-247-6553 (Account rep: Bridget Massie)
E-mail: mel@melona.com
Web site: http://www.melona.com; http://www.onahealthylife.com
Dist(s): **AtlasBooks Distribution**
BookMasters, Inc.

ONA New Body - New Life, Incorporated *See* **ONA Healthy Life, L.L.C.**

Once Upon a Time Creations, *(978-0-615-58304-4; 978-0-615-78978-1; 978-0-692-47489-1; 978-0-692-47911-7; 978-0-692-49075-4)* P.O. Box 583, Ojai, CA 93024 USA Tel 805-448-9998
E-mail: creatingart@aol.com
Web site: http://www.Wishes.bz
Dist(s): **CreateSpace Independent Publishing Platform.**

Once Upon A Time in a Classroom *Imprint of* **Interactive Media Publishing**

Oncekids, *(978-0-9844207; 978-1-938806)* 119 Maono Pl., Honolulu, HI 96821 USA (SAN 859-3574)
E-mail: oncekids@gmail.com
Dist(s): **AtlasBooks Distribution.**

Oncology Nursing Press, Incorporated *See* **Oncology Nursing Society**

Oncology Nursing Society, *(978-1-890504; 978-1-935864)* Subs. of Oncology Nursing Society, 125 Enterprise Dr., Pittsburgh, PA 15275-1214 USA (SAN 689-8041) Tel 412-859-6100
E-mail: jholmes@ons.org
Web site: http://www.ons.org.

One Arm Publishing, *(978-0-9746024)* 3344 Via La Selva, Palos Verdes Estates, CA 90274 USA
E-mail: mariana1969@hotmail.com
Web site: http://www.onearmpublishing.com.

One Armed Operation *See* **One Arm Publishing**

One Coin Publishing, LLC, *(978-0-615-31066-4)* 6876 Towhee, Portage, MI 49024 USA.

One Eyed Pr., *(978-0-9665430; 978-0-615-26684-8)* 272 Rd. 6RT, Cody, WY 82414 USA Tel 307-272-9628; 307-587-6136
E-mail: one_eyed_press@yahoo.com
Web site: http://www.one-eyed-press.com
Dist(s): **Bks. West**
CreateSpace Independent Publishing Platform
Todd Communications.

One Faithful Harp Publishing Co., *(978-0-9666701)* 138 N. 2nd St., Catawissa, PA 17820-1210 USA
E-mail: info@onefaithfulharp.com
Web site: http://www.onefaithfulharp.com.

One Horse Pr., *(978-0-9725650)* 963 Maple Hill Dr., Erie, PA 16509 USA Tel 814-923-4086
E-mail: stephanie@stephaniewincik.com
Web site: http://www.stephaniewincik.com.

One in Me, The, *(978-0-9898437)* 503 Wicklow Pl., Acworth, GA 30102 USA Tel 678-324-8750; Fax: 678-324-8750
E-mail: tgodoy@comcast.net.

One Little Miracle, *(978-0-9743948)* 1449 Highland Ct., Stillwater, MN 55082 USA Tel 651-439-3250
E-mail: allieschield@hotmail.com
Web site: http://www.onelittlemiracle.com.

One Little Spark, *(978-0-615-53981-2; 978-0-578-12711-8)* 239 W. Lime Ave., Monrovia, CA 91016 USA Tel 818-621-3466; Fax: 626-486-9456
E-mail: vicki@oneilspark.com
Web site: oneilspark.com.

One Love Assn. Bks., *(978-0-9776603)* 306 Trillick Ct., Rolesville, NC 27571 USA (SAN 257-8654)
E-mail: ras@newkemet.com; gerald@newkemet.com
Web site: http://www.newkemet.com/gerald.

One Monkey Bks., *(978-0-9777082; 978-1-940722)* 156 Diamond St., San Francisco, CA 94114-2414 USA (SAN 850-0320).

One Night Bks. *Imprint of* **WordWright.biz, Inc.**

One of a Kind Books, Incorporated *See* **Webster Henrietta Publishing**

One Peace Bks., Inc., *(978-0-9785084; 978-1-935548)* 57 Great Jones St., New York, NY 10012 USA (SAN 850-7430) Tel 212-260-4400; Fax: 212-995-2969
E-mail: jun@onepeacebooks.com; mcguire@onepeacebooks.com
Web site: http://www.onepeacebooks.com
Dist(s): **SCB Distributors.**

One Pink Rose, *(978-0-9722991)* 111921 Rawson Rd., Red Bluff, CA 96080 USA
E-mail: pinkwhirlwind@cablespeed.com; squallsknight@yahoo.com
Web site: http://www.darkfedora.com.

One Rib Pubns., *(978-0-9722625; 978-0-9746191)* Orders Addr.: 1811 NW 51st St., Fort Lauderdale, FL 33309 USA Tel 954-489-0141; Edit Addr.: PMB 826, 2001 NW 51st St., Ft. Lauderdale, FL 33309 USA.

1 Sleeve Publishing, *(978-0-9729153)* Orders Addr.: P.O. Box 1865, North Mankato, MN 56002-1865 USA; Edit Addr.: 442 Belgrade Ave., No. 13, North Mankato, MN 56003 USA
E-mail: onesleeve@hotmail.com.

One Source Publishing, LLC, *(978-0-9779374)* 63 Gates St, White River Junction, VT 05001 USA Fax: 802-295-5338
E-mail: hphipps@onesourcefg.com.

One Too Tree Publishing, *(978-0-9820781)* 106 Calendar Ct., No. 108, La Grange, IL 60525-2325 USA (SAN 857-1732)
E-mail: publisher@onetootree.com
Web site: http://www.OneTooTree.com.

One Voice Recordings, *(978-0-9708022)* 16835 Halper St., Encino, CA 91436 USA Tel 818-501-8145 (phone/fax)
E-mail: ddavies858@aol.com.

One Way Bks., *(978-0-9800451; 978-1-936459)* Div. of Waht About You?, Inc., 2269 S. Univ. Dr. #330, Fort Lauderdale, FL 33324 USA Tel 954-680-9095
Web site: http://www.OneWayBooks.org
Dist(s): **MyiLibrary**
Send The Light Distribution LLC
ebrary, Inc.

One Way St., Inc., *(978-1-58302)* Orders Addr.: P.O. Box 5077, Englewood, CO 80155-5077 USA Tel 303-790-1188; Fax: 303-790-2159; Toll Free: 800-569-4537
E-mail: webmaster@onewaystreet.com
Web site: http://www.onewaystreet.com.

OneHope, *(978-1-890525; 978-1-931940; 978-1-59480; 978-1-63049)* 600 SW 3rd St., Pompano Beach, FL 33060-6936 USA Toll Free: 800-448-2425
E-mail: andreadragotas@onehope.net.

ONeill, Gene & Assoc., *(978-0-9747797)* 10163 Potter Rd., Des Plaines, IL 60016 USA.

O'Neill, Hugh & Assocs., *(978-0-9675919; 978-0-615-76348-4)* Orders Addr.: P.O. Box 1297, Nevada City, CA 95959 USA Tel 530-265-4196; Edit Addr.: 227 Prospect St., Nevada City, CA 95959 USA
E-mail: info@bydb.com
Web site: http://www.bydb.com
Dist(s): **CreateSpace Independent Publishing Platform.**

O'Neill, Jan, *(978-0-9746409)* 5681 Rives Junction Rd., Jackson, MI 49201-9413 USA.

OneShare Educational Pr., *(978-0-9788438)* 3450 Third St. Bldg. 1-D, San Francisco, CA 94124 USA (SAN 851-7487) Tel 415-777-1777; Fax: 415-777-1677; Toll Free: 888-777-6919
Web site: http://www.oneshare.com.

Oneworld Pubns. (GBR) *(978-1-85168; 978-1-78074)* *Dist. by* **PerseuPGW.**

Oni Pr., Inc., *(978-0-9667127; 978-1-929998; 978-1-932664; 978-1-934964; 978-1-62010)* 1305 SE Martin Luther King Jr. Blvd., Suite A, Portland, OR 97214 USA Tel 503-233-1377; Fax: 503-233-1477
E-mail: joe@onipress.com
Web site: http://www.onipress.com
Dist(s): **Diamond Comic Distributors, Inc.**
Diamond Bk. Distributors.

Onion River Pr., *(978-0-9657144)* 23 Wildbery Ln., Underhill, VT 05489 USA
E-mail: information@onionriverpress.com
Web site: http://www.onionriverpress.com.

ONLY1EARTH, LLC, *(978-0-9763354)* 3146 The Alameda Suite 7, San Jose, CA 95126 USA
E-mail: only1earthinc@gmail.com
Web site: http://www.theturtlekey.com.

Onondaga Hill Publishing, *(978-0-9794908)* 4586 Bloomsbury Dr., Syracuse, NY 13215 USA Tel 315-420-3025
E-mail: mdunn@imsolv.com; matthew@matthewdunn.net
Web site: http://www.matthewdunn.net
Dist(s): **BookBaby.**

Onstage Publishing, LLC, *(978-0-9700752; 978-0-9753367; 978-0-9790857)* Orders Addr.: 190 Lime Quarry Rd., Suite 106 J, Madison, AL 35758 USA Tel 256-461-0661; Fax: 256-461-0661
E-mail: onstage123@knology.net
Web site: http://www.onstagepublishing.com.

ONTRAK, *(978-0-9765502)* P.O. Box 205, Bethel, CT 06801-0153 USA Do not confuse with Ontrak in Yorba Linda, CA
E-mail: plumtrees@snet.net.

Onyx *Imprint of* **Penguin Publishing Group**

Ooligan Pr., *(978-1-932010)* Div. of Portland State Univ., Dept. of English, Orders Addr.: Dept. of English Portland State Univ. P.O. Box 751, Portland, OR 97207 USA Tel 503-725-9410; Fax: 503-725-3561; Edit Addr.: 630 SW Mill St., 97201, Rm. Nh405, Portland, OR 97201 USA
E-mail: ooligan@ooliganpress.pdx.edu; agaterud@pdx.edu
Web site: http://www.ooliganpress.pdx.edu; http://www.publishing.pdx.edu
Dist(s): **Ingram Pub. Services.**

OPA Author Services, *(978-0-911041)* Div. of Optimum Performance Associates, 777 W. Chandler Blvd., No. 1322, Chandler, AZ 85225-2511 USA (SAN 254-9255) Tel 480-275-5270; 480-393-1646 (phone/fax)
Web site: http://www.opaauthorservices.com; http://www.opapublishing.com
Dist(s): **OPA Publishing & Distributing.**

OPA Publishing *See* **OPA Author Services**

Opacity, Inc., *(978-0-615-14266-1)* 7086 SW Iron Horse St., Wilsonville, OR 97070 USA
Dist(s): **Lulu Enterprises Inc.**

Open Arms Publishing, *(978-0-9770841)* 607 Knob Ct., Fayetteville, NC 28303 USA Tel 910-258-3941
E-mail: sallymander66@earthlink.net; thoglenm@yahoo.com
Web site: http://www.oalm.net.

Open Bk. Publishing, *(978-0-9719167; 978-0-9740321; 978-1-932621)* Rte. 2, Box 2607, Birch Tree, MO 65438 USA Tel 573-292-3368; Fax: 573-292-8115 Do not confuse with Open Book Publishing Company in Huntington beach, CA
E-mail: lfann@socket.net; lfann@socket.net
Web site: http://www.openbookpublishing.com.

Open Bk. Publishing Co., *(978-0-9753349)* P.O. Box 3602, Huntington Beach, CA 92649 USA Tel 714-264-7284; Fax: 714-846-6782 Do not confuse with Open Book Publishing in Birch Tree, MO
E-mail: k.cutt@verizon.net
Web site: http://www.openbookpublishingcompany.com.

†Open Court, *(978-0-8126; 978-0-87548; 978-0-89688; 978-0-912050)* Div. of S R A/McGraw-Hill, 220 E. Daniel

Publisher Name Index

Dale Rd., DeSoto, TX 75115 USA Fax: 972-228-1982; Toll Free: 888-772-4543; 800-442-9685 (orders)
Web site: https://www.sraonline.com
Dist(s): **Libros Sin Fronteras**
Perseus Bks. Group
SRA/McGraw-Hill; *CIP.*

Open Court Publishing Co., *(978-0-8126; 978-0-87548; 978-0-89688; 978-0-912050)* Div. of Carus Publishing Co., Orders Addr.: c/o Publishers Group West, 1700 Fourth St., Berkeley, CA 94710 USA Fax: 510-528-3444; Toll Free: 800-788-3123; Edit Addr.: 70 E. Lake St. Ste. 300, Chicago, IL 60601-5945 USA Toll Free: 800-815-2280
E-mail: opencourt@caruspub.com
Web site: http://www.opencourtbooks.com
Dist(s): **Follett School Solutions**
MyiLibrary
Perseus-PGW
Perseus Bks. Group.

Open Door Publishers, Inc., *(978-0-9841721; 978-1-937138)* 2373 Rte. 9, Mechanicville, NY 12118 USA (SAN 858-625X) Tel 518-899-2097
E-mail: adamiszyn@hotmail.com; ladean@opendoorpublishers.com
Web site: http://www.ladeanwarner.com; http://opendoorpublishers.com/.

Open Gate Publishing, *(978-0-9717036; 978-1-937195)* Div. of Open Gate Sangha, Inc., Orders Addr.: P.O. Box 112107, Campbell, CA 95011-2107 USA; Edit Addr.: 1299 Del Mar Ave., Suite 200, San Jose, CA 95128-3548 USA
E-mail: jerilyn@adyashanti.org
Web site: http://www.adyashanti.org
Dist(s): **New Leaf Distributing Co., Inc.**

Open Gate Sangha Publishing *See* **Open Gate Publishing**

Open Hand Publishing, LLC, *(978-0-940880)* P.O. Box 20207, Greensboro, NC 27420 USA (SAN 219-6174) Tel 336-292-8585; Fax: 336-292-8588
E-mail: info@openhand.com
Web site: http://www.openhand.com.

Open Heaven Pubns., *(978-0-9752622)* P.O. Box 457, Moravian Falls, NC 28654 USA
Web site: http://www.garyoates.com.

Open Mind Pr., *(978-0-9755157)* P.O. Box 1338, Garden Grove, CA 92844 USA Tel 714-322-3049 Do not confuse with Open Mind Press in Garner, NC
E-mail: openmindpress@albalagh.net
Web site: http://www.openmindpress.com.

Open Pages Publishing, *(978-0-9785937)* Orders Addr.: P.O. Box 420788, Houston, TX 77242 USA (SAN 851-0822); Edit Addr.: 3130 Walnut Bend Ln., Unit No. 317, Houston, TX 77042-4778 USA
E-mail: goodstory@openpagespublishing.com.

Open Road Integrated Media, LLC, *(978-1-936317; 978-1-4532; 978-1-4804; 978-1-4976; 978-1-5040)* 180 Varick St. Suite 816, New York, NY 10014 USA Tel 212-691-0900; Fax: 212-691-0901; 345 Hudson St., Suite 6C, New York, NY 10014 Tel 212-691-0900; Fax: 212-691-0901; *Imprints:* Open Road Young Readers (OPEN ROAD YOUN); Open Road Media E-iriginal (OpenRdMedE-rig)
E-mail: acolvin@openroadmedia.com
Web site: http://www.openroadmedia.com
Dist(s): **Follett School Solutions**
Ingram Pub. Services
MyiLibrary.

Open Road Media E-iriginal *Imprint of* **Open Road Integrated Media, LLC**

Open Road Young Readers *Imprint of* **Open Road Integrated Media, LLC**

Open Spaces Publishing (Rupen), LLC, *(978-0-9768752; 978-0-9846494)* 1411 Timberlake Circle, Richardson, TX 75080 USA
E-mail: chistinerhoden@att.net.

Open Texture, *(978-0-9742391; 978-1-933900)* 9457 S. Univ. Blvd. #409, Highlands Ranch, CO 80126 USA Toll Free: 866-546-6459 (phone/fax)
E-mail: sales@opentexture.com
Web site: http://www.opentexture.com.

Open Vision Entertainment Corp., *(978-0-9721825)* 48 Summer St., Stoneham, MA 02180 USA Tel 781-438-7939; Fax: 781-438-8115
Web site: http://www.open-visions.com
Dist(s): **Fell, Frederick Pubs., Inc.**

Open Window Publishing, *(978-0-9798505)* P.O. Box 1436, Clarkston, MI 48347-1436 USA (SAN 854-5642).

Openvein, *(978-0-9764033)* 3760 SE Morrison St., Portland, OR 97214-3210 USA
Web site: http://www.openvein.com/.

Oppenheim Toy Portfolio, Inc., *(978-0-9664823; 978-0-9721050)* 40 E. Ninth St., Suite 14M, New York, NY 10003 USA (SAN 255-2175) Tel 212-598-0502; Fax: 212-598-9709
E-mail: stephanie@toyportfolio.com
Web site: http://www.toyportfolio.com
Dist(s): **Brodart Co.**

Opposable Thumb Pr., *(978-0-9786570)* P.O. Box 409107, Chicago, IL 60640 USA
E-mail: Dawn@opposablethumbpress.com
Web site: http://opposablethumbpress.com.

Options Galore, *(978-0-9801426)* 22890 S. Woodland Rd., Suite 100, Shaker Heights, OH 44122 USA Tel 216-965-8599
Dist(s): **AtlasBooks Distribution.**

Optiview Publishing, *(978-0-9723066)* 7725 Martin Mill Pike, Knoxville, TN 37920 USA
E-mail: mmediajohn@ao.com
Web site: http://www.optiviewpubs.com.

OPUS II Bks., *(978-0-9796210)* Orders Addr.: 1216 Purple Sage Loop, Castle Rock, CO 80104 USA (SAN 853-9367) Tel 720-371-1872
E-mail: egualberto@opusiibooks.com
Web site: http://www.opusiibooks.com.

Oracle Institute Pr., LLC, The, *(978-0-9773929; 978-1-937465)* Div. of The Oracle Institute, Orders Addr.: 1990 Battlefield Dr., Independence, VA 24348 USA (SAN 257-4780) Tel 276-773-3308
E-mail: laura@TheOracleInstitute.org
Web site: http://www.TheOracleInstitute.org
Dist(s): **Lightning Source, Inc.**
New Leaf Distributing Co., Inc.

Orage Publishing, *(978-0-9740901)* 1460 Wren Ct., Punta Gorda, FL 33950 USA Tel 941-639-6144
E-mail: ntoupsschmitt@comcast.net.

Orange Avenue Publishing *See* **Zest Bks.**

Orange County Historical Society, Inc., *(978-1-932547)* 130 Caroline St., Orange, VA 22960 USA Tel 540-672-5366 (Wednesday afternoon)
E-mail: info@orangecohist.org
Web site: http://www.orangecohist.org.

Orange Frazer Pr., *(978-0-9619637; 978-1-882203; 978-1-933197; 978-1-939710)* Orders Addr.: P.O. Box 214, Wilmington, OH 45177 USA (SAN 245-9299)
E-mail: ofrazer@erinet.com
Web site: http://www.orangefrazer.com
Dist(s): **Partners Bk. Distributing, Inc.**

Orange Hat Publishing, *(978-1-937165; 978-1-943331)* 2726 N. 88th St., Milwaukee, WI 53222 USA Tel 414-755-0515
E-mail: orangehatpublishing@gmail.com
Web site: www.orangehatpublishing.com.

Orange, Michael Nicholas, *(978-0-9758877)* Orders Addr.: P.O. Box 236, Half Moon Bay, CA 94019 USA; Edit Addr.: 646 Filbert St., Half Moon Bay, CA 94019-2112 USA.

Orange Ocean Pr., *(978-1-885021)* 127 Bennett Ave., Long Beach, CA 90803-2935 USA; *Imprints:* Tangerine Tide (Tang Tide)
E-mail: nextmag@aol.com.

Orange Palm & Magnificent Magus Pubns., Inc. (CAN) *(978-0-9687048; 978-0-896523; 978-0-9734439; 978-0-9809694; 978-0-9867570; 978-1-928016) Dist. by* **AtlasBooks.**

Orange Spot Publishing, *(978-0-9785191)* P.O. Box 224, Freeland, WA 98249 USA
Web site: http://www.pugetsoundbackyardbirds.com.

OrangeFoot Publishing Co., *(978-0-9760651)* P.O. Box 3694, Pittsburgh, PA 15230-3694 USA
E-mail: orangefootpublishing@zoominternet.net; info@orangefootpublishing.com.

Oratia Media (NZL) *(978-1-877514; 978-0-473-17634-1) Dist. by* **Casemate Pubs.**

Orb Bks. *Imprint of* **Doherty, Tom Assocs., LLC**

Orbis Publications, Incorporated *See* **Bilingual Dictionaries, Inc.**

Orbit, *(978-89-527)* Div. of Hachette Book Group, 237 Park Ave., New York, NY 10017 USA; *Imprints:* Yen Press (YenOr)
Dist(s): **Hachette Bk. Group**
MyiLibrary.

Orca Bk. Pubs. USA, *(978-0-920501; 978-1-55143; 978-1-55469)* Orders Addr.: P.O. Box 468, Custer, WA 98240-0468 USA (SAN 630-9674) Tel 250-380-1229; Fax: 250-380-1892; Toll Free: 800-210-5277
E-mail: orca@orcabook.com
Web site: http://www.orcabook.com.

Orchard Bks. *Imprint of* **Scholastic, Inc.**

Orchard Bks. *Imprint of* **Scholastic Library Publishing**

Orchard House Press *See* **Blue Forge Pr.**

Orchard Pr. *Imprint of* **Point Publishing**

Orchid Isle Publishing Co., *(978-1-887916)* 131 Halai St., Hilo, HI 96720 USA.

Orchid Pr. (THA) *(978-974-8299; 978-974-8304; 978-974-86220; 978-974-87426; 978-974-89229; 978-974-87356; 978-974-89212; 978-974-89218; 978-974-89219; 978-974-89271; 978-974-89272; 978-974-524) Dist. by* **Natl Bk Netwk.**

Orchid Publishing Co., *(978-0-9740898)* 14906 SW 104 St., Miami, FL 33196 USA.

Orchid Publishing, Inc., *(978-0-9831641; 978-0-9838325)* 333 N. Michigan Ave. Suite 222, Chicago, IL 60601 USA Tel 312-332-7200
E-mail: efimova@russianpointe.com.

Oregon Ctr. for Applied Science, Inc., *(978-1-933898)* 260 E. 11th Ave., Eugene, OR 97401-3291 USA (SAN 850-5284) Toll Free: 888-349-5472
E-mail: orcas@orcasinc.com
Web site: http://www.orcasinc.com.

Oregon State Univ. Extension Service, *(978-1-931979)* Extension & Station Communications 422 Kerr Administration, Corvallis, OR 97331 USA Tel 541-737-0807; Fax: 541-737-0817
Web site: http://extension.oregonstate.edu/eesc/.

†Oregon State Univ. Pr., *(978-0-87071)* 500 Kerr Administration Bldg., Corvallis, OR 97331-2122 USA (SAN 202-8328) Tel 541-737-3166; Fax: 541-737-3170; Toll Free: 800-426-3797
E-mail: osu.press@oregonstate.edu
Web site: http://osu.orst.edu/dept/press
Dist(s): **American Society of Civil Engineers**
Chicago Distribution Ctr.
Partners Bk. Distributing, Inc.
University of Arizona Pr.
Univ. of Oklahoma Pr.; *CIP.*

O'Reilly & Associates, Incorporated *See* **O'Reilly Media, Inc.**

O'Reilly Media, Inc., *(978-0-937175; 978-1-56592; 978-3-89721; 978-3-930673; 978-4-900900; 978-0-596; 978-4-87311; 978-1-60033; 978-1-4493; 978-1-4919; 978-1-4920; 978-1-4571)* Orders Addr.: 1005 Gravenstein Hwy. N., Sebastopol, CA 95472 USA (SAN 658-5973) Fax: 707-829-0104; Toll Free: 800-998-9938; Edit Addr.: 10 Fawcett St. Ste. 4, Cambridge, MA 02138-1175 USA Toll Free: 800-775-7731; 4 Castle St, Farnham, GU9 7HR Tel 01252 71 17 76; Fax: 01252 73 42 11
E-mail: order@oreilly.com; information@oreilly.co.uk; nuts@ora.com
Web site: http://www.oreilly.com; http://www.editions-oreilly.fr; http://oreilly.co.uk; http://oreilly.com.tw; http://www.ora.com; http://www.oreilly.fr/; http://www.oreilly.com.cn/
Dist(s): **CreateSpace Independent Publishing Platform**
Ebsco Publishing
Follett School Solutions
Ingram Pub. Services
MyiLibrary.

Oren Village, LLC, *(978-0-9777272)* P.O. Box 1111, Worthington, OH 43085 USA Tel 614-937-8513
E-mail: author@alanstjean.com
Web site: http://www.alanstjean.com.

Oresjozef Pubns., *(978-1-885566)* 167 Canton St., Randolph, MA 02368 USA Tel 781-961-5855; Toll Free: 617-851-0100
E-mail: ojozef@massed.net
Dist(s): **Educa Vision**
Haitiana Pubns., Inc.

Organ Buddies Inc,
Dist(s): **AtlasBooks Distribution.**

OrganWise Guys Inc., The, *(978-0-9648438; 978-1-931212; 978-0-9858048)* 3838 Song River Cir., Duluth, GA 30097 USA Tel 770-844-8686; Fax: 770-844-6580; Toll Free: 800-786-1730 Do not confuse with Wellness, Inc., Boston, MA
E-mail: wellness@abraxis.com
Web site: http://www.organwiseguys.com.

Orion Publishing Group, Ltd. (GBR) *(978-0-304; 978-0-460; 978-0-575; 978-0-7528; 978-1-85797; 978-1-85798; 978-1-85881; 978-1-86047; 978-1-84188; 978-1-84255; 978-1-905619; 978-1-4091; 978-1-78062; 978-0-85782; 978-1-4072; 978-1-4719) Dist. by* **IPG Chicago.**

Orion Publishing Group, Ltd. (GBR) *(978-0-304; 978-0-460; 978-0-575; 978-0-7528; 978-1-85797; 978-1-85798; 978-1-85881; 978-1-86047; 978-1-84188; 978-1-84255; 978-1-905619; 978-1-4091; 978-1-78062; 978-0-85782; 978-1-4072; 978-1-4719) Dist. by* **Trafalgar.**

Orion Publishing Group, Ltd. (GBR) *(978-0-304; 978-0-460; 978-0-575; 978-0-7528; 978-1-85797; 978-1-85798; 978-1-85881; 978-1-86047; 978-1-84188; 978-1-84255; 978-1-905619; 978-1-4091; 978-1-78062; 978-0-85782; 978-1-4072; 978-1-4719) Dist. by* **HachBkGrp.**

Orion Society, The, *(978-0-913098)* Orders Addr.: 187 Main St., Great Barrington, MA 01230-1601 USA (SAN 204-0182) Tel 413-528-4422; Fax: 413-528-0676; Toll Free: 888-909-6568
E-mail: gagne@orionmagazine.org
Web site: http://www.orionmagazine.org.

Orion Wellspring, Inc., *(978-0-9794614)* 20 Blaine St., Seattle, WA 98109 USA Tel 206-931-6556; Fax: 206-374-2149
E-mail: tom.masters@orionwellspring.com; info@orionwellspring.com
Web site: http://www.orionwellspring.com.

Orion-Cosmos, *(978-0-9752725)* 3609 Candleknoll Cir., San Antonio, TX 78244 USA
E-mail: customerservice@orion-cosmos.com
Web site: http://www.orion-cosmos.com.

Orison Pubs., *(978-0-9763800; 978-0-9827944)*
E-mail: marsha@orisonpublishers.com.

Ormond, Jennifer, *(978-0-9792010)* 77 Pkwy., Quincy, MA 02169 USA
E-mail: info@babybinkybooks.com
Web site: http://www.babybinkybooks.com.

Orndee Omnimedia, Inc., *(978-0-9774260; 978-0-9822229)* 36 West 37th St. Penthouse, New York, NY 10018 USA Tel 212-203-0363
E-mail: Publishing@Orndee.com
Web site: http://www.Orndee.com.

ORO Editions, *(978-0-9746800; 978-0-9774672; 978-0-9793801; 978-0-9795395; 978-0-9814628; 978-0-9820607; 978-0-9819857; 978-0-9826226; 978-1-935935; 978-1-941806; 978-1-939621; 978-1-940743; 978-1-943532)* Orders Addr.: P.O. Box 150338, San Rafael, CA 94915 USA Tel 415-663-0678; Fax: 415-457-3650; Edit Addr.: 31 Commercial Blvd., Suite F, Novato, CA 94945 USA Tel 415-883-3300; Fax: 415-883-3309
E-mail: gordon@oroeditions.com; christy@oroeditions.com; info@oroeditions.com
Web site: http://www.oroeditions.com
Dist(s): **D.A.P./Distributed Art Pubs.**
Ingram Pub. Services
Perseus-PGW
Perseus Bks. Group.

Orpen Pr. (IRL) *(978-1-871305; 978-1-909895) Dist. by* **Dufour.**

Orr Bks., *(978-0-9800611; 978-0-9827764; 978-0-9851760)* 608 Seitz St., Easton, PA 18042-6544 USA Tel 610-258-5479
E-mail: derek@beachfrontpress.com; peter@beachfrontpress.com
Web site: http://www.orrbooks.net; http://www.beachfrontpress.com.

Ortells, Alfredo Editorial S.L. (ESP) *(978-84-7189) Dist. by* **Continental Bk.**

Ortiz, Enrique Publishing, *(978-0-615-25622-1; 978-0-615-25637-5; 978-0-615-26124-9; 978-0-578-00134-0; 978-0-578-00135-7)* 1538 Bullbush Way, Oviedo, FL 32765 USA
Dist(s): **Lulu Enterprises Inc.**

Osage Bend Publishing Co., *(978-0-9626245; 978-1-58389)* 213 Belair Dr., Jefferson City, MO 65109 USA Tel 573-635-5580; Toll Free: 888-243-9772
E-mail: OBPC@Socket.net
Dist(s): **Follett School Solutions.**

Osborne Enterprises Publishing, *(978-0-932117)* P.O. Box 255, Port Townsend, WA 98368 USA (SAN 242-7567) Tel 360-385-1200; Toll Free: 800-246-3255 (orders only)
E-mail: jpo@olympus.net
Web site: http://www.jerryosborne.com.

Osborne Pr., *(978-1-928856)* Div. of David M. Osborne, Inc., 16726 Comstock, Livonia, MI 48154 USA Tel 734-464-7002; Fax: 734-464-6837
E-mail: osborne@mich.com
Web site: http://www.mich.com/~osborne.

Osborne/McGraw-Hill *See* **McGraw-Hill Osborne**

Oscar, Erica, *(978-0-9747262)* 20424 Packard, Detroit, MI 48234 USA.

Osherbert Bks., LLC, *(978-0-9885461)* P.O. Box 1591, Gig Harbor, WA 98335 USA Tel 253-651-8997
E-mail: seshell@gmail.com.

Osmosis, LLC, *(978-0-9727886; 978-0-9816281)* 8 Findlay Ave., Hartsdale, NY 10530-2613 USA Tel 914-328-8898; Fax: 914-328-1124; Toll Free: 866-676-6747
E-mail: osmosis@earthlink.net
Web site: http://www.learningbyosmosis.com; http://www.osmosis.tv.

Osprey Pr., *(978-0-9673711)* 2107 Ibis Dr., Buffalo, MN 55313 USA Tel 763-682-4558 Do not confuse with companies with the same or similar names in St. Johnsbury, VT, Wiscasset, ME
E-mail: ospreypress@charter.net
Web site: http://www.planetearthhome.com
Dist(s): **Random Hse., Inc.**

Osteogenesis Imperfecta Foundation, *(978-0-9642189)* 804 W. Diamond Ave., Suite 210, Gaithersburg, MD 20878 USA Tel 301-947-0083; Fax: 301-947-0456; Toll Free: 800-981-2663
E-mail: bonelink@oif.org
Web site: http://www.oif.org.

Ostermeyer Photography, *(978-0-9794226; 978-0-615-74538-1; 978-0-692-02001-2)* 1813 Country Brook Ln., Allen, TX 75002 USA Tel 972-542-7065
E-mail: tim@ostermeyer-photography.com
Web site: http://www.ostermeyer-photography.com.

Ostrageous Publishing, *(978-0-9785144)* P.O. Box 2867, Hot Springs, AK 71914 USA Tel 501-525-4245.

Otago University Pr. (NZL) *(978-0-908569; 978-1-877133; 978-1-877276; 978-1-877372; 978-1-877578) Dist. by* **IPG Chicago.**

Otis & Randolph Pr., *(978-0-9752516)* 1229 Bishop's Lodge Rd., Santa Fe, NM 87501 USA.

Otis, Dorcas Marie *See* **Zion Publishing**

Ottaviano, Christy Bks. *Imprint of* **Holt, Henry & Co.**

Otter Run Bks. LLC, *(978-0-9760796)* 16965 Nicolet Rd., Townsend, WI 54175 USA Tel 715-276-6515 (phone/fax)
E-mail: kathiemarsh@yahoo.com
Web site: http://www.otterrunbooks.com.

OTTN Publishing, *(978-1-59556)* 16 Risler Street, Stockton, NJ 08559 USA Tel 609-397-4005; Fax: 609-397-4007
E-mail: jgallagher@ottnpublishing.com
Web site: http://www.ottnpublishing.com.

Ouattara, Issoufou *See* **International Development Ctr.**

†Our Child Pr., *(978-0-9611872; 978-1-893516)* P.O. Box 4379, Philadelphia, PA 19118 USA (SAN 682-272X) Tel 610-308-8988
E-mail: ourchildpress@aol.com
Web site: http://www.ourchildpress.com; *CIP.*

Our Companions, Inc., *(978-0-9753257)* 84 N. Acoma Blvd., No. 100-33, Lake Havasu City, AZ 86403 USA Tel 928-486-4508.

Our Kids Pr., *(978-0-9660884; 978-0-9860290)* Orders Addr.: P.O. Box 486, Bellingham, WA 98227 USA Tel 360-734-2335; Edit Addr.: 3804 Ridgemont Way, Bellingham, WA 98227 USA
Web site: ourkidspress.com.

Our Lady of Victory Schl., *(978-1-931555)* 103 E. Tenth Ave., Post Falls, ID 83854 USA Tel 208-773-7265; Fax: 208-773-1951
E-mail: lepanto@olvs.org
Web site: http://www.olvs.org.

Our Little Secret Pr., *(978-0-9720978)* 1524 E. Park Rd., Grand Island, NY 14072 USA Tel 716-773-4866.

Our Story Pubns., *(978-0-9765554)* P.O. Box 7514, Round Rock, TX 78683 USA Tel 512-663-1471
E-mail: nicoleeutsey@ourstorypublications.com
Web site: http://www.ourstorypublications.com.

Our Sunday Visitor, Publishing Div., *(978-0-87973; 978-0-9707756; 978-1-931709; 978-1-59276; 978-1-61278; 978-1-68192)* 200 Noll Plaza, Huntington, IN 46750 USA (SAN 202-8344) Tel 260-356-8400; Fax: 260-359-9117; 260-356-8472; Toll Free: 800-348-2440
E-mail: osvbooks@osv.com; ntopp@osv.com
Web site: http://www.osv.com
Dist(s): **Baker & Taylor International**
MyiLibrary
Spring Arbor Distributors, Inc.

Our World of Books, *(978-0-9777979; 978-1-60219)* P.O. Box 218, Yarmouth Port, MA 02675 USA Toll Free: 877-662-5839; 41 Janall Dr., Dennis, MA 02638
E-mail: adam@goodnightourworld.com
Web site: http://www.goodnightourworld.com
Dist(s): **Islander Group**
MyiLibrary
Perseus-PGW
ebrary, Inc.

OurRainbow Pr., LLC, *(978-0-9752860; 978-1-934214)* Orders Addr.: 2600 Penrick Dr., Marietta, GA 30064-1809 USA Tel 770-514-8794; Toll Free: 877-600-7323
E-mail: publisher@ourrainbow.com; ameadows@ourrainbow.com; anthony.meadows@gmail.com; sheila.meadows@gmail.com
Web site: http://www.ourrainbowpress.com.

Out of the Box, *(978-0-9726849)* P.O. Box 24234, Minneapolis, MN 55424 USA Tel 612-822-5151; Fax: 612-823-4164
E-mail: info@ootbooks.com
Web site: http://www.ootbooks.com
Dist(s): **Brodart Co.**
Follett School Solutions
Quality Bks., Inc.

Out of the Box Publishing, Inc., *(978-0-9664517; 978-0-9708554; 978-0-9716729; 978-1-932359)* 609 Bennett Rd., Dodgeville, WI 53533 USA (SAN 760-5269) Toll Free: 800-540-4201 Do not confuse with Out of the Box Publishing, Cincinnati, OH
E-mail: sales@otb-games.com; brad@otb-games.com
Web site: http://www.otb-games.com.

Outcomes Unlimited Pr., Inc., *(978-0-925640)* P.O. Box 8013, Asheville, NC 28814-8497 USA
E-mail: drdossey@drdossey.com
Web site: http://www.drdossey.com.

Outdoor Originals LLC, *(978-0-9762971)* 1052 California Ave. W., Saint Paul, MN 55117 USA.

Outdoor Writing & Photography, Limited *See* **Visions Of Nature**

Outer Banks Pr., *(978-0-9713890; 978-0-9778924)* Div. of OBBC, Inc., P.O. Box 2829, Kitty Hawk, NC 27949 USA (SAN 254-3958) Tel 252-261-0612; Toll Free Fax: 800-215-9648
E-mail: linda@outerbankspress.com
Web site: http://www.outerbankspress.com
Dist(s): **Independent Pubs. Group.**

Outland Communications, LLC, *(978-0-9714102; 978-1-932820)* Orders Addr.: P.O. Box 534, Skaneateles, NY 13152 USA; Edit Addr.: 4022 Mill Rd., Skaneateles, NY 13152-9319 USA
Web site: http://www.outlandbooks.com
Dist(s): **Perseus-PGW.**

Outlaw Bks., *(978-0-9656946)* 419 Centre St., Hereford, TX 79045 USA Tel 806-364-2838; Fax: 806-364-5522; Toll Free: 888-583-9408 Do not confuse with Outlaw Books, Bozeman, MT
Dist(s): **Hervey's Booklink & Cookbook Warehouse.**

Outlaw Pubns., *(978-1-886709)* Orders Addr.: P.O. Box 1424, Red Oak, TX 75154 USA Tel 972-504-6608; Edit Addr.: P.O. Box 3043, Desoto, TX 75115 USA.

Outlet Book Company, Incorporated *See* **Random Hse. Value Publishing**

Outlook Publishing, Inc., *(978-0-9711667; 978-0-9817755)* Orders Addr.: P.O. Box 278, Laurel, MT 59044 USA Tel 406-628-4412; Fax: 406-628-8260; Edit Addr.: 415 E. Main St., Laurel, MT 59044 USA
E-mail: publisher@laureloutlook.com
Web site: http://www.laureloutlook.com.

Outrival Publishing, *(978-0-9885603)* P.O. Box 130345, Houston, TX 77219 USA Tel 832-878-6162; Fax: 713-861-1501
E-mail: kimpedigo@gmail.com.

Outside the Box Publishing, LLC, *(978-0-9817398)* 326 2nd St. No. 3, Brooklyn, NY 11215 USA Tel 202-905-3442
E-mail: info@otbpublishing.com; dax@daxdevlonross.com; daxdevlonross@gmail.com
Web site: http://www.otbpublishing.com
Dist(s): **Lightning Source, Inc.**

Outskirts Pr., Inc., *(978-0-9725874; 978-1-932672; 978-1-59800; 978-1-4327; 978-0-615-20388-1; 978-1-4787)* 10940 S. Parker Rd.- 515, Parker, CO 80134 USA (SAN 256-5420)
Web site: http://www.OutskirtsPress, Inc.com
Dist(s): **Aardvark Global Publishing**
Smashwords.

Outskirts Press, Incorporation *See* **Outskirts Pr., Inc.**

Ovation Bks., *(978-1-933538; 978-0-9790275; 978-0-9814534)* 2100 Kramer Ln., Suite 300, Austin, TX 78758 USA Tel 512-478-2028; Fax: 512-478-2117
E-mail: awillis@bookpros.com; sboulden@ovationbooks.net
Web site: http://www.bookpros.com; http://www.ovationbooks.net.

Over the Rainbow *Imprint of* **Pearn & Assocs. Inc.**

Over The Rainbow Bks. Publishing, *(978-0-9793882)* 1810 New Palm Way, No. 410, Boynton Beach, FL 33435 USA Tel 561-704-6581
E-mail: famuffy@aol.com.

Over the Rainbow Productions, *(978-0-9661330)* 1715 Rosedale, Suite B, Houston, TX 77004 USA Tel 713-523-1276; Fax: 713-526-0571
E-mail: apb3@prodigy.net
Web site: http://www.imneecie.com.

Overdue Bks., *(978-0-9786850)* P.O. Box 259462, Madison, WI 53725 USA Do not confuse with Overdue Books in West Linn, OR
E-mail: theoverduebooks@yahoo.com.

Overdue Media LLC, *(978-0-9740353; 978-1-937914)* 4819 S. Oregon St., Seattle, WA 98118-1449 USA
E-mail: unshelved@overduemedia.com
Web site: http://www.overduemedia.com
Dist(s): **Diamond Comic Distributors, Inc.**
Diamond Bk. Distributors
Ingram Pub. Services.

Overlook Connection Pr., The, *(978-0-9633397; 978-1-892950; 978-1-62330)* Orders Addr.: P.O. Box 1934, Hiram, GA 30141 USA Tel 678-567-9777; Edit Addr.: 364 Valerie Cir., Hiram, GA 30141 USA
E-mail: overlookcn@aol.com
Web site: http://www.overlookconnection.com; http://www.overlookconnection.com
Dist(s): **Diamond Comic Distributors, Inc.**

Overlook Farm, *(978-0-615-48761-8)* 45 E. 89th St. Apt. 22c, New York, NY 10128 USA Tel 646-728-2335
Dist(s): **CreateSpace Independent Publishing Platform**
Dummy Record Do Not USE!!!!.

†Overlook Pr., The, *(978-0-87951; 978-1-58567; 978-1-59020; 978-1-4683)* 141 Wooster St., 4th Flr., New York, NY 10012 USA (SAN 202-8360) Tel 212-673-2210; Fax: 212-673-2296
Web site: http://www.overlookpress.com
Dist(s): **MyiLibrary**
Norton, W. W. & Co., Inc.
Open Road Integrated Media, LLC
Penguin Random Hse., LLC.
Penguin Publishing Group
Perseus Bks. Group; *CIP.*

Overmountain Pr., *(978-0-932807; 978-0-9644613; 978-1-57072; 978-1-935692)* P.O. Box 1261, Johnson City, TN 37605 USA (SAN 687-6641) Tel 423-926-2691; Fax: 423-232-1252; Toll Free: 800-992-2691 (orders only); *Imprints:* Silver Dagger Mysteries (Silver Dagger)
E-mail: beth@overmtn.com
Web site: http://www.silverdaggermysteries.com; http://www.overmountainpress.com
Dist(s): **Independent Pubs. Group**
Partners Pubs. Group, Inc.

Overstreet, Mae *See* **Overstreet Pub. & Mktg.**

Overstreet Pub. & Mktg., *(978-0-9746253)* P.O. Box 3808, Yountville, CA 94599 USA
Web site: http://www.bettyoverstreet.com.

Overview Publishing, *(978-0-9760685)* 1081 Crown River Pkwy., McDonough, GA 30252 USA Tel 678-583-0898
E-mail: cindy@overviewpublishing.com
Web site: http://www.overviewpublishing.com
Dist(s): **Quality Bks., Inc.**

Owen, Richard C. Pubs., Inc., *(978-0-913461; 978-1-57274; 978-1-878450)* P.O. Box 585, Katonah, NY 10536 USA (SAN 285-1814) Tel 914-232-3903; Fax: 914-232-3977; Toll Free: 800-336-5588 (orders); *Imprints:* Meet the Author (Meet Author); Books for Young Learners (Bks Yng Learn); Author at Work (Author at Work)
Web site: http://www.RCOwen.com.

Owens, David A., *(978-0-578-05417-9)* 4253 October Woods Dr., Antioch, TN 37013 USA.

Owensby, Legertha, *(978-0-9742789)* 6820 Chiffview Dr., No. E, Indianapolis, IN 46214 USA
E-mail: legethao@yahoo.com
Web site: http://earvino.tripod.com.

Owl About Books *See* **Owl About Bks. Pub., Inc.**

Owl About Bks. Pub., Inc., *(978-1-937752)* 1632 Royalwood Cir., Joshua, TX 76058 USA Tel 682-553-9078; Fax: 817-558-8983
E-mail: owlaboutbooks@gmail.com
Web site: http://www.owlaboutbooks.com
Dist(s): **Lightning Source, Inc.**

Owl Bks. *Imprint of* **Holt, Henry & Co.**

Owl Creek Farm Bks. *Imprint of* **Owl Tree Pr.**

Owl Creek Media Ltd., *(978-1-60404)* 490 Trego Rd., Waverly, OH 45690 USA Tel 740-493-1939; Toll Free: 800-305-0339 Please leave a message
E-mail: james@owlcreekmedia.com
Web site: http://www.owlcreekmedia.com; http://www.localbookproject.com.

Owl Hollow Publishing, *(978-0-9726826)* 13704 Lawrence 2187, Verona, MO 65769 USA Tel 417-498-6964
E-mail: zona@mo-net.com.

Owl of Minerva Press *See* **Minerva Bks.**

Owl Pals, *(978-0-9799196)* 10210 NE. 12th St. Unit C301, Bellevue, WA 98004 USA Tel 206-948-2629
Web site: http://www.owlpals.com.

Owl Tree Pr., *(978-1-929424)* P.O. Box 292, Saint Helens, OR 97051 USA Tel 503-397-3667; Fax: 503-397-3684; *Imprints:* Owl Creek Farm Books (Owl Creek Farm Bks)
E-mail: jdnyberg@ados.com
Web site: http://www.owltreepress.com.

Owlkids Bks. Inc. (CAN) *(978-0-919872; 978-0-920775; 978-1-895688; 978-2-920660; 978-1-894379; 978-2-89579; 978-1-77147)* *Dist. by* **PerseuPGW.**

Oxbow Bks., *(978-0-9771129)* 76 Presidio Dr., Novato, CA 94949 USA
E-mail: dchaller@horizoncable.com.

Oxfam Publishing (GBR) *(978-0-85598)* *Dist. by* **Stylus Pub VA.**

Oxford Museum Pr., *(978-1-930127)* 5790 Stillwell-Beckett Rd., Oxford, OH 45056 USA Tel 513-756-9386; Fax: 513-756-9123; Toll Free: 877-127-1941
E-mail: omp@oxfordmuseumpress.com
Web site: http://www.oxfordmuseumpress.com.

Oxford Univ. Pr. (GBR) *(978-0-19)* *Dist. by* **OUP.**

Oxford Univ. Pr., Inc., *(978-0-19)* Orders Addr.: 2001 Evans Rd., Cary, NC 27513 USA (SAN 202-5892) Tel 919-677-0977 (general voice); Fax: 919-677-1303 (customer service); Toll Free: 800-445-9714 (customer service - inquiry); 800-451-7556 (customer service - orders); Edit Addr.: 198 Madison Ave., New York, NY 10016-4314 USA (SAN 202-5884) Tel 212-726-6000 (general voice); Fax: 212-726-6440 (general fax)
E-mail: custserv@oup-usa.org; orders@oup-usa.org
Web site: http://www.oup.com/us
Dist(s): **Chicago Distribution Ctr.**
CreateSpace Independent Publishing Platform
Ebsco Publishing
Follett School Solutions
Hancock Hse. Pubs.
ISD
MyiLibrary
World Bank Pubns.
ebrary, Inc.

Oxfordshire Publishing Co., *(978-0-9745895)* 900 Lincoln Hwy., Box 180, East Mckeesport, PA 15035 USA Tel 412-823-1700
E-mail: blissman@pghmail.com.

Oxmoor Hse., Inc., *(978-0-376; 978-0-8487)* Orders Addr.: Leisure Arts 5701 Ranch Dr., Little Rock, AR 72223 USA; Edit Addr.: 2100 Lakeshore Dr., Birmingham, AL 35209 USA Tel 205-445-6000; Fax: 205-445-6078; Toll Free: 800-633-4910; *Imprints:* Sunset Books/Sunset Publishing Corporation (SunsetPublng)
E-mail: allison_lowery@timeinc.com
Web site: http://www.oxmoorhouse.com/
Dist(s): **Hachette Bk. Group**
Leisure Arts, Inc.
MyiLibrary
Perseus Distribution
ebrary, Inc.

Oxton Hse., Pubs., *(978-1-881929)* Orders Addr.: P.O. Box 209, Farmington, ME 04938 USA Tel 207-779-1923; Fax: 207-779-0623; Toll Free: 800-539-7323
E-mail: info@oxtonhouse.com
Web site: http://www.oxtonhouse.com
Dist(s): **Smashwords.**

Ozark Publishing, *(978-1-56763; 978-1-59381)* P.O. Box 228, Prairie Grove, AR 72753 USA (SAN 298-4318) Tel 214-649-0188; Fax: 501-846-2853; Toll Free: 800-321-5671
E-mail: srg304@aol.com
Web site: http://www.ozarkpublishing.com
Dist(s): **Central Programs**
Gumdrop Bks.

Ozone Publishing, Corp., *(978-0-9773285)* PMB 500, RR-8 Box 1995, Bayamon, PR 00956-9676 USA Tel 787-562-5200; Fax: 787-730-0987
E-mail: info@ozonepublishing.net
Web site: http://www.ozonepublishing.net.

Ozten, *(978-0-9752966)* 347 NW 87th St., Seattle, WA 98117 USA
E-mail: shout@ozten.com
Web site: http://www.ozten.com.

P & P Publishing LLC, *(978-0-9797020)* 4957 Lakemont Blvd., SE, Suite C-4, No. 316, Bellevue, WA 98006 USA Tel 425-557-0257 Do not confuse with companies with the same or similar name in Frankermuth, MI, Warren, MI, Temple, TX, Wauwatosa, WI.

P & R Publishing, *(978-0-87552; 978-1-59638; 978-1-62995)* Orders Addr.: 1102 Marble Hill Rd., Harmony, Phillipsburg, NJ 08865 USA (SAN 658-1463) Tel 908-454-0505; Fax: 908-859-2390; Toll Free: 800-631-0094 Do not confuse with P & R Publishing Co. in Sioux Center, IA
E-mail: tara@prpbooks.com; jesse@prpbooks.com
Web site: http://www.prpbooks.com
Dist(s): **CLC Pubns.**

P C I Education, *(978-1-884074; 978-1-58804; 978-1-61975)* 4560 Lockhill-Selma, Suite 100, San Antonio, TX 78265-4270 USA Tel 210-377-1999; Fax: 210-377-1121; Toll Free Fax: 888-259-8284; Toll Free: 800-594-4263
E-mail: lboulet@pcieducation.com
Web site: http://www.pcieducation.com
Dist(s): **Attainment Co., Inc.**

P C I Educational Publishing *See* **P C I Education**

P K I Ds, *(978-1-929524)* P.O. Box 5666, Vancouver, WA 98668 USA Tel 360-695-0293; Fax: 360-695-6941; Toll Free: 877-557-5437
E-mail: pkids@pkids.org
Web site: http://www.pkids.org.

P.O.W. (Pubns. of Worth), *(978-1-877898)* 2561 E. 1980 N., Layton, UT 84040-7928 USA.

PSI & Assocs., *(978-0-938261; 978-1-55993)* 9745 SW 125th Terr., Miami, FL 33176-4941 USA (SAN 659-834X).

P2 Publishing, *(978-0-9856336)* 10455 N. Central Expwy Suite 109-115, Dallas, TX 75231 USA Tel 214-223-0366
E-mail: pickleproductionspc@gmail.com
Web site: www.PiperandPickle.com.

P4K Publishing, *(978-0-9744570)* 5699 Kanan Rd., Suite 373, Agoura Hills, CA 91301 USA Tel 818-991-5764; Fax: 818-879-9646
E-mail: lori@prosperity4kids.com
Web site: http://www.prosperity4kids.com.

Paarmann, Al International, *(978-0-9715963)* 368 El Gaucho Rd., Santa Barbara, CA 93111 USA Tel 805-964-2830 (phone/fax)
E-mail: alpaarmann@aol.com.

Pace Products, Inc., *(978-1-58295; 978-1-880592)* P.O. Box 470970, Lake Monroe, FL 32747-0970 USA Toll Free: 800-541-7670
E-mail: PaceProd@aol.com
Web site: http://www.paceplace.com.

Pacific Bks., *(978-1-885375)* Orders Addr.: P.O. Box 3562, Santa Barbara, CA 93130 USA (SAN 630-2548) Tel 805-687-8340; Fax: 805-687-2514; Edit Addr.: 2573 Treasure Dr., Santa Barbara, CA 93105 USA; *Imprints:* Shore Line Press (Shore Line Pr).

Pacific Heritage Bks., *(978-0-9635906; 978-1-928753)* Orders Addr.: P.O. Box 998, Palos Verdes, CA 90274 USA Tel 310-541-8818; Fax: 310-791-9069; Toll Free: 888-810-9891; Edit Addr.: 532 Via del Monte, Palos Verdes Estates, CA 90274 USA
E-mail: amawong@worldnet.att.net
Web site: http://www.pacificheritagebooks.com
Dist(s): **Distributors, The**
Quality Bks., Inc.

Pacific Learning, Inc., *(978-1-59055; 978-1-60457; 978-1-61391)* Orders Addr.: P.O. Box 2723, Huntington Beach, CA 92647-0723 USA; Edit Addr.: 15342 Graham St., Huntington Beach, CA 92649 USA Tel 714-516-8307; Fax: 714-516-8369; Toll Free: 800-279-0737
E-mail: info@pacificlearning.com
Web site: http://www.pacificlearning.com
Dist(s): **Brightpoint Literacy.**

Pacific Moon Pubns., *(978-0-9729524)* Orders Addr.: 2334 Monroe Blvd. Suite 703, Ogden, UT 84401-1727 USA
Dist(s): **Lightning Source, Inc.**

Pacific Northwest Ballet, *(978-0-9745415)* 301 Mercer St., Seattle, WA 98109 USA Tel 206-441-9411; Fax: 206-441-2440
E-mail: kaolivier@mac.com
Web site: http://www.pnb.org.

Pacific Pr. Pubns., *(978-0-9678122)* 3260 Monument, Ann Arbor, MI 48108 USA Tel 734-975-1877 (phone/fax)
E-mail: hailstormx@aol.com.

†Pacific Pr. Publishing Assn., *(978-0-8163; 978-1-5180)* P.O. Box 5353, Nampa, ID 83653-5353 USA (SAN 202-8409) Tel 208-465-2500; Fax: 208-465-2531; Toll Free: 800-447-7377
E-mail: donlay@pacificpress.com
Web site: http://www.AdventistBookCenter.com; http://www.pacificpress.com; *CIP.*

Pacific Pubs., *(978-0-936521; 978-1-933120)* P.O. Box 480, Bolinas, CA 94924 USA (SAN 697-9335) Tel 415-868-2909; Fax: 415-868-9040
E-mail: tideguy@fastmail.fm
Web site: http://www.tidelog.com.

Pacific Raven Press *See* **Pacific Raven Pr.**

Pacific Raven Pr., *(978-0-9841228; 978-0-9840204; 978-0-9860755)* P.O. Box 195, Wailuku, HI 96793 USA (SAN 931-4946)
E-mail: pacificravenpress@gmail.com
Web site: http://www.pacificravenpress.com.

Pacific Ridge Press, LLC *See* **Parra Grande Pr.**

Pacific View Pr., *(978-1-881896)* 2864 Harrison St., San Francisco, CA 94110 USA Tel 415-285-8538; 510-849-4216; Fax: 415-285-2620; 510-843-5835
E-mail: pvp2@mindspring.com
Web site: http://www.pacificviewpress.com
Dist(s): **Cheng & Tsui Co.**
China Bks. & Periodicals, Inc.
Chinasprout, Inc.

Pacifica Island Art, Inc., *(978-0-9727594; 978-0-9758721; 978-1-933735)* Orders Addr.: P.O. Box 120, Haiku, HI 96708 USA Fax: 808-575-2072; Edit Addr.: 810 Haiku Rd., No. 331, Haiku, HI 96708 USA
E-mail: joseph@islandartcards.com
Web site: http://www.islandartcards.com.

Packard, Boyle & Jackson *See* **Apollo Pubs.**

Padah Pr., *(978-0-9721269)* Orders Addr.: P.O. Box 231285, Gresham, OR 97281 USA Tel 971-219-1861
E-mail: eileen@padah.net; eileen@eileenscott.com
Web site: http://www.eileenscott.com.

Paddle Wheel Publishing, *(978-0-9657612)* Div. of Arabia Steamboat Museum, 400 Grand Blvd., Kansas City, MO 64106 USA Tel 816-471-1856; Fax: 816-471-1616; Toll Free: 800-471-1856
E-mail: greghawley@comcast.net
Web site: http://www.1856.com.

Paddywhack Lane LLC., *(978-0-9794286; 978-1-936169)* 9849 Bluestar Dr., Parker, CO 80138 USA (SAN 858-6497) Tel 303-841-1163; Fax: 888-840-0169; Toll Free: 800-796-1163
E-mail: bob@paddywhacklane.com
Web site: http://www.paddywhacklane.com.

Padwolf Publishing, Inc., *(978-1-890096)* P.O. Box 117, Yulan, NY 12792-0117 USA Toll Free: 800-484-7284 ext. 7239
E-mail: padwolf@padwolf.com
Web site: http://www.padwolf.com.

Pagan Writers Pr. *Imprint of* **Mroczka Media**

Pagan Writers Press *See* **Mroczka Media**

Page Publishing *See* **Page Publishing Inc.**

Page Publishing Inc., *(978-0-9854504; 978-1-62838; 978-1-63417; 978-1-68139; 978-1-68213)* 101 Tyrellan Ave., Suite 100, New York, NY 10309 USA Toll Free: 866-315-2708
E-mail: accounts@pagepublishing.com
Web site: http://www.pagepublishing.com.

PageFree Publishing, Inc., *(978-1-929077; 978-1-930252; 978-1-58961)* P.O. Box 60, Otsego, MI 49078-0060 USA Toll Free: 1-866-GO BOOKS
E-mail: pagefreepublish@aol.com; publisher@pagefreepublishing.com
Web site: http://www.pagefreepublishing.com
Dist(s): **BookBaby**
Lightning Source, Inc.
Midpoint Trade Bks., Inc.
Univ. of Hawaii Pr.

PageMaster Publishing, *(978-0-9797759)* 2884 Britton Rd., B34, Perry, MI 48872 USA (SAN 854-3453)
E-mail: Gwen@pagemasterpublishing.com
Web site: http://www.pagemasterpublishing.com.

Pages of Life, *(978-0-615-24716-8; 978-0-615-48466-2; 978-0-615-48467-9)* Div. of Lavender Belle Enterprises, 6328 Joe Klustch Dr., Fort Washington, MD 20744 USA Tel 202-251-2210
E-mail: LavenderBelle@verizon.net
Web site: http://pagesoflife.wordpress.com.

PageSpring Publishing, *(978-1-939403)* 2671 Bristol Rd., Columbus, OH 43221 USA Tel 614-204-2548
E-mail: rseum@pagespringpublishing.com
Web site: www.pagespringpublishing.com; www.luckymarblebooks.com; www.cupofteabooks.com.

Pageturners Publishing Co., *(978-0-9755102)* Orders Addr.: P.O. Box 6, Jacksonville, FL 32234-0006 USA (SAN 256-1719) Tel 904-266-3393; Fax: 904-266-3394
E-mail: publisher@pageturnerspublishing.com
Web site: http://www.pageturnerspublishing.com.

Paginas de Espuma (ESP) *(978-84-95642; 978-84-931243)* *Dist. by* **Lectorum Pubns.**

Paidea Classics, *(978-0-9749900)* P.O. Box 46, Edwards, CA 93523 USA
E-mail: paideaclassics@aol.com
Web site: http://paideaclassics.org.

Paige Martin Bks., *(978-0-578-06864-0; 978-0-578-08272-1)* 11101 Silver Aspen Ct., Hampton, GA 30228 USA
Dist(s): **Smashwords.**

Paige Publishing, *(978-0-9769375)* 5708 Washington St., Downers Grove, IL 60516 USA Do not confuse with companies with the same or similar name in Lexington, OK, Mesa, AZ La Harba, CA San Antonio, TX .

Paigerac, Patricia & Allan Choi *See* **Paigerac, Patricia M.**

Paigerac, Patricia M., *(978-0-9801137)* 30110 Crown Valley Pkwy., Suite 103, Laguna Niguel, CA 92677 USA.

Paint Creek Press, Limited *See* **Archus Pr., LLC**

Publisher Name Index

Paintbox Pr., *(978-0-9669433; 978-0-9777905)* 208 Glandon Dr., Chapel Hill, NC 27514 USA Tel 919-969-7512; Fax: 919-933-4199; Toll Free: 877-969-7512
E-mail: ppease@paintboxpress.com
Web site: http://www.paintboxpress.com
Dist(s): **Follett School Solutions.**

Paintbrush Tales Publishing, LLC, *(978-0-9846151)* 20 Webber Ave., Beverly, MA 01915 USA Tel 978-239-9895
E-mail: caustin36@yahoo.com.

Painted Daisies Inc., *(978-0-615-34491-1)* 3433 Hwy. 190 PMB 377, Mandeville, LA 70471 USA Tel 985-674-0398; Fax: 985-674-2965; 978 Bald Cypress Dr., Mandeville, LA 70448
E-mail: kborg95@gmail.com
Dist(s): **AtlasBooks Distribution**
BookMasters Distribution Services (BDS).

Painted Horse Pubns., Inc., *(978-0-9708066; 978-0-9729482)* 45 Wingate St., Haverhill, MA 01835 USA Tel 978-521-1740
E-mail: sully@stopforastory.com.

Painted Pony, Inc., *(978-0-9759806)* Orders Addr.: P.O. Box 661, Fort Washakie, WY 82514 USA Tel 307-335-7330; Fax: 307-335-7332; Edit Addr.: 47 N. Fork Rd., Fort Washakie, WY 82514 USA Do not confuse with companies with similar name in Atlanta, GA and La Conner, WA.
E-mail: ppi@wrdf.org.

Painted Sky Productions *See* **Emerald City Publishing**

Painted Turtle *Imprint of* **Wayne State Univ. Pr.**

Painted WORD Studios, *(978-0-9721845; 978-0-9771809; 978-0-9845644)* P.O. Box 1606, Crosby, TX 77532-1606 USA Tel 281-456-8810 Toll Free: 866-241-7510
E-mail: paintedwordstudios@gmail.com
Web site: http://www.paintedwordstudios.com.

Painter, Annie & Assocs., *(978-1-928875)* P.O. Box 2135, Sisters, OR 97759 USA Tel 541-549-9539 (phone/fax)
E-mail: painterannie@msn.com.

Painting the Pages Publishing, *(978-0-9843487)* 673 Potomac Station Dr., No. 628, Leesburg, VA 20176 USA (SAN 859-1393)
Web site: http://www.paintingthepages.com.

Painting With Words, *(978-0-9743080)* 10 B State St., Windsor, VT 05089 USA Tel 802-674-5514; Fax: 802-674-9810.

Pair'a Spurs Pr., *(978-0-9749518)* Rt. 2 Box 20, Hollis, OK 73550 USA.

Paisley Publishing, *(978-0-9761710)* 7240 Sagebrush Dr., Parker, CO 80138 USA Fax: 303-841-5229 Do not confuse with Paisley Publishing in Anchorage, AK
E-mail: mlheinze11@aol.com.

Paizo Publishing, LLC, *(978-0-9770071; 978-0-9776778; 978-1-60125)* 7120 185th Ave NE Ste. 120, Redmond, WA 98052-0577 USA
Web site: http://www.paizo.com
Dist(s): **Diamond Comic Distributors, Inc.**
Diamond Bk. Distributors.

Pajama Pr. (CAN) *(978-0-9869495; 978-1-927485) Dist. by* **IngramPubServ.**

PAJE Publishing Co., *(978-0-9753200)* 267 Henley Rd., Wynnewood, PA 19096 USA Tel 610-642-1729; Fax: 610-642-9891; Toll Free: 877-561-1377
E-mail: jay.scott@verizon.net
Dist(s): **AtlasBooks Distribution**
Quality Bks., Inc.

Pakkins Presents, *(978-0-9700241)* Orders Addr.: P.O. Box 10503, Salinas, CA 93912 USA Tel 831-422-3442; Edit Addr.: 637 Carmelita Dr., No. 23, Salinas, CA 93901 USA
E-mail: Pakkins-Land@worldnet.att.net
Web site: http://www.pakkinsland.com.

Pak's Tang Soo Do Studio *See* **High Mountain Publishing**

Pal Toys, LLC, *(978-0-9726170; 978-0-9763648; 978-0-9841459)* P.O. Box 2531, Palos Verdes Peninsula, CA 90274 USA Tel 310-938-6125 Toll Free: 877-725-8880; 26 Santa Bella Rd., Rolling Hills Estates, CA 90274
E-mail: info@paltoys.com; marymoepal@cox.net
Web site: http://www.paltoys.com.

Palabra, Ediciones S.A. (ESP) *(978-84-7118; 978-84-8239) Dist. by* **Lectorum Pubns.**

Palace Press International *See* **ORO Editions**

Palace Press International *See* **Insight Editions LP**

Paladin Timeless *Imprint of* **Twilight Times Bks.**

Palari Publishing LLP, *(978-1-928662)* Orders Addr.: P.O. Box 9288, Richmond, VA 23227-0288 USA Tel 804-355-1035; Toll Free Fax: 866-570-6724 (on demand); Toll Free: 866-570-6724; *Imprints:* Richmondmom.com Publishing (Richmondmom)
E-mail: dave@palaribooks.com
Web site: http://www.palaribooks.com
Dist(s): **Bookazine Co., Inc.**
Smashwords.

Palazzo Editions, Ltd. (GBR) *(978-0-9545103; 978-0-9553046; 978-0-9564448; 978-0-9564942; 978-0-9571483) Dist. by* **IPG Chicago.**

Pale Silver Rainplop Pr., *(978-0-9794396; 978-0-615-14670-6)* P.O. Box 1285, Sioux City, IA 51102 USA
Web site: http://www.katieandkimbleblog.com
Dist(s): **Lulu Enterprises Inc.**

Palgrave *See* **Palgrave Macmillan**

Palgrave Macmillan, *(978-0-312; 978-0-333; 978-1-4039)* Orders Addr.: 16365 James Madison Hwy., Gordonsville, VA 22942-8501 USA Toll Free Fax: 800-672-2054; Toll Free: 888-330-8477; Edit Addr.: 175 Fifth Ave., New York, NY 10010 USA Tel 212-982-9300; Fax: 212-777-6359; Toll Free Fax: 800 672-2054 (Customer Service); Toll Free: 800-221-7945; 888-330-8477 (Customer Service)
E-mail: customerservice@vhpsva.com
Web site: http://www.palgrave.com
Dist(s): **David Brown Book Company, The**
China Bks. & Periodicals, Inc.
Ebsco Publishing
Independent Pubs. Group
Libros Sin Fronteras
Macmillan
MyiLibrary
Trans-Atlantic Pubns., Inc.
ebrary, Inc.

Palgrave Macmillan Ltd. (GBR) *(978-0-312; 978-0-333; 978-1-4039; 978-0-230; 978-1-137) Dist. by* **Macmillan.**

PALH, *(978-0-9719458)* P.O. Box 5099, Santa Monica, CA 90409 USA
E-mail: palh@aol.com
Web site: http://www.palhbooks.com.

Palibrio, *(978-1-61764; 978-1-5065)* Div. of Author Solutions, Inc., 1663 Liberty Dr., Bloomington, IN 47403 USA Tel 812-674-9757; Fax: 812-355-1576; Toll Free: 877-407-5847
Web site: http://www.palibrio.com
Dist(s): **Author Solutions, Inc.**

Palladium Bks., Inc., *(978-0-916211; 978-1-57457)* 39074 Webb Ct., Westland, MI 48185-7606 USA (SAN 294-9504)
E-mail: palladiumbooks@palladiumbooks.com
Web site: http://www.PalladiumBooks.com.

Pallas Athene (GBR) *(978-1-873429; 978-0-9529986) Dist. by* **IPG Chicago.**

Palm Canyon Pr., *(978-0-9960794)* 24 Crockett St., Rowayton, CT 06853 USA Tel 203-853-1512
E-mail: pmorrison101@gmail.com; pagemcbrier@gmail.com
Web site: www.abracadabratut.com; www.palmcanyonpress.com; www.pagemcbrier.com.

Palm Publishing LLC, *(978-0-9753548)* 1016 N. Dixie Hwy., West Palm Beach, FL 33401 USA Tel 561-833-6333; Fax: 561-833-0070
Web site: http://www.phfpbc.org.

Palm Tree Pubns., *(978-0-9787128; 978-0-9795480; 978-0-9799879; 978-0-9817054; 978-0-9822237; 978-0-9826954; 978-0-9846311; 978-0-9847653; 978-0-9857942; 978-0-9862033)* Div. of Palm Tree Productions, P.O. Box 122, Keller, TX 76244 USA; 4508 Willow Rock ln., Keller, TX 76244 Tel 817-431-8574 Do not confuse with Palm Tree Publications in Baton Rouge, LA
Web site: http://www.palmtreeproductions.net
Dist(s): **BookBaby.**

Palmer, Barbara A., *(978-0-9728228)* 486 Manitou Beach Rd., Hilton, NY 14468 USA Tel 585-392-3391; Fax: 585-392-1322
E-mail: bpforlkart@aol.com.

Palmer Enterprises *See* **Palmer Pr., The**

Palmer Lake Historical Society, *(978-0-9755989)* P.O. Box 662, Palmer Lake, CO 80133 USA.

Palmer Pr., The, *(978-0-912479)* P.O. Box 1347, Loomis, CA 95650 USA (SAN 215-1650) Tel 916-652-3225; Fax: 916-652-8665.

Palmer Publications, Incorporated/Amherst Press *See* **Amherst Pr.**

Palmer Publishing, *(978-0-9744410)* 604 4th N.W., Ardmore, OK 73401 USA Tel 580-504-2609 Do not confuse with companies with the same or similar name in Palmer, AK, Ocala, FL
E-mail: charlsie@duracom.net.

Palmer-Pletsch Assocs., *(978-0-935278; 978-1-61847)* 1801 NW Upshur St. #100, Portland, OR 97209 USA
E-mail: info@palmerpletsch.com; wizbiz@pacifier.com
Web site: http://www.palmerpletsch.com
Dist(s): **Independent Pubs. Group**
MyiLibrary.

Palmetto Street Publishing, *(978-0-615-49043-4; 978-0-9848782)* 106 W. Augusta Pl., Greenville, SC 29605 USA Tel 864-242-3906
E-mail: gabbehoward@gmail.com
Web site: n/a.

Palmetto Tree Pr., *(978-0-9742532)* 821 Calhoun St., Columbia, SC 29201 USA (SAN 255-5832) Tel 803-771-9300; Fax: 803-407-0766
E-mail: follybeech@aol.com.

Palmland Publishing, *(978-0-9666942; 978-1-933678)* Orders Addr.: 7881 Barrancas Ave., Bokeelia, FL 33922 USA (SAN 299-7835) Tel 239-283-3975; Fax: 941-870-2589; Toll Free: 877-725-6782; P.O. Box 478, Pineland, FL 33922 Toll Free: 877-725-6782
Web site: http://www.palmlandpublishing.com.

Palmore, Julie, *(978-0-9722653)* 3203 Harwood, Tyler, TX 75701-7642 USA.

Palo Alto Bks. *Imprint of* **Glencannon Pr.**

Palomina Publishing, *(978-0-9763393)* 338 Napa Rd., Sonoma, CA 95476 USA.

Palomino Publishing, *(978-1-892344)* Div. of Programs for the Arts, Inc., 1535 E. Broadway, Tucson, AZ 85719 USA Tel 520-623-4000; Fax: 520-623-9102
E-mail: madaras@worldnet.att.net
Dist(s): **TNT Media Group, Inc.**

Pamir LLC, *(978-0-9888649)* 460 Jameson Hill Rd., Clinton Corners, NY 12514 USA Tel 845-266-0064
E-mail: natasha_rafi@hotmail.com.

Pampa Publishing, *(978-0-9744675; 978-0-615-11346-3)* Orders Addr.: P.O. Box 3481, Olympia, WA 98509-3481 USA; Edit Addr.: 4613 Shincke Rd. NE, Olympia, WA 98506 USA
E-mail: pampapublishing@comcast.net; ma2ka@home.com.

Pan Asia Pubns. (USA), Inc., *(978-1-57227)* 29564 Union City Blvd., Union City, CA 94587 USA (SAN 173-685X) Tel 510-475-1185; Fax: 510-475-1489; Toll Free: 800-909-8088
E-mail: sales@panap.com; info@panap.com
Web site: http://www.panap.com; http://www.cjkv.com
Dist(s): **China Bks. & Periodicals, Inc.**
Chinasprout, Inc.
Follett School Solutions
Lectorum Pubns., Inc.

Pan Macmillan (GBR) *(978-0-283; 978-0-312; 978-0-330; 978-0-333; 978-0-7522; 978-1-85283; 978-1-4050; 978-1-904633; 978-1-904919; 978-1-905716; 978-1-907360; 978-1-4472; 978-1-909621) Dist. by* **Macmillan.**

Pan Macmillan (GBR) *(978-0-283; 978-0-312; 978-0-330; 978-0-333; 978-0-7522; 978-1-85283; 978-1-4050; 978-1-904633; 978-1-904919; 978-1-905716; 978-1-907360; 978-1-4472; 978-1-909621) Dist. by* **IPG Chicago.**

Pan Macmillan (GBR) *(978-0-283; 978-0-312; 978-0-330; 978-0-333; 978-0-7522; 978-1-85283; 978-1-4050; 978-1-904633; 978-1-904919; 978-1-905716; 978-1-907360; 978-1-4472; 978-1-909621) Dist. by* **Trafalgar.**

Pan Macmillan (GBR) *(978-0-283; 978-0-312; 978-0-330; 978-0-333; 978-0-7522; 978-1-85283; 978-1-4050; 978-1-904633; 978-1-904919; 978-1-905716; 978-1-907360; 978-1-4472; 978-1-909621) Dist. by* **Trans-Atl Phila.**

Panacea Pr., *(978-0-9791309; 978-0-9842147; 978-0-9893645; 978-0-9861012)* P.O. Box 292005, Nashville, TN 37229-2005 USA Tel 615-406-822
E-mail: king2dw@aol.com.

Panacea Publishing, *(978-0-9743432)* Orders Addr.: 5002 Barlow Dr., Round Rock, TX 78681 USA Tel 512-228-1388; Fax: 512-906-1579; Toll Free: 877-723-6110 Do not confuse with Panacea Publishing in North Attleboro MA, South Yarmouth MA
E-mail: sales@panaceabooks.com
Web site: http://www.panaceabooks.com
Dist(s): **Brodart Co.**
Midwest Library Service
Quality Bks., Inc.

Panama Hat Publishing, Ltd., *(978-0-9852202; 978-1-943317)* P.O. Box 343, Green Mountain Falls, CO 80819-0343 USA Tel 970-368-2665
E-mail: admin@panamahatpublishing.com
Web site: http://www.panamahatpublishing.com/.

Pan-American Publishing Co., *(978-0-932906)* P.O. Box 1505, Las Vegas, NM 87701 USA (SAN 212-5366).

Panamericana Editorial (COL) *(978-958-30) Dist. by* **Lectorum Pubns.**

Panda Bear Pr., *(978-0-9724699)* Orders Addr.: 612 Museum Rd., Reading, PA 19611-1427 USA (SAN 255-5328) Tel 610-374-7048; Fax: 610-478-7992
E-mail: HaileJohnJr@msn.com
Web site: http://www.caroljhaile.com
Dist(s): **Firenze Pr.**

Panda Pubns., *(978-0-9818392)* P.O. Box 595, Wilkes Barre, PA 18703 USA
E-mail: pandapublications@verizon.net; antoblanco@msn.com.

Panda Publishing, L.L.C., *(978-0-9740180; 978-1-932724)* Orders Addr.: P.O. Box 670608, Dallas, TX 75367 USA (SAN 255-8165) Toll Free: 800-807-1776; Edit Addr.: 6215 Rex Dr., Dallas, TX 75230 USA; *Imprints:* Bios for Kids (Bios for Kids)
E-mail: info@biosforkids.com.

Pandia Pr., *(978-0-9766057; 978-0-9798496)* 18400 SE Hwy.42, Weirsdale, FL 32195 USA
Web site: http://www.PandiaPress.com.

Pandora *Imprint of* **Highland Pr. Publishing**

Pandora Pr. (GBR) *(978-0-04; 978-0-86358; 978-1-85489) Dist. by* **IPG Chicago.**

PANGAEA, *(978-0-9630180; 978-1-929165)* Orders Addr.: 226 Wheeler St., S., Saint Paul, MN 55105-1927 USA Tel 651-226-2032
E-mail: info@pangaea.org
Web site: http://www.pangaea.org
Dist(s): **Follett School Solutions.**

Pangaea Publishing *See* **PANGAEA**

Pangea Software, Inc., *(978-0-9761505)* 12405 John Simpson Ct., Austin, TX 78732-2112 USA Tel 512-266-9991
Web site: http://www.pangeasoft.net.

Pangloss Publishing, *(978-0-9768586; 978-0-615-12424-7)* 3904 Becker Ave., Austin, TX 78751-5209 USA Fax: 512-453-1486
E-mail: candide@grandecom.net.

Pangus Publishing, *(978-0-9769715)* Orders Addr.: 1637 S. Iseminger St., Philadelphia, PA 19148 USA; Edit Addr.: P.O. Box 15763, Philadelphia, PA 19148 USA.

Pankratz Creations, *(978-0-9742637)* 355 S. Fairlane Dr., Tooele, UT 84074-2623 USA
E-mail: customerservice@pankratzcreations.com; pankratz@mstar2.net
Web site: http://www.pankratzcreations.com.

Panline U.S.A., Inc., *(978-0-9713507; 978-0-615-23938-5; 978-0-9822010; 978-0-9847127)* 251 Union St., Northvale, NJ 07647 USA (SAN 920-5772) Tel 201-750-8010; Fax: 201-750-8030
E-mail: info@alextoys.com
Web site: http://www.alextoys.com.

Pannonia Pr., *(978-0-9657793)* P.O. Box 1062, Palatine, IL 60078-1062 USA Tel 847-277-0806; Fax: 847-228-6847
E-mail: pannoniapress2000@sbcglobal.net
Web site: http://www.pannoniapress.com.

Pannycake Pubn., *(978-0-9769538)* 1710 Vallejo St., Unit B, Seaside, CA 93955 USA Tel 831-393-1358; Fax: 831-753-6085
E-mail: carmelalayne@yahoo.com.

Panoply Pubns., *(978-0-9818391)* P.O. Box 2329, North Hollywood, CA 91610-0329 USA Tel 818-761-8757
E-mail: panoplypub@aol.com
Web site: http://www.panoplypublications.com.

Panorama Pr., Inc., *(978-0-9768642)* P.O. Box 183, Boulder, CO 80306-0183 USA.

Pantheon *Imprint of* **Knopf Doubleday Publishing Group**

Panther Creek Pr., *(978-0-9678343; 978-0-9718361; 978-0-9747839; 978-0-9771797)* Orders Addr.: P.O. Box 130233, Spring, TX 77393-0233 USA (SAN 253-8520); Edit Addr.: 104 Plum Tree Ter. Apt. 115, Houston, TX 77077-5375 USA
E-mail: panthercreek3@hotmail.com; guidamj@juno.com
Web site: http://www.panthercreekpress.com.

Pants On Fire Pr., *(978-0-9827271; 978-0-9860373; 978-0-615-88989-4; 978-0-615-89685-4; 978-0-615-89931-2; 978-0-615-91719-1; 978-0-615-96453-9; 978-0-615-98402-5; 978-0-692-02170-5; 978-0-692-02171-2; 978-0-692-20585-3; 978-0-692-20941-7; 978-0-692-21000-0; 978-0-692-21001-7; 978-0-692-21003-1; 978-0-692-30738-0; 978-0-692-35957-0; 978-0-692-44415-3; 978-0-692-44416-0)* 2062 Harbor Cove Way, Winter Garden, FL 34787 USA
E-mail: david@pantsonfirepress.com; editor@pantsonfirepress.com
Web site: http://www.pantsonfirepress.com
Dist(s): **CreateSpace Independent Publishing Platform**
INscribe Digital
Ingram Pub. Services.

Paon Pubns., *(978-0-9711721)* 608 S. Webik Ave, Clawson, MI 48017 USA Tel 248-288-5621.

Papaloizos Pubns., Inc., *(978-0-932416)* 11720 Auth Ln., Silver Spring, MD 20902-1645 USA (SAN 220-9853) Tel 301-593-0652
E-mail: info@greek123.com
Web site: http://www.greek123.com.

Papas & Nellie Pr., *(978-0-9719925)* 2110 Lakeland Ave., Madison, WI 53704 USA Tel 608-661-0508
E-mail: papasandnellie@tds.net.

Papell, David, *(978-0-615-17531-7; 978-0-615-17931-5; 978-0-615-17932-2)* 5601 Riverdale Ave., Bronx, NY 10471 USA Tel 718-601-3771
E-mail: dpapell@earthlink.net
Web site: http://www.davidpapell.net
Dist(s): **Lulu Enterprises Inc.**

Paper Crane Pr., *(978-0-9650833)* P.O. Box 29292, Bellingham, WA 98228-1292 USA Tel 360-676-0266; Toll Free: 800-356-9315
E-mail: carolrj@nas.com
Dist(s): **Brodart Co.**
New Leaf Distributing Co., Inc.
Unique Bks., Inc.
Upper Access, Inc.

Paper Jam Publishing, *(978-1-888345)* Orders Addr.: P.O. Box 435, Eastsound, WA 98245 USA Tel 360-376-3200 (phone/fax); Toll Free: 877-757-2665; Edit Addr.: 531 Fern St., Eastsound, WA 98245 USA
E-mail: paperjam@rockisland.com
Web site: http://www.rockisland.com/~paperjam.

Paper Kite Pr., *(978-0-9725942; 978-0-9798470; 978-0-615-36742-2; 978-0-9831606)* 443 Main St., Kingston, PA 18704 USA
E-mail: wordpainting@comcast.net
Web site: http://www.wordpainting.com
Dist(s): **SPD-Small Pr. Distribution.**

Paper Posie, *(978-0-9707944; 978-0-9774763)* Orders Addr.: 315a Meigs Rd., #167, Santa Barbara, CA 93109 USA Tel 805-569-2398; Fax: 805-563-0166; Toll Free: 800-360-1761
Web site: http://www.paperposie.com; http://www.kidsatweddings.com
Dist(s): **Greenleaf Book Group.**

Paper Studio Pr., *(978-0-9790668; 978-0-9795053; 978-1-935223; 978-1-942490)* Orders Addr.: P.O. Box 14, Kingfield, ME 04947 USA Tel 207-265-2500
Web site: http://paperstudiopress.com.

Paper Talk, *(978-0-9709537)* 4800 Natrona, Anchorage, AK 99516 USA Tel 907-345-1475
E-mail: kaniut@alaska.net
Web site: http://www.kaniut.com.

Paperbacks for Educators, *(978-0-9702376; 978-1-59721)* 426 W. Front St., Washington, MO 63090 USA (SAN 103-3379) Tel 636-239-1999; Fax: 636-239-4515; Toll Free Fax: 800-514-7323; Toll Free: 800-227-2591
E-mail: paperbacks@usmo.com
Web site: http://www.any-book-in-print.com.

Papercutz, *(978-1-59707; 978-1-62991)* 160 Broadway, E. Wing Suite 700, New York, NY 10038 USA (SAN 850-9670) Tel 646-559-4681
E-mail: nantier@papercutz.com
Web site: http://www.papercutz.com
Dist(s): **Macmillan.**

Papergraphics Printing, *(978-0-9773322)* 4 John Tyler St., Suite 1, Merrimack, NH 03054-3054 USA Tel 603-880-1835; Fax: 603-880-1751; Toll Free: 800-499-1835
E-mail: prepress@papergraphics.biz
Web site: http://www.papergraphics.biz.

Papier-Mache Pr. *Imprint of* **Moyer Bell**

Papillon Pr., *(978-1-884429)* Orders Addr.: P.O. Box 54502, Phoenix, AZ 85078-4502 USA Tel 602-931-0556
E-mail: firstchoiceent05@msn.com.

Papillon Pr., Inc., *(978-0-9667476)* 23 Seagull Pl., Vero Beach, FL 32960-5212 USA
Dist(s): **New Leaf Distributing Co., Inc.**

Papillon Publishing *Imprint of* **Blue Dolphin Publishing, Inc.**

Papillon Publishing, *(978-0-9651048)* P.O. Box 12044, Dallas, TX 75225 USA Tel 214-722-1297 (phone/fax) Do not confuse with Papillon Publishing in Rochester, MN
E-mail: ford.lawrence@sbcglobal.net.

PAPO Brand *Imprint of* **Planet Bronx Productions**

Papyrus & Pen, (978-0-9770687) 2923 Cecil B. Moore Ave., Suite 3, Philadelphia, PA 19121 USA Tel 267-539-7540
E-mail: dmccrary@papyrusandpen.com
Web site: http://www.papyrusandpen.com
Dist(s): **Ingram Pub. Services**
Lightning Source, Inc.

Papyrus Publishing, Inc., (978-0-9675581; 978-0-9882883) Orders Addr.: 7409 Edgewood Ave. N., Brooklyn Park, MN 55428 USA Tel 763-717-8854; Fax: 763-374-7737
Do not confuse with Papyrus Publishing in Missouri City, TX
E-mail: PapyrusPublishing@msn.com
Web site: http://www.mahmoudelkati.com; http://www.papyruspublishinginc.com.

Para-Anchors International, (978-1-878832) Orders Addr.: P.O. Box 19, Summerland, CA 93067 USA Tel 805-966-4837; Fax: 805-966-0782; Toll Free: 800-350-7070; Edit Addr.: 21 E. Canon Perdido, Suite 303, Santa Barbara, CA 93101 USA
E-mail: victor1pai@netscape.com; victor1cnp@netscape.com
Web site: http://www.jerustar.com
Dist(s): **AtlasBooks Distribution**
Quality Bks., Inc.

†Parable Pr., (978-0-917250) P.O. Box 51, Vinalhaven, ME 04863-0051 USA (SAN 208-4449); *CIP.*

Parable Venture Partners, LLC, (978-0-9728501) 12946 SW 133 Ct., Suite B, Miami, FL 33186 USA Tel 305-252-0905; Fax: 305-245-9974
E-mail: info@ethansparables.com
Web site: http://www.ethansparables.com.

Parables & Bks., (978-0-9833188; 978-1-939682) 24 S. Front St., Bergenfield, NJ 07621 USA Tel 201-338-4953
E-mail: sandy@parablesandbooks.com
Web site: www.parablesandbooks.com.

Parabola Bks., (978-0-930407) 656 Broadway, Suite 615, New York, NY 10012-2317 USA (SAN 219-5763) Tel 212-505-6200; Fax: 212-979-7325; Toll Free: 800-560-6984
E-mail: ads-promo@parabola.org; orders@parabola.org; JoeKulin@aol.com; editors@parabola.org
Web site: http://www.parabola.org/; http://www.cinemaofthespirit.org
Dist(s): **Independent Pubs. Group**
New Leaf Distributing Co., Inc.
Perseus-PGW.

Parabola Magazine/Society for Study of Myth & Tradition *See* **Parabola Bks.**

Parachute Jump Publishing, (978-0-9852469; 978-0-9888905; 978-0-9915405; 978-0-9903660) 50 Brighton 1st Rd. Apt. 16D, Brooklyn, NY 11235 USA Tel 718-593-7717
E-mail: kpaulet@verizon.net
Dist(s): **BookBaby**
Lightning Source, Inc.

Parachute Press, Incorporated *See* **Parachute Publishing, LLC**

Parachute Publishing, LLC, (978-0-938753; 978-1-57351) 156 Fifth Ave., New York, NY 10010 USA (SAN 661-5554) Tel 212-691-1421; Fax: 212-645-8769
E-mail: ppibooks@aol.com.

Paraclete Pr., Inc., (978-0-941478; 978-1-55725; 978-1-61261) Orders Addr.: P.O. Box 1568, Orleans, MA 02653 USA (SAN 282-1508) Fax: 508-255-5705; Toll Free: 800-451-5006; Edit Addr.: 36 Southern Eagle Cartway, Brewster, MA 02631 USA (SAN 664-6239) Do not confuse with companies with the same or similar names in Indianapolis, IN, Pentwater, MI
E-mail: srmercy@paracletepress.com; miao@paracletepress.com
Web site: http://www.paracletepress.com
Dist(s): **Follett School Solutions**
Forward Movement Pubns.
MyiLibrary.

Paradigm Accelerated Curriculum, (978-1-928629; 978-1-59476) Div. of Paradigm Alternatives Centers, Inc., Orders Addr.: P.O. Box 200, Dublin, TX 76446-0200 USA Tel 254-445-4272; Fax: 254-445-3947; Edit Addr.: 112 S. Grafton, Dublin, TX 76446-0200 USA
E-mail: learn@pacworks.com
Web site: http://www.pacworks.com.

Paradigm Alternatives Centers, Incorporated *See* **Paradigm Accelerated Curriculum**

Paradigm Publishing, (978-0-9746013) Orders Addr.: P.O. Box 872, LaPorte, CO 80535 USA; Edit Addr.: 3106 Kintzley Ct., D, LaPorte, CO 80535 USA Do not confuse with companies with the same or similar name in Oklahoma City OK, San Dimas CA, Chicago IL, McFarland WI, Saint Paul MN, Midvale UT, Pembroke Pines FL, Pocatello ID, Brookline MA, Boulder CO, Laguna Park, TX , Washington, DC
E-mail: sales@paradigmpublish.com
Web site: http://www.paradigmpublish.com.

Paradise Cay Pubns., (978-0-939837; 978-1-937196) P.O. Box 29, Arcata, CA 95518-0029 USA (SAN 663-690X) Tel 707-822-9063; Fax: 707-822-9163; Toll Free: 800-736-4509 (orders only)
E-mail: jim@paracay.com
Web site: http://www.paracay.com
Dist(s): **Hale, Robert & Co., Inc.**

Paradise Copies, Inc., (978-0-9836716) 21 Conz St., Northampton, MA 01060 USA Tel 413-585-0414; Fax: 413-585-0417
E-mail: Carol@paradisecopies.com
Web site: http://paradisecopies.com.

Paradise Pr. & Assocs., LLC, (978-0-9755970) P.O. Box 783573, Winter Garden, FL 34778-3573 USA Tel 321-354-5881 (phone/fax)
E-mail: bbeehy@gmail.com
Web site: none.

Paradise Pr., Inc., (978-1-57657; 978-1-884907; 978-1-4194) 1776 N. Pine Island Rd. Ste. 218, Plantation, FL 33322-5223 USA Do not confuse with companies with the same or similar names in Crested Butte, CO Corte Madera, CA, Santa Monica, CA, Ridgefield, CA, Chicago, IL, Herdon, VA, Temple Terrace, FL
E-mail: buybooks@paradisepress.us.

Paradise Research Pubns., Inc., (978-1-885803) Orders Addr.: P.O. Box 837, Kihei, HI 96753-0837 USA Tel 808-874-4876 (phone/fax)
E-mail: dickb@dickb.com
Web site: http://www.dickb.com/index.html
Dist(s): **Globe Pequot Pr., The**
Good Bk. Publishing Co.

Paradox *Imprint of* **DC Comics**

Paradoxal Pr., (978-0-9766132) 28916 NE 34th Ct., Redmond, WA 98053-9114 USA
Web site: http://www.paradoxalpress.com.

Paradoxical Pr., The, (978-0-9786663) 48 Cranford Pl., Teaneck, NJ 07666 USA Tel 201-281-8112
E-mail: info@theparadoxicalpress.com
Web site: http://www.theparadoxicalpress.com.

Paraglyph, Inc., (978-1-932111; 978-1-933097) 3533 E. Friess Dr., Phoenix, AZ 85032-5318 USA; 3533 E. Friess Dr., Phoenix, AZ 85032-5318; *Imprints:* Paraglyph Press (Paraglyph Pr)
E-mail: ccaldwell@paraglyphpress.com; stevesayre@paraglyphpress.com
Web site: http://www.paraglyphpress.com
Dist(s): **Ingram Pub. Services**
O'Reilly Media, Inc.

Paraglyph Pr. *Imprint of* **Paraglyph, Inc.**

Paragon Agency, Pubs., The *Imprint of* **Paragon Agency, The**

Paragon Agency, The, (978-1-891030) Orders Addr.: P.O. Box 1281, Orange, CA 92856 USA Tel 714-771-0652; *Imprints:* Paragon Agency, Publishers, The (PAP)
E-mail: Paragon@SpecialBooks.com
Web site: http://www.SpecialBooks.com.

†Paragon Hse. Pubs., (978-0-88702; 978-0-89226; 978-0-913729; 978-0-943852; 978-1-55778; 978-1-61083) Orders Addr.: 3600 Labore Rd., Suite 1, Saint Paul, MN 55110-4144 USA (SAN 286-1704) Tel 651-644-3087; Fax: 651-644-0997; Toll Free Fax: 800-494-0997; Toll Free: 800-447-3709
E-mail: paragon@paragonhouse.com
Web site: http://www.paragonhouse.com
Dist(s): **AtlasBooks Distribution**
Bloomsbury Publishing Inc
Continuum International Publishing Group, Inc.
MPS
Macmillan; *CIP.*

Parallax, Inc., (978-1-928982) 599 Menlo Dr., No. 100, Rocklin, CA 95765-3708 USA Tel 916-624-8333; Fax: 916-624-8003; Toll Free: 888-512-1024
E-mail: info@parallaxinc.com
Web site: http://www.parallaxinc.com.

Parallax Pr., (978-0-938077; 978-1-888375; 978-1-935209; 978-0-9846271; 978-1-937006; 978-1-941529) Orders Addr.: P.O. Box 7355, Berkeley, CA 94707 USA (SAN 663-4494) Tel 510-525-0101; Fax: 510-525-7129; Toll Free: 800-863-5290; Edit Addr.: 2236 6th St., Berkeley, CA 94710-2219 USA; *Imprints:* Plum Blossom Books (Plum Blossom)
E-mail: parallax@parallax.org
Web site: http://www.parallax.org
Dist(s): **MyiLibrary**
Perseus-PGW
Perseus Bks. Group
SPD-Small Pr. Distribution.

Paramance *Imprint of* **MQuills Publishing**

Paramount Market Publishing, Inc., (978-0-9671439; 978-0-9725290; 978-0-9766973; 978-0-9786602; 978-0-9801745; 978-0-9819869; 978-0-9830436; 978-0-9851795; 978-1-941688) 950 Danby Rd., Suite 136, Ithaca, NY 14850 USA (SAN 850-6612) Tel 607-275-8100 (phone/fax); Toll Free: 888-787-8100
E-mail: doris@paramountbooks.com
Web site: http://www.paramountbooks.com.

Paraphrase, LLC, (978-0-9815879) Orders Addr.: P.O. Box 56508, Sherman Oaks, CA 91413 USA (SAN 855-9643) Tel 818-219-4377; Toll Free Fax: 888-863-4377
Web site: http://www.paraphrasellc.com; http://www.espete.com.

Parascension, Inc., (978-0-9729380; 978-0-615-18212-4) 222 Oak Grove Rd., Suite 201, Bradfordwoods, PA 15015-1338 USA; *Imprints:* Parascension Press (Parascen)
E-mail: jameshayhurst@zoominternet.net
Web site: http://www.parascension.com; http://www.badcommandments.com; http://www.adventuresofmercurylane.com.

Parascension Pr. *Imprint of* **Parascension, Inc.**

Parent Brigade Company, The, (978-0-9774998) 530 New Los Angeles Ave., Suite 115-332, Moorpark, CA 93021 USA Fax: 805-523-0119.

Parent Child Pr., Inc., (978-0-939195; 978-0-9601016) Orders Addr.: 11 W 9th St, Santa Rosa, CA 95401 USA (SAN 208-4333) Tel 707-579-3003; Fax: 707-579-1604; Toll Free: 866-727-3682; Edit Addr.: 11 W 9th St, Santa Rosa, CA 95401 USA (SAN 662-7331)
E-mail: smcmath@montessoriservices.com
Web site: http://http://www.montessoriservices.com/parent-child-press.

Parent Perks, Inc., (978-0-9822150) 217 Bellevue St., Newton, MA 02458 USA (SAN 857-569X)
E-mail: parentperks@yahoo.com.

Parent Positive Pr., (978-0-9721502) 446 Willis Ave., No. 118, Williston Park, NY 11596-0118 USA (SAN 257-4438) Tel 516-997-0051
E-mail: Info@parentpositive.com
Web site: http://www.girlsonlyweightloss.com
Dist(s): **Independent Pubs. Group.**

Parental Interventional Tools, Inc, (978-0-9778274) P.O. Box 547, Southbury, CT 06488 USA Tel 203-264-1054
E-mail: pittools@aol.com
Web site: http://www.drketch.com; www.pit-inc.com.

†Parenting Pr., Inc., (978-0-943990; 978-0-9602862; 978-1-884734; 978-1-936903) Orders Addr.: P.O. Box 75267, Seattle, WA 98175 USA (SAN 215-6938) Tel 206-364-2900; Fax: 206-364-0702; Toll Free: 800-992-6657; Edit Addr.: P.O. Box 75267, Seattle, WA 98175 USA (SAN 699-5500)
E-mail: cthreadgill@ParentingPress.com
Web site: http://www.parentingpress.com
Dist(s): **Brodart Co.**
Follett School Solutions
Independent Pubs. Group
Midwest Library Service
MyiLibrary; *CIP.*

ParentMagic, Inc., (978-0-9633861; 978-1-889140) 800 Roosevelt Rd., Glen Ellyn, IL 60137 USA Tel 630-469-0484; Fax: 630-469-4571; Toll Free: 800-442-4453
Web site: http://www.thomasphelan.com
Dist(s): **Independent Pubs. Group**
MAR*CO Products, Inc.
MyiLibrary
ebrary, Inc.

Parents Publishing Group *Imprint of* **Big Tent Bks.**

Parish, Alex (GBR) (978-0-9561613) *Dist. by* **LuluCom.**

Parity Pr., (978-0-9762015) 1450 W. Horizon Ridge Pkwy, B-304-226, Henderson, NV 89012-4480 USA Tel 702-260-8989; Fax: 702-364-8988; Toll Free: 877-260-8989
E-mail: info@paritypress.biz
Web site: http://www.ShiftingRings.com.

Pariyatti Publishing, (978-0-9649484; 978-81-7414; 978-1-928706; 978-1-938754; 978-1-68172) Div. of Pariyatti, 867 Larmon Rd., Onalaska, WA 98570 USA Tel 360-978-4998; Fax: 360-978-4557
E-mail: director@pariyatti.org; admin@pariyatti.org
Web site: http://www.pariyatti.org
Dist(s): **Independent Pubs. Group**
MyiLibrary.

Park Hse. Bks., (978-0-9755097) 838 N. 6th St., Saint Clair, MI 48079 USA
E-mail: parkhousebooks@yahoo.com; mmerkau@yahoo.com
Web site: http://www.familyunity.us.

Park Tutor Schl., (978-0-9612740) 7200 N. College Ave., Indianapolis, IN 46240 USA (SAN 289-7903) Tel 317-415-2700; Fax: 317-254-2714; Toll Free: 888-782-5861
E-mail: info@parktudor.pvt.org
Web site: http://www.parktudor.org.

Parker, Laurie, (978-0-9729615) 111 Dunbrook Dr., Starkville, MS 39759-4149 USA.

Parker Publishing Company *See* **Parker-Wallace Publishing Co., LLC**

Parker Publishing Inc., (978-1-60043) 12523 Limonite Ave. #440-438, Mira Loma, CA 91752 USA Fax: 681-685-8036
E-mail: miriam@parker-publishing.com
Web site: http://www.parker-publishing.com
Dist(s): **AtlasBooks Distribution.**

Parker-Wallace Publishing Co., LLC, (978-0-9654700; 978-1-893091) Orders Addr.: P.O. Box 8654, Fort Lauderdale, FL 33310 USA; *Imprints:* My Ancestors, My Heroes (My Ancestors)
E-mail: thebusiness2@yahoo.com.

Parkhurst Brook Pubs., (978-0-9615664) 303 Perrin Rd., Potsdam, NY 13676 USA (SAN 695-9121) Tel 315-265-9037
E-mail: mhcharle@northnet.org
Dist(s): **AtlasBooks Distribution.**

Parkhurst Brothers, Inc., Pubs., (978-1-935166; 978-1-62491) Orders Addr.: 110 West Main, Marion, MI 49665 USA (SAN 856-7107) Tel 5015153224
E-mail: ted@parkhurstbrothers.com
Web site: www.parkhurstbrothers.com; http://www.parkhurstbrothers.com
Dist(s): **Chicago Distribution Ctr.**

Parkhurst, R.M., (978-0-9770323) Orders Addr.: P.O. Box 1033, Redwood City, CA 94064 USA; Edit Addr.: P.O. Box 1013, Atascadero, CA 93423-1013 USA
E-mail: parkhurst@bigfoot.com.

Parklane Publishing, (978-1-59384) Div. of Book Club of America, 100 Marcus Blvd. Ste. 8, Hauppauge, NY 11788-3749 USA
E-mail: lbaumert@bookclubusa.com
Web site: http://www.parklanepublishing.com.

Parks Publishing *Imprint of* **RBC Publishing Co., Inc.**

Parkside Pubns., Inc., (978-0-9617266; 978-0-9820774) 901 5th Ave. Ste. 4100, Seattle, WA 98164-2001 USA (SAN 663-4907) Do not confuse with Parkside Pubns., Inc., Davis, SD
E-mail: info@parksidepublications.com
Web site: http://www.parksidepublications.com
Dist(s): **Partners Bk. Distributing, Inc.**

Parkway Pr., Ltd., (978-0-9826641; 978-0-9828089) 330 Smith St., Niles, OH 44446-1735 USA Tel 330-505-8113
E-mail: dlbrown88@yahoo.com
Web site: www.parkwaypress.com.

Parkway Pubs., Inc., (978-0-9635752; 978-1-887905; 978-1-933251)
E-mail: parkwaypub@hotmail.com
Web site: http://www.parkwaypublishers.com
Dist(s): **Blair, John F. Pub.**
Julia Taylor Ebel.

Parkwest Pubns., Inc., (978-0-88186) P.O. Box 310251, Miami, FL 33231 USA (SAN 264-6846) Tel 305-256-7880; Fax: 305-256-7816; *Imprints:* DINOSAUR BOOKS (DINOSAURBKS)
E-mail: parkwest@parkwestpubs.com; info@parkwestpubs.com
Web site: http://www.parkwestpubs.com
Dist(s): **Independent Pubs. Group.**

Parlance Publishing, (978-0-9721032) Orders Addr.: P.O. Box 841, Columbus, MS 39703-0841 USA (SAN 255-0806) Tel 662-327-4064; Fax: 662-327-4504; Edit Addr.: 1099 Southdown Pkwy., Columbus, MS 39701 USA
E-mail: parlancepub@aol.com; mail@abookery.com
Web site: http://www.parlancepublishing.com; http://www.abookery.com.

Parra Grande Pr., (978-0-9815541; 978-0-615-19049-5) 211 E. Carrillo St., No. 301, Santa Barbara, CA 93101 USA (SAN 855-8671) Tel 805-899-3210; Fax: 805-899-3211
E-mail: jb657@verizon.net.

Parragon, Inc., (978-0-7525; 978-1-85813; 978-1-4054) Div. of Parragon Publishing, 440 Park Ave. S, 13th Flr., New York, NY 10016 USA (SAN 256-7385) Tel 212-629-9773; Fax: 212-629-9756; *Imprints:* Exclusive Editions (Exclusive Editions); Bright Sparks (Bright Sparks)
Dist(s): **Central Programs.**

Parramon Ediciones S.A. (ESP) (978-84-342) *Dist. by* **Continental Bk.**

Parramon Ediciones S.A. (ESP) (978-84-342) *Dist. by* **Distr Norma.**

Parramon Ediciones S.A. (ESP) (978-84-342) *Dist. by* **Lectorum Pubns.**

Parrhesia Pr. *Imprint of* **Listening Chamber**

Parrot Pr., (978-0-615-17122-7) 6200 Vista Del Mar, Suite 313, Playa del Rey, CA 90293 USA Tel 310-574-0911
E-mail: mira@miramarmango.com
Web site: http://www.parrotstory.com
Dist(s): **Partners Pubs. Group, Inc.**

PARSEC Ink, (978-0-9743231; 978-0-615-15280-6; 978-0-615-23540-0; 978-0-578-03103-3) P.O. Box 3681, Pittsburgh, PA 15230-3681 USA
Web site: http://www.trfn.clpgh.org/parsec
Dist(s): **Lulu Enterprises Inc.**

PARSEC Publishing *See* **PARSEC Ink**

Parson Place Pr., LLC, (978-0-9786567; 978-0-9842163; 978-0-9888528) 10701 Tanner Williams Rd., Mobile, AL 36608-8846 USA (SAN 851-254X); P.O. Box 8277, Mobile, AL 36689-0277 Tel 251-645-9803
E-mail: info@parsonplacepress.com; mlwhite@parsonplacepress.com
Web site: http://www.parsonplacepress.com
Dist(s): **Lightning Source, Inc.**
Spring Arbor Distributors, Inc.

Parsons Porch Bks., (978-0-9826337; 978-0-9829413; 978-1-936912; 978-0-692-25814-9; 978-0-692-30031-2; 978-0-692-30040-4; 978-0-692-30872-1; 978-0-692-32034-1; 978-0-692-32056-3; 978-0-692-32058-7; 978-0-692-32063-1; 978-0-692-32066-2; 978-0-692-32067-9; 978-0-692-32776-0; 978-0-692-33452-2; 978-0-692-33526-0; 978-0-692-33625-0; 978-0-692-33626-7; 978-0-692-35217-5; 978-0-692-35889-4; 978-0-692-35891-7; 978-0-692-35894-8; 978-0-692-36083-5; 978-0-692-36086-6; 978-0-692-38065-9; 978-0-692-38067-3; 978-0-692-380) 121 Holly Trail NW, Cleveland, TN 37311 USA Tel 423-476-4122
E-mail: dtullock@parsonsporch.com
Web site: http://www.parsonsporch.com
Dist(s): **CreateSpace Independent Publishing Platform.**

Parsons Technology, (978-1-57264) Subs. of The Learning Co., Orders Addr.: P.O. Box 100, Hiawatha, IA 52233-0100 USA (SAN 665-6161) Tel 319-395-9626; Fax: 319-378-0335; Toll Free: 800-833-3241
Dist(s): **Spring Arbor Distributors, Inc.**

Partae Pr., (978-0-9662608) 703 Ivinson Ave., Laramie, WY 82070 USA (SAN 254-1688) Tel 307-745-6893
E-mail: press@partae.com
Web site: http://www.partae.com.

Parthenon Pr., (978-0-9718398) 4839 Fullmoon Dr., El Sobrante, CA 94803-2139 USA Tel 510-223-6850 Do not confuse with Parthenon Pr., in New York, NY
E-mail: wakingthetiger@yahoo.com
Web site: http://expage.com/tigerspirit
Dist(s): **CreateSpace Independent Publishing Platform.**

Parthian Bks. (GBR) (978-0-9521558; 978-1-902638; 978-1-905762; 978-1-906998; 978-1-907476) *Dist. by* **IPG Chicago.**

Partners Book Distributing, Incorporated *See* **Partners Pubs. Group, Inc.**

Partners Bk. Distributing, Inc., Orders Addr.: P.O. Box 580, Holt, MI 48842 USA; Edit Addr.: 2325 Jarco Dr., Holt, MI 48842 USA (SAN 630-4559) Tel 517-694-3205; Toll Free: 800-336-3137 (orders).

Partners in Development *See* **Partners in Development Foundation**

Partners in Development Foundation, (978-1-933835) 2040 Bachelot St., Honolulu, HI 96817 USA Tel 808-595-2752; Fax: 808-595-4932
E-mail: admin@pidfoundation.org
Web site: http://www.pidfoundation.org
Dist(s): **Islander Group.**

Partners in Learning, Incorporated *See* **MRN Pubns.**

Partners Pubs. Group, Inc., Orders Addr.: 2325 Jarco Dr., Holt, MI 48842 USA (SAN 631-3418) Tel 517-694-3205; Fax: 517-694-0617; Toll Free: 800-336-3137
E-mail: info@partnerspublishersgroup.com
Web site: http://www.partnerspublishersgroup.com.

Partridge Pub., (978-1-4828) 1663 Liberty Dr., Bloomington, IN 47403 USA Toll Free: 877-655-1722
E-mail: jburns@authorsolutions.com
Web site: http://www.partridgepublishing.com.

PartridgeIndia *Imprint of* **Author Solutions, Inc.**

Pasco Scientific, *(978-1-886998; 978-1-937492)* 10101 Foothills Blvd., Roseville, CA 95678-8905 USA Tel 916-786-3800; Fax: 916-786-8905.

Pascualina Producciones S.A., 150 42nd Ave. E., Seattle, WA 98112 USA Tel 206-940-5412; Fax: 206-621-7956
E-mail: magdelenarossa@aol.com
Dist(s): **Independent Pubs. Group.**

Pasiteles Publishing Co., *(978-0-9785270)* 743 Belmont St., Belmont, MA 02478 USA
Web site: http://www.pasiteles.com.

Passage Publishing, *(978-0-9715926; 978-0-9724619; 978-0-9814833)* Div. of Art by Marianne, P.O. Box 148304, Nashville, TN 37214 USA Tel 615-828-3657 Do not confuse with Passage Publishing in Seattle, WA
E-mail: upcountrygirl@comcast.net; marsydotes1@live.com; upcountrygirl7@msn.com
Web site: http://www.upcountrycreations.com; http://www.artbymarianne.com.

Passion Profit Co., The/NicheMarket, *(978-0-9629202; 978-0-9745313; 978-0-9835808)* Div. of A Company Called W, Orders Addr.: P.O. Box 618, New York, NY 10008 USA Tel 646-219-3565; Fax: 212-658-9232
E-mail: orderdept@passionprofit.com
Web site: http://www.passionprofit.com.

Passionate Purpose, *(978-0-9898579)* 377 Carodon Dr., Ruckersville, VA 22968 USA Tel 850-890-2768
E-mail: wildcatdtt@yahoo.com.

PassionQuest Technologies, LLC, *(978-0-9679338; 978-0-9912611)* P.O. Box 912, Marysville, OH 43040 USA (SAN 254-4326) Tel 707-688-2848; 5055 Business Ctr. Dr. Suite 108, Pmb 110, Fairfield, CA 94534 Tel 707-688-2848; *Imprints:* Wings-on-Disk (Wings Disk)
E-mail: john@earnprofitsfromyourpassion.com
Web site: http://www.OnMyMountain.com.

Passkey Pubns., *(978-0-9818971; 978-0-9822660; 978-1-935664; 978-1-937361)* Orders Addr.: P.O. Box 580465, Elk Grove, CA 95758 USA (SAN 856-8782) Tel 916-712-7446; Fax: 916-427-5765; *Imprints:* Defiant Press (DefiantPr)
E-mail: admin@passkeypublications.com
Web site: http://www.passkeypublications.com; http://www.pineapplepublications.com; http://www.enrolledagentreview.com; http://www.defiantpress.com/
Dist(s): **CreateSpace Independent Publishing Platform**
Lightning Source, Inc.
Lulu Enterprises Inc.

Passport Bks. *Imprint of* **McGraw-Hill Trade**

Pastime Pr., *(978-0-9711632; 978-1-932046)* Div. of CICA Industries, Inc., P.O. Box 741084, Boynton Beach, FL 33474 USA Tel 561-731-3400; Toll Free: 800-370-1174 Do not confuse with Pastime Press in Seattle, WA
E-mail: cicausadotcom@aol.com
Web site: http://www.pastimepress.com.

Pastime Pubns., *(978-0-9760276)* 1370 Trancas St., No. 372, Napa, CA 94558 USA Do not confuse with Pastime Publications in Walnut Creek, CA; Oakhill, VA; Herndon, VA
Web site: http://napavalleypastime.com.

PastWays Inc., *(978-0-9671075)* Orders Addr.: P.O. Box 551, Farmington, MI 48332-0551 USA Tel 248-701-8112; Edit Addr.: 33414 Oakland, Suite 2, Farmington Hills, MI 48335-3571 USA
E-mail: bgolden@pastways.info
Web site: http://www.pastways.info.

Patagonia, *(978-0-9790659; 978-0-9801227; 978-1-938340)* 259 W. Santa Clara St., Ventura, CA 93001-2717 USA Tel 805-643-8616; Fax: 805-643-2367; Toll Free: 800-638-6464
E-mail: karla_olson@patagonia.com
Web site: http://www.Patagonia.com
Dist(s): **D.A.P./Distributed Art Pubs.**
Perseus-PGW.

Patagonia Books *See* **Patagonia**

Patagonia Pr., *(978-1-882695)* P.O. Box 284, Bagdad, FL 32530 USA Tel 904-623-5790 Do not confuse with Patagonia Pr., Inc., Patagonia AZ
E-mail: Patagoniapress@aol.com.

Patchwork Pr., *(978-0-615-88322-9; 978-0-615-91877-8; 978-0-615-93512-6; 978-0-615-98429-2; 978-0-692-20253-1)* 7707 Red Maple Dr., Plainfield, IL 60586 USA Tel 815-416-8236
Dist(s): **CreateSpace Independent Publishing Platform.**

Paterson Museum for Italian Girls Press *See* **Mill Street Forward, The**

Path of Peace Inc., The, *(978-0-9766702)* 6610 Dorel St., Suite B, Philadelphia, PA 19142 USA Tel 215-681-6592
E-mail: blessbango@yahoo.com
Web site: http://www.thepathofpeace.net.

Pathfinder Equine Publications, *(978-0-9819240; 978-0-9915027)* 1908 Glade Rd., Farmington, NM 87401 USA
Dist(s): **Independent Pubs. Group**
MyiLibrary.

Pathway Bks. *Imprint of* **Stone Arch Bks.**

Pathway Pr., *(978-0-87148; 978-1-59684)* Div. of Church of God Publishing Hse., Orders Addr.: P.O. Box 2250, Cleveland, TN 37320-2250 USA (SAN 665-7567); Edit Addr.: 1080 Montgomery Ave., Cleveland, TN 37311 USA (SAN 202-8727) Tel 423-476-4512; Fax: 423-478-7616; Toll Free: 800-546-7590 (music only); 800-553-8506 (trade only) Do not confuse with Pathway Press, San Rafael, CA
E-mail: bill_george@pathwaypress.org
Web site: http://www.pathwaypress.org.

Pathways into Science, *(978-0-9779427)* 7417 River Falls Dr., Potomac, MD 20854 USA (SAN 850-5683) Tel 301-365-7593
Web site: http://pathwaysintoscience.com.

Patio Publishing, *(978-0-9832962)* 302 Santa Anita Rd., Santa Barbara, CA 93105 USA Tel 805-687-6910
E-mail: joan.calder@cox.net
Web site: http://www.airplanesinthegarden.com.

Patmos, Inc., *(978-0-9741748)* P.O. Box 124, Maple Hill, KS 66507-0124 USA
Web site: http://www.patmos.us.

Patmos Publishing, *(978-0-9768545)* 4591 Jernigan Rd., Milton, FL 32571-1921 USA Tel 850-994-0908 (phone/fax) Do not confuse with Patmos Publications in Bristol GBR
E-mail: patmosprinting@gmail.com
Web site: http://www.patmospublishing.com.

Patou Bks., LLC, *(978-0-9767756)* 1550 Larimer St., Suite 459, Denver, CO 80202-1602 USA.

Patrenialla Turner, Queen , *(978-0-578-14812-0)* .

Patria Pr., Inc., *(978-1-882859; 978-1-935731)* P.O. Box 752, Carmel, IN 46082 USA (SAN 153-7504) Tel 317-577-1321; Fax: 413-215-8030; Toll Free: 877-736-7930; *Imprints:* Young Patriots Series (Yng Patriots)
E-mail: info@patriapress.com
Web site: http://www.patriapress.com
Dist(s): **Ebsco Publishing**
Independent Pubs. Group
MyiLibrary.

Patrick Henry College Pr., *(978-0-9714458)* 1 Patrick Henry Cir., Purcellville, VA 20132 USA Tel 540-338-1776; Fax: 540-338-8707
E-mail: info@phc.edu
Web site: http://www.phc.edu.

PatrickGeorge (GBR) *(978-0-9562558; 978-1-908473) Dist. by* **IPG Chicago.**

†Patrick's Pr., *(978-0-944322; 978-0-9609412)* Orders Addr.: P.O. Box 5189, Columbus, GA 31906 USA (SAN 274-466X) Tel 706-322-1584; Fax: 706-322-5806; Toll Free: 800-654-1052; Edit Addr.: 2218 Wynnton Rd., Columbus, GA 31906 USA (SAN 243-2773)
E-mail: quizbowl@aol.com
Web site: http://www.patrickspress.com
Dist(s): **Peller, A. W. & Assocs.**; *CIP.*

Patriot Media, Inc., *(978-0-9791642; 978-0-9845777; 978-0-9846638; 978-0-9888930; 978-0-9905724)* Orders Addr.: P.O. Box 5414, Niceville, FL 32578 USA Tel 850-897-4204 (phone/fax)
E-mail: dari.bradleyceo@patriotmediainc.com; dari@patriotmediainc.com
Web site: http://www.patriotmediapublishing.com; http://www.patriotmediainc.com; http://www.patriotmediainternational.com; http://www.silentbattleground.com; http://www.dmulmer.com; http://www.staffmonkeys.com; http://www.paulsherbo.com; http://www.booksbynelson.com; http://www.those67blues.com
Dist(s): **CreateSpace Independent Publishing Platform.**

Patriot Media Publishing *See* **Patriot Media, Inc.**

Patriot Pr., *(978-0-9796000; 978-1-941020)* 1505 Knoxlyn Rd., Gettysburg, PA 17325 USA (SAN 853-8735)
E-mail: patriotpress@live.com
Web site: http://www.patriotpressbooks.com; http://www.jessicajamesbooks.com
Dist(s): **Independent Pubs. Group.**

Patriot Publishing, *(978-0-9789936)* Ernest Beath, III, 2216 Horn Point Rd., Cambridge, MD 21613-3379 USA Tel 410-228-5771
E-mail: docprb@bluecrab.org.

Patten Point Marketing Services, Incorporated *See* **Liberty Manuals Co.**

Pattern Pr., *(978-0-9729248; 978-1-935559; 978-1-941961)* Orders Addr.: P.O. Box 2737, Fallbrook, CA 92088 USA; Edit Addr.: 40521 De Luz Rd., Fallbrook, CA 92028 USA
E-mail: patternpress1@gmail.com
Web site: http://www.patternpress.com.

Patty's Blooming Words, *(978-0-615-78050-4; 978-0-9893303)* 693 Springlake Dr., Franklin, TN 37064 USA Tel 615-790-0109
E-mail: pattysbloomers@me.com.

†Pauline Bks. & Media, *(978-0-8198)* 50 St. Paul's Ave., Boston, MA 02130-3491 USA (SAN 203-8900) Tel 617-522-8911; Fax: 617-524-8035; Toll Free: 800-876-4463 (orders only)
E-mail: editorial@pauline.org; kcorina@paulinemedia.com
Web site: http://www.PAULINE.org
Dist(s): **MyiLibrary**
O'Reilly Media, Inc.
St Pauls/Alba Hse. Pubs.; *CIP.*

†Paulist Pr., *(978-0-8091; 978-1-893757; 978-1-58768; 978-1-61643)* 997 MacArthur Blvd., Mahwah, NJ 07430-2096 USA (SAN 202-5159) Tel 201-825-7300 (ext. 232); Fax: 201-825-8345; Toll Free Fax: 800-836-3161; Toll Free: 800-218-1903; *Imprints:* HiddenSpring (HidSpring); E T Nedder (ETNedder); Ambassador Books (Ambass Bks)
E-mail: info@paulistpress.com
Web site: http://www.paulistpress.com
Dist(s): **Bookazine Co., Inc.**
Spring Arbor Distributors, Inc.; *CIP.*

Paulsen, Marc Productions, Incorporated *See* **Stance Pubns.**

Paulus Publishing, *(978-0-9744863)* 6115 E. Hillview St., Mesa, AZ 85205 USA.

Pavilion Bks. (GBR) *(978-0-85177; 978-0-86101; 978-0-86283; 978-1-85470; 978-1-85585; 978-1-85753; 978-1-85833; 978-0-947553; 978-1-84138; 978-1-85561; 978-0-904609; 978-1-85028; 978-1-84065; 978-1-85600; 978-1-902616; 978-1-85993; 978-0-86288; 978-1-84333; 978-1-903954; 978-1-84411; 978-1-86222; 978-1-84340; 978-1-84458; 978-0-86124; 978-1-85841; 978-1-906388; 978-1-908449; 978-1-909397) Dist. by* **IPG Chicago.**

Pavilion Bks. (GBR) *(978-0-85177; 978-0-86101; 978-0-86283; 978-1-85470; 978-1-85585; 978-1-85753; 978-1-85833; 978-0-947553; 978-1-84138; 978-1-85561; 978-0-904609; 978-1-85028; 978-1-84065; 978-1-85600; 978-1-902616; 978-1-85993; 978-0-86288; 978-1-84333; 978-1-903954; 978-1-84411; 978-1-86222; 978-1-84340; 978-1-84458; 978-0-86124; 978-1-85841; 978-1-906388; 978-1-908449; 978-1-909397) Dist. by* **Trafalgar.**

Pavilion Bks. (GBR) *(978-0-85177; 978-0-86101; 978-0-86283; 978-1-85470; 978-1-85585; 978-1-85753; 978-1-85833; 978-0-947553; 978-1-84138; 978-1-85561; 978-0-904609; 978-1-85028; 978-1-84065; 978-1-85600; 978-1-902616; 978-1-85993; 978-0-86288; 978-1-84333; 978-1-903954; 978-1-84411; 978-1-86222; 978-1-84340; 978-1-84458; 978-0-86124; 978-1-85841; 978-1-906388; 978-1-908449; 978-1-909397) Dist. by* **Sterling.**

Pavilion Pr., Inc., *(978-1-4145)* 1213 Vine St., Philadelphia, PA 19107 USA Tel 215-569-9779; Fax: 215-569-8814
Web site: http://www.pavilionpress.com.

Pavilion Pubs., *(978-0-88432; 978-1-57970)* Div. of Pavilion Publishers, LLC, P.O. Box 1460, Guilford, CT 06437 USA (SAN 213-957X) Tel 518-605-5179; Toll Free: 800-243-1234
E-mail: Antonydaou@gmail.com; Mcgradylaura@gmail.com
Web site: http://www.audioforum.com
Dist(s): **Bolchazy-Carducci Pubs.**

Paw Print Pubns., *(978-0-9785473)* Orders Addr.: 4206 NE Newbury Ct., Lees Summit, MO 64064-1617 USA (SAN 850-9573) Toll Free: 877-267-9482; *Imprints:* Austin & Charlie Adventures (Austin & Charlie Adventures)
E-mail: lparker154@aol.com; pawfacts@aol.com; linda8000@sbcglobal.net
Web site: http://www.austincharlieadventures.com
Dist(s): **Book Clearing Hse.**

Paw Print Publishing, *(978-0-9770898)* Orders Addr.: P.O. Box 48309, Cumberland, NC 28331-8309 USA
Web site: www.k9fluffy.com.

Paw Prints Press *See* **Heather & Highlands Publishing**

Paws and Claws Publishing, LLC, *(978-0-9846724; 978-0-9906067)* 1586 Skeet Club Rd. Ste 102-175, High Point, NC 27265 USA Tel 336-297-9783
E-mail: jcappoen@pawsandclawspublishing.com
Web site: http://www.pawsandclawspublishing.com.

Paws Four Publishing, *(978-0-934007)* P.O. Box 2364, Homer, AK 99603 USA (SAN 692-7890) Tel 907-235-7697; Fax: 907-235-7698; Toll Free: 800-807-7297
E-mail: pawsiv@ptialaska.net
Dist(s): **Perseus-PGW**
Random Hse., Inc.
Sasquatch Bks.

Paws in the Sand Publishing, *(978-0-9790057)* Orders Addr.: 4644 Pepper Mill St., Moorpark, CA 93021-9302 USA (SAN 852-193X) Fax: 805-553-9253
Web site: http://pawsinthesand.com.

Paxen Learning Corporation *See* **Paxen Publishing LLC**

Paxen Publishing LLC, *(978-1-934350)* 710 Atlantis Rd., Melbourne, FL 32904 USA Tel 321-724-1033; 800-247-2936; Fax: 321-951-1617
E-mail: sales@paxen.com
Web site: http://www.paxen.com.

Paycock Pr., *(978-0-931181; 978-0-9602424)* 3819 N. 13th St., Arlington, VA 22201 USA (SAN 212-5420) Tel 703-525-9296 phone/fax
E-mail: gargoyle@gargoylemagazine.com
Web site: http://www.gargoylemagazine.com.

Payne, Christine, *(978-0-9740643)* P.O. Box 951, Mountain Home, AR 72654-0951 USA.

Payne, Yadira V. Publishing, *(978-0-9747350)* 341 Lamplighter Ln., Martinez, GA 30907 USA Tel 706-414-9566
E-mail: yvppublishing@knology.net.

PAZ Publishing, *(978-0-942253)* Div. of PAZ Percussion, Orders Addr.: 2415 Bevington St. NW, North Canton, OH 44709-2221 USA (SAN 666-8100) Tel 330-493-6661 (phone/fax)
E-mail: PAZPublishing@aol.com
Web site: http://www.PAZPublishing.com.

PB&J OmniMedia *Imprint of* **Takahashi & Black**

PBD, Inc., *(978-0-9846038; 978-0-9837260; 978-1-62219)* 1650 Bluegrass Lakes Pkwy., Alpharetta, GA 30004 USA (SAN 126-6039) Tel 770-442-8633; Fax: 770-442-9742
Web site: http://www.pbd.com.

PBL Stories LLC, *(978-0-9792379)* Orders Addr.: P.O. Box 393, Lynn Haven, FL 32444-4272 USA Tel 850-348-0718; Fax: 850-265-9815; Edit Addr.: 1812 S. Hwy. 77, Suite. 115, Lynn Haven, FL 32444-4272 USA
E-mail: booksales@pblstories.com
Web site: http://www.pblstories.com.

PC Treasures, Inc., *(978-1-933796; 978-1-60072)* 1795 N. Lapeer Rd., Oxford, MI 48371-2415 USA (SAN 857-0930)
E-mail: lthomas@pctreasures.com; jbrandt@pctreasures.com; jadams@pctreasures.com
Web site: http://www.pctreasures.com.

PCS Edventures, Inc., *(978-0-9753193; 978-0-9827203)* 345 Bobwhite Ct., Suite 200, Boise, ID 83706 USA Tel 208-343-3110; Fax: 208-343-1321; Toll Free: 800-429-3110
E-mail: rmwright@pcsedu.com; rgrover@pcsedu.com; agranger@pcsedu.com
Web site: http://www.edventures.com.

PD Hse. Holdings, LLC, *(978-0-9815333)* 4704 Venice Rd., Sandusky, OH 44870 USA (SAN 855-806X)
E-mail: pjgron@pjgrondin.com
Web site: http://www.pjgrondin.com.

P.D. Publishing, Inc., *(978-0-9754366; 978-1-933720; 978-1-61074)* P.O. Box 70, Clayton, NC 27528 USA
E-mail: publisher@pdpublishing.com
Web site: http://www.pdpublishing.com.

PDG *Imprint of* **Publishers Design Group, Inc.**

†Peabody Museum of Archaeology & Ethnology, Harvard Univ., Pubns. Dept., *(978-0-87365)* Orders Addr.: 11 Divinity Ave., Cambridge, MA 02138 USA (SAN 203-1426) Tel 617-496-9922; 617-495-3938; Fax: 617-495-7535
E-mail: ddickers@fas.harvard.edu
Web site: http://www.peabody.harvard.edu/publications
Dist(s): **Harvard Univ. Pr.**
Univ. Pr. of New England
Univ. of New Mexico Pr.; *CIP.*

Peace B Still Ministries Pr., *(978-0-9752665)* 205 Joel Blvd., Suite 107, Lehigh Acres, FL 33972-0202 USA
E-mail: gduncan316@aol.com.

Peace Education Foundation, *(978-1-878227; 978-1-934760)* 1900 Biscayne Blvd., Miami, FL 33132-1025 USA Tel 305-576-5075; Fax: 305-576-3106; Toll Free: 800-749-8838
Web site: http://www.peaceeducation.com.

Peace Evolutions, LLC, *(978-0-9753837; 978-0-9912489)* P.O. Box 256, Glen Echo, MD 20812-0458 USA (SAN 256-2146) Fax: 301-263-9280
E-mail: info@peace-evolutions.com; julie@peace-evolutions.com
Web site: http://www.peace-evolutions.com.

Peace Hill Pr., *(978-0-9714129; 978-0-9728603; 978-1-933339; 978-1-942968)* 18021 The Glebe Ln., Charles City, VA 23030-3828 USA (SAN 254-1726)
E-mail: ptbuff@peacehillpress.net
Web site: http://www.peacehillpress.net
Dist(s): **Norton, W. W. & Co., Inc.**
Penguin Random Hse., LLC.

Peace Love Karma Publishing, *(978-0-9743540)* 607 Elmira Rd., No. 266, Vacaville, CA 95687 USA
E-mail: Carol@peacelovekarma.com; mail@peacelovekarma.com
Web site: http://www.peacelovekarma.com
Dist(s): **New Leaf Distributing Co., Inc.**

Peace Power Pr., *(978-0-9824601)* 6044 Waterloo Rd., Dayton, OH 45402-3015 USA (SAN 858-2254) Tel 937-227-3223
Web site: http://daytonpeacemuseum.org.

Peace Rug Company, Inc., The, *(978-0-9763949)* 407 W. Emery St., Dalton, GA 30720 USA Tel 706-272-0200; Fax: 706-226-2296; Toll Free: 888-732-2378
E-mail: info@peacerug.com
Web site: http://www.peacerug.com.

Peaceable Kingdom Pr., *(978-1-56890; 978-1-59395)* 950 Gilmain, Suite 200, Berkeley, CA 94710 USA Tel 510-558-2051; Fax: 510-558-2052; Toll Free: 800-444-7778 Do not confuse with Peaceable Kingdom Press in Greenville, VA
E-mail: djaffe@pkpress.com
Web site: http://www.pkpress.com.

Peaceable Productions, *(978-0-9709187)* Orders Addr.: P.O. Box 708, Center Hill, FL 33514 USA (SAN 254-4946) Tel 352-793-7516; Edit Addr.: 6698 SE 57th Rd., Center Hill, FL 33514 USA Tel 352-793-7516; Fax: 775-514-8681
E-mail: yvonne@atlantic.net.

Peaceful Thoughts Pr., *(978-0-9725118)* 598 Straton Chase SE, Marietta, GA 30067 USA
Web site: http://www.peacefulthoughts.net.

Peacemakers Press *See* **Positive Spin Pr.**

Peach Blossom Pubns., *(978-0-941367)* 120 E. Beaver Ave. Apt. 212, State College, PA 16801-4991 USA (SAN 665-4800)
E-mail: inezwaterson@prodigy.net
Dist(s): **Quality Bks., Inc.**

PeachMoon Publishing, *(978-0-9795831)* 3915 Bonnett Creek Ln., Hoschton, GA 30548-6204 USA (SAN 853-814X)
E-mail: Alice@peachmoonpublishing.com
Web site: http://luckythelizard.com; http://peachmoonpublishing.com.

Peachtree Junior *Imprint of* **Peachtree Pubs.**

†Peachtree Pubs., *(978-0-931948; 978-0-934601; 978-1-56145; 978-1-68263)* 1700 Chattahoochee Ave., NW, Atlanta, GA 30318-2112 USA (SAN 212-1999) Tel 404-876-8761; Fax: 404-875-2578; Toll Free Fax: 800-875-8909; Toll Free: 800-241-0113; *Imprints:* Peachtree Junior (Peachtree)
E-mail: sales@peachtree-online.com; palermo@peachtree-online.com; McManus@peachtree-online.com
Web site: http://www.peachtree-online.com
Dist(s): **Heinecken & Assoc., Ltd.**
Lectorum Pubns., Inc.
MyiLibrary
Open Road Integrated Media, LLC; *CIP.*

Peachtree Publishers, Limited *See* **Peachtree Pubs.**

Peak City Publishing, LLC, *(978-1-935711)* 104B N. Salem St., Apex, NC 27502 USA Tel 919-758-9516
Web site: http://www.peakcitypublishing.com.

Peak Writing, LLC, *(978-0-9717330; 978-0-9767961)* Orders Addr.: P.O. Box 14196, Savannah, GA 31416 USA Tel 912-398-2987; Toll Free Fax: 888-226-4811; Edit Addr.: 12 Mercer Rd., Savannah, GA 31411 USA Do not confuse with Peak Writing in Frisco, CO
E-mail: info@peakwriting.com
Dist(s): **Quality Bks., Inc.**
Send The Light Distribution LLC
Spring Arbor Distributors, Inc.

Peaks Pr. LLC, *(978-1-938032)* 630 Race St., Denver, CO 80206 USA Tel 720-560-3779
E-mail: info@peakspress.com
Dist(s): **BookBaby.**

Peanut Butter Publishing, *(978-0-89716; 978-1-59849)* 2207 Fairview Ave. E., Houseboat No. 4, Seattle, WA

98102 USA (SAN 212-7881) Tel 206-860-4900 Toll Free: 877-728-8837
E-mail: ewolfpub@aol.com
Web site: http://www.peanutbutterpublishing.com.

Peapod Pr. *Imprint of* **PublishingWorks**

Peapod Publishing, Inc., *(978-0-9729507; 978-0-9894591)* P.O. Box 951599, Lake Mary, FL 32795-1599 USA Tel 407-333-3030
E-mail: info@peapodpublishing.com
Web site: http://www.adventureswithpawpaw.com; http://www.pawpawspals.org; http://www.peapodpublishing.com; http://www.borntoflybook.com; http://www.born2fly.org
Dist(s): **BookBaby.**

Pearl & Dotty, *(978-0-9772441)* Orders Addr.: P.O. Box 2162, Seattle, WA 98111-2162 USA
E-mail: pearlanddotty@gmail.com; holler@pearlanddotty.com
Web site: http://www.pearlanddotty.com.

Pearl Pr., *(978-0-9674525)* Orders Addr.: P.O. Box 266, Eastport, MI 49627 USA (SAN 299-9870) Tel 231-599-2372 (phone/fax); Edit Addr.: 6027 M-88 Hwy., Eastport, MI 49627 USA Do not confuse with Pearl Pr., Nazareth, PA, Sacramento CA
E-mail: Beebystudio@mailbug.com.

Pearl Pr., *(978-0-9741332)* 3104 O St., No. 175, Sacramento, CA 95816 USA Do not confuse with Pearl Press in Nazareth PA, Eastport MI
E-mail: info@pearlpress.net
Web site: http://www.pearlpress.net
Dist(s): **Quality Bks., Inc.**

Pearl Publishing, LLC, *(978-0-9785264; 978-0-9826175; 978-1-937390)* 2587c Southside Blvd., Melba, ID 83641 USA Tel 888-499-9666
E-mail: info@pearlpublishing.net
Web site: http://wupublishing.com; http://666america.com; http://pearlpublishing.net.

Pearlman, Beth, *(978-0-9767522)* 1773 Diane Rd., Mendota Heights, MN 55118 USA.

PearlStone Publishing, Inc., *(978-0-9724586; 978-0-9816883; 978-0-9841899; 978-1-936513)* 514-201 Daniels St., Raleigh, NC 27603 USA
E-mail: publish@pendiumpublishing.com
Web site: http://www.pendiumpublishing.com.

Pearn & Assocs. Inc., *(978-0-9777318; 978-0-9841683; 978-0-9846523; 978-0-9897242)* Orders Addr.: 1600 Edora Ct. Ste. D, Fort Collins, CO 80525-6016 USA; *Imprints:* Over the Rainbow (Over the Rain)
E-mail: happypoet@hotmail.com.

Pearson Education (GBR) *(978-0-15; 978-0-515; 978-0-7466) Dist. by* **ABC-CLIO.**

Pearson Education, *(978-0-582; 978-0-7686; 978-1-5093)* Orders Addr.: 200 Old Tappan Rd., Old Tappan, NJ 07675 USA (SAN 200-2175) Tel 201-767-5000 (Receptionist); Toll Free Fax: 800-445-6991; Toll Free: 800-428-5331; 800-922-0579; Edit Addr.: One Lake St., Upper Saddle River, NJ 07458 USA Tel 201-236-7000; 201-236-5321; Fax: 201-236-6549; 800 E. 96th St., Suite 300, Indianapolis, IN 46240 Toll Free: 800-571-4580; *Imprints:* Microsoft Press (MicrosoftPress)
E-mail: communications@pearsoned.com
Web site: http://www.pearsoned.com; www.pearson.com
Dist(s): **Gaunt, Inc.**
MyiLibrary
Trans-Atlantic Pubns., Inc.

Pearson Education Australia (AUS) *(978-0-7248; 978-0-7342; 978-0-7312; 978-1-86391; 978-0-7339; 978-0-85859; 978-0-86462; 978-1-74009; 978-1-74140; 978-1-876209; 978-1-74085; 978-1-74103; 978-1-74091; 978-1-74081; 978-1-74206; 978-1-4425; 978-0-86911; 978-0-7316-1261-1; 978-0-646-24199-9; 978-0-646-29552-7; 978-0-646-30941-5; 978-0-646-31855-4; 978-0-646-32904-8; 978-0-646-32905-5; 978-1-4860) Dist. by* **Cheng Tsui.**

Pearson Education, Ltd. (GBR) *(978-0-201; 978-0-273; 978-0-321; 978-0-582; 978-0-673; 978-1-4058; 978-1-84479; 978-1-84658; 978-1-84959; 978-1-84878; 978-1-84776; 978-1-4479; 978-1-292) Dist. by* **Trans-Atl Phila.**

Pearson Education, Ltd. (GBR) *(978-0-201; 978-0-273; 978-0-321; 978-0-582; 978-0-673; 978-1-4058; 978-1-84479; 978-1-84658; 978-1-84959; 978-1-84878; 978-1-84776; 978-1-4479; 978-1-292) Dist. by* **Pearson Educ.**

Pearson ESL, *(978-0-582)* Div. of Pearson International, 75 Arlington St., Boston, MA 02116 USA
Dist(s): **Pearson Education.**

Pearson Learning, *(978-0-7652; 978-1-4284)* Div of Pearson Education, Orders Addr.: P.O. Box 2500, Lebanon, IN 46052 USA Toll Free Fax: 800-393-3156; Toll Free: 800-321-3106; Edit Addr.: 1 Lake St., U Saddle Riv, NJ 07458-1813 USA Toll Free: 800-526-9907 (Customer Service)
E-mail: jeff.hoitsma@pearsonlearning.com
Web site: http://www.pearsonlearning.com
Dist(s): **Follett School Solutions.**

Peartree, *(978-0-935343)* P.O. Box 14533, Clearwater, FL 33766 USA Tel 727-531-4973 (phone/fax)
E-mail: martree@aol.com; peartreebooks@yahoo.com
Web site: http://www.peartreebooks.com
Dist(s): **Brodart Co.**
Follett School Solutions
Quality Bks., Inc.

Pebble Beach Pr., Ltd., *(978-1-883740)* P.O. Box 1171, Pebble Beach, CA 93953-1171 USA Tel 408-372-5559; Fax: 408-375-4525.

Pebble Bks. *Imprint of* **Capstone Pr., Inc.**

Pebble Plus *Imprint of* **Capstone Pr., Inc.**

Pebble Plus Bilingue/Bilingual *Imprint of* **Capstone Pr., Inc.**

Pebbleton Pr., *(978-0-9760011)* P.O. Box 1894, Duxbury, MA 02331 USA
E-mail: pebbletonpress@comcast.net
Web site: http://www.pebbletonpress.com.

Pecci Educational Pubs., *(978-0-943220)* 440 Davis Ct., No. 405, San Francisco, CA 94111 USA (SAN 240-558X) Tel 415-391-8579; Fax: 970-493-8781
E-mail: pecci@sirius.com
Web site: http://www.onlinereadingteacher.com.

PeDante Pr., *(978-0-9790199; 978-1-940844)* 4 White Oak, Danbury, CT 06410 USA Tel 203-350-9288
E-mail: erikagrey@rocketmail.com
Web site: www.erikagrey.com.

Peddlers Group, *(978-0-9802257; 978-0-9829177)* 1127 Parrish Rd., Leesville, SC 29070 USA Tel 803-657-5324; Fax: 803-753-9824
E-mail: peddlersgroup@gmail.com
Web site: http://www.peddlersgroup.com.

Pedigree Bks., Ltd. (GBR) *(978-1-874507; 978-1-904329; 978-1-906450; 978-1-907602) Dist. by* **Diamond Book Dists.**

†Pedipress, Inc., *(978-0-914625)* Orders Addr.: 125 Red Gate Ln., Amherst, MA 01002 USA (SAN 287-7570) Tel 413-549-7798 M - Thurs. 8:30 to 4:30 EST; Fax: 413-549-4095; Toll Free: 800-611-6081 M - Thurs. 8:30 to 4:30 EST
E-mail: staceyv@pedipress.com
Web site: http://www.pedipress.com
Dist(s): **INscribe Digital**; *CIP.*

Peebco Publishing Hse., The, *(978-0-9644758)* P.O. Box 45333, Saint Louis, MO 63145 USA (SAN 298-6760) Tel 636-346-7179
E-mail: Info@PeebcoPublishing.com
Web site: http://www.PeebcoPublishing.com.

Peel Productions, Inc., *(978-0-939217; 978-1-943158)* 9415 NE Woodridge, Vancouver, WA 98664 USA
E-mail: ddub@drawbooks.com
Web site: http://www.drawbooks.com; http://www.peelbooks.com; http://www.123draw.com; http://www.1-2-3.draw.com
Dist(s): **F&W Media, Inc.**
Pathway Bk. Service.

Peepal Tree Pr., Ltd. (GBR) *(978-0-948833; 978-1-900715; 978-1-84523) Dist. by* **IPG Chicago.**

Peeper & Friends *Imprint of* **Tree Of Life Publishing**

Peerless Publishing, L.L.C., *(978-0-9666076)* Orders Addr.: P.O. Box 20466, Ferndale, MI 48220 USA Tel 248-542-1930; Fax: 248-542-3895; Edit Addr.: 414 W. Lewiston, Ferndale, MI 48220 USA
E-mail: peerlesspublishing@ameritech.net
Web site: http://www.spannet.org/peerless/index.html.

Pegasus Bks. for Children, *(978-0-9824095; 978-0-615-82835-0)* P.O. Box 681, Flossmoor, IL 60422 USA Tel 708-990-8111; Fax: 708-747-4659
E-mail: stallionbooks@gmail.com
Web site: http://www.stallionbooks.com.

Pegasus Pubns., *(978-0-9747023)* 1055 E., 16th St., Brooklyn, NY 11230 USA Do not confuse with companies with the same name in Point Reyes Statio, CA, San Antonio, TX.

Pegatha Press *See* **Rosasharn Pr.**

Peiffer, Trisha Cousineau *See* **Dream Ridge Pr.**

Peine, Jan *See* **Ashway Pr.**

Pelagia Pr. *Imprint of* **Calm Unity Pr.**

Pelican Lake Pr., *(978-0-9649139)* Div. of Healthy Lifestyle, Inc., 8273 Caminito Lacayo, La Jolla, CA 92037 USA Tel 858-888-2278
E-mail: tomiselin@gmail.com
Web site: http://www.tomiselin.com.

Pelican Press *See* **booksonnet.com**

Pelican Pr., *(978-0-9771102; 978-0-9911640)* Div. of The Pelican Enterprise, LLC, Orders Addr.: P.O. Box 7084, Pensacola, FL 32534 USA Tel 850-475-8179; Edit Addr.: 9121 Carabella St., Pensacola, FL 32514-5878 USA Do not confuse with companies with the same name in Prather, CA, Santa Barbara, CA, Aptos, CA, Saint Augustine, FL, Belvedere, CA
E-mail: pelican.post@att.net
Dist(s): **BookBaby.**

†Pelican Publishing Co., Inc., *(978-0-88289; 978-0-911116; 978-1-56554; 978-1-58980; 978-1-4556)* Orders Addr.: 1000 Burmaster St., Gretna, LA 70053-2246 USA Tel 504-368-1175; Fax: 504-368-1195; Toll Free: 800-843-1724 ordering Do not confuse with companies with the same or similar names in Lowell, MA, Dallas, TX
E-mail: Sales@pelicanpub.com; promo@pelicanpub.com; editorial@pelicanpub.com
Web site: http://www.pelicanpub.com; *CIP.*

Peller, A. W. & Associates, Incorporated *See* **Educational Impressions**

Pelluceo, *(978-0-9851368)* 72 Berry St., No. 5B, Brooklyn, NY 11249 USA Tel 917-825-2232
E-mail: nadine@nadinerubin.com
Web site: www.pelluceo.com
Dist(s): **National Bk. Network.**

Pemblewick Pr., *(978-0-9656557; 978-0-9718507)* Orders Addr.: P.O. Box 321, Lincoln, MA 01773 USA (SAN 254-0886); Edit Addr.: 155 S. Great Rd., Lincoln, MA 01773 USA Tel 781-259-8832 (phone/fax); 617-259-8389; 617 259 8389
E-mail: pemblewick@aol.com
Web site: http://www.pemblewickpress.com.

Pen & Pad Publishing, *(978-0-9769050)* P.O. Box 2995, Orcutt, CA 93457-2995 USA Tel 805-938-1307
E-mail: JBest@BestFamilyAdventures.com
Web site: http://BestFamilyAdventures.com
Dist(s): **Central Coast Bks.**

Pen & Paper Publishing, *(978-0-9703876)* 5450 Saluson Ave., PMB 15, Culver City, CA 90230 USA Fax: 323-933-3851; Toll Free: 800-662-9066 Do not confuse with Pen & Paper Publishing in Horn Lake, MS
E-mail: sixrags@earthlink.net
Web site: http://www.penandpaper.net.

Pen & Publish Inc., *(978-0-9768391; 978-0-9779530; 978-0-9790446; 978-0-9800429; 978-0-9817264; 978-0-9823850; 978-0-9842258; 978-0-9844600; 978-0-9845751; 978-0-9846359; 978-0-9852737; 978-0-9859367; 978-1-941799)* Orders Addr.: 4735 S. State Rd., No. 446, Bloomington, IN 47401 USA Tel 812-837-9226; Toll Free: 866-326-7768
E-mail: info@penandpublish.com; paul@penandpublish.com; info@brickmantelbooks.com
Web site: http://www.penandpublish.com; http://transformationmediabooks.com; http://openbookspress.com; http://brickmantelbooks.com
Dist(s): **Smashwords.**

Pen & Rose Pr. *Imprint of* **Harlin Jacque Pubns.**

Pen & Sword Bks. Ltd. (GBR) *(978-0-7232; 978-0-85052; 978-1-84415; 978-1-84468; 978-1-84832; 978-1-84884; 978-1-78159; 978-1-78383; 978-1-4738) Dist. by* **Casemate Pubs.**

Pen & Sword Publishing Co., The, *(978-0-9745798)* 522 N. Holly St., Philadelphia, PA 19104 USA
E-mail: nancy@theaalamgroup.com; nk81dove@yahoo.com; melodicg2003@hotmail.com.

Pen Row Productions, *(978-0-9766695)* 9461 Charleville Blvd., No. 506, Beverly Hills, CA 90212 USA Tel 310-924-9167
E-mail: bwasz1@verizon.net
Web site: http://www.penrowproductions.com.

Pencil Point Pr., Inc., *(978-1-58108; 978-1-881641)* P.O. Box 634, New Hope, PA 18938-0634 USA Toll Free: 800-356-1299
E-mail: penpoint@ix.netcom.com
Web site: http://www.pencilpointpress.com.

Pendentive Pubns., *(978-0-9853817)* 405 Serrano Dr., Apt. 9-K, San Francisco, CA 94132 USA Tel 415-586-1806
E-mail: mpowers2004@yahoo.com
Dist(s): **Lulu Enterprises Inc.**

Pendleton Publishing, Inc., *(978-0-9654480; 978-0-9711564)* Orders Addr.: P.O. Box 5004, Laurel, MD 20726 USA Tel 301-604-4076; Fax: 301-317-5746; Edit Addr.: 3113 Burning Springs Rd., No.1A, Laurel, MD 20724 USA
E-mail: newauthorsandartists@msn.com; gamjampublishing@yahoo.com.

Pendulum Pr., Inc., *(978-0-87232; 978-0-88301)* Academic Bldg., Saw Mill Rd., West Haven, CT 06516 USA (SAN 202-8808) Tel 203-933-2551 Do not confuse with companies with same or similar names in Jacksonville, FL, Palm Coast, FL, Minneapolis, MN.

Penelope Pipp Publishing, *(978-0-9882369)* 38 McCreedy Dr., McHenry, MS 39561 USA Tel 601-928-4567
E-mail: admin@penelopepipp.com
Web site: www.penelopepipp.com.

Penfield Bks., *(978-0-941016; 978-0-9603858; 978-1-57216; 978-0-9717025; 978-1-932043)* 215 Brown St., Iowa City, IA 52245 USA Tel 319-337-9998; Fax: 319-351-6846
E-mail: penfield@penfieldbooks.com
Web site: http://www.penfieldpress.com; http://www.penfieldbooks.com
Dist(s): **Partners Bk. Distributing, Inc.**
Penfield Pr.

PenGame Publishing LLC, *(978-0-9771444)* Orders Addr.: P.O. Box 341361, Jamaica, NY 11434 USA (SAN 256-8802)
E-mail: PenGameLLC@aol.com
Web site: http://www.PenGamePublishing.com.

Penguin AudioBooks *Imprint of* **Penguin Publishing Group**

Penguin Bks., Ltd. (GBR) *(978-0-14; 978-0-670; 978-1-4059; 978-1-4093) Dist. by* **Penguin Grp USA.**

Penguin Bks., Ltd. (GBR) *(978-0-14; 978-0-670; 978-1-4059; 978-1-4093) Dist. by* **IPG Chicago.**

Penguin Bks., Ltd. (GBR) *(978-0-14; 978-0-670; 978-1-4059; 978-1-4093) Dist. by* **Diamond Book Dists.**

Penguin Bks., Ltd. (GBR) *(978-0-14; 978-0-670; 978-1-4059; 978-1-4093) Dist. by* **Peng Rand Hse.**

Penguin Books Australia (AUS) *(978-0-14; 978-0-670; 978-0-86914; 978-0-7343; 978-1-920989; 978-1-921382; 978-1-921383; 978-1-921384; 978-1-921518; 978-1-74228; 978-1-74253; 978-1-74348; 978-0-85796; 978-0-85797; 978-1-74377; 978-1-76014) Dist. by* **IPG Chicago.**

Penguin Classics *Imprint of* **Penguin Publishing Group**

Penguin Classics Hardcover *Imprint of* **Penguin Publishing Group**

Penguin Family Publishing, *(978-0-9637985)* P.O. Box 471, Orland, CA 95963 USA.

Penguin Global *Imprint of* **Penguin Publishing Group**

Penguin Group India (IND) *(978-0-14; 978-0-670) Dist. by* **Penguin Grp USA.**

Penguin Group New Zealand, Ltd. (NZL) *(978-0-14; 978-0-670) Dist. by* **IPG Chicago.**

Penguin Group (USA) Incorporated *See* **Penguin Publishing Group**

Penguin (Non-Classics) *Imprint of* **Penguin Publishing Group**

Penguin Publishing Group, *(978-0-14; 978-0-399; 978-0-425; 978-0-525; 978-0-698; 978-0-87477; 978-1-58542; 978-1-933438; 978-1-4295; 978-1-934511; 978-1-4362; 978-1-4406; 978-1-101; 978-1-937007)* Orders Addr.: 405 Murray Hill Pkwy., East Rutherford, NJ 07073-2136 USA (SAN 282-5074) Fax: 201-933-2903 (customer service); Toll Free Fax: 800-227-9604; Toll Free: 800-526-0275 (reseller sales); 800-631-8571 (reseller customer service); 800-788-6262 (individual consumer sales); Edit Addr.: 375 Hudson St., New York, NY 10014 USA Tel 212-366-2000; Fax: 212-366-2666; 405 Murray Hill Pkwy., East Rutherford, NJ 07073 (SAN 852-5455) Tel 201-933-9292; *Imprints:* Ace Trade (AceTrade); Minedition (Minedition); Ace Books (Ace Bks); Alpha Books (Alph Bks); Avery (Avr); Berkley (BerkBks); Berkley Hardcover (BerkleHC); Berkley Trade (BrkTrade); DAW Hardcover (DAWHC); D A W Books, Incorporated (D A WBksInc); Dial (Dial); Dutton Adult (Dut); Dutton Juvenile (DuttJuv); Warne (Warne); Putnam Adult (Putnam Adult); Putnam Juvenile (PutnaJuv); Gotham (GotBksHard); Grosset & Dunlap (Gross-Dun); HP Trade (HPTrade); Jove (JovPG); ROC Trade (RocTrade); N A L Hardcover (NALHC); N A L Trade (NewTrade); Onyx (OnyPG); Penguin AudioBooks (PengAudBks); Penguin Classics (PenClassics); Penguin (Non-Classics) (PeNonClass); Perigee Trade (PeriTrade); Philomel (PhilPG); Penguin Classics Hardcover (PengClasHC); Planet Dexter (PlanDext); Plume (PlumPG); Portfolio (Hardcover) (PortHardcover); Portfolio Trade (PortfolTrade); Price Stern Sloan (PSS); Puffin (PufBks); Penguin Global (PenGlobal); Roc (Roc); Razorbill (Razrbl); Riverhead Trade (Paperbacks) (RiverTrade Pap); ROC Hardcover (ROCHC); Sentinel (Senti); Signet (SigBks); Signet Classics (SigClassics); Tarcher (Tarch-Peng); Viking Adult (VikiPG); Viking Juvenile (VCB); DAW Trade (DAWTrade); Prentice Hall Press (PHPP); Celebra (Celebra); Nancy Paulsen Books (Nancy Paulsen); Dawson, Kathy Books (KathyDawson)
E-mail: customer.service@us.penguingroup.com
Web site: http://penguinputnam.custhelp.com; http://booksellers.penguingroup.com; http://www.penguinputnam.com
Dist(s): **Ebsco Publishing**
Follett School Solutions
Independent Pubs. Group
Lectorum Pubns., Inc.
MyiLibrary
Pearson Education
Penguin Random Hse., LLC.
Perfection Learning Corp.
Viking Penguin
ebrary, Inc.

Penguin Random House Audio Publishing Group, *(978-1-61176)* 375 Hudson St., New York, NY 10014 USA Tel 212-366-2000; Fax: 212-366-2873; *Imprints:* Listening Library (Listening Lib)
Web site: http://www.penguin.com
Dist(s): **Follett School Solutions**
Penguin Random Hse., LLC.
Penguin Publishing Group.

Penguin Random House Grupo Editorial (ESP) *Dist. by* **Lectorum Pubns.**

Penguin Random House Grupo Editorial (ESP) *Dist. by* **Casemate Pubs.**

Penguin Random House Grupo Editorial (ESP) *Dist. by* **Perseus Dist.**

Penguin Random Hse., LLC., *(978-1-101)* 375 Hudson St. 3rd Flr., New York, NY 10014 USA Tel 212-366-2424
E-mail: brittany.wienke@us.penguingroup.com
Web site: PenguinRandomHouse.com.

Penguin Young Readers Group, 375 Hudson St., New York, NY 10014 USA; *Imprints:* Speak (SpeakPeng)
Dist(s): **Penguin Random Hse., LLC.**
Penguin Publishing Group.

Penknife Pr., *(978-0-9741949; 978-1-59997)* 1837 N. Oak Pk. Ave., Chicago, IL 60707 USA Tel 773-733-0830
E-mail: publisher@penknifepress.com
Web site: http://www.penknifepress.com
Dist(s): **Lightning Source, Inc.**

Pen-L Publishing, *(978-0-9851274; 978-1-940222; 978-1-942428)* 12 W. Dickson St., No. 4455, Fayetteville, AR 72702 USA Tel 479-871-3330
E-mail: duke@pen-l.com
Web site: Pen-L.com.

Penlight Pubns., *(978-0-9838685)* 572 Empire Blvd., Brooklyn, NY 11225 USA Tel 718-972-5449
E-mail: urim_pub@netvision.net.il
Web site: www.penlightpublications.com
Dist(s): **Independent Pubs. Group.**

Penman Publications *See* **Voice & Vision Pubns.**

Penman Publishing, Inc., *(978-0-9700486; 978-0-9707646; 978-0-9712808; 978-0-9720775; 978-1-932496)* Div. of Pathway Pr., Orders Addr.: P.O. Box 3933, Cleveland, TN 37320-2250 USA; Edit Addr.: 1705 Overhead Bridge Rd., Cleveland, TN 37312 USA Tel 423-478-7613
Web site: http://www.penmanpublishing.com
Dist(s): **AtlasBooks Distribution.**

Pen-Mar News Distributors *See* **Americana Souvenirs & Gifts**

Penner/Lynn Publishing, *(978-0-9763025)* P.O. Box 7393, Naples, FL 34104 USA
E-mail: pennerlynn@msn.com
Web site: http://www.pennerlynn.com.

Pennie Rich Publishing, *(978-0-9820328; 978-0-9824960)* 4755 Cty. Rd. 27, Monte Vista, CO 81144-9314 USA (SAN 857-0884)
E-mail: pennierich@pennierich.com
Web site: http://www.pennierich.com.

Penny Candy Pr. *Imprint of* **Brighter Minds Children's Publishing**

Penny Laine Papers, Inc., *(978-1-890703)* 2211 Century Center Blvd. Ste. 110, Irving, TX 75062-4960 USA Toll Free: 800-456-6484; *Imprints:* Bookmates (Bkmates)
E-mail: cardwhiz1@mindspring.com.

Penny Lane Pubns., Inc., *(978-0-911211)* P.O. Box 3005, New York, NY 10012-0009 USA (SAN 274-4961) Tel 212-570-9666.

Penny Pr. *Imprint of* **Penny Pubns., LLC**

Penny Pubns., LLC, *(978-0-944422; 978-1-55956; 978-1-59238)* 6 Prowitt St., Norwalk, CT 06855 USA (SAN 243-6485); *Imprints:* Penny Press (Penny Pr)
E-mail: ltrutnau@pennypublications.net
Web site: http://www.pennydellpuzzles.com; http://www.analogsf.com; http://www.asimovs.com; http://www.themysteryplace.com; http://www.dellhoroscope.com; http://www.thecrosswordsclub.com.

Publisher Name Index

Penny-Farthing Pr., Inc., *(978-0-9673683; 978-0-9719012; 978-0-9842143)* 2000 W. Sam Houston Pkwy., S., Suite 550, Houston, TX 77042 USA Tel 713-780-0300; Fax: 713-780-4004; Toll Free: 800-926-2669 E-mail: corp@pfpress.com; edit@pfpress.com Web site: http://www.pfpress.com *Dist(s):* **Diamond Comic Distributors, Inc.**

Pennypack Productions, Inc., *(978-0-9704184)* 21 Tree Farm Ct., Glen Arm, MD 21057 USA Tel 410-420-3828; Fax: 410-420-2243 E-mail: ppennypack@comcast.net Web site: http://www.kinderfun.net.

Penny's Publishing *Imprint of* **Balloon Magic**

Pennywhistler's Pr., *(978-0-9623456; 978-0-9727516)* Orders Addr.: P.O. Box 2473, New York, NY 10108 USA Tel 212-247-3231 (phone/fax); Edit Addr.: 467 W. 46th St., New York, NY 10036 USA E-mail: info@pennywhistle.com Web site: http://www.pennywhistle.com *Dist(s):* **Book Clearing Hse. Mel Bay Pubns., Inc.**

Pennywise Pubns., Inc., *(978-0-9702944)* 10550 St. Rd. 84, L98, Davie, FL 33324 USA Tel 954-472-8776 (phone/fax) E-mail: filmpeny@bellsouth.net.

Penrod/Hiawatha Co., *(978-0-942618; 978-1-893624; 978-1-940691)* 10116 M140, Berrien Center, MI 49102 USA (SAN 238-5546) Tel 269-461-6993; Fax: 269-461-4170; Toll Free: 800-632-2823 Web site: http://www.penrodhiawatha.com *Dist(s):* **Partners Bk. Distributing, Inc.**

Pentacle Pr., *(978-0-9604760; 978-0-9763500; 978-0-9825047; 978-1-937313)* Orders Addr.: P.O. Box 9400, Scottsdale, AZ 85252 USA (SAN 255-4860) Tel 480-922-2759; Fax: 480-443-8333; Edit Addr.: 5432 E. Desert Jewel Dr., Paradise Valley, AZ 85253 USA E-mail: djm543@cox.net Web site: http://www.missionscalifornia.com; http://www.pentacle-press.com *Dist(s):* **Sunbelt Pubns., Inc. Univ. of New Mexico Pr.**

Pentatonic Pr., *(978-0-9773712)* 1232 Second Ave., San Francisco, CA 94122 USA Tel 415-564-1597; Fax: 415-566-6828 E-mail: Goodkindg@aol.com Web site: http://www.douggoodkin.com *Dist(s):* **Midpoint Trade Bks., Inc.**

Pen-Tech Professional, *(978-0-9820962)* P.O. Box 67, Greenville, WI 54942 USA Tel 920-203-0563 Web site: http://www.pentechprofessional.com.

Pentland Pr., Inc., *(978-1-57197)* 5122 Bur Oak Cir., Raleigh, NC 27612 USA (SAN 298-5063) Tel 919-782-0281; Fax: 919-781-9042; Toll Free: 800-948-2786; *Imprints:* Ivy House Publishing Group (Ivy Hse Pubng Grp) E-mail: janetevans@ivyhousebooks.com Web site: http://www.ivyhousebooks.com *Dist(s):* **Independent Pubs. Group.**

Penton Kids *Imprint of* **Penton Overseas, Inc.**

Penton Overseas, Inc., *(978-0-939001; 978-1-56015; 978-1-59125; 978-1-60379)* 1958 Kellogg Ave., Carlsbad, CA 92008 USA (SAN 631-0826) Tel 760-431-0060; Fax: 760-431-8110; Toll Free: 800-748-5804; *Imprints:* Penton Kids (Penton Kids); Smart Kids (Smrt Kds) E-mail: kellie@pentonoverseas.com; susan@pentonoverseas.com Web site: http://www.pentonoverseas.com *Dist(s):* **Ideals Pubns.**

Penury Pr., *(978-0-9676344)* 8701 Utah Ave S., Bloomington, MN 55438 USA Tel 952-829-1811 E-mail: penurypress@hotmail.com Web site: http://www.penurypress.com *Dist(s):* **Adventure Pubns., Inc. Adventures Unlimited Pr. Partners Bk. Distributing, Inc.**

People Bks. *Imprint of* **Time Inc. Bks.**

People, Incorporated *See* **People Ink Pr.**

People Ink Pr., *(978-0-9789476; 978-0-9845983)* 1219 N. Forest Rd., Williamsville, NY 14231 USA Tel 716-634-8132; Fax: 716-817-7558 Web site: http://www.people-inc.org.

People Ink Pr., *(978-0-9858052; 978-0-9893267; 978-0-9862182)* 1219 N. Forest, Williamsville, NY 14223 USA Tel 716-629-3602 E-mail: scrocker@people-inc.org; npalumbo@people-inc.org.

People Skills International, *(978-1-881165)* Orders Addr.: 2910 Baily Ave., San Diego, CA 92105 USA Tel 619-262-9951; Fax: 619-262-0505 E-mail: idagreene@earthlink.net Web site: http://www.idagreene.com

People's Literature Publishing Hse. (CHN) *(978-7-02) Dist. by* **China Bks.**

People's Literature Publishing Hse. (CHN) *(978-7-02) Dist. by* **Chinasprout.**

Pep & Olie Publishing, *(978-0-9912023)* 1355 Hilda Ave. No. 6, Glendale, CA 91205 USA Tel 818-552-2642 E-mail: sahin@ersoz.com Web site: www.pepandolie.com.

Peppermint Bks., *(978-0-9828852)* P.O. Box 16512, Edina, MN 55416 USA (SAN 859-9424) Tel 651-815-8137 E-mail: orders@peppermintbooks.com Web site: http://www.peppermintbooks.com.

Peppernut Publishing, *(978-0-9796500)* P.O. Box 31126, Omaha, NE 68131-1126 USA Tel 402-556-5591 E-mail: evyboonyawiroj@yahoo.com.

Peppertree Pr., The, *(978-0-9778525; 978-0-9787740; 978-1-934246; 978-0-9814894; 978-0-9817572; 978-0-9818683; 978-0-9820479; 978-0-9821654; 978-0-9822540; 978-0-9823002; 978-1-936051; 978-1-936343; 978-1-61493)* 1269 First St., Suite 7, Sarasota, FL 34236-5518 USA Web site: http://www.peppertreepublishing.com.

Peppery Pr., *(978-0-9764813)* 504 Springcreek Dr., Longwood, FL 32779 USA Tel 407-786-6113 E-mail: pruben@cfl.rr.com Web site: http://www.pepperypress.com.

Per Aspera Pr., *(978-0-9745734; 978-1-941662)* Div. of Viridian City Media, Orders Addr.: 205 Grandview Dr., San Marcos, TX 78666 USA E-mail: adastra@perasperapress.com Web site: http://www.perasperapress.com/ *Dist(s):* **Brodart Co. Independent Pubs. Group Partners/West Book Distributors.**

Peralta Publishing, LLC, *(978-0-9798620)* 9908 E. Desert Trail Ln., Gold Canyon, AZ 85218 USA Tel 480-288-4306 E-mail: thomaspreiss@msn.com.

Perceval Pr., *(978-0-9721436; 978-0-9747078; 978-0-9763009; 978-0-9774869; 978-0-9819747; 978-0-9895616)* 1223 Wishire Blvd. No. F, Santa Monica, CA 90403 USA E-mail: info@percevelpress.com; michele@percevalpress.com Web site: http://www.percevalpress.com *Dist(s):* **D.A.P./Distributed Art Pubs. SPD-Small Pr. Distribution.**

Peregrine Communications *Imprint of* **Collins, Robert**

Perelandra Publishing Co., *(978-0-9640858)* Orders Addr.: P.O. Box 697, Cardiff, CA 92007 USA; Edit Addr.: 2387 Montgomery, Cardiff, CA 92007 USA Tel 760-753-4469.

Perennial Dreams Pubns., *(978-0-9764779)* P.O. Box 671, Lehi, UT 84043-0671 USA.

Perennis, Sophia, *(978-0-900588; 978-1-59731)* 408 4th St., Petaluma, CA 94952 USA Tel 415-509-6969 E-mail: jameswetmore@mac.com Web site: http://www.sophiaperennis.com *Dist(s):* **Lightning Source, Inc. SPD-Small Pr. Distribution.**

Perennis, Sophia Et Universalis *See* **Perennis, Sophia**

Perfect 4 Preschool, *(978-0-9769239)* 428 N. Nelson St., Arlington, VA 22203 USA (SAN 850-0614) Tel 703-351-5843 E-mail: bjmischel@aol.com Web site: http://www.perfect4preschool.

Perfect Bound Marketing, *(978-0-9887022; 978-1-939614)* P.O. Box 44545, Phoenix, AZ 85064 USA Tel 480-941-8202 E-mail: vickie@perfectboundmarketing.com Web site: www.PerfectBoundMarketing.com *Dist(s):* **eBookit.com.**

Perfect Moment LLC, The, *(978-0-9840039)* 20 Portsmouth Ave. Suite 177, Stratham, NH 03885 USA Tel 603-493-8400 E-mail: theperfectmomentllc@comcast.net Web site: theperfectmomentllc.com *Dist(s):* **Independent Pubs. Group.**

Perfect Praise Publishing, *(978-0-9679240; 978-0-9915735)* 1228 Fourth Ave., E., Williston, ND 58801 USA E-mail: perfectpraise@dia.net Web site: http://www.perfect-praise.com.

Perfecting Parenting Pr., *(978-0-9790420)* 3943 Jefferson Ave, Emerald Hills, CA 94062-3437 USA Tel 650-364-4466; Fax: 650-364-2299 Web site: http://www.perfectingparentingpress.com.

Perfection Form Company, The *See* **Perfection Learning Corp.**

Perfection Learning Corp., *(978-0-7807; 978-0-7891; 978-0-8124; 978-0-89598; 978-1-56312; 978-0-7569; 978-1-60686; 978-1-61563; 978-1-61383; 978-1-61384; 978-1-62299; 978-1-62359; 978-1-62765; 978-1-62766; 978-1-62974; 978-1-63419; 978-1-68064; 978-1-68065; 978-1-68240)* 1000 N. 2nd Ave., Logan, IA 51546 USA (SAN 221-0010) Tel 712-644-2831; Fax: 712-644-2392; Toll Free Fax: 800-543-2745; Toll Free: 800-831-4190 E-mail: orders@perfectionlearning.com Web site: http://www.perfectionlearning.com.

Pergot Pr., *(978-0-936865)* 19 Prospect Ave., Sausalito, CA 94965 USA (SAN 699-9441) Tel 415-332-0279; Fax: 415-332-5588.

Perigee Trade *Imprint of* **Penguin Publishing Group**

Perinatal Loss *See* **Grief Watch**

Perlo Reports, *(978-0-9659236)* Orders Addr.: P.O. Box 30367, Flagstaff, AZ 86003-0367 USA Tel 520-526-2523; Fax: 520-526-0852; Edit Addr.: 1640 N. Spyglass Way, Flagstaff, AZ 86004 USA *Dist(s):* **Jenkins Group, Inc.**

Periplus Editions (HK), Ltd. (HKG) *(978-0-945971; 978-962-593; 978-0-7946; 978-962-8734) Dist. by* **S and S Inc.**

PeriplusEdition *Imprint of* **Tuttle Publishing**

Periscope Film, LLC, *(978-0-9786388; 978-0-9816526; 978-1-935327; 978-1-935700; 978-1-937684; 978-1-940453)* P.O. Box 341474, Los Angeles, CA 90034 USA E-mail: contact@periscopefilm.com Web site: http://www.periscopefilm.com.

Periscope Pr., *(978-0-9718546)* 15736 Horton Ln., Overland Park, KS 66223-3491 USA (SAN 254-9700) Web site: http://www.hearthisorg.com *Dist(s):* **Midwest Library Service Quality Bks., Inc.**

Periscopefilm.com *See* **Periscope Film, LLC**

Periwinkle Studios, *(978-0-9759385)* P.O. Box 5134, Roselle, IL 60172 USA E-mail: periwinklestudios@comcast.net.

Perkins Crawford, *(978-0-9762935)* 2605 Treyburne Ln., Owens Crossroads, AL 35763 USA Tel 256-536-5391 E-mail: e_vroom@bellsouth.net Web site: http://www.perkinscrawford.com.

Perkins Miniatures, *(978-0-9759198)* 1708-59th St., Des Moines, IA 50322 USA Tel 515-279-6639 E-mail: gladon@earthlink.net.

Perkins Schl. for the Blind, *(978-0-9657170; 978-0-9743510; 978-0-615-26039-6; 978-0-9822721; 978-0-9881713)* a/o Publications Dept., 175 N. Beacon St., Watertown, MA 02472 USA Web site: http://www.Perkins.org *Dist(s):* **eBookit.com.**

Perkins-Stell, Crystal, *(978-0-9740705)* P.O. Box 8044, Edmond, OK 73013-8044 USA Tel 405-216-0224; Fax: 405-216-0224 E-mail: cleva@crystalstell.com Web site: http://www.crystalstell.com.

Perks, Brad Lightscapes Photo Gallery, *(978-0-9788442)* 4055 Kimberly Pl., Concord, CA 94521-3359 USA E-mail: bradperks@yahoo.com; bradperks@pcimagenetwork.com Web site: http://pcimagenetwork.com; http://bradperks.com.

Perlycross Pubs., *(978-0-9741743)* Orders Addr.: a/o Bryce D. Gibby, P.O. Box 9725, Ogden, UT 84409 USA Tel 801-732-8600; Fax: 801-732-8602; Edit Addr.: 2711 Centerville Rd., Suite 120, PMB 5544, Wilmington, DE 19808 USA.

PermaGrin Publishing, *(978-0-9717464)* 27758 Santa Margarita Pkwy. No. 379, Mission Viejo, CA 92691 USA (SAN 254-4148) Tel 949-766-1545; Fax: 949-766-0937 E-mail: r2ktrahan@cox.net Web site: http://www.permagrinpublishing.com *Dist(s):* **Independent Pubs. Group.**

Perman, LeAnn, *(978-0-615-79750-2; 978-0-9892677)* 2295 S. Hiawassee Rd. Suite 208, Orlando, FL 32835 USA Tel 801-243-8463 *Dist(s):* **BookBaby CreateSpace Independent Publishing Platform.**

Permanent Productions, Incorporated *See* **Permanent Productions Publishing**

Permanent Productions Publishing, *(978-0-9818204)* Orders Addr.: 904 Silver Spur Rd., No. 510, Rolling Hills Estates, CA 90274 USA (SAN 856-6348) Tel 310-366-4996; Fax: 310-521-9329; Toll Free: 866-698-7376 E-mail: c.jackson@permproductions.com Web site: http://www.permproductions.com.

Permiso Por Favor Publishing Co., *(978-0-9747272)* 8568 Riverwood Farms, Cordova, TN 38016 USA Tel 901-756-0663 E-mail: permisoporfavor@hotmail.com.

Pernell, Pasha, *(978-0-615-82699-8)* 80-84 Berkeley Ave., Newark, NJ 07104 USA Tel 732-535-6676 E-mail: pashapernell@yahoo.com *Dist(s):* **CreateSpace Independent Publishing Platform.**

Perpendicular Pr., *(978-0-9740234)* 64 Estabrook Rd., Carlisle, MA 01741-1724 USA E-mail: info@perpendicularpress.com Web site: http://www.perpendicularpress.com.

Perpetual Motion Machine Publishing, *(978-0-9887488; 978-0-9860594; 978-1-943720)* 152 Dew Fall Trail, Cibolo, TX 78108 USA Tel 210-573-7796 E-mail: pmmpublishing@gmail.com Web site: www.perpetualpublishing.com.

Perri Tales Pubns., *(978-0-9763442)* Orders Addr.: 45 W. 132nd St., Suite 12K, New York City, NY 10037-3123 USA; Edit Addr.: 19601 Kings Hwy., Warrensville Heights, OH 44122 USA E-mail: perrigaffney@aol.com Web site: http://www.perritales.com.

Perrin & Kabel Publishing, *(978-0-9725364)* 145 Waverly Dr., Pasadena, CA 91105 USA Tel 626-577-1023; Fax: 626-577-1024 E-mail: perrinkabel@earthlink.net.

Perry Enterprises, *(978-0-941518)* 3907 N. Foothill Dr., Provo, UT 84604 USA (SAN 171-0281) Tel 801-226-1002.

Perry Heights Pr., *(978-0-9630181)* P.O. Box 102, Georgetown, CT 06829 USA Tel 203-767-6509; *Imprints:* A Road to Discovery Series Guide (Rd Discovery) E-mail: contact@perryheightspress.com; contact@cttrips.com Web site: http://www.cttrips.com.

Pers Publishing, *(978-1-932179)* Div. of Pers Corp., 5255 Stevens Creek Blvd., No. 232-5, Santa Clara, CA 95051-6664 USA (SAN 254-7716) Toll Free Fax: 800-505-7377 E-mail: info@pers.com Web site: http://www.pers.com; http://www.pers.com/wholesale *Dist(s):* **APG Sales & Distribution Services Brodart Co. Emery-Pratt Co. Quality Bks., Inc.**

†**Persea Bks., Inc.,** *(978-0-89255)* 853 Broadway, Suite 604, New York, NY 10003 USA (SAN 212-8233) Tel 212-260-9256; Fax: 212-260-1902 E-mail: info@perseabooks.com Web site: http://www.perseabooks.com *Dist(s):* **Norton, W. W. & Co., Inc. Penguin Random Hse., LLC.;** *CIP.*

Perseus Bks. Group, *(978-0-7382; 978-0-938289; 978-1-58097; 978-1-882810; 978-1-903985)* Orders Addr.: 2465 Central Ave., Suite 200, Boulder, CO 80301-5728 USA Toll Free: 800-343-4499 (customer service); Edit Addr.: 387 Park Ave., S., 12th Flr., New York, NY 10016-8810 USA Tel 212-340-8100; Fax: 212-340-8105; *Imprints:* Weinstein Books (WeinsteinBks) E-mail: perseus.orders@perseusbooks.com Web site: http://www.perseusbooksgroup.com *Dist(s):* **MyiLibrary Perseus-PGW ebrary, Inc.**

Perseus Distribution, Orders Addr.: 210 American Dr., Jackson, TN 38301 USA Toll Free Fax: 800-351-5073 (Customer Service); Toll Free: 800-343-4499 (Customer Service); 800-788-3123 E-mail: ar@perseusbooks.com; celeste.winters@perseusbooks.com; Orderentry@perseusbooks.com Web site: http://www.perseusdistribution.com/.

Perseus-PGW, Orders Addr.: 1094 Flex Dr., Jackson, TN 38301-5070 USA (SAN 631-7715) Tel 731-423-1973; Toll Free Fax: 800-351-5073; Toll Free: 800-343-4499; Edit Addr.: 387 Park Avenue South, New York, NY 10016 USA (SAN 631-760X) Tel 212-340-8100; Fax: 212-340-8195 E-mail: info@pgw.com Web site: http://www.pgw.com/home.

Personal, *(978-0-9756724)* P.O. Box 661, Monticello, IL 61856 USA Tel 217-649-1589 E-mail: flygrl78@gmail.com.

Personal Best Motivional Sciences, Inc., *(978-0-9769988)* P.O. Box 562, Social Circle, GA 30025-0562 USA Web site: http://www.babysimplerecipe.com/.

Personal Genesis Publishing, *(978-0-9747395)* 110 Pacific Ave., No. 204, San Francisco, CA 9411 USA Toll Free: 888-337-7776 Web site: http://www.ForgottenFaces.org.

Personal Power Pr., *(978-0-9616046; 978-0-9772321; 978-0-9821568)* Div. of Institute for Personal Power, P.O. Box 547, Merrill, MI 48637 USA (SAN 698-0155) Tel 989-643-5059; Fax: 989-643-5156; Toll Free: 877-360-1477 E-mail: ipp57@aol.com Web site: http://www.chickmoorman.com *Dist(s):* **Austin & Company, Inc. Partners Pubs. Group, Inc.**

Personal Promise Bible, *(978-0-9759578)* 470 Heritage Hills Dr., Richland, WA 99352 USA Tel 509-627-2607; Fax: 775-402-2106; Toll Free: 866-968-7242 Web site: http://www.personalpromisebible.com.

Personal Security, *(978-0-9675357)* 24366 Falcon, Lake Forest, CA 92630 USA Tel 949-461-9552; Fax: 949-472-8018 E-mail: xwordshicklers@hotmail.com.

Personality Wise *See* **Uniquely You Resources**

Personhood Pr., *(978-1-932181)* P.O. Box 370, Fawnskin, CA 92333 USA Tel 909-866-2912; Fax: 909-866-2961; Toll Free: 800-662-9662 E-mail: blwjalmar@att.net; catwinch@att.net; personhoodpress@att.net Web site: http://www.personhoodpress.com *Dist(s):* **Ebsco Publishing Independent Pubs. Group MyiLibrary ebrary, Inc.**

Personify Pr., *(978-0-9797491)* 1959 Camino a los Cerros, Menlo Park, CA 94025 USA *Dist(s):* **Perseus-PGW.**

Perspective Publishing, Inc., *(978-0-9622036; 978-1-930085)* 2528 Sleepy Hollow Dr., No. A, Glendale, CA 91206 USA Tel 818-502-1270; Fax: 818-502-1272; Toll Free: 800-330-5851 Do not confuse with Perspective Publishing, Memphis, TN E-mail: books@familyhelp.com Web site: http://www.familyhelp.com *Dist(s):* **Independent Pubs. Group Quality Bks., Inc.**

Perspectives Pr., Inc., *(978-0-944934; 978-0-9609504)* P.O. Box 90318, Indianapolis, IN 46290-0318 USA (SAN 262-5059) Tel 317-872-3055 E-mail: patjohnston@perspectivespress.com Web site: http://www.perspectivespress.com *Dist(s):* **Smashwords.**

PES, Inc., *(978-0-9766962)* P.O. Box 5501, Virginia Bch, VA 23471-0501 USA E-mail: sailingthroughbusiness@cox.net Web site: http://www.sailingthroughbusiness.com.

Pesout, Christine, *(978-0-615-47220-1)* 14 Dinan Ct., Lake St. Louis, MO 63367 USA Tel 314-443-6319 E-mail: cpesout@hotmail.com.

Pet Pundit Publishing, *(978-0-9853752)* P.O. Box 91733, Austin, TX 78209-1733 USA Tel 512-358-4515 E-mail: cathy@petpundit.com Web site: www.petpunditpublishing.com.

Petalous Publishing, LLC, *(978-0-9777811)* P.O. Box 338, Montville, NJ 07045-0338 USA.

Peter Pauper Pr. Inc., *(978-0-88088; 978-1-59359; 978-1-4413)* Orders Addr.: 202 Mamaroneck Ave., Suite 400, White Plains, NY 10601 USA (SAN 204-9449) Tel 914-681-0144; Fax: 914-681-0389 E-mail: orders@peterpauper.com; customerservice@peterpauper.com Web site: http://www.peterpauper.com.

Peterman, Melvin G. *See* **Insight Technical Education**

Peters & Pardee Pubs., *(978-0-9626279)* Orders Addr.: 1039 NW Hwy. 101, Lincoln City, OR 97367 USA.

Petersburg Museums, The, *(978-0-9744824)* 15 W. Bank St., Petersburg, VA 23803 USA Tel 804-733-2402 Toll Free: 800-368-3595.

Peterson-Boyce, Linda, *(978-0-9766034)* P.O. Box 2942, North Babylon, NY 11703 USA.

†**Peterson's,** *(978-0-7689; 978-0-87866; 978-1-56079)* Div. of Nelnet, Orders Addr.: P.O. Box 67005, Lawrenceville, NJ 08648-6105 USA (SAN 200-2167); Edit Addr.: 2000 Lenox Dr., 3rd Flr., Lawrenceville, NJ 08648 USA (SAN 297-5661) Tel 609-896-1800; Fax: 609-896-1811; Toll Free: 800-338-3282 X5660;Customer Service; *Imprints:* Arco (Arco) E-mail: custsvc@petersons.com Web site: http://www.petersons.com *Dist(s):* **Hachette Bk. Group Simon & Schuster;** *CIP.*

Petey, Rock & Roo Children's Pubns., *(978-0-9789642)* Orders Addr.: 1657 Broadway, New York, NY 10019 USA (SAN 852-0585) E-mail: tash@timessquarechurch.org Web site: http://www.timessquarechurch.org.

Petit Chou Chou, LLC, *(978-0-615-54492-2; 978-0-9882306)* P.O. Box 470875, Fort Worth, TX 76147 USA Tel 817-793-2594
E-mail: jdrez@att.net
Web site: http://goodnightcowtown.com.

Petite Grande Idée, *(978-0-615-45934-9; 978-0-615-55899-8; 978-0-615-80250-3; 978-0-692-23259-0)* 300 E. Dryden St. No. 37, Glendale, CA 91207 USA Tel 818-468-4669
E-mail: contact@albertocorral.com
Web site: www.petitegrandeidee.com
Dist(s): **CreateSpace Independent Publishing Platform.**

Petra Publishing *See* **Petra Publishing Co.**

Petra Publishing Co., *(978-0-9712429)* 385 S. Lemon Ave., Suite E314, Walnut, CA 91789 USA Tel 404-452-3374
E-mail: admin@petrapublishingcompany.com
Web site: http://www.petrapublishingcompany.com; http://www.positivemag.com.

Pet's Playground *See* **Singing Moon Pr.**

Pex Publishing Co., *(978-0-933767)* 8625 Boysenberry Dr., Tampa, FL 33635 USA (SAN 692-7645).

P.F.B. Publishing, *(978-0-9741273)* P.O. Box 149, Warren, OH 44482-0149 USA Fax: 330-373-0211
E-mail: pat@southparktitle.com.

Pflaum Publishing Group, *(978-0-89837; 978-0-937997; 978-1-933178; 978-1-935042; 978-1-939105)* 2621 Dryden Rd., Suite 300, Dayton, OH 45439 USA (SAN 661-2539) Fax: 937-293-1310; Toll Free Fax: 800-370-4450; Toll Free: 800-543-4383
E-mail: service@pflaum.com
Web site: http://www.pflaum.com
Dist(s): **ACTA Pubns.**

P.F.P. Pubs., *(978-0-615-18028-1; 978-0-615-18027-4; 978-0-615-18157-8; 978-0-615-18343-5; 978-0-615-18415-9; 978-0-615-18648-1; 978-0-615-18873-7; 978-0-615-19123-2; 978-0-615-19266-6; 978-0-615-19773-9; 978-0-615-22198-4)* 35 Stone Ridge Blvd., Hermitage, PA 16148 USA
E-mail: p.f.p.publishers@gmail.com
Web site: http://www.pfpublishers.com
Dist(s): **Lulu Enterprises Inc.**

PGC Publishing *See* **Hope of Vision Publishing**

Phaidon Pr. Ltd. (GBR) *(978-0-7148) Dist. by* **HachBkGrp.**

Phaidon Pr., Inc., *(978-0-7148)* 180 Varick St., 14th Flr., New York, NY 10014-4606 USA (SAN 253-3367) Tel 212-652-5400; Fax: 212-652-5410; Toll Free Fax: 800-286-9471 (Orders only); Toll Free: 800-759-0190 (Orders only); 877-742-4366 (Editorial)
E-mail: ussales@phaidon.com
Web site: http://www.phaidon.com
Dist(s): **Hachette Bk. Group.**

Phantom Horse Publishing, *(978-0-615-76366-6)* 5850 sky pointe dr. #1053, Las Vegas, NV 89130 USA Tel 7028601158
Dist(s): **CreateSpace Independent Publishing Platform.**

Phantom Pubns., Inc., *(978-0-9625372)* 9451 Page Rd., Wattsburg, PA 16442-2005 USA
Dist(s): **AtlasBooks Distribution Empire Publishing Service.**

Pharmasoft Publishing *See* **Hale Publishing**

phazelFOZ Co., LLC., The, *(978-0-9819645; 978-0-9834876; 978-0-9859333; 978-0-9960781)* 858 W. Armitage Ave., No. 365, Chicago, IL 60614 USA.

PHD Ink, *(978-0-9897278; 978-1-941104)* P.O. Box 4295, Sarasota, FL 34230 USA Tel 347-661-2073
E-mail: rkclark@aol.com.

Pheasant Tale Productions, *(978-0-9817001)* P.O. Box 73, Skamokawa, WA 98647-0073 USA (SAN 856-2814)
E-mail: rajj@iinet.com; adventureinborneo@gmail.com
Web site: http://https://sites.google.com/site/adventureinborneo/.

Phelps, Diane *See* **Red Rock Mountain Pr. LLC**

Phenomenal One Pr., *(978-0-9841989; 978-0-9850251)* 1148 Annis Squam Harbour, Pasadena, MD 21122 USA
E-mail: lprstn@hotmail.com
Web site: http://www.phenomenalonepress.com
Dist(s): **AtlasBooks Distribution MyiLibrary.**

Phi Sigma Omega, Alpha Kappa Alpha Sorority, Inc., *(978-0-9785269)* P.O. Box 1784, Gonzales, LA 70707-1784 USA Tel 225-936-1665
Web site: http://phisigmaomega2000.org.

Phidal Publishing, Inc./Editions Phidal, Inc. (CAN) *(978-2-89393; 978-2-920129; 978-2-7643) Dist. by* **AIMS Intl.**

Phil the Pill & Friends *Imprint of* **MAMP Creations**

Philadelphia Folklore Project, *(978-0-9644937)* 735 S. 50th St., Philadelphia, PA 19147 USA Tel 215-726-1106; Fax: 215-726-6250
E-mail: pfp@folkloreproject.org
Web site: http://www.folkloreproject.org.

Philadelphia Inquirer, The, *(978-1-58822)* Div. of Philadelphia Newspapers, Inc., 400 N. Broad St., Philadelphia, PA 19101 USA Tel 215-854-2000
Web site: http://www.philly.com.

†Philadelphia Museum of Art, *(978-0-87633)* 2525 Pennsylvania Ave., Philadelphia, PA 19130 USA (SAN 203-0969) Fax: 215-235-8715
Web site: http://www.philamuseum.org
Dist(s): **Antique Collectors' Club Art Media Resources, Inc. D.A.P./Distributed Art Pubs. National Bk. Network Pennsylvania State Univ. Pr. Yale Univ. Pr.**; *CIP.*

Philio International *See* **Philio Publishing**

Philio Publishing, *(978-0-9622996; 978-0-9964356)* 1138 N. Germantown Pkwy. Suite 101-294, Cordova, TN 38018 USA Tel 901-201-4058
Dist(s): **Lulu Enterprises Inc.**

Philipp, Cathy Publishing, *(978-0-9655848)* P.O. Box 1954, Thousand Oaks, CA 91358-1954 USA Tel 805-498-0611; Fax: 805-498-7331
E-mail: philifam@adelphia.net.

Philippine American Literary House *See* **PALH**

Philippine American Writers & Artists, Inc., *(978-0-9763316; 978-0-9968032)* P.O. Box 31928, San Francisco, CA 94131-0928 USA
E-mail: pawa@pawainc.com
Web site: http://www.pawainc.com.

Philips, Fleur, *(978-0-9889299)* 250 N. College Pk. Dr. No. U33, Upland, CA 91786 USA Tel 909-908-3788
E-mail: fleurphilips@gmail.com
Dist(s): **BookBaby.**

Philograph *Imprint of* **Cascade, Inc.**

Philokalos Pr., *(978-0-9912472)* P.O. Box 3811, McLean, VA 22103 USA Tel 703-586-1353
E-mail: philokalospress@gmail.com
Web site: www.philokalospress.org.

Philomel *Imprint of* **Penguin Publishing Group**

Philos Pr., *(978-0-9831075)* 22545 SW Miami Dr., Tualatin, OR 97062 USA Tel 503-885-8877; Fax: 503-885-1847
E-mail: maryandonian@yahoo.com.

†Philosophical Library, Inc., *(978-0-8022)* P.O. Box 1789, New York, NY 10010 USA (SAN 201-999X) Tel 212-886-1873; Fax: 212-873-6070
Dist(s): **Kensington Publishing Corp.**; *CIP.*

Philothea Pr., *(978-0-9826867)* P.O. Box 1262, West Chester, OH 45071 USA Tel 513-805-6766.

Phlare, Inc., *(978-0-9741147)* 9565 W. 52nd Ave., Arvada, CO 80002 USA Tel 303-513-1565; Toll Free: 888-731-2398
Web site: http://www.phlare.com.

Phoenician Foundry, *(978-0-615-81368-4)* 5129 N saddle rock Ln., phoenix, AZ 85018 USA Tel 4803344403
Dist(s): **CreateSpace Independent Publishing Platform.**

Phoenix Bks., Inc., *(978-1-59777; 978-1-60747; 978-1-61467)* 9465 Wilshire Blvd., Suite 840, Beverly Hills, CA 90212-2609 USA; *Imprints:* Pickwick Press (PickwickPr); Dove Books and Audio (Dove Bks)
Dist(s): **Ingram Pub. Services.**

Phoenix Films & Video, *(978-0-7919)* 2349 Chaffee Dr., Saint Louis, MO 63146 USA (SAN 653-5224) Tel 314-569-0211; Fax: 314-569-2834; Toll Free: 800-221-1274
E-mail: phoenixfilm@worldnet.att.net
Web site: http://www.phoenix-bfa-coronet.com
Dist(s): **Follett School Solutions Weston Woods Studios, Inc.**

Phoenix International, Inc., *(978-0-9650485; 978-0-9713470; 978-0-9768007; 978-0-9824295; 978-0-9835615; 978-0-9899356)* 17762 Summer Rain Rd., Fayetteville, AR 72701 USA Tel 479-521-2204 Do not confuse with companies with the same or similar names in Oxon Hill, MD, Nampa, ID
E-mail: john@phoenixpub.com
Web site: http://www.phoenixbase.com
Dist(s): **Chicago Distribution Ctr. Univ. of Arkansas Pr.**

Phoenix International Publications, Inc., *(978-0-7853; 978-1-4127; 978-1-60553; 978-1-4508; 978-1-5037)* 7373, N. Cicero Ave., Lincolnwood, IL 60712 USA; 7390 Lincoln Ave., Lincolnwood, IL 60712 (SAN 860-424X) Tel 847-676-3518; Fax: 847-676-3528; Toll Free: 800-860-6828
E-mail: ldolan@pikidsmedia.com.

Phoenix Learning Resources, LLC, *(978-0-7915)* Orders Addr.: P.O. Box 510, Honesdale, PA 18431 USA (SAN 246-148X) Tel 570-251-6871; Fax: 570-253-3227; Toll Free: 800-228-9345
E-mail: rich@phoenixlr.com
Web site: http://www.phoenixlr.com.

Phoenix Publishing, *(978-1-928812)* Orders Addr.: P.O. Box 8231, Missoula, MT 59807 USA Fax: 406-721-6195; Toll Free: 800-549-8371; Edit Addr.: 309 SW Higgins, Missoula, MT 59803 USA Do not confuse with companies with the same or similar names in Redmond, WA, W. Kennebunk, ME, Rocklin, CA, Bloomington, IN, Miami, FL, Fairfield, FL, Tolono, IL, Newark, NJ, Lansing, MI, Alpharetta, GA, Custer, WA, Marina del Ray, CA, Half Moon Bay, CA, New York, NY
E-mail: phoenixi@phoenixpub.com
Web site: http://www.phoenixpub.com.

Phoenix Publishing, *(978-0-615-20417-8)* 308 W. Burnside Ave., Fairland, IN 46126 USA
E-mail: kphoenix_3@sbcglobal.net
Dist(s): **Lulu Enterprises Inc.**

Phoenix Rising LLC, *(978-0-9800807)* 11684 Ventura Blvd., Suite 886, Studio City, CA 91604 USA (SAN 855-1464)
E-mail: phoenixrising@earthlink.net.

Phoenix Yard Bks. (GBR) *(978-1-907912) Dist. by* **IPG Chicago.**

Phonics Readers *Imprint of* **Capstone Pr., Inc.**

Phosphene Publishing Co., *(978-0-9796968; 978-0-9851477)* 4019 River Dr., Houston, TX 77017 USA.

PhotoGraphics Publishing, *(978-0-9643844; 978-0-9793813; 978-0-9829730)* 23 Cool Water Ct., Palm Coast, FL 32137 USA Tel 386-246-3672; Fax: 386-445-7365; *Imprints:* Doctor Dolittle's Library (Doctor Dolittle)
E-mail: joycehuber47@hotmail.com
Web site: http://www.photographicspublishing.com.

Photographs Naturally, Inc., *(978-0-9710343)* 57 Laurel Oak, Amelia Island, FL 32034 USA Tel 904-277-4403; Fax: 904-277-0749.

Photographs Naturally, Incorporated *See* **Photographs Naturally, Inc.**

PhotoHutch, *(978-0-9824925)* P.O. Box 482, Alamo, CA 94507 USA
Web site: http://www.bisforbufflehead.com; http://www.photohutch.com.

Photon Pubns., *(978-0-9744128; 978-0-615-11954-0)* 7532 Mason Dells Dr., Dallas, TX 75230-3246 USA
E-mail: j1jagger@aol.com
Dist(s): **BookMasters, Inc.**

Piano Pr, *(978-0-9673325; 978-1-931844)* Orders Addr.: P.O. Box 85, Del Mar, CA 92014-0085 USA Tel 619-884-1401; Fax: 858-755-1104; Edit Addr.: 1425 Ocean Ave., No. 17, Del Mar, CA 92014 USA Tel 619-884-1401
E-mail: eaxford@aol.com; pianopress@pianopress.com; lizaxford@pianopress.com
Web site: http://www.pianopress.com
Dist(s): **Book Wholesalers, Inc. Coutts Information Services Blackwell Wayland Audio-Visual.**

Pianomouse Productions, *(978-0-9889068)* Orders Addr.: 8789 Auburn Folsom Rd. Ste. C416, Granite Bay, CA 95746 USA Tel 916-204-8110
E-mail: kathleen@pianomouse.com
Web site: www.pianomouse.com.

Piñata Books *Imprint of* **Arte Publico Pr.**

Picador, *(978-0-312)* Div. of Holtzbrinck Publishers, Orders Addr.: 16365 James Madison Hwy., Gordonsville, VA 22942-8501 USA Fax: 800-672-2054; Toll Free: 888-330-8477; Edit Addr.: 175 Fifth Ave., New York, NY 10010 USA Tel 212-674-5151; Fax: 540-672-7540 (customer service)
Web site: http://www.picadorusa.com
Dist(s): **Libros Sin Fronteras Macmillan.**

Picaro Press *See* **One Eyed Pr.**

Picarona Editorial (ESP) *(978-84-940745; 978-84-941549; 978-84-16117) Dist. by* **Spanish.**

Piccadilly Bks., Ltd., *(978-0-941599; 978-1-936709)* P.O. Box 25203, Colorado Springs, CO 80936 USA (SAN 665-9969) Tel 719-550-9887
E-mail: info@piccadillybooks.com
Web site: http://www.piccadillybooks.com
Dist(s): **MyiLibrary New Leaf Distributing Co., Inc. Nutri-Bks. Corp.**

Piccolo Tales, *(978-0-9881889)* 10640 Riverlake Dr., Knoxville, TN 37922 USA Tel 865-966-0274; Fax: 865-966-0274
E-mail: bc2bls@yahoo.com.

Pick It Publishing, *(978-0-615-26122-5)* P.O. Box 284, Danville, IA 52623 USA
Dist(s): **Lulu Enterprises Inc.**

Pick Me Up N Go Publishing Co., *(978-0-615-15832-7)* 10312 S. Prospect Ave., Chicago, IL 60643 USA
E-mail: felice@pickmeupngo.com
Dist(s): **Lulu Enterprises Inc.**

Pickering & Chatto Pubs., Ltd. (GBR) *(978-1-85196; 978-1-84893; 978-1-78144) Dist. by* **Ashgate Pub Co.**

Pickering, Todd, *(978-0-615-12910-5)* P.O. Box 907, Pt Reyes Sta, CA 94956-0907 USA
E-mail: todd@toddpickering.com
Web site: http://www.toddpickering.com
Dist(s): **SPD-Small Pr. Distribution.**

Pickett Fennell Group, The, *(978-0-615-31289-7; 978-0-9833864)* 619 Castlewood Dr., Upper Marlboro, MD 20774 USA
E-mail: pfgpublishing@gmail.com.

Pickett Publishing *See* **Pickett Fennell Group, The**

Pickled Eggs Pr., *(978-0-9725311)* Div. of E-Compass Communications, Inc., P.O. Box 9177, Rochester, MN 55903 USA Tel 507-280-1794; Fax: 507-280-4440 (Attn: Pickled Eggs Pr.)
E-mail: pickledeggspress@aol.com
Web site: http://www.pickledeggspress.com
Dist(s): **e-Compass Communications, Inc.**

Pickled Herring Pr., *(978-0-9778276)* 2380 W. Hill Dr., Madison, WI 53711 USA.

Picklesisters, *(978-0-9767542)* 224 Red Oak Dr E. Apt. F, Sunnyvale, CA 94086-6612 USA
E-mail: editor@picklesisters.com
Web site: http://www.picklesisters.com.

Pickup, Terry Lowey *See* **Terry Lowey's Children's Stories, LLC**

Pickwick Pr. *Imprint of* **Phoenix Bks., Inc.**

Picnic Publishing Ltd. (GBR) *(978-0-9556105) Dist. by* **Trans-Atl Phila.**

Pictorial Legends, *(978-0-939031)* Subs. of Event Co., 435 Holland Ave., Los Angeles, CA 90042 USA (SAN 662-8486) Tel 213-254-4416
Dist(s): **Igram Pr.**

Picture Bk. *Imprint of* **Spotlight**

Picture Bk. Learning, Inc., *(978-0-9760725)* P.O. Box 270075, Louisville, CO 80027 USA
E-mail: todd@picturebooklearning.com
Web site: http://www.picturebooklearning.com.

Picture Entertainment *See* **Evening Sun Pr.**

Picture Me Books, Incorporated *See* **Playhouse Publishing**

Picture Window Bks., *(978-1-4048; 978-1-4795; 978-1-5158)* Div. of Coughlan Publishing, 1710 Roe Crest Dr., North Mankato, MN 56003 USA (SAN 254-8828) Toll Free Fax: 888-262-0705; *Imprints:* Chapter Readers (ChapReads); Easy Readers (Easy Readers); Fiction Picture Books (FictPicBks); Nonfiction Picture Books (Nonfiction Pict); My First Classic Story (MY FIRST CLASS); DC Super-Pets (DC SUPER-PETS); Michael Dahl - Super Funny Joke Books (MICHAEL DAHL -); Little Boost (LITTLE BOOST); Kylie Jean (KYLIE JEAN); Monster Street (MONSTER STREET); Max & Zoe (MAX & ZOE); I See (I SEE); Henry Helps (HENRY HELPS); My Little Planet (MY LITTLE PLAN); Zeke Meeks (ZEKE MEEKS); Adventures at Hound Hotel (AdventHound); Charles Reasoners Little Cuddles (ChuckReas); Finley Flowers (FinFlower); Sofia Martinez (SofiMart)
E-mail: k.monyhan@coughlancompanies.com; customerservice@capstonepub.com
Web site: http://www.picturewindowbooks.com; http://www.capstonepub.com; http://www.capstoneclassroom.com
Dist(s): **Capstone Pr., Inc. Capstone Pub.**

Pie in the Sky Publishing, LLC, *(978-1-893815)* 8031 E. Phillips Cir., Centennial, CO 80112 USA
E-mail: PieintheSkyPublishing@msn.com
Web site: http://www.pieintheskypublishing.com
Dist(s): **Bks. West.**

Pie Plate Publishing Co., *(978-0-9855906; 978-1-941175)* P.O. Box 760151, Lathrup Village, MI 48076 USA Tel 248-508-7749
E-mail: joddo@pieplatepublishing.com
Web site: www.pieplatepublishing.com.

Pie Pr., *(978-0-615-76730-7; 978-0-692-02335-8; 978-0-692-32166-9; 978-0-692-32284-0; 978-0-9962480)* 411 Chancellor St., Johnstown, PA 15904-2227 USA Tel 814-525-4783; Fax: 814-262-0235
Web site: www.piepresspublishing.com
Dist(s): **CreateSpace Independent Publishing Platform INscribe Digital.**

Pieces of Learning, *(978-0-9623835; 978-1-880505; 978-1-931334; 978-1-934358; 978-1-937113)* Div. of Creative Learning Consultants, Inc., 1990 Market Rd., Marion, IL 62959 USA (SAN 298-461X) Tel 618-964-9426; Fax: 618-964-1897; Toll Free Fax: 800-844-0455; Toll Free: 800-729-5137
E-mail: piecesoflearning@frontier.com; stan@piecesoflearning.com
Web site: http://www.piecesoflearning.com.

Piedra Santa, Editorial (GTM) *(978-84-8377; 978-99922-1; 978-99922-58) Dist. by* **Libros Fronteras.**

PIEEYE Publishing, Inc., *(978-0-9759435)* 116 Consumer Sq., Suite 333, Plattsburgh, NY 12901 USA Tel 514-684-0434; Toll Free: 888-474-3393
E-mail: jocelyne@pieeyepublishing.com; info@pieeyepublishing.com
Web site: http://www.pieeyepublishing.com/.

Pier Avenue Publishing, *(978-0-9779768)* 1250 6th St., Hermosa beach, CA 90254 USA Tel 310-530-0770
Web site: http://www.educatingamerica.us.

Pier Media, *(978-0-9715980)* Div. of Pier Video, Inc., P.O. Box 190, Gardiner, NY 12525 USA Tel 212-481-0031; Fax: 212-481-0892
E-mail: joe514@aol.com
Web site: http://www.marcusantebi.com.

Pieras Inc. Editorial, *(978-0-9729719)* Div. of Pieras Inc., Y-9 México Ave. and Colorado St. Parkville Extension, Guaynabo, PR 00962-3923 USA (SAN 255-3112) Tel 787-299-4486
E-mail: jorge@elbien.org
Web site: http://www.wakebooks.com
Dist(s): **Lightning Source, Inc.**

Pieras Incorporated *See* **Pieras Inc. Editorial**

Pierce, Paul, *(978-0-9741819)* 1400 15th St., Columbus, GA 31901 USA
E-mail: prpierce@mindspring.com
Dist(s): **Parnassus Bk. Distributors.**

Pierce Pr., *(978-0-9776396; 978-0-9960975)* P.O. Box 206, Arlington, MA 02746 USA Tel 339-368-5656; Fax: 339-368-5656
E-mail: charlotte@piercepress.com
Web site: http://www.piercepress.com; https://www.facebook.com/daytripperbooks; https://plus.google.com/+CharlottePierce; http://peeragogy.org.

Pig Iron Pr., *(978-0-917530)* Orders Addr.: P.O. Box 237, Youngstown, OH 44501 USA (SAN 209-0937) Tel 330-747-6932; Fax: 330-747-0599; Edit Addr.: 26 N. Phelps, Youngstown, OH 44503 USA (SAN 241-8193)
E-mail: pigironpress@cboss.com.

Pig Wing Pr., *(978-0-615-73136-0; 978-0-615-82848-0)* 10 Stoney Hill, Rockport, ME 04856 USA Tel 207-236-0315
E-mail: pwpendleton@yahoo.com
Dist(s): **CreateSpace Independent Publishing Platform.**

Piggy Pr. Bks., *(978-9962-629; 978-9962-690)* PTY 3186 PO Box 025724, Miami, FL 33102-5724 USA Tel 507-720-1072; Dos Bocas, No. 6426, Los Rios, USA.
E-mail: info@piggypress.com
Web site: www.piggypress.com
Dist(s): **Follett School Solutions Smashwords.**

Pike Road Productions *See* **STR8*UP Productions**

Pikes Peak Library District, *(978-1-56735)* 5550 N. Union, Colorado Springs, CO 80918 USA Tel 719-531-6333; Fax: 719-389-8161
E-mail: tblevins@ppld.org.

Pik-Ware Publishing, *(978-0-9744190)* P.O. Box 110, Crisfield, MD 21817 USA Tel 410-968-3873 (phone/fax)
E-mail: pat@funkyseagull.com
Web site: http://www.pik-ware.com.

PIL Kids *Imprint of* **Publications International, Ltd.**

Pilate, Victoria, *(978-0-9759665)* P.O. Box 75433, Washington, DC 20013 USA.

Pilgrim Press *See* **Kinfolk Research Pr.**

Pilgrim Pr., The/United Church Pr., *(978-0-8298)* Div. of United Church Board for Homeland Ministries, Orders Addr.: 226 Sheldon Rd., Berea, OH 44017-1234 USA Toll Free: 800-537-3394; Edit Addr.: 700 Prospect Ave. E., Cleveland, OH 44115-1100 USA Tel 216-736-3764; Fax: 216-736-2207
E-mail: ucpress@ucc.org; pilgrim@ucc.org
Web site: http://www.ucpress.com; http://www.pilgrimpress.com
Dist(s): **BookBaby Women Ink.**

Pilinut Pr., Inc., *(978-0-9779576)* 41 W. Lee Hwy., Suite 59, #808, Warrenton, VA 20186 USA.

Pill Bug Pr., *(978-0-9761623)* 1868 Bridgeport Ave., Claremont, CA 91711 USA Tel 909-624-9985 (phone/fax).

Pill Hill Pr., *(978-0-9842610; 978-1-61706)* 343 W. 4th St., Chadron, NE 69337 USA
E-mail: pillhillpress@gmail.com
Web site: http://www.pillhillpress.com
Dist(s): **BookBaby.**

Pillar of Enoch Ministry Bks., *(978-0-9759131)* 1708 N. 77th Ave., Elmwood Park, IL 60707-4107 USA
E-mail: helena@pillar-of-enoch.com
Web site: http://www.pillar-of-enoch.com
Dist(s): **Lightning Source, Inc.**

Pillar Rock Publishing, *(978-0-9764109)* P.O. Box 86571, Portland, OR 97286 USA
Web site: http://www.zoppa.com.

Pilot Bks. *Imprint of* **Bellwether Media**

Pilot Communications Group, Incorporated *See* **Next Century Publishing**

Pilumeli, Tanya *See* **FAVA Pr.**

Pinata Pubns., *(978-0-934925)* P.O. Box 13252, Oakland, CA 94611 USA (SAN 694-6062) Tel 510-336-0819 (phone/fax)
E-mail: bsalinas@ousd.k12.ca.us
Dist(s): **Lectorum Pubns., Inc.**
Libros Sin Fronteras
Teacher's Discovery.

Pinata Publishing (CAN) *(978-0-9685097; 978-0-9809163)* *Dist. by* **Partners Pubs Grp.**

Pinchey Hse. Pr., *(978-0-9820342)* 1805 Mummasburg Rd., Gettysburg, PA 17325 USA (SAN 857-0655)
Web site: http://www.ofthewing.com
Dist(s): **Follett School Solutions.**

Pine Cone Pr., *(978-0-9791982; 978-0-692-20517-4)* 2870 Callie Still Rd., Lawrenceville, GA 30045 USA
E-mail: marty@donnellan.com
Web site: http://www.frendibles.com.

Pine Hill Graphics, *(978-0-9714103; 978-0-9727279; 978-1-933150; 978-0-615-29527-5)* 85334 Lorane Hwy., Eugene, OR 97405 USA Tel 541-343-1364; Fax: 541-343-0568
E-mail: fred@pinehillgraphics.com
Dist(s): **Leonard, Hal Corp.**

Pine Hill Pr., *(978-1-57579)* Div. of Print Right Printing, 1808 N. K Ave., Sioux Falls, SD 57104 USA Tel 605-362-9200; Fax: 605-362-9222 Do not confuse with Pine Hill Pr., Lafayette, CA8
E-mail: print@pinehillpress.com
Web site: http://www.printrightprinting.com.

Pine Orchard, Inc., *(978-0-9645727; 978-1-930580)* Orders Addr.: 2850 Hwy 95 South. P.O. box 9184, Moscow, ID 83843 USA (SAN 253-4258) Tel 208-882-4838; Fax: 208-882-4845; Toll Free: 877-354-7433; *Imprints:* Ulyssian Publications (Ulyssian Pubns); Luminary Media Group (Luminary Media)
E-mail: orders@pineorchard.com; pineorch@pineorchard.com
Web site: http://www.pineorchard.com
Dist(s): **Brodart Co.**

Pine Orchard Press *See* **Pine Orchard, Inc.**

Pine View Pr., *(978-0-9740151)* Orders Addr.: 42 Central St., Southbridge, MA 01550 USA (SAN 255-3309) Tel 508-764-7415; Fax: 508-765-1963
E-mail: shawnpcormier@aol.com
Web site: http://www.pineviewpress.com
Dist(s): **Partners Bk. Distributing, Inc.**

Pineapple Pr., Inc., *(978-0-910923; 978-1-56164)* P.O. Box 3889, Sarasota, FL 34230-3889 USA (SAN 285-0850) Tel 941-739-2219; Fax: 941-739-2296; Toll Free: 800-746-3275 Do not confuse with companies with same or similar names in Saint Johns, MI, Middletown, RI, Northampton, MA, Wimberley, TX
E-mail: info@pineapplepress.com; editorial@pineapplepress.com
Web site: http://www.pineapplepress.com
Dist(s): **American Wholesale Bk. Co.**
Ingram Pub. Services
MyiLibrary.

Pineapple Publishing and Consulting LLC, *(978-0-9794608; 978-1-938188)* 1046 W. 42nd St., Houston, TX 77018-4314 USA
Web site: http://www.pineapplepublishing.com.

Pineapple Study Guides *See* **Passkey Pubns.**

Pinefield Publishing, *(978-0-9746397)* 9801 Fall Creek Rd., Suite 318, Indianapolis, IN 46256 USA Tel 317-258-6211; Fax: 317-576-9154
E-mail: Pinefieldpublishing@comcast.net
Web site: http://www.Pinefieldpublishing.com.

Pines Publishing, *(978-0-9766820)* 9896 Lincoln Rd., Morrison, KY 61270-9498 USA
E-mail: info@pinespublishing.com
Web site: http://www.pinespublishing.com.

Pinetree Pubns., *(978-0-9709408)* 6523 Oregon Chickadee Rd., Weeki Wachee, FL 34613-8353 USA Tel 352-592-5292 (phone/fax)
E-mail: lwnorris@hitter.net; lwnorris@bellsouth.net.

Pink Angel Pr., *(978-0-9793381)* 168 Hwy. 274, No. 212, Lake Wylie, SC 29710 USA
Web site: http://www.pinkangelpress.com
Dist(s): **Independent Pubs. Group.**

Pink Elephant Pr. The, *(978-0-9772975)* P.O. Box 1153, Jonesboro, GA 30236-1153 USA (SAN 257-2532) Toll Free: 800-583-1439 (phone/fax)
E-mail: info@thepinkelephantpress.com
Web site: http://www.thepinkelephantpress.com.

Pink Granite Pr., *(978-0-9766737)* P.O. Box 231, Thousand Island Park, NY 13692-0231 USA Tel 613-549-6575.

Pink Hyacinth Press *See* **Kelly, Katherine**

Pink Kiss Publishing Co., *(978-0-615-29068-3; 978-0-9828795; 978-0-9835756; 978-0-9847455; 978-0-9851909; 978-0-9858299; 978-0-9885632; 978-0-9895580; 978-0-9904442; 978-0-9962965)* 2316 Greenway Dr., Gautier, MS 39553 USA
E-mail: pinkkisspublishing@pinkkisspublishing.com; glenda099@cableone.net
Web site: http://www.pinkkisspublishing.com.

Pink Lemonade, LLC, *(978-0-9799159)* 297 Sunset Pk. Dr., Prescott, AZ 86303 USA
E-mail: zuzu@cableone.net
Web site: http://www.thecupcakesclub.com.

Pink Pig Pr., *(978-0-9816360)* 980 Broadway, Suite 248, Thornwood, NY 10594 USA Tel 914-747-8188
Dist(s): **AtlasBooks Distribution.**

Pink Stucco Pr., *(978-0-9717796)* 36 Dexter St., Waltham, MA 02453-5017 USA; *Imprints:* Mystic Night Books (Mystic Night Bks)
E-mail: publishing@pinkstucco.net
Web site: http://www.pinkstucco.net/psp/.

Pink&Brown Publishing, LLP, *(978-0-615-36448-3)* 35 E. Main St. Suite 373, Avon, CT 06001 USA Tel 860-674-0292
E-mail: marycashman@comcast.net
Dist(s): **West.**

Pinkney, Gail, *(978-0-9799320)* 1185 Collier Rd NW Apt. 10E, Atlanta, GA 30318-8218 USA
E-mail: pinkneycorey@yahoo.com
Web site: http://www.dreamteambook.com.

Pinkney Wilcox, JoAnn, *(978-0-9764191)* Orders Addr.: 4044 George Busbee Pkwy. #8304, Kennesaw, GA 30144 USA Tel 678-768-5644
E-mail: joannpwilcox@yahoo.com
Web site: http://www.booksbyjpw.com.

Pinkston, Anastasia, *(978-0-9790515)* 500 Moonraker Dr. Apt. 107, Chesapeake, VA 23320-4051 USA
E-mail: anapinkston@yahoo.com
Web site: http://www.cafepress.com/pinkston.

Pinnacle Press *See* **Mountaintop Pr.**

Pinnacle Pr., *(978-0-9745542)* 25 Country Estates W., East Durham, NY 12423 USA Tel 518-239-8003 Do not confuse with companies with the same name in Little Rock, AR, Cary, NC, Spokane, WA, Nashville, TN, Franklin, TN, Saint Louis, MO
E-mail: foxykate2001@yahoo.com.

Pinninti Pubs., *(978-0-9703474)* 120 Carter Rd., Princeton, NJ 08540-2111 USA
E-mail: pkrao@dr.com
Web site: http://www.pinnintipublishers.com.

Pinpoint Color *See* **Pinpoint Printing**

Pinpoint Printing, *(978-0-9702324)* 5115 E. Highland Dr., Jonesboro, AR 72401 USA Tel 870-931-6200; Fax: 870-931-5800
E-mail: dkelley@mkbmarketing.com
Web site: http://www.pinpointprinting.com.

Pinter & Martin Ltd. (GBR) *(978-0-9530964; 978-1-905177; 978-1-78066)* *Dist. by* **Natl Bk Netwk.**

Pinwheel Bks., *(978-0-9832577; 978-0-9854248; 978-1-940741)* Orders Addr.: PO BOX 491470, Key Biscayne, FL 33149 USA Tel 617-794-7976
E-mail: publisher@pinwheelbooks.com
Web site: www.pinwheelbooks.com.

Pinz, Shelley Music, *(978-0-9700251)* Orders Addr.: P.O. Box 275, Atlantic Beach, NY 11509 USA Tel 516-371-4437; Fax: 516-371-4437 (*51); Edit Addr.: 2100 Atlantic Blvd., Atlantic Beach, NY 11509 USA.

Pioneer Clubs, *(978-0-9743503; 978-1-934725; 978-0-9853008; 978-0-9885794)* Orders Addr.: P.O. Box 788, Wheaton, IL 60187-0788 USA (SAN 225-4891) Tel 630-293-1600; Fax: 630-293-3053; Toll Free: 800-694-2582; Edit Addr.: 27 W. 130 St. Charles Rd., Carol Stream, IL 60188-1999 USA (SAN 669-2419)
E-mail: info@pioneerclubs.org
Web site: http://www.pioneerclubs.org.

Pioneer Poet Publishing, *(978-0-615-55095-4; 978-0-615-65742-4)* 10651 MacGregor Dr., Pensacola, FL 32514 USA Tel 850-748-8895
E-mail: gincru@gmail.com
Dist(s): **Lulu Enterprises Inc.**

Pioneer Valley Bks. *Imprint of* **Pioneer Valley Bks.**

Pioneer Valley Bks., *(978-1-58453; 978-1-932570; 978-1-60343)* 155A Industrial Drive, Northhampton, MA 01060 USA Tel 4137273573; Fax: 4137278211; *Imprints:* Pioneer Valley Books (PioValley Bks)
E-mail: Christine@pvep.com; Shanique@pvep.com; lauri@pvep.com; katie@pvep.com
Web site: http://www.pioneervalleybooks.com.

Pioneer Valley Educational Press, Incorporated *See* **Pioneer Valley Bks.**

Piper Verlag GmbH (DEU) *(978-3-492; 978-3-89029; 978-3-8225; 978-3-89521; 978-3-921909)* *Dist. by* **Distribks Inc.**

Pippin & Maxx Arts & Entertain, LLC, *(978-0-9818747)* 533 Choctaw Rd., Jackson, MS 39206-3920 USA (SAN 856-7794) Tel 601-982-9394 (phone/fax)
E-mail: amile@pippinandmaxx.com
Web site: http://www.pippinandmaxx.com.

Pippin Pr., *(978-0-945912)* Orders Addr.: P.O. Box 1347, New York, NY 10028 USA (SAN 247-8366) Tel 212-288-4920; Fax: 732-225-1562; Edit Addr.: 229 E. 85th St., New York, NY 10028 USA.

Pirate Publishing International, *(978-0-9674081)* 6323 St. Andrews Cir., No. 5, Fort Myers, FL 33919-1719 USA Tel 941-939-4845
E-mail: SuperK@juno.com
Dist(s): **ebrary, Inc.**

Piroux, Raymond, *(978-0-9729815)* Orders Addr.: 2014 Holland Ave. #719, Port Huron, MI 48060 USA (SAN 255-3899)
Web site: http://www.raymondpiroux.com.

P.I.T. Pubns., *(978-0-9760608)* 120 Deweese Dr., Waggaman, LA 70094-2480 USA Tel 504-436-7012.

Pitcher, Jan, *(978-0-9795877)* 208 Tait Ave., Los Gatos, CA 95030 USA
E-mail: janpitcher@verizon.net.

Pitspopany Pr. *Imprint of* **Simcha Media Group**

Pittsburgh Literary Arts Network LLC, *(978-0-9727319)* P.O. Box 226, Oakmont, PA 15139 USA Tel 412-820-2507; *Imprints:* Blacktypewriter Press (Blacktypewriter Pr)
E-mail: info@blacktypewriter.com
Web site: http://www.blacktypewriter.com.

PitziGil Pr. *Imprint of* **PitziGil Pubns.**

PitziGil Pubns., *(978-0-9846397; 978-0-9914760)* Orders Addr.: P.O. Box 1315, Gaffney, SC 29342-1315 USA (SAN 860-1550) Tel 864-488-7320; *Imprints:* PitziGil Press (PitziGil Pr)
E-mail: pitzigil@yahoo.com; dl@pitzigilpublications.com
Web site: www.pitzigilpublications.com.

Pivotal Force, *(978-0-9740473)* 632 Skyview Rd., Bellville, TX 77418 USA (SAN 256-4319) Tel 979-865-9213
E-mail: pivotalforce@evl.net
Web site: http://www.pivotalforce.com.

Pixel Mouse Hse., *(978-1-939322)* P.O. Box 20241, Huntington Station, NY 11746 USA Tel 631-850-3497
E-mail: info@pixelmousehouse.com
Web site: www.pixelmousehouse.com.

Pixelated Publishing *Imprint of* **Faithful Publishing**

Pixelpics Publishing, *(978-0-9747826)* 4801 Secret Harbor Dr., Jacksonville, FL 32257 USA
Web site: http://www.pixelpics.net.

Pixels Publishing, *(978-0-9728743)* P.O. Box 10, La Fox, IL 60147 USA
E-mail: customerservice@pixelspublishing.com
Web site: http://www.pixelspublishing.com.

Pixie Stuff LLC, *(978-0-9761421; 978-0-9795832; 978-0-9826081; 978-0-9833364; 978-0-9850897; 978-0-9850898; 978-0-9854666; 978-0-9890806; 978-0-9916167; 978-0-9862115; 978-0-9966836)* Orders Addr.: 18 Brighton Way, Saint Louis, MO 63105 USA Tel 314-721-4107; Fax: 314-721-4107
E-mail: jennifer@thumbsupjohnnie.com; jennifer@hiredink.com
Web site: http://www.thumbsupjohnnie.com; www.hiredink.com.

PixyJack Pr., Inc., *(978-0-9658098; 978-0-9773724; 978-1-936555)* Orders Addr.: P.O. Box 149, Masonville, CO 80541 USA Tel 303-810-2850; Toll Free Fax: 888-273-7499
E-mail: info@pixyjackpress.com
Web site: http://www.pixyjackpress.com.

Pizzazz Publishing, *(978-0-9744936)* Orders Addr.: P.O. Box 415, Victoria, MN 55386 USA Tel 952-368-1903; Fax: 952-944-0399
E-mail: psimenson@aol.com
Web site: http://www.pizzazzpublishing.com
Dist(s): **Quality Bks., Inc.**

PJR Assocs., Ltd., *(978-0-9790796)* Orders Addr.: P.O. Box 2482, Alexandria, VA 22301 USA Fax: 703-683-4348; Edit Addr.: 910 Junior St., Alexandria, VA 22301 USA
E-mail: patrichards@pjrassociates.com
Web site: http://www.pjrassociates.com.

PJs Corner, *(978-0-9745615; 978-1-933158)* P.O. Box 39, Taft, CA 93268 USA Tel 661-765-7216; Fax: 661-770-8608; *Imprints:* Twiglet The Little Christmas Tree (Twiglet)
E-mail: memories@pjscorner.net
Web site: http://www.pjscorner.net.

PJS Publishing, *(978-0-9743177; 978-0-615-40511-7)* 40344 Redbud Dr., Oakhurst, CA 93644 USA Tel 559-641-5994
E-mail: steve@tycooney.com.

PK Bks. Inc., *(978-0-9827347; 978-0-9846799; 978-0-9891177)* 512 Terrace Rd., Bayport, NY 11705-1528 USA
E-mail: jnewbauer6@hotmail.com
Dist(s): **Lightning Source, Inc.**

†Place In The Woods, The, *(978-0-932991)* 3900 Glenwood Ave., Golden Valley, MN 55422-5302 USA (SAN 689-058X) Tel 763-374-2120; Fax: 952-593-5593
E-mail: placewoods@aol.com; differentbooks@aol.com
Dist(s): **Social Studies Schl. Service;** *CIP.*

Placenames Press *See* **Back Channel Pr.**

Plaidswede Publishing, *(978-0-9626832; 978-0-9755216; 978-0-9790784; 978-0-9840650; 978-0-9837400; 978-0-9889176; 978-0-9962182)* P.O. Box 269, Concord, NH 03302-0269 USA Tel 603-226-1020; Toll Free: 800-267-9044
E-mail: gnews@empire.net
Web site: http://www.plaidswede.com.

Plain Vision Publishing, *(978-0-9761628; 978-0-9848234; 978-0-9910594)* 984 Ashford St., Brooklyn, NY 11207 USA Tel 868-704-6397; P.O. Box 2235, Chaguanas, 00000 Tel 868-704-6397 Do not confuse with Plain Vision Publishing in Kihei, HI
E-mail: info@plainvisionpublishing-pvp.com; emguadeloupe@aol.com
Web site: http://www.pvppress.com
Dist(s): **Lightning Source, Inc.**

Plain White Pr., LLC, *(978-0-9760250; 978-0-9777383; 978-0-9815004; 978-0-9815964; 978-1-936005)* Orders Addr.: 17 Chadwick Rd., West Harrison, NY 10604-1802 USA (SAN 850-0886)
E-mail: julie@plainwhitepress.com
Web site: http://www.plainwhitepress.com.

Plan B Bks, *(978-0-9785798)* P.O. Box 300307, University City, MO 63130 USA
E-mail: abby@planbbooks.com
Web site: http://www.planbbooks.com.

Planet Bronx Productions, *(978-0-9765566)* P.O. Box 672146, Bronx, NY 10467-0103 USA; *Imprints:* PAPO Brand (PAPO)
E-mail: ivanvelezjr@planetbronx.com; admin@planetbronx.com
Web site: http://www.planetbronx.com.

Planet Dexter *Imprint of* **Penguin Publishing Group**

Planeta Mexicana Editorial S. A. de C. V. (MEX) *(978-968-406; 978-970-690)* *Dist. by* **Lectorum Pubns.**

Planeta Publishing Corp., *(978-0-9715256; 978-0-9719950; 978-0-9748724; 978-1-933169; 978-0-9795042)* 999 Ponce De Leon Blvd. Ste. 1045, Coral Gables, FL 33134-3047 USA
E-mail: mnorman@planetapublishing.com
Web site: http://www.planeta.es
Dist(s): **Ediciones Universal**
Perseus Distribution.

Plankton Pr., *(978-0-9774074)* 5692 Kalanianaole Hwy., Honolulu, HI 96821 USA Tel 808-373-1016; Fax: 808-373-5381
Web site: www.planktonpress.com.

†Planned Parenthood Federation of America, Inc., *(978-0-934586; 978-1-930996; 978-1-935100)* 434 W. 33rd St., New York, NY 10001 USA (SAN 205-1281) Tel 212-541-4653
E-mail: julia.scheinbeim@ppfa.org
Web site: http://www.plannedparenthood.org/store; *CIP.*

Planning/Communications, *(978-0-9622019; 978-1-884587)* 7215 Oak Ave., River Forest, IL 60305-1935 USA (SAN 253-8717) Tel 708-366-5200; Fax: 708-366-5280; Toll Free: 888-366-5200 (orders only)
E-mail: info@planningcommunications.com; dl@planningcommunications.com
Web site: http://www.jobfindersonline.com; http://www.planningcommunications.com; http://www.dreamitdoit.net.

Plant Kingdom Communications, *(978-0-9834114)* 1503 Gates Ct., Morris Plains, NJ 07950 USA Tel 201-745-5494
E-mail: basia@plantkingdomcommunications.com
Web site: www.PlantKingdomCommunications.com.

Plant the Seed Publishing, *(978-0-9759790)* 4361 Fiesta Ln., Houston, TX 77004 USA Tel 713-747-0026
E-mail: rr4361@aol.com
Web site: http://hometown.aol.com/rr4361/myhomepage/business

Plantain Pr., Inc., *(978-0-9816262)* P.O. Box 37, Cruz Bay, VI 00831-0037 USA (SAN 856-0838) Tel 340-344-6123
E-mail: info@vitaxhelp.com.

Plata Publishing, *(978-1-61268)* 4330 N. Civic Ctr. Plaza Suite 100, Scottsdale, AZ 85251 USA Tel 480-998-6971
E-mail: d.leong@richdad.com
Dist(s): **Perseus Distribution**
Smashwords.

Platinum Bks., *(978-0-9746503)* P.O. Box 660876, Arcadia, CA 91066-0876 USA (SAN 255-7525) Do not confuse with companies with the same name in Alpharetta, GA, Washington, DC
E-mail: hongdenise@yahoo.com
Web site: http://www.happierkids.com.

Platinum Medallion Children's Bks., *(978-1-929489)* Div. of EDS Design & Animation, 2705 Ridge Rd., Huntingtown, MD 20639 USA Tel 410-535-6992; Fax: 410-535-7643
E-mail: doug@dougweb.com; edsdesign@dsmith.com
Web site: http://www.platinum-medallion.com.

Platinum Rose Publishing, *(978-0-9742948)* 16619 W. Sierra Hwy., Canyon Country, CA 91351 USA
Web site: http://www.platinumrose.com.

PlatyPr., *(978-1-62050; 978-1-62407)* 180 S. Madison Ave. No. 6, Pasadena, CA 91101 USA Tel 626-796-8962
E-mail: moodooguru@sbcglobal.net
Dist(s): **BookBaby**
Lulu Enterprises Inc.
SCB Distributors
eBookit.com
ebrary, Inc.

Platypus Media, L.L.C., *(978-1-930775)* Orders Addr.: 725 Eighth St., SE, Washington, DC 20003 USA Tel 202-546-1674; Fax: 202-546-2356; Toll Free: 877-752-8977
E-mail: info@platypusmedia.com
Web site: http://www.platypusmedia.com
Dist(s): **MyiLibrary**
National Bk. Network.

Play Ball Publishing, *(978-0-615-17947-6)* 891 Juliana Cove, Collierville, TN 38017 USA Tel 901-240-1353
E-mail: tmanso9@aol.com.

Play Odyssey Inc., *(978-0-9799441; 978-0-9825931)* 3 Alan Rd., Spring Valley, NY 10977 USA (SAN 854-8463) Tel 520-400-5188; Fax: 310-575-8873
E-mail: mgill@playoi.com
Web site: http://playoi.com; http://worksheetlab.com.

Playdate Kids Publishing, *(978-1-933721)* 1901 Main St., Santa Monica, CA 90405 USA (SAN 257-571X) Toll Free: 800-587-1501
E-mail: info@fmrockskids.com
Web site: http://www.theplaydatekids.com/.

Player Piano Mouse Productions (PPMP), *(978-0-9797794)* 883 S. Iowa St., Suite 105, Dodgeville, WI 53533 USA.

Player Pr., *(978-0-9623966)* 139-22 Caney Ln., Rosedale, NY 11422 USA Tel 718-528-3285 Do not confuse with Player Press LLC in New York, NY.

Players Pr., Inc., *(978-0-88734)* P.O. Box 1132, Studio City, CA 91614-0132 USA (SAN 239-0213) Tel 818-789-4980
E-mail: Playerspress@att.net
Dist(s): **Empire Publishing Service.**

PlayGround *Imprint of* **Forest Hill Publishing, LLC**

Playground Pr., *(978-0-9790033)* 1951 W. Rochelle Ave., Glendale, WI 53209 USA (SAN 852-1832) Tel 414-352-1590
E-mail: trishwilliams@trishwilliams.net
Web site: http://www.trishwilliams.net

Playhouse Publishing, *(978-1-57151; 978-1-878338)* 1566 Akron Peninsula Rd., Akron, OH 44313 USA Tel 330-762-6800; Fax: 330-762-2230; Toll Free: 800-762-6775
E-mail: info@playhousepublishing.com
Web site: http://www.nibble-me-books.com; http://www.playhousepublishing.com; http://www.littlelucyandfriends.com.

Playing Pig Pr., *(978-0-9788324)* 922 S. 87th Ave., Omaha, NE 68114 USA (SAN 851-7452) Tel 402-399-0516
E-mail: bettyhan@cox.net
Web site: http://FrecklesandMaya.com.

PlayInTime Productions, Inc., *(978-1-932895; 978-1-59860)* 19525 Valdez Dr., Tarzana, CA 91356-4946 USA Toll Free: 800-310-0087
E-mail: playintime@aol.com
Web site: http://www.playintime.com.

Playmore, Incorporated, Publishers *See* **Waldman Publishing Corp.**

Playor, Editorial, S.A. (ESP) *(978-84-359) Dist. by* **Continental Bk.**

Playwrights Canada Pr. (CAN) *(978-0-88754; 978-0-919834; 978-1-55155) Dist. by* **Consort Bk Sales.**

Plaza & Janes Editories, S.A. (ESP) *(978-84-01) Dist. by* **Distribks Inc.**

Plaza Joven, S.A. (ESP) *(978-84-7655) Dist. by* **Lectorum Pubns.**

Pleasant Co. *Imprint of* **American Girl Publishing, Inc.**

Pleasant Company Publications *See* **American Girl Publishing, Inc.**

Pleasant Designs, 1204 E. 35th St., Savannah, GA 31404 USA Tel 912-238-1910
E-mail: azamat1@msn.com
Web site: http://www.pleasantart.org.

Pleasant Plains Pr., *(978-0-9790906)* 366 Kingsberry Dr, Suite 100, Annapolis, MD 21409 USA Tel 410-757-1318
E-mail: boaterbrenda@comcast.net
Web site: http://www.pleasantplainspress.com.

Pleasant St. Pr., *(978-0-9792035; 978-1-935025)* P.O. Box 520, Raynham Center, MA 02768 USA (SAN 852-7598) Tel 508-822-3075; Fax: 508-977-2498
E-mail: orders@pleasantstpress.com; info@pleasantstpress.com
Web site: http://www.pleasantstpress.com
Dist(s): **Independent Pubs. Group.**

Pleasure Boat Studio *See* **Pleasure Boat Studio: A Literary Pr.**

Pleasure Boat Studio: A Literary Pr., *(978-0-912887; 978-0-9651413; 978-1-929355)* 201 W. 89th St., New York, NY 10024 USA Tel 212-362-8563; Toll Free: 888-810-5308; 721 Mt. Pleasant Rd., Port Angeles, WA 98362 (SAN 299-0075)
E-mail: pleasboat@nyc.rr.com
Web site: http://www.pleasureboatstudio.com
Dist(s): **Brodart Co.**
Partners/West Book Distributors
SPD-Small Pr. Distribution
Smashwords.

Pleiness Publishing, *(978-0-9742472)* 45937 Duke Dr., Chesterfield Township, MI 48051 USA
E-mail: cpbusy@comcast.net.

PLEO, *(978-0-9660617)* 302 Park Tree Terr Bldg. 1311, Orlando, FL 32825-3474 USA Tel 407-277-3776; 321-297-5531.

pleo leonard productions *See* **PLEO**

Plexus Publishing, Ltd. (GBR) *(978-0-85965) Dist. by* **PerseuPGW.**

Plicata Pr. LLC, *(978-0-9828205; 978-0-9848400; 978-0-9903102)* P.O. Box 32, Gig Harbor, WA 98335 USA Tel 253-851-2444
E-mail: janwalker@centurytel.net; info@plicatapress.com
Web site: http://www.plicatapress.com.

PLMII LLC *See* **McCall, Philip Lee II**

†Plough Publishing Hse., *(978-0-87486)* 151 Bowne Dr., Walden, NY 12586 USA (SAN 202-0092) Tel 845-572-3455; Fax: 845-572-3472; Toll Free: 800-521-8011
E-mail: info@plough.com
Web site: http://www.plough.com
Dist(s): **Ingram Pub. Services**
MyiLibrary
Spring Arbor Distributors, Inc.; *CIP.*

Plowshare Media, *(978-0-9821145; 978-0-9860428)* P.O. Box 278, La Jolla, CA 92038 USA (SAN 857-2933) Tel 858-454-5446
E-mail: tt@plowsharemedia.com
Web site: http://www.plowsharemedia.com.

Pluegl Bks., *(978-0-9760868)* Orders Addr.: P.O. Box 16622, Chapel Hill, NC 27516-6622 USA; Edit Addr.: 114 Waverly Forest Ln., Chapel Hill, NC 27516 USA.

Plum Blossom Bks. *Imprint of* **Parallax Pr.**

Plum Tree Pr., *(978-0-9653535; 978-1-892476)* Orders Addr.: 531 Silcott Rd., Clarkston, WA 99403 USA Tel 509-758-2820; 509-332-1520 (Pine Orchard Distributors)
E-mail: bookinfo@pineorchard.com; gpducky@aol.com
Web site: http://www.pineorchard.com/plumtree; http://www.chinchinian.com
Dist(s): **Partners/West Book Distributors**
Pine Orchard, Inc.

Pluma Productions, *(978-1-889848)* Div. of Southern Dominican Province, USA, Orders Addr.: P.O. Box 1138, Los Angeles, CA 90078-1138 USA Tel 213-463-6488; Fax: 213-466-6645; Edit Addr.: 1977 Carmen Ave., Los Angles, CA 90068 USA
E-mail: pluma@eatrhlink.net.

Plume *Imprint of* **Penguin Publishing Group**

Pluriverse Publishing, *(978-0-9846119)* P.O. Box 3305, Ponte Vedra Beach, FL 32004-3305 USA
E-mail: isbn-registration@epluriverse.com; information@ePluriverse.com
Web site: http://www.ePluriverse.com
Dist(s): **Smashwords.**

Plushy Feely Corp, *(978-0-9837668)* 11 San Rafael Ave., San Anselmo, CA 94960 USA Tel 415-454-4600 (Tel/Fax)
E-mail: kerri@kimochis.com
Web site: www.kimochis.com.

Pluteo Pleno, *(978-1-937847)* 5516 N Linder Ave., Chicago, IL 60630 USA Tel 815-459-2789
E-mail: pete@pluteopleno.com
Web site: http://www.pluteopleno.com.

Pluto Project, *(978-0-9662982)* 601 Van Ness, No. E3801, San Francisco, CA 94102-3200 USA Tel 415-647-5501; Fax: 415-840-0060; Toll Free: 888-227-5886
E-mail: walter@plutoproject.com
Web site: http://www.plutoproject.com
Dist(s): **AtlasBooks Distribution**
New Leaf Distributing Co., Inc.
Quality Bks., Inc.

PM, INK, *(978-0-9753852)* 522 aNDERSON aVE., Rockville, MD 20850 USA (SAN 256-0275) Tel 301-424-0638 (phone/fax)
E-mail: pm.ink@verizon.net
Web site: http://www.pmink.net.

PM Moon Pubs., Ltd., *(978-0-9817777; 978-0-615-15573-9; 978-0-615-15734-4)* Orders Addr.: P.O. Box 110813, Cleveland, OH 44111 USA Tel 216-671-8445; Edit Addr.: 3308 W. 111th St., Cleveland, OH 44111-3642 USA
Dist(s): **Lulu Enterprises Inc.**

PM Pr., *(978-1-60486; 978-1-62963)* P.O. Box 23912, Oakland, CA 94623 USA
Web site: http://www.pmpress.org
Dist(s): **AK Pr. Distribution**
Ebsco Publishing
Follett School Solutions
Independent Pubs. Group
ebrary, Inc.

P.M. Publishing, *(978-0-9798346)* Orders Addr.: P.O. Box 185, Lottsburg, VA 22511 USA (SAN 854-5200); Edit Addr.: 353 Walmsley Rd., Callao, VA 22435 USA
E-mail: pinkie_thecat@yahoo.com.

PMK Press *See* **Dancer's Publishing**

Pneuma Life Publishing, Inc., *(978-1-56229)* Orders Addr.: 12138 Central Ave. #251, Mitchellviille, MD 20721 USA (SAN 297-3057); *Imprints:* Christian Living Books, Inc. (Christian Livng)
E-mail: info@pneumalife.com; Info@christianlivingbooks.com; info@generationa.us
Web site: http://www.pneumalife.com; http://christianlivingbooks.com; http://generationa.us
Dist(s): **Anchor Distributors**
Lightning Source, Inc.
Smashwords
Spring Arbor Distributors, Inc.

POCEE Publishing, *(978-0-9824812)* 1260 Wesley Ave., Pasadena, CA 91104 USA Tel 626-794-8524.

Pocket Books, *(978-1-4165)* 1230 Avenue of the Americas, New York, NY 10020 USA
Dist(s): **Simon & Schuster, Inc.**

Pocket Books/Star Trek *Imprint of* **Pocket Bks./Star Trek**

Pocket Bks./Star Trek, 1230 Avenue of the Americas, New York, NY 10020 USA; *Imprints:* Pocket Books/Star Trek (PockBksStar)
Dist(s): **Simon & Schuster, Inc.**

Pocket Pr., Inc., *(978-1-884493; 978-1-61371)* P.O. Box 25124, Portland, OR 97298 USA Toll Free Fax: 877-643-3732; Toll Free: 888-237-2110
E-mail: sales@pocketpressinc.com
Web site: http://www.pocketpressinc.com.

Pocket Pubn., A, *(978-0-9721333)* 6701 Democracy Blvd., Suite 300, Bethesda, MD 20817 USA Tel 301-468-4905 Do not confuse with Pocket Publications in York, PA
E-mail: david_new@msn.com
Web site: http://www.home.talkcity.com/LibertySt/davidwnew.

PockitBook Publishing, Inc., *(978-0-9761716)* P.O. Box 6753, Athens, GA 30604-4120 USA Tel 706-354-8380
E-mail: pockitbook@bellsouth.net
Web site: http://www.pockitbook.com.

Pocol Pr., *(978-1-929763)* Orders Addr.: 6023 Pocol Dr., Clifton, VA 20124-1333 USA (SAN 253-6021) Tel 703-830-5862; Fax: 703-830-5862
E-mail: chrisandtom@erols.com
Web site: http://www.pocolpress.com.

Poet Tree Pubns., *(978-0-9658926)* P.O. Box 571444, Salt Lake City, UT 84157-1444 USA Tel 801-685-9398; Fax: 801-262-2324
Dist(s): **Tree Hse. Distribution.**

Poet's Passage Pr., The, *(978-0-9841252)* Calle Cruz 203, Old San Juan, PR 00901 USA (SAN 858-4826) Tel 787-567-9235
E-mail: ducart@yahoo.com.

Poets Wear Prada, *(978-0-9817678; 978-0-9841844; 978-0-615-60020-8; 978-0-615-60651-4; 978-0-615-65019-7; 978-0-615-76123-7; 978-0-615-81963-1; 978-0-615-83322-4; 978-0-615-84885-3; 978-0-615-86358-0; 978-0-615-87926-0; 978-0-615-88477-6; 978-0-615-91007-9; 978-0-615-97110-0; 978-0-615-98830-6; 978-0-692-22769-5; 978-0-692-28457-5; 978-0-692-30379-5; 978-0-692-45069-7) 533 Bloomfield St., 2nd Flr., Hoboken, NJ 07030 USA (SAN 856-5031) Tel 201-253-0561 office*
E-mail: poetswearpradanj@att.net; roxy533@yahoo.com
Web site: http://thesmokingbook.blogspot.com; http://poetsweaprada.blogspot.com; http://twitter.com/pradapoet; http://pwpbooks.blogspot.com; http://issuu.com/pradapoet/; http://www.facebook.com/pages/Poets-Wear-Prada/41483895438
Dist(s): **CreateSpace Independent Publishing Platform.**

Pohl, J. Assocs., *(978-0-939332)* 307 N. Shady Ave., Houston, PA 15342 USA (SAN 220-181X) Tel 724-746-1178
E-mail: judepohl@comcast.net.

Pohrte, Dorey Publishing, Inc., *(978-0-9722296)* 917 Maple Rd., Buffalo, NY 14221 USA Tel 716-631-1256
E-mail: kathysue1@adelphia.net.

Point of Grace Entertainment Group, *(978-0-9706112; 978-0-9727644)* 3575 N. Beltline Rd., Suite 345, Irving, TX 75062 USA Tel 972-331-2538; Fax: 972-331-2569; Toll Free: 877-447-2233
E-mail: pgedist@yahoo.com.

Point of Life, Inc., *(978-0-9668069; 978-0-9819367)* 3032 E. Commercial Blvd., Ft. Lauderdale, FL 33308 USA
E-mail: mikmikl@aol.com
Web site: http://www.pointoflife.com.

Point Publishing, *(978-0-9663560)* Orders Addr.: 960 Sage Crest Dr., Wenatchee, WA 98801 USA Tel 509-670-6250; *Imprints:* Orchard Press (Orchard Press) Do not confuse with Point Publishing, Madison, WI
E-mail: thacken@genext.net
Dist(s): **Lulu Enterprises Inc.**

Point To Point Publishing, *(978-0-9714147)* 5108 Brittany Dr., Old Hickory, TN 37138 USA Fax: 615-758-8495.

Poisoned Pen Pr., *(978-1-890208; 978-1-929345; 978-1-59058; 978-1-61595; 978-1-4642; 978-1-62886)* Orders Addr.: 6962 E. First Ave., Suite 103, Scottsdale, AZ 85251 USA (SAN 299-6898) Tel 480-945-3375; Fax: 480-949-1707; Toll Free: 800-421-3976
E-mail: info@poisonedpenpress.com; sales@poisonedpenpress.com
Web site: http://www.poisonedpenpress.com; www.thepoisonedpencil.com
Dist(s): **Ingram Pub. Services**
MyiLibrary.

Pokemon, USA, Inc., *(978-1-933743; 978-1-60438)* 777 108th Ave. NE, Suite 2000, Bellevue, WA 98004 USA
Web site: http://www.pokemon-tcg.com
Dist(s): **Diamond Bk. Distributors**
Simon & Schuster, Inc.

Pokeweed Pr. (CAN) *(978-1-894323) Dist. by* **IngramPubServ.**

Polaire Pubns., *(978-0-9708500; 978-0-9795218; 978-1-936315)* Div. of Polaire Entertainment Group, Inc., 422 Wolf Run Rd., Bartonville, TX 76226 USA (SAN 254-8291)
E-mail: chmeezepal@earthlink.net
Web site: http://www.animalcompanionsandtheirpeople.com
Dist(s): **DeVorss & Co.**

Polar Bear & Co., *(978-1-882190)* Orders Addr.: P.O. Box 311, Solon, ME 04979 USA (SAN 858-8902) Tel 207 643-2795; Edit Addr.: 8 Brook St., Solon, ME 04979 USA
E-mail: polarbear@polarbearandco.com
Web site: http://www.polarbearandco.com; http://www.polarbearandco.org
Dist(s): **AtlasBooks Distribution**
Magazines, Inc.

Polar Club Publishing, *(978-0-615-22038-3)* 635 Sandy Ridge Dr., Glen Burnie, MD 21061 USA
Dist(s): **Lulu Enterprises Inc.**

Polar Surf Enterprises *See* **NORKY AMERICA**

Polaris Bks., *(978-0-9741443)* 11111 W. 8th Ave., Unit A, Lakewood, CO 80215-5516 USA Tel 303-980-0890; Fax: 303-980-0753
E-mail: zubrin@aol.com
Web site: http://www.polarisbooks.net.

Polark, Kelly *See* **Big Smile Pr., LLC**

Polebridge Pr., *(978-0-944344; 978-1-59815)* Orders Addr.: P.O. Box 7268, Santa Rosa, CA 95407 USA Tel 707-523-1323; Fax: 707-523-1350; Toll Free: 877-523-3545
E-mail: accounts@polebridgepress.com
Web site: http://www.polebridgepress.com
Dist(s): **Spring Arbor Distributors, Inc.**

Polistampa (ITA) *(978-88-8304; 978-88-85977) Dist. by* **CasemateAcad.**

Political Status Education Coordinating Commission *See* **Dept. of Chamorro Affairs**

Poll, Michael Publishing, *(978-1-887560; 978-1-934935; 978-1-61342)* Orders Addr.: P.O. Box 24652, New Orleans, LA 70184 USA; *Imprints:* Cornerstone Book Publishers (Cstone Bk Pubs)
E-mail: mpoll@lostword.com
Web site: http://www.cornerstonepublishers.com.

Pollinator Pr., *(978-0-9774410)* P.O. Box 78351, San Francisco, CA 94107 USA (SAN 257-4985) Tel 650-995-6844
E-mail: info@pollinatorpress.com
Web site: http://pollinatorpress.com
Dist(s): **Perseus-PGW.**

PollyRhythm Productions, *(978-0-9701249)* Orders Addr.: P.O. Box 7707, New York, NY 10150 USA Tel 212 688 3900; Toll Free Fax: 800 701 7981
E-mail: prprd@attglobal.net
Web site: http://www.pollyrhythm.com.

Pollywog Bog Bks. (CAN) *(978-0-9810575) Dist. by* **IngramPubServ.**

Polychrome Publishing Corp., *(978-1-879965)* 4509 N. Francisco, Chicago, IL 60625-3808 USA Tel 773-478-4455; Fax: 773-478-0786
E-mail: polypub@earthlink.net
Web site: http://www.home.earthlink.net/~polypub.

Polyglot Pr., Inc., *(978-1-931927; 978-1-4115)* 111 Caenarvon Ln., Haverford, PA 19041-1049 USA Do not confuse with Polyglot Press in Fairfax, VA
E-mail: david@polyglotpress.com
Web site: http://www.polyglotpress.com.

Polygon Publishing, *(978-0-9764768)* 73 Sutton Pl. W., Palm Desert, CA 92211 USA (SAN 256-4521) Tel 760-346-0544; Fax: 760-406-9333
E-mail: polygnpublishing@aol.com
Web site: http://www.polygonpublishing.com/.

Polytope Pr., *(978-0-9670526)* Div. of Tarescent Synductions, Orders Addr.: P.O. Box 1349, Phoenix, AZ 85001 USA Tel 602-271-9922; Fax: 602-230-1991; Edit Addr.: 321 E. Portland, No. 6, Phoenix, AZ 85004 USA
E-mail: polytope@hotmail.com.

Pomegranate Communications, Inc., *(978-0-7649; 978-0-87654; 978-0-917556; 978-1-56640)* Orders Addr.: 19018 NE. Portal Way, Portland, OR 97230 USA (SAN 860-2077) Toll Free: 800-227-1428; Edit Addr.: 19018 NE. Portal Way, Portland, OR 97230 USA Tel 503-328-6500; Fax: 503-328-9330; Toll Free: 800-227-1428; *Imprints:* POMEGRANATE KIDS (POMEGRANATEKID)
E-mail: info@pomegranate.com
Web site: http://www.pomegranate.com.

POMEGRANATE KIDS *Imprint of* **Pomegranate Communications, Inc.**

Pomegranate Publishing, *(978-0-9767377)* P.O. Box 43, Carpinteria, CA 93014 USA Do not confuse with Pomegranate Publishing in Loma Linda, CA
Web site: http://www.pomegranatepublishing.com.

Pontrelli, Jeany, *(978-0-9778456)* 6156 Solstice Dr., Sparks, NV 89436 USA.

PONY *Imprint of* **Stabenfeldt Inc.**

Pony Rock Pr., *(978-0-9759598)* 23484 150th Ave. NE, Thief River Falls, MN 56701 USA.

Poodle Suit Publishing, *(978-0-9728429)* P.O. Box 9844, Phoenix, AZ 85068 USA (SAN 255-1608) Tel 602-943-6766 Toll Free: 800-547-8247
E-mail: lougold@cox.net
Web site: http://www.poodlesuit.com.

Poor Magazine, *(978-0-9742007)* 255 9th St., 3, San Francisco, CA 94103 USA Tel 415-863-6306; Fax: 415-865-1932
E-mail: alex@poormagazine.org
Web site: http://www.poormagazine.org.

PoorHse. Publishing LLC, *(978-0-9896335; 978-1-943468)* 905 Myrtle Ave., Big Bear City, CA 92314 USA (SAN 920-6027) Tel 909-272-0059
E-mail: info@poorhousepublishingllc.com
Web site: poorhousepublishingllc.com
Dist(s): **BookBaby**
Independent Pubs. Group
Small Pr. United.

Pop Pop Pr. *Imprint of* **Micro Publishing Media, Inc.**

Pop Sandbox, Inc. (CAN) *(978-0-9864884) Dist. by* **Diamond Book Dists.**

Pop the Cork Publishing, *(978-0-9741854)* 1629 McGilvra Blvd., E., Seattle, WA 98112 USA Tel 206-720-9779; Fax: 206-720-9771
E-mail: sallyv@isomedia.com
Dist(s): **AtlasBooks Distribution**
Hara Publishing Group.

Popol Vuh Press *See* **Talisman Pr.**

Poppy *Imprint of* **Little, Brown Bks. for Young Readers**

Poppy Blossom Pr., *(978-0-615-24059-6)* 8713 Glenbury Ct., S. Suite 102, Jacksonville, FL 32256 USA
E-mail: hello@poppyblossom.com.

Popular Bk. Co. (Canada) Ltd. (CAN) *(978-0-9698843; 978-1-896477; 978-1-894810; 978-1-897164; 978-1-897457) Dist. by* **IPG Chicago.**

Popular Kinetics Pr., *(978-0-9627752)* 6005 Yale Ave., Glen Echo, MD 20812 USA Tel 301-229-2213
E-mail: cbarton@mindspring.com
Web site: http://www.popularkinetics.com
Dist(s): **Independent Pubs. Group.**

Popular Truth, Inc., *(978-0-9631547)* P.O. Box 40656, Indianapolis, IN 76260 USA Toll Free: 888-342-8156
E-mail: anyike@netscape.net.

Port, Cynthia L., *(978-0-9912278)* 2513 E. Poplar Ct., Bloomington, IN 47401 USA Tel 812-322-7897
E-mail: cynthia.l.port@gmail.com.

Port Hole Pubns., *(978-0-9700274; 978-0-9768107; 978-0-9827627; 978-0-9882659; 978-0-9892608; 978-1-943119)* P.O. Box 205, Westlake, OR 97493-0205 USA
E-mail: porthole@digisys.net
Web site: http://www.ellentaylor.com.

Port Ludlow Bks., *(978-0-9729884)* 20 Keefe Ln., Port Ludlow, WA 98365 USA
E-mail: gldyerjr@waypt.com.

Port Town Publishing, *(978-0-9700544; 978-0-9716239; 978-0-9725990; 978-0-9740833; 978-1-59466)* 5832 Lambom Ave., Superior, WI 54880-6231 USA; *Imprints:* Little Ones (Little Ones); Growing Years (Growing Years)
E-mail: porttownpublish@aol.com
Web site: http://www.porttownpublishing.bigstep.com.

Port Washington Public Library, *(978-0-9615059)* 1 Library Dr., Port Washington, NY 11050 USA (SAN 694-163X) Tel 516-883-4400.

Portable Pr. *Imprint of* **Baker & Taylor Publishing Group**

Portable Press *See* **Akashic Bks.**

Portal Ctr. Pr., *(978-1-936902; 978-0-9834956)* P.O. Box 264, Gleneden Beach, OR 97388 USA; *Imprints:* SpiritBooks (SpiritBooks)
E-mail: editor@portalcenterpress.com; sales@portalcenterpress.com
Web site: portalcenterpress.com.

Portal Pr., *(978-1-933454)* 1327 Irving St., NE, Washington, DC 20017 USA Do not Confuse with Portal Press in Port Washington, NY, Glandale, AZ, Queens Village, NY
E-mail: editor@theportalpress.com
Web site: http://www.theportalpress.com
Dist(s): **SPD-Small Pr. Distribution.**

Porter, Rosanna *See* **Raisykinder Publishing**

Portfolio (Hardcover) *Imprint of* **Penguin Publishing Group**

Portfolio Press *See* **Portfolio Pr. Corp.**

Portfolio Pr. Corp., *(978-0-942620)* Orders Addr.: 130 Wineow St., Suite 3, Cumberland, MD 21502 USA Tel 301-724-2795; Fax: 301-724-2796; Toll Free: 877-737-1200; Edit Addr.: 1107 Broadway, 12th Flr., New York, NY 10010 USA (SAN 238-5554) Tel 212-989-8700; Fax: 212-691-3073
E-mail: portfolio@hereintown.net
Web site: http://www.portfoliopress.com.

Portfolio Trade *Imprint of* **Penguin Publishing Group**

Portico Bks., *(978-0-9664867)* Orders Addr.: P.O. Box 6094, Chesterfield, MO 63006 USA Tel 636-527-2822 (phone/fax); Toll Free: 888-641-5353 (phone/fax); Edit Addr.: 1316 Rusticview Dr., Ballwin, MO 63011 USA
E-mail: info@grammarandmore.com
Web site: http://www.grammarandmore.com.

Portland Press, Incorporated *See* **Chihuly Workshop, Inc.**

Portland State University, Ooligan Press *See* **Ooligan Pr.**

Portland Studios, Inc., *(978-0-9797183)* The Point At Pk. Pl. 112 Poinsett Hwy., Greenville, SC 29609 USA (SAN 854-1744) Tel 864-241-0810; Fax: 864-241-0811
E-mail: jpeterson@portlandstudios.com
Web site: http://www.beowulfthebook.com; http://www.portlandstudios.com
Dist(s): **Pioneer Enterprises.**

Portrait Health Publishing, *(978-0-9853555)* Orders Addr.: 175 E Hawthorn Pkwy. Suite 235, Vernon Hills, IL 60061 USA Tel 847-236-0943
E-mail: info@portraithealthpublishing.com
Web site: http://www.portraithealthpublishing.com.

Portunus Publishing Co., *(978-0-9641330; 978-1-886440)* 27875 Berwick Dr., Carmel, CA 93923 USA Tel 831-622-0604; Fax: 310-399-5644
E-mail: service@portunus.net
Dist(s): **Lectorum Pubns., Inc.**

Positive Action For Christ, *(978-1-929784; 978-0-9719491; 978-1-59557)* 502 W. Pippen St., Whitakers, NC 27891 USA Tel 252-437-7771; Fax: 252-437-3297; Toll Free: 800-688-3008; *Imprints*: ProTeens (ProTeens)
Web site: http://www.positiveaction.org.

Positive Imaging, LLC, *(978-0-615-16787-9; 978-0-615-18693-1; 978-0-9842480; 978-0-9856876; 978-1-944071)* 9016 Palace Pkwy., Austin, TX 78748 USA (SAN 858-8430) Tel 512-217-4803; 512-282-5717; Fax: 877-288-5496
E-mail: bill.benitez@yahoo.com; bill@positive-imaging.com
Web site: http://www.positive-imaging.com; http://www.handyman-business-guide.com/; http://www.woodworking-business.com; http://www.selfpublishingworkbook.com
Dist(s): **CreateSpace Independent Publishing Platform**
Lulu Enterprises Inc.
Smashwords.

Positive Productions, *(978-1-928726)* 934 E. 84th Pl., Suite A, Chicago, IL 60619 USA Tel 773-846-6131; Fax: 773-846-6555; Toll Free: 800-306-3064.

Positive Spin Pr., *(978-0-9773096)* P.O. Box 653, Warren, MI 02885-9998 USA
E-mail: info@positivespinpress.com; lisa@studiocvr.com
Web site: http://www.thehalloweenfairy.com
Dist(s): **Independent Pubs. Group.**

Positive Strokes, *(978-0-9673490)* Orders Addr.: P.O. Box 97271, Raleigh, NC 27624 USA
E-mail: pstrokes@aol.com; healheartsbooks@aol.com.

Positively for Kids, Inc., *(978-0-9634650; 978-0-9765722; 978-0-9778237; 978-0-9786838)* P.O. Box 3283, Kirkland, WA 98083-3283 USA Toll Free: 800-600-5437
E-mail: customerservice@positivelyforkids.com
Web site: http://www.positivelyforkids.com
Dist(s): **American West Bks.**
Brodart Co.
Mackin Bk. Co.

Possum Products, *(978-0-615-12548-0)* 712 Warren Dr., Annapolis, MD 21403 USA Fax: 410-510-1003; 410-263-4473 (call 410-263-1847 first)
E-mail: possumpalette@aol.com.

Post Mortem Pr., *(978-0-615-44412-3; 978-0-615-44413-0; 978-0-615-44414-7; 978-0-615-45262-3; 978-0-615-45562-4; 978-0-615-46517-3; 978-0-615-47440-3; 978-0-615-47960-6; 978-0-615-48012-1; 978-0-615-49431-9; 978-0-615-50034-8; 978-0-615-51257-0; 978-0-615-51652-3; 978-0-615-52194-7; 978-0-615-52504-4; 978-0-615-53662-0; 978-0-615-54009-2; 978-0-615-55202-6; 978-0-615-56286-5; 978-0-615-56340-4; 978-0-615-56657-3; 978-0-615-57441-7; 978-0-615-59185-8; 978-0-615-59369-2; 978-0-615-60381-0; 978-0-615-61676-6;) 601 W. Galbraith Rd. 0, Cincinnati, AE 45215 USA Tel 513-257-2834*
E-mail: info@3d-results.com
Dist(s): **CreateSpace Independent Publishing Platform**
Smashwords.

Post Oak Hill, *(978-0-9636122)* 235 Shady Hill Ln., Double Oak, TX 75067-8270 USA Tel 817-430-1182.

Potenial Psychotherapy Counseling & Remedial Service, *(978-0-9759889)* 1525 E. 53rd St., Suite 516, 11-2, Chicago, IL 60615 USA.

Potential Developing Ministries, Inc., *(978-0-9745554)* 455 Grason Hwy., Suite 111 Box 153, Lawrenceville, GA 30045 USA
E-mail: pdm@winning.com.

Potential Unlimited Publishing, *(978-0-9740003)* 1400 N. Elmhurst Rd. Unit 416, Mount Prospect , IL 60056 USA Tel 630-728-6046
E-mail: screenwriter1914@gmail.com.

Potoma, Alison Elise, *(978-1-940602)* 6234 Avalon Dr., Wilmington, MA 01887 USA Tel 845-461-1065
E-mail: alisonpotoma@gmail.com
Web site: www.alisonpotoma.com.

Potter Assocs., *(978-0-9758672)* 2305 Jacob Dr., Santa Clara, UT 84765 USA Tel 435-986-3886; Fax: 435-986-3887; *Imprints*: Hot Page Press (HotPP)
E-mail: stanpot@sisna.com.

Potter Craft *Imprint of* **Crown Publishing Group**

Potters Publishing LLC, *(978-0-9745810)* Orders Addr.: 2204 Blackjack Oak St., Ocoee, FL 34761 USA Tel 407-877-7444
Web site: http://www.potterspublishing.com.

PottyMD LLC, *(978-0-9762877)* 2216 White Ave., Knoxville, TN 37916 USA Tel 865-525-0000; Fax: 865-525-0262; Toll Free: 877-769-8963
E-mail: support@pottymd.com
Web site: http://www.pottymd.com
Dist(s): **SCB Distributors.**

Poudre Landmarks Foundation, *(978-0-9753849)* 108 N. Meldrum St., Fort Collins, CO 80521 USA Tel 970-221-4220; 970-221-0553
Web site: http://www.poudrelandmarks.com.

Pounce To Success International, Inc., *(978-0-9776074)* 608 1/2 W. Park St., Lamar, CO 81052 USA (SAN 257-7364) Tel 719-201-7470; Toll Free: 800-768-6238.

Pouring the Oil: Poetic Praise Pubns., *(978-0-9760734; 978-0-9841968)* Orders Addr.: P.O. Box 944, Brewster, NY 10509 USA; Edit Addr.: P.O. Box 253, Danbury, CT 06813-0253 USA
E-mail: pouringtheoil@yahoo.com; info@pouringtheoilpublications.com; spoken_word03@yahoo.com
Web site: http://www.pouringtheoilpublications.com.

Powell Hill Pr., *(978-0-9760648)* 8 Packett's Glen, Fairport, NY 14450 USA Tel 585-388-8622
E-mail: scoopwrite@aol.com
Web site: http://www.spiritwolf.info; http://www.powellhillpress.com
Dist(s): **North Country Bks., Inc.**

Power Play Media, *(978-0-9724003; 978-0-9741394; 978-1-934230)* P.O. Box 423, Brandywine, MD 20613 USA Tel 240-375-6908; Fax: 301-579-9913; *Imprints*: Nvision Publishing (NvisPub)
E-mail: tressa428@cs.com
Web site: http://www.nvisionpublishing.com/
Dist(s): **INscribe Digital.**

Power Pr., *(978-0-9748508; 978-0-9825568)* P.O. Box 622, Tyrone, GA 30290 USA Tel 770-486-0758; Fax: 770-486-6687 Do not confuse with Power Press in Torrance CA, Chico CA, Sonoma CA
E-mail: ratto@mindspring.com.

Power Pubns., Inc., *(978-0-9629858; 978-0-9724194; 978-0-615-40283-3; 978-0-615-41417-1)* 185 Randon Terr., Lake Mary, FL 32746 USA (SAN 254-6817) Tel 407-732-4322 (phone/fax) Do not confuse with Power Publications, Inc. in Phoenix, AZ, Mountain City, GA
E-mail: igilbert@cfl.rr.com.

Power Through Faith, *(978-0-9707320)* 1702 Capps St., Durham, NC 27707 USA Tel 919-596-7753.

Power Writings, *(978-0-9641640)* 9019 Wall St., 6F, North Bergen, NJ 07047 USA Fax: 201-869-9179
E-mail: fmelfa02@yahoo.com
Web site: http://www.pharmalanding.com.

Powerband, LLC, *(978-0-9746445)* 16199 Kennedy Rd., Los Gatos, CA 95032-9503 USA Fax: 408-402-0617; 16199 Kennedy Rd., Los Gatos, CA 95032-9503
E-mail: clelliott@mac.com
Web site: http://www.powerbandllc.com.

Power-Glide Foreign Language Courses, *(978-1-58204)* 1682 W. 820 N., Provo, UT 84601 USA Tel 801-373-3973; Fax: 801-343-3912; Toll Free: 800-596-0910
E-mail: deloyh@power-glide.com
Web site: http://www.power-glide.com.

powerHouse Bks. *Imprint of* **powerHouse Cultural Entertainment, Inc.**

powerHouse Cultural Entertainment, Inc., *(978-1-57687)* 37 Main St., Brooklyn, NY 11201 USA (SAN 850-5845); Mercedes Distribution Ctr. Bldg. 3 Brooklyn Navy Yard, Brooklyn, NY 11205 Tel 212-604-9074; Fax: 212-366-5247; *Imprints*: powerHouse Books (pwerHse Bks); PowerHouse Kids (PowerKids)
E-mail: info@powerhousebooks.com
Web site: http://www.powerhousebooks.com
Dist(s): **MyiLibrary**
Penguin Random Hse., LLC.
Random Hse., Inc.

PowerHouse Kids *Imprint of* **powerHouse Cultural Entertainment, Inc.**

PowerKids Pr. *Imprint of* **Rosen Publishing Group, Inc., The**

PowerMark Productions, *(978-0-9705669; 978-0-9713412; 978-0-9717876; 978-0-9729135; 978-0-9747026; 978-0-9749339; 978-0-9795833; 978-0-9827990; 978-1-935980)* Div. of Quest Ministries International, 380 E. Hwy. Cc Suite E104, Nixa, MO 65714 USA Tel 417-724-1222; Fax: 417-724-0119; Toll Free: 877-769-2669
E-mail: linda@qminternational.com
Web site: http://www.powermarkcomics.com
Dist(s): **New Day Christian Distributors Gifts, Inc.**

PowerMoves, *(978-0-9748298)* P.O. Box 92907, Washington, DC 20090 USA Tel 301-568-9111
Web site: http://www.powermoves.org.

Powerstart Pr. *Imprint of* **Rosen Publishing Group, Inc., The**

PowWow Publishing, *(978-0-9819789; 978-0-9859577)* P.O. Box 31855, Tucson, AZ 85751 USA
E-mail: brent@powwowinc.com
Web site: http://www.powwowpublishing.com; http://www.katemathis.net.

P.R.A. Enterprises Incorporated *See* **P.R.A. Publishing**

P.R.A. Publishing, *(978-0-9727703; 978-0-9821407; 978-0-9840142; 978-1-941416)* Orders Addr.: P.O. Box 211701, Martinez, GA 30917 USA Tel 706-855-6173
E-mail: lucindaclark@phoenixrisingarts.com; info@prapublishing.com; ljclark08@gmail.com
Web site: http://www.prapublishing.com; http://www.phoenixrisingarts.com; http://www.phoenixrisingart.wordpress.com
Dist(s): **AtlasBooks Distribution**
BookBaby.

Practical Christianity Foundation, *(978-0-9705996; 978-1-932587; 978-1-60098)* 2514 Aloha Pl., Holiday, FL 34691 USA (SAN 254-4377) Tel 727-934-0927; Fax: 727-934-4241; Toll Free: 888-278-3300
E-mail: cseitz@greenkeybooks.com
Web site: http://www.greenkeybooks.com
Dist(s): **Send The Light Distribution LLC.**

PRACTICAL SOLUTIONS Writing, Editing, Consulting, *(978-0-615-19350-2; 978-0-615-19351-9; 978-0-615-32636-8)* P.O. Box 1484, Wake Forest, NC 27588 USA Tel 919-604-4585; Fax: 901-273-1852
E-mail: Jfaulk28@nc.rr.com
Web site: http://stores.lulu.com/store.php?fAcctID=1906985; http://www.jefferyafaulkerson.com
Dist(s): **Lulu Enterprises Inc.**

Praeger Pubs. *Imprint of* **Greenwood Publishing Group, Inc.**

Pragmatic Bookshelf, The *Imprint of* **Pragmatic Programmers, LLC, The**

Pragmatic Programmers, LLC, The, *(978-0-9745140; 978-0-9766940; 978-0-9776166; 978-0-9787392; 978-1-934356; 978-1-937785; 978-1-941222; 978-1-68050)* 9650 Strickland Rd., Suite 103, No. 255, Raleigh, NC 27615 USA; 2831 El Dorado Pkwy., No. 103-381, Frisco, TX 75033 Toll Free Fax: 800-699-7764; *Imprints*: Pragmatic Bookshelf, The (Pragmatic Bkshelf)
E-mail: andy@pragprog.com
Web site: http://www.pragmaticprogrammer.com
Dist(s): **Ingram Pub. Services**
O'Reilly Media, Inc.

Prairie Arts, Inc., *(978-0-9725382)* 3100 Birch Bark Ln., Oklahoma City, OK 73120 USA Tel 405-755-5432; 405-728-1350; Fax: 405-728-9813
E-mail: dgordonart@aol.com.

Prairie Heart Publishing, *(978-0-9793668)* 8967 W. Driftwood Dr., Coeur d'Alene, ID 83814 USA Tel 208-777-8079 (phone/fax)
E-mail: aprairieheart@earthlink.net; sdianewood@earthlink.net
Web site: http://www.prairievirtuedolls.com.

Prairie Hills Publishing, *(978-0-9821084)* 310 N. Washington St., B5, Groton, SD 57445 USA
Web site: http://www.prairiehillspublishing.com.

Prairie Shore Creative, Inc., *(978-0-9740542)* 2500 S. Corbett, Chicago, IL 60608 USA
E-mail: PSCreative@AOL.com
Web site: http://www.Prairieshorecreative.com.

Prairie Winds Publishing, *(978-0-9778240)* 15154 W. 231st St., Spring Hill, KS 66083 USA Tel 913-592-5002
E-mail: cyndi@gertrudemccluck.com
Web site: http://www.gertrudemccluck.com.

Prairieland Pr., *(978-0-9759829; 978-1-944132)* P.O. Box 2404, Fremont, NE 68026-2404 USA Tel 402-721-0241
E-mail: nlsharpwriter@gmail.com
Web site: http://www.prairielandpress.com; http://writesharp.com.

Pranayama Institute, Inc., The, *(978-0-9724450)* Orders Addr.: P.O. Box 40731, Albuquerque, NM 87196 USA Tel 706-889-5035 (phone/fax); Fax: 505-212-0097
E-mail: ssaranam@pranayama.org; publicity@pranayama.org
Web site: http://www.pranayama.org; http://www.godwithoutreligion.com.

Prancing Pony, The, *(978-0-9763555)* Orders Addr.: 104802 W. Foisy Rd., Prosser, WA 99350 USA
Web site: http://www.herbleonhard.com.

Pratt Ctr. The, *(978-0-9772835)* Orders Addr.: Four Main St., Suite 210, Los Altos, CA 94022 USA Tel 650-949-2997; Fax: 650-949-2442
E-mail: prattcenter@covad.net.

Praxis Pr., Inc., *(978-0-9754305; 978-1-934278)* 1515 Skelton Rd.5-100, Gainesville, GA 30504 USA Tel 770-846-5978
Web site: http://www.praxispress.com.

Prayer Bk. Pr., Inc., *(978-0-87677)* Subs. of Media Judaica, Inc., Orders Addr.: 1363 Fairfield Ave., Bridgeport, CT 06605 USA (SAN 207-0022) Tel 203-384-2284; Edit Addr.: 304 E. 49th St., New York, NY 10017 USA (SAN 282-1788) Tel 212-319-6666.

PRAZZ Pubns., *(978-0-9776356)* Orders Addr.: P.O. Box 636, Upper Marlboro, MD 20773-0636 USA (SAN 257-8212); Edit Addr.: 8419 Thornberry Dr., West Upper Marlboro, MD 20772 USA
E-mail: ycsmallwood@yahoo.com.

Precept Ministries, *(978-1-888655; 978-1-934884; 978-1-62119)* Orders Addr.: P.O. Box 182218, Chattanooga, TN 37422 USA Tel 423-892-6814; Fax: 423-894-2449; Toll Free: 800-763-8280; Edit Addr.: 7324 Noah Reid Rd., Chattanooga, TN 37421 USA
E-mail: info@precept.org; jbundy@precept.org
Web site: http://www.precept.org.

Precious Little Bks., *(978-0-9787235)* 9353 SE. Yardarm Terr., Hobe Sound, FL 33455-3214 USA (SAN 851-3813) Tel 561-307-2367; Fax: 772-545-4944
E-mail: clarke@preciouslittlebooks.com
Web site: http://www.preciouslittlebooks.com.

Precious Moments, Inc., *(978-0-9817159; 978-0-9819885; 978-0-9825809)* 2850 W. Golf Rd., Suite 250, Rolling Meadows, IL 60008 USA (SAN 856-3403)
Web site: http://www.preciousmoments.com
Dist(s): **Midpoint Trade Bks., Inc.**
Perseus-PGW.

Precioustymes Entertainment, LLC, *(978-0-9729325; 978-0-9776507)* 229 Governors Pl., No. 138, Bear, DE 19701 USA Tel 302-294-6980 (office line); Fax: 302-294-6980
E-mail: PrecioustymesEnt@aol.com
Web site: http://www.precioustymes.com; http://www.platinumteen.org
Dist(s): **A & B Distributors & Pubs. Group**
Afrikan World Bk. Distributor.

Precision Cad/Cam Systems, Inc., *(978-0-9707464)* 9564 Deereco Rd., Luthvle Timon, MD 21093-2119 USA
E-mail: info@cadcam4u.com
Web site: http://www.cadcam4u.com.

Preferred Enterprises, *(978-1-885143)* P.O. Box 848, Lakewood, NJ 08701-0848 USA.

Preferred Marketing *See* **American Historical Pr.**

PremaNations Publishing, *(978-1-892176)* Div. of PremaNations, Inc., P.O. Box 321447, Cocoa Beach, FL 32932-1447 USA (SAN 299-5808) Tel 310-417-9195; Fax: 407-784-5372; Toll Free Fax: 877-372-4660; Toll Free: 877-372-4664
E-mail: Paradigm@PremaNations.com
Web site: http://www.PremaNations.com
Dist(s): **New Leaf Distributing Co., Inc.**
Quality Bks., Inc.

Prematurely Yours, *(978-0-9614786)* Orders Addr.: P.O. Box 9141, Chesapeake, VA 23321 USA (SAN 692-9907) Tel 757-483-9879; Fax: 757-484-8267; Toll Free: 800-767-0023
E-mail: kbryant@prematurelyyours.com
Web site: http://www.prematurelyyours.com.

Premier Schl. Agendas, *(978-1-884272; 978-1-59923; 978-1-63080)* 400 Sequoia Dr., Ste. 200, Bellingham, WA 98226 USA Tel 360-734-1153; Fax: 360-734-3014; Toll Free Fax: 800-880-3287; Toll Free: 800-447-2034
E-mail: ruth.richardson@schoolspecialty.com; nancy.fosberg@schoolspecialty.com; arielle.bons@schoolspecialty.com; whitney.ochs@schoolspecialty.com
Web site: http://www.premier.us.

Premiere *Imprint of* **FastPrncil, Inc.**

Premio Publishing & Gozo Bks., LLC, *(978-0-9776065; 978-0-615-43691-3; 978-0-615-44230-3; 978-0-615-44305-8; 978-0-615-49278-0; 978-0-9853988; 978-0-615-68823-7; 978-0-615-68824-4; 978-0-615-69229-6; 978-0-615-85615-5; 978-0-615-85616-2; 978-0-615-85617-9; 978-0-615-87686-3; 978-0-692-22096-2; 978-0-692-22097-9; 978-0-692-22098-6; 978-0-692-22099-3; 978-0-692-40797-4; 978-0-692-42677-7; 978-0-692-43639-4) Div. of Premio Publishing, 648 W. Wasatch St., Midvale, UT 84047 USA Tel 801-953-3793*
E-mail: karl@premiobooks.com; karlbx@gmail.com
Web site: http://gozobooks.com; http://premiobooks.com; http://premiopublishing.com; http://twitter.com/karlbeckstrand
Dist(s): **CreateSpace Independent Publishing Platform**
Smashwords.

Premium Pr. America, *(978-0-9637733; 978-1-887654; 978-1-933725)* Div. of Schnitzer Communications, Inc., Orders Addr.: P.O. Box 159015, Nashville, TN 37215-9015 USA Tel 615-256-8484; Fax: 615-256-8524; Toll Free: 800-891-7323; Edit Addr.: 2606 Eugenia Ave., Suite C, Nashville, TN 37211-2177 USA
E-mail: bbsgcs@aol.com
Web site: http://www.premiumpress.com
Dist(s): **Send The Light Distribution LLC.**

Prentice Hall *Imprint of* **Prentice Hall PTR**

Prentice Hall, ESL Dept., *(978-0-13; 978-0-88345)* 240 Frisch Ct., Paramus, NJ 07652-5240 USA Tel 201-236-7000; Fax: 201-592-0904; Toll Free: 800-922-0579
Dist(s): **Continental Bk. Co., Inc.**
Pearson Education.

Prentice Hall Pr. *Imprint of* **Penguin Publishing Group**

Prentice Hall Pr., *(978-0-13; 978-0-7352)* Orders Addr.: 200 Old Tappan Rd., Old Tappan, NJ 07675 USA; Edit Addr.: 240 Frisch Ct., Paramus, NJ 07652 USA Tel 201-909-6200; Fax: 201-909-6360; Toll Free: 800-288-4745; 800-223-2336 (customer service); a/o Prentice Hall Direct, P.O. Box 11075, Des Moines, IA 50336 Tel 515-284-6719; Toll Free: 800-947-7700
E-mail: pearsoned@eds.com
Web site: http://www.phdirect.com
Dist(s): **Pearson Education**
Penguin Random Hse., LLC.
Penguin Publishing Group
ebrary, Inc.

†Prentice Hall PTR, *(978-0-13; 978-0-201; 978-0-672)* Div. of Pearson Technology Group, Orders Addr.: 200 Old Tappan Rd., Old Tappan, NJ 07675 USA Fax: 416-447-2819 (orders - Canada); Toll Free Fax: 800-835-5327 (individual single copy orders - US); 800-445-6991 (government orders); Toll Free: 800-282-0693 (individual single copy orders - US); 800-922-0579 (government orders); 800-567-3800 (orders - Canada); Edit Addr.: 405 Murray Hill Pkwy., E Rutherford, NJ 07073-2136 USA; *Imprints*: Prentice Hall (Prentice Hall)
Web site: http://www.phptr.com/
Dist(s): **Cambridge Bk. Co.**
Continental Bk. Co., Inc.
Ebsco Publishing
IFSTA
MyiLibrary
Pearson Education
Pearson Technology Group
Rittenhouse Bk. Distributors
Trans-Atlantic Pubns., Inc.; *CIP.*

Prentice Hall (Schl. Div.), *(978-0-13)* Div. of Pearson Education, Orders Addr.: P.O. Box 2500, Lebanon, IN 46052-3009 USA Toll Free: 800-848-9500; P.O. Box 2649, Columbus, OH 43216-2649; Edit Addr.: 160 Gould St. (Northeast Region), Needham Heights, MA 02194-2310 USA Tel 617-455-1300; 8445 Freeport Pkwy., Suite 400 (South Central Region), Irving, TX 75063 Tel 214-915-4255
Web site: http://www.phschool.com/
Dist(s): **Pearson Education.**

Prentice-Hall *See* **Prentice Hall PTR**

Prepare For Rain Pr., *(978-0-9889537)* 4366 S Wagon Train Ln., Boise, ID 83716 USA Tel 208-514-8607
E-mail: Joel@PrepareForRain.com.

Presbeau Publishing, Inc., (*978-0-9831380*) 6533 S. Ouray St., Aurora, CO 80016 USA Tel 303-690-1177
E-mail: carmens222@comcast.net
Web site: www.presbeaupublishing.com.

Presbyterian & Reformed Publishing Company *See* **P & R Publishing**

Presbyterian Publishing Corporation *See* **Curriculum Publishing, Presbyterian Church (U. S. A.)**

Preschool Prep Co., (*978-0-9767008; 978-0-9770215; 978-0-9801717; 978-0-9820331; 978-1-935610*) P.O. Box 1159, Danville, CA 94526 USA Tel 925-743-1400; Fax: 925-886-4843; Toll Free: 866-451-5600
Web site: http://www.preschoolprepco.com
Dist(s): **Follett School Solutions.**

Presence Publishing, (*978-0-9729676*) Orders Addr.: 25909 Plantation Ave., Denham Springs, LA 70726 USA
E-mail: presencepub@bellsouth.net; sharonelliott@bellsouth.net.

Preserving Memories, (*978-0-9742576; 978-0-9817835*) 5809 Stonebridge Ln., Waxhaw, NC 28173 USA
Web site: http://www.preservememories.net.

Presidential Publishing, (*978-0-9729095*) Orders Addr.: P.O. Box 221834, Sacramento, CA 95822 USA (SAN 255-1977) Tel 916-447-2460
E-mail: contactus@presidentialcookies.com; contactus@presidentialpublishing.com
Web site: http://www.presidentialcookies.com; http://www.presidentialpublishing.com.

Press Americana, (*978-0-9789041; 978-0-9829558; 978-0-9967779*) 7095 Hollywood Blvd, 1240, Hollywood, CA 90028-8903 USA (SAN 851-9013) Tel 818-370-1143; Fax: 818-760-1828
E-mail: editor@americanpopularculture.com
Web site: http://www.americanpopularculture.com.

Pr. & Brand Productions, (*978-0-615-25883-6*) 2515 34th St., No. 6, New York, NY 11103 USA Tel 718-267-8771
Dist(s): **Lulu Enterprises Inc.**

Press North America, (*978-0-938271*) P.O. Box 105, Gustavus, AK 99826 USA (SAN 659-8285) Tel 907-697-2303 (phone/fax, press start); Fax: 907-697-2760.

Press of the Camp Pope Bookshop *See* **Camp Pope Publishing**

Press Release Group Corp., (*978-0-9764633*) Orders Addr.: P.O. Box 651, New York, NY 10276 USA
E-mail: info@prgroup.info
Web site: http://www.prgroup.info.

Pr. Room Editions LLC, (*978-1-62143; 978-1-63235; 978-1-63494*) 1686 Cliff Rd. E., Burnsville, MN 55337-1300 USA Tel 952-746-7867; Fax: 952-746-4287
E-mail: btemple@reditorial.com
Dist(s): **Amicus Educational.**

Presses Pocket (FRA) (*978-2-266*) *Dist. by* **Distribks Inc.**

Prestel Publishing, Orders Addr.: c/o VNU, 575 Prospect St., Lakewood, NJ 08701 USA Tel 732-363-5679; Fax: 732-363-0338; Toll Free Fax: 877-227-6564; Toll Free: 888-463-6110; Edit Addr.: 900 Broadway, Suite 603, New York, NY 10003 USA Tel 212-995-2720; Fax: 212-995-2733
E-mail: sales@prestel-usa.com
Web site: http://www.prestel.com; http://www.die-gestalten.de; http://www.scalo.com
Dist(s): **VNU.**

Prestel Verlag GmbH & Co KG. (DEU) (*978-3-7913*) *Dist. by* **Prestel Pub NY.**

Preston-Speed Pubns., (*978-1-887159; 978-1-931587*) 51 Ridge Rd., Mill Hall, PA 17751 USA Tel 570-726-7844; Fax: 570-726-3547
E-mail: doug@prestonspeed.com
Web site: http://www.prestonspeed.com.

Prestwick Hse., Inc., (*978-1-58049; 978-1-60389; 978-1-60843; 978-1-935464; 978-1-935465; 978-1-935466; 978-1-935467; 978-1-935468; 978-0-9823095; 978-0-9823096; 978-0-9823097; 978-0-692-00136-3; 978-0-692-00137-0; 978-1-62019*) Orders Addr.: P.O. Box 658, Clayton, DE 19938 USA Fax: 302-734-0549; Toll Free: 800-932-4593; Edit Addr.: 58 Artisan Dr., Smyrna, DE 19977 USA (SAN 154-5523) Tel 800-983-4593; Fax: 302-659-2792
E-mail: info@prestwickhouse.com; keith@prestwickhouse.com
Web site: http://www.prestwickhouse.com.

Pretty Paper Pr., (*978-0-9746315; 978-0-9858814*) 14 Everett St., East Orange, NJ 07017 USA
E-mail: moody4u@verizon.net
Web site: http://www.moodyholiday.com.

Pretty Please Pr., Inc., (*978-0-9759378*) 105 E. 29th St., 6th Flr., New York, NY 10016 USA.

Prevention Through Puppetry, Inc., (*978-0-9768827*) 468 Boyle Rd., Port Jefferson Station, NY 11776 USA Tel 631-476-3099; Fax: 631-476-7680
Web site: http://www.sunshinepreventionctr.org.

Previn, Lovely Pubns., (*978-0-9847107*) 1810 S. El Camino Real Suite B101, Encinitas, CA 92024 USA Tel 760-632-8288 (phone/fax)
E-mail: lovelyprevinmusic@gmail.com
Web site: www.theearthwormbook.com.

PRF Pubs., (*978-0-578-03405-8; 978-0-578-04719-5*) 221 Hopewell Amwell Rd., Hopewell, NJ 08525 USA
E-mail: s.schwinn1@verizon.net
Web site: http://www.henrythelamb.com
Dist(s): **AtlasBooks Distribution.**

Price, Diane Joan, (*978-0-9789637*) 10508 Courtney Cove, Las Vegas, NV 89144 USA
E-mail: dpcontact@netzero.net.

Price, Mathew Ltd., (*978-1-935021; 978-0-9844366*) 12300 Ford Rd. Ste. 455, Dallas, TX 75234-8136 USA (SAN 856-0471)
Web site: http://www.mathewprice.com
Dist(s): **Consortium Bk. Sales & Distribution.**

Price Stern Sloan *Imprint of* **Penguin Publishing Group**

Priceless Ink Publishing Co., Inc., (*978-0-9778937*) Orders Addr.: P.O. Box 218538, Nashville, TN 37221 USA
E-mail: apricelessgiftcom@yahoo.com; audreylprice@yahoo.com
Web site: http://apricelessgift.com.

Prickly Pear Pr., (*978-0-9764323*) P.O. Box 69, Sahuarita, AZ 85629-0069 USA Tel 520-625-1587; Fax: 520-625-3655 Do not confuse with Pricly Pear Press in San Francisco CA, Cedar Park TX, Scottsdale AZ, Tucson AZ.
E-mail: pricklypearpress@msn.com
Web site: http://pricklypearpress.info.

Prickly Pr., (*978-1-893463*) 11695 Rosehill Rd, Overland Park, KS 66210 USA Tel 913-648-2034 (phone/fax)
E-mail: ikesmith@kc.rr.com
Web site: http://www.readwest.com/flouncesmith.thm.

Priddy Bks. *Imprint of* **St. Martin's Pr.**

Priest, Gerald L., (*978-0-9743871*) 4801 Allen Rd., Allen Park, MI 48101 USA Toll Free: 800-866-0111.

Prima Games *Imprint of* **Random Hse. Information Group**

Primary Concepts/Concepts to Go, (*978-1-893791; 978-1-60184*) 1338 Seventh St., Berkeley, CA 94710 USA Toll Free: 800-660-8646
Web site: www.primaryconcepts.com.

Primary Sources, (*978-1-881849*) 16442 SE 42nd Pl., Issaquah, WA 98027 USA Tel 425-865-0409 (phone/fax)
E-mail: info@primary-sources.com
Web site: http://www.primary-sources.com/
Dist(s): **Smashwords.**

Prime, (*978-0-8095; 978-0-9668968; 978-1-930997; 978-1-894815*) Div. of Wildside Press, P.O. Box 301, Holicong, PA 18928 USA
E-mail: sean@wildsidepress.com
Web site: http://www.primebooks.net
Dist(s): **Diamond Comic Distributors, Inc.**
Diamond Bk. Distributors.

Primedia E-launch LLC, (*978-1-62209; 978-1-62890; 978-0-615-88236-9; 978-0-615-88337-3; 978-0-615-88403-5; 978-1-63173; 978-1-63315; 978-1-63443; 978-1-942526; 978-1-942573; 978-1-942574; 978-1-942748; 978-1-942749; 978-0-692-36411-6; 978-1-942844; 978-1-942845; 978-1-942846; 978-1-943090; 978-1-943091; 978-1-943092; 978-1-943093; 978-1-943274; 978-1-943275; 978-1-943276; 978-1-943277; 978-1-943278; 978-1-943279; 978-1-943280; 978-1-943281; 978-0-692-42561-9; 978-1-943842; 978-1-943843; 978-1-943844; 978-1-943845) 3900 Swiss Ave. No. 205, Dallas, TX 75204 USA (SAN 935-4808) Tel 214-870-5515*
E-mail: josh@primediaelaunch.com
Web site: http://www.primediaelaunch.com
Dist(s): **BookBaby**
Lulu Enterprises Inc.
eBookit.com.

Primordia, (*978-0-9759007*) P.O. Box 2455, Santa Barbara, CA 93120 USA (SAN 256-1018).

Primrose Pr., (*978-0-9673171*) Orders Addr.: P.O. Box 2577, Prescott, AZ 86302 USA (SAN 299-9331) Tel 520-445-4567; Fax: 520-445-0517; Edit Addr.: 815 Bertrand Ave., Prescott, AZ 86303 USA Do not confuse with companies with the same name in Antelope, CA, Alhambra, CA, San Francisco, CA.

Primrose Presses *See* **Scarlet Primrose Pr.**

Princess Joy, (*978-0-615-74323-3*) 1325 Main St. Apt 203, Buffalo, NY 14209 USA Tel 716-464-8913; Toll Free: 1-800-583-8605
Web site: www.expressedentertainment.com
Dist(s): **CreateSpace Independent Publishing Platform.**

Princess Khrystle & Prince Michael, Inc., (*978-0-9772565*) Orders Addr.: P.O. Box 960176, Miami, FL 33296 USA; Edit Addr.: 14631 SW 104 Ct., Miami, FL 33176 USA
E-mail: khrystle19@aol.com
Web site: http://www.princesskhrystle.org
Dist(s): **AtlasBooks Distribution.**

Princeton Architectural Pr., (*978-0-910413; 978-0-9636372; 978-1-56898; 978-1-878271; 978-1-885232; 978-1-61689*) 37 E. Seventh St., New York, NY 10003 USA (SAN 260-1176) Tel 212-995-9720; Fax: 212-995-9454; Toll Free: 800-722-6657
E-mail: sales@papress.com
Web site: http://www.papress.com
Dist(s): **Chronicle Bks. LLC**
Hachette Bk. Group
Metapress
ebrary, Inc.

Princeton Bk. Co. Pubs., (*978-0-87127; 978-0-916622*) Orders Addr.: P.O. Box 831, Hightstown, NJ 08520-0831 USA (SAN 630-1568) Tel 609-426-0602; Fax: 609-426-1344; Toll Free: 800-220-7149; 614 Rte. 130, Hightstown, NJ 08520 (SAN 244-8076); *Imprints:* Dance Horizons (Dance Horizons); Elysian Editions (Elysian Editions)
E-mail: pbc@dancehorizons.com; elysian@aosi.com
Web site: http://www.dancehorizons.com
Dist(s): **Ebsco Publishing**
Follett School Solutions
Independent Pubs. Group
MyiLibrary.

Princeton Health Pr., (*978-0-933665; 978-0-9835782; 978-1-940175*) 711 Westchester Ave., West Harrison, NY 10604-3504 USA (SAN 692-5391) Toll Free: 800-293-4969
E-mail: ksilloway@nhpamail.com
Web site: http://www.lifeskillstraining.com.

Princeton Review *Imprint of* **Random Hse. Information Group**

†Princeton Univ. Pr., (*978-0-691*) Orders Addr.: California-Princeton Fulfillment Services, 1445 Lower Ferry Rd., Ewing, NJ 08618 USA Tel 800-777-4726; Fax: 800-999-1958; Edit Addr.: 41 William St., Princeton, NJ 08540 USA (SAN 202-0254) Tel 609-258-4900; Fax: 609-258-6305; 3 Market Place, Woodstock, OX20 1SY Tel (0) 1993 814501; Fax: (0) 1993 814504
E-mail: webmaster@pupress.princeton.edu
Web site: http://www.pup.princeton.edu
Dist(s): **David Brown Book Company, The**
California Princeton Fulfillment Services
Ebsco Publishing
ISD
MyiLibrary
Perseus Distribution
Perseus Academic
ebrary, Inc.; *CIP.*

Prindle House *See* **Prindle Hse. Publishing Co.**

Prindle House Publishing Co. *Imprint of* **Prindle Hse. Publishing Co.**

Prindle Hse. Publishing Co., (*978-0-9759527; 978-0-9819372; 978-0-9826846; 978-0-9835320; 978-0-9889080*) Orders Addr.: P.O. Box 18761, Jacksonville, FL 32229 USA Tel 904-710-6529; Fax: 904-751-9338; Toll Free: 866-877-4635; Edit Addr.: 1019 Ashton Cove Terr., Jacksonville, FL 32218 USA; *Imprints:* Prindle House Publishing Company (PrinHsePubCo)
E-mail: tp@prindlehouse.com; twylaprindle@yahoo.com
Web site: http://www.prindlehouse.com; http://www.twylaprindle.com; www.childanthology.com.

Prinit Pr., (*978-0-932970*) 211 NW Seventh St., Richmond, IN 47374-4051 USA (SAN 212-680X) Tel 765-966-7130; Fax: 765-966-7131; Toll Free: 800-478-4885
Web site: http://www.printpress.com.

Printing Systems, (*978-0-9767595; 978-1-59916*) Orders Addr.: 2249 14th St SW, Akron, OH 44314-2007 USA Toll Free: 800-231-0521
E-mail: info@48HrBooks.com
Web site: http://www.48HrBooks.com.

Printmedia Bks., (*978-0-9778591; 978-0-9788447; 978-0-9790999; 978-1-934379*) Div. of The Printmedia Cos. of Southern California, 3355 E. Miraloma Ave., Bldg. 165, Anaheim, CA 92806 USA Tel 714-729-0789; Fax: 714-729-0790
E-mail: peter@printmediabooks.com; books@printmediabooks.com
Web site: http://www.printmediabooks.com.

printONDEMANDpublisher.com, (*978-0-9765725*) 325 W. Belden Ave., Chicago, IL 60614-3817 USA Tel 773-988-8619; Fax: 773-935-9967
E-mail: george@georgevalko.com
Web site: http://www.printondemandpublisher.com.

Prints By Mail, (*978-0-9740173*) 33 Jose I Garica Rd., Belen, NM 87002 USA; 33 Jose I Garcia Rd., Belen, NM 87002
E-mail: books@printsbymail.com
Web site: http://www.printsbymail.com.

Prioleau, Jivonne, (*978-0-615-25200-1; 978-0-578-00427-3; 978-0-578-08744-3*) 5701 Rafferty Ave., McClellan, CA 95652 USA
Dist(s): **Lulu Enterprises Inc.**

Prion (GBR) (*978-1-85375*) *Dist. by* **IPG Chicago.**

Prioritybooks Pubns., (*978-0-9753634; 978-0-9792823; 978-0-9816483; 978-0-9819913; 978-0-9834860; 978-0-9896502*) P.O. Box 2535, Florissant, MO 63033 USA (SAN 853-0130) Tel 314-741-6789 (phone/fax); 314-306-2972; Fax: 314-475-5613
E-mail: rosbeav03@yahoo.com
Web site: http://www.prioritybooks.com
Dist(s): **Brodart Co.**
Follet Higher Education Grp
Lightning Source, Inc.
Lushena Bks.

Prism Comics, (*978-0-9759164*) 2621 E. Madison, Seattle, WA 98122-4711 USA Fax: 206-770-6137
Web site: http://www.prismcomics.org.

Prism Hse. Media, (*978-0-9748088*) Orders Addr.: 126 Quail Hollow Dr., San Jose, CA 95128 USA Tel 407-461-4999
E-mail: paulpelley@gmail.com
Dist(s): **Review & Herald Publishing Assn.**

Pristine Pubs., Inc., (*978-0-9716633*) 18 Buckthorn Cove, Jackson, TN 38305 USA (SAN 254-2420) Tel 731-660-3333 Toll Free: 866-565-3311
E-mail: Kathy@pristinepublishers.com
Web site: http://www.readysetgofitness.com; http://www.questforasdin.com; http://www.pristinepublishers.com; http://www.gabrielsmagicornament.com.

†Pritchett & Hull Assocs., Inc., (*978-0-939838; 978-1-933638; 978-1-943234*) 3440 Oakcliff Rd., NE, Suite 110, Atlanta, GA 30340 USA (SAN 216-9258) Tel 770-451-0602; Fax: 770-454-7130; Toll Free: 800-241-4925
E-mail: phsales@p-h.com
Web site: http://www.p-h.com/; *CIP.*

Privacy Trust Group, The, (*978-0-9777457*) Div. of JR The Trust Group Inc., Orders Addr.: 240 S. Elizabeth #h1-116, ELizabeth, CO 80107 USA (SAN 850-122X) Tel 303-648-3496; Fax: 303-648-3205; Toll Free: 877-648-0119; 240 S. Elizabeth #h1-116, Elizabeth, CO 80107 Tel 303-648-3496; Fax: 303-648-3205
Web site: http://www.privacytrustgroup.com.

Private Label Publishing *Imprint of* **Mother's Hse. Publishing**

Privateer Pr., Inc., (*978-0-9706970; 978-1-933362; 978-1-939480; 978-1-943693*) 13434 NE 16th St. Ste. 120, Bellevue, WA 98005-2335 USA Do not confuse with Privateer Pr. in New Orleans, LA
E-mail: mw@privateerpress.com
Web site: http://www.privateerpress.com
Dist(s): **Diamond Bk. Distributors**
PSI (Publisher Services, Inc.).

Privatgaeste Verlag, (*978-0-9712545*) c/o Ute Kruedewagen, 3168 Harrison St., No. 106, Oakland, CA 94611 USA
Web site: http://www.privatgaeste.com.

Privileged Communications, LLC, (*978-0-9802302*) 844 25th St., Santa Monica, CA 90403 USA Fax: 310-828-9590
E-mail: lester310@earthlink.net
Web site: http://www.theboywhowouldntsitstill.com.

Priya's Rhymes, (*978-0-615-43048-5*) 62 Churchill Ave., Palo Alto, CA 94306 USA Tel 650-322-8261
Dist(s): **CreateSpace Independent Publishing Platform**
Dummy Record Do Not USE!!!!.

PRL Publishing, (*978-0-9743957*) 2245 E. Colorado Blvd., No. 104 PMB 243, Pasadena, CA 91107 USA Tel 626-255-1743
E-mail: info@prldesigns.com
Web site: http://www.prlpub.com.

†Pro Lingua Assocs., Inc., (*978-0-86647*) Orders Addr.: P.O. Box 1348, Brattleboro, VT 05302 UMI (SAN 216-0579) Tel 802-257-7779; Fax: 802-257-5117; Toll Free: 800-366-4775; Edit Addr.: P.O. Box 1348, Brattleboro, VT 05302-1348 USA
E-mail: info@prolinguaassociates.com; orders@prolinguaassociates.com
Web site: http://www.prolinguaassociates.com; http://www.lexicarry.com
Dist(s): **Hood, Alan C. & Co., Inc.**; *CIP.*

Proactive Publishing, (*978-0-9767324*) 260 Gateway Dr., Suite 21-C, Bel Air, MD 21014 USA Tel 410-893-9016; Fax: 410-893-9380; *Imprints:* Kids Can (Kids Can)
Web site: http://www.proactive-solutions.net.

Process Inc U. S. *See* **Process Transition International, Inc.**

Process Transition International, Inc., (*978-0-9646008*) P.O. Box 1988, Annapolis, MD 21404 USA Tel 301-261-9921; Fax: 410-295-5037
E-mail: spi@processtransition.com
Web site: http://www.processtransition.com.

Proclaim Publishing, (*978-1-885831*) P.O. Box 415, Palmer, TX 75152-0415 USA
E-mail: jo@awake-ministries.org; mreaves872@earthlink.net.

Production 101, Inc., (*978-0-9729706; 978-0-9767765*)
E-mail: julie@smartkids101.com
Web site: http://www.smartkids101.com
Dist(s): **Big Kids Productions, Inc.**

Production Assocs., Inc., (*978-1-887120*) 1206 W. Collins Ave., Orange, CA 92867 USA Tel 714-771-6519; Fax: 714-771-2456; Toll Free: 800-535-8368
E-mail: mikec@production-associates.com
Web site: http://www.production-associates.com; http://signtospeak.com; http://www.wesign.com
Dist(s): **Brodart Co.**
Follett School Solutions
Independent Pubs. Group.

Products With A Purpose, (*978-0-9641134*) 16430 N. 34th Pl., Phoenix, AZ 85032 USA Tel 602-595-1188
E-mail: maryalice@ev1.net.

Profane Existence, (*978-0-9662035*) P.O. Box 8722, Minneapolis, MN 55408-0722 USA
E-mail: blackened@visi.com
Web site: http://www.propaneexistence.com
Dist(s): **AK Pr. Distribution.**

Professional Book Distributors, Incorporated *See* **PBD, Inc.**

Professional Publishing Hse. LLC, (*978-1-881524; 978-0-9719749; 978-0-9725941; 978-0-9742811; 978-0-9753504; 978-0-9759654; 978-0-9764690; 978-0-9767678; 978-0-9771082; 978-0-9786032; 978-0-9792016; 978-0-9799308; 978-0-9815783; 978-0-9824292; 978-0-9826704; 978-0-9834444; 978-0-9853259; 978-0-9891960; 978-0-9861557) 1425 W. Manchester Ave., Suite B, Los Angeles, CA 90047 USA (SAN 852-7563) Tel 323-750-3592; Fax: 323-750-2886*
Web site: http://www.professionalpublishinghouse.com.

Professional Publishing Services *See* **WayaMedia**

Profile Bks. Ltd. (GBR) (*978-1-86197; 978-0-9536969; 978-0-9535895; 978-0-9541303; 978-1-903942; 978-0-9547913; 978-1-84668; 978-0-9551384; 978-0-9551904; 978-1-84765; 978-0-9556476; 978-1-906994; 978-1-906507; 978-0-9873178; 978-1-78125; 978-1-908990*) *Dist. by* **IPG Chicago.**

Profile Entertainment, Inc., (*978-0-88013; 978-0-931064; 978-0-934551*) 475 Park Ave., S., 8th Flr., New York, NY 10016 USA (SAN 212-1247) Tel 212-689-2830; Fax: 212-889-7933
E-mail: dee.erwine@starloggroup.com
Dist(s): **Kable Media Services.**

Profiles of the Presidents *Imprint of* **Compass Point Bks.**

Profit Publishing, (*978-0-9773757*) 39 W. Trace Creek Dr., Spring, TX 77381 USA
Dist(s): **AtlasBooks Distribution.**

Profitable Publishing *Imprint of* **Thornton Publishing, Inc.**

Profits Publishing, (*978-1-933817*) Orders Addr.: 1300 Boblett St., Unit A-218, Blaine, WA 98230 USA Fax: 604-944-7993; Toll Free: 866-492-6623
E-mail: bwburnham@gmail.com
Web site: http://www.profitspublishing.com
Dist(s): **Lightning Source, Inc.**
Whitewing Pr.

Profound Impact Group, Inc., (*978-0-9760564; 978-0-9887900; 978-1-942151*) Orders Addr.: P.O. Box 370567, Denver, CO 80237 USA Tel 303-437-7827
Web site: http://www.profoundgroup.com; http://www.BusterBlank.com; http://www.DomTesta.com
Dist(s): **Bks. West.**

Progeny Pr., (*978-1-58609*) Div of MG Publishers Group LLC, Orders Addr.: P.O. Box 223, Eau Claire, WI 54702-0223 USA Tel 715-838-0171; Fax:

715-836-0176; Toll Free: 877-776-4369; Edit Addr.: 133 S. State St., Box 100, Fall Creek, WI 54742 USA
E-mail: progeny@progenypress.com
Web site: http://www.progenypress.com.

Progreso Publishing Group , LLC, *(978-1-930584)* 2733 East Battlefield #283, Springfield, MO 65804 USA Tel 417-234-0084
E-mail: sanderson@progresopublishing.com
Web site: www.progresopublishing.com.

Progressive Language, Inc., *(978-0-9758759; 978-0-9899749)* 5804 Lost Dutchman Ave NE, Albuquerque, NM 87111-5901 USA
Web site: http://www.progresssivelangauge.com.

Progressive Rising Phoenix Pr., *(978-0-615-76159-6; 978-0-615-77265-3; 978-0-615-78287-4; 978-0-615-80027-1; 978-0-615-86717-5; 978-0-615-87169-1; 978-0-615-89836-0)* 100 Goldmine Ct., Aledo, TX 68008 USA Tel 817-757-7143
E-mail: thrasher321@sbcglobal.net
Web site: http://www.progressiverisingphoenix.com
Dist(s): **CreateSpace Independent Publishing Platform.**

Project Management Excellence Ctr., Inc., The, *(978-0-9726656; 978-0-9787468)* Div. of Sturgeon Publishing, P.O. Box 30291, Phoenix, AZ 85046-0291 USA Tel 623-321-8068
E-mail: info@perfectscoresoftware.com
Web site: http://www.perfectscoresoftware.com.

Project WET Foundation, *(978-1-888631; 978-0-9857384; 978-0-9903620; 978-0-9907148; 978-1-942416)* 1001 W. Oak St. Suite 210, Bozeman, MT 59715 USA Tel 406-585-2236; Fax: 406-522-0394
E-mail: kristen.read@projectwet.org; linda.hveem@projectwet.org; sandra.deyonge@projectwet.org; stephanie.kaleva@projectwet.org
Web site: http://www.projectwet.org.

Prologo Pubns., *(978-0-9764264)* 4109 N. O Connor Rd., Irving, TX 75062-3748 USA
E-mail: layne@msu.edu; prologo@comcast.net
Web site: http://www.prologopublications.com.

Prom Girl Publishing. Inc., *(978-0-9726917)* 808 Broadway, Penthouse C, New York, NY 10003 USA
Web site: http://www.promgirl.com.

†Prometheus Bks., Pubs., *(978-0-87975; 978-1-57392; 978-1-59102; 978-1-61592; 978-1-61614; 978-1-63388)* Orders Addr.: 59 John Glenn Dr., Amherst, NY 14228-2197 USA (SAN 202-0289) Tel 716-691-0133; Fax: 716-691-0137; Toll Free: 800-421-0351; *Imprints:* Pyr Books (Pyr Bks)
Web site: http://www.prometheusbooks.com
Dist(s): **MyiLibrary
Penguin Random Hse., LLC.
Random Hse., Inc.**; *CIP.*

Promocion Editorial Inca S.A., PEISA (PER) *(978-9972-40; 978-9972-721) Dist. by* **Marluccia Iaconi Bk Imports.**

Promotora de prensa internacional S.A (ESP) *(978-84-936408; 978-84-92810; 978-84-935438; 978-84-935881; 978-84-936508) Dist. by* **Consort Bk Sales.**

ProNailTech.com, *(978-0-9748796)* P.O. Box 260515, Lakewood, CO 80226 USA Tel 720-935-1761
Web site: http://www.pronailtech.com.

Pronghorn Pr., *(978-1-932636; 978-0-9885533; 978-1-941052)* Orders Addr.: P.O. Box 707, Greybull, WY 82426 USA Toll Free: 877-765-2979; Edit Addr.: 335 2nd Ave., N., Greybull, WY 82426 USA
Web site: http://www.pronghornpress.org
Dist(s): **INscribe Digital.**

Prop-Abilities Inc., *(978-0-9827461)* 1502 Fairway Grn, Mamaroneck, NY 10543 USA Tel 914-309-4383.

Propeller Pr., *(978-0-9678577)* P.O. Box 729, Fort Collins, CO 80522 USA (SAN 253-1704) Tel 970-482-8807; Fax: 970-493-1240
E-mail: propress@frii.com
Web site: http://www.propellerpress.com.

Prophecy Pubns., *(978-0-941241)* P.O. Box 7000, Oklahoma City, OK 73153 USA (SAN 665-5319) Tel 405-634-1234; Fax: 405-636-1054; Toll Free: 800-245-5577.

Prophecy, The *Imprint of* **Simon & Son Publishing**

ProQuest Information and Learning *See* **ProQuest LLC**

ProQuest LLC, *(978-0-608; 978-0-7837; 978-0-8357; 978-0-88692; 978-0-89093; 978-0-912380; 978-1-55655; 978-0-591; 978-0-9702937; 978-0-599; 978-1-931694; 978-1-59399; 978-0-496; 978-0-542; 978-1-4247; 978-0-9778091; 978-1-60205; 978-1-4345; 978-0-549; 978-1-109; 978-1-124; 978-1-267; 978-1-303; 978-1-321; 978-1-339)* 5252 N. Edgewood *Dr., Suite 125, Provo, UT 84604 USA Tel 801-765-1737; 789 Eisenhower Pkwy., Ann Arbor, MI 48106-1346 Tel 734-761-4700 Toll Free: 800-521-0600; Imprints:* CultureGrams World Edition (CultureGram Wrld)
E-mail: sales@csa.com
Web site: http://www.culturegrams.com.

ProsePress, *(978-0-9833073; 978-0-9851889; 978-0-9886194; 978-0-9893063; 978-1-941069)* 75 Red Maple Dr., Pawleys Island, SC 29585 USA Tel 843-237-9929
E-mail: prose-cons@outlook.com
Web site: prosepress.biz.

Prospect Palo Alto Publishing, *(978-0-9891043)* 435 Tasso Street, Suite 200, Palo Alto, CA 94301 USA Tel 650-327-8800
E-mail: dschnell@prospectventures.com.

Prospect Park Bks., LLC, *(978-0-9753939; 978-0-9844102; 978-0-9834594; 978-1-938849)* Orders Addr.: 2359 Lincoln Ave., Altadena, CA 91001 USA
E-mail: colleen@prospectparkbooks.com
Web site: http://www.prospectparkbooks.com
Dist(s): **Consortium Bk. Sales & Distribution
Constellation Digital Services
MyiLibrary
Perseus Bks. Group.**

Prospect Park Publishing *See* **Prospect Park Bks., LLC**

Prospecta Pr. *Imprint of* **Easton Studio Pr., LLC**

Prosperity & Profits Unlimited, Distribution Services, P.O. Box 416, Denver, CO 80201-0416 USA (SAN 200-4682) Tel 303-575-5676; Fax: 303-575-1187
E-mail: nonstopsuccess@gmail.com
Web site: http://www.breadpudding.net; http://www.contentprovidermedia.com; http://www.gumbomedia.com.

Prospero's Pr., *(978-0-9727315)* P.O. Box 4616, Boulder, CO 80306-4616 USA (SAN 255-0121) Tel 303-817-5622
Web site: http://www.ahouseforamouse.com.

Protar Hse., LLC, *(978-0-9720910)* 829 Ann St., East Lansing, MI 48823 USA Tel 517-974-7993
E-mail: info@protarhouse.com
Dist(s): **Partners Bk. Distributing, Inc.**

Protea Boekhuis (ZAF) *(978-1-86919; 978-1-919825) Dist. by* **Casemate Pubs.**

Protecting Our Diversity (POD), *(978-0-9727714)* P.O. Box 231598, Encinitas, CA 92023-1598 USA Tel 760-944-0852
E-mail: email@kidspod.com
Web site: http://www.kidspod.com.

Protective Hands Communications, *(978-0-9787394; 978-0-9818990; 978-0-9845161; 978-0-615-57240-6; 978-0-615-60403-9; 978-0-615-63600-9; 978-0-9857105; 978-0-9892028; 978-0-692-32229-1; 978-0-692-40426-3; 978-0-692-46613-1)* Orders Addr.: 1668 Essex Ln., Riviera Beach, FL 33404 USA Toll Free: 866-457-1203
E-mail: info@protectivehands.com; steve@protectivehands.com
Web site: http://protectivehands.com.

ProTeens *Imprint of* **Positive Action For Christ**

ProTips(TM) Media, *(978-0-9740600)* 810 Adair Pl., Del Rey Oaks, CA 93940 USA
E-mail: tom@rivelli.com
Web site: http://www.protipsmedia.com.

Proton Arts, *(978-0-9752647; 978-0-9905028)* 5051 Grand Beech Ct., Haymarket, VA 20169-2586 USA
E-mail: info@protonarts.com
Web site: http://www.protonarts.com.

Proud Peacock Publishing, *(978-0-9859437)* 930 Palm Ave. Apt. 136, West Hollywood, CA 90069 USA Tel 925-520-5528
E-mail: marcelino.rosas@ymail.com.

Proud 2-B Me Publishing!, *(978-0-9655726)* 3653-F Flakes Mill Rd., PMB-F188, Decatur, GA 30034 USA Tel 770-808-2301.

Prous, J. R. S.A. (ESP) *(978-84-499; 978-84-300; 978-84-401; 978-84-86973) Dist. by* **Continental Bk.**

Providence Hse Pubs., *(978-1-57736; 978-1-881576)* 238 Seaboard Ln., Franklin, TN 37067 USA Tel 615-771-2020; Fax: 615-771-2002; Toll Free: 800-321-5692
E-mail: books@providencehouse.com
Web site: http://www.providencehouse.com.

Providence Publishing, *(978-0-9651661; 978-0-9753004; 978-0-9819222; 978-1-60934)* 5744 Bowling Dr., Watauga, TX 76148-3422 USA; 13607 Belinda Ct., Houston, TX 77069 Tel 713-480-7069 Do not confuse with companies with the same or similar name in Salt Lake City, UT, Martinez, CA
E-mail: info@providencepublishing.com
Web site: http://www.providencepublishing.com
Dist(s): **Wilson & Assocs.**

Providence Publishing Corporation *See* **Providence Hse Pubs.**

Provine Pr., *(978-1-889883)* 832 Cerrito St., Albany, CA 94706 USA Tel 510-528-7055
E-mail: jmbartlett@sbcglobal.net.

PRPublishing, *(978-0-9712258)* 2830 N. Fifth St., Kalamazoo, MI 49009 USA Tel 616-375-5909; Fax: 616-375-7649
E-mail: freelanceediting@ameritech.net.

PRS Inc., *(978-0-9768441)* PRS Ctr. Suite 200, PO Box 852, Latrobe, PA 15650 USA Tel 724-539-7820; Fax: 724-539-1388; Toll Free: 800-338-3688
E-mail: prsinfo@prsrx.com; alexr@prsrx.com
Web site: http://www.prsrx.com.

†Pruett Publishing Co., *(978-0-87108)* P.O. Box 2140, Boulder, CO 80306-2140 USA (SAN 205-4035) Toll Free: 800-592-9727 (orders)
Web site: http://www.pruettpublishing.com
Dist(s): **Bks. West
Ingram Pub. Services**; *CIP.*

Prufrock Pr., *(978-1-882664; 978-1-59363; 978-1-61821)* Orders Addr.: P.O. Box 8813, Waco, TX 76714-8813 USA Tel 254-756-3337; Fax: 254-756-3339; Toll Free Fax: 800-240-0333; Toll Free: 800-998-2208; Edit Addr.: 6898 Woodway Dr., Woodway, TX 76712-6158 USA (SAN 851-9188); 1935 Brookdale Rd, Ste 139, Naperville, IL 60563
E-mail: info@prufrock.com
Web site: http://www.prufrock.com
Dist(s): **Follett School Solutions
MyiLibrary
Sourcebooks, Inc.**

Pruggus Publishing, *(978-0-9844037; 978-0-9900225)* P.O. Box 1655, Taos, NM 87571 USA.

Prytania Pr., *(978-0-9742602)* Orders Addr.: P.O. Box 1892, Gray, LA 70359 USA Tel 225-346-8811
E-mail: ameliastreet@go.com.

Psalms for Kidz *Imprint of* **Little Sprout Publishing Hse.**

PSI (Publisher Services, Inc.), 3095 Kingston Ct., Norcross, GA 30071-1231 USA Toll Free: 800-755-9653; 877-578-4774.

PT Publishing, *(978-0-615-21675-1; 978-0-615-27677-9; 978-0-9839147)* P.O. Box 2668, Oak Bluffs, MA 02557 USA
Dist(s): **Lulu Enterprises Inc.**

PTO Pr., *(978-0-9760187)* P.O. Box 5394, Snowmass Village, CO 81615 USA.

P2 Educational Services, Inc., *(978-1-885964)* 4915 S. 146th Cir., Omaha, NE 68137-1402 USA Tel 712-727-3772.

Puarose Publishing, *(978-1-933593)* P.O. Box 1597, Gilroy, CA 95021 USA Tel 408-846-0116
E-mail: admin@puarosepublishing.com
Web site: http://www.puarosepublishing.com.

Public Education Foundation, The, *(978-0-9788980)* 3360 W. Sahara Ave., Suite 160, Las Vegas, NV 89102 USA Tel 702-799-1042; Fax: 702-799-5247
E-mail: dkchristensen@interact.ccsd.net
Web site: http://www.thepef.org.

Public Ink, *(978-0-9772371)* 314 Sandpiper Ct., Novato, CA 94949 USA Fax: 415-883-7669
E-mail: sdunwell@earthlink.net
Dist(s): **AtlasBooks Distribution.**

Public Square Bks., *(978-1-59497)* 307 Seventh Ave., Suite 1601, New York, NY 10001 USA (SAN 255-8149) Tel 212-604-0415; Fax: 212-604-0390; Toll Free: 800-732-3321
Web site: http://www.publicsquarebooks.com
Dist(s): **Diamond Comic Distributors, Inc.
Diamond Bk. Distributors.**

Publicaciones Citem, S.A. de C.V. (MEX) *(978-970-656; 978-968-6792; 978-968-7668) Dist. by* **Lectorum Pubns.**

Publicaciones Educativas, Inc., *(978-0-9767623; 978-0-9767624; 978-0-9779806)* Orders Addr.: P.O. Box 192337, San Juan, PR 00919-2337 USA Tel 787-250-8252; Fax: 787-274-1671; Edit Addr.: 1117 Ave. Munoz Rivera, San Juan, PR 00925 USA Do not confuse with Publicaciones Educativas, Inc. in Hato Rey, PR, Rio Piedras, PR
E-mail: peduc@coqui.net
Web site: http://www.libreriaeducativapr.com.

Publicaciones Fher, S.A. (ESP) *(978-84-243) Dist. by* **AIMS Intl.**

Publicaciones Papelandia, *(978-0-9759194; 978-0-9765805)* 843 Waukee Pass, San Antonio, TX 78260-1919 USA
E-mail: wjconaway@yahoo.com
Web site: http://www.mexicowalkingtours.com.

Publicaciones Puertorriquenas, Inc., *(978-0-929441; 978-1-881713; 978-1-881720; 978-1-932243; 978-1-933485; 978-1-934630; 978-1-935145; 978-1-935606; 978-1-62537)* Orders Addr.: P.O. Box 195064, San Juan, PR 00919-5064 USA; Edit Addr.: 46 Mayaguez St., San Juan, PR 00917-4915 USA (SAN 249-4272) Tel 787-759-9673; Fax: 787-250-6498
Web site: http://www.publicacionespr.com.

Publicaciones Urbanas, *(978-0-615-41660-1)* Garden HIlls PLaza PMB 359, Carr. 19, Guaynabo, PR 00966 USA Tel 787-793-1164 (phone/fax).

Publicaciones y Ediciones Salamandra, S.A. (ESP) *(978-84-7888; 978-84-86033) Dist. by* **Lectorum Pubns.**

Publicaciones y Ediciones Salamandra, S.A. (ESP) *(978-84-9838) Dist. by* **Spanish.**

Publication Consultants, *(978-0-9644809; 978-1-888125; 978-1-59433)* 8370 Eleusis Dr., Anchorage, AK 99502 USA Tel 907-349-2424; Fax: 907-349-2426; *Imprints:* Publishing Consultants (Pubng Consultants)
E-mail: evan@publicationconsultants.com
Web site: http://www.publicationconsultants.com
Dist(s): **INscribe Digital
News Group, The
Todd Communications
Wizard Works.**

Publications International, Ltd., *(978-0-7853; 978-0-88176; 978-1-56173; 978-1-4127; 978-1-60553; 978-1-4508; 978-1-68022)* Orders Addr.: 7373 N. Cicero Ave., Lincolnwood, IL 60641 USA (SAN 263-9823) Tel 847-676-3470; Fax: 847-676-3671; Toll Free: 800-745-9299; *Imprints:* PIL Kids (PIL Kids)
E-mail: customer_service@pubint.com
Web site: http://www.pilbooks.com
Dist(s): **Penguin Publishing Group
Send The Light Distribution LLC.**

Publications Unltd, *(978-0-9767450)* Orders Addr.: 800 Saint Marys St, Ste 201 New St., Raleigh, NC 27605-1458 USA Do not confuse with Publications Unlimited in Lake Worth, FL
Web site: http://www.publicationsunltd.com.

Publish For Christ, Incorporated *See* **Nathaniel Max Rock**

Publish To Go Pubns., *(978-0-9669289; 978-0-9728923; 978-0-9745110)* Orders Addr.: 21539 Hollandaire Dr. E., Boca Raton, FL 33433 USA; Edit Addr.: 21539 Hollandaire Dr. E., Boca Raton, FL 33433 USA Tel 561-350-4770 (phone/fax)
E-mail: marknemcek@comcast.net.

PublishAmerica, Inc., *(978-1-893162; 978-1-58851; 978-1-59129; 978-1-59286; 978-1-4137; 978-1-4241; 978-1-60441; 978-1-60474; 978-1-60563; 978-1-60610; 978-1-60672; 978-1-60703; 978-1-60813; 978-1-60836; 978-1-60749; 978-1-61546; 978-1-61582; 978-1-4489; 978-1-4512;-1-4560; 978-1-4626; 978-1-62709; 978-1-63000; 978-1-63004; 978-1-62772; 978-1-62907; 978-1-63084) Div. of America Hse. Bk. Pubs., Orders Addr.: P.O. Box 151, Frederick, MD 21705 USA Fax: 301-631-9073; Edit Addr.: 230 E Patrick St, Frederick, MD 21701 USA; 230 E. Patrick St., Frederick, MD 21701*
E-mail: pratherm@publishamerica.com; support@publishamerica.com; tina@publishamerica.com; retta@publishamerica.com; alice@publishamerica.com
Web site: http://www.publishamerica.com
Dist(s): **America Hse. Bk. Pubs.**

Published by Westview, Inc., *(978-0-9819172; 978-0-9819325; 978-1-935271; 978-1-937763; 978-1-62880)* P.O. Box 210183, Nashville, TN 37082 USA Tel 615-646-6134; Fax: 615-662-0946.

Publisher Media Services *See* **Independent Publisher Services**

Publisher Page *Imprint of* **Headline Bks., Inc.**

Publisher Plus, *(978-1-888537)* Div. of Montana Ole Store, Orders Addr.: 200 Choteau St., Sun River, MT 59483 USA Tel 406-264-5953; Fax: 406-264-5672
E-mail: rebeccahel2000@yahoo.com
Web site: http://www.montanaolestore.com.

Publishers Design Group, Inc., *(978-1-929170)* Orders Addr.: P.O. Box 37, Roseville, CA 95678 USA Tel 916-784-0500; Fax: 916-773-7421; Toll Free: 800-587-6666; Edit Addr.: 1655 Booth Rd., Roseville, CA 95747 USA; *Imprints:* PDG (PDG)
E-mail: books@publishersdesign.com; orders@publishersdesign.com; admin@publishersdesign.com; marketing@publishersdesign.com
Web site: http://www.publishersdesign.com; http://www.tearoomguide.com
Dist(s): **Quality Bks., Inc.
Send The Light Distribution LLC.**

Publishers' Graphics, L.L.C., *(978-0-9663402; 978-1-930847; 978-1-933556; 978-1-934703; 978-1-935590)* 140 Della Ct., Carol Stream, IL 60188 USA (SAN 990-0241) Toll Free: 888-404-3769
Web site: http://www.pubgraphics.com.

Publishers Place, Inc., *(978-0-9676051; 978-0-9744785; 978-0-9771978; 978-0-9840757; 978-0-9864267)* Div. of Grace Associates, 821 4th Ave., Suite 201, Huntington, WV 25701 USA Tel 304-697-3236; Fax: 304-697-3399; *Imprints:* Mid-Atlantic Highlands Publishing (Mid Atlantic WV)
E-mail: publishersplace@gmail.com
Web site: http://www.publishersplace.org.

Publishers' Pr., *(978-0-943592)* Orders Addr.: P.O. Box 86421, Portland, OR 97286 USA (SAN 240-7558) Do not confuse with Publishers Pr., Salt Lake City, UT.

Publishers@TreeHouse, The, *(978-0-9708816)* 2658 Patapsco Rd., Finksburg, MD 21048 USA Tel 410-848-9306
E-mail: pix4u@qis.net.

Publishing Assocs., Inc., *(978-0-942683)* Subs. of Financial & Commercial Printing Services, 5020 Montcalm Dr., Atlanta, GA 30331 USA (SAN 667-2183) Tel 404-349-4678; Fax: 404-629-5533
E-mail: fcpublish@aol.com.

Publishing Consultants *Imprint of* **Publication Consultants**

Publishing Cooperative, The *Imprint of* **Publishing Factory, The**

Publishing Designs, Inc., *(978-0-929540)* Orders Addr.: P.O. Box 3241, Huntsville, AL 35810 USA (SAN 249-6372) Tel 256-533-4301; Fax: 256-533-4302; Edit Addr.: 517 Killingsworth Cove Rd., Gurley, AL 35748 USA (SAN 249-6380) Tel 205-859-9372
E-mail: info@publishingdesigns.com
Dist(s): **Send The Light Distribution LLC
Twentieth Century Christian Bks.**

Publishing Factory, The, *(978-0-9722741)* 1836 Blake St., Suite 200, Denver, CO 80202 USA Tel 303-297-1233; Fax: 303-297-3997; *Imprints:* Publishing Cooperative, The (Publishing Coop)
E-mail: editorinchief@pencilay.com.

Publishing Hse. Gelany, *(978-0-9712665; 978-0-9728301; 978-0-9747248; 978-0-9777566; 978-0-9817529; 978-0-9827833)* Orders Addr.: P.O. Box 61472, Staten Island, NY 10306 USA Tel 718-668-1375; Edit Addr.: 34 Maple Terr., Staten Island, NY 10306 USA
E-mail: gelany@juno.com
Web site: http://www.zagorizontom20megsfree.com.

Publishing in Motion, *(978-1-61279)* 2502 Canada bld. No. 1, Glendale, CA 91208 USA Tel 818-547-1554
E-mail: publishinginmotion@yahoo.com
Web site: www.publishinginmotion.com.

Publishing Services @ Thomson-Shore, *(978-0-9841658; 978-1-936672; 978-1-943290)* 7300 W. Joy Rd., Dexter, MI 48130 USA Tel 734-426-6248; *Imprints:* Excite Kids Press (ExciteKids); Ignition Press (IgnitionPr)
E-mail: jerryf@tshore.com
Web site: http://thomsonshore.com/publishing/
Dist(s): **Seattle Bk. Co.**

Publishing Syndicate, *(978-0-9824654; 978-0-9850602; 978-1-938778)* Orders Addr.: P.O. Box 607, Orangevale, CA 95662 USA Fax: 916-987-6501
E-mail: ken@publishingsyndicate.com; kenmckowen@gmail.com
Web site: http://www.publishingsyndicate.com
Dist(s): **BookBaby
Independent Pubs. Group
Ingram Pub. Services
Small Pr. United
Smashwords.**

PublishingWorks, *(978-0-9744803; 978-1-933002; 978-1-935557)* 151 Epping Rd., Exeter, NH 03833-4522 USA Toll Free: 800-333-9883; 151 Epping Rd., Exeter, NH 03833-4522 (SAN 850-4806) Toll Free: 800-333-9883; *Imprints:* Townsend, J. N. Publishing (JNTown); Peapod Press (PeapodPr) Do not confuse with The Publishing Works in Waldport, OR
E-mail: bookpub@worldpath.net; jeremy@publishingworks.com
Web site: http://www.publishingworks.com
Dist(s): **MyiLibrary
Perseus-PGW
Perseus Bks. Group.**

PublishNext *See* **Publishing Services @ Thomson-Shore**

Pucci Bks. (GBR) *(978-0-9559352) Dist. by* **IPG Chicago.**

Pucker Art Pubns. *Imprint of* **Pucker Gallery**

Pucker Gallery, *(978-0-9635318; 978-1-879985)* 171 Newbury St., Boston, MA 02116-2897 USA Tel

617-267-9473; Fax: 617-424-9759; *Imprints:* Pucker Art Publications (Pucker Art)
E-mail: contactus@puckergallery.com; destiny@puckergallery.com; tess@puckergallery.com
Web site: http://www.puckergallery.com
Dist(s): **Syracuse Univ. Pr.**
Univ. Pr. of New England
Univ. of Washington Pr.

Pucker Safrai Gallery *See* **Pucker Gallery**

Puckett Publishing, Inc., *(978-0-9764938)* P.O. Box 528, Columbia, IL 62236 USA.

Puddinhead LLC, *(978-0-615-24552-2)* 6470 Fogle Ct., Westerville, OH 43082 USA Tel 614-899-6112
Dist(s): **AtlasBooks Distribution.**

Puddle Jump Pr., Ltd., *(978-0-9726487)* 763 Rte. 9W, Nyack, NY 10960 USA Tel 914-645-6551 (phone/fax)
E-mail: puddlejumppress@gmail.com
Web site: http://www.puddlejumppress.com
Dist(s): **Follett School Solutions.**

Puddledancer Pr., *(978-0-9647349; 978-1-892005; 978-1-934336)* Orders Addr.: P.O. Box 231129, Encinitas, CA 92023-1129 USA Toll Free: 877-367-2849; Edit Addr.: 3245 Rim Rock Cir., Encinitas, CA 92024 USA
E-mail: email@puddledancer.com; neill@puddledancer.com; meiji@puddledancer.com
Web site: http://www.puddledancer.com; http://www.nonviolentcommunication.com
Dist(s): **Ebsco Publishing**
Independent Pubs. Group
MyiLibrary
ebrary, Inc.

Puddletown Publishing Group, Inc., *(978-1-61413)* 4125 SE 63rd, Portland, OR 97206 USA Tel 503-320-1242
E-mail: lachance@puddletowngroup.com
Web site: puddletowngroup.com
Dist(s): **BookBaby.**

Puffin *Imprint of* **Penguin Publishing Group**

Puget Sound Bks., *(978-0-9715019)* Div. of Angel Fire Pr., Orders Addr.: 14403 N. Silverado Dr., Fountain Hls, AZ 85268-3048 USA Tel 480-304-2948
E-mail: almoeblog@yahoo.com.

Pulp Collector Press *See* **Adventure Hse.**

Pulte, Therese Marie, *(978-0-9746557)* 1278 Glenneyre St., Suite 39, Laguna Beach, CA 92651 USA; *Imprints:* Destination Publishers (Destin Pubs)
Web site: http://www.destinationpublishers.com.

Pumpkin Hill Productions, *(978-0-9793602)* P.O. Box 165, Hawleyville, CT 06440 USA
E-mail: nmroddas@aol.com.

Pumpkin House Company *See* **Pumpkin Hse., Ltd.**

Pumpkin Hse., Ltd., *(978-0-9646010)* 3508 La Rochelle Dr., Columbus, OH 43221 USA (SAN 255-0644) Fax: 614-557-9635
E-mail: pumpkinhouse@columbus.rr.com
Web site: http://www.pumpkinhouse.net
Dist(s): **Independent Pubs. Group.**

Pumpkin Patch Publishing, *(978-0-9754823)* 10911 E. Skinner Dr., Scottsdale, AZ 85262 USA.

Pumpkin Ridge Publishing, *(978-0-9754459)* P.O. Box 1668, North Plains, OR 97113-6157 USA (SAN 256-1379) Tel 503-647-5970
E-mail: prpublish@msn.com
Web site: http://www.factoryride.com.

Pumpkin Seed Pr., *(978-0-9700273)* 68335 355th Ave., Humphrey, NE 68642 USA Tel 402-923-1682; Fax: 402-923-9110; Toll Free Fax: 877-923-1682
E-mail: rjnoona@megavision.com; rjnoona@magavision.com
Web site: http://www.usedhomeschoolbooks.com/bgh.htm.

Pumpkin Seeds Pr., *(978-0-615-17159-3)* 24 Uranus Rd., Sewell, NJ 08080 USA
Dist(s): **Lulu Enterprises Inc.**

Pumpkinhead Productions, *(978-0-615-79356-6; 978-0-615-80349-4)* 307 W. Hawthorne Blvd., Mundelein, IL 60060 USA Tel 847 837 0380
Dist(s): **CreateSpace Independent Publishing Platform.**

Pumpkins Pansies Bunnies & Bears, *(978-0-9747367)* Orders Addr.: 19 Treevine Ct., The Woodlands, TX 77381 USA Tel 281-785-0755
E-mail: paklppbb@aol.com; tricialowenfield@gmail.com
Web site: http://www.tricialowenfielddesign.com.

Punch Press Publications *See* **New Growth Pr.**

Punkin Pr., *(978-1-60149)* 1221 S. Sherbourne Dr., Apt. No. 5, Los Angeles, CA 90035 USA
E-mail: punkinpress@hotmail.com
Web site: http://www.punkinpress.net.

Punta Gorda Pr., *(978-1-929528)* 2760 W. Marion Ave., Punta Gorda, FL 33950 USA
E-mail: joeinnovations@gmail.com
Web site: http://www.puntagordapress.com.

Punto de Lectura *Imprint of* **Santillana USA Publishing Co., Inc.**

Puppet Rescue, *(978-0-9799958)* 711 9th St., No. 2, Santa Monica, CA 90402 USA (SAN 854-9516) Tel 310-656-7738
E-mail: darinvents@adelphia.net
Web site: http://www.puppetrescue.com.

Puppetry in Practice, *(978-0-9720183)* 1923 Haring St., Brooklyn, NY 11229-3713 USA
E-mail: tovaa@aol.com
Web site: http://www.puppetryinpractice.com.

Puptattle Pr., Inc., *(978-0-9786947)* 21813 S. Embassy Ave., Carson, CA 90810 USA
Web site: http://www.puptattle.com.

†Purdue Univ. Pr., *(978-0-911198; 978-1-55753; 978-1-61249)* Orders Addr.: P.O. Box 388, Ashland, OH 44805 USA Toll Free: 800-247-6553; Edit Addr.: 504 W. State St. Stewart Ctr. 370, West Lafayette, IN 47907-2058 USA (SAN 203-4026) Tel 765-494-2038; Fax: 765-496-2442 Do not confuse with Purdue Univ. Pubns., same address
E-mail: mchunt@purdue.edu
Web site: http://www.thepress.purdue.edu/
Dist(s): **AtlasBooks Distribution**
BookMasters Distribution Services (BDS)
Ebsco Publishing
Follett School Solutions
MyiLibrary
Trajectory, Inc.; *CIP.*

Pure Joy Pubns., *(978-0-9749578)* P.O. Box 482, Wheat Ridge, CO 80034-0482 USA
E-mail: purejoypublications@comcast.net.

PureLight Pubns., *(978-0-9787597; 978-0-615-23432-8; 978-0-9825988)* Orders Addr.: P.O. Box 720193, Dallas, TX 75372 USA Tel 214-770-0206 weekdays 9am to 5 pm
E-mail: pl.publications@yahoo.com; seaonducote@aol.com
Web site: http://www.seaonducoteproductions.com; http://www.purelightpublications.org
Dist(s): **Lulu Enterprises Inc.**

Pureplay Pr., *(978-0-9714366; 978-0-9765096)* 11353 Missouri Ave., Los Angeles, CA 90025-5553 USA (SAN 852-5404) Tel 310-479-8773; Fax: 310-473-9384
E-mail: editor@pureplaypress.com
Web site: http://www.pureplaypress.com
Dist(s): **BookMasters, Inc.**

pureplaypress.com *See* **Pureplay Pr.**

Purfect Promises, *(978-0-9759343)* 149 Summerhill Dr., Rockwall, TX 75032 USA Tel 972-771-9528; Fax: 972-772-5403
E-mail: purfectpromises@aol.com.

Purgatory Publishing, Inc., *(978-1-932867)* 904 Colonial Ct., Coatesville, PA 19320 USA; *Imprints:* West End Games (W End Games)
Web site: http://www.westendgames.com
Dist(s): **Century Pr.**
Diamond Distributors, Inc.

Purity Pr. Pubs., *(978-0-9728797)* P.O. Box 2896, Decatur, GA 30031 USA.

Purple Bear Bks., Inc., *(978-1-933327)* 300 Park Ave., Suite 1700, New York, NY 10022 USA
Dist(s): **Perseus-PGW.**

Purple Cow Pr., *(978-0-9820983)* 14688 Denmark Ct., Apple Valley, MN 55124 USA Tel 952-322-1419
E-mail: wdwaibel@aol.com
Web site: http://www.rudyslittleworld.com.

Purple Crayon Studios, *(978-0-9706491)* 0-115 Luce, SW, Grand Rapids, MI 49055 USA Tel 616-822-3186; Toll Free Fax: 877-710-2368
E-mail: beryl@pca3d.com
Web site: http://www.mushtons.com.

Purple Haze Pr., *(978-0-9773200; 978-1-935183)* Orders Addr.: 2195 Malibu lake Cir., No. 1134, Naples, FL 34119 USA; Edit Addr.: 2430 Vanderbilt Beach Rd., No. 108, PMB 167, Naples, FL 34109 USA
E-mail: v@purpleV.com; p_tomasello@yahoo.com
Web site: http://www.purplehazepress.com
Dist(s): **AtlasBooks Distribution**
ebrary, Inc.

Purple Hse. Pr., *(978-1-930900)* Orders Addr.: P.O. Box 787, Cynthiana, KY 41031 USA; Edit Addr.: 8100 Us Highway 62 E., Cynthiana, KY 41031-6796 USA
E-mail: jillmorgan@hughes.net
Web site: http://www.purplehousepress.com.

Purple Lady Productions, *(978-0-9714506)* P.O. Box 1277, Tiburon, CA 94920-4277 USA Tel 415-435-0720
E-mail: purpleladybythebay@earthlink.net.

Purple Lizard Pr. LLC, *(978-0-9762902)* Orders Addr.: P.O. Box 68883, Tucson, AZ 85737-7076 USA Tel 520-575-6660
E-mail: Julie@PurpleLizardPress.com
Web site: http://www.purplelizardpress.com.

Purple Mountain Pr., Ltd., *(978-0-916346; 978-0-935796; 978-1-930098)* Orders Addr.: P.O. Box 309, Fleischmanns, NY 12430-0309 USA (SAN 222-3716) Tel 845-254-4062; Fax: 845-254-4476; Toll Free: 800-325-2665; Edit Addr.: 1060 Main St., Fleischmanns, NY 12430 USA Do not confuse with Purple Mountain Pr., Carson City, NV
E-mail: purple@catskill.net
Web site: http://www.catskill.net/purple.

Purple Penguin Publishing, *(978-0-9765473)* 3929 Hummingbird Ln., Roanoke, VA 24018 USA Tel 540-400-7220; Toll Free: 800-788-3196
E-mail: tanyapenguin@aol.com
Web site: http://www.underragingskies.tanyaadams.com.

Purple People, Inc., *(978-0-9707793)* P.O. Box 3194, Sedona, AZ 86340-3194 USA Tel 928-204-6400; Fax: 928-282-1662
E-mail: info@purplepeople.com
Web site: http://www.purplepeople.com.

Purple Pig Publishing, *(978-0-9700380)* Orders Addr.: P.O. Box 1083, Bethel, CT 06801 USA Tel 203-797-1857; Edit Addr.: 7 Wixon Rd., Danbury, CT 06811 USA
E-mail: jshaboo@att.net.

Purple Plume Pr., *(978-0-9744923)* 5980 Peach Ave., Manteca, CA 95337 USA Tel 209-825-7602
E-mail: purpleplumepress@cs.com; purpleplumepress@cs.com.

Purple Toad Publishing, Inc., *(978-1-62469)* 204 S. Union St., Kennett Square, PA 19348 USA Tel 610-444-8259
E-mail: cynthia@purpletoadpublishing.com.

Purple Wings Publishing, *(978-0-9740426)* Orders Addr.: 7473 W. Lake Mead Ste 100, Las Vegas, NV 89128 USA Tel 702-635-2665; Fax: 702-383-8235
Dist(s): **BCH Fulfillment & Distribution.**

PUSH *Imprint of* **Scholastic, Inc.**

Pushkin Pr., Ltd. (GBR) *(978-1-901285; 978-1-906548; 978-1-78227; 978-1-908968) Dist. by* **Random.**

Pushkin Pr., Ltd. (GBR) *(978-1-901285; 978-1-906548; 978-1-78227; 978-1-908968) Dist. by* **Peng Rand Hse.**

Putnam Adult *Imprint of* **Penguin Publishing Group**

Putnam Juvenile *Imprint of* **Penguin Publishing Group**

Putumayo World Music & Crafts, *(978-1-885265; 978-1-58759)* Div. of Putumayo, Inc., 324 Lafayette St., 7th Flr., New York, NY 10012 USA Tel 212-625-1400; Fax: 212-460-0095; Toll Free: 800-995-9588
E-mail: info@putumayo.com
Web site: http://www.putumayo.com
Dist(s): **Follett School Solutions**
Recorded Bks., LLC
Rhino Entertainment Co, A Warner Music Group Co.
Rounder Kids Music Distribution.

Puumakaa Pr., *(978-0-9762387)* Orders Addr.: P.O. Box 500, Na'Alehu, HI 96772 USA; Edit Addr.: 94-6448 Mamalahoa Hwy., Na'Alehu, HI 96772 USA
E-mail: elizabeth@fastnethi.com
Web site: http://www.inka-online.com.

Puwaii International, LLC, *(978-0-9787949)* 7326 N. 61 St., Paradise Valley, AZ 85253 USA
E-mail: jerrelvanier@yahoo.com
Web site: http://www.puwaiiadventures.com.

Puzzlewright *Imprint of* **Sterling Publishing Co., Inc.**

PXL Media, LLC, *(978-0-9749322)* P.O. Box 99, LeClaire, IA 52753-0099 USA
E-mail: pxlmedia@aol.com.

Pyle, Robert Associates *See* **Avocus Publishing, Inc.**

Pyr Bks. *Imprint of* **Prometheus Bks., Pubs.**

Pyramid Dancer Pubns., *(978-0-9659913)* P.O. Box 5263, Colorado Spgs, CO 80931-5263 USA
E-mail: rjb@phoenixbonsai.com
Web site: http://www.phoenixbonsai.com.

Pyramid Educational Products, Inc., *(978-1-928598)* Div of Pyramid Educational Consultants, Incorporated, 13 Garfield Way, Newark, DE 19713-3450 USA
E-mail: dbittner@pyramidproducts.com
Web site: http://www.pyramidproducts.com.

Pyramid Publishing, Inc., *(978-1-885920; 978-1-934008)* Orders Addr.: P.O. Box 129, Zenda, WI 53195-0129 USA Tel 414-275-3384; Fax: 414-275-3584; P.O. Box 129, Zenda, WI 53195 Do not confuse with companies with the same name in Utica, NY, Montgomery, AL
E-mail: pyramid2mail@gmail.com.

Pyrola Publishing, *(978-0-9618348)* P.O. Box 80961, Fairbanks, AK 99708 USA (SAN 667-3503) Tel 907-455-6469 (phone/fax)
E-mail: mshields@mosquitonet.com
Web site: http://www.maryshields.com.

Pyxie Moss Press *See* **Fun Fitness Publishing**

Q & A Books *See* **Paradoxical Pr., The**

Q & J Bird Pr., LLC, *(978-0-615-16566-0)* 141 Morey Pl., Greensburg, PA 15601 USA
E-mail: icanbe@qandjbirdpress.com
Web site: http://www.qandjbirdpress.com.

QA Productions, *(978-0-615-74440-7; 978-0-615-75520-5; 978-0-615-87834-8; 978-0-692-26838-4)*
Dist(s): **CreateSpace Independent Publishing Platform.**

QEB Publishing Inc., *(978-1-59566; 978-1-60992)* Div. of QED Publishing, 23062 La Cadena Dr., Irvine, CA 92653 USA
E-mail: Maxime.boucknooghe@quarto.com
Web site: http://www.qed-publishing.co.uk
Dist(s): **Hachette Bk. Group**
Lerner Publishing Group
Scholastic Bk. Fairs.

QED Publishing *See* **QEB Publishing Inc.**

Quackenbush, Robert Studios, *(978-0-9612518; 978-0-9712757)* Orders Addr.: 460 E. 79th St., Suite 14E, New York, NY 10021 USA (SAN 656-0458) Tel 212-744-3822; Fax: 212-861-2761
E-mail: rqstudios@aol.com
Web site: http://www.rquackenbush.com.

Quackenworth Publishing, *(978-1-933211)* P.O. Box 4747, Culver City, CA 90230-4747 USA Tel 310-945-5634; Fax: 310-945-5709
E-mail: info@quackenworth.com
Web site: http://www.quackenworth.com.

Quadradrillion, LLC - Publishing Division *See* **Transaltar Publishing**

Quail Ridge Pr., Inc., *(978-0-937552; 978-1-893062; 978-1-934193; 978-1-938879)* Orders Addr.: P.O. Box 123, Brandon, MS 39043 USA (SAN 257-8794) Tel 601-825-2063; Fax: 601-825-3091; Toll Free Fax: 800-864-1082; Toll Free: 800-343-1583
E-mail: lward@quailridge.com
Web site: http://www.quailridge.com
Dist(s): **Booklines Hawaii, Ltd.**
Gibson, Dot Pubns.
Forest Sales & Distributing Co.
Islander Group
Southwest Cookbook Distributors.

Quake *Imprint of* **Echelon Press Publishing**

Quaker Press of Friends General Conference *See* **QuakerPress**

QuakerPress, *(978-0-9620912; 978-1-888305; 978-1-937768)* Div. of Friends General Conference, 1216 Arch St., 2B, Philadelphia, PA 19107 USA (SAN 225-4484) Tel 215-561-1700; Fax: 215-561-0759; Toll Free: 800-966-4556
E-mail: publications@fgcquaker.org; bookstore@fgcquaker.org
Web site: http://www.fgcquaker.org/services/fgc-publications.

Quale Pr. LLC, *(978-0-9656161; 978-0-9700663; 978-0-9744503; 978-0-9792999; 978-1-935835; 978-1-939606)* 2 Hillcrest Rd., Niantic, CT 06357 USA Tel 860-739-9153 (phone/fax); P.O. Box 642, Niantic, CT 06357 Tel 860-739-9153
E-mail: central@quale.com
Web site: http://www.quale.com
Dist(s): **ConsuLogic Consulting Services**
SPD-Small Pr. Distribution.

Quality Nature Displays by Eddie Dunbar *See* **Insect Sciences Museum of California**

Quality of Life Publishing Co., *(978-0-9675532; 978-0-9816219)* 6210 Shirley St., Suite 112, Naples, FL 34109-6258 USA Toll Free: 877-513-0099
Web site: http://www.qolpublishing.com
Dist(s): **AtlasBooks Distribution.**

Quality Pubs., *(978-0-9671107)* Orders Addr.: P.O. Box 691546, San Antonio, TX 78269 USA Tel 210-699-9007; Fax: 210-641-6334; Edit Addr.: 11238 Jade Green, San Antonio, TX 78249 USA Toll Free: 888-633-9898
E-mail: aroman@qualitypublishers.com
Web site: http://www.medpress.com.

Quality Publishing Inc., *(978-0-9745741; 978-0-9759309)* 1005 E. Highland Ave., Rome, GA 30161 USA Fax: 706-290-1223; Toll Free: 800-262-4404
E-mail: bbmonday@comcast.net.

Quantum Manifestations Publishing, *(978-0-9718099; 978-1-933505)* 1360 University Ave., W. Suite #104-192, Saint Paul, MN 55104 USA Tel 678-227-3162
E-mail: pm@quantumdatingclub.com
Web site: http://www.quantummanifestationspublishing.com.

Quantum One Publishing, *(978-0-9755681)* 1728 Spruce Ln., Linton, IN 47441 USA Tel 812-847-8708; Fax: 812-847-8712
E-mail: jdsapara@iglide.net.

Quarrier Pr., *(978-0-938985; 978-0-9646197; 978-1-891852; 978-1-942294)* 1125 Central Ave., Charleston, WV 25302 USA Tel 304-342-1848; Fax: 304-343-0594; Toll Free: 888-982-7472; *Imprints:* Mountain Memories Books (Mtn Memories Bks)
E-mail: clemmtstate@gmail.com
Web site: http://www.wvbookco.com
Dist(s): **West Virginia Book Co., The.**

Quarry Bks. *Imprint of* **Quarto Publishing Group USA**

Quarry Bks. *Imprint of* **Indiana Univ. Pr.**

Quarry Books *Imprint of* **Quarto Publishing Group USA**

Quarrystone Bond *See* **Club4Girls Publishing Co.**

Quarter Milestones Publishing, *(978-0-9748216)* Orders Addr.: P.O. Box 441, Milligan College, TN 37682-0441 USA Tel 423-542-0159; Fax: 423-542-9532; Edit Addr.: 1682 Powder Branch Rd., Johnson City, TN 37601-6220 USA
E-mail: qmp@preferred.com
Web site: http://www.quartermilestones.com
Dist(s): **Overmountain Pr.**

Quarterback Press *See* **Why Not Bks.**

Quarto Publishing Group UK (GBR) *(978-0-7112; 978-1-85410; 978-0-948149; 978-0-906053; 978-0-946544; 978-0-906459; 978-1-84092; 978-1-85076; 978-1-84543; 978-1-84507; 978-1-84538; 978-1-84513; 978-1-84780; 978-1-84835; 978-1-78131; 978-1-78171; 978-1-910277) Dist. by* **HachBkGrp.**

Quarto Publishing Group UK (GBR) *(978-0-7112; 978-1-85410; 978-0-948149; 978-0-906053; 978-0-946544; 978-0-906459; 978-1-84092; 978-1-85076; 978-1-84543; 978-1-84507; 978-1-84538; 978-1-84513; 978-1-84780; 978-1-84835; 978-1-78131; 978-1-78171; 978-1-910277) Dist. by* **PerseuPGW.**

Quarto Publishing Group USA, *(978-0-7603; 978-0-86573; 978-0-89738; 978-0-912612; 978-0-929261; 978-0-9640392; 978-1-56010; 978-1-888608; 978-1-930604; 978-1-58923; 978-1-59186; 978-1-59233; 978-1-59253; 978-1-60058; 978-1-61673; 978-1-936309; 978-1-61058; 978-1-61059; 978-1-61060; 978-1-937994; 978-1-939581; 978-1-62788; 978-1-63106; 978-1-63159; 978-1-63322; 978-1-942875) Orders Addr.: Retail Order Dept., Quayside Publishing Group 18705 Lake Dr. E., Chanhassen, MN 55317 USA Tel 1-952-936-4700; Fax: 1-952-099-9101; Toll Free: 1-800-328-0590; Edit Addr.: 3 Wrigley, Suite A, Irvine, CA 92618-2748 USA (SAN 249-051X) Toll Free: 800-426-0099; Imprints:* Motorbooks (Motorbks); Zenith Press (Zenith Press); Creative Publishing International (Creativ Pub); Quarry Books (QuarryBks); Voyageur Press (VoyageurPr); Walter Foster Jr (WalterFostJr); Fair Winds Press (FairWindsPr); Quarry Books (QuarryBksUSA); Creative Publishing International (CreatPubIntl)
E-mail: rebecca.razo@quartous.com
Web site: http://www.walterfoster.com
Dist(s): **Black Rabbit Bks.**
Hachette Bk. Group
Lerner Publishing Group
MyiLibrary.

Quatemion Pr., *(978-0-9672535)* P.O. Box 700564, San Antonio, TX 78270 USA Tel 210-497-1096.

Quattro, Jacquelyn, *(978-0-615-53477-0)* 23 pleasant view way, Flemington, NJ 08822 USA Tel 908-500-9954
E-mail: jakkifoster@gmail.com
Dist(s): **CreateSpace Independent Publishing Platform**
Dummy Record Do Not USE!!!!.

Que, *(978-0-7897; 978-0-88022; 978-1-56529)* Div. of Pearson Technology Group, 201 W. 103rd St., Indianapolis, IN 46290-1094 USA Tel 317-581-3500; Toll Free: 800-428-5331 (orders); 800-858-7674 (customer service) Do not confuse with Que Software, also a division of Macmillan Computer Publishing, same address
E-mail: customerservice@macmillanUSA.com
Web site: http://www.quepublishing.com
Dist(s): **Alpha Bks.**
Ebsco Publishing
MyiLibrary
Pearson Education
Pearson Technology Group
Sams Technical Publishing, LLC.

Quebla, *(978-0-9772738)* P.O. Box 958073, Duluth, GA 30095 USA Tel 404-906-3993
E-mail: support@quebla.com
Web site: http://www.quebla.com.

Queen Alexandra Foundation for Children (CAN) *(978-0-9880536) Dist. by* **Orca Bk Pub.**

Queen's Knight, (978-0-9752810) 8741 Saline Waterworks Rd., Saline, MI 48176 USA.

Queens Museum of Art, (978-0-9604514; 978-1-929641) New York City Bldg., Flushing Meadows Park, Queens, NY 11368-3398 USA (SAN 280-2147) Tel 718-592-9700; Fax: 718-592-5778
Web site: http://www.queensmuseum.org
Dist(s): **D.A.P./Distributed Art Pubs.**
Univ. Pr. of New England.

Quentin Road Ministries *See* **Victory In Grace Ministries**

Quercus (GBR) (978-1-905204; 978-1-906694; 978-1-84916; 978-0-85705; 978-0-85738; 978-1-84866; 978-1-78087; 978-1-78206; 978-1-78429) *Dist. by* **IPG Chicago.**

Quercus *Imprint of* **Quercus NA**

Quercus NA, (978-1-62365; 978-1-63378; 978-1-68144; 978-1-63506) Orders Addr.: 31 W. 57th St. 6th fl, New York, NY 10019 USA; Edit Addr.: 1290 Avenue of the Americas, Flr. 4, New York, NY 10104 USA; *Imprints:* Quercus (Querc); Jo Fletcher Books (Jo Fletcher Bks)
E-mail: nathmaru@gmail.com; eric.price@quercus.com
Dist(s): **Hachette Bk. Group**
MyiLibrary
Random Hse., Inc.

Quercus Pr., (978-0-9793444) P.O. Box 46163, Plymouth, MN 55446-0163 USA (SAN 853-1773)
Web site: http://www.windingoak.com.

Questmarc Publishing, (978-0-9634251; 978-0-9755801; 978-0-9819946; 978-1-939532) Orders Addr.: P.O. Box 340, Yankton, SD 57078 USA Tel 605-660-0335; Fax: 605-260-6873; Edit Addr.: 811 W. 8th, Yankton, SD 57078 USA Tel 605-660-0335
E-mail: questmarc@mail.com
Web site: http://www.questmarc.com.

Quick Book Publishing *See* **FREOMM Publishing**

Quick Quest Pubns. LLC, (978-0-9760372) Orders Addr.: P.O. Box 9934, Alexandria, VA 22306 USA Toll Free Fax: 800-682-6576; Edit Addr.: P.O. Box 9934, Alexandria, VA 22304 USA Tel 978-726-5713
E-mail: nathanialportis@yahoo.com; mnportis@yahoo.com
Web site: http://www.quickquestpub.com.

Quick Wisdom Publishers *See* **Aylen Publishing**

Quickpresspublishing Incorporated *See* **Quick Quest Pubns. LLC**

Quiet Corner Pr., (978-0-615-46682-8; 978-0-615-48009-1; 978-0-615-55460-0; 978-0-615-55956-8; 978-0-615-61782-4; 978-0-615-64603-9; 978-0-615-76331-6; 978-0-615-79336-8; 978-0-615-85947-7)
Dist(s): **CreateSpace Independent Publishing Platform**
Dummy Record Do Not USE!!!!.

Quiet Impact, Inc., (978-0-9713749; 978-0-9754629) 140 Cherry St., No. 388, Hamilton, MT 59840 USA Tel 406-375-9378; Fax: 406-363-5234; *Imprints:* Character-in-Action (Character-in-Action)
E-mail: elhamilton@quietimpact.com; elhamilton@character-in-action.com
Web site: http://www.character-in-action.com; http://www.quietimpact.com.

Quiet Man, (978-0-9744251) 28 W. 44th St., Suite 2105, New York, NY 10036-6600 USA (SAN 255-7150) Tel 212-921-4444; Fax: 212-921-4504
E-mail: dawn@quietman.net
Web site: http://www.quietman.net.

Quiet Man Publishing, (978-0-9742829) 27542 Berkshire Hills Pl., Valencia, CA 91354 USA
E-mail: jh1429@yahoo.com
Web site: http://www.Quietmanpublishing.com.

Quiet Owl Bks., (978-0-615-54891-3; 978-0-615-59366-1; 978-0-615-64284-0; 978-0-615-64677-0; 978-0-615-65835-3; 978-0-9859443; 978-0-615-67800-9; 978-0-9898331) 85 E. Point Rd., Montrose, PA 18801 USA Tel 323-253-1411; 570-278-6332
E-mail: books@quietowl.com
Web site: http://quietowl.com/
Dist(s): **CreateSpace Independent Publishing Platform**
Dummy Record Do Not USE!!!!.

Quiet Storm Publishing Group, (978-0-9714296; 978-0-9728819; 978-0-9744084; 978-0-9749608; 978-0-9758571; 978-0-9770070; 978-0-9787528) Orders Addr.: P.O. Box 1666, Martinsburg, WV 25401 USA; Edit Addr.: 1045 Needmore Rd., Martinsburg, WV 25401 USA
E-mail: quietstormbooks@yahoo.com
Web site: http://www.quietstormpublishing.com.

Quiet Time Pr. *Imprint of* **TKG Publishing**

Quiet Vision Publishing, (978-1-57646; 978-1-891595; 978-1-60545) Orders Addr.: 12155 Mountain Shadow Rd., Sandy, UT 84092-5812 USA Tel 801-572-4018; Fax: 801-571-8625; Toll Free: 800-442-4018
E-mail: john@quietvision.com; info@quietvision.com
Web site: http://www.quietvision.com.

Quiet Waters Pubns., (978-0-9663966; 978-1-931475) Orders Addr.: P.O. Box 0034, Bolivar, MO 65613-0034 USA Tel 417-326-5001; Fax: 617-249-0256; Edit Addr.: 1228 Northwood Cir., Bolivar, MO 65613 USA
E-mail: qwp@usa.net
Web site: http://www.quietwaterspub.com; http://www.fromthescholarsdesk.com.

Quigley, Karen, (978-0-9800449) P.O. Box 535, Blackwood, NJ 08012 USA (SAN 855-076X)
E-mail: loveelwood@comcast.net
Web site: http://www.EveryoneLovesElwood.com.

Quillpen, (978-0-9673504) 1520 Waverly Dr., Trenton, MI 48183 USA Tel 734-676-1285; Fax: 734-676-9822
E-mail: bfquillpen@msn.com.

Quillrunner Publishing LLC, (978-0-9796330; 978-0-9851157) 8423 Los Reyes Ct., NW, Albuquerque, NM 87120 USA (SAN 853-9669) Tel 505-890-0723
E-mail: khickman@comcast.net
Web site: http://www.quillrunner.com.

Quilt In a Day, (978-0-922705; 978-1-891776) 1955 Diamond St., Unit A, San Marcos, CA 92069 USA (SAN 251-5644) Tel 760-591-0081; Fax: 760-591-4424; Toll Free: 800-777-4852
E-mail: qiad@quilt-in-a-day.com
Web site: http://www.quilt-in-a-day.com
Dist(s): **AtlasBooks Distribution**
MyiLibrary
ebrary, Inc.

Quimby & Sneet Pubns., (978-0-9790832) Orders Addr.: 10026 S. Linn Ave, Oklahoma City, OK 73159 USA (SAN 852-3754)
E-mail: gusabaloobooks@yahoo.com.

Quindim *See* **KINJIN Global**

Quinlan Pr., (978-0-933341; 978-0-9611268; 978-1-55770) 1 Devonshire Pl., No. 3108, Boston, MA 02109-3515 USA (SAN 226-4641).

Quinn Entertainment, (978-0-9773099) 7535 Austin Harbour Dr., Cumming, GA 30041 USA (SAN 257-2575) Tel 770-356-3847; Fax: 770-886-1475
E-mail: stephaniequinn@bellsouth.net
Web site: http://www.startabusinessteachingkids.com.

Quinn Micheal Publishing, Incorporated *See* **Rhapsody Branding, Inc.**

†Quintessence Publishing Co., Inc., (978-0-86715; 978-0-931386; 978-1-85097; 978-1-883695) 4350 Chandler Dr., Hanover Park, IL 60133-6763 USA (SAN 215-9783)
E-mail: service@quintbook.com
Web site: http://www.quintpub.com; *CIP.*

Quintessential Corp., (978-0-9715298) P.O. Box 9224, Mclean, VA 22102 USA Tel 703-734-4900
E-mail: info@qproductsarchery.com
Web site: http://qproductsarchery.com.

Quirk Bks., (978-1-931686; 978-1-59474) 215 Church St., Philadelphia, PA 19106 USA Tel 215-627-3581; Fax: 215-627-5220
E-mail: jane@quirkbooks.com
Web site: http://www.quirkbooks.com
Dist(s): **Hachette Bk. Group**
MyiLibrary
Penguin Random Hse., LLC.
Random Hse., Inc.

Quirkles, The *Imprint of* **Creative 3, LLC**

Quist, Harlin Bks., (978-0-8252) 608 Ninth St., S., Virginia, MN 55792 USA
Dist(s): **Alliance Hse., Inc.**
Perseus-PGW.

†Quite Specific Media Group, Ltd., (978-0-89676) Orders Addr.: 7373 Pyramid Pl., Hollywood, CA 90046-1312 USA (SAN 213-5752) Tel 323-851-5797; Fax: 323-851-5798; *Imprints:* Costume & Fashion Press (Costume & Fashion Pr)
E-mail: info@quitespecificmedia.com
Web site: http://www.quitespecificmedia.com; *CIP.*

Quixote Press *See* **Padwolf Publishing, Inc.**

Quixote Pr., (978-1-57166; 978-1-878488) 1854 345th Ave., Wever, IA 52658-9597 USA Tel 319-372-7480; Fax: 319-372-7485; Toll Free: 800-571-2665 Do not confuse with Quixote Pr., Houston, TX, Los Angeles, CA
E-mail: heartsntummies@hotmail.com
Dist(s): **Bookmen, Inc.**

QuotationWorld Pubns., (978-0-9741868) 3035 Shannon Lakes Dr., N., Tallahassee, FL 32309 USA Tel 850-894-1903 (phone/fax)
E-mail: admin@quotationworld.com
Web site: http://www.quotationworld.com.

Quotidian, Incorporated *See* **Quotidian Pubs.**

Quotidian Pubs., (978-0-934391) Orders Addr.: 377 River Rd., Cushing, ME 04563-9502 USA (SAN 693-8094) Tel 207-354-7091
E-mail: judydownmaine@roadrunner.com.

Quranic Educational Society, (978-0-9760681) Orders Addr.: P.O. Box 597969, Chicago, IL 60659 USA; Edit Addr.: 6355 N Claremont Ave., Chicago, IL 60659 USA Tel 773-743-9345
E-mail: qeschicago@sbcglobal.net
Web site: http://www.qesonline.org.

R & D Educational Ctr., (978-0-9725365; 978-0-9774432) 301 Immigrant TL, Windsor, CO 80550 USA
Web site: http://www.rdeducation.home.att.net.

R & D Publishing of Lakeland, Florida, (978-0-9797566) 5709 LaSerena Ave., Lakeland, FL 33809-4262 USA Tel 863-859-2984.

R & J Publishing, (978-0-615-15136-6) 1136 5th Ave. S., Anoka, MN 55303-2726 USA
E-mail: bobhelf.1@juno.com.

R & R Advertising, (978-0-9765225) 3409 Executive Ctr. Dr., No. 202, Austin, TX 78731 USA Tel 512-342-0110; Fax: 512-342-0142
E-mail: info@rradinc.com
Web site: http://www.rradinc.com.

R & R Publishing, LLC, (978-0-9764845; 978-0-615-34449-2; 978-0-9829599; 978-0-9830577) Div. of GlutenFree Passport, Orders Addr.: 80 Burr Ridge Pkwy. Suite 141, Burr Ridge, IL 60527 USA Tel 312-244-3702; Fax: 312-276-8001 Do not confuse with companies with the same or similar name in Torrance, CA, Brimingham, AL, Shelton, WA, San Antonio, TX, Washington, DC, Baldwin City, KS
E-mail: info@mrpublishing.com; kkoeller@glutenfreepassport.com
Web site: http://www.glutenfreepassport.com.

R & S Bks. (SWE) (978-91-29) *Dist. by* **Macmillan.**

RBC Publishing Co., Inc., (978-0-9703178; 978-0-9721547) Orders Addr.: P.O. Box 1330, Elk Grove, CA 95759 USA Tel 916-685-5578; Fax: 916-685-5958; Edit Addr.: 9107 Voos Ct., Elk Grove, CA 95624 USA; *Imprints:* Parks Publishing (Parks Publ)
E-mail: scituate@citlink.net
Web site: http://www.rbcpublishingco.com.

R.B. Media, Inc., (978-0-9700021; 978-0-9797932) 14064 Monterey Estates Dr., Delray Beach, FL 33446-2217 USA Tel 561-498-5922; Fax: 561-498-2369
E-mail: mabudnik@comcast.net
Web site: http://www.rbmediainc.com.

R. E. Farrellbooks, LLC, (978-0-9759116; 978-0-9963587) 18212 N. 130th Ave, Sun City West, AZ 85382-0983 USA
E-mail: info@refarrellbooks.com
Web site: http://www.refarrellbooks.com.

REP Pubs., (978-0-9604876) Orders Addr.: 733 Turrentine Trail, St. Louis, MO 63141 USA (SAN 239-3786) Tel 314-434-1833
E-mail: Richard@reppublishers.com
Web site: www.reppublishers.com
Dist(s): **Unique Bks., Inc.**

R F T Publishing Company *See* **aha! Process, Inc.**

R.H. Boyd Publishing Corp., (978-1-58942; 978-1-68167) 6717 Centennial Blvd., Nashville, TN 37209-1049 USA Tel 615-350-8000; Fax: 615-350-9018
E-mail: dgroves@rhboyd.com
Web site: http://www.rhboydpublishing.com.

R. H. Publishing, (978-0-9772460) 5021 S. 30th St., Lincoln, NE 68516 USA Tel 214-605-0162
Dist(s): **Lightning Source, Inc.**

R J Communications, LLC, (978-0-9700741; 978-1-59664) 51 E. 42nd St., Suite 1202, New York, NY 10017-5404 USA Tel 212-867-1331; Fax: 212-681-8002; Toll Free: 800-621-2556 (New York)
E-mail: ron@rjcom.com
Web site: http://www.selfpublishing.com; http://www.booksjustbooks.com.

R. N. M., Incorporated *See* **Onion River Pr.**

RSVP Pr., (978-0-930865; 978-1-60209) 619 Gay Rd., Monroe, NC 28112-8214 USA (SAN 657-6346)
E-mail: writernet@aol.com
Web site: http://www.rsvpbooks.com; http://www.members.aol.com/writernet/rsvp.htm.

R T A Pr., (978-1-929768) Div. of Rochester Teachers Assn., 30 N. Union St., Suite 301, Rochester, NY 14607 USA Tel 716-546-2681; Fax: 716-546-4123
E-mail: ddsigns@servtech.com.

RVS Bks., Inc., (978-0-9634257) P.O. Box 683, Lebanon, TN 37088-0683 USA (SAN 298-7325) Tel 615-449-6725; Fax: 615-449-6910.

Rabbit Ears Pr. & Co., (978-0-9748922) Orders Addr.: P.O. Box 1952, Davis, CA 95617 USA Tel 530-220-3289
Web site: http://www.rockythemudhen.com
Dist(s): **Partners Bk. Distributing, Inc.**

Rabbit's Foot Pr. *Imprint of* **Blue Mountain Arts Inc.**

Racemaker Pr., (978-0-9766683; 978-1-935240) 39 Church St., Boston, MA 02116 USA (SAN 256-4513) Tel 617-723-6533.

Rach, W. Dennis, (978-0-9792579) 9965 Portofino Dr., Orlando, FL 32832 USA (SAN 852-9299) Tel 407-625-8528
E-mail: dennis@rachfamily.com.

Racing to Joy Pr. LLC, (978-0-9852488; 978-0-9908807) 6103 Centerwood Dr., Crestwood, KY 40014 USA Tel 502-241-7574
E-mail: lindampenn@gmail.com.

Racom Communications, (978-0-9704515; 978-1-933199) 150 N. Michigan Ave. Ste. 2800, Chicago, IL 60601 USA (SAN 852-7210)
E-mail: rahagle@aol.com
Dist(s): **AtlasBooks Distribution.**

Raconteurs, Inc., (978-0-9621758) 1305 W. Wisconsin Ave., No. 114, Oconomowoc, WI 53066-2646 USA (SAN 252-080X) Tel 414-567-4009.

Rada Press, Inc., (978-0-9604212; 978-1-933011) Orders Addr.: 1277 Fairmount Ave., Saint Paul, MN 55105-2701 USA Fax: 888-288-6401
E-mail: rm@radapress.com
Web site: http://www.radapress.com.

Radiance Pubs., (978-0-918224) Div. of S. K. Publications, Orders Addr.: 1042 Maple Ave., Lisle, IL 60532 USA Tel 630-577-7624
E-mail: 'nlarson@radiancepublishers.com
Web site: http://www.radiancepublishers.com.

Radical Reformation Bks., (978-0-9818973) 34 Cindia Ln, Ephrata, PA 17522 USA (SAN 856-8790) Tel 717-738-9099
E-mail: deantaylorfamily@gmail.com; dean@radicalreformation.net
Web site: http://www.radicalreformation.com.

Raedan Bocs *See* **Lire Bks.**

Rafka Pr. LLC, (978-0-9779628; 978-0-9911958) P.O. Box 8099, Phoenix, AZ 85066 USA
Web site: http://www.rafkapress.com.

Rag Mag *See* **Black Hat Pr.**

Ragan, Jewel, (978-0-9853809) 24206 SE 248th St., Maple Valley, WA 98038 USA Tel 425-413-6032
E-mail: jewelragan@gmail.com.

Ragged Sky Pr., (978-0-9633092; 978-1-933974) 270 Griggs Dr., Princeton, NJ 08540 USA
E-mail: ellen_foos@pupress.princeton.edu
Web site: http://Raggedsky.com.

Raging Bull Publishing, LLC *See* **Command Publishing, LLC**

Rai Publishing, (978-0-9765641) P.O. Box 918, Grover Beach, CA 93483 USA Tel 805-473-9025
E-mail: donrai@ix.netcom.com
Dist(s): **AtlasBooks Distribution.**

Raider Publishing International, (978-0-9772054; 978-0-9790799; 978-1-934360; 978-1-935383; 978-1-61667) 350 5th Ave., 59th Flr., New York, NY 10118 USA Tel 917-267-7912; Toll Free: 800-293-1653
E-mail: johnraider@hotmail.com; jraider@raiderpublishing.com
Web site: http://www.raiderpublishing.com.

Rain Tree Bks., (978-0-9764129) Orders Addr.: P.O. Box 1290, DeQueen, AR 71832 USA; Edit Addr.: 146 Treating Plant Rd., DeQueen, AR 71832 USA Tel 870-582-3565.

Rainbow Bks., Inc., (978-0-935834; 978-1-56825) P.O. Box 430, Highland City, FL 33846-0430 USA (SAN 213-5515) Tel 863-648-4420; Fax: 863-647-5951 Do not confuse with companies with the same or similar name in Middleburg, VT, Amstgerdam, NY, New York, NY, Sparks, NV
E-mail: RBIbooks@aol.com
Web site: http://www.RainbowBooksInc.com
Dist(s): **BCH Fulfillment & Distribution**
Book Clearing Hse.
Smashwords.

Rainbow Bridge Publishing, (978-1-887923; 978-1-932210) Div. of Carson-Dellosa Publishing Co., Inc., Orders Addr.: P.O. Box 571470, Salt Lake City, UT 84157-1470 USA Tel 801-268-8887; Fax: 801-268-2770; Toll Free: 800-598-1441; Edit Addr.: P.O. Box 571470, Salt Lake Cty, UT 84157-1470 USA
E-mail: danell@rbpbooks.com
Web site: http://www.rbpbooks.com
Dist(s): **Carson-Dellosa Publishing, LLC**
Midpoint Trade Bks., Inc.

Rainbow Communications, (978-0-9725479; 978-0-9728737; 978-0-9888554) 471 NW Hemlock Ave, Corvallis, OR 97330 USA Tel 541-753-3335
E-mail: varsell4@comcast.net.

†Rainbow Horizons Publishing, Inc., (978-1-55319) Orders Addr.: P.O. Box 19729, San Diego, CA 92159 USA Toll Free Fax: 800-663-3608; Toll Free: 800-663-3609; *Imprints:* Classroom Complete Press (Classrm Comp)
E-mail: paul@classroomcompletepress.com
Web site: http://www.ccpinteractive.com; http://www.rainbowhorizons.com; http://www.classroomcompletepress.com
Dist(s): **Follett School Solutions**
OverDrive, Inc.
ebrary, Inc.; *CIP.*

Rainbow Morning Music Alternatives, (978-0-938663; 978-0-9615696) 2121 Fairland Rd., Silver Spring, MD 20904 USA (SAN 218-2963) Tel 301-384-9207; Fax: 312-337-5985; Toll Free: 800-881-4741
E-mail: barrylou@ziplink.net
Web site: http://www.barrylou.com
Dist(s): **Independent Pubs. Group**
MyiLibrary.

Rainbow Pony Publishing, (978-0-9728871) 368 S. McCaslin Blvd., PMB No. 226, Louisville, CO 80027 USA.

Rainbow Pony Publising *See* **Rainbow Pony Publishing**

Rainbow Publishers *See* **Rainbow Pubs. & Legacy Pr.**

Rainbow Pubs. & Legacy Pr., (978-0-937282; 978-1-885358; 978-1-58411) Orders Addr.: P.O. Box 261129, San Diego, CA 92196 USA (SAN 256-4718) Tel 858-668-3260; Fax: 858-668-3328; Toll Free Fax: 800-331-0297; Toll Free: 800-323-7337; Edit Addr.: P.O. Box 70130, Richmond, VA 23255-0130 USA; *Imprints:* Legacy Press (Lgacy Pr)
E-mail: rainbowed@earthlink.net; drmiley@juno.com
Web site: http://www.rainbowpublishers.com
Dist(s): **Appalachian Bible Co.**
Spring Arbor Distributors, Inc.

Rainbow Resource Ctr., Inc., (978-1-933407; 978-1-942446) P.O. Box 391, Williamsfield, IL 61489 USA; *Imprints:* In the Think of Things (IntheThink).

Rainbow Star Bks., (978-0-9802363) P.O. Box 422, Centereach, NY 11720 USA (SAN 855-5680)
Web site: http://www.rainbowstarbooks.com.

Rainbow Star, Incorporated *See* **Rainbow Star Bks.**

Rainbow Valley Publishing Co., (978-0-9748558) 2189 Hwy. 90 W., Sulphur, LA 70663 USA Tel 337-528-1157.

Rainbows Within Reach, (978-0-9705987; 978-0-578-03944-2; 978-0-578-06631-8) 5765 Westbourne Ave., Columbus, OH 43213 USA
E-mail: debbie@rainbowswithinreach.com
Web site: http://www.rainbowswithinreach.com
Dist(s): **Follett School Solutions**
TNT Media Group, Inc.

Raincoast Bk. Distribution (CAN) (978-0-920417; 978-1-55192; 978-1-895714; 978-1-894542) *Dist. by* **PerseuPGW.**

Raindrop Bks., (978-0-9766129) 423 Hicks St., No. 6-H, Brooklyn, NY 11201 USA Tel 718-855-2918
E-mail: lgliessner@aol.com.

Raindrop Bks., (978-0-9799677) 10 Sunderland St., Melville, NY 11747 USA
Web site: http://www.learnalongwithlily.com; http://www.raindropbooks.com
Dist(s): **Big Tent Bks.**

Raining Popcorn Media, (978-0-9797304) P.O. Box 91244, San Antonio, TX 78209 USA Tel 210-320-0548; Toll Free: 866-503-3088
E-mail: info@rainingopcorn.com; lisa@rainingpopcorn.com
Web site: http://www.RainingPopcorn.com.

Raintree Atomic *Imprint of* **Heinemann-Raintree**

Raintree Freestyle *Imprint of* **Heinemann-Raintree**

Raintree Freestyle en Espanol *Imprint of* **Heinemann-Raintree**

Raintree Freestyle Express *Imprint of* **Heinemann-Raintree**

Raintree Fusion *Imprint of* **Heinemann-Raintree**

Raintree Perspectives *Imprint of* **Heinemann-Raintree**

Raintree Sprouts *Imprint of* **Heinemann-Raintree**

Raintree Steck-Vaughn Publishers *See* **Steck-Vaughn**

Rainy Day Entertainment, LLC *See* **Apologue Entertainment, LLC**

Rairarubia Bks., (978-0-9712206) 1000 San Diego Rd., Santa Barbara, CA 93103 USA Fax: 805-966-4697
E-mail: raira@silcom.com
Web site: http://www.rairarubia.com.

Raisykinder Publishing, (978-0-615-21798-7; 978-0-615-27779-0; 978-0-9825530; 978-0-9907348) 1713 Golden Ct., Bellingham, WA 98226 USA
E-mail: raisykinderpub@aol.com
Web site: http://www.raisykinderpublishing.com.

Rakha, Marwa *See* **Malamih Publishing Hse.**
Rakowski, Diane, *(978-0-9760194)* 11402 W. Parkhill Dr., Littleton, CO 80127-4716 USA
E-mail: dsjsit@juno.com.
Raku Bks., *(978-0-615-12445-2; 978-0-615-12561-9)* Orders Addr.: P.O. Box 51954, Palo Alto, CA 94303 USA
E-mail: rapimus@yahoo.com.
Raku Publishing, *(978-0-9770662)* 30799 Pinetree Rd., No. 411, Pepper Pike, OH 44124 USA Tel 216-299-0613
Dist(s): **AtlasBooks Distribution**
BookBaby.
Ralston Store Publishing, *(978-0-9822585; 978-1-938322)* P.O. Box 4513, Durango, CO 81302-4513 USA
Web site: http://www.ralstonstorepublishing.com
Dist(s): **Smashwords.**
Ramos, Raymond G., *(978-0-9855114)* 11600 Mendel Dr. Apt. 3, Orlando, FL 32826 USA Tel 407-756-5730
E-mail: congabuena@yahoo.com.
Ramsey Dean, Inc., *(978-0-9893372)* 1555 N. Dearborn Pkwy. No. 14A, Chicago, IL 60610 USA Tel 312-860-2021
E-mail: ramseydeaninc@gmail.com
Web site: www.ridingonabeamoflight.com.
Ranch Gate Bks., *(978-0-9618660)* 2409 Dormarion, Austin, TX 78703 USA (SAN 668-4033) Tel 512-476-2185.
†RAND Corp., The, *(978-0-8330)* Orders Addr.: P.O. Box 2138, Santa Monica, CA 90407-2138 USA (SAN 218-9291) Tel 310-393-0411; Fax: 310-393-4818; Edit Addr.: 1776 Main St., Santa Monica, CA 90407-2138 USA (SAN 665-763X)
E-mail: jwarren@rand.org; correspondence@rand.org; randell@rand.org
Web site: http://www.rand.org
Dist(s): **CreateSpace Independent Publishing Platform**
Ebsco Publishing
MyiLibrary
National Bk. Network
ebrary, Inc.; *CIP.*
†Rand McNally, *(978-0-528)* Orders Addr.: 9855 Woods Dr., Skokie, IL 60077-1074 USA Toll Free Fax: 800-934-3479 (Orders); Toll Free: 800-333-0136 (ext. 4771); 800-678-7263 (Orders)
E-mail: Education@randmcnally.com
Web site: http://www.randmcnally.com
Dist(s): **Benchmark LLC**
Bryant Altman Map, Inc.; *CIP.*
Rand Media Co, *(978-0-9818935; 978-0-9824390; 978-0-9841393; 978-0-9844418; 978-0-692-01528-5; 978-0-9852818)* Orders Addr.: 265 Post Rd. W., Westport, CT 06880 USA (SAN 925-4919) Tel 203-226-8727; Fax: 203-221-7677; *Imprints:* Skinny On (tm), The (Skinny on)
E-mail: dhardy@randmediaco.com; daveaweiner7@aol.com; awuqi@randmediaco.com
Web site: http://www.theskinnyon.com; http://randmediaco.com/money/money-book-1/; http://randmediaco.com/
Dist(s): **Lulu Enterprises Inc.**
RAND Publishing *See* **Rand Media Co**
Randall, Charles Inc., *(978-0-9624736; 978-1-890379)* Orders Addr.: 30 Amberwood Pkwy., Ashland, OH 44805 USA Fax: 419-281-6883; Toll Free: 800-247-6553; Edit Addr.: P.O. Box 1656, Orange, CA 92856 USA (SAN 253-7737)
E-mail: peter@randallonline.com
Web site: http://www.randallonline.com; http://www.charlesrandall.com
Dist(s): **AtlasBooks Distribution**
BookMasters Distribution Services (BDS)
BookMasters, Inc.
Follett School Solutions
MyiLibrary
ebrary, Inc.
Randall, Cheri, *(978-0-9767213)* P.O. Box 2176, Belton, TX 76513 USA Tel 254-939-8776 (phone/fax)
E-mail: hrandallmail@aol.com
Web site: http://www.harveyrandall.org.
Randall Fraser Publishing *See* **RandallFraser Publishing**
Randall Hse. Pubns., *(978-0-89265; 978-1-61484)* 114 Bush Rd., Nashville, TN 37217 USA (SAN 207-5040) Tel 615-361-1221; Fax: 615-367-0535; Toll Free: 800-877-7030
E-mail: michelle.orr@randallhouse.com
Web site: http://www.randallhouse.com.
Randall International *See* **Randall, Charles Inc.**
†Randall, Peter E. Pub., *(978-0-914339; 978-1-931807; 978-0-9817898; 978-0-9828236; 978-1-937721; 978-0-692-22144-0; 978-1-942155; 978-0-692-51521-1)* 5 Greenleaf Woods Dr., Unit 102, Portsmouth, NH 03801 USA (SAN 223-0496) Tel 603-431-5667; Fax: 603-431-3566
E-mail: deidre@perpublisher.com; media@perpublisher.com
Web site: http://www.perpublisher.com
Dist(s): **Bondcliff Bks.**
BookBaby
Enfield Publishing & Distribution Co., Inc.
MyiLibrary
National Bk. Network
Univ. Pr. of New England; *CIP.*
RandallFraser Publishing, *(978-0-9745143)* 2082 Business Ctr. Dr., Suite 163, Irvine, CA 92612 USA Fax: 949-250-9020; Toll Free: 866-339-3999
E-mail: algreen51@comcast.net
Web site: http://www.Deweydoolt.com
Dist(s): **National Bk. Network.**
R&B Trading Co., *(978-0-9718784)* 7619 Belmont Stakes Dr., Midlothian, VA 23112 USA (SAN 254-4741) Tel 804-739-8073; Fax: 775-243-6578
E-mail: dwindsofdestiny@aol.com
Web site: http://www.RnBtradingco.net/home.html.
Randle, Ian Pubs., Inc., *(978-0-9729358; 978-0-9742155; 978-0-9753529)* 25 SE Second Ave., Suite 1105, Miami, FL 33131 USA Tel 305-358-1588; Fax: 305-358-1589
E-mail: info@ianrandlepublishers.com
Web site: http://www.ianrandlepublishers.com.
R&N Productions, *(978-0-615-14376-7)* 698 Talbert Ave., Simi Valley, CA 93065 USA
E-mail: norm@kuvina.com
Web site: http://www.troublestreet.com
Dist(s): **Lulu Enterprises Inc.**
Randolph Publishing, *(978-1-932258)* 4125 Braswell Church Rd., Good Hope, GA 30641-160 USA Do not confuse with companies with the same or similar names in Dunnellon, FL, Dallas, TX, Indianapolis, IN, Princeton, TX
E-mail: randolphpublishing@EarthLink.net
Web site: http://www.RandolphPublishing.com.
Random House Adult Trade Publishing Group *See* **Random House Publishing Group**
Random Hse. Audio Publishing Group, Div. of Random House, Inc., Orders Addr.: 400 Hahn Rd., Westminster, MD 21157 USA (SAN 201-3975) Tel 410-848-1900; Toll Free: 800-726-0600; Edit Addr.: 1745 Broadway, New York, NY 10036 USA Tel 212-782-9000; *Imprints:* Listening Library (Listening Lib)
Web site: http://www.randomhouse.com/audio
Dist(s): **Ebsco Publishing**
Follett School Solutions
Penguin Random Hse., LLC.
Random Hse., Inc.
Random House Children's Books (GBR) *Dist. by* **IPG Chicago.**
Random House Children's Books (GBR) *Dist. by* **Trafalgar.**
Random House Children's Books (GBR) *Dist. by* **Perfect Learn.**
Random Hse. Children's Bks., Div. of Random Hse., Inc., Orders Addr.: 400 Hahn Rd., Westminster, MD 21157 USA Tel 410-848-1900; Toll Free: 800-726-0600; Edit Addr.: 1745 Broadway, 10th Flr., New York, NY 10019 USA Tel 212-782-8491; 212-782-9000; Fax: 212-782-9577; Toll Free: 800-200-3552; *Imprints:* Delacorte Books for Young Readers (Delacorte Bks); Yearling (Yearling); Lamb, Wendy (Wendy Lamb); Random House Para Ninos (ParaNinos); Crown Books For Young Readers (CBYR); Dell Books for Young Readers (DBYR); Knopf Books for Young Readers (Knop); RH/Disney (RH Disney); Golden Books (Gold Bks); Random House Books for Young Readers (RHBYR); Bantam Books for Young Readers (BBYngRead); Doubleday Books for Young Readers (Doubleday Bk Yng); Yearling (Year); Dragonfly Books (Dragonfly Bks); Laurel Leaf (LaurelLeaf); Skylark (SkylarkRH); Schwartz & Wade Books (Schwartz & Wade); Golden/Disney (Gold Disney); Robin Corey Books (Robin Corey); Golden Inspirational (Gold Inspir); Delacorte Press (DelacorRHP); Ember (Ember)
E-mail: pmuller@randomhouse.com; kids@random.com
Web site: http://www.randomhouse.com/kids/
Dist(s): **Follett School Solutions**
Libros Sin Fronteras
MyiLibrary
Penguin Random Hse., LLC.
Perseus Bks. Group
Random Hse., Inc.
†Random Hse., Inc., *(978-0-307; 978-0-345; 978-0-375; 978-0-385; 978-0-394; 978-0-440; 978-0-449; 978-0-517; 978-0-553; 978-0-593; 978-0-609; 978-0-676; 978-0-679; 978-0-7364; 978-0-7366; 978-0-7615; 978-0-7679; 978-0-7704; 978-0-8041; 978-0-8052; 978-0-8129; 978-0-8230; 978-0-87637; 978-0-87665; 978-0-87788; 978-0-88070; 978-0-913369; 978-0-914629; 978-0-930014; 978-0-945564; 978-1-57082; 978-1-57673; 978-1-57856; 978-1-878867; 978-1-884536; 978-1-885305; 978-1-58836; 978-1-4000; 978-1-59052; 978-1-4159; 978-) Div. of Penguin Random House LLC, Orders Addr.: 400 Hahn Rd., Westminster, MD 21157 USA (SAN 202-5515) Tel 410 848 1900; Toll Free Fax: 800 659 2436; Toll Free: 800 726 0600 (customer service/orders); Edit Addr.: 1745 Broadway, New York, NY 10019 USA (SAN 202-5507) Tel 212 782 9000; Fax: 212 302 7985; Imprints:* Golden Books (Golden Books)
E-mail: customerservice@randomhouse.com
Web site: http://www.randomhouse.com
Dist(s): **Ebsco Publishing**
Follett School Solutions
Giron Bks.
Libros Sin Fronteras
MyiLibrary
Penguin Random Hse., LLC.
Perfection Learning Corp.; *CIP.*
Random Hse. Information Group, Div. of Random Hse., Inc., Orders Addr.: 400 Hahn Rd., Westminster, MD 21157 USA Tel 410-848-1900; Toll Free: 800-726-0600; Edit Addr.: 1745 Broadway, New York, NY 10019 USA Tel 212-751-2600; Toll Free: 800-726-0600; *Imprints:* Random House Puzzles & Games (RHPG); Prima Games (PrimGames); Living Language (LivingLang); Princeton Review (Prince Review); Sylvan Learning Publishing (Sylvan Random)
E-mail: customerservice@randomhouse.com
Web site: http://www.randomhouse.com/
Dist(s): **Bilingual Pubns. Co., The**
Ediciones Universal
Libros Sin Fronteras
MyiLibrary
Penguin Random Hse., LLC.
Random Hse., Inc.
Simon & Schuster, Inc.
Random Hse. Large Print, Div. of Random House, Inc., Orders Addr.: 400 Hahn Rd., Westminster, MD 21157 USA Tel 410-848-1900 Toll Free: 800-726-0600 (customer service); Edit Addr.: 1745 Broadway, New York, NY 10019 USA Tel 212-782-9000
E-mail: editor@randomhouse.com; customerservice@randomhouse.com
Web site: http://www.randomhouse.com
Dist(s): **Libros Sin Fronteras**
MyiLibrary
Penguin Random Hse., LLC.
Random Hse., Inc.
Thorndike Pr.
Random House Para Ninos *Imprint of* **Random Hse. Children's Bks.**
Random House Publishing Group, Orders Addr.: 400 Hahn Rd., Westminster, MD 21157 USA (SAN 852-5579) Tel 410-848-1900; 410-386-7560; Toll Free: 800-726-0600; Edit Addr.: 1745 Broadway, New York, NY 10019 USA Tel 212-751-2600; Fax: 212-572-4949; Toll Free: 800-726-0600; *Imprints:* Delacorte Books for Young Readers (Delacorte Bks); Random House Trade Paperbacks (RH Trade Bks); Modern Library (Mod Lib); Villard Books (Villard Books); Del Rey (Del Rey); Ballantine Books (Ballantine Bks); Bantam (Bant); Delacorte Press (DelacorRHP); Laurel (LaureRH); Ember (Ember)
E-mail: lstark@randomhouse.com
Dist(s): **Follett School Solutions**
Libros Sin Fronteras
MyiLibrary
Penguin Random Hse., LLC.
Perfection Learning Corp.
Random Hse., Inc.
Random House Reference & Information Publishing *See* **Random Hse. Information Group**
†Random Hse. Value Publishing, Div. of Random House, Inc., Orders Addr.: 400 Hahn Rd., Westminster, MD 21157 USA Tel 410-848-1900 Toll Free: 800-726-0600 (Customer Service); Edit Addr.: 280 Park Ave., 11th Flr., New York, NY 10017 USA Tel 212 572 2400
Web site: http://www.randomhouse.com
Dist(s): **Penguin Random Hse., LLC.**
Random Hse., Inc.; *CIP.*
Random Hse. (GBR) *(978-0-09; 978-0-224; 978-0-7126; 978-1-86046; 978-1-870516; 978-0-85265; 978-1-84657; 978-1-84655; 978-1-84853; 978-1-4881)* *Dist. by* **IPG Chicago.**
Random Hse. (GBR) *(978-0-09; 978-0-224; 978-0-7126; 978-1-86046; 978-1-870516; 978-0-85265; 978-1-84657; 978-1-84655; 978-1-84853; 978-1-4881)* *Dist. by* **Trafalgar.**
Random Hse. Australia (AUS) *(978-1-86359; 978-0-86824; 978-0-947189; 978-1-86325; 978-0-7338; 978-1-74051; 978-0-900882; 978-1-74166; 978-1-86471; 978-1-4230; 978-1-74274; 978-1-74275; 978-0-646-08769-6; 978-0-646-19362-5; 978-0-646-23850-0; 978-0-646-29047-8; 978-0-646-31636-9; 978-0-646-32934-5; 978-0-85798; 978-1-925324)* *Dist. by* **IPG Chicago.**
Random Hse. Bks. for Young Readers *Imprint of* **Random Hse. Children's Bks.**
Random Hse. of Canada (CAN) *(978-0-09; 978-0-307; 978-0-375; 978-0-394; 978-0-676; 978-0-679; 978-0-7704; 978-1-4000)* *Dist. by* **Random.**
Random Hse. Puzzles & Games *Imprint of* **Random Hse. Information Group**
Random Hse. Trade Paperbacks *Imprint of* **Random House Publishing Group**
R&R Endeavors, Inc., *(978-0-9740444)* Orders Addr.: P.O. Box 301, Indianapolis, IN 46217 USA; Edit Addr.: 1350C W. Southport Rd., Indianapolis, IN 46217 USA
E-mail: editor@writerpublishing.com
Web site: http://www.writerpublishing.com.
Rang Jung Yshe Pubns. (HKG) *(978-962-7341)* *Dist. by* **PerseuPGW.**
RAPC - Sparkle & Shine Project, *(978-0-9760282)* 116 Jackson St., Sylva, NC 28779 USA Tel 828-586-0661; Fax: 828-586-0663
Web site: http://www.sparkle-shine.com.
RAPHA, Inc., *(978-0-9740081)* Orders Addr.: P.O. Box 1184, Groton, CT 06340 USA Tel 860-938-2599; Edit Addr.: 45 South Rd., Apt. 9A, Groton, CT 06340 USA Tel 860-514-7266
E-mail: joyindamornin@earthlink.net.
Rapha Publishing, *(978-0-9763686)* 431 Beechwood Ave., Carnegie, PA 15106 USA Tel 412-249-0669
E-mail: raphapublishing@yahoo.com
Web site: http://www.raphapublishing.com/.
Raphel Marketing, Inc., *(978-0-9624808; 978-0-9711542; 978-0-9826644; 978-1-938406)* Orders Addr.: 211 North Ave., St Johnsbury, VT 05819-1626 USA Tel 802-751-8802; *Imprints:* Compass (CompassUSA)
E-mail: neil@raphel.com
Web site: http://www.raphel.com; http://www.brigantinemedia.com; http://compasspublishing.org.
Rapids Christian Pr., Inc., *(978-0-915374)* P.O. Box 717, Ferndale, WA 98248-0717 USA (SAN 205-0986) Tel 360-384-1747
E-mail: gundersonwv@aol.com.
R.A.R.E. TALES, *(978-0-9760303)* 14120 River Rd., Fort Myers, FL 33905-7436 USA
E-mail: kphchance@comcast.net
Web site: http://www.raretales.net.
Rarecity Pr., *(978-0-9760959)* 17 Yardley Dr., Medford, NJ 08055 USA Tel 201-788-9746
E-mail: jason@rarecity.com.
Rasa Music Co., *(978-0-9766219)* 409 Glenview Rd., Glenview, IL 60025-3262 USA Tel 847-486-0416; Fax: 847-657-9459
E-mail: lleifer@northpark.edu
Web site: http://www.admin.northpark.edu/lleifer/.
Rascal Treehouse Publishing, *(978-0-9759321)* 1523 Morris St. - Suite 330, Lincoln Park, MI 48146 USA
E-mail: lscoffman@lscoffman.com
Web site: http://www.lscoffman.com.
Raspberry Bks., *(978-0-9848749)* 4346 Mammoth Ave. No. 4, Sherman Oaks, CA 91423 USA Tel 818-633-9190
E-mail: tammy@tammylaframboise.com.
Ratatat Graphics LLC *See* **Studio Moonfall**
Ratna, Sagar Pvt. Ltd. (IND) *(978-81-7070; 978-81-8332)* *Dist. by* **Midpt Trade.**
Rattle OK Pubns., *(978-0-9626210; 978-1-883965)* Orders Addr.: P.O. Box 5614, Napa, CA 94581 USA (SAN 297-5475) Tel 707-253-9641; Edit Addr.: 296 Homewood Ave., Napa, CA 94558-5617 USA
Dist(s): **Gryphon Hse., Inc.**
Ratway, Michael, *(978-0-9724698)* 216 Midshipman Cir., Stafford, VA 22554-2421 USA
E-mail: yawtar@earthlink.net
Web site: http://www.earthlink.net/~yawtar.
Raven Bks. *Imprint of* **Literations**
Raven Bks. *Imprint of* **Raven Productions**
Raven Mad Studios, *(978-0-9896269)* 16327 197th Ave. NE, Woodinville, WA 98077 USA Tel 206-310-7246
E-mail: randybriley@comcast.net.
Raven Productions, *(978-0-9764091)* 325 E. 2550 N, Suite 117, North Ogden, UT 84414 USA Tel 801-782-0872; *Imprints:* Raven Books (RavenBks) Do not confuse with companies with the same or similar name in Delta Junction, AKEly, MN
E-mail: gshaw@post.harvard.edu
Dist(s): **MyiLibrary.**
Raven Productions, Inc., *(978-0-9677057; 978-0-9766264; 978-0-9794202; 978-0-9801045; 978-0-9819307; 978-0-9835189; 978-0-9883508; 978-0-9914157)* P.O. Box 188, Ely, MN 55731 USA Fax: 218-343-3423 Do not confuse with companies with the same or similar name in Delta Junction, AK, North Ogden, UT
E-mail: raven@ravenwords.com
Dist(s): **Adventure Pubns., Inc.**
MyiLibrary.
Raven Publishing *See* **Raven Publishing Inc. of Montana**
Raven Publishing Inc. of Montana, *(978-0-9714161; 978-0-9772525; 978-0-9820893; 978-0-9827377; 978-1-937849)* P.O. Box 2866, Norris, MT 59745 USA (SAN 254-5861) Tel 406-685-3545; Fax: 406-685-3599; Toll Free: 866-685-3545 Do not confuse with companies with the same or similar name in Bronx, NY, Pittsfield, MA
E-mail: janet@ravenpublishng.net
Web site: http://www.ravenpublishing.net
Dist(s): **Bks. West**
Distributors, The
Follett School Solutions
Partners/West Book Distributors
Quality Bks., Inc.
Smashwords
Wolverine Distributing, Inc.
Western International, Inc.
Raven Rocks Pr., *(978-0-9615961)* 53650 Belmont Ridge, Beallsville, OH 43716 USA (SAN 696-5679) Tel 740-926-1481 (phone/fax)
E-mail: jmrpress@1st.net.
Raven Tree Pr. *Imprint of* **Delta Systems Company, Inc.**
Raven Tree Pr. *Imprint of* **Continental Sales, Inc.**
Raven Tree Pr.,Csi *Imprint of* **Continental Sales, Inc.**
Ravenhawk Bks., *(978-1-893660)* Div. of The 6DOF Group, 7739 E. Broadway Blvd. Suite 95, Tucson, AZ 85710 USA Tel 520-886-9885 (phone/fax); Toll Free: 800-520-9885
E-mail: 76673.3165@compuserve.com
Web site: http://www.ravenhawk.org.
RavenMark, *(978-0-9713998; 978-0-615-55902-5)* 27 E. State St., Montpelier, VT 05602-3011 USA Tel 802-223-5507
E-mail: rebecca@ravenmark.com
Dist(s): **R. C. Brayshaw.**
Ravensburger Buchverlag Otto Maier GmbH (DEU) *(978-3-473)* *Dist. by* **Distribks Inc.**
Ravenstone Pr., *(978-0-9659712)* Orders Addr.: Ravenstone Press 2056 Berry Roberts Dr., Sun City Center, FL 33573-6130 USA Tel 813-633-5759; Fax: 813-633-5759; Edit Addr.: 2056 Berry Roberts Dr., Sun City Ctr, FL 33573-6130 USA
E-mail: raven@ravenstonepress.com
Web site: http://www.ravenstonepress.com.
Ravenwood Publishing, *(978-0-9899275)* 133 Rob Rd., Brooklin, ME 04616 USA Tel 207-359-2451
E-mail: ruthjohnhowell@gmail.com.
Ravenwood Studios, *(978-0-9718604; 978-1-933420)* P.O. Box 197, Diamond Springs, CA 95619 USA
E-mail: ravenwoodstudios@me.com; maureenedgecomb@me.com; todd.ryan@comcast.net
Web site: http://www.maureenedgecomb.com; http://www.ravenwoodstudios.net; http://www.marcyinmanhattan.com.
Ravette Publishing, Ltd. (GBR) *(978-0-948456; 978-1-85304; 978-0-906710; 978-1-84161)* *Dist. by* **Parkwest Pubns.**
Raw Junior, LLC *See* **TOON Books / RAW Junior, LLC**
Ray Greer, Mary Lou, *(978-0-9749161)* P.O. Box 1740, Eagar, AZ 85925 USA Tel 520-850-6209.
Raynestorm Bks. *Imprint of* **Silver Rose Publishing**
Rayo *Imprint of* **HarperCollins Pubs.**
Rayve Productions, Inc., *(978-1-877810)* Orders Addr.: P.O. Box 726, Windsor, CA 95492 USA (SAN 248-4250) Tel 707-838-6200; Fax: 707-838-2220; Toll Free: 800-852-4890
E-mail: rayvepro@aol.com
Web site: http://www.rayveproductions.com; http://www.rayvepro.com
Dist(s): **Brodart Co.**
Follett School Solutions
Quality Bks., Inc.
Unique Bks., Inc.
Razorbill *Imprint of* **Penguin Publishing Group**
RBA Libros, S.A. (ESP) *(978-84-89662; 978-84-7871; 978-84-7901; 978-84-85351; 978-84-9867; 978-84-9006)* *Dist. by* **Lectorum Pubns.**

RBA Libros, S.A. (ESP) *(978-84-89662; 978-84-7871; 978-84-7901; 978-84-85351; 978-84-9867; 978-84-9006) Dist. by* **Santillana.**

RCL Benziger Publishing, *(978-0-89505; 978-0-913592; 978-1-55924)* Orders Addr.: 8805 governor's hill suite 400, cincinnati, OH 45249 USA (SAN 299-0628) Toll Free Fax: 800-688-8356; Toll Free: 877-275-4725
E-mail: cservice@rclbenziger.com
Web site: http://www.rclweb.com/html
Dist(s): **Spring Arbor Distributors, Inc.**

RDM Publishing, *(978-0-9766038)* 605 CR 1040E, Norris City, IL 62869 USA Tel 618-265-3225
E-mail: earthart@midwest.net.

RDR Bks., *(978-0-9636161; 978-1-57143)* 1487 Glen Ave., Muskegon, MI 49441-3101 USA; 960 S. Sherman, Muskegon, MI 49441
E-mail: books@rdrbooks.com
Web site: http://www.rdrbooks.com
Dist(s): **Alpen Bks**
American West Bks.
Book Wholesalers, Inc.
Bookazine Co., Inc.
Brodart Co.
Follett School Solutions
New Leaf Distributing Co., Inc.
Quality Bks., Inc.
Sunbelt Pubns., Inc.
Unique Bks., Inc.
Yankee Bk. Peddler, Inc.

Reaching Beyond, Inc., *(978-0-9741893)* Orders Addr.: P.O. Box 12364, Columbus, GA 31917-2364 USA Tel 706-573-5942; Fax: 706-221-5210; Edit Addr.: P.O. Box 12364, Columbus, GA 31917-2364 USA
E-mail: nccjohnson@hotmail.com
Web site: http://www.reachingbeyond.net
Dist(s): **Book Clearing Hse.**

Reachment Publications *See* **Southeast Media**

Read 2 Children, *(978-0-9755839)* P.O. Box 4113, Warren, NJ 07059 USA Tel 732-805-9073
Web site: http://www.read2children.com.

Read All Over Publishing, *(978-0-9728779)* 17705 Ingleside Rd., Cleveland, OH 44119 USA Tel 216-486-8615 ext. 3
E-mail: readallover@sbcglobal.net.

Read Me! *Imprint of* **Heinemann-Raintree**

Read Publishing, *(978-0-9762868)* Orders Addr.: 3918 Dorcas Dr., Nashville, TN 37215 USA Tel 615-279-9988; Fax: 615-385-2651
E-mail: snea5001@bellsouth.net; jennie0120@aol.com.

Read Street Publishing, Inc., *(978-0-942929)* 133 W. Read St., Baltimore, MD 21201 USA (SAN 667-8505) Tel 410-837-1116; Fax: 410-727-3174; *Imprints:* Omni Arts Publishing (Omni Arts Pubng)
E-mail: editor@omnititles.com; editor@tablespr.com; editor@readstreetpublishing.com
Web site: http://www.omnititles.com; http://www.tablespr.com; http://www.readstreetpublishing.com.

Read Together Bks., *(978-0-9822615)* 8045 230th St, Bellerose Manor, NY 11427-2105 USA Tel 917-757-5868
E-mail: mike@readtogetherbooks.com
Web site: http://www.readtogetherbooks.com
Dist(s): **AtlasBooks Distribution.**

Read Us For Fun Publishing, *(978-0-9820363)* P.O. Box 623, Dover, MA 02030 USA Tel 508-523-9414
E-mail: mking426@msn.com
Web site: http://readusforfun.com.

Read Well Publishing Inc., *(978-0-9630539; 978-0-9703400; 978-1-933873)* Div. of Apodixis, Inc., Orders Addr.: P.O. Box 671053, Dallas, TX 75367 USA Tel 972-241-1366; Fax: 972-241-5345 (call first); Toll Free: 800-522-3341; Edit Addr.: 3975 High Summit Dr., Dallas, TX 75244 USA
E-mail: jillsmithusa@att.net
Web site: http://www.learning-apodixis.com.

ReadaClassic.com, *(978-1-61104)* Orders Addr.: P.O. Box 7, Cedar Lake, MI 48812 USA Tel 989-427-2790; Edit Addr.: 4769 Feather Trail, Cedar Lake, MI 48812 USA Tel 989-427-2790
E-mail: carijhaus@gmail.com
Web site: http://www.readaclassic.com; http://www.clearwords.org.

Reader Publishing Group, *(978-0-9837873)* 1900 E. Ocean Blvd. No. 1001, Long Beach, CA 90802 USA Tel 562-900-0953
E-mail: cunham@aol.com.

Readers Are Leaders, *(978-0-9673625)* 908 Ashland Dr., Mesquite, TX 75149 USA Tel 972-288-5806 (phone/fax)
E-mail: rlgant@airmail.net.

Readers Are Leaders U.S.A., Inc., *(978-0-9768035; 978-0-9800397)* 2315 SW 5th Ave., Miami, FL 33129-1939 USA (SAN 855-0557)
Web site: http://www.readersareleadersusa.net.

†**Reader's Digest Assn., Inc., The,** *(978-0-7621; 978-0-89577; 978-0-86438; 978-1-60652)* One Bedford Rd., Pleasantville, NY 10570 USA (SAN 282-2091) Toll Free: 800-463-8820; 800-334-9599; 800-635-5006
Web site: http://www.readersdigest.com; http://www.rd.com
Dist(s): **Leonard, Hal Corp.**
Penguin Publishing Group
Simon & Schuster, Inc.
Tuttle Publishing; *CIP.*

Reader's Digest Children's Bks. *Imprint of* **Studio Fun International**

Reader's Digest Children's Publishing, Incorporated *See* **Studio Fun International**

Reader's Digest Young Families, Inc. *Imprint of* **Studio Fun International**

READERS to EATERS, *(978-0-9836615)* 12437 SE 26th Pl., Bellevue, WA 98005 USA Tel 206-849-1962
E-mail: philip@readerstoeaters.com
Web site: www.ReadersToEaters.com
Dist(s): **Perseus-PGW.**

Reading Co., The *Imprint of* **Rhoades & Assocs.**

Reading Power *Imprint of* **Rosen Publishing Group, Inc., The**

Reading Reading Bks., LLC, *(978-1-933727; 978-1-60892)* P.O. Box 6654, Reading, PA 19610 USA
E-mail: service@readingreadingbooks.com; orangetabbycat2000@yahoo.com
Web site: http://www.readingreadingbooks.com.

Reading Resc., *(978-0-9755561; 978-0-9795648)* 314 Knowles Hill Rd., Alexandria, NH 03222 USA (SAN 853-7771) Tel 603-744-5803 Do not confuse with Reading Resources, Inc. in Worthington, OH
E-mail: laberge001@gmail.com; readingresources@metrocast.net.

Reading Rock Books *See* **Reading Rock, Inc.**

Reading Rock, Inc., *(978-1-929591)* P.O. Box 67, Athens, MI 49011 USA Tel 616-729-9440
Web site: http://www.Readingrockbook.com.

Reading Room Collection *Imprint of* **Rosen Publishing Group, Inc., The**

Reading Studio Pr., *(978-0-9767506)* 250 W. 90th St., Suite 12F, New York, NY 10024 USA Tel 212-724-6232
E-mail: readingstudio@aol.com
Web site: http://www.alphieandthealphabets.com.

Reading's Fun/Books are Fun, Limited *See* **Bks. Are Fun, Ltd.**

Ready Blade *Imprint of* **Blooming Tree Pr.**

Ready Writer Publishing, LLC, *(978-0-9748748)* P.O. Box 18197, Shreveport, LA 71138 USA Tel 318-470-0538
E-mail: readywriterpublishing@hotmail.com; satbeau1@bellsouth.net.

ReadZone Bks. (GBR) *(978-1-78322) Dist. by* **IPG Chicago.**

Reagent Pr. Bks. for Young Readers *Imprint of* **RP Media**

Reagent Pr. Echo *Imprint of* **RP Media**

Reagent Pr. Signature Editions *Imprint of* **RP Media**

Reagent Press *See* **RP Media**

Reaktion Bks., Ltd. (GBR) *(978-0-948462; 978-1-86189; 978-1-78023) Dist. by* **Chicago Distribution Ctr.**

R.E.A.L. Pubns., *(978-0-9724503; 978-0-9748003)* 109 La Costa Dr., Georgetown, KY 40324 USA (SAN 255-867X) Tel 859-539-2463
E-mail: austinandbelinda@gmail.com
Web site: http://www.arealeducation.com.

R.E.A.L. Publishing *See* **R.E.A.L. Pubns.**

Real Reads Ltd. (GBR) *(978-1-906230) Dist. by* **Casemate Pubs.**

Real World Productions, *(978-1-60855; 978-1-60856)* 131 Ave. B, No. 1B, New York, NY 10009 USA.

Realistically Speaking Publishing Co., *(978-0-9727874)* Orders Addr.: P.O. Box 3566, Cerritos, CA 90703-3566 USA; P.O. Box 3566, cerrito, CA 90703; Edit Addr.: P.O. Box 3566, Cerritos, CA 90703 USA; P.O. Box 3566, cerritos, CA 90703
E-mail: sherea@vejauan.com
Web site: http://www.vejauan.com.

Reality Living Publishing, Inc., *(978-0-9643021; 978-1-888220)* 8720 E. 55th St., Kansas City, MO 64129 USA Tel 816-358-1515 ext 2062; Fax: 816-358-3439 ext 2062
E-mail: sehle@kcbt.org
Web site: http://www.realityliving.org.

RealityIs Bks. *Imprint of* **RealityIsBooks.com, Inc.**

RealityIsBooks.com, Inc., *(978-0-9791317; 978-0-9817137; 978-0-9843883; 978-0-9847390)* 1327 Winslow Dr., Unit 304, Palatine, IL 60074 USA Tel 847-305-4657; Toll Free: 866-534-3366; *Imprints:* RealityIs Books (RealityIs Bks); Green Lady Press, The (GreenLady)
E-mail: publish@realityisbooks.com
Web site: http://www.realityisbooks.com.

Really Big Coloring Bks., Inc., *(978-0-9727833; 978-0-9729753; 978-0-9763186; 978-1-935266; 978-1-61953)* 224 N. Meramec, Saint Louis, MO 63105 USA Tel 314-725-1452; Fax: 314-725-3553; Toll Free: 800-244-2665 (1-800-Big-Book)
E-mail: wayne@bigcoloringbooks.com; ken@bigcoloringbooks.com; derek@bigcoloringbooks.com
Web site: http://www.bigcoloringbook.com; http://www.spanishcoloringbooks.com; http://www.wholesalecoloringbooks.com; http://www.coloringbook.com; http://www.coloringbookpublishers.com
Dist(s): **MeadWestvaco.**

Realms *Imprint of* **Charisma Media**

RealWord Pubns., *(978-0-9743088)* Orders Addr.: P.O. Box 931461, Norcross, GA 30093-1461 USA Fax: 678-406-9178; Edit Addr.: 6450 Indian Acres Trail, Norcross, GA 30093 USA
E-mail: wrcomm@comcast.net
Web site: http://www.climbeveryobstacle.com.

Reasor, Teresa J., *(978-0-615-50243-4; 978-0-9850069; 978-0-9886627; 978-1-940047)* P.O. Box 124, Corbin, KY 40702 USA Tel 606-528-0819
Web site: http://www.teresareasor.com
Dist(s): **CreateSpace Independent Publishing Platform**
Smashwords.

Rebecca Hse., *(978-0-945522)* 1550 California St., Suite 330, San Francisco, CA 94109 USA (SAN 247-1361) Tel 415-752-1453; Toll Free: 800-321-1912 (orders only)
E-mail: Rebeccahse@aol.com
Dist(s): **New Leaf Distributing Co., Inc.**

Rebecca's Bks., *(978-0-9744346)* P.O. Box 644, Watertown, WI 53094 USA.

Rebel Press *See* **Little Dixie Publishing Co.**

Rebellion (GBR) *(978-1-904265; 978-1-906735; 978-1-907519; 978-1-84997; 978-1-907992) Dist. by* **S and S Inc.**

Rebuilding Bks. *Imprint of* **Impact Pubs., Inc.**

Recipe for Success Foundation, *(978-0-692-01183-6; 978-0-9846525)* P.O. Box 56405, Houston, TX 77256 USA Tel 713-520-0443; Fax: 713-520-0453; *Imprints:* S2P Press (STwoP)
Web site: http://www.eatitfoodadventures.com; http://www.recipe4success.org/s2ppress
Dist(s): **Independent Pubs. Group**
Small Pr. United.

Recipe Pubs., *(978-0-9778057; 978-0-9816282; 978-0-9824801; 978-0-9826424; 978-0-9828531; 978-0-9898137)* Orders Addr.: 610 N. Elmwood Ave, Springfield, MO 65802 USA (SAN 930-8873) Tel 417-619-4939; Toll Free: 800-313-5121
E-mail: jec1963@sbcglobal.net; jec@recipepubs.com
Web site: http://www.recipepubs.com.

Reclam, Philipp jun., Verlag GmbH (DEU) *(978-3-15) Dist. by* **Intl Bk Import.**

Recon Academy *Imprint of* **Stone Arch Bks.**

Record Stockman & Coyote Cowboy *See* **Coyote Cowboy Co.**

Recorded Bks., LLC, *(978-0-7887; 978-1-55690; 978-1-84197; 978-1-4025; 978-1-4193; 978-1-84505; 978-1-4281; 978-1-4361; 978-1-4407; 978-1-4498; 978-1-4561; 978-1-4618; 978-1-4640; 978-1-4703; 978-1-4906; 978-1-5019)* Subs. of W. F. Howes Limited, Orders Addr.: 270 Skipjack Rd., Prince Frederick, MD 20678 USA (SAN 111-3984) Fax: 410-535-5499; Toll Free: 800-638-1304; 7257 Pkwy. Dr., Hanover, MD 21076 (SAN 920-7414)
E-mail: thelvey@recordedbooks.com
Web site: http://www.recordedbooks.com
Dist(s): **Ebsco Publishing**
Follett School Solutions.

Rector Pr., Ltd., *(978-0-7605; 978-0-934393; 978-1-57205)* Orders Addr.: The Ledge House 130 Rattlesnake Gutter Rd. Suite 1000, Leverett, MA 01054-9726 USA (SAN 693-8108) Tel 413-367-0303 (International Book Sales); Fax: 413-367-2853
E-mail: info@rectorpress.com; info@runanywhere.com
Web site: http://www.rectorpress.com; http://twitter.com/Lewisxxxusa; http://twitter.com/Rectorpress.

Recursos, Ediciones (ESP) *(978-84-89984; 978-84-921663) Dist. by* **IPG Chicago.**

Red 5 Comics (CAN) *(978-0-9809302) Dist. by* **Diamond Book Dists.**

Red & Black Pubs., *(978-0-9791813; 978-1-934941; 978-1-61001)* P.O. Box 7542, Saint Petersburg, FL 33734 USA
E-mail: info@redandblackpublishers.com
Web site: http://www.redandblackpublishers.com.

Red Barn Reading Inc., *(978-0-9753059)* P.O. Box 540, Alanson, MI 49706 USA
E-mail: thecathy@tm.net.

Red Bird Publishing (GBR) *(978-1-902626) Dist. by* **PerseuPGW.**

Red Brick Learning, *(978-0-7368)* Div. of Coughlan Publishing, 151 Good Counsel Dr., P.O. Box 669, Mankato, MN 56002-0669 USA Toll Free Fax: 888-574-5570; Toll Free: 888-262-6135; *Imprints:* High Five (High Five)
Dist(s): **Capstone Pr., Inc.**

Red Bud Publishing, *(978-0-9759421)* 2425 Lakeshore Ct., Lebanon, IN 46052 USA.

Red CalacArts Publications *Imprint of* **Calaca Pr.**

Red Carpet Publishing, *(978-0-9719657; 978-0-9722829)* P.O. Box 309, Noblesville, IN 46061-0309 USA (SAN 255-755X) Tel 317-847-9553; Fax: 317-773-5375
Web site: http://www.redcarpetpublishing.com.

Red Chair Pr., *(978-1-936163; 978-1-937529; 978-1-939656; 978-1-63440)* P.O. Box 333, South Egremont, MA 01258 USA (SAN 858-6209)
E-mail: redchairpress@gmail.com; info@redchairpress.com
Web site: http://www.redchairpress.com; http://www.lernerbooks.com
Dist(s): **Follett School Solutions**
Lerner Publishing Group
MyiLibrary.

†**Red Crane Bks., Inc.,** *(978-1-878610)* Orders Addr.: P.O. Box 33590, Santa Fe, NM 87954 USA; Edit Addr.: 2008 Rosina St., Suite C, Santa Fe, NM 87505 USA Tel 505-988-7070; Fax: 505-989-7476; Toll Free: 800-922-3392
E-mail: publish@redcrane.com
Web site: http://www.redcrane.com
Dist(s): **Continental Bk. Co., Inc.**
Libros Sin Fronteras; *CIP.*

Red Cygnet Pr., *(978-1-60108)* 2245 Enterprise St. Ste. 110, Escondido, CA 92029-2060 USA; *Imprints:* Bearing Books (Bearing Bks)
E-mail: info@redcygnet.com
Web site: http://www.redcygnet.com
Dist(s): **Rosen Publishing Group, Inc., The**
Soundprints.

Red Deer Pr. (CAN) *(978-0-88995) Dist. by* **Midpt Trade.**

Red Deer Pr. (CAN) *(978-0-88995) Dist. by* **IngramPubServ.**

Red Door Pr., *(978-0-9763770)* 1704 Black Oak Ln., Silver Spring, MD 20910 USA Tel 301-588-7599; Fax: 301-838-9771 Do not confuse with Red Door Press in San Francisco, CA
E-mail: trishbaur@comcast.net.

Red Earth Publishing, *(978-0-9779993)* 2041 NW 20th St., Oklahoma City, OK 73106-1609 USA.

Red Earth Publishing, *(978-0-9767748)* Orders Addr.: 104 Candace Dr., Ponca City, OK 74604 USA Tel 580-763-7003
E-mail: deborahjuckes@gmail.com
Web site: http://www.redearthpub.com.

Red Engine Pr., *(978-0-9663276; 978-0-9743758; 978-0-9745652; 978-0-9785158; 978-0-9800064; 978-0-9800332; 978-0-9827923; 978-0-9834930; 978-1-937958; 978-1-943267)* 18942 State Hwy. 13, Suite F107, Branson West, MO 65737 USA Tel 417-230-5555
E-mail: riverroadpress@yahoo.com
Web site: http://www.redenginepress.com.

Red Giant Entertainment *Imprint of* **Active Media Publishing, LLC**

Red Giant Publishing, *(978-0-9767661)* P.O. Box 5, San Mateo, CA 94401 USA
E-mail: questions@redgiantpublishing.com
Web site: http://www.redgiantpublishing.com.

†**Red Hen Pr.,** *(978-0-931093)* P.O. Box 454, Big Sur, CA 93920 USA (SAN 678-9420) Tel 831-667-2726 (phone/fax) Do not confuse with Red Hen Pr. in Casa Grande, AZ, Granada Hills, CA
E-mail: HopeHen@aol.com
Dist(s): **Book Wholesalers, Inc.**
Brodart Co.
Follett School Solutions; *CIP.*

Red Hen Pr., *(978-1-888996; 978-1-59709; 978-0-9890361)* P.O. Box 3537, Granada Hills, CA 91394 USA Tel 818-831-0649; Fax: 818-831-6659
E-mail: editors@redhen.org
Web site: http://www.redhen.org
Dist(s): **Chicago Distribution Ctr.**
Mintright, Inc.
SPD-Small Pr. Distribution
Valentine Publishing Group.

Red Hills Writers Project, *(978-0-9759339)* 1509 Hasosaw Nene, Tallahassee, FL 32301 USA Tel 850-216-2016; Fax: 831-308-3285
E-mail: info@redhillswritersproject.org
Web site: http://www.redhillswritersproject.org.

Red Ink Pr., *(978-0-9788401)* 1914 N. Roan St., Suite 106-223, Johnson City, TN 37601 USA (SAN 851-724X) Tel 423-741-2835
Web site: http://www.redinkpress.com
Dist(s): **Book Hub, Inc.**

Red Jacket Pr., *(978-0-9748895)* 3099 Maqua Pl., Mohegan Lake, NY 10547-1054 USA
E-mail: info@redjacketpress.com
Web site: http://www.redjacketpress.com
Dist(s): **Pathway Bk. Service.**

Red Letter Pr., *(978-0-9661199; 978-0-9794420; 978-0-692-43517-5)* Orders Addr.: 6148 Rutledge Hill, Columbia, SC 29209-1315 USA Tel 843-344-2221 Do not confuse with Red Letter Pr., Seattle, WA
E-mail: redletterpress@gmail.com
Web site: http://redletterpress.googlepages.com
Dist(s): **CreateSpace Independent Publishing Platform.**

Red Letter Publishing & Media Group *See* **Potential Unlimited Publishing**

Red Men Interprises, *(978-0-9744682)* 8 Boton Rd., Lloyd Harbor, NY 11743 USA Tel 516-769-9720
E-mail: jason@drugfreeteen.com
Web site: http://www.drugfreeteen.com.

Red Mountain Creations, *(978-0-9759858; 978-0-9910804)* P.O. Box 172, High Ridge, MO 63049 USA Tel 636-677-3088; Toll Free: 866-732-4857
E-mail: redmountain@swbell.net
Web site: http://www.byronvonrosenberg.com.

Red Mud Pr., *(978-0-9672996)* Orders Addr.: P.O. Box 1257, Sedona, AZ 86336-4357 USA Tel 520-282-5285; Edit Addr.: 51 Remuda Rd., Sedona, AZ 86336 USA
E-mail: Crawford@sedora.net.

Red Owl Pubns., *(978-0-9754279)* 7857 Sedgewick Dr., Freeland, MI 48623 USA Tel 989-737-4486
E-mail: ckblack@redowlpublications.com
Dist(s): **MyiLibrary.**

Blue Pheonix Bks., *(978-0-9726290; 978-1-937781; 978-1-938969)* 809 W. Dike St., Glendora, CA 91740 USA
E-mail: Service@redphoenixbooks.com; cja@redphoenixbooks.com; claudia.alexander@gmail.com
Web site: http://www.redphoenixbooks.com
Dist(s): **Partners Pubs. Group, Inc.**

Red Planet Adventures, *(978-0-615-83813-7)* 2013 63rd St SE, Auburn, WA 98092 USA Tel 509-338-5626
Dist(s): **CreateSpace Independent Publishing Platform.**

Red Pumpkin Pr., *(978-0-9711572; 978-0-9849284)* P.O. Box 40, Rutledge, TN 37861 USA Tel 865-828-3362; Fax: 865-828-4578
E-mail: centar123@aol.com.

Red River Pr. *Imprint of* **Red River Pr.**

Red River Pr., *(978-0-910653)* 3900 Roy Rd., Suite 37, Shreveport, LA 71107 USA (SAN 270-1774) Fax: 318-309-1653; *Imprints:* Red River Press (Red River Pr)
E-mail: rrp_asi@Bellsouth.net
Web site: http://www.ArchivalServicesInc.com
Dist(s): **AtlasBooks Distribution.**

Red Rock Mountain Pr. LLC, *(978-0-615-30253-9; 978-0-615-40473-8; 978-0-615-73121-6)* 560 Schnebly Rd., Sedona, AZ 86336 USA.

Red Rock Pr., Inc., *(978-0-9669573; 978-0-9714372; 978-1-933176)* 331 W. 57th. Street, suite 175, New York, NY 10019 USA Tel 212-362-8304; Fax: 212-362-6216; Toll Free: 800-488-8040
E-mail: richard@redrockpress.com
Web site: http://www.redrockpress.com
Dist(s): **MyiLibrary.**

Red Sage Publishing, *(978-0-9648942; 978-0-9754516; 978-1-60310)* Div. of Red Sage Publishing, Inc., P.O. Box 4844, Seminole, FL 33775 USA (SAN 859-0249) Tel 727-391-3847 (phone/fax)
E-mail: alekendall@aol.com
Web site: http://www.eRedSage.com
Dist(s): **Brodart Co.**
Cowley Distributing, Inc.
OverDrive, Inc.

Red Tail Publishing, *(978-0-9635757; 978-0-9847756; 978-1-941950)* Orders Addr.: P.O. Box 1477, Anderson, CA 96007 USA Tel 530-365-5863
E-mail: livingston@redtail.com; info@redtail.com
Web site: http://www.redtail.com.

Red Wagon *See* **Magic Wagon**

Red Wagon Bks. *Imprint of* **Harcourt Children's Bks.**

†Red Wheel/Weiser, *(978-0-87728; 978-0-943233; 978-1-57324; 978-1-57863; 978-1-59003; 978-1-60925; 978-1-61283; 978-1-61852; 978-1-61940; 978-1-938875; 978-1-63341; 978-1-942785)* Div. of Weiser Bks., Orders Addr.: 65 Parker St., Suite 7, Newburyport, MA 01950 USA (SAN 255-8610) Tel 978-465-0504; Fax: 978-465-0243; Toll Free Fax: 877-337-3309; Toll Free: 800-423-7087 (orders only)
E-mail: customerservice@redwheelweiser.com
Web site: http://www.redwheelweiser.com
Dist(s): **Abyss Distribution**
Ebsco Publishing
New Leaf Distributing Co., Inc.; *CIP*.

Redcay Publishing, *(978-0-615-17346-7)* 2953 Grandview Blvd ., West LAwn, PA 19609 USA Tel 610-678-5636
E-mail: mwkreitz@msn.com
Web site: http://www.divcothelittlemilktruck.com.

Redding Pr., *(978-0-9658879)* Orders Addr.: c/o Mary Mahony, P.O. Box 366, Belmont, MA 02178 USA Fax: 617-489-9476; Toll Free: 800-267-6012; Edit Addr.: P.O. Box 366, Belmont, MA 02178 USA
E-mail: mary@reddingpress.com
Web site: http://www.channel.com/users/msmahony; http://www.reddingpress.com
Dist(s): **Quality Bks., Inc.**

Redel, Nicole, *(978-0-9769738)* 2125 David Dr., Florissant, MO 63031-4321 USA Tel 314-839-3242
E-mail: gospelpitbull@sbcglobal.net
Web site: http://www.gospelpitbull.com.

Redhawk Publishing, *(978-0-9641861; 978-0-9769267)* Orders Addr.: 602 Pompa St., Carlsbad, NM 88220 USA Tel 505-885-1748; *Imprints:* RWP Books (RWP Bks)
E-mail: randy@rwpbooks.com
Web site: http://www.rwpbooks.com
Dist(s): **CreateSpace Independent Publishing Platform.**

RedJack, *(978-1-892619)* P.O. Box 633, Bayside, CA 95524 USA Tel 707-825-7817
E-mail: heidi@redjack.us
Web site: http://www.redjack.us.

Redleaf Pr., *(978-0-934140; 978-1-884834; 978-1-929610; 978-1-933653; 978-1-60554)* Div. of Resources for Child Caring, Inc., 10 Yorkton Ct., Saint Paul, MN 55117-1065 USA (SAN 212-8691) Toll Free Fax: 800-641-0115; Toll Free: 800-423-8309
E-mail: sales@redleafpress.org
Web site: http://www.redleafpress.org
Dist(s): **Capstone Pr., Inc.**
Capstone Pub.
Consortium Bk. Sales & Distribution
Gryphon Hse., Inc.
Lectorum Pubns., Inc.
MyiLibrary
Perseus Bks. Group.

Redline Bks., *(978-0-9727440)* 2280 Jones Creek Rd., White Bluff, TN 37187 USA Tel 615-797-3043 (phone/fax)
E-mail: redlinebooks@bardyoung.com; bardyoung@bardyoung.com.

RedMEDIA, *(978-0-9721708)* 41 Schermerhorn St., No. 147, Brooklyn, NY 11201 USA Tel 718-857-6638; Fax: 718-857-6427
E-mail: rmedia3@aol.com
Web site: http://www.tgoodlife.com; http://www.ibrooklyn.com/redmedia.

Redmond, Pamela, *(978-0-9760767)* P.O. Box 169, Topping, VA 23169-0169 USA.

Reece, Kim Taylor Prodns. LLC, *(978-0-9660395; 978-1-59779)* 53-866 Kamehameha Hwy., Hauula, HI 96717 USA Tel 808-293-2000; Fax: 808-293-2136; Toll Free: 800-657-7966
E-mail: info@kimtaylorreece.com
Web site: http://www.kimtaylorreece.com
Dist(s): **Booklines Hawaii, Ltd.**
Islander Group.

Reed Business Information, *(978-0-9614276; 978-1-879930; 978-1-931625; 978-0-9764027; 978-0-9851869)* 5900 Wilshire Blvd. Ste. 3100, Los Angeles, CA 90036-5030 USA (SAN 687-3944) Toll Free: 800-545-2411
E-mail: nlongman@reedbusiness.com; steve.atinsky@reedbusiness.com
Web site: http://www.la411.com
Dist(s): **SCB Distributors.**

Reed, Robert D. Pubs., *(978-1-885003; 978-1-931741; 978-1-934759)* P.O. Box 1992, Bandon, OR 97411 USA Tel 541-347-9882; Fax: 541-347-9883
E-mail: 4bobreed@msn.com
Web site: http://www.rdrpublishers.com
Dist(s): **Midpoint Trade Bks., Inc.**
Todd Communications.

Reedswain, Inc., *(978-0-9651020; 978-1-890946; 978-1-59164)* Orders Addr.: 88 Wells Rd., Spring City, PA 19475-8628 USA Toll Free: 800-331-5191
E-mail: bryan@reedswain.com
Web site: http://www.reedswain.com
Dist(s): **Cardinal Pubs. Group.**

Reedy Pr., *(978-0-9753180; 978-1-933370; 978-1-935806; 978-1-68106)* Orders Addr.: P.O. Box 5131, Saint Louis, MO 63139 USA Toll Free Fax: 866-999-6916 fax
E-mail: jstevens@reedypress.com; dkorte@reedypress.com
Web site: http://www.reedypress.com
Dist(s): **Partners Bk. Distributing, Inc.**

Reel Productions, LLC, *(978-0-9675010; 978-0-9707422)* P.O. Box 1069, Monument, CO 80132 USA Toll Free: 800-964-0439
E-mail: support@reelproductions.net; jolene@explorationfilms.com
Web site: http://www.explorationfilms.com; http://www.reelproductions.net
Dist(s): **Exploration Films**
Send The Light Distribution LLC.

Reeves, Emily, *(978-0-9821506)* P.O. Box 15861, Savannah, GA 31416 USA.

Reference Service Pr., *(978-0-918276; 978-1-58841)* 5000 Windplay Dr., Suite 4, El Dorado Hills, CA 95762 USA (SAN 210-2633) Tel 916-939-9620; Fax: 916-939-9626
E-mail: findaid@aol.com; info@rspfunding.com
Web site: http://www.rspfunding.com.

ReferencePoint Pr., Inc., *(978-1-60152)* P.O. Box 27779, San Diego, CA 92198 USA (SAN 858-6845) Tel 858-618-1314; 17150 Via Del Campo. Ste. 205, San Diego, CA 92127-2138
E-mail: dan@referencepointpress.com; orders@referencepointpress.com
Web site: http://www.referencepointpress.com.

Refined Savage Editions / Ediciones El Salvaje Refinado, The, *(978-0-9713175; 978-0-9746855; 978-0-9761940; 978-0-9768868; 978-0-9791011; 978-0-9802008; 978-0-9816968)* 10 Delaware Ave., Charleston, WV 25302-1950 USA
E-mail: esrefinado@aol.com
Web site: http://www.esrefinado.net.

Reflection Pr., *(978-0-9671543)* 3430 W. 98th Pl. Unit A, Westminster, CO 80031 USA Tel 303-862-4868 Do not confuse with companies with the same name in Huntsville, AL, Berkeley, CA
E-mail: mbsmith48@gmail.com.

Reflection Publishing, *(978-0-9797618; 978-1-936629)* P.O. Box 2182, Citrus Heights, CA 95621-2182 USA Fax: 916-726-2768
E-mail: contact@reflectpublishing.com
Web site: http://www.reflectpublishing.com.

Reflection Publishing Company *See* **Imprints**

Reflection Publishing Co., *(978-0-9657561; 978-0-9712142)* 1813 4th St W., Palmetto, FL 34221-4303 USA (SAN 299-2787) Toll Free: 888-677-0101
E-mail: lakepm@msn.com
Web site: http://www.reflectionpublishing.com
Dist(s): **Brodart Co.**
Spring Arbor Distributors, Inc.

Reflections Publishing, Inc., *(978-0-9792132; 978-0-9840789)* P.O. Box 294, Inglewood, CA 90306 USA (SAN 858-2297) Tel 310-695-9800 Do not confuse with companies with the same or similar name in Odenton, MD, Cove, OR, Livingston, TX, Dallas, TX, Dunlap, TN, Hume, CA
E-mail: writray@aol.com
Web site: http://www.reflectionspublishings.net.

Reformation Herald Publishing Assn., *(978-0-9745295; 978-1-934308)* P.O. Box 7240, Roanoke, VA 24019-0240 USA
Web site: http://www.sdarm.org.

Reformation Heritage Bks., *(978-1-892777; 978-1-60178)* 2965 Leonard St., NE, Grand Rapids, MI 49525-5828 USA
E-mail: jay.collier@heritagebooks.org
Web site: http://www.heritagebooks.org
Dist(s): **Send The Light Distribution LLC**
christianaudio.

Reformation Pubs., *(978-1-933304; 978-1-60416)* 242 University Dr., Prestonsburg, KY 41653-1058 USA Tel 606-886-7222; Fax: 606-886-8222; Toll Free Fax: 800-765-2464
E-mail: rpublisher@aol.com
Web site: http://www.reformationpublishers.com
Dist(s): **Lightning Source, Inc.**

Reformed Church Pr., Reformed Church in America, *(978-0-916466)* 4500 60th St., SE, Grand Rapids, MI 49512-9670 USA Tel 616-698-7071; Fax: 616-698-6606; Toll Free: 800-968-7221 (orders); 475 Riverside Dr., 18th Flr., New York, NY 10115 (SAN 207-4508).

Reformed Free Publishing Assn., *(978-0-916206; 978-1-936054)* Orders Addr.: 1894 Georgetown Ctr. Dr., Jenison, MI 49428-7137 USA Tel 616-457-5970
E-mail: mail@rfpa.org; evelyn@rfpa.org
Web site: http://www.rfpa.org.

Regal Bks. *Imprint of* **Gospel Light Pubns.**

Regal Enterprises, *(978-0-9727771; 978-0-9729960)* 16310 Garfield Ave., Paramount, CA 90723-4806 USA (SAN 255-2477)
Dist(s): **Timberwolf Pr., Inc.**

ReganBooks *Imprint of* **HarperCollins Pubs.**

Regency Hse., Ltd., *(978-0-9716923)* 6538 Pardee, Taylor, MI 48180-1771 USA Tel 313-291-9242
Dist(s): **BookMasters, Inc.**

Regenold Publishing, *(978-0-9773085)* P.O. Box 621967, Littleton, CO 80162-1967 USA (SAN 257-2583) Tel 303-797-8881
Web site: http://www.regenoldpublishing.com.

Regent Pr., *(978-0-916147; 978-1-889059; 978-1-58790)* 2747 Regent St., Berkeley, CA 94705-1212 USA (SAN 294-9717) Tel 510-845-1196 Do not confuse with Regent Pr., Oxnard, CA
E-mail: regentpress@mindspring.com
Web site: http://www.regentpress.net
Dist(s): **Consortium Bk. Sales & Distribution**
Lightning Source, Inc.
New Village Pr.
Quality Bks., Inc.

Regina Orthodox Pr., *(978-0-9649141; 978-1-928653)* Orders Addr.: P.O. Box 5288, Salisbury, MA 01952 USA Fax: 978-462-5079; Toll Free: 800-636-2470; Edit Addr.: 6 Second St., Salisbury, MA 01952 USA
E-mail: reginaorthodoxpress@comcast.net
Web site: http://www.reginaorthodoxpress.com
Dist(s): **National Bk. Network.**

Regina Pr., Malhame & Co., *(978-0-88271)* Orders Addr.: P.O. Box 608, Melville, NY 11747-0608 USA (SAN 203-0853) Tel 631-694-8600; Edit Addr.: 10 Hub Dr., Melville, NY 11747 USA
E-mail: customerservice@malhame.com
Web site: http://www.malhame.com/.

Region IV Education Service Ctr., *(978-1-932524; 978-1-932797; 978-1-933049; 978-1-933521; 978-1-934950; 978-1-937403)* 7145 W. Tidwell, Houston, TX 77092-2096 USA Tel 713-462-7708; Fax: 713-744-6514
E-mail: dharvey@esc4.net
Web site: http://www.esc4.net
Dist(s): **Consortium Bk. Sales & Distribution.**

Regional Laboratory for Educational Improvement of the Northeast & Islands *See* **NETWORK Inc., The**

Regnery Gateway, Incorporated *See* **Regnery Publishing, Inc., An Eagle Publishing Co.**

Regnery Kids *Imprint of* **Regnery Publishing, Inc., An Eagle Publishing Co.**

†Regnery Publishing, Inc., An Eagle Publishing Co., *(978-0-89526; 978-1-59698; 978-1-62157)* Subs. of Phillips Publishing International, One Massachusetts Ave., NW, Suite 600, Washington, DC 20001 USA (SAN 210-5578) Tel 202-216-0600; *Imprints:* Little Patriot Press (LittlePatriot); Regnery Kids (REGNERY KIDS)
Web site: http://www.regnery.com
Dist(s): **Continental Bk. Co., Inc.**
MyiLibrary
Perseus-PGW
Perseus Bks. Group
Perseus Distribution
Send The Light Distribution LLC
ebrary, Inc.; *CIP*.

†Regular Baptist Pr., *(978-0-87227; 978-1-59402; 978-1-60776; 978-1-62940)* Div. of General Assn. of Regular Baptist Churches, 1300 N. Meacham Rd., Schaumburg, IL 60173-4806 USA (SAN 205-2229) Tel 847-843-1600 (foreign orders); 708-843-1600; Fax: 847-843-3757; Toll Free: 800-727-4440 (orders only)
E-mail: rbporders@garbc.org
Web site: http://www.regularbaptistpress.org; *CIP*.

Reiki Blessings, *(978-0-9743679)* P.O. Box 2000, Byron, GA 31008-2000 USA (SAN 255-7045) Fax: 801-705-1802
E-mail: reikiblessings@earthlink.net
Web site: http://www.rbpress.com.

Reimann Bks., *(978-0-9820941; 978-0-9838148; 978-0-9852254; 978-1-938743)* Orders Addr.: 305 Parkton Dr, Richlands, NC 28574 USA
E-mail: reimannbooks@gmail.com
Web site: http://www.reimannbooks.com.

Rein Designs, Inc., *(978-0-9758704; 978-0-9859684)* 2400 Central Ave., Suite 1, Boulder, CO 80301-3099 USA Toll Free: 800-432-7346 (phone/fax)
E-mail: ricd@reindesigns.com
Dist(s): **Bookazine Co., Inc.**

Reinoso, Marta, *(978-0-9676203)* World Educational Guild, Inc. 1330 E. 223rd., Suite 501, Carson, CA 90745 USA Tel 310-816-1100; Fax: 310-816-1103
E-mail: wegi@earthnet.com.

Reisman, Dave *See* **Jumping Cow Pr.**

Rejoyce Pubns., *(978-0-9661564)* 5205 Aryshire Dr., Dublin, OH 43017 USA Tel 614-766-2771; Fax: 614-766-1731.

Relationship Resources, Inc., *(978-0-9721728)* P.O. Box 63383, Colorado Springs, CO 80962 USA
E-mail: gaylyn@relationshipresources.org
Web site: http://www.relationshipresources.org
Dist(s): **Send The Light Distribution LLC.**

Relde Publishing, *(978-0-9701863)* Subs. of Solutions Training & Development LLC, P.O. Box 21304, Jackson, MS 39289 USA Tel 601-926-4375; Fax: 601-926-4374; Toll Free: 800-489-3439
E-mail: solut2000@aol.com.

Relevant Graces Productions, *(978-0-9822375)* 1044 Cresswood Dr., Richlands, VA 24641 USA.

Relevant Media Group, Inc., *(978-0-9714576; 978-0-9729276; 978-0-9746942; 978-0-9760357; 978-0-9763642; 978-0-9768175; 978-0-9776167; 978-0-9777480)* 1220 Alden Rd., Orlando, FL 32803-2546 USA; 600 Rinehart Rd., Lake Mary, FL 32746
E-mail: nick@relevantmediagroup.com
Web site: http://www.relevantbooks.com/
Dist(s): **Charisma Media.**

Relevant Ventures, LLC, *(978-0-9760259)* 4279 Roswell Rd., Suite 102-273, Atlanta, GA 30342-4145 USA (SAN 256-4483) Tel 404-842-1930; Fax: 404-842-1021
E-mail: td3@mac.com; tom@relevantventures.com
Web site: http://www.relevantventures.com.

Reliant Energy, *(978-0-9791383)* 1000 Main St., Houston, TX 77002 USA
E-mail: jmolholt@reliant.com.

Religion Res. Institute, *(978-0-9765024)* P.O. Box 7505, Prospect Heights, IL 60070 USA Tel 773-396-0147
E-mail: info@religionresearchinstitute.org
Web site: http://www.religionresearchinstitute.org.

Reluctant Reader Bks. *Imprint of* **Cronus College**

Remarco Publishing, *(978-0-9770762)* P.O. Box 644, Ames, IA 50010 USA (SAN 256-6958) Tel 515-203-0358
Web site: http://www.remarcopublishing.com.

RemarkableMe, *(978-0-9776642)* 3905 W 10260 N, CEDAR HILLS, UT 84062 USA Tel 801-796-6486; Fax: 801-796-6486
E-mail: charless@utahweb.com
Web site: http://www.remarkableme.com.

Remedia Pubns., *(978-1-56175; 978-1-59639; 978-1-61394)* 15887 N. 76th St., Suite 120, Scottsdale, AZ 85260-1696 USA Tel 602-661-9900; Fax: 602-661-9901; Toll Free: 800-826-4740
E-mail: Becky@rempub.com
Web site: http://www.rempub.com.

Remey, Lisa, *(978-0-9855445)* PSC 2 Box 6496, APO, AE 85718 USA
E-mail: rlremey@aol.com.

Reminders Of Faith, Inc., *(978-0-9748160; 978-0-9763691)* 518 Overhead Dr., Moon Township, PA 15108 USA Fax: 412-264-7857
E-mail: kathyb@remindersoffaith.com
Dist(s): **Send The Light Distribution LLC.**

Remnant Pubns., *(978-1-883012; 978-1-933291; 978-0-9777445; 978-1-937718; 978-1-62913)* Orders Addr.: 649 E. Chicago Rd., Coldwater, MI 49036-9497 USA Tel 517-279-1304 (ext. 23); Fax: 517-279-1804; Toll Free: 800-423-1319
Web site: http://www.remnantpublications.com.

Renaissance Bks. *Imprint of* **St. Martin's Pr.**

Renaissance Books *See* **New Millennium Bks.**

Renaissance Learning, Inc., *(978-0-9646404; 978-1-893751; 978-0-9708138; 978-1-931731; 978-1-931819; 978-1-932299; 978-1-59455)* 2911 Peach St., Wisconsin Rapids, WI 54494 USA Tel 715-424-3636; Toll Free: 800-338-4204; P.O. Box 8036, Wisconsin Rapids, WI 54495-8036
E-mail: answers@renlearn.com
Web site: http://www.renlearn.com.

Renaissance Printing *See* **Bookends Pr.**

Renaissance Pubns., *(978-1-929473)* Div. of Mission Renaissance, 5744 San Fernando Rd., Glendale, CA 91202-2104 USA Toll Free: 800-430-4278 Do not confuse with Renaissance Publications, Worthington, OH.

Renegado Pr., The, *(978-0-9754616)* Orders Addr.: 29 Lynn Way, Indiana, PA 15701 USA Tel 724-388-3958
E-mail: mackelly@renegadopress.com
Web site: http://www.theavatarthenovel.com.

Reney Editions, Inc., *(978-0-9752688)* 35 Sands Brook Dr., New Hemstead, NY 10977 USA Tel 845-548-4029
E-mail: ethan@reney.com
Web site: http://www.reney.com.

Renovo Partners LLC, *(978-1-935310)* 8220 Jones Rd., Suite 100, Houston, TX 77065-5375 USA (SAN 857-1163) Tel 281-677-9568; Fax: 281-677-9480; Toll Free: 877-773-6686
E-mail: customers@renovopartners.com; barhorw@nationwide.com
Web site: http://www.renovopartners.com.

Repko, Marya *See* **ECity Publishing**

Repressed Publishing LLC, *(978-1-4622; 978-1-5042)* P.O. Box 1242, Provo, UT 84603 USA; 223 W. Bulldog Blvd., Number 420, Provo, UT 84604 Tel 385-204-4408
E-mail: orders@repressedpublishing; customerservice@repressedpublishing.com
Web site: http://www.repressedpublishing.com/.

†Reprint Services Corp., *(978-0-7812; 978-0-932051; 978-1-4227)* P.O. Box 130, Murrieta, CA 92564-0130 USA (SAN 686-2640) Fax: 951-699-5065
E-mail: Reprintservices@gmail.com; *CIP*.

Requiem Pr., *(978-0-9758542; 978-0-9788687)* Orders Addr.: 3271 Timrod Rd., Bethune, SC 29009 USA Toll Free: 888-708-7675; P.O. Box 7, Bethune, SC 29009 Tel 843-334-6222; Toll Free: 888-708-7675
E-mail: info@requiempress.com
Web site: http://www.requiempress.com.

Research & Education Assn., *(978-0-7386; 978-0-87891)* Div. of Courier Corporation, Orders Addr.: 61 Ethel Rd., W., Piscataway, NJ 08854 USA (SAN 204-6814) Tel 732-819-8880; Fax: 732-819-8808; Toll Free: 800-822-0830
E-mail: jcording@rea.com; info@rea.com
Web site: http://www.rea.com
Dist(s): **Dover Pubns., Inc.**
INscribe Digital
MyiLibrary.

†Research Centre of Kabbalah, *(978-0-924457; 978-0-943688; 978-1-57189)* 83-84 115th St., Richmond Hill, NY 11418 USA (SAN 210-9484) Tel 718-805-9122; Fax: 718-805-5899; Toll Free: 888-522-2252
Web site: http://www.kabbalah.com/kabbalah/
Dist(s): **MyiLibrary**
Perseus-PGW
Perseus Bks. Group; *CIP*.

Research Evaluation & Statistics *See* **Image Cascade Publishing**

Research In Time Publications, *(978-0-9764341)* 101 Hotchkiss Grove Rd., No. 4, Branford, CT 06405 USA
E-mail: raradune@comcast.net
Dist(s): **AtlasBooks Distribution.**

Research In Time Publishers *See* **Research In Time Publications**

Research Institute Pr., The, *(978-0-9752986)* 5000 Enighed Pmb 356, Saint John, VI 00830 USA Tel 340-998-9597
E-mail: asewer@triinformation.com; info@triinformation.com
Web site: www.triinformation.com.

Research Pr., *(978-0-87822)* Orders Addr.: P.O. Box 7886, Champaign, IL 61826-9177 USA (SAN 282-2490) Toll Free: 800-519-2707; Edit Addr.: 2612 N. Mattis Ave., Champaign, IL 61822 USA (SAN 282-2482) Tel 217-352-3273; Fax: 217-352-1221 Do not confuse with Research Pr., Prairie Village, KS
E-mail: products@researchpress.com; permissions@researchpress.com
Web site: http://www.researchpress.com.

Resort Gifts Unlimited, Incorporated *See* **RGU Group, The**

ReSource Guides, Inc., *(978-0-9755370)* 13110 Vista del Mundo, San Antonio, TX 78216-2200 USA Tel 210-493-3974
E-mail: resource@resourceguides.com
Web site: http://www.resourceguides.com.

†Resource Pubns., Inc., *(978-0-89390)* 160 E. Virginia St., No. 290, San Jose, CA 95112-5876 USA (SAN 209-3081) Tel 408-286-8505; Fax: 408-287-8748; Toll Free: 888-273-7782 Do not confuse with Resource Pubns. in Los Angeles, CA
E-mail: info@rpinet.com
Web site: http://www.rpinet.com
Dist(s): **Empire Publishing Service**
Feldheim Pubs.; *CIP.*

Resource Publishing, *(978-0-9706429; 978-0-615-22022-2; 978-0-692-49159-1)* 3736 Brookwood Rd., Birmingham, AL 35223 USA Tel 205-967-3446 Do not confuse company with same or similar name in Greensboro, NC, Baton Rouge, LA, San Francisco, CA
E-mail: hoytwilson1@charter.net.

Resource Pubns.(OR) *Imprint of* **Wipf & Stock Pubs.**

Resources for Children with Special Needs, Inc., *(978-0-9678365; 978-0-9755716)* 116 E. 16th St., 5th Flr., New York, NY 10003 USA
E-mail: dlittwin@resourcesnyc.org
Web site: http://www.resourcesnyc.org.

Resources for Christian Living *See* **RCL Benziger Publishing**

Resources on the Net Publishing, *(978-0-9722803)* 250 32 St., No. 307, Bellingham, WA 98225-0943 USA.

RESPONDER911, Inc., *(978-0-9746186)* 17011 Beach Blvd., Suite No. 900, Huntington Beach, CA 92647 USA Tel 714-375-6693; Fax: 714-375-6694
Web site: http://www.responder911.com.

Resurrected Pr. *Imprint of* **Intrepid Ink, LLC**

Resurrecting Faith, *(978-0-9729876)* P.O. Box 43217, Minneapolis, MN 55443-0217 USA
E-mail: admin@churchofminneapolis.org; cerise.lewis@comcast.net
Web site: http://www.resurrectingfaith.org; http://www.churchofminneapolis.org.

Resurrection Pr. *Imprint of* **Catholic Bk. Publishing Corp.**

Resurrection Resources LLC, *(978-0-9653723; 978-0-9710950; 978-0-9792338)* 8362 Tamarack Village, Ste. 119, Woodbury, MN 55125 USA
E-mail: editor@thefathersbooks.com; sales@thefathersbooks.com
Web site: http://www.thefathersbooks.com
Dist(s): **Send The Light Distribution LLC.**

Retriever Pr., *(978-0-9760718; 978-0-615-55790-8)* 3689 Ridge Line Dr., San Bernardino, CA 92407 USA.

Retro Recess, *(978-0-9785425)* 3939 Lavista Rd., Suite E, PMB 327, Tucker, GA 30084 USA
E-mail: retrorecess@comcast.net
Web site: http://www.retrorecess.net.

Return To The Word, *(978-0-9709763)* Div of LIFE Fellowship Family Bible Church, 11500 Sheridan Blvd., Westminster, CO 80020 USA Tel 303-451-5433; Fax: 303-469-1787
E-mail: truthquester@aol.com
Web site: http://www.returntotheworld.org.

Return to Titanic *Imprint of* **Stone Arch Bks.**

Retzlaff Publishing Co., *(978-0-9752525)* 1516 Piedmont Pl., Savannah, TX 76227 USA Tel 817-975-1115
E-mail: DonRetzlaff@gmail.com
Web site: http://RPC.macroenterprisesinc.com.

Revelation Products LLC, *(978-0-9792510)* 11746 Manhattan Ave., Saint Louis, MO 63131-4625 USA Tel 314-984-8180; Fax: 314-984-8194; Toll Free: 888-344-0606
E-mail: info@rpideas.com.

†Revell, *(978-0-8007)* Div. of Baker Publishing Group, Orders Addr.: P.O. Box 6287, Grand Rapids, MI 49516-6287 USA Toll Free Fax: 800-398-3111; Toll Free: 800-877-2665; Edit Addr.: 6030 E. Fulton, Ada, MI 49301 USA Tel 616-676-9185; Fax: 616-676-9573
E-mail: sharlow@bakerbooks.com
Web site: http://www.bakerbooks.com
Dist(s): **Baker Publishing Group**; *CIP.*

Revell, Fleming H. Company *See* **Revell**

Reverence for Life, *(978-1-880757)* P.O. Box 222, Rectortown, VA 20140 USA Tel 540-364-1282; Fax: 540-364-7636
E-mail: sananda@erols.com
Web site: http://www.1spirit.com/sananda.

Reverie Publishing Co., *(978-1-932485)* Orders Addr.: 130 South Wineow St., Suite 3, Cumberland, MD 21502 USA Tel 301-722-2373; Fax: 301-722-2374; Toll Free: 888-721-4999; Edit Addr.: 127 West 96th St., 6-D, New York, NY 10025 USA Tel 212-662-7627
E-mail: info@reveriepublishing.com
Web site: http://www.reveriepublishing.com.

†Review & Herald Publishing Assn., *(978-0-8127; 978-0-8280)* 55 W. Oak Ridge Dr., Hagerstown, MD 21740 USA (SAN 203-3798) Tel 301-393-3000
E-mail: smulkern@rhpa.org
Web site: http://www.reviewandherald.com/
Dist(s): **Spring Arbor Distributors, Inc.**; *CIP.*

Revivalist Pr., The, *(978-0-9749186; 978-0-9891979)* Div. of God's Bible School & College, 1810 Young St., Cincinnati, OH 45202 USA
E-mail: president@gbs.edu
Web site: http://www.gbs.edu.

Revolutionary Strategies, *(978-0-9769354; 978-0-9825493; 978-0-9883527)* P.O. Box 900, Dripping Springs, TX 78620 USA Tel 512-858-0974
Web site: http://www.rickgreen.com.

Rexroad, Frederick, *(978-0-9817742)* 616 Upham Pl. NW, Vienna, VA 22180 USA; *Imprints:* Rexroad International (Rexroad Int)
E-mail: fred_rexroad@yahoo.com; fred.rexroad@yahoo.com
Web site: http://www.FredRexroad.com.

Rexroad International *Imprint of* **Rexroad, Frederick**

Reyes, Jose, *(978-0-9794731)* 422 Sabal Palm Ln., Pearland, TX 77584-7770 USA
E-mail: thelordsfield@sbcglobal.net; riff28@sbcglobal.net.

Reynolds & Hearn (GBR) *(978-1-903111; 978-1-905287)* *Dist. by* **Trafalgar.**

Reynolds, Morgan Inc., *(978-1-883846; 978-1-931798; 978-1-59935)* 620 S. Elm St., Suite 223, Greensboro, NC 27406 USA (SAN 858-4680) Tel 336-275-1311; Fax: 336-275-1152; Toll Free Fax: 800-535-5725; Toll Free: 800-535-1504; *Imprints:* First Biographies (First Biographies)
E-mail: sales@morganreynolds.com; editorial@morganreynolds.com
Web site: http://www.morganreynolds.com
Dist(s): **Follett School Solutions.**

RGC Pr., LLC, *(978-0-9728876; 978-0-9779886)* P.O. Box 2921, Indianapolis, IN 46206-2921 USA (SAN 255-4747) Tel 317-926-0541
E-mail: info@RGCPress.com
Web site: http://www.RGCPress.com.

RGU Group, The, *(978-1-891795)* 560 W. Southern Ave., Tempe, AZ 85282 USA (SAN 299-9366) Tel 480-736-9862; Fax: 480-736-9863; Toll Free: 800-266-5265
E-mail: mpagnozzi@theRGUgroup.com
Web site: http://www.thergugroup.com
Dist(s): **Send The Light Distribution LLC.**

RGZ Consulting, *(978-0-615-80196-4)* P.O. Box 153, South Woodstock, VT 05071 USA Tel 802-457-5861
E-mail: zamenhof@alum.mit.edu.

Rhapsody Branding, Inc., *(978-0-9667232)* Orders Addr.: 14027 N. Miami Ave., Miami, FL 33168 USA Tel 305-681-0489
E-mail: pumba66@yahoo.com; Don@notw8.com; Don@nightofthewitches.com
Web site: http://www.nightofthewitches.com
Dist(s): **Bk. Warehouse**
Distributors, The
Southern Bk. Service.

RH/Disney *Imprint of* **Random Hse. Children's Bks.**

Rhemalda Publishing, *(978-0-615-32885-0; 978-0-9827437; 978-1-936850)* P.O. Box 1790, Moses Lake, WA 98837 USA
E-mail: emmaline@rhemalda.com
Web site: http://www.rhemalda.com; http://shop.rhemalda.com/
Dist(s): **MyiLibrary**
Smashwords.

Rhino Entertainment Co, A Warner Music Group Co., *(978-0-7379; 978-0-930589; 978-1-56826; 978-0-9797278)* 3400 W. Olive Ave., Burbank, CA 91505 USA (SAN 677-5454) Tel 818-238-6110; Fax: 818-562-9239
E-mail: gladys.sanchez@wmg.com; tracie.bowers@wmg.com
Web site: http://www.rhino.com.

Rhizoo Publishing, *(978-0-9762723)* P.O. Box 1249, Stephenville, TX 76401 USA.

Rhoades & Assocs., *(978-1-930006; 978-0-9841378)* 8070 19th St., No. 326, Alta Loma, CA 91701 USA (SAN 858-5369) Tel 909-297-3436; Fax: 909-657-5446; Toll Free: 888-699-0685; *Imprints:* Reading Company, The (Reading Co)
E-mail: jacquie@readingcompany.us
Web site: http://www.readingcompany.us.

Rhode Island State Council, International Reading Assn., *(978-0-9664455)* 4 Gardner Ave., North Providence, RI 02911 USA.

Rhode, Steve Inc., *(978-0-9742781; 978-1-59840)* 310 Watkins Pond Blvd., Rockville, MD 20850 USA
E-mail: steve@steverhode.com
Web site: http://www.steverhode.com.

Rhodes Educational Pubns., *(978-0-9743214)* P.O. Box 501155, Dallas, TX 75250 USA
Web site: http://www.nativeamericanrhymes.com.

Rhodes, Edwin Books LLC *See* **Rhodes, EL. Bks., LLC**

Rhodes, EL. Bks., LLC, *(978-0-615-24550-8; 978-0-578-01988-8; 978-0-578-03719-6)* 7710 Tinkers Creek Dr., Clinton, MD 20735 USA.

Rhymeglow.com, *(978-0-9786912; 978-0-578-15239-4)* Orders Addr.: 14625 Baltimore Ave., Laurel, MD 20707 USA; Edit Addr.: P.O. Box 869, Laurel, MD 20707 USA.

Rialp, Ediciones, S.A. (ESP) *(978-84-320; 978-84-321)* *Dist. by* **Lectorum Pubns.**

R.I.C. Publications Asia Co, Inc. (JPN) *(978-4-902216)* *Dist. by* **CEG.**

R.I.C. Pubns. (AUS) *(978-1-86311; 978-1-74126; 978-1-921750; 978-1-922116; 978-1-925201)* *Dist. by* **SCB Distributo.**

Rich List *See* **Rich Register, The**

Rich Pr., *(978-1-933914)* 4330 N. Civic Center Plaza, #100, Scottsdale, AZ 85251 USA (SAN 850-5209)
E-mail: kathy@richdad.com
Dist(s): **Perseus Distribution.**

Rich Publishing, *(978-0-9726670)* 4175 W. 5345 S., Salt Lake City, UT 84118 USA Tel 801-965-6200; Fax: 801-965-6199; Toll Free: 800-224-3221 Do not confuse with companies with the same or similar name in Houston, TX, Temecula, CA
E-mail: milton@zeestlouis.com
Web site: http://www.miltonrich.com.

Rich Register, The, *(978-0-9633933; 978-0-9831368)* P.O. Box 29955, Austin, TX 78755 USA Tel 512-477-8871
Web site: www.richregister.com.

Richardson, Lilith, *(978-0-578-00920-9; 978-0-578-04792-8; 978-0-578-07481-8)* 360 Dusty Rd., St. Augustine, FL 32095 USA
Dist(s): **Lulu Enterprises Inc.**

Richardson Production, Inc., *(978-0-9761222)* Orders Addr.: P.O. Box 543, Marietta, OH 45750 USA Tel 740-373-0861; Edit Addr.: 177 Acme St., Marietta, OH 45750 USA
Web site: http://www.richardsonproductions.tv.

Richardson Publishing, Inc., *(978-0-9637991; 978-1-935683)* Orders Addr.: P.O. Box 162115, Altamonte Springs, FL 32716-2115 USA Tel 407-862-5037
E-mail: coachrik@aol.com
Web site: http://www.gymnastictrainingtips.com; http://www.AmericanDreamPublishing.com.

Richer Life, LLC, *(978-0-9744617; 978-0-9855699; 978-0-9892884; 978-0-9899001; 978-0-9903291; 978-0-9863544)* 5725 S. 21st Pl., Phoenix, AZ 85040 USA Tel 602-708-4268; Fax: 602-772-4910
E-mail: earlcobb@earthlink.net; earlcobb1@gmail.com; earl@richerlifellc.com; charlotte@richerlifellc.com; cobbcare@yahoo.com
Web site: http://www.richerlifellc.com.

Richer Life, LLC (dba RICHER Publications) *See* **Richer Life, LLC**

Richer Resources Pubns., *(978-0-9776269; 978-0-9797571; 978-0-9818162; 978-1-935238; 978-1-63464)* 1926 N. Woodrow St., Arlington, VA 22207-2410 USA (SAN 853-2931) Tel 800-856-3060; Fax: 703-276-0193
E-mail: info@richerresourcespublications.com; publisher@richerresourcespublications.com
Web site: http://www.richerresourcespublications.com.

Riches Publishing Co., *(978-0-9728219)* P.O. Box 02232, Detroit, MI 48202 USA
E-mail: klrich@sbcglobal.net
Web site: http://www.klrich.com.

Richeson, John W., *(978-0-9675315)* P.O. Box 710371, San Diego, CA 92171 USA
E-mail: john@VBAtech.com
Web site: http://vbatech.com.

Richlee Publishing, *(978-0-9796265)* 2898 Morning Creek Rd., Chula Vista, CA 91914-4311 USA
E-mail: jmacgregor@cadencemarketinggroup.com
Dist(s): **AtlasBooks Distribution.**

Richlyn Publishing, *(978-0-9722264)* 12045 W Brandt Pl, Littleton, CO 80127-4572 USA Tel 303-979-8609
E-mail: richlyn2@msn.com
Web site: http://www.richlynpublishing.com.

Richmond *Imprint of* **Santillana USA Publishing Co., Inc.**

Richmondmom.com Publishing *Imprint of* **Palari Publishing LLP**

Rickshaw Press *See* **Ragged Sky Pr.**

Riddering, Marggie, *(978-0-9765977)* P.O. Box 770, Hormigueros, PR 00660 USA Tel 787-833-2260.

Riddle Creek Publishing, *(978-0-9725894; 978-0-9835009)* 232 Cty. Rd. 19, Haleyville, AL 35565-7416 USA
E-mail: riddlecreek@centurytel.net
Web site: http://www.riddlecreekpublishing.com.

Rider Franklin Reynolds Publishing *See* **Belisarian Bks.**

Riders Elite Academy, Inc., *(978-0-9741628)* 23120 Garrison Rd., Corcoran, MN 55340-9103 USA Tel 763-498-6565 (phone/fax)
E-mail: books@riderselite.com
Web site: http://www.riderselite.com.

Ridge Rock Pr., *(978-0-9670177)* Div. of Ridge Rock, Inc., Orders Addr.: P.O. Box 255, Healy, AK 99743 USA (SAN 253-6595) Tel 907-322-8185 (cell); 907-683-7737 (phone/fax); Edit Addr.: Mile 261 Parks Hwy., Box 255, Healy, AK 99743 USA
E-mail: ridgerock@gtemail.net
Dist(s): **Todd Communications.**

Ridge Row Press *See* **Univ. of Scranton Pr.**

Ridgewood Group, The, *(978-0-9716907)* P.O. Box 8011, Manchester, CT 06040 USA (SAN 254-3419) Tel 860-432-4537 (phone/fax); *Imprints:* Ridgewood Publishing (Ridgewood Pub)
E-mail: info@theridgewoodgroup.com
Web site: http://www.hermanthecrab.com.

Ridgewood Pr., *(978-0-9650434)* 2160 Aztec Dr., dyersburg, TN 38024 USA Do not confuse with Ridgewood Pr., Jefferson City, MO
E-mail: bartonsn@mac.com.

Ridgewood Publishing *Imprint of* **Ridgewood Group, The**

†Rienner, Lynne Pubs., *(978-0-89410; 978-0-931477; 978-1-55587; 978-1-56549; 978-1-58826; 978-1-62637)* 1800 30th St., Suite 314, Boulder, CO 80301-1026 USA (SAN 683-1869) Tel 303-444-6684; Fax: 303-444-0824
E-mail: cservice@rienner.com; sglover@rienner.com; questions@rienner.com
Web site: http://www.rienner.com; http://https://www.kpbooks.com/; http://www.firstforumpress.com; *CIP.*

Rigby Education, *(978-0-7635; 978-0-7578; 978-1-4189)* Div. of Houghton Mifflin Harcourt Supplemental Pubs., Orders Addr.: 6277 Sea Harbor Dr., 5th Flr., Orlando, FL 32887 USA Toll Free Fax: 877-578-2638; Toll Free: 888-363-4266; Edit Addr.: 10801 N. Mopac Expressway, Bldg. 3, Austin, TX 78759 USA Toll Free Fax: 800-699-9459; Toll Free: 800-531-5015
Web site: http://www.harcourtachieve.com
Dist(s): **Follett School Solutions**
Houghton Mifflin Harcourt Supplemental Pubs.

Riggott, Dean Photography, *(978-0-9659875)* 831 10 1/2 St., SW, Rochester, MN 55902 USA Tel 507-285-5076; Fax: 253-540-6093
Web site: http://www.riggottphoto.com
Dist(s): **Partners Bk. Distributing, Inc.**

Riggs, Theresia, *(978-0-9746132)* 8910 Dogwood Dr., Tomball, TX 77375 USA Tel 281-351-2329 (phone/fax)
E-mail: Ohringen@aol.com
Web site: http://www.CosmicSisters.com.

Right On Programs, Inc., *(978-0-933426)* 522 E. Broadway, Suite 101, Glendale, CA 91205 USA (SAN 212-5099) Tel 818-240-1683; Fax: 818-240-2858.

Right Stuff Kids Bks., *(978-0-9704597; 978-1-932317)* 5600 Claire Rose Ln., Atlanta, GA 30327 USA
E-mail: satiller@bellsouth.net
Web site: http://www.michaelsmind.com.

Right Track Reading LLC, *(978-0-9763290)* P.O. Box 1952, Livingston, MT 59047 USA
E-mail: mmgagen@earthlink.net.

Right-Away, Inc., *(978-0-9709095)* P.O. Box 741993, Riverdale, GA 30274 USA Tel 404-798-7508
E-mail: jakiharris2004@yahoo.com; rightaway1@hotmail.com.

Righteous Bks., *(978-0-9883634)* 2801 W. 83rd St., Chicago, IL 60652 USA Tel 773-744-8162
E-mail: righteousrayray@gmail.com.

Righter Publishing Co., Inc., *(978-0-9706823; 978-0-9747735; 978-0-9766032; 978-0-9778948; 978-0-9796209; 978-1-934936; 978-1-938527)* Orders Addr.: 410 River Oaks Pkwy., Timberlake, NC 27583 USA Fax: 336-597-8881
E-mail: righterpub@esinc.net
Web site: http://www.righterbooks.com
Dist(s): **CreateSpace Independent Publishing Platform.**

Riker, Dale, *(978-0-9771621)* 6937 W. Country Club Dr. N, Unit 152, Sarasota, FL 34243-3507 USA.

Riley Pr., *(978-0-9728958)* P.O. Box 202, Eagle, MI 48822 USA Tel 517-626-7027
E-mail: rileypress@yahoo.com
Web site: http://rileypress.hypermart.net.

Rilly Silly Bk. Co., The, *(978-0-9747054)* 11130 W. Heatherbrae Dr., Phoenix, AZ 85037 USA Tel 623-877-6020
Web site: http://www.rillysilly.com.

Rincon Publishing Co., *(978-0-9660858)* Orders Addr.: 1913 Skyline Dr., Orem, UT 84097 USA Tel 801-377-7657; Fax: 801-356-2733
E-mail: RinconPub@Utahtrails.com
Web site: http://www.utahtrails.com
Dist(s): **Partners/West Book Distributors.**

Rind, Sherry, *(978-0-9674729)* Orders Addr.: 959 Evonshire Ln., Great Falls, VA 22066 USA; Edit Addr.: 8419 NE 144th St., Bothell, WA 98011-5055 USA
E-mail: AIREBIRD@hotmail.com; KCBROOM@erols.com
Web site: http://www.airedaleterriers.org.

Rinehart, Roberts Pubs., *(978-0-911797; 978-0-943173; 978-1-57098; 978-1-57140; 978-1-879373; 978-1-58979)* Div. of Rowman & Littlefield Pubs., Inc., Orders Addr.: 15200 NBN Way, Blue Ridge Summit, PA 17214 USA Tel 717-794-3800 (Customer Service &/or orders); Fax: 717-794-3803 (Customer Service &/or orders only); 717-794-3857 (Sales & MIS); 717-794-3856 (Royalties, Inventory Mgmt., & Dist.); Toll Free Fax: 800-338-4550 (Customer Service &/or orders); Toll Free: 800-462-6420 (Customer Service &/or orders); Edit Addr.: 4501 Forbes Blvd., Suite 200, Lanham, MD 20706 USA Tel 301-459-3366; Toll Free: 800-462-6420
E-mail: nrothschild@rowman.com
Web site: http://www.robertsrinehart.com
Dist(s): **Ebsco Publishing**
Follett School Solutions
National Bk. Network
Rowman & Littlefield Publishers, Inc.
ebrary, Inc.

Rio Grande Bks. *Imprint of* **LPD Pr.**

Rio Nuevo Pubs., *(978-0-918080; 978-1-887896; 978-0-9700750; 978-1-933855; 978-1-940322)* Orders Addr.: P.O. Box 5250, Tucson, AZ 85703-0250 USA (SAN 209-3251) Tel 520-623-9558; Fax: 520-624-5888; Toll Free Fax: 800-715-5888; Toll Free: 800-969-9558; Edit Addr.: 451 N. Bonita Ave., Tucson, AZ 85745 USA Tel 602-623-9558; *Imprints:* Rio Nuevo Publishers (Rio Nuevo)
E-mail: info@rionuevo.com; info@treasurechestbooks.com; suzang@rionuevo.com
Web site: http://www.treasurechestbooks.com; http://www.rionuevo.com/
Dist(s): **Treasure Chest Bks.**

Rio Nuevo Pubs. *Imprint of* **Rio Nuevo Pubs.**

Rio Wildflower Pubns., *(978-0-9786168)* P.O. Box 246, Almont, CO 81210 USA Tel 970-642-0272
E-mail: wildflowercd@peoplepc.com.

Rip Squeak, Inc., *(978-0-9672422; 978-0-9747825)* Orders Addr.: c/o Raven Tree Press, 1400 Miller Pkwy., McHenry, IL 60050 USA Tel 815-363-3582; Fax: 815-363-2948; Edit Addr.: 840 Capitolio Way, Suite B, San Luis Obispo, CA 93401-7130 USA Tel 805-594-0184; Fax: 805-543-5782; Toll Free: 800-251-0654; *Imprints:* Rip Squeak Press (Rip Squeak Pr)
E-mail: Beda@RipSqueak.com; dawnj@delta-systems.com
Web site: http://www.RipSqueak.com; http://www.raventreepress.com
Dist(s): **Delta Systems Company, Inc.**

Rip Squeak Pr. *Imprint of* **Rip Squeak, Inc.**

Ripley Entertainment, Inc., *(978-1-893951; 978-1-60991)* Div. of The Jim Pattison Group, 7576 Kingspointe Pkwy., Suite. 188, Orlando, FL 32819-6510 USA (SAN 299-9498)
E-mail: meyer@ripleys.com; dula@ripleys.com
Web site: http://www.ripleys.com
Dist(s): **Mint Pubs. Group**
Simon & Schuster, Inc.

Ripple Grove Pr., *(978-0-9913866)* P.O. Box 86740, Portland, OR 97286 USA Tel 774-230-3556
E-mail: amanda@ripplegrovepress.com
Web site: www.ripplegrovepress.com
Dist(s): **Midpoint Trade Bks., Inc.**

Riptide Pr., Inc., *(978-0-9723456)* 233 Walnut Creek Dr., Clayton, NC 27520 USA Tel 919-359-2852; Fax: 919-882-9924 Do not confuse with companies with the same or similar name in New York, NY, Fredericksburg, VA
E-mail: info@riptidebooks.com; info@riptidepress.com
Web site: http://www.riptidebooks.com; http://www.riptidepress.com.

Risa Publications, *(978-0-9771404)* 8424-A Santa Monica Blvd., Suite 175, West Hollywood, CA 90069 USA
Web site: http://www.lisahaisha.com.

Risen Heart Pr., *(978-0-9764497)* 554 Bruns Dr., Rossford, OH 43460 USA Tel 419-666-6269
E-mail: rjbaden@wcnet.org.

Rising Bks., *(978-0-9644456)* P.O. Box 1408, Conyers, GA 30012 USA (SAN 298-5438) Tel 404-378-7464; Fax: 770-761-9865
E-mail: chadfoster@mindspring.com
Web site: www.chadfoster.com.

Rising Moon Bks. for Young Readers *Imprint of* **Northland Publishing**

Rising Phoenix Pr., *(978-0-615-68352-2; 978-0-615-68666-0; 978-0-615-68667-7; 978-0-615-69091-9; 978-0-615-70515-6; 978-0-615-74990-7; 978-0-9888568)* 100 Goldmine Ct., Aledo, TX 68008 USA Tel 817-757-7143
Web site: www.progressiverisingphoenix.com
Dist(s): **CreateSpace Independent Publishing Platform.**

Rising Star Publishers *See* **WeWrite LLC**

Rising Star Studios, LLC., *(978-1-936086; 978-1-936770)* 5251 W. 73rd St. Suite C, Edina, MN 55439 USA Tel 952-831-8532; Fax: 952-831-5809
E-mail: mark@risingstarstudios.com; info@risingstarstudios.com; sales@risingstarstudios.com
Web site: http://www.risingstarstudios.com
Dist(s): **Follett School Solutions.**

Rising Sun Publishing, Inc., *(978-1-880463)* P.O. Box 70906, Marietta, GA 30007-0906 USA Tel 770-518-0369; Fax: 770-587-0862; Toll Free: 800-524-2813 Do not confuse with Rising Sun Pubng in Fairfield, OH
E-mail: info@rspublishing.com; sholland@rspublishing.com
Web site: http://www.rspublishing.com.

Rising Tide Pr., *(978-0-913844)* Div. of American-Canadian Pubs., Inc., P.O. Box 6136, Santa Fe, NM 87502-4595 USA (SAN 298-217X) Do not confuse with Rising Tide Pubs., Tucson, AZ.

Rissylyn, *(978-0-9894933)* 2 12th St. Apt. 1012, Hoboken, NJ 07030 USA Tel 917-859-4751
E-mail: info@dreambigacademy.com.

Ritchie Unlimited Pubns., *(978-0-939656)* 1427 Anderson Rd. Suite B, Springfield, OR 97477 USA (SAN 216-6461) Tel 541-741-0794 (phone/fax)
E-mail: ralph-ritchie@comcast.net
Web site: http://www.ritchieunlimitedpublications.com.

Rite Lite Limited, *(978-0-9772560)* 333 Stanley Ave., Brooklyn, NY 11207 USA Tel 718-498-1700; Fax: 718-498-1251; Toll Free: 800-942-0707
E-mail: mail@riteliteltd.com
Web site: http://www.riteliteltd.com.

Rite Quest, *(978-0-9801484)* 1308 Turnberry Ct., Chesapeake, VA 23320-9445 USA.

Ritz, Lee Pubns., *(978-1-940840)* 2934 Ames St., Wheat Ridge, CO 80214 USA Tel 303-330-2477
E-mail: leeritz@leeritzpublications.com
Web site: www.leeritzpublications.com.

Rivendell Bk. Factory, *(978-0-944353)* 217 Country Club Park Crestline Village, PMB321, Mountain Brook, AL 35213 USA Tel (205) 871-5915; Fax: (205) 871-5945
Dist(s): **Cardinal Pubs. Group.**

River Canyon Pr., *(978-0-9815914; 978-0-9827531)* Orders Addr.: P.O. Box 191, Oakland, OR 97462 USA (SAN 855-9651) Tel 541-530-2061
Web site: http://www.rivercanyonpress.com
Dist(s): **CreateSpace Independent Publishing Platform**
River Canyon Distributing.

River City Kids *Imprint of* **River City Publishing**

River City Pr., *(978-0-9706962; 978-0-9764232; 978-0-9776713)* 4301 Emerson Ave. N., Minneapolis, MN 55412 USA Tel 612-521-9633 (phone/fax); Toll Free: 888-234-3559 Do not confuse with River City Pr. in New Orleans, LA
E-mail: bwolf@rivercitypress.net
Web site: http://www.rivercitypress.net.

River City Publishing, *(978-0-913515; 978-0-9622815; 978-1-57966; 978-1-880216; 978-1-881320)* 1719 Mulberry St., Montgomery, AL 36106 USA (SAN 631-4910) Tel 334-265-6753; Fax: 334-265-8880; Toll Free: 877-408-7078; *Imprints:* River City Kids (River City Kids) Do not confuse with companies with the same or similar names in Richland, WA, South Bend, IN
E-mail: sales@rivercitypublishing.com
Web site: http://www.rivercitypublishing.com.

River Lake Pr., *(978-0-615-36951-8)* 1799 Ashland Ave., Saint Paul, MN 55104 USA Tel 651-646-2915
E-mail: bethanymasters@riverlakepress.com
Web site: http://www.bethanymasters.com.

River of Life Publishing, *(978-0-9746345)* 3700 Chestnut Lake Ct., Jonesboro, GA 30236-5502 USA Do not confuse with River of Life Publishing in Kremmling, CO.

River Pointe Pubns., *(978-0-9758805; 978-0-9817258; 978-0-9848103)* 612 River Pointe Ct., Milan, MI 48160 USA Tel 734-439-8031
E-mail: riverptpub@sbcglobal.net.

River Pr., *(978-0-9725796; 978-0-9849909)* Div. of OCRS, Inc., Orders Addr.: 52 Tuscan Way Ste 202 # 404, Saint Augustine, FL 32092 USA (SAN 850-5098) Tel 904-563-6277; Fax: 904-940-5178; Edit Addr.: P.O. Box 551627, Jacksonville, FL 32255 USA
E-mail: wrcsacriver@comcast.net
Web site: http://randycribbsauthor.com.

River Road Pubns., Inc., *(978-0-938682)* 1433 Fulton St., Grand Haven, MI 49417-1572 USA (SAN 253-8172) Toll Free: 800-373-8762
E-mail: Pandex@prodigy.net
Web site: http://www.riverroadpublications.com.

River Sanctuary Publishing, *(978-0-9841140; 978-1-935914)* P.O. Box 1561, Felton, CA 95018 USA (SAN 858-4532) Tel 831-335-7283
Web site: http://www.riversanctuarypublishing.com.

River Styx Publishing Co., *(978-0-9788997; 978-1-61704)* 1400 Ash St., Terre Haute, IN 47804 USA; P.O. Box 3246, Terre Haute, IN 47803
E-mail: pessy74@aol.com
Web site: http://fixitprogram.zoomshare.com.

Rivera Engineering, *(978-0-9801695)* 227 Brahan Blvd., San Antonio, TX 78215 USA (SAN 855-3874) Tel 210-771-2662; Fax: 210-226-9027
E-mail: alanegarivera@yahoo.com
Web site: http://www.rivera-engineering.com
Dist(s): **AtlasBooks Distribution.**

Riverbank Publishing, *(978-0-9753320)* 1917 Winterport Cluster, Reston, VA 20191 USA
Web site: http://www.riverbankpublishing.com.

Riverbend Publishing, *(978-1-931832; 978-1-60639)* Orders Addr.: P.O. Box 5833, Helena, MT 59604 USA Tel 406-449-0200; Fax: 406-449-0330; Toll Free: 866-787-2363; Edit Addr.: 1660 B St., Helena, MT 59601 USA (SAN 254-5020) Do not confuse with companies with the same or similar names in Elizabeth, CO, Marion, KY, Knoxville, TN
Web site: http://www.riverbendpublishing.com
Dist(s): **Bks. West**
High Peak Bks.
Partners Bk. Distributing, Inc.
Smashwords
TNT Media Group, Inc.
Wolverine Distributing, Inc.

Rivercity Pr. *Imprint of* **Amereon LTD.**

RiverCreek Bks., Inc., *(978-0-9745171)* Orders Addr.: P.O. Box 1146, Buies Creek, NC 27506 USA Tel 910-893-8853.

Riverdale Bks. *Imprint of* **Riverdale Electronic Bks.**

Riverdale Electronic Books *See* **Riverdale Electronic Bks.**

Riverdale Electronic Bks., *(978-0-9712207; 978-1-932606)* 4420 Bonneville Dr., Cumming, GA 30041 USA Tel 770-891-2710; *Imprints:* Riverdale Books (RiverdBks)
E-mail: jtm@riverdalebooks.com
Web site: http://www.riverdaleebooks.com.

Riverdeep, Incorporated *See* **Houghton Mifflin Harcourt Learning Technology**

RiverEarth, *(978-0-9787722)* Orders Addr.: P.O. Box 245, Southern Pines, NC 28388 USA (SAN 851-5824) Tel 910-795-2285; Edit Addr.: P.O. Box 245, Southern Pines, NC 28388 USA
E-mail: bernie@riverearth.com
Web site: http://riverearth.com.

Riverhead Trade (Paperbacks) *Imprint of* **Penguin Publishing Group**

RiverPlace Development Corp., *(978-0-9785538)* Orders Addr.: P.O. Box 6218, Reading, PA 19610-0218 USA
E-mail: info@RiverPlacePA.com
Web site: http://www.RiverPlacePA.com.

RIVERRUN BOOKSTORE INC, *(978-0-9856073; 978-0-9885370; 978-1-939739)* 142 Fleet St, Portsmouth, NH 03801 USA Tel 603-431-2100
E-mail: riverrunbookstore@gmail.com.

Rivers, Swannee, *(978-0-9749216; 978-0-578-04160-5)* 1629 Index Ave. Se, Suite No. 400, Renton, WA 98058 USA Fax: 425-277-2950
E-mail: swanneerivers@mindspring.com
Web site: http://www.swanneerivers.com.

Riverside Art Museum, *(978-0-9802207; 978-0-692-41917-5)* 3425 Mission Inn Ave., Riverside, CA 92501-3304 USA
E-mail: mcarlson@riversideartmuseum.org.

Riverstone Group Publishing, *(978-0-9706117; 978-0-9763092; 978-0-9906166)* 1245 Scott Rd., Canton, GA 30114 USA; 1245 Scott Rd., Canton, GA 30115 Tel 770-720-1008
E-mail: epulleu@riverstonegroup.com
Web site: http://www.riverstonegroup.com.

RiverStream Publishing, *(978-1-62243)* 123 S. Broad St., Mankato, MN 56001 USA Tel 414-378-2480
E-mail: jstrick@hickorytech.net
Dist(s): **Child's World, Inc., The.**

Rivertide Publishing, *(978-0-9826252)* 890 Kensington Ave., Astoria, OR 97103 USA Tel 503-325-8818
E-mail: karenleedom@q.com.

Rivertree Productions, Inc., *(978-1-882412)* P.O. Box 410, Bradford, NH 03221 USA Tel 603-938-5120; Fax: 603-938-5616; Toll Free: 800-554-1333; *Imprints:* Odds Bodkin Storytelling Library, The (Odds Bodkin)
E-mail: rivertree@conknet.com
Web site: http://www.oddsbodkin.com
Dist(s): **Penton Overseas, Inc.**

Riverview Foundation, *(978-0-9771639)* Orders Addr.: P.O. Box 310, Topsham, ME 04086 USA (SAN 256-8357) Tel 207-729-7399; Fax: 207-797-5676; Edit Addr.: 610 Augusta Rd., Tomsham, ME 04086 USA
E-mail: office@riverviewfoundation.com
Web site: http://www.riverviewfoundation.com.

Riverwood Bks. *Imprint of* **White Cloud Pr.**

Rivet Bks. *Imprint of* **Feral Pr., Inc.**

RIXKIN, *(978-0-9842069)* P.O. Box 11922, Atlanta, GA 30355 USA Tel 888-674-1679; Fax: 888-674-2577
E-mail: info@rixkin.com; pr@rixkin.com; orders@rixkin.com
Web site: http://www.rixkin.com
Dist(s): **Quality Bks., Inc.**

†Rizzoli International Pubns., Inc., *(978-0-8478; 978-0-941807; 978-1-932183; 978-1-59962)* Subs. of RCS Rizzoli Editore Corp., 300 Park Ave., S., 3rd Flr., New York, NY 10010 USA (SAN 111-9192) Tel 212-387-3400; Fax: 212-387-3535; *Imprints:* White Star (White Star NY); Rizzoli Universe Promotional Books (RUPB); Skira (Skira); Welcome Books (Welcome)
Web site: http://www.rizzoliusa.com/
Dist(s): **MyiLibrary**
Penguin Random Hse., LLC.
Random Hse., Inc.; *CIP.*

Rizzoli Universe Promotional Bks. *Imprint of* **Rizzoli International Pubns., Inc.**

R.J. Bob Chavez Images, *(978-0-9778110)* 5537 Lewis Ct. Unit 201, Arvada, CO 80002 USA Tel 303-423-6982
E-mail: rjbcimages@aol.com.

RJ Pubns., *(978-0-9769277; 978-0-9786373; 978-0-9817773; 978-0-9819998; 978-1-939284)* 290 Dune St., Far Rockaway, NY 11691-2714 USA (SAN 256-5919); P.O. Box 300771, Jamaica, NY 11430
Web site: http://www.rjpublications.com.

RJI Publishing, *(978-1-885184)* Orders Addr.: 2800 N. Roadrunner Pkwy. # 701, Las Cruces, NM 88011 USA Tel 575-521-1336
E-mail: rjipublishing@aol.com
Web site: http://www.rjipublishing.com.

RK Enterprises, Inc., *(978-0-9743775)* 22581 NE State Route 3., Belfair, WA 98528-9303 USA
E-mail: rkilsby@wavecable.com
Web site: http://www.gooshu.com.

Roach, Patricia, *(978-0-9817680)* 17 Hillside Ave., Winsted, CT 06098 USA.

Road Tunes Media, *(978-0-9721725)* Orders Addr.: 534 Hidden Way, Homer, AK 99603 USA (SAN 852-5188)
E-mail: roadtunes@gci.net
Web site: http://www.berniejones.com
Dist(s): **Follett School Solutions.**

Roadracing World Publishing, Inc., *(978-0-9749615)* P.O. Box 1428, Lake Elsinore, CA 92531 USA Tel 951-245-6411 Toll Free: 800-464-8336
E-mail: custsvc@roadracingworld.com
Web site: http://www.roadracingworld.com.

Roadrunner Pr., *(978-0-9636346)* Orders Addr.: 2815 Lake Shore Dr., Michigan City, IN 46360-1619 USA Tel 219-879-0133; 2815 Lake Shore Dr., Michigan City, IN 46360-1619
E-mail: roadrunnerpress@comcast.net
Web site: http://www.halhigdon.com.

RoadRunner Pr., *(978-1-937054)* P.O. Box 2564, Oklahoma City, OK 73101 USA Tel 405-524-6205; Fax: 405-524-6312
E-mail: jeanne@theroadrunnerpress.com
Web site: www.TheRoadRunnerPress.com.

Roald Publishing, *(978-0-578-12595-4; 978-0-578-12602-9)* 1139 West Ave., J-9, Lancaster, CA 93534 USA.

Roaring Brook Pr., *(978-0-7613; 978-1-59643)* 115 West 18th Street, New York, NY 10011 USA Tel 212-886-1030; *Imprints:* First Second Books (First Second); Kingfisher (Kingfsh); Macaulay, David Studio (D Macaulay)
Web site: http://www.henryholt.com; http://us.macmillan.com/splash/publishers/roaring-brook-press.html
Dist(s): **Follett School Solutions**
Macmillan
MyiLibrary.

Robbie Dean Pr., *(978-0-9630608; 978-1-889743; 978-0-9892303; 978-0-9916017)* 2910 E. Eisenhower Pkwy., Ann Arbor, MI 48108 USA Tel 734-973-9511; Fax: 734-973-9475
E-mail: fairyha@aol.com.

Robe Communications, Inc., *(978-0-9817403; 978-1-935831)* 5138 S. Clifton Ave., Springfield, MO 65810 USA Tel 417-887-8793
E-mail: krobe@mchsi.com
Web site: http://www.robbietherabbit.com.

Robello, Kimberly, *(978-0-615-75525-0)* 1100 S. Hidalgo Ave., Alhambra, CA 91801 USA Tel 6262897144
Web site: www.planetkimberly.blogspot.com
Dist(s): **CreateSpace Independent Publishing Platform.**

Roberts & Ross Publishing, *(978-1-936449)* 3361 W. Monmouth Ave., Englewood, CO 80110-6336 USA Tel 303-762-1469; Fax: 303-993-5639
E-mail: Patricia@RobertsRossPublishing.com.

Roberts, Michele, *(978-0-9760188)* P.O. Box 271611, Houston, TX 77277-1611 USA.

Roberts Publishing Co., *(978-0-931764)* 738 32nd St., S. E., Grand Rapids, MI 49548 USA Tel 616-245-1560; Fax: 616-245-1561 (orders can be sent by fax) Do not confuse with companies with the same or similar names in Sacramento, CA, San Marcos, CA, Great Lake, WI, Blaine, WA
E-mail: robertspublishingco@juno.com
Web site: http://www.scoliosishelp.com; http://www.scoliosishelp.org; http://www.robertsbookshelf.comw.

Robertson Publishing, *(978-0-9727721; 978-0-9796251; 978-0-9798633; 978-0-9801675; 978-1-935125; 978-1-61170)* 59 N. Santa Cruz Ave., Suite B, Los Gatos, CA 95030 USA Tel 408-354-5957 Toll Free: 888-354-5957
E-mail: alicia.r@robertsonpubblishing.com
Web site: http://www.RobertsonPublishing.com.

Robillard, Kristy, *(978-0-9800870)* 15110 S Oakleigh Ln., Prairieville, LA 70769 USA Fax: 225-744-3276
E-mail: robillard1@eatel.net.

Robin Corey Bks. *Imprint of* **Random Hse. Children's Bks.**

Robinbook, Ediciones S.L. (ESP) *(978-84-7927; 978-84-9917) Dist. by* **Lectorum Pubns.**

Robinson, Beth, *(978-0-9799092)* P.O. Box 100, New Deal, TX 79350 USA (SAN 854-7378)
Web site: http://www.drbethrobinson.com.

Robinson, Consuelo, *(978-0-9786767)* P.O. Box 8662, Delray Beach, FL 33482 USA (SAN 851-2868)
E-mail: math1on1@math1on1.com
Web site: www.math1on1.com.

Robinson, Francesca *See* **Francesca Studios**

Robison Gamble Creative, *(978-1-933497)* 1420 W. Skyline Ave., Ozark, MO 65721 USA Tel 417-581-6008; Fax: 417-581-4542; Toll Free: 877-335-2735
E-mail: carrie@robisongamble.com
Web site: http://www.robisongamble.com.

Robot Playground, Inc., *(978-0-615-51355-3; 978-0-615-57232-1; 978-0-615-67487-2; 978-0-9862926)* 9471 Villa way, Miamisburg, OH 45342 USA Tel 937-371-1240
E-mail: rita@ritajwebb.com
Dist(s): **CreateSpace Independent Publishing Platform.**

Robus, Debbie, *(978-0-9762034)* 31 Timberline Dr., Heber Springs, AR 72543-9417 USA
E-mail: firecrackerbaby57@yahoo.com
Web site: http://firecrackerbaby57.blogspot.com; http://www.workamper.com
Dist(s): **Workamper Bookstore.**

Robyn Z Moon Publishing, *(978-0-615-15292-9; 978-0-615-20370-6)* 3021 Eads Ave., Saint Lois, MO 63104 USA Toll Free: 877-544-0102
E-mail: robynzmoon@gmail.com
Dist(s): **Lulu Enterprises Inc.**

Roc *Imprint of* **Penguin Publishing Group**

ROC Hardcover *Imprint of* **Penguin Publishing Group**

ROC Trade *Imprint of* **Penguin Publishing Group**

Roca Bolsillo (ESP) *(978-84-96940; 978-84-92833; 978-84-15729; 978-84-16240) Dist. by* **Spanish.**

Roca Editorial De Libros (ESP) *(978-84-96284; 978-84-96544; 978-84-96791; 978-84-9918; 978-84-92429) Dist. by* **Ediciones.**

Roca Editorial De Libros (ESP) *(978-84-96284; 978-84-96544; 978-84-96791; 978-84-9918; 978-84-92429) Dist. by* **Spanish.**

Rocco, Editora, Ltda (BRA) *(978-85-325; 978-85-62500) Dist. by* **Distribks Inc.**

Rock & Learn Educational Products *See* **Rock 'N Learn, Inc.**

Rock Cliff Media, *(978-0-9791384)* 553 Staci Ct., Ogden, UT 84404 USA
E-mail: info@rockcliffmedia.com
Web site: http://www.rockcliffmedia.com.

Rock Hse. Method, The *Imprint of* **Russell, Fred Publishing**

Rock Ink, *(978-0-9726979)* 2826 Cory Creek Rd., Oroville, CA 95965 USA Tel 530-894-7743; Fax: 530-892-8293
E-mail: mlrock@mariarock.com
Web site: http://www.mariarock.com.

Rock, James A. & Co. Pubs., *(978-0-918736; 978-1-59663)* 900 S. Irby St., #508, Florence, SC 29505-6357 USA (SAN 211-4690) Toll Free: 800-411-2230; 9710 Traville Gateway Dr., No. 305, Rockville, MD 20850; *Imprints:* Castle Keep Press (Castle Keep Pr); Sense of Wonder Press (Sense of Wonder); Mount Helicon Press (Mt Helicon MD)
E-mail: jarrock@sprintmail.com
Web site: http://www.rockpublishing.com; http://www.senseofwonderpress.com.

Rock 'N Learn, Inc., *(978-1-878489; 978-1-934312; 978-1-941722)* Orders Addr.: P.O. Box 3595, Conroe, TX 77305-3595 USA Tel 936-539-2731; Fax: 936-539-2659; Toll Free Fax: 800-801-5481; Toll Free: 800-348-8445; Edit Addr.: 105 Commercial Cir., Conroe, TX 77304 USA
E-mail: info@rocknlearn.com
Web site: http://www.rocknlearn.com
Dist(s): **Big Kids Productions, Inc.**
Follett School Solutions
Rounder Kids Music Distribution.

Rock Village Publishing, *(978-0-9674204; 978-0-9721389; 978-0-9766356; 978-1-934400)* 41 Walnut St., Middleborough, MA 02346 USA Tel 508-946-4738
E-mail: rockvillage@verizon.net.

Rockbott'm *See* **Spring Hollow Bks., LLC**

Rocket Ride Bks., *(978-0-9823322)* P.O. Box 1046, Somerset, PA 15501 USA
E-mail: anthonyrotoolo@yahoo.com.

Rockhill Bks. *Imprint of* **Kansas City Star Bks.**

Rockmill Publishing Co., *(978-0-9764012)* Rockmill Management, Inc., 17360 Hunter Ct., Lake Oswego, OR 97035 USA (SAN 256-5722) Tel 503-989-2590 (phone/fax); 503-806-3970
E-mail: energiesinc@msn.com; tammystamermotsch@msn.com.

Rockon Publishing, *(978-0-9726255)* 210 Hy Rd., Buda, TX 78610 USA Tel 512-295-4889
E-mail: wermundj@mail.utexas.edu.

Rocksand, LLC, *(978-1-931552)* 238 Greenbrier Dr., Cape Girardeau, MO 63701 USA Tel 877-625-7263
E-mail: bethprints@gmail.com
Web site: http://www.rainbowindow.com.

Rockshow Comedy, Inc., *(978-0-9854699)* 130 Old Town Blvd. N., Argyle, TX 76226 USA Tel 817-915-4296
E-mail: todd@rockshowcomedy.com
Web site: www.rockshowcomedy.com.

RockTuff, *(978-0-9800754)* Orders Addr.: P.O. Box 133, Roscoe, SD 57471 USA (SAN 855-1308) Tel 605-287-4133; Fax: 605-287-4188; Edit Addr.: 34240 Hwy. 12, Roscoe, SD 57471 USA
E-mail: rocktuff@venturecomm.net
Web site: http://www.andreabeyers.com.

Rocky Mountain Bks. (CAN) *(978-0-921102; 978-0-9690038; 978-1-894765; 978-1-897522; 978-1-926855; 978-1-927330; 978-1-77160) Dist. by* **PerseuPGW.**

Rod & Staff Pubs., Inc., *(978-0-7399)* P.O. Box 3, 14193 Hwy. 172, Crockett, KY 41413 USA (SAN 206-7633) Tel 606-522-4348; Fax: 606-522-4896; Toll Free Fax: 800-643-1244
Web site: http://www.rodstaff.com/.

Rodaian Pr., *(978-1-935436; 978-0-9847167; 978-0-9847986; 978-0-9893251)* P.O. Box 3128, Palm Springs, CA 92263 USA
Web site: http://www.rodaian.com.

Publisher Name Index

†**Rodale Pr., Inc.**, *(978-0-87596; 978-0-87857; 978-1-57954; 978-1-4050; 978-1-59486; 978-1-60529; 978-1-60961; 978-1-62336)* Orders Addr.: 16365 James Madison Hwy., Gordonsville, VA 22942-8501 USA Toll Free Fax: 800-672-2054; Toll Free: 888-330-8477; Edit Addr.: 400 S. Tenth St., Emmaus, PA 18098-0099 USA (SAN 200-2477) Tel 610-967-5171; Fax: 215-967-8961; Toll Free: 800-222-4997
E-mail: sara.cox@rodale.com
Web site: rodale.com
Dist(s): **Bilingual Pubns. Co., The**
Lectorum Pubns., Inc.
MBI Distribution Services/Quayside Distribution
Macmillan
Send The Light Distribution LLC
St. Martin's Pr.
TNT Media Group, Inc.; *CIP*.

Rodgers, Alan Bks., *(978-1-59818; 978-0-60312; 978-1-60664; 978-1-4638)* 23511 Aliso Creek Rd., No. 120, Alsio Viejo, CA 92656-1341 USA
E-mail: AlanRodg@aol.com; amysterlingcasil@gmail.com; lmdegange@yahoo.com
Web site: http://www.aegypan.com; www.chameleonpublishers.com; http://www.chameleonmedia.co.

Rodgers & Nelsen Publishing Company *See* **Loveland Pr., LLC**

Rodmell Pr., *(978-0-9627138; 978-1-930485)* 2147 Blake St., Berkeley, CA 94704-2715 USA Tel 510-841-3123; Fax: 510-841-3191; Toll Free: 800-841-3123
E-mail: rodmellprs@aol.com
Web site: http://www.rodmellpress.com
Dist(s): **MyiLibrary**
Perseus-PGW
Perseus Bks. Group.

Rodrigue & Sons Company *See* **Rodrigue & Sons Co./Double R Books Publishing**

Rodrigue & Sons Co./Double R Books Publishing, *(978-0-9749026; 978-0-9833975; 978-1-938319)* Orders Addr.: 740 N. H St., Suite 170, Lompoc, CA 93436 USA Tel 805-735-7103 10am - 5pm PST; Fax: 805-737-9846; Edit Addr.: 740 N. H St., Suite 170, Lompoc, CA 93436 Tel 805-735-7103 10am - 5pm PST; Fax: 805-737-9846; *Imprints*: DOUBLE-R BOOKS (DOUBLE-R)
E-mail: publisher@double-Rbooks.com
Web site: http://Double-Rbooks.com
Dist(s): **INscribe Digital**
Ingram Bk. Co.

Rodriguez, Estela, *(978-0-9772631)* Orders Addr.: 2050 NW 16th Terr., Apt. E111, Miami, FL 33125 USA Tel 305-549-3039; Edit Addr.: Jose Marti Stat. 27 & 4th St., Miami, FL 33135 USA
E-mail: colorama@bellsouth.net.

Rodriguez, Michelle, *(978-0-9900061)* 38-33 147th St., Flushing, NY 11354 USA Tel 646-217-9177
E-mail: maliperto1@gmail.com.

Rodriguez, Raul, *(978-0-9912750)* 9619 Judalon Ln., Houston, TX 77063 USA Tel 281-467-6992
E-mail: raul6992@yahoo.com.

Rodro, *(978-0-9744770)* 52 Richmond Blvd., No. 3B, Ronkonkoma, NY 11779-3629 USA
Web site: http://www.rodro.com.

Roedway Pr., *(978-0-9659650)* P.O. Box 903, La Quinta, CA 92253 USA Tel 760-771-9818; Fax: 760-771-9618; Toll Free: 888-694-2248.

Roehm, Nancy Jean, *(978-0-9745591)* 210 Stoney Ridge Dr., Alpharetta, GA 30022-7668 USA
E-mail: njroehm4116@aol.com.

Rogers, Al M. Jr., *(978-0-9760159)* 48151 N. Laura Rogers Rd., Tickfaw, LA 70466 USA
Web site: http://www.lasttrumpgathering.com.

Rogers, Siobain K., *(978-0-615-13289-1)* 103 Harris Cir., Carthage, TX 75633 USA
Web site: http://www.lulu.com/siobainrogers
Dist(s): **Lulu Enterprises Inc.**

Rogue Bear Pr., *(978-0-9789512)* PO Box #513, Ardsley, NY 10502 USA (SAN 852-0275)
Web site: http://monsterdetectiveagency.com
Dist(s): **Partners Pubs. Group, Inc.**

Rogue Wave Publishing *See* **Tonepoet Publishing**

Rohrer Design, *(978-0-9721138)* 725-17th St., Kenosha, WI 53140-1329 USA
Web site: http://www.rohrer-design.com.

Roland & Eleanor Bergthold, *(978-0-9741193)* 9133 N. Stoneridge Ln., Fresno, CA 93720 USA Tel 559-434-4137
E-mail: rolbergthold@prodigy.net; embergthold@prodigy.net.

Rolemommy, *(978-0-9822974)* 36 Rutledge Rd., Scarsdale, NY 10583 USA
E-mail: beth@rolemommy.com; mail@plainwhitepress.com.

Rolling Hills Pr., *(978-0-943978)* 17 Olive Ave., Novato, CA 94945-3428 USA (SAN 282-2601) Do not confuse with Rolling Hills Pr., in Alexandria, VA
E-mail: rhpressllc@aol.com.

Romain, Trevor Co., The, *(978-0-9762843; 978-0-9787783; 978-1-934365; 978-0-9819804; 978-1-936407)* 4412 Spicewood Springs Rd. Suite 705, Austin, TX 78759-8567 USA Toll Free: 877-876-6246
E-mail: sabrina@trevorromain.com
Web site: http://www.TrevorRomain.com; http://www.comicalsense.com.

Roman Catholic Bks., *(978-0-912141; 978-1-929291; 978-0-9793540; 978-1-934888)* Div. of Catholic Media Apostolate, Orders Addr.: P.O. Box 2286, Fort Collins, CO 80522 USA Fax: 970-493-8781; Edit Addr.: 1331 Red Cedar Cir., Fort Collins, CO 80524 USA
Web site: http://www.booksforcatholics.com.

Romancing Cathay, *(978-1-932592)* 10050 Montgomery Rd., No. 315, Cincinnati, OH 45242 USA Tel 513-290-7419; Fax: 949-266-8395
E-mail: business@romancingcathay.com
Web site: http://www.romancingcathay.com.

Romani, Gabriella *See* **BBM Bks.**

Romoulous *Imprint of* **MIROGLYPHICS**

Romoulous Enterprises *See* **MIROGLYPHICS**

Ronald, George Pub., Ltd., *(978-0-85398)* 8325 17th St., N., Saint Petersburg, FL 33702-2843 USA (SAN 679-1859); 3 Rosecroft Ln. Oaklands, Welwyn, AL6 0UB
E-mail: sales@grbooks.com
Web site: www.grbooks.com
Dist(s): **Cambridge Univ. Pr.**

Ronan Enterprises, Inc., *(978-0-9821110)* P.O. Box 574, Richmond, MI 48062 USA.

Rondo Bks., *(978-0-9826717)* 264 Country Club Dr., Avila Beach, CA 93424 USA Tel 805-627-1765.

Ronin Publishing, *(978-0-914171; 978-1-57951)* P.O. Box 22900, Oakland, CA 94609 USA (SAN 287-5365) Tel 510-420-3669; Fax: 510-420-3672; Toll Free: 800-858-2665 (orders) Do not confuse with Ronin Publishing in Cambridge, MA
E-mail: orders@roninpub.com
Web site: http://www.roninpub.com
Dist(s): **MyiLibrary**
New Leaf Distributing Co., Inc.
Perseus-PGW
Perseus Bks. Group
ebrary, Inc.

RonJon Publishing, Incorporated *See* **Hewell Publishing**

Ronsdale Pr. (CAN) *(978-0-921870; 978-1-55380)* *Dist. by* **SPD-Small Pr Dist.**

Roost Books *Imprint of* **Shambhala Pubns., Inc.**

Rooster Pubns., *(978-0-9792135)* Orders Addr.: 101 S. Page St., Morrisonville, IL 62546-6746 USA; Edit Addr.: 101 S. Page St., Morrisonville, IL 62546-6746 USA
E-mail: grandmotherstewart@msn.com.

RoosterBugglePue Bks. *Imprint of* **Eupanapue-Auntella's Rooster Pubns.**

Roots & Wings, *(978-0-9703319)* 20114 Illinois Rte. 16, Nokomis, IL 62075 USA Tel 217-594-7300; Fax: 217-563-2111 Do not confuse with companies with the same name in Lake Forest, IL, New Paltz, NY, Boulder, CO
E-mail: beltpulley@ccipost.net.

Roots, Robert, *(978-0-9715336)* 11820 Miramar Pkwy. No. 212, Miramar, FL 33025 USA
E-mail: rbroots22@yahoo.com; rr@robertroots.com
Web site: http://www.robertroots.com.

Rope Ferry Press *See* **Anemone Publishing**

Roque-Velasco, Dr. Ismael, *(978-0-9706319)* P.O. Box 432804, Miami, FL 3243 USA Tel 305-667-6230; 305-740-6724
E-mail: northemismael@aol.com
Web site: http://www.cubaforkids.com
Dist(s): **Lectorum Pubns., Inc.**

Rorschach Entertainment, *(978-0-9748654)* 15806 18th Ave W. Apt. F203, Lynnwood, WA 98087-8755 USA
E-mail: info@rorschachentertainment.com
Web site: http://www.rorschachentertainment.com.

Rosales, Irene, *(978-0-9824348)* PMB 154, 3118 FM 528, Webster, TX 77598 USA.

Rosasharn Pr., *(978-0-615-96746-2; 978-0-9916496; 978-0-692-50595-3)* 1011 Serenity Cir., Auburn, AL 36830 USA Tel 334-750-6280
E-mail: info@pegathapress.com.

Rose Art Industries, Inc., *(978-1-57041)* 6 Regent St., Livingston, NJ 07039 USA Toll Free: 800-272-9667.

Rose Bud Publishing Co. LLC, *(978-0-9836913)* 8245 N. 27th Ave., Apt. 1048, Phoenix, AZ 85051 USA Tel 602-501-4533.

Rose Publishing, *(978-0-9655082; 978-1-890947; 978-1-59636; 978-1-62862)* 4733 Torrance Blvd., No. 259, Torrance, CA 90503-4100 USA (SAN 253-0120) Tel 310-353-2100; Fax: 310-353-2116; Toll Free: 800-532-4278 Do not confuse with companies with same or similar names in Flagtown, NJ, Arcadia, CA, Keystone Heights, FL, Salem, OR, Santa Cruz, CA, Tucson, AZ, Alameda, CA, Grand Rapids, MI, Little Rock, AR, Boulder, CO
Web site: http://www.rose-publishing.com
Dist(s): **Firebrand Technologies**
INscribe Digital
Spring Arbor Distributors, Inc.

Rose River Publishing Co., *(978-0-9707976)* P.O. Box 19864, Alexandria, VA 22320 USA Tel 703-768-2380 (phone/fax)
E-mail: herbpuscheck@cs.com.

Rose Valley Publishing, *(978-0-9765905)* 53762 Kristin Ct., Shelby Township, MI 48316 USA
E-mail: manitoumagic@aol.com
Web site: http://www.rosevalleypublishing.com.

Rose Water Cottage Pr., *(978-0-9853223; 978-0-9961393)* 308 Stewart St., Franklin, TN 37064 USA Tel 615-476-6717
E-mail: tray296@att.net.

Rose Wind Pr., *(978-0-9631232)* Div. of Compass Rose Corp., 1701 Broadway, No. 345, Vancouver, WA 98663 USA Tel 360-693-7742; Fax: 360-693-0950
E-mail: galenahk@aol.com
Web site: http://www.compassart.

RoseDog Bks. *Imprint of* **Dorrance Publishing Co., Inc.**

RoseFountain Pr., LLC, *(978-0-9768051)* 65 High Ridge Rd., No. 163, Stamford, CT 06905-3814 USA (SAN 858-4664)
Dist(s): **BookBaby**
Enfield Publishing & Distribution Co., Inc.

RoseKnows, Inc., *(978-0-9755889)* P.O. Box 5448, McLean, VA 22103-5448 USA
Web site: http://www.playgeist.com.

Rosemaling & Crafts, *(978-0-9674583)* Orders Addr.: 3208 Snowbrush Pl., Fort Collins, CO 80521 USA Tel 970-229-9846; Fax: 970-229-5683
E-mail: diaedwards@cs.com
Web site: http://www.nordic-arts.com.

Rosemont, Ltd., *(978-0-9635811)* 1620 Belmont St., Jackson, MS 39202-1203 USA Tel 601-355-1233.

Rosen & Assocs., Inc., *(978-0-9746811; 978-0-9778973)* P.O. Box 17173, Chapel Hill, NC 27516 USA Tel 919-264-5976; Fax: 919-929-7119
E-mail: info@cashworkbooks.com
Web site: http://www.cashworkbooks.com.

Rosen Central *Imprint of* **Rosen Publishing Group, Inc., The**

Rosen Classroom *Imprint of* **Rosen Publishing Group, Inc., The**

†**Rosen Publishing Group, Inc., The**, *(978-0-8239; 978-1-4042; 978-1-4358; 978-1-60851; 978-1-60852; 978-1-60853; 978-1-60854; 978-1-61511; 978-1-61512; 978-1-61513; 978-1-61514; 978-1-61530; 978-1-61531; 978-1-61532; 978-1-61533; 978-1-4488; 978-1-4777; 978-1-4824; 978-1-4994; 978-1-68048; 978-1-5081) a/o Dept. C234561, 29 E. 21st St., New York, NY 10010 USA (SAN 203-3720) Tel 212-777-3017; Fax: 212-358-9588; Toll Free Fax: 888-436-4643; Toll Free: 800-237-9932; Imprints*: Everett Press (Everett Pr); PowerKids Press (PowerKids Pr); Rosen Reference (RosenRef); Editorial Buenas Letras (EditBuenas); Powerstart Press (Powerstart Pr); Reading Power (Reading Power); Reading Room Collection (RRC); Dance & Movement Press (Dance); Rosen Classroom (RosenClassrm); Britannica Educational Publishing (BritEducPub); Rosen Young Adult (RosenYA); Windmill Books (WindmillBks); Rosen Central (RosenCent)
E-mail: info@rosenpub.com; customerservice@rosenpub.com; deang@rosenpub.com
Web site: http://www.rosenpublishing.com; http://www.rosendigital.com; http://www.rosenclassroom.com
Dist(s): **Ebsco Publishing**
Follett School Solutions
Lectorum Pubns., Inc.
ebrary, Inc.; *CIP*.

Rosen Publishing, Inc., *(978-1-881930)* 3000 Chestnut Ave., Suite 300, Baltimore, MD 21211 USA Tel 800-237-9932; Fax: 410-889-1320.

Rosen Reference *Imprint of* **Rosen Publishing Group, Inc., The**

Rosen Young Adult *Imprint of* **Rosen Publishing Group, Inc., The**

Rosenberg Publishing Pty, Ltd. (AUS) *(978-1-877058; 978-1-921719; 978-1-922013; 978-1-925078)* *Dist. by* **Intl Spec Bk.**

Rosenberger, Matthew, *(978-0-9760047; 978-0-9909415)* Div. of ABC Publishing for Kids, One Summit St., Philadelphia, PA 19118 USA (SAN 858-9887) Tel 215-242-4011; Fax: 215-242-9421
E-mail: mgr@kidstravelguides.com
Web site: http://www.kidstravelguides.com.

Roses Are READ Productions, *(978-0-9703489; 978-0-9755093)* P.O. Box 7844, Saint Paul, MN 55107 USA Tel 651-686-8418; Fax: 651-340-5333; *Imprints*: Little Petals (Little Petals)
E-mail: admin@rosesareread.cc.

Rosetta Stone Communications, *(978-0-9759331)* 1971 N. Nowak Ave., Thousand Oaks, CA 91360 USA (SAN 256-1549) Tel 805-370-0010; Fax: 805-435-1541
E-mail: johngriffith@maggio-associates.com
Web site: http://www.scientificgolfer.com.

Rosetta Stone Ltd., *(978-1-58022; 978-1-883972; 978-1-60391; 978-1-60717; 978-1-60829; 978-1-61716; 978-1-62821)* 135 W. Market St., Harrisonburg, VA 22801 USA Toll Free: 800-788-0822
E-mail: info@trstone.com; help@RosettaStone.com
Web site: http://www.rosettastone.com.

Rosmen-Izdat (RUS) *(978-5-8451)* *Dist. by* **Distribks Inc.**

Ross, Alan Publications *See* **Ross Pubns.**

Ross & Perry, Inc., *(978-1-931641; 978-1-931839; 978-1-932080; 978-1-932109; 978-0-9849531)* 3 S. Haddon Ave., Suite 4, Haddonfield, NJ 08003 USA (SAN 253-8555) Tel 856 427-6135; Fax: 856-427-6136
E-mail: grfisherii@gmail.com
Web site: http://www.rossperry.com; http://www.gporeprints.com
Dist(s): **TextStream.**

Ross, Cathy, *(978-0-9797832)* 1509 Cypress Rd., Olney, IL 62450 USA Tel 618-393-7732; Fax: 618-395-0123
E-mail: devspecinc@yahoo.com.

Ross Pubns., *(978-0-9617038)* 1438 W. Lantana Rd., No. 401, Lantana, FL 33462 USA (SAN 662-8230)
E-mail: alanross@aol.com
Web site: http://www.thegenuinejesus.com.

Rossi, Debra, *(978-0-9758982)* 813 Wentwood, Southlake, TX 76092 USA.

Rotaplast Pr., *(978-0-9706901)* Orders Addr.: P.O. Box 1100, Kennebunkport, ME 04046 USA Tel 207-967-0118; Edit Addr.: 4 East Ave., Kennebunkport, ME 04046 USA.

Roth Pubs., *(978-0-9832102; 978-1-938428)* P.O. Box 1058, Monsey, NY 10952 USA Tel 845-474-0022; Fax: 845-770-3382
E-mail: solomon@rothpublishers.com
Web site: www.rothpublishers.com.

Roth Publishing *See* **HELORO Publishing Group**

Rothwell Digital Imagery, *(978-0-615-18912-3)* Orders Addr.: P.O. Box 383, Westfield, NY 14787 USA Tel 716-326-4319; 716-969-4088 (cell)
E-mail: tlroth@fairpoint.net; tlrothwell@gmail.com; lewisthedragon@live.com
Web site: http://lewisthedragon.com
Dist(s): **R J Communications, LLC.**

Rough Draft Printing, *(978-1-933998; 978-1-60386)* 1280 Queen St., Seaside, OR 97138 USA; *Imprints*: Merchant Books (Merchant Bks).

Rough Guides, Ltd. (GBR) *(978-1-85828; 978-1-84353; 978-1-906063; 978-1-84836)* *Dist. by* **Peng Rand Hse.**

Round Cow Media Group, *(978-0-9745218)* Orders Addr.: P.O. Box 87, Alpharetta, GA 30009-0087 USA Tel 678-762-9053; Edit Addr.: 2822 Ashleigh Ln., Alpharetta, GA 30004 USA; *Imprints*: Biz4Kids (Biz4Kids)
E-mail: christian@biz4kids.com
Web site: http://www.biz4kids.com.

Round Tower Pr., *(978-0-9765964)* P.O. Box 2942, Paradise, CA 95969-2942 USA Tel 530-872-9705; Fax: 530-872-7732; Toll Free: 888-737-9705
E-mail: thor@roundtowerpress.com
Web site: http://www.roundtowerpress.com.

Rounder Bks., *(978-1-57940)* 1 Rounder Way, Burlington, MA 01803-5157 USA Toll Free: 800-768-6337
E-mail: info@rounderbooks.com
Web site: http://www.rounderbooks.com/
Dist(s): **Leonard, Hal Corp.**

Roundsquare Pr., *(978-0-9717280)* 295 Marble St., Suite 303, Broomfield, CO 80020-2171 USA
E-mail: rs_press@msn.com.

Rourke Educational Media, *(978-0-86592; 978-0-86593; 978-0-86625; 978-1-55916; 978-1-57103; 978-1-58952; 978-1-59515; 978-1-60044; 978-1-60472; 978-1-60694; 978-1-61590; 978-1-61741; 978-1-61236; 978-1-61810; 978-1-62169; 978-1-62717; 978-1-63155; 978-1-63430; 978-1-68191) Orders Addr.: P.O. Box 3328, Vero Beach, FL 32963 USA (SAN 857-0825) Fax: 772-234-6622; Toll Free: 800-394-7055; Edit Addr.: 1701 Hwy. A1A S., Ste 300, Vero Beach, FL 32963 USA Toll Free Fax: 1-888-355-6270; Toll Free: 800-394-7055*
E-mail: rourke@rourkepublishing.com; rbrady@rourkepublishing.com; renee@roukeeducationalmedia.com
Web site: http://www.rourkeeducationalmedia.com
Dist(s): **Findaway World, LLC**
Follett School Solutions
Ideals Pubns.
MyiLibrary.

Rourke Enterprises, Inc., *(978-0-86592)* Div. of Rourke Publishing Group, P.O. Box 3328, Vero Beach, FL 32964-3328 USA Tel 561-234-6001; Fax: 561-234-6622
E-mail: rourke@sunet.net
Web site: http://www.rourkepublishing.com.

Rourke Publishing, LLC *See* **Rourke Educational Media**

Rourke, Ray Publishing Company, Incorporated *See* **Rourke Enterprises, Inc.**

†**Routledge**, *(978-0-04; 978-0-413; 978-0-415; 978-0-7100; 978-0-86861; 978-0-87830; 978-1-317)* Mem. of Taylor & Frances Group, Orders Addr.: 7625 Empire Dr., Florence, KY 41042 USA Toll Free Fax: 800-248-4724 (orders, customer serv.); Toll Free: 800-634-7064 (orders, customer serv.); Edit Addr.: 270 Madison Ave. # 3, New York, NY 10016-0601 USA (SAN 213-196X)
E-mail: cserve@routledge-ny.com; info@routledge-ny.com
Web site: http://www.routledge-ny.com
Dist(s): **Ebsco Publishing**
MyiLibrary
Oxford Univ. Pr., Inc.
Taylor & Francis Group
Women Ink; *CIP*.

Rowe, Kysha, *(978-0-9769339)* 605 Crested View Ct., Loganville, GA 30052-8926 USA
E-mail: kysha_r@yahoo.com
Web site: http://www.whatcreaturesteachus.com; http://www.focusontheyouth.com.

Rowe Publishing and Design, *(978-0-9833971; 978-0-9851196; 978-1-939054)* 1080 15 Rd., Stockton, KS 67669 USA Tel 785-425-7350
E-mail: info@rowepublishingdesign.com
Web site: www.rowepublishingdesign.com
Dist(s): **Smashwords.**

Rowles, Louis, *(978-0-9708748)* 204 12th Ave., N., Amory, MS 38821-1206 USA Tel 662-256-3865
E-mail: glrowles@network-one.com.

Rowman & Littlefield Education, *(978-0-8108; 978-1-56676; 978-1-57886; 978-1-60709; 978-1-61048; 978-1-4758)* Orders Addr.: 15200 NBN Way, Blue Ridge Summit, PA 17214 USA Tel 717-794-3800 (Sales, Customer Service, MIS, Royalties Inventory); Fax: 717-794-3803 (Customer Service & orders only); 717-794-3857 (Sales & MIS); 717-794-3856 (Royalties, Inventory Mgmt. & Distribution); Toll Free Fax: 800-338-4550 (Customer Service & orders); Toll Free: 800-462-6420 (Customer Service & orders); Edit Addr.: 4501 Forbes Blvd., Suite 200, Lanham, MD 20706 USA Tel 301-459-3366; Fax: 301-459-5748; Toll Free Fax: 800-338-4550; Toll Free: 800-462-6420; 4501 Forbes Blvd Suite 200, Lanham, MD 20706 Short Discount, contact rlpgsales@rowman.com
E-mail: mmcmenamin@rowman.com; tkoerner@rowman.com
Web site: http://www.rlpgbooks.com; http://www.scarecroweducation.com; http://www.rowman.com
Dist(s): **CreateSpace Independent Publishing Platform**
Ebsco Publishing
Follett School Solutions
MyiLibrary
National Bk. Network
Rowman & Littlefield Publishers, Inc.
ebrary, Inc.

†**Rowman & Littlefield Publishers, Inc.**, *(978-0-8476; 978-0-87471; 978-0-9632978; 978-1-56699; 978-1-888052; 978-0-7425; 978-1-931890; 978-1-933494; 978-1-4422; 978-1-936283; 978-1-61281; 978-1-4616; 978-1-4617; 978-1-62093)* Mem. of Rowman & Littlefield Publishing Group, Inc., Orders Addr.: 15200 NBN Way, Blue Ridge Summit, PA 17214 USA Tel 717-794-3800 (Sales, Customer Service, MIS, Royalties, Inventory; Fax: 717-794-3803

(Customer Service & orders only); 717-794-3857 (Sales & MIS); 717-794-3856 (Royalties, Inventory Mgmt. & Distribution); Toll Free Fax: 800-338-4550 (Customer Service & orders); Toll Free: 800-462-6420 (Customer Service & orders); Edit Addr.: 4501 Forbes Blvd., Suite 200, Lanham, MD 20706 USA Tel 301-459-3366; Fax: 301-459-5749; *Imprints:* Scholarly Resources, Incorporated (ScholRes); Gooseberry Patch (GooseberP) Short Discount, please contact rlpgsales@rowman.com
E-mail: rlpgsales@rowman.com; lweston@rowman.com
Web site: http://www.rowmanlittlefield.com; http://www.rlpgbooks.com/bookseller/index.shtml
Dist(s): **CreateSpace Independent Publishing Platform**
Ebsco Publishing
Follett School Solutions
MyiLibrary
National Bk. Network
National Film Network LLC
Perseus Distribution
Send The Light Distribution LLC
ebrary, Inc.; *CIP.*

Rowohlt Taschenbuch Verlag GmbH (DEU) *(978-3-499) Dist. by* **Distribks Inc.**

Rowohlt Taschenbuch Verlag GmbH (DEU) *(978-3-499) Dist. by* **Continental Bk.**

Roxbury Park Juvenile *Imprint of* **Lowell Hse. Juvenile**

Roxby Media Ltd. (GBR) *(978-1-900521; 978-0-9848539) Dist. by* **LaurusCo.**

Roy, Wendy, *(978-0-615-59502-3)* 18 Haviland St. No. 15, Boston, MA 02115 USA Tel 617-645-9018
E-mail: contactwendynow@yahoo.com
Web site: http://www.glamgranola.com.

Royal Academy of Arts (GBR) *(978-0-900946; 978-1-903973; 978-1-905711; 978-1-907533; 978-1-910350) Dist. by* **HachBkGrp.**

Royal Council of the Real Fairyland, LLC, *(978-0-9841188)* 1332 Landfall Dr., Wilmington, NC 28405-2840 USA (SAN 858-4621)
Web site: http://www.therealtoothfairies.com.

Royal Fireworks Publishing Co., *(978-0-88092; 978-0-89824)* Orders Addr.: P.O. Box 399, Unionville, NY 10988 USA (SAN 240-2394) Tel 845-726-4444; Fax: 845-726-3824; Edit Addr.: 1 First Ave., Unionville, NY 10988 USA
E-mail: rfpress@frontiernet.net
Web site: http://www.rfwp.com/.

Royal Guard Dragon Society, The, *(978-0-9791733)* 706 Hall Ave., White Bear Lake, MN 55110 USA
E-mail: trgdspublications@trgds.com
Web site: http://trgds.com.

Royal Hse. Publishing, *(978-0-9772671)* 2315 Market Pl., Suite E, Huntsville, AL 35801 USA Tel 256-519-2291; Fax: 256-519-2292.

Royal Imprint Pr., Inc., *(978-0-9798624)* P.O. Box 342403, Austin, TX 78734 USA
Web site: http://http:www.TheRoyalYacht.net.

Royal Knight Inc., *(978-0-9777110)* 1204 Harbor Dr SE # 100, Rochester, MN 55904-5923 USA
Web site: http://www.royalknightresearch.com.

Royal Limited Partnership, *(978-0-9714798)* P.O. Box 448, Eugene, OR 97440-0448 USA
E-mail: fun@funnix.com
Web site: http://www.funnix.com.

Royal Peacock Publications *See* **Satin Finish Publishing**

Royal Penny Pr., The, *(978-0-9912370)* 9300 Colesville Rd., Silver Spring, MD 20901 USA Tel 240-372-1670
E-mail: sales@royalpennypress.com.

Royal Swan Enterprises, Inc., *(978-0-9793000)* 201 Orchard Ln., Carrboro, NC 27510-2530 USA (SAN 853-0521); *Imprints:* Alazar Press (Alazar Pr)
E-mail: rse@nc.rr.com; alazar.press@gmail.com
Web site: http://www.royal-swan-enterprises.com; http://www.alazar-press.com
Dist(s): **Independent Pubs. Group.**

Royal Tropical Institute Pr. (KIT (Koninklijk Instituut voor de Tropen) (NLD) *(978-90-6832; 978-90-74822; 978-94-6022) Dist. by* **Stylus Pub VA.**

Royall World Productions, *(978-0-9768115)* 1608 N. 13th St., Kansas City, KS 66102 USA Toll Free: 800-331-7668
E-mail: royallworldproductions@unoi.org.

Royalty Bks. International, Inc., *(978-0-9705458)* Orders Addr.: 2047 Gees Mill Rd. Suite 210, Conyers, GA 30013 USA
E-mail: royaltybooks@gmail.com
Web site: http://www.royaltybooksonline.com.

Royalty Company Two-Thousand, The *See* **Royalty Bks. International, Inc.**

Royalty Patrenia Turner Publications, *(978-0-578-15322-3)* 211 South Clark St, Chicago, IL 60690 USA.

Royalty Publishing Co., *(978-0-910487)* P.O. Box 2125, Bedford, IN 47421 USA (SAN 260-1265) Fax: 812-278-8785
E-mail: nitaspeaks@nitascoggan.com
Web site: http://www.the-maximum-zone.com.

RP Media, *(978-1-57545; 978-1-62716)* Div. of RP Bks., Orders Addr.: P.O. Box 362, East Olympia, WA 98540 USA; *Imprints:* Ruin Mist Publications (Ruin Mist Pubns); Reagent Press Signature Editions (Reagent Pr Sig Edns); Reagent Press Echo (Reagent Pr Echo); Reagent Press Books for Young Readers (RPBTR)
E-mail: sales@reagentpress.com; service@reagentpress.com; rights@reagentpress.com; emma.spring@reagentpress.com
Web site: http://www.reagentpress.com/; http://www.ruinmist.com/; http://books.reagentpress.com/; http://audio.reagentpress.com/; http://video.reagentpress.com/; http://graphics.reagentpress.com/; http://www.wizardsofskyhall.com/; http://www.ruinmistmovie.com/; http://www.themagiclands.com/; http://www.tvpress.com; http://www.bugvillecritters.com/
Dist(s): **CreateSpace Independent Publishing Platform**
EBSCO Media
Lightning Source, Inc.
MyiLibrary
OverDrive, Inc.
ebrary, Inc.

RPG Objects, *(978-0-9724826; 978-0-9743067; 978-1-935432)* 9275 Cedar Forest Rd., Eden Prairie, MN 55347 USA
E-mail: chris@rpgobjects.com
Web site: http://www.rpgobjects.com.

RPJ & Co., Inc., *(978-0-9761122; 978-0-615-27121-7; 978-0-9819980; 978-0-9828277; 978-1-937770)* 1080 Princewood Dr., Orlando, FL 32810-4542 USA; *Imprints:* SPC Books (SPCBks)
E-mail: kathy@rpjandco.com
Web site: http://www.rpjandco1417.com; http://www.rpjandco.com
Dist(s): **Advocate Distribution Solutions**
Ingram Content Group Inc.
Send The Light Distribution LLC
Smashwords.

RPM Publishing, *(978-0-9764085; 978-0-9795126)* P.O. Box 1417, Maple Valley, WA 98038 USA Tel 425-281-8045; Fax: 425-996-0614
E-mail: sarahg@bmginc.com
Web site: http://www.sarahgerdes.com.

RRJ Publishing, Inc., *(978-0-9857095)* 2073 SilverCrest Dr. unit C, Myrtle Beach, SC 29579 USA Tel 864-497-8392
E-mail: Mstnwright@yahoo.com.

RS Art Studio, *(978-0-9787729)* PO Box 64, Big Bear City, CA 92314 USA Tel 714-724-1480
E-mail: rsart@aol.com
Web site: http://www.rsartstudio.com.

RS Publishing *See* **JD Entertainment**

RTC Publishing, *(978-1-939418)* P.O. Box 511, Highland Park, IL 60035-0511 USA Tel 949.375.1006; Fax: 815.346.2398.

RTI Publishing, LLC, *(978-0-9769086)* 5685 S. Topaz Pl., Chandler, AZ 85249-5804 USA (SAN 256-6338)
E-mail: rtipublishing@cox.net.

RTMC Organization, LLC, *(978-1-934316)* P.O. Box 15105, Baltimore, MD 21282 USA (SAN 852-6923) Tel 410-900-7834
E-mail: Sales@RTMC.org
Web site: http://www.rtmc.org.

Ruach Publishing, *(978-0-9669910)* 1507 Central Ave., Deerfield, IL 60015 USA Tel 847-945-6421; Fax: 847-607-0217; Toll Free: 877-647-8224
E-mail: larry@ruachbooks.com
Web site: http://www.ruachbooks.com
Dist(s): **Independent Pubs. Group.**

Rubicon Bks., *(978-0-9771676)* P.O. Box 1167, Silver City, NM 88062-1167 USA Tel 505-388-4585 Do not confuse with companies with the same name in Montrose, CA, Glendale, AZ
E-mail: badarmstrong@signalpeak.net.

Ruby Tuesday Books Limited (GBR) *(978-1-909673) Dist. by* **Bearport Pubng.**

Rugg's Recommendations, *(978-0-9608934; 978-1-883062)* P.O. Box 417, Fallbrook, CA 92088-0417 USA (SAN 237-9694) Tel 760-728-4558; Fax: 760-728-4467
E-mail: frugg@thegrid.net
Web site: http://www.ruggsrecommendations.com.

Ruin Mist Pubns. *Imprint of* **RP Media**

Run With Me Publishing, *(978-0-9776835)* 15447 W. Monterey Ln., Kerman, CA 93630 USA Tel 559-846-6432
E-mail: runwithmepublishing@yahoo.com.

Runamuck Publishing, *(978-0-615-16220-1)* 221 Academy St., Mexico, NY 13114 USA
Dist(s): **Lulu Enterprises Inc.**

Running Moose Publications, *(978-0-9777210)* 42400 Garfield Road, Clinton Township, MI 48038 USA
Dist(s): **Adventure Pubns., Inc.**
AtlasBooks Distribution.

Running Pr. *Imprint of* **Running Pr. Bk. Pubs.**

Running Pr. Kids *Imprint of* **Running Pr. Bk. Pubs.**

Running Pr. Minature Editions *Imprint of* **Running Pr. Bk. Pubs.**

†Running Pr. Bk. Pubs., *(978-0-7624; 978-0-89471; 978-0-914294; 978-1-56138)* Div. of Perseus Books Group, 125 S. 22nd St., Philadelphia, PA 19103-4399 USA (SAN 204-5702) Tel 215-567-5080; Fax: 215-568-2919; Toll Free Fax: 800-453-2884; Toll Free: 800-345-5359 customer service; *Imprints:* Courage Books (Courage); Running Press (RunPr); Running Press Kids (RunningKids); Running Press Miniature Editions (RunMinEdns)
E-mail: support@runningpress.com
Web site: http://www.runningpress.com
Dist(s): **MyiLibrary**
Perseus-PGW
Perseus Bks. Group
Zondervan
ebrary, Inc.; *CIP.*

Runny Nose Press L.L.C., *(978-0-9788542)* 24111 Beierman, Warren, MI 48091-1714 USA
Web site: http://www.runnynosepress.com.

Rupa & Co. (IND) *(978-81-7167; 978-81-291) Dist. by* **S Asia.**

Rupanuga Vedic College, *(978-0-9650899; 978-0-9728372; 978-1-934405)* Div. of Iskcon Krishnafest, Inc., Orders Addr.: 5201 Paseo Blvd, Kansas City, MO 64110 USA Tel 224-558-8868; Edit Addr.: 5201 Paseo, Kansas City, MO 64110 USA Tel 816-924-5619; Fax: 816-924-5640
E-mail: eternityknowledgebliss@gmail.com; danavir.goswami@pamho.net
Web site: RVC.edu; DanavirGoswami.com; RVC.edu/RVC_BOOKS.html.

Rural Farm Productions, *(978-0-9753542)* 6538 Germanton Rd., Rural Hall, NC 27045 USA Tel 336-969-2202.

RUSH Pubns. & Educational Consultancy, LLC, *(978-0-9748222; 978-0-9748868; 978-0-9814958)* 1901 60th Pl. E., Suite L7432, Bradenton, FL 34203-5076 USA Tel 941-227-4444
E-mail: meylani@superonline.com
Web site: http://www.rushsociety.com
Dist(s): **AtlasBooks Distribution**
Cardinal Pubs. Group.

Rush, Ricki, *(978-0-9674292)* 123 Gregory Dr., Fairfax, CA 94930 USA Tel 415-457-6422; Fax: 415-456-4459
E-mail: rickicoach@aol.com
Web site: http://lifeworks-coaching.com.

Russell, Fred Publishing, *(978-0-9764347; 978-0-9789832; 978-0-9796229)* 52 Collis St., West Haven, CT 06516 USA Tel 203-934-2501; Fax: 203-934-8723; Toll Free: 866-968-7685; *Imprints:* Rock House Method, The (The Rock)
E-mail: jp@rockhousemethod.com
Web site: http://www.rockhousemethod.com
Dist(s): **Leonard, Hal Corp.**
Music Sales Corp.

Russet & Kensington Pr., *(978-1-940114)* 2066 Russet Dr. Suite 200, Troy, MI 48098 USA Tel 248-515-4247
E-mail: time4equilibrium@hotmail.com.

Russian Information & Business Center, Incorporated *See* **International Business Pubns., USA**

Ruth, A. Creations, *(978-0-9656306; 978-0-9907390)* 1860 Wynnewood Ln., Cincinnati, OH 45237 USA Tel 513-821-9027; Fax: 513-821-7762
E-mail: annieruth@fuse.net
Web site: http://www.annieruth.com.

Rutigliano, Joe, *(978-0-9767769)* 178 Ramona Ave., Staten Island, NY 10312-2717 USA.

Ruwanga Trading, *(978-0-9615102; 978-0-9701528)* P.O. Box 1027, Puunene, HI 96784 USA (SAN 694-2776)
Dist(s): **Booklines Hawaii, Ltd.**

RWP Bks. *Imprint of* **Redhawk Publishing**

Rx Humor, *(978-0-9639002; 978-1-892157)* 2272 Vistamont Dr., Decatur, GA 30033 USA Tel 404-321-0126; Fax: 404-633-9198
E-mail: nshulma@emory.edu.

Ryan Ave Publishing, *(978-0-9760759)* Div. of J. C. Melvin Seminars, Inc., 5738 Hedgeford Ct., Las Vegas, NV 89120 USA Tel 702-454-9822; Fax: 702-454-9821.

Ryan, Karlene Kay Author, *(978-0-9888843)* 5154 N. Woodson, Fresno, CA 93711 USA Tel 559-304-9737; Fax: 559-446-0565
E-mail: karleneryan@comcast.net
Web site: karleneryan.com.

Ryan, Shirley, *(978-0-9754196)* 6480 Havenside Dr., Sacramento, CA 95831-1504 USA
E-mail: shirley@workingtogether1.com
Web site: http://www.workingtogether1.com.

Rye Grass Roots Publishing, *(978-0-9788713)* Orders Addr.: P.O. Box 291382, Port Orange, FL 32129-1382 USA (SAN 851-8289) Tel 386-212-1800
E-mail: jamesmhunt@ryegrassroots.com.

Ryherd, Tim Publishing, *(978-0-9749974)* 21479 FM 365, Beaumont, TX 77705 USA.

Ryland, John B. Publishing *See* **DJ Blues Publishing**

Rymer Bks., *(978-0-934723; 978-0-9600792)* P.O. Box 153, Tollhouse, CA 93667-0153 USA (SAN 207-1010) Tel 209-298-8845.

Ryzewski, Deborah, *(978-0-9765302)* 240 Crabapple Ln., Valparaiso, IN 46383 USA.

R.Z. Enterprises of Florida, *(978-0-9792031)* 7640 Prospect Hill Cir., New Port Richey, FL 34654-6376 USA
Web site: http://www.RobertzHicks.com.

S & S Pr., *(978-0-615-14271-5; 978-0-615-14642-3; 978-0-615-14930-1; 978-0-615-14931-8; 978-0-615-14954-7)* 35221 SE Kinsey, Suite 101, Snoqualmie, WA 98065 USA
Web site: http://www.gloriabond.com
Dist(s): **Lulu Enterprises Inc.**

SMS Cos., Inc., *(978-0-9669595)* P.O. Box 1184, Smyrna, GA 30081 USA Tel 678-339-0626; Fax: 678-339-0726
E-mail: JMBryant@bellsouth.net
Web site: http://www.smsbooks.com
Dist(s): **Follett School Solutions.**

S.O.C.O. Pubns., *(978-0-910119)* 276 Ward Rd., Mohawk, NY 13407 USA (SAN 241-5720) Tel 315-866-7445
E-mail: copress@borg.com.

S P I E-International Society for Optical Engineering *See* **SPIE**

S V E & Churchill Media, *(978-0-7932; 978-0-89290; 978-1-56357)* 6465 N. Avondale Ave., Chicago, IL 60631-1909 USA (SAN 208-3930) Toll Free Fax: 800-624-1678; Toll Free: 800-829-1900
E-mail: custserv@svemedia.com
Web site: http://www.svemedia.com
Dist(s): **Video Project, The**
Weston Woods Studios, Inc.

†SYDA Foundation, *(978-0-911307; 978-0-914602; 978-1-930939)* 371 Brickman Rd., South Fallsburg, NY 12779 USA (SAN 206-5649) Tel 845-434-2000 Toll Free Fax: 888-422-2339 (ordering); Toll Free: 888-422-3334 (ordering); P.O. Box 600, South Fallsburg, NY 12779
Web site: http://www.siddhayoga.org
Dist(s): **Bookpeople**
Independent Pubs. Group
New Leaf Distributing Co., Inc.; *CIP.*

S2 Services, *(978-0-9770928)* 9006 Friars Rd., Bethesda, MD 20817 USA (SAN 257-3377) Tel 301-493-4982
E-mail: socrtwo@s2services.com
Web site: http://www.socrtwo.info/portfolio.htm; http://people.lulu.com/users/index.php?fHomepage=179563; http://s2press.com
Dist(s): **CafePress.com**
Lulu Enterprises Inc.

S2P Pr. *Imprint of* **Recipe for Success Foundation**

S.A. Kokinos (ESP) *(978-84-88342; 978-84-96629) Dist. by* **IPG Chicago.**

S.A. Kokinos (ESP) *(978-84-88342; 978-84-96629) Dist. by* **Lectorum Pubns.**

Saberlee Bks., *(978-0-9815836; 978-0-9909606)* 171 N. Wilson Ave. Apt. 205, Pasadena CA, CA 91106 USA
E-mail: saberleebooks@yahoo.com
Web site: http://www.lisettebrodey.com.

Sable Creek Pr. LLC, *(978-0-9766823; 978-0-9828875; 978-0-9890667)* P.O. Box 12217, Glendale, AZ 85318 USA Tel 602-803-4065
E-mail: sablecreekpress@cox.net
Web site: http://www.sablecreekpress.com; http://www.ohiofrontierhistorylady.com; http://www.sandrawaggoner.com; http://donnabraymer.com; http://rowdyraccoon.com; http://rickhuntress.org; http://janetclarkshay.com; http://bethanynwallace.com.

Sabledrake Enterprises, *(978-0-9702189; 978-0-9771005; 978-0-9844032)* P.O. Box 30751, Seattle, WA 98113 USA Tel 425-317-9241; Fax: 772-673-2381
E-mail: tim@sabledrake.com
Web site: http://www.sabledrake.com.

Sabre Publishing Hse., Inc., *(978-0-9746213)* 201 Huff Lake Ct., Ortonville, MI 48462 USA Tel 248-627-1112; Fax: 248-627-1113
E-mail: mikeatsabre@aol.com.

Sabyr Pr., *(978-0-9746463)* 2999 Allmon Ln., Missouri Vly, IA 51555-5057 USA
E-mail: info@sabyr.com
Web site: http://www.sabyr.com.

Sachedina, Dr. Shenin Medical Education Products, *(978-0-9778648)* 2200 Glenwood Dr., Winter Park, FL 32792 USA (SAN 850-4377) Tel 407-740-5127
E-mail: Metuandlee@aol.com
Web site: http://www.metuandlee.com
Dist(s): **AtlasBooks Distribution.**

Sacred Garden Fellowship, *(978-1-932746)* 279 Troy Rd. Suite 9, Box No. 225, Rensselaer, NY 12144 USA Tel 802-363-5579
E-mail: sacredgf@gmail.com
Web site: www.sacredgardenfellowship.org.

Sacred Truth Publishing, *(978-1-58840)* Div. of Sacred Truth Ministries, Orders Addr.: P.O. Box 18, Mountain City, TN 37683 USA
E-mail: sacredtruthministries@mounet.com.

Saddle & Bridle, Inc., *(978-0-9655501)* 375 Jackson Ave., Saint Louis, MO 63130-4243 USA Tel 314-725-9115; Fax: 314-725-6440
E-mail: saddlebr@saddleandbridle.com
Web site: http://www.saddleandbridle.com.

Saddle Pal Creations, Inc., *(978-0-9663495; 978-1-931353)* Orders Addr.: P.O. Box 872127, Wasilla, AK 99687-2127 USA Tel 907-357-3235; Fax: 907-357-3446
Web site: http://www.alaskachildrensbooks.com
Dist(s): **Partners Bk. Distributing, Inc.**
Partners/West Book Distributors
Wizard Works.

Saddleback Educational Publishing *See* **Saddleback Educational Publishing, Inc.**

Saddleback Educational Publishing, Inc., *(978-1-56254; 978-1-59905; 978-1-60291; 978-1-61651; 978-1-61247; 978-1-62250; 978-1-62670; 978-1-63078; 978-1-68021)* 3120-A Pullman St., Costa Mesa, CA 92626-4564 USA (SAN 860-0902) Toll Free Fax: 888-734-4010; Toll Free: 800-637-8715
E-mail: contact@saddleback.com; amchugh@sdlback.com; cpizer@sdlback.com
Web site: http://www.saddlebackpublishing.com
Dist(s): **Findaway World, LLC**
Follett School Solutions
ebrary, Inc.

Sadie Bks., *(978-0-9816047; 978-0-615-55525-6; 978-0-615-74503-9)* 215 E. Camden Ave., H11, Moorestown, NJ 08057 USA (SAN 856-017X) Tel 856-234-2676; 856-313-0548
E-mail: info@sadie-books.com
Web site: http://www.sadie-books.com
Dist(s): **CreateSpace Independent Publishing Platform**
Dummy Record Do Not USE!!!!
Smashwords.

Sadlier *Imprint of* **Sadlier, William H. Inc.**

Sadlier, William H. Inc., *(978-0-8215; 978-0-87105; 978-1-4217)* 9 Pine St., New York, NY 10005-1002 USA (SAN 204-0948) Tel 212-227-2120; Fax: 212-267-8696; Toll Free: 800-221-5175; *Imprints:* Sadlier (Sadlier)
Web site: http://www.sadlier.com.

†SAE Intl., *(978-0-7680; 978-0-89883; 978-1-56091; 978-1-4686)* 400 Commonwealth Dr., Warrendale, PA 15096 USA (SAN 232-5721) Tel 724-776-4970; Fax: 724-776-0790
E-mail: customerservice@sae.org
Web site: http://www.sae.org; http://books.sae.org/; *CIP.*

Saeligstone, *(978-0-615-15984-3; 978-0-615-15985-0)* 13110 Moselle Forest, helotes, TX 78023 USA
E-mail: peirce1@saeligstone.com
Dist(s): **Lulu Enterprises Inc.**

Safari, Ltd., *(978-1-881469)* Orders Addr.: P.O. Box 630685, Miami, FL 33163 USA Tel 305-621-1000; Fax: 305-621-6894; Toll Free: 800-554-5414; Edit Addr.: 1400 NW 159th St., Miami, FL 33169 USA
Web site: http://www.toydirectory.com.

Safari Pr., Inc., *(978-0-940143; 978-1-57157)* 15621 Chemical Ln., Suite B, Huntington Beach, CA 92649

Publisher Name Index

USA (SAN 663-0723) Tel 714-894-9080; Fax: 714-894-4949; Toll Free: 800-451-4788 (orders only)
E-mail: info@safaripress.com
Web site: http://www.safaripress.com
Dist(s): **National Bk. Network.**

Safe Harbor Pubns., *(978-0-9760416)* P.O. Box 396, Titusville, FL 32781 USA
E-mail: admin@rikerbooks.com
Web site: http://www.rikerbooks.com.

Safeblade, Evelyn Collins, *(978-0-9670655)* W8504 Jellen Rd., Spooner, WI 54801 USA Tel 715-635-7536.

Safer Society Pr., *(978-1-884444; 978-1-940234)* Div. of Safer Society Foundation, Inc., Orders Addr.: P.O. Box 340, Brandon, VT 05733-0340 USA Tel 802-247-3132; Fax: 802-247-4233; Edit Addr.: 8-10 Conant Sq., Brandon, VT 05733-1121 USA
E-mail: Theream@saver.net
Web site: http://www.safersociety.org.

Safety Always Matters, Inc., *(978-0-9620584; 978-1-883994)* 222 Wildwood Ct., Bloomingdale, IL 60108 USA (SAN 248-9759) Tel 630-894-1229
Dist(s): **Syndistar, Inc.**

Safeworld Publishing Co., *(978-0-9655604; 978-0-578-15130-4; 978-0-692-31823-2; 978-0-692-31827-0; 978-0-692-31835-5)* 3 Greenshire Ln., Owings Mills, MD 21117-4813 USA Tel 410-356-7233
E-mail: janisraf4@aol.com
Web site: www.declineandfallofallevil.org.

SAGA Press *Imprint of* **Simon & Schuster Bks. For Young Readers**

Sagaponack Bks., *(978-0-9668845)* Orders Addr.: 101 South Walk Pl., Saint Augustine, FL 32086 USA Tel 904-429-7209
E-mail: fran@sagbooks.com
Web site: http://www.SagaponackBooks.com
Dist(s): **Follet Higher Education Grp**
Partners Bk. Distributing, Inc.

Saga-Whyte Pr. (NLD) *(978-90-8885)* *Dist. by* **AtlasBooks.**

Sage, David, *(978-0-9894210)* 67 N. Piney PO Box 208, Story, WY 82842 USA Tel 303-883-4148
E-mail: davesageinstory@gmail.com.

Sage Hill Pubs., LLC, *(978-0-913205)* Orders Addr.: P.O. Box 866, Yerington, NV 89447 USA (SAN 283-0493) Tel 775-463-4188 (phone/fax)
E-mail: booksbysagehill@aol.com.

Sage Pr., *(978-0-9799972)* P.O. Box 981432, Park City, UT 84098 USA (SAN 854-9494) Tel 435-658-1238 Do not confuse with companies with similar name in Evergreen, CO, Phonenix, AZ, Murrieta, CA, Glenwood Springs, CO, San Diego, CA
E-mail: rudyandcoco@hotmail.com
Web site: http://www.rudyandcoco.com.

†SAGE Pubns., Inc., *(978-0-7619; 978-0-8039; 978-1-4129; 978-1-4522; 978-1-4462; 978-1-4833; 978-1-5063)* 2455 Teller Rd., Thousand Oaks, CA 91360 USA (SAN 204-7217) Tel 800-818-7243; Fax: 800-583-2665; 805-499-0871
E-mail: info@sagepub.com; deborah.vaughn@sagepub.com
Web site: http://www.sagepub.com; http://www.sagepub.co.uk; http://www.pineforge.com; http://sagepub.com
Dist(s): **Ambassador Bks. & Media**
Coutts Information Services
Cranbury International
Ebsco Publishing
Emery-Pratt Co.
MBS Textbook Exchange, Inc.
Midwest Library Service
MyiLibrary
Blackwell
NACSCORP, Inc.
Yankee Bk. Peddler, Inc.
ebrary, Inc.; *CIP.*

SAGE Pubns., Ltd. (GBR) *(978-0-7619; 978-0-8039; 978-1-903300; 978-1-4129; 978-1-84445; 978-1-84641; 978-1-84860; 978-1-4462; 978-0-85725; 978-0-85702; 978-1-84787; 978-1-4739; 978-1-84920)* *Dist. by* **SAGE.**

Sagebrush Entertainment, Inc., *(978-0-9766557)* P.O. Box 261187, Encino, CA 91426-1187 USA Toll Free Fax: 800-881-4577; Toll Free: 800-711-4677
E-mail: info@hopalong.com
Web site: http://www.hopalong.com.

SageBrush Exchange, *(978-0-9762728)* P.O. Box 525, Buckner, MO 64016 USA Tel 816-305-6916
E-mail: toby@homeisp.com
Web site: http://www.prairielabyrinth.com; http://www.chakralabyrinth.com.

Saint Andrew Pr., Ltd. (GBR) *(978-0-7152; 978-0-86153)* *Dist. by* **Westminster John Knox.**

Saint Anthony Messenger Press & Franciscan Communications *See* **Franciscan Media**

St. Augustine Pr., *(978-0-9819634)* 809 Copperhead Cir., St. Augustine, FL 32092 USA
Dist(s): **Chicago Distribution Ctr.**

St. Augustine's Pr., Inc., *(978-1-890318; 978-1-58731)* P.O. Box 2285, South Bend, IN 46680 USA Tel 574-291-3500; Fax: 574-291-3700; Toll Free: 888-997-4994
E-mail: bruce@staugustine.net
Web site: http://www.staugustine.net
Dist(s): **Chicago Distribution Ctr.**
Univ. of Chicago Pr.

St. Bob Pr., *(978-0-9796988)* 2095 Poplar Ave., Suite 54, Memphis, TN 38104 USA (SAN 854-1523) Tel 901-412-7362
E-mail: murff@saintbobpress.com
Web site: http://www.saintbobpress.com.

St. Clair Pubns., *(978-0-9801704; 978-0-9826302; 978-1-935786)* P.O. Box 727, Mc Minnville, TN 37111-0726 USA Tel 931-668-2860; Fax: 931-668-2861; Toll Free: 888-248-0192
E-mail: stan@stclair.net
Web site: http://stan.stclair.net/StClairPublications.html#books.

St. Clair Publishing, *(978-0-615-17629-1)* 3103 Fleece Flower, Austin, TX 78735 USA
Web site: http://www.richardshenderson.com.

Saint Mary's Press *See* **St. Mary's Pr. of MN**

St. Mary's Pr. of MN, *(978-0-88489; 978-1-59982)* 702 Terrace Heights, Winona, MN 55987-1320 USA (SAN 203-073X) Tel 507-457-7900; Fax: 507-457-7990; Toll Free Fax: 800-344-9225; Toll Free: 800-533-8095
E-mail: smpress@smp.org; hwilliams@smp.org
Web site: http://www.smp.org.

St. Nectarios Pr., *(978-0-913026)* 10300 Ashworth Ave., N., Seattle, WA 98133-9410 USA (SAN 203-3542) Tel 206-522-4471; Fax: 206-523-0550; Toll Free: 800-643-4233
E-mail: orders@stnectariospress.com; anneborozan@live.com
Web site: http://www.stnectariospress.com.

St. Nicholas Monastery, *(978-0-9773579)* 1340 Piney Rd., North Fort Myers, FL 33903-3822 USA.

Saint Paul Books & Media *See* **Pauline Bks. & Media**

Saint Paul Brotherhood, *(978-0-9721698; 978-0-9800065; 978-1-940661)* Div. of Coptic Orthodox Church - Diocese of Los Angeles, P.O. Box 4467, Diamond Bar, CA 91765 USA
E-mail: theophiluspaul@lacopts.org
Web site: http://www.lacopts.org.

St. Vincent Archabbey Pubns., *(978-0-9708216; 978-0-9773909; 978-0-9906855)* 300 Fraser Purchase Rd., Latrobe, PA 15650-2690 USA Tel 724-805-2601; Fax: 724-805-2775
E-mail: kim.metzgar@email.stvincent.edu
Web site: http://www.stvincentstore.com
Dist(s): **Distributors, The.**

St. Vincent College Ctr. for Northern Appalachian Studies, *(978-1-885851)* 300 Fraser Purchase Rd., Latrobe, PA 15650 USA Tel 724-805-2316; Fax: 724-537-4554
E-mail: rwissolik@stvincent.edu
Web site: http://www.stvincent.edu/napp.

†St. Vladimir's Seminary Pr., *(978-0-88141; 978-0-913836; 978-0-9618545; 978-0-9622536; 978-1-879038; 978-1-891295)* 575 Scarsdale Rd., Yonkers, NY 10707 USA (SAN 204-6296) Tel 914-961-8313 x 348; Fax: 914-961-5456 Bookstore fax; 914-961-4507 Press fax; Toll Free: 800-204-2665 Bookstore
E-mail: benedict@svots.edu; ghatrak@svots.edu
Web site: http://www.svspress.com; *CIP.*

Saints Of Glory Church, *(978-0-9673342)* Orders Addr.: P.O. Box 8957, Anaheim, CA 92812-0957 USA Tel 714-846-0401; Fax: 714-846-3395; Edit Addr.: 16102 Warmington Ln., Huntington Beach, CA 92649 USA
E-mail: sgcgow@aol.com.

Sakthi Bks., Inc., *(978-0-9752586)* Orders Addr.: 1507 Lone Oak Cir., Fairfield, IA 52556 USA
E-mail: pradheepkumar@hotmail.com
Web site: http://www.matrixjourney.com; http://www.rightawareness.com.

Sakura Pr., *(978-0-9660583)* Hesta Roach 227 Croatan Dr., Oriental, NC 28571 USA Tel 252-249-1929 (phone/fax) Do not confuse with Sakura Pr., Pleasant Hill, OR
E-mail: roachdj@hotmail.com.

Salado Pr., LLC, *(978-0-9663870; 978-0-9835342; 978-0-9913118)* Orders Addr.: P.O. Box 470171, Fort Worth, TX 76147 USA Tel 972-215-6116
E-mail: lee@saladopress.com
Web site: http://www.salaodpress.com.

Salani (ITA) *(978-88-7782; 978-88-8451)* *Dist. by* **Distribks Inc.**

Salaud Publishing, *(978-0-9713167)* P.O. Box 11681, Portland, OR 97211 USA Tel 919-963-9135
E-mail: jesse@hastardrecords.com; jesse@bastardrecords.com; jordan_lari@highcountrystudentpublishers.org
Web site: http://www.highcountrystudentpubishers.org; http://www.bastardrecords.com/salaud.htm.

Salch, Megan F., *(978-0-9776154)* 3106 Lawrence St., Houston, TX 77018 USA Tel 713-864-1344.

Salem Academy & College, *(978-0-9789608)* P.O. Box 10548, Winston-Salem, NC 27108 USA
Web site: http://www.salem.edu.

†Salem Pr., Inc., *(978-0-89356; 978-1-58765)* Div. of EBSCO Publishing, Orders Addr.: 10 Estes St, IPSWICH, MA 01938 USA (SAN 241-841X) Tel 800-758-5995; Fax: 201-968-1411; Toll Free: 800-221-1592; *Imprints*: Magill's Choice (Magills Choice)
E-mail: csr@salempress.com
Web site: http://www.salempress.com; http://salempress.com/Store/pages/hwwilson.htm
Dist(s): **Ebsco Publishing**
Grey Hse. Publishing
ebrary, Inc.; *CIP.*

Salem Publishing Solutions, Inc., *(978-1-931232; 978-1-59160; 978-1-59467; 978-1-59781; 978-0-9769668; 978-1-60034; 978-1-60266; 978-1-60477; 978-1-60647; 978-1-60791; 978-1-61579; 978-1-60957; 978-1-61215; 978-1-61379; 978-1-61904; 978-1-61996; 978-1-62230; 978-1-62419; 978-1-62509; 978-1-62697; 978-1-62839; 978-1-62871; 978-1-62952; 978-1-63050; 978-1-63129; 978-1-63221; 978-1-4984) 2301 Lucien Way No. 415, Maitland, FL 32751 USA Fax: 407-339-9898; Toll Free: 866-381-2665*
E-mail: sscott@christianpublishing.com; cclark@christianpublishing.com
Web site: http://www.xulonpress.com
Dist(s): **INscribe Digital**
eBookit.com.

Salem Ridge Press LLC, *(978-0-9776786; 978-1-934671)* 4263 Salem Dr., Emmaus, PA 18049 USA
E-mail: customerservice@slaemridgepress.com.

Sales Effectiveness, Inc., *(978-0-9676255)* 570 W. Crossville Rd., Suite 103, Roswell, GA 30075 USA Tel 770-552-6612; Fax: 770-643-8205
E-mail: info@saleseffectiveness.com
Web site: http://www.saleseffectiveness.com.

Salih, Sara *See* **Harlan Rose Publishing**

Salina Bookshelf *See* **Salina Bookshelf Inc**

Salina Bookshelf Inc, *(978-0-9644189; 978-1-893354)* 3120 N. Caden Ct. Ste. 4, Flagstaff, AZ 86004 USA (SAN 253-0503) Tel 928-527-0070; Fax: 928-526-0386; Toll Free: 877-527-0070
E-mail: elockard@salinabookshelf.com
Web site: http://www.salinabookshelf.com.

Salish Kootenia College Pr., *(978-1-934594)* Orders Addr.: P.O. Box 70, Pablo, MT 59855 USA Tel 406-275-4882; Fax: 406-275-4801; Edit Addr.: 52000 Hwy.93, Pablo, MT 59855 USA
E-mail: bob-bigant@skc.edu
Dist(s): **Stoneydale Pr. Publishing Co.**
Univ. of Nebraska Pr.

Sally Ride Science, *(978-0-9753920; 978-1-933798; 978-1-940073; 978-1-941094)* 9191 Towne Centre Dr. Ste. L101, San Diego, CA 92122-6204 USA Tel 858-638-1432; Fax: 858-638-1419; Toll Free: 800-561-5161
E-mail: tam@sallyridescience.com; bleck@sallyridescience.com
Web site: http://www.sallyridescience.com.

Salmon Hole Poetry Press *See* **Minimal Pr., The**

Salmon Publishing (IRL) *(978-0-948339; 978-1-897648; 978-1-903392)* *Dist. by* **Dufour.**

Salmon Run Pr., *(978-0-9634000; 978-1-887573)* Orders Addr.: P.O. Box 672130, Chugiak, AK 99567-2130 USA Tel 907-688-4268
E-mail: salmonrp@aol.com
Dist(s): **Partners/West Book Distributors**
SPD-Small Pr. Distribution
Todd Communications
Wizard Works.

Salmon Run Publishing Company *See* **Salmon Run Pr.**

Salt City Books, *(978-0-9776332)* P.O. Box 6, Farmington, UT 84025-0006 USA (SAN 257-8522) Tel 801-309-7820; Fax: 801-485-2654
E-mail: saltcitybooks@msn.com.

Salt City Systems *See* **Salt Pubs.**

Salt of the Earth Pr., *(978-0-9816949; 978-0-9849183)* W. 4456 Hwy. 63, Springbrook, WI 54875 USA (SAN 856-2555) Fax: 715-318-6417
Web site: http://www.saltpress.com.

Salt Pubs., *(978-0-9709940; 978-0-9725804)* 6163 E. Molloy Rd., East Syracuse, NY 13057 USA Tel 315-437-1139; Fax: 315-463-2055; Toll Free: 800-324-2607
E-mail: salt@twcny.rr.com.

Salt Publishing (GBR) *(978-1-876857; 978-1-901994; 978-1-84471; 978-1-907773; 978-1-78463)* *Dist. by* **SPD-Small Pr Dist.**

SaltRiver *Imprint of* **Tyndale Hse. Pubs.**

Salty Dog, Inc., The, *(978-0-9793560)* Orders Addr.: a/o Mark Yarbrough, The Salty Dog Inc., 69 Arrow Rd., Hilton Head Island, SC 29928-2992 USA (SAN 853-2338)
Web site: http://www.saltydog.com.

Salty Pond Pubs., *(978-0-615-45705-5; 978-0-615-56089-2)* 10 Edward Kelly Rd., East Sandwich, MA 02537 USA Tel 781-715-5014; Fax: 508-833-8923
E-mail: jglinehan@comcast.net.

Salty Splashes Collection *Imprint of* **Balcony 7 Media and Publishing**

Salvation Army, *(978-0-89216)* 120 W. 14th St., New York, NY 10011 USA (SAN 237-2649) Tel 212-337-7200 Do not confuse with Salvation Army Supplies, Southern, Des Plaines, IL (Southern Territory) or Salvation Army Supplies & Purchasing Dept., Des Plaines, IL or Salvation Army, Des Plaines, IL.

Salvo Pr. *Imprint of* **Start Publishing LLC**

Salzman Bks. LLC, *(978-0-9842632)* Orders Addr.: P.O. Box 189, Winfield, KS 67156 USA (SAN 858-8910) Tel 620-262-7280; Edit Addr.: 2106 Kickapoo, Winfield, KS 67156 USA
E-mail: jsalzman@salzmanbooks.com
Web site: http://www.salzmanbooks.com
Dist(s): **AtlasBooks Distribution.**

Saman Publishing, *(978-0-9728020)* 751 Lemonwood Ct., San Jose, CA 95120 USA.

Samara Pr., *(978-0-9577556)* c/o Trillium Hse., 241 Bonita, Los Trancos Woods, Portola Valley, CA 94028-8103 USA Tel 650-851-1847.

Sambodh Society, Inc., The, *(978-0-9785969)* 6363 N 24th St., Kalamazoo, MI 49004 USA (SAN 851-0849)
Web site: http://www.sambodh.us.

Samhain Publishing, LTD, *(978-1-59998; 978-1-60504; 978-1-60928; 978-1-61921; 978-1-61922; 978-1-61923; 978-1-5139)* Orders Addr.: 11821 Mason Montgomery Rd. 4B, Cincinnati, OH 45249 USA; Edit Addr.: 11821 Mason Montgomery Rd. Suite 4b, Cincinnati, OH 45249 USA (SAN 257-7488) Tel 513-453-4688; Fax: 513-583-0191
E-mail: contracts@samhainpublishing.com
Web site: http://www.samhainpublishing.com.

Sams, II, Carl R. Photography, Inc., *(978-0-9671748; 978-0-9770108; 978-0-9827625)* 361 Whispering Pines, Milford, MI 48380-3807 USA (SAN 859-435X) Tel 248-685-2422; Fax: 248-685-1643; Toll Free: 800-552-1867
E-mail: carlsams@ameritech.net
Web site: http://www.carlsams.com; http://www.strangerinthewoods.com
Dist(s): **Follett School Solutions**
Partners Bk. Distributing, Inc.

San Diego Business Accounting Solutions a Non CPA Firm, *(978-0-9746093; 978-0-9794124)* Subs. of SDBAS Publishing, Orders Addr.: P.O. Box 7275, Loveland, CO 80537 USA Tel 970-776-8395; Fax: 970-692-2492
E-mail: julieaydlott@gmail.com
Web site: http://www.sdbas.biz; http://www.businessbudgetinghelp.com; http://www.messages-from-beyond.com
Dist(s): **Emery-Pratt Co.**
Midwest Library Service.

San Diego County Regional Airport Authority, *(978-0-9745294)* P.O. Box 82776, San Diego, CA 92138-2776 USA Tel 619-400-2400; Fax: 619-400-2866
Web site: http://www.san.org.

San Diego Museum of Man, *(978-0-937808)* 1350 El Prado, Balboa Pk., San Diego, CA 92101-1616 USA Tel 619- 239-2001; Fax: 619- 239-2749
E-mail: khedges@museumofman.org
Web site: http://www.museumofman.org
Dist(s): **Casemate Academic.**

San Francisco Art Commission, The, *(978-1-888048)* 800 Chestnut St., San Francisco, CA 94133 USA Tel 415-771-7020; Fax: 415-252-2595; *Imprints*: WritersCorps Books (WrtrsCorps Bks)
Dist(s): **SPD-Small Pr. Distribution.**

San Francisco Story Works, *(978-0-9774227)* 386 Union St., San Francisco, CA 94133-3516 USA (SAN 257-5248)
Web site: http://www.pengey.com.

San Francisco Study Ctr., *(978-0-936434; 978-1-888956)* 1095 Market St., Rm. 602, San Francisco, CA 94103 USA (SAN 214-4654) Tel 415-626-1650; Fax: 415-626-7276; Toll Free: 888-281-3757; *Imprints*: Study Center Press (Study Ctr Pr)
E-mail: marjorie@studycenter.org
Web site: http://www.studycenter.org
Dist(s): **Parent Services Project.**

San Juan Publishing, *(978-0-9707399; 978-0-9858897)* Orders Addr.: P.O. Box 923, Woodinville, WA 98072 USA
E-mail: sanjuanbooks@yahoo.com
Dist(s): **Partners Bk. Distributing, Inc.**

San Val, Incorporated *See* **Turtleback Bks.**

Sananda Publications *See* **Reverence for Life**

Sancho Storybooks *See* **Joseph Pubns.**

Sanctuary Bks., *(978-0-9753334)* P.O. Box 1623, New York, NY 10028 USA Do not confuse with companies with the same or similar name in Mount Juliet, TN, Tampa, FL
E-mail: sanctuarybooks@earthlink.net
Web site: http://www.sanctuarybks.com.

Sanctuary Publishing, Inc., *(978-0-9746995; 978-0-9785334; 978-0-9843754; 978-0-9830018; 978-0-9840392)* 40 Red Butte Rd., Sedona, AZ 86351-7765 USA (SAN 920-1122) Tel 928-284-2269; 928-284-1154; Fax: 928-284-4782
Web site: http://www.SanctuaryPublications.com
Dist(s): **MyiLibrary.**

Sanctuary Publishing, Ltd. (GBR) *(978-1-86074; 978-1-898141)* *Dist. by* **H Leonard.**

Sand Dreams Pr., LLC, *(978-0-9798656)* P.O. Box 24, Whitehouse Station, NJ 08889-0024 USA (SAN 854-6134) Tel 908-256-4834
E-mail: imre@sanddreamspress.com
Web site: http://www.sanddreamspress.com.

Sand Sage Pr., *(978-0-9793474)* Orders Addr.: P.O. Box 60812, Canyon, TX 79016 USA (SAN 853-1935) Toll Free: 888-655-0875 (phone/fax)
E-mail: psallison@earthlink.net
Web site: http://www.SandSagePress.com.

Sandbox Bks., *(978-0-9755184)* 6561 Portage Rd., DeForest, WI 53532-0000 USA
Web site: http://www.sandboxbooks.com.

Sandbridge Sons Publishing, *(978-0-9796039)* 2577 Sandpiper Rd., Virginia Beach, VA 23456 USA.

SandCastle *Imprint of* **ABDO Publishing Co.**

Sandcastle Publishing, *(978-0-9627756; 978-1-883995)* Orders Addr.: P.O. Box 3070, South Pasadena, CA 91031-6070 USA Fax: 323-255-3616; Edit Addr.: 1723 Hill Dr., South Pasadena, CA 91030 USA Tel 213-255-3616 Do not confuse with Sandcastle Publishing, Orleans, MA
E-mail: info@sandcastle-online.com; rwhatley@sandcastle-online.com
Web site: http://www.sandcastle-online.com
Dist(s): **Quality Bks., Inc.**
Unique Bks., Inc.

†Sandlapper Publishing Co., Inc., *(978-0-87844)* Orders Addr.: P.O. Box 730, Orangeburg, SC 29115 USA (SAN 203-2678) Toll Free Fax: 800-337-9420 (orders); Toll Free: 800-849-7263 (orders); Edit Addr.: 1281 Amelia St., NE., Orangeburg, SC 29116 USA Tel 803-533-1658; Fax: 803-534-5223
E-mail: agallman1@bellsouth.net
Web site: http://www.sandlapperpublishing.com
Dist(s): **Follet Higher Education Grp**; *CIP.*

Sandner-Petersen International Bks., *(978-0-9744852)* 5112 Coronado Pkwy., No.11, Cape Coral, FL 33904 USA Tel 739-549-3028; Fax: 239-549-5547.

Sandpiper *Imprint of* **Houghton Mifflin Harcourt Trade & Reference Pubs.**

Sandramantos Publishing, *(978-0-9887848)* 1550 Alpine Trail, San Marcos, TX 78666 USA Tel 512-462-9670
E-mail: manager@Sandramantos.com
Web site: http://princessapril.com.

Sands, Monty, *(978-0-9788038; 978-0-615-25788-4; 978-0-578-15474-9)* P.O. Box 6463, Visalia, CA 93291 USA
E-mail: monger15@juno.com; montysands@yahoo.com.

S&S Publishing LLC, *(978-0-9794710)* 1609 Dublin Dr., Silver Spring, MD 20902 USA Tel 301-681-8729
E-mail: xsalinas21@gmail.com.

Sandvik Innovations, LLC, *(978-1-932915; 978-1-935868)* 460 E. Swedesford Rd., Suite 2030, Wayne, PA 19087 USA Tel 610-975-3585; Fax: 610-975-3587
Web site: http://www.sandvikinnovations.com.

Sandvik Publishing, *(978-1-58048; 978-1-881445)* Div. of Sandviks Bokforlag, Norway, 3729 Knights Rd., Bensalem, PA 19020-2908 USA Toll Free: 800-843-2445
E-mail: Nicole@sandvikpublishing.com; cust-serv@sandvikpublishing.com
Web site: http://www.sandviks.com.

Sandy Bay Publishing, *(978-0-9701285)* Orders Addr.: P.O. Box 580, Hatteras, NC 27943-0580 USA Tel 252-986-2195; Fax: 252-986-2372; Edit Addr.: 56187 Pamlico Dr., Hatteras, NC 27973-0580 USA Tel 252-986-2195
E-mail: joannewhale@earthlink.net.

Sandy Putter Pr., *(978-0-578-05153-6)* 9 Meadowview Rd., Asheville, NC 28804 USA.

SangFroid Pr., *(978-0-917939)* 34 Water St., Excelsior, MN 55331 USA (SAN 657-0178) Tel 952-474-6220; Fax: 952-474-6221 Do not confuse with Sang Froid in New York, NY
Dist(s): **Independent Pubs. Group.**

Sankofa Bks. *Imprint of* **Just Us Bks., Inc.**

Sankofa Pr., *(978-0-9654009)* Orders Addr.: P.O. Box 3144, Jacksonville, FL 32206 USA Tel 904-355-0126 (phone/fax); Edit Addr.: 239 W. 40th St., Jacksonville, FL 32206 USA
E-mail: sankofa@leading.net
Web site: http://www.users.southeast.net/~sankofa.

Sankofa Productions *See* **Sankofa Pr.**

SanPaul Group, LLC, The, *(978-0-9670875)* 209 Josephine St., Detroit, MI 48202-1811 USA (SAN 253-6013)
E-mail: gtpspg@cs.com
Web site: http://www.qtpieworld.com.

Sanpitch Pr., *(978-0-9760607)* 141 S. Main, Manti, UT 84642 USA Tel 435-835-6271; Fax: 435-835-8431; Toll Free: 800-748-4660
E-mail: sanman@horseshoetrader.com.

Sansom & Co. Ltd. (GBR) *(978-0-905459; 978-0-948265; 978-1-872971; 978-1-900178; 978-1-904537)* *Dist. by* **Natl Bk Netwk.**

Santa Ana River Pr., *(978-0-9747638)* P.O. Box 5473, Norco, CA 92860 USA (SAN 255-7568)
E-mail: admin@santaanariverpress.com
Web site: http://www.santaanariverpress.com
Dist(s): **Sunbelt Pubns., Inc.**

Santa Fe Writers Project, *(978-0-9776799; 978-0-9819661; 978-0-9882252; 978-1-939650)* No. 350, 369 Montezuma Ave., Santa Fe, NM 87501 USA (SAN 257-9588)
E-mail: agifford@sfwp.com
Web site: http://www.sfwp.com
Dist(s): **Ebsco Publishing**
Independent Pubs. Group
MyiLibrary
ebrary, Inc.

Santa Monica Pr., *(978-0-9639946; 978-1-891661; 978-1-59580)* Orders Addr.: P.O. Box 1076, Santa Monica, CA 90406 USA (SAN 298-1459) Tel 310-230-7759; Fax: 310-230-7761; Toll Free: 800-784-9553; Edit Addr.: 513 Wilshire Blvd., No. 321, Santa Monica, CA 90401 USA
E-mail: books@santamonicapress.com
Web site: http://www.santamonicapress.com
Dist(s): **Ebsco Publishing**
Independent Pubs. Group
Legato Pubs. Group
MyiLibrary
Perseus-PGW
ebrary, Inc.

Santacroce, John, *(978-0-615-76887-8; 978-0-9899916)* 2066 Rivers Edge Dr., Rio Rancho, NM 87144 USA Tel 505-450-7096
E-mail: johnpsantacroce@gmail.com.

Santiago, Claribel, *(978-0-9744726)* P.O. Box 25345, Tamarac, FL 33320 USA
E-mail: claribel_santiago@hotmail.com
Web site: http://www.claribelsantiago.com.

Santillana (COL) *(978-958-24)* *Dist. by* **Santillana.**

Santillana Ecuador (ECU) *(978-9978-07; 978-9942-05; 978-9942-19; 978-9978-29)* *Dist. by* **Santillana.**

Santillana Ediciones Generales, S.A. de C.V. (MEX) *(978-607-11; 978-607-01)* *Dist. by* **Santillana.**

Santillana, Editorial, S.A. de C.V. (MEX) *(978-970-29; 978-968-430; 978-970-642)* *Dist. by* **Santillana.**

Santillana S. A. (URY) *(978-9974-590; 978-9974-671)* *Dist. by* **Santillana.**

Santillana USA Publishing Co., Inc., *(978-0-88272; 978-1-56014; 978-1-58105; 978-1-58986; 978-1-59437; 978-1-59820; 978-1-60396; 978-1-61605; 978-1-61435; 978-1-62263; 978-1-63113)* Div. of Grupo Santillana, 2023 NW 84th Ave., Doral, FL 33122 USA (SAN 205-1133) Tel 305-591-9522 Toll Free Fax: 888-248-9518 (orders); Toll Free: 800-245-8584; Av. Rio Mixcoac No. 274 Col. Acacias, C.P. 0324 Benito Juarez, Ciudad de Mexico, DF,; *Imprints:* Richmond (Richmond); Alfaguara (Alfaguara); Punto de Lectura (Punto de Lectura); Alfaguara Juvenil (AlfaguaraJuv)
E-mail: dpena@santillanausa.com; esanta@santillanausa.com
Web site: http://www.santillanausa.com/
Dist(s): **Barnes & Noble, Inc.**
Bilingual Pubns. Co., The
Continental Bk. Co., Inc.
CreateSpace Independent Publishing Platform
EMC/Paradigm Publishing
Follett School Solutions
Lectorum Pubns., Inc.
Libros Sin Fronteras
Perseus-PGW
Perseus Distribution.

Santoon Bks., *(978-0-9744905)* 13533 1/2 Village Dr., Cerritos, CA 90703 USA Tel 562-926-3361; Fax: 562-802-7680
E-mail: santoon@santoon.com.

Santoon Productions, Incorporated *See* **Santoon Bks.**

Sapling Bks. *Imprint of* **Cedar Grove Bks.**

Saqi Bks. (GBR) *(978-0-86356; 978-1-908906)* *Dist. by* **Consort Bk Sales.**

Sarah & David LLC, *(978-0-9761648; 978-0-9796785)* P.O. Box 5894, Englewood, NJ 07631-5894 USA Fax: 201-221-7879
Web site: http://www.sarahdavid.com.

SarahRose Children's Bks. *Imprint of* **SarahRose Publishing**

SarahRose Publishing, *(978-0-9745865)* Orders Addr.: 1220 Wing Point Way NE, Bainbridge Island, WA 98110 USA Tel 253-232-9561; Edit Addr.: 1220 Wing Point Way NE, Bainbridge Island, WA 98110 USA Tel 253-232-9561; *Imprints:* SarahRose Children's Books (SarahRose Child Bks)
E-mail: melodycurtiss@gmail.com
Web site: http://www.melodycurtiss.com; http://sarahrosepublishing.tumblr.com.

Sarah's Daughters Publishing *See* **Fidelity Heart Publishing**

Sarajames Poetry, Inc., *(978-0-9767395)* 88 Lawrence Ave., Brooklyn, NY 11230 USA Tel 718-972-2944
E-mail: jamestronan@yahoo.com.

Saranjon Publishing, *(978-0-9665282)* Orders Addr.: P.O. Box 980, Homer, AK 99603-0980 USA Tel 907-235-8200; Fax: 907-235-8699; Edit Addr.: 385 E. Fairview St., Homer, AK 99603-0980 USA
E-mail: saranjon@alaska.net
Dist(s): **Wizard Works.**

Saseen, Sharon, *(978-0-9748425)* 403 E. 46th St., Savannah, GA 31405 USA Tel 912-233-1341
E-mail: saseenart@aol.com
Web site: http://www.saseen.com.

Sasquatch Bks., *(978-0-912365; 978-1-57061; 978-0-9821188; 978-1-63217)* 1904 Third Avenue, Suite 710, Seattle, WA 98101 USA (SAN 289-0208) Toll Free: 800-775-0817; *Imprints:* Little Bigfoot (Little Bigfoot)
E-mail: custserv@SasquatchBooks.com
Web site: http://www.sasquatchbooks.com
Dist(s): **MyiLibrary**
Penguin Random Hse., LLC.
Perseus-PGW
Perseus Bks. Group
Random Hse., Inc.

Sasscer, Abby, *(978-0-9854729)* 158 Nazareth Dr., Fort Valley, VA 22652 USA Tel 540-933-6496
E-mail: projectnazareth@yahoo.com.

Satellite Studio, *(978-0-9743968)* P.O. Box 32457, Knoxville, TN 37930-2457 USA Tel 865-691-1450; Fax: 865-691-2464
E-mail: dwilson@dannywilson.com.

Satin Finish Publishing, *(978-0-9764930; 978-0-9800209)* P.O. Box 481351, Kansas City, MO 64131 USA
E-mail: slfoster0826@kc.rr.com.

Satin Sheet Memoirs Publishing *See* **Nowata Press Publishing Consultants**

Saturn International, *(978-0-9764957)* 126 Herricks Rd., Mineola, NY 11501 USA Fax: 516-214-0154.

Satya Hse. Pubns., *(978-0-9729191; 978-0-9818720; 978-1-935874)* Orders Addr.: 22 Turkey St., Hardwick, MA 01037 USA; Edit Addr.: P.O. Box 122, Hardwick, MA 01037 USA Tel 413-477-8743
E-mail: julie@satyahouse.com
Web site: http://www.satyahouse.com; http://www.iseethesunbooks.com
Dist(s): **Midpoint Trade Bks., Inc.**
OverDrive, Inc.
Smashwords.

Sauerlander AG (CHE) *(978-3-7941)* *Dist. by* **Distribks Inc.**

Sauls, Lynn, *(978-0-615-74910-5; 978-0-615-78903-3; 978-0-9893216)* 14 Alexander St., Alexandria, VA 22314 USA Tel 703-549-5799
E-mail: lynnbsauls@aol.com.

Saunders Bk. Co. (CAN) *(978-1-895058; 978-1-897563; 978-1-926660; 978-1-926722; 978-1-926853; 978-1-77092)* *Dist. by* **Creative Co.**

Saunders Bk. Co. (CAN) *(978-1-895058; 978-1-897563; 978-1-926660; 978-1-926722; 978-1-926853; 978-1-77092)* *Dist. by* **RiverStream.**

Sauvignon Pr., *(978-0-9889618)* 1459 Brookcliff Dr., Marietta, GA 30062 USA Tel 404-435-6507
E-mail: rewrites1@gmail.com.

Savage Books *See* **Blue Thunder Bks.**

Savage Pr., *(978-1-886028; 978-1-937706)* P.O. Box 115, Superior, WI 54880 USA Tel 218-391-3070 (phone/fax)
E-mail: mail@savpress.com
Web site: http://www.savpress.com
Dist(s): **Partners Bk. Distributing, Inc.**

Savanna Pr., *(978-0-9759440)* Orders Addr.: P.O. Box 777, Monte Vista, CO 81144 USA Tel 719-850-2255; Fax: 719-852-2211; Edit Addr.: 67 Gold Cir., Pagosa Springs, CO 81147 USA; P.O. Box 1806, Vryburg, 8600
E-mail: riovista@rmi.net.

Savannah College of Art & Design Exhibitions, *(978-0-9654682; 978-1-893974; 978-0-9797440; 978-0-615-22202-8)* Orders Addr.: P.O. Box 3146, Savannah, GA 31401-3146 USA Tel 912-525-5287; Fax: 912-525-4952; Edit Addr.: 212 W. Hall St., Garden Apt., Savannah, GA 31401 USA; *Imprints:* Design Press Books (Design Press Bks)
E-mail: asalgado@scad.edu
Web site: http://www.scadexhibitions.com
Dist(s): **D.A.P./Distributed Art Pubs.**

Savas, Bachtsoglou, *(978-0-9771020)* 139-02 97th Ave., Jamaica, NY 11435 USA Tel 718-793-0107
E-mail: aviprem1all@gmail.com.

Save Our Seas, Ltd., *(978-0-9800444)* 626 Elvira Ave., Redondo Beach, CA 90277-9027 USA Tel 310-792-0338; Fax: 310-792-9273
E-mail: jonr@jokarproductions.com
Web site: http://www.saveourseas.com
Dist(s): **National Bk. Network.**

Savor Publishing Hse., Inc., *(978-0-9708296)* 6020 Broken Bow Dr., Citrus Heights, CA 95621 USA Tel 718-846-7277
E-mail: Smarties@SavorPublishing.com; SavorPubHouse@aol.com
Web site: http://www.savorpublishing.com
Dist(s): **Book Clearing Hse.**
Book Wholesalers, Inc.
Follett School Solutions.

Savory Palate, Inc., *(978-1-889374)* 8174 S. Holly, No. 404, Centennial, CO 80122-4004 USA Tel 303-741-5408; Fax: 303-741-0339; Toll Free: 800-741-5418
E-mail: info@savorypalate.com
Web site: http://www.savorypalate.com
Dist(s): **Brodart Co.**
New Leaf Distributing Co., Inc.
Quality Bks., Inc.
Royal Pubns., Inc.

Savvy Cyber Kids, Inc., *(978-0-9827968)* 4780 Ashford Dunwoody Rd. Suite A 312, Atlanta, GA 30338 USA Tel 404-955-7233
E-mail: info@savvycyberkids.org
Web site: http://www.savvycyberkids.org.

Savvy Pr., *(978-0-9669877; 978-0-9826069; 978-0-9852115; 978-1-939113)* Orders Addr.: P.O. Box 63, Salem, NY 12865 USA Tel 518-633-4778; Fax: 815 346-2659
E-mail: info@savvypress.com; info@gowanusbooks.com
Web site: http://www.savvypress.com; http://www.sagasf.com; http://www.gowanusbooks.com
Dist(s): **Quality Bks., Inc.**

Sawmill Publishing, *(978-0-9749915)* 6444 E. Spring St., No. 215, Long Beach, CA 90815 USA
Web site: www.sawmillpublishing.com.

Sawmill Ridge Publishing, *(978-0-9761924)* 183 Post Oak Dr., Roanoke, VA 24019 USA Tel 540-966-5706.

Saxon Pubs., Inc., *(978-0-939798; 978-1-56577; 978-1-59141)* Div. of Houghton Mifflin Harcourt Supplemental Pubs., Orders Addr.: 6277 Sea Harbor Dr., 5th Flr., Orlando, FL 32887 USA Toll Free Fax: 877-578-2638; Toll Free: 888-363-4266; Edit Addr.: 10801 N. Mopac Expressway, Bldg. 3, Austin, TX 78759 USA (SAN 216-8960) Toll Free: 800-531-5015
Web site: http://www.saxonpublishers.com
Dist(s): **Follett School Solutions**
Houghton Mifflin Harcourt Publishing Co.

Say It Loud! Readers & Writers Series, *(978-0-9779499)* 1507 E. 53rd St., No. 841, Chicago, IL 60615 USA.

Say It Right, *(978-0-9723457; 978-0-9760490; 978-0-9770418; 978-1-934701)* Orders Addr.: P.O. Box 651, Tybee Island, GA 31328 USA Tel 912-228-4556; Fax: 912-480-4214; Toll Free: 888-811-0759
E-mail: jim@sayitright.org
Web site: http://www.sayitright.org.

Say Out Loud, LLC, *(978-0-9799127)* Orders Addr.: 885 Woodstock Rd. Suite 430-373, Roswell, GA 30075 USA (SAN 854-7483) Tel 404-428-7935; Fax: 404-506-9823
E-mail: author@wordstosayoutloud.com
Web site: http://www.wordstosayoutloud.com.

SBA Bks., LLC, *(978-0-9711404)* Orders Addr.: P.O. Box 3019, Daphne, AL 36526 USA Tel 251-232-9927; Fax: 251-621-1834; Edit Addr.: 12655-a Dominion Dr., Fairhope, AL 36532 USA
E-mail: sheila@sbabooks.com
Web site: http://www.sbabooks.com
Dist(s): **Emerald Bk. Co.**
Greenleaf Book Group.

SC & FC Publications, *(978-0-9860794)* P.O. Box 124, Interlochen, MI 49643 USA.

Scafe, Claire, *(978-0-9787695)* 7918 John Dr., Cheyenne, WY 82009 USA Tel 307-632-1702
E-mail: skir2@aol.com.

Scandinavia Publishing Hse. (DNK) *(978-87-7247; 978-87-87732)* *Dist. by* **Destiny Image Pubs.**

Scandora,
Dist(s): **AtlasBooks Distribution.**

Scanlan, John M., *(978-0-9755405)* 5 Gumtree Rd., No. F-20, Hilton Head, SC 29926 USA (SAN 256-0771) Tel 843-342-2793; Fax: 419-281-6883 (orders); Toll Free: 800-247-6553 (orders)
E-mail: ping1@hargray.com; order@bookmasters.com
Web site: http://www.speedislife.us; http://www.atlasbooks.com
Dist(s): **AtlasBooks Distribution.**

Scanlan, John M. Literary Services *See* **Scanlan, John M.**

†Scarecrow Pr., Inc., *(978-0-8108; 978-1-57886)* Div. of Rowman & Littlefield Publishing Group, Orders Addr.: 15200 NBN Way, Blue Ridge Summit, PA 17214 USA Tel 717-794-3800 (Sales, Customer Service, MIS, Royalties, Inventory Mgmt., Dist., Credit & Collection); Fax: 717-794-3803 (Customer Service &/or orders); 717-794-3857 (Sales & MIS); 717-794-3856 (Royalties, Inventory Mgmt. & Dist.); Toll Free Fax: 800-338-4550 (Customer Service &/or orders); Toll Free: 800-462-6420 (Customer Service &/or orders); Edit Addr.: 4501 Forbes Blvd., Suite 200, Lanham, MD 20706-4310 USA Tel 301-459-3366; Fax: 301-429-5747 Short Discount, please contact rlpgsales@rowman.com
E-mail: custserv@rowman.com
Web site: http://www.scarecrowpress.com; http://www.rlpgbooks.com
Dist(s): **CreateSpace Independent Publishing Platform**
Ebsco Publishing
Follett School Solutions
MyiLibrary
National Bk. Network
Rowman & Littlefield Publishers, Inc.
ebrary, Inc.; *CIP.*

ScarecrowEducation *See* **Rowman & Littlefield Education**

Scarlet Primrose Pr., *(978-0-9851678)* 308 Blue Heron Cir., Simpsonville, SC 29680 USA Tel 585-545-0032
E-mail: andreacefalo4@gmail.com; scarletprimrosepress@gmail.com
Web site: http://www.andreacefalo.com
Dist(s): **CreateSpace Independent Publishing Platform**
Lightning Source, Inc.
Smashwords.

Scarletta *See* **Mighty Media Pr.**

Scars Pubns. & Design, *(978-1-891470)* 829 Brian Ct., Gurnee, IL 60031 USA
E-mail: Editor@scars.tv
Web site: http://scars.tv.

Scavenger's Pubns., *(978-0-9798792)* 3443 Remington Ct., Eau Claire, WI 54703 USA Tel 715-456-3909
E-mail: ggparadox@hotmail.com.

SCB Distributors, Orders Addr.: 15608 S. New Century Dr., Gardena, CA 90248-2129 USA (SAN 630-4818) Tel 310-532-9400; Fax: 310-532-7001; Toll Free: 800-729-6423 (orders only)
E-mail: info@scbdistributors.com
Web site: http://www.scbdistributors.com.

Schafer-Post Entomology Pubns., *(978-0-9766855)* Entomology Dept. Hultz Hall, North Dakota State Univ., Fargo, ND 58105 USA Tel 701-231-7582; Fax: 701-231-8557
E-mail: david.rider@ndsu.edu.

Schallert, Ann, *(978-0-578-03425-6)* 10047 Hwy. 104, Tucumcari, NM 88401 USA
E-mail: crossann@shipleysystems.com.

Schaub, Stephen M. Photography *See* **Indian Hill Gallery of Fine Photography**

Scheer Delight Publishing, *(978-0-9671761)* 4030 E. Christy, Wichita, KS 67220-2540 USA (SAN 253-908X) Tel 316-683-2001; Fax: 316-636-1268
E-mail: schdelight@cox.net
Web site: http://scheerdelightpub.com.

Schermerhorn, Walters Co., *(978-0-9741746; 978-0-9824987)* 740 Purdue Dr., Claremont, CA 91711-3418 USA Tel 909-398-1228
E-mail: lilly.walters@verizon.net
Web site: http://www.motivational-keynote-speakers.com.

Schiavi, Sherry *See* **Celltrition**

Schiffer Publishing, Ltd., *(978-0-7643; 978-0-87033; 978-0-88740; 978-0-89538; 978-0-916838; 978-0-9787278; 978-1-5073)* Orders Addr.: 4880 Lower Valley Rd., Atglen, PA 19310 USA (SAN 208-8428) Tel 610-593-1777; Fax: 610-593-2002; *Imprints:* Cornell Maritime Press/Tidewater Publishers (CornellTide); Schiffer Publishing Ltd (SCHIFFER PUBLI)
E-mail: info@schifferbooks.com; karen@schifferbooks.com
Web site: http://www.schifferbooks.com.

Schiffer Publishing Ltd *Imprint of* **Schiffer Publishing, Ltd.**

Schiffner, Frederick A., *(978-0-9765782)* P.O. Box 1047, Spring Mt., PA 19478 USA Tel 610-287-5827
E-mail: fschiffner@fast.net.

Schiller Institute, Inc., *(978-0-9621095; 978-1-882985)* Orders Addr.: P.O. Box 20244, Washington, DC 20041-0244 USA (SAN 250-4944) Tel 703-777-9451 ext 541; Fax: 703-771-3099
E-mail: swelsh@schillerinstitute.org
Web site: http://www.schillerinstitute.org.

Schirmer Trade Bks. *Imprint of* **Music Sales Corp.**

Schleich, James, *(978-0-615-12142-0)* 105 Woodland Dr., Zelienople, PA 16063-9316 USA
E-mail: james@the-soundman.org
Web site: http://www.the-soundman.org.

Schlessinger Media, *(978-1-57225; 978-1-879151)* Div. of Library Video Co., Orders Addr.: P.O. Box 580, Wynnewood, PA 19096 USA Tel 610-645-4000; Fax: 610-645-4050; Toll Free: 800-843-3620; Edit Addr.: 7 Wynnewood Rd., Wynnewood, PA 19096 USA
E-mail: sales@libraryvideo.com
Web site: http://www.libraryvideo.com
Dist(s): **Follett School Solutions**
Library Video Co.
Video Project, The.

Schlessinger Video Productions *See* **Schlessinger Media**

Schley, Michael, *(978-0-9759645)* 2 Oak Pk. Ave., Darien, CT 06820 USA
E-mail: mike_schley@yahoo.com.

Schmitt, Steven E. *See* **Global Partnership, LLC**

Schmul Publishing Co., Inc., *(978-0-88019)* Orders Addr.: P.O. Box 716, Salem, OH 44460-0716 USA (SAN 180-2771) Tel 330-222-2249; Fax: 330-222-0001; Toll Free: 800-772-6657; Edit Addr.: 3583 Newgarden Rd., Salem, OH 44460 USA
E-mail: spchale@valunet.com
Web site: http://www.wesleyanbooks.com.

Schnitzelbank Press *See* **BeerBooks.com**

Schocken *Imprint of* **Knopf Doubleday Publishing Group**

Schoenberg & Assocs., *(978-0-9748208)* 8033 W. Sunset Blvd., No. 944, Los Angeles, CA 90046 USA
Web site: http://www.rdsphotos.com.

Schoenhof's Foreign Bks., Inc., *(978-0-87774)* 76a Mount Auburn St., Cambridge, MA 02138-5051 USA (SAN 212-0062)
E-mail: info@schoenhofs.com
Web site: http://www.schoenhofs.com.

Scholargy Custom Publishing, Incorporated *See* **Scholargy Publishing, Inc.**

Scholargy Publishing, Inc., *(978-1-58666; 978-1-59247)* 17855 N. Black Cnyon Hwy., Phoenix, AZ 85023 USA (SAN 254-7295) Tel 602-548-5833 (phone/fax); Fax: 602-353-0680
E-mail: stephanie@scholargy.com
Web site: http://www.scholargy.com.

Scholarly Resources, Inc. *Imprint of* **Rowman & Littlefield Publishers, Inc.**

Scholastic *Imprint of* **Scholastic, Inc.**

Scholastic Canada, Ltd. (CAN) *(978-0-439; 978-0-590; 978-0-7791; 978-1-4431)* Dist. by **Scholastic Inc.**
Scholastic en Espanol *Imprint of* **Scholastic, Inc.**
Scholastic, Inc. *Imprint of* **Scholastic, Inc.**
†Scholastic, Inc., *(978-0-439; 978-0-590; 978-0-545; 978-1-338)* 557 Broadway, New York, NY 10012-3999 USA (SAN 202-5442) Fax: 212-343-6802; Toll Free: 800-325-6149 (customer service); *Imprints:* Cartwheel Books (Cartwheel); Scholastic Reference (Scholastic Ref); Blue Sky Press, The (Blue Sky Press); Scholastic (Scholastic); Levine, Arthur A. Books (A A Levine); Orchard Books (Orchard Bks); Scholastic Press (Scholastic Pr); Chicken House, The (Chick Hse); PUSH (PUSH); Scholastic en Espanol (Scholastic en Espanol); Scholastic Nonfiction (Schol Nonfic); Scholastic Paperbacks (Schol Pbk); Sidekicks TM (Sidekicks); Tangerine Press (Tang Pr Sch); Teaching Resources (Teach Res Sch); Graphix (Graphx); Scholastic, Incorporated (SchInc); Teaching Strategies (TeachStrategi); Theory & Practice (Theory & Prac); Little Shepherd (Little Shepard); Di Capua, Michael (Michael DiCapua); WestBow Press (WestBowPr)
E-mail: info@scholastic.com
Web site: http://www.scholastic.com
Dist(s): **Ebsco Publishing**
Follett School Solutions
Hachette Bk. Group
HarperCollins Pubs.
Lectorum Pubns., Inc.
MyiLibrary
Open Road Integrated Media, LLC
Perfection Learning Corp.; *CIP.*
Scholastic Library Publishing, *(978-0-516; 978-0-531; 978-0-7172; 978-1-60631)* 90 Old Sherman Tpke., Danbury, CT 06816 USA (SAN 253-8865) Tel 203-797-3500; Fax: 203-797-3657; Toll Free: 800-621-1115; *Imprints:* Orchard Books (Orchard Bks); Grolier Online (Grolier Online); Children's Press (Childrens Pr); Grolier (Grolier Schol); Watts, Franklin (Frank Watts)
E-mail: agraham@grolier.com; kbreen@scholastic.com
Web site: http://librarypublishing.scholastic.com
Dist(s): **Booksource, The**
Hachette Bk. Group
Lectorum Pubns., Inc.
Scholastic Nonfiction *Imprint of* **Scholastic, Inc.**
Scholastic Paperbacks *Imprint of* **Scholastic, Inc.**
Scholastic Pr. *Imprint of* **Scholastic, Inc.**
Scholastic Reference *Imprint of* **Scholastic, Inc.**
Schonwalder, Helmut, *(978-0-9763287)* P.O. Box 1390, Monterey, CA 93940 USA Tel 831-375-7737
E-mail: helmut@schonwalder.org; helmut@schonwalder.com
Web site: http://www.schonwalder.com; http://www.gastronomical.net; http://www.kaufhouse.info.
School Age Notes *Imprint of* **Gryphon Hse., Inc.**
School Days, *(978-0-9744302)* Orders Addr.: P.O. Box 454, North Carrollton, MS 38947 USA
E-mail: schooldaysmemorybook@yahoo.com
Web site: http://www.schooldaysmemorybook.com
Dist(s): **Wimmer Cookbooks.**
†School for Advanced Research Pr./SAR Pr., *(978-0-933452; 978-1-930618; 978-1-934691; 978-1-938645)* P.O. Box 2188, Santa Fe, NM 87504-2188 USA (SAN 212-6222) Tel 505-954-7206; Fax: 505-954-7241; Toll Free: 888-390-6070
E-mail: press@sarsf.org
Web site: http://www.sarpress.sarweb.org; *CIP.*
School of American Research Press *See* **School for Advanced Research Pr./SAR Pr.**
School of Color Publishing, *(978-0-9679628; 978-1-931780)* Div. of The Michael Wilcox School of Color, Inc., P.O. Box 4793, Pinehurst, NC 28374 USA Toll Free: 888-794-5269
E-mail: wilcoxschool@earthlink.net; anne.m.gardner@worldnet.att.net
Web site: http://www.schoolofcolor.com
Dist(s): **F&W Media, Inc.**
Schl. of Government, *(978-1-56011)* CB 3330 UNC Chapel Hill, Chapel Hill, NC 27599-3330 USA (SAN 204-8752) Tel 919-966-4119; Fax: 919-962-2707
E-mail: khunt@iogmail.iog.unc.edu
Web site: http://www.sog.unc.edu.
School of Music Publishing Hse. (RUS) *(978-5-9500)* Dist. by **Coronet Bks.**
Schl. Services of California, Inc., *(978-0-9708628; 978-0-9748487; 978-0-9848031)* 1121 L St., No. 1060, Sacramento, CA 95814 USA Tel 916-446-7517; Fax: 916-446-2011
E-mail: susanm@sscal.com
Web site: http://www.sscal.com.
Schl. Tools, *(978-0-9754578)* 23418 28th Ave. W, Brier, WA 98036 USA.
School Zone Publishing Co., *(978-0-88743; 978-0-938256; 978-1-58947; 978-1-60041; 978-1-60159; 978-1-68147)* P.O. Box 777, Grand Haven, MI 49417 USA (SAN 289-8314) Tel 616-846-5030; Fax: 616-846-6181; Toll Free: 800-253-0564; 1819 Industrial Dr., Grand Haven, MI 49417
E-mail: Bobb@schoolzone.com
Web site: http://www.schoolzone.com.
Schoolhouse Publishing, *(978-0-9758543; 978-0-9845335; 978-0-9834657)* Orders Addr.: 659 Schoolhouse Rd., Telford, PA 18969-2449 USA Toll Free: 877-747-4711
Web site: http://www.shpublishing.com.
Schoolside Pr, *(978-0-9785100)* 7039 Sacred Cir., Sparks, NV 89437 USA Tel 818-884-7349
E-mail: eamartonyi@schoolsidepress.com
Web site: http://Schoolsidpress.com
Dist(s): **Midpoint Trade Bks., Inc.**
Schooner Pubns., *(978-1-929234)* 1610-D Church St. Coastal Ctr., PMB 360, Conway, SC 29526 USA Tel 843-347-9792.
Schott Music Corp., *(978-0-930448)* 35 E 21st ST., 8th Flr., New York, NY 10010 USA
E-mail: scott.wollschleger@eamdllc.com
Dist(s): **Leonard, Hal Corp.**
Schott Musik International GmbH & Co. KG (DEU) *(978-3-7957; 978-3-95983)* Dist. by **H Leonard.**
Schrader, Racheal, *(978-0-9815274)* P.O. Box 15603, Colorado Springs, CO 80935-5603 USA
E-mail: inspired-ink@hotmail.com
Web site: http://inspired-ink.net.
Schroeder, Patrick A. Publications: Civil War Books *See* **Schroeder Pubns.: Civil War Bks.**
Schroeder Pubns.: Civil War Bks., *(978-1-889246)* Orders Addr.: 131 Tanglewood Dr., Lynchburg, VA 24502 USA Tel 434-525-4431; Fax: 434-525-7293
E-mail: civilwarbooks@yahoo.com
Web site: http://www.civilwar-books.com.
Schwarcz, Editora Ltda, Companhia das Letrinhas (BRA) *(978-85-7406)* Dist. by **Distribks Inc.**
Schwartz & Wade Bks. *Imprint of* **Random Hse. Children's Bks.**
Schwartz, Arthur & Company, Incorporated/Woodstocker Books *See* **Woodstocker Books/Arthur Schwartz & Company**
Schwartz, Joel, *(978-0-9785885)* 1315 Cinnamon Dr., Fort Washington, PA 19034-2818 USA
E-mail: jshrink@comcast.net
Web site: http://www.stresslessshrink.com.
Schwarz Pauper Pr., *(978-0-9621505)* 88 Winwood Dr., Barnstead, NH 03225 USA (SAN 251-4540) Tel 603-776-5680
E-mail: Granitesunset@aol.com.
Sci Fi-Arizona, Inc., *(978-1-929381)* 1931 E. Libra Dr., Tempe, AZ 85283 USA Tel 480-838-6558; *Imprints:* Third Millennium Publishing (Third Millen Pubng)
E-mail: mccollum@scifi-az.com
Web site: http://www.scifi-az.com; http://www.3mpub.com.
Science Academy Software, *(978-0-9623926)* 600 Baychester Ave., Apt 5B, Bronx, NY 10475-4457 USA Tel 718-561-4048.
Science & God, Inc., *(978-0-9745861)* P.O. Box 2036, Labelle, FL 33975-2036 USA Tel 239-218-4543.
Science & Humanities Pr., *(978-1-888725; 978-1-59630)* Subs. of Banis & Assocs., Orders Addr.: P.O. Box 7151, Chesterfield, MO 63006-7151 USA (SAN 299-8459) Tel 636-394-4950; Fax: 800-706-0585; P.O. Box 7151, Chesterfield, MO 63006-7151; Edit Addr.: 1023 Stuyvesant Ln., Manchester, MO 63011-3601 USA Tel 636-394-4950; Toll Free Fax: 800-706-0585; 1023 Stuyvesant Ln., Manchester, MO 63011-3601 Tel 636-394-4950; Toll Free Fax: 800-706-0585; *Imprints:* BeachHouse Books (BeachHouse Bks)
E-mail: banis@sciencehumanitiespress.com; banis@banis-associates.com
Web site: http://www.banis-associates.com; http://www.sciencehumanitiespress.com; http://www.macroprintbooks.com; http://www.stressmyth.com; http://www.normajeanebook.com; http://www.route66book.com; http://www.accessible-travel.com.
Science and Technology Concepts (STC) *Imprint of* **Smithsonian Science Education Ctr. (SSEC)**
Science Curriculum, Inc., *(978-1-882057)* Orders Addr.: 200 Union Blvd. Ste. G18, Lakewood, CO 80228-1845 USA (SAN 248-3637) Toll Free: 888-501-0957; 24 Stone Rd., Belmont, MA 04278
E-mail: marketing@sci-ips.com
Web site: http://www.sci-ips.com.
Science Enterprises, Inc., *(978-0-930116)* 402 N. Blackford St., Indianapolis, IN 46202-3272 USA (SAN 210-6639).
Science, Naturally!, *(978-0-9678020; 978-0-9700106; 978-1-938492)* 725 Eighth St., SE., Washington, DC 20003 USA Tel 202-465-4798; Fax: 202-558-2132; Toll Free: 866-724-9876
E-mail: dia@sciencenaturally.com
Web site: http://www.sciencenaturally.com
Dist(s): **MyiLibrary**
National Bk. Network
ebrary, Inc.
Science of Knowledge Pr., *(978-1-59620)* P.O. Box 324, Little Falls, NJ 07424 USA Fax: 973-272-1102
Web site: http://www.scienceok.com
Dist(s): **Majors, J. A. Co.**
Science of Mind Publishing, *(978-0-911336; 978-0-917849; 978-0-9727184)* Div. of United Church of Religious Science, Orders Addr.: 573 Park Point Dr., Golden, CO 80401-7042 USA (SAN 203-2570) Tel 720-279-1643; 720-496-1370; Fax: 303-526-0913
E-mail: ahubbard@csl.org
Web site: http://www.scienceofmind.com; http://www.spirituallivingpress.com
Dist(s): **DeVorss & Co.**
Red Wheel/Weiser.
Science Pubs., *(978-0-9700733; 978-0-9716445; 978-0-9749755; 978-1-938024)* Div. of BrainMind.com, 677 Elm St., San Jose, CA 95126 USA Do not confuse with companies with the same name in Hudson, WI, Flushing, NY, San Francisco, CA, Missoula, MT, Wolf City, TX
E-mail: BookMoviesOrders@BrainMind.com
Web site: http://www.UniversityPress.Info; http://BrainMind.com; http://Cosmology.com
Dist(s): **MyiLibrary.**
Science Square Publishing, *(978-0-9740861)* 2845 Bowen St., Graton, CA 95444-9347 USA
E-mail: info@sciencesquare.com
Web site: http://www.sciencesquare.com.
Science2Discover, Inc., *(978-0-9673811)* P.O. Box 2435, Del Mar, CA 92014-1735 USA Fax: 858-793-0410; Toll Free: 888-359-6075; 2015 Seaview Ave., Del Mar, CA 92014 Do not confuse with MetaMetrix, Inc., Norcross, GA
E-mail: info@science2discover.com
Web site: http://www.science2discover.com.
Sciencenter, *(978-0-578-00196-8; 978-0-578-00197-5)* 601 First St., Ithaca, NY 14850 USA Tel 607-272-0600
Dist(s): **Lulu Enterprises Inc.**
Scientia Est Vox Pr., *(978-0-578-02353-3; 978-0-578-05385-1; 978-0-578-07089-6; 978-0-578-12511-4; 978-0-578-16302-4)* 2338 8th Ave., Terre Haute, IN 47804 USA Tel 812-917-4182; 812-917-4384
E-mail: magicianofoz@hotmail.com
Web site: http://www.magicianofoz.blogspot.com
Dist(s): **Lulu Enterprises Inc.**
Sci-Hi *Imprint of* **Heinemann-Raintree**
Scion Publishing Ltd. (GBR) *(978-1-904842; 978-1-907904)* Dist. by **Chicago Distribution Ctr.**
Scobre Pr. Corp., *(978-0-9708992; 978-0-9741695; 978-0-9741997; 978-0-9766240; 978-1-933423; 978-1-934713; 978-1-61570; 978-1-62920)* 2255 Calle Clara, La Jolla, CA 92037 USA Toll Free: 877-726-2734
E-mail: Scott@bookbuddyaudio.com
Web site: http://www.scobre.com
Dist(s): **Lerner Publishing Group**
MyiLibrary.
SCOJO ENTERTAINMENT, *(978-0-9651306; 978-0-9786488)* Orders Addr.: P.O. Box 1225, New York, NY 10008 USA
Web site: theportalinthepark.com.
Scooby-Doo *Imprint of* **Stone Arch Bks.**
SCOPE Pubns., *(978-0-9759955)* Orders Addr.: 100 Lawrence Ave., Smithtown, NY 11787 USA Tel 631-360-0800; Fax: 631-360-8489 Do not confuse with Scope Publications, Fairfax, OK
E-mail: bkauffman@scopeonline.us
Web site: http://www.scopeonline.us.
Scotland Gate, Inc., *(978-0-9830084; 978-0-9837523; 978-0-9839550; 978-0-9888972; 978-0-9888973)* 176 Edgecliff Dr., Highland Park, IL 60035 USA Tel 847-432-1947
E-mail: mskemp@sbcglobal.net.
Scott, Cassandra Dr Ministries, *(978-0-9882936)* 3802 Hanberry, Pearland, TX 77584 USA Tel 713-550-3370
E-mail: cescott1@aol.com.
Scott, D.& F. Publishing, Inc., *(978-0-941037; 978-1-930566)* Orders Addr.: P.O. Box 821653, North Richland Hills, TX 76182-1653 USA (SAN 665-2875) Tel 817-788-2280; Fax: 817-788-9232; Toll Free: 888-788-2280; Edit Addr.: P.O. Box 821653, N Richlnd Hls, TX 76182-1653 USA; *Imprints:* WestWind Press (WstWind)
E-mail: info@dfscott.com
Web site: http://www.dfscott.com.
Scott Foresman *Imprint of* **Addison-Wesley Educational Pubs., Inc.**
Scott Foresman *Imprint of* **Addison-Wesley Educational Pubs., Inc.**
Scott Foresman *Imprint of* **Addison Wesley Schl.**
Scott, J & N Pubs., *(978-0-9719868)* 10461 NW 20 St., Pembroke Pines, FL 33026 USA Tel 954-432-6578
E-mail: nscott2000@aol.com.
Scott, James *See* **Scott, J & N Pubs.**
Scott, Josephine, *(978-0-9718582; 978-0-9746600)* P.O. Box 55127, Bridgeport, CT 06610 USA
E-mail: jartist@optonline.net
Web site: http://www.ethnicitycards.com
Dist(s): **BookMasters Distribution Services (BDS)**
MyiLibrary
ebrary, Inc.
†Scott Pubns., Inc., *(978-0-916809; 978-1-893625; 978-0-9787419)* 2145 W. Sherman Blvd., Muskegon, MI 49441-3434 USA Toll Free: 866-733-9382 Do not confuse with Scott Pubns. in Indianapolis, IN
E-mail: contactus@scottpublications.com
Web site: http://www.scottpublications.com; *CIP.*
Scott Publishing Co., *(978-0-9617626; 978-1-930043; 978-0-9908913)* Orders Addr.: P.O. Box 9707, Kalispell, MT 59901 USA (SAN 664-6948) Tel 406-755-0099; Fax: 406-756-0098; Edit Addr.: 1845 Helena Flats Rd., Kalispell, MT 59901-6525 USA (SAN 664-6956) Do not confuse with companies with the same or similar name in Sidney, OH, Houston, TX, Edmonds, WA
E-mail: scott@scottcompnay.net.
Scottish Children's Pr. (GBR) *(978-1-898218; 978-1-899827)* Dist. by **Wlsn Assocs.**
Scottish Christmas, *(978-0-9726114)* 2369 Joslyn Ct., Lake Orion, MI 48360 USA.
Scottwall Assocs., *(978-0-942087; 978-0-9612790; 978-0-578-01245-2)* 95 Scott St., San Francisco, CA 94117 USA (SAN 289-8322) Tel 415-861-1956; Fax: 415-863-7273
E-mail: scotwall@pacbell.net
Web site: http://www.scottwallpub.com
Dist(s): **Sunbelt Pubns., Inc.**
Todd Communications.
Scott-Waters, Marilyn, *(978-0-9759884)* 1589 Baker St., Costa Mesa, CA 92626 USA
E-mail: msw@scottwatersdesign.com
Web site: http://www.thetoymaker.com.
SCR, Inc., *(978-0-9747582; 978-1-63227)* Orders Addr.: P.O. Box 803338 #46673, Chicago, IL 60680 USA (SAN 255-7509) Tel 815-642-0848
E-mail: isbn@spamex.com
Web site: http://www.scrbooks.com
Dist(s): **Lulu Enterprises Inc.**
SCR Publications *See* **SCR, Inc.**
S.C.R.A.P. Gallery, *(978-0-9708135)* 46-350 Arabia St., Indio, CA 92201 USA Tel 760-863-7777; Fax: 760-863-8973; Toll Free: 866-717-2727 (866-71-SCRAP)
E-mail: scrapgallery@earthlink.net
Web site: http://www.infoteam.com/nonprofit/scrapgallery.
Scrap Paper Pr., *(978-0-9745493)* 6 Manor Dr., Goldens Bridge, NY 10526 USA Tel 914-997-1692; Fax: 914-997-2253.
Scribbler's Sword, *(978-0-9761186)* 1640 Halfacre Rd., Newberry, SC 29108 USA.
Scribe Publishing, *(978-0-9727077)* 132 Bainbridge St., Philadelphia, PA 19147 USA Tel 215-592-7266 Do not confuse with companies with the same or similar name in King City, CA, Murray, UT, Welsh, LA, Seattle, WA, Redan, GA
E-mail: scribe@scribenet.com
Web site: http://www.scribenet.com.
Scribe Publishing & Consulting Services, The, *(978-0-9793516)* Div. of TrueLight Ministries, P.O. Box 11013, Tacoma, WA 98411 USA Tel 253-312-9377; Fax: 253-238-6041; *Imprints:* Writing The Vision (Writing The Vision)
E-mail: missmillie59@yahoo.com
Web site: http://www.truelightmin.org.
Scribe Publishing Co., *(978-0-9859562; 978-1-940368; 978-0-9916021)* 29488 Woodward Suite 426, Royal Oak, MI 48073 USA Tel 248-259-0090
E-mail: jennifer@scribe-publishing.com
Web site: http://scribe-publishing.com.
Scribe Pubns. (AUS) *(978-0-908011; 978-1-920769; 978-1-921215; 978-1-921372; 978-1-921640; 978-1-921753; 978-1-921844; 978-1-921863; 978-1-921864; 978-1-921942; 978-1-922070; 978-1-922072; 978-1-922247; 978-1-925106; 978-1-925113; 978-1-925228; 978-1-925292; 978-1-925293; 978-1-925307; 978-1-925321; 978-1-925322)* Dist. by **IPG Chicago.**
Scribe's Closet Pubns., The, *(978-0-9801269; 978-0-9832570; 978-0-9884125; 978-0-9912487; 978-1-943058)* 702 South Missouri, Macon, MO 63552 USA
E-mail: scribescloset@gmail.com
Web site: http://www.thescribesclosetpublications.com.
Scribez, Scarebz & Vibez, *(978-0-9853406)* 689 Macon St., Brooklyn, NY 11233 USA Tel 646-267-1459
E-mail: bedstuybelle1@gmail.com.
Scribner *Imprint of* **Scribner**
Scribner, *(978-0-684; 978-0-7432)* Orders Addr.: 100 Front St., Riverside, NJ 08075 USA; Edit Addr.: 1230 Ave. of the Americas, New York, NY 10020 USA; *Imprints:* Scribner (ScribImp)
Dist(s): **Simon & Schuster**
Simon & Schuster, Inc.
Scribolin, *(978-0-9746226)* 10107 Copeland Dr., Manassas, VA 20109 USA Tel 703-257-7683
E-mail: books@scribolin.com
Web site: http://www.scribolin.com.
Scripts Publishing, *(978-1-889826)* Orders Addr.: 638 Hennepin Ter., Mcdonough, GA 30253-5965 USA
E-mail: AtaxiaBooks@aol.com
Web site: http://www.hometown.aol.com/pathamilto/myhomepage/profile.html.
Scripture Mastery Resources!, *(978-1-933589)* 1814 Cranberry Way, Springville, UT 84663-3930 USA
E-mail: scripturemastery@kenalford.com
Web site: http://www.kenalford.com.
Scripture Memory Fellowship International, *(978-1-880960)* Orders Addr.: P.O. Box 411551, Saint Louis, MO 63141 USA Tel 314-569-0244; Fax: 314-569-0025; Toll Free: 888-569-2560; Edit Addr.: P.O. Box 568, Hannibal, MO 63401-0568 USA
E-mail: memorize@stlnet.com
Web site: http://www.scripturememory.com.
Scripture Union (GBR) *(978-0-85421; 978-0-86201; 978-1-85999; 978-1-873824; 978-1-84427)* Dist. by **STL Dist.**
Scripture Union (GBR) *(978-0-85421; 978-0-86201; 978-1-85999; 978-1-873824; 978-1-84427)* Dist. by **Gabriel Res.**
†Scroll Pr., Inc., *(978-0-87592)* 2858 Valerie Ct., Merrick, NY 11566 USA (SAN 206-796X) Tel 516-379-4283; *CIP.*
Scroll Publishing Co., *(978-0-924722)* Orders Addr.: P.O. Box 4714, Tyler, TX 75712 USA; Edit Addr.: 22012 Indian Spring Tr., Amberson, PA 17210 USA Tel 717-349-7033; Fax: 717-349-7558
E-mail: customerservice@scrollpublishing.com
Web site: http://www.scrollpublishing.com.
Scrumps Entertainment, Inc., *(978-0-9672279)* 19320 NW. 47th Ave., Miami, FL 33055 USA Tel 305-624-7231
E-mail: climbcrick@aol.com.
SDP Publishing, *(978-0-9824461; 978-0-9829256; 978-0-9885157; 978-0-9889381; 978-0-9899723; 978-0-9911597; 978-0-9913167; 978-0-9905596; 978-0-9862896; 978-0-9964345; 978-0-9968426)* Div. of SDP Publishing Solutions, LLC, Orders Addr.: P.O. Box 26, East Bridgewater, MA 02333 USA (SAN 858-1762)
E-mail: lross@SDPPublishing.com
Web site: http://www.sdppublishingsolutions.com; http://www.PublishAtSweetDreams.com; http://www.sdppublishing.com
Dist(s): **Lightning Source, Inc.**
SDP Publishing Solutions *See* **SDP Publishing**
SE PrinTech, *(978-0-615-33647-3; 978-0-615-48019-0; 978-0-9847344)* 315 E. Banks St., Glennville, GA 30427 USA Tel 912-654-3610
E-mail: bill@welovetoprint.com.
Se7enth Swan Publishing Group, LLC, *(978-0-615-14849-6)* P.O. Box 16874, Chapel Hill, NC 27516 USA
Web site: http://www.se7enthswan.com
Dist(s): **Lulu Enterprises Inc.**
Sea Chest Bks., *(978-0-9742909)* 11573 Viking Ave., Northridge, CA 91326 USA
E-mail: info@beverlyhillsvideographer.com
Web site: http://www.seachestbooks.com.
Sea Keepers Publishing, *(978-0-9846251)* 936 N. Main St., Akron, OH 44310 USA.

Sea Lion Bks., *(978-0-578-06080-4; 978-0-9828186; 978-0-9836131; 978-0-9857691)* 6070 Autumn View Trail, Acworth, GA 30101 USA
E-mail: david@sealionbooks.com
Dist(s): **BookBaby**
Diamond Bk. Distributors.

Sea Oats Publishing, *(978-0-9798143)* 699-A Sterling Dr., James Island, SC 29412-9135 USA Tel 843-762-2606
E-mail: seaoatspublishing@yahoo.com.

Sea Raven Enterprises *See* **Sea Raven Pr.**

Sea Raven Pr., *(978-0-9768707; 978-0-9821899; 978-0-9827700; 978-0-9838185; 978-0-9858632; 978-0-9913779; 978-1-943737)* Orders Addr.: P.O. Box 1054, Franklin, TN 37065 USA Tel 615-349-1345; P.O. Box 1054, Franklin, TN 37065
E-mail: searavenpress@nii.net
Web site: http://www.searavenpress.com.

Seabury Bks. *Imprint of* **Church Publishing, Inc.**

Seachild, *(978-0-9787881)* P.O. Box 2600, Petaluma, CA 94952 USA (SAN 851-6499) Tel 707-762-7316
E-mail: judiegerber@earthlink.net
Web site: http://www.seachild.net.

Seacoast Publishing, Inc., *(978-1-878561; 978-1-59421)* Orders Addr.: 3115 Northington Ct Ste 114, Birmingham, AL 35260 USA Tel 256-349-5020 Do not confuse with companies with the same name in Monterey, CA, East Hampton, NY
E-mail: info@seacoast.pub
Web site: http://www.seacoast.pub.

Seaforth Publishing, *(978-0-9725706)* 5818 Three Ponds Ct., West Bloomfield, MI 48324-3124 USA
Dist(s): **MyiLibrary.**

Seagull Books (GBR) *(978-1-905422; 978-1-906497; 978-0-85742) Dist. by* **Chicago Distribution Ctr.**

Seagull Pr., *(978-0-9753709)* 375-A Maxham Rd., No. 414, Austell, GA 30168 USA Fax: 770-944-3799 Do not confuse with companies with the same name in Oakland, CA, Owings, MD.

Seal Pr, *(978-0-931188; 978-1-58005; 978-1-878067)* Div. of Perseus Bks. Grp., 387 Park Ave., S., 12th Flr., New York, NY 10016-8810 USA Tel 212-340-8100
Dist(s): **Ebsco Publishing**
Follett School Solutions
Perseus-PGW
Perseus Bks. Group
ebrary, Inc.

Seal Publishing, LLC, *(978-0-9774062)* P.O. Box 435, Odessa, FL 33556 USA
Web site: http://www.sealswimschool.com.

Seal Rock Publishing, LLC, *(978-0-9763778)* 834 Marshall Rd., Boulder, CO 80305-7337 USA
E-mail: sealrockpub@yahoo.com.

Seaman, P. David, *(978-0-9755066)* 2645 E. Southern Ave. Apt. A679, Tempe, AZ 85282-7532 USA.

Sean Tigh Pr., *(978-0-9851200)* 1799 Ivy Oak Sq., Reston, VA 20190 USA Tel 321-446-1483
E-mail: kristen@kristenandjoe.com.

Search Institute, *(978-1-57482)* 615 First Ave. NE, Suite 125, Minneapolis, MN 55413 USA Tel 612-376-8955; Fax: 612-376-8956; Toll Free: 800-888-7828
Web site: http://www.search-institute.org
Dist(s): **Ebsco Publishing**
Independent Pubs. Group
MyiLibrary
ebrary, Inc.

Search Pr., Ltd. (GBR) *(978-0-85532; 978-1-903975; 978-1-84448; 978-1-78126; 978-1-78221) Dist. by* **PerseuPGW.**

Searchlight Pr., *(978-0-9644609; 978-0-9824802; 978-1-936497)* Orders Addr.: 5634 Ledgestone Dr., Dallas, TX 75214-2026 USA Tel 214-662-5494; Toll Free: 888-896-6081
E-mail: searchlight@johncunyus.com; info@searchlight-press.com
Web site: http://www.johncunyus.com; http://www.searchlight-press.com.

SearlStudio Publishing, *(978-0-9883670; 978-0-9895062)* 18331 Pines Blvd., No. 322, Pembroke Pines, FL 33029 USA Tel 305-517-7261
E-mail: searlstudio@me.com
Web site: http://www.searlstudio.com.

Sears, M.A., *(978-0-9639785)* 16809 Superior, North Hills, CA 91343 USA; 555 W. Sierra Hwy., Acton, CA 93510 Tel 818-891-8632.

Sears, Stanley, *(978-0-9770067)* Rte. 1 Box 215, Hickman, NE 68372-9686 USA.

Seascape Pr., *(978-0-9769510)* P.O. Box 13132, Jekyll Island, GA 31527 USA Tel 912-635-3263; Fax: 912-635-3264 Do not confuse with Seascape Press, LLC in Santa Barbara, CA.

SeaScape Pr., Ltd., *(978-0-9669741; 978-0-9852381)* 5717 Tanner Ridge Ave., Westlake Vlg, CA 91362-5238 USA (SAN 299-8386) Tel 818-707-3080 Toll Free: 800-929-2906 do not confuse with Seascape Press in Jekyll Island, GA
E-mail: seapress@aol.com; llamensdor@aol.com
Web site: http://www.lenlamensdorf.com.

Seascay Productions, *(978-0-9764152)* 11 Ventnor Dr. Suite 906, Edison, NJ 08820 USA Tel 732-242-3902
E-mail: corporate@seascay.com
Web site: http://www.seascay.com.

Seashell Pr., The, *(978-0-9768866)* 28 Skytop Rd, Ipswich, MA 01938 USA
E-mail: mailbag@theseashellpress.com
Web site: http://www.theseashellpress.com.

Seaside Books *See* **Ladd, David Pr.**

Seasoning Quilting (Arts & Crafts), *(978-1-888413)* 806 Elvie St., Wilson, NC 27893-6116 USA Tel 919-291-7705.

SeaSquirt Pubns. (GBR) *(978-1-905470) Dist. by* **Basic Dist.**

SeaStar Bks. *Imprint of* **Chronicle Bks. LLC**

Seastory Pr., *(978-0-9673704; 978-0-9768370; 978-0-9799474; 978-0-9821151; 978-1-936818)* 305 Whitehead St., No. 1, Key West, FL 33040 USA Tel 305-296-5762; Toll Free: 877-454-6282
E-mail: sheri@seastorypress.com
Web site: http://www.seastorypress.com
Dist(s): **BookMasters Distribution Services (BDS)**
MyiLibrary
ebrary, Inc.

Sea-To-Sea Pubns., *(978-1-932889; 978-1-59771)* Div. of Creative Co., 2140 Howard Dr., W., North Mankato, MN 56003 USA
Dist(s): **Creative Co., The**
RiverStream Publishing.

SeaWorld Education Dept. *Imprint of* **SeaWorld, Inc.**

SeaWorld, Inc., *(978-1-893698)* Div. of Anheuser-Busch Adventure Parks, 500 SeaWorld Dr., San Diego, CA 92109 USA (SAN 255-576X) Tel 619-225-4275; Fax: 619-226-3634; Toll Free: 800-237-4268; *Imprints:* SeaWorld Education Department (SeaWorld Educ)
E-mail: swc.education@seaworld.com; debbie.nuzzolo@seaworld.com
Web site: http://www.seaworld.org
Dist(s): **Book Wholesalers, Inc.**
Brodart Co.
Carolina Biological Supply Co.

Second Adam Publishing, *(978-0-615-60098-7; 978-0-615-63443-2; 978-0-615-77942-3)* P.O. Box 2813, Westminster, MD 21158 USA Tel 443-463-2789
Dist(s): **CreateSpace Independent Publishing Platform.**

Second Ark Pubns., *(978-1-889667)* 2907 Kevin Ln., Houston, TX 77043 USA.

Second Base Publishing, *(978-0-9793562)* 6197 Hinterlong Ct, Lisle, IL 60532 USA (SAN 853-2206)
Dist(s): **Ebsco Publishing**
Independent Pubs. Group
MyiLibrary
ebrary, Inc.

Second Sight Enterprises, Inc., *(978-0-9785222)* P.O. Box 251248, Plano, TX 75025 USA (SAN 850-7996)
Web site: http://www.asktheinventors.com
Dist(s): **Independent Pubs. Group.**

Second Star Creations, *(978-0-9725977)* 12120 State Line Rd., No. 190, Leawood, KS 66209 USA Tel 913-681-2252
E-mail: jan@secondstar.us
Web site: http://www.secondstar.us.

Second Story Pr. (CAN) *(978-0-921299; 978-0-929005; 978-1-896764; 978-1-897187) Dist. by* **Orca Bk Pub.**

Second Time Media & Communications, *(978-0-9727498; 978-0-9815162; 978-0-9840660; 978-0-9831743)* P.O. Box 401367, Redford, MI 48240 USA Tel 800-377-7497
E-mail: secondtimemedia@yahoo.com
Web site: http://www.secondtimemedia.com.

Second Wind Publishing, LLC *See* **Indigo Sea Pr., LLC**

Secret Corners Publishing, *(978-0-615-24083-1; 978-0-615-24084-8)* 12917 Brookcrest Pl., Riverview, FL 33578 USA
E-mail: info@secret-corners.com
Web site: http://www.secret-corners.com.

Secret Garden Bookworks, *(978-0-9766283)* Orders Addr.: P.O. Box 1506, Oak Bluffs, MA 02557-1506 USA Tel 508-693-4759; Fax: 508-693-4867; Edit Addr.: 41 Circuit Ave., Oak Bluffs, MA 02557-1506 USA
E-mail: secretgardenmv@peoplepc.com
Web site: http://www.secretgardenbookworks.com.

Secret Passage Pr., *(978-1-888695)* 26 Tucker Hollow Rd., North Scituate, RI 02857 USA Tel 401-647-0440; Toll Free: 877-863-4622 (Orders Only)
E-mail: lucindalandon@verizon.net
Web site: http://www.megmackintosh.com
Dist(s): **Ebsco Publishing**
Enfield Publishing & Distribution Co., Inc.
Independent Pubs. Group
MyiLibrary.

Security Studies Pr., *(978-0-9797539)* 650 J St., Suite 405, Lincoln, NE 68508 USA
E-mail: rlund@securitystudies.us
Web site: http://www.securitystudies.us.

Sedell, Kirsten, *(978-0-9800838)* 3 John R's Bend, Berkley, MA 02779 USA
E-mail: ksedell@norton.k12.ma.us.

Sedwick, Daniel Frank LLC, *(978-0-9820818)* P.O. Box 1964, Winter Park, FL 32790-1964 USA Tel 407-975-3325; Fax: 407-975-3327
E-mail: info@sedwickcoins.com
Web site: http://www.sedwickcoins.com.

See abc's LC, *(978-1-890566)* Orders Addr.: P.O. Box 276, Smithfield, UT 84335 USA; Edit Addr.: 9 S. 490 E., Smithfield, UT 84335 USA.

See Sharp Pr., *(978-0-9613289; 978-1-884365; 978-1-937276)* P.O. Box 1731, Tucson, AZ 85702-1731 USA (SAN 653-8134) Tel 520-628-8720 (phone/fax)
E-mail: cb@seesharppress.com
Web site: http://www.seesharppress.com
Dist(s): **Ebsco Publishing**
Independent Pubs. Group
MyiLibrary
ebrary, Inc.

See The Wish, *(978-0-9822134; 978-0-9857676; 978-0-9886716)* 246 Main St., Cold Spring, NY 10516 USA Tel 845-797-9183
Web site: http://www.seethewish.com
Dist(s): **Follett School Solutions.**

Seed Faith Bks, *(978-1-60101)* P.O. Box 12227, Portland, OR 97212-0227 USA (SAN 850-6795)
Web site: http://seedfaithbooks.com.

SeeDEGA, *(978-0-9746586)* Orders Addr.: P.O. Box 588, Rhinebeck, NY 12572 USA Tel 845-876-0609
E-mail: info@seedega.com
Web site: http://seedega.com.

Seedling Pubns. *Imprint of* **Continental Pr., Inc.**

SeeHearDo Co., LLC, The, *(978-0-9788089)* 3011 E. 7145 S., Salt Lake City, UT 84121 USA.

Seelcraft Publishing, *(978-0-9728380)* 63 Church St., Suite 201, High Bridge, NJ 08829-1516 USA
Web site: http://www.seelcraft.com.

See-More's Workshop, *(978-1-882601)* Div. of Shadow Box Theatre, 325 West End Ave., New York, NY 10023 USA Tel 212-724-0677; Fax: 212-724-0767
E-mail: sbt@shadowboxtheatre.org
Web site: http://www.shadowboxtheatre.org
Dist(s): **Follett School Solutions**
Professional Media Service Corp.

Segal, Berty Inc., *(978-0-938395)* 1749 E. Eucalyptus St., Brea, CA 92821 USA (SAN 630-0553) Tel 714-529-5359; Fax: 714-529-3882
E-mail: bertytprsource@earthlink.net
Web site: http://www.tprsource.com
Dist(s): **Continental Bk. Co., Inc.**

Segal, Robin *See* **Murray Hill Bks., LLC**

Segarra, Angelo, *(978-0-9752664)* 422 Gregg Ave., Santa Fe, NM 87501-1600 USA
Dist(s): **Greenleaf Book Group.**

Seglie, Susan M., *(978-0-9747243)* 1 Deer Run Ln., Pittsburg, KS 66762 USA Fax: 620-232-5819.

Segue Pubs., *(978-0-9671796)* 527 arbor Rd., Cheltenham, PA 19012 USA Tel 215-277-5525 phone
E-mail: seguepublishing@aol.com; kbradford@seguepublishing.com
Web site: seguepublishing.com.

Selah Publishing Group, LLC, *(978-0-9679371; 978-1-58930)* 162 Crescent Dr., Bristol, TN 37620 USA Toll Free Fax: 866-777-8909; Toll Free: 877-616-6451 Do not confuse with the same name in Kingston, NY, Berkley, MI
E-mail: garlen@selahbooks.com
Web site: http://www.selahbooks.com.

Selah Publishing, Incorporated *See* **Selah Publishing Group, LLC**

Selby Dean Ventures, Inc., *(978-0-9716479)* P.O. Box 246, Kure Beach, NC 28449 USA (SAN 852-7539) Tel 910-279-2486
E-mail: fishinstructor@aol.com
Web site: http://www.gullswatch.com; http://www.SelbyDeanVentures.com.

Selective Mutism Anxiety Research & Treatment Ctr., *(978-0-9714800)* 1130 Herkness Dr., Meadowbrook, PA 19046 USA Tel 215 -887-5748; Fax: 215-827-5722
E-mail: dreshiponblum@aol.com
Web site: http://www.selectivemutismcenter.org.

Selector, S.A. de C.V. (MEX) *(978-968-403; 978-970-643; 978-607-453) Dist. by* **Libros Fronteras.**

Selector, S.A. de C.V. (MEX) *(978-968-403; 978-970-643; 978-607-453) Dist. by* **AIMS Intl.**

Selector, S.A. de C.V. (MEX) *(978-968-403; 978-970-643; 978-607-453) Dist. by* **Lectorum Pubns.**

Self-Counsel Pr., Inc. (CAN) *(978-0-88908; 978-1-55180; 978-1-77040) Dist. by* **Midpt Trade.**

Self-Esteem Adventures Pr., *(978-0-9747597)* P.O. Box 2145, Universal City, TX 78148 USA Tel 210-595-6952
E-mail: daddybooks@grandecom.net
Web site: http://www.daddybooks.com.

Self-Mastery Press *See* **Love & Blessings**

Self-Realization Fellowship Pubs., *(978-0-87612)* Orders Addr.: 3208 Humboldt St., Los Angeles, CA 90031 USA (SAN 204-5788) Tel 323-276-6002; Fax: 323-276-6003; Toll Free: 888-773-8680; Edit Addr.: 3880 San Rafael Ave., Los Angeles, CA 90065 USA Tel 323-276 6000; 215 K. St., Encinitas, CA 92024 Tel 760-753-2888 ext 471; Fax: 323-276-6003
E-mail: sales@srfpublishers.org
Web site: http://www.srfpublishers.org
Dist(s): **Distributors, The**
TNT Media Group, Inc.

Sellers, Amy, *(978-0-9787632)* 5151 Round Lake Rd., Apopka, FL 32712 USA (SAN 851-5425)
E-mail: amycsellers@yahoo.com
Web site: http://www.amysellers.com.

Sellers Publishing, Inc., *(978-1-56906; 978-1-4162)* Orders Addr.: P.O. Box 818, Portland, ME 04104 USA (SAN 858-1258) Tel 207-772-6833; Fax: 207-772-6814; Toll Free: 800-625-3386 (800-MAKE-FUN); Edit Addr.: 161 John Roberts Rd., South Portland, ME 04106 USA
E-mail: rsp@rsvp.com
Web site: http://www.rsvp.com
Dist(s): **Bookazine Co., Inc.**
MBI Distribution Services/Quayside Distribution
New Leaf Distributing Co., Inc.
Partners Bk. Distributing, Inc.

Sellers, Ronnie Productions, Incorporated *See* **Sellers Publishing, Inc.**

Sem Fronteiras Pr., Ltd., *(978-0-9642333)* 1530 Palisade Ave., Suite 2F, Fort Lee, NJ 07024 USA (SAN 253-4959) Toll Free Fax: 800-433-5193
E-mail: semfront@superlink.net.

Sem, Gilmore, *(978-0-9742299)* 1822 Carl St., Lauderdale, MN 55113-5203 USA.

SEMAR (ITA) *(978-88-7778) Dist. by* **SPD-Small Pr Dist.**

Semele Bks., *(978-0-9764937)* 40 Cedar Ln., Princeton, NJ 08540 USA Tel 609-924-6481; Fax: 609-924-0549; Toll Free: 866-967-3835
E-mail: eva@evasiroka.com
Web site: http://www.evasiroka.com.

Semper Studio, *(978-0-9778420)* 4416 Rte. 47, Delmont, NJ 08314 USA (SAN 850-3885) Tel 609-501-3341
E-mail: Catherine@semperstudiosus.com
Web site: http://www.semperstudiosus.com.

Send The Light Distribution LLC, *(978-0-9835608; 978-1-939900)* Orders Addr.: 129 Mobilization Dr., Waynesboro, GA 30830 USA (SAN 631-8894) Tel 706-554-5827; Toll Free Fax: 877-323-4551; Toll Free: 877-323-4550; 100 Biblica Way, Elizabethton, TN 37643-6070 (SAN 630-7388) Tel 423-547-5131 editorial Toll Free Fax: 800-759-2779
E-mail: Customerservice@stl.org
Web site: http://www.stl-publisherservices.com.

Seneca Mill Pr. LLC, *(978-0-9768986; 978-0-9899595)* P.O. Box 1423, Great Falls, VA 22066 USA
E-mail: senecamillpress@aol.com.

Sensational Bks., *(978-0-9770054)* P.O. Box 261085, Lakewood, CO 80226 USA (SAN 256-6265) Tel 303-238-4760; Fax: 303-205-0614
Web site: http://www.sensationalbooks.com.

Sensational Pubns., *(978-0-9888003; 978-0-9912808)* P.O. Box 661, Oswego, IL 60543 USA Tel 630-800-4254
E-mail: cindyjusino@ymail.com
Web site: www.cindyjusino.com; http://www.sensationalpublications.com.

Sensational Publishing *See* **Sensational Pubns.**

Sense of Wonder Pr. *Imprint of* **Rock, James A. & Co. Pubs.**

Senshu, Noriko *See* **Studio Cherry Publishing**

Sensory Resources, *(978-1-893601; 978-1-931615)* Div. of Future Horizons, Inc., P.O. Box 530790, Henderson, NV 89053-0790 USA (SAN 253-8288) Toll Free: 888-357-5867
E-mail: orders@sensoryresources.com
Web site: http://www.sensoryresources.com
Dist(s): **Ingram Pub. Services**
MyiLibrary.

Sentient Pubns., *(978-0-9710786; 978-1-59181)* 1113 Spruce St., Boulder, CO 80302 USA Tel 303-443-2188; Fax: 303-447-1511; Toll Free: 866-588-9846
E-mail: cshaw@sentientpublications.com; dialagzone@aol.com
Web site: http://www.sentientpublications.com/
Dist(s): **National Bk. Network.**

Sentinel *Imprint of* **Penguin Publishing Group**

Sentinel Publishing, *(978-0-9728291)* 1131 Rossiter Ln., Wayne, PA 19087-2812 USA Tel 610-687-5908; Fax: 610-687-5909 Do not confuse with Sentinel Publishing in Ogden, UT
E-mail: orchidman@snip.net
Web site: http://www.linenpostcards.com.

Sentry Bks. *Imprint of* **Great West Publishing**

Sentry Pr., Inc., *(978-1-889574)* 424 E. Call St., Tallahassee, FL 32301-7693 USA
E-mail: wwrogers@peoplepc.com
Web site: http://sentry-press.com/
Dist(s): **Polk County Historical Assn.**

Seoul Selection, *(978-1-62412)* 4199 Campus Dr., Suite 550, Irvine, CA 92612 USA Tel 949-509-6584; Fax: 949-509-6599
E-mail: sales@seoulselection.com
Web site: www.seoulselection.com
Dist(s): **SPD-Small Pr. Distribution.**

Sephyrus *See* **Sephyrus Pr.**

Sephyrus Pr., *(978-0-615-23982-8; 978-0-9830137)* Orders Addr.: 28 Daggett St., Milford, CT 06460 USA Tel 203-414-5694
E-mail: rachel@sephyrus.com
Web site: http://www.sephyruspress.blogspot.com.

SepSha Publishing, *(978-0-9727885)* P.O. Box 462075, Aurora, CO 80046 USA (SAN 255-3007)
Web site: http://www.endtimebooks.com.

Sequent Media, Inc., *(978-0-9746531)* P.O. Box 126325, San Diego, CA 92112 USA
Web site: http://www.sequentmedia.com.

Seraph Publishing, *(978-1-934948)* 7660 Fay Ave., La Jolla, CA 92037-4843 USA
E-mail: info@markmlittle.com.

Seraphemera Bks *See* **Seraphemera Bks.**

Seraphemera Bks., *(978-0-9778989; 978-0-9815516; 978-0-9844441; 978-0-9846464)* P.O. Box 73562, Houston, TX 77273-7727 USA Tel 832-515-9539
E-mail: three@seraphemera.org
Web site: http://www.seraphemera.org.

Seraphic Pr., *(978-0-9754382)* 1531 Cardiff Ave., Los Angeles, CA 90035 USA (SAN 256-0496) Tel 310-557-0132; Fax: 310-286-9534
E-mail: robert@seraphicpress.com; rjaprod@aol.com
Web site: http://www.seraphicpress.com
Dist(s): **David, Jonathan Pubs., Inc.**

Seraphim Pubns., *(978-0-615-21071-1)* 17641 Gilmore St., Van Nuys, CA 91406 USA
E-mail: toni@seraphimpublications.com
Web site: http://www.seraphimpublications.com.

Seraphina *Imprint of* **Bonita and Hodge Publishing Group, LLC**

Seren Bks. (GBR) *(978-0-907476; 978-1-85411; 978-1-78172) Dist. by* **IPG Chicago.**

Serena Bocchino/In His Perfect Time Collection, *(978-0-9767674; 978-0-9838660; 978-0-9961443)* 82 Haas Rd., Basking Ridge, NJ 07920 USA
E-mail: serena@serenaboocchino.com
Web site: http://www.serenaboocchino.com.

Serendib Pr., *(978-0-615-18889-8)* 1611 N. Bell, No. 3N, Chicago, IL 60647 USA
Dist(s): **Lulu Enterprises Inc.**

Serendipity Hse. *Imprint of* **LifeWay Christian Resources**

Serenity Pr., *(978-0-9787981)* 500 SW. 21st Terr., Fort Lauderdale, FL 33312 USA (SAN 851-6251)
E-mail: marty@mwpr.com
Web site: http://www.mwpr.com/Splash.html.

Serenity Pubs. *Imprint of* **Arc Manor**

Serey/Jones Pubs., *(978-1-881276)* 7413 W. Oraibi Dr., Glendale, AZ 85308 USA Tel 623-561-0240; Fax: 623-561-8441
E-mail: info@sereyjones.com.

Serpent's Tale Natural History Bk. Distributors, Inc., *(978-1-885209)* Orders Addr.: P.O. Box 405, Lanesboro, MN 55949-0405 USA (SAN 630-6101) Tel 507-467-8734; Fax: 507-467-8735
E-mail: zoobooks@acegroup.cc
Web site: http://www.zoobooksales.com.

Serres, Ediciones, S. L. (ESP) *(978-84-88061; 978-84-95040; 978-84-8488) Dist. by* **Lectorum Pubns.**

Serve Man Pr., *(978-0-9768517)* P.O. Box 1445, Easthampton, MA 01027 USA Tel 413-209-1029
E-mail: rokari@hotmail.com
Web site: http://www.seanwang.com; www.runnersuniverse.com.

Servilibro Ediciones, S.A. (ESP) *(978-84-7971) Dist. by* **Giron Bks.**

Serving Jesus Christ with Joy Ministries, *(978-0-9770078; 978-0-9774426)* Div. of Serving Jesus Christ with Joy, Orders Addr.: 316 E. Ajo, Tucson, AZ 85713 USA Tel 520-406-1674 (Publishing Phone) 520-889-0215 (Publishing Fax)
E-mail: pastorrandy@sjcwj.org; info@sjcwj.org
Web site: http://christianbooks1.com.

Session Family, *(978-0-9658006)* Orders Addr.: P.O. Box 841, Florissant, MO 63032 USA Tel 314-972-7705 (phone/fax); Edit Addr.: 16856 Heather Moor Dr., Florissant, MO 63034 USA
E-mail: denise.session@att.net
Web site: http://www.sessionfamily.com.

Seton Pr., *(978-1-60704)* 1350 Progress Dr., Front Royal, VA 22630 USA Tel 540-636-9990; Fax: 540-636-1602
Web site: http://setonhome.org.

Setubandh Pubns., *(978-0-9623674)* 1 Lawson Ln., Great Neck, NY 11023 USA Tel 516-482-6938
Web site: http://www.setubandh.com.

Seven C's Productions, Inc., *(978-0-9910345)* 311 W. 43rd St. Penthouse, New York, NY 10036 USA Tel 212-757-7555
E-mail: marc@7csproductions.com
Web site: www.7csproductions.com.

Seven Footer Pr., *(978-0-9740439; 978-0-9788178; 978-1-934734)* 184 Kendrick Pl., Apt. 28, Gaithersburg, MD 20878-5662 USA; 247 W. 30th St., New York, NY 10001-2824
E-mail: david@wouldyourather.com; jnheimberg@aol.com
Web site: http://www.wouldyourather.com; http://www.movieplotgenerator.com
Dist(s): **Perseus-PGW**
Perseus Bks. Group.

Seven Guns Pr., *(978-0-615-70006-9; 978-0-9884259; 978-0-615-82838-1; 978-0-9899461)* 2405 Jennieville Dr., Davidsonville, MD 21035 USA Tel 4433066691
Dist(s): **CreateSpace Independent Publishing Platform.**

†Seven Locks Pr., *(978-0-929765; 978-0-932020; 978-0-9615964; 978-1-931643; 978-0-9790950; 978-0-9795852; 978-0-9801270; 978-0-9822293; 978-0-9824957)* P.O. Box 25689, Santa Ana, CA 92799-5689 USA (SAN 211-9781) Toll Free: 800-354-5348
E-mail: sevenlocks@aol.com
Web site: http://www.sevenlockspublishing.com; *CIP.*

Seven Rivers Publishing, *(978-0-9728768; 978-0-615-63339-8)* P.O. Box 682, Crowley, TX 76036-0682 USA Toll Free: 800-544-3770 (Order line: Hendrick-Long)
E-mail: hendrick-long@att.net; djls@sevenriverspublishing.com; sales@sevenriverspublishing.com; seven-rivers@earthlink.net
Web site: http://www.hendricklongpublishing.com; http://www.sevenriverspublishing.com; http://www.smashwords.com/books/view/93148
Dist(s): **CreateSpace Independent Publishing Platform**
Hendrick-Long Publishing Co.
Lightning Source, Inc.
Smashwords.

Seven Seas Entertainment, LLC, *(978-1-933164; 978-1-934876; 978-1-935934; 978-1-937867; 978-1-62692)* 3463 State St., Suite 545, Santa Barbara, CA 93105 USA
Web site: http://www.gomanga.com
Dist(s): **Diamond Comic Distributors, Inc.**
Diamond Bk. Distributors
Macmillan.

Seven Stars Trading Co., *(978-0-9743999; 978-0-9863464)* 3543 Marvin St., Annandale, VA 22003 USA Tel 703-573-2939.

Seven Stories Pr., *(978-1-58322; 978-1-888363; 978-1-60980)* 140 Watts St., New York, NY 10013 USA Tel 212-226-8760; Fax: 212-226-1411; Toll Free: 800-596-7437; *Imprints*: Triangle Square (Triangle Sq)
E-mail: info@sevenstories.com
Web site: http://www.sevenstories.com
Dist(s): **Independent Pubs. Group**
MyiLibrary
Penguin Random Hse., LLC.
Random Hse., Inc.

SevenHorns Publishing, *(978-0-9838427)* P.O. Box 269, Randolph, MA 02368 USA Tel 856-269-2852
E-mail: admin@sevenhornspublishing.com
Web site: http://www.sonsofcaasi.com; http://www.biffprice.com; http://www.sevenhornspublishing.com; http://www.adventuresofjackandmax.com.

Seventh Street Pr., Div. of Malone-Ballard Book Pubs., 2215 6th Ave. Apt D, Moline, IL 61265 USA
E-mail: bookwoman1110@hotmail.com.

Severn Hse. Pubs., Ltd. (GBR) *(978-0-7278; 978-1-78029; 978-0-9560566; 978-1-78010) Dist. by* **IngramPubServ.**

Seymour, Dale Pubns., *(978-0-201; 978-0-7690; 978-0-86651; 978-1-57232)* Div. of Pearson Learning, Orders Addr.: P.O. Box 2500, Lebanon, OH 43216 USA Toll Free Fax: 800-393-3156; Toll Free: 800-321-3106 (Customer Service); Edit Addr.: 10 Bank St., White Plains, NY 10602-5026 USA (SAN 200-9781) Toll Free Fax: 800-393-3156; Toll Free: 800-237-3142
E-mail: pearson_learning2@prenhall.com
Web site: http://www.pearsonlearning.com; http://www.pearsonlearning.com/rightsPerm.rtf
Dist(s): **Addison-Wesley Educational Pubs., Inc.**

SFT Pubns., *(978-0-9724384)* Orders Addr.: 3915 S. Cramer Cir., Bloomington, IN 47403 USA (SAN 254-8283) Tel 812-333-8902
E-mail: leilarandle@sbcglobal.net.

Sgian Enterprises, *(978-0-9771197; 978-0-615-12814-6)* 4349 W. Tomahawk Dr., Beverly Hills, FL 34465-4871 USA.

Shaar Pr. *Imprint of* **Mesorah Pubns., Ltd.**

Shade Bks. *Imprint of* **Stone Arch Bks.**

Shades of Me Publishing, *(978-0-9718307)* 3969 Strandhill Rd., Cleveland, OH 44128 USA
E-mail: marybury1927@msn.com.

Shades of White, *(978-0-9796834)* 301 Tenth Ave., Crystal City, MO 63019 USA Tel 314-740-0361; *Imprints*: Magical Child Books (Magical Child)
Web site: http://www.magicalchildbooks.com
Dist(s): **Abyss Distribution**
New Leaf Distributing Co., Inc.

ShadeTree Publishing, LLC, *(978-0-9822632; 978-1-937331)* 1038 N. Eisenhower Dr., No. 274, Beckley, WV 25801 USA (SAN 857-6971)
E-mail: jennifer.minigh@shadetreepublishing.com
Web site: http://www.shadetreepublishing.com.

Shadow Canyon Graphics, *(978-0-9857420)* 454 Somerset Dr., Golden, CO 80401 USA Tel 303 278 0949; Fax: 303-279-5831
E-mail: dnshadow@earthlink.net.

Shadow Mountain *Imprint of* **Deseret Bk. Co.**

Shadow Mountain *Imprint of* **Shadow Mountain Publishing**

Shadow Mountain Publishing, *(978-0-87579; 978-1-57345; 978-1-59038; 978-1-60907)* Div. of Deseret Book Company, P.O. Box 30178, Salt Lake City, UT 84130 USA Tel 801-517-3223; *Imprints*: Shadow Mountain (ShadowMountain); Ensign Peak (EnsPeak)
E-mail: info@shadowmountain.com
Web site: http://www.shadowmountain.com
Dist(s): **Deseret Bk. Co.**

Shadow Pubns., *(978-0-9771424)* P.O. Box 1151, Valley Forge, PA 19482-1151 USA
Web site: http://www.olliedude.com.

ShadowPlay Pr., *(978-0-9638819)* P.O. Box 647, Forreston, IL 61030 USA Tel 815-938-3151; Fax: 815-371-1440
E-mail: sheilawelch@juno.com; ericwelch2@juno.com
Web site: http://www.shadowplay.userworld.com.

Shady Tree Productions, *(978-0-9747352)* 5383 Iron Pen Pl., Columbia, MD 21044 USA Tel 410-997-6337 (phone/fax)
E-mail: shadytreepro@hotmail.com; bigtree_75@msn.com; ronfullwood@returningsoldiers.us.

Shaffer, Dale E., *(978-0-915060)* 478 Jennings Ave., Salem, OH 44460-2732 USA (SAN 206-9067).

Shaffer, Earl Foundation, Inc., *(978-0-9795659)* 1635 Haft Dr., Reynoldsburg, OH 43068-3059 USA Tel 614-751-0029
E-mail: spur@mac.com
Web site: http://www.earlshaffer.org.

Shaffner, Randolph P. *See* **Faraway Publishing**

Shaggy Dog Pr., *(978-0-9722007)* P.O. Box 318, Westport, NY 12993 USA Tel 518-962-2278; Fax: 518-962-2393
E-mail: sdp78@aol.com; shaggydogpress@aol.com.

ShaGru Entertainment, LLC, *(978-0-9724621)* P.O. Box 689, Darby, PA 19023 USA
E-mail: sag@shawnagrundy.com
Web site: http://www.shawnagrundy.com.

Shah, Meera, *(978-0-9774219)* 7003 Westminster Ln., Germantown, TN 38138 USA Tel 901-754-7197
E-mail: meeds_46@yahoo.com; merra.meeds46@gmail.com.

Shakalot High Entertainment, *(978-0-9721067; 978-0-9796219)* 20687 White Dove Ln., Bend, OR 97702 USA Tel 541-788-4011; 13019 SW 154th Ave., Tigard, OR 97223 Tel 503-548-3336; *Imprints*: Writing Wild & Crazy (Writing Wild)
E-mail: shakalothighentertainment@yahoo.com
Web site: http://www.shakalothigh.com
Dist(s): **Lulu Enterprises Inc.**

Shake the Moon Bks., *(978-0-615-25125-7; 978-0-615-53638-5)* 6216 Denny Ave., N. Hollywood, CA 91606 USA Tel 818-903-4112
E-mail: scott@shakethemoonbooks.com
Web site: http://www.shakethemoonbooks.com
Dist(s): **AtlasBooks Distribution.**

ShakeB Co., *(978-0-615-24232-3; 978-0-615-41353-2)* 1189 Masselin Ave., Los Angeles, CA 90019 USA.

Shakespeare Graphics *Imprint of* **Stone Arch Bks.**

Shalako Pr., *(978-0-9798898; 978-0-9830608; 978-0-9846811; 978-0-9892917; 978-0-9908878; 978-0-9974235)* P.O. Box 371, Oakdale, CA 95361-0371 USA (SAN 854-6622)
E-mail: major@majormitchell.net
Web site: http://www.shalakopress.com
Dist(s): **Smashwords.**

Shalhout, Ahlam LLC *See* **Expressions Woven**

Shamber Pubns., *(978-0-9771326)* P.O. Box 470321, Lake Monroe, FL 32747-0321 USA
E-mail: unbrokencirclebymcghee@gmail.com.

Shambhala Publications, Incorporated *See* **Shambhala Pubns., Inc.**

†Shambhala Pubns., Inc., *(978-0-8348; 978-0-87773; 978-0-937938; 978-1-55939; 978-1-56957; 978-1-57062; 978-1-59030; 978-1-61180)* Horticultural Hall, 300 Massachusetts Ave., Boston, MA 02115 USA (SAN 203-2481) Tel 617-424-0030; Fax: 617-236-1563; *Imprints*: Weatherhill, Incorporated (Weathill); Trumpeter (Trumpeter); Roost Books (Roost Bks); Snow Lion Publications, Incorporated (SnowLion)
E-mail: editors@shambhala.com
Web site: http://www.shambhala.com
Dist(s): **MyiLibrary**
Penguin Random Hse., LLC.
Random Hse., Inc.; *CIP.*

Shammah Ministries, *(978-0-9725944)* Orders Addr.: 1346 Oak Pk. Dr., Aransas Pass, TX 78336 USA Tel 361-226-4918
E-mail: tonia@shammah.org
Web site: http://www.shammah.org.

Shamrock Pr., *(978-0-9675410)* Orders Addr.: P.O. Box 58186, Charleston, WV 25358 USA Tel 304-744-4259 (phone/fax) Do not confuse with Shamrock Pr. in Chattanooga, TN
E-mail: shamrockpress@frontier.com
Web site: www.shamrockpress.com.

Shamrock Publishing, Inc., *(978-0-9743244; 978-0-9759703)* 400 Corey Ave., Wachovia Bldg., 2nd Flr., Saint Pete Beach, FL 33706 USA Tel 727-363-4747; Fax: 727-363-4848; 1220 S. State St., Chicago, IL 60605 Tel 312-212-1143; Fax: 708-371-9576 Do not confuse with Shamrock Publishing, Incorporated in New Orleans, LA
E-mail: tpmac@sprynet.com; bksemmer@blueshamrockpublishing.com.

Shamus B. Publishing, *(978-0-9753671)* 18533 Pond Dr., Abingdon, VA 24211 USA.

Shamwari Publishing (ZAF) *(978-0-620-40992-6) Dist. by* **AtlasBooks.**

Shan Jen Publishing Co., Ltd. (TWN) *(978-986-7517; 978-957-2041; 978-957-8298; 978-957-9658; 978-957-99079) Dist. by* **Chinasprout.**

Shanahan, John Francis Publishing, *(978-0-9618275)* 6727 N. Lightfoot Ave., Chicago, IL 60646 USA (SAN 667-0490) Tel 773-631-6344; Fax: 773-631-6372
E-mail: REPSbooks@aol.com.

Shanbhag, Arun, *(978-0-9790081)* 32 Chatham St., Arlington, MA 02474-2008 USA
E-mail: arun@shanbhag.org.

Shangri-La Pubns., *(978-0-9677201; 978-0-9714683; 978-0-9719496)* Orders Addr.: P.O. Box 65, Warren Center, PA 18851-0065 USA Toll Free: 866-966-6288; Edit Addr.: 3 Coburn Hill Rd., PMB 65, Warren Center, PA 18851 USA Tel 570-395-3423; Fax: 570-395-0146
E-mail: gosline@egypt.net; shangrila@egypt.net; shangri_la_book@hotmail.com
Web site: http://www.shangri-la.0catch.com/.

Shannon Road Pr., *(978-0-9788785; 978-0-9846101)* 16330 Shannon Rd., Los Gatos, CA 95032 USA
E-mail: info@shannonroadpress.com
Web site: http://www.shannonroadpress.com.

Shapato Publishing, LLC, *(978-0-9821058; 978-0-9826992; 978-0-9833526; 978-0-615-50457-5; 978-0-615-50918-1; 978-0-615-50920-4; 978-0-615-50921-1; 978-0-615-51306-5; 978-0-615-53431-2; 978-0-615-53435-0; 978-0-615-56643-6; 978-0-615-55791-1; 978-0-615-60650-7; 978-0-615-72638-0; 978-0-615-83271-5; 978-0-615-91943-0; 978-0-692-25479-0; 978-0-692-30027-5) Orders Addr.: P.O. Box 476, Everly, IA 51338 USA Tel 712-490-5165; Edit Addr.: 503 E 2nd St., Everly, IA 51338 USA*
E-mail: Jean@midwestwriter.com
Web site: http://www.shapatopublishing.com
Dist(s): **CreateSpace Independent Publishing Platform**
Smashwords.

Share & Care Society, *(978-0-9722025)* 2105 55th Ln., NW, Olympia, WA 98502 USA Tel 760-819-9174; *Imprints*: True Lightening (True Lght)
E-mail: london_pain@hotmail.com
Web site: http://www.shareandcaresociety.org.

Share Publishing, *(978-0-9633705)* Orders Addr.: 313 Laurel Ave., Menlo Park, CA 94025 USA Tel 650-321-5947 (phone/fax)
E-mail: pamelalaw@sbcglobal.net
Web site: http://sharepublishing.com.

Sharif, Mboya *See* **Doses of Reality, Inc.**

Shark Press *See* **Lemon Shark Pr.**

†Sharp & Dunnigan, *(978-0-918495)* 2700 Richards Rd., Suite 110, Bellevue, WA 98005 USA (SAN 657-3029) Tel 425-467-6565; Fax: 425-467-6564
E-mail: ecovepress@aol.com
Web site: http://elfincovepress.com
Dist(s): **Elfin Cove Pr.**; *CIP.*

Sharp & Dunnigan, Publications, Incorporated *See* **Sharp & Dunnigan**

Sharp, Diana Consulting, *(978-0-9762626)* 5954 Fishhawk Crossing Blvd., Lithia, FL 33547-5878 USA.

SHARP Literacy, Inc., *(978-0-9770816; 978-0-9836222)* 750 N. Lincoln Memorial Dr. Suite 311, Milwaukee, WI 53202 USA Tel 414-270-3388
Web site: http://www.sharpliteracy.org.

Sharpe, Jeannie W., *(978-0-9763117)* 373 Langford Rd., Blythewood, SC 29016 USA Fax: 803-786-4557
E-mail: jws415@aol.com.

†Sharpe, M.E. Inc., *(978-0-7656; 978-0-87332; 978-1-56324)* 80 Business Park Dr., Armonk, NY 10504 USA (SAN 202-7100) Tel 914-273-1800; Fax: 914-273-2106; Toll Free: 800-541-6563; *Imprints*: Sharpe Reference (Sharpe Ref)
Web site: http://www.mesharpe.com
Dist(s): **Follett School Solutions**
Metapress
MyiLibrary
Taylor & Francis Group
Women Ink
ebrary, Inc.; *CIP.*

Sharpe Reference *Imprint of* **Sharpe, M.E. Inc.**

Shauger, Daniel, *(978-0-9746114)* 12438 Moorpark St., No. 241, Studio City, CA 91605 USA Tel 818-693-6231
E-mail: dan@aperfectswing.com
Web site: http://www.aperfectswing.com.

Shaw, Dana, *(978-0-9791091)* Orders Addr.: P.O. Box 91, Franklin, ME 04634 USA (SAN 852-4815) Tel 207-565-4445; Edit Addr.: 206 Georges Pond Rd., Franklin, ME 04634 USA
E-mail: myfriendzundel@yahoo.com
Web site: http://myfriendzundel.com.

Shawnee Pr., Inc., *(978-0-8256; 978-0-9603394; 978-1-59235)* Subs. of Music Sales Corp., Orders Addr.: P.O. Box 1250, Marshalls Creek, PA 18335 USA Toll Free Fax: 800-345-6842; Toll Free: 800-962-8584; Edit Addr.: 9 Dartmouth Dr., Bldg. 4, Marshalls Creek, PA 18335 USA (SAN 202-084X) Tel 212-254-2100 (copyright & licensing information); 570-476-0550; Fax: 570-476-5247
E-mail: shawnee-info@shawneepress.com
Web site: http://www.shawneepress.com
Dist(s): **Leonard, Hal Corp.**
Music Sales Corp.

Shayach Comics *Imprint of* **Judaica Pr., Inc., The**

Shaymaa Publishing Corp., *(978-0-9719581)* P.O. Box 501, Lodi, NJ 07644-0501 USA (SAN 255-738X) Fax: 973-237-0537
E-mail: elhewiemf@juno.com; todaysgy@todaysgym.com; elhewie@lift-4-life.com
Web site: http://www.lift-4-life.com; http://www.todaysgym.com; http://www.shaymaa-publishing.com.

Shayne Publishing, *(978-0-9771192)* 4895 SE 40th St., Des Moines, IA 50320 USA (SAN 256-7997) Tel 515-263-2784
E-mail: dlhuston01@aol.com.

Shazak Productions *Imprint of* **Torah Excel**

†Shearer Publishing, *(978-0-940672)* 406 Post Oak Rd., Fredericksburg, TX 78624 USA Tel 830-997-6529; Fax: 830-997-9752; Toll Free: 800-458-3808
E-mail: shearer@shearerpub.com
Web site: http://www.shearerpub.com
Dist(s): **Bk. Marketing Plus**
Texas A&M Univ. Pr.; *CIP*

Shechinah Third Temple, Inc., *(978-0-9723866; 978-0-9817212; 978-0-9895128)* 11583 Pamplona Blvd., Boynton Beach, FL 33437 USA Tel 561-735-7958; Fax: 561-738-1535
E-mail: thirdtemple@bellsouth.net; jerrypollock@bellsouth.net
Web site: http://www.shechinahthirdtemple.org.

Sheepdog Pr., *(978-0-9742205)* P.O. Box 60, Onancock, VA 23417 USA Tel 888-787-1951; Fax: 888-787-2675
E-mail: publisher@sheepdogpress.com
Web site: http://www.sheepdogpress.com.

Sheets, Judy, *(978-0-9726451)* 2526 Brune Rd., Farmington, MO 63640 USA Tel 573-756-6254
E-mail: judys@i1.net.

Shekinah Productions, *(978-0-9802250; 978-0-578-04316-6; 978-0-578-05243-4; 978-0-578-05610-4; 978-0-578-05834-4; 978-0-578-07417-7; 978-0-578-08092-5; 978-0-578-08093-2; 978-0-578-08094-9; 978-0-578-08182-3; 978-0-578-08415-2; 978-0-578-08869-3; 978-0-578-10324-2; 978-0-578-11645-7; 978-0-578-13210-5; 978-0-578-13328-7; 978-0-578-13499-4; 978-0-578-13962-3; 978-0-578-14057-5; 978-0-578-14114-5) 8111 Windersgate Drive, Olive Branch, MS 38654 USA Fax: 662-504-4234; P.O. Box 209, Olive Branch, MS 38654*
E-mail: shekinah.productions@yahoo.com
Web site: http://www.skpseminars.com.

Shekinah Publishing Hse., *(978-0-9700976; 978-1-940153)* Orders Addr.: P.O. Box 156423, Fort Worth, TX 76155 USA Tel 817-538-1363; 2140 E. Southlake Blvd. Suite L642, Southlake, TX 76092; *Imprints*: Shekinah Publishing House (Shek Pub Hse) Do not confuse with companies with the same or similar names in Cameron, NC, Cameron, NC
E-mail: patadams@ureach.com; author@oneheartseries.com.

Shekinah Publishing Hse. *Imprint of* **Shekinah Publishing Hse.**

Shelby, Lloyd *See* **Painted WORD Studios**

Shelbykay Publishing Co., *(978-0-9744407)* 525 Greenhill Ln., Philadelphia, PA 19128 USA Tel 215-483-6688
E-mail: cdkae@aol.com.

Shelf-Life Bks., *(978-1-880042)* Div. of M.A.P.S., Inc., 2132 Fordem, Madison, WI 53704-0599 USA Tel 608-244-7767; Fax: 608-244-8394.

Shell Beach Publishing, LLC, *(978-0-9706732)* 677 Shell Beach Dr., Lake Charles, LA 70601-5732 USA Tel 433-439-2110
E-mail: kkblake@compuserve.com.

Shell Educational Publishing, *(978-1-4258)* 5301 Oceanus Dr., Huntington Beach, CA 92649 USA Tel 714-489-2080; Fax: 714-230-7070; Toll Free: 888-877-7606; 877-777-3450
E-mail: cmiller2@tcmpub.com; LShill@seppub.com; pkoehl@tcmpub.com; CMiller2@teachercreatedmaterials.com
Web site: http://www.seppub.com; http://www.tcmpub.com
Dist(s): **Follett School Solutions**
Teacher Created Materials, Inc.

Shelle, Carole Creative Arts, *(978-0-9792641)* P.O. Box 52972, Irvine, CA 92619 USA (SAN 852-9493) Toll Free: 800-929-1634.

Shelley Adina, *(978-0-615-52095-7; 978-0-615-62675-8; 978-1-939087)* P.O. Box 752, Redwood Estates, CA 95044 USA Tel 408-761-1195; *Imprints*: Moonshell Books, Inc. (MoonshellBks)
Web site: http://www.shelleyadina.com
Dist(s): **CreateSpace Independent Publishing Platform.**

Shelly's Adventures LLC, *(978-0-9851845)* P.O. Box 2632, Land O Lakes, FL 34639 USA Tel 352-219-7199
E-mail: kentrell@shellysadventuresllc.com; kentrell.martin15@gmail.com; kentrell@shellysadventures.com
Web site: www.shellysadventuresllc.com; www.shellysadventures.com
Dist(s): **Partners Pubs. Group, Inc.**

Shelter of Flint, Inc., *(978-0-9740929)* 902 E. 6th St., Flint, MI 48503-2787 USA
E-mail: sof@shelterofflint.com
Web site: http://www.shelterofflint.com.

†Shelter Pubns., Inc., *(978-0-936070)* Orders Addr.: P.O. Box 279, Bolinas, CA 94924 USA (SAN 122-8463) Tel 415-868-0280; Fax: 415-868-9053; Toll Free: 800-307-0131; Edit Addr.: 285 Dogwood Rd, Bolinas, CA 94924 USA
E-mail: shelter@shelterpub.com
Web site: http://www.shelterpub.com
Dist(s): **Bk. Express**
Bookmen, Inc.
Distributors, The
Koen Pacific
Partners/West Book Distributors
Perseus-PGW; *CIP.*

shelterpetsink, *(978-0-9740980)* 16457 Gledhill St., North Hills, CA 91343 USA Fax: 818-892-2112
E-mail: shelterpetsink@shelterpetsink.com; remilove2002@yahoo.com
Web site: http://www.shelterpetsink.com.

Shenandoah County Historical Society, Inc., *(978-0-9795924)* P.O. Box 506, Edinburg, VA 22824 USA Tel 540-465-5570
E-mail: adamsons@shentel.net.

Shenango River Bks., *(978-1-888836)* P.O. Box 631, Sharon, PA 16146 USA Tel 412-342-3811; Fax: 412-342-1583.

Shenanigan Bks., *(978-0-9726614; 978-1-934860)* 84 River Rd., Summit, NJ 07901-1443 USA (SAN 915-7085)
Web site: http://www.shenaniganbooks.com
Dist(s): **Jobson, Oliver H.**

Shenanigans Series,

Shen's Bks. *Imprint of* **Lee & Low Bks., Inc.**

Shepard Pubns., *(978-0-938497; 978-1-62035; 978-0-9849616; 978-0-9898649)* P.O. Box 280, Friday Harbor, WA 98250 USA (SAN 661-0536); *Imprints:* Skyhook Press (Skyhook Pr)
Web site: http://www.shepardpub.com
Dist(s): **CreateSpace Independent Publishing Platform**
Lightning Source, Inc.

Shepherd Mountain Pr., *(978-0-9749282)* 21 Cargill Rd., Liberty, ME 04949 USA Tel 207-589-4772.

Shepherd Pr. Inc., *(978-0-9663786; 978-0-9723046; 978-0-9767582; 978-0-9815400; 978-0-9824387; 978-0-9830990; 978-1-936908; 978-1-63342)* Orders Addr.: P.O. Box 24, Wapwallopen, PA 18660 USA Tel 570-379-2101; Fax: 570-379-2071; Toll Free: 800-338-1445; Edit Addr.: 437 S. River St., Wapwallopen, PA 18660 USA Do not confuse with companies with the same or similar names in Tappan, NJ, S. Hackensack, NJ, Birmingham, AL, Amityville, NY
E-mail: info@shepherdpress.com
Web site: http://www.shepherdpress.com.

Shepherd's Workshop, LLC, The, *(978-0-9752895)* 8213 Otis Ct., Arvada, CO 80003 USA Toll Free: 888-257-4673
E-mail: info@tsworkshop.com
Web site: http://www.tsworkshop.com.

Sheppard Publishing, *(978-0-9725286)* 3371 Old Forge Rd., Kent, OH 44240 USA Tel 330-325-9658
E-mail: sheppardpublishing@neo.rr.com.

Sher-A-Craft, *(978-0-9670612)* Div. of Bell Blueprint Co., Inc., 7888 Othello Ave., San Diego, CA 92111 USA Tel 619-278-4830; Fax: 619-278-6830; Toll Free: 877-235-5877.

Sherian Publishing, *(978-0-9795676)* 2700 Braselton Hwy., Suite 10-390, Dacula, GA 30019-3207 USA Tel 888-276-6730; Fax: 888-209-8212; Toll Free: 888-276-6730
E-mail: sherri.sheusi@sherianinc.com
Web site: http://www.sherianinc.com.

Sheridan Books *See* **KEYGARD**

Sheridan County Historical Society Pr., *(978-0-9792871)* Orders Addr.: 850 Sibley Cir., Sheridan, WY 82801-9626 USA
Web site: http://www.sheridancountyhistory.org
Dist(s): **Greenleaf Book Group.**

Sherman Asher Publishing, *(978-0-9644196; 978-1-890932)* P.O. Box 31725, Santa Fe, NM 87594-1725 USA
E-mail: westernedge@santa-fe.net
Web site: http://www.shermanasher.com
Dist(s): **Partners/West Book Distributors**
SCB Distributors.

Sherman, Linda, *(978-0-615-16017-7)* 31557 W. 10 Mile Rd., Farmington, MI 48336 USA Tel 248-476-3433; Fax: 248-476-4307
E-mail: grandmalouie@hotmail.com
Web site: http://grandmalouie.com.

Sheron Enterprises, Inc., *(978-1-891877)* 1035 S. Carley Ct., N Bellmore, NY 11710-2051 USA
E-mail: sheron@concentric.net.

Sherriffmatt9 Publishing Company *See* **Second Time Media & Communications**

Sherry Gansle *See* **Little Big Tomes**

Sheva, Marie, *(978-0-9741736)* 301 Main St., Apt. 8, East Greenwich, RI 02818 USA
E-mail: mariesheva@yearofthedogs.com
Web site: http://www.yearofthedogs.com.

Shields, Kathleen J. *See* **Erin Go Bragh Publishing**

Shiloh Children's Bks., *(978-0-9777923; 978-0-615-81504-6)* P.O. Box 954, Polson, MT 59860 USA Tel 406-531-2281
E-mail: oxman@blackfoot.net.

Shiloh Group *See* **Shiloh Children's Bks.**

Shine On Pubns., *(978-0-9749806)* 12325 Kosich Pl., Saratoga, CA 95070 USA; 12325 Kosich Pl., Saratoga, CA 95070-3575
Web site: http://www.shineonpublications.com.

Shine Publishing Hse., *(978-0-9749467)* 1811 Abbey Oak Dr., Suite 12879, Vienna, VA 22182 USA (SAN 255-9269) Tel 571-432-8922; Fax: 703-448-8443
E-mail: sales@shinepublishing.com
Web site: http://www.shinepublishing.com
Dist(s): **CreateSpace Independent Publishing Platform**
Global Bk. Distributors.

Shine Time Records & Bks., *(978-0-9712398)* Orders Addr.: P.O. Box 331941, Nashville, TN 37203 USA Tel 615-242-9857 (phone/fax); Toll Free: 888-807-4463 (888-80-SHINE)
E-mail: chucwhit@usit.net; info@shinetime.com; info@littleststar.com
Web site: http://www.littleststar.com; http://www.shinetime.com.

Shining Tramp Pr., *(978-0-9749352; 978-0-615-46043-7)* 2114 Harbor View Dr., Rocky Hill, CT 06067 USA Tel 860-563-1899
E-mail: kjrmurphy@sbcglobal.net
Dist(s): **CreateSpace Independent Publishing Platform.**

Shiny Red Ball Publishing, *(978-0-9773608)* 105 Lakeover Dr., Athens, GA 30607 USA
Web site: http://www.shinyredball.com.

Shires Press *Imprint of* **Northshire Pr.**

Shirley's Girl Pubns., *(978-0-578-06605-9)* 2165 Silverado St., San Marcos, CA 92078 USA Tel 619-723-8492
E-mail: LVa2thpro@gmail.com.

Shirt Tales *Imprint of* **Brookteam Corp.**

Shively, Lisa Cookbooks, *(978-0-9766756)* P.O. Box 2123, Eden, NC 27289 USA
E-mail: loopi3@earthlink.net; kitchenhelpers@earthlink.net
Web site: http://www.fromourhometoyours.net; http://www.cookingwithlisa.com.

Shiver Hill Bks., *(978-0-9747417)* 1220 Tico Rd., Ojai, CA 93023 USA; 79 S Canyon Diablo Rd. Unit 11, Sedona, AZ 86351 Tel 805-908-1651
E-mail: geraldstanek@yahoo.com
Dist(s): **Lulu Enterprises Inc.**

Shnoozles, LLC, *(978-0-9768852; 978-0-9770292)* 8 Canyon Ridge, Irvine, CA 92603 USA
Web site: http://www.shnoozles.com
Dist(s): **AtlasBooks Distribution.**

Shoemaker & Hoard *See* **Counterpoint LLC**

Shoetree Publishers, Inc., *(978-0-9785521)* P.O. Box 2122, Chandler, AZ 85244 USA (SAN 850-9859) Fax: 480-812-0182
Web site: http://www.shoetreepublishers.com.

Shogakukan (JPN) *(978-4-09) Dist. by* **S and S Inc.**

Shonda *See* **Sole Reason Publishing, LLC**

Shooting Star Edition *Imprint of* **American Literary Pr.**

Shooting Star Publishing, *(978-0-9762835)* 1305 E. Fort King St. # 100, Ocala, FL 34471-2443 USA Do not confuse with companies with the same name in Dearborn, MI, Moses Lake, WA
Web site: http://www.shootingstarpublishing.com.

Shope, E. Raymond *See* **Flutter-By Productions**

Shore Line Pr. *Imprint of* **Pacific Bks.**

Shorebird Media, *(978-0-9745737)* Orders Addr.: P.O. Box 372, Mukilteo, WA 98275-0372 USA (SAN 255-6359)
E-mail: jeanie.james@verizon.net.

Shorefront N.F.P., *(978-0-9765232)* Orders Addr.: P.O. Box 1894, Evanston, IL 60204 USA Tel 847-475-5321; Edit Addr.: P.O. Box 1894, Evanston, IL 60204 USA
Web site: http://shorefrontlegacy.org
Dist(s): **Lulu Enterprises Inc.**

Shoreline Pr., *(978-1-887671)* P.O. Box 555, Jamestown, RI 02835 USA Do not confuse with Shoreline Press in Soquel, CA
E-mail: kennethproudfoot@hotmail.com.

Shore Publishing Co., *(978-0-9746846)* PMB 123, 7485 Rush River Dr., Suite 710, Sacramento, CA 95831-5260 USA Tel 916-442-4883; Fax: 916-428-9542.

Shorey Publications *See* **Shorey's Bookstore**

Shorey's Bookstore, *(978-0-8466)* P.O. Box 77316, Seattle, WA 98177-0316 USA (SAN 204-5958) Tel 206-633-2990
E-mail: shorey@serv.net
Web site: http://www.serv.net/shorey.

Short Books *See* **Half-Pint Kids, Inc.**

Short Tales *Imprint of* **Magic Wagon**

Short Term Mission Language Program, *(978-0-9746182)* 3612 Mary Elizabeth Church Rd., Waxhaw, NC 28173-9273 USA
E-mail: info@missionlanguage.com
Web site: http://www.missionlanguage.com.

Shortbread Hill Bk. Co., *(978-0-9799162)* P.O. Box 1565, Veradale, WA 99037 USA (SAN 854-7599)
E-mail: shortbreadhill@hotmail.com.

Shortland Pubns. (U. S. A.) Inc., *(978-0-7699; 978-1-57257)* 19201 120th Ave NE Ste. 100, Bothell, WA 98011-9507 USA
Dist(s): **Heinemann-Raintree**
Wright Group/McGraw-Hill.

Show n' Tell Publishing,
Dist(s): **AtlasBooks Distribution.**

Showcase Writers, *(978-0-9753340)* P.O. Box 13757, Richmond, VA 23225 USA Tel 804-398-1138
E-mail: editor@showcasewriters.com
Web site: http://www.showcasewriters.com.

Shrewsbury Publishing, *(978-0-9678182)* 3624 Livingston, New Orleans, LA 70118 USA Tel 504-488-5249.

Shulemite Christian Crusade, *(978-0-9714361)* 1420 Armstrong Valley Rd., Halifax, PA 17032-8383 USA (SAN 254-3931) Tel 717-896-8383; Fax: 717-896-8386
E-mail: sherrerd@epix.net
Web site: http://www.chrissherrerd.com.

Shulenberger Publishing, *(978-0-9767355)* 3912 NE 127th St., Seattle, WA 98125 USA (SAN 256-5935) Tel 206-367-5886
E-mail: ericshul@hotmail.com.

Shumpert, Sharon *See* **SYS Publishing**

ShuNu Publishing, *(978-0-9742329)* P.O. Box 2636, Saintfford, TX 77497 USA Tel 281-208-1687
E-mail: kmitchellthomas@aol.com.

Shurley Instructional Materials, Inc., *(978-1-881940; 978-1-58561)* 366 Sim Dr., Cabot, AR 72023 USA Tel 501-843-3869; Fax: 501-843-0583; Toll Free: 800-566-2966; Ballad Rd., Cabot, AR 72023
E-mail: shurley@shurley.com
Web site: http://www.shurley.com.

SIA Publishing, LLC, *(978-0-9787344; 978-1-936820)* 204 Wyndom Ct., Goodlettsville, TN 37072-2176 USA
E-mail: donbloomquist@siapublishing.com
Web site: http://www.siapublishing.com
Dist(s): **Smashwords.**

SIA Software, LLC *See* **SIA Publishing, LLC**

Sibyl Merritt, *(978-0-9824565)* 25 Western Ledge Rd., Corea, ME 04624 USA (SAN 858-2157)
E-mail: bparks@maine.edu
Web site: http://sibylmerritt.com
Dist(s): **Lightning Source, Inc.**

Sidedoor Publishing LLC, *(978-0-9770248)* P.O. Box 18271, San Jose, CA 95158-8271 USA
E-mail: isbn@sidedoorpublishing.com
Web site: http://www.sidedoorpublishing.com.

Sidekicks TM *Imprint of* **Scholastic, Inc.**

Sidewalk Publishing, *(978-0-9766418)* Inform Design, 2809 Forest Hill Cir., SE, Olympia, WA 98501 USA Tel 360-570-9398
E-mail: informbarb@qwest.net
Web site: http://www.sidewalkpublishing.net.

Sidewalk Univ. Pr., *(978-0-9759962)* 1739 Springfield Ave., Maplewood, NJ 07040 USA Tel 973-885-0860
E-mail: sidewalku@msn.com
Web site: http://www.sidewalkuniversity.org.

Sidewinder Publishing LLC, *(978-0-914001)* 4609 Kinney St. SE, Albuquerque, NM 87105 USA Tel 505-998-8000
Web site: http://www.sidewinderpublishing.com/.

Sidran Institute Pr., *(978-0-9629164; 978-1-886968)* Div. of Sidran Institute, P.O. Box 436, Brooklandville, MD 21022 USA Tel 410-825-8888; Fax: 410-560-0134
E-mail: esther.giller@sidran.org
Web site: http://www.sidran.org
Dist(s): **New Leaf Distributing Co., Inc.**
Quality Bks., Inc.

Siegrist, Vicky, *(978-0-615-21676-8; 978-0-9820977; 978-0-9824444)* 1478 E. Buder Ave., Millington, MI 48529 USA
Web site: http://www.vickisiegrist.com
Dist(s): **Lulu Enterprises Inc.**

Siemers, Robert, *(978-0-9744723)* P.O. Box 549, Koloa, HI 96756-0549 USA Toll Free: 888-233-8365
Web site: http://www.teok.com.

Siems, D.R., *(978-0-9794483)* Orders Addr.: P.O. Box 83, Daniel, WY 83115 USA; Edit Addr.: 19 School House Ln., Daniel, WY 83115 USA.

Sierra Club Bks. for Children, *(978-0-87156; 978-1-57805)* Div. of Sierra Club Bks., 85 Second Street, San Francisco, CA 94105 USA Tel 415-977-5500; Fax: 415-977-5792
E-mail: Books.Publishing@sierraclub.org
Web site: http://www.sierraclub.org/books
Dist(s): **Gibbs Smith, Publisher**
Perseus-PGW.

Sierra Nevada Publishing Hse., *(978-0-9765697)* P.O. Box 50366, Henderson, NV 89016 USA Tel 702-991-1383; Fax: 702-953-8973; Toll Free: 800-254-6266
Web site: http://www.climbonsuccess.com.

Sierra Pr., *(978-0-939365; 978-0-9617651; 978-1-58071)* Div. of Panorama International Productions, Inc., Orders Addr.: 4988 Gold Leaf Dr., Mariposa, CA 95338 USA (SAN 662-6955) Tel 209-966-5071; Fax: 209-966-5073; Toll Free: 800-745-2631; *Imprints:* Wish You Were Here (Wish You Were Here)
E-mail: siepress@sti.net
Web site: http://www.nationalparksusa.com
Dist(s): **Smashwords.**

Sierra Raconteur Publishing, *(978-1-58365; 978-1-58582)* Orders Addr.: P.O. Box 97, Memphis, IN 47143 USA Tel 812-294-4693
E-mail: Lori_soard@yahoo.com.

Sierra Vista Junior High *See* **Sierra Vista Pubns.**

Sierra Vista Pubns., *(978-0-9711314; 978-0-615-11784-3)* Alpine Sports, Orders Addr.: P.O. Box 55391, Valencia, CA 91385 USA Fax: 661-259-8941; Toll Free: 800-330-7734; Edit Addr.: P.O. Box 186, Crystal Bay, NV 89402 USA (SAN 411-5961)
E-mail: alpinesport@earthlink.net
Web site: http://www.alpinebasketball.com
Dist(s): **American West Bks.**
Brigham Distribution.

Sigel Pr., *(978-1-905941)* Orders Addr.: 4403 Belmont Ct., Medina, OH 44256 USA (SAN 853-960X) Tel 330-722-2541 (phone/fax); 51a Victoria Rd., Cambridge, CB4 3BW Tel 01223 30 33 03
E-mail: tsigel@sigelpress.com
Web site: http://www.sigelpress.com
Dist(s): **MyiLibrary.**

Sights Productions, *(978-0-9629978; 978-1-886366)* Orders Addr.: 15130 Black Ankle Rd., Mount Airy, MD 21771 USA Tel 410-795-4582; Fax: 410-795-5054
E-mail: eric@sights-productions.com
Web site: http://sights-productions.com
Dist(s): **Brodart Co.**
Follett School Solutions
Kamkyi Bks.
New Leaf Distributing Co., Inc.
Quality Bks., Inc.

Sigil Publishing, *(978-0-9728461; 978-0-9785642; 978-0-9846528; 978-0-9860323)* P.O. Box 824, Leland, MI 49654- USA (SAN 255-1667)
Web site: http://www.knightscares.com; www.realheroesread.com
Dist(s): **Partners Bk. Distributing, Inc.**
Quality Bks., Inc.

Sigler Printing & Publishing, Incorporated *See* **McMillen Publishing**

Sigmar (ARG) *(978-950-11) Dist. by* **Continental Bk.**

Sigmar (ARG) *(978-950-11) Dist. by* **Mariuccia Iaconi Bk Imports.**

Sigmar (ARG) *(978-950-11) Dist. by* **AIMS Intl.**

Sigmar (ARG) *(978-950-11) Dist. by* **Lectorum Pubns.**

Sign Up Learning, Incorporated *See* **Language Quest Corp.**

Sign2Me *Imprint of* **Sign2Me Early Learning / Northlight Communications, Inc.**

Sign2Me Early Learning / Northlight Communications, Inc., *(978-0-9668367; 978-1-932354)* Orders Addr.: 11112 47th Ave. W., Mukilteo, WA 98275 USA (SAN 850-7902) Tel 425-493-1903; Fax: 425-493-1904; Edit Addr.: 11112 4th Ave. W., Mukilteo, WA 98275 USA Tel 425-493-1903; Fax: 425-493-1904; Toll Free: 877-744-6263; *Imprints:* Sign2Me (Sign Two Me)
E-mail: btarcea@sign2me.com; acrain@sign2me.com
Web site: http://sign2me.com
Dist(s): **American Wholesale Bk. Co.**

Signal Fire Pr., *(978-0-9764128)* 25260 Terr. Grove Rd., Los Gatos, CA 95033 USA (SAN 256-4351)
Web site: http://www.signalfirepress.com.

Signator Publishing Group Inc., *(978-0-9728472)* 1725 I St. NW., Suite 300, Washington, DC 20006 USA Tel 202-349-3896; Fax: 202-349-3915
E-mail: info@signatorpublishing.com
Web site: http://www.signatorpublishing.com.

Signature Lives *Imprint of* **Compass Point Bks.**

Signet *Imprint of* **Penguin Publishing Group**

Signet Classics *Imprint of* **Penguin Publishing Group**

Significant Faith Ministries *See* **SignificantFaith.com**

SignificantFaith.com, *(978-0-9848314)* 6742 Millstone Pl., Highlands Ranch, CO 80130 USA Tel 303-591-6530
E-mail: hwhitmore12@icloud.com
Web site: http://www.significantfaith.com.

Sigueme, Ediciones, S.A. (ESP) *(978-84-301) Dist. by* **Augsburg Fortress.**

Sikes Sports Concepts *See* **Old Bay Publishing**

Sikh Research Institute, *(978-1-60411)* P.O. Box 690504, San Antonio, TX 78269 USA (SAN 854-0403)
E-mail: info@sikhri.org
Web site: http://www.sikhri.org.

Sikorski, Lorna D. & Associates *See* **LDS & Assocs., LLC**

Silent Devil Productions, *(978-0-9752582; 978-0-9786451; 978-0-9789281; 978-0-9791192; 978-0-9796902)* 3777 Center Way, Fairfax, VA 22033 USA
E-mail: silentdevilproductions@hotmail.com
Web site: http://www.silentdevil.com.

Silent Hse. Pr., *(978-0-615-66700-3)* 115 Orange Tree Dr., Orange, OH 44022 USA Tel 216-970-1899
E-mail: sap2006@gmail.com.

Silent Moon Bks., *(978-0-9721457)* P.O. Box 1280, Seeley Lake, MT 59868 USA
E-mail: bschieber@yahoo.com.

Silhouette Pond Productions, *(978-0-9761169)* P.O. Box 778, Palm Harbor, FL 34682-0778 USA (SAN 256-3886) Tel 727-771-1691
E-mail: ceceenter@tampabay.rr.com
Web site: http://www.silhouettepond.com.

Silk Waters Mooney, *(978-0-9776608)* 316 E. El Paso St., Brackettville, TX 78832 USA Tel 830-563-3443; P.O. Box 393, Brackettville, TX 78832
E-mail: swmooney@pukathemoose.com.

Silly Goose Productions, LLC, *(978-0-9711500)* 525 Cutty Trl. Apt. A, Lakeway, TX 78734-4836 USA
E-mail: sallysue678@yahoo.com; sally@onmyown.com
Web site: http://www.starfishpublishing.com; http://www.onmyown.com
Dist(s): **Follett School Solutions.**

Silly String Media, *(978-0-615-25193-6)* P.O. Box 884, Ross, CA 94957 USA
Web site: http://www.sillystringmedia.com
Dist(s): **Lulu Enterprises Inc.**

Siloam Pr. *Imprint of* **Charisma Media**

Silver Bells Publishing Hse., *(978-0-9793517)* 19415 150th Ave., Tustin, MI 49688 USA Tel 231-829-3898
E-mail: dgbelleville@yahoo.com.

†Silver, Burdett & Ginn, Inc., *(978-0-382; 978-0-663; 978-1-4182)* Orders Addr.: P.O. Box 2500, Lebanon, IN 46052 USA Toll Free Fax: 800-841-8939; Toll Free: 800-552-2259; Edit Addr.: P.O. Box 480, Parsippany, NJ 07054 USA (SAN 204-5982); 108 Wilmot Rd., Suite 380, Midwest Div., Deerfield, IL 60015 (SAN 111-6517) Tel 708-945-1240
E-mail: customerservice@scottforesman.com
Web site: http://www.scottforesman.com/; *CIP.*

Silver Cloak Pubns., *(978-0-9777677)* P.O. Box 1027, Carpinteria, CA 93014-1027 USA
E-mail: SilverCloak@aol.com.

Silver Dagger Mysteries *Imprint of* **Overmountain Pr.**

Silver Dolphin Bks. *Imprint of* **Baker & Taylor Publishing Group**

Silver Knight Publishing, LLC, *(978-0-615-55725-0; 978-0-615-58405-8; 978-1-938083)* PO Box 721254, Orlando, FL 32872 USA Tel 407-668-3103
Web site: http://www.silverknightpublishing.com
Dist(s): **CreateSpace Independent Publishing Platform.**

Silver Lake Publishing, *(978-0-930868; 978-1-56343)* 1119 N. Broadway St., Aberdeen, WA 98520-2433 USA (SAN 203-8110) Toll Free: 800-663-3091 Do not confuse with Silver Lake Publishing, Morton, PA
E-mail: publisher@silverlakepublishing.com; SCRIBERE@aol.com; mthorpe@silverlakepub.com
Web site: http://www.silverlakepub.com
Dist(s): **SCB Distributors.**

Silver Leaf Bks., LLC, *(978-0-9744354; 978-0-9787782; 978-1-60975)* Orders Addr.: P.O. Box 6460, Holliston, MA 01746 USA Tel 508-740-6270; Toll Free:

888-823-6450; Edit Addr.: 13 Temi Rd., Holliston, MA 01746 USA
E-mail: Sales@SilverLeafBooks.com
Web site: http://www.silverleafbooks.com.

Silver Moon Pr., *(978-1-881889; 978-1-893110)* 400 E. 85th St. Apt. 15K, New York, NY 10028-6324 USA Toll Free: 800-874-3320
E-mail: mail@silvermoonpress.com
Web site: http://www.silvermoonpress.com.

Silver Print Pr., Inc., *(978-0-9628064; 978-0-9749890)* Div. of Peter Miller LLC, Orders Addr.: 20 Crossroad, Suite #1, Colbyville, VT 05676 USA (SAN 299-0350) Tel 802-244-5339
E-mail: peter@petermillerphotography.com
Web site: http://www.silverprintpress.com.

Silver Rim Pr., *(978-1-878611)* 2759 Park Lake Dr., Boulder, CO 80301 USA Tel 303-666-4290 (phone/fax)
E-mail: Sybilset@aol.com.

Silver Rose Publishing, *(978-0-9778211)* P.O. Box 462174, Aurora, CO 80046 USA Tel 303-946-2183; Toll Free: 800-431-1579; *Imprints:* Raynestorm Books (Raynestorm Bks)
E-mail: contact@silverrosepublishing.com
Web site: http://www.silverrosepublishing.com; http://www.bookch.com
Dist(s): **BCH Fulfillment & Distribution.**

Silver Snowflake Publishing, *(978-0-9778476)* P.O. Box 1256, East Greenwich, RI 02818 USA (SAN 850-394X)
E-mail: exteriordesigner@cox.net
Web site: http://www.themagicsceptre.com; http://www.silversnowflakepublishing.com.

Silver Whistle *Imprint of* **Harcourt Trade Pubs.**

SilverBrown Bks., *(978-0-9840922)* 9355 54th Ave., S., Seattle, WA 98118 USA Tel 206-721-3794.

SilverhawkCorp., *(978-0-9772933)* 618 Draper Heights Way, Draper, UT 84020 USA.

Silverman, Toby, *(978-0-9793475)* 1611 Hemlock Farms, Lords Valley, PA 18428 USA
E-mail: tsilverman@noln.com.

Silvermine International Bks., LLC, *(978-0-692-35528-2)* 25 Perry Ave., Suite 11, Norwalk, CT 06850 USA (SAN 760-6338) Tel 203-451-2396
E-mail: jatkin@silvermineinternational.com
Dist(s): **INscribe Digital.**

Silvey Bk. Publishing, *(978-0-9762446)* P.O. Box 5171, Goodyear, AZ 85338-5171 USA Fax: 623-853-9172
E-mail: silveybooks@earthlink.net.

Simakan Group, The, *(978-0-9767812)* P.O. Box 492496, Atlanta, GA 30349 USA Fax: 770-981-1046
E-mail: info@playingyouragame.com
Web site: http://www.playingyourAgame.com.

Simba Publishing Co., *(978-0-9765982)* 5413 Whistler Dr., Tallahassee, FL 32317 USA (SAN 256-4270) Tel 850-878-7741
E-mail: gladys_gikiri@simbapublishingcompany.com
Web site: http://www.simbapublishingcompany.com.

Simba's Publishing, *(978-0-9765475)* P.O. Box 27634, Fresno, CA 93729-7634 USA.

Simcha Media Group, *(978-0-943706; 978-965-465; 978-1-930143; 978-1-932687; 978-1-934440; 978-1-936068)* 94 Dwight Pl., Englewood, NJ 07631 USA Tel 201-503-1151; Fax: 201-503-9761; *Imprints:* Devora Publishing (DevorPubng); Pitspopany Press (Pitspopany Pr)
Web site: http://www.pitspopany.com
Dist(s): **Coronet Bks.**
Lulu Enterprises Inc.

Simmons, Kristina, *(978-0-9769843)* 40 Christopher Cir., Middletown, CT 06457 USA.

Simmons, Sukether Williams *See* **Shrewsbury Publishing**

Simms, Laura Storyteller, *(978-0-9911692)* 814 Broadway, New York, NY 10003 USA Tel 212-674-3479
E-mail: storymentor2010@gmail.com
Web site: http://www.laurasimms.com.

Simon & Barklee, Inc./ExplorerMedia, *(978-0-9704661; 978-0-9714502)* 2280 E. Whidbey Shores Rd., Langley, WA 98260 USA Tel 360-730-2360; Fax: 360-730-2355; *Imprints:* Explorer Media (Explorer Media)
E-mail: cwsch@whidbey.com
Web site: http://simonandbarklee.com
Dist(s): **Quality Bks., Inc.**

Simon & Brown, *(978-0-9814843; 978-1-936041; 978-1-61382)* 540 S. Park Rd., Suite 934, Hollywood, FL 33021 USA Tel 305-610-7128
E-mail: info@simonandbrown.com
Web site: http://www.simonandbrown.com.

Simon & Northrop of Cal, Incorporated *See* **Martell Publishing Co**

Simon & Schuster, *(978-0-671; 978-0-684; 978-0-689; 978-0-914676; 978-0-7432; 978-1-4165; 978-1-4391; 978-1-4516; 978-1-4767; 978-1-5011)* Div. of Simon & Schuster, Inc., Orders Addr.: 100 Front St., Riverside, NJ 08075 USA (SAN 200-2442) Toll Free Fax: 800-943-9831; Toll Free: 800-223-2336 (ordering); 800-223-2348 (customer service); Edit Addr.: a/o Subsidiary Rights, 11th Flr., 1230 Avenue of the Americas, New York, NY 10020 USA (SAN 200-2450) Tel 212-698-7000; Fax: 212-698-7007; 212-632-8099 (Rights & Permissions); 212-698-1269 (Pocket Bks. Rights & Permissions); Toll Free: 800-897-7650 (customer financial services); 100 Front St., Riverside, NJ 08075 (SAN 852-5471) Tel 856-824-2115; *Imprints:* Atria Books (Atria)
E-mail: ssonline_feedback@simonsays.com; consumer.customerservice@simonandschuster.com
Web site: http://www.simonsays.com; http://www.oasis.simonandschuster.com; http://www.simonandschuster.com/ebooks
Dist(s): **Cengage Gale**
Giron Bks.
Libros Sin Fronteras
Simon & Schuster, Inc.
Studio Fun International
TextStream
Thorndike Pr.
Ulverscroft Large Print Bks., Ltd.

Simon & Schuster Audio, *(978-0-671; 978-0-7435; 978-1-4423)* Orders Addr.: 100 Front St., Riverside, NJ 08075 USA Toll Free Fax: 800-943-9831 (orders); Toll Free: 800-223-2336 (customer service); Edit Addr.: a/o Sub Rights Manager, 11th flr., 1230 Avenue of the Americas, New York, NY 10020 USA Tel 212-698-7000; Fax: 212-698-2370; 212-632-8091 (Rights & Permissions)
Web site: http://www.simonsays.com/subs/index.cfm?areaid=45
Dist(s): **Follett School Solutions**
Simon & Schuster
Simon & Schuster, Inc.

Simon & Schuster Bks. For Young Readers *Imprint of* **Simon & Schuster/Paula Wiseman Bks.**

Simon & Schuster Bks. For Young Readers *Imprint of* **Simon & Schuster Bks. For Young Readers**

Simon & Schuster Bks. For Young Readers, Div. of Simon & Schuster Children's Publishing, 1230 Ave. of the Americas, New York, NY 10020 USA; *Imprints:* Simon & Schuster Books For Young Readers (S&SBFYng); Simon & Schuster/Paula Wiseman Books (S&SPaulaW); SAGA Press (SAGA Press)
Dist(s): **Simon & Schuster, Inc.**

Simon & Schuster Children's Publishing, *(978-0-02; 978-0-671; 978-0-684; 978-0-689; 978-0-7434; 978-1-4169; 978-1-4424; 978-0-85707)* Orders Addr.: 100 Front St., Riverside, NJ 08075 USA Toll Free Fax: 800-943-9831; Toll Free: 800-223-2336; Edit Addr.: a/o Subsidiary Rights, 4th floor, 1230 Avenue of the Americas, New York, NY 10020 USA Tel 212-698-7200; Fax: 212-698-2797 (Rights & Permissions); *Imprints:* Aladdin Library (AlaLib); Atheneum Books for Young Readers (AthenSS); Atheneum/Anne Schwartz Books (Anne Schwart); Atheneum/Richard Jackson Books (Rich Jack); Simon & Schuster/Paula Wiseman Books (S&SPaulaW); Aladdin Paperbacks (AladdinPaperbcks)
Web site: http://www.simonsays.com
Dist(s): **Follett School Solutions**
Lectorum Pubns., Inc.
Simon & Schuster
Simon & Schuster, Inc.

†**Simon & Schuster, Inc.,** *(978-0-02; 978-0-671; 978-0-684; 978-0-689; 978-0-914676; 978-0-7432; 978-0-7434; 978-0-7435; 978-1-4165; 978-1-4169; 978-1-4391; 978-1-4423; 978-1-4424; 978-1-4516; 978-0-85707; 978-1-4814; 978-1-5082)* Div. of Viacom Co., Orders Addr.: 100 Front St., Riverside, NJ 08075 USA Toll Free Fax: 800-943-9831; Toll Free: 800-223-2336 (orders); 800-223-2348 (customer service); Edit Addr.: 1230 Ave. of the Americas, New York, NY 10020 USA Tel 212-698-7000
E-mail: Consumer.CustomerService@simonandschuster.com
Web site: http://www.simonsays.com
Dist(s): **Follett School Solutions;** *CIP.*

Simon & Schuster, Ltd. (GBR) *(978-0-671; 978-0-684; 978-0-689; 978-0-7432; 978-0-7434; 978-1-84738; 978-1-84737; 978-0-85720; 978-0-85707; 978-1-84983; 978-1-4711)* *Dist. by* **IPG Chicago.**

Simon & Schuster, Ltd. (GBR) *(978-0-671; 978-0-684; 978-0-689; 978-0-7432; 978-0-7434; 978-1-84738; 978-1-84737; 978-0-85720; 978-0-85707; 978-1-84983; 978-1-4711)* *Dist. by* **S and S Inc.**

Simon & Schuster Trade *See* **Simon & Schuster**

Simon & Schuster/Paula Wiseman Bks. *Imprint of* **Simon & Schuster Children's Publishing**

Simon & Schuster/Paula Wiseman Bks. *Imprint of* **Simon & Schuster/Paula Wiseman Bks.**

Simon & Schuster/Paula Wiseman Bks. *Imprint of* **Simon & Schuster Bks. For Young Readers**

Simon & Schuster/Paula Wiseman Bks., Div. of Simon & Schuster Children's Publishing, 1230 Ave. of the Americas, New York, NY 10020 USA; *Imprints:* Simon & Schuster Books For Young Readers (S&SBFYng); Simon & Schuster/Paula Wiseman Books (S&SPaulaW)
Dist(s): **Simon & Schuster, Inc.**

Simon & Simon, LLC *See* **Maestro Classics**

Simon & Son Publishing, *(978-0-9773665)* 4995 Paist Rd., Doylestown, PA 18901 USA; *Imprints:* Prophecy, The (Prophecy)
E-mail: frankfsp1@comcast.net
Web site: http://www.simonsonpublishing.com.

Simon, Les, *(978-0-9761914)* Orders Addr.: P.O. Box 57274, Washington, DC 20037-0274 USA Tel 202-659-3639; Fax: 202-457-1155; Edit Addr.: 1400 20th St., NW, No. 805, Washington, DC 20036 USA
E-mail: lessim2003@yahoo.com.

Simon Peter Pr., Inc., *(978-0-9761533; 978-0-9777430; 978-1-936159)* P.O. Box 2187, Oldsmar, FL 34677 USA Fax: 727-772-0368
E-mail: theaben@aol.com
Web site: http://www.simonpeterpress.com
Dist(s): **eBookit.com.**

Simon Pulse *Imprint of* **Simon Pulse**

Simon Pulse, Div.of Simon & Schuster Children's Publishing, 1230 Ave. of the Americas, New York, NY 10020 USA; *Imprints:* Simon Pulse (SimonPulse)
Dist(s): **Simon & Schuster, Inc.**

Simon Pulse/Beyond Words, 1230 Avenue of the Americas, New York, NY 10020 USA
Dist(s): **Simon & Schuster, Inc.**

Simon Pulse/Mercury Ink *Imprint of* **Simon Pulse/Mercury Ink**

Simon Pulse/Mercury Ink, 1230 Avenue of the Americas, New York, NY 10020 USA; *Imprints:* Simon Pulse/Mercury Ink (SimoPulseMer)
Dist(s): **Simon & Schuster, Inc.**

Simon Scribbles *Imprint of* **Simon Scribbles**

Simon Scribbles, Div. of Simon & Schuster Children's Publishing, 1230 Ave. of the Americas, New York, NY 10020 USA; *Imprints:* Simon Scribbles (SScribbles)
Dist(s): **Simon & Schuster, Inc.**

Simon Spotlight *Imprint of* **Simon Spotlight**

Simon Spotlight, Div. of Simon & Schuster Children's Publishing, 1230 Ave. of the Americas, New York, NY 10020 USA; *Imprints:* Simon Spotlight (SimonSpotlight)
Dist(s): **Simon & Schuster, Inc.**

Simon Spotlight/Nickelodeon *Imprint of* **Simon Spotlight/Nickelodeon**

Simon Spotlight/Nickelodeon, Div.of Simon & Schuster Children's Publishing, 1230 Ave. of the Americas, New York, NY 10020 USA; *Imprints:* Simon Spotlight/Nickelodeon (SSpotNick)
Dist(s): **Simon & Schuster, Inc.**

Simone's Bks., *(978-0-615-18719-8; 978-0-615-20614-1)* 65 Winding Wood Dr., Apt. 4A, Sayreville, NJ 08872 USA
Dist(s): **Lulu Enterprises Inc.**

Simpatico Bks., *(978-0-9771322)* P.O. Box 201, Heber Springs, AR 72543 USA Tel 501-362-2858
Web site: http://www.simpaticobooks.com.

Simple Faith Bks. *Imprint of* **Sunrise Mountain Bks.**

Simple Fish Bk. Co., LLC, *(978-0-9817598; 978-0-9837932)* 5500 Abercorn St., Suite 32, Savannah, GA 31405 USA
E-mail: bbrooks@simplefishbookco.com
Web site: http://www.simplefishbookco.com
Dist(s): **AtlasBooks Distribution.**

Simple Ink, LLC, *(978-0-9794167)* P.O. Box 1825, Hays, KS 67601 USA
E-mail: gmarconette@simpleink.net; gameck@gmail.com
Web site: http://www.simpleink.net.

Simple Productions *See* **Shepard Pubns.**

Simple Thoughts Pr., LLC, *(978-0-9768557)* Orders Addr.: P.O. Box 759, Northfield, MN 55057 USA; Edit Addr.: 14345 Falk Ave., Northfield, NJ 55057 USA
Web site: http://www.backandforthjournal.com.

Simplemente Maria Pr., *(978-0-9766811)* 2611 Samarkand Dr., Santa Barbara, CA 93105 USA Tel 805-962-2497
E-mail: mary@maryheebner.com
Web site: http://www.simplementemariapress.com; http://www.maryheebner.com.

Simpler Life Pr., *(978-0-9619806)* 1599 S. Uinta Way, Denver, CO 80231 USA (SAN 246-5809) Tel 303-751-2454; Fax: 303-671-5200
E-mail: avs@vansteenhouse.com
Web site: http://www.vansteenhouse.com.

Simplex Pubns., *(978-0-9623113; 978-1-929304)* Orders Addr.: 575 Larkspur Plaza Dr., Unit 4, Larkspur, CA 94939-1476 USA
E-mail: gosmith@pacbell.net
Web site: http://www.simplexpublications.com
Dist(s): **Bookpeople.**

SimpliFun Studios, *(978-1-932839)* 2070 Stratford Dr., Milpitas, CA 95035 USA Tel 408-946-8632; Toll Free: 800-850-4-FUN
E-mail: mail@simplifun.com
Web site: http://www.childrenspartygames.com.

Simply Read Bks. (CAN) *(978-0-9688768; 978-1-894965; 978-1-897476; 978-1-927018)* *Dist. by* **IngramPubServ.**

Simply Silly Stories, *(978-0-9838964)* 3603 Forsythia Dr., Wylie, TX 75098 USA Tel 214-597-8999
E-mail: bewilson@simplysillystories.com.

Simpson, Charles B., *(978-0-9703818)* 234 Faulkner Ave., Hazard, KY 41701 USA Tel 606-436-4652
E-mail: cngsimpson@earthlink.net
Web site: http://www.appalachianwriter.com.

Simsand Publishing, *(978-0-9765580)* 8 Huntington Pl. Dr., Atlanta, GA 30350 USA Tel 678-458-0759
E-mail: timsanders01@aol.com.

Sinanan, Cindy, *(978-0-9769004)* 10169 New Hampshire Ave., No. 155, Silver Spring, MD 20903 USA
E-mail: mybook@mris.com.

Sinclair/Polk, *(978-0-615-20281-5)* 1717 W. Green Tree Rd., No. 204, Glendale, WI 53209 USA Tel 414-704-3207
E-mail: janpolk@janpolk.com; margerysinclair@juno.com
Web site: http://www.janpolk.com; http://www.margerysinclair.com; http://www.ayearofgoodmanners.com
Dist(s): **Signature Bks., LLC.**

SingaporeMath.com, Inc., *(978-0-9741573; 978-1-932906)* 19535 SW 129th Ave., Tualatin, OR 97062 USA (SAN 255-6510) Tel 503-557-8100; Fax: 503-557-8103
E-mail: accounting@singaporemath.com; dthomas@singaporemath.com
Web site: http://www.singaporemath.com.

SingaporeMath.com, Incorporated *See* **SingaporeMath.com, Inc.**

Singing Moon Pr., *(978-0-9770497)* Singing Moon Press #239 2601 S. Minnesota Ave., Ste 105, Sioux Falls, SD 57105-4750 USA; *Imprints:* Itty Bitty Kitty (Itty Bitty Kitty)
E-mail: editor@singingmoonpress.com
Web site: http://www.singingmoonpress.com.

Singing River Pubns., *(978-0-9709575; 978-0-9759953; 978-0-9774831; 978-0-9789870; 978-0-9822596)* Orders Addr.: P.O. Box 72, Ely, MN 55731 USA (SAN 254-136X) Tel 218-365-3498; Fax: 218-365-5792; Edit Addr.: 3365 Wolf Lake Rd., Ely, MN 55731 USA
E-mail: cmoroni@singingriverpublications.com; info@singingriverpublications.com
Web site: http://www.singingriverpublications.com
Dist(s): **Adventure Pubns., Inc.**
Partners Bk. Distributing, Inc.

Singing Tree Pr., *(978-0-9708005)* P.O. Box 722, Auburn, CA 95604 USA (SAN 255-4011) Tel 530-823-9284
E-mail: editor@mail.singingtreepress.com; orders@singingtreepress.com
Web site: http://www.singingtreepress.com.

Singing Turtle Pr., *(978-0-9659113; 978-0-9846381)* 942 Vuelta Del Sur., Santa Fe, NM 87507-7755 USA Toll Free: 888-308-6284
E-mail: kathy@mathkits.com
Web site: http://www.mathkits.com
Dist(s): **Blessing Way Publishing Co.**
Midpoint Trade Bks., Inc.

Singing Winds Pr., *(978-1-61955)* 1331 SE Ellis, Dallas, OR 97338 USA Tel 503-551-7241 (phone/fax)
E-mail: singingwindspress@gmail.com
Web site: www.singingwindspress.com.

Siniff Publishing *See* **Country Messenger Pr. Publishing Group, LLC**

Sinolingua (CHN) *(978-7-80052)* *Dist. by* **China Bks.**

Sinonexus Publishing Co., *(978-0-9767664)* 65 Wethersfield Rd., Bellingham, MA 02019-1045 USA Tel 508-966-4423
E-mail: sinonexus@yahoo.com
Web site: http://www.sinonexus.org.

Sinsinawa Dominicans, Inc., *(978-0-9774934)* 585 Cty. Rd., Z, Sinsinawa, WI 53824-9701 USA Tel 608-748-4411; Fax: 608-748-4491
E-mail: communication@sinsinawa.org
Web site: http://www.sinsinawa.org.

Sioux City Lewis & Clark Interpretive Ctr., The, *(978-0-9753860; 978-0-9785063)* 900 Larsen Pk. Rd., Sioux city, IA 51103 USA Tel 712-224-5242; Fax: 712-224-5244
E-mail: mpoole@siouxcitylcic.com
Web site: http://www.siouxcitylcic.com.

Sir Wrinkles Pr., *(978-0-9766639)* 30692 Fox Run Ln., San Juan Capistrano, CA 92675 USA
Web site: http://www.sirwrinklesthebulldog.com.

Siren-BookStrand, Inc., *(978-1-933563; 978-1-60601; 978-1-61034; 978-1-61926; 978-1-62241; 978-1-62242; 978-1-62740; 978-1-62741; 978-1-63258; 978-1-63259)* 2500 S. Lamar Blvd., Austin, TX 78704 USA (SAN 256-6869) Toll Free: 866-887-4736
E-mail: diana.debalko@sirenpublishing.com
Web site: http://www.sirenpublishing.com.

Sirius Entertainment, Inc., *(978-1-57989)* Orders Addr.: P.O. Box X, Unadilla, NY 13849 USA Tel 607-369-2620; Fax: 607-369-2623; Edit Addr.: P.O. Box X, Unadilla, NY 13849-0723 USA
E-mail: sirent@aol.com
Dist(s): **Diamond Comic Distributors, Inc.**
Diamond Bk. Distributors.

SIRS Mandarin *See* **SIRS Publishing, Inc.**

†**SIRS Publishing, Inc.,** *(978-0-89777; 978-0-9678914)* Div. of ProQuest Information and Learning, 5201 Congress Ave., Suite 250, Boca Raton, FL 33487 USA (SAN 222-8920) Tel 561-994-0079; Fax: 561-995-4074; Toll Free: 800-521-0600
Web site: http://www.proquestK12.com; *CIP.*

Siruela, Ediciones S.A. (ESP) *(978-84-7844; 978-84-85876)* *Dist. by* **Lectorum Pubns.**

Sistemas Tecnicos de Edicion, S.A. de C.V. (MEX) *(978-968-6579; 978-970-629; 978-968-6048; 978-968-6135; 978-968-6394)* *Dist. by* **AIMS Intl.**

Sisterhaus Publishing, *(978-0-578-05291-5)* 40555 La Colima Rd., Suite 100, Temecula, CA 92591 USA
E-mail: lisaharding4@yahoo.com.

Sisters of Providence, *(978-1-893789; 978-0-9897397)* a/o Ann Casper, SP, Sisters of Providence Owens Hall, Saint Mary-of-the-Woods, IN 47876 USA Tel 812-535-2800; Fax: 812-535-1009 Do not confuse with Sisters of Providence in Holyoke, MA
E-mail: acasper@spsmw.org
Web site: http://www.sistersofprovidence.org.

Sisters Three Publishing Inc., *(978-0-9787375)* 5026 SW. 94th Ave., Cooper City, FL 33328 USA Fax: 954-885-8007
Web site: http://www.sistersthreeseries.com.

Sisu Home Entertainment, Inc., *(978-1-56086; 978-1-884857)* 340 W. 39th St., 6th Fl., New York, NY 10018 USA Tel 212-779-1559; Fax: 212-779-7115; Toll Free Fax: 888-221-7478; Toll Free: 800-223-7478
E-mail: sisu@sisuent.com
Web site: http://www.sisuent.com
Dist(s): **Follett School Solutions.**

Sitare, Ltd., *(978-0-940178)* Orders Addr.: 1101 N. Rainbow Blvd., No. 52, Las Vegas, NV 89108 USA (SAN 217-0833) Tel 702-990-0688
E-mail: editor@dlvmagazine.com
Web site: http://www.dlvmagazine.com.

Six Seconds, *(978-0-9629123; 978-0-9716772; 978-0-9797343; 978-1-935667)* Orders Addr.: P.O. Box 1985, Freedom, CA 95019 USA Tel 831-763-1800
E-mail: staff@6seconds.org; jenny@6seconds.org
Web site: http://www.6seconds.org.

Six Suns Publishing, *(978-0-9654200)* P.O. Box 112852, Anchorage, AK 99511 USA Tel 907-344-2905
Dist(s): **Todd Communications**
Wizard Works.

Sixth Avenue Bks. *Imprint of* **Grand Central Publishing**

Sixth&Spring Bks., *(978-1-931543; 978-1-933027; 978-1-936096)* 233 Spring St., 3rd Fl., New York, NY 10013 USA; *Imprints:* Hart, Chris Books (Chris Hart)
E-mail: wendy@sohopublishing.com
Web site: http://sixthandspringbooks.com
Dist(s): **Sterling Publishing Co., Inc.**

Skandisk, Inc., *(978-0-9615394; 978-1-57534)* 6667 W. Old Shakopee Rd., Suite 109, Bloomington, MN 55438-2622 USA (SAN 695-4405) Tel 952-829-8998; Fax: 952-829-8992; Toll Free: 800-468-2424 (orders)
E-mail: lhamnes@skandisk.com; tomten@skandisk.com
Web site: http://www.skandisk.com.

SkateRight Publishing, *(978-0-9798876)* 2913 Cummings, Berkley, MI 48072-4807 USA.

Skeete, D., *(978-0-9769012)* P.O. Box 737, New York, NY 10030 USA
E-mail: msdss@aol.com
Web site: http://www.hiphopwordsearch.com.

Skeezel Pr., *(978-0-9747217)* 2624 Lakeside Dr., Erie, PA 16511 USA
E-mail: pmerski@roadrunner.com; patricia@skeezelpress.com
Web site: http://www.skeezelpress.com
Dist(s): **Independent Pubs. Group**
MyiLibrary.

Skeptical Guitarist Pubns., *(978-0-9665029; 978-0-9788609; 978-1-944210)* Orders Addr.: P.O. Box 5824, Raleigh, NC 27650-5824 USA Tel 919-834-2031; Edit Addr.: 714 Faircloth St., Raleigh, NC 27607-4013 USA
E-mail: bruceemery@mindspring.com
Web site: http://www.skepticalguitarist.com/.

Sketch Publishing, *(978-0-9726764)* 414 S. 43rd St, Philadelphia, PA 19104 USA Tel 215-243-0644
E-mail: msand227@aol.com.

Sketches From The Heart Publishing, *(978-0-9759300)* P.O. Box 3431, Boulder, CO 80307 USA
Web site: www.sketchesfromtheheart.com
Dist(s): **Bks. West**
Common Ground Distributors, Inc.
Partners/West Book Distributors
Quality Bks., Inc.

Skinder-Strauss Assocs., *(978-1-57741)* Orders Addr.: P.O. Box 50, Newark, NJ 07101 USA Tel 973-642-1440; Fax: 973-242-1905; Toll Free: 800-444-4041; Edit Addr.: 240 Mulberry St., Newark, NJ 07101 USA
E-mail: ed@elaw.com
Web site: http://lawdiary.com; http://elaw.com.

Skinner Hse. Bks. *Imprint of* **Unitarian Universalist Assn.**

Skinner, Kerry L., *(978-0-9648743; 978-1-931080)* Div. of Think Life/Change, Orders Addr.: 67 N. Marshside Pl., The Woodlands, TX 77389 USA; *Imprints:* KLS LifeChange Ministries (KLS LifeChge)
E-mail: kerry@kerryskinner.com
Web site: http://www.kerryskinner.com.

Skinny On (tm), The *Imprint of* **Rand Media Co**

Skira *Imprint of* **Rizzoli International Pubns., Inc.**

Skirvan, Pamela, *(978-0-9742943)* P.O. Box 484, New Harbor, ME 04554-0484 USA.

Sky Blue Pr., *(978-0-9652364; 978-0-9774851; 978-0-9889170)* 4514 Spotted Oak Woods, San Antonio, TX 78249 USA Tel 505-603-5738
E-mail: orders@skybluepress.com; skybluepress@skybluepress.com
Web site: http://www.skybluepress.com
Dist(s): **Smashwords.**

Sky Carrier Pr., *(978-1-880589)* P.O. Box 442, Fayetteville, NY 13066 USA Tel 605-486-4310; 315-637-9511
E-mail: swagner711@aol.com.

Sky Pony Pr. *Imprint of* **Skyhorse Publishing Co., Inc.**

†Sky Publishing, *(978-0-933346; 978-1-931559; 978-0-615-38976-9)* Div. of New Track Media, 90 Sherman St. Ste. D, Cambridge, MA 02140-3264 USA (SAN 212-4556) Toll Free: 800-253-0245
E-mail: orders@SkyandTelescope.com
Web site: http://www.skyandtelescope.com
Dist(s): **F&W Media, Inc.**
Sterling Publishing Co., Inc.; *CIP*

Sky Publishing Corporation *See* **Sky Publishing**

Sky Rocket Pr., *(978-0-9724637)* Orders Addr.: 2104 Old York Dr., Keller, TX 76248-5497 USA Tel 817-498-4300; Fax: 757-299-3608
E-mail: robert@rocketvilletexas.com
Web site: http://www.rocketvilletexas.com.

Skyhook Pr. *Imprint of* **Shepard Pubns.**

Skyhorse Publishing Co., Inc., *(978-0-934672; 978-0-941873; 978-1-56148; 978-1-892389; 978-1-59780; 978-1-60239; 978-1-61608; 978-1-61145; 978-1-936697; 978-1-61321; 978-1-62087; 978-1-62153; 978-1-62636; 978-1-62872; 978-1-62873; 978-1-62914; 978-1-940456; 978-1-63144; 978-1-63158; 978-1-63220; 978-1-63450; 978-1-68099; 978-1-5107)* 307 W. 36th Street, Flr. 11, New York, NY 10018 USA Tel 212-643-6816; 212-648-6819; *Imprints:* Arcade Publishing (ARCADE PUBLISH); Sky Pony Press (SKY PONY PRESS); Allworth Press (Allwrth Pr); Yucca Publishing (Yucca Pub); Good Books (GoodBksUSA)
E-mail: info@skyhorsepublishing.com
Web site: http://www.skyhorsepublishing.com
Dist(s): **Follett School Solutions**
MBI Distribution Services/Quayside Distribution
MyiLibrary
Perseus Bks. Group
Perseus Distribution
Random Hse., Inc.
Sterling Publishing Co., Inc.

Skylark *Imprint of* **Random Hse. Children's Bks.**

Skylight Paths Publishing *Imprint of* **LongHill Partners, Inc.**

Skylight Publishing, *(978-0-9654853; 978-0-9727055; 978-0-9824775)* Orders Addr.: 9 Bartlet St., Suite 70, Andover, MA 01810-3655 USA Tel 978-475-1431 (phone/fax); Toll Free: 888-476-1940
E-mail: support@skylit.com
Web site: http://www.skylit.com.

Skyline Pubn., *(978-0-9723493; 978-0-9815846; 978-0-9843602; 978-0-615-66773-7)* P.O. Box 295, Stormville, NY 12582-0295 USA; *Imprints:* Water Forest Press (Wtr Forest) Do not confuse with companies with the same or similar name in Lancaster, OH, Oakland Park, FL
E-mail: skylineeditor@aol.com
Web site: http://www.skylinemagazines.com
Dist(s): **CreateSpace Independent Publishing Platform.**

Skyline Publishing, *(978-0-918981)* Orders Addr.: P.O. Box 1118, Columbia Falls, MT 59912 USA (SAN 669-8662) Tel 406-892-5560; Fax: 406-892-1922; Edit Addr.: a/o Skyline Publishing, 3101 Hwy. 206, Columbia Falls, MT 59912 USA Do not confuse with companies with similar names in Londonderry, NH, Saint George, UT
E-mail: carolynj@rolandcheek.com
Web site: http://www.rolandcheek.com
Dist(s): **Partners/West Book Distributors.**

Skylo, Inc, *(978-0-9774615; 978-0-615-54774-9; 978-0-615-56103-5)* Orders Addr.: P.O. Box 2815, Murfreesboro, TN 37133-2815 USA Tel 615-893-7800; Fax: 615-848-1693; Edit Addr.: 4082 E. Compton Rd., Murfreesboro, TN 37130 USA
E-mail: jjaques@bellsouth.net
Web site: http://www.skyloinc.com
Dist(s): **CreateSpace Independent Publishing Platform.**

SkyMacSyd Publishing, *(978-0-9767244)* P.O. Box 56363, Little Rock, AR 72215 USA.

SkyMark Corp., *(978-0-9769873)* 7300 Penn Ave., Pittsburgh, PA 15208 USA Tel 412-371-0680; Fax: 412-371-0681
E-mail: marie.routledge@skymark.com
Web site: http://www.theseus.biz.

Skyscraper Pr. (children's) *Imprint of* **Windy City Pubs.**

Skyward Bks., *(978-0-9777902)* Orders Addr.: P.O. Box 56734, Riverside, CA 92517 USA Tel 951-782-0711
E-mail: skywardbooks@msn.com.

Skyward Press *See* **Skyward Bks.**

Skyward Publishing Co., *(978-1-881554)* Div. of Paragon Media Corp., 813 Michael St., Kennett, MO 63857 USA (SAN 297-9705) Tel 573-888-5589
E-mail: nfo@skywardpublishing.com
Web site: http://www.skywardpublishing.com; http://www.bransonozarks.com; http://www.brandywineswar.com.

Skyword Pr., *(978-0-9740202)* Orders Addr.: P.O. Box 1714, Hood River, OR 97031 USA; Edit Addr.: 555 Highline Rd., Hood River, OR 97031 USA.

SL Conradt, LLC, *(978-0-615-37381-2)* N1685 Amies Ln., Greenville, WI 54942 USA Tel 920-427-0512
E-mail: shanaleeconradt@gmail.com
Web site: http://www.getfitwithfood.com.

SL Resources, *(978-1-935040; 978-1-935808)* Orders Addr.: P.O. Box 36040, Birmingham, AL 35236 USA Tel 205-985-0760; Fax: 205-403-3969; Toll Free: 800-718-2267; Edit Addr.: 2183 Pkwy. Lake Dr., Hoover, AL 35242 USA
E-mail: products@studentlife.net; bradford@studentlife.net
Web site: http://www.studentlifestore.com.

SLABYPRESS, *(978-0-9774118; 978-0-9792622)* W25952 State Rd., 95, Arcadia, WI 54612 USA Tel 608-323-7335
E-mail: john@slabypress.com
Web site: http://www.slabypress.com.

SLACK, Inc., *(978-0-913590; 978-0-943432; 978-1-55642; 978-1-61711; 978-1-63091)* 6900 Grove Rd., Thorofare, NJ 08086-9447 USA (SAN 201-8632) Tel 856-848-1000; Fax: 856-853-5991; Toll Free: 800-257-8290
E-mail: orders@slackinc.com; lplummer@slackinc.com
Web site: http://www.slackbooks.com
Dist(s): **Barnes & Noble Bks.-Imports**
Coutts Information Services
Ebsco Publishing
Emery-Pratt Co.
Holt, Henry & Co.
Majors, J. A. Co.
Macmillan
Matthews Medical Bk. Co.
Rittenhouse Bk. Distributors.

Slangman Publishing, *(978-1-891888)* Orders Addr.: 12206 Hillslope St., Studio City, CA 91604 USA Tel 818-752-6462; Fax: 413-647-1589
E-mail: info@slangman.com
Web site: http://www.slangman.com
Dist(s): **Delta Systems Company, Inc.**

Slate Falls Pr., LLC, *(978-0-578-04697-6; 978-0-578-07199-2; 978-0-578-10560-4; 978-0-578-12468-1)* P.O. Box 7062, Loveland, CO 80537 USA
Web site: http://www.slatefallspress.com.

Slater Software, Inc., *(978-0-9743149)* 351 Badger Ln., Guffey, CO 80820-9106 USA Tel 719-479-2255 Toll Free: 877-306-6968
E-mail: jim@slatersoftware.com
Web site: http://www.slatersoftware.com.

Slave Labor Bks., *(978-0-943151; 978-1-59362)* 577 S. Market St., San Jose, CA 95113 USA (SAN 668-1204) Tel 408-971-8929; Fax: 408-279-0451; Toll Free: 800-866-8929; *Imprints:* Slave Labor Graphics (Slave Labor Graph)
E-mail: dan@slavelabor.com
Web site: http://www.slavelabor.com
Dist(s): **Diamond Comic Distributors, Inc.**
Diamond Bk. Distributors.

Slave Labor Graphics *Imprint of* **Slave Labor Bks.**

Slavens Enterprises & Marketing Services, LLP *See* **Slavens Enterprises, LLC.**

Slavens Enterprises, LLC., *(978-0-9740348)* 13335 SW Violet Ct., Beaverton, OR 97008-5015 USA Toll Free: 877-526-0904; *Imprints:* Special Editions — Customized Biographies (Special Edns)
E-mail: ricks@slavensmarketing.com.

Sleep Garden, Inc., *(978-0-9752988)* P.O. Box 2365, Menlo Park, CA 94025-2365 USA Toll Free: 877-475-3376
E-mail: marykelley@amsiventures.com
Web site: http://www.zzonesleep.com.

Sleeping Bear Pr., *(978-1-57504; 978-1-886947; 978-1-58536)* Orders Addr.: P.O. Box 20, Chelsea, MI 48118 USA (SAN 253-8466) Tel 734-475-4411; Fax: 734-475-0787; Toll Free: 800-487-2323; Edit Addr.: 27500 Drake Rd., Farmington Hills, MI 48331 USA
E-mail: customerservice@sleepingbearpress.com
Web site: http://www.sleepingbearpress.com
Dist(s): **Booklines Hawaii, Ltd.**
Cherry Lake Publishing
Follett School Solutions
Keith Distributors
MyiLibrary
Partners Bk. Distributing, Inc.
Southern Bk. Service
Urban Land Institute.

Sleepless Warrior Publishing, *(978-0-9747707)* 14989 Grassy Knoll Ct., Woodbridge, VA 22193 USA (SAN 256-1069) Tel 703-897-9394; Fax: 703-897-0696
E-mail: cynthia.little@comcast.net
Web site: http://www.sleeplesswarrior.com.

Sleepy Creek Music, *(978-0-9754633)* P.O. Box 2652, Bloomington, IN 47402-2652 USA Tel 812-334-9901
E-mail: grey@greylarsen.com
Web site: http://www.greylarsen.com.

Sleepy Dog Publishing, *(978-0-9842560)* P.O. Box 2033, Turlock, CA 95381 USA
E-mail: swolsen@sbcglobal.net
Web site: http://sleepydogpublishing.com.

Sleepytown Pr., *(978-0-9826344; 978-0-9831738; 978-1-937260)* 1709 Valley Creek Rd., Anniston, AL 36207 USA Tel 256-365-1416
E-mail: artnbooks73@yahoo.com
Web site: http://www.sleepytownpress.com.

SLG, *(978-0-615-12907-5)* 128 C Main St., Agawam, MA 01001 USA
E-mail: slg_gallery@yahoo.com
Web site: http://geocities.com/slg_gallery/about.

Slhoetree Publishers, Incorporated *See* **Shoetree Publishers, Inc.**

Slice of Lime Publishing, *(978-0-9789475)* 1415 Easy St., New Iberia, LA 70560 USA Tel 337-365-4136; Fax: 337-365-4137
E-mail: jady@sliceoflime.net
Web site: http://www.sliceoflime.net
Dist(s): **Partners Bk. Distributing, Inc.**

Slim Goodbody Corp., *(978-1-887028; 978-0-9708230)* Orders Addr.: P.O. Box 242, Lincolnville, ME 04850 USA Tel 207-230-0399; Fax: 207-230-0795; Toll Free: 888-484-1100
E-mail: john@slimgoodbody.com
Web site: http://www.slimgoodbody.com
Dist(s): **INscribe Digital.**

Slippery Slope Press *See* **Ideate Prairie**

SLM Bk. Publishing, *(978-0-9830039)* Orders Addr.: 21204 Pontiac Trail, No. 16, South Lyon, MI 48178 USA
E-mail: joanna@slmbookpublishing.com
Web site: http://www.slmbookpublishing.com.

Slow on the Draw Productions, *(978-0-615-48469-3; 978-0-615-74591-6)* 12826 Ironstone Way No. 304, Parker, CO 80134 USA Tel 720-838-5176
E-mail: swpaulding@msn.com
Web site: lifelessonsfromandywink.com.

Sluser Publishing, *(978-0-578-03599-4; 978-0-578-03634-2; 978-0-578-04034-9; 978-0-578-06031-6; 978-0-578-08065-9; 978-0-578-10299-3; 978-0-578-10318-1; 978-0-578-12746-0; 978-0-578-12986-0)* 324 Stonegate Cir. N., Chambersburg, PA 17201 USA.

Slusser, Jan *See* **RiverCreek Bks., Inc.**

SM Ediciones (ESP) *(978-84-348; 978-84-404; 978-84-398; 978-84-675) Dist. by* **Continental Bk.**

SM Ediciones (ESP) *(978-84-348; 978-84-404; 978-84-398; 978-84-675) Dist. by* **Mariuccia Iaconi Bk Imports.**

SM Ediciones (ESP) *(978-84-348; 978-84-404; 978-84-398; 978-84-675) Dist. by* **AIMS Intl.**

SM Ediciones (ESP) *(978-84-348; 978-84-404; 978-84-398; 978-84-675) Dist. by* **Lectorum Pubns.**

SM Ediciones (ESP) *(978-84-348; 978-84-404; 978-84-398; 978-84-675) Dist. by* **IBD Ltd.**

Small Bear Publishing, *(978-0-9801662)* P.O. Box 842, Livingston, MT 59047 USA
E-mail: BarringtonBear@q.com
Web site: http://www.travelswithbarrington.com.

Small Beer Pr., *(978-1-931520; 978-1-61873)* 150 Pleasant St. #306, Easthampton, MA 01027 USA Fax: 413-203-1636; *Imprints:* Big Mouth House (BigMouthHse)
E-mail: info@smallbeerpress.com; info@bigmouthhouse.net; info@lcrw.net
Web site: http://www.smallbeerpress.com; http://www.bigmouthhouse.net; http://www.lcrw.net; http://www.weightlessbooks.com
Dist(s): **Consortium Bk. Sales & Distribution**
MyiLibrary
Perseus Bks. Group
ebrary, Inc.

Small Fry Beginnings, *(978-0-9651690; 978-1-892703)* Affil. of LightVision Films, Inc., 6625 Hwy. 53 E. Suite No. 410-212, Dawsonville, GA 30534 USA Tel 770-451-7000
E-mail: dennis@smallfrybeginnings.com
Web site: http://www.smallfrybeginnings.com
Dist(s): **Follett School Solutions**
Ingram Entertainment, Inc.
VPD, Inc.
Valley Media, Inc.

Small Fry Productions *See* **Small Fry Beginnings**

Small Horizons *Imprint of* **New Horizon Pr. Pubs., Inc.**

Small Press Distribution *See* **SPD-Small Pr. Distribution**

Small Pr., The, *(978-1-933651)* Div. of Brown Bks. Publishing Group, 16200 N. Dallay Pkwy., No. 170, Dallas, TX 75248 USA Tel 972-381-0009; Fax: 972-248-4336
Dist(s): **BookBaby.**

Small Waters Publishing, *(978-0-9765621)* 14251 75th Ave. SE, Atwater, MN 56209 USA Tel 320-894-7904; Fax: 320-235-6418
E-mail: markp@lakesideprintingandadvertising.com.

Small Wonder Publishing, *(978-0-9899964)* 130 Boniface Dr., Rochester, NY 14620 USA Tel 585-271-3492
E-mail: hdm@smallwonderpublishing.com.

Small Wonders Enterprises, *(978-0-9741888)* 12210 Fairfax Towne Ctr., PMB No. 901, Fairfax, VA 22033 USA Tel 703-352-0226 Do not confuse with Small Wonders Enterprises in Farmington, NM
E-mail: snickerdoodle@erols.com
Web site: http://www.snickerdoodleforkids.com.

Small World Toys, *(978-0-9774677; 978-0-9776034; 978-0-9795081)* P.O. Box 3620, Culver City, CA 90231-3620 USA
Web site: http://www.smallworldtoys.com.

Smallbag Bks., *(978-0-9761631)* Orders Addr.: 2000 Del Sol, Bowie, MD 20721 USA
E-mail: konaapub@yahoo.com
Web site: http://www.younganddebtfree.com.

Smallfellow Pr. *Imprint of* **Tallfellow Pr.**

SmallHorse Pr. *Imprint of* **Equine Graphics Publishing Group**

Smallwood, Edward, *(978-0-9741282)* 1609 Mountain Ashe Ct., Matthews, NC 28105 USA
Web site: http://www.jfrankles.com.

SmallWorld Books *See* **Kudakon Publishing**

Smart & Smarter Publishing, *(978-0-9713530)* P.O. Box 1815, Zillah, WA 98953 USA (SAN 255-3104) Tel 877-807-3703 (phone/fax)
E-mail: daviddunham@smartandsmarter.com; services@smartandsmarter.com
Web site: http://www.smartandsmarter.com.

Smart Data Processing, Inc., *(978-0-9718439)* 14 Molly Pitcher Dr., Manalapan, NJ 07726 USA Tel 732-598-4027; Fax: 732-409-1364
E-mail: info@smartdataprocessing.com
Web site: http://www.smartdataprocessing.com.

Smart Kids *Imprint of* **Penton Overseas, Inc.**

Smart Kids Publishing *See* **Smart Kidz Media, Inc.**

Smart Kidz Media, Inc., *(978-1-891100; 978-1-939658)* 2460 Hobbit Ln., Fallbrook, CA 92028 USA Tel 760-468-1891
Dist(s): **APG Sales & Distribution Services.**

smart Life Ministries, Inc., The, *(978-0-9741091)* 1649 Springhill St., Chillicothe, MO 64601 USA.

Smart Love Pr., LLC, *(978-0-9838664)* 400 E. Randolph St. Suite 1905, Chicago, IL 60601 USA Tel 312-856-0918; Fax: 312-278-0441
E-mail: smartlovepress@gmail.com; marthapieper@smartlovepress.com
Web site: http://www.smartlovepress.com; http://www.mommydaddyihadabaddream.com.

Smart Picks, Inc., *(978-0-9764785)* P.O. Box 771440, Lakewood, OH 44107 USA Tel 216-226-6173; Fax: 216-226-5413
E-mail: games@smartpicks.com.

Smart Poodle Publishing, *(978-0-9800307)* 3436 Pierce St., Hollywood, FL 33021 USA
E-mail: debbie.glade@comcast.net
Web site: http://www.smartpoodlepublishing.com.

Smart Publishing, *(978-0-9761819)* P.O. Box 410894, Chicago, IL 60641 USA Tel 773-616-0267
E-mail: halfbakedsistas@aol.com
Web site: http://www.halfbakedsistas.com.

Smart Smiles Co., The, *(978-0-9722792; 978-0-9723727; 978-0-9762740; 978-0-9763328)* 380 S. Mizner Blvd., No. 1709, Boca Raton, FL 33432 USA Tel 561-347-3075; *Imprints:* Flat Kids (Flat Kids)
Web site: http://www.smartsmilescompany.com.

SmartBook Media, Inc., *(978-1-5105)* 350 5th Ave, 59th Floor, New York, NY 10118 USA Toll Free Fax: 866-449-3445; Toll Free: 866-649-3445
E-mail: linda@weigl.com; samantha.nugent@weigl.com
Web site: http://www.asmartbook.com.

Smartinbooks, Inc., *(978-0-9761765)* Orders Addr.: P.O. Box 729, Paducah, KY 42002-0729 USA; Edit Addr.: 1441 HC Mathis Dr., Paducah, KY 42001 USA
E-mail: hmartin@paducah.com
Web site: http://www.smartinbooks.com.

SmartInk Bks., LLC, *(978-1-932403)* 413 6th Ave., Brooklyn, NY 11215 USA Tel 718-768-3696; Fax: 718-369-0844
E-mail: publisher@smartinkbooks.com
Web site: http://ww.smartinkbooks.com
Dist(s): **Hachette Bk. Group**
Ideals Pubns.
Penton Overseas, Inc.

SmartiPantz Publishing, *(978-0-9747563)* P.O. Box 24014, Minneapolis, MN 55424 USA (SAN 256-0720).

SmartLab *Imprint of* **becker&mayer! books**

S.M.A.R.T.S. Learning System, *(978-0-9709634)* 3208 Eldon Ln., Waco, TX 76710-1204 USA Fax: 254-776-3136
E-mail: edavis5024@worldnet.att.net
Dist(s): **Capstone Pub.**

SMARTseeds Co., LLC, The, *(978-0-9790931)* P.O. Box 100028, Cudahy, WI 53110 USA (SAN 852-4068) Tel 414-433-0500
E-mail: carlos@thesmartseedscompany.com; info@thesmartseedscompany.com
Web site: http://www.thesmartseedscompany.com.

Smartypants Bks., *(978-0-9773550)* P.O. Box 1014, Logandale, NV 89021-1014 USA (SAN 257-3423)
Web site: http://www.smartypants-books.com.

Smartypants Publishing, *(978-0-9792897)* Orders Addr.: P.O. Box 1548, Buckley, WA 98321 USA Tel 253-278-6612
E-mail: christa@smartypantspublishing.com
Web site: http://smartypantspublishing.com.

SmatteringsBks., *(978-0-9800130)* P.O. Box 556, Clarence, NY 14031 USA (SAN 854-9931) Tel 716-818-0324
Web site: http://smatteringsbooks.com/books.html.

SMC Pubns., LLC, *(978-0-9729546)* P.O. Box 2684, Branchville, NJ 07826 USA Tel 973-948-7441 (phone/fax) Do not confuse with companies with the same name in Houston, TX, Garden Grove, CA, Corona, CA, West Long Branch, NJ
E-mail: smcpublications@embarqmail.com
Web site: http://www.magi-call.com.

SMC Publishing *See* **SMC Pubns., LLC**

Publisher Name Index

Smile Time Publishing, (*978-0-9785961*) P.O. Box B, Del Mar, CA 92014 USA
E-mail: ps@peterstrunk.com
Web site: http://www.smile-time.com.

Smile-a-Lot, LLP, (*978-0-9785132*) 1050 Walnut St. #201, Boulder, CO 80302 USA Tel 303-443-2006; Fax: 303-443-9475; *Imprints:* Smiletown Books (Smiletown Bks)
E-mail: chris@smiletownbooks.com
Web site: http://smiletownbooks.com.

SMiles Productions (SMP), LLC, (*978-0-9768456*) 14241 NE Woodinville-Duvall Rd., Woodinville, WA 98072 USA Tel 425-481-8817; Fax: 425-481-8179
E-mail: language@smilesprod.com
Web site: http://www.smilesprod.com.

Smiletown Bks. *Imprint of* **Smile-a-Lot, LLP**

Smiley Co., (*978-0-9629001*) 401 Anglin St., Smiley, TX 78159-0099 USA (SAN 297-4045) Tel 830-587-6623; Fax: 830-587-6113; Toll Free: 800-584-3655
E-mail: npattesonsmiley@the-cia.net.

Smiley Originals *See* **Smiley Co.**

Smith & Assocs., (*978-0-9790817*) 70 Goodwin Cir., Hartford, CT 06105 USA (SAN 852-3886) Tel 860-543-0279; Fax: 860-586-8718
Web site: http://www.morningdovepress.com
Dist(s): **Connecticut River Pr.**

Smith & Daniel, (*978-0-9630463; 978-1-889668*) P.O. Box 8097, Jacksonville, FL 32239-0097 USA Toll Free: 800-330-1325.

Smith & Kraus Pubs., Inc., (*978-0-9622722; 978-1-57525; 978-1-880399; 978-1-936232; 978-1-937738; 978-1-943511*) Orders Addr.: P.O. Box 127, Lyme, NH 03768 USA (SAN 255-1454) Tel 603-643-6431; Toll Free: 877-866-8680; Edit Addr.: 177 Lyme Rd., Hanover, NH 03755 USA
E-mail: marisasmithkraus@gmail.com; boda@sover.net
Web site: http://www.smithandkraus.com.

Smith, Andrea Joy, (*978-0-9764396*) 2447 Mission Ave, Suite B, Carmichael, CA 95608 USA
E-mail: smithfamdent@aol.com
Web site: http://smileagainnow.com; http://inthechairwithdrsmith.com.

Smith, Barbara Maxine, (*978-0-578-11939-7; 978-0-615-85722-0*) 21103 Gary Dr., Apt 114, Castro Valley, CA 94546 USA.

Smith, Bill O., (*978-0-615-56972-7; 978-0-9895238*) 8489 Timbers Trail, Traverse City, MI 49685 USA Tel 313-515-4328
E-mail: bill@billosmith.com.

Smith, Brenda J. Few *See* **Tall Through Bks.**

Smith, C. Brandt, (*978-0-9768020*) 1910 Scenic Rd., Jonesboro, AR 72401-0220 USA Tel 870-933-1908
E-mail: brandt@walnutstreetbaptist.org.

Smith, Deanna *See* **Annade Publishing**

Smith, Debra, (*978-0-9747754*) 1934 Donna Dr., Coupeville, WA 98239 USA.

Smith, Ernest, (*978-0-9729154*) Orders Addr.: 3155 Sharpe Ave. Apt. 304, Memphis, TN 38111-3784 USA
E-mail: ernest725@Hotmail.com.

Smith, Florence B. *See* **Prickly Pr.**

Smith, George Publishing, (*978-0-9740434*) Orders Addr.: 11 Amberwinds Ct., Lakewood, NJ 08701 USA (SAN 255-3716)
E-mail: customer_support@georgesmithpublishing.com
Web site: http://www.georgesmithpublishing.com
Dist(s): **Mountain Bk. Co.**

Smith, Gibbs Publisher *See* **Gibbs Smith, Publisher**

Smith Island Foundation, (*978-0-9754170*) 44108 Bristow Cir., Ashburn, VA 20147 USA Tel 703-729-4462 Phone/Fax
E-mail: books@smithislandfoundation.org; heather@pneumabooks.com
Web site: http://www.smithislandfoundation.org.

Smith, Joseph L., (*978-0-9754985*) 38118 Village 38, Camarillo, CA 93012 USA
E-mail: cayusekid@earthlink.net.

Smith, Kasper, (*978-0-9744519*) 4251 Fischer, Detroit, MI 48214 USA Tel 313-922-1728
E-mail: pastorsmith@dominionintl.org
Web site: http://www.dominionintl.org.

Smith, Keith Bks., (*978-0-9637682; 978-0-9740764*) 1115 E. Main St., Suite 219, Box 8, Rochester, NY 14609 USA Tel 585-473-6776; Fax: 585-482-2496
E-mail: keith@keithsmithbooks.com
Web site: http://www.keithsmithbooks.com.

Smith, Mason, (*978-0-692-02010-4*) 107 Southland Dr., Richmond, KY 40475-2413 USA Tel 859-582-5960
E-mail: mason.smith@eku.edu.

Smith, Michael *See* **East West Discovery Pr.**

Smith, Mildred C., (*978-0-9778641*) 4200 Cathedral Ave, NW, Apt. 610, Washington, DC 20016 USA Tel 202-363-5352
E-mail: mcs29@georgetown.edu.

Smith Novelty Co., Inc., (*978-0-938765; 978-1-59099; 978-1-934954*) Div. of Smith News Co., Inc., 460 Ninth St., San Francisco, CA 94103-4418 USA (SAN 216-2326) Tel 415-861-4900; Fax: 415-861-5683
E-mail: ken@smithnovelty.com; matt@smithnovelty.com
Web site: http://www.smithnovelty.com.

Smith, Patricia, (*978-0-615-74446-9; 978-0-615-76267-8; 978-0-615-76268-5; 978-0-615-87216-2*) 1626 Parkwood Rd, Lakewood, OH 44107 USA Tel 2163769094
Dist(s): **CreateSpace Independent Publishing Platform.**

Smith, Peter Pub., Inc., (*978-0-8446*) Five Lexington Ave., Magnolia, MA 01930 USA (SAN 206-8885) Tel 978-525-3562; Fax: 978-525-3674.

Smith, Ronald J. Sr., (*978-0-9749390*) 1123 S. Thomas St., Apt. 22, Arlington, VA 22204-3640 USA
E-mail: ronaldjay50@gmail.com
Dist(s): **Morris Publishing.**

Smith, S. Pubns., (*978-0-9769320*) P.O. Box 122, Severna Park, MD 21146 USA Tel 410-271-0837; Fax: 410-544-0059
E-mail: stew@stewsmith.com
Web site: http://www.stewsmith.com.

Smith, Sharon, (*978-0-9817615*) 13611 SW 285th Terr., Homestead, FL 33033 USA Tel 786-317-0267
E-mail: dexavior1@msn.com.

Smith, Tyjauna, (*978-0-9760112*) P.O. Box 2230 Misty Woods Rd., Lake Cormorant, MS 38641 USA
E-mail: tyjauna@bellsouth.net
Web site: http://www.authorsden.com/tyjaunalsmith.

Smith, Viveca Publishing, (*978-0-9740551*) PMB No. 131, 3001 S. Hardin Blvd., Suite 110, McKinney, TX 75070-9028 USA Tel 214-793-0089; Fax: 972-562-7559
E-mail: vsmithpublishing@aol.com
Web site: http://www.vivecasmithpublishing.com
Dist(s): **BookBaby**
ebrary, Inc.

Smithfield Capital Corp., (*978-0-9764670*) 219 S. D. St., Hamilton, OH 45013 USA
E-mail: smithfieldcap@msn.com.

Smithfield Press *See* **Princeton Health Pr.**

Smithsonian Institution *Imprint of* **United States Government Printing Office**

†Smithsonian Institution Pr., (*978-0-87474; 978-1-56098; 978-1-58834*) Div. of Smithsonian Institution, Orders Addr.: 22883 Quicksilver Dr., Dulles, VA 20166 USA (SAN 253-3383); Edit Addr.: 750 Ninth St. NW, Suite 4300, Washington, DC 20560-0950 USA (SAN 206-8044) Tel 202-275-2300; Fax: 202-275-2245; 202-275-2274; Toll Free: 800-233-4830 (orders)
Web site: http://www.sipress.si.edu/
Dist(s): **CreateSpace Independent Publishing Platform**
Ebsco Publishing
Penguin Random Hse., LLC.
Random Hse., Inc.
Rowman & Littlefield Publishers, Inc.
Wittenborn Art Bks.; *CIP.*

Smithsonian National Museum of the American Indian, (*978-0-9719163; 978-1-933565*) MRC 590 PO Box 37012, Washington, DC 20013-7012 USA; 4th St. & Independence Ave., SW, Washington, DC 20024
E-mail: nmai-pubs@si.edu
Web site: http://www.americanindian.si.edu
Dist(s): **Consortium Bk. Sales & Distribution**
D.A.P./Distributed Art Pubs.
Fulcrum Publishing.

Smithsonian Science Education Ctr. (SSEC), (*978-1-933008*) 901 D St. SW, Suite 704B, Washington, DC 20024 USA; *Imprints:* Science and Technology Concepts (STC) (Sci & Tech)
E-mail: campbellc@si.edu
Web site: http://www.nsrconline.org; http://carolinacurriculum.com
Dist(s): **Carolina Biological Supply Co.**

Smokestack Bks. (GBR) (*978-0-9548691; 978-0-9551061; 978-0-9554028; 978-0-9575747; 978-0-9571722; 978-0-9927409; 978-0-9560341; 978-0-9564175; 978-0-9568144; 978-0-9929581*) *Dist. by* **Dufour.**

Smooth Sailing Pr., LLC, (*978-1-933660; 978-0-578-01793-8; 978-1-61899*) Orders Addr.: 20519 Sunshine Ln. Suite B, Spring, TX 77388 USA (SAN 257-2680) Tel 281-826-4026 (phone/fax); *Imprints:* Tadpole Press 4 Kids (Tadpole Pr)
E-mail: fwilmoth@smoothsailingpress.com; cmcginnis@smoothsailingpress.com
Web site: http://www.smoothsailingpress.com
Dist(s): **Follett Higher Education Grp.**

SMPR, (*978-0-9767898*) 4800 S. Westshore Blvd., Suite 411, Tampa, FL 33611 USA Tel 813-831-8206 (phone/fax); Toll Free Fax: 866-958-1323 (phone/fax)
E-mail: sonja.moffett@smpr.info
Web site: http://www.smpr.info.

Snake Country Publishing, (*978-0-9635828*) 16748 W. Linden St., Caldwell, ID 83607-9270 USA Tel 208-459-9233
E-mail: snakecountry@mindspring.com
Dist(s): **Caxton Pr.**

Snake Goddess Bks., (*978-0-9744910*) 11431/2 Gladsy Ave., Long Beach, CA 90804 USA.

Snap Bks. *Imprint of* **Capstone Pr., Inc.**

Snapshots in History *Imprint of* **Compass Point Bks.**

Snelsonbks.com, (*978-0-9723935*) 355 N. Diamond Ave., Canon City, CO 81212 USA
E-mail: bs@ris.net
Web site: http://www.snelsonbooks.com.

SNL Publishing, (*978-0-615-48221-7; 978-0-9848368*) 9 Spring Hill Ave., Norwalk, CT 06850 USA Tel 914-671-2252
E-mail: davidalara@aol.com; snlpublishing@aol.com.

Snodgrass, Ruth M., (*978-0-9754867*) 160 Polaris Dr., Dover, OH 44622 USA.

Snojoy Publishing, (*978-0-9743913*) 4509 14th St., Greeley, CO 80634 USA
E-mail: snojoy1@hotmail.com; gnojoy1@hotmail.com.

Snow In Sarasota Publishing, (*978-0-9663335; 978-0-9824611; 978-0-9830362; 978-0-9837685; 978-0-9893840; 978-0-9862979*) 5170 Central Sarasota Pkwy., No.309, Sarasota, FL 34238 USA Tel 941-923-9201; Fax: 941-926-8739
E-mail: sarasota58@aol.com
Web site: http://www.snowinsarasota.com
Dist(s): **AtlasBooks Distribution**
BookMasters Distribution Services (BDS)
Follett School Solutions
MyiLibrary
ebrary, Inc.

Snow Lion Publications, Inc, *Imprint of* **Shambhala Pubns., Inc.**

Snow Tree Bks., (*978-0-9749006*) Orders Addr.: P.O. Box 546, Peabody, MA 01960-7564 USA (SAN 255-965X) Tel 781-592-9866
E-mail: info@snowtreebooks.com
Web site: http://snowtreebooks.com.

Snowbound Bks., (*978-0-9722570*) Orders Addr.: P.O. Box 281327, Lamoille, NV 89828 USA; Edit Addr.: 1291 Country Ln., Lamoille, NV 89828 USA.

Snowbound Pr., Inc., (*978-1-932362*) P.O. Box 698, Littleton, CO 80160-0698 USA Tel 303-347-2869; Fax: 303-386-3232
E-mail: info@snowboundpress.com
Web site: http://www.snowboundpress.com
Dist(s): **Independent Pubs. Group**
Quality Bks., Inc.

Snowman Learning Center, The, (*978-0-9674666*) 6 Carver St., Plymouth, MA 02360-3301 USA Tel 508-746-5993; Fax: 508-746-8097
E-mail: S.Snowmanph.d@worldnet.att.net.

Snowy Day Distribution & Publishing, A, (*978-0-9844681; 978-1-936615*) P.O. Box 2014, Merrimack, NH 03054 USA Tel 603-493-2276
E-mail: salspiritosr@asnowyday.com
Web site: http://www.asnowyday.com.

Snowy Night Pub., (*978-0-9860324*) 44240 Riverview Ridge Dr., Clinton Township, MI 48038 USA
E-mail: yroehler@bookpublishing.com.

Snowy Plains, (*978-0-9791367*) 270 Flodin Rd., Gwinn, MI 49841 USA
E-mail: jwsnowyplains@yahoo.com.

Snuggle Up Bks., (*978-0-9655530*) 3145 Claremore Ave., Long Beach, CA 90808-4421 USA
E-mail: judybelshe@aol.com.

SnuggleBugzzz Pr., (*978-0-615-38169-5*) 21328 Independence Ave., Lakeville, MN 55044 USA Tel 612-910-0190; Fax: 952-985-4151
E-mail: kathylucilejohnson@att.net
Web site: http://www.snugglebugzzz.com
Dist(s): **West.**

Snyder, Vicki, (*978-0-9773187*) 4349 Cimarron Ct., NW, Rochester, MN 55901 USA
E-mail: cctraining@prodigy.net.

Snyder-Winston Pr., (*978-0-9752749*) 23679 Calabasas Rd., No. 186, Calabasas, CA 91302 USA Tel 818-876-0188; Fax: 818-876-0133
E-mail: tedafed@earthlink.net
Web site: http://www.midaskids.com.

SNZ Publishing, (*978-0-9758815*) P.O. Box 32190, Cincinnati, OH 45232 USA (SAN 256-1255)
E-mail: doug@snzpublishing.com
Web site: http://www.snzpublishing.com.

So Pretty In Pink LLC *See* **King Production, A**

So Simple Learning, (*978-0-9772158*) 12463 Rancho Bernardo Rd., PMB 253, San Diego, CA 92128 USA Tel 858-530-5055
E-mail: info@sosimplelearning.com
Web site: http://www.sosimplelearning.com.

Soar Publishing, LLC, (*978-0-9721142; 978-0-9825450; 978-0-9838220; 978-0-9888650; 978-0-9962052*) 16 Austree Ct., Columbia, SC 29229-7581 USA (SAN 255-4437) Tel 803-699-0633 phone; Fax: 803-699-0634 (phone/fax)
E-mail: smithser@bellsouth.net; smithser1@bellsouth.net
Web site: http://www.soarpublishing.com; http://www.titlewave.com; http://titletales.com
Dist(s): **Follett School Solutions.**

Soaring Sparrow Pr., (*978-1-891262*) 11795 SW Crater Loop, Beaverton, OR 97008 USA Tel 503-644-5960
E-mail: sparrowman@earthlink.net
Web site: www.marvinmallard.com.

Social Skill Builder, Inc., (*978-0-9819585*) P.O. Box 2430, Leesburg, VA 20177 USA.

Social Studies Collections *Imprint of* **Capstone Pr., Inc.**

Social Studies Schl. Service, (*978-1-56004; 978-1-57596*) Orders Addr.: 10200 Jefferson Blvd., P.O. Box 802, Culver City, CA 90232-0802 USA (SAN 168-9592) Tel 310-839-2436; Fax: 310-839-2249; Toll Free: 800-421-4246
E-mail: access@socialstudies.com
Web site: http://socialstudies.com
Dist(s): **Follett School Solutions.**

Sociedad de San Pablo (COL) (*978-958-607*) *Dist. by* **St Pauls Alba.**

Sociedad de San Pablo (ESP) *Dist. by* **St Pauls Alba.**

Sociedad General Espanola de Libreria (ESP) (*978-84-7143; 978-84-9778*) *Dist. by* **Distribks Inc.**

Sociedad General Espanola de Libreria (ESP) (*978-84-7143; 978-84-9778*) *Dist. by* **Continental Bk.**

Society for Developmental Education *See* **Staff Development for Educators**

Society For The Understanding Of Early Child Development, (*978-0-9762509*) 39741 Lynn St., Canton, MI 48187 USA (SAN 256-260X) Tel 734-416-0480; Fax: 734-459-5280
E-mail: rsawhney@infotreeservice.com.

Society for Visual Education, Incorporated *See* **S V E & Churchill Media**

Society of Automotive Engineers, Incorporated *See* **SAE Intl.**

Sofia Martinez *Imprint of* **Picture Window Bks.**

Soft Saints, Inc., (*978-0-9769519*) 5753-G Santa Ana Canyon Rd., No. 378, Anaheim Hills, CA 92807 USA Tel 714-505-3127; Fax: 714-838-5857
E-mail: teri@softsaints.com
Web site: http://www.softsaints.com.

Soft Skull Pr. *Imprint of* **Counterpoint LLC**

SoftPlay, Inc., (*978-1-931312; 978-1-59292*) 3535 W. Peterson Ave., Chicago, IL 60659 USA (SAN 858-4982) Tel 773-509-0707; Fax: 773-509-0404
E-mail: sales@softplayforkids.com
Web site: http://www.softplayforkids.com.

SoGo Creation, (*978-0-9852052; 978-1-941006*) 6830 Via Marinero, Carlsbad, CA 92009 USA Tel 760-710-7144
E-mail: sogocreation@yahoo.com.

Soho Pr., Inc., (*978-0-939149; 978-1-56947; 978-1-61695*) 853 Broadway, New York, NY 10003 USA (SAN 662-5088) Tel 212-260-1900; Fax: 212-260-1902; *Imprints:* Soho Teen (Soho Teen)
E-mail: soho@sohopress.com
Web site: http://www.sohopress.com
Dist(s): **MyiLibrary**
Penguin Random Hse., LLC.
Random Hse., Inc.

Soho Publishing Company *See* **Sixth&Spring Bks.**

Soho Teen *Imprint of* **Soho Pr., Inc.**

Soil Science Society of America *See* **ASA-CSSA-SSSA**

SoJam Pr., (*978-0-9761477*) P.O. Box 25163, Woodbury, MN 55125-9998 USA (SAN 256-2359)
E-mail: sojam@comcast.net
Web site: http://www.sojampress.com.

Sojourner Publishing, Inc., (*978-0-9701726; 978-0-9773156; 978-0-9824741*) Orders Addr.: P.O. Box 1575, Wake Forest, NC 27588 USA; Edit Addr.: 1208 Chilmark Ave., Wake Forest, NC 27587 USA Do not confuse with companies with the same name in Arlington, WA, Clarkston, MI
E-mail: wandam123@yahoo.com
Web site: http://www.thepaperjourney.com.

Sojourner Stories, (*978-0-9896660*) 4225 Piedmont Mesa Rd., Claremont, CA 91711 USA Tel 562-305-9119
E-mail: sojournerstories@gmail.com.

Sol de Oro Pubns., (*978-0-9754261*) 1004 S. Quinn Ct., Gilbert, AZ 85296-8818 USA Tel 480-892-0582
E-mail: SoldeOroPublications@yahoo.com
Web site: http://www.SoldeOroPublications.50megs.com.

Solar Publishing LLC, (*978-0-9785326*) P.O. Box 2116, Ellicott City, MD 21041 USA (SAN 850-8089) Tel 410-493-1872
E-mail: robyn@solarpub.com
Web site: http://www.solarpub.com
Dist(s): **BookBaby.**

Sole Bks., (*978-0-9844257; 978-1-938591*) P.O. Box 10445, Beverly Hills, CA 90213 USA Tel 424-283-4299
E-mail: info@wildsoccer.com; sales@solebooks.com; tally@wildsoccer.com
Web site: http://www.wildsoccerbunch.com; http://www.solebooks.com.

Sole Reason Publishing, LLC, (*978-0-615-43937-2; 978-0-615-58759-2; 978-0-615-69104-6*) PO Box 78313, Indianapolis, IN 46278 USA Tel 317-847-1884
E-mail: shonda@shondasbookshelf.com
Web site: http://www.shondasbookshelf.com; www.boldensmith.com; www.sabrinahfaith.com; www.solereasonpublishing.com
Dist(s): **CreateSpace Independent Publishing Platform.**

Solebury Press *See* **Thompson Mill Pr.**

Solel Pubns., (*978-0-9748332*) 309 Concord Ave., Oceanside, NY 11572 USA Tel 516-678-9778.

Solemn Word Publishing, (*978-0-9759717*) P.O. Box 301, Grant City, MO 64456 USA
E-mail: cjblanchard@solemnword.com
Web site: http://www.solemnword.com.

Soler, Michael, (*978-0-9795469*) 74 Sashington Heights Rd., Washington, NH 03280 USA (SAN 853-6996).

Solibros, (*978-0-9755945*) 2215 Peachtree N. Ct., Atlanta, GA 30338 USA
Web site: http://www.solibros.com.

Solid Ground Christian Bks., (*978-0-9710169; 978-1-932474; 978-1-59925*) Orders Addr.: P.O. Box 660132, Vestavia Hills, AL 35266 USA Tel 205-443-0311; Fax: 775-822-5917; Toll Free: 877-666-9469; Edit Addr.: 715 Oak Grove Rd., Birmingham, AL 35209-6503 USA
E-mail: solid-ground-books@juno.com; solid_ground_books@yahoo.com; scgbclassics@juno.com; sgcb@charter.net
Web site: http://www.solid-ground-books.com.

Solid Rock Bks. *Imprint of* **Trumpet In Zion Publishing**

Solid Rock Publishing *See* **Trumpet In Zion Publishing**

SolidA, Inc., (*978-0-9677328*) 9339 Paradise Rd., Kewaskum, WI 53040 USA Tel 262-692-9609
E-mail: deanne@solida.net
Web site: http://www.solida.net.

Solitude Pr., (*978-1-928874*) 212 Brooks St., Williamsburg, VA 23185 USA Tel 757-564-1365
E-mail: zander67@cox.net.

Solomon Schechter Day Schl. of Greater Boston, (*978-0-9836623*) 60 Stein Cir., Newton, MA 02459 USA Tel 617-964-7765
E-mail: amy.bardack@ssdsboston.org
Web site: www.ssdsboston.org.

Solomon Waterwine, LLC, (*978-1-934195*) 30 Westgate Pkwy. Suite No. 336, Asheville, NC 28806 USA
E-mail: solomonwaterwine@yahoo.com
Web site: http://www.solomonwaterwine.com.

Solomon's Bks., (*978-0-9763871; 978-0-9827949; 978-0-9838687; 978-0-615-67340-0*) 885 New Hope Dr., Suite 100, Hampton, GA 30228 USA.

Solovisions *Imprint of* **Comic Library International**

Solsidan Hse., (*978-0-9741620*) Orders Addr.: 104 7th St., Colorado Springs, CO 80906 USA; Edit Addr.: 475 Sunnyside Ave., Eugene, OR 97404 USA
E-mail: solsidanhouse@yahoo.com
Web site: http://www.solsidanhouse.com.

Soltz, Sheri, (*978-0-615-43389-9; 978-0-615-48117-3; 978-0-615-52334-7; 978-0-615-57118-8*) 1847 Puterbaugh St., San Diego, CA 92103 USA Tel 619-295-5581
Dist(s): **CreateSpace Independent Publishing Platform**
Dummy Record Do Not USE!!!!.

Solutions for Human Services, LLC, (*978-0-9764802*) 25 Vernon Dr., Warren, PA 16365 USA Tel 814-726-1228
E-mail: lindab@westpa.net.

Solving Light Bks., (*978-0-9705438; 978-0-692-26013-5*) 727 Mountalban Dr., Annapolis, MD 21409-4646 USA Tel 410-757-4630
E-mail: rbowlej@comcast.net; nancygjohnson@comcast.net
Web site: http://www.solvinglight.com; http://www.theparthenoncode.com
Dist(s): **BookBaby**
Send The Light Distribution LLC.

Some Kids I Know, (*978-0-9768230*) Div. of Some Kids I Know, LLC, W323 N8164 Northcrest Dr., Hartland, WI 53029 USA Tel 262-966-2582
E-mail: thorst@wi.rr.com.

Some Kids I Know, LLC, (*978-0-9768230*) W323 N8164 Northcrest Dr., Hartland, WI 53029 USA.

Someday Ranch, (*978-0-9910180*) P.O. Box 414, Wauna, WA 98395 USA Tel 253-380-0663
E-mail: zookeeper99@comcast.net.

†**Somerset Pubs., Inc.**, (*978-0-403*) 1532 State St., Santa Barbara, CA 93101 USA (SAN 204-6105) Toll Free: 800-937-7947
Dist(s): **North American Bk. Distributors**; *CIP*.

Somerville Hse. Bks., Ltd. (CAN) (*978-0-921051; 978-1-58184; 978-1-895897; 978-1-55286; 978-1-894042*) *Dist. by* **Penguin Grp USA.**

Something Else Publishing, (*978-0-615-55445-7; 978-0-615-60346-9; 978-0-9856877*) 20031 NW 5th St., Pembroke Pines, FL 33029 USA Tel 954-435-8171
Dist(s): **CreateSpace Independent Publishing Platform**
Dummy Record Do Not USE!!!!.

Sonfire Media, LLC, (*978-0-9825773; 978-0-9891064*) 974 E. Stuart Dr. Suite D, PMB 232, Galax, VA 24333 USA; *Imprints:* Taberah Press (Taberah Pr)
Web site: http://www.sonfiremedia.com.

Song Revival Fellowship & Ministries, (*978-0-9673093; 978-0-9823344*) Div. of LaVerne Tripp Ministries, Orders Addr.: P.O. Box 899, Gallatin, TN 37066 USA Tel 615-230-7577; Fax: 615-230-7939; Edit Addr.: 2105 Cages Bend Rd., Gallatin, TN 37066 USA
E-mail: kim@lavernetripp.com
Web site: http://www.lavernetripp.com.

Songadh, Jain Swadhyay Mandir, (*978-0-9748681*) 304 Tall Oak Trail, Tarpon Springs, FL 34688 USA Tel 602-863-1073; 727-376-7290; Fax: 602-863-3557; 727-843-8157
E-mail: kahanguru@hotmail.com.

Songbird Pr., (*978-0-9720913*) Orders Addr.: P.O. Box 99, Freeport, ME 04032 USA Fax: 207-373-1128
Web site: http://www.songbirdpress.biz.

Sonic Sword Productions, (*978-0-9797715*) 1089-A Alice Dr., Suite 327, Sumter, SC 29150 USA Tel 803-983-5084
E-mail: john@jhollandbooks.com
Web site: http://jhollandbooks.com; http://rjwargames.com.

Sonnenschein Bks. *Imprint of* **Black Forest Pr.**

Sono Nis Pr. (CAN) (*978-0-919203; 978-0-919462; 978-0-9690282; 978-1-55039*) *Dist. by* **Orca Bk Pub.**

SonoMagnetics, (*978-1-930216*) P.O. Box 22, Rumney, NH 03266-0022 USA Tel 603-204-5273
E-mail: bap@sonomagnetics.com
Web site: http://www.nuenergy.org; http://www.sonomagnetics.com.

Son-Rise Pubns. & Distribution Co., (*978-0-936369*) 51 Greenfield Rd., New Wilmington, PA 16142 USA (SAN 698-0031) Tel 724-946-9057; Fax: 724-946-8700; Toll Free: 800-358-0777
Web site: http://www.softspace.com/steelvalley; http://www.sonrisepublications.com.

Sonrise Publishing, (*978-0-9724458; 978-0-9845663; 978-0-9914347*) 131 Galleon St. # 2B, Marina Dl Rey, CA 90292-5973 USA (SAN 254-8348) Do not confuse with companies with the same or similar names in Corte Madera, CA, Ashland, OH
E-mail: annsonrise@aol.com
Web site: http://www.sonrisepublishing.com; http://www.annhamiltonwallace.com
Dist(s): **BookMasters, Inc.**

Sonship Pr. *Imprint of* **21st Century Pr.**

†**Sophia Institute Pr.**, (*978-0-918477; 978-1-928832; 978-1-933184; 978-1-62282*) Orders Addr.: P.O. Box 5284, Manchester, NH 03108 USA (SAN 657-7172) Tel 603-641-9344; Fax: 603-641-8108; Toll Free: 800-888-9344 Do not confuse with Sophia Pr., Durham, NH
E-mail: production@sophiainstitute.com
Web site: http://www.sophiainstitute.com
Dist(s): **eBookit.com**; *CIP*.

Sophie's Tales, LLC, (*978-0-578-03818-6; 978-0-9851575*) 665 S Skinker Blvd, Saint Louis, MO 63105 USA Tel 516-242-1466
E-mail: mpaticoff@sophiestales.com
Web site: www.sophiestales.com.

Sophrose Entertainment Inc., (*978-0-9800736*) P.O. Box 1989, Cape Canaveral, FL 32920-1989 USA (SAN 855-1286) Tel 321-459-3442 Toll Free: 888-599-7483
E-mail: mail@sophrose.com
Web site: http://www.sophrose.com.

Sopris West Educational Services *See* **Cambium Education, Inc.**

Sora Publishing, (*978-0-9765756*) 1800 Atlantic Blvd., A-405, Key West, FL 33040-5708 USA (SAN 256-4157) Tel 305-296-6699
E-mail: sorapublishing@comcast.net
Web site: http://www.sorapublishing.com.

Sorcerer's Pr., The, (*978-0-9667747*) 6 Berks St., Catasauqua, PA 18032-1532 USA.

Sorella Bks., (*978-0-9767351*) P.O. Box 454, Plantsville, CT 06479 USA
E-mail: sorellabooks@yahoo.com
Web site: http://www.sorellabooks.com.

Sorenson, E. Randy, (*978-0-615-16939-2*) 3053 Frederick Pl., West Valley City, UT 84119 USA
Web site: http://www.firstreindeer.com.

Sortis Publishing, (*978-0-9772025; 978-0-9827986*) 2193 E. Claxton Ave., Gilbert, AZ 85297 USA (SAN 256-923X) Tel 480-310-8316; Fax: 480-279-5851
E-mail: tradewebb@wydebeam.com
Web site: http://www.sortispublishing.com.

Soul Attitude Press, (*978-0-578-06870-1; 978-1-939181*) P.O. Box 1656, Pinellas Park, FL 33782 USA
Web site: http://www.johnrehg.com.

Soul Family Travels *See* **SFT Pubns.**

Soul Pubns., (*978-0-937327*) 232 Rockford St., Mt. Airy, NC 27030 USA (SAN 658-8050) Tel 336-786-4118 (phone/fax); 3220 Lazelle St. #114, STURGIS, SD 57785 Tel 605-720-0986
Dist(s): **Lulu Enterprises Inc.**

Soul Vision Works Publishing, (*978-0-9659538; 978-0-9816254*) P.O. Box 360063, Brooklyn, NY 11236 USA Tel 718-493-7981; Toll Free: 888-789-6757; *Imprints:* Vision Works Publishing (Vis Wrks)
E-mail: info@visionworksonline.net
Web site: http://www.visionworksonline.net.

Soulful Storytellers, Inc., (*978-0-9851628*) 3263 Ave. H, Brooklyn, NY 11210 USA Tel 718-781-7560
E-mail: soulmuze@gmail.com.

Soulo Communications, (*978-0-9778209; 978-0-9825607*) Div. of Soulo Communications, Orders Addr.: 2112 Broadway St., NE Suite 100, Minneapolis, MN 55413-3036 USA Tel 612-788-4341; Fax: 612-788-4347
E-mail: tomh@soulocommunications.com
Web site: http://www.soulocommunications.com
Dist(s): **Partners Pubs. Group, Inc.**

SoulSong Publishing, (*978-0-9793113*) Div. of SoulSong Enterprises, Orders Addr.: P.O. Box 715, Crestone, CO 81131 USA
E-mail: soulsongpublishing@yahoo.com
Web site: http://www.soulsong.org.

Sound Concepts, Inc., (*978-1-887938; 978-1-933057; 978-1-936631*) 782 S. Automall Dr. Unit A, American Fork, UT 84003 USA Tel 801-225-9520; Fax: 801-343-3301; Toll Free: 800-544-7044
E-mail: mjo@soundconcepts.com; jca@soundconcepts.com; jason@soundconcepts.com; vs@soundconcepts.com; edr@soundconcepts.com
Web site: http://www.soundconcepts.com.

Sound Craft Designs, (*978-0-9771357*) P.O. Box 1563, Poway, CA 92074-1563 USA Tel 858-842-1985
E-mail: info@exploreguitar.com
Web site: http://www.exploreguitar.com.

Sound Library *Imprint of* **AudioGO**

Sound Reading *Imprint of* **Sound Reading Solutions**

Sound Reading Solutions, (*978-0-9704183; 978-0-9742485; 978-0-9743384*) 379 Turkey Hill Rd., Ithaca, NY 14850 USA Tel 607-273-1370 (phone/fax); Toll Free: 800-801-1954; *Imprints:* Sound Reading (Sound Read)
E-mail: info@soundreading.com
Web site: http://www.soundreading.com.

Sound Room Pubs., Inc., (*978-1-883049; 978-1-58472*) Orders Addr.: P.O. Box 3168, Falls Church, VA 22043 USA Tel 540-722-2535; Fax: 540-722-0903; Toll Free: 800-643-0295; Edit Addr.: 100 Weems Ln., Winchester, VA 22601 USA; *Imprints:* In Audio (In Aud)
E-mail: commuterslib@worldnet.att.net
Web site: http://www.inaudio.biz/
Dist(s): **Distributors, The**
Findaway World, LLC
Follett Media Distribution
Follett School Solutions.

Sound View Press *See* **Falk Art Reference**

Soundcheck Bks. LLP (GBR) (*978-0-9566420; 978-0-9575700; 978-0-9571442*) *Dist. by* **SCB Distributo.**

Soundprints, (*978-0-924483; 978-1-56899; 978-1-931465; 978-1-59249; 978-1-60727*) Div. of Trudy Corp., 353 Main Ave., Norwalk, CT 06851 USA Fax: 203-846-1776; Toll Free: 800-228-7839; *Imprints:* Little Soundprints (Little Sound)
Web site: http://www.soundprints.com
Dist(s): **Follett School Solutions**
Cengage Gale
Learning Connection, The.

Sounds True, Inc., (*978-1-56455; 978-1-59179; 978-1-60407; 978-1-62203*) Orders Addr.: P.O. Box 8010, Boulder, CO 80306-8010 USA; Edit Addr.: 413 S. Arthur Ave., Louisville, CO 80027 USA (SAN 850-3532) Tel 303-665-3151; Fax: 303-665-5292; Toll Free: 800-333-9185
E-mail: rhiannonh@soundstrue.com; jaimes@soundstrue.com
Web site: http://www.soundstrue.com.

Sounds Write Productions, Inc., (*978-0-9626286; 978-1-890161*) 6685 Norman Ln., San Diego, CA 92120 USA Tel 619-697-6120; Fax: 619-697-6124; Toll Free: 800-976-8639
E-mail: soundswrite@aol.com; info@soundswrite.com
Web site: http://www.soundswrite.com.

SourceAid, LLC, (*978-0-9771957*) Orders Addr.: P.O. Box 430, Osterville, MA 02655 USA Tel 508-428-3150 Toll Free: 877-687-2324; Edit Addr.: 1284 A Main St., Osterville, MA 02655 USA
E-mail: info@sourceaid.com
Web site: http://www.sourceaid.com
Dist(s): **Independent Pubs. Group.**

Sourcebook Project, The, (*978-0-915554; 978-0-9600712*) P.O. Box 107, Glen Arm, MD 21057 USA (SAN 201-7652) Tel 410-668-6047
Web site: http://www.science-frontiers.com.

Sourcebooks Casablanca *Imprint of* **Sourcebooks, Inc.**

†**Sourcebooks, Inc.**, (*978-0-942061; 978-0-9629162; 978-0-9629803; 978-1-57071; 978-1-57248; 978-1-58182; 978-1-883518; 978-1-887166; 978-1-888952; 978-1-4022; 978-1-932783; 978-1-62047; 978-1-4926*) 1935 Brookdale Rd., Suite 139, Naperville, IL 60563 USA (SAN 666-7864) Tel 630-961-3900; Fax: 630-961-2168; Toll Free: 800-727-8866; *Imprints:* Sourcebooks Casablanca (Casablanca); Sourcebooks Landmark (Sourcebks Land); Sourcebooks MediaFusion (MediaFusion); Sourcebooks Jabberwocky (Srcbks Jabber); Marianne Richmond Studios, Incorporated (MarianneRich); Cumberland House (Cumberland)
E-mail: info@sourcebooks.com
Web site: http://www.sourcebooks.com/
Dist(s): **Ebsco Publishing**
Follett School Solutions
MyiLibrary; *CIP*.

Sourcebooks Jabberwocky *Imprint of* **Sourcebooks, Inc.**

Sourcebooks Landmark *Imprint of* **Sourcebooks, Inc.**

Sourcebooks MediaFusion *Imprint of* **Sourcebooks, Inc.**

South Asia Bks., (*978-0-8364; 978-0-88386*) P.O. Box 502, Columbia, MO 65205 USA (SAN 207-4044) Tel 573-474-0116; Fax: 573-474-8124
E-mail: sabooks@juno.com
Web site: http://www.southasiabooks.com.

South Carolina Geographic Alliance, (*978-0-9768247*) Ctr. of Excellence for Geographic Education, Orders Addr.: Department of Geography, Univ. of S. C., Columbia, SC 29208 USA Toll Free: 888-895-2023
Web site: http://www.cas.sc.edu/cege/.

South Dakota State Historical Society Pr. *Imprint of* **South Dakota State Historical Society Pr.**

South Dakota State Historical Society Pr., (*978-0-9622621; 978-0-9715171; 978-0-9749195; 978-0-9777955; 978-0-9798940; 978-0-9822749; 978-0-9845041; 978-0-9846505; 978-0-9852817; 978-0-9852905; 978-0-9860355; 978-1-941813*) 900 Governors Dr., Pierre, SD 57501 USA; *Imprints:* South Dakota State Historical Society Press (S Dak St Hist Soc Pr)
E-mail: sdshspress@state.sd.us; rodger.hartley@state.sd.us
Web site: http://www.sdshspress.com
Dist(s): **BookBaby.**

South Florida Art Ctr., Inc., (*978-0-9719492*) 924 Lincoln Rd., Suite 205, Miami Beach, FL 33139-2609 USA
Web site: http://www.artcentersf.org.

South Hadley Publishing, (*978-0-9761844*) Orders Addr.: P.O. Box 681, South Hadley, MA 01075 USA Tel 413-433-6456; Edit Addr.: 18 Maria Dr., South Hadley, MA 01075 USA
E-mail: price@bookshappen.com
Web site: http://bookshappen.com.

South River Pr., (*978-0-9770764*) P.O. Box 392, Indianola, IA 50125-5012 USA (SAN 256-6982) Tel 515-962-9375.

Southall, Twyla, (*978-0-9765501*) 5837 Karric Sq. Dr., Dublin, OH 43016 USA
E-mail: twyla@tsouthall.com
Web site: http://www.tsouthall.com.

Southeast Media, (*978-1-888141*) 87 Piedmont Dr., Palm Coast, FL 32164-7085 USA
E-mail: Reachment@msn.com
Web site: http://www-gout-haters.com.

Southern Acres Academy, (*978-0-615-17522-5*) 4955 Hwy. 4, Davenport, NE 68335ed USA
Dist(s): **Lulu Enterprises Inc.**

Southern Girl Media, (*978-0-9744423*) Orders Addr.: P.O. Box 373, Festus, MO 63028 USA Tel 760-535-2640
Web site: http://www.masonweaver.com
Dist(s): **Executive Bks.**

Southern Lion Bks., (*978-0-9662454; 978-0-9794203; 978-1-935272*) 1070 Jordan Rd., Madison, GA 30650 USA Tel 706-474-1667 (Tel. & Fax)
E-mail: taniamcclain@yahoo.com; mcclain2@bellsouth.net
Web site: http://www.southernlionbooks.com.

Southfarm Pr., (*978-0-913337*) Div. of Haan Graphic Publishing Services, Ltd., P.O. Box 1296, Middletown, CT 06457 USA (SAN 283-4146) Tel 860-346-8798
E-mail: southfar@ix.netcom.com
Web site: http://www.war-books.com; http://www.wandahaan.com.

Southgate Pubs. (GBR) (*978-1-85741*) *Dist. by* **Parkwest Pubns.**

Southpaw Books LLC, (*978-0-9777720*) Southpaw Books LLC, Maplewood, NJ 07040 USA (SAN 850-1017) Tel 973-313-0843; Fax: 973-313-0843
E-mail: info@southpawbooks.com
Web site: http://southpawbooks.com.

Southport Historical Society, Inc., (*978-1-892444*) P.O. Box 10014, Southport, NC 28461-0014 USA Tel 910-457-6940
E-mail: Furstenau@earthlink.net.

Southwest guns & stuff, (*978-0-9747407*) 4212 Lanshire Ct., Grand Prairie, TX 75052-3164 USA.

Southwest Legal Services, (*978-0-9644908; 978-0-9843383*) Div. of Charlynn Publishing Co., Inc., Orders Addr.: P.O. Box 57091, Tucson, AZ 85732 USA Tel 520-795-1414; Edit Addr.: 4152 E. Fifth St., Tucson, AZ 85711 USA
E-mail: swlsorders@yahoo.com
Web site: http://www.southwestlegalservices.com; http://www.bustedbythefeds.com
Dist(s): **Charlynn Publishing Co., Inc.**

Southwest Parks & Monuments Association *See* **Western National Parks Assn.**

SouthWest Pubns., (*978-1-934345*) Div. of NF Publishing, P.O. Box 782, Kingsport, TN 37662 USA Tel 423-765-1416; Fax: 800-807-9203; Toll Free Fax: 800-807-9203; Toll Free: 800-807-9203
Web site: http://www.southwestpublications.net.

Southwestern Pr., Inc, (*978-0-923176*) Orders Addr.: P.O. Box 4297, Carlsbad, CA 92018-4297 USA (SAN 251-5601) Tel 760-434-8858; Fax: 760-434-8888
E-mail: sharon@southwesternpress.com
Web site: http://www.southwesternpress.com/.

Souvenir Pr. Ltd. (GBR) (*978-0-285*) *Dist. by* **IPG Chicago.**

Sovereign Grace Pubs., Inc., (*978-1-878442; 978-1-58960*) P.O. Box 4998, Lafayette, IN 47903-4998 USA (SAN 299-6847) Toll Free: 800-447-9142 Do not confuse with Sovereign Grace Pubns., Lexington, KY
E-mail: jaygreenxx@quest.net
Web site: http://www.sovgracepub.com.

Sovereign Press *See* **Margaret Weis Productions, Ltd.**

Sow Forth Publishing LLC, (*978-0-9822262*) P.O. Box 303, Lewis Center, OH 43035-9462 USA (SAN 857-7358)
E-mail: sowforth@insight.rr.com
Dist(s): **AtlasBooks Distribution.**

Sowash, Rick Publishing Co., (*978-0-9762412*) 338 Milton St. # 1, Cincinnati, OH 45202-0971 USA Toll Free: 888-255-2764
E-mail: rick@sowash.com
Web site: http://www.sowash.com.

Soxwings Publishing, (*978-0-615-20974-6*) 414 Executive Ctr. Blvd., Suite 105, El Paso, TX 79902 USA Tel 915-533-3827; Fax: 915-533-3745; Toll Free: 866-416-3827
E-mail: bobtjr@yahoo.com.

SP Family Productions, LLC, (*978-0-9773134*) 5 Knute Drive, Andover, NJ 07821-3912 USA Tel 973-479-6111
E-mail: seancanning@hotmail.com
Web site: http://www.seancanning.com.

Space Penguins *Imprint of* **Stone Arch Bks.**

Spalding Education International, (*978-1-935289*) 23335 N. 18th Dr., Suite 102, Phoenix, AZ 85027-6301 USA (SAN 857-0310) Tel 623-434-1204; Fax: 623-434-1208
E-mail: jsexton@spalding.org; kporter@spalding.org
Web site: http://www.spalding.org.

Spanish Language Texts, Inc., (*978-0-9710710*) Orders Addr.: P.O. Box 1088, New York, NY 10040 USA; Edit Addr.: 19 Seaman Ave. 2M, New York, NY 10034 USA
Web site: http://www.spanishlanguagetexts.com
Dist(s): **Lectorum Pubns., Inc.**

Spanish Pubs., LLC., 8871 SW 129 Terr., Miami, FL 33176 USA Tel 305-233-3365; Fax: 305-251-1310
E-mail: mariela@spanishpublishers.net
Web site: www.spanishpublishers.net.

Spanish-Live, (*978-0-9816973*) 1033 Imperial Dr., Morgantown, WV 26508 USA
E-mail: lorena@spanish-live.com
Web site: http://www.spanish-live.com.

Spann Productions, (*978-0-9772209*) P.O. Box 10412, Bakersfield, CA 93389 USA Tel 661-832-2135 (phone/fax)
E-mail: spannlake@aol.com.

SpanPress, Inc., (*978-1-58045; 978-1-887578*) 5722 S. Flamingo Rd., Suite 277, Cooper City, FL 33330 USA Tel 305-592-7913; Fax: 305-477-5632; Toll Free: 800-585-8384
Dist(s): **Continental Bk. Co., Inc.**
Lectorum Pubns., Inc.

Spark Notes *Imprint of* **Sterling Publishing Co., Inc.**

Spark Publishing Group *Imprint of* **Sterling Publishing Co., Inc.**

Sparkhouse Family *Imprint of* **Augsburg Fortress, Pubs.**

Sparkledoll Productions, (*978-0-9747832*) P.O. Box 56173, Virginia Beach, VA 23456 USA Tel 757-718-3095
E-mail: books@sparkledoll.com
Web site: http://www.sparkledoll.com/publishing.

Sparklesoup LLC, (*978-0-9714776; 978-1-932379; 978-1-59748; 978-1-61814*) 11700 W. Charleston Blvd., Ste. 170-95, Las Vegas, NV 89135 USA; *Imprints:* The Edge (TheEdge)
E-mail: sparklesoup@aol.com
Web site: http://www.sparklesoup.com; http://www.theedgebooks.com; http://www.kailingowbooks.com
Dist(s): **CreateSpace Independent Publishing Platform**
Lightning Source, Inc.

Sparklesoup Studios, Incorporated *See* **Sparklesoup LLC**

Sparkling Bks. (GBR) (*978-1-907230*) *Dist. by* **Silvermine Int.**

Sparkling Pr., (*978-0-9774855*) 137 E. Curtice St., St. Paul, MN 55107 USA Tel 651-227-5248.

SparkNotes *Imprint of* **Barnes & Noble, Inc.**

Sparks Fly, (*978-0-9789445*) 609 Myrtle Ave., Apt 3A, Brooklyn, NY 11205-1470 USA Toll Free: 866-556-2432
E-mail: info@sparksfly.org
Web site: http://www.sparksfly.org.

Sparrow Media Group, Inc., (*978-0-9719304; 978-0-9786018; 978-0-9829526*) P.O. Box 44272, Eden Prairie, MN 55344-4272 USA Tel 952-953-9166
Web site: http://www.sparrowmediagroup.com.

SPC Bks. *Imprint of* **RPJ & Co., Inc.**

SPCK Publishing (GBR) (*978-0-281; 978-0-7459; 978-0-85969; 978-1-902694*) *Dist. by* **Pilgrim OH.**

SPD-Small Pr. Distribution, (*978-0-914068*) 1341 Seventh St., Berkeley, CA 94710-1409 USA (SAN 204-5826) Tel 510-524-1668; Fax: 510-524-0852; Toll Free: 800-869-7553 (orders)
E-mail: orders@spdbooks.org
Web site: http://www.spdbooks.org.

Speak *Imprint of* **Penguin Young Readers Group**

Speakeasy Comics (CAN) (*978-0-9737039; 978-0-9738386*) *Dist. by* **Diamond Book Dists.**

Speak-Easy Publishing, LLC, (*978-0-9714433; 978-0-9754977*) Orders Addr.: P.O. Box 11377, Takoma Park, MD 20913 USA Tel 202-723-1317
E-mail: jgduarte@speakeasypublishing.com; info@speakeasypublishing.com
Web site: http://www.speakeasypublishing.com
Dist(s): **Lyrical Liquor Productions.**

Special Edition Studios, Inc., (*978-0-9759013*) P.O. Box 7216, Sebring, FL 33872-0104 USA
Web site: http://www.sestudios.com.

Special Editions — Customized Biographies *Imprint of* **Slavens Enterprises, LLC.**

Special Kids Company, Incorporated *See* **Anythings Possible, Inc.**

Special Reads for Special Needs, (*978-0-9702698; 978-0-9795922*) 12025 Merganser Dr., Cincinnati, OH

45246-1542 USA Tel 513-541-7617; Fax: 513-541-2543; Toll Free: 866-553-2042
E-mail: specialreads@aol.com
Web site: http://www.specialreads.com.

Specialized Printing, LLC, *(978-0-615-38944-8)* 2430 NW Broadway St., Albany, OR 97321 USA Tel 800-282-6621
E-mail: ericbrunsvold@gmail.com.

Specialized Quality Pubns., *(978-0-9634906; 978-0-9789582)* 921 11th St., S., Wisconsin Rapids, WI 54494 USA (SAN 299-299X) Tel 715-423-7476; *Imprints:* SQP (SQP)
Web site: http://www.specializedqualitypublications.com/index.htm

Specialty Educational Pubs., *(978-0-9718488)* P.O. Box 161, New Oxford, PA 17350 USA
E-mail: specialtypublishers@hotmail.com.

Specialty Greetings, *(978-0-9860024)* 2225 Grant St., Eugene, OR 97405 USA Tel 541-344-6400
E-mail: orders@specialtygreetings.com
Web site: http://www.SpecialtyGreetings.com.

Specialty Pr., Inc., *(978-0-9621629; 978-1-886941; 978-1-937761)* 300 NW 70th Ave., Suite 102, Plantation, FL 33317 USA (SAN 251-6977) Tel 954-792-8100; Fax: 954-792-8545; Toll Free: 800-233-9273 Do not confuse with Specialty Pr., Inc., in Ocean, NJ
E-mail: sales@addwarehouse.com
Web site: http://www.addwarehouse.com
Dist(s): **Ebsco Publishing**
Independent Pubs. Group
MyiLibrary.

Specialty Publishing Co., *(978-0-9755199)* 135 E. Saint Charles Rd., Caol Stream, IL 60188 USA (SAN 256-0569) Tel 630-933-0844; Fax: 630-933-0845
Web site: http://www.specialtypub.com.

Spectacle Films, Inc., *(978-0-9767771)* 2021 Commonwealth Ave. #2, Boston, MA 02135 USA Tel 212-807-0290
E-mail: spectaclefilms@gmail.com; csoling@gmail.com
Web site: http://www.Rumpleville.com; http://www.SpectacleFilms.com
Dist(s): **AtlasBooks Distribution**
BookMasters Distribution Services (BDS).

Spectre Publishing, *(978-0-9709191)* 22316 Haig St., Taylor, MI 48180 USA
E-mail: publisher@spectrepublishing.com
Web site: http://www.spectrepublishing.com
Dist(s): **CreateSpace Independent Publishing Platform.**

Spectrum *Imprint of* **Carson-Dellosa Publishing, LLC**

Spectrum Films Inc., *(978-0-9760906)* 4319 Salisbury Rd., Suite 4, Jacksonville, FL 32216 USA
Web site: http://www.spectrumfilms.tv.

SpeculativeFictionReview.com, *(978-0-9785232)* 22281 Letur, Mission Viejo, CA 92691-1406 USA
Web site: http://www.speculativefictionreview.com.

Speech Bin, Inc., The, *(978-0-937857)* 1965 25th Ave., Vero Beach, FL 32960 USA (SAN 630-1657) Tel 772-770-0007; Fax: 772-770-0006
E-mail: info@speechbin.com
Web site: http://www.speechbin.com.

Speech Kids Texas Pr., *(978-1-933319)* 3802 Beaconsdale Dr., Austin, TX 78727-2951 USA (SAN 256-4122)
E-mail: info@speechkidstexaspress.com
Web site: http://www.speechkidstexaspress.com.

Speech Place Publishing, The, *(978-0-9794102)* 1810-A York Rd., No. 432, Lutherville, MD 21093 USA (SAN 853-3679) Tel 410-517-9026
E-mail: cs@thespeechplace.com
Web site: http://www.thespeechplace.com.

Speech Publishing Hse., *(978-0-9770483)* 1115 Cordova St., Suite 318, Pasadena, CA 91106-3013 USA Tel 626-372-1195
E-mail: jonandspeech@prodigy.net.

Speedwitch Media, *(978-0-9749508)* 645 Tanner Marsh Rd., Guilford, CT 06437-2106 USA
Web site: http://www.speedwitch.com.

Speedy Kids (Children's Fiction) *Imprint of* **Speedy Publishing LLC**

Speedy Publishing Books (General) *Imprint of* **Speedy Publishing LLC**

Speedy Publishing LLC, *(978-1-939643; 978-1-62884; 978-1-63022; 978-1-63187; 978-1-63287; 978-1-63383; 978-1-63428; 978-1-68032; 978-1-63501; 978-1-68127; 978-1-68145; 978-1-68185; 978-1-68212; 978-1-68260; 978-1-68280)* 7914 Raven Creek Ln., Cypress, TX 77433 USA (SAN 920-6620) Tel 954-379-7796; Fax: 954-379-7796; 40 E. Main St., Newark, DE 19711; *Imprints:* Speedy Kids (Children's Fiction) (Speedy Kids); Baby Professor (Education Kids) (Baby Profes); Speedy Publishing Books (General) (SpeedyPub)
Web site: http://www.speedypublishing.co
Dist(s): **Lulu Enterprises Inc.**

Speight, Theresa , L.L.C., *(978-0-9795007)* P.O. Box 45100, Baton Rouge, LA 70895 USA
E-mail: tspeightpublish@cox.net
Web site: http://www.tspeightpublish.com.

†Speller, Robert & Sons, Pubs., Inc., *(978-0-8315)* Orders Addr.: P.O. Box 411, New York, NY 10159 USA (SAN 203-2295) Tel 646-334-8008; P.O. Box 461, New York, NY 10108 (SAN 203-2309); *CIP.*

Spence City *Imprint of* **Spencer Hill Pr.**

Spence Publishing Co., *(978-0-9653208; 978-1-890626)* 5646 Milton St. Ste. 314, Dallas, TX 75206-3923 USA (SAN 257-9383) Toll Free: 888-773-6782
E-mail: tspence@spencepublishing.com
Web site: http://www.spencepublishing.com
Dist(s): **Chicago Distribution Ctr.**
Vigilante, Richard Bks.

Spence, Stephen Mark, *(978-0-9705324)* 211 Moore Ave., Buffalo, NY 14223 USA Tel 716-836-5178
E-mail: spence@buffalo.edu
Web site: http://www.acsu.buffalo.edu/~spence/.

Spencer Hill Contemporary *Imprint of* **Spencer Hill Pr.**

Spencer Hill Middle Grade *Imprint of* **Spencer Hill Pr.**

Spencer Hill Pr., *(978-0-9845311; 978-0-9831572; 978-1-937053; 978-1-939392; 978-1-63392)* 27 W. 20th St., New York, NY 10011 USA (SAN 859-6573); *Imprints:* Spence City (Spence City); Spencer Hill Contemporary (SpencerHill); Spencer Hill Middle Grade (SpencHill Middl)
E-mail: kate@katekaynak.com; jporteous@spencerhillpress.com; karenahughes@me.com
Web site: http://www.spencerhillpress.com; http://www.spencecity.com/
Dist(s): **INscribe Digital**
Midpoint Trade Bks., Inc.

Spencer, Russell & Kathlynn, *(978-0-9664055)* Orders Addr.: 2484 Dewberry Ln., Oxnard, CA 93030 USA Tel 805-981-2820
E-mail: RSpencer@windshieldadventures.com
Web site: http://www.windshieldadventures.com
Dist(s): **Gem Guides Bk. Co.**

Spencer's Mill Pr., *(978-0-9771666)* 555 Church St. No. 1501, Nashville, TN 37219 USA (SAN 256-8225) Tel 615 477-2044
E-mail: trudychoices@aol.com
Web site: http://www.spencersmillpress.com
Dist(s): **BookBaby.**

Spending Solutions Pr., *(978-0-9729732)* 4347 W. NW Hwy., Suite 120, PMB 283, Dallas, TX 75220-3864 USA
Web site: http://www.spendingsolutions.com.

Speranza's Pr., *(978-0-9800327)* P.O. Box 2404, Glenview, IL 60025 USA.

Sphinx Publishing, *(978-0-9725951; 978-0-9762875; 978-0-9770912; 978-0-9776711; 978-1-934144; 978-1-935921)* 7400 Airport Dr., Macon, GA 31216 USA Toll Free: 866-311-9578; *Imprints:* Blue Marble Books (Blu Marble Bks)
E-mail: gpulliam@indigopublishing.us
Web site: http://www.indigopublishing.us
Dist(s): **American Wholesale Bk. Co.**
Parnassus Bk. Distributors.

SPI Bks., *(978-0-944007; 978-1-56171)* 99 Spring St., 3rd Flr., New York, NY 10012 USA Tel 212-431-5011; Fax: 212-431-8646
E-mail: ian@spibooks.com
Web site: http://www.spibooks.com
Dist(s): **APG Sales & Distribution Services**
Perseus Distribution.

Spica Bks., *(978-0-9728531)* 9742 N. 105th Dr., Sun City, AZ 85351 USA Tel 623-583-6764 (phone/fax)
E-mail: marilyn@dreamlady.com
Web site: http://www.dreamlady.com.

Spicka, Jana Incorporated *See* **Tree of Life Pr.**

Spider Comics, *(978-0-9859884)* 1489 Wallace Dr., Springville, UT 84663 USA Tel 678-386-5550
E-mail: michael@spidercomics.com
Web site: www.spidercomics.com.

SPIE, *(978-0-8194; 978-0-89252; 978-1-62841; 978-1-5106)* Orders Addr.: P.O. Box 10, Bellingham, WA 98227-0010 USA (SAN 224-1706) Tel 360-676-3290; Fax: 360-647-1445; Edit Addr.: 1000 20th St., Bellingham, WA 98225 USA (SAN 669-1323) Tel 360-676-3290; Fax: 360-647-1445; Toll Free: 888-504-8171
E-mail: spie@spie.org
Web site: http://www.spie.org/bookstore
Dist(s): **Wiley, John & Sons, Inc.**
ebrary, Inc.

Spina, Janice, *(978-0-615-83653-9; 978-0-615-88107-2; 978-0-615-96697-7; 978-0-615-98936-5; 978-0-692-20511-2; 978-0-692-31717-4; 978-0-692-38880-8; 978-0-692-43327-0; 978-0-692-45229-5; 978-0-692-51084-1)* 63 Sawgrass Cir., Londonderry, NH 03053 USA Tel 603-434-6463
Web site: http://www.jemsbooks.com
Dist(s): **CreateSpace Independent Publishing Platform.**

Spineless Bks., *(978-0-9724244; 978-0-9801392; 978-0-9853578)* P.O. Box 91, Urbana, IL 61803 USA Tel 217-722-1033
E-mail: william@spinelessbooks.com
Web site: http://www.spinelessbooks.com.

Spinelli, Patti, *(978-0-9742328)* 87 Portland Ave., Dover, NH 03820-3525 USA
E-mail: pasbug1010@aol.com.

Spinifex Pr. (AUS) *(978-1-875559; 978-0-908205; 978-1-876756; 978-1-74219; 978-0-646-04196-4) Dist. by* **IPG Chicago.**

Spinner Bks., *(978-1-59653)* 2030 Harrison St., San Francisco, CA 94110-1310 USA Tel 415-503-1600; Fax: 415-503-0085.

Spinner Pubns., Inc., *(978-0-932027)* 164 William St., New Bedford, MA 02740-6022 USA (SAN 686-0826) Tel 508-994-4564; Fax: 508-994-6925; Toll Free: 800-292-6062
E-mail: spinner@spinnerpub.com
Web site: http://www.spinnerpub.com.

SpinSmart Software, *(978-0-9743434)* Orders Addr.: 4717 S. Hydraulic, Wichita, KS 67216 USA
E-mail: support@spinsmart.com
Web site: http://www.spinsmart.com.

Spinsters Ink *See* **Spinsters Ink Bks.**

†Spinsters Ink Bks., *(978-1-883523; 978-1-935226)* Div. of Southern Belle Bks., P.O. Box 242, Midway, FL 32343 USA (SAN 212-6923) Tel 850-576-2370; Fax: 850-576-3498; Toll Free: 800-301-6860
E-mail: Linda@SpinstersInk.com
Web site: http://www.spinstersink.com
Dist(s): **Bella Distribution**
Perseus-PGW
Perseus Bks. Group
Perseus Distribution
SPD-Small Pr. Distribution; *CIP.*

Spirit & Life Productions, *(978-0-9788928)* Orders Addr.: 2260 Grand Ave., Baldwin, NY 11510 USA Tel 866-430-3801.

Spirit Arm Publishing *See* **Solemn Word Publishing**

Spirit Pr. *Imprint of* **Bendon, Inc.**

Spirit Pr., LLC, *(978-1-893075)* Orders Addr.: 1323 SE. 49th Ave., Portland, OR 97215 USA Tel 503-954-0012
suzannedeak@gmail.com Do not confuse with companies with the same name in Santa Cruz, CA, Raleigh, NC
E-mail: suzannedeak@gmail.com; onespiritpress@gmail.com; spiritpresspublishing@gmail.com
Web site: http://www.onespiritpress.com
Dist(s): **CreateSpace Independent Publishing Platform**
Lightning Source, Inc.

Spirit Publishing LLC, *(978-0-9770967)* 819 Marcy Ave., Brooklyn, NY 11216 USA (SAN 256-7636) Tel 718-230-5605.

SpiritBooks *Imprint of* **Portal Ctr. Pr.**

Spiritbuilding, *(978-0-9774754; 978-0-9821376; 978-0-9829811)* 15591 N. State Rd., 9, Summitville, IN 46070 USA Tel 765-623-2238
E-mail: mcmurray@spiritbuilding.com
Web site: http://www.SpiritBuilding.com.

Spirited Presentations, *(978-0-9790017)* 4249 Peak Ln., Grand Rapids, MI 49525 USA
E-mail: Kathey@spiritedpresentations.com
Web site: http://Spiritedpresentations.com.

Spirited Publishing, LLC, *(978-0-9768513)* Orders Addr.: P.O. Box 1796, Appleton, WI 54912-1796 USA Tel 920-419-3340
E-mail: kris@spiritedpublishing.com
Web site: http://www.spiritedpublishing.com.

Spiritpoint Press *See* **Bitty Book Pr.**

Spiritual Hse. Pr., The, *(978-0-9656847)* 24 Old Milford Rd., Brookline, NH 03033 USA Tel 603-672-8550
E-mail: blueskies@myfairpoint.net
Web site: http://www.TheSpiritualHouse.com.

Spitzer, Lance, *(978-0-615-72525-3)* 226 Crestmoor Cir., Pacifica, CA 94044 USA Tel 650-922-8554
E-mail: lancesherwood@comcast.net.

Spizzirri Pr., Inc., *(978-0-86545)* P.O. Box 9397, Rapid City, SD 57709 USA (SAN 215-2851) Tel 605-348-2749; Fax: 605-348-6251 (orders); Toll Free: 800-325-9819; 800-322-9819
E-mail: spizzpub@aol.com
Web site: http://www.spizzirri.com.

Splendid Benedict, *(978-0-615-90023-0; 978-0-9910809)* 5094 N Agave Trl, Flagstaff, AZ 86001 USA Tel 303-455-1835
Dist(s): **CreateSpace Independent Publishing Platform.**

Splendid Torch, *(978-0-9788027; 978-0-615-16717-6; 978-0-615-16784-8)* 2000 St. Regis Dr. #6d, Lombard, IL 60148 USA (SAN 851-6588)
Web site: http://www.puglish.com
Dist(s): **Lulu Enterprises Inc.**

Splendors Publishing, *(978-0-9717228)* P.O. Box 1155, Soquel, CA 95073 USA Fax: 831-464-1854
E-mail: lalo@lalofiorelli.com
Web site: http://www.lalofiorelli.com.

Split Level of the Blessed Suburbs Publishing, *(978-0-9761515)* 56 Arbor St., Hartford, CT 06106-1201 USA Tel 860-586-8448 (phone/fax)
Web site: http://www.tedpaulsen.com.

Spoken Arts, Inc., *(978-0-8045)* 195 S. White Rock Rd., Holmes, NY 12531-5406 USA (SAN 205-079X) Toll Free: 800-326-4090
Web site: http://www.spokenartsmedia.com/home.htm
Dist(s): **AudioGO**
Follett Media Distribution
Follett School Solutions
Lectorum Pubns., Inc.
Weston Woods Studios, Inc.

Spoken Word, The, *(978-0-9637644)* 1031 Michigan Ave. NE, No. 205, Washington, DC 20017 USA Tel 202-832-2368 Do not confuse with Spoken Word, The, Arlington , TX.

SpokenVizions Entertainment Group, LLC, *(978-0-9773834)* P.O. Box 373, Florissant, MO 63032 USA Tel 314-517-8764
E-mail: info@spokenvizions.com
Web site: http://www.spokenvizions.com.

Spoon Publishing Hse., *(978-0-615-11213-8)* Div. of A Corpus Polymedia Monolith, 440 E. Broadway, Executive Suite 51, Salt Lake City, UT 84111-2651 USA
E-mail: spoonpublishing@corpuspolymedia.com
Web site: http://www.corpuspolymedia.com/spoonpublishing/; http://www.spoonpublishing.com.

Spoonbender Bks., *(978-0-9725750)* Div. of Holahan, Inc., 419 N. Larchmont Blvd., No. 4, Los Angeles, CA 90004 USA (SAN 254-9123) Tel 323-933-0253 (phone/fax)
E-mail: jgrist@mac.com; publisher@spoonbenderbooks.com
Web site: http://www.spoonbenderbooks.com
Dist(s): **Follett School Solutions**
Quality Bks., Inc.
SCB Distributors.

Spooners Publishing, *(978-0-9766179)* 98 Onteora Ct., Shokan, NY 12481-5610 USA Tel 845-657-8737
E-mail: ecurtis@hvc.rr.com.

Sport Story Publishing, *(978-0-9702216)* 740 Lakeview Dr., Palm Harbor, FL 34683 USA Fax: 727-447-3587
E-mail: thoover@tampabay.rr.com.

Sport Workbooks, *(978-0-9787458)* P.O. Box 1623, Pacifica, CA 94044 USA (SAN 851-5093) Tel 650-270-3200
E-mail: baseballmath@hotmail.com.

Sport Your Stuff Corp., *(978-1-931746)* 5025 Longbrook Rd., Winston Salem, NC 27105 USA.

SportAmerica, *(978-1-879498)* P.O. Box 95030, South Jordan, UT 84095 USA Tel 801-253-3360; Fax: 801-253-3361; Toll Free: 800-467-7885
Web site: http://www.sportamerica.com.

Sportime International, *(978-0-9793506)* 3175 Northwoods Pkwy. # A, Norcross, GA 30071-1539 USA
E-mail: dkissel@sportime.com
Web site: http://www.sportime.com.

Sports Challenge Network, *(978-0-615-15195-3; 978-0-615-21091-9; 978-0-578-00861-5; 978-0-9819861; 978-1-935592)* Orders Addr.: 1420 Locust St., No. 10F, Philadelphia, PA 19102 USA (SAN 913-4190) Tel 1-267-847-9018
E-mail: elik@sportschallengenetwork.com
Web site: www.sportschallengenetwork.com.

Sports Illustrated For Kids, *(978-0-316; 978-0-553; 978-1-886749; 978-1-930623)* Div. of Time, Inc., 135 W. 50th St. , New York, NY 10020-1393 USA Tel 212-522-1212; Fax: 212-522-0926
E-mail: joe_nunziata@sikids.com
Web site: http://www.sikids.com
Dist(s): **Hachette Bk. Group.**

Sports In Mind, *(978-0-9745066; 978-0-9765074)* 3603 Palm Harbor Blvd., Unit C, Palm Harbor, FL 34683 USA Fax: 727-942-3339
Web site: http://www.ravesystems.com.

Sports Marketing International, Inc., *(978-0-9743082)* 27 E. Housatonic St., Pittsfield, MA 01201-4121 USA Tel 413-499-1733; Fax: 413-499-3820; Toll Free: 800-320-1733; *Imprints:* Moscow Ballet (Moscow Ballet)
E-mail: smi@nutcracker.com
Web site: http://www.nutcracker.com.

Sports Masters, *(978-1-58382)* Div. of Sports Publishing, Inc., 804 N. Neil St., Champaign, IL 61820 USA Tel 217-363-2072; Fax: 217-363-2073; Toll Free: 877-424-2665
E-mail: choffman@sagamorepub.com
Dist(s): **Ingram Pub. Services.**

Sports Publishing, LLC, *(978-1-57167; 978-1-58261; 978-1-58382; 978-1-59670)* 804 N. Neil St., Champaign, IL 61820 USA Tel 217-363-2072; Fax: 217-353-2073; Toll Free: 877-424-2665 Do not confuse with Sports Publishing, Champaign, IL
E-mail: info@sportspublishingllc.com
Web site: http://www.sportspublishingllc.com
Dist(s): **Hachette Bk. Group**
Ingram Pub. Services
MyiLibrary.

Sports Touch *See* **Sports Touch/Kate Montgomery**

Sports Touch/Kate Montgomery, *(978-1-878069)* 1625 E. Jackson Blvd., Elkhart, IN 46516 USA
E-mail: kate@sportstouch.com
Web site: http://www.lulu.com; http://www.sportstouch.com; http://www.createspace.com
Dist(s): **Lulu Enterprises Inc.**

Sportsman's Connection, *(978-1-885010)* Div. of Sportsman's Marketing, Inc., Orders Addr.: P.O. Box 852, Lake Elmo, MN 55042 USA Tel 800-264-0474; Fax: 651-773-3320; Toll Free: 800-777-7461; Edit Addr.: 1810 N. 16th St. Ste. 1, Superior, WI 54880-2597 USA
E-mail: info@sportsmansconnection.com
Web site: http://www.sportsmansconnection.com
Dist(s): **Partners Bk. Distributing, Inc.**

SportsZone *Imprint of* **ABDO Publishing Co.**

Spotlight *Imprint of* **ABDO Publishing Co.**

Spotlight, *(978-1-59961)* Div. of ABDO Publishing Group, Orders Addr.: P.O. Box 398166, Edina, MN 55439-8166 USA Fax: 952-831-1632; Toll Free: 877-877-5939; Edit Addr.: 8000 W. 78th St., Suite 310, Edina, MN 55439 USA; *Imprints:* Chapter Books (ChapterBks); Graphic Novels (GraphNvls); Picture Book (PicBook)
E-mail: info@abdopublishing.com
Web site: http://www.abdopublishing.com
Dist(s): **ABDO Publishing Co.**

Spotlight Books *See* **Hannacroix Creek Bks., Inc.**

Spotlight News Publications *See* **Autumn Hse. Publishing**

Spotted Dog Pr., Inc., *(978-0-9647530; 978-1-893343)* Orders Addr.: P.O. Box 1721, Bishop, CA 93515 USA (SAN 257-9936) Tel 760-872-1524; Fax: 800-872-0681; Toll Free: 800-417-2790 Do not confuse with Spotted Dog Pr., Ashland, OR
E-mail: wbenti@spotteddogpress.com; store@spotteddogpress.com
Web site: http://www.spotteddogpress.com
Dist(s): **Gem Guides Bk. Co.**
Partners/West Book Distributors
Treasure Chest Bks.

Spreeda Publishing, *(978-0-9748979)* Div. of SPREEDA, 14204 W. 72nd St., Shawnee, KS 66216 USA Do not confuse with Maple Leaf Publishing in Minneapolis, MN
E-mail: karen@spreeda.com
Web site: http://www.spreeda.com.

Spriitelee Enterprises, *(978-0-9773460)* P.O. Box 207, Westwood, MA 02090 USA.

Spring Arbor Distributors, Inc., Subs. of Ingram Industries Inc., 4271 Edison Ave., Chino, CA 91710 USA; 7315 Innovation Blvd., Fort Wayne, IN 46818-1371; Edit Addr.: 1 Ingram Blvd., La Vergne, TN 37086-1976 USA Fax: 615-213-5192; Toll Free: 800-395-4340; 800-395-7234 (customer service)
E-mail: orders@springarbor.com.

Spring Creek Bk. Co., *(978-1-932898; 978-0-9960974)* P.O. Box 50355, Provo, UT 84606-0355 USA
Web site: http://www.springcreekbooks.com
Dist(s): **Brigham Distribution.**

Spring Ducks Bks., LLC, *(978-0-9761076)* Orders Addr.: P.O. Box 44847, Madison, WI 53744-4847 USA Toll Free: 800-342-4404; Edit Addr.: 222 Carillon Dr., Madison, WI 53705 USA
E-mail: kathy@springducks.com
Web site: http://www.springducks.com.

Spring Harbor Pr., *(978-0-935891)* Div. of Spring Harbor, Ltd., Orders Addr.: P.O. Box 346, Delmar, NY 12054 USA (SAN 695-9768) Tel 518-478-7817 (phone/fax) E-mail: springharbor@springharborpress.com; info@springharborpress.com Web site: http://www.springharborpress.com.

Spring Hollow Bks., LLC, *(978-0-9665389)* P.O. Box 115, Cave Spring, GA 30124-0115 USA Tel 706-235-5113; Fax: 706-235-0742 Do not confuse with Spring Hollow Bks., Richfield, MN E-mail: jbcjmc@aol.com.

Spring Tide Publishing, *(978-0-9765578)* 1281 N. Ocean Dr. Suite 151, Singer Island, FL 33404 USA Tel 561-632-2278 E-mail: delores@springtidepublishing.com Web site: www.springtidepublishing.com.

Spring Tree Pr., *(978-0-9785007)* P.O. Box 461, Atlantic Highlands, NJ 07716 USA (SAN 850-8429) Tel 732-872-8002; Fax: 732-872-6967 Web site: http://www.springtreepress.com *Dist(s):* **New Leaf Distributing Co., Inc.**

†Springer, *(978-0-387; 978-0-8176; 978-3-211; 978-3-540; 978-3-7908; 978-4-431; 978-1-85233; 978-1-84628; 978-1-4419; 978-1-4612; 978-1-4613; 978-1-4614; 978-1-4615; 978-1-4684; 978-1-4757; 978-1-4899; 978-1-4939; 978-1-5041)* Subs. of Springer Science+Business Media, Orders Addr.: P.O. Box 2485, Secaucus, NJ 07096-2485 USA Tel 201-348-4033; Fax: 201-348-4505; Toll Free: 800-777-4643; Edit Addr.: 233 Spring St., New York, NY 10013-1578 USA (SAN 203-2228) Tel 212-815-0249; 212-460-1500; Fax: 212-460-1575; Toll Free: 1-800-777-4643 Thomson Delmar Learning Distributes Blanchard & Loeb Nursing Videos Only E-mail: Slu@Springer-ny.com; service-ny@springer.com Web site: http://www.springeronline.com; http://www.springer.com *Dist(s):* **Ebsco Publishing**
Metapress
MyiLibrary
Rittenhouse Bk. Distributors
ebrary, Inc.; *CIP.*

†Springer Publishing Co., Inc., *(978-0-8261; 978-0-939957; 978-1-888799; 978-1-932603; 978-0-9771597; 978-1-933864; 978-1-935281; 978-1-936287; 978-1-936303; 978-1-61705; 978-1-62070)* 11 W. 42nd St., 15th Fl., New York, NY 10036 USA (SAN 203-2236) Tel 212-431-4370; Fax: 212-941-7842; Toll Free: 877-687-7476 E-mail: Springer@springerpub.com; journals@springerpub.com; Editorial@springerpub.com; cs@springerpub.com Web site: http://www.springerpub.com *Dist(s):* **CreateSpace Independent Publishing Platform**
Ebsco Publishing
Independent Pubs. Group
MyiLibrary
Rittenhouse Bk. Distributors
ebrary, Inc.; *CIP.*

Springer-Verlag New York, Incorporated *See* **Springer**

SpringTree *Imprint of* **Forest Hill Publishing, LLC**

Sprite Pr., *(978-0-9706654; 978-0-9764295)* 2118 Sycamore Cove Cir., Miamisburg, OH 45343 USA Tel 740-767-2470 E-mail: spritepress@aol.com Web site: http://www.members.aol.com/spritepress.

Sproing Books *See* **Gripper Products**

Sprouting Peanut Pubs., *(978-0-615-22222-6)* P.O. Box 2606, Gilroy, CA 95021 USA Web site: http://www.whatsupwillie.com.

Spruce Gulch Pr., *(978-0-9625714; 978-0-9841259)* Orders Addr.: P.O. Box 4347, Rome, NY 13442-4347 USA (SAN 297-3014) Tel 315-337-3626 E-mail: SprGulch@aol.com *Dist(s):* **North Country Bks., Inc.**

Spuyten Duyvil Publishing, *(978-0-923389; 978-0-9661242; 978-1-881471; 978-0-9720662; 978-1-933132; 978-1-941550)* 385 E. 18th St. 5J, Brooklyn, NY 11226 USA (SAN 237-9481) Toll Free: 800-886-5304 (phone/fax) E-mail: editors@spuytenduyvil.net Web site: http://www.spuytenduyvil.net *Dist(s):* **SPD-Small Pr. Distribution.**

SpyGirls Pr., *(978-0-9852273)* P.O. Box 1537, Fairfax, VA 22038 USA Tel 571-213-1586 E-mail: melissamahle@verizon.net Web site: www.anatoliasteppe.com.

Spyrou-Andriotis, Vicky, *(978-0-615-24795-3; 978-0-9821808)* 3919 Old Town Rd., Bridgeport, CT 06606 USA E-mail: info@vickyandriotis.com Web site: http://www.vickyandriotis.com.

SQP *Imprint of* **Specialized Quality Pubns.**

Square Circle Pr., LLC *See* **Square Circle Pr. LLC**

Square Circle Pr. LLC, *(978-0-9789066; 978-0-9833897; 978-0-9856926)* P.O. Box 913, Schenectady, NY 12301 USA (SAN 851-9145) Tel 518-432-6657 Do not confuse with Square Circle Press in Corte Madera, CA E-mail: bookinfo@squarecirclepress.com Web site: http://www.squarecirclepress.com *Dist(s):* **Lightning Source, Inc.**
North Country Bks., Inc.

Square Deal Pr., *(978-0-9754941)* 368 S. McCaslin Blvd., Box 206, Louisville, CO 80027 USA.

Square Fish, *(978-0-312)* 175 Fifth Ave., New York, NY 10010 USA Tel 646-307-5770 E-mail: squarefish.market@hbpub.com Web site: http://www.squarefishbooks.com *Dist(s):* **Macmillan.**

Square Halo Bks., *(978-0-9658798; 978-0-9785097; 978-1-941106)* Orders Addr.: P.O. Box 18954, Baltimore, MD 21206 USA Tel 410-485-6227; Edit Addr.: 4310 Southern Ave., Baltimore, MD 21206 USA E-mail: square_halo@yahoo.com; ned@squarehalobooks.com Web site: http://www.squarehalobooks.com.

Square One Pubs., *(978-0-9664202; 978-0-7570; 978-0-9792746)* 115 Herricks Rd., Garden City Park, NY 11040 USA Tel 516-535-2010; Fax: 516-535-2014; *Imprints:* Vital Health Publishing (Vital Hlth) E-mail: sq1info@aol.com Web site: http://squareonepublishers.com *Dist(s):* **Athena Productions, Inc.**

Squarey Head, Inc., *(978-0-9742003)* 6362 W. Cross Dr., Littleton, CO 80123 USA Tel 303-798-1877; Fax: 303-794-4639.

Squid Works, *(978-0-9755041)* P.O. Box 480463, Denver, CO 80248-0463 USA Web site: http://www.squidworks.com.

Squires Publishing, *(978-0-9816048)* 7224 S. Yates Blvd., Suite 3N, Chicago, IL 60649 USA Tel 773-667-0039 E-mail: tanyacloud@comcast.net.

Squirrel Bks., *(978-0-615-48109-8; 978-0-615-50653-1)* 7 Park Blvd., Hyde Park, NY 12538 USA Tel 845-625-3637 *Dist(s):* **CreateSpace Independent Publishing Platform**
Dummy Record Do Not USE!!!!.

SRA/McGraw-Hill, *(978-0-07; 978-0-383)* Div. of The McGraw-Hill Education Group, Orders Addr.: 220 E. Daniel Dale Rd., DeSoto, TX 75115-2490 USA Fax: 972-228-1982; Toll Free: 800-843-8855; Edit Addr.: 8787 Orion Pl., Columbus, OH 43240-4027 USA Tel 614-430-6600; Fax: 614-430-6621; Toll Free: 800-468-5850 E-mail: sra@mcgraw-hill.com Web site: https://www.sraonline.com *Dist(s):* **Libros Sin Fronteras**
Weston Woods Studios, Inc.

Sri Ramakrishna Math (IND) *(978-81-7120; 978-81-86465; 978-81-7823) Dist. by* **Vedanta Pr.**

Sroda, George, *(978-0-9604486)* P.O. Box 97, Amherst Junction, WI 54407 USA (SAN 210-8607) Tel 715-824-3868; Fax: 715-824-5344.

SRT Publishing, *(978-0-9771248)* 530 Moon Clinton Rd., Moon Township, PA 15108 USA Tel 412-741-0581; Fax: 412-264-1103 E-mail: merch@silverringthing.com Web site: http://www.silverringthing.com.

Sruvis Publishing, *(978-0-9889907)* 2219 Pear Blossom, San Antonio, TX 78247 USA Tel 210-219-2156; Fax: 210-494-1994 E-mail: lyndasdavis8@aol.com.

Ssorgsoft, LLC, *(978-0-9765240)* P.O. Box 771192, Orlando, FL 32877 USA.

St. Aidan Pr., Inc., *(978-0-9719230)* 96 Dunlap Dr., Charles Town, WV 25414 USA E-mail: michael_rabjohns@hotmail.com Web site: http://www.staidanpress.com.

St. Augustine Academy Pr., *(978-1-936639)* 12050 Rambling Rd., Homer Glen, IL 60491 USA Tel 708-645-4691 E-mail: Lbergman2@sbcglobal.net Web site: www.staugustineacademypress.com.

St. Bernard Publishing, LLC, *(978-0-9741269)* P.O. Box 2218, Bay City, MI 48707-2218 USA Tel 989-892-1348 (phone/fax) E-mail: bcgirl@charter.net Web site: http://www.lifeongrannysfarm.com/.

St. Germain, Mark *See* **Three Cups, LLC**

St. Hope Academy, *(978-0-9759548)* Orders Addr.: P.O. Box 5447, Sacramento, CA 95817 USA Tel 916-649-7900; Fax: 916-452-7177; Edit Addr.: 3400 3rd Ave., Sacramento, CA 95817 USA Web site: http://40acresartgallery.org.

St. John's Pr., *(978-0-9710551; 978-0-615-83132-9; 978-0-9916014)* Orders Addr.: 5318 Torri Park Dr., Cottondale, AL 35453 USA Tel 205-242-4422; Fax: 205-553-9459 Do not confuse with Saint John's Press in Los Angeles, CA E-mail: charleysix@gmail.com.

St. Martin's Griffin *Imprint of* **St. Martin's Pr.**

St. Martin's Paperbacks *Imprint of* **St. Martin's Pr.**

†St. Martin's Pr., *(978-0-312; 978-0-8050; 978-0-940687; 978-0-9603648; 978-1-55927; 978-1-58063; 978-1-58238; 978-1-4299; 978-1-250)* Div. of Holtzbrinck Pubs., Orders Addr.: 16365 James Madison Hwy., Gordonville, VA 22942 USA Tel 540-672-7600; Fax: 540-672-7540 (customer service); Toll Free Fax: 800-672-2054; Toll Free: 888-330-8477; Edit Addr.: 175 Fifth Ave., 20th Flr., New York, NY 10010 USA (SAN 200-2132) Tel 212-674-5151 (Trade Div.); 212-726-0200 (College Div.); Fax: 212-674-3179 (Trade Div.); 212-686-9491 (College Div.); Toll Free: 800-221-7945 (Trade Div.); 800-470-4767 (College Div.); *Imprints:* Saint Martin's Griffin (St Martin Griffin); Saint Martin's Paperbacks (St Martins Paperbacks); Dunne, Thomas Books (Thomas Dunne); Minotaur Books (Minotaur); Golden Books Adult Publishing Group (Golden Adult); Golden Guides from Saint Martin's Press (Gldn Guides); Priddy Books (Priddy); Renaissance Books (Rena Bks) E-mail: webmaster@stmartins.com; enquiries@stmartins.com Web site: http://www.stmartins.com; http://www.smpcollege.com *Dist(s):* **Comag Marketing Group**
CreateSpace Independent Publishing Platform
Ediciones Universal
Kaplan Publishing
Libros Sin Fronteras
Macmillan
MyiLibrary
ebrary, Inc.; *CIP.*

St Mary's Church, *(978-0-9763902)* 429 Central Ave., Sandusky, OH 44870 USA Tel 419-625-7465 Web site: http://www.stmarysandusky.org.

St. Michael's Abbey, *(978-0-9742298)* 19292 El Toro Rd., Silverado, CA 92676-9710 USA E-mail: frnorbertw@yahoo.com Web site: http://www.abbeynews.com.

St. Nicholas Pr. *Imprint of* **CrossBearers Publishing**

St. Pauls *Imprint of* **St Pauls/Alba Hse. Pubs.**

St Pauls Pubns. (AUS) *(978-0-909986; 978-0-949080; 978-1-875570; 978-1-876295; 978-1-921032; 978-1-921472; 978-1-921963) Dist. by* **St Pauls Alba.**

†St Pauls/Alba Hse. Pubs., *(978-0-8189)* Div. of Society of St. Paul, 2187 Victory Blvd., Staten Island, NY 10314-6603 USA (SAN 201-2405) Tel 718-761-0047; Fax: 718-761-0057; 718-698-8390; Toll Free: 800-343-2522; *Imprints:* Saint Pauls (Saint Pauls) E-mail: albabooks@aol.com Web site: http://www.albahouse.org; *CIP.*

St. Roux Pr., *(978-0-9718433)* 308 Montmartre St., Folsom, LA 70437 USA E-mail: faucheux@msn.com.

Stabenfeldt Inc., *(978-1-933343; 978-1-934983)* Orders Addr.: 225 N. Main St., Bristol, CT 06011 USA Toll Free: 800-410-4145; *Imprints:* PONY (Pny) Web site: http://www.pony4kids.com.

Stacey Publishing (GBR) *(978-1-906768) Dist. by* **CasemateAcad.**

†Stackpole Bks., *(978-0-8117)* 5067 Ritter Rd., Mechanicsburg, PA 17055 USA (SAN 202-5396) Tel 717-796-0411; Fax: 717-796-0412; Toll Free: 800-732-3669 E-mail: ccraley@stackpolebooks.com Web site: http://www.stackpolebooks.com/ *Dist(s):* **MyiLibrary**; *CIP.*

Staff Development for Educators, *(978-0-9627389; 978-1-884548; 978-1-934026; 978-1-935502; 978-1-63133)* Div. of Highlights for Children, Orders Addr.: P.O. Box 577, Peterborough, NH 03458 USA Tel 603-924-9621; Fax: 603-924-6688; Toll Free Fax: 800-337-9929; Toll Free: 800-321-0401; Edit Addr.: 10 Sharon Rd., Peterborough, NH 03458 USA; *Imprints:* Crystal Springs Books (Crystal Spgs) E-mail: dfredericks@sde.com Web site: http://www.sde.com; http://www.crystalsprings.com; http://www.barnesandnoble.com *Dist(s):* **Follett School Solutions**
Stenhouse Pubs.

Stafford House, *(978-0-9822587)* P.O. Box 291, Pacific Palisades, CA 90272 USA Web site: http://www.abcyogaforkids.com *Dist(s):* **AtlasBooks Distribution.**

Stagecast Software, Inc., *(978-1-929721)* 580 College Ave., Palo Alto, CA 94306 USA Tel 650-354-0735; Fax: 650-354-0739; Toll Free: 888-782-4322 E-mail: info@stagecast.com Web site: http://www.stagecast.com.

Stahl Pubns., *(978-0-9755174)* P.O. Box 201, Ashley, IN 46705-0201 USA.

Staige Productions, *(978-0-9641375)* 290 Orrin St., Winona, MN 55987-2083 USA Tel 507-452-3627.

Stairway Pubns., *(978-0-9740061)* P.O. Box 518, Huntington, NY 11743-0518 USA (SAN 255-3422) Fax: 631-351-2142 E-mail: publisher@stairwaypub.com Web site: http://www.stairwaypub.com *Dist(s):* **Quality Bks., Inc.**

Stairway Publishing, *(978-0-9761953)* 1332 Anacapa St., Suite 200, Santa Barbara, CA 93101 USA; 230 E. Pedregosa St., Santa Barbara, CA 93101 (SAN 256-761X) Tel 805-451-5070; Fax: 805-962-1404 Do not Confuse with Shoreline Publishing in Bayside, NY E-mail: purnoff@seedmackall.com.

Stampley, C. D. Enterprises, Inc., *(978-0-915741; 978-1-58087)* Orders Addr.: P.O. Box 33172, Charlotte, NC 28233 USA (SAN 294-1325) Tel 704-333-6631; Fax: 704-336-6932; Edit Addr.: 1135 N. Tryon St., Charlotte, NC 28206 USA E-mail: info@stampley.com; rick@stampley.com Web site: http://www.stampley.com *Dist(s):* **Follett School Solutions**
Giron Bks.

Stance Pubns., *(978-0-615-18108-0; 978-0-9821047)* 4510 Seashore Dr., #A, Newport Beach, CA 92663-2520 USA E-mail: marcpent@msn.com Web site: http://www.stancepublications.com *Dist(s):* **AtlasBooks Distribution**
Lightning Source, Inc.

Standard International Media, *(978-1-58279; 978-1-888777; 978-1-86091; 978-1-60081)* Orders Addr.: 568 9th St. South, Suite 201, Naples, FL 34105 USA Tel 239-595-5516; Fax: 239-649-5832 E-mail: orders@standardinternationalmedia.com Web site: http://www.standardinternationalmedia.com.

Standard Pubns., Inc., *(978-0-9709788; 978-0-9722691; 978-1-59462; 978-1-60424; 978-1-60597; 978-1-4385; 978-1-61742)* P.O. Box 2226, Champaign, IL 61825 USA (SAN 912-9251) Tel 217-898-7825; Fax: 630-214-0564; *Imprints:* Book Jungle (Book Jungle) E-mail: spi@standardpublications.com *Dist(s):* **MyiLibrary.**

†Standard Publishing, *(978-0-7847; 978-0-87239; 978-0-87403; 978-0-933657; 978-1-58170)* 8805 Governors Hill Dr. Ste. 400, Cincinnati, OH 45249-3319 USA (SAN 110-5515) Toll Free Fax: 877-867-5751 (customer service); Toll Free: 800-543-1301; 800-543-1353 (customer service); *Imprints:* Bean Sprouts (Bean Sprouts) Do not confuse with Standard Publishing Corp., Boston, MA E-mail: customerservice@standardpub.com; trolfes@standardpub.com; dlewis@standardpub.com Web site: http://www.standardpub.com *Dist(s):* **B&H Publishing Group**; *CIP.*

Standard Publishing Company *See* **Standard Publishing**

Standing For Christ, Inc., *(978-0-9754834)* P.O. Box 28468, Cleveland, OH 44128 USA Tel 216-299-4523 E-mail: kelvinsfc@yahoo.com Web site: http://www.standingforchrist.org.

Stanek, Mary Beth, *(978-0-9747556)* 291 Lothrop Rd., Grosse Pointe, MI 48236 USA.

Stanfield, James Co., *(978-1-56304; 978-1-941264)* P.O. Box 41058, Santa Barbara, CA 93140 USA Tel 805-897-1185; Fax: 805-897-1187; Toll Free: 800-421-6534 E-mail: maindesk@stanfield.com Web site: http://www.stanfield.com.

Stanford Center for Research in Disease Prevention (S C R D P) *See* **Stanford Prevention Research Ctr.**

Stanford Prevention Research Ctr., *(978-1-879552)* Div. of Stanford Univ. Schl. of Medicine, Hoover Pavilion, Rm. N 229 211 Quarry Rd., Stanford, CA 94305-5705 USA Tel 650-723-0003; Fax: 650-498-4828 E-mail: askhprc@med.stanford.edu Web site: http://hprc.stanford.edu.

Stanger, Robert *See* **Club Pro Products**

Stanley, Donna Lacy, *(978-0-9766894)* 244 Sunset Dr., Waynesboro, VA 22980 USA Tel 540-949-5474 E-mail: dlstanle@yahoo.com.

Stanley Publishing Co., *(978-0-9790350; 978-0-615-55295-8; 978-0-9856495)* 810 Agua Caliente Dr., El Paso, TX 79912-1705 USA (SAN 852-257X) E-mail: info@stanleypublishing.com Web site: http://stanleypublishing.com *Dist(s):* **AtlasBooks Distribution.**

Stansbury Publishing, *(978-0-9708922; 978-0-9766269; 978-1-935807)* Subs. of Heidelberg Graphics, Orders Addr.: 2 Stansbury Ct., Chico, CA 95928 USA E-mail: spublishing@heidelberggraphics.com Web site: http://www.heidelberggraphics.com.

Stanton, Ilene J., *(978-0-615-82206-8)* 17 Canterbury Dr., Endicott, NY 13760 USA Tel 6077869128 *Dist(s):* **CreateSpace Independent Publishing Platform.**

Star Bible & Tract Corp., *(978-0-933672; 978-0-940999; 978-1-56794)* Orders Addr.: P.O. Box 821220, Fort Worth, TX 76182 USA (SAN 203-3518) Tel 817-416-5889; Fax: 817-251-0129; Toll Free: 800-433-7507; Edit Addr.: P.O. Box 821220, N Richlnd Hls, TX 76182-1220 USA (SAN 664-6247) E-mail: starbible@starbible.com Web site: http://www.starbible.com *Dist(s):* **Twentieth Century Christian Bks.**

Star Bright Bks., Inc., *(978-1-887734; 978-1-932065; 978-1-59572)* Orders Addr.: 30-19, 48th Ave., Long Island City, NY 11101 USA (SAN 254-5225) Tel 718-784-9112; Fax: 718-784-9012; Toll Free: 800-788-4439 E-mail: info@starbrightbooks.com Web site: http://www.starbrightbooks.com.

Star Cross'd Destiny *Imprint of* **Bohemian Trash Studios**

Star Dome Publishing, LLC, *(978-0-9766662)* P.O. Box 411300, Melbourne, FL 32941 USA E-mail: fcavalli@bellsouth.net Web site: http://www.stardomepublishing.com.

Star Light Pr., *(978-1-879817)* 1811 S. First St., Austin, TX 78704-4299 USA Tel 512-441-0588; 512-441-0062 (phone/fax); *Imprints:* Children (Children) E-mail: info@starlightpress.com Web site: http://www.starlightpress.com *Dist(s):* **Book Wholesalers, Inc.**
lLeon.

Star Pr., The, *(978-0-9676189)* Div. of Indiana Newspapers, Inc., Orders Addr.: P.O. Box 2408, Muncie, IN 47307-0408 USA (SAN 169-2437) Tel 765-213-5799; Fax: 765-213-5703; Toll Free: 800-783-7827; Edit Addr.: 345 S. High St., Muncie, IN 47305 USA E-mail: rfarmer@thestarpress.com Web site: http://www.thestarpress.com.

Star Publish LLC, *(978-1-932993; 978-1-935188)* E-mail: tcmcmullen@starpublishllc.com Web site: http://www.starpublishllc.com *Dist(s):* **Smashwords.**

Star Quest Publishing Phx, *(978-0-9767035)* 3030 E. Shangri-La Rd., Phoenix, AZ 85028 USA Tel 602-621-3431; Fax: 602-926-2484 E-mail: karen@starquestpublishingphx.com Web site: http://www.starquestpublishing.com.

Star Write Creations, *(978-0-9743851)* P.O. Box G, Birnamwood, WI 54414 USA Toll Free: 888-999-6609.

Starbell Bks., *(978-0-9747774)* 2507 LaBrecque Dr., Plainfield, IL 60544 USA Tel 815-254-9495 E-mail: starbellbooks@comcast.net Web site: http://www.starbellbooks.com.

Starborne Hse., *(978-0-9671701)* Orders Addr.: 1262 SR 257 S., Delaware, OH 43015-7821 USA (SAN 254-4024) Tel 740-369-4952 E-mail: david@davidredding.com; starbourne53@mac.com; info@davidredding.com Web site: http://www.davidredding.com.

Starbound Bks. *Imprint of* **Wheatmark**

Starbound Publishing Company *See* **Collectors Pr., Inc.**

Starbucks Coffee Co., *(978-0-9726394)* 2401 Utah Ave. S., Seattle, WA 98134 USA Tel 206-447-1575; Toll Free: 800-235-2883 E-mail: info@starbucks.com Web site: http://www.starbuckscollectibles.com.

Stardust Stables *Imprint of* **Stone Arch Bks.**

STAReviews *Imprint of* **N&N Publishing Co., Inc.**

Starfall Education, *(978-1-59577)* Div. of Pancil, LLC, P.O. Box 359, Boulder, CO 80306 USA Toll Free Fax: 800-943-6666; Toll Free: 888-857-8990 Web site: http://www.starfall.com *Dist(s):* **Blue Mountain Arts Inc.**

Starfall Publications *See* **Starfall Education**

Starfish Aquatics Institute, *(978-0-9746613; 978-0-578-13105-4; 978-0-578-13448-2;*

Publisher Name Index

978-0-578-13449-9) 10 Ramshorn Ct., Savannah, GA 31411 USA Tel 912-692-1173
E-mail: sara@sai-intl.org; jill@sai-intl.org
Web site: http://www.starfishaquatics.org.

Stargazer Bks. *Imprint of* **Black Rabbit Bks.**

Stargazer Publishing Co., (*978-0-9643853; 978-0-9713756; 978-1-933277*) Orders Addr.: P.O. Box 77002, Corona, CA 92877-0100 USA (SAN 298-6566) Tel 951-898-4619; Fax: 951-898-4633; Toll Free: 800-606-7895; Edit Addr.: 958 Stanislaus Dr., Corona, CA 92881 USA Do not confuse with Stargazer Publishing in Neenah, WI
E-mail: stargazer@stargazerpub.com
Web site: http://www.stargazerpub.com.

Stark Productions Inc., (*978-1-936592*) 109 Orange Ave., St. Cloud, FL 34769 USA Tel 407-957-8502 (Tel/Fax) Do not confuse with Stark Productions Inc in OaklandCA
E-mail: stark109@hotmail.com
Web site: www.starkproductioninc.com.

Starks, Shirley *See* **Inspirational Hse. of America**

StarLineage Pubns., (*978-1-885226*) P.O. Box 1630, McCloud, CA 96057-1630 USA Tel 530-964-2496.

Starling Publishing, (*978-0-9857394*) 71 S. 1300 E., Hyrum, UT 84319 USA Tel 435-881-4812
E-mail: amberargyle@yahoo.com.

Starlit Publishing LLC, (*978-0-9792946*) 1750 Powder Springs Rd. Suite 190, Marietta, GA 30064 USA.

Starlog Group, Incorporated *See* **Profile Entertainment, Inc.**

StarProse Corp., (*978-0-9721071*) 17445 Roosevelt Rd., Hemlock, MI 48626 USA
E-mail: webmaster@starprose.com
Web site: http://www.starprose.com.

Starr, Joyce *See* **Dr. Joyce STARR Publishing**

StarryBks., (*978-0-9882113; 978-0-692-27075-2; 978-0-692-34543-6*) P.O. Box 1788, Yelm, WA 98597 USA Tel 360-894-3592
E-mail: dreamscapes@ywave.com
Dist(s): **CreateSpace Independent Publishing Platform.**

Starscape *Imprint of* **Doherty, Tom Assocs., LLC**

Starshell Pr., Ltd., (*978-0-9707110*) 210 Ridge Rd., Watchung, NJ 07069 USA Tel 908-755-7050; Fax: 212-983-5271
E-mail: starshellpress@yahoo.com
Web site: http://www.starshellpress.com.

Start Publishing LLC, (*978-0-9664520; 978-1-930486; 978-1-60977; 978-1-62558; 978-1-62793; 978-1-63355; 978-1-68146*) 375 Hudson St. Flr. 12th Flr., New York, NY 10014 USA Tel 646-502-5309; *Imprints*: Salvo Press (SalvoPr)
E-mail: weisfeld@start-media.com
Web site: http://www.start-publishing.com
Dist(s): **MyiLibrary**
Perseus-PGW.

State Historical Society of North Dakota, (*978-1-891419; 978-0-9796796; 978-0-9801993*) Orders Addr.: 612 E. Blvd. Ave., Bismarck, ND 58505-0830 USA Tel 701-205-7802; Fax: 701-328-3710
E-mail: nhowe@nd.gov
Web site: http://www.history.nd.gov.

State Historical Society of Wisconsin *See* **Wisconsin Historical Society**

State Hse. Pr., (*978-0-938349; 978-1-880510; 978-1-933337*) S. 14th & Sayles Blvd., Austin, TX 79697 USA (SAN 660-966X); McMurry University, Box 637, Abilene, TX 79697-0637 Tel 325-793-4697; Fax: 325-793-4754 Do not confuse with State House Publishing in Madison, WI
E-mail: ckahl@mcm.edu
Web site: http://www.mcwhiney.org
Dist(s): **Encino Pr.**
Texas A&M Univ. Pr.

State of Growth Publishing Co., (*978-0-9740289*) P.O. Box 38633, Colorado Springs, CO 80937 USA
Web site: http://www.stateofgrowth.com.

State Standards Publishing, LLC, (*978-1-935077; 978-1-935884; 978-1-938813*) 1788 Quail Hollow, Hamilton, GA 31811 USA (SAN 856-292X) Tel 706-643-0043; Fax: 706-643-0042; Toll Free: 866-740-3056
E-mail: jward@statestandardspublishing.com
Web site: http://www.statestandardspublishing.com.

State Street Pr. *Imprint of* **Borders Pr.**

†State Univ. of New York Pr., (*978-0-7914; 978-0-87395; 978-0-88706; 978-1-4384*) Orders Addr.: P.O. Box 960, Herndon, VA 20172-0960 USA (SAN 203-3496) Tel 703-661-1575; Fax: 703-996-1010; Toll Free Fax: 877-204-6074; Toll Free: 877-204-6073 (customer service); Edit Addr.: 22 Corporate Woods Blvd., 3rd Flr., Albany, NY 12211-2504 USA (SAN 658-1730) Tel 518-472-5000; Fax: 518-472-5038; Toll Free: 866-430-7869; *Imprints*: Suny Press (Suny Pr)
E-mail: info@sunypress.edu; suny@presswarehouse.com
Web site: http://www.sunypress.edu
Dist(s): **Books International, Inc.**
CreateSpace Independent Publishing Platform
Ebsco Publishing
Pegasus Pr.
SPD-Small Pr. Distribution
TNT Media Group, Inc.
ebrary, Inc.; *CIP.*

Station Hill Press *See* **Barrytown/Station Hill Pr.**

Staying Healthy Media, Inc., (*978-0-9763237*) 4409 Summer Grape Rd., Pikesville, MD 21208 USA Tel 410-484-0457
E-mail: healthy@stayinghealthymedia.com
Web site: http://www.stayinghealthymedia.com.

STE Pubs. (ZAF) (*978-1-919855; 978-1-920222*) *Dist. by* **IPG Chicago.**

Steam Crow Pr., (*978-0-9774173*) 7233 W. Cottontail Ln., Peoria, AZ 85383 USA
E-mail: sales@steamcrow.com
Web site: http://www.steamcrow.com.

Steam Passages Pubns., (*978-0-9758584*) 508 Lakeview Ave., Wake Forest, NC 27587 USA
E-mail: sdegaetano@steampassages.com
Web site: http://www.dlrcad.com/book.

†Steck-Vaughn, (*978-0-8114; 978-0-8172; 978-0-8393; 978-0-7398; 978-1-4190*) Div. of Houghton Mifflin Harcourt Supplemental Pubs., Orders Addr.: 6277 Sea Harbor Dr., 5th Flr., Orlando, FL 32887 USA Toll Free Fax: 877-578-2638; Toll Free: 888-363-4266; Edit Addr.: 10801 N. Mopac Expressway, Bldg. 3, Austin, TX 78759 USA (SAN 658-1757) Toll Free: 800-531-5015
E-mail: ecare@harcourt.com
Web site: http://www.harcourtachieve.com
Dist(s): **Follett School Solutions**
Houghton Mifflin Harcourt Publishing Co.
Houghton Mifflin Harcourt Supplemental Pubs.; *CIP.*

Stedjee Publishing *See* **Lawe Street Bks.**

Steel Bridge Pr., (*978-0-9764415*) 610 Briarcliff, Bardstown, KY 40004-8941 USA Tel 502-348-7447; Fax: 502-350-1126
E-mail: john@steelbridgepress.com.

Steel Rooster Pr., (*978-0-615-77887-7; 978-0-615-78508-0*) 22 Rockaway Trail, Ridge, NY 11961 USA Tel 631-559-9259
Dist(s): **CreateSpace Independent Publishing Platform.**

Steele, Eugene *See* **E-BookTime LLC**

Steele Studios, (*978-0-9716811*) Orders Addr.: P.O. Box 3093, Glenwood Springs, CO 81602 USA (SAN 254-3230); Edit Addr.: 125 Ctr. Dr., No.18, Glenwood Springs, CO 81601 USA.

Steerforth Pr., (*978-0-944072; 978-1-58195; 978-1-883642; 978-1-58642*) 45 Lyme Rd. # 208, Hanover, NH 03755-1219 USA; *Imprints*: Zoland Books, Incorporated (Zoland)
E-mail: helga@steerforth.com; info@steerforth.com
Web site: http://www.steerforth.com
Dist(s): **MyiLibrary**
Penguin Random Hse., LLC.
Random Hse., Inc.
Red Wheel/Weiser.

†SteinerBooks, Inc., (*978-0-8334; 978-0-88010; 978-0-89345; 978-0-910142; 978-1-58420; 978-1-85584; 978-0-9701097; 978-0-9831984; 978-1-62148; 978-1-62151; 978-1-938685*) Orders Addr.: P.O. Box 960, Herndon, VA 20172-0960 USA Tel 703-661-1594 (orders); Fax: 702-661-1501; Toll Free Fax: 800-277-7947 (orders); Toll Free: 800-856-8664 (orders); Edit Addr.: 610 Main St., Suite 1, Great Barrington, MA 01230 USA Tel 413-528-8233; Fax: 413-528-8826; Fulfillment Addr.: 22883 Quicksilver Dr., Dulles, VA 20166 USA (SAN 253-9519) Tel 703-661-1529; Fax: 703-996-1010; *Imprints*: Bell Pond Books (Bell Pond); Lindisfarne Books (Lindisfarne)
E-mail: service@steinerbooks.org
Web site: http://www.steinerbooks.org
Dist(s): **New Leaf Distributing Co., Inc.**
Red Wheel/Weiser; *CIP.*

Steingart, Nathan Publishing, (*978-0-9769321*) 617 N. Kensington Dr., No. 1, Appleton, WI 54915 USA
E-mail: nathansteingart@new.rr.com
Web site: http://www.santastories.net.

Steinschneider, Bernadetta, (*978-0-9790026*) 205 Georgetown Rd., Weston, CT 06883 USA Tel 203-454-8907; Fax: 203-227-0184
E-mail: swigutb@gmail.com.

Stejskal, Susan M., (*978-0-615-13395-9; 978-0-615-81867-2*) 15095 S. 18th St., Vicksburg, MI 49097 USA.

Stella Bks, Inc., (*978-0-9746932*) P.O. Box 4707, Edwards, CO 81632-4707 USA Tel 970-926-7827 (phone/fax)
E-mail: info@astellabook.com
Dist(s): **Partners/West Book Distributors.**

Stellar Learning, (*978-0-9763833*) P.O. Box 64, Guildrind Ctr, NY 12085-0064 USA
E-mail: admin@stellarlearn.com
Web site: http://www.stellarlearn.com.

Stellar Pubns., (*978-0-9761224*) 3767 Forest Ln., Suite 124 - MBX 1231, Dallas, TX 75244 USA Toll Free: 866-840-4378
E-mail: info@stellarpublishers.com; maymathis@msn.com
Web site: http://www.stellarpublishers.com.

Stellar Publishing, (*978-0-9703041; 978-0-9849660*) Div. of M & M Enterprises, Orders Addr.: 2114 S. Live Oak Pkwy., Wilmington, NC 28403 USA (SAN 860-2298) Tel 910-269-7444
E-mail: info@stellar-publishing.com
Web site: http://www.stellar-publishing.com
Dist(s): **Distributors, The.**

Stellinga, Mark, (*978-0-9762011; 978-0-9796421; 978-0-9817101*) 42 Lancester Pl., Iowa City, IA 52240 USA Tel 319-354-7287
E-mail: mark@writerofbooks.com
Web site: http://www.writerofbooks.com.

Stellium Pr., (*978-1-883376*) P.O. Box 82834, Portland, OR 97282-0834 USA.

Stelucan Pr., (*978-0-9601454*) 2129 State Hwy. 79 S., Wichita Falls, TX 76302 USA (SAN 221-3176).

†Stemmer Hse. Pubs., (*978-0-88045; 978-0-916144*) P.O. Box 89, Gilsum, NH 03448 USA (SAN 207-9623) Tel 603-357-0236; Fax: 603-357-2073; *Imprints*: NaturEncyclopedia (Naturencyclop)
E-mail: pbs@pathwaybook.com
Web site: http://stemmer.com
Dist(s): **Pathway Bk. Service**; *CIP.*

Stenhouse Pubs., (*978-1-57110; 978-1-62531*) Div. of Highlights for Children, Orders Addr.: P.O. Box 11020, Portland, ME 04104-7020 USA (SAN 298-1580) Tel 207-253-1600; Fax: 207-253-5121; Toll Free Fax: 800-833-9164; Toll Free: 800-988-9812 (orders)
E-mail: jkilburn@stenhouse.com
Web site: http://www.stenhouse.com
Dist(s): **Ebsco Publishing**
Follett School Solutions
MyiLibrary.

Stensland Bks., (*978-0-9759456*) 6011 S. 102 St., Omaha, NE 68127 USA
E-mail: info@stenslandbooks.com
Web site: http://www.stenslandbooks.com.

Stephi /Lee, (*978-0-578-11938-0*) 2884 Blairmont Dr., Danville, VA 24540 USA
Web site: http://www.wheredomyprayersgo.com; http://www.stephileebooks.com.

Steps To Literacy, LLC, (*978-0-9728803; 978-1-59564; 978-1-60015; 978-1-60881; 978-1-60923; 978-1-61267; 978-1-62038; 978-1-63395; 978-1-63502; 978-1-68136*) Orders Addr.: P.O. Box 6737, Bridgewater, NJ 08807 USA (SAN 858-3005) Toll Free: 800-895-2804
Web site: http://www.stepstoliteracy.com.

Sterli Publishing, (*978-0-9790014*) 986 Gable Cove, Collierville, TN 38017 USA (SAN 852-1638) Tel 352-753-4335 (sales office)
E-mail: admin@sterlipublishing.com
Web site: http://www.sterlipublishing.com.

Sterling & Ross Pubs., (*978-0-9766372; 978-0-9779545; 978-0-9787213; 978-0-9814535; 978-0-9814536; 978-0-9821391; 978-0-9821392; 978-0-9827588; 978-1-937802*) 1221 Ave. of the Americas Suite 4200, New York City, NY 10020 USA; *Imprints*: Cambridge House Press (CambridgeHse)
E-mail: contact@sterlingandross.com
Web site: http://www.sterlingandross.com
Dist(s): **Perseus-PGW**
Perseus Bks. Group.

Sterling Innovation *Imprint of* **Sterling Publishing Co., Inc.**

Sterling Investments I, LLC DBA Twins Magazine, (*978-0-9636745; 978-0-9655442; 978-1-891846*) 30799 Pinetree Rd., #256, Cleveland, OH 44124 USA Tel 855-758-9467; Fax: 855-758-9467; Toll Free: 855-758-9467; *Imprints*: Twins Books (Twins Bks)
E-mail: bill@twinsmagazine.com
Web site: http://www.twinsmagazine.com; http://www.twinsmagazine.com/theBookshelf.shtml.

Sterling Pr., Inc., (*978-0-9637735*) 6811 Old Canton Rd., Apt. 3802, Ridgeland, MS 39157-1248 USA Tel 602-957-9265 Do not confuse with companies with similar names in Bulverde, TX, Chicago, IL, Marysville, WA, Bedford, TX, Kihei,HI.

†Sterling Publishing Co., Inc., (*978-0-8069; 978-1-4027; 978-1-60582; 978-1-4549; 978-1-61837*) 387 Park Ave., S., New York, NY 10016-8810 USA (SAN 211-6324) Tel 212-532-7160 212-213-2495; Toll Free Fax: 800-775-8736 (warehouse); *Imprints*: Sterling/Main Street (Sterling-Main St); Chapelle (Chapelle); Balloon Books (Balloon Books); Sterling Innovation (SterInnov); Puzzlewright (Puzzlewright); Fall River (FallRiver); Spark Notes (Spark Notes); Spark Publishing Group (SparkPubng) Do not confuse with companies with similar names in Falls Church, VA, Fallbrook, CA, Lewisville, TX
E-mail: custservice@sterlingpub.com; tradesales@sterlingpub.com
Web site: http://www.sterlingpublishing.com/
Dist(s): **Booklines Hawaii, Ltd.**
Follett School Solutions
Hachette Bk. Group
MBI Distribution Services/Quayside Distribution
Music Sales Corp.
MyiLibrary
Partners Bk. Distributing, Inc.; *CIP.*

Sterling/Main St. *Imprint of* **Sterling Publishing Co., Inc.**

Stern, Frederick *See* **Stern Math, LLC**

Stern Math, LLC, (*978-0-9779132; 978-0-9845392*) 754 N. Hollow Rd., Box 172, Rochester, VT 05767 USA (SAN 850-6027) Tel 212-874-4530
E-mail: sternmath@gmail.com; fredstern@gmail.com; emilyalison@gmail.com
Web site: http://sternmath.com.

Sterner, Hilda, (*978-0-615-22164-9*) P.O. Box 713071, Santee, CA 92072-3071 USA
E-mail: hilda@momsauthenticassyrianrecipes.com
Web site: http://www.momsauthenticassyrianrecipes.com.

Steve Diet Goedde, (*978-1-890836*) 2807 W. Sunset Blvd., Los Angeles, CA 90026 USA Tel 323-377-0235
E-mail: stevedg@gmail.com
Web site: http://www.stevedietgoedde.com.

Steveedee Publishing Co,
Dist(s): **AtlasBooks Distribution.**

Stevens, Gareth Incorporated *See* **Stevens, Gareth Publishing LLLP**

†Stevens, Gareth Publishing LLLP, (*978-0-8368; 978-0-918831; 978-1-55532; 978-1-4339*) Orders Addr.: P.O. Box 360140, Strongsville, OH 44136-0140 USA Fax: 877-542-2596; Toll Free: 800-542-2595; Edit Addr.: 111 East 14th St., Suite 349, New York, NY 10003 USA (SAN 696-1592) Toll Free: 877-444-0210; *Imprints*: World Almanac Library (Wrld Almanac Lib); Weekly Reader Leveled Readers (Weekly Read); Gareth Stevens Secondary Library (G S Sec Lib); Gareth Stevens Learning Library (G S Lrning Lib); Gareth Stevens Hi-Lo Must Reads (G S Hi-Lo)
E-mail: customerservice@gspub.com; hollyc@rosenpub.com
Web site: http://www.garethstevens.com; http://www.garethstevensclassroom.com
Dist(s): **Bound to Stay Bound Bks.**
Davidson Titles, Inc.
Follett School Solutions
Lectorum Pubns., Inc.; *CIP.*

Stevens Publishing, (*978-0-9632054; 978-1-885529*) Orders Addr.: P.O. Box 160, Kila, MT 59920 USA Tel 406-756-0307; Fax: 406-257-5051; Edit Addr.: 1550 Rogers Ln. Rd., Kila, MT 59920 USA Do not confuse with Stevens Publishing Corp. in Waco, TX.

Steward & Wise Publishing *See* **Acclaim Pr., Inc.**

Stewart Education Services, (*978-0-9764154*) 3722 Bagely Ave., No. 19, Los Angeles, CA 90034-4113 USA Tel 310-838-6247; Fax: 310-838-6769
E-mail: info@stewarteducationservices.com
Web site: http://www.stewarteducationservices.com.

Stewart, Mary *See* **Rooster Pubns.**

Stewart, R. J. Bks., (*978-0-9791402; 978-0-9819246; 978-0-9856006*) P.O. Box 507, milton, WA 98354 USA (SAN 852-5382)
E-mail: rjspeak@gmail.com
Web site: http://www.rjstewart.net.

†Stewart, Tabori & Chang, (*978-0-941434; 978-0-941807; 978-1-55670; 978-1-899791; 978-1-58479*) Div. of Harry N. Abrams, Inc., 115 W. 18th St., 5th Flr., New York, NY 10011 USA (SAN 293-4000) Tel 212-519-1200; Fax: 212-519-1210
E-mail: trudi@stcbooks.com
Web site: http://www.abramsbooks.com
Dist(s): **Abrams**
Hachette Bk. Group
MyiLibrary
Open Road Integrated Media, LLC; *CIP.*

Stickysoft Corp., (*978-0-9740384*) Orders Addr.: P.O. Box 7855, Buffalo Grove, IL 60089 USA Tel 847-229-9999; Fax: 847-808-8777; Toll Free: 800-366-8448; Edit Addr.: 620 Silver Rock Ln., Buffalo Grove, IL 60089 USA
E-mail: euclid@stickysoft.com
Web site: http://www.blackjack678.com.

Still Water Publishing, (*978-0-9740855*) Orders Addr.: 1093 Kiva Cir., Windsor, CO 80550 USA
E-mail: chein8@attbi.com
Web site: http://www.stillwaterpublishing.com.

Stillman, Steve, (*978-0-9740508*) 251 Green St., Shrewsbury, MA 01545-4708 USA.

Stillwater Publishing, (*978-0-9709754; 978-0-9837671*) Div. of Stillwater Enterprises, Inc., P.O. Box 500, Lionville, PA 19335 USA (SAN 253-7931) Tel 610-458-4000; Fax: 610-458-4001; *Imprints*: Take a Walk Book (Take a Walk Bk) Do not confuse with companies with the same or similar name in Stillwater,MN
E-mail: jane@takeawalk.com
Web site: http://www.takeawalk.com
Dist(s): **Common Ground Distributors, Inc.**
Independent Pubs. Group
MyiLibrary.

STL Distribution North America *See* **Send The Light Distribution LLC**

Stockade Bks., (*978-0-9731570; 978-0-9863983*) P.O. Box 30, Woodsville, NH 03785 USA Toll Free: 866-799-4500
E-mail: orders@stockadebooks.com
Web site: http://www.stockadebooks.com.

Stockcero, Inc., (*978-1-934768*) 3785 NW 82nd Ave., Doral, FL 33166 USA Tel 305-722-7628; Fax: 305-477-5794
E-mail: pagrest@stockcero.com; stockcero@stockcero.com
Web site: http://www.stockcero.com.

Stockwell Publishing, (*978-0-9785594*) 84 State St. Suite 300, Boston, MA 02109 USA Tel 617-290-3039; Fax: 617-720-0761
E-mail: pel.stockwell@lpl.com
Web site: http://www.followthefox.com.

Stoddart Kids (CAN) (*978-0-7736; 978-0-7737*) *Dist. by* **IngramPubServ.**

Stoke Books *Imprint of* **Lerner Publishing Group**

Stoke Bks.,
Dist(s): **Lerner Publishing Group.**

Stone Acres Publishing Co., (*978-0-9765478; 978-1-937480*) P.O. Box 407, Waverly, PA 18471-0407 USA (SAN 850-0940) Fax: 570-319-1675
E-mail: gmiltony@yahoo.com
Web site: http://www.stoneacrespublishing.com.

Stone & Scott Pubs., (*978-0-9627031; 978-1-891135*) Orders Addr.: P.O. Box 56419, Sherman Oaks, CA 91413-1419 USA (SAN 297-3030) Tel 818-904-9088; Fax: 818-787-1431
E-mail: Friday@StoneandScott.com; BostonLesPaul@adelphia.net
Web site: http://www.stoneandscott.com.

Stone, Anne Publishing, (*978-0-9858811*) 1158 26th St. Suite 440, Santa Monica, CA 90403 USA Tel 310-418-4674; Fax: 310-828-8057
E-mail: JulieK.AnneStone@gmail.com
Web site: www.annestonepublishing.com.

Stone Arch Bks., (*978-1-59889; 978-1-4342; 978-1-4965*) Div. of Coughlan Publishing, Orders Addr.: 1710 Roe Crest Dr., North Mankato, MN 56003 USA (SAN 257-3148) Tel 800-747-4992; Fax: 888-262-0705; Edit Addr.: 5050 Lincoln Dr, Edina, MN 55436 USA Fax: 952-933-2410; Toll Free: 1-888-517-8977; 1710 Roe Crest Dr., North Mankato, MN 56003; *Imprints*: Claudia Cristina Cortez (CCCortez); David Mortimore Baxter (DMB); Graphic Flash (Graphic Flash); Graphic Quest (Graph Quest); Graphic Revolve (GraRevolve); Graphic Sparks (GraphiSparks); Impact Books (ImpacBks); Keystone Books (KeystonBks); Pathway Books (PathwaBks); Shade Books (Shade Bks); Vortex Books (Vortex Bks); Zone Books (ZoneBks); After Happily Ever After (After Happily); DC Super Heroes (DC Super Hero); My First Graphic Novel (First Graph Nov); Recon Academy (Recon Acad); Graphic Revolve en Español (GRAPHIC REVOLV); Shakespeare Graphics (SHAKESPEARE GR); Team Cheer (TEAM CHEER); Good vs Evil (GOOD VS EVIL); Myth-O-Mania (MYTH-O-MANIA); Tony Hawk's 900 Revolution (TONY HAWKS 900); Stone Arch Novels (STONE ARCH NOV); Graphic Spin en Español (GRAPHIC SPIN E); Bilingual Stone Arch Readers (BILINGUAL STONE); DC

Super-villains (DC SUPER-VILLA); Return to Titanic (RETURN TO TITA); Troll Hunters (TROLL HUNTERS); Faerieground (FAERIEGROUND); Claudia & Monica: Freshman Girls (CLAUDIA & MONI); Echo & the Bat Pack (ECHO & THE BAT); Connect (Connect2); Dino-Mike! (Dino-Mike); Far Out Fairy Tales (Far Out FT); Museum Mysteries (Museum Myst); Scooby-Doo (Scooby-Doo2); Space Penguins (Space Peng); Stardust Stables (Stardust Stabl) Do not confuse with Stone Arch Books in Afton, MN
E-mail: k.monyhan@coughlancompanies.com; customerservice@capstonepub.com
Web site: http://stonearchbooks.com; http://www.capstonepub.com
Dist(s): **Capstone Pr., Inc.**
Capstone Pub.
Follett School Solutions.

Stone Arch Novels *Imprint of* **Stone Arch Bks.**

Stone Arrow Bks., *(978-0-9825528)* P.o. Box 221, Draper, UT 84020 USA Tel 801-699-2844
E-mail: komarkris@gmail.com
Dist(s): **Coutts Information Services**
Lightning Source, Inc.
NACSCORP, Inc.
Spring Arbor Distributors, Inc.

†Stone Bridge Pr., *(978-0-9628137; 978-1-880656; 978-1-933330; 978-1-61172)* P.O. Box 8208, Berkeley, CA 94707 USA Tel 510-524-8732; Fax: 510-524-8711; Toll Free: 800-947-7271 (orders) Do not confuse with Stone Bridge Press in Naples, FL
Web site: http://www.stonebridge.com
Dist(s): **Art Media Resources, Inc.**
Consortium Bk. Sales & Distribution
MyiLibrary
Perseus Bks. Group
SPD-Small Pr. Distribution; *CIP.*

Stone Castle Publishing, *(978-0-578-00171-5)* 2602 Skyline Dr., Sedalia, MO 65301 USA
Dist(s): **Lulu Enterprises Inc.**

Stone Cottage Bks., *(978-0-9822503)* Orders Addr.: P.O. Box 962497, Riverdale, GA 30296 USA (SAN 857-6734)
E-mail: info@stonecottagebooks.com; orders@stonecottagebooks.com
Web site: http://www.stonecottagebooks.com; http://www.bigandgrown.com; http://www.bigandgrown.com.

Stone Pine Pr., *(978-0-9728929)* Orders Addr.: P.O. Box 585, Marcola, OR 97454-0585 USA; Edit Addr.: 92985 Marcola Rd., Marcola, OR 97454 USA.

Stone Publishing Co., *(978-1-880991)* Orders Addr.: P.O. Box 711, Mendocino, CA 95460 USA Tel 707-937-0239; Edit Addr.: 10491 Wheeler St., Mendocino, CA 95460 USA.

Stonebridge Pubns., *(978-0-9896904; 978-1-940473)* 25036 Meadowdale Ln., Veneta, OR 97487 USA Tel 626-629-0195 Do not confuse with Stonebridge Publications in Chesapeake, VA
E-mail: stonebridgepublications@outlook.com.

Stonechester, Inc., *(978-0-9759014)* 4894 Lone Mountain Rd., No. 311, Las Vegas, NV 89130-2239 USA.

StoneGarden.net Publishing, *(978-0-9765426; 978-1-60076)* 3851 Cottonwood Dr., Danville, CA 94506 USA Tel 925-984-7867
E-mail: theshop@stonegarden.net
Web site: http://www.stonegarden.net.

Stonehorse Publishing, LLC, *(978-0-9764199)* Orders Addr.: 6528 E. 101st St. S., Ste D1 Rm. 296, Tulsa, OK 74133 USA (SAN 256-3797) Toll Free Fax: 888-867-1927; Toll Free: 888-867-1927
E-mail: generalinfo@stonehorsepublishing.com
Web site: http://www.stonehorsepublishing.com
Dist(s): **Educational Distribution Corp.**

StoneHouse Ink, *(978-0-9826078; 978-0-9827705; 978-0-615-52573-0; 978-0-615-52575-4; 978-0-615-53802-0; 978-0-615-54333-8; 978-0-615-54337-6; 978-0-615-54696-4; 978-0-615-54711-4; 978-0-615-54901-9; 978-0-615-56858-4; 978-0-615-56861-4; 978-0-615-56900-0; 978-0-615-57160-7; 978-0-615-57163-8; 978-0-615-57164-5; 978-0-615-57165-2; 978-0-615-57168-3; 978-0-615-57222-2; 978-0-615-57225-3; 978-0-615-57624-4; 978-0-615-58014-2; 978-0-615-61352-9; 978-0-615-61354-3; 978-0-615-61786-2; 978-1-938426; 978-0-615-626) 12235 W. Briarwood Dr, Boise, ID 83713 USA Tel 208-514-6631*
E-mail: Pattersonbooks@hotmail.com; stonehousepress@hotmail.com; StoneHouseMgr@gmail.com
Web site: http://www.stonegateink.com/; http://www.stonehouseink.net
Dist(s): **CreateSpace Independent Publishing Platform**
Smashwords
Wesscott Marketing, Inc.

StonesThrow Publishing, LLC, *(978-0-9793823)* P.O. Box 1898, Mount Dora, FL 32756 USA Tel 208-610-0431
Web site: http://stonesthrowpublishing.com.

Stoneydale Pr. Publishing Co., *(978-0-912299; 978-1-931291; 978-1-938707)* Orders Addr.: P.O. Box 188, Stevensville, MT 59870 USA Tel 406-777-2729; Fax: 406-777-2521; Toll Free: 800-735-7006; Edit Addr.: 523 Main St., Stevensville, MT 59870 USA (SAN 265-3168)
E-mail: stoneydale@stoneydale.com
Web site: http://www.stoneydale.com
Dist(s): **Partners Bk. Distributing, Inc.**

Stony Meadow Publishing, *(978-0-9787925; 978-0-9834335; 978-0-9850290; 978-0-9885569; 978-0-9894090; 978-0-9962834)* 3412 Imperial Palm Dr., Largo, FL 33771 USA
E-mail: stonymeadowbooks@aol.com; darkmoondigest@gmail.com
Web site: http://www.stonymeadowpublishing.com; http://www.inspiration4songwriters.net; http://www.books4songwriters.com; http://htto://www.darkmoondigest.com.

Stop N Go Fitness, *(978-0-9800091)* 13518 L St., Omaha, NE 68137 USA Fax: 413-669-8870
E-mail: angelinsights@conciergemarketing.com
Web site: http://www.anangeltowatchover.com.

Storer, Mark *See* **Little River Bookshelf**

Storey Books *See* **Storey Publishing, LLC**

†Storey Publishing, LLC, *(978-0-88266; 978-1-58017; 978-0-9674717; 978-1-60342; 978-1-61212)* Subs. of Workman Publishing Co., Inc., Orders Addr.: 210 Mass Moca Way, North Adams, MA 01247 USA (SAN 203-4158) Fax: 413-346-2198; Toll Free Fax: 800-865-3429; Toll Free: 800-827-7444; c/o Workman Publishing, 225 Varick St., New York, NY 10014-4381 Tel 212-614-7700; Toll Free Fax: 800-521-1832; Toll Free: 800-722-7202
E-mail: info@storey.com; sales@storey.com
Web site: http://www.storey.com
Dist(s): **MBI Distribution Services/Quayside Distribution**
Workman Publishing Co., Inc.; *CIP.*

Stori Tyme Hugggs, Inc., *(978-1-890925)* Div. of T.L.B. Publishing, 827 N. Hollywood, #202, Burbank, CA 91505 USA Tel 770-987-5547; 894 Roberts Way, Lawrenceville, GA 30043
E-mail: tenabrown@thejpak.com.

Storie Tree, Inc., The, *(978-0-9679014)* Orders Addr.: P.O. Box 441048, Aurora, CO 80044-1048 USA Tel 303-690-6493; Fax: 303-758-7792; Edit Addr.: 3952 S. Joplin Way, Aurora, CO 80044-1048 USA.

Stories From Four Publishing Co., *(978-0-9742288)* 558 N. Nash St., Hortonville, WI 54944 USA Tel 920-779-9995
E-mail: fourinspirations@aol.com
Web site: http://www.storiesfromfour.com.

Stories of My Life, The, *(978-0-9741215)* Div. of Frontsiders Marketing Strategists, P.O. Box 1478, Summerland, CA 93067 USA Tel 805-969-3597
Web site: http://www.thestoriesofmylife.com.

Storm Leaf, *(978-0-9858325)* 6041 S Valdai Way, Aurora, CO 80015 USA Tel 303-408-3838
E-mail: david@stormleaf.com
Web site: www.stormleaf.com.

Storm Moon Pr., LLC, *(978-0-9827008; 978-1-937058; 978-1-62757)* 5705 Fishermans Dr., Bradenton, FL 34209 USA
E-mail: editor@stormmoonpress.com
Web site: http://www.stormmoonpress.com
Dist(s): **Smashwords.**

Storm Peak Pr., *(978-0-9641357; 978-1-928990)* 2502 4th Ave N., Seattle, WA 98109-2149 USA.

Story and Logic Media Group, *(978-0-615-72436-2; 978-0-615-74806-1; 978-0-9897549; 978-1-941622)* 12386 W. National Rd., New Carlisle, OH 45344 USA Tel 9374783002
Web site: http://storyandlogic.blogspot.com/
Dist(s): **CreateSpace Independent Publishing Platform.**

Story Direction, *(978-0-9675940)* 39650 Us Hwy. 19 N. Apt. 583, Tarpon Spgs, FL 34689-3950 USA Tel 727-939-8466
E-mail: angelface12@earthlink.net.

Story of Your Life Publishing Co., The, *(978-0-9771667)* 528 Palisades Dr., No. 711, Pacific Palisades, CA 90272 USA (SAN 256-8241) Tel 310-230-8510.

Story Plant, The, *(978-0-9816087; 978-0-9819568; 978-0-9841905; 978-1-61188)* P.O. Box 4331, Stamford, CT 06907 USA (SAN 856-0234)
Web site: http://www.thestoryplant.com
Dist(s): **MyiLibrary**
Perseus Distribution.

Story Road Publishing, Inc., *(978-1-939898)* 16564 SW 47th Ter., Miami, FL 33185 USA Tel 818-590-3991
E-mail: zachary@zcbolger.com.

Story Store Collection Publishing, *(978-0-9764798)* 11040 Hickman Rd. # 226, Clive, IA 50325-3740 USA.

Story Stuff, Inc., *(978-1-928811)* P.O. Box 501372, Indianapolis, IN 46250-6372 USA Fax: 317-913-1777
E-mail: jmferrone@storystuff.com
Web site: http://www.storystuff.com.

Story Time Stories That Rhyme, *(978-1-56820)* P.O. Box 416, Denver, CO 80201-0416 USA Tel 303-575-5676; *Imprints:* folder leaf (folder leaf)
E-mail: emailstreet@gmail.com
Web site: http://www.storytimestoriesthatrhyme.net; http://www.storytimestoriesthatrhyme.com/; http://www.storytimestoriesthatrhyme.org; http://www.storiesforschools.com; http://www.kidsrhymenewsletter.com.

Storybook Acres, *(978-0-9761675)* 4309 Creek Rd., Conneaut, OH 44030 USA (SAN 256-2219) Tel 440-593-2780 (phone/fax)
E-mail: storybookacres@adelphia.net
Web site: http://storybookacres.org.

Storybook Meadow Publishing, *(978-0-9704621; 978-0-9845236)* 7700 Timbers Trail, Traverse City, MI 49684 USA; *Imprints:* Bower Books (Bower Bks)
E-mail: garybower@charter.net
Web site: http://www.bowerbooks.com
Dist(s): **Partners Bk. Distributing, Inc.**

Storybook Pr. & Productions, *(978-1-887683)* 467 Central Park W., Apt. 6E, New York, NY 10025 USA Tel 212-975-2473; 212-749-7178 (phone/fax); Fax: 212-975-2026; Toll Free: 800-779-4341
E-mail: storybookp@aol.com.

Storycraft Publishing, *(978-0-9638339)* Orders Addr.: P.O. Box 205, Masonville, CO 80541-0205 USA Tel 970-669-3755 (phone/fax); Edit Addr.: 8600 Firethorn Dr., Loveland, CO 80538 USA
E-mail: Vivian@storycraft.com
Web site: http://www.storycraft.com
Dist(s): **Book Wholesalers, Inc.**
Brodart Co.
Follett School Solutions
Quality Bks., Inc.
Unique Bks., Inc.

Storydog, Inc., *(978-0-9722690)* 3510 N. Bell Ave., Chicago, IL 60618 USA (SAN 254-9786) Tel 773-327-1588
Web site: http://www.storydog.com.

StoryGirl Productions, LLC, *(978-0-9762587)* 213 W. Montebello, Phoenix, AZ 85013 USA
E-mail: jaime@ding-a-lings.net
Web site: http://www.ding-a-lings.net.

StoryMaster Pr., *(978-0-9761179)* 15420 Memorial Dr., Suite M -141, Houston, TX 77079 USA Tel 281-920-0443; Fax: 281-920-1629
E-mail: info@storymasterpress.com
Web site: http://www.storymasterpress.com
Dist(s): **AtlasBooks Distribution.**

StoryRobin Co., *(978-1-937489)* 849 Durshire Way, Sunnyvale, CA 94087 USA Tel 408-905-7543
E-mail: suechen78@gmail.com
Web site: www.storyrobin.com.

Storytime Ink International, *(978-0-9628769; 978-0-9897371)* P.O. Box 470505, Broadview Heights, OH 44147 USA Tel 440-584-0018; Fax: 270-573-4913; 10001 Gatewood Dr., Brecksville, OH 44141
E-mail: storytimeink@att.net
Web site: http://storytimeink.com.

Storytime Pr., Inc., *(978-0-9754942)* 427 W. Main, Suite D, Brighton, MI 48116 USA
E-mail: monroestudio@yahoo.com
Web site: http://www.michaelglennmonroe.com
Dist(s): **Ann Arbor Editions LLC.**

Storytime Works, *(978-0-9886984)* 904 Winter Dr., El Paso, TX 79912 USA Tel 915-248-9658
E-mail: storytimeworks@gmail.com
Web site: www.storytimeworks.com
Dist(s): **Greenleaf Book Group.**

StoryTime World Publishing Hse., *(978-0-9792800)* 5268g Nicholson Ln., Suite 380, Kensington, MD 20895 USA Tel 301-672-4296
Web site: http://storytimeworld.com.

StoryTyme Publishing, *(978-0-9753699)* 7909 Walerga Rd., Suite 112, PMB 178, Antelope, CA 95843 USA (SAN 256-0763)
Web site: http://www.storytymepublishing.com.

Stott, Darrel Ministry, *(978-0-9755564)* 1885 Nancy Ave., Central Point, OR 97502-1627 USA Tel 541-840-7171
E-mail: Dstottmin@yahoo.com
Web site: www.DarrelStott.com.

Stourbridge Distributors, Inc., *(978-0-9753758)* 812 Ct. St., Honesdale, PA 18431-1965 USA
E-mail: rich@stourbridgedist.com
Web site: http://www.stourbridgedist.com
Dist(s): **Phoenix Learning Resources, LLC.**

Stout, William Inc., *(978-0-9712716; 978-0-9743638)* 1468 Loma Vista St., Pasadena, CA 91104-4709 USA Tel 626-798-6490; Fax: 626-798-3756
E-mail: wmstout@altrionet.com
Web site: http://www.williamstout.com.

STR8*UP Productions, *(978-0-9795862)* Orders Addr.: P.O. Box 640173, Pike Road, AL 36064 USA.

Strack, Beth, *(978-0-9898991)* 2594 Hastings Ave., Redwood City, CA 94061 USA Tel 650-368-6158
E-mail: hummingbirdhmmmm@aol.com.

Straight Edge Pr., The, *(978-1-883043)* Subs. of Straight Edge, Inc., 386 Clinton St., Brooklyn, NY 11231-3603 USA (SAN 254-9395) Toll Free: 800-732-3628
E-mail: info@straightedgeinc.com
Web site: http://www.straightedgeinc.com.

Straight Forward Technologies, *(978-0-9718515)* P.O. Box 102, Valley Center, KS 67147 USA Tel 316-207-3211; Toll Free Fax: 877-766-8566
E-mail: info@straightforwardtech.com
Web site: http://www.bakingwithmommy.com; http://www.straightforwardtech.com; http://www.gardeningwithmommy.com.

Straight Paths Pr., *(978-0-9759871)* 17450 SW Viking St., Beaverton, OR 97007 USA (SAN 256-1468) Tel 503-259-9764 (phone/fax); Toll Free: 800-348-2346 ext. 23
E-mail: info@straightpathspress.com
Web site: http://www.straightpathspress.com.

Strang Communications Company *See* **Charisma Media**

StrangeDays Publishing, *(978-0-9747581)* P.O. Box 587, Merton, WI 53056 USA.

Strategic Bk. Publishing *Imprint of* **Strategic Book Publishing & Rights Agency (SBPRA)**

Strategic Book Publishing & Rights Agency (SBPRA), *(978-0-9795935; 978-1-934925; 978-1-60693; 978-1-60911; 978-1-60976; 978-1-61204; 978-1-61897; 978-1-62212; 978-1-62516; 978-1-62857; 978-1-63135; 978-1-63410; 978-1-943204; 978-1-68181)* 14493 SPID Ste. A # 317, Corpus Christi, TX 78418 USA (SAN 853-8492) Toll Free: 888-808-6187; *Imprints:* Eloquent Books (Eloquent Bks); Strategic Book Publishing (Strat Bk)
E-mail: support@sbpra.net
Web site: http://sbpra.net.

Strategic Educational Tools, *(978-0-9842863)* 293 Center St., East Aurora, NY 14052 USA (SAN 858-9666) Tel 716-445-9609.

Strategic Media Group, *(978-0-9824157)* 9800 De Soto Ave., Chatsworth, CA 91311 USA (SAN 858-0979)
Web site: http://www.hospitalcritterz.com.

Strategic Partners Press *See* **Strategic Media Group**

Strategic Visions, Inc., *(978-0-9769069)* Orders Addr.: 337 Turnberry Rd., Birmingham, AL 35244 USA Tel 205-995-8495
E-mail: jom@strategicvisionsinc.com
Web site: http://www.strategicvisionsinc.com.

Strategies Publishing Co., *(978-0-9769662)* Orders Addr.: P.O. Box 5588, Cary, NC 27512 USA Do not confuse with companies with the same or similar name in Sahuarita, AZ, Tampa, FL, New Augusta, MS
E-mail: jjohnson0710@yahoo.com; strategiespublishing@nc.rr.com.

Stratford Road Pr., Ltd., *(978-0-9743221; 978-0-9835480)* 128 S. Camden Dr., Suite 201, Beverly Hills, CA 90212-3232 USA Fax: 310-550-8926
E-mail: peasonions@aol.com
Dist(s): **AtlasBooks Distribution.**

Strathmoor *Imprint of* **Tabby Hse. Bks.**

Strathmoor Pr., *(978-0-9740718)* 1710 Tyler Pkwy., Louisville, KY 40204 USA Tel 502-479-3287.

Stratten, Lou, *(978-0-9747173)* Orders Addr.: 3144 S. Barrington Ave. #c, Los Angeles, CA 90066 USA; Edit Addr.: 3144 S. Barrington Ave. Apt. C, Los Angeles, CA 90066-1146 USA.

Straub, Rick, *(978-0-9793269; 978-0-9842209; 978-0-9913726)* Orders Addr.: 493 Ridgecrest Dr., Blairsville, GA 30512 USA Tel 706-781-6551
E-mail: csddata@windstream.net
Web site: http://www.straubpublishing.com/.

Strauberry Studios, *(978-0-9830321)* 11000 NE 10th St. No. 230, Bellevue, WA 98004 USA Tel 425-821-7007
E-mail: susan@strauberrystudios.com
Web site: http://www.strauberrystudios.com.

Straus, Jane, *(978-0-9667221)* Orders Addr.: P.O. Box 472, Mill Valley, CA 94942 USA (SAN 253-8202) Toll Free: 800-644-3222
E-mail: jane@grammarbook.com
Web site: http://www.grammarbook.com; http://www.thebluebooks.com.

Strauss Consultants, 48 W. 25th St., 11th Flr., New York, NY 10010-2708 USA Toll Free Fax: 888-528-8273; Toll Free: 800-236-7918
E-mail: strausscon@aol.com
Dist(s): **Smashwords.**

Strawbery Banke, Incorporated *See* **Strawbery Banke Museum**

Strawbery Banke Museum, *(978-0-9603896)* Orders Addr.: P.O. Box 300, Portsmouth, NH 03802-0300 USA (SAN 221-6515) Tel 603-433-1100; Fax: 603-433-1115; Edit Addr.: 454 Court St., Portsmouth, NH 03802-0300 USA
E-mail: deidre@perpublisher.com
Web site: http://www.strawberybanke.org
Dist(s): **Univ. Pr. of New England.**

Streams Publishing Co., *(978-1-933358)* P.O. Box 260, Sidney, OH 45365-0260 USA Tel 937-492-4586; Fax: 937-492-7633
E-mail: budford@bright.net
Web site: http://www.cityreaching.net.

Strebor Bks. *Imprint of* **Strebor Bks.**

Strebor Bks., *(978-0-9674601; 978-0-9711953; 978-1-59309)* 1230 Ave. of the Americas, New York, NY 10020 USA; *Imprints:* Strebor Books (Strebor Imp)
Dist(s): **Simon & Schuster, Inc.**

Streetside Stories, Inc., *(978-0-9646977; 978-0-9710606)* 3130 20th St. Ste. 311, San Francisco, CA 94110-2700 USA
E-mail: contact@streetside.org
Web site: http://www.streetside.org.

StreetTalk Publishing Co., *(978-0-9770009)* 187 N. Garfield Ave., Columbus, OH 43203 USA
E-mail: amazingteistreet@gmail.com.

Strelecky, John *See* **Aspen Light Publishing**

Stress Free Kids, *(978-0-9708633; 978-0-9787781; 978-0-9800328; 978-0-9836256; 978-1-937985)* 2561 Chimney Springs Dr, Marietta, GA 30062 USA
E-mail: rick@StressFreeKids.com
Web site: www.stressfreekids.com
Dist(s): **Ingram Pub. Services**
Lightning Source, Inc.

Strickland, Wilton, *(978-0-9747035)* 618 Pk. Ave., Goldsboro, NC 27530 USA (SAN 255-8114) Tel 919-734-2830 (phone/fax)
E-mail: wilton@esn.net
Web site: http://www.wiltonstrickland.com.

Striking Presence Pubns., *(978-0-9724935)* Orders Addr.: P.O. Box 475, Moorestown, NJ 08057 USA Tel 609-936-7278; Fax: 609-936-9651; Edit Addr.: 49-13 Quail Ridge Dr., Plainsboro, NJ 08536 USA
E-mail: jc@strikingpresence.com
Web site: http://www.strikingpresence.com.

String of Beads Pubns., *(978-0-9672012)* 9297 Avignon Pl., West Jordan, UT 84088 USA Fax: 801-566-0406
E-mail: jepp@fiber.net
Web site: http://www.stringofbeads.com.

Strong Corner Publishing, LCC, *(978-0-9754755)* 5331 Talavero Pl., Parker, CO 80134-2799 USA
E-mail: spencerj@broncos.nfl.com.

Strong, Louise dev, *(978-0-9770950)* P.O. Box 197, Morristown, NY 13664 USA Tel 315-375-4238
E-mail: riverstrong@gisco.net.

Structured Learning, *(978-0-9787800; 978-0-9845881; 978-0-9893690; 978-1-942101)* 27062 Lost Colt, Laguna Hills, CA 92653 USA
Web site: http://www.structuredlearning.net.

Struggle Against the Odds, *(978-0-9778318)* 3929 Clay Pl., NE, Washington, DC 20019 USA Tel 202-397-5310 (phone/fax)
E-mail: satocommunications@rcn.com
Web site: http://www.satocommunication.com.

Struik Christian Media (ZAF) *(978-1-4153) Dist. by* **Casemate Pubs.**

Stryker Illustrations, *(978-0-9821038)* 18011 Biscayne Blvd. Apt. 1901, Aventura, FL 33160-5239 USA Toll Free: 888-710-2513
E-mail: strykercards@bellsouth.net.

Publisher Name Index

STS Publishing, *(978-0-9798806)* 1125 E. Second St., Casper, WY 82601 USA Tel 307-577-4227.

Stuart & Weitz Publishing Group, *(978-0-9769949)* Div. of EQ Pubns., Orders Addr.: 674 Triunfo Canyon Rd., Westlake Village, CA 91361 USA
E-mail: contact@stuartweitzpublishing.com
Web site: http://www.stuartweitzpublishing.com
Dist(s): **BookBaby.**

Stuart, Jesse Foundation, The, *(978-0-945084; 978-1-931672; 978-1-938471)* 1645 Winchester Ave., Ashland, KY 41101 USA (SAN 245-8845)
Web site: http://www.jsfbooks.com.

Student Pr. Initiative, *(978-1-932948)* 509 W. 121st St., Suite 406, New York, NY 10027 USA Tel 212-678-8339; Fax: 212-678-3746
E-mail: epg10@columbia.edu.

Studio 37 Pubns., *(978-0-615-73166-7; 978-0-615-79740-3; 978-0-615-92329-1)* 502 Leonard St, Madison, WI 53711 USA Tel 503-449-2821
Dist(s): **CreateSpace Independent Publishing Platform.**

Studio 403, *(978-0-9633943; 978-1-933129)* 399 Shoreland Dr., Lopez Island, WA 98261-8412 USA Tel 360-468-4347
E-mail: mark@studio403.com
Web site: http://www.studio403.com.

Studio 9 Bks. and Music, 162 Margaret St., Plattsburgh, NY 12901 USA Tel 518-298-8595
E-mail: studio9@rdppub.com.

Studio Cherry Publishing, *(978-0-9793360)* 3697 Rt.75, Huntington, WV 25704-9011 USA Tel 304-697-2051
E-mail: studio_cherry@verizon.net.

Studio Foglio, LLC, *(978-1-889061; 978-1-890856)* 2400 NW 80th St., Suite 129, Seattle, WA 98117-4449 USA (SAN 254-5128) Tel 206-782-8739; Fax: 206-783-3931
E-mail: foglio@studiofoglio.com; savannah@studiofoglio.com; foglio@xxxenophile.com
Web site: http://www.studiofoglio.com
Dist(s): **Berkeley Game Distributors**
Chessex
Cold Cut Comics Distribution
Diamond Comic Distributors, Inc.
Diamond Bk. Distributors
FM International
Rip Off Pr.
Syco Distribution.

Studio Fun International, *(978-0-276; 978-0-7621; 978-0-88705; 978-0-88850; 978-0-89577; 978-1-57584; 978-1-57619; 978-0-7944)* Subs. of Reader's Digest Assn., Inc., Reader's Digest Rd., Pleasantville, NY 10570-7000 USA (SAN 283-2143) Tel 914-244-4800; Fax: 914-244-4841; *Imprints:* Reader's Digest Children's Books (RD Childrens); Reader's Digest Young Families, Incorporated (RDYF)
Web site: http://www.readersdigestkids.com; http://www.studiofun.com/
Dist(s): **Continental Bk. Co., Inc.**
MyiLibrary
Simon & Schuster, Inc.
Simon & Schuster Children's Publishing
Simon & Schuster Children's Publishing.

Studio Indiana, *(978-0-9745186)* 430 N. Sewell Rd., Bloomington, IN 47408 USA Tel 812-223-5073 (phone/fax)
E-mail: john@studioindiana.com
Web site: http://www.studioindiana.com.

Studio Ironcat L.L.C. *See* **International Comics & Entertainment L.L.C.**

Studio Moonfall, *(978-0-9841746; 978-1-942811)* 5605 Sheridan Rd. No. 1172, Kenosha, WI 53141-1172 USA
Web site: http://www.fearandsunshine.com; http://www.ratatatgraphics.com
Dist(s): **Lightning Source, Inc.**

Studio Mouse LLC, *(978-1-59069)* 353 Main Ave., Norwalk, CT 06851 USA Tel 203-846-2274; Fax: 203-846-1776; Toll Free: 800-228-7839
E-mail: chelsea.shriver@soundprints.com
Dist(s): **Soundprints.**

Studio See *See* **Studio See Publishing, LLC**

Studio See Publishing, LLC, *(978-0-9796974)* P.O. Box 7013, Sheridan, WY 82801 USA Tel 307-673-1207
E-mail: psee@fiberpipe.net
Web site: http://www.studiosee.com.

Studio4264, *(978-0-9721327)* 4264 Main St., Chincoteague Island, VA 23336 USA
E-mail: acanfld@gmail.com; andrea@studio4264.com
Web site: http://studio4264.com.

StudioLine Photo *Imprint of* **H&M Systems Software, Inc.**

Studios West Publications *See* **Ritchie Unlimited Pubns.**

Study Ctr. Pr. *Imprint of* **San Francisco Study Ctr.**

Stuff on Paper, *(978-0-578-01210-0; 978-0-578-05355-4; 978-0-578-13881-7)* 21849 Erdahl Ct. NE, Tenstrike, MN 56683 USA
Dist(s): **Aardvark Global Publishing.**

Stull, Judy, *(978-0-9765738)* 16401 96th St., Lexington, OK 73051-8208 USA Tel 405-527-7467
E-mail: puppetlady@valornet.com.

Stunt Publishing, *(978-0-9745930)* 22287 Mulholland Why, No. 281, Calabasas, CA 91302 USA Tel 818-312-5157
E-mail: stuntpublishing@earthlink.net
Dist(s): **Independent Pubs. Group.**

Stuttering Foundation of America *See* **Stuttering Foundation, The**

Stuttering Foundation, The, *(978-0-933388; 978-1-930244)* Orders Addr.: P.O. Box 11749, Memphis, TN 38111-0749 USA (SAN 282-3330) Tel 901-452-7343; Fax: 901-452-3931; Toll Free: 800-992-9392
E-mail: stutter@stutteringhelp.org
Web site: http://www.stutteringhelp.org.

Stylewriter Pubns., *(978-0-9718288; 978-0-9721653; 978-0-9729411; 978-0-9748771)* Div. of Stylewriter, Inc., 4395 N. Windsor Dr., Provo, UT 84604-6301 USA Toll Free: 866-802-7888
E-mail: customerservice@spllc.rog
Web site: http://www.spllc.org.

Stylus Publishing, LLC, *(978-0-931816; 978-1-57922; 978-1-887208; 978-1-62036)* Orders Addr.: P.O. Box 605, Herndon, VA 20172-0605 USA; Edit Addr.: 22883 Quicksilver Dr., Sterling, VA 20166-2012 USA (SAN 299-1853) Tel 703-661-1581; Fax: 703-661-1501 Do not confuse with companies with the same name in Sunnyvale, CA, Quakertown, PA
E-mail: stylusmail@presswarehouse.com; jean.westcott@styluspub.com
Web site: http://www.styluspub.com
Dist(s): **ebrary, Inc.**

Subcomission Literature Christiana *See* **Libros Desafio**

Subterranean Pr., *(978-0-9649890; 978-1-892284; 978-1-931081; 978-1-59606)* P.O. Box 190106, Burton, MI 48519 USA Tel 810-232-1489; Fax: 810-232-1447 Do not confuse with Subterranean Pr., San Francisco, CA
E-mail: subpress@gmail.com
Web site: http://www.subterraneanpress.com
Dist(s): **Diamond Comic Distributors, Inc.**
Diamond Bk. Distributors.

Success Empowering Techniques, Inc., *(978-0-9753415)* 5500 S. Eastern Ave., Las Vegas, NV 89119 USA Tel 702-893-0042
E-mail: set@setsuccess.com
Web site: http://www.setsuccess.com.

Success for All Foundation, *(978-0-9767850; 978-1-941010)* 300 E. Joppa Rd. 5th Flr., Baltimore, MD 21286 USA Tel 800-548-4998; Fax: 410-324-4458
E-mail: jworrell@successforall.org; tkoromah@successforall.org
Web site: http://www.successforall.org.

Suckerfish Bks., *(978-0-9764659)* 23700 NW Skyline Blvd., North Plains, OR 97133 USA Tel 503-957-1554
Web site: http://www.suckerfishbooks.com.

Sugar Creek Publishing, *(978-0-9712571)* 4126 N. London Rd., Fairland, IN 46126 USA Tel 727-399-0342.

Sugar Ducky Bks., Inc., *(978-0-9727388)* P.O. Box 56954, Jacksonville, FL 32241-6954 USA (SAN 255-1403)
E-mail: service@sugarduckybooks.com
Web site: http://www.sugarduckybooks.com.

Sulby Hall Publishing, *(978-0-615-84593-7; 978-0-615-86133-3; 978-0-615-89846-9)* P.O. Box 8687, Malibu, CA 90264 USA Tel 310-457-0439
Dist(s): **CreateSpace Independent Publishing Platform.**

Sullivan, Kelley Enterprises, *(978-0-9728556)* c/o L. Leon, KSE, P.O. Box 1843, Lemon Grove, CA 91946-1843 USA
E-mail: ll@mykse.com
Web site: http://www.mykse.com.

Suma de Letras, S.L. (ESP) *(978-84-663; 978-84-95501; 978-84-96463) Dist. by* **Distribks Inc.**

Summa Bks., *(978-0-932423)* P.O. Box 2095, Darien, IL 60561-6895 USA (SAN 687-4096).

Summa Publishing Company *See* **Summa Bks.**

Summer Camp Stories LLC, *(978-0-9863743)* 35 Toilsome Brook Rd., Stamford, CT 06905 USA Tel 203-705-1600
E-mail: elliotsloyer@yahoo.com
Web site: www.summercampstories.com.

Summer Day Publishing, LLC, *(978-0-9768653)* 14747 San Marsala Ct., Tampa, FL 33626 USA Tel 727-224-9874; Fax: 813-926-8215
E-mail: baflorida@aol.com
Web site: http://www.thebreakawaykid.com.

Summer Fit Learning, Inc., *(978-0-9762800; 978-0-9853526)* 2795 S. 2300 E., Salt Lake City, UT 84152 USA Tel 801-466-4272; *Imprints:* Monkeyfeather (Monkeyfeather)
E-mail: george@summerfitlearning.com
Web site: www.summerfitlearning.com; www.mikeandthebike.com
Dist(s): **Brigham Distribution**
Midpoint Trade Bks., Inc.

Summer Street Pr., *(978-0-9766367; 978-0-9822541)* 460 Summer St., Stamford, CT 06901 USA Tel 203-325-2217; Fax: 203-325-2218 Do not confuse with Summer Street Press in Santa Barbara, CA
E-mail: Cathy@summerstreetpress.com
Web site: http://www.summerstreetpress.com.

Summerbook Co., *(978-1-933055)* 305 Lyndale Dr., Hartsville, SC 29550 USA Tel 843-383-5554 (phone/fax)
E-mail: angela@summerbookcompany.com
Web site: http://www.summerbookcompany.com.

Summerdale Pubs. (GBR) *(978-1-84024; 978-1-873475; 978-1-84953; 978-0-85764; 978-0-85765; 978-1-78372) Dist. by* **IPG Chicago.**

Summerhill Pr., *(978-0-9801861)* P.O. Box 79684, Fort Worth, TX 76179 USA; *Imprints:* Summertime Books (Summertime Bk) Do not confuse with Summerhill Pr., Naperville, IL
E-mail: summerhillpress@charter.net
Web site: http://www.summertimebooks.com.

Summerland Publishing, *(978-0-9794585; 978-0-9794863; 978-0-9795444; 978-0-9824870; 978-0-9837923; 978-0-9891121; 978-0-9893996; 978-0-9905886; 978-0-9963736)* Orders Addr.: 625 SE Summit Dr., ROSEBURG, OR 97470 USA (SAN 853-4497) Tel 307-399-7744
E-mail: SummerlandPubs@aol.com
Web site: http://www.SummerlandPublishing.com.

Summerside Lane, *(978-0-9777570)* 179 Highlands Dr., Williston, VT 05495 USA (SAN 850-1793)
Web site: http://www.Summersidelane.com.

Summerthought Publishing Ltd. (CAN) *(978-0-919934; 978-0-9782375; 978-0-9811491; 978-1-926983) Dist. by* **Alpen Bks.**

Summertime Bks. *Imprint of* **Summerhill Pr.**

Summertime Books *See* **Summerhill Pr.**

Summit Hse. Pubs., *(978-0-9746735)* Orders Addr.: P.O. Box 15478, Chicago, IL 60615 USA Tel 847-379-8822 (phone/fax); *Imprints:* Ijiwola Press, Gregory (G Ijiwola Pr)
Web site: http://www.summitpublishers.com; http://thecitylight.org.

Summit Interactive, *(978-1-57458)* Orders Addr.: 302 Albany Ave., Shreveport, LA 71105 USA Tel 318-865-8232; Fax: 318-865-6227; Toll Free: 877-843-0277
E-mail: mhenry@sieducation.com; scavel@sieducation.com; kbriley@sieducation.com
Web site: http://www.sieducation.com; http://www.AscendEdu.com.

Summit Univ. Pr., *(978-0-916766; 978-0-922729; 978-0-9720402; 978-1-932890; 978-1-60988)* Orders Addr.: 63 Summit Way, Gardiner, MT 59030 USA Tel 406-848-9500; Fax: 406-848-9605; Toll Free: 800-245-5445
E-mail: info@summituniversitypress.com
Web site: http://www.summituniversitypress.com
Dist(s): **National Bk. Network.**

Sun Break Publishing, *(978-0-9815557; 978-1-60916)* 1037 NE 65th St., No. 164, Seattle, WA 98115 USA
Web site: http://sunbreakpublishing.com
Dist(s): **Smashwords.**

Sun on Earth Bks., *(978-1-883378)* P.O. Box 704, Heathsville, VA 22473 USA Tel 804-435-5195
E-mail: books@sunonearth.com
Web site: http://www.sunonearth.com.

Sun Pubns., *(978-0-9665932; 978-1-931034)* Div. of Success Unleashed, Inc., 300 Carlsbad Village Dr., Suite 108A-7B, Carlsbad, CA 92008 USA (SAN 253-4444) Tel 619-884-7505; Fax: 760-434-7076 Do not confuse with Sun Publications, Charlottesville, VA
E-mail: eagles10@pacbell.net
Dist(s): **Insight Publishing.**

Sun Rose Pubs., *(978-0-9712781)* P.O. Box 2314, East Orange, NJ 07019 USA
E-mail: carolineilo@yahoo.com; eph-llogienboh@worldnet.att.net.

Sun Sings Pubns., *(978-0-9721429; 978-0-9832053)* 4144 Lafayette Pl., Culver City, CA 90232-2818 USA Tel 310-837-1313; Fax: 802-609-2959
E-mail: alan-alanlindgren@hotmail.com.

Sun Sprite Publishing, *(978-0-9745712)* 19 Milton Ave, Cranston, RI 02905 USA Toll Free: 877-883-4798
E-mail: kwanyin@ureach.com
Web site: http://www.mykwanyin.com/sunsprite.html.

Sunbelt Media, Incorporated *See* **Eakin Pr.**

†Sunbelt Pubns., Inc., *(978-0-916251; 978-0-932653; 978-0-9606704; 978-0-9620402; 978-1-941384)* 1256 Fayette St., El Cajon, CA 92020-1511 USA (SAN 630-0790) Tel 619-258-4911; Fax: 619-258-4916; Toll Free: 800-626-6579
E-mail: info@sunbeltpub.com; sales@sunbeltpub.com; dyoung@sunbeltpub.com; mail@sunbeltpub.com
Web site: http://www.sunbeltpub.com; http://www.sunbeltbooks.com
Dist(s): **Pacific Bks.**
Quality Bks., Inc.; *CIP.*

Sunburst *Imprint of* **Farrar, Straus & Giroux**

Sunbury Press, Inc., *(978-0-9760925; 978-1-934597; 978-1-62006)* Orders Addr.: 50 W. Main St. Unit A, Mechanicsburg, PA 17055 USA Tel 1-855-338-8359
E-mail: orders@sunburypress.com
Web site: http://www.sunburypress.com.

Sundance Entertainment, *(978-0-9729847)* P.O. Box 418, New York, NY 10035 USA Tel 646-431-9334.

Sundance Media Group, Inc./VASST, *(978-0-9762380)* P.O. Box 3, Stockton, UT 84071 USA Tel 435-882-8494; Fax: 435-882-8508
E-mail: info@sundancemediagroup.com
Web site: http://www.vasst.com.

SunDance Press *See* **Bk. Pubs. of El Paso**

Sundance/Newbridge Educational Publishing, *(978-0-7608; 978-0-88741; 978-0-940146; 978-1-56784; 978-1-56801; 978-1-58273; 978-1-4007; 978-1-4207)* P.O. Box 740, Northborough, MA 01532 USA (SAN 169-3484) Tel 888-200-2720; Fax: 508-303-2015; Toll Free: 800-343-8204
E-mail: info@sundancepub.com; lroman@sundancepub.com
Web site: http://www.sundancepub.com; http://www.newbridgeonline.com.

Sunday School Board of the Southern Baptist Convention *See* **LifeWay Christian Resources**

Sunday School Publishing Board *See* **Townsend Pr. - Sunday Schl. Publishing Board**

SundaySchoolNetwork.com, *(978-0-9665124)* Div. of SA Keith of Creative Imaginations, 438 E. Ilex Dr., Lake Park, FL 33403-2606 USA Tel 561-281-5033
E-mail: orders@Bible-4-Life.com; orders@SundaySchoolNetwork.com; orders@christiancrafters.com
Web site: http://www.christiancrafters.com; http://www.Bible-4-Life.com; http://www.SundaySchoolNetwork.com; http://www.creativeimaginations.net.

Sundback, Ruth, *(978-0-9776850)* 10430 Perla Bello Ct., Las Vegas, NV 89135 USA (SAN 850-9719)
E-mail: ruthslv@earthlink.net.

SunDog Enterprises, *(978-0-9854677)* 119 Persimmon Ridge Rd., Cleveland, SC 29635 USA Tel 864-836-2668
E-mail: gail.mcdiarmid@furman.edu.

Sundog, Ltd., *(978-1-932203; 978-1-59744)* Orders Addr.: 35 W. 92nd St., 5e, New York, NY 10025 USA.

Sunergos Bible Studies, *(978-1-932934)* 2485 Morse Rd., Sebastopol, CA 95472 USA Tel 707-829-2956
E-mail: rich@sunergosbible.org; jan@sunergosbible.org
Web site: http://www.sunergosbible.org.

Sunflower Education, *(978-1-937166)* 15044 Haley Hollow, Austin, TX 78728 USA Tel 512-310-2215
E-mail: cynthia.hannon@gmail.com
Web site: sunflowereducation.net.

Sunflower Pr., *(978-0-9616586; 978-0-9768507; 978-0-9832659)* P.O. Box 750733, Forest Hills, NY 11375 USA (SAN 659-7785) Fax: 718-830-9616
E-mail: order@chutaichi.com.

Sunflower Publishing *See* **Growing Field Bks.**

Sunflower Seeds Pr., *(978-0-9743627; 978-0-9830089)* 9470 Hwy 96 W., Franklin, TN 37064 USA
E-mail: bill@rondafriend.com
Web site: http://www.sunflowerseedspress.com; http://www.downonfriendlyacres.com.

Sunflower Univ. Pr., *(978-0-89745)* Subs. of Journal of the West, Inc., 2961 Nevada St., Manhattan, KS 66502-2355 USA (SAN 218-5075) Toll Free: 800-258-1232 (orders)
E-mail: pub@sunflower-univ-press.org
Web site: http://www.sunflower-univ-press.org.

SunHill Pubs., *(978-0-9673189)* Orders Addr.: P.O. Box 4921, Atlanta, GA 30302 USA Tel 404-627-9025; Fax: 678-623-8237 Do not confuse with Hill Publishing in Marina, CA
E-mail: ehill111@comcast.net.

Sunlight Publishing, *(978-0-9818190)* 339 E. Weller St., Ansonia, OH 45303 USA (SAN 924-7130) Tel 937-671-8511; 419-925-4121; *Imprints:* Candy Cane Books (CandyCane).

Sunny & The Chocolate Dog, LLC, *(978-0-9725945)* 5 Palm Row, Saint Augustine, FL 32084 USA Tel 904-808-7144; Fax: 904-808-7142
E-mail: josh@sunnyandthechocolatedog.com
Web site: http://www.sunnyandthechocolatedog.com.

Sunny Bks. *Imprint of* **J B Communications, Inc.**

Sunny Day Publishing, LLC, *(978-0-9825480; 978-0-9903823)* 3800 Rosemont Blvd. 117 C, Fairlawn, OH 44333 USA (SAN 920-8232) Tel 330-289-1052 Do not confuse with Sunny Day Publishing in Richardson, TX
E-mail: mjporrata@gmail.com
Web site: http://www.sunnydaypublishing.com.

Sunny Future Pr., *(978-0-9754980)* 890 Bruce Dr., Wantagh, NY 11793-1116 USA
E-mail: canivan@optonline.net
Web site: http://www.jc-solarhomes.com.

Sunny Hollow Pr., *(978-0-9755818)* 2517 N. 62nd St., Mesa, AZ 85215 USA Tel 480-830-7634; Toll Free: 800-442-0046
E-mail: rjvb@sunnyhollowpress.com
Web site: http://www.sunnyhollowpress.com.

Sunny Smiles, *(978-0-615-78712-1; 978-0-692-25693-0; 978-0-692-36794-0; 978-0-692-41456-9; 978-0-692-44513-6; 978-0-692-53065-8)* 2515 Muscory Dr., Humble, TX 77396 USA Tel 832-202-7818
Dist(s): **CreateSpace Independent Publishing Platform.**

Sunnyfields Publishing, *(978-0-578-06095-8; 978-0-578-06541-0; 978-0-578-06574-8; 978-0-615-75133-7; 978-0-615-76128-2; 978-0-615-76235-7)* 1746 N. Gramercy Pl., No. 15, Los Angeles, CA 90028 USA Tel 323-960-2563
E-mail: Daviddayan666@aol.com.

Sunnyside Pr., *(978-0-9742566)* 902 E. 10th St., Jeffersonville, IN 47130 USA Tel 812-282-8832; Fax: 812-282-4057 Do not confuse with companies with the same or similar name in Saint Johnsville, NY, San Marcos, CA, Washington, DC
E-mail: bprintcenter@cs.com.

Sunphone, Ltd., *(978-0-9652458)* 427 Sippewissett Rd., Falmouth, MA 02540 USA Tel 508-540-6899; Fax: 508-540-8226
E-mail: sunfal@aol.com.

Sunraehealing, *(978-0-9896218; 978-0-9908374)* 3906 Cherrywood Rd., Austin, TX 78722 USA Tel 512-547-2454
E-mail: raedoman@hotmail.com.

SunRaSon Production Co., *(978-0-9677644)* 882 E. 57th St., Brooklyn, NY 11234 USA
E-mail: info@sunrason.com
Web site: http://www.sunrason.com.

Sunray Publishing, *(978-1-934478)* 25123 22nd Ave., Saint Cloud, MN 56301 USA Tel 320-253-8808; Fax: 320-253-9683; Toll Free: 888-253-8808
E-mail: jwindschitl@sunrayprinting.com
Web site: http://www.sunrayprinting.com
Dist(s): **Partners Bk. Distributing, Inc.**

Sunrise Bks., *(978-0-940652)* P.O. Box 7003, Eureka, CA 95502-7003 USA (SAN 665-7893) Do not confuse with with companies with the same name in Lebanon, VA, Lake Bluff, IL
E-mail: Sunrise-2004@sbcglobal.net.

Sunrise Mountain Bks., *(978-0-9842362; 978-1-940728)* Div. of Sunrise Services Distributing, LLC, 13347 W. Tapatio Dr., Boise, ID 83713 USA (SAN 858-8139) Fax: 208-938-8338; *Imprints:* Simple Faith Books (SimpleFaith)
Web site: http://www.sunrisemountainbooks.com; http://www.sunrisedistrib.com; http://www.youcandoitart.com.

Sunrise Publications *See* **Prematurely Yours**

SunRise Publishing, *(978-0-9644552; 978-1-57636)* Orders Addr.: P.O. Box 1001, Orem, UT 84059 USA Tel 801-860-2665; Fax: 801-705-0124; Edit Addr.: P.O. Box 1001, Orem, UT 84059-1001 USA Do not confuse with companies with the same or similar names in Lake Forest, IL, Niagara Falls, NY, Lincoln City, OR, Santa Barbara, CA, Hatfield, PA, Maryland Heights, MD, Austinburg, OH, Inman, SC, Fort Lauderdale, FL, Albuquerque, NM
E-mail: brian@sunrisebooks.com
Web site: http://www.sunrisebooks.com
Dist(s): **Granite Publishing & Distribution**
Village Marketing.

Sunrise Selections, *(978-0-9656307)* Orders Addr.: P.O. Box 51602, Provo, UT 84605-1602 USA Tel

801-852-6141; Fax: 801-489-9517; Edit Addr.: 1102 N. Main, Mapleton, UT 84664 USA
E-mail: bbriggs@provo.utah.gov
Web site: http://www.sunrise-selections.com
Dist(s): **Granite Publishing & Distribution.**

SunriseHouse Pubs., *(978-0-9770783)* 5181 Blackpool Rd., Westminster, CA 92683 USA
E-mail: dawn@dawnwilliams.net
Web site: http://www.sunrisehousepublishers.com.

Sunseri, Heather, *(978-0-9887153; 978-1-943165)* P.O. Box 1264, Versailles, KY 40383 USA
E-mail: heather@heathersunseri.com.

Sunset Beach Music, *(978-0-9639279)* P.O. Box 159, Haleiwa, HI 96712 USA
E-mail: msmusic@hula.net.

Sunset Bks./Sunset Publishing Corp. *Imprint of* **Oxmoor Hse., Inc.**

Sunset Readers Publishing, *(978-0-9749333)* 220 W., 400 N., American Fork, UT 84003-1567 USA
E-mail: beb1@sisna.com
Web site: http://www.bennetthbracken.com.

Sunshine Bks. for Children, *(978-0-9745116)* 8127 E. Weldon Ave., Scottsdale, AZ 85251 USA.

Sunshine Center, Incorporated *See* **Prevention Through Puppetry, Inc.**

Sunshine Publishing, *(978-0-9749844)* 1421 Washington St., Lincoln, NE 68502-2455 USA Do not confuse with companies with the same or similar names in Carthage, NY, Buffalo Grove, IL, Bristol, TN, Columbus, GA, Raleigh, NC, Ft Worth, TX.

SunSprouts *Imprint of* **ETA hand2mind**

Sunstar Publishing *Imprint of* **1st World Publishing, Inc.**

†Sunstone Pr., *(978-0-86534; 978-0-913270; 978-1-61139; 978-1-63293)* Div. of The Sunstone Corporation, Orders Addr.: 239 Johnson St., Santa Fe, NM 87504-2321 USA; Edit Addr.: P.O. Box 2321, Santa Fe, NM 87504-2321 USA (SAN 214-2090) Tel 505-988-4418; Fax: 505-988-1025; Toll Free: 800-243-5644 (Orders Only)
E-mail: jsmith@sunstonepress.com
Web site: http://www.sunstonepress.com
Dist(s): **Brodart Co.**
Lightning Source, Inc.
New Leaf Distributing Co., Inc.
Quality Bks., Inc.
Rio Nuevo Pubs.; *CIP.*

Suny Pr. *Imprint of* **State Univ. of New York Pr.**

Super Dentists, The, *(978-0-9798506)* 2226 Otay Lakes Rd., Chula Vista, CA 91915 USA (SAN 854-5650)
Web site: http://www.thesuperdentists.com.

Super Duper Pubns., *(978-1-58650; 978-1-60723)* Div. of Super Duper, Inc., Orders Addr.: P.O. Box 24997, Greenville, SC 29616 USA Tel 864-288-3536; Fax: 864-288-3380; Toll Free: 800-277-8737; Edit Addr.: 5201 Pelham Rd., Greenville, SC 29615-5723 USA
E-mail: lgranger@superduperinc.com
Web site: http://www.superduperinc.com; http://www.handyhandouts.com; http://www.hearbuilder.com; http://www.superduperlearning.com.

Super SandCastle *Imprint of* **ABDO Publishing Co.**

Super Source The *Imprint of* **ETA hand2mind**

SuperKids Nutrition Inc., *(978-0-9801148)* 375 S. Grand Oaks Ave., Pasadena, CA 91107 USA (SAN 855-2436) Tel 626-818-6299
E-mail: melissa@superkidsnutrition.com
Web site: http://www.superkidsnutrition.com.

Supreme Design, LLC, *(978-0-9816170; 978-1-935721)* P.O. Box 10887, Atlanta, GA 30310 USA Tel 404-759-8799
E-mail: sujandass@ymail.com
Web site: http://www.supremedesignllc.com.

Surber, Shawn-Michelle *See* **Mornin' Light Media**

Surface Communications LLC *See* **Books by Kids LLC**

Surfing Group, The, *(978-0-9770730)* Primedia, 236 Avenida Fabricante. Ste. 201, San Clemente, CA 92672-7557 USA
E-mail: ross.garrett@primedia.com.

Sur-Mount Pubs., *(978-0-9673517; 978-0-9740107)* P.O. Box 99396, Emeryville, CA 94662-9396 USA Tel 510-559-8797
E-mail: cs@surmountpublishersincorporated.com; sales@surmountpublishersincorporated.com
Web site: http://www.surmountpublishersincorporated.com.

Suromex, Ediciones, S.A. (MEX) *(978-968-855) Dist. by* **Giron Bks.**

Susaeta Ediciones, S.A. (ESP) *(978-84-305; 978-84-677) Dist. by* **IPG Chicago.**

Susaeta Ediciones, S.A. (ESP) *(978-84-305; 978-84-677) Dist. by* **AIMS Intl.**

Susaeta Ediciones, S.A. (ESP) *(978-84-305; 978-84-677) Dist. by* **Lectorum Pubns.**

Susaeta Ediciones, S.A. (ESP) *(978-84-305; 978-84-677) Dist. by* **Giron Bks.**

Susi B. Marketing, Inc., *(978-0-9773653)* 188 Wentworth St., Charleston, SC 29401 USA Tel 843-822-7676; Fax: 843-958-8444
Web site: http://www.angietheant.com.

Susquehanna Univ. Pr., *(978-0-941664; 978-0-945636; 978-1-57591)* Affil. of Associated Univ. Presses, Orders Addr.: 2010 Eastpark Blvd., Cranbury, NJ 08512 USA Tel 609-655-4770; Fax: 609-655-8366
Web site: http://www.susqu.edu/su_press
Dist(s): **Associated Univ. Presses**
Rowman & Littlefield Publishers, Inc.
ebrary, Inc.

Susy Dorn Productions, LLC, *(978-0-9764010)* P.O. Box 111393, Campbell, CA 95011-1393 USA
Web site: http://www.juguemosenespanol.com.

Sutton, Robin, *(978-0-9755098)* P.O. Box 79174, Saginaw, TX 76179 USA
Web site: http://www.therobinsnestbooks.com.

Suzalooz Pr., *(978-0-9660350)* 139 S. Eighth St., Brooklyn, NY 11211 USA Tel 718-387-3384; Fax: 212-475-4442
E-mail: zhour@inx.net.

Suzeteo Enterprises, *(978-0-9791276; 978-1-936830)* P.O. Box 436, Holmen, WI 54636 USA (SAN 852-5234)
E-mail: publisher@suzeteo.com
Web site: http://www.suzeteo.com.

Suzuki *Imprint of* **Alfred Publishing Co., Inc.**

Susy & Livy Pubns., *(978-0-9727757)* Orders Addr.: P.O. Box 449, Virginia City, NV 89440 USA Tel 775-847-0454; Fax: 775-847-9010; Edit Addr.: 111 S. C St., Virginia City, NV 89440-0449 USA
E-mail: info@marktwainbooks.com
Web site: http://www.marktwainbooks.com.

Svoboda, David *See* **BooksbyDave Inc.**

†Swallow Pr., *(978-0-8040)* Ohio Univ. Pr., Scott Quadrangle, Athens, OH 45701 USA (SAN 202-5663) Tel 740-593-1158; Fax: 740-593-4536; Toll Free: 800-621-2736
E-mail: arnold@ohio.edu
Web site: http://www.ohio~.edu/oupress/
Dist(s): **Chicago Distribution Ctr.**
Ohio Univ. Pr.
Univ. of Chicago Pr.
ebrary, Inc.; *CIP.*

Swampland Publishing Co., *(978-0-9754785)* P.O. Box 1311, Larose, LA 70373 USA
E-mail: alces@cajunswampland.com.

Swan Creek Pr., *(978-0-9753216)* 3736 Linden Green Dr., Toledo, OH 43614 USA Tel 419-381-0115
E-mail: swancreekpress@buckeye-express.com
Dist(s): **Lightning Source, Inc.**

Swan Hill Pr. (GBR) *(978-1-84037; 978-1-85310; 978-0-906393; 978-0-9504543; 978-1-904057) Dist. by* **IPG Chicago.**

Swan-Jones Production, *(978-1-882238)* 8362 San Critobal Dr., Dallas, TX 75218 USA Tel 214-319-7049.

Swannee Rivers *See* **Rivers, Swannee**

Swanson, David, *(978-0-9830830)* 707 Gillespie Ave., Charlottesville, VA 22902 USA Tel 434-296-4228
E-mail: david@davidswanson.org.

SWC Editions *Imprint of* **Wayne, Steven Co.**

Sweden Trade, Inc., *(978-0-9744088)* 9-11 South Blvd. of Presidents, Sarasota, FL 34236 USA; *Imprints*: Sweden Trade Publishing (Sweden Trd Pub)
Web site: http://TheRoadToHappinessBook.com.

Sweden Trade Publishing *Imprint of* **Sweden Trade, Inc.**

Swedenborg Foundation, Inc., *(978-0-87785)* 320 N. Church St., West Chester, PA 19380 USA (SAN 111-7920) Tel 610-430-3222; Fax: 610-430-7982
E-mail: editor@swedenborg.com
Web site: http://www.swedenborg.com
Dist(s): **AtlasBooks Distribution**
Chicago Distribution Ctr.

Sweet 76 Bakery, *(978-0-615-80672-3)* 8709 58th Ave. SW Apt. D, Lakewood, WA 98499 USA Tel 253-205-1373
E-mail: dineensmith@yahoo.com.

Sweet Dreams Pr. *Imprint of* **Bier Brothers, Inc.**

Sweet, Joanne, *(978-0-9774881)* 228 Westin Hls., New Braunfels, TX 78132-2328 USA.

Sweet Potato Brown, *(978-0-9788158)* Orders Addr.: 5208 S. Drexel Ave., 2w, Chicago, IL 60615 USA Tel 773-752-3521
E-mail: sofiapenelopebrown@sbcglobal.net
Web site: http://www.at3619.com
Dist(s): **Lulu Enterprises Inc.**

Sweet Punkin Pr., *(978-0-9755078)* 43 Riverside Ave., No. 405, Medford, MA 02155-4605 USA Tel 781-389-0693; Fax: 781-396-8052
E-mail: cvenez@aol.com
Web site: http://www.sweetpunkinpress.com.

Sweet Success Pr., *(978-0-9700127)* P.O. Box 351564, Westminster, CO 80035-1564 USA
E-mail: Vkrudwig@aol.com
Web site: http://www.members.aol.com/vkrudwig
Dist(s): **Bks. West.**

Sweetbriar Crafts & Pubns., *(978-0-9802015)* 3390 40th St., Mandan, ND 58554 USA Tel 701-663-6941
E-mail: swcandp@gmail.com.

Sweetgrass Bks. *Imprint of* **Farcountry Pr.**

Sweetwater Bks. *Imprint of* **Cedar Fort, Inc./CFI Distribution**

Sweetwater Pr., *(978-1-58173; 978-1-889372; 978-1-60196)* Div. of Books-A-Million, Orders Addr.: 3608 Clairmont Ave., Birmingham, AL 035222 USA Do not confuse with companies with the same name in Ault, CO, Raleigh, NC Miami FL, Little Rock AR
Dist(s): **Independent Pubs. Group.**

Sweetwater Stagelines *Imprint of* **Old West Co., The**

Swell Gal, *(978-0-9701812; 978-0-615-45460-3; 978-0-615-49231-5)* 1770 Bryant Ave. So. #108, Minneapolis, MN 55403 USA
E-mail: mary@maryhirsch.net
Dist(s): **CreateSpace Independent Publishing Platform.**

Swift Learning Resources, *(978-0-944991; 978-1-56861)* Div. of Swift Printing Corp., 1520 N. State St., Lehi, UT 84043-1079 USA (SAN 245-6737) Toll Free: 800-292-2831
E-mail: swift@swift-net.com
Web site: http://www.swiftlearning.com.

Swingset Pr., LLC, *(978-0-9658167; 978-1-930680)* Orders Addr.: P.O. Box 18701, Encino, CA 91416-8701 USA Tel 818-779-1413; Fax: 818-779-1411; Toll Free: 888-543-9366; Edit Addr.: 5987 S. High Dr., Morrison, CO 80465-2608 USA
E-mail: info@swingsetpress.com
Web site: http://www.swingsetpress.com.

Swiss Creek Pubns., *(978-0-9702276)* Orders Addr.: 15565 Swiss Creek Ln., Cupertino, CA 95014-5452 USA Tel 408-741-5809; Fax: 408-741-5231
E-mail: bob@zeidman.net
Web site: http://www.zeidman.net.

Switch Pr., *(978-1-63079)* Div. of Capstone Publishers, Orders Addr.: 1710 Roe Crest Dr., North Mankato, MN 56003 USA; Edit Addr.: 5050 Lincoln Dr., Edina, MN 55436 USA Tel 952-224-0558; *Imprints*: WestBow Press (WestBowPr).

Switzer Land Enterprises, *(978-0-9642663)* Orders Addr.: P.O. Box 3800, Estes Park, CO 80517 USA Tel 303-586-4624; Fax: 907-577-0775; Edit Addr.: 1236 Glacier View, Estes Park, CO 80517 USA
E-mail: philalpaca@aol.com.

Sword of the Lord Pubs., *(978-0-87398)* Orders Addr.: P.O. Box 1099, Murfreesboro, TN 37133 USA (SAN 203-5642) Tel 615-893-6700; Fax: 615-895-7447
Web site: http://www.swordbooks.com/; http://www.swordofthelord.com
Dist(s): **Dake Publishing.**

Sword of the Spirit Publishing, *(978-0-615-20617-2; 978-0-615-20810-7; 978-0-615-21223-4; 978-0-615-21437-5; 978-0-615-22183-0; 978-0-615-22348-3; 978-0-615-24292-7; 978-0-578-01560-6; 978-0-578-03282-5; 978-0-9825870; 978-0-9838836; 978-1-939219)* Orders Addr.: 219 Lakewood Dr., Crossville, TN 38558 USA Tel 931-287-0280
E-mail: scaramouche9999@yahoo.com
Web site: http://www.swordofspirit.net
Dist(s): **Lulu Enterprises Inc.**
Send The Light Distribution LLC.

Swordfish Communications, LLC, *(978-0-9741955)* Orders Addr.: 1748 Ohlen Rd. #67, Austin, TX 78757 USA
E-mail: orders@swordfishcommunications.com
Web site: http://www.swordfishcommunications.com.

Sy Publishing, *(978-0-9761613)* 7720 E. Redfield Rd., Suite No. 7, Scottsdale, AZ 85260 USA Tel 480-596-9226; Fax: 480-967-8736
E-mail: devinsper@yahoo.com
Web site: http://www.devinsper.com.

Sybertooth, Inc. (CAN) *(978-0-9688024; 978-0-9739505; 978-0-9810244; 978-0-9864974; 978-1-927592) Dist. by* **LightSource CS.**

Sycuan Pr., *(978-0-9790951)* 5401 Sycuan Rd., El Cajon, CA 92019 USA Tel 619-445-6917; Fax: 619-445-5176
E-mail: jbathke@sycuan.org.

Sydney Pr., LLC, *(978-0-9724577)* Orders Addr.: 2035 Fanning Ct., Leland, NC 28451 USA Tel 910-632-7778
E-mail: buckaloha@gmail.com.

Syentek Books Company, Incorporated *See* **Syentek, Inc.**

Syentek, Inc., *(978-0-914082)* P.O. Box 26588, San Francisco, CA 94126 USA (SAN 202-7534) Tel 415-928-0471.

Sylables, *(978-0-9724394)* 2105 Sheldon Rd., Saint Albans, VT 05478 USA (SAN 255-1500) Tel 802-524-0262
E-mail: sylables@earthlink.net
Web site: http://www.sylables.com.

Syllabets, LLC, *(978-0-9794543)* 3740 30th Ave. S., Suite 307, Grand Forks, ND 58201-5820 USA (SAN 853-4632)
Web site: http://www.syllabets.com.

Syllogism Pr., *(978-0-9638001)* 875 Emory Shield Rd., Murphy, NC 28906 USA Tel 732-290-7901
E-mail: spress@dnet.net.

Sylph Pubns., *(978-0-9673004; 978-0-9760742)* 1248 E. Edison St., W., Tucson, AZ 85719 USA Tel 520-882-3794
E-mail: eliotbooks@aol.com
Web site: http://www.eliotbooks.com.

Sylvan Dell Publishing *See* **Arbordale Publishing**

Sylvan Learning Publishing *Imprint of* **Random Hse. Information Group**

Sylvestre, Gibson Publishing, *(978-0-615-21166-4; 978-0-578-01878-2; 978-0-578-01879-9; 978-0-578-03784-4; 978-0-578-04150-6)* P.O. Box 934741, Margate, FL 33093 USA
E-mail: info@mylifeonpurpose.org
Web site: http://www.mylifeonpurpose.org.

Symmetry Learning Systems, *(978-1-58447)* Div. of Symmetry Research, Inc., 5 Bretton Rd., Dover, MA 02030 USA (SAN 299-7967)
E-mail: info@symmetrylearning.com; prberget@symmetrylearning.com
Web site: http://www.symmetrylearning.com.

Symtalk, Inc., *(978-1-932770; 978-1-933209)* 875 Montreal Way, Saint Paul, MN 55102-4245 USA Toll Free: 877-796-8255
E-mail: info@symtalk.com
Web site: http://www.symtalk.com.

Symtext Media, *(978-0-9768379)* 21538 N. 65th Ave., Glendale, AZ 85308-6410 USA Tel 623-362-1947
E-mail: fullschedule@symtextmedia.com
Web site: http://www.symtextmedia.com.

Synaptic Wammy Works *See* **Loose In The Lab**

Synaxis Pr., *(978-0-911523)* P.O. Box 689, Lynden, WA 98264 USA (SAN 685-4338) Tel 604-826-9336; Fax: 604-820-9758.

Syndistar, Inc., *(978-1-56230)* P.O. Box 3027, Hammond, LA 70404-3027 USA (SAN 298-007X) Toll Free: 800-841-9532
E-mail: webmaster@syndistar.com
Web site: http://www.syndistar.com.

SynergEbks., *(978-0-7443; 978-0-9702385; 978-1-931540)* Orders Addr.: 948 New Hwy 7, Columbia, TN 38401 USA (SAN 254-4962) Tel 931-548-2494
E-mail: synergebooks@aol.com
Web site: http://www.synergebooks.com; http://www.yourspecs.media; http://www.synerotica.com.

Synergetic Pubns., Inc., *(978-0-9632248)* Orders Addr.: P.O. Box 1506, Hendersonville, TN 37075 USA (SAN 297-6129) Tel 615-264-3405; Edit Addr.: 205 Applewood Valley Dr., Hendersonville, TN 37075 USA.

†Syracuse Univ. Pr., *(978-0-8156; 978-0-615-28768-3)* 621 Skytop Rd., Suite 110, Syracuse, NY 13244-5290 USA (SAN 206-9776) Tel 315-443-2597; Fax: 315-443-5545
E-mail: supress@syr.edu
Web site: http://www.SyracuseUniversityPress.syr.edu
Dist(s): **Gryphon Hse., Inc.**
Longleaf Services
ebrary, Inc.; *CIP.*

Syren Bk. Co., *(978-0-929636)* Orders Addr.: 5120 Cedar Lake Rd., S., Minneapolis, MN 55416 USA (SAN 249-7719) Tel 763-398-0030; Fax: 763-398-0198; Toll Free: 800-901-3480 Do not confuse with BookMobile in Port Ludlow WA
E-mail: dleeper@bookmobile.com; jogren@bookmobile.com
Web site: http://www.itascabooks.com
Dist(s): **BookMobile**
Itasca Bks.

SYS Publishing, *(978-0-9794871)* P.O. Box 868, Montclair, NJ 07042 USA Tel 973-951-7490; 2142 Blackwolf Run Ln., Raleigh, NC 27604 Toll Free: 800-994-3683
E-mail: SYSPublishing@aol.com
Web site: http://www.sadieshero.com.

Systems Group, Inc., The, *(978-0-9847740)* 4618 Granite Rock Ct., Chantilly, VA 20151 USA Tel 703-378-4193
E-mail: Oliver.Franklin@verizon.net.

†TAB Bks., Div. of The McGraw-Hill Cos., 11 W. 19th St., New York, NY 10011 USA (SAN 202-568X)
E-mail: bookstore@mcgraw-hill.com; customer.service@mcgraw-hill.com
Web site: http://www.mcgraw-hill.com/; *CIP.*

T. A. S. Enterprises, Incorporated *See* **Lit Torch Publishing**

T & T Roberts Publishing, *(978-0-9723868)* 3105 S. Trenton Cir., Sioux Falls, SD 57103 USA
E-mail: tom.roberts@chssd.org
Web site: www.chssd.org/books.

TBM, Inc., *(978-0-9647096)* 280 N. Latah St., Boise, ID 83706 USA Tel 208-853-0555; Fax: 208-383-9010; 9295 Esterbrook, Boise, ID 83703
E-mail: realbows@aol.com
Web site: http://www.tradbow.com.

TCR Pr., *(978-0-9714465)* P.O. Box 12011, Raleigh, NC 27605 USA
E-mail: newplants@angelfire.com
Web site: http://www.tcrpress.com.

T. E. Publishing, Inc., *(978-0-9722036)* P.O. Box 823, Bath, NY 14810 USA Tel 607-76-1307
E-mail: pcarlton@tepublishing.com.

THINC Corp., *(978-0-9655026)* Orders Addr.: P.O. Box 14, Batesville, MS 38606 USA Tel 601-563-1162; Fax: 601-563-6640; Toll Free: 888-837-7606; Edit Addr.: 150 Hwy. 35 N., Batesville, MS 38606 USA.

TM Photography, Inc., *(978-0-9660144)* 82 King St., Charleston, SC 29401 USA Tel 843-577-3237.

T.Y.M. Publishing, *(978-0-9641274)* 409 Melville Ave., Palo Alto, CA 94301 USA Tel 415-325-1130.

Tabby Hse. Bks., *(978-0-9627974; 978-1-881539)* Orders Addr.: P.O. Box 544, Mineral, VA 23117 USA Tel 540-895-9093 (phone/fax); Edit Addr.: 12004 Sycamore Shoals Dr. Bumpass, Va 23034, Bumpass, VA 23024 USA; *Imprints*: Strathmoor (Strathmoor)
E-mail: tabbyhouse@gmail.com; publisher@tabbyhouse.com
Web site: http://www.tabbyhouse.com
Dist(s): **Distributors, The.**

Taberah Pr. *Imprint of* **Sonfire Media, LLC**

Table Rock Bks., *(978-0-9726869)* 69 Woodland Ave., Smithfield, RI 02917 USA.

Tabor Pr., *(978-0-9745799)* Orders Addr.: P.O. Box 470842, Brookline Village, MA 02447 USA Tel 617-784-6561; Edit Addr.: 278 Warren St., Brookline, MA 02445 USA
E-mail: ephraim541@hotmail.com.

Tachyon Pubns., *(978-0-9648320; 978-1-892391; 978-1-61696)* 1459 18th St., No. 139, San Francisco, CA 94107 USA Tel 415-285-5615
E-mail: tachyonsf@aol.com
Web site: http://www.tachyonpublications.com/
Dist(s): **Ebsco Publishing**
Firebird Distributing, LLC
Follett School Solutions
Legato Pubs. Group
MyiLibrary
Perseus-PGW
ebrary, Inc.

Tackett, Viti, *(978-0-9769963)* 85 Pond St., Cabot, AR 72023-3741 USA Toll Free: 877-518-9575.

Tadpole Pr. 4 Kids *Imprint of* **Smooth Sailing Pr., LLC**

TAE Nazca Resources, *(978-0-9749745)* P.O. Box 7592, Broomfield, CO 80021 USA
E-mail: anitajg5@aol.com
Web site: http://www.nazcaresources.com
Dist(s): **Mountain Bk. Co.**

Taffey Pop Kids Publishing, *(978-0-9771438)* Div. of Taffey Pop Kids, LLC, Orders Addr.: P.O. Box 571973, Dallas, TX 75357-1973 USA Tel 214-704-7307
E-mail: js@taffeypopkids.com
Web site: http://www.taffeypopkids.com.

TAG Publishing, LLC, *(978-1-934606)* Orders Addr.: P.O. Box 8975, Amarillo, TX 79109 USA (SAN 853-9251); Edit Addr.: 2618 Lipscomb, Amarillo, TX 79109 USA Do not confuse with companies with the same name in Hanover, VA, Camerillo. CA
E-mail: deaitra@suddenlink.net
Web site: www.tagbookpublishing.com.

Tahrike Tarsile Quran, Inc., *(978-0-940368; 978-1-879402)* 80-08 51st Ave., Elmhurst, NY 11373 USA (SAN 658-1870) Tel 718-446-6472; Fax: 718-446-4370
E-mail: read@koranusa.org
Web site: http://www.koranusa.org
Dist(s): **BookBaby**
Perseus-PGW.

Tai Chi Chuan Center of New York *See* **Sunflower Pr.**

Publisher Name Index

Taiji Arts Publishing, *(978-0-9728192)* 50 Bates Rd., Hillsborough, CA 94010-7016 USA
E-mail: ben@TaijiArts.com
Web site: http://www.TaijiArts.com
Dist(s): **China Bks. & Periodicals, Inc.**

Tail Wagging Productions, *(978-0-9752887)* P.O. Box 1357, Brea, CA 92822-1357 USA
E-mail: contact@tailwaggingproductions.us
Web site: http://www.tailwaggingproductions.us.

Tailwind Press, *(978-0-9799473)* 58 Brookshire Dr., Warrenton, VA 20186-3033 USA
E-mail: loribakewell@gmail.com.

Takahashi & Black, *(978-0-9723247)* Orders Addr.: 8725 Roswell Rd., Suite O-129, Atlanta, GA 30350 USA; *Imprints:* PB&J OmniMedia (PB&J)
E-mail: orders@pbjomnimedia.com; credit@pbjomnimedia.com; returns@pbjomnimedia.com; domo@takahashiblack.com
Web site: http://www.pbjomnimedia.com
Dist(s): **Book Wholesalers, Inc.**
Brodart Co.

Take a Walk Bk. *Imprint of* **Stillwater Publishing**

Take Five Pubs., *(978-0-930099)* P.O. Box 1094, Arlington, IL 60006 USA (SAN 670-1884) Tel 847-253-4370
E-mail: m.shaughnessy@comcast.net.

Takhar's, Jodi Spilt Milk Collection, *(978-1-886000)* Orders Addr.: P.O. Box 1005, Bemidji, MN 56601 USA Tel 218-759-2089; Fax: 218-759-2088; Edit Addr.: 403 4th St., NW, No. 200, Bemidji, MN 56601 USA.

Taking Grades Publishing Co., *(978-1-934538)* 1110 4th St., Dr., S.E., Conover, NC 28613-1825 USA Tel 866-511-8378; Fax: 828-466-0025; Toll Free: 866-511-8378
E-mail: takinggrades@charter.net
Web site: http://www.takinggrades.com
Dist(s): **Follett School Solutions.**

Taku Graphics, *(978-0-9717820; 978-0-9772297; 978-0-9801616; 978-0-9823450; 978-0-9846318; 978-0-9899679)* 5763 Glacier Hwy., Juneau, AK 99801 USA Tel 907-780-6310; Fax: 907-780-6314; Toll Free: 800-278-3291
E-mail: adele@takugraphics.com
Web site: http://www.takugraphics.com.

Talaris Research Institute, *(978-0-9742761; 978-0-615-40953-5)* P.O. Box 45040, Seattle, WA 98145 USA Tel 206-859-5604; Fax: 206-859-5699
E-mail: tinam@talaris.org
Web site: http://www.talaris.org.

Ta-La-Vue Pub., *(978-0-9797521)* 316 Rowan Alley, Apt. 6, Pottstown, PA 19464 USA (SAN 854-2376).

Talented *See* **Cantemos-bilingual bks. and music**

Tales Alive *See* **Words & Music**

Talicor, Inc., *(978-1-57057; 978-0-9674871)* 901 Lincoln Pkwy., Plainwell, MI 49080 USA (SAN 253-0406) Tel 269-685-2345; Fax: 269-685-6789; Toll Free: 800-433-4263
E-mail: webmaster@talicor.com; orders@talicor.com
Web site: http://www.talicor.com.

Talisman Pr., *(978-0-9670848)* 7036 Lyndale Cir., Elk Grove, CA 95758 USA Tel 916-683-1749
E-mail: talismanpress@aol.com.

TALK, *(978-0-9741182)* Orders Addr.: P.O. Box 9226, Peoria, IL 61612 USA Tel 309-224-9665; Edit Addr.: 5001 N. Big Hollow Rd., Peoria, IL 61615 USA Tel 309-694-5444
E-mail: dsymo92699@aol.com
Web site: http://www.doristalk.com.

TALKAIDS, Inc., *(978-0-9659046)* Orders Addr.: P.O. Box 112, New York, NY 10113 USA Tel 212-465-2646; Fax: 212-675-7291; Edit Addr.: 305 W. 13th St., 1K, New York, NY 10014 USA
E-mail: talkaids@aol.com.

Talking Crow Publishing, *(978-0-9860287)* P.O. Box 1356, Haines, AK 99827 USA.

Talking Drum Pr., Ltd., *(978-0-9662428)* Div. of Oversoul Theater Collective, Inc., P.O. Box 190028, Roxbury, MA 02119 USA
E-mail: talkingdrumpress@gmail.com.

Talking Drum Press/OTC, Incorporated *See* **Talking Drum Pr., Ltd.**

Talking Hands, Incorporated *See* **Time to Sign, Incorporated**

TalkTools/Innovative Therapists International, *(978-1-932460)* 2209 Mechanic St., Charleston, SC 29405 USA Tel 843-789-3672; Fax: 843-206-0590; Toll Free: 888-529-2879
E-mail: info@talktools.com
Web site: http://www.talktools.com.

Tall Tails Publishing Hse., *(978-0-9823519)* 902 Arlington Box 113, Ada, OK 74820 USA (SAN 857-9288)
E-mail: talltailspublishing@gmail.com
Web site: http://www.talltailspublishing.com.

Tall Through Bks., *(978-0-9744549)* P.O. Box 6723, Virginia Beach, VA 23456 USA Tel 757-635-6174; Fax: 757-563-6277
E-mail: tallthroughbooks@aol.com
Web site: http://www.tallthroughbooks.com.

Tallfellow Pr., *(978-0-9676061; 978-1-931290)* 9454 Wilshire Blvd. Ste. 550, Beverly Hills, CA 90212-2905 USA; *Imprints:* Smallfellow Press (Smallfellow Pr)
E-mail: Tallfellow@pacbell.net
Web site: http://TallfellowPress.com
Dist(s): **Parklane Publishing**
SCB Distributors.

Tallulah & Bear (GBR) *(978-0-9559752) Dist. by* **LuluCom.**

Talmage Publishing, *(978-0-9773010)* 4820 Strack Rd., Houston, TX 77069 USA (SAN 257-2370) Tel 281-440-1106.

Tamaja Pr., *(978-0-9841260; 978-0-9863753)* Div. of Artees / Tamaja, Orders Addr.: 126 Cherry Hill Dr., Saltillo, MS 38866 USA Tel 662-251-7841
E-mail: tam3artees@yahoo.com.

Tamarin Pr. *Imprint of* **Ekklesia Pr.**

Tameme, Inc., *(978-0-9674093)* 199 First St. Suite 335, Los Altos, CA 94022 USA Tel 650-941-2037; Fax: 650-941-5338
E-mail: Sales@tameme.org
Web site: http://www.tameme.org.

Tamerac Publishing, *(978-0-9621292)* 402 Conestoga Dr., Moscow, ID 83843 USA (SAN 250-9466) Tel 208-883-7761
Web site: www.tameracpub.com
Dist(s): **Lightning Source, Inc.**

Tamerac Publishing Company *See* **Tamerac Publishing**

Tamos Bks., Inc. (CAN) *(978-1-895569) Dist. by* **Sterling.**

TAN Bks., *(978-0-89555; 978-0-911845; 978-0-9675978; 978-1-930873; 978-1-939094)* Div. of Saint Benedict Prerss, LLC, 13315 Carowinds Blvd Suite Q, Charlotte, NC 28273 USA; *Imprints:* Neumann Press (Neumann NC)
E-mail: rick@tanbooks.com; mara@tanbooks.com
Web site: https://tanbooks.com/; https://neumann.benedictpress.com/
Dist(s): **Saint Benedict Pr.**

Tana Lake Publishing, *(978-0-9651007)* P.O. Box 44595, Fort Washington, MD 20749 USA Tel 301-292-3636; P.O. Box P.O. Box 44595, Fort Washington, MD 20749
E-mail: xnate333@aol.com
Web site: http://www.tanalakepublishing.com
Dist(s): **Evanston Publishing, Inc.**

T&N Children's Publishing, *(978-1-55971; 978-1-58728)* Div. of Rowman & Littlefield Publishing Group, Orders Addr.: 8500 Normandale Lake Blvd., Minneapolis, MN 55437-3813 USA Toll Free: 888-255-9989; Fulfillment Addr.: SDS-12-2462, P.O. Box 86, Minneapolis, MN 55486-2462 USA; *Imprints:* NorthWord Books for Young Readers (NrthWrd Bks); Two-Can Publishing (TCan Pubng)
E-mail: sales@tnkidsbooks.com
Web site: http://www.tnkidsbooks.com
Dist(s): **Follett School Solutions**
National Bk. Network.

Tandora's Box Pr., *(978-0-9627337)* Orders Addr.: P.O. Box 8073, Vallejo, CA 94590 USA
E-mail: barbara@tangrammit.com
Web site: http://www.tangrammit.com.

Tangela Publishing, *(978-0-615-18297-1)* 8093 Miller Cir., Arvada, CO 80005 USA
E-mail: a.newell@comcast.net.

Tangerine Pr. *Imprint of* **Scholastic, Inc.**

Tangerine Tide *Imprint of* **Orange Ocean Pr.**

TangleTown Media Inc., *(978-0-9724022)* 713 Minnehaha Ave. E. Suite 210, Saint Paul, MN 55106 USA (SAN 254-8054)
E-mail: todd.berntson@tangletownmedia.com
Web site: http://www.tangletownmedia.com.

Tanglewood Pr., *(978-0-9749303; 978-1-933718; 978-1-939100)* P.O. Box 3009, Terre Haute, IN 47803 USA Do not confuse with Tanglewood Press in Portland, OR, Raleigh, NC
E-mail: ptierney@tanglewoodbooks.com
Web site: http://www.tanglewoodbooks.com
Dist(s): **Lectorum Pubns., Inc.**
MyiLibrary
Perseus-PGW
Perseus Bks. Group.

Tango Bks. (GBR) *(978-1-85707) Dist. by* **IPG Chicago.**

Tango Latin, *(978-0-9663572)* 325 N. Maple Dr., Beverly Hills, CA 90209 USA Tel 213-381-5820; P.O. Box 16111, Beverly Hills, CA 90209
E-mail: tangomediagroup@yahoo.com.

Tango Publishing International, Incorporated *See* **Tango Latin**

TankerToys, *(978-0-615-16200-3)* 387 C Bergin Dr., Monterey, CA 93940 USA
E-mail: tanker@tankertoys.com
Web site: http://www.tankertoys.com
Dist(s): **Lulu Enterprises Inc.**

Tanner, David, *(978-0-9767287; 978-0-578-00817-2)* P.O. Box 140, Avon, CT 06001-0140 USA; 3 David Dr., Simsbury, CT 06070
E-mail: collectiblesodacans@comcast.net
Web site: http://www.collectiblesodacans.com.

Tanner, Matt J., *(978-0-9885253)* 27 Amherst Dr., Basking Ridge, NJ 07920 USA Tel 908-581-9822
E-mail: mtanner07@msn.com.

Tanner, Ralph Assocs., Inc., *(978-0-942078)* P.O. Box 3400, Prescott, AZ 86302-3400 USA (SAN 239-9857).

TanosBooks Publishing, *(978-0-9764666; 978-0-9788520; 978-0-9815522; 978-0-9822543; 978-0-9844865; 978-0-9846540)* 1110 W. 5th St., Coffeyville, KS 67337 USA
Web site: http://www.tanosbookspublishing.com.

Tantan Publishing, 4005 W Olympic Blvd., Los Angeles, CA 90019-3258 USA
Dist(s): **Independent Pubs. Group.**

Tao of Golf *See* **DVTVFilm**

Tapis & Assocs., Inc., *(978-0-9729610; 978-0-9741172)* 1950 N. 6900 E., Croydon, UT 84018-9707 USA Tel 801-829-3295; Fax: 509-984-2718
E-mail: info@tapisinc.com
Web site: http://www.tapisinc.com.

Tapper Records Inc., *(978-0-9747465)* P.O. Box 5241, Hollywood, FL 33083-5241 USA Tel 954-483-5093; Fax: 954-961-9049
E-mail: thespeakingsax@juno.com
Web site: http://www.thespeakingsax.com.

Tapper Seminars *See* **Tapper Records Inc.**

Taqwa Images *See* **Early Rise Pubns.**

Tara Books Agency (IND) *(978-81-85403; 978-81-907546) Dist. by* **PerseuPGW.**

Tara Publishing (IND) *(978-81-86211; 978-81-906756) Dist. by* **Consort Bk Sales.**

Tara Publishing (IND) *(978-81-86211; 978-81-906756) Dist. by* **PerseuPGW.**

Tarbutton Pr., *(978-0-9714086; 978-1-933094)* 951 Snug Harbor St., Salinas, CA 93906 USA (SAN 254-4989) Tel 831-443-5694
E-mail: info@tarbuttonpress.com
Web site: http://www.tarbuttonpress.com
Dist(s): **CreateSpace Independent Publishing Platform**
Lightning Source, Inc.

Tarcher *Imprint of* **Penguin Publishing Group**

Targum Pr., Inc., *(978-0-944070; 978-1-56871)* 22700 W. Eleven Mile Rd., Southfield, MI 48034 USA (SAN 242-8997) Tel 248-355-2266; Toll Free Fax: 888-298-9992
E-mail: targum@elronet.co.il
Web site: http://www.targum.com
Dist(s): **Feldheim Pubs.**
Lulu Enterprises Inc.
SPD-Small Pr. Distribution.

Targum Press USA Incorporated *See* **Menucha Pubs. Inc.**

TARK Classic Fiction *Imprint of* **Arc Manor**

Tarquin Pubns. (GBR) *(978-0-906212; 978-1-899618) Dist. by* **Parkwest Pubns.**

Tarver, Monroe, *(978-0-9743568)* 7904 Calibre Crossing Dr. Apt. 205, Charlotte, NC 28227-6781 USA
E-mail: monroetarver@msn.com
Web site: http://www.worldoftarver.com.

TASCHEN (DEU) *(978-3-8228; 978-3-89450; 978-3-8365) Dist. by* **IngramPubServ.**

Tastica, Suanne Creations Inc., *(978-0-9769348)* 1621 25th St., PMB No. 337, San Pedro, CA 90732 USA.

Tasty Minstrel Games, *(978-0-9841558; 978-1-938146)* P.O. Box 64794, Tucson, AZ 85728 USA Tel 520-275-8913
E-mail: michael@tastyminstrelgames.com
Web site: http://tastyminstrelgames.com.

Tate Publishing & Enterprises, LLC, *(978-0-9740939; 978-0-9748244; 978-0-9752572; 978-0-9753933; 978-0-9759124; 978-0-9759973; 978-1-933148; 978-1-933290; 978-1-59886; 978-1-60247; 978-1-60462; 978-1-60604; 978-1-60696; 978-1-60799; 978-1-61566; 978-1-61663; 978-1-61739; 978-1-61777; 978-1-61346; 978-1-61862; 978-1-62024; 978-1-62147; 978-1-62295; 978-1-62463; 978-1-62510; 978-1-62563; 978-1-62746; 978-1-62854; 978-1-62902; 978-1-62994; 978-1-63063; 978-1-63122; 978-1-63185; 978-1-63268; 978-1-63306; 978-1-63367; 978-1-63418; 127 E. Trade Center Terr., Mustang, OK 73064 USA Fax: 405-376-4401; Toll Free: 888-361-9473)*
E-mail: rachael@tatepublishing.com; accounts.payable@tatepublishing.net
Web site: http://www.tatepublishing.com
Dist(s): **Send The Light Distribution LLC.**

Tate Publishing, Ltd. (GBR) *(978-0-900874; 978-0-905005; 978-1-85437; 978-0-946590; 978-1-84976) Dist. by* **Abrams.**

Tate Publishing, Ltd. (GBR) *(978-0-900874; 978-0-905005; 978-1-85437; 978-0-946590; 978-1-84976) Dist. by* **HachBkGrp.**

Tattered Essence Publishing LLC, *(978-0-9766130)* P.O. Box 290996, Nashville, TN 37229 USA Tel 615-360-6117
E-mail: info@cinderellasrebellion.com
Web site: http://www.tatteredessence.com.

Tau Publishing *See* **Vesuvius Pr. Inc.**

Tau Publishing *Imprint of* **Vesuvius Pr. Inc.**

†Taunton Pr., Inc., *(978-0-918804; 978-0-942391; 978-1-56158; 978-1-60085; 978-1-62113; 978-1-62710; 978-1-63186)* 63 S. Main St., P. O. Box 5506, Newtown, CT 06470-5506 USA (SAN 210-5144) Tel 203-426-8171; Fax: 203-426-7184; Toll Free: 800-477-8727 (orders)
E-mail: tt@taunton.com; cmandarano@taunton.com
Web site: http://www.taunton.com
Dist(s): **Ingram Pub. Services**
Linden Publishing Co., Inc.
Simon & Schuster, Inc.; *CIP.*

Taven Hill Studio, *(978-0-9765321)* 5214n 325w, LaPorte, IN 46350 USA
E-mail: mhill@mc123.com
Web site: http://www.tavenhill.com.

Tavine'ra Publishing, LLC, *(978-0-9713953)* 270 Doug Baker Blvd Suite 700-316, Birmingham, AL 35242 USA Tel 205-218-7678; Toll Free: 888 234-7256
E-mail: tahiera@gmail.com
Web site: www.tahieramoniquebrown.com
Dist(s): **AtlasBooks Distribution.**

Tawa Productions, *(978-0-9718741)* Orders Addr.: 2186 Buffalo Dr., Grand Junction, CO 81503 USA
E-mail: information@poepal.com
Web site: http://www.poepal.com.

Tawnsy Publishing, *(978-0-9887612)* 1212 N. Wuthering Hills Dr., Janesville, WI 53546 USA Tel 608-754-2024
E-mail: tawnsy@charter.net.

Tayes Bks., *(978-0-9743207)* Orders Addr.: P.O. Box 50973, Fort Myers, FL 33994-0973 USA; Edit Addr.: 813 Dellena Ln., Fort Myers, FL 33905 USA
E-mail: tayesbooks@yahoo.com
Web site: http://www.tayesbooks.com.

Tayler Corp., The, *(978-0-9779074; 978-0-9835746)* Orders Addr.: 1066 N. 440 W., Orem, UT 84057 USA Tel 801-426-5714
Web site: http://www.schlockmercenary.com.

Taylor & Francis Group (GBR) *(978-0-389; 978-0-7484; 978-0-85066; 978-0-905273; 978-1-85000; 978-1-85728; 978-1-84142; 978-0-203; 978-1-84872; 978-1-134; 978-1-136) Dist. by* **Taylor and Fran.**

†Taylor & Francis Group, *(978-0-335; 978-0-415; 978-0-8448; 978-0-85066; 978-0-89116; 978-0-903796; 978-0-905273; 978-1-56032; 978-1-85000; 978-1-59169)* Orders Addr.: 7625 Empire Dr., Florence, KY 41042-2919 USA Toll Free Fax: 800-248-4724; Toll Free: 800-634-7064; 74 Rolark Dr., Scarborough, ON M1R 4G2 Tel 416-299-5388; Fax: 416-299-7531; Toll Free: 877-226-2237; Edit Addr.: 325 Chestnut St., Philadelphia, PA 19106 USA (SAN 241-9246) Tel 215-625-8900; Fax: 215-625-2940; 270 Madison Ave., 4th Flr., New York, NY 10016-0601
Web site: http://www.routledge-ny.com; http://www.crcpress.com; http://www.garlandscience.com; http://www.taylorandfrancis.com
Dist(s): **CRC Pr. LLC**
Ebsco Publishing
MyiLibrary
Oxford Univ. Pr., Inc.; *CIP.*

Taylor & Francis, Incorporated *See* **Taylor & Francis Group**

Taylor and Seale Publishers *See* **Taylor and Seale Publishing, LLC**

Taylor and Seale Publishing, LLC, *(978-0-9846558; 978-0-9887836; 978-1-940224; 978-1-943789)* Orders Addr.: 2 Oceans West Blvd. Unit 406, Daytona Beach Shores, FL 32118 USA Tel 386-760-8987.

Taylor, Ann, *(978-0-9800059)* 4319 Candlewood Ln., Ponce Inlet, FL 32127 USA
E-mail: taboka@aol.com; anntaylor@cfl.rr.com.

Taylor, Dale *See* **Barton Publications**

Taylor, Dorothy Loring, *(978-0-9610640)* R. R. 2, Box 152, Virginia, IL 62691 USA (SAN 265-3567) Tel 217-458-2506.

Taylor, Keary Bks., *(978-0-615-76980-6; 978-0-615-82770-4)* 117 Candlewood Ln, Eastsound, WA 98245 USA Tel 3603768200
Web site: www.kearytaylor.com
Dist(s): **CreateSpace Independent Publishing Platform.**

Taylor Productions *Imprint of* **G R M Assocs.**

Taylor Publishing Company *See* **Taylor Trade Publishing**

Taylor Publishing Grp., *(978-0-9762933)* 1605 E. Elizabeth St., Pasadena, CA 91104 USA Tel 626-398-2341
E-mail: tp@finishthetask.org
Web site: http://www.taylorpublishing.info.

Taylor Street Publishing LLC, *(978-0-9892854; 978-0-9911621)* 575 O'Farrell St. Suite 904, San Francisco, CA 94102 USA Tel 415-374-4846
E-mail: timhewtson@gmail.com
Web site: http://www.taylorstreetbooks.com.

†Taylor Trade Publishing, *(978-0-87833; 978-0-925190; 978-1-57749; 978-1-58979; 978-1-63076)* Orders Addr.: 15200 NBN Way, Blue Ridge Summit, PA 17214 USA Tel 717-794-3800 (Sales, Customer Service, MIS, Royalties, Inventory Mgmt., Dist., Credit & Collections); Fax: 717-794-3803 (Customer Service &/or orders only); 717-794-3857 (Sales & MIS); 717-794-3856 (Royalties, Inventory Mgmt. & Dist.); Toll Free Fax: 800-338-4550 (Customer Service &/or orders); Toll Free: 800-462-6420 (Customer Service &/or orders); Edit Addr.: 4501 Forbes Blvd., Suite 200, Lanham, MD 20706 USA Tel 301-459-3366; Fax: 301-459-5743 Do not confuse with companies with the same or similar names in Rochester, MI, Bellingham, WA, St. Petersburg, FL, Owatonna, MN, Eureka, CA
Web site: http://www.rlpgbooks.com; http://www.taylortradepublishing.com
Dist(s): **Ebsco Publishing**
Follett School Solutions
MyiLibrary
National Bk. Network
Rowman & Littlefield Publishers, Inc.
Smashwords
ebrary, Inc.; *CIP.*

Taylor, Y. H., *(978-0-9788386)* P.O. Box 9618, Philadelphia, PA 19131-3315 USA.

Taylor-Dth Publishing, *(978-0-9712923; 978-0-9727583; 978-0-9747532; 978-0-9774431; 978-0-9834780)* Orders Addr.: P.O. Box 216, Fairfax, CA 94978 USA Tel 415-299-1087
E-mail: ncardinali@taylor-dth.com
Web site: http://www.taylor-dth.com.

TaySysCo Publishing, *(978-0-9773236)* 808 White Ivy Pl. NE, Cedar Rapids, IA 52402 USA
E-mail: taysysco@msn.com
Web site: http://taysysco.com.

TazTales, *(978-0-9742178)* P.O. Box 48031, Oak Park, MI 48237-5731 USA
E-mail: taztales@lycos.com
Web site: http://www.taztales.com.

TBG.LLC *See* **Gilliam, T. & Associates, LLC**

Tbooks Publishing Co., *(978-0-9789449)* 324 E. 2nd St., Benicia, CA 94510-3249 USA (SAN 852-0135) Tel 707-342-2280
E-mail: terrie@tbookspublishing.com
Web site: http://tbookspublishing.com.

TBSM Publishing, *(978-0-9860056)* P.O. Box 6314, Traverse City, MI 49686 USA.

T.C. McSears Publishing, *(978-0-9787015)* P.O. Box 341, Linconton, NC 28093 USA
E-mail: tryloc@tryloc.com
Web site: http://www.tryloc.com
Dist(s): **Big Tent Bks.**

TCB-Cafe Publishing, *(978-0-9674898; 978-0-9767682; 978-0-9798640; 978-0-9822200; 978-0-9911208)* Orders Addr.: P.O. Box 471706, San Francisco, CA 94147 USA Tel 415-263-6800
Web site: http://www.cafeandre.com; http://www.tastetv.com
Dist(s): **Perseus-PGW**
Quality Bks., Inc.

TdB Pr. LLC, *(978-0-9740494)* P.O. Box 6348, Altadena, CA 91003-6348 USA (SAN 255-3147)
E-mail: mail@tdbpress.com
Web site: http://www.tdbpress.com.

TDO Enterprises, *(978-0-9787624)* Orders Addr.: 92 N. Yale St., Nampa, ID 83651-2347 USA (SAN 851-6553)
E-mail: jscott@tdoent.com
Web site: http://www.tdoent.com; http://www.booksbyjeffscott.com.

Te Papa Pr. (NZL) *(978-0-909010; 978-0-908953; 978-0-9582371; 978-0-9582432; 978-1-877385; 978-0-9941041)* *Dist. by* **IPG Chicago.**

Tea Party Pr., *(978-0-9749173)* P.O. Box 767425, Atlanta, GA 30076 USA Tel 770-649-4434 Do not confuse with Tea Party Press in Cincinnati, OH
E-mail: paula_taylor@bellsouth.net
Web site: http://www.teapartypress.com.

Teach Me Tapes, Inc., *(978-0-934633; 978-1-59972)* P.O. Box 698, Mequon, WI 53092 USA (SAN 693-9309) Tel 262-518-6060; Toll Free: 800-456-4656
E-mail: renee@teachmetapes.com
Web site: http://www.teachmetapes.com.

TEACH Ministries, *(978-0-9740328)* Orders Addr.: 891 Ted Ln., Elgin, IL 60120 USA
E-mail: marylou@empoweringdiversity.com
Web site: http://www.empoweringdiversity.com/anna.

Teach My Children Pubns., *(978-0-9668891)* 258 Bahia Ln., E., Litchfield Park, AZ 85340-4728 USA Tel 602-935-0386
E-mail: oldbaha@goodnet.com.

Teach Services *See* **TEACH Services, Inc.**

TEACH Services, Inc., *(978-0-945383; 978-1-57258; 978-1-4796)* P.O. Box 954, Ringgold, GA 30736 USA (SAN 246-9863) Tel 706-504-9187; Fax: 866-757-6023; Toll Free: 800-367-1844; 8300 Highway 41, Unit 107, Ringgold, GA 30736 Tel 800-367-1844; Fax: 866-757-6023; *Imprints:* Aspect Book (AspectBk)
E-mail: publisher@teachservices.com
Web site: http://www.teachservices.com; http://www.AspectBooks.com.

Teacher Created Materials, Inc., *(978-0-87673; 978-0-7439; 978-1-4333; 978-1-60401; 978-1-4807; 978-1-4938; 978-1-5164)* 5301 Oceanus Dr., Huntington Beach, CA 92649 USA (SAN 665-5270) Tel 714-891-2273; Fax: 714-230-7070; Toll Free Fax: 888-877-7606; Toll Free: 800-858-7339
E-mail: sozbat@tcmpub.com
Web site: http://www.tcmpub.com; http://www.teachercreated.com
Dist(s): **Ebsco Publishing**
Follett School Solutions
MyiLibrary
Shell Educational Publishing.

Teacher Created Resources, Inc., *(978-1-55734; 978-1-57690; 978-1-4206; 978-1-4570)* 6421 Industry Way, Westminster, CA 92683 USA Tel 714-891-7895; Fax: 714-892-0283; Toll Free: 888-343-4335
E-mail: dlytle@teachercreated.com
Web site: http://www.teachercreated.com
Dist(s): **Austin & Company, Inc.**
Follett School Solutions
Partners Pubs. Group, Inc.

Teacher Ideas Pr. *Imprint of* **Libraries Unlimited, Inc.**

Teacher Press, Incorporated *See* **Teaching Point, Inc.**

†Teachers College Pr., Teachers College, Columbia Univ., *(978-0-8077)* Orders Addr.: c/o AIDC, P.O. Box 20, Williston, VT 05495-0020 USA (SAN 248-3904) Fax: 802-864-7626; Toll Free: 800-575-6566; Edit Addr.: 1234 Amsterdam Ave., New York, NY 10027 USA (SAN 282-3985) Tel 212-678-3929; Fax: 212-678-4149
E-mail: tcpress@tc.columbia.edu
Web site: http://www.teacherscollegepress.com
Dist(s): **American International Distribution Corp.**
Ebsco Publishing
MyiLibrary; *CIP.*

Teacher's Discovery, *(978-1-884473; 978-0-7560)* Div. of American Eagle Co., Inc., 2741 Paldan Dr., Auburn Hills, MI 48326 USA (SAN 631-4570) Tel 248-340-7210; Fax: 248-340-7212; Toll Free: 800-832-2437
Web site: http://www.teachersdiscovery-science.com; http://www.teachersdiscovery-english.com; http://www.teachersdiscovery-social studies.com; http://www.teachersdiscovery-foreignlanguage.com; http://www.teachersdiscovery.com
Dist(s): **American Eagle Pubns., Inc.**
Follett School Solutions.

Teacher's Friend Pubns., Inc., *(978-0-943263; 978-1-57882)* Div. of Scholastic, Inc., 2155 Chicago Ave. Ste. 304, Riverside, CA 92507-2209 USA (SAN 668-3177) Toll Free Fax: 800-307-8176; Toll Free: 800-343-9680
E-mail: info@teachersfriend.com
Web site: http://www.teachersfriend.com
Dist(s): **Scholastic, Inc.**

Teachers' Handbooks, *(978-0-9634938)* P.O. Box 2778, San Rafael, CA 94912 USA (SAN 297-8326) Tel 415-461-0871; Fax: 415-461-5357.

Teacher's Treasure *See* **Perfect 4 Preschool**

Teaching & Learning Co., *(978-1-57310)* Div. of Lorenz Corp., 501 E. Third St., Dayton, OH 45401 USA Tel 937-228-6118; Fax: 937-223-2042; Toll Free: 800-444-1144
E-mail: customerservice@teachinglearning.com
Web site: http://www.teachinglearning.com.

Teaching Christ's Children Publishing, *(978-0-9855423; 978-0-615-80614-3; 978-0-692-20138-1; 978-0-692-20142-8; 978-0-692-20166-4)* 7404 Forrest Ave., Parkville, MD 21234 USA Tel 410-665-2655
E-mail: teachingchristschildren@yahoo.com
Web site: www.teachingchristschildren.com
Dist(s): **CreateSpace Independent Publishing Platform.**

Teaching Point, Inc., *(978-0-9629357; 978-1-931680; 978-1-59657)* Orders Addr.: 6950 Philips Hwy. Ste. 46, Jacksonville, FL 32216-6087 USA Toll Free: 877-494-0550; *Imprints:* Expert Systems for Teachers (Expert Systms Teach)
Web site: http://www.teaching-point.net.

Teaching Resources *Imprint of* **Scholastic, Inc.**

Teaching Strategies *Imprint of* **Scholastic, Inc.**

Teaching Strategies, Inc., *(978-0-9602892; 978-1-879537; 978-1-933021; 978-1-60617)* Orders Addr.: P.O. Box 42243, Washington, DC 20015 USA Toll Free: 800-637-3652; Edit Addr.: 7101 Wisconsin Ave., NW, Bethesda, MD 20814 USA (SAN 222-240X) Tel 301-634-0818; Fax: 301-657-0250; Toll Free: 800-637-3652
E-mail: MatthewM@teachingstrategies.com
Web site: http://www.teachingstrategies.com; http://www.EdPro.com; http://www.MindNurture.com
Dist(s): **Delmar Cengage Learning**
Gryphon Hse., Inc.

Teahouse of Danger, *(978-0-9801054)* P.O. Box 1361, Tucson, AZ 85702 USA (SAN 855-2193) Toll Free: 877-663-3324
E-mail: teahouseofdanger@gmail.com
Web site: http://www.teahouseofdanger.com.

Team B Creative LLC, *(978-0-9774119; 978-1-937665)* 9864 E. Grand River, Suite 110, No. 244, Brighton, MI 48116 USA
E-mail: mickmorrisinfo@yahoo.com; teambcreative@yahoo.com; karen@teambcreative.com
Web site: http://www.mickmorris.net; http://www.ghostboardposse.com; http://www.mickmorris.com; http://www.totallyunrehearsed.com
Dist(s): **Follett School Solutions**
Partners Bk. Distributing, Inc.

Team Cheer *Imprint of* **Stone Arch Bks.**

Team Dawg Productions, Inc., *(978-0-9749378)* Orders Addr.: P.O. Box 105, Nesconset, NY 11767 USA Tel 718-926-5984; Edit Addr.: 1 Mayfair Rd., Apt. 1, Nesconset, NY 11767 USA
E-mail: bobby@teamdawg.com
Web site: http://www.teamdawg.com.

Team EEKI, *(978-0-9767646)* Orders Addr.: 413 Bella St., Hollidaysburg, PA 16648 USA Tel 814-695-7631
E-mail: gimmygum@gimmygum.com
Web site: http://www.gimmygum.com.

Team Jilli Dog, *(978-0-615-47477-9)* 209 Jackson Crescent, Centerport, NY 11721 USA Tel 621-875-2669; 631-875-2660
E-mail: rickcaran@hotmail.xom
Web site: http://www.jillidog.com
Dist(s): **CreateSpace Independent Publishing Platform**
Dummy Record Do Not USE!!!!.

Team Kidz, Inc., *(978-0-9793833)* P.O. Box 2111, Voorhees, NJ 08043-8111 USA Tel 856-768-2181
E-mail: jgkeega@aol.com.

Team Reach, Inc., *(978-0-9767610)* 8448 Summit St., Lenexa, KS 66215-5388 USA Fax: 913-312-8872
E-mail: troy@krystal-planet.com; troy@troyhelming.com
Web site: http://www.troyhelming.com; http://www.teamreach.com.

TechArts International LLC, *(978-0-9726326)* 7638 S. Carroll Rd., Indianapolis, IN 46259 USA.

Technical Data Freeway, Inc., *(978-0-9841600)* P.O. Box 308, Poway, CA 92074 USA.

Technology & Imagination Pr., *(978-0-9798991; 978-1-944273)* 1970 Chalon Glen Ct., Livermore, CA 94550-8206 USA (SAN 854-7068) Tel 925-606-1285; Fax: 925-606-1297
E-mail: books@siliconmap.net.

Technology Education Concepts Inc., *(978-0-9740796; 978-0-9777525)* 32 Commercial St., Concord, NH 03301-5031 USA Tel 603-224-8324; Fax: 603-225-7766; Toll Free: 800-338-2238
E-mail: justyn@tecedu.com
Web site: http://www.tecedu.com.

Tecknl-Corp, Ltd., *(978-0-9724178)* P.O. Box 866, Bettendorf, IA 52722-1955 USA Tel 563-359-4388; Fax: 563-359-4671
E-mail: patrickm@studentsafe.com
Web site: http://www.studentsafe.com.

Tecolote, Ediciones, S.A. de C.V. (MEX) *(978-968-7381)* *Dist. by* **Mariuccia Iaconi Bk Imports.**

Tecolote, Ediciones, S.A. de C.V. (MEX) *(978-968-7381)* *Dist. by* **Lectorum Pubns.**

Tectum B.V.B.A. (BEL) *(978-90-76886; 978-90-79761)* *Dist. by* **InnovativeLog.**

Teddy Bear Pr., Inc., *(978-1-880017)* 5470 Van Ness, Bloomfield Hills, MI 48302 USA Tel 248-851-8607 Do not confuse with Teddy Bear Pr., Las Vegas, NV.

Teddy Traveler Co., *(978-0-9748954)* P.O. Box 3223, Manhattan Beach, CA 90266 USA
Web site: http://www.teddytraveler.com
Dist(s): **Beyda for Bks., LLC.**

Tedesco, James *See* **JBT Publishing**

Teen Winners, LLC, *(978-0-9740356)* 19 Quail Run, Berlin, CT 06037 USA Tel 860-829-2067; Fax: 860-829-8067
E-mail: info@teenwinners.com
Web site: http://www.teenwinners.com.

TEG Publishing, *(978-0-9707208; 978-0-9727410)* Orders Addr.: P.O. Box 12737, Tempe, AZ 85284 USA Tel 310-919-3013
E-mail: microlawyers@aol.com; tegpublishing@wwsws.com
Web site: http://www.tegpublishing.com.

Tegen, Katherine Bks *Imprint of* **HarperCollins Pubs.**

Tehabi Bks., *(978-1-887656; 978-1-931688)* 4920 Carroll Canyon Rd., Suite 200, San Diego, CA 92121 USA Tel 858-450-9100; Fax: 858-450-9146; Toll Free: 800-243-7259
E-mail: Emily.Henning@tehabi.com
Web site: http://www.tehabi.com.

Telemachus Pr., LLC, *(978-0-9841083; 978-1-935670; 978-1-937387; 978-1-937698; 978-1-938135; 978-1-938701; 978-1-939337; 978-1-939927; 978-1-940745; 978-1-941536; 978-1-942899)* Orders Addr.: 5883 Dunabbey Loop, Dublin, OH 43017 USA (SAN 858-4508) Tel 941-993-5816; 941-993-5987; Fax: 941-296-7873; 5883 Dunabbey Loop, Dublin, OH 43017 (SAN 858-4508) Tel 941-993-5816; 941-993-5987; Fax: 941-296-7873
E-mail: Steve.himes@telemachuspress.com
Web site: http://www.telemachuspress.com
Dist(s): **Lightning Source, Inc.**
Smashwords.

Tell Me Pr., LLC, *(978-0-9816453; 978-0-9819835; 978-0-9829421; 978-0-9906453)* 98 Mansfield St., New Haven, CT 06511 USA (SAN 857-8508) Tel 203-562-4215; Fax: 203-562-4225
E-mail: lisa@tellmepress.com
Web site: http://www.tellmepress.com
Dist(s): **Greenleaf Book Group.**

Tell-a-Vision Bks., *(978-0-9727706)* Orders Addr.: P.O. Box 396, Lexington, VA 24450 USA; Edit Addr.: 272 Dogwood Rise, Lexington, VA 24450 USA
Web site: http://www.tell-a-visionbooks.com.

Telling Family Tales, *(978-1-940379)* 12129 S. 2160 W., Riverton, UT 84065 USA Tel 801-787-5673
E-mail: raelyn@tellingfamilytales.com.

Temenos Pr., *(978-0-9701319)* Orders Addr.: P.O. Box 477, Ashfield, MA 01330 USA Tel 413-625-9148; Edit Addr.: 989 Apple Valley Rd., Ashfield, MA 01330 USA Do not confuse with Temenos Pr., in Cloverdale, CA.

Tempest Bk. Shop, *(978-0-9632484)* Orders Addr.: 5031 Main St., Waitsfield, VT 05673-7111 USA Tel 802-496-2022; Fax: 802-496-3299
E-mail: rayfieldvt@aol.com.

Tempest Pr., *(978-0-9790232)* P.O. Box 3504, New York, NY 10008-3504 USA (SAN 852-2340)
E-mail: info@tempestpress.com
Web site: http://www.tempestpress.com
Dist(s): **Greenfield Distribution, Inc.**

Templar *Imprint of* **Candlewick Pr.**

Temple Care: Body, Mind & Spirit, *(978-0-9773759)* P.O. Box 1221 Ring Bill Loop, Upper Marlboro, MD 20774-7170 USA Tel 301-218-5941; Fax: 719-218-5948
E-mail: templecare@verizon.com.

Temple Street Pr., *(978-0-9896231)* P.O. Box 7071, Halcyon, CA 93421 USA Tel 805-243-8144
E-mail: eva@templestreetpress.com
Web site: http://templestreetpress.com.

†Temple Univ. Pr., *(978-0-87722; 978-1-56639; 978-1-59213; 978-1-4399)* 1601 N. Broad St., Univ. Services Bldg., Rm. 305, Philadelphia, PA 19122-6099 USA (SAN 202-7666) Tel 215-204-3389; Fax: 215-204-4719; Toll Free: 800-447-1656
E-mail: charles.ault@temple.edu
Web site: http://www.temple.edu/tempress
Dist(s): **Chicago Distribution Ctr.**
Ebsco Publishing
Follett School Solutions
MyiLibrary
Univ. of Chicago Pr.
ebrary, Inc.; *CIP.*

Templeton Foundation Press *See* **Templeton Pr.**

Templeton Pr., *(978-1-890151; 978-1-932031; 978-1-59947)* Div. of John Templeton Foundation, 300 Conshohocken State Rd., Conshohocken, PA 19428-3801 USA
E-mail: info@templetonpress.org; lbarrett@templeton.org
Web site: http://www.templetonpress.org
Dist(s): **Chicago Distribution Ctr.**
Ebsco Publishing
MyiLibrary
ebrary, Inc.

Temporal Mechanical Pr., *(978-1-928878)* Div. of Enos Mills Cabin, Orders Addr.: 6760 Hwy. 7, Estes Park, CO 80517-6404 USA Tel 970-586-4706
E-mail: info@enosmills.com
Web site: http://www.enosmills.com.

Ten Gallon Pr., *(978-0-615-69261-6; 978-0-9883021)* 2896 Bardy Rd., Santa Rosa, CA 95404 USA Tel 415-713-8386
E-mail: hsedwick@gmail.com
Web site: www.tengallonpress.com
Dist(s): **CreateSpace Independent Publishing Platform.**

Ten Minas Publishing, *(978-0-9716786)* P.O. Box 8984, Reston, VA 20195 USA Fax: 703-834-1176
Web site: http://www.crowsofhiddencreek.

†Ten Speed Pr., *(978-0-89815; 978-0-913668; 978-1-58008; 978-1-60774)* Div. of Crown Publishing Group, Orders Addr.: P.O. Box 7123, Berkeley, CA 94707 USA (SAN 202-7674) Fax: 510-559-1629 (orders); Toll Free: 800-841-2665; 555 Richmond St., W. Suite 405, Box 702, Toronto, ON M5V 3B1 Tel 416-703-7775; Fax: 416-703-9992; *Imprints:* Celestial Arts (CelestialArts); Tricycle Press (TricyclePress)
E-mail: order@tenspeed.com; alan@tenspeed.ca
Web site: http://www.tenspeed.com
Dist(s): **Fujii Assocs.**
MyiLibrary
Penguin Random Hse., LLC.
Random Hse., Inc.; *CIP.*

Tender Heart Pr., *(978-0-9741401)* 15448 S. Jasper, Bldg. G, Odessa, TX 79766 USA
Web site: http://www.tenderheartpress.com.

Tender Learning Concepts, *(978-0-9708796)* 5362 Rockledge Dr., Buena Pk., CA 90621 USA Tel 714 739 2145; 714-739-2145; Fax: 714-739-0593; Toll Free: 877 886-7091; *Imprints:* TLConcepts, Incorporated (TLCPTS)
E-mail: whm@iqboosters.com
Web site: http://www.iqboosters.com; http://tenderlearning.econgo.com.

Tendril Pr., LLC, *(978-0-9763706; 978-0-9802190; 978-0-9822394; 978-0-9841543; 978-0-9831587; 978-0-9858933)* Orders Addr.: P.O. Box 441110, Aurora, CO 80044 USA Tel 303-696-9227; Fax: 303-873-6766; 2215 S. Oakland Way, Aurora, CO 80014 Tel 720-275-8371 Direct
E-mail: publisher@tendrilpress.com
Web site: http://www.tendrilpress.com
Dist(s): **Brigham Distribution.**

teNeues Publishing Co., *(978-3-570; 978-3-8238; 978-3-929278; 978-3-8327; 978-1-933427; 978-1-60160; 978-1-62325)* 7 W. 18th St., New York, NY 10011 USA (SAN 245-176X) Tel 212-627-9090; Fax: 212-627-9511; Toll Free: 800-352-0305; 12 Ferndene Rd., London, SE24 0AQ
E-mail: tnp@teneues-usa.com
Web site: http://www.teneues.com.

Tengan, G. Shay Service Group, *(978-0-9883478)* 2229 Orange Grove Pl., Escondido, CA 92027 USA Tel 760-443-9069
E-mail: stengan@cox.net.

Tenley Circle Pr., *(978-0-9773536)* Orders Addr.: P.O. Box 5625, Washington, DC 20016 USA
Dist(s): **AtlasBooks Distribution.**

Tennessee Valley Publishing, *(978-1-882194; 978-1-932604)* Orders Addr.: P.O. Box 52527, Knoxville, TN 37950-2527 USA Tel 865-584-5235; Fax: 865-584-0113; Toll Free: 800-762-7079; Edit Addr.: 5227 N. Middlebrook Pike., Knoxville, TN 37921-5963 USA
E-mail: info@tvp1.com
Web site: http://www.tvp1.com
Dist(s): **Chicago Distribution Ctr.**

Tenney, Bob Solutions, LLC, *(978-0-9763485)* 160 Hamburg Mountain Rd., Weaverville, NC 28787-9432 USA
E-mail: bobtenney@earthlink.net
Web site: http://www.tenneypubs.com.

Tensaw Pr., Inc., The, *(978-0-9746444)* 158 S. Jefferson St., Mobile, AL 36602-1119 USA Fax: 251-438-4545
E-mail: tensawpress@aol.com.

Teora USA LLC, *(978-1-59496)* Orders Addr.: 505 Hampton Park Blvd. Ste. G, Capitol Hgts, MD 20743-3862 USA (SAN 256-1220)
E-mail: welcome@teora.com
Web site: http://www.teorausa.com.

Terabyte Pr. LLC, *(978-0-9839877)* 223A S. Durkee Hill Ln., Southbury, CT 06488 USA Tel 203-448-8142
E-mail: cbaileysims@gmail.com.

Terminal Pr., LLC, *(978-0-9753683)* 27 June Walk., Long Beach, NY 11561-2884 USA
E-mail: bferrara@terminalpress.com
Web site: http://www.terminalpress.com.

Terra Denuo, Inc., *(978-1-933232)* P.O. Box 485, Rocklin, CA 95677 USA
E-mail: mark@terradenuo.com
Web site: http://www.terradenuo.com.

Terra Linda Publishing, *(978-0-9746710)* 593 Tamarack Dr., San Rafael, CA 94903 USA Tel 415-491-1042
E-mail: rneolson@earthlink.net
Web site: http://www.terralindapublishing.com.

Terra Niños *See* **Solibros**

Terra Nova Publishing Company *See* **Dream Ship Publishing Co.**

Terra Tales, *(978-0-9771804)* 101 Lattice Ln., Collegeville, PA 19426-3374 USA.

Terrapin Pr., *(978-0-9753087)* 2094 Arthur St., Eugene, OR 97405-1519 USA Do not confuse with companies with the same name in Marina del Rey, CA, Aiken, SC.

Terrific Science Pr., *(978-1-883822)* Miami Univ. Middletown, 4200 E. University Blvd., Middletown, OH 45042 USA Fax: 513-727-3328
E-mail: cse@muohio.edu
Web site: http://www.terrificscience.org
Dist(s): **Carolina Biological Supply Co.**
Nasco Math Eighty-Six
Science Kit & Boreal Labs
Teacher's Discovery.

Terrific Twins LLC, *(978-0-9769910)* 659 Kensington Ave., Severna Park, MD 21146 USA Tel 410-647-8923 (phone/fax)
E-mail: carpenterzyla@hotmail.com
Web site: http://terrifictwins.com.

Terry Lowey's Children's Stories, LLC, *(978-0-9792695)* 1325 Airmotive Way, Suite 175, Reno, NV 89502 USA Tel 775-322-1924; Fax: 775-322-1937
Web site: http://www.lifesamagicaljourney.com.

Tertulia Pubns., *(978-0-9785988)* P.O. Box 2450, Nevada City, CA 95959 USA (SAN 851-0962)
Web site: http://www.tertuliapress.com.

Terumah Publishing, *(978-0-9744277)* Orders Addr.: 5 Pipe Hill Ct., Unit C, Baltimore, MD 21209 USA Tel 410-486-0950
E-mail: info@terumah.com
Web site: http://www.terumah.com.

Tesoro Publishing, *(978-0-9797419; 978-1-941346)* P.O. Box 528, Fullerton, CA 92836 USA (SAN 854-2279)
E-mail: Info@Tesoropublishing.com
Web site: http://www.TesoroPublishing.com.

Tetoca Pr., *(978-0-9788085)* P.O. Box 337, Puyallup, WA 98371 USA Tel 253-845-1256; 253-845-5090; Toll Free: 888-483-8622
E-mail: thhunter@earthlink.net; tetoca@tetocapress.net
Web site: http://www.tetocapress.net
Dist(s): **Pathway Bk. Service**
Quality Bks., Inc.

Tetrahedron, Incorporated *See* **Tetrahedron Publishing LLC**

Tetrahedron Publishing LLC, *(978-0-923550; 978-0-9609386)* Orders Addr.: c/o Healthy World Distributing, LLC, 206 N. Fourth Ave., Suite 147, Sandpoint, ID 83864 USA Tel 208-265-2575; Fax: 208-265-2775; Toll Free: 888-508-4787; Edit Addr.: P.O. Box 2033, Sandpoint, ID 83864-0906 USA (SAN 260-2717) Toll Free: 888-508-4787 (orders)
E-mail: tetra@tetrahedron.org
Web site: http://www.tetrahedron.org
Dist(s): **New Leaf Distributing Co., Inc.**

Publisher Name Index

Texas Agricultural Extension Service *See* **Texas Cooperative Extension**

†Texas Christian Univ. Pr., *(978-0-87565; 978-0-912646; 978-0-87565-510-9)* P.O. Box 298300, Fort Worth, TX 76129 USA (SAN 202-7690) Tel 817-257-7822; Fax: 817-257-5075
E-mail: j.alter@tcu.edu; s.petty@tcu.edu
Web site: http://www.prs.tcu.edu
Dist(s): **Ebsco Publishing**
MyiLibrary
Texas A&M Univ. Pr.
ebrary, Inc.; *CIP.*

Texas Cooperative Extension, *(978-0-9672990; 978-0-9721049)* c/o Texas A & M University, 2112 TAMU, College Station, TX 77843-2112 USA Fax: 979-862-1202
E-mail: d-bowen@tamu.edu
Dist(s): **Texas A&M Univ. Pr.**

†Texas State Historical Assn., *(978-0-87611)* 2-306 Richardson Hall, University Sta., Austin, TX 78712 USA (SAN 202-7704) Tel 512-471-1525; Fax: 512-471-1551; Toll Free: 800-687-8132
Web site: http://www.tshaonline.org
Dist(s): **MyiLibrary**
Texas A&M Univ. Pr.
ebrary, Inc.; *CIP.*

†Texas Tech Univ. Pr., *(978-0-89672)* Affil. of Texas Tech Univ., P.O. Box 41037, Lubbock, TX 79409-1037 USA (SAN 218-5989) Tel 806-742-2982; Fax: 806-742-2979; Toll Free: 800-832-4042
E-mail: ttup@ttu.edu; barbara.brannon@ttu.edu
Web site: http://www.ttup.ttu.edu
Dist(s): **Chicago Distribution Ctr.**
MyiLibrary; *CIP.*

†Texas Woman's Univ. Pr., *(978-0-9607488; 978-0-9712104)* Orders Addr.: P.O. Box 425858, Denton, TX 76204 USA (SAN 238-4833) Tel 940-898-3123; Fax: 940-898-3127; Edit Addr.: 1200 Frame St., Denton, TX 76205 USA
E-mail: wbenson@twu.edu; *CIP.*

Text 4m Publishing, *(978-0-9779207; 978-0-9795691)* P.O. Box 12586, Milwaukee, WI 53212-0586 USA (SAN 850-6299)
E-mail: info@text4mpublishing.com; teresarae@msn.com
Web site: http://www.text4mpublishing.com.

Text N Tone, Inc., *(978-0-9764429)* 1500 King William Woods Rd., Midlothian, VA 23113-9119 USA
E-mail: mchekel@dslextreme.com.

Text Publishing Co. (AUS) *(978-1-875847; 978-1-876485; 978-1-86372; 978-1-877008; 978-1-920885; 978-1-921145; 978-1-921351; 978-1-921520; 978-1-921656; 978-1-921758; 978-1-921776; 978-1-921799; 978-1-921834; 978-1-921921; 978-1-921922; 978-1-921961; 978-1-922079; 978-1-922147; 978-1-922148; 978-1-922182; 978-1-925095; 978-1-922253; 978-1-925240; 978-1-925355; 978-1-925410) Dist. by* **Consort Bk Sales.**

Textbook Pubs., *(978-0-7581; 978-1-60630; 978-1-62583)* Orders Addr.: 17853 Santiago Blvd. Suite 107-133, Villa Park, CA 92861 USA Fax: 951-767-0133
E-mail: reprintservices@gmail.com.

Textbooks On Demand *See* **Reprint Services Corp.**

Texture Pr., *(978-0-9641837; 978-0-9712061; 978-0-9797573; 978-0-9850081; 978-0-615-69474-0; 978-0-615-71148-5; 978-0-615-71503-2; 978-0-615-75380-5; 978-0-615-77101-4; 978-0-615-78283-6; 978-0-615-81691-3; 978-0-615-82399-7; 978-0-615-85856-2; 978-0-615-87735-8; 978-0-615-90534-1; 978-0-615-95462-2; 978-0-615-95463-9; 978-0-692-21272-1; 978-0-692-30003-9; 978-0-692-30004-6; 978-0-692-31702-0; 978-0-692-35682-1; 978-0-692-35683-8; 978-0-692-36138-2; 978-0-692-39578-3; 978-0-692-40157-6; 978-0-692-52042-) 1108 Westbrooke Terr., Norman, OK 73072 USA Tel 405-314-7730; Fax: 405-310-6617*
E-mail: susan@beyondutopia.com; texturepress@beyondutopia.com
Web site: http://www.beyondutopia.com/texturepress; http://www.texturepress.org
Dist(s): **SPD-Small Pr. Distribution.**

TFG, *(978-0-9884132)* P.O. Box 91452, Portland, OR 97291 USA Tel 503-629-5045; Fax: 503-531-9175
E-mail: kimball@kimballfisher.com; info@thefishergroup.com
Web site: www.kimballfisher.com; www.thefishergroup.com.

TFG Pr., *(978-0-9743521; 978-0-9748553)* 244 Madison Ave., No. 254, New York, NY 10016 USA Tel 877-822-2504 do nto confuse with TGF Press in New York, NY.

†TFH Pubns., Inc., *(978-0-7938; 978-0-86622; 978-0-87666; 978-1-85279)* Orders Addr.: One TFH Plaza, Third & Union Aves., Neptune City, NJ 07753 USA (SAN 202-7720) Tel 732-988-8400; Fax: 732-988-5466; Toll Free: 800-631-2188 (outside New Jersey); Edit Addr.: P.O. Box 427, Neptune, NJ 07753 USA (SAN 658-1862)
E-mail: info@tfh.com
Web site: http://www.tfh.com; *CIP.*

Th1nk Bks. *Imprint of* **NavPress Publishing Group**

Th3rd World Studios, *(978-0-9818694; 978-0-9832161; 978-0-9895744)* 290 Powell Cir., Berlin, MD 21811 USA
Web site: http://www.th3rdworld.com
Dist(s): **Diamond Comic Distributors, Inc.**
Diamond Bk. Distributors.

Thacker Hse. Enterprises, *(978-0-9801919)* 1840 Thacker Ave., Jacksonville, FL 32207 USA Tel 904-398-8332
E-mail: 22dwebb@comcast.net
Web site: http://www.debrawebbrogers.com.

Thames & Hudson, *(978-0-500)* 500 Fifth Ave., New York, NY 10110 USA Tel 212-354-3763; Fax: 212-398-1252; Toll Free: 800-233-4830 (orders)
E-mail: bookinfo@thames.wwnorton.com
Web site: http://www.thamesandhudsonusa.com
Dist(s): **Hachette Bk. Group**
ISD
Norton, W. W. & Co., Inc.
Penguin Random Hse., LLC.

Thameside Press *See* **Chrysalis Education**

Thandi's Place, A Billo Communication Company *See* **Youth Popular Culture Institute, Inc.**

Tharpa Pubns. (GBR) *(978-0-948006; 978-1-899996; 978-0-9548790; 978-1-906665; 978-0-9558667) Dist. by* **IngramPubServ.**

That Patchwork Place *Imprint of* **Martingale & Co.**

That's Life, Incorporated *See* **That's Life Publishing, Inc.**

That's Life Publishing, Inc., *(978-0-9722304)* 3431 Thunderbird Rd., No. 200, Phoenix,, AZ 85053 USA Toll Free: 877-896-9500; *Imprints:* ZZ Dogs Press (ZZ Dogs Pr)
Web site: http://www.zzdogs.com.

That's Me Publishing, LLC, *(978-1-933843)* Hc 62 Box 488., Salem, MO 65560-8819 USA
E-mail: mary@thatsmepublishing.com
Web site: http://www.thatsmepublishing.com.

ThatsMyLife Co., *(978-0-9760419)* 5516 Challis View Ln., Charlotte, NC 28226 USA Tel 704-752-0935; Toll Free: 866-752-0935
E-mail: customerservice@thatsmytale.com
Web site: http://www.thatsmytale.com.

The Argonauts *See* **Argonauts, The**

The Edge *Imprint of* **Sparklesoup LLC**

The Old West Company *See* **Old West Co., The**

The Publishing Place LLC, *(978-0-9754307; 978-0-9760129; 978-0-9763423; 978-0-9776554; 978-0-9788002; 978-0-9840555; 978-0-9845794; 978-0-9835095; 978-0-9849172)* 2330 Hickory Ridge, Ashland, KY 41101 USA Do not confuse with Avant-garde Publishing Company in Mableton, GA
E-mail: info@avantgardepublishing.com
Web site: http://www.avantgardepublishing.com
Dist(s): **Smashwords.**

The Wisdom Pages, Inc., *(978-0-9706482)* Div. of Bullies to Buddies, Inc., 65 Fraser St., Staten Island, NY 10314 USA (SAN 255-1217) Tel 718-983-1333; Fax: 718-983-3851
E-mail: miriam@bullies2buddies.com; izzy@bullies2buddies.com
Web site: http://www.bullies2buddies.com; http://www.thewisdompages.com.

†Theatre Communications Group, Inc., *(978-0-88754; 978-0-913745; 978-0-930452; 978-1-55936; 978-1-84002; 978-1-85459; 978-1-870259; 978-1-899791)* 355 Lexington Ave., New York, NY 10017-6603 USA (SAN 210-9387) Tel 212-697-5230; Fax: 212-983-4847
Web site: http://www.tcg.org
Dist(s): **Abraham Assocs. Inc.**
Consortium Bk. Sales & Distribution
MyiLibrary
Perseus Bks. Group
ebrary, Inc.; *CIP.*

Theatre of Innocence, A, L.L.C., *(978-0-9760283)* 1212 Hull St., No. 1, Louisville, KY 40204 USA.

Theee Hole Punch Publishing, *(978-0-9771678)* P.O. Box 4488, Midlothian, VA 23112 USA
E-mail: threeholepunchpublishing@verizon.net; vzentja9@verizon.net
Web site: http://threeholepunchpublishing.com.

Theisen, Patricia, *(978-0-9793076)* 10520 11th Ave. NW, Seattle, WA 98177 USA
E-mail: ptheisen@gmail.com.

Them Potatoes, *(978-0-9772564)* 7318 21st Ave NW, Seattle, WA 98117-5623 USA (SAN 257-1285)
E-mail: kbrown@thempotatoes.com
Web site: http://www.thempotatoes.com.

Theme Perks, Inc., *(978-0-9729777)* 3300 S. Hiawassee Rd., Bldg. 105, Orlando, FL 32835 USA (SAN 852-6435) Tel 407-296-5800; Fax: 407-296-5801
E-mail: salcorn@alcorn.com
Web site: http://www.themeperks.com
Dist(s): **Smashwords.**

TheNetworkAdministrator.com, *(978-0-9744630; 978-1-937485)* Orders Addr.: 201 W. Cottesmore Cir., Longwood, FL 32779 USA
E-mail: douglaschick@thenetworkadministrator.com
Web site: http://www.thenetworkadministrator.com.

Theodore Berlin Publishing, *(978-0-9769196)* Div. of Theodore Berlin LLC, Orders Addr.: 8221 Provident St., Philadelphia, PA 19150 USA Tel 215-327-8212; Fax: 615-704-4422
E-mail: berlintheodore@yahoo.com.

Theory & Practice *Imprint of* **Scholastic, Inc.**

ThePaintedWord, Ltd., *(978-0-9846473)* P.O. Box 4132, Lutherville, MD 21094 USA
Dist(s): **AtlasBooks Distribution**
BookMasters Distribution Services (BDS).

Theragogy.com, *(978-0-9749862)* 301 1/2 Crescent NE, Grand Rapids, MI 49503 USA
E-mail: drperkins@theragogy.com
Web site: http://www.theragogy.com.

TheWhippetyWood, *(978-0-9897216)* S9305 Slotty Rd., Prairie du Sac, WI 53578 USA Tel 608-544-2242
E-mail: pj.pixie1@gmail.com
Web site: www.theWhippetyWood.com.

Thimble Mouse Publishing, Inc., *(978-0-9794522)* 1619 Saddle Creek Cir., No. 1312, Arlington, TX 76015 USA (SAN 853-4942).

ThingsAsian Pr., *(978-0-9715940; 978-1-934159)* 3230 Scott St., San Francisco, CA 94123 USA Tel 415-921-1316; Fax: 415-921-3432
E-mail: info@thingsasian.com; albert@thingsasian.com
Web site: http://www.thingsasianpress.com; http://www.toasiawithlove.com; http://www.thingsasian.com
Dist(s): **Ingram Pub. Services.**

Think-Outside-the-Book Publishing, Inc., *(978-0-9770751; 978-0-9896781)* 311 N. Robertson Blvd., Suite 323, Beverly Hills, CA 90211 USA
Web site: http://www.thinkoutsidethebook.com.

Thinkus Pubs., *(978-0-9818449)* Orders Addr.: 13109 SW 43rd St., Davie, FL 33330 USA
E-mail: loriflorido@aol.com
Web site: http://www.Dezzerthebook.com; http://www.HugothePunk.com
Dist(s): **Brodart Co.**
Follet Higher Education Grp
Quality Bks., Inc.

Third Axe Publishing, *(978-0-9765547)* 1150 McFarland, HR 26, Morristown, TN 37814 USA Tel 423-736-0884
E-mail: thirdaxepub@yahoo.com
Web site: http://www.brotherhoodofdwarves.com.

Third Dimension Publishing, *(978-0-9777041)* Div. of Third Dimension Group, Inc., Orders Addr.: P.O. Box 1845, Calhoun, GA 30703-1845 USA Tel 706-602-0398; Fax: 706-625-8712; Edit Addr.: 167 Richardson Rd., Calhoun, GA 30701 USA
E-mail: jeffcompton@msn.com
Web site: http://www.areyouawriter.com; http://www.thirddimensiongroup.com; http://www.thirddimensionpublishing.com.

Third Millennium Pr., *(978-0-9795608; 978-0-9833308)* 1845 Avondale Dr., Baton Rouge, LA 70808-1913 USA (SAN 853-7496) Tel 805-217-3109; Toll Free: 800-891-0390
E-mail: ellenhbrown@gmail.com
Web site: http://www.webofdebt.com; http://www.forbiddenmedicine.org; http://www.ellenbrown.com
Dist(s): **Lightning Source, Inc.**

Third Millennium Pubns., *(978-1-932657; 978-1-934805)* Sci Fi - Arizona, Inc., 1931 E. Libra Dr., Tempe, AZ 85283-5117 USA Tel 602-740-0569; Fax: 480-619-6202
E-mail: mccollum@3mpub.com
Web site: http://www.3mpub.com; http://www.scifi-az.com.

Third Millennium Publishing *Imprint of* **Sci Fi-Arizona, Inc.**

3rd Party Publishing Co., *(978-0-89914)* Div. of Third Party Assocs., Inc., P.O. Box 13306, Oakland, CA 94661-0306 USA (SAN 127-7294) Tel 510-339-2323; Fax: 510-339-6729; Toll Free: 888-339-2323
E-mail: paulmico@tpaserver.com
Web site: http://www.tpaserver.com.

Third Week Bks., *(978-0-9712816; 978-0-9829948)* 1112 W. 66th St., No.1, Richfield, MN 55423-2280 USA Tel 612-990-6011
E-mail: TheBabyReader@yahoo.com
Web site: http://ThirdWeekBooks.com.

Third World Games, Inc., *(978-0-9728526)* P.O. Box 667, Westminster, CA 92684-0667 USA Tel 714-357-2967
E-mail: companyisbn-dir@thirdworldgames.com
Web site: http://www.thirdworldgames.com.

Third World Press, *(978-0-88378)* P.O. Box 19730, Chicago, IL 60619 USA (SAN 202-778X) Tel 773-651-0700; Fax: 773-651-7286
E-mail: TWPress3@aol.com
Web site: http://www.thirdworldpressinc.com
Dist(s): **Austin & Company, Inc.**
Chicago Distribution Ctr.
Independent Pubs. Group
Ingram Pub. Services.

Thirsty(?) *Imprint of* **Tyndale Hse. Pubs.**

Thirsty Horse LLC, *(978-0-9723127)* 1220 N. Market St., Suite 606, Wilmington,, DE 19801-2598 USA (SAN 254-7767) Tel 302-428-1222
E-mail: orders@thirsty-horse.com
Web site: http://www.thirsty-horse-media.com.

Thirsty Sponge Publishing Co., *(978-0-9797960)* 898 Southgate Dr., Cookeville, TN 38501 USA.

Thirty-Three Hundred Pr., *(978-0-9646017)* 3300 Mission St., San Francisco, CA 94110 USA Tel 415-826-6886; 300 Vicksburg St., No. 5, San Francisco, CA 94114
Dist(s): **SPD-Small Pr. Distribution.**

This Joy Bks., *(978-0-9821835; 978-0-9834546)* 1117 S. Milwaukee Ave., Suite A4, Libertyville, IL 60048 USA Tel 847-247-4350
E-mail: info@thisjoybooks.com
Web site: http://www.thisjoybooks.com.

Thistledown Pr., Ltd. (CAN) *(978-0-920066; 978-0-920633; 978-1-895449; 978-1-894345; 978-1-897235) Dist. by* **IngramPubServ.**

Thistlewood Publishing, *(978-0-9821507; 978-0-9853600)* 92 Wayside Ln., Apalachin, NY 13732 USA
E-mail: gnw@stny.rr.com; gwestover@thistlewoodpublishing.com
Web site: http://www.thistlewoodpublishing.com.

Thomas & Kay, LLC, *(978-0-9729505)* N37w26805 Kopmeier Dr., Pewaukee, WI 53072 USA (SAN 255-7576) Tel 414-581-0449
E-mail: susan@solutionsbysusan.com
Web site: http://www.solutionsbysusan.com.

Thomas & Mercer *Imprint of* **Amazon Publishing**

Thomas & Sons Bks., *(978-0-9758800)* 33 Greenwich Ave., Suite 7L, New York, NY 10014 USA
E-mail: willysthom@rcn.com.

Thomas, Brandis, *(978-0-9792526)* P.O. Box 690162, Houston, TX 77269 USA.

†Thomas, Charles C. Pub., Ltd., *(978-0-398)* 2600 S. First St., Springfield, IL 62704 USA (SAN 201-9485) Tel 217-789-8980; Fax: 217-789-9130; Toll Free: 800-258-8980
E-mail: books@ccthomas.com; dmccarty@ccthomas.com; editorial@ccthomas.com
Web site: http://www.ccthomas.com
Dist(s): **Follett School Solutions**
MyiLibrary
ebrary, Inc.; *CIP.*

Thomas, Duerre, *(978-0-9793877; 978-0-9857798)* 23505 Ferndale Ave., Port Charlotte, FL 33980 USA
E-mail: d_jacel@yahoo.com; madpastor1@gmail.com
Web site: http://www.madpastor.tripod.com.

Thomas Expressions, Incorporated *See* **Thomas Expressions, LLC**

Thomas Expressions, LLC, *(978-0-9713573; 978-0-9771059)* Orders Addr.: 390 S. Tyndall Pkwy., #294, Panama City, FL 32404 USA Fax: 850-785-6408; Toll Free: 866-570-5560
E-mail: thomasexpressions@gmail.com
Web site: http://www.thomasexpressions.com; http://www.didyano.com
Dist(s): **Follett School Solutions.**

Thomas, Frederic Inc., *(978-0-9747133; 978-1-933443)* 5621 Strand Blvd. Ste. 301, Naples, FL 34110-7307 USA (SAN 255-8157); *Imprints:* Values to Live By Classic Stories (ValLiveByClass)
E-mail: freimer@fredericthomas.com; bmichalowski@fredericthomas.com
Web site: http://fredericthomas.com; http://www.healthylivingforkids.com; http://www.valuestoliveby.com.

Thomas, Kevin *See* **Catch 22 Publishing Inc.**

Thomas Max Publishing, *(978-0-9764052; 978-0-9788571; 978-0-9799950; 978-0-9822189; 978-0-9842626; 978-0-9846347)* P.O. Box 250054, Atlanta, GA 30325-1054 USA Tel 404-794-6588
E-mail: LeeC@thomasmax.com; bee.ell.cee@comcast.net
Web site: http://www.thomasmax.com.

Thomas Pubns., *(978-0-939631; 978-1-57747)* 3245 Fairfield Rd., Gettysburg, PA 17325 USA (SAN 663-7213) Tel 717-642-6600; Fax: 717-642-5555; Toll Free: 800-840-6782 Do not confuse with companies with the same name in Austin, TX, La Crescenta, CA
E-mail: info@thomaspublications.com
Web site: http://www.thomaspublications.com.

Thomas, R. E., *(978-0-9761077)* P.O. Box 53091, Houston, TX 77052 USA.

Thomas, Richard Kayeen *See* **MarWel Enterprises, Inc.**

Thomas, Sheldon Wade, *(978-0-9670539)* 1091 Thomas S. Boyland St., Brooklyn, NY 11236 USA Tel 718-495-6002 (phone/fax).

Thomastar Publishing, *(978-0-615-17087-9)* 14241 NE Wood-Duvall Rd Suite 406, Woodinville, WA 98072 USA Tel 425-703-8807
E-mail: thomastar.publishing@hotmail.com
Dist(s): **Lulu Enterprises Inc.**

Thompson, Alyce C. Books, Inc., *(978-0-9746411)* Orders Addr.: 6105 W.master St., Philadelphia, PA 19151-0827 USA; Edit Addr.: P.O. Box 664, Havertown, PA 19083 USA
E-mail: emailalyce8@aol.com; info@alycecthompsonbooksinc.com
Web site: http://alycecthompsonbooksinc.com; http://www.myspace.com/alycecthompson; http://www.myspace.com/alycecthompsonbooksinc
Dist(s): **A & B Distributors & Pubs. Group**
Afrikan World Bk. Distributor
Culture Plus Bk. Distributors
Lushena Bks.

Thompson, Angela Bolden, *(978-0-615-14774-1)* 9501 W. 171st St. Ste. Q, Tinley Park, IL 60487 USA
Web site: http://angelathompson1.tripod.com/
Dist(s): **Lulu Enterprises Inc.**

Thompson Mill Pr., *(978-0-9883269)* 2865 S. Eagle Rd., #368, Newtown, PA 18940 USA
E-mail: bob.regan@thompsonmillpress.com
Web site: http://www.thompsonmillpress.com; http://www.KobeeManatee.com
Dist(s): **Independent Pubs. Group.**

Thompson Original Productions LLC, *(978-0-9799216)* 11997 Youngtree Ct., Bristow, VA 20136 USA (SAN 854-7203)
Web site: http://www.chickenboybooks.com.

Thomson Custom Solutions *See* **CENGAGE Learning Custom Publishing**

Thomson, D.C., & Co., Ltd. (GBR) *(978-0-85116; 978-1-84535) Dist. by* **APG.**

Thomson Delmar Learning *See* **Delmar Cengage Learning**

Thomson ELT, *(978-1-4240; 978-1-4282)* 25 Thomson Pl., 5th Flr., Boston, MA 02210 USA Tel 617-289-7700 Toll Free: 800-237-0053
E-mail: reply@heinle.com
Web site: http://www.elt.thomson.com
Dist(s): **CENGAGE Learning.**

Thomson Gale *See* **Cengage Gale**

Thomson, J P, *(978-0-9754365)* P.O. Box 377, Exton, PA 19341 USA Tel 610-594-1707; Fax: 610-594-1866
E-mail: montanapino@comcast.net.

Thomson Learning *See* **CENGAGE Learning**

Thomson Peterson's *See* **Peterson's**

Thomson South-Western *See* **Cengage South-Western**

Thornapple Farms, LLC, *(978-0-9749728)* 13010 W. Darrow Rd., Vermilion, OH 44089 USA Tel 440-967-2680; Fax: 440-967-2696
E-mail: ashar@hbr.net
Web site: http://www.thornapplefarms.com.

Thorncrown Publishing *Imprint of* **Yorkshire Publishing Group**

†Thorndike Pr., *(978-0-7838; 978-0-7862; 978-0-8161; 978-0-89621; 978-1-56054; 978-1-4104)* Div. of Gale Group, 295 Kennedy Memorial Dr., Waterville, ME 04901 USA Tel 207-859-1053; 207-859-1020; 207-859-1000; Toll Free Fax: 800-558-4676; Toll Free:

800-223-1244 (ext. 15); 800-877-4253 (customer resource ctr.); *Imprints:* Large Print Press (Lrg Print Pr)
E-mail: jamie.knobloch@gale.com;
barb.littfield@galegroup.com;
Betsy.M.Brown@thomson.com;
jamie.knobloch@cengage.com
Web site: http://www.gale.com/thorndike
Dist(s): **Cengage Gale**; *CIP.*

Thornton Publishing, *(978-1-882913)* 1504 Howard St., New Iberia, LA 70560 USA Tel 337-364-2752; Fax: 318-365-0316; Toll Free: 800-551-3076 Do not confuse with companies with the same or similar names in Littleton, CO, Forest Grove, OR, Burley, ID.

Thornton Publishing, Inc., *(978-0-9670242; 978-0-9719597; 978-0-9723309; 978-1-932344; 978-0-9774761; 978-0-9779960; 978-0-9801941; 978-0-9820838; 978-0-9824705; 978-0-9844838; 978-0-9845417; 978-0-9846342; 978-0-9856151; 978-0-9889816)* 17011 Lincoln Ave., No. 408, Parker, CO 80134 USA Tel 303-794-8888; Fax: 720-863-2013; *Imprints:* Profitable Publishing (Profitable Pubng); Books To Believe In (Bks To Believe In) Do not confuse with companies with the same or similar names in New Iberia, LA, Forest Grove, OR, Burley, ID
E-mail: publisher@bookstobelievein.com
Web site: http://bookstobelievein.com;
http://www.getting-published.com
Dist(s): **Follett School Solutions.**

Thorogood (GBR) *(978-1-85418) Dist. by* **Stylus Pub VA.**

Thorpe, Sandy, *(978-0-9764147)* 20205 NE 3rd Ct., No. 3, N. Miami Beach, FL 33179 USA
E-mail: sthorpe@trekstuff.com.

Thotsup LLC, *(978-0-9883420)* Orders Addr.: 305 NE 6th St. Suite 588, Grants Pass, OR 97526 USA Tel 541-792-0212.

ThoughtRockets, Inc., *(978-0-9766793)* 2033 Ralston Ave., No. 114, Belmont, CA 94002 USA Tel 650-592-3169 (phone/fax)
E-mail: laura@thoughtrockets.com
Web site: http://www.thoughtrockets.com.

Threatt, Cedric L., *(978-0-9720543)* Div. of Ahava Publishing, LLC, 65 Twisted Oak Cir., Odenville, AL 35120 USA
E-mail: cl3tt@windstream.net
Web site: http://www.Ahavapublishing.org.

Three Angels Broadcasting Network, *(978-0-9718083; 978-0-9720888; 978-1-934869; 978-1-942455)* Orders Addr.: P.O. Box 220, West Frankfort, IL 62896 USA Tel 618-627-4651; Edit Addr.: 3391 Charley Good Rd., West Frankfort, IL 62896 USA
Web site: http://www.3abn.org
Dist(s): **Pacific Pr. Publishing Assn.**

Three Bean Pr., *(978-0-9767276; 978-0-9882212; 978-0-9903315)* P.O. Box 301711, Jamaica Plain, MA 02130 USA (SAN 256-5137) Tel 617-584-5759; 617-827-2042
E-mail: seneca@threebeanpress.com
Web site: http://www.threebeanpress.com
Dist(s): **Partners Bk. Distributing, Inc.**

Three Cents Publishing, *(978-0-9746697)* Orders Addr.: 177 Ocean St.: PO Box 339 Brant Rock Ma02020 Usa, Boston, MA 02020 USA.

Three Conditions Pr., *(978-0-9721241)* Drawer H, Baltimore, MD 21228 USA
Web site: http://www.marylandpoetry.org.

Three Cups, LLC, *(978-0-9794563)* 36 S. Pennsylvania St. Suite 190, Indianapolis, IN 46204 USA Tel 317-633-1456
E-mail: trt@hokansoninc.com;
Scott@360GroupOnline.com
Web site: http://www.3cupsbook.com
Dist(s): **Ingram Pub. Services.**

Three Flower Farm Pr., *(978-0-615-67849-8)* 24 Brooks Rd, Wayland, MA 01778 USA Tel 508-653-9307
E-mail: kjlin306@gmail.com.

Three Four Three Publishing Co., *(978-0-9675286)* 3738 Victoria Dr., West Palm Beach, FL 33406 USA Tel 917-407-2270
E-mail: paulnison@mindspring.com
Web site: http://www.rawlife.com.

Three Hermits Pr., *(978-0-9753906)* P.O. Box 99099, Bennington, VT 05201 USA
E-mail: threehermits@mail.com.

Three Legged Toad Pr., *(978-0-615-60236-3; 978-0-615-61476-2; 978-0-615-61477-9; 978-0-615-62499-0; 978-0-615-62500-3; 978-0-615-65260-3; 978-0-615-65424-9; 978-0-615-65425-6; 978-0-615-67142-0; 978-0-615-71817-0; 978-0-615-71818-7; 978-0-615-71940-5; 978-0-615-72276-4; 978-0-615-72485-0; 978-0-615-72486-7; 978-0-615-72487-4; 978-0-615-72488-1) 3510 Red River St., Austin, TX 78705 USA Tel 512-542-9741*
E-mail: russin@alumni.utexas.net
Web site: http://www.thecorneback.co.uk
Dist(s): **CreateSpace Independent Publishing Platform.**

Three Moons Media, *(978-0-9725164; 978-0-9747440; 978-1-933514)* 1610 Valley Brook Ln., Longview, TX 75605-2676 USA
E-mail: marilyn@threemoonsmedia.com
Web site: http://www.threemoonsmedia.com
Dist(s): **CreateSpace Independent Publishing Platform.**

Three Part Harmony LLC, *(978-0-9800577)* Orders Addr.: 538 Eagle Blvd., Kingsland, GA 31548 USA (SAN 855-0972) Tel 386-717-4583; 912-882-7008
E-mail: threepartharmony@earthlink.net.

Three Pebble Pr., LLC, *(978-0-9799289; 978-0-9960219)* 10040 SW 25th Ave., Portland, OR 97219-6325 USA (SAN 854-7777) Tel 503-977-0944
E-mail: info@yogacalm.org
Web site: http://www.threepebblepress.com
Dist(s): **Follett School Solutions**
Independent Pubs. Group
MyiLibrary.

Three River Rambler, *(978-0-615-20131-3)* 422 W. Cumberland Ave., Knoxville, TN 37901 USA Tel 865-524-9411; Fax: 865-546-3717
E-mail: kac@gulfandohio.com
Web site: http://threeriversrambler.com.

Three Rivers Council, BSA, Incorporated *See* **Alchemy Creative, Inc.**

Three Rivers Pr. *Imprint of* **Crown Publishing Group**

Three Sisters Communication, LLC, *(978-0-9771204)* P.O. Box 280, Star, ID 83669-5015 USA (SAN 256-7970)
E-mail: sfunk624@heritagewifi.com.

Three Sisters Pr., *(978-0-9722999)* P.O. Box 17061, Golden, CO 80402 USA Tel 720-231-6540; Fax: 303-561-0626 Do not confuse with Three Sisters Pr., in Washington, DC
E-mail: violeta134@hotmail.com;
sjbrehm@comcast.net.

Three Sisters Publishing Hse., Ltd., *(978-0-9785570)* 32104 Cty. Rd., 1, Saint Cloud, MN 56303 USA Tel 320-654-0001.

Three Socks Publishing, *(978-0-9789631)* 3351 Charlotte, Brighton, MI 48114 USA.

Three Spots Productions, *(978-0-9744509)* 67 Rutz St., Stamford, CT 06906 USA
E-mail: rarruzza@optonline.net;
rarruzza@sparkyswalk.com
Web site: http://www.sparkyswalk.com.

Three Trees, Inc., *(978-0-9789426)* P.O. Box 92, Cottleville, MO 63368-6336 USA Tel 636-561-9184; Fax: 636-561-9184
Web site: http://Petalwinkthefairy.com.

Three Willows Pr., *(978-0-9770279)* 4680 S. 1000 W., Rensselaer, IN 47978 USA.

Three Wishes Publishing Co., *(978-0-9796380)* 26500 W. Agoura Rd., Suite 102-754, Calabasas, CA 91302 USA Tel 818-878-0902; Fax: 818-878-1805
E-mail: alva710@aol.com
Web site: http://www.alvasachs.com;
http://www.threewishespublishing.com.

Three-D Vision Productions *See* **Soul Vision Works Publishing**

Threshold Editions *Imprint of* **Threshold Editions**

Threshold Editions, Div. of Simon & Schuster, 1230 Ave. of the Americas, New York, NY 10020 USA; *Imprints:* Threshold Editions (ThresholdEdit)
Dist(s): **Simon & Schuster, Inc.**

Thriving Churches International, *(978-0-9716489; 978-0-9831958)* P.O. Box 230, Genoa, NV 89411 USA Tel 775-450-1625
E-mail: john@thrivingchurches.com
Web site: http://www.thrivingchurches.com.

Throwback Publishing, *(978-0-9771630)* P.O. Box 33792, Washington, DC 20033 USA
Web site: http://www.throwbackpublishing.com.

Thule Ediciones, S. L. (ESP) *(978-84-933734; 978-84-96473) Dist. by* **IPG Chicago.**

Thumbprint Publishing, *(978-0-9741833)* P.O. Box 9972, Cincinnati, OH 45209 USA Tel 513-207-7550 Do not confuse with Thumbprint Publishing in Studio City, CA
E-mail: rdavis_art@fuse.net
Web site: http://www.connectionssp.org/.

Thumbs Up Pr., *(978-0-9772513)* 3731 Reed's Landing Cir., Midlothian, VA 23113 USA Tel 804-320-8331
E-mail: thumbsuppress@earthlink.net.

Thunder Bay Pr. *Imprint of* **Baker & Taylor Publishing Group**

Thunder Bay Pr., *(978-1-882376; 978-1-933272; 978-1-62026)* 2325 Jarco Dr., Holt, MI 48842 USA Tel 517-694-3205; Fax: 517-694-0617; Toll Free: 800-336-3137 Do not confuse with Thunder Bay Pr, San Diego, CA
E-mail: sspeigel@partners-east.com;
saraspeigel@partners-east.com;
longstad@partners-east.com;
jtaylor@partners-east.com
Dist(s): **Partners Bk. Distributing, Inc.**
Perseus Bks. Group.

Thunder Enlightening, *(978-0-9832491)* 11 Cherokee Camp Trail No. 20451, JASPER, GA 30143 USA Tel 706-692-2199
E-mail: chrisrumble@gmail.com
Web site: www.chrisrumble.com.

ThunderBolt Pubns., *(978-0-615-16040-5; 978-0-578-00692-5)* 14785 Kay Ln., Atlanta, GA 30306 USA
E-mail: medemach@bellsouth.net
Web site: http://www.kenmedemach.com
Dist(s): **Lulu Enterprises Inc.**

Thunderbolt Publishing, *(978-0-9715390; 978-0-9826165; 978-0-9910777)* 1750 Ben Franklin Dr. #11g, Sarasota, FL 34236 USA (SAN 254-8119); *Imprints:* We Do Listen (WE DO LISTEN)
E-mail: howardb@wedolisten.com
Web site: http://www.wedolisten.org
Dist(s): **Lerner Publishing Group.**

ThunderBolt Publishing, *(978-0-9799671)* 113 14th Ave. S., Nampa, ID 83651 USA Tel 208-466-0122; Fax: 208-466-5294
E-mail: arlette@thunder-bolt.com.

ThunderHousePress, *(978-0-9771154)* Div. of ThunderHouse Entertainment, 6709 La Tijera Blvd., No. 141, Los Angeles, CA 90045 USA
E-mail: reggiecook@yahoo.com
Web site: http://www.thunderhousepress.com.

Thundermist Consulting and Research Co., *(978-0-9759494)* P.O. Box 7023, Cumberland, RI 02864-7023 USA
E-mail: book-sales@thundermist.com
Web site: http://www.thundermist.com;
http://thundermist.blogspot.com.

Thurman Hse., LLC, *(978-1-58989)* 5 Park Ctr. Ct., Suite 300, Owings Mills, MD 21117 USA Tel 410-902-9100; Fax: 410-902-7210
E-mail: thurmanhouse@ottenheimerpub.com.

Thynne, Garry R. *See* **Garry & Donna, LLC**

Tianjin Education Pr.,
Dist(s): **Chinasprout, Inc.**

Tiaanya Literature Pr., *(978-0-9768679; 978-1-60508)* 613 151st St. Pl., NE, Bellevue, WA 98007 USA
E-mail: tianyapress@hotmail.com
Web site: http://www.tianyapress.com.

Tiara Bks. LLC, *(978-0-9729846)* 62 Birchall Dr., Scarsdale, NY 10583-4503 USA Tel 914-723-9133.

Tickling Keys, Inc., *(978-0-9724258; 978-1-932802; 978-1-61547)* 13386 Judy Ave., NW, Uniontown, OH 44685 USA Tel 330-715-2875; Fax: 707-220-4510; *Imprints:* Holy Macro! Books (Holy Macro Bks)
E-mail: consult@mrexcel.com; pub@mrexcel.com
Web site: http://www.holymacrobooks.com
Dist(s): **Ebsco Publishing**
Independent Pubs. Group
MyiLibrary
ebrary, Inc.

TICO Publishing, *(978-0-9777688)* 25045 Jaclyn Ave., Moreno Valley, CA 92557 USA (SAN 850-167X) Tel 562-292-0796
E-mail: tijerin@yahoo.com; books@ticopublishing.com.

Tidal Press, Incorporated *See* **Mushgush Pr.**

Tidal Wave Bks., *(978-0-9724770)* 4476 Wedgewood Dr., Pleasant Grove, UT 84062 USA Tel 801-785-5555; Fax: 801-785-9676
E-mail: sgraham@tidalwavebooks.com
Web site: http://www.tidalwavebooks.com
Dist(s): **Send The Light Distribution LLC.**

Tidal Wave Productions *See* **Black, Judith Storyteller**

Tide-Mark Pr., Ltd, *(978-0-936846; 978-1-55949; 978-1-59490; 978-1-63114)* Orders Addr.: 22 Prestige Park Cir., East Hartford, CT 06108-1917 USA (SAN 222-1802) Tel 860-683-4499; Fax: 860-683-4055; Toll Free: 800-338-2508; Edit Addr.: 22 Prestige Park Cir., East Hartford, CT 06108-1917 USA (SAN 665-794X)
E-mail: carol@tide-press.com
Web site: http://www.tidemarkpress.com
Dist(s): **BookBaby.**

Tiffin Pr. of Maine, *(978-0-9646018)* Div. of Tiffin Pr., 110 Jones Point Rd., Brooksville, ME 04617-3570 USA Tel 207-326-0916
E-mail: joanmacc@aol.com
Dist(s): **Bilingual Pubns. Co., The**
Perseus-PGW.

Tiger Iron Pr., *(978-0-9787263; 978-0-9851745)* Orders Addr.: 4 Hopscotch Ln., Savannah, GA 31411 USA Tel 478-474-2323
E-mail: Sales@TigerIronPress.com
Web site: http://www.TigerIronPress.com;
http://Http://www.TI-Holdings.com
Dist(s): **TI-Holdings Distribution Co.**

Tiger Lily Publishing, *(978-1-880883)* Six Swift Ct., Newport Beach, CA 92663 USA Tel 949-645-5907; Toll Free: 800-950-3237 (800-950-DADS)
E-mail: janedrew@home.com.

Tiger Publishing *See* **Tiger Tale Publishing Co.**

Tiger Tale Publishing Co., *(978-0-9787533; 978-0-9859579)* 522 N. Grant Ave., Odessa, TX 79761 USA Tel 432-337-8511; Fax: 432-337-1035
E-mail: cynthia.l.clack@gmail.com
Dist(s): **BookBaby.**

Tiger Tales, *(978-1-58925; 978-1-68010)* Orders Addr.: P.O. Box 411037, Kansas City, MO 64141-1037 USA Fax: 913-362-7401; Toll Free: 888-454-0097
E-mail: barbknight@tigertalesbooks.com
Web site: http://www.tigertalesbooks.com
Dist(s): **Midpoint National, Inc.**

Tiger Tales Pubns., *(978-0-9610576)* 103 Monte Cresta, Oakland, CA 94611 USA (SAN 264-4347) Tel 510-653-8422.

Tigermoth Pubns., *(978-0-9844785)* P.O. Box 4367, Tulsa, OK 74159 USA (SAN 859-4953)
Web site: http://www.tigermothpublications.com.

Tightrope Bks. (CAN) *(978-0-9738645; 978-1-926639) Dist. by* **IPG Chicago.**

TIGO & Co., *(978-0-9761167)* P.O. Box 210066, Dallas, TX 75211-0066 USA Tel 214-330-4420
E-mail: thekingskid1982@sbcglobal.net.

Tike Time, Inc., *(978-0-9729093)* Orders Addr.: 872 S. Milwaukee, No. 125, Libertyville, IL 60048 USA (SAN 255-3058)
E-mail: info@tiketime.com
Web site: http://www.tiketime.com.

Tiki Machine, LLC, *(978-0-615-39785-6; 978-0-615-49510-1; 978-0-615-54715-2; 978-0-615-65028-9; 978-0-9894507; 978-0-692-22851-7)* 160 W. Foothill Pkwy. Suite 105 No. 171, Corona, CA 92882 USA Tel 818-237-6325
Web site: www.tikimachine.blogspot.com;
www.tikimachine.com.

Tiki Tales, *(978-0-9740582)* P.O. Box 1194, Haiku, HI 96708 USA
Dist(s): **Booklines Hawaii, Ltd.**

Tikva Corp., *(978-0-615-12595-4)* 40 W. 23rd St., New York, NY 10010-5215 USA
E-mail: emilyl@mkugodessa.org.

Tilbury Hse. Pubs., *(978-0-88448; 978-0-937966; 978-1-937644)* 12 Starr St., Thomaston, ME 04861 USA Toll Free: 800-582-1899 (orders); *Imprints:* Harpswell Press (Hrpswel Pr)
E-mail: tilbury@tilburyhouse.com;
mariellen@tilburyhouse.com
Web site: http://www.tilburyhouse.com
Dist(s): **INscribe Digital**
Lectorum Pubns., Inc.
SPD-Small Pr. Distribution
Univ. Pr. of New England.

†Timber Pr., Inc., *(978-0-88192; 978-0-917304; 978-0-931146; 978-0-931340; 978-1-60469)* Div. of Workman Publishing Co., Inc., 133 SW Second Ave., Suite 450, Portland, OR 97204-3527 USA (SAN 216-082X) Tel 503-227-2878; Fax: 503-227-3070; Toll Free: 800-327-5680; 20 Lonsdale Rd Swavesey, London, NW6 6RD Tel (01954) 232959; Fax: (01954) 206040
E-mail: info@timberpress.co.uk;
publicity@timberpress.com
Web site: http://www.timberpress.com
Dist(s): **Ebsco Publishing**
Meredith Bks.
Workman Publishing Co., Inc.; *CIP.*

Timberwood Pr., *(978-0-9745454)* 112 NW 156th St., Shoreline, WA 98177 USA Tel 206-295-6186
E-mail: kearney@timberwoodpress.com
Web site: http://www.timberwoodpress.com
Dist(s): **Partners Bk. Distributing, Inc.**

Time & Chance Publishing, *(978-0-9748274)* Orders Addr.: P.O. Box 488, New York, NY 10116 USA Tel 718-370-3655 [phone/fax]
E-mail: tandchpublishing@yahoo.com;
timeandchancepublishing@yahoo.com
Dist(s): **Culture Plus Bks.**

Time Bks. *Imprint of* **Time Inc. Bks.**

Time Dancer Press *See* **5 Star Stories, Inc.**

Time Home Entertainment, Incorporated *See* **Time Inc. Bks.**

Time Inc. Bks., *(978-1-883013; 978-1-929049; 978-1-931933; 978-1-932273; 978-1-932994; 978-1-933405; 978-1-933821; 978-1-60320; 978-1-61893)* Div. of Time, Inc., 1271 Avenue of the Americas, New York, NY 10020-1201 USA (SAN 227-3209); *Imprints:* Time Books (Time Bks); People Books (People Bks); LIFE Books (LIFEBooks); Liberty Street (LibertySt)
Dist(s): **Hachette Bk. Group**
MyiLibrary
National Bk. Network.

Time to Organize, *(978-0-9786733)* 1414 Willow Creek Ln., Shoreview, MN 55126 USA Tel 651-717-1284
E-mail: sara@time2organize.net.

Time to Sign, Incorporated, *(978-0-9713666; 978-0-9765364)* Orders Addr.: P.O. Box 110308, Palm Bay, FL 32911 USA Tel 321-723-6997; Fax: 321-723-6896; Edit Addr.: 426 Olsmar St., Palm Bay, FL 32908 USA Do not confuse with Talking Hands, Inc., in Bangor, ME
E-mail: contact@timetosign.com
Web site: http://www.timetosign.com.

Time Warner Book Group *See* **Hachette Bk. Group**

Time Warner Custom Publishing, *(978-1-931722; 978-1-59995)* 1271 Ave. of the Americas, New York, NY 10020 USA Tel 212-522-7381
Dist(s): **Hachette Bk. Group.**

†Timeless Bks., *(978-0-931454; 978-1-932018)* Div. of Assn. for the Development of Human Potential, Orders Addr.: P.O. Box 3543, Spokane, WA 99220-3543 USA (SAN 211-6502) Fax: 509-838-6652; Toll Free: 800-251-9273; P.O. Box 9, Kootenay Bay, BC V0B 1X0 Tel 250-227-9224 (Business Office); Fax: 250-227-9494 (orders); Toll Free: 800-661-8711 (orders) Do not confuse with Timeless Books in Pickerington, OH
E-mail: info@timeless.org; orders@timeless.org;
bookstore@timeless.org; Contact@timeless.org
Web site: http://timeless.org
Dist(s): **Lulu Enterprises Inc.**
New Leaf Distributing Co., Inc.; *CIP.*

Timeless Voyager Pr., *(978-1-892264)* Orders Addr.: 249 Iris Ave., Goleta, CA 93117 USA; Edit Addr.: P.O. Box 6678, Santa Barbara, CA 93160 USA (SAN 253-9233) Tel 805-455-8895; Fax: 805-683-4456; Toll Free: 800-576-8463
E-mail: bsh@timelessvoyager.com
Web site: http://www.timelessvoyager.com.

Time-Life Education, Inc., *(978-0-7054; 978-0-7370; 978-0-7835; 978-0-8094)* Orders Addr.: P.O. Box 85026, Richmond, VA 23285-5026 USA Toll Free Fax: 800-449-2011; Edit Addr.: 2000 Duke St., Alexandria, VA 22314 USA Tel 703-838-7000; Fax: 703-518-4124; Toll Free: 800-449-2010
E-mail: education@timelifecs.com
Web site: http://www.timelifeedu.com/
Dist(s): **Hachette Bk. Group.**

†Time-Life, Inc., *(978-0-7835; 978-0-8094)* Div. of Time Warner Co., Orders Addr.: Three Center Plaza, Boston, MA 02108-2084 USA Toll Free Fax: 800-308-1083; 800-286-9471; Toll Free: 800-277-8844; 800-759-0190; Edit Addr.: 8280 Willow Oaks Corporate Dr., Fairfax, VA 22031-4511 USA (SAN 202-7836) Toll Free: 800-621-7026
Web site: http://www.timelifeedu.com
Dist(s): **Hachette Bk. Group**
Time-Life Publishing Warehouse
Worldwide Media Service, Inc.; *CIP.*

Times Bks. *Imprint of* **Holt, Henry & Co.**

Times Square Church *See* **Petey, Rock & Roo Children's Pubns.**

Time-Together Pr., *(978-1-888384)* Orders Addr.: P.O. Box 11689, Saint Paul, MN 55111 USA Tel 612-827-1639; Fax: 612-823-6404.

T.I.M.M.-E. Co., Inc., *(978-0-9718232)* Div. of NYC Department of Education, 230 E. 25th St, Suite 2E, New York, NY 10010 USA
E-mail: tbellavia@weareallthesameinside.com; tools4tolerance@aol.com
Web site: http://www.weareallthesameinside.com
Dist(s): **Bookazine Co., Inc.**

Timothy Lane Pr., *(978-0-9744751)* 3211 Rosewood Dr., Hattiesburg, MS 39401-4517 USA
Web site: http://www.robynjackson.com.

Timshel Literature, *(978-0-9708317)* P.O. Box 751, Portsmouth, RI 02871 USA Tel 401-835-7156
E-mail: jkatz@timshelarts.com
Web site: http://www.timshelarts.com.

Timtu Ink., *(978-0-9742460)* 11 Via Acuatica, Rancho Santa Margarita, CA 92688-1482 USA (SAN 255-6146); 31441 Santa Margarita Pkwy., Suite A, No. 341, Rancho Santa Margarita, CA 92688
E-mail: timtuink@dslextreme.com
Web site: http://www.dragonopolis.com; http://www.dragonia.net.

Timun Mas, Editorial S.A. (ESP) *(978-84-480; 978-84-7176; 978-84-7722)* *Dist. by* **AIMS Intl.**

Timun Mas, Editorial S.A. (ESP) *(978-84-480; 978-84-7176; 978-84-7722)* *Dist. by* **Lectorum Pubns.**

Tingley, Megan Bks. *Imprint of* **Little, Brown Bks. for Young Readers**

TINK INK Publishing, *(978-0-9840916)* 6817 W. Lariat Ln., Peoria, AZ 85383 USA Toll Free: 888-829-5117
Web site: http://www.tinkinkpublishing.com.

Tinkertown Museum, *(978-0-9793124)* Orders Addr.: P.O. Box 303, Sandia Park, NM 87047 USA (SAN 853-1161) Tel 505-281-5233; Edit Addr.: 121 Sandia Crest Rd., Sandia Park, NM 87047-0303 USA
E-mail: tinker4u@tinkertown.com
Web site: http://www.tinkertown.com.

Tino Turtle Travels, LLC, *(978-0-9793158; 978-0-9816297)* 8550 W. Charleston Blvd., Suite 102-398, Las Vegas, NV 89117 USA (SAN 853-0920) Tel 702-499-4477; Toll Free Fax: 800-656-4641
E-mail: info@tinoturtletravels.com
Web site: http://www.tinoturtletravels.com.

Tintagel Publications, *(978-0-9743718)* 45 Lapeer St., Lake Orion, MI 48362 USA.

Tintinatie Publishing Hse., *(978-0-9842625; 978-0-9830884; 978-0-9966540)* 32315 Corte Zamora, Temecula, CA 92592 USA Tel 888-998-4684
E-mail: natalie.tinti@tintinatie.com
Web site: http://tintinatiepublishing.com; http://www.sewingafriendship.com
Dist(s): **Lightning Source, Inc.**
Smashwords.

Tiny Stachel Pr., *(978-0-9845318; 978-0-9849146)* 311 W. Seymour St., Philadelphia, PA 19144 USA Tel 215-266-9587
E-mail: TinySatchelPress@gmail.com
Web site: http://www.TinySatchelPress.com
Dist(s): **Perseus Distribution.**

Tiny Scribbles Publishing, *(978-0-615-74146-8)* 6212 Englewood Ave., Cincinnati, OH 45237 USA Tel 513-349-8259
Dist(s): **CreateSpace Independent Publishing Platform.**

Tiny Tales, *(978-0-9627661)* P.O. Box 12212, Wilmington, DE 19850 USA
Dist(s): **Capstone Pub.**

Tiny Tortoise Publishing, LLC, *(978-0-9787477)* Orders Addr.: P.O. Box 752123, Las Vegas, NV 89136 USA Tel 702-798-6646.

Tip-Of-The-Moon Publishing Co., *(978-0-9657047; 978-0-9746372; 978-0-9829121)* Orders Addr.: 175 Crescent Rd., Farmville, VA 23901 USA; Edit Addr.: c/o Francis E. Wood, Jr., Rte. 2, Box 1725, Farmville, VA 23901 USA Tel 434-392-4195; Fax: 434-392-5724
E-mail: fewwords@moonstar.com
Web site: http://www.tipofthemoon.com.

Tisdale, Edward W., *(978-0-9744166)* 3420 SW 1st Pl., Cape Coral, FL 33914 USA.

Tish & Co. LLC, *(978-0-9793419)* 10 Twin Pines Ln. No. 205, Belmont, CA 94002-3889 USA (SAN 853-182X)
Web site: http://www.tishandcompany.com
Dist(s): **Big Tent Bks.**
Music, Bks. & Business, Inc.

Tishomingo Tree Pr., The, *(978-0-9768861)* 606 Bay St., Hattiesburg, MS 39401 USA
E-mail: info@tishomingotree.com
Web site: http://www.tishomingotree.com.

Titan Bks. Ltd. (GBR) *(978-0-907610; 978-1-84023; 978-1-85286; 978-1-900097; 978-1-84576; 978-1-84856; 978-0-85768; 978-1-78116; 978-1-78329; 978-1-78585; 978-1-78565)* *Dist. by* **Random.**

Titan Bks. Ltd. (GBR) *(978-0-907610; 978-1-84023; 978-1-85286; 978-1-900097; 978-1-84576; 978-1-84856; 978-0-85768; 978-1-78116; 978-1-78329; 978-1-78585; 978-1-78565)* *Dist. by* **Peng Rand Hse.**

Titan Publishing, *(978-0-9770680)* P.O. Box 2457, Glen Allen, VA 23058 USA (SAN 256-6737)
E-mail: sales@titan-media.com
Web site: http://www.titan-media.com.

Titletown Publishing, LLC, *(978-0-9820009; 978-0-9837547; 978-0-9888605; 978-0-9910699; 978-0-9911938)* Orders Addr.: P.O. Box 12093, Green Bay, WI 54304 USA Tel 920-737-8051; Edit Addr.: 1581 Forest Glen Dr., Green Bay, WI 54304 USA
E-mail: tracy.ertl@titletownpublishing.com
Web site: http://www.titletownpublishing.com
Dist(s): **Midpoint Trade Bks., Inc.**
MyiLibrary.

Titlewaves Publishing, *(978-1-57077)* 1579 Kuhio Hwy., Suite 104, Kapaa, HI 96746 USA (SAN 152-1357) Tel 808-822-7449; Fax: 808-822-2312; Toll Free: 800-835-0583
E-mail: transform@hshawaii.com
Web site: http://www.bestbookshawaii.com; http://www.writersdirect.com.

Titus Institute of California, *(978-0-9747452)* P.O. Box 77023, Corona, CA 92877 USA
E-mail: titusbooks@titusinstitute.com
Web site: http://www.titusinstitute.com.

Tiville Press *See* **MiraQuest**

Tixlini Scriptorium, Inc., *(978-0-9723720)* 681 Grove St., San Luis Obispo, CA 93401 USA Tel 805-543-3540; Fax: 805-543-5195
E-mail: tixlini@yahoo.com.

Tizbit Books, LLC, *(978-0-9760553)* 304 Rte. 22 W., Springfield, NJ 07081 USA Tel 973-564-7200; Fax: 973-564-8895
E-mail: jill@tizbitbooks.com
Web site: http://www.tizbitbooks.com.

T.J. Publishing, *(978-0-9760811)* 1099 E. Champlain, Suite A, No. 152, Fresno, CA 93720 USA Tel 559-297-5559
E-mail: tjpub@aol.com.

TJG Management Services, Inc., *(978-0-9762347; 978-1-62193)* 194 Brantley Pl. Dr., Mooresville, NC 28117 USA Tel 702-349-7718
E-mail: tjgmanage@gmail.com
Web site: http://www.theresagonsalves.com
Dist(s): **BCH Fulfillment & Distribution.**

TJMF Publishing, *(978-0-9759314; 978-0-9789705; 978-0-9801003; 978-0-9829447; 978-0-9910671)* P.O. Box 2923, Clarksville, IN 47131-2923 USA Tel 812-288-7597; Fax: 812-288-1329
E-mail: jimf@dialinn.com
Web site: http://www.tjmfpublishing.com.

TJMF Publishing Daylight Enterprises *See* **TJMF Publishing**

Tkac, John Enterprises LLC, *(978-0-9794454)* Orders Addr.: P.O. Box 7813, Delray Beach, FL 33482 USA Tel 954-632-6360; Fax: 561-330-6917; Edit Addr.: 1095 Hibiscus Ln., Delray Beach, FL 33444 USA
E-mail: adstkac@aol.com
Web site: http://www.jtack.com.

TKG Publishing, *(978-1-884743; 978-0-9755812; 978-0-9825090)* 1800 S. Robertson Blvd., Suite 125, Los Angeles, CA 90035 USA Tel 310-827-9060; Fax: 310-827-9460; *Imprints:* Quiet Time Press (QuietTimePr)
E-mail: cgreco@earthlink.net
Web site: http://www.buyamilliondollars.com.

TLC, *(978-0-9853560)* 12 W. End Ave., Old Greenwich, CT 06870 USA Tel 203-344-9548
E-mail: tanyalcecc@optonline.net.

TLC Information Services, *(978-0-9771594)* Orders Addr.: P.O. Box 944, Yorktown Heights, NY 10598 USA Tel 914-248-6770; Edit Addr.: 3 Louis Dr., Katonah, NY 10536-3122 USA
E-mail: ifaywanli@yahoo.com
Web site: http://www.mwsearch.com.

TLC Publishing, *(978-0-9721517)* c/o Tiller Lactation Consulting, 5221 Rushbrook Dr., Centreville, VA 20120 USA Tel 703-266-3823 Do not confuse with TLC Publishing in Paonia, CO
E-mail: stiller@breastfeeding101.com
Web site: http://www.breastfeeding101.com.

TLConcepts, Inc. *Imprint of* **Tender Learning Concepts**

TLK Pubns., *(978-0-9752558)* Div. of TLK Enterprise, 762 Heather Ln., Easton, PA 18040 USA Tel 973-906-2814
E-mail: ugochuik@yahoo.com
Web site: http://www.tlkenterprise.com
Dist(s): **Lulu Enterprises Inc.**

TLM Publishing Hse., *(978-0-9748829)* P.O. Box 123, Ozark, MO 65721 USA
E-mail: booksellers@tlmpublishinghouse.com
Web site: http://tlmpublishinghouse.com.

TLS Consulting *See* **TLS Publishing**

TLS Publishing, *(978-0-9716244)* P.O. Box 403, Dobbs Ferry, NY 10522 USA Tel 914-674-2257 Do not confuse with TLS Publishing in Irvine, CA
E-mail: tls@nvbb.net.

TMD Enterprises, *(978-0-9789297; 978-0-9842980)* 76 E. Blvd., Suite 11, Rochester, NY 14610-1536 USA (SAN 851-9617)
E-mail: dbeerse@tmd-enterprises.com
Web site: www.tmd-enterprises.com.

TNJ Ministries, *(978-0-9762770)* 8214 SW 52nd Ln., Gainesville, FL 32608 USA Tel 352-376-8930
E-mail: tnj_ministries@yahoo.com
Web site: http://www.wtswlg.bravehost.com.

TNMG Publishing, *(978-0-9768297)* P.O. Box 1032, Winter Park, FL 32790-1032 USA
Web site: http://www.tnmg.ws.

TNT Bks., *(978-1-885227)* Orders Addr.: 3657 Cree Dr., Salt Lake City, UT 84120-2867 USA
E-mail: twixom@msn.com.

TNT Publishing *See* **Reasor, Teresa J.**

TNT Publishing Co., *(978-0-9800860)* P.O. Box 456, Richmond, CA 94808-9991 USA (SAN 855-1634) Tel 510-334-2533
E-mail: tanithtyler@yahoo.com
Web site: http://tntpublishing.com.

Toasted Coconut Media LLC, *(978-1-934906)* 200 Second Ave., 4th Flr., Suite 40, New York, NY 10003 USA (SAN 855-4862) Fax: 646-434-1102
E-mail: donuts@toastedcoconutmedia.com; sales@toastedcoconutmedia.com
Web site: http://www.toastedcoconutmedia.com
Dist(s): **Diamond Comic Distributors, Inc.**
Diamond Bk. Distributors.

Toby & Tutter Publishing, *(978-0-9847812)* 817 W. End Ave. No. 5E, New York, NY 10025-5319 USA (SAN 920-6868) Tel 212-663-8416; Fax: 212-663-8715
E-mail: laura@laurадwightphoto.com
Web site: http://www.tobyandtutter.com.

Todazebooks.com, *(978-0-615-48741-0)* 68 Crystal Cove Ave., Winthrop, MA 02152 USA Tel 617-645-0051
Dist(s): **CreateSpace Independent Publishing Platform**
Dummy Record Do Not USE!!!!.

Todd Communications, *(978-1-57833; 978-1-878100)* 611 E. 12th Ave. Ste. 102, Anchorage, AK 99501-4663 USA (SAN 298-6280)
E-mail: info@toddcom.com
Dist(s): **Ingram Pub. Services**
Wizard Works.

Toe The Line, *(978-0-9792820)* 7071 Warner Ave., Suite F-497, Huntington Beach, CA 92647-5495 USA
E-mail: toetheline@earthlink.net
Web site: http://Toetheline.org.

Tofte Literary Enterprises *See* **Creative Quill Publishing, Inc.**

Together in the Harvest Ministries, Incorporated *See* **Together in the Harvest Pubns./Productions**

Together in the Harvest Pubns./Productions, *(978-0-9637090; 978-1-892853)* Div. of Together In The Harvest Ministries, Inc., Orders Addr.: P.O. Box 612288, Dallas, TX 75261 USA Tel 817-849-8773; Fax: 888-800-1509
E-mail: contact@stevehill.org
Web site: http://www.stevehill.org.

Together, Inc., *(978-0-9764572; 978-1-933463)* 3205 Roosevelt St., NE, Saint Anthony, MN 55418 USA Tel 612-706-7836; Fax: 612-789-8008
E-mail: info@togetherinc.com; pesellors@minn.net
Web site: http://www.togetherinc.com.

Toki Productions, *(978-0-9729527)* P.O. Box 88216, Los Angeles, CA 90009-6888 USA
Web site: http://www.betteroffthan.com.

TokoBooks, LLC, *(978-0-9720436)* 1863c Brattleboro Ct., Kettering, OH 45440 USA (SAN 254-573X) Tel 937-231-4193.

Tokyopop Adult *Imprint of* **TOKYOPOP, Inc.**

TOKYOPOP, Inc., *(978-1-892213; 978-1-931514; 978-1-59182; 978-1-59532; 978-1-59816; 978-1-4278)* Div. of Mixx Entertainment, Inc., People's Bank Building 5900 Wilshire Blvd., Suite 2000, Los Angeles, CA 90036 USA Tel 323-692-6700; Fax: 323-692-6701; *Imprints:* TOKYOPOP Manga (Tokyopop Manga); Tokyopop Kids (TokyoKids); Tokyopop Adult (TokyoAdult)
Web site: http://www.tokyopop.com/
Dist(s): **Diamond Bk. Distributors**
MyiLibrary.

Tokyopop Kids *Imprint of* **TOKYOPOP, Inc.**

TOKYOPOP Manga *Imprint of* **TOKYOPOP, Inc.**

Tokyopop Press *See* **TOKYOPOP, Inc.**

Tolana Publishing, *(978-0-9773912; 978-1-935208)* Orders Addr.: P.O. Box 719, Teaneck, NJ 07666 USA
E-mail: tolanapub@yahoo.com
Web site: http://www.tolanapublishing.com
Dist(s): **CreateSpace Independent Publishing Platform**
Lightning Source, Inc.

Toledo Zoo, The, *(978-0-9776974)* P.O. Box 140130, Toledo, OH 43614 USA Tel 419-385-5721; Fax: 419-724-0068
E-mail: tzgift@toledozoo.org
Web site: http://www.toledozoo.org.

Tolstoy Dom Press, LLC *See* **Vernissage Pr., LLC**

Tom & Susan Allen *See* **Dean's Bks., Inc.**

Tomato Enterprises, *(978-0-9617357)* P.O. Box 73892, Davis, CA 95617 USA (SAN 664-0427) Tel 530-750-1832; Fax: 530-759-9741
E-mail: info@tomatoenterprises.com
Web site: http://www.tomatoenterprises.com.

Tommy Bks. Pubng., *(978-0-9762690)* Div. of C4 Kids, 1220 N. Las Palmas, No. 201, Los Angeles, CA 90038 USA Tel 323-974-8249
E-mail: renegadepic@earthlink.net
Web site: http://www.tommybooks.net
Dist(s): **C4 Kids.**

Tommye-music Corp. DBA Tom eMusic, *(978-1-62321)* 157-17 Willets Point Blvd., Whitestone, NY 11357 USA Tel 718-609-9420
E-mail: office@tommye-music.com.

Tomoka Pr., *(978-0-9657211)* Orders Addr.: 115 Coquina Ave., Ormond Beach, FL 32174 USA Tel 386-677-4219
E-mail: yvonnewpunnett@aol.com
Web site: http://www.tomokapress.com.

Tomorrow's Forefathers, Inc., *(978-0-9719405; 978-1-940793)* Orders Addr.: P.O. Box 11451, Cedar Rapids, IA 52410-1451 USA
E-mail: info@tomorrowsforefathers.com
Web site: http://www.tomorrowsforefathers.com
Dist(s): **Send The Light Distribution LLC.**

TOMY International, Inc., *(978-1-887327; 978-1-890647)* Orders Addr.: 2021 9th St., SE, Dyersville, IA 52040 USA Tel 563-875-5653; Fax: 563-875-5633; Edit Addr.: 1111 W. 22nd St., Oak Brook, IL 60523-1940 USA
E-mail: rcs@rc2corp.com; credit@rc2corp.com
Web site: http://www.learningcurve.com.

Tonepoet Publishing, *(978-0-922224)* 3069 Alamo Dr., Suite 146, Vacaville, CA 95687 USA (SAN 250-3654)
E-mail: tonepoet@jackshiner.com
Web site: http://www.jackshiner.com.

Tongue Untied Publishing, *(978-0-9745783)* Orders Addr.: P.O. Box 822, Jackson, GA 30233 USA; Edit Addr.: 2571 Hwy. 36 E., Jackson, GA 30233 USA
E-mail: maseyree2001@yahoo.com
Web site: http://www.tongueuntiedpublishing.com
Dist(s): **A & B Distributors & Pubs. Group**
Culture Plus Bk. Distributors.

Tony Franklin Cos., The, *(978-0-9714280)* 521 Ridge Rd., Lexington, KY 40503-1229 USA (SAN 254-2145)
E-mail: tlf3c@aol.com; ed@crystalcommunications.biz
Web site: www.thetonyfranklin.com.

Tony Hawk's 900 Revolution *Imprint of* **Stone Arch Bks.**

Tony Tales, *(978-0-9791362)* 6024 Cottontail Cove, Las Vegas, NV 89130 USA (SAN 852-5285) Tel 702-245-8624; Fax: 702-898-1359
E-mail: barbarites@aol.com
Web site: www.Tony.

Too Fun Publshing, *(978-0-9773317)* P.O. Box 2098, Vashon Island, WA 98070 USA; 1055 SW 178th St., Vashon Island, WA 98070
E-mail: toofunpublishing@gmail.com.

Toobeez Project-Connect Joint Venture, *(978-0-9765670)* Div. of Connectable Color Tubes, LLC, Orders Addr.: Project Connect JV 1204 Thomas Rd., Wayne, PA 19087 USA Tel 610-975-0102 (phone/fax)
E-mail: jdonahue@toobeez.com
Web site: http://www.toobeez.com; http://www.project-connect.net.

Toodle-oo Innovative Products, *(978-0-9793145)* 2166 E. Wellington Ave., Santa Ana, CA 92701 USA (SAN 853-0890) Tel 714-558-9537
E-mail: w.kawamoto@cox.net; suszanales@adelphia.net
Web site: http://www.makebubblesgrow.com.

Tool Kits For Kids LLC, *(978-0-9819483)* Orders Addr.: P.O. Box 173, Glen Rock, NJ 07452 USA
Web site: http://www.toolkitsforkids.com.

Tools For Young Historians *Imprint of* **BrimWood Pr.**

TOON Books / RAW Junior, LLC, *(978-0-9799238; 978-1-935179; 978-1-943145)* 27 Greene St., New York, NY 10013 USA (SAN 854-7246) Tel 212-226-0146; Fax: 212-343-9296
E-mail: raw.junior@gmail.com
Web site: http://www.toon-books.com
Dist(s): **Consortium Bk. Sales & Distribution**
Diamond Comic Distributors, Inc.
Diamond Bk. Distributors.

Toonhound Studios, LLC, *(978-0-615-37908-1; 978-0-9833944)* 2761 Peach Dr., Little Elm, TX 75068 USA Tel 214-726-2875
E-mail: kurtz@pvponline.com
Web site: http://www.pvponline.com
Dist(s): **Diamond Comic Distributors, Inc.**

Toot and Moo, *(978-0-615-62256-9)* 1253 Hillwood Cir., East Lansing, MI 48823 USA Tel 517-803-3576
Dist(s): **CreateSpace Independent Publishing Platform.**

Tootle Time Publishing Co., *(978-0-9721706)* Orders Addr.: P.O. Box 62, Cade, LA 70519 USA Tel 337-364-6410; Fax: 337-364-6415; Edit Addr.: 1031 Mary Rd., New Iberia, LA 70560 USA
E-mail: marycelesteclement@yahoo.com.

TOP *Imprint of* **Top Pubns., Ltd.**

Top5 Co., The, *(978-0-9746760)* Div. of Bucc Wild LLC, Orders Addr.: 785 E. Tibet Rd., Columbus, OH 43211 USA Tel 614-372-3367
E-mail: bzumfelde@hotmail.com.

Top Choice Pr., LLC., *(978-0-9761396)* 28 Worcester Sq., Unit No. 1, Boston, MA 02118-2943 USA Tel 617-424-9726; Fax: 617-262-0702
E-mail: tberkan@mindspring.com
Web site: http://topchoicebooks.com.

Top Pubns., Ltd., *(978-0-9666366; 978-1-929976; 978-1-935722)* Div. of Top Ventures, Ltd., Orders Addr.: 12221 Merit Dr., Suite 950, Dallas, TX 75251 USA; Edit Addr.: 3100 Independence Pkwy., No. 311-349, Plano, TX 75075-9152 USA Tel 972-960-2240; Fax: 972-233-0713; *Imprints:* TOP (TOP USA)
E-mail: bill@toppub.com
Web site: http://toppub.com.

Top Quality Pubns., *(978-0-9726311)* Orders Addr.: 3925 Americana Dr., Tampa, FL 33634 USA
E-mail: parfisher@yahoo.com
Web site: http://www.topqualitypublications.org.

Top Shelf *Imprint of* **Jawbone Publishing Corp.**

Top Shelf Productions, *(978-1-891830; 978-1-60309)* Orders Addr.: P.O. Box 1282, Marietta, GA 30061-1282 USA Fax: 770-427-6395; Edit Addr.: 1109 Grand Oaks Glen, Marietta, GA 30064 USA Fax: 770-427-6395
E-mail: staros@bellsouth.net; chris@topshelfcomix.com
Web site: http://www.topshelfcomix.com
Dist(s): **Consortium Bk. Sales & Distribution**
Diamond Comic Distributors, Inc.
Diamond Bk. Distributors.

Top Shelf Publishing, *(978-0-9770443)* 4124 W. Fremont Rd., Spokane, WA 99224 USA
Web site: http://www.melodramerica.com/html/grammar_keys.html.

Tor Bks. *Imprint of* **Doherty, Tom Assocs., LLC**

Tor Teen *Imprint of* **Doherty, Tom Assocs., LLC**

†Torah Aura Productions, *(978-0-933873; 978-1-891662; 978-1-934527)* 4423 Fruitland Ave., Los Angeles, CA 90058 USA (SAN 692-7025) Fax: 323-585-0327; Toll Free: 800-238-6724
E-mail: jane@torahaura.com
Web site: http://torahaura.com; *CIP.*

Torah Excel, *(978-1-930925)* 6415 N. Sacramento, Chicago, IL 60645 USA Tel 773-743-7915; Fax: 773-508-9874; *Imprints:* Shazak Productions (Shazak Prods)
E-mail: torahxl@megsinet.com
Web site: http://torahxl.com.

Torah Institute of Baltimore, *(978-0-9767505)* 35 Rosewood Ln., Owings Mills, MD 21117-3704 USA Tel 410-654-3500 ext. 3; Fax: 443-394-5999
E-mail: tibexec@comcast.net
Web site: http://www.torahinstitute.org.

Torah Umesorah Pubns., *(978-0-914131; 978-1-878895)* 1090 Coney Island Ave. 3rd Flr., Brooklyn, NY 11230 USA (SAN 218-9992) Tel 718-259-1223; Fax: 718-259-1795.

Torch Legacy Pubns., *(978-0-9763487; 978-0-9785333; 978-0-615-26544-5; 978-0-615-30182-2; 978-0-615-30191-4; 978-0-615-37024-8; 978-0-9830141; 978-0-9849441)* P.O. Box 165046, Irving, TX 75016 USA
E-mail: torchlegacypublications@msn.com
Web site: http://www.torchlegacy.com
Dist(s): **Send The Light Distribution LLC**
Smashwords.

Torchlight Publishing, (*978-1-887089; 978-0-9779785; 978-0-9817273; 978-1-937731*) Orders Addr.: P.O. Box 52, Badger, CA 93603 USA Tel 559-337-2200; Fax: 559-337-2354; Toll Free: 888-867-2458 Do not confuse with Torchlight Publishing in Colorado Springs, CO
E-mail: torchlightpublishing@yahoo.com
Web site: http://www.torchlight.com
Dist(s): **AtlasBooks Distribution**
BookMasters.

Torgerson Meadows Publishing, (*978-0-9767116*) 37492 Outpost Rd., NW, Grygla, MN 56727 USA Tel 218-294-6644
E-mail: sstorg@webtv.net
Web site: http://www.taolc.com.

Tornado Creek Pubns., (*978-0-9652219; 978-0-9740881; 978-0-9821529*) P.O. Box 8625, Spokane, WA 99203-8625 USA Tel 509-838-7114; Fax: 509-455-6798; 1308 E. 29th Ave., Spokane, WA 99203 Tel 509-838-7114; Fax: 509-445-6798
E-mail: tcpoffice@comcast.net
Web site: http://www.tornadocreekpublications.com.

Torque Bks. *Imprint of* **Bellwether Media**

Torquere Pr., (*978-0-9748202; 978-0-9749923; 978-0-9762389; 978-1-933389; 978-1-934166; 978-1-60370; 978-1-61040*) P.O. Box 37, Waldo, AR 71770 USA
E-mail: torquere@torquerepress.com
Web site: http://www.torquerepress.com.

Torres, Eliseo & Sons, (*978-0-88303*) P.O. Box 2, Eastchester, NY 10709 USA (SAN 207-0235).

Tortuga Pr., (*978-1-889910*) Orders Addr.: PMB 181, 2777 Yulupa Ave., Santa Rosa, CA 95405 USA (SAN 299-1756) Tel 707-544-4720; Fax: 707-544-5609; Toll Free: 866-4 TORTUGA
E-mail: info@tortugapress.com
Web site: http://www.tortugapress.com
Dist(s): **Follett School Solutions.**

Toshia Shaw *See* **Purple Wings Publishing**

Total Career Resources, (*978-0-615-24214-9; 978-0-9849970*) 2000 Bering Dr., Suite 460, Houston, TX 77057 USA Tel 713-784-3197.

Total Outreach for Christ Ministries, Inc., (*978-0-9745834*) 3411 Asher Ave., Little Rock, AR 72204 USA Tel 501-663-0362; Fax: 501-663-0390
E-mail: tofchristm@aol.com
Web site: http://theonenewman.org.

Total Publishing & Media *Imprint of* **Yorkshire Publishing Group**

Total Wellness *See* **Total Wellness Publishing**

Total Wellness Publishing, (*978-0-9744585*) 14545 Glenoak Pl., Fontana, CA 92337 USA
E-mail: micheleiqbal@netzero.net
Web site: http://www.Totalwellnesspublishing.com; http://www.micheleiqbal.com
Dist(s): **Distributors, The.**

Totally Outdoors Publishing, Inc., (*978-0-9726653*) 7284 Raccoon Rd., Manning, SC 29102 USA
Web site: http://www.totallyoutdoorspublishing.com.

TotalRecall Pubns., (*978-0-9704684; 978-1-59095*) P.O. Box 1497, Friendswood, TX 77549 USA Tel 281-992-3131
E-mail: corby@totalrecallpress.com
Web site: http://www.totalrecallpress.com
Dist(s): **MyiLibrary**
ebrary, Inc.

Totem Tales Publishing, (*978-0-9843228*) 219 Salzedo St., Royal Palm Beach, FL 33411 USA Tel 561-537-2522
E-mail: books@totemtales.com; danbodenstein@yahoo.com
Web site: http://www.totemtales.com
Dist(s): **BookBaby.**

Toucan Pr., Inc., (*978-0-9744926*) 307 Sweet Bay Pl., Carrboro, NC 27510-2378 USA.

Toucan Valley Pubns., Inc., (*978-0-9634017; 978-1-884925*) Orders Addr.: P.O. Box 15520, Fremont, CA 94539-2620 USA Tel 510-498-1009; Fax: 510-498-1010; Toll Free Fax: 888-391-6943; Toll Free: 800-236-7946
E-mail: ben@toucanvalley.com; query@toucanvalley.com
Web site: http://www.toucanvalley.com
Dist(s): **Grey Hse. Publishing.**

Touch Books, Incorporated *See* **Minardi Photography**

Touch the Music, (*978-0-9837585*) 110 Konner Ave., Pine Brook, NJ 07058 USA (SAN 860-2794) Tel 973-220-9785
E-mail: Claudia@Touchthemusic.us
Web site: www.Touchthemusic.us.

TouchSmart Publishing, LLC, (*978-0-9765060; 978-0-9787517*) 167 Old Richmond Rd., Swanzeyti, NH 03446 USA (SAN 256-3835) Tel 603-352-7282; a/o Touchsmart Publishing (Distributor), LLC, 6522 Waldorf Pl., Cincinnati, OH 45230 (SAN 631-8703) Tel 513-225-8765; Fax: 206-666-4856
E-mail: ccardine@touchsmart.net
Web site: http://www.touchsmart.net.

Touchstone *Imprint of* **Touchstone**

Touchstone, (*978-0-7432*) 1230 Avenue of the Americas, New York, NY 10020 USA; *Imprints:* Touchstone (TouchImp)
Dist(s): **Simon & Schuster, Inc.**

Touchstone Center for Children, Incorporated, The *See* **Touchstone Ctr. Pubns.**

Touchstone Ctr. Pubns., (*978-1-929299*) Div. of Touchstone Center for Children, Inc., Orders Addr.: 141 E. 88th St., New York, NY 10028 USA (SAN 265-3664) Tel 212-831-7717
E-mail: rlewis212@aol.com
Web site: http://www.touchstonecenter.net
Dist(s): **AtlasBooks Distribution**
State Univ. of New York Pr.

Touchstone Communications, (*978-0-9790775*) Orders Addr.: P.O. Box 396, Oneonta, NY 13820-0396 USA (SAN 852-3835); 291 Chestnut St., Box 396, Oneonta, NY 13820
E-mail: Touchstonecom@stny.rr.com; Clerk@touchstone-com.com
Web site: http://Touchstone-com.com.

Touchstones Discussion Project, (*978-1-878461; 978-1-937742*) PO Box 2329, Annapolis, MD 21404-2329 USA Toll Free: 800-456-6542
Web site: http://www.touchstones.org.

Tower Pr., (*978-0-615-67490-2*) 7211 Brickyard Rd., Potomac, MD 20854 USA Tel 202 944 3810; Fax: 202 944 3826
Dist(s): **CreateSpace Independent Publishing Platform.**

Towers Maguire Publishing *Imprint of* **Local History Co., The**

Town & Country Reprographics, (*978-0-9725808; 978-0-9754383; 978-0-9771894; 978-0-9794860; 978-0-9801439; 978-0-9825067; 978-0-9835219; 978-0-9896702; 978-0-9968302*) 230 N. Main St., Concord, NH 03301 USA (SAN 254-959X)
Web site: http://www.reprographic.com
Dist(s): **Smashwords.**

Townsend, Diana, (*978-0-615-15882-2; 978-0-615-16214-0*) 3432 Briaroaks Dr., Garland, TX 75044 USA Tel 214-703-9718
E-mail: dianatownsend@aol.com
Dist(s): **Lulu Enterprises Inc.**

Townsend, J. N. Publishing *Imprint of* **PublishingWorks**

Townsend Pr., (*978-0-944210; 978-1-59194*) 439 Kelly Dr., West Berlin, NJ 08091-9284 USA (SAN 243-0444) Toll Free Fax: 800-225-8894; Toll Free: 800-772-6410
E-mail: townsendcs@aol.com; orderstp@aol.com; emily@townsend.press
Web site: http://www.townsendpress.com.

Townsend Pr. - Sunday Schl. Publishing Board, (*978-0-910683; 978-1-932972; 978-1-939225*) 330 Charlotte Ave., Nashville, TN 37201-1188 USA (SAN 275-8598) Tel 615-256-2480; Fax: 615-242-4929; Toll Free: 800-359-9398
E-mail: byron217@lycos.com.

Toy Box Productions, (*978-1-887729; 978-1-932332*) Div. of CRT, Custom Products, Inc., 7532 Hickory Hills Ct., Whites Creek, TN 37189 USA Tel 615-299-0822; 615-876-5490; Fax: 615-876-3931; Toll Free: 800-750-1511
E-mail: leeann@crttoybox.com
Dist(s): **Christian Bk. Distributors.**

Toy Quest, (*978-0-9767325; 978-0-9786246*) Manley, 2229 Barry Ave., Los Angeles, CA 90064-1401 USA.

Toy Rocket Studios, LLC, (*978-0-615-23521-9; 978-0-578-15192-2*) Orders Addr.: 5410 Fallen Timbers Dr., West Chester, OH 45069 USA; Edit Addr.: 814 St.Clair Ave, Hamilton, OH 45015 USA
E-mail: ToyRocketLaunch@gmail.com
Web site: http://www.ToyRocketStudiosLLC.com; http://www.ToyRocketLaunch.com.

Toy Truck Publishing, (*978-0-9764983*) 4602 Lilac Ln., Lake Elmo, MN 55042 USA (SAN 256-3754) Tel 612-716-8383; Fax: 651-275-1279
E-mail: sales@toytruckpublishing.com
Web site: http://www.toytruckpublishing.com.

Toys 'n Things Press *See* **Redleaf Pr.**

Tpprince Esquire *See* **Tpprince Esquire International**

Tpprince Esquire International, (*978-0-9790110; 978-0-692-22159-4; 978-1-63365*) 6429 Printz Ct. Apt 237, Saint Louis, MO 63116 USA (SAN 852-2219) Tel 41794299891 (swiss portable); 41218821971 (swiss main office); 314-843-0451 st.Louis, Mo. USA; Cretillon 9, Froideville, ch 1055 Fax: +41218821971
E-mail: tpprince_esq@yahoo.com; dan.sekarski@bluewin.ch; tpprince@tpprince-esquire.com; dan.sekarski@bluewin.ch; sandrinesekarski@bluewin.ch
Web site: http://stores.lulu.com/tpprince_esquire; http://tpprince-esquire.com.

TPRS Publishing, Inc., (*978-0-9777911; 978-1-934958; 978-1-935575; 978-1-940408*) P.O. Box 11624, Chandler, AZ 85248 USA Tel 480-821-8608; Fax: 480-963-3463; Toll Free: 800-877-4738
E-mail: patgaab@gmail.com
Web site: http://www.tprstorytelling.com.

TR Bks., (*978-0-9788969*) 2430 N. Penn Ave., Independence, KS 67301 USA (SAN 851-8882) Tel 620-331-4486; *Imprints:* Exhibit A (Exhibit A).

Tracepaper Bks. Inc., (*978-0-9792728*) 68 Ridgewood Ave., Selden, NY 11784 USA
Web site: http://www.tracepaper.net.

Trachtman, Joseph, (*978-0-9795170*) 5008 Pullman Ave. NE, Seattle, WA 98105 USA.

Tracks Publishing, (*978-1-884654; 978-1-935937*) 140 Brightwood Ave., Chula Vista, CA 91910 USA Tel 619-476-7125; Fax: 619-476-8173; Toll Free: 800-443-3570
E-mail: tracks@cox.net
Web site: http://www.startupsports.com
Dist(s): **Ebsco Publishing**
Independent Pubs. Group
MyiLibrary
ebrary, Inc.

Tractor Mac Inc., (*978-0-9788496; 978-0-9826870; 978-0-9888329*) 121 Transylvania Rd., Roxbury, CT 06783 USA Tel 860-210-9805; Fax: 260-210-9805
E-mail: bsteers@tractormac.com
Web site: http://tractormac.com.

Tracy, Jean A. *See* **KidsDiscuss.com**

TracyTrends, (*978-0-9708226; 978-0-9814737; 978-0-615-11462-0*) 7710-C Somerset Bay, Indianapolis, IN 46240-3336 USA Toll Free: 800-840-6118
E-mail: tracytrends@aol.com
Web site: http://www.tracytrends.com.

Tradewind Bks. (CAN) (*978-1-896580*) *Dist. by* **Orca Bk Pub.**

Tradition Publishing, (*978-0-9789969*) 1823 Hart Leonard Rd., Cornerville, TN 37047 USA (SAN 852-1603)
Web site: http://www.carouselcarving.com.

Trafalgar Square Bks., (*978-0-943955; 978-1-57076*) Orders Addr.: P.O. Box 257, North Pomfret, VT 05053 USA Tel 802-457-1911; Fax: 802-457-1913; Edit Addr.: Howe Hill Rd., North Pomfret, VT 05053 USA
E-mail: kimcook@sover.net
Web site: http://www.horseandriderbooks.com; http://www.trafalgarbooks.com/
Dist(s): **Follett School Solutions**
Legato Pubs. Group
MyiLibrary
Perseus-PGW.

Trafalgar Square Publishing, (*978-0-943955; 978-1-57076*) Orders Addr.: P.O. Box 257, North Pomfret, VT 05053-0257 USA (SAN 213-8859) Tel 802-457-1911; Fax: 802-457-1913; Toll Free: 800-423-4525; Edit Addr.: 388 Howe Hill Rd., North Pomfret, VT 05053 USA Tel 802-423-4525; 802-457-1913
E-mail: tsquare@sover.net
Web site: http://www.trafalgarbooks.com; http://www.horseandriderbooks.com
Dist(s): **Independent Pubs. Group**
MyiLibrary
Perseus-PGW.

Trafford Publishing, (*978-1-55212; 978-1-55369; 978-1-55395; 978-1-4120; 978-1-4122; 978-1-4251; 978-1-4269; 978-1-4669; 978-1-4907*) 1663 Liberty Dr., Suite 200, Bloomington, IN 47403 USA Tel 812-334-5345; 888-232-4444; Fax: 812-339-6554
E-mail: orders@trafford.com; editorial@trafford.com; info@trafford.com
Web site: http://www.trafford.com
Dist(s): **AtlasBooks Distribution**
Author Solutions, Inc.
CreateSpace Independent Publishing Platform
DecisionPro, Inc.
Ediciones Universal
Wizard Works
Zondervan.

Trail, George (GBR) (*978-0-9559927*) *Dist. by* **LuluCom.**

Trail Media, (*978-0-615-72790-5; 978-0-615-79866-0; 978-0-615-83231-9; 978-0-615-92942-2; 978-0-615-93203-3; 978-0-615-93205-7; 978-0-692-39548-6; 978-0-692-39549-3; 978-0-692-42791-0; 978-0-692-44492-4; 978-0-692-52132-8*) 1320 Ynez Pl. No. 181306, Coronado, CA 92178 USA Tel 760-212-6519
E-mail: ChisholmAuthor@gmail.com
Web site: Chisholm_TrailMedia.com
Dist(s): **CreateSpace Independent Publishing Platform.**

Trail Trotters Bk. Ranch, (*978-0-9763209*) 616 N. Aurelius Rd., Mason, MI 48854 USA Tel 517-244-0727
E-mail: rosewoodbouz@aol.com
Web site: http://www.ponypointers.com.

Trails Bks. *Imprint of* **Big Earth Publishing**

Trails Media Group, Incorporated *See* **Big Earth Publishing**

Trails of Discovery, (*978-0-9788926*) 31071 Marbella Vista, San Juan Capistrano, CA 92675 USA.

Training Grounds, (*978-0-9729057*) P.O. Box 5631, Tucson, KY 85703 USA
E-mail: sjrose@plantagriculture.org
Web site: http://www.plantagriculture.org.

Train-Up A Child, LLC, (*978-0-9703069*) P.O. Box 1122, Jenks, OK 74037 USA Tel 918-299-8178 (phone/fax)
E-mail: TrainUpStudies@aol.com
Web site: http://www.trainupstudies.com.

Traitor Dachshund, LLC *See* **Minted Prose, LLC**

Trammel, Crystal, (*978-0-9746327*) 133 Montego Dr., Mesquite, TX 75149-1708 USA
E-mail: minc34@hotmail.com.

Tranquility Publishing *See* **Tranquility Ranch Publishing**

Tranquility Ranch Publishing, (*978-0-9747425*) 25796 Tranquility Ln., Magnolia, TX 77355 USA
E-mail: gcadwalder@aol.com.

†Transaction Pubs., (*978-0-7658; 978-0-87855; 978-0-88738; 978-1-56000; 978-1-4128*) Raritan Ctr., 300 McGaw Dr., Edison, NJ 08837 USA; Edit Addr.: 10 Corporate Pl., S., Piscataway, NJ 08854 USA (SAN 202-7941) Toll Free: 888-999-6778
E-mail: orders@transactionpub.com
Web site: http://www.transactionpub.com
Dist(s): **MyiLibrary**
ebrary, Inc.; *CIP.*

Transaltar Publishing, (*978-0-9771802; 978-0-615-20263-1; 978-0-615-20419-2; 978-0-615-20678-3; 978-0-615-20814-5*) 5517 E St., Sacramento, CA 95819 USA
E-mail: publisher@transaltar.com
Web site: http://www.transaltar.com; http://www.heathbuckmaster.com/
Dist(s): **CreateSpace Independent Publishing Platform**
Lulu Enterprises Inc.

Transatlantic Arts, Inc., (*978-0-693*) P.O. Box 6086, Albuquerque, NM 87197 USA (SAN 202-7968) Tel 505-898-2289 Do not confuse with Trans-Atlantic Pubns., Inc., Philadelphia, PA.
E-mail: books@transatlantic.com
Web site: http://www.transatlantic.com/direct.

Trans-Atlantic Pubns., Inc., 311 Bainbridge St., Philadelphia, PA 19147 USA (SAN 694-0234) Tel 215-925-5083; Fax: 215-925-1912 Do not confuse with Transatlantic Arts, Inc., Albuquerque, NM
E-mail: order@transatlanticpub.com
Web site: http://www.transatlanticpub.com.

Transcontinental Music Pubns., (*978-0-8074*) Div. of URJ, 633 Third Ave., 6th Flr., New York, NY 10017-6778 USA Tel 212-650-4101; Fax: 212-650-4109
E-mail: tmp@uahc.org
Web site: http://www.eTranscon.com
Dist(s): **Leonard, Hal Corp.**

Trans-Galactic Pubns., (*978-0-9616078*) 20 Sunnyside Ave. Suite A134, Mill Valley, CA 94941 USA (SAN 698-0899)
E-mail: transpubls@aol.com.

Transworld Publishers Ltd. (GBR) (*978-0-552*) *Dist. by* **IPG Chicago.**

Trapper Creek Museum Sluice Box Productions, (*978-0-9718302*) Orders Addr.: P.O. Box 13011, Trapper Creek, AK 99683 USA Tel 907-733-2555; Edit Addr.: Mile 3/4 Petersville Rd., Trapper Creek, AK 99683 USA
E-mail: info@trappercreekmuseum.com
Web site: http://www.trappercreekmuseum.com; http://www.sluiceboxproductions.com.

Trash, Steve Enterprises, (*978-0-9652542*) 975 Old Dirt Rd., Spruce Pine, AL 35585 USA.

Travel 4 Life I, (*978-0-9749441*) 2040 E. 22nd St., Box 911, Fremont, NE 68025 USA Tel 402-727-1559
E-mail: deanjcbs4u@yahoo.com
Web site: http://www.travel4life.org.

Travel America Bks., (*978-0-9795867*) 64 Vanderbilt Ave., Floral Park, NY 11001 USA Tel 516-354-2615
E-mail: shajovin@aol.com.

TravelBrains, Inc., (*978-0-9705809; 978-1-933763*) 360 Rte. 101, Unit 13a, Bedford, NH 03110-5660 USA
Web site: http://www.travelbrains.com.

Traveler's Trunk Publishing LLC, (*978-0-9841496*) 15071 Hanna Ave. NE, Cedar Springs, MI 49319 USA (SAN 858-558X) Tel 937-903-9233
E-mail: amanda@travelerstrunkpublishing.com
Web site: http://www.travelerstrunkpublishing.com/.

Trawick, Gary E., (*978-0-615-66181-0*) 202 N. McNeil St., Burgaw, NC 28425 USA Tel 910-602-0993
E-mail: jenningstrawick@hotmail.com.

Traylor, Waverley Publishing, (*978-0-9715068*) Div. of Waverley Traylor Photography, 3407 Longwood Dr., Smithfield, VA 23430 USA Tel 757-356-9119 (phone/fax)
E-mail: wlfoto@aol.com.

Treadle Pr., (*978-0-935143*) Div. of Binding & Printing Co., Box D, Sheperdstown, WV 25443 USA (SAN 695-2070) Tel 304-876-2557.

Treasure Bay, Inc., (*978-1-891327; 978-1-60115*) 5 Ash Ct., Novato, CA 94949 USA (SAN 859-0958)
E-mail: customerservice@webothread.com; donpanec@comcast.net
Web site: http://www.webothread.com.

Treasure Chest Books *See* **Rio Nuevo Pubs.**

Treasure Hunt Adventures, Inc., (*978-0-9749809*) P.O. Box 1049, Carmel, NY 10512-9998 USA Tel 845-225-2539
E-mail: info@treasurehuntadventures.com
Web site: http://www.treasurehuntadventures.com.

Treasure Trove, Inc., (*978-0-9760618; 978-0-9772314*) P.O. Box 459, Pound Ridge, NY 10576 USA Fax: 203-801-0099
Web site: http://www.atreasuretrove.com.

Treasured Images, (*978-0-9728770*) P.O. Box 361, Milton, WA 98354-0361 USA
E-mail: snspubs@aol.com.

Treasured Legacies, (*978-0-9819217*) 1589 Althouse Rd., Cochranville, PA 19330 USA Tel 610-593-2053
E-mail: anjoy@epix.net.

Treble Heart Bks., (*978-0-9711882; 978-1-931742; 978-1-932695; 978-1-936127; 978-1-938370*) 1284 Overlook Dr., Sierra Vista, AZ 85635-5512 USA (SAN 254-7120) Tel 520-458-5602; Fax: 520-459-0162; *Imprints:* MountainView (MtnView)
Web site: http://www.trebleheartbooks.com
Dist(s): **Smashwords.**

Tree Branch Publishing, (*978-0-9772578*) Orders Addr.: P.O. Box 421004, Summerland Key, FL 33042 USA Tel 305-872-4600; Fax: 305-832-0156; Toll Free: 866-454-6525; Edit Addr.: 19769 Date Palm Dr., Summerland Key, FL 33042 USA
E-mail: info@treeoflifepublishing.com.

Tree Musketeers, Inc., (*978-0-9770196*) Orders Addr.: 136 Main St., El Segundo, CA 90245 USA
E-mail: gail@treemusketeers.org
Web site: http://www.treemusketeers.org.

Tree of Life Pr., (*978-0-9727103*) 7212 Dogwood Dr., Knoxville, TN 37919-8828 USA
E-mail: jana@janaspicka.com
Web site: http://www.janaspicka.com.

Tree Of Life Publishing, (*978-0-9745052*) P.O. Box 421004, Summerland Key, FL 33042 USA Tel 305-744-0330; Fax: 305-744-0320; Toll Free: 866-454-6525; *Imprints:* Peeper & Friends (Peep & Friends)
E-mail: peeper@peeperandfriends.com
Web site: http://www.peeperandfriends.com.

Tree of Life Publishing Hse., (*978-0-9801357; 978-0-9822060*) 730 Gladstone St., La Verne, CA 91750 USA Tel 626-825-5539
E-mail: shaynah@treeoflifepublishinghouse.com
Web site: http://www.treeoflifepublishinghouse.com.

Tree Tunnel Pr., (*978-0-9841037*) P.O. Box 733, Capitola, CA 95010 USA (SAN 931-3931) Tel 831-427-5551; Toll Free: 800-213-1885
E-mail: contact@treetunnelpress.com
Web site: http://www.treetunnelpress.com.

Treehaus Communications, Inc., (*978-0-929496; 978-1-886510*) Orders Addr.: P.O. Box 249, Loveland, OH 45140 USA (SAN 249-5325) Tel 513-683-5716; Fax: 513-683-2882; Toll Free: 800-638-4287; Edit Addr.: 906 W. Loveland Ave., Loveland, OH 45140 USA (SAN 249-5333)
E-mail: treehaus1@fuse.net
Dist(s): **ACTA Pubns.**

TreeHse. Publishing Group, (*978-0-9892079; 978-0-9963901*) Div. of Amphorae Publishing Group,

Publisher Name Index

3963 Flora Pl., St. Louis, MO 63110 USA Tel 314-363-4546
E-mail: kbmakansi@blankslatecommunications.com
Web site: http://www.treehousepublishinggroup.com
Dist(s): **Midpoint Trade Bks., Inc.**

Trefry, Deana, *(978-0-9798193)* 587 Essex St., Beverly, MA 01915 USA
E-mail: deanat@comcast.net.

Tremendous Life Bks. *Imprint of* **Executive Bks.**

Trend Enterprises, Inc., *(978-1-889319; 978-1-58792; 978-1-60912; 978-1-62807)* Orders Addr.: P.O. Box 64073, Saint Paul, MN 55164 USA Tel 651-631-2850; Fax: 651-582-3500; Toll Free Fax: 800-845-4832; Toll Free: 800-328-5540; Edit Addr.: 300 Ninth Ave., SW, New Brighton, MN 55112 USA
Web site: http://www.trendenterprises.com.

Trend Factor Pr., *(978-0-9818669)* 8101 Timber Valley Ct., Dunn Loring, VA 22027 USA (SAN 856-7468) Tel 571-723-5645
E-mail: publisher@trendfactorpress.com; avanderbilt@vanderbilt-consulting.com
Web site: http://www.trendfactorpress.com
Dist(s): **Blu Sky Media Group.**

Trenton Creative Enterprises, *(978-0-9754958)* 731 Springdale Dr., Spartanburg, SC 29302 USA
E-mail: trentoncreativeenterprises@charter.net
Web site: http://www.vintagegastonia.com.

Trent's Prints, *(978-0-9728872; 978-0-9762389; 978-0-9773723; 978-1-934035; 978-1-937000)* 3754 Willard Norris Rd., Pace, FL 32571 USA Tel 850-994-1421 Toll Free: 866-275-7124
Web site: http://www.trentsprints.com.

Treorca Pr., *(978-0-9766559)* 1718 W. 102nd St., Chicago, IL 60643-2147 USA
E-mail: joga9@aol.com
Web site: http://www.treorcapress.com.

Tres Canis Publishing Co., *(978-0-9659065)* P.O. Box 163, Nanticoke, PA 18634 USA Tel 570-735-0328
E-mail: rjanosov@verizon.net.

Tres Clavas Pr., *(978-0-615-37077-4; 978-0-9855731)* 626 N. 6th Ave., Tucson, AZ 85705 USA Tel 480-433-0597
E-mail: zaa@dexterandstray.com
Web site: http://dexterandstray.com.

Trevor Romain Company, The *See* **Romain, Trevor Co., The**

Tri I Pubns., *(978-0-9793683; 978-0-9821674)* 100 Taylor Pl., Southport, CT 06890 USA Tel 203-254-7631; Fax: 203-254-7826
E-mail: thompson@triist.com; linda@lindasworlds.com
Web site: http://www.triist.com; http://www.lindasworlds.com; http://www.iammyowndragon.com
Dist(s): **AtlasBooks Distribution.**

TRI LIFE Pr., *(978-0-9755938)* P.O. Box 2174, Clinton, MD 20735 USA Tel 602-561-1354; Toll Free: 888-786-7526
Web site: http://www.byrongarrett.com.

Tri Valley Children's Publishing, *(978-0-9790962)* 512 Briarwood Ct., Livermore, CA 94551 USA Tel 925-413-0546
E-mail: stephanierutledge@comcast.net.

†Triad Publishing Co., *(978-0-937404)* Imprint of Triad Communications, Inc., Orders Addr.: P.O. Box 13355, Gainesville, FL 32604 USA (SAN 205-4574) Tel 352-373-5800 editorial office; Fax: 352-373-1488 editorial office; Toll Free Fax: 800-854-4947 orders & queries Do not confuse with companies iwth the same or similar name in Tujuga, CA, Sequim, WA, Parker, CO, Marlton, NJ, West Hartford, CT,Raleigh, NC , Sarasota, Fl
E-mail: lorna@triadpublishing.com
Web site: http://www.triadpublishing.com; *CIP.*

Tri-Ad veterans League, Inc., *(978-0-9720404)* 31 Heath St., Jamaica Plain, MA 02130-1650 USA
E-mail: triadveterans@hotmail.com
Web site: http://www.triadveteransleague.org.

Triangle Square *Imprint of* **Seven Stories Pr.**

Tribute Bks., *(978-0-9765072; 978-0-9795045; 978-0-9814619; 978-0-9822565; 978-0-9837418; 978-0-9857922)* P.O. Box 95, Archbald, PA 18403 USA (SAN 256-4416) Tel 570-876-2416 (phone/fax)
E-mail: info@tribute-books.com
Web site: http://www.tribute-books.com
Dist(s): **Lightning Source, Inc.**

Trice, B.E. Publishing, *(978-0-9631925; 978-1-890885)* 2727 Prytania St., New Orleans, LA 70130 USA Tel 504-895-0111
E-mail: betbooks@aol.com.

Trickle Creek Bks., *(978-0-9640742; 978-1-929432)* Orders Addr.: 500 Andersontown Rd., Mechanicsburg, PA 17055 USA Tel 717-766-2638; Fax: 717-766-1343; Toll Free: 800-353-2791
E-mail: tonialbert@aol.com
Web site: http://www.TrickleCreekBooks.com.

Tricolor Bks., *(978-0-9754641)* P.O. Box 24811, Tempe, AZ 85285 USA
E-mail: tricolorbrian@hotmail.com
Web site: http://www.mountainkingsnake.com.

Tricycle Pr. *Imprint of* **Ten Speed Pr.**

Trident, Inc., *(978-1-887801; 978-1-58978)* Orders Addr.: 885 Pierce Butler Rte., Saint Paul, MN 55104 USA; *Imprints*: Atlas Games (Atlas Games)
E-mail: info@atlas-games.com
Web site: http://www.atlas-games.com
Dist(s): **PSI (Publisher Services, Inc.).**

Trident Press International *See* **Standard International Media**

TriEclipse, Inc., *(978-0-9704512)* P.O. Box 7763, Jacksonville, FL 32238 USA Tel 904-778-1841
E-mail: vtaylor4@bellsouth.net
Web site: http://www.trieclipse.com.

Trigger Memory Systems, *(978-0-9762024; 978-0-9863000)* P.O. Box 24, Waitsburg, WA 99361 USA
E-mail: timestalesmj@msn.com
Web site: http://www.triggermemorysystem.com.

Trillas Editorial, S. A. (MEX) *(978-968-24) Dist. by* **Continental Bk.**

Trillas Editorial, S. A. (MEX) *(978-968-24) Dist. by* **Lectorum Pubns.**

Trilogy Pubns. LLC, *(978-0-9772799; 978-0-615-80854-3)* Orders Addr.: 560 Sylvan Ave. Suite 1240, Englewood Cliffs, NJ 07632 USA (SAN 257-2044) Tel 201-816-1211; Fax: 201-816-8424
Web site: http://www.trilogypublications.com.

Trinity Bks., *(978-0-9743669)* P.O. Box 401, Cascade, ID 83611 USA.

Trinity Pr., *(978-0-9822113)* 303 Park Ave., New York, NY 10010 USA
E-mail: yroehker@bookoublishing.com
Dist(s): **AtlasBooks Distribution.**

†Trinity Univ. Pr., *(978-0-911536; 978-0-939980; 978-0-9651507; 978-1-893271; 978-1-59534)* One Trinity Pl., San Antonio, TX 78212 USA (SAN 205-4590) Tel 210-999-8881; Fax: 210-999-8182; *Imprints*: Maverick Books (MaverickBks) Do not confuse with Trinity University Press in Bannockburn, IL
E-mail: sarah.nawrocki@trinity.edu
Dist(s): **Bilingual Pr./Editorial Bilingue**
MyiLibrary
Perseus-PGW
Perseus Bks. Group; *CIP.*

Triple Crown Pubns., *(978-0-9702472; 978-0-9747895; 978-0-9762349; 978-0-9767894; 978-0-9778804; 978-0-9799517; 978-0-9820996; 978-0-9825888; 978-0-9832095)* P.O. Box 247378, Columbus, OH 43219 USA (SAN 914-3815) Tel 614-478-9402
E-mail: editor@triplecrownpublications.com
Web site: http://www.triplecrownpublications.com
Dist(s): **Ambassador Bks. & Media**
Brodart Co.
MyiLibrary.

Triple Exposure Publishing, Incorporated *See* **T. E. Publishing, Inc.**

Triple Seven Pr., *(978-0-9710486)* P.O. Box 70552, Las Vegas, NV 89170-0552 USA Do not confuse with Triple Seven International, Gaston, IN
E-mail: wendy@777press.com
Web site: http://www.777press.com.

Triple Tail Publishing *See* **Farcountry Pr.**

Triple Tulip Pr., *(978-0-9754825; 978-0-615-11380-7)* Orders Addr.: P.O. Box 250, Sanbornville, NH 03872 USA Tel 603-522-3398; Fax: 603-218-6502; 2717 Wakefield Rd., Sanbornville, NH 03872 Tel 603-522-3398; Fax: 603-218-6502
E-mail: tripletulip@roadrunner.com
Web site: http://www.tripletulippress.com.

TripleCrown Pubns. *See* **Triple Crown Pubns.**

Trisar, Inc., *(978-1-886386)* 804 W. Town & Country Rd., Orange, CA 92868-4712 USA.

TRISTAN Publishing, Inc., *(978-0-931674; 978-0-9726504; 978-1-939881)* 2355 Louisiana Ave N. Ste. 2, Minneapolis, MN 55427-3646 USA Toll Free: 866-545-1383; *Imprints*: Waldman House Press (WaldmanHse)
E-mail: bwaldman@tristanpublishing.com; swaldman@tristanpublishing.com
Web site: http://www.tristanpublishing.com.

Tritium Pr., *(978-0-9761726)* 8690 Aero Dr., No. 339, San Diego, CA 92123 USA
E-mail: tritium@n2.net.

Triumph Bks., *(978-0-9624436; 978-1-57243; 978-1-880141; 978-1-60078; 978-1-61749)* Orders Addr.: 542 S. Dearborn St., Suite 750, Chicago, IL 60605 USA (SAN 852-6826) Tel 312-939-3330; Fax: 312-663-3557; Toll Free: 800-335-5323; Edit Addr.: c/o Kaplan Logistics, 901 Bilter Rd., Aurora, IL 60502 USA
E-mail: Ordering@TriumphBooks.com; J_Martini@triumphbooks.com; s_kaufman@triumphbooks.com; orders@triumphbooks.com; w.swanson@triumphbooks.com
Web site: http://www.triumphbooks.com
Dist(s): **Detroit Free Pr., Inc.**
Independent Pubs. Group
MyiLibrary.

Triumph Publishing, *(978-1-890430)* 10415 219th St., Queens Village, NY 11429-2020 USA Do not confuse with companies with a similar name in Omal, WA, College park, GA.

Trivium Pubns., *(978-0-9713671)* Orders Addr.: Dept. of Humanities & Human Sciences Point Park Univ., 201 Wood St., Pittsburgh, PA 15222 USA (SAN 254-5152) Tel 716-982-8591
E-mail: bdeanrob@janushead.org
Web site: http://www.janushead.org.

Trivium Pursuit, *(978-0-9743616; 978-1-933228)* 429 Lake Park Blvd., PMB 168, Muscatine, IA 52761 USA Tel 309-537-3641
E-mail: bluedom@triviumpursuit.com
Web site: http://www.triviumpursuit.com
Dist(s): **Send The Light Distribution LLC.**

Troll Hetta Publishing Company *See* **SBA Bks., LLC**

Troll Hunters *Imprint of* **Stone Arch Bks.**

Trolley (GBR) *(978-0-9542079; 978-0-9542648; 978-1-904563; 978-1-907112) Dist. by* **Dist Art Pubs.**

Trolley Press *See* **Ignite Reality**

Trotman, Kay L., *(978-0-615-13350-8)* P.O. Box 1501, Lake Elsinore, CA 92531 USA Tel 951-898-6094; Fax: 951-898-6094
E-mail: njeri@mac.com
Web site: http://www.onsafariwithkay.com.

Trouble Street Productions, *(978-0-615-79451-8)* 10735 Bloomfield St. #6, North Hollywood, CA 91602 USA Tel 2139496676
Web site: troublestreet.com
Dist(s): **CreateSpace Independent Publishing Platform.**

Troublemaker Publishing, LP, *(978-1-933104)* P.O. Box 608, Spicewood, TX 78669 USA Tel 512-334-7777.

truckerkidzPr., *(978-0-9856770)* 121 Overhill Rd., Warwick, RI 02818 USA Tel 401-480-3403
E-mail: ckmellor@cox.net
Web site: http://www.grandpaandthetruck.com.

Trudgian, Sherri *See* **Little Sprout Publishing Hse.**

True Exposures Publishing, Inc., *(978-0-9642595; 978-0-9771762)* Orders Addr.: P.O. Box 5066, Brandon, MS 39047 USA Tel 601-829-1222; Fax: 601-829-1656; Toll Free: 800-323-3398; Edit Addr.: 106 Shenandoah Estates Cir., Brandon, MS 39047 USA
E-mail: trueexposures@bellsouth.net
Web site: http://www.trueexposures.com.

True Friends Bk. Club, LLC, *(978-0-9797165)* 3708 142nd Pl. NE, Bellevue, WA 98007 USA (SAN 854-1833) Tel 425-556-4319
E-mail: laurawreeves@yahoo.com
Web site: http://www.truefriendsbookclub.com.

True Gifts Publishing, *(978-0-9796701)* 14 Clark St., Belmont, MA 02478 USA (SAN 854-056X) Fax: 617-741-4013
Web site: http://truegifts.net.

True Horizon Publishing, *(978-0-9818396)* 12306 Fox Lake Pl., Fairfax, VA 22033 USA Toll Free: 866-601-4106 (phone/fax)
E-mail: montgomerylm@gmail.com
Web site: http://www.truehorizonpublishing.com.

True Light Publishing, *(978-0-9656670)* Orders Addr.: P.O. Box 1284, Boulder, CO 80308-0734 USA Tel 303-447-2547; Fax: 303-443-4373; Edit Addr.: 411 Wild Horse Cir., Boulder, CO 80304-0459 USA Do not confuse with True Light Publishing in Homewood, IL
E-mail: tlpub@ecentral.com; orders@truelightpub.com; amber@truelightmusic.com
Web site: http://www.truelightpub.com; http://www.truelightpublishing.com; http://www.truelightmusic.com
Dist(s): **New Leaf Distributing Co., Inc.**
Gangaji Foundation, The.

True Lightening *Imprint of* **Share & Care Society**

True North Studio, *(978-0-9845798)* 518 W. 8th St., Traverse City, MI 49684 USA.

True Path Pubs., *(978-0-9830978)* 9620 Smoot Ln., Argyle, TX 76226 USA Tel 817-879-8229
E-mail: ronda@ronda-ray.com.

True Vine Publishing Co., *(978-0-9760914; 978-0-9786088; 978-0-9822087; 978-0-9826694; 978-0-9894869; 978-0-9905326)* P.O. Box 22448, Nashville, TN 37202 USA Tel 615-585-0143
E-mail: timbond@truevinepublishing.org
Web site: http://www.truevinepublishing.org.

True You Inc,
Dist(s): **AtlasBooks Distribution.**

Truman Pr., Inc., *(978-0-9637846; 978-0-9798599)* 5 NW. Ave., Fayetteville, AR 72701 USA Tel 479-521-4999; Fax: 479-575-9393; *Imprints*: Hannover House (Hann Hse)
E-mail: hannoverhouse@aol.com
Web site: http://www.HannoverHouse.com
Dist(s): **Follett School Solutions**
National Bk. Network.

Truman State Univ. Pr., *(978-0-943549; 978-1-931112; 978-1-935503; 978-1-61248)* 100 E. Normal Ave., Kirksville, MO 63501-4221 USA (SAN 253-4231) Tel 660-785-7336; Fax: 660-785-4480; Toll Free: 800-916-6802
E-mail: tsup@truman.edu
Web site: http://tsup.truman.edu
Dist(s): **INscribe Digital**
ISD.

Trumpet In Zion Publishing, *(978-0-9716355)* Div. of Spring of Hope Church of God in Christ, P.O. Box 51163, Indian Orchard, MA 01151 USA Tel 413-733-1032; Fax: 413-241-6132; *Imprints*: Solid Rock Books (Solid Rock Bks).

Trumpeter *Imprint of* **Shambhala Pubns., Inc.**

Trumpold, Brenda Lee Cadett, *(978-0-615-77397-1)* 290 Preston Ave., Westfield, CT 06457 USA Tel 860-347-6369
Dist(s): **CreateSpace Independent Publishing Platform.**

Truth Bk. Pubs., *(978-0-9778261; 978-0-9794861; 978-0-9815203; 978-1-935298; 978-1-937089; 978-1-940725)* 824 Bills Rd., Franklin, IL 62638 USA (SAN 912-2834) Tel 217-675-2191; Toll Free: 877-649-9092
E-mail: faithprinting77@yahoo.com; truthbookpublishers@yahoo.com
Web site: http://www.faithprinting.net; http://www.itseasywithjesus-printing.com; http://www.truthbookpublishers.com
Dist(s): **BCH Fulfillment & Distribution**
BookBaby
eBooks2go.

Truth For Eternity Ministries, *(978-1-889520)* Div. of Reformed Baptist Church of Grand Rapids, 860 Peachcrest Ct NE, Grand Rapids, MI 49505-6435 USA
E-mail: office@girbc.org
Web site: www.girbc.org.

Truth Publishers *See* **Truth Bk. Pubs.**

Truthful Pr. Publishing, *(978-0-9799707)* P.O. Box 240, Statesville, NC 28687 USA Tel 704-287-8378; Fax: 704-878-8972
E-mail: author@daphinerobinson.com
Web site: http://www.daphinerobinson.com.

Tsaba Hse., *(978-0-9725486; 978-1-933853)* 2252 12th St., Reedly, CA 93654 USA (SAN 254-9441) Tel 559-643-8575; Fax: 559-638-2640
E-mail: ps@tsabahouse.com
Web site: http://www.tsabahouse.com
Dist(s): **Send The Light Distribution LLC.**

T.S.I. Strategies, LLC, *(978-0-9772609)* 140 SE 8th St., Cape Coral, FL 33990 USA Fax: 866-761-4233
E-mail: jim@jamesroach.com
Web site: http://www.producevideos.com.

TSM Publishing Group, LLC *See* **Autumn Publishing Group, LLC**

Tsui Wong-Avery, Sally, *(978-0-9798874; 978-0-9819358; 978-0-9855246)* 2618 W. Canyon Ave., San Diego, CA 92123 USA.

Tu Bks. *Imprint of* **Lee & Low Bks., Inc.**

Tualen (GBR) *(978-0-9556798) Dist. by* **LuluCom.**

Tubbs, Stephen P., *(978-0-9659446; 978-0-9819753)* 1344 Firwood Dr., Pittsburgh, PA 15243-1861 USA Tel 412-279-4866
E-mail: electrpow@aol.com
Web site: http://www.members.aol.com/electrpow/power.htm.

Tucker, Peggy *See* **Heritage Publishing**

Tucker, Peter E. *See* **PT Publishing**

Tucker, Terra, *(978-0-9794578)* P.O. Box 682371, Franklin, TN 37068 USA (SAN 853-5027).

Tucson Botanical Gardens, *(978-0-9792253)* 2150 N. Alvernon Way, Tucson, AZ 85712 USA Tel 520-326-9686; Fax: 520-324-0166
E-mail: execdirector@tucsonbotanical.org
Web site: http://www.tucsonbotanical.org.

Tucu Pr., *(978-0-9766572)* Orders Addr.: P.O. Box 447, Bozeman, MT 59771-0447 USA Tel 406-586-5084 (phone/fax); Edit Addr.: 3150 Graf St., No. 8, Bozeman, MT 59715 USA
E-mail: anndiberardinis@msn.com.

Tudor Assocs. Pr., *(978-0-9760939)* P.O. Box 1804, Payson, AZ 85547-1804 USA Tel 928-978-5799
E-mail: press@tudorassociates.com
Web site: http://www.tudorassociates.com.

Tudor Hse. (GBR) *(978-0-9530676) Dist. by* **Orca Bk Pub.**

Tudor Pubs., Inc., *(978-0-936389; 978-0-9778026)* Orders Addr.: P.O. Box 38366, Greensboro, NC 27438 USA; Edit Addr.: 3109 Shady Lawn Dr., Greensboro, NC 27408 USA (SAN 697-3035) Tel 336-288-5395
E-mail: tudorpublishers@triad.rr.com
Dist(s): **Brodart Co.**

Tuesday's Child, *(978-0-9772795)* Orders Addr.: P.O. Box 2512, Cookeville, TN 38502-2512 USA (SAN 257-2060)
E-mail: tuesdayschildpub@charter.net
Web site: http://tuesdayschildpub.com.

Tughra Bks., *(978-0-9720654; 978-1-932099; 978-1-59784; 978-1-68236)* 345 Clifton Ave., Clifton, NJ 07011 USA Tel 973-777-2704; Fax: 973-457-7334 Do not confuse with Light, Inc., in Lemont, IL
E-mail: info@tughrabooks.com; senturk@tughrabooks.com
Web site: http://www.tughrabooks.com/
Dist(s): **Independent Pubs. Group**
National Bk. Network.

Tulip Books (GBR) *(978-1-900149) Dist. by* **IPG Chicago.**

Tullycrine, LLC, *(978-0-9746554)* P.O. Box 178, Heisson, WA 98622-0178 USA
E-mail: tullycrineinc@aol.com; tullycrinellc@aol.com
Web site: http://www.tullycrine.com; http://www.book.traditionalcats.com.

Tumbleweed Publishing, *(978-0-9720132)* P.O. Box 194, Valley City, OH 44280 USA Do not confuse with Tumbleweed Publishing Company in Eugene, OH
E-mail: tumbleweedbooks@aol.com.

Tundra Bks. (CAN) *(978-0-88776; 978-0-89541; 978-0-912766; 978-1-77049) Dist. by* **Random.**

Tundra Bks. (CAN) *(978-0-88776; 978-0-89541; 978-0-912766; 978-1-77049) Dist. by* **Peng Rand Hse.**

Tuned In to Learning, *(978-0-9768881)* P.O. Box 221016, San Diego, CA 92192 USA (SAN 256-5803) Tel 858-453-0590; Fax: 858-777-3626
E-mail: mlazar@coastmusictherapy.com
Web site: http://www.tunedintolearning.com.

Turley, Sandy *See* **Helps4Teachers**

Turman, E., *(978-0-9753042)* 1321 Singingwood Ct., No. 1, Walnut Creek, CA 94595 USA Tel 925-944-5743
E-mail: shihtze1@msn.com.

Turn the Page Publishing, *(978-0-9832148; 978-1-938501)* Memorial Sta., Upper Montclair, NJ 07043 USA (SAN 860-0864) Tel 973-202-8979
E-mail: rlentin@turnthepagepublishing.com
Web site: www.turnthepagepublishing.com
Dist(s): **Lightning Source, Inc.**

Turnapaige & Reed Moore, *(978-0-9725231)* P.O. Box 412, Scottsdale, AZ 85252 USA
E-mail: reedmoore@turnapaige.com
Web site: http://www.turnapaige.com.

Turnaround Bk. Publishing Corp., *(978-0-9753028)* 5047 W. Main St., Suite 212, Kalamazoo, MI 49001 USA.

Turner, Barbara, *(978-0-9747019)* P.O. Box 893493, Temecula, CA 92589 USA Tel 951-699-3933
E-mail: adayinsanfrancisco@yahoo.com
Dist(s): **Lulu Enterprises Inc.**

Turner, Blaine, *(978-0-615-25688-7; 978-0-578-00165-4; 978-0-578-00497-6; 978-0-578-09035-1; 978-0-578-12843-6; 978-0-578-14952-3)* 26626 Lily Lake Inn Rd., Webster, WI 54893 USA
E-mail: blaine_turner@tsco.org
Dist(s): **Lulu Enterprises Inc.**

Turner Publishing Co., *(978-0-89793; 978-0-938021; 978-0-940069; 978-1-56311; 978-1-59652; 978-1-61858; 978-1-62045; 978-1-63026; 978-1-68162)* 200 4th Ave N. Ste. 950, Nashville, TN 37219-2145 USA; 424 Church St., Suite 2240, Nashville, TN 37219 Tel 615-255-2665; Fax: 615-255-5081; *Imprints*: Hunter House (HunterHse) Do not confuse with companies with the same or similar name in Atlanta, GA, Eastchester, NY, Houston, TX
E-mail: info@turnerpublishing.com; editorial@turnerpublishing.com
Web site: http://www.turnerpublishing.com
Dist(s): **Ingram Pub. Services**
MyiLibrary
Partners Bk. Distributing, Inc.
Perseus-PGW.

Turner, Rich Photographs, *(978-0-9762410)* 305 Fyffe Ave., Suite 158, Stockton, CA 95203 USA Tel 209-460-1050; Fax: 209-460-1051
E-mail: richt@turnerphoto.com
Web site: http://www.turnerphoto.com.

Turngroup Technologies, LLC, *(978-0-9794377)* 2811 Locust St., Saint Louis, MO 63103-1308 USA
Web site: http://www.hisforhopebooks.com
Dist(s): **Big River Distribution.**

Turning a New Page, *(978-0-9762030)* Orders Addr.: P.O. Box 91603, Tucson, AZ 85752-1603 USA Tel 520-579-7183; Fax: 520-407-6524
E-mail: rick4758@turninganewpage.com
Web site: http://www.turninganewpage.com.

Turning Point LLC, *(978-0-9745745)* 1339 Indiana Ave., Connersville, IN 47331 USA Tel 765-825-9835; 765-265-3207 (Mobile)
E-mail: lsfitzg@aol.com
Web site: http://www.stellarstar.biz.

Turning Point Pubns., LLC, *(978-0-9752742; 978-0-9840986)* Orders Addr.: 2822 Cashwell Dr., No. 233, Goldsboro, NC 27534 USA Tel 615-562-1540
Order books at www.turningpointstore.org Do not confuse with Turning Point Publications in Eureka, CA
E-mail: info@turningpointpublications.com
Web site: http://www.turningpointpublications.com.

Turnstyle, *(978-0-9668541)* Orders Addr.: P.O. Box 810, Portland, IN 47371 USA; Edit Addr.: 1601 W. 100 S., Portland, IN 47371 USA
E-mail: rogdomingo@gmail.com.

Turquoise Lake *See* **FireFly Lights**

Turquoise Morning Pr., *(978-1-935817; 978-1-937389; 978-1-62237)* PO Box 43958, Louisville, KY 40253 USA Tel 859-940-6816
E-mail: kim@turquoisemorning.com; kim.tmpress@gmail.com
Web site: http://www.maddiejames.com; http://www.bellamasters.com
Dist(s): **Smashwords.**

Turtle Bks. *Imprint of* **Jason & Nordic Pubs.**

Turtle Bks., *(978-1-890515)* 897 Boston Post Rd., Madison, CT 06443-3155 USA
E-mail: turtlebook@aol.com
Web site: http://www.turtlebooks.com
Dist(s): **Lectorum Pubns., Inc.**
Perseus-PGW.

Turtle Gallery Editions, *(978-0-9626935)* P.O. Box 219, Deer Isle, ME 04627-0219 USA Tel 207-348-9977 (phone/fax)
E-mail: person@turtlegallery.com
Web site: http://www.turtlegallery.com.

Turtle Point Pr., *(978-0-9627987; 978-1-885586; 978-1-885983; 978-1-933527)* 233 Broadway, Rm. 946, New York, NY 10279 USA Tel 212-285-1019 (phone/fax)
E-mail: countomega@aol.com
Web site: http://www.turtlepoint.com
Dist(s): **Consortium Bk. Sales & Distribution**
Lightning Source, Inc.
MyiLibrary
Perseus Bks. Group
SPD-Small Pr. Distribution
Sprout, Inc.

Turtle Pr., *(978-1-880336; 978-1-934903; 978-1-938585; 978-0-9895971)* Orders Addr.: 500 N Washington St No. 1545, Rockville, MD 20849 USA Toll Free: 800-778-8785 (orders only)
E-mail: orders@turtlepress.com; turtlepress@gmail.com
Web site: http://www.turtlepress.com.

Turtle Press Corporation *See* **Turtle Pr.**

Turtle Time Bks., *(978-0-9770957)* P.O. Box 809, San Luis Obispo, CA 93406 USA.

Turtleback *Imprint of* **Turtleback Bks.**

Turtleback Bks., *(978-0-613; 978-0-7857; 978-0-8085; 978-0-8335; 978-0-88103; 978-1-4176; 978-1-4177; 978-1-4178; 978-0-606)* Sub. of GL group, Inc., 1230 Macklind Ave., Saint Louis, MO 63110-1432 USA (SAN 159-947X) Tel 314-644-6100; Fax: 314-647-2845; Toll Free: 800-458-8438; *Imprints*: Turtleback (TurtleMO)
E-mail: info@sanval.com; rheflin@turtleback.com
Web site: http://www.Turtleback.com
Dist(s): **Booksource, The**
MyiLibrary.

Tuscarora Publishing Company, *(978-0-9860321)* 3199 Sherman Rd, Mansfield, OH 44903 USA Tel 419-529-5596
Dist(s): **AtlasBooks Distribution.**

Tush People, The, *(978-0-9722514)* P.O. Box 950100, Mission Hills, CA 91395 USA Tel 661-298-2293; 818-897-1734; Fax: 818-899-4455
E-mail: dfav218@aol.com.

Tuttle Publishing, *(978-0-8048; 978-1-4629)* Orders Addr.: 364 Innovation Dr., North Clarendon, VT 05759 USA (SAN 213-2621) Tel 802-773-8930; Fax: 802-773-6993; Toll Free Fax: 800-329-8885; Toll Free: 800-526-2778; *Imprints*: PeriplusEdition (PeriplEdns)
E-mail: info@tuttlepublishing.com
Web site: http://www.tuttlepublishing.com
Dist(s): **Cheng & Tsui Co.**
MyiLibrary
Perseus-PGW
Perseus Bks. Group
Simon & Schuster
Simon & Schuster, Inc.
ebrary, Inc.

Tuvott Publishing, *(978-0-9723974)* P.O. Box 18276, Erlanger, KY 41018 USA (SAN 255-3341) Tel 859-341-6004; Fax: 859-341-6033
E-mail: tuvott@fuse.net
Web site: http://www.trinityunveiled.com
Dist(s): **Book Clearing Hse.**
Spring Arbor Distributors, Inc.

Tuxedo Blue, LLC, *(978-0-9754056)* Orders Addr.: P.O. Box 2008, Lenox, MA 01240 USA Tel 413-637-2190; Edit Addr.: 455 W. 43rd St., No. 1A, New York, NY 10036 USA Tel 212-262-5113
E-mail: billiamsw@earthlink.net
Web site: http://www.spacenicks.com.

Tuxedo Pr., *(978-0-9774486; 978-1-936161)* 546 E. Springville Rd., Carlisle, PA 17015 USA
E-mail: info@Tuxedo-Press.com
Web site: http://Tuxedo-Press.com.

TV Acres Bks., *(978-0-9794133; 978-0-615-14014-8)* Div. of TV Acres.com, 1965 Broadway St., Saintckport, OH 43787 USA
Web site: http://www.tvacres.com
Dist(s): **CreateSpace Independent Publishing Platform**
Lulu Enterprises Inc.

Twain, Mark Media, Inc. Pubs., *(978-1-58037)* 100 E. Main St., Lewistown, MO 63452 USA Tel 573-497-2202; Fax: 573-497-2507
Dist(s): **Carson-Dellosa Publishing, LLC.**

Twain's Huckleberry Press *See* **Huckleberry Pr.**

Tweener Pr. *Imprint of* **Baker Trittin Pr.**

Twelve Star Pr., *(978-0-9797232)* 1105 2nd Ave. NE, Clarion, IA 50525 USA Tel 515-689-9157
E-mail: duncalf@goldfieldaccess.net.

Twelve Stones Publishing LLC, *(978-0-9712363; 978-0-692-30050-3)* Orders Addr.: P.O. Box 921, Eufaula, AL 36072 USA Tel 334-687-4491 Do not confuse with Twelve Stones Publishing in Grandville, MI
E-mail: brittbooks@msn.com
Web site: http://www.poemsfromthefast.com
Dist(s): **CreateSpace Independent Publishing Platform.**

Twentieth Century Christian Bks., *(978-0-89098)* 2809 Granny White Pike, Nashville, TN 37204 USA (SAN 206-2550) Tel 615-383-3842.

Twenty First Century Bks., *(978-0-9636012; 978-1-893817)* P.O. Box 2001, 507 SCR 528, Breckenridge, CO 80424-2001 USA (SAN 298-248X) Tel 970-453-9293; Fax: 970-453-6692; Toll Free: 877-453-9293 Do not confuse with Twenty First Century Bks., Inc. in New York, NY
E-mail: order_desk03@tfcbooks.com; g.peterson@tfcbooks.com
Web site: http://www.tfcbooks.com; http://www.teslabooks.com
Dist(s): **MyiLibrary.**

Twenty-First Century Bks. *Imprint of* **Lerner Publishing Group**

Twenty-First Century Co., The, *(978-0-933451; 978-1-888264)* 2201 Rockbrook Dr., No. 1916, Lewisville, TX 75067-3830 USA Tel 972-459-6327 (phone/fax)
E-mail: t21cenco@flash.net
Web site: http://www.cleareducation.com.

Twenty-fourth Street Bks, LLC, *(978-0-9726939)* 215 E. 24th St., New York, NY 10010 USA
E-mail: cz@yiddishcat.com
Web site: http://www.yiddishcat.com.

Twenty-Third Pubns./Bayard, *(978-0-89622; 978-1-58595; 978-1-62785)* 1 Montauk Ave. No. 20, New London, CT 06320-4967 USA (SAN 658-2052) Toll Free Fax: 800-572-0788; Toll Free: 800-321-0411
E-mail: kerry.moriarty@bayard-inc.com
Web site: http://www.23rdpublications.com
Dist(s): **Forward Movement Pubns.**

twhiteart, *(978-0-9639670)* 5290 Meadville St., Excelsior, MN 55331-8792 USA Tel 952-474-2083
E-mail: madonna@twhiteart.com
Web site: http://www.twhiteart.com.

Twice PI Pr., *(978-0-615-76345-3; 978-0-615-76383-5; 978-0-615-76385-9; 978-0-9890004; 978-0-9860571; 978-0-692-28089-8; 978-1-942360)* 1161 York Ave. Apt. 12C, New York, NY 10065 USA Tel 646-639-3618
E-mail: erecstebbins@gmail.com
Dist(s): **CreateSpace Independent Publishing Platform.**

Twiglet The Little Christmas Tree *Imprint of* **PJs Corner**

Twilight Tales, Inc., *(978-0-9711309; 978-0-9779856)* Orders Addr.: 331 Berkshire Terrace, Roselle, IL 60172 USA Tel 630-351-9311 Sales; Edit Addr.: 2339 N. Commonwealth, No. 4C, Chicago, IL 60614 USA (SAN 851-772X) Tel 773-472-8722
E-mail: sales@twilighttales.com
Web site: http://www.twilighttales.com.

Twilight Times Bks., *(978-1-931201; 978-1-933353; 978-1-60619)* Orders Addr.: P.O. Box 3340, Kingsport, TN 376643340 USA; *Imprints*: Paladin Timeless (PalaTimeless)
E-mail: publisher@twilighttimes.com
Web site: http://www.twilighttimesbooks.com
Dist(s): **Book Clearing Hse.**

Twin Lights Pubs., Inc., *(978-1-885435; 978-1-934907)* 8 Hale St., Rockport, MA 01966 USA (SAN 257-8867) Tel 978-546-7398; Fax: 978-546-5803; 6 Tide St., Boston, MA 02210
E-mail: info@twinlightspub.com; orders@twinlightspub.com
Web site: http://www.twinlightspub.com
Dist(s): **Strisik, Nancy**
Windhover Performing Arts Ctr.

Twin Monkeys Pr., *(978-0-9768602)* 146 First St., Dunellen, NJ 08812 USA Tel 732-752-3285
E-mail: storytellerjt@optonline.net
Web site: http://www.twinmonkeyspress.com.

Twin Peacocks Publishing, *(978-0-9839047)* 29911 Niguel Rd., 6654, Laguna Niguel, CA 92607 USA Tel 949-412-7182; Fax: 949-272-3217
E-mail: contact@andsoyouwereborn.com
Web site: http://www.AndSoYouWereBorn.com
Dist(s): **Independent Pubs. Group.**

Twin Peaks Publishing, Inc., *(978-0-9722259)* 4708 Mountain Vista Ct., Loveland, CO 80537 USA
E-mail: Twinpeakspublish@aol.com
Web site: http://www.bookmasters.com/marktplc/rr00979.htm; http://www.atlasbooks.com/authorspotlight/asdmiller.htm; http://hometown.aol.com/TwinPeaksPublish/TwinPeaks.htm.

Twin Sisters IP, LLC, *(978-0-9632249; 978-1-57583; 978-1-882331; 978-1-59922; 978-1-61938; 978-1-62002; 978-1-62581)* Orders Addr.: 1653 Merriman Rd. Suite L-1, Akron, OH 44313 USA (SAN 859-8460) Toll Free: 800-248-8946; 800-480-8946
E-mail: doug.kline@twinsisters.com; melissa.chase@twinsisters.com.

Twin Sisters Productions, LLC *See* **Twin Sisters IP, LLC**

Twin Sisters Publishing Co., *(978-0-615-23714-5; 978-0-615-24258-3; 978-0-578-00651-2)* 1805 Breckenridge Dr., Del City, OK 73115 USA Tel 405-882-9606
E-mail: twinsisterspublishing@yahoo.com
Web site: http://www.oklahomawriter/tripod.com
Dist(s): **Lulu Enterprises Inc.**

TwinAtaa Studio, *(978-1-889926)* P.O. Box 1162, Stone Mountain, GA 30086 USA Tel 770-469-5138; Fax: 770-469-5139
E-mail: twinataa@twinataa.com; srw@twinataa.com
Web site: http://www.twinataa.com.

TwinAtaa/Sanaa Village Publications *See* **TwinAtaa Studio**

Twinbrook Publishing, *(978-0-9759086)* P.O. Box 355, Bedminster, NJ 07921 USA Tel 908-534-6799
Web site: http://www.pleasantdreaming.com/.

Twinkle Bks., *(978-0-9792992)* 1415 Riverbank St., Lincoln Park, MI 48146-3880 USA (SAN 853-0483) Tel 313-381-2082
E-mail: Treasurecloud@msn.com
Web site: http://Twinkleblink.com.

Twinkle Twinkle Little Bks., *(978-0-9771447)* 131 E. Wilson St., Centre Hall, PA 16828-8703 USA Tel 814-364-2237
E-mail: nicole@twinkletwinklelittlebooks.com
Web site: http://www.twinkletwinklelittlebooks.com.

Twins Bks. *Imprint of* **Sterling Investments I, LLC DBA Twins Magazine**

TwinsBooks, *(978-0-615-35370-8; 978-0-615-60112-0)* 14590 Ludlow St., Oak Park, MI 48237 USA Tel 248-968-2135
E-mail: deanna41969@hotmail.com.

Twisted Spice, *(978-0-9893075)* 2873 SW 85th Ave., Miramar, FL 33025 USA Tel 954-391-7520
E-mail: Crimpy79@hotmail.com.

Twisted Tree Pr, *(978-0-9778865)* 1232 Grant Rd, Harlem, GA 30814 USA Tel 706-306-9503
E-mail: twisted_tree_press@hotmail.com.

Two Bear Publishing *See* **Cracker the Crab LLC**

Two Chicks, *(978-0-9899544)* 2063 White Horse Rd, Berwyn, PA 19312 USA Tel 610-408-8688
E-mail: ayfriday@gmail.com.

Two Dogz, *(978-0-9767072)* Orders Addr.: 775 Lefort By Pass Rd., Thibodaux, LA 70301 USA
E-mail: zsagabby@yahoo.com
Web site: http://www.two-dogz.com.

Two Dolphins Publishing Group, *(978-0-615-47819-7; 978-0-9836920)* 28494 Westinghouse Pl. No. 201, Valencia, CA 91355 USA Tel 818-266-8210
E-mail: info@twodolphinspublishing.com
Web site: www.twodolphinspublishing.com; www.wendylewisbooks.com.

Two Harbors Press *Imprint of* **Hillcrest Publishing Group, Inc.**

Two Lakes Pr., Inc., *(978-1-59885)* P.O. Box 384, Saint Joseph, MN 56374-0384 USA Tel 616-822-1865
E-mail: s@twolakespress.com
Web site: http://www.twolakespress.com.

Two Lands, *(978-1-933984)* 1631 Lakefield North Ct., Wellington, FL 33414-1066 USA
E-mail: twolandsoffice@yahoo.com.

Two Lines Pr.,
Dist(s): **Perseus-PGW**
Perseus Bks. Group.

Two Lions *Imprint of* **Amazon Publishing**

Two Little Birds Bks., *(978-0-9912935)* 58 Cutts Rd., Kittery, ME 03904 USA Tel 603-828-7343
E-mail: birdie@twolittlebirdsbooks.com
Web site: www.twolittlebirdsbooks.com
Dist(s): **Ingram Pub. Services.**

Two Little Hands Productions LLC, *(978-1-933543; 978-1-936859)* Orders Addr.: 870 E. 7145 S., Midvale, UT 84047 USA
E-mail: rose@signingtime.com
Web site: http://www.signingtime.com.

Two Lives Publishing, *(978-0-9674468)* Orders Addr.: 2500 Painter Ct., Annapolis, MD 21401 USA; Edit Addr.: 2500 Painter Ct., Annapolis, MD 21401 USA
E-mail: bcombs@TwoLives.com
Web site: http://www.TwoLives.com
Dist(s): **Book Wholesalers, Inc.**
Brodart Co.

Two Saints Publishing, *(978-0-9625782)* 615 Mennonite Church Rd., Kalispell, MT 59901-7753 USA Tel 406-756-1959.

Two Seed Planters Inc., *(978-0-9755789)* 141 Tall Pines Dr., Leesburg, GA 31763-3143 USA
E-mail: twoseedplanters@aol.com
Web site: http://www.twoseedplanters.com.

Two Small Fish Pubns., *(978-0-9826582)* 109 W. Market St., Freeburg, PA 17827 USA Tel 570-374-1363
E-mail: brendakhendricks@verizon.net
Web site: http://www.twosmallfish.org.

Two Sons Pr., Inc., *(978-0-9748995)* 14 Red Tail Dr., Highlands Ranch, CO 80126-5001 USA Tel 303-346-3003; Fax: 303-791-2226
E-mail: McAdamfam@aol.com
Dist(s): **Westcliffe Pubs.**

Two Tired Teachers Connection, Inc., The, *(978-0-9786835)* 151 Michael Ln., Aberdeen, NC 28315 USA (SAN 851-3090) Tel 910-944-8857
E-mail: bevlashley@nc.rr.com
Web site: http://www.twotiredteachers.com.

Two Way Bilingual, Inc., *(978-0-941911)* Cond The Falls, No. 405, Guaynabo, PR 00657 USA (SAN 666-0169).

Two-Can Publishing *Imprint of* **T&N Children's Publishing**

TwoDot *Imprint of* **Globe Pequot Pr., The**

TwoMorrows Publishing, *(978-1-893905; 978-1-60549)* Div. of TwoMorrows Advertising & Design, 10407 Bedfordtown Dr., Raleigh, NC 27614-8058 USA Tel 919-449-0344; Fax: 919-449-0327
E-mail: twomorrow@aol.com
Web site: http://www.twomorrows.com
Dist(s): **Diamond Comic Distributors, Inc.**
Diamond Bk. Distributors.

TwoPenny Pubns., *(978-0-9755671)* 205 Rainbow Dr., No. 10503, Livingston, TX 77399-2005 USA
E-mail: samnalice@twopennytravels.com
Web site: http://www.79scenario.com.

Two's Company, *(978-0-9742862)* Div. of Threaded Images, 303 Wrenn Ave., New Paris, OH 45347 USA Tel 937-437-0095; 513-933-9207; Toll Free Fax: 877-217-0700; Toll Free: 800-487-0095
E-mail: sgray6@cinci.rr.com; timages@aol.com
Web site: http://www.twos-company.biz.

Two-Ten Bk. Pr., *(978-0-578-05661-6; 978-0-9827799; 978-0-9884642; 978-0-9896216; 978-1-941208)* 5 Gibson Kees Way, Sissonville, WV 25320 USA; P.O. Box 4215, Charleston, WV 25364 Tel 304-419-4169
Web site: http://www.thedarkslayer.com; http://www.thedarkslayer.net
Dist(s): **Smashwords.**

TyBook, *(978-0-9779631)* 5504 Nieman Rd., Shawnee, KS 66203 USA Tel 503-407-1217
E-mail: clayme@claytonpixton.com
Web site: http://www.tybookinc.com.

TYL Publishing, *(978-0-9753902)* 1902 Spillers Ln., Houston, TX 77043 USA Tel 713-647-9501; Fax: 713-647-9410
E-mail: tylnwt@gmail.com
Dist(s): **Partners/West Book Distributors**
Quality Bks., Inc.

Tyler, J. Publishing *See* **Crush Publishing**

Tyndale Entertainment *Imprint of* **Tyndale Hse. Pubs.**

Tyndale Espanol *Imprint of* **Tyndale Hse. Pubs.**

†Tyndale Hse. Pubs., *(978-0-8423; 978-1-4143; 978-1-4964)* Orders Addr.: 370 Executive Dr., Carol Stream, IL 60188 USA; Edit Addr.: 351 Executive Dr., Carol Stream, IL 60188 USA (SAN 206-7749) Tel 630-668-8310; Fax: 630-668-3245; Toll Free: 800-323-9400; *Imprints*: Tyndale Kids (Tyndale Kids); Tyndale Entertainment (Tyndale Ent); Thirsty(?) (Thirsty); SaltRiver (SaltRiver); Tyndale Espanol (Tyndale Espanol); Happy Day (HappyDay)
E-mail: international@tyndale.com; permission@tyndale.com
Web site: http://www.tyndale.com
Dist(s): **Anchor Distributors**
Brodart Co.
Christian Bk. Distributors
Cokesbury
CreateSpace Independent Publishing Platform
Editorial Unilit
Follett School Solutions
Ingram Entertainment, Inc.
Spring Arbor Distributors, Inc.; *CIP.*

Tyndale Kids *Imprint of* **Tyndale Hse. Pubs.**

Type F, *(978-0-9768733)* P.O. Box 1045, Lodi, CA 95241-1045 USA
E-mail: info@enduranceguide.com
Web site: http://www.enduranceguide.com.

Tyr Publishing, *(978-0-9723473)* P.O. Box 19895, Fountain Hills, AZ 85269-9895 USA (SAN 254-7775) Tel 480-836-4261
E-mail: info@tyrpublishing.com
Web site: http://www.tyrpublishing.com
Dist(s): **Midpoint Trade Bks., Inc.**

Tyson, Sandi *See* **Christiangela Productions**

Tytam Publishing, *(978-0-9758602)* 111 Lincoln Ave., Suite A-9, Newark, NJ 07104-4607 USA
E-mail: Tygoode1@aol.com
Web site: http://www.tygoode.com.

Tzipora Pubns., Inc., *(978-0-9722595)* Orders Addr.: P.O. Box 115, New York, NY 10185 USA Tel 347-562-8727; Toll Free Fax: 775-414-2940
E-mail: tziporapub@msn.com
Web site: http://www.tziporapub.us.

U A H C Press *See* **URJ Pr.**

U H H Hale Kuamo'o Hawaiian Language Center *See* **Hale Kuamo'o Hawaiian Language Ctr. at UHH**

U. S. Capitol Historical Society, *(978-0-916200)* 200 Maryland Ave., NE, Washington, DC 20002 USA (SAN 226-6601) Tel 202-543-8919; Fax: 202-544-8244; Toll Free: 800-887-9318
E-mail: uschs@uschs.org
Web site: http://www.uschs.org
Dist(s): **Univ. Pr. of Virginia.**

U. S. ISBN Agency, *(978-0-317; 978-0-318; 978-0-614; 978-0-615; 978-0-685; 978-0-686; 978-0-615-17190-6; 978-0-578; 978-0-692)* R. R. Bowker, 630 Central Ave., New Providence, NJ 07974 USA Fax: 908-219-0188; Toll Free: 877-310-7333
E-mail: ISBN-SAN@Bowker.com
Web site: http://www.isbn.org.

Ubaviel's Gifts, *(978-0-9713589)* 1550 Scenic View Dr., Loudon, TN 37774 USA
Web site: http://www.angelicgift.com.

UBUS Communications Systems, *(978-1-56411)* Div. of Khalifah's Booksellers & Associates, Orders Addr.: 26070 Barhams Hill Rd., Drewryville, VA Southhampton 23844 USA (SAN 630-6748) Tel 434-378-2140;

704-390-0663; *Imprints:* CB Publishing & Design (CB Pubng & Design)
E-mail: khalifah@khabooks.com
Web site: http://www.khabooks.com; http://www.khabooks.com; http://www.blackbooksaward.com; http://www.black-e-books.com; http://www.black-e-books.com
Dist(s): **Khalifah's Booksellers & Assocs.**

Uccello Rosso, *(978-0-9819187)* 328 Windsor St., Reading, PA 19601-2124 USA (SAN 856-955X)
E-mail: mail@uccellorosso.com
Web site: http://uccellorosso.com.

UFO Photo Archives, *(978-0-934269; 978-0-9608558)* Orders Addr.: 27341 Stanford St., Hemet, CA 92544 USA (SAN 240-7949) Tel 520-907-0102; Fax: 951-652-8605
Web site: http://www.UFOPhotoArchives.com.

Ufodike, Ekwutosi, *(978-0-9800538)* 3987 Nemours Trail, Kennesaw, GA 30152 USA Tel 404-574-0193
E-mail: tosi.ufodike@ge.com.

Uitti, Daniel, *(978-0-9708430; 978-0-9819478)* Div. of DaSum Company LLC, 223 Buckingham St., Oakville, CT 06779 USA Tel 860-274-9065; Fax: 860-417-0609
E-mail: dan@uitti.net
Web site: http://www.uitti.net/DaSum/.

UK Abrams Bks. for Young Readers,
Dist(s): **Abrams.**

Ullstein-Taschenbuch-Verlag (DEU) *(978-3-548) Dist. by* **Distribks Inc.**

Ultimacy Pr., *(978-0-9760205)* 11409 Parkside Pl., Bradenton, FL 34202 USA Tel 941-753-6560; Fax: 941-753-6561
E-mail: info@ultimatefinancialadvisor.com
Web site: http://www.ultimatefinancialadvisor.com.

Ultimate Bks., *(978-0-9725953; 978-0-9788430)* 104 Oakhill Key Ct., Valrico, FL 33594 USA Do not confuse with Ultimate Bks., in Glendale, CA
E-mail: info@opynyon.com
Web site: http://www.opynyon.com.

Ultimate Martial Arts CD, The *See* **Black Belt Training**

Ulverscroft Large Print Bks. (GBR) *(978-0-7089; 978-0-85456; 978-1-84395; 978-1-84617) Dist. by* **Ulverscroft US.**

Ulverscroft Large Print Bks., Ltd., *(978-0-7089; 978-1-84617)* Orders Addr.: P.O. Box 1230, West Seneca, NY 14224-1230 USA; Edit Addr.: 950 Union Rd., West Seneca, NY 14224-3438 USA (SAN 208-3035) Toll Free: 800-955-9659
E-mail: enquiries@ulverscroft.co.uk; sales@ulverscroft.com
Web site: http://www.ulverscroft.co.uk.

Ulysses Pr., *(978-0-915233; 978-1-56975; 978-1-61243)* Orders Addr.: P.O. Box 3440, Berkeley, CA 94703-3440 USA (SAN 289-8764) Tel 510-601-8301; Fax: 510-601-8307; Toll Free: 800-377-2542; Edit Addr.: 3286 Adeline St., Suite 1, Berkeley, CA 94703 USA (SAN 289-8772)
E-mail: ulysses@ulyssespress.com
Web site: http://www.ulyssespress.com
Dist(s): **MyiLibrary**
Perseus-PGW
Perseus Bks. Group
ebrary, Inc.

Ulyssian Pubns. *Imprint of* **Pine Orchard, Inc.**

Umbrelly Bks., *(978-0-9791127; 978-0-615-14064-3; 978-0-615-14065-0; 978-0-615-15448-0; 978-0-615-20654-7; 978-0-692-53594-3)* P.O. Box 2703, Saratoga, CA 95070-5608 USA
E-mail: umbrelly_books@yahoo.com
Web site: http://www.umbrellybooks.com
Dist(s): **Lulu Enterprises Inc.**

UMI *Imprint of* **UMI (Urban Ministries, Inc.)**

UMI (Urban Ministries, Inc.), *(978-0-940955; 978-1-932715; 978-1-934056; 978-1-60352; 978-1-60997; 978-1-63038)* 1551 Regency Ct., Calumet City, IL 60409-5448 USA (SAN 665-2247) Fax: 708-868-7105; Toll Free: 800-860-8642; *Imprints:* UMI (UMI)
Web site: http://www.urbanministries.com
Dist(s): **Midpoint Trade Bks., Inc.**

Umina, Lisa M. *See* **Halo Publishing International**

Unaluna Ediciones (ARG) *(978-987-1296) Dist. by* **Lectorum Pubns.**

Unbridled Bks., *(978-1-932961; 978-1-936071; 978-1-60953)* 2000 Wadsworth Blvd., No. 195, Lakewood, CO 80214 USA Toll Free: 888-732-3822 (phone/fax)
E-mail: alexa@unbridledbooks.com; swallace@unbridledbooks.com
Web site: http://www.unbridledbooks.com
Dist(s): **Intrepid Group, Inc., The**
MyiLibrary
Perseus-PGW
Perseus Bks. Group.

Unchained Spirit Enterprises, *(978-0-9717790; 978-0-615-94962-8)*
Dist(s): **CreateSpace Independent Publishing Platform.**

Uncle Henry Bks., *(978-1-932568)* P.O. Box 41310, Long Beach, CA 90853-1310 USA Tel 562-987-9165; Fax: 562-439-5924
E-mail: unclehenrybooks@aol.com.

Uncle Jim's Publishing, *(978-0-9800764)* Orders Addr.: c/o Potomac Adventist Bookstore, 12004 Cherry Hill Rd., Silver Spring, MD 20904 USA Tel 301-572-0700; Toll Free: 800-325-8492; P.O. Box 410, Chino Valley, AZ 86323 Tel 928-636-9419 (wholesale orders only); Fax: 928-636-1216 (wholesale orders only)
E-mail: soonchin@freezees.com
Web site: http://www.freezees.com; http://www.potomacabc.com.

Under the Green Umbrella, *(978-1-929701)* 5808 Westmont Dr., Austin, TX 78731-3836 USA Tel 512-454-2414
E-mail: janesbauld@aol.com
Web site: http://www.uts.cc.utexas.edu/~jbauld.

Underland Pr., *(978-0-9802260; 978-0-9826639; 978-1-937163)* 833 SE Main St., Box 122, Portland, OR 97214 USA
E-mail: victoria@underlandpress.com
Web site: http://www.underlandpress.com
Dist(s): **MyiLibrary**
Perseus-PGW
Perseus Bks. Group.

Understanding For Life Ministries, Inc., *(978-0-9714584; 978-0-9721504; 978-0-9749019; 978-0-9797019; 978-0-9822938; 978-0-9833673; 978-0-9850813; 978-0-9904982)* 3665 Kirby Pkwy., Suite 6, Memphis, TN 38115 USA Tel 901-844-3962; Fax: 901-844-3944
E-mail: info@understandingforlife.org
Web site: http://www.understandingforlife.org
Dist(s): **BookBaby.**

Understanding Nutrition, PC, *(978-0-9764002; 978-0-9800334)* Orders Addr.: 505 N. College St., McKinney, TX 75069 USA Tel 214-503-7100
E-mail: info@understandingnutrition.com; jessica@understandingnutrition.com
Web site: http://www.understandingnutrition.com.

Underwood Books, *(978-0-88733; 978-0-934438; 978-1-887424; 978-1-59929)* Orders Addr.: P.O. Box 1919, Nevada City, CA 95945 USA Tel 530-470-9095; Fax: 530-470-9049; Edit Addr.: 12514 Cavanaugh Ln., Nevada City, CA 95959 USA
E-mail: tim@underwoodbooks.com; contact@underwoodbooks.com
Web site: http://www.underwoodbooks.com
Dist(s): **Perseus-PGW.**

Unfurl, *(978-0-615-64051-8; 978-0-9909669)* 1393 Knight Rd., Ann Arbor, MI 48103 USA Tel 734-663-9129
Dist(s): **CreateSpace Independent Publishing Platform.**

Unicorn Pr., *(978-0-937004)* 3300 Chestnut St., Reading, PA 19605 USA Tel 610-929-8306 Do not confuse with Unicorn Pr. in Northville, MI
E-mail: kthynoll@aol.com
Web site: http://hometown.aol.com/kthynoll.

Uniformology, *(978-0-9815078; 978-1-935344)* 105 Coates Trail, Weatherford, TX 76087 USA Tel 817-629-9205
E-mail: uniformology@mac.com
Web site: http://www.uniformology.com.

Union Creek Communications, Inc., *(978-0-9721404)* P.O. Box 1811, Bryson City, NC 28713 USA Tel 828-488-3596; Fax: 828-488-1018
E-mail: info@researchpaperstation.com
Web site: http://researchpaperstation.com.

Unique Executive Pubs., *(978-0-9744978)* Div. of Unique Executive.com, 1653 Georgia Hwy. 257, Suite A, Cordele, GA 31015 USA Tel 229-273-8121; Fax: 229-273-7289; *Imprints:* Healthful Living Books (Living Books)
E-mail: harvardg@sowega.net
Web site: http://upublish.uniqueexecutive.com.

Uniquely You Resources, *(978-0-9627245; 978-1-888846)* P.O. Box 490, Blue Ridge, GA 30513 USA Tel 706 492 4709; 706-492-5490
E-mail: drmels@myuy.com
Web site: http://www.myuy.com; http://www.uyprofiler.com
Dist(s): **Send The Light Distribution LLC.**

Unisystems, Inc., *(978-0-7666; 978-0-87449; 978-1-56144)* 155 55th St., New York, NY 10022 USA Tel 212-826-0850; Fax: 212-758-4166
Web site: http://www.modernpublishing.com.

†Unitarian Universalist Assn., *(978-0-933840; 978-1-55896)* 25 Beacon St., Boston, MA 02108-2800 USA (SAN 225-4840) Tel 617-742-2100; Fax: 617-742-7025; Toll Free: 800-215-9076; *Imprints:* Skinner House Books (Skinner Hse)
Web site: http://www.uua.org
Dist(s): **Red Wheel/Weiser;** *CIP.*

United Bible Societies Association Inc., *(978-1-57697; 978-1-930564; 978-1-931471; 978-1-931952; 978-1-932507; 978-1-933218; 978-1-59877)* 1989 NW 88th Ct., Miami, FL 33172 USA Tel 305-702-1824; Fax: 305-702-0424 Do not confuse with United Bible Societies, New York, NY
E-mail: Pteixeira@sbb.org.br; Bdehoyos@biblesocieties.org
Web site: http://www.labibliaweb.com
Dist(s): **American Bible Society.**

United Bible Societies/Americas Service Center *See* **United Bible Societies Association Inc.**

United Christian Fellowship of Chapel Hill, North Carolina *See* **Armour of Light Publishing**

United Comics, *(978-0-9743086)* Div. of Obsidian Entertainment, P.O. Box 401, Milford, CT 06460-0401 USA Toll Free: 800-546-3249 (phone/fax)
E-mail: unitedcomicworks@gmail.com
Web site: http://www.unitedcomicworks.com.

United Educators, Inc., *(978-0-87566)* 900 W. North Shore Dr. Ste. 279, Lake Bluff, IL 60044-2210 USA (SAN 204-8795).

United InnoWorks Academy, *(978-0-9771380; 978-1-936478)* 9721 Conestoga Way, Potomac, MD 20854-4711 USA
E-mail: executive@innoworks.org; staff@innoworks.org
Web site: http://www.innoworks.org.

United Nation of Islam, The, *(978-0-9768502)* 1608 N. 13th St., Kansas City, KS 66102 USA Tel 913-342-0758; Fax: 913-342-0340; Toll Free: 800-331-7668
E-mail: unoi@unoi.org
Web site: http://www.unoi.org.

United Network for Organ Sharing, *(978-1-886651)* Orders Addr.: P.O. Box 2484, Richmond, VA 23218 USA Tel 804-782-4800; Edit Addr.: 700 N. 4th St., Richmond, VA 23219 USA
Web site: http://www.unos.org.

United Optical Publishing Co., *(978-0-9764337)* 9147 Millbranch Rd., Southaven, MS 38671 USA
Web site: http://www.steelguitarbyhughjeffreys.com.

United Research Publishers, *(978-0-9614924; 978-1-887053)* Div. of Solor Products, Inc., 2233 Faraday Ave., Suite G, Carlsbad, CA 92008-7214 USA (SAN 693-5834) Tel 760-930-8937; Fax: 760-930-4291 Do not confuse with United Research, Black Mountain, NC
Web site: http://www.unitedresearchpubs.com.

†United States Government Printing Office, *(978-0-16; 978-0-18)* Orders Addr.: P.O. Box 371954, Pittsburgh, PA 15250-7954 USA (SAN 658-0785) Tel 202-512-1800; Fax: 202-512-2250; Toll Free: 866-512-1800; Edit Addr.: USGPO Stop SSMB, Washington, DC 20401 USA (SAN 206-152X) Tel 202-512-1705 (bibliographic information only); 202-512-2268 (book dealers only); Fax: 202-512-1655; *Imprints:* Defense Department (Defense Dept); Environmental Protection Agency (Envir Protect); Interior Department (Interior Dept); Department of the Army (Dept Army); Forest Service (Forest Service); Joint Committee on Printing (Joint ComPrint); National Marine Fisheries Service (NMFS); Smithsonian Institution (SmithsonInst)
E-mail: orders@gpo.gov; rdavis@gpo.gov; ContactCenter@gpo.gov
Web site: http://bookstore.gpo.gov; http://www.gpoaccess.gov/index.html
Dist(s): **Bernan Assocs.**
MyiLibrary
Trucatriche
ebrary, Inc.; *CIP.*

United States Judo Federation, Inc., *(978-0-9729790)* P.O. Box 338, Ontario, OR 97914-0338 USA Tel 541-889-8753; Fax: 541-889-5836
E-mail: natofc@usjf.com
Web site: http://www.usjf.com.

United States Power Squadrons, *(978-1-891148; 978-1-938405)* Orders Addr.: P.O. Box 30423, Raleigh, NC 27622 USA Tel 919-821-0281; Fax: 919-836-0813; Toll Free: 888-367-8777; Edit Addr.: 1504 Blue Ridge Rd., Raleigh, NC 27607 USA
Web site: http://www.usps.org.

United States Trotting Association, *(978-0-9793891)* 750 Michigan Ave., Columbus, OH 43215 USA Tel 614-224-2291 Toll Free: 877-800-8782 (ext. 3260)
E-mail: jamie.rucker@ustrotting.com; HRCNews@ustrotting.com
Web site: http://www.ustrotting.com.

United Synagogue of America Bk. Service, *(978-0-8381)* Subs. of United Synagogue of America, 820 2nd Ave., New York, NY 10017-4504 USA (SAN 203-0551)
E-mail: booksvc@uscj.org
Web site: http://www.uscj.org/booksvc.

United Writers Pr., *(978-0-9725197; 978-0-9760824; 978-1-934216)* Orders Addr.: 17 Willow Tree Run, Asheville, NC 28803 USA
E-mail: vsharpe@unitedwriterspress.com
Web site: http://www.unitedwriterspress.com.

Unitrust Design, *(978-0-9752775)* P.O. Box 653, Loma Linda, CA 92354 USA
E-mail: unitrustdesign@aol.com
Web site: http://www.unitrustdesign.com.

Unity Books & Multimedia Publishing (Unity School of Christianity) *See* **Unity Schl. of Christianity**

Unity Hse. *Imprint of* **Unity Schl. of Christianity**

Unity Schl. of Christianity, *(978-0-87159)* Orders Addr.: 1901 NW Blue Pkwy., Unity Village, MO 64065-0001 USA (SAN 204-8817) Tel 816-524-3550; 816 251-3571 (ordering); Fax: 816-251-3551; *Imprints:* Unity House (Unity Hse)
E-mail: unity@unityworldhq.org
Web site: http://www.unity.org
Dist(s): **BookBaby**
DeVorss & Co.
New Leaf Distributing Co., Inc.

Univ. of Queensland Pr. (AUS) *(978-0-7022; 978-1-875491) Dist. by* **IPG Chicago.**

Universal Flag Publishing, *(978-1-933426)* Div. of Universal Flag Cos., 1440 W. Maple Ave., Suite 6B, Lisle, IL 60532 USA Tel 630-245-8500
E-mail: publishing@universalflag.com
Web site: www.universalflag.com.

Universal Handwriting *See* **Universal Publishing**

Universal Life Matters, Incorporated *See* **Quality of Life Publishing Co.**

Universal Marketing Media, Inc., *(978-0-9764272)* Orders Addr.: P.O. Box 7575, Pensacola, FL 32534-0575 USA Toll Free: 877-437-7811
E-mail: sales@universalmarketingmedia.com
Web site: http://www.universalmarketingmedia.com.

Universal Messengers Pubns., *(978-0-9768879)* P.O. Box 9039, Wilmington, DE 19809 USA Tel 302-764-4293; Toll Free: 866-207-9301
E-mail: phdfoxx@msn.com; phdfoxx@verizon.net
Web site: http://mysite.verizon.net/vze0488v.

Universal Pubs., *(978-0-9658564; 978-1-58112; 978-1-59942; 978-1-61233; 978-1-62734)* 23331 Water Cir., Boca Raton, FL 33486-8540 USA (SAN 299-3635) Tel 561-750-4344; Fax: 561-750-6797; Toll Free: 800-636-8329
E-mail: bookorders@upublish.com; bookorders@universal-publishers.com
Web site: http://www.dissertation.com; http://www.universal-publishers.com; http://www.BrownWalker.com.

Universal Publishing, *(978-1-883421; 978-1-931181; 978-1-934732)* Subs. of Gutenberg, Inc., 100 4th St., Honesdale, PA 18431 USA Tel 570-251-0260; Fax: 570-251-0264; Toll Free: 800-940-2270 Do not confuse with companies with the same or similar name in Ecino, CA, Egg Harbor Township, NJ, Gainesville, FL, Newport Beach, CA, Stoughton, MA, Pasadena, CA, Oak Park, IL, Jacksonville, FL
E-mail: tom@upub.net; larry@upub.net
Web site: http://www.upub.net; http://www.universalpublishing.net.

Universal Publishing LLC, *(978-0-9840456)* P.O. Box 99491, Emeryville, CA 94606 USA Tel 510-485-1183
E-mail: universalpublishingllc@gmail.com
Web site: www.universalpublishingllc@gmail.com.

Universal Reference Pubns. *Imprint of* **Grey Hse. Publishing**

Universal Values Media, LLC, *(978-0-9729821; 978-1-60210)* 3800 Powell Ln., No. 823, Falls Church, VA 22041 USA
Web site: http://www.onceandfuturebooks.com.

Universe Publishing, *(978-0-7893; 978-0-87663; 978-1-55550)* Div. of Rizzoli International Pubns., Inc., 300 Park Ave. S., 3rd Flr., New York, NY 10010 USA (SAN 202-537X) Tel 212-387-3400; Fax: 212-387-3444 Do not confuse with similar names in North Hollywood, CA, Englewood, NJ, Mendocino, CA
Dist(s): **Andrews McMeel Publishing**
MyiLibrary
Penguin Random Hse., LLC.
Random Hse., Inc.
Rizzoli International Pubns., Inc.

Univ. At Buffalo, Child Care Ctr., *(978-0-9712349)* Butler Annex A, 3435 Main St., Buffalo, NY 14214-3011 USA Tel 716-829-2226
E-mail: rorrange@buffalo.edu.

Univ. Editions, *(978-0-9711659; 978-0-615-11379-1)* 1003 W. Centennial Dr., Peoria, IL 61614-2828 USA Tel 309-692-0621; Fax: 309-693-0628 Do not confuse with University Editions in Huntington, WV
E-mail: mikruc@aol.com
Web site: http://www.terrythetractor.com.

Univ. Games, *(978-0-935145; 978-1-57528)* 2030 Harrison St., San Francisco, CA 94110-1310 USA (SAN 695-2321) Tel 415-503-1600; Fax: 415-503-0085
E-mail: info@ugames.com
Web site: http://www.ugames.com.

†Univ. of Alabama Pr., *(978-0-8173)* Orders Addr.: 11030 S. Langley, Chicago, IL 60628 USA Tel 773-702-7000; Toll Free: 800-621-2736; Edit Addr.: P.O. Box 870380, Tuscaloosa, AL 35487-0380 USA (SAN 202-5272) Tel 205-348-5180; Fax: 205-348-9201
Web site: http://www.uapress.ua.edu
Dist(s): **Chicago Distribution Ctr.**
Univ. of Chicago Pr.
ebrary, Inc.; *CIP.*

Univ. of Alaska Pr., *(978-0-912006; 978-1-889963; 978-1-60223)* P.O. Box 756240, Fairbanks, AK 99775-6240 USA (SAN 203-3011) Tel 907-474-5831; Fax: 907-474-5502; Toll Free: 888-252-6657
E-mail: fypress@uaf.edu; sue.mitchell@alaska.edu
Web site: http://www.alaska.edu/uapress
Dist(s): **Chicago Distribution Ctr.**
Wizard Works
ebrary, Inc.

Univ. of Arizona, Poetry Ctr., Arizona Board of Regents, *(978-0-9727635)* c/o Univ. of Arizona Poetry Ctr.,, 1216 N. Cherry Ave., Tucson, AZ 85719 USA Tel 520-626-3765; Fax: 520-621-5566
E-mail: poetry@u.arizona.edu
Web site: http://www.poetrycenter.arizona.edu.

†University of Arizona Pr., *(978-0-8165; 978-1-941451)* 355 S. Euclid Ave., Suite 103, Tucson, AZ 85719 USA (SAN 205-468X) Tel 520-621-1441; Fax: 520-621-8899; Toll Free: 800-426-3797 (orders)
E-mail: orders@uapress.arizona.edu
Web site: http://www.uapress.arizona.edu
Dist(s): **Chicago Distribution Ctr.**
Continental Bk. Co., Inc.
Many Feathers Bks. & Maps
MyiLibrary
Univ. of Chicago Pr.
Univ of Arizona Critical Languages Program
ebrary, Inc.; *CIP.*

†Univ. of Arkansas Pr., *(978-0-938626; 978-1-55728; 978-1-61075; 978-1-68226)* 105 N. McIlroy Ave., Fayetteville, AR 72701 USA (SAN 239-3972) Tel 479-575-7544; Fax: 479-575-6044; Toll Free: 800-626-0090
E-mail: info@uapress.com
Web site: http://www.uapress.com; http://www.uark.edu/~uaprinfo
Dist(s): **Chicago Distribution Ctr.**
MyiLibrary
Yankee Peddler Bookshop
ebrary, Inc.; *CIP.*

Univ. of California, Berkeley, Lawrence Hall of Science, *(978-0-912511; 978-0-924886; 978-1-931542)* U of CA, Lawrence Hall of Science, Berkeley, CA 94720-5200 USA (SAN 271-9754) Tel 510-642-7771; Fax: 510-643-0309; *Imprints:* GEMS (GEMS); EQUALS (EQUALS)
E-mail: gems@berkeley.edu
Web site: http://www.lhs.berkeley.edu; http://www.lhsgems.org
Dist(s): **Distributors, The.**

†Univ. of Chicago Pr., *(978-0-226; 978-0-89065; 978-0-943056; 978-1-892850)* Orders Addr.: 11030 S. Langley Ave., Chicago, IL 60628 USA (SAN 202-5280) Tel 773-702-7000; Fax: 773-702-7212; Toll Free Fax: 800-621-8476 (US & Canada); Toll Free: 800-621-2736 (US & Canada); Edit Addr.: 1427 E. 60th St., Chicago, IL 60637 USA (SAN 202-5299) Tel 773-702-7700; 773-702-7748 (Marketing & Sales); Fax: 773-702-9756
E-mail: general@press.uchicago.edu; kh@press.uchicago.edu; custserv@press.uchicago.edu; sales@press.uchicago.edu;

marketing@press.uchicago.edu; publicity@press.uchicago.edu
Web site: http://www.press.uchicago.edu
Dist(s): **Chicago Distribution Ctr.**
CreateSpace Independent Publishing Platform
Ebsco Publishing
Giron Bks.
MyiLibrary
Oxford Univ. Pr., Inc.
TNT Media Group, Inc.
ebrary, Inc.; *CIP*.

Univ. of Denver, Ctr. for Teaching International Relations Pubns., *(978-0-943804)* 2201 S. Gaylord St., Denver, CO 80208 USA (SAN 241-0877) Tel 303-871-2697; Fax: 303-871-2456
E-mail: ctir-press@du.edu; pubsinfo@du.edu
Web site: http://www.du.edu/ctir
Dist(s): **Lightning Source, Inc.**
Social Studies Schl. Service
Teacher's Discovery.

†Univ. of Georgia, Carl Vinson Institute of Government, *(978-0-89854)* 201 N. Milledge Ave., Athens, GA 30602 USA (SAN 212-8012) Tel 706-542-2736; Fax: 706-542-6239
E-mail: pou@cviog.uga.edu
Web site: http://www.cviog.uga.edu; *CIP*.

†Univ. of Georgia Pr., *(978-0-8203)* Orders Addr.: 4435 Atlanta Hwy. West Dock, Athens, GA 30602 USA; Edit Addr.: Main Library, Third Flr. 320 S. Jackson St., Athens, GA 30602 USA (SAN 203-3054) Fax: 706-542-2558; Toll Free: 800-266-5842
E-mail: books@uga.edu
Web site: http://www.ugapress.org
Dist(s): **Ebsco Publishing**
MyiLibrary
ebrary, Inc.; *CIP*.

Univ. of Guam, Micronesian Area Research Ctr., *(978-1-878453; 978-0-9800331; 978-1-935198)* 303 University Dr., UOG Sta., Mangilao, GU 96923 USA Tel 671-735-2150; Fax: 671-734-7403
Web site: http://www.uog.edu/marc.

†Univ. of Hawaii Pr., *(978-0-8248; 978-0-87022)* Orders Addr.: 2840 Kolowalu St., Honolulu, HI 96822-1888 USA (SAN 202-5353) Tel 808-956-8255; Fax: 808-988-6052; Toll Free Fax: 800-650-7811; Toll Free: 888-847-7377; *Imprints*: Latitude Twenty Book (Latitude Twenty)
E-mail: uhpmkt@hawaii.edu; uhpbooks@hawaii.edu
Web site: http://www.uhpress.hawaii.edu
Dist(s): **Booklines Hawaii, Ltd.**; *CIP*.

†Univ. of Iowa Pr., *(978-0-87745; 978-1-58729; 978-1-60938)* Div. of The University of Iowa, Orders Addr.: c/o Chicago Distribution Ctr. 11030 S. Langley Ave., Chicago, IL 60628 USA Toll Free Fax: 800-621-8476; Toll Free: 800-621-2736; Edit Addr.: 100 Kuhl Hse. 119 W. Park Rd., Iowa City, IA 52242-1000 USA (SAN 203-3070) Tel 319-335-2000; Fax: 319-335-2055 Do not confuse with Univ. of Iowa, Pubns. Dept. at same address
E-mail: uipress@uiowa.edu
Web site: http://www.uiowapress.org
Dist(s): **Chicago Distribution Ctr.**
Ebsco Publishing
Univ. of Chicago Pr.
ebrary, Inc.; *CIP*.

University of Kwazulu-Natal Press (ZAF) *(978-0-86980; 978-1-86840; 978-1-874897; 978-1-86914)* *Dist. by* **Intl Spec Bk.**

University of Louisiana at Lafayette *See* **Univ. of Louisiana at Lafayette Pr.**

Univ. of Louisiana at Lafayette Pr., *(978-0-940984; 978-1-887366; 978-1-935754)* P.O. Box 40831, Lafayette, LA 70504 USA (SAN 630-9755) Tel 337-482-6027; Fax: 337-482-6028
E-mail: cls@louisiana.edu
Web site: http://www.ulpress.org
Dist(s): **Forest Sales & Distributing Co.**

†Univ. of Massachusetts Pr., *(978-0-87023; 978-1-55849; 978-1-61376; 978-1-62534)* Orders Addr.: P.O. Box 429, Amherst, MA 01004 USA (SAN 203-3089) Tel 413-545-2217 (editorial); Fax: 413-545-1226; Toll Free Fax: 800-537-5487; P.O. Box 50370, Baltimore, MD 21211 Tel 800-537-5487; Fax: 410-516-6998
E-mail: info@umpress.umass.edu
Web site: http://www.umass.edu/umpress
Dist(s): **Hopkins Fulfillment Services**
INscribe Digital
MyiLibrary; *CIP*.

†Univ. of Michigan Pr., *(978-0-472)* Orders Addr.: c/o Chicago Distribution Center, Perseus Distribution 1094 Flex Dr., Jackson, TN 38301 USA (SAN 282-4884) Toll Free Fax: 800-351-5073; Toll Free: 800-343-4499 , ext. 165; Edit Addr.: 839 Greene St., Ann Arbor, MI 48104-3209 USA Tel 734-764-4388; Fax: 734-615-1540
E-mail: um.press@umich.edu
Web site: http://www.press.umich.edu/
Dist(s): **Chicago Distribution Ctr.**
Ebsco Publishing
MyiLibrary
Palgrave Macmillan
ebrary, Inc.; *CIP*.

†Univ. of Minnesota Pr., *(978-0-8166; 978-1-4529; 978-1-5179)* Affil. of Univ. of Minnesota, 111 Third Ave. S., Suite 290, Minneapolis, MN 55401-2520 USA (SAN 213-2648) Tel 612-627-1970; Fax: 612-627-1980
E-mail: ump@umn.edu
Web site: http://www.upress.umn.edu
Dist(s): **David Brown Book Company, The**
Chicago Distribution Ctr.
Ebsco Publishing
MyiLibrary
Univ. of Chicago Pr.
ebrary, Inc.; *CIP*.

Univ. of Missouri, Extension, *(978-0-933842)* c/o Extension Pubns., Univ. of Missouri, 2800 Maguire Blvd., Columbia, MO 65211 USA (SAN 688-427X) Tel 573-882-7216; Fax: 573-884-5038; Toll Free: 800-292-0969; 2800 Maguire Blvd., Columbia, MO 65211
E-mail: extpubs@missouri.edu; umccafnrexplore@missouri.edu; muextensionweb@missouri.edu
Web site: http://www.muextension.missouri.edu/xplor.

†Univ. of Missouri Pr., *(978-0-8262)* 2910 LeMone Blvd., Columbia, MO 65201 USA (SAN 203-3143) Tel 573-882-7641; Fax: 573-884-4498; Toll Free: 800-828-1894 (orders only)
E-mail: rennerk@umsystem.edu; deandj@umsystem.edu
Web site: http://press.umsystem.edu
Dist(s): **Chicago Distribution Ctr.**
East-West Export Bks.
Ebsco Publishing
Lulu Enterprises Inc.
Univ. of Chicago Pr.
ebrary, Inc.; *CIP*.

Univ. of Montana Pr., The, *(978-0-9754009; 978-0-9815760; 978-0-9837259; 978-0-9894031; 978-0-9909748)* Div. of The Univ. of Montana, The University of Montana 32 Campus Dr. Todd Bldg., Lower Level, Missoula, MT 59812-0792 USA (SAN 255-9994) Tel 406-243-2711; Fax: 406-243-2615
E-mail: ken.price@umontana.edu
Web site: http://www.umt.edu/printingandgraphics.com.

†Univ. of Nebraska Pr., *(978-0-8032; 978-1-4962)* Orders Addr.: 1111 Lincoln Mall, Lincoln, NE 68588-0630 USA Tel 402-472-3581; 402-472-7702; Fax: 402-472-6214; Toll Free Fax: 800-526-2617; Toll Free: 800-755-1105; Edit Addr.: P.O. Box 880630, Lincoln, NE 68588-0630 USA (SAN 202-5337); *Imprints*: Bison Books (Bison Books)
E-mail: pressmail@unl.edu
Web site: http://www.nebraskapress.unl.edu; http://www.bisonbooks.com
Dist(s): **Continental Bk. Co., Inc.**
Ebsco Publishing
MyiLibrary
ebrary, Inc.; *CIP*.

Univ. of Nebraska-Lincoln, GPN, *(978-0-7941)* Orders Addr.: P.O. Box 80669, Lincoln, NE 68501-0669 USA (SAN 179-1699) Tel 402-472-2007; Fax: 402-472-4076; Toll Free: 800-228-4630; Edit Addr.: 1800 N. 33rd St., Lincoln, NE 68583 USA
E-mail: gpn@unl.edu
Web site: http://gpn.unl.edu; http://shopgpn.com/.

†Univ. of New Mexico Pr., *(978-0-8263)* Orders Addr.: 1312 Basehart Rd., SE, Albuquerque, NM 87106-4363 USA (SAN 213-9588) Tel 505-277-2346; 505-272-7777 (orders); Toll Free Fax: 800-622-8667; Toll Free: 800-249-7737 (orders)
E-mail: unmpress@unm.edu
Web site: http://www.unmpress.com
Dist(s): **Bks. West**
Continental Bk. Co., Inc.
D.A.P./Distributed Art Pubs.
MyiLibrary
Rio Nuevo Pubs.
ebrary, Inc.; *CIP*.

†Univ. of North Carolina Pr., *(978-0-8078; 978-1-4696)* c/o Longleaf Services, 116 S. Boundary sT., Chapel Hill, NC 27514-3808 USA (SAN 203-3151) Tel 919-966-3561; Fax: 919-966-3829; Toll Free Fax: 800-272-6817; Toll Free: 800-848-6224
E-mail: uncpress@unc.edu
Web site: http://www.uncpress.unc.edu
Dist(s): **CreateSpace Independent Publishing Platform**
Ebsco Publishing
ebrary, Inc.; *CIP*.

†Univ. of Oklahoma Pr., *(978-0-8061)* Orders Addr.: 2800 Venture Dr., Norman, OK 73069-8218 USA Tel 405-325-2000; Fax: 405-364-5798; Toll Free Fax: 800-735-0476; Toll Free: 800-627-7377
E-mail: presscs@ou.edu
Web site: http://www.oupress.com
Dist(s): **Ebsco Publishing**
ebrary, Inc.; *CIP*.

†Univ. of Pennsylvania Pr., *(978-0-8122; 978-1-5128)* Orders Addr.: c/o Hopkins Fulfillment Srvc., Hopkins Fulfillment Service, Baltimore, MD 21211-4370 USA Tel 410-516-6948; Fax: 410-516-6998; Toll Free: 800-537-5487; Edit Addr.: 3905 Spruce St., Philadelphia, PA 19104-4112 USA (SAN 202-5345) Tel 215-898-6261; Fax: 215-898-0404; Toll Free: 800-537-5487 (book orders)
E-mail: custserv@pobox.upenn.edu
Web site: http://www.upenn.edu/pennpress
Dist(s): **Hopkins Fulfillment Services**
MyiLibrary
TNT Media Group, Inc.; *CIP*.

†Univ. of Pittsburgh Pr., *(978-0-8229)* 3400 Forbes Ave., Eureka Bldg., Fifth Flr., Pittsburgh, PA 15260 USA (SAN 203-3216) Tel 412-383-2456; Fax: 412-383-2466
E-mail: press@pitt.edu
Web site: http://www.upress.pitt.edu
Dist(s): **Chicago Distribution Ctr.**
MyiLibrary; *CIP*.

†Univ. of Puerto Rico Pr., *(978-0-8477)* Subs. of Univ. of Puerto Rico, Orders Addr.: P.O. Box 23322, Rio Piedras, PR 00931-3322 USA (SAN 208-1245) Tel 787-250-0435 Administrative Offices; 787-250-8996 Administrative Offices; 787-758-8345 Sales Office and Warehouse; 787-751-8251 Sales Office and Warehouse; 787-934-3400 Sales Office and Warehouse; Fax: 787-753-9116 Administrative Offices; 787-751-8785 Sales/Warehouse, Ordering fax
E-mail: info@laeditorialupr.com
Web site: http://www.laeditorialupr.com
Dist(s): **Ediciones Universal**
Lectorum Pubns., Inc.
Libros Sin Fronteras; *CIP*.

Univ. of Rhode Island, Sea Grant Pubns. Unit, *(978-0-938412)* Narragansett Bay Campus, Narragansett, RI 02882-1197 USA (SAN 209-0708) Tel 401-874-6800
E-mail: tkennedy@mail.uri.edu
Web site: http://www.seagrant.gso.uri.edu/riseagrant
Dist(s): **Chicago Distribution Ctr.**

Univ. of Scranton Pr., *(978-0-940866; 978-1-58966)* Orders Addr.: c/o Univ. of Scranton Pr., St. Thomas Hall, Linden & Monroe Sts., Scranton, PA 18510 USA Toll Free Fax: 800-941-8804; Toll Free: 800-941-3081; Edit Addr.: Linden & Monroe Sts., Scranton, PA 18510 USA (SAN 688-4067) Tel 570-941-7955; Fax: 570-941-4309
E-mail: richard.rousseau@uofs.edu
Web site: http://www.scrantonpress.com
Dist(s): **Associated Univ. Presses**
Chicago Distribution Ctr.

†Univ. of South Carolina Pr., *(978-0-87249; 978-1-57003; 978-1-61117)* Orders Addr.: 718 Devine St., Columbia, SC 29208 USA Tel 803-777-1774; Fax: 803-777-0026; Toll Free Fax: 800-868-0740; Toll Free: 800-768-2500; Edit Addr.: 1600 Hampton St., 5th Flr., Columbia, SC 29208 USA (SAN 203-3224) Tel 803-777-5243; Fax: 803-777-0160; Toll Free Fax: 800-868-0740; Toll Free: 800-768-2500
E-mail: jhaupt@sc.ed
Web site: http://www.sc.edu/uscpress/
Dist(s): **Ebsco Publishing**
MyiLibrary
ebrary, Inc.; *CIP*.

Univ. St. Mary of the Lake, Mundelein Seminary, *(978-0-9774733)* 1000 E. Maple Ave., Mundelein, IL 60060 USA Tel 847-566-6401; Fax: 847-566-7330
E-mail: info@usml.edu
Web site: http://www.usml.edu.

Univ. of Temecula Pr., Inc., *(978-0-936283)* 42730 De Luz Ave., Murrieta, CA 92562-7214 USA (SAN 697-9793) Tel 951-698-0059; Fax: 951-698-3676; *Imprints*: UTP (UTP)
E-mail: mikeray@utem.com
Web site: http://www.utem.com.

†Univ. of Texas Pr., *(978-0-292; 978-1-4773)* Orders Addr.: P.O. Box 7819, Austin, TX 78713-7819 USA (SAN 212-9876) Tel 512-471-7233; Fax: 512-232-7178; Toll Free: 800-252-3206; Edit Addr.: University of Texas at Austin 2100 Comal, Austin, TX 78722 USA
E-mail: info@utpress.utexas.edu
Web site: http://www.utexas.edu/utpress
Dist(s): **Continental Bk. Co., Inc.**
Ebsco Publishing
Urban Land Institute
ebrary, Inc.; *CIP*.

†Univ. of Utah Pr., *(978-0-87480; 978-1-60781)* 1795 E. South Campus Dr., Rm. 101, Salt Lake City, UT 84112-9402 USA (SAN 220-0023) Tel 801-581-6771; Fax: 801-581-3365; Toll Free: 800-773-6672
E-mail: info@upress.utah.edu
Web site: http://www.upress.utah.edu
Dist(s): **Chicago Distribution Ctr.**
Partners Bk. Distributing, Inc.
Rio Nuevo Pubs.
ebrary, Inc.; *CIP*.

†Univ. of Washington Pr., *(978-0-295; 978-1-902716)* Orders Addr.: P.O. Box 50096, Seattle, WA 98145-5096 USA (SAN 212-2502) Tel 206-543-4050; Fax: 206-543-3932; Toll Free Fax: 800-669-7993; Edit Addr.: P.O. Box 50096, Seattle, WA 98145-5096 USA Toll Free Fax: 800-669-7993; 1126 N. 98th St., Seattle, WA 98103
E-mail: uwpord@u.washington.edu
Web site: http://www.washington.edu/uwpress
Dist(s): **Ebsco Publishing**
Hopkins Fulfillment Services
MyiLibrary
Partners Bk. Distributing, Inc.
Urban Land Institute
ebrary, Inc.; *CIP*.

Univ. of West Florida Foundation, Inc., *(978-0-9659142; 978-0-9798292)* 11000 University Pkwy., Pensacola, FL 32514 USA
E-mail: cmarse@uwf.edu.

†Univ. of Wisconsin Pr., *(978-0-299)* Orders Addr.: c/o Chicago Dist Ctr., 11030 S. Langley Ave., Chicago, IL 60628 USA Tel 773-568-1550; Fax: 773-660-2235; Toll Free Fax: 800-621-8476 (orders only); Toll Free: 800-621-2736 (orders only); Edit Addr.: 1930 Monroe St., 3rd Flr., Madison, WI 53711 USA Tel 608-263-1110; Fax: 608-263-1132
E-mail: uwiscpress@uwpress.wisc.edu
Web site: http://www.wisc.edu/wisconsinpress/
Dist(s): **Chicago Distribution Ctr.**
East-West Export Bks.
Ebsco Publishing
Follett School Solutions
MyiLibrary
ebrary, Inc.; *CIP*.

†Univ. Pr. of America, Inc., *(978-0-7618; 978-0-8191; 978-1-879691)* Member of Rowman & Littlefield Publishing Group, Inc., Orders Addr.: 15200 NBN Way, Blue Ridge Summit, PA 17214-0190 USA Tel 717-794-3800 (Sales, Customer Service, MIS, Royalties, Inventory Mgmt, Dist., Credit & Collections); Fax: 717-794-3803 (Customer Service & orders); 717-794-3857 (Sales & MIS); 717-794-3856 (Royalties, Inventory Mgmt. & Dist.); Toll Free Fax: 800-338-4550 (Customer Service & /or orders); Toll Free: 800-462-6420 (Customer Service &/or orders); Edit Addr.: 4501 Forbes Blvd., Suite 200, Lanham, MD 20706 USA Tel 301-459-3366; Fax: 301-459-5748 Short Discount, please contact rlpgsales@rowman.com
E-mail: custserv@rowman.com
Web site: http://www.univpress.com; http://www.rlpgbooks.com
Dist(s): **CreateSpace Independent Publishing Platform**
Ebsco Publishing
MyiLibrary
National Bk. Network
Rowman & Littlefield Publishers, Inc.
Yale Univ. Pr.
ebrary, Inc.; *CIP*.

Univ. Pr. of Colorado, *(978-0-87081; 978-0-87421; 978-1-60732)* Orders Addr.: 2800 Venture Dr., Norman, OK 73069-8218 USA Toll Free Fax: 800-735-0476; Toll Free: 800-627-7377; Edit Addr.: 5589 Arapahoe Ave., Suite 206C, Boulder, CO 80303 USA (SAN 658-0343) Tel 720-406-8849
Web site: http://www.upcolorado.com
Dist(s): **Bks. West**
Chicago Distribution Ctr.
Ctr. for Literary Publishing, Colorado State Univ.
Ebsco Publishing
Follett School Solutions
MyiLibrary
O'Reilly Media, Inc.
Univ. of Oklahoma Pr.
ebrary, Inc.

†Univ. Pr. of Kentucky, *(978-0-8131; 978-0-912839; 978-0-916968)* Orders Addr.: P.O. Box 4680, Lexington, KY 40544-4680 USA Tel 859-257-8400; Fax: 859-257-8481; Toll Free: 800-839-6855; Edit Addr.: 663 S. Limestone St., Lexington, KY 40508-4008 USA (SAN 203-3275) Tel 859-257-5200; Fax: 859-323-4981; Toll Free Fax: 800-870-4981
Web site: http://www.kentuckypress.com
Dist(s): **Ebsco Publishing**
MyiLibrary
Oxford Univ. Pr., Inc.
ebrary, Inc.; *CIP*.

†Univ. Pr. of Mississippi, *(978-0-87805; 978-1-57806; 978-1-934110; 978-1-60473; 978-1-61703; 978-1-62103; 978-1-62674; 978-1-62846; 978-1-4968)* 3825 Ridgewood Rd., Jackson, MS 39211-6492 USA (SAN 203-1914) Tel 601-432-6205; Fax: 601-432-6217; Toll Free: 800-737-7788 (orders only)
E-mail: kburgess@ihl.state.ms.us; press@mississippi.edu
Web site: http://www.upress.state.ms.us
Dist(s): **CreateSpace Independent Publishing Platform**
East-West Export Bks.
Ebsco Publishing
MyiLibrary
ebrary, Inc.; *CIP*.

†Univ. Pr. of New England, *(978-0-87451; 978-0-915032; 978-1-58465; 978-1-61168; 978-1-5126)* Orders Addr.: One Court St., Suite 250, Lebanon, NH 03755 USA Tel 603-448-1533 (ext. 255); Fax: 603-448-9429; Toll Free: 800-421-1561
E-mail: University.Press@Dartmouth.edu
Web site: http://www.upne.com
Dist(s): **David Brown Book Company, The**
MyiLibrary
Smashwords
ebrary, Inc.; *CIP*.

Univ. Pr. of the Pacific, *(978-0-89875; 978-1-4102)* 4440 NW 73rd Ave., PTY 362, Miami, FL 33166-6437 USA Tel 407-650-2537 (phone/fax)
E-mail: bip@universitypressofthepacific.com
Web site: http://www.universitypressofthepacific.com.

†Univ. Pr. of Virginia, *(978-0-8139; 978-0-912759; 978-1-57814)* Orders Addr.: P.O. Box 400318, Charlottesville, VA 22904-4318 USA (SAN 202-5361) Tel 804-924-3468; Fax: 804-982-2655
E-mail: upress@virginia.edu
Web site: http://www.upress.virginia.edu
Dist(s): **Ediciones Universal**
MyiLibrary; *CIP*.

University Publishing Associates, Incorporated *See* **National Film Network LLC**

Univ. Publishing Co., *(978-0-8346)* P.O. Box 80298, Lincoln, NE 68501 USA (SAN 206-0582) Tel 402-476-2761.

Univ. Science Bks., *(978-0-935702; 978-1-891389; 978-1-938787; 978-1-940380)* 20 Edgehill Rd., Mill Valley, CA 94941-1113 USA (SAN 213-8085); 111 Prospect Pl., South Orange, NJ 07079 Tel 973-378-3900; Fax: 973-378-3925
E-mail: univscibks@igc.org; bjellis@igc.org; deskcopy@uscibooks.com
Web site: http://www.uscibooks.com
Dist(s): **RedShelf.**

UniversityPress.Info *See* **Science Pubs.**

Unlimited Horizons, *(978-0-9753817)* 427 S. Fraser Dr., Mesa, AZ 85204-2605 USA.

Unlimited Publishing LLC, *(978-0-9677649; 978-1-58832)* P.O. Box 3007, Bloomington, IN 47402 USA Fax: 425-928-5465
E-mail: jaymasp@aol.com; paradoxofthesoul@aol.com
Web site: http://www.unlimitedpublishing.com
Dist(s): **CreateSpace Independent Publishing Platform**
TextStream.

Unlock A Bk. Pubs., LLC, *(978-0-9796456)* 225 S. Bishop, San Angelo, TX 76901 USA
Web site: http://unlockabook.com.

Unmistakably C K C, *(978-0-9742064)* 3244 Kingswood Glen, Decatur, GA 30034 USA Tel 404-244-8113; 404-242-2690; Fax: 678-418-3056
E-mail: info@billyzany.com
Web site: http://www.billyzany.com.

Publisher Name Index

Unseen Gallery, (*978-0-9795206*) Orders Addr.: P.O. Box 6065, Albuquerque, NM 87197 USA Tel 505-232-2161
E-mail: webmaster@unseengallery.com
Web site: http://www.unseengallery.com.

Unshackled Publishing, (*978-0-9708688*) Orders Addr.: P.O. Box 44216, Indianapolis, IN 46244 USA; P.O. Box 44216, Indianapolis, IN 46244
E-mail: lexthewriter@yahoo.com; treks-journey@yahoo.com
Web site: http://www.unshackledpublishing.com; http://www.alexusrhone.com.

Unspeakable Joy Pr., (*978-0-9761538*) Orders Addr.: 499 Adams St., #252, Milton, MA 02186 USA; Edit Addr.: 233 Eliot St., Milton, MA 02186 USA
E-mail: roybue@aol.com; adoptionis@aol.com
Web site: http://www.adoptionis.com.

Untold Pr., LLC, (*978-0-615-63143-1; 978-0-615-64153-9; 978-0-615-70336-7; 978-0-615-76650-8; 978-0-615-77270-7; 978-0-615-77291-2; 978-0-615-82504-5; 978-0-615-83855-7; 978-0-615-85098-6; 978-0-615-88514-8; 978-0-615-89925-1; 978-0-615-99550-2; 978-0-615-99820-6; 978-0-692-02234-4; 978-0-692-02235-1; 978-0-692-25607-7; 978-0-692-25608-4; 978-0-692-27650-1; 978-0-692-28090-4; 978-0-692-28728-6; 978-0-692-28729-3; 978-0-692-30590-4; 978-0-692-31882-9; 978-0-692-31886-7; 978-0-692-34932-8; 978-0-692-40306-8;) 114 NE Estia Ln., Port Saint Lucie, FL 34983 USA Tel 772-607-2203*
Web site: http://untoldpress.com
Dist(s): **CreateSpace Independent Publishing Platform.**

Untreed Reads Publishing, LLC, (*978-1-61187*) 506 Kansas St., San Francisco, CA 94107 USA Tel 415-621-0465; Toll Free Fax: 800-318-6037
E-mail: jhartman@untreedreads.com; kdsullivan@untreedreads.com
Web site: http://www.untreedreads.com.

Unveiled Media, LLC, (*978-0-9776385*) P.O. Box 930463, Verona, WI 53593 USA (SAN 257-8093); *Imprints:* Cotton Candy Press (CottonCandy Pr)
Web site: http://www.unveiledmedia.com
Dist(s): **Consortium Bk. Sales & Distribution**
CreateSpace Independent Publishing Platform
Lightning Source, Inc.

UP *See* **Infobus, Inc.**

UPfirst.com Bks., (*978-0-9800222*) Div. of UPfirst.com, 2803 Us Hwy. 41 W. Suite 100, Marquette, MI 49855-2291 USA (SAN 855-0271)
E-mail: michaeleen@upfirst.com
Web site: http://www.upfirst.com.

UPfirst.com Picture Books for Children *See* **UPfirst.com Bks.**

Upheaval Media, Inc., (*978-0-615-19321-2; 978-0-578-03360-0; 978-0-615-36266-3; 978-0-9829610*) P.O. Box 241488, Detroit, MI 48224 USA Tel 877-429-2370; Fax: 313-556-1669; Toll Free: 877-429-2370
E-mail: info@upheavalmedia.net
Web site: http://www.upheavalmedia.net
Dist(s): **Lulu Enterprises Inc.**

Uphoff, Pamela Ann *See* **Iron Ax Pr.**

Upland Public Library Foundation *See* **Citrus Roots - Preserving Citrus Heritage Foundation**

Uplift Pr., (*978-0-9622834*) 295 Lenox Ave., #105, Oakland, CA 94610 USA Do not confuse with Uplift Pr. in Los Angeles, CA.

Upper Deck Co., LLC,The, (*978-1-931860; 978-1-932241; 978-1-932669; 978-1-932825; 978-1-932939; 978-1-933103; 978-1-933252; 978-1-933489; 978-1-59945; 978-1-60806*) 5909 Sea Otter Pl., Carlsbad, CA 92010 USA Tel 760-929-6500; Fax: 760-929-6548; Toll Free: 800-873-7332
Web site: http://www.upperdeck.com
Dist(s): **Diamond Bk. Distributors.**

Upper Room Bks., (*978-0-8358; 978-0-88177; 978-1-935205*) Div. of The Upper Room, 1908 Grand Ave., Nashville, TN 37212 USA (SAN 203-3364) Tel 615-340-7256; Toll Free: 800-972-0433 (customer service, orders); *Imprints:* Discipleship Resources (DiscipleshipRes) Do not confuse with Upper Room Education for Parenting, Inc. in Derry, NH
E-mail: jneely@gbod.org; lbruner@gbod.org; atrudel@gbod.org
Web site: http://www.upperroom.org; http://books.upperroom.org; http://bookstore.upperroom.org
Dist(s): **Abingdon Pr.**
Smashwords.

Upper Strata Ink, Incorporated *See* **Crowder, Jack L.**

Upside Down Tree Publishing, (*978-0-9802329*) 1605 N. Grand Ave., Maryville, MO 64468 USA.

Upstart Bks. *Imprint of* **Highsmith Inc.**

Upstart Pr. (NZL) (*978-1-927262*) *Dist. by* **IPG Chicago.**

UpTree Publishing, (*978-0-9787248*) P.O. Box 212863, Columbia, SC 29221 USA (SAN 851-447X) Toll Free: 800-905-2157 (phone/fax)
E-mail: sales@uptreepublishing.com; info@uptreepublishing.com
Web site: http://www.uptreepublishing.com.

Upublish.com *See* **Universal Pubs.**

Upword Pr., (*978-0-9654140*) Orders Addr.: P.O. Box 974, Atmore, AL 36504-0974 USA; 1879 Old Bratt Rd., Atmore, AL 36504 Tel 251-609-2918 Do not confuse with Upword Pr., Yelm, WA
Web site: http://www.scattersunshine.com
Dist(s): **American Wholesale Bk. Co.**

Urban Advocacy, (*978-0-9745122*) 917 Columbia Ave. Suite 123, Lancaster, PA 17603 USA Tel 717-490-6148
E-mail: vuuhu02@yahoo.com
Web site: http://www.urbanadvocacy.org.

Urban Bks., LLC, (*978-1-893196; 978-0-9743636; 978-0-9747025; 978-1-60162; 978-1-62286*) 78 E. Industry Ct., Deer Park, NY 11729-4704 USA Do not confuse with Urban Books in Berkeley, CA
E-mail: urbanbooks@optonline.net
Web site: http://www.urbanbooks.net
Dist(s): **Kensington Publishing Corp.**
MyiLibrary
Penguin Random Hse., LLC.
Penguin Publishing Group
Random Hse., Inc.

Urban Edge Publishing Co., (*978-0-9743781*) 16209 Victory Blvd., Suite 207, Van Nuys, CA 91406 USA Tel 818-786-3700; Fax: 818-786-3737
E-mail: willcon@pacbell.net.

Urban, Keith Studios, (*978-0-9815370*) P.O. Box 4572, Wayne, NJ 07474 USA (SAN 855-8280)
Web site: http://www.keithurban.com.

Urban Ministries, Incorporated *See* **UMI (Urban Ministries, Inc.)**

Urban Moon Publishing, (*978-0-9787913; 978-0-9800101*) 931 Monroe Dr., Suite 276, Atlanta, GA 30308 USA Toll Free: 866-205-9228
E-mail: kinglistens@aol.com.

Urban Spirit!, (*978-0-9638127; 978-0-9845359; 978-0-9846480; 978-0-9881958; 978-0-9884572*) 753 Walden Blvd., Atlanta, GA 30349 USA Tel 770-969-7891
E-mail: melbanks2002@yahoo.com
Web site: http://www.urbanspirit.biz.

Urbanik, Karen L., (*978-0-9759031*) 2285 Marsh Hawk Ln. Apt. 302, Orange Park, FL 32003-6366 USA.

Ure, Daylene, (*978-0-615-25326-8*) 160 E. 200 S., Washington, UT 84780 USA
Dist(s): **Lulu Enterprises Inc.**

Urim Pubns. (ISR) (*978-965-7108; 978-965-524*) *Dist. by* **IPG Chicago.**

Urim Pubns. (ISR) (*978-965-7108; 978-965-524*) *Dist. by* **Lambda Pubs.**

Urim Pubns. (ISR) (*978-965-7108; 978-965-524*) *Dist. by* **Coronet Bks.**

Urim Pubns. (ISR) (*978-965-7108; 978-965-524*) *Dist. by* **AtlasBooks.**

†**URJ Pr.,** (*978-0-8074*) 633 Third Ave., New York, NY 10017 USA (SAN 203-3291) Tel 212-650-4120; Fax: 212-650-4119; Toll Free: 888-489-8242
E-mail: press@urj.org
Web site: http://www.urjbooksandmusic.com
Dist(s): **Leonard, Hal Corp.**
MyiLibrary; *CIP.*

URON Entertainment Corp. (CAN) (*978-0-9738652; 978-0-9781386; 978-1-897376; 978-1-926778; 978-1-927925*) *Dist. by* **Diamond Book Dists.**

Ursu Pubns., (*978-0-9741634*) PMB 429, 5250 Grand Ave., Suite 14, Gurnee, IL 60031-1877 USA
E-mail: info@grandmaursu.com
Web site: http://www.grandmaursu.com.

Urtext, (*978-0-9790573; 978-1-940121*) 39 Longwood Dr., San Rafael, CA 94901-1026 USA (SAN 852-3061).

U.S. Games Systems, Inc., (*978-0-88079; 978-0-913866; 978-1-57281*) 179 Ludlow St., Stamford, CT 06902 USA (SAN 158-6483) Tel 203-353-8400; Fax: 203-353-8431; Toll Free: 800-544-2637
E-mail: usgames@aol.com
Web site: http://www.usgamesinc.com
Dist(s): **New Leaf Distributing Co., Inc.**

US Super Teen, (*978-0-615-84742-9*) 8784 Pointe Dr, Broadview Heights, OH 44147 USA Tel 518-956-4651; Fax: 440-627-6291
Dist(s): **CreateSpace Independent Publishing Platform.**

Usborne *Imprint of* **EDC Publishing**

Usera, Christian, (*978-0-615-14618-8; 978-0-615-14645-4; 978-0-615-31319-1*) 7818 S. Zeno St., Centennial, CO 80016-1849 USA
Dist(s): **Lulu Enterprises Inc.**

Utopia Pr., (*978-0-9661060*) 126 1/2 E. Front St., Traverse City, MI 49684 USA Tel 231-922-2234 editorial office
E-mail: pub@fimg.net.

UTP *Imprint of* **Univ. of Temecula Pr., Inc.**

Utterly Global, (*978-0-9891338*) 44 Lenhome Dr., Cranford, NJ 07016 USA Tel 908-272-0631
E-mail: info@antibullyingprograms.com
Web site: www.antibullyingprograms.com.

UWA Publishing (AUS) (*978-0-85564; 978-0-86422; 978-0-909751; 978-1-875560; 978-1-876268; 978-1-920694; 978-0-9802964; 978-0-9802965; 978-1-921401; 978-1-920964; 978-1-74258; 978-0-7316-0213-1; 978-0-7316-1196-6; 978-0-7316-1212-3; 978-0-7316-3945-8; 978-0-646-15226-4; 978-0-646-31692-5; 978-0-646-39116-8; 978-0-646-43446-9) Dist. by* **Intl Spec Bk.**

UXL *Imprint of* **Cengage Gale**

Uxor Pr., Inc., (*978-0-932555*) One Blackfield Dr. #174, Tiburon, CA 94920 USA Tel 415-383-8481
E-mail: bobzimmerman@usa.com.

V V C Publishing *See* **Vic-Vincent Publishing**

Vabella Publishing, (*978-0-9712204; 978-0-9834332; 978-1-938230; 978-1-942766*) Orders Addr.: P.O. Box 1052, Carrollton, GA 30112 USA (SAN 920-1858) Tel 770-328-8355; Edit Addr.: 222 Hampton Way, Carrollton, GA 30116 USA (SAN 860-1682) Tel 770-328-8355
E-mail: belljg@aol.com
Web site: www.vabella.com.

Vacation Spot Publishing, (*978-0-9637688; 978-1-893622*) Orders Addr.: P.O. Box 1723, Lorton, VA 22199-1723 USA Tel 703-684-8142; Fax: 703-684-7955; Toll Free: 800-441-1949; Edit Addr.: 1903 Duffield Ln., Alexandria, VA 22307 USA; *Imprints:* VSP Books (VSP Bks)
E-mail: mail@VSPBooks.com
Web site: http://www.vspbooks.com
Dist(s): **Follett School Solutions.**

Vadeboncoeur, Jim, (*978-0-9724697*) 3809 Laguna Ave., Palo Alto, CA 94306-2629 USA Fax: 650-493-1145
E-mail: images@bpib.com
Web site: http://www.bpib.com/images.htm.

Valenti, Robert A., (*978-0-9773119*) 3500 Galt Ocean Dr.2401, Fort Lauderdale, FL 33308-6809 USA Tel 954-563-0069; Fax: 954-563-4503
E-mail: rvalenti@bellsouth.net.

Valerie Bendt, (*978-1-885814*) Orders Addr.: 333 W. Rio Vista Ct., Tampa, FL 33604 USA
E-mail: ValerieBendt@verizon.net; ValerieBendt@gmail.com
Web site: http://www.ValerieBendt.com
Dist(s): **Follett School Solutions.**

Vallentine Mitchell Pubs. (GBR) (*978-0-85303; 978-1-910383*) *Dist. by* **Intl Spec Bk.**

Valley Publishing *See* **Karosa Publishing**

Values of America Co., (*978-0-9765868*) P.O. Box 1534, Merchantville, NJ 08109 USA Toll Free: 866-467-7304
E-mail: orders@quipman.com
Web site: http://www.quipman.com.

Values to Live By Classic Stories *Imprint of* **Thomas, Frederic Inc.**

Van der Westhuizen, Kevin Ministries International, Incorporated *See* **JMC Printing**

van der Zande, Irene, (*978-0-9796191*) P.O. Box 1212, Santa Cruz, CA 95061 USA Tel 831-426-4407 Toll Free: 800-467-6997
E-mail: safety@kidpower.org
Web site: http://www.kidpower.org
Dist(s): **Romeii LLC.**

Van Steenhouse, Andrea L. *See* **Simpler Life Pr.**

Vandalia Pr. *Imprint of* **West Virginia Univ. Pr.**

Vandam Pr., Inc., (*978-0-9702383; 978-1-937010*) P.O. Box 155, Brooklyn, NY 11230 USA Tel 212-969-0286; Fax: 212-858-5720
E-mail: publisher@vandampress.com
Web site: http://www.vandampress.com.

Vandamere Pr., (*978-0-918339*) Subs. of AB Assocs., Orders Addr.: P.O. Box 149, St. Petersburg, FL 33731 USA (SAN 657-3088) Tel 727-556-0950; Fax: 727-556-2560; Toll Free: 800-551-7776
Web site: www.vandamere.com.

V&R Editoras,
Dist(s): **Lectorum Pubns., Inc.**

Vanguard Pr., (*978-1-59315*) 425 Madison Ave., 3rd Flr., New York, NY 10017 USA Do not confuse with CDS Books in Paso Robles, CA Durham, NC
Dist(s): **Ebsco Publishing**
Perseus-PGW
Perseus Bks. Group
ebrary, Inc.

Vanguard Productions, (*978-1-887591; 978-1-934331*) 186 Center St., Suite 200, Clinton, NJ 08809 USA Tel 732-748-8895
E-mail: vanguardpub@att.net
Web site: http://vanguardproductions.net
Dist(s): **Innovative Logistics**
Watson-Guptill Pubns., Inc.

Vanir Bks., (*978-0-615-28865-9*) 351 Salem St., No. 2, Glendale, CA 91203 USA Tel 818-669-4070
Web site: http://rickandbobo.com.

Vanishing Horizons, (*978-0-9823445*) Orders Addr.: P.O. Box PO Box 2118, Pueblo, CO 81004 USA Tel 719-561-0993
E-mail: vanishinghorizons1@me.com
Web site: http://www.vanishinghorizons.com.

Vanissery, Matthew, (*978-0-9759906*) P.O. Box 1056, Guasti, CA 91743-1056 USA; 175 Mountain View Ave., Scotch Plains, NJ 07076 Tel 908-889-7930; Fax: 908-889-6281
E-mail: chemplavil@aol.com.

VanitaBooks, (*978-0-9800162; 978-0-9819714; 978-0-9826366*) 3875 Embassy Pkwy., Suite 250, Akron, OH 44333 USA
Web site: http://www.vanitabooks.com
Dist(s): **Ingram Pub. Services.**

Vanwell Publishing, Ltd. (CAN) (*978-0-920277; 978-1-55068; 978-1-55125*) *Dist. by* **Casemate Pubs.**

VAO Publishing, (*978-0-615-48066-4; 978-0-615-54442-7; 978-0-615-54756-5; 978-0-615-55670-3; 978-0-615-57119-5; 978-0-615-58097-5; 978-0-615-59535-1; 978-0-615-65178-1; 978-0-615-71107-2; 978-0-615-72376-1; 978-0-615-77825-9; 978-0-615-78183-9; 978-0-615-79117-3; 978-0-615-79424-2; 978-0-615-95618-3) Div. of Valley Artistic Outreach, 4717 N. FM 493, Donna, TX 78537 USA Tel 956-351-2384; 956-246-0353*
E-mail: publishing@valartout.org
Web site: http://www.publishing.valartout.org
Dist(s): **CreateSpace Independent Publishing Platform**
Dummy Record Do Not USE!!!!
Smashwords.

Varas, Reny, (*978-0-9726946*) 918 Cortney Dr., Carpentersville, IL 60110 USA (SAN 255-3333) Tel 847-428-7852; Fax: 847-428-7880
E-mail: lionan2@msn.com.

Variance Publishing, LLC, (*978-1-935142*) P.O. Box 612, Cabot, AR 72023-7577 USA (SAN 856-6259) Tel 501-259-6102; *Imprints:* Breakneck Books (Breakneck)
E-mail: tpaulschulte@variancepublishing.com
Web site: http://www.variancepublishing.com
Dist(s): **Bookazine Co., Inc.**
Smashwords.

Vaughanworks *Imprint of* **Vaughanworks Publishing**

Vaughanworks Publishing, (*978-0-9771160*) Div. of Vaughanworks, Orders Addr.: P.O. Box 44224, West Allis, WI 53214 USA; *Imprints:* Vaughanworks (Vaughanworks)
E-mail: vaughanworks@sbcglobal.net
Web site: http://www.vaughanworks.com.

Vaughn, Jerry T., (*978-0-9772507*) 1921 Ashford Cir., Longmout, CO 80501 USA Tel 303-776-9134
E-mail: vaughn.jc@gmail.com.

Vedanta Pr., (*978-0-87481*) Div. of Vedanta Society of Southern California, Orders Addr.: 1946 Vedanta Pl., Hollywood, CA 90068-3996 USA (SAN 202-9340) Tel 323-960-1728 (general manager); 323-960-1727 (orders and customer service); Fax: 323-465-9568 (orders)
E-mail: bob@vedanta.com; orders@vedanta.org
Web site: http://www.vedanta.com.

vegaslocal.com, (*978-0-9752804*) 4329 Talofa Ave., Toluca Lake, CA 91602-2917 USA
E-mail: info@vegaslocal.com
Web site: http://www.vegaslocal.com.

Veillette, Sally *See* **Pop the Cork Publishing**

Veiva Bks., (*978-0-615-83152-7*) 1709 W. 1375 S., Syracuse, UT 84075 USA Tel 801-661-2203
Dist(s): **CreateSpace Independent Publishing Platform.**

Velazquez de Leon, Mauricio *See* **Duo Pr. LLC**

Velesquious Studios, (*978-0-9754232*) P.O. Box 72, Blakeslee, PA 18610-0072 USA Tel 610-360-8946
E-mail: webmaster@velesquious.com
Web site: http://www.velesquious.com.

Velichko, Vera, (*978-0-9754433*) Orders Addr.: 12671 SE 169th Pl., Renton, WA 98058 USA Tel 253-237-2271; Fax: 253-444-4916; *Imprints:* Language Transformer Books (LangTransforBks)
E-mail: talkinrussian@gmail.com
Web site: http://www.lulu.com/talkinrussian1; http://www.languagetransformer.com/.

Velikanje, Kathryn *See* **Levity Pr.**

Vellum *Imprint of* **New Academia Publishing, LLC**

Velocity Pr., (*978-1-938804*) 49 Twin Lakes Rd. Suite 1000, South Salem, NY 10590 USA Tel 914-763-8333 (phone/fax)
E-mail: yesmail@aol.com
Web site: www.Velocity-Press.com
Dist(s): **National Bk. Network.**

VeloPress, (*978-0-9622630; 978-1-884737; 978-1-931382; 978-1-934030*) Div. of Inside Communications, Inc., 1830 N. 55th St., Boulder, CO 80301-2700 USA Tel 303-440-0601; Fax: 303-444-6788; Toll Free: 800-811-4210
E-mail: velopress@7dogs.com
Web site: http://www.velogear.com
Dist(s): **Ingram Pub. Services.**

Velvet Pony Pr., (*978-0-615-26652-7*) 409 Denniston St., Pittsburgh, PA 15206 USA
E-mail: Betsybinder@yahoo.com
Web site: http://www.velvetponypress.com.

Vendera Publishing, (*978-0-9749411; 978-1-936307*) 61 Big Pete Rd., Franklin Furnace, OH 45629 USA Tel 740-531-2122; *Imprints:* 711Press (SevenElev)
E-mail: admin@venderapublishing.com
Web site: http://www.venderapublishing.com.

Vengco, Aletha Fulton, (*978-0-578-00613-0; 978-0-578-00778-6; 978-0-578-00890-5; 978-0-578-02728-9*) 2224 O St., Apt. 4, Sacramento, CA 95816 USA
Dist(s): **Lulu Enterprises Inc.**

Venture Development Group, (*978-0-9748030*) 1114 Blue Lake Sq., Mountain View, CA 94040-4561 USA Tel 650-967-3403; Fax: 650-965-0320.

Venture Publishing, (*978-0-9761694*) 750 Tabor St., No. 64, Golden, CO 80401 USA Tel 303-239-6531 (phone/fax).

Venture Publishing, Inc., (*978-0-910251; 978-1-892132; 978-1-939476*) 1999 Cato Ave., State College, PA 16801 USA (SAN 240-897X) Tel 814-234-4561; Fax: 814-234-1651 Do not confuse with companies with the same name in Andover, MA, Ho-Ho-Kus, NJ
E-mail: vpublish@venturepublish.com
Web site: http://www.venturepublish.com.

Verbal Images Pr., (*978-0-9625136; 978-1-884281; 978-0-9821982*) 46 Duncott Rd., Fairport, NY 14450-3150 USA
Web site: http://www.verbalimagespress.com
Dist(s): **Gryphon Hse., Inc.**
Independent Pubs. Group.

Veritas Pr., Inc., (*978-1-930710; 978-1-932168; 978-1-936648*) 1829 William Penn Way, Lancaster, PA 17601 USA (SAN 255-9617) Tel 717-519-1974; Fax: 717-519-1978; Toll Free: 800-922-5082 Do not confuse with companies with same name in Santa Barbara CA, Santa Monica CA, Bronx NY, Clearwater Fl, Sioux Falls SD, West Hartford CT, West Allis,MI
E-mail: info@veritaspress.com
Web site: http://www.veritaspress.com.

Veritas Publishing, (*978-0-9643261; 978-0-9715007; 978-1-933297; 978-0-9765742; 978-1-933391; 978-1-933885; 978-1-938033*) Orders Addr.: P.O. Box 3516, Sedona, AZ 86340 USA (SAN 254-3613) Tel 928-282-8722; Fax: 928-282-4789; *Imprints:* Axial Publishing (Axial Pub) Do not confuse with companies with the same or similar names in Cranbrook, WA, Rockwall, TX, McMinnville, MN, Mountain View, CA, Prescott, AZ
E-mail: veritaspublish@postmark.net; info@veritaspub.com; eventcoordinator@veritaspub.com
Web site: http://www.veritaspub.com
Dist(s): **AtlasBooks Distribution**
DeVorss & Co.
Hay Hse., Inc.
New Leaf Distributing Co., Inc.
Partners Bk. Distributing, Inc.

Veritas Pubns. (IRL) (*978-1-85390; 978-0-901810; 978-0-905092; 978-0-86217; 978-1-84730*) *Dist. by* **Dufour.**

Verlag Wilhelm Heyne (DEU) (*978-3-453*) *Dist. by* **Distribks Inc.**

For full information on wholesalers and distributors, refer to the Wholesaler and Distributor Name Index

Vermont Bookworks, (*978-0-9745931*) 12 Perry Ln., Rutland, VT 05701 USA
E-mail: digbysworld@comcast.net
Web site: http://www.digbysworld.com
Dist(s): **North Country Bks., Inc.**

Vermont Council on the Arts, Incorporated *See* **Vermont Folklife Ctr.**

†Vermont Folklife Ctr., (*978-0-916718; 978-0-692-00433-3*) Orders Addr.: 88 Main St., Middlebury, VT 05753 USA (SAN 208-9092) Tel 802-388-4964; Fax: 802-388-1844
E-mail: bbjorkman@vermontfolklifecenter.org
Web site: http://www.vermontfolklifecenter.org
Dist(s): **Thistle Hill Pubns.**
Univ. Pr. of New England; *CIP.*

†Vermont Life Magazine, (*978-0-936896; 978-1-931389; 978-1-941730*) Div. of State of Vermont, Agency on Development & Community Affairs, 1 National Life Drive, 6th fl, Montpelier, VT 05620-0501 USA (SAN 215-8213) Tel 802-828-3241; Fax: 802-828-3366; Toll Free: 800-455-3399
E-mail: info@vtlife.com; products@vtlife.com; subs@vtlife.com
Web site: http://www.vermontlife.com; http://www.VermontLifeCatalog.com
Dist(s): **Hood, Alan C. & Co., Inc.**
TNT Media Group, Inc.; *CIP.*

Vernacular Pr., (*978-0-9740266*) 197 Grand St. Ste. 2W, New York, NY 10013-3859 USA (SAN 255-3945)
E-mail: hthamann@vernacularpress.com; cvecoli@vernacularpress.com
Web site: http://www.vernacularpress.com.

Verney, Jeff *See* **JRV Publishing**

Vernier Software *See* **Vernier Software & Technology**

Vernier Software & Technology, (*978-0-918731; 978-1-929075*) 13979 SW Millikan Way, Beaverton, OR 97005-2886 USA (SAN 293-1753) Tel 503-277-2299; Fax: 503-277-2440
E-mail: info@vernier.com
Web site: http://www.vernier.com.

Vernissage Pr., LLC, (*978-0-9725027*) 2200 Central Ave., Boulder, CO 80301 USA Tel 303-440-8102; Toll Free: 888-849-8697
E-mail: info@vernissagepress.com
Web site: http://www.vernissagepress.com.

Verona (Bk.) Publishing, Inc., (*978-0-9667037; 978-0-9769031*) P.O. Box 24071, Edina, MN 55426 USA
Web site: http://www.veronapublishing.com.

Versait Pr. LLC, (*978-0-9746810*) P.O. Box 644332, Vero Beach, FL 32964-4332 USA
E-mail: info@versaitpress.com
Web site: http://VersaitPress.com.

Versal Editorial Group *See* **Cambridge BrickHouse, Inc.**

Versal Technologies, Inc., (*978-0-9749460*) One Cranberry Hill, Suite 102, Lexington, MA 02421 USA.

Versary Pubns., (*978-0-9641429*) 984 Brownsville Rd., Wernersville, PA 19565 USA Tel 610-693-5920.

Verso Bks. (GBR) (*978-0-86091; 978-0-902308; 978-1-85984; 978-1-84467; 978-1-78168; 978-1-78478*) *Dist. by* **Random.**

Vertical *Imprint of* **Vertical, Inc.**

Vertical Connect Pr., (*978-0-9769087*) 120 N. Magnolia St., Summerville, SC 29483-6836 USA; *Imprints:* Grand Kidz, The (Grand Kidz)
E-mail: kate@verticalconnectpress.com
Web site: http://www.verticalconnectpress.com.

Vertical, Inc., (*978-1-932234; 978-1-934287; 978-1-935654; 978-1-939130; 978-1-941220; 978-1-942993*) 451 Park Ave. S. 7th Flr., New York, NY 10016 USA; *Imprints:* Vertical (Vrtical)
E-mail: info@vertical-inc.com
Web site: http://www.vertical-inc.com
Dist(s): **MyiLibrary**
Penguin Random Hse., LLC.
Random Hse., Inc.

Vertigo *Imprint of* **DC Comics**

Vertigo Publishing, (*978-0-9764463*) P.O. Box 2683, Dearborn, MI 48123 USA
E-mail: vertigopublish@cs.com
Web site: http://www.vertigopublishing.com.

Vescori, Laura, (*978-0-9762965*) 28 Fir Tree Dr., Bradford, CT 06405 USA.

Vesper Enterprises, Inc., (*978-0-9663730*) Orders Addr.: P.O. Box 565, Hingham, MA 02043 USA Tel 781-749-5378; Fax: 781-740-2391; Edit Addr.: 102 Central St., Hingham, MA 02043 USA.

Vessel Ministries, (*978-0-9713345; 978-0-9816463; 978-0-615-11148-3*) 1974 E. Mcandrews Rd., Medford, OR 97504-5510 USA
E-mail: vesselmin@cox.net
Dist(s): **Todd Communications.**

Vesta Bks., LLC, (*978-0-9791065*) 3624 Lone Wolf Trail, Saint Augustine, FL 32086-5316 USA.

Vesta Publishing, (*978-1-60481*) 3750 Priority Way S. Dr., Suite 114, Indianapolis, IN 46240 USA
E-mail: customerservice@vestapublishing.com
Web site: http://www.vestapublishing.com.

Vested Owl, (*978-0-9767926*) Div. of IRM, 3217 Wisconsin Ave., NW #5c, Washington, DC 20016 USA
E-mail: nino@irm360.com
Web site: http://www.vestedowl.com; http://www.kit4marketing.com.

Vesuvius Pr. Inc., (*978-0-9719921; 978-0-9796766; 978-0-9815190; 978-1-935257; 978-1-61956*) Orders Addr.: 4727 N. 12th St., Phoenix, AZ 85014 USA (SAN 255-2981) Tel 602-651-1873; Fax: 602-651-1875; *Imprints:* Tau Publishing (TauPubng)
E-mail: jeffcampbell@vesuviuspress.com
Web site: http://www.taupublishing.com; http://Amordeus.com; http://http:/WellnessandEducation.com; http://Vesuviuspressincorporated.com; http://VesuviusPress.com.

VG Publishing, (*978-0-9785900*) 51613 Sass Rd., Chesterfield, MI 48047-5935 USA (SAN 851-0482)
Web site: http://www.voyagergroupllc.com.

Via Media, Incorporated *See* **Via Media, Pr.**

Via Media, Pr., (*978-0-9646362*) 3112 James St., San Diego, CA 92106 USA Tel 619-884-6440
E-mail: via_media_press@pacbell.net.

Vibatorium LLC, (*978-0-9742495*) 419 N. Larchmont Blvd., No. 3265, Los Angeles, CA 90004 USA Tel 323-460-4441; Fax: 323-935-0225
E-mail: info@backyardwonders.com
Web site: http://www.vibatorium.com; http://www.backyardwonders.com.

Vibrante Pr., (*978-0-935301*) P.O. Box 51853, Albuquerque, NM 87181-1853 USA (SAN 696-2351)
E-mail: Lonnie@vibrante.com
Web site: http://www.vibrante.com.

Vice Press Publishing Company *See* **Ascension Education**

Vicens-Vives, Editorial, S.A. (ESP) (*978-84-316*) *Dist. by* **Lectorum Pubns.**

Vickery Bks., (*978-1-928531*) 3012 Anchor Dr., Ormond Beach, FL 32176-2304 USA
E-mail: kvv145@gte.net.

Victoria Univ. Pr. (NZL) (*978-0-86473; 978-1-77656*) *Dist. by* **IPG Chicago.**

Victor's Crown Publishing, (*978-0-9761188*) 3322 N. 900 E., Ogden, UT 84414 USA Fax: 801-782-3864
E-mail: steve@victorscrown.com
Web site: http://www.victorscrown.com.

Victory Belt Publishing, (*978-0-9777315; 978-0-9815044; 978-0-9825658; 978-1-936608; 978-1-62860*) 32245 Old Ranch Pk. Ln., Auberry, CA 93602 USA (SAN 850-0819) Tel 559-355-4188
Web site: http://www.victorybelt.com
Dist(s): **Simon & Schuster**
Simon & Schuster, Inc.
Tuttle Publishing.

Victory by Any Means Games, (*978-0-9764048; 978-1-935074*) Orders Addr.: P.O. Box 329, Lusk, WY 82225-0329 USA Tel 307-334-3190; Edit Addr.: 315 S. Iron, Lusk, WY 82225-0329 USA
E-mail: tyrel@vbamgames.com
Web site: http://www.vbamgames.com.

Victory Graphics & Media *See* **Yorkshire Publishing Group**

Victory Hse. Pr., (*978-1-935571*) 3836 Tradition Dr., Fort Collins, CO 80526 USA Tel 970-226-1078.

Victory In Grace Ministries, (*978-0-9679145; 978-0-9719262; 978-0-9858764*) 60 Quentin Rd., Lake Zurich, IL 60047 USA Tel 847-438-4494 ext 1071; Fax: 847-438-4232; Toll Free: 800-784-7223
E-mail: feedback@victoryingrace.org
Web site: http://www.victoryingrace.org.

Victory Pr., (*978-0-9753818*) P.O. Box 118, Massillon, OH 44648 USA Do not confuse with companies with the same name in Carlton OR, Chesterfield MO, Monterey CA
E-mail: rabteach2001@aol.com
Web site: http://www.ruthann.faithweb.com.

Victory Publishing Co., (*978-0-9778925*) 3797 N. Ashley Ct., Decatur, IL 62526 USA (SAN 850-4458) Do not confuse with companies with the same or similar name in Hampton, VA, Redwood City, CA, MOunt Pleasant, SC, Inglewood, CA, Banco, VA, Pama, ID, New Orleans, LA, Littleton, CO
E-mail: edmar84@aol.com.

Victory WW 2 Publishing Ltd., (*978-0-9700567*) 18140 Zane St. NW - 200, Elk River, MN 55330 USA (SAN 253-2476) Tel 763-753-5200; Fax: 763-753-2862
E-mail: victorypub@aol.com
Dist(s): **MyiLibrary**
ebrary, Inc.

Vic-Vincent Publishing, (*978-0-9646817*) Div. of Vic-Vincent Corp., Orders Addr.: 362 Gulf Breeze Pkwy., Suite 151, Gulf Breeze, FL 32561 USA (SAN 257-4039) Tel 850-476-7673; Toll Free: 800-772-3343
E-mail: inventorz@aol.com
Web site: http://www.inventorsfreehelp.com
Dist(s): **Distributors, The.**

Vida Life Publishers International *See* **Vida Pubs.**

Vida Pubs., (*978-0-8297*) 8410 NW 53rd Ter. Ste. 103, Miami, FL 33166-4510 USA Toll Free: 800-843-2548
E-mail: vidapubsales@harpercollins.com
Web site: http://www.editorialvida.com
Dist(s): **Follett School Solutions**
Zondervan.

Vidro, Kenneth *See* **Gilbert Square Bks.**

Vidya Bks., (*978-1-878099*) P.O. Box 7788, Berkeley, CA 94707-0788 USA Tel 510-527-9932.

Viet Baby, LLC, (*978-0-9776482*) Orders Addr.: P.O. Box 750074, Las Vegas, NV 89136-0074 USA Tel 702-234-5127
E-mail: an@viet-baby.com
Web site: http://www.viet-baby.com.

Vietnamese International Poetry Society, (*978-0-9746300*) Orders Addr.: P.O. Box 246958, Sacramento, CA 95824 USA; Edit Addr.: 3067 Harrison St., NW, Washington, DC 20015 USA.

Viewpoint Pr., (*978-0-943962*) Orders Addr.: P.O. Box 1090, Tehachapi, CA 93581 USA Tel 661-821-5110; Fax: 661-821-7515; Edit Addr.: 785 Tucker Rd., Apt. G400, Tehachapi, CA 93561 USA Do not confuse with companies with the same name in San Diego, CA, Portland, ME
E-mail: joie99@aol.com.

Viewpoints Research Institute, Inc., (*978-0-9743131*) 1209 Grand Central Ave., Glendale, CA 91201 USA
Web site: http://www.viewpointsresearch.org.

Vikasam, (*978-0-615-46456-5*) 23355 N. Empress Dr., Hawthorn Woods, IL 60047 USA Tel 847-815-1978
E-mail: dollysap@gmail.com.

Viking Adult *Imprint of* **Penguin Publishing Group**

Viking Juvenile *Imprint of* **Penguin Publishing Group**

Viking Juvenile *Imprint of* **Holt, Henry & Co.**

VILA Group, Inc., The, (*978-0-9635047*) V2947 S. Atlantic Ave., Apt. 1906, Daytona Beach, FL 32118-6029 USA Tel 904-767-8245.

Vilasa Pr., (*978-0-9762809; 978-1-937927*) Orders Addr.: 2835 Long Valley Rd., Santa Ynez, CA 93460 USA (SAN 256-2995) Tel 805-688-6116; Fax: 805-456-3340
E-mail: vilasapress@gmail.com
Web site: http://www.vilasapress.com; http://sandynathan.com
Dist(s): **BookBaby**
Lightning Source, Inc.
Smashwords.

Villa Serena Publishing, (*978-0-9753326*) 15657 Westbrook Rd., Livonia, MI 48154 USA
Dist(s): **AtlasBooks Distribution.**

Village Earth Pr. *Imprint of* **Harding Hse. Publishing Sebice Inc.**

Village Monkey LLC, The, (*978-0-9789633*) 7760 McWhorter Rd., Martinsville, IN 46151 USA Tel 765-352-1718
E-mail: zenmonkey@thevillagemonkey.com
Web site: http://www.thevillagemonkey.com.

Village Monkey, The *See* **Village Monkey LLC, The**

Village Museum, (*978-0-9740091*) Orders Addr.: 401 Pinckney St., McClellanville, SC 29458 USA Tel 843-887-3030; Edit Addr.: P.O. Box 595, McClellanville, SC 29458 USA Tel 843-887-3030
Web site: http://www.villagemuseum.com.

Village Publishing, (*978-0-9857741*) 2924 W.132nd Pl., Gardena, CA 90249 USA Tel 310-922-6562
E-mail: wwilson150@gmail.com.

Village Tales Publishing, (*978-0-9753609; 978-0-9853625*) 662 Lookout Point, Lawrenceville, GA 30043 USA
E-mail: publisher@villagetalespublishing.com; villagetalespublishing@yahoo.com; villagetalespub@gmail.com
Web site: http://villagetalespublishing.com; http://www.villagetalespublishing.com.

Villager Bk. Publishing, (*978-1-934643*) Orders Addr.: P.O. Box 222 W. Las Colinas Blvd, Suite 1650, Irving, TX 75039 USA (SAN 854-0969)
E-mail: semerick@villagerdustbunnies.com; jbloom@villagerdustbunnies.com; lrinn@villagerdustbunnies.com; jfox@villagerdustbunnies.com
Web site: http://villagerpublishers.com; http://www.villagerdustbunnies.com.

Villard Bks. *Imprint of* **Random House Publishing Group**

Vilnius Pr., (*978-0-615-80054-7; 978-0-615-80223-7; 978-1-940136*) 152 Ct. St. Suite 2E, Portsmouth, NH 03801 USA Tel 8552607535
Web site: http://vilnius-press.com/
Dist(s): **CreateSpace Independent Publishing Platform.**

Vincent, Thomas J. Foundation Inc., (*978-0-9759284*) 44-447 Kaneohe Bay Dr., Kaneohe, HI 96744 USA
E-mail: vincentfoundation@yahoo.com.

Vincero Enterprises, (*978-0-9675329*) 490 Marin Oaks Dr., Novato, CA 94949 USA Tel 800-715-1492; Fax: 415-883-4115; Toll Free: 800-715-1492
E-mail: heritage1492@earthlink.net
Web site: http://www.italianheritage.net; http://www.hispaniclatino.net.

Vindof Publishing, (*978-0-9759310*) 410 N. 3rd St., Ft. Atkinson, WI 53538 USA.

Vineyard Publishing, LLC *See* **Ampelon Publishing, LLC**

Vineyard Stories, (*978-0-9771384; 978-0-615-26606-0; 978-0-615-34267-2; 978-0-9827146; 978-0-9849136; 978-0-9915028; 978-0-692-40086-9*) Orders Addr.: RR 1, Box 65-B9, Edgartown, MA 02539 USA Tel 598-221-2338; Fax: 508-627-6909; Edit Addr.: 52 Bold Meadow Rd., Edgartown, MA 02539 USA
Web site: http://www.vineyardstories.com
Dist(s): **Ingram Pub. Services.**

Vinland Pr., (*978-0-9721410*) P.O. Box 927, North Bend, OR 97459 USA Tel 541-751-1566
E-mail: s_coons@charter.net.

Vinland Publishing, (*978-0-9801601; 978-0-9889455*) 661 Tamarron Dr., Grand Jct, CO 81506-4911 USA (SAN 855-3564)
E-mail: jahunsinger@vinlandpublishing.com; info@vinlandpublishing.com
Web site: http://www.vinlandpublishing.com
Dist(s): **Follett School Solutions**
MyiLibrary
ebrary, Inc.

Vinspire Publishing LLC, (*978-0-9752868; 978-0-9770107; 978-0-9785368; 978-0-9793327; 978-0-9815592; 978-0-9819896; 978-0-9834198; 978-0-9851232; 978-0-9890632; 978-0-9903042; 978-0-9964423*) P.O. Box 1165, Ladson, SC 29456 USA
Web site: http://www.vinspirepublishing.com.

Vintage *Imprint of* **Knopf Doubleday Publishing Group**

Vintage Romance Publishing, LLC *See* **Vinspire Publishing LLC**

Violet Bks., (*978-0-615-19128-7*) 306 Edgewater Dr., Anderson, SC 29626 USA
Dist(s): **Lulu Enterprises Inc.**

Violette Editions (GBR) (*978-1-900828*) *Dist. by* **Dist Art Pubs.**

VIP Ink Publishing, L.L.C., (*978-1-939670*) 140 Belle Terre Dlvd. Ste. D 211, LaPlace, LA 70068 USA Tel 985-359-2337
E-mail: info@vipinkpublishing.com
Web site: http://www.vipinkpublishing.com.

Vipassana Research Publications *See* **Pariyatti Publishing**

Viper Comics, (*978-0-9754193; 978-0-9777883; 978-0-9793680; 978-0-9802385; 978-0-9827117; 978-0-9833670*) Div. of Viper Entertainment Inc., 9400 N. MacArthur Blvd., Suite 124-215, Irving, TX 75063 USA Tel 214-638-1400; 469-682-9331; Fax: 817-741-3758
E-mail: jessie@vipercomics.com
Web site: http://www.vipercomics.com
Dist(s): **Diamond Comic Distributors, Inc.**

Virginia Museum of Natural History, (*978-0-9625801; 978-1-884549*) 21 Starling Ave., Martinsville, VA 24112-2921 USA
E-mail: dgreytak@vmnh.org.

Virginia Publishing Corp., (*978-0-9631448; 978-1-891442; 978-0-9914806*) P.O. Box 4538, Saint Louis, MO 63108 USA Tel 314-367-6612 (ext. 22); Fax: 314-367-0727 Do not confuse with Virginia Publishing Co. in Lynchburg, VA
E-mail: jfister@westendword.com
Web site: http://www.stl-books.com; http://bluebirdbookpub.com
Dist(s): **Big River Distribution**
Partners Bk. Distributing, Inc.

Virginian Pilot, (*978-0-9648308*) Div. of Landmark Communcations, Inc., 150 W. Brambleton Ave., Norfolk, VA 23501 USA Tel 757-481-4777; Fax: 757-446-2963
E-mail: linda.hollingsworth@pilotonline.com; pam.smithrodden@pilotonline.com
Dist(s): **Parnassus Bk. Distributors.**

VirTru Powers, (*978-0-9778798; 978-0-9779497*) Orders Addr.: P.O. Box 9404, Tavernier, FL 33070 USA; Edit Addr.: 10S073 Clarendon Hills Rd., Willowbrook, IL 60527 USA (SAN 850-492X) Tel 630-986-5262; Fax: 630-986-5262
E-mail: nomorewast@aol.com.

Virtual Baby Nurse LLC, (*978-0-9755180*) P.O. Box 881296, Port Saint Lucie, FL 34988-1296 USA (SAN 256-1239)
Web site: http://www.virtualbabynurse.com.

Virtual Tales *See* **BRP Publishing Group**

Virtual Word Publishing, (*978-0-9787930*) 1660 Cathedral Dr., Margate, FL 33063 USA Tel 954-971-4025; Fax: 954-971-4025
E-mail: diana@virtualwordpublishing.com
Web site: http://www.virtualwordpublishing.com.

Virtualbookworm.com Publishing, Inc., (*978-0-9703682; 978-1-58939; 978-1-60264; 978-1-62137*) P.O. Box 9949, College Station, TX 77842 USA (SAN 852-6575) Toll Free: 877-376-4955 (phone/fax)
E-mail: info@virtualbookworm.com
Web site: http://www.virtualbookworm.com.

Virtue Bks., (*978-0-9746440*) Div. of Virtue Products, Inc., 197 Woodland Pkwy., No. 104-476, San Marcos, CA 92069 USA Tel 760-471-5511; Fax: 760-471-5515; Toll Free: 800-201-5200
E-mail: kenwilcox3@cox.net; ken@virtueproducts.com
Web site: http://www.virtueproducts.com.

Viselman, Kenn Presents.., (*978-0-9722361*) P.O. Box 195, New York, NY 10113 USA (SAN 254-7783) Tel 212-929-1234
E-mail: viselmanpresents@aol.com.

Visible Ink Pr., (*978-0-7876; 978-0-8103; 978-1-57859*) Orders Addr.: 1094 Flex Dr., Jackson, TN 38301-5070 USA Toll Free Fax: 800-351-5073; Toll Free: 800-343-4499; Edit Addr.: 43311 Joy Rd., Canton, MI 48187-2075 USA (SAN 860-2271) Tel 734-667-3211; Fax: 734-667-4311
E-mail: inquiries@visibleink.com
Web site: http://www.visibleink.com
Dist(s): **Ebsco Publishing**
Follett School Solutions
Legato Pubs. Group
Mint Pubs. Group
MyiLibrary
Perseus-PGW.

Visikid Bks. *Imprint of* **GSVQ Publishing**

Vision *Imprint of* **Grand Central Publishing**

Vision Bk. Co., (*978-0-9886402*) 6919 Roswell Rd. NE Apt F, Sandy Springs, GA 30328 USA Tel 404-293-2556
E-mail: kimg@visionbookcompany.com
Web site: www.visionbookcompany.com.

Vision Chapters Publishing Co., (*978-0-9860169*) 932 Homestead Park Dr., Apex, NC 27502 USA.

Vision Forum, Inc., The, (*978-0-9665233; 978-1-929241; 978-0-9755263; 978-0-9787559; 978-1-934554*) 4719 Blanco Rd., San Antonio, TX 78212 USA Tel 210-340-5250; Fax: 210-340-8577; Toll Free: 800-440-0022
E-mail: orders@visionforum.com
Web site: http://www.visionforum.com
Dist(s): **Send The Light Distribution LLC.**

Vision Harmony Publishing, (*978-0-9748715*) 4195 Chino Hills Pkwy., #393, Chino Hills, CA 91709 USA Tel 951-505-2503; Toll Free Fax: 866-855-1476
E-mail: info@visionharmony.com
Web site: http://www.visionharmony.com.

Vision Life Pubns, (*978-0-9717065*) P.O. Box 153691, Irving, TX 75015 USA Tel 469-549-0730; Fax: 469-549-0736
E-mail: vlm@visionlife.org
Web site: http://www.visionlife.org
Dist(s): **Send The Light Distribution LLC.**

Vision Pubns., (*978-0-9746161; 978-1-933260*) P.O. Box 71532, Marietta, GA 30007-1532 USA Fax: 770-973-9446; Toll Free: 800-862-5264 Do not confuse with companies with the same name in Southfield, MI, Saint Louis, MO, Boise, ID
E-mail: visionpublications@earthlink.net; dvandewalker@earlink.net.

Vision Publishers, Incorporated *See* **Vision Pubs., LLC**

Vision Pubs., LLC, (*978-0-9717054; 978-1-932676; 978-1-63100*) Orders Addr.: P.O. Box 190, Harrisonburg, VA 22803 USA Fax: 540-437-1969; Toll Free: 877-488-0901; Edit Addr.: 755 Cantrell Ave., Suite

Publisher Name Index

C, Harrisonburg, VA 22801 USA Do not confuse with Vision Publishers, Fort Lauderdale, FL
E-mail: visionpubl@ntelos.net
Web site: www.vision-publishers.com
Dist(s): **AtlasBooks Distribution**
ebrary, Inc.

Vision Publishing, *(978-0-9651783; 978-0-9762730)* Orders Addr.: P.O. Box 11166, Carson, CA 90746-1166 USA Tel 310-537-0791; Toll Free: 800-478-7925; Edit Addr.: 20123 Harlan Ave., Carson, CA 90746 USA Tel 310-367-0641 Do not confuse with companies with the same name in Sandy, UT, Huntsville, AL, Ramona, CA, Southfield, MI, Griffen, GA, Phoenix, MD, Detroit, MI
E-mail: visionpub@rcn.com
Web site: http://www.visionpublishing.net
Dist(s): **Send The Light Distribution LLC**
Smashwords.

Vision Tree, Ltd., The, *(978-1-933334)* 216 Waterbury Cir., Lake Villa, IL 60046 USA (SAN 256-5072) Tel 847-833-2546; Fax: 847-356-3783
E-mail: jo@thevisiontree.com
Web site: http://www.thevisiontree.com.

Vision Unlimited Pr., *(978-0-9746385)* 3832 Radnor Ave., Long Beach, CA 90808 USA Tel 562-537-1397 Do not confuse with Vision Unlimited in Spartanburg, SC
E-mail: joachung@msn.com; susan@newhopegrief.org.

Vision Video, *(978-1-56364)* Orders Addr.: P.O. Box 540, Worcester, PA 19490 USA Tel 610-584-3500; Fax: 610-584-4610; Toll Free: 800-523-0226; Edit Addr.: 2030 Wentz Church Rd., Worcester, PA 19490 USA (SAN 298-7392)
E-mail: info@gatewayfilms.com; info@visionvideo.com
Web site: http://www.gatewayfilms.com
Dist(s): **BJU Pr.**
Christian Bk. Distributors
Follett Media Distribution
Follett School Solutions
Midwest Tape
Spring Arbor Distributors, Inc.
Tapeworm Video Distributor, Inc.

Vision Works Publishing *Imprint of* **Soul Vision Works Publishing**

Vision Works Publishing, *(978-0-9678529; 978-0-9728840)* P.O. Box 217, Boxford, MA 01921 USA (SAN 253-3758) Fax: 630-982-2134; Toll Free: 888-821-3135
E-mail: visionworksbooks@email.com
Web site: http://www.VisionWorksPublishing.com
Dist(s): **AtlasBooks Distribution.**

Visionary Play Pr., *(978-0-615-21946-2; 978-0-615-40324-3)* 5098 Reed Rd., Columbus, OH 43220 USA
Web site: http://www.InspiredFlying.com
Dist(s): **Lightning Source, Inc.**

VisionQuest Kids *Imprint of* **GSVQ Publishing**

VisionQuest Ministries *See* **Thriving Churches International**

Visions Given Life Publishing Co., *(978-0-9842468)* 1514 Parker Pointe Blvd., Odessa, FL 33556-4022 USA Tel 724-561-9426
E-mail: gdgregdixon@gmail.com.

Visions Of Nature, *(978-0-9656051; 978-0-9749570)* 460 E. 56th St., Suite A, Anchorage, AK 99518 USA Tel 907-561-4062
E-mail: robolson@gci.com
Web site: http://robertolson.com.

Visit to Hawaii, A, *(978-0-9772200)* 445 Kaiolu St., No. 807, Honolulu, HI 55303 USA Tel 808-921-2440
E-mail: hawaiiholm@aol.com
Dist(s): **Booklines Hawaii, Ltd.**

Visor Bks., *(978-0-9771994)* 62 W. Gaslight Pl., The Woodlands, TX 77382 USA (SAN 256-9752)
E-mail: rosszilla@sbcglobal.net
Web site: http://www.visorbooks.com
Dist(s): **AtlasBooks Distribution.**

Visor Libros (ESP) *(978-84-7522) Dist. by* **AIMS Intl.**

Vista Press Ventures, Incorporated *See* **Eaglemont Pr.**

Visual Education Productions, *(978-1-56916)* 1020 SE Loop 289, Lubbock, TX 79404 USA Tel 806-745-8820; Toll Free: 800-922-9965
E-mail: cev@cevmultimedia.com
Web site: http://www.cevmultimedia.com
Dist(s): **Follett School Solutions.**

Visual Manna, *(978-0-9677386; 978-0-9715970; 978-0-9816093)* Orders Addr.: P.O. Box 553, Salem, MO 65560 USA Tel 573-729-2100; Edit Addr.: 1403 Dent County Rd., 502A, Salem, MO 65560 USA
E-mail: visualmanna@gmail.com.

Visual Velocity, *(978-0-9884679)* 22106 Chesapeake Cir., Commerce Twp., MI 48390 USA Tel 248-345-0789
E-mail: visualvelocityllc@gmail.com.

Vital Health Publishing *Imprint of* **Square One Pubs.**

Vital Link Orange County, *(978-0-9765880)* Orders Addr.: P.O. Box 12064, Costa Mesa, CA 92627 USA Tel 949-646-2520; Fax: 949-646-2523; Edit Addr.: 1701 E. 16th St., Newport Beach, CA 92663 USA
E-mail: kathy@vitallinkoc.org
Web site: http://www.vitallinkoc.org.

Vital Links, *(978-0-9717653)* 6613 Seybold Rd., Suite E, Madison, WI 53719 USA Tel 608-270-5424; Fax: 608-278-9363; Toll Free: 866-829-6331
Web site: http://vitallinks.net.

Vives, Luis Editorial (Edelvives) (ESP) *(978-84-263) Dist. by* **Lectorum Pubns.**

Viz Comics *Imprint of* **Viz Media**

Viz Communications, Incorporated *See* **Viz Media**

Viz Media, *(978-0-929279; 978-1-56931; 978-1-59116; 978-1-4215)* Subs. of Shogakukan, Inc., 295 Bay St., San Francisco, CA 94133 USA (SAN 248-8604) Tel 415-546-7073; Fax: 415-546-7086; P.O. Box 77010, San Francisco, CA 94107 Fax: 415-546-7086; *Imprints*: Viz Comics (Viz Comics)
E-mail: scott@viz.com
Web site: http://www.viz.com
Dist(s): **AAA Anime Distribution**
Diamond Comic Distributors, Inc.
Follett School Solutions
Simon & Schuster, Inc.
Simon & Schuster Children's Publishing.

Vizione Productions Inc., *(978-0-9758863)* P.O. Box 54838, Atlanta, GA 30312 USA (SAN 256-1158) Tel 404-538-9424.

VK Publishing, Inc., *(978-0-9777171)* 464 Ridgewood Ln., Buffalo Grove, IL 60089 USA (SAN 850-0509)
E-mail: vkofman@vkpublishing.com.

Vocal Power Inc., *(978-0-934419)* 2123 N. Topanga Canyon Blvd., Topanga, CA 90290 USA (SAN 693-4471) Toll Free: 800-829-7664
E-mail: info@vocalpowerinc.com
Web site: http://www.vocalpowerinc.com
Dist(s): **Alfred Publishing Co., Inc.**

Vocalis, Ltd., *(978-0-9665743; 978-0-9709948; 978-1-932653)* 100 Avalon Cir., Waterbury, CT 06710 USA Tel 203-753-5244; Fax: 203-574-5433
E-mail: vocalis@sbcglobal.net; info@VocalisESL.com
Web site: http://www.vocalisltd.com; http://www.vocalisesl.com; http://www.vocalis.com
Dist(s): **Follett School Solutions**
ebrary, Inc.

Vogel, Robert, *(978-0-9768455)* P.O. Box 551, Chesterton, IN 46304 USA Tel 219-688-5895; Toll Free: 800-815-7685 (phone/fax) Do not confuse with Robert Vogel in South Burlington, VT
E-mail: contact@azarovmemories.com
Web site: http://www.garrythegroundhog.com.

Voice & Vision Pubns., *(978-1-888251)* 902 Fletcher Ave., Indianapolis, IN 46203 USA Tel 317-262-4030; Fax: 317-262-4029
E-mail: voicevision@apostolic.edu.

Voice Connection/Vendera Publishing, The *See* **Vendera Publishing**

Voice of Light Pubns., *(978-0-9785623)* P.O. Box 1437, Fair Oaks, CA 95628 USA (SAN 850-9905) Tel 916-965-3046
E-mail: voiceoflight@comcast.net.

Voice of Truths Publishing, *(978-0-9666777; 978-0-9742357; 978-0-9818992; 978-0-9916280)* P.O. Box 34, Donalds, SC 29638-9039 USA
E-mail: publishers@charter.net; robert@voiceoftruths.com
Web site: http://www.voiceoftruths.com.

Voigt, J. M. Incorporated *See* **MindWare Holdings, Inc.**

Volare, LLC *See* **Dividion Group, LLC, The**

†volcano pr., *(978-0-912078; 978-1-884244)* Orders Addr.: P.O. Box 270, Volcano, CA 95689 USA (SAN 220-0015) Tel 209-296-4991; Fax: 209-296-4995; Toll Free: 800-879-9636; Edit Addr.: 21496 National St., Volcano, CA 95689 USA
E-mail: info@volcanopress.com; sales@volcanopress.com; adam@volcanopress.com
Web site: http://www.volcanopress.com
Dist(s): **New Leaf Distributing Co., Inc.**
Quality Bks., Inc.; *CIP*.

Volo *Imprint of* **Hyperion Bks. for Children**

Volunteers of the Colorado Historical Society, *(978-0-9770423)* 1560 Broadway, Ste. 400, Denver, CO 80202-5133 USA
E-mail: angela.caudill@chs.state.co.us.

von Buchwald, Martin Farina, *(978-0-9777266)* 1158 5th Ave., New York, NY 10029 USA Tel 212-348-5580
E-mail: martin@farina.com.

von Klan, Laurene, *(978-0-578-00322-1)* 4532 N. Albany, Chicago, IL 60625 USA
E-mail: chicagoriver@hotmail.com
Dist(s): **Lulu Enterprises Inc.**

Vorndran, Judith Clay, *(978-0-9772439)* 6431 Antoinette Dr., Mentor, OH 44060-3431 USA
E-mail: jclayvorndran05@sbcglobal.net; jclayvorndran@aol.com
Web site: http://www.hometown.aol.com/jclayvorndran/myhomepage.

Vorpal Words, LLC, *(978-0-9881969)* 2840 W Hwy. 101, Wellsville, UT 84339 USA Tel 435-764-7052
E-mail: dcolemanbooks@gmail.com
Web site: http://www.dcolemanbooks.com.

Vortex Bks. *Imprint of* **Stone Arch Bks.**

Voss, Dawn L., *(978-0-615-15324-7; 978-0-615-15581-4)* 481 Hallman St., Berlin, WI 54923 USA
E-mail: wr1t3r@yahoo.com
Dist(s): **Lulu Enterprises Inc.**

Vox Dei *Imprint of* **Booktrope**

Voyageur Pr *Imprint of* **Quarto Publishing Group USA**

VSP Bks. *Imprint of* **Vacation Spot Publishing**

WAMY International, Inc., *(978-1-882837)* P.O. Box 8096, Falls Church, VA 22041-8096 USA Tel 703-916-0924; Fax: 703-916-0925.

WCS Corp., *(978-0-9639350)* Orders Addr.: P.O. Box 900, Lander, WY 82520 USA Tel 307-332-2881; Fax: 307-332-9332; Toll Free: 800-656-8762.

WGBH Boston Video, *(978-0-9636881; 978-1-57807; 978-1-884738; 978-1-59375)* Orders Addr.: P.O. Box 2284, South Burlington, VT 05407-2284 USA Fax: 802-864-9846; 617-300-1050; Toll Free: 800-255-9424
Web site: http://www.wgbh.org
Dist(s): **Follett School Solutions**
Midwest Tape.

W.J. Fantasy, Inc., *(978-1-56021)* 120 Long Hill Cross Rd., Shelton, CT 06484-6125 USA Toll Free Fax: 800-200-3000; Toll Free: 800-222-7529
E-mail: wjfantasy@erols.com.

WJH Publishing, *(978-0-9674864)* 1445 Ross St., Suite 5400, Dallas, TX 75202-2785 USA Tel 214-978-8520; Fax: 214-978-8526.

W M Books *See* **Sierra Raconteur Publishing**

W M C Publishing *See* **Milestone Pr., Inc.**

WP Pr., Inc., *(978-0-9633019; 978-1-884837)* 525 N. Norris Ave., Tucson, AZ 85719-5239 USA.

W Q E D Multimedia, *(978-0-9713080; 978-0-9769936; 978-0-9816697)* 4802 Fifth Ave., Pittsburgh, PA 15213 USA
Web site: http://www.wqed.org.

W Q E D Pittsburgh *See* **W Q E D Multimedia**

W S Publishing, *(978-0-9773520)* 213 Levant Way, Oceanside, CA 92057 USA (SAN 257-3180)
E-mail: elaine@elaineswann.com
Web site: http://www.elaineswann.com.

W. St. James Pr., *(978-0-9672818)* 2683 W. St. James Pkwy., Cleveland Heights, OH 44106 USA Tel 216-932-0290 (phone/fax)
E-mail: marcjaffe@aol.com.

WW West, Inc., *(978-0-9653924; 978-0-9727921; 978-0-9758960)* 20875 Sholes Rd., Bend, OR 97702 USA (SAN 299-2574) Tel 541-385-8911 (phone/fax)
E-mail: wwwest@bendbroadband.com
Web site: http://www.nationalparkspopup.com
Dist(s): **Farcountry Pr.**

W Y Publishing *See* **Bluewood Bks.**

W3 Publishing, *(978-0-9801322)* P.O. Box 1255, Suitland, MD 20752-2075 USA Tel 240-354-7077
E-mail: kellum_ent@verizon.net.

W5YI Group, Incorporated, The *See* **Master Publishing, Inc.**

Wachob, Chuck, *(978-0-578-15467-1)* 311 Rigas Ct, Americas, GA 31709 USA.

Wack, Nancy, *(978-0-615-16634-6)* 600 Fairwick Dr., saint Louis, MO 63129 USA
Dist(s): **Lulu Enterprises Inc.**

Wackophoto, *(978-0-9798532)* P.O. Box 14843, Richmond, VA 23221 USA (SAN 854-5529)
E-mail: info@coolingthesouth.com
Web site: http://www.wackophoto.com; http://www.coolingthesouth.com.

Wacky World Studios LLC, *(978-0-9742997)* 148 E. Douglas Rd., Oldsmar, FL 34677-2939 USA Tel 813-818-8277; Fax: 813-818-8396; Toll Free: 877-429-2259
E-mail: info@wackyworld.tv
Web site: http://www.wackyworld.tv.

Wade & Kayak Fishing Bks., *(978-0-9742253)* 702 Balmoral Ct., Friendswood, TX 77546 USA
E-mail: flyfisher@ev1.net
Web site: http://www.texascoastalfishingbooks.com/pages/1/index.htm.

Wade, John Pub., *(978-0-9623934; 978-1-882425)* Orders Addr.: P.O. Box 303, Phillips, ME 04966 USA Tel 207-639-2501 (phone/fax); 1413 Hwy. 17 S., PMB 154, Surfside Beach, SC 29575 Tel 843-215-1097; Edit Addr.: 193 Weld Rd., Phillips, ME 04966 USA
E-mail: wadecjs@yahoo.com
Web site: http://www.johnwadepublisher.com.

Wadhams! Pr., *(978-0-9754987)* c/o Cordelia Sand, P.O. Box 264, Essex, NY 12936 USA.

Wading River Bks., LLC., *(978-0-9791463)* P.O. Box 361, Calverton, NY 11933 USA Tel 516-527-6283
E-mail: robert@wrbooks.com
Web site: http://www.wrbooks.com.

†Wadsworth, *(978-0-15; 978-0-314; 978-0-534; 978-0-8185; 978-0-8273; 978-0-942728; 978-1-928916; 978-1-4163; 978-0-495)* Div. of CENGAGE Learning, Orders Addr.: 7625 Empire Dr., Florence, KY 41042-2978 USA (SAN 200-2663) Tel 859 525 2230; Toll Free Fax: 800-487-8488; Toll Free: 800 354 9706; 10650 Toebben Dr., Independence, KY 41051 Toll Free Fax: 800-487-8488; Toll Free: 800-354-9706; Edit Addr.: 10 Davis Dr., Belmont, CA 94002 USA Tel 650 595 2350; Fax: 606 592 9081
Web site: http://www.brookscole.com; http://www.wadsworth.com
Dist(s): **CENGAGE Learning**
Follett School Solutions
MyiLibrary; *CIP*.

Wadsworth Publishing *See* **Wadsworth**

Wagging Tails Publishing *See* **Wagging Tales Publishing**

Wagging Tales Publishing, *(978-0-9715224)* 727 Lincoln Ave., Carbondale, CO 81623 USA.

Wagner Entertainment, *(978-0-9754515)* Orders Addr.: 3640 Loadstone Dr., Sherman Oaks, CA 91403-4558 USA
Web site: http://www.wagnerentertainment.com.

WainWave Media, *(978-0-9789319)* P.O. Box 11037, Lexington, KY 40512-1037 USA (SAN 853-6953) Tel 859-294-9033; Fax: 859-233-1999
E-mail: dougwain@earthlink.net
Web site: http://www.waragainstviolence.com.

WainWave Publishing *See* **WainWave Media**

Waiting Room to Heaven *Imprint of* **Loucks-Christenson Publishing**

Wajsbort, Rochel, *(978-0-9749491)* 1431 E9, Brooklyn, NY 11230 USA Tel 718-339-5070; Fax: 718-998-1615.

Wakefield Connection, The, *(978-0-9703632)* 5201 Kingston Pike, Suite 6-302, Knoxville, TN 37919-5026 USA Tel 304-624-3901
E-mail: richard@wakefieldconnection.com; wendy@wakefieldconnection.com
Web site: http://www.wakefieldconnection.com
Dist(s): **Independent Pubs. Group.**

Wakinglion Studio, *(978-0-9767413)* P.O. Box 624, Bayfield, CO 81122 USA.

Walch Education, *(978-0-8251)* 40 Walch Dr., Portland, ME 04103 USA (SAN 669-6562) Fax: 207-828-8818; Toll Free Fax: 888-991-5755; Toll Free: 800-341-6094
E-mail: customerservice@walch.com
Web site: http://www.walch.com
Dist(s): **Follett School Solutions.**

Walch Publishing *See* **Walch Education**

Waldenhouse Pubs., Inc., *(978-0-9705214; 978-0-9761033; 978-0-9779189; 978-0-9793712; 978-0-9814996; 978-1-935186)* 100 Clegg St., Signal Mountain, TN 37377 USA (SAN 856-8111) Toll Free: 888-222-8228
E-mail: karenstone@waldenhouse.com
Web site: http://waldenhouse.com
Dist(s): **eBookIt.com.**

Waldman House Pr. *Imprint of* **TRISTAN Publishing, Inc.**

Waldman Publishing Corp., *(978-0-86611; 978-1-59060; 978-1-60340)* P.O. Box 1587, New York, NY 10028-0013 USA (SAN 219-340X)
E-mail: info@waldmanbooks.com
Web site: http://www.waldmanbooks.com/.

Waldon Pond Pr. *Imprint of* **HarperCollins Pubs.**

Waldorf Early Childhood Assn. Of North America, *(978-0-9722238; 978-0-9796232; 978-0-9816159; 978-1-936849)* 285 Hungry Hollow Rd., Chestnut Ridge, NY 10977 USA Tel 845-352-1690
E-mail: mlyons@wardolfearlychildhood.org; publications@waldorfearlychildhood.org.

Waldorf Pubns., *(978-0-9623978; 978-1-888365; 978-1-936367)* Div. of Research Institute for Waldorf Education, Orders Addr.: Publications Office 38 Main St., Chatham, NY 12037 USA Tel 303-545-9486; Edit Addr.: 575 Quail Cir., Boulder, CO 80304 USA
E-mail: ann_erwin@hotmail.com
Web site: http://www.whywaldorfworks.org; http://www.waldorfeducation.org; http://www.waldorfresearchinstitute.org
Dist(s): **SteinerBooks, Inc.**

Walford Pr., *(978-0-9787671; 978-0-615-35161-2; 978-0-9826629; 978-0-9826969)* 11693 San Vicente Blvd. Suite 393, Los Angeles, CA 90049 USA (SAN 851-4941) Tel 310-487-3552
E-mail: ericweinsteinl@walfordpress.com; sambabyhead@aol.com
Web site: http://www.walfordpress.com
Dist(s): **AtlasBooks Distribution.**

Walkabout Publishing, *(978-0-9802086; 978-0-9821799)* P.O. Box 151, Kansasville, WI 53139 USA Tel 262-878-0448
E-mail: publisher@walkaboutpublishing.com
Web site: http://www.walkaboutpublishing.com
Dist(s): **Smashwords.**

†Walker & Co., *(978-0-8027)* 175 Fifth Ave., New York, NY 10010 USA (SAN 202-5213) Tel 646-438-6056; Fax: 212-780-0115 (orders); Toll Free Fax: 800-218-9367; Toll Free: 800-289-2553 (orders); *Imprints*: Bloomsbury USA Childrens (Bloom Child)
Web site: http://www.walkerbooks.com
Dist(s): **Macmillan**
Perfection Learning Corp.
Beeler, Thomas T. Pub.; *CIP*.

Walker, Esther, *(978-0-9716071)* 80-000 Ave. 48, Suite 131, Indio, CA 92201 USA Tel 760-347-4352
E-mail: strwalkr@easyfeed.com.

Walker, Fay Alice *See* **Favortwou Publishing**

Walker, J.W. Ministries *See* **LightHouse Pr.**

Walker Large Print *Imprint of* **Cengage Gale**

Walker Publishing Company *See* **Walker & Co.**

Walking Elk Pubns., *(978-1-59648; 978-0-615-41705-9; 978-0-9881775)* 81 Portsmouth Ave. No. 5, Stratham, NH 03885 USA Tel 603-772-9300
E-mail: ajkitt@kripara.com.

Walking the Line Pubns., *(978-0-9714540; 978-0-9816247; 978-0-9846299)* 4612 S. Jordan Pkwy., South Jordan, UT 84009 USA
E-mail: kclawson@walkingthelinebooks.com
Web site: http://www.walkingthelinebooks.com.

Walking Tree, Inc., *(978-0-9749832)* P.O. Box 468, Crystal Beach, FL 34681 USA Tel 727-784-5016
E-mail: art@halstowers.com
Web site: http://www.halstowers.com; http://www.lifeblending.com.

Wall, Mary Joanne, *(978-0-9644283)* 601 Ingomar Rd., Pittsburgh, PA 15237-4983 USA Tel 412-364-2598; Fax: 412-314-0862.

Walling, Emma *See* **Emma's Pantry**

Walls Tumbling Down Publishing, *(978-0-9770098)* Manhttanville Station, 871, New York, NY 10027-9998 USA Tel 212-865-6008
E-mail: antonioj365@aol.com
Web site: http://www.hometown.aol.com.

wallymeets, *(978-0-9843648)* Div. of wallymeets ltd., Orders Addr.: Hans Memlingdreef 50, LOMMEL, 3920 BEL
Web site: http://wallymeets.com/.

Walnut Cracker Publishing, LLC, *(978-0-9800571)* Orders Addr.: P.O. Box 2707, Loveland, CO 80539 USA
E-mail: mwalker@walnutcrackerpublishing.com
Web site: http://www.walnutcrackerpublishing.com
Dist(s): **Independent Pubs. Group.**

Walnut Grove Press *See* **Freeman-Smith LLC**

Walnut Springs Bks., *(978-1-933317; 978-1-59992; 978-1-934393; 978-1-935217)* 4110 Highland Dr. Ste. 300, Salt Lake Cty, UT 84124-2676 USA
E-mail: editorial@leatherwoodpress.com
Web site: http://www.leatherwoodpress.com
Dist(s): **Brigham Distribution**
Deseret Bk. Co.
Independent Pubs. Group.

Walsh, Joseph, *(978-0-9818019)* P.O. Box 34105, Granada Hills, CA 91394 USA
Web site: http://www.gambierontheloose.com.

Walt Disney Home Video, 3333 N. Pagosa Ct., Indianapolis, IN 46226 USA Tel 317-890-3030; Fax: 818-560-1930
Web site: http://disney.go.com/DisneyVideos/
Dist(s): **Buena Vista Home Video**
Critics' Choice Video
Follett Media Distribution
Midwest Tape.

Walt Disney Records, *(978-0-7634; 978-1-55723)* Div. of Walt Disney Co., 3333 N. Pagosa Ct., Indianapolis, IN 46226 USA Tel 317-890-3030; Fax: 317-897-4614
Web site: http://disneymusic.disney.go.com/index.html
Dist(s): **Follett School Solutions**
Ingram Pub. Services
Rounder Kids Music Distribution.

Walter Foster Jr *Imprint of* **Quarto Publishing Group USA**

Water Shoe Pr., *(978-0-9759499)* P.O. Box 928, Langley, WA 98260 USA.

Walter, Wendy D., *(978-0-9857147)* 301 Hillcrest Rd., San Carlos, CA 94070 USA Tel 650-598-0178; *Imprints:* Angry Bicycle (AngryBicycle)
Web site: ambrils-tale.com.

Walterick Pubs., Inc., *(978-0-937396; 978-1-884838)* Orders Addr.: P.O. Box 2216, Kansas City, KS 66110-0216 USA (SAN 211-9366) Tel 913-334-0100; Fax: 913-334-0153; Toll Free: 800-255-4097 (US only); Edit Addr.: 6549 State Ave., Kansas City, KS 66110 USA Toll Free: 800-648-0443 (Canada only).

Walters, Jack C., *(978-0-9754658)* 2850 Airport Rd., No. 1, Carson City, NV 89706 USA Tel 775-882-0518
E-mail: waltersjc@charter.net.

Walters, Steve Ministries, *(978-0-9719767)* 3633 Corners Way, Norcross, GA 30092 USA Tel 770-409-1633; Fax: 770-300-9636; *Imprints:* Crowned Warrior Publishing (Crowned Warr)
E-mail: holyspiritinfo@stevewaltersministries.com
Web site: http://www.stevewaltersministries.com.

Wampum Bks., LLC, *(978-0-9842012)* 115a Pine St., Greenwich, CT 06830 USA (SAN 858-7116) Tel 203-531-8111
E-mail: sgalfas@itoinc.net.

Wand In Magic, *(978-0-9761921)* P.O. Box 58068, Nashville, TN 37205 USA Fax: 615-269-6820.

Wandering Sage Bookstore & More, LLC *See* **Wandering Sage Pubns., LLC**

Wandering Sage Pubns., LLC, *(978-0-9725230; 978-1-933300)* Orders Addr.: 614 Rivers Bend Estates Dr., Saint Charles, MO 63303 USA Tel 314-623-6647
E-mail: valkpub@yahoo.com
Web site: http://www.wanderingsagebooks.com
Dist(s): **Valkyrie Distribution.**

WannaBees Media LLC, *(978-0-9767670)* 118 E. 25th St., Suite LL, New York, NY 10010 USA Tel 212-253-9874
E-mail: kdonovan@nvmagazine.com
Web site: http://www.theDobees.com.

Wanniarachchige, Somiruwan, *(978-0-615-17026-8)* 20700 San Jose Hills Rd., Suite 115, Walnut, CA 91789 USA
E-mail: ruwangotu@hotmail.com
Dist(s): **Lulu Enterprises Inc.**

Waquis *See* **Black Ship Publishing**

Warbelow, Willy Lou, *(978-0-9618314)* P.O. Box 252, Tok, AK 99780 USA (SAN 667-2639) Tel 907-883-2881.

Warbranch Pr., Inc., *(978-0-9667114; 978-0-692-52275-2)* 329 Warbranch Rd., Central, SC 29630 USA Tel 864-654-6180
E-mail: kspalmer@aol.com; salley.ouellette@gmail.com; jhpalmer42@aol.com
Web site: http://www.warbranchpress.com
Dist(s): **Follett School Solutions**
Partners Bk. Distributing, Inc.

Warburton and Gorman Publishing *See* **BareBones Publishing**

Ward, Jason E., *(978-0-9662366)* P.O. Box 719, Bronx, NY 10475 USA Tel 718-379-6285
E-mail: Jason@aiyahlevene.com.

Ward, John H., *(978-0-615-21017-9; 978-0-9834038)* 6606 Deerwood Dr., Crystal Lake, IL 60012 USA.

Warehousing & Fulfillment Specialists, LLC (WFS, LLC), *(978-1-57102; 978-1-58029; 978-1-59093)* 7344 Cockrill Bend Blvd., Nashville, TN 37209-1043 USA Toll Free Fax: 800-510-3650; Toll Free: 800-327-5113; *Imprints:* Eager Minds Press (Eager Minds)
E-mail: vhill@apgbooks.com
Web site: http://www.apgbooks.com
Dist(s): **APG Sales & Distribution Services.**

Ware-Pak, Inc., Orders Addr.: 2427 Bond St., University Park, IL 60466 USA Tel 708-534-2600; Fax: 708-534-7803
E-mail: kshay@ware-pak.com
Web site: http://www.ware-pak.com.

Warne *Imprint of* **Penguin Publishing Group**

Warner Books, Incorporated *See* **Grand Central Publishing**

Warner Bros. Pubns. *Imprint of* **Alfred Publishing Co., Inc.**

Warner Brothers Records, *(978-1-880528)* Div. of Creative Enterprises, 3300 Warner Blvd., Burbank, CA 91505 USA Tel 818-953-3467; Fax: 818-953-3797.

†**Warner Pr. Pubs.,** *(978-0-87162; 978-1-59317)* Orders Addr.: P.O. Box 2499, Anderson, IN 46018-2499 USA (SAN 691-4241) Tel 765-648-2116; Fax: 765-622-9511; Toll Free: 800-848-2464; Edit Addr.: 1201 E. Fifth St., Anderson, IN 46012 USA (SAN 111-8110) Tel 765-648-2116; Fax: 765-622-9511; Toll Free: 800-741-7721 (orders only)
E-mail: jallison@warnerpress.org; rjackson@warnerpress.org
Web site: http://www.warnerpress.org; http://www.francisasburypress.org
Dist(s): **Anchor Distributors**
Lightning Source, Inc.
OverDrive, Inc.
Potter's House Book Service
SPD-Small Pr. Distribution
Send The Light Distribution LLC
Spring Arbor Distributors, Inc.; *CIP.*

Warren Machine Co., *(978-0-9729410; 978-1-934866)* 3 Taylor St., Portland, OR 04102 USA
E-mail: ari.meil@warren-machine.com
Web site: http://www.warren-machine.com
Dist(s): **Independent Pubs. Group.**

Warren Publishing, Inc., *(978-1-886057; 978-0-9853094; 978-0-9884170; 978-0-9894814; 978-0-9960506; 978-0-9908136; 978-1-943258)* 3440 Toringdon Way Suite 205, CHARLOTTE, NC 28277 USA Tel 704-992-2829 Do not confuse with companies with the same or similar name in Indianapolis, IN, Pomona, CA, Washington, DC, Loomis, CA, Roseville, CA, Chesterfield, VA
E-mail: warrenpublish@gmail.com
Web site: http://warrenpublishing.net
Dist(s): **BookBaby.**

Warrington Pubns., *(978-0-9889698; 978-0-9890974)* 11100 SE Petrovitsky Apt. A-104, Renton, WA 98055 USA Tel 425-793-9629; *Imprints:* Oceanus Books (Oceanus Bks)
E-mail: WarringtonPress@aol.com
Web site: WarringtonPublications.com.

Warrior Schl. Pr., *(978-0-9715289)* P.O. Box 768, Sonoita, AZ 85637 USA
E-mail: info@warriorschool.com
Web site: http://www.warriorschool.com.

Warwick Hse. Publishing, *(978-0-9638455; 978-1-890306; 978-0-9786369; 978-0-9790367; 978-0-9795258; 978-0-9801315; 978-0-9823004; 978-0-9842516; 978-0-9845166; 978-1-936553)* 720 Court St., Lynchburg, VA 24504 USA Tel 434-846-1200
E-mail: whp720@aol.com
Web site: http://www.warwickpublishers.com.

Warwick Publishing (CAN) *(978-1-894020; 978-1-895629; 978-1-894622) Dist. by* **Perseus Dist.**

Washington Pubs., *(978-0-9715721)* P.O. Box 12517, Tallahassee, FL 32317-2517 USA (SAN 254-2366) Do not confuse with Washington Publishers in Renton, WA
E-mail: info@washingtonpublishers.com
Web site: http://www.washingtonpublishers.com.

†**Washington State Univ. Pr.,** *(978-0-87422)* P.O. Box 645910, Pullman, WA 99164-5910 USA (SAN 206-6688) Tel 509-335-3518; Fax: 509-335-8568; Toll Free: 800-354-7360
E-mail: wsupress@wsu.edu; lawton@wsu.edu
Web site: http://wsupress.wsu.edu
Dist(s): **Ebsco Publishing**
MyiLibrary
Partners Bk. Distributing, Inc.
Todd Communications; *CIP.*

Washington University, Gallery of Art *See* **Washington Univ., Mildred Lane Kemper Art Museum**

Washington Univ., Mildred Lane Kemper Art Museum, *(978-0-936316)* Campus Box 1214, 1 Brookings Dr., Saint Louis, MO 63130 USA (SAN 214-4859) Tel 314-935-7460; Fax: 314-935-7282
E-mail: Jane_Neidhardt@wustl.edu
Web site: http://www.kemperartmuseum.wustl.edu
Dist(s): **Chicago Distribution Ctr.**
D.A.P./Distributed Art Pubs.
Univ. of Chicago Pr.

WasiWorks Studio LLC, *(978-0-9845203)* 6109 Piping Rock Rd., Madison, WI 53711 USA Tel 608-239-2526
E-mail: odalo@wasiworks.com
Web site: http://www.wasiworks.com.

Wasteland Pr., *(978-0-9715811; 978-0-9724289; 978-0-9729186; 978-0-9740725; 978-0-9742342; 978-0-9744368; 978-0-9746290; 978-0-9748230; 978-1-932852; 978-1-933265; 978-1-60047; 978-1-68111)* Orders Addr.: 18 Village Plz Pmb 177, Shelbyville, KY 40065 USA
Dist(s): **Lightning Source, Inc.**
SPD-Small Pr. Distribution.

Watch & Learn, Inc., *(978-1-893907; 978-1-940301)* 1882 Queens Way, Atlanta, GA 30341 USA Tel 404-762-7760; Fax: 770-457-2132; Toll Free: 800-416-7088
E-mail: bc@cvls.com
Web site: http://www.cvls.com
Dist(s): **Music, Bks. & Business, Inc.**

Watch Me Grow Kids, *(978-1-932555)* P.O. Box 4405, Carson, CA 90749 USA (SAN 255-5093) Fax: 310-532-4536
E-mail: panderson@watchmegrowkids.com
Web site: http://www.watchmegrowkids.com.

Watchmaker Publishing *Imprint of* **Wexford College Pr.**

Water Daughter Publishing, *(978-0-9753089)* P.O. Box 930031, Rockaway Beach, NY 11693 USA Toll Free: 888-778-2928
E-mail: info@waterdaughter.com
Web site: http://www.waterdaughter.com.

Water Forest Pr. *Imprint of* **Skyline Pubn.**

Water Lily Pr., Inc., *(978-0-9772168; 978-0-9860394)* 17214 Hillview Ln., Spring, TX 77379 USA
E-mail: hfwynn@outlook.com
Web site: waterlilypress.com.

WaterBrook Pr. *Imprint of* **Doubleday Religious Publishing Group, The**

Waterbrook Press *See* **Doubleday Religious Publishing Group, The**

Watercourse, The *See* **Project WET Foundation**

Waterfall Ridge, *(978-0-9725485)* 40497 Cty. Rd. 20, Saint Peter, MN 56082 USA.

Waterford Pr., Inc., *(978-0-9640225; 978-1-58355; 978-1-889903)* 1123 Overcash Dr., Dunedin, FL 34698 USA Tel 602-681-3333
E-mail: info@waterfordpress.com
Web site: http://www.waterfordpress.com
Dist(s): **Legato Pubs. Group**
Perseus-PGW.

Waterford Press, Limited *See* **Waterford Pr., Inc.**

Waterfront Productions, *(978-0-9759185; 978-0-692-26375-4; 978-0-692-29262-4)* Orders Addr.: P.O. Box 607085, Chicago, IL 60660 USA
E-mail: jb@johnborowski.com
Web site: http://www.strangecase.com; http://www.hhholmesthefilm.com; http://www.johnborowski.com; http://www.albertfishfilm.com; http://www.panzram.com; http://www.serialkillerculture.com.

Waterhouse Publishing, *(978-0-9764082)* 40 Sheridan Ave., Congers, NY 10920 USA Tel 646-391-6669; Toll Free Fax: 877-260-5758 Do not confuse with Waterhouse Publishing in Scottsdale, AZ
E-mail: dfighter@msn.com
Web site: http://www.devonharris.com.

Watering Can, *(978-0-9759868; 978-0-9826416)* 351 W. 19th St., New York, NY 10011 USA
E-mail: info@wateringcanpress.com
Web site: http://www.wateringcanpress.com.

Watering the Seed Productions *See* **Grace & Mercy Publishing**

Watermark Cruises, *(978-0-9754400)* P.O. Box 3350, Annapolis, MD 21403 USA
Web site: http://www.watermarkcruises.com.

WaterMark, Inc., *(978-1-882077)* 5281 Mount Juliet Farm, Crozet, VA 22932 USA (SAN 248-2010) Fax: 434-823-1187; Toll Free: 888-490-0100 Do not confuse with Watermark Assocs. in New York, NY or Watermark Pr., Inc. in Wichita, KS
E-mail: agary242@aol.com
Web site: http://www.picture-book.com; http://wmibooks.com/.

Watermark Publishing, LLC, *(978-0-9631154; 978-0-9705787; 978-0-9720932; 978-0-9742672; 978-0-9753740; 978-0-9779143; 978-0-9790647; 978-0-9796769; 978-0-9815086; 978-0-9821698; 978-0-9844212; 978-1-935690)* Orders Addr.: 1000 Bishop St., Suite 806, Honolulu, HI 96813 USA (SAN 253-7427) Tel 808-587-7766; Fax: 808-521-3461; Toll Free: 866-900-2665 (866-900-BOOK) Do not confuse with confuse with companies with the same or similar names in San Diego, CA, Beverly Hills, CA, Seattle, WA
E-mail: info@bookshawaii.net
Web site: http://www.bookshawaii.net
Dist(s): **Booklines Hawaii, Ltd.**
Islander Group.

Waterside Productions, Inc., *(978-0-9627145; 978-1-939116; 978-1-941768; 978-1-943625)* 2055 Oxford Ave., Cardiff-by-the-Sea, CA 92007-1719 USA
Dist(s): **INscribe Digital**
Midpoint Trade Bks., Inc.
Perseus Bks. Group.

Waterside Publishing, *(978-0-9766801; 978-1-933754)* 2376 Oxford Ave., Cardiff-by-the-Sea, CA 92007 USA
E-mail: admin@waterside.com
Web site: http://www.waterside.com
Dist(s): **Perseus Bks. Group**
Perseus Distribution.

Waterwood Publishing Group, *(978-0-9769044)* Orders Addr.: P.O. Box 12540, Charlotte, NC 28220 USA (SAN 257-1072) Tel 704-477-0708
Web site: http://www.waterwoodpublishing.com.

Watkins Media Limited (GBR) *(978-1-900131; 978-1-903296; 978-1-84293; 978-1-904292; 978-1-84483; 978-1-906787; 978-0-85766; 978-1-907486; 978-1-78028; 978-1-84899) Dist. by* **Peng Rand Hse.**

Watling St., Ltd. (GBR) *(978-1-904153) Dist. by* **IPG Chicago.**

Watling St., Ltd. (GBR) *(978-1-904153) Dist. by* **Trafalgar.**

Watosh Publishing, *(978-0-9611954)* P.O. Box 11231, Las Vegas, NV 89111 USA (SAN 286-1976) Tel 702-896-4108
E-mail: gecfly@aol.com
Web site: http://www.watoshpublishing.com; http://www.angietheaviator.com.

†**Watson-Guptill Pubns., Inc.,** *(978-0-8230; 978-1-60569)* Div. of Crown Publishing Grp., 575 Prospect St., Lakewood, NJ 08701 USA Tel 732-363-5679; Toll Free Fax: 877-227-6564; Edit Addr.: 1745 Broadway # 124, New York, NY 10019-4305 USA (SAN 282-5384)
E-mail: aalexander@watsonguptill.com
Web site: http://www.watsonguptill.com
Dist(s): **Follett School Solutions**
Leonard, Hal Corp.
MyiLibrary
Penguin Random Hse., LLC.
Random Hse., Inc.
ebrary, Inc.; *CIP.*

Watts, Franklin *Imprint of* **Scholastic Library Publishing**

Watts, Katherine (GBR) *(978-0-9556878) Dist. by* **LuluCom.**

Wave Publishing, *(978-0-9642359; 978-0-9722430)* Div. of Caroy, Inc., 4 Yawl St., Venice, CA 90292 USA (SAN 298-3788) Tel 310-306-0699; Fax: 310-822-4921 Do not confusw with Wave Publishing in Virginia Beach, VA.

WaveCloud Corp., *(978-1-62217)* 8055 E. Tufts Ave. Suite 250, Denver, CO 80237 USA Tel 303-904-1376; *Imprints:* Evergreen House Publishing LLC (EvergreenHse)
E-mail: Bill.VanOrsdel@WaveCloud.com; publishing.manager@wavecloud.com
Web site: www.WaveCloud.com.

Waves of Bliss, *(978-0-9821302)* 6909 VT Rt. 15, Jeffersonville, VT 05464 USA
E-mail: nasrin@nasrinsafai.com
Web site: http://www.wavesofbliss.com.

Wawa Pr. *Imprint of* **Adisoft, Inc.**

Way Out Comics, *(978-0-9742386)* P.O. Box 642218, Los Angeles, CA 90064 USA
E-mail: julieyeh@sbcglobal.net
Web site: http://www.wayoutcomics.com.

Way With Words Publishing Company *See* **W3 Publishing**

WayaMedia, *(978-0-9765700)* 391 Watson Br. Rd., Cullowhee, NC 28723 USA (SAN 256-503X) Do not confuse with PPS Publishing Inc. in Lake in the Hills, IL
Web site: http://www.wayamedia.com.

Wayfarer Pr., LLC, *(978-0-9789965)* P.O. Box 948, Union Lake, MI 48387-0948 USA Do not confuse with Wayfarer Press in Plymouth, NH
E-mail: wayfarerpress@sbcglobal.net
Web site: http://www.wayfarerbooks.com.

Wayland Historical Society, *(978-0-9762756)* Orders Addr.: P.O. Box 56, Wayland, MA 01778 USA Tel 508-358-7959; Edit Addr.: 12 Cochituate Rd., Wayland, MA 01778 USA
E-mail: jane_sciacca@comcast.net
Web site: http://j.w.d.home.comcast.net/whs.

†**Wayne State Univ. Pr.,** *(978-0-8143)* Leonard N. Simons Bldg., 4809 Woodward Ave., Detroit, MI 48201-1309 USA (SAN 202-5221) Tel 313-577-6120; Fax: 313-577-6131; Toll Free: 800-978-7323 (customer orders); *Imprints:* Great Lakes Books (Great Lks Bks); Painted Turtle (Painted Turtle)
E-mail: theresa.martinelli@wayne.edu; Kristina.Stonehill@wayne.edu
Web site: http://wsupress.wayne.edu
Dist(s): **East-West Export Bks.**
INscribe Digital
ebrary, Inc.; *CIP.*

Wayne, Steven Co., *(978-0-9713154; 978-0-9727696)* 3940 Laurel Canyon Blvd., No. 698, Studio City, CA 91604 USA Tel 323-654-9339; Fax: 323-656-7324; Toll Free: 866-446-1201; *Imprints:* SWC Editions (SWC Editions)
E-mail: wschoenfeld@stevenwaynecompany.com; schoenfeld@swceditions.com
Web site: http://www.stevenwaynecompany.com; http://www.swceditions.com.

Wayside Pubns., *(978-0-9749749)* P.O. Box 318, Goreville, IL 62939 USA (SAN 255-898X)
E-mail: belletrist.1@gmail.com.

Wayside Publishing, *(978-1-877653; 978-1-938026; 978-1-942400)* Orders Addr.: 50 Downeast Dr., Yarmouth, ME 04096 USA Toll Free: 888-302-2519
E-mail: sales@waysidepublishing.com
Web site: http://www.waysidepublishing.com.

Waywiser Pr., The (GBR) *(978-1-904130) Dist. by* **Dufour.**

WCI Pr., *(978-0-9745480)* 6161 7th Ave N., St Petersburg, FL 33710-7015 USA
E-mail: clauberfl@aol.com
Web site: http://www.SoccerDreamsBook.com.

WD/GBGM Bks. *Imprint of* **General Board of Global Ministries, The United Methodist Church**

We Do Listen *Imprint of* **Thunderbolt Publishing**

We the People *Imprint of* **Compass Point Bks.**

Wealth of Wisdom LLC, A, *(978-0-9843125; 978-1-941635)* P.O. Box 390038, Keauhou, HI 96739 USA Tel 808-896-3950
Web site: http://www.awealthofwisdom.com.

Weapons of Mass Instruction, *(978-0-9766978; 978-0-9769266)* P.O. Box 1299, Freedom, CA 95019 USA Tel 831-728-0600
Web site: http://www.bilingualnation.com.

Wear-A-Book *Imprint of* **Capstone Young Readers**

Weatherhill, Inc. *Imprint of* **Shambhala Pubns., Inc.**

Weatherstock, Inc., *(978-0-9728107)* P.O. Box 31808, Tucson, AZ 85751 USA.

Weaver *Imprint of* **Alpha Omega Pubns., Inc.**

Weaver, Jack R. Company, *(978-0-9773370)* 375 A Donald Rd., Canton, GA 30114 USA Tel 770-479-1342
E-mail: jackweaver426@tds.net.

Web of Life Children's Bks., *(978-0-9773795; 978-0-9777539; 978-0-9883302; 978-0-9883303)* P.O. Box 2726, Berkeley, CA 94702-0726 USA
E-mail: mdunphy@weboflifebooks.com
Web site: http://www.weboflifebooks.com
Dist(s): **Perseus-PGW**
Perseus Bks. Group.

Web Wise Services, Inc., *(978-0-9748237; 978-1-933404)* 305 Woodstock Rd, Eastlake, OH 44095 USA Tel 440-953-2443; Toll Free: 866-232-7032
Web site: http://www.webwiseseniors.com.

Webb, Dirk E, *(978-0-578-01867-6; 978-0-578-05527-5)* 3367 E. 150 N., Anderson, IN 46012 USA Tel 765-378-7025
E-mail: dirk.webb@comcast.net
Web site: http://lulu.com/dirkwebb
Dist(s): **Lulu Enterprises Inc.**

Webb, Jack, *(978-0-9640275; 978-0-9719906; 978-0-615-99047-7)* Div. of San Diego State Univ. Research Foundation, Orders Addr.: 7618 Stevenson, San Diego, CA 92120 USA Tel 619-723-5371
E-mail: jackwebb1@cox.net
Web site: http://www.bordervoices.com.

Webb Ministries, Inc., *(978-0-9632226)* Orders Addr.: P.O. Box 520729, Longwood, FL 32752-0729 USA Tel 407-834-5233; Fax: 407-332-6277
E-mail: Webbministries@cfl.rr.com
Dist(s): **CreateSpace Independent Publishing Platform**
Spring Arbor Distributors, Inc.

WebbWorks, *(978-0-9791076)* P.O. Box 985, Semmes, AL 36575-0985 USA (SAN 852-4629)
E-mail: duet2sisters@bellsouth.net.

WebCartoons, LLC, *(978-0-9743215)* 3727 W. Magnilia Blvd., Suite No. 141, Burbank, CA 91510 USA Tel 818-620-4256; Fax: 818-598-1842
E-mail: jerryching@earthlink.net
Web site: http://www.thegreatestkingbok.com.

WeBeANS Corp., *(978-0-9740115)* 466 S. Spruce Ave., Galloway, NJ 08205 USA Tel 609-652-5778; Fax: 877-589-3184; Toll Free Fax: 877-589-3184; Toll Free: 888-867-8838
E-mail: john@webeans.net
Web site: http://www.webeans.net.

Webster Henrietta Publishing, *(978-0-9726222)* P.O. Box 50044, Myrtle Beach, SC 29579 USA Tel 843-251-8867; Fax: 843-236-0260
E-mail: mhetzer@websterhenrietta.com
Web site: http://www.websterhenrietta.com
Dist(s): **Independent Pubs. Group.**

Webster House Publishing LLC, *(978-1-932635)* 309 Florida Hill Rd., Ridgefield, CT 06877 USA Tel 203-438-0345; Fax: 203-438-0379
E-mail: fred@websterhousepub.com
Web site: http://www.websterhousepub.com.

Wedding Solutions Publishing, Incorporated *See* **WS Publishing**

Publisher Name Index

Wedgeworth, Anthony G., *(978-0-615-20879-4; 978-0-615-25816-4; 978-0-615-26007-5; 978-0-578-00695-6; 978-0-578-03617-5; 978-0-578-04710-2; 978-0-578-05827-6; 978-0-578-06337-9)* Orders Addr.: P.O. Box 621, Monona, IA 52159-0621ed USA; Edit Addr.: 104 N. Anderson St., Monona, IA 52159-0621 USA
E-mail: anthonywedgeworth@hotmail.com; thorlk@alteredcreatures.com
Web site: http://www.anthonywedgeworth.com
Dist(s): **Lulu Enterprises Inc.**
Smashwords.

WeDream.com, *(978-0-9764351)* P.O. Box 6020, Dillon, CO 80435-6020 USA
E-mail: climbing@wedream.com
Web site: http://www.wedream.com; http://discgolfguides.com

Wee Read Publishing, *(978-0-9723122)* 2269 Ginger Hill Loop., Lincoln, CA 95648-8719 USA
E-mail: lindamarchus@yahoo.com; vmarchus@hotmail.com
Web site: http://www.weereadpublishing.com.

Weebie Publishing *See* **Susi B. Marketing, Inc.**

Weekly Reader Corp., *(978-0-8374)* Affil. of WRC Media, Orders Addr.: P.O. Box 120023, Stamford, CT 06912-0023 USA (SAN 207-060X) Tel 203-705-3569; Fax: 203-705-3483; Toll Free: 800-446-3355; 3001 Cindel Dr., Delran, NJ 08370 (SAN 207-0618); Edit Addr.: 1 Readers Digest Rd., Pleasantville, NY 10570-7000 USA
E-mail: cpekar@weeklyreader.com
Web site: http://www.weeklyreader.com.

Weekly Reader Leveled Readers *Imprint of* **Stevens, Gareth Publishing LLLP**

Weekly Reader Teacher's Pr *Imprint of* **iUniverse, Inc.**

Weeks, Kermit *See* **KWIP, Inc.**

Weem, Nadia *See* **Weems, Madia**

Weems, Madia, *(978-0-615-19289-5)* 1343 Stevens Rd. SE, Washington, DC 20020 USA Tel 202-889-5239
E-mail: thewriter1115@yahoo.com.

Weeping Willow Publishing, *(978-0-9789227)* Orders Addr.: 405 Redwater Rd., Wake Village, TX 75501 USA Tel 903-293-4433; 2416 Connecticut Ln. Ste. A, Dallas, TX 75214
E-mail: tomcgreer@gmail.com
Web site: http://www.tomcgreer.com.

Wehner, Adrienna, *(978-0-9653866)* P.O. Box 6196, San Jose, CA 95150-6196 USA
E-mail: Awehner408@hotmail.com.

Wehr Animations, *(978-0-9748093)* 3890 CloverLeaf Dr., Boulder, CO 80304 USA
Web site: http://www.wehranimations.com.

Wehrley, Susan K. & Associates, Incorporated *See* **Thomas & Kay, LLC**

Weight Loss Buddy, Inc., *(978-0-9754448)* P.O. Box 488, Tenafly, NJ 07670 USA Toll Free: 877-283-3987
Web site: http://www.weightlossbuddy.com.

Weightman, Bud, *(978-0-9821035)* PMB#103, 5315 FM 1960 W., Suite B, Houston, TX 77069 USA (SAN 857-247X) Tel 281-444-4950; Fax: 281-966-1769
E-mail: budqsi@isoconsultants.com; piggytales.press@gmail.com
Web site: http://www.piggytalespress.com.

Weigl Pubs., Inc., *(978-1-930954; 978-1-59036; 978-1-60596; 978-1-61690; 978-1-61913; 978-1-62127; 978-1-4896)* Orders Addr.: 350 5th Ave., Suite 3304, PMB 6G 59th Flr., New York, NY 10118 USA Tel 866-649-3445; Fax: 866-449-3445; 6325 Tenth St., SE, Calgary, AB T2H 2ZP Tel 403-233-7747; Fax: 403-233-7769; *Imprints*: AV2 by Weigl (AVTwo Weigl)
E-mail: editorial3@weigl.com
Web site: http://www.weigl.com
Dist(s): **Follett School Solutions**
MyiLibrary.

Weinstein Bks. *Imprint of* **Perseus Bks. Group**

Wei's Publishing Co., *(978-0-9747284)* 116 W. Donald St., South Bend, IN 46613 USA
E-mail: liuwei82@hotmail.com
Web site: http://www.weispublishing.com.

Weiser, Samuel Incorporated *See* **Red Wheel/Weiser**

Weiss, Janet Bruschetti, *(978-0-9747716)* P.O. Box 8411, Longboat Key, FL 34228 USA
E-mail: jentajean@aol.com.

Welcome Bks *Imprint of* **Rizzoli International Pubns., Inc.**

Weldon Owen, Inc., *(978-1-875137; 978-1-892374; 978-1-61628; 978-1-68188)* 1045 Sansome St. Suite 100, San Francisco, CA 94117 USA Tel 415-291-0111 Do not confuse with Weldon Owen Reference, Inc. also at the same address
E-mail: info@weldonowen.com; customer_service@weldonowen.info
Web site: http://www.weldonowen.com/
Dist(s): **Chain Sales Marketing, Inc.**
INscribe Digital
Simon & Schuster, Inc.

Weldon Pubns., Inc., *(978-0-9724175)* 432 Pennsylvania Ave., Waverly, NY 14892 USA
E-mail: weldon@cqservices.com; sales@cqservices.com
Web site: http://www.Marchintotheendlessmountains.com.

Well Fire Pubns., *(978-0-9701912; 978-0-615-11133-9; 978-0-615-11146-9)* Orders Addr.: 100 Markley St., Port Reading, NJ 07064-1897 USA Tel 732-636-2060; Fax: 732-636-2538
E-mail: sherryross@home.com
Web site: http://www.sherryross.com.

WellFire Publications *See* **Well Fire Pubns.**

Wellman, Patrick *See* **MrDuz.com**

Wellness, Incorporated *See* **OrganWise Guys Inc., The**

Wellness Institute, Incorporated *See* **Wellness Institute/Self-Help Bks., LLC**

Wellness Institute/Self-Help Bks., LLC, *(978-0-9617202; 978-1-58741)* 515 W. N. St., Pass Christian, MS 39571 USA (SAN 663-382X) Tel 228-452-0770; Fax: 228-452-0775 YES NAME CHANGE CORRECT H DAWLEY
E-mail: publisher@selfhelpbooks.com
Web site: http://www.selfhelpbooks.com.

Wellness pH, *(978-1-933559)* 757 Gue Rd., Orangeburg, SC 29115 USA (SAN 256-6753) Tel 855-327-6624
E-mail: christine@wellnessph.net
Web site: www.wellnessph.net.

Wellness Pubn., *(978-0-9701490; 978-0-9748581; 978-0-9906147)* 624 Marsat Ct., Chula Vista, CA 91911-4646 USA Toll Free: 800-755-4656; *Imprints*: Bayport Press (Bayport Pr) Do not confuse with companies with the same or similar name in Rockport, TX, Omaha, NE, Holland, MI, Ft. Lauderdale, FL, Santa Barbara, CA
E-mail: malan1208@sbcglobal.net; ted@soriano.com
Web site: http://www.drjwallach.com.

Welt, Rich & Assocs., *(978-0-9706529)* 8401 Heron Cir., Huntington Beach, CA 92646 USA Tel 866-742-4935
E-mail: richwelt@aol.com
Web site: http://richwelt.com.

Wenner Bks., *(978-1-932958)* 1290 Ave. of the Americas, 2nd Flr., New York, NY 10104 USA Tel 212-484-1696; Fax: 212-484-3433
E-mail: kate.rockland@wennermedia.com.

We-Publish.com, *(978-1-931335)* 6311 Gulf Freeway #4201, Houston, TX 77023 USA Tel 713-448-0720 phone
E-mail: admin@banmex.com
Web site: http://www.we-publish.com.

WeShine Pr. Co., *(978-0-9818113)* 12 Lake Mist Dr., Sugar Land, TX 77479 USA
Web site: http://www.weshinepress.com.

Wesleyan Publishing Hse., *(978-0-89827; 978-1-63257)* Div. of The Wesleyan Church, P.O. Box 50434, Indianapolis, IN 46250-0434 USA (SAN 162-7104) Tel 317-774-3853; Fax: 317-774-3860; Toll Free Fax: 800-788-3535; Toll Free: 800-493-7539 (orders only)
E-mail: wph@wesleyan.org; lebarons@wesleyan.org
Web site: http://www.wesleyan.org/wph.

West Coast Learning Development Center, *(978-0-615-19154-6; 978-0-615-19269-7; 978-0-578-12128-4)* P.O. Box 194, Torrance, CA 90507 USA
E-mail: westcoastlearningdevelopmentcenter@yahoo.com
Web site: http://www.westcoastlearningdevelopmentcenter.org
Dist(s): **R J Communications, LLC.**

West, Dave Corporation *See* **Aztec 5 Publishing**

West End Games *Imprint of* **Purgatory Publishing, Inc.**

West End Games, Inc., *(978-0-87431)* Subs. of Bucci Imports, R.D. 3, Box 2345, Honesdale, PA 18431 USA (SAN 687-8466) Tel 717-253-6990; Fax: 717-253-5104
E-mail: dspweg@hotmail.com
Web site: http://www.westendgames.net.

West Highland Pr., *(978-0-9721486)* P.O. Box 10040, Alexandria, VA 22310 USA
E-mail: westhighlandpress@earthlink.net
Web site: http://www.westhighlandpress.com.

West, Mary, *(978-0-578-02740-1)* 733 Avenida Tercera, Apt 109, Clermont, FL 34714 USA
E-mail: sales@hecalledianswered.com
Web site: http://www.hecalledianswered.com
Dist(s): **Lulu Enterprises Inc.**

West Virginia Univ. Pr., *(978-0-937058; 978-1-933202; 978-1-935978; 978-1-938228; 978-1-940425; 978-1-943665)* Orders Addr.: P.O. Box 6295, Morgantown, WV 26506-6295 USA (SAN 205-5163) Tel 304-293-8400; Fax: 304-293-6585; Toll Free: 866-988-7737; *Imprints*: Vandalia Press (Vandalia Pr)
E-mail: carrie.mullen@mail.wvu.edul
Web site: http://www.wvupress.com
Dist(s): **BookMobile**
Chicago Distribution Ctr.
ebrary, Inc.

West Winds Pr. *Imprint of* **Graphic Arts Ctr. Publishing Co.**

West Woods Pr., *(978-0-9776837)* 3905 Westwood Cir., Flagstaff, AZ 86001 USA (SAN 257-9375)
Web site: http://www.WestWoodsPress.com.

WestBow Pr. *Imprint of* **Scholastic, Inc.**

WestBow Pr. *Imprint of* **Author Solutions, Inc.**

WestBow Pr. *Imprint of* **Switch Pr.**

Westchester Publishing, *(978-0-9891504)* 280 Mamaroneck Ave., White Plains, NY 10605 USA Tel 914-761-1894
E-mail: dhampton@newshelves.com.

Westcliffe Pubs., *(978-0-929969; 978-0-942394; 978-1-56579)* Div. of Big Earth Publishing, Orders Addr.: 1637 Pearl St. Ste. 201, Boulder, CO 80302-5447 USA Toll Free: 800-258-5830 Do not confuse with Westcliff Publications in Newport Beach, CA
E-mail: sales@westcliffepublishers.com
Web site: http://www.westcliffepublishers.com
Dist(s): **Bks. West.**

Westcom Press *See* **Cathedrall Pr./Encycloware**

Western Images Pubns., Inc., *(978-0-9627600; 978-1-887302)* 2249 Marion St., Denver, CO 80205 USA.

Western Michigan University, New Issues Press *See* **New Issues Poetry & Prose, Western Michigan Univ.**

Western National Parks Assn., *(978-0-911408; 978-1-877856; 978-1-58369)* 12880 N. Vistoso Village Dr., Tucson, AZ 85755 USA (SAN 202-750X) Tel 520-622-1999; Fax: 520-623-9519
E-mail: abby@wnpa.org; derek@wnpa.org
Web site: http://www.wnpa.org
Dist(s): **Canyonlands Pubns.**
Rio Nuevo Pubs.
Sunbelt Pubns., Inc.

Western New York Wares, Inc., *(978-0-9620314; 978-1-879201)* Orders Addr.: P.O. Box 733, Buffalo, NY 14205 USA (SAN 248-6911) Tel 716-832-6088; Edit Addr.: 419 Parkside Ave., Buffalo, NY 14216 USA (SAN 248-692X) Tel 716-832-6088
E-mail: wnywares@gateway.net.

Western Psychological Services, *(978-0-87424)* Div. of Manson Western Corp., 12031 Wilshire Blvd., Los Angeles, CA 90025 USA (SAN 160-8002) Tel 310-478-2061; Fax: 310-478-7838; Toll Free: 800-648-8857
E-mail: weinberg@wpspublish.com
Web site: http://www.wpspublish.com.

Western Reflections Publishing Co., *(978-1-890437; 978-1-932738; 978-1-937851)* Orders Addr.: P.O. Box 1149, Lake City, CO 81235 USA Tel 970-944-0110 Toll Free: 800-993-4490
Web site: http://www.westernreflectionspub.com
Dist(s): **Bks. West**
Hinsdale County Historical Society
Lake City Downtown Improvement and Revitalization Team
Partners/West Book Distributors
Quality Bks., Inc.
Rio Nuevo Pubs.

Westigan Review Press *See* **Ephemeron Pr.**

†Westminster John Knox Pr., *(978-0-664; 978-0-8042; 978-1-61164)* Div. of Presbyterian Publishing Corp., Orders Addr.: 100 Witherspoon St., Louisville, KY 40202-1396 USA (SAN 202-9669) Tel 502-569-5052 (outside U.S. for ordering); Fax: 502-569-5113 (outside U.S. for faxed orders); Toll Free Fax: 800-541-5113 (toll-free U.S. faxed orders); Toll Free: 800-227-2872 (customer service)
E-mail: orders@wjkbooks.com
Web site: http://www.wjkbooks.com
Dist(s): **Presbyterian Publishing Corp.**; *CIP.*

Weston Priory, *(978-0-9763005)* 58 Priory Hill Rd., Weston, VT 05161-6400 USA Tel 802-824-5409; Fax: 802-824-3573
E-mail: brjohn@westonpriory.org
Web site: http://www.westonpriory.org.

Weston Woods Studios, Inc., *(978-0-7882; 978-0-89719; 978-1-55592; 978-1-56008)* Div. of Scholastic, Inc., 143 Main St., Norwalk, CT 06851 USA (SAN 630-3838) Tel 203-845-0197; Fax: 203-845-0498; Toll Free: 800-243-5020
E-mail: questions@Scholastic.com
Web site: http://www.scholastic.com/westonwoods
Dist(s): **Findaway World, LLC**
Follett School Solutions.

Westphalia Thoroughbreds, LLC, *(978-0-9754103)* 1231 Latigo Ln., Flower Mound, TX 75022 USA Tel 817-368-6981
E-mail: arazielf@yahoo.com
Web site: http://www.westphaliathoroughbreds.com.

Westrim Crafts, *(978-0-9819053)* 7855 Hayvenhurst Ave., Van Nuys, CA 91406 USA Fax: 469-362-8016
E-mail: lisa.groshek@creativityinc.com
Web site: http://www.creativityinc.com.

Westry Wingate Group, Inc., *(978-1-935323)* 2708 Wet Stone Way Unit 108, Charlotte, NC 28208-4794 USA (SAN 857-183X)
E-mail: gabriel@westrywingate.com
Web site: http://www.westrywingate.com.

Westside Bks., *(978-1-934813)* Div. of Marco Bk. Co., 60 Industrial Rd., Lodi, NJ 07644 USA (SAN 855-0166) Tel 973-458-0485; Fax: 973-458-5289; Toll Free: 800-842-4234
Web site: http://www.westside-books.com
Dist(s): **Bks. & Media, Inc.**
Marco Bk. Co.
MyiLibrary.

Westside Press *See* **Wordsmith Pr.**

Westside Studio, *(978-0-9786147)* P.O. Box 703, Trumansburg, NY 14886-0703 USA.

†Westview Pr., *(978-0-8133; 978-0-86531; 978-0-89158)* A Member of Perseus Books Group, 2465 Central Ave. Ste. 200, Boulder, CO 80301-5728 USA (SAN 219-970X) Toll Free: 800-343-4499 orders only
E-mail: westview.orders@perseusbooks.com; meegan.finnegan@perseusbooks.com
Web site: http://www.perseusbooksgroup.com; http://www.westviewpress.com
Dist(s): **MyiLibrary**
Perseus-PGW
Perseus Bks. Group
ebrary, Inc.; *CIP.*

Westview Publishing Co., Inc., *(978-0-9744322; 978-0-9748730; 978-0-9755646; 978-0-9764940; 978-0-9773179; 978-0-9776207; 978-1-933912; 978-0-9816172)* P.O. Box 210183, Nashville, TN 37221 USA
Web site: http://www.westviewpublishing.com.

Westview Publishing, Incorporated *See* **Westview Publishing Co., Inc.**

WestWind Pr. *Imprint of* **Scott, D.& F. Publishing, Inc.**

Westwood Pr., Inc., *(978-0-936159)* 116 E. 16th St., New York, NY 10003-2112 USA (SAN 696-7183) Tel 212-420-8008 Do not confuse with Westwoods Press, Darien, CT.

Wever Books *See* **Red Engine Pr.**

WeWrite LLC, *(978-1-57635; 978-1-884987)* Orders Addr.: P.O. Box 593, Ben Lomond, CA 95005 USA Tel 831-336-3382; Fax: 831-336-8592; Toll Free: 800-295-9037; Edit Addr.: 11040 Alba Rd., Ben Lomond, CA 95005-9220 USA
E-mail: info@wewrite.net
Web site: http://www.wewrite.net.

Wexford College Pr., *(978-0-9709917; 978-0-9721786; 978-0-9726596)* 401 Merito Pl., Journalism Bldg., Palm Springs, CA 92262 USA; *Imprints*: Watchmaker Publishing (Watchmaker Pub)
E-mail: books@wexfordcollegepress.com
Web site: http://www.wexfordcollegepress.com.

WGH Arts LLC, *(978-0-9776562)* P.O. Box 215, Lisbon, IA 52253-0215 USA
E-mail: bill@wgharts.com
Web site: http://www.wgharts.com.

WHA Publishing, *(978-0-9773228)* P.O. Box 20818, Wickenburg, AZ 85358 USA Tel 520-877-7860; Fax: 520-877-7869
E-mail: jerry@datssoftware.com.

Whale Tale Pr., *(978-0-9824784)* 343 Hertford Cir., Decatur, GA 30030 USA
Web site: http://www.whaletalepress.com
Dist(s): **AtlasBooks Distribution.**

Whaleback Pr, *(978-0-9785465)* P.O. Box 865, Leland, MI 49654 USA
E-mail: whalebackpress@gmail.com
Web site: http://www.petoskeystonesoup.com.

Whaleback Publishing, *(978-0-9725938)* 4 Captain's Way, Exeter, NH 03833 USA Fax: 603-772-5416; Toll Free: 800-207-2580
Web site: http://www.whalebackpublishing.com.

Whale's Jaw Publishing, *(978-0-9740778)* 11 Dennison St., Gloucester, MA 01930 USA Tel 978-281-9684
E-mail: info@whalesjaw.com; chetbrig@comcast.net
Web site: http://www.whalesjaw.com.

Whale's Library, The *See* **Mindsong Math**

What The Flux Media, Incorporated *See* **Ark Watch Holdings LLC**

Whatever Publishing, Incorporated *See* **New World Library**

Wheat State Media LLC, *(978-0-9882892)* 21606 W. 52nd St., Shawnee, KS 66226 USA Tel 816-668-8400
E-mail: bhowell@wheatstatemedia.com
Web site: http://www.wheatstatemedia.com
Dist(s): **Anchor Distributors.**

Wheatmark, *(978-1-58736; 978-1-60494; 978-1-62787)* 1760 E. River Rd. Ste 145, Tucson, AZ 85718 USA (SAN 253-1054) Tel 520-798-0888; Fax: 520-798-3394; Toll Free: 888-934-0888; *Imprints*: Hats Off Books (Hats Off Bks); Starbound Books (Starbound Bks)
E-mail: bookstore@wheatmark.com; avekony@wheatmark.com; shenrie@wheatmark.com
Web site: http://www.wheatmark.com
Dist(s): **INscribe Digital.**

Wheaton-Smith, Simon, *(978-0-9765286)* 810 W. 6th St., Silver City, NM 88061 USA
E-mail: illustratingshadows@yahoo.com
Web site: http://www.illustratingshadows.com/.

WHEEL Council, Inc., The, *(978-0-9656732; 978-0-9728889)* P.O. Box 22517, Flagstaff, AZ 86002 USA Tel 928-214-0120
E-mail: info@wheelcouncil.org
Web site: http://www.wheelcouncil.org.

Wheeler Publishing, Inc. *Imprint of* **Cengage Gale**

wheels comics, *(978-0-615-48451-8)* P.O. Box 1964, Dallas, GA 30132 USA Tel 404-590-8006
Web site: www.wheelscomics.com
Dist(s): **CreateSpace Independent Publishing Platform.**

Where? Pr., Inc., *(978-0-9719144)* Orders Addr.: P.O. Box 154, Paintsville, KY 41240 USA Tel 606-789-9423; Edit Addr.: 830 Robin Ct., Paintsville, KY 41240 USA
E-mail: wherepress@mail.com
Web site: http://www.wherepress.netfirms.com.

Where-I-Live / Foster Pr., *(978-0-9764893)* 430 91st Ave., NE, Suite 3, Everett, WA 98205 USA Tel 425-334-9317; Fax: 425-334-8155
E-mail: vern@fosterpress.com
Web site: http://www.fosterpress.com.

Whimble Designs, *(978-0-9773523)* 1540/42 Monroe Dr., NE, Atlanta, GA 30324 USA.

WhipperSnapper Bks., *(978-0-9657218)* P.O. Box 3186, Los Altos, CA 94024 USA 925-249-0709 (orders/general); Toll Free: 800-910-4482.

Whippoorwill, LLC, *(978-0-9741968)* 9601 Linden St., Overland Park, KS 66207 USA (SAN 255-6553) Tel 913-341-7104; Fax: 913-385-2453
E-mail: schase@mischomeloans.com.

Whirling Dirvish Publishing, *(978-0-9768870)* 26895 Aliso Creek Rd., Suite B591, Aliso Viejo, CA 92656 USA Tel 949-643-1865; Fax: 949-606-7180; Toll Free: 800-993-1291
E-mail: info@whirlingdirvish.com
Web site: http://www.whirlingdirvish.com/.

Whirlwhim, *(978-0-9800274)* 12930 Ventura Blvd., Studio City, CA 91604 USA
E-mail: whirlwhim@yahoo.com
Web site: http://www.blunderbrothers.com.

Whiskey Creek Pr., LLC, *(978-1-59374; 978-1-60313; 978-1-61160)* Orders Addr.: 609 Greenwich St. 6th Fl, New York, NY 10014 USA Tel 212-431-5455; Fax: 917-464-6394
E-mail: publishing@start-media.com
Web site: http://www.whiskeycreekpress.com; http://www.whiskeycreekpresstorrid.com
Dist(s): **All Romance Ebooks, LLC**
OverDrive, Inc.

Whiskey Creek Restorations, *(978-0-9625756)* Orders Addr.: P.O. Box 69, Barnesville, MN 56514-0069 USA Tel 218-354-2251; Edit Addr.: 419 Fourth Ave., NE, Barnesville, MN 56514 USA.

Whispering Pine Press, Incorporated *See* **Whispering Pine Pr. International, Inc.**

Whispering Pine Pr. International, Inc., *(978-0-9679368; 978-1-930948; 978-1-59210; 978-1-59434; 978-1-59649; 978-1-59808)* Orders Addr.: 2510 N. Pines Rd. Suite 206, Sales Rm., Spokane, WA 99206-7636 USA (SAN 253-200X) Tel 509-928-7888; Fax: 509-922-9949; Edit Addr.: 2510 N. Pines Rd. Suite 206, Sales Rm., Spokane Valley, WA 99206 USA
E-mail: whisperingpinepress@outlook.com
Web site: http://www.whisperingpinepress.com; http://www.whisperingpinepressbookstore.com.

Whispering Wind Publishing Inc., *(978-0-9721640)* Orders Addr.: 11089 Utica Ct., Westminster, CO 80031-2057 USA Tel 303-717-6442
E-mail: KaKillam@cs.com; publisher@whisperingwind.org
Web site: http://www.whisperingwind.org
Dist(s): **Quality Bks., Inc.**

Whistle Pr., The, *(978-0-9624893)* P.O. Box 1006, Petal, MS 39465-8618 USA Tel 601-544-8486 (phone/fax)
E-mail: contact@whistlepress.com
Web site: www.whistlepress.com.

Whitaker Hse., *(978-0-88368; 978-1-60374; 978-1-62911)* Div. of Whitaker Corp., 1030 Hunt Valley Cir., New Kensington, PA 15068 USA (SAN 203-2104) Tel 724-334-7000 Whitaker House/Anchor Distributors; Fax: 724-334-1200 Anchor Distributors; Toll Free Fax: 866-773-7001 Whitaker House; 800-765-1960 Anchor Distributors; Toll Free: 877-793-9800 Whitaker House; 800-444-4484 Whitaker House/Anchor Distributors
E-mail: sales@whitakerhouse.com
Web site: http://www.whitakerhouse.com/; http://www.anchordistributors.com/; http://www.amazon.com/
Dist(s): **Anchor Distributors.**

Whitaker, Thurston Information Services, LLC, *(978-0-9758940; 978-0-9892525)* P.O. Box 271743, West Hartford, CT 06127-1743 USA Tel 860-922-4719
E-mail: gwhit@twisbiz.com
Web site: http://www.thurstonwhitaker.com.

Whitcombe, Renee *See* **Budding Family Publishing**

White Cloud Pr., *(978-1-883991; 978-0-9745245; 978-0-9793840; 978-1-935952; 978-1-940468)* Orders Addr.: P.O. Box 3400, Ashland, OR 97520 USA; Edit Addr.: 300 E. Hersey St., #11, Ashland, OR 97520-6200 USA Fax: 541-482-7708; Toll Free: 800-380-8286; *Imprints:* Riverwood Books (RiverwoodBks) Do not confuse with White Cloud Pr. in Hobbs, NM
Web site: http://www.whitecloudpress.com
Dist(s): **MyiLibrary**
Perseus-PGW
Perseus Bks. Group.

White Dog Studio, *(978-0-9667286; 978-0-9897882)* Orders Addr.: P.O. Box 189, Louisville, TN 37777 USA Tel 865-776-9886; Edit Addr.: 3825 Island Path, Louisville, TN 37777 USA
E-mail: jprince1@mac.com
Web site: http://www.newcooksinamerica.com; www.missjanetsglutenfreeamerica.

White Eagle Publishing Trust (GBR) *(978-0-85487) Dist. by* **DeVorss.**

White Feather Press, LLC, *(978-0-9766083; 978-0-9822487; 978-0-9831751; 978-1-61808)* 579 119th Ave, Martin, MI 49070 USA
E-mail: skip@whitefeatherpress.com
Web site: http://www.whitefeatherpress.com
Dist(s): **AtlasBooks Distribution**
Smashwords.

White Feather Publishing, *(978-0-9740413)* 5595 White Feather Way, Placerville, CA 95667 USA
E-mail: whitefeather@directcom.net.

White Hat Communications, *(978-0-9653653; 978-1-929109; 978-0-615-62872-1)* Orders Addr.: P.O. Box 5390, Harrisburg, PA 17110-0390 USA Tel 717-238-3787; Fax: 717-238-2090; Edit Addr.: 2793 Old Post Rd., Suite 13, Harrisburg, PA 17110 USA
E-mail: Linda.grobman@paonline.com; lindagrobman@gmail.com
Web site: http://www.whitehatcommunications.com; http://www.socialworker.com
Dist(s): **CreateSpace Independent Publishing Platform**
Smashwords.

White Heat Ltd., *(978-0-9740149; 978-0-9799108)* 901 N. Mcdonald St. Ste. 503, Mckinney, TX 75069-2166 USA
E-mail: info@whiteheatltd.com
Web site: http://www.whiteheatltd.com.

White Horse Bks., *(978-0-9744860; 978-0-9801406)* 1347 Glenmare St., Salt Lake City, UT 84105-2707 USA
Web site: http://www.whitehorsebooks.net.

White Hse. Historical Assn., *(978-0-912308; 978-1-931917)* 740 Jackson Pl., NW, Washington, DC 20503 USA (SAN 226-8108) Tel 202-737-8292; Fax: 202-789-0440
Web site: http://whitehousehistory.org
Dist(s): **Ingram Pub. Services.**

White, Howard Ray, *(978-0-9746875; 978-0-9837192)* Orders Addr.: 6012 Lancelot Dr., Charlotte, NC 28270 USA Tel 704-846-4411 Ask for Howard
E-mail: howardraywhite@gmail.com
Web site: http://www.southernhistorians.org; http://www.amazon.com.

White, James C., *(978-0-9747752)* 7020 E. 28th Ter., Kansas City, MO 64129-1209 USA Do not confuse with James C. White in Ruston, LA
E-mail: jcwhite08@yahoo.com
Web site: http://www.jcwhite08.com.

White Kiser, Dolores, *(978-0-9766648)* 212 Quail Creek Rd., Durant, OK 74701-7543 USA
E-mail: wobblywh@yahoo.com.

White Knight Printing and Publishing, *(978-0-9725916)* 187 E. 670 S., Kamas, UT 84036 USA (SAN 853-3539) Tel 801-955-4504; Fax: 801-955-5324
E-mail: johnmsimmons@whiteknightpublish.com; brigdist@sisna.com; careenlancaster@whiteknightpublish.com
Web site: http://www.brighamdistributing.com; http://www.whiteknightpublish.com
Dist(s): **Brigham Distribution.**

White Line Productions Inc., *(978-0-9729965)* P.O. Box 248411, Coral Gables, FL 33124 USA Tel 305-663-3235
E-mail: lcoll@bewaretheunknown.com
Web site: http://www.bewaretheunknown.com.

White Lion Pr., *(978-0-9615707; 978-1-886942)* 225 E. Fifth St., No. 4D, New York, NY 10003 USA (SAN 695-7919) Tel 212-982-5518; Toll Free: 800-243-9642
Dist(s): **New Leaf Distributing Co., Inc.**

White Mane Kids *Imprint of* **White Mane Publishing Co., Inc.**

White Mane Publishing Co., Inc., *(978-0-942597; 978-1-57249)* Orders Addr.: P.O. Box 708, Shippensburg, PA 17257 USA (SAN 667-1926) Tel 717-532-2237; Fax: 717-532-6110; Toll Free: 888-948-6263; *Imprints:* White Mane Kids (WM Kids)
E-mail: marketing@whitemane.com
Web site: http://www.whitemane.com.

White Oak Creative, *(978-0-9763562)* 26415 W. Stonebriar Way, Channahon, IL 60410-8740 USA Tel 815-922-2890; Fax: 815-521-0042 Do not confuse with White Oak Publishing in Reed Springs, MO; Galena, MO; Sewickley, PA; Portland, OR
E-mail: kashmir37@aol.com.

White Owl Manuscripts, *(978-0-615-77659-0)* 100 State Rte. 39, New Fairfield, CT 06812 USA Tel 203-746-0709
Web site: http://www.thedeliverersseries.com
Dist(s): **CreateSpace Independent Publishing Platform.**

White Owl Publishing, *(978-1-891691)* P.O. Box 1180, Redding, CA 96001 USA Tel 530-241-1921 Do not confuse with White Owl Publishing, Wellington, KS,
E-mail: editor@whiteowlweb.com
Web site: http://whiteowlweb.com
Dist(s): **Smashwords.**

White Pelican Pr., *(978-0-9625544)* 1805 Cedar Ridge Dr., Austin, TX 78741 USA Tel 512-477-5211 Do not confuse with companies with the same name in Windsor, CO, Sharpsburg, GA.

White Rhino Pr., *(978-0-9704122)* Div. of The Patnaude Corp., Orders Addr.: 6068 Windsor Farm Rd., Summerfield, NC 273589053 USA Tel 336-253-8987; Fax: 336-644-7849
E-mail: joy@patnaude.com.

White Rhino Publishing *See* **White Rhino Pr.**

White, Russ, *(978-0-9742885)* 122 E. Oak Hill Dr., Florence, AL 35633 USA.

White Stag Pr., *(978-0-9792583; 978-0-9828216)* Div. of Publishers Design Group, Inc., P.O. Box 37, Roseville, CA 95678 USA (SAN 852-9353) Tel 916-784-0500; Fax: 916-773-7421; Toll Free: 800-587-6666
E-mail: orders@publishersdesign.com
Web site: http://www.publishersdesign.com.

White Star (ITA) *(978-88-8095; 978-88-544; 978-88-7844; 978-88-540) Dist. by* **Random.**

White Star *Imprint of* **Rizzoli International Pubns., Inc.**

White Star (ITA) *(978-88-8095; 978-88-544; 978-88-7844; 978-88-540) Dist. by* **Sterling.**

White Stone Bks., *(978-1-59379)* P.O. Box 35035, Tulsa, OK 74153 USA Toll Free: 866-253-8622 Do not confuse with White Stone Books in Atlanta, MI
E-mail: amandap@whitestonebooks.com
Web site: http://www.whitestonebooks.com
Dist(s): **Distributors, The**
Harrison House Pubs.

White Stone Publications *See* **Fair Havens Pubns.**

White, T. *See* **twhiteart**

White, Terry, *(978-0-9755835)* P.O. Box 760399, Southfield, MI 48076-0399 USA.

White Tiger Pr. *Imprint of* **Homes for the Homeless Institute, Inc.**

White Tulip Publishing, *(978-0-9746890)* Orders Addr.: P.O. Box 645, Brewster, NY 10509 USA Tel 917-514-7701
E-mail: wtime2write@aol.com
Web site: http://www.whitetulippublishing.com
Dist(s): **Quality Bks., Inc.**

White Turtle Bks., *(978-1-933482)* P.O. Box 2113, North Mankato, MN 56003 USA Tel 605-770-5385
E-mail: info@whiteturtlebooks.com.

White Willow Bks., *(978-0-615-69534-1; 978-0-615-85810-4; 978-0-615-88498-1)* 1323 Kermit Dr., Nashville, TN 37217 USA Tel 615-589-9117
Web site: www.gregoryleewhite.com
Dist(s): **CreateSpace Independent Publishing Platform.**

White Wolf Publishing, Inc., *(978-0-9627790; 978-1-56504; 978-1-58846)* 2075 W. Park Place Blvd. Ste. G, Stone Mtn, GA 30087-3542 USA (SAN 299-1349) Toll Free: 800-454-9653 Do not confuse with White Wolf Publishing, Cresson, TX
E-mail: dianez@white-wolf.com
Web site: http://www.white-wolf.com
Dist(s): **PSI (Publisher Services, Inc.).**

White Wolf Studio, Inc., *(978-0-9760654)* P.O. Box 490, Windermere, FL 34786 USA Tel 407-909-0889; Fax: 407-876-8462
E-mail: whitewolfstudio@aol.com
Web site: http://www.whitewolfstudio.com.

White-Boucke Publishing, *(978-0-9625006; 978-1-888580)* Orders Addr.: P.O. Box 1463, Oakhurst, CA 93644 USA Tel 559-641-5444
E-mail: orders@white-boucke.com
Web site: http://www.white-boucke.com.

Whitecap Bks., Ltd. (CAN) *(978-0-920620; 978-0-921061; 978-0-921396; 978-1-55110; 978-1-895099; 978-1-55285; 978-1-77050) Dist. by* **Midpt Trade.**

Whitecap Bks., Ltd. (CAN) *(978-0-920620; 978-0-921061; 978-0-921396; 978-1-55110; 978-1-895099; 978-1-55285; 978-1-77050) Dist. by* **Wizard Works.**

Whitecaps Media, *(978-0-9758577; 978-0-9826353; 978-0-9836825; 978-0-9883628; 978-1-942732)* P.O. Box 680568, Houston, TX 77268-0568 USA
Web site: http://www.whitecapsmedia.com
Dist(s): **Partners Bk. Distributing, Inc.**

Whitedove Pr., *(978-0-9714908; 978-0-615-11118-6; 978-0-615-11600-6)* Orders Addr.: 401 Thornton Rd, Lithia Springs, GA 30112 USA Tel 800-326-2665; Edit Addr.: 2728 Davie Blvd. 226, Fort Lauderdale, FL 33312 USA Tel 954-981-2828; 954-981-2828; 2728 Davie Blvd No. 226, fort Lauderdale, FL 33312 Tel 954-981-2828
E-mail: mail@michellewhitedove.com
Web site: http://www.michellewhitedove.com
Dist(s): **New Leaf Distributing Co., Inc.**

Whitegate Bks., *(978-0-9767570)* The Appletree, 903 26 Rd., Grand Junction, CO 81506 USA
E-mail: lyn@appletreedesigns.com
Web site: http://www.appletreedesigns.com.

Whitehead, Judith, *(978-0-615-23987-3)* 5686 Fieldbrook Dr., East Amherst, NY 14051 USA Tel 716-238-5547
E-mail: juju8451@yahoo.com
Web site: http://myspace.com.

Whitehouse Publishing, *(978-0-9644171)* 6556 Mckenna Way, Alexandria, VA 22315-5571 USA Do not confuse with Whithouse Publishing in Corning, NY
E-mail: erw192@hotmail.com
Web site: http://users.starpower.net/whitee/bookcover/treasure.html.

Whitehouse Publishing, *(978-1-933031)* P.O. Box 16, Corning, NY 14830 USA Toll Free: 800-784-0537 Do not confuse with Whitehouse Publishing in Alexandria, VA
E-mail: elizabeth@whitehouse-publishing.com
Web site: http://www.whitehouse-publishing.com.

WhiteWalls, Inc., *(978-0-945323)* Orders Addr.: P.O. Box 8204, Chicago, IL 60647 USA (SAN 246-9952); Edit Addr.: 2845 W. Altgeld, Chicago, IL 60647 USA (SAN 246-9960)
E-mail: aeelms@aol.com
Web site: http://www.whitewalls.org
Dist(s): **Chicago Distribution Ctr.**
SPD-Small Pr. Distribution.

Whitis, Cindy, *(978-0-615-17079-4)* 9018 Imperial Dr., Indianapolis, IN 46239 USA
E-mail: jim.whitis@sbcglobal.net.

Whitline Ink, Inc., *(978-1-930154)* Orders Addr.: P.O. Box 668, Boonville, NC 27011 USA Tel 336-367-6914; Fax: 336-367-6913; Edit Addr.: Hwy. 601 S., Boonville, NC 27011 USA
E-mail: whitlineink@yadtel.net
Dist(s): **Parnassus Bk. Distributors.**

†**Whitman, Albert & Co.,** *(978-0-8075)* 250 S. Northwest Hwy. # 320, Park Ridge, IL 60068-4237 USA (SAN 201-2049) Toll Free: 800-255-7675
E-mail: mail@awhitmanco.com
Web site: http://www.albertwhitman.com
Dist(s): **Follett School Solutions**
MyiLibrary
Open Road Integrated Media, LLC
Perfection Learning Corp.; *CIP.*

Whitman Publishing LLC, *(978-0-937458; 978-1-930849; 978-0-7948)* Div. of Anderson Press Inc., Orders Addr.: 4001 Helton Dr., Florence, AL 35030 USA Tel 256-246-1166; Toll Free: 800-528-3992; Edit Addr.: 3101 Clairmont Rd., NE, Suite C, Atlanta, GA 30329 USA (SAN 253-522X) Tel 404-214-4300; Fax: 404-214-4391; Toll Free: 800-528-3992
E-mail: info@whitmanbooks.com
Web site: http://www.whitmanbooks.com.

†**Whitmore Publishing Co.,** *(978-0-87426)* 1144 Riverview Ln., West Conshohocken, PA 19428-2964 USA (SAN 203-2112)
E-mail: production@whitmorepublishing.com; *CIP.*

Whittet Bks., Ltd. (GBR) *(978-0-905483; 978-1-873580) Dist. by* **Diamond Farm Bk.**

Who Am I Pr., *(978-0-9774174)* 4444 Hazeltine Ave., No. 229, Sherman Oaks, CA 91423 USA Tel 818-501-5908
E-mail: lea@godwhoami.com
Web site: http://www.godwhoami.com.

Whole Heart Ministries, *(978-1-888692)* Orders Addr.: P.O. Box 3445, Monument, CO 80132-8506 USA; *Imprints:* Whole Heart Press (WholeHeart)
E-mail: whm@wholeheart.org; admin@wholeheart.org
Web site: http://www.wholeheart.org/
Dist(s): **BookBaby.**

Whole Heart Pr. *Imprint of* **Whole Heart Ministries**

Whole Spirit Pr., *(978-1-892857)* 1905 S. Clarkson St., Denver, CO 80210 USA Tel 303-979-5820; 303-246-9554; Fax: 303-979-6151; Toll Free: 877-488-3774
E-mail: sales@wholespiritpress.com
Web site: http://www.wholespiritpress.com.

Whole Systems Support *See* **WiseWoman Pr.**

Wholemovement Pubns., *(978-0-9766773)* Orders Addr.: 4606 N. Elston No. 3, Chicago, IL 60630 USA Tel 773-794-9764
E-mail: bradhs@interaccess.com
Web site: http://www.wholemovement.com.

Wholesome Puppy Tales, *(978-0-9762466)* 13432 San Pasqual Rd., Escondido, CA 92025-7834 USA
E-mail: cmodicagraphics@aol.com
Web site: http://www.wholesomepuppytales.com.

Whorl Bks., *(978-0-9778850; 978-0-615-70205-6; 978-0-615-71111-9; 978-0-615-72898-8; 978-0-615-99191-7; 978-0-692-21281-3; 978-0-692-30046-6; 978-0-692-37390-3; 978-0-692-47723-6)* 5658 NW Pioneer Cir., Norman, OK 73072 USA (SAN 850-5713); *Imprints:* Dark Passages (Dark Passages); WhorlBooks Thumbprints (WhorlBks)
E-mail: whorlbooks@gmail.com; marilynahudson@yahoo.com
Web site: http://www.freewebs.com/whorlbooks/
Dist(s): **CreateSpace Independent Publishing Platform.**

WhorlBooks Thumbprints *Imprint of* **Whorl Bks.**

Who's There, Inc., *(978-1-60106)* 1633 Electric Ave., Venice, CA 90291 USA Tel 310-396-4132; Fax: 310-396-4385
E-mail: info@knockknock.biz
Web site: http://www.knockknock.biz.

Who's Who in Sports *Imprint of* **Guidry Assocs., Inc.**

Why Mom Deserves a Diamond, Incorporated *See* **Moon Over Mountains Publishing (M.O.M.)**

Why Not Bks., *(978-0-9849919; 978-0-9962422)* 831 Spruce Ave., Pacific Grove, CA 93950 USA Tel 831-238-1849
E-mail: info@whynotbooks.com; amyherzog@sbcglobal.net
Web site: http://www.bradherzog.com; http://www.whynotbooks.com
Dist(s): **Partners Pubs. Group, Inc.**

Wickenburg Healthcare Alliance *See* **WHA Publishing**

Wicker Pk. Pr., Ltd., *(978-0-9789676; 978-1-936679)* 440 DeKalb Ave No. B, Sycamore, IL 60178 USA Tel 773-391-1199; Toll Free: 877-751-5033 (orders)
E-mail: eric@3ibooks.com
Web site: http://www.wickerparkpress.us.

Wicks, Valerie, *(978-0-615-71556-8; 978-0-9912594)* 831 1/2 Silver Lake Blvd., Los Angeles, CA 90026 USA Tel 678 3613895
Web site: www.sevenspectral.com
Dist(s): **CreateSpace Independent Publishing Platform.**

Wide World Publishing/Tetra, *(978-0-933174; 978-1-884550)* Orders Addr.: P.O. Box 476, San Carlos, CA 94070 USA (SAN 211-1462) Tel 650-593-2839; Fax: 650-595-0802
E-mail: wwpbl@aol.com
Web site: http://www.wideworldpublishing.com
Dist(s): **Booklines Hawaii, Ltd.**
Islander Group
Perseus-PGW
Perseus Bks. Group.

WideThinker Bks., *(978-0-9728195)* P.O. Box 30144, Philadelphia, PA 19146 USA Tel 215-985-0322; Toll Free: 866-236-1077
E-mail: wtb@widethinker.com
Web site: http://www.widethinkerbooks.com.

WiDo Publishing, *(978-0-9796070; 978-0-9830238; 978-1-937178)* Orders Addr.: P.O. Box 22675, Salt Lake City, UT 84122 USA (SAN 853-8786) Tel 801-280-5317; Fax: 801-280-0594
E-mail: information@widopublishing.com
Web site: http://www.widopublishing.com.

Wiggles, Piggy, *(978-1-939076)* 150 Ocean Pk. Blvd. Ste 418, Santa Monica, CA 90405 USA Tel 310-666-0069
E-mail: emma@emmalouisebooks.com.

Wiggles Pr., *(978-0-9823906; 978-1-935706)* Orders Addr.: 23 Athens St. Suite 2, Cambridge, MA 02138 USA Tel 617-895-7698; 617-981-0285
E-mail: rochelle.thorpe@yahoo.com.

Wighita Pr., *(978-0-9786648)* P.O. Box 30399, Little Rock, AR 72260-0399 USA
E-mail: info@wighitapress.com
Web site: www.wighitapress.com.

Wigu Publishing *Imprint of* **Wigu Publishing**

Wigu Publishing, *(978-1-939973)* P.O. Box 1800, Sun Valley, ID 83353 USA Tel 208-928-6287; *Imprints:* Wigu Publishing (WiguPubng)
E-mail: beressler@wigupublishing.com
Web site: www.wigupublishing.com; www.whenigrowupbooks.com.

Wigwam Publishing, *(978-0-9721022)* Orders Addr.: P.O. Box 574, Weyauwega, WI 54983 USA; Edit Addr.: 410 S. Harlon St., No. 2, Weyauwega, WI 54983 USA Do not confuse with companies with the same or similar names in Villa Park, IL, Cheyenne, WY.

WigWam Publishing Co., *(978-1-930076)* Orders Addr.: P.O. Box 6992, Villa Park, IL 60181 USA; *Imprints:* New Leaf Books (New Leaf Books); Agrippina Press (Agrippina Pr) Do not confuse with companies with the same or similar names in Weyauwega, WI, Cheyenne, WY
E-mail: info@newleafbooks.net
Web site: http://www.newleafbooks.net.

Wilander Publishing Co., *(978-0-9628335)* Orders Addr.: P.O. Box 56121, Portland, OR 97238 USA.

Wild About Learning, Inc., *(978-0-9789880)* 964 John St., Joliet, IL 60435 USA Tel 815-740-1173; Fax: 815-740-1174
E-mail: info@wildaboutlearning.org
Web site: http://wildaboutlearning.org.

Wild Animal Publishing, *(978-0-9769555)* 246 Meridian St., Westerly, RI 02891 USA
E-mail: sciarrajb@aol.com; keith@wildanimalpublishing.com
Web site: http://www.wildanimalpublishing.com.

Wild Child Publishing, *(978-0-9771314; 978-1-934069; 978-1-935013; 978-1-936222; 978-1-61798)* P.O. Box 4897, Culver City, CA 90231 USA
E-mail: mgbaun@wildchildpublishing.com; mbaun@freyasbower.com
Web site: http://www.wildchildpublishing.com; http://www.freyasbower.com
Dist(s): **All Romance Ebooks, LLC.**

Wild Flower USA, *(978-0-9646698)* 26614 Oak Ridge Dr., Suite 110, The Woodlands, TX 77380 USA Tel 281-363-2360; Fax: 281-367-4480.

Wild Goose Publishing, *(978-0-9792657; 978-0-9799255)* Orders Addr.: P.O. Box 386, Charlotte, MI 48813 USA
E-mail: wildgoosepub@sbcglobal.net.

Wild Hare Publishing, *(978-0-9772096)* P.O. Box 2144, Ridgeland, MS 39158-2144 USA (SAN 256-9639) Tel 601-853-8120; Fax: 601-853-8121
E-mail: dgibbes@wildharepublishing.com.

Wild Heart Ranch, Inc., *(978-0-9761768)* 1385 Gulf Rd., Suite 102, Point Roberts, WA 98281 USA Toll Free Fax: 866-735-3518; Toll Free: 888-889-9215
E-mail: dawn@wildheartranch.com
Web site: http://www.wildheartranch.com; http://www.iseahorses.com.

Wild Horses Publishing Co., *(978-0-937148; 978-0-9601088)* Orders Addr.: P.O. Box 1373, Los Altos, CA 94022 USA (SAN 211-8289)
E-mail: pwalatka@earthlink.net
Dist(s): **TNT Media Group, Inc.**

Publisher Name Index

Wild Mind Creations, *(978-0-615-15138-0)* P.O. Box 1935, Fairview, OR 97024-1806 USA
E-mail: jmm1965mionda_4@msn.com.

Wild Plum Woods Bks., *(978-0-9745581)* 39042 Ruann Ct., Zephyrhills, FL 33540 USA.

Wild Rose *Imprint of* **Mayhaven Publishing, Inc.**

Wild Rose Pr., Inc., The, *(978-1-60154; 978-1-61217; 978-1-62830; 978-1-5092)* P.O. Box 708, Adams Basin, NY 14410 USA Tel 585-880-0819
E-mail: info@thewildrosepress.com
Web site: http://www.thewildrosepress.com.

Wilder Pubns., Corp., *(978-0-9773040; 978-1-934451; 978-1-60459; 978-1-61720; 978-1-62755; 978-1-63384; 978-1-5154)*.

Wilder Publications, Limited *See* **Wilder Pubns., Corp.**

Wildfire Enterprises, *(978-0-9771969)* Orders Addr.: P.O. Box 402, Viola, AR 72583-0402 USA Tel 870-458-3600 (phone/fax); Edit Addr.: P O Box 402, Viola, AR 72583-0402 USA
E-mail: wfenterprises@hotmail.com
Web site: http://www.wildfireenterprises.iceryder.net.

Wildflower Pr., The, *(978-0-9714343; 978-0-9779933)* P.O. Box 4757, Albuquerque, NM 87196-4757 USA Tel 505-296-0691; Fax: 505-296-6124 Do not confuse with companies with the same or similar name in Oceanside, CA ,Phoenix, AZ ,Littleton, CO
E-mail: jspoetry@aol.com
Dist(s): **Smashwords.**

Wildflower Run, *(978-0-9667086)* Orders Addr.: P.O. Box 9656, College Station, TX 77842 USA Tel 979-764-0166
E-mail: atmgold@aol.com
Web site: http://www.aggiegoose.com.

Wildlife Education, Ltd., *(978-0-937934; 978-1-888153; 978-1-932396; 978-1-938811)* 1260 Audubon Rd., Park Hills, KY 41011-1904 USA (SAN 215-8299) Toll Free: 800-477-5034; *Imprints:* Zoo Books (Zoo Bks); Critters Up Close (Critters Up Close)
E-mail: sales@zoobooks.com
Web site: http://www.zoobooks.com.

Wildlife Tales Publishing, *(978-0-9793207)* Div. of Ark R.A.I.N. Wildlife Sanctuary, Inc., P.O. Box 721, Brownsville, TN 38012-0721 USA Toll Free: 877-352-6657
E-mail: books@wildlifetalespublishing.com
Web site: http://www.wildlifetalespublishing.com.

Wildly Austin, *(978-0-9753990)* P.O. Box 161987, Austin, TX 78716-1987 USA
E-mail: vikki@wildlyaustin.com; vl@intersourcesearch.com
Web site: http://www.wildlyaustin.com.

Wildot Pr., *(978-0-9789043; 978-0-9797933)* 4402 W. Creedance Blvd., Glendale, AZ 85310-3921 USA Tel 623-434-2636
E-mail: wildotpress@cox.net
Web site: http://www.wildotpress.com.

Wildside Pr., LLC, *(978-0-8095; 978-0-913960; 978-1-880448; 978-1-58715; 978-1-59224; 978-1-4344; 978-1-4794)* Orders Addr.: 9710 Traville Gateway Dr., No. 234, Rockville, MD 20850 USA Tel 301-762-1305; Fax: 301-762-1306
E-mail: customerservice@wildsidepress.com; wildsidepress@gmail.com
Web site: http://www.wildsidepress.com; http://www.weirdtales.net; http://www.wildsidebooks.com
Dist(s): **Diamond Comic Distributors, Inc.**
Diamond Bk. Distributors
MyiLibrary
NACSCORP, Inc.

Wildstone Media, *(978-1-882467)* Orders Addr.: P.O. Box 511580, Saint Louis, MO 63151 USA Tel 314-482-8472; Fax: 314-487-1910; Toll Free: 800-296-1918
E-mail: wildstone@mlc.net
Web site: http://www.wildstonemedia.com
Dist(s): **Anderson News, LLC**
Big River Distribution
BookBaby.

Wildstorm *Imprint of* **DC Comics**

WildWest Publishing, *(978-0-9721800)* P.O. Box 11658, Olympia, WA 98508 USA
E-mail: clamityJan@aol.com
Web site: http://www.CalamityJan.com.

Wiley *Imprint of* **Wiley, John & Sons, Inc.**

†Wiley, John & Sons, Inc., *(978-0-470; 978-0-471; 978-0-7645; 978-0-7821; 978-0-8260; 978-0-87605; 978-0-88422; 978-0-937721; 978-0-939246; 978-1-55828; 978-1-56561; 978-1-56884; 978-1-57313; 978-1-58245; 978-1-878058; 978-3-527; 978-1-118; 978-1-119)* Orders Addr.: c/o John Wiley & Sons, Inc., United States Distribution Ctr., 1 Wiley Dr., Somerset, NJ 08875-1272 USA Tel 732-469-4400; Fax: 732-302-2300; Toll Free Fax: 800-597-3299; Toll Free: 800-225-5945 (orders); Edit Addr.: 111 River St., Hoboken, NJ 07030 USA (SAN 200-2272) Tel 201-748-6000; 201-748-6276 (Retail and Wholesale); Fax: 201-748-6088; 201-748-6641 (Retail and Wholesale); *Imprints:* Wiley-VCH (Wiley-VCH); Jossey-Bass (Jossey-Bass); For Dummies (For Dummies); Howell Book House (HBH); Capstone (CapstW); Wiley (JWiley); Wiley-Blackwell (WileyBlack)
E-mail: compbks@wiley.com; bookinfo@wiley.com; custserv@wiley.com
Web site: http://www.wiley.com/compbooks; http://www.interscience.wiley.com; http://www.wiley.com
Dist(s): **Ebsco Publishing**
Follett School Solutions
Leonard, Hal Corp.
Ingram Pub. Services
Lightning Source, Inc.
Lippincott Williams & Wilkins
MBI Distribution Services/Quayside Distribution
Mel Bay Pubns., Inc.
MyiLibrary
Pearson Education
Peoples Education
TNT Media Group, Inc.
Urban Land Institute
ebrary, Inc.; *CIP.*

Wiley OBrien Worksapce *See* **OBrien, Wiley Workspace**

Wiley-Blackwell *Imprint of* **Wiley, John & Sons, Inc.**

Wiley-VCH *Imprint of* **Wiley, John & Sons, Inc.**

Wilfrid Laurier Univ. Pr. (CAN) *(978-0-88920; 978-0-921821; 978-1-55458) Dist. by* **IngramPubServ.**

Wilkes Publishing Co., Inc., *(978-0-9747755)* P.O. Box 340, Washington, GA 30673 USA Tel 706-678-2636; Fax: 706-678-3857
E-mail: editor@news-reporter.com
Web site: http://www.news-reporter.com.

Wilkins Farago Pty, Ltd. (AUS) *(978-0-9585571; 978-0-9804165; 978-0-9806070; 978-0-9871099) Dist. by* **IPG Chicago.**

Will Hall Bks., *(978-0-9630310; 978-0-9801257)* 611 Oliver Ave., Fayetteville, AR 72701 USA
E-mail: rharriso@uark.edu
Web site: http://www.willhallbooks.com.

Will to Print Pr., *(978-0-9772985)* 234 Hyde St., San Francisco, CA 94102-3324 USA Tel 415-474-0508; Fax: 415-673-1027
E-mail: willtoprintpress@faithfulfools.org
Web site: http://www.faithfulfools.org.

WillGo Pr., *(978-0-9828231)* 2874 Arcade St., Maplewood, MN 55109 USA Tel 651-774-2558
E-mail: gdesigns@comcast.net.

William Askel Art, *(978-0-9752528)* 21665 Wallace Dr., Southfield, MI 48075-7570 USA
E-mail: waksel@provide.net
Web site: http://fieldguidetomonsters.com.

William M. Gaines Agent, INC. *Imprint of* **Diamond Bk. Distributors**

William Morrow Paperbacks *Imprint of* **HarperCollins Pubs.**

William Works, Inc., *(978-0-9745244)* P.O. Box 2709, Washington, DC 20013 USA Toll Free: 877-335-2057.

Williams, Angela Claudette, *(978-0-615-15833-4; 978-0-615-16052-8; 978-0-615-16098-6; 978-0-615-16138-9; 978-0-615-17571-3; 978-0-615-17889-9)* 3645 Watkins Ridge Ct., Raleigh, NC 27616 USA
E-mail: claudetteexpressiona@yahoo.com
Web site: http://www.claudetteexpressions.com
Dist(s): **Lulu Enterprises Inc.**

Williams, Benjamin Publishing, *(978-0-9764945; 978-0-9796180; 978-0-9802398; 978-0-9850233; 978-0-9909650)* 18525 S. Torrence Ave. Suite D3, Lansing, IL 60438 USA Tel 1-888-757-0007
E-mail: ben@bwpublishing.com
Web site: http://www.bwpublishing.com
Dist(s): **AtlasBooks Distribution.**

Williams, Benny Publishing *See* **Williams, Benjamin Publishing**

Williams, Darnell *See* **Williams, Darnell L. Foundation, The**

Williams, Darnell L. Foundation, The, *(978-0-9747771)* 2402 Magnolia Dr., Harrisburg, PA 17104 USA Tel 717-233-1511
E-mail: WDarn44243@aol.com.

Williams, David Michael, *(978-0-9910562)* 1122 Carriage Cir., Fond du Lac, WI 54935 USA Tel 920-904-5249
E-mail: onemillionwords@hotmail.com
Web site: www.david-michael-williams.com.

Williams, Dontez *See* **MySheri Enterprises, LLC**

Williams Enterprises, Inc., *(978-0-9755478)* 500 5th Ave., N., Greybull, WY 82426 USA.

Williams, Gary, *(978-0-9743000)* 574 Falcon Fork Way, Jacksonville, FL 32259 USA
Web site: http://www.fbcofmand.org.

Williams, Geoffrey T., *(978-0-9771381; 978-0-9801671)* 3119 Redwood St., San Diego, CA 92104 USA
Web site: http://wildvoices.com
Dist(s): **Audible.com**
Smashwords.

Williams, James E., *(978-0-9746310)* P.O. Box 6921, Atlanta, GA 30315-0921 USA Fax: 404-691-0726.

Williams, Morgan, *(978-0-9762768)* 3243 Cloverwood Dr., Nashville, TN 37214-3428 USA
E-mail: mandj@magiclink.com
Web site: http://www.thestandards.com.

Williams, Rozalia *See* **Hidden Curriculum Education**

Williams, Thomas, *(978-0-9763633)* 358 Homestead Rd., NW, Willis, VA 24380 USA Tel 540-789-4295
E-mail: tomwill@swva.net
Web site: http://www.santacares.org.

Williamson Bks. *Imprint of* **Ideals Pubns.**

Williamson County Public Library, *(978-0-9911915)* Williamson Cty. Public Library, Franklin, TN 37064 USA Tel 615-595-1240; *Imprints:* Academy Park Press (AcadParkPr)
E-mail: dgreenwald@williamson-tn.org
Web site: wcpltn.org.

Williamspublishing, *(978-0-615-19121-8)* 317 E. Oakgrove, Kalamazoo, MI 49004 USA
E-mail: starowl1@hotmail.clm
Dist(s): **Lulu Enterprises Inc.**

Willie & Willie, *(978-0-9754126)* P.O. Box 26071, Saint Louis, MO 63136 USA.

Willis Music Co., *(978-0-87718)* Orders Addr.: P.O. Box 548, Florence, KY 41022-0548 USA (SAN 294-6947) Tel 606-283-2050 ext 859; Fax: 606-283-1784; Toll Free: 800-354-9799; Edit Addr.: 7380 Industrial Rd., Florence, KY 41040 USA
E-mail: willis@willis-music.com; orderdpt@willis-music.com
Web site: http://www.willismusic.com
Dist(s): **Leonard, Hal Corp.**

Willow Bend Publishing, *(978-0-9709002; 978-0-9831138)* 111 West St., P.O. Box 304, Goshen, MA 01032 USA Tel 413-230-1514 Do not confuse with Willow Bend Publishing in Lakeland, FL
E-mail: info@willowbendpublishing.com
Web site: http://www.willowbendpublishing.com.

Willow Brook Publishing, *(978-0-9817636)* 19600 W. Shore Dr., Suite 101, Mundelein, IL 60060 USA (SAN 856-4914)
E-mail: Info@willowBrookPublishing.com
Web site: http://www.willowbrook-publishing.com/
Dist(s): **Pathway Bk. Service.**

†Willow Creek Pr., Inc., *(978-0-932558; 978-1-57223; 978-1-59543; 978-1-60755; 978-1-62343; 978-1-68234)* Orders Addr.: P.O. Box 147, Minocqua, WI 54548-0147 USA (SAN 255-4038) Tel 715-358-7010; Fax: 715-358-2807; Toll Free: 800-850-9453; P.O. Box 147 / EDI Orders, Minoqua, WI 54548 (SAN 920-8070) Tel 715-358-7010; Fax: 715-358-2807; Edit Addr.: 9931 Hwy. 70 W., Minocqua, WI 54548 USA Tel 715-358-7010; Fax: 715-358-2807; Toll Free: 800-850-9453 Do not confuse with Willowcreek Pr. in Aloha, OR
E-mail: info@willowcrewpress.com; info@wcpretail.com
Web site: http://www.wcpretail.com
Dist(s): **MyiLibrary**
Perseus Bks. Group
Perseus Distribution
Strauss Consultants; *CIP.*

Willow Creel Publishing Co., *(978-0-9729655)* 35 Willow Creek, 820 9th Ave. S., North Myrtle Beach, SC 29582 USA Tel 843-272-1096 Do not confuse with Willow Creek Publishing in Canton, MI, Pine River, MN
E-mail: grayfox.43@att.net
Web site: http://www.chinquawhere.com.

Willow Dance Pubns., *(978-0-9768750)* Orders Addr.: P.O. Box 71, Hillsdale, WY 82060 USA Tel 307-631-0236; Edit Addr.: 1370 CR 142, Hillsdale, WY 82060 USA
E-mail: willowdancepublishing@yahoo.com.

Willow Mountain Publishing, *(978-0-615-43583-1)* 6920 Buckhead Dr., Raleigh, NC 27615 USA Tel 919-747-9062
E-mail: hallstuff@gmail.com
Dist(s): **CreateSpace Independent Publishing Platform**
Dummy Record Do Not USE!!!!.

Willow Publishing, *(978-0-9825212)* 1000 Kinsley Ave., No. 32, Winslow, AZ 86047 USA Toll Free Fax: 800-643-9527.

Willow Tree Books *See* **Apricot Pr.**

Willow Tree Press *See* **Little Willow Tree Bks.**

Willowgate Pr., *(978-1-930008)* P.O. Box 6529, Holliston, MA 01746 USA (SAN 253-0376); 120 Brook Rd., Port Jefferson, NY 11777-1665
E-mail: willowgatepress@yahoo.com
Web site: http://www.willowgatepress.com
Dist(s): **AtlasBooks Distribution.**

WillowSpring Downs, *(978-0-9648525; 978-0-9742716)* 1582 N. Falcon, Hillsboro, KS 67063 USA Tel 620-367-8432; Fax: 620-367-8218; Toll Free: 888-551-0973
E-mail: willowspringdowns@juno.com.

WillowTree Pr., L.L.C., *(978-0-9678221; 978-0-9794533; 978-1-937778)* Orders Addr.: P.O. Box 142414, St. Louis, MO 63114 USA Tel 314-423-3634; Edit Addr.: P.O. Box 142414, Saint Louis, MO 63114 USA (SAN 253-1178); *Imprints:* Full Circle Press (Full Circle MO)
E-mail: info@willowtreepress.com
Web site: http://www.willowtreepress.com
Dist(s): **Smashwords.**

Willy Waw wees, LLC, *(978-0-9785103)* Orders Addr.: PO Box 390593, Deltona, FL 32739 USA
E-mail: artgallerymeris@aol.com
Web site: http://www.willywawwees.com.

Wilmington Today LLC, *(978-0-9729573; 978-0-9916642)* 1213 Culbreth Dr., Wilmington, NC 28405 USA Tel 910-509-7195
E-mail: hwjones@wilmingtontoday.com
Web site: http://www.wilmingtontoday.com.

Wilshire House of Arkansas *See* **Ozark Publishing**

Wilson & Assocs., *(978-0-9710427)* P.O. Box 2569, Alvin, TX 77512 USA Tel 281-388-0196; Fax: 413-683-8503 Do not confuse with Wilson & Associates, Gig Harbor, WA
E-mail: john@wilsonpublishing.com; pwilson@wilsonpublishing.com
Web site: http://www.orsapress.com; http://www.thebookdistributor.com; http://www.wilsonpublishing.com.

Wilson, Gerrard (IRL) *(978-0-9561553) Dist. by* **LuluCom.**

†Wilson, H.W., *(978-0-8242)* 950 University Ave., Bronx, NY 10452-4224 USA (SAN 203-2961) Tel 718-588-8400; Fax: 718-681-1511 (Outside of the U.S. & Canada); Toll Free: 800-367-6770 ext 2272
E-mail: custserv@hwwilson.com
Web site: http://www.hwwilson.com
Dist(s): **Ebsco Publishing**
Grey Hse. Publishing
MyiLibrary; *CIP.*

Wilson Language Training, *(978-1-56778)* 47 Old Webster Rd., Oxford, MA 01540-2705 USA Toll Free: 800-899-8454.

Wilson Place Comics, *(978-0-9744235)* P.O. Box 435, Oceanside, NY 11572 USA
E-mail: Wilplace@optonline.net
Web site: http://www.wjhc.com
Dist(s): **Brodart Co.**
Diamond Comic Distributors, Inc.
Diamond Bk. Distributors
Follett School Solutions
Mackin Library Media
Midwest Library Service.

Wilson, Rebecca, *(978-0-9760569)* 450 Massachusetts Ave NW Apt. 1004, Washington, DC 20001-6222 USA
E-mail: info@sunfishmanuals.com
Web site: http://www.sunfishmanuals.com.

Wilson, W. Shane, *(978-0-578-00301-6; 978-0-578-00634-5; 978-0-578-00797-7; 978-0-578-01639-9; 978-0-578-02119-5; 978-0-578-02550-6; 978-0-578-03095-1; 978-0-578-03299-3)* 7600 NE 64th Cir., Vancouver, WA 98662 USA Tel 360-521-1584
E-mail: redtimberwolf67@yahoo.com
Web site: http://stores.lulu.com/shanesbooks
Dist(s): **Lulu Enterprises Inc.**

Wilson-Barnett Publishing, *(978-1-888840)* P.O. Box 345, Tustin, CA 92781-0345 USA Tel 949-380-5748; Fax: 714-730-6140
E-mail: mrcalc@usa.net.

Wilson-Crawford & Co., *(978-0-9752948)* P.O. Box 809, Island Lake, IL 60042-0809 USA Fax: 847-487-1591
E-mail: freecellmax@aol.com
Web site: http://www.freecellsecrets.com.

Wilstonian, *(978-0-9772122)* 3603 Whitaker Dr., Melvindale, MI 48122 USA (SAN 257-0106)
Web site: http://www.wilstonian.com.

Wilt, Lisa, *(978-0-9770053)* Orders Addr.: 1072 Frye Rd., Jeannette, PA 15644-4717 USA
E-mail: thankyoumousie@comcast.net.

Wimabi Pr., *(978-0-578-02359-5; 978-0-578-03340-2; 978-0-578-05718-7)* 7102 Lakewood Dr., Richmond, VA 23229 USA
E-mail: inquiries@wimabi.com
Web site: http://www.wimabi.com
Dist(s): **Lulu Enterprises Inc.**

Win Publishing, LLC, *(978-0-9826865)* 35 E. Main St., Suite 337, Avon, CT 06001 USA Tel 860-651-6859; Fax: 203-413-4409
Dist(s): **Outskirts Pr., Inc.**

Winchester Pr., *(978-0-9745279)* P.O. Box 711, Hollis, NH 03049-0711 USA Tel 603-880-9559 Do not confuse with companies with the same or similar name in Southhampton, NY, Howell, NJ, LaFox, IL.

Winck, Stephanie *See* **One Horse Pr.**

Wind Pubns., *(978-0-9636545; 978-1-893239; 978-1-936138)* Orders Addr.: 600 Overbrook Dr., Nicholasville, KY 40356 USA
E-mail: books@windpub.com
Web site: http://www.windpub.com.

Windblown Enterprises, *(978-0-9752576)* 12207 243rd Pl NE, Redmond, WA 98053-5685 USA
E-mail: windblowne@msn.com.

Windblown Media, *(978-0-9647292; 978-1-935170; 978-1-61871)* 4680 Calle Norte, Newbury Park, CA 91320 USA Tel 805-498-2484; Fax: 805-499-4260
E-mail: office@windblownmedia.com
Web site: http://www.windblownmedia.com
Dist(s): **Hachette Bk. Group.**

Windcall Enterprises *See* **Windcall Publishing**

Windcall Publishing, *(978-0-9745884; 978-0-9845934; 978-0-9847607)* Div. of Windcall Enterprises, Orders Addr.: 75345 Rd. 317, Venango, NE 69168 USA Tel 308-447-5566 (phone/fax); Fax: 308-447-5566
E-mail: windcall@chase3000.com
Web site: http://www.windcallenterprises.com; http://www.windcallpublishing.com
Dist(s): **Smashwords.**

Windchimes Publishing, *(978-0-9763253)* P.O. Box 1433, Palm City, FL 34991-6433 USA Tel 772-285-5429
E-mail: wchimes@gate.net
Web site: http://www.wchimes.com.

Windfeather Pr., *(978-0-9620122)* 4545 W. Heart Rd., Bismarck, ND 58504-4257 USA (SAN 247-7246); 1203 N. 27th St., Bismarck, ND 58501 (SAN 247-7254) Tel 701-258-5047
Dist(s): **Duebbert, Harold F.**

Windhill Bks. LLC, *(978-0-9844828)* 939 Windhill St., Onalaska, WI 54650-2081 USA (SAN 859-5135)
E-mail: jeanna@windhillbooks.com
Web site: http://www.windhillbooks.com
Dist(s): **Midpoint Trade Bks., Inc.**

Winding Road Pubs., *(978-0-615-21989-9; 978-0-578-04819-2; 978-0-578-07274-6; 978-0-578-09900-2; 978-0-578-10413-3; 978-0-578-10703-5; 978-0-578-10929-9; 978-0-578-11074-5; 978-0-578-11693-8; 978-0-578-12821-4; 978-0-578-13843-5)* 2904 Giles St., West Des Moines, IA 50265 USA Tel 515-226-1179
Dist(s): **Lulu Enterprises Inc.**

Windjammer Adventure Publishing, *(978-0-9768477; 978-0-615-29130-7; 978-0-615-33790-6; 978-0-615-36411-7; 978-0-615-38745-1; 978-0-9831300; 978-0-9898232)* 289 S. Franklin St., Chagrin Falls, OH 44022-3449 USA Tel 440-247-6610
E-mail: windjammerpub@mac.com
Web site: http://windjammerpublishing.com.

Windmill Bks. *Imprint of* **Rosen Publishing Group, Inc., The**

Windmill Bks., *(978-1-60754; 978-1-62275)* 303 Pk. Ave. S., Suite No. 1280, NEW YORK, NY 10010-3657 USA Tel 646-205-7415
Dist(s): **Rosen Publishing Group, Inc., The.**

Windoggle, *(978-0-615-64557-5)* 27 Pinecrest Cir, Bailey, CO 80421 USA Tel 303-838-3634
Dist(s): **CreateSpace Independent Publishing Platform.**

Window Bks., *(978-1-889829)* Orders Addr.: 1425 Broadway #513, Seattle, WA 98122 USA Tel 206-351-9993
E-mail: orders@windowbooksonline.com
Web site: http://www.meetmarcadams.com; http://www.windowbooksonline.com.

Window Box Pr. LLC, *(978-0-9793738)* Orders Addr.: 13516 Fillmore Ct., Thornton, CO 80241-1330 USA (SAN 853-2958) Tel 303-255-9432
E-mail: windowboxpress@q.com
Web site: http://windowboxpress.com
Dist(s): **Independent Pubs. Group.**

For full information on wholesalers and distributors, refer to the Wholesaler and Distributor Name Index

Window Seat Publishing, *(978-0-9721949)* 82 Marlborough Rd., West Hempstead, NY 11552 USA Tel 516-481-5969
E-mail: aferrant@optonline.net.

Windows of Discovery, *(978-0-9785399)* P.O. Box 9085, Spokane, WA 99209-9085 USA
Web site: http://theprofessorstelescope.com.

Windrad Press *See* **Pinwheel Bks.**

WinDruid Publishing, *(978-0-9758943)* Orders Addr.: 220 Walworth Dr., St. Louis, MO 63125-5008 USA; Edit Addr.: P.O. Box 25008, Saint Louis, MO 63125-5008 USA
E-mail: orders@LukeCarter.com; info@windruidpublishing.com; susan@windruidpublishing.com
Web site: http://www.LukeCarter.com; http://www.windruidpublishing.com
Dist(s): **Book Clearing Hse.**
Quality Bks., Inc.

Windsong Publishing Co., *(978-0-9655078)* P.O. Box 588, Rimrock, AZ 86335 USA Do not confuse with companies with the same or similar names in Eugene, OR, San Diego, CA, Staunton, VA, Lake Patagonia, AZ
Dist(s): **New Leaf Distributing Co., Inc.**

Windsor Media Enterprises, Inc., *(978-0-9765304; 978-0-9777297; 978-1-934229)* 5412 Wolf St., Longmont, CO 80504-3432 USA Toll Free: 877-947-2665
E-mail: collins@wmebooks.com
Web site: http://www.wmebooks.com.

WindSpirit Publishing, *(978-0-9643407)* Orders Addr.: 220 Compass Ave., Beachwood, NJ 08722-2919 USA Fax: 732-240-7860
E-mail: windspiritpub@earthlink.net
Web site: http://www.windspiritpublishing.net.

Windsurf Publishing LLC, *(978-1-936509)* 14 Ctr. Dr., Old Greenwich, CT 06870 USA Tel 203-698-2975
E-mail: m.lagana@att.net.

Windswept Productions, *(978-0-9764825)* Orders Addr.: P.O. Box 167, Felton, PA 17322-0167 USA Tel 717-244-7700; Edit Addr.: 11525 High Point Rd., Felton, PA 17322 USA
E-mail: wpebs@earthlink.net.

Windward Publishing *Imprint of* **Finney Co., Inc.**

Windward Publishing, *(978-0-9758597)* 112 N. St., New Bedford, MA 02740-6513 USA Do not confuse with Windward Publishing in Minneapolis, MN
E-mail: windwardpublish@aol.com; josettefernandes@hotmail.com.

Windy City Pubs., *(978-0-9819505; 978-1-935766; 978-1-941478)* 2118 Plum Grove Rd., No. 349, Rolling Meadows, IL 60008 USA Tel 888-673-7126; *Imprints:* Skyscraper Press (children's) (Skyscraper Pr)
E-mail: dawn@windycitypublishers.com
Dist(s): **BookBaby.**

Windy City Publishing *See* **Windy City Pubs.**

Windy Hill Pr., *(978-0-9662983)* Orders Addr.: 22 Hilltop Ave., Barrington, RI 02806 USA Tel 401-247-2707 Do not confuse with Windy Hill Pr., in Menlo Park, CA
E-mail: windyhillpress@cox.net
Web site: http://www.windyhillpress.net.

Windy Hills Press *See* **Old Stone Pr.**

Windy Press International Publishing Hse., LLC, *(978-1-890568)* 29W 424 Tanglewood Ln, Warrenville, IL 60555-2663 USA; P.O. Box 5131, Wheaton, IL 60189-4383 Fax: 630-604-0490; Toll Free Fax: 888-508-5577; *Imprints:* A-BA-BA-HA-LA-MA-HA Publishers (A-BA-BA-HA-LA-MA-HA)
E-mail: interhouse@comcast.net
Web site: http://www.snowqueen.us.

Wineries by County, *(978-0-615-18047-2)* 3373 Silver Rapids Rd., Valley Spgs, CA 95252-9573 USA
E-mail: info@wineriesbycounty.com
Web site: http://www.wineriesbycounty.com.

Winfrey Inc., *(978-0-9818526)* Orders Addr.: 14525 SW. Millikan Way #23515, Beaverton, OR 970052343 USA (SAN 856-7263) Tel 404-993-0532; 228 Pk. Ave. S. #23515, New York, NY 10003; Edit Addr.: 4480 S. Cobb Dr. Ste H Pmb 451, Smyrna, GA 30080 USA
E-mail: info@shakeetawinfrey.com
Web site: http://www.shakeetawinfrey.com
Dist(s): **APG Sales & Distribution Services**
AtlasBooks Distribution
BCH Fulfillment & Distribution
Bella Distribution
Book Hub, Inc.
BookMasters Distribution Services (BDS)
Bks. Plus, U.S.A.
C & B Bk. Distribution
Cardinal Pubs. Group
Greenleaf Book Group
Independent Pubs. Group
Lightning Source, Inc.
Midpoint Trade Bks., Inc.
Mint Pubs. Group
New Leaf Distributing Co., Inc.
Partners Bk. Distributing, Inc.
Penton Overseas, Inc.
Perseus Distribution
Quality Bks., Inc.
SCB Distributors
SPD-Small Pr. Distribution
Send The Light Distribution LLC.

Wing Dam Pr., *(978-0-9758615)* P.O. Box 200, Ferryville, WI 54628 USA Tel 608-734-3292 (phone/fax)
E-mail: nlichter@mwt.net.

Wing Lane Pr., *(978-0-9792430)* 19 Exeter Ln., Morristown, NJ 07960 USA
E-mail: tazni@optonline.net.

Winged Willow Pr., *(978-0-9664805)* Orders Addr.: P.O. Box 92, Carrboro, NC 27510 USA Tel 919-942-4689; Fax: 919-933-3555
E-mail: info@sudierakusin.com
Web site: http://www.sudierakusin.com
Dist(s): **Parnassus Bk. Distributors.**

WingedChariot Pr. (GBR) *(978-1-905341) Dist. by* **IPG Chicago.**

Winger Publishing, *(978-0-9805263)* P.O. Box 20991, Juneau, AK 99802 USA
E-mail: wingerpublishing@gmail.com.

Wings Above, *(978-0-9768403)* 1607 Market St., Galveston, TX 77550 USA Tel 409-750-9176.

Wings ePress, Inc., *(978-1-59088; 978-1-59705; 978-1-61309)* 403 Wallace Crt., Richmond, KY 82225 USA Do not confuse with companies with the same or similar name in Northhampton, MA, Union, ME, San Antonio, TX
E-mail: mkapp2@roadrunner.com; lady0@earthlink.net
Web site: http://www.wings-press.com
Dist(s): **Smashwords.**

Wings, Inc., *(978-0-9705018)* 4790 Caughlin Pkwy., Suite 143, Reno, NV 89509 USA
E-mail: glebeck@wingsnv.com
Web site: http://www.wingsnv.com.

Wings Pr., *(978-0-916727; 978-0-930324; 978-1-60940)* 627 E. Guenther, San Antonio, TX 78210 USA (SAN 209-4975) Tel 210-271-7805 Do not confuse with companies with the same or similar name in Northhampton, MA, UNion, ME, Lusk, WY
E-mail: milligan@wingspress.com
Web site: http://www.wingspress.com
Dist(s): **Brodart Co.**
Ebsco Publishing
Follett School Solutions
Independent Pubs. Group
MyiLibrary
SCB Distributors
ebrary, Inc.

Wings Press, Limited *See* **Wings ePress, Inc.**

Wings-on-Disk *Imprint of* **PassionQuest Technologies, LLC**

Wingspan Pr. *Imprint of* **WingSpan Publishing**

WingSpan Publishing, *(978-1-59594)* P.O. Box 631665, Nacogdoches, TX 75963 USA Toll Free: 866-735-3782; *Imprints:* Wingspan Press (Wingspan Pr)
Web site: http://www.wingspanpress.com
Dist(s): **BookBaby**
CreateSpace Independent Publishing Platform.

WingSpread Publishers, *(978-1-60066)* Div. of Zur LTD, 820 N. LaSalle, Chicago, IL 60610 USA Tel 312-329-2101; Fax: 312-329-2144; Toll Free: 800-678-8812
E-mail: pbrossman@zurltd.com
Web site: http://www.wingspreadpublishers.com
Dist(s): **Anchor Distributors**
Moody Pubs.
Send The Light Distribution LLC.

Wink Publishing, *(978-0-9702572)* P.O. Box 9957, Richmond, VA 23228 USA.

Winking Moon Pr., *(978-0-9764175)* 4130 S. Splendor Ct., Gilbert, AZ 85297 USA Do not confuse with Winking Moon Press in Cleveland OH .

Winn, Lynnette, *(978-0-9791884)* 2617 Claudia Dr., Leander, TX 78641 USA (SAN 852-7040)
Web site: http://www.butterpodjerome.com.

Winnow Pr., *(978-0-9764726)* 3505 El Dorado Trail, Suite A, Austin, TX 78739 USA (SAN 256-4017) Tel 512-280-4483
E-mail: publisher@winnowpress.com
Web site: http://winnowpress.com.

Winoca Bks. & Media, *(978-0-9755910; 978-0-9789736; 978-1-935619)* 1923 29th St., Suite 2, Lubbock, TX 79411-1515 USA
Web site: http://www.winocapress.com
Dist(s): **Parnassus Bk. Distributors.**

Winoca Press *See* **Winoca Bks. & Media**

Winslow's Art, *(978-0-9748505)* P.O. Box 2099, Avalon, CA 90704-2099 USA Tel 310-510-1613 (phone/fax)
E-mail: winslow@catalinaisp.com.

Winsor Corporation *See* **Winsor Learning, Inc.**

Winsor Learning, Inc., *(978-1-891602; 978-1-935450)* 1620 W. Seventh St., Saint Paul, MN 55102 USA Tel 651-222-3922; Fax: 651-222-3969; Toll Free: 800-321-7585
E-mail: sondaysystem@winsorcorp.net
Web site: http://www.sondaysystem.com.

Winstead Pr., Ltd., *(978-0-940787)* 202 Slice Dr., Stamford, CT 06907 USA (SAN 664-6913) Tel 203-322-4941
E-mail: winstead.press@gte.net.

Winter Goose Publishing, *(978-0-9836764; 978-0-9851548; 978-0-9881845; 978-0-9889049; 978-0-9894792; 978-1-941058)* 2701 Del Paso Rd., 130-92, Sacramento, CA 95835 USA Tel 530-771-7058
E-mail: jordan@wintergoosepublishing.com
Web site: wintergoosepublishing.com; graceinspiredpress.com
Dist(s): **Lightning Source, Inc.**

Winter Light Bks., Inc., *(978-0-9797372)* 734 Franklin Ave., No. 675, Garden City, NY 11530-4525 USA (SAN 854-2163)
Web site: http://www.winterlightbooks.com; http://www.winterlightbooks.org.

Wintergreen Orchard Hse., *(978-1-933119; 978-1-936035)* Div. of Alloy Education, 2 Lan Dr., Suite 100, Westford, MA 01886 USA Tel 978-692-9708; Fax: 978-692-2304
E-mail: info@wintergreenorchardhouse.com; mjd@alloyeducation.com
Web site: http://www.wintergreenorchardhouse.com.

Winterlake Pr., *(978-0-9816003)* P.O. Box 1274, Buffalo, NY 14231-1274 USA (SAN 856-0013)
E-mail: info@winterlakepress.com
Web site: http://www.winterlakepress.com
Dist(s): **Independent Pubs. Group.**

Wintermantel Group, LLC, The, *(978-0-9767418)* 316 Saddle Back Dr., Saint Louis, MO 63129-3449 USA
Web site: http://www.theangelchildren.com.

Winters Publishing, *(978-0-9625329; 978-1-883651)* Orders Addr.: P.O. Box 501, Greensburg, IN 47240 USA (SAN 298-1645) Tel 812-663-4948 (phone/fax); Toll Free: 800-457-3230; Edit Addr.: 705 E. Washington, Greensburg, IN 47240 USA Do not confuse with Winters Publishing, Wichita, KS
E-mail: tmwinters@juno.com
Web site: http://www.winterspublishing.com
Dist(s): **Partners Bk. Distributing, Inc.**
Partners/West Book Distributors
Send The Light Distribution LLC
Spring Arbor Distributors, Inc.

Winterwolf Publishing, *(978-0-9744831; 978-0-9752711; 978-0-9762471; 978-0-9772632)* Orders Addr.: P.O. Box 1373, Westerville, OH 43086-1373 USA; Edit Addr.: 5446 Highbrook Ct., Westerville, OH 43081 USA
Web site: http://www.winterwolfpublishing.com.

Wipf and Stock *Imprint of* **Wipf & Stock Pubs.**

Wipf & Stock Pubs., *(978-0-9653517; 978-1-55635; 978-1-57910; 978-1-59244; 978-1-59752; 978-1-60608; 978-1-60899; 978-1-61097; 978-1-62032; 978-1-62189; 978-1-62564; 978-1-63087; 978-1-4982)* 199 W. 8th Ave., Suite 3, Eugene, OR 97401 USA Tel 541-344-1528; Fax: 541-344-1506; *Imprints:* Resource Publications (OR) (Resource Pubcns); Wipf and Stock (Wipf and Stock)
Web site: http://wipfandstock.com/; http://slantbooks.com
Dist(s): **CreateSpace Independent Publishing Platform**
MyiLibrary
Spring Arbor Distributors, Inc.

Wire Rim Bks., *(978-0-9802253; 978-0-615-15357-5; 978-1-935236)* 188 Spring Valley St., Hutto, TX 78634 USA (SAN 913-5960)
E-mail: hmelton@mac.com
Web site: http://www.wirerimbooks.com.

Wisconsin Dept. of Public Instruction, *(978-1-57337)* Orders Addr.: Drawer 179, Milwaukee, WI 53293-0179 USA Tel 608-266-2188; Fax: 608-267-9110; Toll Free: 800-243-8782; Edit Addr.: 125 S. Webster St., Box 7841, Madison, WI 53702 USA
Web site: http://www.dpi.state.wi.us.

†Wisconsin Historical Society, *(978-0-87020)* 816 State St., Madison, WI 53706 USA (SAN 203-350X) Tel 608-264-6584; Fax: 608-264-6486
E-mail: diane.drexler@wisconsinhistory.org
Web site: http://www.wisconsinhistory.org
Dist(s): **Chicago Distribution Ctr.**
Hoover Institution Pr.
Univ. of Chicago Pr.; *CIP.*

Wisdom Audio-Books *Imprint of* **BloomingFields**

Wisdom Foundation Publishing, *(978-1-932590)* 796 Isenberg St., Suite 19E, Honolulu, HI 96826 USA Tel 808-944-3113; Fax: 808-988-4212
E-mail: wisdomfactors@hawaii.rr.com.

†Wisdom Pubns., *(978-0-86171; 978-1-61429)* 199 Elm St., Somerville, MA 02144 USA (SAN 246-022X) Tel 617-776-7416 ext 24; Fax: 617-776-7841; Toll Free Fax: 800-338-4550 (orders only); Toll Free: 800-462-6420 (orders only)
E-mail: marketing@wisdompubs.org
Web site: http://www.wisdompubs.org
Dist(s): **MyiLibrary**
Simon & Schuster, Inc.; *CIP.*

Wisdom Tales *Imprint of* **World Wisdom, Inc.**

Wisdom Tree (IND) *(978-81-86685; 978-81-8328) Dist. by* **SCB Distributo.**

Wisdom Tree Records *See* **Rivertree Productions, Inc.**

Wise Guides, LLC, *(978-0-9768772; 978-1-935237)* 1924 W. Montrose, PMB No. 206, Chicago, IL 60613 USA Toll Free: 866-262-3842
E-mail: info@wiseguidebooks.com
Web site: http://www.wiseguidebooks.com
Dist(s): **Zagat Survey.**

Wise Owl Printing Plus, Incorporated *See* **Deziner Media International**

Wise Pubns. (GBR) *(978-0-7119; 978-0-86001) Dist. by* **Music Sales.**

Wise Words Publications *See* **EPI Bks.**

Wisecracker Press, Inc., *(978-0-9752657)* 2735 April Hill Ln., Dallas, TX 75287 USA
Web site: http://www.wisecrackerpress.com.

WiseWoman Pr., *(978-0-945385)* 1521 N. Jantzen Ave., No. 143, Portland, OR 97217 USA (SAN 247-0039) Tel 1-800-603-3005; 1408 NE 65th St., Vancouver, WA 98665 Tel 503 310-0105
E-mail: web@wisewomanpress.com
Web site: http://www.wisewomanpress.com
Dist(s): **DeVorss & Co.**
Lulu Enterprises Inc.

Wish Publishing, *(978-1-930546; 978-0-9835754; 978-0-615-74522-0)* P.O. Box 10337, Terre Haute, IN 47801 USA (SAN 253-4320) Fax: 928-447-1836
E-mail: holly@wishpublishing.com
Web site: http://www.wishpublishing.com
Dist(s): **Cardinal Pubs. Group**
Lightning Source, Inc.

Wish You Were Here *Imprint of* **Sierra Pr.**

Wishful Penny Books *See* **The Wish**

Wishing Star Children's Bks., *(978-0-615-16077-1; 978-0-615-16078-8; 978-0-615-16079-5)* 12755 Eurels Rd., Southgate, MI 48195 USA Tel 734-754-3168
E-mail: mgrazi@wowway.com
Web site: http://www.wishingstarchildrensbooks.com
Dist(s): **Lulu Enterprises Inc.**

Wishing U Well Publishing, *(978-0-9769524)* 1560 Gulf Blvd., Unit 1202, Clearwater, FL 33767 USA.

Wishingstone Enterprises *See* **Wishingstone Publishing**

Wishingstone Publishing, *(978-0-9779701)* 1640 Hartley Ave., Henderson, NV 89052 USA Tel 702-617-7325
E-mail: dapwishingstone@earthlink.net.

Witcher Productions, *(978-0-925159; 978-1-55942)* Div. of Marsh Film Enterprises, Inc., P.O. Box 8082, Shawnee Mission, KS 66208 USA Tel 816-523-1059; Fax: 816-333-7421; Toll Free: 800-821-3303 (for orders/customer service only)
E-mail: info@marshmedia.com
Web site: http://www.marshmedia.com
Dist(s): **Follett School Solutions.**

Witherspoon Pr. *Imprint of* **Curriculum Publishing, Presbyterian Church (U. S. A.)**

Within Reach, Inc., *(978-0-9718864)* P.O. Box 6217, Harrisburg, PA 17112 USA Tel 717-657-8689
E-mail: wreach@epix.net
Web site: http://www.boatingsidekicks.com.

WithinU Life Coaching LLC, *(978-0-9890134)* 39 Skunk Hollow Rd., Jericho, VT 05495 USA Tel 802-238-0822
E-mail: hchipp@comcast.net
Web site: www.withinulifecoaching.com.

Witness Impulse *Imprint of* **HarperCollins Pubs.**

Witness Productions, *(978-0-9627653; 978-1-891390)* Box 34, Church St., Marshall, IN 47859 USA Tel 765-597-2487.

Witty Bit World, Inc., *(978-0-9770548)* 1009 Basil Dr., New Bern, NC 28562 USA
E-mail: deborah@wittybitworld.com
Web site: http://www.wittybitworld.com.

Witty Fools Productions, *(978-0-9745179)* 19 Le Grande Ave., No.14, Greenwich, CT 06830 USA Toll Free: 877-733-0528 (phone/fax)
E-mail: wittyfools@aol.com; flierlp@bww.com
Web site: http://www.wittyfools.com; http://www.prayerlaughterandbroccoli.com.

Witty Publishing, *(978-0-9785571)* 2875 F Northtowne, Box 232, Reno, NV 89512 USA Toll Free: 866-948-8948.

Wiyd, Lewis, *(978-0-9650637)* 47 Glen Park Rd., East Orange, NJ 07017-1813 USA Tel 973-673-0094; Fax: 973-673-0095.

Wizard Academies, LLC, *(978-0-615-18398-5; 978-0-615-18505-7; 978-0-615-18594-1; 978-0-615-18712-9; 978-0-615-18713-6)* 57485 170th St., Ames, IA 50010-9425 USA
E-mail: rivals@interdrama.com
Web site: http://www.interdrama.com/wiz/
Dist(s): **Lulu Enterprises Inc.**

Wizard Academy Pr., *(978-0-9714769; 978-1-932226)* 16621 Crystal Hills Dr., Austin, TX 78737 USA Tel 512-295-5700; Fax: 512-295-5701; Toll Free: 800-425-4769
E-mail: publisher@wizardofads.com; sean@wizardofads.com
Web site: http://www.wizardacademypress.com
Dist(s): **BookBaby.**

Wizard of Baum, *(978-0-615-74707-1; 978-0-615-74778-1; 978-0-615-74844-3; 978-0-615-74921-1; 978-0-615-75023-1; 978-0-615-75107-8; 978-0-615-75528-1)* PO Box 2536, Victorville, CA 92393-2536 USA
Web site: www.WizardOfBaum.com
Dist(s): **CreateSpace Independent Publishing Platform.**

Wizard Works, *(978-0-9621543; 978-1-890692)* Orders Addr.: P.O. Box 1125, Homer, AK 99603-1125 USA Toll Free: 877-210-2665
E-mail: wizard@xyz.net
Web site: http://www.xyz.net/~wizard.

Wizarding World Pr., *(978-0-9723936)* 8926 N. Greenwood Ave., Suite 133, Niles, IL 60714 USA
E-mail: wizardingworld@waycoolstuffonline.com
Web site: http://www.wizardingworldpress.com
Dist(s): **SCB Distributors.**

Wizards of the Coast, *(978-0-7869; 978-1-57530; 978-1-880992; 978-0-7430)* Subs. of Hasbro, Inc., Orders Addr.: P.O. Box 707, Renton, WA 98057-0709 USA Toll Free: 800-821-8028; Edit Addr.: 1801 Lind Ave., SW, Renton, WA 98055 USA (SAN 299-4410) Tel 425-226-6500; *Imprints:* Mirrorstone (Mirrorstone)
E-mail: angella@wizards.com
Web site: http://www.wizards.com
Dist(s): **Diamond Bk. Distributors**
MyiLibrary
PSI (Publisher Services, Inc.)
Penguin Random Hse., LLC.
Random Hse., Inc.
Doherty, Tom Assocs., LLC.

WizdomInc, *(978-0-9764829; 978-0-9767958; 978-0-9768053; 978-0-9778512; 978-0-9785170; 978-0-9786574; 978-0-9820173; 978-0-9840885)* Orders Addr.: 273 Candlelight Dr., Santa Rosa, CA 95403 USA Tel 707-578-1866; Fax: 707-578-4978; Toll Free: 866-607-4510
E-mail: aswan@wizdominc.com
Web site: http://www.wizdominc.com.

WizKids, LLC, *(978-0-9703934; 978-1-931462; 978-1-59041)* Subs. of Topps Europe Ltd., 2002 156th Ave. NE, #300, Bellevue, WA 98007-3827 USA
E-mail: jenny@wizkidsgames.com; customerservice@wizkidsgames.com
Web site: http://www.mageknight.com
Dist(s): **Diamond Bk. Distributors.**

Wms-Ashe, Marcella *See* **Allecram Publishing**

WND Bks, Inc., *(978-0-9746701; 978-0-9767269; 978-0-9778984; 978-0-9790451; 978-0-9792671; 978-1-935071; 978-1-936488; 978-1-938067; 978-1-942475; 978-1-944212; 978-1-944229)* 2020 Pennsylvania Ave NW No. 351, Washington, DC 20006 USA (SAN 255-7304) Tel 571-612-8600; Fax: 571-612-8619; *Imprints:* Kids Ahead Books (Kids Ahead)
E-mail: marketing@wndbooks.com; gstone@wnd.com
Web site: http://www.wnd.com; http://www.wndbooks.com
Dist(s): **Follett School Solutions**
McLemore, Hollern & Assocs.
Midpoint Trade Bks., Inc.
MyiLibrary
Quality Bks., Inc.
ebrary, Inc.

Wobblefoot Ltd., *(978-0-9747149)* 1662 Mars Ave., Lakewood, OH 44107-3825 USA
E-mail: wblft1@sbcglobal.net
Web site: http://wobblefoot.com.

Wocto Publishing, *(978-1-934867)* 7486 La Jolla Blvd., Pmb 559, La Jolla, CA 92037 USA (SAN 855-2754) Tel 858-551-5585; Fax: 858-731-4082; Toll Free: 888-551-5010
E-mail: lin@wocto.com; sales@wocto.com
Web site: http://www.wocto.com.

Wohlers Assocs., Inc., *(978-0-9754429; 978-0-9913332)* OakRidge Business Pk., 1511 River Oak Dr., Fort Collins, CO 80525-5537 USA
Web site: http://www.wohlersassociates.com.

Wold Creative Group, *(978-0-615-24135-7)* 1392 S. 1100 E., Suite 201, Salt Lake City, UT 84105 USA Tel 801-783-4502
Web site: http://www.woldcreative.com
Dist(s): **Lulu Enterprises Inc.**

Wold, Kelly, *(978-0-9768944)* 398 Ricketts Rd. Apt. D, Monterey, CA 93940-7420 USA
E-mail: kmwold@hotmail.com.

Wolf Creek Publishing, *(978-0-9768983)* 193 Tenby Chase Dr., Apt. S-233, Delran, NJ 08075 USA
Web site: http://www.photosfromthewild.com.

Wolf Jump Publications, *(978-0-9820440)* 2217 Princess Anne St., Suite 101-1A c/o R.R.R., Fredericksburg, VA 22401 USA
E-mail: rrr@marstel-day.com.

Wolf Pirate Publishing, *(978-0-9798372; 978-0-9822343)* 337 Lost Lake Dr., Divide, CO 80814 USA
E-mail: wolfpirateprop@aol.com
Web site: http://www.wolf-pirate.com.

Wolfenden, *(978-0-9642521; 978-0-9786951)* 780-a Redwood Dr., Garberville, CA 95542 USA (SAN 298-4571)
E-mail: dai@asis.com
Web site: http://wolfendenpublishing.com.

Wolfhound Pr. (IRL) *(978-0-86327; 978-0-905473; 978-0-9503454) Dist. by* **Interlink Pub.**

Wolfhound Pr. (IRL) *(978-0-86327; 978-0-905473; 978-0-9503454) Dist. by* **Irish Amer Bk.**

Wolfhound Pr. (IRL) *(978-0-86327; 978-0-905473; 978-0-9503454) Dist. by* **Irish Bks Media.**

Wolfmont, LLC, *(978-0-9778402; 978-1-60364)* 238 Park Dr., NE, Ranger, GA 30734 USA Fax: 702-543-8386; P.O. Box 205, Ranger, GA 30734; *Imprints:* Honey Locust Press (Honey Locust)
E-mail: tony@wolfmont.com; editor@honeylocustpress.com
Web site: http://www.wolfmont.com; http://www.honeylocustpress.com
Dist(s): **Smashwords.**

Wolfmont Publishing *See* **Wolfmont, LLC**

Wolfs Corner Publishing, *(978-0-9779921)* 20 Primrose Ln., Sparta, NJ 07871 USA (SAN 856-4191) Tel 973-579-5305
E-mail: jmd_inc007@hotmail.com
Web site: http://www.wolfscornerpublishing.com.

Wollaston Pr., *(978-0-9657005)* Div. of Ctr. for Learning Abilities, 4013 Coyte Ct., Marietta, GA 30062 USA Tel 678-318-3518; Fax: 208-474-9521
E-mail: morewords@comcast.net.

Wolsak & Wynn Pubs., Ltd. (CAN) *(978-0-919897; 978-1-894987; 978-1-928088) Dist. by* **IPG Chicago.**

Woman's Missionary Union, *(978-0-936625; 978-1-56309; 978-1-59669; 978-1-62591)* Orders Addr.: c/o Carol Causey, P.O. Box 830010, Birmingham, AL 35283 USA (SAN 699-7015) Tel 205-991-8100; Fax: 205-995-4825; Toll Free: 800-968-7301; Edit Addr.: 100 Missionary Ridge, Birmingham, AL 35242 USA (SAN 699-7023)
E-mail: cwhite@wmu.org
Web site: http://www.wmu.com
Dist(s): **Send The Light Distribution LLC.**

Wombacher, Michael, *(978-0-9713033)* 2412 Valley St., Berkeley, CA 94702-2136 USA
E-mail: michael_wombacher@excite.com
Web site: http://www.doggonegood.org.

Women & Addiction Counseling & Educational Services, *(978-0-9663144)* 43522 Modena Dr., Temecula, CA 92592-9235 USA Tel 951-303-0235 (phone/fax)
E-mail: info@wacespublishing.com
Web site: http://www.wacespublishing.com.

Women in Aviation, International, *(978-0-9749190)* 3647 State Route 503 S., W Alexandria, OH 45381-9354 USA
Web site: http://www.wai.org.

Women's Pr., Ltd., The (GBR) *(978-0-7043) Dist. by* **Trafalgar.**

Wonder Chess LLC, *(978-0-9771787)* 2622 10th Ave E., Seattle, WA 98102-3901 USA
E-mail: info@wonderchess.com
Web site: http://www.wonderchess.com.

Wonder Forge LLC, The, *(978-0-9797123; 978-0-9819248; 978-1-935595)* 300 E. Pike St., Seattle, WA 98122 USA
E-mail: brant@thewonderforge.com
Web site: http://www.thewonderforge.com.

Wonder Readers *Imprint of* **Capstone Pr., Inc.**

Wonder Realms Bks., *(978-0-615-86175-3; 978-0-615-87453-1; 978-0-615-87731-0; 978-0-615-98143-7; 978-0-692-27842-0; 978-0-692-30193-7; 978-0-692-41215-2; 978-0-692-45067-3; 978-0-692-50052-1)* 3740 W. 3850 N., Beryl, UT 84714 USA Tel 385-282-8598
Dist(s): **CreateSpace Independent Publishing Platform.**

Wonder Toast Arts, Incorporated *See* **WonderToast**

Wonder Workshop, *(978-1-56919)* Div. of Stephens Group, Inc., 1123 Brookstone Blvd., Mount Juliet, TN 37122-3274 USA Toll Free: 800-627-6874.

Wonderbooks Publishing, *(978-0-9773809)* P.O. Box 770741, Orlando, FL 32877 USA (SAN 257-4535)
Web site: http://www.wonderbookspublishing.com.

Wonderful Publishing, *(978-0-9798421)* 150 Brewster Rd., Scarsdale, NY 10583 USA (SAN 854-5006)
Web site: http://www.madelineart.com
Dist(s): **Partners Pubs. Group, Inc.**

Wonderstrand Pr., *(978-0-9818295)* P.O. Box 156, North Eastham, MA 02651-0156 USA (SAN 856-6585) Tel 508-240-0432; Fax: 508-240-0432
E-mail: michael@successonyourownterms.com
Web site: http://www.wonderstrandpress.com.

WonderToast, *(978-0-9761606)* Orders Addr.: 3075 E. Bates Ave., Denver, CO 80210 USA Tel 303-330-4770
E-mail: anna@wondertoast.com
Web site: http://www.wondertoast.com.

Wood Designs, Inc., *(978-0-9729454)* P.O. Box 1790, New Waverly, TX 77358-1790 USA Toll Free Fax: 877-612-8306; Toll Free: 877-612-8306; *Imprints:* MomGeek.com (MomGeek.com)
E-mail: sales@pegrack.com
Web site: http://www.flamencoguide.com.

Wood, Ella Sue, *(978-0-9774937)* 3229 Regatta Pointe Ct., Midlothian, VA 23112 USA.

Wood Lake Publishing, Inc. (CAN) *(978-0-919599; 978-0-929032; 978-0-929599; 978-1-55145; 978-1-895562) Dist. by* **Westminster John Knox.**

†Woodbine Hse., *(978-0-933149; 978-1-890627; 978-1-60613)* 6510 Bells Mill Rd., Bethesda, MD 20817 USA (SAN 630-4052) Tel 301-897-3570; Fax: 301-897-5838; Toll Free: 800-843-7323
E-mail: info@woodbinehouse.com
Web site: http://www.woodbinehouse.com; *CIP*

Woodburn Graphics, Inc., *(978-0-9707547)* P.O. Box 490, Terre Haute, ID 47807 USA Tel 812-232-0323; Fax: 812-232-2733; Toll Free: 800-457-0674
E-mail: len@woodburngraphics.com
Web site: http://www.woodburngraphics.com.

Wooded Hill Productions, *(978-1-886635)* Orders Addr.: 7480 Esplin Way, Flagstaff, AZ 86004 USA Tel 928-522-0058 (phone/fax)
E-mail: sig@boloz.com; sigmund.boloz@nau.edu
Web site: http://www.boloz.com.

Wooden Nickel Pr., *(978-0-615-25177-6; 978-0-9882891)* 2189 N. 55th St., Milwaukee, WI 53208 USA
Web site: http://www.woodennickelpress.com.

Wooden Shoe Pr., *(978-0-9762852)* N3566 Cty. Rd., GG, Hancock, WI 54943 USA Do not confuse with Wooden Shoe Press in Philadelphia, PA
E-mail: woodenshoepress@yahoo.com
Web site: http://www.woodenshoepress.com.

WoodenBoat Pubns., *(978-0-937822; 978-1-934982)* P.O. Box 78, Brooklin, ME 04616 USA Tel 207-359-4651; Fax: 207-359-2058; Toll Free: 800-273-7447
E-mail: books@woodenboat.com; wbstore@woodenboat.com
Web site: http://www.woodenboat.com.

Woodglen Publishing LLC, *(978-0-9827951)* P.O. Box 122, Califon, NJ 07830 USA Tel 908-638-5338; Fax: 908-638-0368
E-mail: stephanie@woodglenpublishing.com
Web site: http://www.woodglenpublishing.com
Dist(s): **AtlasBooks Distribution.**

Woodland Health Books *See* **Woodland Publishing, Inc.**

Woodland Pr., *(978-0-9755822)* 605 Timber Ln., Lake Forest, IL 60045-3117 USA Tel 847-295-3514; 847-924-0324 Do not confuse with companies with the same name in Minneapolis, MN, Lapeer MI, Salt Lake City, UT.

Woodland Pr., LLC, *(978-0-9724867; 978-0-9793236; 978-0-9824939; 978-0-9829937; 978-0-9852640; 978-0-9912301)* 118 Woodland, Suite 1102, Chapmanville, WV 25508 USA (SAN 254-9999) Tel 304-752-7500; Fax: 304-752-9002 Do not confuse with companies with the same or similar names in Minneapolis, MN, Lapeer, MI, Salt Lake City, UT, Florance, AL, Moscow, ID
E-mail: info@woodlandpress.com; woodlandpressllc@mac.com; fkeithdavis@me.com
Web site: http://www.woodlandpress.com
Dist(s): **New Day Christian Distributors Gifts, Inc.**
Quality Bks., Inc.
West Virginia Book Co., The
Woodland Distribution.

Woodland Publishing, Inc., *(978-0-913923; 978-1-58054; 978-1-885670)* Orders Addr.: 1500 Kearns Blvd., Park City, UT 84060-7226 USA (SAN 286-9063) Toll Free: 800-777-2665
E-mail: hpackham@woodlandpublishing.com
Web site: http://www.woodlandpublishing.com
Dist(s): **Integral Yoga Pubns.**
New Leaf Distributing Co., Inc.
Nutri-Bks. Corp.
Royal Pubns., Inc.

Woodland Scenics, *(978-1-887436)* Div. of Osment Models, Inc., Orders Addr.: P.O. Box 98, Linn Creek, MO 65052 USA Tel 573-346-5555; Toll Free: 800-346-6642; Edit Addr.: 101 E. Valley Dr., Linn Creek, MO 65052 USA
E-mail: sales@woodlandscenics.com.

Woodruff, David Roberts, *(978-0-9716806)* 4075 Carmel View Rd., No.9, San Deigo, CA 92130 USA
E-mail: drbts@att.net.

Woodruff, Paul, *(978-0-9764327)* 58048 Inglewood Ln., Glenwood, IA 51534 USA.

Woods, Emmett L., *(978-0-615-12589-3)* 4016 Monterey Ct., Montgomery, AL 36116 USA Tel 334-288-1380.

Woods N' Water, Incorporated *See* **Woods N' Water Pr., Inc.**

Woods N' Water Pr., Inc., *(978-0-9707493; 978-0-9722804; 978-0-9769233; 978-0-9795131; 978-0-9820414; 978-0-9828228; 978-0-615-38124-4)* Orders Addr.: P.O. Box 10, South New Berlin, NY 13843 USA (SAN 254-3869) Tel 607-548-4011; Fax: 607-548-4013; Toll Free: 800-652-7527; Edit Addr.: 3312 State Hwy. 8, South New Berlin, NY 13843 USA Tel 607-548-4011; Fax: 607-548-4013; Toll Free: 800-652-7527
E-mail: kate@fiduccia.com
Web site: http://www.woodsnwaterpress.com; http://www.atabooks.com
Dist(s): **Cardinal Pubs. Group.**

Woodstocker Books/Arthur Schwartz & Company, *(978-1-879504)* 15 Meads Mountain Rd., Woodstock, NY 12498-1016 USA (SAN 630-0464) Tel 845-679-4024; Fax: 845-679-4093; Toll Free: 800-669-9080 (orders only)
E-mail: woodstockerbooks@woodstockerbooks.com
Web site: http://www.aschwartzbooks.com
Dist(s): **Antique Collectors' Club**
National Bk. Network.

Woolfolk Publications *See* **Gye Nyame Hse.**

Wooster Bk. Co., The, *(978-1-888683; 978-1-59098)* 205 W. Liberty St., Wooster, OH 44691-4831 USA Tel 330-262-1688; Fax: 330-264-9753; Toll Free: 800-982-6651 (800-WUBook-1)
E-mail: mail@woosterbook.com
Web site: http://www.woosterbook.com.

Wo-Pila Publishing, *(978-1-886340)* Orders Addr.: P.O. Box 8966, Erie, PA 16505-0966 USA Tel 814-868-5331; Fax: 814-868-1711; Toll Free: 888-567-8267; Edit Addr.: 3324 Charlotte St., Erie, PA 16508-2224 USA
E-mail: WopilaPublishing@aol.com
Web site: http://www.MannyTwofeathers.com.

Word Aflame Pr., *(978-0-912315; 978-0-932581; 978-1-56722; 978-0-7577)* Subs. of Pentecostal Publishing Hse., 8855 Dunn Rd., Hazelwood, MO 63042 USA (SAN 212-0046) Tel 314-837-7300; Fax: 314-837-6574
E-mail: pph@upci.org
Web site: http://www.upci.org/pph.

Word Among Us Pr., *(978-0-932085; 978-1-59325)* 7115 Guilford Dr. Suite 100, Frederick, MD 21704 USA (SAN 686-4651) Tel 301-831-1262; Fax: 301-831-1188; Toll Free: 800-775-9673
E-mail: pmm@wall.org
Web site: http://www.wau.org
Dist(s): **Spring Arbor Distributors, Inc.**

Word Assocs., Inc., *(978-0-939153; 978-1-57265)* 3226 Robincrest Dr., Northbrook, IL 60062 USA (SAN 679-7792) Tel 847-291-1101; Fax: 847-291-0931
E-mail: microlm@aol.com
Web site: http://www.wordassociates.com.

Word Association Pubs., *(978-1-891231; 978-1-932205; 978-1-59571; 978-1-63385)* 205 Fifth Ave., Tarentum, PA 15084 USA Tel 724-226-4526; Fax: 724-226-3974; Toll Free: 800-827-7903
E-mail: publish@wordassociation.com
Web site: http://www.wordassociation.com.

Word Circus *See* **Chanda Hahn**

Word Distribution *See* **Word Entertainment**

Word Entertainment, *(978-0-9644619; 978-1-933876)* 25 Music Sq. W., Nashville, TN 37203 USA Tel 615-726-7900; Toll Free Fax: 800-671-6601; Toll Free: 800-876-9673; *Imprints:* Word Music (Word Music)
E-mail: matt.taylor@wordentertainment.com
Web site: http://www.wordentertainment.com
Dist(s): **Christian Bk. Distributors.**

Word For Word Publishing Co., *(978-1-889732)* 144 Quincy St. Apt. 1, Brooklyn, NY 11216-1393 USA; *Imprints:* A & E Sivells Publications (A & E Sivells Pubns)
E-mail: word4wrd@aol.com.

Word Gift Pubns., *(978-0-9788381)* 6641 Cty. Rd. 912, Joshua, TX 76058 USA (SAN 851-7223)
E-mail: peregrina@wordgift.org
Web site: http://www.wordgift.org.

Word Music *Imprint of* **Word Entertainment**

Word of Life Fellowship, Inc., *(978-1-931235; 978-1-935475)* Orders Addr.: P.O. Box 600, Schroon Lake, NY 12870-0600 USA Fax: 518-494-6312; Toll Free: 888-932-5827; Edit Addr.: 71 Olmstedville Rd., Pottersville, NY 12860 USA Do not confuse with Word of Life Fellowship, Sand Springs, OK
E-mail: timf@wol.org; DReichard@wol.org
Web site: http://www.wol.org.

Word of Mouth Bks. *Imprint of* **KA Productions, LLC**

Word of Mouth Pr., *(978-0-615-24213-2; 978-0-578-03631-1; 978-0-578-05051-5; 978-0-578-05113-0; 978-0-578-12825-2)* 406 Shelby St., Kingsport, TN 37660 USA Tel 423-245-1199
E-mail: electragraphics@earthlink.net.

Word on Da Street Publishing, *(978-0-615-52643-0; 978-0-615-64869-9; 978-0-9885056)* 252 W. Westfield Ave. 252 W. Westfield Ave, Roselle Park, NJ 07204 USA Tel 973-445-1690
E-mail: llperry803@gmail.com.

Word Prodns., *(978-0-9728590; 978-0-9765010; 978-0-9827998; 978-0-9909245)* P.O. Box 11865, Albuquerque, NM 87192 USA Tel 505-750-2748; Fax: 505-292-5999; *Imprints:* KID-E Books (KID-E Bks)
Web site: http://www.wordproductions.org
Dist(s): **Bridge-Logos Foundation**
CreateSpace Independent Publishing Platform.

Word Prostitute, *(978-0-9728465)* 3434 SE 13th Ave., Portland, OR 97202 USA
E-mail: kalabjoster@wordprostitute.com
Web site: http://www.wordprostitute.com.

Word Riot Pr., *(978-0-9728200; 978-0-9779343)* P.O. Box 414, Middletown, NJ 07748 USA
E-mail: editor@wordriot.org
Web site: http://www.wordriot.org
Dist(s): **Pathway Bk. Service.**

Word Seed Publishing, *(978-0-9755232)* 650 NE 2nd St., Hermiston, OR 97838 USA Tel 541-567-0886; Fax: 541-481-7500
E-mail: hashcraftz1@charter.net.

Word Supremacy Pr., *(978-0-9747231)* 910 St., Paul St., No. C, Baltimore, MD 21202 USA Tel 443-414-4600; Fax: 877-504-3140
E-mail: taalam@aol.com
Web site: http://www.taalamacey.com.

Word Weaver Bks., Inc., *(978-0-9670600)* 9743 W. Bray Creek St., Star, ID 83669-5815 USA
E-mail: tidegirl32@aol.com
Web site: http://www.wordweaverbooks.com.

Word Weaver Media, *(978-1-940350)* 7410 SW Oleson Rd No. 254, Portland, OR 97223-7475 USA Tel 503-297-3262
E-mail: KarenM@WordWeaverMedia.com.

Word with You Pr., A, *(978-0-9843064; 978-0-9829094; 978-0-9884646)* 802 S. Tremont St., Oceanside, CA 92054 USA Tel 760-500-5409; 310 E. A St. Suite B, Moscow, ID 83843 Tel 760-500-5409
E-mail: thorn@awordwithyoupress.com
Web site: http://awordwithyoupress.com.

Word Wright International *See* **WordWright.biz, Inc.**

WordFire, Incorporated *See* **WordFire Pr.**

WordFire Pr. *Imprint of* **WordFire Pr.**

WordFire Pr., *(978-0-9673548; 978-1-61475; 978-1-68057)* Div. of WordFire, Inc., P.O. Box 1840, Monument, CO 80132-1840 USA; *Imprints:* WordFire Press (WrdFire Pr)
E-mail: reb@wordfire.com
Web site: http://wordfire.com; http://wordfirepress.com.

WordMaster Publishing, *(978-0-9740410)* 4317 W. Farrand Rd., Clio, MI 48420 USA (SAN 255-3325) Tel 810-686-2047; Fax: 810-564-9929
E-mail: wordmasterpub@aol.com.

Wordminder Pr., *(978-0-9729103)* Orders Addr.: 1008 Norview Ave., Norfolk, VA 23513-3410 USA Tel 757-853-4775
E-mail: sma@wordminderpress.com; wp@wordminderpress.com
Web site: http://www.wordminderpress.com
Dist(s): **CreateSpace Independent Publishing Platform.**

Wordpainting/Paper Kite Press *See* **Paper Kite Pr.**

WordPlay Multimedia, LLC, *(978-0-9755444)* Orders Addr.: P.O. Box 9303, Jacksonville, FL 32208 USA Tel 904-683-8032
E-mail: jjfrederick98@aol.com
Web site: http://www.frederickpreston.com
Dist(s): **A & B Distributors & Pubs. Group.**

Words & Music, *(978-0-9800880; 978-0-615-15540-1)* 13967 Amber Pl., San Diego, CA 92130 USA Do not confuse with Words & Music, Gig Harbor, CA
E-mail: info@talesalive.com
Web site: http://www.talesalive.com.

Words & Pictures Publishing, Inc., *(978-0-9621280)* P.O. Box 61444, Honolulu, HI 96839 USA (SAN 250-9326) Tel 808-955-4742; Fax: 808-951-6541
E-mail: gecko@aloha.net
Web site: http://www.brucehale.com
Dist(s): **Booklines Hawaii, Ltd.**
Sunbelt Pubns., Inc.

Words of Essence Publishing, *(978-0-9768133)* P.O. Box 13182, Durham, NC 27709 USA Tel 919-624-4138
E-mail: godslove232@yahoo.com
Web site: http://www.wordsofessence.com.

words4u, *(978-0-9740419)* P.O. Box 641257, San Francisco, CA 94164-1257 USA
E-mail: info@words4u.com
Web site: http://www.words4u.com.

WordsBright, *(978-1-940229)* 501-I S. Reino Rd, No. 365, Newbury Park, CA 91320 USA Tel 805-413-4525
E-mail: contactus@wordsbright.com
Web site: www.wordsbright.com
Dist(s): **Pathway Bk. Service.**

Wordshed, *(978-0-942684)* 5118 Glendale St., Duluth, MN 55804-1107 USA (SAN 239-6246) Tel 218-525-3266.

Wordsmith Bks., *(978-1-882646)* 1418 Manchester Dr., Eugene, OR 97401 USA Tel 541-341-4687 Do not confuse with Wordsmith Bks. in Auburn, AL
E-mail: wordsmithbooks@comcast.net.

Wordsmith Pr., *(978-1-893972)* 11462 East Ln., Whitmore Lake, MI 48189 USA Tel 810-231-5435
E-mail: info@thewordsmithpress.com
Web site: http://www.thewordsmithpress.com.

Wordsmiths, *(978-0-9632774; 978-1-886061)* 1355 Ferry Rd., Grants Pass, OR 97526 USA Tel 541-476-3080; Fax: 541-474-9756 Do not confuse with the Wordsmiths in Evergreen, CO
E-mail: frodej@chatlink.com
Web site: http://www.jsgrammar.com.

Wordsong *Imprint of* **Boyds Mills Pr.**

Wordsworth Editions, Ltd. (GBR) *(978-1-85326; 978-1-84022) Dist. by* **LBMayAssocs.**

WORDSWORTH Publishing Co., *(978-0-9672491; 978-0-9754351)* Orders Addr.: P.O. Box 7132, Santa Rosa, CA 95407 USA Tel 707-829-2316 (phone/fax); Edit Addr.: 2524 S. Edison St., Graton, CA 95444 USA
E-mail: wwinfo@getyourwordsworth.com
Web site: http://www.getyourwordsworth.com.

WordThunder Pubns., *(978-0-9745268; 978-1-59790)* P.O. Box 540931, Merritt Island, FL 32954 USA (SAN 256-3770)
E-mail: books@wordthunder.com
Web site: http://wordthunder.com/books/.

Wordwindow LLC, *(978-0-9774484)* 2125 Jackson Bluff Rd. Apt. V-204, Tallahassee, FL 32304 USA Toll Free: 877-967-3946
Web site: http://www.wordwindow.com.

WordWorks Publishing, *(978-0-9831557)* 1081 Rosedale Dr., Atlanta, GA 30306 USA Tel 404-664-5256 Do not confuse with WordWorks Publishing in Austin, TX, Westfield, IN
E-mail: laurelannd@gmail.com
Dist(s): **BookBaby.**

Wordwright Communications, *(978-0-9718838)* 4900 Randall Pkwy. Ste, F, Wilmington, NC 28403-2831 USA Toll Free: 888-235-0248.

WordWright.biz, Inc., *(978-0-9700615; 978-0-9713832; 978-0-9717868; 978-1-932196; 978-1-934335)* P.O. Box 1785, Georgetown, TX 78627 USA Fax: 512-260-3080 (phone/fax); *Imprints*: Legacy (Lgcy TX); One Night Books (One Night Bks)
E-mail: joan@wordwright.biz; snwriter@earthlink.net; jnwriter@aol.com
Web site: http://www.wordwright.biz.

Workhouse Road Productions, *(978-0-615-74249-6; 978-0-615-78551-6; 978-0-692-41154-4)* 1321 S. CLOVERDALE AVE, LOS ANGELES, CA 90019 USA Tel 323-528-7495
E-mail: Bettykbynum@gmail.com
Web site: www.theimagirlcollection.com
Dist(s): **Midpoint Trade Bks., Inc.**

Working Parents, LLC, *(978-0-9711040)* P.O. Box 715, Santa Clara, CA 95052-0715 USA Tel 408-554-0280 (phone/fax)
E-mail: info@workingparents.com
Web site: http://www.workingparents.com.

Working Title Publishing, *(978-1-59344; 978-0-9776440)* P.O. Box 384, Lodi, CA 95241 USA
Web site: http://www.workingtitlepublishing.com.

Working Words & Graphics *See* **Lockman, James Consulting**

†Workman Publishing Co., Inc., *(978-0-7611; 978-0-89480; 978-0-911104; 978-1-56305)* Orders Addr.: 225 Varick St., New York, NY 10014-4381 USA (SAN 203-2821) Tel 212-254-5900; Fax: 212-254-8098; Toll Free: 800-722-7202
E-mail: info@workman.com
Web site: http://www.workman.com; *CIP*.

World Ahead Media *See* **WND Bks, Inc.**

World Almanac Bks. *Imprint of* **Facts On File, Inc.**

World Almanac Library *Imprint of* **Stevens, Gareth Publishing LLLP**

World Audience Pubs., *(978-0-9788086; 978-1-934209; 978-0-9820540; 978-1-935444)* 303 Pk. Ave. S., Suite 1440, New York, NY 10010 USA
E-mail: worldaudience@gmail.com; info@worldaudience.org
Web site: http://www.worldaudience.org; http://www.worldaudience.mobi; http://www.worldaudience.co.uk.

World Awake Bks., *(978-0-615-26795-1)* 15508 W. Bell Rd., Suite 101,, Surprise, AZ 85374 USA.

†World Bank Pubns., *(978-0-8213; 978-1-4648)* Orders Addr.: P.O. Box 960, Herndon, VA 20172-0960 USA Toll Free: 800-645-7247; Edit Addr.: 1818 H St., NW, Mail Stop: U11-1104, Washington, DC 20433 USA (SAN 219-0648) Tel 703-661-1580; 202-473-1000 (Head Office); Fax: 202-614-1237
E-mail: books@worldbank.org
Web site: http://www.worldbank.org/publications
Dist(s): **Bernan Assocs.**
Ebsco Publishing
Independent Pubs. Group
MyiLibrary
Oxford Univ. Pr., Inc.
ebrary, Inc.; *CIP*.

World Bk., Inc., *(978-0-7166)* Div. of Scott Fetzer Co., 233 N. Michigan, Suite 2000, Chicago, IL 60601 USA (SAN 201-4815) Tel 312-729-5800; Fax: 312-729-5600; 312-729-5614; Toll Free Fax: 800-433-9330 (US orders); 888-690-4002 (Canadian orders); Toll Free: 800-975-3250 (US orders); 800-967-5325; 800-837-5365 (Canadian orders)
Web site: http://www.worldbook.com
Dist(s): **MyiLibrary.**

World CARP, *(978-0-9722946)* 4 W. 43rd St., New York, NY 10036-7408 USA
E-mail: yyk21@worldcarp.org
Web site: http://www.worldcarp.org.

World Cycling Pr., *(978-0-9745842)* 3910 Chapman St., San Diego, CA 92110-5694 USA Tel 619-224-1050; Fax: 619-224-0530
E-mail: team_mallory@hotmail.com.

World Famous Children's Bks., *(978-0-9725398)* 4455 Torrance Blvd, No. 153, Torrance, CA 90503 USA
Web site: http://www.worldfamouschildrensbooks.com
Dist(s): **Quality Bks., Inc.**

World Health Organization, Orders Addr.: 49 Sheridan Ave., Albany, NY 12210 USA (SAN 221-6310) Tel 518-436-9686; Fax: 518-436-7433; Edit Addr.: Av Appia, Geneva, 1211 CHE Tel 41-22) 7912111; Fax: 41-22) 7910746
E-mail: publications@who.int
Web site: http://www.who.ch
Dist(s): **Balogh International, Inc.**
Bernan Assocs.
MyiLibrary
Stylus Publishing, LLC
Women Ink.

World Leisure Marketing Ltd (GBR) *(978-1-84006; 978-1-899026) Dist. by* **Midpt Trade.**

World Library Pubns., *(978-0-937690; 978-1-58459)* Div. of J. S. Paluch Co., Inc., 3708 River Rd. Suite 400, Franklin Park, IL 60131-2158 USA (SAN 203-0036) Tel 847-233-2767; Toll Free Fax: 888-957-3291; Toll Free: 800-621-5197
E-mail: wlpcs@jspaluch.com
Web site: http://www.wlpmusic.com
Dist(s): **Ingram Pub. Services**
Spring Arbor Distributors, Inc.

World Nouveau, *(978-0-9828865; 978-1-938208)* P.O. Box 571, Torrance, CA 90508 USA Tel 310-776-5510
E-mail: WorldNouveau@Gmail.com
Web site: http://www.WorldNouveau.com.

World of Angels, A, *(978-0-9743964)* 97 Main St., Belfast, ME 04915 USA Tel 207-338-8900
E-mail: aworldofangels@prexar.com
Web site: http://www.aworldofangels.com.

World of Imagination, *(978-0-9761228)* 200 N. Maryland Ave., Suite 101, Glendale, CA 91206 USA Tel 818-547-5541; Fax: 818-543-1889; Toll Free: 800-266-5255.

World of Learning Publishing *See* **Swift Learning Resources**

World of Reading, Ltd., P.O. Box 13092, Atlanta, GA 30324-0092 USA Tel 404-233-4042; Fax: 404-237-5511; Toll Free: 800-729-3703.

World of Whimsy Productions, LLC, *(978-0-9702675)* 409 N. Pacific Coast Hwy., No. 594, Redondo Beach, CA 90277 USA (SAN 256-1077) Fax: 310-542-9297; Toll Free: 1-888-4-WHIMSY
E-mail: info@worldofwhimsy.com
Web site: http://worldofwhimsy.com.

World Pubns. Group, Inc., *(978-0-7669; 978-0-9640034; 978-1-57215; 978-0-7429; 978-1-4132; 978-1-4279; 978-1-4376; 978-1-4513; 978-1-4643; 978-1-4785)* Orders Addr.: P.O. Box 509, East Bridgewater, MA 02333 USA (SAN 631-7014); *Imprints*: JG Press (JG Pr)
E-mail: sales@wrldpub.net
Web site: http://www.wrldpub.com
Dist(s): **Hachette Bk. Group.**

World Publications, Incorporated *See* **World Pubns. Group, Inc.**

World Quest Learning, *(978-1-933248)* P.O. Box 654, Lewis Center, OH 43035 USA Tel 740-548-3857; Toll Free Fax: 866-722-7521; Toll Free: 866-722-7520
E-mail: info@worldquestlearning.com
Web site: http://www.worldquestlearning.com.

World Thoughts Publishing, Co., *(978-0-9711018)* P.O. Box 3206, Saint Augustine, FL 32084-3206 USA
E-mail: beebes@aug.com
Web site: http://www.energeticawakening.com; http://www.worldthoughts.com.

World Tribune Pr., *(978-0-915678; 978-1-932911; 978-1-935523)* Orders Addr.: 8811 Aviation Blvd., Inglewood, CA 90301 USA Tel 310-337-0055; Fax: 310-642-4625; Toll Free: 800-626-1313; Edit Addr.: 606 Wilshire Blvd., Santa Monica, CA 90401 USA (SAN 683-230X) Tel 310-260-8900; Fax: 310-260-8910
E-mail: dmcneill@sgi-usa.org
Dist(s): **PCE International.**

World Wide Distributors, Limited *See* **Island Heritage Publishing**

World Wisdom, Inc., *(978-0-941532; 978-1-933316; 978-1-935493; 978-1-936597; 978-1-937786)* Orders Addr.: P.O. Box 2682, Bloomington, IN 47402-2682 USA (SAN 239-1406) Tel 812-330-3232; Fax: 812-333-1642; Toll Free: 888-992-6651; Edit Addr.: 1501 E. Hillside Dr., Bloomington, IN 47401 USA; *Imprints*: Wisdom Tales (WisdomTales)
Web site: http://www.worldwisdom.com
Dist(s): **Follett School Solutions**
MyiLibrary
National Bk. Network
New Leaf Distributing Co., Inc.
Send The Light Distribution LLC
ebrary, Inc.

Worlds In Ink *See* **Worlds In Ink Publishing, Inc.**

Worlds In Ink Publishing, Inc., *(978-0-9745568)* 4812 Ridgecrest Cir SE, Albuquerque, NM 87108-4435 USA
E-mail: info@WorldsInInk.com
Web site: http://www.WorldsInInk.com.

WorldTrek Publishing, *(978-1-936376)* 121 E. Vermijo, Colorado Springs, CO 80903 USA (SAN 859-7154).

Worldview Publishing, Inc., *(978-1-889995)* 521 Herchel Dr., Tampa, FL 33617 USA Tel 813-985-9344; Fax: 813-985-4505; Toll Free: 800-987-9444 Do not confuse with companies with same or similar names in Tiburon, CA, Colorado Springs, CO
E-mail: drlindahf@aol.com
Web site: http://www.worldviewpub.com.

Worldwide United Publishing *See* **Pearl Publishing, LLC**

Worthwhile Bks. *Imprint of* **Idea & Design Works, LLC**

Worthy Media, Incorporated *See* **Worthy Publishing**

Worthy Publishing, *(978-1-936034; 978-1-61795)* Div. of Worthy Media, Inc., One Franklin Pk. 6100 Tower Cir. Suite 210, Franklin, TN 37067 USA Tel 615-932-7605 Do not confuse with Worthy Publishing in Birmingham, AL
E-mail: jeana@worthymedia.com
Web site: http://worthypublishing.com/
Dist(s): **CreateSpace Independent Publishing Platform**
EMI CMG Distribution
MyiLibrary.

Worthy Shorts, *(978-1-935340; 978-1-937503; 978-1-937504; 978-1-937505; 978-1-937506; 978-1-937507)* P.O. Box 177, Malden on Hudson, NY 12453 USA Tel 845-246-2336; 15 Bostan Rd., Malden on Hudson, NY 12453
Web site: http://www.worthyshorts.com
Dist(s): **Smashwords.**

WowZee Works Inc, *(978-0-9778858)* 2217 Green Mountain Ct., Las Vegas, NV 89135 USA (SAN 850-5128).

WPR Publishing, *(978-1-889379)* 3445 Catalina Dr., Carlsbad, CA 92010 USA Tel 760-434-1223; Fax: 760-434-7476 Do not confuse with WPR Publishing, Dillon, MT
E-mail: kirk@whisler.com
Web site: http://www.WPRbooks.com
Dist(s): **Lightning Source, Inc.**

WRB Pub., *(978-0-9844198; 978-0-9838832; 978-0-9856762; 978-0-9896247; 978-0-9909040)* 1260 SW 25 LN, Palm City, FL 34990 USA Tel 772-463-0928; Fax: 267-220-1541
E-mail: wrb1174@att.net
Dist(s): **Ingram Pub. Services**
Smashwords.

WRDSMTH Productions, *(978-0-9744562)* Orders Addr.: P.O. Box 1406, Lawton, OK 73502-1406 USA (SAN 255-7282) Tel 580-353-4710; Fax: 580-357-9787; Toll Free: 800-357-9854; Edit Addr.: 130 SW B Ave., Lawton, OK 73501 USA
E-mail: okteller@juno.com
Web site: http://www.stringfigurestore.com.

Wren Song Pr., *(978-0-9769827)* 233 Poors Mill Rd., Belfast, ME 04915 USA Toll Free: 800-943-7664 Do not confuse with Wren Song Press in Ripton, VT
E-mail: jennifer@jenniferarmstrong.com
Web site: http://www.jenniferarmstrong.com.

Wren's Nest Publishing, Inc., *(978-0-9744111)* 177 Rabbit Farm Trail, Advance, NC 27006 USA Tel 336-998-2858
E-mail: rickyp@yadtel.net.

Wright Bk. Publishing, *(978-0-615-23176-1; 978-0-9822822)* 4188 Defoors Farm Dr., Powder Springs, GA 30127 USA
Web site: http://www.wrightbookpublishing.com; http://www.earthsavergirl.com.

Wright, Dr. Author O., *(978-0-9679676)* 4524 Portland Ave., S., Minneapolis, MN 55407-3550 USA Tel 612-822-8032
E-mail: Awright@email.usps.gov.

Wright Group/McGraw-Hill, *(978-0-322; 978-0-7802; 978-0-940156; 978-1-55624; 978-1-55911; 978-1-4045)* Div. of Mcgraw-Hill School Education Group, Orders Addr.: P.O. Box 545, Blacklick, OH 43004-0545 USA Tel 614-755-5645; Toll Free: 800-722-4726; 800-442-9685 (customer service)
Web site: http://www.wrightgroup.com/.

Wright, Lacie, *(978-0-615-20657-8; 978-0-615-20658-5)* 413 Acorn Grove Ln. Apt. C, Chesapeake, VA 23320-6561 USA
E-mail: paulndlacie@gmail.com
Dist(s): **Lulu Enterprises Inc.**

Wright Publishing, Inc., *(978-0-935087; 978-0-9652368)* Orders Addr.: P.O. Box 1956, Fayetteville, GA 30214 USA Tel 770-460-5525; Fax: 770-460-8998; Edit Addr.: 320 Devilla Trace, Fayetteville, GA 30214 USA (SAN 695-0507) Do not confuse with companies with same or similar name in Los Angeles, CA, Virgina Beach, VA, West Seneca, NY, Torrance, CA,.

Wright, Robert, *(978-0-9763223)* 272 Horse Hill Rd., Ashford, CT 06278 USA.

Wright's Way Inc., *(978-0-9767483)* 210 Henderson Dr., Jacksonville, NC 28540 USA Tel 910-989-0000 (phone/fax)
E-mail: sensei@bizec.rr.com
Web site: http://www.wrightskarate.com.

Write Away, *(978-0-615-26181-2)* 242 Hyle Ave., Murfreesboro, TN 37128 USA Tel 615-848-0247
Dist(s): **AtlasBooks Distribution.**

Write Bloody Publishing, *(978-0-9789989; 978-0-9815213; 978-0-9821488; 978-0-9842515; 978-0-9845031; 978-1-935904; 978-1-938912)* 235 E. Broadway, Sixth Flr., No. 609, Long Beach, CA 90802 USA
E-mail: writebloody@gmail.com
Web site: http://www.writebloody.com
Dist(s): **SCB Distributors.**

Write Designs, Ltd., *(978-0-9661661; 978-0-9741627; 978-0-9772614; 978-0-9826838; 978-0-9838033)* 2959 Sudderth Dr., Ruidoso, NM 88345-6323 USA (SAN 257-067X) Tel 575-257-3777; Fax: 575-257-4865
E-mail: books@wdltdpublishing.com; laura@printwritenow.com; laura.reynolds@wdltdpublishing.com
Web site: http://www.wdltdpublishing.com.

Write On!, *(978-0-9753870; 978-0-9825722; 978-0-9890688)* Orders Addr.: 704 Norwalk Ct., Nashville, TN 37214 USA Tel 615-415-9861 Do not confuse with companies with a similar name in Albuquerque, NM, Estes Park, CO
E-mail: writer@yvonneperry.net
Web site: http://writersinthesky.com; http://weare1inspirit.com/bookstore.htm.

Write Solution Ink, *(978-0-615-82067-5)* 46 Montgomery Ave., Morgantown, WV 26505 USA Tel 304-284-0958
Web site: www.WriteSolutionInk.com
Dist(s): **CreateSpace Independent Publishing Platform.**

Write Way Publishing, *(978-1-885173)* Orders Addr.: P.O. Box 441278, Aurora, CO 80044 USA Tel 303-617-0497; Fax: 303-617-1440; Toll Free: 800-680-1493 Do not confuse with Write Way Publishing, Charleston, WV
E-mail: staff@writewaypub.com; writewy@aol.com
Web site: http://www.writewaypub.com.

Write Words, Inc., *(978-0-9706152; 978-1-59431; 978-1-61386)* 2934 Old Rte. 50, Cambridge, MD 21613 USA (SAN 254-0304) Fax: 410-221-7510; *Imprints*: Cambridge Books (CB); Ebooks On The Net (Ebks on the Net) Do not confuse with The Write Words Inc., in Arlington, VA
E-mail: arline@mail.com; ArlineChase@comcast.net
Web site: http://www.ebooksonthe.net; http://www.cambridgebooks.us
Dist(s): **CreateSpace Independent Publishing Platform.**

Write World, Inc., *(978-0-9722173)* 3839 McKinney Ave. No. 155-373, Dallas, TX 75204 USA (SAN 254-8445)
E-mail: writeworld@cs.com.

Write Your Own *Imprint of* **Compass Point Bks.**

Write Your Way Through Publishing *See* **Urban Moon Publishing**

WriteGirl Pubns., *(978-0-9741251; 978-0-9837081)* 1330 Factory Pl. Unti 104, Los Angeles, CA 90013 USA Tel 213-253-2655
E-mail: info@writegirl.org
Web site: http://www.writegirl.org
Dist(s): **SPD-Small Pr. Distribution.**

WriteLife Publishing *Imprint of* **Boutique of Quality Books Publishing Co.**

WRITER for HIRE!, *(978-0-9701356; 978-0-9854623)* Orders Addr.: P.O. Box 1143, Decatur, GA 30031 USA Tel 404-315-7740 (9am-5pm EST); Fax: 770-454-0029 (24 hour)
E-mail: angeladurden@msn.com
Web site: http://www.angeladurden.com; http://www.mikeandhisgrandpa.com.

Writers Advantage Pr. *Imprint of* **iUniverse, Inc.**

Writers Cafe Pr., The, *(978-1-934284)* 418 S. Brookfield Dr., Lafayette, IN 47905-7299 USA (SAN 852-5498)
E-mail: admin@thewriterscafe.com
Web site: http://www.thewriterscafe.com.

Writers Club Pr. *Imprint of* **iUniverse, Inc.**

Writer's Coffee Shop, The, *(978-1-61213)* P.O. Box 2116, Waxahachie, TX 75168 USA (SAN 860-0112)
E-mail: publishing@thewriterscoffeeshop.com; amhayward@thewriterscoffeeshop.com
Web site: http://www.thewriterscoffeeshop.com; http://ph.thewriterscoffeeshop.com/
Dist(s): **Lulu Enterprises Inc.**

Writers Collective, The *Imprint of* **Day to Day Enterprises**

Writers' Collective, The, *(978-0-9716734; 978-1-932133; 978-1-59411)* 780 Reservoir Ave., Suite 243, Cranston, RI 02910 USA Toll Free: 800-497-0037
E-mail: factotum@writerscollective.org
Web site: http://www.writerscollective.org
Dist(s): **Midpoint Trade Bks., Inc.**

Writer's Cramp, Inc., *(978-0-9645983)* 711 San Juan Dr., Coral Gables, FL 33143-6224 USA
E-mail: JandyPF@aol.com.

Writer's Digest Bks. *Imprint of* **F&W Media, Inc.**

Writers in the Schools (WITS), *(978-0-9747704)* 1523 W. Main, Houston, TX 77006 USA
E-mail: mail@writersintheschools.org
Web site: http://www.writersintheschools.org.

Writer's Ink. Studios, Inc., *(978-0-9704460)* P.O. Box 952, Windermere, FL 34786 USA Tel 407-876-3399; Fax: 270-964-5984; Toll Free: 888-229-9200
E-mail: cat@brownbagbooks.com; writersinkstudios@cfl.rr.com
Web site: http://www.brownbagbooks.com.

Writers Marketplace:Consulting, Critiquing & Publishing, *(978-1-928632)* P.O. Box 21218, Carson City, NV 89721 USA Tel 775-544-0909; Fax: 775-884-3103.

Writer of the Round Table Pr., *(978-0-9814545; 978-0-9822206; 978-1-61066)* P.O. Box 511, Highland Park, IL 60035-0511 USA (SAN 855-6067)
Web site: http://www.writersoftheroundtable.com
Dist(s): **National Bk. Network.**

Writer's Publishing Cooperative *Imprint of* **Beech River Bks.**

Writer's Showcase Pr. *Imprint of* **iUniverse, Inc.**

WritersCorps Bks. *Imprint of* **San Francisco Art Commission, The**

Writing as a Ghost *See* **Jots & Tittles Publishing**

Writing Bench LLC., The, *(978-0-9818374)* P.O. Box 775037, Saint Louis, MO 63177-5037 USA
E-mail: backwardkingdom@yahoo.com.

Writing Center, The *See* **Full Court Pr.**

Writing etc. *See* **Etcetera Pr. LLC**

Writing for the Lord Ministries, *(978-0-9705902; 978-0-9883038; 978-0-9893188)* 6400 Shannon Ct., Clarksville, MD 21029 USA
E-mail: kevin@writingforthelord.com; kgj27@aol.com
Web site: http://www.writingforthelord.com; http://www.writingforthelord.org.

Writing The Vision *Imprint of* **Scribe Publishing & Consulting Services, The**

Writing Wild & Crazy *Imprint of* **Shakalot High Entertainment**

Writing-Right, *(978-0-9772196)* 27 Somerset Dr., Holbrook, NY 11741 USA
E-mail: lori@writing-right.org.

Written By Clark, Publishing, *(978-0-9795102)* Orders Addr.: P.O. Box 874023, Vancouver, WA 98687 USA Tel 323-447-9676
E-mail: jthomasclark@gmail.com; info@writtenbyclark.com
Web site: http://www.writtenbyclark.com
Dist(s): **Lightning Source, Inc.**

Written Expressions Enterprise, Inc., *(978-0-9728674)* 2276 Griffin Way, Suite 105-161, Corona, CA 92879 USA Tel 951-371-0160.

Written Images, Inc., *(978-0-9705721)* 1300 E. Lafayette, Suite 1104, Detroit, MI 48207 USA (SAN 253-7591) Tel 248-356-8310; Fax: 248-356-8311 Do not confuse with Written Image, The in Lancaster, NY
E-mail: writtenimages@aol.com
Web site: http://www.adiaryofjoseph.com.

Written in Black Publishing *See* **WordPlay Multimedia, LLC**

Written World Communications, *(978-0-9829377; 978-1-938679)* Orders Addr.: 4725 Splendid Cir. S., Colorado Springs, CO 80917 USA (SAN 859-9696) Tel 719-947-2181
E-mail: kristinepratt@gmail.com
Web site: http://www.writtenworldcommunications.com/.

WS Publishing, *(978-0-9639654; 978-1-887169; 978-1-934386; 978-1-936061; 978-1-61351)* 7290 Navajo Rd., Suite 207, San Diego, CA 92119 USA Tel 619-589-1919
E-mail: sarah@weddingsolutions.com; info@wspublishinggroup.com
Web site: http://wspublishinggroup.com
Dist(s): **Perseus Distribution.**

WT Melon Publishing, *(978-0-615-68671-4; 978-0-615-68782-7; 978-0-615-69346-0; 978-0-615-69810-6; 978-0-615-70474-6; 978-0-615-70475-3; 978-0-615-70525-5; 978-0-615-70531-6; 978-0-615-70715-0; 978-0-615-71033-4; 978-0-615-75767-4; 978-0-615-75775-9; 978-0-615-76301-9; 978-0-615-76302-6; 978-0-615-76867-0; 978-0-615-77035-2; 978-0-615-77246-2; 978-0-615-80660-0; 978-0-615-83940-0; 978-0-615-83947-9; 978-0-615-83980-6; 978-0-615-84316-2; 978-0-615-85818-0;*

978-0-615-90351-4) 2819 Piedmont Ave., Berkeley, CA 94705 USA Tel 510-848-3925
E-mail: devans@wtmelon.com
Web site: wtmelon.com
Dist(s): **CreateSpace Independent Publishing Platform.**

Wu Li Turtle Corp., (*978-0-9741176*) 3885 S. Decatur Blvd., Suite 2010, Las Vegas, NV 89103 USA Tel 703-864-3769; Fax: 702-920-8118; Toll Free: 888-381-6864
E-mail: rbraye@wuliturtle.com
Web site: http://www.wuliturtle.com.

Wunderlannd Pr., (*978-0-615-62918-6; 978-0-9893166*) 3141 Elmer St., Sarasota, FL 34231 USA Tel 443-742-7039
E-mail: wunderlanndpress@hotmail.com.

www.margaretmouse.com publishing co., (*978-0-9761326*) Orders Addr.: 41953 20th St., W., Palmdale, CA 93551-0000 USA Please allow four weeks for delivery. Shipments come direct from printer in China. Invoiced at order. Shipping free for all orders over 5000. Dolls are available as well. Please contact me direct at email Lparnold@verizon.net or call US 661-943-0275 with any questions or concerns or special orders.
E-mail: info@margaretmouse.com
Web site: http://www.margaretmouse.com
Dist(s): **Follett School Solutions.**

www.pmptools.com *See* **Project Management Excellence Ctr., Inc., The**

www.underdogpublishing.com, (*978-0-9754420*) 124 Titleist Cir., Savannah, GA 31419 USA
Web site: http://www.underdogpublishing.com.

Wyatt Hse. Publishing, (*978-0-9882209; 978-0-9896119; 978-0-9915798*) 399 Lakeview Dr. W., Mobile, AL 36695 USA Tel 251-421-1296
E-mail: editor@wyattpublishing.com
Web site: www.wyattpublishing.com.

Wyatt Pr., (*978-0-9718161*) 15005 W. 167th Terr., Olathe, KS 66062 USA Tel 913-768-1917; Fax: 913-768-4307.

Wyatt-MacKenzie Publishing, (*978-0-9673025; 978-1-932279; 978-0-9743832; 978-0-9820518; 978-1-936214; 978-1-939288; 978-1-942545*) 15115 Hwy. 36, Deadwood, OR 97430-9700 USA Tel 541-964-3314; Fax: 541-964-3315
E-mail: info@wymacpublishing.com; nancy@wymacpublishing.com
Web site: http://www.wymacpublishing.com
Dist(s): **BookBaby.**

Wybel Marketing Group, Orders Addr.: 213 W. Main St., Barrington, IL 60010 USA Tel 847-382-0384.

Wycliffe Bible Translators, (*978-0-938978*) P.O. Box 628200, Orlando, FL 32862-8200 USA (SAN 211-5484)
Web site: http://www.wycliffe.org.

Wyer Pearce Press *See* **SangFroid Pr.**

Wyland Galleries *See* **Wyland Worldwide, LLC**

Wyland Worldwide, LLC, (*978-0-9631793; 978-1-884840; 978-1-60586*) 6 Mason, Irvine, CA 92618 USA Tel 949-643-7070; Fax: 949-643-7082
E-mail: valeries@wyland.com
Web site: http://www.wyland.com
Dist(s): **Booklines Hawaii, Ltd.**

Wynden *Imprint of* **Canmore Pr.**

Wyoming Historical & Geological Society, (*978-0-937537*) 49 S. Franklin St., Wilkes-Barre, PA 18701 USA (SAN 281-2061) Tel 717-823-6244; Fax: 717-823-9011
E-mail: lchs@epix.net
Web site: http://www.luzernecountyhistory.com.

Wyson, Dan, (*978-0-9771522*) 1173 S. 250 W. Suite 305, Saint George, UT 84770 USA Tel 435-229-6713 Toll Free: 877-827-0710.

Wysteria, Limited *See* **Wysteria Publishing**

Wysteria Publishing, (*978-0-9651162; 978-0-9677839; 978-1-932412*) P.O. Box 1250, Bellmore, NY 11710 USA Toll Free Fax: 888-434-7979; Toll Free: 888-997-8300
E-mail: wysteria@wysteria.com
Web site: http://www.wysteria.com.

X, Y, & Me LLC, (*978-0-9755028; 978-0-9773441*) 21409 138th St., Webster, IA 52355-9079 USA
E-mail: customerservice@xyandme.com
Web site: http://www.xyandme.com.

Xanadu Metaphysical *See* **Xanadu New Age Products & Services, LLC**

Xanadu New Age Products & Services, LLC, (*978-0-9759752*) Orders Addr.: 1011 S. Lake St., Neenah, WI 54956 USA; Edit Addr.: 1011 S. Lake St., Neenah, WI 54956 USA
E-mail: parisdrake@parisdrake.com
Web site: http://www.parisdrake.com.

xbks publishing, (*978-0-9626458*) c/o Arturo Watlington Station, P.O. Box 568, Saint Thomas, VI 00804 USA
E-mail: llrush@viaccess.net; mail@xbkspublishing.net
Web site: http://www.xbkspublising.net.

Xbooks *See* **xbks publishing**

Xerces Society, The, (*978-0-9744475*) 4828 SE Hawthorne Blvd., Portland, OR 97215 USA Tel 503-232-6639; Fax: 503-233-6794
E-mail: mdshepherd@xerces.org
Web site: http://www.xerces.org.

Xist Publishing, (*978-0-615-49153-0; 978-0-9838428; 978-1-62395; 978-1-68195*) 16604 Sonora St., Tustin, CA 92782 USA Tel 949-842-5296; P.O. Box 61593, Irvine, CA 92692
E-mail: calee@xistpublishing.com
Web site: http://xistpublishing.com
Dist(s): **CreateSpace Independent Publishing Platform**
Follett School Solutions
Ingram Pub. Services
Mackin Educational Resources.

Xlibris, 1663 Liberty Dr., Bloomington, IN 47403 USA Tel 888-795-4274
E-mail: Johnnyline.Jagdon@xlibris.com
Web site: http://www2.xlibris.com/.

Xlibris Corporation *See* **Xlibris Corp.**

Xlibris Corp., (*978-0-7388; 978-0-9663501; 978-1-4010; 978-1-4134; 978-1-59926; 978-1-4257; 978-1-4363; 978-1-4415; 978-1-4500; 978-1-4535; 978-1-4568; 978-1-4628; 978-1-4653; 978-1-4691; 978-1-4771; 978-1-4797; 978-1-4836; 978-1-4931; 978-1-4990; 978-1-5035;-1-5144) Orders Addr.: 1663 S. Liberty Dr. Suite 200, Bloomington, IN 47403 USA (SAN 299-5522) Tel 812-334-5223; Fax: 812-334-5223; Toll Free: 888-795-4274*
E-mail: info@xlibris.com; orders@xlibris.com; dave.weinman@xlibris.com; customersupport@xlibris.com; digitalcontent@authorsolutions.com
Web site: http://www2.xlibris.com
Dist(s): **AtlasBooks Distribution**
Author Solutions, Inc.
CreateSpace Independent Publishing Platform
International Pubns. Service
Lulu Enterprises Inc.
Smashwords
TextStream.

Xophix, (*978-0-9754173*) P.O. Box 12081, Scottsdale, AZ 85267 USA Fax: 586-461-1712
E-mail: books@xophix.com
Web site: http://www.xophix.com.

X-treme Reviews *Imprint of* **N&N Publishing Co., Inc.**

Xulon Press, Incorporated *See* **Salem Publishing Solutions, Inc.**

Y Lolfa (GBR) (*978-0-86243; 978-0-904864; 978-0-9500178; 978-0-9555272; 978-1-84771; 978-0-9567031; 978-0-9560125; 978-1-78461*) *Dist. by* **Dufour.**

YA Angst *Imprint of* **Norilana Bks.**

YA Bks., (*978-0-615-72187-3; 978-0-615-79766-3; 978-0-9899934*) 211 Oxford St., Martin, TN 38237 USA Tel 7315875993
Web site: merrybrown.com
Dist(s): **CreateSpace Independent Publishing Platform.**

Yabitoon Bks., (*978-0-578-05342-4*) 1679 Bluffhill Dr., Monterey Park, CA 91754 USA.

Yacos Pubns., (*978-0-9653734*) Orders Addr.: 90-20 169th St., Apt. 4D, Jamaica, NY 11432 USA Tel 718-523-8911 (phone/fax)
E-mail: Drltgrant@yahoo.com
Web site: http://www.yacos.org.

Yad Vashem Pubns. (ISR) (*978-965-308*) *Dist. by* **Coronet Bks.**

Yadda Yadda Pr., (*978-0-9791387*) 1748 Donwell Dr., South Euclid, OH 44121-3734 USA
E-mail: williamecook@gmail.com
Web site: http://www.yaddayaddapress.com.

Yadeeda.com, (*978-0-9747122*) P.O. Box 38642, Colorado Springs, CO 80937 USA Tel 719-520-5125
E-mail: yadeeda@hotmail.com
Web site: http://www.yadeeda.com.

†Yale Univ. Pr., (*978-0-300*) Orders Addr.: c/o Triliteral LLC, 100 Maple Ridge Dr., Cumberland, RI 02864 USA Tel 401-531-2800; Fax: 401-531-2801; Toll Free Fax: 800-406-9145; Toll Free: 800-405-1619; Edit Addr.: 302 Temple St., New Haven, CT 06511 USA (SAN 203-2740) Tel 203-432-0960; Fax: 203-432-0948
E-mail: yupmkt@yale.edu
Web site: http://www.yale.edu/yup/; http://www.yale.edu/yup/index.html
Dist(s): **Cheng & Tsui Co.**
Ebsco Publishing
ISD
MyiLibrary
TriLiteral, LLC
Yale Univ., Far Eastern Pubns.
ebrary, Inc.; *CIP.*

Yana's Kitchen, (*978-0-9670982*) 5256 Pizzo Ranch Rd., La Canada, CA 91011 USA Tel 818-790-8381 (phone/fax)
E-mail: yana119@yahoo.com
Web site: http://yanasplace.com.

Yang, Jennifer, (*978-0-578-06384-3; 978-0-578-09356-7; 978-0-578-12358-5; 978-0-578-14107-7*) P.O. Box 22204, San Francisco, CA 94122 USA
E-mail: jenniyang@aol.com
Dist(s): **Lulu Enterprises Inc.**

Yankee Cowboy, (*978-0-9708530; 978-0-9836149*) P.O. Box 123, Keller, TX 76244 USA Tel 800-557-8166; Toll Free: 800-557-8166
E-mail: publisher@yankeecowboy.com
Web site: http://www.yankeecowboy.com; http://www.watchdognation.com; http://www.davelieber.org
Dist(s): **BCH Fulfillment & Distribution.**

Yankee Publishing, Inc., (*978-0-89909; 978-1-57198*) Orders Addr.: P.O. Box 520, Dublin, NH 03444 USA Tel 603-563-8111; Fax: 603-563-8252; Edit Addr.: Main St., Dublin, NH 03444 USA Do not confuse with Yankee Publishing, Saint Petersburg, FL
E-mail: almanac@yankeepub.com
Web site: http://www.almanac.com
Dist(s): **Houghton Mifflin Harcourt Publishing Co.**
Houghton Mifflin Harcourt Trade & Reference Pubs.
MyiLibrary.

Yari Publishing, (*978-0-578-06838-1*) P.O. Box 142624, Austin, TX 78714-2624 USA.

Yaroslavskaya, Lyudmila, (*978-0-9791248*) 600 W. Diversey Parkaway, Rm. 1410, Chicago, IL 60614 USA.

Yarrow, Peter Bks. *Imprint of* **Charlesbridge Publishing, Inc.**

Yarrow Pr., (*978-0-9741562*) Orders Addr.: P.O. Box 665, Rainelle, WV 25962 USA Tel 304-438-1040 Do not confuse with Yarrow Press in Pelham, NY
E-mail: kate@yarrowpress.com
Web site: http://www.yarrowpress.com.

Yasgur, Abigail *See* **Change the Universe Pr.**

YAV, (*978-0-9790221; 978-1-937449*) Orders Addr.: 1950 Hendersonville Rd. No. 243, Skyland, NC 28776 USA
E-mail: books@yav.com
Web site: http://InterestingWriting.com; http://ScienceOfWriting.com; http://YAVpublications.com.

Yawn's Bks. & More, Inc., (*978-0-9818673; 978-0-9830190; 978-1-936815; 978-1-940395; 978-1-943529*) 198 North St., Canton, GA 30114 USA (SAN 856-7476) Tel 678-880-1922; Fax: 678-880-1923
E-mail: fyawn@yawnsbooks.com
Web site: http://www.yawnspublishing.com.

YBK Pubs., Inc., (*978-0-9703923; 978-0-9764359; 978-0-9790972; 978-0-9800508; 978-0-9824012; 978-1-936411*) 39 Crosby St. Apt. 2N, New York, NY 10013-3254 USA
E-mail: obarz@ybkpublishers.com
Web site: http://www.ybkpublishers.com.

Ye Hedge Schl., (*978-0-9723239; 978-0-9825521*) Orders Addr.: 24934 478 Ave., Garretson, SD 57030 USA
E-mail: mod61047@alliancecom.net
Web site: http://www.hedgeschool.com.

Ye Olde Font Shoppe, (*978-1-889289*) Orders Addr.: P.O. Box 8328, New Haven, CT 06708 USA Tel 203-575-9385; Edit Addr.: 35 Ferndale, Waterbury, CT 06708 USA Tel 860-870-9741
E-mail: varivas@yahoo.com
Web site: http://www.yeolde.org.

Yearling *Imprint of* **Random Hse. Children's Bks.**

Yearling *Imprint of* **Random Hse. Children's Bks.**

Yehuda, Ben Pr., (*978-0-9769862; 978-0-9789980; 978-1-934730*) 122 Ayers Ct. No. 1B, Teaneck, NJ 07666 USA Tel 201-833-5145; Fax: 201-917-1278
E-mail: yudel@benyehudapress.com
Web site: http://www.BenYehudaPress.com.

Yellow Brick Road Publishing, (*978-0-615-24159-3*) 35 Fiske St., No. 1, Waltham, MA 02451 USA.

Yellow Daffodil Pr., (*978-0-9824943*) 17939 Chatsworth St., No. 241, Granada Hills, CA 91344 USA
E-mail: mdesannoy@gmail.com.

Yellow Umbrella Bks. *Imprint of* **Capstone Pr., Inc.**

Yellow Umbrella en espanol *Imprint of* **Capstone Pr., Inc.**

Yen Pr. *Imprint of* **Orbit**

Yen Pr., (*978-0-7595; 978-89-527*) Div. of Hachette Book Group, 237 Park Ave., New York, NY 10017 USA
Dist(s): **Hachette Bk. Group**
MyiLibrary.

Yeoman Hse., (*978-0-9754676; 978-0-9822659; 978-0-9852537*) 10 Old Bulgarmarsh Rd., Tiverton, RI 02878 USA Tel 401-816-0061
E-mail: yeomanhouse@cox.net
Web site: http://www.yeomanhouse.com.

YES - Your Emergency Safety, (*978-0-9740670*) 1302 W. Adams Ave., Saint Louis, MO 63122 USA Tel 314-822-8895; Fax: 775-458-7717
E-mail: info@youremergencysafety.org
Web site: http://www.youremergencysafety.org.

Yesterday's Classics, (*978-1-59915; 978-1-63334*) Orders Addr.: P.O. Box 3418, Chapel Hill, NC 27515 USA Tel 919-967-3119; Toll Free: 866-497-3729 (phone/fax); Edit Addr.: 1705 Audubon Rd., Chapel Hill, NC 27514 USA
Web site: http://www.yesterdaysclassics.com.

Yestermorrow, Inc., (*978-1-56723*) Orders Addr.: P.O. Box 700, Princess Anne, MD 21853 USA.

Yewtree Pr. LLC, (*978-1-933029*) P.O. Box 110 671, Brooklyn, NY 11211 USA Toll Free: 800-939-7404
E-mail: info@yewtreepress.com
Web site: http://www.yewtreepress.com.

Yhabbut Publishing, (*978-0-9724292*) Orders Addr.: P.O. Box 23032, Seattle, WA 981 USA; Edit Addr.: 2111 15th Ave., S., Suite A, Seattle, WA 98144-4271 USA
E-mail: benthoven@qwest.net
Web site: http://www.1stbooks.com/bookview/20054.

Y-IREAD Publishing, (*978-0-9728549*) Orders Addr.: P.O. Box 33248, Indianapolis, IN 46203 USA Tel 317-294-3423
E-mail: kenyawash@sbcglobal.net.

Yisrael, Sean Publishing Co., (*978-0-9772424*) 11769 Kenn Rd., Cincinnati, OH 45240 USA Tel 513-266-1158
E-mail: syisrael@dps.k12.oh.us.

YNR Media L.L.C., (*978-0-9753262*) 338 Streeter Dr., McCook Lake, SD 57049 USA Tel 310-422-1662.

Yo Puedo Publishing, (*978-0-9714533*) P.O. Box 940895, Houston, TX 77094 USA (SAN 254-3729) Tel 281-496-2015; 866-YO-PUEDO; Fax: 281-558-3773
E-mail: kathryn@yopuedo.com
Web site: http://www.yopuedo.com.

Yofi Bk. Publishing, Inc., (*978-1-931387; 978-1-60046*) 199 Lee Ave. Unit #397, Brooklyn, NY 11211 USA Tel 718-694-9040; Fax: 718-694-9062
E-mail: yofi@yeshivanet.com.

Yoga Life *See* **Love Your Life**

yomitobi, (*978-0-9799470*) 403 Knight Dr., Apt 9, Statesboro, GA 30458 USA
E-mail: yoko_6@hotmail.com
Web site: http://www.yomitobi.com.

Yonay, Shahar, (*978-0-927580; 978-0-9616783*) 126 Dover St., Brooklyn, NY 11235 USA (SAN 661-0544) Tel 718-615-0027.

Yoon-il Auh/Intrepid Pixels, (*978-1-882858*) 820 West End Ave., No. 9E, New York, NY 10025 USA Tel 212-662-6891.

Yoot Pr., (*978-0-9764611*) 17-47 Chandler Dr., Fair Lawn, NJ 07410 USA
Web site: http://www.yootpress.com.

York House Pr., Ltd., (*978-0-9791956; 978-0-9855508*) 1266 E. Main St, suite 700R,, Stamford, CT 06902 USA Tel 203-539-6180; Fax: 914-764-5159
E-mail: pholt@yorkhousepress.com
Dist(s): **Lightning Source, Inc.**

Yorkshire Publishing Group, (*978-0-88144; 978-1-936750; 978-0-9883786; 978-0-9889281; 978-0-9896518; 978-1-942451*) Orders Addr.: 9731 E. 54th St., Tulsa, OK 74147 USA (SAN 260-0285) Tel 918-394-2665; *Imprints:* Thorncrown Publishing (Thorncrown); Total Publishing & Media (Total Pubng)
E-mail: todd.rutherford@yorkshirepublishing.com
Web site: http://www.yorkshirepublishing.com
Dist(s): **BookBaby**
INscribe Digital.

Yorkville Pr., (*978-0-9729427; 978-0-9767442*) Orders Addr.: 1202 Lexington Ave., No. 315, New York, NY 10028 USA (SAN 255-3139) Tel 212-650-9154; Fax: 212-650-9157; 1202 Lexington Ave. # 315, New York, NY 10028 Tel 212-650-9154
E-mail: editors@yorkvillepress.com
Web site: http://www.yorkvillepress.com.

Yoroson Publishing *See* **Young-Robinson, Christine**

Yosemite Assn., (*978-0-939666; 978-1-930238*) Orders Addr.: P.O. Box 230, El Portal, CA 95318 USA (SAN 662-197X) Tel 209-379-2648; Fax: 209-379-2486; Edit Addr.: 5020 El Portal Rd., El Portal, CA 95318 USA
E-mail: dguy@yosemite.org
Web site: http://www.yosemite.org
Dist(s): **MyiLibrary**
Perseus-PGW
Sunbelt Pubns., Inc.

Yosoy Publishing, (*978-0-9763503*) 4141 Linden Ave, Long Beach, CA 90807 USA Tel 714-271-7667; Fax: 562-989-2031
E-mail: goodbooks@yeomanhouse.com
Web site: http://www.ginaspoems.com; http://www.yosoypublishing.com.

Yost-Haynes, Melissa, (*978-0-9760909*) RR1, 115C, Ravenswood, WV 26164 USA.

You Can Do It! Productions, (*978-0-9744306*) 106 Paradise Rd., Havana, FL 32333-4236 USA
E-mail: infinipede@juno.com
Web site: http://www.infinipede.com.

You Can Do It! ART Publications *See* **Sunrise Mountain Bks.**

you can too publishing, (*978-0-615-80082-0*) 2316 N. 19th St., Boise, ID 83702 USA Tel 208-336-2039
Dist(s): **CreateSpace Independent Publishing Platform.**

You Choose Bks. *Imprint of* **Capstone Pr., Inc.**

You Come Too Publishing, (*978-0-9816836*) 3138 NW Colonial Dr., Bend, OR 97701 USA Tel 541-317-4912 (phone/fax)
E-mail: imkehoe@msn.com
Web site: http://youcometoo.com
Dist(s): **Smashwords.**

You Publishing Group, (*978-0-9764472*) 2500 S. Lamar Blvd., Austin, TX 78704 USA.

Young Advent Pilgrim's Bookshelf *See* **Barnes Printing**

Young, Beth, (*978-0-9760180*) 124 Chestnut St. Apt. 201, Englewood, OH 45322-1410 USA
E-mail: 369beth@bellsouth.net
Web site: http://www.saintlukespress.com.

Young Patriots Series *Imprint of* **Patria Pr., Inc.**

Young Patronesses of the Opera, The, (*978-0-9785364; 978-0-9795725*) P.O. Box 3471616, Miami, FL 33234-7616 USA Tel 305-665-3470; Fax: 305-667-9265
Web site: www.ypo-miami.org.

Young Readers Publications, (*978-0-9789525*) 47 W. Schuyler St., Oswego, NY 13126 USA
E-mail: sabistonart@yahoo.com
Web site: http://jguntherphotography.com.

Young Scholars Pr., (*978-0-9787138*) 354 1/2 Calle Loma Norte, Santa Fe, NM 87501 USA Tel 505-989-7116; Fax: 505-820-2367
E-mail: MsAnnett1@aol.com
Web site: http://oneworldmanypeople.com.

Young Women Books *See* **Harper Kids Hse.**

Young Women Programming *Imprint of* **Harper Kids Hse.**

Young Writer's Contest Foundation *See* **Miracle Pr.**

Youngheart Music, (*978-0-945267; 978-1-57471*) Affil. of Creative Teaching Pr., Orders Addr.: P.O. Box 2723, Huntington, CA 92647-0723 USA Tel 714-895-5047; Fax: 714-895-5087; Toll Free Fax: 800-229-9929; Toll Free: 800-444-4287; Edit Addr.: 15342 Graham St., Huntington Beach, CA 92649-1111 USA
E-mail: webmaster@creativeteaching.com; rebecca.cleland@creativeteaching.com
Web site: http://www.youngheartmusic.com; http://www.creativeteaching.com
Dist(s): **Creative Teaching Pr., Inc.**
Follett School Solutions
Rounder Kids Music Distribution.

Youngheart Records *See* **Youngheart Music**

Youngjin (Singapore) Pte Ltd. (SGP) *Dist. by* **IPG Chicago.**

Young-Robinson, Christine, (*978-0-9706985*) 10120 Two Notch Rd., No. 143, Columbia, SC 29223 USA Fax: 803-865-9001
E-mail: miraclewriter4u@aol.com
Web site: http://www.christineyoungrobinson.com.

Youngs, Bettie Bks., (*978-0-9843081; 978-1-936332; 978-0-9836045; 978-0-9882848; 978-1-940784*) Div. of Bettie Youngs Book Publishers, 532 1/2 Via De La Valle No. C Suite C, Solana Beach, CA 92075 USA Tel 858-350-6360; *Imprints:* Kendahl House Press (KendahlHse)
E-mail: Bettie@BettieYoungs.com
Web site: http://www.BettieYoungsBooks.com
Dist(s): **Brodart Co.**
Coutts Information Services
Quality Bks., Inc.
Smashwords.

Youngs, C. R., (*978-0-9760451*) 11687 Sugar Creek Ave., Mount Carmel, IL 62863 USA
E-mail: ronyoungs@davidbook.com
Web site: http://www.davidbook.com/.

Your Culture Gifts, (*978-0-9797637*) P.O. Box 1245, Ellicott City, MD 21041 USA (SAN 854-3208) Tel 410-461-5799
E-mail: info@yourculturegifts.com
Web site: http://www.yourculturegifts.com.

For full information on wholesalers and distributors, refer to the Wholesaler and Distributor Name Index

Your Story Hour Recordings, P.O. Box 511, Medina, OH 44258 USA Tel 216-725-5767; 717 St. Jospeh Dr. #254, Saint Joseph, MI 49085 Tel 269-471-3701
Web site: http://www.yourstoryhour.org.

You're On!, Inc., *(978-0-9760280)* P.O. Box 101071, Fort Worth, TX 76185 USA.

Youth Communication - New York Center, *(978-0-9661256; 978-1-933939; 978-1-935552; 978-1-938970)* 244 W. 27th St., 2nd Flr., New York, NY 10001 USA Tel 212-279-0708 ext. 115; Fax: 212-279-8856
E-mail: khefner@youthcomm.org
Web site: http://www.youthcomm.org
Dist(s): **Follett School Solutions.**

Youth Cultural Publishing Co. (CHN) *(978-957-530; 978-957-574) Dist. by* **Chinasprout.**

Youth Development & Research Fund, *(978-0-9659130)* P.O. Box 2188, Germantown, MD 20875-2188 USA
E-mail: ed@ydrf.com
Web site: http://www.ydrf.com.

Youth Inkwell Publishing, *(978-0-9773451)* 155 S. El Molino Ave., Suite 102, Paadena, CA 91101 USA Tel 626-449-6884; Fax: 626-449-6885
E-mail: info@youthinkwell.org
Web site: http://youthinkwell.org; http://www.youthinkwell.org.

Youth Popular Culture Institute, Inc., *(978-1-887191)* 8906 Fox Park Rd., Clinton, MD 20735 USA Tel 301-877-1525.

Youth Quest Institute, *(978-0-9748994)* 5515 Azalea Trail Ln., Sugar Land, TX 77479 USA
Web site: http://youthquestinstitute.com; http://getagripbooks.com.

Youthleadership.com, *(978-0-9677981)* 5593 Golf Course Dr., Morrison, CO 80465 USA Tel 303-358-1563; Fax: 303-393-9066
E-mail: support@youthleadership.com; mariam@youthleadership.com
Web site: http://www.youthleadership.com.

Youthlight, Inc., *(978-1-889636; 978-1-59850)* Orders Addr.: P.O. Box 115, Chapin, SC 29036 USA (SAN 256-6400) Tel 803-345-1070; Fax: 803-345-0888; Toll Free: 800-209-9774; Edit Addr.: 105 Fairway Pond Dr., Chapin, SC 29036 USA
E-mail: yl@sc.rr.com; yl@youthlightbooks.com
Web site: http://www.youthlight.com; http://www.youthlightbooks.com.

Ysanti *See* **Lion's Crest Pr.**

Yucca Publishing *Imprint of* **Skyhorse Publishing Co., Inc.**

Yudcovitch, Lorne, *(978-0-9749781)* 6905 S.W. 7th Ave., Portland, OR 97219 USA Tel 503-293-6923
E-mail: yudcovil@pacificu.edu.

Yumcha Studios LLC, *(978-0-9881899)* 33-59 Farrington St., 2nd Flr., Flushing, NY 11354 USA Tel 917-332-8931; Fax: 917-332-8931
E-mail: yenyen@dimsumwarriors.com; colin@dimsumwarriors.com
Web site: www.dimsumwarriors.com
Dist(s): **Diamond Comic Distributors, Inc.**
Diamond Bk. Distributors.

YWAM Publishing, *(978-0-927545; 978-0-9615534; 978-1-57658)* Div. of Youth With A Mission International, P.O. Box 55787, Seattle, WA 98155 USA (SAN 248-4021)
E-mail: customerservice@ywampublishing.com
Web site: http://www.ywampublishing.com.

ZEM Pr., *(978-0-9634168)* 8220 Stone Trail Dr., Bethesda, MD 20817-4556 USA Tel 301-365-4585; Fax: 301-365-4586
E-mail: zem@wbh.com
Web site: http://www.wb4.com.

Z Health Bks. *Imprint of* **New Win Publishing**

Z Pr., *(978-0-615-14380-4)* P.O. Box 6556, Woodland Hills, CA 91365 USA Tel 717-337-9968
E-mail: amy@amyleecoy.com
Dist(s): **Lulu Enterprises Inc.**

Zach Feuer Gallery, *(978-0-9768533)* 530 W 24th St., New York, NY 10011 USA Tel 212-989-7700
E-mail: zach@zachfeuer.com
Web site: http://www.zachfeuer.com
Dist(s): **D.A.P./Distributed Art Pubs.**

Zachmeyer, Mary L., *(978-0-9646864)* 1008 County Road 105., Columbus, TX 78934-1606 USA.

Zadunajsky, Donna M. *See* **Little T's Corner**

Zagat Survey, *(978-0-943421; 978-0-9612574; 978-1-57006; 978-1-60478)* 4 Columbus Cir., New York, NY 10019 USA (SAN 289-4777) Tel 212-977-6000; Fax: 212-765-9438; Toll Free: 866-999-0991
E-mail: tradesales@justzagat.com; theinz@zagat.com
Web site: http://www.zagat.com
Dist(s): **Perseus Distribution.**

Zagorski, Steve, *(978-0-578-05364-6)* Orders Addr.: P.O. Box 50196, Austin, TX 78763 USA Tel 517-789-3259; Edit Addr.: 1009 W. 6th St., Suite 206, Austin, TX 78703 USA
E-mail: swzagorski@gmail.com.

Zahir Publishing, *(978-0-9741311; 978-0-9786041; 978-0-9831090)* 315 S. Coast Hwy. 101, Suite U8, Encinitas, CA 92024 USA
Web site: http://www.zahirtales.com.

Zahrob Publishing Co., *(978-0-9753641)* Orders Addr.: P.O. Box 5825, Rochester, MN 55903-5825 USA; Edit Addr.: 1445 Valley High Dr., NW, Rochester, MN 55903-5825 USA.

Zaloll, LLC, *(978-0-9857047; 978-0-9897380)* 4065 Sleeping Indian Ln., Colorado Springs, CO 80904 USA Tel 719-685-6505
E-mail: goldflagstudios@gmail.com.

Zaner-Bloser, Inc., *(978-0-7367; 978-0-88085; 978-0-88309; 978-1-4531)* Subs. of Highlights for Children, Orders Addr.: P.O. Box 16764, Columbus, OH 43216-6764 USA (SAN 282-5678) Tel 614-486-0221; Fax: 614-487-2263; Toll Free Fax: 800-992-6087; Toll Free: 800-421-3018; 1201 Dublin Rd., Columbus, OH 43215-1026
Web site: http://www.zaner-bloser.com/.

Zangadoo Entertainment, *(978-0-9847428)* 14101 19th Dr. SE, Mill Creek, WA 98102 USA Tel 206-234-8123
E-mail: dean@zangadoo.com
Web site: www.zangadoo.com.

Zangadoo LLC *See* **Zangadoo Entertainment**

Zany Angel Projects LLC, *(978-0-9769234)* P.O. Box 1411, New York, NY 10159 USA Tel 212-686-4206.

Zardoz Pr. *Imprint of* **Life Force Bks.**

Zarraonandia, Anne, *(978-0-9741070)* P.O. Box 151435, San Rafael, CA 94915 USA Tel 415-456-4070; Toll Free: 877-892-6974 (phone/fax)
E-mail: annezarra@aol.com
Web site: http://www.cowboyluke.com.

Zarrella, Sharon *See* **Lizzy Anne's Adventures**

Zarrika, Ltd., *(978-0-9758663; 978-1-934252)* P.O. Box 488, Unionville, PA 19375 USA Fax: 610-486-6501; Toll Free: 888-369-3366
Web site: http://www.zarrika.com.

ZC Horses Series of Children's Bks., *(978-0-9721496; 978-0-9791719)* 8 Hokanson Ln., Salmon, ID 83467 USA Tel 208-756-7947
E-mail: zchorses@hotmail.com
Web site: http://www.zchorses.com.

ZCR Pr., *(978-0-9763926)* 4912 Woodman Ave., No. 3, Sherman Oaks, CA 91423 USA (SAN 256-3479) Tel 818-995-3032 (phone/fax)
E-mail: zaldy80@aol.com.

Zebra Ginkgo, *(978-0-9891510)* 310 Frieda Ave., Kirkwood, MO 63122 USA Tel 314-292-9452
E-mail: edchen7@zebraginkgo.com
Web site: www.zebraginkgo.com.

Zeezok Publishing *See* **Zeezok Publishing, LLC**

Zeezok Publishing, LLC, *(978-0-9746505; 978-1-933573; 978-1-61006)* P.O. Box 1960, Elyria, OH 44036 USA (SAN 179-4493) Fax: 440-323-9494; Toll Free: 800-749-1681
E-mail: info@zeezok.com
Web site: http://www.zeezok.com.

Zeidman Consulting *See* **Swiss Creek Pubns.**

Zeke & Me Bks., *(978-0-9883042)* 2415 Outlook St., Kalamazoo, MI 49001 USA Tel 269-344-7757
E-mail: sstamm625@gmail.com.

Zeke Meeks *Imprint of* **Picture Window Bks.**

Zellmann Publishing, LLC, *(978-0-9763325)* 420 Springwood Ct., Canton, GA 30115-8287 USA Tel 770-345-7265; Fax: 770-345-7265
E-mail: zellmann@zellmannpublishing.com.

Zemi Comics, *(978-0-9745825)* SDQ 17, 4440 NW, 73rd Ave., Miami, FL 33166 USA Tel 787-748-4567
E-mail: fans@zemicomics.com
Web site: http://www.zemicomics.com.

Zen Care, *(978-0-9747334)* 212 Merchant St., Suite 5, Honolulu, HI 96813 USA Tel 808-523-3622
E-mail: elithe@hawaii.rr.com
Dist(s): **Booklines Hawaii, Ltd.**
Native Bks.

Zendrera Zariquiey, Editorial (ESP) *(978-84-89675; 978-84-8418) Dist. by* **Marluccia Iaconi Bk Imports.**

Zendrera Zariquiey, Editorial (ESP) *(978-84-89675; 978-84-8418) Dist. by* **Lectorum Pubns.**

Zenescope Entertainment, *(978-0-9786874; 978-0-9817550; 978-0-9823630; 978-0-9825826; 978-0-9827507; 978-0-615-40679-4; 978-0-9830404; 978-1-937068; 978-0-9853378; 978-1-939683; 978-1-942275)* 433 Caredean Dr Suite C, Horsham, PA 19044 USA (SAN 851-2760)
E-mail: jbrusha@zenscope.com
Web site: http://www.zenescope.com
Dist(s): **Diamond Comic Distributors, Inc.**
Diamond Bk. Distributors.

Zenga Publishing, *(978-0-9765484)* Orders Addr.: P.O. Box 39, New York, NY 10113 USA; Edit Addr.: 48 W. 22nd St., Suite 2, New York, NY 10010 USA
E-mail: zenga@nyc.rr.com
Web site: http://www.zengapublishing.com.

Zenith Pr. *Imprint of* **Quarto Publishing Group USA**

Zephyr Pr. *Imprint of* **Chicago Review Pr., Inc.**

Zephyr Pr., *(978-0-939010; 978-0-9815521; 978-0-9832970; 978-1-938890)* 50 Kenwood St., No. 2, Brookline, MA 02446 USA (SAN 239-7668) Do not confuse with companies with the same name in New York, NY, Tucson, AZ, Kansas City, MO, Canton, OH
E-mail: editors@zephyrpress.org
Web site: http://www.zephyrpress.org
Dist(s): **Consortium Bk. Sales & Distribution**
MyiLibrary
Perseus Bks. Group
SPD-Small Pr. Distribution.

Zero To Three Pr., *(978-0-943657; 978-1-934019; 978-1-938558)* Div. of Zero To Three: National Ctr. for Infants, Toddlers & Families, Orders Addr.: P.O. Box 960, Herndon, VA 20172 USA Toll Free: 800-899-4301; Edit Addr.: 1255 23RD St. NW, Suite 350, Washington, DC 20037 USA (SAN 242-5084) Tel 202-638-1144; Fax: 202-638-0851
E-mail: n.guadagno@zerotothree.org; jenniferli@zerotothree.org
Web site: http://www.zerotothree.org.

Zeromayo Studios, LLP, *(978-0-9661985)* Orders Addr.: P.O. Box 417, Haydenville, MA 01039 USA Tel 413-584-9372; Fax: 413-665-2312; Edit Addr.: 16 Market St., Northampton, MA 01060 USA; *Imprints:* Empty Sky (Empty Sky)
E-mail: planetrace@aol.com
Web site: http://www.ninjaturtles.com
Dist(s): **Diamond Comic Distributors, Inc.**

ZeroTo Three: National Center for Instants, Toddlers & Families *See* **Zero To Three Pr.**

Zest Bks., *(978-0-9772660; 978-0-9790173; 978-0-9800732; 978-0-9819733; 978-0-9827322; 978-1-936976; 978-1-942186)* 35 Stillman St., Suite 121, San Francisco, CA 94107 USA
Web site: http://zestbooks.net
Dist(s): **Books International, Inc.**
Houghton Mifflin Harcourt Publishing Co.
Houghton Mifflin Harcourt Trade & Reference Pubs.
Independent Pubs. Group
MyiLibrary.

Zest Publishing, *(978-0-9758861)* Orders Addr.: P.O. Box 484, Edgar, NE 68935-0484 USA; Edit Addr.: R.R. 1, Edgar, NE 68935-0484 USA Do not confuse with Zest Publishing Company in Southfield, MI.

Zeus Media LLC, *(978-0-9765840)* 12900 Canterbury, Leawood, KS 66209 USA
Web site: http://www.wisdomofzeus.com.

Zeus Sports Florida LLC, *(978-0-9777437)* Orders Addr.: 2312 SE 23rd Rd., Homestead, FL 33035-1900 USA Tel 786-417-9197
E-mail: habbook@msn.com.

JYZ Bks., LLC, *(978-0-9743272; 978-0-9906905)* 5816 White Pebble Path, Clarksville, MD 21029 USA Fax: 443-535-9664
E-mail: jianyi.zhang@chickensfirst.net
Web site: http://chickensfirst.net.

Zhera Pubns., *(978-0-9618904)* Orders Addr.: 2605 E. Flora Pl., Denver, CO 80210-6827 USA (SAN 242-231X) Tel 303-753-0384
E-mail: Zhera@msn.com; zhera@msn.com.

Zielinski, David, *(978-0-615-69214-2)* 2849 NE 13 Ave, Pompano Beach, FL 33064 USA Tel 754-366-4622
Dist(s): **CreateSpace Independent Publishing Platform.**

Ziert, Paul Assocs., Inc., *(978-0-9666104)* Orders Addr.: P.O. Box 721020, Norman, OK 73070 USA Tel 405-447-9988; Fax: 405-447-5810; Edit Addr.: 3214 Bart Conner Dr., Norman, OK 73072 USA
E-mail: paul@intlgymnast.com; IGDwight@aol.com.

Zig the Pig, *(978-0-9761700)* 815 Poinsettia St., Columbia, SC 29205 USA.

Ziker, Andrew, *(978-0-9762147)* 1788 E. Indigo St., Gilbert, AZ 85298-3222 USA.

Zilber, Jeremy, *(978-0-9786688)* P.O. Box 5543, Madison, WI 53705 USA
E-mail: jzilber@littledemocrats.net
Web site: http://www.littledemocrats.net.

Zimmerman, W. Frederick *See* **Nimble Bks. LLC**

Zinka Pr., Inc., *(978-0-9647171)* 1480 Pulaski Ln., Wayne, PA 19087 USA Tel 610-688-2113; Fax: 610-688-0753
E-mail: zinkapress@aol.com
Web site: http://www.zinkapress.com.

Zino Pr. Children's Bks., *(978-1-55933)* Div. of Knowledge Unlimited, Inc., P.O. Box 52, Madison, WI 53701-0052 USA Tel 608-836-6660; Fax: 608-831-1570; Toll Free Fax: 800-618-1570; Toll Free: 800-356-2303
E-mail: madzino@zinopress.com
Web site: http://www.zinopress.com
Dist(s): **Brodart Co.**
Follett School Solutions.

Zion Publishing, *(978-0-9627147)* 1500 Crown Colony Ct., Suite 540, Des Moines, IA 50315 USA Tel 515-282-5940; Toll Free: 800-996-2777 Do not confuse with companies with the same name in Monarch Beach, CA, Vallejo, CA
E-mail: maryenilsen@aol.com
Web site: http://www.zionpublishing.org.

Zion Publishing, *(978-0-9714844)* 17 Harding Ln., Sumiton, AL 35148 USA Tel 205-648-6741
E-mail: driverdm@aol.com.

Zip Line Publishing, *(978-0-9883792)* P.O. Box 78134, Charlotte, NC 28271 USA Tel 704-516-4287
E-mail: bethsmith@zipintoreading.com
Web site: zipintoreading.com
Dist(s): **Independent Pubs. Group.**

Zo Publishing, *(978-0-938465)* Orders Addr.: P.O. Box 61335, Honolulu, HI 96839 USA (SAN 660-9864) Tel 808-988-7111; Edit Addr.: 2918 Manoa Rd., Honolulu, HI 96822 USA (SAN 660-9872)
E-mail: dyen@lava.net.

Zoe Life Publishing, *(978-0-9748251; 978-0-9779445; 978-1-934363; 978-1-938807)* P.O. Box 871066, Canton, MI 48187 USA (SAN 256-1735) Tel 734-404-5485; Fax: 734-981-0251; Toll Free: 877-841-3400
E-mail: info@zoelifepub.com
Web site: http://www.zoelifepub.com
Dist(s): **Send The Light Distribution LLC.**

Zoland Bks., Inc. *Imprint of* **Steerforth Pr.**

Zonderkidz, *(978-0-310)* Div. of Zondervan, 5300 Patterson Ave., SE, Grand Rapids, MI 49530 USA Tel 1-800-727-3480
E-mail: zprod@zondervan.com
Web site: http://www.zondervan.com
Dist(s): **Zondervan.**

†Zondervan, *(978-0-00; 978-0-310; 978-0-937336)* Subs. of HarperCollins Publishers US, Orders Addr.: c/o Zondervan XNET Ordering Dept., 5249 Corporate Grove, Grand Rapids, MI 49512 USA (SAN 298-9107); Edit Addr.: 5300 Patterson Ave., SE, Grand Rapids, MI 49530 USA (SAN 203-2694) Tel 616-698-6900; Fax: 616-698-3439
E-mail: zprod@zondervan.com
Web site: http://www.zondervan.com
Dist(s): **Ebsco Publishing**
Follett School Solutions
Send The Light Distribution LLC
Vida Pubs.; *CIP.*

Zondervan bibles *See* **Zondervan Bibles**

Zondervan Bibles, *(978-0-310)* 5300 Patterson Ave., SE, Grand Rapids, MI 49530 USA Tel 800-727-3480
E-mail: zprod@zondervan.com
Web site: http://www.zondervan.com
Dist(s): **Zondervan.**

Zondervan Bks., *(978-0-310)* 5300 Patterson Ave., SE, Grand Rapids, MI 49530 USA Tel 1-800-727-3480
E-mail: zprod@zondervan.com
Web site: http://www.zondervan.com
Dist(s): **Zondervan.**

Zondervan Publishing House *See* **Zondervan**

Zone Bks. *Imprint of* **Stone Arch Bks.**

Zonk Galleries *See* **Zonk Galleries and Pubns.**

Zonk Galleries and Pubns., *(978-0-9706537)* 2909 Hansen Rd., Hayward, CA 94541 USA (SAN 254-3443) Tel 510-530-2681
E-mail: davidhoobler@sbcglobal.net
Web site: http://zonktheturtle.com.

Zoo Bks. *Imprint of* **Wildlife Education, Ltd.**

Zoombird Bks., *(978-0-615-32691-7)* Orders Addr.: 2734 Carisbrook Dr., Oakland, CA 94611 USA Tel 510-530-2737
Web site: http://www.zoombirdbooks.com.

Zoo-phonics, Inc., *(978-0-9617342; 978-1-886441)* Orders Addr.: 20950 Ferretti Rd., Groveland, CA 95321 USA (SAN 663-8589) Tel 209-962-5030; Fax: 209-962-4320; Toll Free: 800-622-8104
E-mail: zoo-info@zoo-phonics.com; shirley@zoo-phonics.com
Web site: http://www.zoo-phonics.com.

Zora, *(978-0-9714039; 978-1-59898)* Orders Addr.: 450 Stedman Pl., Monrovia, CA 91016 USA Tel 626-359-6071
E-mail: emil@zorapubs.com.

Zottola Publishing, Inc., *(978-0-9725880; 978-0-9823907)* Orders Addr.: 4212 Boone Ave. N., New Hope, MN 55428-0001 USA
E-mail: zottolaj@comcast.net
Web site: http://www.zotpub.com.

zReyomi Publishing, *(978-0-9670712)* Div. of Reyomi Global Media Group, Inc., P.O. Box 51928, Durham, NC 27717 USA Tel 919-321-2573; Fax: 919-489-3913
E-mail: Reyomi@aol.com
Dist(s): **Bk. Hse., The**
Brodart Co.

Zu Bks., *(978-0-615-15267-7)* 1813 Comet, Altus, OK 73521 USA Tel 580-477-0819
Web site: http://zuopolis.com
Dist(s): **Lulu Enterprises Inc.**

'Zubaan Bks. (IND) *(978-93-81017) Dist. by* **Chicago Distribution Ctr.**

Zuber Publishing, *(978-0-9785551)* 52180 Tammy Dr., Granger, IN 46530 USA Tel 574-272-8914
E-mail: admin@zuberpublishing.com
Web site: http://www.zuberpublishing.com
Dist(s): **Distributors, The.**

Zuiho, *(978-0-9743474)* 11628 82nd Ave. NE, Kirkland, WA 98034-3400 USA.

Zulema Enterprises Publishing, *(978-1-881223)* 7715 Yardley Dr., Tamarac, FL 33321 USA Tel 954-724-5204
E-mail: peopleteachers@aol.com
Web site: http://www.zulemabooks.com.

Zulu Planet Pubs. (ZAF) *(978-1-920070; 978-1-920153) Dist. by* **APG.**

Zumaya Embraces *Imprint of* **Zumaya Pubns. LLC**

Zumaya Otherworlds *Imprint of* **Zumaya Pubns. LLC**

Zumaya Pubns. LLC, *(978-1-894869; 978-1-894942; 978-1-55410; 978-1-934135; 978-1-934841; 978-1-936144; 978-1-61271)* Orders Addr.: 3209 S. Interstate 35 APT 1086, Austin, TX 78741-6905 USA Tel 512-537-3145; 512-931-4594; Fax: 512-276-6745; *Imprints:* Zumaya Otherworlds (Zumaya Otherworlds); Zumaya Embraces (Zumaya Embraces); Zumaya Thresholds (ZumThresh)
E-mail: production@zumayapublishing.com; business@zumayapublishing.com
Web site: http://www.zumayapublications.com; http://www.zumayapublishing.com.

Zumaya Thresholds *Imprint of* **Zumaya Pubns. LLC**

Zy Iman Pubng, *(978-0-9779130)* P.O. Box 367, Brooklyn, NY 11221 USA
Web site: http://www.ucanspeakup.com.

Zygote Games LLC, *(978-0-9770419)* 100 Venture Way, Flr. 3, Suite 4, Hadley, MA 01035 USA Tel 413-303-9031; Fax: 253-540-5054
E-mail: orders@zygotegames.com
Web site: http://www.zygotegames.com.

Zyrro, Roggen, *(978-0-9762580)* 5841 Wornall Rd., Kansas City, MO 64113 USA
Web site: http://www.bunsta.com.

ZZ Dogs Pr. *Imprint of* **That's Life Publishing, Inc.**

Publisher Name Index

WHOLESALER & DISTRIBUTOR NAME INDEX

1stBooks Library, *See* **AuthorHouse**

2Learn-English, *(978-0-9627878; 978-1-891077; 978-1-934637)* Div. of Authors & Editors, Orders Addr.: 10736 Jefferson Blvd., No. 604, Culver City, CA 90230-4969 USA Tel 310-251-3931 Arthur Rubin; 310-836-2014 General/Messages; Fax: 310-836-1845
E-mail: info@2learn-english.com
Web site: http://www.2learn-english.com.

3M Sportsman's Video Collection, 3M Ctr., Bldg. 223-4NE-05, Saint Paul, MN 55144-1000 USA (SAN 159-8929) Tel 612-733-7412; Fax: 612-736-7479; Toll Free: 800-940-8273 (orders only).

A & B Books, *See* **A & B Distributors & Pubs. Group**

A & B Distributors & Pubs. Group, *(978-1-881316; 978-1-886433)* Div. of A&B Distributors, 1000 Atlantic Ave., Brooklyn, NY 11238 USA (SAN 630-9216) Tel 718-783-7808; Fax: 718-783-7267; Toll Free: 877-542-6657; 146 Lawrence St., Brooklyn, NY 11201 (SAN 631-385X)
E-mail: maxtay@webspan.net.

A & M Church Supplies, 3535 Bay Rd., Saginaw, MI 48603-2464 USA (SAN 157-0145) Toll Free: 800-345-4694.

A B C-Clio Information Services, *See* **ABC-CLIO, LLC**

A B S Corporation, *See* **Budgetext**

A K J Educational Services, Incorporated, *See* **AKJ Bks.**

AAA Anime Distribution, 4509 Shirley Ave., Unit D, El Mone, CA 91731 USA Tel 626-575-8922
E-mail: vince@aaaanime.com.

Aardvark Global Publishing, *(978-0-9770328; 978-1-933570; 978-1-59971; 978-1-4276)* 9587 S. Grandview Dr., Sandy, UT 84092 USA Do not confuse with Aardvark Global Publishing, Atlanta, GA
E-mail: info@eckohousepublishing.com
Web site: http://eckohousepublishing.com/; http://aardvarkglobalpublishing.com/; http://eckobooks.com.

ABC-CLIO, LLC, *(978-0-87436; 978-0-903450; 978-1-57607; 978-1-85109; 978-1-59884; 978-1-61069)* 130 Cremona Dr., Santa Barbara, CA 93117 USA (SAN 301-5467) Tel 805-968-1911; Fax: 805-685-9685; Toll Free: 800-368-6868; P.O. Box 93116, Goleta, CA 93116 (SAN 857-7099)
E-mail: customerservice@abc-clio.com; service@abc-clio.com; salesuk@abc-clio.com
Web site: http://www.abc-clio.com.

ABC'S Bk. Supply, Inc., 7319 W. Flagler St., Miami, FL 33144 USA Toll Free: 877-383-4240
E-mail: abcbooks@abcbooks.com.

Abdo & Daughters Publishing, *See* **ABDO Publishing Co.**

ABDO Publishing Co., *(978-0-939179; 978-1-56239; 978-1-57765; 978-1-59197; 978-1-59679; 978-1-59928; 978-1-59961; 978-1-60270; 978-1-60453; 978-1-61613; 978-1-61714; 978-1-61758; 978-1-61783; 978-1-61784; 978-1-61785; 978-1-61786; 978-1-61787; 978-1-61478; 978-1-61479; 978-1-61480; 978-1-62401; 978-1-62402; 978-1-62403; 978-1-62968; 978-1-62969; 978-1-62970; 978-1-68076; 978-1-68077; 978-1-68078; 978-1-68079; 978-1-68080) Div. of ABDO Publishing Group, Orders Addr.: 8000 W. 78th St. Suite 310, Edina, MN 55439 USA (SAN 662-9172) Tel 952-831-2120; Fax: 952-831-1632; Toll Free Fax: 800-862-3480; Toll Free: 800-800-1312*
E-mail: info@abdopublishing.com
Web site: http://www.abdopublishing.com.

Abel Love, Inc., Orders Addr.: P.O. Box 2250, Newport News, VA 23609 USA (SAN 158-4081) Tel 757-877-2939; Toll Free: 800-520-2939; Edit Addr.: 935 Lucas Creek Rd., Newport News, VA 23608 USA Fax: 804-877-2939.

Abingdon Pr., *(978-0-687; 978-1-4267; 978-1-63088; 978-1-5018)* Div. of United Methodist Publishing House, Orders Addr.: P.O. Box 801, Nashville, TN 37202-3919 USA (SAN 201-0054) Tel 615-749-6409; Fax: 615-749-6056; Toll Free: 800-627-1789; Edit Addr.: 201 Eighth Ave., S., Nashville, TN 37202 USA (SAN 699-9956) Tel 615-749-6000; Toll Free Fax: 800-445-8189; Toll Free: 800-672-1789
E-mail: cokes_serv@cokesbury.com
Web site: http://www.abingdonpress.com/; http://www.umph.org.

Abraham Assocs. Inc., 5120-A Cedar Lake Rd., Minneapolis, MN 55416 USA Tel 952-927-7920; Fax: 952-927-8089; Toll Free: 800-701-2489
E-mail: stu@abrahamassociatesinc.com.

Abrams, *(978-0-8109; 978-1-4197; 978-1-61769; 978-1-61312)* Orders Addr.: The Market Building Third Floor, 72-82 Rosebery Ave., London, EC1R 4RW GBR Tel 020 7713 2060; Fax: 020 7713 2061; Edit Addr.: 115 West 18th St., New York, NY 10011 USA (SAN 200-2434) Tel 212-206-7715; Fax: 212-519-1210
E-mail: webmaster@abramsbooks.com
Web site: http://www.hnabooks.com.

Abrams, Harry N. Incorporated, *See* **Abrams**

Abrams Learning Trends, Orders Addr.: 16310 Bratton Ln., Suite 250, Austin, TX 78728 USA Tel 512-735-2863
E-mail: billt@abramslearningtrends.com.

Abyss Distribution, *(978-1-932548)* P.O. Box 48, Middlefield, MA 01243-0048 USA (SAN 630-9925) Tel 413-623-2155; Fax: 413-623-2156; Toll Free: 800-326-0804
E-mail: abyssdist@aol.com
Web site: http://www.azuregreen.com.

Academic Bk. Ctr., Inc., P.O. Box 1320, Lake Oswego, OR 97035-0320 USA (SAN 169-7145) Toll Free: 800-547-7704
E-mail: orders@acbc.com
Web site: http://www.abc.com.

Academic Bk. Services, Inc., 5490 Fulton Industrial Blvd., Atlanta, GA 30336 USA (SAN 631-0591) Tel 404-344-8317; Fax: 404-349-2127.

Academi-Text Medical Wholesalers, P.O. Box 1080, Monroe, MI 48161-6080 USA (SAN 135-2415) Toll Free: 800-552-8398 (out of state)
E-mail: dyourist@academi-text.com.

ACCESS Pubs. Network, 6893 Sullivan Rd., Grawn, MI 49637 USA.

Acorn Alliance, 549 Old North Rd., Kingston, RI 02881-1220 USA Tel 401-783-5480; Fax: 401-284-0959; Fulfillment Addr.: Client Distribution Services 193 Edwards Dr., Jackson, TN 38301 USA Toll Free Fax: 800-351-5073; Toll Free: 800-343-4499
E-mail: moyerbellbooks@yahoo.com
Web site: http://www.moyerbellbooks.com.

ACTA Pubns., *(978-0-87946; 978-0-914070; 978-0-915388)* 5559 Howard St., Skokie, IL 60077-2621 USA (SAN 204-7489) Toll Free Fax: 800-397-0079; Toll Free: 800-397-2282; 4848 N. Clark St., Chicago, IL 60640
E-mail: actapublications@aol.com
Web site: http://www.actapublications.com.

Action Products International, Inc., 344 Cypress Rd., Ocala, FL 34472-3108 USA (SAN 630-8805) Tel 352-687-4961; Toll Free: 800-772-2846
E-mail: sales@apii.com.

ACW Pr., *(978-0-9656749; 978-1-892525; 978-1-932124; 978-1-934668)* Orders Addr.: P.O. Box 110390, Nashville, TN 37222 USA Tel 615-834-0450; Toll Free: 800-219-7483; Edit Addr.: 4854 Aster Dr., Nashville, TN 37211 USA
E-mail: regaforder@aol.com.

Adams Bk. Co., Inc., 140 58th Street, Unit 6G, Box 39, Brooklyn, NY 11220-2523 USA (SAN 107-7171) Tel 718-875-5464; Fax: 718-852-3212; Toll Free: 800-221-0909
E-mail: sales@adamsbook.com
Web site: http://www.adamsbook.com.

Adams News, 1555 W. Galer St., Seattle, WA 98119 USA (SAN 169-8842) Tel 206-284-7617; Fax: 206-284-7599; Toll Free: 800-533-7617.

Adams, Robert Henry Fine Art, *(978-0-9713010)* 2146 W. Sunnyside Ave., Chicago, IL 60625-1626 USA (SAN 159-6918)
E-mail: info@adamsfineart.com
Web site: http://www.adamsfineart.com.

Addicus Bks., *(978-1-886039; 978-1-936374; 978-1-938803; 978-1-940495; 978-1-943886)* Orders Addr.: P.O. Box 45327, Omaha, NE 68145 USA Tel 402-330-7493; Fax: 402 330-1707; Toll Free: 800-352-2873; Edit Addr.: 814 N. Franklin St., Chicago, IL 60610 USA
E-mail: addicusbks@aol.com; info@addicusbooks.com
Web site: http://www.AddicusBooks.com.

Addison-Wesley Educational Pubs., Inc., *(978-0-321; 978-0-328; 978-0-673)* Div. of Addison Wesley Longman, Inc., 75 Arlington St., Boston, MA 02116 USA Tel 617-848-7500; Toll Free: 800-447-2226
Web site: http://www.awl.com.

Addison-Wesley Longman, Inc., *(978-0-201; 978-0-321; 978-0-582; 978-0-673; 978-0-8013; 978-0-8053; 978-0-9654123)* Orders Addr.: 200 Old Tappan Rd., Old Tappan, NJ 07675 USA (SAN 299-4739) Toll Free: 800-922-0579; Edit Addr.: 75 Arlington St., Suite 300, Boston, MA 02116 USA (SAN 200-2000) Tel 617-848-7500; Toll Free: 800-447-2226
E-mail: pearsoned@eds.com; orderdeptnj@pearsoned.com
Web site: http://www.awl.com.

Addison-Wesley Publishing Company, Incorporated, *See* **Addison-Wesley Longman, Inc.**

Adelman, Joseph, 530 N. 40th St., Allentown, PA 18104-4558 USA (SAN 285-8002).

Adler, Leo, P.O. Box 10308, Eugene, OR 97440-2308 USA (SAN 169-7021).

Adler's Foreign Bks., Inc., *(978-0-8417)* 915 Foster St., Evanston, IL 60201 USA (SAN 111-3089) Tel 847-864-0664; Fax: 847-864-0804; Toll Free: 800-235-3771
E-mail: info@afb-adlers.com
Web site: http://www.afb-adlers.com.

Advanced Global Distribution Services, 5880 Oberlin Dr., San Diego, CA 32121 USA Toll Free Fax: 800-499-3822; Toll Free: 800-284-3580.

Advantage Publishers Group, *See* **Baker & Taylor Publishing Group**

Adventure Pubns., Inc., *(978-0-934860; 978-1-885061; 978-1-59193)* Orders Addr.: 820 Cleveland St., S., Cambridge, MN 55008 USA (SAN 212-7199) Tel 763-689-9800; Fax: 763-689-9039; Toll Free Fax: 877-374-9016; Toll Free: 800-678-7006
E-mail: orders@adventurepublications.net; custservice@adventurepublications.net
Web site: http://www.adventurepublications.net.

Adventures Unlimited Pr., *(978-0-932813; 978-1-931882; 978-1-935487; 978-1-939149)* Orders Addr.: P.O. Box 74, Kempton, IL 60946 USA (SAN 630-1126) Tel 815-253-6390; Fax: 815-253-6300; Edit Addr.: 303 Main St., Kempton, IL 60946 USA (SAN 250-3484)
E-mail: auphq@frontiernet.net
Web site: http://www.adventuresunlimitedpress.com.

Advertising Specialties, Inc., 4920 River Rd., Pascagoula, MS 39567 USA (SAN 108-6316) Tel 601-769-7904
Web site: http://www.advmkt.com; http://www.advantagebooksonline.com.

Advocate Distribution Solutions, Div. of Send The Light Distribution LLC, 100 Biblica Way, Elizabethton, TN 37643 USA Tel 423-767-1100; Fax: 423-547-5199; Toll Free Fax: 800-759-2779; Toll Free: 800-289-2772
Web site: http://www.stl-distribution.com; http://www.advocatedistribution.com.

Affiliated Bk. Distributor, Div. of North Shore Distributors, Inc., 1200 N. Branch St., Chicago, IL 60622 USA (SAN 169-2267).

Africa World Pr., *(978-0-86543; 978-1-59221)* 541 W. Ingham Ave., Suite B, Trenton, NJ 08638 USA (SAN 692-3925) Tel 609-695-3200; Fax: 609-695-6466
E-mail: customerservice@africaworldpressbooks.com
Web site: http://www.africaworldpressbooks.com.

African World Bks., 2217 Pennsylvania Ave., Baltimore, MD 21217 USA (SAN 631-3868) Tel 410-383-2006.

Afrikan World Bk. Distributor, Orders Addr.: P.O. Box 16447, Baltimore, MD 21217 USA; Edit Addr.: 2217 Pennsylvania Ave., Baltimore, MD 21217 USA (SAN 631-2020) Tel 410-383-2006.

Afro-American Bk. Distributor, 2537 Prospect, Houston, TX 77004 USA (SAN 169-8257).

Agencia de Publicaciones de Puerto Rico, GPO Box 4903, San Juan, PR 00936 USA (SAN 169-9296).

Agritech Publishing Group, Inc., Div. of Agritech Corp., 825 W. Samalayuca Dr., Tucson, AZ 85704-3912 USA (SAN 174-612X) Tel 520-544-2542.

AHA, Inc., *(978-0-918545)* P.O. Box 8405, Santa Cruz, CA 95061-8405 USA (SAN 295-5059) Tel 408-458-9119.

AIMS International Bks., Inc., *(978-0-922852)* 7709 Hamilton Ave., Cincinnati, OH 45231-3103 USA (SAN 630-270X) Tel 513-521-5590; Fax: 513-521-5592; Toll Free: 800-733-2067
E-mail: aimsbooks@fuse.net
Web site: http://www.aimsbooks.com.

A-K News Company, *See* **Aramark Magazine & Bk. Co.**

AK Pr. Distribution, *(978-1-873176; 978-1-902593; 978-0-9830597; 978-1-939202)* 674-A 23rd St., Oakland, CA 94612-1163 USA (SAN 298-2234) Tel 510-208-1700; Fax: 510-208-1701
E-mail: akpress@akpress.org
Web site: http://www.akpress.org.

AKJ Bks., 4702 Benson Ave., Halethorpe, MD 21227-1411 USA (SAN 170-5431) Toll Free: 800-922-6066
E-mail: info@akjbooks.com
Web site: www.akjbooks.com; http://store.akjbooks.com; www.akjebooks.com.

Alabama Bookstore, Orders Addr.: P.O. Box 1279, Tuscaloosa, AL 35401-1626 USA Tel 205-758-4532; Fax: 205-758-5525; Toll Free: 800-382-2665 (orders only)
E-mail: ABS@AlabamaBook.com
Web site: http://www.AlabamaBook.com.

Alamo Square Distributors, P.O. Box 14543, San Francisco, CA 94114 USA Fax: 415-863-7456
E-mail: alamosqdist@earthlink.net.

Alba House, *See* **St Pauls/Alba Hse. Pubs.**

Alexander News Company, *See* **Blue Ridge News Co.**

Alfonsi Enterprises, 8621 Gavinton Ct., Dublin, OH 43017-9615 USA (SAN 169-4227).

Alfred Publishing Co., Inc., *(978-0-7390; 978-0-87487; 978-0-88284; 978-1-58951; 978-1-4574; 978-1-4706)* Orders Addr.: P.O. Box 10003, Van Nuys, CA 91410-0003 USA; Edit Addr.: 123 Dry Rd., Oriskany, NY 13424 USA Tel 315-736-1572; Fax: 315-736-7281
E-mail: customerservice@alfred.com; permissions@alfred.com; submissions@alfred.com
Web site: http://www.alfred.com.

Alibris, *(978-0-9702763)* 1250 45th St., Suite 100, Emeryville, CA 94608 USA Fax: 510-550-6052; Toll Free: 877-254-2747 (877-ALIBRIS, option 1)
E-mail: libraries@alibris.com
Web site: http://www.alibris.com/library.

Alive Books, *See* **Books Alive**

All Electronics Corp., 14928 Oxnard St., Van Nuys, CA 91411 USA.

All Romance Ebooks, LLC, *(978-1-936387; 978-1-943576)* 334 E. Lake Rd., Suite 286, Palm Harbor, FL 34685 USA
E-mail: info@allromanceebooks.com.

Allegro New Sound Distribution, Subs. of Allegro Distribution, 20048 NE San Rafael St., Portland, OR 97230-7459 USA.

Allentown News Agency, Inc., Orders Addr.: P.O. Box 446, Allentown, PA 18105 USA; Edit Addr.: 719-723 Liberty

St., Allentown, PA 18105 USA (SAN 169-7226) Tel 610-432-4441; Fax: 610-432-2708.

Alliance Bk. Co., P.O. Box 7884, Hilton Head, SC 29938-7884 USA
E-mail: alliancebk@mindspring.com.

Alliance Game Distributors, Centennial Dr., Fort Wayne, IN 46808 USA Tel 260-482-5490 (ext. 253); Fax: 260-471-9539
E-mail: jjh@alliance-games.com
Web site: http://www.alliance-games.com.

Alliance Hse., Inc., *(978-0-9665234)* 220 Ferris Ave., Suite 201, White Plains, NY 10603 USA Tel 914-328-5456; Fax: 914-946-1929
E-mail: alliancehs@aol.com.

Alonso Bk. & Periodical Services, Inc., 2316 2nd St S., Arlington, VA 22204-2010 USA (SAN 170-7035).

Alpen Bks, 4602 Chennault Beach Rd. Ste. B1, Mukilteo, WA 98275-5016 USA.

Alpenbooks, *See* **Alpenbooks Pr. LLC**

Alpenbooks Pr. LLC, *(978-0-9669795)* 4602 Chennault Beach Rd, B1, Mukilteo, WA 98275 USA (SAN 113-5309) Tel 425-415-4560; Fax: 425-493-6381
E-mail: rkoch@alpenbooks.com
Web site: http://www.alpenbooks.com.

Alpha & Omega Distributor, P.O. Box 36640, Colorado Springs, CO 80936-3664 USA (SAN 169-0515).

Alpha Bks., *(978-0-02; 978-0-672; 978-0-7357; 978-0-7897; 978-1-56761; 978-1-57595; 978-0-7431; 978-1-59257; 978-1-61564)* Div. of Pearson Technology Group, 800 E 96th St., 3rd Flr., Indianapolis, IN 46290 USA (SAN 219-6298) Tel 317-581-3500 Toll Free: 800-571-5840 (orders)
Web site: http://www.idiotsguides.com.

Alpine News Distributors, Div. of Mountain States Distributors, 0105 Marand Rd., Glenwood Springs, CO 81601 USA Tel 970-945-2269; Fax: 970-945-2260.

Alta Book Center Publishers, *See* **Alta English Publishers**

Alta English Publishers, *(978-1-878598; 978-1-882483; 978-1-932383)* 1775 E. Palm Canyon Dr. Suite 110-275, Palm Springs, CA 92264 USA (SAN 630-9240) Tel 760-459-2603; Fax: 760-464-0588
E-mail: info@altaenglishpublishers.com
Web site: http://www.altaenglishpublishers.com; http://www.altaenglishonline.com.

Amacom, *(978-0-7612; 978-0-8144)* Div. of American Management Association, Orders Addr.: 600 AMA Way, Saranac Lake, NY 12983 USA (SAN 227-3578) Tel 518-891-5510; Fax: 518-891-2372; Toll Free: 800-250-5308 (orders & customer service); Edit Addr.: 1601 Broadway, New York, NY 10019-7420 USA (SAN 201-1670) Tel 212-586-8100; Fax: 212-903-8168; 1 Ingram Blvd., La Vergne, TN 37086
E-mail: pubservice@amanet.org
Web site: http://www.amacombooks.org.

Amarillo Periodical Distributors, P.O. Box 3823, Lubbock, TX 70404 USA (SAN 156-4986) Tel 806-745-6000.

Amato, Frank Pubns., Inc., *(978-0-936608; 978-1-57188; 978-1-878175)* Orders Addr.: P.O. Box 82112, Portland, OR 97282 USA (SAN 214-3372) Tel 503-653-8108; Fax: 503-653-2766; Toll Free: 800-541-9498; Edit Addr.: 4040 SE Wister St., Milwaukie, OR 97222 USA (SAN 858-5741)
E-mail: wholesale@amatobooks.com; Lorraine@amatobooks.com
Web site: http://www.amatobooks.com.

Amazon.Com, *(978-1-58060)* 1200 12th Ave. S., Suite 1200, Seattle, WA 98144 USA (SAN 179-4205) Tel 206-266-6817; Orders Addr.: P.O. Box 80387, Seattle, WA 98108-0387 USA (SAN 156-143X) Tel 206-622-2335; Fax: 206-622-2405; 1 Centerpoint Blvd., non-carton, New Castle, DE 19720 (SAN 155-3992); 1 Centerpoint Blvd., carton, New Castle, DE 19720 (SAN 156-1405); 520 S. Brandon, non-carton, Seattle, WA 98108 (SAN 152-6642); 520 S. Brandon, carton, Seattle, WA 98108 (SAN 156-1383); 1600 E. Newlands Dr., carton, Fernley, NV 89408 (SAN 156-5982); 1600 E. Newlands Dr., non-carton, Fernley, NV 89408 (SAN 156-6008); Edit Addr.: 520 Pike St., Seattle, WA 98101 USA (SAN 155-3984); P.O. Box 81226, Seattle, WA 98108-1226; 705 Boulder Dr. Carton, Breinigsville, PA 18031
E-mail: catalog-dept@amazon.com
Web site: http://www.amazon.com.

Ambassador Bks. & Media, 42 Chasner St., Hempstead, NY 11550 USA (SAN 120-064X) Tel 516-489-4011; Fax: 516-489-5661; Toll Free: 800-431-8913
E-mail: ambassador@absbook.com
Web site: http://www.absbook.com.

Ambassador Book Service, *See* **Ambassador Bks. & Media**

America Hse. Bk. Pubs., *(978-1-893162; 978-1-58851; 978-1-59129)* Orders Addr.: P.O. Box 151, Frederick, MD 21705-0151 USA; Edit Addr.: 113 E. Church St., Frederick, MD 21701 USA
Web site: http://www.publishamerica.com.

American Assn. for Vocational Instructional Materials, *(978-0-89606; 978-0-914452)* 220 Smithonia Rd., Winterville, GA 30683 USA (SAN 225-8811) Tel 706-742-5355; Fax: 706-742-7005; Toll Free: 800-228-4689
E-mail: ksseab@aavim.com; sales@aavim.com
Web site: http://www.aavim.com.

American Bible Society, *(978-0-8267; 978-1-58516; 978-1-937628; 978-1-941448; 978-1-941449)* Orders Addr.: 6201 E. 43rd St., Tulsa, OK 74135-6562 USA (SAN 662-7129) Toll Free Fax: 866-570-2877; Edit Addr.: 1865 Broadway, New York, NY 10023-9980 USA (SAN 203-5189) Tel 212-408-1200; Fax: 212-408-1305; 700 Plaza Dr., 2nd Flr., Secaucus, NJ 07094
E-mail: info@americanbible.org
Web site: http://www.bibles.org; http://www.americanbible.org.

American Buddhist Shim Gum Do Assn., Inc., *(978-0-9614427)* 203 Chestnut Hill Ave., Brighton, MA 02135 USA (SAN 113-2873) Tel 617-787-1506; Fax: 617-787-2708
E-mail: marystackhouse@shimgumdo.org
Web site: http://www.shimgumdo.org.

American Business Systems, Inc., 315 Littleton Rd., Chelmsford, MA 01824 USA (SAN 264-8229) Tel 508-250-9600; Fax: 508-250-8027; Toll Free: 800-356-4034.

American Eagle Pubns., Inc., *(978-0-929408)* Orders Addr.: P.O. Box 5111, Sun City West, AZ 85376 USA (SAN 249-2415) Tel 623-556-2925; Fax: 623-556-2926; Toll Free: 866-764-2925; Edit Addr.: 12647 Crystal Lake Dr., Sun City West, AZ 85375 USA
E-mail: custservice@ameaglepubs.com
Web site: http://www.ameaglepubs.com.

American Education Corp., The, *(978-0-87570; 978-1-58636; 978-0-9841672; 978-0-9841972)* 7506 N. Broadway, Suite 505, Oklahoma City, OK 73116-9016 USA (SAN 654-6250) Tel 405-840-6031; Toll Free: 800-222-2811
E-mail: jamesr@amered.com
Web site: http://www.amered.com.

American Educational Computer, Incorporated, *See* **American Education Corp., The**

American Heritage Magazine, 90 Fifth Ave., New York, NY 10011 USA.

American International Distribution Corp., Orders Addr.: P.O. Box 574, Williston, VT 05495-0020 USA Tel 800-390-3149; Fax: 802-864-7626; Toll Free: 888-822-9942; Edit Addr.: 50 Winter Sport Ln., Williston, VT 05495 USA (SAN 630-2238) Toll Free: 800-488-2665
E-mail: jmacon@aidcvt.com
Web site: http://www.aidcvt.com/Specialty/Home.asp.

American Kennel Club Museum of the Dog, *(978-0-9615072)* 1721 S. Mason Rd., Saint Louis, MO 63131 USA (SAN 110-8751) Tel 314-821-3647; Fax: 314-821-7381.

American Magazine Service, *See* **Prebound Periodicals**

American Marketing & Publishing Company, *See* **Christian Publishing Network**

American Micro Media, 19 N. Broadway, Box 306, Red Hook, NY 12571 USA (SAN 653-9920) Tel 914-758-5567.

American Overseas Bk. Co., Inc., 550 Walnut St., Norwood, NJ 07648 USA (SAN 169-4863) Tel 201-767-7600; Fax: 201-784-0263
E-mail: books@aobc.com
Web site: http://www.aobc.com.

American Pharmacists Assn., *(978-0-914768; 978-0-917330; 978-1-58212)* 2215 Constitution Ave., NW, Washington, DC 20037-2907 USA (SAN 202-4446) Tel 202-628-4410; Fax: 202-783-2351; Toll Free: 800-878-0729
E-mail: kanderson@aphanet.org
Web site: http://www.pharmacist.com.

American Society of Agronomy, *(978-0-89118)* 5585 Guilford Rd., Fitchburg, WI 53711-5801 USA (SAN 107-5683)
Web site: http://www.agronomy.org.

American Society of Civil Engineers, *(978-0-7844; 978-0-87262)* 1801 Alexander Bell Dr., Reston, VA 20191-4400 USA (SAN 204-7594) Tel 703-295-6300; Fax: 703-295-6211; Toll Free: 800-548-2723
E-mail: pubsful@asce.org
Web site: http://www.asce.org/bookstore.

American Technical Pubs., Inc., *(978-0-8269)* 10100 Orland Pkwy., Orland Park, IL 60467-5756 USA (SAN 206-8141) Toll Free: 800-323-3471
E-mail: service@americantech.net
Web site: http://www.americantech.net.

American West Bks., Orders Addr.: 14190 N. Washington Hwy., Ashland, VA 23005 USA (SAN 920-5233); Edit Addr.: 1254 Commerce Way, Sanger, CA 93657 USA (SAN 630-8570) Toll Free: 800-497-4909 Do not confuse with American West Bks., Albuquerque, NM
E-mail: JBM12@CSUFresno.edu.

American Wholesale Bk. Co., Subs. of Books-A-Million, Orders Addr.: 402 Industrial Ln., Birmingham, AL 35211-4465 USA (SAN 631-7391).

Americana Publishing, Inc., *(978-1-58807; 978-1-58943)* 195 Us Highway 9. Ste. 204, Englishtown, NJ 07726-8294 USA Toll Free: 888-883-8203; 303 San Mateo Blvd, Ne, Albuquerque, NM 87108
E-mail: editor@americanabooks.com
Web site: http://www.americanabooks.com.

Americana Souvenirs & Gifts, *(978-1-890541)* 206 Hanover St., Gettysburg, PA 17325-1911 USA (SAN 169-7366) Toll Free: 800-692-7436.

America's Cycling Pubns., 6425 Capitol Ave., Suite F, Diamond Springs, CA 95619 USA.

America's Hobby Ctr., 146 W. 22nd St., New York, NY 10011 USA (SAN 111-0403) Tel 212-675-8922.

Ames News Agency, Inc., 2110 E. 13th St., Ames, IA 50010 USA (SAN 169-2550).

Amicus Educational, *(978-1-60753; 978-1-68151)* Div. of Amicus Publishing, P.O. Box 1329, Mankato, MN 56002 USA Tel 507-388-5164; Fax: 507-388-4797
E-mail: info@amicuspublishing.us
Web site: http://www.amicuspublishing.us.

Amicus Publishing, *See* **Amicus Educational**

Amigos Book Co., Orders Addr.: 5401 Bissonnet, Houston, TX 77081-6605 USA.

Amoskeag News Agency, 92 Allard Dr., Manchester, NH 03102 USA (SAN 169-4537) Tel 603-623-5343.

AMS Pr., Inc., *(978-0-404)* Brooklyn Navy Yard Bldg. 292, Suite 417, 63 Flushing Ave., New York, NY 11205 USA (SAN 106-6706) Tel 718-875-8100; Fax: 212-995-5413 Do not confuse with companies with the same or similar name in Los Angeles, CA, Pittsburgh, PA
E-mail: amserve@earthlink.net
Web site: http://www.amspressinc.com/.

Analos Magazine, 475 Park Ave. S., New York, NY 10016 USA.

Anchor Distributors, 30 Hunt Valley Cir., New Kensington, PA 15068 USA (SAN 631-077X) Tel 724-334-7000; Fax: 724-334-1200; Toll Free: 800-444-4484
E-mail: customerservice@anchordistributors.com
Web site: http://www.anchordistributors.com.

Anderson Merchandisers, 421 E. 34th St., Amarillo, TX 79103 USA (SAN 169-8028) Tel 806-376-6251
E-mail: hanleyg@amerch.com.

Anderson News - Tacoma, 9914 32nd Ave., S., Lakewood, WA 98499 USA (SAN 108-1322) Tel 253-581-1940; Fax: 253-584-5941; Toll Free: 800-552-2000 (in Washington).

Anderson News, LLC, 211 Industrial Dr., Roanoke, VA 24019 USA (SAN 168-9223); 6016 Brookvale Ln. Ste. 110B, Knoxville, TN 37919-4003 (SAN 168-9363); 2541 Westcott Blvd., Knoxville, TN 37931 Tel 423-966-7575; 3911 Volunteer Dr., Chattanooga, TN 37416 (SAN 169-7862) Tel 423-894-3945; 6301 Forbing Rd., Little Rock, AR 72219 Tel 501-562-7360; 1185a Commerce Blvd., Midway, FL 32343-6629; 1857 W. Grant Rd., Tucson, AZ 85745-1203; 5184 Sullivan Gardens Pkwy., Kingsport, TN 37660-8104 (SAN 241-6131); 390 Exchange St., Box 1624, New Haven, CT 06506 (SAN 241-6158) Tel 203-777-5545; 5000 Moline St., Denver, CO 80239-2622 Tel 303-321-1111; 1709 N. East St., Flagstaff, AZ 86002 (SAN 168-9290) Tel 520-774-6171; Fax: 520-779-1958; 6016 Brookvale Ln. Ste. 110B, Knoxville, TN 37919-4003; P.O. Box 22968, Chattanooga, TN 37422; P.O. Box 36003, Knoxville, TN 37930-6003; P.O. Box 280077, Memphis, TN 38168-0077; P.O. Box 6660, Pensacola, FL 32503 Do not confuse with Anderson News Company, Pinellas Park, FL.

Anderson-Austin News Co., LLC, 808 Newtown Cir., No. B, Lexington, KY 40511-1230 USA (SAN 169-2836) Tel 606-254-2765; Fax: 606-254-3328.

Andich Brothers News Company, *See* **Tobias News Co.**

Andrews McMeel Publishing, *(978-0-8362; 978-0-939251; 978-1-57939; 978-0-7407; 978-1-4494)* Orders Addr.: c/o Simon & Schuster, Inc., 100 Front St., Riverside, NJ 08075 USA Toll Free Fax: 800-943-9831; Toll Free: 800-943-9839 (Customer Service); 800-897-7650 (Credit Dept.); Edit Addr.: 1130 Walnut St., Kansas City, MO 64106-2109 USA (SAN 202-540X) Toll Free: 800-851-8923
Web site: http://www.AndrewsMcMeel.com.

Andrzejewski's Marian Church Supply, *See* **A & M Church Supplies**

Angler's Bk. Supply, 1380 W. Second Ave., Eugene, OR 97402 USA (SAN 631-4546) Tel 541-342-8355; Fax: 541-342-1785; Toll Free: 800-260-3869.

Ann Arbor Editions LLC, *(978-1-58726)* 2500 S. State St., Ann Arbor, MI 48104 USA Tel 734-913-1302; Fax: 734-913-1249; 1094 Flex Dr., Jackson, TN 38301
E-mail: ljohnson@aaeditions.com
Web site: http://www.annarbormediagroup.com; http://www.mittenpress.com; http://www.aaeditions.com.

Ann Arbor Media Group, LLC, *See* **Ann Arbor Editions LLC**

answers period, Inc., *(978-0-917875)* Orders Addr.: P.O. Box 427, Goliad, TX 77963 USA (SAN 112-6431) Tel 361-645-2268; Toll Free: 800-852-4752
Web site: http://www.answersbook.com.

Anthracite News Company, *See* **Great Northern Distributors, Inc.**

Anthroposophic Press, Incorporated, *See* **SteinerBooks, Inc.**

Antipodes Bks. & Beyond, 9707 Fairway Ave., Silver Spring, MD 20901-3001 USA Tel 301-602-9519; Fax: 301-565-0160
E-mail: Antipode@antipodesbooks.com
Web site: http://www.antipodesbooks.com.

Antiquarian Bookstore, The, 1070 Lafayette Rd., Portsmouth, NH 03801 USA (SAN 158-9938) Tel 603-436-7250.

Antique Collectors' Club, *(978-0-902028; 978-0-907462; 978-1-85149)* Orders Addr.: Eastworks, 116 Pleasant St., Easthampton, MA 01027 USA (SAN 630-7787) Tel 413-529-0861; Fax: 413-529-0862; Toll Free: 800-252-5231 (orders)
E-mail: info@antiquecc.com; sales@antiquecc.com
Web site: http://www.antiquecollectorsclub.com.

AOAC International, *(978-0-935584)* 481 N. Frederick Ave., Suite 500, Gaithersburg, MD 20877-2417 USA (SAN 260-3411) Tel 301-924-7077; Fax: 301-924-7089; Toll Free: 800-379-2622
E-mail: aoac@aoac.org
Web site: http://www.aoac.org.

A-One Bk. Distributors, Inc., 1555 Ocean Ave. Ste. D, Bohemia, NY 11716-1933 USA (SAN 630-7981).

APG Sales & Distribution Services, Div. of Warehousing and Fulfillment Specialists, LLC (WFS, LLC), 7344 Cockrill Bend Blvd., Nashville, TN 37209-1043 USA (SAN 630-818X) Toll Free: 800-327-5113
E-mail: sswift@agpbooks.com
Web site: http://www.apgbooks.com.

APG Sales & Fulfillment, *See* **APG Sales & Distribution Services**

Apollo Bks., *(978-0-938290)* 91 Market St., Wappingers Falls, NY 12590-2333 USA (SAN 170-0928).

Apollo Library Bk. Supplier, 865 Kent Ln., Philadelphia, PA 19115 USA (SAN 159-8031).

Appalachian Bible Co., *(978-1-889049)* Orders Addr.: 522 Princeton Rd., Johnson City, TN 37605 USA (SAN 169-7889) Tel 423-282-9475; Fax: 423-282-9110; Toll Free: 800-289-2772; Edit Addr.: P.O. Box 1573, Johnson City, TN 37601 USA
E-mail: appainc@aol.com.

Appalachian Bk. Distributors, Div. of Send The Light Distribution LLC, Orders Addr.: 100 Biblica Way, Elizabethton, TN 37643-6070 USA Toll Free Fax: 800-759-2779; Edit Addr.: 506 Princeton Rd., Johnson City, TN 37601 USA.

Appalachian, Incorporated, *See* **Appalachian Bible Co.**

Applause Learning Resources, *(978-0-9655052; 978-0-9786746; 978-0-9788527; 978-0-9790091; 978-1-60713)* 85 Fernwood Ln., Roslyn, NY 11576 USA Tel 516-625-1145; Fax: 516-625-7392; Toll Free Fax: 877-365-7484; Toll Free: 800-277-5287
E-mail: info@applauselearning.com
Web site: http://www.applauselearning.com.

Applause Productions, *See* **Applause Learning Resources**

Apple Bk. Co., Div. of Scholastic Bk. Fairs, Inc., Orders Addr.: P.O. Box 217156, Charlotte, NC 28221-0156 USA Tel 704-596-6641; Fax: 704-599-1738; Toll Free: 800-331-1993; Edit Addr.: 5901 N. Northwoods Business Pkwy., Charlotte, NC 28269 USA (SAN 108-4569).

Applewood Bks., *(978-0-918222; 978-1-55709; 978-1-889833; 978-1-933212; 978-1-4290; 978-0-9819430; 978-1-60889; 978-0-9844156; 978-0-9836416; 978-1-938700; 978-0-9882885; 978-1-5162)* 1 River Rd., Carlisle, MA 01741-1820 USA (SAN 210-3419) Toll Free: 800-277-5312; 1 Ingram Blvd., La Vergne, TN 37086
E-mail: applewood@awb.com; svec@awb.com
Web site: http://www.awb.com.

Arabic & Islamic Univ. Pr., 4263 Fountain Ave., Los Angeles, CA 90029 USA (SAN 107-6299) Tel 323-665-1000; Fax: 323-665-3107.

Aramark, 18825 67th Ave., NE, Arlington, WA 98223-9656 USA (SAN 631-3507) Tel 360-435-2524; Fax: 360-435-6805 Do not confuse with Aramark, Albuquerque, NM.

Aramark Magazine & Bk. Co., P.O. Box 25489, Oklahoma City, OK 73125 USA (SAN 169-6971) Tel 405-843-9383; Fax: 405-843-0379 Do not confuse with Aramark Magazine & Bk. Services, Inc., Norfolk, VA.

Aramark Magazine & Bk. Services, Inc., P.O. Box 2240, Norfolk, VA 23501 USA (SAN 169-8680) Do not confuse with Aramark Magazine & Book Co., Oklahoma City, OK.

Arbit Bks., Inc., *(978-0-930038)* 8050 N. Port Washington Rd., Milwaukee, WI 53217 USA (SAN 169-913X) Tel 414-352-4404.

Ardic Bk. Distributors, Inc., 331 High St., 2nd Flr., Burlington, NJ 08016-4411 USA (SAN 170-5415).

Argus International Corp., Subs. of ICS International Group, Skypark Business Pk., P.O. Box 4082, Irvine, CA 92716-4082 USA (SAN 681-9761) Tel 714-552-8494 (phone/fax).

Aries Pr., *(978-0-933646)* P.O. Box 30081, Chicago, IL 60630 USA (SAN 111-9168) Tel 312-725-8300.

Aries Productions, Inc., *(978-0-910035)* Orders Addr.: P.O. Box 29396, Sappington, MO 63126 USA (SAN 669-0009); Edit Addr.: 6935 Tholozan Ave., Saint Louis, MO 63109-1130 USA (SAN 241-2004)
E-mail: uspsisquad@aol.com
Web site: http://ww.ussisquad.com.

Arizona Periodicals, Inc., P.O. Box 5780, Yuma, AZ 85366-5780 USA Tel 520-782-1822.

Arkansas Bk. Co., 1207 E. Second St., Little Rock, AR 72202-2732 USA (SAN 168-9940) Tel 501-375-1184.

Arlington Card Co., Bk. Dept., 140 Gansett Ave., Cranston, RI 02910 USA (SAN 108-5794) Tel 401-942-3188.

Armstrong, J. B. News Agency, *See* **News Group, The**

Arrow, G. H. Co., P.O. Box 676, Bala Cynwyd, PA 19004 USA (SAN 111-3771) Tel 215-227-3211; Fax: 215-221-0631; Toll Free: 800-775-2776.

Arrowhead Magazine Co., Inc., P.O. Box 5947, San Bernardino, CA 92412 USA (SAN 169-0094) Tel 909-799-8294; Fax: 909-799-3774; 1055 Cooley Ave., San Bernardino, CA 92408 (SAN 249-2717) Tel 909-370-4420.

Ars Obscura, *(978-0-9623780)* P.O. Box 4424, Seattle, WA 98104-0424 USA (SAN 113-5368) Tel 206-324-9792.

Art Institute of Chicago, *(978-0-86559)* Orders Addr.: a/o Museum Shop Mail Order Dept., 950 N. North Branch St., Chicago, IL 60622-4276 USA; Edit Addr.: 111 S. Michigan Ave., Chicago, IL 60603-6110 USA (SAN 204-479X) Tel 312-443-3540; Fax: 312-443-1334
Web site: http://www.artic.edu.

Art Media Resources, Inc., *(978-1-878529; 978-1-58886)* 1507 S. Michigan Ave., Chicago, IL 60605 USA (SAN 253-8199) Tel 312-663-5351; Fax: 312-663-5177
E-mail: info@artmediaresources.com
Web site: http://www.artmediaresources.com.

Artisan, *(978-1-57965; 978-1-885183)* Div. of Workman Publishing Co., Inc., 225 Varick St. Flr. 9, New York, NY 10014-4381 USA Toll Free: 800-967-5630 Do not confuse with Artisan, Wheaton, IL
E-mail: artisan@workman.com.

Artisan House, *See* **Artisan**

ARVEST, P.O. Box 200248, Denver, CO 80220 USA (SAN 159-8694) Tel 303-388-8486; Fax: 303-355-4213; Toll Free: 800-739-0761
E-mail: copy@concentric.net.

Asia Bk. Corp. of America, *(978-0-940500)* 45-77 157th St., Flushing, NY 11355 USA (SAN 214-493X) Tel 718-762-7204; Fax: 718-460-5030.

ASM International, *(978-0-87170; 978-1-61503; 978-1-62708)* 9639 Kinsman Rd., Materials Park, OH 44073-0002 USA (SAN 204-7586) Tel 440-338-5151; Fax: 440-338-4634; Toll Free: 800-336-5152 0 Do not

confuse with ASM International, Inc., Fort Lauderdale, FL
E-mail: memberservicecenter@asminternational.org
Web site: http://asmcommunity.asminternational.org; http://www.asminternational.org.

ASP Wholesale, c/o A&A Quality Shipping Services 3623 Munster Ave, Unit B, Hayward, CA 94545 USA Tel 510-732-6521 (Voice).

Aspen West Publishing, *(978-0-9615390; 978-1-885348)* P.O. Box 522151, Salt Lake Cty, UT 84152-2151 USA (SAN 112-7993) Toll Free: 800-222-9133 (orders only)
E-mail: kent@aspenwest.com
Web site: http://www.aspenwest.com.

Assn. of Energy Engineers, Orders Addr.: P.O. Box 1026, Lilburn, GA 30048 USA Tel 770-925-9558; Fax: 770-381-9865; Edit Addr.: 4025 Pleasantdale Rd., Suite 420, Atlanta, GA 30340 USA Tel 770-447-5083.

Associated Univ. Presses, *(978-0-8453)* 2010 Eastpark Blvd., Cranbury, NJ 08512 USA (SAN 281-2959) Tel 609-655-4770; Fax: 609-655-8366
E-mail: aup440@aol.com
Web site: http://www.aupresses.com.

Association of Official Analytical Chemists, *See* **AOAC International**

Astran, Inc., 6995 NW 82nd Ave. Ste. 40, Miami, FL 33166-2783 USA (SAN 169-1082) Toll Free: 800-431-4957
E-mail: sales@astranbooks.com
Web site: http://www.astranbooks.com.

ATEXINC, Corp., *(978-0-9702332; 978-1-60405)* Orders Addr.: 17738 Vintage Oak Dr., Glencoe, MO 63038-1478 USA (SAN 631-774X) Toll Free Fax: 866-346-9515 Do not confuse with Atex, Inc., Bedford, MA
E-mail: mail@atexinc.com
Web site: http://www.atexinc.com; http://www.thetextilekit.com; http://www.itextiles.com.

Athelstan Pubns., *(978-0-940753)* Orders Addr.: 5925 Kirby Dr. Suite E. 464, Houston, TX 77005 USA (SAN 663-5318) Tel 713-371-2107; Fax: 713-524-1159
E-mail: info@athel.com; barlow@athel.com
Web site: http://www.athel.com.

Athena Productions, Inc., 5500 Collins Ave., No. 901, Miami Beach, FL 33140 USA Tel 305-868-8482; Fax: 305-868-8891.

Atlas News Co., Div. of Hudson News Co., P.O. Box 779, Boylston, MA 01505-0779 USA (SAN 169-3360).

Atlas Publishing Co., *(978-0-930575)* 1464 36th St., Ogden, UT 84403 USA (SAN 110-3873) Tel 801-627-1043.

AtlasBooks, *See* **AtlasBooks Distribution**

AtlasBooks Distribution, Div. of BookMasters, Inc., Orders Addr.: 30 Amberwood Pkwy., Ashland, OH 44805 USA (SAN 631-936X) Fax: 419-281-6883; Toll Free: 800-247-6553; 800-537-6727; 800-266-5564
E-mail: orders@atlasbooks.com
Web site: http://www.atlasbooksdistribution.com.

Attainment Co., Inc., *(978-0-934731; 978-1-57861; 978-1-943148)* Orders Addr.: P.O. Box 930160, Verona, WI 53593 USA (SAN 694-1656) Tel 608-845-7880; Fax: 608-845-8040; Toll Free: 800-327-4269; Edit Addr.: 504 Commerce Pkwy., Verona, WI 53953 USA (SAN 631-6174)
E-mail: info@attainmentcompany.com; sue@attainmentcompany.com; ameyer@attainmentcompany.com
Web site: http://www.attainmentcompany.com/.

Audible.com, One Washington Pk., Newark, NJ 07102 USA Tel 973-820-0400 (International); Fax: 973-890-2442; Toll Free: 888-283-5051 (USA & Canada)
E-mail: content-requests@audible.com
Web site: http://www.audible.com.

Audio Bk. Co., *(978-0-89926)* 235 Bellefontaine St., Pasadena, CA 91105-2921 USA (SAN 158-1414) Toll Free: 800-423-8273
E-mail: sales@audiobookco.com
Web site: http://www.audiobookco.com.

AudioGO, *(978-0-563; 978-0-7540; 978-0-7927; 978-0-89340; 978-1-55504; 978-1-60283; 978-1-60998; 978-1-62064; 978-1-62460; 978-1-4815; 978-1-4821)* Orders Addr.: c/o Perseus, 1094 Flex Dr., Jackson, TN 38301 USA; Edit Addr.: 42 Whitecap Dr., North Kingstown, RI 02852-7445 USA (SAN 858-7701) Toll Free: 800-621-0182
E-mail: laura.almeida@audiogo.com
Web site: http://www.audiogo.com/us/.

Audubon Prints & Bks., 9720 Spring Ridge Ln., Vienna, VA 22182 USA (SAN 111-820X).

Augsburg Fortress Publishers, Publishing House of The Evangelical Lutheran Church in America, *See* **Augsburg Fortress, Pubs.**

Augsburg Fortress, Pubs., *(978-0-8006; 978-0-8066; 978-1-4514; 978-1-5064)* Orders Addr.: P.O. Box 1209, Minneapolis, MN 55440-1209 USA (SAN 169-4081) Toll Free Fax: 800-722-7766; Toll Free: 800-328-4648 (orders only); Edit Addr.: 510 Marquette 8th Fl., Minneapolis, MN 55402 USA Tel 800-328-4648 800-722-7766
E-mail: customerservice@augsburgfortress.org; info@augsburgfortress.org; subscriptions@augsburgfortress.org; copyright@augsburgfortress.org; international@augsburgfortress.org
Web site: http://www.augsburgfortress.org.

Augusta News Co., 25 Second St., Apt. 124, Hallowell, ME 04347-1481 USA (SAN 169-3026).

Auromere, Inc., *(978-0-89744)* 2621 W. US Hwy. 12, Lodi, CA 95242-9200 USA (SAN 169-0043) Fax: 209-339-3715; Toll Free: 800-735-4691
E-mail: sasp@lodinet.com
Web site: http://www.auromere.com.

Austin & Company, Inc., *(978-0-9657153)* 104 S. Union St., Suite 202, Traverse City, MI 49684 USA (SAN 631-1466) Tel 231-933-4649; Fax: 231-933-4659
E-mail: aandn@aol.com
Web site: http://www.austinandcompanyinc.com.

Austin & Nelson Publishing, *See* **Austin & Company, Inc.**

Austin Management Group, Orders Addr.: P.O. Box 3206, Paducah, KY 42002-3206 USA (SAN 135-3349); Edit Addr.: P.O. Box 300, Paducah, KY 42002-0300 USA (SAN 249-6844).

Author Solutions, Inc., Div. of Penguin Group (USA) Inc., 1663 Liberty Dr., Bloomington, IN 47403 USA Tel 812-334-5223; Toll Free: 877-655-1722
E-mail: sfurr@authorsolutions
Web site: http://www.authorsolutions.com.

AuthorHouse, *(978-1-58500; 978-0-9675669; 978-1-58721; 978-1-58820; 978-0-7596; 978-1-4033; 978-1-4107; 978-1-4140; 978-1-4184; 978-1-4208; 978-1-4259; 978-1-4343; 978-1-4389; 978-1-4490; 978-1-4520; 978-1-61764; 978-1-4567; 978-1-4582; 978-1-4624; 978-1-4633; 978-1-4634; 978-0-9846457; 978-1-4670; 978-1-4678; 978-1-4685; 978-1-4772; 978-1-4817; 978-1-4918; 978-1-4969; 978-1-5049; 978-1-5065) Div. of Author Solutions, Inc., 1663 Liberty Dr, Suite 200, Bloomington, IN 47403 USA (SAN 253-7605) Fax: 812-336-5449; Toll Free: 888-519-5121*
E-mail: authorsupport@authorhouse.com; emilyguldin@yahoo.com; sfurr@authorsolutions.com; jburns@authorsolutions.com
Web site: http://www.facebook.com/daveywizzletooth1; http://www.authorhouse.com.

Authors & Editors, *See* **2Learn-English**

Auto-Bound, Inc., 909 Marina Village Pkwy., No. 67B, Alameda, CA 94501-1048 USA (SAN 170-0782) Tel 510-521-8655; Fax: 510-521-8755; Toll Free: 800-523-5833.

Avanti Enterprises, Inc., P.O. Box 3563, Hinsdale, IL 60522-3563 USA (SAN 158-3727) Toll Free: 800-799-6464.

Avenue Bks., 2270 Porter Way, Stockton, CA 95207-3339 USA (SAN 122-4158).

Avery BookStores, Inc., 516 Asharoken Ave., Northport, NY 11768-1176 USA (SAN 169-510X).

Aviation Bk. Co., *(978-0-911720; 978-0-911721; 978-0-916413)* 7201 Perimeter Rd., S., No. C, Seattle, WA 98108-3812 USA (SAN 120-1530) Tel 206-767-5232; Fax: 206-763-3428; Toll Free: 800-423-2708
E-mail: sales@aviationbook.com.

Avonlea Bks., Inc., Orders Addr.: P.O. Box 74, White Plains, NY 10602-0074 USA (SAN 680-4446) Tel 914-946-5923; Fax: 914-761-3119; Toll Free: 800-423-0622
E-mail: avonlea@bushkin.com
Web site: http://www.bushkin.com.

B. P. I. Communications, *See* **VNU**

B T P Distribution, 4135 Northgate Blvd., Suite 5, Sacramento, CA 95834-1226 USA (SAN 631-2489) Tel 916-567-2496; Fax: 916-441-6749.

Baggins Bks., 3560 Meridian St., Bellingham, WA 98225-1731 USA (SAN 156-501X).

Baha'i Distribution Service, *(978-0-87743)* Orders Addr.: P.O. Box 1759, Powder Springs, GA 30127-7522 USA (SAN 213-7496) Toll Free: 800-999-9019; Edit Addr.: 415 Linden Ave., Wilmette, IL 60091 USA Tel 847-251-1854; Fax: 847-251-3652
E-mail: bds@usbnc.org.

Baker & Taylor Bks., *(978-0-8480; 978-1-222; 978-1-223)* Orders Addr.: Commerce Service Ctr., 251 Mt. Olive Church Rd., Commerce, GA 30599 USA (SAN 169-1503) Tel 404-335-5000; Toll Free: 800-775-1200 (customer service); 800-775-1800 (orders); Reno Service Ctr., 1160 Trademark Dr., Suite 111, Reno, NV 89511 (SAN 169-4464) Tel 775-850-3800; Fax: 775-850-3826 (customer service); Toll Free Fax: 800-775-1700 (orders); Edit Addr.: Bridgewater Service Ctr. 1120 US Hwy. 22, E., Bridgewater, NJ 08807 USA (SAN 169-4901) Toll Free: 800-775-1500 (customer service); Momence Service Ctr., 501W. Gladiolus St., Momence, IL 60954-1799 (SAN 169-2100) Tel 815-472-2444 (international customers); Fax: 815-472-9886 (international customers); Toll Free: 800-775-2300 (customer service, academic libraries)
E-mail: btinfo@btol.com
Web site: http://www.btol.com.

Baker & Taylor Fulfillment, Inc., 2550 W. Tyvola Rd., Suite 370, Charlotte, NC 28217 USA (SAN 760-8772) Tel 704-236-9553
E-mail: johnsod@btol.com.

Baker & Taylor International, 1120 US Hwy. 22 E., Box 6885, Bridgewater, NJ 08807 USA (SAN 200-6804) Tel 908-541-7000; Fax: 908-729-4037.

Baker & Taylor Publishing Group, *(978-0-934429; 978-1-57145; 978-1-59223; 978-1-60710; 978-1-62686)* Div. of Baker & Taylor Bks., 10350 Barnes Canyon Rd. Suite 100, San Diego, CA 92121 USA (SAN 630-8090) Toll Free: 800-284-3580
Web site: http://www.silverdolphinbooks.com; http://www.baker-taylorpublishing.com; http://www.thunderbaybooks.com/; http://www.bathroomreader.com; http://www.baker-taylor.com.

Baker Bks., *(978-0-8010; 978-0-913686)* Div. of Baker Publishing Group, Orders Addr.: P.O. Box 6287, Grand Rapids, MI 49516-6287 USA (SAN 299-1500) Toll Free Fax: 800-398-3111 (orders only); Toll Free: 800-877-2665 (orders only); Edit Addr.: 6030 E. Fulton, Ada, MI 49301 USA (SAN 201-4041) Tel 616-676-9185; Fax: 616-676-9573
Web site: http://www.bakerpublishinggroup.com.

Baker Book House, Incorporated, *See* **Baker Publishing Group**

Baker Publishing Group, *(978-0-8007; 978-0-8010; 978-1-58743; 978-1-4412; 978-1-4934; 978-1-68196)* Orders Addr.: P.O. Box 6287, Grand Rapids, MI 49516-6287 USA Tel 616-676-9573; Toll Free Fax: 800-398-3111 (orders only); Toll Free: 800-877-2665 (orders only); Edit Addr.: 6030 E. Fulton, Ada, MI 49301 USA Tel 616-676-9185; Fax: 616-676-9573; Toll Free Fax: 800-398-3111; Toll Free: 800-877-2665
E-mail: webmaster@bakerpublishinggroup.com
Web site: http://www.bakerbooks.com; http://www.bakerpublishinggroup.com.

Balogh International, Inc., *(978-1-878762; 978-1-891770)* 1911 N. Duncan Rd., Champaign, IL 61822 USA (SAN 297-2344) Tel 217-355-9331; Fax: 217-355-9413
E-mail: balogh@balogh.com
Web site: http://www.balogh.com.

Balogh Scientific Books, *See* **Balogh International, Inc.**

Balzekas Museum of Lithuanian Culture, 6500 S. Pulaski Rd., Chicago, IL 60629 USA (SAN 110-8522) Tel 773-582-6500; Fax: 773-582-5133.

Banner of Truth, The, *(978-0-85151)* Orders Addr.: P.O. Box 621, Carlisle, PA 17013 USA Tel 717-249-5747; Fax: 717-249-0604; Toll Free: 800-263-8085; Edit Addr.: 63 E. Louther St., Carlisle, PA 17013 USA (SAN 112-1553)
E-mail: info@banneroftruth.org
Web site: http://www.banneroftruth.co.uk.

Banta Packaging & Fulfillment, 1071 Willow Spring Rd., Harrisonburg, VA 22801 USA (SAN 631-7731) Tel 540-442-1333; Fax: 540-434-3541; N9234 Lake Park Rd., Appleton, WI 54915 (SAN 631-8290) Tel 920-969-6400; Fax: 920-751-7794
E-mail: jfair@banta.com.

Banyan Tree Bks., *(978-0-9604320)* 1963 El Dorado Ave., Berkeley, CA 94707 USA (SAN 207-3862) Fax: 510-524-2690
E-mail: banyan@uclink.berkeley.edu.

Barbour & Company, Incorporated, *See* **Barbour Publishing, Inc.**

Barbour Publishing, Inc., *(978-0-916441; 978-1-55748; 978-1-57748; 978-1-58660; 978-1-59310; 978-1-59789; 978-1-60260; 978-1-60742; 978-1-61626; 978-1-62029; 978-1-62416; 978-1-62836; 978-1-63058; 978-1-63409)* Orders Addr.: P.O. Box 719, Uhrichsville, OH 44683 USA (SAN 295-7094) Tel 740-922-6045; Fax: 740-922-5948; Toll Free Fax: 800-220-5948; Toll Free: 800-852-8010
E-mail: info@barbourbooks.com
Web site: http://www.barbourbooks.com.

Barnes & Noble Bks.-Imports, *(978-0-389)* 4720 Boston Way, Lanham, MD 20706 USA (SAN 206-7803) Tel 301-459-3366; Toll Free: 800-462-6420.

Barnes & Noble, Inc., *(978-0-7607; 978-0-88029; 978-1-4028; 978-1-4114; 978-1-4351; 978-1-61551; 978-1-61552; 978-1-61553; 978-1-61554; 978-1-61555; 978-1-61556; 978-1-61557; 978-1-61558; 978-1-61559; 978-1-61560; 978-1-61679; 978-1-61680; 978-1-61681; 978-1-61682; 978-1-61683; 978-1-61684; 978-1-61685; 978-1-61686; 978-1-61687; 978-1-61688) 76 Ninth Ave., 9th Flr., New York, NY 10011 USA (SAN 141-3651) Tel 212-414-6385*
E-mail: smcculloch@bn.com.

Barnes&Noble.com, *(978-1-4005; 978-1-4006)* c/o Merch Accounts Payable/NR Dept., 76 Ninth Ave., 9th Flr., New York, NY 10011 USA (SAN 192-6551) Tel 212-414-6000
Web site: http://www.bn.com.

Basic Crafts Co., 6001 66th Ave., No. 10, Riverdale, MD 20737-1717 USA (SAN 169-5622) Toll Free: 800-847-4127 (outside New York).

Basin News Co., P.O. Box 300, Paducah, KY 42002-0300 USA (SAN 169-2860).

Bassett Printing Corp., *(978-0-9632415)* Orders Addr.: P.O. Box 866, Bassett, VA 24055 USA Fax: 540-629-3416; Toll Free: 800-336-5102 (outside Virginia); Edit Addr.: 101 Main St., Bassett, VA 24055 USA Tel 540-629-2541.

Bay News, Inc., 3333 NW 35th Ave., Portland, OR 97210 USA Tel 503-219-3001; Fax: 503-241-1877.

Bayou Bks., 1005 Monroe St., Gretna, LA 70053 USA (SAN 120-1913) Tel 504-368-1171; Toll Free: 800-843-1724.

BBC Audiobooks America, *See* **AudioGO**

BCH Fulfillment & Distribution, 46 Purdy St., Harrison, NY 10528 USA
E-mail: info@bookch.com
Web site: http://www.bookch.com/.

Beagle Bay Bks., *(978-0-9679591; 978-0-9749610)* Div. of Beagle Bay, Inc., 2325 Homestead Pl., Reno, NV 89509-3657 USA
E-mail: info@beaglebay.com
Web site: http://www.beaglebay.com.

Beaver News Co., Inc., 230 W. Washington St., Rensselaer, IN 47978 USA (SAN 630-8864).

Beck's Bk. Store, 4520 N. Broadway, Chicago, IL 60640 USA (SAN 159-8139) Tel 773-784-7963; Fax: 773-784-0066
E-mail: rsvltrd@aol.com
Web site: http://www.aol.members/becks.html.

Beechwood Pubns., Inc., P.O. Box 1158, Kennett Square, PA 19348 USA (SAN 107-5853) Tel 610-444-5991; Fax: 215-566-4178.

Beekman Bks., Inc., *(978-0-8464)* 300 Old All Angels Hill Rd., Wappingers Falls, NY 12590 USA (SAN 170-1622) Tel 845-297-2690; Fax: 845-297-1002
E-mail: manager@beekmanbooks.com
Web site: http://www.beekmanbooks.com.

Beeler, Thomas T. Pub., *(978-1-57490)* Orders Addr.: P.O. Box 310, Rollinsford, NH 03869 USA Toll Free Fax: 888-222-3396; Toll Free: 800-818-7574; Edit Addr.: 710 Main St., Suite 300, Rollinsford, NH 03869 USA Tel 603-749-0392; Fax: 603-749-0395
E-mail: tombeeler@beelerpub.com
Web site: http://www.beelerpub.com.

Before Columbus Foundation, 655 13th St. Ste. 302, Oakland, CA 94612-1225 USA (SAN 159-2955).

Beijing Bk. Co., Inc., 701 E. Linden Ave., Linden, NJ 07036-2495 USA (SAN 169-5673) Tel 908-862-0909; Fax: 908-862-4201.

Bell Magazine, Orders Addr.: P.O. Box 1957, Monterey, CA 93940 USA (SAN 159-7221); Edit Addr.: 3 Justin Ct., Monterey, CA 93940 USA (SAN 169-0353) Tel 408-642-4668.

Bella Distribution, Orders Addr.: P.O. Box 10543, Tallahassee, FL 32302 USA; Edit Addr.: 1041 Aenon Church Rd., Tallahassee, FL 32304 USA Fax: 850-576-3498; Toll Free: 800-533-1973
E-mail: info@belladistribution.com
Web site: http://www.belladistribution.com.

Benchmark LLC, *(978-0-7834; 978-0-929591)* 559 San Ysidro Rd. Suite I, Santa Barbara, CA 93108 USA (SAN 249-7522) Tel 805-565-8911; Toll Free: 888-797-9377
E-mail: bridger@benchmarkmaps.com; teri@benchmarkmaps.com; curtis@benchmarkmaps.com
Web site: http://www.benchmarkmaps.com.

Benjamin News Group, Orders Addr.: 2131 International St., Columbus, OH 43228 USA (SAN 660-9406) Tel 614-777-9768; Fax: 7=614-777-9766; Edit Addr.: 1701 Rankin St., Missoula, MT 59808-1629 USA (SAN 169-4391) Tel 406-721-7801; Fax: 406-721-7802.

Bennett & Curran, Inc., *(978-1-879607)* 1280 Cherryville Rd., Greenwood Vlg, CO 80121-1222 USA
E-mail: Jeff@bennettandcurran.com.

Berkeley Educational Paperbacks, 2480 Bancroft Way, Berkeley, CA 94704 USA (SAN 168-9509) Tel 510-848-7907.

Berkeley Game Distributors, 5850 Hollis St., Emeryville, CA 94608-2016 USA (SAN 631-2934) Toll Free: 800-424-4263; 1164 E. Sandhill Ave., Carson, CA 90746
E-mail: bgdnorth@ix.netcom.com.

Bernan Assocs., *(978-0-400; 978-0-527; 978-0-89059; 978-1-59610; 978-1-59888; 978-1-60175; 978-1-60946; 978-1-63005)* Div. of Kraus Organization, The, Orders Addr.: 15200 NBN Way, P.O. Box 190, Blue Ridge Summit, PA 17214 USA (SAN 169-3182) Tel 301-459-7666; Fax: 301-459-6988; Toll Free Fax: 800-865-3450; Toll Free: 800-865-3457; Edit Addr.: 4501 Forbes Blvd., Suite 200, Lanham, MD 20706 USA (SAN 760-7253) Tel 301-459-2255; Fax: 301-459-0056; Toll Free: 800-416-4385; 15200 Nbn Way, Blue Ridge Summ, PA 17214
E-mail: query@bernan.com; order@bernan.com; info@bernan.com; jkemp@bernan.com; jculley@rowman.com
Web site: http://www.bernan.com.

Berrett-Koehler Pubs., Inc., *(978-1-57675; 978-1-58376; 978-1-881052; 978-1-60509; 978-1-60994; 978-1-62656)* Orders Addr.: c/o AIDC, P.O. Box 565, Williston, VT 05495 USA Fax: 802-864-7626 (orders); Toll Free: 800-929-2929 (orders); Edit Addr.: 1333 Broadway, Suite 1000, Oakland, CA 94612 USA Tel 510-817-2277; Fax: 415-362-2512
E-mail: bkpub@bkpub.com
Web site: http://www.bkconnection.com.

Bess Pr., Inc., *(978-0-935848; 978-1-57306; 978-1-880188)* 3565 Harding Ave., Honolulu, HI 96816 USA (SAN 239-4111) Tel 808-734-7159; Fax: 808-732-3627
E-mail: kelly@besspress.com
Web site: http://www.besspress.com.

Best Bk. Ctr., Inc., 1016 Ave. Ponce De Leon, San Juan, PR 00926 USA (SAN 132-4403) Tel 809-727-7945; Fax: 809-268-5022.

Best Continental Bk. Co., Inc., P.O. Box 615, Merrifield, VA 22116 USA (SAN 107-3737) Tel 703-280-1400.

Bethany Hse. Pubs., *(978-0-7642; 978-0-87123; 978-1-55661; 978-1-56179; 978-1-57778; 978-1-880089; 978-1-59066)* Div. of Baker Publishing Group, Orders Addr.: P.O. Box 6287, Grand Rapids, MI 49516-6287 USA Toll Free Fax: 800-398-3111 (orders); Toll Free: 800-877-2665 (orders); Edit Addr.: 11400 Hampshire Ave., S., Bloomington, MN 55438-2455 USA (SAN 201-4416) Tel 952-829-2500; Fax: 952-996-1393
E-mail: orders@bakerbooks.com
Web site: http://www.bethanyhouse.com.

Better Homes & Gardens Books, *See* **Meredith Bks.**

Betty Segal, Inc., 1749 Eucalyptus St., Brea, CA 92621 USA Tel 714-529-5359; Fax: 714-529-3882
E-mail: BertySegal@aol.com
Web site: http://www.agoralang.com/trp-bertysegal.html.

Beyda & Associates, Incorporated, *See* **Beyda for Bks., LLC**

Beyda for Bks., LLC, P.O. Box 2535, Montclair, CA 91763-1035 USA (SAN 169-0426) Toll Free: 800-422-3932 (orders only)
E-mail: info@beydaforbooks.com
Web site: http://www.beydaforbooks.com.

B&H Publishing Group, *(978-0-8054; 978-0-87981; 978-1-55819; 978-1-58640; 978-0-8400; 978-1-4336)* Div. of LifeWay Christian Resources of the Southern Baptist Convention, One LifeWay Plaza MSN 114, Nashville, TN 37234-0114 USA (SAN 201-937X) Tel 615-251-2520; Fax: 615-251-5026 (Books Only); 615-251-2036 (Bibles Only); 615-251-2413 (Gifts/Supplies Only); Toll Free: 800-725-5416; 800-251-3225 (retailers); 800-296-4036 (orders/returns); 800-448-8032 (consumers); 800-458-2772 (churches)
E-mail: broadmanholman@lifeway.com; heather.counsellor@bhpublishinggroup.com; wes.banks@bhpublishinggroup.com
Web site: http://www.bhpublishinggroup.com.

BHB Fulfillment, Div. of Weatherhill, Inc., 41 Monroe Tpke., Trumbull, CT 06611 USA.

BHB International, Incorporated, *See* **Continental Enterprises Group, Inc. (CEG)**
Bibliotech, Inc., P.O. Box 720459, Dallas, TX 75372-0459 USA (SAN 631-8312) Tel 214-221-0002; Fax: 214-221-1794
E-mail: metatron@airmail.net
Web site: http://www.bibliotechincorporated.com.
Biddy Bks., 1235 168 Model Rd., Manchester, TN 37355 USA (SAN 157-8561) Tel 931-728-6967.
Big Earth Publishing, *(978-0-915024; 978-1-879483; 978-1-931599; 978-1-934553)* Orders Addr.: 3005 Ctr. Green Dr., Suite 200, Boulder, CO 80301 USA (SAN 209-2425) Fax: 608-259-8370; Toll Free: 800-258-5830; Edit Addr.: 1637 Pearl St. Ste. 201, Boulder, CO 80302-5447 USA
E-mail: books@bigearthpublishing.com
Web site: http://www.bigearthpublishing.com.
Big Kids Productions, Inc., *(978-1-885627)* 2120 Oxford Ave., Austin, TX 78704-4014 USA (SAN 631-340X) Toll Free: 800-477-7811
E-mail: customerservice@bigkidsvideo.com
Web site: http://www.awardvids.com.
Big River Distribution, *(978-0-9795944; 978-0-9823575; 978-0-9845519)* Orders Addr.: 8214 Exchange Way, Saint Louis, MO 63144 USA (SAN 631-9114) Tel 314-918-9800; Fax: 314-918-9804
E-mail: info@bigriverdist.com; randy@bigriverdist.com
Web site: http://www.bigriverdist.com.
Big Tent Bks., *(978-1-60131)* 115 Bluebill Dr., Savannah, GA 31419 USA (SAN 851-1136)
E-mail: admin@dragonpencil.com; admin@bigtentbooks.com
Web site: http://www.bigtentbooks.com.
Bilingual Educational Services, Inc., *(978-0-86624; 978-0-89075)* 2514 S. Grand Ave., Los Angeles, CA 90007 USA (SAN 218-4680) Tel 213-749-6213; Fax: 213-749-1820; Toll Free: 800-448-6032
E-mail: sales@besbooks.com
Web site: http://www.besbooks.com.
Bilingual Pr./Editorial Bilingue, *(978-0-916950; 978-0-927534; 978-1-931010; 978-1-939743)* Orders Addr.: Hispanic Research Ctr. Arizona State Univ. P.O. Box 875303, Tempe, AZ 85287-5303 USA (SAN 208-5526) Fax: 480-965-8309; Toll Free: 800-965-2280; Edit Addr.: Bilingual Review Pr. Administration Bldg. Rm. B-255 Arizona State Univ., Tempe, AZ 85281 USA
E-mail: brp@asu.edu
Web site: http://www.asu.edu/brp.
Bilingual Pubns. Co., The, 270 Lafayette St., New York, NY 10012 USA (SAN 164-8993) Tel 212-431-3500; Fax: 212-431-3567 Do not confuse with Bilingual Pubns., in Denver, CO
E-mail: lindagoodman@juno.com; spanishbks@aol.com.
Birdlegs Christian Apparel, P.O. Box 189, Duluth, GA 30136-0189 USA (SAN 631-3280) Toll Free: 800-545-0790.
BJU Pr., *(978-0-89084; 978-1-57924; 978-1-59166; 978-1-60682; 978-1-62856)* 1700 Wade Hampton Blvd., Greenville, SC 29614 USA (SAN 223-7512) Tel 864-242-5731; 864-370-1800 (ext. 4397; Fax: 864-298-0268; Toll Free Fax: 800-525-8398; Toll Free: 800-845-5731
E-mail: bjup@bjup.com
Web site: http://www.bjupress.com.
Bk. Box, Inc., 3126 Purdue Ave., Los Angeles, CA 90066 USA (SAN 243-2285) Tel 310-391-2313.
Bk. Buy Back, 5150 Candlewood St., No. 6, Lakewood, CA 90712 USA (SAN 631-7251) Tel 562-461-9355; Fax: 562-461-9445.
Bk. Co., The, 145 S. Glencoe St., Denver, CO 80222-1152 USA (SAN 200-2809).
Bk. Distribution Ctr., *(978-0-941722)* Div. of Free Islamic Literatures, Inc., Orders Addr.: P.O. Box 35844, Houston, TX 77235 USA (SAN 241-6395); Edit Addr.: P.O. Box 31669, Houston, TX 77231 USA (SAN 226-2770).
Bk. Distribution Ctr., Inc., Orders Addr.: P.O. Box 64631, Virginia Beach, VA 23467-6431 USA (SAN 134-8019) Tel 757-456-0005; Fax: 757-552-0837; Edit Addr.: 5321 Cleveland St., No. 203, Virginia Beach, VA 23462-6552 USA (SAN 169-8672)
E-mail: sales@bookdist.com
Web site: http://www.bookdist.com.
Bk. Dynamics, Inc., *(978-0-9612440)* 18 Kennedy Blvd., East Brunswick, NJ 08816 USA (SAN 169-5649) Tel 732-545-5151; Fax: 732-545-5959; Toll Free: 800-441-4510.
Bk. Express, *(978-0-9612322; 978-1-890308)* Orders Addr.: P.O. Box 1249, Bellflower, CA 90706 USA (SAN 289-1301) Tel 562-865-1226; Edit Addr.: 12122 E. 176th St., Artesia, CA 90701-4013 USA
E-mail: carbks4u@escapenet.net.
Bk. Home, The, 119 E. Dale St., Colorado Springs, CO 80903-4701 USA (SAN 249-3055) Tel 719-634-5885.
Bk. Hse., Inc., The, 208 W. Chicago St., Jonesville, MI 49250-0125 USA (SAN 169-3859) Tel 517-849-2117; Fax: 517-849-9716; Toll Free Fax: 800-858-9716; Toll Free: 800-248-1146
E-mail: bhinfo@thebookhouse.com.
Bk. Hse., The, 9719 Manchester Rd., Saint Louis, MO 63119 USA Toll Free: 800-513-4491.
Bk. Margins, Inc., 7100 Valley Green Rd., Fort Washington, PA 19034-2206 USA (SAN 106-7788) Tel 215-223-5300
E-mail: paul.gross@bookmargins.com
Web site: http://www.bookmargins.com.
Bk. Marketing Plus, 406 Post Oak Rd., Fredericksburg, TX 78624 USA (SAN 630-6543) Tel 830-997-4776; Fax: 830-997-9752; Toll Free: 800-356-2445.
Bk. Mart, The, 1153 E. Hyde Pk., Inglewood, CA 90302 USA (SAN 168-969X).
Bk. Service of Puerto Rico, 102 De Diego, Santurce, PR 00907 USA (SAN 169-9326) Tel 809-728-5000; Fax: 809-726-6131
E-mail: bellbook@coqui.net
Web site: http://home.coqui.net/bellbook.
Bk. Service Unlimited, P.O. Box 31108, Seattle, WA 98103-1108 USA (SAN 169-877X) Toll Free: 800-347-0042.
Bk. Services International, Orders Addr.: P.O. Box 1434-SMS, Fairfield, CT 06430 USA (SAN 157-9541) Tel 203-374-4939; Fax: 203-384-6099; Toll Free: 800-243-2790.
Bk. Shelf, The, 222 Crestview Dr., Fort Dodge, IA 50501-5708 USA (SAN 169-2658).
Bk. Warehouse, 5154 NW 165th St., Hialeah, FL 33014-6335 USA.
Bk. World, 311 Sagamore Pkwy., N., Lafayette, IN 47904 USA (SAN 135-4051) Tel 765-448-1131 Do not confuse with companies with the same or similar name in Sun Lakes, AZ, Roanoke, VA
E-mail: fsjintl@pworld.net.ph.
Bks. & Media, Inc., *(978-0-7848; 978-0-88483; 978-1-55744)* Div. of Marco Bk. Co., Orders Addr.: P.O. Box 695, Lodi, NY 07644 USA (SAN 206-3352) Tel 973-458-8153; Fax: 973-458-5289; Toll Free: 800-901-8150; Edit Addr.: 60 Industrail Rd., Lodi, NJ 07644 USA.
Bks. & Research, Inc., 145 Palisade St. Ste. 389, Dobbs Ferry, NY 10522-1628 USA (SAN 130-1101)
E-mail: brinc@ix.netcom.com
Web site: http://www.books-and-research.com.
Bks. Are Fun, Ltd., *(978-0-9649777; 978-1-58209; 978-1-890409; 978-1-59795; 978-1-60626)* 1 Readers Digest Rd., Pleasantville, NY 10570-7000 USA
E-mail: msmall@booksarefun.com
Web site: http://www.booksarefun.com.
Bks. Plus, U.S.A., 20171 Kelso Rd., Walnut, CA 91789-1922 USA (SAN 630-8473).
Bks. to Grow On, 826 S. Aiken Ave., Pittsburgh, PA 15232 USA (SAN 128-438X); 210 S. Highland Ave., Pittsburgh, PA 15206 Fax: 412-621-5324.
Bks. West, 11111 E. 53rd Ave., Unit D2, Boulder, CO 80239 USA (SAN 631-4724) Tel 303-449-5995; Fax: 303-449-5951; Toll Free: 800-378-4188; 6340 E. 58Th Ave, Commerce City, CO 80022 Do not confuse with Books West, San Diego, CA
E-mail: wnack@rmi.net
Web site: http://www.bookswest.net/.
Black Box Corp., 1000 Park Dr., Lawrence, PA 15055 USA (SAN 277-1985) Tel 412-746-5500; Fax: 412-746-0746.
Black Christian Bk. Distributors, 1169 North Burleson Blvd. Suite 107-246, Burleson, TX 76028 USA.
Black Magazine Agency, 4515 Fleur Dr. Ste. 301, Des Moines, IA 50321-2369 USA (SAN 107-0819) Toll Free: 800-782-9787.
Black Rabbit Bks., *(978-1-58340; 978-1-887068; 978-1-59920; 978-1-62310; 978-1-62588; 978-1-68071; 978-1-68072)* Orders Addr.: P.O. Box 3263, Mankato, MN 56002 USA (SAN 925-4862); Edit Addr.: 123 S. Broad St., Mankato, MN 56001 USA (SAN 858-902X)
E-mail: info@blackrabbitbooks.com; production@blackrabbitbooks.com
Web site: http://www.blackrabbitbooks.com.
Blackburn News Agency, P.O. Box 1039, Kingsport, TN 37662 USA (SAN 169-7900).
Blackhawk Hobby Distributors, Incorporated, 5600 N. 2nd St., Loves Park, IL 61111-4602 USA.
Blackstone Audio Books, Incorporated, *See* **Blackstone Audio, Inc.**
Blackstone Audio, Inc., *(978-0-7861; 978-1-4332; 978-1-4417; 978-1-4551; 978-1-4708; 978-1-4829; 978-1-4830; 978-1-5046; 978-1-5047)* 31 Mistletoe Rd., Ashland, OR 97520 USA (SAN 173-2811) Fax: 800-482-9294; Toll Free Fax: 800-482-9294; Toll Free: 800-729-2665
E-mail: sales@blackstoneaudio.com; megan.wahrenbrock@blackstoneaudio.com
Web site: http://www.blackstoneaudio.com.
Blackwell, *(978-0-913262; 978-0-916472)* Orders Addr.: 6024 SW Jean Rd., Bldg. G, Lake Oswego, OR 97034 USA (SAN 169-7048) Tel 503-684-1140; Fax: 503-639-2481; Toll Free: 800-547-6426 (in Oregon); Edit Addr.: 100 University Ct., Blackwood, NJ 08012 USA (SAN 169-4596) Tel 856-228-8900; Toll Free: 800-257-7341
Web site: http://www.blackwell.com/.
Blackwell North America, *See* **Blackwell**
Blair, John F. Pub., *(978-0-89587; 978-0-910244)* Orders Addr.: 1406 Plaza Dr., Winston-Salem, NC 27103 USA (SAN 201-4319) Tel 336-768-1374; Fax: 336-768-9194; Toll Free: 800-222-9796
E-mail: harwood@blairpub.com
Web site: http://www.blairpub.com.
Blessing Way Publishing Co., *(978-0-9627324)* 1131 Villa Dr., Suite 003, Atlanta, GA 30306-2593 USA (SAN 297-3251).
Blooming Twig Books LLC, *(978-0-9777736; 978-1-933918; 978-1-61343; 978-1-937753)* Orders Addr.: 320 S. Boston Suite 1026, Tulsa, OK 74103 USA Tel 866-389-1482; Fax: 866-298-7260
Web site: http://www.bloomingtwig.com.
Bloomington News Agency, P.O. Box 3757, Bloomington, IL 61702-3757 USA (SAN 169-1732).
Bloomsbury Publishing Inc, *(978-0-225; 978-0-264; 978-0-304; 978-0-485; 978-0-567; 978-0-7136; 978-0-7185; 978-0-7201; 978-0-7220; 978-0-8044; 978-0-8264; 978-0-86187; 978-1-56338; 978-1-85567; 978-1-85805; 978-1-84127; 978-0-223; 978-0-86012; 978-1-84371; 978-1-4411; 978-1-84706; 978-1-62356; 978-1-62892; 978-1-5013) Orders Addr.: 1385 Broadway, 5th Flr., New York, NY 10018 USA (SAN 213-8220) Tel 212-419-5300*
E-mail: info@continuumbooks.com
Web site: http://www.continuumbooks.com; http://www.thoemmes.com; http://www.bloomsbury.com.
Blu Sky Media Group, P.O. Box 10069, Murfreesboro, TN 37129-0002 USA
Web site: http://www.bluskymediagroup.com.
Blue Cat, *(978-0-932679; 978-0-936200)* 469 Barbados, Walnut, CA 91789 USA (SAN 214-0322) Tel 909-594-3317.
Blue Mountain Arts Inc., *(978-0-88396; 978-1-58786; 978-1-59842; 978-1-68088)* Orders Addr.: P.O. Box 4549, Boulder, CO 80306 USA (SAN 299-9609) Tel 303-449-0536; Fax: 303-417-6434; 303-417-6496; Toll Free Fax: 800-943-6666; 800-545-8573; Toll Free: 800-525-0642
Web site: http://www.sps.com/.
Blue Mountain Arts (R) by SPS Studios, Incorporated, *See* **Blue Mountain Arts Inc.**
Blue Ridge News Co., 21 Westside Dr., No. B, Asheville, NC 28806-2846 USA (SAN 169-6335).
BMI Educational Services, *(978-0-922443; 978-1-60884; 978-1-60933; 978-1-63071)* Orders Addr.: 26 Haypress Rd., Cranbury, NJ 08512 USA (SAN 760-7032); Edit Addr.: P.O. Box 800, Dayton, NJ 08810-0800 USA (SAN 169-4669) Tel 732-329-6991; Fax: 732-329-6994; Toll Free Fax: 800-986-9393 (orders only); Toll Free: 800-222-8100 (orders only)
E-mail: info@bmionline.com
Web site: http://www.bmionline.com/.
Bolchazy-Carducci Pubs., *(978-0-86516; 978-1-61041)* 1570 Baskin Rd., Mundelein, IL 60060-4474 USA (SAN 219-7685) Toll Free: 800-392-6453
E-mail: jcull@bolchazy.com
Web site: http://www.bolchazy.com.
Boley International Subscription Agency, Inc., 1001 Fries Mill Rd., Blackwood, NJ 08012 USA (SAN 159-6225) Tel 609-629-2500.
Bondcliff Bks., *(978-0-9657475; 978-1-931271)* Orders Addr.: P.O. Box 385, Littleton, NH 03561 USA Toll Free: 800-859-7581; Edit Addr.: 8 Bluejay Ln., Littleton, NH 03561 USA
E-mail: bondcliff@ncia.net.
Bonneville News Co., 965 Beardsley Pl., Salt Lake City, UT 84119 USA Tel 801-972-5454; Fax: 801-972-1075; Toll Free: 800-748-5453.
Book Clearing Hse., 46 Purdy St., Harrison, NY 10528 USA (SAN 125-5169) Tel 914-835-0015; Fax: 914-835-0398; Toll Free: 800-431-1579
E-mail: bookch@aol.com.
Book Gallery, *(978-1-878382)* 632 S. Quincy Ave., Apt. 1, Tulsa, OK 74120-4635 USA (SAN 630-9321).
Book Hub, Inc., 903 Pacific Ave., Suite 207A, Santa Cruz, CA 95060 USA Tel 831-466-0145; Fax: 831-515-5955.
Book Publishing Co., *(978-0-913990; 978-1-57067; 978-0-9669317; 978-0-9673108; 978-0-9779183; 978-1-939053)* P.O. Box 99, Summertown, TN 38483 USA (SAN 202-439X) Tel 931-964-3571; Fax: 931-964-3518; Toll Free: 888-260-8458
E-mail: info@bookpubco.com
Web site: http://www.bookpubco.com.
Book Sales, Inc., *(978-0-7628; 978-0-7858; 978-0-89009; 978-1-55521; 978-1-57715; 978-1-4161)* Orders Addr.: 400 1st Ave N. Ste. 300, Minneapolis, MN 55401-1721 USA (SAN 169-488X) Toll Free: 800-526-7257; Edit Addr.: 276 Fifth Ave., Suite 206, New York, NY 10001 USA (SAN 299-4062) Tel 212-779-4972; Fax: 212-779-6058
E-mail: sales@booksalesusa.com
Web site: http://www.booksalesusa.com/.
Book Wholesalers, Inc., *(978-0-7587; 978-1-4046; 978-1-4131; 978-1-4155; 978-1-4156; 978-1-4287)* 1847 Mercer Rd., Lexington, KY 40511-1001 USA (SAN 135-5449) Toll Free: 800-888-4478
E-mail: jcarrico@bwibooks.com; lison@bwibooks.com
Web site: http://www.bwibooks.com.
Bookazine Co., Inc., 75 Hook Rd., Bayonne, NJ 07002 USA (SAN 169-5665) Tel 201-339-7777; Fax: 201-339-7778; Toll Free: 800-221-8112.
BookBaby, *(978-0-60984; 978-1-61792; 978-1-61842; 978-1-62095; 978-1-62309; 978-1-62488; 978-1-62675; 978-1-4835)* 13909 NE. Airport Way, Portland, OR 97230 USA Tel 503-961-6878; Toll Free: 877-961-6878; 13909 NE. Airport Way, Portland, OR 97230 Toll Free: 877-961-6878
E-mail: books@bookbaby.com; mj@cdbaby.com; phil@cdbaby.com
Web site: http://www.bookbaby.com.
Bookhouse, The, 10505 N. May Ave., Oklahoma City, OK 73120-2611 USA (SAN 200-8467) Tel 405-755-0020.
Booklegger, The, *(978-0-936421)* Orders Addr.: P.O. Box 2626, Grass Valley, CA 95945 USA (SAN 697-9548); Edit Addr.: 13100 Grass Valley Ave., Suite D, Grass Valley, CA 95945 USA (SAN 120-6125) Tel 530-272-1556; Fax: 530-272-2133; Toll Free Fax: 800-250-2199; Toll Free: 800-262-1556
E-mail: order@booklegger.com
Web site: http://www.booklegger.com/.
Bookline, Div. of Michiana News Service, Inc., 2232 S. 11th St., Niles, MI 49120 USA (SAN 169-3948) Tel 616-684-3013; Fax: 616-684-8740.
Booklines Hawaii, Ltd., *(978-1-929844; 978-1-58849; 978-1-60274)* Div. of Islander Group, 269 Pali'i St., Mililani, HI 96789 USA (SAN 630-6624) Tel 808-676-0116; Fax: 808-676-0634
E-mail: customerservice@booklines.com
Web site: http://www.booklineshawaii.com.
BookLink, *(978-0-9797436)* 465 Broad Ave., Leonia, NJ 07605-1637 USA (SAN 854-2473) Tel 201-947-3471; Fax: 201-947-6321
E-mail: booklink@es1booklink.com.
BookLink, Inc., 444 Broad St., Camden, SC 29020 USA (SAN 631-5291) Tel 803-432-5169; Fax: 803-424-8418
E-mail: sam@thebooklink.com
Web site: http://www.thebooklink.com.
Bookman Bks., 138 Elena St., Santa Fe, NM 87501 USA (SAN 630-933X) Tel 505-982-5964.
Bookmark, Inc., The, 1445 N. Winchester St., Olathe, KS 66061-5881 USA (SAN 131-4017) Toll Free: 800-642-1288.
BookMasters, 6745 FM 2738, Burleson, TX 76028-1167 USA (SAN 630-8406) Do not confuse with BookMasters Inc., Ashland, OH.
BookMasters Distribution Services (BDS), Div. of Bookmasters, Inc., 30 Amberwood Pkwy., Ashland, OH 44805 USA (SAN 760-6680) Fax: 419-281-6883; Toll Free: 800-537-6727; 800-266-5564; 800-247-6553.
BookMasters, Inc., *(978-0-9717889)* Orders Addr.: P.O. Box 388, Mansfield, OH 44903 USA (SAN 631-3566) Tel 419-281-1802; Fax: 419-281-6883; Toll Free: 800-247-6553; 30 Amberwood Pkwy., Ashland, OH 44805 (SAN 760-9264) Tel 419-281-1802; Fax: 419-281-6886 Do not confuse with BookMasters, Burleson, TX
E-mail: info@bookmasters.com; order@bookmaster.com
Web site: http://www.bookmasters.com.
Bookmen, Inc., Orders Addr.: 2300 Louisiana Ave N. # B, Minneapolis, MN 55427-3631 USA (SAN 169-409X) Toll Free Fax: 800-266-5636; Toll Free: 800-328-8411 (customer service)
Web site: http://www.bookmen.com.
BookMobile, Orders Addr.: 5120 Cedar Lake Rd., Saint Louis Park, MN 55416 USA (SAN 760-7245) Fax: 763-398-0198
E-mail: dleeper@bookmobile.com
Web site: http://www.bookmobile.com.
BookPartners, Inc., *(978-0-9622269; 978-1-58151; 978-1-885221)* Orders Addr.: P.O. Box 345, Portland, OR 97205 USA; Edit Addr.: 620 SW Main, Portland, OR 97205 USA Tel 503-225-9900; Fax: 503-225-9901
Web site: http://www.amicapublishing.com.
Books Alive, *(978-0-920470; 978-1-55312)* Div. of Book Publishing Co., Orders Addr.: P.O. Box 99, Summertown, TN 38483 USA (SAN 115-7078) Tel 931-964-3571; Fax: 931-964-3518; Toll Free: 888-260-8458 (orders and customer service)
E-mail: Cynthia@bookpubco.com
Web site: http://www.bookpubco.com.
Books International, Inc., *(978-1-891078)* Orders Addr.: P.O. Box 605, Herndon, VA 20172-0605 USA (SAN 131-761X) Tel 703-661-1500; Fax: 703-661-1501
E-mail: bimail@presswarehouse.com.
Booksellers Order Service, 828 S. Broadway, Tarrytown, NY 10591-5112 USA (SAN 106-5181) Tel 914-591-2665; Fax: 914-591-2720; Toll Free: 800-637-0037.
Booksmith Promotional Co., 100 Paterson Plank Rd., Jersey City, NJ 07307 USA (SAN 664-5364) Tel 201-659-2768; Fax: 201-659-3631.
Booksource, The, *(978-0-7383; 978-0-8335; 978-0-911891; 978-0-9641084; 978-1-886379; 978-1-890760; 978-0-7568; 978-1-4117; 978-1-4178; 978-1-60446; 978-1-4364)* Div. of GL group, Inc., Orders Addr.: 1230 Macklind Ave., Saint Louis, MO 63110-1432 USA (SAN 169-4324) Tel 314-647-0600 Toll Free Fax: 800-647-1923; Toll Free: 800-444-0435
E-mail: shankins@booksource.com
Web site: http://www.booksource.com.
BookWorksUSA, 385 Freeport Blvd., Suite 3, Sparks, NV 89431 USA
E-mail: bookworksusa@mac.com.
Bookworld Cos., P.O. Box 2260, Sarasota, FL 34230-2260 USA.
Bookworm, 14 Griffin St., Northport, ME 04849-4446 USA (SAN 170-8074).
Bookworm Bookfairs, P.O. Box 306, Simsbury, CT 06070-0306 USA (SAN 156-5621).
Bookworm, The, 417 Monmouth Dr., Cherry Hill, NJ 08002 USA (SAN 120-9531) Tel 609-667-5884.
Borchardt, G. Inc., 136 E. 57th St., New York, NY 10022 USA (SAN 285-8614) Tel 212-753-5785; Fax: 212-838-6518.
Borders, Inc., 9910 N. By NE Blvd., Bldg. 4, Fishers, IN 46038 USA (SAN 152-5352); Space 497, 1st Level 525 F D Roosevelt Ave. Plaza Las Americas, Hato Rey, PR 00917 (SAN 193-2314); 455 Industrial Blvd., Suite E, La Vergne, TN 37086 (SAN 156-6474); Edit Addr.: 100 Phoenix Dr., Ann Arbor, MI 48108 USA (SAN 152-3546) Tel 734-477-1100; Fulfillment Addr.: a/o Fulfillment Center, 100 Phoenix Dr., Ann Arbor, MI 48108-2202 USA (SAN 197-0917).
Bored Feet Pr., *(978-0-939431)* Orders Addr.: P.O. Box 1832, Mendocino, CA 95460 USA (SAN 661-6992) Tel 707-964-6629; Fax: 707-964-5953; Edit Addr.: 16630 Mitchell Creek Dr., Fort Bragg, CA 95437 USA (SAN 663-3226)
E-mail: Boredft@mcn.org.
Bored Feet Publications, *See* **Bored Feet Pr.**
Bottman Design, Inc., *(978-1-884741)* 1081 S. 300 W., No. A, Salt Lake City, UT 84101 USA (SAN 860-2166) Tel 801-487-1949; Fax: 801-973-6746; Toll Free: 800-365-5564.
Bottom Dog Pr., *(978-0-933087; 978-1-933964)* c/o Firelands College, P.O. Box 425, Huron, OH 44839 USA (SAN 689-5492) Tel 419-433-3573; Fax: 419-616-3966
E-mail: LSmithDog@aol.com; lsmithdog@smithdocs.net
Web site: http://smithdocs.net; http://smithdocs.net/recent_bottom_dog_press_titles.
Bound to Stay Bound Bks., *(978-0-9718238)* 1880 W. Morton Rd., Jacksonville, IL 62650 USA (SAN

169-1996) Toll Free Fax: 800-747-2872; Toll Free: 800-637-6586
Web site: http://www.btsb.com.

Bowers & Merena Galleries, Inc., *(978-0-943161)* Orders Addr.: P.O. Box 1224, Wolfeboro, NH 03894 USA (SAN 168-9746) Tel 603-569-5095; Fax: 603-569-5319; Toll Free: 800-222-5993; Edit Addr.: 18061 Fitch., Irvine, CA 92614-6018 USA (SAN 668-2561).

Bowker LLC, R. R., *(978-0-8352; 978-0-911255)* Subs. of Proquest LLC, Orders Addr.: P.O. Box 32, New Providence, NJ 07974 USA Tel 908-286-1090; Fax: 908-219-0098; Toll Free: 888-269-5372; Edit Addr.: 630 Central Ave., New Providence, NJ 07974 USA (SAN 214-1191); 630 Central Ave., B&T box, New Providence, NJ 07974 (SAN 857-8516)
E-mail: info@bowker.com; pad@bowker.com; customerservice@bowker.com; specialtytitles@bowker.com
Web site: http://www.bowker.com.

Bowling Green State University, Philosophy Documentation Center, *See* **Philosophy Documentation Ctr.**

Boydell & Brewer, Inc., *(978-0-85115; 978-0-85991; 978-0-907239; 978-0-938100; 978-1-57113; 978-1-58046; 978-1-85566; 978-1-870252; 978-1-878822; 978-1-879751; 978-1-900639; 978-1-84384; 978-1-84383)* Div. of Boydell & Brewer Group, Ltd., Orders Addr.: 668 Mount Hope Ave., Rochester, NY 14620-2731 USA (SAN 013-8479) Tel 585-275-0419; Fax: 585-271-8778
E-mail: boydell@boydellusa.net; boydell@boydell.co.uk
Web site: http://www.boydellandbrewer.com.

Boyds Mills Pr., *(978-1-56397; 978-1-878093; 978-1-886910; 978-1-59078; 978-1-932425; 978-1-62091; 978-1-62979; 978-0-9961172; 978-0-9961173; 978-1-943283; 978-1-68238)* Div. of Highlights For Children, Inc., 815 Church St., Honesdale, PA 18431-1877 USA (SAN 852-3177) Tel 570-251-4513 Toll Free: 800-490-5111 Admin line; 877-512-8366; 800-874-8817 Cust Svc Columbus, OH
E-mail: admin@boydsmillspress.com; honesdale-cs@boydsmillspress.com; marketing@boydsmillspress.com
Web site: http://www.boydsmillspress.com; http://www.wordsongpoetry.com; http://www.calkinscreekbooks.com; http://www.frontstreetbooks.com.

BPDI, 1000 S. Lynndale Dr., Appleton, WI 54914 USA (SAN 631-6859) Tel 920-830-7897; Fax: 920-830-3857.

Bridge Pubns., Inc., *(978-0-88404; 978-1-57318; 978-1-4031; 978-1-61177; 978-1-4572)* Orders Addr.: 5600 E. Olympic Blvd., Commerce, CA 90022 USA (SAN 208-3884) Tel 323-888-6200; Fax: 323-888-6210; Toll Free: 800-722-1733; Edit Addr.: 4751_Fountain Ave., Los Angeles, CA 90029 USA
E-mail: annarnow@bridgepub.com; daniellem@bridgepub.com; donarnow@bridgepub.com
Web site: http://www.bridgepub.com; http://www.clearbodyclearmind.com; http://www.scientology.org; http://www.dianetics.org.

Bridge-Logos Foundation, *(978-0-88270; 978-0-912106; 978-0-9841034; 978-1-61036)* Orders Addr.: 17750 NW 115th Ave., Bldg. 200 Suite 220, Alachua, FL 32615 USA (SAN 253-5254) Tel 386-462-2525; Fax: 386-462-2535; Toll Free: 800-935-6467 (orders only); 800-631-5802 (orders only)
E-mail: info@bridgelogos.com; mail@bridgelogos.com; phildebrand@bridgelogos.com; lhildebrand@bridgelogos.com
Web site: http://www.bridgelogos.com.

Bridge-Logos Publishers, *See* **Bridge-Logos Foundation**

Brigham Distribution, 110 S. 800 W., Brigham City, UT 84302 USA (SAN 760-7652) Tel 435-723-6611; Fax: 435-723-6644
E-mail: brigdist@sisna.com.

Brigham, Kay, Orders Addr.: 9500 Old Cutler Rd., Miami, FL 33156 USA Tel 305-666-3844; Fax: 305-661-4843
Web site: http://www.kaybrigham.com.

Brigham Young Univ. Print Services, 205 UPB, Provo, UT 84602 USA Tel 801-378-2809; Fax: 801-378-3374
E-mail: denise@upb.byu.edu
Web site: http://www.upb.byu.edu.

Bright Horizons Specialty Distributors, Inc., 206 Riva Ridge Dr., Fairview, NC 28730-9764 USA (SAN 110-4101) Toll Free: 800-437-3959 (orders only).

Brightpoint Literacy, 299 Market St., Saddle Brook, NJ 07663 USA Tel 201-708-6498.

Brill, E. J. U. S. A., Incorporated, *See* **Brill USA, Inc.**

Brill USA, Inc., Subs. of Brill Academic Publishing Co., The Netherlands, 2 Liberty Square, Eleventh Flr., Boston, MA 02109 USA (SAN 254-6922) Tel 617-263-2323; Fax: 617-263-2324; Toll Free: 800-962-4406
E-mail: cs@brillusa.com; brillonline@brillusa.com
Web site: http://www.brill.nl.

Brilliance Audio, *See* **Brilliance Publishing**

Brilliance Publishing, *(978-0-930435; 978-1-56100; 978-1-56740; 978-1-58788; 978-1-59086; 978-1-59355; 978-1-59600; 978-1-59710; 978-1-59737; 978-1-4233; 978-1-4418; 978-1-61106; 978-1-4558; 978-1-4692; 978-1-4805; 978-1-4915; 978-1-5012; 978-1-5113)* Orders Addr.: P.O. Box 887, Grand Haven, MI 49417 USA (SAN 690-1395) Tel 616-846-5256; Fax: 616-846-0630; Toll Free: 800-648-2312 (phone/fax, retail & library orders); Edit Addr.: 1704 Eaton Dr., Grand Haven, MI 49417 USA (SAN 858-138X) Toll Free: 800-648-2312 x330
E-mail: sales@brillianceaudio.com; customerservice@brillianceaudio.com; jcraig@brilliancepublishing.com
Web site: http://www.brilliancepublishing.com.

Brisco Pubns., *(978-0-9603576)* P.O. Box 2161, Palos Verdes Peninsula, CA 90274 USA (SAN 133-0268) Tel 310-534-4943; Fax: 310-534-8437.

Bristlecone Publishing Co., 2560 Brookridge Ave., Golden Valley, MN 55422 USA
E-mail: davej@jblcompanies.com.

Broadman & Holman Publishers, *See* **B&H Publishing Group**

Brodart Co., *(978-0-87272; 978-1-62844)* Orders Addr.: 500 Arch St., Williamsport, PA 17705 USA (SAN 169-7684) Tel 570-326-2461 (International); Fax: 570-326-1479; 717-326-2461; 519-759-1144 (Canada); Toll Free Fax: 800-999-6799; Toll Free: 800-233-8467 (US & Canada)
E-mail: bookinfo@brodart.com
Web site: http://www.brodart.com.

Brookes, Paul H. Publishing Co. Inc., *(978-0-933716; 978-1-55766; 978-1-59857; 978-1-68125)* Orders Addr.: P.O. Box 10624, Baltimore, MD 21285-0624 USA (SAN 212-730X) Tel 410-337-9580; Fax: 410-337-8539; Toll Free: 800-638-3775 (customer service/ordering/billing/fulfillment); Edit Addr.: 409 Washington Ave., Suite 500, Baltimore, MD 21204 USA (SAN 666-6485)
E-mail: custserv@brookespublishing.com
Web site: http://www.brookespublishing.com.

Brotherhood of Life, Inc., *(978-0-914732)* P.O. Box 46306, Las Vegas, NV 89114-6306 USA (SAN 111-3674) Fax: 702-319-5577
E-mail: brotherhoodoflife@hotmail.com
Web site: http://www.brotherhoodoflife.com.

Brown, David Book Company, The, *See* **Casemate Academic**

Brown Enterprises, Inc., *(978-0-9711451)* P.O. Box 11447, Durham, NC 27703 USA Tel 919-680-2288 Do not confuse with companies with the same or similar names in Pasadena, CA, Bellingham, WA
E-mail: brown.enterprisesinc@verizon.net.

Brunner News Agency, 217 Flanders Ave., P.O. Box 598, Lima, OH 45801 USA (SAN 169-6777) Tel 419-225-5826; Fax: 419-225-5537; Toll Free: 800-998-1727
E-mail: brunnews@aol.com
Web site: http://www.readmoreshallmark.com.

Bryan, R. L., *(978-0-934870)* P.O. Box 368, Columbia, SC 29202 USA Tel 803-779-3560.

Bryant Altman Map, Inc., Endicott St., Bldg. 26, Norwood, MA 02062 USA (SAN 630-2475) Tel 781-762-3339; Fax: 781-769-9080
E-mail: JPG63@aol.com.

Bryant-Altman Book & Map Distributors, *See* **Bryant Altman Map, Inc.**

Buckeye News Co., 6800 W. Central Ave., Suite F, Toledo, OH 43617-1157 USA (SAN 169-6874).

Budget Bk. Service, Inc., Div. of LDAP, Inc., 386 Park Ave. S., Suite 1913, New York, NY 10016-8804 USA (SAN 169-5762) Fax: 212-679-2247.

Budget Marketing, Inc., P.O. Box 1805, Des Moines, IA 50306 USA (SAN 285-8754).

Budgetext, Orders Addr.: P.O. Box 1487, Fayetteville, AR 72702 USA (SAN 111-3321) Tel 501-443-9205; Fax: 501-442-3064; Toll Free: 800-643-3432; Edit Addr.: 1936 N. Shiloh Dr., Fayetteville, AR 72704 USA (SAN 249-3330)
E-mail: wmorgan@absc.com; scaldwell@budgetext.com
Web site: http://www.budgetext.com.

Buena Vista Home Video, *(978-0-7888; 978-1-55890)* Div. of Walt Disney Studios, 500 S. Buena Vista St., Burbank, CA 91521-1120 USA (SAN 249-2342) Tel 818-295-4841; Fax: 818-972-2845; Toll Free: 800-723-4763
Web site: http://www.disney.com.

Burlington News Agency, 382 Hercules Dr., Colchester, VT 05446-5836 USA (SAN 169-8583).

Burns News Agency, P.O. Box 1211, Rochester, NY 14603-1211 USA (SAN 169-5320).

B.W. Bks. on Wings, Orders Addr.: 581 Market St., San Francisco, CA 94105-2847 USA.

BWI, 1340 Ridgeview Dr., Mchenry, IL 60050-7047 USA.

Byeway Bks., *(978-1-85997; 978-1-904586; 978-1-933581; 978-1-934004; 978-1-60176)* 15941 W. 65th St., Shawnee, KS 66217-9342 USA Toll Free Fax: 866-426-3929; Toll Free: 866-429-3929
E-mail: customerservice@byewaybooks.com
Web site: http://www.byewaybooks.com/how_to_order.html.

Byrrd Enterprises, Inc., *(978-1-886715)* 1302 Lafayette Dr., Alexandria, VA 22308 USA (SAN 169-8605) Tel 703-765-5626; Fax: 703-768-4086; Toll Free: 800-628-0901
E-mail: byrrdbooks@aol.com.

C & B Bk. Distribution, 65-77 160th St., Flushing, NY 11365 USA Tel 718-591-4525
Web site: http://www.cbbooksdistribution.com.

C & B Bk. Hse., 21 Oak Ridge Rd., Monroe, CT 06468 USA (SAN 159-8279).

C & H News Co., P.O. Box 2768, Corpus Christi, TX 78403-2768 USA (SAN 169-8249).

C & T Publishing, *(978-0-914881; 978-1-57120; 978-1-60705; 978-1-61745)* Orders Addr.: 1651 Challenge Dr., Concord, CA 94520 USA (SAN 289-0720) Tel 925-677-0377; Fax: 925-677-0374; Toll Free: 800-284-1114
E-mail: ctinfo@ctpub.com
Web site: http://www.ctpub.com.

C4 Kids, Orders Addr.: 1220 N. Las Palmas, No. 201, Los Angeles, CA 90038 USA.

Cadmus Communications, a Cenveo Co., Publisher Services Group 136 Carlin Rd., Conklin, NY 13748 USA Tel 607-762-5555; Fax: 607-762-6774.

Cafepress, 127 Brockmoore Dr., East Amherst, NY 14051 USA.

CafePress.com, *(978-1-4148)* 1850 Gateway Dr. Ste. 300, Foster City, CA 94404-4061 USA Toll Free: 877-809-1659
E-mail: mystore@cafepress.com
Web site: http://www.cafepress.com.

Calico Subscription Co., P.O. Box 640337, San Jose, CA 95164-0337 USA (SAN 285-9173) Tel 408-432-8700; Fax: 408-432-8813; Toll Free: 800-952-2542.

California Princeton Fulfillment Services, 1445 Lower Ferry Rd., Ewing, NJ 08618 USA (SAN 630-639X) Tel 609-883-1759 ext 536; Toll Free: 800-777-4726
E-mail: donnaw@cpfs.pupress.princeton.edu.

Calliope Bks., *(978-0-9620187)* 2115 Chadbourne Ave., Madison, WI 53705 USA (SAN 247-9370) Tel 608-238-9258 Do not confuse with Calliope Books in Santa Barbara, CA
E-mail: wcoleman@facstaff.wisc.edu; calliopebooks@hotmail.com
Web site: http://www.execpc.com/~calliope.

Cambium Education, Inc., *(978-0-944584; 978-1-57035; 978-1-59318; 978-1-932282; 978-1-4168; 978-1-60218; 978-1-60697)* 4093 Specialty Pl., Longmont, CO 80504 USA (SAN 243-945X) Tel 303-651-2829; Fax: 303-907-8694; Toll Free: 800-547-6747 (orders only)
E-mail: publishing@sopriswest.com; customerservice@cambiumlearning.com
Web site: http://www.sopriswest.com.

Cambridge Bk. Co., *(978-0-8428)* Div. of Simon & Schuster, Inc., 4350 Equity Dr., Box 249, Columbus, OH 43216 USA (SAN 169-5703) Toll Free: 800-238-5833
Web site: http://www.simonsays.com/.

Cambridge Univ. Pr., *(978-0-521; 978-0-511)* Orders Addr.: 100 Brook Hill Dr., West Nyack, NY 10994-2133 USA (SAN 281-3769) Tel 845-353-7500; Fax: 845-353-4141; Toll Free: 800-872-7423 (orders, returns, credit & accounting); 800-937-9600; Edit Addr.: 32 Avenue of the Americas, New York, NY 10013-2473 USA (SAN 200-206X) Tel 212-924-3900; Fax: 212-691-3239
E-mail: customer_service@cup.org; orders@cup.org; information@cup.org
Web site: http://www.cambridge.org/.

Canyonlands Pubns., *(978-0-9702595)* Orders Addr.: P.O. Box 16175, Bellemont, AZ 86015-6175 USA (SAN 114-3824) Tel 520-779-3888; Fax: 520-779-3778; Toll Free: 800-283-1983; Edit Addr.: 4860 N. Ken Morey, Bellemont, AZ 86015 USA
E-mail: books@infomagic.com.

Cape News Co., P.O. Box 568680, Rockledge, FL 32955 USA Tel 407-636-5909.

Capital Business Systems, Div. of Capital Business Service, Orders Addr.: P.O. Box 2088, Napa, CA 94558 USA (SAN 698-3146) Tel 707-252-8844; Fax: 707-252-6368; Edit Addr.: 2033 First St., Napa, CA 94558 USA.

Capital News Co., 961 Palmyra, Jackson, MS 39203 USA Tel 601-355-8341; Fax: 601-352-1343.

Capitol News Agency, P.O. Box 7886, Richmond, VA 23231 USA (SAN 249-2768); 5203 Hatcher St., Richmond, VA 23231-0271 Tel 804-222-7252.

Capper Pr., 1503 SW 42nd, Topeka, KS 66609 USA (SAN 285-8886) Tel 913-274-4324; Fax: 913-274-4305; Toll Free: 800-678-5779 (ext. 4324).

Capstone Pr., Inc., *(978-0-7368; 978-1-56065; 978-1-4296; 978-1-62065; 978-1-4765; 978-1-4914; 978-1-5157)* Div. of Coughlan Publishing, 1905 Lookout Dr., North Mankato, MN 55033 USA Tel 507-385-8215; Fax: 507-388-3752; Orders Addr.: 1710 Roe Crest Dr., North Mankato, MN 56003 USA (SAN 254-1815) Toll Free Fax: 888-262-0705; Toll Free: 800-747-4992; Edit Addr.: 5050 Lincoln Dr Suite 200, Edina, MN 55436 USA Fax: 952-933-2410; Toll Free: 888-517-8977 Do not confuse with Capstone Pr., Inc. in Decatur, IL
E-mail: customerservice@capstonepub.com
Web site: http://www.capstone-press.com; http://www.capstonepub.com; http://www.capstoneclassroom.com.

Cardinal Pubs. Group, 2402 N. Shadeland Ave. Ste. A, Indianapolis, IN 46219-1746 USA (SAN 631-7936)
E-mail: tdoherty@in.net.

Cards Bks. N Things, 1446 St., Rd. 2 West, La Porte, IN 46350 USA (SAN 159-8295).

Carlex, Orders Addr.: 1545 W. Hamlin, Rochester Hills, MI 48309 USA (SAN 631-5615) Tel 810-852-5422; Fax: 810-852-7142.

Carolina Biological Supply Co., *(978-0-89278; 978-1-4350)* 2700 York Rd., Burlington, NC 27215-3398 USA (SAN 249-2784) Tel 336-584-0381; Fax: 910-584-3399; Toll Free Fax: 800-222-7112; Toll Free: 800-334-5551
E-mail: carolina@carolina.com
Web site: http://www.carolina.com.

Carolina Cassette Distributors, Orders Addr.: P.O. Box 429, New Bern, NC 28560 USA (SAN 110-8395) Fax: 919-638-1291; Edit Addr.: 2600 Oaks Rd., New Bern, NC 28560 USA (SAN 659-2155) Tel 919-638-5583.

Carolina News Co., Orders Addr.: P.O. Box 10, Fayetteville, NC 28302 USA; Edit Addr.: 245 Tillinghast St., Fayetteville, NC 28301 USA Tel 910-483-4135.

Carson-Dellosa Publishing Company, Incorporated, *See* **Carson-Dellosa Publishing, LLC**

Carson-Dellosa Publishing, LLC, *(978-0-88724; 978-1-57156; 978-1-57332; 978-1-59441; 978-1-60022; 978-1-60418; 978-1-936022; 978-1-936023; 978-1-936024; 978-0-9823625; 978-0-9823626; 978-0-9823627; 978-0-692-00200-1; 978-1-60996; 978-1-62057; 978-1-62223; 978-1-62399; 978-1-62442; 978-1-62648; 978-1-4838) Orders Addr.: P.O. Box 35665, Greensboro, NC 27425 USA Tel 336-632-0084; Fax: 336-808-3249; Toll Free: 800-321-0943*
Web site: http://www.carsondellosa.com.

Casa Del Libro, Orders Addr.: P.O. Box 3853, La Mesa, CA 91944-3853 USA.

Cascade News, Inc., 1055 Commerce Ave., Longview, WA 98632 USA (SAN 169-8761) Tel 360-425-2450; Fax: 360-425-2451.

Casemate Academic, *(978-0-9774094; 978-1-935488)* Orders Addr.: P.O. Box 511, Oakville, CT 06779 USA (SAN 630-9461) Tel 860-945-9329; Fax: 860-945-9468; Toll Free: 800-791-9354; Edit Addr.: 20 Main St., Oakville, CT 06779 USA
E-mail: queries@dbbconline.com
Web site: http://www.oxbowbooks.com.

Casemate Pubs. & Bk. Distributors, LLC, *(978-0-9711709; 978-1-932033; 978-1-935149; 978-1-61200)* Orders Addr.: 908 Darby Rd., Havertown, PA 19083-4608 USA; 22883 Quicksilver Dr., Herndon, VA 20166 (SAN 631-9386) Tel 703-661-1500; Edit Addr.: 180 Varick St. Suite 816, New York, NY 10014 USA
E-mail: casemate@casematepublishing.com
Web site: http://www.casematepublishing.com.

Casino Distributors, Orders Addr.: P.O. Box 849, Pleasantville, NJ 08232 USA (SAN 169-457X) Tel 609-646-4165; Fax: 609-645-0152; Edit Addr.: 10 Canale Dr., Pleasantville, NJ 08234 USA (SAN 249-3276).

Casper Magazine Agency, P.O. Box 2340, Casper, WY 82602 USA (SAN 159-8325).

Cassette Book Company, *See* **Audio Bk. Co.**

Castlebridge Distribution, 115 Bluebill Dr., Savannah, GA 31419 USA Toll Free: 888-300-1961 (phone/fax)
E-mail: orders@castlebridgedistribution.com.

Catholic Bookrack Service, 700 E. Elm St., La Grange, IL 60525 USA (SAN 169-2178) Tel 708-482-0044; Fax: 708-482-9644.

Catholic Heritage Curricula, *(978-0-9788376; 978-0-9824585; 978-0-9836832; 978-0-9851642; 978-0-9858343; 978-0-9883797; 978-0-9913264)* P.O. Box 579090, Modesto, CA 95357 USA
Web site: https://www.chcweb.com.

Catholic Literary Guild, Inc., 200 Hamilton Ave., White Plains, NY 10601 USA (SAN 285-8908) Tel 914-949-4444.

Catweasel Productions, *See* **Ars Obscura**

Caxton Pr., *(978-0-87004)* Div. of Caxton Printers. Ltd., 312 Main St., Caldwell, ID 83605-3299 USA (SAN 201-9698) Tel 208-459-7421; Fax: 208-459-7450; Toll Free: 800-657-6465
E-mail: publish@caxtonprinters.com; wcornell@caxtonpress.com; sgipson@caxtonpress.com
Web site: http://www.caxtonpress.com.

Caxton Printers, Limited, *See* **Caxton Pr.**

CBLS Pubs., *(978-1-878907; 978-1-59529)* 119 Brentwood St., Marietta, OH 45750 USA (SAN 169-5517) Tel 740-374-9458; Fax: 740-374-8029
E-mail: cbls@cbls.com
Web site: http://www.cbls.com.

CD Baby, Orders Addr.: 5925 NE 80th Ave., Portland, OR 97218-2891 USA Tel 503-595-3000; Fax: 503-296-2370; Toll Free: 800-289-6923 (CD orders only)
E-mail: cdbaby@cdbaby.com
Web site: http://www.cdbaby.com.

CD Distributing, Inc., P.O. Box 4965, Missoula, MT 59806-4965 USA (SAN 169-4367) Fax: 406-454-0415.

Cedar Fort, Inc./CFI Distribution, *(978-0-88290; 978-0-934126; 978-1-55517; 978-1-59955; 978-1-4621)* 2373 West 700 South, Springville, UT 84663 USA (SAN 170-2858) Tel 801-489-4084; Fax: 801-489-1097; Toll Free: 800-759-2665
E-mail: skybook@cedarfort.com
Web site: http://www.cedarfort.com.

Cedar Graphics, *See* **Igram Pr.**

Cengage Gale, *(978-0-13; 978-0-7876; 978-0-8103; 978-0-936474; 978-1-57302; 978-1-878623; 978-1-59413; 978-1-59414; 978-1-59415; 978-1-4144; 978-1-4205; 978-1-59722; 978-1-4328)* Subs. of Cengage Learning, Orders Addr.: P.O. Box 9187, Farmington Hills, MI 48333-9187 USA Toll Free Fax: 800 414 5043; Toll Free: 800 877 4253; Edit Addr.: 27500 Drake Rd., Farmington Hills, MI 48331-3535 USA (SAN 213-4373) Tel 248 699 4253; a/o Wheeler Publishing, 295 Kennedy Memorial Dr., Waterville, ME 04901 Toll Free: 800 223 1244
E-mail: gale.salesassistance@thomson.com
Web site: http://www.gale.com.

CENGAGE Learning, Orders Addr.: 10650 Toebben Dr., Independence, KY 41051 USA (SAN 200-2213) Tel 859-525-6620; Fax: 859-525-0978; Toll Free Fax: 800-487-8488; Toll Free: 800-354-9706
Web site: http://www.cengage.com/.

Centennial Pubns., 1400 Ash Dr., Fort Collins, CO 80521 USA (SAN 630-494X) Tel 970-493-2041 Do not confuse with Centennial Pubns., Grand Junction, CO.

Central Arizona Distributing, 4932 W. Pasadena Ave., Glendale, AZ 85301 USA (SAN 170-6128) Tel 602-939-6511.

Central Coast Bks., 1195 Al Sereno Ln., Los Osos, CA 94302-4413 USA Tel 805-534-0307 (phone/fax)
E-mail: ccbooks@charter.net.

Central European Univ. Pr., *(978-1-85866; 978-963-9116; 978-963-9241; 978-963-7326; 978-963-9776; 978-615-5211)* Orders Addr.: c/o Books International, P.O. Box 605, Herndon, VA 20172 USA; Edit Addr.: 2 River Rd. Apt. 18, Highland Park, NJ 08904 USA Tel 732-763-8816; Október 6 utca 14, Budapest, 1051 Tel 36-1-327-3000; Fax: 36-1-327-3183
E-mail: abel.meszaros@gmail.com; ceupress@ceu.hu; MeszarosA@ceu.hu
Web site: http://www.ceupress.com.

Central Illinois Periodicals, P.O. Box 3757, Bloomington, IL 61701 USA (SAN 630-8945) Tel 309-829-9405.

Central Kentucky News Distributing Company, *See* **Anderson-Austin News Co., LLC**

Wholesaler & Distributor Name Index

Central News of Sandusky, 5716 McCartney Rd., Sandusky, OH 44870-1538 USA (SAN 169-684X).

Central Programs, 802 N. 41st St., Bethany, MO 64424 USA Tel 660-425-7777.

Central South Christian Distribution, 3730 Vulcan Dr., Nashville, TN 37211 USA (SAN 631-2543) Tel 615-833-5960; Toll Free Fax: 800-220-0194; Toll Free: 800-757-0856.

Centralia News Co., 232 E. Broadway, Centralia, IL 62801 USA (SAN 159-8341) Tel 618-532-5601.

CentroLibros de Puerto Rico, Inc., Santa Rosa Unit, Bayamon, PR 00960 USA (SAN 631-1245) Tel 787-275-0460; Fax: 787-275-0360.

Century Bk. Distribution, 814 Boon, Traverse City, MI 49686 USA Tel 231-933-6405 (phone/fax).

Century Pr., *(978-0-9659417)* Div. of Conservatory of American Letters, P.O. Box 298, Thomaston, ME 04861 USA Tel 207-354-0998; Fax: 207-354-8953 Do not confuse with companies with the same name in Arroyo Seco, NM, Oklahoma City, OK
E-mail: cal@americanletters.org
Web site: http://www.americanletters.org.

Ceramic Book & Literature Service, *See* **CBLS Pubs.**

Chain Sales Marketing, Inc., *(978-1-55836)* 149 Madison Ave., Suite 810, New York, NY 10016 USA (SAN 245-1328) Tel 212-696-4230; Fax: 212-696-4391.

Chambers Kingfisher Graham Publishers, Incorporated, *See* **Larousse Kingfisher Chambers, Inc.**

Champaign-Urbana News Agency, Orders Addr.: P.O. Box 793, Champaign, IL 61824 USA (SAN 630-8953) Tel 217-351-7047; Edit Addr.: 503 Kenyon, Champaign, IL 61820 USA.

Charisma Media, *(978-0-88419; 978-0-930525; 978-1-59185; 978-1-59979; 978-1-61638; 978-1-62136; 978-1-62998; 978-1-62999)* Div. of Creation House Pr., 600 Rinehart Rd., Lake Mary, FL 32746 USA (SAN 677-5640) Tel 407-333-0600; Fax: 407-333-7100; Toll Free: 800-283-8494
Web site: http://www.charismamedia.com/.

Charlesbridge Publishing, Inc., *(978-0-88106; 978-0-935508; 978-1-57091; 978-1-58089; 978-1-879085; 978-1-60734; 978-0-9822939; 978-0-9823064; 978-1-936140; 978-1-63289)* Orders Addr.: 85 Main St., Watertown, MA 02472 USA (SAN 240-5474) Tel 617-926-0329; Fax: 617-926-5720; Toll Free Fax: 800-926-5775; Toll Free: 800-225-3214
E-mail: orders@charlesbridge.com
Web site: http://www.charlesbridge.com.

Charlynn Publishing Co., Inc., 4152 E. Fifth St., Tucson, AZ 85711 USA.

Checker Distributors, 400 W. Dussel Dr. Ste. B, Maumee, OH 43537-1636 USA (SAN 631-1431) Toll Free: 800-537-1060.

Chelsea Green Publishing, *(978-0-930031; 978-1-890132; 978-1-931498; 978-1-933392; 978-1-60358)* Orders Addr.: P.O. Box 428, White River Junction, VT 05001 USA (SAN 669-7631) Tel 802-295-6300; Fax: 802-295-6444; Toll Free: 800-639-4099; Edit Addr.: 85 N. Main St., Suite 120, White River Junction, VT 05001 USA
E-mail: info@chelseagreen.com
Web site: http://www.chelseagreen.com.

Cheng & Tsui Co., *(978-0-88727; 978-0-917056; 978-1-62291)* 25 West St., Boston, MA 02111-1213 USA (SAN 169-3387) Tel 617-988-2401; Fax: 617-426-3669
E-mail: service@cheng-tsui.com
Web site: http://www.cheng-tsui.com.

Cherry Lake Publishing, *(978-1-60279; 978-1-61080; 978-1-62431; 978-1-62753; 978-1-63137; 978-1-63188; 978-1-63362; 978-1-63470; 978-1-63471; 978-1-63472)* 1215 Overidgeview Ct., Ann Arbor, MI 48103 USA Tel 248-705-2045; 1750 Northway Dr., Suite 101, North Mankato, MN 56003 (SAN 858-9275) Tel 866-918-3956; Toll Free Fax: 866-489-6490
E-mail: customerservice@cherrylakepublishing.com; benmondloch@me.com; amy.lennex@sleepingbearpress.com
Web site: http://cherrylakepublishing.com.

Chesbro Music Co., 327 Broadway, Idaho Falls, ID 83403 USA (SAN 631-0850) Tel 208-522-8691.

Chicago Distribution Ctr., Orders Addr.: 11030 S. Langley Ave., Chicago, IL 60628 USA (SAN 630-6047) Tel 773-702-7000 (International); Fax: 773-702-7212 (International); Toll Free Fax: 800-621-8476 (USA/Canada); Toll Free: 800-621-2736 (USA/Canada); 800-621-8471 (credit & collections)
E-mail: custserv@press.uchicago.edu; orders@press.uchicago.edu
Web site: http://www.press.uchicago.edu; http://www.press.uchicago.edu/presswide/cdc/.

Chicago Review Pr., Inc., *(978-0-89733; 978-0-912777; 978-0-913705; 978-0-914090; 978-0-914091; 978-0-915864; 978-1-55652; 978-1-56976; 978-1-61373; 978-1-61374)* 814 N. Franklin St., Chicago, IL 60610 USA (SAN 213-5744) Tel 312-337-0747; Toll Free: 800-888-4741 (orders only)
E-mail: frontdesk@chicagoreviewpress.com; orders@ipgbook.com
Web site: http://www.ipgbook.com; http://www.chicagoreviewpress.com.

Chico News Agency, P.O. Box 690, Chico, CA 95927 USA (SAN 168-9533) Tel 530-895-1000; Fax: 530-895-0158.

Children's Bookfair Co., The, 700 E. Grand Ave., Chicago, IL 60611-3472 USA (SAN 630-6705) Tel 312-477-7323; 837 W. Altgeld St., Chicago, IL 60614 (SAN 630-6713).

Children's Plus, Inc., 1387 Dutch American, Beecher, IL 60401 USA Tel 708-946-4100; Fax: 709-946-4199
E-mail: danw@childrensplusinc.com
Web site: http://www.childrensplusinc.com.

Child's World, Inc., The, *(978-0-89565; 978-0-913778; 978-1-56766; 978-1-59296; 978-1-60253; 978-1-60954; 978-1-60973; 978-1-61473; 978-1-62323; 978-1-62687; 978-1-63143; 978-1-63407; 978-1-5038)* 1980 Lookout Dr., Mankato, MN 56003 USA (SAN 858-5385) Tel 507-385-1044; Fax: 888-320-2329; Toll Free Fax: 800-599-7323
E-mail: info@childsworld.com; mary.berendes@childsworld.com; mike.peterson@childsworld.com
Web site: http://www.childsworld.com.

China Bks. & Periodicals, Inc., *(978-0-8351)* 360 Swift Ave., Suite 48, South San Francisco, CA 94080 USA (SAN 145-0557) Tel 800-818-2017; 650-872-7076; Fax: 650-872-7808
E-mail: chris@chinabooks.com
Web site: http://www.chinabooks.com.

China Cultural Ctr., 3535 Dunn Dr. Apt. 303, Los Angeles, CA 90034-4977 USA (SAN 111-8161).

China House Gallery, China Institute in America, *See* **China Institute Gallery, China Institute in America**

China Institute Gallery, China Institute in America, *(978-0-9654270; 978-0-9774054; 978-0-9893776)* Div. of China Institute in America, 125 E. 65th St., New York, NY 10065 USA (SAN 110-8743) Tel 212-744-8181; Fax: 212-628-4159
E-mail: gallery@chinainstitute.org
Web site: http://www.chinainstitute.org.

Chinasprout, Inc., *(978-0-9707332; 978-0-9747302; 978-0-9820227)* 110 W. 32nd St., Flr. 6, New York, NY 10001-3205 USA Toll Free: 800-644-2611
E-mail: info@chinasprout.com
Web site: http://www.chinasprout.com.

Chinese American Co., 44 Kneeland St., Boston, MA 02111 USA (SAN 159-7248) Fax: 617-451-2318.

Christian Bk. Distributors, Orders Addr.: P.O. Box 7000, Peabody, MA 01961 USA (SAN 630-5458) Tel 978-977-5000; Fax: 978-977-5010
Web site: http://www.christianbook.com.

Christian Literature Crusade, Incorporated, *See* **CLC Pubns.**

Christian Printing Service, 4861 Chino Ave., Chino, CA 91710-5132 USA (SAN 108-2647) Tel 714-871-5200.

Christian Publishing Network, *(978-0-9628406)* P.O. Box 405, Tulsa, OK 74101 USA (SAN 631-2756) Tel 918-296-4673 (918-296-HOPE); Toll Free: 888-688-8125
E-mail: vpsales@olp.net.

christianaudio, *(978-1-59644; 978-1-61045; 978-1-61843; 978-1-63389)* 2235 Enterprise ,Ste. 140, Escondido, CA 92029 USA (SAN 851-4577) Tel 760-745-2411; Fax: 760-745-3462
E-mail: todd@eChristian.com
Web site: http://christianaudio.com.

Chronicle Bks. LLC, *(978-0-8118; 978-0-87701; 978-0-938491; 978-1-4521)* Orders Addr.: 680 Second St., San Francisco, CA 94107 USA (SAN 202-165X) Tel 415-537-4200; Fax: 415-537-4460; Toll Free Fax: 800-286-9471; Toll Free: 800-759-0190 (orders only); Edit Addr.: 3 Center Plaza, Boston, MA 2108 USA
E-mail: order.desk@hbgusa.com; customer.service@hbgusa.com
Web site: http://www.chroniclebooks.com.

Chulain Publishing Corp., Orders Addr.: 8241 Sweet Water Rd., Lone Tree, CO 80124-3017 USA.

Church Hymnal Corporation, *See* **Church Publishing, Inc.**

Church of Scientology Information Service-Pubns., *(978-0-915598)* c/o Bridge Pubns., Inc., 1414 N. Catalina, Los Angeles, CA 90029 USA (SAN 268-9774).

Church Publishing, Inc., *(978-0-89869; 978-1-59627; 978-1-59628)* 445 Fifth Ave., New York, NY 10016-0109 USA (SAN 857-0140) Tel 212-592-1800; Fax: 212-779-3392; Toll Free: 800-242-1918
E-mail: churchpublishing@cpg.org
Web site: http://www.churchpublishing.org; http://morehousepublishing.org.

Church Richards Co., 10001 Roosevelt Rd., Westchester, IL 60154 USA (SAN 285-8975) Toll Free: 800-323-0227.

Circa Pubns., Inc., 415 Fifth Ave., Pelham, NY 10803-0408 USA (SAN 169-6122) Tel 914-738-5570; Toll Free: 800-582-5952 (orders only).

Circle Bk. Service, Inc., *(978-0-87397)* P.O. Box 626, Tomball, TX 77377 USA (SAN 158-2526) Tel 281-255-6824; Fax: 281-255-8158; Toll Free: 800-227-1591
E-mail: orders@circlebook.com
Web site: http://www.circlebook.com.

City News Agency, Orders Addr.: P.O. Box 561129, Charlotte, NC 28256-1129 USA (SAN 169-782X); Edit Addr.: P.O. Box 2069, Newark, OH 43055 USA (SAN 169-6947); 220 Cherry Ave., NE, Canton, OH 44702-1198 USA (SAN 169-6602); 303 E. Lasalle St., South Bend, IN 46617 (SAN 159-9992); 417 S. McKinley, Harrisburg, IL 62946 (SAN 169-1961).

Clarks Out of Town News, 303 S. Andrews Ave., Fort Lauderdale, FL 33301 USA (SAN 159-8384) Tel 954-467-1543.

Class Pubns., Inc., *(978-0-913031)* 71 Bartholomew Ave., Hartford, CT 06106 USA (SAN 283-0302) Tel 860-951-9200.

Classroom Reading Service, P.O. Box 2708, Santa Fe Spgs, CA 90670-0708 USA (SAN 131-3959) Toll Free: 800-422-6657
E-mail: crsbooks@aol.com.

CLC Pubns., *(978-0-87508; 978-1-936143; 978-1-61958)* Div. of CLC Ministries International, Orders Addr.: P.O. Box 1449, Fort Washington, PA 19034-8449 USA Tel 215-542-1242; Fax: 215-542-7580; Toll Free: 800-659-1240; 701 Pennsylvania Ave., Fort Washington, PA 19034 (SAN 169-7358) Tel 215-542-1242; Fax: 215-542-7580; Toll Free: 800-659-1240
E-mail: orders@clcpublications.com; churd@clcpublications.com
Web site: http://www.clcusa.org; http://www.clcpublications.com.

CLEARVUE/eav, Inc., 6465 N. Avondale Ave., Chicago, IL 60631-1996 USA (SAN 204-1669) Tel 773-775-9433; Fax: 773-775-9855; Toll Free Fax: 800-444-9855 (24 Hours); Toll Free: 800-253-2788 (8:00 am to 4:30 pm Central Time M-F); P.O. Box 2284, S Burlington, VT 05407-2287
E-mail: custserv@clearvue.com
Web site: http://www.clearvue.com.

Client Distribution Services, *See* **Perseus-PGW**

Closet Case Bks., P.O. Box 16116, Saint Paul, MN 55116 USA
Web site: http://www.closetcasebooks.com.

Clover Bk. Service, 1220 S. Monroe St., Covingtons, LA 70433-3639 USA (SAN 106-472X) Tel 504-875-0038.

Cobblestone Publishing Co., *(978-0-382; 978-0-942389; 978-0-9607638)* Div. of Cricket Magazine Group, 30 Grove St., Suite C, Peterborough, NH 03458 USA (SAN 237-9937) Tel 603-924-7209; Fax: 603-924-7380; Toll Free: 800-821-0115; P.O. Box 487, Effingham, IL 62401
E-mail: custsvc@cobblestone.mv.com
Web site: http://www.cobblestonepub.com.

Cogan Bks., *(978-0-940688)* P.O. Box 579, Hudson, OH 44236-0579 USA (SAN 168-9649) Toll Free: 800-733-3630.

Cokesbury, 201 Eighth Ave., S., Nashville, TN 37203 USA (SAN 200-6863) Tel 615-749-6409; Toll Free: 800-672-1789
Web site: http://www.cokesbury.com.

Cold Cut Comics Distribution, 475-D Stockton Ave., San Jose, CA 95126 USA (SAN 631-6409) Tel 408-293-3844; Fax: 408-293-6645
E-mail: comics@coldcut.com
Web site: http://www.coldcut.com.

Cole, Bill Enterprises, Inc., P.O. Box 60, Randolph, MA 02368-0060 USA (SAN 685-6373) Tel 617-986-2653.

Collector Bks., *(978-0-89145; 978-1-57432; 978-1-60460)* Div. of Schroeder Publishing Co., Inc., Orders Addr.: P.O. Box 3009, Paducah, KY 42003 USA (SAN 157-5368) Tel 270-898-6211; 270-898-7903; Fax: 270-898-8890; 270-898-1173; Toll Free: 800-626-5420 (orders only); Edit Addr.: 5801 Kentucky Dam Rd., Paducah, KY 42003 USA (SAN 200-7479)
E-mail: Info@collectorbooks.com; info@AQSquilt.com
Web site: http://www.collectorbooks.com; http://www.americanquilter.com/.

College Bk. Co. of California, Inc., 181 W. Orangethorpe Ave. Ste. C, Placentia, CA 92870-6931 USA (SAN 269-0802).

Collegedale Distributors, *See* **Tree of Life Midwest**

Colonial Williamsburg Foundation, *(978-0-87935; 978-0-910412)* P.O. Box 3532, Williamsburg, VA 23187-3532 USA (SAN 128-4630) Fax: 757-565-8999 (orders only); Toll Free: 800-446-9240 (orders only)
Web site: http://www.colonialwilliamsburg.com.

Colorado Periodical Distributor, Inc., 1227 Pitkin St., Grand Junction, CO 81502 USA Tel 970-242-3865; Fax: 970-242-3760.

Colorado State University, Center for Literary Publishing, *See* **Ctr. for Literary Publishing, Colorado State Univ.**

Columbia County News Agency, Inc., 49 Bender Blvd., Ghent, NY 12075-3327 USA (SAN 169-5339).

Columbia Univ. Pr., *(978-0-231)* Orders Addr.: 61 W. 62nd St., New York, NY 10023-7015 USA (SAN 212-2480) Toll Free Fax: 800-944-1844; Toll Free: 800-944-8648 x 6240 (orders); Edit Addr.: 61 W. 62nd St., New York, NY 10023 USA (SAN 212-2472) Tel 212-459-0600; Fax: 212-459-3678; 387 Pk. Ave., S., New York, NY 10016; 1094 Flex Dr., Jackson, TN 38301
E-mail: cupbooks@columbia.edu
Web site: http://www.columbia.edu/cu/cup.

Comag Marketing Group, 1790 Broadway, Suite 401, New York, NY 10019 USA (SAN 169-5800) Tel 212-841-8365; Fax: 212-977-9401.

Comics Hawaii Distributors, *See* **Hobbies Hawaii Distributors**

Common Ground Distributors, Inc., Orders Addr.: P.O. Box 25249, Asheville, NC 28813-1249 USA Toll Free: 800-654-0626; Edit Addr.: 115 Fairview Rd., Asheville, NC 28803-2307 USA (SAN 113-8006) Tel 828-274-5575; Fax: 828-274-1955
E-mail: orders@comground.com.

Communication Service Corporation, *See* **Gryphon Hse., Inc.**

Communications Technology, Inc., *(978-0-918232)* P.O. Box 209, Rindge, NH 03461 USA (SAN 159-8198) Tel 603-899-6957.

Complete Book & Media Supply, 10700 Ashton Cove, Austin, TX 78750 USA Fax: 512-249-0720; Toll Free: 800-986-1775
E-mail: books@completebook.com; bradm@completebook.com.

Computer & Technical Bks., 6338 Ranchview Ln., N., Osseo, MN 55311-3924 USA (SAN 630-8120).

Conde Nast Pubns., Inc., *(978-1-878494)* Four Times Sq., 20th Flr., New York, NY 10036 USA (SAN 285-905X) Tel 212-880-8800; Fax: 212-880-8289.

Connecticut River Pr., *(978-0-9706573)* 111 Holmes Rd., Newington, CT 06111 USA Tel 860-666-1200; 203-254-0147; Fax: 860-594-6037
E-mail: wolftalk@ziplink.net.

Consortium Bk. Sales & Distribution, Div. of Perseus Bks. Group, Orders Addr.: 1094 Flex Dr., Jackson, TN 38301-5070 USA; Edit Addr.: 34 13th Ave NE, Suite 100, Minneapolis, MN 55413-1007 USA (SAN 200-6049) Toll Free: 800-283-3572 (orders)
E-mail: info@cbsd.com
Web site: http://www.cbsd.com/.

Constellation Digital Services, Div. of Perseus Books Group, 2465 Central Ave., Suite 200, Boulder, CO 80301 USA
Web site: http://www.constellationdigital.com.

ConsuLogic Consulting Services, 276 Longhouse Ln., Slingerlands, NY 12159-3012 USA Tel 518-452-9228; Fax: 518-452-9216.

Contemporary Arts Pr., *(978-0-931818)* Div. of La Mamelle, Inc., P.O. Box 3123, San Francisco, CA 94119-3123 USA (SAN 170-5423) Tel 415-282-0286.

Continental Bk. Co., Inc., *(978-0-9626800)* Eastern Div., 80-00 Cooper Ave., Bldg. No. 29, Glendale, NY 11385 USA (SAN 169-5436) Tel 718-326-0560; Fax: 718-326-4276; Toll Free: 800-364-0350; Western Div., 625 E. 70th Ave., No. 5, Denver, CO 80229 (SAN 630-2882) Tel 303-289-1761; Fax: 303-289-1764
E-mail: hola@continentalbook.com; esl@continentalbook.com; bonjour@continentalbook.com; tag@continentalbook.com
Web site: http://www.continentalbook.com.

Continental Enterprises Group, Inc. (CEG), Orders Addr.: 108 Red Row St., Easley, SC 29640-2820 USA (SAN 631-0915)
E-mail: ContactUs@centerprisesgrp.com.

Continental Sales, 213 W. Main St., Barrington, IL 60010-0010 USA Tel 847-381-6530.

Continuum International Publishing Group, Limited, *See* **Bloomsbury Publishing Inc**

Cook, David C., *(978-0-7814; 978-0-88207; 978-0-89191; 978-0-89693; 978-0-912692; 978-1-55513; 978-1-56476; 978-1-4347)* 4050 Lee Vance View, Colorado Springs, CO 80918 USA (SAN 206-0981) Tel 719-536-0100; Fax: 719-536-3244; Toll Free: 800-708-5550; 800-323-7543 (Customer Service)
E-mail: wendi.lord@davidccook.com
Web site: http://www.davidccook.com.

Cook, David C. Publishing Company, *See* **Cook, David C.**

Cookbook Marketplace, The, P.O. Box 305142, Nashville, TN 37230 USA (SAN 631-4201) Tel 615-391-2656; Toll Free: 800-358-0560.

Coos Bay Distributors, 131 N. Schoneman St., Coos Bay, OR 97420 USA (SAN 169-7064) Tel 541-888-5912.

Copper Island News, 1010 Wright St., Marquette, MI 49855-1834 USA (SAN 169-3824).

Copyright Clearance Ctr., Inc., 222 Rosewood Dr, Danvers, MA 01923 USA Tel 978-750-8400; Fax: 978-750-4343
Web site: http://www.copyright.com.

Cornell Univ. Pr., *(978-0-8014; 978-0-87546; 978-1-5017)* Orders Addr.: P.O. Box 6525, Ithaca, NY 14851 USA (SAN 281-5680) Tel 607-277-2211; Toll Free Fax: 800-688-2877; Toll Free: 800-666-2211; Edit Addr.: Sage House, 512 E. State St., Ithaca, NY 14851 USA (SAN 202-1862) Tel 607-277-2338
E-mail: cupressinfo@cornell.edu; orders@nbninternational.com; cupress-sales@cornell.edu
Web site: http://www.cornellpress.cornell.edu.

Coronet Bks., *(978-0-89563)* 311 Bainbridge St., Philadelphia, PA 19147 USA (SAN 210-6043) Tel 215-925-2762; Fax: 215-925-1912 Do not confuse with Coronet Bks. & Pubns., Eagle Point, OR
E-mail: ronsmolin@earthlink.net; order@coronetbooks.com
Web site: http://www.coronetbooks.com.

Country News Distributors, Div. of Bakers, Inc., P.O. Box 1258, Brattleboro, VT 05302-1258 USA (SAN 169-8575).

Countryside Bks., *(978-0-88453)* 2430 Estancia Blvd. Ste. 100, Clearwater, FL 33761-2644 USA (SAN 107-4415).

Coutts Information Services, Div. of ProQuest LLC, Orders Addr.: 7309 Innovation BLVD, Fort Wayne, IN 46818 USA (SAN 920-6779); Edit Addr.: 7309 Innovation BLVD, Fort Wayne, IN 46818 USA (SAN 169-5401) Toll Free: 800-263-1686
E-mail: joanne.rattie@ingramcontent.com.

Coutts Library Service, Incorporated, *See* **Coutts Information Services**

Cove Distributors, 6325 Erdman Ave., Baltimore, MD 21205 USA (SAN 158-9814) Toll Free: 800-622-5656 (Orders).

Cowley Distributing, Inc., 732 Heisinger Rd., Jefferson City, MO 65109 USA (SAN 169-426X) Tel 573-636-6511; Fax: 573-636-6262; Toll Free: 800-346-5950 (orders).

Cox Subscriptions, Inc., 201 Village Rd., Shallotte, NC 28470 USA (SAN 107-0061) Tel 800-571-9554; Fax: 877-755-6274; Toll Free: 800-553-8088
E-mail: dknox@wtcox.com
Web site: http://www.wtcox.com.

CQ Products, 507 Industrial St., Waverly, IA 50677 USA (SAN 631-5216) Tel 319-352-2086; Fax: 319-352-5338
E-mail: gifts@cqproducts.com
Web site: http://www.cqproducts.com.

Crabtree Publishing, *(978-0-937070)* P.O. Box 3451, Federal Way, WA 98063 USA (SAN 214-3615) Tel 253-925-9300; 59Th Flr., New York, NY 10118 Do not confuse with Crabtree Publishing Co. in New York, NY.

Cram, George F. Co., Inc., *(978-0-87448)* 301 S. LaSalle St., P.O. Box 426, Indianapolis, IN 46201 USA (SAN 204-2630) Tel 317-635-5564; Fax: 317-635-2720; Toll Free: 800-227-4199
E-mail: cram-services@iquest.net.

Cranbury International, Orders Addr.: 7 Clarendon Ave., Suite 2, Montpelier, VT 05602 USA.

CRC Pr. LLC, *(978-0-8493; 978-0-87762; 978-0-87819; 978-0-935184; 978-1-56676; 978-1-57491; 978-1-58488; 978-1-58716; 978-1-4200; 978-1-4398;*

978-1-4665; 978-1-4822; 978-1-4987) Subs. of Taylor & Francis, Inc., Orders Addr.: 6000 Broken Sound Pkwy., NW, Ste. 300, Boca Raton, FL 33487 USA Tel 800-272-7737 Toll Free Fax: 800-374-3401; Edit Addr.: 270 Madison Ave., New York, NY 10016 USA
E-mail: orders@crcpress.com; Theresa.Gutierrez@taylorandfrancis.com
Web site: http://www.crcpress.com; http://www.taylorandfrancis.com.

CreateSpace, *See* **CreateSpace Independent Publishing Platform**

CreateSpace Independent Publishing Platform, (*978-1-58898; 978-1-59109; 978-1-59456; 978-1-59457; 978-1-4196; 978-1-4348; 978-1-4382; 978-1-4392; 978-1-4404; 978-1-4414; 978-1-4421; 978-1-61550; 978-1-4486; 978-1-4495; 978-1-4499; 978-1-4505; 978-1-4515; 978-1-4528; 978-1-4536; 978-1-4537; 978-1-4538; 978-1-4563; 978-1-4564; 978-1-4565; 978-1-61789; 978-1-4609; 978-1-4610; 978-1-4611; 978-1-61396; 978-1-61397; 978-1-4635; 978-1-4636; 978-1-4637; 978-1-4662; 978-1-4663; 978-1-4664; 978-1-61914; 978-1-61915; 978-1-61916; 978-1-4679; 978) Orders Addr.: 4900 LaCross Rd., North Charleston, SC 29406 USA (SAN 255-2132) Tel 843-225-4700 (Ask for ordering department); Fax: 843-577-7506; Toll Free: 866-308-6235; 4900 LaCross Rd., North Charleston, SC 29406*
E-mail: info@createspace.com
Web site: http://www.createspace.com.

Creative Co., The, (*978-0-87191; 978-0-88682; 978-0-89812; 978-1-56660; 978-1-56846; 978-1-58341; 978-1-60818; 978-1-62832; 978-1-68277*) 123 S. Broad St., Mankato, MN 56001 USA Tel 507-388-2109; Fax: 507-388-2746; Toll Free: 800-445-6209 Do not confuse with The Creative Co., Lawrenceburg, IN
E-mail: info@thecreativecompany.us; lmaker@thecreativecompany.us
Web site: http://www.thecreativecompany.us.

Creative Homeowner, (*978-0-932944; 978-1-58011; 978-1-880029*) Div. of Courier Corporation, 24 Park Way, Upper Saddle River, NJ 07458-9960 USA (SAN 213-6627) Tel 201-934-7100; Fax: 201-934-8971; Toll Free: 800-631-7795
E-mail: info@creativehomeowner.com
Web site: http://www.creativehomeowner.com.

Creative Teaching Pr., Inc., (*978-0-88160; 978-0-916119; 978-1-57471; 978-1-59198; 978-1-60689; 978-1-61601; 978-1-62186; 978-1-63445*) Orders Addr.: P.O. Box 2723, Huntington Beach, CA 92647-0723 USA Tel 714-895-5047; Fax: 714-895-6547; Toll Free Fax: 800-444-4287; Edit Addr.: 6262 Katella Ave., Cypress, CA 90630-5204 USA (SAN 294-9180) Tel 714-895-5047; Toll Free Fax: 800-229-9929; Toll Free: 800-444-4287
E-mail: webmaster@creativeteaching.com; we.listen@creativeteaching.com
Web site: http://www.creativeteaching.com; http://www.thelearningworks.com; http://www.learntoreadkidsclub.com.

Crescent Imports & Pubns., (*978-0-933127*) P.O. Box 7827, Ann Arbor, MI 48107-7827 USA (SAN 111-3976) Tel 734-665-3492; Fax: 734-677-1717; Toll Free: 800-521-9744
E-mail: crescentus@aol.com
Web site: http://www.crescentimports.com.

Crescent International, Inc., 2238 Otranto Rd., Charleston, SC 29418 USA (SAN 110-0777) Tel 803-797-6363; Fax: 803-797-6367.

Critics' Choice, *See* **Critics' Choice Video**

Critics' Choice Video, (*978-1-932566; 978-1-933240*) 900 N. Rohlwing Rd., Itasca, IL 60143 USA Tel 630-775-3300; Fax: 603-775-3340
E-mail: rterry@ccvideo.com
Web site: http://www.ccvideo.com.

Cromland, 964 Marcon Blvd, Suite 190, Allentown, PA 18109 USA (SAN 254-6736) Tel 610-266-6610; Fax: 610-266-8987; Toll Free: 800-944-5554 (U.S. & Canada)
Web site: http://www.cromland.com.

CrossLife Expressions, (*978-0-9636049; 978-1-57838*) Div. of Exchanged Life Ministries, Inc., 10610 E. Bethany Dr., Suite A, Aurora, CO 80014 USA (SAN 169-0590) Tel 303-750-0440; Fax: 303-750-1228; Toll Free: 800-750-6818
E-mail: info@crosslifebooks.com
Web site: http://www.crosslifebooks.com.

Crowley Distributors, *See* **Sunburst Bks., Inc., Distributor of Florida Bks.**

Crowley, Inc., 16120 U.S. Hwy. 19 N., Suite 220, Clearwater, FL 34624-6862 USA (SAN 285-9130) Tel 813-531-5889.

Crown Agents Service, Ltd., 3100 Massachusetts Ave., NW, Washington, DC 20008 USA (SAN 285-919X).

Ctr. for Literary Publishing, Colorado State Univ., (*978-1-885635*) Center for Literary Publishing, Department of English, Colorado State University, Fort Collins, CO 80523 USA Tel 970-491-5449; Fax: 970-491-0283
E-mail: creview@colostate.edu
Web site: http://coloradoreview.colostate.edu/.

Cultural Hispana/Ameriketako Liburuak, Orders Addr.: P.O. Box 7729, Silver Spring, MD 20907 USA (SAN 159-2823); Edit Addr.: 1413 Crestridge Dr., Silver Spring, MD 20910 USA (SAN 249-3063) Tel 301-585-0134
E-mail: mokordo@erols.com
Web site: http://www.coloquio.com/libros.html.

Culture Plus Bk. Distributors, 44 Willoughby St., Brooklyn, NY 11201-5200 USA.

Culture Plus Bks., 209 N. La Brea Ave., Inglewood, CA 90301-1247 USA (SAN 631-3876).

CUP Services, 750 Cascadilla St., Ithaca, NY 14851 USA (SAN 630-6519) Tel 607-277-2211; Fax: 607-277-6292; Toll Free: 800-666-2211.

Curran Assocs., Inc., (*978-1-60423; 978-1-60560; 978-1-61567; 978-1-61738; 978-1-61782; 978-1-61839; 978-1-62276; 978-1-62748; 978-1-62993; 978-1-63266; 978-1-63439; 978-1-5108*) 57 Morehouse Ln., Red Hook, NY 12571 USA Tel 845-758-0400; Fax: 845-758-2633
E-mail: curran@proceedings.com
Web site: http://www.proceedings.com.

Curreri, Michelle Morrow, 3 Eagle Ln., Beverly, MA 01915 USA Tel 978-921-8020; Fax: 978-921-7577
E-mail: michelle@curreriworldsvs.net.

Curtis, Ralph Books, *See* **Curtis, Ralph Publishing**

Curtis, Ralph Publishing, (*978-0-88359*) P.O. Box 349, Sanibel, FL 33957 USA (SAN 121-1323) Tel 239-454-0010; Fax: 239-395-2727; Toll Free: 888-454-0011
E-mail: rcurtisbks@yahoo.com
Web site: http://www.ralphcurtisbooks.com.

CustomFlix Labs, Inc., (*978-0-9774415*) 100 Enterprise Way Ste. A200, Scotts Valley, CA 95066-3266 USA.

Cybernetics Technology Corp., (*978-0-923458*) 1370 Port Washington Blvd., Port Washington, NY 11050-2628 USA (SAN 295-933X) Tel 516-883-7676.

Cypress Bk. Co., Inc., (*978-0-934643*) Subs. of China International Bk. Trading Corp., 360 Swift Ave. Ste. 42, S San Fran, CA 94080-6220 USA (SAN 112-1162) Toll Free: 800-383-1688
E-mail: sales@cypressbook.com; info@cypressbook.com; cypbook@pacbell.net
Web site: http://www.cypressbook.com.

Cypress Hse., (*978-1-879384*) 155 Cypress St., Fort Bragg, CA 95437 USA (SAN 297-9004) Tel 707-964-9520; Fax: 707-964-7531; Toll Free: 800-773-7782
E-mail: cypresshouse@cypresshouse.com; forms@cypresshouse.com
Web site: http://www.cypresshouse.com.

D & H News Co., Inc., 79 Albany Post Rd., Montrose, NY 10548 USA (SAN 169-5533) Tel 914-737-3152.

D & J Bk. Distributors, (*978-1-883080*) 229-21B Merrick Blvd., Laurelton, NY 11413 USA (SAN 630-5091) Tel 718-949-5400; Fax: 718-949-6161; Toll Free: 800-446-4707.

D K Publishing, Incorporated, *See* **Dorling Kindersley Publishing, Inc.**

Daedalus Bks., 9645 Gerwig Ln., Columbia, MD 21046-1520 USA (SAN 158-9202) Tel 410-309-2700
E-mail: tstock@daedalus-books.com; custserv@daedalus-books.com
Web site: http://www.daedalus-books.com.

Dahlstrom, Carol Field Inc., (*978-0-9679764; 978-0-9768446*) 7952 NE. Berwick Dr., Ankeny, IA 50021 USA Tel 515-964-1777; Fax: 515-964-1788
E-mail: braveink@aol.com
Web site: http://www.braveink.com.

Dake Bible Sales, *See* **Dake Publishing**

Dake Publishing, (*978-0-9655968; 978-1-55829*) Orders Addr.: P.O. Box 1050, Lawrenceville, GA 30046 USA (SAN 212-0828) Tel 770-963-1611; Fax: 770-963-7700; Toll Free: 800-241-1239; Edit Addr.: 764 Martins Chapel Rd., Lawrenceville, GA 30246 USA (SAN 243-2684)
E-mail: derrick@dake.com
Web site: http://www.dake.com.

Dakota News, Inc., 221 Petro Ave., Box 1310, Sioux Falls, SD 57101 USA (SAN 169-7854) Tel 605-336-3000; Fax: 605-336-7279; Toll Free: 800-658-5498.

Dakota West Bks., P.O. Box 9324, Rapid City, SD 57701 USA (SAN 630-351X) Tel 605-348-1075; Fax: 605-348-0615.

Danforth Bk. Distribution, Orders Addr.: 3220 228th St., S. E., Bothell, WA 98021 USA Tel 206-351-5872
E-mail: Danfothbookdist@gmail.com.

D.A.P./Distributed Art Pubs., (*978-1-881616; 978-1-891024; 978-1-933045; 978-1-935202; 978-1-938922; 978-1-942884*) Orders Addr.: 155 Sixth Ave., 2nd Flr., New York, NY 10013-1507 USA (SAN 630-6446) Tel 212-627-1999; Fax: 212-627-9484; Toll Free Fax: 800-478-3128; Toll Free: 800-338-2665
E-mail: dap@dapinc.com
Web site: http://www.artbook.com/.

Darr Subscription Agency, P.O. Box 575, Louisburg, KS 66053-0575 USA (SAN 285-9149) Toll Free: 800-850-3741
E-mail: lgriff@midusa.net.

David Brown Book Company, The, P.O. Box PO Box 511, Oakville, CT 06779 USA
E-mail: david.brown.bk.co@snet.net.

David, Jonathan Pubs., Inc., (*978-0-8246*) 68-22 Eliot Ave., Middle Village, NY 11379 USA (SAN 169-5274) Tel 718-456-8611; Fax: 718-894-2818
E-mail: jondavpub@aol.com
Web site: http://www.jdbooks.com.

Davidson Titles, Inc., (*978-1-884756*) Orders Addr.: 2345 Dr. F.E. Wright Dr., Jackson, TN 38303 USA; Edit Addr.: P.O. Box 3538, Jackson, TN 38303-3538 USA (SAN 255-9129) Tel 731-988-5333; Fax: 731-988-5080; Toll Free Fax: 800-787-7935; Toll Free: 800-433-3903 Do not confuse with companies of the same name in Sugar Hill NH, Windsor CT, Redmond & Kirkland WA, Newark NJ, Fairfield & Reddick FL, East Lansing MI, Rocklin CA, Tolono IL, Missoula MT, Ann Arbor MI, Half Moon Bay CA
E-mail: brian@davidsontitles.com
Web site: http://www.davidsontitles.com.

Dawson Subscription Service, *See* **Faxon Illinois Service Ctr.**

Day School Magazine Service, P.O. Box 262, Brooklyn, NY 11219 USA (SAN 285-9157) Tel 718-871-1486; Fax: 718-435-2342
E-mail: Elciv@juno.com.

De Gruyter, Walter Inc., (*978-0-89925; 978-1-56445; 978-3-11; 978-1-934078; 978-1-61451; 978-1-5015*) Subs. of Walter de Gruyter & GmbH & Co. KG, Orders Addr.: P.O. Box 960, Herndon, VA 20172-0960 USA Tel 703-661-1589; Fax: 703-661-1501; Toll Free: 800-208-8144; Edit Addr.: 121 High St., Third Flr., Boston, MA 02110 USA Tel 857-284-7073; Fax: 857-284-7358
E-mail: info@deGruyterny.com; kruehle@degruyterny.com; USinfo@degruyter.com; info@degruyter.com
Web site: http://www.degruyter.com; http://www.mouton-publishers.com; http://www.mouton-online.com.

De Vore Group/Carla Bks. & More, Orders Addr.: P.O. Box 10276, San Juan, PR 00922 USA (SAN 159-8309) Tel 809-721-7645; Fax: 809-722-9216; Edit Addr.: 1409 Ave. Ponce De Leon, San Juan, PR 00907-4023 USA (SAN 249-2776).

Dearborn Financial Publishing, Inc., (*978-0-7931; 978-0-88462; 978-0-913864; 978-0-936894; 978-1-57410*) 30 South Wacker Dr., Chicago, IL 60606-1719 USA (SAN 201-3622) Tel 312-836-4400 ext 282429; Fax: 312-836-1021
Web site: http://www.dearborn.com.

Dearborn Trade, A Kaplan Professional Company, *See* **Kaplan Publishing**

DecisionPro, Inc., 2452 General Potter Hwy., Centre Hall, PA 16828-9022 USA.

DeHoff Christian Bookstore, (*978-1-933965*) 749 N. W. Broad St., Murfreesboro, TN 37129-3797 USA (SAN 184-4202) Tel 615-893-8322; Fax: 615-896-7447; Toll Free: 800-695-5385
E-mail: dehoff@bellsouth.net; fakesb@yahoo.com
Web site: http://www.dehoffbooks.com.

Dehoff Publications, *See* **DeHoff Christian Bookstore**

Delmar Cengage Learning, (*978-0-314; 978-0-7668; 978-0-7693; 978-0-8273; 978-0-87350; 978-0-916032; 978-0-944132; 978-0-9653629; 978-1-56253; 978-1-56593; 978-1-56930; 978-1-4018; 978-1-4180; 978-1-4283; 978-1-4354*) Div. of Cengage Learning, Orders Addr.: c/o Thomson Learning Order Fulfilment, P.O. Box 6904, Florence, KY 41022 USA Toll Free Fax: 800 487 8488; Toll Free: 800 347 7707; c/o Thomson Delmar Learning Clinical Health Care Series, P.O. Box 3419, Scranton, PA 18505-0419 Fax: 570-347-9072; Toll Free: 888-427-5800; Edit Addr.: P.O. Box 15015, Albany, NY 12212-5015 USA (SAN 206-7544) Tel 518-348-2300; Fax: 518-373-6345; Toll Free: 800-998-7498; 5 Maxwell Dr., Clifton Park, NY 12065-(SAN 658-0440) Tel 518-348-2300; Fax: 518-881-1256; Toll Free: 800-998-7498
E-mail: matthew.grover@thomson.com; clinicalmanuals@thomson.com
Web site: http://www.delmarlearning.com; http://www.clinicalmanuals.com/.

Delmar News Agency, Inc., P.O. Box 7169, Newark, DE 19714-7169 USA (SAN 169-0892) Tel 302-455-9922; Toll Free: 800-441-7025.

DeLong Subscription Agency, P.O. Box 806, Lafayette, IN 47902 USA (SAN 285-9246) Toll Free: 800-992-2092.

Delphi Distribution Inc., Orders Addr.: 1263 SW Blvd., Kansas City, KS 66103 USA (SAN 760-7989) Tel 913-362-7400; Fax: 913-362-7401
E-mail: kent@delphidistribution.com; linda@midpt.com.

Delta Education, Incorporated, *See* **Delta Education, LLC**

Delta Education, LLC, (*978-0-87504; 978-1-58356; 978-1-59242; 978-1-59821; 978-1-60395; 978-1-60902; 978-1-62571*) 80 Northwest Blvd., Nashua, NH 03063 USA (SAN 630-1711) Toll Free: 800-442-5444
E-mail: ngosselin@delta-edu.com
Web site: http://www.delta-education.com.

Delta Systems Company, Inc., (*978-0-937354; 978-1-887744; 978-1-932748; 978-1-934960; 978-1-936299; 978-1-936402; 978-1-62167*) Orders Addr.: 1400 Miller Pkwy., McHenry, IL 60050-7030 USA (SAN 220-0457) Tel 815-363-3582; Fax: 815-363-2948; Toll Free Fax: 800-909-9901; Toll Free: 800-323-8270
E-mail: d.patchin@DeltaPublishing.com; L.Bruell@DeltaPublishing.com; j.patchin@deltapublishing.com
Web site: http://www.deltapublishing.com; http://www.raventreepress.com.

Deltiologists of America, (*978-0-913782*) P.O. Box 8, Norwood, PA 19074 USA (SAN 170-3072) Tel 610-485-8572.

Derstine, Roy Bk. Co., 14 Birch Rd., Kinnelon, NJ 07405 USA (SAN 130-822X) Tel 973-838-1109.

DeRu's Fine Arts, (*978-0-939370*) 9100 E. Artesia Blvd., Bellflower, CA 90706 USA (SAN 159-3862) Tel 562-920-1312; Fax: 562-920-3077
E-mail: derusgal@aol.com
Web site: http://www.derusfinearts.com.

Deseret Bk. Co., (*978-0-87579; 978-0-87747; 978-1-57345; 978-1-59038; 978-1-60641; 978-1-60907; 978-1-60908; 978-1-62972; 978-1-62973*) Div. of Deseret Management Corp., P.O. Box 30178, Salt Lake City, UT 84130 USA (SAN 150-763X) Tel 801-517-3165 (Wholesale Dept.); 801-534-1515; Fax: 801-517-3338; Toll Free: 800-453-3876
E-mail: wholesale@deseretbook.com; dbwhsale@deseretbook.com
Web site: http://www.deseretbook.com; http://www.shadowmountain.com.

Destiny Image Pubs., (*978-0-7684; 978-0-914903; 978-1-56043; 978-0-9716036*) 167 Walnut Bottom Rd., Shippensburg, PA 17257 USA (SAN 253-4339) Tel 717-532-3040; Fax: 717-532-9291; Toll Free: 800-722-6774
E-mail: dnj@destinyimage.com
Web site: http://www.destinyimage.com.

Detroit Free Pr., Inc., (*978-0-937247; 978-0-9605692*) Div. of Gannett, 615 W. Lafayette Blvd., Detroit, MI 48226 USA (SAN 239-6998) Tel 313-223-4575; Fax: 313-222-5982; Toll Free: 800-678-6400
E-mail: ajhartley@freepress.com; ldelves@freepress.com
Web site: http://www.freep.com.

Devin-Adair Pubs., Inc., (*978-0-8159*) P.O. Box A, Old Greenwich, CT 06870 USA (SAN 112-062X) Tel 203-531-7755; Fax: 718-359-8568.

DeVorss & Co., (*978-0-87516*) Orders Addr.: P.O. Box 1389, Camarillo, CA 93011-1389 USA (SAN 168-9886) Tel 805-322-9010; Fax: 805-322-9011; Toll Free: 800-843-5743; Edit Addr.: 553 Constitution Ave., Camarillo, CA 93012-8510 USA
E-mail: service@devorss.com
Web site: http://www.devorss.com.

Diamond Bk. Distributors, Div. of Diamond Comic Distributors, Inc., Orders Addr.: 1966 Greenspring Dr., Suite 300, Timonium, MD 21093 USA (SAN 110-9502) Tel 410-560-7100; Fax: 410-560-2583; Toll Free: 800-452-6642
E-mail: books@diamondbookdistributors.com
Web site: http://www.diamondcomics.com; http://www.diamondbookdistributors.com/.

Diamond Book Distributors Inc., *See* **Diamond Comic Distributors, Inc.**

Diamond Comic Distributors, Inc., (*978-1-59396; 978-1-60584*) 1966 Greenspring Dr., Suite 300, Timonium, MD 21093 USA Tel 410-560-7100; Fax: 410-560-2583; Toll Free: 800-452-6642
E-mail: books@diamondbookdistributors.com
Web site: http://www.diamondbookdistributors.com/.

Diamond Distributors, Inc., Orders Addr.: 1966 Greenspring Dr., Suite 300, Timonium, MD 21093 USA Tel 410-560-7100.

Digital Manga Distribution, *See* **Digital Manga Publishing**

Digital Manga Publishing, (*978-1-56970*) Div. of Digital Manga, Inc., 1487 W. 178th St. Ste. 300, Gardena, CA 90248-3253 USA (SAN 111-817X) Toll Free: 866-897-7300
E-mail: contact@emanga.com
Web site: http://www.dmpbooks.com/.

Digi-Tall Media, (*978-0-9837334; 978-0-9850007; 978-0-9894024*) Orders Addr.: 6205 Oregon Ct., Plano, TX 75023 USA Tel 972-517-6513.

Dillon Bk., Subs. of Harold Dillon, Inc., 460 S. Marion Pkwy., Apt. 851B, Denver, CO 80209-2508 USA (SAN 169-0493) Tel 303-442-5323; Toll Free: 800-525-0842.

Discount Bk. Distributors, 1854 Wallace School Rd., No. E, Charleston, SC 29407-4822 USA (SAN 107-2250) Tel 843-556-6582.

Disney Publishing Worldwide, (*978-1-892309; 978-1-931580; 978-1-4231; 978-1-4847*) Subs. of Walt Disney Productions, 44 S. Broadway, 10th Flr., White Plains, NY 10601 USA Tel 914-288-4316
Web site: http://www.disney.go.com; http://www.hyperionbooksforchildren.com.

Distribooks, Inc., Div. of MED, Inc., 8124 N. Ridgeway, Skokie, IL 60076 USA (SAN 630-9763) Tel 847-676-1596; Fax: 847-676-1195
E-mail: info@distribooks.com.

Distribuidora Escolar, Inc., 2250 SW 99th Ave., Miami, FL 00165-7569 USA (SAN 169-1104).

Distribuidora Norma, Inc., (*978-1-881700; 978-1-935164*) Div. of Carvajal International, Orders Addr.: P.O. Box 195040, San Juan, PR 00919-5040 USA Tel 787-788-5050; Fax: 787-788-7161; Edit Addr.: Carretera 869 Km 1.5 Barrio Palmas Royal Industrial, Catano, PR 00962 USA
Web site: http://www.norma.com.

Distribuidora Plaza Mayor, 1500 Ave. Ponce de Leon Local 2 El Cinco, San Juan, PR 1 USA.

Distribution Solutions Group, 1120 Rte. 22 E., Bridgewater, NJ 08807-0885 USA Toll Free: 866-374-4748.

Distributors International, Div. of Dennis-Landman Pubs., 1150 18th St., Santa Monica, CA 90403 USA (SAN 129-8089) Tel 310-828-0680
E-mail: info@moviecraft.com
Web site: http://www.moviecraft.com.

Distributors, The, (*978-0-942520*) 702 S. Michigan, South Bend, IN 46601 USA (SAN 169-2488) Tel 574-232-8500; Fax: 312-803-0887; Toll Free: 800-348-5200
E-mail: info@thedistributors.com
Web site: http://thedistributors.com/.

Diversion Bks., (*978-0-9845151; 978-0-9829050; 978-0-9833371; 978-0-9838395; 978-0-9839885; 978-1-938120; 978-1-62681; 978-1-68230*) 443 Park Aveue S., Ste. 1008, New York, NY 10016 USA Tel 212-675-5556; 212-961-6390
E-mail: info@diversionbooks.com; charles@efit.com
Web site: http://www.diversionbooks.com.

Diversion Media, *See* **Diversion Bks.**

Divine, Inc., (*978-0-87305*) 1600 Providence Hwy., Walpole, MA 02081-2553 USA (SAN 159-8619) Toll Free: 800-766-0039
E-mail: pubservices@faxon.com; helpdesk@faxon.com
Web site: http://www.faxon.com.

Dixie News Co., P.O. Box 561129, Charlotte, NC 28256-1129 USA (SAN 169-636X) Tel 704-376-0140; Fax: 704-335-8604; Toll Free: 800-532-1045.

DKE Toys, (*978-0-9915790*) 8568 Walnut Dr., Los Angeles, CA 90046 USA Tel 323-656-3262
E-mail: dkelemer@aol.com
Web site: dketoys.com.

Docustar, 1325 Glendale-Milford Rd., Cincinnati, OH 45215 USA Tel 513-772-5400; Fax: 513-772-5410.

Dog Museum, The, *See* **American Kennel Club Museum of the Dog**

Doherty, Tom Assocs., LLC, *(978-0-312; 978-0-7653; 978-0-8125)* Div. of Holtzbrinck Publishers, Orders Addr.: 16365 James Madison Hwy., Gordonsville, VA 22942-8501 USA Toll Free Fax: 800-672-2054; Toll Free: 888-330-8477; Edit Addr.: 175 Fifth Ave., New York, NY 10010 USA Tel 212-674-5151; Fax: 540-672-7540 (customer service)
E-mail: inquiries@tor.com
Web site: http://www.tor.com/.

Donars Spanish Bks., P.O. Box 808, Lafayette, CO 80026 USA (SAN 108-1586) Tel 303-666-9175; Toll Free: 800-552-3316
E-mail: donars@prolynx.com.

Dorling Kindersley Publishing, Inc., *(978-0-7894; 978-1-56458; 978-1-879431; 978-0-7566; 978-1-4654)* Div. of Penguin Publishing Group, 375 Hudson St., 2nd Flr., New York, NY 10014 USA (SAN 253-0791) Tel 212-213-4800; Fax: 212-213-5240; Toll Free: 877-342-5357 (orders only)
E-mail: Annemarie.Cancienne@dk.com; customer.service@dk.com
Web site: http://www.dk.com.

Dot Gibson Distribution, Div. of Dot Gibson Pubns., P.O. Box 117, Waycross, GA 31502 USA Tel 912-285-2848.

Dover Pubns., Inc., *(978-0-486; 978-1-60660)* Div. of Courier Corporation, 31 E. Second St., Mineola, NY 11501 USA (SAN 201-338X) Tel 516-294-7000; Fax: 516-873-1401 (orders only); Toll Free: 800-223-3130 (orders only)
E-mail: rights@doverpublications.com
Web site: http://www.doverdirect.com; http://www.doverpublications.com.

Downtown Bk. Ctr., Inc., *(978-0-941010)* 247 SE First St., Suites 236-237, Miami, FL 33131 USA (SAN 169-1112) Tel 305-377-9941
E-mail: raxdown@aol.com.

Draft2Digital, *(978-1-4977; 978-1-4989; 978-1-5014; 978-1-5022; 978-1-5070; 978-1-5130; 978-1-5163; 978-1-5199)* 5629 SE 67th St., Oklahoma City, OK 73135 USA Fax: 866-358-6413
E-mail: support@draft2digital.com
Web site: www.draft2digital.com.

Dreams In Action Distribution, P.O. Box 1894, Sedona, AZ 86339 USA Tel 928-204-1560; 70 Yucca St., Sedona, AZ 86351
E-mail: sales@dreamsinaction.us; pamela@deamsinaction.us.

Drown News Agency, P.O. Box 2080, Folsom, CA 95763-2080 USA (SAN 169-0450).

Duebbert, Harold F., P.O.B. 629 E. Adolphus Ave., Fergus Falls, MN 56537 USA Tel 218-736-4312.

Dufour Editions, Inc., *(978-0-8023)* Orders Addr.: P.O. Box 7, Chester Springs, PA 19425-0007 USA (SAN 201-341X) Tel 610-458-5005; Fax: 610-458-7103; Toll Free: 800-869-5677
E-mail: info@dufoureditions.com
Web site: http://www.dufoureditions.com.

Dumont, Charles Son, Inc., *(978-1-61727)* 1085 Dumont Cir. PO Box 1017, Voorhees, NJ 08043 USA (SAN 631-0842) Tel 856-346-9100; Fax: 856-346-3452; Toll Free: 800-257-8283
E-mail: info@dumontmusic.com
Web site: http://www.dumontmusic.com.

Durst, Sanford J., *(978-0-915262; 978-0-942666; 978-1-886720)* 106 Woodcleft Ave., Freeport, NY 11520 USA (SAN 211-6987) Tel 516-867-3333; Fax: 516-867-3397
E-mail: sjdbooks@verizon.net.

Duval News Co., Orders Addr.: P.O. Box 61297, Jacksonville, FL 32203 USA (SAN 169-1015); Edit Addr.: 5638 Commonwealth Ave., Jacksonville, FL 32205 USA (SAN 249-2865) Tel 904-783-2350.

Duval-Bibb Publishing Co., *(978-0-937713)* Div. of Mareeco Enterprises, Inc., Orders Addr.: P.O. Box 24168, Tampa, FL 33623-4168 USA (SAN 111-8641) Tel 813-281-0091; Fax: 813-282-0220; 1808 B St. NW, Suite 140, Auburn, WA 98001 Toll Free: 800-548-1169; Toll Free: 800-518-3541
E-mail: reese.cop@gte.net
Web site: http://lonepinepublishing.com/ordering.

E Learn Aid, Orders Addr.: P.O. Box 39545, Los Angeles, CA 90039-0545 USA Fax: 323-665-8875.

E M C Publishing, *See* **EMC/Paradigm Publishing**

Eagle Business Systems, *(978-0-928210)* P.O. Box 1240, El Toro, CA 92630-1240 USA (SAN 285-7510) Tel 714-859-9622.

Eagle Feather Trading Post, Inc., 168 W. 12th St., Ogden, UT 84404 USA (SAN 630-8996) Tel 801-393-3991; Fax: 801-745-0903; Toll Free: 800-547-3364 (orders only).

Eaglecrafts, Orders Addr.: 168 W. 12th St., Ogden, UT 84404 USA (SAN 630-6381) Tel 801-393-3991; Fax: 801-745-0903; Toll Free: 800-547-3364 (orders only)
E-mail: porsturbo@aol.com.

EAL Enterprises, Inc., Div. of Ambassador Bk. Service, 42 Chasner St., Hempstead, NY 11550 USA (SAN 169-6645) Toll Free: 800-431-8913.

East Kentucky News, Inc., 416 Teays Rd., Paintsville, KY 41240 USA (SAN 169-2879) Tel 606-789-8169.

East Texas Distributing, 7171 Grand Blvd., Houston, TX 77054 USA (SAN 169-8265) Tel 713-748-2520; Fax: 713-748-2504.

Eastern Bk. Co., Orders Addr.: P.O. Box 4540, Portland, ME 04112-4540 USA Fax: 207-774-0331; Toll Free Fax: 800-214-3895; Toll Free: 800-937-0331; Edit Addr.: 55 Bradley Dr., Westbrook, ME 04092-2013 USA (SAN 169-3050)
E-mail: info@ebc.com
Web site: http://www.ebc.com.

Eastern News Distributors, Subs. of Hearst Corp., 250 W. 55th St., New York, NY 10019 USA (SAN 169-5738) Tel 212-649-4484; Fax: 212-265-6239; Toll Free: 800-221-3148; 1 Media Way, 12406 Rte. 250, Milan, OH 44846-9705 (SAN 200-7711); 227 W. Trade St., Charlotte, NC 28202 (SAN 631-600X) Tel 704-348-8427
E-mail: enews@hearst.com.

Eastern Subscription Agency, 231 Moria Ct., Aston, PA 19014-1264 USA (SAN 285-9467).

Easton News Co., 2601 Dearborn St., Easton, PA 18042 USA (SAN 169-7315).

Eastview Editions, *(978-0-89860)* P.O. Box 247, Bernardsville, NJ 07924 USA (SAN 169-4952) Tel 908-204-0535.

East-West Export Bks., c/o Univ. of Hawaii Pr., 2840 Kolowalu St., Honolulu, HI 96822 USA Tel 808-956-8830; Fax: 808-988-6052
E-mail: royden@hawaii.edu
Web site: http://eastwestexportbooks.wordpress.com.

Eastwind Bks. & Arts, Inc., 1435-A Stockton St., San Francisco, CA 94133 USA (SAN 127-3159) Tel 415-772-5888; Fax: 415-772-5885
E-mail: info@eastwindsf.com
Web site: http://www.eastwindsf.com.

Eau Claire News Co., Inc., 8100 Partridge Rd., Eau Claire, WI 54703-9646 USA (SAN 169-9059) Tel 715-835-5437.

eBookIt.com, *(978-1-4566)* Div. of Archieboy Holdings, LLC, 365 Boston Post Rd., No. 311, Sudbury, MA 01776 USA
Web site: http://www.ebookit.com.

eBooks2go, *(978-1-61813)* 1111 N. Plaza Dr., Suite 652, Schaumburg, IL 60173 USA Tel 847-598-1145
E-mail: ram@gantecsolutions.com
Web site: www.gantecpublishing.com; http://www.ebooks2go.com/.

ebrary, Inc., 318 Cambridge Ave., Palo Alto, CA 94306 USA (SAN 760-7741) Tel 650-475-8700; Fax: 650-475-8881
E-mail: info@ebrary.com
Web site: http://www.ebrary.com.

ebrary.com, *See* **ebrary, Inc.**

EBS, Inc. Bk. Service, 290 Broadway, Lynbrook, NY 11563 USA (SAN 169-5487) Tel 516-593-1195; Fax: 516-596-2911.

EBSCO Media, *(978-1-885860)* Div. of EBSCO Industries, Inc., 801 Fifth Ave., S., Birmingham, AL 35233 USA Tel 205-323-1508; Fax: 205-226-8400; Toll Free: 800-765-0852
Web site: http://www.ebsco.com.

Ebsco Publishing, *(978-1-882248; 978-0-585; 978-1-4175; 978-1-4237; 978-1-4294; 978-1-4298; 978-1-4356; 978-1-4416; 978-1-4619)* Orders Addr.: 10 Estes St., Ipswich, MA 01938 USA (SAN 253-9497) Tel 978-356-6500; 800-653-2726; Fax: 978-356-6565
E-mail: information@ebscohost.com
Web site: http://www.ebscohost.com.

EBSCO Subscription Services, 5724 Hwy. 280 E., Birmingham, AL 35242-6818 USA (SAN 285-9394) Tel 205-991-6000; Fax: 205-991-1479
E-mail: jacomo@ebsco.com
Web site: http://www.ebsco.com.

Ecompass Business Ctr., 3125 Wellner Dr. NE, Rochester, MN 55906 USA Tel 507-280-0787.

e-Compass Communications, Inc., P.O. Box 9177, Rochester, MN 55903 USA.

Economical Wholesale Co., 6 King Philip Rd., Worcester, MA 01606 USA (SAN 169-3646).

EDC Publishing, *(978-0-7460; 978-0-86020; 978-0-88110; 978-1-58086; 978-0-7945; 978-1-60130)* Orders Addr.: P.O. Box 470663, Tulsa, OK 74147-0663 USA (SAN 658-0505); Edit Addr.: 10302 E. 55th Pl., Tulsa, OK 74146-6515 USA (SAN 107-5322) Tel 918-622-4522; Fax: 918-665-7919; Toll Free Fax: 800-747-4509; Toll Free: 800-475-4522
E-mail: edc@edcpub.com
Web site: http://www.edcpub.com.

Ediciones del Norte, *(978-0-910061)* P.O. Box 5130, Hanover, NH 03755 USA (SAN 241-2993).

Ediciones Enlace de PR, Inc., *(978-0-9904869)* 159 Calle Las Flores, San Juan, PR 00911-2223 USA Tel 787-725-7252; Fax: 787-725-7231
E-mail: info@edenlacepr.com; gramirez@edenlacepr.com
Web site: www.edenlacepr.com.

Ediciones Universal, *(978-0-89729; 978-1-59388)* Orders Addr.: P.O. Box 450353, Miami, FL 33245-0353 USA (SAN 658-0548); Edit Addr.: 3090 SW Eighth St., Miami, FL 33135 USA (SAN 207-2203) Tel 305-642-3355; Fax: 305-642-7978
E-mail: marta@ediciones.com; ediciones@ediciones.com
Web site: http://www.ediciones.com.

Editorial Betania, *See* **Grupo Nelson**

Editorial Cernuda, Inc., 1040 27th Ave., SW, Miami, FL 33135 USA (SAN 158-8850) Tel 305-264-9400.

Editorial Cultural, Inc., *(978-1-56758; 978-84-399)* Orders Addr.: P.O. Box 21056, San Juan, PR 00928 USA; Edit Addr.: Calle Robles, No. 51, San Juan, PR 00928 USA
E-mail: angiev@editorialculturalpr.com; alamo48@gmail.com
Web site: http://www.editorialculturalpr.com.

Editorial Unilit, *(978-0-7899; 978-0-945792; 978-1-56063)* Div. of Spanish Hse., Inc., 1360 NW 88th Ave., Miami, FL 33172-3093 USA (SAN 247-5979) Tel 305-592-6136; Fax: 305-592-0087; Toll Free: 800-767-7726
E-mail: sales1@unidial.com
Web site: http://www.editorialunilit.com/.

Educa Vision, *(978-1-881839; 978-1-58432; 978-1-62632)* 7550 NW 47th Ave., Coconut Creek, FL 33073 USA (SAN 760-873X) Tel 954-968-7433; Fax: 954-970-0330
E-mail: educa@aol.com
Web site: http://www.educavision.com; http://www.educabrazil.org/; http://www.caribbeanstudiespress.com/; www.educalanguage.com.

Education Guide, Inc., *(978-0-914880)* P.O. Box 421, Randolph, MA 02368 USA (SAN 201-4580) Tel 617-376-0066; Fax: 617-376-0067.

Educational Audio Visual, Incorporated, *See* **CLEARVUE/eav, Inc.**

Educational Bk. Distributors, P.O. Box 2510, Novato, CA 94948 USA (SAN 158-2259) Tel 415-883-3530; Fax: 415-883-4280; Toll Free: 800-761-5501
E-mail: PblshrSvcs@aol.com.

Educational Development Corporation, *See* **EDC Publishing**

Educational Distribution Corp., 10302 E. 55th Pl., Tulsa, OK 74146 USA Tel 918-622-4522.

Educational Media Corp., *(978-0-932796; 978-1-930572)* Orders Addr.: 1443 Old York Rd., Warminster, PA 18974 USA Fax: 215-956-9041; Toll Free: 800-448-2197; Edit Addr.: 4256 Central Ave. NE, Minneapolis, MN 55421-2920 USA (SAN 212-4203) Tel 763-781-0088; Fax: 763-781-7753; Toll Free: 800-966-3382
E-mail: emedia@educationalmedia.com
Web site: http://www.educationalmedia.com.

Educational Record Ctr., Inc., 3233 Burnt Mill Dr., Suite 100, Wilmington, NC 28403-2698 USA (SAN 630-592X) Tel 910-251-1235; Fax: 910-343-0311; Toll Free Fax: 888-438-1637; Toll Free: 800-438-1637
E-mail: info@erc-inc.com
Web site: http://www.erc-inc.com.

Educational Resources, 1550 Executive Dr., Elgin, IL 60123 USA (SAN 631-5674) Tel 847-888-8300; Toll Free: 800-624-2926 Do not confuse with companies with same or similar name in Shawnee Mission, Columbia, SC, Saint Paul, MN
E-mail: gmhardeman@aol.com.

Educational Showcase, 3571 Newgate Dr., Troy, MI 48084-1042 USA Toll Free: 800-213-3671.

Edumate-Educational Materials, Inc., P.O. Box 711174, San Diego, CA 92171-1174 USA (SAN 630-2955)
E-mail: GusBus@aol.com.

Edu-Tech Corp., The, 65 Bailey Rd., Fairfield, CT 06432 USA (SAN 157-5392) Tel 203-374-4212; Fax: 203-374-8050; Toll Free: 800-338-5463
E-mail: edutcorp@aoc.com.

Edward Weston Graphic, Incorporated, *See* **Weston, Edward Fine Arts**

Eisenbrauns, Inc., *(978-0-931464; 978-1-57506)* Orders Addr.: P.O. Box 275, Winona Lake, IN 46590-0275 USA (SAN 200-7835) Tel 574-269-2011; Fax: 574-269-6788; Edit Addr.: 600 N. Bay Dr., Warsaw, IN 46580 USA
E-mail: ghannah@eisenbrauns.com; Orders@eisenbrauns.com
Web site: http://www.eisenbrauns.com.

El Qui-Jote Bk., Inc., 12651 Monarch, Houston, TX 77047 USA (SAN 107-8666) Tel 713-433-3388.

Elder's Bk. Store, 2115 Elliston Pl., Nashville, TN 37203 USA (SAN 112-6091) Tel 615-327-1867.

Elkins, C. J., 400 S. Beverly Dr. Suite 214, Beverly Hills, CA 90212 USA Toll Free: 800-769-2120
E-mail: sitare@aol.com; sitare@zwallet.com.

Ellis News Co., Affil. of L-S Distributors, 130 E. Grand Ave., South San Francisco, CA 94080 USA (SAN 169-0183) Tel 415-873-2094; Fax: 415-873-4222; Toll Free: 800-654-7040 (orders only).

ELS Educational Services, *(978-0-87789; 978-0-89285; 978-0-89318)* Orders Addr.: 200 Old Tappan Rd., Old Tappan, NJ 07675 USA; Edit Addr.: 1357 Second St., Santa Monica, CA 90401-1102 USA (SAN 281-6326).

Elsevier, *(978-0-444; 978-0-7204; 978-0-916086; 978-1-85617; 978-1-59278; 978-0-08; 978-1-4831; 978-1-4832; 978-1-4933)* Orders Addr.: P.O. Box 945, New York, NY 10159-0945 USA (SAN 251-2564) Toll Free: 888-437-4636; P.O. Box 28430, Saint Louis, MO 63146-0930 Toll Free Fax: 800-535-9935; Toll Free: 800-460-3110 (Outside US); 800-545-2522; Edit Addr.: 360 Park Ave S. Flr. 11, New York, NY 10010-1710 USA (SAN 200-2051); 525 B St., Suite 1800, San Diego, CA 92101-4475 Tel 800-894-3434; 1-619-231-6616
E-mail: usinfo-f@elsevier.com; custserv@elsevier.com; d.gomez@elsevier.com
Web site: http://www.elsevier.com.

Elsevier - Health Sciences Div., *(978-0-323; 978-0-443; 978-0-444; 978-0-7020; 978-0-7216; 978-0-7234; 978-0-7236; 978-0-7506; 978-0-8016; 978-0-8151; 978-0-920513; 978-0-932883; 978-1-55664; 978-1-56053; 978-1-898507; 978-1-932141; 978-1-4160; 978-1-4377; 978-1-4557)* Subs. of Elsevier Science, Orders Addr.: a/o Customer Service, 3251 Riverport Ln., Maryland Heights, MO 63043 USA Tel 314-453-7010; Fax: 314-447-8030; Toll Free Fax: 800-535-9935; Toll Free: 800-545-2522; 800-460-3110 (Customers Outside US); 1799 Highway 50, Linn, MO 65051 (SAN 200-2280); Edit Addr.: 1600 John F. Kennedy Blvd., Suite 1800, Philadelphia, PA 19103-2899 USA Tel 215-239-3900; Fax: 215-239-3990; Toll Free: 800-523-4069
E-mail: usbkinfo@elsevier.com
Web site: http://www.elsevier.com; http://www.us.elsevierhealth.com/.

Elsevier Science, *See* **Elsevier**

Elsevier Science - Health Sciences Division, *See* **Elsevier - Health Sciences Div.**

EMC/Paradigm Publishing, *(978-0-7638; 978-0-8219; 978-0-88436; 978-0-912022; 978-1-56118)* Div. of EMC Corp., 875 Montreal Way, Saint Paul, MN 55102-4245 USA (SAN 201-3800) Tel 651-290-2800; Fax: 651-290-2828
E-mail: publish@emcp.com; educate@emcp.com
Web site: http://www.emcp.com.

Emerald Bk. Co., *(978-1-934572; 978-1-937110)* Div. of Greenleaf Bk. Group, 4425 Mo Pac Expy., Suite 600, Austin, TX 78735 USA.

Emery-Pratt Co., Orders Addr.: 1966 W. M 21, Owosso, MI 48867-1397 USA (SAN 170-1401) Tel 989-723-5291; Fax: 989-723-4677; Toll Free Fax: 800-523-6379; Toll Free: 800-762-5683 (library orders only); 800-248-3887 (customer service only) Distributor to Libraries & Hospitals
E-mail: custserv@emery-pratt.com
Web site: http://www.emery-pratt.com.

Empire Comics, 375 Stone Rd., Rochester, NY 14616 USA (SAN 110-943X) Tel 716-442-0371; Fax: 716-442-7807
E-mail: empires@frontiernet.net.

Empire News of Jamestown, Foot Ave. & Extension St., Box 2029, Sta. A, Jamestown, NY 14702 USA (SAN 169-5371).

Empire Publishing Service, *(978-1-58690)* P.O. Box 1344, Studio City, CA 91614-0344 USA (SAN 630-5687) Tel 818-784-8918
E-mail: empirepubsvc@att.net.

Empire State News Corp., Orders Addr.: P.O. Box 1167, Buffalo, NY 14240-1167 USA Tel 716-681-1100; Fax: 716-681-1120; Toll Free: 800-414-6247; Edit Addr.: 316 Forestview Dr., Buffalo, NY 14221-1461 USA (SAN 169-5177)
Web site: http://www.esnc.com.

Empowerment Technologies, *See* **Empowerment Technologies/Neuro-Semantics Publns.**

Empowerment Technologies/Neuro-Semantics Publns., *(978-1-890001; 978-1-899836)* Orders Addr.: P.O. Box 8, Clifton, CO 81520 USA Tel 704-864-3585; Fax: 970-523-5790; Edit Addr.: P.O. Box 9231, Grand Junction, CO 81501 USA Tel 970-523-7877
E-mail: meta@acsol.net
Web site: http://www.neurosemantics.com.

Encino Pr., *(978-0-88426)* 510 Baylor St., Austin, TX 78703 USA (SAN 201-3843) Tel 512-476-6821; Fax: 512-476-9393.

Enfield Publishing & Distribution Co., Inc., *(978-0-9656184; 978-1-893598)* Orders Addr.: P.O. Box 699, Enfield, NH 03748 USA Tel 603-632-7377; Fax: 603-632-5611; Edit Addr.: 234 May St., Enfield, NH 03748 USA
E-mail: info@enfieldbooks.com
Web site: http://www.enfielddistribution.com; http://www.enfieldbooks.com.

Entrepreneur Media Inc/Entrepreneur Pr., *(978-0-916378; 978-1-55571; 978-1-891984; 978-1-932156; 978-1-932531; 978-1-59918; 978-1-61308)* 2445 McCabe Way, Suite 400, Irvine, CA 92614-6244 USA Tel 949-261-2325; Fax: 949-261-7729; Toll Free: 800-864-6864
E-mail: jmctigue@entrepreneur.com
Web site: http://www.entrepreneur.com; http://www.entrepreneurpress.com.

Entrepreneur Press, *See* **Entrepreneur Media Inc/Entrepreneur Pr.**

Entrepreneur Start a Business Store, 9114 River Look Ln., Fair Oaks, CA 95628-6565 USA (SAN 133-1485) Fax: 916-863-0361.

Epic Book Promotions, 914 Nolan Way, Chula Vista, CA 91911-2408 USA Tel 619-498-8547; Fax: 619-498-8540
E-mail: gvjack@pacbell.net.

Epicenter Pr., Inc., *(978-0-945397; 978-0-9708493; 978-0-9724944; 978-0-9745014; 978-0-9790470; 978-0-9800825; 978-1-935347)* Orders Addr.: 6524 NE 181st ST No. 2, Kenmore, WA 98028 USA; Edit Addr.: 6524 NE 181st ST No. 2, Kenmore, WA 98028 USA (SAN 246-9405) Do not confuse with companies with similar names in Kanehoe, HI, Long Beach, CA, Oakland, CA
E-mail: slay@epicenterpress.com; phil@epicenterpress.com; aubrey@epicenterpress.com
Web site: http://www.epicenterpress.com.

E-Pros DG, 32 N. Goodwin Ave., Elmsford, NY 10523 USA Toll Free: 866-377-6700
E-mail: sales@e-pros.ws.

Epson Mid-Atlantic, Subs. of Epson America, Inc., 8 Neshaminy Interplex, Suite 319, Trerose, PA 19053 USA (SAN 285-7243) Tel 215-245-2180.

Equinox, Ltd., 1307 Park Ave., Williamsport, PA 17701 USA.

Eriksson Enterprises, 126 Sunset Dr., Farmington, UT 84025-3426 USA (SAN 110-5892).

Erlbaum, Lawrence Assocs., Inc., *(978-0-8058; 978-0-86377; 978-0-89859; 978-1-880393; 978-1-4106)* 270 Madison Ave. Flr. 4, New York, NY 10016-0601 USA (SAN 213-960X) Toll Free: 800-926-6579 (orders only)
E-mail: orders@erlbaum.com
Web site: http://www.erlbaum.com.

ETA hand2mind, *(978-0-7406; 978-0-914040; 978-0-923832; 978-0-938587; 978-1-57162; 978-1-57452; 978-1-63406)* Div. of A. Daigger & Company, 500 Greenview Ct., Vernon Hills, IL 60061 USA (SAN 285-7553) Tel 847-816-5050; Fax: 847-816-5066; Toll Free: 800-445-5985
E-mail: info@hand2mind.com
Web site: http://www.hand2mind.com.

ETAhand2mind, *See* **ETA hand2mind**

ETD KroMar Temple, P.O. Box 535695, Grand Prairie, TX 75053-5625 USA (SAN 169-8435) Tel 254-778-5261; Fax: 254-778-5267.

European Bk. Co., Inc., 925 Larkin St., San Francisco, CA 94109 USA (SAN 169-0191) Tel 415-474-0626; Fax: 415-474-0630; Toll Free: 877-746-3666
E-mail: info@europeanbook.com.

European Press Service - PBD America Wholesalers, 30 Edison Dr., Wayne, NJ 07470-4713 USA (SAN 630-7825).

Evans Bk. Distribution & Pubs., Inc., *(978-0-9654884; 978-1-56684)* 895 W. 1700 S., Salt Lake City, UT 84104 USA.

Evans Book, *See* **Evans Bk. Distribution & Pubs., Inc.**

Evanston Publishing, Inc., *(978-1-879260)* 4824 Brownsboro Ctr. Arcade, Louisville, KY 40207-2342 USA Tel 502-899-1919; Fax: 502-896-0246; Toll Free: 800-594-5190
E-mail: EvanstonPB@aol.com; info@evanstonpublishing.com
Web site: http://www.EvanstonPublishing.com.

Everbind/Marco Book Company, *See* **Marco Bk. Co.**

Excaliber Publishing Co., *(978-1-881353)* 7954 W. Bury Ave., San Diego, CA 92126 USA (SAN 297-6412) Tel 619-695-3091; Fax: 619-695-3095.

Exciting Times, 17430C Crenshaw Blvd., Torrance, CA 90504 USA (SAN 114-4642) Tel 310-515-2676; Fax: 310-515-1382.

Executive Bks., *(978-0-937539; 978-1-933715; 978-1-936354)* Div. of Life Management Services, Inc., 206 West Allen St., Mechanicsburg, PA 17055-6240 USA (SAN 156-5419) Tel 717-766-9499; Fax: 717-766-6565; Toll Free: 800-233-2665
E-mail: JLiller@TremendousLifeBooks.com
Web site: http://www.TremendousLifeBooks.com.

Exploration Films, P.O. Box 1069, Monument, CO 80132 USA Tel 719-481-4599; Fax: 719-481-1399; Toll Free: 800-964-0439
E-mail: jolene@explorationfilms.com
Web site: http://www.explorationfilms.com.

Explorations, 360 Interlocken Blvd., Suite 300, Broomfield, CO 80021 USA Toll Free Fax: 800-456-1139; Toll Free: 800-720-2114
E-mail: customerservice@gaiam.com
Web site: http://www.gaiam.com.

Express Media, *(978-0-9723163)* 127 Rankin Rd., Columbia, MS 37202 USA Tel 615-360-6400
Web site: http://www.authorsexpress.com.

Faber & Faber, Inc., *(978-0-571)* Affil. of Farrar, Straus & Giroux, LLC, Orders Addr.: c/o Van Holtzbrinck Publishing Services, 16365 James Madison Hwy., Gordonsville, VA 22942 USA Fax: 540-572-7540; Toll Free: 888-330-8477; Edit Addr.: 19 Union Sq., W, New York, NY 10003-3304 USA (SAN 218-7256) Tel 212-741-6900; Fax: 212-633-9385
E-mail: sales@fsgbooks.com
Web site: http://www.fsgbooks.com.

Fairfield Bk. Service Co., 150 Margherita Lawn, Stratford, CT 06615 USA (SAN 131-0976) Tel 203-375-7607.

Falk Bks. Inc., W.E., 7491 N. Federal Hwy., PMB 267, Boca Raton, FL 33487 USA.

Falk, W. E., *See* **Falk Bks. Inc., W.E.**

Fall River News Co., Inc., 144 Robeson St., Fall River, MA 02720-4925 USA (SAN 169-3425) Tel 508-679-5266.

Family History World, P.O. Box 129, Tremonton, UT 84337 USA (SAN 159-673X) Fax: 801-250-6727; Toll Free: 800-377-6058
E-mail: genealogy@utahlinx.com
Web site: http://www.genealogical-institute.com.

Family Reading Service, 1601 N. Slappey Blvd., Albany, GA 31701-1431 USA (SAN 169-1376).

Fantaco Pubns., *(978-0-938782)* Affil. of Fantaco Enterprises, Inc., 17810 Poppy Trails Ln., Houston, TX 77084-1070 USA (SAN 158-5134).

Far West Bk. Service, 3515 NE Hassalo, Portland, OR 97232 USA (SAN 107-6760) Tel 503-234-7664; Fax: 503-231-0573; Toll Free: 800-964-9378.

Farcountry Pr., *(978-0-938314; 978-1-56037; 978-1-59152)* Orders Addr.: P.O. Box 5630, Helena, MT 59604 USA (SAN 220-0732) Tel 406-422-1263; Fax: 406-443-5480; Toll Free: 800-821-3874; 2750 Broadwater, Helena, MT 59602
E-mail: books@farcountrypress.com
Web site: http://www.farcountrypress.com.

Farrar, Straus & Giroux, *(978-0-374)* Div. of Holtzbrinck Publishers, Orders Addr.: c/o Holtzbrinck Publishers, 16365 James Madison Hwy., Gordonsville, VA 22942 USA Toll Free Fax: 800-672-2054; Toll Free: 888-330-8477; Edit Addr.: 18 W. 18th St., New York, NY 10011-4607 USA (SAN 206-782X)
E-mail: sales@fsgee.com; fsg.editorial@fsgee.com
Web site: http://www.fsgbooks.com/.

Faxon Company, The, *See* **Divine, Inc.**

Faxon Illinois Service Ctr., Affil. of Dawson Holdings PLC, 1600 Providence Hwy., Walpole, MA 02081-2553 USA (SAN 286-0147) Toll Free: 800-852-7404
E-mail: postmaster@dawson.com; sandy.nordman@dawson.com
Web site: http://www.faxon.com.

Fayette County News Agency, Orders Addr.: P.O. Box 993, Uniontown, PA 15401 USA Tel 724-437-1181; Edit Addr.: Cherry Tree Square 42 Matthew Dr., Uniontown, PA 15401 USA (SAN 169-765X).

FEC News Distributing, 2201 Fourth Ave., N., Lake Worth, FL 33461-3835 USA (SAN 169-1341) Tel 407-547-3000; Fax: 407-547-3080.

Feldheim, Philipp Incorporated, *See* **Feldheim Pubs.**

Feldheim Pubs., *(978-0-87306; 978-1-58330; 978-1-59826; 978-1-68025)* 208 Airport Executive Park., Nanuet, NY 10954-5262 USA (SAN 106-6307) Toll Free: 800-237-7149
E-mail: sales@feldheim.com; eli@feldheim.com
Web site: http://www.feldheim.com.

Fell, Frederick Pubs., Inc., *(978-0-8119; 978-0-88391; 978-0-936320)* Orders Addr.: 1403 Shoreline Way, Hollywood, FL 33019-5007 USA (SAN 215-0670)
Web site: http://www.fellpub.com.

Fennell, Reginald F. Subscription Service, 1002 W. Michigan Ave., Jackson, MI 49202 USA (SAN 159-6071) Tel 517-782-3132; Fax: 517-782-1109.

FEP, A Booksource Co., 1230 Macklind Ave., Saint Louis, MO 63110 USA (SAN 169-1317) Tel 314-647-0600; Fax: 314-647-6850; Toll Free: 800-444-0435
Web site: http://www.booksource.com.

Fiddlecase Bks., HC 63 Box 104, East Alstead, NH 03602 USA (SAN 200-7495) Tel 603-835-7889.

Fiesta Bk. Co., *(978-0-88473)* P.O. Box 490641, Key Biscayne, FL 33149 USA (SAN 201-8470) Tel 305-858-4843.

Fiesta Publishing Corporation, *See* **Fiesta Bk. Co.**

Films for the Humanities & Sciences, *See* **Films Media Group**

Films Media Group, *(978-0-7365; 978-0-89113; 978-1-56950; 978-1-4213; 978-1-60467)* Div. of Infobase Learning, Orders Addr.: 132 W. 31st St., 17th Flr., New York, NY 10001 USA (SAN 653-2705) Toll Free Fax: 800-678-3633; Toll Free: 800-322-8755
E-mail: mgallo@infobaselearning.com
Web site: http://www.films.com.

Findaway World, LLC, *(978-1-59895; 978-1-60252; 978-1-60514; 978-1-60640; 978-1-60775; 978-1-60812; 978-1-60847; 978-1-61545; 978-1-61574; 978-1-61587; 978-1-61637; 978-1-61657; 978-1-61707; 978-1-4676; 978-1-5094)* 31999 Aurora Rd., Solon, OH 44139 USA (SAN 853-8778)
Web site: http://www.findawayworld.com; http://www.playawaydigital.com.

Fine Assocs., One Farragut Sq., S., Washington, DC 20006 USA (SAN 169-0914) Tel 202-628-2609.

Finn News Agency, Inc., 4415 State Rd. 327, Auburn, IN 46706-9542 USA (SAN 169-2356).

Finney Co., Inc., *(978-0-89317; 978-0-912486; 978-0-933855; 978-0-9617767; 978-0-9639705; 978-1-880654; 978-1-893272)* Orders Addr.: 8075 215th St. W., Lakeville, MN 55044 USA (SAN 206-412X) Tel 952-469-6699; Fax: 952-469-1968; Toll Free Fax: 800-330-6232; Toll Free: 800-846-7027
E-mail: feedback@finneyco.com
Web site: http://www.finneyco.com; http://www.ecopress.com; http://www.pogopress.com; http://www.astragalpress.com.

Fire Protection Publications, *See* **IFSTA**

Firebird Distributing, LLC, 1945 P St., Eureka, CA 95501-3007 USA (SAN 631-1229) Toll Free: 800-353-3575
E-mail: sales@firebirddistributing.com
Web site: http://www.firebirddistributing.com.

Firebrand Technologies, 44 Merrimac St., Newburyport, MA 01950 USA.

Firefly Bks., Ltd., *(978-0-920668; 978-1-55209; 978-1-895565; 978-1-896284; 978-1-55297; 978-1-55407)* Orders Addr.: c/o Frontier Distributing, 1000 Young St., Suite 160, Tonawanda, NY 14150 USA (SAN 630-611X) Tel 203-222-9700; Toll Free Fax: 800-565-6034; Toll Free: 800-387-5085; Edit Addr.: 8514 Long Canyon Dr., Austin, TX 78730-2813 USA
E-mail: service@fireflybooks.com
Web site: http://www.fireflybooks.com/.

Firenze Pr., *(978-0-9711236)* Orders Addr.: P.O. Box 6892, Wyomissing, PA 19610-0892 USA (SAN 254-315X); Edit Addr.: 612 Museum Rd., Reading, PA 19610-0892 USA Tel 610-374-7048; Fax: 610-478-7992 Do not confuse with Leonardo Pr., Camden, ME
E-mail: hailejohnjr@msn.com; HaileJohnJr@msn.com; InkPenCJH@msn.com
Web site: http://caroljhaile.com.

Fischer, Carl LLC, *(978-0-8258)* Orders Addr.: 588 N. Gulph Rd. Ste. B, Kng Of Prussa, PA 19406-2831 USA Toll Free: 800-762-2328; Edit Addr.: 65 Bleeker St., New York, NY 10012-2420 USA (SAN 107-4245) Tel 212-772-0900; Fax: 212-477-6996; Toll Free: 800-762-2328
E-mail: cf-info@carlfischer.com
Web site: http://www.carlfischer.com.

Fish, Enrica Medical Bks., 1208 W. Minnehaha Pkwy., Minneapolis, MN 55419-1163 USA (SAN 157-8588) Toll Free: 800-728-8398.

Fisher King Bks., 316 Mid Valley Ctr., #194, Carmel, CA 93923 USA Tel 831-238-7799; Toll Free: 800-228-9316 (Canada & US).

Flannery Co., 16430 Beaver Rd., Adelanto, CA 92301-3904 USA (SAN 168-9754) Toll Free: 800-456-3400.

Flannery, J. F. Company, *See* **Flannery Co.**

Fleming, Robert Hull Museum, *(978-0-934658)* Div. of Univ. of Vermont, Univ. of Vermont, 61 Colchester Ave., Burlington, VT 05405 USA (SAN 110-8824) Tel 802-656-0750; Fax: 802-656-8059
Web site: www.upne.com.

Flora & Fauna Bks., P.O. Box 15718, Gainesville, FL 32604 USA (SAN 133-1221) Tel 352-373-5630; Fax: 352-373-3249
E-mail: ffbks@aol.com
Web site: http://www.ffbooks.com.

Florida Academic Pr., *(978-1-890357)* P.O. Box 540, Gainesville, FL 32602-0540 USA (SAN 299-3643) Tel 352-332-5104; Fax: 352-331-6003
E-mail: fapress@worldnet.att.net.

Florida Classics Library, *(978-0-912451)* P.O. Drawer 1657, Port Salerno, FL 34992-1657 USA (SAN 265-2404) Tel 561-546-9380 (orders); Fax: 561-546-7545 (orders).

Florida Schl. Bk. Depository, 1125 N. Ellis Rd., Jacksonville, FL 32236 USA (SAN 161-8423) Tel 904-781-7191; Fax: 904-781-3486; Toll Free: 800-447-7957
Web site: http://www.fsbd.com.

Flury & Co., 322 First Ave S., Seattle, WA 98104 USA (SAN 107-5748) Tel 206-587-0260.

FM International, P.O. Box 91, Waunakee, WI 53597-0091 USA.

Fodor's Travel Guides, *See* **Fodor's Travel Pubns.**

Fodor's Travel Pubns., Div. of Random Hse., Information Group, Orders Addr.: 400 Hahn Rd., Westminster, MD 21157 USA Tel 410-848-1900; Toll Free: 800-726-0600; Edit Addr.: 1745 Broadway, New York, NY 10019 USA Tel 212-782-9000
Web site: http://www.fodors.com.

Follet Higher Education Grp, P.O. Box 3488, Oak Brook, IL 60522-3488 USA Tel 630-279-0123.

Follett Audiovisual Resources, *See* **Follett Media Distribution**

Follett Library Resources, *See* **Follett School Solutions**

Follett Media Distribution, 1847 Mercer Rd., Lexington, KY 40511-1001 USA (SAN 631-7316) Toll Free: 888-281-1216.

Follett School Solutions, *(978-0-329; 978-0-88153; 978-0-924917; 978-1-4898; 978-1-5160; 978-1-5181)* Div. of the Follett Corp., Orders Addr.: a/o McHenry Warehouse, 1340 Ridgeview Dr., McHenry, IL 60050 USA (SAN 169-1902) Toll Free: 888-511-5114; a/o Patti Hall: R & R Bindery Services, 499 Rachel Rd., Girard, IL 62640 (SAN 155-8412) Tel 815-759-1700; a/o Formerly FES, 1433 Internationale Pkwy. DOCK Door 30, Woodridge, IL 60517 (SAN 631-7901) Tel 630-972-5600; Fax: 630-972-4673; Toll Free: 800-621-4272; a/o Russell Henning (Formerly FSC), 1391 Corporate Dr., McHenry, IL 60050-7041 (SAN 298-587X) Fax: 815-344-8774; a/o Formerly FLR, 1340 Ridgeview Dr., Suite EDI, McHenry, IL 60050-0000 (SAN 760-7164)
Web site: http://www.follett.com.

Fondo de Cultura Economica USA, 2293 Verus St., San Diego, CA 92154 USA (SAN 860-1380) Tel 619-429-0455; Fax: 619-429-0827; Toll Free: 800-532-3872
E-mail: drazo@fceusa.com; fondosales@fceusa.com; dbase@fceusa.com
Web site: http://www.fceusa.com.

Forest Hse. Publishing Co., Inc., *(978-1-56674; 978-1-878363)* P.O. Box 738, Lake Forest, IL 60045 USA Tel 847-295-8287; Fax: 847-295-8201; Toll Free: 800-394-7323.

Forest Sales & Distributing Co., *(978-0-9712183)* 139 Jean Marie St., Reserve, LA 70084 USA (SAN 157-5511) Toll Free: 800-347-2106
E-mail: tbooks2@juno.com.

Forsa Editores, *(978-1-881714)* Orders Addr.: P.O. Box 11249, San Juan, PR 00922-1249 USA Tel 787-707-1792; Fax: 787-707-1797; Toll Free: 888-225-8984; Edit Addr.: No. 1594 J.T. Pinero Ave., Caparra Heights, PR 00920 USA
E-mail: forsa@forsaeditores.com
Web site: http://www.forsaeditores.com.

Forsyth Travel Library, Inc., *(978-0-9614539)* 1750 E. 131st St., P.O. Box 480800, Kansas City, MO 64148-0800 USA (SAN 169-2755) Tel 816-942-9050; Fax: 816-942-6969; Toll Free: 800-367-7984 (orders only)
E-mail: forsyth@gvi.net
Web site: http://www.forsyth.com.

Forward Movement Pubns., *(978-0-88028)* 300 West Fourth St., Cincinnati, OH 45202 USA (SAN 208-3841) Tel 513-721-6659; Fax: 513-721-0729; Toll Free: 800-543-1813 (orders only)
E-mail: Orders@forwarddaybyday.com
Web site: http://www.forwardmovement.org.

Four Winds Trading Co., *(978-0-9672383)* 6355 Joyce Dr., Golden, CO 80403-7568 USA (SAN 631-1989) Toll Free: 800-456-5444
E-mail: Paul@Fourwinds-trading.com; sales@fourwinds-trading.com
Web site: http://www.fourwinds-trading.com.

Franklin Bk. Co., Inc., P.O. Box 451, Newtown Sq, PA 19073-0451 USA (SAN 121-4160)
E-mail: service@franklinbook.com
Web site: http://www.franklinbook.com.

Franklin Readers Service, P.O. Box 662, Dunn Loring, VA 22027-0662 USA (SAN 285-9599).

Franklin Square Overseas, 17-19 Washington St., Tenafly, NJ 07670-2084 USA (SAN 285-9637) Tel 201-569-2500; Fax: 201-569-5141
E-mail: esstn@ebsco.com.

Fraser Publishing Co., *(978-0-87034; 978-0-918632)* Div. of Alvin Q. Garbanzo, Inc., Orders Addr.: P.O. Box 217, Flint Hill, VT 22747 USA (SAN 213-9537)
E-mail: info@fraserpublishing.com
Web site: http://www.fraserpublishing.com.

Freeman Family Ministries, Orders Addr.: P.O. Box 593, Waldo, FL 32694 USA Tel 352-468-2785
E-mail: freemanfamily9@msn.com.

Freihofer, A. G., 175 Fifth Ave., New York, NY 10010 USA (SAN 285-9602) Tel 272-460-7500; Fax: 272-473-6272.

French & European Pubns., Inc., *(978-0-320; 978-0-7859; 978-0-8288)* 425 E. 58th St., Suite 27D, New York, NY 10022-2379 USA (SAN 206-8109) Fax: 212-265-1094
E-mail: frenchbookstore@aol.com
Web site: http://www.frencheuropean.com.

Fresno Bk. Fairs, 1030 Bonita Ave., La Verne, CA 91750 USA (SAN 630-6225) Tel 909-593-0697; 1650 W. Orange Grove Ave., Pomona, CA 91768-2153 (SAN 299-2434)
Web site: http://www.mrsnelsons.com.

Friendly Hills Fellowship, *See* **Health and Growth Assocs.**

Fris News Co., 194 River Ave., Holland, MI 49423 USA (SAN 159-8643).

Frontline Communications, *See* **YWAM Publishing**

Fujii Assocs., 1400 W. 47th St. Ste. 4, La Grange, IL 60525-6148 USA (SAN 631-5305).

Fulcrum Publishing, *(978-0-912347; 978-1-55591; 978-1-56373; 978-1-936218; 978-1-938486; 978-1-68275)* Orders Addr.: 4690 Table Mountain Dr. Suite 100, Golden, CO 80403 USA (SAN 200-2825) Toll Free Fax: 800-726-7112; Toll Free: 800-992-2908
E-mail: info@fulcrumbooks.com
Web site: http://www.fulcrumbooks.com.

Fulmont News Co., Affil. of Rubin Periodical Group, P.O. Box 1211, Rochester, NY 14603-1211 USA (SAN 169-5029) Tel 518-843-2421.

Fultz News Agency, 2008 Woodbrook, Denton, TX 76205 USA (SAN 169-8168).

Futech Educational Products, Inc., *(978-0-9627001; 978-1-889192)* 2999 N. 44th St., Suite 225, Phoenix, AZ 85018-7248 USA Tel 602-808-8765; Fax: 602-278-5667; Toll Free: 800-597-6278.

F&W Media, Inc., *(978-0-89134; 978-0-89879; 978-0-932620; 978-1-55870; 978-1-58180; 978-1-58297; 978-1-884910; 978-1-892127; 978-1-59963; 978-1-60061; 978-1-4402; 978-1-4403; 978-0-578-03300-6; 978-1-940038)* Orders Addr.: 10151 Carver Rd., Ste 200, Blue Ash, OH 45242 USA Tel 513-531-2690; Fax: 513-531-1843; Toll Free Fax: 888-590-4082; Toll Free: 800-289-0963; Edit Addr.: Brunel House Forde Close, Newton Abbot, TQ12 4PU GBR Tel 01626 323200; Fax: 01626 323319
E-mail: amber.ziegler@fwmedia.com; mark.griffin@fwmedia.com
Web site: http://www.artistsmagazine.com; http://www.artistsnetwork.com; http://www.davidandcharles.co.uk; http://www.krause.com; http://www.familytreemagazine.com; http://www.howdesign.com; http://www.idonline.com; http://www.memorymakersmagazine.com; http://www.popularwoodworking.com; http://www.writersdigest.com; http://www.writersmarket.com; http://www.writersonlineworkshops.com; http://www.fwpublications.com; http://www.fwmedia.co.uk.

F+W Media, Incorporated, *See* **F&W Media, Inc.**

G A M Printers & Grace Christian Bookstore, *See* **GAM Pubn.**

Gabriel Resources, Orders Addr.: P.O. Box 1047, Waynesboro, GA 30830 USA Tel 706-554-1594; Fax: 706-554-7444; Toll Free: 800-732-6657 (8MORE-BOOKS); Edit Addr.: 129 Mobilization Dr., Waynesboro, GA 30830 USA.

Galda Library Services, Inc., 33 Richdale Ave., Cambridge, MA 02140 USA (SAN 630-5806) Tel 617-864-8232.

Gale Virtual Reference Library, 27500 Drake Rd., Farmington Hills, MI 48331 USA Toll Free: 800-877-4253
Web site: http://www.gale.cengage.com/servlet/GvrlMS?msg=ma.

Galesburg News Agency, Inc., Five E. Simmons St., Galesburg, IL 61401 USA (SAN 169-1945).

Galveston News Agency, P.O. Box 7608, San Antonio, TX 78207-0608 USA (SAN 169-8230).

GAM Pubn., P.O. Box 25, Sterling, VA 20167 USA (SAN 158-7218) Tel 703-450-4121; Fax: 703-450-5311.

Gamboge International, Inc., 18 Brittany Ave., Trumbull, CT 06611 USA (SAN 631-046X) Tel 203-261-2130; Fax: 203-452-0180
E-mail: gamboge@pcaet.com.

Gangaji Foundation, The, *(978-0-9632194; 978-1-887984)* P.O. Box 716, Ashland, OR 97520-0024 USA Toll Free: 800-267-9205
E-mail: order@Gangaji.org; info@gangaji.org
Web site: http://www.gangaji.org.

Gannon Distributing Co., *(978-0-88307)* 100 La Salle Cir., No. A, Santa Fe, NM 87505-6916 USA (SAN 201-5889).

Gardner's Bk. Service, 11226 N. 23rd Ave., Ste. 103, Phoenix, AZ 85029 USA (SAN 106-9322) Tel 602-863-6000; Fax: 602-863-2400 (orders only); Toll Free: 800-851-6001 (orders only)
E-mail: gbsbooks@bgsbooks.com
Web site: http://www.gbsbooks.com.

Garrett Educational Corp., *(978-0-944483; 978-1-56074)* Orders Addr.: P.O. Box 1588, Ada, OK 74820 USA (SAN 169-6955) Tel 580-332-6884; Fax: 580-332-1560; Toll Free: 800-654-9366; Edit Addr.: 130 E. 13th St., Ada, OK 74820 USA (SAN 243-2722)
E-mail: mail@garrettbooks.com
Web site: http://www.garrettbooks.com.

Gasman News Agency, 2211 Third Ave., S., Escanaba, MI 49829 USA (SAN 169-3794).

Gaunt, Inc., *(978-0-912004; 978-1-56169; 978-1-60449)* 3011 Gulf Dr., Holmes Beach, FL 34217-2199 USA (SAN 202-9413) Tel 941-778-5211; Fax: 941-778-5252
E-mail: info@gaunt.com; sales@gaunt.com
Web site: http://www.gaunt.com.

Gaunt, William W. & Sons, Incorporated, *See* **Gaunt, Inc.**

GBGM Service Ctr., P.O. Box 691328, Cincinnati, OH 45269 USA.

Gefen Bks., *(978-0-86343)* 11 Edison Pl., Springfield, NJ 07081 USA (SAN 856-8065)
E-mail: gefenny@gefenpublishing.com
Web site: http://www.gefenpublishing.com.

Gem Guides Bk. Co., *(978-0-935182; 978-0-937799; 978-1-889786)* Orders Addr.: 1275 W. 9th St., Upland, CA 91786 USA (SAN 221-1637) Tel 626-855-1611; Fax: 626-855-1610
E-mail: info@gemguidesbooks.com
Web site: http://www.gemguidesbooks.com.

Gemini Enterprises, P.O. Box 8251, Stockton, CA 95208 USA (SAN 128-1402).

Genealogical Sources, Unlimited, *(978-0-913857)* 407 Ascot Ct., Knoxville, TN 37923-5807 USA (SAN 170-8058) Tel 865-690-7831.

Genealogy Digest, 960 N. 400 E., North Salt Lake, UT 84054-1920 USA (SAN 110-389X); 420 S. 425 W., Bountiful, UT 84010 (SAN 243-2439).

General Medical Pubs., *(978-0-935236)* P.O. Box 210, Venice, CA 90294-0210 USA (SAN 215-689X) Tel 310-392-4911.

Generic Computer Products, Inc., *(978-0-918611)* P.O. Box 790, Marquette, MI 49855 USA (SAN 284-8856) Tel 906-226-7600; Fax: 906-226-8309.

GenPop Bks., *(978-0-9823594)* Orders Addr.: P.O. Box 189, Grafton, VT 05146 USA
Web site: http://www.genpopbooks.com.

Geographia Map Co., Inc., *(978-0-88433)* 75 Moore St., Hackensack, NJ 07601-7107 USA (SAN 132-5566).

Gerold International Booksellers, Inc., 35-23 Utopia Pkwy., Flushing, NY 11358 USA (SAN 129-959X) Tel 718-358-4741; Fax: 718-358-3688.

Gibbs Smith, Publisher, *(978-0-87905; 978-0-941711; 978-1-58685; 978-1-4236)* Orders Addr.: P.O. Box 667, Layton, UT 84041 USA (SAN 201-9906) Tel 801-544-9800; Fax: 801-544-5582; Toll Free Fax: 800-213-3023 (orders); Toll Free: 800-748-5439 (orders); 800-835-4993 (Customer Service order only); Edit Addr.: 1877 E. Gentile St., Layton, UT 84040 USA Tel 801-544-9800; Fax: 801-546-8853
E-mail: info@gibbs-smith.com; tradeorders@gibbs-smith.com
Web site: http://www.gibbs-smith.com.

Gibson, Dot Pubns., *(978-0-941162)* Orders Addr.: P.O. Box 117, Waycross, GA 31502-0117 USA (SAN 200-4143) Tel 912-285-2848; Fax: 912-285-0349; Toll Free: 800-336-8095; Edit Addr.: 383 Bonneyman Rd., Blackshear, GA 31516 USA (SAN 200-9676)
E-mail: info@dotgibson.com
Web site: http://www.dotgibson.com.

Gilmore-Howard, P.O. Box 1268, Arlington, TX 76004-1268 USA (SAN 157-485X).

Giron Bks., *(978-0-9741393; 978-0-9915442)* 2141 W. 21st St., Chicago, IL 60608-2608 USA Tel 773-847-3000; Fax: 773-847-9197; Toll Free: 800-405-4276
E-mail: juanmanuel@gironbooks.com
Web site: http://www.gironbooks.com.

G-Jo Institute/DeerHaven Hills, *(978-0-916878)* P.O. Box 1460, Columbus, NC 28722-1460 USA (SAN 111-0004)
E-mail: officesupport@g-jo.com
Web site: http://www.g-jo.com.

G-Jo Institute/Falkyn, Incorporated, *See* **G-Jo Institute/DeerHaven Hills**

GL Services, 4588 Interstate Dr., Cincinnati, OH 45246 USA Tel 805-677-6815.

Global Bk. Distributors, P.O. Box 192629, Dallas, TX 75219 USA.

Global Engineering Documents-Latin America, 3909 NE 163rd St., Suite 110, North Miami Beach, FL 33160 USA (SAN 630-7868) Tel 305-944-1099; Fax: 305-944-1028
E-mail: global.csa@ihs.com.

Global Info Centres, *See* **Global Engineering Documents-Latin America**

Global Publishing Associates, Inc., *See* **Jobson, Oliver H.**

Globe Pequot Pr., The, *(978-0-7627; 978-0-87106; 978-0-88742; 978-0-914788; 978-0-933469; 978-0-934802; 978-0-941130; 978-1-56440; 978-1-57034; 978-1-58574; 978-1-59228; 978-1-59921; 978-1-4779; 978-1-4930)* Orders Addr.: P.O. Box 480, Guilford, CT 06437-0480 USA (SAN 201-9892) Tel 888-249-7586; Toll Free Fax: 800-820-2329 (in Connecticut); Toll Free: 800-243-0495 (24 hours); 800-336-8334; Edit Addr.: 246 Goose Ln., Guilford, CT 06437 USA Tel 203-458-4500; Fax: 203-458-4600; Toll Free Fax: 800-336-8334
E-mail: info@globepequot.com
Web site: http://www.globepequot.com.

Gluesing & Gluesing, *(978-0-9631357)* 10301 Bren Rd W. Ste. 165, Hopkins, MN 55343-9129 USA (SAN 630-0022) Toll Free: 800-747-0227.

Goldberg, Louis Library Bk. Supplier, 45 Belvidere St., Nazareth, PA 18064 USA (SAN 169-7536) Tel 610-759-9458; Fax: 610-759-8134.

Goldenrod Music, Inc., 1310 Turner Rd., Lansing, MI 48906-4342 USA (SAN 630-5962) Tel 517-484-1777
E-mail: music@goldenrod.com
Web site: http://www.goldenrod.com.

Goldenrod/Horizon Distribution, *See* **Goldenrod Music, Inc.**

Goldman, S. Otzar Hasefarim, Inc., 125 Ditmas Ave., Brooklyn, NY 11218 USA (SAN 169-5770) Tel 718-972-6200; Fax: 718-972-6204; Toll Free: 800-972-6201.

Good Bk. Publishing Co., *(978-1-881212)* P.O. Box 837, Kihei, HI 96753-0837 USA (SAN 297-9578) Tel 808-874-4876 (phone/fax)
E-mail: dickb@dickb.com
Web site: http://www.dickb.com/index.shtml.

Good News Magazine Distributors, 6332 Saunders St., Rego Park, NY 11374-2031 USA (SAN 113-7271) Toll Free: 800-624-7257.

Gopher News Co., 9000 10th Ave N., Minneapolis, MN 55427-4322 USA (SAN 169-4138).

Gopher News Company, *See* **St. Marie's Gopher News Co.**

Gospel Light Pubns., *(978-0-8307)* Orders Addr.: 1957 Eastman Ave., Ventura, CA 93003 USA (SAN 299-0873) Tel 805-644-9721; Fax: 805-289-0200; Toll Free: 800-446-7735 (orders only) Do not confuse with companies with similar names in Brooklyn, NY, Delight, AR
E-mail: info@gospellight.com; kyleloffelmacher@gospellight.com
Web site: http://www.gospellight.com.

Gospel Mission, Inc., *(978-1-62813)* Orders Addr.: P.O. Box 318, Choteau, MT 59422 USA (SAN 170-3196) Tel 406-466-2311; Edit Addr.: 316 First St., NW, Choteau, MT 59422 USA (SAN 243-2455).

Gospel Publishing Hse., *(978-0-88243; 978-1-60731)* Div. of General Council of the Assemblies of God, 1445 N. Boonville Ave., Springfield, MO 65802-1894 USA (SAN 206-8826) Tel 417-862-2781; Fax: 417-862-5881; Toll Free Fax: 800-328-0294; Toll Free: 800-641-4310 (orders only)
E-mail: webmaster@gph.com
Web site: http://www.gospelpublishing.com.

Goyescas Corp. of Florida, P.O. Box 524207, Miami, FL 33152-4207 USA (SAN 169-1120).

Graham Services, Inc., 180 James Dr., E., Saint Rose, LA 70087-9481 USA (SAN 169-2895) Tel 504-467-5863; Fax: 504-464-6196; Toll Free: 800-457-7323 (in Los Angeles only)
E-mail: gsi@aol.com.

Grand Central Publishing, *(978-0-445; 978-0-446; 978-0-7595; 978-1-4555)* Orders Addr.: c/o Little Brown & Co., 3 Center Plaza, Boston, MA 02108-2084 USA Toll Free Fax: 800-286-9471; Toll Free: 800-759-0190; Edit Addr.: 237 Park Ave., New York, NY 10017 USA (SAN 281-8892) Fax: 800-331-1664; Toll Free Fax: 800-759-0190
E-mail: renee.supriano@twbg.com
Web site: http://www.hbgusa.com.

Granite Publishing & Distribution, *(978-1-890558; 978-1-930980; 978-1-932280; 978-1-59936)* 868 N. 1430 W., Orem, UT 84057 USA (SAN 631-0605) Tel 801-229-9023; Fax: 801-229-1924; Toll Free: 800-574-5779 Do not confuse with companies with same or similar names in Madison, WI, Columbus, NC
E-mail: granite@granitepublishing.biz; gregg@granitepublishing.biz
Web site: http://granitepublishing.biz.

Granta, *(978-0-9645611; 978-1-86207; 978-1-929001; 978-1-84708)* 62 E. Starrs Plain Rd., Danbury, CT 06810-8319 USA
E-mail: granta@nybooks.com; jhederman@nybooks.com
Web site: http://www.nybooks.com.

Granta U. S. A., Limited, *See* **Granta**

Graphic Arts Ctr. Publishing Co., Orders Addr.: P.O. Box 10306, Portland, OR 97296-0306 USA (SAN 201-6338) Tel 503-226-2402; Fax: 503-223-1410 (executive & editorial); Toll Free Fax: 800-355-9685 (sales office); Toll Free: 800-452-3032
E-mail: sales@gacpc.com
Web site: http://www.gacpc.com.

Great American Book Fairs, *See* **Scholastic Bk. Fairs**

Great Lakes Reader's Service, Inc., Orders Addr.: P.O. Box 1078, Detroit, MI 48231 USA (SAN 285-9912) Tel 313-965-4577; Fax: 313-965-2445.

Great Northern Distributors, Inc., 634 South Ave., Rochester, NY 14620-1316 USA (SAN 169-7676) Tel 717-342-8159.

Greathall Productions, Inc., *(978-1-882513; 978-1-940916)* Orders Addr.: P.O. Box 5061, Charlottesville, VA 22905-5061 USA Tel 434-296-4288; Fax: 434-296-4490; Toll Free: 800-477-6234
E-mail: greathall@greathall.com
Web site: http://www.greathall.com.

Green Dragon Bks., *(978-0-89334; 978-1-62386)* Orders Addr.: P.O. Box 7400, Atlanta, GA 30357-0400 USA (SAN 208-3833) Tel 561-533-6231; Fax: 404-874-1976; Toll Free: 888-874-8844; Edit Addr.: 12 S. Dixie Hwy., Suite 203, Lake worth, FL 33460 USA (SAN 658-0882) Tel 561-533-6231; Fax: 561-533-6233; Toll Free Fax: 888-874-8844; Toll Free: 800-874-8844 Do not confuse with Humanics ErgoSystems, Inc., Reseda, CA
E-mail: humanics@mindspring.com
Web site: http://www.humanicspub.com; http://www.humanicslearning.com; http://www.humanicsdealer.com.

Green Gate Bks., 6700 W. Chicago St., Chandler, AZ 85226 USA (SAN 169-6785) Tel 480-961-5176; Fax: 480-961-5256; Toll Free: 800-228-3816
E-mail: ggb@wcoil.com
Web site: http://www.greengatebooks.com.

Greenfield Distribution, Inc., Orders Addr.: c/o IDS, 400 Bedford St., Suite 322, Manchester, NH 03101 USA Tel 413-772-2976; Edit Addr.: 20 Blaine St., Manchester, NH 03102 USA
E-mail: Findikzade1@aol.com; Gdibooks@aol.com
Web site: http://www.gdibooks.com.

Greenleaf Book Group, *(978-0-9665319; 978-1-929774; 978-0-9790842; 978-1-60832; 978-1-61486; 978-1-62634)* Orders Addr.: 4005-B Banister Ln., Austin, TX 78704 USA Tel 512-891-6100; Fax: 512-891-6150; Toll Free: 800-932-5420; Edit Addr.: P.O. Box 91869, Austin, TX 78709 USA
E-mail: tanya@greenleafbookgroup.com
Web site: http://www.greenleafbookgroup.com.

Greenwood Press, Incorporated, *See* **Greenwood Publishing Group, Inc.**

Greenwood Publishing Group, Inc., *(978-0-275; 978-0-313; 978-0-8371; 978-0-86569; 978-0-89789; 978-0-89930; 978-1-56720; 978-1-4408)* Orders Addr.: P.O. Box 6926, Portsmouth, NH 03802 USA (SAN 213-2028) Fax: 603-431-2214 (customer service and sales); Toll Free: 800-225-5800 (orders only); Linacre House Jordan Hill Bus Pk, Banbury Rd, Oxford, OX2 8DP Tel 01865 888181; Fax: 01865 314981 Do not confuse with Greenwood Publishing in Glenview, IL
E-mail: customer-service@greenwood.com; celeste.bilyard@greenwood.com; Greenwood.enquiries@harcourteducation.co.uk
Web site: http://www.greenwood.com.

Grey Hse. Publishing, *(978-0-939300; 978-1-891482; 978-1-930956; 978-1-59237; 978-1-61925; 978-1-68217)* 4919 Rte. 22, Amenia, NY 12501 USA Tel 518-789-8700; Fax: 518-789-0556; Toll Free: 800-562-2139; 4919 Rte. 22, Amenia, NY 12501 Tel 518-789-8700; Fax: 518-789-0556; Toll Free: 800-562-2139; 4919 Rte. 22, Amenia, NY 12501 Tel 518-789-8700; Fax: 518-789-0556; Toll Free: 800-562-2139
E-mail: books@greyhouse.com
Web site: http://www.greyhouse.com.

Grey Owl Indian Craft Co., Inc., 132-05 Merrick Blvd., P.O. Box 468, Jamaica, NY 11434 USA (SAN 132-9979) Tel 718-341-4000.

Grolier Americana, 1111 Crandon Blvd., Apt. C501, Key Biscayne, FL 33149-2734 USA (SAN 108-1764) Tel 305-551-6711.

Grupo Nelson, *(978-0-8499; 978-0-88113; 978-0-89922; 978-1-60255)* Div. of Thomas Nelson, Inc., 501 Nelson Pl., Nashville, TN 37217 USA (SAN 240-6349) Tel 615-889-9000; Fax: 615-883-9376; Toll Free: 800-251-4000
Web site: http://www.editorialcaribe.com.

Gryphon Hse., Inc., *(978-0-87659; 978-0-917505; 978-1-58904)* Orders Addr.: 6848 Leon's Way, Lewisville, NC 27023 USA (SAN 169-3190) Tel 800-638-0928; Fax: 800-638-7576; Toll Free: 800-638-0928
E-mail: info@ghbooks.com
Web site: http://www.gryphonhouse.com.

GSG & Assocs., *(978-0-945001; 978-1-933355)* Orders Addr.: P.O. Box 590, San Pedro, CA 90733 USA (SAN 245-7792) Tel 310-548-3455; Fax: 310-548-5802; Edit Addr.: 831 S. Palos Vereds St., San Pedro, CA 90731 USA
E-mail: gsgbooks@earthlink.net.

Guardian Bk. Co., P.O. Box 202, Ottawa Lake, MI 49267-0202 USA (SAN 163-7355).

Gulf States Book Fairs, *See* **Gulf States Educational Bks.**

Gulf States Educational Bks., Orders Addr.: 368 Laurel Dr., Satsuma, AL 36572 USA (SAN 158-7870) Toll Free: 800-533-1189.

Gumdrop Bks., Div. of Central Programs, Inc., Orders Addr.: P.O. Box 505, Bethany, MO 64424 USA (SAN 631-4988) Tel 660-425-3923; Fax: 660-425-3970; Toll Free: 800-821-7199; Edit Addr.: P.O. Box 505, Bethany, MO 64424-0505 USA (SAN 131-0860)
E-mail: wecare@gumdropbooks.com
Web site: http://www.gumdropbooks.com.

H & H Distribution, 1634 Stilesgate, Grand Rapids, MI 49508 USA Tel 616-248-7990; Fax: 616-248-0016.

Hachette Bk. Group, *(978-0-446; 978-1-60941; 978-1-61113; 978-1-61969; 978-1-4789)* Div. of Hachette Groupe Livre, Orders Addr.: 3 Center Plaza, Boston, MA 02108 USA (SAN 852-5463) Tel 617-263-1828; Toll Free Fax: 800-286-9471; Toll Free: 800-759-0190; Edit Addr.: 237 Park Ave., New York, NY 10017 USA Tel 212-363-1100; P.O. Box 2146, Johannesburg, 2196 Tel 2711 783-7565; Fax: 2711 883-6866
Web site: http://www.hachettebookgroup.com.

Hagerstown News Distributors, *See* **Mid-States Distributors**

Haitiana Pubns., Inc., *(978-0-944987)* 3740 81st St. Apt. B3, Jackson Hts, NY 11372-6947 USA (SAN 245-7059)
E-mail: haitiana@idt.net
Web site: http://www.idtnet/haitiana/.com.

Halalco Bks., 108 E. Fairfax St., Falls Church, VA 22046 USA
E-mail: halalco@halalco.com.

Hale, Robert & Co., Inc., 1803 132nd Ave., NE, Suite 4, Bellevue, WA 98005 USA (SAN 200-6995) Tel 425-881-5212; Fax: 425-881-0731; Toll Free: 800-733-5330.

Ham Radio's Bookstore, *See* **Radio Bookstore**

Hamakor Judaica, Inc., 7777 Merrimac Ave., Niles, IL 60714 USA (SAN 169-1791) Tel 847-966-4040; Fax: 847-966-4033; Toll Free: 800-552-4088.

Hamel, Bernard H. Spanish Bk. Corp., 10977 Santa Monica Blvd., Los Angeles, CA 90025 USA (SAN 111-8862) Tel 310-475-0453; Fax: 310-473-6132
E-mail: spanish@primenet.com
Web site: http://www.BernardHamel.com; http://www.SpanishBooksUSA.com.

Hamilton News Co., Ltd., 41 Hamilton Ln., Glenmont, NY 12077 USA (SAN 169-5312) Tel 518-463-1135; Fax: 518-463-3154.

Hammond, Incorporated, *See* **Hammond World Atlas Corp.**

Hammond Publishing Co., Inc., *(978-1-883882)* P.O. Box 279, G7166 N. Saginaw St., Mount Morris, MI 48458 USA (SAN 185-142X) Tel 810-686-8881; Fax: 810-686-0561; Toll Free: 800-521-3440 (orders only)
E-mail: hammondpub@juno.com.

Hammond World Atlas Corp., *(978-0-7230; 978-0-8437)* Subs. of Langenscheidt Pubs., Inc., 193 Morris Ave., Springfield, NJ 07081-1211 USA (SAN 202-2702)
E-mail: rstrung@americanmap.com
Web site: http://www.Hammondmap.com.

Hamon, Gerard Incorporated, *See* **Lafayette Bks.**

Hancock Hse. Pubs., *(978-0-88839; 978-0-919654; 978-1-55205)* 1431 Harrison Ave., Blaine, WA 98230-5005 USA (SAN 665-7079) Tel 604-538-1114; Fax: 604-538-2262; Toll Free Fax: 800-983-2262; Toll Free: 800-938-1114; 19313 Zero Ave., Surrey, BC V3S 9R9 (SAN 115-3730)
E-mail: sales@hancockhouse.com
Web site: http://www.hancockhouse.com.

Handleman, 500 Kirts Blvd., Troy, MI 48084-5225 USA (SAN 106-4886).

Handler News Agency, P.O. Box 27007, Omaha, NE 68127-0007 USA (SAN 169-4405).

Hansen Hse., 1842 West Ave., Miami Beach, FL 33139 USA (SAN 200-7908) Tel 305-532-5461; Toll Free: 800-327-8202.

Harcourt Achieve, *See* **Houghton Mifflin Harcourt Supplemental Pubs.**

Harcourt Brace & Company, *See* **Harcourt Trade Pubs.**

Harcourt Trade Pubs., *(978-0-15)* Div. of Houghton Mifflin Harcourt Trade & Reference Pubs., Orders Addr.: 6277 Sea Harbor Dr., Orlando, FL 32887 USA (SAN 200-285X) Tel 619-699-6707; Toll Free Fax: 800-235-0256; Toll Free: 800-543-1918 (trade orders, inquiries, claims); Edit Addr.: 15 E. 26th St., New York, NY 10010 USA Tel 212-592-1000; Fax: 212-592-1011; 525 B St., Suite 1900, San Diego, CA 92101-4495 (SAN 200-2736) Tel 619-231-6616
E-mail: andrewporter@harcourt.com
Web site: http://www.HarcourtBooks.com.

Harness, Miller, 750 Route 73 S. Ste. 110, Marlton, NJ 08053-4142 USA (SAN 169-5789) Toll Free: 800-526-6310.

HarperCollins Pubs., *(978-0-00; 978-0-06; 978-0-380; 978-0-688; 978-0-690; 978-0-694; 978-0-87795; 978-1-55710)* Div. of News Corp., Orders Addr.: 1000 Keystone Industrial Pk., Scranton, PA 18512-4621 USA (SAN 215-3742) Tel 570-941-1500; Toll Free Fax: 800-822-4090; Toll Free: 800-242-7737 (orders only); Edit Addr.: 10 E. 53rd St., New York, NY 10022-5299 USA (SAN 200-2086) Tel 212-207-7000
Web site: http://www.harpercollins.com; http://www.harpercollinschildrens.com.

Harrisburg News Co., 980 Briarsdale Rd., Harrisburg, PA 17109 USA (SAN 169-7420) Tel 717-561-8377; Fax: 717-561-1466
E-mail: jmurphy@harrisburgnewsco.com
Web site: http://www.harrisburgnewsco.com.

Harrison House, Incorporated, *See* **Harrison House Pubs.**

Harrison House Pubs., *(978-0-89274; 978-1-57794; 978-1-60683; 978-1-68031)* Orders Addr.: P.O. Box 35035, Tulsa, OK 74153 USA (SAN 208-676X) Tel 918-523-5700; Toll Free Fax: 800-830-5688; Toll Free: 800-888-4126; Edit Addr.: 7498 E. 46th Pl., Tulsa, OK 74145 USA Tel 918-523-5700; Toll Free Fax: 800-830-5688; Toll Free: 800-888-4126
E-mail: lisad@harrisonhouse.com; juliew@harrisonhouse.com
Web site: http://www.harrisonhouse.com.

Harry-Young Pubn. Services Agency, Inc., 6261 Manchester Blvd., Buena Park, CA 90621-2259 USA (SAN 110-8832).

Harvard Assocs., Inc., *(978-0-924346)* 10 Holworthy St., Cambridge, MA 02138 USA (SAN 170-2939) Tel 617-492-0660; Fax: 617-492-4610; Toll Free: 800-774-5646
E-mail: info@harvassoc.com
Web site: http://www.harvassoc.com.

Harvard Business Review Pr., *(978-0-87584; 978-1-57851; 978-1-59139; 978-1-4221; 978-1-62527; 978-1-63369)* 60 Harvard Way, Boston, MA 02163 USA (SAN 202-277X) Tel 617-783-7400; 617 495 6181; Fax: 617-783-7492; Toll Free: 888-500-1016 6-19-01 faxed 2nd prefix app, charge, KC
E-mail: corpcustserv@hbsp.harvard.edu
Web site: http://www.hbsp.harvard.edu; http://www.harvardbusinessonline.com.

Harvard Business School Press, *See* **Harvard Business Review Pr.**

Harvard Univ. Art Museums Shop, 32 Quincy St., Cambridge, MA 02138 USA (SAN 111-3372) Tel 617-495-8286; Fax: 617-495-9985
E-mail: appleyar@fas.harvard.edu
Web site: http://www.artmuseums.harvard.edu.

Harvard Univ. Pr., *(978-0-674; 978-0-916724; 978-0-935617)* Orders Addr.: c/o Triliteral LLC, 100 Maple Ridge Dr., Cumberland, RI 02864 USA Tel 401-531-2800; Fax: 401-531-2801; Toll Free Fax: 800-406-9145; Toll Free: 800-405-1619; 800-448-2242; Edit Addr.: 79 Garden St., Cambridge, MA 02138 USA (SAN 200-2043) Tel 617-495-2600; Fax: 617-495-5898
E-mail: contact_hup@harvard.edu
Web site: http://www.hup.harvard.edu.

Harvest Distributors, *See* **ARVEST**

Hastings Bks., *(978-0-940846)* 116 N. Wayne Ave., Wayne, PA 19087 USA (SAN 205-048X).

Haven Distributors, 5456 N. Damen Ave., Chicago, IL 60625 USA.

Hawaiian Magazine Distributor, 3375 Koapaka St., No. D180, Honolulu, HI 96819-1865 USA (SAN 169-1619).

Hay Hse., Inc., *(978-0-937611; 978-0-945923; 978-1-56170; 978-1-891751; 978-1-58825; 978-1-4019)* Orders Addr.: P.O. Box 5100, Carlsbad, CA 92018-5100 USA (SAN 630-477X) Tel 760-431-7695 ext 112; Fax: 760-431-6948; Toll Free Fax: 800-650-5115 (orders only); Toll Free: 800-654-5126 (orders only); 2776 Loker Ave. W, Carlsbad, CA 92010 USA (SAN 257-3024) Tel 800-654-5126; Fax: 800-650-5115; 2776 Loker Ave. W., Carlsbad, CA 92010
E-mail: kjohnson@hayhouse.com; pcrowe@hayhouse.com
Web site: http://www.hayhouse.com.

Hazelden, *(978-0-89486; 978-0-89638; 978-0-935908; 978-0-942421; 978-1-56246; 978-1-56838; 978-1-59285; 978-1-61649)* 15251 Pleasant Valley Rd., P.o. Box 176, Center City, MN 55012-0176 USA (SAN 209-4010) Fax: 651-213-4044; Toll Free: 800-328-9000; P.O. Box 176, RW4, Center City, MN 55012 Tel 651-213-4000; Toll Free: 800-328-9000
E-mail: bosterbauer@hazelden.org
Web site: http://www.hazelden.org.

Hazelden Publishing & Educational Services, *See* **Hazelden**

Health and Growth Assocs., *(978-0-9630266)* Orders Addr.: 28195 Fairview Ave., Hemet, CA 92544 USA Tel 951-927-1768; Fax: 951-927-1548
E-mail: flloomis@earthlink.net.

Health Communications, Inc., *(978-0-932194; 978-1-55874; 978-0-7573; 978-0-9910732)* Orders Addr.: 3201 SW 15th St., Deerfield Beach, FL 33442-8190 USA (SAN 212-100X) Tel 954-360-0909; Fax: 954-360-0034; Toll Free: 800-441-5569 Do not confuse with Health Communications, Inc., Edison, NJ
E-mail: terip@hcibooks.com; lorig@hcibooks.com
Web site: http://www.hcibooks.com.

Hearst Distribution Group, Incorporated, Book Division, *See* **Comag Marketing Group**

Heartland Bk. Co., 10195 N. Lake Ave., Olathe, KS 66061 USA (SAN 631-2497) Tel 913-829-1784.

Heffernan Audio Visual, Orders Addr.: P.O. Box 5906, San Antonio, TX 78201-0906 USA Tel 210-732-4333; Fax:

210-732-5906; Edit Addr.: 435 Isom Rd. Ste. 210, San Antonio, TX 78216-5144 USA (SAN 166-8722) E-mail: sales@heffernanav.com Web site: http://www.heffernanav.com.

Heffernan School Supply, *See* **Heffernan Audio Visual**

Heinecken & Assoc., Ltd., 1733 N. Mohawk, Chicago, IL 60614 USA Toll Free Fax: 800-947-5694; Toll Free: 800-449-0138.

.Heinemann-Raintree, *See* **Heinemann-Raintree**

Heinemann-Raintree, *(978-0-431; 978-1-57572; 978-1-58810; 978-1-4034; 978-1-4109; 978-1-4329; 978-1-4846)* Div. of Capstone, Orders Addr.: 1710 Roe Crest Dr., North Mankato, MN 56003 USA Toll Free Fax: 888-844-5329; Toll Free: 800-747-4992; Halley Court Freepost PO Box 1125, Oxford, OX2 8YY E-mail: k.monyhan@coughlancompanies.com; customerservice@capstonepub.com Web site: http://www.heinemannlibrary.com/; http://www.capstonepub.com; http://www.capstoneclassroom.com.

Heirloom Bible Pubs., *(978-0-9817263)* Orders Addr.: P.O. Box 118, Wichita, KS 67201-0118 USA (SAN 630-2793) Fax: 316-267-1850; Toll Free: 800-676-2448; Edit Addr.: 9020 E. 35th St. N., Wichita, KS 67226-2017 USA.

Helix, 310 S. Racine St., Chicago, IL 60607 USA (SAN 111-915X) Tel 312-421-6000; Fax: 312-421-1586.

Hemed Books, Incorporated, *See* **Lambda Pubs., Inc.**

Hendrick-Long Publishing Co., *(978-0-937460; 978-1-885777)* Orders Addr.: 10635 Tower Oaks, Suite D, Houston, TX 77070 USA (SAN 281-7756) Toll Free: 800-544-3770; Edit Addr.: 10635 Tower Oaks Blvd., Houston, TX 77070-5927 USA (SAN 281-7748) E-mail: hendrick-long@worldnet.att.net Web site: http://www.hendricklongpublishing.com.

Herald Pr., *(978-0-8361; 978-1-5138)* Div. of MennoMedia, Inc., Orders Addr.: 1251 Virginia Ave., Harrisonburg, VA 22802 USA (SAN 202-2915) Fax: 1-316-283-0454; Toll Free: 1-800-245-7894; 800-631-6535 (Canada only) Do not confuse with Herald Pr., Charlotte, NC E-mail: info@mennomedia.org Web site: http://www.mennomedia.org.

Herald Publishing Hse., *(978-0-8309)* Orders Addr.: P.O. Box 390, Independence, MO 64051-0390 USA Tel 816-521-3015; Fax: 816-521-3066 (customer services); Toll Free: 800-767-8181; Edit Addr.: 1001W. Walnut St., Independence, MO 64051-0390 USA (SAN 111-7556) Tel 816-257-0200 E-mail: sales@HeraldHouse.org Web site: http://www.heraldhouse.org.

Heritage Bookstore, Orders Addr.: P.O. Box 6007, Springfield, MO 65801-6007 USA (SAN 111-7696).

Hertzberg-New Method Inc., 617 E. Vandalia Rd., Ebooks, Jacksonville, IL 62650 USA (SAN 780-0479) Tel 217-243-5451.

Hervey's Booklink & Cookbook Warehouse, P.O. Box 831870, Richardson, TX 75083 USA (SAN 630-9747).

Hesteria Records & Publishing Co., 124 Hagar Ct., Santa Cruz, CA 95064 USA Tel 831-459-2575; Fax: 831-457-2917 E-mail: alissa@aainnovators.com Web site: http://www.aainnovators.com.

Hi Jolly Library Service, 150 N. Gay St., Susanville, CA 96130-3902 USA (SAN 133-5944).

Hibel, Edna Studio, P.O. Box 9967, Riviera Beach, FL 33419 USA (SAN 111-1574) Tel 561-848-9640; Toll Free: 800-275-3426.

Hicks News Agency, Incorporated, *See* **NEWSouth Distributors**

High Peak Bks., *(978-1-884709)* Orders Addr.: P.O. Box 703, Wilson, WY 83014 USA (SAN 299-4232); Edit Addr.: 355 N. Bar Y Rd., Jackson, WY 83011 USA Tel 307-739-0147 Do not confuse with High Peak Pr. in Schenectady, NY.

Hill City News Agency, Inc., 3228 Odd Fellow Rd., Lynchburg, VA 24501 USA (SAN 169-8656) Tel 804-845-4231; Fax: 804-845-0864.

Hillcrest Publishing Group, Inc., *(978-0-9723806; 978-0-9744668; 978-0-9754803; 978-0-9764981; 978-1-934248; 978-0-9798246; 978-0-9798467; 978-0-9799120; 978-1-934937; 978-1-934938; 978-0-9802455; 978-0-9802456; 978-1-935097; 978-1-935098; 978-1-935204; 978-0-9820938; 978-1-935456; 978-1-936107; 978-1-936183; 978-0-9841965; 978-1-936198; 978-1-936400; 978-1-936401; 978-0-9846204; 978-0-9846205; 978-1-937003; 978-1-936780; 978-1-936782; 978-1-937293; 978-1-937563; 978-1-937600; 978-1-937860; 978-0-9848028; 978-1-937928; 978-) 212 3rd Ave. N., Suite 290, Minneapolis, MN 55401-2420 USA Toll Free: 888-645-2489* E-mail: paigen@twoharborspress.com; paigen@jabberwocky-books.com; paigen@seraphinapress.com Web site: http://www.seraphinapress.com; http://www.jabberwocky-books.com; http://www.langdonstreetpress.com; http://www.bascomhillpublishing.com; http://www.twoharborspress.com; http://www.millicitypress.net/.

Hillsboro News, Orders Addr.: P.O. Box 25738, Tampa, FL 33622-5738 USA Tel 813-622-8087; Edit Addr.: 7002 Parke E. Blvd., Tampa, FL 33610 USA.

Himber Bks., Div. of F. C. Himber & Son's, Inc., 1380 W. Second Ave., Eugene, OR 97402 USA Tel 541-686-8003; Toll Free: 800-888-5904.

Himber, F. C., *See* **Himber Bks.**

Hinrichs, E. Louis, P.O. Box 1090, Lompoc, CA 93438-1090 USA (SAN 133-1493) Tel 805-736-7512 E-mail: booklompoc@aol.com.

Hinsdale County Historical Society, P.O. Box 353 130 N. Silver St., Lake City, CO 81235 USA Tel 970-944-2050.

Historic Aviation Bks., 121 Fifth Ave., Suite 300, New Brighton, MN 55112 USA (SAN 129-5284) Tel 651-635-0100; Fax: 651-635-0700.

Historic Cherry Hill, *(978-0-943366)* 523 1/2 S. Pearl St., Albany, NY 12202 USA (SAN 110-8859) Tel 518-434-4791; Fax: 518-434-4806.

Hobbies Hawaii Distributors, 4420 Lawehana St., No. 3, Honolulu, HI 96818 USA (SAN 630-8619) Tel 808-423-0265; Fax: 808-423-1635.

Holiday Enterprises, Inc., 3328 US Hwy. 123, Rochester Bldg., Greenville, SC 29611 USA (SAN 169-779X) Tel 864-220-3161; Fax: 864-295-9757.

Holt, Henry & Co., *(978-0-03; 978-0-8050)* Div. of Holtzbrinck Publishers, Orders Addr.: 16365 James Madison Hwy., Gordonsville, VA 22942-8501 USA Toll Free Fax: 800-672-2054; Toll Free: 888-330-8477; Edit Addr.: 115 W. 18th St., 5th Flr., New York, NY 10011 USA (SAN 200-6472) Tel 212-886-9200; Fax: 540-672-7540 (customer service) E-mail: info@hholt.com Web site: http://www.henryholt.com.

Holtzbrinck Publishers, *See* **Macmillan**

Holyoke News Co., Inc., 720 Main St., P.O. Box 990, Holyoke, MA 01041 USA (SAN 169-3468) Tel 413-534-4537; Fax: 413-538-7161; Toll Free: 800-628-8372 E-mail: sales@holyoke-news.com.

Homestead Book Co., *(978-0-930180)* Orders Addr.: P.O. Box 31608, Seattle, WA 98103 USA (SAN 662-037X); Edit Addr.: 6101 22nd Ave., NW, Seattle, WA 98107 USA (SAN 169-8796) Tel 206-782-4532; Fax: 206-784-9328; Toll Free: 800-426-6777 (orders only) E-mail: info@homesteadbook.com Web site: http://www.homesteadbook.com.

Homestead Book, Incorporated, *See* **Homestead Book Co.**

Hood, Alan C. & Co., Inc., *(978-0-911469)* P.O. Box 775, Chambersburg, PA 17201 USA (SAN 270-8221) Tel 717-267-0867; Fax: 717-267-0572; Toll Free Fax: 888-844-9433; 4501 Forbes Blvd., Lanham, MD 20706 E-mail: hoodbooks@pa.net Web site: http://www.hoodbooks.com.

Hoover Institution Pr., *(978-0-8179)* Stanford Univ., Stanford, CA 94305-6010 USA (SAN 202-3024) Tel 650-723-3373; Fax: 650-723-8626; Toll Free: 800-935-2882 E-mail: scott.harrison@stanford.edu Web site: http://www.hooverpress.org.

Hopkins Fulfillment Services, P.O. Box 50370, Baltimore, MD 21211-4370 USA Fax: 410-516-6998; Toll Free: 800-537-5487.

Hotho & Co., P.O. Box 9738, Fort Worth, TX 76147-2738 USA (SAN 169-8192).

Houghton Mifflin Company, *See* **Houghton Mifflin Harcourt Publishing Co.**

Houghton Mifflin Company Trade & Reference Division, *See* **Houghton Mifflin Harcourt Trade & Reference Pubs.**

Houghton Mifflin Harcourt Publishing Co., *(978-0-395; 978-0-87466; 978-0-9631591; 978-1-57630; 978-1-881527; 978-0-618; 978-0-544; 978-0-547; 978-1-328)* Orders Addr.: 9205 Southpark Ctr. Loop, Orlando, FL 32819 USA Toll Free: 800-225-3362; Edit Addr.: 222 Berkeley St., Boston, MA 02116 USA (SAN 215-3793) Tel 617-351-5000 Web site: http://www.hmco.com.

Houghton Mifflin Harcourt Supplemental Pubs., *(978-1-60032; 978-1-60277)* 10801 N. Mopac Expressway, Bldg. 3, Austin, TX 78759 USA Web site: http://www.harcourtachieve.com.

Houghton Mifflin Harcourt Trade & Reference Pubs., *(978-0-395; 978-0-89919; 978-0-618)* Orders Addr.: 9205 Southpark Ctr. Loop, Orlando, FL 32819 USA Tel 978-661-1300; Toll Free: 800-225-3362; Edit Addr.: 222 Berkeley St., Boston, MA 02116 USA (SAN 200-2388) Tel 617-351-5000; Fax: 617-227-5409; 215 Park Ave S., 12th Flr., New York, NY 10003-1621 E-mail: trade_sub_rights@hmco.com Web site: http://www.hmco.com/; http://www.houghtonmifflinbooks.com.

Houston Paperback Distributor, 4114 Gairloch Ln., Houston, TX 77025-2912 USA (SAN 169-8273).

Hovel Audio, Incorporated, *See* **christianaudio**

How-2 Bks., P.O. Box 5793, Denver, CO 80217 USA (SAN 631-1369) Tel 303-778-8383; Toll Free: 800-279-7323.

HPK Educational Resource Ctr., *(978-0-89895)* Div. of H. P. Koppelmann, Inc., 140 Van Block Ave., Hartford, CT 06141 USA (SAN 169-071X) Tel 860-549-6210; Toll Free: 800-243-7724.

Hubbard, P.O. Box 100, Defiance, OH 43512 USA (SAN 169-6726) Tel 419-784-4455; Fax: 419-782-1662; Toll Free: 800-582-0657 E-mail: hubbard@bright.net.

Hudson County News Co., 1305 Paterson Plank Rd., North Bergen, NJ 07047 USA (SAN 169-4782) Tel 201-867-3600.

Hudson Hills Pr. LLC, *(978-0-933920; 978-0-9646042; 978-1-55595)* Orders Addr.: P.O. Box 205, Manchester, VT 05254 USA; Edit Addr.: 74-2 Union St., Manchester, VT 05254 USA (SAN 213-0815) Tel 802-362-6450; Fax: 802-362-6459 E-mail: artbooks@hudsonhills.com Web site: http://www.hudsonhills.com/.

Hudson Hills Press, Incorporated, *See* **Hudson Hills Pr. LLC**

Hudson Valley News Distributors, P.O. Box 1236, Newburgh, NY 12550 USA (SAN 169-6084) Tel 914-562-3399; Fax: 914-562-6010.

Humanics Publishing Group, *See* **Green Dragon Bks.**

Hyperion Pr., *(978-0-7868; 978-1-56282; 978-1-4013)* Div. of Disney Bk. Publishing, Inc., A Walt Disney Co., Orders Addr.: c/o HarperCollins Publishers, 1000 Keystone Industrial Park, Scranton, PA 18512-4621 USA Toll Free: 800-242-7737; Edit Addr.: 114 Fifth Ave., New York, NY 110011 USA Tel 917-661-2000 Web site: http://www.hyperionbooks.com.

I. b. d., Ltd., *(978-0-88431)* 24 Hudson St., Kinderhook, NY 12106 USA (SAN 630-7779) Tel 518-758-1755; Fax: 518-758-6702 E-mail: lankhof@ibdltd.com Web site: http://www.ibdltd.com.

I S H K, *(978-0-86304; 978-0-900860; 978-1-883536; 978-1-933779; 978-1-942698)* Div. of Institute for the Study of Human Knowledge, Orders Addr.: P.O. Box 381069, Cambridge, MA 02238-1069 USA (SAN 226-4536) Tel 617-497-4124; Fax: 617-500-0268; Toll Free Fax: 800-223-4200; Toll Free: 800-222-4745; Edit Addr.: P.O. Box 176, Los Altos, CA 94023 USA Tel 650-948-9428 E-mail: ishkbooks@aol.com Web site: http://www.ishkbooks.com.

Iaconi, Mariuccia Bk. Imports, *(978-0-9628720)* P.O. Box 77023, San Francisco, CA 94107-0023 USA (SAN 161-1364) Toll Free: 800-955-9577 E-mail: mibibook@ixnetcom.com Web site: http://www.mibibook.com.

ICG Muse, Inc., 420 W. 42nd St. Apt. 35B, New York, NY 10036-6863 USA (SAN 631-7200).

Icon Distribution, 3325 Donnell Dr., Forestville, MD 20747 USA.

ID International Bk. Service, 126 Old Ridgefield Rd., Wilton, CT 06897-3017 USA (SAN 630-8074) Tel 203-834-2272; Fax: 203-762-9725 E-mail: orders@idintl.com.

Idaho News Agency, 2710 Julia St., Coeur D'Alene, ID 83814 USA (SAN 169-1651) Tel 208-664-3444.

Ideal Foreign Bks., Inc., 132-10 Hillside Ave., Richmond Hill, NY 11418 USA (SAN 169-6173) Tel 718-297-7477; Fax: 718-297-7645; Toll Free: 800-284-2490 (orders only).

Ideals Publishing Corporation, *See* **Ideals Pubns.**

Ideals Pubns., *(978-0-8249; 978-0-89542)* Div. of Guideposts, Orders Addr.: 2630 Elm Hill Pike., Suite 100, Nashville, TN 37214 USA E-mail: hhulse@guideposts.org Web site: http://www.idealsbooks.com.

IFSTA, *(978-0-87939; 978-1-56916)* Orders Addr.: c/o Oklahoma State Univ., Fire Protection Pubns., 930 N. Willis, Stillwater, OK 74078-8045 USA Tel 405-744-5723; Fax: 405-744-8204; Toll Free: 800-654-4055 (orders only) Web site: http://www.ifsta.org/.

Ignatius Pr., *(978-0-89870; 978-1-58617; 978-1-62164; 978-1-68149)* Orders Addr.: P.O. Box 1339, Fort Collins, CO 80522-1339 USA (SAN 855-3556) Tel 970-221-3920; Fax: 970-221-3964; Toll Free Fax: 800-278-3566; Toll Free: 877-320-9276 (bookstore orders); 800-651-1531 (credit card orders, no minimum, individual orders); Edit Addr.: 1348 10th Ave., San Francisco, CA 94122 USA (SAN 214-3887) Toll Free: 800-651-1531 E-mail: info@ignatius.com Web site: http://www.ignatius.com.

Igram Pr., *(978-0-911119; 978-1-930279)* 311 Parsons Dr., Hiawatha, IA 52233 USA (SAN 263-1709) Tel 319-393-3600; Fax: 319-393-3934; Toll Free: 800-393-2399 E-mail: clabarr@cedargraphicsinc.com.

Illinois News Service, *See* **News Group - Illinois, The**

Ilmhouse Inc., P.O. Box 74, Haverford, PA 19041-0074 USA E-mail: admin@ilmhouse.com Web site: http://www.ilmhouse.com.

Image Processing Software, Inc., *(978-0-924507)* 6409 Appalachian Way, Madison, WI 53705 USA (SAN 265-5977) Tel 608-233-5033; 4414 Regent St., Madison, WI 53705 (SAN 249-3020).

Impact Photographics, *(978-0-918327; 978-1-56540; 978-1-60068)* 4961 Windplay Dr., Eldorado Hills, CA 95630 USA (SAN 657-3126) Tel 916-939-9333; Fax: 916-939-9334; Toll Free: 800-950-0110 E-mail: juliem@impactphotographics.com Web site: http://www.impactphotographics.com.

Imperial News Co., Inc., 5131 Post Rd., Dublin, OH 43017-1160 USA (SAN 169-5509) Fax: 516-752-8515.

Imported Bks., Orders Addr.: St., Dallas, TX 75208 USA (SAN 169-8095) Tel 214-941-6497.

Incor Periodicals, 32150 Hwy. 34, Tangent, OR 97389-9704 USA (SAN 169-7072) Tel 541-926-8889; Fax: 541-926-9553.

Independent Magazine Co., 2970 N. Ontario St., Burbank, CA 91504-2016 USA (SAN 159-8783).

Independent Pubs. Group, *(978-1-4956)* Subs. of Chicago Review Pr., 814 N. Franklin, Chicago, IL 60610 USA (SAN 201-2936) Tel 312-337-0747; Fax: 312-337-5985; Toll Free: 800-888-4741 E-mail: frontdesk@ipgbook.com Web site: http://www.ipgbook.com; http://www.trafalgarsquarepublishing.com.

Indiana Periodicals, Inc., 2120 S. Meridian St., Indianapolis, IN 46225 USA (SAN 169-2380) Tel 317-786-1488; Fax: 317-782-4999.

Indiana Univ. Pr., *(978-0-253; 978-0-86196)* 601 N. Morton St., Bloomington, IN 47404-3797 USA (SAN 202-5647) Fax: 812-855-7931; Toll Free: 800-842-6796 E-mail: iuporder@indiana.edu Web site: http://www.iupress.indiana.edu.

Indig, Stanley M. Specialty Pubn., *(978-0-945815; 978-1-57767)* 2173 E. 38th St., Brooklyn, NY 11234 USA (SAN 248-0719) Tel 718-692-0648; Fax: 718-677-9542 E-mail: indigpublishing@yahoo.com; indigpublishing@aol.com Web site: http://www.indigpublishing.com.

Ingenix, Incorporated, *See* **OptumInsight, Inc.**

Ingham Publishing, Inc., *(978-0-9611804; 978-1-891130)* Orders Addr.: P.O. Box 12642, Saint Petersburg, FL 33733-2642 USA Tel 813-343-4811; Fax: 813-381-2807; Edit Addr.: 5650 First Ave., N., Saint Petersburg, FL 33710 USA (SAN 112-8930) E-mail: ftreflex@concentric.net.

Ingram Bk. Co., *(978-1-61522; 978-1-60894)* Subs. of Ingram Industries, Inc., Orders Addr.: 1 Ingram Blvd., P.O. Box 3006, La Vergne, TN 37086-1986 USA (SAN 169-7978) Tel 615-213-5000; Fax: 615-213-3976 (Electronic Orders); Toll Free Fax: 800-285-3296 (fax inquiry US & Canada); 800-876-0186 (orders); 877-663-5367 (Canadian orders); Toll Free: 800-937-8000 (orders only); 800-937-8200 (customer service US & Canada); 800-289-0687 (Canadian orders only customer service); 800-234-6737 (electronic orders US & Canada)) Do not confuse with Ingram Pr., Sacramento, CA E-mail: flashback@ingrambook.com; customerservice@ingrambook.com; ics-sales@ingrambook.com Web site: http://www.ingrambook.com.

Ingram Content Group Inc., 1 Ingram Blvd., La Vergne, TN 37086 USA Tel 615-793-5000; Toll Free: 800-937-8000 (option 3) E-mail: inquiry@ingramcontent.com; customerservice@ingramcontent.com Web site: http://www.ingramcontent.com.

Ingram Entertainment, Inc., Two Ingram Blvd. (Corp. Headquarters), La Vergne, TN 37089-7006 USA (SAN 630-6780) Tel 615-287-4000; Fax: 615-287-4995; Toll Free: 800-759-5000; 12000 Ridgemont Dr., Urbandale, IA 50323-2317 (SAN 630-6950); 26391 Curtiss Wright Pkwy. Ste. 106, Cleveland, OH 44143-4401 (SAN 630-6896) Toll Free: 800-621-1333; 15002 Sommermeyer, Houston, TX 77041-5333 (SAN 630-7000) Tel 713-937-3600; Fax: 713-466-4316; 382 E. Lies Rd., Carol Stream, IL 60188-9418 (SAN 630-690X) Toll Free: 800-621-1333; 7911 NE 33rd Dr., Suite 270, Portland, OR 97211-1920 (SAN 630-7116) Tel 503-281-2673; Fax: 503-284-6046; 23 Monte Vista Ave., Larkspur, CA 94939-2120 (SAN 630-6993) Toll Free: 800-621-1333; 2611 S. Roosevelt, Suite 102, Tempe, AZ 85282-2017 (SAN 630-7094) Tel 602-966-6691; Fax: 602-894-0329; 4703 Fulton Industrial Blvd., Atlanta, GA 30336-2017 (SAN 630-6845) Tel 404-691-6280; Fax: 404-696-3944; 400 Airport Executive Pk., Spring Valley, NY 10977-7404 (SAN 630-7078) Tel 914-425-3191; Fax: 914-425-7521; 7949 Woodley Blvd., Van Nuys, CA 91406 (SAN 630-7183) Tel 818-375-5027; Fax: 818-375-5001; 1293 Heil Quaker Blvd., Suite B, P.O. Box 7006, La Vergne, TN 37086-7006 (SAN 630-7051) Fax: 615-793-6196; Toll Free: 800-688-3110; 3675 Crestwood Pkwy NW Ste. 105, Duluth, GA 30096-5045 (SAN 630-6853) Toll Free: 800-876-0832; 3114 S. 24th St., Kansas City, KS 66106-4709 (SAN 630-7027) Tel 913-362-0391; Fax: 913-362-0605; Toll Free: 800-621-1333; 6635 NE 59th Pl., Portland, OR 97218-2709 (SAN 630-7124) Tel 503-284-3313; Fax: 503-284-3876; Toll Free: 800-876-0834; 7319 Innovation Blvd., Fort Wayne, IN 46818-1371 (SAN 630-6985) Fax: 219-489-8850; Toll Free: 800-759-5588; 8779 Greenwood Pl., Savage, MD 20763 (SAN 630-7019) Tel 301-490-1166; Fax: 301-490-0031; Toll Free: 800-621-1333; 1521 W. Copans Rd., Suite 105, Pompano Beach, FL 33064 (SAN 630-7108) Tel 954-971-5412; Fax: 954-971-3113; Toll Free: 800-888-3876; 20435 E. Business Pkwy., Walnut, CA 91789-2999 (SAN 630-7191) Tel 714-594-6569; Fax: 714-595-0735; Toll Free: 800-759-4422; 2 Ingram Blvd., La Vergne, TN 37086-3638 (SAN 630-6837) Toll Free: 800-621-1333; 1349 Charwood Rd., Hanover, MD 21076-3114 (SAN 630-6861) Tel 410-850-9191; Fax: 410-850-9229; 110 Shawmut Rd., Canton, MA 02021-1412 (SAN 630-687X) Tel 617-575-9585; Fax: 617-575-9586; 100 Dobbs Ln., Suite 206, Cherry Hill, NJ 08034-1435 (SAN 630-6888) Tel 609-428-8668; Fax: 609-428-8536; Toll Free: 800-288-7565; 11235 Knott Ave., Suite C, Cypress, CA 90630-5401 (SAN 630-6918) Tel 714-373-8855; Fax: 714-373-8858; Toll Free: 800-759-4422; 1430 Bradley Ln., No. 102, Carrollton, TX 75007-4855 (SAN 630-6926) Tel 214-245-6088; Fax: 214-323-3890; Toll Free: 800-621-1333; 2259 Merritt Dr., Garland, TX 75041-6138 (SAN 630-6934) Tel 214-840-6621; Fax: 214-840-3357; Toll Free: 800-727-0688; 10990 E. 55th Ave., Denver, CO 80239-2007 (SAN 630-6942) Tel 303-371-8372; Fax: 303-373-4583; 35245 Schoolcraft, Livonia, MI 48150-1209 (SAN 630-6969) Tel 313-422-9955; Fax: 313-422-1171; 3540 NW 56th St., Fort Lauderdale, FL 33309-2260 (SAN 630-6977) Tel 305-733-7440; Fax: 305-735-7752; 6733 S. Sepulveda, Suite 108, Los Angeles, CA 90045-1525 (SAN 630-7035) Tel 213-410-4067; Fax: 213-410-0919; Toll Free: 800-759-4422; 9549 Penn Ave S. Ste. 200, Minneapolis, MN 55431-2565 (SAN 630-7043) Toll Free: 800-825-3112; 25 Branca Rd., East Rutherford, NJ 07073-2121 (SAN 630-706X) Tel 201-933-9797; Fax: 201-933-5139; Toll Free: 800-621-1333; 5576 Inland Empire Blvd, Bldg. G, Suite A, Ontario, CA 91764-5117 (SAN 630-7086) Tel 714-948-7998; Fax: 714-948-9778; Freeport Ctr., Bldg. H-12 N., P.O. Box 1387, Clearfield, UT 84016-1387 (SAN 630-7132) Tel 801-775-0555; Fax: 801-773-8172; 2700 Merchantile Dr., Suite 100, Rancho Cordova, CA 95742-6574 (SAN 630-7140) Tel 916-638-8090; Fax: 916-638-8021; Toll Free: 800-866-1568; 4660 Viewridge Ave., Suite B, San Diego, CA 92123-1638 (SAN 630-7159) Tel 619-569-9816; Fax: 619-569-1542; Toll Free: 800-365-5229; 6411 S. 216th, Bldg. F, Kent, WA 98032-1392 (SAN 630-7167) Tel 206-395-3515; Fax: 206-395-0650; 445 W. Freedom Ave., Orange, CA 92865 (SAN 630-7175) Tel 714-282-1232; Fax: 714-282-2245; 201 Ingram Dr., Roseburg, OR 97470;

Wholesaler & Distributor Name Index

12600 SE Hwy. 212, Bldg. B, Clackamas, OR 97015-9081 Tel 615-287-4000
Web site: http://www.ingramentertainment.com.

Ingram Pub. Services, Orders Addr.: Customer Services, Box 512 1 Ingram Blvd., LaVergne, TN 37086 USA Toll Free Fax: 800-838-1149; Edit Addr.: 1 Ingram Blvd., LaVergne, TN 37086 USA (SAN 631-8630) Tel 615-793-5000; Fax: 615-213-5811
E-mail: customer.service@ingrampublisherservices.com; Publisher@ingrampublisherservices.com; Retailer@ingrampublisherservices.com
Web site: http://www.ingrampublisherservices.com.

Ingram Software, Subs. of Ingram Distribution Group, Inc., 1759 Wehrle, Williamsville, NY 14221 USA (SAN 285-760X) Toll Free: 800-828-7250; 900 W. Walnut Ave., Compton, CA 90220 (SAN 285-7073).

INgrooves, *See* **INscribe Digital**

Inland Empire Periodicals, *See* **Incor Periodicals**

Inner Traditions International, Ltd., *(978-0-89281; 978-1-59477; 978-1-62055)* Orders Addr.: P.O. Box 388, Rochester, VT 05767-0388 USA Tel 802-767-3174; Fax: 802-767-3726; Toll Free Fax: 800-246-8648; Edit Addr.: One Park St., Rochester, VT 05767 USA (SAN 208-6948) Tel 802-767-3174; Fax: 802-767-3726
E-mail: customerservice@innertraditions.com; info@innertraditions.com
Web site: http://www.innertraditions.com.

Innovative Logistics, Orders Addr.: 575 Prospect St., Lakewood, NJ 08701 USA (SAN 760-6532) Tel 732-534-7001; 732-363-5679; Fax: 732-363-0338
E-mail: innlogorders@innlog.net
Web site: http://www.innlog.net.

INscribe Digital, *(978-1-61750; 978-1-62517)* 55 Francisco St. Suite 710, San Francisco, CA 94105 USA
E-mail: digitalpublishing@ingrooves.com
Web site: http://www.INscribeDigital.com.

Insight Guides, *(978-0-88729; 978-1-58573)* 46-35 54th Rd., Maspeth, NY 11378 USA Tel 718-784-0055; Fax: 718-784-1246
E-mail: customerservice@americanmap.com
Web site: http://www.americanmap.com.

Insight Publishing, *(978-0-9663550)* Orders Addr.: P.O. Box 32383, Jacksonville, FL 32237 USA Tel 904-262-9975; Fax: 904-262-3220; Edit Addr.: 5417 Autumnbrook Trail, N., Jacksonville, FL 32258 USA Do not confuse with companies with the same name in Yreka, CA, Parker, CO, Woodbridge, VA, Salt Lake City, UT, Tulsa, OK
E-mail: 102502.2561@compuserve.com.

Instructional Video, 2219 C St., Lincoln, NE 68502 USA (SAN 631-6115) Tel 402-475-6570; 402 475 6570; Fax: 402-475-6500; Toll Free: 800-228-0164 Do not confuse with Instructional Video in Golden, CO
E-mail: Kathy@insvideo.com
Web site: http://www.insvideo.com.

Integral Yoga Pubns., *(978-0-932040; 978-1-938477)* Satchidananda Ashram-Yogaville, 108 Yogaville Way, Buckingham, VA 23921 USA (SAN 285-0338) Tel 434-969-3121 ex 102; Fax: 434-969-1303; Toll Free: 800-262-1008 (orders)
Web site: http://www.yogaville.org.

Interlink Publishing Group, Inc., *(978-0-940793; 978-1-56656; 978-1-62371)* 46 Crosby St., Northampton, MA 01060-1804 USA (SAN 664-8908) Tel 413-582-7054; Fax: 413-582-6731; Toll Free: 800-238-5465
E-mail: info@interlinkbooks.com; editor@interlinkbooks.com
Web site: http://www.interlinkbooks.com.

InterMountain Periodical Distributors, *See* **Majic Enterprises**

International Bk. Ctr., Inc., *(978-0-86685; 978-0-917062)* 2007 Laurel Dr., P.O. Box 295, Troy, MI 48099 USA (SAN 169-4014) Tel 248-879-7920; 586-254-7230; Fax: 586-254-7230
E-mail: ibc@ibcbooks.com
Web site: http://www.ibcbooks.com.

International Magazine Service, Div. of Periodical Pubs. Service Bureau, 1 N. Superior St., Sandusky, OH 44870 USA (SAN 285-9955) Tel 419-626-0623.

International Networking Assn., 4130 Citrus Ave., Suite 5, Rocklin, CA 95677 USA (SAN 631-1857).

International Periodical Distributors, 674 Via de la Valle, Suite 204, Solana Beach, CA 92075 USA (SAN 250-5290) Tel 619-481-5928; Toll Free: 800-999-1170; 800-228-5144 (in Canada).

International Pubns. Service, *(978-0-8002)* Div. of Taylor & Francis, Inc., Orders Addr.: 325 Chestnut St., 8th Flr., Levittown, PA 19057-4700 USA Fax: 215-785-5515; Toll Free: 800-821-8312.

International Readers League, Div. of Periodical Pubs. Service Bureau, 1 N. Superior St., Sandusky, OH 44870 USA (SAN 285-9971) Tel 419-626-0633.

International Service Co., International Service Bldg., 333 Fourth Ave., Indialantic, FL 32903-4295 USA (SAN 169-5134) Tel 407-724-1443 (phone/fax).

International Specialized Bk. Services, 920 NE 58th Ave., Suite 300, Portland, OR 97213-3786 USA (SAN 169-7129) Tel 503-287-3093; Fax: 503-280-8832; Toll Free: 800-944-6190
E-mail: info@isbs.com
Web site: http://www.isbs.com.

International Thomson Computer Pr., *(978-1-85032)* Orders Addr.: 7625 Empire Dr., Florence, KY 41042-2978 USA Tel 606-525-6600; Fax: 606-525-7778; Toll Free: 800-842-3636; Edit Addr.: 20 Park Plaza, 13th Flr., Boston, MA 02116 USA Fax: 617-695-1615
E-mail: itcp@itp.thomson.com
Web site: http://www.itcpmedia.com.

Internet Systems, Inc., Subs. of Internet Systems, Inc., 20250 Century Blvd., Germantown, MD 20874 USA (SAN 129-9611) Tel 301-540-5100; Fax: 301-540-5522; Toll Free: 800-638-8725
Web site: http://www.pwl.com/Internet.

Interstate Distributors, 150 Blackstone River Rd. Ste. 4, Worcester, MA 01607-1455 USA (SAN 170-4885) Toll Free: 800-365-6430.

Interstate Periodical Distributors, 201 E. Badger Rd., Madison, WI 53713 USA (SAN 169-9105) Tel 608-277-2407; Fax: 608-277-2410; Toll Free: 800-752-3131.

Intertech Bk. Services, Inc., 25971 Sarazen Dr., South Riding, VA 20152-1741 USA (SAN 630-5253).

Intrepid Group, Inc., The, 1331 Red Cedar Cir., Fort Collins, CO 80524 USA (SAN 631-5429) Tel 970-493-3793; Fax: 970-493-8781
E-mail: intrepid@frii.com.

Iowa & Illinois News, 8645 Northwest Blvd., Davenport, IA 52806-6418 USA (SAN 169-2607).

Irish American Bk. Co., Subs. of Roberts Rinehart Pubs., Inc., P.O. Box 666, Niwot, CO 80544-0666 USA Tel 303-652-2710; Fax: 303-652-2689; Toll Free: 800-452-7115
E-mail: irishbooks@aol.com
Web site: http://www.irishvillage.com.

Irish Bks. & Media, Inc., *(978-0-937702)* Orders Addr.: 2904 41st Ave S., Minneapolis, MN 55406-1814 USA (SAN 111-8870) Toll Free: 800-229-3505 Do not confuse with Irish Bks. in New York, NY
E-mail: Irishbook@aol.com
Web site: http://www.irishbook.com.

Ironside International Pubs., Inc., *(978-0-935554)* Orders Addr.: P.O. Box 1050, Lorton, VA 22199-1050 USA (SAN 206-2380) Tel 703-493-9120; Fax: 703-493-9424; Edit Addr.: P.O. Box 1050, Lorton, VA 22199-1050 USA (SAN 663-656X)
E-mail: info@ironsidepub.com.

ISD, 70 Enterprise Dr., Bristol, CT 06010 USA Tel 860-584-6546; Fax: 860-540-1001.

Islamic Bk. Service, 1209 Cleburne, Hoston, TX 77004 USA (SAN 169-2453) Tel 713-528-1440; Fax: 713-528-1085.

Island Heritage Publishing, *(978-0-89610; 978-0-931548; 978-1-59700)* Div. of The Madden Corp., 94-411 Koaki St., Waipahu, HI 96797 USA (SAN 211-1403) Tel 808-564-8800; Fax: 808-564-8888; Toll Free: 800-468-2800
E-mail: ihorders@welcometotheislands.com
Web site: http://www.welcometotheislands.com.

Islander Group, 269 Pali'i St., Mililani, HI 96789 USA Tel 808-676-0116.

Israel Book Shop, *See* **Israel Bookshop Pubns.**

Israel Bookshop Pubns., *(978-0-9670705; 978-1-931681; 978-1-60091)* 501 Prospect St., No. 97, Lakewood, NJ 08701 USA Tel 732-901-3009; Fax: 732-901-4012; Toll Free: 888-536-7427
E-mail: sales@israelbookshoppublications.com
Web site: http://www.israelbookshoppublications.com.

Itasca Bks., *(978-0-9767054)* Orders Addr.: 5120 Cedar Lake Rd. S., Minneapolis, MN 55416 USA (SAN 855-3823) Tel 952-345-4488; Fax: 952-920-0541; Toll Free: 800-901-3480
E-mail: mjung@itascabooks.com
Web site: http://www.itascabooks.com.

iUniverse, Inc., *(978-0-9665514; 978-1-58348; 978-0-9668591; 978-1-893652; 978-0-595; 978-0-9795279; 978-1-60528; 978-1-4401; 978-1-936236; 978-1-4502; 978-1-4620; 978-1-4697; 978-1-4759; 978-1-4917)* Orders Addr.: 1663 Liberty Dr., Suite 300, Bloomington, IN 47403 USA (SAN 254-9425) Toll Free: 800-288-4677
E-mail: post.production@iuniverse.com; book.orders@iuniverse.com; bethany.dirks@iuniverse.com
Web site: http://www.iUniverse.com; http://iuniverse.com.

iUniverse.com, Incorporated, *See* **iUniverse, Inc.**

J & J Bk. Sales, 24871 Pylos Way, Mission Viejo, CA 92691-4668 USA (SAN 253-8075)
E-mail: jacki@hydrasystems.com
Web site: http://www.divanet.com/matilda.

J & L Bk. Co., Orders Addr.: P.O. Box 13100, Spokane, WA 99213 USA (SAN 129-6817) Fax: 509-534-0152; 509-534-7713; Toll Free: 800-288-9756; Edit Addr.: 1710 Trent, Spokane, WA 99220 USA (SAN 243-2145).

J & N Creations, LLC, 48 First St., N., Sauk Centre, MN 56304 USA Tel 320-352-6260.

Jacobob Pr. Distributing, 11035 Ridge Forest Ct., Saint Louis, MO 63126 USA.

JAGCO & Associates Inc., Orders Addr.: 596 Indian Trail Rd. South #227, Indian Trail, NC 28079 USA Tel 802-223-6565.

Jalmar Pr., *(978-0-915190; 978-0-935266; 978-1-880396; 978-1-931061)* Subs. of B. L. Winch & Assocs., P.O. Box 370, Fawnskin, CA 92333-0370 USA (SAN 113-3640) Toll Free: 800-662-9662 (orders)
E-mail: jalmarpress@att.net
Web site: http://jalmarpress.com.

James & Law Co., Orders Addr.: P.O. Box 2468, Clarksburg, WV 26302-2468 USA (SAN 169-894X); Edit Addr.: Middletown Mall I-79 & U. S. 250, Fairmont, WV 26554 USA (SAN 169-8966) Tel 304-624-7401.

James Trading Group, Limited, The, 13 Highview Ave., Orangeburg, NY 10962-2125 USA Toll Free: 800-541-5004
E-mail: sales@thejamestradinggroup.com.

Janway, 11 Academy Rd., Cogan Station, PA 17728 USA (SAN 108-3708) Tel 717-494-1239; Fax: 717-494-1350; Toll Free: 800-877-5242.

Jawbone Publishing Corp., *(978-0-9702959; 978-1-59094)* 1540 Happy Valley Cir., Newnan, GA 30263-4035 USA (SAN 253-5335)
E-mail: marketing@jawbonepublishing.com
Web site: http://www.jawbonepublishing.com.

Jeanies Classics, *(978-0-9609672)* Orders Addr.: 2123 Oxford St., Rockford, IL 61103 USA (SAN 271-7409); Edit Addr.: 2123 Oxford St., Rockford, IL 61103 USA (SAN 271-7395) Tel 815-968-4544.

Jean's Dulcimer Shop & Crying Creek Pubs., P.O. Box 8, Hwy. 32, Cosby, TN 37722 USA (SAN 249-9282) Tel 423-487-5543.

Jech Distributors, 674 Via De La Valle, No. 204, Solana Beach, CA 92075-2462 USA (SAN 107-0258) Tel 619-452-7251.

Jellyroll Productions, *See* **Osborne Enterprises Publishing**

Jenkins Group, Inc., *(978-1-890587; 978-0-9860224)* 121 E. Front St., 4th Flr., Traverse City, MI 49684 USA Tel 231-933-0445; Fax: 231-933-0448; 1129 Woodmere Ave., Traverse City, MI 49686
Web site: http://www.bookpublishing.com.

JIST Publishing, *(978-0-942784; 978-1-56370; 978-1-57112; 978-1-59357; 978-1-63332)* Div. of EMC Publishing, 875 Montreal Way, Saint Paul, MN 55102 USA (SAN 240-2351) Tel 651-290-2800 Toll Free Fax: 800-547-8329
E-mail: info@jist.com
Web site: http://www.jist.com.

JIST Works, Incorporated, *See* **JIST Publishing**

JMS Distribution, 2017 San Mateo St., Richmond, CA 94804 USA.

Jobson, Oliver H., *(978-0-9764988)* 12171 SW 123rd Pl., Miami, FL 33186 USA (SAN 256-5463) Tel 954-260-4914
E-mail: ojobson@gmail.com
Web site: http://www.gpaonline.com.

Johns Hopkins Univ. Pr., *(978-0-8018; 978-1-4214)* Div. of Johns Hopkins Univ., Orders Addr.: P.O. Box 50370, Baltimore, MD 21211-4370 USA; Edit Addr.: 2715 N. Charles St., Baltimore, MD 21218-4319 USA (SAN 202-7348) Fax: 410-516-4189; Toll Free: 800-537-5487
E-mail: webmaster@press.jhu.edu
Web site: http://muse.jhu.edu/; http://www.press.jhu.edu/books/.

Johnson Bks., *(978-0-917895; 978-0-933472; 978-1-55566)* Div. of Big Earth Publishing Co., Orders Addr.: 1637 Pearl St. Ste. 201, Boulder, CO 80302-5447 USA (SAN 201-0313) Toll Free: 800-258-5830
E-mail: books@bigearthpublishing.com
Web site: http://www.johnsonbooks.com.

Johnson News Agency, P.O. Box 9009, Moscow, ID 83843 USA (SAN 169-1678).

Johnson, Walter J. Inc., *(978-0-8472)* 1 New York Plaza 28th Flr., New York, NY 10004-1901 USA (SAN 209-1828).

Jones, Bob University Press, *See* **BJU Pr.**

Joseph Ruzicka, Incorporated, *See* **Southeast Library Bindery, Inc.**

Journey Pubns., LLC, *(978-0-9671696)* 3443 Esplanade Ave. Apt. 511, New Orleans, LA 70119 USA Do not confuse with companies with the same or similar names in Woodstock, NY, Summerland, CA, Savannah, GA, Avon Park, FL, lacey, WA
E-mail: msl3393@yahoo.com; mlewis@simmonswhite.com.

Joyce Media, Inc., *(978-0-917002)* P.O. Box 57, Acton, CA 93510 USA (SAN 208-7197) Tel 805-269-1169; Fax: 805-269-2139
E-mail: joycemed@pacbell.net
Web site: http://joycemedia.com.

Julia Taylor Ebel, P.O. Box 11, Jamestown, NC 27282 USA
E-mail: ebel@northstate.net.

Junior League of Greensboro Pubns., *(978-0-9605788)* 3101 W. Friendly Ave., Greensboro, NC 27408-7801 USA (SAN 112-9597)
E-mail: Jlgso@aol.com.

Just Us Bks., Inc., *(978-0-940975; 978-1-933491)* 356 Glenwood Ave., 3rd Flr., East Orange, NJ 07017-2108 USA (SAN 664-7413) Tel 973-672-7701
E-mail: justusbook@aol.com
Web site: http://www.justusbooks.com.

K. F. Enterprises, *See* **Production Assocs., Inc.**

K. M. R. Enterprises, *(978-0-9656379)* 5731 Pony Express Trail, Pollock Pines, CA 95726 USA (SAN 299-237X) Tel 530-644-1410.

Kable Media Services, Subs. of AMREP Corp., 505 Park Ave. 7th Fl., New York, NY 10022 USA Tel 212-705-4600; Fax: 212-705-4666; Toll Free: 800-223-6640
E-mail: info@kable.com
Web site: http://www.kable.com/.

Kable News Company, Incorporated, *See* **Kable Media Services**

Kalispell News Agency, P.O. Box 4965, Missoula, MT 59806-4965 USA (SAN 169-4383) Toll Free: 800-955-1266.

Kamkin, Victor, P.O. Box 34583, Bethesda, MD 20827-0583 USA Toll Free: 800-852-6546; 925 Broadway, New York, NY 10010 (SAN 113-7395) Tel 212-673-0776; Fax: 212-673-2473.

Kamkyi Bks., *(978-0-9675031)* Div. of Source International Technology Corp., 939 E. 156th St., Bronx, NY 10455 USA (SAN 630-8392) Tel 718-378-3878 (phone/fax); Toll Free: 888-729-5117
E-mail: source.Intl.Tech@erols.com
Web site: http://www.kamkyibooks.

Kampmann, Kump & Bell, LLC, Orders Addr.: 27 W. 20th St., Suite 1102, New York, NY 10011 USA Tel 212-727-0190; Fax: 212-727-0195
E-mail: midpointny@aol.com.

Kane Miller, *(978-0-916291; 978-1-929132; 978-1-933605; 978-1-935279; 978-1-61067)* Div. of EDC Publishing, Orders Addr.: P.O. Box 470663, Tulsa, OK 74146 USA (SAN 295-8945) Tel 858-456-0540; Fax: 858-456-9641; Edit Addr.: P.O. Box 8515, La Jolla, CA 92038 USA Tel 858-456-0540
E-mail: info@kanemiller.com
Web site: http://www.kanemiller.com; http://www.edcpub.com.

Kane/Miller#Book Publishers, Incorporated, *See* **Kane Miller**

Kansas City Periodical Distributing, Orders Addr.: P.O. Box 14948, Lenexa, KS 66285-4948 USA (SAN 107-9433); Edit Addr.: 9605 Dice Ln., Lenexa, KS 66215 USA Tel 913-541-8600.

Kansas State Reading Circle, 715 W. Tenth St., C-170, Topeka, KS 66601 USA (SAN 169-2771).

Kaplan Publishing, *(978-0-7931; 978-0-88462; 978-0-913864; 978-0-936894; 978-0-942103; 978-1-57410; 978-1-60714; 978-1-60978; 978-1-61865; 978-1-62523; 978-1-5062)* 395 Hudson St., New York, NY 10014 USA (SAN 211-2280); 395 Hudson St., New York, NY 10014
E-mail: deb.darrock@kaplan.com; shayna.webb@kaplan.com; alexander.noya@kaplan.com
Web site: http://www.kaplanpublishing.com.

Kaybee Montessori, Inc., 157 Lagrange Ave., Rochester, NY 14613-1511 USA (SAN 133-1256) Toll Free: 800-732-9304.

Kazi Pubns., Inc., *(978-0-933511; 978-0-935782; 978-1-56744; 978-1-871031; 978-1-930637)* 3023 W. Belmont Ave., Chicago, IL 60618 USA (SAN 162-3397) Tel 773-267-7001; Fax: 773-267-7002
E-mail: info@kazi.org
Web site: http://www.kazi.org.

Kehot Pubn. Society, *(978-0-8266)* Div. of Merkos L'Inyonei Chinuch, Orders Addr.: 291 Kingston Ave., Brooklyn, NY 11213 USA Tel 718-778-0226; Fax: 718-778-4148; Toll Free: 877-463-7567 (877-4MERKOS); Edit Addr.: 770 Eastern Pkwy., Brooklyn, NY 11213 USA (SAN 220-7060) Tel 718-604-2785
E-mail: orders@kehotonline.com; info@kehot.com
Web site: http://www.kehotonline.com.

Keith Distributors, 1230 Macklind Ave., Saint Louis, MO 63110-1432 USA (SAN 112-6377) Toll Free: 800-373-2366
E-mail: keithsbooks@juno.com.

Kensington Publishing Corp., *(978-0-7860; 978-0-8065; 978-0-8184; 978-0-8217; 978-1-55817; 978-1-57566; 978-0-7582; 978-1-4201; 978-1-59983; 978-1-60183; 978-0-9817144; 978-0-9818905; 978-0-9824170; 978-0-9841132; 978-1-61650; 978-1-61773; 978-1-4967; 978-1-5161)* 119 W. 40th St., New York, NY 10018 USA Tel 212-407-1500; Fax: 212-935-0699; Toll Free: 800-221-2647; 499 North Canon Dr., Beverly Hills, CA 90210 Tel 310-887-7082
E-mail: jmclean@kensingtonbooks.com; melley@kensingtonbooks.com
Web site: http://www.kensingtonbooks.com.

Kent News Agency, Inc., P.O. Box 1828, Scottsbluff, NE 69363-1828 USA (SAN 169-4448) Tel 303-286-9694; 308-635-2225; Fax: 308-635-1563; Toll Free: 877-290-4740
E-mail: kentrob@prairieweb.com.

Keramos, P.O. Box 7500, Ann Arbor, MI 48107 USA (SAN 169-3670) Tel 313-439-1261.

Kerem Publishing, *(978-1-889727)* 723 N. Orange Dr., Los Angeles, CA 90038 USA (SAN 299-1209).

Kerhulas News Co., P.O. Box 751, Union, SC 29379 USA (SAN 169-7838).

Ketab Corp., *(978-1-883819; 978-1-59584)* Orders Addr.: 1419 Westwood Blvd., Los Angeles, CA 90024 USA (SAN 107-7791) Tel 310-477-7477; Fax: 310-444-7176; Toll Free: 800-367-4726
E-mail: ketab@ketab.com
Web site: http://www.ketab.com.

Key Bk. Service, Inc., *(978-0-934636)* P.O. Box 1434, Fairfield, CT 06430 USA (SAN 169-0671) Tel 203-374-4939; Fax: 203-384-6099.

Keystone Bks. & Media LLC, 12526 Cutten Rd., Suite C, Houston, TX 77066 USA (SAN 990-0160) Tel 281-893-2665; 888-670-2665; Fax: 281-549-2500; Toll Free: 888-670-2665
E-mail: books@keystonebooksmedia.com; matthew@keystonebooksmedia.com
Web site: http://www.keystonebooksmedia.com/.

Khalifah's Booksellers & Assocs., Orders Addr.: 210 East Arrowhead Dr. #2, Charlotte, NC 28213 USA.

Kidsbooks, Inc., 220 Monroe Tpke., No. 560, Monroe, CT 06468-2247 USA (SAN 169-0795).

King Electronics Distributing, 1711 Southeastern Ave., Indianapolis, IN 46201-3990 USA (SAN 107-6795) Tel 317-639-1484; Fax: 317-639-4711.

Kingdom, Inc., P.O. Box 506, Mansfield, PA 16933 USA.

Kinokuniya Bookstores of America Co., Ltd., 1581 Webster St., San Francisco, CA 94115 USA (SAN 121-8441) Tel 415-567-7625; Fax: 415-567-4109.

Kinokuniya Pubns. Service of New York, 1075 Avenue Of The Americas., New York, NY 10018-3701 USA (SAN 157-5414)
E-mail: kinokuniya@kinokuniya.com
Web site: http://www.kinokuniya.com.

Kirkbride, B.B. Bible Co., Inc., *(978-0-88707; 978-0-934854)* P.O. Box 606, Indianapolis, IN 46206-0606 USA (SAN 169-2372) Tel 317-633-1900; Fax: 317-633-1444; Toll Free: 800-428-4385
E-mail: hyperbible@aol.com
Web site: http://www.kirkbride.com.

Kitrick Management Co., Ltd., P.O. Box 15523, Cincinnati, OH 45215 USA (SAN 132-6236) Tel 513-782-2930; Fax: 513-782-2936
E-mail: bachb@aol.com.

Klein's Booklein, Orders Addr.: P.O. Box 968, Fowlerville, MI 48836 USA (SAN 631-3329) Tel 517-223-3964; Fax: 517-223-1314; Toll Free: 800-266-5534; Edit Addr.: One Klein Dr., Fowlerville, MI 48836 USA (SAN 631-3337).

Knopf, Alfred A. Inc., Div. of The Knopf Publishing Group, Orders Addr.: 400 Hahn Rd., Westminster, MD 21157 USA Tel 410-848-1900; Toll Free: 800-726-0600 (orders); Edit Addr.: 1745 Broadway, New York, NY 10019 USA (SAN 202-5825) Tel 212-782-9000; Toll Free: 800-726-0600
E-mail: customerservice@randomhouse.com
Web site: http://www.randomhouse.com/knopf.

Knox, John Press, *See* **Westminster John Knox Pr.**

KOCH Entertainment, LLC, *(978-0-9721700; 978-1-4172)* 740 Broadway, New York, NY 10003 USA Tel 212-353-8800; Fax: 212-505-3095; 22 Harbor Park Dr., Port Washington, NY 11050 Tel 516-484-1000; Fax: 516-484-4746; Toll Free: 800-332-7553
E-mail: nives@kochent.com; videosales@kochent.com
Web site: http://www.kochvision.com; http://www.kochlorberfilms.com; http://www.kochentertainment.com.

Kodansha America, Inc., *(978-0-87011; 978-1-56836; 978-1-935429; 978-1-61262; 978-1-63236)* 451 Park Ave S. Flr. 7, New York, NY 10016-7390 USA (SAN 201-0526) Toll Free: 800-451-7556
E-mail: t-sumi@kodansha-usa.com; ka-koide@kodansha.co.jp
Web site: http://kodanshacomics.com/; www.kodanshausa.com.

Kodansha USA Publishing, *See* **Kodansha America, Inc.**

Koen Pacific, Orders Addr.: P.O. Box 600, Moorestown, NJ 08057-0600 USA (SAN 631-5593) Toll Free: 800-995-4840
E-mail: info@koenpacific.com.

Kraus Reprint, *See* **Periodicals Service Co.**

Kregel Pubns., *(978-0-8254)* Div. of Kregel, Inc., Orders Addr.: P.O. Box 2607, Grand Rapids, MI 49501-2607 USA (SAN 206-9792) Tel 616-451-4775; Fax: 616-451-9330; Toll Free: 800-733-2607; Edit Addr.: 733 Wealthy St., SE., Grand Rapids, MI 49503-5553 USA (SAN 298-9115)
E-mail: kregelbooks@kregel.com; acquisitions@kregel.com
Web site: http://www.kregel.com.

Krullstone Distributing, LLC, 8751 Clayton Cove Rd., Springville, AL 35146 USA
E-mail: charlotte@krullstonepublishing.com
Web site: http://www.krullstonepublishing.com.

KSG Distributing, 1121 W. Flint Meadow Dr., Kaysville, UT 84037 USA.

Kurian, George Reference Bks., *(978-0-914746)* Orders Addr.: P.O. Box 519, Baldwin Place, NY 10505 USA (SAN 203-1981); Edit Addr.: 3689 Campbell Ct., Yorktown Heights, NY 10598 USA (SAN 110-6236) Tel 914-962-3287.

Kurtzman Bk. Sales Co., 17348 W. 12 Mile Rd., Southfield, MI 48076 USA (SAN 114-0787) Tel 248-557-7230; Fax: 248-557-8705; Toll Free: 800-869-0505.

Kuykendall's Pr., Bookstore Div., P.O. Box 627, Athens, AL 35612-0627 USA (SAN 168-9185) Tel 256-232-1754; Toll Free: 800-781-1754.

L I M Productions, LLC, *(978-1-929617)* 3553 Northdale St., NW, Uniontown, OH 44685-8004 USA Toll Free: 877-628-4532
E-mail: customerservice@limproductions.com
Web site: http://www.limproductions.com.

L L Co., *(978-0-937892)* 1647 Manning Ave., Los Angeles, CA 90024 USA (SAN 110-0009) Tel 310-615-0116; Fax: 310-640-6863; Toll Free: 800-473-3699
E-mail: wallacelab@aol.com.

L M C Source, P.O. Box 720400, San Jose, CA 95172-0400 USA (SAN 631-189X) Tel 408-630-0589; Fax: 408-634-1456; Toll Free: 800-873-3043
E-mail: lmcs@pacbell.net
Web site: http://www.csn.net/~davidl/.

L P C Group, c/o CDS, 193 Edwards Dr., Jackson, TN 38305 USA (SAN 630-5644) Fax: 731-423-1973; 731-935-7731; Toll Free Fax: 800-351-5073; Toll Free: 800-343-4499
E-mail: lpc-info@lpcgroup.com
Web site: http://www.lpcgroup.com.

La Belle News Agency, 814 University Blvd., Steubenville, OH 43952 USA (SAN 169-6858) Tel 740-282-9731.

La Cite French Bks., Div. of The La Cite Group, Inc., P.O. Box 64504, Los Angeles, CA 90064-0504 USA (SAN 168-9789)
E-mail: lacite@aol.com.

La Moderna Poesia, Inc., 5739 NW 7th St., Miami, FL 33126-3105 USA (SAN 169-1139).

Lafayette Bks., P.O. Box 758, Mamaroneck, NY 10543-0758 USA (SAN 135-292X) Tel 914-833-0248.

Lake City Downtown Improvement and Revitalization Team, P.O. Box 973 231 N. Silver St., Lake City, CO 81235 USA Tel 970-944-3478
E-mail: ed@lakecitydirt.com.

Lakeport Distributors, Inc., 139 W. 18th St., P.O. Box 6195, Erie, PA 16501 USA (SAN 169-734X).

Lambda Pubs., Inc., *(978-0-915361; 978-1-55774)* 3709 13th Ave., Brooklyn, NY 11218-3622 USA (SAN 291-0640) Tel 718-972-5449; Fax: 718-972-6307
E-mail: judaica@email.msn.com.

Lambert Bk. Hse., Inc., *(978-0-89315)* 4139 Parkway Dr., Florence, AL 35630-6347 USA (SAN 180-5169) Tel 256-764-4098; 256-764-4090; Fax: 256-766-9200; Toll Free: 800-551-8511
E-mail: info@lambertbookhouse.com
Web site: http://www.lambertbookhouse.com.

Landmark Audiobooks, 4865 Sterling Dr., Boulder, CO 80301 USA Fax: 303-443-3775
Web site: http://www.landmarkaudio.com.

Landmark Bk. Co., *(978-0-929194)* 131 Hicks St., Brooklyn, NY 11201-2318 USA (SAN 169-5843).

Lang, Peter Publishing, Inc., *(978-0-8204; 978-1-4331; 978-1-4539; 978-1-4540; 978-1-4541; 978-1-4542)* Subs. of Verlag Peter Lang AG (SZ), 29 Broadway, New York, NY 10006 USA (SAN 241-5534) Tel 212-647-7700; 212-647-7706 (Outside USA); Fax: 212-647-7707; Toll Free: 800-770-5264
E-mail: customerservice@plang.com
Web site: http://www.peterlangusa.com.

Langenscheidt Publishing Group, *(978-0-88729; 978-1-58573)* Subs. of Langenscheidt KG, Orders Addr.: 15 Tyger River Dr., Duncan, SC 29334 USA Fax: 888-773-7979; Toll Free: 800-432-6277; Edit Addr.: 36-36 33rd St., Long Island City, NY 11106 USA
Web site: http://www.americanmap.com; http://www.langenscheidt.com.

Larousse Kingfisher Chambers, Inc., *(978-0-7534; 978-1-85697)* 215 Park Ave., S., New York, NY 10003 USA (SAN 297-7540); 181 Ballardvale St., Wilmington, MA 01887.

Las Vegas News Agency, 2312 Silver Bluff Ct., Las Vegas, NV 89134-6092 USA.

Lash Distributors, 7106 Geoffrey Way, Frederick, MD 21704 USA (SAN 169-3131).

Last Gasp Eco-Funnies, Incorporated, *See* **Last Gasp of San Francisco**

Last Gasp of San Francisco, *(978-0-86719)* Orders Addr.: 777 Florida St., San Francisco, CA 94110 USA (SAN 216-8308); Edit Addr.: 777 Florida St., San Francisco, CA 94110-2025 USA (SAN 170-3242) Tel 415-824-6636; Fax: 415-824-1836; Toll Free: 800-366-5121
E-mail: colin@lastgasp.com
Web site: http://www.lastgasp.com.

Laster, Larry D. Old & Rare Bks., Prints & Maps, 2416 Maplewood Ave., Winston-Salem, NC 27103 USA (SAN 112-9600) Tel 336-724-7544; Fax: 336-724-9055.

Latcorp, Ltd., 10 Norden Ln., Huntington Station, NY 11746 USA (SAN 159-8910) Tel 516-271-0548; Fax: 516-549-8849.

Latin American Book Source, Inc., 681 Anita St., Suit 102, Chula Vista, CA 91911-4663 USA
Web site: http://www.latambooks.com/.

Latin Trading Corp., 539 H St., Chula Vista, CA 91910 USA (SAN 630-2963) Tel 619-427-7867; Fax: 619-476-1817; Toll Free: 800-257-7248
E-mail: info@latintradingbooks.com
Web site: http://www.latintradingbooks.com.

Latta, J. S. Incorporated, *See* **Latta's**

Latta's, 1502 Fourth Ave., P.O. Box 2668, Huntington, WV 25726 USA (SAN 169-8982) Fax: 304-525-5038; Toll Free: 800-624-3501.

Laurus Co., The, Orders Addr.: 524 Guinevere Court, McDonough, GA 30252 USA (SAN 858-608X) Tel 678-814-4047; Fax: 678-272-7255; Toll Free: 800-596-7370
E-mail: thelaurusco@charter.net
Web site: http://www.thelauruscompany.com.

LD Bks., Inc., *(978-0-9772669; 978-0-9785897; 978-1-939048; 978-1-940281; 978-1-943387)* 8313 NW 68th St., Miami, FL 33166 USA (SAN 631-8088) Tel 305-406-2292; Fax: 305-406-2293
E-mail: vilmac@ldbooks.com; sales@ldbooks.com
Web site: http://www.sinlimites.net; http://www.ldbooks.com.

LEA Bk. Distributors (Libros Espana y America), *(978-1-883110)* 170-23 83rd Ave., Jamaica Hills, NY 11432 USA (SAN 170-5407) Tel 718-291-9891; Fax: 718-291-9830
E-mail: leabook@idt.net
Web site: http://www.leabooks.com.

Learning Collection, The, 145 S. Glencoe St., Denver, CO 80246-1152 USA (SAN 630-8287).

Learning Connection, The, *(978-1-56831)* Orders Addr.: 4100 Silver Star Rd. Ste. D, Orlando, FL 32808-4618 USA Toll Free: 800-218-8489
Web site: http://www.tlconnection.com.

Learning Services, 2095 Laura St. Ste. H, Springfield, OR 97477-2285 USA Toll Free: 800-877-3278.

Lectorum Pubns., Inc., *(978-0-9625162; 978-1-880507; 978-1-930332; 978-1-931932; 978-1-941802; 978-1-63245)* 205 Chubb Ave., Lyndhurst, NJ 07071 USA (SAN 860-0597) Tel 201-559-2200; Fax: 201-559-2201; Toll Free Fax: 877-532-8676; Toll Free: 800-345-5946
E-mail: acorrea@lectorum.com
Web site: http://www.lectorum.com; http://www.librerialectorum.com.

Lee Bks., *(978-0-939818)* Div. of Lee S. Cole & Assocs., Inc., 524 San Anselmo Ave., No 215, San Anselmo, CA 94960-2614 USA (SAN 110-649X) Tel 415-456-4388; Fax: 415-456-7532; Toll Free: 800-828-3550 Do not confuse with other companies with the same or similar names in Jacksonville, FL, Columbia, SC
E-mail: lcs@lsc-associates.com
Web site: http://www.lsc-associates.com.

Left Bank Bks., 92 Pike St., Seattle, WA 98101 USA
Web site: http://www.leftbankbooks.com.

Left Bank Books Distribution & Publishing, *See* **Left Bank Distribution**

Left Bank Distribution, *(978-0-939306)* 92 Pike St., Seattle, WA 98101-2025 USA (SAN 216-5368)
E-mail: leftbank@leftbankbooks.com
Web site: http://www.leftbankbooks.com.

Legato Pubs. Group, Orders Addr.: , Chicago, IL 33333 USA
Web site: http://www.legatopublishersgroup.com/.

Leisure Arts, Inc., *(978-0-942237; 978-1-57486; 978-1-60140; 978-1-60900; 978-1-4647)* Orders Addr.: 5701 Ranch Dr., Little Rock, AR 72223 USA (SAN 666-9565) Tel 501-868-8800; Fax: 501-868-1001; Toll Free Fax: 877-710-5603; Toll Free: 800-643-8030 (customer service); 800-526-5111
E-mail: hermine_linz@leisurearts.com
Web site: http://www.leisurearts.com.

Leman Pubns., Inc., *(978-0-943721; 978-0-9602970)* Div. of Rodale Pr. Co., Box 4100, 741 Corporate Cir., Suite A, Golden, CO 80401-5622 USA (SAN 213-3415) Fax: 303-277-0370; Toll Free: 800-877-3775.

Leonard, Hal Corp., *(978-0-634; 978-0-7935; 978-0-87910; 978-0-87930; 978-0-88188; 978-0-931340; 978-0-9607350; 978-1-56516; 978-1-57467; 978-1-4234; 978-1-61713; 978-1-61774; 978-1-61780; 978-1-4584; 978-1-4768; 978-1-4803; 978-1-4950)* Orders Addr.: P.O. Box 13819, Milwaukee, WI 53213-0819 USA Tel 414-774-3630; Fax: 414-774-3259; Toll Free: 800-524-4425; Edit Addr.: 7777 W. Bluemound Rd., Milwaukee, WI 53213 USA (SAN 239-250X)
E-mail: halinfo@halleonard.com
Web site: http://www.halleonard.com.

Leonardo Press, *See* **Firenze Pr.**

Lerner Publishing Group, *(978-0-7613; 978-0-8225; 978-0-87406; 978-0-87614; 978-0-929371; 978-0-930494; 978-1-57505; 978-1-58013; 978-1-58196; 978-1-4677; 978-1-5124)* Orders Addr.: 1251 Washington Ave. N., Minneapolis, MN 55401 USA (SAN 256-0283) Tel 612-332-3344; Fax: 612-204-9208; Edit Addr.: 241 First Ave., N., Minneapolis, MN 55401 USA (SAN 201-0828) Tel 612-332-3344; Fax: 612-215-6230; Toll Free Fax: 800-332-1132; Toll Free: 800-328-4929
E-mail: info@lernerbooks.com; custserve@lernerbooks.com
Web site: http://www.lernerbooks.com; http://www.karben.com.

Levant Distributors, Incorporated, *See* **Levant USA, Inc.**

Levant USA, Inc., 145 Hook Creek Blvd. BLDG B6B3, Valley Stream, NY 11581-2223 USA (SAN 631-1970)
E-mail: levantusa@cs.com.

Levine, J. Religious Supplies, Five W. 30th St., New York, NY 10001 USA (SAN 169-5878) Tel 212-695-6888; Fax: 212-643-1044
E-mail: sales@levine.judica.com.

Levy, Charles Company, *See* **Levy Home Entertainment, Ltd.**

Levy Home Entertainment, *See* **Readerlink Distribution Services, LLC**

Levy Home Entertainment, Ltd., Div. of Charles Levy Co., 1420 Kensington Rd. Ste. 300, Oak Brook, IL 60523-2164 USA (SAN 159-835X).

Lewis International, Inc., *(978-0-9666771; 978-1-930983)* 2201 NW 102nd Pl., No. 1, Miami, FL 33172 USA Tel 305-436-7984; Fax: 305-436-7985; Toll Free: 800-259-5962.

Lewis, John W. Enterprises, 168 Perez St., P.O. Box 3375, Santurce, PR 00936 USA (SAN 169-9334) Tel 809-722-0104.

Lexicon Pubns., Inc., P.O. Box 1737, Danbury, CT 06810 USA (SAN 205-664X) Tel 203-796-2540.

LEXIS Law Publishing, *See* **LEXIS Publishing**

LEXIS Publishing, *(978-0-327; 978-0-406; 978-0-409; 978-0-672; 978-0-87215; 978-0-87473; 978-0-88063; 978-0-930273; 978-1-55834; 978-1-56257)* Div. of Reed Elsevier, Orders Addr.: P.O. Box 7587, Charlottesville, VA 22906-7587 USA Tel 434-972-7600; Fax: 434-972-7686; Toll Free Fax: 800-643-1280; Toll Free: 800-446-3410; Edit Addr.: 701 E. Water St., Charlottesville, VA 22902 USA Do not confuse with Lexis Publishing, Malabar, FL
Web site: http://www.lexisnexis.com.

Liberation Distributors, *(978-0-89928)* P.O. Box 5341, Chicago, IL 60680 USA (SAN 169-880X) Tel 773-248-3442.

Libraries Unlimited, Inc., *(978-0-313; 978-0-87287; 978-1-56308; 978-1-59158)* Div. of Greenwood Publishing Group, Orders Addr.: a/o Customer Service Group, Dept. 2229, P.O. Box 5007, Westport, CT 06881 USA Fax: 603-431-2214; Toll Free: 800-225-5800; Edit Addr.: 88 Post Rd W., Westport, CT 06880-4208 USA
E-mail: lubooks@lu.com
Web site: http://www.lu.com.

Library & Educational Services, P.O. Box 288, Berrien Springs, MI 49103 USA Tel 269-695-1800; Fax: 616-695-8500
E-mail: libraryanded@juno.com.

Library Bk. Selection Service, P.O. Box 277, Bloomington, IL 61702-0277 USA (SAN 169-1740).

Library Integrated Solutions & Assocs., P.O. Box 6189, Mckinney, TX 75071-5105 USA
Web site: http://www.llibs.com.

Library Sales of N.J., *(978-1-888032)* Orders Addr.: P.O. Box 335, Garwood, NJ 07027-0335 USA Tel 908-232-1446; Edit Addr.: 607 S. Chestnut St., Westfield, NJ 07090-1369 USA
E-mail: Librarysalesofnj@aol.com.

Library Video Co., *(978-1-4171)* P.O. Box 580, Wynnewood, PA 19096 USA (SAN 631-3205) Fax: 610-645-4050; Toll Free: 800-843-3620
E-mail: cs@libraryvideo.com
Web site: http://www.libraryvideo.com.

LibreDigital, 1835-B Kramer Ln. Suite 150, Austin, TX 78758 USA; 18 Soho Sq., London, W1D3QL
E-mail: support@libredigital.com.

Libreria Bereana, 1825 San Alejandro, Urb San Ignacio, Rio Piedras, PR 00927-6819 USA (SAN 169-9288) Tel 809-764-6175.

Libreria Distribuidora Universal, 3090 SW 8th St., Miami, FL 33135 USA Tel 305-642-3234.

Libreria Universal, Inc., *(978-1-881375)* Orders Addr.: P.O. Box 1480, Mayaguez, PR 00680 USA; Edit Addr.: 55 N. Post St., Mayaguez, PR 00680 USA Tel 787-832-6041; Fax: 787-832-8477
E-mail: colom@coqui.net; nikkynicole2004@gmail.com.

Libros de Espana y America, *See* **LEA Bk. Distributors (Libros Espana y America)**

Libros Sin Fronteras, P.O. Box 2085, Olympia, WA 98507 USA Tel 360-357-4332; Fax: 360-357-4964
E-mail: info@librossinfronteras.com
Web site: http://www.librossinfronteras.com.

Light & Life Publishing Co., *(978-0-937032; 978-1-880971; 978-1-933654)* Orders Addr.: 4808 Park Glen Rd., Minneapolis, MN 55416 USA (SAN 213-8565) Tel 952-925-3888; Fax: 888-925-3918; Toll Free Fax: 888-925-3918
E-mail: ivy@light-n-life.com
Web site: http://www.light-n-life.com.

Light Impressions Corp., *(978-0-87992)* Orders Addr.: P.O. Box 940, Rochester, NY 14603-0940 USA (SAN 169-619X) Toll Free Fax: 800-826-5539; Toll Free: 800-828-6216; Edit Addr.: P.O. Box 22708, Rochester, NY 14692-2708 USA
Web site: http://www.lightimpresionsdirect.com.

Light Technology Publishing, *See* **Light Technology Publishing, LLC**

Light Technology Publishing, LLC, *(978-0-929385; 978-1-891824; 978-1-62233)* Orders Addr.: P.O. Box 3540, Flagstaff, AZ 86003 USA (SAN 249-1389) Tel 928-526-1345; Toll Free: 800-450-0985; Edit Addr.: 4030 E. Huntington Dr., Flagstaff, AZ 86004 USA (SAN 990-0101)
E-mail: publishing@lighttechnology.net; art@lighttechnology.net; newmedia@lighttechnology.com
Web site: http://www.sedonajournal.com; http://lighttechnology.com.

Lightning Source, Inc., Orders Addr.: 150 Fieldcrest Ave. Lightning Source, Edison, NJ 08837 USA (SAN 920-4288); 4260 Port Union Rd. No. 100 Lightning Source, Fairfield, OH 45011 (SAN 920-4296); 150 Fieldcrest Ave Ingram Book - IBC, Edison, NJ 08837 (SAN 920-430X) Tel 615-413-4476; 4260 Port Union Rd. No. 100 Ingram Book - IBC, Fairfield, OH 45011 (SAN 920-4318); 150 Fieldcrest Ave Ingram Publisher Services, Edison, NJ 08837 (SAN 920-4431); 4260 Port Union Rd. No 100 Ingram Publisher Services, Fairfield, OH 45011 (SAN 920-444X); 860 Nestle Way - IBC, Breinigsville, PA 18031 (SAN 920-6264); 860 Nestle Way-IPS, Breinigsville, PA 18031 (SAN 920-6272); 3145 S. Northpointe Dr. N. Pointe Business Pk., Fresno, CA 93725 (SAN 920-6280); 3145 S Northpointe Dr - IPS, Fresno, CA 93725 (SAN 920-7937); 3145 S Northpointe Dr - IBC, Fresno, CA 93725 (SAN 920-7945); Edit Addr.: 1246 Heil Quaker Blvd., LaVergne, TN 37086 USA (SAN 179-6976) Tel 615-213-4595; Fax: 615-213-4426.

Liguori Pubns., *(978-0-7648; 978-0-89243)* One Liguori Dr., Liguori, MO 63057-9999 USA (SAN 202-6783) Tel 636-464-2500; Fax: 636-464-8449; Toll Free Fax: 800-325-9526; Toll Free: 800-325-9521 (orders)
E-mail: liguori@liguori.org
Web site: http://www.liguori.org.

Likely Story Bookfairs, A, 7210 SW 57th Ave., Suite 207-A, South Miami, FL 33143 USA (SAN 631-1210) Tel 305-668-9183; Fax: 305-667-3323.

Lilly News Agency, P.O. Box 280077, Memphis, TN 38168-0077 USA (SAN 168-9452).

Limerock Bks., Inc., P.O. Box 57, New Canaan, CT 06840 USA (SAN 630-8708) Tel 203-322-5352; Fax: 203-322-2182 Do not confuse with Limerock Books, Thomaston, ME
E-mail: limerockbk@aol.com
Web site: http://www.netpocus.com/limerock.

Linden Publishing Co., Inc., *(978-0-941936; 978-1-933502; 978-1-61035)* 2006 S. Mary, Fresno, CA 93721 USA (SAN 238-6089) Tel 559-233-6633 (phone/fax); Toll Free: 800-345-4447 (orders only) Do not confuse with Linden Publishing in Avon, NY
E-mail: richard@lindenpub.com
Web site: http://www.lindenpub.com.

Linden Tree Children's Records & Bks., 265 State St., Los Altos, CA 94022 USA (SAN 131-744X) Tel 415-949-3390; Fax: 415-949-0346.

Linden Tree Children's Records & Books, *See* **Linden Tree Children's Records & Bks.**

Lindsay News & Photo Service, Inc., 868 Lockport Rd., Youngstown, NY 14174-1139 USA (SAN 169-6092).

Ling's International Bks., Orders Addr.: P.O. Box 82684, San Diego, CA 92138 USA (SAN 169-0116) Tel 619-292-8104; Fax: 619-292-8207; Edit Addr.: 3396 Via Cabo Verde., Escondido, CA 92029-7459 USA.

Linx Educational Publishing, Inc., *(978-1-891818; 978-0-9797510)* P.O. Box 50009, Jacksonville Beach, FL 32240 USA Tel 904-241-1861; Fax: 904-241-3279; Toll Free Fax: 888-546-9338; Toll Free: 800-717-5469
E-mail: mimi@lixedu.com; info@linxedu.com
Web site: http://www.linxedu.com.

Lippincott Williams & Wilkins, *(978-0-316; 978-0-397; 978-0-683; 978-0-7817; 978-0-8067; 978-0-8121; 978-0-88167; 978-0-89004; 978-0-89313; 978-0-89640; 978-0-911216; 978-1-881063; 978-1-60547; 978-1-60831; 978-1-60929; 978-1-4698)* Orders Addr.: P.O. Box 1620, Hagerstown, MD 21741 USA Fax: 301-223-2400; Toll Free: 800-638-3030; Edit Addr.: 530 Walnut St., Philadelphia, PA 19106-3621 USA (SAN 201-0933) Tel 215-521-8300; Fax: 215-521-8902; Toll Free: 800-638-3030; 351 W. Camden St., Baltimore, MD 21201 Tel 410-528-4000; 410-528-4209; 345 Hudson St., 16th Flr., New York, NY 10014 Tel 212-886-1200; 16522 Hunters Green Pkwy., Hagerstown, MD 21740 Tel 301-223-2300; Fax: 301-223-2398; Toll Free: 800-638-3030
E-mail: custserv@lww.com; orders@lww.com
Web site: http://www.lww.com.

Lippincott-Raven Publishers, *See* **Lippincott Williams & Wilkins**

Literal Bk. Distributors: Bks. in Spanish, Orders Addr.: P.O. Box 7113, Langley Park, MD 20787 USA; Edit Addr.: 7705 Georgia Ave. NW, Suite 102, Washington, DC 20012 USA (SAN 113-2784) Tel 202-723-8688; Fax: 202-882-6592; Toll Free: 800-366-8680.

Little Brown & Co., *(978-0-316; 978-0-8212; 978-0-7595)* Div. of Hachette Bk. Group, Orders Addr.: 3 Center Plaza, Boston, MA 02108-2084 USA (SAN 630-7248) Tel 617-227-0730; Toll Free Fax: 800-286-9471; Toll Free: 800-759-0190; Edit Addr.: 237 Park Ave., New York, NY 10017 USA (SAN 200-2205) Tel 212-364-0600; Fax: 212-364-0952
E-mail: customer.service@hbgusa.com
Web site: http://www.hachettebookgroup.com.

Little Dania's Juvenile Promotions, Div. of Booksmith Promotional Co., 100 Paterson Plank Rd., Jersey City, NJ 07307 USA (SAN 169-5681) Tel 201-659-2317; Fax: 201-659-3631
E-mail: hochberga@aol.com.

Little Professor Bk. Ctrs., Inc., P.O. Box 3160, Ann Arbor, MI 48106-3160 USA (SAN 144-2503) Toll Free: 800-899-6232.

Llewellyn Worldwide Ltd., Orders Addr.: 2143 Wooddale Dr., Woodbury, MN 55125-2989 USA Tel 651-291-1970; Fax: 651-291-1908
E-mail: sales@llewellyn.com
Web site: http://www.llewellyn.com.

Login Fulfillment Services, *See* **L P C Group**

Lone Pine Publishing USA, *(978-0-919433; 978-1-55105)* Orders Addr.: 1808 B St., NW Suite 140, Auburn, WA 98001 USA (SAN 859-0427) Tel 253-394-0400; Fax: 253-394-0405; Toll Free Fax: 800-548-1169; Toll Free: 800-518-3541
E-mail: mikec@lonepinepublishing.com
Web site: http://www.lonepinepublishing.com; http://www.companyscoming.com/; http://overtimebooks.com/; http://www.folklorepublishing.com/.

Long Beach Bks., Inc., P.O. Box 179, Long Beach, NY 11561-0179 USA (SAN 164-632X) Tel 718-471-5934.

Longleaf Services, Orders Addr.: P.O. Box 8895, Chapel Hill, NC 27515-8895 USA Tel 800-848-6224; Fax: 800-272-6817
E-mail: customerservice@longleafservices.org.

Longstreet Pr., Inc., *(978-0-929264; 978-1-56352)* Subs. of Cox Newspapers, Inc., 325 N. Milledge Ave., Athens, GA 30601-3805 USA (SAN 248-7640)
E-mail: scottbard@gmail.com.

Looseleaf Law Pubns., Inc., *(978-0-930137; 978-1-889031; 978-1-932777; 978-1-60885)* Orders Addr.: P.O. Box 650042, Fresh Meadows, NY 11365-0042 USA Tel 718-359-5559; Fax: 718-539-0941; Toll Free: 800-647-5547
E-mail: info@looseleaflaw.com; lynette@looseleaflaw.com
Web site: http://www.looseleaflaw.com.

Lord's Line, *(978-0-915952)* 1065 Lomita Blvd., No. 434, Harbor City, CA 90710-1944 USA (SAN 169-0051).

Lorenz Corp., The, *(978-0-7877; 978-0-88335; 978-0-89328; 978-1-55863; 978-1-57310; 978-1-885564; 978-1-4291)* 501 E. Third St., Dayton, OH 45401-0802 USA (SAN 208-7413) Tel 937-228-6118; Fax: 937-223-2042; Toll Free: 800-444-1144
E-mail: service@lorenz.com
Web site: http://www.lorenz.com.

Los Angeles Mart, The, 1933 S. Broadway, Suite 665, Los Angeles, CA 90007 USA (SAN 168-9797) Tel 213-748-6449; Fax: 714-523-0796.

Lotus Lights Publications, *See* **Lotus Pr.**

Lotus Pr., *(978-0-910261; 978-0-914955; 978-0-940676; 978-0-940985; 978-0-941524; 978-1-60869)* Div. of Lotus Brands, Inc., P.O. Box 325, Twin Lakes, WI 53181 USA (SAN 239-1120) Tel 262-889-2461; Fax: 262-889-8591; Toll Free: 800-824-6396 Do not confuse with companies with the same or similar name in Lotus, CA, Westerville, OH, Bokeelia, FL, Brattleboro, VT, Detroit, MI, Tobyhanna, PA
E-mail: lotuspress@lotuspress.com
Web site: http://www.lotuspress.com.

Louisville Distributors, *See* **United Magazine**

Louisville News Co., P.O. Box 36, Columbia, KY 42728 USA (SAN 169-281X) Tel 502-384-3444; Fax: 502-384-9324.

Lubrecht & Cramer, Ltd., *(978-0-934454; 978-0-945345)* P.O. Box 3110, Port Jervis, NY 12771-0176 USA; Orders Addr.: 2749 Albany Post Rd., Montgomery, NY 12549 USA (SAN 214-1256) Toll Free: 800-920-9334; Edit Addr.: 350 Fifth Ave., Suite 3304, New York, NY 10118-0069 USA
E-mail: lubrecht@frontiernet.net; books@lubrechtcramer.com
Web site: http://www.lubrechtcramer.com.

Luciano Bks., 13111 NW Le Jeune, Opa Locka, FL 33054 USA (SAN 631-2829) Tel 305-769-3103.

Ludington News Co., 1600 E. Grand Blvd., Detroit, MI 48211-3195 USA (SAN 169-3751) Tel 313-929-7600.

Lukeman Literary Management, Ltd., *(978-0-9829537; 978-0-9839778; 978-0-9849753; 978-1-939416; 978-1-63291)* 157 Bedford Ave., Brooklyn, NY 11211 USA Tel 718-599-8988; Fax: 775-264-2189.

Lulu Enterprises Inc., *(978-1-4116; 978-1-84728; 978-1-4303; 978-1-4357; 978-1-60552; 978-0-557; 978-1-4583; 978-1-257; 978-1-105; 978-1-300; 978-1-4834; 978-1-304; 978-1-312; 978-1-329)* 3101 Hillsborough St., Raleigh, NC 27607 USA; 26-28 Hammersmith Grove, London, W6 7BA Tel 0208 834 1020
E-mail: sparker@lulu.com.

Lulu.com, *See* **Lulu Enterprises Inc.**

Lushena Bks., *(978-1-930097; 978-1-63182)* 607 Country Club Dr., Unit E, Bensenville, IL 60106 USA (SAN 630-5105) Tel 630-238-8708; Fax: 630-238-8824
E-mail: Lushenabks@yahoo.com
Web site: http://www.lushenabks.com/.

Lyrical Liquor Productions, Orders Addr.: 7212 15th Ave., Takoma Park, MD 20912 USA Tel 202-723-1317
E-mail: llp@speakeasypublishing.com.

M & J Bk. Fair Service, 2307 Sherwood Cir., Minneapolis, MN 55431 USA (SAN 169-4030).

M & M News Agency, Orders Addr.: P.O. Box 1129, La Salle, IL 61301 USA (SAN 169-2062) Fax: 815-223-2828; Toll Free: 800-245-6247.

M L E S, *See* **Pathway Bk. Service**

Ma'ayan, *See* **WellSpring Bks.**

MacGregor News Agency, 1733 Industrial Park Dr., Mount Pleasant, MI 48858 USA (SAN 169-3921) Toll Free: 800-626-1982.

Mackin Bk. Co., 615 Travelers Trail W., Burnsville, MN 55337 USA (SAN 631-3442).

Mackin Educational Resources, *(978-1-62170; 978-1-62353)* 3505 CR 42 W., Burnsville, MN 55306 USA Tel 800-245-9540
E-mail: developers@mackin.com
Web site: http://www.mackin.com/.

Mackin Library Media, 3505 County Rd. 42 W., Burnsville, MN 55306-3804 USA (SAN 134-8795) Toll Free: 800-245-9540
E-mail: mackin@mackin.com
Web site: http://www.mackin.com.

Macmillan, *(978-0-374; 978-1-4668; 978-1-68274)* Div. of Holtzbrinck Publishing, Orders Addr.: 16365 James Madison Hwy., Gordonsville, VA 22942 USA (SAN 631-5011) Tel 540-672-7600; Fax: 540-672-7664; 540-672-7540 (Customer Service); Toll Free Fax: 800-672-2054 (Order Dept.); Toll Free: 888-330-8477; Edit Addr.: 175 Fifth Ave., 20th Flr., New York, NY 10010 USA Tel 212-674-5151; Fax: 212-677-6487; Toll Free Fax: 800-258-2769; Toll Free: 800-488-5233
E-mail: customerservice@mpsvirginia.com
Web site: http://www.macmillan.com.

Macmillan USA, *See* **Alpha Bks.**

MacRae's Indian Bk. Distributor, 1605 Cole St., P.O. Box 652, Enumclaw, WA 98022 USA (SAN 157-5473) Tel 360-825-3737.

Madden Corp., The, *(978-1-61710)* 94-411 Koaki St., Waipahu, HI 96797 USA.

Madison Art Ctr., Inc., *(978-0-913883)* 222 W. Washington Ave. Ste. 350, Madison, WI 53703-2719 USA
E-mail: mac@itis.com
Web site: http://www.madisonartcenter.org.

Magazine Distributors, Inc., 15 Sparks St., Plainville, CT 06062 USA (SAN 169-0817).

Magazines, Inc., 1135 Hammond St., Bangor, ME 04401 USA (SAN 169-3034) Tel 207-942-8237; Fax: 207-942-9226; Toll Free: 800-649-9224 (in Maine)
E-mail: pam@mint.net.

Mahoning Valley Distributing Agency, Inc., 2556 Rush Blvd., Youngstown, OH 44507 USA Tel 330-788-6162; Fax: 330-788-9046.

Main Trail Productions, P.O. Box 365, Clearwater, MN 55320 USA.

Maine Writers & Pubs. Alliance, *(978-0-9618592)* P.O. Box 9301, Portland, ME 04104-9301 USA (SAN 224-2303).

Majic Enterprises, 2232 S. 11th St., Niles, MI 49120-4410 USA (SAN 169-8508).

Majors, J. A. Co., Orders Addr.: 1401 Lakeway Dr., Lewisville, TX 75057 USA (SAN 169-8117) Tel 972-353-1100; Fax: 972-353-1300; Toll Free: 800-633-1851
E-mail: dallas@majors.com
Web site: http://www.majors.com.

Majors Scientific Bks., Inc., P.O. Box 35705, Dallas, TX 75235-0705 USA Toll Free: 800-633-1851
E-mail: dallas@majors.com
Web site: http://www.majors.com.

Manchester News Co., Inc., P.O. Box 4838, Manchester, NH 03108-4838 USA (SAN 169-4480).

Manhattan Publishing Co., Div. of U.S. & Europe Bks., Inc., P.O. Box 850, Croton-on-Hudson, NY 10520 USA (SAN 113-7476) Tel 914-271-5194; Fax: 914-271-5856
Web site: http://www.manhattanpublishing.com.

Manitowoc News Agency, 907 S. Eighth St., Manitowoc, WI 54220 USA (SAN 159-9046).

Manning's Bks. & Prints, 580M Crespi Dr., Pacifica, CA 94044 USA (SAN 157-5384) Fax: 650-355-1851
E-mail: manningsbks@aol.com
Web site: http://www.printsoldandrare.com.

Many Feathers Bks. & Maps, 2626 W. Indian School Rd., Phoenix, AZ 85017 USA (SAN 158-8877) Tel 602-266-1043; Toll Free: 800-279-7652.

Map Link, *See* **Benchmark LLC**

Marangio, Charles F. Distribution, Orders Addr.: P.O. Box 3643, Sonoro, CA 95370 USA (SAN 631-3965) Tel 209-533-0997; Edit Addr.: 659 Sanguinetti Rd., Sonoro, CA 95370 USA (SAN 631-3973).

Marco Bk. Co., *(978-0-9710756; 978-0-9729765)* 60 Industrail Rd., Lodi, NJ 07644 USA Tel 973-458-0485; Fax: 973-458-5289; Toll Free: 800-842-4234
E-mail: everbind5@aol.com.

Marco Bk. Distributors, *(978-0-88298)* 60 Industrial Rd., Lodi, NJ 07644 USA (SAN 169-5142) Tel 973-458-0485; Fax: 973-458-5289; Toll Free: 800-842-4234
Web site: http://www.everbind.com.

MAR*CO Products, Inc., *(978-1-57543; 978-1-884063)* Orders Addr.: 1443 Old York Rd., Warminster, PA 18974 USA Tel 215-956-0313; Fax: 215-956-9041; Toll Free: 800-448-2197
E-mail: csfunk@marcoproducts.com; marcoproducts@comcast.net
Web site: http://www.store.yahoo.com/marcoproducts; http://www.marcoproducts.com.

Marcus Wholesale, P.O. Box 1618, R49 E. Hwy. 4, Murphys, CA 95247 USA (SAN 185-0296).

Mardelva News Co., Inc., 8999 Ocean Hwy., Delmar, MD 21875 USA (SAN 169-3247) Tel 410-742-8613; Fax: 410-742-2616.

Mariposa Pr., *(978-0-9666899)* 551 W. Cordova Rd., Santa Fe, NM 87501 USA Tel 505-471-7846; Fax: 505-986-0690 Do not confuse with companies with same or similar names in Gainesville, FL, Chicago, IL, Hurleyville, NY, Boulder, CO, Abilene TX.

Marshall Cavendish Corp., *(978-0-7614; 978-0-85685; 978-0-86307; 978-1-85435; 978-1-60870)* Member of Times Publishing Group, 99 White Plains Rd., Tarrytown, NY 10591-9001 USA (SAN 238-437X) Tel 914-332-8888; Fax: 914-332-8882; Toll Free: 800-821-9881
E-mail: npalazzo@marshallcavendish.com
Web site: www.MCEducation.us.

Marshall-Mangold Distribution Co., Inc., 4805 Nelson Ave., Baltimore, MD 21215-2507 USA (SAN 169-3115) Toll Free: 800-972-2665.

Maruzen International Co., Ltd., 145 Hook Creek Blvd., Bldg. C5A, Valley Strwam, NY 11581 USA (SAN 630-6012) Tel 516-561-8900.

Marvin Law Bk., 11020 27th Ave., S., Burnsville, MN 55337 USA (SAN 163-898X) Tel 612-644-2236.

Master Bks., *(978-0-89051; 978-1-61458)* P.O. Box 726, Green Forest, AR 72638-0726 USA (SAN 205-6119) Tel 870-438-5288; Fax: 870-438-5120; Toll Free: 800-999-3777
E-mail: nlp@newleafpress.net
Web site: http://www.masterbooks.net; NLPG.com.

Master Communications, Inc., *(978-1-888194; 978-1-60480)* 2692 Madison Rd., Suite N1-307 N1-307, Cincinnati, OH 45208 USA (SAN 299-2140) Tel 513-563-3100; Fax: 513-563-3105; Toll Free: 800-765-5885
E-mail: sales@master-comm.com
Web site: http://www.worldculturemedia.com; http://www.master-comm.com.

Mastery Education Corporation, *See* **Charlesbridge Publishing, Inc.**

Matagiri Sri Aurobindo Ctr., *(978-0-89071)* 2288 Fulton St., No. 310, Berkeley, CA 94704-1449 USA (SAN 169-5541).

Matthews Medical Bk. Co., Orders Addr.: 10 Old Bloomfield Ave., Pine Brook, NJ 07058 USA; 11559 Rock Island Ct., Maryland Heights, MO 63043 (SAN 146-4655) Tel 314-432-1400; Fax: 314-432-7044
E-mail: mlc@mattmccoy.com
Web site: http://www.mattmccoy.com.

Maus Tales, 77-490 Loma Vista, La Quinta, CA 92253 USA Fax: 760-564-6669
E-mail: maustales@aol.com.

Maxwell Scientific International, Inc., *(978-0-8277)* Div. of Pergamon Pr., Inc., 1345 Ave. of the Americas, No. 1036C, New York, NY 10105-0302 USA (SAN 169-524X) Tel 914-592-9141.

May, L. B. & Assocs., 3517 Neal Dr., Knoxville, TN 37918 USA Tel 865-922-7490; Fax: 865-922-7492
E-mail: lbmay@aol.com.

MBI Distribution Services/Quayside Distribution, *(978-0-7603; 978-0-87938; 978-0-912612; 978-1-85010)* Div. of MBI Publishing Co. LLC, Orders Addr.: P.O. Box 1, Osceola, WI 54020-0001 USA (SAN 169-9164) Toll Free: 800-458-0454; Edit Addr.: 400 First Ave., N, Suite 300, Minneapolis, MN 55401 USA Toll Free: 800-328-0590
Web site: http://www.motorbooks.com.

MBS Textbook Exchange, Inc., Orders Addr.: 2711 W. Ash St., Columbia, MO 65203-4613 USA (SAN 140-7015) Tel 573-445-2243; Fax: 573-446-5254; Toll Free: 800-325-0929 (orders); 800-325-0530 (customer service); Edit Addr.: 2711 W. Ash St., Columbia, MO 65203 USA
E-mail: kyates@mbsbooks.com
Web site: http://www.mbsbooks.com.

McCaslin, Boyce, 3 Greenbriar Dr., Saint Louis, MO 63124-1819 USA (SAN 110-8298).

McCoy Church Goods, 1010 Howard Ave., San Mateo, CA 94401 USA (SAN 107-2315) Tel 415-342-0924.

McCrory's Books, *See* **McCrory's Wholesale Bks.**

McCrory's Wholesale Bks., Orders Addr.: P.O. Box 2032, Alexandria, LA 71301 USA (SAN 108-5999); Edit Addr.: 1808 Rapides Ave., Alexandria, LA 71301 USA.

McGraw-Hill Cos., The, *(978-0-07)* 6480 Jimmy Carter Blvd., Norcross, GA 30071-1701 USA (SAN 254-881X) Tel 614-755-5637; Fax: 614-755-5611; Orders Addr.: 860 Taylor Station Rd., Blacklick, OH 43004-0545 USA (SAN 200-254X) Fax: 614-755-5645; Toll Free: 800-722-4726 (orders & customer service); 800-338-3987 (college); 800-525-5003 (subscriptions); 800-352-3566 (books - US/Canada orders); P.O. Box 545, Blacklick, OH 43004-0545 Fax: 614-759-3759; Toll Free: 877-833-5524; a/o General Customer Service, P.O. Box 182604, Columbus, OH 43272 Fax: 614-759-3759; Toll Free: 877-833-5524
E-mail: customer.service@mcgraw-hill.com
Web site: http://www.mcgraw-hill.com; http://www.ebooks.mcgraw-hill.com/.

McGraw-Hill Create (TM), *(978-0-390)* Div. of McGraw-Hill Higher Education, 148 Princeton-Hightstown Rd., Hightstown, NJ 08520-1450 USA Tel 609-426-5721; Toll Free: 800-962-9342
Web site: http://www.mhhe.com.

McGraw-Hill Health Professions Division, *See* **McGraw-Hill Medical Publishing Div.**

McGraw-Hill Medical Publishing Div., *(978-0-07)* Div. of The McGraw-Hill Cos., Orders Addr.: P.O. Box 545, Blacklick, OH 43004-0545 USA Fax: 614-755-5645 (customer service); Toll Free: 800-262-4729 (customer service); 800-722-4726 (bookstores & libraries)
E-mail: customerservice@mcgraw-hill.com
Web site: http://www.mghmedical.com.

McGraw-Hill Osborne, *(978-0-07; 978-0-88134; 978-0-931988)* Div. of The McGraw-Hill Professional, 160 Spear St. Flr. 7, San Francisco, CA 94105-1544 USA (SAN 274-3450) Toll Free: 800-227-0900
E-mail: customer.service@mcgraw-hill.com
Web site: http://www.osborne.com.

McGraw-Hill Primis Custom Publishing, *See* **McGraw-Hill Create (TM)**

McGraw-Hill Professional Publishing, *(978-0-07)* Div. of McGraw-Hill Higher Education, Orders Addr.: P.O. Box 545, Blacklick, OH 43004-0545 USA Fax: 614-755-5645; Toll Free: 800-722-4726; Edit Addr.: 2 Penn Plaza, New York, NY 10121-2298 USA Tel 212-904-2000.

McGraw-Hill Trade, *(978-0-07; 978-0-658; 978-0-8442)* Div. of McGraw-Hill Professional, Orders Addr.: P.O. Box 545, Blacklick, OH 43004-0545 USA Tel 800-722-4726; Fax: 614-755-5645; Edit Addr.: 2 Penn Plaza, New York, NY 10121 USA Tel 212-904-2000
E-mail: Jeffrey_Krames@mcgraw-hill.com
Web site: http://www.books.mcgraw-hill.com/.

McGraw-Hill/Contemporary, *(978-0-658; 978-0-8092; 978-0-8325; 978-0-8442; 978-0-88499; 978-0-89061; 978-0-913327; 978-0-940279; 978-0-941263; 978-0-9630646; 978-1-56626; 978-1-56943; 978-1-57028)* Div. of McGraw-Hill Higher Education, Orders Addr.: P.O. Box 545, Blacklick, OH 43004-0545 USA Toll Free Fax: 800-998-3103; Toll Free: 800-621-1918; Edit Addr.: 4255 W. Touhy Ave., Lincolnwood, IL 60712 USA (SAN 169-2208) Tel 847-679-5500; Fax: 847-679-2494; Toll Free Fax: 800-998-3103; Toll Free: 800-323-4900
E-mail: ntcpub@tribune.com
Web site: http://www.ntc-cb.com.

McKay, David Co., Inc., *(978-0-679; 978-0-88326; 978-0-89440)* Subs. of Random Hse., Inc., Orders Addr.: 400 Hahn Rd., Westminster, MD 21157 USA Tel 410-848-1900; Toll Free: 800-733-3000 (orders only); Edit Addr.: 201 E. 50th St., MD 4-6, New York, NY 10022 USA (SAN 200-240X) Tel 212-751-2600; Fax: 212-872-8026.

McKnight Sales Co., P.O. Box 4138, Pittsburgh, PA 15202 USA (SAN 169-7587) Tel 412-761-4443; Fax: 412-761-0122; Toll Free: 800-208-8078
E-mail: sales@mscmags.com
Web site: http://www.mscmags.com.

McLemore, Hollern & Assocs., 3538 Maple Park Dr., Kingwood, TX 77339 USA Tel 281-360-5204.

McMillen Bk. Distributors, 304 Main St., Ames, IA 50010 USA Fax: 515-232-0402; Toll Free: 866-385-2027.

MeadWestvaco, Orders Addr.: 4751 Hempstead Sta., Kettering, OH 45429 USA Tel 937-495-6323
Web site: http://us.meadwestvaco.com.

MediaTech Productions, *(978-0-9702309)* 917 E. Prospect Rd. Unit B, Fort Collins, CO 80525-1364 USA Toll Free: 800-816-7566 Do not confuse with companies with the same or similar name in Chicago, IL
E-mail: maury@mediatechproductions.com
Web site: http://mediatechproductions.com.

Medicina Biologica, 2937 NE Flanders St., Portland, OR 97232 USA (SAN 113-0226) Tel 503-287-6775; Fax: 503-235-3520
E-mail: med_bio@imagina.com.

Mel Bay Pubns., Inc., *(978-0-7866; 978-0-87166; 978-1-56222; 978-1-60974; 978-1-61065; 978-1-61911; 978-1-5134)* 4 Industrial Dr., Pacific, MO 63069-0066 USA (SAN 657-3630) Tel 636-257-3970; Fax: 636-257-5062; Toll Free: 800-863-5229
E-mail: email@melbay.com; sharon@melbay.com
Web site: http://www.melbay.com; www.melbaydealers.com.

Melton Book Company, Incorporated, *See* **Nelson Direct**

Menasha Ridge Pr., Inc., *(978-0-89732; 978-1-63404)* Div. of Keen Communications, 2204 First Ave., S., Suite 102, Birmingham, AL 35233 USA (SAN 219-7294) Tel 205-322-0439; Fax: 205-326-1012
E-mail: info@menasharidge.com
Web site: http://www.menasharidge.com.

Mentor Bks., 5318 Lowell Blvd., Denver, CO 80221 USA Fax: 303-975-1936; Toll Free: 800-795-6198
E-mail: blair@mentorbooks.com.

Merced News Co., 1324 Coldwell Ave., Modesto, CA 95350-5702 USA (SAN 168-9894) Tel 209-722-5791.

Mercedes Book Distributors Corporation, *See* **Mercedes Distribution Ctr., Inc.**

Mercedes Distribution Ctr., Inc., Brooklyn Navy Yard, Bldg. No. 3, Brooklyn, NY 11205 USA (SAN 169-5150) Tel 718-534-3000; Fax: 718-935-9647; Toll Free: 800-339-4804
E-mail: contact@mdist.com.

Meredith Bks., *(978-0-696; 978-0-89721; 978-0-917102)* Div. of Meredith Corp., Orders Addr.: 1716 Locust St., LN-110, Des Moines, IA 50309-3023 USA (SAN 202-4055) Tel 515-284-2363; 515-284-2126 (sales); Fax: 515-284-3371; Toll Free: 800-678-8091 Do not confuse with Meredith Pr. in Skaneateles, NY
E-mail: John.OBannon@meredith.com
Web site: http://www.bhgstore.com.

Merkos Pubns., Div. of Merkos L'Inyonei Chinuch, 291 Kingston Ave., Brooklyn, NY 11213 USA (SAN 631-1040) Tel 718-778-0226; Fax: 718-778-4148.

Merry Thoughts, *(978-0-88230)* 364 Adams St., Bedford Hills, NY 10507 USA (SAN 169-5061) Tel 914-241-0447; Fax: 914-241-0247.

Meta Co., LLC, P.O. Box 2667, Columbia, MD 21045 USA.

Metamorphosis Publishing Company, *See* **Metamorphous Pr., Inc.**

Metamorphous Pr., Inc., *(978-0-943920; 978-1-55552)* Orders Addr.: P.O. Box 10616, Portland, OR

97296-0616 USA (SAN 110-8786) Tel 503-228-4972; Fax: 503-223-9117; Toll Free: 800-937-7771 (orders only); Edit Addr.: P.O. Box 10616, Portland, OR 97296-0616 USA
E-mail: metabooks@metamodels.com
Web site: http://www.metamodels.com.

Metro Systems, 3381 Stevens Creek Blvd., Suite 209, San Jose, CA 95117 USA (SAN 631-1016) Tel 408-247-4050; Fax: 408-247-4236.

Metropolitan News Co., 47-25 34th, Long Island City, NY 11101 USA (SAN 159-9089) Do not confuse with Metropolitan News Co. in Los Angeles, CA.

Mi Lybro, 9775 Marconi Dr., Suite D, San Diego, CA 92154 USA Tel 619-900-7624
E-mail: sales@milybro.com.

Miami Bks., Inc., 17842 State Rd. 9, Miami, FL 33162 USA (SAN 106-8997) Tel 305-652-3231.

Miami Valley News Agency, 2127 Old Troy Pike, Dayton, OH 45404 USA (SAN 169-6718) Fax: 513-233-8544; Toll Free: 800-791-5137.

Michiana News Service, 2232 S. 11th St., Niles, MI 49120 USA (SAN 110-5051) Tel 616-684-3013; Fax: 616-684-8740.

Michigan Church Supply, P.O. Box 279, Mount Morris, MI 48458-0279 USA (SAN 184-413X) Toll Free: 800-521-3440.

Michigan State Univ. Pr., *(978-0-87013; 978-0-937191; 978-1-60917; 978-1-61186; 978-1-938065; 978-1-62895; 978-1-62896; 978-1-941258; 978-0-9967252)* Orders Addr.: 1405 S. Harrison Rd. Suite 25, East Lansing, MI 48823 USA (SAN 202-6295) Tel 517-355-9543; Fax: 517-432-2611; Toll Free: 800-678-2120
E-mail: msupress@msu.edu
Web site: http://www.msupress.msu.edu.

Mickler's Bks., Inc., 61 Alafaya Woods Blvd., No. 197, Oviedo, FL 32765 USA Tel 407-365-8500; Toll Free Fax: 800-726-0585
E-mail: orders@micklers.com
Web site: http://www.micklers.com.

Micklers Floridiana, Incorporated, *See* **Mickler's Bks., Inc.**

Microdistributors International, Inc., *(978-0-918025)* Subs. of Medcomp Technologies, Inc., 34 Maple Ave., P.O. Box 8, Armonk, NY 10504 USA (SAN 296-158X) Tel 914-273-6480.

Mid Penn Magazine Agency, 100 Eck Cir., Williamsport, PA 17701 USA (SAN 169-7692).

Mid South Manufacturing Agency, Incorporated, *See* **Mid-South Magazine Agency, Inc.**

Mid-Cal Periodical Distributors, P.O. Box 245230, Sacramento, CA 95824-5230 USA (SAN 169-0078).

Midpoint National, Inc., 1263 Southwest Blvd., Kansas City, MO 66103-1901 USA (SAN 630-9860) Tel 913-831-2233; Fax: 913-362-7401; Toll Free: 800-228-4321.

Midpoint Trade Bks., Inc., *(978-1-940416)* Orders Addr.: 1263 Southwest Blvd., Kansas City, KS 66103 USA (SAN 631-3736) Tel 913-831-2233; Fax: 913-362-7401; Toll Free: 800-742-6139 (consumer orders); Edit Addr.: 27 W. 20th St., No. 1102, New York, NY 10011 USA (SAN 631-1075) Tel 212-727-0190; Fax: 212-727-0195
E-mail: info@midpointtrade.com
Web site: http://www.midpointtrade.com; http://www.midpointtradebooks.com/.

Mid-South Magazine Agency, Inc., P.O. Box 4585, Jackson, MS 39296-4585 USA (SAN 286-0163) Toll Free: 800-748-9444.

Mid-State Periodicals, Inc., P.O. Box 3455, Quincy, IL 62305-3455 USA Tel 217-222-0833; Fax: 217-222-1256.

Mid-States Distributors, P.O. Box 1374, Chambersburg, PA 17201-5374 USA (SAN 169-3166).

Midtown Auto Bks., 212 Burnet Ave., Syracuse, NY 13203 USA (SAN 169-6289).

Midwest European Pubns., 915 Foster St., Evanston, IL 60201 USA (SAN 169-1937) Tel 847-866-6289; Fax: 847-866-6290; Toll Free: 800-380-8919
E-mail: info@mep-eli.com
Web site: http://www.mep-eli.com.

Midwest Library Service, 11443 St. Charles Rock Rd., Bridgeton, MO 63044-2789 USA (SAN 169-4243) Tel 314-739-3100; Fax: 314-739-1326; Toll Free Fax: 800-962-1009; Toll Free: 800-325-8833
E-mail: hudson@midwestls.com.

Midwest Tape, Orders Addr.: P.O. Box 820, Holland, OH 43528-0820 USA (SAN 254-9913) Toll Free Fax: 800-444-6645; Toll Free: 800-875-2785
E-mail: randys@midwesttapes.com
Web site: http://www.midwesttapes.com.

Military History Assocs., 407B E. Sixth St., No. 200, Austin, TX 78701-3739 USA (SAN 111-7866).

Mill City Press, Incorporated, *See* **Hillcrest Publishing Group, Inc.**

Miller Educational Materials, *(978-1-934274)* Orders Addr.: P.O. Box 2428, Buena Park, CA 90621 USA Fax: 714-562-0237; Toll Free: 800-636-4375; Edit Addr.: 3294 Cherry Ave., Long Beach, CA 90807-5214 USA (SAN 631-5445)
E-mail: MillerEdu@aol.com
Web site: http://www.millereducational.com.

Miller Trade Bk. Marketing, 363 W. Erie St. Ste. 700E, Chicago, IL 60610-6996 USA (SAN 631-4287)
E-mail: millertrade@sbcglobal.net.

Milligan News Co., Inc., 150 N. Autumn St., San Jose, CA 95110 USA (SAN 169-0272) Tel 408-286-7604; Fax: 408-298-0235; Toll Free: 800-873-2387.

Millmark Education, *(978-1-4334; 978-1-61618)* Orders Addr.: 7272 Wisconsin Ave. Suite 300, Bethesda, MD 20814-2081 USA (SAN 852-4912) Tel 301-941-1974; Fax: 301-656-0183; Edit Addr.: 7272 Wisconsin Ave. Suite 300, Bethesda, MD 20814-2081 USA
E-mail: rachel.moir@millmarkeducation.com; info@millmarkeducation.com
Web site: http://www.millmarkeducation.com/.

Mind Trip Pr., P.O. Box 489, Georgetown, TX 78626 USA Tel 513-428-9278.

Minerva Science Bookseller, Inc., 175 Fifth Ave., New York, NY 10010 USA (SAN 286-0171).

Mint Pubs. Group, Orders Addr.: 62 June Rd., Suite 241, North Salem, NY 10560 USA Tel 914-276-6576; Fax: 914-276-6579; Edit Addr.: 1220 Nicholson Rd., Newmarket, ON I3Y 7VI CAN Toll Free Fax: 800-363-2665; Toll Free: 800-399-6858
E-mail: info@mintpub.com
Web site: http://www.mintpub.com.

Mintright, Inc., *(978-1-4687)* 55 W. 26th St., Suite 36D, New York, NY 10010 USA (SAN 935-4840) Tel 646-368-8090; Fax: 646-368-8099
E-mail: content@mintright.com
Web site: http://mintright.com/.

Mission Resource Ctr., 1221 Profit Dr., Dallas, TX 75247 USA Toll Free: 800-305-9857.

Mississippi Library Media & Supply Co., P.O. Box 108, Brandon, MS 39043-0108 USA (SAN 169-4189) Tel 601-824-1900; Fax: 601-824-1999; Toll Free: 800-257-7566 (in Mississippi).

Mistco, Inc., P.O. Box 694854, Miami, FL 33269 USA (SAN 630-8384) Tel 305-653-2003; Fax: 305-653-2037; Toll Free: 800-552-0446
E-mail: mistco@worldnet.att.net
Web site: http://www.mistco.com.

Mobile News Co., 1118 14th St., Tuscaloosa, AL 35401-3318 USA (SAN 169-924X) Tel 334-479-1435.

Modern Curriculum Pr., *(978-0-7652; 978-0-8136; 978-0-87895)* Div. of Pearson Education, Orders Addr.: P.O. Box 2500, Lebanon, IN 46052-3009 USA (SAN 206-6572) Toll Free: 800-526-9907 (Customer Service)
Web site: http://www.pearsonlearning.com.

Modesto News Co., 1324 Coldwell Ave., Modesto, CA 95350-5702 USA (SAN 168-9908) Tel 209-577-5551.

Montfort Pubns., *(978-0-910984)* Div. of Montfort Missionaries, 26 S. Saxon Ave., Bay Shore, NY 11706-8993 USA (SAN 169-5053) Tel 631-665-0726; Fax: 631-665-4349
E-mail: montfort@optonline.net
Web site: http://www.montfortmissionaries.com; http://www.montfortmissionaries.org; http://www.montfortpublications.com.

Moody Pubs., *(978-0-8024)* Div. of Moody Bible Institute, Orders Addr.: 210 W. Chestnut, Chicago, IL 60610 USA; Edit Addr.: 820 N. LaSalle, Chicago, IL 60610 USA (SAN 202-5604) Tel 312-329-2101; Fax: 312-329-2144; Toll Free: 800-678-8812
E-mail: mpcustomerservice@moody.edu
Web site: http://www.moodypublishers.com.

Mook & Blanchard, P.O. Box 4177, La Puente, CA 91747-4177 USA (SAN 168-9703) Toll Free: 800-875-9911
E-mail: mookbook@ix.netcom.com
Web site: http://www.mookandblanchard.com.

Moon Over the Mountain Publishing Company, *See* **Leman Pubns., Inc.**

More, Thomas Assn., 205 W. Monroe St., 5th Flr., Chicago, IL 60606-5097 USA (SAN 169-1880) Tel 312-609-8880; Toll Free: 800-835-8965.

Morlock News Co., Inc., 496 Duanesburg Rd., Schenectady, NY 12306 USA (SAN 169-6246).

Morris Publishing, *(978-0-7392; 978-0-9631249; 978-1-57502; 978-1-885591; 978-0-9863567)* Orders Addr.: P.O. Box 2110, Kearney, NE 68848 USA Fax: 308-237-0263; Toll Free: 800-650-7888 Do not confuse with companies with the same Wesley Chapel, FL; Elkhart, IN
Web site: http://www.morrispublishing.com.

Moshy Brothers, Inc., 127 W. 25th St., New York, NY 10001 USA (SAN 169-5886) Tel 212-255-0613.

Mother Lode Distributing, 17890 Lime Rock Dr., Sonora, CA 95370-8707 USA (SAN 169-0361).

Motorbooks International Wholesalers & Distributors, *See* **MBI Distribution Services/Quayside Distribution**

Mountain Bk. Co., P.O. Box 778, Broomfield, CO 80038-0778 USA Tel 303-436-1982; Fax: 917-386-2769
E-mail: wordguise@aol.com
Web site: http://www.mountainbook.org.

Mountain n' Air Bks., *(978-1-879415)* Div. of Mountain n' Air Sports, Inc., Orders Addr.: P.O. Box 12540, La Crescenta, CA 91224 USA (SAN 630-5598) Tel 818-248-9345; Toll Free Fax: 800-303-5578; Toll Free: 800-446-9696; Edit Addr.: 2947-A Hololulu Ave., La Crescenta, CA 91214 USA (SAN 631-4198)
E-mail: books@mountain-n-air.com
Web site: http://mountain-n-air.com.

Mountain Pr. Publishing Co., Inc., *(978-0-87842)* Orders Addr.: P.O. Box 2399, Missoula, MT 59806-2399 USA (SAN 202-8832) Tel 406-728-1900; Fax: 406-728-1635; Toll Free: 800-234-5308; Edit Addr.: 1301 S. Third West, Missoula, MT 59801 USA (SAN 662-0868)
E-mail: jrimel@mtnpress.com; info@mtnpress.com; anne@mtnpress.com
Web site: http://www.mountain-press.com.

Mountain States News Distributor, P.O. Drawer P, Fort Collins, CO 80522 USA Tel 970-221-2330; Fax: 970-221-1251.

Mouse Works, *(978-0-7364; 978-1-57082)* Div. of Disney Bk. Publishing, Inc., A Walt Disney Co., 114 Fifth Ave., New York, NY 10011 USA (SAN 298-0797) Tel 212-633-4400; Fax: 212-633-4811
Web site: http://www.disneybooks.com.

MPS, 16365 James Madison Hwy., Gordonsville, VA 22942-8501 USA Toll Free Fax: 800-672-2054; Toll Free: 888-330-8477.

Mr. Paperback/Publishers News Co., 6030 Fostoria Ave., Findlay, OH 45840 USA (SAN 169-393X) Tel 419-424-6774; Fax: 419-420-1805; Toll Free: 800-872-0031.

M-S News Co., Inc., P.O. Box 13278, Wichita, KS 67213-0278 USA Fax: 316-267-5405.

Mullare News Agency, Inc., P.O. Box 578, Brockton, MA 02401 USA (SAN 169-3379) Tel 508-580-1000; Fax: 508-586-0968.

Multi-Cultural Bks. & Videos, Inc., *(978-0-9656274)* 30007 John R. Rd., Madison Hts, MI 48071-2526 USA (SAN 760-6796) Toll Free: 800-567-2220
E-mail: service@multiculbv.com
Web site: http://www.multiculbv.com.

Multilingual Bks., Orders Addr.: P.O. Box 440632, Miami, FL 33144 USA (SAN 169-1155) Tel 305-471-9847 Do not confuse with Multilingual Bks., Seattle, WA.

Mumford Library Bks., Inc., 7847 Bayberry Rd., Jacksonville, FL 32256 USA (SAN 156-7721) Fax: 904-730-8913; Toll Free: 800-367-3927.

Mumford Library Book Sales, *See* **Mumford Library Bks., Inc.**

Murr's Library Service, 4045 E. Palm Ln., No. 5, Phoenix, AZ 85008-3116 USA (SAN 107-3222) Fax: 602-273-1217; Toll Free: 888-273-0279.

Music, Bks. & Business, Inc., Orders Addr.: 4305 32nd St W Suite A, Bradenton, FL 34205 USA (SAN 760-5986) Fax: 941-752-8994; Toll Free: 888-876-7716
E-mail: info@musicbooksbusiness.com
Web site: http://www.musicbooksbusiness.com.

Music Design, Inc., 4650 N. Port Washington Rd., Milwaukee, WI 53212 USA (SAN 200-7649) Tel 414-961-8380; Fax: 414-961-8381; Toll Free: 800-862-7232
E-mail: order@musicdesign.com
Web site: http://www.musicdesign.com.

Music in Motion, P.O. Box 869231, Plano, TX 75086-9231 USA (SAN 631-4589) Fax: 972-943-8906; Toll Free Fax: 866-943-8906; Toll Free: 800-445-0649 Do not confuse with Music in Motion, Ithaca, NY
Web site: http://www.musicmotion.com.

Music is Elementary, *(978-0-9721085; 978-0-9910656; 978-0-9966913)* P.O. Box 24263, Cleveland, OH 44124 USA Tel 440-442-4475; Fax: 440-461-3631; Toll Free: 800-888-7502
E-mail: music@en.com
Web site: http://www.musiciselementary.com.

Music Sales Corp., *(978-0-7119; 978-0-8256; 978-1-84609)* Orders Addr.: 445 Bellvale Rd., P.O. Box 572, Chester, NY 10918 USA (SAN 662-0876) Tel 845-469-2271; Fax: 845-469-7544; Toll Free Fax: 800-345-6842; Toll Free: 800-431-7187; Edit Addr.: 257 Park Ave., S., 20th Flr., New York, NY 10010 USA (SAN 282-0277) Tel 212-254-2100; Fax: 212-254-2103
E-mail: info@musicsales.com
Web site: http://www.musicroom.com; http://www.musicsales.com.

Musicart West, P.O. Box 1900, Orem, UT 84059-1900 USA (SAN 110-1250) Tel 801-225-0859; Toll Free: 800-950-1900 (orders only).

MVP Wholesales, 9301 W. Hwy. 290, No. D, Austin, TX 78736-7817 USA (SAN 630-9550) Tel 512-416-1452; Toll Free: 800-328-7931 (phone/fax).

MyiLibrary, *(978-1-280; 978-1-281; 978-1-282; 978-1-283; 978-1-299; 978-1-306; 978-1-322; 978-1-336)* Div. of Coutts Information Services, 14 Ingram Blvd., La Vergne, TN 37086 USA Tel 615-213-5400; Fax: 615-213-5111
E-mail: wendell.lotz@ingramcontent.com.

NACSCORP, Inc., Orders Addr.: 528 E. Lorain St., Oberlin, OH 44074-1298 USA (SAN 134-2118) Tel 440-775-7777; Toll Free Fax: 800-344-5059; Toll Free: 800-321-3883 (orders only); 800-458-9303 (backorder status only); 800-334-9882 (support programs/technical support)
E-mail: service@nacscorp.com; orders@nacscorp.com
Web site: http://www.nacscorp.com.

Najarian Music Co., Inc., 236 Partridge Ln., Concord, MA 01742-2651 USA (SAN 169-3344).

Napa Book Company, *See* **Napa Children's Bk. Co.**

Napa Children's Bk. Co., 1239 First St., Napa, CA 94559 USA (SAN 122-2732) Tel 707-224-3893; Fax: 707-224-1212.

Nasco Math Eighty-Six, 901 Janesville Ave., Fort Atkinson, WI 53538 USA (SAN 679-7512).

National Academies Pr., *(978-0-309)* Orders Addr.: 8700 Spectrum Dr., Landover, MD 20785 USA; Edit Addr.: 500 Fifth St., NW Lockbox 285, Washington, DC 20001 USA (SAN 202-8891) Tel 202-334-3313; Fax: 202-334-2451; Toll Free: 888-624-7654
E-mail: zjones@nas.edu
Web site: http://www.nap.edu.

National Academy Press, *See* **National Academies Pr.**

National Assn. of the Deaf, *(978-0-913072)* 8630 Fenton St. Ste. 820, Silver Spring, MD 20910-3819 USA (SAN 159-4974)
E-mail: donna.morris@nad.org
Web site: http://www.nad.org.

National Bk. Co., Keystone Industrial Pk., Scranton, PA 18512 USA Tel 717-346-2020; Toll Free: 800-233-4830 Do not confuse with National Book Company, Portland, OR.

National Bk. Network, Div. of Rowman & Littlefield Pubs., Inc., Orders Addr.: 15200 NBN Way, Blue Ridge Summit, PA 17214 USA (SAN 630-0065) Tel 717-794-3800; Fax: 717-794-3828; Toll Free Fax: 800-338-4550 (Customer Service); Toll Free: 800-462-6420 (Customer Service); a/o Les Petriw, 67 Mowat Ave., Suite 241, Toronto, ON M6P 3K3 Tel 416-534-1660; Fax: 416-534-3699
E-mail: custserv@nbnbooks.com
Web site: http://www.nbnbooks.com.

National Catholic Reading Distributor, 997 Macarthur Blvd., Mahwah, NJ 07430 USA (SAN 169-4855) Tel 201-825-7300; Fax: 201-825-8345; Toll Free: 800-218-1903
E-mail: paulistp@pipeline.com.

National Educational Systems, Inc., *(978-1-893493)* P.O. Box 691450, San Antonio, TX 78269-1450 USA Toll Free: 800-442-2604.

National Film Network LLC, *(978-0-8026)* Orders Addr.: 4501 Forbes Blvd., Lanham, MD 20706 USA (SAN 630-1878) Tel 301-459-8020 ext 2066
E-mail: info@nationalfilmnetwork.com
Web site: http://www.nationalfilmnetwork.com.

National Health Federation, Box 688, Monrovia, CA 91016 USA (SAN 227-9266) Tel 626-357-2181; Fax: 818-303-0642
E-mail: nhf@earthlink.net
Web site: http://www.healthfreedom.net.

National Learning Corp., *(978-0-8293; 978-0-8373)* 212 Michael Dr., Syosset, NY 11791 USA (SAN 206-8869) Tel 516-921-8888; Fax: 516-921-8743; Toll Free: 800-645-6337
E-mail: sales@passbooks.com.

National Magazine Service, Orders Addr.: P.O. Box 834, Mars, PA 16046 USA (SAN 169-7595); Edit Addr.: 535 Linden Way, Pittsburgh, PA 15202 USA Tel 412-898-0001.

National Organization Service, Inc., P.O. Box 2007, Birmingham, AL 35201-2007 USA (SAN 107-1548) Toll Free: 800-747-3032.

National Rifle Assn., *(978-0-935998)* a/o Office of the General Counsel, 11250 Waples Mill Rd., Fairfax, VA 22030 USA (SAN 213-859X) Tel 703-267-1250; Fax: 703-267-3985; Toll Free: 800-672-3888
E-mail: ndowd@nrahq.org.

National Sales, Inc., 1818 W. 2300 South, Salt Lake City, UT 84119 USA (SAN 159-9127) Tel 801-972-2300; Fax: 801-972-2883.

National Technical Information Service, U.S. Dept. of Commerce, *(978-0-934213; 978-1-935239)* Orders Addr.: 5285 Port Royal Rd., Springfield, VA 22161 USA (SAN 205-7255) Tel 703-605-6000; Fax: 703-605-6900; Toll Free: 800-553-6847
E-mail: orders@ntis.gov; info@ntis.gov
Web site: http://www.ntis.gov; http://wnc.fedworld.gov.

Native Bks., P.O. Box 37095, Honolulu, HI 96837 USA (SAN 631-1121) Tel 808-845-8949; Fax: 808-847-6637; Toll Free: 800-887-7751.

Naval Institute Pr., *(978-0-87021; 978-1-55750; 978-1-59114; 978-1-61251; 978-1-68247; 978-1-68269)* Orders Addr.: 291 Wood Rd, Annapolis, MD 21402-5034 USA (SAN 662-0930) Tel 410-268-6110; Fax: 410-295-1084; Toll Free: 800-233-8764; Edit Addr.: 291 Wood Rd., Beach Hall, Annapolis, MD 21402-5034 USA (SAN 202-9006)
E-mail: tskord@usni.org; books@usni.org
Web site: http://www.usni.org.

Nazarene Publishing Hse., *(978-0-8341)* Orders Addr.: 2923 Troost Ave., Kansas City, MO 64109 USA (SAN 253-0902); Edit Addr.: P.O. Box 419527, Kansas City, MO 64141 USA (SAN 202-9022) Tel 816-931-1900; Fax: 816-531-0923; Toll Free Fax: 800-849-9827; Toll Free: 800-877-0700
E-mail: heather@nph.com
Web site: http://www.bhillkc.com; http://www.nph.com.

Neal-Schuman Pubs., Inc., *(978-0-918212; 978-1-55570)* Div. of American Library Assn., 100 William St., Suite 2004, New York, NY 10038 USA (SAN 210-2455) Tel 212-925-8650; Fax: 212-219-8916; Toll Free Fax: 800-584-2414
E-mail: info@neal-schuman.com
Web site: http://www.neal-schuman.com.

Neeland Media, LLC, 3921 Harvard Rd., Lawrence, KS 66049 USA Tel 913-548-6825.

Neighborhood Periodical Club, Inc., P.O. Box 830, Clementon, NJ 08021-0860 USA (SAN 285-9262).

Nelson Direct, P.O. Box 140300, Nashville, TN 37214 USA (SAN 169-8133) Toll Free: 800-441-0511 (sales); 800-933-9673
E-mail: csalazar@thomasnelson.com
Web site: http://www.nelsondirect.com.

Nelson News, Inc., P.O. Box 27007, Omaha, NE 68127-0007 USA (SAN 169-443X) Tel 402-734-3333; Fax: 402-731-0516.

Nelson, Thomas Inc., *(978-0-529; 978-0-7852; 978-0-8407; 978-0-8499; 978-0-86605; 978-0-88113; 978-0-89840; 978-0-89922; 978-0-918956; 978-0-7180; 978-1-4002; 978-1-4003; 978-1-4016; 978-1-59145; 978-1-4041; 978-1-59554; 978-1-59555; 978-1-4185; 978-1-59951; 978-1-4261; 978-1-60255; 978-1-4845; 978-1-5000) Orders Addr.: P.O. Box 141000, Nashville, TN 37214-1000 USA (SAN 209-3820) Fax: 615-902-1866; Toll Free: 800-251-4000; Edit Addr.: 501 Nelson Pl., Nashville, TN 37214 USA*
Web site: http://www.thomasnelson.com.

Nelson's Bks., *(978-0-9612188)* P.O. Box 2302, Santa Cruz, CA 95063 USA (SAN 289-4858) Tel 831-465-9148.

Ner Tamid Bk. Distributors, P.O. Box 10401, Riviera Beach, FL 33419-0401 USA (SAN 169-135X) Tel 561-686-9095.

Net Productions, 210 Elm Cir., Colorado Springs, CO 80906-3348 USA (SAN 159-9143).

NetLibrary, Incorporated, *See* **Ebsco Publishing**

NetSource Distribution, Orders Addr.: 675 Dutchess Tpke., Poughkeepsie, NY 12603 USA Tel 845-463-1100 x314; Fax: 845-463-0018; Toll Free: 800-724-1100
Web site: http://www.hudsonhousepub.com.

Wholesaler & Distributor Name Index

New Alexandrian Bookstore, 110 N Cayuga St., Ithaca, NY 14850-4331 USA (SAN 159-4958) Tel 607-272-1163.
New Concepts Bks. & Tapes Distributors, Orders Addr.: P.O. Box 55068, Houston, TX 77255 USA (SAN 114-2682) Tel 713-465-7736; Fax: 713-465-7106; Toll Free: 800-842-4807; Edit Addr.: 9722 Pine Lake, Houston, TX 77055 USA (SAN 630-7531).
New Day Christian Distributors, *See* **New Day Christian Distributors Gifts, Inc.**
New Day Christian Distributors Gifts, Inc., 124 Shivel Dr., Hendersonville, TN 37075 USA (SAN 631-2551) Tel 615-822-3633; Fax: 615-822-5829; Toll Free: 800-251-3633; 126 Shivel Dr., Hendersonville, TN 37075 (SAN 920-6604).
New England Bk. Service, Inc., 7000 Vt Route 17 W., Vergennes, VT 05491-4408 USA (SAN 170-0952) Toll Free: 800-356-5772
E-mail: nebs@together.net.
New England Mobile Bk. Fair, 82 Needham St., P.O. Box 610159, Newton Highlands, MA 02461 USA (SAN 169-3530) Tel 617-527-5817; Fax: 617-527-0113.
New Harbinger Pubns., *(978-0-934986; 978-1-57224; 978-1-879237; 978-1-60882; 978-1-62625)* Orders Addr.: 5674 Shattuck Ave., Oakland, CA 94609 USA (SAN 205-0587) Tel 510-652-2002; 510-652-0215; Fax: 510-652-5472; Toll Free: 800-652-1613
E-mail: customerservice@newharbinger.com
Web site: http://www.newharbinger.com.
New Jersey Bk. Agency, Orders Addr.: P.O. Box 144, Morris Plains, NJ 07950 USA (SAN 106-861X) Tel 973-267-7093; Fax: 973-292-3177; Edit Addr.: 7 Somerset Hills Ct. Apt. D, Bernardsville, NJ 07924-2619 USA (SAN 243-2307).
New Jersey Bks., Inc., 59 Market St., Newark, NJ 07102 USA Tel 973-624-8070; Toll Free: 800-772-3678.
New Leaf Distributing Co., Inc., *(978-0-9627209)* Div. of Al-Wali Corp., 401 Thornton Rd., Lithia Springs, GA 30122-1557 USA (SAN 169-1449) Tel 770-948-7845; Fax: 770-944-2313; Toll Free Fax: 800-326-1066; Toll Free: 800-326-2665
E-mail: santoshk@msn.com; alimt@bellsouth.net
Web site: http://www.NewLeaf-dist.com.
New Leaf Pr., Inc., *(978-0-89221)* P.O. Box 726, Green Forest, AR 72638 USA (SAN 207-9518) Tel 870-438-5288; Fax: 870-438-5120 Toll Free: 800-643-9535 Do not confuse with companies with the same or similar name in Los Angeles, CAStone Mountain, GA
E-mail: nlp@newleafpress.net
Web site: http://www.newleafpress.net.
New Leaf Resources, 2102 Button Ln., Unit 2, Lagrange, KY 40031 USA Toll Free: 800-346-3087
E-mail: info@newleaf-resources.com
Web site: http://www.www.newleaf-resources.com.
New Life Foundation, *(978-0-911203; 978-1-934162)* P.O. Box 2230, Pine, AZ 85544-2230 USA (SAN 170-3986) Tel 928-476-3224; Fax: 928-476-4743; Toll Free: 800-293-3377 (wholesale only)
E-mail: info@anewlife.org
Web site: http://www.anewlife.org.
New Shelves Distribution, 103 Remsen St., Cohoes, NY 12047 USA Tel 518-391-2300; Fax: 518-391-2365
Web site: http://www.newshelvesdistribution.com.
New Tradition Bks., *(978-0-9728473; 978-1-932420; 978-0-9845418)* 627 Brickle Ridge Rd., Decatur, TN 37322 USA
E-mail: newtraditionbooks@yahoo.com.
New Village Pr., *(978-0-9766054; 978-0-9815593; 978-1-61332)* Div. of Architects/Designers/Planners for Social Responsibility, 400 Central Pk. W, 12B, New York, NY 10025 USA Tel 510-717-3101
E-mail: lynne@newvillagepress.net
Web site: http://www.newvillagepress.net.
New World Library, *(978-0-931432; 978-0-945934; 978-1-57731; 978-1-880032; 978-1-60868)* 14 Pamaron Way, Novato, CA 94949 USA (SAN 211-8777) Tel 415-884-2100; Fax: 415-884-2199; Toll Free: 800-972-6657 (retail orders only) Do not confuse with New World Library Publishing Co., Los Altos, CA
E-mail: escort@nwlib.com
Web site: http://www.newworldlibrary.com.
New World Resource Ctr., P.O. Box 25310, Chicago, IL 60625-0310 USA (SAN 169-1848).
New York Periodical Distributors, P.O. Box 29, Massena, NY 13662-0029 USA (SAN 169-6149).
New York Review of Bks., Inc., The, *(978-0-940322; 978-1-59017; 978-1-68137)* 435 Hudson St., 3rd Flr. Suite 300, New York, NY 10014 USA (SAN 220-3448) Tel 212-757-8070; Fax: 212-333-5374
E-mail: mail@nybooks.com; nyrb@nybooks.com
Web site: http://www.nyrb.com.
New York Univ. Pr., *(978-0-8147; 978-1-4798)* Div. of New York Univ., Orders Addr.: 838 Broadway, 3rd Flr., New York, NY 10003-4812 USA (SAN 658-1293) Tel 212-998-2575; Fax: 212-995-3833; Toll Free: 800-996-6987 (ordering)
E-mail: orders@nyupress.org
Web site: http://www.nyupress.org.
Newborn Enterprises, Inc., P.O. Box 1713, Altoona, PA 16603 USA (SAN 169-7242) Tel 814-944-3593; Fax: 814-944-1881; Toll Free: 800-227-0285 (in Pennsylvania).
NewLife Bk. Distributors, 2969 Spalding Dr., Suite 100, Atlanta, GA 30350 USA (SAN 169-121X) Tel 404-207-5280
E-mail: lifebooks@mindspring.com
Web site: http://www.newlifebookdistributors.com.
News Group, 15 N. Spring St., #2, Bloomfield, NJ 07003 USA.
News Group - Illinois, The, 1301 SW Washington St., Peoria, IL 61602 USA (SAN 169-216X) Tel 309-673-4549; Fax: 309-673-8883.
News Group, The, 325 W. Potter Dr., Anchorage, AK 99518 USA (SAN 168-9274) Tel 907-563-3251; Fax: 907-261-8523 Do not confuse with companies with the same name in Winston-Salem, NC, Elizabeth, NC.
News Supply Co., 216 S. La Huerta Cir., Carlsbad, NM 88220-9620 USA (SAN 159-9151).
Newsdealers Supply Co., Inc., P.O. Box 3516, Tallahassee, FL 32315-3516 USA.
NewSound, LLC, 81 Demeritt Pl., Waterbury, VT 05676 USA Tel 802-244-7858; Fax: 802-244-1808; Toll Free: 800-342-0295 (wholesale orders)
E-mail: sales@newsoundmusic.com.
NEWSouth Distributors, P.O. Box 61297, Jacksonville, FL 32236-1297 USA (SAN 159-8732).
Newsstand Distributors, 155 W. 14th St., Ogden, UT 84404 USA (SAN 169-8494) Fax: 810-621-7336; Toll Free: 800-283-6247; 800-231-4834 (in Utah).
Ng Hing Kee, 648 Jackson St., San Francisco, CA 94133 USA (SAN 107-1084) Tel 415-781-8330; Fax: 415-397-9766.
Niagara County News, 70 Nicholls St., Lockport, NY 14094 USA (SAN 169-541X) Tel 716-433-6466.
Ninety & Nine Records, *See* **Blooming Twig Books LLC**
Noelke, Carl B., 529 Main, Box 563, La Crosse, WI 54602 USA (SAN 111-8315) Tel 608-782-8544.
Nonagon, 1556 Douglas Dr., El Cerrito, CA 94530 USA (SAN 654-0503) Tel 510-237-5290.
Nonetheless Pr., *(978-1-932053)* 20332 W. 98th St., Lenexa, KS 66220-2650 USA Tel 913-254-7266; Fax: 913-393-3245
E-mail: mschutte@nonethelesspress.com
Web site: http://www.nonethelesspress.com; http://www.lookingglasspress.com.
Nor-Cal News Co., 2040 Petaluma Blvd., P.O. Box 2508, Petaluma, CA 94953 USA (SAN 169-0035) Tel 707-763-2606; Fax: 707-763-3905.
Norfolk SPCA, 916 Ballentine Blvd., Norfolk, VA 23504 USA Tel 757-622-3319
Web site: http://www.norfolkspca.com.
North American Bk. Distributors, P.O. Box 510, Hamburg, MI 48139 USA (SAN 630-4680) Tel 810-231-3728.
North Carolina News Co., P.O. Box 1051, Durham, NC 27702-1051 USA Tel 919-682-5779.
North Carolina Schl. Bk. Depository, Inc., P.O. Box 950, Raleigh, NC 27602-0950 USA (SAN 169-6467) Tel 919-833-6615.
North Central Bk. Distributors, N57 W13636 Carmen Ave., Menomonee Falls, WI 53051 USA (SAN 173-5195) Tel 414-781-3299; Fax: 414-781-4432; Toll Free: 800-966-3299.
North Country Bks., Inc., *(978-0-925168; 978-0-932052; 978-0-9601158; 978-1-59531)* 220 Lafayette Street, Utica, NY 13502 USA (SAN 110-828X) Tel 315-735-4877; Fax: (315) 738-4342
E-mail: ncbooks@verizon.net
Web site: http://www.northcountrybooks.com.
North Shore Distributors, 1200 N. Branch, Chicago, IL 60622 USA (SAN 169-2275).
North Shore News Co., Inc., 150 Blossom St., Lynn, MA 01902 USA (SAN 169-3492).
North Texas Periodicals, Inc., Orders Addr.: P.O. Box 3823, Lubbock, TX 79452 USA Tel 806-745-6000; Fax: 806-745-7028; Edit Addr.: 118 E. 70th St., Lubbock, TX 79404 USA
E-mail: ntp@hts-online.net.
Northern News Co., P.O. Box 467, Petoskey, MI 49770-0467 USA (SAN 169-3964) Toll Free: 800-632-7138 (Michigan only).
Northern Schl. Supply Co., P.O. Box 2627, Fargo, ND 58108 USA (SAN 169-6548) Fax: 800-891-5836.
Northern Sun, 2916 E. Lake St., Minneapolis, MN 55406 USA (SAN 249-9290) Tel 612-729-2001; Fax: 612-729-0149; Toll Free: 800-258-8579.
Northern Sun Merchandising, *See* **Northern Sun**
North-South Bks., Inc., *(978-0-7358; 978-1-55858; 978-1-58717)* 350 7th Ave. Rm. 1400, New York, NY 10001-5013 USA
E-mail: mnavarro@northsouth.com
Web site: http://www.northsouth.com.
Northwest News, 1560 NE First St., No. 13, Bend, OR 97701 USA (SAN 111-8587) Tel 541-382-6065; 3100 Merriman Rd., Medford, OR 97501 Tel 541-779-5225.
Northwest News Company, Incorporated, *See* **Benjamin News Group**
Northwest Textbook Depository, Orders Addr.: P.O. Box 5608, Portland, OR 97228 USA Toll Free: 800-676-6630; Edit Addr.: 17970 SW McEwan Rd., Portland, OR 97224 USA (SAN 631-4481) Tel 503-639-3193; Fax: 503-639-2559.
Norton News Agency, 905 Kelly Ln., Dubuque, IA 52003-8526 USA (SAN 169-2631); 1467 Service Dr., Winona, MN 55987 (SAN 156-4889).
Norton, W. W. & Co., Inc., *(978-0-393; 978-1-324)* Orders Addr.: c/o National Book Company, 800 Keystone Industrial Pk., Scranton, PA 18512 USA (SAN 157-1869) Tel 570-346-2020; Fax: 570-346-1442; Toll Free: 800-233-4830; Edit Addr.: 500 Fifth Ave., New York, NY 10110-0017 USA (SAN 202-5795) Tel 212-354-5500; Fax: 212-869-0856; Toll Free: 800-223-2584
Web site: http://www.wwnorton.com.
Notions Marketing, 1500 Buchanan Ave., SW, Grand Rapids, MI 49507-1613 USA.
NTC/Contemporary Publishing Company, *See* **McGraw-Hill/Contemporary**
Nueces News Agency, 5130 Commerce Pkwy., San Antonio, TX 78218-5523 USA (SAN 169-8079).
Nueva Vida Distributors, 4300 Montana Ave., El Paso, TX 79903-4503 USA (SAN 107-8615) Tel 915-565-6215; Fax: 915-565-1722.
Nutri-Bks. Corp., Div. of Royal Pubns., Inc., 790 W. Tennessee Ave., P.O. Box 5793, Denver, CO 80223 USA Tel 303-778-8383; Fax: 303-744-9383; Toll Free: 800-279-2048 (orders only).
Oak Knoll Pr., *(978-0-938768; 978-1-884718; 978-1-58456; 978-1-872116)* 310 Delaware St., New Castle, DE 19720 USA (SAN 216-2776) Tel 302-328-7232; Fax: 302-328-7274; Toll Free: 800-996-2556 Do not confuse with Oak Knoll Press in Hardy, VA
E-mail: oakknoll@oakknoll.com
Web site: http://www.oakknoll.com.
Octagon Pr./ISHK Bk. Service, *See* **I S H K**
Ohio Periodical Distributors, P.O. Box 145449, Cincinnati, OH 45250-5449 USA (SAN 169-6904) Fax: 513-853-6245; Toll Free: 800-777-2216.
Ohio Univ. Pr., *(978-0-8214)* Orders Addr.: 11030 S. Langley Ave., Chicago, IL 60628 USA Tel 773-702-7000; Fax: 773-702-7212; Toll Free Fax: 800-621-8476; Toll Free: 800-621-2736; Edit Addr.: 19 Circle Dr. The Ridges, Athens, OH 45701 USA (SAN 282-0773) Tel 740-593-1154; Fax: 740-593-4536
Web site: http://www.ohiou.edu/oupress/.
Oil City News Co., 112 Innis St., Oil City, PA 16301-2930 USA (SAN 169-7501).
Oleand Pubns., P.O. Box 375, Lyons, WI 53148 USA Tel 262-342-0018 (phone/fax)
E-mail: wings@oleand.com.
Ollis Bk. Corp., Orders Addr.: P.O. Box 258, Steger, IL 60475 USA (SAN 658-1323); Edit Addr.: 28 E. 35th St., Steger, IL 60475 USA (SAN 169-2224) Tel 312-755-5151; Fax: 708-755-5153; Toll Free: 800-323-0343.
Olson, D & Company, *See* **Nelson's Bks.**
Olson News Agency, P.O. Box 129, Ishpeming, MI 49849 USA (SAN 169-3832).
Omega Pubns., Inc., *(978-0-930872; 978-1-941810)* 34 Amity Pl., Amherst, MA 01002-2255 USA (SAN 214-1493) Toll Free: 888-443-7107 (orders only) Do not confuse with companies with the same name in Medford, OR, Indianapolis, IN
E-mail: sufibooks@omegapub.com
Web site: http://www.omegapub.com.
Omnibooks, 456 Vista Del Mar Dr., Aptos, CA 95003-4832 USA (SAN 168-9487) Tel 408-688-4098; Toll Free: 800-626-6671.
Omnibus Pr., *(978-0-7119; 978-0-8256; 978-0-86001; 978-1-84449)* Div. of Music Sales Corp., Orders Addr.: 445 Bellvale Rd., Chester, NY 10918-0572 USA Tel 845-469-4699; Fax: 845-469-7544; Toll Free Fax: 800-345-6842; Toll Free: 800-431-7187; Edit Addr.: 257 Park Ave., S., 20th Flr., New York, NY 10010 USA Tel 212-254-2100; Fax: 212-254-2013 Do not confuse with Omnibus Pr., Menasha, WI
E-mail: info@musicsales.com
Web site: http://www.musicsales.com.
One Small Voice Foundation, P.O. Box 644, Elmhurst, IL 60126 USA Tel 630-620-6634
E-mail: onesmallvoice@earthlink.net
Web site: http://www.onesmallvoicefoundation.org.
Onondaga News Agency, P.O. Box 6445, Syracuse, NY 13217-6445 USA (SAN 169-6297).
OPA Publishing & Distributing, Orders Addr.: P.O. Box 1764, Chandler, AZ 85244-1764 USA; Edit Addr.: 777 W. Chandler Blvd., Suite 1322, Chandler, AZ 85244-1764 USA.
Open Road Integrated Media, LLC, *(978-1-936317; 978-1-4532; 978-1-4804; 978-1-4976; 978-1-5040)* 180 Varick St. Suite 816, New York, NY 10014 USA Tel 212-691-0900; Fax: 212-691-0901; 345 Hudson St., Suite 6C, New York, NY 10014 Tel 212-691-0900; Fax: 212-691-0901
E-mail: acolvin@openroadmedia.com
Web site: http://www.openroadmedia.com.
Options Unlimited, 550 Swan Creek Ct., Suwanee, GA 30174 USA (SAN 631-3949) Tel 770-237-3282 Do not confuse with Options Unlimited, Inc., Green Bay, WI.
OptumInsight, Inc., *(978-1-56329; 978-1-56337; 978-1-60151; 978-1-62254)* 2525 Lake Park Blvd., West Valley City, UT 84120 USA (SAN 630-5482) Tel 801-982-3000; Toll Free: 800-464-3649 (phone/fax)
E-mail: jeni.smith@ingenix.com; chris.smith@ingenix.com; jean.parkinson@ingenix.com
Web site: http://www.ingenix.com; http://www.IngenixOnline.com.
Orange News Company, *See* **Anderson News, LLC**
Orbit Bks. Corp., 43 Timberline Dr., Poughkeepsie, NY 12603 USA (SAN 169-6157) Tel 914-462-5653; Fax: 914-462-8409.
Orca Bk. Pubs. USA, *(978-0-920501; 978-1-55143; 978-1-55469)* Orders Addr.: P.O. Box 468, Custer, WA 98240-0468 USA (SAN 630-9674) Tel 250-380-1229; Fax: 250-380-1892; Toll Free: 800-210-5277
E-mail: orca@orcabook.com
Web site: http://www.orcabook.com.
Oregon State Univ. Pr., *(978-0-87071)* 500 Kerr Administration Bldg., Corvallis, OR 97331-2122 USA (SAN 202-8328) Tel 541-737-3166; Fax: 541-737-3170; Toll Free: 800-426-3797
E-mail: osu.press@oregonstate.edu
Web site: http://osu.orst.edu/dept/press.
O'Reilly & Associates, Incorporated, *See* **O'Reilly Media, Inc.**
O'Reilly Media, Inc., *(978-0-937175; 978-1-56592; 978-3-89721; 978-3-930673; 978-4-900900; 978-0-596; 978-4-87311; 978-1-60033; 978-1-4493; 978-1-4919; 978-1-4920; 978-1-4571)* Orders Addr.: 1005 Gravenstein Hwy. N., Sebastopol, CA 95472 USA (SAN 658-5973) Fax: 707-829-0104; Toll Free: 800-998-9938; Edit Addr.: 10 Fawcett St. Ste. 4, Cambridge, MA 02138-1175 USA Toll Free: 800-775-7731; 4 Castle St, Farnham, GU9 7HR Tel 01252 71 17 76; Fax: 01252 73 42 11; c/o Madeleine Fakhoury Editions O'Reilly, 18, rue Seguier, Paris, F-75006 Tel 33 1 40 51 52 30; Fax: 33 1 40 51 52 31; c/o Michelle Chen, SIGMA Building, Suite B809 No. 49 Zhichun Rd. Haidian District, Beijing, 100080 Tel 86-10-88097476; 86-10-88097475; Fax: 86-10-88097463; c/o O'Reilly Verlag, Gerd Miske, Balthasarstr. 81, Köln, D-50670 Tel 49 221 973160 0; Fax: 49 221 973160 8; 1Fl, No. 21, Lane 295 Section 1, Fu-Shing South Rd., Taipei, Tel 886 2 27099669; Fax: 886 2 27038802; Intelligent Plaza Bldg. 1F 26 Banchi 27, Sakamachi, Shinjuku-ku, Tokyo, 160-0002 Tel 81 3 3356 5227; Fax: 81 3 3356 5261
E-mail: order@oreilly.com; information@oreilly.co.uk; nuts@ora.com
Web site: http://www.oreilly.com; http://www.editions-oreilly.fr; http://oreilly.co.uk; http://oreilly.com.tw; http://www.ora.com; http://www.oreilly.fr/; http://www.oreilly.com.cn/.
Original Pubns., *(978-0-942272)* Subs. of Maximo, Inc., 129 Forest Dr., Jericho, NY 11753-2324 USA (SAN 133-0225) Toll Free: 888-622-8581.
Osborne Enterprises Publishing, *(978-0-932117)* P.O. Box 255, Port Townsend, WA 98368 USA (SAN 242-7567) Tel 360-385-1200; Toll Free: 800-246-3255 (orders only)
E-mail: jpo@olympus.net
Web site: http://www.jerryosborne.com.
Osborne/McGraw-Hill, *See* **McGraw-Hill Osborne**
Oslander Bk. Trade, 7483H Candlewood Rd., Hanover, MD 21076-3102 USA (SAN 130-0970).
Outbooks, Incorporated, *See* **Vistabooks**
Outdoorsman, The, Orders Addr.: P.O. Box 268, Boston, MA 02134 USA (SAN 169-3352).
Outskirts Pr., Inc., *(978-0-9725874; 978-1-932672; 978-1-59800; 978-1-4327; 978-0-615-20388-1; 978-1-4787)* 10940 S. Parker Rd.- 515, Parker, CO 80134 USA (SAN 256-5420)
Web site: http://www.OutskirtsPress, Inc.com.
Outskirts Press, Incorporation, *See* **Outskirts Pr., Inc.**
OverDrive, Inc., Valley Tech Ctr. 8555 Sweet Valley Dr., Cleveland, OH 44125-4210 USA (SAN 245-0658) Tel 216-573-6886; Fax: 216-573-6888
Web site: http://www.overdrive.com.
OverDrive Systems, Incorporated, *See* **OverDrive, Inc.**
Overmountain Pr., *(978-0-932807; 978-0-9644613; 978-1-57072; 978-1-935692)* P.O. Box 1261, Johnson City, TN 37605 USA (SAN 687-6641) Tel 423-926-2691; Fax: 423-232-1252; Toll Free: 800-992-2691 (orders only)
E-mail: beth@overmtn.com
Web site: http://www.silverdaggermysteries.com; http://www.overmountainpress.com.
Oxford Univ. Pr., Inc., *(978-0-19)* Orders Addr.: 2001 Evans Rd., Cary, NC 27513 USA (SAN 202-5892) Tel 919-677-0977 (general voice); Fax: 919-677-1303 (customer service); Toll Free: 800-445-9714 (customer service - inquiry); 800-451-7556 (customer service - orders); Edit Addr.: 198 Madison Ave., New York, NY 10016-4314 USA (SAN 202-5884) Tel 212-726-6000 (general voice); Fax: 212-726-6440 (general fax)
E-mail: custserv@oup-usa.org; orders@oup-usa.org
Web site: http://www.oup.com/us.
Oxmoor Hse., Inc., *(978-0-376; 978-0-8487)* Orders Addr.: Leisure Arts 5701 Ranch Dr., Little Rock, AR 72223 USA; Edit Addr.: 2100 Lakeshore Dr., Birmingham, AL 35209 USA Tel 205-445-6000; Fax: 205-445-6078; Toll Free: 800-633-4910
E-mail: allison_lowery@timeinc.com
Web site: http://www.oxmoorhouse.com/.
Ozark Bk. Distributors, 1802 Van Buren Ave., Mountain Home, AR 72653 USA.
Ozark Magazine Distributing, Incorporated, *See* **Ozark News Distributor, Inc.**
Ozark News Agency, Inc., P.O. Box 1150, Fayetteville, AR 72702 USA.
Ozark News Distributor, Inc., 1630 N. Eldon Ave., Springfield, MO 65803 USA (SAN 169-4332) Tel 417-862-9224; Fax: 417-862-6642; Toll Free: 800-743-0380.
P & G Wholesale, P.O. Box 1548, Fargo, ND 58102 USA (SAN 156-4536).
P & R Publishing, *(978-0-87552; 978-1-59638; 978-1-62995)* Orders Addr.: 1102 Marble Hill Rd., Harmony, Phillipsburg, NJ 08865 USA (SAN 658-1463) Tel 908-454-0505; Fax: 908-859-2390; Toll Free: 800-631-0094 Do not confuse with P & R Publishing Co. in Sioux Center, IA
E-mail: tara@prpbooks.com; jesse@prpbooks.com
Web site: http://www.prpbooks.com.
P C I Education, *(978-1-884074; 978-1-58804; 978-1-61975)* 4560 Lockhill-Selma, Suite 100, San Antonio, TX 78265-4270 USA Tel 210-377-1999; Fax: 210-377-1121; Toll Free Fax: 888-259-8284; Toll Free: 800-594-4263
E-mail: lboulet@pcieducation.com
Web site: http://www.pcieducation.com.
P C I Educational Publishing, *See* **P C I Education**
P. D. Music Headquarters, Inc., Orders Addr.: P.O. Box 252, New York, NY 10014 USA (SAN 282-5880) Tel 212-242-5322.
Pacific Bks., *(978-1-885375)* Orders Addr.: P.O. Box 3562, Santa Barbara, CA 93130 USA (SAN 630-2548) Tel 805-687-8340; Fax: 805-687-2514; Edit Addr.: 2573 Treasure Dr., Santa Barbara, CA 93105 USA.
Pacific Island Bks., 2802 E. 132nd Cir., Thornton, CO 80241 USA Fax: 603-368-6628; Toll Free: 888-492-6657 (888-49-BOOKS)
E-mail: pacificbks@aol.com
Web site: http://www.pacificislandbooks.com.
Pacific Learning, Inc., *(978-1-59055; 978-1-60457; 978-1-61391)* Orders Addr.: P.O. Box 2723, Huntington Beach, CA 92647-0723 USA; Edit Addr.: 15342 Graham St., Huntington Beach, CA 92649 USA Tel 714-516-8307; Fax: 714-516-8369; Toll Free: 800-279-0737
E-mail: info@pacificlearning.com
Web site: http://www.pacificlearning.com.

Pacific Magazine-Bk. Wholesaler, 1515 NW 51st St., Seattle, WA 98107 USA (SAN 274-3884) Tel 206-789-5333.

Pacific Periodical Services, LLC, *See* **Anderson News - Tacoma**

Pacific Pr. Publishing Assn., (*978-0-8163; 978-1-5180*) P.O. Box 5353, Nampa, ID 83653-5353 USA (SAN 202-8409) Tel 208-465-2500; Fax: 208-465-2531; Toll Free: 800-447-7377
E-mail: donlay@pacificpress.com
Web site: http://www.AdventistBookCenter.com; http://www.pacificpress.com.

Pacific Trade Group, 68-309 Crozier Dr., Waialua, HI 96791 USA (SAN 169-1635) Tel 808-636-2300; Fax: 808-636-2301.

Paladin Pr., (*978-0-87364; 978-1-58160; 978-1-891268; 978-1-61004*) Orders Addr.: c/o Gunbarrel Tech Ctr., 7077 Winchester Cir., Boulder, CO 80301 USA (SAN 662-1066) Tel 303-443-7250; Fax: 303-442-8741; Toll Free: 800-392-2400 (Credit Card Orders Only)
E-mail: sales@paladin-press.com; editorial@paladin-press.com; service@paladin-press.com
Web site: http://www.paladin-press.com; http://www.flying-machines.com; http://www.sycamoreisland.com.

Palgrave, *See* **Palgrave Macmillan**

Palgrave Macmillan, (*978-0-312; 978-0-333; 978-1-4039*) Orders Addr.: 16365 James Madison Hwy., Gordonsville, VA 22942-8501 USA Toll Free Fax: 800-672-2054; Toll Free: 888-330-8477; Edit Addr.: 175 Fifth Ave., New York, NY 10010 USA Tel 212-982-9300; Fax: 212-777-6359; Toll Free Fax: 800 672-2054 (Customer Service); Toll Free: 800-221-7945; 888-330-8477 (Customer Service)
E-mail: customerservice@vhpsva.com
Web site: http://www.palgrave.com.

Palmer News Co., Inc., 534 S. Kansas Ave. Ste. 700, Topeka, KS 66603-3429 USA.

Palmer News, Inc., 9605 Dice Ln., Lenexa, KS 66215 USA Tel 913-541-8600; Fax: 913-541-9413
E-mail: palmerco@oni.com.

Palmetto News Co., 200 Sunbelt Ct., Greer, SC 29650-9349 USA.

Pan American Publishing, Inc., (*978-1-889867*) 420 E. Ohio St., Suite 4-F, Chicago, IL 60611-3355 USA (SAN 299-1977) Tel 773-404-7282.

Pan Asia Pubns. (USA), Inc., (*978-1-57227*) 29564 Union City Blvd., Union City, CA 94587 USA (SAN 173-685X) Tel 510-475-1185; Fax: 510-475-1489; Toll Free: 800-909-8088
E-mail: sales@panap.com; info@panap.com
Web site: http://www.panap.com; http://www.cjkv.com.

Pan De Vida Distributors, (*978-1-934811*) 5507 Brooks St., Montclair, CA 91763 USA (SAN 631-0753) Tel 909-510-5219; 909-510-5200; Fax: 909-510-5210
Web site: http://www.pandevida.com.

Panamericana Publishing LLC, 12902 SW 133 Ct., Suite D, Miami, FL 33186 USA (SAN 256-1409) Tel 305-278-2648; Fax: 305-436-7264
E-mail: operez@panamericana.com.co
Web site: http://panamericanaeditorial.com.

Pantheon Bks., (*978-0-375; 978-0-394; 978-0-676; 978-0-679*) Orders Addr.: 400 Hahn Rd., Westminster, MD 21157 USA Toll Free: 800-733-3000 (orders); Edit Addr.: 299 Park Ave, New York, NY 10171 USA (SAN 202-862X).

Paperback Books, Incorporated, *See* **Bk. Distribution Ctr., Inc.**

Paperbacks for Educators, (*978-0-9702376; 978-1-59721*) 426 W. Front St., Washington, MO 63090 USA (SAN 103-3379) Tel 636-239-1999; Fax: 636-239-4515; Toll Free Fax: 800-514-7323; Toll Free: 800-227-2591
E-mail: paperbacks@usmo.com
Web site: http://www.any-book-in-print.com.

Paradise Cay Pubns., (*978-0-939837; 978-1-937196*) P.O. Box 29, Arcata, CA 95518-0029 USA (SAN 663-690X) Tel 707-822-9063; Fax: 707-822-9163; Toll Free: 800-736-4509 (orders only)
E-mail: jim@paracay.com
Web site: http://www.paracay.com.

Parent Services Project, 79 Belvedere St., Suite 101, San Rafael, CA 94901 USA Tel 415-454-1870
E-mail: family@parentservices.org.

Parklane Publishing, (*978-1-59384*) Div. of Book Club of America, 100 Marcus Blvd. Ste. 8, Hauppauge, NY 11788-3749 USA
E-mail: lbaumert@bookclubusa.com
Web site: http://www.parklanepublishing.com.

Parkwest Pubns., Inc., (*978-0-88186*) P.O. Box 310251, Miami, FL 33231 USA (SAN 264-6846) Tel 305-256-7880; Fax: 305-256-7816
E-mail: parkwest@parkwestpubs.com; info@parkwestpubs.com
Web site: http://www.parkwestpubs.com.

Parliament News Co., Inc., P.O. Box 910, Santa Clarita, CA 91380-9010 USA (SAN 168-9924).

Parnassus Bk. Distributors, 200 Academy Way, Columbia, SC 29206-1445 USA (SAN 631-0680) Tel 803-782-7748; Toll Free: 800-782-7760.

Partners Bk. Distributing, Inc., Orders Addr.: P.O. Box 580, Holt, MI 48842 USA; Edit Addr.: 2325 Jarco Dr., Holt, MI 48842 USA (SAN 630-4559) Tel 517-694-3205; Toll Free: 800-336-3137 (orders).

Partners Book Distributing, Incorporated, *See* **Partners Pubs. Group, Inc.**

Partners Distributing, Orders Addr.: 13089 Root Rd., Columbia Station, OH 44028 USA Tel 216-236-3744.

Partners Pubs. Group, Inc., Orders Addr.: 2325 Jarco Dr., Holt, MI 48842 USA (SAN 631-3418) Tel 517-694-3205; Fax: 517-694-0617; Toll Free: 800-336-3137
E-mail: info@partnerspublishersgroup.com
Web site: http://www.partnerspublishersgroup.com.

Partners/West Book Distributors, 1901 Raymond Ave., SW, Suite C, Renton, WA 98055 USA (SAN 631-421X) Tel 425-227-8486; Fax: 425-204-1448; Toll Free: 800-563-2385.

Pathfinder Pr., (*978-0-87348; 978-0-913460; 978-1-60488*) Orders Addr.: P.O. Box 162767, Atlanta, GA 30321-2767 USA Tel 404-669-0600 (voice mail only); Fax: 707-667-1141; Pathfinder Books/Livres Pathfinder 6362 Fraser St. Suite 264, VANCOUVER, BC V5W 0A1 Tel 888-692-4939; Fax: 888-692-4939; 120 Bethnal Green Rd., London, E2 6DG; P.O. Box 10130,75723, Paris, Cedex 15 FRANCE Tel 014-010-2837; Fax: 014-010-2837; Australia Pathfinder Level 1, 3/281-287 Beamish St., Campsie, NSW, NSW 2194 Tel 029-718-9698; Fax: 029-718-9698; Unit 4, 125 Grafton Rd., Grafton, Auckland, none; Edit Addr.: 306 W. 37th St., 10th Flr., New York, NY 10018 USA (SAN 202-5906) Do not confuse with companies with the same or similar names in Alameda, CA, Battle Ground, WA, Elicott City, MD, Midland, MI
E-mail: pathfinder@pathfinderpress.com; permissions@pathfinderpress.com; orders@pathfinderpress.com
Web site: http://www.pathfinderpress.com.

Pathway Bk. Service, Div. of MLES, Inc., Orders Addr.: 4 White Brook Rd., Gilsum, NH 03448 USA (SAN 170-0545) Tel 603-357-0236; Fax: 603-357-2073; Toll Free: 800-345-6665; P.O. Box 89, Gilsum, NH 03448
E-mail: pbs@pathwaybook.com
Web site: http://www.pathwaybook.com.

Pathway Bks., (*978-0-935538*) P.O. Box 27790, Golden Valley, MN 55427-0790 USA (SAN 213-4241) Tel 612-694-9434; Toll Free: 800-958-3375 (Pin 32) Do not confuse with Pathway Books, Gilsum, NH
E-mail: shermjim@aol.com
Web site: http://www.caregiver911.com.

Paul & Co. Pubs. Consortium, Inc., Div. of Independent Publishers Group, Orders Addr.: 814 N. Franklin St., Chicago, IL 60610 USA Tel 312-337-0747; Fax: 312-337-5985; Toll Free: 800-888-4741
E-mail: frontdesk@ipgbook.com
Web site: http://www.ipgbook.com.

Paulsen, G. Co., 27 Sheep Davis Rd., Pembroke, NH 03275 USA (SAN 169-4499) Tel 603-225-9787.

PBD, Inc., (*978-0-9846038; 978-0-9837260; 978-1-62219*) 1650 Bluegrass Lakes Pkwy., Alpharetta, GA 30004 USA (SAN 126-6039) Tel 770-442-8633; Fax: 770-442-9742
Web site: http://www.pbd.com.

PCE International, 8811 Aviation Blvd., Inglewood, CA 90301 USA Tel 310-337-0055; Fax: 310-642-4625; Toll Free: 800-626-1313.

PDR Network, LLC, (*978-0-87489; 978-0-942036; 978-1-56363; 978-1-880080*) 5 Paragon Dr., Montvale, NJ 07645-1742 USA (SAN 253-0562) Tel 201-358-7522; Fax: 201-722-2686; Toll Free Fax: 877-737-3535; Toll Free: 800-442-6657
Web site: http://www.pdr.net; http://www.pdrnetwork.net/.

Peabody Essex Museum, (*978-0-87577; 978-0-88389*) Orders Addr.: East India Sq., Salem, MA 01970 USA Tel 978-745-9500 ext 3047; Fax: 978-740-3622; Toll Free: 800-745-4054 ext 3047
E-mail: wholesale@pem.org
Web site: http://www.pem.org.

Pearson Education, (*978-0-582; 978-0-7686; 978-1-5093*) Orders Addr.: 200 Old Tappan Rd., Old Tappan, NJ 07675 USA (SAN 200-2175) Tel 201-767-5000 (Receptionist); Toll Free Fax: 800-445-6991; Toll Free: 800-428-5331; 800-922-0579; Edit Addr.: One Lake St., Upper Saddle River, NJ 07458 USA Tel 201-236-7000; 201-236-5321; Fax: 201-236-6549; 800 E. 96th St., Suite 300, Indianapolis, IN 46240 Toll Free: 800-571-4580
E-mail: communications@pearsoned.com
Web site: http://www.pearsoned.com; www.pearson.com.

Pearson Learning, (*978-0-7652; 978-1-4284*) Div of Pearson Education, Orders Addr.: P.O. Box 2500, Lebanon, IN 46052 USA Toll Free Fax: 800-393-3156; Toll Free: 800-321-3106; Edit Addr.: 1 Lake St., U Saddle Riv, NJ 07458-1813 USA Toll Free: 800-526-9907 (Customer Service)
E-mail: jeff.hoitsma@pearsonlearning.com
Web site: http://www.pearsonlearning.com.

Pearson Technology Group, One Lake St., Upper Saddle River, NJ 07458 USA.

Pee Dee News Co., 2321 Lawrens Cir., Florence, SC 29501-9408 USA.

Pegasus Pr., (*978-1-889818*) 2641 S. Emerson St., Chandler, AZ 85248-3248 USA Do not confuse with companies with the same name in Vashon Island, WA, San Diego, CA, Kerrville, TX, Lake Forest, IL
E-mail: pegpress@hotmail.com
Web site: http://www.pegpress.org.

Pegram, Christine, 1901 Upper Cove Terr., Sarasota, FL 33581 USA (SAN 110-0254) Tel 941-921-2467.

Pekin News Agency, 1637 Monroe St., Madison, WI 53711-2021 USA (SAN 169-2151).

Pelican Publishing Co., Inc., (*978-0-88289; 978-0-911116; 978-1-56554; 978-1-58980; 978-1-4556*) Orders Addr.: 1000 Burmaster St., Gretna, LA 70053-2246 USA Tel 504-368-1175; Fax: 504-368-1195; Toll Free: 800-843-1724 ordering Do not confuse with companies with the same or similar names in Lowell, MA, Dallas, TX
E-mail: Sales@pelicanpub.com; promo@pelicanpub.com; editorial@pelicanpub.com
Web site: http://www.pelicanpub.com.

Peller, A. W. & Assocs., 210 Sixth Ave., P.O. Box 106, Hawthorne, NJ 07507-0106 USA (SAN 631-1563) Tel 973-423-4666; Fax: 973-423-5569; Toll Free: 800-451-7450
E-mail: awpeller@worldnet.att.net
Web site: http://www.awpeller.com.

Pen Notes, Inc., (*978-0-939564*) 10111 NW 24th Pl. Apt. 201, Sunrise, FL 33322-6882 USA (SAN 107-3621)
E-mail: pennotes@worldnet.att.net.

Penguin Group (USA) Incorporated, *See* **Penguin Publishing Group**

Penguin Publishing Group, (*978-0-14; 978-0-399; 978-0-425; 978-0-525; 978-0-698; 978-0-87477; 978-1-58542; 978-1-933438; 978-1-4295; 978-1-934511; 978-1-4362; 978-1-4406; 978-1-101; 978-1-937007*) Orders Addr.: 405 Murray Hill Pkwy., East Rutherford, NJ 07073-2136 USA (SAN 282-5074) Fax: 201-933-2903 (customer service); Toll Free Fax: 800-227-9604; Toll Free: 800-526-0275 (reseller sales); 800-631-8571 (reseller customer service); 800-788-6262 (individual consumer sales); Edit Addr.: 375 Hudson St., New York, NY 10014 USA Tel 212-366-2000; Fax: 212-366-2666; 405 Murray Hill Pkwy., East Rutherford, NJ 07073 (SAN 852-5455) Tel 201-933-9292
E-mail: customer.service@us.penguingroup.com
Web site: http://penguingroup.custhelp.com; http://booksellers.penguingroup.com; http://www.penguinputnam.com.

Penguin Random Hse., LLC., (*978-1-101*) 375 Hudson St. 3rd Flr., New York, NY 10014 USA Tel 212-366-2424
E-mail: brittany.wienke@us.penguingroup.com
Web site: PenguinRandomHouse.com.

Peniel Productions, 73 Smith Hill Rd., Monsey, NY 10952-4131 USA (SAN 631-2837).

Pen-Mar News Distributors, *See* **Americana Souvenirs & Gifts**

Penmarch Publishing, 3932 S. Willow Ave., Sioux Falls, SD 57105 USA Toll Free: 800-282-2399.

Penn News Co., 944 Franklin St., Johnstown, PA 15905 USA (SAN 169-7390).

Pennsylvania State Univ. Pr., (*978-0-271*) Orders Addr.: 820 N. University Dr., USB-1 Suite C, University Park, PA 16802 USA (SAN 213-5760) Tel 814-865-1327; Fax: 814-863-1408; Toll Free Fax: 877-778-2665 (orders only); Toll Free: 800-326-9180 (orders only)
E-mail: info@psupress.org; log-ins@press.psu.edu
Web site: http://www.psupress.org.

Pentecostal Publishing Hse., (*978-0-912315*) Subs. of United Pentecostal Church International, 8855 Dunn Rd., Hazelwood, MO 63042-2299 USA (SAN 219-3817) Tel 314-837-7300; (314) 837-7300; Fax: 314-837-4503
E-mail: PPHpublish@aol.com.

Penton Overseas, Inc., (*978-0-939001; 978-1-56015; 978-1-59125; 978-1-60379*) 1958 Kellogg Ave., Carlsbad, CA 92008 USA (SAN 631-0826) Tel 760-431-0060; Fax: 760-431-8110; Toll Free: 800-748-5804
E-mail: kellie@pentonoverseas.com; susan@pentonoverseas.com
Web site: http://www.pentonoverseas.com.

Peoples Education, (*978-1-56256; 978-1-58984; 978-1-4138; 978-1-61526; 978-1-61527; 978-1-936025; 978-1-936026; 978-1-936027; 978-1-936028; 978-1-936029; 978-1-936030; 978-1-936031; 978-0-692-00207-0; 978-0-692-00208-7; 978-0-692-00209-4; 978-0-692-00210-0; 978-1-61602; 978-1-61734; 978-1-60979) Orders Addr.: P.O. Box 513, Saddle Brook, NJ 07633 USA Tel 201-712-0090; Fax: 201-712-1534; Toll Free: 800-822-1080; Edit Addr.: 299 Market St. Suite 240, Saddle Brook, NJ 07663 USA (SAN 857-9873)*
E-mail: solvier@peoplesed.com; sales@peoplesed.com; customersupport@peoplesed.com; editorial@peoplesed.com
Web site: http://www.peopleseducation.com/.

Peoples Publishing Group, Incorporated, The, *See* **Peoples Education**

Peregrine Outfitters, Orders Addr.: P.O. Box 1500, Williston, VT 05495 USA (SAN 631-1059) Tel 802-860-2977; Fax: 802-860-2978; Toll Free: 800-222-3088; Edit Addr.: 25 Omega Dr., Suite A, Williston, VT 05482 USA.

Perelandra, Ltd., (*978-0-927978; 978-0-9617713*) Orders Addr.: P.O. Box 3603, Warrenton, VA 20188 USA (SAN 665-0198) Tel 540-937-2153; Fax: 540-937-3360; Toll Free: 800-960-8806
E-mail: email@perelandra-ltd.com
Web site: http://www.perelandra-ltd.com.

Perfection Form Company, The, *See* **Perfection Learning Corp.**

Perfection Learning Corp., (*978-0-7807; 978-0-7891; 978-0-8124; 978-0-89598; 978-1-56312; 978-0-7569; 978-1-60686; 978-1-61563; 978-1-61383; 978-1-61384; 978-1-62299; 978-1-62359; 978-1-62765; 978-1-62766; 978-1-62974; 978-1-63419; 978-1-68064; 978-1-68065; 978-1-68240*) 1000 N. 2nd Ave., Logan, IA 51546 USA (SAN 221-0010) Tel 712-644-2831; Fax: 712-644-2392; Toll Free Fax: 800-543-2745; Toll Free: 800-831-4190
E-mail: orders@perfectionlearning.com
Web site: http://www.perfectionlearning.com.

Perfume River Pubns., 1420 2nd Ave., N., Suite 304, Sauk Rapids, MN 56379 USA Tel 320-761-1229.

Periodical Distributors, Incorporated, *See* **North Texas Periodicals, Inc.**

Periodical Marketing Services, 1065 Bloomfield Ave., Clifton, NJ 07012 USA (SAN 250-5304) Tel 201-342-6334.

Periodical Pubs. Service Bureau, One N. Superior St., Sandusky, OH 44870 USA (SAN 285-9351) Tel 419-626-0623.

Periodicals Service Co., (*978-0-527; 978-0-8115; 978-3-262; 978-3-601*) 11 Main St., Germantown, NY 12526 USA (SAN 164-8608) Tel 518-537-4700; Fax: 518-537-5899
E-mail: psc@periodicals.com
Web site: http://www.periodicals.com.

Perma-Bound Bks., (*978-0-605; 978-0-7804; 978-0-8000; 978-0-8479*) Div. of Hertzberg-New Method, Inc., 617 E. Vandalia Rd., Jacksonville, IL 62650 USA (SAN 169-202X) Tel 217-243-5451; Fax: 217-243-7505; Toll Free Fax: 800-551-1169; Toll Free: 800-637-6581 (customer service)
E-mail: books@permabound.com
Web site: http://www.perma-bound.com.

Perrone, Calle 11. #372-A Urb. Hill Brothers, San Juan, PR 00924 USA Tel 787-764-6112; Fax: 787-754-2374 Do not confuse with Perrone in Franklin, TN
E-mail: ecruz@perroneimporters.com
Web site: http://www.perroneimporters.com.

Perry Enterprises, (*978-0-941518*) 3907 N. Foothill Dr., Provo, UT 84604 USA (SAN 171-0281) Tel 801-226-1002.

Perseus Academic, Div. of Perseus Books Group, Orders Addr.: c/o Perseus Books Group, 210 American Dr., Jackson, TN 38301 USA Toll Free Fax: 800-351-5073; Toll Free: 800-343-4499; c/o Publishers Group Canada, 76 Stafford St., Unit 300, Toronto, ON M6J 2S1 Tel 416-934-9900; Fax: 416-934-1410; Toll Free Fax: 800-565-3770; Toll Free: 800-663-5714
E-mail: academicorders@perseusbooks.com; client.info@perseusbooks.com
Web site: http://www.perseusacademic.com.

Perseus Bks. Group, (*978-0-7382; 978-0-938289; 978-1-58097; 978-1-882810; 978-1-903985*) Orders Addr.: 2465 Central Ave., Suite 200, Boulder, CO 80301-5728 USA Toll Free: 800-343-4499 (customer service); Edit Addr.: 387 Park Ave., S., 12th Flr., New York, NY 10016-8810 USA Tel 212-340-8100; Fax: 212-340-8105
E-mail: perseus.orders@perseusbooks.com
Web site: http://www.perseusbooksgroup.com.

Perseus Distribution, Orders Addr.: 210 American Dr., Jackson, TN 38301 USA Toll Free Fax: 800-351-5073 (Customer Service); Toll Free: 800-343-4499 (Customer Service); 800-788-3123
E-mail: ar@perseusbooks.com; celeste.winters@perseusbooks.com; Orderentry@perseusbooks.com
Web site: http://www.perseusdistribution.com/.

Perseus-PGW, Orders Addr.: 1094 Flex Dr., Jackson, TN 38301-5070 USA (SAN 631-7715) Tel 731-423-1973; Toll Free Fax: 800-351-5073; Toll Free: 800-343-4499; Edit Addr.: 387 Park Avenue South, New York, NY 10016 USA (SAN 631-760X) Tel 212-340-8100; Fax: 212-340-8195
E-mail: info@pgw.com
Web site: http://www.pgw.com/home.

Peterson's, (*978-0-7689; 978-0-87866; 978-1-56079*) Div. of Nelnet, Orders Addr.: P.O. Box 67005, Lawrenceville, NJ 08648-6105 USA (SAN 200-2167); Edit Addr.: 2000 Lenox Dr., 3rd Flr., Lawrenceville, NJ 08648 USA (SAN 297-5661) Tel 609-896-1800; Fax: 609-896-1811; Toll Free: 800-338-3282 X5660;Customer Service
E-mail: custsvc@petersons.com
Web site: http://www.petersons.com.

Petterson Antiques, 379 Clayton Dr., Charleston, SC 29414-5048 USA (SAN 114-2399).

Philosophy Documentation Ctr., (*978-0-912632; 978-1-889680; 978-1-63435*) Orders Addr.: P.O. Box 7147, Charlottesville, VA 22906-7147 USA (SAN 218-6586) Tel 434-220-3300; Fax: 434-220-3301; Toll Free: 800-444-2419
E-mail: order@pdcnet.org
Web site: http://www.pdcnet.org.

Phoenix Distributors, Orders Addr.: P.O. Box 1589, Blaine, WA 98231 USA Toll Free Fax: 800-298-4422.

Phoenix Learning Resources, LLC, (*978-0-7915*) Orders Addr.: P.O. Box 510, Honesdale, PA 18431 USA (SAN 246-148X) Tel 570-251-6871; Fax: 570-253-3227; Toll Free: 800-228-9345
E-mail: rich@phoenixlr.com
Web site: http://www.phoenixlr.com.

Phoenix Rising Pr., (*978-0-9840521; 978-1-936429*) 70 S. Val Vista Dr. Suite A3, Box 217, Gilbert, AZ 85296 USA (SAN 631-838X)
E-mail: support@phoenixrisingpress.com; lynnames@lynnames.com
Web site: http://www.phoenixrisingpress.com.

Physician's Desk Reference, *See* **PDR Network, LLC**

Pictorial Histories Distribution, *See* **West Virginia Book Co., The**

Pilgrim Pr., The/United Church Pr., (*978-0-8298*) Div. of United Church Board for Homeland Ministries, Orders Addr.: 226 Sheldon Rd., Berea, OH 44017-1234 USA Toll Free: 800-537-3394; Edit Addr.: 700 Prospect Ave. E., Cleveland, OH 44115-1100 USA Tel 216-736-3764; Fax: 216-736-2207
E-mail: ucpress@ucc.org; pilgrim@ucc.org
Web site: http://www.ucpress.com; http://www.pilgrimpress.com.

Pine Orchard, Inc., (*978-0-9645727; 978-1-930580*) Orders Addr.: 2850 Hwy 95 South. P.O. box 9184, Moscow, ID 83843 USA (SAN 253-4258) Tel 208-882-4838; Fax: 208-882-4845; Toll Free: 877-354-7433
E-mail: orders@pineorchard.com; pineorch@pineorchard.com
Web site: http://www.pineorchard.com.

Pine Orchard Press, *See* **Pine Orchard, Inc.**

Pioneer Enterprises, W10085 Pike Plain Rd., Dunbar, WI 54119 USA.

Pitsco Education, 1002 E. Adams St., Pittsburg, KS 66762-6050 USA Tel 620-231-0010.

Pittsfield News Co., Inc., 6 Westview Rd., Pittsfield, MA 01201 USA (SAN 124-2768) Tel 413-445-5682; Fax: 413-445-5683.

PixyJack Pr., Inc., (*978-0-9658098; 978-0-9773724; 978-1-936555*) Orders Addr.: P.O. Box 149, Masonville, CO 80541 USA Tel 303-810-2850; Toll Free Fax: 888-273-7499
E-mail: info@pixyjackpress.com
Web site: http://www.pixyjackpress.com.

Plains Distribution Service, P.O. Box 931, Moorhead, MN 56561 USA (SAN 169-6556).

Planeta Publishing Corp., (*978-0-9715256; 978-0-9719950; 978-0-9748724; 978-1-933169; 978-0-9795042*) 999 Ponce De Leon Blvd. Ste. 1045, Coral Gables, FL 33134-3047 USA
E-mail: mnorman@planetapublishing.com
Web site: http://www.planeta.es.

Plank Road Publishing, Orders Addr.: 3540 J N. 126 St., Brookfield, WI 53005 USA Tel 262-790-5210; Fax: 262-781-8818.

Players Pr., Inc., (*978-0-88734*) P.O. Box 1132, Studio City, CA 91614-0132 USA (SAN 239-0213) Tel 818-789-4980
E-mail: Playerspress@att.net.

Plough Publishing Hse., (*978-0-87486*) 151 Bowne Dr., Walden, NY 12586 USA (SAN 202-0092) Tel 845-572-3455; Fax: 845-572-3472; Toll Free: 800-521-8011
E-mail: info@plough.com
Web site: http://www.plough.com.

Plymouth Press, Limited, *See* **Plymouth Toy & Book**

Plymouth Toy & Book, (*978-1-882663*) 101 Panton Rd., Vergennes, VT 05491 USA Tel 802-877-2150; Fax: 802-877-2116; Toll Free: 800-350-1007 Do not confuse with Plymouth Pr. in Miami Beach, FL
E-mail: plymouth@together.net
Web site: http://www.plymouthtoyandbook.com.

PMG Bks. Ltd., P.O. Box 7608, San Antonio, TX 78207-0608 USA (SAN 631-3183).

Polk County Historical Assn., c/o UrbanDog Communications, Inc., P.O. Box 25474, Tampa, FL 33622 USA Tel 813-832-4538; Fax: 813-832-1759
E-mail: cbrownfl@earthlink.net.

Polybook Distributors, Orders Addr.: P.O. Box 109, Mount Vernon, NY 10550 USA Tel 914-664-1633; Fax: 904-428-3953; Edit Addr.: 501 Mamaroneck Ave., White Plains, NY 10605 USA (SAN 169-5568) Tel 914-328-6364
E-mail: mainstreetbook@gmail.com.

Pomona Valley News Agency, 10736 Fremont Ave., Ontario, CA 91762 USA (SAN 169-0019) Tel 909-591-3885.

Pop-M Company, *See* **Bk. Margins, Inc.**

Popular Subscription Service, P.O. Box 1566, Terre Haute, IN 47808 USA (SAN 285-9386) Tel 812-466-1258; Fax: 812-466-9443; Toll Free: 800-466-5038
E-mail: info@popularsubscriptionsvc.com
Web site: http://www.popularsubscriptionsvc.com.

Portland News Co., Orders Addr.: P.O. Box 6970, Scarborough, ME 04070-6970 USA (SAN 169-3093) Toll Free: 800-639-1708 (in Maine); Edit Addr.: 18 Hutcherson Dr., Gorham, ME 04038-2643 USA.

Potter's House Book Service, (*978-1-928717*) 1658 Columbia Rd., NW, Washington, DC 20009 USA Tel 202-232-5483; Fax: 202-328-7483
E-mail: pottershse@aol.com
Web site: http://www.pottershousebooks.com.

Potter's House Church, *See* **Potter's House Book Service**

Powells.com, Orders Addr.: 2720 NW 29th Ave., Portland, OR 97210 USA Tel 800-291-2676
Web site: http://www.powells.com/.

Practice Ring, (*978-0-929758*) Div. of Beeman Jorgensen, Inc., 7510 Allisonville Rd., Indianapolis, IN 46250 USA (SAN 630-6144) Tel 317-841-7677; Toll Free: 800-553-5319.

Pratz News Agency, Orders Addr.: P.O. Box 892, Deming, NM 88030 USA (SAN 159-9275).

Prebound Periodicals, 631 SW Jewell Ave., Topeka, KS 66606-1606 USA (SAN 285-8037).

Premier Pubs., Inc., (*978-0-915665*) P.O. Box 330309, Fort Worth, TX 76163 USA (SAN 292-5966) Tel 817-293-7030; Fax: 817-293-3410.

Presbyterian & Reformed Publishing Company, *See* **P & R Publishing**

Presbyterian Publishing Corp., (*978-0-664*) 100 Witherspoon St., Louisville, KY 40202-1396 USA Tel 502-569-5052; Fax: 502-569-8308; Toll Free Fax: 800-541-5113; Toll Free: 800-227-2872
E-mail: rpinotti@presbypub.com; customer_service@presbypub.com
Web site: http://www.ppcbooks.com.

Prestel Publishing, Orders Addr.: c/o VNU, 575 Prospect St., Lakewood, NJ 08701 USA Tel 732-363-5679; Fax: 732-363-0338; Toll Free Fax: 877-227-6564; Toll Free: 888-463-6110; Edit Addr.: 900 Broadway, Suite 603, New York, NY 10003 USA Tel 212-995-2720; Fax: 212-995-2733
E-mail: sales@prestel-usa.com
Web site: http://www.prestel.com; http://www.die-gestalten.de; http://www.scalo.com.

Princeton Architectural Pr., (*978-0-910413; 978-0-9636372; 978-1-56898; 978-1-878271; 978-1-885232; 978-1-61689*) 37 E. Seventh St., New York, NY 10003 USA (SAN 260-1176) Tel 212-995-9720; Fax: 212-995-9454; Toll Free: 800-722-6657
E-mail: sales@papress.com
Web site: http://www.papress.com.

Princeton Bk. Co. Pubs., (*978-0-87127; 978-0-916622*) Orders Addr.: P.O. Box 831, Hightstown, NJ 08520-0831 USA (SAN 630-1568) Tel 609-426-0602; Fax: 609-426-1344; Toll Free: 800-220-7149; 614 Rte. 130, Hightstown, NJ 08520 (SAN 244-8076)
E-mail: pbc@dancehorizons.com; elysian@aosi.com
Web site: http://www.dancehorizons.com.

Print & Ship, 1412 Greenbrier Pkwy., Suite 145-B, Norfolk, VA 23320 USA Tel 757-424-5868.

Printed Matter, Inc., (*978-0-89439*) 195 10th Ave. FRNT, New York, NY 10011-4739 USA (SAN 169-5924)
E-mail: Keith@printedmatter.org; Max@printedmatter.org
Web site: http://www.printedmatter.org.

Production Assocs., Inc., (*978-1-887120*) 1206 W. Collins Ave., Orange, CA 92867 USA Tel 714-771-6519; Fax: 714-771-2456; Toll Free: 800-535-8368
E-mail: mikec@production-associates.com
Web site: http://www.production-associates.com; http://signtospeak.com; http://www.wesign.com.

Productivity, Incorporated, *See* **Productivity Pr.**

Productivity Pr., (*978-0-527; 978-0-915299; 978-1-56327*) Orders Addr.: 7625 Empire Dr., Florence, KY 41042-2919 USA (SAN 290-036X) Toll Free Fax: 800-248-4724; Toll Free: 800-634-7064 (orders).

PRO-ED, Inc., (*978-0-88744; 978-0-89079; 978-0-933014; 978-0-936104; 978-0-944480; 978-1-4164*) Orders Addr.: 8700 Shoal Creek Blvd., Austin, TX 78757-6897 USA (SAN 222-1349) Tel 512-451-3246 Toll Free Fax: 800-397-7633; Toll Free: 800-897-3202
E-mail: cheri@proedinc.com
Web site: http://www.proedinc.com.

Professional Book Distributors, Incorporated, *See* **PBD, Inc.**

Professional Media Service Corp., 1160 Trademark Dr., Suite 109, Reno, NV 89511 USA (SAN 630-5776) Toll Free Fax: 800-253-8853; Toll Free: 800-223-7672.

Project Patch, 2404 E. Mill Plain Blvd., Vancouver, WA 98661-4334 USA.

ProQuest Information and Learning, *See* **ProQuest LLC**

ProQuest LLC, (*978-0-608; 978-0-7837; 978-0-8357; 978-0-88692; 978-0-89093; 978-0-912380; 978-1-55655; 978-0-591; 978-0-9702937; 978-0-599; 978-1-931694; 978-1-59399; 978-0-496; 978-0-542; 978-1-4247; 978-0-9778091; 978-1-60205; 978-1-4345; 978-0-549; 978-1-109; 978-1-124; 978-1-267; 978-1-303; 978-1-321; 978-1-339) 5252 N. Edgewood Dr., Suite 125, Provo, UT 84604 USA Tel 801-765-1737; 789 Eisenhower Pkwy., Ann Arbor, MI 48106-1346 Tel 734-761-4700 Toll Free: 800-521-0600; 7500 Old Georgetown Rd. Suite 1400, Bethesda, MD 20814*
E-mail: sales@csa.com
Web site: http://www.culturegrams.com.

Prosperity Publishing Hse., 1405 Autumn Ridge Dr., Durham, NC 27712 USA Tel 919-767-9620.

Provident Music Distribution, 1 Maryland Farms, Brentwood, TN 37027 USA Tel 615-373-3950; Fax: 615-373-0386; Toll Free: 800-333-9000
E-mail: gmiller@pmgsonybmg
Web site: http://www.providentmusic.com.

PSI (Publisher Services, Inc.), 3095 Kingston Ct., Norcross, GA 30071-1231 USA Toll Free: 800-755-9653; 877-578-4774.

Public Lands Interpretive Assn., (*978-1-879343; 978-0-9863666*) 6501 Fourth St., NW, No. 1, Albuquerque, NM 87107-5800 USA (SAN 133-3119) Tel 505-345-9498; Fax: 505-344-1543.

Publication Consultants, (*978-0-9644809; 978-1-888125; 978-1-59433*) 8370 Eleusis Dr., Anchorage, AK 99502 USA Tel 907-349-2424; Fax: 907-349-2426
E-mail: evan@publicationconsultants.com
Web site: http://www.publicationconsultants.com.

Publications Unlimited, 7512 Coconut Dr., Lake Worth, FL 33467-6511 USA (SAN 285-9432) Tel 407-434-4688 Do not confuse with Publications Unlimited in Raleigh, NC.

Publishers Business Service, Inc., P.O. Box 25674, Chicago, IL 60625 USA (SAN 285-9459) Tel 312-561-5552.

Publishers Clearing Hse., 382 Channel Dr., Port Washington, NY 11050 USA (SAN 285-9440) Tel 516-883-5432.

Publishers Continental Sales Corp., 613 Franklin Sq., Michigan City, IN 46360 USA (SAN 285-9475) Tel 219-874-4245; Fax: 219-872-8961.

Publishers' Graphics, L.L.C., (*978-0-9663402; 978-1-930847; 978-1-933556; 978-1-934703; 978-1-935590*) 140 Della Ct., Carol Stream, IL 60188 USA (SAN 990-0241) Toll Free: 888-404-3769
Web site: http://www.pubgraphics.com.

Publishers Group International, Inc., (*978-0-9633653*) 1506 27th St. NW, No. 1, Washington, DC 20007 USA Tel 202-342-0886; Fax: 202-338-1940
E-mail: issbooks@aol.com.

Publishers Media, (*978-0-934064*) 1447 Valley View Rd., Glendale, CA 91202-1716 USA (SAN 159-6683) Tel 818-548-1998.

Publishers News Company, *See* **Mr. Paperback/Publishers News Co.**

Publishers Services, Orders Addr.: P.O. Box 2510, Novato, CA 94948 USA (SAN 201-3037) Tel 415-883-3530; Fax: 415-883-4280.

Publishers Storage & Shipping, 46 Development Rd. 231 Industrial Pk., Fitchburg, MA 1420 USA Tel 508-345-2121; 313 487 9720.

Publishers Wholesale Assocs., Inc., Orders Addr.: P.O. Box 2078, Lancaster, PA 17608-2078 USA (SAN 630-7450) Fax: 717-397-9253; Edit Addr.: 231 N. Shippen St., Lancaster, PA 17608 USA.

Puerto Rico Postcard, P.O. Box 79710, Carolina, PR 00984-9710 USA.

Pulley Learning Assocs., 210 Alpine Meadow Rd., Winchester, VA 22602-6701 USA (SAN 133-1434).

Purple Unicorn Bks., (*978-0-931998*) 1928 W. Kent Rd., Duluth, MN 55812-1154 USA (SAN 111-0071) Tel 218-525-4781 Do not confuse with Purple Unicorn in Augusta, ME.

Puzzle Piece Pubns., 846 36th Ave., N., Saint Cloud, MN 56303 USA Tel 320-656-5361.

Quality Bks., Inc., (*978-0-89196*) 1003 W. Pines Rd., Oregon, IL 61061-9680 USA (SAN 169-2127) Tel 815-732-4450; Fax: 815-732-4499; Toll Free: 800-323-4241 (libraries only)
E-mail: info@quality-books.com.

Quality Book Fairs, 5787 Ryan Rd., Medina, OH 44256-8823 USA (SAN 630-7752).

Quality Schl. Plan, Inc., P.O. Box 10203, Des Moines, IA 50381-0001 USA (SAN 285-953X).

R & W Distribution, Inc., 87 Bright St., Jersey City, NJ 07302 USA (SAN 169-4723) Tel 201-333-1540; Fax: 201-333-1541
E-mail: rwmag@mail.idt.net.

R. C. Brayshaw, P.O. Box 91, Warner, NH 03278 USA Tel 603-456-3101.

R J Communications, LLC, (*978-0-9700741; 978-1-59664*) 51 E. 42nd St., Suite 1202, New York, NY 10017-5404 USA Tel 212-867-1331; Fax: 212-681-8002; Toll Free: 800-621-2556 (New York)
E-mail: ron@rjcom.com
Web site: http://www.selfpublishing.com; http://www.booksjustbooks.com.

R T R Publishing Company, *See* **Red Toad Road Co.**

Radio Bookstore, P.O. Box 209, Rindge, NH 03461-0209 USA (SAN 111-3496) Tel 603-899-6957 Do not confuse with Radio Bookstore Pr., Bellevue, WA.

Raimond Graphics Inc., Orders Addr.: 360 Sylvan Ave., Englewd Clfs, NJ 07632-2712 USA.

Rainbow Bk. Co., (*978-1-932834; 978-1-60117; 978-1-60447*) 500 E. Main St., Lake Zurich, IL 60047 USA (SAN 920-2935) Tel 800-255-0965; Fax: 847-726-9935 Do not confuse with Rainbow Book Company in Mt. Mourne, NC
E-mail: mike@rainbowbookcompany.com
Web site: http://www.rainbowbookcompany.com.

Rainbow Re-Source Ctr., P.O. Box 491, Kewanee, IL 61443 USA (SAN 631-4007) Tel 309-937-3385; Fax: 309-937-3382
E-mail: rainbowres@aol.com.

Rainier News, Inc., 3400-D Industry Dr., E., Fife, WA 98424-1853 USA (SAN 169-8745) Toll Free: 800-843-2995 (in Washington).

RAM Pubns. & Distribution, (*978-0-9630785; 978-0-9703860; 978-0-9897315*) Bergamot Sta., 2525 Michigan Ave., No. A2, Santa Monica, CA 90404 USA (SAN 298-2641) Tel 310-453-0043; Fax: 310-264-4888
E-mail: rampub@gte.net.

Rand McNally, (*978-0-528*) Orders Addr.: 9855 Woods Dr., Skokie, IL 60077-1074 USA Toll Free Fax: 800-934-3479 (Orders); Toll Free: 800-333-0136 (ext. 4771); 800-678-7263 (Orders)
E-mail: Education@randmcnally.com
Web site: http://www.randmcnally.com.

Random House Adult Trade Publishing Group, *See* **Random House Publishing Group**

Random House Publishing Group, Orders Addr.: 400 Hahn Rd., Westminster, MD 21157 USA (SAN 852-5579) Tel 410-848-1900; 410-386-7560; Toll Free: 800-726-0600; Edit Addr.: 1745 Broadway, New York, NY 10019 USA Tel 212-751-2600; Fax: 212-572-4949; Toll Free: 800-726-0600
E-mail: lstark@randomhouse.com.

Random Hse. Bks. for Young Readers, (*978-0-375; 978-0-394; 978-0-517; 978-0-679; 978-1-4000*) Orders Addr.: 400 Hahn Rd., Westminster, MD 21157 USA; Edit Addr.: 1540 Broadway, New York, NY 10036 USA.

Random Hse., Inc., (*978-0-307; 978-0-345; 978-0-375; 978-0-385; 978-0-394; 978-0-440; 978-0-449; 978-0-517; 978-0-553; 978-0-593; 978-0-609; 978-0-676; 978-0-679; 978-0-7364; 978-0-7366; 978-0-7615; 978-0-7679; 978-0-7704; 978-0-8041; 978-0-8052; 978-0-8129; 978-0-8230; 978-0-87637; 978-0-87665; 978-0-87788; 978-0-88070; 978-0-913369; 978-0-914629; 978-0-930014; 978-0-945564; 978-1-57082; 978-1-57673; 978-1-57856; 978-1-878867; 978-1-884536; 978-1-885305; 978-1-58836; 978-1-4000; 978-1-59052; 978-1-4159; 978-) Div. of Penguin Random House LLC, Orders Addr.: 400 Hahn Rd., Westminster, MD 21157 USA (SAN 202-5515) Tel 410 848 1900; Toll Free Fax: 800 659 2436; Toll Free: 800 726 0600 (customer service/orders); Edit Addr.: 1745 Broadway, New York, NY 10019 USA (SAN 202-5507) Tel 212 782 9000; Fax: 212 302 7985*
E-mail: customerservice@randomhouse.com
Web site: http://www.randomhouse.com.

Raven West Coast Distribution, 767 W. 18th St., Costa Mesa, CA 92627 USA
E-mail: ken@ravenwcd.com.

Read News Agency, 2501 Greensboro Ave., Tuscaloosa, AL 35401-6520 USA Tel 205-752-3515.

Readerlink Distribution Services, LLC, Div. of Charles Levy Co., 1420 Kensington Rd. Ste. 300, Oak Brook, IL 60523-2164 USA (SAN 176-2478)
E-mail: jstamborski@readerlink.com
Web site: http://www.readerlink.com.

Reader's Digest Assn., Inc., The, (*978-0-7621; 978-0-89577; 978-0-86438; 978-1-60652*) One Bedford Rd., Pleasantville, NY 10570 USA (SAN 282-2091) Toll Free: 800-463-8820; 800-334-9599; 800-635-5006
Web site: http://www.readersdigest.com; http://www.rd.com.

Reader's Digest Children's Publishing, Incorporated, *See* **Studio Fun International**

Readex Bk. Exchange, Box 1125, Carefree, AZ 85377 USA (SAN 159-9291).

Reading Circle, The, 7858 Industrial Pkwy., Plain City, OH 43064-9468 USA (SAN 169-670X).

Reading Matters, Inc., (*978-1-930654*) 806 Main St., Akron, PA 17501 USA Tel 717-859-5608; Fax: 717-859-3469; Toll Free: 888-255-6665 Do not confuse with companies with the same name in Brookline, MA, Denver, CO
E-mail: office@readingmatters.net
Web site: http://readingmatters.net.

Reading Peddler Bk. Fairs, 10580 3/4 W. Pico Blvd., Los Angeles, CA 90064 USA (SAN 157-9770) Tel 310-559-2665.

Reading's Fun/Books are Fun, Limited, *See* **Bks. Are Fun, Ltd.**

Readmor, Orders Addr.: P.O. Box 7264, Grand Rapids, MI 49508 USA (SAN 169-3875); Edit Addr.: 301 S. Rath Ave., Ludington, MI 49431 USA Tel 231-843-2537.

Readmore Academic Services, Orders Addr.: P.O. Box 1459, Blackwood, NJ 08012 USA (SAN 630-5741) Tel 609-227-1100; Fax: 609-227-8322; Toll Free: 800-645-6595; Edit Addr.: 700 Black Horse Pike, Suite 207, Blackwood, NJ 08012 USA.

Readmore, Inc., 22 Cortlandt St., New York, NY 10007 USA (SAN 159-9313) Tel 212-349-5540; Fax: 212-233-0746; Toll Free: 800-221-3306.

Recorded Bks., LLC, (*978-0-7887; 978-1-55690; 978-1-84197; 978-1-4025; 978-1-4193; 978-1-84505; 978-1-4281; 978-1-4361; 978-1-4407; 978-1-4498; 978-1-4561; 978-1-4618; 978-1-4640; 978-1-4703; 978-1-4906; 978-1-5019*) Subs. of W. F. Howes Limited, Orders Addr.: 270 Skipjack Rd., Prince Frederick, MD 20678 USA (SAN 111-3984) Fax: 410-535-5499; Toll Free: 800-638-1304; 7257 Pkwy. Dr., Hanover, MD 21076 (SAN 920-7414)
E-mail: thelvey@recordedbooks.com
Web site: http://www.recordedbooks.com.

Red Sea Pr., (*978-0-932415; 978-1-56902*) Affil. of Africa World Pr., 541 W. Ingham Ave., Suite B, Trenton, NJ 08638 USA (SAN 630-1983) Tel 609-695-3200; Fax: 609-695-6466
E-mail: awprsp@verizon.net
Web site: http://www.africaworldpressbooks.com.

Red Toad Road Co., (*978-1-889287*) Orders Addr.: P.O. Box 642, Havre de Grace, MD 21078 USA Tel 410-939-4092; Fax: 410-939-5614; Edit Addr.: 223 Heather Way, Havre de Grace, MD 21078 USA
E-mail: redtoadroad@aol.com
Web site: http://www.amazon.com/shops/redtoadroad.

Red Wheel/Weiser, (*978-0-87728; 978-0-943233; 978-1-57324; 978-1-57863; 978-1-59003; 978-1-60925; 978-1-61283; 978-1-61852; 978-1-61940; 978-1-938875; 978-1-63341; 978-1-942785*) Div. of Weiser Bks., Orders Addr.: 65 Parker St., Suite 7, Newburyport, MA 01950 USA (SAN 255-8610) Tel 978-465-0504; Fax: 978-465-0243; Toll Free Fax: 877-337-3309; Toll Free: 800-423-7087 (orders only)
E-mail: customerservice@redwheelweiser.com
Web site: http://www.redwheelweiser.com.

RedShelf, Orders Addr.: 747 N LaSalle, Suite 220, Chicago, IL 60654 USA Tel 312-878-8586
E-mail: help@virdocs.com
Web site: http://redshelf.com/.

Redwing Bk. Co., Orders Addr.: 202 Bendix Dr., Taos, NM 87571 USA Tel 505-758-7758; Fax: 505-758-7768; Toll Free: 800-873-3946 (USA); 888-873-3947 (Canada); Edit Addr.: P.O. Box 470688, Brookline Vlg, MA 02447-0688 USA (SAN 163-3597) Toll Free: 800-873-3946
E-mail: bob@redwingbooks.com
Web site: http://www.redwingbooks.com.

Reference Bk. Ctr., 175 Fifth Ave., New York, NY 10010 USA (SAN 159-9356) Tel 212-677-2160; Fax: 212-533-0826.

Regent Bk. Co., Inc., Orders Addr.: P.O. Box 750, Lodi, NJ 07644-0750 USA Tel 973-574-7600; Fax: 973-574-7605; Toll Free: 800-999-9554; Edit Addr.: 101 E. Main St. BLDG 5, Little Falls, NJ 07424-1659 USA (SAN 169-4715)
E-mail: info@regentbook.com
Web site: http://www.regentbook.com.

Renaissance News, 5232 Clairton Blvd., Pittsburgh, PA 15236 USA Tel 412-881-4848; Fax: 412-881-5422.

Replica Books, *See* **TextStream**

Representaciones Borinquenas, Inc., (*978-0-9727750; 978-0-9755107*) P.O. Box 139, Aguas Buenas, PR 00703-0139 USA Tel 787-309-9047; Fax: 787-780-5835
E-mail: rborinquenas@centennialpr.net.

Reprint Services Corp., (*978-0-7812; 978-0-932051; 978-1-4227*) P.O. Box 130, Murrieta, CA 92564-0130 USA (SAN 686-2640) Fax: 951-699-5065
E-mail: Reprintservices@gmail.com.

Research Bks., Inc., P.O. Box 555, Old Saybrook, CT 06475-0555 USA
E-mail: info@researchbooks.com.

Resource Software International, Inc., (*978-0-87539*) Affil. of Datamatics Management, 330 New Brunswick Ave., Fords, NJ 08863 USA (SAN 264-8628) Tel 732-738-8500; Fax: 732-738-9603; Toll Free: 800-673-0366
E-mail: info@datamaticsinc.com
Web site: http://www.tc-1.com.

Resurgam Publishing Company, *See* **Blessing Way Publishing Co.**

Reveal Entertainment, Inc., (*978-0-9712633*) 1250 Petroleum Dr. Ste. B6, Abilene, TX 79602-7957 USA
E-mail: revealgames@aol.com
Web site: http://www.revealgames.com.

Review & Herald Publishing Assn., (*978-0-8127; 978-0-8280*) 55 W. Oak Ridge Dr., Hagerstown, MD 21740 USA (SAN 203-3798) Tel 301-393-3000
E-mail: smulkern@rhpa.org
Web site: http://www.reviewandherald.com/.

Revolution Booksellers, 60 Winter St., Exeter, NH 03833 USA Tel 603-772-7200; Fax: 603-772-7200; Toll Free: 800-738-6603.

Rhinelander News Agency, 314 Courtney, Crescent Lake, WI 54501 USA (SAN 159-9372) Tel 715-362-6397.

Rhino Entertainment Co, A Warner Music Group Co., *(978-0-7379; 978-0-930589; 978-1-56826; 978-0-9797278)* 3400 W. Olive Ave., Burbank, CA 91505 USA (SAN 677-5454) Tel 818-238-6110; Fax: 818-562-9239
E-mail: gladys.sanchez@wmg.com; tracie.bowers@wmg.com
Web site: http://www.rhino.com.

Rhodes News Agency, *See* **Treasure Valley News**

Richardson's Bks., Inc., 2014 Lou Ellen Ln., Houston, TX 77018 USA (SAN 169-829X) Tel 713-688-2244; Fax: 713-688-8420; Toll Free: 800-392-8562.

Richardson's Educators, *See* **Richardson's Bks., Inc.**

Right Start, Inc., 5388 Sterling Center Dr., Suite C, Westlake Village, CA 91361-4687 USA (SAN 631-7022).

Rio Grande Bk. Co., P.O. Box 2795, McAllen, TX 78502-2795 USA (SAN 169-8354).

Rio Nuevo Pubs., *(978-0-918080; 978-1-887896; 978-0-9700750; 978-1-933855; 978-1-940322)* Orders Addr.: P.O. Box 5250, Tucson, AZ 85703-0250 USA (SAN 209-3251) Tel 520-623-9558; Fax: 520-624-5888; Toll Free Fax: 800-715-5888; Toll Free: 800-969-9558; Edit Addr.: 451 N. Bonita Ave., Tucson, AZ 85745 USA Tel 602-623-9558
E-mail: info@rionuevo.com; info@treasurechestbooks.com; suzang@rionuevo.com
Web site: http://www.treasurechestbooks.com; http://www.rionuevo.com/.

Rip Off Pr., *(978-0-89620)* Orders Addr.: P.O. Box 4686, Auburn, CA 95604 USA (SAN 207-7671) Tel 530-885-8183; Toll Free: 800-468-2669
E-mail: mail@ripoffpress.com
Web site: http://www.ripoffpress.com.

Rishor News Co., Inc., 109 Mountain Laurel Dr., Butler, PA 16001-3921 USA (SAN 159-9402).

Rittenhouse Bk. Distributors, *(978-0-87381)* Orders Addr.: P.O. Box 61565, Kng Of Prussa, PA 19406-0965 USA (SAN 213-4454) Toll Free Fax: 800-223-7488; Toll Free: 800-345-6425
E-mail: alan.yockey@rittenhouse.com; joan.townshend@rittenhouse.com
Web site: http://www.rittenhouse.com.

Ritter Bk. Co., 7011 Foster Pl., Downers Grove, IL 60516-3446 USA (SAN 169-1856).

River Canyon Distributing, P.O. Box 70643, Eugene, OR 97401 USA.

River Road Recipes Cookbook, 9523 Fenway Dr., Baton Rouge, LA 70809 USA (SAN 132-7852) Tel 504-924-0300; Fax: 504-927-2547; Toll Free: 800-204-1726.

RiverStream Publishing, *(978-1-62243)* 123 S. Broad St., Mankato, MN 56001 USA Tel 414-378-2480
E-mail: jstrick@hickorytech.net.

Rizzoli International Pubns., Inc., *(978-0-8478; 978-0-941807; 978-1-932183; 978-1-59962)* Subs. of RCS Rizzoli Editore Corp., 300 Park Ave., S., 3rd Flr., New York, NY 10010 USA (SAN 111-9192) Tel 212-387-3400; Fax: 212-387-3535
Web site: http://www.rizzoliusa.com/.

Roadrunner Library Service, c/o Kerbs, 700 Highview Ave., Glen Ellyn, IL 60137-5504 USA.

Roberts, F.M. Enterprises, *(978-0-912746)* P.O. Box 608, Dana Point, CA 92629-0608 USA (SAN 201-4688) Tel 714-493-1977; Fax: 714-493-7124.

Rockbottom Bks., Pentagon Towers, P.O. Box 398166, Minneapolis, MN 55439 USA (SAN 108-4402) Tel 612-831-2120.

Rockland Catskill, Inc., 26 Church St., Spring Valley, NY 10977 USA (SAN 169-6254) Tel 914-356-1222; Fax: 914-356-8415; Toll Free: 800-966-6247.

Rocky Mount News Agency, Two Great State Ln., Rocky Mount, NC 27801 USA.

Rogue Valley News Agency, Inc., 550 Airport Rd., Medford, OR 97504-4156 USA (SAN 169-7137).

Rohr, Hans E., 76 State St., Newburyport, MA 01950-6616 USA (SAN 113-8804).

Roig Spanish Bks., 146 W. 29th St., No. 3W, New York, NY 10001-5303 USA (SAN 165-1021) Fax: 212-695-6811.

Romeil LLC, *(978-0-9830484; 978-1-937391)* 1050 Sommers St. N, Hudson, WI 54016 USA Tel 651-204-3753
E-mail: steve@romeil.com
Web site: Romeil.com.

Rosen Publishing Group, Inc., The, *(978-0-8239; 978-1-4042; 978-1-4358; 978-1-60851; 978-1-60852; 978-1-60853; 978-1-60854; 978-1-61511; 978-1-61512; 978-1-61513; 978-1-61514; 978-1-61530; 978-1-61531; 978-1-61532; 978-1-61533; 978-1-4488; 978-1-4777; 978-1-4824; 978-1-4994; 978-1-68048; 978-1-5081) a/o Dept. C234561, 29 E. 21st St., New York, NY 10010 USA (SAN 203-3720) Tel 212-777-3017; Fax: 212-358-9588; Toll Free Fax: 888-436-4643; Toll Free: 800-237-9932*
E-mail: info@rosenpub.com; customerservice@rosenpub.com; deang@rosenpub.com
Web site: http://www.rosenpublishing.com; http://www.rosendigital.com; http://www.rosenclassroom.com.

Rosenblum's, *See* **Rosenblum's World of Judaica, Inc.**

Rosenblum's World of Judaica, Inc., 2906 W. Devon Ave., Chicago, IL 60659 USA (SAN 169-1864) Tel 773-262-1700; Fax: 773-262-1930; Toll Free: 800-626-6536.

Rosewood Foundation, The, Orders Addr.: P.O. Box 252, Archer, FL 32618 USA Tel 352-495-2197; Fax: 352-495-8313
E-mail: lizziePRJ@aol.com.

Rounder Kids Music Distribution, Orders Addr.: P.O. Box 516, Montpelier, VT 05602 USA (SAN 630-6675) Tel 802-223-5825; Fax: 802-223-5303; Toll Free: 800-223-6357; Edit Addr.: 80 W. Harvey Farm Rd., Waterbury Ctr, VT 05677-7132 USA
E-mail: Pauls@rounder.com.

Rowman & Littlefield Publishers, Inc., *(978-0-8476; 978-0-87471; 978-0-9632978; 978-1-56699; 978-1-888052; 978-0-7425; 978-1-931890; 978-1-933494; 978-1-4422; 978-1-936283; 978-1-61281; 978-1-4616; 978-1-4617; 978-1-62093)* Mem. of Rowman & Littlefield Publishing Group, Inc., Orders Addr.: 15200 NBN Way, Blue Ridge Summit, PA 17214 USA Tel 717-794-3800 (Sales, Customer Service, MIS, Royalties, Inventory; Fax: 717-794-3803 (Customer Service & orders only); 717-794-3857 (Sales & MIS); 717-794-3856 (Royalties, Inventory Mgmt. & Distribution); Toll Free Fax: 800-338-4550 (Customer Service & orders); Toll Free: 800-462-6420 (Customer Service & orders); Edit Addr.: 4501 Forbes Blvd., Suite 200, Lanham, MD 20706 USA Tel 301-459-3366; Fax: 301-459-5749 Short Discount, please contact rlpgsales@rowman.com
E-mail: rlpgsales@rowman.com; lweston@rowman.com
Web site: http://www.rowmanlittlefield.com; http://www.rlpgbooks.com/bookseller/index.shtml.

Royal Pubns., Inc., *(978-0-918738)* Orders Addr.: P.O. Box 5793, Denver, CO 80217 USA (SAN 244-7193) Tel 303-778-8383; Toll Free: 800-279-2048 (orders only); Edit Addr.: 790 W. Tennessee Ave., Denver, CO 80223 USA (SAN 169-054X).

Rumpf, Raymond & Son, Orders Addr.: P.O. Box 319, Sellersville, PA 18960 USA (SAN 631-5259).

Rushmore News, Inc., 924 East St. Andrew, Rapid City, SD 57701 USA (SAN 169-7846) Tel 605-342-2617; Fax: 605-342-9091; Toll Free: 800-423-0501
E-mail: afreese911@aol.com.

Russell News Agency, Inc., P.O. Box 158, Sarasota, FL 33578 USA (SAN 169-1287).

Russica Bk. & Art Shop, Inc., 799 Broadway, New York, NY 10003 USA (SAN 165-1072) Tel 212-473-7480; Fax: 212-473-7486.

S & L Sales Co., Inc., Orders Addr.: P.O. Box 2067, Waycross, GA 31502 USA (SAN 107-413X) Tel 912-283-0210; Fax: 912-283-0261; Toll Free: 800-243-3699 (orders only).

S & S News & Greeting, 5304 15th Ave., S., Minneapolis, MN 55417-1812 USA (SAN 159-9453) Tel 612-224-8227; Toll Free: 800-346-9892.

S & W Distributors, Inc., 1600-H E. Wendover Ave., Greensboro, NC 27405 USA.

S. A. V. E. with Victor Hotho, *See* **S.A.V.E. Suzie & Vic Enterprises**

S V E & Churchill Media, *(978-0-7932; 978-0-89290; 978-1-56357)* 6465 N. Avondale Ave., Chicago, IL 60631-1909 USA (SAN 208-3930) Toll Free Fax: 800-624-1678; Toll Free: 800-829-1900
E-mail: custserv@svemedia.com
Web site: http://www.svemedia.com.

SAAN Corp., 189-01 Springfield Ave., Suite 201, Flossmoor, IL 60422 USA (SAN 631-0419) Tel 708-799-5225; Fax: 708-799-8713.

Saddleback Educational Publishing, *See* **Saddleback Educational Publishing, Inc.**

Saddleback Educational Publishing, Inc., *(978-1-56254; 978-1-59905; 978-1-60291; 978-1-61651; 978-1-61247; 978-1-62250; 978-1-62670; 978-1-63078; 978-1-68021)* 3120-A Pullman St., Costa Mesa, CA 92626-4564 USA (SAN 860-0902) Toll Free Fax: 888-734-4010; Toll Free: 800-637-8715
E-mail: contact@saddleback.com; amchugh@sdlback.com; cpizer@sdlback.com
Web site: http://www.saddlebackpublishing.com.

Sadler, Dale, 209 Foster Dr., White House, TN 37188 USA.

Safari Museum Pr., 111 N. Lincoln Ave., Chanute, KS 66720 USA Tel 630-431-2730; Fax: 630-431-3848.

SAGE Pubns., Inc., *(978-0-7619; 978-0-8039; 978-1-4129; 978-1-4522; 978-1-4462; 978-1-4833; 978-1-5063)* 2455 Teller Rd., Thousand Oaks, CA 91360 USA (SAN 204-7217) Tel 800-818-7243; Fax: 800-583-2665; 805-499-0871
E-mail: info@sagepub.com; deborah.vaughn@sagepub.com
Web site: http://www.sagepub.com; http://www.sagepub.co.uk; http://www.pineforge.com; http://sagepub.com.

Sagebrush Pr., *(978-0-930704)* P.O. Box 87, Morongo Valley, CA 92256 USA (SAN 113-387X) Tel 760-363-7398 Do not confuse with companies with same name in Cedarville, CA, Salt Lake City, UT.

Saint Benedict Pr., Div. of Saint Benedict Press, LLC, Orders Addr.: P.O. Box 410487, Charlotte, NC 28241 USA Toll Free: 800-437-5876
Web site: https://books.benedictpress.com/.

Saint George Book Service, Incorporated, *See* **Steiner, Rudolf College Pr./St. George Pubns.**

Saks News, Inc., P.O. Box 1857, Bismarck, ND 58502 USA (SAN 169-653X).

Sams Technical Publishing, LLC, *(978-0-7906; 978-0-578-12070-6)* 9850 E. 30th St., Indianapolis, IN 46229 USA Toll Free Fax: 800-552-3910; Toll Free: 800-428-7267
E-mail: samstech@samswebsite.com
Web site: http://www.samswebsite.com.

San Diego Museum of Art, *(978-0-937108; 978-0-9845555)* Orders Addr.: P.O. Box 122107, San Diego, CA 92112-2107 USA Tel 619-696-1970; Fax: 619-232-9367
E-mail: sward@sdmart.org
Web site: http://www.sdmart.org.

San Francisciana, *(978-0-934715)* P.O. Box 590955, San Francisco, CA 94159 USA (SAN 161-1607) Tel 415-751-7222.

San Val, Incorporated, *See* **Turtleback Bks.**

Sandlapper Publishing Co., Inc., *(978-0-87844)* Orders Addr.: P.O. Box 730, Orangeburg, SC 29115 USA (SAN 203-2678) Toll Free Fax: 800-337-9420 (orders); Toll Free: 800-849-7263 (orders); Edit Addr.: 1281 Amelia St., NE., Orangeburg, SC 29116 USA Tel 803-533-1658; Fax: 803-534-5223
E-mail: agallman1@bellsouth.net
Web site: http://www.sandlapperpublishing.com.

Sandvik Publishing, *(978-1-58048; 978-1-881445)* Div. of Sandviks Bokforlag, Norway, 3729 Knights Rd., Bensalem, PA 19020-2908 USA Toll Free: 800-843-2445
E-mail: Nicole@sandvikpublishing.com; cust-serv@sandvikpublishing.com
Web site: http://www.sandviks.com.

Santa Barbara Botanic Garden, *(978-0-916436)* 1212 Mission Canyon Rd., Santa Barbara, CA 93105 USA (SAN 208-8398) Tel 805-682-4726; Fax: 805-563-0352
E-mail: info@sbbg.org
Web site: http://www.sbbg.org.

Santa Barbara News Agency, 725 S. Kellogg Ave., Goleta, CA 93117-3806 USA (SAN 168-9665) Tel 805-564-5200.

Santa Monica Software, Inc., 30018 Zenith Point Rd., Malibu, CA 90265-4264 USA (SAN 630-6764) Tel 310-457-8381; Fax: 310-395-7635.

Santillana USA Publishing Co., Inc., *(978-0-88272; 978-1-56014; 978-1-58105; 978-1-58986; 978-1-59437; 978-1-59820; 978-1-60396; 978-1-61605; 978-1-61435; 978-1-62263; 978-1-63113)* Div. of Grupo Santillana, 2023 NW 84th Ave., Doral, FL 33122 USA (SAN 205-1133) Tel 305-591-9522 Toll Free Fax: 888-248-9518 (orders); Toll Free: 800-245-8584; Av. Rio Mixcoac No. 274 Col. Acacias, C.P. 0324 Benito Juarez, Ciudad de Mexico, DF,
E-mail: dpena@santillanausa.com; esanta@santillanausa.com
Web site: http://www.santillanausa.com/.

Saphrograph Corp., *(978-0-87557)* 5409 18th Ave., Brooklyn, NY 11204 USA (SAN 110-4128) Tel 718-331-1233; Fax: 718-331-8231
E-mail: saphrograph@verizon.net.

Sasquatch Bks., *(978-0-912365; 978-1-57061; 978-0-9821188; 978-1-63217)* 1904 Third Avenue, Suite 710, Seattle, WA 98101 USA (SAN 289-0208) Toll Free: 800-775-0817
E-mail: custserv@SasquatchBooks.com
Web site: http://www.sasquatchbooks.com.

Sathya Sai Bk. Ctr. of America, *(978-1-57836)* 305 W. First St., Tustin, CA 92780 USA (SAN 111-3542) Tel 714-669-0522; Fax: 714-669-9138
Web site: http://www.sathyasaibooks.com.

Satsang Press, *See* **Gangaji Foundation, The**

Savant Bk. Distribution Co., 3107 E 62nd Ave., Spokane, WA 99223-6934 USA (SAN 631-9203) Tel 509-443-7057; Fax: 509-448-2191
E-mail: service@savant-books.com
Web site: http://www.savant-books.com.

S.A.V.E. Suzie & Vic Enterprises, 303 N. Main, P.O. Box 30, Schulenburg, TX 78956 USA (SAN 630-6365) Tel 409-743-4145; Fax: 409-743-4147.

SCB Distributors, Orders Addr.: 15608 S. New Century Dr., Gardena, CA 90248-2129 USA (SAN 630-4818) Tel 310-532-9400; Fax: 310-532-7001; Toll Free: 800-729-6423 (orders only)
E-mail: info@scbdistributors.com
Web site: http://www.scbdistributors.com.

Schmul Publishing Co., Inc., *(978-0-88019)* Orders Addr.: P.O. Box 716, Salem, OH 44460-0716 USA (SAN 180-2771) Tel 330-222-2249; Fax: 330-222-0001; Toll Free: 800-772-6657; Edit Addr.: 3583 Newgarden Rd., Salem, OH 44460 USA
E-mail: spchale@valunet.com
Web site: http://www.wesleyanbooks.com.

Schoenhof's Foreign Bks., Inc., *(978-0-87774)* 76a Mount Auburn St., Cambridge, MA 02138-5051 USA (SAN 212-0062)
E-mail: info@schoenhofs.com
Web site: http://www.schoenhofs.com.

Scholar's Bookshelf, *(978-0-678; 978-0-945726; 978-1-60105)* Orders Addr.: 110 Melrick Rd., Cranbury, NJ 08512 USA (SAN 110-8360) Tel 609-395-6933; Fax: 609-395-0755
E-mail: books@scholarsbookshelf.com
Web site: http://www.scholarsbookshelf.com.

Scholastic Bk. Fairs, P.O. Box 958411, Lake Mary, FL 32795-8411 USA (SAN 173-7457) Tel 407-829-2600.

Scholastic, Inc., *(978-0-439; 978-0-590; 978-0-545; 978-1-338)* 557 Broadway, New York, NY 10012-3999 USA (SAN 202-5442) Fax: 212-343-6802; Toll Free: 800-325-6149 (customer service)
E-mail: info@scholastic.com
Web site: http://www.scholastic.com.

Scholium International, Inc., *(978-0-87936)* P.O. Box 1519, Port Washington, NY 11050-0306 USA (SAN 169-5282) Tel 516-767-7171; Fax: 516-944-9824
E-mail: info@scholium.com
Web site: http://www.scholium.com.

School Aid Co., *(978-0-87385)* 911 Colfax Dr., P.O. Box 123, Danville, IL 61832 USA (SAN 158-3719) Tel 217-442-6855; Toll Free: 800-447-2665.

School Aids, 9335 Interline Ave., Baton Rouge, LA 70809-1910 USA (SAN 169-2909) Tel 504-926-4498.

School Bk. Service, 3650 Coral Ridge Dr., Suite 112, Coral Springs, FL 33065-2559 USA (SAN 158-6963) Tel 954-341-7207; Fax: 954-341-7303; Toll Free: 800-228-7361
E-mail: compedge@ix.netcom.com.

School of Metaphysics, 163 Moonvalley Rd., Windyville, MO 65783 USA (SAN 159-5423) Tel 417-345-8411; Fax: 417-345-6668
E-mail: som@som.org
Web site: http://www.som.org.

Schroeder News Company, *See* **Merced News Co.**

Schroeder's Bk. Haven, 104 Michigan Ave., League City, TX 77573 USA (SAN 122-7998) Tel 281-332-5226; Fax: 281-332-1695; Toll Free: 800-894-5032
E-mail: schroedr@interloc.com.

Schulze News Co., 2451 Eastman Ave., Suite 13, Oxnard, CA 93030-5193 USA (SAN 169-0434) Tel 805-642-9759.

Schuylkill News Service, 1801 W. Market St., Pottsville, PA 17901-2001 USA (SAN 159-9518).

Schwartz, Arthur & Company, Incorporated/Woodstocker Books, *See* **Woodstocker Books/Arthur Schwartz & Company**

Schwartz Brothers, Inc., 822 Montgomery Ave., No. 204, Narberth, PA 19072-1937 USA (SAN 285-7529) Fax: 301-459-6418; Toll Free: 800-638-0243.

Science Kit & Boreal Labs, P.O. Box 5003, Tonawanda, NY 14151-5003 USA (SAN 631-2314)
E-mail: sk@sciencekit.com.

Scientific & Medical Pubns. of France, Inc., P.O. Box 3490, New York, NY 10163-3490 USA (SAN 169-5940).

SCPBooks, *See* **Phoenix Rising Pr.**

Seaboard Sub Agency, 215 S. Ott St., Allentown, PA 18104-6147 USA (SAN 285-9718).

Seaburn Bks., P.O. Box 2085, Long Island City, NY 11102 USA (SAN 631-2799) Tel 718-274-7040
E-mail: info@seaburn.com.

Seattle Bk. Co., Orders Addr.: P.O. Box 2222, Poulsbo, WA 98370 USA Tel 206-922-0418; Edit Addr.: 18864 Front St., Suite 200, Poulsbo, WA 98370 USA
E-mail: sales@seattlebookcompany.com.

Selective Bks., Inc., *(978-0-912584)* P.O. Box 1140, Clearwater, FL 34617 USA (SAN 204-577X) Tel 813-447-0100.

Selective Publishers, Incorporated, *See* **Selective Bks., Inc.**

Semler News Agency, Orders Addr.: P.O. Box 350, New Castle, PA 16101 USA (SAN 169-7471); Edit Addr.: P.O. Box 526, Morgantown, WV 26505 USA (SAN 169-8990).

Send The Light Distribution LLC, *(978-0-9835608; 978-1-939900)* Orders Addr.: 129 Mobilization Dr., Waynesboro, GA 30830 USA (SAN 631-8894) Tel 706-554-5827; Toll Free Fax: 877-323-4551; Toll Free: 877-323-4550; 100 Biblica Way, Elizabethton, TN 37643-6070 (SAN 630-7388) Tel 423-547-5131 editorial Toll Free Fax: 800-759-2779
E-mail: Customerservice@stl.org
Web site: http://www.stl-publisherservices.com.

Seneca News Agency, 800 Pre Emption Rd., Geneva, NY 14456-2010 USA (SAN 169-5304).

Sental Distributors, 8839 Shirley Ave., Northridge, CA 91324 USA (SAN 168-9959) Tel 818-886-3113; Fax: 818-886-0423
Web site: http://www.plasticmodels.com.

Sepher-Hermon Pr., *(978-0-87203)* 1153 45th St., Brooklyn, NY 11219 USA (SAN 169-5959) Tel 718-972-9010; Fax: 718-972-6935.

Serendipity Couriers, Inc., P.O. Box 5897, Vallejo, CA 94591-5897 USA (SAN 169-0329) Toll Free: 800-459-4005 (Bay area only)
E-mail: dipity@14.netcom.com.

Serpent's Tale Natural History Bk. Distributors, Inc., *(978-1-885209)* Orders Addr.: P.O. Box 405, Lanesboro, MN 55949-0405 USA (SAN 630-6101) Tel 507-467-8734; Fax: 507-467-8735
E-mail: zoobooks@acegroup.cc
Web site: http://www.zoobooksales.com.

Service News Co., 1306 N. 23rd St., Wilmington, NC 28406 USA (SAN 169-6491) Tel 910-762-0837; Fax: 910-762-9539; Toll Free: 800-552-8238; P.O. Box 5027, Macon, GA 31208; Pope's Island, Box D-629, New Bedford, MA 02742 (SAN 169-3514).

Seven Locks Pr., *(978-0-929765; 978-0-932020; 978-0-9615964; 978-1-931643; 978-0-9790950; 978-0-9795852; 978-0-9801270; 978-0-9822293; 978-0-9824957)* P.O. Box 25689, Santa Ana, CA 92799-5689 USA (SAN 211-9781) Toll Free: 800-354-5348
E-mail: sevenlocks@aol.com
Web site: http://www.sevenlockspublishing.com.

Seymour, Dale Pubns., *(978-0-201; 978-0-7690; 978-0-86651; 978-1-57232)* Div. of Pearson Learning, Orders Addr.: P.O. Box 2500, Lebanon, OH 43216 USA Toll Free Fax: 800-393-3156; Toll Free: 800-321-3106 (Customer Service); Edit Addr.: 10 Bank St., White Plains, NY 10602-5026 USA (SAN 200-9781) Toll Free Fax: 800-393-3156; Toll Free: 800-237-3142
E-mail: pearson_learning2@prenhall.com
Web site: http://www.pearsonlearning.com; http://www.pearsonlearning.com/rightsPerm.rtf.

Shambhala Publications, Incorporated, *See* **Shambhala Pubns., Inc.**

Shambhala Pubns., Inc., *(978-0-8348; 978-0-87773; 978-0-937938; 978-1-55939; 978-1-56957; 978-1-57062; 978-1-59030; 978-1-61180)* Horticultural Hall, 300 Massachusetts Ave., Boston, MA 02115 USA (SAN 203-2481) Tel 617-424-0030; Fax: 617-236-1563
E-mail: editors@shambhala.com
Web site: http://www.shambhala.com.

Sharon News Agency Co., 527 Silver St., Sharon, PA 16146 USA (SAN 169-7633).

Sharpe, M.E. Inc., *(978-0-7656; 978-0-87332; 978-1-56324)* 80 Business Park Dr., Armonk, NY 10504 USA (SAN 202-7100) Tel 914-273-1800; Fax: 914-273-2106; Toll Free: 800-541-6563
Web site: http://www.mesharpe.com.

Shea Bks., 1563 Solano Ave., Suite 206, Berkeley, CA 94707 USA (SAN 159-9720) Tel 510-528-5201; Fax: 510-528-4987.

Shell Educational Publishing, *(978-1-4258)* 5301 Oceanus Dr., Huntington Beach, CA 92649 USA Tel

714-489-2080; Fax: 714-230-7070; Toll Free: 888-877-7606; 877-777-3450
E-mail: cmiller2@tcmpub.com; LShill@seppub.com; pkoehl@tcmpub.com; CMiller2@teachercreatedmaterials.com
Web site: http://www.seppub.com; http://www.tcmpub.com.

Shelter Pubns., Inc., *(978-0-936070)* Orders Addr.: P.O. Box 279, Bolinas, CA 94924 USA (SAN 122-8463) Tel 415-868-0280; Fax: 415-868-9053; Toll Free: 800-307-0131; Edit Addr.: 285 Dogwood Rd, Bolinas, CA 94924 USA
E-mail: shelter@shelterpub.com
Web site: http://www.shelterpub.com.

Shenanigan Bks., *(978-0-9726614; 978-1-934860)* 84 River Rd., Summit, NJ 07901-1443 USA (SAN 915-7085)
Web site: http://www.shenaniganbooks.com.

Shoppers Guide Pr., 706 N. Fifth, Alpine, TX 79830 USA (SAN 159-9550) Tel 915-837-7426.

Sierra News Co., 2136 Pony Express Ct., Stockton, CA 95215-7946 USA (SAN 169-4472).

Signature Bks., LLC, *(978-0-941214; 978-1-56085)* 564 W. 400 N., Salt Lake City, UT 84116-3411 USA (SAN 217-4391) Tel 801-531-1483; Fax: 801-531-1488; Toll Free: 800-356-5687 (orders only)
E-mail: people@signaturebooks.com
Web site: http://www.signaturebooks.com.

Silky Way, Inc., 1227 38th Ave., San Francisco, CA 94122-1334 USA (SAN 169-3328).

Silver Bow News Distributing Co., Inc., 219 E. Park St., Butte, MT 59701 USA (SAN 169-4359) Tel 406-782-6995.

Silver, Burdett & Ginn, Inc., *(978-0-382; 978-0-663; 978-1-4182)* Orders Addr.: P.O. Box 2500, Lebanon, IN 46052 USA Toll Free Fax: 800-841-8939; Toll Free: 800-552-2259; Edit Addr.: P.O. Box 480, Parsippany, NJ 07054 USA (SAN 204-5982); 108 Wilmot Rd., Suite 380, Midwest Div., Deerfield, IL 60015 (SAN 111-6517) Tel 708-945-1240; 1925 Century Blvd. NE, Suite 14, Southeast Div., Atlanta, GA 30345 (SAN 111-6509); 8445 Freeport Pkwy., Suite 400, South Div., Irving, TX 75063 (SAN 108-0458) Tel 214-915-4200; 2001 The Alameda, West Div., San Jose, CA 95126 (SAN 111-6525) Tel 408-248-6854; 160 Gould St., East Div., Needham Heights, MA 02194-2310; 1900 E. Lake Ave., Glenview, IL 60025
E-mail: customerservice@scottforesman.com
Web site: http://www.scottforesman.com/.

Simon & Schuster, *(978-0-671; 978-0-684; 978-0-689; 978-0-914676; 978-0-7432; 978-1-4165; 978-1-4391; 978-1-4516; 978-1-4767; 978-1-5011)* Div. of Simon & Schuster, Inc., Orders Addr.: 100 Front St., Riverside, NJ 08075 USA (SAN 200-2442) Toll Free Fax: 800-943-9831; Toll Free: 800-223-2336 (ordering); 800-223-2348 (customer service); Edit Addr.: a/o Subsidiary Rights, 11th Flr., 1230 Avenue of the Americas, New York, NY 10020 USA (SAN 200-2450) Tel 212-698-7000; Fax: 212-698-7007; 212-632-8099 (Rights & Permissions); 212-698-1269 (Pocket Bks. Rights & Permissions); Toll Free: 800-897-7650 (customer financial services); 100 Front St., Riverside, NJ 08075 (SAN 852-5471) Tel 856-824-2115
E-mail: ssonline_feedback@simonsays.com; consumer.customerservice@simonandschuster.com
Web site: http://www.simonsays.com; http://www.oasis.simonandschuster.com; http://www.simonandschuster.com/ebooks.

Simon & Schuster Children's Publishing, *(978-0-02; 978-0-671; 978-0-684; 978-0-689; 978-0-7434; 978-1-4169; 978-1-4424; 978-0-85707)* Orders Addr.: 100 Front St., Riverside, NJ 08075 USA Toll Free Fax: 800-943-9831; Toll Free: 800-223-2336; Edit Addr.: a/o Subsidiary Rights, 4th floor, 1230 Avenue of the Americas, New York, NY 10020 USA Tel 212-698-7200; Fax: 212-698-2797 (Rights & Permissions)
Web site: http://www.simonsays.com.

Simon & Schuster, Inc., *(978-0-02; 978-0-671; 978-0-684; 978-0-689; 978-0-914676; 978-0-7432; 978-0-7434; 978-0-7435; 978-1-4165; 978-1-4169; 978-1-4391; 978-1-4423; 978-1-4424; 978-1-4516; 978-0-85707; 978-1-4814; 978-1-5082)* Div. of Viacom Co., Orders Addr.: 100 Front St., Riverside, NJ 08075 USA Toll Free Fax: 800-943-9831; Toll Free: 800-223-2336 (orders); 800-223-2348 (customer service); Edit Addr.: 1230 Ave. of the Americas, New York, NY 10020 USA Tel 212-698-7000
E-mail: Consumer.CustomerService@simonandschuster.com
Web site: http://www.simonsays.com.

Simon & Schuster Trade, *See* **Simon & Schuster**

Skandisk, Inc., *(978-0-9615394; 978-1-57534)* 6667 W. Old Shakopee Rd., Suite 109, Bloomington, MN 55438-2622 USA (SAN 695-4405) Tel 952-829-8998; Fax: 952-829-8992; Toll Free: 800-468-2424 (orders)
E-mail: lhamnes@skandisk.com; tomten@skandisk.com
Web site: http://www.skandisk.com.

Sky Oaks Productions, Inc., *(978-0-940296; 978-1-56018)* P.O. Box 1102, Los Gatos, CA 95031 USA (SAN 217-5843) Tel 408-395-7600; Fax: 408-395-8440
E-mail: TRPWorld@aol.com
Web site: http://www.tpr-world.com.

Slatner, Thomas & Co., Inc., 193 Palisade Ave., 3rd Flr., Jersey City, NJ 07306-1112 USA (SAN 130-9862) Tel 201-420-6700; Fax: 201-420-6787.

Slavica Pubs., *(978-0-89357)* c/o Indiana University, 2611 E. Tenth St., Bloomington, IN 47408-2618 USA (SAN 208-8576) Tel 812-856-4186; Fax: 812-856-4187
E-mail: slavica@indiana.edu
Web site: http://www.slavica.com.

Sleeper, Dick Distribution, 18680-B Langensand Rd., Sandy, OR 97055-6426 USA (SAN 631-0273) Tel 503-668-3454; Fax: 503-668-5314; Toll Free: 800-699-9911
E-mail: sleepydick@bigfoot.com.

Sleuth Pubns., Ltd., *(978-0-915341)* 3398 Washington, San Francisco, CA 94118 USA (SAN 130-9374) Tel 415-771-2689.

Small Pr. United, Div. of Independent Pubs. Group, 814 N. Franklin St., Chicago, IL 60610 USA Tel 312-337-0747 (ext. 274)
Web site: http://www.smallpressunited.com.

Small Press Distribution, *See* **SPD-Small Pr. Distribution**

Smashwords, *(978-1-4523; 978-1-4524; 978-1-4580; 978-1-4581; 978-1-4657; 978-1-4658; 978-1-4659; 978-1-4660; 978-1-4661; 978-1-4760; 978-1-4761; 978-1-4762; 978-1-4763; 978-1-4764; 978-1-301; 978-1-310; 978-1-311)* 15951 Gatos Blvd., Suite 16, Los Gatos, CA 95032 USA Tel 408-358-1824; Fax: 408-358-1921; ziya gokalp mah. cimen sk. no:1/1 ikitelli koyu, basaksehir-istanbul, 34306 Tel 90 0538 8939727
Web site: http://www.smashwords.com.

Smith, Gibbs Publisher, *See* **Gibbs Smith, Publisher**

Smith News Agency, 118 S. Mitchell St., Cadillac, MI 49601 USA (SAN 169-3727).

SMMA Distributors, 6609 Brooks Dr., Temple, TX 76502 USA Tel 254-773-4884.

Snyder Magazine Agency, 3050 S. 9th Terr., Kansas City, KS 66103-2629 USA (SAN 285-9750).

Social Studies Schl. Service, *(978-1-56004; 978-1-57596)* Orders Addr.: 10200 Jefferson Blvd., P.O. Box 802, Culver City, CA 90232-0802 USA (SAN 168-9592) Tel 310-839-2436; Fax: 310-839-2249; Toll Free: 800-421-4246
E-mail: access@socialstudies.com
Web site: http://socialstudies.com.

Sociedad Biblica de Puerto Rico, Orders Addr.: P.O. Box 2548, Bayamon, PR 00960-2548 USA; Edit Addr.: Carr. 167, Km 14.7 Bo, Bayamon, PR 00960-2548 USA.

Society for Visual Education, Incorporated, *See* **S V E & Churchill Media**

Sopris West Educational Services, *See* **Cambium Education, Inc.**

Sort Card Co., The, 400 S. Summit View Dr., Fort Collins, CO 80524-1424 USA (SAN 159-9607).

Soundprints, *(978-0-924483; 978-1-56899; 978-1-931465; 978-1-59249; 978-1-60727)* Div. of Trudy Corp., 353 Main Ave., Norwalk, CT 06851 USA Fax: 203-846-1776; Toll Free: 800-228-7839
Web site: http://www.soundprints.com.

Sounds True, Inc., *(978-1-56455; 978-1-59179; 978-1-60407; 978-1-62203)* Orders Addr.: P.O. Box 8010, Boulder, CO 80306-8010 USA; Edit Addr.: 413 S. Arthur Ave., Louisville, CO 80027 USA (SAN 850-3532) Tel 303-665-3151; Fax: 303-665-5292; Toll Free: 800-333-9185
E-mail: rhiannonh@soundstrue.com; jaimes@soundstrue.com
Web site: http://www.soundstrue.com.

Source Bks., *(978-0-940147; 978-0-85650)* Orders Addr.: 204 E. Fourth St., Suite O, Santa Ana, CA 92701 USA (SAN 248-2231) Tel 714-558-8944 (phone/fax); Toll Free: 800-695-4237 Do not confuse with Source Bks., Nashville, TN
E-mail: studio185@earthlink.net.

Source International Technology Corporation, *See* **Kamkyi Bks.**

Sourcebooks, Inc., *(978-0-942061; 978-0-9629162; 978-0-9629803; 978-1-57071; 978-1-57248; 978-1-58182; 978-1-883518; 978-1-887166; 978-1-888952; 978-1-4022; 978-1-932783; 978-1-62047; 978-1-4926)* 1935 Brookdale Rd., Suite 139, Naperville, IL 60563 USA (SAN 666-7864) Tel 630-961-3900; Fax: 630-961-2168; Toll Free: 800-727-8866
E-mail: info@sourcebooks.com
Web site: http://www.sourcebooks.com/.

South Asia Bks., *(978-0-8364; 978-0-88386)* P.O. Box 502, Columbia, MO 65205 USA (SAN 207-4044) Tel 573-474-0116; Fax: 573-474-8124
E-mail: sabooks@juno.com
Web site: http://www.southasiabooks.com.

South Atlantic News, Orders Addr.: P.O. Box 61297, Jacksonville, FL 32236-1297 USA; Edit Addr.: 1426 NE Eighth Ave., Ocala, FL 32678 USA.

South Carolina Bookstore, Orders Addr.: P.O. Box 4767, West Columbia, SC 29171 USA (SAN 131-2294) Tel 803-796-8200; Fax: 803-794-6927; Toll Free: 800-845-8200; Edit Addr.: 523 Jasper St., West Columbia, SC 29169 USA (SAN 243-2390).

South Central Bks., Inc., 1106 S. Strong Blvd., McAlester, OK 74501-6952 USA (SAN 108-1144) Tel 405-275-4522; Toll Free: 800-548-9858.

South Eastern Bk. Co., Inc., 3333 Hwy. 641 N., P.O. Box 309, Murray, KY 42071 USA (SAN 630-4869) Tel 270-753-0732; Fax: 270-759-4742; Toll Free Fax: 800-433-6966 (orders); Toll Free: 800-626-3952 (orders)
E-mail: orders@sebook.com
Web site: http://www.sebook.com.

South Louisiana News Company, *See* **Southern Periodicals, Inc.**

Southeast Library Bindery, Inc., P.O. Box 35484, Greensboro, NC 27425-5484 USA (SAN 159-9445) Tel 336-931-0800
E-mail: 70304.3023@compuserve.com
Web site: http://www.webmasters.net/bookbinding/.

Southeast Periodical & Bk. Sales, Inc., 10100 NW 25th St., Box 520155-Biscayne Annex, Miami, FL 33152 USA.

Southeastern Educational Toy & Bk. Distributors, Orders Addr.: 3215 Wellington Court Suite 113, Raleigh, NC 27615 USA (SAN 630-8104) Tel 704-364-6988; Edit Addr.: 4217 Park Rd., Charlotte, NC 28209 USA Tel 704-527-1921; Fax: 704-527-1653.

Southeastern Library Service, Subs. of Haskins Hse., P.O. Box 44, Gainesville, FL 32602-0044 USA (SAN 159-9615) Tel 352-372-3823.

Southern Bk. Service, *(978-0-9663836)* 5154 NW 165th St., Palmetto Lakes Industrial Pk., Hialeah, FL 33014-6335 USA (SAN 169-0981) Tel 305-624-4545; Fax: 305-621-0425; Toll Free: 800-766-3254.

Southern Cross Pubns., 1734 W. Roseberry Rd., P.O. Box 717, Donnelly, ID 83615 USA (SAN 110-8549) Tel 208-325-8606; Fax: 208-325-3400
E-mail: scp@cyberhighway.net
Web site: http://www.thoughtlines.com/southerncross/.

Southern Library Bindery Co., 2952 Sidco Dr., Nashville, TN 37204 USA (SAN 169-7986).

Southern Michigan News Co., 2571 Saradan, P.O. Box 908, Jackson, MI 49204 USA (SAN 169-3697) Tel 517-784-7163; Toll Free: 800-248-2213 (in Michigan); 800-828-2140.

Southern Periodicals, Inc., P.O. Box 407, Rayne, LA 70578-0407 USA (SAN 113-2520); 180 James Dr E., Saint Rose, LA 70087-4005.

Southern Tier News Co., P.O. Box 2128, Elmira Heights, NY 14903 USA (SAN 169-5223).

Southern Wisconsin News, 58 Artisan Dr., Edgerton, WI 53534 USA (SAN 169-9121) Tel 608-884-2600; Fax: 608-756-2357
E-mail: ndewar@southernwisconsinnews.com.

Southwest Cookbook Distributors, Orders Addr.: P.O. Box 707, Bonham, TX 75418 USA (SAN 200-4925) Tel 903-583-8898; Fax: 903-583-2522; Toll Free: 800-725-8898 (orders); Edit Addr.: P.O. Box 707, Bonham, TX 75418-0707 USA (SAN 630-8325).

Southwest Natural Cultural Heritage Association, *See* **Public Lands Interpretive Assn.**

Southwest News Co., Box 5465, Tucson, AZ 85704 USA (SAN 159-9631).

Southwestern Bk. Distributors, c/o Kerbs, 700 Highview Ave., Glen Ellyn, IL 60137-5504 USA (SAN 160-2373).

Sovereign News Company, *See* **Trans World News**

Spama, Inc., 78 Lake St., Jersey City, NJ 07306-3407 USA (SAN 169-5967).

Spanish & European Bookstore, Inc., 3102 Wilshire Blvd., Los Angeles, CA 90010 USA Tel 213-739-8899; Fax: 213-739-0087.

Spanish Bookstore-Wholesale, The, 10977 Santa Monica Blvd., Los Angeles, CA 90025-4538 USA (SAN 168-9835) Tel 310-475-0453; Fax: 310-473-6132
E-mail: BernardHamel@SpanishbooksUSA.com
Web site: http://www.BernardHamel.com.

Spanish Hse. Distributors, 1360 NW 88th Ave., Miami, FL 33172-3093 USA (SAN 169-1171) Tel 305-592-6136; Fax: 305-592-0087; Toll Free: 800-767-7726.

Spanish Language Bk. Services, Inc., Orders Addr.: 7855 N.W. 12th St., Suite 211, Miami, FL 33126 USA.

Spanish Pubs., LLC., 8871 SW 129 Terr., Miami, FL 33176 USA Tel 305-233-3365; Fax: 305-251-1310
E-mail: mariela@spanishpublishers.net
Web site: www.spanishpublishers.net.

Spanishtech, Inc., Div. of Editor's Bureau, Ltd., P.O. Box 68, Westport, CT 06881 USA (SAN 289-9620) Tel 203-452-7655.

SPD-Small Pr. Distribution, *(978-0-914068)* 1341 Seventh St., Berkeley, CA 94710-1409 USA (SAN 204-5826) Tel 510-524-1668; Fax: 510-524-0852; Toll Free: 800-869-7553 (orders)
E-mail: orders@spdbooks.org
Web site: http://www.spdbooks.org.

SpeakWare, 2836 Stephen Dr., Richmond, CA 94803 USA Tel 510-222-2455
E-mail: leds@speakware.com
Web site: http://www.speakware.com.

Specialized Bk. Service, Inc., 307 Autumn Ridge Rd., Fairfield, CT 06432-1003 USA (SAN 166-9788) Tel 203-377-6510; Fax: 203-377-4792.

Specialty Bk. Services, 1150 N. San Francisco, Flagstaff, AZ 86001 USA (SAN 130-8114) Tel 520-779-7843.

Specialty Promotions, 4516 S. Vincennes Ave. # 1S, Chicago, IL 60653-3470 USA (SAN 110-9987).

Speech Bin, Inc., The, *(978-0-937857)* 1965 25th Ave., Vero Beach, FL 32960 USA (SAN 630-1657) Tel 772-770-0007; Fax: 772-770-0006
E-mail: info@speechbin.com
Web site: http://www.speechbin.com.

Speedimpex U.S.A., Inc., 35-02 48th Ave., Long Island City, NY 11101-2421 USA (SAN 169-5479) Tel 718-392-7477; Fax: 718-361-0815
E-mail: nsalvatore@speedimpex.com
Web site: http://www.speedimpex.com.

Spencer Museum of Art, *(978-0-913689)* Affil. of Univ. of Kansas, Univ. of Kansas 1301 Mississippi St., Lawrence, KS 66045-7500 USA (SAN 111-347X) Tel 785-864-4710; Fax: 785-864-3112
E-mail: spencerart@ku.edu
Web site: http://www.ukans.edu/~sma.

SPI Bks., *(978-0-944007; 978-1-56171)* 99 Spring St., 3rd Flr., New York, NY 10012 USA Tel 212-431-5011; Fax: 212-431-8646
E-mail: ian@spibooks.com
Web site: http://www.spibooks.com.

Spirit Filled Pr., Inc., *(978-0-9656668)* 2549 Tallavana Trail, Havana, FL 32333 USA Tel 850-539-3843 (phone/fax)
E-mail: 2549@bellsouth.net
Web site: http://www.mindspring.com/~spiritfilled.

Spirit Rising, c/o Nicole Heyward, 1505 Hadley St., Houston, TX 77002 USA Tel 713-772-5175; Fax: 713-772-3034
E-mail: nicole.heyward@musicworldent.com.

Spring Arbor Distributors, Inc., Subs. of Ingram Industries Inc., 4271 Edison Ave., Chino, CA 91710 USA; 7315 Innovation Blvd., Fort Wayne, IN 46818-1371; 201 Ingram Dr., Roseburg, OR 97470-7148; Newbury Rd., East Windsor, CT 06088; 25420 Weakley Rd., Petersburg, VA 23803; 11333 E. 53rd Ave., Denver, CO 80239-2108; Edit Addr.: 1 Ingram Blvd., La Vergne, TN 37086-1976 USA Fax: 615-213-5192; Toll Free: 800-395-4340; 800-395-7234 (customer service)
E-mail: orders@springarbor.com.

Springer, *(978-0-387; 978-0-8176; 978-3-211; 978-3-540; 978-3-7908; 978-4-431; 978-1-85233; 978-1-84628; 978-1-4419; 978-1-4612; 978-1-4613; 978-1-4614; 978-1-4684; 978-1-4757; 978-1-4899; 978-1-4939; 978-1-5041)* Subs. of Springer Science+Business Media, Orders Addr.: P.O. Box 2485, Secaucus, NJ 07096-2485 USA Tel 201-348-4033; Fax: 201-348-4505; Toll Free: 800-777-4643; Edit Addr.: 233 Spring St., New York, NY 10013-1578 USA (SAN 203-2228) Tel 212-815-0249; 212-460-1500; Fax: 212-460-1575; Toll Free: 1-800-777-4643 Thomson Delmar Learning Distributes Blanchard & Loeb Nursing Videos Only
E-mail: Slu@Springer-ny.com; service-ny@springer.com
Web site: http://www.springeronline.com; http://www.springer.com.

Springer-Verlag New York, Incorporated, *See* **Springer**

Springwater Bks., Orders Addr.: P.O. Box 194, Springwater, NY 14560-0194 USA (SAN 111-8900); Edit Addr.: Main St. & East Ave., Springwater, NY 14560-0194 USA (SAN 243-2412) Tel 716-669-2450.

Sprout, Inc., Orders Addr.: 430 Tenth St., NW, Suite 007, Atlanta, GA 30318 USA Tel 404-892-9600; Fax: 404-881-1383.

Square Deal Records, 303 Higuera St., San Luis Obispo, CA 93401-4209 USA (SAN 170-6799) Tel 805-543-3636; Fax: 805-543-3938; Toll Free: 800-253-4114
E-mail: sdrsslo@aol.com.

SRA/McGraw-Hill, *(978-0-07; 978-0-383)* Div. of The McGraw-Hill Education Group, Orders Addr.: 220 E. Daniel Dale Rd., DeSoto, TX 75115-2490 USA Fax: 972-228-1982; Toll Free: 800-843-8855; Edit Addr.: 8787 Orion Pl., Columbus, OH 43240-4027 USA Tel 614-430-6600; Fax: 614-430-6621; Toll Free: 800-468-5850
E-mail: sra@mcgraw-hill.com
Web site: https://www.sraonline.com.

Sri Aurobindo Association, Incorporated, *See* **Matagiri Sri Aurobindo Ctr.**

St. Marie's Gopher News Co., 9000 Tenth Ave., N., Minneapolis, MN 55427 USA (SAN 169-4103) Tel 612-546-5300; Fax: 612-546-1487.

St. Martin's Pr., *(978-0-312; 978-0-8050; 978-0-940687; 978-0-9603648; 978-1-55927; 978-1-58063; 978-1-58238; 978-1-4299; 978-1-250)* Div. of Holtzbrinck Pubs., Orders Addr.: 16365 James Madison Hwy., Gordonville, VA 22942 USA Tel 540-672-7600; Fax: 540-672-7540 (customer service); Toll Free Fax: 800-672-2054; Toll Free: 888-330-8477; Edit Addr.: 175 Fifth Ave., 20th Flr., New York, NY 10010 USA (SAN 200-2132) Tel 212-674-5151 (Trade Div.); 212-726-0200 (College Div.); Fax: 212-674-3179 (Trade Div.); 212-686-9491 (College Div.); Toll Free: 800-221-7945 (Trade Div.); 800-470-4767 (College Div.)
E-mail: webmaster@stmartins.com; enquiries@stmartins.com
Web site: http://www.stmartins.com; http://www.smpcollege.com.

St. Mary Seminary Bookstore, 28700 Euclid Ave., Wyckliffe, OH 44092 USA (SAN 169-667X) Tel 216-943-7600.

St Pauls/Alba Hse. Pubs., *(978-0-8189)* Div. of Society of St. Paul, 2187 Victory Blvd., Staten Island, NY 10314-6603 USA (SAN 201-2405) Tel 718-761-0047; Fax: 718-761-0057; 718-698-8390; Toll Free: 800-343-2522
E-mail: albabooks@aol.com
Web site: http://www.albahouse.org.

Stackpole Bks., *(978-0-8117)* 5067 Ritter Rd., Mechanicsburg, PA 17055 USA (SAN 202-5396) Tel 717-796-0411; Fax: 717-796-0412; Toll Free: 800-732-3669
E-mail: ccraley@stackpolebooks.com
Web site: http://www.stackpolebooks.com/.

Star Bright Bks., Inc., *(978-1-887734; 978-1-932065; 978-1-59572)* Orders Addr.: 30-19, 48th Ave., Long Island City, NY 11101 USA (SAN 254-5225) Tel 718-784-9112; Fax: 718-784-9012; Toll Free: 800-788-4439
E-mail: info@starbrightbooks.com
Web site: http://www.starbrightbooks.com.

StarCrossed Productions, *(978-0-9668483)* 14552 NW., 88 Pl., Miami, FL 33018 USA Tel 305-828-2619 Phone/Fax
E-mail: tinami@msn.com
Web site: http://www.cookiesisters.com.

Starkmann, Inc., 25-u Olympia Ave., Woburn, MA 01801 USA (SAN 126-6128) Tel 781-938-9643; Fax: 781-938 9647
E-mail: biggs@starkmann.co.uk.

Starmaster Co., 6911 Haverhill Dr., Knoxville, TN 37909 USA (SAN 108-1217) Tel 423-588-6661.

State Mutual Bk. & Periodical Service, Ltd., *(978-0-7855; 978-0-89771)* Orders Addr.: P.O. Box 1199, Bridgehampton, NY 11932-1199 USA.

State News Agency, 2750 Griffith Rd., Winston Salem, NC 27103-6418 USA (SAN 169-6424).

State Univ. of New York Pr., *(978-0-7914; 978-0-87395; 978-0-88706; 978-1-4384)* Orders Addr.: P.O. Box 960, Herndon, VA 20172-0960 USA (SAN 203-3496) Tel 703-661-1575; Fax: 703-996-1010; Toll Free Fax: 877-204-6074; Toll Free: 877-204-6073 (customer service); Edit Addr.: 22 Corporate Woods Blvd., 3rd Flr., Albany, NY 12211-2504 USA (SAN 658-1730) Tel

518-472-5000; Fax: 518-472-5038; Toll Free: 866-430-7869
E-mail: info@sunypress.edu; suny@presswarehouse.com
Web site: http://www.sunypress.edu.

Steerforth Pr., *(978-0-944072; 978-1-58195; 978-1-883642; 978-1-58642)* 45 Lyme Rd. # 208, Hanover, NH 03755-1219 USA
E-mail: helga@steerforth.com; info@steerforth.com
Web site: http://www.steerforth.com.

Steiner, Rudolf College Pr./St. George Pubns., *(978-0-916786; 978-0-945803; 978-0-9818095)* 9200 Fair Oaks Blvd., Fair Oaks, CA 95628 USA (SAN 208-8371) Tel 916-961-3722; Fax: 916-961-3032
E-mail: claude.julien@steinercollege.edu; cblatch@comcast.net
Web site: http://www.steinercollege.edu.

SteinerBooks, Inc., *(978-0-8334; 978-0-88010; 978-0-89345; 978-0-910142; 978-1-58420; 978-1-85584; 978-0-9701097; 978-0-9831984; 978-1-62148; 978-1-62151; 978-1-938685)* Orders Addr.: P.O. Box 960, Herndon, VA 20172-0960 USA Tel 703-661-1594 (orders); Fax: 702-661-1501; Toll Free Fax: 800-277-7947 (orders); Toll Free: 800-856-8664 (orders); Edit Addr.: 610 Main St., Suite 1, Great Barrington, MA 01230 USA Tel 413-528-8233; Fax: 413-528-8826; Fulfillment Addr.: 22883 Quicksilver Dr., Dulles, VA 20166 USA (SAN 253-9519) Tel 703-661-1529; Fax: 703-996-1010
E-mail: service@steinerbooks.org
Web site: http://www.steinerbooks.org.

Stenhouse Pubs., *(978-1-57110; 978-1-62531)* Div. of Highlights for Children, Orders Addr.: P.O. Box 11020, Portland, ME 04104-7020 USA (SAN 298-1580) Tel 207-253-1600; Fax: 207-253-5121; Toll Free Fax: 800-833-9164; Toll Free: 800-988-9812 (orders)
E-mail: jkilburn@stenhouse.com
Web site: http://www.stenhouse.com.

Sterling Publishing Co., Inc., *(978-0-8069; 978-1-4027; 978-1-60582; 978-1-4549; 978-1-61837)* 387 Park Ave., S., New York, NY 10016-8810 USA (SAN 211-6324) Tel 212-532-7160 212-213-2495; Toll Free Fax: 800-775-8736 (warehouse) Do not confuse with companies with similar names in Falls Church, VA, Fallbrook, CA, Lewisville, TX
E-mail: custservice@sterlingpub.com; tradesales@sterlingpub.com
Web site: http://www.sterlingpublishing.com/.

Stevens, Gareth Incorporated, *See* **Stevens, Gareth Publishing LLLP**

Stevens, Gareth Publishing LLLP, *(978-0-8368; 978-0-918831; 978-1-55532; 978-1-4339)* Orders Addr.: P.O. Box 360140, Strongsville, OH 44136-0140 USA Fax: 877-542-2596; Toll Free: 800-542-2595; Edit Addr.: 111 East 14th St., Suite 349, New York, NY 10003 USA (SAN 696-1592) Toll Free: 877-444-0210
E-mail: customerservice@gspub.com; hollyc@rosenpub.com
Web site: http://www.garethstevens.com; http://www.garethstevensclassroom.com.

Stevens International, Orders Addr.: P.O. Box 126, Magnolia, NJ 08049 USA (SAN 631-3612) Tel 856-435-1555; Edit Addr.: 706 N. White Horse Pike, Magnolia, NJ 08049 USA
Web site: http://www.stevenshobby.com.

Stevens, Mark Industries, Div. of Christian World, Inc., 304 N. Meridian Ave., Suite 6, Oklahoma City, OK 73107 USA (SAN 631-127X) Toll Free: 800-654-6760.

STL Distribution North America, *See* **Send The Light Distribution LLC**

Stoneydale Pr. Publishing Co., *(978-0-912299; 978-1-931291; 978-1-938707)* Orders Addr.: P.O. Box 188, Stevensville, MT 59870 USA Tel 406-777-2729; Fax: 406-777-2521; Toll Free: 800-735-7006; Edit Addr.: 523 Main St., Stevensville, MT 59870 USA (SAN 265-3168)
E-mail: stoneydale@stoneydale.com
Web site: http://www.stoneydale.com.

Storey Books, *See* **Storey Publishing, LLC**

Storey Publishing, LLC, *(978-0-88266; 978-1-58017; 978-0-9674717; 978-1-60342; 978-1-61212)* Subs. of Workman Publishing Co., Inc., Orders Addr.: 210 Mass Moca Way, North Adams, MA 01247 USA (SAN 203-4158) Fax: 413-346-2198; Toll Free Fax: 800-865-3429; Toll Free: 800-827-7444; c/o Workman Publishing, 225 Varick St., New York, NY 10014-4381 Tel 212-614-7700; Toll Free Fax: 800-521-1832; Toll Free: 800-722-7202
E-mail: info@storey.com; sales@storey.com
Web site: http://www.storey.com.

Strang Communications Company, *See* **Charisma Media**

Strauss Consultants, 48 W. 25th St., 11th Flr., New York, NY 10010-2708 USA Toll Free Fax: 888-528-8273; Toll Free: 800-236-7918
E-mail: strausscon@aol.com.

Streamwood Distribution, P.O. Box 91011, Mobile, AL 36691 USA Tel 334-665-0022; Fax: 334-665-0570.

Strelow, James C., 12588 Ivy Glen Ln., Garden Grove, CA 92841-4563 USA (SAN 132-4144).

Strisik, Nancy, 10 Main St., Rockport, MA 01966 USA Tel 978-546-7653.

Studio 2 Publishing, Inc., *(978-0-9763601; 978-0-9792455; 978-0-9819281; 978-0-9819874; 978-0-9826427; 978-0-9828175; 978-1-937013)* 1828 Midpark Dr., Suite I, Knoxville, TN 37921 USA Tel 865-637-0616
E-mail: contact@studio2publishing.com
Web site: http://www.studio2publishing.com.

Studio Fun International, *(978-0-276; 978-0-7621; 978-0-88705; 978-0-88850; 978-0-89577; 978-1-57584; 978-1-57619; 978-0-7944)* Subs. of Reader's Digest Assn., Inc., Reader's Digest Rd., Pleasantville, NY 10570-7000 USA (SAN 283-2143) Tel 914-244-4800; Fax: 914-244-4841
Web site: http://www.readersdigestkids.com; http://www.studiofun.com/.

Stylus Publishing, LLC, *(978-0-931816; 978-1-57922; 978-1-887208; 978-1-62036)* Orders Addr.: P.O. Box 605, Herndon, VA 20172-0605 USA; Edit Addr.: 22883 Quicksilver Dr., Sterling, VA 20166-2012 USA (SAN 299-1853) Tel 703-661-1581; Fax: 703-661-1501 Do not confuse with companies with the same name in Sunnyvale, CA, Quakertown, PA
E-mail: stylusmail@presswarehouse.com; jean.westcott@styluspub.com
Web site: http://www.styluspub.com.

Subscription Account, 84 Needham, Newton Highlands, MA 02161 USA (SAN 285-9424).

Subscription Hse., Inc., 209 Harvard St., Suite 407, Brookline, MA 02146-5005 USA (SAN 285-9343).

Subterranean Co., Orders Addr.: P.O. Box 160, Monroe, OR 97456 USA Fax: 541-847-6018
E-mail: subco@clipper.net.

Success Education Assn., Box 175, Roanoke, VA 24002 USA (SAN 159-9690).

Sun Life, *(978-0-937930)* 2399 Cool Springs Rd., Thaxton, VA 24174 USA (SAN 240-8333) Tel 540-586-4898.

Sunbelt Pubns., Inc., *(978-0-916251; 978-0-932653; 978-0-9606704; 978-0-9620402; 978-1-941384)* 1256 Fayette St., El Cajon, CA 92020-1511 USA (SAN 630-0790) Tel 619-258-4911; Fax: 619-258-4916; Toll Free: 800-626-6579
E-mail: info@sunbeltpub.com; sales@sunbeltpub.com; dyoung@sunbeltpub.com; mail@sunbeltpub.com
Web site: http://www.sunbeltpub.com; http://www.sunbeltbooks.com.

Sunburst Bks., Inc., Distributor of Florida Bks., 700 S. John Rodes Blvd., #D8, West Melbourne, FL 32904 USA Tel 321-409-0225; Fax: 321-728-2742
Web site: http://www.sunburstbooks.com.

Sunburst Communications, Inc., *(978-0-7805; 978-0-911831; 978-1-55636; 978-1-55826)* 400 Columbus Ave., Valhalla, NY 10595-1335 USA (SAN 213-5620) Toll Free: 800-431-1934
E-mail: webmaster@nysunburst.com
Web site: http://www.sunburst.com.

Sunburst Visual Media, *(978-1-59520)* Orders Addr.: P.O. Box 4455, Scottsdale, AZ 85261 USA Toll Free: 800-262-8837; Edit Addr.: P.O. Box 9120, Plainview, NY 11803-9020 USA
Web site: http://www.schoolspecialty.com.

Sundaykool Bulletins, *(978-1-888824)* Div. of Griffin Publishing Co., 18022 Cowan, Suite 202, Irvine, CA 92614 USA (SAN 631-5046) Toll Free: 800-472-9741
E-mail: griffinbooks@earthlink.net
Web site: http://www.griffinpublishing.com.

Sunshine Harbor, 825 Glen Arden Way, Altamonte Springs, FL 32701 USA (SAN 159-6640) Tel 407-339-0401.

Swedenborg Foundation, Inc., *(978-0-87785)* 320 N. Church St., West Chester, PA 19380 USA (SAN 111-7920) Tel 610-430-3222; Fax: 610-430-7982
E-mail: editor@swedenborg.com
Web site: http://www.swedenborg.com.

Swenson, Jim, 2610 Riverside Ln., NE, Rochester, MN 55901 USA (SAN 285-9505).

Swift News Agency, Orders Addr.: P.O. Box 160, Poncha Springs, CO 81242 USA (SAN 282-3810); Edit Addr.: 338 E. Hwy. 50, Poncha Springs, CO 81242 USA (SAN 169-0639).

Syco Distribution, 9208A Venture Ct., Manassas, VA 20111-4804 USA.

Symmes Systems, *(978-0-916352; 978-0-9907312)* 3977 Briarcliff Rd., NE, Atlanta, GA 30345-2647 USA (SAN 169-1465) Tel 404-876-7260.

Syndistar, Inc., *(978-1-56230)* P.O. Box 3027, Hammond, LA 70404-3027 USA (SAN 298-007X) Toll Free: 800-841-9532
E-mail: webmaster@syndistar.com
Web site: http://www.syndistar.com.

Syracuse Univ. Pr., *(978-0-8156; 978-0-615-28768-3)* 621 Skytop Rd., Suite 110, Syracuse, NY 13244-5290 USA (SAN 206-9776) Tel 315-443-2597; Fax: 315-443-5545
E-mail: supress@syr.edu
Web site: http://www.SyracuseUniversityPress.syr.edu.

T A Bookstore, *See* **Shea Bks.**

Taku Graphics, *(978-0-9717820; 978-0-9772297; 978-0-9801616; 978-0-9823450; 978-0-9846318; 978-0-9899679)* 5763 Glacier Hwy., Juneau, AK 99801 USA Tel 907-780-6310; Fax: 907-780-6314; Toll Free: 800-278-3291
E-mail: adele@takugraphics.com
Web site: http://www.takugraphics.com.

Tales of Wonder.com, 3037 Summer Oak Pl., Buford, GA 30518 USA (SAN 920-1246) Tel 770-904-2221; 770-904-2221; Toll Free: 866-796-6337
E-mail: service@towdistribution.com; rob@towdistribution.com
Web site: www.talesofwonder.com; http://www.towdistribution.com.

Tallahassee News Co., Inc., 3777 Hartsfield Rd., Tallahassee, FL 32303-1120 USA.

Tapeworm Video Distributor, Inc., 27833 Avenue Hopkins, Unit 6, Valencia, CA 91355-3407 USA (SAN 630-8767) Tel 805-257-4904; Fax: 805-257-4820; Toll Free: 800-367-8437
E-mail: sales@tapeworm.com
Web site: http://www.tapeworm.com.

Tatnuck BookSeller, The, 335 Chandler St., Worcester, MA 01602-3402 USA (SAN 169-3654) Tel 508-756-7644.

Tattered Cover Bookstore, 1628 16th St., Denver, CO 80202-1308 USA (SAN 631-0214) Toll Free: 800-833-9327 (ext. 250)
E-mail: roy@tatteredcover.com.

Taylor & Francis Group, *(978-0-335; 978-0-415; 978-0-8448; 978-0-85066; 978-0-89116; 978-0-903796; 978-0-905273; 978-1-56032; 978-1-85000; 978-1-59169)* Orders Addr.: 7625 Empire Dr., Florence, KY 41042-2919 USA Toll Free Fax: 800-248-4724; Toll Free: 800-634-7064; 74 Rolark Dr., Scarborough, ON M1R 4G2 Tel 416-299-5388; Fax: 416-299-7531; Toll Free: 877-226-2237; Edit Addr.: 325 Chestnut St., Philadelphia, PA 19106 USA (SAN 241-9246) Tel 215-625-8900; Fax: 215-625-2940; 270 Madison Ave., 4th Flr., New York, NY 10016-0601
Web site: http://www.routledge-ny.com; http://www.crcpress.com; http://www.garlandscience.com; http://www.taylorandfrancis.com.

Taylor & Francis, Incorporated, *See* **Taylor & Francis Group**

TBN Enterprises, *See* **Ironside International Pubs., Inc.**

Teacher Created Materials, Inc., *(978-0-87673; 978-0-7439; 978-1-4333; 978-1-60401; 978-1-4807; 978-1-4938; 978-1-5164)* 5301 Oceanus Dr., Huntington Beach, CA 92649 USA (SAN 665-5270) Tel 714-891-2273; Fax: 714-230-7070; Toll Free Fax: 888-877-7606; Toll Free: 800-858-7339
E-mail: sozbat@tcmpub.com
Web site: http://www.tcmpub.com; http://www.teachercreated.com.

Teacher Created Resources, Inc., *(978-1-55734; 978-1-57690; 978-1-4206; 978-1-4570)* 6421 Industry Way, Westminster, CA 92683 USA Tel 714-891-7895; Fax: 714-892-0283; Toll Free: 888-343-4335
E-mail: dlytle@teachercreated.com
Web site: http://www.teachercreated.com.

Teacher's Discovery, *(978-1-884473; 978-0-7560)* Div. of American Eagle Co., Inc., 2741 Paldan Dr., Auburn Hills, MI 48326 USA (SAN 631-4570) Tel 248-340-7210; Fax: 248-340-7212; Toll Free: 800-832-2437
Web site: http://www.teachersdiscovery-science.com; http://www.teachersdiscovery-english.com; http://www.teachersdiscovery-social studies.com; http://www.teachersdiscovery-foreignlanguage.com; http://www.teachersdiscovery.com.

Technical Bk. Co., P.O. Box 25934, Los Angeles, CA 90025-8994 USA (SAN 168-9851) Toll Free: 800-233-5150.

Techno Mecca, Inc., 4201 Wilshire Blvd., No. 620, Los Angeles, CA 90019 USA (SAN 631-7812) Tel 323-634-1650; Fax: 323-634-1655
E-mail: tjkim@tmecca.com
Web site: http://www.tmecca.com.

Temme Haus Pr., *(978-0-9727036)* 1784 Palm Ave., Stockton, CA 95205 USA (SAN 253-1925) Fax: 209-463-5527
E-mail: temmehans1953@sbcglobal.net.

Temple News Agency, *See* **ETD KroMar Temple**

Tempo Bookstore, 4905 Wisconsin Ave., NW, Washington, DC 20016 USA Tel 202-363-6683; Fax: 202-363-6686
E-mail: Tempobookstore@usa.net; tempobookstore@usa.net.

Ten Speed Pr., *(978-0-89815; 978-0-913668; 978-1-58008; 978-1-60774)* Div. of Crown Publishing Group, Orders Addr.: P.O. Box 7123, Berkeley, CA 94707 USA (SAN 202-7674) Fax: 510-559-1629 (orders); Toll Free: 800-841-2665; 555 Richmond St., W. Suite 405, Box 702, Toronto, ON M5V 3B1 Tel 416-703-7775; Fax: 416-703-9992
E-mail: order@tenspeed.com; alan@tenspeed.ca
Web site: http://www.tenspeed.com.

teNeues Publishing Co., *(978-3-570; 978-3-8238; 978-3-929278; 978-3-8327; 978-1-933427; 978-1-60160; 978-1-62325)* 7 W. 18th St., New York, NY 10011 USA (SAN 245-176X) Tel 212-627-9090; Fax: 212-627-9511; Toll Free: 800-352-0305; 12 Ferndene Rd., London, SE24 0AQ
E-mail: tnp@teneues-usa.com
Web site: http://www.teneues.com.

Territory Titles, 22 Camino Real, Sandia Park, NM 87047 USA.

Tesla Bk. Co., *(978-0-914119; 978-0-9603536)* P.O. Box 121873, Chula Vista, CA 91912-6573 USA (SAN 241-8703) Tel 619-585-8487; Toll Free: 800-398-2056
E-mail: bfeuling@teslabook.com.

Teva Nature, 2344 Black Oak Ct., Sarasota, FL 34232 USA (SAN 631-4619) Tel 941-377-7414; Fax: 941-371-6237; Toll Free: 800-924-8382.

Texas A&M Univ. Pr., *(978-0-89096; 978-1-58544; 978-1-60344; 978-1-62349)* 4354 TAMU John H. Lindsey Bldg., Lewis St., College Station, TX 77843-4354 USA (SAN 658-1919) Tel 979-458-3978; Fax: 979-847-8752; Toll Free Fax: 888-617-2421 (orders); Toll Free: 800-826-8911 (orders)
E-mail: tamupresscontact@gmail.com
Web site: http://www.tamupress.com.

Texas Art Supply, 2001 Montrose Blvd., Houston, TX 77006 USA (SAN 169-8303) Tel 713-526-5221; Fax: 713-524-7474; Toll Free: 800-888-9278
E-mail: info@texasart.com
Web site: http://www.texasart.com.

Texas Bk. Co., Orders Addr.: 2601 King, Greenville, TX 75401 USA (SAN 103-4308) Tel 903-455-6969; Fax: 903-454-4775; US Naval Academy/TBC, 5th Wing Bancroft Hall/Textbook, 101 Wilson Rd., Anapolis, MD 21402 (SAN 920-8461) Tel 903-455-6969 ext 642; TBC-NWLTC Bookstore-810 8501 Technology Cir. Unit 810, Greenville, TX 75402 (SAN 920-9050) Tel 903-455-6969; TBC-SOWELA Tech Comm College Bookstore-820 8501 Technology Cir. - Unit 820, Greenville, TX 75402 (SAN 920-9069) Tel 903-455-6969; TBC-Trenholm State Tech. Coll Bookstore-830 8501 Technology Circle-Unit 830, Greenville, TX 75402 (SAN 920-9077) Tel 903-455-6969; TBC-Drake State Tech College Bookstore-831 8501 Technology Circle-Unit 831, Greenville, TX 75402 (SAN 920-9085) Tel 903-455-6969; Edit Addr.: P.O. Box 212, Greenville, TX 75403 USA Fax: 903-454-2442; Toll Free: 800-527-1016
E-mail: monica@texasbook.com; diana@texasbook.com; molson@texasbook.com.

Texas Bookman, The, *(978-1-931040)* 2700 Lone Star Dr., Dallas, TX 75212-6209 USA (SAN 106-875X) Toll Free: 800-566-2665
E-mail: texas.bookman@halfpricebooks.com.

Texas Hill Country Cookbook, P.O. Box 126, Round Mountain, TX 78663 USA (SAN 110-831X) Tel 210-825-3242; Fax: 210-825-3244; Toll Free: 800-231-3553.

Texas Library Bk. Sales, 1408 West Koenig Lane, Austin, TX 78756 USA (SAN 169-8044) Tel 512-452-4140.

Textbooks On Demand, *See* **Reprint Services Corp.**

TextStream, *(978-0-7351)* Div. of Baker & Taylor Bks., Orders Addr.: c/o Baker & Taylor Digital Media Services, 1120 US Hwy., 22 E., Bridgewater, NJ 08807 USA Tel 908-541-7035; Toll Free Fax: 800-648-0541; Toll Free: 800-775-1800; Edit Addr.: P.O. Box 6885, Bridgewater, NJ 08807-0885 USA
E-mail: btinfo@baker-taylor.com
Web site: http://www.baker-taylor.com/textstream.

TFH Pubns., Inc., *(978-0-7938; 978-0-86622; 978-0-87666; 978-1-85279)* Orders Addr.: One TFH Plaza, Third & Union Aves., Neptune City, NJ 07753 USA (SAN 202-7720) Tel 732-988-8400; Fax: 732-988-5466; Toll Free: 800-631-2188 (outside New Jersey); Edit Addr.: P.O. Box 427, Neptune, NJ 07753 USA (SAN 658-1862)
E-mail: info@tfh.com
Web site: http://www.tfh.com.

Thames Bk. Co., 1 Quarry Rd., Mystic, CT 06355-3200 USA (SAN 169-0760).

Theme Stream, Inc., P.O. Box 142, Broomfield, CT 06002 USA Tel 860-243-5200
Web site: http://www.themestream.com.

Theological Bk. Service, P.O. Box 509, Barnhart, MO 63012 USA (SAN 631-6662) Tel 636-464-2500; Fax: 636-464-8449; Toll Free Fax: 800-325-9526; Toll Free: 877-484-1600
E-mail: tbs@execpc.com
Web site: http://www.theobooks.org.

Thieme Medical Pubs., Inc., *(978-0-86577; 978-0-913258; 978-1-58890; 978-1-60406; 978-1-62623)* Subs. of Georg Thieme Verlag Stuttgart, 333 Seventh Ave., 5th Flr., New York, NY 10001 USA (SAN 169-5983) Tel 212-760-0888; Fax: 212-947-1112; Toll Free: 800-782-3488 (orders only)
E-mail: customerservice@thieme.com
Web site: http://www.thieme.com.

Thieme-Stratton, Inc., *See* **Thieme Medical Pubs., Inc.**

Thinkers' Pr., Inc., *(978-0-938650; 978-1-888710)* Orders Addr.: P.O. Box 8, Davenport, IA 52805-0008 USA Tel 319-323-1226; Fax: 319-323-0511; Toll Free: 800-397-7117 (orders only); Edit Addr.: 1524 Leclaire St., Davenport, IA 52803-4428 USA (SAN 162-7759)
E-mail: tpi@chessco.com
Web site: http://www.chessco.com.

Thistle Hill Pubns., *(978-0-9705511)* 477 Thistle Hill Rd., North Pomfret, VT 05053-0307 USA Tel 802-457-2050; Fax: 802-457-3653; Fulfillment Addr.: P.O. Box 428, White River Junction, VT 05001 USA
E-mail: thp@together.net
Web site: http://www.thistlehillpub.com.

Thomas Brothers Maps, *(978-0-88130; 978-1-58174)* Div. of Rand McNally & Co., 17731 Cowan, Irvine, CA 92614 USA (SAN 158-8192) Fax: 949-757-1564; Toll Free: 800-899-6277
Web site: http://www.thomas.com.

Thompson Schl. Bk. Depository, Orders Addr.: P.O. Box 60160, Oklahoma City, OK 73146 USA (SAN 159-9747) Tel 405-525-9458; Fax: 405-525-5443; Edit Addr.: 39 NE 24th St., Oklahoma City, OK 73143 USA.

Thomson Delmar Learning, *See* **Delmar Cengage Learning**

Thomson Gale, *See* **Cengage Gale**

Thomson Learning, *See* **CENGAGE Learning**

Thomson, Linda, P.O. Box 1225, Orem, UT 84059-1225 USA (SAN 110-3881) Tel 801-226-0155; Fax: 801-226-0166; Toll Free: 800-226-0155.

Thomson Peterson's, *See* **Peterson's**

Thomson West, *See* **West**

Thorndike Pr., *(978-0-7838; 978-0-7862; 978-0-8161; 978-0-89621; 978-1-56054; 978-1-4104)* Div. of Gale Group, 295 Kennedy Memorial Dr., Waterville, ME 04901 USA Tel 207-859-1053; 207-859-1020; 207-859-1000; Toll Free Fax: 800-558-4676; Toll Free: 800-223-1244 (ext. 15); 800-877-4253 (customer resource ctr.)
E-mail: jamie.knobloch@gale.com; barb.littfield@galegroup.com; Betsy.M.Brown@thomson.com; jamie.knobloch@cengage.com
Web site: http://www.gale.com/thorndike.

Tiffin News Agency, 34 Kennat Blvd., Tiffin, OH 44883-4604 USA (SAN 169-6866).

Tiger Bk. Distributors, Ltd., 328 S. Jefferson, Chicago, IL 60661 USA (SAN 631-0672) Tel 312-382-1160; Fax: 312-382-0323.

TI-Holdings Distribution Co., 4 Hopscotch Ln., Savannah, GA 31411 USA.

Timber Pr., Inc., *(978-0-88192; 978-0-917304; 978-0-931146; 978-0-931340; 978-1-60469)* Div. of Workman Publishing Co., Inc., 133 SW Second Ave., Suite 450, Portland, OR 97204-3527 USA (SAN 216-082X) Tel 503-227-2878; Fax: 503-227-3070; Toll Free: 800-327-5680; 20 Lonsdale Rd Swavesey, London, NW6 6RD Tel (01954) 232959; Fax: (01954) 206040
E-mail: info@timberpress.co.uk; publicity@timberpress.com
Web site: http://www.timberpress.com.

Time Home Entertainment, Incorporated, *See* **Time Inc. Bks.**

Time Inc. Bks., *(978-1-883013; 978-1-929049; 978-1-931933; 978-1-932273; 978-1-932994; 978-1-933405; 978-1-933821; 978-1-60320; 978-1-61893)* Div. of Time, Inc., 1271 Avenue of the Americas, New York, NY 10020-1201 USA (SAN 227-3209).

Time Warner Book Group, *See* **Hachette Bk. Group**

Time-Life Publishing Warehouse, 5240 W. 76th, Indianapolis, IN 43268-4137 USA (SAN 631-1504) Fax: 717-348-6409; Toll Free: 800-277-8844
Web site: http://www.timelifecs.com; http://www.timelifeedu.com.

TIS, Inc., *(978-0-89917; 978-1-56581; 978-0-7421)* Orders Addr.: P.O. Box 669, Bloomington, IN 47402 USA Tel 812-332-3307; Fax: 812-331-7690; Toll Free: 800-367-4002; Edit Addr.: 5005 N. State Rd. 37 Business, Bloomington, IN 47404 USA.

Titan Bookstore, P.O. Box 34080, Fullerton, CA 92634-9480 USA (SAN 106-4851).

Title Bks., Inc., 3013 Second Ave. S, Birmingham, AL 35233 USA (SAN 168-9207) Tel 205-324-2596.

Tobias News Co., 130 18th St., Rock Island, IL 61201 USA (SAN 169-2186) Tel 309-788-7517.

Todd Communications, *(978-1-57833; 978-1-878100)* 611 E. 12th Ave. Ste. 102, Anchorage, AK 99501-4663 USA (SAN 298-6280)
E-mail: info@toddcom.com.

Topical Review Bk Co., Inc., *(978-1-929099; 978-1-939246)* P.O. Box 328, Onsted, MI 49265 USA Tel 517-547-8072; Fax: 517-547-7512
E-mail: topicalrbc@aol.com
Web site: www.topicalrbc.com.

Total Information, Inc., 844 Dewey Ave., Rochester, NY 14613 USA (SAN 123-7373) Tel 716-254-0621.

T.R. Bks., Orders Addr.: P.O. Box 310279, New Braunfels, TX 78131 USA (SAN 630-4885) Tel 830-625-2665; Fax: 830-620-0470; Toll Free: 800-659-4710; Edit Addr.: P.O. Box 310279, New Braunfels, TX 78131-0279 USA
E-mail: trbooks@trbooks.com
Web site: http://www.trbooks.com.

T.R. Trading Co., *See* **T.R. Bks.**

Tracor Technology Resources (TTR), Specialized Bk. Distributors, 1601 Research Blvd., Rockville, MD 20850 USA (SAN 169-3220) Tel 301-251-4970.

Trafalgar Square Publishing, *(978-0-943955; 978-1-57076)* Orders Addr.: P.O. Box 257, North Pomfret, VT 05053-0257 USA (SAN 213-8859) Tel 802-457-1911; Fax: 802-457-1913; Toll Free: 800-423-4525; Edit Addr.: 388 Howe Hill Rd., North Pomfret, VT 05053 USA Tel 802-423-4525; 802-457-1913
E-mail: tsquare@sover.net
Web site: http://www.trafalgarbooks.com; http://www.horseandriderbooks.com.

Trails Media Group, Incorporated, *See* **Big Earth Publishing**

Trajectory, Inc., *(978-1-62028; 978-1-62665; 978-1-62978; 978-1-63209; 978-1-68100; 978-1-68124)* 50 Doaks Lane, Marblehead, MA 01945 USA Tel 781-476-2100
E-mail: info@trajectory.com; bob@trajectory.com
Web site: http://www.trajectory.com.

Trans World News, 3700 Kelley Ave., Cleveland, OH 44114-4533 USA (SAN 169-6688) Tel 216-391-4800; Fax: 216-391-9911; Toll Free: 800-321-9858.

Transaction Pubs., *(978-0-7658; 978-0-87855; 978-0-88738; 978-1-56000; 978-1-4128)* Raritan Ctr., 300 McGaw Dr., Edison, NJ 08837 USA; Edit Addr.: 10 Corporate Pl., S., Piscataway, NJ 08854 USA (SAN 202-7941) Toll Free: 888-999-6778
E-mail: orders@transactionpub.com
Web site: http://www.transactionpub.com.

Transamerican & Export News Co., 12345 World Trade Dr., San Diego, CA 92128-3743 USA (SAN 169-0140).

Trans-Atlantic Pubns., Inc., 311 Bainbridge St., Philadelphia, PA 19147 USA (SAN 694-0234) Tel 215-925-5083; Fax: 215-925-1912 Do not confuse with Transatlantic Arts, Inc., Albuquerque, NM
E-mail: order@transatlanticpub.com
Web site: http://www.transatlanticpub.com.

Traveler Restaurant, 741 Buckley Hwy., Union, CT 06076 USA (SAN 111-8218) Tel 860-684-4920.

Treasure Chest Bks., P.O. Box 5250, Tucson, AZ 85703-0250 USA Tel 520-623-9558; Fax: 520-624-5888; Toll Free Fax: 800-715-5888; Toll Free: 800-969-9558.

Treasure Chest Books, *See* **Rio Nuevo Pubs.**

Treasure Valley News, 4242 S. Eagleson Rd. Ste. 108B, Boise, ID 83705-4985 USA.

Tree Frog Trucking Co., 7983 SE 13th Ave., Portland, OR 97202-6665 USA (SAN 169-7188).

Tree Hse. Distribution, 1007 Perrywill Ave., Salt Lake City, UT 84124-2428 USA (SAN 631-6603) Fax: 801-262-2324; Toll Free: 888-299-7895.

Tree of Life Midwest, P.O. Box 2629, Bloomington, IN 47402-2629 USA (SAN 169-7994) Toll Free: 800-999-4200.

Tres Americas Bks., Orders Addr.: 4336 N. Pulaski Rd., Chicago, IL 60641 USA Tel 773-481-9090.

T-Rex Products, 2391 Boswell Rd., Chula Vista, CA 91914-3509 USA.

Triangle News Co., Inc., 3498 Grand Ave., Pittsburgh, PA 15225 USA (SAN 169-7447).

Tri-County News Co., Inc., 1376 W. Main St., Santa Maria, CA 93458 USA (SAN 169-0345) Tel 805-925-6541; Fax: 805-925-3565
E-mail: trico2000@aol.com
Web site: http://tri-countynews.com.

TriLiteral, LLC, 100 Maple Ridge Dr., Cumberland, RI 02864-1796 USA (SAN 631-8126) Tel 401-531-2800; 401-531-2804 (Credit & Collections); Fax: 401-531-2801; 401-531-2803 (Credit & Collections); Toll Free Fax: 800-406-9145; Toll Free: 800-405-1619
E-mail: rich.swafford@triliteral.org; customer.care@Triliteral.org.

Trinity Pr. International, *(978-1-56338)* Orders Addr.: P.O. Box 1321, Harrisburg, PA 17105-1321 USA; Edit Addr.: 4775 Linglestown Rd., Harrisburg, PA 17112 USA (SAN 253-8156).

Triple Tail Publishing, *See* **Farcountry Pr.**

Tri-State News Agency, P.O. Box 778, Johnson City, TN 37601 USA (SAN 169-7897) Tel 423-926-8159; 604 Rolling Hills Dr., Johnson City, TN 37601 (SAN 282-4744).

Tri-State Periodicals, Inc., Orders Addr.: P.O. Box 1110, Evansville, IN 47706-1110 USA Tel 812-867-7416; Edit Addr.: 9844 Heddon Rd., Evansville, IN 47711 USA (SAN 241-7537) Tel 812-867-7419.

Trucatriche, Orders Addr.: 3800 Main St., Suite 8, Chula Vista, CA 91911 USA Tel 619-426-2690; Fax: 619-426-2695
E-mail: info@trucatriche.com
Web site: http://www.trucatriche.com.

Truth Pubns., Orders Addr.: 8105 NW 23rd Ave., Gainesville, FL 32606 USA Tel 352-376-6320; Fax: 352-376-7105 Do not confuse with companies with the same or similar name in Paris, TX, Lombard, IL, Philadelphia, PA, Springfield, MO, Woodstock, MO
E-mail: upgflorida@juno.com.

Tulare County News, 13595 El Nogal Ave., Visalia, CA 93292-9352 USA (SAN 169-0442) Toll Free: 800-479-6006.

Turner Subscription Agency, Subs. of Dawson Holdings PLC, 15 S. West Park., Westwood, MA 02090-1524 USA (SAN 107-7112) Toll Free: 800-847-4201
E-mail: postmaster@dawson.com.

Turtleback Bks., *(978-0-613; 978-0-7857; 978-0-8085; 978-0-8335; 978-0-88103; 978-1-4176; 978-1-4177; 978-1-4178; 978-0-606)* Sub. of GL group, Inc., 1230 Macklind Ave., Saint Louis, MO 63110-1432 USA (SAN 159-947X) Tel 314-644-6100; Fax: 314-647-2845; Toll Free: 800-458-8438
E-mail: info@sanval.com; rheflin@turtleback.com
Web site: http://www.Turtleback.com.

Tuttle Publishing, *(978-0-8048; 978-1-4629)* Orders Addr.: 364 Innovation Dr., North Clarendon, VT 05759 USA (SAN 213-2621) Tel 802-773-8930; Fax: 802-773-6993; Toll Free Fax: 800-329-8885; Toll Free: 800-526-2778
E-mail: info@tuttlepublishing.com
Web site: http://www.tuttlepublishing.com.

Twentieth Century Christian Bks., *(978-0-89098)* 2809 Granny White Pike, Nashville, TN 37204 USA (SAN 206-2550) Tel 615-383-3842.

Twenty First Century Pubns., *(978-0-933278)* Orders Addr.: P.O. Box 702, Fairfield, IA 52556-0702 USA Tel 515-472-5105; Fax: 515-472-8443; Toll Free: 800-593-2665; Edit Addr.: 401 N. Fourth St., Fairfield, IA 52556 USA Do not confuse with Twenty First Century Pubns., Tolland, CT
E-mail: books21st@lisco.com
Web site: http://www.21stbooks.com.

Twenty-First Century Antiques, Orders Addr.: P.O. Box 70, Hatfield, MA 01038 USA (SAN 110-8085); Edit Addr.: 11 1/2 Main St., Hatfield, MA 01038 USA (SAN 243-248X) Tel 413-247-9396.

Twenty-Third Pubns./Bayard, *(978-0-89622; 978-1-58595; 978-1-62785)* 1 Montauk Ave. No. 20, New London, CT 06320-4967 USA (SAN 658-2052) Toll Free Fax: 800-572-0788; Toll Free: 800-321-0411
E-mail: kerry.moriarty@bayard-inc.com
Web site: http://www.23rdpublications.com.

Twin City News Agency, Inc., P.O. Box 466, Lafayette, IN 47902-0466 USA Tel 765-742-1051.

Tyndale Hse. Pubs., *(978-0-8423; 978-1-4143; 978-1-4964)* Orders Addr.: 370 Executive Dr., Carol Stream, IL 60188 USA; Edit Addr.: 351 Executive Dr., Carol Stream, IL 60188 USA (SAN 206-7749) Tel 630-668-8310; Fax: 630-668-3245; Toll Free: 800-323-9400
E-mail: international@tyndale.com; permission@tyndale.com
Web site: http://www.tyndale.com.

Ubiquity Distributors, Inc., 607 Degraw St., Brooklyn, NY 11217 USA (SAN 200-7428) Tel 718-875-5491; Fax: 718-875-8047.

Ultra Bks., P.O. Box 945, Oakland, NJ 07436 USA (SAN 112-9074) Tel 201-337-8787.

Ulverscroft Large Print Bks., Ltd., *(978-0-7089; 978-1-84617)* Orders Addr.: P.O. Box 1230, West Seneca, NY 14224-1230 USA; Edit Addr.: 950 Union Rd., West Seneca, NY 14224-3438 USA (SAN 208-3035) Toll Free: 800-955-9659
E-mail: enquiries@ulverscroft.co.uk; sales@ulverscroft.com
Web site: http://www.ulverscroft.co.uk.

Unarius Academy of Science Pubns., *(978-0-932642; 978-0-935097)* Orders Addr.: 145 S. Magnolia Ave., El Cajon, CA 92020-4522 USA (SAN 168-9614) Tel 619-444-7062; Fax: 619-444-9637; Toll Free: 800-475-7062
E-mail: uriel@unarius.org
Web site: http://www.unarius.org.

Underground Railroad, The, 2769 Club House Rd., Mobile, AL 36605-4373 USA (SAN 630-7892) Tel 334-432-8811.

Unifacmanu International Trading Co., Inc., 22 Cross Ridge Rd., Chappaqua, NY 10514 USA (SAN 631-743X)
E-mail: unifacmanu@att.net
Web site: http://www.bookvariety.com.

UNIPUB, *See* **Bernan Assocs.**

Unique Bks., Inc., 5010 Kemper Ave., Saint Louis, MO 63139 USA (SAN 630-0472) Tel 314-776-6695; Fax: 314-776-0841; Toll Free: 800-533-5446.

United Magazine, Orders Addr.: P.O. Box 36, Columbia, KY 42728-0036 USA (SAN 169-2852) Tel 502-384-3444; Fax: 502-384-9324; Edit Addr.: 361 Industrial Park Rd., Louisville, KY 42728-0036 USA (SAN 250-3336).

United News Co., Inc., 111 Lake St., P.O. Box 3426, Bakersfield, CA 93305 USA (SAN 169-7579) Tel 805-323-7864.

United Society of Shakers, *(978-0-915836)* 707 Shaker Rd., New Gloucester, ME 04260 USA (SAN 158-619X) Tel 207-926-4597; Fax: 207-926-3559
E-mail: sdlshakers@aol.com
Web site: http://www.shaker.lib.me.us.

United States Government Printing Office, *(978-0-16; 978-0-18)* Orders Addr.: P.O. Box 371954, Pittsburgh, PA 15250-7954 USA (SAN 658-0785) Tel 202-512-1800; Fax: 202-512-2250; Toll Free: 866-512-1800; Edit Addr.: USGPO Stop SSMB, Washington, DC 20401 USA (SAN 206-152X) Tel 202-512-1705 (bibliographic information only); 202-512-2268 (book dealers only); Fax: 202-512-1655
E-mail: orders@gpo.gov; rdavis@gpo.gov; ContactCenter@gpo.gov
Web site: http://bookstore.gpo.gov; http://www.gpoaccess.gov/index.html.

United Subscription Service, 527 Third Ave., No. 284, New York, NY 10016-4100 USA (SAN 286-0104).

Univ of Arizona Critical Languages Program, 1230 N. Park Ave., Suite 102, Tucson, AZ 85719 USA.

Univ. of Arkansas Pr., *(978-0-938626; 978-1-55728; 978-1-61075; 978-1-68226)* 105 N. McIlroy Ave., Fayetteville, AR 72701 USA (SAN 239-3972) Tel 479-575-7544; Fax: 479-575-6044; Toll Free: 800-626-0090
E-mail: info@uapress.com
Web site: http://www.uapress.com; http://www.uark.edu/~uaprinfo.

Univ. of California Pr., *(978-0-520)* 155 Grand Ave., Suite 400, Oakland, CA 94612-3758 USA Tel 510-883-8232 (Books & Journals); Fax: 510-836-8910
E-mail: journals@ucpress.edu; orders@cpfsinc.com; askucp@ucpress.edu
Web site: http://www.ucpress.edu.

Univ. of Chicago Pr., *(978-0-226; 978-0-89065; 978-0-943056; 978-1-892850)* Orders Addr.: 11030 S. Langley Ave., Chicago, IL 60628 USA (SAN 202-5280) Tel 773-702-7000; Fax: 773-702-7212; Toll Free Fax: 800-621-8476 (US & Canada); Toll Free: 800-621-2736 (US & Canada); Edit Addr.: 1427 E. 60th St., Chicago, IL 60637 USA (SAN 202-5299) Tel 773-702-7700; 773-702-7748 (Marketing & Sales); Fax: 773-702-9756
E-mail: general@press.uchicago.edu; kh@press.uchicago.edu; custserv@press.uchicago.rdu; sales@press.uchicago.edu; marketing@press.uchicago.edu; publicity@press.uchicago.edu
Web site: http://www.press.uchicago.edu.

Univ. of Georgia Pr., *(978-0-8203)* Orders Addr.: 4435 Atlanta Hwy. West Dock, Athens, GA 30602 USA; Edit Addr.: Main Library, Third Flr. 320 S. Jackson St., Athens, GA 30602 USA (SAN 203-3054) Fax: 706-542-2558; Toll Free: 800-266-5842
E-mail: books@uga.edu
Web site: http://www.ugapress.org.

Univ. of Hawaii Pr., *(978-0-8248; 978-0-87022)* Orders Addr.: 2840 Kolowalu St., Honolulu, HI 96822-1888 USA (SAN 202-5353) Tel 808-956-8255; Fax: 808-988-6052; Toll Free Fax: 800-650-7811; Toll Free: 888-847-7377
E-mail: uhpmkt@hawaii.edu; uhpbooks@hawaii.edu
Web site: http://www.uhpress.hawaii.edu.

Univ. of Missouri Pr., *(978-0-8262)* 2910 LeMone Blvd., Columbia, MO 65201 USA (SAN 203-3143) Tel 573-882-7641; Fax: 573-884-4498; Toll Free: 800-828-1894 (orders only)
E-mail: rennerk@umsystem.edu; deandj@umsystem.edu
Web site: http://press.umsystem.edu.

Univ. of Nebraska Pr., *(978-0-8032; 978-1-4962)* Orders Addr.: 1111 Lincoln Mall, Lincoln, NE 68588-0630 USA Tel 402-472-3581; 402-472-7702; Fax: 402-472-6214; Toll Free Fax: 800-526-2617; Toll Free: 800-755-1105; Edit Addr.: P.O. Box 880630, Lincoln, NE 68588-0630 USA (SAN 202-5337)
E-mail: pressmail@unl.edu
Web site: http://www.nebraskapress.unl.edu; http://www.bisonbooks.com.

Univ. of New Mexico Pr., *(978-0-8263)* Orders Addr.: 1312 Basehart Rd., SE, Albuquerque, NM 87106-4363 USA (SAN 213-9588) Tel 505-277-2346; 505-272-7777 (orders); Toll Free Fax: 800-622-8667; Toll Free: 800-249-7737 (orders)
E-mail: unmpress@unm.edu
Web site: http://www.unmpress.com.

Univ. of Oklahoma Pr., *(978-0-8061)* Orders Addr.: 2800 Venture Dr., Norman, OK 73069-8218 USA Tel 405-325-2000; Fax: 405-364-5798; Toll Free Fax: 800-735-0476; Toll Free: 800-627-7377
E-mail: presscs@ou.edu
Web site: http://www.oupress.com.

Univ. of Pennsylvania Pr., *(978-0-8122; 978-1-5128)* Orders Addr.: c/o Hopkins Fulfillment Srvc., Hopkins Fulfillment Service, Baltimore, MD 21211-4370 USA Tel 410-516-6948; Fax: 410-516-6998; Toll Free: 800-537-5487; Edit Addr.: 3905 Spruce St., Philadelphia, PA 19104-4112 USA (SAN 202-5345) Tel 215-898-6261; Fax: 215-898-0404; Toll Free: 800-537-5487 (book orders)
E-mail: custserv@pobox.upenn.edu
Web site: http://www.upenn.edu/pennpress.

Univ. of Tennessee Pr., *(978-0-87049; 978-1-57233; 978-1-62190)* Div. of Univ. of Tennessee & Member of Assn. of American Univ. Presses, Orders Addr.: 11030 S. Langley, Chicago, IL 60628 USA Tel 773-568-1550; Toll Free Fax: 800-621-8471; Toll Free: 800-621-2736 (orders only); Edit Addr.: 110 Conference Ctr. Bldg., Knoxville, TN 37996-0325 USA (SAN 212-9930) Tel 865-974-3321; Fax: 865-974-3724
E-mail: tpost@utk.edu; ccarson3@utk.edu
Web site: http://www.utpress.org.

Univ. of Texas Pr., *(978-0-292; 978-1-4773)* Orders Addr.: P.O. Box 7819, Austin, TX 78713-7819 USA (SAN 212-9876) Tel 512-471-7233; Fax: 512-232-7178; Toll Free: 800-252-3206; Edit Addr.: University of Texas at Austin 2100 Comal, Austin, TX 78722 USA
E-mail: info@utpress.utexas.edu
Web site: http://www.utexas.edu/utpress.

Univ. of Washington Pr., *(978-0-295; 978-1-902716)* Orders Addr.: P.O. Box 50096, Seattle, WA 98145-5096 USA (SAN 212-2502) Tel 206-543-4050; Fax: 206-543-3932; Toll Free Fax: 800-669-7993; Edit Addr.: P.O. Box 50096, Seattle, WA 98145-5096 USA Toll Free Fax: 800-669-7993; 1126 N. 98th St., Seattle, WA 98103
E-mail: uwpord@u.washington.edu
Web site: http://www.washington.edu/uwpress.

Univ. of Wisconsin Pr., *(978-0-299)* Orders Addr.: c/o Chicago Dist Ctr., 11030 S. Langley Ave., Chicago, IL 60628 USA Tel 773-568-1550; Fax: 773-660-2235; Toll Free Fax: 800-621-8476 (orders only); Toll Free: 800-621-2736 (orders only); Edit Addr.: 1930 Monroe St., 3rd Flr., Madison, WI 53711 USA Tel 608-263-1110; Fax: 608-263-1132
E-mail: uwiscpress@uwpress.wisc.edu
Web site: http://www.wisc.edu/wisconsinpress/.

Univ. Pr. of Florida, *(978-0-8130; 978-0-942084; 978-0-9760555; 978-1-61610; 978-1-942852)* Orders Addr.: 15 NW 15th St., Gainesville, FL 32611-0279 USA (SAN 207-9275) Tel 352-392-1351; Fax: 352-392-7302; Toll Free Fax: 800-680-1955; Toll Free: 800-226-3822
E-mail: press@upf.com; orders@upf.com
Web site: http://www.upf.com.

Univ. Pr. of Mississippi, *(978-0-87805; 978-1-57806; 978-1-934110; 978-1-60473; 978-1-61703; 978-1-62103; 978-1-62674; 978-1-62846; 978-1-4968)* 3825 Ridgewood Rd., Jackson, MS 39211-6492 USA (SAN 203-1914) Tel 601-432-6205; Fax: 601-432-6217; Toll Free: 800-737-7788 (orders only)
E-mail: kburgess@ihl.state.ms.us; press@mississippi.edu
Web site: http://www.upress.state.ms.us.

Univ. Pr. of New England, *(978-0-87451; 978-0-915032; 978-1-58465; 978-1-61168; 978-1-5126)* Orders Addr.: One Court St., Suite 250, Lebanon, NH 03755 USA Tel 603-448-1533 (ext. 255); Fax: 603-448-9429; Toll Free: 800-421-1561
E-mail: University.Press@Dartmouth.edu
Web site: http://www.upne.com.

Univ. Pr. of Virginia, *(978-0-8139; 978-0-912759; 978-1-57814)* Orders Addr.: P.O. Box 400318, Charlottesville, VA 22904-4318 USA (SAN 202-5361) Tel 804-924-3468; Fax: 804-982-2655
E-mail: upress@virginia.edu
Web site: http://www.upress.virginia.edu.

Univelt, Inc., *(978-0-87703; 978-0-912183)* Orders Addr.: P.O. Box 28130, San Diego, CA 92198 USA; Edit Addr.: 740 Metcalf St., Suite 13, Escondido, CA 92025-1671 USA (SAN 658-2095)
E-mail: sales@univelt.com
Web site: http://www.univelt.com.

Universal Subscription Service, P.O. Box 35445, Houston, TX 77035 USA (SAN 287-4768).

Universe Publishing, *(978-0-7893; 978-0-87663; 978-1-55550)* Div. of Rizzoli International Pubns., Inc., 300 Park Ave. S., 3rd Flr., New York, NY 10010 USA (SAN 202-537X) Tel 212-387-3400; Fax: 212-387-3444 Do not confuse with similar names in North Hollywood, CA, Englewood, NJ, Mendocino, CA.

University Book Service, Orders Addr.: P.O. Box 608, Grove City, OH 43123 USA (SAN 169-6912); Edit Addr.: P.O. Box 607, Grove City, OH 43123-0607 USA (SAN 282-4841) Toll Free: 800-634-4272.

University of Arizona Pr., *(978-0-8165; 978-1-941451)* 355 S. Euclid Ave., Suite 103, Tucson, AZ 85719 USA (SAN 205-468X) Tel 520-621-1441; Fax: 520-621-8899; Toll Free: 800-426-3797 (orders)
E-mail: orders@uapress.arizona.edu
Web site: http://www.uapress.arizona.edu.

University of Nevada Pr., *(978-0-87417; 978-1-943859)* Orders Addr.: Mail Stop 166, Reno, NV 89557 USA (SAN 203-316X) Tel 775-784-6573; Fax: 775-784-6200; Toll Free: 877-682-6657 (orders only)
E-mail: vfontana@unpress.nevada.edu
Web site: http://www.unpress.nevada.edu.

University Publishing Associates, Incorporated, *See* **National Film Network LLC**

Untreed Reads Publishing, LLC, *(978-1-61187)* 506 Kansas St., San Francisco, CA 94107 USA Tel 415-621-0465; Toll Free Fax: 800-318-6037
E-mail: jhartman@untreedreads.com; kdsullivan@untreedreads.com
Web site: http://www.untreedreads.com.

Upper Access, Inc., *(978-0-942679)* Orders Addr.: 87 Upper Access Rd., Hinesburg, VT 05461 USA (SAN 667-1195) Tel 802-482-2988; Fax: 802-304-1005; Toll Free: 800-310-8320 (orders only)
E-mail: info@upperaccess.com
Web site: http://www.upperaccess.com.

Urban Land Institute, *(978-0-87420)* 1025 Thomas Jefferson St., NW, Suite 500 W., Washington, DC 20007-5201 USA (SAN 203-3399) Tel 202-624-7000; Fax: 202-624-7140; Toll Free: 800-321-5011
E-mail: bookstore@uli.org
Web site: http://www.uli.org/.

U.S. Games Systems, Inc., *(978-0-88079; 978-0-913866; 978-1-57281)* 179 Ludlow St., Stamford, CT 06902

USA (SAN 158-6483) Tel 203-353-8400; Fax: 203-353-8431; Toll Free: 800-544-2637 E-mail: usgames@aol.com Web site: http://www.usgamesinc.com.

US PubRep, Inc., 5000 Jasmine Dr., Rockville, MD 20853 USA Tel 301-838-9276; Fax: 301-838-9278 E-mail: craigfalk@aya.yale.edu.

Val Publishing, 16 S. Terrace Ave., Mount Vernon, NY 10551 USA (SAN 107-6876) Tel 914-664-7077.

Valentine Publishing Group, Orders Addr.: P.O. Box 902582, Palmdale, CA 93590-2582 USA; Edit Addr.: 18543 Devonshire St., Northridge, CA 91324 USA Tel 818-831-0649; Fax: 818-831-6659 E-mail: sales@vpg.net.

Valiant International Multi-Media Corp., 55 Ruta Ct., South Hackensack, NJ 07606 USA (SAN 652-8813) Tel 201-229-9800; Fax: 201-814-0418.

Valjean Pr., 721 Shadowlawn Ct., Franklin, TN 37069 USA E-mail: pastorforthemoment@gmail.com.

Valkyrie Distribution, 43 New Hope Ct., Florissant, MO 63033 USA Tel 314-623-6639 E-mail: valkpub@yahoo.com.

Valley Distributors, Inc., 2947 Felton Rd., Norristown, PA 19401 USA (SAN 169-7498) Tel 610-279-7650; Fax: 610-279-9093; Toll Free: 800-355-2665 (orders only).

Valley Media, Inc., 1276 Santa Anita Ct., Woodland, CA 95776 USA Tel 530-661-6600; Fax: 530-661-5472 E-mail: valley@valley-media.com Web site: http://www.valsat.com.

Valley Record Distributors, *See* **Valley Media, Inc.**

Van Dyke News Agency, 2238 W. Pinedale Ave., Fresno, CA 93711-0453 USA (SAN 168-9630) Tel 209-291-7768; Fax: 209-291-7770.

Van Khoa Bks., 14601 Moran St., Westminster, CA 92683-5629 USA (SAN 110-7534) E-mail: vankhoa@vinet.com.

Vandamere Pr., *(978-0-918339)* Subs. of AB Assocs., Orders Addr.: P.O. Box 149, St. Petersburg, FL 33731 USA (SAN 657-3088) Tel 727-556-0950; Fax: 727-556-2560; Toll Free: 800-551-7776 Web site: www.vandamere.com.

Verham News Corp., 75 Main St., West Lebanon, NH 03784 USA (SAN 169-4561) Fax: 603-298-8843.

VHPS Distribution Center, *See* **MPS**

Victory Multimedia, *(978-0-9661850)* Div. of Victory Audio Video Services, Inc., 460 Hindry Ave., Suite D, Inglewood, CA 90301-2045 USA (SAN 631-4112) E-mail: sbvictory@juno.com.

Vida Life Publishers International, *See* **Vida Pubs.**

Vida Pubs., *(978-0-8297)* 8410 NW 53rd Ter. Ste. 103, Miami, FL 33166-4510 USA Toll Free: 800-843-2548 E-mail: vidapubsales@harpercollins.com Web site: http://www.editorialvida.com.

Video Project, The, 200 Estates Dr., Ben Lomond, CA 95005-9444 USA Toll Free: 800-475-2638 E-mail: videoproject@videoproject.org Web site: http://www.videoproject.org.

Vigilante, Richard Bks., *(978-0-9800763; 978-0-9827163)* 7400 Metro Blvd. Suite 217, Minneapolis, MN 55439 USA.

Village Marketing, 145 W. 400 N., Richfield, UT 84701 USA (SAN 631-6751) Toll Free: 800-982-6683.

Vinabind, P.O. Box 340, Steelville, MO 65565 USA (SAN 159-9828).

Vincennes News Agency, P.O. Box 1110, Evansville, IN 47706-1110 USA (SAN 169-2518).

Virginia Periodical Distributors, *See* **Aramark Magazine & Bk. Services, Inc.**

Virginia Pubns., 16 W. Washington St., Lexington, VA 24450 USA Tel 540-462-3993 E-mail: vapublications@rockbridge.net.

Visible Ink Pr., *(978-0-7876; 978-0-8103; 978-1-57859)* Orders Addr.: 1094 Flex Dr., Jackson, TN 38301-5070 USA Toll Free Fax: 800-351-5073; Toll Free: 800-343-4499; Edit Addr.: 43311 Joy Rd., Canton, MI 48187-2075 USA (SAN 860-2271) Tel 734-667-3211; Fax: 734-667-4311 E-mail: inquiries@visibleink.com Web site: http://www.visibleink.com.

Vision Distributors, *(978-0-9626732)* Div. of Infinite Creations, Inc., Orders Addr.: P.O. Box 9839, Santa Fe, NM 87504 USA Tel 505-986-8221.

Vision Press, *See* **Vision Distributors**

Vision Video, *(978-1-56364)* Orders Addr.: P.O. Box 540, Worcester, PA 19490 USA Tel 610-584-3500; Fax: 610-584-4610; Toll Free: 800-523-0226; Edit Addr.: 2030 Wentz Church Rd., Worcester, PA 19490 USA (SAN 298-7392) E-mail: info@gatewayfilms.com; info@visionvideo.com Web site: http://www.gatewayfilms.com.

Vistabooks, *(978-0-89646)* 0637 Blue Ridge Rd., Silverthorne, CO 80498-8931 USA (SAN 211-0849) Tel 970-468-7673 (phone/fax) E-mail: vistabooks@compuserve.com Web site: http://www.vistabooks.com.

Vital Source Technologies, Inc., *(978-0-9651916; 978-1-59377)* 227 Fayetteville St., Suite 400, Raleigh, NC 27601 USA Tel 919-755-8110 E-mail: hayesbarton@vitalbook.com.

Vitality Distributors, 940 NW 51st Pl., Fort Lauderdale, FL 33309 USA (SAN 169-0973) Toll Free: 800-226-8482.

VNU, Div. of Prestel Publishing, 575 Prospect Ave., Lakewood, NJ 08701 USA (SAN 631-7758) Tel 732-363-5679; Fax: 732-363-0338; Toll Free: 888-463-6110.

volcano pr., *(978-0-912078; 978-1-884244)* Orders Addr.: P.O. Box 270, Volcano, CA 95689 USA (SAN 220-0015) Tel 209-296-4991; Fax: 209-296-4995; Toll Free: 800-879-9636; Edit Addr.: 21496 National St., Volcano, CA 95689 USA E-mail: info@volcanopress.com; sales@volcanopress.com; adam@volcanopress.com Web site: http://www.volcanopress.com.

VPD, Inc., 150 Parkshore Dr., Folsom, CA 95630-4710 USA (SAN 631-287X) Toll Free: 800-366-2111 Web site: http://www.vpdinc.com/.

Vroman's, A. C., *(978-0-9639197)* 695 E. Colorado Blvd., Pasadena, CA 91101 USA (SAN 169-0027) Tel 626-449-5320; Fax: 626-792-7308.

W5YI Group, Inc., P.O. Box 565101, Dallas, TX 75356 USA.

WA Bk. Service, P.O. Box 514, East Islip, NY 11730-0514 USA (SAN 107-2943).

Wabash Valley News Agency, 2200 N. Curry Pike, No. 2, Bloomington, IN 47404-1486 USA (SAN 169-250X).

Waffle, O. G. Bk. Co. (The Bookhouse), P.O. Box 586, Marion, IA 52302 USA (SAN 112-8817) Tel 319-373-1832.

Waldenbooks Company, Incorporated, *See* **Waldenbooks, Inc.**

Waldenbooks, Inc., *(978-0-681)* Div. of Borders Group, Inc., a/o Calendar Orders, 455 Industrial Blvd., Suite C, LaVergne, TN 37086 USA (SAN 179-3373); Orders Addr.: One Waldenbooks Dr., LaVergne, TN 37096 USA; 11625 Venture, Mira Loma, CA 91752 Tel 951-361-4025; Edit Addr.: 100 Phoenix Dr., Ann Arbor, MI 48108-2202 USA (SAN 200-8858) Tel 734-477-1100 E-mail: customerservice@waldenbooks.com Web site: http://www.waldenbooks.com; http://www.preferredreader.com.

Walker Art Ctr., *(978-0-935640; 978-1-935963)* Orders Addr.: 1750 Hennepin Ave., Minneapolis, MN 55403 USA (SAN 206-1880) Tel 612-375-7638; Fax: 612-375-7565 E-mail: paul.schumacher@walkerart.org; lisa.middag@walkerart.org.

Wallace's College Bk. Co., P.O. Box 689, Nicholasville, KY 40340-0689 USA (SAN 169-2844) Tel 606-255-0886; Fax: 606-259-9892; Toll Free Fax: 800-433-9329 (orders only); Toll Free: 800-354-9590 (orders only); 800-354-9500 E-mail: orders@wallaces.com.

Walthers, William K. Inc., *(978-0-941952)* 5601 W. Florist Ave., Milwaukee, WI 53201-3039 USA (SAN 238-4868) Tel 414-527-0770; Fax: 414-527-4423; Toll Free: 800-877-7171.

Ware-Pak, Inc., Orders Addr.: 2427 Bond St., University Park, IL 60466 USA Tel 708-534-2600; Fax: 708-534-7803 E-mail: kshay@ware-pak.com Web site: http://www.ware-pak.com.

Warner Books, Incorporated, *See* **Grand Central Publishing**

Warner Bros. Pubns., *(978-0-7604; 978-0-7692; 978-0-87487; 978-0-89724; 978-0-89898; 978-0-910957; 978-1-55122; 978-1-57623; 978-0-7579)* Div. of AOL Time Warner, 15800 NW 48th Ave., Miami, FL 33014-6422 USA (SAN 203-0586).

Warner Pr. Pubs., *(978-0-87162; 978-1-59317)* Orders Addr.: P.O. Box 2499, Anderson, IN 46018-2499 USA (SAN 691-4241) Tel 765-648-2116; Fax: 765-622-9511; Toll Free: 800-848-2464; Edit Addr.: 1201 E. Fifth St., Anderson, IN 46012 USA (SAN 111-8110) Tel 765-648-2116; Fax: 765-622-9511; Toll Free: 800-741-7721 (orders only) E-mail: jallison@warnerpress.org; rjackson@warnerpress.org Web site: http://www.warnerpress.org; http://www.francisasburypress.org.

Washington Bk. Distributors, 4930A Eisenhower Ave., Alexandria, VA 22304 USA (SAN 631-0095) Tel 703-212-9113; Fax: 703-212-9114; Toll Free: 800-699-9113 E-mail: zacwbd@prodigy.net Web site: http://www.washingtonbk.com.

Washington Toy Co., 2163 28th Ave., San Francisco, CA 94116-1732 USA (SAN 107-1718).

Watson, W. R. & Staff, 150 Mariner Green Ct., Corte Madera, CA 94925 USA (SAN 286-0155) Tel 510-524-6156; Fax: 510-526-5023.

Watson-Guptill Pubns., Inc., *(978-0-8230; 978-1-60569)* Div. of Crown Publishing Grp., 575 Prospect St., Lakewood, NJ 08701 USA Tel 732-363-5679; Toll Free Fax: 877-227-6564; Edit Addr.: 1745 Broadway # 124, New York, NY 10019-4305 USA (SAN 282-5384) E-mail: aalexander@watsonguptill.com Web site: http://www.watsonguptill.com.

Waverly News Co., 17 State St., Newburyport, MA 01950 USA (SAN 169-3522).

Wayland Audio-Visual, 210 E. 86th St., Suite 405, New York, NY 10028 USA Toll Free: 800-813-1271 E-mail: jm@waylandav.com.

Waymont Bk. Co., 136 Steuben St., Jersey City, NJ 07302 USA (SAN 630-768X) Tel 201-434-4268; Fax: 201-432-1293 E-mail: waymont@worldnet.att.net.

Wayne State Univ. Pr., *(978-0-8143)* Leonard N. Simons Bldg., 4809 Woodward Ave., Detroit, MI 48201-1309 USA (SAN 202-5221) Tel 313-577-6120; Fax: 313-577-6131; Toll Free: 800-978-7323 (customer orders) E-mail: theresa.martinelli@wayne.edu; Kristina.Stonehill@wayne.edu Web site: http://wsupress.wayne.edu.

Weiner News Co., 1011 N. Frio, P.O. Box 7608, San Antonio, TX 78207 USA (SAN 169-8427) Tel 210-226-9333; Fax: 210-226-8679.

Weiser, Samuel Incorporated, *See* **Red Wheel/Weiser**

WellSpring Bks., P.O. Box 2765, Woburn, MA 01888-1465 USA (SAN 111-3399) Do not confuse with companies with the same or similar names in Albuquerque, NM, Ukiah, CA, Adelphia, NJ, Woburn, MA, Groton, VT.

Wenatchee News Agency, 434 Rock Island Rd., East Wenatchee, WA 98802-5360 USA (SAN 169-8885) Tel 509-662-3511.

Wesscott Marketing, Inc., *(978-0-9764077)* P.O. Box 26144, Saint Louis Park, MN 55426 USA Fax: 952-541-4905; Toll Free: 800-375-3702.

West, *(978-0-314; 978-0-7620; 978-0-8321; 978-0-8366; 978-0-87632)* Orders Addr.: 610 Opperman Dr., Eagan, MN 55123-1396 USA Tel 657-687-6849; Fax: 651-687-6857; Toll Free: 800-328-2209; 800-328-9378 (Editorial) Do not confuse with The West Group in Prairie Village, KS E-mail: west.bookstore@thomson.com; customer.service@westgroup.com; janet.linkert@thompson.com Web site: http://west.thomson.com; http://westacademic.com.

West Music Co., 1212 Fifth St., Coralville, IA 52241 USA Toll Free: 800-397-9378.

West Texas News Co., Orders Addr.: 1214 Barranca, El Paso, TX 79935 USA; Edit Addr.: P.O. Box 26488, El Paso, TX 79926 USA (SAN 169-8184) Tel 915-594-7586; Fax: 915-594-7589.

West Virginia Book Co., The, 1125 Central Ave., Charleston, WV 25302 USA (SAN 920-9956) Tel 304-342-1848; Fax: 304-343-0594; Toll Free: 888-982-7472 E-mail: wvbooks@wvbookco.com.

Westcliffe Pubs., *(978-0-929969; 978-0-942394; 978-1-56579)* Div. of Big Earth Publishing, Orders Addr.: 1637 Pearl St. Ste. 201, Boulder, CO 80302-5447 USA Toll Free: 800-258-5830 Do not confuse with Westcliff Publications in Newport Beach, CA E-mail: sales@westcliffepublishers.com Web site: http://www.westcliffepublishers.com.

Western Book Distributors/Booksource, *See* **Western Booksource, Inc.**

Western Booksource, Inc., 4935 Metart Shwayn, Tillamook, OR 97141 USA (SAN 158-4332) Toll Free: 800-825-0100; 230 Fifth Ave., No. 1104, New York, NY 10001 Tel 212-889-9339; Fax: 212-889-9572.

Western International, Inc., *(978-0-9665194)* 2220 Delaware St., Lawrence, KS 66046-3150 USA (SAN 631-1695) Toll Free: 800-634-6737.

Western Library Bks., 560 S. San Vicente Blvd., Los Angeles, CA 90048 USA (SAN 168-9878) Tel 213-653-8880.

Western Merchandisers, 2900 Airport Rd., Denton, TX 76207-2102 USA (SAN 156-4633).

Western Michigan News, *See* **Readmor**

Western Pubns. Service, 2128 Sun Valley Rd., San Marcos, CA 92069 USA (SAN 630-6241) Tel 760-295-2231; Fax: 760-295-3978.

Western Record Sales, 2991 Saint Andrews Rd., Fairfield, CA 94533-7839 USA (SAN 630-6667).

Western Reserve Historical Society, *(978-0-911704; 978-0-9967844)* 10825 East Blvd., Cleveland, OH 44106 USA (SAN 110-8387) Tel 216-721-5722; Fax: 216-721-0645.

Westminster John Knox Pr., *(978-0-664; 978-0-8042; 978-1-61164)* Div. of Presbyterian Publishing Corp., Orders Addr.: 100 Witherspoon St., Louisville, KY 40202-1396 USA (SAN 202-9669) Tel 502-569-5052 (outside U.S. for ordering); Fax: 502-569-5113 (outside U.S. for faxed orders); Toll Free Fax: 800-541-5113 (toll-free U.S. faxed orders); Toll Free: 800-227-2872 (customer service) E-mail: orders@wjkbooks.com Web site: http://www.wjkbooks.com.

Weston, Edward Fine Arts, P.O. Box 3098, Chatsworth, CA 91313-3098 USA (SAN 168-9967) Tel 818-885-1044; Fax: 818-885-1021.

Weston Woods Studios, Inc., *(978-0-7882; 978-0-89719; 978-1-55592; 978-1-56008)* Div. of Scholastic, Inc., 143 Main St., Norwalk, CT 06851 USA (SAN 630-3838) Tel 203-845-0197; Fax: 203-845-0498; Toll Free: 800-243-5020 E-mail: questions@Scholastic.com Web site: http://www.scholastic.com/westonwoods.

Westwater Bks., *(978-0-916370; 978-1-941406)* Div. of Belknap Photographic Services, Inc., P.O. Box 2560, Evergreen, CO 80437 USA (SAN 208-3698) Tel 303-674-5410; Fax: 303-670-0586; Toll Free: 800-628-1326.

WFiveYI Group, Inc., The, 7101 N. Ridgeway Ave., Lincolnwood, IL 60712 USA Tel 847-763-0916; Fax: 847-763-0918.

Whatever Publishing, Incorporated, *See* **New World Library**

Whitaker Distributors, *See* **Anchor Distributors**

Whitaker Hse., *(978-0-88368; 978-1-60374; 978-1-62911)* Div. of Whitaker Corp., 1030 Hunt Valley Cir., New Kensington, PA 15068 USA (SAN 203-2104) Tel 724-334-7000 Whitaker House/Anchor Distributors; Fax: 724-334-1200 Anchor Distributors; Toll Free Fax: 866-773-7001 Whitaker House; 800-765-1960 Anchor Distributors; Toll Free: 877-793-9800 Whitaker House; 800-444-4484 Whitaker House/Anchor Distributors E-mail: sales@whitakerhouse.com Web site: http://www.whitakerhouse.com/; http://www.anchordistributors.com/; http://www.amazon.com/.

Whitewing Pr., P.O. Box 1561, Hemphill, TX 75948 USA Tel 409-787-1526 E-mail: books@whitewingpress.com.

Whiting News Co., 1011 Azalea Dr., Munster, IN 46321-3501 USA (SAN 169-2542).

Whitlock & Co., 10001 Roosevelt Rd., Westchester, IL 60153 USA (SAN 285-9645).

Whitman Distribution Co., Orders Addr.: P.O. Box 513, Lebanon, NH 03766 USA (SAN 631-0540) Fax: 603-448-2576; Toll Free: 800-353-3730; Edit Addr.: 10 Water St., Lebanon, NH 03766 USA E-mail: distribution@whitmancommunications.com.

Whitman Publishing & Distribution Company, *See* **Whitman Distribution Co.**

Wholesale Distributors, P.O. Box 126, Burlington, IA 52601 USA (SAN 145-8051) Tel 319-753-1683; Fax: 319-753-5988; Toll Free: 800-272-1556.

Wickel, W. W. Co., Inc., 520 N. Exchange Ct., Aurora, IL 60504 USA (SAN 135-1230) Tel 630-820-0044; Fax: 630-820-0057; Toll Free: 800-728-0708.

Wicker Pk. Pr., Ltd., *(978-0-9789676; 978-1-936679)* 440 DeKalb Ave No. B, Sycamore, IL 60178 USA Tel 773-391-1199; Toll Free: 877-751-5033 (orders) E-mail: eric@3ibooks.com Web site: http://www.wickerparkpress.us.

Wilcor International Bk. Dept., 161 Drive In Rd., Frankfort, NY 13340-5238 USA (SAN 107-7023).

Wild Dog Bks., Orders Addr.: Seven Balsa Ct., Sante Fe, NM 87508 USA E-mail: WildDogBooks@att.net.

Wilderness Pr., *(978-0-89997; 978-0-911824)* Div. of Keen Communications, Orders Addr.: 2204 First Ave. South Suite 102, Birmingham, AL 35233 USA (SAN 854-7289) Fax: 205-326-1012; Toll Free: 800-443-7227 E-mail: mail@wildernesspress.com; info@wildernesspress.com Web site: http://www.wildernesspress.com.

Wiley, John & Sons, Inc., *(978-0-470; 978-0-471; 978-0-7645; 978-0-7821; 978-0-8260; 978-0-87605; 978-0-88422; 978-0-937721; 978-0-939246; 978-1-55828; 978-1-56561; 978-1-56884; 978-1-57313; 978-1-58245; 978-1-878058; 978-3-527; 978-1-118; 978-1-119)* Orders Addr.: c/o John Wiley & Sons, Inc., United States Distribution Ctr., 1 Wiley Dr., Somerset, NJ 08875-1272 USA Tel 732-469-4400; Fax: 732-302-2300; Toll Free Fax: 800-597-3299; Toll Free: 800-225-5945 (orders); Edit Addr.: 111 River St., Hoboken, NJ 07030 USA (SAN 200-2272) Tel 201-748-6000; 201-748-6276 (Retail and Wholesale); Fax: 201-748-6088; 201-748-8641 (Retail and Wholesale) E-mail: compbks@wiley.com; bookinfo@wiley.com; custserv@wiley.com Web site: http://www.wiley.com/compbooks; http://www.interscience.wiley.com; http://www.wiley.com.

William Thomson, *See* **Thomson, Linda**

Williamson, Darcy, *See* **Southern Cross Pubns.**

Willman Productions, P.O. Box 272345, Fort Collins, CO 80527 USA Tel 970-224-5911; Toll Free: 800-816-7566.

Wilshire Bk. Co., *(978-0-87980)* 9731 Variel Ave., Chatsworth, CA 91311-4315 USA (SAN 168-9932) E-mail: mpowers@mpowers.com Web site: http://www.mpowers.com.

Wilson & Assocs., *(978-0-9710427)* P.O. Box 2569, Alvin, TX 77512 USA Tel 281-388-0196; Fax: 413-683-8503 Do not confuse with Wilson & Associates, Gig Harbor, WA E-mail: john@wilsonpublishing.com; pwilson@wilsonpublishing.com Web site: http://www.orsapress.com; http://www.thebookdistributor.com; http://www.wilsonpublishing.com.

Wilson & Sons, P.O. Box 996, Bellevue, WA 98009 USA (SAN 129-0010) Tel 425-392-1965 E-mail: dchief@seanst.com.

Wimmer Companies, The, *See* **Wimmer Cookbooks**

Wimmer Cookbooks, *(978-0-918544; 978-0-939114; 978-1-879958)* 4650 Shelby Air Dr., Memphis, TN 38118 USA Tel 901-362-8900; 800-727-1034; Fax: 901-795-9806; Toll Free Fax: 800-794-9806; Toll Free: 800-727-1034 Do not confuse with Wimmer Cooksbooks in Atlanta, GA E-mail: wimmer@wimmerco.com Web site: http://www.wimmerco.com.

Windham County News Co., P.O. Box 8127, Brattleboro, VT 05304 USA (SAN 159-9917) Tel 802-254-2373.

Windhover Performing Arts Ctr., 257 Granite St., Rockport, MA 01966 USA Tel 978-546-3611 Web site: http://www.windhover.org.

Wine Appreciation Guild, Ltd., *(978-0-932664; 978-1-891267; 978-1-934259; 978-1-935879)* 360 Swift Ave., Unit 30, South San Francisco, CA 94080-6220 USA (SAN 169-0264) Tel 650-866-3020; Fax: 650-866-3513; Toll Free: 800-242-9462 (orders only) E-mail: Jim@wineappreciation.com; bryan@wineappreciation.com Web site: http://www.wineappreciation.com.

Winebaum News, Inc., P.O. Box 1620, Raymond, NH 03077-3620 USA (SAN 169-4529).

Wisdom Pubns., *(978-0-86171; 978-1-61429)* 199 Elm St., Somerville, MA 02144 USA (SAN 246-022X) Tel 617-776-7416 ext 24; Fax: 617-776-7841; Toll Free Fax: 800-338-4550 (orders only); Toll Free: 800-462-6420 (orders only) E-mail: marketing@wisdompubs.org Web site: http://www.wisdompubs.org.

Wittenborn Art Bks., *(978-0-8150; 978-0-89648)* Div. of Alan Wofsy Fine Arts, Orders Addr.: 1109 Geary Blvd., San Francisco, CA 94109 USA Tel 415-292-6500; Fax: 415-292-6594; Edit Addr.: P.O. Box 2210, San Francisco, CA 94126 USA Tel 510-482-3677; Toll Free: 800-660-6403 E-mail: art-books.com@jps.net Web site: http://www.art-books.com.

Wizard Works, *(978-0-9621543; 978-1-890692)* Orders Addr.: P.O. Box 1125, Homer, AK 99603-1125 USA Toll Free: 877-210-2665 E-mail: wizard@xyz.net Web site: http://www.xyz.net/~wizard.

Wolper Sales Agency, Inc., 6 Centre Sq., Suite 302A, Easton, PA 18042-3606 USA (SAN 285-9785) Tel 610-559-9550; Fax: 610-559-9898.

Wolverine Distributing, Inc., *(978-0-941875)* P.O. Box 503, Powell, WY 82435 USA (SAN 666-1211) Tel 307-754-2948; Fax: 307-754-2968; Toll Free: 800-967-1633 E-mail: wolverine@tctwest.net.

Wolverine Gallery, *See* **Wolverine Distributing, Inc.**

Women Ink, 777 United Nations Plaza, New York, NY 10017 USA (SAN 630-8309) Tel 212-687-8633; Fax: 212-661-2704
E-mail: wink@womenink.org
Web site: http://www.womenink.org.

Woodbine Publishing Co., The, 15621 Chemical Ln., No. B, Huntington Beach, CA 92649 USA (SAN 114-4243) Tel 714-894-9080; Fax: 714-894-4949; Toll Free: 800-451-4788
Web site: http://www.safaripress.com.

Woodcrafters Lumber Sales, Inc., 212 NE Sixth Ave., Portland, OR 97232 USA (SAN 112-6075) Tel 503-231-0226; Toll Free: 800-777-3709.

Woodland Distribution, Orders Addr.: 118 Woodland Dr., Chapmanville, WV 25508 USA Tel 304-752-7152; Fax: 304-752-9002.

Woodstocker Books/Arthur Schwartz & Company, (*978-1-879504*) 15 Meads Mountain Rd., Woodstock, NY 12498-1016 USA (SAN 630-0464) Tel 845-679-4024; Fax: 845-679-4093; Toll Free: 800-669-9080 (orders only)
E-mail: woodstockerbooks@woodstockerbooks.com
Web site: http://www.aschwartzbooks.com.

Word Distribution, *See* **Word Entertainment**

Word Entertainment, (*978-0-9644619; 978-1-933876*) 25 Music Sq. W., Nashville, TN 37203 USA Tel 615-726-7900; Toll Free Fax: 800-671-6601; Toll Free: 800-876-9673
E-mail: matt.taylor@wordentertainment.com
Web site: http://www.wordentertainment.com.

Word For Today, The, (*978-0-936728; 978-1-931713; 978-1-932941; 978-1-59751*) Div. of Calvary Chapel Costa Mesa, Orders Addr.: P.O. Box 8000, Costa Mesa, CA 92628 USA (SAN 110-8379) Tel 714-825-9673 Toll Free: 800-272-9673; Edit Addr.: 3232 W. MacArthur Blvd., Santa Ana, CA 92704 USA (SAN 214-2260) Tel 714-825-9673 Toll Free: 800-272-9637
E-mail: info@twft.com
Web site: http://www.twft.com.

Word of Life Distributors, 2707 W. Olympic Blvd. Ste. 100, Los Angeles, CA 90006-2850 USA (SAN 108-433X) Toll Free: 800-347-7057.

WordWorks Publishing, (*978-1-887913*) Orders Addr.: 207 E. Pine Ridge Dr., Westfield, IN 46074 USA Tel 317-867-1879 (phone/fax) Do not confuse with Wordworks Publishing, Austin, TX
E-mail: joanetta.hendel@comcast.net.

Workamper Bookstore, 201 Hiram Rd., Heber Springs, AR 72543-8747 USA (SAN 631-547X) Tel 501-362-2637; Toll Free: 800-446-5627 (orders only)
Web site: http://www.workamper.com.

Workman Publishing Co., Inc., (*978-0-7611; 978-0-89480; 978-0-911104; 978-1-56305*) Orders Addr.: 225 Varick St., New York, NY 10014-4381 USA (SAN 203-2821) Tel 212-254-5900; Fax: 212-254-8098; Toll Free: 800-722-7202
E-mail: info@workman.com
Web site: http://www.workman.com.

World Bank Pubns., (*978-0-8213; 978-1-4648*) Orders Addr.: P.O. Box 960, Herndon, VA 20172-0960 USA Toll Free: 800-645-7247; Edit Addr.: 1818 H St., NW, Mail Stop: U11-1104, Washington, DC 20433 USA (SAN 219-0648) Tel 703-661-1580; 202-473-1000 (Head Office); Fax: 202-614-1237
E-mail: books@worldbank.org
Web site: http://www.worldbank.org/publications.

World of Reading, Ltd., P.O. Box 13092, Atlanta, GA 30324-0092 USA Tel 404-233-4042; Fax: 404-237-5511; Toll Free: 800-729-3703.

World Publications, Incorporated, *See* **World Pubns. Group, Inc.**

World Pubns. Group, Inc., (*978-0-7669; 978-0-9640034; 978-1-57215; 978-0-7429; 978-1-4132; 978-1-4279; 978-1-4376; 978-1-4513; 978-1-4643; 978-1-4785*) Orders Addr.: P.O. Box 509, East Bridgewater, MA 02333 USA (SAN 631-7014)
E-mail: sales@wrldpub.net
Web site: http://www.wrldpub.com.

World Univ., (*978-0-941902*) P.O. Box 2470, Benson, AZ 85602 USA (SAN 239-7943) Tel 520-586-2985; Fax: 520-586-4764
E-mail: desertsanctuary@theriver.com
Web site: http://worlduniversity.org.

World Wide Distributors, Limited, *See* **Island Heritage Publishing**

World Wide Hunting Books, *See* **Woodbine Publishing Co., The**

World Wide Pubns., (*978-0-89066*) P.O. Box 668089, Charlotte, NC 28266-8089 USA (SAN 159-9941) Toll Free: 800-788-0442.

World Wisdom, Inc., (*978-0-941532; 978-1-933316; 978-1-935493; 978-1-936597; 978-1-937786*) Orders Addr.: P.O. Box 2682, Bloomington, IN 47402-2682 USA (SAN 239-1406) Tel 812-330-3232; Fax: 812-333-1642; Toll Free: 888-992-6651; Edit Addr.: 1501 E. Hillside Dr., Bloomington, IN 47401 USA
Web site: http://www.worldwisdom.com.

Worldwide Media Service, Inc., Affil. of Hudson County News Agency, 30 Montgomery St., Jersey City, NJ 07302-3821 USA (SAN 630-4826) Tel 201-332-7100; Fax: 201-332-0265; Toll Free: 800-345-6478
Web site: http://www.americanmagazine.com.

Worthy Media, Incorporated, *See* **Worthy Publishing**

Worthy Publishing, (*978-1-936034; 978-1-61795*) Div. of Worthy Media, Inc., One Franklin Pk. 6100 Tower Cir. Suite 210, Franklin, TN 37067 USA Tel 615-932-7605 Do not confuse with Worthy Publishing in Birmingham, AL
E-mail: jeana@worthymedia.com
Web site: http://worthypublishing.com/.

Wright Bk./Educational, 2195 Owendale Dr., Dayton, OH 45439 USA (SAN 159-9968).

Wright Group/McGraw-Hill, (*978-0-322; 978-0-7802; 978-0-940156; 978-1-55624; 978-1-55911; 978-1-4045*) Div. of Mcgraw-Hill School Education Group, Orders Addr.: P.O. Box 545, Blacklick, OH 43004-0545 USA Tel 614-755-5645; Toll Free: 800-722-4726; 800-442-9685 (customer service)
Web site: http://www.wrightgroup.com/.

Writers & Bks., (*978-0-9618487; 978-0-9863305*) 740 University Ave., Rochester, NY 14607-1259 USA (SAN 156-9678).

Wybel Marketing Group, Orders Addr.: 213 W. Main St., Barrington, IL 60010 USA Tel 847-382-0384.

Wyoming Periodical Distributor, P.O. Box 2340, Casper, WY 82601 USA (SAN 169-9245).

Xlibris Corp., (*978-0-7388; 978-0-9663501; 978-1-4010; 978-1-4134; 978-1-59926; 978-1-4257; 978-1-4363; 978-1-4415; 978-1-4500; 978-1-4535; 978-1-4568; 978-1-4628; 978-1-4653; 978-1-4691; 978-1-4771; 978-1-4797; 978-1-4836; 978-1-4931; 978-1-4990; 978-1-5035;-1-5144) Orders Addr.: 1663 S. Liberty Dr. Suite 200, Bloomington, IN 47403 USA (SAN 299-5522) Tel 812-334-5223; Fax: 812-334-5223; Toll Free: 888-795-4274*
E-mail: info@xlibris.com; orders@xlibris.com; dave.weinman@xlibris.com; customersupport@xlibris.com; digitalcontent@authorsolutions.com
Web site: http://www2.xlibris.com.

Xlibris Corporation, *See* **Xlibris Corp.**

X-S Bks., Inc., 81 Brookside Ave., Amsterdam, NY 12010-0740 USA (SAN 169-4634).

Yale Univ., Far Eastern Pubns., (*978-0-88710*) 340 Edwards St., Box 208252, New Haven, CT 06520-8252 USA (SAN 219-0710) Tel 203-432-3109; Fax: 203-432-3111
Web site: http://www.yale.edu/fep.

Yale Univ. Pr., (*978-0-300*) Orders Addr.: c/o Triliteral LLC, 100 Maple Ridge Dr., Cumberland, RI 02864 USA Tel 401-531-2800; Fax: 401-531-2801; Toll Free Fax: 800-406-9145; Toll Free: 800-405-1619; Edit Addr.: 302 Temple St., New Haven, CT 06511 USA (SAN 203-2740) Tel 203-432-0960; Fax: 203-432-0948
E-mail: yupmkt@yale.edu
Web site: http://www.yale.edu/yup/; http://www.yale.edu/yup/index.html.

Yankee Bk. Peddler, Inc., 999 Maple St., Contoocook, NH 03229 USA (SAN 169-4510) Tel 603-746-3102; Fax: 603-746-5628; Toll Free: 800-258-3774
E-mail: ybp@office.ybp.com
Web site: http://www.ybp.com.

Yankee Paperback & Textbook Co., P.O. Box 18880, Tucson, AZ 85731 USA (SAN 112-1073) Tel 520-325-7229 (phone/fax); Toll Free: 800-340-2665 (in Arizona, California, Nevada, Colorado, New Mexico and Utah only).

Yankee Paperback Distributors, *See* **Yankee Paperback & Textbook Co.**

Yankee Peddler Bookshop, (*978-0-918426*) 4299 Lake Rd., Williamson, NY 14589-9615 USA (SAN 209-925X)
E-mail: byankeep@rochester.rr.com
Web site: http://www.shoprochester.com//yankeepeddler-abc.

YBP Library Services, 999 Maple St., Contocook, NH 03229 USA.

Ye Olde Genealogie Shoppe, (*978-0-932924; 978-1-878311*) Orders Addr.: P.O. Box 39128, Indianapolis, IN 46239 USA (SAN 200-7010) Tel 317-862-3330; Toll Free: 800-419-0200 (orders)
E-mail: yogs@iquest.net
Web site: http://www.yogs.com.

Young News, Inc., 1600 E. Grand Blvd., Detroit, MI 48211-3144 USA (SAN 169-3999) Fax: 517-753-7774.

Youthlight, Inc., (*978-1-889636; 978-1-59850*) Orders Addr.: P.O. Box 115, Chapin, SC 29036 USA (SAN 256-6400) Tel 803-345-1070; Fax: 803-345-0888; Toll Free: 800-209-9774; Edit Addr.: 105 Fairway Pond Dr., Chapin, SC 29036 USA
E-mail: yl@sc.rr.com; yl@youthlightbooks.com
Web site: http://www.youthlight.com; http://www.youthlightbooks.com.

Yuma News, Incorporated, *See* **Arizona Periodicals, Inc.**

YWAM Publishing, (*978-0-927545; 978-0-9615534; 978-1-57658*) Div. of Youth With A Mission International, P.O. Box 55787, Seattle, WA 98155 USA (SAN 248-4021)
E-mail: customerservice@ywampublishing.com
Web site: http://www.ywampublishing.com.

Zabel, C. & W. Co., Orders Addr.: P.O. Box 953, East Brunswick, NJ 08816-0953 USA (SAN 169-4731) Tel 732-254-1000; Fax: 732-254-0121; Edit Addr.: 76 Pennsbury Way, E Brunswick, NJ 08816-5278 USA (SAN 241-6441).

Zagat Survey, (*978-0-943421; 978-0-9612574; 978-1-57006; 978-1-60478*) 4 Columbus Cir., New York, NY 10019 USA (SAN 289-4777) Tel 212-977-6000; Fax: 212-765-9438; Toll Free: 866-999-0991
E-mail: tradesales@justzagat.com; theinz@zagat.com
Web site: http://www.zagat.com.

Zeitlin Periodicals Co., Inc., 7917 Lark Meadow Ave., Las Vegas, NV 89131-4710 USA (SAN 160-8088).

Zondervan, (*978-0-00; 978-0-310; 978-0-937336*) Subs. of HarperCollins Publishers US, Orders Addr.: c/o Zondervan XNET Ordering Dept., 5249 Corporate Grove, Grand Rapids, MI 49512 USA (SAN 298-9107); Edit Addr.: 5300 Patterson Ave., SE, Grand Rapids, MI 49530 USA (SAN 203-2694) Tel 616-698-6900; Fax: 616-698-3439
E-mail: zprod@zondervan.com
Web site: http://www.zondervan.com.

Zondervan Publishing House, *See* **Zondervan**

Zubal, John T. Inc., (*978-0-939738*) 2969 W. 25th St., Cleveland, OH 44113 USA (SAN 165-5841) Tel 216-241-7640; Fax: 216-241-6966.